FOUR COLOR COMICS
BUY
WHY YOU SHOULD CALL US BEFORE YOU SELL YOUR COLLECTION OF COMICS, ARTWORK OR MEMORABILIA:
SELL
We make it easy! No waiting for payment, No song and dance about grading. We'll come to you: Anywhere, Anytime! FOUR COLOR COMICS takes the risk out of selling. Treat yourself to an honest, straight-forward experience—Sell your collection to us and walk away with more money in your pocket and a smile on your face.
And if you're looking to buy comics, original artwork or memorabilia, give us a call first! We probably already have that elusive issue or object you've been searching for—and at a price you'll like!
CALL ROBERT ROGOVIN!
(914) 722-4696
Detective Comics
Action Comics
Detective Comics
P.O.BOX 1399, Scarsdale, NY 10583 TEL:(914) 722-4696, FAX (914) 722-7656
NEW!
Visit our on-line
SEARCHABLE DATABASE!
1000's of Golden and Silver Age comics available without scrolling thru endless listings!
www.fourcolorcomics.com
ORIGINAL COMIC ART
SEARCH COMICS!
MOVIE POSTERS

CGC
It just makes sense.

34th Edition

COMICS FROM 1828-PRESENT INCLUDED
FULLY ILLUSTRATED CATALOGUE & EVALUATION GUIDE

by ROBERT M. OVERSTREET

GEMSTONE PUBLISHING

J.C. Vaughn, **Executive Editor**
Arnold T. Blumberg, **Editor** • Brenda Busick, **Creative Director**
Mark Huesman, **Production Coordinator** • Tom Gordon, **Managing Editor**
Jamie David, **Office Manager** •Sara Ortt, **Assistant Office Manager**
Stacia Brown, **Editorial Coordinator**

SPECIAL CONTRIBUTORS TO THIS EDITION

Robert L. Beerbohm • Arnold T. Blumberg • Douglas Gillock
Matt Nelson • Richard D. Olson, Ph.D. • J.C. Vaughn • Doug Wheeler

SENIOR OVERSTREET ADVISORS FOR OVER 25 YEARS

Dave Alexander • Steve Geppi • Bruce Hamilton • Paul Levitz • Michelle Nolan • Ron Pussell • Rick Sloane
John K. Snyder Jr. • Terry Stroud • Doug Sulipa • Harry B. Thomas • Raymond S. True

SENIOR OVERSTREET ADVISORS FOR OVER 20 YEARS

Gary M. Carter • Bill Cole • Stan Gold • M. Thomas Inge
Phil Levine • Richard Olson • Gene Seger • David R. Smith

SPECIAL ADVISORS

Lon Allen • Dave Anderson • David J. Anderson, D.D.S. • Robert L. Beerbohm • Jon Berk • Steve Borock
Michael Browning • John Chruscinski • Gary Colabuono • Carl De La Cruz • Peter Dixon • Gary Dolgoff • Joe Dungan
Bruce Ellsworth • Conrad Eschenberg • Richard Evans • D'Arcy Farrell • Stephen Fishler • Dan Fogel
Chris Foss • Philip J. Gaudino • Steve Gentner • Michael Goldman • Tom Gordon • Jamie Graham
Daniel Greenhalgh • Eric Groves • Gary Guzzo • John Grasse • Jim Halperin • Mark Haspel • John Hauser
Greg Holland • John Hone • George Huang • Bill Hughes • Rob Hughes • William Insignares • Ed Jaster
Joe Mannarino • Rick Manzella • Patrick Marchbanks • Harry Matetsky • Jon McClure • Mike McKenzie
Fred McSurley • Dale Moore • Michael Naiman • Josh Nathanson • Matt Nelson • Terry O'Neill • George Pantela
James Payette • John Petty • Jim Pitts • Yolanda Ramirez • Jo Ann Reisler • Todd Reznik • "Doc" Robinson
Israel Rodriguez • Robert Rogovin • Rory Root • Robert Roter • Chuck Rozanski • Matt Schiffman • Dave Smith
Laura Sperber • Tony Starks • Bob Storms • Joel Thingvall • Joe Vereneault • Frank Verzyl • John Verzyl
Rose Verzyl • Bob Wayne • Jerry Weist • Mark Wilson • Anthony Yamada • Harley Yee • Vincent Zurzolo, Jr.

House of Collectibles
New York

Gemstone Publishing

Cover illustrations: *Incredible Hulk* #1 re-creation by John K. Snyder III; *Special Edition Comics* #1 re-creation by Joe Simon; Donald Duck's 70th anniversary by Daan Jippes.

THE OFFICIAL OVERSTREET COMIC BOOK PRICE GUIDE (34th Edition) is an original publication of Gemstone Publishing, Inc. and House of Collectibles. Distributed by Random House Information Group, a division of Random House, Inc., New York and simultaneously in Canada by Random House of Canada Limited, Toronto. This edition has never before appeared in book form.

House of Collectibles
Random House Information Group
1745 Broadway
New York, New York 10019

www.houseofcollectibles.com

Overstreet is a registered trademark of Gemstone Publishing, Inc.

House of Collectibles is a registered trademark and the H colophon is a trademark of Random House, Inc.

Published by arrangement with Gemstone Publishing.

ISBN: 1-4000-4669-6
ISSN: 0891-8872

Printed in the United States of America

10 9 8 7 6 5 4 3 2 1

Thirty-Fourth Edition: May 2004

www.ComicCollectors.net
for high grade quality rare vintage comic books!!!
IT IS TIME, ONCE AGAIN, MY DEFENDERS OF FREEDOM, TO CRUSH THE EVILDOERS!!!
All characters ©2004 respective holders. All rights reseved
DEFENDERS OF FREEDOM

Table of Contents

Acknowledgements

Mark Arnold (Harvey data); Larry Bigman (Frazetta-Williamson data); Glenn Bray (Kurtzman data); Gary Carter (DC data); J. B. Clifford Jr. (EC data); Gary Coddington (Superman data); Wilt Conine (Fawcett data); Dr. S. M. Davidson (Cupples & Leon data); Al Dellinges (Kubert data); David Gerstein (Walt Disney Comics data); Kevin Hancer (Tarzan data); Charles Heffelfinger and Jim Ivey (March of Comics listing); R. C. Holland and Ron Pussell (Seduction and Parade of Pleasure data); Grant Irwin (Quality data); Richard Kravitz (Kelly data); Phil Levine (giveaway data); Dan Malan & Charles Heffelfinger (Classic Comics data); Jon McClure (Whitman data); Fred Nardelli (Frazetta data); Michelle Nolan (love comics); Mike Nolan (MLJ, Timely, Nedor data); George Olshevsky (Timely data); Chris Pedrin (DC War data); Scott Pell ('50s data); Greg Robertson (National data); Don Rosa (Late 1940s to 1950s data); Matt Schiffman (Bronze Age data); Frank Scigliano (Little Lulu data); Gene Seger (Buck Rogers data); Rick Sloane (Archie data); David R. Smith, Archivist, Walt Disney Productions (Disney data); Tony Starks (Silver and Bronze Age data); Don and Maggie Thompson (Four Color listing); Mike Tiefenbacher & Jerry Sinkovec (Atlas and National data); Raymond True & Philip J. Gaudino (Classic Comics data); Jim Vadeboncoeur Jr. (Williamson and Atlas data); Kim Weston (Disney and Barks data); Cat Yronwode (Spirit data); Andrew Zerbe and Gary Behymer (M. E. data).

We thank John Snyder III for his "incredible" cover re-creation of Jack Kirby's *Incredible Hulk* #1, appearing on our book store edition. I would also like to thank Joe Simon for his re-creation of his own *Special Edition Comics* #1 cover, and to noted Disney artist Daan Jippes for his tribute cover for Donald Duck's 70th anniversary.

Credit is due my two grading advisors, Steve Borock and Mark Haspel of Comics Guaranty Corp., for their ongoing input on grading. A special "thanks" is also given to Chuck Rozanski for his many years of support.

Thanks again to Doug Sulipa, Jon McClure, Fred McSurley and Tony Starks for continuing to provide detailed Bronze Age data. To Dave Alexander, Dave Anderson-Oklahoma, Dave Anderson-Virginia, Lauren Becker, Michael Browning, Conrad Eschenberg, Dan Fogel, Stephen Gentner, Jamie Graham, Eric Groves, Jef Hinds, Bill Hughes, Pat Marchbanks, Josh Nathanson, Terry O'Neil, Jim Payette, Ron Pussell, Rob Rogovin, Michael Tierney, John Verzyl, Frank Verzyl and Vincent Zurzolo Jr., who supplied detailed pricing data, market reviews or other material in this edition.

My gratitude is given to Chris Pedrin for his advice on DC war comics data and to Stephen Fishler and Marc Patten for "How to Sell Your Comic Collection;" to Stephen Fishler for inspiring and helping develop the new 10 point grading system adopted in the 30th Edition; to Dr. Richard Olson for grading and Yellow Kid information; to Matt Nelson for his new update to the restored comics section; to Arnold T. Blumberg for his introduction to the Promotional Comics section; to Bill Blackbeard of the San Francisco Academy of Comic Art for his Platinum Age cover photos; to Bill Spicer and Zetta DeVoe (Western Publishing Co.) for their contribution of data; and especially to Bill for his kind permission to reprint portions of his and Jerry Bails' America's Four Color Pastime.

Special Recognition is due Bob Beerbohm and Doug Wheeler who spent months researching the Platinum and Victorian Sections in this edition. Bob organized a team of experts from around the world who sent him detailed data for updating this section. My hat is off to Bob and his colleagues for a job well done.

Acknowledgement is also due to the following people who generously contributed much needed data for this edition: Mark Arnold, John Aston, Stephen Baer, Jonathan Bennett, Mike Bromberg, Dr. Bruce C. Brumfield, Chris Boyko, Jonathan Calure, Reggie Conner, Bob Conway, Matthew Hawes, Greg Holland, John M. Jackson, Bradley Keen, Dan Lega, Rod Matlack, Rick McQuaig, David Pascoe, Jeremy Patrick, Schultz Riggs, Robert J. Simpson, T. L. Steed, Mark Squirek, Jeff Walker, Bob Wayne, Mike Wilbur and Stanley Wong.

Finally, special credit is due our talented production staff for their assistance with this edition; to Arnold T. Blumberg (Editor), Brenda Busick (Creative Director), Mark Huesman (Production Coordinator), Tom Gordon (Managing Editor), Jamie David (Office Manager), Sara Ortt (Assistant Office Manager) and Stacia Brown (Editorial Coordinator), as well as to our Executive Editor, J.C. Vaughn, for their valuable contributions to this edition. Thanks to my wife, Caroline, for her encouragement and support on such a tremendous project, and to all who placed ads in this edition.

Comics Guaranty. The technical grade applied to each comic book has now become the standard used for buying and selling."

(Robert M. Overstreet, Overstreet Price Guide, 32nd Edition)

Benefits of CGC Grading

▲ **CGC has an Established and Trusted Grading Standard.** CGC's grading team includes the most experienced and recognized experts in the field.

▲ **CGC provides an Expert restoration check for each book submitted.** When detected, restoration is noted on CGC's purple label.

▲ **Better Protection for your Comic Books.** The CGC holder is made with state-of-the-art materials and is designed to meet the needs and demands of comic book collectors.

▲ **Holder can be Safely Opened.** The CGC holder is designed to allow optimal visibility of the comic book, while still keeping it safe from the elements. It can be opened carefully, allowing safe removal. We strongly recommend you call for instructions on the proper way to open the CGC holder. Due to the fragile nature of comic books, we also recommend immediate recertification.

▲ **Access to the Message Boards.** Talk to the experts and collectors who have similar interests to yours. Do you have a question about a rare piece? Ever wondered who's collecting what? Maybe you want to share a bit of interesting information? Speak out on the Message Boards, get your answers and become a more knowledgeable collector today!

▲ **Access to the Comic Population Reports.** A comprehensive database that lists submitted items graded by our companies. Watch for the updates and see the trends shift week-by-week.

For information on submitting your comic books call us or visit our website at CGCcomics.com!

1-877-NM-COMIC • P.O. Box 4738 • Sarasota, FL 34230 • fax 941-360-2558 • www.CGCcomics.com

12¢
the AMAZING SPIDER-MAN
1 MAR.
2 GREAT FEATURE-LENGTH SPIDER-MAN THRILLERS!
THE FANTASTIC FOUR THINK I'M TRAPPED! BUT THEY DON'T SUSPECT MY REAL POWER!
No. 1
JUNE, 1938
ACTION COMICS
10¢

12¢
THE INCREDIBLE HULK
1 MAY
THE STRANGEST MAN OF ALL TIME!!
IS HE MAN OR MONSTER OR... IS HE BOTH
FANTASY AS YOU LIKE IT!
NO. 16
Introducing THE GREEN LANTERN!

No. 27
64 PAGES OF ACTION!
Detective COMICS

STARTING THIS ISSUE: THE AMAZING AND UNIQUE ADVENTURES OF THE BATMAN!

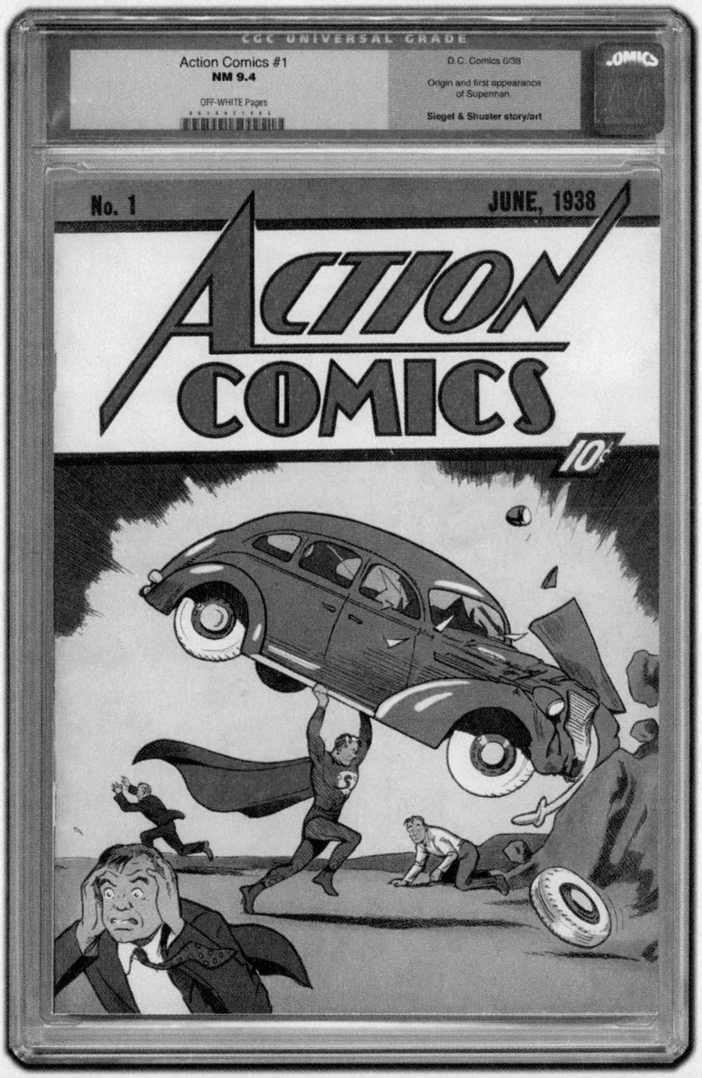

© DC
Jay Parrino's
The
MINT
L.L.C.
The Rarest and The Finest
Post Office Drawer 9326 • Kansas City, MO 64133
(816) 373-7744 Fax
www.jp-themint.com • info@jp-themint.com

GREEN
...IS ALL YOU WILL SEE WHEN YOU
BRING YOUR COMICS TO YEE!
• Over 15 years of Experience as One the Top Dealers in the Industry.
• Senior Advisor to the Overstreet Comic Book Price Guide.
• We will Travel Anywhere to view your comics.
• No Collection is too Small or too Large for Our Attention.
• Highest Prices Paid and Immediate Cash Available.
• Courteous Prompt and Professional Service.
• Complete Customer Satisfaction
• Accurate Grading and Competitive Pricing.
© Marvel
HARLEY YEE
P.O. Box #51758
Livonia, MI
48151-5758 USA
(800) 731-1029 or
(734) 421-7921
(734) 421-7928 Fax
Cash in the Hand is Quite Grand
www.HarleyYeeComics.com • HarleyComx@aol.com
Call, email or write us for a Free Catalog

The Southeast's Coolest Shop
HEROES AND DRAGONS .COM
BUYING
LOTS OF COMICS
Woder Women ©DC Comics 2004
Paying SUPER sums for Gold & Silver Age, ALL grades and titles, through 1970.
Now purchasing collections, store/convention stock, and bulk comics from 1970 to today.
Have cash, will travel anywhere to make offers on large and/or quality collections.
Be assured, all transactions are handled reliably and with the utmost professionalism.
1-803-731-4376
Batman symbol © DC Comics 2004
Spider-man © Marvel Comics 2004

HEROES
AND
DRAGONS
.COM

Walt Disney's
DONALD DUCK
ADVENTURES
1
BIG
Disney
Thrills
in a Small
package
Walt Disney's
DONALD DUCK
ADVENTURES
2
3
Walt Disney's
DONALD DUCK
ADVENTURES
Sometimes the most excitement takes up the least amount of space. That's certainly the case with *Donald Duck Adventures*, the first of Gemstone Publishing's squarebound "Take-Along" comic books, published bimonthly.
©2004 Disney Enterprises, Inc.

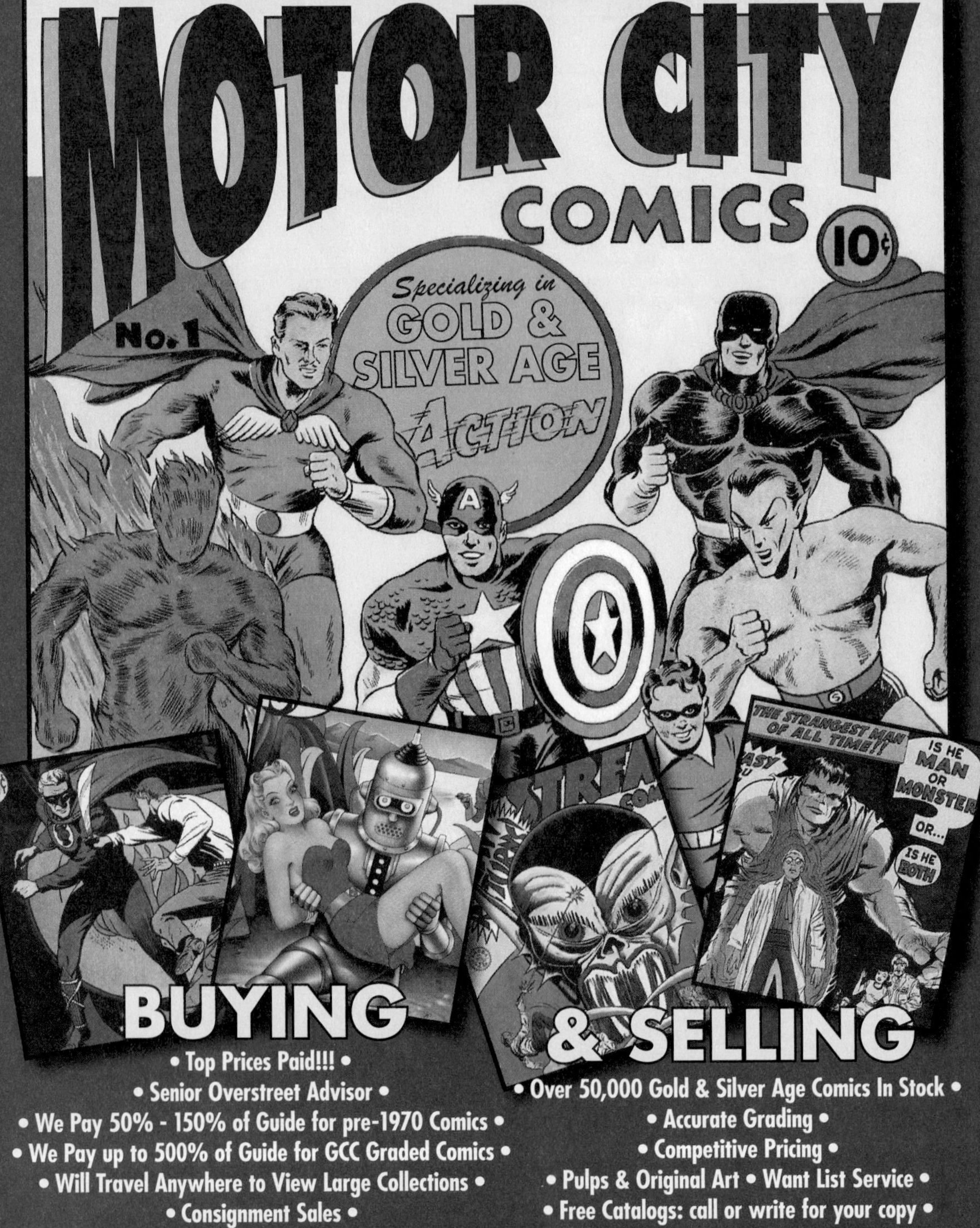
MOTOR CITY
COMICS
10¢
No. 1
Specializing in
GOLD &
SILVER AGE
ACTION
THE STRANGEST MAN OF ALL TIME!!
IS HE MAN OR MONSTER OR...
IS HE BOTH
BUYING
• Top Prices Paid!!! •
• Senior Overstreet Advisor •
• We Pay 50% - 150% of Guide for pre-1970 Comics •
• We Pay up to 500% of Guide for GCC Graded Comics •
• Will Travel Anywhere to View Large Collections •
• Consignment Sales •
& SELLING
• Over 50,000 Gold & Silver Age Comics In Stock •
• Accurate Grading •
• Competitive Pricing •
• Pulps & Original Art • Want List Service •
• Free Catalogs: call or write for your copy •

FLIPPABLE! FACTUAL! FUNCTIONAL!

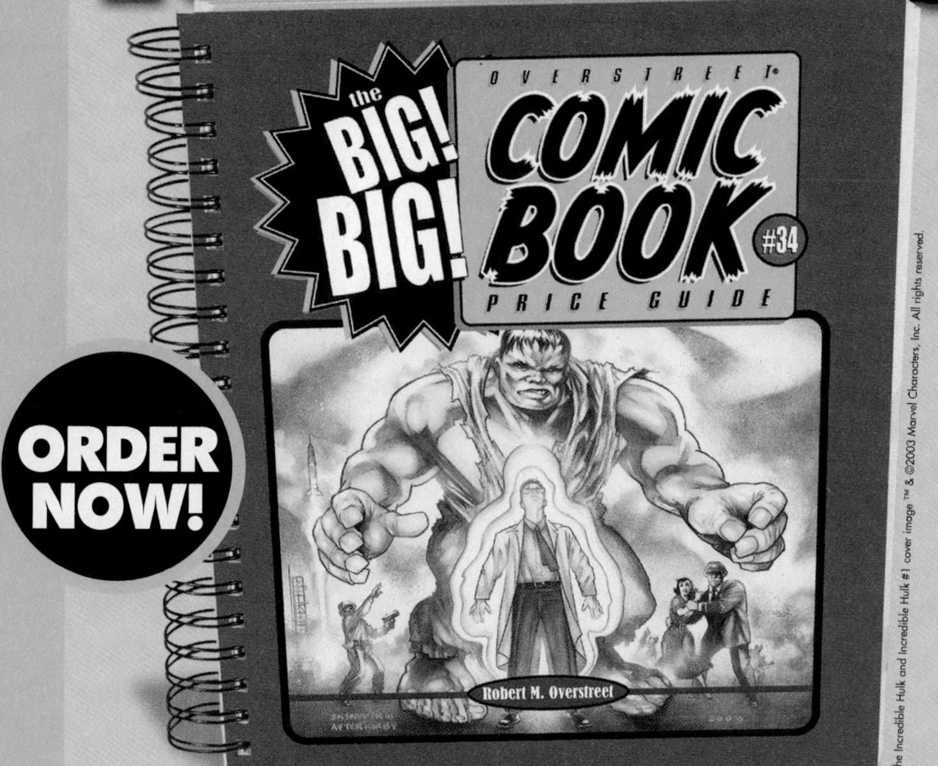

It's ***The Official Overstreet Comic Book Price Guide #34*** in a special limited edition! Featuring a stunning re-creation of Jack Kirby's cover for *Incredible Hulk* #1 by John K. Snyder III (*Green Lantern: Brightest Day/Darkest Night*), this edition contains only the pricing, Top Ten charts, selected glossary and text from the regular edition of the *Guide*.

SPECIAL FEATURES

Stay-Flat Spiral Binding ▼ Larger Print ▼ Room For Notes ▼ A Must For Serious Collectors

Call Sara at 888-375-9800 ext. 410 to order!

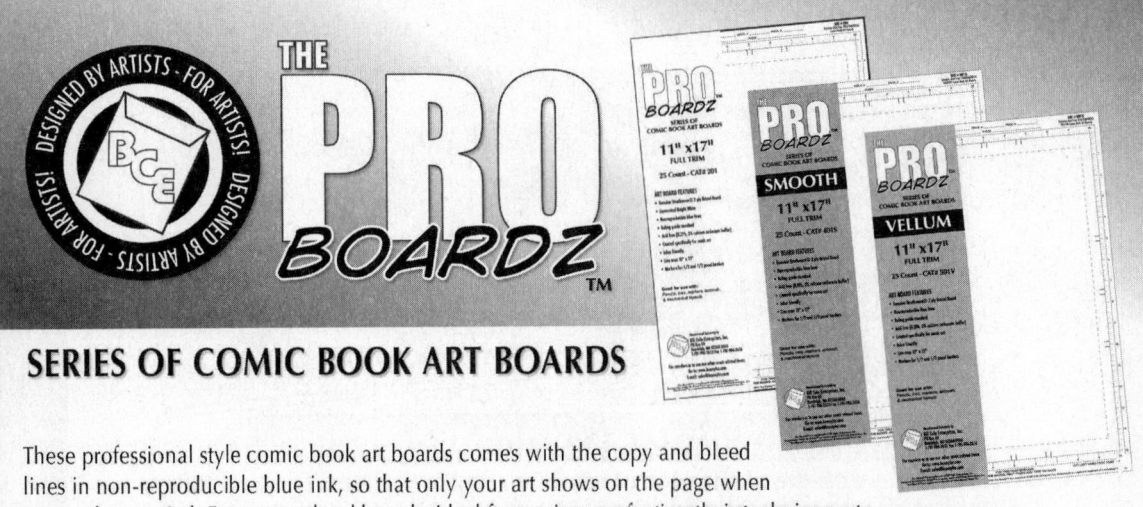

RUSS COCHRAN'S COMIC ART AUCTION

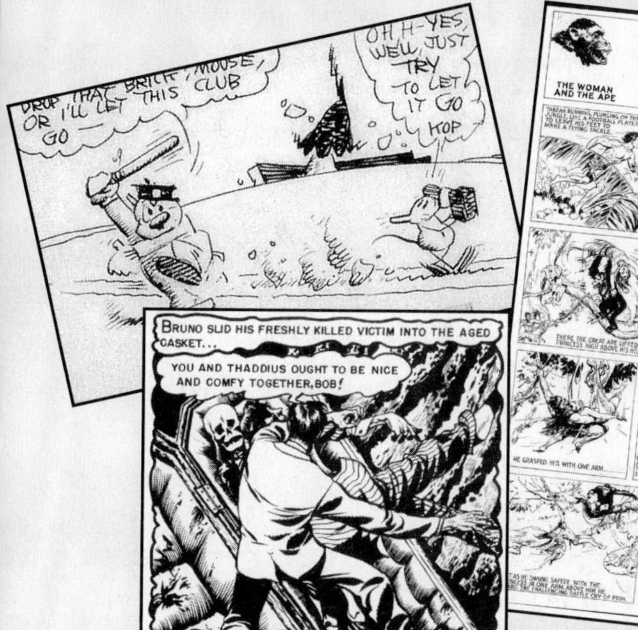

Russ Cochran's Comic Art Auction

started in 1973 with the publication of his illustrated art catalog, Graphic Gallery. Soon after that, it became the main source of comic strip and comic book art, as well as paintings by Carl Barks and Frank Frazetta. It is safe to say that Russ Cochran sold more Barks and Frazetta paintings than all the other dealers in comic art combined.

At the same time, auctions were being held for the EC original art, all of which passed through Russ's Comic Art Auction. Dozens of important originals by Hal Foster, Alex Raymond, George Herriman, George McManus, Milton Caniff, and virtually every comic artist have passed through the pages of this auction catalog, finding their way to comic art collections all over the western world.

In all, a total of 13 issues of Graphic Gallery were published, and to date, 67 issues of the Comic Art Auction.

If you are a collector of comic art, or if you have art to consign, contact

Russ Cochran at
1-800-EC CRYPT, or at
cruss@gemstonepub.com

Buying & Sell

SILVER STREAK COMICS
DAREDEVIL BATTLES CLAW
10c
SHADOW COMICS
10¢
THE SHADOW FINDS
The Ghost-Guarded Treasure of the Haunted Glen Proving
"Crime Does Not Pay"
BLUE BOLT
JUNE
10¢
BLUE BOLT
SUB-ZERO MAN
SERGEANT SPOOK
SUPERHORSE
PHANTOM SUB
DICK COLE
And Others
THE GREEN HORNET
See 'em MOVE just flip the pages
CRACKS DOWN
HOWDY DOODY comics
10c
HOWDINI
No. 1
JOE PALOOKA
10c
JOE PALOOKA!
Thrilling...Humorous Entertaining!
DELL
12¢
K.A.O.S. CAPTURES MAXWELL SMART...
THEY GAVE HIM BACK...
"SORRY ABOUT THAT CHIEF!"

ing!
TALES TO ASTONISH
ANT-MAN BECOMES GIANT MAN
THE LIVING ERASER!
GNEY
ERIDAN
CITY FOR CONQUEST
FRANK CRAVEN
DONALD CRISP
FRANK McHUGH
ARTHUR KENNEDY
WARNER BROS.
No. 30
ACTION COMICS
NOV.
10¢
DIAMOND
INTERNATIONAL GALLERIES

Introduction: About This Book

Welcome to the hobby of comic book collecting! This book, now in its 34rd consecutive year of publication, remains the most comprehensive reference work available on comic book pricing and history, and is respected and used by dealers and collectors everywhere. The Overstreet pricing and grading standards are the accepted foundations of the comic book marketplace around the world, and we have not earned this privilege easily. Through hard work, diligence and constant contact with the market for decades, Overstreet has become the most trusted name in comics.

How To Use This Book

This volume is a detailed alphabetical list of comic books and their market values. Comic books are listed by title, regardless of company. Prices listed are shown in Good, Very Good, Fine, Very Fine, Very Fine/Near Mint, and Near Mint condition. The older true Mint books usually bring a premium over the Near Mint price. Books in Fair bring 50 to 70% of the Good price. Some books only show a Very Fine price as the highest grade. The author has not been able to determine if these particular books exist in better than Very Fine condition, thus the omission of a Near Mint price.

Many of the comic books are listed in groups, i.e., 11-20, 21-30, 31-50, etc. The prices listed opposite these groupings represent the value of each issue in that group. More detailed information is given for individual comic books where warranted, such as publication dates, creators, and significant story and/or character notations.

This book also contains hundreds of advertisements covering all aspects of this hobby. Whether you are buying or selling, the advertising sections can be of tremendous benefit to you.

IMPORTANT: When pricing your books, keep in mind that over 90% of existing older comic books are in the good to fine range. Do not automatically jump to the conclusion that your books are worth the NM price listed before first trying to accurately grade the collection.

New Comic Books

This book lists all new comic books at cover price, regardless of their performance in the secondary market. In many cases, new comics are not worth their cover price in the secondary market, and collectors may pay pennies on the dollar for copies of these issues. Nevertheless, since these comics have yet to establish themselves as collectors' items, they are listed at full cover price. It should also be noted that regarding polybagged comics, it is the official policy of **The Overstreet Comic Book Price Guide** to grade comics regardless of whether they are still sealed in their polybag or not. If opened, the polybag and its contents should be preserved separately so that all components of the original package remain together.

Comic Book Values

It is important to understand that values listed in this book are approximations or guidelines, presenting an average range of what one might expect to pay for the corresponding items. This listing acknowledges but in no way can determine the final effect of regional differences, differences in condition, rarity and/or demand. In the marketplace, buyers and sellers determine prices asked and prices paid. This is not a price list of items for sale or items wanted by the author or publisher, and neither the author nor the publisher shall be held responsible for losses that may occur in the purchase, sale or other transaction of property because of information contained herein.

With input from a network of experienced advisors including well established collectors, dealers and historians of popular culture, we have undertaken significant effort to assemble this pricing information. The resulting listings come through the observation and documentation of prices realized through hobby and trade shows, catalog sales, retail sales, and Internet, live and mail-in auctions. Documented personal sales may also be included. We have earned our reputation for our cautious, conservative approach to pricing. We are proud of that reputation and our track record, and we actively encourage readers who believe they have discovered an error to mail related information to the author, Robert M. Overstreet, Gemstone Publishing, Inc., 1966 Greenspring Drive, Timonium, MD 21093. Verified corrections will be incorporated into future editions of this book.

How Comics Are Listed

Comic books are listed alphabetically by title. The true title of a comic book can usually be found listed with the publisher's information, or indicia, often found at the bottom of the first page. Titles that appear on the front cover can vary from the official title listed inside.

Comic book titles, sequence of issues, dates of first and last issues, publishing companies, origin and special issues are listed when known. Prominent and collectible artists are also pointed out (usually in footnotes). Page counts will always include covers. Most comic books began with a #1, but occasionally many titles began with an odd number. There is a reason for this - publishers had to register new titles with the post office for 2nd class permits, but the registration fee was expensive. To avoid this expense, many publishers would continue the numbering of new titles from old defunct series. For instance, EC Comics' **Weird Science** #12 (1st issue) was continued from the defunct **Saddle Romances** #11 (the last issue). In doing this, the publishers hoped to avoid having to register new titles. However, the post office would soon discover the new title and force the publisher to pay the registration fee as well as to list the correct number. For instance, **Weird Science** continued from #12 through #15. Issue #5 followed after the Post Office correction. Now the sequence of published issues (see the listings) is #12-15, #5-on. This created a problem in early fandom for the collector because the issue numbers #12-15 in this title were duplicated. This Guide offers a roadmap to these sometimes confusing twists and turns in the publishing history of many comic book series.

What Comics Are Listed

The Guide lists primarily American comic books due to space limitations. The earliest verifiable comic books date back to 1828; comics predating the Golden Age and the birth of the comic book in its most familiar physical form in the 1930s are listed in their own sections under the Victorian And Platinum Ages. Prior to that, we list a wide variety of promotional, giveaway and premium comics in a section of their own. Finally, the main alphabetical listings of the book are comprised of comic books released between 1938 and the present.

New Comic Listings

Every effort is made to incorporate as many new comics into this Guide as possible during the course of a given year. Unfortunately, not all comics released each year may be listed in this book for reasons of space limitation or even the human error of simple oversight. We attempt to list complete information wherever possible, and we encourage readers to contact us with any information that may enhance the accuracy of our listings. We're also interested in review copies of any new comic books that are published.

Grading

Comic book grading has evolved over the past several decades from a much looser interpretation of standards in the beginning to the very tight professional scrutiny in use by the market today. In recent years, grading criteria have become even tighter, especially in Silver and Bronze Age books, due to their higher survival rate.

Several events have impacted grading over the years. The first has to be the arrival of comic book conventions. Here, collectors could easily compare and discuss grading with dealers. The second major event was the discovery of the Mile High collection in 1977, which showed fandom true NM/MT Golden Age books.

Probably the most important event to date, however, was the arrival of comic book certification with Comics Guaranty, LLC (CGC), which has transformed much of the industry and introduced many die-hard and casual collectors alike to the subtle distinctions involved in grading comic books.

This year, the release of the all-new second edition of **The Official Overstreet Comic Book Grading Guide** has re-established Gemstone as the purveyors of a grading standard embraced by the vast majority of the comic book collecting community. The Overstreet standards, long relied upon by collectors from the professional to the casual level, describe a method for evaluating the condition of all comic books from the Victorian through the Modern Age.

However, there are a group of special books, known as "pedigrees," that have high cover gloss, brilliant cover inks and white, fresh, supple pages that place them far above other books that might receive the same technical grade. Books from these pedigree collections actually transcend their technical grade. Of these, many collectors and dealers agree that the most important collections are the Mile High (Edgar Church) collection, the San Francisco (Reilly) collection, and the Gaines file copies. They are the most sought after and generally the most well-documented, making it easier to ascertain identity or provenance. Books from these collections all exhibit the extra qualities mentioned above.

This striking difference becomes apparent when comparing two comic books of the same grade, one pedigree and one generic. In most cases, the pedigree book will far outshine the generic one. This is the reason why Mile Highs, San Franciscos and Gaines file copies bring multiples of Guide. Many also agree that a book from one of these collections could very well be one of, if not the, best surviving copies.

To the beginner, it may seem odd that a 9.2 Mile High will bring a higher price than a non-pedigree 9.4, but to the seasoned collector with a good understanding of the hobby and its historical background, it makes perfect sense. The novice collector should understand these facts and acquire as much knowledge as possible about all the other pedigree collections and their place in the market before paying large multiples of Guide for books that are not of pedigree quality.

For much more information on grading and restoration, as well as full-color photographs of many major defects and conditions, consult **The Official Overstreet Comic Book Grading Guide**. Copies are available through all normal distribution channels or can be ordered direct from Gemstone by sending $24 plus $4 postage and handling. You can also call Gemstone toll free at 1-888-375-9800.

How To Grade

Before a comic book's true value can be assessed, its condition or state of preservation must be determined. In all cases, the better the condition of the comic, the more desirable and valuable the book will be. Comic books in Mint condition will bring several times the price of the same book in Poor condition. Therefore, it is very important to be able to properly grade your books. Comics should be graded from the exterior (the covers) to the interior (the pages) and thoroughly examined before assigning a final grade.

Carefully remove the comic from its plastic bag or Mylar sleeve (if it's stored in one), and lay the comic down on a flat, clean surface. Under normal incandescent lighting, examine the exterior of the comic from front to back, identifying any defects, loss of cover reflectivity or other significant attributes. Check the spine for rusted staples, stress lines, tears, and spine roll.

Check to make sure that the centerfold and all interior pages are still present. The whiteness level of the pages is of major importance in determining the final grade as well. Locate and identify interior defects such as chipping, flaking, possible brittleness, and other flaws.

After all the above steps have been taken, then the collector can begin to consider an overall grade for his or her book, which may range from absolutely perfect Gem Mint condition to Poor, where a comic is extremely worn, dirty and even falling apart.

Numerous variables influence the evaluation of a comic book's condition and all must be considered in the final determination of a grade. Although the grade of a comic book is based upon an accumulation of defects, some defects may be more extreme for a particular grade as long as other acceptable listed defects are absent or less severe. As grading is the most subjective aspect of determining a comic's value - more of an art than a science - it is very important for the grader to take care not to allow wishful thinking to influence what the choice of grade. It is also very important to realize that older comics in Mint condition are extremely scarce and are rarely advertised for sale; most of the higher grade comics advertised range from Very Fine to Near Mint.

GRADING DEFINITIONS

10.0 GEM MINT (GM): An exceptional example of a given book - the best ever seen. Only the slightest bindery or printing defects are allowed. Cover is flat with no surface wear. Inks are bright with high reflectivity. Corners are cut square and sharp. Spine is tight and flat. Staples must be original, centered and clean with no rust. Paper is white, supple and fresh. No interior autographs or owner signatures.

9.9 MINT (MT): Near perfect in every way. Only subtle bindery or printing defects are allowed. Cover is flat with no surface wear. Inks are bright with high reflectivity and minimal fading. Corners are cut square and sharp. Small, inconspicuous, lightly penciled, stamped or inked arrival dates are acceptable as long as they are in an unobtrusive location. Spine is tight and flat. Staples must be original, generally centered and clean with no rust. Paper is white, supple and fresh.

9.8 NEAR MINT/MINT (NM/MT): Nearly perfect in every way with only minor imperfections that keep it from the next higher grade. Only subtle bindery or printing defects are allowed. Cover is flat with no surface wear. Inks are bright with high reflectivity and minimal fading. Corners are cut square and sharp. Small, inconspicuous, lightly penciled, stamped or inked arrival dates are acceptable as long as they are in an unobtrusive location. Spine is tight and flat. Staples must be original, generally centered and clean with no rust. Paper is white, supple and fresh. Only the slightest interior tears are allowed.

9.6 NEAR MINT+ (NM+): Nearly perfect with a minor additional virtue or virtues that raise it from Near Mint. Only subtle bindery or printing defects are allowed. No bindery tears are allowed, although on Golden Age books bindery tears of up to 1/8" have been noted. Cover is flat with no surface wear. Inks are bright with high reflectivity and a minimum of fading. One corner may be almost imperceptibly blunted, but still almost sharp and cut square. Almost imperceptible indentations are permissible, but no creases, bends, or color break. Small, inconspicuous, lightly penciled, stamped or inked arrival dates are acceptable as long as they are in an unobtrusive location. Spine is tight and flat. Staples must be original, generally centered, with only the slightest discoloration. Paper is off-white, supple and fresh. Only the slightest interior tears are allowed.

9.4 NEAR MINT (NM): Nearly perfect with only minor imperfections that keep it from the next higher grade. Subtle bindery/printing defects are allowed. Bindery tears must be less than 1/16" on Silver Age and later books, although on Golden Age books bindery tears of up to 1/4" have been noted. Cover is flat with no surface wear. Inks are bright with high reflectivity and a minimum of fading. Corners are cut square and sharp with ever-so-slight blunting permitted. A 1/16" bend is permitted with no color break. Small, inconspicuous, lightly penciled, stamped or inked arrival dates are acceptable as long as they are in an unobtrusive location. Slight foxing. Spine is tight and flat. Staples are generally centered; may have slight discoloration. Almost no stress lines. Paper is off-white to cream, supple and fresh. Slight interior tears are allowed.

9.2 NEAR MINT– (NM–): Nearly perfect with only a minor additional defect or defects that keep it from Near Mint. A limited number of minor bindery/printing defects are allowed. Cover is flat with no surface wear. Inks are bright with only the slightest dimming of reflectivity. Corners are cut square and sharp with ever-so-slight blunting permitted. A 1/16-1/8" bend is permitted with no color break. Small, inconspicuous, lightly penciled, stamped or inked arrival dates are acceptable as long as they are in an unobtrusive location. Slight foxing. Spine is tight and flat. Staples may show some discoloration. Almost no stress lines. Paper is off-white to cream, supple and fresh. Slight interior tears are allowed.

9.0 VERY FINE/NEAR MINT (VF/NM): Nearly perfect with outstanding eye appeal. A limited number of bindery/printing defects are allowed. Cover is almost flat with almost imperceptible wear. Inks are bright with slightly diminished reflectivity. An 1/8" bend is allowed if color is not broken. Corners are cut square and sharp with ever-so-slight blunting permitted but no creases. Several lightly penciled, stamped or inked arrival dates are acceptable. Very minor foxing. Spine is tight and flat. Staples may show some discoloration. Only the slightest staple tears are allowed. A very minor accumulation of stress lines may be present if they are nearly imperceptible. Paper is off-white to cream and supple. Very minor interior tears may be present.

8.5 VERY FINE+ (VF+): Fits the criteria for Very Fine but with an additional virtue or small accumulation of virtues that improves the book's appearance by a perceptible amount.

8.0 VERY FINE (VF): An excellent copy with outstanding eye appeal. A limited accumulation of minor bindery/printing defects is allowed. Cover is relatively flat with minimal surface wear beginning to show, possibly including some minute wear at corners. Inks are generally bright with moderate to high reflectivity. An unnoticeable 1/4" crease is acceptable if color is not broken. Stamped or inked arrival dates may be present. Minor foxing. Spine is almost completely flat with a possible minor color break. Staples may show some discoloration. Very slight staple tears and a few almost insignificant stress lines may be present. Paper is cream to tan and supple. Centerfold is mostly secure. Minor interior tears at the margin may be present.

7.5 VERY FINE– (VF–): Fits the criteria for Very Fine but with an additional defect or small accumulation of defects that detracts from the book's appearance by a perceptible amount.

7.0 FINE/VERY FINE (FN/VF): An above-average copy that shows minor wear but is still relatively flat and clean with outstanding eye appeal. A small accumulation of minor bindery/printing defects is allowed. Minor cover wear beginning to show, possibly including minor creases. Corners may be blunted. Inks are generally bright with a moderate reduction in reflectivity. Stamped or inked arrival dates may be present. Minor foxing. The slightest spine roll may be present, as well as a possible moderate color break. Staples may show some discoloration. Slight staple tears and a small accumulation of light stress lines may be present. Slight rust migration. Paper is cream to tan. Centerfold is mostly secure. Minor interior tears at the margin may be present.

6.5 FINE+ (FN+): Fits the criteria for Fine but with an additional virtue or small accumulation of virtues that improves the book's appearance by a perceptible amount.

6.0 FINE (FN): An above-average copy that shows minor wear but is still relatively flat and clean with no significant creasing or other serious defects. Some accumulation of minor bindery/printing defects is allowed. Minor cover wear apparent, with minor to moderate creases. Inks show a significant reduction in reflectivity. Blunted corners are more common, as is minor staining, soiling, discoloration, and/or foxing. Stamped or inked arrival dates may be present. A minor spine roll is allowed. There can also be a 1/4" spine split or severe color break. Staples may show minor discoloration. Minor staple tears and a few slight stress lines may be present, as well as minor rust migration. Paper is tan to brown and fairly supple with no signs of brittleness. Minor interior tears at the margin may be present. Centerfold may be loose.

5.5 FINE– (FN–): Fits the criteria for Fine but with an additional defect or small accumulation of defects that detracts from the book's appearance by a perceptible amount.

5.0 VERY GOOD/FINE (VG/FN): An above-average but well-used comic book. An accumulation of bindery/printing defects is

10.0	GM	Gem Mint	
9.9		MT	Mint
9.8		NM/MT	Near Mint/Mint
9.6		NM+	Near Mint+
9.4		NM	Near Mint
9.2		NM-	Near Mint-
9.0		VF/NM	Very Fine/Near Mint
8.5		VF+	Very Fine+
8.0		VF	Very Fine
7.5		VF-	Very Fine-
7.0		FN/VF	Fine/Very Fine
6.5		FN+	Fine+
6.0		FN	Fine
5.5		FN-	Fine-
5.0		VG/FN	Very Good/Fine
4.5		VG+	Very Good+
4.0		VG	Very Good
3.5		VG-	Very Good-
3.0		GD/VG	Good/Very Good
2.5		GD+	Good+
2.0		GD	Good
1.8		GD-	Good-
1.5		FR/GD	Fair/Good
1.0		FR	Fair

allowed. Minor to moderate cover wear apparent, with minor to moderate creases and/or dimples. Inks have moderate to low reflectivity. Blunted corners are increasingly common, as is minor to moderate staining, discoloration, and/or foxing. Stamped or inked arrival dates may be present. A minor to moderate spine roll is allowed. A spine split of up to 1/2" may be present. Staples may show minor discoloration. Minor staple tears and minor stress lines may also be present, as well as minor rust migration. Paper is tan to brown with no signs of brittleness. Centerfold may be loose. Minor interior tears may also be present.

4.5 VERY GOOD+ (VG): Fits the criteria for Very Good but with an additional virtue or small accumulation of virtues that improves the book's appearance by a perceptible amount.

4.0 VERY GOOD (VG): The average used comic book. Cover shows moderate to significant wear, and may be loose but not completely detached. Cover reflectivity is low. Can have moderate creases or dimples. Corners may be blunted. Store stamps, name stamps, arrival dates, initials, etc. have no effect on this grade. Some discoloration, fading, foxing, and even minor soiling is allowed. As much as a 1/4" triangle can be missing out of the corner or edge; a missing 1/8" square is also acceptable. Only minor unobtrusive tape and other amateur repair allowed on otherwise high grade copies. Moderate spine roll may be present and/or a 1" spine split. Staples may be discolored. Minor to moderate staple tears and stress lines may be present, as well as some rust migration. Paper is brown but not brittle. Minor to moderate interior tears may be present. Centerfold may be loose or detached at one staple.

3.5 VERY GOOD– (VG–): Fits the criteria for Very Good but with an additional defect or small accumulation of defects that detracts from the book's appearance by a perceptible amount.

3.0 GOOD/VERY GOOD (GD/VG): A used comic book showing some substantial wear. Cover shows significant wear, and may be loose or even detached at one staple. Cover reflectivity is very low. Can have a book-length crease and/or dimples. Corners may be blunted or even rounded. Discoloration, fading, foxing, and even minor to moderate soiling is allowed. A triangle from 1/4" to 1/2" can be missing out of the corner or edge; a missing 1/8" to 1/4" square is also acceptable. Tape and other amateur repair may be present. Moderate spine roll likely. May have a spine split of anywhere from 1" to 1-1/2". Staples may be rusted or replaced. Minor to moderate staple tears and moderate stress lines may be present, as well as some rust migration. Paper is brown but not brittle. Centerfold may be loose or detached at one staple. Minor to moderate interior tears may be present.

2.5 GOOD+ (GD+): Fits the criteria for Good but with an additional virtue or small accumulation of virtues that improves the book's appearance by a perceptible amount.

2.0 GOOD (GD): Shows substantial wear; often considered a "reading copy." Cover shows significant wear and may even be detached. Cover reflectivity is low and in some cases completely absent. Book-length creases and dimples may be present. Rounded corners are more common. Moderate soiling, staining, discoloration and foxing may be present. The largest piece allowed missing from the front or back cover is usually a 1/2" triangle or a 1/4" square, although some Silver Age books such as 1960s Marvels have had the price corner box clipped from the top left front cover and may be considered Good if they would otherwise have graded higher. Tape and other forms of amateur repair are common in Silver Age and older books. Spine roll is likely. May have up to a 2" spine split. Staples may be degraded, replaced or missing. Moderate staple tears and stress lines may be present, as well as rust migration. Paper is brown but not brittle. Centerfold may be loose or detached. Moderate interior tears may be present.

1.8 GOOD– (GD–): Fits the criteria for Good but with an additional defect or small accumulation of defects that detracts from the book's appearance by a perceptible amount.

1.5 FAIR/GOOD (FR/GD): Shows substantial to heavy wear. Books in this grade are commonly creased, scuffed, abraded, soiled, and possibly unattractive, but still generally readable. Cover shows considerable wear and may be detached. Almost no cover reflectivity remaining. Book-length creases, tears and folds may be present. Rounded corners are increasingly common. Soiling, staining, discoloration and foxing is generally present. Up to 1/10 of the back cover may be missing. Tape and other forms of amateur repair are increasingly common in Silver Age and older books. Spine roll is common. May have a spine split between 2" and 2/3 the length of the book. Staples may be degraded, replaced or missing. Staple tears and stress lines are common, as well as rust migration. Paper is brown and may show brittleness around the edges. Acidic odor may be present. Centerfold may be loose or detached. Interior tears are common.

1.0 FAIR (FR): Shows heavy wear. Some collectors consider this the lowest collectible grade because comic books in lesser condition are usually incomplete and/or brittle. Cover may be detached, and inks have lost all reflectivity. Creases, tears and/or folds are prevalent. Corners are commonly rounded or absent. Soiling and staining is present. Books in this condition generally have all pages and most of the covers, although there may be up to 1/4 of the front cover missing or no back cover, but not both. Tape and other forms of amateur repair are more common. Spine roll is more common; spine split can extend up to 2/3 the length of the book. Staples may be missing or show rust and discoloration. An accumulation of staple tears and stress lines may be present, as well as rust migration. Paper is brown and may show brittleness around the edges but not in the central portion of the pages. Acidic odor may be present. Accumulation of interior tears. Chunks may be missing. The centerfold may be missing if readability is generally preserved. Coupons may be cut.

0.5 POOR (PR): Sufficiently degraded to the point where there is little or no collector value; easily identified by a complete absence of eye appeal. Brittle almost to the point of turning to dust with a touch, and usually incomplete. Extreme fading may render the cover almost indiscernible. May have extremely severe stains, mildew or heavy cover abrasion to the point that some cover inks are indistinct/absent. Covers may be detached with large chunks missing. Can have extremely ragged edges and extensive creasing. Corners are rounded or virtually absent. Covers may have been defaced with paints, varnishes, glues, oil, indelible markers or dyes, and may have suffered heavy water damage. Can also have extensive amateur repairs such as laminated covers. Extreme spine roll present; can have extremely ragged spines or a complete, book-length split. Staples can be missing or show extreme rust and discoloration. Extensive staple tears and stress lines may be present, as well as extreme rust migration. Paper exhibits moderate to severe brittleness (where the comic book literally falls apart when examined). Extreme acidic odor may be present. Extensive interior tears. Multiple pages, including the centerfold, may be missing that affect readability. Coupons may be cut.

COVERLESS COMICS: The exception to the "not collectible in Poor" rule. Many collectors want clean, readable, coverless comics that are priced fairly. Coverless copies of key and/or rare comics are often in demand by collectors. These enthusiasts also seek coverless comics to retrieve centerfolds, first wraparounds, coupons and even staples in order to restore other copies of the same or a similar incomplete comic.

INCOMPLETE/UNCOLLECTABLE: At the very bottom of the range, comics with the absolute maximum number of defects, heavy degradation, and significant portions of the book missing might not even be considered Poor any longer, but may be termed "incomplete." These books are so ruined as to be rendered unreadable and virtually uncollectable.

Dust Jackets

Many of the early strip reprint comics, as well as many modern graphic novels and collections, were published with hard covers and dust jackets, which can also suffer damage common to comic book covers and may even be absent on some copies if removed by a previous owner or lost. The condition of the dust jacket should be graded independently of the book. Books with dust jackets are worth more. The value can increase from 20 to 50 percent depending on the rarity of book. Usually, the earlier the book, the greater the percentage. Unless noted, prices listed are without dust jackets.

Restored Comics - Update for 2004 by Matt Nelson

The Market for Restored Comics

Professional restoration became a legitimate enterprise in the 1970s, but was initially ignored as a profit tool and was used mainly by collectors who wished to make their comics look as perfect as possible. There was no consideration given to candidacy or the effect on value.

Restoration reached a fever pitch in the '80s and early '90s, evidenced by the increasing number of comics being restored and the high prices paid for them regardless of the extent and quality of work. The resultant profit made it an extremely lucrative business, but one critical factor was missing; full disclosure was largely ignored, and many buyers were deceived into buying books under the false pretense that they were unrestored or restored to a lesser degree. As a result, restoration developed a tarnished image by the end of the decade.

With the advent of independent grading (CGC) in 2000, collectors' trust began to build again, although bloated prices of the '90s still lingered. The market has seen an adjustment of restored values since then, eliminating the large profit margins enjoyed in the prior years. This has proven essential to re-establishing a strong market, because restoration should not be viewed strictly as a money-making device but as a way to preserve our treasures for future generations.

Understanding a Restored Grade

Currently there are three factors involved when grading a restored comic. They are: A. Apparent Grade; B. Extent of Restoration (Slight, Moderate, Extensive); C. Quality of Work (Amateur or Professional)

A. Apparent Grade: No two restored comics are alike. Technically speaking, a fully restored comic should be NM, because the book exhibits no tears, missing pieces, spine splits, tape, or loose centerfolds. All defects have been repaired, and yet each restored book can receive a different "apparent" grade. Two factors contribute to this: the prior grade of the book and the quality of restoration.

The lower a book's grade, the more restoration will be required, and the less chance it has to restore to a high grade. Some defects cannot be completely repaired and made invisible, such as creases, stains and writing. This is one reason why a fully restored comic may only grade as high as a Fine.

Another measurement used to determine grade is the quality of work. Color touch is the best indicator of quality, followed by piece replacement and cleaning. What most determines grade when evaluating restored comics is the "feel"; the closer a restored comic feels to an unrestored copy, the higher the apparent grade. Acquiring the ability to grade by feel takes time and requires handling many restored comics.

B. Extent of Restoration: It makes sense that the more restoration a book has, the lower grade it was to begin with, and therefore it is subsequently worth less than another book with slight restoration. Below is a breakdown of the three categories currently used in grading, and some of the allowable repairs for each:

Slight
Cover cleaned
Cover re-glossed (amateur)
Color touch (very light, a few hits on the spine or edges)
Minor support or seals using glue (amateur)
Minor support or seals using rice paper and adhesive (pro)
Tiny piece replacement (bindery chips or Marvel chip)

Moderate
Color touch (along spine and edges, for piece replacement)
Small piece replacement (small and few in nature)
Numerous support areas or tear seals

Extensive
Large piece replacement
Color touch (large areas impainted, whole areas recreated)

Reconstructed interiors

Recreated pages or parts of cover

It is possible that a book may only have repairs in the Slight category, and yet receive a Moderate label. This is due to the cumulative amount of work exceeding what is allowable in the Slight range.

C. Quality of Work: This is indicated with a "P" (Professional) or "A" (Amateur), and refers to the materials and techniques used when restoring the comic book. A professional restoration job utilizes archival materials such as rice paper, water-soluble adhesive and acrylic or water based paint for color touch. Amateur work indicates unsafe or crude materials, including irreversible adhesive (white glue, wood glue, etc.), non-archival paper replacement, and color touch that is non-archival (crayon, chalk) or results in bleedthrough (pen, marker).

Restoration Removal

Since certification began, the market has seen an even greater demand for unrestored comics, pushing some to consider removing restoration from their books in order to achieve the coveted "blue label." While this may prove to be financially beneficial in the short run, one must consider the long-term effects of removal, including defacement and changing market conditions. Even when removing slight restoration, it is sometimes necessary to scrape, dig, cut, and obliterate parts of the comic itself. This is especially true for removing amateur restoration, such as glue and color touch that has bled through the paper. The grade of a comic will almost always suffer upon removal of restoration.

Considering how young the certified market is, patience should be exercised when considering a candidate for restoration removal. As the number of certified comics compounds over the coming years, the true rarity of pre-1960 comics in unrestored condition will become obvious, making slightly restored copies more desirable, especially considering their relative value.

However, if removal is desired, the best candidates exhibit professional restoration that can be safely removed with minimal risk to the book itself. This includes tear seals and support using rice paper and water-soluble adhesive, and acrylic and water-based color touch. Cleaned covers are irreversible, as well as trimming, re-glossing, and replaced staples. Removal should not be attempted on comics with Moderate or Extensive restoration due to the damage that could occur and the resulting significant decrease in grade. It is safe to say that 90% of restored comics are not worthy candidates for removal.

Valuing Restored Comics

Below are general formulae that can be used to determine the value of restored comics. Multiply the number given with the unrestored value in the *Guide* to determine an estimated value. These numbers are based on professionally restored comics – books with amateur work would be worth 15-20% less. But remember: These formulae serve only as a benchmark. Each book is unique and may vary in value.

Scarcity of Comics

Victorian and Platinum Age comics (1828-1933): Many of these books were bound with thick cardboard covers and are extremely rare to non-existent in VF or better condition. Due to their extreme age, paper browning is very common. Brittleness could also be a problem.

Late Platinum and early Golden Age comics (1933-1940): There are many issues from this period that are very scarce in any condition, especially from the early to mid-1930s. Surviving copies of any particular issue range from a handful to several hundred. Near Mint to Mint copies are virtually non-existent with known examples of any particular issue limited to five or fewer copies. Most surviving copies are in FN-VF or less condition. Brittleness or browning of paper is fairly common and could be a problem.

Golden Age comics (1941-1952): Surviving comic books would number from less than 100 to several thousand copies of each issue. Near Mint to Mint copies are a little more common but are still relatively scarce, with only a dozen or so copies in this grade existing of any particular issue. Exceptions would be recent warehouse finds of most Dell comics (6-100 copies, but usually 30 or less), and Harvey comics (1950s-1970s) surfacing. Due to low paper quality of the late 1940s and 1950s, many comics from this period are rare in Near Mint to Mint condition. Most remaining copies are VF or less. Browning of paper could be a problem.

Late Golden Age and early Silver Age comics (1953-1959): As comic book sales continued to drop during the 1950s, production values were lowered resulting in cheaply printed comics. For this reason, high grade copies are extremely rare. Many Atlas and Marvel comics have chipping along the trimmed edges (Marvel chipping) which reduces the number of surviving high grade copies even more.

Silver Age and early Bronze Age comics (1960-1979): Early '60s comics are rare in Near Mint to Mint condition. Most copies of early '60s Marvels and DCs grade no higher than VF. Many early keys in NM or MT exist in numbers less than 10-20 of each. Mid-'60s to late '70s books in high grade are more common due to the hoarding of comics that began in the mid-'60s.

'80s and '90s comics (1980-1992): Collectors are only now beginning to discover that 10-15 years spent in quarter boxes have rendered many '80s comics scarce in NM condition, and as modern collecting shifts its focus ever closer to the present, these will become increasingly sought-after and harder to locate in high grade as a result, but not nearly as difficult as earlier era comics that are genuinely rare in high grade.

'90s and Modern Age comics (1992-Present): Comics of today are common in high grade. VF to NM is the standard rather than the exception.

When you consider how few Golden and Silver Age books exist compared to the current market, you will begin to appreciate the true rarity of these early books. In many cases less than 5-10 copies exist of a particular issue in Near Mint to Mint condition, while most of the 1930s books do not exist in this grade at all.

Silver Age (1956-1970)

	Slight	Moderate	Extensive
app NM 9.4	0.15	0.10	0.05
app VF 8.0	0.25	0.20	0.10
app FN 6.0	0.50	0.40	0.30
app VG 4.0	0.70	0.50	0.40
app GD 2.0	0.80	0.60	0.50

Golden Age Comics (pre-1956)

	Slight	Moderate	Extensive
app NM 9.4	0.25	0.20	0.125
app VF 8.0	0.50	0.35	0.20
app FN 6.0	0.70	0.60	0.40
app VG 4.0	0.80	0.70	0.50
app GD 2.0	0.90	0.80	0.60

Collecting Comics

New comic books are available in many different venues, but principally in your local comic book shop and book store chains. However, comics can also be found in grocery stores; drug stores; newsstands; collectibles specialty shops; through mail order catalogs; and online from individual retailers and in some cases from the publishers themselves. Local flea markets and, of course, comic book conventions in your area, are also excellent sources for new and old comic books.

Many collectors begin by buying new issues in Near Mint condition directly from their local comic shop or off the newsstand, or perhaps they obtain comics via subscriptions with retailers and/or the publishers. Every week, new comics appear on the stands that are destined to become true collectors' items. The trick is to locate a store that carries a complete line of comics, but this may be difficult. Most collectors have to make use of several venues, from "brick and mortar" stores to online retailers, in order not to miss something they want. Even then, it pays to keep in close contact with collectors in other areas. Sooner or later, nearly every collector has to rely upon a friend in fandom or a dealer (such as those who placed ads in this book) to obtain an item that is unavailable locally.

Before you buy any comic to add to your collection, you should carefully inspect its condition. Unlike stamps and coins, defective comics are generally not highly prized. Remember that every blemish or sign of wear depreciates the beauty and value of your comics. For more detailed information on this aspect of collecting, consult **The Official Overstreet Comic Book Grading Guide**, which features a wealth of material on how to evaluate the condition of your comic books.

Some collectors not only collect comics because they enjoy the stories or have fond memories of a particular title and/or character, but because they're interested in "playing the market." A collector may even buy extra copies of popular titles in the hope that this investment will enable him to make a profit by selling the additional copies at some future date. He may also trade these multiples for desired items that are unavailable locally - for example, foreign comics. Such speculation is, of course, a gamble. Selecting the right investment books is a tricky business that requires specialized knowledge. With experience, the beginner will improve his buying skills. Remember, if you play the new comics market, be prepared to buy and sell fast; values can rise and fall rapidly as a character, title, or specific storyline garners enough attention to drive the price up or falls out of favor and sends the price down.

Today's comic books offer a wide variety of subjects, art styles and writers to satisfy even the most discriminating fan. Whether it's the latest new hot title or company, or one of many popular titles that have been around for a long time, the comic book fan has a broad range from which to pick. Print runs of many popular titles have dropped over the past few years, creating the possibility of a true rarity occurring when demand outstrips supply. Less "gimmicky" covers are seen these days - they were all the rage through most of the '90s and have come to symbolize a time when flash was more important than substance. However, some comic books are still released with variant covers.

In terms of genre, "Bad Girl" and horror titles have often proven popular in addition to the ubiquitous superhero fare, but many series delving into less fanciful subjects, like crime comics and real-world relationship-based series, have also found some measure of success and a solid fan following. The collector should always stay informed about the new trends developing in this fast-moving market. Since the market fluctuates greatly, and there is a vast array of comics to choose from, it's recommended first and foremost that you collect what you enjoy reading; that way, despite any value changes, you will always maintain a sense of personal satisfaction with your collection.

Polybagged Comics

It is the official policy of this Guide to grade comics regardless of whether they are still sealed in their polybag or not. Sealed comics in bags are not always in Mint condition and could even be damaged. The value should not suffer as long as the bag (opened) and all of its original manufactured contents are preserved and kept together.

Collecting on a Budget

Collectors usually check out their local comic shop or book store for the latest arrivals. Hundreds of brand new comic books are displayed each week for the collector, much more than anyone can afford to purchase. Today's reader must be careful and budget his money wisely in choosing what to buy. If a collector cannot find a way to logically limit his spending, there are a few basic approaches to collecting comics on a budget, listed below, that may offer a solution.

Collecting Artists or Companies

Many collectors enjoy favorite artists and follow their work from issue to issue, title to title, or company to company. Over the years, some artists have achieved "star" status. Autograph signings occur at all major comic conventions as well as special promotions with local stores. Fans line up by the hundreds at such events to meet these superstars. Some of the top artists of the past several years include Alex Ross, Jim Lee, Michael Turner, Chris Bachalo, J. Scott Campbell, Humberto Ramos, and Adam and Andy Kubert. Original artwork from these artists bring record prices at auctions and from dealers' lists.

Some collectors become loyal to a particular company and only collect its titles. It's another way to specialize and collect in a market that expands faster than your wallet.

Collecting #1 issues

For decades, comic enthusiasts have collected first (#1) issues.

This is yet another way to control spending and build an interesting collection for the future. #1 issues have a lot going for them - some introduce new characters, while others are under-printed, creating a rarity factor (underprinting frequently becomes a factor with last issues as well, another focus of some collectors). #1 issues cross many subjects as well as companies, and make for an intriguing collection.

Back Issues

A back issue is any comic currently not available on the stands. Collectors of current titles often want to find the earlier issues in order to complete a run; thus a back issue collector is born. Comic books have been published and collected for over 100 years, but the earliest known comic book dealers didn't appear until the late 1930s. Today, there are hundreds of dealers that sell old comic books, and many of them advertise in this Guide. The hunt begins!

A good place to begin looking is with your collector friends who may have unwanted back issues or duplicates for sale. Look in the yellow pages, or call the Comic Shop Locator Service at 1-888-COMIC-BOOK, to see if you have a comic book store in your area. Advertising in local papers or trade publications can often get good results. These publications can also put you in touch with out-of-town dealers. This Guide has many advertisements for buying and selling old comic books. Some dealers also publish regular price lists of old comic books for sale.

Of course, one of the best sources for information today is the Internet. Search online for local comic shops, dealers with mailing lists and catalogs, or simply order from countless retailers who operate through the web. Auction sites like eBay also provide an enormous forum for finding desired comics, selling comics of your own, or just communicating with other collectors who share your interests.

Putting a quality collection of old comics together takes a lot of time, effort and money. Many old comics are not easy to find. Persistence and luck play a big part in acquiring needed issues. Most quality collections are put together over a long period of time by placing mail orders with dealers and other collectors, networking online and bidding in Internet auctions, and/or visiting conventions to find those elusive issues.

Comics of early vintage are extremely expensive if they are purchased through a regular dealer or collector. Unless you have unlimited funds to invest in your hobby, you will find it necessary to restrict your collecting in certain ways. However you define your collection, you should be careful to set your goals well within affordable limits.

Preservation & Storage

Comic books were built to last but a short time - utilizing acidic newsprint paper, thin covers, inconsistent inks, occasionally damaging bindery machinery - and bound not for a Mylar snug or a CGC slab but for a child's back pocket and eventually the nearest rubbish bin. Comics were intended as disposable fare, but collectors now apply the most stringent archival regulations on a class of collectible that was ephemeral at best.

Some of the best advice for preserving a comic is simply to handle it carefully. Most dealers and collectors hesitate to let anyone personally handle their rare comics, and it is common courtesy to ask permission before handling another person's comic book. Most dealers would prefer to remove the comic from its bag and show it to the customer themselves. In this way, if the book is damaged, it would be the dealer's responsibility and not the customer's.

When handling high grade comics, always wash your hands first, eliminating harmful oils from the skin before coming into contact with the books. Lay the comic on a flat surface or in the palm of your hand and slowly turn the pages. This will minimize the stress to the staples and spine. In basic handling situations:

Step 1: Remove the comic from its protective sleeve or bag very carefully (more detail can be found in "How to Grade")

Step 2: Gently lay the comic unopened in the palm of your hand so that it will stay relatively flat and secure.

Step 3: Leaf through the book by carefully rolling or flipping the pages with the thumb and forefinger of your other hand. Be sure the book always remains relatively flat or slightly rolled. Avoid creating stress points on the covers with your fingers and be particularly cautious in bending covers back too far.

Step 4: After examining the book, carefully insert it back into the bag or protective sleeve. Watch corners and edges for folds or tears as you replace the book. Always keep tape completely away while inserting a comic in a bag.

Careful handling of an exceptional book can go a long way to preserving its condition for some time to come, but careful storage is also a key element. Comic books must be protected from the elements, as well as the dangers of light, heat, and humidity. This can be accomplished with certain storage methods, but remember: improper storage methods will be detrimental to the "health" of your collection, and may even quicken its deterioration.

Store comic books away from direct light sources, especially florescent light, which contains high levels of ultraviolet (UV) radiation. UV lights are like sunlight, and will quickly fade the cover inks. Tungsten filament lighting is safer than florescent lighting, but should still be used at brief intervals. Remember, exposure to light accumulates damage, so store your collection in a cool, dark place away from windows.

Room temperature must also be carefully regulated. Fungus and mold thrives in higher temperatures, so the lower the temperature, the longer the life of your collection. Like UV, high relative humidity (rh) can also be damaging to paper. Maintaining a low and stable relative humidity, around 50%, is crucial. Varying humidity will only damage your collection.

Atmospheric pollution is another problem associated with long term storage of paper. Sulfuric dioxide, which can occur from automobile exhaust, will cause paper to turn yellow over a period of time. For this reason, it is best not to store your valuable comics close to a garage. Some of the best preserved comic books known were protected from exposure to the air, such as the Gaines EC collection. These books were carefully wrapped in paper at the time of publication and completely sealed from the air. Each package was then sealed in a box and stored in a closet in New York. After over 40 years of storage, when the packages were opened, you could instantly catch the odor of fresh newsprint; the paper was snow white and supple, and the cover inks were as brilliant as the day they were printed. This illustrates how important it is to protect your comics from the atmosphere.

Care must also be taken when choosing materials for storing your comics. Many common items such as plastic bags, boards, and boxes may not be as safe as they seem; some contain chemicals that will actually help to destroy your collection rather than save it. Always purchase materials designed for long-term storage, such as Mylar sleeves and acid-free backing boards and boxes. Polypropylene and polyethylene bags, while safe for temporary storage, should be changed every three to five years.

Comics are best stored vertically in boxes to preserve flatness and spine tightness. If you choose to store your comics on shelves, make sure that the books do not come into direct contact with the shelving surface. Use acid-free boards as a buffer between the shelves and the comics. Also, never store comics directly on the floor; elevate them 6-10 inches to allow for flooding. Similarly, never store your collection directly against a wall, particularly an outside wall. Condensation and poor air circulation will encourage mold and fungus growth.

Ultimately, nothing will prevent the deterioration of a comic book collection, but as examples like the Gaines collection have proven, there are occasions when even unintentionally well-stored comics can avoid the aging process for a considerable length of time. With some care in handling and attention to the materials used for comic book storage, your collection can enjoy a long life and maintain a reasonable condition for years to come.

Buying & Selling Comics

Whether you're a new collector just starting to acquire comics or a long-time collector now interested in selling a collection, by purchasing this Guide you have begun the long process necessary to successfully buy and sell comics.

Selling Your Comics

If you are planning to sell a collection, you must first decide what category listed below best describes the comics you wish to sell. As a rule of thumb, the lower categories will not require you to offer as much detail in your inventory list as the upper categories. A collection of key late '30s DCs will require you to list exact titles, numbers, and grades, as well as possible restoration information. If, however, you have 20,000 miscellaneous '80s and '90s comics for sale, a rough list of the number of books and publishers should be enough. Keep in mind that this can vary depending on what your potential buyers are seeking; those who are keen to fill in gaps in a collection of Bronze Age books, for example, might demand the same level of detail that another potential buyer might want regarding the Golden Age books you're offering for sale. The categories are:

1. Victorian & Platinum Age (1828-1938): The supply is very scarce. More people are becoming interested in these early books as research turns up more and more detailed information. Moderate interest among average dealers, but high interest with dealers that specialize in this material. A detailed list will be necessary paying attention to brittleness, damage and pages missing. Dealers will pay up to a high percentage of Guide for key titles.

2. Golden Age, All Grades (1938-1956): A detailed inventory will be necessary. Key higher grade books are easier to sell, but lower grades in most titles show the best selling potential due to the fact that many collectors cannot afford a $20,000 VF book but may be able to afford a GD copy for only $2,000. Highest demand is for the superhero titles such as **Batman**, **Superman**, **Human Torch**, etc. The percentage of Guide that dealers will pay for your collection will vary depending on condition and contents. A collection of low demand titles will not bring the same percentage as a collection of prime titles.

3. High Grade Silver Age: A detailed inventory will be necessary. There are always investors looking for VF or better books from this period. Dealers will usually pay a high percentage of Guide list for these high grade books. Silver Age below VF will fall into category #4.

4. Low Grade Silver Age: Spanning books lower than VF from the late '50s to the early '70s, this category exhibits the average grade of most collections. Consequently, the supply of this material is much more common than category #2. This means that you could be competing with many other similar collections being offered at the same time. You will have to shop this type of collection to get the best price, and be prepared to sell at a significant discount if you find a willing buyer with good references.

5. Bronze Age and Beyond: Many titles from the 1970s in high grade are showing increasing demand, and 1980s books are showing signs of interest as well. However, many books from the '80s to the '90s are in low demand, with the supply for the most part consisting of high grade books. These collections are typified by long runs of certain titles and/or publishers; a detailed inventory will not be necessary. Contact local comic stores or buyers first to gauge their level of interest. Dealing with buyers outside your area should be avoided if possible. **IMPORTANT:** Many of the 1980s and 1990s books are listed at cover price; this indicates that these books have not established a collector's value as yet. When selling books of this type, the true market value could be 20-50% of cover price or less.

9. Bulk (in quantities greater than 5,000): These collections usually contain multiple copies of the same issues. It is advisable to price on a per-book basis (for example, 25¢ or 50¢ each). Do NOT attempt an inventory list, and only contact buyers who advertise buying in bulk quantity.

You should never deal with a buyer without fully checking their references. For additional verification, consult The Better Business Bureau; the local BBB may be able to help you in establishing a buyer's credibility, as well as assisting in resolving any disputes. **The Overstreet Comic Book Price Guide** and **Comic Book Marketplace** are also recognized authorities. Advertised dealers will likely have a more established reputation.

Potential buyers will be most concerned with the retail value of your entire collection, which may be more or less than Guide depending on what you have and the current demand for many of the individual issues in your collection. Some rare early books in VF or NM may bring a price well over Guide while other titles in lower grades may sell for a price well under Guide. Most vintage books, though, will sell for around the Guide price.

However, since many '80s and '90s books that list at cover price may only be worth a percentage of that price, you must decide on what percentage you would be willing to accept for your collection, taking into account how the collection breaks down into fast, moderate and slow-moving books. To expect someone to pay full retail for books that usually sell at considerably lower prices is unrealistic. You will have to be flexible in order to close a deal.

Many buyers may want to purchase only certain key or high grade books from your collection, almost always favoring the buyer. While you may be paid a high percentage of retail for their selections, you will find that "cherry-picked" collections are much more difficult to sell, since all of the most desired books will be sold by the time the second or third potential buyer examines your collection. Furthermore, the percentage of retail that you will receive for a cherry-picked collection will be much lower than if the collection had been left intact. Remember, key issues and/or high grade issues make or break a collection and often set the value for the collection as a whole. Selling on consignment, another popular option, could become another breeding ground for cherry-pickers, so again, always check a dealer's references thoroughly.

Of course, while these rules apply to any transaction between collectors and potential buyers in most physical or "brick and mortar" retailer/dealer situations, there is a far more popular option available to collectors today who wish to sell part or all of their collection. With the advent of eBay and other online auction and store venues, collectors can now bypass the traditional routes and sell directly to other collectors rather than to retailers and/or dealers. As a result, realized prices for individual issues or entire collections can be much higher, since potential buyers are now often drawn from a pool of equally enthused collectors rather than dealers with a desire to resell their aquisitions for profit. On the other hand, even individual collectors seeking to buy comics on the web may be into the speculation game, so all the old rules about being a cautious buyer or seller still apply.

If you do choose to sell your comics on a piecemeal basis through eBay or other means, the process will require much greater care and detail in preparing an inventory list and grading comics for sale. As noted above, you will probably be able to realize a higher final price by selling your collection this way, but the key books will certainly sell first, leaving a significant portion of your collection unsold. You will need to keep repricing and discounting your books to encourage buyers on books that do not initially sell.

Entire books have been written about how best to achieve sales success through eBay and other Internet sites, so rather than dwell on all the possible strategies here, we will simply say that online auctions are the fastest-growing and most convenient venues for many private collectors to engage in the buying and selling of vintage comics of all Ages. It behooves anyone who chooses to use this method to educate themselves thoroughly about the intricacies of online auctions and transactions.

You can also advertise your collection in trade publications or through mass mailings, but whether selling books through the mail by traditional means or when shipping books at the close of an Internet auction, you should establish a reasonable return policy, as some books will unquestionably be returned. Close attention to detail when presenting accurate descriptions of the books in your sales information, and use of very clear pictures - particularly in Internet auction listings - will go a long way to preventing misunderstandings and arguments later on. Check the local post office and/or UPS regarding the various rates and services available for shipping your books.

Marketing your books at conventions is another option, but as a dealer, you will naturally also incur overhead expenses such as table rental if setting up at a show, postage, mailing and display supplies, advertising costs, etc.

In all cases, be willing to establish trust with a prospective buyer. By following the procedures outlined here, you will be able to sell your collection successfully, for a fair price, with both parties walking away satisfied. After all, collecting comic books is supposed to be fun; it only becomes a chore if you let it.

Where to Buy and Sell

Throughout this book you will find the advertisements of many reputable dealers who sell back-issue comics. If you are an inexperienced collector, be sure to compare prices before you buy. When a dealer is selected (ask for references), send him a small order (under $100) first to check out his grading accuracy, promptness in delivery, guarantees of condition advertised, and whether he will accept returns when dissatisfied. Never send cash through the mail. Send money orders or checks for your personal protection. Beware of bargains, as the items advertised sometimes do not exist but are only a fraud to get your money.

Many dealers also maintain an Internet presence, and a quick search can turn up a number of sites from which you can purchase comics of all eras. Of course, you can also locate comics for sale by searching auction sites like eBay, but given the complexity of that world and its uniuqe policies and practices, it would be wise to learn everything you can about the online auction process in order to safeguard yourself as a buyer before bidding on any comics or making a purchase.

The Guide is indebted to everyone who placed advertisements in this volume. Mentioning this book when dealing with the advertisers would be greatly appreciated.

Comic Conventions

The first comic book conventions, or cons, were originally conceived as the comic book counterpart to science fiction fandom conventions. There were many attempts to form successful national cons, but they were all stillborn. It is interesting that after only three relatively organized years of existence, the first comic con was held. Of course, its magnitude was nowhere near as large as most established cons held today.

What is a comic con? Dealers, collectors, fans, publishers, distributors, manufacturers, and other enthusiasts can be found buying, selling and trading the adventures of their favorite characters for hours on end. Additionally, most cons have guests of honor, usually professionals in the field of comic art - writers, artists, editors, or other production personnel. The committees that run these conventions put together panels for the con attendees in which the assembled pros talk about certain aspects of comic book production and history, and often these guests field questions from the assembled audience as well.

At cons, one can usually find displays of various and sundry items for purchase, including toys, comic books of course, original art, and much more. Larger cons often serve as a launching platform for comic- or genre-related films and television shows, and there can be showings of movie trailers, video presentations, and special personal appearances by media stars. Of course, there is always the chance to get together with friends at cons and just talk about comics. One also has a good opportunity to make new friends who have similar interests and with whom one can correspond after the convention is over.

It is difficult to describe accurately what goes on at a con. The best way to find out is to go to one and see for yourself. The largest cons are WonderCon (April), Pittsburgh (April), San Diego (July), Chicago (July), and Atlanta (July). For accurate dates and addresses, consult advertisements in this edition or visit the convention websites themselves for details. Please remember when writing for convention information to include a self-addressed, stamped envelope for reply.

Comic Book Fandom

It's possible to discern two distinct and largely unrelated movements in the history of Comics Fandom. The first began around 1953 as a response to the the trend-setting EC lines of comics. The first true comics fanzines of this movement were short-lived. Bob Stewart's **EC FAN BULLETIN** was a hectographed newsletter that ran two issues about six months apart; Jimmy Taurasi's **FANTASY COMICS**, a newsletter devoted to all science-fiction comics of the period, was a monthly that ran for about six months. These were followed by other newsletters such as Mike May's **EC FAN JOURNAL**, and George Jennings' **EC WORLD PRESS**. EC fanzines of a wider and more critical scope appeared somewhat later. Two of the finest were **POTRZEBIE**, from a number of fans, and Ron Parker's **HOOHAH**. Gauging from the response that **POTRZEBIE** received from an EC letter column plug, Ted White estimated the average age of EC fans at 9 to 13, while many were actually in their mid-teens. This was discouraging to many fanzine editors hoping to reach an older audience. Consequently, many gave up their efforts on behalf of Comics Fandom, especially with the demise of the EC groups, and turned to SF (science fiction) fandom with its longer tradition and older membership. While the flourish of fan activity in response to the EC comics was certainly noteworthy, it never developed into a full-fledged, independent, and self-sustaining movement.

The second movement began in 1960, largely as a response to (and later stimulus for) the reappearance of the costumed hero and the Second Heroic Age of Comics. Most historians date the Second Heroic Age from **Flash** #105, February 1959. The letter departments of Julius Schwartz (editor at National Periodicals), and later those of Stan Lee (Marvel Group) and Bill Harris (Gold Key) were influential in bringing comics readers into Fandom. Sparks were lit among SF fans first, when experienced fan writers, who were part of an established tradition, produced the first in a series of articles on '40s comics–ALL IN COLOR FOR A DIME. The series was introduced in **XERO** #1 (September 1960), a general SF fanzine edited and published by Dick Lupoff.

Meanwhile, outside SF fandom, Jerry Bails and Roy Thomas, two comics fans of long-standing, conceived the first true comics fanzine in response to the Second Heroic Age, **ALTER EGO**, appearing in March 1961. The first issues were widely circulated, and profoundly influenced the comics fan movement, attracting many fans in their twenties and thirties, unlike the earlier EC fan following. Many of these older fans had been collectors for years but were largely unknown to each other. Joined by scores of new, younger fans, this group formed the nucleus of a self-sustaining and still growing movement. Although it has borrowed a few appropriate SF terms, Comics Fandom of the '60s was an independent movement without the advantages and disadvantages of a longer tradition. What Comics Fandom did derive from SF fans was largely thanks to fanzines produced by so-called double fans, the most notable being **COMIC ART**, edited and published by Don and Maggie Thompson.

The **ROCKET'S BLAST COMIC COLLECTOR** by G.B. Love was the first sucessful adzine in the early 1960s and was instrumental in the development of the comics market. G.B. remembers beginning his fanzine **THE ROCKET'S BLAST** in late 1961. Only six copies of the first 4 page issue were printed. Soon after Mr. Love had a letter published in **MYSTERY IN SPACE**, telling all about his new fanzine. His circulation began to grow. Buddy Saunders, a well known comic book store owner, designed the first **ROCKET'S BLAST** logo and was an artist on the publication for many years thereafter. With issue #29 he took over **THE COMICOLLECTOR** fanzine from Biljo White and combined it with **ROCKET'S BLAST** to form the **RBCC**. He remembers that the **RBCC** hit its highest circulation of 2,500 around 1971. Many people who wrote, drew or otherwise contributed to the **RBCC** went on to become well known writers, artists, dealers and store-owners in the comics field.

Related Collectibles

Foreign Edition Comics

One interesting and relatively inexpensive source of early vintage comics is the foreign market. Many American newspaper and magazine strips are reprinted abroad (in English and other languages) months and even years after they appear in the States. By arranging trades with foreign collectors, one can obtain substantial runs of American comic book reprints and newspaper strips dating back years. These reprints are often in black and white, and sometimes the reproduction is poor. Once interest in foreign-published comics has been piqued, a collector might become interested in original strips from these countries.

Newspaper Strips

Collecting newspaper comic strips is somewhat different than collecting comic books, although it can be equally satisfying. Most strip collectors begin by clipping strips from their local paper, but soon branch out to out-of-town papers. Naturally this can become more expensive and more frustrating, as it is easy to miss out-of-town editions. Consequently, most strip collectors work out trade agreements with collectors in other cities. This usually means saving local strips for trade only.

Back issues of some newspaper comic strips are also occasionally available from dealers. Prices vary greatly depending on age, condition, and demand.

Original Art

Some enthusiasts collect original comic book and strip art. These mostly black and white, inked drawings are usually done on illustration paper at about 30 percent larger than the original printed panels. Because original art is a one-of-a-kind article, it is highly prized and can be difficult to obtain.

Interest in original comic art has increased in the past few years because more current art is available now that companies return originals to the artists, who then either sell the work themselves at cons, or through agents and dealers. The best way to find the piece you want is to scour cons and get on as many art dealers' mailing lists as possible. Although Golden and Silver Age art brings fine art prices, most current work is available at moderate prices, with something for everyone at various costs, from Kirby to McFarlane, Ditko to Bachalo.

Toys and More

In the past ten years or so, interest in collecting comic-related merchandise has soared. Comic book and toy shows are often dominated by toys and related products.

Action figures and limited edition statues based on comic characters are currently the most popular. Highly successful toy action figure lines based on Batman, Spawn, Spider-Man, and many others cram toy store shelves. Statues and figurines, either painted or in kit form, are very popular higher-end collectibles. Statues of characters like Witchblade, Sandman, Shi, and many more draw collector attention through print, web, and convention advertising.

Numerous other tie-in products based on comic characters are released every year and seem to represent a large percentage of the collectible market today. Books like **Hake's Price Guide to Character Toys**, and periodicals like **Collecting Figures** and **Toyfare** track the collectibility of these items.

Cover Bar Codes

Today's comic books are cover-coded for the direct sales (comic shop, newsstand, and foreign markets). They are all first printings, with the special coding being the only difference. The comics sold to the comic shops have to be coded differently, as they are sold on a no-return basis while newsstand comics are not. The Price Guide has not detected any price difference between these versions. Currently, the difference is easily detected by looking at the front cover bar code (a box located at the lower left). The bar code used to be filled in for newsstand sales and left blank or contain a character for comic shop sales. Now, as you can see below, direct sale editions are clearly marked, both versions containing the bar code.

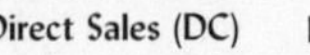

Direct Sales (DC)

Direct Edition (Marvel)

Newsstand

Comic Book Reprints

Over the years, many publishers have reprinted comic books, from individual stories collected under new covers to entire issues published with facsimile covers that may be indistiguishable from the original. Some did not re-present old material but were successive printings generated at the time of an original comic's release to satisfy demand for more copies. Whatever the reason for the reprint, distinguishing a reprint from an original edition can be tricky.

Many such reprints carry a notation somewhere in the indicia indicating that it is a "reprint," or "2nd printing," etc., and perhaps even a later copyright date. Still others even feature a variation in cover coloring or issue number information to distinguish it from the original. Fantastic Four #371, for example, featured an all-white embossed cover in its original printing, but the second printing changed to an all-red embossed cover. In the 1990s, many Marvel reprints sported a gold logo.

Unfortunately, many reprints were never marked as such. For example, a few of the Marvel movie books, such as **Star Wars**, the **Marvel Treasury Editions**, and tie-ins such as **G.I. Joe**, were reprinted and not identified as reprints. The **Star Wars** reprints have a large diamond with no date and a blank UPC symbol on the cover. Others had cover variations such as a date missing or different colors.

Gold Key and other comics were also sold with a Whitman label. Although collectors may prefer one label over the other, the Price Guide does not differentiate in price. Beginning in 1980, all comics produced by Western carried the Whitman label.

Recently, DC Comics reprinted many key issues with a gold foil "Millennium Edition" stamp. There is little difficulty in distinguishing the reprint, however, due to the distinctive modern trade dress and border surrounding the original cover art.

Publishers' Codes

The following abbreviations are used with cover reproductions throughout the book for copyright purposes:

ABC-America's Best Comics
AC-AC Comics
ACE-Ace Periodicals
ACG-American Comics Group
AJAX-Ajax-Farrell
AP-Archie Publications
ATLAS-Atlas Comics (see below)
AVON-Avon Periodicals
BP-Better Publications
C & L-Cupples & Leon
CC-Charlton Comics
CEN-Centaur Publications
CCG-Columbia Comics Group
CG-Catechetical Guild
CHES-Harry 'A' Chesler
CLDS-Classic Det. Stories
CM-Comics Magazine
CN-Condé Nast
DC-DC Comics, Inc.
DEF-Defiant Comics
DELL-Dell Publishing Co.
DH-Dark Horse
DMP-David McKay Publishing
DS-D. S. Publishing Co.
EAS-Eastern Color Printing Co.
EC-E. C. Comics
ECL-Eclipse Comics
ENWIL-Enwil Associates
EP-Elliott Publications
ERB-Edgar Rice Burroughs
FAW-Fawcett Publications
FC-First Comics
FF-Famous Funnies
FH-Fiction House Magazines
FOX-Fox Features Syndicate
GIL-Gilberton
GK-Gold Key
GP-Great Publications
HARV-Harvey Publications
H-B-Hanna-Barbera
HILL-Hillman Periodicals
HOKE-Holyoke Publishing Co.
IM-Image Comics
KING-King Features Syndicate
LEV-Lev Gleason Publications
MAL-Malibu Comics
MAR-Marvel Characters, Inc.
ME-Magazine Enterprises
MLJ-MLJ Magazines
MS-Mirage Studios
NOVP-Novelty Press
NYNS-New York News Syndicate
PG-Premier Group
PINE-Pines
PMI-Parents' Magazine Institute
PRIZE-Prize Publications
QUA-Quality Comics Group
REAL-Realistic Comics
RH-Rural Home
S & S-Street and Smith Publishers
SKY-Skywald Publications
STAR-Star Publications
STD-Standard Comics
STJ-St. John Publishing Co.
SUPR-Superior Comics
TC-Tower Comics
TM-Trojan Magazines
TMP-Todd McFarlane Prods.
TOBY-Toby Press
TOPS-Tops Comics
UFS-United Features Syndicate
VAL-Valiant
VITL-Vital Publications
WB-Warner Brothers.
WDC-The Walt Disney Company
WEST-Western Publishing Co.
WHIT-Whitman Publishing Co.
WHW-William H. Wise
WMG-William M. Gaines (E. C.)
WP-Warren Publishing Co.
YM-Youthful Magazines
Z-D-Ziff-Davis Publishing Co.

Timely/Marvel/Atlas Codes

"A Marvel Magazine" and "Marvel Group" were the designations used between December 1946 and May 1947 for the Timely/Marvel/Atlas group of comics during that period, although these taglines were not used on all of the titles/issues during that time. The Timely Comics symbol was used between July 1942 and September 1942, although again not on all titles/issues during the period. The round "Marvel Comic" symbol was used between February 1949 and June 1950. An early Comics Code symbol (star and bar) was used between April 1952 and February 1955. The Atlas globe symbol was used between December 1951 and September 1957. The M over C symbol (signifying the beginning of Marvel Comics as we know it today) was introduced in July 1961 and remained until the price increased to 12 cents in February 1962. We present here the publishers' codes for the Timely/Marvel/Atlas group of comics:

ACI-Animirth Comics, Inc.
AMI-Atlas Magazines, Inc.
ANC-Atlas News Co., Inc.
BPC-Bard Publishing Corp.
BFP-Broadcast Features Pubs.
CBS-Crime Bureau Stories
CLDS-Classic Detective Stories
CCC-Comic Combine Corp.
CDS-Current Detective Stories
CFI-Crime Files, Inc.
CmPI-Comedy Publications, Inc.
CmPS-Complete Photo Story
CnPC-Cornell Publishing Corp.
CPC-Chipiden Publishing Corp.
CPI-Crime Publications, Inc.
CPS-Canam Publishing Sales Corp.
CSI-Classics Syndicate, Inc.
DCI-Daring Comics, Inc.
EPC-Euclid Publishing Co.
EPI-Emgee Publications, Inc.
FCI-Fantasy Comics, Inc.
FPI-Foto Parade, Inc.
GPI-Gem Publishing, Inc.
HPC-Hercules Publishing Corp.
IPS-Interstate Publishing Corp.
JPI-Jaygee Publications, Inc.
LBI-Lion Books, Inc.
LCC-Leading Comic Corp.
LMC-Leading Magazine Corp.
MALE-Male Publishing Corp.
MAP-Miss America Publishing Corp.
MCI-Marvel Comics, Inc.
MgPC-Margood Publishing Corp.
MjMC-Marjean Magazine Corp.
MMC-Mutual Magazine Corp.
MPC-Medalion Publishing Corp.
MPI-Manvis Publications, Inc.
NPI-Newsstand Publications, Inc.
NPP-Non-Pareil Publishing Corp.
OCI-Official Comics, Inc.
OMC-Official Magazine Corp.
OPI-Olympia Publications, Inc.
PPI-Postal Publications, Inc.
PrPI-Prime Publications, Inc.
RCM-Red Circle Magazines, Inc.
SAI-Sports Actions, Inc.
SePI-Select Publications, Inc.
SnPC-Snap Publishing Co.
SPC-Select Publishing Co.
SPI-Sphere Publications, Inc.
TCI-Timely Comics, Inc.
TP-Timely Publications
20 CC-20th Century Comics Corp.
USA-U.S.A. Publications, Inc.
VPI-Vista Publications, Inc.
WFP-Western Fiction Publishing
WPI-Warwick Publications, Inc.
YAI-Young Allies, Inc.
ZPC-Zenith Publishing Co., Inc.

Comic Book Artists

Many of the more popular artists in the business are specially noted in the listings. When more than one artist worked on a story, their names are separated by a (/), with the penciler first and the inker second. When two or more artists worked on a story, only the most prominent will be noted in some cases. Due to space limitations, only the most popular artists can be listed.

The following artists are considered to be either the most collected in the comic field or otherwise historically significant. Artists designated below with an (*) indicate that only their most noted work will be listed. The rest will eventually have all their work shown as the information becomes available. This list could change from year to year as new artists come into prominence:

Adams, Arthur
Adams, Neal
Aragonés, Sergio
Anderson, Murphy
Aparo, Jim
Bachalo, Chris
Bagley, Mark
Baker, Matt
Barks, Carl
Beck, C. C.
*Brunner, Frank
*Buscema, John
Byrne, John
Campbell, J. Scott
Capullo, Greg
*Check, Sid
Colan, Gene
Cole, Jack
Cole, L. B.
Craig, Johnny
Crandall, Reed
Darrow, Geof
Davis, Jack
Disbrow, Jayson
*Ditko, Steve
Eisner, Will
*Elder, Bill
Evans, George
Everett, Bill
Feldstein, Al
Fine, Lou
Foster, Harold
Fox, Matt
Frazetta, Frank
Gibbons, Dave
*Giffen, Keith
Golden, Michael
Gottfredson, Floyd
*Guardineer, Fred
Gustavson, Paul
*Heath, Russ
Howard, Wayne
Hughes, Adam
*Infantino, Carmine
Ingels, Graham
Jones, Jeff
Kamen, Jack
Kane, Bob
*Kane, Gil
Kelly, Walt
Kieth, Sam
Kinstler, E. R.
Kirby, Jack
Krenkel, Roy
Krigstein, Bernie
Kubert, Adam
Kubert, Andy
*Kubert, Joe
Kurtzman, Harvey
Lapham, Dave
Larsen, Erik
Lee, Jae
Lee, Jim
Liefeld, Rob
Madureira, Joe
Manning, Russ
McFarlane, Todd
McWilliams, Al
Meskin, Mort
Mignola, Mike
Miller, Frank
Moreira, Ruben
*Morisi, Pete
*Newton, Don
Nostrand, Howard
Orlando, Joe
Pakula, Mac
*Palais, Rudy
*Perez, George
Portacio, Whilce
Powell, Bob
Quesada, Joe
Quitely, Frank
Raboy, Mac
Ramos, Humberto
Raymond, Alex
Ravielli, Louis
*Redondo, Nestor
Rogers, Marshall
Romita Sr., John
Ross, Alex
Schaffenberger, Kurt
Schomburg, Alex
Sears, Bart
Siegel & Shuster
Silvestri, Marc
Simon & Kirby (S&K)
*Simonson, Walt
Smith, Paul
Stanley, John
*Starlin, Jim
Steranko, Jim
Stevens, Dave
Swan, Curt
Texeira, Mark
Thibert, Art
Torres, Angelo
Toth, Alex
Turner, Michael
Tuska, George
Ward, Bill
Williamson, Al
Windsor-Smith, Barry
Woggon, Bill
Wolverton, Basil
Wood, Wallace
Wrightson, Bernie
Zeck, Mike

ARTISTS' FIRST WORK:

Adams, Neal - (1 pg.) **Archie's Jokebook Mag.** #41, 9/59; (1st on Batman, cvr only) **Detective Comics** #370, 12/67; (1st Warren art) **Creepy** #14
Aparo, Jim - Go-Go #1, 6/66
Balent, Jim - Sgt. Rock #393, 10/84
Barks, Carl - (art only) **Donald Duck Four Color** #9, 8/42; (scripts only) **Large Feature Comic** #7, ca. Spring 1942
Broderick, Pat - (cover & art) **Planet of Vampires** #1, 2/75
Brunner, Frank - (fan club sketch) **Creepy** #10, 1965
Buckler, Rich - Flash Gordon #10, 11/67
Burnley, Jack - (cover & art) **NY World's Fair** nn, '40
Buscema, John - (1st at Marvel) **Strange Tales** #150, 11/66
Byrne, John - Nightmare #20, 8/74; (1st at DC) **Untold Legend of the Batman** #1, 7/80; (1st at Marvel) **Giant-Size Dracula** #5, 6/75
Capullo, Greg - (1st on X-Force) **X-Force Annual** #1, '92
Colan, Gene - Wings Comics #53, 1/45
Cole, Jack - (1 pg.) **Star Comics** #11, 4/38
Crandall, Reed - Hit Comics #10, 4/41
Davis, Jack - (cartoon) **Tip Top Comics** #32, 12/38
Ditko, Steve - (1st publ.) **Black Magic** V4#3, 11-12/53 (1st drawn story), **Fantastic Fears** #5, 1-2/54
Everett, Bill - Amazing Mystery Funnies V1#2, 9/38
Fine, Lou - (1st cvr) **Wonder Comics** #2, 6/39; **Jumbo Comics** #4, 12/38
Frazetta, Frank - Tally-Ho Comics nn, 12/44
Garney, Ron - G. I. Joe, A Real American Hero #110, 3/91
Giffen, Keith - (1 pg.) **Deadly Hands of Kung-Fu** #17, 11/75; (1st story) **Deadly Hands of Kung-Fu** #22, 4?/76; (tied w/Deadly Hands) **Amazing Adventures** #35, 3/76
Golden, Michael - Marvel Classics Comics #28, '77
Grell, Mike - Adventure Comics #435, 9-10/74
Hamner, Cully - Green Lantern: Mosaic #1, 6/92
Hughes, Adam - Blood of Dracula #1, 11/87
Ingels, Graham art at E.C. - Saddle Justice #4, Sum '48
Jurgens, Dan - Warlord #53, 1/82
Kaluta, Michael - Teen Confessions #59, 12/69
Kelly, Walt - New Comics #1, 12/35
Keown, Dale - Samurai #13, 1987; **Nth Man the Ultimate Ninja** #8, 1/90; (1st at Marvel); (1st on Hulk) **Incredible Hulk** #367, 3/90
Kieth, Sam - Primer #5, 11?/83
Kirby, Jack - Jumbo Comics #1, 9/38;
Kubert, Adam/Andy/Joe art - Sgt. Rock #422, 7/88
Kurtzman, Harvey - Tip Top Comics #36, 4/39; (1st at E.C.) **Lucky Fights It Through** nn, 1949
Larsen, Erik - Megaton #1, 11/83
Lee, Jae - Marvel Comics Presents #85, '91
Lee, Jim - (1st at Marvel) **Alpha Flight** #51, 10/87; (1st on X-Men) **X-Men** #248?, ?/89; (art on Punisher) **Punisher War Journal** #1, 11/88
Liefeld, Rob - (1st at DC) **Warlord** #131, 9/88; (1st at Marvel) **X-Factor** #40, 4?/89; (1st full story) **Megaton** #8, 8/87; (inside front cover only) **Megaton** #5, 6/86
Lim, Ron - (art on Silver Surfer) **Silver Surfer Ann.** #1, '88
Matsuda, Jeff - Brigade #0, 9/93
Mayer, Sheldon - New Comics #1, 12/35
McFarlane, Todd - Coyote #11, ?/85; (1st full story) **All Star Squadron** #47, 7/85; (1st on Hulk) **Incredible Hulk** #330, 4/87
Medina, Angel - (pin-up only) **Megaton** #3, 2/86
Mignola, Mike - Marvel Fanfare #15, 5/83
Miller, Frank - (1st on Batman) **DC Special Series** #21, Spr '80; (1st on Daredevil) **Spectacular Spider-Man** #27, 2/79
Newton, Don - Many Ghosts of Dr. Graves #45, 5/74
Perez, George - (1st at DC) **Flash** #289, 9/80; (2 pgs.) **Astonishing Tales** #25, 8/74
Portacio, Whilce - (1st on X-Men) **X-Men** #201, 1/86
Pulido, Brian - Evil Ernie #1, 12/91
Quesada, Joe - (1st on X-Factor) **X-Factor Ann.** #7, '92
Raboy, Mac - (1st cover for Fawcett) **Master Comics** #21, 12/41
Ramos, Humberto - (1st U.S. work) **Hardwire** #15, 6/94
Romita, John - Strange Tales #4, 12/51; (1st at Marvel) **Daredevil** #12, 1/66
Romita, John Jr. - (1st complete story) **Iron Man** #115, 10/78
Ross, Alex - The Terminator: The Burning Earth V2#1, 3/90
Shuster, Joe - (cover) **New Adv. Comics** #16, 6/37
Siegel & Shuster - New Fun Comics #6, 10/35
Simon & Kirby - Blue Bolt #2, 7/40
Simonson, Walter - Magnus, Robot Fighter #10, 5/65
Smith, Paul - (1 pg. pin-up) **King Conan** #7, 9/81; (1st full story) **Marvel Fanfare** #1, 3/82
Steranko, Jim - Spyman #1, Sep '66; (1st at Marvel) **Strange Tales** #151, 12/66
Swan, Curt - Dick Cole #1, 12-1/48-49
Talbot, Bryan - (1st U.S. work) **Hellblazer Annual** #1, Summer '89
Thomas, Roy - (scripts) **Son of Vulcan** #50, 1/66
Torres, Angelo - Crime Mysteries #13, 5/54
Turner, Mike - Cyberforce Origins-Stryker, 2/95
Weeks, Lee - Tales of Terror #5, 11/85
Weiss, Alan - (illo) **Blue Beetle** #5, 3-4/65
Williamson, Al - (1st at E.C.) **Tales From the Crypt** #31, 9/52; (text illos) **Famous Funnies** #169, 8/48
Windsor-Smith, Barry - X-Men #53, 2/69
Wood, Wally - (1st at E.C.) **Saddle Romances** #10, 1-2/50
Wrightson, Bernie - House of Mystery #179, 4/68; (1st at Marvel) **Chamber of Darkness** #7, 10/70; (1st cover) **Web of Horror** #3, 4/70
Zeck, Mike - (illos) **Barney and Betty Rubble** #11, 2/75

Market Report 2004

With the improving economy...

BE ANOTHER BANNER YEAR?

by Robert M. Overstreet

The stock market boom in 2003 reversed the previous three years of the worst stock market in over 60 years. The sagging economy began showing signs of life towards the year's end. Many businesses began reporting increased profits and interest rates remained low. With billions of dollars of wealth restored to investors throughout last year as the Dow and NASDAQ spiraled upward, will the comic book market also enjoy a rally in 2004?

Incredible Hulk #1 in CGC 9.0, $26,000!

© MAR

Certified Comics: Professionally graded and certified comics by Comics Guaranty Corp. expanded to grading magazine size books last year. Certification continued to be important to the market as we all began to see in the population reports what really does exist and in what grade.

Target Comics #7 (Mile High) in CGC 9.6, $57,500!

© NOVP

Changes in this Guide: The six price columns and the larger format size are again provided in this edition, but with one major change. Starting with this edition, the top grade priced will be the NM- or 9.2 grade. This change has been contemplated and discussed with our advisors for several years now. Finally, due to the continued volatility of the 9.4 grade, it was decided to institute the change with this edition.

Auction Houses: Heritage Comics Auctions and MastroNet held large successful comics auctions last year as in the past. There were also many other auctions during the year, such as Hakes Americana, All-Star, John Verzyl, eBay, etc.

Record Sales: Thousands of noteworthy sales were reported last year and a few noted certified sales are: **Action Comics** #63 (Mile High) in 9.6 – $14,950, #81 (Mile High) in 9.6 – $7,187; **Adventure Comics** #79 (Mile High) in 9.6 – $29,900; **All Select** #1 in 8.5 – $11,557; **All Star** #36 (Spokane) in 9.6 – $9,200, #38 (Pennsylvania) in 9.6 – $7,350; **Amazing Spider-Man** #8 in 9.6 – $7,187, #19 in 9.9 – $12,650, #121 in 9.8 – $6,612, #122 in 9.8 – $5,635, #129 in 9.6 – $2,449; **Avengers** #1 in 9.0 – $4,200, #4 in 9.2 – $3,400; **Batman** #6 in 9.2 – $12,500, #6 (Allentown) in 9.6 – $39,100;

Suspense Comics #3 in CGC 4.5, $11,100!

© Cont. Mags.

© MAR

X-Men #1 in CGC 9.4, $45,000!!

Blackhawk #9 (Mile High) in 9.6 – $11,000; **Crypt of Terror** #17 (Gaines) in 9.6 – $13,800; **Daredevil Comics** #1 (1941) in 9.0 – $13,225; **Daredevil** #2 in 9.4 – $3,001; **Detective Comics** #1 (Lost Valley) in 6.0 – $42,000; #118 (Mile High) in 9.6 – $12,650, #140 in 9.4 – $19,607; **Fantastic Four** #48 in 9.6 – $3,277; **Flash Comics** #15 in 9.6 – $9,200, #26 (Mile High) in 9.6 – $14,950; **Frontline Combat** #1 (Gaines) 9.6 – $3680; **Green Hornet** #1 (Mile High) in 9.2 – $18,400; **Incredible Hulk** #1 in 9.0 – $26,000, #181 in 9.8 – $17,825; **Mad** #1 (Gaines) in 9.6 – $24,150; **Marvel Mystery Comics** #7 (Larson) in 9.2 – $12,650; **Mary Marvel** #1 in 9.6 – $7,762; **More Fun Comics** #65 (Mile High) in 9.2 – $22,500; **Our Army At War** #81 in 8.5 – $4,370; **Richie Rich** #1 (File copy) in 9.4 – $5,635; **Sad Sack** #1 (File copy) in 9.0 – $3,910; **Shock SuspenStories** #6 (Gaines) in 9.8 – $3,220; **Sub-Mariner** #1 in 8.5 – $25,000; **Superboy** #1 in 9.0 – $12,000; **Suspense Comics** #3 in 4.5 – $11,100; **Target Comics** #1 (Mile High in 9.4 – $20,700, #7 (Mile High) in 9.6 – $57,500; **Terrifying Tales** #13 in 9.6 – $4,550; **Tomb of Dracula** #10 in 9.8 – $1,575; **Uncle Scrooge** #1 (FC #386) in 9.4 – $8,337; **Vault of Horror** #13 (Gaines) in 9.6 – $4,600; **Weird Science** #13/2 (Gaines) in 9.6 – $5,750; **X-Men** #1 in 9.4 – $45,000, #3 in 9.4 – $5,650, #4 in 9.4 – $4,082, #94 in 9.6 – $6,612, in 9.4 – $2,213; **Wonder World Comics** #3 in 9.4 – $20,000; **Young Allies** #1 (San Francisco) in 9.6 – $57,500.

© HOKE

***Green Hornet Comics #1** (Mile High) in CGC 9.2, $18,400!*

© WMG

***Shock SuspenStories #6** in CGC 9.8, (Gaines) $3,220!*

The Victorian Age section has been a work in progress and this edition has been expanded to include more history, more listings, and more pricing than ever before.

A new section pricing Big Little Books has been added to this edition for the first time. Since these books are so closely related to comic books, we felt our readers would enjoy the addition of this listing.

Important: The following market reports were submitted by some of our many advisors and are published here for your information only. The opinions in these reports belong to each contributor and do not necessarily reflect the views of the publisher.

RECORD SALES! RECORD SALES! RECORD SALES! RECORD SALES!

© MAR

***Incredible Hulk** #181 in CGC 9.8, $17,825!*

© EC Publ.

***Mad** #1 (Gaines) in CGC 9.6, $24,150!*

© MAR

***Sub-Mariner Comics** #1 in CGC 8.5, $25,000!*

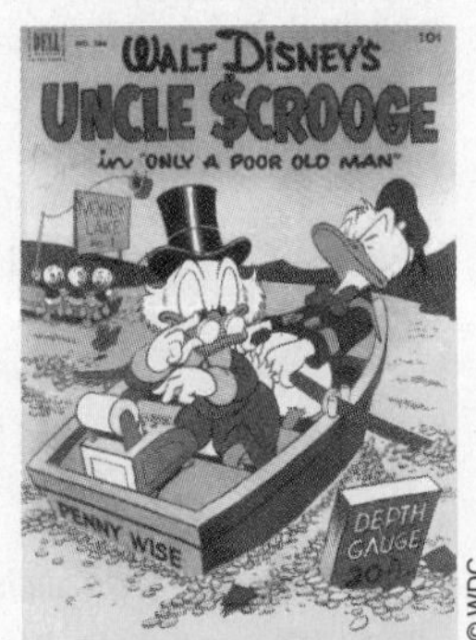

© WDC

***Uncle Scrooge** #1 (FC #386) in CGC 9.4, $8,337!!*

David T. Alexander & Tyler Alexander (Cultureandthrills.com)

Demand for quality collectibles has fueled the heart of the comic book market. We have seen increasing demand for almost all comic books from the mid-1970s and earlier. Is this caused by more collectors seeking original material or by fewer dealers consistently offering new acquisitions? The Internet does have an influence, but lacks consistent offerings. A collector can sell his collection, or some fortunate individual can unearth a horde and will sell 'til all is gone, never to be heard from again.

Over a period of time collectors are driven to dealers with extensive track records for constantly increasing their offerings. The local comic store with an extensive Golden/Silver Age inventory is almost a thing of the past. Certainly a few are still surviving, but most collectors will look to national mail order dealers or auctions to fill their wants.

Acquisitions: We have obtained several impressive collections during the past twelve months. The volume of incoming material has been so large that we have had to add additional staff to continue to process material on a timely basis. The warehouse that we built two years ago is almost filled and we are looking at expansion plans in the early part of 2004.

The most impressive of the collections that came in this year is without a doubt the biggest find of Golden Age comics in the 21st century. You often hear about collectors lamenting the fact that Mom threw their comics out; we hear this story several times a month. This collection and this Mom were different. Not only did the Mom keep the comics, she helped her son collect them. She was a savvy antique collector who was way, way ahead of her time; she saved everything, and when the son lost interest in the comics, she put them away.

A few months ago the son called me; he was liquidating everything. In 50 years of collecting and dealing I have never seen anything like this – thousands of Golden Age comics, with heavy multiples of key Golden Age issues. Single copies of *Action* #1 (since graded a CGC 4.0), *Red Raven* #1, and *Flash* #1 were among the highlights. The eye-popping factor was the multiples which included several copies each of: *Batman* #1-4, *Captain America* #1, *Sub-Mariner* #1, *World's Best* #1, *All-Winners* #1, *World's Finest* #2-5, *New York World's Fair 1939* and *1940*, *All-Flash* #1, *Green Lantern* #1, *America's Greatest* #1, *Superboy* #1 and 2, *Captain Marvel* #1-4, *Bulletman* #1, *Flame* #1, *Looney Tunes* #1, *Leading* #1, *Military* #1, *Superman* #2-10, *USA Comics* #1, *Science Comics* #1, *Walt Disney's Comics and Stories* #1, *Rangers* #1, *Samson* #1, *Comic Cavalcade* #1, *Daredevil Battles Hitler* #1, *U.S. Jones* #1, *Victory* #1, *Catman* #1, and much more. This was the collection we have all dreamed about; most of the early books range around VG. It appears that Mom started hitting the newsstands in 1946 as most of the copies from that era seem to be around VF.

When I went for my second visit, another huge horde of Golden Age with some pre-Code horror and ECs had been unearthed. More multiple copies were there with lots of Timely, DC, Fawcett, Fiction House, etc. I was overwhelmed. Some books have been sent to CGC, while others will be offered on our catalog and website.

Victorian Age: There continues to be some real sleepers in this area of comic collecting. The average collector has not been looking into this area, so while supplies are limited, there are still fabulous buying opportunities; this will not always be the case. *Judge Magazine* produced a lot of one-shots and annual type issues. Buy any that you can find, and don't get prissy about condition of books from this era. Be happy if you can secure anything.

Promotional Comics: A huge number of undocumented giveaway comics have started to surface this year; the most valuable ones have some connection to newsstand comics of the same era. Often the work of well-known artists is found in various giveaways, so don't pass these up if you get a chance at them. The best giveaway that we came across was published by EC for The Museum of Natural History. We sold a very low grade copy for $500.

CGC: The status of graded comics has not changed in the last year. High grade and key issues continue to get a boost in value from CGC authentication. Common material may not bring back the costs of grading. The restoration check is the most valuable service that CGC can provide.

Pulps: Comic book collectors continued to jump into the pulp area this year. Prices are still relatively inexpensive on pulps when compared to Golden Age comics. *Marvel Science Stories* #1 from Aug 1938 is the holy grail for Timely collectors; it features the first appearance of the *Marvel Mystery* logo and appeared over one year before *Marvel Comics* #1 hit the stands. The pulp, which features a Norman Saunders bondage cover, sells for about 2% of the price of *Marvel Comics* #1. Do you see any potential for appreciation in this pulp? Pulps that are on fire now are: all issues of *Lone Ranger*, *Weird Tales* issues with Conan stories, all issues of *Captain Future*, and *Hopalong Cassidy* pulps which feature stories by Louis L'Amour. All of these and many others have strong tie-ins with comic books. A lot more comic book dealers are making an effort to carry pulps, but there are just not that many available. It seems you have to do a lot more work to build up a pulp collection, but the prices are well below equivalent comics, so you will be rewarded for your efforts.

Golden Age: Everybody loves them. Top publishers by dollar sales volume are: D.C., Timely, Fawcett, Fiction House, and Fox. Fawcett hangs with the big boys because these comics have a much lower average selling price. People who collect Fawcett gobble up stacks at a time, while Timely and DC collectors are picking and choosing. This trend is definitely cost generated. It seems every Golden Age comic is on someone's want list; every publisher and every genre are desirable. This type of demand keeps us jumping to find material to fill our customers' want lists. Properly priced Golden Age is a hot commodity, and proper pricing is the key. Some books will move but not at *Guide* values. Internet sales have increased availability on some titles causing prices to dip. We don't feel that this will be a long-term event, as all these books will find a home, which will cause the next wave of buyers to up the ante. Hot items in this category are comics with boxing covers and comics with paper dolls inside. These have been selling to crossover collectors and have been bringing 3-10 times *Guide*.

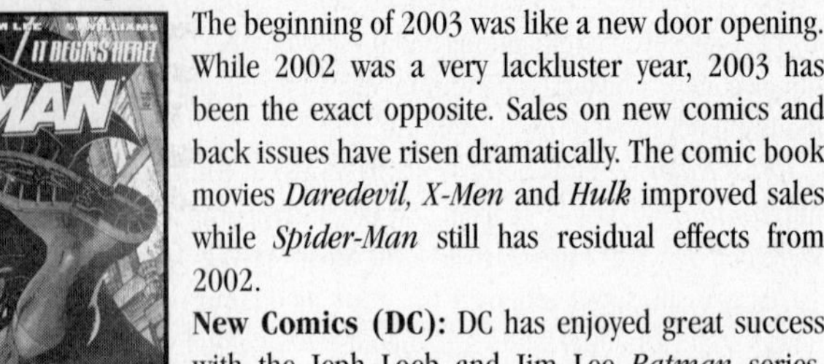

Jim Lee's ***Batman*** *#608 started a successful 12-issue run. The artist tackles* ***Superman*** *in 2004.*

Funny Animals: If we were going to have a category titled "Going Up," funny animals would be at the top of this list. We have been receiving an incredible amount of action on formerly dormant titles such as *New Funnies, Looney Tunes,* Disney titles, and many Harvey titles. We have had multiple orders for copies of *Casper, Wendy, Richie Rich*, and *Little Lotta* that we have offered on our price lists; these are selling for well over *Guide*. This is an area that has been relatively weak in sales for years. Could it be that we are only a few years away from seeing all the Dell Comics in permanent collections?

Unusual Formats: We have noticed a huge increase in interest in this area since our market report in the last *Guide*. Magazines that have comic book type stories are totally undocumented and continue to be a fertile ground for treasure hunters. Art by such greats as Wally Wood, Frank Frazetta, Jack Davis, Bob Powell, Basil Wolverton, Bill Ward, Jack Kirby, Graham Ingles, and many others often appeared in various magazines of the 1940s, 1950s, and 1960s; many have actual comic book stories in them. Popular yet elusive items in this category are the early 1970s NFL programs with Marvel Comics characters on the covers by Jack Kirby and John Romita. Now is an excellent time to seek them out.

David J. Anderson

The comic book market is currently experiencing what all collectible markets experience from time to time: a bit of a cooling off or leveling period. This was almost predictable after last year's influx of such an enormous amount of quality material. Collectors find themselves regrouping and re-evaluating their collections (and pocketbooks) as a result of last year's activity and have slowed down their buying. The big money buyers are still willing and able to buy expensive books for very high prices, but only if they are extremely high grade and unrestored. There is high resistance on these buyers' parts if the books are less than 9.4 or restored or touched in any way. Since there is so little material better than 9.4 available at any given time, this contributes to less overall spending. The biggest bargains in the comic book market right now are VF books (which sell for *Guide* or slightly less) or VF+ and better books with very minor restoration (which sell for around fine *Guide*).

Stephen Barrington

*Michael Haller and John Schmidt also contributed to this report.

The beginning of 2003 was like a new door opening. While 2002 was a very lackluster year, 2003 has been the exact opposite. Sales on new comics and back issues have risen dramatically. The comic book movies *Daredevil, X-Men* and *Hulk* improved sales while *Spider-Man* still has residual effects from 2002.

New Comics (DC): DC has enjoyed great success with the Jeph Loeb and Jim Lee *Batman* series. *Batman* sales quadrupled with this team-up. A lot of collectors are waiting for Jim Lee's stint on *Superman* in 2004. *Teen Titans* seems to have caught a lot of people off guard but caught up after DC offered second prints on #1 and #2. Other success stories have been DC's Vertigo titles, *Fables* and *Y: The Last Man*.

JLA and *JSA* are still selling great, and DC's special projects *Superman Red Son* and *Superman Birthright* came on strong. Limited series *Batgirl Year One, Human Defense Corps* and *Doctor Fate* were surprise sellers. The DC/Marvel effort of *JLA/Avengers* was a winner right out of the gate. Also making a big splash was the *Superman-Batman* title.

Back Issues (DC): DC Comics from the 1950s and 1960s sell well when priced right. *Batman* and *Detective* bring close to *Guide* prices in all grades as well as *Superman* and *Action. World's Finest* is right behind them with *Wonder Woman* from the 1960s and early '70s moving quickly. The market for 1980s and 1990s is slow at *Guide* but move well in the $1 and quarter boxes.

Silver Age *Green Lantern, Flash,* and *Atom* are slow but the *Justice League of America* issues sell fast and can be hard to find. *Lois Lane* and *Jimmy Olsen* are slow except for the very early issues; the first ten of these series can be very hard to find in any decent condition. Demand for *My Greatest Adventure/Doom Patrol* is rising because collectors are finding out that these quirky characters have fun stories.

New Comics (Marvel): Marvel's much anticipated and publicized titles *Rawhide Kid* and *Truth (Red, White and Black)* were huge flops. *Marvel: The End* did well but wasn't exactly a barn-burner. All of the *Ultimate* titles sell very well but *The Ultimates* title has been hurt by a chronically late production schedule. *The New X-Men, Uncanny X-Men* and *Amazing Spider-Man* are all extremely good sellers. *Fantastic Four, Daredevil, Captain America, Iron Man* and *Thor* are pretty much middle of the road sellers. Marvel's MAX line is nothing to write home about. Decent sellers were *Marvel 1602* and *Supreme Power.*

Back Issues (Marvel): *X-Men*, Silver Age to present, have become bloated price-wise in the *Guide*. Almost all issues are hard to sell even at half *Guide*. The exceptions, of course, are *Giant-Size X-Men* #1 (this book sells in any grade); *Uncanny*

X-Men #94, #101 and #266 (first Gambit). My dollar box has nice copies of *X-Men* going back over twenty years but they do move well at this price as well as *Amazing Spider-Man* in its own dollar section. The print runs on many of the 1970s and 1980s issues were tremendous and a good number of collectors are always bringing them in to sell. Unfortunately, I have thousands of these in my warehouse.

Ghost Rider remains popular (both series) at *Guide* prices but *Tomb of Dracula* (except for Blade appearances) and *Werewolf By Night* are hard to sell. Most Marvels from the 1970s are still low enough in price for nice copies to keep newer collectors interested. And then there is a good segment of collectors who aren't terribly concerned about condition; they just want a copy to read. Marvel's anthology monster reprints (*Where Creatures Roam, Where Monsters Dwell*, etc.) fall into this category.

The *Daredevil* and *Hulk* movies (the *Hulk* movie was panned by almost all of my customers) sparked some interest in these series but it was more like a flash-in-the-pan than a trend. The *X-Men* movie impact was almost non-existent since the *X-Men* franchise is so well known.

Marvels from the 1960s and 1970s move well at the $5 and under level. A lot of collectors are being more price conscious with the economy fluctuating so much in this area. *Amazing Spider-Man* seems to be the leader, though, with #129 (1st Punisher), #121 and #122, #100, and #50 the most sought after issues, especially in high grade.

Golden Age: This is an area that doesn't do well on the Alabama Gulf Coast. Golden Age comics, for the most part, are too pricey for my clientele. Low grade 1950s books do well, though. Oddball comics from across the spectrum from the late 1940s and into the '50s sell well.

Other Publishers: Dark Horse, Image and CrossGen do poorly around here; there is very little demand for most of the titles published by these companies. The exceptions are *Lady Death* and *G.I. Joe*. Even *Spawn* has fallen on hard times; his issues from #1 on up are winding up the $1 box. His spinoff titles fare even worse and are in the quarter boxes. Dreamwave has done very well with its *Transformers* line but its other titles are not as fortunate.

Gemstone EC Reprints: I wish I could get my hands on a few hundred of the classic EC reprints done by Gemstone several years ago. I can't keep these in stock and the number of readers wanting these issues is growing every day. Fans are discovering what a great line of comics these were and they want more and more issues to read.

eBay Sales: For the first time, I started selling on eBay last spring and the results have been interesting to say the least. High grade books can be hard to sell on eBay while some dogs will fetch high prices. Silver Age DC lots (*Flash, Atom, Adventure* and *Aquaman*) sell well but at well below *Guide. Amazing Spider-Man* issues move very quickly, but again at below *Guide*. Low grade *Superman* family titles sell quickly and close to *Guide*. About 80% of what I post, from Valiant to miscellaneous titles, do sell.

San Diego Comic Con: As usual, the San Diego International Comic Con was the main event of the year. With 400,000 square feet of main exhibition space and around 70,000 in attendance, it turned out to be the most exhausting convention I have ever attended. Every facet of the hobby and then some was represented there. It was just about impossible to see everything. Of course there was a huge selection of comics and related material with prices ranging from reasonable to the ridiculous.

Lauren Becker

The market seems to be getting stronger each year. This year is no exception with Marvel leading the way in most ordered, but DC is quickly gaining. Our best selling Marvel titles are *Ultimates, Ultimate Spider-Man*, and *Amazing Spider-Man*. DC has *Batman* (which will taper off once Jim Lee leaves), *JSA*, and *League of Extraordinary Gentlemen*. However, it should be pointed out that many of DC's newer titles are selling as much if not more than the aforementioned Marvels; most noticeably *Teen Titans* and *Superman/Batman*. Demand exceeded supply and we were stunned (our orders for *Teen Titans* #1 were five times the amount we normally ordered for *Titans* and *Young Justice, combined*). Some of our independent sales have risen, most noticeably *Dark Days, Criminal Macabre* and *Hellboy*. The big sleeper will be Eric Powell's *The Goon*. Early back issues – before the Dark Horse jump – will be huge.

The big loser though, and there's always a loser, is Image. With the exception of *Powers* and *Rex Mundi*, if we run out of an Image title that is not connected to the big guns (i.e. *Spawn, G.I. Joe*), then drinks are on the boss (me). Also, all the hype for the *Hulk* movie quickly died when the movie lacked action, and sales of *all* Hulk books went down. The next big license, *The Punisher*, has been met with trepidation. The silver lining though might lie with the new *Hellboy* movie. Buzz on the movie has created demand on *all* Hellboy back issues and graphic novels. If *Hellboy* becomes the hit that it should be, expect more independent comics to make it to the big screen. I would love to see big screen adaptations of

© MAR

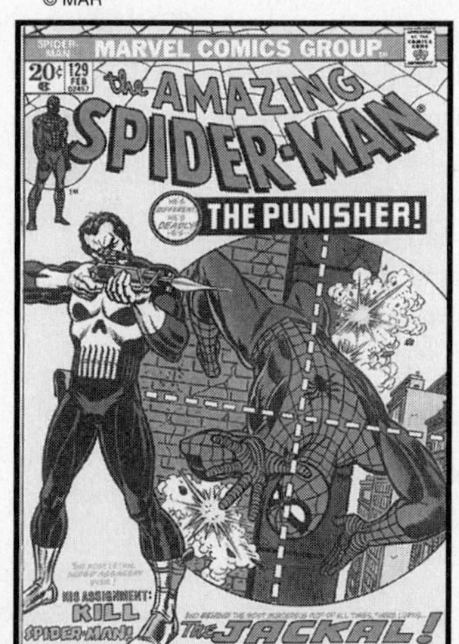

With the Punisher's highly anticipated new movie debuting in 2004, collectors are making ***Amazing Spider-Man*** *#129*, the 1st comic appearance of the character, a leading seller.

Grendel, Strangers in Paradise and *The Goon*.

Back issues, especially Silver Age, have increased in sales. There has been big demand for *Avengers* and *Fantastic Four* in low to mid-grade. *Captain America* is slowly gaining in sales. Silver Age DC, which was very big for us before, has now slowed, especially *Batman* and *Wonder Woman*.

Recent back issues (1990-present) sell extremely well at our store. *Ultimate Spider-Man, Ultimates*, and Jim Lee's *Batman* are going gangbusters. *Daredevil* has slowed a bit after the movie (*ala Hulk*), but *League of Extraordinary Gentlemen* has much more anticipation between issues than for the actual movie.

Michael Browning

What decade is this? The 1990s? It would seem that way, as comics are once again soaring in value with variants leading the way. Anyone remember Valiant's gold and platinum books and how high their prices rose? One national newspaper called them better than gold, and speculators took heed of the growing interest in the low print run books and jumped on the bandwagon. Prices on regular editions and variant retailer editions soared and a lot of people made a lot of money. Then, when it was all over, a lot of speculators were stuck with a load of books they couldn't move and the market imploded. That's the same thing that's happening with today's variant editions. DC's retailer-only limited editions are the hottest. Variant covers equal big bucks for retailers, who are selling these "rare" editions for astronomical prices. Collectors are snapping them up and shelling out some major cash for these editions.

Batman #608 retailer editions have reportedly gone for as high as $1,000, and one sold recently on eBay for $722.50 in Near Mint; that's a lot of money for a book that was released a little more than a year ago.

The other big retailer edition is the *Superman/Batman* #1, which has been going for upwards of $400 online. Four copies sold in September for $425 each and eight sold for $400; two others sold for $406 and $405. One of the lowest prices realized on the *Superman/Batman* retailer edition was $172.50, a bargain compared to other sales of the same book. That book was only two months old when it sold for those prices. How far can these go and what effect will it have on the comic market?

A bigger question may be: Are we seeing the return of the speculator crowd, the same crowd who brought about the boom and bust of comics in the mid-1990s? We should all hope this isn't the case, but there are a lot of "low print run" comics that are soaring in value.

As was the case back in the mid-1990s, "low print run" variants, such as gold and platinum comics with slight variants to their covers, saw huge price hikes. These days, new covers on later printings and retailer-only editions mean more money as variant editions rake in big bucks online and in stores.

Reprints were hot late in 2003 with *Batman* #612 second printings (the Jim Lee sketch cover) selling for as much as $112.50 in CGC 9.8. Another *Batman* #612, not CGCed, sold online for $20.56.

Jim Lee's work on *Batman* lit a hot streak for the Caped Crusader's comics with a full set of *Batman* #608-619 (regular editons) selling on some sites for $144.

And speaking of the speculator market of the mid-'90s, Valiant Comics, the leader of the trend of that era, are seeing a surge in prices with an *X-O Manowar* #1/2 gold selling for $255 and the Diamond *Unity* Trade Paperback set selling for $299.99. A *Chaos Effect* Alpha Red sold online for $127.50 and a CGCed *Rai* #3 in 9.8 NM+ sold for $108.05. Copies of *Unity* #0 Red sold in NM for $57.01, $52.01 and $51. Two *Bloodshot* #0 platinums, thought to be non-existent, sold for an average of $599 according to www.valiantcomics.com. Copies of *Harbinger* #0, once Valiant's highest-priced and hardest to find comic, sold in NM for $38.01, $36, $34.97, $33 and $31. These books are going to get hotter as they get older. Last issues of Valiant Comics are rising in value, as are the Valiant Validated Signature Series, which were each signed by the creators and stamped with an official Valiant seal on the front covers. Some of these books had print runs lower than 1,000 and are highly sought after by Valiant collectors.

Batman isn't the only hero with a variant cover rising in value. A *Wolverine* #145 Nabisco variant sold for $113.50. A *Daredevil* #132 (30 cent variant and the first appearance of Bullseye) sold in CGC 9.0 for $153.51. An *X-Men* #25 with a black and white cover sold in NM for $49.99. Another example of how speculators are once again flooding the market is *Teen Titans* #1 (2003) with the Michael Turner variant cover selling in CGC 9.8 for $79.99.

Last issues were again hot this year, with *Vampirella* #113, the scarce last Harris issue, selling for $275. A *Conan the Barbarian* #275 sold in NM for $99.99, and copies of *G.I. Joe* #155 sold for $50 and $42 in VF and NM, respectively.

Some rare Golden Age books that sold were *Sure-Fire* #3 (G- $190.50), *Superworld* #2 (CGC 7.0 $711 without restoration), *Canteen Kate* #3 (VG+ $95.05) and *Flash Comics* #103 (G $265).

A Charlton ashcan of *Fightin' Air Force* with a black and white cover and a *Hot Rods and Racing* interior, sold with browning edges for $350.

A big sale happened in December of 2002 when a copy of *Miracleman Gold* #1 sold in Portland, Oregon, for $1,500. The *MM Gold*, No. 11 of 400 signed and numbered by Alan Moore, was sold by Excalibur Books and Comics of Portland, a store which has been in business since 1974. It was found in a collection of independent comics which contained a bunch of *Miraclemans*. Each *MM* #1 came with either a gold or a blue card. The golds were signed on the first page by Moore and numbered 1-400 and the blues were signed on the same page by Eclipse owners and editors Cat Yronwode and Dean Mullaney and were not numbered. They were sold through American Comics as the first copies distributed and were sold at the 1985 San Diego Comicon. It is believed there were 600 blues sold at the convention. Many didn't believe the books even existed. It wasn't until this reporter, after several years of searching, unearthed a gold and a blue copy. Another copy of *Miracleman Gold* #1 sold online in the Spring of 2003 for big bucks, but didn't get the cash the No. 11 copy sold for in late 2002. The copy, No. 325 of 400, was sold on eBay. As with nearly all copies of *Miracleman* #1, there are printing defects on the cover of the No. 325 copy. Other copies that have surfaced, including the No. 11 copy that recently sold for $1,500, also have the cover defects, such as a crease near the bottom of the right side of the Miracleman logo near Miracleman's head.

A set of the *Miracleman* gold and blue editions which were signed but had no numbering were recently put up for sale online, but no information concerning the sale was available. The unnumbered issues were sold after the San Diego Comicon. Extras were signed but not numbered after the initial 400 signed and numbered were sold. Eclipse Comics sold these from their ads in their books. Two copies sold on eBay in the past year: a No. 360 for $41 and a No. 90 for $138. Two copies sold since for $500 and another has been for sale on eBay several times with a reserve of $1,500. A couple copies of *Miracleman Blue* #1s have sold online for $130 each.

Another *Miracleman* rarity, a copy of the non-3-D 3-D edition, sold for nearly $150, but *Miracleman* wasn't the only Alan Moore book to climb in price. Leatherbound copies of *Supreme: The Story of the Year* and *Supreme: The Return* had print runs of 400 each, making the books extremely rare. They sold as a set from Checker Books Publishing Group for $125 and were selling online for nearly $100 each. *Supreme: The Story of the Year* trade paperback, published early in 2002 and with an error on the back cover (stating that Alan Moore's *Swamp Thing* had been published by Marvel instead of DC), had a low print run of nearly 30,000 and sold out almost immediately from the company. A second printing was published late in the year, and although the first error was corrected, a second error appeared on the front cover (which read: Moore•Sprouse•Veitch rather than the correct Moore•Bennett•Veitch). The company confirmed that this was an error on the second printing.

Tim Collins (RTS Unlimited, Inc.)

The current market has been extremely resilient in the face of a sluggish economy. This is partly due to the convergence of the following factors: third party grading, eBay, large scale and well managed auction houses, Marvel's success at the box office, low interest rates, and the stock market bubble.

Third party grading, primarily through CGC, took some of the risk out of buying comics. CGC's excellent staff is renowned for finding restoration and the encapsulation helps eliminate some of the risk of buying from an unknown party. No longer does a buyer wanting a NM 9.4 comic wonder if a dealer's NM 9.4 comes under the same interpretation as the collector's. eBay has revolutionized the way a lot of people buy and sell comics, whether it be their personal collection or a dealer's overstock or even regular inventory. Now the "average Joe" collector can reach an audience of thousands of collectors without the need of a dealer.

The advent of eBay has helped explain why comic conventions are no longer just comics but a showcase for all kinds of exciting entertainment possibilities. Most dealers have lost customers to eBay and it is their job to create and add value for the customer in order to survive against the online auction powerhouse.

The entry of Mastronet and Heritage Comic Auctions into the hobby has added a new level of excitement and encouraged more people to enter the hobby. My good friends at Heritage should be commended for the publicity they have generated in making John Q. Public aware of the comics market.

Of course, Marvel's success with their *Spider-Man* and *X-Men* movies has brought the superhero genre to the forefront of an admiring public. Like the *Batman* and *Superman* movies from a few years ago, Marvel has ensured that these costumed wonders are trapped in the public's mind. Now, it's the retailers job to continue the momentum and bring these potential customers into the fold.

The current low interest rates coupled with the uncertainty of the stock market have many investors seeking higher returns outside of more traditional investment fare and are looking at collectibles as an alternative investment. As others have noted, record-breaking prices have been realized in the comics market at the auction houses. Over time, the returns on investment grade comics have been much higher than the DOW Jones Industrial Average. Furthermore, having a tangible asset in one's hands is far more appealing than a stock whose value may be obliterated with an accounting scandal. These converging factors have helped shape a very strong comics market that should last for quite some time.

Dealing in a wide variety of merchandise has enabled us at RTS Unlimited, Inc. to become friends with a wide variety of collectors. As we tend to deal more with the collector than investor, we get the chance to appreciate what comics were meant to be: imaginative and creative works of art that tell a story. As such, we find that a comic with a famous artist or writer will almost always sell for a premium. To wit, artists of the likes of L.B. Cole, Basil Wolverton, Alex Schomburg (aka Xela), Wally Wood, Berni Wrightson, and many others continually sell and at above *Guide* too.

Of course popular characters also sell. For instance, we have seen a huge increase in demand for Spider-Man, Daredevil, and X-Men comics. The 'Baby Boomers' are now in their prime earning years and want to reconnect with their childhood memories from the 1960s. As mentioned above, Marvel's success with their movies has helped to rekindle this desire. Early and key issues from nearly all titles published in the 1960s sell at or even above *Guide*. Later issues continue to command a premium in high grade. Fast sellers include *Amazing Fantasy* #15, *Amazing Spider-Man* #1, *Fantastic Four* #1, and *X-Men* #1 in all grades. The Bronze Age is gaining momentum for most issues in VF and higher. Most requested issues from the Bronze Age include *Amazing Spider-Man* #129, *Giant Size X-Men* #1, *Incredible Hulk* #181, *Iron Man* #1 (yes, Iron Man!), and *X-Men* #94.

As with any hobby where significant amounts of money are involved, the comics market will have its ups and downs. We are definitely in an up cycle and should remain so for quite some time. This is good news for collectors, dealers and all those that love comics indeed.

Peter Dixon (Paradise Comics)

2003 has been a year of expansion for Paradise Comics. Located in North Toronto, Canada, Paradise Comics has been in business for over a decade and we have been Toronto's consistent source for Silver and Bronze Age comics throughout those years.

New Books: Marvel's titles are still very strong for us. *Ultimate* Marvel books are still among our top sellers, and *Ultimate X-Men* is definitely catching up to *Ultimate Spider-Man* sales since Bendis and Finch took over in issue #34. *Ultimate Six* was a strong launch and we have high hopes for *Ultimate Fantastic Four*. August saw the release of three huge first issues from Marvel: Neil Gaiman's *Marvel 1602, Supreme Power*, and *JLA/Avengers*. *Thanos* #1 has been a strong seller for us, especially after the word-of-mouth success of *Marvel: The End*, which was a sleeper hit for us. As for other new Marvels, *Amazing Spider-Man* has been selling well, as has *New X-Men,* whose sales went up as soon as fan-favorite Phil Jimenez came on board to illustrate "Murder at Xavier's" and "Planet X."

The long-awaited **JLA/Avengers** #1 was a huge first issue in a summer of hot debuts.

Incredible Hulk seems to be losing momentum as the storyline has been crawling along. Mike Deodato's return with #60 is starting to get people interested again after a slow summer. *Daredevil, Alias, Avengers* and *Fantastic Four* are also fairly strong sellers, and people are excited to hear that Mark Waid is back on *FF*. Of the 'Tsunami' launches, only *Mystique* was a hit, while *Runaways* and *Sentinel* are books with decent word of mouth. *Spider-Man: Blue* lost steam as the issues crawled out, and was DOA when the last issue arrived; the hardcover came out almost right away and deflated sales. Many Marvel readers have clued in and wait for the inevitable trade paperback reprint. Reviving the *Marvel Masterworks* line has been very warmly received.

DC, for the first time in a long time, has begun to give Marvel a run for their money. Others will have discussed the success of Jim Lee and Jeph Loeb's *Batman* at great length, but it is noting that putting top talent on top books creates top sales–something that DC wasn't doing for a long time. Hopefully the Azzarello/Risso and Lapham/Sienkiewicz follow-ups will keep up the momentum. *Superman/Batman* by Loeb and McGuinness is another successful application of this formula and sales have been through the roof. *Teen Titans* took everyone by surprise, and the first issue is a tough find, with most collectors looking for the Michael Turner cover. *Outsiders* was another successful relaunch. The former *Titans* and *Young Justice* series (and the *Graduation Day* mini-series) were largely ignored, so it was truly surprising to see successful launches out of life-support titles. *Formerly Known as the Justice League* was another hit for us, but not as big a surprise as our customers have been looking forward to it since the project was announced nearly a year before; it deserves to be an ongoing title. Most other DC titles are limping along, but the best sellers of the remaining titles are *JSA, Green Arrow, Hawkman, Green Lantern* and *Flash*. Superman titles are not great sellers, and *Wonder Woman* did not really benefit from the media exposure her "haircut" brought. As for DC/Vertigo, *100 Bullets, Fables* and *Y: The Last Man* are quite popular. DC/WildStorm books are not selling well. The *Authority* revival was met with collective yawns, but some readers are excited about the return of *Planetary*.

Image comics are not big sellers, and aside from *Powers*, there's little interest. Top Cow titles have a devoted group of followers, but sales are not great; *Darkness* by Dale Keown and Paul Jenkins is probably the most popular of the bunch. *G.I. Joe* comics have a small but devoted group of buyers. We had some fun with an in-store promotion with the *Witchblade Animated Special* and artists Darwyn Cooke, J. Bone and regular *Witchblade* artist Francis Manapul. *Thirty Days of Night* and *Dark Days* did very well. The eighties cartoon revival is on life-support, and sales have definitely been declining on the Dreamwave *Transformers* comics. *Battle of the Planets* never met anyone's expectations, and the overuse of fan-favorites *The Thundercats* by DC/WildStorm killed the momentum it had going for it. CrossGen has been building a reliable fan base, and *El Cazador* was very well received, but their financial troubles seem to be affecting fence-sitters from committing to a line that may go the way of Valiant.

Back Issue Sales: Modern back issue sales are quite strong, and it's a real mixed bag of books that people are looking for. I wish I had more access to mid-1990s Marvels, as the return of many collectors to the main Marvel line over the last three years has caused new interest in the final issues of *Avengers, Fantastic Four* and *Amazing Spider-Man* before their "reboots" that they didn't buy when the Marvel books were selling poorly. The announced return of Volume One numbering on those titles is making completists scramble to catch up on what they didn't get, and since the print runs were not high on those books, they go for premium prices when I get them in. Kevin Smith and Brian Michael Bendis *Daredevil* issues are still strong back issue sellers. Bendis' *Alias* has a loyal following and the title sells well as a back issue. *Ultimate* Marvel titles have been consistent back issue sellers, as have Straczynski *Amazing Spider-Man* comics and Bruce Jones *Hulks*. High grade copies of back issues by popular creators remain easy back issue sellers. I get asked regularly for Valiant Comics, especially the hard-to-find premium comics and the last six to twelve issues of the major Valiant titles before the Acclaim relaunches.

Bronze Age comics remain strong back issue sellers as collectors are beginning to realize the scarcity of some 1970s comics; 20¢, 25¢, 30¢ and 35¢ Marvels and DCs are gaining momentum. Spider-Man and X-Men comics are traditionally the books in the highest demand, but there are many collectors looking for lesser known books and first appearances of Bronze Age characters. Notable Marvel keys that I get asked for regularly include: *Daredevil* #131 (Bullseye), *Daredevil* #168 (Elektra), *Incredible Hulk* #141 (Doc Samson), *Incredible Hulk* #181 (Wolverine), *Marvel Spotlight* #5 (Ghost Rider), and *Amazing Spider-Man* #129 (Punisher). Early issues of *Cerebus* are hard to find and command higher than *Guide* prices in any grade.

Whether they are Silver or Bronze, Neal Adams DC Comics are still solid sellers, and I picked up some nice copies of his DC books including *Strange Adventures, Batman, Detective, Green Lantern/Green Arrow* and *Brave and the Bold*.

© MAR

Captain America Comics *is a most desirable 1940s title. (#3 shown)*

Silver sales remain solid, with consistent interest in Marvel Comics titles across the board and DC keys.

CGC Graded Comics: I rarely sell non-graded comic books on eBay, so CGC is a valuable part of my online presence in the marketplace; it is the single most important selling tool for online comics sales, period. Despite the arrival of poorly thought-out imitators, CGC has yet to have any reasonable competition in the grading marketplace. eBay is still the best way to connect buyers with the books they are looking for. Buyers are still looking for high grade and tend to avoid mid- to low grade copies of graded comics (Golden Age and hard-to-find keys being the exceptions). Modern books tend to sell well right out of the gate, especially if the book has received a 9.8 or higher. CGC's on-site grading was a real success at the Wizard World Chicago convention, and we received two 10.0 Gem Mint books back that received shocking premium prices on eBay (*Supreme Power* #1 for $266 and *Thor: Vikings* #1 for $305.)

Conventions: In addition to travelling to most of the major conventions in North America, we have also set up at the Canadian National Comic Book Expo in Toronto. Paradise has been putting on successful one-day shows in Toronto for over six years, but we recently decided to expand and we will be putting on our first three-day Toronto Comicon show in November. The response from the fan, professional, artistic and dealer communities has been very positive and we hope that this will lead to further shows in 2004 and beyond.

Gary Dolgoff

2003 was a year for strong sales in all grades. The Guide's large price spread has produced three types of buyers: 1) Those who want mainly low grade reading copies so they can proudly state 'I own these books!' and for relatively cheap reading (in those grades, many '60s comics cost only $2-3 and many '50s books aren't much more); 2) Those who desire mid-grade comics (strict G+ to Fine) – these collectors get solid very collectible copies at a fraction of the Very Fine or better price; 3) High grade collectors – a great idea for investment, but difficult to obtain for the most part if your collecting tastes are pre-1965.

Golden Age Superhero (1940s): Almost all are solid sellers (plus I personally treasure them) in all grades. Anyone who says they sell slower in the lower grades just doesn't grade them strictly enough. Timelys sell best and are getting tougher for me to wrest from collectors' eager clutches – can't blame them really. The next time I get offered a collection of Timelys for 80% of Guide I think I'll take them up on it. 1940s *Captain America*s are probably the most desirable '40s title of them all. DCs, however, should not be taken for granted. Though they do not in general have the high-octane, rapid sales that Timelys do, nevertheless they never sit around long in my experience. I find that late '30s/early '40s sell best in all DC titles, especially early *Superman, Action, Detective, Flash, More Fun* and early '40s *Adventure* comics.

Mid- to late '40s DCs are also solid sellers, especially those later *Flash* comics with Black Canary. Her first appearance in #86 and her first solo story in #92 are very requested. Fawcett comics, especially Capt. Marvel titles – *Master, Whiz, Capt. Marvel Jr., Marvel Family, Mary Marvel, Wow* – and *Spy Smasher* sell well. In particular, early '40s issues and affordable Fawcetts – those selling for under $30 – sell well, and are well worth the money.

MLJ comics sell well. I haven't had any *Hangman* comics in a long time. Those covers are works of art – I want them! Quality Comics sell solidly from the early 1940s. I particularly love those *Smash* issues in the #18-40 range, loaded with great art and characters like *The Ray, Wildfire,* and *The Jester*. Crandall, Gustavson, Eisner – you can't beat them. Early *Police* are real cool too. Later '40s issues are OK though not thrilling sellers. Fiction House: *Planets* are best, and early *Jungles* and *Jumbos* are also compelling. Later issues are also solid sellers.

Other Golden Age: It's all good, especially if they are superhero comics. I can never see turning down a Golden Age collection no matter what the grades or size.

1950s Superhero: Relatively little superhero stuff was produced in this decade. However, it had: 1) The end run for a number of Golden Age titles, among them *All-Star, Capt. Marvel, Whiz*, and *Sensation*, plus those fabled short runs of Timelys (called Atlas in the '50s), *Capt. America* #76-78, *Sub-Mariner* #33-42, *Human Torch* #36-38; 2) A few very long-running DC superheroes continued throughout the '50s and are still going, like *Batman, Superman,* and *Wonder Woman*); and 3) The intros of some major DC heroes – Flash, Challengers of the Unknown, Adam Strange – plus a couple of major Superman supporting character titles began, like *Superboy* (actually 1949), *Jimmy Olsen* ('54), and *Lois Lane* ('58). A few minor and short-lived heroes prevailed, like The Avenger.

1950s DC superhero books are consistent sellers, although *Guide* values have increased slowly but surely over the years to the point where I can no longer get over *Guide* for strictly graded copies of these books, especially pre-Code issues. I cannot keep early *Jimmy Olsen*s in stock and the choice early *Showcase*s (#1, 4, 6-14) seem tougher to buy.

In 2003, I sold several runs of '50s superhero DCs, most with a crease through the middle of the book and some as runs, for strictly graded Guide. They were part of the 27,000 book collection I got from Montana (I love these big collections – such variety). Early *Flash* (#105-120) are selling better then ever in all grades.

'40s-'60s Crime: Sells well enough though not brilliantly. Of particular interest are the more grisly theme covers, such as electrocution covers.

'40s-'60s Horror: Very solid, especially in higher grades, which are tough to get.

EC: Horror ECs sell best. *Crime* and *Shock Suspenstories* are also movers. Some of those 1953-54 *CSS* have some uniquely gritty covers. Sci-fi ECs also sell well. I got in a near complete run of low to mid-grade ECs this year; 80% of them went right away. Since then, many of the remaining 20% have dribbled out even in somewhat tattered but quite affordable shape. I was only too happy to pay 50% of *Guide* for the collection – I knew they'd move. I've found the war ECs (*Frontline Combat* and *Two-Fisted Tales*) to be pretty slow-moving outside of the first issues. Believe it or not, *MAD*s – except for the good-selling #s 1 and 5 – are in my experience the slowest selling ECs despite great art, near-universal title recognition, and entertaining, clever story-lines. As we say in New York, 'go figure.' 'New direction' ECs – *Psychoanalysis, Piracy, Valor, M.D.* – move decently however. The pre-trend ECs – *Moon Girl, War Against Crime* – are also solid.

Romance: Sells well. In that Montana Run, I had long runs of *Millie The Model* and *Patsy & Hedy*, as well as DC romance titles, and they're all gone. I always enjoy obtaining romance books. Charlton '60s romance books seem slower than their romantic brethren. I got in some boxes (multiples of an issue #) of 1960s *Millie The Model*, *Patsy & Hedy*, plus some Iws – various issue #s. Offering copies ranging from a strict G/VG to strict VF, they have been moving all right at my discounted prices. I CGCd some of the best ones and got 9.4s, 9.6s, and some 9.8s. Because they are not superhero Marvels, I cannot get the same multiples of *Guide* that I would otherwise, but that's OK.

Science-Fiction: These imagination-provoking '50's comics have mostly great covers and are quite popular.

Prestigious One-Shots: *Reform School Girl, Teen-Age Dope Slaves, Kidnapped, Mask of Dr. Fu-Manchu* – these titles are exotic, cool and always brisk sellers. I had a Fair copy of *Mask of* that sold at the first comic convention I took it to.

Western and *Tarzan*: Though not selling as briskly as they were a couple of years ago, they still sell OK. *Red Ryder*s are among the better-selling westerns; I sold a lot of them this year. Sometimes they move better in runs as it makes less work for a collector (or dealer for that matter). One dealer bought a lower grade run of *Tarzan* #1-30 for a customer of his. Sometimes folks also want a general package of strictly graded westerns, or they select titles. I have no problem with providing such a service.

War: Those early '50s 'gritty cover' war comics move solidly for the most part. Best of all are the early appearances of Sgt. Rock in *Our Army At War*. A few years ago, I bought a large collection with complete and near complete runs of DC '50s and '60s war comics (*Star Spangled War Stories, G.I. Combat, Our Army*). I sold them as strictly graded sets and sold them well.

Sgt. Fury: Despite having some great story-lines – what *Sgt. Fury* reader can forget the chilling "Death of Pamela Hawley" story about Fury's girlfriend in #18-19? – they move relatively slowly with the exception of the undervalued #1. For many '60s issues, I've had to resort to selling them at $3-5 each.

Classics Comics/Illustrated: Traditionally the best sellers of these are later editions at $3 each or so in FR to G/VG, but lately sales on these are picking up' somewhat. First editions of #43 and earlier have been moving better, as well as line-drawn covers in general, many of which seem undervalued. Many of my fellow dealers underestimate *Classics*. I recently outbid others and obtained a complete run of *Classics* #1-121 – mostly originals.

Archie: My favorite comics as a kid. I still get some good laughs when I reread the oldies. I can't keep 10¢ cover price Archie titles in stock, though the Jokebook titles sell somewhat slower. I sold a run of *Betty & Veronica* #5-40, as well as a long run of *Katy Keene*s, to a fellow last year at Guide, graded strictly; he was quite happy. I find *Archie* #1 & *Pep* #22 almost impossible to obtain and would happily pay 100% of Guide for those two books just to own them.

Humor and Funny Animal (non-Dell/Gold Key): Of these, I find Harveys to be picking up and selling quite well. This year, I have sold runs of *Friendly Ghost Casper* #1-29 plus long runs of *Baby Huey & Poppa, Hot Stuff*, etc., for Guide graded strictly. I was lucky enough to obtain a large collection of these. As for other humor titles: *MAD* spin offs from the early '50s (*Wild, Unsane*) are both fun to look at, have nice art for the most part, and are decent sellers. Titles like *Goofy, HaHa,* and *Happy Comics* are on and off sellers; though I buy them, it can take a while to sell them. They have cool and funny covers. I recommend them just for fun.

Dell & Gold Key: Many of these have improved in sales over the last year or two, though for the most part I find 10¢ cover price superhero comics sell better than most Dells and GKs.

TV/Movie Dell & GKs: The better-known sell pretty solidly. *I Love Lucy* and Ricky Nelsons sell very well. *Three Stooges* is a steady seller. Generally, I like getting them in. *Howdy Doody*s also sell.

Westerns: They move OK but not consistently in my experience, except *Red Ryder*, particularly early issues. Those look great and sell well. TV/movie westerns also sell OK.

Hero/Superhero: *Magnus, Robot-Fighter* always move; I recently sold a run of *Magnus* #1-46. *Dr. Solar* is not as fast, but with those great painted covers, they occasionally compel collectors to purchase them. *Mighty Samson* sells moderately.

Disney, Bugs Bunny: As usual, early '40s of these sell well. I never have much trouble selling *WDC&S* #1-39 or *Looney Tunes* #1-10, *Donald Duck FC* #49,62,108, etc. I always have ready customers for *March Of Comics* #4 (Maharajah Donald) and #20 (also D. Duck). Later '40s Dells are a lot slower: '50s and '60s funny animal Dell and GKs are quite slow. I am often willing to sell strictly graded batches of these at 25-50% off Guide as that seems the only way to move them decently.

Other Dells: *Little Lulu* continues to sell well, especially the early issues. They've got style, and I'm not ashamed to say that I've enjoyed reading a few. In general, late '30s/early '40s Dells are solid sellers. Early is good!

1960s Superhero DCs: The top tier titles – *Action, Adventure, Batman, Superman, Detective, Flash, GL, JLA., HOM* & *HOS* (non-superhero), DC war, *Brave & Bold*, some *Showcase* – sell quite well in all grades, especially in strict VG/F and better, which are tougher to get than mid/late '60s high-grade Marvels as '60s DCs were not warehoused and kept. Many of them are quite affordable in strict Fair to G/VG and are being increasingly bought through my website by collectors who want to fill in holes in their collections. I recently filled in all but two of a *Rip Hunter, Time Master* want list from #1-20. Some DC titles sell slowly: *Metal Men, Metamorpho, Secret Six*, 'Dial H'- *House Of Mystery, Anthro,* etc. *Aquaman, Atom*, and *Hawkman* are spotty sellers, but fine titles all – I like to stock them to sell whenever.

1960s Marvels: Yes! These are the mainstays of the comics biz. The whole country – nay, the western world – who grew up on these formed the nucleus of our present comics' collecting industry. 1964 and before: They all sell in all grades. Early *Fantastic Four* and *Spider-Man* plus the #1s and first appearances of this era are the selling emperors of this genre. Early *X-Men* and *Avengers* are also solid sellers. *Tales Of Suspense* has picked up in sales, especially #39-50. *Tales to Astonish* (Ant-Man) and *Strange Tales* (Human Torch) don't sell as swiftly. *Sgt. Fury* #2 and up don't move too fast. 1965 and up: High grade – strict VG/F and better – sell well across the board, with *Amazing Spider-Man* leading the pack. In fact, *ASM* – which has always sold well – is now a blistering seller in all grades. *Avengers* #57-100 also sell very well; that great late '60s revival of the title boasted great art, compelling and original storylines, plus the early Vision appearances. They are also priced relatively low in the Guide. In general, the best sellers are *Avengers, Fantastic Four, Spider-Man*, and *X-Men,* plus those 1968 #1s and premiere issues – *Captain America, Captain Marvel, Incredible Hulk, Iron Man, Silver Surfer*. Also, *Silver Surfer* #4 (vs. Thor – what a great issue) sells very well. *Conan* #1 is a great seller. Mid/late '60s: *Sgt. Fury, Strange Tales, Tales of Suspense, Tales to Astonish*, and *Sub-Mariner* sell slowly. As a result I sometimes discount them for larger buyers.

1970s DCs and Marvels: In general, 20¢ cover comics sell well, with some exceptions – DC *Tarzan*, for instance, sell slowly – as do the 100-page DC comics *Tomb Of Dracula* #1-10, *Marvel Team-Up* #1-10, *Defenders* #1-10, and *Marvel Spotlight* #5 (first Ghost Rider) are consistent solid sellers. *Amazing Spider-Man* #100-150 sell very well in all grades as do *Avengers* #101-140. *Fantastic Four* #100-150 are always being bought. Early '70s DC horror are always being sought after. *Jonah Hex* sells well in high grade; I recently sold an eager buyer a complete run of #1-92 in VF or so at Guide graded strictly. 1970s *Batman* and *Detective* are consistent sellers in G/VG to VG/F. *Hulk* #181 consistently sells for 2-3 times Guide on eBay for lower grade, strictly graded comics. *X-Men* #94 and *Giant-Size* #1 sell well in all grades. *X-Men* #95-142 are decent movers, but not blistering like they were years ago. Many late '70s Marvels sell slow at Guide in F/VF or less. Consequently, I sometimes sell them at discount – 300 for $300. At the right price, they seem to sell OK as they are about 25 years old. Must-read: The 1970s *Tomb Of Dracula* series, with spine-chilling, well-written stories by Marv Wolfman; characters that you can care about; marvelous art that really helps tell the story well by Gene Colan; atmosphere, mood, tempo – this series has it all. Collect the set (#1-70)!

'80s/'90s: Often I am tempted to sell out my 400,000 or so '80s/'90s books, and yet this year they've really picked up. If I let buyers (dealers and spending collectors) select titles and broad number ranges at 50¢-75¢, they start selling pretty well. My opinion if they are not moving – charge 25-33% of NM Guide for nice copies or you have no right to complain about lack of sales in those eras. Frank Milller *Daredevil*s (#150-181) sell well. There is also a small but enthusiastic following for early Alan Moore *Swamp Thing* (#20-40) and *Hellblazer*. *Amazing Spider-Man* sells OK. In general, comics from the late '90s to 2003 sell well due to their low print runs.

CGC: I've always looked at CGC as a non-permanent-value market, though I must give them credit for their strict grading on most 9.4 or better comics. However, early 1960s superhero Marvels seem to sell for big bucks in CGC 9.2 and above.

What can I say? Mid- to late '60s seems to sell in CGC high grade but often for less than a couple of years ago. I CGCd a few each of some high grade *Millie The Model Annual* #4-5, plus a few other *Millie*s and *Patsy & Hedy*s, a few IW romance, and *Rawhide Kid* #50. I found 9.6 getting about double *Guide* or so on these, and 9.8 getting four times *Guide* or so.

Magazines ('60s and '70s): Warrens like *Creepy*s and *Eerie*s sell well enough. The early issues were loaded with good art, like Williamson, Crandall, Ditko, plus those fantastic Frazetta covers on some. *Vampirella*s are tougher for me to obtain multiples of and sell well, especially #1s in all grades. *Blazing Combat* #1 is very tough to get. *Famous Monsters* #1-30 are solid sellers in all grades.

***Creepy* #4 is loaded with good art, and a Frazetta cover too.**

Marvel Magazines: I haven't tried actively in years to offer out some of my huge inventory of these; I will do so soon. I know that the '70s Marvel horror titles in particular are quite requested.

***MAD* Magazines:** These are only moderate sellers, except for the first magazine issue, #24, which sells great.

'30s and '40s Movie Magazines: When I'm lucky enough to get the occasional collection, they really sell.

Original Art: Although I don't get it in much these days – collectors love to keep their treasured pieces – I have complete confidence in the saleability of most superhero art. As soon as I get offered a large original art collection, I may just use that as a basis to form a 'Dolgoff Original Art & Old Comics Auction.' Complete stories and covers as well as splashes of 1960s and earlier Marvel and DC art are the most quickly saleable in general.

Pulps: The best sellers are superhero and horror pulps, *Weird Tales*, plus the exotic titles. I'm asked for *Shadow, Spider, Doc Savage, G-8 & his Battle Birds, Operator 5, Horror Stories, Terror Tales, Strange Tales* pulps, *Wu-Fang, Yen Sin, Zeppelin Stories*, plus those early '30s Clayton Pub. *Astounding*s. Pulps in truly high grade are beginning to command higher prices, as they are genuinely tough to get in nice nick (a British phrase for nice shape).

Shows: Throughout the years, I sell comics – plus magazines and some original art – to dealers and collectors, mostly from my humble warehouse. When folks call me up with wants, I have my entire inventory – about 900,000+ pieces – to draw from. Most of the callers realize that it's the grading and the pricing, not the so-called discount, that matters.

When I go to most shows, however, many of the attendees are more interested in discount even if it's overpriced at first than in good value for the money. Sadly, they often end up paying someone more for the same book in the same actual condition. In other words, they would rather have you come down from $15 to $10 than get the same book in the same shape for $8 with no further discount. In effect, this bargain mentality costs them money.

I am not dissing shows; they are wonderful venues for meeting the people of comics, plus you get to eyeball the books you are thinking of buying. The discerning buyer can then select the books that are graded and priced properly or pay extra for that scarce, cool oldie that they've been looking for. It's just that I prefer to sell to folks who recognize values as opposed to discounts. One comic book web-selling rival often doubles and quadruples many of his prices over the *Guide* value, grades them at a mediocre standard, and then gives '40-50% off.' I prefer to sell at a straightforward price where the grading is strict enough that dealers and collectors alike can enjoy. Plus, I like to sell many '80s/'90s books at 75¢-$1 each just to move them. At a convention, I can't give them over 100,000 comics to choose from as I can on my website. Also, it's good for the industry if buyers know unequivocally that they can trust your grading; it helps keep collectors collecting and dealers buying. I also feel that an informed buyer is a happier buyer, thus my pictorial grading samples on my homepage.

Website Sales: I've found some aspects of traditional comic book websites to be annoying, mostly the fact that the listings are mostly one book per line, which means endless scrolling for browsers. I've found that my new condensed inventory option saves the browser tons of scrolling. Convenience for the buyer is key to good website sales. My package deals are also helpful to the dealer/collector who wants to get it in one shot. eBay is a decent selling venue; in my experience, if you grade strictly enough, 90-100% of Guide is often forthcoming there.

To all in comics, a happy and healthy four-color year!

Conrad Eschenberg

The comic book and original comic book art markets continue to march to the tune of increased demand and record prices. High grade condition comics, pedigree comics, CGC graded comics, rare and esoteric comics and original comic art covers and splashes are at the forefront of this upward trend. In most cases, we are seeing prices increasing at astounding geometric proportions. Case in point: on eBay, *Incredible Hulk* #181 CGC 9.8 sold for about $18,000; *Marvel Spotlight* #5 CGC 9.4 sold for about $1200; and *Amazing Spider-Man* #129 CGC 9.6 sold for about $3000. At the San Diego Comicon, the original art for the cover of *Hulk Annual* #1 by Jim Steranko sold for about $70,000 in cash and trade, and *X-Men* #2 page one splash sold for approximately $38,000. The list goes on and on and on. This is stupid money, folks, and I don't mean literally. The good and bad part of this trend is that in five years, these prices, in most cases, will be bargains.

CGC graded comics have been the fuel for this upswing in prices, particularly the higher grade comics that are in demand. The range of multiples of *Guide* Near Mint for Golden, Silver and early Bronze Age comics that are in demand varies but here is an approximation: CGC 9.0 1x to 3x; CGC 9.2 2x to 4x; CGC 9.4 3x to 6x; CGC 9.6 4x to 12x; CGC 9.8 8x to 20x.

The best sellers are Marvels, Marvels, and Marvels. From the Golden Age Timelys to the pre-hero Marvels to the Silver Age Marvels to the Bronze Age Marvels, and even the current comics, Marvel comics are king. Make no mistake about it.

Over in the original comic book art market, covers and splashes are in the most demand, followed by any art by those artists whose work is most wanted. Some of these artists are Frazetta, Kirby, Ditko, Wally Wood, Swan, Murphy Anderson, Gil Kane, Steranko, Byrne, Wrightson, B. Smith, Kaluta, Miller, etc.

Finally, we must all remember that comics and art are fun, and if you buy what you really like without re-financing your house, then "face it tiger, you just hit the jackpot!"

D'Arcy Farrell (Pendragon Comics)

Who needs the Internet when in-store and convention sales are at a fifteen-year high? We at Pendragon do not! Since the big *Batman* boom of the late 1980s, I have not seen such a demand for quality back issue sales. Perhaps this is due to high grade CGC books attaining unfathomable heights never seen before? Maybe it is due to major Marvel motion pictures such as *Spider-Man, X-Men, Daredevil* and the *Hulk*? It could just be that this year we have obtained numerous collections of Silver and even Golden Age books unseen by my eyes in years. All these points matter in the equation, but I beleive in another point. The past two to three years has seen an influx of new collectors and speculators. Many of these were teens from the late 1980s to the mid-'90s. They left with Marvel's near death and have come back with Marvel's revival. They are readers, collectors and speculators. These aged teenagers are the new home-owners, stock investors and parents that want to see their children reading the same books they did as youths. Just wait till the next *Batman* movie hits.

Modern Age Marvel: Where the 1990s lost the youth market to Nintendo and *Pokémon*, the new millennia has recaptured them, mostly thanks to Marvel with Marvel Knights, *Ultimate* titles, and major revivals starting in 1998–titles such as Kevin Smith's *Daredevil*, Bendis' many *Ultimate* titles, the *Punisher* et al.

Modern Age DC: We cannot forget DC, whose main hero, Batman, is number one, period. When Marvel nearly died in the 1990s, DC maintained its loyal audience through it all. Just like Marvel, DC has in this current year created a major uplift in the market with the "Hush" storyline from Jeph Loeb and Jim Lee. Well drawn and written, this story took the length of a year. Remember Spider-Man's "Clone Saga" of the 1990s? No one had the patience for a story of that length. "Hush" was different, and it was also *Batman*. Spider-Man may be amazing, but no one comes close to the Bat. No other hero has so many one-shots, minis, and ongoing titles; no customer of mine complains about it either.

Image: What can I say? Every year, *Spawn* numbers dwindle and Top Cow is just as bad. This is a dead company to me. I look more forward to a Dark Horse revival (will it come?) because it won't happen here. Marvel figured out in the late 1990s what DC always knew, and that is that substance (story) matters. It's not just about art and gimmicks, #1s and variant covers. Being monthly and on time helps too.

CrossGen: I really do not sell as much of this as I should. This comic book company has decent art, good stories, no gimmicks, a monthly on-time schedule, and the titles don't end in three issues just to restart a new volume for more #1s. They do their work well and at a fair cost to the reader, especially with their graphic novels, which I recommend highly. They offer a good product at a fair price. Their purchase of *Lady Death* from Chaos was very smart. Titles I would recommend are *Ruse, Solus* (by Perez), *Sojourn* and *Lady Death.*

Tokyopop/Manga: This is where many teenagers, especially girls, flock. *Chobbits, Clamp, Sailor Moon* all sell well. This market is growing quickly. VIZ and Antarctic Press do OK, but Tokyopop rules. Their well-priced manga graphic novels at $9.99 (5x7, b&w) are a great read for the buck. Teens have limited funds and can't spend $30-40 a week like adults purchasing new comics.

Modern Age Hot Titles: Most Marvel, especially *Ultimate* titles. *Batman, Nightwing*, low run Vertigo titles like *Y: The Last Man* and *Fables*.

Modern Age Dead Titles: Most Image titles, with Top Cow slowing way down.

Copper Age (1980s): Various Marvel and DC titles had fairly small print runs in the early 1980s (1979-85). These mainstay core titles began in the 1950s and 1960s, lasting easily 20-30 years. Nearing the end, the print runs had diminished. These titles are now 20+ years old going on 30. Most are still readily available at $3-5 in decent shape with off-white to white pages. Looking hard, you may pick up a NM copy with white pages. Those are great investments, especially if something key (minor or major) occurs. Store these for 5-10 years and I'm sure you will reap rewards. Remember, ten years ago the Bronze Age was barely considered an investment; think of ten years from now. There is a big difference between the Ages, but a low print run is still worthy of note. My top picks from this Age would be *Green Lantern* #120-200, *Wonder Woman* #250-329, and *Flash* #300-350.

Copper Age Hot Titles: Miller *Daredevils*, *Dark Knight Returns*, *G.I. Joe*, Elektra and Bullseye appearances.

Copper Age Dead Titles: Most items are actually slow except the mainstream ongoing series. If the title ended in the 1980s, anyone who wished to complete runs did so ten years ago, hence there isn't much back issue action. Titles like *Batman* and even *Superman* always sell as their titles have continued. This will change within a few years though, so watch out.

Bronze Age: This is still the area with the most action for speculators. Why? These are extremely affordable (compared to Silver Age) with loads of minor keys and some major keys. For example, a few years ago, *Tomb of Dracula* #10 (1st Blade) and *Daredevil* #131 (1st Bullseye) were minor books valued barely as much as a new graphic novel; now they are front and center in an immense storm of investors. High grade copies of these fetch easily over $200. These same investors realize there is much more to be seen with other titles and keys. *Marvel Spotlight* has numerous key first appearances, such as #2 (1st Werewolf by Night) and #5 (1st Ghost Rider) and are currently coming close to red hot. Mr. N. Cage is rumored to be Ghost Rider in an upcoming movie and will escalate *Marvel Spotlight* #5 to new heights. These comics are getting truly harder to find in nice shape with their black or red covers and 30+ years of aged paper. There are plenty out there, but not that many in higher grades. Silver Age has gone beyond the reach of many budgets, but not the Bronze Age. There's so much potential. DC made fantastic horror and war titles during this period, the best titles being *Swamp Thing, Weird War Tales, Jonah Hex, Weird Western Tales, Witching Hour*, and of course Joe Kubert's Sgt.Rock in *Our Army At War*. Most superhero titles get all the attention, but these underrated titles are worth buying. Amazing art and stories, low print runs.

Bronze Age Hot Titles: *Marvel Spotlight* #1-12, *Tomb of Dracula* #1 and 10, *Hero For Hire* #1, *Swamp Thing* #1-10, any *Jonah Hex, Werewolf by Night* #32, *Amazing Spider-Man* (especially #121, 122, 129, 136), *X-Men* #94-109, *House of Secrets* #92, tons of *Batman* such as #232 and anything Neal Adams. This list can go on. Basically, any affordable minor/major key goes fast.

Bronze Age Dead Titles: Marvel horror reprints, *Sgt.Fury, Star Wars.*

Silver Age Marvel: Everyone wants *Amazing Spider-Man* and *X-Men*. The other Marvel titles sell well, such as *Fantastic Four* #1-100 and in most grades. The mid-grades sell well due to high grade costs being out of reach. I feel too much attention is being given *Spider-Man*. It is their strongest character and has a hit movie, but *AMZ* #1 should not be higher in value than *FF* #1. True, more people *want* an *AMZ* #1, but *Amazing Fantasy* #15 is alike in key quality to *FF* #1, being the character's first appearance. *AMZ* #1 is *not* a first appearance. There is a large amount of Marvels that should be listed here as fast movers; almost *all* Marvels are moving in any grade. The biggest movers after Marvel's big three of *AMZ, FF,* and *X-Men* are *Daredevil, Avengers, Iron Man, TOS* #49-66, and *TTA* #44-60.

Silver Age DC: Much of DC is overlooked with exceptions like *Batman* and *Detective*. Trying to sell mid-grade DC titles like *Aquaman* or *Atom* is almost impossible. Mainstream titles in mid-grades sell OK (like *Batman, Wonder Woman*) but nowhere near Marvel levels. Low grades move great as readers seem to be truer fans to the art and stories and do not need F+ or VF/NM copies, unlike Marvel fans. Anything Neal Adams sells all the time. Major titles like *Green Lantern, Flash, Wonder Woman, Showcase, Adventure* and all *Supermans* generally sell very well.

Silver Age Hot Titles: *Amazing Spider-Man* (especially #3, 6, 14, 25, 28, 41, 50), *Fantastic Four* (especially #5, 12, 25, 26, 52, 53) any *Wonder Woman* (extremelly hard to find), any Neal Adams art (even ads), of course *Batman* and *Detective, Action* #242 (1st Braniac) and #252 (1st Supergirl), *Superboy* #89 (1st Monel) and *Detective* #359 (1st Batgirl, real HOT!) are some examples.

Silver Age Dead Titles: *Blackhawk* and *Sgt. Fury* rarely sell any more.

Golden/Atom Age: I have a fair amount of superheroes in stock and some do move. Timelys are the hardest to come by and definitely sell over *Guide* in any grade. DCs sell well, with *Batman* and *Detective, Action* and *Superman, Adventure* and *Wonder Woman* leading the way. Fawcetts are slow with *Master Comics* (especially Raboy covers) being the exception. Ducks and *Lulus* sell all the time. *Looney Tunes* is selective but does OK. Westerns like *Lone Ranger, Gene Autry* and *Roy Rogers* do well but the rest hang around. *MAD* does very well, and most EC horror does average. Romance and sci-fi seems dead, but horror is red hot. Horror is very affordable with *Mysterious Adventures* leading the way. Crime does near nothing for me. Less speculators are in this market compared to the hot Silver or Bronze Age keys.

Golden/Atom Age Hot Titles: All Timelys, *All-Star, Batman, Detective, Action*.

Golden/Atom Age Dead Titles: Crime genre.

Gold Keys/Dells/Whitman/Other Non-Superheroes: I mention this separately from the various Ages for a good reason. Superhero titles like *Batman* will always be in demand because they hang around and never end. These books, all non-super-heroes, are in the same realm. Will *The Munsters* never again be a rerun on TV? Or *Star Trek, Gunsmoke, Bonanza*? These TV shows are all part of Americana that will always be on the air, on DVD, and even in new movies. Gold Key, Dell and Whitman made many fantastic TV and movie and funny comics, lots of them featuring photo covers. There is plenty of talk about revivals like *Transformers, G. I. Joe* and so on, so it won't stop there. I have plenty of these books, and I sell plenty of them as well. Photo covers lead the way in popularity. Clayton Moore photos in *Lone Ranger* and *Three Stooges* are extremely hot in this field of collecting. Non-photo covers sell OK, with Disney stuff overall doing better than the rest, especially Barks material. *Archies*, especially early books, do well. Unfortunately, most Dells and non-photo covers are somewhat dead in our store.

© DC

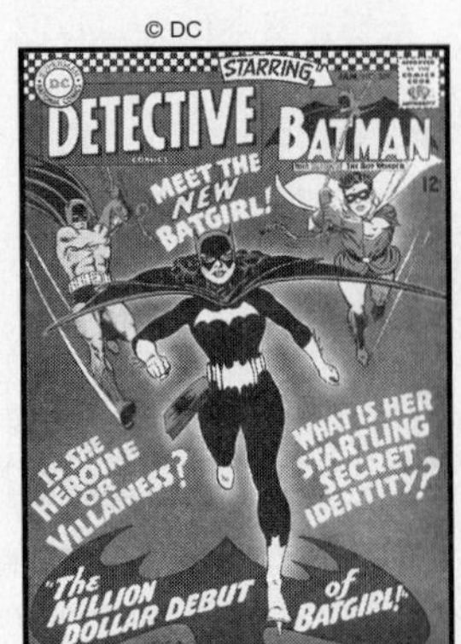

Detective Comics *#359, the debut of Batgirl, is a hot issue from the Silver Age.*

CGC: A necessity for restoration checks and for some investors of bigger books. I never recommend Modern Age books to be slabbed unless you expect a 9.8 or better as anything else seems undesirable. Some items make sense, such as *Amazing Spider-Man* #300 (1st Venom) as a 9.8 will get you $400+, but a 9.4 maybe $80-90. If you happen to have Bronze Age or older books that would make 9.4 or better, that is reasonable as well, as you can attain two times *Guide* or better. If you invest in an expensive Golden Age or key Silver Age book, it is smart to send it off to CGC. Afterall, when you look at a used vehicle that will run you $1000s, why not bring it to your mechanic for an inspection prior to purchase? It may cost you $50-100 for piece of mind, but you will be safer to do so. The cost is negligible compared to the book, it gets a restoration check and a third party grading approximation.

eBay and Internet Auctions: If you have a collection, and need to sell, this is a place to go. If you are a buyer, I'm not so sure. There's too much bad grading, lack of descriptions, fuzzy pictures and shill bidding. Many stores staved off death by selling their wares this way. I prefer to sell in person, be it at the store or at a convention; that way a customer can not only see the book he/she is interested in, but all of them. The collector, to be safe, should always buy that way. Many Internet sellers are not professional graders and at best guess or over-grade. So be safe, have fun, and remember, bidding on the Internet is a bit like an empty Visa card in Vegas–you see chips, not the hours you worked to make that money, and it's too easy to bid.

Investing: Here is my formula and hints about good investing, even if you know zip about comics. #1: Buy the current *Guide*; #2: Buy a *Guide* that is three, four or five years old; #3: Look at mainstream titles that anyone anywhere in the world would recognize, like *Batman*; #4: Track a few affordable key issues and even some non-keys and/or #1s. From this, you see a fair track record of the #1s, keys and overall normal issues increase over a period of time. Big gains would show *Daredevil* #1-10, 131, 168 for example as smart investments. With anything old, say 1939-1974 titles with big names like *Batman, Superman, Spider-Man,* or *X-Men* (these are the big 4), you can't go wrong. If a key issue, major or minor, of a major title or hero, goes up a measily 10% or 15% or 20% yearly, your return doubles in 6.8 or 5.5 or 3.8 years respectively. I know of no stock or bank that gives that interest.

Conclusion: Watch out for high grade horror mags. Marvel is mega-hot in all Ages. Comics are fun to collect, especially when April comes around–new *Guide*!–and comics can make you money. Patience is a virtue in any investment, and comics prove every year the worth of holding on to them. Buy books in front of you, and know what you are buying. There are good buys out there for sure, but be careful. The year at our store has been one of non-stop great collections. In the summer, we had a collection of Silver Age (1965-69) Marvels, 400 total, and most fell in the 8.5-9.6 area. Our best books sold would include *Amazing Fantasy* #15, *Captain America Weird Tales* #74 (I still have a copy), *Star Spangled* run. Best books currently would be *Captain America* #2, *Marvel Mystery* #7 (9.0), *Human Torch* #3 (#2) and #5 (fall). Shop around!

Early ***Uncle Scrooge*** *issues are steady sellers. (#4 shown)*

Dan Fogel & Jim Pitts (Hippy Comix Inc.)

On the national comic convention scene, we've seen increased sales in the following categories and titles:

Golden/Silver/Bronze Age Misc. Publishers: Archie: *That Wilkins Boy*, Charlton: *War Heroes*, *Classics Illustrated*: all printings and conditions are steady sellers; Dell: *Bugs Bunny, New Funnies, Red Ryder, Uncle Scrooge, Walt Disney's Comics & Stories;* Eastern: *Jingle Jangle*; Gold Key: *Space Family Robinson, Star Trek, Tom & Jerry;* Quality: *Marmaduke Mouse*, later humor issues of *National Comics*.

Magazines: *MAD* is a consistent seller, mainly pre-'80s issues, paperbacks, and giants. Warren mags, especially *Vampirella* and *Famous Monsters of Filmland* also sell. Skywald black and white horror mags from the '70s: *Nightmare, Psycho, Shriek*, etc.

DC Golden Age: Mid- to low grade *Sensation Comics, Wonder Woman, Flash Comics*, and *Green Lantern*. People are buying these in any shape now, like Timelys.

DC Silver/Bronze Age: *All-American Men of War, Aquaman, Atom & Hawkman, Batman, Batman Family, Blackhawk, Brave and the Bold, Detective Comics, The Flash, Forever People, Heart Throbs, House of Mystery, House of Secrets, Peter Porkchops, Showcase, Superboy, Superman, Superman's Girlfriend Lois Lane, Superman's Pal Jimmy Olsen, Tales of the Unexpected,* and *Witching Hour*.

DC Modern Age: The new, post-"No-Man's Land" *Batgirl* is selling well in her own title and earlier appearances. Jeph Loeb and Jim Lee's *Batman* is red-hot, and Geoff John's scripts on *Flash* are popular among DC fans. Trade paperbacks and hardcover collected editions continue steady growth in market share.

Marvel Silver/Bronze Age: *Amazing Spider-Man, Arrgh!, Avengers, Captain America, Conan, Daredevil, Fantastic Four, Marvel Spotlight* (Ghost Rider appearances), *Monsters on the Prowl, Punisher, Savage Sword of Conan, Sgt. Fury and his Howling Commandos, Sub-Mariner, Tomb of Dracula, The Mighty Thor, Tales to Astonish*, and *What If?*

Marvel Modern Age: There's been a big upsurge in *X-Men* titles from the early to mid-1980s. Is this a newer, younger, movie-mutated audience looking for titles the older collector takes for granted?

Misc. Modern Age Publishers: *American Splendor*

(thanks to the movie?), *Tug & Buster* #1-7 (by Marc Hempel), Dave Sim's *Cerebus* (as it nears its historic 300th issue), Tim Vigil's *Faust,* and J. Michael Straczynski's *Rising Stars.*

Underground and adult titles sell in general, especially R. Crumb, S. Clay Wilson, and Spain titles.

Stephen Gentner

Golden Age: I feel a bit repetitive in my assessment of Golden Age material, but the trends I see still favor icon covers and characters. *Hit Comics* #5, *Silver Streak* #6, *More Fun Comics* #73, *Human Torch* #12 & #13, *Startling Comics* #49, etc. These books and many more icons like them are strong in upper mid- and better grades; they are still liquid in lower grades when priced fairly. There are those times when even a GD+ copy of *Superman* #14 or #17 will beat *Guide* pricing easily. The lesser covers or crime covers in most of the major titles do not bring the same interest or money from the speculator or savvy collector. This opens a window of opportunity for collectors who aren't concerned with cover content and would like a taste of gold for a reasonable amount of money. I am not aware of many completists in the Golden Age arena who will chase entire runs. This is a function of money and opportunity cost. Silver, Atom Age and Bronze are available, and the question is, do you want a run-of-the-mill *Superman* from 1947, or several Bronze Age keys? The speculator would probably go for the Bronze due to the growth potential, thinking the price of the *Superman* isn't going anywhere fast. Each has its attraction. Timelys, *Batman* titles, and Schomburg rule.

Atom Age/Good Girl: Matt Baker, Jack Kamen, Poolin, Renee and Bob Lubbers give 'good girl' a good name. Fiction House titles like *Fight, Rangers, Wings* and *Planet* are great books to chase, as are Fox titles such as *All Top, Zoot, Rulah. Junior, Phantom Lady* and the smattering of *My Love Secret*, "My Love" everything–i.e. *Secret Confessions, Stories*, all have great icon covers. All of these comics from 1947-49 push the limits of acceptable content; can you say 'racy?' Prices for icons here, when they infrequently appear, are over *Guide* from FN on up.

Silver Age: Anyone with access to eBay can see the high values placed on high grade Silver material, especially Marvel. The pendulum has swung strongly over to *Spider-Man, FF, X-Men, Tales of Suspense* and *Journey Into Mystery*. To a lesser degree but rising are *Strange Tales, Tales to Astonish, Hulk, Avengers,* et al. Over at DC, the *Batman* titles, *Flash, Showcase,* and to a lesser degree *Justice League of America, Atom, Hawkman, Green Lantern, Mystery in Space* et al are also rising. As the Marvel material becomes too pricey, many of those DC titles look like a bargain in comparison, and deserve a look. The "Big Five" war titles are hard to get and cool. *Sgt. Rock* and the *Haunted Tank* with *Enemy Ace* rule. I have found the war titles are nearly impossible to find in grade, and a nice VG/FN is pretty good. Prices are climbing.

Bronze Age: In which titles and odd numbers do the Bronze heroes first appear and older characters become reborn? Which ones are going to stand out? Which ones will languish? The answers are still elusive. Many savvy collectors aren't taking chances and are buying it all so as not to miss out. I repeat myself on this era, often noting that at the time this stuff came out, virtually everybody said it would never be valuable. Notable exceptions would be *Conan, Swamp Thing*, and a few others, but now all bets are off. Prices for some titles and numbers like *Tomb of Dracula* #1, *Special Marvel Edition* #15, *Marvel Team-Up* #1, *Amazing Adventures* #11 and others in highest grade are well over $1,000 and more. It's almost too late to catch anybody napping.

Since Bronze has come on with a vengeance, many collectors are dusting off their long-boxes of '80s and '90s material to reaquaint themselves with what's there. Many print runs in this time frame are low, and if there's a hot-button icon or title, they could be tough. Seasoned collectors would be wise to toss out their prejudices against this era, because it's coming on. Artists like Frank Miller and titles like *Batman: Year One*, *Year Two*, and the first *Dark Knight* series are great.

Just as in guns, cars, watches and coins, as the market rises way up in one area, the cost and scarcity of traditionally accepted icon material moves out of peoples' monetary range. The collector then refocuses on second and third tier areas for the next winner, based on lower cost and availability. What fun is it to chase high grade *Junior Comics* when none ever show up, and when they do, they are too expensive? Affection for recent material, affordability, and availability are all strong demand factors, and this bodes well for renewed interest in our entire comic collecting continuum.

John Hauser

This has been a great year for sales. Golden Age has been tougher to get and easier to sell. Bronze and Silver Age Marvel comics have been in hot demand all year. I have purchased several large Silver Age collections this year and sales of these have been brisk.

Golden Age: Tough to get and easy to sell. Carl Barks' Disneys and Westerns have been hot all year.

Silver Age: Sells well in any grade. High grade Marvels top the list.

Bronze Age: This Age has become very popular in the last couple of years. The readers that grew up with these books now have disposable income.

Modern Age: The '80s are becoming desirable and many collectors are actively looking for these.

CGC: Modern Age has slowed down. Everything else is going strong.

Greg Holland (ValiantComics.com)

It's been a dozen years since a small company revived a couple of Gold Key's Silver Age titles, crafted a new Modern Age universe around them, and changed comic collecting forever. Even though it's also been seven years since the last issue was published, the words "Valiant Comics" still raise eyebrows whenever they're mentioned. For some, Valiant still represents the worst aspects of the hobby – speculation, over-production, and hoarding, which are all, in essence, greed. For others, the story of Valiant is a tragedy – a meteoric rise from humble beginnings to unrivaled success, and then with the blink of an eye, they're gone. While speculators of Valiant, Marvel, DC, and Image books in 1993 lost money across the board, since none of those books held their values until the next year, Valiant is the easiest to blame because the company itself didn't even survive the decade.

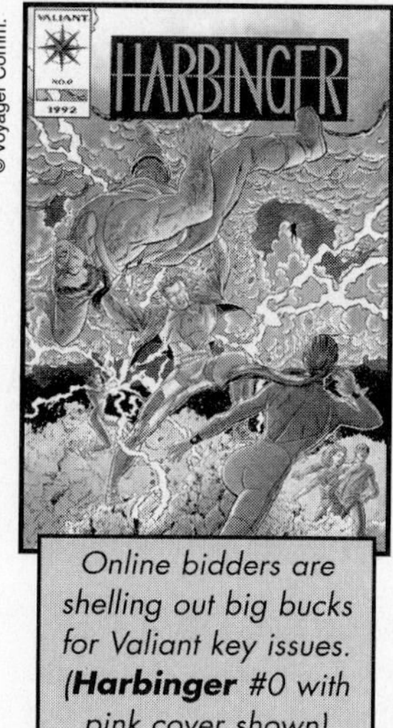

Online bidders are shelling out big bucks for Valiant key issues. (**Harbinger** #0 with pink cover shown)

Today's back issue market, which is primarily online auctions, has established that comic books from the 1990s rarely sell for even one half of *Guide* prices, particularly raw (non-CGC graded) copies. However, a handful of Valiant comics surprisingly and frequently sell for multiples of *Guide*, even without CGC slabs. Among these you will find the first six issues of *Harbinger* (with unclipped coupons), the first five *Rai*, Valiant "key issues" such as *Solar* #10, *Magnus* #12, *Harbinger* #0 (pink cover), and the final issues of titles from 1996. Bidders regularly shell out $50-100 each for *Unity* #0 (red cover), *Chaos Effect Alpha* (red cover), and *X-O Manowar* #1/2 Gold, regardless of the printed *Guide* values. These three books are among the most wanted of the 800 issues needed for a complete Valiant set (1991-1996).

Many dealers reading this might want to disagree, believing they can't sell their Valiant books at any price, but they may be surprised to find that they actually have none of the issues mentioned above. Yes, there are many Valiant issues lingering in bargain bins everywhere, but those issues are from 1993-94. Issues from 1991-92 and 1995-96 are much harder to find, and the market has demonstrated the increasing demand, though prices over the past five years have been driven mainly by back issue collectors and not new issue speculators. Hindsight has allowed collectors to easily differentiate between books which are truly harder to find and those which are not. Slow, steady growth is the new story for early Valiant issues and hopefully this time it will be a happy ending.

And now, back issue sales tracking (raw, non-CGC prices for NM issues). Frozen in time (far below cover price): 1993 issues, *Turok* #1, *Magnus* #25, *Deathmate*. Still cold (at or below cover price): *Archer & Armstrong, Armorines, HARDCorps, Geomancer, Ninjak, PSI-Lords, Second Life of Dr. Mirage, Secret Weapons,* and *Timewalker*. Thawing: *Unity* 1992 issues, post-1995 and/or issues numbers higher than #40. Warming up: pre-*Unity* issues, incentive variants, the "last issue" of 1996 titles. Hot: *Chaos Effect Alpha* red cover ($75), *Unity* #0 red ($50), *Solar* #0 hardcover ($45), *Harbinger* #0 pink ($40), *Harbinger* #1 with coupon ($25), *Magnus* #0 ($20), *Rai* #3-4 ($18 each), *Magnus* #12 ($15), and *Solar* #10 first printing ($12).

William Insignares (Demolitioncomics.com)

This past year was a very busy and great year in sales for us as we kicked off the world's first multi-lingual comic book website. At the click of a button, customers can shop our website in five languages: English, Spanish, German, Italian, and French. We were lucky enough to pull in many new monthly international comic subscriptions and are happy to report that we mailed packages to eighteen different countries. From Aruba to the Netherlands to Venezuela, you guys would not believe what the trends in comic book shopping are in different countries. We even shipped an *Overstreet Comic Book Price Guide* #33 to as far away as Belgium. We were very honored to accept a prestigious award from the Tampa Hispanic Chamber Of Commerce for our remarkable work in the marketing of comics to the Spanish speaking market. We are currently working on our live-action commercial for international TV spots in Spain and Italy (so far). Our goal is to reach those who used to be the unreachable, to promote and distribute American comics to as far away as burros or planes will travel. We are working on several exciting projects associated with this agenda and we will be happy to share those with you in next year's *Guide*.

Meanwhile back at the ranch, Modern Age sales were stronger this year for us than in the past four years. DC and Marvel did an incredible job at promoting and releasing new and exciting projects; it seemed like there was something hot and sold-out coming in every week. DC and Marvel Comics accounted for 70% of our new comics sales, and CrossGen sales did amazingly well for us. Marvel and DC seemed to be in very close competition all year, with each trying to outdo the other in market share, topping Diamond sales charts, and in announcing sell-outs of their new ongoing titles. Both giants also tried desperately to, and often succeeded in, signing hit artists and writers to exclusive contracts, moreso than in the past several years. We really had to keep on our toes and we enjoyed the challenge. As the end of the year closed in, our store sales for new comics were up considerably compared to last year.

The most important change we noticed in the modern new comics market was DC's incredible acceptance in the collectable comic and certified comic markets. It seemed like eons since a new DC comic had sold out immediately and been reprinted once, let alone twice, as was the case with *Teen Titans* #1. Other notable mentions are: *Teen Titans* #2, *Batman* #608 and #612 (2nd printing), *Outsiders* #1-2, *Superman/Batman* #1, *Superman Red Son* #1, and *Formerly Known As The Justice League* #1. These books all sold out fast and most were selling on the secondary market for over three times their cover price in as little as five weeks from their original release date. This was most impressive for DC, as it seemed like only Marvel Comics could claim this amazing feat in the past.

Even more astounding was collectors' acceptance of new DC Comics as being valuable enough to pay to be professionally certified. Many collectors bought them certified directly from their local comic dealers, comic websites (I know many customers enjoyed getting 15% of submissions by submitting from our website), conventions, or online from auction sites such as eBay and Yahoo. Some notable closing prices on online auctions in this classification are: *Superman Red Son* #1 CGC 9.8 $85, *Teen Titans* #1 (Michael Turner cover) CGC 9.8 $117, *Batman* #608 (1st printing) $80, *Batman* #608 RRP variant CGC 9.8 $2,300 (and the reserve was not even met), *Batman* #612 (2nd printing) $119. This unbelievable list could go on and on.

Comic related movies continue to influence back issues sales for titles like *Punisher, Namor, Fantastic Four* and *Hellboy.*

As we celebrate our ten year anniversary, we would like to thank all of our loyal customers who have helped us grow and succeed throughout the years. Thanks to all the comic industry professionals that have shopped with us and those who continue to do so including the guys from CrossGen and CGC. Thanks to all the industry celebrities who appear on our website via video and introduce our company. See you all next time.

Nadia Mannarino (All Star Auctions)

2003 was a great one for All Star Auctions. We held our catalogue sale early in the year, with many record setting results. We also held 1000s of Internet/eBay auctions, and we also held our annual San Diego Comic Con sale.

As always, our sales include high end, pedigree CGC-graded Golden Age and Silver Age comics as well as important non-pedigree, non-CGC graded books. We have found through the year that the pedigree CGC-graded books do realize multiples of their *Guide* value but that multiple has decreased over last year. This is due, in our opinion, to the extensive amount of material that has surfaced this year. The market is in the midst of a correction, as prices were spiraling and now there is more of an equilibrium; this is not a bad thing. All markets go through this process and are usually the better for it as the market solidifies.

What is interesting is the change of venue our hobby/business has taken. Conventions don't seem to be the gathering places they once were. With eBay, it is a convention a day; this is a double-edged sword. Selling material has never been easier, but it is securing large important collections of prime Golden and Silver Age comics that has become a challenge. This will obviously affect prices – as material becomes harder to get, prices for existing items will rise.

2004 promises to be another strong year, and with the many movie adaptations of comic books continuing, we think comics will continue to grow in their nostalgic value. Comic books are a very big part of America's popular culture and as such their visibility will continue to increase. These are very exciting times and we are fortunate to be a part of them.

Patrick Marchbanks (Golden Age Comics & Games)

This year, much as it has been in the past few years, the market for vintage comic books and original artwork has flourished, from the astounding, record-breaking prices being set for some of the best material in the world, to smooth and consistent prices being realized for books of all grades and genres. Sales have been steady from our website, Internet auctions and convention exploits throughout the year. There has also been a decent amount of material available to us to purchase. For the most part, purchases have included smaller collections of Golden and Silver Age books along with some very interesting pieces of Silver Age comic artwork.

CGC: Throughout the year encapsulated books in NM 9.4 or better continue to command extreme premium prices regardless of the book's age. While the monetary price will of course always be greater for an encapsulated NM 9.4 Golden Age key as opposed to a Modern Age NM 9.4, the multiples of *Guide* being paid seem to remain for the most part the same. There is however the off occasion when Modern Age books in CGC NM 9.4 or higher have reached upwards of ten to twelve times the actual value of the book itself while a Golden Age book in the same high grade may only realize two to three times the *Guide* value of that particular issue. This is somewhat odd considering the rarity of a Near Mint sixty-year-old book as opposed to a Near Mint five-year-old book.

Another key change in 2003 has been the label that CGC places inside their slab. Overall opinions are that it was a good improvement to enlarge the numerical grade of the book and have it boldly displayed on the left side of the label. Now individuals can clearly see the grade of an encapsulated book if it is resting on a convention or store wall, not to mention knowing the grade of a book by a mere glance at the slab. Also improved is the arrangement of important information on the label such as the year of publication, artist, grader notes and bar code. With all these improvements, many people, including myself, were a little disappointed that CGC removed the actual word of the grade from the label (i.e., VG, VF, NM). The concern about the removal of the grade title from the label is that it is imperative that people be able to associate the numerical grade with the grade title. So many new people are constantly entering the world of comic collecting that it is important that they understand that a grade title goes right along with a numerical representation of that grade. I have already seen it happen where a customer comes up to me and asks if I have any 7.5s or 8.0s. When told that I do have their particular request in Very Fine, I will get a blank stare back and then a response such as, "No, I wanted an 8.0., What is a Very Fine?" With the removal of the grade title from the CGC label, many feel this may become a common occurrence.

Newcomers to our business/hobby must become aware that a 4.0 is also known as a Very Good or a 6.0 is also called a Fine. Hopefully CGC will at some point reconsider this removal and place the grade title back on the labels along with the numerical representation of that grade.

Restoration: This is a controversial topic in our business in the past few years, and I have noticed a major increase in the realized sale prices of professionally restored Golden Age books. This past year in particular, we have sold a vast array of restored Golden Age at prices higher then we have been able to in the past. As I have stated in previous market reports, I continue to feel the true reason for this seems to be an ever-growing number of collectors that desire a nice looking solid copy of a book that is unrestored would for the most part be out of their reach. While restored Golden Age books are swiftly sold in today's market, any book printed after 1955 regardless of being a key issue or not will sell either slowly or not at all if it has been restored. Also it has come to my attention that most individuals who purchase restored books prefer to purchase them raw and not slabbed by CGC.

Original Comic Art: While we do offer a small selection of comic art for sale on our website, the majority of all comic art that is purchased by Golden Age Comics & Games remains stored in our vault. Throughout 2003 there has been a sudden abundance of vintage original comic art that has become available to us, particularly Silver Age. Only time will tell if the surge of availability will help or hurt the value of these usually difficult to locate comic art pages. I do not believe that the value of these prices will fall at all, and after these current offerings are bought up and placed into private collections, their rarity will again become apparent and prices should again boom.

Conventions: 2003 was again a year of exciting and action-filled comic conventions. While we were unable to set up at all of the events we had originally planned, I and few staff members attended a large number of shows simply to walk the floor, talk with fellow dealers and to buy material. This flip of positions (we usually set up in the dealer area) enabled us to get a unique perspective of this past year's shows. The conventions seem to be significantly stronger for selling than buying this year. Most attributed this to strong Internet and auction sales throughout the year. The majority of dealers report brisk sales at practically all major shows. Overall it seems convention sales from 2003 surpassed sales from 2002.

Conclusion: As we look on into the future, I expect that unrestored books that have been encapsulated and graded CGC VF/NM 9.0 or higher will continue their upward climb and remain selling for above *Guide* prices, especially as the best copies are sold and placed into permanent collections. Sales through the Internet (eBay and website) should remain steady, with most raw books realizing prices right at or slightly above the *Guide* value. Vintage comic books overall should continue to sell well regardless of grade. Their investment potential is greater then most stocks of today, as practically all Golden and Silver Age books steadily increase in value annually. This fact continues to attract new investors and collectors which in turn aids in values rising even more. Exciting times truly await all who are involved in this fast-paced, ever-changing yet constantly growing marketplace.

Jon McClure

With the 2003 economy sluggish at best, sales of general comics were slow again this year, continuing the pattern of rare, key and especially high grade comics selling best. Lower grade Silver and Bronze bring 150-200% of *Guide* for "reading copies," where collectiblity is negligible to collectors who want to enjoy perusing affordable issues. It is also easy to sell your low grade older comics as a collector with little risk financially, unlike books in the FN/VF range, which tend to be slow movers. Every region is unique for sales; in Durango, Colorado I sell *Red Ryder* at 250-300% *Guide* and with no resistance (the Red Ryder Museum is one hour away in Pagosa Springs.) *Archie*s sell at double *Guide*, and 1970s Charlton romance bring 125-150% *Guide*. 20¢ cover Marvel and DC are heating up, especially the 1972 DCs with the larger 20¢ page opposite the DC symbol, in all grades. Skywald and other black and white horror mags are often requested but impossible to restock, and sell quickly at 150% *Guide* in any grade.

Dale Moore (www.comics4kids.org)

There has been activity in all areas, as investors hunting for high grade comics are finding that they are reunited with stories that captivated them previously. Others are discovering new gems regularly. Identifying writers and artists is a challenge to the casual collector. The gears are grinding and players are assembling in the fields as the anticipation mounts for third party grading to attack the comic book magazine megalith. Even dog-eared, tattered examples are being voraciously consumed by collectors, investors and speculators as they ace to glean all the knowledge they can. Future fruits of labor possibly include a coveted high grade, relevant appearance, or artist's first work or key issue. This feeding frenzy will continue to fuel challenges for high ranking in third party grading services such as CGC. What treasure will census placement bring? Only time will tell.

Terry O'Neill (Terry's Comics)

The end of 2002 and most of 2003 was a good market for comic sales. Strong demand continues for high grade Bronze and Silver Age comics. This is starting to be seen for DC titles as well as Marvels. As always, locating enough high grade Silver and Bronze Age to satisfy collector demand proved challenging.

Golden Age: There is a large quantity of this material available for sale through the auction houses and eBay. Timely Comics have been slow to sell but as elusive as ever to acquire, while *Captain America* is still the most requested title. Comics with Alex Schomberg war covers such as *Thrilling,*

Exciting, All Select and others are always in demand. Most Golden Age superhero books priced below $50 continue to sell well at, or slightly above *Guide*. About a year ago, I purchased a small group of lower grade superheroes (most publishers), and half of them are still in my inventory. I believe that DC Golden Age, especially early *Batman, Superman* and pre-hero titles such as *Adventure, More Fun* and *Detective*, in lower to mid-grade are overpriced in the *Guide*. On the other hand, I bought some Centaurs and Fox superhero books a few months ago, most of which sold quickly at or slightly above *Guide*. *Sensation Comics* also sell well at or slightly above *Guide*. Overall, Golden Age comics are moving within a year or two of purchase when priced according to market.

Red Ryder Comics *is a best-selling western title from the Atom Age. (#13 shown)*

Atom Age: It seems that I can never find enough material from this era. Pre-Code horror is on the move again, with the classic covers always getting top dollar. Most EC titles are on the upswing after many years of decline. Crime titles are steady sellers but almost never selling above *Guide;* however, they are a good and less expensive alternative to horror. Western comics also continue to move; *John Wayne, White Indian, Durango Kid* and *Tim Holt* always sell. The old serial cowboys such as *Gene Autry* and *Roy Rogers* sell well, but *Red Ryder* is my best-selling western title. DC war titles are slow sellers unless they have Sergeant Rock or dinosaurs in them. Atlas war titles continue to sell well for three main reasons: they are cheap, they have good artwork, and they have good stories. Science fiction titles such as *House of Mystery, House of Secrets* and *Mystery in Space* sell at a steady pace but at slightly below *Guide*. Atlas science fiction titles such as *Journey into Unknown Worlds* and *Space Squadron* tend to be a little pricey and continue to sell at a slower pace. *Journey into Mystery, Strange Tales* and *Menace* always sell well. ACG titles tend to be a little bland in art and stories, but they trickle out when discounted. High demand continues for romance and teen comics, such as *Kilroys* and *Tissue*, selling mostly at or slightly above *Guide*. Even higher priced books are moving well, especially if they have Matt Baker, Bill Ward or Jack Kamen art in them. Early *Archie* titles are a little slower, but *Katy Keene* is an exception. Funny animal comics sell but must be discounted to move. There are some exceptions to this, such as *Walt Disney's Comics* before #50, early *Four Color Comics*, and *Looney Tunes* before #40. Most cartoon comics such as *Casper, Bullwinkle* and *Popeye* are selling well. *Tarzan, Marge's Little Lulu* and *Dick Tracy* are always in demand with *Mutt and Jeff* making a comeback. Over all, the Atom Age comics are good, steady sellers, but there are no price records being set within this group.

Silver Age: This era is the backbone for almost all back issue collectors and dealers. *Amazing Spider-Man* continues to be the best seller, and demand has increased for *Tales of Suspense* and *Fantastic Four. Fantastic Four* issues below #20 in high grade are extremely hard to find, and quick to sell over *Guide*. *Rawhide Kid* and other Marvel westerns are selling well at or slightly above *Guide*. I've been getting a lot of requests for a nice copy of *Silver Surfer* #1, but I rarely find one above a VG. The pre-hero titles of *Amazing Adventures, Amazing Adult Fantasy, Journey into Mystery, Strange Tales, Tales of Suspense* and *Tales to Astonish* are hard to find in Fine or better and sell fast in all grades. DC titles in high demand are *Wonder Woman* and *Adventure Comics* with either Superboy and the Legion of Super-Heroes or Supergirl in them. Superman family titles are reliable sellers, but sales of Batman titles are showing some decline. *Green Lantern, House of Mystery,* and *House of Secrets* are steady second-string titles, as is (much to my surprise) *Angel and the Ape*. DC romance titles are selling well if priced near *Guide*. I purchased a large selection of Tower Comics; they sell at regular intervals, but haven't set any price records. Charltons continue to be slow sellers unless they are very cheap; the exception is *The Phantom*. Dell and Gold Key TV/movie titles are selling quite well at or slightly below *Guide*. *Doctor Solar* and *Turok* are steady sellers, and back from the "dead titles" box is *Star Trek*. I recently picked up a large collection with many DC Silver and Bronze Age comics; there were full runs of almost every title, especially some hard-to-find romance titles. Two of the Super DC Specials sold above *Guide*.

Bronze Age: This era is finally giving my Silver Age inventory competition for volume of books sold, but they still have a way to go before they reach the higher *Guide* prices of Silver. There are certainly many more books from this era in high grade, however there seems to be a lot less key books from this era in high grade than one would expect. Once again, the book with the highest demand is *Hulk* #181. This book always sells fast and over *Guide* in any grade. Also, *Amazing Spider-Man* #129 is again a close runner-up for a high demand book. Most of Marvel's long-running horror titles such as *Tomb of Dracula, Werewolf by Night* and *Frankenstein* are good sellers. DC titles are a little slower, but steady with *Adventure* (with The Spectre), *Phantom Stranger, Witching Hour* and *Weird War Tales* leading in sales. Oddball Marvel romance, western, teen and kid titles are selling well if you can find them. *X-Men* titles have slowed down a bit despite a relatively successful second movie. *Justice League, Batman* and *Wonder Woman* from this era are sought after in high grade. As for funny animals, titles by Whitman sell, but not much else from the other publishers of the era.

Magazines: *Savage Sword of Conan* is still a top seller. *Creepy, Eerie, Vampirella* and other Warren magazines in higher grade continue to sell very well; this may have to do with CGC now offering grading services for magazine-size books. Selling at or over *Guide* are *Deadly Hands of Kung-Fu* and *Planet of the Apes* in higher numbers, although they are very hard to locate. Overall, the illustrated magazine market is quite healthy.

Modern Age & Independents: *Daredevil* #132, #158 and #181 were my best selling Modern Age books this year, probably due to the movie association. *Wolverine* V1#1-4 were good sellers as well. *Hulk* #340 is on the upswing, and *Amazing Spider-Man* #300 continues to do well. I picked up a run of *Miracleman*, most of which sold quickly. The scarce issue #15 sold above *Guide* in mid-grade. *Spawn* continues to sell well, as do EC reprints. Most early 1980s independents by Eclipse, PC and First are well drawn and written. They all sell at very reasonable prices and I would consider most of them to be bargains, except for the large supply that exists.

CGC: I have been generally satisfied with this service; I use it mostly for high grade and expensive key comics. I believe they have tightened up their grading in the past year and their turnaround time has greatly improved. I was particularly happy to see same day grading offered at the Chicago Comic Con. I had been requesting this for a long while now. There has been talk of some competing companies, but I have yet to see their product.

Internet Sales: I have finally transferred my website to a database compatible host. I have had an increase in sales from my website as a result of keeping it updated. I was also a little happier with the eBay sales I did this year. They were still below show sales, but some of the better material sold close to *Guide*.

In summary, most comic book sales this year have been better than the same titles sold last year, comic fan attendance at all conventions appears to have been up, and my last catalog was my most successful ever. In short, the comic market seems to be stable, and even in some areas, expanding.

Josh Nathanson

ComicLink (**www.comiclink.com** and **www.comiclinkexpress.com**) is a full-service, automated exchange for investment quality Golden Age, Silver Age, Bronze Age and CGC-graded comic books and original comic book art. This is the market I am specifically commenting on in this report; the state of the Modern Age back issue market may be very different.

2003 has been another banner year for the vintage comic book industry. Thanks to a steady influx of new buyers and a solid base of sellers, there is a lot of vintage material on the market and prices generally remain strong. As has increasingly become the trend, and has been solidified even more by Hollywood this year, the most buyers exist for Silver and Bronze Age Marvel comic books. That is not to say that other areas are not strong as well; it just means that this area is currently stronger. There is more volume in this category than ever before.

The strength of Silver and Bronze Age comic books is a result of a broad market surge caused by many aggressive buyers. This is especially true for CGC-graded comic books in the right grade. Existing collectors are willing to pay more money than ever before in order to fill in their runs. New collectors continue to enter the market at higher prices. Many other collectors and dealers provide strong price support at low retail levels. Many collectors and dealers have driven the rise in prices because it indicates that the risk of the bottom falling out when a few major players leave the market is minimal. There is a lot of support for Silver and Bronze Age Marvel comic books and I do not expect this to change anytime soon.

Other categories, such as Golden Age and pre-Code horror and science fiction, have shown less support. A few major players moving the market caused price increases in the recent past. They paid prices that were much higher than what the average collector in the field was willing to pay and then stopped buying as aggressively. Some have become sellers, increasing supply without an offsetting increase in demand. Combined, these two factors have resulted in a drop in prices. The good news for collectors and investors is that prices have already dropped and settled for most items within these categories. Having settled in at relatively affordable levels, collectors are once again able to buy without much downside risk and with significant upside. It only takes a few big money players to come in to lift this market. When this occurs, it will once again create lofty profits for collectors and investors. Although many great books have surfaced over the last few years, there is not enough supply to handle a strong influx of big money without resulting in price increases. It may take a few more years for this to occur, but patient investors will most likely be rewarded.

©ECL

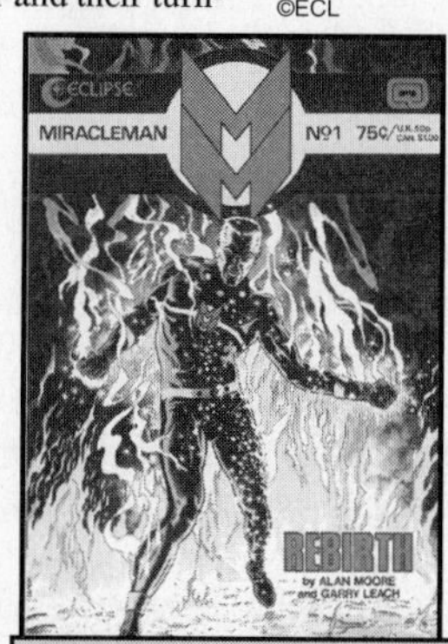

Modern Age issues like Alan Moore's ***Miracleman*** *#1 will sell quickly.*

As a result of the strong market for investment-quality material and advances in our comic book exchange, this year was a landmark year for ComicLink. Among other improvements to the website infrastructure, the bid/ask system of the exchange is automated in real-time, and an automated Wantlist Service, traditional online auctions and a sophisticated search engine have been added. Across the board, the response from buyers and sellers, dealers and collectors has been overwhelmingly positive. Users have been extremely active by buying, bidding, listing, and consigning comic books and comic art. Sellers on the site are obtaining great prices for Golden, Silver and Bronze Age keys. A few key sales this year include:

All-Star Comics #11 CGC 9.4 $8,500; *Amazing Fantasy* #15 CGC VF 8.0 $17,250; *Amazing Spider-Man* #14 CGC 9.6 $17,000; *Batman* #12 CGC 9.2 $6,500; *Brave and the Bold* #34 CGC 9.4 $12,800; *Detective Comics* #1 CGC 6.0 $42,000;

Flash Comics #1 VGF 5.0 $14,100; *Incredible Hulk* #1 CGC 8.5 $11,500; *Incredible Hulk* #3 CGC 9.4 $10,025; *Journey Into Mystery* #83 CGC VF 8.0 $5,275; *Sub-Mariner Comics* #1 CGC 8.5 $25,000; *X-Men* #1 CGC 9.4 $45,000; *X-Men* #1 CGC 9.2 $20,000.

Most new collectors and investors that are spending a lot of money on comic books are interested in buying CGC-graded material. The CGC market is still relatively new but it has evolved significantly over the past few years. When CGC first started, the same multiples of Guide were being charged for nearly all high grade books depending upon their condition. A 9.4 Silver Age Spider-Man would sell for the same price as a 9.4 Golden Age Batman; this is no longer the case. Now, not only do *Spider-Man* comic books generally sell for different multiples of Guide than *Batman*, but the multiples vary from issue to issue within these titles. Across the board, market prices are now dependent upon the specific grade and the specific item. *Amazing Spider-Man* #31 and *Amazing Spider-Man* #33 were published within two months of each other, yet on ComicLink.com a 9.6 copy of #33 sold for $900 while a 9.6 copy of #31 sold for $2,750. This has nothing to do with the contents or the fact that one cover is better than another; this is a result of the fact that #33 is a "warehouse book" – dealers found many of this issue in stacks and there are a lot of high grade copies around. As of this date, there are 31 of these issues in 9.6 as compared with only 7 in 9.6 for the #31. The fourfold difference in scarcity resulted in a threefold difference in price.

Pricing is generally determined by the combination of supply and demand factors, previously realized prices for the same or similar issue in a specific grade, and the established Guide price. The way these four factors interact also differ from book to book. Although it's not rocket science, it is notably difficult for a novice investor/collector to know what to pay for a specific item. It is not always easy to know which items are good deals at the listed price and which items are to be avoided. Buyers investing in comic books also need to understand a bit about market timing and have a realistic time horizon in mind in order to make a profit. A common mistake made by new investors is that they do not know when to get in and when to get out of a purchase. They either liquidate too soon for a loss, or take the opposite approach and hold out for too long after getting an excellent one-time offer that would have led to a significant profit. It is worthwhile for any novice collector or investor to talk to an experienced (and honest) professional in the field prior to making significant purchases. It is also completely necessary to accurately state one's objectives. The advice given will be totally different if a buyer wants to make a profit in two years instead of ten. I offer confidential advice free of charge to ComicLink clients interested in investing significant sums of money. If a buyer is able to make an educated decision before purchasing an item, it is more likely that buyer will be happy in the future and continue to stay in the hobby.

What is ahead for 2004? We are in for more of the same. High grade Silver and Bronze Age Marvel will lead the way in dollar sales and will continue to set record prices. Silver and Bronze Age Marvel will also lead the way in volume. Having settled in price, key Golden Age and pre-Code horror and science fiction comic books look like sleepers; some buyers are already starting to recognize this. That said, it may be another year or two before demand for these categories is sufficient enough to absorb supply and lead to further price escalation.

Redbeard's Book Den

Prices remained strong during the past year in the comic book marketplace as the recovery of the national economy continues. Within the marketplace, price increases varied. As the Golden Age slowed, the Silver Age caught fire. This is an all too familiar trend and one that has proved very healthy for the marketplace in previous years. The last three major increases in Golden Age prices were preceded by large increases in the Silver Age segment.

Golden Age: As the year progressed, increases in this area became more restricted, more of a mixed bag than prior years as the buyers' market continued. Increases were not defined by genre or publisher as much as by specific titles or specific issues.

1930s Titles: This category experienced slower sales as current prices have met resistance in the marketplace. DC titles were the most requested, with renewed interest in early Dell titles.

1940s Titles: Superhero titles are still the favorite, with Timely and DC as the hottest areas.

DC: These saw record prices for almost all books in 9.4 or higher. Sales on lower grade issues for most titles have met resistance at current price levels. Key cover issues still command above Guide in all grades. *Action, Superman,* and *Wonder Woman* sold well at above Guide in all grades. *Batman* in lesser grade has met some resistance due to current price levels. There were slower sales for earlier issues of *Leading, Comic Cavalcade* and *Star Spangled*. Offbeat title sales were slower than superhero titles.

Timely: Sales remained strong throughout the year, with record prices for 9.2 or higher books. *Captain America, Marvel Mystery, Sub-Mariner* and *Human Torch* were the most active with very good sales in all grades. Other superhero titles had good sales at or above current Guide levels. There were slower sales for offbeat titles.

Fawcett: These saw slower sales throughout. The best-selling title is still *Captain Marvel*. Key covers brought higher prices on all titles.

Centaur: Sales slowed for this publisher, while record prices continued for 9.4 or higher books. Key covers are still in demand at higher prices, with slower sales for their non-superhero titles.

Fox: These saw good sales at current Guide levels for most superhero titles. Lou Fine issues are still the most demanded with 9.4 copies or higher bringing record prices. Offbeat title sales were slower.

Gleason: Slower sales overall were observed for this publisher. Good sales on *Silver Streak* and earlier issues of *Daredevil* were seen, but slower sales were noted on earlier issues of *Boy*. Offbeat title sales slowed.

Fiction House: Slower sales on earlier, more expensive issues were seen. "Good Girl" art still helps this publisher's sales. There were slow sales on offbeat titles.

Quality: Lou Fine titles are still the most popular, but there were slow sales for this publisher.

MLJ: Sales have also slowed for this publisher, with record prices for 9.4 or better copies. Key covers are still in strong demand.

Nedor: Good sales were seen, as Schomberg covers are still very popular, including his work on offbeat titles.

Classic Comics: Slower sales were also noted for this publisher.

Funny Animal: The most requested publisher is once again Dell with good sales above current Guide levels. There were record prices for 9.2 or higher early Dells and record prices for early high grade *Comics & Stories*. Timely and DC are also popular, but overall there were slow sales for this category.

Misc. Publishers: Keys and first issues of superhero titles are the most requested. Key covers are very important in determining demand. There were slower sales overall for most publishers.

Atom Age: This Age saw mixed sales throughout. Demand varied as to titles or particular issues versus across the board as in previous years. Still, sales remained somewhat better than Golden Age books.

Dell/GK: Where are all those high grade duck one-shot file copies from yesteryear? As an old timer, I can tell you there were a lot of them, but only a very small amount have entered the market over the past few years. I won't begin to speculate how much 9.2 or better duck one-shots will bring at auction currently. Disney has always had a solid following. A special thank you to Steve Geppi for helping make sure another generation of kids has the opportunity to grow up with those great Disney characters. Barks is still very popular. There were good sales in low grade and slow sales in mid-grade above Fine. 9.2 or higher copies are bringing record prices.

Atlas: Mixed sales were seen for this publisher, with record prices for 9.2 or higher copies. Key covers are very important, and there were good sales for crime, romance, war and horror/SF titles. There was lesser demand for offbeat titles.

DC: This publisher has also had mixed sales. The most popular areas are war and western titles followed by horror/SF titles.

TV/Movie Titles: Lesser condition title sales were good at current Guide levels. Medium grade titles are still slower. Photo covers are the most popular.

EC: Horror and SF titles are still very strong. Gaines file copies continue to bring record prices. There were also strong sales for *MAD* comic books and very good sales for *Shock SS, Crime SS, Frontline* and *Two-Fisted*. *Picto-Fiction* titles sell very well in all grades above current Guide levels. There were slower sales for *MAD* magazines, but they still remain popular.

Westerns: There were mixed sales led by the photo cover issues. Key covers and issues are very important in determining demand.

Dell Giants: In lower grade, sales remain strong, with record prices for 9.4 or higher copies. Mid-grade sales in Fine and above remain slow.

Romance: Good sales continue across the board for most titles in this genre. Key covers bring record prices. 9.2 or higher copies are selling for record prices.

Humor, Funny Animal, Teen-Age, Strip Reprints: All these categories saw slow sales at current Guide levels.

"Good Girl" Art: Good demand continues for this genre in all grades, with record prices for Schomberg covers and Nedor titles in 9.2 or higher. *Phantom Lady* is still very popular, with record prices for *Phantom Lady* #17 and *Blue Beetle* #54. Key covers sell very well over current Guide levels.

Avon: Horror, science fiction, romance and crime titles continue to sell well. Western and war titles are still selling a bit slower for this publisher. Offbeat title sales were slower.

Horror/Science Fiction: Good sales continue for this genre, with record prices for books in 9.2 or higher. Key covers range from strong demand to hot. Interior content is also important in determining a title's demand.

Sports: There were slower sales here versus prior years. Fawcett one-shots sell well over current Guide levels.

Art Titles: These saw record prices for 9.2 or higher copies. Strong demand continues for Baker with good sales over current Guide. There was also good demand for LB Cole books and increased sales for Wolverton horror/science fiction titles. Ditko and Kirby books still sell very well above current Guide. Frazetta continues to sell very well. Kubert, Krigstein, Toth and Williamson are requested at a slower rate than those previously mentioned. Katz and Torres demand was slight in comparison to others.

Silver Age: How about those Silver Age DCs in 9.0 or higher? Gary and Lane Carter, where are you? Wow! To say that this area is hot is an understatement. Sales throughout the Silver Age are on the rise with record prices for high grade copies. There were good sales in all grades. Early *Spider-Man, FF, X-Men* and *Hulk* were very strong.

Bronze Age: Record prices continue to be realized for very high-grade copies of mid-'70s books. Sales of better condition books from this period sell very well at both conventions and Internet websites. The most popular are new *X-Men* titles.

Israel Rodriguez (Midgard Comic Den)

2003 has been the best year for comic books that I have seen in a very long time. With blockbuster movies like *The Hulk, X2* and *League of Extraordinary Gentlemen*, it comes as no surprise. Many of the collectors from the early '90s are beginning to reappear for the first time in ten years and are picking up comic books like *Spawn* and *Spider-Man* #1. Batman titles are on fire with the Jim Lee/Jeph Loeb "Hush" storyline and with this, all of the Jim Lee penciled books from earlier in his career are white hot. Many of the independent comics are gaining recognition. My best indy seller by far is *Johnny the*

Homicidal Maniac, followed by *Squee* and *Lenore.*

Bronze Age: Bronze Age books are selling extremely well with record sales on books like *Incredible Hulk* #181 and *X-Men* #94 as well as *Giant-Size X-Men* #1. Bronze Age kung-fu books like *Iron Fist* and *Master of Kung-Fu* are selling extremely well. Bronze Age DC and Marvel horror like *Swamp Thing, Ghosts, Unexpected, Tomb of Dracula,* and *Werewolf By Night* are selling well at *Guide.*

Silver Age: Silver Age comics are becoming the younger collector's Golden Age. I have seen a 25% sales increase in the last year. Any *Amazing Spider-Man* or (*Uncanny*) *X-Men* below #100 sell out. I cannot keep Silver Age *Captain America, Justice League, G.I. Combat, Our Army at War* and *Star Spangled War Stories* in VF condition or better.

Atom Age: EC war and horror books are selling good with high demand.

With upcoming movies like *The Punisher, Spider-Man 2* and *Hellboy*, I hope 2004 will be as good a year as 2003.

Matt Schiffman

Platinum Age: I am seeing more and more low grade books show up in collections, for sale and in antique malls. Is this a viable market? Is it still in its infancy or in its decline? I find myself with quite a few of the "scarce" issues, and find it difficult to get around 30% of *Guide*. Cool as they might be, finding active collectors that can find these bygone characters still relevant is a tough task.

Pulps: The injection of comic book collectors into this genre has only helped flush out some great books that have languished in long time collections. Prices for the "Spicy" titles have escalated over the past year, as well as the continued strength in the *Shadow* and *Spider* titles. Key Louis L'Amour/Mayo appearances as well as Agatha Christie and other crossover authors drive key issues in the more moribund titles. As a market still in transition, demand still far outweighs supply as collectors have yet to find enough to keep them actively interested.

Golden Age: I still cannot think of a year where more quality material turned up for sale at auction, eBay and with dealers. Deep runs of Timely and mainstream DC allowed collectors to pick from a wide range of prices and grades. Although many of these new books that had higher grades found a welcome reception and well deserved multiples, this enthusiastic injection did not seem to help the market overall. More and more, we are seeing lower prices from online sales, with only slightly higher fractions of *Guide* being achieved at conventions. The market does indeed seem poised for a correction, especially at the mid- to lower grade levels. Pockets of strength continue to be many of the Fiction House titles, odd keys, high grade Timely, Flash, and early *Detective*. We still see continued strength in the low grade keys, with auction prices for books in GD nearing *Guide* prices for VG, while the VG price stands still and the FN price lowers toward the VG price. This is by no means a new trend, but one that has been developing over the past three years and continues to cement.

© FH

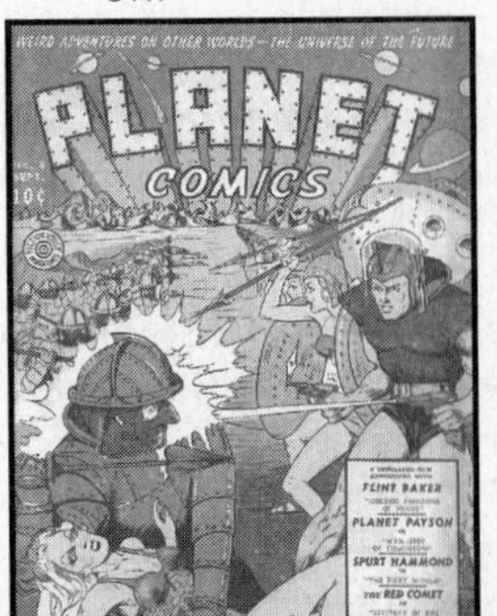

Planet Comics *is one of the pockets of strength in the Golden Age market. (#8 shown)*

Atom Age: As a genre that continues to show strength across the board in all grades, only a few pockets continue to remain soft while more new highs continue to be set. Fox 'Good Girl,' St. John Romance, Fiction House, and most of the pre-Code horror titles still retain their popularity, growth and price levels. This seems to still be the only genre where you see the ungraded books being sold for more than *Guide* prices. Scarcity drives the success of this era more than anything else. Collectors know that some of these books are so difficult to find in any grade that they are willing to step up and pay. The crossover from other hobbies into the western titles, Dell movie/TV and *Peanuts* issues continues as strong as ever. Even if they are not willing to pay *Guide* prices, at least they bring some activity to these slower moving titles.

Silver Age: This continues to be where the market reigns supreme and continues to bring headlines. *The New York Times, Economist, Forbes*, and more have latched onto the newfound explosion of high end CGC Silver Age keys. Still leading the way is *Amazing Fantasy* #15 and *Amazing Spider-Man* #1, but a truly high grade *FF* #1 or *X-Men* #1 just might pose a good challenge to these two top titles. The DC keys have been lagging behind for the past four years and have yet to see the rebound that most everyone expected. Although bidding on the Heritage high grade *Showcase* #4 was active, it still fell short of expectations placed on it by the market. Although no true breakout DC book has emerged, there is plenty of action in the other titles. *Brave and the Bold* #65-105, *Showcase* #45-90, *Adventure* #300-400, and high grade *Detective* and *Batman* issues all bring multiples of *Guide* when receiving a 9.2 or better. The *Hulk* and *Daredevil* movies brought a smallish spike to the Silver Age issues but could not sustain those highs after the poor showing of each. Unfortunately, the growing rift between these 9.0 and better books and those falling below that continues to spread.

Once hot titles even in the lower grades, such as *Amazing Spider-Man, Fantastic Four* and *X-Men*, find it difficult to come close to *Guide* in 8.5 and lower. Mere fractions of *Guide* are becoming the norm and DC titles in lower grade suffer even more.

Bronze Age: The explosive growth in this section has redefined the entire hobby. The dramatic price escalation brought in a whole new collector that had not previously collected these long-ignored books. Even those of us who have been collecting these books for years were like deer in the headlights when it came to the huge multiples that are being paid for the emerging keys. The traditional triumph rate of *Hulk* #181, *Giant-Size X-Men* #1 and *X-Men* #94 continued to lead the way and set new highs that most thought not possible, but it was the emergence of a few new keys that set the market alight. *Tomb of Dracula* #1, *Marvel Team-Up* #1, *Amazing Adventures* #11, *Dark Mansion of Forbidden Love* #1, *Detective* #400, and *Avengers* #93 all brought new vigor to the genre. In addition, plenty of other books are bringing incredible multiples that are just not seen in the other segments of our hobby. Even those books and titles long thought irredeemable are finding new life after receiving a high grade from CGC. DC issues show an overall strength not found elsewhere in our hobby. With such passion and still a lack of complete artist attribution and cover knowledge, surprises are plenty and do drive the overall excitement needed and appreciated over the entire hobby.

Modern Age: In a word: speculation. Collectors realize that this long-maligned segment of the hobby is now 20-25 years old and has really taken abuse in the bargain bins over that timeframe. This is the golden age of the black and whites and independents, with low prints runs, poor distribution and complete lack of collectivity at the time of their release. Now, we are seeing collectors digging deep and coming up with some true gems and perhaps even a few future keys. Leading the way in the era is *TMNT* #1, followed closely by *Cerebus* and the early *Grendel* incarnations, along with the first two *Crow* appearances. Collectors are also having fun by digging into long-running but sparsely documented crossover and key appearances in such runs as *Micronauts, G.I. Joe, Rom, Action, Adventure, Detective*, and *Warlord*. Watching this segment of the hobby come to life should be fun and quite an education for us all.

Magazines: Everyone loved them but few collected them. Now they are the new flavor for collectors, investors, and speculators. Even before the first releases of the CGC-graded issues, the market is poised to see just how nice these books have been preserved over the past few decades. Difficult to store, never distributed with care, and often sitting for great lengths of time on the shelf, these books are hard to find in high grade. Also, the collecting circles are alive with speculation on which issues besides the obvious ones are going to be the emerging keys. Neal Adams, Frank Miller, Wrightson, early *Conan, Punisher, Vampirella* and *Kiss* are safe bets, but many are digging deeper. Just the anticipation of the potential success of the new graded magazines has given a true shot in the arm to the hobby.

Dave Sincere (Sincere Comics)

It's been a real roller coaster of a year. All the new movies based on comic book superheroes coming out of Hollywood and the History Channel doing the *History of Comic Books* documentary have made a big impact on the new comic book market into the third and fourth quarters of 2003. The big winners in the new comic book market are Marvel and DC. We're experiencing sellouts on 60% of the mainstream lines on an ongoing basis for Marvel and DC, with some sellouts happening on Dark Horse, CrossGen, Image, IDW, and Slave Labor. There do not seem to be any mainstream books going over the 150,000 mark, and 80% of the print runs are somewhere between 30,000 and 70,000. This means old laws of supply and demand are starting to kick in. I expect these books from the last three years to shoot up significantly. Most of the low print runs are due to dealers not over-buying because it is too expensive to speculate on books.

It appears that the market has been jump-started by all the media coverage that has drawn old and new collectors into the market. We still have a lot of younger collectors 15 and younger coming in through the back door, buying manga and eventually branching out into independents, i.e. *Johnny the Homicidal Maniac, Lenore, Criminal Macabre, Dark Days*, and finally breaking into Marvels and DCs.

© IDW

Younger collectors cut their teeth on independents like **Dark Days** before breaking into Marvels and DCs.

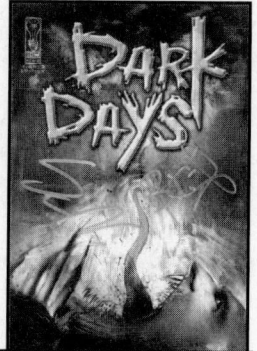

Marvel 1602 is a shining example, and the *Sandman Endless Night* graphic novel is still packing them in. I was lucky enough to obtain copies of *Knights of the Dinner Table* #1-3 and put them on eBay. I sold the #1 for $85, and #2 & 3 went for $28.50 each. The publisher stated in the book that the print run was only 3000 copies. The variant white cover *Ultimate Spider-Man* #1 seems to be going for $225. We also had a run of the Gladstone Disneys, for which we have been able to get upwards of $3 apiece on eBay. Once again, low print run equals high demand.

Most books from the late '70s through the '90s are pretty much dead in the water. There needs to be some major corrections on these books; the supply far outstrips the demand. Most of these books, when they are sold, are bought by people who have sold their collections and are now getting back into the market, newcomers who want to catch up on these books for the cheap prices they're going for, storeowners that do not have access to them in their area and have a demand, and people who buy to sell on eBay as a side-line or as an ongoing business. The average price for these books is around 50¢ a copy, with *X-Men, Wolverine, Amazing Spider-Man,* and *Spider-Man* bringing upwards of a dollar each. These books are easily had on eBay any day of the week and can be at your local convention for the same price. This trend has yet to play itself out, but the source of these books is drying up, causing it to be more of a buyers market than a sellers market at this time. There are other exceptions: *X-Men, Amazing Spider-Man*, and Frank Miller *Daredevil* books from the late '70s and early '80s list between $10 to $30. *Amazing Spider-Man* #190 in *Guide* goes for around $15, but in actuality brings in only around $4. *X-Men* #136-138 are $25 in *Guide*, but are difficult to sell even at $10. This was not a problem for the X-Men during the period of the *X-Men* movie's run, but it has slowed down significantly since. Most of the books from this time period need to come down by at least half due to the large availability of these books on the Internet, where people are finding it more convenient to sell their collections online themselves rather than to a dealer. This is making it increasingly harder for the long-term dealers to be your sources for these products.

Stuff from 1970 to 1977 has been in demand. Books like *Marvel Comics Presents* featuring Ghost Rider, *Amazing Spider-Man*, the reprint *X-Men*, westerns, horror, and monster comics have shown a significant increase. People are actually starting to pay *Guide* for these books and not having reservations about doing it. They're lucky just to be able to find them in any grade, especially Fine or better. It's a cheap way to get the westerns and horror comics without having to pay the bottom price of $20 and the top prices of $150 each, when you can find them on eBay or at your local show. These books used to be in everybody's 25-cent and 50-cent boxes, and now they're nearly nonexistent. We've been able to sell war comics, *Phantoms*, *Turok: Son of Stone, Mighty Samson*, and DC horror comics. *Detective, Batman* and *Superman* from this period are difficult to sell, going for only about half *Guide,* but the only *Detectives* moving for half are the 100-page giants in low grade. Higher grades seem to go for full price. *Daredevil, Incredible Hulk*, and *Fantastic Four* are going for about a third of *Guide*. Believe it or not, we seem to be able to sell *Richie Rich* and *Sad Sacks* for about 50% of *Guide*, and are increasingly harder to find. The DC westerns, *Jonah Hex* and *Weird Western Tales,* from this period are still in big demand, but there's not enough supply to meet it; I still see these going up.

Silver Surfers from this period are moving quite well. Of course, this is going to bleed over into the late '60s, but they are getting difficult to find in any grade. I still see the prices on these going up in the near future, and I don't think they are going to level off anytime soon. I really feel we're going to see a lot of significant increases in these books over the next five years, and I don't think getting twice *Guide* for these in the next year or two is unreasonable.

Most of the books from the Silver Age can be broken down into key issues and non-key issues for mainstream books. If it's not a key Marvel or DC, it's only going to sell for 35-50% of *Guide*, no matter what the condition is. The Justice League appearances in *Brave and the Bold*, and *Justice Leagues* up to about #118 are doing extremely well for us in any grade. Apparently there are not that many people listing them anymore because supply has dwindled; I think the same could be said for most DC comics. There are more Marvel buyers than DC buyers, but DCs are easier to sell. Supply of these books has really dried up. The Legion of Super-Heroes and their appearances in *Adventure* comics still do extremely well; for us, they are the hottest selling DC comics. *Superman* has been doing extremely well, with *Action* having about one-third of the interest that *Superman* does. Most have been selling for $10 to $25 for mid-grade, and the 10-cent issues sell just as soon as we can list them. This is the same for *Batman*; 10-cent *Batmans* are extremely hot right now in any grade. It is not so on the 12-cent *Batmans*, which have become very sluggish this year, along with *Detective, Brave and the Bold*, and *World's Finest*, which all seem to be taking a nose-dive. The major exceptions are 10-cent issues, which seem to move very well as long as they are reasonably priced. Believe it or not, we have had good luck with 10-cent *Tomahawks*. The few we've had seem to be moving quickly, although the 12-cent ones are still sluggish, and the same can be said for *Blackhawk*.

Flashs from the '60s have done poorly for us this year, although *Green Lantern, Atom, Hawkman*, and believe it or not, *Aquaman*, have done extremely well for us. *Wonder Womans* have also been extremely hot this year, with the demand outstripping the supply. It seems that one month we can't seem to move them, but the next month we blow out of everything we have. One of the general rules for a lot of the '60s books seem to be the weirder it is, the easier it is to sell online, because most people don't put them up, but they do go. Good examples are books like *Mystery in Space, Metal Men*, and *Doom Patrol* (the last two books always sell for us online). It seems that the demand for DC is increasing, while the demand for Marvel seems to be waning. That's not to say that nobody wants Marvel anymore; it's just that there seems to be ten Marvel books for every DC book, whether it's a single or a lot. When it comes to Marvel, people seem to be extremely picky, and they don't want to buy unless it's Near Mint, so lower and mid-grades seem to be going for 50-75% of *Guide*. In most cases, if it's not a key, we've been lucky to get a third of *Guide* for it. My opinion is that Marvel Silver Age has pretty much topped off when it comes to superheroes. Pre-superhero Marvels, westerns and monster comics still show significant interest. The prices on these books are not going to spike in the foreseeable future, i.e. the next five years.

As far as magazines go, Warrens are moving very slowly. They are not getting anywhere near *Guide*, and we have to heavily discount them to move them. I think another reason for this is that a lot of people coming into the market don't know these books exist, or of the quality of the stories in them. The Marvel magazines aren't too far behind. *The Savage Sword of Conans* along with the *Hulks* also have to be heavily discounted to move. There is some glimmer of hope, though – we have been able to achieve *Guide* on the *Master of Kung-Fu* magazines; I think the general interest in martial arts has a lot to do with it. *MAD, Cracked*, and *Crazy* don't seem to move past $3 unless they're older than 25 years (for *MAD*), and in those cases, they still don't achieve anywhere near *GUIDE*. *Heavy Metals* are difficult to move too; people are looking for them, they just don't want to pay for them. This is a good time if you are looking to buy them, because everybody's willing to get rid of them cheap.

Last but not least is Golden Age. We had a selection of about 265 westerns from 1944 to 1955, most of which sold for about half *Guide*, except for the lower grade ones, which achieved a little over *Guide*. This means that most of these books even in low grade will go for around $10, even if listed at $5-6 in the *Guide*. I used to think that kiddie comics were tough sells for the '40s, but I was proven wrong this year. We had a run of *Walt Disney's Comics & Stories* #32-66 with Carl Barks art which all achieved *Guide* with no problem. They generally sold on the first attempt on eBay. We also sold *Candy Comics* #1 with Wolverton artwork in about a 4.0. We also sold some other books with his artwork, all of which were scooped up just as fast as we could put them up. We had some early issues of *Looney Tunes* with Carl Barks art and *Walt Kelly's Brownies*. All these books were well received because of the artists that were in them, the age of the books (1940s), and the fact that they were relatively cheap compared to other Golden Age books. These were also off-the-wall books that don't pop up too often, and we were lucky enough to get them in about mid-grade, which is hard to achieve for any Golden Age book. This proves once again that good quality books from the Golden Age, no matter what they are, will find a buyer.

© WDC

Carl Barks' artwork makes **Walt Disney's Comics & Stories** #32-#66 easy to sell. (#33 shown)

In closing, we find that the CGC graded books have both helped and hurt the market. It's difficult to sell key books in mid- to upper grades unless they have been graded. On the other hand, having them graded makes it easier for the novice seller to sell them on his own. The only problem with buying a graded book and paying ten times *Guide* is, at what point do you sell a book that you paid ten times *Guide* for? eBay has proved once again that it dominates the market when it comes to selling books in general. It has helped a lot of dealers move back room inventory and slow-moving merchandise, and put a convention at anybody's fingertips anywhere on the globe. It has made the art of selling comic books an international phenomenon, now more so than ever. It is becoming more difficult to find complete collections without the keys missing. This seems to be bringing the price down on books from the '60s to the '90s, since there are so many being offered on eBay on a daily basis. The more popular books are being listed more often than the obscure titles, so between store sales, show sales, auction houses and eBay, more comic books exchange hands on a daily basis than ever before.

I want to thank Melissa Mallett, a highly valued employee, for once again typing my report and interjecting some additional feedback to help make this report possible.

Tony Starks (Comics Ina Flash)

It's been a rough year for the business, or my business anyway. The last six months of 2002 and the first nine months of 2003 saw my business down by at least a third, and this at a time when I had nicer than normal inventory. After careful consideration, I attribute this to the following: The weak economy; the entrance of a couple of major auction services – they have sucked up a lot of the available dollars; the continued impact of the online person-to-person (P2P) auction services such as eBay; and what I'd call the CGC factor. The first, the weak economy, speaks for itself. If one can believe the forward leaning prognostications by politicians and economists, the economy is looking up. However, the other three issues combine in a synergistic fashion to create a powerful impact.

The major auction houses, online P2P auction services and CGC combine to focus an extraordinary amount of attention on a relatively small number of books. The first two manage to regularly set "record" sale prices, mostly of CGC-graded high grade material. I am sorry to say that I see a mentality developing amongst an increasing number of collectors that only key issues – excuse me, high grade key issues as certified by CGC – are worth owning. If the issue is key enough, and the grade high enough, it's worth owning at many, many multiples of *Guide*. Some collectors get caught up in the chase, competing with investors from outside the hobby who possess deep pockets. Others simply give up on owning what should be affordable minor keys in NM (*Amazing Spider-Man* #121 and 122, for instance). Either way, NM books – excuse me, CGC graded NM or better books – continue to escalate to unaffordable prices for most collectors. Meanwhile, everything between the grades of VG/FN to VF/NM languishes. At this moment in time, I'd rather have most books that Guide over $50 in NM in either NM, NM-, GD or VG. VF is definitely the hardest sell. In very few cases will a VF book bring more than 50% of the NM price. On big keys, it's a lot less than that.

Over a period of time, I believe that the online auctions, the big auction houses, mail order catalogues (me), and comic shops will come into a balance. Buyers will discover that there are more questionable dealings – items not as described, items don't show up, seller reneges and poor packaging – in the online P2P auctions than the services care to admit. Sellers have and will continue to learn that the auction houses only are interested in their nicest items and that the online P2P auction services are a labor intensive and frustrating way to go about selling a large collection. Hopefully, collectors will rediscover that there are a lot of mid-grade, non-key books worth owning and that they can be had at very reasonable prices.

So it's a tough market right now. My Christmas catalogue has been out about ten days as of this writing, and it is looking a little more positive than last Christmas. Maybe there is hope. So what else is of interest?

The mid-'70s Marvel titles like *Devil Dinosaur, Omega the Unknown, Machine Man* (1 NM at $18), *Red Sonja, Eternals, Human Torch* (1 NM at 15), *Invaders* (1 NM at $55, 1 CGC 9.2 at $60), *Spider-Woman, Super-Villain Team-Up* and the like are showing a definite increase in interest. They're still very affordable and getting older everyday, all bringing a modest premium in NM. Marvel Westerns from the '70s like *Outlaw Kid, Gunhawks* and *Tex Dawson, Gun-Slinger* sell very quickly at above Guide in NM. *Howard the Duck* #1 (NM at $30) sells very well in NM but is a lot harder to find in NM than one would think. On the DC side, a lot of their mid-'70s books – *Tales of Ghost Castle, Blitzkrieg, Sherlock Holmes* – have already gone up in Guide. A few titles showing increased interest include *Freedom Fighters* (1 NM at $15), *Warlord* (1 NM- at $20), *Man Bat, Secret Society of Super-Villains* (1 NM at $20), *Firestorm, Shade the Changing Man* and *Karate Kid*. Titles like *Tor* and *Stalker* are not quite there yet. Not all prices need to go up or even stay the same. *Nova* #25, the last issue, is the only issue of *Nova* for which I can get Guide price. On the DC side, *First Issue Special* is slow for all issues except Warlord's first appearance in #8.

The Punisher's first appearance, and to a lesser degree his second and third, are hot again on the anticipation of his big screen debut. I sold a VG and a FN copy of *AMZ* #129 at 1.25x Guide, and could have sold many copies at those prices. Collectors should reflect on the fact that *AMZ* #129 may be vastly under-priced. For over a decade, Wolverine and Punisher's first appearances were valued virtually the same. Both introduce important, much copied characters – Wolverine the grim and gritty anti-hero, Punisher the armed vigilante. Punisher's value crashed due to Marvel's over-exposure of the character: four ongoing comic books plus a magazine in addition to crossovers galore. I look for Punisher to make up a lot of ground. *Iron Fist* (1 NM at $75) is also stirring with his movie possibly due out sometime late in 2004 – the date is uncertain.

I have nothing of great importance to note in Silver Age sales. I sell a lot (and I'd like to sell a lot more) of Silver Age books at $50 or less, and most at $20 or less. Given the market conditions I've described, most of those sales have been for less than *Guide*. The occasional NM books do bring a modest premium. GD condition doesn't usually require a significant discount because they are often nice and inexpensive anyway. On most of the rest, price does matter and lower is better.

***Archie's Girls Betty and Veronica** is the most-requested of Archie titles. (#1 shown)*

Doug Sulipa
(Doug Sulipa's Comic World)

ACG Comics: All 10-cent cover price issues are in demand, especially horror titles. The 1960s superhero titles are in demand. The most consistent best-seller is still Herbie and his early appearances in *Forbidden Worlds*. This year all the love and humor titles sold well too. The 3-D effect titles sold as fast as we found them.

Alternative Comics: From nowhere, demand has skyrocketed for almost all pre-1990 alternative comics thought to be scarce or undervalued. By far the most undervalued is *Albedo Anthropomorphics*, with #2 (1st Usagi Yojimbo) in VG/FN regularly bringing $200+, and NM copies at the $1000+ range for the last one to two years. The various printings of #0 bring 300-500% of *Guide*, while the yellow 50-copy version would bring $1000+ in NM if you could find one. *Dark Red* #1 brings $70-$120 and *Bright Red* sells in the $20-$40 range. *Cerebus the Aardvark* #1 (1st), *Teenage Mutant Ninja Turtles* #1(1st), and *Gobbledygook* #1-2 (1984) are in huge demand, with *Guide* prices being below wholesale. Unslabbed VF copies bring $400-$600, and CGC NMs would be an easy $1000-$1500 each. *Cerebus* #2-30 are all hot, bringing 150-200% *Guide* in any grade. *TMNT* #2-10 and many of the '80s one-shots are up in demand and undervalued.

The ultra-rare self-published black and white *Elflord* #1 (6/1980) by Nightwynd Pub. with Barry Blair-s-c/a is unfindable and an easy sale at $200+ in VF. *Fantasy Quarterly* #1 is suddenly in big demand and we expect high grade copies to break the $100 level in the near future. *Grendels* (1983/84 Comico series) are hard to come by and bring 150%+ *Guide*. The scarcer Valiant titles that once had high value are back in demand and almost gone with very few noticing. Still great reading and again due for price increases are: *Magnus* #0, 1-12, *Harbinger* #0, 1-10, *Rai* #1-10, *Solar* #1-10, etc.

Other hot and under-valued titles to watch include: *Caliber Presents* #1, *Cody Starbuck, Crow* #1-3, *Crusaders* #1(Southern Knights), *Flaming Carrot* #1-16, *Galaxia, Gasm, Imagine, Justice Machine* (Noble) #1-3 and Annual #1, *Love & Rockets* #1-20, *Macross* #1(1984), *Mage* #1-7, *Mangazine* #1-4, *Megaton, Nexus* (Capital) #1-3, *Ninja High School* (1986/87), *Nucleus, Oktoberfest, Omen* (Vigil), *Orb, Phantacea, Primer* (Comico), *Quadrant, Rock Comics* (Adams-a), *Star Reach, Tick, Uncensored Mouse,* and *Zen* (1987).

Archie: We got in several *Archie* collections and this has been our best year ever for selling back issues. The single most requested *Archie* title this year has consistently been *Archie's Girls Betty & Veronica* from 1950-1987 and also the current series. Issues #310-347 are the most requested, hard to find and due for a big increase. This is right in the low print run era that spawned Cheryl Blossom. All 1940s/'50s *Archie* teen character title issues are very fast sellers and are not possible for dealers to restock on eBay, as overgraded copies typically sell well over *Guide* in FN or lower grades. We have had to restock the hard way by buying from other dealers and paying high *Guide* percentages.

Katy Keene is again selling well. In fact, many who have completed their *Katy Keene* sets now want the backup stories in *B&V, Laugh, Wilbur, Archie* and *Pep*. Everything with Dan DeCarlo art sells well, *Archie* or not. Most buyers of pre-1980 issues prefer G to FN range copies, but we have many recent requests for 1960s-1980s issues in VF or better. This is no easy task on most pre-1980 issues, as most were well read by the general public and not in the hands of collectors. *Archie Giant Series Magazine* #26 (6/64) and #32 (6/65) are hot, as both are all pin-up issue Betty & Veronica spectaculars with Classic Dan DeCarlo-c/a. Circa 1960 *Archie* titles with the SF/horror covers are hot and in short supply, as are all issue #1-10s and all giants. 1984-2002 comics all had low print runs and can be quite difficult runs to complete if issues were missed. Digest issues of the 1984-2002 period are more plentiful and are highly collected, often by otherwise non-comic collectors, thus price is often more important than condition. All early appearances of Cheryl Blossom from 1982-1990 are in demand and many are undervalued. *B&V* #320 and *Jughead* #325 easily bring 200-300% *Guide*. Josie and Sabrina in *Archie Giant* mags are in demand. *Red Circle* and *Archie Adventure* series superhero and horror titles of the 1970s-'80s are in steady demand, with *Archie Adventure* series having low print runs and being scarcer. The 1960s superhero appearances in *Laugh* and *Pep* are in very high demand at 150% *Guide* if you can find them at all.

© KING

Many highly collectible characters can be found in Big Little Books. ***(Flash Gordon and the Power Men of Mongo** #1469 shown)*

Atlas Marvel: Pre-hero horror/SF, especially if they had Kirby or prototypes, were the top sellers this year. Many grew up on the 1970s reprints of these and remember them fondly, now wanting to sample originals. *Millie the Model, Patsy*, and teen titles were in demand, especially with paper dolls and pinups. Love and western titles sold well due to still low prices. Crime, sports, spy and funny animal titles were slower. Parody titles sold as fast as we could find them and are full of nice characters and art. We had a hard time stocking and keeping the undervalued war titles in stock. *Kid Colt, Rawhide Kid, Ringo Kid* and *Two-Gun Kid* were the best sellers this year, as many fans stretched their Marvel runs back to the Atlas years and discovered some truly wonderful comics. Compared to 1960s Marvels, these are infinitely scarcer especially in nice condition and a definite "must try" for fans.

Atlas/Seaboard: All titles sold well, as many still want to complete all product from this publisher. The biggest obstacle is always the rare *Gothic Romances* #1 which sells instantly in the 200% *Guide* range. *Blazing Battle* #1, *Savage Combat* #1-3, *Vicki* #1-2 and *Western Action* #1 are in lower supplies. *Devilina, Thrilling Adventure* and *Weird Tales of the Macabre* #2 all remain scarcer and bring 25-50% over *Guide*. *Movie Monsters* #1 is around, but #2-4 are scarce, bringing $20+ in VF.

Big Little Books: BLBs have picked up in demand of late because they remain a relative bargain when compared to their comic counterparts. Supplies from all eras are depleted in most dealer stocks. Pre-1960 BLBs are quite scarce in VF or better and are typically found in G or VG. Most are full of original material, many of highly collectible characters, usually never reprinted and not found anywhere else. Even most of the prized GA issues, quite rare in high grade, are very undervalued and selling for less than a NM Silver Age Marvel comic. The taller 1950s TV westerns sold well for us this year at $25-$50 each in mid-grades, but I specialize in the post-1960 issues. The 1960s Whitman color hardcover issues are in high demand at $15-$25 each in VG-FN due to the finite quantity of issues in the numbered series (36 different?). The most requested from the 1960s were: *Aquaman, Batman, Fantastic Four, Frankenstein Jr., Lone Ranger, Tarzan,* Hanna-Barbera's *Shazam* and *Space Ghost*. Many were later reprinted in the '70s Whitman softcover editions, which also contained much new material, including *Grimm's Ghost* and *Spider-Man*. They sold well at $6-12 each for FN-VF copies. The Marigold Press reprints of 1980-up are scarcer than the '70s editions and had several scarce new material issues. The Gold Star Library hardcover series of 1966-1970 contained fairy tales (many with early Richard Scarry art), classics, and Walt Disney (*Pinocchio, Peter Pan*). The Gold Stars remain scarce and sold steady at $7-$15 each in G-VG.

The illustrated classics editions by Moby Books, #4501-4536 (1977/83), sold well in VG-FN copies at $4-$9 each, with the most requested being: *Wizard of Oz, Sherlock Holmes* (2 different), *War of the Worlds* and *The Time Machine.*

The Hanna-Barbera softcover titles published by Modern circa 1977 had low print runs and all are scarce with VG copies bringing $9-$12 range. The Young Reader's Christian Library and *Zaanan* series are highly collected by Christian comic collectors at $5-$12 each. The Chronicle Books series from the 1990s has suprisingly disappeared swiftly, with NM copies bringing $10-$15. *Xena* was most requested, followed by *Legendary Journeys of Hercules, Star Wars* and *Zorro*. The wise buyer would look again at BLBs as we do not anticipate the low price levels to remain much longer.

British/UK Items: We now likely have the biggest selection of UK comics this side of the 'Big Pond.' Marvel UK comics are the most collected in North America. The strange formats –

black and white in mag and digest sizes, oblong, thick and thin – tend to fascinate buyers.

Many hidden gems are there to be found, including: original UK comic stories of the Hulk and others; Alan Moore stories, new front and back cover and pin-up art by UK artists; new art by US artists like Austin; text stories; games/puzzles; articles; and more. Then there is: *Action Force*, the UK Version of *G.I. Joe*, 300+ issues of *Doctor Who*, 666 issues of *Spider-Man Weekly* with loads of cool covers and contents, 122 issues of *Planet of the Apes* with loads of cool covers and contents, 330+ issues of *Transformers* and 180+ Marvel digests. These are loaded with the artists that collectors love, like Kirby, Starlin, Byrne, Perez and more. Alan Class, Miller and other 1950s-1980s black and white squarebound giant reprints sell great, as they are an inexpensive alternative to buying the 1950s and '60s US horror and SF titles they reprint, including: Atlas, Archie, ACG, DC, and Charlton.

Rosnock, Spencer, Strato, and Top Seller Pub. reprints of US western, TV, cartoon, war, love, and crime titles sold well but were harder to find. The original material UK war comic digests like *Commando* and *War Picture Library* are in demand and still rising in value as war comic fans discover superb stories and art not seen in the US at still low prices. *Warrior, 2000AD* and other titles with Alan Moore, *Miracleman*, Talbot, and Bolland were hot. The UK *Starblazer* digest was in good demand. The 1970s UK full color *Vampirella* mags #1-4 and UK paperbacks #1-6 with different painted covers were in high demand at $20-$50 each in FN to VF. The original UK *Classics Illustrated* titles #143, 146-150, 156, 157, 159, 161-163 sold out at $75-$125+ each in FN-VF, with #158A (*Dr. No*) impossible to find and worth about $400+ in VF. The UK hardcover annuals of the 1950s-1990s were hot sellers in North America and supplies are dwindling in the UK. They are packed with great covers, comics, art, text stories, photos, puzzles and games, and much of it is new material not seen in the US. The most requested in the $15-$35 price range included: *A-Team, Avengers* (TV), *Avengers* (Marvel), *Batman, Battlestar Galactica, Bionic Woman, Charlie's Angels, Danger Man, Doctor Who,* Hanna-Barbera titles, *Hulk, Knight Rider, Lone Ranger,* Madonna, Marvel Annuals, *Planet of the Apes, Roy Rogers, Scooby Doo, Six Million Dollar Man, Space 1999, Spider-Man, Superman, Tarzan, Thunderbirds, Transformers, X-Men* and *Zoids.*

In the 1960s and 1970s there were UK cover price variants of US Marvel comics. These were printed at the same time as the original US edition, thus these are also scarce variant originals and should *not* be considered reprints. These were also not produced for all issues. The bottom inside front cover of *Amazing Spider-Man* #1, for example, states "Sole Distributors in United Kingdom – Thorpe & Porter Ltd" and printed in the USA. UK publishers instead chose to print 90% of all UK Marvels in magazine-sized black and white comics, often with stories serialized in weekly issues and often with new UK cover art.

Canadian Comics: Golden Age "Canadian Whites" saw perhaps their biggest demand and higest price increases ever this year, especially the pre-1947 Canadian Whites of Fawcett hero titles, including *Captain Marvel, Bulletman, Golden Arrow* and others, with US comics redrawn by Canadian artists. All original material Canadian story and art titles were in even greater demand. Canadian Whites were typically found in FR to VG and sold for $40-$100 each. FN copies were scarce and sold for $75-$150 each, and finally VF copies are usually the best you can hope for, bringing $100-$250 each. Early numbers on all were bringing 200-300% or more of above. The Most valuable #1 issues which would bring $300-$1000 in VG-VF include: *Active, Better, Bing Bang, Canadian Heroes, Capt. Commando, Colossal, Commando, Dime, Freelance, Grand Slam, Joke, Lightning, Lucky, Nelvana, Red Rover, Robin Hood, Rocket/Name-It, Slam-Bang, Space Nomad, Speed Savage, Spy Smasher, Super Funnies, Three Aces, Triumph, Whiz, Wow*, and *Zor the Mighty. Nelvana of the Northern Lights* and her appearances in *Triumph* and other comics are in huge demand, with VG copies starting at $100-up. *Weird SuspenStories* #1-3 (Superior; 1951; Color; Canadian variant editions of EC's *Crime SuspenStories* #1-3; by law, the word "Crime" was not allowed in the titles of Canadian comics; no copies known in FN or better; very rare; less than five copies of each known) are selling in the $750-$1500 each price range for VG-FN copies if you can find them.

The rare Canadian Timely 132-page *Marvel Mystery* variant with *MM* #41 contents sold for US $3000 in Fair and will be pro restored as I write this. The Canadian editions that are vintage variants of US comics are bringing higher percentages than their US equivalents. Canada has 10% of the population of the US, thus Canadian editions had 5-10% of the print runs and survival rates of their US counterparts. Variant collectors have started to dabble in the more desirable tiltes. These GA Canadian variant issues survive in quantites of 1-20 copies each. Publishers included are: Archie, Atlas, Avon, Classics, DC, Dell, EC, Fawcett, Fiction House, Lev Gleason, Quality, Timely, Toby, and others. US collector awareness of their scarcity, CGC graded copies and good prices at major auction houses has made these rare items even more collectible. The Timely Canadian variants were printed circa 1946 through the 1950s Atlas issues, with the Timely superhero issues remaining among the scarcest and most valuable. Titles like *Captain America* and *Marvel Mystery* are almost impossible to find. It is likely that a Canadian run of 1946-up Timely would be impossible to assemble at any price.

Fuddle Duddle (black and white comics humor magazine) #4-5 features *Captain Canada* (1st appearance?). The Canadian cover price newsstand edition variants are still in high demand, especially with completionists and variant collectors at 150%-300% US copy prices. Especially popular variants are: *Spider-Man, Hulk, Daredevil, Batman, JLA,* Byrne-a and Perez-a. Known Canadian cover price variant eras include: Archie Comics digests (1/1984-12/1997), Charlton (2/1983-8/1984), DC (10/1982-9/1988), Dell (random, 1960-1962), Gold Key (5-8/1968, and 4/72-4/73), MAD (some 1964 and 7/1978-7/1979), Marvel (all newsstand comics, magazines and digests 10/1982-8/1986), Warren

(3/1977-3/1983), Whitman (4/1980-1984).

We bought and sold several collections of Canadian French language comics out of Quebec on Archie, DC and Marvel from the late 1960s-1990. These had very small print runs for newstand comics, as they were mainly distributed only in one province. They had a bizarre mix of contents and are cool variant items for fans of *Archie, Avengers, Batman, Conan, Flash, Hulk, Spider-Man, Superman,* and *X-Men*. The many rare large softcover giants containing Rebound French comics with new outer covers are getting scarcer and sell rather fast.

Finally there are a vast quantity of low valued $3-$6 range new material French language comic digests from the 1950s-1970s, with western, war, adventure, jungle and love themes; all are scarce and may be lost to history if more collectors do not snap up the dwindling supplies being lost daily to non-collectors. The 1970s horror digest issues sell best at $6-$15 each, as they have amazing sex and violence, covers, stories and art not seen in North American comics.

Cartoon and Comics Paperbacks: This remains one of the fastest growing areas on the Internet yet one of the most overlooked by comic collectors. The mass market paperback format virtually ceased to exist for cartoon and comic paperbacks in the early 1990s. The format was very popular from 1950-1980, but slowed and died by 1990. Instead, publishers went to the new and higher priced trade paperback, especially the oblong type (like the *Garfield* books), as the new format of choice. Most were sold to the general public and not collectors, and most would be suprised to see how many of these are now scarce to even rare. *Peanuts* paperbacks remain common and low valued, but the titles first issued in 1985-1990 had low print runs and often retail between $8-$20 each. Already scarce and getting expensive in high grade is the *Peanuts Parade* (1970s to late 1980s) trade paperback series #1-29 with VF copies starting at $35 for #1-10, #11-20 at $40-$50 each, and #21-27 at $60 and up. The rare #28 and #29 sell at well over $100 each in high grade if you can find them at all. Once one gets to about 50% of the known existing titles of a larger series, the remaining titles get scarcer and scarcer to downright rare.

These are mass market paperback series that many fans are now trying to complete (many with an approximate number of different titles known): *Addams Family, Andy Capp* (50+ different titles), *Archie, B.C.* (33+ titles), *Beetle Bailey* (70+ different titles), *Berensteins* (pre-Bears; 20+), *Blondie, Broomhilda* (21+), *Casper, Dennis the Menace* (50+), *Doonesbury* (35+), *Family Circus* (43+), *Flash Gordon, Flintstones & Pebbles* (19+), *Hagar* (47+), *Heathcliff* (29+), *Hi and Lois* (27+), *MAD* (220+), *Marmaduke* (14+), *Peanuts,* Pocket Classics (70 different titles), *Richie Rich, Tiger, Tumbleweeds* (16+), *Tiger, Vampirella* (6 each US and UK), *Wizard of ID* (24+), *Ziggy* (14+), and many more. Count the books in your collection to see how many you are missing. There is a general rule of thumb: older issues had higher print runs, are common and often only sell for $3-$10 in the VG-FN range. Later and last issues in the various series often have small print runs, are scarce, and often bring $12-$25+ in FN or better.

Playboy and other vintage adult cartoon paperbacks are very low in supply, highly collected and gaining value fast, with most in the $10-$20 each range for VG-FN copies. Noteable scarcer titles of value: *Autumn People, Barnaby, Christopher Lee's Treasury of Terror, Cracked, Creepy, Eggbert,* Harvey Kurtzman titles, *High Camp Superheroes, Jimmy Hatlo, Luann, Modesty Blaise, Nellie the Nurse, Sick, Tales from Crypt, Thunder Agents*, and *U.S. Acres* by Jim Davis. Hatlo's *Inferno* is rare and brings $50+ in higher grades. All the Marvel and DC superhero titles are in high demand (1960s, $20-$50 each; 1975-1985, $8-$20 each) and are scarce in VF or better.

CGC: CGC graded comics are how all higher grade and valuable comics will be sold in our market for the forseeable future. Lower priced items, however, as well as 1975-up items and items with too many copies graded, have lost steam; many are dead sellers and money losers for their sellers. On these items, we have found collectors still want them but do not want to pay the $15+ premium for the slab, plus high per-item shipping costs. I have found it more profitible to keep cheaper items in regular inventory and sell them unslabbed. We sold 100s of properly graded 1975-1984 comics in 9.0-9.6 unslabbed, comics from the "Manitoba" collection in the 150-300% *Guide* price ranges, to very happy buyers. Over 50% of them were under the $15 minimum slab cost. CGC buyers seem to want mainly Marvel and mostly the big mainstream titles. We experimented with Gold Key, Charlton, Dell and DC war CGC comics with poor results; these buyers prefer them unslabbed. But we did find many buyers for all high grade Harvey comics, with all performing well. Superhero books are where most of the CGC big multiples are achieved. We had a few good large batches of high grade Marvel and DC 1965-1974 superhero comics and were able to sell over 50% of them offline to ready buyers at good multiples. We eventually sold the remaining issues on eBay, also at good multiples.

Buyers are still trying to find the highest graded copies, and they are getting harder to locate. We had a few buyers who are trying to complete runs of comics that *Guide* under $10 in 9.8 or better, but will not touch 9.6s. The CGC census has both helped and hurt sales as what exists is now in front of you. Many collectors no longer understand how strict NM 9.4 is in the current market and constantly ask for unslablled copies in NM of items that regularly bring 300-500% *Guide*, such as *Marvel Spotlight* #5. It is now a process of explaining the strict grading and finding if they truly need NM copies, or if what they really want are reasonably priced VFs. Many have lowered their expectations to the strictly graded and beautiful VF range copies. This has become one of our best years for selling unslabbed VF to VF/NM comics.

CGC has just begun slabbing magazines as I write this and it is too early to judge results. It has caused a lot of demand for Marvel, Skywald and Warren mags in high grades. Once slabbed copies become more common, these undervalued mags should be driven up in value by the CGC copies.

Charlton: All types of Charlton titles sold well in all grades as few other sellers have a decent selection. This time, horror titles were the most requested, with many many buyers trying to complete runs. We had many requests for higher grade issues, and this usually means VF copies from this publisher as VF/NM and up copies are quite scarce due to distribution and printing problems. Also popular were war, Hanna-Barbera, western and TV cartoon, John Byrne art, and western titles. The best sellers and still undervalued titles which brought 20-35% over *Guide* include: *Beetle Bailey, Bionic Woman, Bobby Sherman, Cheyenne Kid, Creepy Things, David Cassidy, Dudley Do-Right, E-Man, Go-Go, Great Gazoo, Gunfighters, Haunted, Haunted Love,* hot rod comics, *Kid Montana,* love comics, *Many Ghosts of Dr. Graves, Midnight Tales, Outlaws of the West, Partridge Family, Phantom, Scary Tales, Underdog, Wyatt Earp.*

Hot titles which brought 35-60% over *Guide: Blondie, Bugaloos, Hong Kong Phooey, Jungle Tales of Tarzan, Ponytail, Popeye, Ronald McDonald, Scooby Doo, Speed Buggy, Wheelie & the Chopper Bunch. Charlton Bullseye, Emergency, Six Million Dollar Man*, and *Space: 1999* are selling faster in both comic and magazine formats. Buyers still need many of the low distribution 1984-86 issues to finish runs.

Religious/Christian Comics: These are consistent good sellers. Spire is the most collected series with about 37 regular comic titles and about 19 *Archie*-related titles. Those titles with a single printing in the 1980s are scarce and command about double the earlier issues. The hottest Spire is *Hansi, the Girl who Loved the Swastika*, with strict NM copies starting to break the $100 barrier. *Sunday Pix* of 1957-63 vintage by David C. Cook were hot in the $5-10 each range. The 1949-1954 issues are very tough to find and sport good competition on eBay when they appear. *Sunday Pix* was preceded by *What to Do, Boys World* and *Girls Companion* from 12/1943-2/1949. They all carried the very popular "Tullus" feature, later to Continue in *Sunday Pix*; the "Tullus" feature is the most collected part of *Sunday Pix*, thus 1943-1945 era appearances are very desirable but near impossible to find.

Dennis the Menace and *The Bible Kids* were in huge demand, with the regionally distributed only #7-10 remaining very scarce. All the Marvel and DC Christian titles sold steady, with *Francis* and *Pope Paul* the best sellers. Now highly collected are the *Jack Chick* tracts (3"x5"; b&w; oblong mini-comics). Chick is best known in fandom for his over-the-top 'fire and brimstone' *Crusaders* series. There are about 80 common tracts still in print that sell for about $1 each, but earlier pre-1985 printings bring $3-$10 each. There are many pre-1985 tracts that are long out of print and are in big demand to completionists, commanding $20-$35 each. All issues of *Topix* sold extremely well this year and are hard to restock.

All these religious comics sold well at 135-200% *Guide*: *Bible Tales, Bible Visualized, Catechetical Guild, Cosmics, Crusaders* (#16-17 are rare), *Dan Red Eagle, Logos Pub, Open Door, Oral Roberts, Picture Stories from the Bible, Tales from the Great Book, United Bible, Young Reader's Christian Library* and *Zaanan* BLBs.

All pre-1955 *Treasure Chest* are scarce and in low supply, with newer issues selling steady. We also bought and sold a nice batch of circa 1980 *Amar Chitra Katha* Comics (India-related, English language, religion, history, mythology and legend) in the $10 each range for VG-FN copies. We sold many issues of *Adventures of Mendy and the Golem* (Jewish-related) of the 1982-1985 era at $5-10 each. *Marx, Lenin, Mao & Christ* #nn (1977; one-shot; superb Redondo studio art; scarce) is a beautiful comic and sells as fast as we find them in the VF $25 each range.

Classics Illustrated and Related Comics: *Classics* collectors seemed to want line-drawn cover issues more than ever this year and they remain a bargain for comics of their vintage, with most still under $10 in low grades. Since the story adaptions and art are different in the painted vs line-drawn cover versions, more and more buyers now want both versions. Low grade copies still sell best. We did see a notable increased demand for nicer FN or better copies. These issues are always in biggest demand: #8, 14, 20, 21, 33, 40, 43, 44, 53, 66, 71, 73, 74, 84, 110, 113-118, 129, 161-169; they bring premiums of 25-35% over *Guide*.

The first appearance of new art or first new cover issues are a different type of original and remain top sellers. Once collectors complete their main runs, they look to complete *World Around Us* and *Classics Special Series*, with #162A *War Between The States* in low supply and big demand. Once we listed them all on our website, we found many new homes for the various miscellaneous *Classics*, including: Berkley/First, Big Little Books, Catechetical Guild, Famous Authors, Foreign, Golden Picture Classics, King Classics, Marvel Classics, Pendulum, Pocket Classics, Power Records, UK Marvel Classics Digests, and all others.

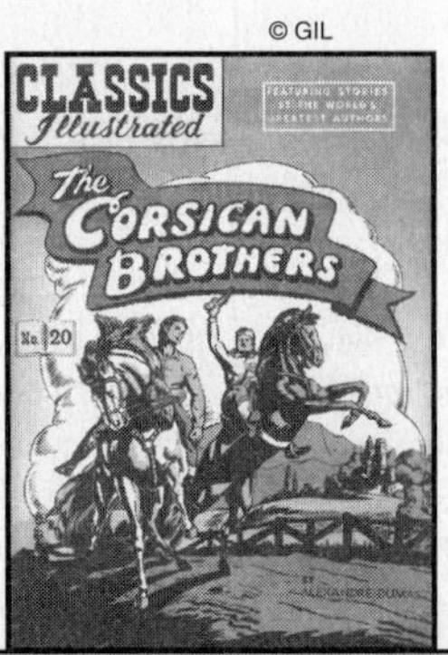

***Classics Illustrated** #20 is one of the issues always in biggest demand.*

*Classics Junior*s sold about twice as fast as in previous years. With about 50% of the issues being common, 25% uncommon and 25% scarcer, it is not as easy a series to complete, as the low *Guide* prices would indicate. Among the toughest issues to keep in stock, and bringing 50-100% over *Guide*, are: #514, 525, 527, 528, 531, 537, 542, 543, 547, 552, 555, 558, 559, 564,565, 568, 571, 572, 575, 576.

Canadian variant edition *Classics* are quite scarce and most contain illustrated text stories on the inside cover that aren't see in any US editions. When we listed these facts on our website, it immediately caused almost double the sales on these issues.

Comic Digests: Gold Key digests were especially hot, with

Mystery Comics Digest still the best seller. But this year we had more requests for high grade copies of all pre-1980 digests than ever before. Most pre-1975 issues are scarce in strict FN or better, but we managed to find an original owner collection of VF-NM copies of Gold Key digests and sold them at 150-200% *Guide*.

Most Gold Key digest #1-10s are hard to keep in stock in any grade. All Harvey digests sold better than any previous year, with 1970s issues scarce in high grades. All the Harvey digests from the 1986-1993 era had low print runs and are easily the scarcest and most difficult runs to complete. Harvey digests from about 1990-up are non-existent in strict NM as they had thin cover stock and too much glue, causing wrinkling on almost all the covers. *Dennis the Menace Pocket Full of Fun* #1-20, *Archie Comics Digest* #1-20 and *Jughead With Archie* #1-10 are becoming scarce in any condition and are impossible to keep in stock at 150-200% *Guide*. The Marvel *Dennis The Menace* digests with DC logos are steady sellers. *Best of DC* #41-71 and *Blue Ribbon* #20-24 remain in short supply and brought 135-150% *Guide*. The rare Skylark digests (*Doc Savage* and *Twilight Zone*) and Charlton digests (*Barney & Betty, Flinstones, Jetsons, Scooby Doo, Space-1999, Yogi Bear*) were near impossible to find in any grade, and are a bargain at 200% current *Guide*. Most digests were originally sold to non-collectors, so strict VF or better pre-1980 issues are scarce, with strict NM copies being rare. *Katy Keene, Jokebook* and *Madhouse Comics Digests* were all in higher demand and lower supply. Low grade copies of all titles by all publishers sold well, as many buyers just want to read them.

DC Comics: All superhero books were in high demand, but in less supply than Marvels. The 1970-1974 issues are getting harder to keep in stock, especially in VF or better. *Wonder Woman* #50-170 were impossible to keep in stock, and #171-220 were also hot. Everything from 1960 through the 1985/86 "Crisis" era sold well; 1987-1995 issues were slower. 1998-2003 issues are low in most dealer stocks and most can be sold for over *Guide*. All issues with Neal Adams and Wrightson cover/art were in high demand, especially in VF or better. All oddball material sold well as usual, most at 20-35% over *Guide*, including: *Amazing World of DC*, digests, fanzines, Fireside books, giveaways, magazines, paperbacks, and treasuries. Horror and SF were especially popular this year. Cartoon, humor/parody, romance, teen, TV, war, and western still sell well and we filled in many runs for buyers. The romance titles were hardest to keep in stock. All artist issue love comics were in very high demand at about 35-50% over *Guide*. Best-selling were 1970s, followed by 1980s, then 1960s and 1950s issues, probably because Bronze Age titles fit most budgets.

Our most requested issues included: *Action* #300-420, *Adventure* #300-440, 491-503 (Supergirl issues most requested and in lower supply; Spectre issues were hot), all issues of *Adv. of Bob Hope & Jerry Lewis*, all *New Collectors Edition* (scarce in VF+ or better; hot issues were C-54-56, 58), *All Star* #58-74 (58 and 69 were hot), *Amazing World of DC* (hot issues were1-4, 9, 14-17), *Aquaman* #50-52, *Authority, Batgirl* (2000-up), *Batman* #150-350 (hot issues were 250-300), *Batman Family, Bat Lash, Best of DC Digest* (41-71 were scarce), *Birds of Prey, Brave & Bold* #59-120 (esp. Adams), *DC Special, DC Special* series, *Detective* #330-500, *Flash* #200-300, 341-350, *Flex Mentallo, Forbidden Tales of Dark Mansion, Forever People* #1-9, *Fox & Crow, Freedom Fighters, Ghosts, GI Combat, Green Lantern* #76-125 (#76 is red hot in VF and better), *Hot Wheels* (hot at 25-35% over *Guide*), *House of Mystery* #174-259, 291-300 (Wrightson is hot), *House of Secrets* #81-140, (Wrightson again), *Inferior Five, Jonah Hex* #1-20, 81-92 (#90-92 hot at 50% over *Guide*), *Justice League* #71-160, 183-185, 200, 260, 261 (#71-120 in low supply; JSA crossovers were hot), *Leave it to Binky, Limited Collectors Edition* (C#23-25, 32-34, 37, 39, 41, 43-46, 48-52, 57 are hot and scarce in VF+ or better), *Mr. Miracle* #1-9, *New Gods* #1-9, *Our Army at War* #83-250, *Phantom Stranger* #1-20, *Planetary, Scooby Doo, Secret Society of Super Villians, Sinister House, Spectre* #1-5, 9, *Star Spangled War* #90-163, *Strange Advs.* #205-236, *Superboy* #197-245, *Supergirl* (all), *Super Friends, Superman* #150-300, *Lois Lane* #79-137, *Jimmy Olsen* #100-150, *Superman Family* #164-180, *Swamp Thing* (1982) #20-40, *Tomahawk* #100-125 (Adams-c are hot), *Unexpected* #105-162, *Weird Mystery* #1-10, *Weird War* #1-50, *Weird Western* #12-39, *Witching Hour* #1-40, *Wonder Woman* (old) #51-220, 300-329, *World's Finest* #200-230, 244-282, 300, 323, *Young Love & Romance*. These sold in all grades, often bought by buyers in the condition that matches their existing collection as they fill in runs.

© ERB

***Tarzan** is one of the Four Color titles that is way up in demand. (Four Color #161 shown)*

Dell: Dell is always a steady seller as they remain affordable and have loads of popular characters. Westerns and most *Four Colors* were especially popular this time with almost all requested in G-FN. *Tarzan* and *Turok* are way up in demand, with a very low supply of early issues. We tried a few high grade CGC Dells and found they did not perform well, as high grade buyers want only major keys and only in 9.4 or better and were not willing to pay the premiums required to stock them at a profit. We will gladly stick to good-selling G-FN copies.

The best-sellers at 20-35% over *Guide* included: *Air War, Andy Griffith, Animal Comics, Beep Beep, Beetle Bailey, Ben Bowie, Beverly Hillbillies, Bewitched, Bugs Bunny, Cheyenne, Chilly Willy, Cisco Kid, Combat, Dracula, Flintstones, Flying Saucers, Frankenstein, F-Troop, Gene*

Autry & Champion, Get Smart, Ghost Stories, Hogans Heroes, Howdy Doody, Huckleberry Hound, Indian Chief, all *John Wayne, Jungle Jim, King of Royal Mounted, Kookie, Lassie* #39-58, *Little Lulu, Lone Ranger, Looney Tunes, Melvin Monster, Mighty Heroes, Monkees, Peanuts, Pogo, Ponytail, Popeye, Raggedy Ann, Red Ryder, Roy Rogers, Sgt Preston, Smokey Stover, Tarzan, Thirteen, Tonto, Top Cat, Turok, Western Roundup, Yogi Bear* and *Zorro. Huck & Yogi Jamboree* and *Flinstone On the Rocks* remain among the rarest items for both Hanna-Barbera and Dell collectors, bringing 200-400% over current low *Guide* prices.

Dennis the Menace: *Dennis* was a great seller, with 1950s issues and all giants still top sellers at 25-50% over *Guide*. All issues are scarce in VF or better. *Pocketful of Fun* #1-20 are getting scarce in any grade and sold at 200% *Guide*. The Marvel comics and digests also sold well.

Buyers are now trying to complete their mass market paperback series of 50+ different books, with about 15+ titles having only one printing and being scarcer. The scarcer *Dennis* #143 (3/76; Olympic issue) was hard to find. We found no copies of *Bible Kids* #7-10 at reasonable prices for resale but had many requests. #7-9 in FN-VF bring $25-$50 each, with #10 bringing $50-$100 if you can find it at all.

Fanzines: Scarce fanzines are on many want lists and can be very difficult to locate in any grade. We finally got in a couple nice fanzine collections and many issues sold fast. Some of the better titles sold included: *Art of Neal Adams* (VF+ $35 ea), *Alter Ego* (1962-69; $25-$50), *Back for More* (VF $60), *Badtime Stories* (VF $75), *Berni Wrightson Treasury* (VF/NM $60), *Cartoonists and Illustrators Portfolio* #1-3 (VF $35 ea), *Chronicle* #3 (1973; BYRNE-a; FN $75), *Colour Your Dreams* (1972; VF- $30), *Comic Art Convention Program Book* (New York, Phil Seuling, 1971, VF $60; 1972-1977, VF $30-$40), Richard Corben's *Funny Book* (1976; HC; VF+ $125), *CPL* #7, 8, 12 (all Byrne $25-$40 ea), *Doctor Weird* #1 (1970; Starlin; FN/VF $49), *Eagle* #1(1971; Starlin; VF $59), *Fantasy Illustrated* #5 (1966; ERB, Crandall, Jeff Jones art; VF US $125), *Focus on John Byrne* (TPB; VF/NM $25), *Focus on George Perez* (TPB; VF $25), *Infinity* #2 (Wrightson, Frazetta, FN/VF $59), *Illustrated Harvey Kurtzman Index* 1939-1975 (TPB; VF+ $149.00), *RBCC* #114 (Wrightson-c; FN $22), and *Star Studded Comics* #6-16 (1965-69; Starlin issues $50; others $30).

Many fanzines from the 1970s-1990s are loaded with great articles and art, and many are great sellers in the $5-$15 each price range. Some great-selling titles include: *Amazing Heroes, Comics Feature, Comics Interview, Comics Journal, Comics Revue,* Dragon Lady Press mags, *Flashback* (series by Alan Light from 1970s; low print runs), *Monster Times, Nostalgia Journal* (#32 up becomes *The Comics Journal*), (Diamond) *Previews*, and *RBCC*.

Foreign Language: We bought a huge collection of French language comics from the 1960s-1980s, including many original material digests. The Marvel and DC superhero reprint books of the 1970s are the best sellers to completionists of Spider-Man, Hulk, Batman, Byrne, Starlin, Kirby, Perez, etc. We also moved a few batches of the adventure, jungle, war, western and love digests. We are getting lower in stock on the 1970s French/France gore horror comic digests with sex, bondage, nudity and violence. The European Disney digests – *Donald Duck & Uncle Scrooge*, and also *Mickey Mouse* and others – sold steady and in several good size batches to fans who have grown to appreciate them. We got in some large collections of the Belgium/French Phantom and Mandrake digests of the 1960s and '70s, selling many in the $5-$10 each range.

Giveaways: This was a strange year for giveaways. The best-sellers turned out to be a few buyers who picked up a lot of issues that are not yet listed in the *Guide*. We also had buyers who wanted any issues published in Canada, as it's a very unknown territory. *March of Comics, Kite Fun, Comics Reading Library, Whitman Mini Comics* and Dan Curtis titles were in demand from people with favorite characters, but most pre-1970 issues were hard to find anywhere. All the DC mini-comics like *Swordquest, Centipede*, and *Atari Force* #4-5 sold well. All Power Records sold well, especially Marvel and DC titles. We also sold a bunch of *Classics* titles. The superhero records without comics are also up in demand but low in supply. But the biggest increase in demand was for non-comic promotional items, like advance news items, catalogues, ephemera, distributor-only items, publisher and retailer displays, flyers, handouts, posters, calendars, publisher shareholder items, *Dark Horse Insider, Marvel Age* (newsprint), *Marvel Requirer, Marvel Spotlight, Comic Shop News, Previews, DC Currents*, etc. Many completionists seem to grab these items first, as they judge that they may never see them again.

Gold Key: *Scooby Doo* (GK) #1 remains at the top of many want lists and easily brings 200-300% *Guide*, especially in the elusive high grades. All issues of *Tarzan* and *Turok* sold in all grades. *Tarzan* by Manning and those with Ron Ely photo covers were the best sellers. *Turok* #100-130 seem to have less than half the supply of #71-99 and sell quite fast. Notable good and still undervalued sellers: Whitman variant editions are possible for all Gold Key comics and digests published from 11/1971-3/1980, but might only exist on 30-50% of all titles. These and the 1968 Canadian newstand variant cover price issues sold mostly to completionists.

The top-selling titles at 120-135% *Guide* included: *Addams Family, Amazing Chan, Banana Splits, Battle of the Planets, Boris Karloff* #1-50, 80-86, *Bugs Bunny* #86-110, *Bullwinkle, Dagar, Dark Shadows* #1-20, *Doc Savage, Dr. Solar, Fat Albert, Flash Gordon, Fun-In, Funky Phantom, Grimm's Ghost, Happy Days, Land of Giants, Kroft Supershow, Looney Tunes, Magnus, Mighty Mouse* #156-172 (esp. *Mighty Heroes* issues), *Mighty Samson, Mars Patrol, Munsters, Nancy & Sluggo* (for the *Peanuts* strip), *Occult Files of Dr. Spector*, most #1s, *Phantom* #1-10, *Popeye* #66-80, *Ripley's* #1-30, *Space Family Robinson* #1-20, *Space Ghost, Star Trek* #1-9, TV superheroes, *Tarzan* #132-206, *Turok* #30-50, 101-130, *Twilight Zone* #1-30, 83, 84, *UFO*

Flying Saucers, Underdog, Wacky Witch, Wild Wild West and *Zody the Mod Rob*.

These undervalued and low supply titles sold well at 135-150% *Guide*: *Beetle Bailey* #39-53, *Golden Comics Digest, Inspector, Lancelot Link, Little Monsters, Lone Ranger, Mystery Comics Digest, Peanuts, Phantom, Pink Panther, Scooby Doo, Smokey Bear,* and *Wacky Races.*

Harvey Comics: Demand went through the roof for almost all cartoon Harvey titles this year from all eras, but especially those from 1950-1970. We sold more this year than in the previous six-seven years combined. The greatest difficulty is restocking, which cannot be done on eBay as prices go too high for non-strict graded copies. Even most of our 1970s and 1980s titles are greatly depleted this year.

For the first half year, *Hot Stuff* was by far the most requested title, but in the third quarter all pre-1976 *Richie Rich* titles tripled in demand and became the new bestselling Harveys once again. When compared to the much more common Marvels, everything from Harvey seems quite the bargain, especially for very popular characters that two generations of fans grew up on. The few existing CGC 9.4 early and key issues that exist can bring 300-800% *Guide*.

A new trend is buyers who, having completed their favorite characters, now hunt down back-up stories in other titles of the same characters. This is especially true for Richie Rich, who for example appears in *Mutt & Jeff* #116-131. These are the approximate order of most requested titles: *Hot Stuff, Wendy, Devil Kids, Richie Rich Poor Little Rich Boy*, all squarebound giants, *Hot Stuff Sizzlers*, all #1s, *Baby Huey, Stumbo, Richie Rich Millions & Success, Harvey Hits, Sad Sack, Playful Little Audrey, Spooky, Little Dot*, 1970s *Richie Rich* titles, *Blondie, Casper, Scooby Doo, Dagwood, Felix the Cat*, Hanna-Barbera Titles, *Bunny, Little Max, Mutt & Jeff,* and *Joe Palooka*.

Li'l Abner and *Dick Tracy* were slower. Many buyers were filling in sets and would take any grade availiable, with the VG-FN range the most requested. Those looking for pre-1970 strict NM copies were pretty much out of luck, as very few exist with even most file copies being in the VF thru VF/NM condition range. The low print run comics and digests from 1988-1993 plus the Alfred Harvey titles are all consistent sellers at 150% *Guide*.

Humor/Parody Comics and Magazines: *MAD, Crazy, Sick* and *Cracked* are not around in big supplies like a decade back. Cover and contents affect the value and ability to sell these titles. Most buyers preferred cheaper G-VG range copies. *Sick* and *Cracked* #1-100 are hard to restock and are fast sellers at 125-150% *Guide*. We encountered a few *Cracked* completionists who are having a hard time with un-numbered specials, series that did not begin at #1, and series where the last issue number is not known. There are also various digests, paperbacks, specials and other items on the above. At 220+ different titles, the *MAD* mass market paperback series just might be more difficult to complete than the complete comic and magazine series. Many of the 1980s paperbacks had just one short and finite printing.

The early fold-in issues *MAD* #86-150 remain scarce in unfolded high grade and bring premiums. It seems that most of the 1975 and older *MAD* specials have the bonuses missing, thus they can be tough to complete intact. Warren's *Help* mags and Harvey Kurtzman paperbacks sold very fast at around 135% *Guide* and are hard to restock. Well up in demand and bringing 120-150% *Guide* are all the obscure parody titles, like *Ape, Apple Pie, Ballyhoo, Berford Seaman's Flabby Thighs & Butter, Brother Billy the Pain from Plains, CARtoons, Cycletoons, Eh, Fuddle Duddle, Grin, Humbug, International Insanity, Laugh-In, Nuts, Panic, Parody, Rump, Surftoons, Thimk, Trash, Trump, Up Your Nose, Whack, Wacko, Wild, Yell, You Don't Say* (Marvel), and *Zany*.

IW and Super Reprints: IW and Super reprints now date 40-50 years old. There are perhaps about 250-300 different comics in total. About one hundred of them are fairly easy to get, but once you get past that point they get scarcer. I have been told by collectors that once you get down to the last 50 needed, many are quite scarce to rare and must be purchased one at a time with lots of searching. They are cool titles to collect, as they contain great variety of genres with lots of artists from many publisher sources. In the early Comic Code era, they published their titles without the Code. Many issues contain pre-Code reprints in an era where they were not allowed. 90% of their output can be purchsed at under $10 per item in lower grades. Apparently some have previously unpublished Golden and Atom Age stories, like *Dynamic Adventures* #12(Unpublished Chestler GA material?; Canada's *Zor the Mighty* -c/s; Letkeman-a). All this probably explains why they sold so well in the last couple of years. They are affordable, lots of fun, interesting and a challenging series to collect.

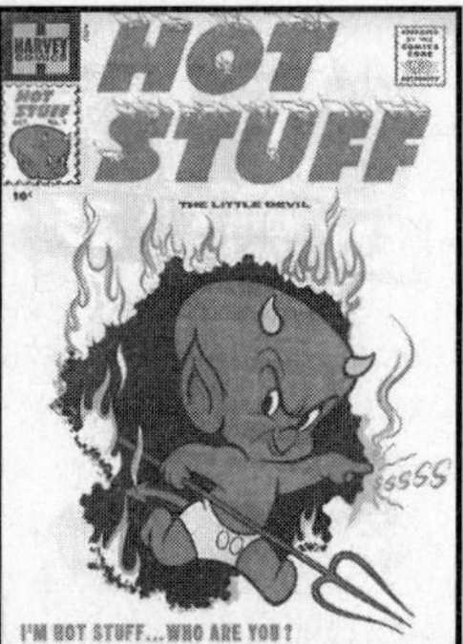

***Hot Stuff** #1 is indeed "Hot Stuff" in the market*

Love Comics: It still amazes superhero fans how love comics have become so popular. The biggest appeal seems to be the low survival rates. Most sellers do not or will not carry them; thus, when buyers find us, they are very happy and place nice-sized orders.

Most buyers of non-Marvel and non-DC titles want lower grade copies in FA, G or VG, but higher grades move too. Marvel and DC titles sell fast in all grades, but the FN-up issues are in short supply and are now the fastest sellers. *My Love* and *Our Love Story* are constantly asked for, as many Marvel Bronze Age completionists need these. Any issue from any publisher that is judged a key issue, minor key, giant, or popular artist issue sells at least twice as fast. Neal Adams issues are red hot and cannot be kept in stock at 150-200% *Guide* in any grade. A small warehouse find of about a hundred different issues of 1960s Charlton love comics turned up, mostly in VF condition range, thus over-supplying the market on these issues for a short time. One must remember that the other hundreds of Charlton love comics are still quite scarce in better than FN condition. All in G-FN still moved very well.

Demand for 1940s and 1950s romance is still strong and steady, with artist issues still the most sought after. Steranko's *Our Love Story* #5 is now one of our most requested of all Bronze Age Marvels. *Gothic Romances* #1 and *Gothic Tales of Love* #1-2 sell at double *Guide* but were near impossible to find. Skywald's *Tender Love* was also much requested by completionists. *Teen Love Stories* #1-3 (1969/70) has also been hot with Warren completionists.

Marvel Comics: The Marvels from 1970-1974 were the most requested and remain in short supply. Issues from 1961-1964 were in demand, but high prices have scared off buyers with smaller budgets. All major and moderate key issues of the 1970-1974 period more than doubled in demand as compared to last year. *Amazing Spider-Man* #129 is red hot and even on eBay, unslabbed copies bring over *Guide* with CGC copies bringing good multiples. The other 10-15 earliest appearances of Punisher are hot too. The shortage of 20-cent era Marvels continues, especially in high grades. Strict high grade copies bring well over *Guide*, slabbed or not. This was perhaps the best year ever for Bronze and Silver Age in strictly graded 8.0, VF/NM and better. All superhero titles were in large demand as everyone wanted to complete everything from 1961-1985.

These Marvel key issues bringing 135-150% *Guide* saw their highest demand in many years: *Amazing Adventures* #11, *Amazing Spider-Man* #3, 11, 12, 53-56, 119-122, 124, 129, 134, 135, 161, 162, *Avengers* #101-125, *Daredevil* #50-53, 77, 81, 100, 131, 158, 168, *Deadly Hands of Kung-Fu* #28, *Defenders* #1-5, 10, *Evel Knievel, Fear* #10, 19, 20, 24, *Ghost Rider* #1-10, *GS Spidey* #4, *G.I. Joe* #21, 93, 150-155, *Incredible Hulk* #122, 126, 140, 141, 161, 162, 180, 181, *Iron Fist* #14, 15, *Marvel Feature* #1-3, *Marvel Preview* #2, *Marvel Spotlight* #2, 5-11, *Marvel Team-Up* #1-11, *Planet of the Apes* (mag) #29, *Pussycat* #1 (scarce and sells instantly at 150% *Guide*), *Savage Sword* #231-235, *Savage Tales* #1, *Sub-Mariner* #34, 35, *Tomb of Dracula* #1-10, *Transformers* #61-80, *Werewolf by Night* #1-10, 32, *GS X-Men* #1.

All Marvel 1970s to early 1980s magazines have finally seen a good rise in demand, especially for strict high grade copies. Now that CGC grades them, they will likely not stay inexpensive as compared to color comics for much longer. It will be interesting to see how CGC handles grading mags, as they are traditionally much tougher in strict NM than their color comic counterparts. TNC (Traditionally Non-Collected) titles are still big sellers, but were overshadowed this year by superhero titles and are good long-term buys; they brought 120%-135% *Guide*. Some of them are: cartoon, digests, fanzines, giveaway/promo items, magazines, memorabilia, paperbacks, reprint titles, romance, teenage, treasuries, TV/movie, war, and western.

The Marvel adult cartoon mags (*Cartoons & Gags, Cartoon Capers/Laughs/Parade*, etc.) are hard to find in any grade and sell fast. Those with the *Pussycat* strip or Bill Ward art typically sell for about double the others.

Also in heavy demand and bringing 120%-135% *Guide* were: *Amazing Adv.* #11-17, *Amazing Spider-Man* #91-200, *Avengers* #71-99, 126-200, *Beware, Bizarre Adventures, Capt. America* #131-200, *Capt. Marvel* #25-35, *Chamber of Chills, Chili, Conan* #26-100, 270-275, *Daredevil* #50-181, *Dead of Night* #1-11, *Deadly Hands of Kung-Fu, Dracula Lives, Epic, Fantastic Four* #100-200, Fireside books, *Foom, Fraggle Rock* #7, 8 (non-reprinted issues), *Frankenstein,* all *Giant Size* titles, *G.I. Joe* #1-27, 94-120, 141-149, *Haunt of Horror* (magazine and digest), *Howard the Duck* mag, *Hulk* mag, *Incredible Hulk* #121-200, *Invaders* #1-10, *Iron Man* #31-100, *Kazar* #12 (variant), Kull #1-10, *Kull & Barbarians* #1-3, *L'il Kids, L'il Pals, Mad about Millie, M. Comics Super Special* #1-10, 31-41, *Marvel Fun & Games, Marvel Preview* #1-10, *M. Treasury* #1-28, *M. Two-in-One* #1-10, Ann. 2, *Masters of the Universe, Master of Kung-Fu* #15-50, *Mighty Marvel Western* #1-15, all *Millie the Model, Monsters on the Prowl* #9-16, *Monsters Unleashed, My Love, Nick Fury* #1-5, *Night Nurse, Our Love Story, Pizzazz, Planet of the Apes* mags #21-28, *Savage Sword* #1-20, 200-230, *Savage Tales* #2-5, *Scooby Doo, Shanna, Spectacular Spider-Man* #26-28, 64, 81-83, *Spidey Super Stories* #1-20, *Sub-Mariner* #8, 21-50, *Supernatural Thrillers, Tales of the Zombie, Thor* #180-230, *Tomb of Dracula* mags #1-6, *Uncanny Tales, Unknown Worlds of SF, Vampire Tales, Vault of Evil, What If* (1st series) #1-31, *X-Men* #50-66, 94-121.

Low grade reading copies were again in big demand. Early appearances of the Abomination were hot for the previous six months, now upstaged by demand for Doctor Octopus items due to the next Spidey film. Due to small print runs, most Marvels from 1996 up sell well. "Onslaught" issues still sell, with only the "Heroes Return" era selling slow. Marvel Knights and many titles from 2000-2003 are hot and are actually tough to keep in stock. It is nice to see again – new comics that hold their value and even legitimately rise in value.

National Lampoon: *National Lampoon* took over the helm from *MAD* in 1970 as the greatest humor mag on the market. Every issue in the 1970s had comics, and the appeal of a Comics Code-free mag with huge creative freedom and higher wages drew almost all the major talent of the time. Artists appearing (many regularly) include: Neal Adams, Bode, Frazetta, Jeff Jones, Kaluta, Morrow, Orlando, Rodrigues, Romita, Arnold Roth, Springer, Barry Windsor-Smith, Gahan Wilson, Wrightson, and many more. Issue #1-16 (4/1970-7/1971) are scarce in FN or better, but also in any grade. #17-33(12/1972) are in low supply, but especially in VF or better.

The hottest issues are: #1, which sells at $150-$200 in FN/VF; #2-10 at $40-$75 each in FN range; #13 (Frazetta-c; VF $50); #16 (7/1971; pornography issue); #19 (Beatles parody); #20 (horror issue; Wilson-c; "Dragula," with Frazetta inner-c and nine pages of Neal Adams art; VF $50); #22 (1/72; "Nothing Sacred;" first "Son-O-God," ten pages of Neal Adams art, Robert Crumb art; classic M. Gross painted-c, first 'funny pages' section; VF $40); #26 (*Conan* parody by Barry

Windsor-Smith; VF $30); #27 (SF issue; classic Frazetta-c; VF $35); #31 (*Rolling Stones* parody, Neal Adams; VF $30); #33 (Adams-a; VF $25); #34 (1/1973; "Death" issue; "Buy this Magazine, or we will shoot this Dog;" scarce and hot; VF $50); and many more.

The *1964 High School Yearbook* parody is the single hottest of anything they published with reading copies bringing $35-$50 and nice VF copies selling very fast at $100 each. Most of the specials on the market are only G to VG+ copies, with VF or better copies being scarce, as most were not bagged and-most were well read and loved by their owners.

Some of the highest demand or scarcer specials include: *Best of National Lampoon* #1 (VF $50), 3, 7-9, *Breast of NL* (#2), *Cartoons Even We Wouldn't Dare Print, Comics, Encyclopedia of Humor* (Wrightson-c; VF $30), *Foto Funnies* (VF $25), *French Comics* (VF $25), *Gentlemen's Bathroom Companion* Vol.1, 2 (VF $25+ each), *Hitler's Favorite Cartoons* (VF $25), *True Facts* (VF$30), *Up Yourself Book* (VF $30), *Very Large Book of Comical Funnies* (VF $22), and others.

The classic paperback *Bored of the Rings* has been in print since the 1960s and is a best-seller in any grade at $4-$10 each. From 1981-1985 the print runs dropped sharply and the remaining copies on the market are getting scarcer. From 1986-1993, it seems almost no one bought them and there are almost no copies on the market. Prices are rising on this era and they will be tough to complete. *National Lampoon* remains one of the most overlooked and undervalued collectibles in our entire hobby. Perhaps one day consumer demand will get them listed in the *Guide*; they rightly deserve to be listed. We highly recommend you buy them now while prices are still relatively low and before all supplies are gone. They remained one of our top sellers consistently all year.

Treasury Editions: All treasury-sized comics are on the rise in demand. Previous buyers were buying special artist and favorite character issues, but recent buyers are now filling in their runs. The scarcest issues bringing 135-200% *Guide* are: *Annie, Christmas & Archie, Rudolph* (1972), *G.I. Joe, Golden Picture Story Book, King Kong,* and *Smurfs*. We even sold a couple nice sets and some singles of the six-issue *Walt Disney Paint Book* series (1975) at *Guide* prices. Due to their large size, treasuries tend to become damaged easily, coupled with the fact that treasury-sized comic bags have never been widely availiable; this means that true strict VF+ and better copies are quite scarce on the market. Since CGC does not grade this size, it makes it even tougher for fans to get true high grade copies. Strict NM and better copies are nearly non-existent. Red and black colored covers are ever tougher as the colors rub so easily on these giant comics. *Marvel Treasury* #1, and *LCE* C-23 and C-25 for example, are 'condition sensitive' and extra tough in high grade.

The hottest issues bringing 120-135% *Guide* are: *All-New Collectors Edition* C#53-56,58, *Captain America's Bicentennial Battles, DC Special Series* #27, *Famous First Edition, Funtastic World of Hanna-Barbera* #1-3, *Limited Collectors Edition* C#23-25, 32-34, 37-39, 41-52, *Marvel Treasury* #1-10, 14, 18, 26, 28, *Marvel Special Edition* (Spectacular Spider-Man) #1 (1975), *Superman vs. The Amazing Spider-Man* #1.

Underground Comics: Interest has picked up on undergrounds, with Robert Crumb topping most requests in any printings. Many are looking for impossibly scarce low print 1960s issues and we could not help. We do have a large 1970s to early 1980s selection and sold about double what we did in previous years. Artist issues like Corben and Bode were most requested, followed by well known characters and titles. Bestsellers included: *Air Pirates Funnies, Anomaly, Bijou Funnies, Cocaine Comix, Dr Atomic, Fat Freddy's Cat, Grim Wit, Rip Off, Rowlf, Skull, Slow Death, Snarf, Wonder Wart Hog* and *Zap*. Most pre-1975 issues are scarce in strict VF/NM or better. When the next *Underground Price Guide* is eventually released, we should see a sharp rise in prices and demand, especially with the scarcer early issues.

Variants and Limited Editions: Marvel's 30 and 35-cent variants saw big increased demand and price increases. We sold almost all we could get our hands on in spite of the very low *Guide* prices. There are now many buyers after these.

Value is determined by character popularity and implied scarcity. Spider-Man is hands down the most requested. The Marvel 30-cent price variants, with 100-500 copies each estimated to exist, brought 400%-1500% regular issue prices in grade. *Amazing Spider-Man* #155-159 variants are most requested and VF copies would bring in the $100+ each range for VF copies. *Omega the Unknown* #3 is among the more common of the 30-cent variants and reflects our minimum price on these variants: G $7; VG $14; FN $20; VF $30; NM $40 (minimum for 35-cent variants begins at double these prices).

Marvel western and horror reprint titles are among the scarcest issues and bring higher percentages. The much scarcer Marvel 35-cent price variants, with 10-100 copies each estimated to exist, brought 1000-5000% regular issue prices. *Amazing Spider-Man* #169-173 variants are most requested and VF copies would bring in the $200+ each range for VF copies. The most common 35-cent variant is *Star Wars* #1 with an estimated 200 copies existing. Because it has been listed in the *Guide* for about twenty years, it has reached legendary status, thus the high *Guide* value and large demand. Over 3.5% of CGC graded copies of *Star Wars* #1s are variants.

Canadian Variants were again popular; see our Canadian comics section in this report. Limited edition comics like Dynamic Forces signed copies, hologram-c, gold, platinum, signed & numbered, polybagged specials, and cover variants, are expensive to stock and collect. They seem to be most popular when relatively new, but as they get older they get lost in a vast sea of such limited editions and become hard to move. The only exception seems to be long proven characters such as Vampirella.

Warren, Skywald and Other Horror Comic Magazines: Horror mags were again one of our strongest sellers. Marvel and Warren are espacially hot in VF/NM or better, as many expect CGC grading mags to cause price increases. It will be interesting to see how many undervalued *Dracula Lives* #1s and *Vampire Tales* #1s exist in 9.4 or better as compared to the higher priced *Tomb of Dracula* #1s. How long will the mags with early Blade and Punisher appearances stay low-priced? Many fans will soon realize how scarce mags truly are in strict grades of VF/NM or higher.

We still have huge demand for low grade copies, as a lot of readers want these mags while they are still affordable. The mags from Eerie the publisher, Modern Day and Stanley had over-the-top gory covers/stories, but still sell better to readers than to higher grade collectors. These were scarcer and sold fast at 120-135% *Guide*: *Ghoul Tales, Shock, Terrors of Dracula, Web of Horror* and *Weird Vampire Tales*.

In the last two years, we sold over 25 copies of *Creepshow* 1st printing in VF/NM range at $50 average, mainly to ready buyers in the Stephen King collectible market. We finally got in some nice Skywald mag collections (*Psycho, Nightmare* and *Scream*), and all numbers sold fast and furious. Previously low grade was most requested, but this year high grades were on most want lists. We had some amazing high grade copies in the "Manitoba" collection that brought 150-300% *Guide*. Many buyers told me they got tired of bidding on overgraded VF-NM copies on eBay and having FN-F/VF copies arrive.

Early issues of **Vampirella** are among the most requested. (#12 shown)

There are still some dwindling supplies of only a few issues (perhaps under 100 different in total) of Warren warehouse leftovers, but they are not high grade copies, as many are now only VG+ to FN+ after over 20 years of handling wear. The Warren warehouse copies are what is holding back Warren prices from exploding. As fans realize they all need the same issue numbers no longer commonly available, they begin to pay better prices to fill in their runs. We found a few each of Skywald's 1971 adult mag *King*, with #1s selling fast with Boris Vallejo art at $20 in FN. We sold a VF *After Hours* #1 (1957, first Warren mag and *Playboy* imitator with a two-page centerfold b&w nude photo pinup of Bettie Page) for $500. Later in this four-issue series, Jim Warren asked Forrest J. Ackerman to do a feature on Hollywood monsters and thus this became a very rare precursor to *Famous Monsters*. These mags are rarely offered for sale in any condition, much less in high grade. Also, *Eerie* #17 is blazing hot, with current values of about VG $75, FN $150, VF $250. *Blazing Combat* #1 easily brings 200% of *Guide* in any grade.

The most requested issues at 120-150% *Guide: Blazing Combat* #1-2 and *Anthology*, *Comix International* #1, *Cracked Monster Party* and *For Monsters Only*, *Creepy* #9, 10, 14, 17-19, 29, 32, 50, 76, 78, 113, 132-146 and 1968 Yearbook, *Devilina* #2, *Dracula Lives* #1-3, 10-13, *Eerie* #5, 8, 17, 18, 23-25, 28, 38, 40, 45, 60, 81, 94, 95, 98, 108, 125, 128, 130-139 and 1970 Yearbook, *Famous Monsters* #1-32, and paperbacks, *Haunt of Horror* #3-5, *King* (Skywald) #1-2, *Marvel Preview* #3, 7, 8, 12, *Monsters to Laugh With* #1-3, *Monsters Unleashed* #1-4, 9-11, *Monster World* (replaces *Famous Monsters* #70-79) #2, 3, 4, 9, 10, *Movie Monsters* (Skywald) #2-4, *Odd World of Richard Corben, Screen Thrills* (Warren), *Spacemen* (Warren), *Spirit Special, Tales of the Zombie* #1, 10 and Annual, *Thrilling Adv.* #2, *Vampirella* #1-8, 12, 16, 19, 33, 36, 41, 45, 46, 48, 52, 61, 63, 64, 77, 78, 100-113, *Annual* #1, *Special* #1, UK mags #1-4, paperbacks (UK and USA) #1-6, *Vampire Tales* #1-5, 8, 9, *Warren Presents* #13(*Sword & Sorcery Comix*), 14 (11/81, Rex Havoc), *Web of Horror* #1-3, *Weird Tales of the Macabre* #2 and westerns (aka *Wildest Westerns of Filmland*).

Websites Vs. eBay: eBay prices were low on many unslabbed comics. Buyers often now assume bad grading and bid accordingly. There are many sellers willing to accommodate this market. We bought a lot less material off eBay this year as off-graded copies offset profits on many purchases. We did sucessfully sell a few batches of nice comics by using large scans so buyers could see they were properly graded. In general I found it too much labor to sell items that would bring decent prices. Most of what we sold on eBay this year was CGC graded comics and they did quite well. To me eBay is a huge flea market and I prefer a more controlled market, thus I really concentrated on listing items on my website. Our website now has about 100 categories to choose from, with 10-150 pages of items listed in each category. We had a very stong return of previous buyers, plus many new buyers who preferred to buy many well graded items all at once from one seller over buying single items via auction. We gain more international buyers each year. eBay accounted for under 5% of our sales. Both my customers and I are finding endless items that even I didn't know I had. We have literally thousands of items that no one else on the Internet has in stock, and buyers find these items many times per day. We abandoned our traditional snail mail catalogued lists in 1997. We still sell to many buyers who do not have Internet access, mainly through phone calls, want lists, ads and word of mouth. It seems our website and our regular repeat buyers will be our main avenue for selling collectibles in the years to come.

Whitman Comics: Whitmans from 8-12/1980 are confirmed to be sold only in pre-packs and with very low distribution. *Porky Pig* #99 might be the scarcest of all the Whitman 8-12/1980 issues and would bring $100+ in VF if it exists at all. The current market rarest issues in approximate order from rarest to moderately rare are: *Porky Pig* #99, *Winnie the Pooh* #22, *Looney Tunes* #34-35, *Tom & Jerry* #332, *Super Goof* #61, *Pink Panther* #76-77, *Chip & Dale* #69, *Little Lulu* #260, *Daffy Duck* #130-131, *Tweety &*

Slyvester #107, *Yosemite Sam* #70, *Popeye* #158, *Woody Woodpecker* #190, *Porky Pig* #98, *Chip and Dale* #68, *Tweety & Slyvester* #106, *Yosemite Sam* #69, *Bugs Bunny* #221, *WDC&S* #480, *Battle of the Planets* #7, *Mickey Mouse* #208, *Donald Duck* #222, and *Uncle Scrooge* #179. Our minimum price for 8-12/80 Whitmans begins at G $6, VG $10, FN $18, and VF $25, and we are nearly sold out. The Big Three – *Uncle Scrooge* #179, *Donald Duck* #222 and *WDC&S* #480 – are finding their way into the market because of high and still rising prices. *Little Lulu* #260 is apparently still not high enough in the *Guide* as they are not coming onto the market and would easily bring $500-$1000 in VF/NM. The books on the list above might start to hit the market more as prices rise. At current price levels, sellers are not hunting them down that hard. We have a waiting list for *Battle of the Planets* #7, *Porky Pig* #99, *Winnie the Pooh* #22, *Super Goof* #61 and *Pink Panther* #77. The 1983/84 no-date, no Code issues are also confirmed distributed only in pre-packs and bring $15 minimum in VF. Whitman variants of Gold Keys 11/71-2/80 are possible and they sell to completionists for 150-300% of GK issue values. The 163+ known DC Whitman variants in sixteen titles sell well to completionists and variant collectors in the $6-$15 range for VG-VF copies.

Michael Tierney

(Collector's Edition - North Little Rock, Arkansas)
(The Comic Book Store - Little Rock, Arkansas)

Comic books as a cash equivalent? The perception of comics as a negotiable currency has always been lurking around in the back of collectors' minds, but after the boom of comic-related movies in 2003, this concept has really taken hold of the general public. This kind of perception has both problems and benefits. The benefits become obvious when old collections are saved from being thrown into trash bins when the original owners are preparing to move; I saw several examples of that this year. But the problem with people thinking of comic book stores in terms of a bank comes from a lack of education in condition in relation to value. A person once argued that he felt that bends and creases should increase the value of a certain book, because all the flaws gave it 'character.' I countered with the fact that you can find a lot of classic cars with 'character' in the local junkyard. This year a fellow came into one store expecting to be paid $19,000 cash for a $900 copy of *Hulk* #1. This book was part of a collection being brought in for the third time. Because of poor storage conditions, the state of the books was tragically worse each time that I saw them, and this time my offer was half of what I'd made previously. He finally understood the importance of condition in relation to a book's value.

Last year there was also a big shakeup in the publisher rankings as DC pushed Marvel out of the #1 spot for overall new comics sales, thanks in part to their aggressive program of overprinting. This was particularly evident with sales of the Jim Lee run on *Batman* from #608-619. Where the normal sales model for a comic series is one of strong early sales that subsequently decline, with this run the sales were actually much stronger at the conclusion than they were at the start. By the time #619 shipped, #608 was selling for $12 and #612 (with a Superman cover) was selling for $8, with the second printing of #612 selling for three times that amount.

Another shakeup in the echelon of comic publishers came at the #3 spot, with CrossGen moving past both Dark Horse and Image in total sales at my stores this year. At one location, CrossGen outsells both of those established premier publishers by a firm margin of three to one and growing. That's quite an accomplishment for a young publisher, despite having a year filled with financial difficulties. Customers bought multiple copies of *El Cazador* #1 to give away to new readers; that's a lot of faith and consumer support. Watch for value increases on the CrossGen early issues and the first printing of *El Cazador* #1 in particular.

A big reason for CrossGen's success is due to their dedication to maintaining titles and reliable shipping dates. Many publishers have decided not to print the last issues of failing mini-series, or cancelled titles before they finished the storylines; this leads to an erosion of consumer faith, and is damaging to the hobby as a whole. Once consumers have invested their time and their money in a series and then are left without closure, they are less likely to try new series from publishers that have disappointed them in the past.

Golden/Atom Age: This year we discovered some new promotional *Blue Bird* issues of the *Masked Raider* and *Freddy*, plus the previously unknown *Eager Beaver Space Activity Book*. The adventures of the Space Beaver is loaded with lots of interesting, although dated, astronomical facts and details about space exploration. There are probably still a lot of wonderful discoveries to be made in this pivotal time period of comics publishing.

Sgt. Rock in **Our Army at War** remains timeless. (#138 shown)

On a sad note concerning the Golden Age, as the years continue to roll by, western comics are currently dropping in demand. The exception to this are comics featuring still recognized names like John Wayne and Chuck Conners, especially issues that feature photo covers, or issues containing artwork by the ever-legendary Frank Frazetta.

On the other hand, war comics like *Our Army* remain timeless and seem to be rising in demand. Horror and adventure comics from EC and Fiction House also sustain very strong demand, and early Marvel comics containing prototype characters are blistering hot.

Silver Age: As always, what is selling in the new category directly affects the sale of older comics. After the phenomenal success of the *Spider-Man* movie, demand for all appearances of the movie's villain, the Green Goblin, is way up, garnering prices 20% above *Guide* values. This kind of increased demand is an example of the effect that a popular movie can have. However, the release of the *Hulk* movie had the exact opposite result. Interest in Silver Age *Hulk*s was strong right up to the moment that the movie opened; then the negative feedback from moviegoers started and sales went into the tank on both classic and new comics, with current issue sales dropping more than 25% and still declining. Thanks to buzz about the 2004 movie, interest is already stirring on *Punisher* comics; how good the movie is will determine if that new demand continues.

Modern Age: With the revival of *Conan the Barbarian*, interest has rekindled in this classic Robert E. Howard character. But interest in the black and white magazines, *Savage Sword of Conan* and *Conan Saga,* have always been there. They've always been in demand even when the color comics languished in my back issue bins and sell as rapidly as I can restock them.

Books that I refer to as the 'Millennium Age,' published after 2000, are already starting to reveal a lot of titles with value, even when followed by second and third printings. *Origin* and early issues of *Ultimate X-Men, Ultimate Spider-Man*, *Teen Titans* (2003), and *Outsiders* (2003) have all jumped dramatically in value. This is partially due to incredibly low print runs that resulted from the drop in demand after the over-inflated print runs of the '90s.

Only pre-*Unity* Valiants from the early '90s have remained strong in a time period that has few issues still in demand. There is definitely a hardcore group of fans out there, still looking to finish their collections...which is what collecting is all about! Good luck to everyone endeavoring to complete your childhood goals. After all, just because you might have grown up, it doesn't mean that you have to stop being a child at heart.

Harley Yee

2003 was a very good year for the comic book market and I expect 2004 to be even better. With the multiple movies coming out next year after three comic book-themed films in 2003, the industry is getting wider exposure than ever with the general public. This and the general improvement to the economy has brought many new collections into the market. This can only improve as the economy continues to improve and *Spider-Man 2* and *Punisher* open in 2004.

Also fueling the market is the incredible success of CGC. No single event has occurred since the *Guide* came out that has changed the industry as much. Third party grading was the one thing that separated the comic book market from most other collectibles. This has brought many new investors into the market. This along with their population reports, which truly reflect how scarce books are in truly high grade, have brought in incredible multiples on many books.

2004 is shaping up as a follow up to 2003, which was 'Follow the Movie.' Golden Age will be steady, led by Timely and DC. High grade Silver Age DC is trending up as the population report will continue to show how scarce in grade they are. However, Silver Age and Bronze Age Marvels again will dominate sales. If *Hulk* #181 is the *Action* #1 and *Giant-Size X-Men* #1 the *Detective* #27 of the Bronze Age collector, then what will *Amazing Spider-Man* #129 be in 2004?

Vincent Zurzolo

In the fast paced world in which we live, it's very easy to get caught up in the day-to-day and not realize how fortunate we are. Before I begin my comic book market analysis, I would like to thank my partner Stephen Fishler, my entire staff and all of my customers for a truly successful year.

It is amazing for me to look back on my career in comics, which started when I was merely sixteen years of age. Since that time, the hobby, market and the world have changed a great deal. One thing that hasn't changed is the type of questions collectors ask. I can remember for as long as I have been involved in this hobby collectors asking me questions about whether I thought the comic market would ever come to an end, will prices ever get higher than they already are, and who would win in a fight – Hulk or Superman? The answers have always been and always will be: no, yes and Hulk, because the more he gets beaten up, the angrier he gets, and the angrier he gets, the stronger he gets...and because I'm a Marvel guy.

Internet Sales: Internet sales have nearly doubled from last year. I believe this trend will continue, especially after the addition of the "Metropolis Gallery Section" on our website (www.metropoliscomics.com), which will showcase thousands of actual scans of comics for sale. The number of first time buyers/new collectors that find Metropolis through our website never ceases to amaze me. It is very reassuring to see so much new blood entering the market. This includes customers spending twenty-five dollars a month to twenty five thousand dollars a month.

eBay Sales: I still use eBay as a way to market low, mid and high- end collectibles, and to attract new customers. However, I find my return on time and investment continually diminishing. This, coupled with eBay's never ending fee increases, poor customer service and allowance of fraudulent key comic sellers to continually rip off unsuspecting customers just begs for someone to come into the market and offer a viable alternative.

Conventions: As usual, San Diego was my biggest show of the year. Sales as well as attendance were up. The Las Vegas Comic Con, which debuted this past October, was quite impressive. Not only was it professionally run, but sales-wise it was my second best show of the year. The Madison Square Garden Convention in NYC, another great show, ranked third. One thing all of these conventions have in common is the ability to draw customers who are serious about buying comics.

CGC: Dealers/collectors/investors continue to utilize the variety of services offered by CGC. The grading service is used for several reasons, including the following: to increase the value of a comic book; to learn CGC's opinion of the condition of a comic book; to protect or preserve a comic book; and to make certain a comic book is unrestored. While I have no problem with any of these reasons for paying for CGC's service, I still find it discouraging to watch buyers simply looking at the number grade on a label instead of looking at the book itself. Whether a novice or a seasoned pro, it is extremely important to actually look at the comic book itself. You may find books that you think look better than the numeric grade on the label or vice versa. Remember, it is *your* opinion that really counts.

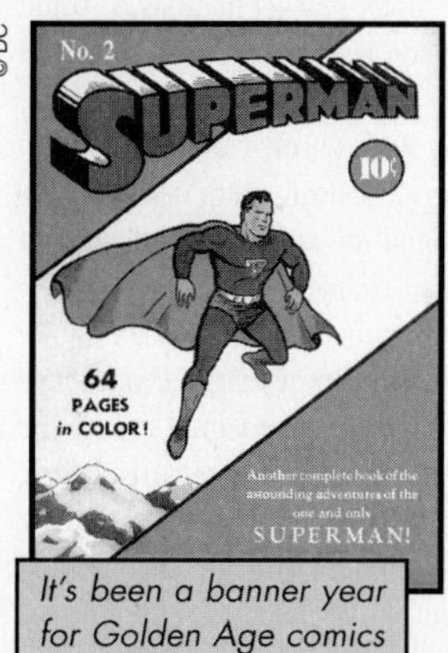

© DC

It's been a banner year for Golden Age comics like **Superman** #2 in all conditions and price ranges

If I had to point to one area of the market that has been disappointing over the last year, it would be the low and mid- grade CGC Golden Age market. I would like to believe there is a market for collectors who want to buy low and mid-grade CGC books, but time will tell.

Golden Age: This has been a banner year for Golden Age comics of all conditions and price ranges. The usual suspects like *Captain America, Marvel Mystery, Superman, Batman, Action* and *Detective* sold quite well. The surprise here was increased demand for esoteric funny animal comics, westerns, Disney and *Classic Comics*. High-ticket price Golden Age keys sold extremely well. I sold low, mid and high-grade copies of *Action* #1, *Detective* #27, *Superman* #1, *Batman* #1 and *Captain America* #1. Interest in Edgar Church/Mile High Comics was at all-time high with books selling for many multiples of Guide.

Silver Age: Due to the continued success of the Marvel superhero movies, Silver Age Marvels once again lead the pack. The release of *Daredevil*, *Hulk* and *X-Men 2* helped to boost sales of all three titles. Very Fine or better early Silver Age DCs are increasingly difficult to find in comparison to Marvels and make great investments. Look for *Amazing Spider-Man* #3 to jump in price this year as it is Doctor Octopus' first appearance and he is the villain for the second movie.

Collectors and investors alike should continue to look beyond Marvel and DC, as there are many great stories and deals to be had. Titles from Charlton with Ditko art, *Magnus* and *Doctor Solar* from Gold Key, and the *Thunder Agents* from Tower Comics are all undervalued.

Bronze Age: Interest continues to grow for 1970s comic books. The two hottest issues are *Amazing Spider-Man* #129 (first appearance of the Punisher), and of course, *Incredible Hulk* #181 (first full Wolverine appearance). The #129 price increase is fueled by the upcoming movie, while Wolverine is simply one of the most popular characters in the hobby. Prices will fluctuate on these books from time to time, but they are consistent sellers.

Promoting the Hobby: Spreading the word about comic book collecting and investing is the responsibility of every person actively involved in the hobby. Everyone can do something! In 2003, Metropolis sent out press releases espousing the profitability of investing in comic books. The results were fantastic; articles and interviews appeared in over fifty newspapers across the country.

Our website, **www.metropoliscomics.com**, has once again proven itself to be the premiere site for Golden, Silver and Bronze Age comic books. The site, aside from having the deepest inventory for vintage comics, is content rich. The "Market Report" section contains over five years of analysis. The "In the Press" section contains dozens of articles about collecting and investing in comic books. The "Feature" section contains dozens of articles about publishers, comic titles, genres and the history of comics. The site also offers a free grading guide, free appraisal service, online want list service, an incredible array of original art on display, time payments, gift certificates, a consignment program and a twenty percent discount on CGC grading fees.

Metropolis Director of Marketing, Ben Smith, created The Metropolis Index, comparing the long-term compound annual growth rates of "blue chip" comics with the DJIA. The data was first presented at a Bloomberg Seminar, and a second conference is planned in 2004. The data proved once again that comic books, while great entertainment, are also truly viable investments. Make sure to take a look at this year's comparison right here in the *Guide*.

My partner, Stephen Fishler, appeared on several national and international TV and radio shows talking about the virtues of comic collecting. Reuters News Group produced business segments at the Metropolis Showroom in Manhattan on collecting and investing in comic books. These segments were shown in Japan as well as the USA.

In conjunction with the release of the sequel to the *Spider-Man* Movie, the Discovery Channel is producing a documentary about comic books. Upon meeting the producers, I scheduled a shoot at my showroom. The interview focused on the popularity of Marvel Comics. Keep an eye out for it this summer.

Metropolis continues to support MOCCA, the Museum of Cartoon and Comic Art located in New York City. Their exhibits are spectacular and should not be missed.

I am now hosting a weekly online radio show called "The Comic Zone." The show can be heard live or archived by clicking on the Comic Zone icon at the top of the Metropolis' home page. Past guests include comic greats Jim Steranko, Terry Austin, Peter David, Larry Hama, Steve Borock of CGC and comic historians John Snyder and Arlen Schumer.

Whether it is giving your niece or nephew comic books as a present, simply sharing a fond story of your childhood reading comics, or how much your *Incredible Hulk* #1 went up in value, there are many easy ways to help promote the hobby. Sharing the hobby we cherish dearly is a good way to ensure it will continue well into the future.

Market Comparison [illegible] Metropolis Collectible[illegible]

	1994	2004	Price Appreciation	CAGR
DOW JONES IND. AVG.	3754.09	10453.92	241.76%*	13.07%
METROPOLIS INDEX	$704,185	$2,588,750	267.6%	13%

* DJIA Price Appreciation & CAGR increased to include reinvested dividends.

In early 2002, Metropolis Collectibles noticed customers increasingly soliciting help from partners **Vincent Zurzolo** and **Stephen Fishler** in creating financial strategies for comic book investment. While Metropolis advises any enthusiast to collect out of love for the art form first, and monetary returns second, they were nevertheless interested to see comics become an en vogue "counter-cyclical" investment option during the past two years. With many collectors redirecting funds from their stock portfolios to comic books, comics became nationally recognized in news and media as a "safe equity" alternative in today's unpredictable economy. Encouraged by this new attention to the hobby, Metropolis decided to conduct a formal comparative analysis of comic book valuations to the returns of the stock market. In doing so, they found comics weren't simply an overnight phenomenon during times of a depressed economy. A well-balanced portfolio of vintage comics can consistently outpace the market in the long-term.

On June 10th, 2003, Stephen Fishler and **Ben Smith (Metropolis' Director of Marketing)** conducted a seminar on comic book investment at Bloomberg headquarters in Manhattan. Inspired by the Dow Jones Industrial Average (DJIA), Fishler & Smith presented **"The Metropolis Index,"** a portfolio of 30 "blue-chip" vintage comics. Comics are selected for the Index based upon good-standing reputation, sustainable growth and collector-driven demand. Additionally, the index is diversified across a large number of comic industry market sectors, including superhero, humor, crime, horror and funny animal. Research is compiled using publicly available stock market data, and current and historical comic valuations as compiled by **Gemstone Publishing**.

Sources: Bloomberg; Factset; Official Overstreet Comic Book Price Guide "top of guide" prices 1994, 2004.

On January 1, 2004, the **DJIA** stood at **10453.92.** Ten years prior in 1994, the **DJIA** was **3754.09.** If dividends paid are considered to have been reinvested into the index, over the 10 year period, an investor's **Compound Annual Growth Rate (CAGR)** is **13.07%** with a **price appreciation** of **241.76%.** Comparatively, the **Metropolis Index** total value in 1994 was **$704,185**, and is **$2,588,750** in 2004. The **CAGR** of the Metropolis Index is **13%** with a **price appreciation** of **267.6%**.

Although numerous factors make an apples-to-apples comparison of comic books and stocks a difficult proposition, evidence lends itself to the long-term stability of the comic book market, and the security of comic book investments. Additional information can be found in the Press Section of **www.metropoliscomics.com**. Serious investors interested in consultation should contact **Vincent Zurzolo** of **Metropolis Collectibles** at **212.260.4147** or email **vincentz@metropolisent.com.**

THE METROPOLIS INDEX — 30 Handpicked Blue Chip Comics

	1994	2004	CAGR
ACTION COMICS #1	$ 90,000	$ 440,000.0[illegible]	[illegible]7.2%
ALL-AMERICAN COMICS #16	$ 37,000	$ 160,000.00	15.8%
ALL STAR COMICS #3	$ 20,000	$ 55,000.0[illegible]	[illegible]0.6%
AMAZING FANTASY #15	$ 20,000	$ 42,500.00	[illegible]8.0%
AMAZING SPIDER-MAN #1	$ 13,500	$ 32,000.0[illegible]	[illegible].0%
BATMAN #1	$ 36,000	$ 125,000.00	13.3%
BRAVE AND THE BOLD #28	$ 3,070	$ 8,000.0[illegible]	[illegible]0.1%
CAPTAIN AMERICA COMICS #1	$ 36,000	$ 125,000.00	13.3%
DETECTIVE COMICS #1	$ 24,000	$ 58,000.0[illegible]	[illegible].2%
DETECTIVE COMICS #27	$ 92,000	$ 375,000.00	15.1%
FANTASTIC FOUR #1	$ 12,000	$ 34,000.0[illegible]	[illegible]1.0%
FLASH COMICS #1	$ 23,000	$ 97,000.00	15.5%
GIANT-SIZE X-MEN #1	$ 230	$ 1,200.0[illegible]	[illegible]8.0%
INCREDIBLE HULK #1	$ 7,100	$ 23,000.00	12.5%
INCREDIBLE HULK #181	$ 255	$ 1,250.0[illegible]	[illegible]7.2%
JOURNEY INTO MYSTERY #83	$ 2,730	$ 9,000.00	12.7%
MAD #1	$ 2,500	$ 7,000.0[illegible]	[illegible]0.8%
MARVEL COMICS #1	$ 75,000	$ 330,000.00	16.0%
MORE FUN COMICS #52	$ 28,000	$ 84,000.0[illegible]	[illegible]1.6%
NEW FUN COMICS #1	$ 20,000	$ 43,500.00	8.1%
PEP #22	$ 3,500	$ 20,000.0[illegible]	[illegible]9.0%
SENSATION COMICS #1	$ 6,000	$ 40,000.00	20.9%
SHOWCASE #4	$ 18,000	$ 41,000.0[illegible]	[illegible].6%
SHOWCASE #22	$ 3,300	$ 7,000.00	7.8%
SUPERMAN #1	$ 70,000	$ 270,000.0[illegible]	[illegible]4.5%
VAULT OF HORROR #12	$ 2,500	$ 6,300.00	9.7%
WALT DISNEY COMICS & STORIES #1	$ 7,000	$ 23,000.0[illegible]	[illegible]2.6%
WHIZ COMICS #2 (1)	$ 42,000	$ 84,000.00	7.2%
WONDER WOMAN #1	$ 6,500	$ 34,000.0[illegible]	[illegible]8.0%
X-MEN #1	$ 3,000	$ 13,000.00	15.8%
TOTAL COMIC PORTFOLIO	$ 704,185	$ 2,588,75[illegible]	[illegible]3.0%

Editor's Note: *The above information was graciously provided by Metropolis Collectibles Inc.*

Key Comics Sold in 2003

The following lists of sales were reported to Gemstone during the year and represent only a small portion of the total amount of important books that have sold.

PLATINUM AGE - GOLDEN AGE - ATOM AGE SALES

Action Comics #1 Fair+ $26,000
Action Comics #4 FN+ (restored) $2,900
Action Comics #7 Fair/GD $3,000
Action Comics #11 (restored) app. FN $1,265
Action Comics #12 (restored) app. FN $1,265
Action Comics #18 VG $575
Adventure Comics #59 GD+ $288
Adventure Comics #121 FN $150
Adventures of Alan Ladd #7 VG $68
All-American Comics #70 FN+ $250
All Funny Comics #6 VG $30
All Select Comics #10 FN+ $607
Archie's Rival Reggie #1 VG $155
Batman #1 FN/VF(restored) $11,500
Batman #3 G/VG $1,450
Batman #4 FN+ $2,370
Blackhawk #12 GD- $105
Blackhawk #17 VG+ $375
Blue Bolt #105 VG/F+ $185
Blue Bolt #106 VG+ $160
Brown's Blue Ribbon Book of Jokes & Jingles Bk. 1 FN $785
Brown's Blue Ribbon Book of Jokes & Jingles Bk. 1 FN/VF (7.0) $1,667.50
Buster Brown's Blue Ribbon Book of Jokes & Jingles Bk. 2 FN $677.87
Buster Brown Plays Indian Muslin Series FN $101
Buster Brown Quick Meal Steel Ranges VF+ $224.75
Captain Aero Comics #25 VF $410
Captain America Comics #35 G+ $225
Captain America Comics #49 G $240
Captain America Comics #74 VG/FN $1,550
Captain Marvel, Jr. #1 VF $5,250
Champion Comics ashcan $4,000
Charlie Chaplin #317 GD $150
Charlie Chaplin Funny Stunts VG $299
Crash Comics #4 CGC 2.5 $480
Cyclone Comics ashcan $1,000
Detective Comics #12 VF/NM (rest.) $2,300
Detective Comics #13 VF/NM (rest.) $2,200
Detective Comics #127 FN/VF $325
Detective Comics #200 VG+ $105
Detective Comics #221 VG/FN $110
Dick Tracy FC Series 1 #1 VF/NM $12,600
Flash Comics #6 GD $925
Flash Comics #21 VG+ $180
Flash Gordon FC #190 FN- $35
Four Color #178 VF $900
Funny Stuff #13 VG $32
Heroic #40 VF #125
I Love Lucy #1 FN $180
Journey Into Mystery #1 VG $700
Leading Comics #4 VG $180
Legend of Daniel Boone #1 VG/FN $150
Little Orphan Annie #9 FN+ $120.75
Mad #49 FN+ $40
Marvel Mystery #2 VF/NM $47,600
Marvel Mystery Comics #72 VG+ $230
Marvel Mystery Comics #90 VG/FN $300
Master Comics #42 VG $65
More Fun #101 GD+ $900
More Fun #107 VG+ $125
The Newlyweds and Their Baby VG $99.99
OK Comics ashcan $1,000
Pep #22 VG+ $7,000
Phantom Lady #15 GD- $315
Police Comics #102 VG $60
Real Fact Comics #2 GD $40
Roy Rogers FC #129 VG/FN $45
Sensation Comics #28 G/VG $110
Sensation Comics #93 VG/FN $88
Skyman #2 FN $80
Star-Spangled Comics #32 VG- $110
Startling Terror Tales #11 Fr/G $250
Strange Tales #7 G/VG $185
Sub-Mariner Comics #10 G+ $250
Sub-Mariner Comics #17 VF+ $775
Superboy #1 VF+ $10,000
Superboy #1 VG $600
Superman #2 VG $2,600
Superman #3 GD $500
Tarzan of the Apes to Color GD- $300
Terrors of the Jungle #17 FN+ $200
Terrors of the Jungle #18 VF- $300
Tillie the Toiler #8 VF- $305
Treasure Box of Famous Comics, How Dick Tracy & Dick Tracy Jr. Caught The Racketeers VG $120.75
Uncle Scrooge FC #386 VG/FN $235
Weird Chills #1 VG $250
Weird Fantasy #15 FN $90
Whiz Comics #11 VG+ $146.50
Wonder Woman #21 FN/VF $390
World's Finest #30 VG $150
Zoot #14 VG- $149
Zorro FC #495 VG/FN $110

Adventure Comics #245 VG/FN $77
Adventure Comics #260 FN- $200
Adventure Comics #267 VG $170
Adventure Comics #300 FN+ $162
All-American Men of War #46 FN/VF $75
Amazing Adult Fantasy #8 FN- $135
Amazing Adult Fantasy #12 FN- $125
Amazing Fantasy #15 VF $33,600
Amazing Fantasy #15 VG+ $3,350
Amazing Spider-Man #1 VG+ $1800
Amazing Spider-Man #2 VG $500
Amazing Spider-Man #3 VF- $1,225
Amazing Spider-Man #4 VF $2,000
Amazing Spider-Man #13 VG $125
Amazing Spider-Man #14 FN/VF $1,090
Amazing Spider-Man #14 FN- $335
Amazing Spider-Man #14 VG- $350
Amazing Spider-Man #14 G+ $250
Amazing Spider-Man #17 F/VF $500
Amazing Spider-Man #28 VF/NM $1,000
Amazing Spider-Man #28 FN+ $225
Amazing Spider-Man #34 VF+ $325
Amazing Spider-Man #35 VG $44
Amazing Spider-Man #38 VF+ $200
Amazing Spider-Man #38 FN- $60
Amazing Spider-Man #42 VF+ $300
Amazing Spider-Man #47 VF+ $185
Amazing Spider-Man #48 VF/NM $210
Amazing Spider-Man #50 VF/NM $870
Amazing Spider-Man #55 VF+ $145
Amazing Spider-Man #64 NM- $145
Amazing Spider-Man #65 VF/NM $130
Amazing Spider-Man #69 FN+ $28
Amazing Spider-Man #119 NM- $120
Amazing Spider-Man #129 VF/NM $400
Amazing Spider-Man #129 VF+ $270
Amazing Spider-Man #136 VF/NM $90
Amazing Spider-Man Annual #4 NM- $250
Aquaman #5 FN $50
Atom #25 VF $38
Avengers #1 FN+ $500
Avengers #2 FN+ $150
Avengers #3 FN- $110
Avengers #4 VF/NM $1,800
Avengers #4 VG/FN $400
Avengers #32 VF $29
Avengers Annual #1 VF+ $155
Batman #109 VG/FN $100
Batman #117 FN/VF $170
Batman #171 G/VG $70
Batman #197 FN+ $170
Brave and the Bold #28 FN+ $845
Brave and the Bold #30 VG+ $230
Brave and the Bold #40 FN $45
Brave and the Bold #41 FN/VF $75
Bullwinkle #01-090-209 FN/VF $80
Captain America #100 FN/VF $250
Captain America #102 FN+ $20
Captain America #117 NM $110
Creepy #1 NM- $175
Creepy #14 VF/NM $75
Daredevil #2 VG- $150
Daredevil #3 VF- $295
Daredevil #5 VF $140
Detective Comics #186 G/VG $75
Detective Comics #360 VF $30
Doctor Solar #1 VF- $125
Doom Patrol #110 VF $25
Eerie (mag.) #2 NM- $140
Fantastic Four #1 VF $13,500
Fantastic Four #1 G $950
Fantastic Four #3 GD $170
Fantastic Four #5 VG+ $550
Fantastic Four #6 GD- $195
Fantastic Four #7 VG $125
Fantastic Four #8 VG- $110
Fantastic Four #9 VG- $125
Fantastic Four #10 GD+ $110
Fantastic Four #12 VF $1,200
Fantastic Four #17 VG $75
Fantastic Four #19 VG $62
Fantastic Four #22 VG/FN $40
Fantastic Four #23 VG $32
Fantastic Four #25 VF+ $420
Fantastic Four #25 FN/VF 260
Fantastic Four #26 FN+ $180
Fantastic Four #28 VG $62
Fantastic Four #48 VG $180
Fantastic Four #52 VF+ $175
Fantastic Four #61 NM $120
Fantastic Four #67 VF+ $90
Fantastic Four #95 VF/NM $35
Fantastic Four #66 NM- $285
Fantastic Four #68 NM- $110
Fantastic Four #105 NM $75
Fantastic Four #107 NM $75
Fantastic Four #108 NM $75
Fantastic Four #112 NM- $150
Green Lantern #4 VG+ $70
Hanna-Barbera Super TV Heroes #6 F/VF $85
Huck & Yogi Jamboree #1 Fair/GD $35
Incredible Hulk #1 GD+ (pressed) $950
Incredible Hulk #2 VF $3,000
Incredible Hulk #2 VG/FN $477
Incredible Hulk #102 VF+ $300
Iron Man #1 VF/NM $675

Journey Into Mystery #109 VG $25
Journey Into Mystery #116 VG $16
Justice League of America #1 VF $5,565
Justice League of America #2 VF $200
Justice League of America #6 FN $84
Justice League of America #21 VF $250
Metal Men #1 VG/FN $125
Millie The Model Annual #3 NM $120
Mystery in Space #53 VG $175
Sea Devils #1 VG+ $90
Sgt. Fury Annual #2 NM- $44
Showcase #8 VF+ $12,000
Showcase #73 VF $75
Strange Tales #68 VG/FN $55
Strange Tales #72 VG/FN $55
Strange Tales #75 VG/F $90
Strange Tales #93 FN- $55
Strange Tales #123 VF $50
Superman #132 FN- $57
Superman Annual #1 VG $66
Tales of Suspense #5 G/VG $95
Tales of Suspense #39 NM- $16,000
Tales of Suspense #42 VF/NM- $510
Tales of Suspense #51 NM $225
Tales of Suspense #54 VF $70
Tales of Suspense #84 NM $85
Tales to Astonish #5 VG/F $145
Tales to Astonish #27 VF+ $5,250
Tales to Astonish #56 VG+ $90
Tales to Astonish #58 NM- $190
Turok #30 (1st Gold Key) VF/NM $90
Wonder Woman #131 FN $25
World's Finest #145 FN+ $18
X-Men #1 VF+ $8,500
X-Men #1 FN $1,200
X-Men #1 GD- $650
X-Men #2 VG $270
X-Men #3 VF/NM $625
X-Men #9 FN+ $30
X-Men #12 F/VF- $235
X-Men #15 NM $225
X-Men #16 VF/NM- $200

BRONZE AGE TO MODERN AGE SALES

Bronze Age Sales:

Amazing Spider-Man #129 VF $129
Amazing Spider-Man #300 VF/NM $60
Batman #232 VF- $95
Batman #255 NM- $120
Batman #332 NM $25
Batman #366 NM $25
Batman #404 NM $25
Batman Family #1 NM- $40
Captain America #193 NM $40
Daredevil #131 NM- $250
Daredevil #131 FN $150
Daredevil #158 NM $200
Daredevil #158 VF/NM $60
Daredevil #168 NM $250
Daredevil #168 NM $150
Daredevil #168 NM- $190
Daredevil #168 VF+ $60
Defenders #10 VG $19
Detective Comics #440 NM- $55
Fear #10 NM $55
For Lovers Only #60 VG $38
Ghosts #3 NM $45
Giant Size Super-Heroes #1 NM- $60
Giant Size X-Men #1 VF+ $850
Giant-Size X-Men #1 FN $400
Incredible Hulk #181 VF $800
Invaders #1 NM $75
Invaders #1 NM $40
Invaders Annual #1 NM $50
Iron Fist #1 NM $85
Iron Fist #14 NM- $125
Marvel Premiere #3 NM- $75
Marvel Premiere #15 VF/NM $95
Marvel Premiere #50 NM $25
Marvel Preview (mag.) #2 VF/NM $150
Marvel Spotlight #2 VF+ $150
Marvel Spotlight #5 VF/NM $250
Marvel Spotlight #12 NM- $65
Marvel Spotlight #28 NM $50
Night Nurse #1 VF/NM $125
Omega Men #3 NM $12
Showcase #88 NM $22
Wolverine (1982 mini) #1 NM $15
X-Men #94 VF+ $575

Modern Age Sales:

Amazing Spider-Man #36 NM $30
Batman #608 NM $10
Batman #612 NM $8
Batman #612 (2nd printing) NM $15
Batman: Dark Knight Returns #1 NM $80
Daredevil V2 #1 NM $35
Hulk: The End NM $25
League of Extraordinary Gentlemen #2 NM $20
League of Extraordinary Gentlemen Vol. 2#1 NM $12
Mystique #1 NM $8
Outsiders #1 NM $8
Spawn #1 NM $12
Superman: Red Son #1 NM $25
Teen Titans #1 (2003 w/Turner-c) NM $15
Wolverine #145 (Nabisco) NM $100

Aces High #1 (Gaines file) NM+(9.6) $1,380
Action Comics ashcan VF/NM(9.0) $22,000
Action Comics #1 GD+(2.5) $40,307.50
Action Comics #4 VF(8.0) $9,775
Action Comics #32 (Lost Valley) VF-(7.5) $1,125
Action Comics #38 NM-(9.2) $3,335
Action Comics #50 (Mile High) NM(9.4) $12,650
Action Comics #61 (Mile High) NM(9.4) $13,225
Action Comics #63 (Mile High) NM+(9.6) $14,950
Action Comics #70 (Mile High) NM/MT(9.8) $12,075
Action Comics #87 VF+(8.5) $575
Action Comics #102 (Mile High) NM+(9.6) $8,625
Action Comics #150 (Mile High) VF/NM-(9.0) $1,610
Adventure Comics #40 VG/FN(5.0) $11,390
Adventure Comics #51 NM-(9.2) $6,618
Adventure Comics #79 (Mile High) NM+(9.6) $29,900
Adventure Comics #100 NM(9.4) $2,300
Adventure Comics #105 VF+(8.5) $900
All-American Comics #65 VF/NM-(9.0) $862
All Select Comics #1 VF+(8.5) $11,557
All Star Comics #2 FN+(6.5) $1,495
All Star Comics #6 NM-(9.2) $2,400
All Star Comics #12 (Rockford) NM(9.4) $7,762
All Star Comics #14 (Rockford) NM-(9.2) $2,990
All Star Comics #19 (Rockford) NM+(9.6) $6,612
All Star Comics #32 NM(9.4) $3,849
All Star Comics #36 (Spokane) NM+(9.6) $9,200
All Winners Comics #1 FN/VF(7.0) $8,050
All-Winners Comics #21 FN(6.0) $1150
Amazing Willie Mays nn (File copy) NM-(9.2) $1,207
America's Best Comics #29 (Mile High) NM+(9.6) $1,667
Annie Oakley #1 NM(9.4) $747
Archie's Pal Jughead #1 VF/NM(9.0) $1,955
Batman #1 VG/F(5.0) $16,995
Batman #1 Fair/GD(1.5) $4,600
Batman #6 (Allentown) NM+(9.6) $39,100
Batman #6 NM-(9.2) $12,500
Batman #20 VF/NM(9.0) $3,000
Batman # 24 VF(8.0) $1,000
Big All-American Comic Book #1 VF+(8.5) $6,037.50
Black Cat Comics #24 NM(9.4) $290
Blackhawk #9 (Mile High) NM+(9.6) $11,000
Blonde Phantom #16 NM(9.4) $2,587
Boy Comics #4 (Mile High) NM(9.4) $6,000
Boy Commandos #2 (Pennsylvania) NM-(9.2) $3,800
Captain America Comics #5 VF-(7.5) $3,250
Captain America Comics #7 FN(6.0) $1,667
Captain America Comics #8 NM-(9.2) $10,350
Captain America Comics #9 NM-(9.2) $9,775
Captain America Comics #39 (Okajima) VF+(8.5) $1,782
Captain Marvel Adventures #47 NM(9.4) $1,500
Captain America Comics #49 NM(9.4) $3,653
Casper the Friendly Ghost #10 (File) VF/NM-(9.0) $862.50
Catman #1 VG(4.0) $736
Classic Comics #3 (Lost Valley) FN-(5.5) $550
Crimes Incorporated #12 NM+(9.6) $1000.00 (Double-c)
Crime SuspenStories #3 (Gaines file) NM/MT(9.8) $2,587
Crime SuspenStories #9 (Gaines file) NM/MT(9.8) $2,012
Crime SuspenStories #22 (Gaines file) VF/NM-(9.0) $2,357
Crime Suspenstories #24 (Gaines file) NM(9.4) $650
Crime SuspenStories #27 (Gaines file) NM-(9.2) $488
Crypt of Terror #17 (Gaines file) NM+(9.6) $13,800
Crypt of Terror #17 (River City) VF/NM-(9.0) $2,990
Crypt of Terror #18 (Gaines file) NM/MT(9.8) $10,062
Crypt of Terror #19 (Gaines file) NM/MT(9.8) $8,625
Cyclone Comics #1 (Mile High) NM+(9.6) $6,000
Cyclone Comics #2 (Mile High) NM-(9.2) $2,127
Dale Evans Comics #6 (Mile High) NM/MT(9.8) $1,840
Daredevil Comics #1 VF/NM-(9.0) $13,225
Daring Comics #9 VF(8.0) $805
Detective Comics #1 (Lost Valley) FN(6.0) $42,000
Detective Comics #27 FN-(5.5) $100,000 (trade)
Detective Comics #27 GD/VG(3.0) $47,500
Detective Comics #54 VF/NM(9.0) $1,950
Detective Comics #57 VF/NM(9.0) $1,797
Detective Comics #99 (Mile High) NM/MT(9.8) $16,100
Detective Comics #109 (Mile High) NM/MT(9.8) $12,650
Detective Comics #118 (Mile High) NM+(9.6) $12,650
Detective Comics #152 (Twilight) VF/NM(9.0) $760
Detective Picture Stories #1 (Lost Valley) FN-(5.5) $2,000
Detective Picture Stories #2 (Lost Valley) VF(8.0) $1,925
Doc Savage Comics #9 (Mile High) NM(9.4) $1,575
Don Winslow #37 (Mile High) NM/MT(9.8) $900
Fight Comics #36 (Lost Valley) VF-(7.5) $180
Fight Comics #43 (Big Apple) NM+(9.6) $632
Flash Comics ashcan NM+(9.6) $11,500
Flash Comics #1 FN-(5.5) $11,212
Four Color #108 Donald Duck NM(9.4) $4,140
Four Color #129 Walt Disney's Uncle Remus and His Tales of Brer Rabbit NM(9.4) $1,236.25
Four Color #159 Donald Duck NM+(9.6) $6000
Four Favorites #29 (Crowley) NM(9.4) $450
Frontline Combat #1 (Gaines file) NM+(9.6) $3,680
Gene Autry (Dell) #7 NM-(9.2) $500
Gene Autry (Dell) #51 NM+(9.6) $650
Green Hornet Comics #1 (Mile High) NM-(9.2) $18,400
Green Hornet Comics #6 (Mile High) NM(9.4) $3,565
Green Lantern #1 VF-(7.5) $34,500
Green Lantern #27 VF-(7.5) $900
Haunt of Fear #4 (Gaines file) NM+(9.6) $3,450
Haunt of Fear #7 (Gaines file) NM/MT(9.8) $3,000
Haunt of Fear #15 (Gaines file) NM/MT(9.8) $2,500
Hit Comics #1 FN-(5.5) $1,552
Human Torch #2 (#1) VG(4.0) $3,450
Human Torch #6 VF/NM(9.0) $2,702
Human Torch #11 VF(8.0) $1,840

Human Torch #13 VF/NM(9.0) $2,500
Human Torch #19 VF(8.0) $1,075
Jo-Jo Comics #14 FN(6.0) $166
Joker Comics #6 (Mile High) NM+(9.6) $1,380
Joker Comics #11 (Mile High) NM+(9.6) $1,380
Joker Comics #19 (Mile High) NM+(9.6) $1,265
Jumbo Comics #94 (Lost Valley) VF+(8.5) $300
Junior Miss #27 (Mile High) NM+(9.6) $529
Jungle Tales #5 (Mile High) NM(9.4) $750
Little Dot #1 (File copy) VF-(7.5) $2,185
Looney Tunes and Merrie Melodies #1 VG-(3.5) $1,860
Mad #1 (Gaines file) NM+(9.6) $24,150
Mad #3 (Gaines file) NM+(9.6) $5,520
Mad #4 NM-(9.2) $2,200
Mad #8 (Gaines file) NM-(9.2) $2,760
Magic Comics #1 (Mile High) FN(6.0) $2,357
March of Comics #41 Donald Duck VF(8.0) $2,357
Marvel Mystery Comics #7 Larson NM-(9.2) $12,650
Marvel Mystery Comics #8 Larson VF(8.0) $7,475
Marvel Mystery Comics #9 FN+(6.5) $8,768
Marvel Mystery Comics #83 (D copy) VF+(8.5) $1,326
Mary Marvel Comics #1 NM+(9.6) $7,762.50
Master Comics #39 (Mile High) VF/NM-(9.0) $1,897
Master Comics #95 (Mile High) NM-(9.2) $575
Mighty Mouse #1 VF/NM(9.0) $1,124
Military Comics #22 (Mile High) VF/NM-(9.0) $2,016
Military Comics #27 (Mile High) VF/NM-(9.0) $2,016
Miss Fury #6 (Twilight) VF+(8.5) $575
Mister Mystery #6 VF(8.0) $1,265
More Fun Comics #52 FN+(6.5) (sl. rest.) $23,000
More Fun Comics #68 (Mile High) NM-(9.2) $11,500
More Fun Comics #69 VF/NM-(9.0) $4,750
More Fun Comics #69 VF(8.0) $1,800
Mystic Comics #1 FN+(6.5) $3,450
Mystic Comics #2 (Nova Scotia) VF(8.0) $2,990
Mystic Comics #8 VF+(8.5) $1,532
Panic #3 (Gaines file) NM+(9.6) $805
Pep Comics #36 FN/VF(7.0) $1600
Phantom Lady #15 FN+(6.5) $747.50
Picture Stories from the Bible Old Testament #3
(Gaines file) NM/MT(9.8) $1,380
Planet Comics #51 VF/NM-(9.0) $550
Plastic Man #9 (Mile High) NM+(9.6) $1,725
Prize Comics #5 (Mile High) NM+(9.6) $3,220
Rangers Comics #29 (Lost Valley) NM(9.4) $1,400
Real Life #34 (Big Apple) NM/MT(9.8) $580
Red Ryder #29 NM+(9.6) $900
Red Ryder #37 NM-(9.2) $250
Red Ryder #118 NM+(9.6) $375
Rin Tin Tin #7 NM(9.4) $400
Rin Tin Tin #30 NM(9.4) $250
Roy Rogers Comics #1 NM-(9.2) $1,380
Roy Rogers Comics #2 NM-(9.2) $250
Roy Rogers Comics #72 NM+(9.6) $650
Roy Rogers Comics #95 NM(9.4) $350
Roy Rogers Comics #96 NM+(9.6) $550
Roy Rogers Comics #103 NM-(9.2) $250
Roy Rogers Comics #131 NM(9.4) $500
Sad Sack Comics #1 (File copy) VF/NM-(9.0) $3,910
Sad Sack Comics #2 (File copy) NM(9.4) $1,150
Sad Sack Comics #3 (File copy) NM+(9.6) $1,380
Sad Sack Comics #4 (File copy) NM(9.4) $1,035
Sad Sack Comics #6 (File copy) NM+(9.6) $1,150
Sad Sack Comics #8 (File copy) NM+(9.6) $1,035
Sensation Comics #53 VF/NM-(9.0) $449
Sergeant Preston #14 NM-(9.2) $125
Shock SuspenStories #1 (Gaines file) NM/MT(9.8) $6,250
Shock SuspenStories #2 (Gaines file) NM+(9.6) $1,667
Shock SuspenStories #6 (Gaines file) NM/MT(9.8) $5,060
Shock SuspenStories #7 (Gaines file) NM/MT(9.8) $4,715
Shock SuspenStories #8 (Gaines file) NM/MT(9.8) $2,600
Shock SuspenStories #9 (Gaines file) NM/MT(9.8) $2,200
Showcase #1 FN+(6.5) $1,200
Showcase #2 VF+(8.5) $2,200
Sparkler Comics #3 (Mile High) NM+(9.6) $2,000
Sparky Watts #1 VF/NM-(9.0) $920
Spooky #1 (File copy) VF+(8.5) $1,955
Spy Smasher #1 F/VF(7.0) $1,665
Star Spangled Comics #50 (Mile High) NM-(9.2) $2,240
Startling Comics #40 VF/NM(9.0) $460
Sub-Mariner Comics #1 VF+(8.5) $25,000
Sub-Mariner Comics #1 G/VG(3.0) $3,700
Sub-Mariner Comics #22 VF(8.0) $645
Superboy #1 VF/NM-(9.0) $12,000
Superman #1 VF-(7.5) $186,000
Superman #2 FN/VF(7.0) $6,395
Superman #9 (Lost Valley) VF-(7.5) $1,700
Suspense Comics #3 FN-(5.5) $11,100
Tales of Terror Annual #3 VF/NM-(9.0) $1,495
Terrifying Tales #13 NM+(9.6) $4550
Thrill Comics #1 Ashcan (Fawcett, 1940) VF(8.0) $10,925
Tom Corbett, Space Cadet #5 (Dell) NM(9.4) $350
Tom Mix Western #1 NM-(9.2) $1,380
Torchy #2 NM-(9.2) $651
Two-Fisted Tales #19 (Gaines file) NM+(9.6) $2,500
Uncle Scrooge #13 NM-(9.2) $322.77
Valor #5 (Gaines file) NM(9.4) $612
Vault of Horror #19 (Gaines file) NM/MT(9.8) $3,450
Vault of Horror #22 (Gaines file) NM(9.4) $1,725
Walt Disney's Comics and Stories #1 VF+(8.5) $19,600
Walt Disney's Comics and Stories #9 VF-(7.5) $1,063
Walt Disney's Comics and Stories #26 VF(8.0) $450
War Against Crime #10 (Gaines file) NM/MT(9.8) $10,074
War Against Crime #10 (Gaines file) NM+(9.6) $10,062
Weird Science #13 (#2) (Gaines file) NM+(9.6) $5,750
Weird Science #19 (Gaines file) NM+(9.6) $2,012
Wonder Comics #1 GD(2.0) $1,500
Wonder Woman #1 VF(8.0) $16,200
Wonder World Comics #3 NM(9.4) $20,000
World's Finest Comics #8 NM-(9.2) $3,600
Young Allies Comics #1 (San Francisco) NM+(9.6) $57,500
Young Allies Comics #1 G/VG(3.0) $2,200

Action Comics #300 NM(9.4) $1,063
Action Comics #344 NM+(9.6) $575
Action Comics #363 NM(9.4) $275
Action Comics #366 NM(9.4) $275
Action Comics #369 NM(9.4) $175
Action Comics #398 (Oakland) NM+(9.6) $250
Adventure Comics #349 (Boston) NM(9.4) $335
Advs. of Jerry Lewis #89 (Pacific Coast) NM+(9.6) $250
Adventures Of The Jaguar #2 NM(9.4) $350
All American Men Of War #104 NM(9.4) $300
Amazing Adult Fantasy #10 VF/NM-(9.0) $805
Amazing Fantasy #15 VF+(8.5) $28,000
Amazing Fantasy #15 VF(8.0) $17,250
Amazing Fantasy #15 FN/VF(7.0) $10,493
Amazing Spider-Man #2 VF/NM-(9.0) $4,255
Amazing Spider-Man #5 VF+(8.5) $1,850
Amazing Spider-Man #6 VF(8.0) $900
Amazing Spider-Man #8 NM+(9.6) $4,975
Amazing Spider-Man #9 NM(9.4) $4,830
Amazing Spider-Man #10 NM(9.4) $5,500
Amazing Spider-Man #10 VF+(8.5) $900
Amazing Spider-Man #11 NM-(9.2) $4,255
Amazing Spider-Man #14 NM-(9.2) $3,680
Amazing Spider-Man #14 NM-(9.2) $4,250
Amazing Spider-Man #15 NM(9.4) $3,795
Amazing Spider-Man #17 NM(9.4) $3,750
Amazing Spider-Man #17 NM(9.4) $3,350
Amazing Spider-Man #17 NM(9.4) $3,220
Amazing Spider-Man #18 NM+(9.6) $4,500
Amazing Spider-Man #19 NM(9.4) $2,150
Amazing Spider-Man #19 VF/NM(9.0) $575
Amazing Spider-Man #28 NM(9.4) $6,037
Amazing Spider-Man #29 NM+(9.6) $2,200
Amazing Spider-Man #31 NM+(9.6) $2,750
Amazing Spider-Man #33 NM+(9.6) $1,050
Amazing Spider-Man #39 VF/NM(9.0) $550
Amazing Spider-Man #40 VF/NM(9.0) $450
Amazing Spider-Man #43 NM+(9.6) $1,590
Amazing Spider-Man #43 NM(9.4) $725
Amazing Spider-Man #50 VF/NM-(9.0) $1,207.50
Amazing Spider-Man #53 NM(9.4) $575
Amazing Spider-Man #59 NM(9.4) $300
Amazing Spider-Man #59 NM(9.4) $750
Amazing Spider-Man #63 NM+(9.6) $3,000
Amazing Spider-Man #64 NM/MT(9.8) $1,265
Amazing Spider-Man #69 NM(9.4) $450
Amazing Spider-Man #76 NM+(9.6) $1,050
Amazing Spider-Man #90 NM+(9.6) $790
Amazing Spider-Man #97 NM(9.4) $525
Amazing Spider-Man #100 NM/MT(9.8) $2,300
Amazing Spider-Man #100 NM(9.4) $475
Amazing Spider-Man Annual #1 NM(9.4) $4,775
Aquaman #1 VF/NM(9.0) $1025

Atom #1 VF/NM(9.0) $1,000
Atom #2 VF/NM(9.0) $390
Atom #5 VF/NM(9.0) $270
Atom #7 NM-(9.2) $356.50
Avengers #1 VF/NM-(9.0) $4,200
Avengers #2 NM(9.4) $4,500
Avengers #4 NM+(9.6) $850 (1966 reprint)
Avengers #4 NM-(9.2) $4,000
Avengers #4 NM-(9.2) $3,400
Avengers #11 NM(9.4) $1,495
Avengers #11 NM-(9.2) $500
Avengers #12 NM+(9.6) $2150
Avengers #25 NM(9.4) $400
Avengers #58 NM/MT(9.8) $816
Batman #119 VF+(8.5) $405
Batman #171 NM-(9.2) $737
Batman #171 VF/NM(9.0) $700
Batman #176 (Pacific Coast) NM+(9.6) $1,035
Batman #181 VF/NM(9.0) $370
Batman #200 NM/MT(9.8) $2,995
Blackhawk #199 (Pacific Coast) NM+(9.6) $150
Brave and the Bold #28 VG/FN(5.0) $965
Brave and the Bold #28 VG-(3.5) $356.50
Brave and the Bold #35 VF(8.0) $356
Brave and the Bold #42 VF+(8.5) $355
Brave and the Bold #56 (Pacific Coast) NM+(9.6) $747.50
Captain America #100 NM/MT(9.8) $4,950
Captain America #100 NM(9.4) $621
Captain America #106 Double Cover NM/MT(9.8) $611
Captain America #117 NM(9.4) $625
Captain Marvel #1 (Marvel, 1968) NM/MT(9.8) $1,300
Captain Marvel #1 (Marvel, 1968) NM/MT(9.8) $1,265
Captain Marvel #2 (Marvel, 1968) NM/MT(9.8) $460
Captain Marvel #3 (Marvel, 1968) NM/MT(9.8) $603.75
Captain Venture #1 NM+(9.6) $350
Daredevil #1 NM(9.4) $12,000
Daredevil #1 NM-(9.2) $6,800
Daredevil #1 NM-(9.2) $6,500
Daredevil #1 NM-(9.2) $5,600
Daredevil #1 G/VG(3.0) $390
Daredevil #2 NM(9.4) $3,001
Daredevil #2 VF+(8.5) $865
Daredevil #4 NM(9.4) $1,610
Daredevil #17 NM(9.4) $460
Dark Shadows #6 NM+(9.6) $410
Dark Shadows #7 NM+(9.6) $410
Dell Giant #39 NM(9.4) $600
Detective Comics #321 NM(9.4) $600
Detective Comics #327 NM(9.4) $1,100
Detective Comics #359 NM-(9.2) $500
Detective Comics #382 NM+(9.6) $550
Doctor Solar #11 NM+(9.6) $295
Doctor Solar #18 NM(9.4) $285

Doctor Solar #25 NM+(9.6) $225
Doctor Strange #169 NM/MT(9.8) $811
Doom Patrol #86 NM/MT(9.8) $3,750
80 Page Giant #2 (Pacific Coast) NM+(9.6) $1,350
80 Page Giant #15 NM(9.4) $600
Fantastic Four #1 NM+(9.6) $1,100 (1966 reprint)
Fantastic Four #2 NM-(9.2) $8,400
Fantastic Four #2 VF(8.0) $3,000
Fantastic Four #5 VF/NM(9.0) $5,000
Fantastic Four #6 VF+(8.5) $1,345
Fantastic Four #7 NM-(9.2) $3,335
Fantastic Four #8 NM(9.4) $6,612.50
Fantastic Four #8 VF+(8.5) $765
Fantastic Four #16 VF/NM(9.0) $990
Fantastic Four #46 NM(9.4) $449
Fantastic Four #48 NM(9.4) $1,495
Fantastic Four #48 NM-(9.2) $1,125
Fantastic Four #48 FN+(6.5) $212.75
Fantastic Four #50 NM-(9.2) $670
Fantastic Four #52 NM(9.4) $1,232
Fantastic Four #53 NM+(9.6) $1,325
Fantastic Four #55 NM(9.4) $900
Fantastic Four #55 NM(9.4) $875
Fantastic Four #93 NM+(9.6) $350
Fantastic Four #98 NM+(9.6) $350
Fantastic Four Annual #1 NM(9.4) $3,400
Fantastic Four Annual #1 VF/NM-(9.0) $805
Fantastic Four Annual #4 NM+(9.6) $860
Flash #122 VF/NM(9.0) $368
Flash #123 VF/NM(9.0) $2,070
Flash #144 NM+(9.6) $1,250
Flash #168 NM+(9.6) $603.75
Flintstones #27 NM(9.4) $175
Flintstones Bigger And Boulder #1 NM(9.4) $350
Forbidden Worlds #131 NM(9.4) $150
Green Hornet #1 (Gold Key) NM+(9.6) $1950
Green Hornet #3 (Gold Key) NM/MT(9.8) $1350
Green Lantern #1 VF/NM(9.0) $6,900
Green Lantern #2 (Bethlehem)VF/NM(9.0) $1,150
Green Lantern #12 NM(9.4) $1,325
Green Lantern #16 NM+(9.6) $2,075
Green Lantern #29 NM-(9.2) $356.50
Green Lantern #30 NM+(9.6) $1,200
Green Lantern #34 NM-(9.2) $195
Green Lantern #59 NM(9.4) $500
Harvey Hits #3 Richie Rich File Copy NM(9.4) $4,370
Hawkman #15 NM+(9.6) $650 (Double cover)
Hot Stuff #1 (File copy) VF/NM-(9.0) $2,070
House of Secrets #78 NM+(9.6) $290
Incredible Hulk #1 VF-(7.5) $10,062
Incredible Hulk #1 VG-(3.5) $1,100
Incredible Hulk #2 VF/NM(9.0) $4,000
Incredible Hulk #2 G/VG(3.0) $275
Incredible Hulk #5 VF(8.0) $1,000
Incredible Hulk #102 NM+(9.6) $1,150
Incredible Hulk #104 NM(9.4) $350
Incredible Hulk #117 NM/MT(9.8) $632
Incredible Hulk Annual #1 NM+(9.6) $700
Incredible Hulk Annual #1 NM+(9.6) $647
Iron Man #1 NM+(9.6) $1,897
Iron Man #1 NM+(9.6) $1,495
Iron Man #1 NM-(9.2) $1,400
Iron Man #1 NM/MT(9.8) $4,500
Iron Man #2 NM/MT(9.8) $575
I Spy #1 NM(9.4) $1550
John Carter Warlord Of Mars #1 Marvel NM/MT(9.8) $225
Journey Into Mystery #83 VF/NM-(9.0) $13,000
Journey Into Mystery #84 VF/NM-(9.0) $2,675
Journey into Mystery #105 VF/NM-(9.0) $253
Journey Into Mystery #114 NM(9.4) $1,050
Justice League of America #21 NM-(9.2) $862.50
Justice League of America #22 NM-(9.2) $718.75
Justice League of America #48 NM+(9.6) $1,092
Land Of The Giants #1 NM+(9.6) $750 (Double cover)
Land Of The Giants #2 NM+(9.6) $300
Lone Ranger #130 NM(9.4) $600
Lone Ranger #132 NM(9.4) $550
Lone Ranger #134 NM(9.4) $550
Lone Ranger #136 NM+(9.6) $850
Man From U.N.C.L.E. #9 NM+(9.6) $550
Man From U.N.C.L.E. #17 NM+(9.6) $300
Man From U.N.C.L.E. #18 NM+(9.6) $300
Man From U.N.C.L.E. #20 NM+(9.6) $300
Metal Men #1 NM+(9.6) $3,500
Metamorpho #13 (Pacific Coast) NM(9.4) $100
Monkees #10 VF/NM-(9.0) $100
Movie Comics - Yellow Submarine NM+(9.6) $2,150
My Favorite Martian #1 NM+(9.6) $1150
My Greatest Adventure #80 NM+(9.6) $3,500
Mystery In Space #90 NM+(9.6) $1,199
Nick Fury, Agent of Shield #1 NM(9.4) $210
Nick Fury, Agent of Shield #15 NM+(9.6) $454
Our Army At War #81 VF+(8.5) $4,370
Our Army At War #81 VF-(7.5) $3,105
Plastic Man #1 (Western Penn) VF/NM(9.0) $190
Rawhide Kid #50 NM/MT(9.8) $177.50
Richie Rich #1 File Copy NM-(9.2) $5,635
Richie Rich #30 NM(9.4) $335
Richie Rich #65 NM+(9.6) $350
Richie Rich & Jackie Jokers #1 NM(9.4) $200
Rip Hunter #29 NM/MT(9.8) $700
Secret Agent #1 (Gold Key) NM+(9.6) $900
Sgt Fury #1 VF+(8.5) $1800
Sgt Fury #22 NM+(9.6) $450
Sgt Fury #28 NM(9.4) $250
Showcase #4 VF+(8.5) $18,400
Showcase #4 FN-(5.5) $3,795
Showcase #7 VF(8.0) $1600
Showcase #19 NM+(9.6) $12700 (Double cover)
Showcase #20 VF(8.0) $810

Showcase #34 NM(9.4) $12,000
Showcase #34 VF/NM-(9.0) $2,990
Showcase #37 VF-(7.5) $350
Showcase #38 VF/NM(9.0) $500
Showcase #45 NM(9.4) $1,500
Showcase #50 NM+(9.6) $560
Showcase #53 NM+(9.6) $1260
Showcase #54 NM(9.4) $600
Showcase #55 NM(9.4) $1,100
Showcase #55 NM(9.4) $1,050
Showcase #60 NM(9.4) $1,350
Showcase #61 NM(9.4) $356
Showcase #80 NM(9.4) $400
Silver Surfer #1 NM/MT(9.8) $3,220
Silver Surfer #1 NM(9.4) $1,075.65
Silver Surfer #1 NM(9.4) $1,000
Silver Surfer #1 NM(9.4) $949
Silver Surfer #1 NM-(9.2) $510
Silver Surfer #5 NM(9.4) $250
Space Family Robinson #7 NM-(9.2) $175
Space Family Robinson #22 NM+(9.6) $205
Space Family Robinson #32 NM+(9.6) $185
Strange Adventures #151 NM+(9.6) $750
Strange Adventures #180 NM/MT(9.8) $3750
Strange Tales #102 NM(9.4) $2250
Strange Tales #114 NM-(9.2) $1100
Strange Tales #129 NM(9.4) $450
Strange Tales #130 NM(9.4) $525
Strange Tales #133 NM-(9.2) $185
Strange Tales #133 NM(9.4) $350
Strange Tales #141 NM(9.4) $275
Strange Tales #149 NM(9.4) $250
Strange Tales Annual #1 VF+(8.5) $602
Sub-Mariner #1 NM/MT(9.8) $1,035
Sub-Mariner #1 NM+(9.6) $550
Sub-Mariner #4 NM+(9.6) $500
Sub-Mariner #6 NM+(9.6) $275
Sub-Mariner #7 NM+(9.6) $275
Sub-Mariner #15 NM/MT(9.8) $500
Superboy #117 NM+(9.6) $700
Superboy #123 NM(9.4) $300
Superboy #127 NM+(9.6) $585
Superboy #136 NM+(9.6) $525
Superman #196 NM(9.4) $400
Superman's Girlfriend Lois Lane #52 NM-(9.2) $250
Superman's Girlfriend Lois Lane #53 NM+(9.6) $650
Superman's Girlfriend Lois Lane #54 NM+(9.6) $650
Superman's Pal Jimmy Olsen #64 VF/NM(9.0) $110
Superman's Pal Jimmy Olsen #93 NM/MT(9.8) $850
Tales of Suspense #11 FN/VF(7.0) $300
Tales of Suspense #12 VF(8.0) $375
Tales of Suspense #13 VF+(8.5) $425
Tales of Suspense #26 VF+(8.5) $370
Tales of Suspense #39 VF+(8.5) $4,100
Tales of Suspense #40 VF/NM(9.0) $2,200
Tales of Suspense #41 VF+(8.5) $600
Tales of Suspense #48 NM(9.4) $1,400.55
Tales of Suspense #49 NM(9.4) $4,000
Tales Of Suspense #49 NM(9.4) $3050
Tales of Suspense #58 NM(9.4) $2,500
Tales of Suspense #58 NM-(9.2) $1,150
Tales of Suspense #59 NM-(9.2) $1,725
Tales to Astonish #38 NM-(9.2) $625
Tales to Astonish #39 VF/NM(9.0) $500
Tales to Astonish #42 NM-(9.2) $450
Tales to Astonish #49 NM(9.4) $800
Tales to Astonish #52 NM-(9.2) $210
Teen-In #1 NM+(9.6) $250
Teen Titans #1 VF+(8.5) $225
Teen Titans #8 NM(9.4) $159
Teen Titans #17 NM(9.4) $250
Thor Annual #2 NM(9.4) $529
Turok #6 VF+(8.5) $150
Turok #49 NM+(9.6) $323
Unknown Worlds #1 VF/NM(9.0) $265
Voyage To The Bottom Of The Sea #12 NM+(9.6) $260
Voyage To The Bottom Of The Sea #13 NM+(9.6) $225
Wild Wild West #1 NM+(9.6) $1325
Wild Wild West #7 NM+(9.6) $450
Witching Hour #1 NM(9.4) $450
Wonder Woman #105 NM(9.4) $10,000
Wonder Woman #151 NM(9.4) $490
Wonder Woman #152 NM(9.4) $490
Wonder Woman #155 NM(9.4) $490
Wonder Woman #156 NM(9.4) $475
Wonder Woman #162 NM(9.4) $475
Wonder Woman #171 NM+(9.6) $575
Wonder Woman #175 NM+(9.6) $450
Wonder Woman #200 NM(9.4) $290
X-Men #1 NM(9.4) $45,000
X-Men #1 VF+(8.5) $7,000
X-Men #1 VF(8.0) $4,800
X-Men #2 VF(8.0) $1,400
X-Men #3 NM(9.4) $5,701
X-Men #3 NM(9.4) $5,650
X-Men #3 VF+(8.5) $700
X-Men #4 NM(9.4) $3,565
X-Men #5 NM(9.4) $3,151
X-Men #10 NM-(9.2) $600
X-Men #12 NM(9.4) $2,200
X-Men #16 VF/NM(9.0) $250.05
X-Men #18 NM-(9.2) $425
X-Men #19 NM+(9.6) $1,200
X-Men #20 NM+(9.6) $1032.27
X-Men #23 NM+(9.6) $950
X-Men #24 NM+(9.6) $925
X-Men #29 (Northland) NM+(9.6) $1,025
X-Men Annual #1 NM(9.4) $152.50
Zorro #2 NM(9.4) $350
Zorro #9 NM(9.4) $350

BRONZE AGE - SALES OF CGC GRADED COMICS

Action Comics #398 NM+(9.6) $150
Action Comics #404 NM/MT(9.8) $274.77
Adventure Comics #420 NM+(9.6) $200
Adventure Comics #428 NM-(9.2) $49.99
Adventure Comics #436 NM+(9.6) $225
All Star Comics #58 NM/MT(9.8) $499
All Star Western #10 NM(9.4) $1,026
All Star Western #10 NM-(9.2) $499
Amazing Adventures #11 NM+(9.6) $1,009.99
Amazing Spider-Man #120 NM(9.4) $154.50
Amazing Spider-Man #121 NM/MT(9.8) $6,612.50
Amazing Spider-Man #121 NM+(9.6) $1,255.01
Amazing Spider-Man #121 NM-(9.2) $400
Amazing Spider-Man #122 NM/MT(9.8) $5,635
Amazing Spider-Man #122 NM+(9.6) $800
Amazing Spider-Man #122 NM(9.4) $862.50
Amazing Spider-Man #122 NM-(9.2) $380
Amazing Spider-Man #123 NM+(9.6) $285
Amazing Spider-Man #129 NM+(9.6) $2,449
Amazing Spider-Man #129 NM+(9.6) $2,050
Amazing Spider-Man #129 NM+(9.6) $1,851.76
Amazing Spider-Man #129 NM(9.4) $1,207.50
Amazing Spider-Man #129 NM(9.4) $1,050
Amazing Spider-Man #129 NM-(9.2) $700
Amazing Spider-Man #129 NM-(9.2) $560
Amazing Spider-Man #129 VF(8.0) $185
Amazing Spider-Man #136 NM/MT(9.8) $1,840
Avengers #95 NM+(9.6) $400
Batman #232 NM(9.4) $375
Batman #232 NM(9.4) $316
Batman #251 NM+(9.6) $500
Battlestar Galactica #1 NM/MT(9.8) $39.95
Black Panther #1 VF/NM(9.0) $25
Captain America #286 MT(9.9) $150
Captain Marvel #1 NM(9.4) $326
Cerebus #6 NM/MT(9.8) $227.50
Cerebus #7 NM/MT(9.8) $306
Champions #1 NM+(9.6) $100
Conan the Barbarian #1 NM+(9.6) $1,437.50
Conan the Barbarian #1 NM+(9.6) $1,200
Conan the Barbarian #1 NM(9.4) $611
Conan the Barbarian #1 NM(9.4) $500
Conan the Barbarian #1 NM(9.4) $410
Conan the Barbarian #1 VF+(8.5) $187.50
Conan the Barbarian #2 NM-(9.2) $322
Conan the Barbarian #7 NM+(9.6) $230
Conan the Barbarian #24 NM/MT(9.8) $475
Creatures on the Loose #10 NM/MT(9.8) $373.75
Creepy #91 NM/MT(9.8) $78
Crisis on Infinite Earths #7 NM/MT(9.8) $50
Daredevil #168 NM+(9.6) $590
Daredevil #168 NM-(9.2) $124.50
Daredevil #181 NM+(9.6) $40
Dark Mansion of Forbidden Love #1 NM(9.4) $776.25
DC 100 Page Super Spectacular #6 NM(9.4) $585
DC 100 Pg Super Spectacular #16 NM/MT(9.8) $300
Deadliest Heroes of King Fu #1 NM(9.4) $72.23
Deadly Hands of Kung Fu #1 NM+(9.6) $171.50
Defenders #1 NM(9.4) $402.50
Defenders #4 NM-(9.2) $75
Defenders #10 NM+(9.6) $437.65
Defenders #10 NM(9.4) $350
Defenders #13 NM+(9.6) $135
Detective Comics #408 NM+(9.6) $350
Detective Comics #442 NM+(9.6) $300
Doc Savage #1 NM(9.4) $27
Dr. Strange #1 NM/MT(9.8) $405
Fantastic Four #110 (Green Printing Error) NM(9.4) $460
Flash #213 NM/MT(9.8) $350
Flash Gordon #30 Whitman NM(9.4) $125
Ghost Rider #1 NM-(9.2) $188.06
Ghost Rider #11 NM/MT(9.8) $560
Giant-Size Spider-Man #4 NM-(9.2) $175
Giant-Size Super Stars #1 NM+(9.6) $122.50
Giant-Size X-Men #1 NM/MT(9.8) $11,500
Giant-Size X-Men #1 NM+(9.6) $2,000
Giant-Size X-Men #1 NM(9.4) $1,719.30
Giant-Size X-Men #1 NM(9.4) $1,575
Giant-Size X-Men #1 NM(9.4) $1,525
Giant-Size X-Men #1 NM(9.4) $1,320.08
Giant-Size X-Men #1 NM(9.4) $1,610
Giant Size-X-Men #1 NM-(9.2) $866
Giant-Size X-Men #1 VF-(7.5) $900
Giant-Size X-Men #2 NM(9.4) $150
Green Lantern #76 NM(9.4) $1,653.82
Green Lantern #76 VF+(8.5) $200
Green Lantern #76 VF-(7.5) $600
Green Lantern #80 VF-(7.5) $475
Green Lantern #85 NM+(9.6) $400
Green Lantern #86 NM(9.4) $150
Green Lantern #87 NM+(9.6) $510
Green Lantern #116 NM/MT(9.8) $149
Hero For Hire #1 NM(9.4) $380
House of Secrets #93 NM-(9.2) $40
House of Secrets #96 NM/MT(9.8) $456.50
Howard the Duck #12 NM/MT(9.8) $114.50
Incredible Hulk #180 NM/MT(9.8) $3,105
Incredible Hulk #180 VF/NM-(9.0) $215.50
Incredible Hulk #181 NM/MT(9.8) $17,825
Incredible Hulk #181 NM+(9.6) $4,000
Incredible Hulk #181 NM(9.4) $2,530
Incredible Hulk #181 NM(9.4) $2,512
Incredible Hulk #181 NM(9.4) $2,200
Incredible Hulk #181 NM-(9.2) $1,425
Incredible Hulk #181 NM-(9.2) $1,725
Incredible Hulk #181 NM-(9.2) $1,259

Incredible Hulk #181 VF/NM(9.0) $1,001
Incredible Hulk #181 VF/NM(9.0) $955
Incredible Hulk #181 VF+(8.5) $699.99
Incredible Hulk #181 FN/VF(7.0) $800
Incredible Hulk #181 FN(6.0) $1,400
Incredible Hulk #181 FN-(5.5) $304
Incredible Hulk #250 NM+(9.6) $49.95
Incredible Hulk #300 GM(10.0) $760
Iron Fist #1 NM+(9.6) $249
Iron Fist #14 NM+(9.6) $503
Iron Fist #14 NM+(9.6) $500
Iron Fist #14 NM(9.4) $355
Iron Fist #14 NM(9.4) $315.99
Iron Fist #14 NM(9.4) $300
Iron Fist #14 NM(9.4) $275
Iron Fist #14 NM(9.4) $257.03
Iron Fist #15 NM+(9.6) $272.50
Invaders #1 NM/MT(9.8) $355
Joker #1 NM(9.4) $31
Justice League of America #107 NM+(9.6) $125.50
Justice League of America #116 NM+(9.6) $300
Justice League of America #138 NM+(9.6) $105.84
Kamandi #1 NM/MT(9.8) $256.50
Kamandi #1 NM-(9.2) $40
Kull and the Barbarians #1 NM(9.4) $37
Kull The Conqueror #1 NM+(9.6) $138.51
Legion of Monsters #1 NM/MT(9.8) $305
Legion of Super-Heroes #300 GM(10.0) $308
Man-Thing #1 NM(9.4) $95
Man-Thing #1 NM-(9.2) $86
Marvel Comics Presents #83 NM/MT(9.8) $45
Marvel Feature #1 NM+(9.6) $810
Marvel Feature #1 NM(9.4) $565
Marvel Movie Premiere #1 NM/MT(9.8) $58.53
Marvel Premiere #15 NM/MT(9.8) $1,940.13
Marvel Premiere #15 NM/MT(9.8) $1,795
Marvel Premiere #15 NM+(9.6) $710
Marvel Spotlight #2 NM+(9.6) $1,150
Marvel Spotlight #5 NM(9.4) $875 (Ghost Rider)
Marvel Spotlight #5 NM-(9.2) $405
Marvel Spotlight #5 NM-(9.2) $395
Marvel Spotlight #6 NM(9.4) $106.17
Marvel Spotlight #32 NM+(9.6) $150 (Spider-Woman)
Marvel Super-Heroes Secret Wars #8 NM/MT(9.8) $115
Marvel Super Heroes Secret Wars #8 NM+(9.6) $46
Marvel Team-Up #2 NM/MT(9.8) $349.95
Master of Kung-Fu #21 NM/MT(9.8) $151.07
Ms. Marvel #16 NM/MT(9.8) $335
New Gods #1 VF/NM(9.0) $40
Omac #1 NM/MT(9.8) $126.50
Punisher (Limited series) #1 NM/MT(9.8) $255.50
Punisher (Limited series) #1 NM(9.4) $45
Raiders of the Lost Ark #1 NM/MT(9.8) $43
Richie Rich & Jackie Jokers #1 NM(9.4) $200
Sandman #1 (DC, 1974) MT(9.9) $1,207.50
Sandman #1 (DC, 1974) NM/MT(9.8) $235.75
Savage Sword of Conan #16 NM/MT(9.8) $171.50
Shazam! #1 NM/MT(9.8) $228
Shazam! #1 NM/MT(9.8) $170.49
Shazam! #1 VF/NM(9.0) $39.99
Special Marvel Edition #15 NM(9.4) $145
Spectacular Spider-Man #1 NM/MT(9.8) $255
Spectacular Spider-Man #1 NM+(9.6) $80.50
Spider-Woman #1 NM/MT(9.8) $130
Star Spangled War Stories #152 NM+(9.6) $250
Star Wars #2 NM/MT(9.8) $58
Star Wars Annual #1 NM/MT(9.8) $116
Super Friends #1 NM+(9.6) $69
Supernatural Thrillers #5 NM/MT(9.8) $393.88
Super Powers #2 MT(9.9) $43
Swamp Thing #1 NM+(9.6) $429
Swamp Thing #1 NM-(9.2) $135
Swamp Thing #1 NM+(9.6) $1150
Swamp Thing #1 NM/MT(9.8) $1950
Swamp Thing #5 NM(9.4) $125
Swamp Thing #9 NM/MT(9.8) $475
Tomb of Dracula #1 NM+(9.6) $632.50
Tomb of Dracula #1 NM(9.4) $270
2001: A Space Odyssey #1 NM+(9.6) $45
Vampirella #7 NM-(9.2) $102.50
Vampirella #13 NM/MT(9.8) $456
Vampirella #44 NM+(9.6) $205
Vampirella #77 NM/MT(9.8) $251
Vampirella #90 NM+(9.6) $202.50
Web of Spider-Man #1 NM/MT(9.8) $105.49
Weird War Tales #1 NM+(9.6) $1,200
Weird War Tales #12 NM+(9.6) $400
Werewolf By Night #1 NM/MT(9.8) $2,250
Werewolf By Night #1 NM+(9.6) $805
Wolverine (limited series) #1 GM(10.0) $3,550
Wolverine (limited series) #1 MT(9.9) $875
Wolverine (limited series) #1 NM/MT(9.8) $222.50
Wolverine (limited series) #1 NM/MT(9.8) $405
Wolverine (limited series) #2 NM/MT(9.8) $138
Wolverine #10 NM/MT(9.8) $260
Wolverine #10 NM/MT(9.8) $106
Wonder Woman #210 NM/MT(9.8) $270
X-Men #94 NM+(9.6) $6,900
X-Men #94 NM+(9.6) $6,612.50
X-Men #94 NM(9.4) $2,448
X-Men #94 NM-(9.2) $960
X-Men #94 VF(8.0) $1,300
X-Men #94 VF(8.0) $425
X-Men #95 NM+(9.6) $711
X-Men #95 NM+(9.6) $650
X-Men #97 NM(9.4) $275
X-Men #101 NM+(9.6) $660
X-Men #101 VF/NM-(9.0) $122.50
X-Men #137 NM+(9.6) $80
X-Men #140 NM(9.4) $90
X-Men #141 NM+(9.6) $102.50
Yogi Bear #5 (Marvel) 9.9 MT- Double cover $225

Albedo #2 NM/MT(9.8) $1,280
Albedo #2 NM(9.4) $560
Amazing Spider-Man #298 NM/MT(9.8) $350
Amazing Spider-Man #299 NM/MT(9.8) $240
Amazing Spider-Man #300 NM/MT(9.8) $625
Amazing Spider-Man #300 NM/MT(9.8) $565
Amazing Spider-Man #300 NM+(9.6) $225
Amazing Spider-Man #500 NM/MT(9.8) $41
Amazing Spider-Man V2 #36 NM/MT(9.8) $110
Amazing Spider-Man V2 #36 MT(9.9) $295
Amazing Spider-Man Vol.2 #36 MT(9.9) $300
Aspen #1 NM/MT(9.8) $34.95
Aspen Signature Series #1 NM/MT(9.8) $250
Avengers/JLA #2 GM(10.0) $149.95
Batman #411 MT(9.9) $51
Batman #428 NM+(9.6) $99
Batman #608 (1st pr.) NM/MT(9.8) $65
Batman #608 (2nd pr.) NM/MT(9.8) $85
Batman #608 RRP NM/MT(9.8) $2,425
Batman #608 RRP NM+(9.6) $885.99
Batman #608 RRP Signature Series NM/MT(9.8) $2,950
Batman #612 (1st pr.) NM/MT(9.8) $30
Batman #612 (2nd pr.) NM/MT(9.8) $105
Batman #612 (2nd pr.) NM/MT(9.8) $85
Batman #619 (Riddler-c) GM(10.0) $611
Batman: Dark Knight Returns #2 NM/MT(9.8) $102.50
Batman: The Long Halloween #1 NM+(9.6) $75
Caliber Presents #1 NM/MT(9.8) $282
CSI: Crime Scene Investigation #1 MT(9.9) $49.95
Daredevil V2 #1 (reg. -c) NM/MT(9.8) $80
Daredevil V2 #1 (Campbell-c) NM/MT(9.8) $65
Dark Days #1 NM/MT(9.8) $35
Dark Knight Strikes Again #1 MT(9.9) $44
Emma Frost #1 NM/MT(9.8) $34.95
Fantastic Four #500 NM/MT(9.8) $53
G.I. Joe #1 NM/MT(9.8) $232.50
G.I. Joe #1 NM/MT(9.8) $195
Green Arrow #101 NM/MT(9.8) $115
Harbinger #0 Pink NM/MT(9.8) $105
Incredible Hulk #340 NM/MT(9.8) $250
Incredible Hulk #340 NM/MT(9.8) $197.50
Incredible Hulk #340 NM-(9.2) $45.33
JLA/Avengers #1 MT(9.9) $99.95
JLA/Avengers #3 NM/MT(9.8) $40
John Byrne's Next Men #21 NM/MT(9.8) $275
John Byrne's Next Men #21 NM/MT(9.8) $202
League of Extraordinary Gentlemen #1 NM+(9.6) $55
Marvel 1602 #1 NM/MT(9.8) $50
Marvel 1602 #2 MT(9.9) $109.95
Marvel 1602 #3 MT(9.9) $79.95
Mystique #1 NM/MT(9.8) $29.95
Nightwing #1 NM/MT(9.8) $150
NYX #1 NM/MT(9.8) $35.52
Outsiders #1 NM/MT(9.8) $60
Punisher #1 NM/MT(9.8) $80
Punisher Kills the Marvel Universe #1 NM/MT(9.8) $227
Rai #0 NM/MT(9.8) $50
Sandman #1 (Vertigo) NM/MT(9.8) $155
Solar #1 NM/MT(9.8) $305
Spawn #1 MT(9.9) $147.50
Spawn #1 NM/MT(9.8) $57
Spawn #1 NM/MT(9.8) $51
Spider-Man #1 Gold UPC NM/MT(9.8) $300
Spider-Man #1 Platinum NM(9.4) $150
Spider-Man: Blue #1 NM/MT(9.8) $41
Superman/Batman #1 NM/MT(9.8) $60
Superman/Batman #1 NM/MT(9.8) $54.99
Superman/Batman #1 (Retailer Ed.) NM/MT(9.8) $638
Superman/Batman #1 (Retailer Ed.) NM+(9.6) $315
Superman: Red Son #1 NM/MT(9.8) $91
Superman: Red Son #1 NM/MT(9.8) $85
Supreme Power #1 GM(10.0) $266
Teen Titans #1 (McKone-c) NM/MT(9.8) $60
Teen Titans #1 (Turner-c) NM/MT(9.8) $90
Teen Titans #1 (Turner-c) NM/MT(9.8) $79.99
Titans/Young Justice Grad. Day #1 NM/MT(9.8) $49.95
30 Days of Night #3 MT(9.9) $89.99
Thor: Vikings #1 GM(10.0) $305
Trouble #1 (1st printing) NM/MT(9.8) $55
Ultimates #1 MT(9.9) $122.50
Ultimates #1 MT(9.9) $75
Ultimate Six #1 MT(9.9) $132.50
Ultimate Spider-Man #1 NM/MT(9.8) $685
Ultimate Spider-Man #1 NM/MT(9.8) $350
Ultimate Spider-Man #1 White Cover NM/MT(9.8) $1,175
Ultimate Spider Man #1 White Cover NM/MT(9.8) $1,100
Ultimate Spider-Man #2 NM/MT(9.8) $225
Ultimate Spider-Man #2 (car cover) NM/MT(9.8) $190
Ultimate Spider-Man #2 (car cover) NM/MT(9.8) $95
Ultimate Spider-Man #3 NM/MT(9.8) $90
Ultimate Spider-Man #5 NM/MT(9.8) $355
Ultimate Spider-Man #15 GM(10.0) $349.95
Ultimate Spider-Man #50 NM/MT(9.8) $50
Ultimate X-Men #1 NM/MT(9.8) $133.72
Ultimate X-Men #1 (DFE-cover) NM/MT(9.8) $250
Ultimate X-Men #2 NM/MT(9.8) $76
Ultimate War #1 NM/MT(9.8) $23
Unity #0 NM/MT(9.8) $88
Venom: Lethal Protector #1 (Black-c) NM/MT(9.8) $500
Witchblade #1 NM/MT(9.8) $71
Wolverine: The End #1 NM/MT(9.8) $35
Wolverine: The Origin #1 GM(10.0) $961.75
Wolverine: The Origin #1 NM/MT(9.8) $90
X-Men #1 MT(9.9) $56
X-O Manowar #5 NM/MT(9.8) $144.92
Y The Last Man #1 NM(9.4) $50

The following tables denote the rate of appreciation of the top Golden Age, Platinum Age, Silver Age and Bronze Age books, as well as selected genres over the past year. The retail value for a Near Mint- copy of each book (or VF where a Near Mint- copy is not known to exist) in 2004 is compared to its Near Mint- value in 2003. The rate of return for 2004 over 2003 is given. The place in rank is given for each comic by year, with its corresponding value in highest known grade. These tables can be very useful in forecasting trends in the market place. For instance, the investor might want to know which book is yielding the best dividend from one year to the next, or one might just be interested in seeing how the popularity of books changes from year to year. For instance, *Sub-Mariner Comics* #1 was in 21st place in 2003 and has increased to 18th place in 2004. Premium books are also included in these tables and are denoted with an asterisk(*).

The following tables are meant as a guide to the investor. However, it should be pointed out that trends may change at anytime and that some books can meet market resistance with a slowdown in price increases, while others can develop into real comers from a presently dormant state. In the long run, if the investor sticks to the books that are appreciating steadily each year, he shouldn't go very far wrong.

Top Golden Age Books

2004 over 2003 Guide Values

TITLE/ISSUE#	2004 RANK	2004 NM- PRICE	2003 RANK	2003 NM- PRICE	$ INCR.	% INCR.
Action Comics #1	1	$440,000	1	$352,500	$87,500	25%
Detective Comics #27	2	$375,000	2	$308,750	$66,250	21%
Marvel Comics #1	3	$330,000	3	$258,750	$71,250	28%
Superman #1	4	$270,000	4	$210,000	$60,000	29%
All-American Comics #16	5	$160,000	5	$118,125	$41,875	35%
Batman #1	6	$125,000	6	$98,515	$26,485	27%
Captain America Comics #1	6	$125,000	6	$98,515	$26,485	27%
Flash Comics #1	8	$97,000	8	$80,500	$16,500	20%
More Fun Comics #52	9	$84,000	10	$68,250	$15,750	23%
Whiz Comics #2 (#1)	10	$84,000	9	$70,000	$14,000	20%
Adventure Comics #40	11	$64,000	12	$50,750	$13,250	26%
Detective Comics #33	12	$60,000	13	$48,125	$11,875	25%
Detective Comics #1	13	VF $58,000	11	VF $56,000	$2,000	4%
All Star Comics #3	14	$55,000	14	$43,750	$11,250	26%
Detective Comics #38	14	$55,000	14	$43,750	$11,250	26%
Green Lantern #1	16	$50,000	16	$40,250	$9,750	24%
Action Comics #2	17	$46,000	18	$37,380	$8,620	23%
Detective Comics #29	18	$45,000	19	$35,875	$9,125	25%
Detective Comics #31	18	$45,000	19	$35,875	$9,125	25%
Sub-Mariner Comics #1	18	$45,000	21	$35,000	$10,000	29%
All Star Comics #8	21	$44,000	21	$35,000	$9,000	26%
Human Torch #2 (#1)	21	$44,000	21	$35,000	$9,000	26%
New Fun Comics #1	23	VF $43,500	16	VF $43,000	$500	1%
More Fun Comics #53	24	$43,000	24	$34,375	$8,625	25%
Captain Marvel Adventures #1	25	$42,000	25	$34,125	$7,875	23%
Sensation Comics #1	26	$40,000	26	$31,500	$8,500	27%
Marvel Mystery Comics #2	27	$38,000	28	$29,750	$8,250	28%
Marvel Mystery Comics #9	28	$36,000	29	$28,000	$8,000	29%
Action Comics #7	29	$35,000	31	$26,700	$8,300	31%
Adventure Comics #48	29	$35,000	29	$28,000	$7,000	25%
Wonder Woman #1	31	$34,000	32	$26,250	$7,750	30%
All Winners Comics #1	32	$30,000	34	$23,625	$6,375	27%
Marvel Mystery Comics #5	32	$30,000	34	$23,625	$6,375	27%
New York World's Fair 1939	32	VF/NM $30,000	27	VF/NM $30,000	$0	0%
Daring Mystery Comics #1	35	$29,000	34	$23,625	$5,375	23%
Action Comics #3	36	$28,000	38	$23,410	$4,590	20%
* Motion Picture Funnies Weekly #1	36	$28,000	34	$23,625	$4,375	19%
Detective Comics #28	38	$27,000	41	$21,875	$5,125	23%
Famous Funnies-Series 1 #1	38	VF $27,000	33	VF $26,000	$1,000	4%
* Century Of Comics nn	40	VF $24,000	40	VF $22,000	$2,000	9%

TITLE/ISSUE#	004 RANK	2004 NM- PRICE	2003 RANK	2003 NM- PRICE	$ INCR.	% INCR.
*Marvel Mystery Comics 132 pg.	41	VF $23,000	39	VF $22,000	$1,000	5%
Walt Disney's Comics & Stories #1	41	$23,000	48	$18,375	$4,625	25%
Action Comics #10	43	$22,000	51	$17,800	$4,200	24%
All-American Comics #19	43	$22,500	49	$17,938	$4,062	23%
All Flash #1	43	$22,000	52	$17,500	$4,500	26%
Amazing Man Comics #5	43	$22,000	49	$17,938	$4,062	23%
World's Best Comics #1	47	VF $21,500	52	VF $17,500	$4,000	23%
Captain America Comics 132 pg.	48	$21,000	43	$20,000	$1,000	5%
Wonder Comics #1	48	$21,000	54	$17,063	$3,937	23%
Young Allies Comics #1	48	$21,000	62	$15,750	$5,250	33%
New Fun Comics #6	51	VF $20,700	42	VF $20,500	$200	1%
All-American Comics #17	52	$20,500	56	$16,625	$3,875	23%
Archie Comics #1	52	$20,500	58	$16,188	$4,312	27%
Jumbo Comics #1	52	VF $20,500	43	VF $20,000	$500	3%
Mystic Comics #1	52	$20,500	56	$16,625	$3,875	23%
Famous Funnies #1	56	VF $20,000	45	VF $19,000	$1,000	5%
Pep Comics #22	56	$20,000	58	$16,188	$3,812	24%
Wow Comics #1	56	$20,000	58	$16,188	$3,812	24%
Batman #2	59	$19,500	62	$15,750	$3,750	24%
New Comics #1	59	VF $19,500	45	VF $19,000	$500	3%
Silver Streak Comics #6	59	$19,500	62	$15,750	$3,750	24%
Captain America Comics #2	62	$19,000	67	$14,875	$4,125	28%
Marvel Mystery Comics #3	62	$19,000	67	$14,875	$4,125	28%
More Fun Comics #55	62	$19,000	65	$15,314	$3,686	24%
New Fun Comics #2	65	VF $18,700	47	VF $18,500	$200	1%
All Star Comics #1	66	$18,000	67	$14,875	$3,125	21%
Daredevil Comics #1	66	$18,000	76	$14,000	$4,000	29%
More Fun Comics #73	66	$18,000	76	$14,000	$4,000	29%
Suspense Comics #3	66	$18,000	67	$14,875	$3,125	21%
USA Comics #1	66	$18,000	72	$14,438	$3,562	25%
Action Comics #4	71	$17,500	73	$14,240	$3,260	23%
Action Comics #5	71	$17,500	73	$14,240	$3,260	23%
Action Comics #6	71	$17,500	73	$14,240	$3,260	23%
Adventure Comics #73	71	$17,500	76	$14,000	$3,500	25%
Superman #2	71	$17,500	76	$14,000	$3,500	25%
Adventure Comics #61	76	$17,000	81	$13,562	$3,438	25%
All-Select Comics #1	76	$17,000	81	$13,562	$3,438	25%
Double Action Comics #2	76	$17,000	71	$14,625	$2,375	16%
More Fun Comics #54	76	$17,000	83	$13,125	$3,875	30%
Red Raven Comics #1	76	$17,000	83	$13,125	$3,875	30%
New York World's Fair 1940	81	VF/NM $16,800	55	VF/NM $16,800	$0	0%
Marvel Mystery Comics #4	81	$16,500	83	$13,125	$3,375	26%
Planet Comics #1	81	$16,500	83	$13,125	$3,375	26%
Detective Comics #2	84	VF $16,300	61	VF $16,000	$300	2%
Adventure Comics #72	85	$16,000	83	$13,125	$2,875	22%
Detective Comics #35	85	$16,000	97	$11,813	$4,187	35%
Green Giant Comics #1	85	$16,000	83	$13,125	$2,875	22%
Looney Tunes and Merrie Melodies #1	85	$16,000	91	$12,667	$3,333	26%
Mickey Mouse Magazine #1	85	VF/NM $16,000	66	VF/NM $15,000	$1,000	7%
Captain America Comics #3	90	$15,500	94	$12,250	$3,250	27%
Four Color Ser. 1 (Donald Duck) #4	90	$15,500	96	$12,141	$3,359	28%
Silver Streak Comics #1	90	$15,500	94	$12,250	$3,250	27%
* Funnies on Parade nn	93	$14,500	92	$12,615	$1,885	15%
Marvel Mystery Comics #8	93	$14,500	99	$11,563	$2,937	25%
Mystery Men Comics #1	93	$14,500	97	$11,813	$2,687	23%
All-American Comics #18	96	$14,000	-	$10,250	$3,750	37%
Big Book of Fun Comics #1	96	VF $14,000	76	VF $14,000	$0	0%
Pep Comics #1	96	$14,000	-	$10,500	$3,500	33%
Tough Kid Squad Comics #1	96	$14,000	-	$11,375	$2,625	23%
Big All-American #1	100	$13,500	-	$10,937	$2,563	23%

Top 10 Platinum Age Books

TITLE/ISSUE#	2004 RANK	2004 PRICE	2003 RANK	2003 PRICE	$ INCR.	% INCR.
Mickey Mouse Book (2nd printing)-variant	1	FN $12,000	1	FN $12,000	$0	0%
Mickey Mouse Book (1st printing)	2	VF $11,000	2	VF $11,000	$0	0%
Mickey Mouse Book (2nd printing)	3	VF $10,000	3	VF $10,000	$0	0%
Yellow Kid in McFadden Flats	4	FN $8,700	4	FN $8,700	$0	0%
Pore Li'l Mose	5	FN $5,250	5	FN $5,250	$0	0%
Buster Brown and His Resolutions 1903	6	FN $5,000	6	FN $4,600	$400	9%
Little Sammy Sneeze	7	FN $3,900	7	FN $3,400	$500	15%
Little Nemo 1906	8	FN $3,200	8	FN $3,000	$200	7%
Yellow Kid #1	8	FN $3,000	8	FN $3,000	$0	0%
Little Nemo 1909	10	FN $2,600	-	FN $2,500	$100	4%

Top 10 Silver Age Books

TITLE/ISSUE#	2004 RANK	2004 NM- PRICE	2003 RANK	2003 NM- PRICE	$ INCR.	% INCR.
Amazing Fantasy #15	1	$42,500	1	$39,500	$3,000	8%
Showcase #4 (The Flash)	2	$41,000	2	$31,750	$9,250	29%
Fantastic Four #1	3	$34,000	3	$26,338	$7,663	29%
Amazing Spider-Man #1	4	$32,000	3	$26,338	$5,663	21%
Incredible Hulk #1	5	$23,000	5	$15,988	$7,013	44%
Showcase #8 (The Flash)	6	$16,800	6	$13,800	$3,000	22%
X-Men #1	7	$13,000	7	$9,375	$3,625	39%
Showcase #9 (Lois Lane)	8	$10,500	8	$8,400	$2,100	25%
The Flash #105	9	$8,500	9	$6,492	$2,008	31%
Brave and the Bold #28	10	$8,000	9	$6,492	$1,508	23%

Top 10 Bronze Age Books

TITLE/ISSUE#	2004 RANK	2004 NM- PRICE	2003 RANK	2003 NM- PRICE	$ INCR.	% INCR.
Incredible Hulk #181	1	$1,250	1	$1,012	$238	24%
Giant-Size X-Men #1	2	$1,200	2	$997	$203	20%
X-Men #94	3	$1,025	3	$836	$189	23%
House of Secrets #92	4	$800	5	$640	$160	25%
Star Wars #1 (35¢ cover price variant)	4	$800	4	$663	$137	21%
DC 100 Page Super Spectacular #5	6	$700	6	$574	$126	22%
All-Star Western #10	7	$560	7	$443	$117	27%
Vampirella Special HC	8	$525	8	$420	$105	25%
Cerebus #1	9	$500	9	$334	$166	50%
Gobbledygook #1	10	$450	-	$232	$218	94%
Teenage Mutant Ninja Turtles #1	10	$450	-	$214	$236	111%

Top 10 Crime Books

TITLE/ISSUE#	2004 RANK	2004 NM- PRICE	2003 RANK	2003 NM- PRICE	$ INCR.	% INCR.
Crime Does Not Pay #22	1	$3,100	1	$2,480	$620	25%
True Crime Comics #2	2	$1,800	2	$1,461	$339	23%
Crime Does Not Pay #23	3	$1,650	3	$1,329	$321	24%
Crimes By Women #1	4	$1,540	4	$1,307	$233	18%
The Killers #1	5	$1,340	5	$1,085	$255	24%
True Crime Comics #3	5	$1,340	5	$1,085	$255	24%
Crime Does Not Pay #24	7	$1,300	7	$1,063	$237	22%
True Crime Comics #4	8	$1,175	8	$952	$223	23%
The Killers #2	9	$1,100	9	$886	$214	24%
Crime Smashers #1	10	$1,060	10	$864	$196	23%
True Crime Comics Vol. 2 #1	10	$1,060	10	$864	$196	23%

Top 10 Horror Books

TITLE/ISSUE#	2004 RANK	2004 NM- PRICE	2003 RANK	2003 NM- PRICE	$ INCR.	% INCR.
Vault of Horror #12	1	$6,300	1	$5,157	$1,143	22%
Eerie #1	2	$5,000	3	$3,938	$1,062	27%
Tales of Terror Annual #1	3	VF $4,400	2	VF $4,200	$200	5%
Journey into Mystery #1	4	$4,000	4	$3,244	$756	23%
Strange Tales #1	5	$3,900	7	$3,169	$731	23%
Crypt of Terror #17	6	$3,800	5	$3,200	$600	19%
Haunt of Fear #15	6	$3,800	5	$3,200	$600	19%
Crime Patrol #15	8	$3,500	8	$2,933	$567	19%
House of Mystery #1	9	$2,850	9	$2,304	$546	24%
Tales to Astonish #1	10	$2,400	10	$1,934	$466	24%

Top 10 Romance Books

TITLE/ISSUE#	2004 RANK	2004 NM- PRICE	2003 RANK	2003 NM- PRICE	$ INCR.	% INCR.
Giant Comics Edition #12	1	$1,400	1	$1,050	$350	33%
Intimate Confessions #1	2	$950	2	$775	$175	23%
Romance Trail #1	3	$750	4	$606	$144	24%
Young Lovers #18	3	$750	3	$608	$142	23%
DC 100 Page Super Spectacular #5	5	$700	5	$574	$126	22%
Giant Comics Edition #9	6	$675	6	$547	$128	23%
Giant Comics Edition #15	6	$675	6	$547	$128	23%
Secret Hearts #1	8	$660	8	$533	$127	24%
Personal Love #32	9	$650	9	$519	$131	25%
Women in Love - 1952	10	$635	10	$510	$125	25%

Top 10 Sci-Fi Books

TITLE/ISSUE#	2004 RANK	2004 NM- PRICE	2003 RANK	2003 NM- PRICE	$ INCR.	% INCR.
Strange Adventures #1	1	$4,500	1	$3,719	$781	21%
Mystery In Space #1	2	$4,400	2	$3,575	$825	23%
Showcase #17 (Adam Strange)	3	$3,500	3	$2,789	$711	26%
Journey Into Unknown Worlds #36	4	$2,900	4	$2,347	$553	24%
Fawcett Movie #15 (Man From Planet X)	5	$2,850	5	$2,304	$546	24%
Showcase #15 (Space Ranger)	6	$2,750	9	$2,197	$553	25%
Strange Adventures #9	7	$2,700	6	$2,238	$462	21%
Weird Science-Fantasy Annual 1952	8	$2,650	10	$2,166	$484	22%
Weird Fantasy #13 (#1)	9	$2,600	7	$2,222	$378	17%
Weird Science #12 (#1)	9	$2,600	7	$2,222	$378	17%

Top 10 Western Books

TITLE/ISSUE#	2004 RANK	2004 NM- PRICE	2003 RANK	2003 NM- PRICE	$ INCR.	% INCR.
Gene Autry Comics #1	1	$11,000	1	$8,750	$2,250	26%
*Lone Ranger Ice Cream 1939 2nd	2	VF $7,000	2	VF $6,800	$200	3%
Hopalong Cassidy #1	3	$6,800	4	$5,513	$1,287	23%
*Lone Ranger Ice Cream 1939	4	VF $6,500	3	VF $6,200	$300	5%
*Red Ryder Victory Patrol '42	5	$5,000	5	$4,350	$650	15%
*Red Ryder Victory Patrol '43	6	$4,600	6	$3,975	$625	16%
*Red Ryder Victory Patrol '44	6	$4,600	6	$3,975	$625	16%
*Tom Mix Ralston #1	8	$4,000	8	$3,400	$600	18%
Red Ryder Comics #1	9	$3,800	9	$3,107	$693	22%
Roy Rogers Four Color #38	10	$3,500	10	$2,789	$711	26%

FIRST NATIONAL PICTURES, INC. presents

BABE RUTH

IN "BABE COMES HOME"

With ANNA Q. NILSSON and LOUISE FAZENDA

BY ARRANGEMENT WITH CHRISTY WALSH

ADAPTED FROM GERALD BEAUMONT'S "SAID WITH SOAP"

DIRECTED BY TED WILDE

PRODUCED BY WID GUNNING

A FIRST NATIONAL PICTURE

Morgan

Home of the $250,000 "Babe Comes Home" One Sheet Poster

WE'RE CONFUSED!

**THE FOLLOWING IS A TRUE STORY.
WE HOPE THAT SOMEONE WHO READS THIS
WILL BE ABLE TO EXPLAIN WHY THIS KIND OF
THING HAPPENS, BECAUSE WE DON'T GET IT !**

At one of the biggest conventions of the year, a dealer who traveled hundreds of miles to set up, sold a high-grade Fantastic Four #1 for roughly 1/2 the price that we would have paid. After that book passed through the hands of several dealers, we did in fact buy it. The fellow who initially sold it at the convention could easily have made ***Seven Thousand Dollars more*** if he had he sold it to us.

SHOULDN'T THESE GUYS KNOW BETTER?

SHOULDN'T EVERYONE? IS IT STILL BETTER TO GET MORE MONEY FOR YOUR BOOKS THAN LESS? DOES THE EARTH STILL REVOLVE AROUND THE SUN? ARE THERE STILL PEOPLE OUT THERE WHO ARE NOT OFFERING THEIR BOOKS TO METROPOLIS AND LOSING MONEY SELLING TO THE WRONG GUY?

If anyone out there can shed any light on why this still happens in this day and age, could you please let us know?

COLLECTIBLES
873 Broadway, Suite 201
New York, NY 10003
Call Toll Free: 1-800-229-6387
ph: (212) 260-4147 fax: (212) 260-4304
email: buying@metropoliscomics.com
web: www.metropoliscomics.com

FOUR COLOR
COMICS
BUYING PRE-1980 LINE-ART
I buy, sell, and collect original comic art. I can and will pay you the highest price for your art. Call me before you sell.
•
Of particular interest:
GOLDENAGE ART
DC SILVERAGE ART
MARVEL SILVERAGE ART
EC COVER ART
FRAZETTA, KIRBY, DITKO, BARKS
P.O. Box 1399
Scarsdale, NY 10583
Tel: (914) 722-4696
Fax: (914) 722-7656
www.fourcolorcomics.com
SPIDER-MAN
SPIDER-MAN NO MORE
THOR BATTLES THE INCREDIBLE HULK
GYRO GEARLOOSE
BROUGHT THE ROC TO LIFE!
TALES CALCULATED TO DRIVE YOU
MAD
NICK FURY, AGENT OF S.H.I.E.L.D.
"TO FREE A BRAIN SLAVE"

The REDISTRIBUTOR

No. 1

HINDS FINDS ALL KINDS

Jef Hinds COMICS

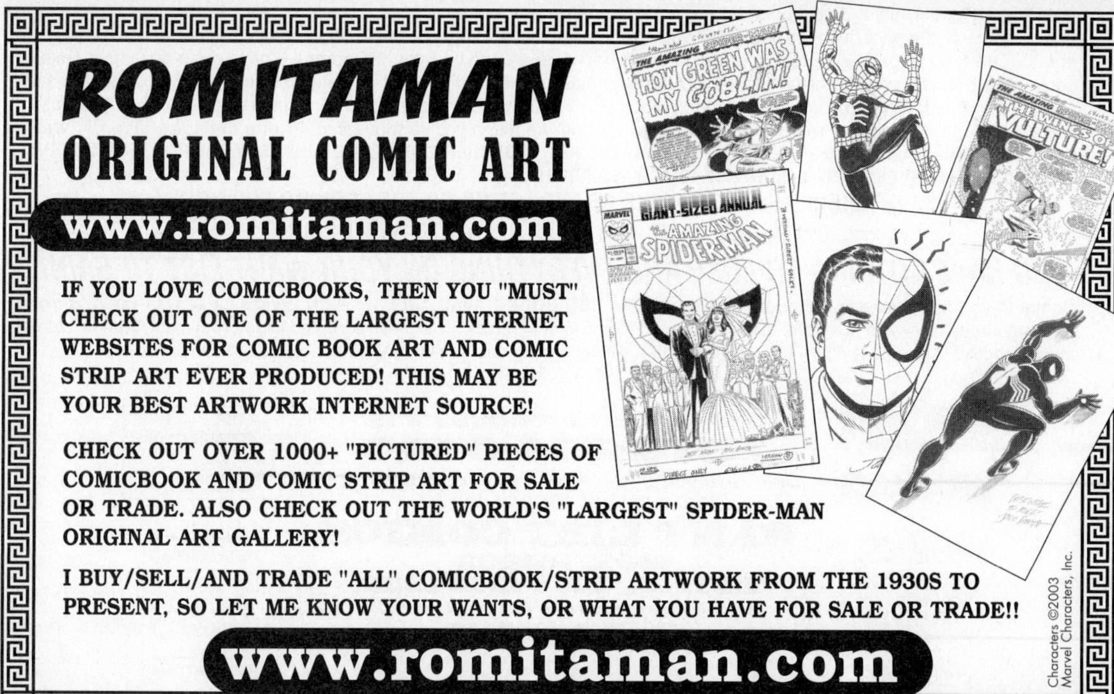
ROMITAMAN
ORIGINAL COMIC ART
www.romitaman.com
HOW GREEN WAS MY GOBLIN!
THE WINGS OF VULTURE!
GIANT-SIZED ANNUAL
THE AMAZING SPIDER-MAN
IF YOU LOVE COMICBOOKS, THEN YOU "MUST" CHECK OUT ONE OF THE LARGEST INTERNET WEBSITES FOR COMIC BOOK ART AND COMIC STRIP ART EVER PRODUCED! THIS MAY BE YOUR BEST ARTWORK INTERNET SOURCE!
CHECK OUT OVER 1000+ "PICTURED" PIECES OF COMICBOOK AND COMIC STRIP ART FOR SALE OR TRADE. ALSO CHECK OUT THE WORLD'S "LARGEST" SPIDER-MAN ORIGINAL ART GALLERY!
I BUY/SELL/AND TRADE "ALL" COMICBOOK/STRIP ARTWORK FROM THE 1930S TO PRESENT, SO LET ME KNOW YOUR WANTS, OR WHAT YOU HAVE FOR SALE OR TRADE!!
www.romitaman.com
Characters ©2003 Marvel Characters, Inc.

BEDROCK CITY
COMIC COMPANY
TM
Girl trouble
PHANTOM Lady
APR. 10¢
PHANTOM LADY
CRIME NEVER PAYS!
WINGS COMICS
No.93 MAY 10¢
'Kidnap Cargo'
Captain Wings
The GHOST SQUADRON
STRANGE STORIES OF THE SUPERNATURAL
Venus
10¢
19
"THE KISS OF DEATH! THE MOST TERRIFYING HORROR THAT EVER EXISTED!"
You'll find *hellcats* and *headlights* on-line at *www.bedrockcity.com*
Check out the cheesecake at store #1:
6517 Westheimer (at Hillcroft)
Houston, Texas 77057
Phone (713) 780-0675 Fax (713) 780-2366
Or these *drop-dead gorgeous* stores:
2204-B FM 1960 W.
Houston, Texas 77090
Phone (281) 444-9763
106 W. Bay Area Blvd.
Webster, Texas 77598
Phone (281) 557-2748

BAGS Unlimited INC 800-767-2247

www.bagsunlimited.com . E-mail: info@bagsunlimited.com

your ONE STOP SHOP for COMIC SUPPLIES

Economy to Archival

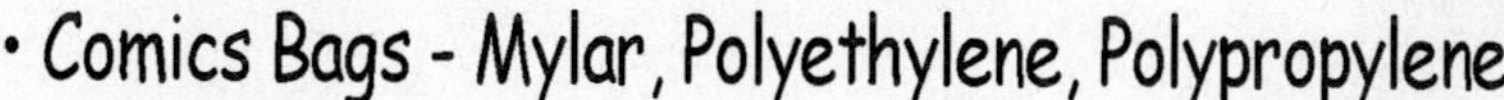

- Archival Frame Kits
- Binder Pages
- Dividers
- Storage Boxes
- Graded Comic Supplies
- Mailers
- Backings

Protecting Collections Since 1975

WHOLESALE / RETAIL • FREE PHONE CALL • FREE CATALOG

BAGS UNLIMITED INC. 1-800-767-BAGS

7 CANAL ST • ROCHESTER, NY 14608 • (585)436-9006 • FAX(585)328-8526

BUYING/SELLING
COMIC BOOKS & ORIGINAL ART
$$ TOP DOLLAR PAID $$

Golden Age and Silver Age comic books and original art

I have been a collector since 1959. I am an accurate grader, and I know how you want to be treated.

I will **Buy** both small and large collections. Send your list today for a prompt reply, **and remember** - before you sell, contact me.
Also, please send me your **want list.**

CONRAD ESCHENBERG
108 HUSTIS ROAD
COLD SPRING, NY 10516
PHONE/FAX: (914) 265-2649
E-MAIL: COMICART@PCREALM.NET
INTERNET SITE:
WWW.COMICSNART.PCREALM.NET

ABSOLUTE TOP DOLLAR FOR DITKO & KIRBY ORIGINAL ART!!!!!!!!!!

		FAIR	GOOD	V. GOOD
WANTED:	ACTION #1	14,000	25,000	48,000
	DETECTIVE #27	12,000	21,000	44,000

PARADISE COMICS (WWW.PARADISECOMICS.COM)
THE ULTIMATE SOURCE
FOR SILVER AGE COMICS IN TORONTO
3278 Yonge Street,
Toronto Ontario, Canada, M4N 2L6
Tel: 416-487-9807
Fax: 416-487-9907
e-mail: info@paradisecomics.com
ASK ABOUT OUR MEMBERSHIP DISCOUNTS
COMICS PARADISE CONVENTIONS
SPECIALIZING IN:
Comic Books of All Kinds
From New Releases to Golden Age
Always Buying, come in for a competitive quote!
CGC Comics & Signature Series
Graphic Novels & Original Artwork
Gaming & Figurines
Supplies
COMICS GUARANTY, LLC Charter Member Dealer
PARADISE CONVENTIONS PRESENTS:
THE TORONTO COMICON
Web: WWW.TORONTOCOMICON.COM
e-mail: info@torontocomicon.com
Toronto's Only Conventions Devoted
to Comic Books and Sequential
Art From All Comic Ages!
Lots of Dealers!
Great Guests!
Panels & Seminars!
Charity Art Auction!
Check out our
website for
dates, locations,
guest list and
other information!
Batman © and ™ DC Comics, 2003. Artwork BY J. Fiore after Jim Lee.

Tales of Terror!

Tales of Terror! **is a fully illustrated visual checklist, creator index, guidebook and more! Celebrate the legend of EC's "New Trend" titles with this full-color, exhaustively researched and meticulously detailed book! It's the perfect addition to any comics or pop culture library, and it's an absolute "must have" for even the casual EC enthusiast.**

Hardcover $39.95 • Soft Cover $24.95

TERROR
TOMORROWS TREASURES
SINCE 1971
Does The Prospect Of Selling Your Collection SCARE You?!?
There Is No Mystery!
I have over 30 years of professional experience, and I have purchased Thousands of books from various sources, INCLUDING MOST OF THE DEALERS advertised in this book!
Simply contact me with details of the Golden Age / Silver Age Comics (1933-1976 ONLY), Incomplete Comics, Original Art, or Pulps you have for sale.
Visit our web site of over 25,000 vintage books.
Serving the NE with Distinction!
MASS.
CT.
R.I.
PENN.
NEW YORK
LONG ISLAND
NEW JERSEY
Contact Richard Muchin At:
Address: PO Box 925 Commack, LI NY 11725
24 hr. Phone/Fax: 631-543-5737
Email: comics@tomorrowstreasures.com
Web: www.tomorrowstreasures.com
Send $3 for Catalog.
Housecleaning?
Wolf at the Door?
Out of Options?

Canada's Number One Buyer

Buying Pre-1975

We have Bought From Virtually Every Major Dealer In This Book

Cut Out The MIddle Man

No Collection Too Big Or Too Small

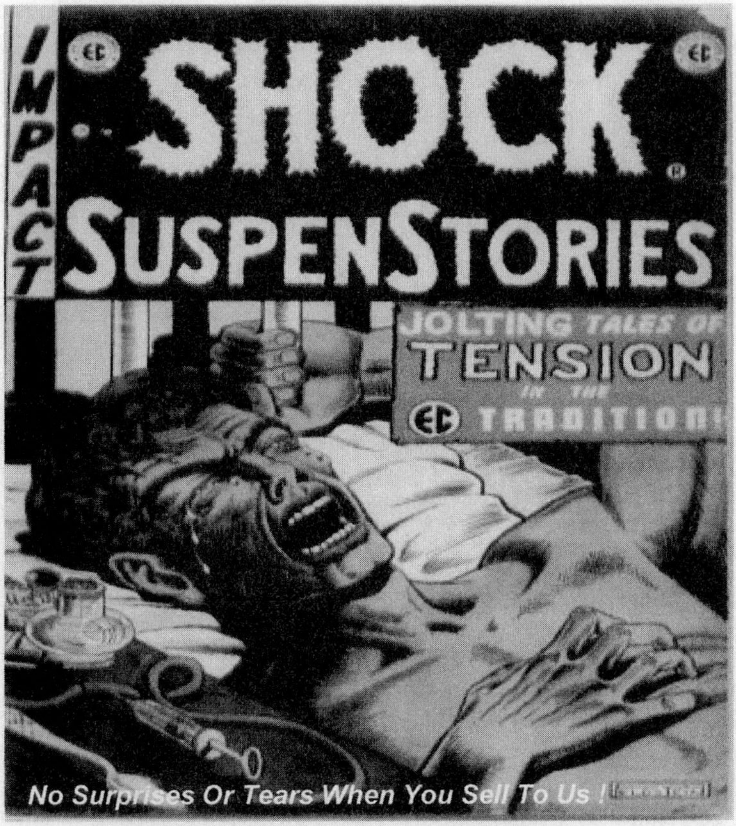

IMPACT
EC SHOCK EC
SUSPENSTORIES
JOLTING TALES OF TENSION IN THE EC TRADITION!

No Surprises Or Tears When You Sell To Us !

Tel 519 679-9995 OR Email n8kcomics@rogers.com
119 Dundas Street London Ontario

For Instant Results

We Are Members Of CGC

Disney
COMIC BOOKS
ARE HERE!
Since Gemstone Publishing's line of Disney Standard Character comic books hit the stands last June, many fans have commented that the product has never looked better. And we must humbly agree!
After all, we're stepping up to the plate with a team of professionals who both know and love the characters and who are committed to producing a product that we would like to have for ourselves and our children. When this is coupled with some of the finest freelance talent available today, and the most sophisticated production methods in history, how can you go wrong?
If you're a Disney enthusiast or just a comics fan in general, you owe it to yourself to check out this great line-up:
◆ Walt Disney's Comics and Stories and Uncle Scrooge – 64-page comic books in the sturdy squarebound prestige format that collector's love. These books will feature stories and art by Pat Block, Don Rosa, William Van Horn, and many other favorites. Published monthly.
◆ Donald Duck and Friends and Mickey Mouse and Friends – 32-page standard comic books aimed especially at kids and featuring the finest stories available from both North American and European talent. Published monthly.
◆ Donald Duck Adventures – 128-page squarebound comic books in the handy new "Take-Along" format (5" X 7½"), containing long adventures of your favorite Disney stars by North American and European creators. Published bimonthly.
Walt Disney's Comics
$6.95
Walt Disney's Uncle Scrooge
$6.95
Walt Disney's Donald Duck Adventures
4
Blue Rain
©2004 Disney Enterprises, Inc.
GEMSTONE PUBLISHING
COMIC SHOP LOCATOR SERVICE
888-COMIC-BOOK
888-266-4226
Look for them at you local comic shop. If you can't find a comic shop, try our toll-free Comic Shop Locator Service at 888-COMIC-BOOK for the shop nearest you. Or you may subscribe to each title at no extra cost and we'll pay for postage. For further information call 800-322-7978 or visit our website at www. gemstonepub.com.
www.gemstonepub.com/disney

BUNKY
BROTHERS
COMICS - CARDS - ORIGINAL ART - TOYS

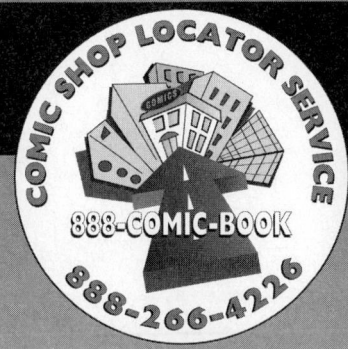

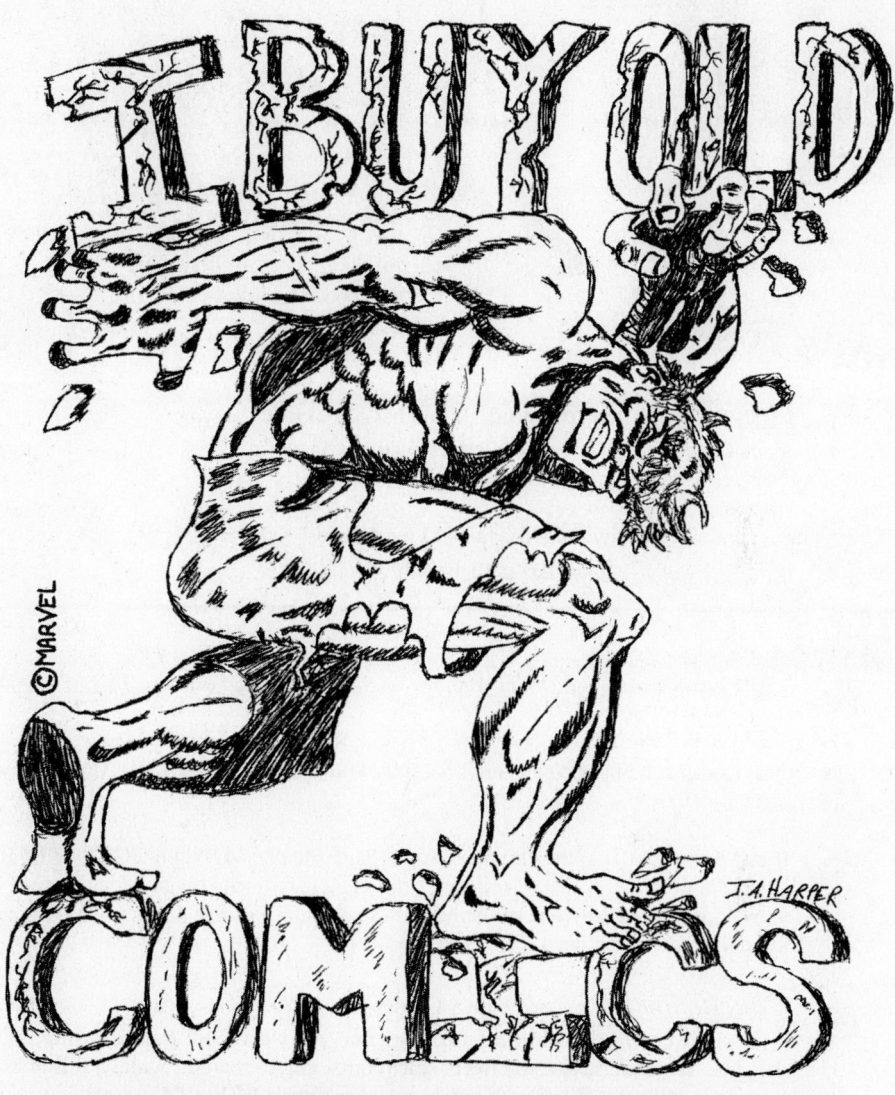

Visit Our
Warehouse
by appointment only
MOTOR CITY COMICS
Gold & Silver Age
WE ALSO DEAL IN PULPS
AND ORIGINAL ART

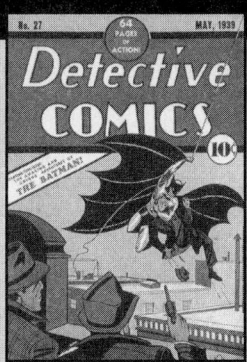

Where were you when Ultimate Spider-Man started to climb?

OVERSTREET'S COMIC REVIEW PRICE

January 2004

Vol. 1 Issue 4

Single Issue Price: $6.25

Featuring other high profile character memorabilia!

MARKET SNAPSHOT: HOW MANY 10.0?

As the number of comics certified in 10.0 accumulate, it is possible to get the mistaken perception that the grade is becoming more common. With one reported 10.0 sale since last issue – and with a snapshot look at the comics certified 10.0 this year and since the inception of CGC, it's clear that the magic number may actually be harder to obtain than first thought.

Ultimate Spider-Man #15, which sold for $349.95, was the one 10.0 sale this time.

The next grade down, 9.9, was a lot more fruitful, including *Batman #612* ($220), *Fantastic Four #500* ($81), *JLA/Avengers #1* ($99.95), *Marvel 1602 #2* *JLA/Avengers #2* ($39.95), *1602 #3* ($79.95), *Spawn #1* ($109.95, $79.95), *Ultimate Six #1* ($132.50), *Ultimate* ($113.61), *Spider-Man #19* ($139.95), and *Wolverine Limited Series #1* ($875, $759.99).

In 9.8, the independents scored a major hit with *Albedo #2* which sold for $1,280. *Amazing Spider-Man* continued strong with numerous sales including *ASM #168* ($177.50), *#182* ($370) and *#300* ($805.57).

Additional notables in 9.8 include *Aspen #1* Signature Series ($250), *Aurora Comic Scenes #182* ($49.99), *Avengers Annual #7* ($350), *Batman #608* *2nd Prim* ($139), *Flash #292* ($139.95), *Four Color #417* ($243.50), *Howard The Duck #12* ($114.50), *Next Men #21* ($202.50), *Nick Fury Agent of SHIELD #1* ($799.99), *Omega Men #3* ($59), *Rai #1* ($130), *Solar Man of the Atom #3* ($82), *Spider-Woman #1* ($129.95), *Star Wars Annual #1* ($116.01), *Sub-Mariner #2* ($700), *Superman/Batman #1* Batman cover ($46.95-$49.95), *Superman: Red Son #1* ($52.36), *Teen Titans #1* Turner Variant ($89.95), *Tomb of Dracula #10* ($1,575), *Ultimate Spider-Man #1* White Variant ($845.95), *Ultimate Spider-Man #6* ($179.95), *Unity #0* ($88), *Venom: Lethal Protector #1* Black Cover ($499.99), *X-Men #109* ($800) and *X-O*

continued on page 4

*Logan claws his way to the top with the most-graded single issue, **Wolverine: The Origin #1**.*

TOP 10 CERTIFIED 10.0 BY CGC
January 2000 to Present

Aurora Comic Scenes #192-140 (Capt. America)	10
Aurora Comic Scenes #193-140 (Robin)	10
Transformers: Generation 1 #1 Holofoil Edition	10
Venom: Lethal Protector #1	9
X-Men: Prime #1	9
Marvel Authentix: Daredevil #1	7
Amazing Spider-Man v2 #36	6
Spawn #1	6
Aurora Comic Scenes #185-140	5
Darkness v2 #1 Holofoil Edition	5

Source: 10/13/2003 CGC Census Update/ValiantComics.com

SPIDER-MAN #1 5.0 HITS $12,000

A Signature Series file copy of *Amazing Spider-Man #1* in 5.0 signed by Stan Lee has been sold for $12,000 by Ideal Collectables of Hawaii.

"This is the book that collectors associate with Stan Lee more than any other comic. It is not only signed by Stan Lee, but was his file copy," said Ideal's Bryce Iwamoto.

Pointing to the issue's pop culture appeal beyond the comic market, Iwamoto said Ideal had found continued developing interest based on the ultra-successful hit film.

"*Amazing Spider-Man #1* also features the famous phrase, 'With great power comes great responsibility,' since the Spider-Man movie this phrase has become well know outside the comic book industry," he said.

This issue was one of two copies of *Amazing Spider-Man #1* from the Stan Lee Collection originally offered by Heritage Comics Auctions. *Spider-Man 2* is set to debut July 2, 2004.

DIRECT SALES 00411>

7 14899 21152 1

TEEN TITANS . . . TITANIC!

Now that it once again seems common place for new issues of *Teen Titans* to sell out – as common as it can seem after just five issues – more sales data regarding the title and its predecessors is definitely beginning to become available.

Teen Titans debuted as its own title in 1966 following the team's appearances in *Brave & the Bold #54*, *#60* and *Showcase #59*. The original title, teaming the sidekicks Robin, Kid Flash, Speedy, Aqualad, and Wonder Girl, lasted until 1973. It returned in 1976 and ran until 1978.

The New Teen Titans, perhaps the best-known incarnation of the title, debuted in 1980 with writer Marv Wolfman and artist George Perez, with Beast Boy/Changling,

continued on page 6

WE WERE WATCHING IT.

Overstreet's Comic Price Review is the monthly newsletter for certified comics pricing. Also featuring other high profile comic character collectibles.

TO ORDER CALL SARA AT (888)375-9800 ext. 410

CAPTAIN MARVEL
MARVEL COMICS GROUP
THE ALL NEW ALL-DIFFERENT X-MEN
HERE COMES... DAREDEVIL
THE MAN WITHOUT FEAR!
SPIDER MAN
CONAN THE BARBARIAN
COMING OF CONAN!
THE AMAZING SPIDER-MAN
CHAMELEON STRIKES!
EARTH'S MIGHTIEST
Fantastic Four
AMAZING FANTASY
SPIDER MAN
THE STRANGEST SUPER-HEROES OF ALL!
the X-MEN
THE INCREDIBLE HULK
IS HE MAN OR MONSTER OR... IS HE BOTH?
ALL HERO COMICS
SUPERMAN
THE COMPLETE STORY OF THE DARING EXPLOITS OF THE ONE AND ONLY SUPERMAN
WALT DISNEY'S MICKEY MOUSE OUTWITS THE PHANTOM BLOT
68 PAGES IN FULL COLOR
SPRING ISSUE
BATMAN
ALL GRAND NEW ADVENTURES OF THE BATMAN AND ROBIN

GEPPI'S
COMIC WORLD
ASTOUNDING SPACE THRILLS
MORE FUND COMICS
BENEFITTING THE COMIC BOOK LEGAL DEFENSE FUND!
Teen Titans
DAREDEVIL
BRIAN MICHAEL BENDIS • ALEX MALEEV
THE SHIELD
FRANKENSTEIN MOBSTER
HE'S NOT AFRAID TO DIE... AGAIN!
"HANDS OFF MY CORPSE!!"
Discover new worlds you didn't know existed and revisit your favorite box office hits in entirely new ways with a trip to Geppi's Comic World. Our new location is fully stocked and ready to offer you the ride of your life!
Spider-Man! Star Wars! Blade! Star Trek! Batman! And much more!
Comics, Games, Statues, Storage Supplies, Mini-busts, Lunch Boxes, Magazines & More!
New and Back Issues
Special Orders, Hardcovers, Trade Paperbacks
Buying & Selling
Subscription Service
GEPPI'S COMIC WORLD
1116 N. Rolling Road
Baltimore, MD 21228
(410) 788-0900
All characters ©2003 respective copyright holders. All rights reserved.

RUSS COCHRAN'S COMIC ART AUCTION

Russ Cochran's Comic Art Auction

started in 1973 with the publication of his illustrated art catalog, Graphic Gallery. Soon after that, it became the main source of comic strip and comic book art, as well as paintings by Carl Barks and Frank Frazetta. It is safe to say that Russ Cochran sold more Barks and Frazetta paintings than all the other dealers in comic art combined.

At the same time, auctions were being held for the EC original art, all of which passed through Russ's Comic Art Auction. Dozens of important originals by Hal Foster, Alex Raymond, George Herriman, George McManus, Milton Caniff, and virtually every comic artist have passed through the pages of this auction catalog, finding their way to comic art collections all over the western world.

In all, a total of 13 issues of Graphic Gallery were published, and to date, 67 issues of the Comic Art Auction.

If you are a collector of comic art, or if you have art to consign, contact

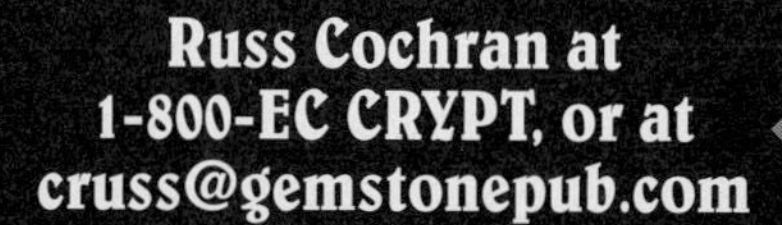

COMIC

BUY

- Timelys
- MLJs
- Golden Age DCs
- "Mile High" Copies (Church Collection)
- "San Francisco," "Bethlehem" and "Larson" Copies
- 1950s Horror and Sci-Fi Comics
- Fox/Quality/ECs
- Silver Age Marvels and DCs
- Most other brands and titles from the Golden and Silver Age

Specializing In Large Silver And Golden Age Collections

HEAVEN

I N G

Comic Heaven
John and Nanette Verzyl
P.O. Box 900
Big Sandy, TX 75755
1-903-636-5555

JOHN VERZYL AND DAUGHTER ROSE, "HARD AT WORK."

John Verzyl started collecting comic books in 1965, and within ten years he had amassed thousands of Golden and Silver Age comic books. In 1979, with his wife Nanette, he opened "COMIC HEAVEN," a retail store devoted entirely to the buying and selling of comic books.

Over the years, John Verzyl has come to be recognized as an authority in the field of comic books. He has served as a special advisor to the "Overstreet Comic Book Price Guide" for the last ten years. Thousands of his "mint" comics were photographed for Ernst Gerber's newly-released "Photo-Journal Guide to Comic Books." His tables and displays at the annual San Diego Comic Convention and the Chicago Comic Convention draw customers from all over the country.

The first COMIC HEAVEN AUCTION was held in 1987, and today his Auction Catalogs are mailed out to more than ten thousand interested collectors and dealers.

Big Little Books

INTRODUCTION

In 1932, at the depths of the Great Depression, comic books were not selling despite their successes in the previous two decades. Desperate publishers had already reduced prices to 25¢, but this was still too much for many people to spend on entertainment. This necessitated a smaller, less expensive format.

Comic books evolved into two newer formats. The first was the comics magazine (today's term, comic book, remains an anachronism referring to the earlier sturdier publications) as represented by **Funnies on Parade**. The second was the format we now know as the Big Little Book. Both types retailed for 10¢. Very quickly, the traditionally successful characters we now identify as Classic Characters migrated to these formats.

Big Little Books began by reprinting the art (and adapting the stories) from newspaper comics. As their success grew and publishers began commissioning original material, movie adaptations and other entertainment-derived stories became commonplace.

GRADING

Before a Big Little Book's value can he assessed, its condition or state of preservation must be determined. A book in **Near Mint** condition will bring many times the price of the same book in **Poor** condition. Many variables influence the grading of a Big Little Book and all must be considered in the final evaluation. Due to the way they are constructed, damage occurs with very little use - usually to the spine, book edges and binding. Consequently, books in **Near Mint** or better are scarce. More important defects that affect grading are: Split spines, pages missing, page browning or brittleness, writing, crayoning, loose pages, color fading, chunks missing, and rolling or out of square. The following grading guide is given to aid the novice:

9.4 Near Mint: The overall look is as if it was just purchased and maybe opened once; only subtle defects are allowed; paper is cream to off-white, supple and fresh; cover is flat with no surface wear or creases; inks and colors are bright; small penciled or inked arrival dates are acceptable; very slight blunting of corners at top and bottom of spine are common; outside corners are cut square and sharp. Books in this grade could bring prices of guide and a half or more.

9.0 Very Fine/Near Mint: Limited number of defects; full cover gloss with only very slight wear on book corners and edges; very minor foxing; very minor tears allowed, binding still square and tight with no pages missing; paper quality still fresh from cream to off-white. Dates, stamps or initials allowed on cover or inside.

8.0 Very Fine: Most of the cover gloss retained with minor wear appearing at corners and around edges; spine tight with no pages missing; cream/tan paper allowed if still supple; up to 1/4" bend allowed on covers with no color break; cover relatively flat; minor tears allowed.

6.0 Fine: Slight wear beginning to show; cover gloss reduced but still clean, pages tan/brown but still supple (not brittle); up to 1/4" split or color break allowed; minor discoloration and/or foxing allowed.

4.0 Very Good: Obviously a read copy with original printing luster almost gone; some fading and discoloration, but not soiled; some signs of wear such as corner splits and spine rolling; paper can be brown but not brittle; a few pages can be loose but not missing; no chunks missing; blunted corners acceptable.

2.0 Good: An average used copy complete with only minor pieces missing from the spine, which may be partially split; slightly soiled or marked with spine rolling; color flaking and wear around edges, but perfectly sound and legible; could have minor tape repairs but otherwise complete.

1.0 Fair: Very heavily read and soiled with small chunks missing from cover; most or all of spine could be missing; multiple splits in spine and loose pages, but still sound and legible, bringing 50 to 70 percent of good price.

0.5 Poor: Damaged, heavily weathered, soiled or otherwise unsuited for collecting purposes.

IMPORTANT

Most BLBs on the market today will fall in the **Good** to **Fine** grade category. Rarely will **Very Fine** to **Near Mint** BLBs be offered for sale. When they are, they usually bring premium prices.

A WORD ON PRICING

The prices are given for **Good**, **Fine** and **Very Fine/ Near Mint** condition. A book in **Fair** would be 50-70% of the **Good** price. **Very Good** would be halfway between the **Good** and **Fine** price, and **Very Fine** would be halfway between the **Fine** and **Very Fine/ Near Mint** price. The prices listed were averaged from convention sales, dealers' lists, adzines, auctions, and by special contact with dealers and collectors from coast to coast. The prices and the spreads were determined from sales of copies in available condition or the highest grade known. Since most available copies are in the **Good** to **Fine** range, neither dealers nor collectors should let the **Very Fine/Near Mint** column influence the prices they are willing to charge or pay for books in less than near perfect condition.

In the past, the BLB market has lacked a point of focus due to the absence of an annual price guide that accurately reports sales and growth in the market. Due to this, current prices for BLBs still vary considerably from region to region. It is our hope that this section will contribute to the stability of the BLB market. The prices listed reflect a six times spread from **Good** to **Very Fine/ Near Mint** (1 - 3 - 6). We feel this spread accurately reflects the current market, especially when you consider the scarcity of books in **Very Fine/Near Mint** condition. When one or both end sheets are missing, the book's value would drop about a half grade.

Books with movie scenes are of double importance due to the high crossover demand by movie collectors.

Abbreviations: a-art; c-cover; nn-no number; p-pages; r-reprint.

Publisher Codes: BRP-Blue Ribbon Press; **ERB**-Edgar Rice Burroughs; **EVW**-Engel van Wiseman; **FAW**-Fawcett Publishing Co.; **Gold**-Goldsmith Publishing Co.; **Lynn**-Lynn Publishing Co.; **McKay**-David McKay Co.; **Whit**-Whitman Publishing Co.; **World**-World Syndicate Publishing Co.

Terminology: ***All Pictures Comics***-no text, all drawings; ***Fast-Action***-A special series of Dell books highly collected; ***Flip Pictures***-upper right corner of interior pages contain drawings that are put into motion when rifled; ***Movie Scenes***-book illustrated with scenes from the movie. ***Soft Cover***-A thin single sheet of cardboard used in binding most of the give-away versions.

"Big Little Book" and "Better Little Book" are registered trademarks of Whitman Publishing Co. "Little Big Book" is a registered trademark of the Saalfield Publishing Co.

"Pop-Up" is a registered trademark of Blue Ribbon Press. "Little Big Book" is a registered trademark of the Saalfield Co.

Top 20 Big Little Books and related size books*

Issue#	Rank	Title	Price
731	1	Mickey Mouse the Mail Pilot (variant version of Mickey Mouse #717) (Fine copy sold at auction for $5,090)	
nn	2	Mickey Mouse and Minnie Mouse at Macy's	$2,200
nn	3	Mickey Mouse and Minnie March to Macy's	$1,600
717	4	Mickey Mouse	$1,600
W-707	5	Dick Tracy The Detective	$1,600
725	6	Big Little Mother Goose HC	$1,500
4063	7	Popeye Thimble Theater Starring... (2nd printing)	$1,200
725	8	Big Little Mother Goose SC	$1,000
721	9	Big Little Paint Book	$1,000
4062	10	Mickey Mouse and the Smugglers	$1,000
725	11	Mickey Mouse, The Story of...	$1,000
4063	12	Popeye Thimble Theater Starring... (1st printing)	$1,000
nn	13	Buck Rogers	$850
nn	14	Mickey Mouse Silly Symphonies	$850
4057	15	Buck Rogers, The Adventures of...	$800
4071	16	Dick Tracy and the Mystery of the Purple Cross	$800
nn	17	Tarzan	$800
4057	18	Dick Tracy, The Adventures of...	$750
4054	19	Little Orphan Annie, The Story of...	$750
770	20	Tarzan Twins, 1934	$600

*Includes only the various sized BLBs; no premiums, giveaways or other divergent forms are included.

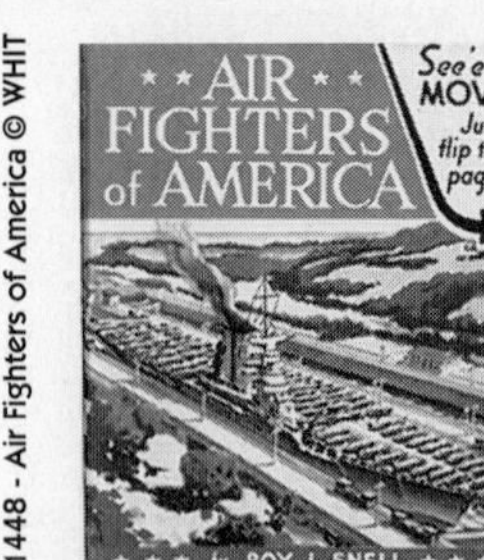

1448 - Air Fighters of America © WHIT

1469 - Bambi © WDC

1119 - Betty Boop in Snow White © WHIT

GD FN VF/NM

1175-0- Abbie an' Slats, 1940, Saalfield, 400 pgs. 10.00 30.00 60.00
1175-0- Abbie an' Slats, 1940, Saalfield, 400 pgs. 10.00 30.00 60.00
1182- Abbie an' Slats-and Becky, 1940, Saalfield, 400 pgs. 10.00 30.00 60.00
1177- Ace Drummond, 1935, Whitman, 432 pgs. 15.00 30.00 60.00
Admiral Byrd (See Paramount Newsreel ...)
nn- Adventures of Charlie McCarthy and Edgar Bergen, The, 1938, Dell, 194 pgs., Fast-Action Story, soft-c 20.00 64.00 128.00
1422- Adventures of Huckleberry Finn, The, 1939, Whitman, 432 pgs., Henry E. Vallely-a 10.00 25.00 50.00
1648- Adventures of Jim Bowie (TV Series), 1958, Whitman, 280 pgs. 5.00 15.00 30.00
1056- Adventures of Krazy Kat and Ignatz Mouse in Koko Land, 1934, Saalfield, 160 pgs., oblong size, hard-c, Herriman-c/a 50.00 200.00 400.00
1306- Adventures of Krazy Kat and Ignatz Mouse in Koko Land, 1934, Saalfield, 164 pgs., oblong size, soft-c, Herriman-c/a 50.00 200.00 400.00
1082- Adventures of Pete the Tramp, The, 1935, Saalfield, hard-c, by C. D. Russell 10.00 35.00 70.00
1312- Adventures of Pete the Tramp, The, 1935, Saalfield, soft-c, by C. D. Russell 10.00 35.00 70.00
1053- Adventures of Tim Tyler, 1934, Saalfield, hard-c, oblong size, by Lyman Young 20.00 70.00 140.00
1303- Adventures of Tim Tyler, 1934, Saalfield, soft-c, oblong size, by Lyman Young 20.00 70.00 140.00
1058- Adventures of Tom Sawyer, The, 1934, Saalfield, 160 pgs., hard-c, Park Sumner-a 10.00 30.00 60.00
1308- Adventures of Tom Sawyer, The, 1934, Saalfield, 160 pgs., soft-c, Park Sumner-a 10.00 30.00 60.00
1448- Air Fighters of America, 1941, Whitman, 432 pgs., flip picture 10.00 30.00 60.00
Alexander Smart, ESQ. (See Top Line Comics)
759- Alice in Wonderland, 1933, Whitman, 160 pgs., hard-c, photo-c, movie scenes 15.00 75.00 150.00
1481- Allen Pike of the Parachute Squad U.S.A., 1941, Whitman, 432 pgs. 10.00 30.00 60.00
763- Alley Oop and Dinny, 1935, Whitman, 384 pgs., V. T. Hamlin-a 15.00 50.00 100.00
1473- Alley Oop and Dinny in the Jungles of Moo, 1938, Whitman, 432 pgs., V. T. Hamlin-a 15.00 50.00 100.00
nn- Alley Oop and the Missing King of Moo, 1938, Whitman, 36 pgs., 2 1/2" x 3 1/2", Penny Book 10.00 30.00 60.00
nn- Alley Oop in the Kingdom of Foo, 1938, Whitman, 68 pgs., 3 1/4" x 3 1/2", Pan-Am premium 15.00 75.00 150.00
nn- "Alley Oop the Invasion of Moo," 1935, Whitman, 260 pgs., Cocomalt premium, soft-c; V. T. Hamlin-a 16.00 55.00 110.00
Andy Burnette (See Walt Disney's...)
Andy Panda (Also see Walter Lantz ...)
531- Andy Panda, 1943, Whitman, 3 3/4x8 3/4", Tall Comic Book, All Pictures Comics 32.00 100.00 200.00
1425- Andy Panda and Tiny Tom, 1944, Whitman, All Pictures Comics 10.00 32.00 65.00
1431- Andy Panda and the Mad Dog Mystery, 1947, Whitman, 288 pgs., by Walter Lantz 10.00 28.00 60.00
1441- Andy Panda in the City of Ice, 1948, Whitman, All Picture Comics, by Walter Lantz 10.00 32.00 65.00
1459- Andy Panda and the Pirate Ghosts, 1949, Whitman, 88 pgs., by Walter Lantz 10.00 28.00 60.00
1485- Andy Panda's Vacation, 1946, Whitman, All Pictures Comics, by Walter Lantz 12.00 32.00 65.00
15- Andy Panda (The Adventures of), 1942, Dell, Fast-Action Story 25.00 80.00 160.00
707-10 - Andy Panda and Presto the Pup, 1949, Whitman 10.00 28.00 60.00
1130- Apple Mary and Dennie Foil the Swindlers, 1936, Whitman, 432 pgs. (Forerunner to Mary Worth) 10.00 30.00 60.00
1403- Apple Mary and Dennie's Lucky Apples, 1939, Whitman, 432 pgs. 10.00 30.00 60.00
2017- (#17)-Aquaman-Scourge of the Sea, 1968, Whitman, 260 pgs., 39 cents, hard-c, color illos 5.00 15.00 30.00
1192- Arizona Kid on the Bandit Trail, The, 1936, Whitman, 432 pgs. 10.00 25.00 50.00
1469- Bambi (Walt Disney's), 1942, Whitman, 432 pgs. 20.00 68.00 135.00
1497 Bambi's Children (Disney), 1943, Whitman, 432 pgs., Disney Studios-a 20.00 68.00 135.00
1138- Bandits at Bay, 1938, Saalfield, 400 pgs. 10.00 25.00 50.00
1459- Barney Baxter in the Air with the Eagle Squadron, 1938, Whitman, 432 pgs. 10.00 30.00 60.00
1083- Barney Google, 1935, Saalfield, hard-c 15.00 50.00 100.00
1313- Barney Google, 1935, Saalfield, soft-c 15.00 50.00 100.00
2031- Batman and Robin in the Cheetah Caper, 1969, Whitman, 258 pgs. 5.00 15.00 30.00
5771-2- Batman and Robin in the Cheetah Caper, 1975?, Whitman, 258 pgs. 2.00 5.00 10.00
nn- Beauty and the Beast, nd (1930s), np (Whitman), 36 pgs., 3" x 3 1/2" Penny Book 4.00 10.00 20.00
760- Believe It or Not!, 1933, Whitman, 160 pgs., by Ripley (c. 1931) 10.00 30.00 60.00
Betty Bear's Lesson (See Wee Little Books)
1119- Betty Boop in Snow White, 1934, Whitman, 240 pgs., hard-c; adapted from Max Fleischer Paramount Talkartoon 42.00 163.00 325.00
1158- Betty Boop in "Miss Gullivers Travels," 1935, Whitman, 288 pgs., hard-c 40.00 150.00 300.00
1432- Big Chief Waboo and the Lost Pioneers, 1942, Whitman, 432 pgs., Elmer Woggon-a 10.00 30.00 60.00
1443- Big Chief Wahoo and the Great Gusto, 1938, Whitman, 432 pgs., Elmer Woggon-a 10.00 30.00 60.00
1483- Big Chief Wahoo and the Magic Lamp, 1940, Whitman, 432 pgs., flip pictures, Woggon-c/a 10.00 30.00 60.00
725- Big Little Mother Goose, The, 1934, Whitman, 580 pgs. (Rare) Hardcover 150.00 750.00 1500.00
725- Big Little Mother Goose, The, 1934, Whitman, 580 pgs. (Rare) Softcover 100.00 500.00 1000.00
1006- Big Little Nickel Book, 1935, Whitman, 144 pgs., Blackie Bear stories, folk tales in primer style 10.00 25.00 50.00
1007- Big Little Nickel Book, 1935, Whitman, 144 pgs., Wee Wee Woman, etc. 10.00 25.00 50.00
1008- Big Little Nickel Book, 1935, Whitman, 144 pgs., Peter Rabbit, etc. 10.00 25.00 50.00
721- Big Little Paint Book, The, 1933, Whitman, 336 pgs., 3 3/4" x 8 1/2", for crayoning (Rare) 140.00 500.00 1000.00
1178- Billy of Bar-Zero, 1940, Saalfield, 400 pgs. 10.00 25.00 50.00
773- Billy the Kid, 1935, Whitman, 432 pgs., Hal Arbo-a 10.00 30.00 60.00
1159- Billy the Kid on Tall Butte, 1939, Saalfield, 400 pgs. 10.00 25.00 50.00
1174- Billy the Kid's Pledge, 1940, Saalfield, 400 pgs. 10.00 25.00 50.00
nn- Billy the Kid, Western Outlaw, 1935, Whitman, 260 pgs., Cocomalt premium, Hal Arbo-a, soft-c 10.00 32.00 65.00
1057- Black Beauty, 1934, Saalfield, hard-c 10.00 25.00 50.00
1307- Black Beauty, 1934, Saalfield, soft-c 10.00 25.00 50.00
1414- Black Silver and His Pirate Crew, 1937, Whitman, 300 pgs. 10.00 28.00 55.00
1447- Blaze Brandon with the Foreign Legion, 1938, Whitman, 432 pgs. 10.00 28.00 55.00
1410- Blondie and Dagwood in Hot Water, 1946, Whitman, 352 pgs., by Chic Young 10.00 30.00 60.00
1415- Blondie and Baby Dumpling, 1937, Whitman, 432 pgs., by Chic Young 10.00 32.00 65.00
1419- Oh, Blondie the Bumsteads Carry On, 1941, Whitman, 432 pgs., flip pictures, by Chic Young 10.00 32.00 65.00
1423- Blondie Who's Boss?, 1942, Whitman, 432 pgs., flip pictures,

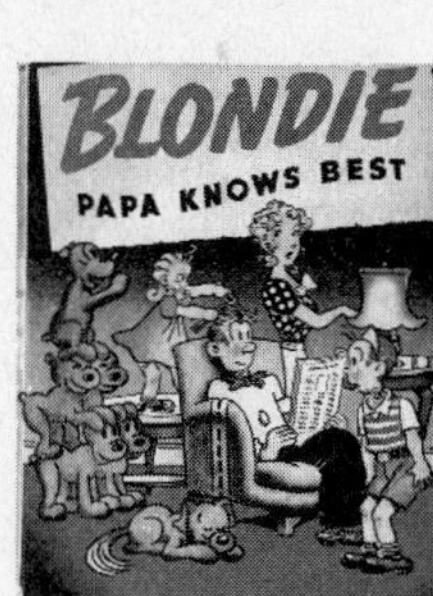

1490 - Blondie Papa Knows Best © WHIT

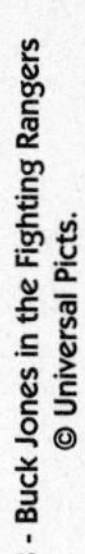

1188 - Buck Jones in the Fighting Rangers © Universal Picts.

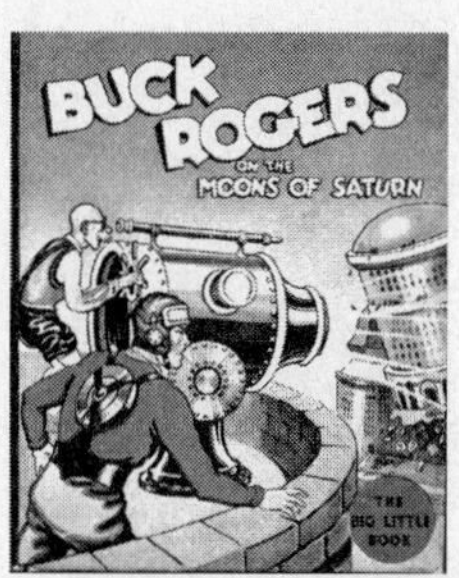

1143 - Buck Rogers on the Moons of Saturn © KING

	GD	FN	VF/NM
by Chic Young	10.00	32.00	65.00
1429- **Blondie with Baby Dumpling and Daisy**, 1939, Whitman, 432 pgs., by Chic Young	10.00	32.00	65.00
1430- **Blondie Count Cookie in Too!**, 1947, Whitman, 288 pgs., by Chic Young	10.00	30.00	60.00
1438- **Blondie and Dagwood Everybody's Happy**, 1948, Whitman, 288 pgs., by Chic Young	10.00	30.00	60.00
1450- **Blondie No Dull Moments**, 1948, Whitman, 288 pgs., by Chic Young	10.00	30.00	60.00
1463- **Blondie Fun For All**, 1949, Whitman, 288 pgs., by Chic Young	10.00	30.00	60.00
1466- **Blondie or Life Among the Bumsteads**, 1944, Whitman, 352 pgs., by Chic Young	10.00	32.00	65.00
1476- **Blondie and Bouncing Baby Dumpling**, 1940, Whitman, 432 pgs., by Chic Young	10.00	32.00	65.00
1487- **Blondie Baby Dumpling and All!**, 1941, Whitman, 432 pgs. flip pictures, by Chic Young	10.00	32.00	65.00
1490- **Blondie Papa Knows Best**, 1945, Whitman, 352 pgs., by Chic Young	10.00	30.00	60.00
1491- **Blondie-Cookie and Daisy's Pups**, 1943, Whitman, 432 pgs.	10.00	32.00	65.00
703-10- **Blondie and Dagwood Some Fun!**, 1949, Whitman, by Chic Young	10.00	25.00	50.00
21- **Blondie and Dagwood**, 194?, Lynn, by Chic Young	15.00	50.00	100.00
1108- **Bobby Benson on the H-Bar-O Ranch**, 1934, Whitman, 300 pgs., based on radio serial	10.00	38.00	75.00
Bobby Thatcher and the Samarang Emerald (See Top-Line Comics)			
1432- **Bob Stone the Young Detective**, 1937, Whitman, 240 pgs., movie scenes	10.00	32.00	65.00
2002- **(#2)-Bonanza-The Bubble Gum Kid**, 1967, Whitman, 260 pgs., 39 cents, hard-c, color illos	5.00	15.00	30.00
1139- **Border Eagle, The**, 1938, Saalfield, 400 pgs.	10.00	25.00	50.00
1153- **Boss of the Chisholm Trail**, 1939, Saalfield, 400 pgs.	10.00	25.00	50.00
1425- **Brad Turner in Transatlantic Flight**, 1939, Whitman, 432 pgs.	10.00	25.00	50.00
1058- **Brave Little Tailor, The** (Disney), 1939, Whitman, 5" x 5 1/2", 68 pgs., hard-c (Mickey Mouse)	12.00	43.00	85.00
1427- **Brenda Starr and the Masked Impostor**, 1943, Whitman, 352 pgs., Dale Messick-a	10.00	38.00	75.00
1426- **Brer Rabbit** (Walt Disney's ...), 1947, Whitman, All Picture Comics, from "Song Of The South" movie	15.00	50.00	100.00
704-10- **Brer Rabbit**, 1949, Whitman	12.00	48.00	95.00
1059- **Brick Bradford in the City Beneath the Sea**, 1934, Saalfield, hard-c, by William Ritt & Clarence Gray	12.00	48.00	95.00
1309- **Brick Bradford in the City Beneath the Sea**, 1934, Saalfield, soft-c, by Ritt & Gray	12.00	48.00	95.00
1468- **Brick Bradford with Brocco the Modern Buccaneer**, 1938, Whitman, 432 pgs., by Wrn. Ritt & Clarence Gray	10.00	32.00	65.00
1133- **Bringing Up Father**, 1936, Whitman, 432 pgs., by George McManus	12.00	43.00	85.00
1100- **Broadway Bill**, 1935, Saalfield, photo-c, 4 1/2" x 5 1/4", movie scenes (Columbia Pictures, horse racing)	10.00	32.00	65.00
1580- **Broadway Bill**, 1935, Saalfield, soft-c, photo-c, movie scenes	10.00	32.00	65.00
1181- **Broncho Bill**, 1940, Saalfield, 400 pgs.	10.00	28.00	55.00
nn- **Broncho Bill in Suicide Canyon** (See Top-Line Comics)			
1417- **Bronc Peeler the Lone Cowboy**, 1937, Whitman, 432 pgs., by Fred Harman, forerunner of Red Ryder	10.00	30.00	60.00
1470- **Buccaneer, The**, 1938, Whitman, 240 pgs., photo-c, movie scenes	10.00	35.00	70.00
1646- **Buccaneers, The** (TV Series), 1958, Whitman, 4 1/2" x 5 1/4", 280 pgs., Russ Manning-a	5.00	15.00	30.00
1104- **Buck Jones in the Fighting Code**, 1934, Whitman, 160 pgs., hard-c, movie scenes	12.00	43.00	85.00
1116- **Buck Jones in Ride 'Em Cowboy** (Universal Presents), 1935, Whitman, 240 pgs., photo-c, movie scenes	12.00	43.00	85.00
1174- **Buck Jones in the Roaring West** (Universal Presents), 1935, Whitman, 240 pgs., movie scenes	12.00	43.00	85.00
1188- **Buck Jones in the Fighting Rangers** (Universal Presents), 1936, Whitman, 240 pgs., photo-c, movie scenes	12.00	43.00	85.00
1404- **Buck Jones and the Two-Gun Kid**, 1937, Whitman, 432 pgs.	10.00	30.00	60.00
1451- **Buck Jones and the Killers of Crooked Butte**, 1940, Whitman, 432 pgs.	10.00	30.00	60.00
1461- **Buck Jones and the Rock Creek Cattle War**, 1938, Whitman, 432 pgs.	10.00	30.00	60.00
1486- **Buck Jones and the Rough Riders in Forbidden Trails**, 1943, Whitman, flip pictures, based on movie; Tim McCoy app.	10.00	38.00	75.00
3- **Buck Jones in the Red Ryder**, 1934, EVW, 160 pgs., movie scenes	16.00	55.00	110.00
15- **Buck Jones in Rocky Rhodes**, 1935, EVW, 160 pgs., photo-c, movie scenes	16.00	55.00	110.00
4069- **Buck Jones and the Night Riders**, 1937, Whitman, 7" x 9", 320 pgs., Big Big Book	80.00	250.00	500.00
nn- **Buck Jones on the Six-Gun Trail**, 1939, Whitman, 36 pgs., 2 1/2" x 3 1/2", Penny Book	10.00	30.00	60.00
nn- **Buck Jones Big Thrill Chewing Gum**, 1934, Whitman, 8 pgs., 2 1/2" x 3 1/2" (6 diff.) each...	15.00	50.00	100.00
742- **Buck Rogers in the 25th Century A.D.**, 1933, Whitman, 320 pgs., Dick Calkins-a	40.00	150.00	300.00
nn- **Buck Rogers in the 25th Century A.D.**, 1933, Whitman, 204 pgs.,Cocomalt premium, Calkins-a	32.00	100.00	200.00
765- **Buck Rogers in the City Below the Sea**, 1934, Whitman, 320 pgs., Dick Calkins-a	30.00	87.00	175.00
765- **Buck Rogers in the City Below the Sea**, 1934, Whitman, 324 pgs., soft-c, Dick Calkins-c/a	40.00	150.00	300.00
1143- **Buck Rogers on the Moons of Saturn**, 1934, Whitman, 320 pgs., Dick Calkins-a	30.00	87.00	175.00
nn- **Buck Rogers on the Moons of Saturn**, 1934, Whitman, 324 pgs., premium w/no ads, soft 3-color-c, Dick Calkins-a	40.00	150.00	300.00
1169- **Buck Rogers and the Depth Men of Jupiter**, 1935, Whitman, 432 pgs., Calkins-a	30.00	87.00	175.00
1178- **Buck Rogers and the Doom Comet**, 1935, Whitman, 432 pgs., Calkins-a	28.00	85.00	170.00
1197- **Buck Rogers and the Planetoid Plot**, 1936, Whitman, 432 pgs., Calkins-a	28.00	85.00	170.00
1409- **Buck Rogers Vs. the Fiend of Space**, 1940, Whitman, 432 pgs., Calkins-a	28.00	85.00	170.00
1437- **Buck Rogers in the War with the Planet Venus**, 1938, Whitman, 432 pgs., Calkins-a	28.00	85.00	170.00
1474- **Buck Rogers and the Overturned World**, 1941, Whitman, 432 pgs., flip pictures, Calkins-a	28.00	85.00	170.00
1490- **Buck Rogers and the Super-Dwarf of Space**, 1943, Whitman, 11 Pictures Comics, Calkins-a	28.00	85.00	170.00
4057- **Buck Rogers, The Adventures of**, 1934, Whitman, 7" x 9 1/2", 320 pgs., Big Big Book, "The Story of Buck Rogers on the Planet Eros," Calkins-c/a	120.00	400.00	800.00
nn- **Buck Rogers**, 1935, Whitman, 4" x 3 1/2", Tarzan Ice Cream cup premium (Rare)	125.00	425.00	850.00
nn- **Buck Rogers in the City of Floating Globes**, 1935, Whitman, 258 pgs., Cocomalt premium, soft-c, Dick Calkins-a	80.00	250.00	500.00
nn- **Buck Rogers Big Thrill Chewing Gum**, 1934, Whitman, 8 pgs., 2 1/2" x 3 " (6 diff.) each...	16.00	55.00	110.00
1135- **Buckskin and Bullets**, 1938, Saalfield, 400 pgs.	10.00	25.00	50.00
Buffalo Bill (See Wild West Adventures of ...)			
nn- **Buffalo Bill**, 1934, World Syndicate, All pictures, by J. Carroll Mansfield	10.00	25.00	50.00
713- **Buffalo Bill and the Pony Express**, 1934, Whitman, 384 pgs., Hal Arbo-a	10.00	30.00	60.00

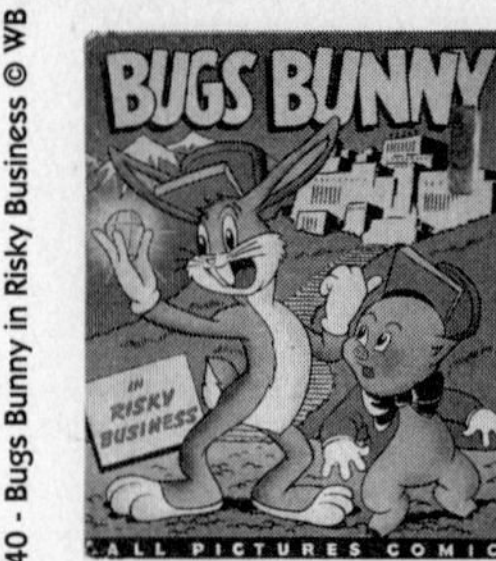

1440 - Bugs Bunny in Risky Business © WB

1452 - Captain Midnight and the Moon Woman © FAW

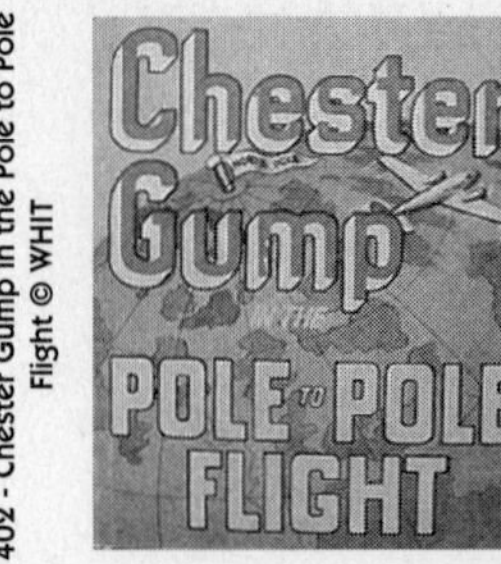

1402 - Chester Gump in the Pole to Pole Flight © WHIT

GD FN VF/NM

1194- Buffalo Bill Plays a Lone Hand, 1936, Whitman, 432 pgs., Hal Arbo-a 10.00 25.00 50.00
530- Bugs Bunny, 1943, Whitman, All Pictures Comics, Tall Comic Book, 3 1/4" x 8 1/4", reprints/Looney Tunes 1 & 5 32.00 100.00 200.00
1403- Bugs Bunny and the Pirate Loot, 1947, Whitman, All Pictures Comics 10.00 30.00 60.00
1435- Bugs Bunny, 1944, Whitman, All Pictures Comics 10.00 35.00 70.00
1440- Bugs Bunny in Risky Business, 1948, Whitman, All Pictures & Comics 10.00 30.00 60.00
1455- Bugs Bunny and Klondike Gold, 1948, Whitman, 288 pgs. 10.00 30.00 60.00
1465- Bugs Bunny The Masked Marvel, 1949, Whitman, 288 pgs. 10.00 30.00 60.00
1496- Bugs Bunny and His Pals, 1945, Whitman, All Pictures Comics; r/Four Color Comics #33 10.00 35.00 70.00
13- Bugs Bunny and the Secret of Storm Island, 1942, Dell,194 pgs., Fast-Action Story 30.00 87.00 175.00
706-10- Bugs Bunny and the Giant Brothers, 1949, Whitman 10.00 25.00 50.00
2007- (#7)-Bugs Bunny-Double Trouble on Diamond Fountain, 1967, Whitman, 260 pgs., 39 cents, hard-c, color illos 5.00 15.00 30.00
2952- Bugs Bunny's Mistake, 1949, Whitman, 3 1/4" x 4", 24 pgs., Tiny Tales, full color (5 cents) 10.00 28.00 55.00
2029-(#29)- Bugs Bunny, Accidental Tourist, 1969, Whitman, 256 pgs., hard-c, color illos. 4.00 10.00 20.00
5757-2- Bugs Bunny in Double Trouble on Diamond Island,1967, (1980-reprints #2007), Whitman, 260 pgs., soft-c, 79 cents, B&W 4.00 10.00 20.00
5772-2- Bugs Bunny the Last Crusader, 1975, Whitman, 79 cents, flip-it book 1.00 3.00 8.00
1169- Bullet Benton, 1939, Saalfield, 400 pgs. 10.00 25.00 50.00
nn- Bulletman and the Return of Mr. Murder, 1941, Fawcett, 196 pgs., Dime Action Book 35.00 130.00 260.00
1142- Bullets Across the Border (A Billy The Kid story), 1938, Saalfield, 400 pgs. 10.00 25.00 50.00
Bunky (See Top-Line Comics)
837- Bunty (Punch and Judy), 1935, Whitman, 28 pgs., Magic-Action with 3 pop-ups 10.00 38.00 75.00
1091- Burn 'Em Up Barnes, 1935, Saalfield, hard-c, movie scenes 10.00 38.00 75.00
1321- Burn 'Em Up Barnes, 1935, Saalfield, soft-c, movie scenes 10.00 38.00 75.00
1415- Buz Sawyer and Bomber 13,1946, Whitman, 352 pgs., Roy Crane-a 10.00 38.00 75.00
1412- Calling W-I-X-Y-Z, Jimmy Kean and the Radio Spies, 1939, Whitman, 300 pgs. 10.00 32.00 65.00
Call of the Wild (See Jack London's...)
1107- Camels are Coming, 1935, Saalfield, movie scenes 10.00 30.00 60.00
1587- Camels are Coming, 1935, Saalfield, movie scene 10.00 30.00 60.00
nn- Captain and the Kids, Boys Will Be Boys, The, 1938, 68 pgs., Pan-Am Oil premium, soft-c 10.00 38.00 75.00
1128- Captain Easy Soldier of Fortune, 1934, Whitman, 432 pgs., Roy Crane-a 12.00 40.00 80.00
nn- Captain Easy Soldier of Fortune, 1934, Whitman, 436 pgs., Premium, no ads, soft 3-color-c, Roy Crane-a 20.00 68.00 135.00
1474- Captain Easy Behind Enemy Lines, 1943, Whitman, 352 pgs., Roy Crane-a 10.00 35.00 70.00
nn- Captain Easy and Wash Tubbs, 1935, 260 pgs., Cocomalt premium, Roy Crane-a 10.00 35.00 70.00
1444- Captain Frank Hawks Air Ace and the League of Twelve, 1938, Whitman, 432 pgs. 10.00 30.00 60.00
nn- Captain Marvel, 1941, Fawcett, 196 pgs., Dime Action Book 45.00 175.00 350.00
1402- Captain Midnight and Sheik Jomak Khan, 1946, Whitman, 352 pgs. 22.00 75.00 150.00
1452- Captain Midnight and the Moon Woman, 1943, Whitman, 352 pgs. 22.00 75.00 150.00
1458- Captain Midnight Vs. The Terror of the Orient, 1942, Whitman, 432 pgs., flip pictures, Hess-a 22.00 75.00 150.00
1488- Captain Midnight and the Secret Squadron, 1941, Whitman, 432 pgs. 22.00 75.00 150.00
Captain Robb of.. (See Dirigible ZR90 ...)
L20- Ceiling Zero, 1936, Lynn, 128 pgs., 7 1/2" x 5", hard-c, James Cagney, Pat O'Brien photos on-c, movie scenes, Warner Bros. Pictures 10.00 30.00 60.00
1093- Chandu the Magician, 1935, Saalfield, 5" x 5 1/4", 160 pgs., hard-c, Bela Lugosi photo-c, movie scenes 12.00 43.00 85.00
1323- Chandu the Magician, 1935, Saalfield, 5" x 5 1/4", 160 pgs., soft-c, Bela Lugosi photo-c 12.00 43.00 85.00
Charlie Chan (See Inspector ...)
1459- Charlie Chan Solves a New Mystery (See Inspector..), 1940, Whitman, 432 pgs., Alfred Andriola-a 12.00 40.00 80.00
1478- Charlie Chan of the Honolulu Police, Inspector, 1939, Whitman, 432 pgs., Andriola-a 12.00 40.00 80.00
Charlie McCarthy (See Story Of ...)
734- Chester Gump at Silver Creek Ranch, 1933, Whitman, 320 pgs., Sidney Smith-a 12.00 40.00 80.00
nn- Chester Gump at Silver Creek Ranch, 1933, Whitman, 204 pgs., Cocomalt premium, soft-c, Sidney Smith-a 12.00 45.00 90.00
nn- Chester Gump at Silver Creek Ranch, 1933, Whitman, 52 pgs., 4" x 5 1/2", premium-no ads, soft-c, Sidney Smith-a 20.00 65.00 130.00
766- Chester Gump Finds the Hidden Treasure, 1934, Whitman, 320 pgs., Sidney Smith-a 12.00 40.00 80.00
nn- Chester Gump Finds the Hidden Treasure, 1934, Whitman, 52 pgs., 3 1/2" x 5 3/4", premium-no ads, soft-c, Sidney Smith-a 20.00 65.00 130.00
nn- Chester Gump Finds the Hidden Treasure, 1934, Whitman, 52 pgs., 4" x 5 1/2", premium-no ads, Sidney Smith-a 20.00 65.00 130.00
1146- Chester Gump in the City Of Gold, 1935, Whitman, 432 pgs., Sidney Smith-a 12.00 40.00 80.00
nn- Chester Gump in the City Of Gold, 1935, Whitman, 436 pgs., premium-no ads, 3-color, soft-c, Sidney Smith-a 25.00 80.00 160.00
1402- Chester Gump in the Pole to Pole Flight, 1937, Whitman, 432 pgs. 10.00 35.00 70.00
5- Chester Gump and His Friends, 1934, Whitman, 132 pgs., 3 1/2" x 3 1/2", soft-c, Tarzan Ice Cream cup lid premium 22.00 75.00 150.00
nn- Chester Gump at the North Pole, 1938, Whitman, 68 pgs. soft-c, 3 3/4" x 3 1/2", Pan-Am giveaway 22.00 75.00 150.00
nn- Chicken Greedy, nd(1930s), np (Whitman), 36 pgs., 3" x 2 1/2", Penny Book 4.00 10.00 20.00
nn- Chicken Licken, nd (l 930s), np (Whitman), 36 pgs., 3" x 2 1/2", Penny Book 4.00 10.00 20.00
1101- Chief of the Rangers, 1935, Saalfield, hard-c, Tom Mix photo-c, movie scenes from "The Miracle Rider" 16.00 55.00 110.00
1581- Chief of the Rangers, 1935, Saalfield, soft-c, Tom Mix photo-c, movie scenes 16.00 55.00 110.00
Child's Garden of Verses (See Wee Little Books)
L14- Chip Collins'Adventures on Bat Island, 1935, Lynn, 192 pgs. 10.00 35.00 70.00
2025- Chitty Chitty Bang Bang, 1968, Whitman, movie photos 4.00 12.00 25.00
Chubby Little Books, 1935, Whitman, 3" x 2 1/2", 200 pgs.
W803- Golden Hours Story Book, The 5.00 15.00 30.00
W803- Story Hours Story Book, The 5.00 15.00 30.00
W804- Gay Book of Little Stories, The 5.00 15.00 30.00
W804- Glad Book of Little Stories, The 5.00 15.00 30.00
W804- Joy Book of Little Stories, The 5.00 15.00 30.00
W804- Sunny Book of Little Stories, The 5.00 15.00 30.00

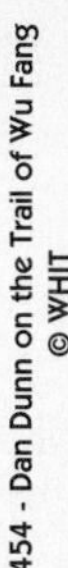
1410 - Clyde Beatty Daredevil Lion and Tiger Tamer © WHIT

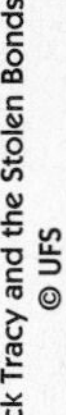
1454 - Dan Dunn on the Trail of Wu Fang © WHIT

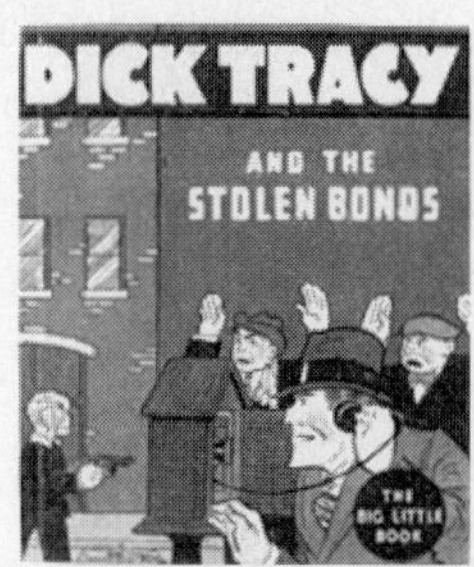

1105 - Dick Tracy and the Stolen Bonds © UFS

	GD	FN	VF/NM
1453- **Chuck Malloy Railroad Detective on the Streamliner**, 1938, Whitman, 300 pgs.	10.00	25.00	50.00
Cinderella (See Walt Disney's...)			
Clyde Beatty (See The Steel Arena)			
1410- **Clyde Beatty Daredevil Lion and Tiger Tamer**, 1939, Whitman, 300 pgs.	10.00	35.00	70.00
1480- **Coach Bernie Bierman's Brick Barton and the Winning Eleven**, 1938, 300 pgs.	10.00	25.00	50.00
1446- **Convoy Patrol** (A Thrilling U.S. Navy Story), 1942, Whitman, 432 pgs., flip pictures	10.00	25.00	50.00
1127- **Corley of the Wilderness Trail**, 1937, Saalfield, hard-c	10.00	27.00	52.00
1607- **Corley of the Wilderness Trail**, 1937, Saalfield, soft-c	10.00	27.00	52.00
1- **Count of Monte Cristo**, 1934, EVW, 160 pgs., (Five Star Library), movie scenes, hard-c	15.00	50.00	100.00
1457- **Cowboy Lingo Boys' Book of Western Facts**, 1938, Whitman, 300 pgs., Fred Harman-a	10.00	27.00	52.00
1171- **Cowboy Malloy**, 1940, Saalfield, 400 pgs.	10.00	25.00	50.00
1106- **Cowboy Millionaire**, 1935, Saalfield, movie scenes with George O'Brien, photo-c, hard-c	10.00	38.00	75.00
1586- **Cowboy Millionaire**, 1935, Saalfield, movie scenes with George O'Brien, photo-c, soft-c	10.00	38.00	75.00
724- **Cowboy Stories**, 1933, Whitman, 300 pgs., Hal Arbo-a	10.00	32.00	65.00
nn- **Cowboy Stories**, 1933, Whitman, 52 pgs., soft-c, premium-no ads, 4" x 5 1/2" Hal Arbo-a	10.00	38.00	75.00
1161- **Crimson Cloak, The**, 1939, Saalfield, 400 pgs.	10.00	25.00	50.00
L19- **Curley Harper at Lakespur**, 1935, Lynn, 192 pgs.	10.00	27.00	52.00
5785-2- **Daffy Duck in Twice the Trouble**, 1980, Whitman, 260 pgs., 79 cents soft-c	1.00	3.00	6.00
2018-(#18)-**Daktari-Night of Terror**, 1968, Whitman, 260 pgs., 39 cents, hard-c, color illos	4.00	12.00	25.00
1010- **Dan Dunn And The Gangsters' Frame-Up**, 1937, Whitman, 7 1/4" x 5 1/2", 64 pgs., Nickel Book	36.00	144.00	250.00
1116- **Dan Dunn "Crime Never Pays,"** 1934, Whitman, 320 pgs., by Norman Marsh	10.00	35.00	70.00
1125- **Dan Dunn on the Trail of the Counterfeiters**, 1936, Whitman, 432 pgs., by Norman Marsh	10.00	35.00	70.00
1171- **Dan Dunn and the Crime Master**, 1937, Whitman, 432 pgs., by Norman Marsh	10.00	35.00	70.00
1417- **Dan Dunn and the Underworld Gorillas,** 1941, Whitman, All Pictures Comics, flip pictures, by Norman Marsh	10.00	35.00	70.00
1454- **Dan Dunn on the Trail of Wu Fang**, 1938, Whitman, 432 pgs., by Norman Marsh	12.00	43.00	85.00
1481- **Dan Dunn and the Border Smugglers**, 1938, Whitman, 432 pgs., by Norman Marsh	10.00	35.00	70.00
1492- **Dan Dunn and the Dope Ring**, 1940, Whitman, 432 pgs., by Norman Marsh	10.00	35.00	70.00
nn- **Dan Dunn and the Bank Hold-Up**, 1938, Whitman, 36 pgs., 2 1/2" x 3 1/2", Penny Book	10.00	27.00	52.00
nn- **Dan Dunn and the Zeppelin Of Doom**, 1938, Dell, 196 pgs., Fast-Action Story, soft-c	30.00	87.00	175.00
nn- **Dan Dunn Meets Chang Loo**, 1938, Whitman, 66 pgs., Pan-Am premium, by Norman Marsh	22.00	75.00	150.00
nn- **Dan Dunn Plays a Lone Hand**, 1938, Whitman, 36 pgs., 2 1/2" x 3 1/2", Penny Book	10.00	27.00	52.00
3 3/4" x 3 1/2", Buddy book	32.00	100.00	200.00
9- **Dan Dunn's Mysterious Ruse**, 1936, Whitman, 132 pgs., soft-c, 3 1/2" x 3 1/2", Tarzan Ice Cream cup lid premium	32.00	100.00	200.00
1177- **Danger Trail North**, 1940, Saalfield, 400 pgs.	10.00	25.00	50.00
1151- **Danger Trails in Africa**, 1935, Whitman, 432 pgs.	10.00	27.00	52.00
nn- **Daniel Boone**, 1934, World Syndicate, High Lights of History Series, hard-c, All in Pictures	10.00	25.00	50.00
1160- **Dan of the Lazy L**, 1939, Saalfield, 400 pgs.	10.00	25.00	50.00
1148- **David Copperfield**, 1934, Whitman, hard-c, 160 pgs., photo-c, movie scenes (W. C. Fields)	15.00	50.00	100.00
nn- **David Copperfield**, 1934, Whitman, soft-c, 164 pgs., movie scenes	15.00	50.00	100.00
1151- **Death by Short Wave**, 1938, Saalfield	10.00	30.00	60.00
1156- **Denny the Ace Detective**, 1938, Saalfield, 400 pgs.	10.00	25.00	50.00
1431- **Desert Eagle and the Hidden Fortress, The**, 1941, Whitman, 432 pgs., flip pictures	10.00	27.00	52.00
1458- **Desert Eagle Rides Again, The**, 1939, Whitman, 300 pgs.	10.00	27.00	52.00
1136- **Desert Justice**, 1938, Saalfield, 400 pgs.	10.00	25.00	50.00
1484- **Detective Higgins of the Racket Squad**, 1938, Whitman, 432 pgs.	10.00	27.00	52.00
1124- **Dickie Moore in the Little Red School House**, 1936, Whitman, 240 pgs., photo-c, movie scenes (Chesterfield Motion Picts. Corp)	10.00	35.00	70.00
W-707- **Dick Tracy the Detective, The Adventures of**, 1933, Whitman, 320 pgs. (The 1st Big Little Book), by Chester Gould (Scarce)	266.00	800.00	1600.00
nn- **Dick Tracy Detective, The Adventures of**, 1933, Whitman, 52 pgs., 4" x 5 1/2", premium-no ads, soft-c, by Chester Gould	80.00	250.00	500.00
710- **Dick Tracy and Dick Tracy, Jr.** (The Advs. of ...), 1933, Whitman, 320 pgs., by Chester Gould	52.00	212.00	425.00
nn- **Dick Tracy and Dick Tracy, Jr.** (The Advs. of ...), 1933, Whitman, 52 pgs., premium-no ads, soft-c, 4" x 5 1/2", by Chester Gould	52.00	212.00	425.00
nn- **Dick Tracy the Detective and Dick Tracy, Jr.**, 1933, Whitman, 52 pgs., premium-no ads, 3 1/2"x 5 1/4", soft-c, by Chester Gould	52.00	212.00	425.00
723- **Dick Tracy Out West**, 1933, Whitman, 300 pgs., by Chester Gould	33.00	125.00	250.00
749- **Dick Tracy from Colorado to Nova Scotia**, 1933, Whitman, 320 pgs., by Chester Gould	32.00	105.00	210.00
nn- **Dick Tracy from Colorado to Nova Scotia**, 1933, Whitman, 204 pgs., premium-no ads, soft-c, by Chester Gould	33.00	125.00	250.00
1105- **Dick Tracy and the Stolen Bonds**, 1934, Whitman, 320 pgs., by Chester Gould	20.00	68.00	135.00
1112- **Dick Tracy and the Racketeer Gang**, 1936, Whitman, 432 pgs., by Chester Gould	16.00	55.00	110.00
1137- **Dick Tracy Solves the Penfield Mystery**, 1934, Whitman, 320 pgs., by Chester Gould	20.00	70.00	140.00
nn- **Dick Tracy Solves the Penfield Mystery**, 1934, Whitman, 324 pgs., premium-no ads, 3-color, soft-c, by Chester Gould	33.00	125.00	250.00
1163- **Dick Tracy and the Boris Arson Gang**, 1935, Whitman, 432 pgs., by Chester Gould	16.00	55.00	110.00
1170- **Dick Tracy on the Trail of Larceny Lu**, 1935, Whitman, 432 pgs., by Chester Gould	16.00	55.00	110.00
1185- **Dick Tracy in Chains of Crime**, 1936, Whitman, 432 pgs., by Chester Gould	16.00	55.00	110.00
1412- **Dick Tracy and Yogee Yamma**, 1946, Whitman, 352 pgs., by Chester Gould	15.00	52.00	105.00
1420- **Dick Tracy and the Hotel Murders**, 1937, Whitman, 432 pgs., by Chester Gould	16.00	55.00	110.00
1434- **Dick Tracy and the Phantom Ship**, 1940, Whitman, 432 pgs., by Chester Gould	16.00	55.00	110.00
1436- **Dick Tracy and the Mad Killer**, 1947, Whitman, 288 pgs., by Chester Gould	12.00	45.00	90.00
1439- **Dick Tracy and His G-Men**, 1941, Whitman, 432 pgs., flip pictures, by Chester Gould	16.00	55.00	110.00
1445- **Dick Tracy and the Bicycle Gang**, 1948, Whitman, 288 pgs., by Chester Gould	12.00	45.00	90.00
1446- **Detective Dick Tracy and the Spider Gang**, 1937, Whitman, 240 pgs., movie scenes from "Adventures of Dick Tracy" (Republic serial)			

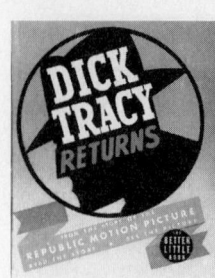

1495 - Dick Tracy Returns © UFS

1486 - Donald Duck Up in the Air © WDC

1107 - Don Winslow, U.S.N. © WHIT

	GD	FN	VF/NM
	22.00	75.00	150.00
1449- Dick Tracy Special F.B.I. Operative, 1943, Whitman, 432 pgs. by Chester Gould	16.00	55.00	110.00
1454- Dick Tracy on the High Seas, 1939, Whitman, 432 pgs., by Chester Gould	16.00	55.00	110.00
1460- Dick Tracy and the Tiger Lily Gang, 1949, Whitman, 288 pgs., by Chester Gould	12.00	45.00	90.00
1478- Dick Tracy on Voodoo Island, 1944, Whitman, 352 pgs., by Chester Gould	12.00	45.00	90.00
1479- Detective Dick Tracy Vs. Crooks in Disguise, 1939, Whitman, 432 pgs., flip pictures, by Chester Gould	16.00	55.00	110.00
1482- Dick Tracy and the Wreath Kidnapping Case, 1945, Whitman, 352 pgs.	12.00	45.00	90.00
1488- Dick Tracy the Super-Detective, 1939, Whitman, 432 pgs., by Chester Gould	16.00	55.00	110.00
1491- Dick Tracy the Man with No Face, 1938, Whitman, 432 pgs.	16.00	55.00	110.00
1495- Dick Tracy Returns, 1939, Whitman, 432 pgs., based on Republic Motion Picture serial, Chester Gould-a	16.00	55.00	110.00
2001- (#1)-Dick Tracy-Encounters Facey, 1967, Whitman, 260 pgs., 39 cents, hard-c, color illos	5.00	15.00	30.00
4055- Dick Tracy, The Adventures of, 1934, Whitman, 7" x 9 1/2", 320 pgs., Big Big Book, by Chester Gould	125.00	375.00	750.00
4071- Dick Tracy and the Mystery of the Purple Cross, 1938, 7" x 9 1/2", 320 pgs., Big Big Book, by Chester Gould (Scarce)	150.00	400.00	800.00
nn- Dick Tracy and the Invisible Man, 1939, Whitman, 3 1/4" x 3 3/4", 132 pgs., stapled, soft-c, Quaker Oats premium; NBC radio play script, Chester Gould-a	32.00	105.00	210.00
Vol. 2- Dick Tracy's Ghost Ship, 1939, Whitman, 3 1/2" x 3 1/2", 132 pgs., soft-c, stapled, Quaker Oats premium; NBC radio play script episode from actual radio show; Gould-a	32.00	105.00	210.00
3- Dick Tracy Meets a New Gang, 1934, Whitman, 3" x 3 1/2", 132 pgs., soft-c, Tarzan Ice Cream cup lid premium	46.00	190.00	380.00
11- Dick Tracy in Smashing the Famon Racket, 1938, Whitman, 3 3/4" x 3 1/2", Buddy Book-ice cream premium, by Chester Gould	46.00	190.00	380.00
nn- Dick Tracy Gets His Man, 1938, Whitman, 36 pgs., 2 1/2" x 3 1/2", Penny Book	10.00	32.00	65.00
nn- Dick Tracy the Detective, 1938, Whitman, 36 pgs., 2 1/2" x 3 1/2", Penny Book	10.00	32.00	65.00
9- Dick Tracy and the Frozen Bullet Murders, 1941, Dell, 196 pgs., Fast-Action Story, soft-c, by Gould	33.00	112.00	225.00
6833- Dick Tracy Detective and Federal Agent, 1936, Dell, 244 pgs., Cartoon Story Books, hard-c, by Gould	33.00	125.00	250.00
nn- Dick Tracy Detective and Federal Agent, 1936, Dell, 244 pgs., Fast-Action Story, soft-c, by Gould	33.00	120.00	240.00
nn- Dick Tracy and the Blackmailers, 1939, Dell, 196 pgs., Fast-Action Story, soft-c, by Gould	33.00	120.00	240.00
nn- Dick Tracy and the Chain of Evidence, Detective, 1938, Whitman, 196 pgs., Fast-Action Story, soft-c, by Chester Gould	33.00	120.00	240.00
nn- Dick Tracy and the Crook Without a Face, 1938, Whitman, 68 pgs., 3 1/4" x 3 1/2", Pan-Am giveaway, Gould-c/a	34.00	130.00	260.00
nn- Dick Tracy and the Maroon Mask Gang, 1938, Dell, 196 pgs., Fast-Action Story, soft-c, by Gould	33.00	120.00	240.00
nn- Dick Tracy Cross-Country Race, 1934, Whitman, 8 pgs., 2 1/2" x 3", Big Thrill chewing gum premium (6 diff.)	12.00	43.00	85.00
nn- Dick Whittington and his Cat, nd(1930s), np(Whitman), 36 pgs., Penny Book	4.00	12.00	25.00
Dinglehoofer und His Dog Adolph (See Top-Line Comics)			
Dinky (See Jackie Cooper in ...)			
1464- Dirigible ZR90 and the Disappearing Zeppelin (Captain Robb of ...), 1941, Whitman, 300 pgs., Al Lewin-a	15.00	50.00	100.00
1167- Dixie Dugan Among the Cowboys, 1939, Saalfield, 400 pgs.	10.00	27.00	52.00
1188- Dixie Dugan and Cuddles, 1940, Saalfield, 400 pgs., by Striebel & McEvoy	10.00	27.00	52.00
Doctor Doom (See Foreign Spies... & International Spy...)			
Dog of Flanders, A (See Frankie Thomas in ...)			
1114- Dog Stars of Hollywood, 1936, Saalfield, photo-c, photo-illos	12.00	40.00	80.00
1594- Dog Stars of Hollywood, 1936, Saalfield, photo-c, soft-c, photo-illos	12.00	40.00	80.00
Donald Duck (See Silly Symphony... & Walt Disney's ...)			
1404- Donald Duck (Says Such a Life) (Disney), 1939, Whitman, 432 pgs., Taliaferro-a	22.00	75.00	150.00
1411- Donald Duck and Ghost Morgan's Treasure (Disney), 1946, Whitman, All Pictures Comics, Barks-a; reprints Four Color #9	30.00	87.00	175.00
1422- Donald Duck Sees Stars (Disney), 1941, Whitman, 432 pgs., flip pictures, Taliaferro-a	22.00	75.00	150.00
1424- Donald Duck Says Such Luck (Disney), 1941, Whitman, 432 pgs., flip pictures, Taliaferro-a	22.00	75.00	150.00
1430- Donald Duck Headed For Trouble (Disney), 1942, Whitman, 432 pgs., flip pictures, Taliaferro-a	22.00	75.00	150.00
1432- Donald Duck and the Green Serpent (Disney), 1947, Whitman, All Pictures Comics, Barks-a; reprints Four Color #108	25.00	80.00	160.00
1434- Donald Duck Forgets To Duck (Disney), 1939, Whitman, 432 pgs., Taliaferro-a	22.00	75.00	150.00
1438- Donald Duck Off the Beam (Disney), 1943, Whitman, 352 pgs., flip pictures, Taliaferro-a	22.00	75.00	150.00
1438- Donald Duck Off the Beam (Disney), 1943, Whitman, 432 pgs., flip pictures, Taliaferro-a	22.00	75.00	150.00
1449- Donald Duck Lays Down the Law, 1948, Whitman, 288 pgs.	22.00	75.00	150.00
1457- Donald Duck in Volcano Valley (Disney), 1949, Whitman, 288 pgs., Barks-a	22.00	75.00	150.00
1462- Donald Duck Gets Fed Up (Disney), 1940, Whitman, 432 pgs.,Taliaferro-a	22.00	75.00	150.00
1478- Donald Duck-Hunting For Trouble (Disney), 1938, Whitman, 432 pgs., Taliaferro-a	22.00	75.00	150.00
1484- Donald Duck is Here Again!, 1944, Whitman, All Pictures Comics, Taliaferro-a	22.00	75.00	150.00
1486- Donald Duck Up in the Air (Disney), 1945, Whitman, 352 pgs., Barks-a	26.00	82.00	165.00
705-10- Donald Duck and the Mystery of the Double X, (Disney), 1949, Whitman, Barks-a	10.00	38.00	75.00
2023-(#23)- Donald Duck, Luck of the Ducks, 1969, Whitman, 256 pgs., hard-c, color illos.	4.00	12.00	25.00
2009-(#9)-Donald Duck-The Fabulous Diamond Fountain, (Walt Disney), 1967, Whitman, 260 pgs., 39 cents, hard-c, color illos	5.00	15.00	30.00
nn- Donald Duck and the Ducklings, 1938, Whitman, 194 pgs., Fast-Action Story, soft-c, Taliaferro-a	40.00	150.00	300.00
nn- Donald Duck Out of Luck (Disney), 1940, Dell, 196 pgs., Fast-Action Story, has Four Color #4 on back-c, Taliaferro-a	40.00	150.00	300.00
8- Donald Duck Takes It on the Chin (Disney), 1941, Dell, 196 pgs., Fast-Action Story, soft-c, Taliaferro-a	40.00	150.00	300.00
5760-2- Donald Duck in Volcano Valley (Disney), 1973, Whitman, 79 cents, flip-it book	3.00	8.00	15.00
L13- Donnie and the Pirates, 1935, Lynn, 192 pgs.	10.00	32.00	65.00
1438- Don O'Dare Finds War, 1940, Whitman, 432 pgs.	10.00	25.00	50.00
1107- Don Winslow, U.S.N., 1935, Whitman, 432 pgs.	12.00	43.00	85.00
nn- Don Winslow, U.S.N., 1935, Whitman, 436 pgs., premium-no ads, 3-color, soft-c	22.00	75.00	150.00
1408- Don Winslow and the Giant Girl Spy, 1946, Whitman, 352 pgs.	10.00	32.00	65.00
1418- Don Winslow Navy Intelligence Ace, 1942, Whitman, 432 pgs., flip pictures	12.00	43.00	85.00
1419- Don Winslow of the Navy Vs. the Scorpion Gang,			

1406 - Ellery Queen the Master Detective © WHIT

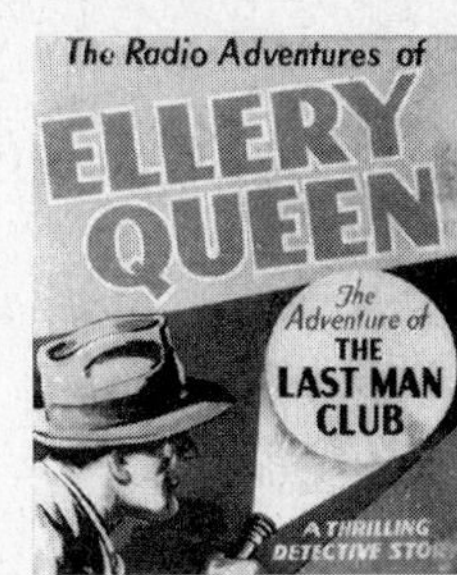

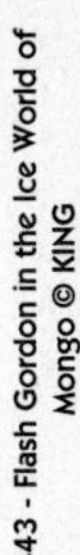
1443 - Flash Gordon in the Ice World of Mongo © KING

1108 - Flying the Sky Clipper with Winsie Atkins © WHIT

GD FN VF/NM

1938, Whitman, 432 pgs. 12.00 43.00 85.00

1453- Don Winslow of the Navy and the Secret Enemy Base, 1943, Whitman, 352 pgs. 12.00 43.00 85.00

1489- Don Winslow of the Navy and the Great War Plot, Whitman, 432 pgs. 12.00 43.00 85.00

nn- Don Winslow U.S. Navy and the Missing Admiral, 1938, Whitman, 36 pgs., 2 1/2" x 3 1/2", Penny Book 10.00 27.00 52.00

1137- Doomed To Die, 1938, Saalfield, 400 pgs. 10.00 25.00 50.00

1140- Down Cartridge Creek, 1938, Saalfield, 400 pgs. 10.00 25.00 50.00

1416- Draftie of the U.S. Army, 1943, Whitman, All Pictures Comics 10.00 27.00 52.00

1100B- Dreams (Your dreams & what they mean), 1938, Whitman, 36 pgs., 2 1/2" x 3 1/2", Penny Book 4.00 10.00 20.00

L24- Dumb Dora and Bing Brown, 1936, Lynn 10.00 38.00 75.00

1400- Dumbo, of the Circus - Only His Ears Grew! (Disney), 1941, Whitman, 432 pgs., based on Disney movie 22.00 75.00 150.00

10- Dumbo the Flying Elephant (Disney), 1944, Dell, 194 pgs., Fast-Action Story, soft-c 36.00 137.00 275.00

nn- East O' the Sun and West O' the Moon, nd (1930s), np (Whitman), 36 pgs., 3" x 2 1/2", Penny Book 4.00 10.00 20.00

774- Eddie Cantor in an Hour with You, 1934, Whitman, 154 pgs., 4 1/4" x 5 1/4", photo-c, movie scenes 12.00 43.00 85.00

nn- Eddie Cantor in Laughland, 1934, Goldsmith, 132 pgs., soft-c, photo-c, Vallely-a 12.00 43.00 85.00

1106- Ella Cinders and the Mysterious House, 1934, Whitman, 432 pgs. 10.00 36.00 72.00

nn- Ella Cinders and the Mysterious House, 1934, Whitman, 52 pgs., premium-no ads, soft-c, 3 1/2" x 5 3/4" 18.00 60.00 120.00

nn- Ella Cinders, 1935, Whitman, 148 pgs., 3 1/4" x 4", Tarzan Ice Cream cup lid premium 30.00 92.00 185.00

nn- Ella Cinders Plays Duchess, 1938, Whitman, 68 pgs., 3 3/4" x 3 1/2", Pan-Am Oil premium 12.00 43.00 85.00

nn- Ella Cinders Solves a Mystery, 1938, Whitman, 68 pgs., Pan-Am Oil premium, soft-c 12.00 43.00 85.00

11- Ella Cinders' Exciting Experience, 1934, Whitman, 3 1/2" x 3 1/2", 132 pgs., Tarzan Ice Cream cup lid giveaway 30.00 92.00 185.00

1406- Ellery Queen the Adventure of the Last Man Club, 1940, Whitman, 432 pgs. 10.00 35.00 70.00

1472- Ellery Queen the Master Detective, 1942, Whitman, 432 pgs., flip pictures 10.00 35.00 70.00

1081- Elmer and his Dog Spot, 1935, Saalfield, hard-c 10.00 25.00 50.00

1311- Elmer and his Dog Spot, 1935, Saalfield, soft-c 10.00 25.00 50.00

722- Erik Noble and the Forty-Niners, 1934, Whitman, 384 pgs. 10.00 27.00 52.00

nn- Erik Noble and the Forty-Niners, 1934, Whitman, 386 pgs., 3-color, soft-c 12.00 40.00 80.00

2019-(#19)- Fantastic Four in the House of Horrors, 1968, Whitman, 256 pgs., hard-c, color illos. 4.00 12.00 24.00

1058- Farmyard Symphony, The (Disney), 1939, 5" X 5 1/2", 68 pgs., hard-c 10.00 36.00 72.00

1129- Felix the Cat, 1936, Whitman, 432 pgs., Messmer-a 25.00 80.00 160.00

1439- Felix the Cat, 1943, Whitman, All Pictures Comics, Messmer-a 20.00 68.00 135.00

1465- Felix the Cat, 1945, Whitman, All Pictures Comics, Messmer-a 18.00 60.00 120.00

nn- Felix (Flip book), 1967, World Retrospective of Animation Cinema, 188 pgs., 2 1/2" x 4" by Otto Messmer 4.00 12.00 25.00

nn- Fighting Cowboy of Nugget Gulch, The, 1939, Whitman, 2 1/2" x 3 1/2", Penny Book 8.00 20.00 40.00

1401- Fighting Heroes Battle for Freedom, 1943, Whitman, All Pictures Comics, from "Heroes of Democracy" strip, by Stookie Allen 10.00 25.00 50.00

6- Fighting President, The, 1934, EVW (Five Star Library), 160 pgs., photo-c, photo ill., F. D. Roosevelt 10.00 32.00 65.00

nn- Fire Chief Ed Wynn and "His Old Fire Horse," 1934, Goldsmith, 132 pgs., H. Vallely-a, photo, soft-c 10.00 32.00 65.00

1464- Flame Boy and the Indians' Secret, 1938, Whitman, 300 pgs., Sekakuku-a (Hopi Indian) 10.00 25.00 50.00

22- Flaming Guns, 1935, EVW, with Tom Mix, movie scenes 15.00 50.00 100.00

1110- Flash Gordon on the Planet Mongo, 1934, Whitman, 320 pgs., by Alex Raymond 32.00 105.00 210.00

1166- Flash Gordon and the Monsters of Mongo, 1935, Whitman, 432 pgs., by Alex Raymond 32.00 100.00 200.00

nn- Flash Gordon and the Monsters of Mongo, 1935, Whitman, 436 pgs., premium-no ads, 3-color, soft-c, by Alex Raymond 40.00 150.00 300.00

1171- Flash Gordon and the Tournaments of Mongo, 1935, Whitman, 432 pgs., by Alex Raymond 32.00 100.00 200.00

1190- Flash Gordon and the Witch Queen of Mongo, 1936, Whitman, 432 pgs., by Alex Raymond 32.00 100.00 200.00

1407- Flash Gordon in the Water World of Mongo, 1937, Whitman, 432 pgs., by Alex Raymond 30.00 90.00 180.00

1423- Flash Gordon and the Perils of Mongo, 1940, Whitman, 432 pgs., by Alex Raymond 25.00 80.00 160.00

1424- Flash Gordon in the Jungles of Mongo, 1947, Whitman, 352 pgs., by Alex Raymond 16.00 55.00 110.00

1443- Flash Gordon in the Ice World of Mongo, 1942, Whitman, 432 pgs., flip pictures, by Alex Raymond 25.00 80.00 160.00

1447- Flash Gordon and the Fiery Desert of Mongo, 1948, Whitman, 288 pgs., Raymond-a 16.00 55.00 110.00

1469- Flash Gordon and the Power Men of Mongo, 1943, Whitman, 352 pgs., by Alex Raymond 25.00 80.00 160.00

1479- Flash Gordon and the Red Sword Invaders, 1945, Whitman, 352 pgs., by Alex Raymond 22.00 75.00 150.00

1484- Flash Gordon and the Tyrant of Mongo, 1941, Whitman, 432 pgs., flip pictures, by Alex Raymond 25.00 80.00 160.00

1492- Flash Gordon in the Forest Kingdom of Mongo, 1938, Whitman, 432 pgs., by Alex Raymond 32.00 100.00 200.00

12- Flash Gordon and the Ape Men of Mor, 1942, Dell, 196 pgs., Fast-Action Story, by Alex Raymond 40.00 150.00 300.00

6833- Flash Gordon Vs. the Emperor of Mongo, 1936, Dell, 244 pgs., Cartoon Story Books, hard-c, Alex Raymond-c/a 45.00 180.00 360.00

nn- Flash Gordon Vs. the Emperor of Mongo, 1936, Dell, 244 pgs., Fast-Action Story, soft-c, Alex Raymond-c/a 40.00 150.00 300.00

1467- Flint Roper and the Six-Gun Showdown, 1941, Whitman, 300 pgs. 10.00 25.00 50.00

2014-(#14)- Flintstones-The Case of the Many Missing Things, 1968, Whitman, 260 pgs., 39 cents, hard-c, color illos 4.00 12.00 25.00

2003-(#3)- Flipper-Killer Whale Trouble, 1967, Whitman, 260 pgs., hard-c, 39 cents, color illos 4.00 10.00 20.00

2032-(#32)- Flipper, Deep-Sea Photographer, 1969, Whitman, 256 pgs., hard-c, color illos. 4.00 10.00 20.00

1108- Flying the Sky Clipper with Winsie Atkins, 1936, Whitman, 432 pgs. 10.00 25.00 50.00

1460- Foreign Spies Doctor Doom and the Ghost Submarine, 1939, Whitman, 432 pgs., Al McWilliams-a 10.00 31.00 62.00

1100B- Fortune Teller, 1938, Whitman, 36 pgs., 2 1/2" x 3 1/2", Penny Book 4.00 12.00 25.00

1175- Frank Buck Presents Ted Towers Animal Master, 1935, Whitman, 432 pgs. 10.00 27.00 52.00

2015-(#15)-Frankenstein, Jr. - The Menace of the Heartless Monster, 1968, Whitman, 260 pgs., 39 cents, hard-c, color illos. 4.00 12.00 25.00

16- Frankie Thomas in A Dog of Flanders, 1935, EVW, movie scenes 12.00 43.00 85.00

1121- Frank Merriwell at Yale, 1935, 432 pgs. 10.00 27.00 52.00

Freckles and His Friends in the North Woods (See Top-Line Comics)

nn- Freckles and His Friends Stage a Play, 1938, Whitman, 36 pgs., 2 1/2" x 3 1/2", Penny Book 10.00 27.00 52.00

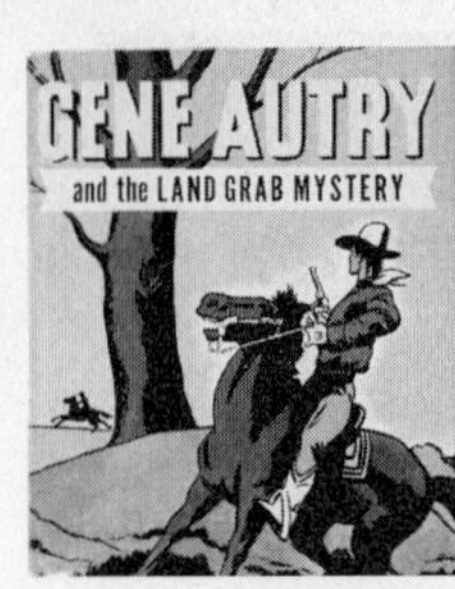

1430 - Gene Autry and the Land Grab Mystery © WHIT

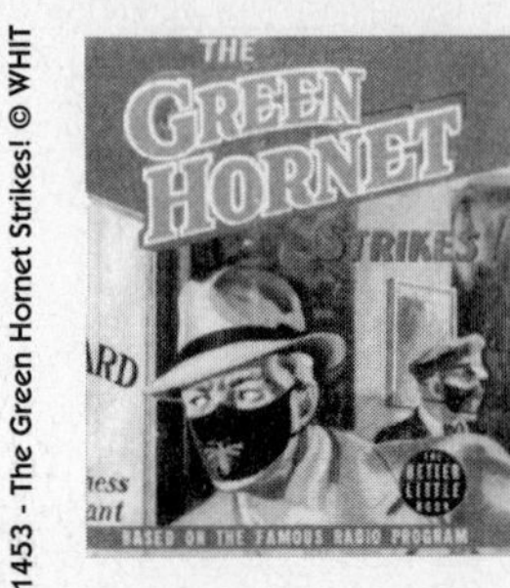

1453 - The Green Hornet Strikes! © WHIT

1647 - Gunsmoke © CBS

GD FN VF/NM

1164- **Freckles and the Lost Diamond Mine**, 1937, Whitman, 432 pgs., Merrill Blosser-a 10.00 31.00 62.00
nn- **Freckles and the Mystery Ship**, 1935, Whitman, 66 pgs., Pan-Am premium 12.00 40.00 80.00
1100B- **Fun, Puzzles, Riddles**, 1938, Whitman, 36 pgs., 2 1/2" x 3 1/2", Penny Book 4.00 12.00 25.00
1433- **Gang Busters Step In**, 1939, Whitman, 432 pgs., Henry E. Vallely-a 10.00 35.00 70.00
1437- **Gang Busters Smash Through**, 1942, Whitman, 432 pgs. 10.00 35.00 70.00
1451- **Gang Busters in Action!**, 1938, Whitman, 432 pgs. 10.00 35.00 70.00
nn- **Gangbusters and Guns of the Law**, 1940, Dell, 4" x 5", 194 pgs., Fast-Action Story, soft-c 32.00 100.00 200.00
nn- **Gang Busters and the Radio Clues**, 1938, Whitman, 36 pgs., 2 1/2" x 3 1/2", Penny Book 10.00 27.00 52.00
1409- **Gene Autry and Raiders of the Range**, 1946, Whitman, 352 pgs. 10.00 35.00 70.00
1425- **Gene Autry and the Mystery of Paint Rock Canyon**, 1947, Whitman, 288 pgs. 10.00 35.00 70.00
1428- **Gene Autry Special Ranger**, 1941, Whitman, 432 pgs., Erwin Hess-a 12.00 43.00 85.00
1430- **Gene Autry and the Land Grab Mystery**, 1948, Whitman, 288 pgs. 10.00 32.00 65.00
1433- **Gene Autry in Public Cowboy No. 1**, 1938, Whitman, 240 pgs., photo-c, movie scenes (1st Autry BLB) 25.00 80.00 160.00
1434- **Gene Autry and the Gun-Smoke Reckoning**, 1943, Whitman, 352 pgs. 12.00 40.00 80.00
1456- **Gene Autry in Special Ranger Rule**, 1945, Whitman, 352 pgs., Henry E. Vallely-a 12.00 40.00 80.00
1461- **Gene Autry and the Red Bandit's Ghost**, 1949, Whitman, 288 pgs. 10.00 30.00 60.00
1483- **Gene Autry in Law of the Range**, 1939, Whitman, 432 pgs. 12.00 43.00 85.00
1493- **Gene Autry and the Hawk of the Hills**, 1942, Whitman, 428 pgs., flip pictures, Vallely-a 12.00 43.00 85.00
1494- **Gene Autry Cowboy Detective**, 1940, Whitman, 432 pgs., Erwin Hess-a 12.00 43.00 85.00
700-10- **Gene Autry and the Bandits of Silver Tip**, 1949, Whitman 10.00 25.00 50.00
714-10- **Gene Autry and the Range War**, 1950, Whitman 10.00 25.00 50.00
nn- **Gene Autry in Gun-Smoke**, 1938, Dell, 196 pgs., Fast-Action story, soft-c 33.00 120.00 240.00
2035-(#35)- **Gentle Ben, Mystery of the Everglades**, 1969, Whitman, 256 pgs., hard-c, color illos. 4.00 10.00 20.00
1176- **Gentleman Joe Palooka**, 1940, Saalfield, 400 pgs. 12.00 43.00 85.00
George O'Brien (See The Cowboy Millionaire)
1101- **George O'Brien and the Arizona Badman**, 1936?, Whitman 10.00 38.00 75.00
1418- **George O'Brien in Gun Law**, 1938, Whitman, 240 pgs., photo-c, movie scenes, RKO Radio Pictures 10.00 38.00 75.00
1457- **George O'Brien and the Hooded Riders**, 1940, Whitman, 432 pgs., Erwin Hess-a 10.00 27.00 52.00
nn- **George O'Brien and the Arizona Bad Man**, 1939, Whitman, 36 pgs., 2 1/2" x 3 1/2", Penny Book 10.00 27.00 52.00
1462- **Ghost Avenger**, 1943, Whitman, 432 pgs., flip pictures, Henry Vallely-a 10.00 25.00 50.00
nn- **Ghost Gun Gang Meet Their Match, The**, 1939. Whitman, 2 1/2" x 3 1/2", Penny Book 10.00 25.00 50.00
nn- **Gingerbread Boy, The**, nd(1930s), np(Whitman), 36 pgs., Penny Book 4.00 10.00 20.00
1173- **G-Man in Action, A**, 1940, Saalfield, 400 pgs., J.R. White-a 10.00 25.00 50.00
1118- **G-Man on the Crime Trail**, 1936, Whitman, 432 pgs. 10.00 32.00 65.00
1147- **G-Man Vs. the Red X**, 1936, Whitman, 432 pgs. 10.00 35.00 70.00
1162- **G-Man Allen**, 1939, Saalfield, 400 pgs. 10.00 25.00 50.00
1173- **G-Man in Action, A**, 1940, Saalfield, 400 pgs. 10.00 25.00 50.00
1434- **G-Man and the Radio Bank Robberies**, 1937, Whitman, 432 pgs. 10.00 32.00 65.00
1469- **G-Man and the Gun Runners, The**, 1940, Whitman, 432 pgs. 10.00 32.00 65.00
1470- **G-Man vs. the Fifth Column**, 1941, Whitman, 432 pgs., flip pictures 10.00 32.00 65.00
1493- **G-Man Breaking the Gambling Ring**, 1938, Whitman, 432 pgs., James Gary-a 10.00 32.00 65.00
4- **G-Men Foil the Kidnappers**, 1936, Whitman, 132 pgs., 3 1/2" x 3 1/2", soft-c, Tarzan Ice Cream cup lid premium 30.00 90.00 180.00
nn- **G-Man on Lightning Island**, 1936, Dell, 244 pgs., Fast-Action Story, soft-c, Henry E. Vallely-a 25.00 80.00 160.00
6833- **G-Man on Lightning Island**, 1936, Dell, 244 pgs., Cartoon Story Book, hard-c, Henry E. Vallely-a 22.00 75.00 150.00
1157- **G-Men on the Trail**, 1938, Saalfield, 400 pgs. 10.00 25.00 50.00
1168- **G Men on the Job**, 1935, Whitman, 432 pgs. 10.00 30.00 60.00
nn- **G-Men on the Job Again**, 1938, Whitman, 36 pgs., 2 1/2" x 3 1/2", Penny Book 10.00 27.00 52.00
nn- **G-Men and Kidnap Justice**, 1938, Whitman, 68 pgs., Pan-Am premium, soft-c 10.00 32.00 65.00
nn- **G-Men and the Missing Clues**, 1938, Whitman, 36 pgs., 2 1/2"x 3 1/2", Penny Book 10.00 27.00 52.00
1097- **Go Into Your Dance**, 1935, Saalfield, 160 pgs.. photo-c, movie scenes with Al Jolson & Ruby Keeler 10.00 38.00 75.00
1577- **Go Into Your Dance**, 1935, Saalfield, 160 pgs., photo-c, movie scenes, soft-c 10.00 38.00 75.00
5751- **Goofy in Giant Trouble** (Walt Disney's ...), 1968, Whitman, 260 pgs., 39 cents, soft-c, color illos. 4.00 10.00 20.00
5751-2- **Goofy in Giant Trouble**, 1968 (1980-reprint of '67 version), Whitman, 260 pgs., 79 cents, soft-c, B&W 1.00 3.00 6.00
8- **Great Expectations**, 1934, EVW, (Five Star Library), 160 pgs., photo-c, movie scenes 15.00 50.00 100.00
1453- **Green Hornet Strikes!, The**, 1940, Whitman, 432 pgs., Robert Weisman-a 35.00 130.00 260.00
1480- **Green Hornet Cracks Down, The**, 1942, Whitman, 432 pgs., flip pictures, Henry Vallely-a 33.00 120.00 240.00
1496- **Green Hornet Returns, The**, 1941, Whitman, 432 pgs., flip pictures 33.00 120.00 240.00
1172- **Gullivers' Travels**, 1939, Saalfield, 320 pgs., adapted from Paramount Pict. Cartoons 15.00 50.00 100.00
nn- **Gumps In Radio Land, The** (Andy Gump and the Chest of Gold), 1937, Lehn & Fink Prod. Corp., 100 pgs., 3 1/4" x 5 1/2", Pebeco Tooth Paste giveaway, by Gus Edson 18.00 60.00 120.00
nn- **Gunmen of Rustlers' Gulch, The**, 1939, Whitman, 36 pgs., 2 1/2" x 3 1/2", Penny Book 10.00 27.00 52.00
1426- **Guns in the Roaring West**, 1937, Whitman, 300 pgs. 10.00 25.00 50.00
1647- **Gunsmoke** (TV Series), 1958, Whitman, 280 pgs., 4 1/2" x 5 3/4" 8.00 20.00 40.00
1101- **Hairbreath Harry in Department QT**, 1935, Whitman, 384 pgs., by J. M. Alexander 10.00 31.00 62.00
1413- **Hal Hardy in the Lost Land of Giants**, 1938, Whitman, 300 pgs., "The World 1,000,000 Years Ago" 10.00 27.00 52.00
1159- **Hall of Fame of the Air**, 1936, Whitman, 432 pgs., by Capt. Eddie Rickenbacker 10.00 25.00 50.00
nn- **Hansel and Grethel, The Story of**, nd (1930s), no publ., 36 pgs., Penny Book 4.00 10.00 20.00
1145- **Hap Lee's Selection of Movie Gags**, 1935, Whitman, 160 pgs., photos of stars 10.00 35.00 70.00
Happy Prince, The (See Wee Little Books)
1111- **Hard Rock Harrigan-A Story of Boulder Dam**, 1935, Saalfield, photo-c, photo illos. 10.00 25.00 50.00
1591- **Hard Rock Harrigan-A Story of Boulder Dam**, 1935, Saalfield, photo-c, photo illos. 10.00 25.00 50.00

Houdini's Big Little Book of Magic © WHIT

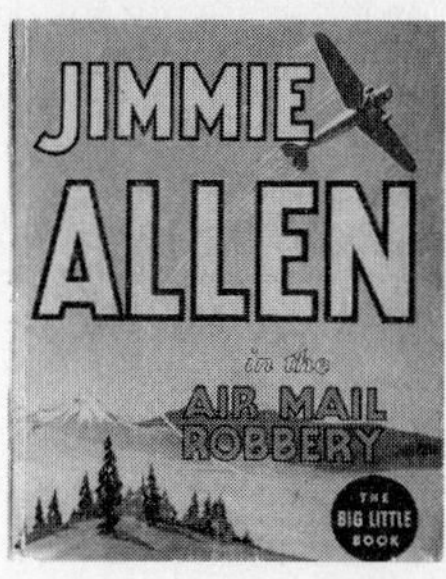

1143 - Jimmie Allen in the Air Mail Robbery © WHIT

1402 - John Carter of Mars © ERB

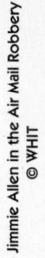

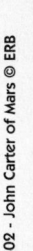

	GD	FN	VF/NM
1418- Harold Teen Swinging at the Sugar Bowl, 1939, Whitman, 432 pgs., by Carl Ed	10.00	30.00	60.00
1100B- Hobbies, 1938, Whitman, 36 pgs., 2 1/2" x 3 1/2", Penny Book	4.00	10.00	20.00
1125- Hockey Spare, The, 1937, Saalfield, sports book	8.00	20.00	40.00
1605- Hockey Spare, The, 1937, Saalfield, soft-c	8.00	20.00	40.00
728- Homeless Homer, 1934, Whitman, by Dee Dobbin, for young kids	4.00	12.00	24.00
17- Hoosier Schoolmaster, The, 1935, EVW, movie scenes	12.00	40.00	80.00
715- Houdini's Big Little Book of Magic, 1927 (1933), 300 pgs.	12.00	45.00	90.00
nn- Houdini's Big Little Book of Magic, 1927 (1933), 196 pgs., American Oil Co. premium, soft-c	12.00	45.00	90.00
nn- Houdini's Big Little Book of Magic, 1927 (1933), 204 pgs., Cocomalt premium, soft-c	12.00	45.00	90.00
Huckleberry Finn (See The Adventures of...)			
1644- Hugh O'Brian TV's Wyatt Earp (TV Series), 1958, Whitman, 280 pgs.	8.00	20.00	40.00
1424- Inspector Charlie Chan Villainy on the High Seas, 1942, Whitman, 432 pgs., flip pictures	12.00	40.00	80.00
1186- Inspector Wade of Scotland Yard, 1940, Saalfield, 400 pgs.	10.00	25.00	50.00
1448- Inspector Wade Solves the Mystery of the Red Aces, 1937, Whitman, 432 pgs.	10.00	25.00	50.00
1148- International Spy Doctor Doom Faces Death at Dawn, 1937, Whitman, 432 pgs., Arbo-a	10.00	31.00	62.00
1155- In the Name of the Law, 1937, Whitman, 432 pgs., Henry E. Vallely-a	10.00	25.00	50.00
2012-(#12)-Invaders, The-Alien Missile Threat (TV Series), 1967, Whitman, 260 pgs., hard-c, 39 cents, color illos.	4.00	12.00	25.00
1403- Invisible Scarlet O'Neil, 1942, Whitman, All Pictures Comics, flip pictures	10.00	30.00	60.00
1406- Invisible Scarlet O'Neil Versus the King of the Slums, 1946, Whitman, 352 pgs.	10.00	27.00	52.00
1098- It Happened One Night, 1935, Saalfield, 160 pgs., Little Big Book, Clark Gable, Claudette Colbert photo-c, movie scenes from Academy Award winner	16.00	55.00	110.00
1578- It Happened One Night, 1935, Saalfield, 160 pgs., soft-c	16.00	55.00	110.00
Jack and Jill (See Wee Little Books)			
1432- Jack Armstrong and the Mystery of the Iron Key, 1939, Whitman, 432 pgs., Henry E. Vallely-a	10.00	32.00	65.00
1435- Jack Armstrong and the Ivory Treasure, 1937, Whitman, 432 pgs., Henry Vallely-a	10.00	32.00	65.00
Jackie Cooper (See Story Of..)			
1084- Jackie Cooper in Peck's Bad Boy, 1934, Saalfield, 160 pgs., hard, photo-c, movie scenes	12.00	40.00	80.00
1314- Jackie Cooper in Peck's Bad Boy, 1934, Saalfield, 160 pgs., soft, photo-c, movie scenes	12.00	40.00	80.00
1402- Jackie Cooper in "Gangster's Boy," 1939, Whitman, 240 pgs., photo-c, movie scenes	10.00	35.00	70.00
13- Jackie Cooper in Dinky, 1935, EVW, 160 pgs., movie scenes	10.00	38.00	75.00
nn- Jack King of the Secret Service and the Counterfeiters, 1939, Whitman, 36 pgs., 2 1/2" x 3 1/2", Penny Book, by John G. Gray	10.00	25.00	50.00
L11- Jack London's Call of the Wild, 1935, Lynn, 20th Cent. Pic., movie scenes with Clark Gable	12.00	43.00	85.00
nn- Jack Pearl as Detective Baron Munchausen, 1934, Goldsmith, 132 pgs., soft-c	10.00	32.00	65.00
1102- Jack Swift and His Rocket Ship, 1934, Whitman, 320 pgs.	15.00	50.00	100.00
1498- Jane Arden the Vanished Princess, Whitman, 300 pgs.	10.00	30.00	60.00
1179- Jane Withers in This is the Life (20th Century-Fox Presents...), 1935, Whitman, 240 pgs., photo-c, movie scenes	10.00	38.00	75.00
1463- Jane Withers in Keep Smiling, 1938, Whitman, 240 pgs., photo-c, movie scenes	10.00	38.00	75.00
Jaragu of the Jungle (See Rex Beach's ...)			
1447- Jerry Parker Police Reporter and the Candid Camera Clue, 1941, Whitman, 300 pgs.	10.00	25.00	50.00
Jim Bowie (See Adventures of ...)			
nn- Jim Bryant of the Highway Patrol and the Mysterious Accident, 1939, Whitman, 36 pgs., 2 1/2" x 3 1/2", Penny Book	10.00	25.00	50.00
1466- Jim Craig State Trooper and the Kidnapped Governor, 1938, Whitman, 432 pgs.	10.00	25.00	50.00
nn- Jim Doyle Private Detective and the Train Hold-Up, 1939, Whitman, 36 pgs., 2 1/2" x 3 1/2", Penny Book	10.00	27.00	52.00
1180- Jim Hardy Ace Reporter, 1940, Saalfield, 400 pgs., Dick Moores-a	10.00	27.00	52.00
1143- Jimmy Allen in the Air Mail Robbery, 1936, Whitman, 432 pgs.	10.00	25.00	50.00
L15- Jimmy and the Tiger, 1935, Lynn, 192 pgs.	10.00	27.00	52.00
Jimmy Skunk's Justice (See Wee Little Books)			
1428- Jim Starr of the Border Patrol, 1937, Whitman, 432 pgs.	10.00	25.00	50.00
Joan of Arc (See Wee Little Books)			
1105- Joe Louis the Brown Bomber, 1936, Whitman, 240 pgs., photo-c, photo-illos.	18.00	60.00	120.00
Joe Palooka (See Gentleman ...)			
1123- Joe Palooka the Heavyweight Boxing Champ, 1934, Whitman, 320 pgs., Ham Fisher-a	12.00	75.00	150.00
1168- Joe Palooka's Great Adventure, 1939, Saalfield	12.00	75.00	150.00
nn- Joe Penner's Duck Farm, 1935, Goldsmith, Henry Vallely-a	10.00	32.00	65.00
1402- John Carter of Mars, 1940, Whitman, 432 pgs., John Coleman Burroughs-a	52.00	210.00	420.00
nn- John Carter of Mars, 1940, Dell, 194 pgs., Fast-Action Story, soft-c	54.00	230.00	460.00
1164- Johnny Forty Five, 1938, Saalfield, 400 pgs.	10.00	25.00	50.00
John Wayne (See Westward Ho!)			
1100B- Jokes (A book of laughs galore), 1938, Whitman, 36 pgs., 2 1/2" x 3 1/2", Penny Book	4.00	10.00	20.00
1100B- Jokes (A book of side-splitting funny stories), 1938, Whitman, 36 pgs., 2 1/2" x 3 1/2", Penny Book	4.00	10.00	20.00
2026- Journey to the Center of the Earth, The Fiery Foe, 1968, Whitman	4.00	12.00	24.00
Jungle Jim (See Top-Line Comics)			
1138- Jungle Jim, 1936, Whitman, 432 pgs., Alex Raymond-a	15.00	50.00	100.00
1139- Jungle Jim and the Vampire Woman, 1937, Whitman, 432 pgs., Alex Raymond-a	16.00	55.00	110.00
1442- Junior G-Men, 1937, Whitman, 432 pgs., Henry E. Vallely-a	10.00	27.00	52.00
nn- Junior G-Men Solve a Crime, 1939, Whitman, 36 pgs., 2 1/2" x 3 1/2", Penny Book	10.00	27.00	52.00
1422- Junior Nebb on the Diamond Bar Ranch, 1938, Whitman, 300 pgs., by Sol Hess	10.00	27.00	52.00
1470- Junior Nebb Joins the Circus, 1939, Whitman, 300 pgs. by Sol Hess	10.00	27.00	52.00
nn- Junior Nebb Elephant Trainer, 1939, Whitman, 68 pgs., Pan-Am Oil premium, soft-c	10.00	35.00	70.00
1052- "Just Kids" (Adventures of ...), 1934, Saalfield, oblong size, by Ad Carter	18.00	60.00	120.00
1094- Just Kids and the Mysterious Stranger, 1935, Saalfield, 160 pgs., by Ad Carter	10.00	36.00	72.00
1184- Just Kids and Deep-Sea Dan, 1940, Saalfield, 400 pgs., by Ad Carter	10.00	30.00	60.00
1302- Just Kids, The Adventures of, 1934, Saalfield, oblong size, soft-c, by Ad Carter	18.00	60.00	120.00
1324- Just Kids and the Mysterious Stranger, 1935, Saalfield, 160 pgs., soft-c, by Ad Carter ,	10.00	36.00	72.00

14 - Katzenjammer Kids © DELL

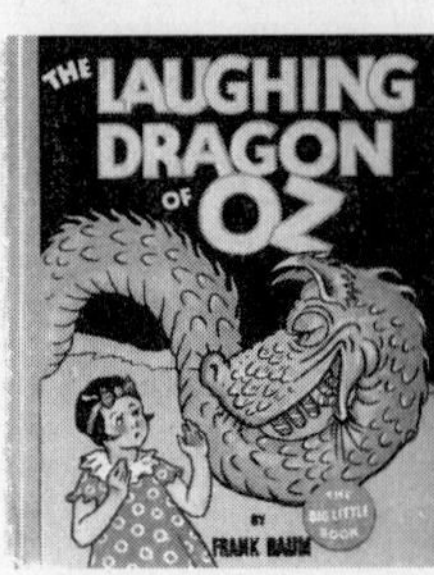

1126 - The Laughing Dragon of Oz © WHIT

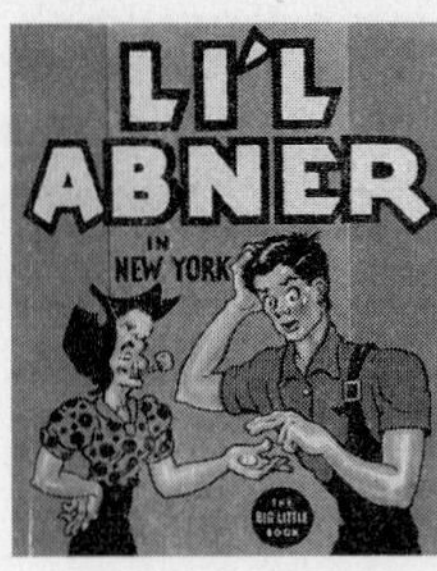

1198 - Li'l Abner in New York © UFS

GD FN VF/NM

1401- **Just Kids**, 1937, Whitman, 432 pgs., by Ad Carter 10.00 36.00 72.00

1055- **Katzenjammer Kids in the Mountains**, 1934, Saalfield, oblong, H. H. Knerr-a 16.00 55.00 110.00

14- **Katzenjammer Kids, The**, 1942, Dell, 194 pgs., Fast-Action Story, H. H. Knerr-a 18.00 60.00 120.00

1411- **Kay Darcy and the Mystery Hideout**, 1937, Whitman, 300 pgs., Charles Mueller-a 10.00 30.00 60.00

1180- **Kayo in the Land of Sunshine** (With Moon Mullins), 1937, Whitman, 432 pgs., by Willard 10.00 38.00 75.00

1415- **Kayo and Moon Mullins and the One Man Gang**, 1939, Whitman, 432 pgs., by Frank Willard 10.00 32.00 65.00

7- **Kayo and Moon Mullins 'Way Down South**, 1938, Whitman, 132 pgs., 3 1/2" x 3 1/2", Buddy Book 26.00 82.00 165.00

1105- **Kazan in Revenge of the North** (James Oliver Curwood's...), 1937, Whitman, 432 pgs., Henry E. Vallely-a 10.00 25.00 50.00

1471- **Kazan, King of the Pack** (James Oliver Curwood's...), 1940, Whitman, 432 pgs. 8.00 22.00 45.00

1420- **Keep 'Em Flying! U.S.A. for America's Defense**, 1943, Whitman, 432 pgs., Henry E. Vallely-a, flip pictures 10.00 25.00 50.00

1133- **Kelly King at Yale Hall**, 1937, Saalfield 8.00 22.00 45.00

Ken Maynard (See Strawberry Roan, Western Frontier & Wheels of Destiny)

776- **Ken Maynard in "Gun Justice,"** 1934, Whitman, 160 pgs., movie scenes (Universal Pic.) 16.00 55.00 110.00

1430- **Ken Maynard in Western Justice**, 1938, Whitman, 432 pgs., Irwin Myers-a 10.00 30.00 60.00

1442- **Ken Maynard and the Gun Wolves of the Gila**, 1939, Whitman, 432 pgs. 10.00 30.00 60.00

nn- **Ken Maynard in Six-Gun Law**, 1938, Whitman, 36 pgs., 2 1/2" x 3 1/2", Penny Book 10.00 27.00 52.00

1134- **King of Crime**, 1938, Saalfield, 400 pgs. 10.00 25.00 50.00

King of the Royal Mounted (See Zane Grey)

1010- **King of the Royal Mounted in Arctic Law**, 1937, Whitman, 7 1/4" x 5 1/2", 64 pgs., Nickel Book 10.00 36.00 72.00

nn- **Kit Carson**, 1933, World Syndicate, by J. Carroll Mansfield, High Lights Of History Series, hard-c 10.00 25.00 50.00

nn- **Kit Carson**, 1933, World Syndicate, same as hard-c above but with a black cloth-c 10.00 25.00 50.00

1105- **Kit Carson and the Mystery Riders**, 1935, Saalfield, hard-c, Johnny Mack Brown photo-c, movie scenes 12.00 48.00 95.00

1585- **Kit Carson and the Mystery Riders**, 1935, Saalfield, soft-c, Johnny Mack Brown photo-c, movie scenes 12.00 48.00 95.00

Krazy Kat (See Adventures of...)

2004- **(#4)-Lassie-Adventure in Alaska** (TV Series), 1967, Whitman, 260 pgs., 39 cents hard-c, color illos 4.00 12.00 24.00

2027- **Lassie and the Shabby Sheik** (TV Series), 1968, Whitman 4.00 12.00 24.00

1132- **Last Days of Pompeii, The**, 1935, Whitman, 5 1/4" x 6 1/4", 260 pgs., photo-c, movie scenes 12.00 40.00 80.00

1128- **Last Man Out** (Baseball), 1937, Saalfield, hard-c 10.00 25.00 50.00

L30- **Last of the Mohicans, The**, 1936, Lynn, 192 pgs., movie scenes with Randolph Scott, United Artists Pictures 12.00 43.00 85.00

1126- **Laughing Dragon of Oz, The**, 1934, Whitman 432 pgs., by Frank Baum (scarce) 85.00 260.00 520.00

1086- **Laurel and Hardy**, 1934, Saalfield, 160 pgs., hard-c, photo-c, movie scenes 15.00 50.00 100.00

1316- **Laurel and Hardy**, 1934, Saalfield, 160 pgs. soft-c, photo-c, movie scenes 15.00 50.00 100.00

1092- **Law of the Wild, The**, 1935, Saalfield, 160 pgs., photo-c, movie scenes of Rex, The Wild Horse & Rin-Tin-Tin Jr. 10.00 30.00 60.00

1322- **Law of the Wild, The**, 1935, Saalfield, 160 pgs., photo-c, movie scenes, soft-c 10.00 30.00 60.00

1100B- **Learn to be a Ventriloquist**, 1938, Whitman, 36 pgs. 2 1/2" x 3 1/2", Penny Book 4.00 10.00 20.00

1149- **Lee Brady Range Detective**, 1938, Saalfield, 400 pgs. 8.00 22.00 45.00

GD FN VF/NM

L10- **Les Miserables** (Victor Hugo's ...), 1935, Lynn, 192 pgs., movie scenes 10.00 38.00 75.00

1441- **Lightning Jim U.S. Marshall Brings Law to the West**, 1940, Whitman, 432 pgs., based on radio program 10.00 30.00 60.00

nn- **Lightning Jim Whipple U.S. Marshall in Indian Territory**, 1939, Whitman, 36 pgs., 2 1/2" x 3 1/2", Penny Book 10.00 31.00 62.00

653- **Lions and Tigers** (With Clyde Beatty), 1934, Whitman, 160 pgs., photo-c movie scenes 12.00 40.00 80.00

1187- **Li'l Abner and the Ratfields**, 1940, Saalfield, 400 pgs., by Al Capp 15.00 50.00 100.00

1193- **Li'l Abner and Sadie Hawkins Day**, 1940, Saalfield, 400 pgs., by Al Capp 15.00 50.00 100.00

1198- **Li'l Abner in New York**, 1936, Whitman, 432 pgs., by Al Capp 15.00 50.00 100.00

1401- **Li'l Abner Among the Millionaires**, 1939, Whitman, 432 pgs., by Al Capp 15.00 50.00 100.00

1054- **Little Annie Rooney**, 1934, Saalfield, oblong - 4" x 8", All Pictures Comics, hard-c 15.00 52.00 105.00

1304- **Little Annie Rooney**, 1934, Saalfield, oblong - 4" x 8", All Pictures, soft-c 15.00 52.00 105.00

1117- **Little Annie Rooney and the Orphan House**, 1936, Whitman, 432 pgs. 10.00 30.00 60.00

1406- **Little Annie Rooney on the Highway to Adventure**, 1938, Whitman, 432 pgs. 10.00 30.00 60.00

1149- **Little Big Shot** (With Sybil Jason), 1935, Whitman, 240 pgs., photo-c, movie scenes 10.00 38.00 75.00

nn- **Little Black Sambo**, nd (1930s), np (Whitman), 36 pgs., 3" x 2 1/2", Penny Book 10.00 35.00 70.00

Little Bo-Peep (See Wee Little Books)

Little Colonel, The (See Shirley Temple)

1148- **Little Green Door, The**, 1938, Saalfield, 400 pgs. 8.00 27.00 55.00

1112- **Little Hollywood Stars**, 1935, Saalfield, movie scenes (Little Rascals, etc.), hard-c 10.00 35.00 70.00

1592- **Little Hollywood Stars**, 1935, Saalfield, movie scenes, soft-c 10.00 35.00 70.00

1087- **Little Jimmy's Gold Hunt**, 1935, Saalfield, 160 pgs., hard-c, Little Big Book, by Swinnerton 15.00 50.00 100.00

1317- **Little Jimmy's Gold Hunt**, 1935,Saalfield, 160 pgs., 4 1/4" x 5 3/4", soft-c, by Swinnerton 15.00 50.00 100.00

Little Joe and the City Gangsters (See Top-Line Comics)

Little Joe Otter's Slide (See Wee Little Books)

1118- **Little Lord Fauntleroy**, 1936, Saalfield, movie scenes, photo-c, 4 1/2" x 5 1/4", starring Mickey Rooney & Freddie Bartholomew, hard-c 10.00 31.00 62.00

1598- **Little Lord Fauntleroy**, 1936, Saalfield, photo-c, movie scenes, soft-c 10.00 31.00 62.00

1192- **Little Mary Mixup and the Grocery Robberies**, 1940, Saalfield 10.00 27.00 52.00

8- **Little Mary Mixup Wins A Prize**, 1936, Whitman, 132 pgs., 3 1/2" x 3 1/2", soft-c, Tarzan Ice Cream cup lid premium 30.00 90.00 180.00

1150- **Little Men**, 1934, Whitman, 4 3/4" x 5 1/4", movie scenes (Mascot Prod.), photo-c, hard-c 10.00 31.00 62.00

9- **Little Minister, The**,-Katherine Hepburn, 1935, 160 pgs., 4 1/4" x 5 1/2", EVW (Five Star Library), movie scenes (RKO) 12.00 43.00 85.00

1120- **Little Miss Muffet**, 1936, Whitman, 432 pgs., by Fanny Y. Cory 10.00 30.00 60.00

708- **Little Orphan Annie**, 1933, Whitman, 320 pgs., by Harold Gray, the 2nd Big Little Book 46.00 190.00 380.00

nn- **Little Orphan Annie**, 1928('33), Whitman, 52 pgs., 4" x 5 1/2", premium-no ads, soft-c, by Harold Gray 32.00 100.00 200.00

716- **Little Orphan Annie and Sandy**, 1933, Whitman, 320 pgs., by Harold Gray 25.00 80.00 160.00

716- **Little Orphan Annie and Sandy**, 1933, Whitman, 300 pgs., by Harold Gray 25.00 80.00 160.00

nn- **Little Orphan Annie and Sandy**, 1933, Whitman, 52 pgs.,

1162 - Little Orphan Annie and Punjab the Wizard © WHIT

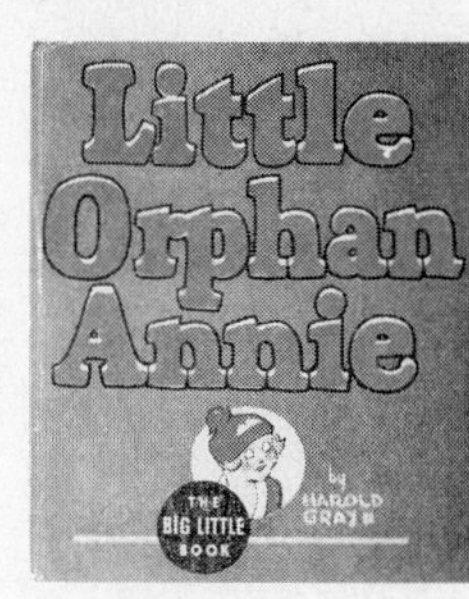

Little Orphan Annie
by HAROLD GRAY
THE BIG LITTLE BOOK

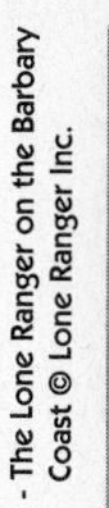
1421 - The Lone Ranger on the Barbary Coast © Lone Ranger Inc.

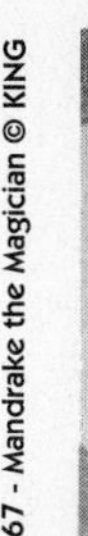
1167 - Mandrake the Magician © KING

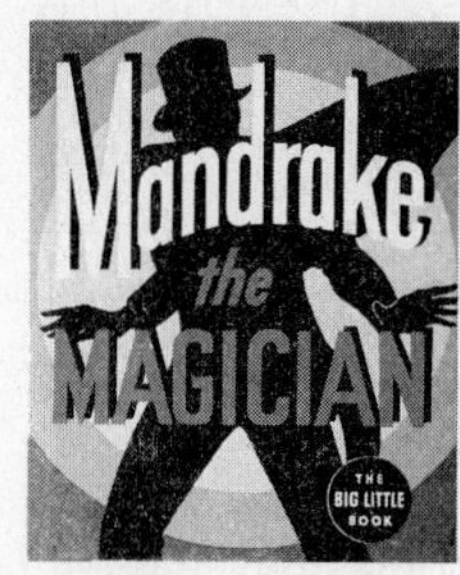

GD FN VF/NM

premium-no ads, 4" x 5 1/2", soft-c by Harold Gray 32.00 100.00 200.00
748- Little Orphan Annie and Chizzler, 1933, Whitman, 320 pgs., by Harold Gray 20.00 70.00 140.00
1010- Little Orphan Annie and the Big Town Gunmen, 1937, 7 1/4" x 5 1/2", 64 pgs., Nickel Book 10.00 38.00 75.00
1103- Little Orphan Annie with the Circus, 1934, Whitman, 320 pgs., by Harold Gray 15.00 50.00 100.00
1140- Little Orphan Annie and the Big Train Robbery, 1934, Whitman, 300 pgs., by Gray 15.00 50.00 100.00
1140- Little Orphan Annie and the Big Train Robbery, 1934, Whitman, 300 pgs., premium-no ads, soft-c, by Harold Gray 30.00 92.00 185.00
1154- Little Orphan Annie and the Ghost Gang, 1935, Whitman, 432 pgs. by Harold Gray 15.00 50.00 100.00
nn- Little Orphan Annie and the Ghost Gang, 1935, Whitman, 436 pgs., premium-no ads, 3-color, soft-c, by Harold Gray 30.00 92.00 185.00
1162- Little Orphan Annie and Punjab the Wizard, 1935, Whitman, 432 pgs., by Harold Gray 15.00 50.00 100.00
1186- Little Orphan Annie and the $1,000,000 Formula, 1936, Whitman, 432 pgs., by Gray 12.00 45.00 90.00
1414- Little Orphan Annie and the Ancient Treasure of Am, 1939, Whitman, 432 pgs., by Gray 10.00 38.00 75.00
1416- Little Orphan Annie in the Movies, 1937, Whitman, 432 pgs., by Harold Gray 10.00 38.00 75.00
1417- Little Orphan Annie and the Secret of the Well, 1947,Whitman, 352 pgs., by Gray 10.00 32.00 65.00
1435- Little Orphan Annie and the Gooneyville Mystery, 1947, Whitman, 288 pgs., by Gray 10.00 32.00 65.00
1446- Little Orphan Annie in the Thieves' Den, 1949, Whitman, 288 pgs., by Harold Gray 10.00 32.00 65.00
1449- Little Orphan Annie and the Mysterious Shoemaker, 1938, Whitman, 432 pgs., by Harold Gray 10.00 38.00 75.00
1457- Little Orphan Annie and Her Junior Commandos, 1943, Whitman, 352 pgs., by H. Gray 10.00 32.00 65.00
1461- Little Orphan Annie and the Underground Hide-Out, 1945, Whitman, 352 pgs., by Gray 10.00 32.00 65.00
1468- Little Orphan Annie and the Ancient Treasure of Am, 1949 (Misdated 1939), 288 pgs., by Gray 10.00 38.00 75.00
1482- Little Orphan Annie and the Haunted Mansion, 1941, Whitman, 432 pgs., flip pictures, by Harold Gray 12.00 40.00 80.00
3048- Little Orphan Annie and Her Big Little Kit, 1937, Whitman, 384 pgs., 4 1/2" x 6 1/2" box, includes miniature box of 4 crayons-red, yellow, blue and green 80.00 250.00 500.00
4054- Little Orphan Annie, The Story of, 1934, 7" x 9 1/2", 320 pgs., Big Big Book, Harold Gray-c/a 150.00 400.00 750.00
nn- Little Orphan Annie Gets into Trouble, 1938, Whitman, 36 pgs., 2 1/2" x 3 1/2", Penny Book 10.00 27.00 52.00
nn- Little Orphan Annie in Hollywood, 1937, Whitman, 3 1/2" x 3 1/4", Pan-Am premium, soft-c 22.00 75.00 150.00
nn- Little Orphan Annie in Rags to Riches, 1939, Dell, 194 pgs., Fast-Action Story, soft-c 32.00 100.00 200.00
nn- Little Orphan Annie Saves Sandy, 1938, Whitman, 36 pgs., 2 1/2" x 3 1/2", Penny Book 10.00 27.00 52.00
nn- Little Orphan Annie Under the Big Top, 1938, Dell, 194 pgs., Fast-Action Story, soft-c 32.00 100.00 200.00
nn- Little Orphan Annie Wee Little Books (In open box)
nn, 1934, Whitman, 44 pgs., by H. Gray
L.O.A. And Daddy Warbucks 10.00 27.00 52.00
L.O.A. And Her Dog Sandy 10.00 27.00 52.00
L.O.A. And The Lucky Knife 10.00 27.00 52.00
L.O.A. And The Pinch-Pennys 10.00 27.00 52.00
L.O.A. At Happy Home 10.00 27.00 52.00
L.O.A. Finds Mickey 10.00 27.00 52.00
Complete set with box 45.00 175.00 350.00
nn- Little Polly Flinders, The Story of, nd (1930s), no publ., 36 pgs., 2 1/2" x 3", Penny Book 4.00 10.00 20.00

GD FN VF/NM

nn- Little Red Hen, The, nd(1930s), np(Whitman), 36 pgs., Penny Book 4.00 10.00 20.00
nn- Little Red Riding Hood, nd(1930s), np(Whitman), 36 pgs., 3" x 2 1/2", Penny Book 4.00 10.00 20.00
nn- Little Red Riding Hood and the Big Bad Wolf (Disney), 1934, McKay, 36 pgs., stiff-c, Disney Studio-a 25.00 80.00 160.00
757- Little Women, 1934, Whitman, 4 3/4" x 5 1/4", 160 pgs., photo-c, movie scenes, starring Katharine Hepburn 15.00 50.00 100.00
Littlest Rebel, The (See Shirley Temple)
1181- Lone Ranger and his Horse Silver, 1935, Whitman, 432 pgs., Hal Arbo-a 22.00 75.00 150.00
1196- Lone Ranger and the Vanishing Herd, 1936, Whitman, 432 pgs. 16.00 55.00 110.00
1407- Lone Ranger and Dead Men's Mine, The, 1939, Whitman, 432 pgs. 15.00 50.00 100.00
1421- Lone Ranger on the Barbary Coast, The, 1944, Whitman, 352 pgs., Henry Vallely-a 12.00 43.00 85.00
1428- Lone Ranger and the Secret Weapon, The, 1943, Whitman, 12.00 43.00 85.00
1431- Lone Ranger and the Secret Killer, The, 1937, Whitman 432 pgs., H. Anderson-a 16.00 55.00 110.00
1450- Lone Ranger and the Black Shirt Highwayman, The, 1939, Whitman, 432 pgs. 15.00 50.00 100.00
1465- Lone Ranger and the Menace of Murder Valley, The, 1938, Whitman, 432 pgs., Robert Wiseman-a 15.00 50.00 100.00
1468- Lone Ranger Follows Through, The, 1941, Whitman, 432 pgs., H.E. Vallely-a 15.00 50.00 100.00
1477- Lone Ranger and the Great Western Span, The, 1942, Whitman, 424 pgs., H. E. Vallely-a 12.00 43.00 85.00
1489- Lone Ranger and the Red Renegades, The, 1939, Whitman, 432 pgs. 16.00 55.00 110.00
1498- Lone Ranger and the Silver Bullets, 1946, Whitman, 352 pgs., Henry E. Vallely-a 12.00 43.00 85.00
712-10- Lone Ranger and the Secret of Somber Cavern, The, 1950, Whitman 10.00 25.00 50.00
2013- (#13)-Lone Ranger Outwits Crazy Cougar, The, 1968, Whitman, 260 pgs., 39 cents, hard-c, color illos 4.00 12.00 24.00
nn- Lone Ranger and the Lost Valley, The, 1938, Dell, 196 pgs., Fast-Action Story, soft-c 32.00 100.00 200.00
1405- Lone Star Martin of the Texas Rangers, 1939, Whitman, 432 pgs. 15.00 50.00 100.00
19- Lost City, The, 1935, EVW, movie scenes 12.00 40.00 80.00
1103- Lost Jungle, The (With Clyde Beatty), 1936, Saalfield, movie scenes, hard-c 12.00 40.00 80.00
1583- Lost Jungle, The (With Clyde Beatty), 1936, Saalfield, movie scenes, soft -c 10.00 36.00 72.00
753- Lost Patrol, The, 1934, Whitman, 160 pgs., photo-c, movie scenes with Boris Karloff 10.00 36.00 72.00
1189- Mac of the Marines in Africa, 1936, Whitman, 432 pgs. 10.00 30.00 60.00
1400- Mac of the Marines in China, 1938, Whitman, 432 pgs. 10.00 30.00 60.00
1100B- Magic Tricks (With explanations), 1938, Whitman, 36 pgs., 2 1/2" x 3 1/2", Penny Book 4.00 10.00 20.00
1100B- Magic Tricks (How to do them), 1938, Whitman, 36 pgs., 2 1/2" x 3 1/2", Penny Book 4.00 10.00 20.00
Major Hoople (See Our Boarding House)
2022-(#22)- Major Matt Mason, Moon Mission, 1968, Whitman, 256 pgs., hard-c, color illos. 5.00 15.00 30.00
1167- Mandrake the Magician, 1935, Whitman, 432 pgs., by Lee Falk & Phil Davis 18.00 60.00 120.00
1418- Mandrake the Magician and the Flame Pearls, 1946, Whitman, 352 pgs., by Lee Falk & Phil Davis 10.00 38.00 75.00
1431- Mandrake the Magician and the Midnight Monster, 1939, Whitman, 432 pgs., by Lee Falk & Phil Davis 12.00 41.00 82.00
1454- Mandrake the Magician Mighty Solver of Mysteries, 1941, Whitman, 432 pgs., by Lee Falk & Phil Davis, flip pictures

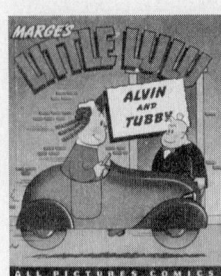

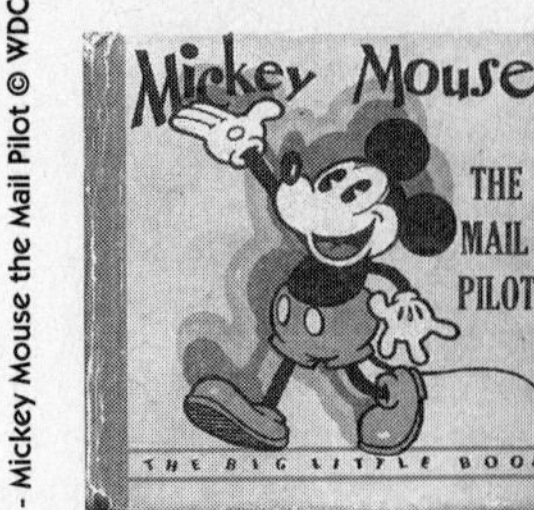
1429 - Marge's Little Lulu Alvin and Tubby © WHIT

731 - Mickey Mouse the Mail Pilot © WDC

Mickey Mouse and Minnie at Macy's © WDC

GD FN VF/NM

12.00 41.00 82.00

2011-(#11)-Man From U.N.C.L.E., The-The Calcutta Affair (TV Series), 1967, Whitman, 260 pgs., 39 cents, hard-c, color illos 5.00 15.00 30.00

1429- Marge's Little Lulu Alvin and Tubby, 1947, Whitman, All Pictures Comics, Stanley-a 22.00 75.00 150.00

1438- Mary Lee and the Mystery of the Indian Beads, 1937, Whitman, 300 pgs. 10.00 25.00 50.00

1165- Masked Man of the Mesa, The, 1939, Saalfield, 400 pgs. 8.00 22.00 45.00

1436- Maximo the Amazing Superman, 1940, Whitman, 432 pgs., Henry E. Vallely-a 10.00 35.00 70.00

1444- Maximo the Amazing Superman and the Crystals of Doom, 1941, Whitman,432 pgs., Henry E. Vallely-a 10.00 35.00 70.00

1445- Maximo the Amazing Superman and the Supermachine, 1941, Whitman, 432 pgs. 10.00 35.00 70.00

755- Men of the Mounted, 1934, Whitman, 320 pgs. 10.00 35.00 70.00

nn- Men of the Mounted, 1933, Whitman, 52 pgs., 3 1/2" x 5 3/4", premium-no ads; other versions with Poll Parrot & Perkins ad; soft-c 16.00 55.00 110.00

nn- Men of the Mounted, 1934, Whitman, Cocomalt premium, soft-c, by Ted McCall 10.00 31.00 62.00

1475- Men With Wings, 1938, Whitman, 240 pgs., photo-c, movie scenes (Paramount Pics.) 10.00 30.00 60.00

1170- Mickey Finn, 1940, Saalfield, 400 pgs., by Frank Leonard 10.00 30.00 60.00

717- Mickey Mouse (Disney), 1933, Whitman, 320 pgs., Gottfredson-a 150.00 800.00 1600.00

731- Mickey Mouse the Mail Pilot (Disney), 1933, Whitman, (This is the same book as the 1st Mickey Mouse BLB #717 but with "The Mail Pilot" printed on the front. Lower left of back cover has a small box printed over the existing "No. 717." "No. 731" is printed next to it.) (sold at auction in 2001 in Fine condition for $5,090)

726- Mickey Mouse in Blaggard Castle (Disney), 1934, Whitman, 320 pgs., Gottfredson-a 32.00 100.00 200.00

731- Mickey Mouse the Mail Pilot (Disney), 1933, Whitman, 300 pgs., Gottfredson-a 32.00 100.00 200.00

nn- Mickey Mouse the Mail Pilot (Disney), 1933, Whitman, 292 pgs., American Oil Co. premium, soft-c, Gottfredson-a; another version 3 1/2" x 4 3/4" 32.00 100.00 200.00

750- Mickey Mouse Sails for Treasure Island (Disney), 1933 Whitman, 320 pgs., Gottfredson-a 32.00 100.00 200.00

nn- Mickey Mouse Sails for Treasure Island (Disney), 1935, Whitman, 196 pgs., premium-no ads, soft-c, Gottfredson-a (Scarce) 40.00 140.00 280.00

nn- Mickey Mouse Sails for Treasure Island (Disney), 1935, Whitman, 196 pgs., Kolynos Dental Cream premium (Scarce) 40.00 140.00 280.00

756- Mickey Mouse Presents a Walt Disney Silly Symphony (Disney), 1934, Whitman, 240 pgs., Bucky Bug app. 30.00 90.00 180.00

1111- Mickey Mouse Presents Walt Disney's Silly Symphonies Stories, 1936, Whitman, 432 pgs., Donald Duck app. 30.00 90.00 180.00

1128- Mickey Mouse and Pluto the Racer (Disney), 1936, Whitman, 432 pgs., Gottfredson-a 26.00 82.00 165.00

1139- Mickey Mouse the Detective (Disney), 1934, Whitman, 300 pgs., Gottfredson-a 30.00 90.00 180.00

1139- Mickey Mouse the Detective (Disney), 1934, Whitman, 304 pgs., premium-no ads, soft-c, Gottfredson-a (Scarce) 40.00 140.00 280.00

1153- Mickey Mouse and the Bat Bandit (Disney), 1935, Whitman, 432 pgs., Gottfredson-a 28.00 85.00 170.00

nn- Mickey Mouse and the Bat Bandit (Disney), 1935, Whitman, 436 pgs., premium-no ads, 3-color, soft-c, Gottfredson-a (Scarce) 40.00 140.00 280.00

1160- Mickey Mouse and Bobo the Elephant (Disney), 1935, Whitman, 432 pgs., Gottfredson-a 28.00 85.00 170.00

1187- Mickey Mouse and the Sacred Jewel (Disney), 1936, Whitman, 432 pgs., Gottfredson-a 25.00 80.00 160.00

1401- Mickey Mouse in the Treasure Hunt (Disney), 1941, Whitman, 430 pgs., flip pictures of Pluto, Gottfredson-a 22.00 75.00 150.00

1409- Mickey Mouse Runs His Own Newspaper (Disney), 1937, Whitman, 432 pgs., Gottfredson-a 22.00 75.00 150.00

1413- Mickey Mouse and the "Lectro Box" (Disney), 1946, Whitman, 352 pgs., Gottfredson-a 15.00 50.00 100.00

1417- Mickey Mouse on Sky Island (Disney), 1941, Whitman, 432 pgs., flip pictures, Gottfredson-a; considered by Gottfredson to be his best Mickey story 22.00 75.00 150.00

1428- Mickey Mouse in the Foreign Legion (Disney), 1940, Whitman, 432 pgs., Gottfredson-a 22.00 75.00 150.00

1429- Mickey Mouse and the Magic Lamp (Disney), 1942, Whitman, 432 pgs., flip pictures 22.00 75.00 150.00

1433- Mickey Mouse and the Lazy Daisy Mystery (Disney), 1947, Whitman, 288 pgs. 15.00 50.00 100.00

1444- Mickey Mouse in the World of Tomorrow (Disney), 1948, Whitman, 288 pgs., Gottfredson-a 25.00 80.00 160.00

1451- Mickey Mouse and the Desert Palace (Disney), 1948, Whitman, 288 pgs. 15.00 50.00 100.00

1463- Mickey Mouse and the Pirate Submarine (Disney), 1939, Whitman, 432 pgs., Gottfredson-a 22.00 75.00 150.00

1464- Mickey Mouse and the Stolen Jewels (Disney), 1949, Whitman, 288 pgs. 20.00 70.00 140.00

1471- Mickey Mouse and the Dude Ranch Bandit (Disney), 1943, Whitman, 432 pgs., flip pictures 22.00 75.00 150.00

1475- Mickey Mouse and the 7 Ghosts (Disney), 1940, Whitman, 432 pgs., Gottfredson-a 22.00 75.00 150.00

1476- Mickey Mouse in the Race for Riches (Disney), 1938, Whitman, 432 pgs., Gottfredson-a 22.00 75.00 150.00

1483- Mickey Mouse Bell Boy Detective (Disney), 1945, Whitman, 352 pgs. 20.00 70.00 140.00

1499- Mickey Mouse on the Cave-Man Island (Disney), 1944, Whitman, 352 pgs. 20.00 70.00 140.00

2004- Mickey Mouse, Here Comes (Disney), 1936, Whitman, (Very Rare), 224 pgs., 12" x 8 1/4" box, with red, yellow and blue crayons, contains 224 loose pages to color, reprinted from early Mickey Mouse related movie and strip reprints 600.00 1200.00 2400.00

2020-(#20)- Mickey Mouse, Adventure in Outer Space, 1968, Whitman, 256 pgs.,hard-c, color illos. 4.00 12.00 25.00

3049- Mickey Mouse and His Big Little Kit (Disney), 1937, Whitman, 384 pgs., 4 1/2" x 6 1/2" box, includes miniature box of 4 crayons-red, yellow, blue and green 125.00 375.00 750.00

4062- Mickey Mouse, The Story Of, 1935, Whitman, 7" x 9 1/2", 320 pgs., Big Big Book, Gottfredson-a 180.00 500.00 1000.00

4062- Mickey Mouse and the Smugglers, The Story Of, 1935, Whitman, (Scarce), 7" x 9 1/2", 320 pgs., Big Big Book, same contents as above version; Gottfredson-a 180.00 500.00 1000.00

708-10- Mickey Mouse on the Haunted Island (Disney), 1950, Whitman, Gottfredson-a 10.00 38.00 75.00

nn- Mickey Mouse and Minnie at Macy's, 1934 Whitman, 148 pgs., 3 1/4" x 3 1/2", soft-c, R. H. Macy & Co. Christmas giveaway (Rare, less than 20 known copies) 550.00 1100.00 2200.00

nn- Mickey Mouse and Minnie March to Macy's, 1935, Whitman, 148 pgs., 3 1/2" x 3 1/2", soft-c, R. H. Macy & Co. Christmas giveaway (scarce) 300.00 800.00 1600.00

nn- Mickey Mouse and the Magic Carpet, 1935, Whitman, 148 pgs., 3 1/2"x 4", soft-c, giveaway, Gottfredson-a, Donald Duck app. 80.00 250.00 500.00

nn- Mickey Mouse Silly Symphonies, 1934, Dean & Son, Ltd (England), 48 pgs., with 4 pop-ups, Babes In The Woods, King Neptune
With dust jacket 125.00 425.00 850.00
Without dust jacket 100.00 300.00 600.00

3061- Mickey Mouse to Draw and Color (The Big Little Set), nd (early 1930s), Whitman, with crayons; box contains 320 loose pages to color, reprinted from early Mickey Mouse BLBs 100.00 300.00 600.00

1113 - Mutt and Jeff © WHIT

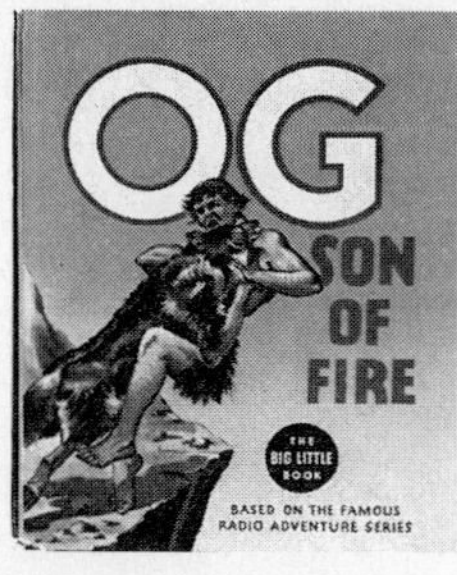

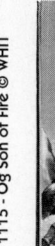

1115 - Og Son of Fire © WHIT

1416 - The Phantom and the Girl of Mystery © KING

GD FN VF/NM

16- **Mickey Mouse and Pluto** (Disney), Dell, 196 pgs., Fast-Action story 40.00 150.00 300.00

nn- **Mickey Mouse the Sheriff of Nugget Gulch** (Disney) 1938, Dell, 196 pgs., Fast-Action Story, soft-c, Gottfredson-a 40.00 150.00 300.00

nn- **Mickey Mouse with Goofy and Mickey's Nephews**, 1938, Dell, 196 pgs., Fast-Action Story, Gottfredson-a 40.00 150.00 300.00

Series A-**Mickey Mouse** (In actual Motion Pictures), nd (1932?), Moviescope Corp., 50 pgs., stapled, 1 3/4" x 2 1/2" flip book. Earliest known M. Mouse flip book 22.00 75.00 150.00

512- **Mickey Mouse Wee Little Books** (In open box), nn, 1934, 44 pgs., small size, soft-c
- Mickey Mouse and Tanglefoot 10.00 38.00 75.00
- Mickey Mouse at the Carnival 10.00 38.00 75.00
- Mickey Mouse Will Not Quit! 10.00 38.00 75.00
- Mickey Mouse Wins the Race! 10.00 38.00 75.00
- Mickey Mouse's Misfortune 10.00 38.00 75.00
- Mickey Mouse's Uphill Fight 10.00 38.00 75.00
- Complete set with box 80.00 250.00 500.00

1493- **Mickey Rooney and Judy Garland and How They Got into the Movies**, 1941, Whitman, 432 pgs., photo-c 10.00 35.00 70.00

1427- **Mickey Rooney Himself**, 1939, Whitman, 240 pgs., photo-c, movie scenes, life story 10.00 35.00 70.00

532- **Mickey's Dog Pluto** (Disney), 1943, Whitman, All Picture Comics, A Tall Comic Book , 3 3/4" x 8 3/4" 30.00 90.00 180.00

2113- **Midget Jumbo Coloring Book**, 1935, Saalfield 30.00 90.00 180.00

21- **Midsummer Night's Dream**, 1935, EVW, movie scenes 12.00 40.00 80.00

nn- **Minute-Man** (Mystery of the Spy Ring), 1941, Fawcett, Dime Action Book 40.00 150.00 300.00

710- **Moby Dick the Great White Whale, The Story of**, 1934, Whitman, 160 pgs., photo-c, movie scenes from "The Sea Beast" 10.00 35.00 70.00

746- **Moon Mullins and Kayo** (Kayo and Moon Mullins-inside), 1933, Whitman, 320 pgs., Frank Willard-c/a 12.00 43.00 85.00

nn- **Moon Mullins and Kayo**, 1933, Whitman, Cocomalt premium, soft-c, by Willard 12.00 43.00 85.00

1134- **Moon Mullins and the Plushbottom Twins**, 1935, Whitman, 432 pgs., Willard-c/a 12.00 40.00 80.00

nn- **Moon Mullins and the Plushbottom Twins**, 1935, Whitman, 436 pgs., premium-no ads, 3-color, soft-c, by Willard 22.00 75.00 150.00

1058- **Mother Pluto** (Disney), 1939, Whitman, 68 pgs., hard-c 10.00 36.00 72.00

1100B- **Movie Jokes** (From the talkies), 1938, Whitman, 36 pgs., 2 1/2" x 3 1/2", Penny Book 4.00 10.00 20.00

1408- **Mr. District Attorney on the Job**, 1941, Whitman, 432 pgs., flip pictures 10.00 25.00 50.00

nn- **Musicians of Bremen, The**, nd (1930s), np (Whitman), 36 pgs., 3" x 2 1/2", Penny Book 4.00 10.00 20.00

1113- **Mutt and Jeff**, 1936, Whitman, 300 pgs., by Bud Fisher 20.00 70.00 140.00

1116- **My Life and Times** (By Shirley Temple), 1936, Saalfield, Little Big Book, hard-c, photo-c/illos 12.00 40.00 80.00

1596- **My Life and Times** (By Shirley Temple), 1936, Saalfield, Little Big Book, soft-c, photo-c/illos 12.00 40.00 80.00

1497- **Myra North Special Nurse and Foreign Spies**, 1938, Whitman, 432 pgs. 10.00 30.00 60.00

1400- **Nancy and Sluggo**, 1946, Whitman, All Pictures Comics, Ernie Bushmiller-a 10.00 30.00 60.00

1487- **Nancy has Fun**, 1944, Whitman, All Pictures Comics 10.00 30.00 60.00

1150- **Napoleon and Uncle Elby**, 1938, Saalfield, 400 pgs., by Clifford McBride 10.00 30.00 60.00

1166- **Napoleon Uncle Elby And Little Mary**, 1939, Saalfield, 400 pgs., by Clifford McBride 10.00 30.00 60.00

1179- **Ned Brant Adventure Bound**, 1940, Saalfield, 400 pgs. 10.00 27.00 52.00

GD FN VF/NM

1146- **Nevada Rides The Danger Trail**, 1938, Saalfield, 400 pgs., J.R. White-a 10.00 25.00 50.00

1147- **Nevada Whalen, Avenger**, 1938, Saalfield, 400 pgs. 10.00 25.00 50.00

Nicodemus O'Malley (See Top-Line Comics)

1115- **Og Son of Fire**, 1936, Whitman, 432 pgs. 10.00 35.00 70.00

1419- **Oh, Blondie the Bumsteads** (See Blondie)

11- **Oliver Twist**, 1935, EVW (Five Star Library), movie scenes, starring Dickie Moore (Monogram Pictures) 12.00 40.00 80.00

718- **Once Upon a Time**, 1933, Whitman, 364 pgs., soft-c 12.00 40.00 80.00

712- **100 Fairy Tales for Children, The**, 1933, Whitman, 288 pgs., Circle Library 10.00 25.00 50.00

1099- **One Night of Love**, 1935, Saalfield, 160 pgs., hard-c, photo-c, movie scenes, Columbia Pictures, starring Grace Moore 10.00 35.00 70.00

1579- **One Night of Love**, 1935, Sat, 160 pgs., soft-c, photo-c, movie scenes, Columbia Pictures, starring Grace Moore 10.00 35.00 70.00

1155- **$1000 Reward**, 1938, Saalfield, 400 pgs. 10.00 25.00 50.00

Orphan Annie (See Little Orphan ...)

L17- **O'Shaughnessy's Boy**, 1935, Lynn, 192 pgs., movie scenes, w/Wallace Beery & Jackie Cooper (Metro-Goldwyn-Mayer) 10.00 31.00 62.00

1109- **Oswald the Lucky Rabbit**, 1934, Whitman, 288 pgs. 15.00 50.00 100.00

1403- **Oswald Rabbit Plays G-Man**, 1937, Whitman, 240 pgs., movie scenes by Walter Lantz 16.00 55.00 110.00

1190- **Our Boarding House, Major Hoople and his Horse**, 1940, Saalfield, 400 pgs. 10.00 32.00 65.00

1085- **Our Gang**, 1934, Saalfield, 160 pgs., photo-c, movie scenes, hard-c 10.00 38.00 75.00

1315- **Our Gang**, 1934, Saalfield, 160 pgs., photo-c, movie scenes, soft-c 10.00 38.00 75.00

1451- **"Our Gang" on the March**, 1942, Whitman, 432 pgs., flip pictures, Vallely-a 10.00 38.00 75.00

1456- **Our Gang Adventures**, 1948, Whitman, 288 pgs. 10.00 32.00 65.00

nn- **Paramount Newsreel Men with Admiral Byrd in Little America**, 1934, Whitman, 96 pgs., 6 1/4" x 6 1/4", photo-c, photo ill. 15.00 50.00 100.00

nn- **Patch**, nd (1930s), np (Whitman), 36 pgs., 3" x 2 1/2", Penny Book 4.00 10.00 20.00

1445- **Pat Nelson Ace of Test Pilots**, 1937, Whitman, 432 pgs. 10.00 25.00 50.00

1411- **Peggy Brown and the Mystery Basket**, 1941, Whitman, 432 pgs., flip pictures, Henry E. Vallely-a 10.00 27.00 52.00

1423- **Peggy Brown and the Secret Treasure**, 1947, Whitman, 288 pgs., Henry E. Vallely-a 10.00 27.00 52.00

1427- **Peggy Brown and the Runaway Auto Trailer**, 1937, Whitman, 300 pgs., Henry E. Vallely-a 10.00 27.00 52.00

1463- **Peggy Brown and the Jewel of Fire**, 1943, Whitman, 352 pgs., Henry E. Vallely-a 10.00 27.00 52.00

1491- **Peggy Brown in the Big Haunted House**, 1940, Whitman, 432 pgs., Vallely-a 10.00 27.00 52.00

1143- **Peril Afloat**, 1938, Saalfield, 400 pgs. 10.00 25.00 50.00

1199- **Perry Winkle and the Rinkeydinks**, 1937, Whitman, 432 pgs., by Martin Branner 10.00 35.00 70.00

1487- **Perry Winkle and the Rinkeydinks get a Horse**, 1938, Whitman, 432 pgs., by Martin Branner 10.00 35.00 70.00

Peter Pan (See Wee Little Books)

nn- **Peter Rabbit**, nd(1930s), np(Whitman), 36 pgs., Penny Book, 3" x 2 1/2" 4.00 12.00 24.00

Peter Rabbit's Carrots (See Wee Little Books)

1100- **Phantom, The**, 1936, Whitman, 432 pgs., by Lee Falk & Ray Moore 32.00 100.00 200.00

1416- **Phantom and the Girl of Mystery, The**, 1947, Whitman, 352 pgs. by Falk & Moore 12.00 45.00 90.00

1421- **Phantom and Desert Justice, The**, 1941, Whitman, 432 pgs.,

1466 - Pilot Pete Dive Bomber © WHIT

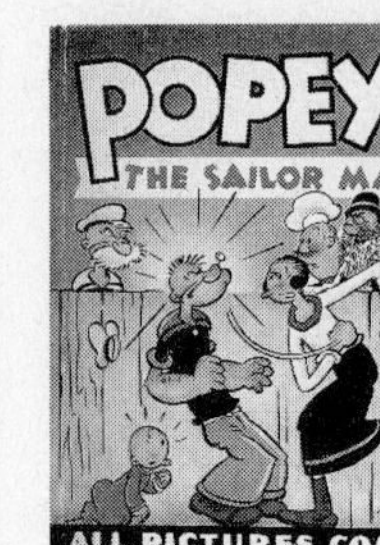

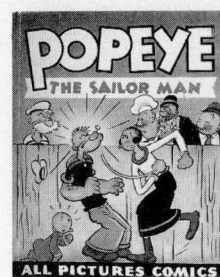

1422 - Popeye the Sailor Man © KING

203 - The Pop-Up Mother Goose © BRP

	GD	FN	VF/NM
flip pictures, by Falk & Moore	18.00	60.00	120.00
1468- Phantom and the Sky Pirates, The, 1945, Whitman, 352 pgs., by Falk & Moore	16.00	55.00	110.00
1474- Phantom and the Sign of the Skull, The, 1939, Whitman, 432 pgs., by Falk & Moore	20.00	65.00	130.00
1489- Phantom, Return of the..., 1942, Whitman, 432 pgs., flip pictures, by Falk & Moore	18.00	60.00	120.00
1130- Phil Barton, Sleuth (Scout Book), 1937, Saalfield, hard-c	8.00	20.00	40.00
Pied Piper of Hamlin (See Wee Little Books)			
1466- Pilot Pete Dive Bomber, 1941, Whitman, 432 pgs., flip pictures	10.00	25.00	50.00
5783-2- Pink Panther at Castle Kreep, The, 1980, Whitman, 260 pgs., soft-c, 79 cents, B&W	1.00	3.00	6.00
Pinocchio and Jiminy Cricket (See Walt Disney's ...)			
nn- Pioneers of the Wild West (Blue-c), 1933, World Syndicate, High Lights of History Series	10.00	25.00	50.00
nn- Pioneers of the Wild West (Red-c), 1933, World Syndicate, High Lights of History Series	10.00	25.00	50.00
1123- Plainsman, The, 1936, Whitman, 240 pgs., photo-c, movie scenes with Gary Cooper (Paramount Pics.)	15.00	75.00	150.00
Pluto (See Mickey's Dog ... & Walt Disney's ...)			
2114- Pocket Coloring Book, 1935, Saalfield	32.00	100.00	200.00
1060- Polly and Her Pals on the Farm, 1934, Saalfield, 164 pgs., hard-c, by Cliff Sterrett	12.00	40.00	80.00
1310- Polly and Her Pals on the Farm, 1934, Saalfield, soft-c	12.00	40.00	80.00
1051- Popeye, Adventures of..., 1934, Saalfield, oblong-size, E.C. Segar-a, hard-c	40.00	150.00	300.00
1088- Popeye in Puddleburg, 1934, Saalfield, 160 pgs., hard-c, E. C. Segar-a	16.00	55.00	110.00
1113- Popeye Starring in Choose Your Weppins, 1936, Saalfield, 160 pgs., hard-c, Segar-a	16.00	55.00	110.00
1117- Popeye's Ark, 1936, Saalfield, 4 1/2" x 5 1/2", hard-c, Segar-a	16.00	55.00	110.00
1163- Popeye Sees the Sea, 1936, Whitman, 432 pgs., Segar-a	18.00	60.00	120.00
1301- Popeye, Adventures of..., 1934, Saalfield, oblong-size, Segar-a	40.00	150.00	300.00
1318- Popeye in Puddleburg, 1934, Saalfield, 160 pgs., soft-c, Segar-a	16.00	55.00	110.00
1405- Popeye and the Jeep, 1937, Whitman, 432 pgs., Segar-a	18.00	60.00	120.00
1406- Popeye the Super-Fighter, 1939, Whitman, All Pictures Comics, flip pictures, Segar-a	16.00	55.00	110.00
1422- Popeye the Sailor Man, 1947, Whitman, All Pictures Comics	12.00	40.00	80.00
1450- Popeye in Quest of His Poopdeck Pappy, 1937, Whitman, 432 pgs., Segar-c/a	18.00	60.00	120.00
1458- Popeye and Queen Olive Oyl, 1949, Whitman, 288 pgs., Sagendorf-a	12.00	40.00	80.00
1459- Popeye and the Quest for the Rainbird, 1943, Whitman, Winner & Zaboly-a	12.00	45.00	90.00
1480- Popeye the Spinach Eater, 1945, Whitman, All Pictures Comics	12.00	40.00	80.00
1485- Popeye in a Sock for Susan's Sake, 1940, Whitman, 432 pgs., flip pictures	12.00	45.00	90.00
1497- Popeye and Caster Oyl the Detective, 1941, Whitman, 432 pgs. flip pictures, Segar-a	16.00	55.00	110.00
1499- Popeye and the Deep Sea Mystery, 1939, Whitman, 432 pgs., Segar-c/a	16.00	55.00	110.00
1593- Popeye Starring in Choose Your Weppins, 1936, Saalfield, 160 pgs., soft-c, Segar-a	16.00	55.00	110.00
1597- Popeye's Ark, 1936, Saalfield, 4 1/2" x 5 1/2", soft-c, Segar-a	16.00	55.00	110.00
2008-(#8)- Popeye-Ghost Ship to Treasure Island, 1967, Whitman, 260 pgs., 39 cents, hard-c, color illos	4.00	12.00	24.00
2034-(#34)- Popeye, Danger Ahoy!, 1969, Whitman, 256 pgs., hard-c, color illos.	4.00	12.00	24.00
4063- Popeye, Thimble Theatre Starring, 1935, Whitman, 7" x 9 1/2", 320 pgs., Big Big Book, Segar-c/a; (Cactus cover w/yellow logo)	180.00	500.00	1000.00
4063- Popeye, Thimble Theatre Starring, 1935, Whitman, 7" x 9 1/2", 320 pgs., Big Big Book, Segar-c/a; (Big Balloon-c with red logo), (2nd printing w/same contents as above)	200.00	600.00	1200.00
5761-2- Popeye and Queen Olive Oyl, 1973 (1980-reprint of 1973 version), 260 pgs., 79 cents, B&W, soft-c	1.00	3.00	6.00
103- "Pop-Up" Buck Rogers in the Dangerous Mission (with Pop-Up picture), 1934, BRP, 62 pgs., The Midget Pop-Up Book w/Pop-Up in center of book, Calkins-a	120.00	400.00	800.00
206- "Pop-Up" Buck Rogers - Strange Adventures in the Spider Ship, The, 1935, BRP, 24 pgs., 8" x 9", 3 Pop-Ups, hard-c, by Dick Calkins	120.00	400.00	800.00
nn- "Pop-Up" Cinderella, 1933, BRP, 7 1/2" x 9 3/4", 4 Pop-Ups, hard-c			
With dustjacket ($2.00)	100.00	300.00	600.00
Without dustjacket	80.00	250.00	500.00
207- "Pop-Up" Dick Tracy-Capture of Boris Arson, 1935, BRP, 24 pgs., 8" x 9", 3 Pop-Ups, hard-c, by Gould	100.00	300.00	600.00
210- "Pop-Up" Flash Gordon Tournament of Death, The, 1935, BRP, 24 pgs., 8" x 9", 3 Pop-Ups, hard-c, by Alex Raymond	120.00	400.00	800.00
202- "Pop-Up" Goldilocks and the Three Bears, The, 1934, BRP, 24 pgs., 8" x 9", 3 Pop-Ups, hard-c	33.00	125.00	250.00
nn- "Pop-Up" Jack and the Beanstalk, 1933, BRP, hard-c (50 cents), 1 Pop-Up	33.00	125.00	250.00
nn- "Pop-Up" Jack the Giant Killer, 1933, BRP, hard-c (50 cents), 1 Pop-Up	33.00	125.00	250.00
nn- "Pop-Up" Jack the Giant Killer, 1933, BRP, 4 Pop-Ups, hard-c			
With dustjacket ($2.00)	100.00	300.00	600.00
Without dust jacket	80.00	250.00	500.00
nn- "Pop-Up" Little Black Sambo, (with Pop-Up picture), 1934, BRP, 62 pgs., The Midget Pop-Up Book, one Pop-Up in center of book	50.00	200.00	400.00
208- "Pop-Up" Little Orphan Annie and Jumbo the Circus Elephant, 1935, BRP, 24 pgs., 8x9% 3 Pop-Ups, hard-c, by H. Gray	100.00	300.00	600.00
nn- "Pop-Up" Little Red Ridinghood, 1933, BRP, hard-c (50 cents), 1 Pop-Up	22.00	75.00	150.00
nn- "Pop-Up" Mickey Mouse, The, 1933, BRP, 34 pgs., 6 1/2" x 9", 3 Pop-Ups, hard-c, Gottfredson-a (75 cents)	100.00	300.00	600.00
nn- "Pop-Up" Mickey Mouse in King Arthur's Court, The,1933, BRP, 56 pgs., 7 1/2" x 9 1/4", 4 Pop-Ups, hard-c, Gottfredson-a			
With dust jacket ($2.00)	400.00	750.00	1500.00
Without dustjacket	275.00	550.00	1100.00
101- "Pop-Up" Mickey Mouse in "Ye Olden Days" (with Pop-Up picture), 1934, 62 pgs., BRP, The Midget Pop-Up Book, one Pop-Up in center of book, Gottfredson-a	80.00	250.00	500.00
nn- "Pop-Up" Minnie Mouse, The, 1933, BRP, 36 pgs., 6 1/2" x 9", 3 Pop-Ups, hard-c (75 cents), Gottfredson-a	100.00	300.00	600.00
203- "Pop-Up" Mother Goose, The, 1934, BRP, 24 pgs., 8" x 9 1/4", 3 Pop-Ups, hard-c	40.00	150.00	300.00
nn- "Pop-Up" Mother Goose Rhymes, The, 1933, BRP, 96 pgs., 7 1/2" x 9 1/4", 4 Pop-Ups, hard-c			
With dustjacket ($2.00)	80.00	250.00	500.00
Without dustjacket	53.00	217.00	435.00
209- "Pop-Up" New Adventures of Tarzan, 1935, BRP, 24 pgs., 8" x 9", 3 Pop-Ups, hard-c	100.00	300.00	600.00
104- "Pop-Up" Peter Rabbit, The (with Pop-Up picture), 1934, BRP, 62 pgs., The Midget Pop-Up Book, one Pop-Up in center of book	33.00	125.00	250.00
nn- "Pop-Up" Pinocchio, 1933, BRP, 7 1/2" x 9 3/4", 4 Pop-Ups, hard-c			
With dustjacket ($2.00)	102.00	305.00	610.00
Without dust jacket	86.00	265.00	530.00
102- "Pop-Up" Popeye among the White Savages (with Pop-Up picture), 1934, BRP, 62 pgs., The Midget Pop-Up Book, one Pop-Up in center of book, E. C. Segar-a	45.00	180.00	360.00

1408 - Porky Pig and Petunia © WB

1400 - Red Ryder and Little Beaver on Hoofs of Thunder © WHIT

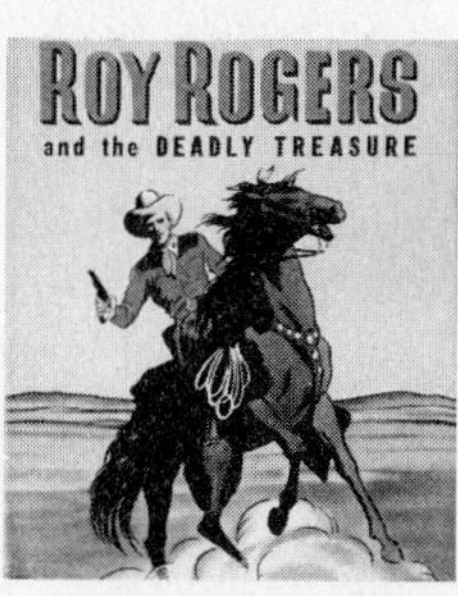

1437 - Roy Rogers and the Deadly Treasure © WHIT

GD FN VF/NM

205- **"Pop-Up" Popeye with the Hag of the Seven Seas, The**, 1935, BRP, 24 pgs., 8" x 9", 3 Pop-Ups, hard-c, Segar-a 100.00 300.00 600.00

201- **"Pop-Up" Puss In Boots, The**, 1934, BRP, 24 pgs., 3 Pop-Ups, hard-c 32.00 100.00 200.00

nn- **"Pop-Up" Silly Symphonies, The** (Mickey Mouse Presents His ...), 1933, BRP, 56 pgs., 9 3/4" x 7 1/2", 4 Pop-Ups, hard-c
With dust jacket ($2.00) 135.00 450.00 900.00
Without dust jacket 120.00 400.00 800.00

nn- **"Pop-Up" Sleeping Beauty**, 1933, BRP, hard-c, (50 cents), 1 Pop-up 33.00 120.00 240.00

212- **"Pop-Up" Terry and the Pirates in Shipwrecked, The**, 1935, BRP, 24 pgs., 8" x 9", 3 Pop-Ups, hard-c 80.00 250.00 500.00

211- **"Pop-Up" Tim Tyler in the Jungle, The**, 1935, BRP, 24 pgs., 8" x 9", 3 Pop-Ups, hard-c 40.00 150.00 300.00

1404- **Porky Pig and His Gang**, 1946, Whitman, All Pictures Comics, Barks-a, reprints Four Color #48 18.00 60.00 120.00

1408- **Porky Pig and Petunia**, 1942, Whitman, All Pictures Comics, flip pictures, reprints Four Color #16 & Famous Gang Book of Comics 12.00 40.00 80.00

1176- **Powder Smoke Range**, 1935, Whitman, 240 pgs., photo-c, movie scenes, Hoot Gibson, Harey Carey app. (RKO Radio Pict.) 10.00 35.00 70.00

1058- **Practical Pig!, The** (Disney), 1939, Whitman, 68 pgs., 5" x 5 1/2", hard-c 10.00 31.00 62.00

758- **Prairie Bill and the Covered Wagon**, 1934, Whitman, 384 pgs., Hal Arbo-a 10.00 30.00 60.00

nn- **Prairie Bill and the Covered Wagon**, 1934, Whitman, 390 pgs., premium-no ads, 3-color, soft-c, Hal Arbo-a 12.00 45.00 90.00

1440- **Punch Davis of the U.S. Aircraft Carrier**, 1945, Whitman, 352 pgs. 8.00 22.00 45.00

nn- **Puss in Boots**, nd(1930s), np(Whitman), 36 pgs., Penny Book 4.00 10.00 20.00

1100B- **Puzzle Book**, 1938, Whitman, 36 pgs., 2 1/2" x 3 1/2", Penny Book 4.00 12.00 24.00

1100B- **Puzzles**, 1938, Whitman, 36 pgs., 2 1/2" x 3 1/2", Penny Book 4.00 12.00 24.00

1100B- **Quiz Book, The**, 1938, Whitman, 36 pgs., 2 1/2" x 3 1/2", Penny Book 4.00 12.00 24.00

1142- **Radio Patrol**, 1935, Whitman, 432 pgs., by Eddie Sullivan & Charlie Schmidt (#1) 10.00 31.00 62.00

1173- **Radio Patrol Trailing the Safeblowers**, 1937, Whitman, 432 pgs. 10.00 27.00 52.00

1496- **Radio Patrol Outwitting the Gang Chief**, 1939, Whitman, 432 pgs. 10.00 27.00 52.00

1498- **Radio Patrol and Big Dan's Mobsters**, 1937, Whitman, 432 pgs. 10.00 27.00 52.00

1441- **Range Busters, The**, 1942, Whitman, 432 pgs., Henry E. Vallely-a 10.00 27.00 52.00

1163- **Ranger and the Cowboy, The**, 1939, Saalfield, 400 pgs. 10.00 25.00 50.00

1154- **Rangers on the Rio Grande**, 1938, Saalfield, 400 pgs. 10.00 25.00 50.00

1447- **Ray Land of the Tank Corps, U.S.A.**, 1942, Whitman, 432 pgs., flip pictures, Hess-a 10.00 25.00 50.00

1157- **Red Barry Ace-Detective**, 1935, Whitman, 432 pgs., by Will Gould 10.00 35.00 70.00

1426- **Red Barry Undercover Man**, 1939, Whitman, 432 pgs., by Will Gould 10.00 30.00 60.00

20- **Red Davis**, 1935, EVW, 160 pgs. 10.00 30.00 60.00

1449- **Red Death on the Range, The**, 1940, Whitman, 432 pgs., Fred Harman-a (Bronc Peeler) 10.00 30.00 60.00

nn- **Red Hen and the Fox, The**, nd(1930s), np(Whitman), 36 pgs., 3" x 2 1/2", Penny Book 4.00 10.00 20.00

1145- **Red Hot Holsters**, 1938, Saalfield, 400 pgs. 10.00 25.00 50.00

1400- **Red Ryder and Little Beaver on Hoofs of Thunder**, 1939, Whitman, 432 pgs., Harman-c/a 12.00 45.00 90.00

1414- **Red Ryder and the Squaw-Tooth Rustlers**, 1946, Whitman, 352 pgs., Fred Harman-a 10.00 35.00 70.00

GD FN VF/NM

1427- **Red Ryder and the Code of the West**, 1941, Whitman, 432 pgs., flip pictures, by Harman 10.00 41.00 82.00

1440- **Red Ryder the Fighting Westerner**, 1940, Whitman, Harman-a 10.00 41.00 82.00

1443- **Red Ryder and the Rimrock Killer**, 1948, Whitman, 288 pgs., Harman-a 10.00 31.00 62.00

1450- **Red Ryder and Western Border Guns**, 1942, Whitman, 432 pgs., flip pictures, by Harman 10.00 41.00 82.00

1454- **Red Ryder and the Secret Canyon**, 1948, Whitman, 288 pgs., Harman-a 10.00 31.00 62.00

1466- **Red Ryder and Circus Luck**, 1947, Whitman, 288 pgs., by Fred Harman 10.00 31.00 62.00

1473- **Red Ryder in War on the Range**, 1945, Whitman, 352 pgs., by Fred Harman 10.00 35.00 70.00

1475- **Red Ryder and the Outlaw of Painted Valley**, 1943, Whitman, 352 pgs., by Harman 10.00 31.00 62.00

702-10- **Red Ryder Acting Sheriff**, 1949, Whitman, by Fred Hannan 10.00 30.00 60.00

nn- **Red Ryder Brings Law to Devil's Hole**, 1939, Dell, 196 pgs., Fast-Action Story, Harman-c/a 26.00 100.00 200.00

nn- **Red Ryder and the Highway Robbers**, 1938, Whitman, 36 pgs., 2 1/2" x 3 1/2", Penny Book 10.00 31.00 62.00

754- **Reg'lar Fellers**, 1933, Whitman, 320 pgs., by Gene Byrnes 10.00 36.00 72.00

nn- **Reg'lar Fellers**, 1933, Whitman, 202 pgs., Cocomalt premium, by Gene Byrnes 12.00 40.00 80.00

1424- **Rex Beach's Jaragu of the Jungle**, 1937, Whitman, 432 pgs. 10.00 25.00 50.00

12- **Rex, King of Wild Horses in "Stampede,"** 1935, EVW, 160 pgs., movie scenes, Columbia Pictures 10.00 30.00 60.00

1100B- **Riddles for Fun**, 1938, Whitman, 36 pgs., 2 1/2" x 3 1/2", Penny Book 4.00 12.00 24.00

1100B- **Riddles to Guess**, 1938, Whitman, 36 pgs., 2 1/2" x 3 1/2", Penny Book 4.00 12.00 24.00

1425- **Riders of Lone Trails**, 1937, Whitman, 300 pgs. 10.00 30.00 60.00

1141- **Rio Raiders** (A Billy The Kid Story), 1938, Saalfield, 400 pgs. 10.00 30.00 60.00

2023-(#23)- **The Road Runner, The Super Beep Catcher**, 1968, Whitman, 256 pgs., hard-c, color illos. 2.00 5.00 10.00

5767-2- **Road Runner, The Lost Road Runner Mine, The**, 1974 (1980), 260 pgs., 79 cents, B&W, soft-c 1.00 3.00 6.00

Robin Hood (See Wee Little Books)

10- **Robin Hood**, 1935, EVW, 160 pgs., movie scenes w/Douglas Fairbanks (United Artists), hard-c 15.00 50.00 100.00

719- **Robinson Crusoe** (The Story of...), nd (1933), Whitman, 364 pgs., soft-c 10.00 36.00 72.00

1421- **Roy Rogers and the Dwarf-Cattle Ranch**, 1947, Whitman, 352 pgs., Henry E. Vallely-a 10.00 43.00 85.00

1437- **Roy Rogers and the Deadly Treasure**, 1947, Whitman, 288 pgs. 10.00 40.00 80.00

1448- **Roy Rogers and the Mystery of the Howling Mesa**, 1948, Whitman, 288 pgs. 10.00 40.00 80.00

1452- **Roy Rogers in Robbers' Roost**, 1948, Whitman, 288 pgs. 10.00 40.00 80.00

1460- **Roy Rogers Robinhood of the Range**, 1942, Whitman, 432 pgs., Hess-a (1st) 10.00 43.00 85.00

1462- **Roy Rogers and the Mystery of the Lazy M**, 1949, Whitman 10.00 35.00 70.00

1476- **Roy Rogers King of the Cowboys**, 1943, Whitman, 352 pgs., Irwin Myers-a, based on movie 12.00 48.00 95.00

1494- **Roy Rogers at Crossed Feathers Ranch**, 1945, Whitman, 320 pgs., Erwin Hess-a , 3 1/4" x 5 1/2" 10.00 40.00 80.00

701-10- **Roy Rogers and the Snowbound Outlaws**, 1949, 3 1/4" x 5 1/2" 10.00 30.00 60.00

715-10- **Roy Rogers Range Detective**, 1950, Whitman, 2 1/2" x 5" 10.00 30.00 60.00

nn- **Sandy Gregg Federal Agent on Special Assignment**, 1939, Whitman,

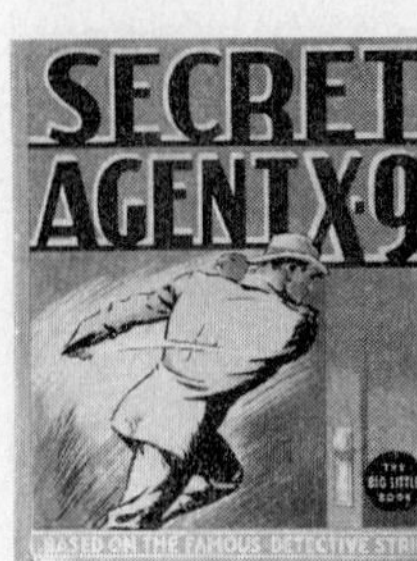

1144 - Secret Agent X-9 © WHIT

1430 - The Shadow and the Living Death © CN

1460 - Snow White and the Seven Dwarfs © WDC

GD FN VF/NM

36 pgs., 2 1/2" x 3 1/2", Penny Book 10.00 31.00 62.00
Sappo (See Top-Line Comics)
1122- **Scrappy**, 1934, Whitman, 288 pgs. 15.00 50.00 100.00
L12- **Scrappy** (The Adventures of...), 1935, Lynn, 192 pgs., movie scenes 15.00 50.00 100.00
1191- **Secret Agent K-7**,1940, Saalfield, 400 pgs., based on radio show 10.00 25.00 50.00
1144- **Secret Agent X-9**, 1936, Whitman, 432 pgs., Charles Flanders-a 10.00 36.00 72.00
1472- **Secret Agent X-9 and the Mad Assassin**, 1938, Whitman, 432 pgs., Charles Flanders-a 10.00 36.00 72.00
1161- **Sequoia**, 1935, Whitman, 160 pgs., photo-c, movie scenes 10.00 35.00 70.00
1430- **Shadow and the Living Death, The**, 1940, Whitman, 432 pgs., Erwin Hess-a 40.00 180.00 360.00
1443- **Shadow and the Master of Evil, The**, 1941, Whitman, 432 pgs., flip pictures, Hess-a 40.00 180.00 360.00
1495- **Shadow and the Ghost Makers, The**, 1942, Whitman, 432 pgs., John Coleman Burroughs-c 40.00 180.00 360.00
2024- **Shazzan, The Glass Princess**, 1968, Whitman 4.00 12.00 24.00
Shirley Temple (See My Life and Times & Story of..)
1095- **Shirley Temple and Lionel Barrymore Starring In "The Little Colonel,"** 1935, Saalfield, photo-c, movie scenes 15.00 50.00 100.00
1115- **Shirley Temple in the Littlest Rebel**, 1935, Saalfield, photo-c, movie scenes, hard-c 15.00 50.00 100.00
1595- **Shirley Temple in the Littlest Rebel**, 1935, Saalfield, photo-c, movie scenes, soft-c 15.00 50.00 100.00
1195- **Shooting Sheriffs of the Wild West**, 1936, Whitman, 432 pgs. 10.00 25.00 50.00
1169- **Silly Symphony Featuring Donald Duck** (Disney), 1937, Whitman, 432 pgs., Taliaferro-a 25.00 80.00 160.00
1441- **Silly Symphony Featuring Donald Duck and His (MIS) Adventures** (Disney), 1937, Whitman, 432 pgs., Taliaferro-a 25.00 80.00 160.00
1155- **Silver Streak, The**, 1935, Whitman, 160 pgs., photo-c, movie scenes (RKO Radio Pict.) 10.00 30.00 60.00
Simple Simon (See Wee Little Books)
1649- **Sir Lancelot** (TV Series), 1958, Whitman, 280 pgs. 8.00 20.00 40.00
1112- **Skeezix in Africa**, 1934, Whitman, 300 pgs., Frank King-a 12.00 40.00 80.00
1408- **Skeezix at the Military Academy**, 1938, Whitman, 432 pgs., Frank King-a 10.00 35.00 70.00
1414- **Skeezix Goes to War**, 1944, Whitman, 352 pgs., Frank King-a 10.00 35.00 70.00
1419- **Skeezix on His Own in the Big City**, 1941, Whitman, All Pictures Comics, flip pictures, Frank King-a 10.00 37.00 74.00
761- **Skippy**, 1934, Whitman, 320 pgs., by Percy Crosby 12.00 40.00 80.00
4056- **Skippy, The Story of**, 1934, Whitman, 320 pgs., 7" x 9 1/2", Big Big Book, Percy Crosby-a 50.00 200.00 400.00
nn- **Skippy, The Story of**, 1934, Whitman, Phillips Dental Magnesia premium, soft-c, by Percy Crosby 10.00 35.00 70.00
1439- **Skyroads with Clipper Williams of the Flying Legion**, 1938, Whitman, 432 pgs., by Lt. Dick Calkins, Russell Keaton-a 10.00 30.00 60.00
1127- **Skyroads with Hurricane Hawk**, 1936, Whitman, 432 pgs., by Lt. Dick Calkins, Russell Keaton-a 10.00 30.00 60.00
Smilin' Jack and his Flivver Plane (See Top-Line Comics)
1152- **Smilin' Jack and the Stratosphere Ascent**, 1937, Whitman, 432 pgs., Zack Mosley-a 12.00 40.00 80.00
1412- **Smilin' Jack Flying High with "Downwind,"** 1942, Whitman, 432 pgs., Zack Mosley-a 10.00 36.00 72.00
1416- **Smilin' Jack in Wings over the Pacific**, 1939, Whitman, 432 pgs., Zack Mosley-a 10.00 36.00 72.00
1419- **Smilin' Jack and the Jungle Pipe Line**, 1947, Whitman, 352 pgs., Zack Mosley-a 10.00 32.00 65.00

GD FN VF/NM

1445- **Smilin' Jack and the Escape from Death Rock**, 1943, Whitman, 352 pgs., Mosley-a 10.00 32.00 65.00
1464- **Smilin' Jack and the Coral Princess**, 1945, Whitman, 352 pgs., Zack Mosley-a 10.00 32.00 65.00
1473- **Smilin' Jack Speed Pilot**, 1941, Whitman, 432 pgs., Zack Mosley-a 10.00 36.00 72.00
2- **Smilin' Jack and his Stratosphere Plane**, 1938, Whitman, 132 pgs., Buddy Book, soft-c, Zack Mosley-a 32.00 100.00 200.00
nn- **Smilin' Jack Grounded on a Tropical Shore**, 1938, Whitman, 36 pgs., 2 1/2" x 3 1/2", Penny Book 10.00 27.00 52.00
11- **Smilin' Jack and the Border Bandits**, 1941, Dell, 196 pgs., Fast-Action Story, soft-c, Zack Mosley-a 30.00 90.00 180.00
745- **Smitty Golden Gloves Tournament**, 1934, Whitman, 320 pgs., Walter Berndt-a 10.00 36.00 72.00
nn- **Smitty Golden Gloves Tournament**, 1934, Whitman, 204 pgs., Cocomalt premium, soft-c, Walter Berndt-a 12.00 43.00 85.00
1404- **Smitty and Herbie Lost Among the Indians**, 1941, Whitman, All Pictures Comics 10.00 27.00 52.00
1477- **Smitty in Going Native**, 1938, Whitman, 300 pgs., Walter Berndt-a 10.00 27.00 52.00
2- **Smitty and Herby**, 1936, Whitman, 132 pgs., 3 1/2" x 3 1/2", soft-c, Tarzan Ice Cream cup lid premium 30.00 90.00 180.00
9- **Smitty's Brother Herby and the Police Horse**, 1938, Whitman, 132 pgs., 3 1/4" x 3 1/2", Buddy Book-ice cream premium, by Walter Berndt 30.00 90.00 180.00
1010- **Smokey Stover Firefighter of Foo**, 1937, Whitman, 7 1/4" x 5 1/2", 64 pgs., Nickel Book, Bill Holman-a 10.00 35.00 70.00
1413- **Smokey Stover**, 1942, Whitman, All Pictures Comics, flip pictures, Bill Holman-a 10.00 30.00 60.00
1421- **Smokey Stover the Foo Fighter**, 1938, Whitman, 432 pgs., Bill Holman-a 10.00 30.00 60.00
1481- **Smokey Stover the Foolish Foo Fighter**, 1942, Whitman, All Pictures Comics 10.00 30.00 60.00
1- **Smokey Stover the Fireman of Foo**, 1938, Whitman, 3 3/4" x 3 1/2", 132 pgs., Buddy Book-ice cream premium, by Bill Holman 30.00 90.00 180.00
1100A- **Smokey Stover**, 1938, Whitman, 36 pgs., 2 1/2" x 3 1/2", Penny Book 10.00 27.00 52.00
nn- **Smokey Stover and the Fire Chief of Foo**, 1938, Whitman, 36 pgs., 2 1/2" x 3 1/2", Penny Book, yellow shirt on-c 10.00 27.00 52.00
nn- **Smokey Stover and the Fire Chief of Foo**, 1938, Whitman, 36 pgs., Penny Book, green shirt on-c 10.00 30.00 60.00
1460- **Snow White and the Seven Dwarfs** (The Story of Walt Disney's ...), 1938, Whitman, 288 pgs. 22.00 75.00 150.00
1136- **Sombrero Pete**, 1936, Whitman, 432 pgs. 10.00 25.00 50.00
1152- **Son of Mystery**, 1939, Saalfield, 400 pgs. 10.00 25.00 50.00
1191- **SOS Coast Guard**, 1936, Whitman, 432 pgs., Henry E. Vallely-a 10.00 25.00 50.00
2016-(#16)-**Space Ghost-The Sorceress of Cyba-3** (TV Cartoon), 1968, Whitman, 260 pgs., 39¢-c, hard-c, color illos 10.00 25.00 50.00
1455- **Speed Douglas and the Mole Gang-The Great Sabotage Plot**, 1941, Whitman, 432 pgs., flip pictures 10.00 25.00 50.00
5779-2- **Spider-Man Zaps Mr. Zodiac**, 1976 (1980), 260 pgs., 79¢-c, soft-c, B&W 1.00 3.00 6.00
1467- **Spike Kelly of the Commandos**, 1943, Whitman, 352 pgs. 8.00 22.00 45.00
1144- **Spook Riders on the Overland**, 1938, Saalfield, 400 pgs. 8.00 22.00 45.00
768- **Spy, The**, 1936, Whitman, 300 pgs. 10.00 30.00 60.00
nn- **Spy Smasher and the Red Death**, 1941, Fawcett, 4" x 5 1/2", Dime Action Book 40.00 150.00 300.00
1120- **Stan Kent Freshman Fullback**, 1936, Saalfield, 148 pgs., hard-c 8.00 25.00 50.00
1132- **Stan Kent, Captain**, 1937, Saalfield 8.00 25.00 50.00
1600- **Stan Kent Freshman Fullback**, 1936, Saalfield, 148 pgs., soft-c 8.00 25.00 50.00
1123- **Stan Kent Varsity Man**, 1936, Saalfield, 160 pgs., hard-c 8.00 25.00 50.00

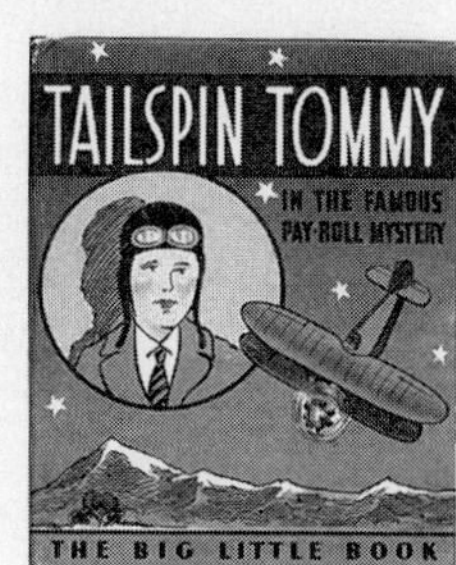

747 - Tailspin Tommy in the Famous Pay-Roll Mystery © WHIT

nn - Tarzan of the Apes © ERB

770 - The Tarzan Twins © ERB

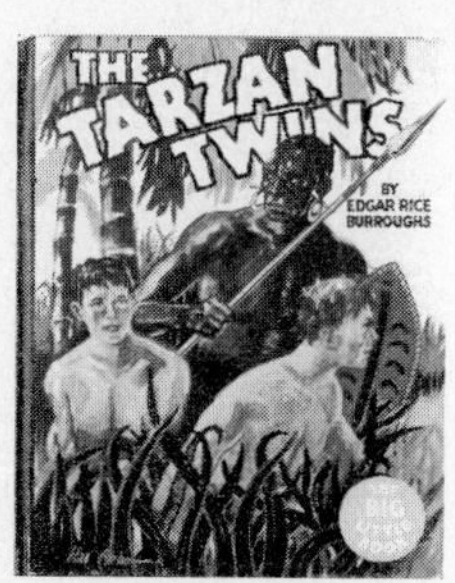

GD FN VF/NM

1603- Stan Kent Varsity Man, 1936, Saalfield, 160 pgs., soft-c 8.00 25.00 50.00
1104- Steel Arena, The (With Clyde Beatty), 1936, Saalfield, hard-c, movie scenes adapted from "The Lost Jungle" 10.00 32.00 65.00
1584- Steel Arena, The (With Clyde Beatty), 1936, Saalfield, soft-c, movie scenes 10.00 32.00 65.00
1426- Steve Hunter of the U.S. Coast Guard Under Secret Orders, 1942, Whitman, 432 pgs. 8.00 22.00 45.00
1456- Story of Charlie McCarthy and Edgar Bergen, The, 1938, Whitman, 288 pgs. 10.00 38.00 75.00
Story of Daniel, The (See Wee Little Books)
Story of David, The (See Wee Little Books)
1110- Story of Freddie Bartholomew, The, 1935, Saalfield, 4 1/2" x 5 1/4", hard-c, movie scenes (MGM) 10.00 30.00 60.00
1590- Story of Freddie Bartholomew, The, 1935, Saalfield, 4 1/2" x 5 1/4", soft-c, movie scenes (MGM) 10.00 30.00 60.00
Story of Gideon, The (See Wee Little Books)
W714- Story of Jackie Cooper, The, 1933, Whitman, 240 pgs., photo-c, movie scenes, "Skippy" & "Sooky" movie 10.00 37.00 74.00
Story of Joseph, The (See Wee Little Books)
Story of Moses, The (See Wee Little Books)
Story of Ruth and Naomi (See Wee Little Books)
1089- Story of Shirley Temple, The, 1934, Saalfield, 160 pgs., hard-c, photo-c, movie scenes 12.00 40.00 80.00
1319- Story of Shirley Temple, The, 1934, Saalfield, 160 pgs., soft-c, photo-c, movie scenes 12.00 40.00 80.00
1090- Strawberry-Roan, 1934, Saalfield, 160 pgs., hard-c, Ken Maynard photo-c, movie scenes 12.00 40.00 80.00
1320- Strawberry-Roan, 1934, Saalfield, 160 pgs., soft-c, Ken Maynard photo-c, movie scenes 12.00 40.00 80.00
Streaky and the Football Signals (See Top-Line Comics)
5780-2- Superman in the Phantom Zone Connection, 1980, 260 pgs., 79¢-c, soft-c, B&W 2.00 5.00 10.00
582- "Swap It" Book, The, 1949, Samuel Lowe Co., 260 pgs., 3 1/2" x 4 1/2"
1. Little Tex in the Midst of Trouble 5.00 20.00 40.00
2. Little Tex's Escape 5.00 20.00 40.00
3. Little Tex Comes to the XY Ranch 5.00 20.00 40.00
4. Get Them Cowboy 5.00 20.00 40.00
5. The Mail Must Go Through! A Story of the Pony Express 5.00 20.00 40.00
6. Nevada Jones, Trouble Shooter 5.00 20.00 40.00
7. Danny Meets the Cowboys 5.00 20.00 40.00
8. Flint Adams and the Stage Coach 5.00 20.00 40.00
9. Bud Shinners and the Oregon Trail 5.00 20.00 40.00
10. The Outlaws' Last Ride 5.00 20.00 40.00
Sybil Jason (See Little Big Shot)
747- Tailspin Tommy in the Famous Pay-Roll Mystery, 1933, Whitman, 320 pgs., Hal Forrest-a (# 1) 12.00 40.00 80.00
nn- Tailspin Tommy the Pay-Roll Mystery, 1934, Whitman, 52 pgs., 3 1/2" x 5 1/4", premium-no ads, soft-c; another version with Perkins ad, Hal Forrest-a 18.00 60.00 120.00
1110- Tailspin Tommy and the Island in the Sky, 1936, Whitman, 432 pgs., Hal Forrest-a 10.00 32.00 65.00
1124- Tailspin Tommy the Dirigible Flight to the North Pole, 1934, Whitman, 432 pgs., H. Forrest-a 10.00 36.00 72.00
nn- Tailspin Tommy the Dirigible Flight to the North Pole, 1934, Whitman, 436 pgs., 3-color, soft-c, premium-no ads, Hal Forrest-a 30.00 87.00 175.00
1172- Tailspin Tommy Hunting for Pirate Gold, 1935, Whitman, 432 pgs., Hal Forrest-a 10.00 32.00 65.00
1183- Tailspin Tommy Air Racer, 1940, Saalfield, 400 pgs., hard-c 10.00 32.00 65.00
1184- Tailspin Tommy in the Great Air Mystery, 1936, Whitman, 240 pgs., photo-c, movie scenes 12.00 40.00 80.00
1410- Tailspin Tommy the Weasel and His "Skywaymen," 1941, Whitman, All Pictures Comics, flip pictures 10.00 30.00 60.00
1413- Tailspin Tommy and the Lost Transport, 1940, Whitman, 432 pgs., Hal Forrest-a 10.00 30.00 60.00
1423- Tailspin Tommy and the Hooded Flyer, 1937, Whitman, 432 pgs., Hal Forrest-a 10.00 32.00 65.00
1494- Tailspin Tommy and the Sky Bandits, 1938, Whitman 432 pgs., Hal Forrest-a 10.00 32.00 65.00
nn- Tailspin Tommy and the Airliner Mystery, 1938, Whitman, 196 pgs., Fast-Action Story, soft-c, Hal Forrest-a 33.00 120.00 240.00
nn- Tailspin Tommy in Flying Aces, 1938, Dell, 196 pgs., Fast-Action Story, soft-c, Hal Forrest-a 33.00 120.00 240.00
nn- Tailspin Tommy in Wings Over the Arctic, 1934, Whitman, Cocomalt premium, Forrest-a 15.00 50.00 100.00
nn- Tailspin Tommy Big Thrill Chewing Gum, 1934, Whitman, 8 pgs., 2 1/2" x 3 " (6 diff.) each.. 10.00 35.00 70.00
3- Tailspin Tommy on the Mountain of Human Sacrifice, 1938, Whitman, soft-c, Buddy Book 32.00 105.00 210.00
7- Tailspin Tommy's Perilous Adventure, 1934, Whitman, 132 pgs., 3 1/2" x 3 1/2" soft-c, Tarzan Ice Cream cup premium 32.00 110.00 220.00
L16- Tale of Two Cities, A, 1935, Lynn, movie scenes 12.00 40.00 80.00
744- Tarzan of the Apes, 1933, Whitman, 320 pgs., by Edgar Rice Burroughs (1st) 33.00 120.00 240.00
nn- Tarzan of the Apes, 1935, Whitman, 52 pgs., 3 1/2" x 5 1/4", soft-c, stapled, premium, no ad; another version with a Perkins ad 40.00 150.00 300.00
769- Tarzan the Fearless, 1934, Whitman, 240 pgs., Buster Crabbe photo-c, movie scenes, ERB 25.00 80.00 160.00
770- Tarzan Twins, The, 1934, Whitman, 432 pgs., ERB 100.00 300.00 600.00
770- Tarzan Twins, The, 1935, Whitman, 432 pgs., ERB 40.00 150.00 300.00
nn- Tarzan Twins, The, 1935, Whitman, 52 pgs., 3 1/2" x 5 3/4", premium-no ads, soft-c, ERB 47.00 195.00 390.00
nn- Tarzan Twins, The, 1935, Whitman, 436 pgs., 3-color, soft-c, premium-no ads, ERB 52.00 210.00 420.00
778- Tarzan of the Screen (The Story of Johnny Weissmuller), 1934, Whitman, 240 pgs., photo-c, movie scenes, ERB 30.00 87.00 175.00
1102- Tarzan, The Return of, 1936, Whitman, 432 pgs., Edgar Rice Burroughs 18.00 60.00 120.00
1180- Tarzan, The New Adventures of, 1935, Whitman, 160 pgs., Herman Brix photo-c, movie scenes, ERB 20.00 70.00 140.00
1182- Tarzan Escapes, 1936, Whitman, 240 pgs., Johnny Weissmuller photo-c, movie scenes, ERB 30.00 87.00 175.00
1407- Tarzan Lord of the Jungle, 1946, Whitman, 352 pgs., ERB 12.00 45.00 90.00
1410- Tarzan, The Beasts of, 1937, Whitman, 432 pgs., Edgar Rice Burroughs 16.00 55.00 110.00
1442- Tarzan and the Lost Empire, 1948, Whitman, 288 pgs., ERB 12.00 48.00 95.00
1444- Tarzan and the Ant Men, 1945, Whitman, 352 pgs., ERB 12.00 48.00 95.00
1448- Tarzan and the Golden Lion, 1943, Whitman, 432 pgs., ERB 16.00 55.00 110.00
1452- Tarzan the Untamed, 1941, Whitman, 432 pgs., flip pictures, ERB 16.00 55.00 110.00
1453- Tarzan the Terrible, 1942, Whitman, 432 pgs., flip pictures, ERB 16.00 55.00 110.00
1467- Tarzan in the Land of the Giant Apes, 1949, Whitman, ERB 12.00 48.00 95.00
1477- Tarzan, The Son of, 1939, Whitman, 432 pgs., ERB 16.00 55.00 110.00
1488- Tarzan's Revenge, 1938, Whitman, 432 pgs., ERB 16.00 55.00 110.00
1495- Tarzan and the Jewels of Opar, 1940, Whitman, 432 pgs. 16.00 55.00 110.00
4056- Tarzan and the Tarzan Twins with Jad-Bal-Ja the Golden Lion, 1936, Whitman, 7" x 9 1/2", 320 pgs., Big Big Book 100.00 300.00 600.00
709-10- Tarzan and the Journey of Terror, 1950, Whitman, 2 1/2" x 5", ERB, Marsh-a 10.00 27.00 52.00

10 - Terry and the Pirates Meet Again © WHIT

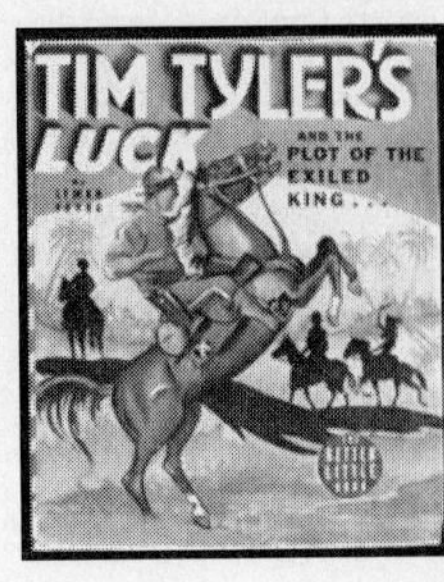

1479 - Tim Tyler's Luck and the Plot of the Exiled King © WHIT

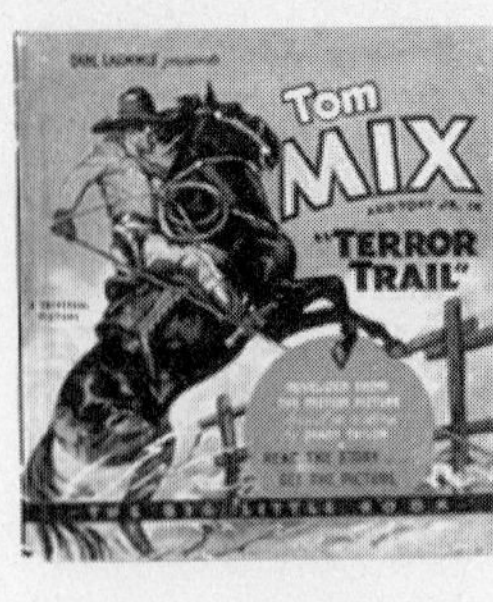

762 - Tom Mix and Tony Jr. in "Terror Trail" © WHIT

	GD	FN	VF/NM
2005- **(#5)-Tarzan: The Mark of the Red Hyena**, 1967, Whitman, 260 pgs., 39 cents, hard-c, color illos	4.00	12.00	25.00
nn- **Tarzan**, 1935, Whitman, 148 pgs., soft-c, 3 1/2" x 4", Tarzan Ice Cream cup premium, ERB (scarce)	120.00	400.00	800.00
nn- **Tarzan and a Daring Rescue**, 1938, Whitman, 68 pgs., Pan-Am premium, soft-c, ERB	37.00	120.00	240.00
nn- **Tarzan and his Jungle Friends**, 1936, Whitman, 132 pgs., soft-c, 3 1/2" x 3 1/2", Tarzan Ice Cream cup premium, ERB (scarce)	90.00	275.00	550.00
nn- **Tarzan in the Golden City**, 1938, Whitman, 68 pgs., Pan-Am premium, soft-c, ERB	25.00	80.00	160.00
nn- **Tarzan The Avenger**, 1939, Dell, 194 pgs., Fast-Action Story, ERB, soft-c	33.00	120.00	240.00
nn- **Tarzan with the Tarzan Twins in the Jungle**, 1938, Dell, 194 pgs., Fast-Action Story, ERB	33.00	120.00	240.00
1100B- **Tell Your Fortune**, 1938, Whitman, 36 pgs., 2 1/2" x 3 1/2", Penny Book	4.00	14.00	28.00
1156- **Terry and the Pirates**, 1935, Whitman, 432 pgs., Milton Caniff-a (#1)	15.00	50.00	100.00
nn- **Terry and the Pirates**, 1935, Whitman, 52 pgs., 3 1/2" x 5 1/4", soft-c, premium, Milton Caniff-a; 3 versions: No ad, Sears ad & Perkins ad	22.00	80.00	160.00
1412- **Terry and the Pirates Shipwrecked on a Desert Island**, 1938, Whitman, 432 pgs., Milton Caniff-a	10.00	36.00	72.00
1420- **Terry and War in the Jungle**, 1946, Whitman, 352 pgs., Milton Caniff-a	10.00	32.00	65.00
1436- **Terry and the Pirates the Plantation Mystery**, 1942, Whitman, 432 pgs., flip pictures, Milton Caniff-a	10.00	36.00	72.00
1446- **Terry and the Pirates and the Giant's Vengeance**, 1939, Whitman, 432 pgs., Caniff-a	10.00	36.00	72.00
1499- **Terry and the Pirates in the Mountain Stronghold**, 1941, Whitman, 432 pgs., Caniff-a	10.00	36.00	72.00
4073- **Terry and the Pirates, The Adventures of**, 1938, Whitman, 7" x 9 1/2", 320 pgs., Big Big Book, Milton Caniff-a	80.00	250.00	500.00
10- **Terry and the Pirates Meet Again**, 1936, Whitman, 132 pgs., 3 1/2" x 3 1/2", soft-c, Tarzan Ice Cream cup lid premium	40.00	150.00	300.00
nn- **Terry and the Pirates, Adventures of**, 1938, 36 pgs., 2 1/2" x 3 1/2", Penny Book, Caniff-a	10.00	30.00	60.00
nn- **Terry and the Pirates and the Island Rescue**, 1938, Whitman, 68 pgs., 3 1/4" x 3 1/2", Pan-Am premium	20.00	75.00	150.00
nn- **Terry and the Pirates on Their Travels**, 1938, 36 pgs., 2 1/2" x 3 1/2", Penny Book, Caniff-a	10.00	30.00	60.00
nn- **Terry and the Pirates and the Mystery Ship**, 1938, Dell, 194 pgs., Fast-Action Story, soft-c	32.00	100.00	200.00
1492- **Terry Lee Flight Officer U.S.A.**, 1944, Whitman, 352 pgs., Milton Caniff-a	10.00	32.00	65.00
7- **Texas Bad Man, The** (Tom Mix), 1934, EVW, 160 pgs., (Five Star Library), movie scenes	18.00	60.00	120.00
1429- **Texas Kid, The**, 1937, Whitman, 432 pgs.	10.00	25.00	50.00
1135- **Texas Ranger, The**, 1936, Whitman, 432 pgs., Hal Arbo-a	10.00	25.00	50.00
nn- **Texas Ranger, The**, 1935, Whitman, 260 pgs., Cocomalt premium, soft-c, Hal Arbo-a	10.00	30.00	60.00
nn- **Texas Ranger and the Rustler Gang, The**, 1936, Whitman, Pan-Am giveaway	20.00	75.00	150.00
nn- **Texas Ranger in the West, The**, 1938, Whitman, 36 pgs., 2 1/2" x 3 1/2", Penny Book	10.00	27.00	52.00
nn- **Texas Ranger to the Rescue, The**, 1938, Whitman, 36 pgs., 2 1/2" x 3 1/2", Penny Book	10.00	27.00	52.00
12- **Texas Rangers in Rustler Strategy, The**, 1936, Whitman, 132 pgs., 3 1/2" x 3 1/2", soft-c, Tarzan Ice Cream cup lid premium	30.00	90.00	180.00
Tex Thorne (See Zane Grey)			
Thimble Theatre (See Popeye)			
L26- **13 Hours By Air**, 1936, Lynn, 128 pgs., 5" x 7 1/2", photo-c, movie scenes (Paramount Pictures)	12.00	40.00	80.00
nn- **Three Bears, The**, nd (1930s), np (Whitman), 36 pgs., 3" x 2 1/2", Penny Book	4.00	10.00	20.00
1129- **Three Finger Joe** (Baseball), 1937, Saalfield, Robert A. Graef-a	10.00	25.00	50.00
nn- **Three Little Pigs, The**, nd (1930s), np (Whitman), 36 pgs., 3" x 2 1/2", Penny Book	4.00	10.00	20.00
1131- **Three Musketeers**, 1935, Whitman, 182 pgs., 5 1/4" x 6 1/4", photo-c, movie scenes	12.00	45.00	90.00
1409- **Thumper and the Seven Dwarfs** (Disney), 1944, Whitman, All Pictures Comics	15.00	50.00	100.00
1108- **Tiger Lady, The** (The life of Mabel Stark, animal trainer), 1935, Saalfield, photo-c, movie scenes, hard-c	10.00	30.00	60.00
1588- **Tiger Lady, The**, 1935, Saalfield, photo-c, movie scenes, soft-c	10.00	30.00	60.00
1442- **Tillie the Toiler and the Wild Man of Desert Island**, 1941, Whitman, 432 pgs., Russ Westover-a	10.00	32.00	65.00
1058- **"Timid Elmer"** (Disney), 1939, Whitman, 5" x 5 1/2", 68 pgs., hard-c	10.00	31.00	62.00
1152- **Tim McCoy in the Prescott Kid**, 1935, Whitman, 160 pgs., hard-c, photo-c, movie scenes	15.00	50.00	100.00
1193- **Tim McCoy in the Westerner**, 1936, Whitman, 240 pgs., photo-c, movie scenes	12.00	48.00	95.00
1436- **Tim McCoy on the Tomahawk Trail**, 1937, Whitman, 432 pgs., Robert Weisman-a	10.00	30.00	60.00
1490- **Tim McCoy and the Sandy Gulch Stampede**, 1939, Whitman, 424 pgs.	10.00	30.00	60.00
2- **Tim McCoy in Beyond the Law**, 1934, EVW, Five Star Library, photo-c, movie scenes (Columbia Pictures)	18.00	60.00	120.00
10- **Tim McCoy in Fighting the Redskins**, 1938, Whitman, 130 pgs., Buddy Book, soft-c	30.00	87.00	175.00
14- **Tim McCoy in Speedwings**, 1935, EVW, Five Star Library, 160 pgs., photo-c, movie scenes (Columbia Pictures)	18.00	60.00	120.00
nn- **Tim the Builder**, nd (1930s), np (Whitman), 36 pgs., 3" x 2 1/2", Penny Book	4.00	10.00	20.00
Tim Tyler (See Adventures of ...)			
1140- **Tim Tyler's Luck Adventures in the Ivory Patrol**, 1937, Whitman, 432 pgs., by Lyman Young	10.00	30.00	60.00
1479- **Tim Tyler's Luck and the Plot of the Exiled King**, 1939, Whitman, 432 pgs., by Lyman Young	10.00	27.00	52.00
767- **Tiny Tim, The Adventures of**, 1935, Whitman, 384 pgs., by Stanley Link	10.00	36.00	72.00
1172- **Tiny Tim and the Mechanical Men**, 1937, Whitman, 432 pgs., by Stanley Link	10.00	32.00	65.00
1472- **Tiny Tim in the Big, Big World**, 1945, Whitman, 352 pgs., by Stanley Link	10.00	30.00	60.00
2006- **(#6)-Tom and Jerry Meet Mr. Fingers**, 1967, Whitman, 39¢-c 260 pgs., hard-c, color illos.	4.00	12.00	24.00
2030-**(#30)- Tom and Jerry, The Astro-Nots**, 1969, Whitman, 256 pgs., hard-c, color illos.	4.00	10.00	20.00
5787-2- **Tom and Jerry Under the Big Top**, 1980, Whitman, 79¢-c, 260 pgs., soft-c, B&W	1.00	3.00	6.00
723- **Tom Beatty Ace of the Service**, 1934, Whitman, 256 pgs., George Taylor-a	10.00	32.00	65.00
nn- **Tom Beatty Ace of the Service**, 1934, Whitman, 260 pgs., soft-c	10.00	32.00	65.00
1165- **Tom Beatty Ace of the Service Scores Again**, 1937, Whitman, 432 pgs., Weisman-a	10.00	30.00	60.00
1420- **Tom Beatty Ace of the Service and the Big Brain Gang**, 1939, Whitman, 432 pgs.	10.00	30.00	60.00
nn- **Tom Beatty Ace Detective and the Gorgon Gang**, 1938?, Whitman, 36 pgs., 2 1/2" x 3 1/2", Penny Book	10.00	27.00	52.00
nn- **Tom Beatty Ace of the Service and the Kidnapers**, 1938?, Whitman, 36 pgs., 2 1/2" x 3 1/2", Penny Book	10.00	27.00	52.00
1102- **Tom Mason on Top**, 1935, Saalfield, 160 pgs., Tom Mix photo-c, from Mascot serial "The Miracle Rider," movie scenes, hard-c	12.00	48.00	95.00
1582- **Tom Mason on Top**, 1935, Saalfield, 160 pgs., Tom Mix photo-c, movie scenes, soft-c	12.00	48.00	95.00
Tom Mix (See Chief of the Rangers, Flaming Guns & Texas Bad Man)			
762- **Tom Mix and Tony Jr. in "Terror Trail,"** 1934, Whitman, 160 pgs., movie scenes	12.00	48.00	95.00

541 - Top-Line Comics © WHIT

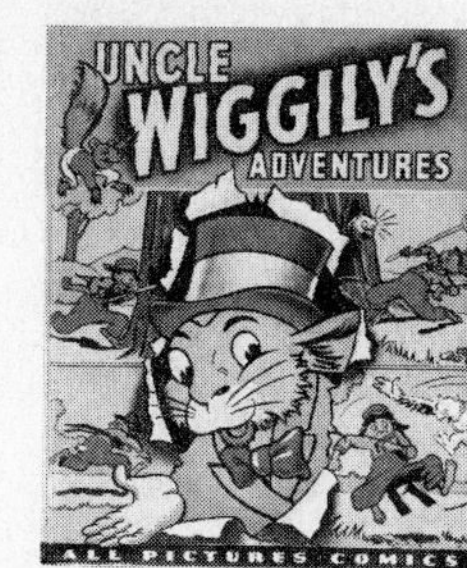

1405 - Uncle Wiggily's Adventures © WHIT

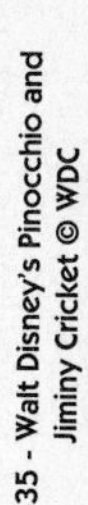
1435 - Walt Disney's Pinocchio and Jiminy Cricket © WDC

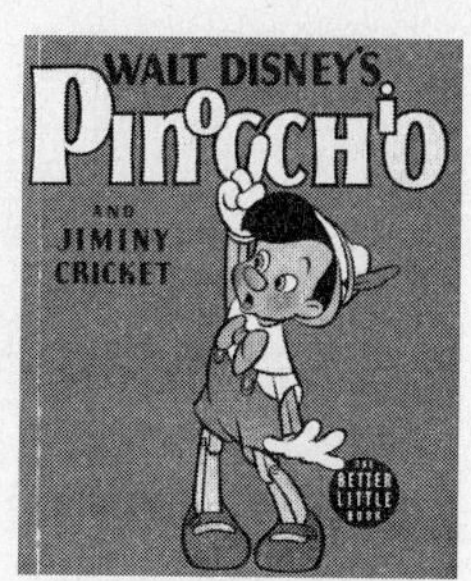

	GD	FN	VF/NM
1144- **Tom Mix in the Fighting Cowboy**, 1935, Whitman, 432 pgs., Hal Arbo-a	10.00	35.00	70.00
nn- **Tom Mix in the Fighting Cowboy**, 1935, Whitman, 436 pgs., premium-no ads, 3 color, soft-c, Hal Arbo-a	22.00	75.00	150.00
1166- **Tom Mix in the Range War**, 1937, Whitman, 432 pgs., Hal Arbo-a	10.00	32.00	65.00
1173- **Tom Mix Plays a Lone Hand**, 1935, Whitman, 288 pgs., hard-c, Hal Arbo-a	10.00	32.00	65.00
1183- **Tom Mix and the Stranger from the South**, 1936, Whitman, 432 pgs.	10.00	32.00	65.00
1462- **Tom Mix and the Hoard of Montezuma**, 1937, Whitman, H. E. Vallely-a	10.00	32.00	65.00
1482- **Tom Mix and His Circus on the Barbary Coast**, 1940, Whitman, 432 pgs., James Gary-a	10.00	32.00	65.00
3047- **Tom Mix and His Big Little Kit**, 1937, Whitman, 384 pgs., 4 1/2" x 6 1/2" box, includes miniature box of 4 crayons-red, yellow, blue and green	80.00	250.00	500.00
4068- **Tom Mix and the Scourge of Paradise Valley**, 1937, Whitman, 7" x 9 1/2", 320 pgs., Big Big Book, Vallely-a	50.00	200.00	400.00
6833- **Tom Mix in the Riding Avenger**, 1936, Dell, 244 pgs., Cartoon Story Book, hard-c	25.00	80.00	160.00
nn- **Tom Mix Riders to the Rescue**, 1939, 36 pgs., 2 1/2" x 3", Penny Book	10.00	27.00	52.00
nn- **Tom Mix Avenges the Dry Gulched Range King**, 1939, Dell, 196 pgs., Fast-Action Story, soft-c	25.00	80.00	160.00
nn- **Tom Mix in the Riding Avenger**, 1936, Dell, 244 pgs., Fast-Action Story	25.00	80.00	160.00
nn- **Tom Mix the Trail of the Terrible 6**, 1935, Ralston Purina Co., 84 pgs., 3" x 3 1/2", premium	16.00	55.00	110.00
4- **Tom Mix and Tony in the Rider of Death Valley**, 1934, EVW, Five Star Library, 160 pgs., movie scenes (Universal Pictures), hard-c	18.00	60.00	120.00
7- **Tom Mix in the Texas Bad Man**, 1934, EVW, Five Star Library, 160 pgs., movie scenes	18.00	60.00	120.00
10- **Tom Mix in the Tepee Ranch Mystery**, 1938, Whitman, 132 pgs., Buddy Book, soft-c	30.00	87.00	175.00
1126- **Tommy of Troop Six** (Scout Book), 1937, Saalfield, hard-c	8.00	22.00	45.00
1606- **Tommy of Troop Six** (Scout Book), 1937, Saalfield, soft-c	8.00	22.00	45.00
Tom Sawyer (See Adventures of ...)			
1437- **Tom Swift and His Magnetic Silencer**, 1941, Whitman, 432 pgs., flip pictures	12.00	40.00	80.00
1485- **Tom Swift and His Giant Telescope**, 1939, Whitman, 432 pgs., James Gary-a	12.00	40.00	80.00
540- **Top-Line Comics** (In Open Box), 1935, Whitman, 164 pgs., 3 1/2" x 3 1/2", 3 books in set, all soft-c:			
Bobby Thatcher and the Samarang Emerald	12.00	45.00	90.00
Broncho Bill in Suicide Canyon	12.00	45.00	90.00
Freckles and His Friends in the North Woods	12.00	45.00	90.00
Complete set with box	43.00	165.00	330.00
541- **Top-Line Comics** (In Open Box), 1935, Whitman, 164 pgs., 3 1/2" x 3 1/2", 3 books in set; all soft-c:			
Little Joe and the City Gangsters	12.00	45.00	90.00
Smilin' Jack and His Flivver Plane	12.00	45.00	90.00
Streaky and the Football Signals	12.00	45.00	90.00
Complete set with box	43.00	165.00	330.00
542- **Top-Line Comics** (In Open Box), 1935, Whitman, 164 pgs., 3 1/2" x 3 1/2", 3 books in set; all soft-c:			
Dinglehoofer Und His Dog Adolph by Knerr	12.00	45.00	90.00
Jungle Jim by Alex Raymond	18.00	60.00	120.00
Sappo by Segar	18.00	60.00	120.00
Complete set with box	50.00	202.00	405.00
543- **Top-Line Comics** (In Open Box), 1935, Whitman, 164 pgs., 3 1/2" x 31/2", 3 books in set; all soft-c:			
Alexander Smart, ESQ by Winner	12.00	45.00	90.00
Bunky by Billy de Beck	12.00	45.00	90.00
Nicodemus O'Malley by Carter	12.00	45.00	90.00

	GD	FN	VF/NM
Complete set with box	43.00	165.00	330.00
1158- **Tracked by a G-Man**, 1939, Saalfield, 400 pgs.	10.00	25.00	50.00
L25- **Trail of the Lonesome Pine, The**, 1936, Lynn, movie scenes	12.00	40.00	80.00
nn- **Trail of the Terrible 6** (See Tom Mix ...)			
1185- **Trail to Squaw Gulch, The**, 1940, Saalfield, 400 pgs.	10.00	25.00	50.00
720- **Treasure Island**, 1933, Whitman, 362 pgs.	15.00	50.00	100.00
1141- **Treasure Island**, 1934, Whitman, 160 pgs., 4 1/4" x 5 1/4", Jackie Cooper photo-c, movie scenes	12.00	43.00	85.00
1100B- **Tricks Easy to Do** (Slight of hand & magic), 1938, Whitman, 36 pgs., 2 1/2" x 3 1/2", Penny Book	4.00	10.00	20.00
1100B- **Tricks You Can Do**, 1938, Whitman, 36 pgs., 2 1/2" x 3 1/2", Penny Book	4.00	10.00	20.00
1104- **Two-Gun Montana**, 1936, Whitman, 432 pgs., Henry E. Vallely-a	10.00	25.00	50.00
nn- **Two-Gun Montana Shoots it Out**, 1939, Whitman, 36 pgs., 2 1/2" x 3 1/2", Penny Book	10.00	27.00	52.00
1058- **Ugly Duckling, The** (Disney), 1939, Whitman, 68 pgs., 5" x 5 1/2", hard-c	10.00	36.00	72.00
nn- **Ugly Duckling, The**, nd (1930s), np (Whitman), 36 pgs., 3" x 2 1/2", Penny Book	4.00	10.00	20.00
Unc' Billy Gets Even (See Wee Little Books)			
1114- **Uncle Don's Strange Adventures**, 1935, Whitman, 300 pgs., radio star-Uncle Don Carney	10.00	27.00	52.00
722- **Uncle Ray's Story of the United States**, 1934, Whitman, 300 pgs.	10.00	30.00	60.00
1461- **Uncle Sam's Sky Defenders**, 1941, Whitman, 432 pgs., flip pictures	10.00	25.00	50.00
1405- **Uncle Wiggily's Adventures**, 1946, Whitman, All Pictures Comics	12.00	40.00	80.00
1411- **Union Pacific**, 1939, Whitman, 240 pgs., photo-c, movie scenes	10.00	32.00	65.00
1189- **Up Dead Horse Canyon**, 1940, Saalfield, 400 pgs.	8.00	22.00	45.00
1455- **Vic Sands of the U.S. Flying Fortress Bomber Squadron**, 1944, Whitman, 352 pgs.	10.00	30.00	60.00
1645- **Walt Disney's Andy Burnett on the Trail** (TV Series), 1958, Whitman, 280 pgs.	4.00	12.00	24.00
711-10- **Walt Disney's Cinderella and the Magic Wand**, 1950, Whitman, 2 1/2" x 5", based on Disney movie	10.00	25.00	50.00
845- **Walt Disney's Donald Duck and his Cat Troubles** (Disney), 1948, Whitman, 100 pgs., 5" x 5 1/2", hard-c	10.00	30.00	60.00
845- **Walt Disney's Donald Duck and the Boys**, 1948, Whitman, 100 pgs., 5" x 5 1/2", hard-c, Barks-a	20.00	70.00	140.00
2952- **Walt Disney's Donald Duck in the Great Kite Maker**, 1949, Whitman, 24 pgs., 3 1/4" x 4", Tiny Tales, full color (5 cents)	10.00	25.00	50.00
804- **Walt Disney's Mickey and the Beanstalk**, 1948, Whitman, hard-c	10.00	30.00	60.00
2952- **Walt Disney's Mickey Mouse and the Night Prowlers**, Whitman, 1949, 24 pgs., 3 1/4" x 4", Tiny Tales, full color (5 ¢)	10.00	25.00	50.00
845- **Walt Disney's Mickey Mouse and the Boy Thursday**, 194 pgs., Whitman, 5" x 5 1/2", 100 pgs.	10.00	30.00	60.00
845- **Walt Disney's Mickey Mouse the Miracle Maker**, 1948, Whitman, 5" x 5 1/2", 100 pgs.	10.00	30.00	60.00
845- **Walt Disney's Minnie Mouse and the Antique Chair**, 194 pgs., Whitman, 5" x 5 1/2", 100 pgs.	10.00	30.00	60.00
1435- **Walt Disney's Pinocchio and Jiminy Cricket**, 1940, Whitman, 432 pgs.	15.00	50.00	100.00
845- **Walt Disney's Poor Pluto**, 1948, Whitman, 5" x 5 1/2", 100 pgs., hard-c	10.00	30.00	60.00
1467- **Walt Disney's Pluto the Pup** (Disney), 1938, Whitman, 432 pgs., Gottfredson-a	12.00	48.00	95.00
1066- **Walt Disney's Story of Clarabelle Cow** (Disney), 1938, Whitman, 100 pgs.	10.00	30.00	60.00
66- **Walt Disney's Story of Dippy the Goof** (Disney), 1938, Whitman, 100 pgs.	10.00	30.00	60.00

1407 - Wings of the U.S.A. © WHIT

779 - The World War in Photographs © WHIT

1452 - Zane Grey's King of the Royal Mounted Gets His Man © WHIT

GD FN VF/NM

1066- **Walt Disney's Story of Donald Duck** (Disney), 1938, Whitman, 100 pgs., hard-c, Taliaferro-a 10.00 30.00 60.00

1066- **Walt Disney's Story of Mickey Mouse** (Disney), 1938, Whitman, 100 pgs., hard-c, Gottfredson-a, Donald Duck app. 10.00 30.00 60.00

1066- **Walt Disney's Story of Minnie Mouse** (Disney), 1938, Whitman, 100 pgs., hard-c 10.00 30.00 60.00

1066- **Walt Disney's Story of Pluto the Pup**, (Disney), 1938, Whitman, 100 pgs., hard-c 10.00 30.00 60.00

2952- **Walter Lantz Presents Andy Panda's Rescue**, 1949, Whitman, Tiny Tales, full color (5 cents) 10.00 25.00 50.00

751- **Wash Tubbs in Pandemonia**, 1934, Whitman, 320 pgs., Roy Crane-a 10.00 32.00 65.00

1455- **Wash Tubbs and Captain Easy Hunting For Whales**, 1938, Whitman, 432 pgs., Roy Crane-a 10.00 30.00 60.00

6- **Wash Tubbs in Foreign Travel**, 1934, Whitman, soft-c, 3 1/2" x 3 1/2", Tarzan Ice Cream cup premium 30.00 87.00 175.00

nn- **Wash Tubbs**, 1934, Whitman, 52 pgs., 4" x 5 1/2", premium-no ads, soft-c, Roy Crane-a 15.00 50.00 100.00

513- **Wee Little Books** (In Open Box), 1934, Whitman, 44 pgs., small size, 6 books in set
Child's Garden of Verses 4.00 10.00 20.00
The Happy Prince (The Story of) 4.00 10.00 20.00
Joan of Arc (The Story of) 4.00 10.00 20.00
Peter Pan (The Story of) 5.00 15.00 30.00
Pied Piper Of Hamlin 4.00 10.00 20.00
Robin Hood (A Story of...) 4.00 10.00 20.00
Complete set with box 25.00 80.00 160.00

514- **Wee Little Books** (In Open Box), 1934, Whitman, 44 pgs., small size, 6 books in set
Jack And Jill 4.00 10.00 20.00
Little Bo-Peep 4.00 10.00 20.00
Little Tommy Tucker 4.00 10.00 20.00
Mother Goose 4.00 10.00 20.00
Simple Simon 4.00 10.00 20.00
Complete set with box 20.00 70.00 140.00

518- **Wee Little Books** (In Open Box), 1933, Whitman, 44 pgs., small size, 6 books in set, written by Thornton Burgess
Betty Bear's Lesson-1930 4.00 11.00 22.00
Jimmy Skunk's Justice-1933 4.00 11.00 22.00
Little Joe Otter's Slide-1929 4.00 11.00 22.00
Peter Rabbit's Carrots-1933 4.00 12.00 24.00
Unc' Billy Gets Even-1930 4.00 11.00 22.00
Whitefoot's Secret-1933 4.00 11.00 22.00
Complete set with box 26.00 82.00 164.00

519- **Wee Little Books** (In Open Box) (Bible Stories), 1934, Whitman, 44 pgs., small size, 6 books in set, Helen Janes-a
The Story of David 4.00 10.00 20.00
The Story of Gideon 4.00 10.00 20.00
The Story of Daniel 4.00 10.00 20.00
The Story of Joseph 4.00 10.00 20.00
The Story of Ruth and Naorrii 4.00 10.00 20.00
The Story of Moses 4.00 10.00 20.00
Complete set with box 20.00 70.00 140.00

1471- **Wells Fargo**, 1938, Whitman, 240 pgs., photo-c, movie scenes 10.00 35.00 70.00

L18- **Western Frontier**, 1935, Lynn, 192 pgs., starring Ken Maynard, movie scenes 16.00 55.00 110.00

1121- **West Pointers on the Gridiron**, 1936, Saalfield, 148 pgs., hard-c, sports book 10.00 25.00 50.00

1601- **West Pointers on the Gridiron**, 1936, Saalfield, 148 pgs., soft-c, sports book 10.00 25.00 50.00

1124- **West Point Five, The**, 1937, Saalfield, 4 3/4" x 5 1/4", sports book, hard-c 10.00 25.00 50.00

1604- **West Point Five, The**, 1937, Saalfield, 4 1/4" x 5 1/4", sports book, soft-c 10.00 25.00 50.00

1164- **West Point of the Air**, 1935, Whitman, 160 pgs., photo-c, movie scenes 10.00 30.00 60.00

18- **Westward Ho!**, 1935, EVW, 160 pgs., movie scenes, starring John Wayne (Scarce) 35.00 130.00 260.00

1109- **We Three**, 1935, Saalfield, 160 pgs., photo-c, movie scenes, by John Barrymore, hard-c 10.00 27.00 52.00

1589- **We Three**, 1935, Saalfield, 160 pgs., photo-c, movie scenes, by John Barrymore, soft-c 10.00 27.00 52.00

5- **Wheels of Destiny**, 1934, EVW, 160 pgs., movie scenes, starring Ken Maynard 16.00 55.00 110.00

Whitefoot's Secret (See Wee Little Books)

nn- **Who's Afraid of the Big Bad Wolf**, "Three Little Pigs" (Disney), 1933, McKay, 36 pgs., 6" x 8 1/2", stiff-c, Disney studio-a 32.00 100.00 200.00

nn- **Wild West Adventures of Buffalo Bill**, 1935, Whitman, 260 pgs., Cocomalt premium, soft-c, Hal Arbo-a 10.00 35.00 70.00

1096- **Will Rogers, The Story of**, 1935, Saalfield, photo-hard-c 10.00 30.00 60.00

1576- **Will Rogers, The Story of**, 1935, Saalfield, photo-soft-c 10.00 30.00 60.00

1458- **Wimpy the Hamburger Eater**, 1938, Whitman, 432 pgs., E.C. Segar-a 15.00 50.00 100.00

1433- **Windy Wayne and His Flying Wing**, 1942, Whitman, 432 pgs., flip pictures 10.00 25.00 50.00

1131- **Winged Four, The**, 1937, Saalfield, sports book, hard-c 10.00 25.00 50.00

1407- **Wings of the U.S.A.**, 1940, Whitman, 432 pgs., Thomas Hickey-a 10.00 25.00 50.00

nn- **Winning of the Old Northwest, The**, 1934, World Syndicate, High Lights of History Series 10.00 30.00 60.00

1122- **Winning Point, The**, 1936, Saalfield, (Football), hard-c 8.00 22.00 45.00

1602- **Winning Point, The**, 1936, Saalfield, soft-c 8.00 22.00 45.00

710-10- **Woody Woodpecker Big Game Hunter**, 1950, Whitman, by Walter Lantz 10.00 25.00 50.00

2010-(#10)-**Woody Woodpecker-The Meteor Menace**, 1967, Whitman, 260 pgs., 39¢-c, hard-c, color illos. 4.00 12.00 24.00

2028- **Woody Woodpecker-The Sinister Signal**, 1969, Whitman 4.00 10.00 20.00

23- **World of Monsters, The**, 1935, EVW, Five Star Library, movie scenes 12.00 43.00 85.00

779- **World War in Photographs, The**, 1934, photo-c, photo illus. 10.00 25.00 50.00

Wyatt Earp (See Hugh O'Brian ...)

nn- **Zane Grey's Cowboys of the West**, 1935, Whitman, 148 pgs., 3 3/4" x 4", Tarzan Ice Cream Cup premium, soft-c, Arbo-a 32.00 100.00 200.00

Zane Grey's King of the Royal Mounted (See Men of the Mounted)

1103- **Zane Grey's King of the Royal Mounted**, 1936, Whitman, 432 pgs. 10.00 36.00 72.00

nn- **Zane Grey's King of the Royal Mounted**, 1935, Whitman, 260 pgs., Cocomalt premium, soft-c 12.00 48.00 95.00

1179- **Zane Grey's King of the Royal Mounted and the Northern Treasure**, 1937, Whitman, 432 pgs. 10.00 35.00 70.00

1405- **Zane Grey's King of the Royal Mounted the Long Arm of the Law**, 1942, Whitman, All Pictures Comics 10.00 35.00 70.00

1452- **Zane Grey's King of the Royal Mounted Gets His Man**, 1938, Whitman, 432 pgs. 10.00 35.00 70.00

1486- **Zane Grey's King of the Royal Mounted and the Great Jewel Mystery**, 1939, Whitman, 432 pgs. 10.00 35.00 70.00

5- **Zane Grey's King of the Royal Mounted in the Far North**, 1938, Whitman, 132 pgs., Buddy Book, soft-c 30.00 92.00 185.00

nn- **Zane Grey's King of the Royal Mounted in Law of the North**, 1939, Whitman, 36 pgs., 2 1/2" x 3 1/2", Penny Book 10.00 25.00 50.00

nn- **Zane Grey's King of the Royal Mounted Policing the Frozen North**, 1938, Dell, 196 pgs., Fast-Action Story, soft-c 20.00 70.00 140.00

1440- **Zane Grey's Tex Thorne Comes Out of the West**, 1937, Whitman, 432 pgs. 10.00 25.00 50.00

1465- **Zip Saunders King of the Speedway**, 1939, 432 pgs., Weisman-a 10.00 25.00 50.00

The American Comic Book: 1842-2003

THE MARKETING OF A MEDIUM

by Arnold T. Blumberg

with new material and additional research by Sol M. Davidson, PhD, and Robert L. Beerbohm

Starting with the 30th edition of ***The Official Overstreet Comic Book Price Guide****, we now list premium and giveaway comics (now collectively referred to as "promotional comics" in this edition) in their own section. This article has appeared in previous editions in a shorter form, but now contains even more detailed information on this often overlooked corner of the comic book collecting universe. We hope that by setting promotional comics apart, we can draw attention to this fertile but still poorly represented area of comic book history.*

A very rare piece indeed, this represents one of the few existing examples of Palmer Cox's signature, as Cox always printed his name on his art. The character depicted in the upper left, "The Dude," represents a typical New Yorker and was Cox's favorite. "Brownieland" was the name of Cox's studio.

Everyone wants something for free. It's in our nature to look for the quick fix, the good deal, the complimentary gift. We long to hit the lottery and quit our job, to win the trip around the world, or find that pot of gold at the end of the proverbial rainbow. Collectors in particular are certainly built to appreciate the notion of the "free gift," since it not only means a new item to collect and enjoy, but no risk or obligation in order to acquire it.

Ah, but there's the rub. Because things are not always what they seem, and "free gifts" usually come with a price. As the saying goes, "there's no such thing as a free lunch," so if it seems too good to be true, it probably is. This is the case even in the world of comics, where premiums and giveaways have a familiar agenda hidden behind the bright colors and fanciful stories. But where did it all begin?

EXTRA EXTRA

As we learn more about the early history of the comic book industry through continual investigation and the publishing of articles like those regularly featured in this book, we gain a much greater understanding of the financial and creative forces at work in shaping the medium, but perhaps one of the most intriguing and least recognized factors that influenced the dawn of comics is the concept of the premium or giveaway. (Note: Some of the historical information referenced in this article is derived from material also presented in Robert L. Beerbohm's introductory articles to the Platinum Age and Modern Age sections.)

The birth of the comic book as we know it today is intimately connected with the development of the comic strip in American newspapers and their use as an advertising and marketing tool for staple products such as bread, milk, and cereal. From the very beginning, comic characters have played several roles in pop culture, entertaining the youth of the country while also (sometimes none too subtly) acting as hucksters for whatever corporation foots the bill. From important staples to frivolous material produced simply to make a buck, these products have utilized the comics medium to sell, sell, sell. And what better way to hook a prospective customer than to give them "something for nothing?"

Starting in the 1850s, comics were being used in free almanacs such as **Elton's**, **Hostetter's** and **Wright's** to lure readers for the little booklets to sell patent medicine, farm products, tobacco, shoe polish, etc. Most of these are exceedingly rare today, hence it is difficult to compile an accurate history. More mention of these early precursors can be found in the Victorian Comics Era essay following this one. But although comic characters themselves were already being aggressively merchandised all around the world by the mid-1890s--as with, for example, Palmer Cox's **The Brownies**--the real starting point for the success of comics as a giveaway marketing mechanism can be traced to the introduction of **The Yellow Kid**, Richard Outcault's now legendary newspaper strip.

Newspaper publishers had already recognized that comic strips could boost circulation as well as please sponsors and advertisers by drawing more eyes to the page, so Sunday "supplements" were introduced to entice fans. Outcault's creation cemented the theory with proof of comic characters' marketing and merchandising power.

Soon after, Outcault (who had most likely been inspired by Cox's merchandising success with **The Brownies** in the first place) caught lightning in a bottle once more with **Buster Brown**, who has the distinction of being America's first nationally licensed comic strip character. Soon, comic strips proliferated throughout the nation's newspapers as tycoons like Hearst and Pulitzer recognized the drawing power of the new medium and fought circulation wars to capture the pennies of the nouveau readership. They paid exorbitant salaries to comic strip artists such as Rudolph Dirks (**Katzenjammer Kids**), and used the funnies as newspaper supplements and as premiums to attract readers. Corporations soon had the chance to license recognizable personas as their own personal pitchmen (or women or animals...). Comic character merchandise wasn't far behind, resulting in a boom of future collectibles now catalogued in volumes like **Hake's Price Guide to Character Toys**.

TWO BIRTHS FOR THE PRICE OF ONE

Comic books themselves were at the heart of this movement, and giveaway and premium collections of comic strips not only appealed to children and adults alike, but provided the impetus for the birth of the modern comic book format itself. It could be said that without the concept of the giveaway comic or the marketing push behind it, there would be no comic book industry as we have it today. Well-known now is the story of how in spring 1933 Harry Wildenberg of Eastern Color Printing Company convinced Proctor & Gamble to sponsor the first modern comic book, **Funnies on Parade**, as a premium. Its success led to the first continuing comic book, **Famous Funnies**, and the rest, as they say, is history.

One of the best examples of the Brownies' proliferation into all kinds of merchandise. This rare Luden's Cough Drop ad (1890s) is the earliest known character die-cut sign.

In 1935, while working on the printing presses of Eastern Color developing how modern comic books get printed, Juliun J. Proskauer came up with an idea for printing "Comic-Books-For-Industry." In July 1936 he made his first sale through his newly formed William C. Popper & Co. to David M. Davies, then advertising manager for Seagram's Distillers Corp. for three million copies of **Seagram's Merrymakers** in time for the 1936-37 Christmas season. "Thus was a new industry born," wrote **Printing News** in August 1945.

Even a casual perusal of the listings in this section of the Guide will dazzle the reader with the endless variety of purposes that this medium has served. Yes, promos have been used to hawk products from athletic equipment to zithers and zip codes, but comics are too versatile an art form to be confined to a few uses. They've swayed elections in cities (**The O'Dwyer Story**, 1949), in states (**Giant for a Day**: Jacob Javits, 1946) and nationwide (**The Story of Harry Truman**, 1948); solicited for charities (**Donald Duck and the Red Feather**, 1948); addressed health issues (**Blondie**, 1949, mental hygiene); discouraged kids from smoking (**Captain America Meets the Asthma Monster**, 1987); coached youngsters in sports skills (**Circling the Bases**, 1947, A.G. Spaulding); explained scientific complexities (**Adventures in Science**, 1946-61, GE); pleaded for social justice (**Consumer Comics**, 1975); espoused religious causes (**Oral Roberts' True Stories**, 1950s); protected the environment (**Our Spaceship Earth**, 1947); encouraged tourism (**Wyoming, The Cowboy State**, 1954); conveyed a sense of history (**Louisiana Purchase**, 1953); taught about computers (**Superman Radio Shack Giveaway**, 1980);

trained employees (**Dial Finance Dialogues**, 1961-70) and executives (**Beneficial Finance System, Managing New Employees**, 1950s); cautioned safety (**Willy Wing Flap**, 1944(?)); announced corporate annual results (**Motorola Annual Report**, 1952); defended free enterprise (**Steve Merritt**, 1949); hammered communism (**How Stalin Hopes to Destroy America**, 1951); fought discrimination (**Mammy Yokum & the Great Dogpatch Mystery**, 1956, B'nai Brith); aided young workers in job-hunting (**The Job Scene**, 1969); battled the scourge of sickle cell anemia (**Where's Herbie**, 1972, U.S. H.E.W.); inspired the overcoming of adversity (**Al Capp by Li'l Abner**, 1946); fostered reading (**Linus Gets a Library Card**, 1960); recruited for the armed forces (**Li'l Abner Joins the Navy**, 1950); beguiled readers into learning languages (**Blondie**, 1949, Philadelphia public schools); and even instructed in such delicate matters as birth control (**Escape from Fear**, 1950 (revised 1959, etc.), for Planned Parenthood).

READ ALL ABOUT IT

The impact of this new approach to advertising was not lost on the business world. Contrary to modern belief, comic books were hardly discounted by the adults of the time...at least not those who had the marketing savvy to recognize an opportunity - or a threat - when they saw one. In the April 1933 issue of **Fortune** magazine, an article titled "The Funny Papers" trumpeted the arrival of comics as a force to be reckoned with in the world of advertising and business, and what's more, a force to fear as well. At first providing a brief survey of the newspaper comic strip business (which for many of the magazine's readers must have seemed a foreign topic for serious discussion), the article goes on to examine the incredible financial draw of comics and their characters:

"Between 70 and 75 per cent {sic} of the readers of any newspaper follow its comic sections regularly...Even the advertiser has succumbed to the comic, and in 1932 spent well over $1,000,000 for comic-paper space."

"**Comic Weekly** is the comic section of seventeen Hearst Sunday papers...Advertisers who market their wares through balloon-speaking manikins {sic} may enjoy the proximity of Jiggs, Maggie, Barney Google, and other funny Hearst headliners."

Although the article continues to cast the notion of relying on comic strip material to sell product in a negative light, actually suggesting that advertisers who utilize comics are violating unspoken rules of "advertising decorum" and bringing themselves "down to the level" of comics (and since when have advertisers been stalwart preservers of good taste and high moral standards), there is no doubt that they are viewing comics in a new light. The comic characters have arrived by 1933...and they're ready to help sell your merchandise too.

Fortune wasn't the only one to take notice as World War II came and went. In 1948, Louis P. Birk, the head of Brevity, Inc., an important promotional comics publisher said, "Comics are serious business." In an article in **Printers' Ink** magazine, he estimated that more than 80 different "comic booklets" had been produced and more than 45,000,000 million copies distributed in the five years before 1948. But of course, comics were serious business long before businessman/historian Birk noted the fact for posterity.

THE MARCH OF WAR AND BEYOND

Through the relentless currents of time, comic strips, books, and the characters that starred in them became more and more an intrinsic part of American culture. During the turmoil of the Great Depression and World War II, comic characters in print and celluloid form entertained while informing and selling at the same time, and premium and giveaway comics came well and truly into their own, pushing everything from loaves of bread to war bonds.

In the 1950s and '60s, there was a shift in focus as the power of giveaway and premium comics was applied to more altruistic endeavors than simply selling something. Comic book format pamphlets, fully illustrated and often inventively written, taught children about banking, money, the dangers of poison and other household products, and even chronicled moments in American history. The comic book as giveaway was now not only a marketing gimmick--it was a tool for educating as well.

One of the earliest examples of the business world acknowledging and investigating the influence of the comic book on modern pop culture and American enterprise. ***FORTUNE Magazine****, April 1933.*

The 1970s and '80s saw another boom in premium and giveaway comics. Every product imaginable seemed to have a licensing deal with a comic book character, usually one of the prominent flag bearers of the Big Two, Marvel or DC. Spider-Man fought bravely against the Beetle for the benefit of All Detergent; Captain America allied himself with the Campbell Kids; and Superman helped a class of computer students beat a disaster-conjuring foe at his own game with the help of Radio Shack Tandy computers.

Newspapers rediscovered the power of comics, not just with enlarged strip supplements but with actual comic books. Spider-Man, the Hulk, and others turned up as giveaway comic extras in various American newspapers (including Chicago and Dallas publications), while a whole series of public information comics like those produced decades earlier used superheroes to caution children about the dangers of smoking, drugs, and child abuse.

Comics also turned up in a plethora of other toy products as the 1980s introduced kids to the joy of electronic games and action figures. Supplementary comics provided "free" with action figure and video game packages told the backstory about the product, adding depth to the play experience while providing an extra incentive to buy. Comics became an intrinsic part of the Atari line of video cartridges, for example, eventually spawning its own full-blown newsstand series as well.

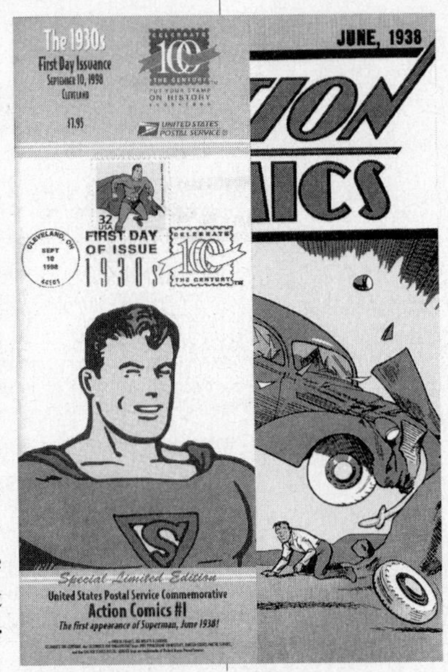

This 1998 U.S. Postal Service premium is one of the most recent examples of the continuing popularity of promotional comics.

As the twentieth century gave way to the twenty-first, giveaway comics were still being produced for inclusion in action figure and video game packages, as well as in conjunction with countless consumer items and corporations. It seems that the medium still has a lot to offer for all those companies desperate to make the most of their market share.

A COMIC BY ANY OTHER NAME

One of the earliest names for promotional comics was "special purpose comics." In their pursuit of superheroes, collectors have allowed promotional comics to lie fallow - underappreciated and uncollected. Without a legitimate name, these products were given sundry other appellations - industrial comics, promos, giveaways, premiums, promics - each accurate but only for a small segment of the unorganized but lusty and lively medium. Perhaps no one name can cover all the variations and purposes of this branch of comic art, but for practical reasons if we accept the general premise that these comics were created to promote an idea, a product or a person, then "Promotional Comics" is probably as convenient a catch-all title as we can come up with.

We used the phrase "for practical reasons" because the word "practical" goes to the heart of promotional comics more than it does for any other comics product. What greater testimony is there to the medium's impact on American culture than to note their use by hard-headed, profit-minded business people and corporations? They invest their money and they expect results.

Today, premium comics continue to thrive and are still utilized as a valuable marketing and promotional tool. "Free" comics are still packaged with action figures and video games, and offered as mail-away premiums from a variety of product manufacturers. The comic industry itself has expanded its use of giveaway comics to self-promote as well, with "ashcan" and other giveaway editions turning up at conventions and comic shops to advertise upcoming series and special events. Many of these function as old-fashioned premiums, with a coupon or other response required from the reader to receive the comic.

As for the supplements and giveaways printed all those years ago, they have spawned a collectible fervor all their own, thanks to their atypical distribution and frequent rarity. For that and the desire to delve deeper into comics history, we hope that by focusing more directly on this genre, we can enhance our understanding of this vital component in the development and history of the modern comic book.

Whether you're a collector or not, we're all motivated by that desire to get something for nothing. For as long as consumers are enticed by the notion of the "free gift," promotional comics will remain a vital marketing component in many business models, but they will also continue to fight the stigma that has long been associated with the industry as a whole. "Respectable" sources like **Fortune** may have taken notice of the power of comic-related advertising 71 years ago, but after all this time comics still fight an uphill battle to establish some measure of dignity for the medium. Perhaps the higher visibility of promotional comics will eventually prove to be a deciding factor in that intellectual war.

See ya in the funny papers.

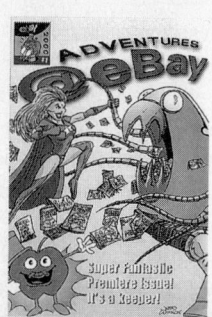

Adventures @ eBay #1 © eBay Inc.

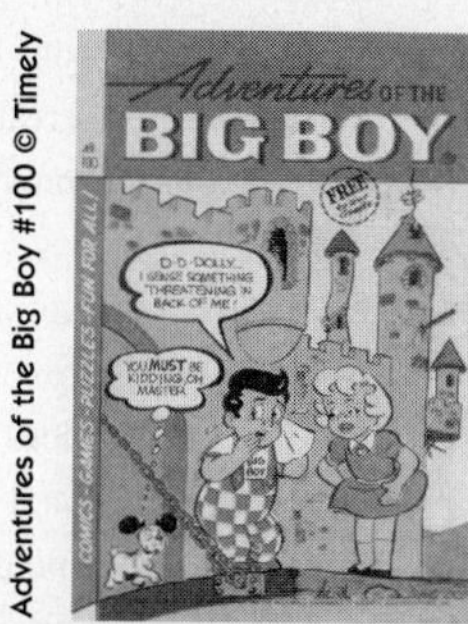

Adventures of the Big Boy #100 © Timely

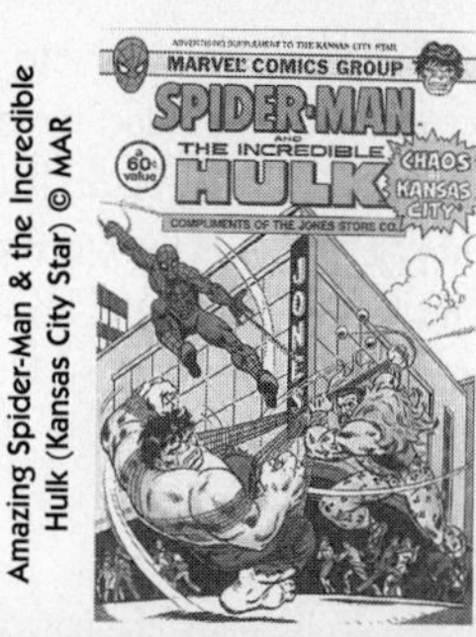

Amazing Spider-Man & the Incredible Hulk (Kansas City Star) © MAR

GD 2.0 | VG 4.0 | FN 6.0 | VF 8.0 | VF/NM 9.0 | NM- 9.2

ACTION COMICS
DC Comics: 1947 - 1998 (Giveaway)
1 (1976, 1983) paper cover w/10¢ price, 16 pgs. in color; reprints complete Superman story from #1 ('38) 3 6 9 16 20 24
1 (1976) Safeguard Giveaway; paper cover w/"free", 16 pgs. in color; reprints complete Superman story from #1 ('38) 3 6 9 17 21 26
1 (1987 Nestle Quik; 1988, 50¢) 1 2 3 5 6 8
1 (1993)-Came w/Reign of Superman packs 3.00
1 (1998 U.S. Postal Service, $7.95) Reprints entire issue; extra outer half-cover contains First Day Issuance of 32¢ Superman stamp with Sept. 10, 1998 Cleveland, OH postmark 1 2 3 5 6 8
Theater (1947, 32 pgs., 6-1/2 x 8-1/4", nn)-Vigilante story based on Columbia Vigilante serial; no Superman-c or story 66 132 198 413 619 700

ACTION ZONE
CBS Television: 1994 (Promotes CBS Saturday morning cartoons)
1-WildC.A.T.s, T.M.N.Turtles, Skeleton Warriors stories; Jim Lee-c 2.00

ADVENTURE COMICS
IGA: No date (early 1940s) (Paper-c, 32 pgs.)
Two diff. issues; Super-Mystery-r from 1941 25 50 75 144 198 255

ADVENTURE IN DISNEYLAND
Walt Disney Productions (Dist. by Richfield Oil): May, 1955 (Giveaway, soft-c., 16 pgs)
nn 10 20 30 58 73 90

ADVENTURES @ EBAY
eBay: 2000 (6 3/4" x 4 1/2", 16 pgs.)
1-Judd Winick-a/Rucka & Van Meter-s; intro to eBay comic buying 2.25

ADVENTURES OF BIG BOY
Timely Comics/Webs Adv. Corp./Illus. Features: 1956 - Present (Giveaway) (East & West editions of early issues)
1-Everett-a 140 280 420 600 825 1050
2-Everett-a 40 80 120 180 278 375
3-5: 4-Robot-c 20 40 60 95 133 170
6-10: 6-Sci/fic issue 10 20 30 73 107 140
11-20 6 12 18 43 59 75
21-30 4 8 12 24 32 40
31-50 3 6 9 16 20 25
51-100 2 4 6 9 11 14
101-150 1 3 4 6 8 10
151-240 1 2 3 5 6 8
241-265,267-269,271-300: 5.00
266-Superman x-over 3 7 10 21 28 35
270-TV's Buck Rogers-c/s 3 6 9 16 20 25
301-400 3.50
401-500 2.75
1-(2nd series - '76-'84,Paragon Prod.) (...Shoney's Big Boy) 1 2 3 5 6 8
2-20 4.00
21-50 2.50
Summer, 1959 issue, large size 10 20 30 56 78 100

ADVENTURES OF G. I. JOE
1969 (3-1/4x7") (20 & 16 pgs.)
First Series: 1-Danger of the Depths. 2-Perilous Rescue. 3-Secret Mission to Spy Island. 4-Mysterious Explosion. 5-Fantastic Free Fall. 6-Eight Ropes of Danger. 7-Mouth of Doom. 8-Hidden Missile Discovery. 9-Space Walk Mystery. 10-Fight for Survival. 11-The Shark's Surprise.
Second Series: 2-Flying Space Adventure. 4-White Tiger Hunt. 7-Capture of the Pygmy Gorilla. 12-Secret of the Mummy's Tomb.
Third Series: Reprinted surviving titles of First Series. Fourth Series: 13-Adventure Team Headquarters. 14-Search For the Stolen Idol.
each.... 2 4 6 14 18 22

ADVENTURES OF KOOL-AID MAN
Marvel Comics: 1983; 1984 (Mail order giveaway)
1,2 6.00

ADVENTURES OF MARGARET O'BRIEN, THE
Bambury Fashions (Clothes): 1947 (20 pgs. in color, slick-c, regular size) (Premium)
In "The Big City" movie adaptation (scarce) 20 40 60 112 156 200

ADVENTURES OF QUIK BUNNY
Nestle's Quik: 1984 (Giveaway, 32 pgs.)
nn-Spider-Man app. 2 4 6 8 10 12

ADVENTURES OF STUBBY, SANTA'S SMALLEST REINDEER, THE
W. T. Grant Co.: nd (early 1940s) (Giveaway, 12 pgs.)
nn 6 12 18 31 38 45

ADVENTURES OF VOTEMAN, THE
Foundation For Citizen Education Inc.: 1968
nn 5 10 15 36 48 60

ADVENTURES WITH SANTA CLAUS
Promotional Publ. Co. (Murphy's Store): No date (early 50's) (9-3/4x 6-3/4", 24 pgs., giveaway, paper-c)
nn-Contains 8 pgs. ads 5 10 15 24 30 35
16 pg. version 6 12 18 28 34 40

AIR POWER (CBS TV & the U.S. Air Force Presents)
Prudential Insurance Co.: 1956 (5-1/4x7-1/4", 32 pgs., giveaway, soft-c)
nn-Toth-a? Based on 'You Are There' TV program by Walter Cronkite 10 20 30 56 73 90

ALICE IN BLUNDERLAND
Industrial Services: 1952 (Paper cover, 16 pgs. in color)
nn-Facts about government waste and inefficiency 14 28 42 79 107 135

ALICE IN WONDERLAND
Western Printing Company/Whitman Publ. Co.: 1965; 1969; 1982
Meets Santa Claus(1950s), nd, 16 pgs. 6 12 18 28 34 40
Rexall Giveaway(1965, 16 pgs., 5x7-1/4) Western Printing (TV, Hanna-Barbera) 3 6 9 18 24 30
Wonder Bakery Giveaway(1969, 16 pgs, color, nn, nd) (Continental Baking Company) 3 6 9 18 23 28

ALICE IN WONDERLAND MEETS SANTA
No publisher: nd (6-5/8x9-11/16", 16 pgs., giveaway, paper-c)
nn 9 18 27 52 66 80

ALL ABOARD, MR. LINCOLN
Assoc. of American Railroads: Jan, 1959 (16 pgs.)
nn-Abraham Lincoln and the Railroads 6 12 18 28 34 40

ALL NEW COMICS
Harvey Comics: Oct, 1993 (Giveaway, no cover price, 16 pgs.)(Hanna-Barbera)
1-Flintstones, Scooby Doo, Jetsons, Yogi Bear & Wacky Races previews for upcoming Harvey's new Hanna-Barbera line-up 5.00
NOTE: Material previewed in Harvey giveaway was eventually published by Archie.

AMAZING SPIDER-MAN, THE
Marvel Comics Group
Acme & Dingo Children's Boots (1980)-Spider-Woman app. 2 4 6 11 14 18
Adventures in Reading Starring... (1990,1991) Bogdanove & Romita-c/a 3.00
Aim Toothpaste Giveaway (36 pgs., reg. size)-1 pg. origin recap; Green Goblin-c/story 2 4 6 9 11 14
Aim Toothpaste Giveaway (16 pgs., reg. size)-Dr. Octopus app. 2 4 6 10 13 16
All Detergent Giveaway (1979, 36 pgs.), nn-Origin-r 2 4 6 10 13 16
Amazing Fantasy #15 (8/02) reprint included in Spider-Man DVD Collector's Gift Set 2.25
Amazing Spider-Man nn (1990, 6-1/8x9", 28 pgs.)-Shan-Lon giveaway; r/ Amazing Spider-Man #303 w/McFarlane-c/a 1 2 3 5 7 9
...& Power Pack (1984, nn)(Nat'l Committee for Prevention of Child Abuse) (two versions, mail offer & store giveaway)-Mooney-a; Byrne-c
Mail offer 2 4 6 8 10 12
Store giveaway 4.00
...& The Hulk (Special Edition)(6/8/80; 20 pgs.)-Supplement to Chicago Tribune 2 4 6 10 13 16
...& The Incredible Hulk (1981, 1982; 36 pgs.)-Sanger Harris or May D&F supplement to Dallas Times, Dallas Herald, Denver Post, Kansas City Star, Tulsa World; Foley's supplement to Houston Chronicle (1982, 16 pgs.)- "Great Rodeo Robbery"; The Jones Store-giveaway (1983, 16 pgs.) 2 4 6 12 16 20
...and the New Mutants Featuring Skids nn (National Committee for Prevention of Child Abuse/K-Mart giveaway)-Williams-c(i) 5.00
...Captain America, The Incredible Hulk, & Spider-Woman (1981) (7-11 Stores giveaway; 36 pgs.) 2 4 6 10 12 15
...: Christmas in Dallas (1983) (Supplement to Dallas Times Herald) giveaway 2 4 6 10 12 15
...: Danger in Dallas (1983) (Supplement to Dallas Times Herald) giveaway 2 4 6 10 12 15
...: Danger in Denver (1983) (Supplement to Denver Post) giveaway for May D&F stores 2 4 6 10 12 15
..., Fire-Star, And Ice-Man at the Dallas Ballet Nutcracker (1983; supplement to Dallas Times Herald)-Mooney-p 2 4 6 10 12 15
Giveaway-Esquire Magazine (2/69)-Miniature-Still attached 12 24 36 84 125 165

Archie & Friends Monster Bash 2003 © AP

Aurora Comic Scenes Instruction Booklet - Superman © DC

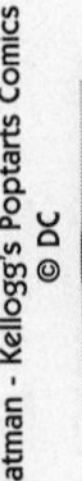

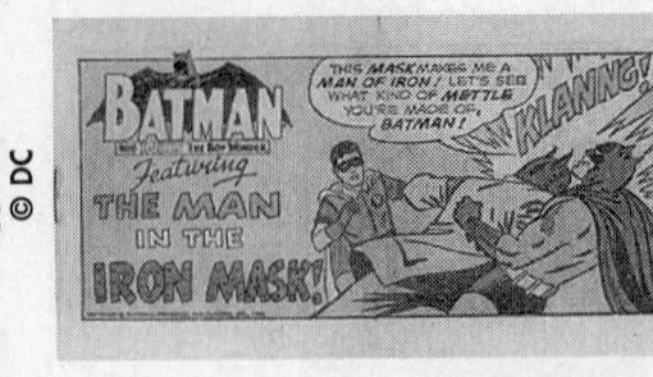

Batman - Kellogg's Poptarts Comics © DC

GD VG FN VF VF/NM NM-
2.0 4.0 6.0 8.0 9.0 9.2

Giveaway-Eye Magazine (2/69)-Miniature-Still attached 10 20 30 67 96 125

...: Riot at Robotworld (1991; 16 pgs.)(National Action Council for Minorities in Engineering, Inc.) giveaway; Saviuk-c 5.00

..., Storm & Powerman (1982; 20 pgs.)(American Cancer Society) giveaway 1 2 3 5 6 8

...Vs. The Hulk (Special Edition; 1979, 20 pgs.)(Supplement to Columbus Dispatch) 2 4 6 12 16 20

...Vs. The Prodigy (Giveaway, 16 pgs. in color (1976, 5x6-1/2")-Sex education; (1 million printed; 35-50¢) 2 4 6 14 18 22

Spidey & The Mini-Marvels Halloween 2003 Ashcan (12/03, 8 1/2"x 5 1/2") Giarusso-s/a; Venom and Green Goblin app. 2.25

AMERICA MENACED!
Vital Publications: 1950 (Paper-c)

nn-Anti-communism 35 70 105 175 250 325

AMERICAN COMICS
Theatre Giveaways (Liberty Theatre, Grand Rapids, Mich. known): 1940's

Many possible combinations. "Golden Age" superhero comics with new cover added and given away at theaters. Following known: Superman #59, Capt. Marvel #20, Capt. Marvel Jr. #5, Action #33, Classics Comics #8, Whiz #39. Value would vary with book and should be 70-80 percent of the original.

ANDY HARDY COMICS
Western Printing Co.:

...& the New Automatic Gas Clothes Dryer (1952, 5x7-1/4", 16 pgs.) Bendix Giveaway (soft-c) 6 12 18 31 38 45

ANIMANIACS EMERGENCY WORLD
DC Comics: 1995

nn-American Red Cross 4.00

APACHE HUNTER
Creative Pictorials: 1954 (18 pgs. in color) (promo copy) (saddle stitched)

nn-Severin, Heath stories 16 32 48 92 126 160

AQUATEERS MEET THE SUPER FRIENDS
DC Comics: 1979

nn 1 3 4 6 8 10

ARCHIE AND HIS GANG (Zeta Beta Tau Presents...)
Archie Publications: Dec. 1950 (St. Louis National Convention giveaway)

nn-Contains new cover stapled over Archie Comics #47 (11-12/50) on inside; produced for Zeta Beta Tau 15 30 45 86 118 150

ARCHIE COMICS
Archie Publications

... And Friends and the Shield (10/02, 8 1/2"x 5 1/2") Diamond Comic Dist. 2.50
... And Friends - A Halloween Tale (10/98, 8 1/2"x 5 1/2") Diamond Comic Dist.; Sabrina and Sonic app.; Dan DeCarlo-a 2.50
... And Friends - A Timely Tale (10/01, 8 1/2"x 5 1/2") Diamond Comic Dist. 2.50
... And Friends Monster Bash 2003 (8 1/2"x 5 1/2") Diamond Comic Dist. Halloween 2.25
...And His Friends Help Raise Literacy Awareness In Mississippi nn (3/94) 5.50
...And His Pals in the Peer Helping Program nn (2/91, 7"x4 1/2") produced by the FBI 5.50
...And the History of Electronics nn (5/90, 36 pgs.)-Radio Shack giveaway; Bender-c/a 5.50
Fairmont Potato Chips Giveaway-Mini comics 1970 (8 issues-nn's., 8 pgs. each) 3 6 9 16 20 24
Fairmont Potato Chips Giveaway-Mini comics 1970 (6 issues-nn's.,6 7/8" x 2 1/4", 8 pgs. each) 3 6 9 16 20 24
Fairmont Potato Chips Giveaway-Mini comics 1971 (4 issues-nn's.,6 7/8" x 5", 8 pgs. each) 3 6 9 16 20 24
... Free Comic Book Day Edition 1 (7/03) 2.25
Official Boy Scout Outfitter (1946, 9-1/2x6-1/2, 16 pgs.)-B. R. Baker Co. (Scarce) 47 94 141 282 424 565
Shoe Store giveaway (1948, Feb?) 17 34 51 95 130 165
...'s Ham Radio Adventure (1997) Morse code instruction; Goldberg-a 5.00
...'s Weird Mysteries (9/99, 8 1/2"x 5 1/2") Diamond Comic Dist. Halloween giveaway 2.25

ARCHIE SHOE-STORE GIVEAWAY
Archie Publications: 1944-49 (12-15 pgs. of games, puzzles, stories like Superman-Tim books, No nos. - came out monthly)

	GD 2.0	VG 4.0	FN 6.0	VF 8.0	VF/NM 9.0	NM- 9.2
(1944-47)-issues	14	28	42	79	107	135
2/48-Peggy Lee photo-c	14	28	42	79	107	135
3/48-Marylee Robb photo-c	12	24	36	71	96	120
4/48-Gloria De Haven photo-c	14	28	42	79	107	135
5/48,6/48,7/48	12	24	36	71	96	120
8/48-Story on Shirley Temple	14	28	42	81	111	140
10/48-Archie as Wolf on cover	13	26	39	76	103	130
5/49-Kathleen Hughes photo-c	10	20	30	60	80	100
7/49	10	20	30	58	77	95
8/49-Archie photo-c from radio show	16	32	48	92	126	160
10/49-Gloria Mann photo-c from radio show	13	26	39	76	103	130
11/49,12/49	10	20	30	58	77	95

ARCHIE'S JOKE BOOK MAGAZINE (See Joke Book ...)
Archie Publications

Drug Store Giveaway (No. 39 w/new-c) 6 12 18 31 38 45

ARCHIE'S TEN ISSUE COLLECTOR'S SET (Title inside of cover only)
Archie Publications: June, 1997 - No. 10, June, 1997 ($1.50, 20 pgs.)

1-10: 1,7-Archie. 2,8-Betty & Veronica. 3,9-Veronica. 4-Betty. 5-World of Archie. 6-Jughead. 10-Archie and Friends each... 4.00

ASTRO COMICS
American Airlines (Harvey): 1968 - 1979 (Giveaway)

Reprints of Harvey comics. 1968-Hot Stuff. 1969-Casper, Spooky, Hot Stuff, Stumbo the Giant, Little Audrey, Little Lotta, & Richie Rich reprints. 1970-r/Richie Rich #97 (all scarce) 3 6 9 19 25 32
1973-r/Richie Rich #122. 1975-Wendy. 1975-Richie Rich & Casper. 1977-r/Richie Rich & Casper #20. 1978-r/Richie Rich & Casper #25. 1979-r/Richie Rich & Casper #30 (scarce) 3 6 9 16 20 24

ATARI FORCE
DC Comics: 1982 - No. 5, 1983

1-3 (1982, 5X7", 52 pgs.)-Given away with Atari games 6.00
4,5 (1982-1983, 52 pgs.)-Given away with Atari games (scarcer) 1 3 4 6 8 10

AURORA COMIC SCENES INSTRUCTION BOOKLET (Included with superhero model kits)
Aurora Plastics Co.: 1974 (6-1/4x9-3/4," 8 pgs., slick paper)

181-140-Tarzan; Neal Adams-a 3 6 9 19 25 32
182-140-Spider-Man. 4 8 12 27 36 45
183-140-Tonto(Gil Kane art). 184-140-Hulk. 185-140-Superman. 186-140-Superboy. 187-140-Batman. 188-140-The Lone Ranger(1974-by Gil Kane). 192-140-Captain America(1975). 193-140-Robin 3 6 9 18 23 28

BACK TO THE FUTURE
Harvey Comics

Special nn (1991, 20 pgs.)-Brunner-c; given away at Universal Studios in Florida 4.00

BALTIMORE COLTS
American Visuals Corp.: 1950 (Giveaway)

nn-Eisner-c 45 90 135 250 375 500

BAMBI (Disney)
K. K. Publications (Giveaways): 1941, 1942

1941-Horlick's Malted Milk & various toy stores; text & pictures; most copies mailed out with store stickers on-c 45 90 135 240 345 450
1942-Same as 4-Color #12, but no price (Same as '41 issue?) (Scarce) 70 140 280 437 619 800

BATMAN
DC Comics: 1966 - Present

Act II Popcorn mini-comic(1998) 2.50
Batman #121 Toys R Us edition (1997) r/1st Mr. Freeze 2.50
Batman #362 Mervyn's edition (1989) 2.50
Batman Adventures #1 Free Comic Book Day edition (6/03) Timm-c 2.50
Batman Adventures #25 Best Western edition (1997) 2.50
Batman and Other DC Classics 1 (1989, giveaway)-DC Comics/Diamond Comic Distributors; Batman origin-r/Batman #47, Camelot 3000-r, Justice League-r('87), New Teen Titans-r 2.50
Batman Beyond Six Flags edition 5.50
Batman: Canadian Multiculturalism Custom (1992) 3.00
Batman Claritan edition (1999) 2.50
Kellogg's Poptarts comics (1966, Set of 6, 16 pgs.); All were folded and placed in Poptarts boxes. Infantino art on Catwoman and Joker issues.
"The Man in the Iron Mask", "The Penguin's Fowl Play", "The Joker's Happy Victims", "The Catwoman's Catnapping Caper", "The Mad Hatter's Hat Crimes", "The Case of the Batman II"
each.... 5 10 15 33 44 55
Mask of the Phantasm (1993) Mini-comic released w/video 6.00
Onstar - Auto Show Special Edition (OnStar Corp., 2001, 8 pgs.) Riddler app. 2.50
Pizza Hut giveaway (12/77)-exact-r of #122,123; Joker-c/story 1 3 4 6 8 10
Prell Shampoo giveaway (1966, 16 pgs.)- "The Joker's Practical Jokes" (6-7/8x3-3/8") 4 8 12 29 40 50
Revell in pack (1995) 2.50
...: The 10-Cent Adventure (3/02, 10¢) intro. to the "Bruce Wayne: Murderer" x-over; Rucka-s/ Burchett & Janson-a/Dave Johnson-c; these are alternate copies with special outer half-covers (at least 10 different) promoting comics, toys and games shops 2.50

The Blazing Forest © WEST

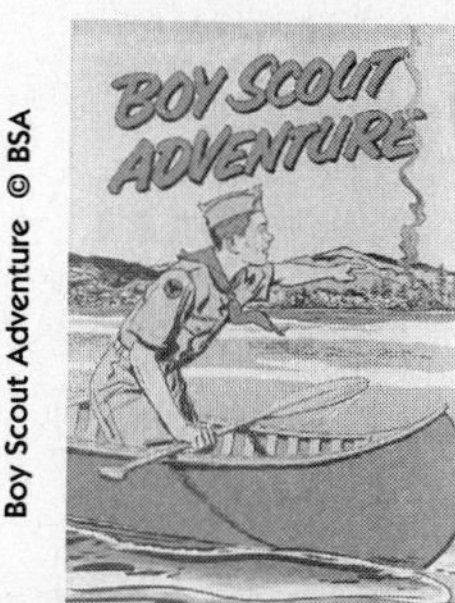

Boy Scout Adventure © BSA

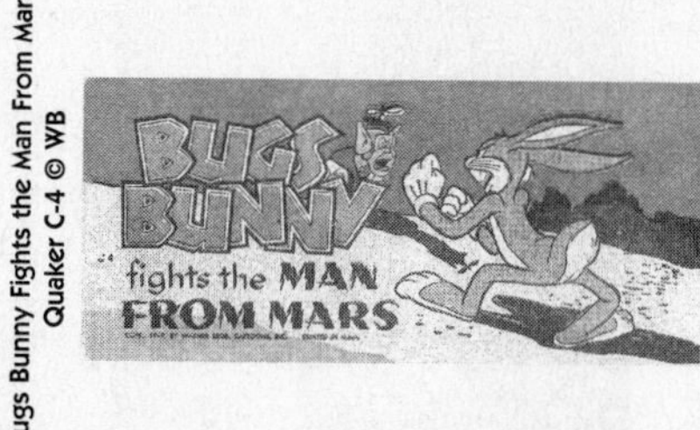

Bugs Bunny Fights the Man From Mars
Quaker C-4 © WB

GD 2.0 | VG 4.0 | FN 6.0 | VF 8.0 | VF/NM 9.0 | NM- 9.2

BATMAN RECORD COMIC
National Periodical Publications: 1966 (one-shot)
1-With record (still sealed) 15 30 45 104 152 200
Comic only 8 16 24 55 78 100

BEETLE BAILEY
Charlton Comics: 1969-1970 (Giveaways)
Armed Forces ('69)-same as regular issue (#68) 2 4 6 10 12 15
Bold Detergent ('69)-same as regular issue (#67) 2 4 6 10 12 15
Cerebral Palsy Assn. V2#71('69) - V2#73(#1,1/70) 2 4 6 10 12 15
Red Cross (1969, 5x7", 16 pgs., paper-c) 2 4 6 10 12 15

BEST WESTERN GIVEAWAY
DC Comics: 1999
nn-Best Western hotels 2.25

BETTER LIFE FOR YOU, A
Harvey Publications Inc.: (16 pgs., paper cover)
nn-Better living through higher productivity 3 6 9 16 20 25

B-FORCE (Milwaukee Brewers and Wisconsin Dental Asso.)
Dark Horse Comics: 2001 (School and stadium giveaway)
nn-Brewers players combat the evils of smokeless tobacco 2.50

BIG BOY (see Adventures of...)

BIG JIM'S P.A.C.K.
Mattel, Inc. (Marvel Comics): No date (1975) (16 pgs.)
nn-Giveaway with Big Jim doll; Buscema/Sinnott-c/a 4 8 12 24 32 40

"BILL AND TED'S EXCELLENT ADVENTURE" MOVIE ADAPTATION
DC Comics: 1989 (No cover price)
nn-Torres-a 3.00

BLACK GOLD
Esso Service Station (Giveaway): 1945? (8 pgs. in color)
nn-Reprints from True Comics 6 12 18 27 33 38

BLAZING FOREST, THE (See Forest Fire and Smokey Bear)
Western Printing: 1962 (20 pgs., 5x7", slick-c)
nn-Smokey The Bear fire prevention 2 4 6 11 14 18

BLESSED PIUS X
Catechetical Guild (Giveaway): No date (Text/comics, 32 pgs., paper-c)
nn 5 10 15 24 29 34

BLIND JUSTICE (Also see Batman: Blind Justice)
DC Comics/Diamond Comic Distributors: 1989 (Giveaway, squarebound)
nn-Contains Detective #598-600 by Batman movie writer Sam Hamm, w/covers; published same time as originals? 6.00

BLONDIE COMICS
Harvey Publications: 1950-1964
1950 Giveaway 7 14 21 35 43 50
1962,1964 Giveaway 3 6 9 16 20 25
N. Y. State Dept. of Mental Hygiene Giveaway-(1950) Regular size; 16 pgs.; no # 4 8 12 24 32 40
N. Y. State Dept. of Mental Hygiene Giveaway-(1956) Regular size; 16 pgs.; no # 3 6 9 18 23 28
N. Y. State Dept. of Mental Hygiene Giveaway-(1961) Regular size; 16 pgs.; no # 2 4 6 14 18 22

BLOOD IS THE HARVEST
Catechetical Guild: 1950 (32 pgs., paper-c)
(Scarce)-Anti-communism (13 known copies) 128 256 384 800 1200 1600
Black & white version (5 known copies), saddle stitched 50 100 150 300 450 600
Untrimmed version (only one known copy); estimated value-$600
NOTE: *In 1979 nine copies of the color version surfaced from the old Guild's files plus the five black & white copies.*

BLUE BIRD CHILDREN'S MAGAZINE, THE
Graphic Information Service: V1#2, 1957 - No. 10 1958 (16 pgs., soft-c, regular size)
V1#2-10: Pat, Pete & Blue Bird app. 2 4 6 8 10 12

BLUE BIRD COMICS
Various Shoe Stores/Charlton Comics: Late 1940's - 1964 (Giveaway)
nn(1947-50)(36 pgs.)-Several issues; Human Torch, Sub-Mariner app. in some 18 36 54 101 138 180
1959-Li'l Genius, Timmy the Timid Ghost, Wild Bill Hickok (All #1) 3 6 9 17 21 26
1959-(6 titles; all #2) Black Fury #1,4,5, Freddy #4, Li'l Genius, Timmy the Timid Ghost #4, Masked Raider #4, Wild Bill Hickok (Charlton) 3 6 9 16 20 25

GD 2.0 | VG 4.0 | FN 6.0 | VF 8.0 | VF/NM 9.0 | NM- 9.2

1959-(#5) Masked Raider #21 3 6 9 16 20 25
1960-(6 titles)(All #4) Black Fury #8,9, Masked Raider, Freddy #8,9, Timmy the Timid Ghost #9, Li'l Genius #7,9 (Charlt.) 2 4 6 14 18 22
1961,1962-(All #10's) Atomic Mouse #12,13,16, Black Fury #11,12, Freddy, Li'l Genius, Masked Raider, Six Gun Heroes, Texas Rangers in Action, Timmy the Ghost, Wild Bill Hickok, Wyatt Earp #3,11-13,16-18 (Charlton) 2 4 6 12 16 20
1963-Texas Rangers #17 (Charlton) 2 4 6 10 12 15
1964-Mysteries of Unexplored Worlds #18, Teenage Hotrodders #18, War Heroes #18 (Charlton) 2 4 6 10 12 15
1965-War Heroes #18 1 3 4 6 8 10
NOTE: *More than one issue of each character could have been published each year. Numbering is sporadic.*

BOB & BETTY & SANTA'S WISHING WHISTLE
Sears Roebuck & Co.: 1941 (Christmas giveaway, 12 pgs.)
nn 11 22 33 63 84 105

BOBBY BENSON'S B-BAR-B RIDERS (Radio)
Magazine Enterprises/AC Comics
...in the Tunnel of Gold-(1936, 5-1/4x8"; 100 pgs.) Radio giveaway by Hecker-H.O. Company (H.O. Oats); contains 22 color pgs. of comics, rest in novel form 10 20 30 58 77 95
...And The Lost Herd-same as above 10 20 30 58 77 95

BOBBY SHELBY COMICS
Shelby Cycle Co./Harvey Publications: 1949
nn 4 8 12 18 22 25

BOY SCOUT ADVENTURE
Boy Scouts of America: 1954 (16 pgs., paper cover)
nn 4 8 12 17 21 24

BOYS' RANCH
Harvey Publications: 1951
Shoe Store Giveaway #5,6 (Identical to regular issues except Simon & Kirby centerfold replaced with ad) 20 40 60 110 137 175

BOZO THE CLOWN (TV)
Dell Publishing Co.: 1961
Giveaway-1961, 16 pgs., 3-1/2x7-1/4", Apsco Products 5 10 15 36 48 60

BRER RABBIT IN "ICE CREAM FOR THE PARTY"
American Dairy Association: 1955 (5x7-1/4", 16 pgs., soft-c) (Walt Disney) (Premium)
nn-(Scarce) 45 90 135 230 315 400

BUCK ROGERS (In the 25th Century)
Kelloggs Corn Flakes Giveaway: 1933 (6x8", 36 pgs)
370A-By Phil Nowlan & Dick Calkins; 1st Buck Rogers radio premium & 1st app. in comics (tells origin) (Reissued in 1995) 100 200 350 700 - -
with envelope 175 350 500 800 - -

BUGS BUNNY (Puffed Rice Giveaway)
Quaker Cereals: 1949 (32 pgs. each, 3-1/8x6-7/8")
A1-Traps the Counterfeiters, A2-Aboard Mystery Submarine, A3- Rocket to the Moon, A4-Lion Tamer, A5-Rescues the Beautiful Princess, B1-Buried Treasure, B2-Outwits the Smugglers, B3-Joins the Marines, B4-Meets the Dwarf Ghost, B5-Finds Aladdin's Lamp, C1-Lost in the Frozen North, C2-Secret Agent, C3-Captured by Cannibals, C4-Fights the Man from Mars, C5-And the Haunted Cave
each.... 8 16 24 46 58 70
Mailing Envelope (has illo of Bugs on front)(Each envelope designates what set it contains, A,B or C on front) 8 16 24 46 58 70

BUGS BUNNY (3-D)
Cheerios Giveaway: 1953 (Pocket size) (15 titles)
each.... 10 20 30 56 73 90
Mailing Envelope (has Bugs drawn on front) 10 20 30 56 73 90

BUGS BUNNY
DC Comics: May, 1997 ($4.95, 24 pgs., comic-sized)
1-Numbered ed. of 100,000; "1st Day of Issue" stamp cancellation on-c 6.00

BUGS BUNNY POSTAL COMIC
DC Comics: 1997 (64 pgs., 7.5" x 5")
nn -Mail Fan; Daffy Duck app. 4.50

BULLETMAN
Fawcett Publications
Well Known Comics (1942)-Paper-c, glued binding; printed in red (Bestmaid/Samuel Lowe giveaway) 17 34 51 95 130 165

BULLS-EYE (Cody of The Pony Express No. 8 on)
Charlton: 1955

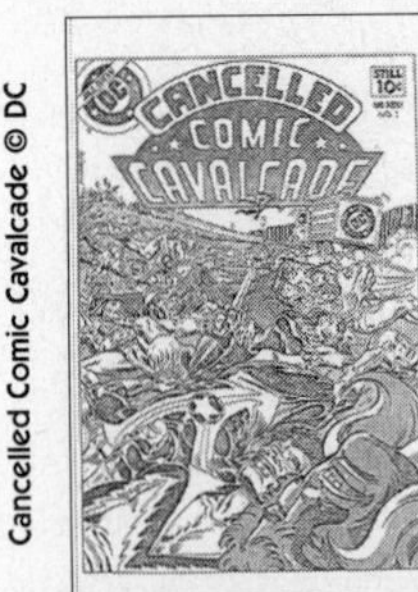
Cancelled Comic Cavalcade © DC

Captain Marvel Adventures Well Known Comics © FAW

Casper's Dental Health Activity Book © HARV

	GD 2.0	VG 4.0	FN 6.0	VF 8.0	VF/NM 9.0	NM- 9.2
Great Scott Shoe Store giveaway-Reprints #2 with new cover	19	38	57	107	149	190

BUSTER BROWN COMICS (Radio)(Also see My Dog Tige in Promotional sec.)
Brown Shoe Co: 1945 - No. 43, 1959 (No. 5: paper-c)

	GD	VG	FN	VF	VF/NM	NM-
nn, nd (#1,scarce)-Featuring Smilin' Ed McConnell & the Buster Brown gang "Midnight" the cat, "Squeaky" the mouse & "Froggy" the Gremlin; covers mention diff. shoe stores. Contains adventure stories	62	124	187	388	582	775
2	19	38	57	106	146	185
3,5-10	11	22	33	63	84	105
4 (Rare)-Low print run due to paper shortage	16	32	48	89	122	155
11-20	8	16	24	43	54	65
21-24,26-28	6	12	18	29	36	42
25,33-37,40,41-Crandall-a in all	10	20	30	56	73	90
29-32-"Interplanetary Police Vs. the Space Siren" by Crandall (pencils only #29)	10	20	30	56	73	90
38,39,42,43	6	12	18	29	36	42

BUSTER BROWN COMICS (Radio)
Brown Shoe Co: 1950s

	GD	VG	FN	VF	VF/NM	NM-
...Goes to Mars (2/58-Western Printing), slick-c, 20 pgs., reg. size	11	22	33	63	84	105
...In "Buster Makes the Team!" (1959-Custom Comics)	8	16	24	43	54	65
...In The Jet Age ('50s), slick-c, 20 pgs., 5x7-1/4"	10	20	30	58	77	95
...Of the Safety Patrol ('60-Custom Comics)	3	7	10	21	28	35
...Out of This World ('59-Custom Comics)	7	14	21	35	43	50
...Safety Coloring Book ('58, 16 pgs.)-Slick paper	7	14	21	35	43	50

CALL FROM CHRIST
Catechetical Educational Society: 1952 (Giveaway, 36 pgs.)

	GD	VG	FN	VF	VF/NM	NM-
nn	5	10	15	22	26	30

CANCELLED COMIC CAVALCADE
DC Comics, Inc.: Summer, 1978 - No. 2, Fall, 1978 (8-1/2x11", B&W)
(Xeroxed pgs. on one side only w/blue cover and taped spine)(Only 35 sets produced)

1-(412 pgs.) Contains xeroxed copies of art for: Black Lightning #12, cover to #13; Claw #13, 14; The Deserter #1; Doorway to Nightmare #6; Firestorm #6; The Green Team #2,3.

2-(532 pgs.) Contains xeroxed copies of art for: Kamandi #60 (including Omac), #61; Prez #5; Shade #9 (including The Odd Man); Showcase #105 (Deadman), 106 (The Creeper); Secret Society of Super Villains #16 & 17; The Vixen #1; and covers to Army at War #2, Battle Classics #3, Demand Classics #1 & 2, Dynamic Classics #3, Mr. Miracle #26, Ragman #6, Weird Mystery #25 & 26, & Western Classics #1 & 2.

(A set of Number 1 & 2 was sold in 2002 for $2127.50, then resold for $2590 a month later)

NOTE: *In June, 1978, DC cancelled several of their titles. For copyright purposes, the unpublished original art for these titles was xeroxed, bound in the above books, published and distributed. Only 35 copies were made.*

CAP'N CRUNCH COMICS (See Quaker Oats)
Quaker Oats Co.: 1963; 1965 (16 pgs.; miniature giveaways; 2-1/2x6-1/2")

	GD	VG	FN	VF	VF/NM	NM-
(1963 titles)- "The Picture Pirates", "The Fountain of Youth", "I'm Dreaming of a Wide Isthmus". (1965 titles)- "Bewitched, Betwitched, & Betweaked", "Seadog Meets the Witch Doctor", "A Witch in Time"	6	12	18	40	55	70

CAPTAIN ACTION (Toy)
National Periodical Publications

	GD	VG	FN	VF	VF/NM	NM-
...& Action Boy('67)-Ideal Toy Co. giveaway (1st app. Captain Action)	14	28	42	99	145	190

CAPTAIN AMERICA
Marvel Comics Group

	GD	VG	FN	VF	VF/NM	NM-
...& The Campbell Kids (1980, 36pg. giveaway, Campbell's Soup/U.S. Dept. of Energy)	2	4	6	8	10	12
...Goes To War Against Drugs(1990, no #, giveaway)-Distributed to direct sales shops; 2nd printing exists						6.00
...Meets The Asthma Monster (1987, no #, giveaway, Your Physician and Glaxo, Inc.)						6.00
Return of The Asthma Monster Vol. 1 #2 (1992, giveaway, Your Physician & Allen & Hanbury's)						6.00
...Vs. Asthma Monster (1990, no #, giveaway, Your Physician & Allen & Hanbury's)						6.00

CAPTAIN AMERICA COMICS
Timely/Marvel Comics: 1954

	GD	VG	FN	VF	VF/NM	NM-
Shoestore Giveaway #77	56	112	168	350	525	700

CAPTAIN ATOM
Nationwide Publishers

	GD	VG	FN	VF	VF/NM	NM-
...- Secret of the Columbian Jungle (16 pgs. in color, paper-c, 3-3/4x5-1/8")-Fireside Marshmallow giveaway	5	10	15	24	30	35

CAPTAIN BEN DIX
Bendix Aviation Corporation: 1943 (Small size)

	GD	VG	FN	VF	VF/NM	NM-
nn	8	16	24	43	54	65

CAPTAIN BEN DIX IN ACTION WITH THE INVISIBLE CREW
Bendix Aviation Corp.: 1940s (nd), (20 pgs, 8-1/4"x11", heavy paper)

	GD	VG	FN	VF	VF/NM	NM-
nn-WWII bomber-c; Jap app.	6	12	18	28	34	40

CAPTAIN FORTUNE PRESENTS
Vital Publications: 1955 - 1959 (Giveaway, 3-1/4x6-7/8", 16 pgs.)

	GD	VG	FN	VF	VF/NM	NM-
"Davy Crockett in Episodes of the Creek War", "Davy Crockett at the Alamo", "In Sherwood Forest Tells Strange Tales of Robin Hood" ('57), "Meets Bolivar the Liberator" ('59), "Tells How Buffalo Bill Fights the Dog Soldiers" ('57), "Young Davy Crockett"	4	7	9	14	16	18

CAPTAIN GALLANT (...of the Foreign Legion) (TV)
Charlton Comics

	GD	VG	FN	VF	VF/NM	NM-
Heinz Foods Premium (#1?)(1955; regular size)-U.S. Pictorial; contains Buster Crabbe photos; Don Heck-a	1	2	3	5	6	8
Mailing Envelope						20.00

CAPTAIN MARVEL ADVENTURES
Fawcett Publications

	GD	VG	FN	VF	VF/NM	NM-
Bond Bread Giveaways-(24 pgs.; pocket size-7-1/4x3-1/2"; paper cover): "...& the Stolen City" ('48), "The Boy Who Never Heard of Capt. Marvel", "Meets the Weatherman" (1950) (reprint) each....	30	60	90	165	220	275
...Well Known Comics (1944; 12 pgs.; 8-1/2x10-1/2")-printed in red & in blue; soft-c; glued binding - (Bestmaid/Samuel Lowe Co. giveaway)	20	40	60	110	149	190

CAPTAIN MARVEL ADVENTURES (Also see Flash and Funny Stuff)
Fawcett Publications (Wheaties Giveaway): 1945 (6x8", full color, paper-c)

	GD	VG	FN	VF	VF/NM	NM-
nn- "Captain Marvel & the Threads of Life" plus 2 other stories (32 pgs.)	100	250	400	-	-	-

NOTE: *All copies were taped at each corner to a box of Wheaties and are never found in Fine or Mint condition. Prices listed for each grade include tape.*

CAPTAIN MARVEL AND THE LTS. OF SAFETY
Ebasco Services/Fawcett Publications: 1950 - 1951 (3 issues - no No.'s)

	GD	VG	FN	VF	VF/NM	NM-
nn (#1) "Danger Flies a Kite" ('50, scarce),	233	466	700	1400	-	-
nn (#2)"Danger Takes to Climbing" ('50),	183	366	550	1000	-	-
nn (#3)"Danger Smashes Street Lights" ('51)	183	366	550	1000	-	-

CAPTAIN MARVEL, JR.
Fawcett Publications: (1944; 12 pgs.; 8-1/2x10-1/2")

	GD	VG	FN	VF	VF/NM	NM-
...Well Known Comics (Printed in blue; paper-c, glued binding)-Bestmaid/Samuel Lowe Co. giveaway	14	28	42	79	107	135

CARDINAL MINDSZENTY (The Truth Behind the Trial of...)
Catechetical Guild Education Society: 1949 (24 pgs., paper cover)

	GD	VG	FN	VF	VF/NM	NM-
nn-Anti-communism	8	16	24	43	54	65
Press Proof-(Very Rare)-(Full color, 7-1/2x11-3/4", untrimmed) Only two known copies						185.00
Preview Copy (B&W, stapled), 18 pgs.; contains first 13 pgs. of Cardinal Mindszenty and was sent out as an advance promotion. Only one known copy						170.00 - 240.00

NOTE: *Regular edition also printed in French. There was also a movie released in 1949 called "Guilty of Treason" which is a fact-based account of the trial and imprisonment of Cardinal Mindszenty by the Communist regime in Hungary.*

CARNIVAL OF COMICS
Fleet-Air Shoes: 1954 (Giveaway)

	GD	VG	FN	VF	VF/NM	NM-
nn-Contains a comic bound with new cover; several combinations possible; Charlton's Eh! known	4	8	12	18	22	25

CARTOON NETWORK
DC Comics: 1997 (Giveaway)

	GD	VG	FN	VF	VF/NM	NM-
nn-reprints Cow and Chicken, Scooby-Doo, & Flintstones stories						3.00

CARVEL COMICS (Amazing Advs. of Capt. Carvel)
Carvel Corp. (Ice Cream): 1975 - No. 5, 1976 (25¢; #3-5: 35¢) (#4,5: 3-1/4x5")

	GD	VG	FN	VF	VF/NM	NM-
1-3	1	2	3	5	6	8
4,5(1976)-Baseball theme	2	4	6	8	10	12

CASE OF THE WASTED WATER, THE
Rheem Water Heating: 1972? (Giveaway)

	GD	VG	FN	VF	VF/NM	NM-
nn-Neal Adams-a	4	8	12	29	40	50

CASPER SPECIAL
Target Stores (Harvey): nd (Dec, 1990) (Giveaway with $1.00 cover)

	GD	VG	FN	VF	VF/NM	NM-
Three issues-Given away with Casper video						5.00

CASPER, THE FRIENDLY GHOST (Paramount Picture Star...)(2nd Series)
Harvey Publications

American Dental Association (Giveaways):

	GD	VG	FN	VF	VF/NM	NM-
...'s Dental Health Activity Book-1977	1	3	4	6	8	10
...Presents Space Age Dentistry-1972	2	4	6	8	10	12

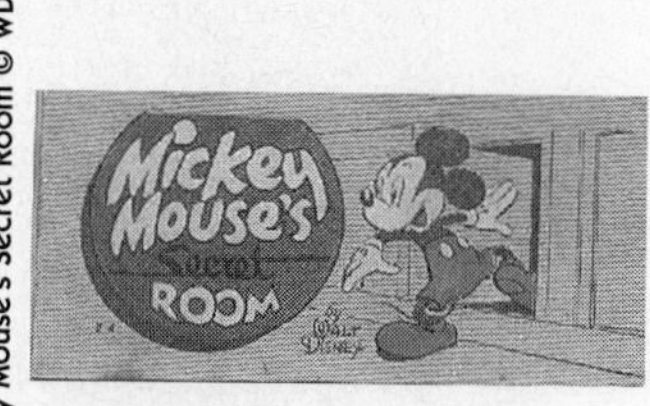

Cheerios Premiums Z-4
Mickey Mouse's Secret Room © WDC

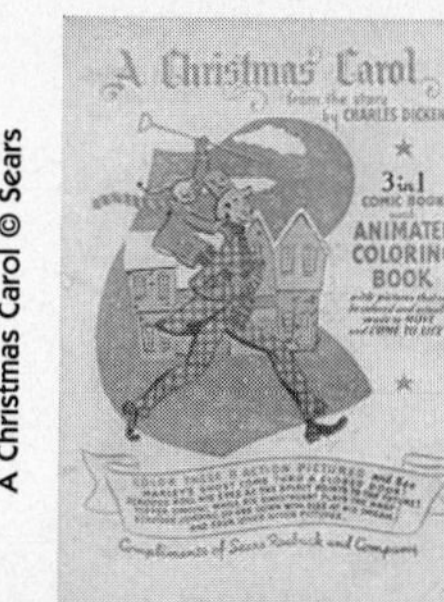

A Christmas Carol © Sears

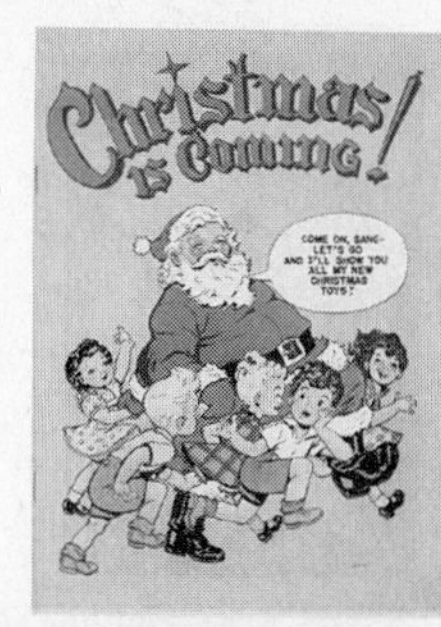

Christmas is Coming

GD VG FN VF VF/NM NM-
2.0 4.0 6.0 8.0 9.0 9.2

..., His Den, & Their Dentist Fight the Tooth Demons-1974
2 4 6 8 10 12

CELEBRATE THE CENTURY SUPERHEROES STAMP ALBUM
DC Comics: 1998 - No. 5, 2000 (32 pgs.)
1-5: Historical stories hosted by DC heroes 3.00

CENTIPEDE
DC Comics: 1983
1-Based on Atari video game 6.00

CENTURY OF COMICS
Eastern Color Printing Co.: 1933 (100 pgs.) (Probably the 3rd comic book)
Bought by Wheatena, Milk-O-Malt, John Wanamaker, Kinney Shoe Stores, & others to be used as premiums and radio giveaways. No publisher listed.
nn-Mutt & Jeff, Joe Palooka, etc. reprints 3670 7335 11,000 24,000 - -

CHEERIOS PREMIUMS (Disney)
Walt Disney Productions: 1947 (16 titles, pocket size, 32 pgs.)
Mailing Envelope for each set "W,X,Y & Z" (has Mickey illo on front)(each envelope designates the set it contains on the front) 10 20 30 56 73 90
Set "W"
W1-Donald Duck & the Pirates 10 20 30 56 73 90
W2-Bucky Bug & the Cannibal King 6 12 18 31 38 45
W3-Pluto Joins the F.B.I. 6 12 18 31 38 45
W4-Mickey Mouse & the Haunted House 7 14 21 37 46 55
Set "X"
X1-Donald Duck, Counter Spy 10 20 30 56 73 90
X2-Goofy Lost in the Desert 6 12 18 31 38 45
X3-Br'er Rabbit Outwits Br'er Fox 6 12 18 31 38 45
X4-Mickey Mouse at the Rodeo 7 14 21 37 46 55
Set "Y"
Y1-Donald Duck's Atom Bomb by Carl Barks. Disney has banned reprinting this book
85 170 255 530 765 1000
Y2-Br'er Rabbit's Secret 6 12 18 31 38 45
Y3-Dumbo & the Circus Mystery 6 12 18 31 38 45
Y4-Mickey Mouse Meets the Wizard 7 14 21 37 46 55
Set "Z"
Z1-Donald Duck Pilots a Jet Plane (not by Barks) 10 20 30 56 73 90
Z2-Pluto Turns Sleuth Hound 6 12 18 31 38 45
Z3-The Seven Dwarfs & the Enchanted Mtn. 7 14 21 37 46 55
Z4-Mickey Mouse's Secret Room 7 14 21 37 46 55

CHEERIOS 3-D GIVEAWAYS (Disney)
Walt Disney Productions: 1954 (24 titles, pocket size) (Glasses came in envelopes)
Glasses only... 7 14 21 35 43 50
Mailing Envelope (no art on front) 8 16 24 43 54 65
(Set 1)
1-Donald Duck & Uncle Scrooge, the Firefighters 9 18 27 52 66 80
2-Mickey Mouse & Goofy, Pirate Plunder 8 16 24 46 58 70
3-Donald Duck's Nephews, the Fabulous Inventors 9 18 27 52 66 80
4-Mickey Mouse, Secret of the Ming Vase 8 16 24 46 58 70
5-Donald Duck with Huey, Dewey, & Louie; ...the Seafarers (title on 2nd page)
9 18 27 52 66 80
6-Mickey Mouse, Moaning Mountain 8 16 24 46 58 70
7-Donald Duck, Apache Gold 9 18 27 52 66 80
8-Mickey Mouse, Flight to Nowhere 8 16 24 46 58 70
(Set 2)
1-Donald Duck, Treasure of Timbuktu 9 18 27 52 66 80
2-Mickey Mouse & Pluto, Operation China 8 16 24 46 58 70
3-Donald Duck in the Magic Cows 9 18 27 52 66 80
4-Mickey Mouse & Goofy, Kid Kokonut 8 16 24 46 58 70
5-Donald Duck, Mystery Ship 9 18 27 52 66 80
6-Mickey Mouse, Phantom Sheriff 8 16 24 46 58 70
7-Donald Duck, Circus Adventures 9 18 27 52 66 80
8-Mickey Mouse, Arctic Explorers 8 16 24 46 58 70
(Set 3)
1-Donald Duck & Witch Hazel 9 18 27 52 66 80
2-Mickey Mouse in Darkest Africa 8 16 24 46 58 70
3-Donald Duck & Uncle Scrooge, Timber Trouble 9 18 27 52 66 80
4-Mickey Mouse, Rajah's Rescue 8 16 24 46 58 70
5-Donald Duck in Robot Reporter 9 18 27 52 66 80
6-Mickey Mouse, Slumbering Sleuth 8 16 24 46 58 70
7-Donald Duck in the Foreign Legion 9 18 27 52 66 80
8-Mickey Mouse, Airwalking Wonder 8 16 24 46 58 70

CHESTY AND COPTIE (Disney)
Los Angeles Community Chest: 1946 (Giveaway, 4pgs.)
nn-(One known copy) by Floyd Gottfredson 85 170 255 525 725 950

GD VG FN VF VF/NM NM-
2.0 4.0 6.0 8.0 9.0 9.2

CHESTY AND HIS HELPERS (Disney)
Los Angeles War Chest: 1943 (Giveaway, 12 pgs., 5-1/2x7-1/4")
nn-Chesty & Coptie 55 110 165 350 488 625

CHOCOLATE THE FLAVOR OF FRIENDSHIP AROUND THE WORLD
The Nstle Company: 1955
nn 4 8 12 24 32 40

CHRISTMAS ADVENTURE, THE
S. Rose (H. L. Green Giveaway): 1963 (16 pgs.)
nn 2 4 6 10 13 16

CHRISTMAS AT THE ROTUNDA (Titled Ford Rotunda Christmas Book 1957 on) (Regular size)
Ford Motor Co. (Western Printing): 1954 - 1961 (Given away every Christmas at one location)
1954-56 issues (nn's) 5 10 15 24 30 35
1957-61 issues (nn's) 5 10 14 20 24 28

CHRISTMAS CAROL, A
Sears Roebuck & Co.: No date (1942-43) (Giveaway, 32 pgs., 8-1/4x10-3/4", paper cover)
nn-Comics & coloring book 18 36 54 104 142 180

CHRISTMAS CAROL, A
Sears Roebuck & Co.: 1940s ? (Christmas giveaway, 20 pgs.)
nn-Comic book & animated coloring book 16 32 48 92 126 160

CHRISTMAS CAROLS
Hot Shoppes Giveaway: 1959? (16 pgs.)
nn 4 8 11 16 19 22

CHRISTMAS COLORING FUN
H. Burnside: 1964 (20 pgs., slick-c, B&W)
nn 2 4 6 10 13 16

CHRISTMAS DREAM, A
Promotional Publishing Co.: 1950 (Kinney Shoe Store Giveaway, 16 pgs.)
nn 5 10 15 22 26 30

CHRISTMAS DREAM, A
J. J. Newberry Co.: 1952? (Giveaway, paper cover, 16 pgs.)
nn 4 8 12 18 22 25

CHRISTMAS DREAM, A
Promotional Publ. Co.: 1952 (Giveaway, 16 pgs., paper cover)
nn 4 8 12 18 22 25

CHRISTMAS FUN AROUND THE WORLD
No publisher: No date (early 50's) (16 pgs., paper cover)
nn 5 10 15 22 26 30

CHRISTMAS IS COMING!
No publisher: No date (early 50's?) (Store giveaway, 16 pgs.)
nn 4 8 12 18 22 25

CHRISTMAS JOURNEY THROUGH SPACE
Promotional Publishing Co.: 1960
nn-Reprints 1954 issue Jolly Christmas Book with new slick cover
3 6 9 18 24 30

CHRISTMAS ON THE MOON
W. T. Grant Co.: 1958 (Giveaway, 20 pgs., slick cover)
nn 8 16 24 43 54 65

CHRISTMAS PLAY BOOK
Gould-Stoner Co.: 1946 (Giveaway, 16 pgs., paper cover)
nn 0 10 24 40 54 05

CHRISTMAS ROUNDUP
Promotional Publishing Co.: 1960
nn-Marv Levy-c/a 2 4 6 10 13 16

CHRISTMAS STORY CUT-OUT BOOK, THE
Catechetical Guild: No. 393, 1951 (15¢, 36 pgs.)
393-Half text & half comics 7 14 21 35 43 50

CHRISTMAS USA (Through 300 Years) (Also see Uncle Sam's...)
Promotional Publ. Co.: 1956 (Giveaway)
nn-Marv Levy-c/a 3 6 8 12 14 16

CHRISTMAS WITH SNOW WHITE AND THE SEVEN DWARFS
Kobackers Giftstore of Buffalo, N.Y.: 1953 (16 pgs., paper-c)
nn 7 14 21 37 46 55

Cinema Comics Herald - Thunder Birds © 20th Century Fox

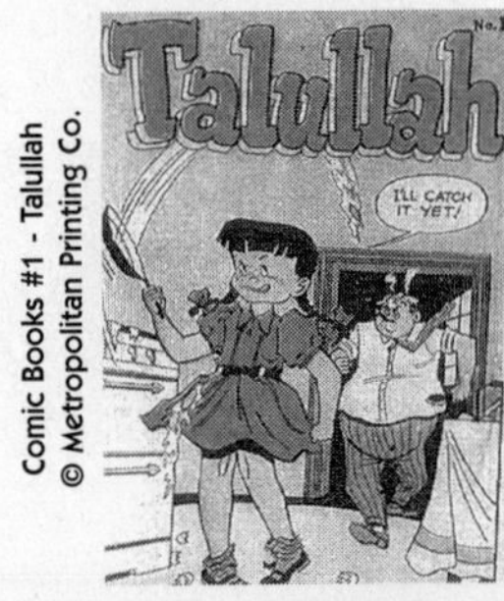

Comic Books #1 - Talullah © Metropolitan Printing Co.

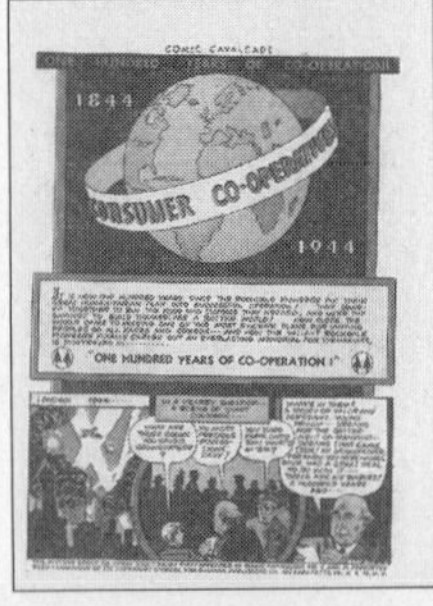

Comic Cavalcade 1944 © DC

CHRISTOPHERS, THE
Catechetical Guild: 1951 (Giveaway, 36 pgs.) (Some copies have 15¢ sticker)

	GD 2.0	VG 4.0	FN 6.0	VF 8.0	VF/NM 9.0	NM- 9.2
nn-Stalin as Satan in Hell	23	46	69	132	186	240

CINDERELLA IN "FAIREST OF THE FAIR"
American Dairy Association (Premium): 1955 (5x7-1/4", 16 pgs., soft-c) (Walt Disney)

	GD 2.0	VG 4.0	FN 6.0	VF 8.0	VF/NM 9.0	NM- 9.2
nn	9	18	27	56	70	85

CINEMA COMICS HERALD
Paramount Pictures/Universal/RKO/20th Century Fox/Republic:
1941 - 1943 (4-pg. movie "trailers", paper-c, 7-1/2x10-1/2")(Giveaway)

	GD 2.0	VG 4.0	FN 6.0	VF 8.0	VF/NM 9.0	NM- 9.2
"Mr. Bug Goes to Town" (1941)	11	22	33	63	84	105
"Bedtime Story"	8	16	24	46	58	70
"Lady For A Night", John Wayne, Joan Blondell ('42)	14	28	42	79	107	135
"Reap The Wild Wind" (1942)	9	18	27	49	62	75
"Thunder Birds" (1942)	8	16	24	46	58	70
"They All Kissed the Bride"	8	16	24	46	58	70
"Arabian Nights" (nd)	9	18	27	49	62	75
"Bombardie" (1943)	8	16	24	46	58	70
"Crash Dive" (1943)-Tyrone Power	9	18	27	49	62	75

NOTE: *The 1941-42 issues contain line art with color photos. 1943 issues are line art.*

CLASSICS GIVEAWAYS (Classic Comics reprints)

	GD 2.0	VG 4.0	FN 6.0	VF 8.0	VF/NM 9.0	NM- 9.2
12/41–Walter Theatre Enterprises (Huntington, WV) giveaway containing #2 (orig.) w/new generic-c (only 1 known copy)	90	180	270	550	775	1000
1942–Double Comics containing CC#1 (orig.) (diff. cover) (not actually a giveaway) (very rare) (also see Double Comics) (only one known copy)	175	350	525	1100	1525	1950
12/42–Saks 34th St. Giveaway containing CC#7 (orig.) (diff. cover) (very rare; only 6 known copies)	640	1280	1920	2700	3850	5000
2/43–American Comics containing CC#8 (orig.) (Liberty Theatre giveaway) (different cover) (only one known copy) (see American Comics)	145	290	435	800	1100	1400
12/44–Robin Hood Flour Co. Giveaway - #7-CC(R) (diff. cover) (rare) (edition probably 5 [22])	250	500	750	1300	1850	2400

NOTE: How are above editions determined without CC covers? 1942 is dated 1942, and CC#1-first reprint did not come out until 5/43. 12/42 and 2/43 are determined by blue note at bottom of first text page only in original edition. 12/44 is estimated from page width each reprint edition had progressively slightly smaller page width.

	GD 2.0	VG 4.0	FN 6.0	VF 8.0	VF/NM 9.0	NM- 9.2
1951–Shelter Thru the Ages (C.I. Educational Series) (actually Giveaway by the Ruberoid Co.) (16 pgs.) (contains original artwork by H. C. Kiefer) (there are 5 diff. back cover ad variations: "Ranch" house ad, "Igloo" ad, "Doll House" ad, "Tree House" ad & blank) (scarce)	75	150	225	450	600	750
1952–George Daynor Biography Giveaway (CC logo) (partly comic book/pictures/newspaper articles) (story of man who built Palace Depression out of junkyard swamp in NJ) (64 pgs.) (very rare; only 3 known copies, one missing back-c)	800	1600	2400	3500	4900	6300
1953–Westinghouse/Dreams of a Man (C.I. Educational Series) (Westinghousebio./ Westinghouse Co. giveaway) (contains original artwork by H. C. Kiefer) (16 pgs.) (also French/Spanish/Italian versions) (scarce)	70	140	210	430	565	700
NOTE: Reproductions of 1951, 1952, and 1953 exist with color photocopy covers and black & white photocopy interior ("W.C.N. Reprint")	2	4	5	7	8	10
1951-53–Coward Shoe Giveaways (all editions very rare); 2 variations of back-c ad exist: With back-c photo ad: 5 (87), 12 (89), 22 (85), 32 (85), 49 (85), 69 (87), 72 (no HRN), 80 (0), 91 (0), 92 (0), 96 (0), 98 (0), 100 (0), 101 (0), 103-105 (all Os)	38	76	114	220	292	365
With back-c cartoon ad: 106-109 (all 0s), 110 (111), 112 (0)	40	80	120	240	320	400
1956–Ben Franklin 5-10 Store Giveaway (#65-PC with back cover ad) (scarce)	34	68	102	180	248	315
1956–Ben Franklin Insurance Co. Giveaway (#65-PC with diff. back cover ad) (very rare)	65	130	195	400	550	700
11/56–Sealtest Co. Edition - #4 (135) (identical to regular edition except for Sealtest logo printed, not stamped, on front cover) (only two copies known to exist)	40	80	120	225	300	375
1958–Get-Well Giveaway containing #15-CI (new cartoon-type cover) (Pressman Pharmacy) (only one copy known to exist)	35	70	105	200	263	325
1967-68–Twin Circle Giveaway Editions - all HRN 166, with back cover ad for National Catholic Press.						
2(R68), 4(R67), 10(R68), 13(R68)	3	6	9	19	25	32
48(R67), 128(R68), 535(576-R68)	4	8	12	22	30	38
16(R68), 68(R67)	4	8	12	29	40	50
12/69–Christmas Giveaway ("A Christmas Adventure") (reprints Picture Parade #4-1953, new cover) (4 ad variations)						
Stacey's Dept. Store	3	6	9	18	23	28
Anne & Hope Store	5	10	15	33	44	55
Gibson's Dept. Store (rare)	5	10	15	33	44	55
"Merry Christmas" & blank ad space	3	6	9	18	23	28

CLIFF MERRITT SETS THE RECORD STRAIGHT
Brotherhood of Railroad Trainsmen: Giveaway (2 different issues)

	GD 2.0	VG 4.0	FN 6.0	VF 8.0	VF/NM 9.0	NM- 9.2
...and the Very Candid Candidate by Al Williamson	1	2	3	5	7	9
...Sets the Record Straight by Al Williamson (2 different-c: one by Williamson, the other by McWilliams)	1	2	3	5	7	9

CLYDE BEATTY COMICS (Also see Crackajack Funnies)
Commodore Productions & Artists, Inc.

	GD 2.0	VG 4.0	FN 6.0	VF 8.0	VF/NM 9.0	NM- 9.2
...African Jungle Book('56)-Richfield Oil Co. 16 pg. giveaway, soft-c	9	18	27	54	70	85

C-M-O COMICS
Chicago Mail Order Co.(Centaur): 1942 - No. 2, 1942 (68 pgs., full color)

	GD 2.0	VG 4.0	FN 6.0	VF 8.0	VF/NM 9.0	NM- 9.2
1-Invisible Terror, Super Ann, & Plymo the Rubber Man app. (all Centaur costume heroes)	84	168	253	525	788	1050
2-Invisible Terror, Super Ann app.	55	110	165	330	495	660

COCOMALT BIG BOOK OF COMICS
Harry 'A' Chesler (Cocomalt Premium): 1938 (Reg. size, full color, 52 pgs.)

	GD 2.0	VG 4.0	FN 6.0	VF 8.0	VF/NM 9.0	NM- 9.2
1-(Scarce)-Biro-c/a; Little Nemo by Winsor McCay Jr., Dan Hastings; Jack Cole, Guardineer, Gustavson, Bob Wood-a	215	430	645	1350	1950	2600

COMIC BOOK (Also see Comics From Weatherbird)
American Juniors Shoe: 1954 (Giveaway)
Contains a comic rebound with new cover. Several combinations possible. Contents determine price.

COMIC BOOK MAGAZINE
Chicago Tribune & other newspapers: 1940 - 1943 (Similar to Spirit sections) (7-3/4x10-3/4"; full color; 16-24 pgs. ea.)

	GD 2.0	VG 4.0	FN 6.0	VF 8.0	VF/NM 9.0	NM- 9.2
1940 issues	7	14	21	37	46	55
1941, 1942 issues	6	12	18	28	34	40
1943 issues	5	10	15	24	30	35

NOTE: *Published weekly. Texas Slim, Kit Carson, Spooky, Josie, Nuts & Jolts, Lew Loyal, Brenda Starr, Daniel Boone, Captain Storm, Rocky, Smokey Stover, Tiny Tim, Little Joe, Fu Manchu appear among others. Early issues had photo stories with pictures from the movies; later issues had comic art.*

COMIC BOOKS (Series 1)
Metropolitan Printing Co. (Giveaway): 1950 (16 pgs.; 5-1/4x8-1/2"; full color; bound at top; paper cover)

	GD 2.0	VG 4.0	FN 6.0	VF 8.0	VF/NM 9.0	NM- 9.2
1-Boots and Saddles; intro The Masked Marshal	6	12	18	29	36	42
1-The Green Jet; Green Lama by Raboy	27	54	81	155	218	280
1-My Pal Dizzy (Teen-age)	4	9	13	18	22	26
1-New World; origin Atomaster (costumed hero)	10	20	30	56	73	90
1-Talullah (Teen-age)	4	9	13	18	22	26

COMIC CAVALCADE
All-American/National Periodical Publications

	GD 2.0	VG 4.0	FN 6.0	VF 8.0	VF/NM 9.0	NM- 9.2
Giveaway (1944, 8 pgs., paper-c, in color)-One Hundred Years of Co-operation-r/Comic Cavalcade #9	70	140	210	425	600	800
Giveaway (1945, 16 pgs., paper-c, in color)-Movie "Tomorrow The World" (Nazi theme); r/Comic Cavalcade #10	90	180	270	550	760	1000
Giveaway (c. 1944-45; 8 pgs, paper-c, in color)-The Twain Shall Meet-r/Comic Cavalcade #8	70	140	210	425	600	800

COMIC SELECTIONS (Shoe store giveaway)
Parents' Magazine Press: 1944-46 (Reprints from Calling All Girls, True Comics, True Aviation, & Real Heroes)

	GD 2.0	VG 4.0	FN 6.0	VF 8.0	VF/NM 9.0	NM- 9.2
1	5	10	15	22	26	30
2-5	4	7	10	14	17	20

COMICS FROM WEATHER BIRD (Also see Comic Book, Edward's Shoes, Free Comics to You & Weather Bird)
Weather Bird Shoes: 1954 - 1957 (Giveaway)
Contains a comic bound with new cover. Many combinations possible. Contents would determine price. Some issues do not contain complete comics, but only parts of comics. Value equals 40 to 60 percent of contents.

COMICS READING LIBRARIES (Educational Series)
King Features (Charlton Publ.): 1973, 1977, 1979 (36 pgs. in color) (Giveaways)

	GD 2.0	VG 4.0	FN 6.0	VF 8.0	VF/NM 9.0	NM- 9.2
R-01-Tiger, Quincy	1	3	4	6	8	10
R-02-Beetle Bailey, Blondie & Popeye	2	4	6	9	11	14
R-03-Blondie, Beetle Bailey	1	3	4	6	8	10
R-04-Tim Tyler's Luck, Felix the Cat	3	6	9	16	20	24
R-05-Quincy, Henry	1	3	4	6	8	10
R-06-The Phantom, Mandrake	3	6	9	16	20	24
1977 reprint(R-04)	2	4	6	8	10	12
R-07-Popeye, Little King	2	4	6	11	14	18
R-08-Prince Valiant (Foster), Flash Gordon	3	6	9	18	24	30
1977 reprint	2	4	6	10	13	16
R-09-Hagar the Horrible, Boner's Ark	2	4	6	9	11	14
R-10-Redeye, Tiger	1	3	4	6	8	10
R-11-Blondie, Hi & Lois	1	3	4	6	8	10

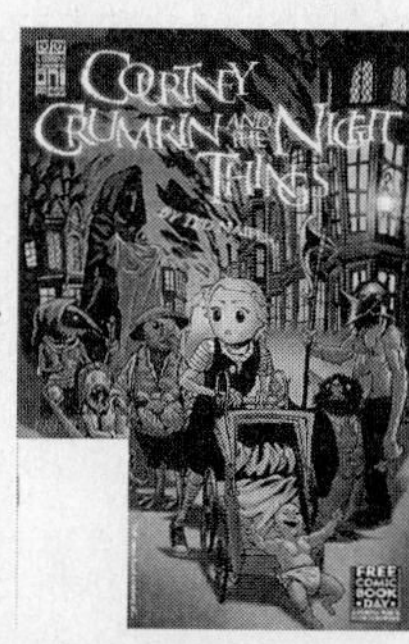

Courtney Crumrin & The Night Things Free Comic Book Day Ed. © Ted Naifeh

Dan Curtis Giveaways #7 © WEST

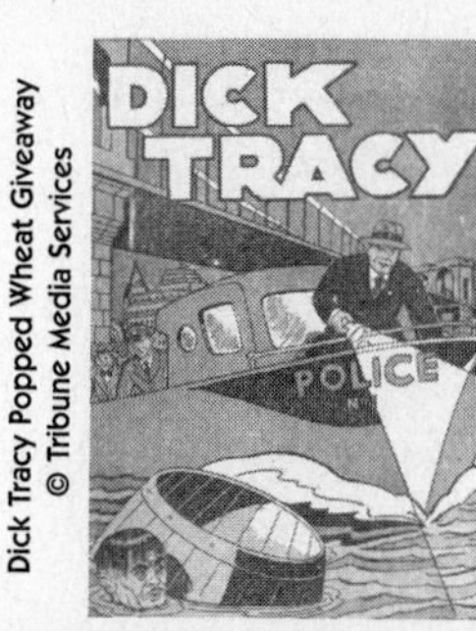

Dick Tracy Popped Wheat Giveaway © Tribune Media Services

	GD 2.0	VG 4.0	FN 6.0	VF 8.0	VF/NM 9.0	NM- 9.2
R-12-Popeye-Swee'pea, Brutus	2	4	6	11	14	18
R-13-Beetle Bailey, Little King	1	3	4	6	8	10
R-14-Quincy-Hamlet	1	3	4	6	8	10
R-15-The Phantom, The Genius	2	4	6	11	14	18
R-16-Flash Gordon, Mandrake	3	6	9	18	24	30
1977 reprint	2	4	6	9	11	14
Other 1977 editions....						7.00
1979 editions (68 pgs.)						7.00

NOTE: *Above giveaways available with purchase of $45.00 in merchandise. Used as a reading skills aid for small children.*

COMMANDMENTS OF GOD
Catechetical Guild: 1954, 1958

	GD	VG	FN	VF	VF/NM	NM-
300-Same contents in both editions; diff-c	4	8	12	17	21	24

COMPLIMENTARY COMICS
Sales Promotion Publ.: No date (1950's) (Giveaway)

	GD	VG	FN	VF	VF/NM	NM-
1-Strongman by Powell, 3 stories	7	14	21	37	46	55

COURTNEY CRUMRIN & THE NIGHT THINGS
Oni Press: 2003

	GD	VG	FN	VF	VF/NM	NM-
Free Comic Book Day Edition (5/03) Naifeh-s/a						2.25

CRACKAJACK FUNNIES (Giveaway)
Malto-Meal: 1937 (Full size, soft-c, full color, 32 pgs.)(Before No. 1?)

	GD	VG	FN	VF	VF/NM	NM-
nn-Features Dan Dunn, G-Man, Speed Bolton, Buck Jones, The Nebbs, Clyde Beatty, Freckles, Major Hoople, Wash Tubbs	90	180	270	575	825	1100

CROSLEY'S HOUSE OF FUN (Also see Tee and Vee Crosley...)
Crosley Div. AVCO Mfg. Corp.: 1950 (Giveaway, paper cover, 32 pgs.)

	GD	VG	FN	VF	VF/NM	NM-
nn-Strips revolve around Crosley appliances	5	10	14	20	24	28

DAGWOOD SPLITS THE ATOM (Also see Topix V8#4)
King Features Syndicate: 1949 (Science comic with King Features characters) (Giveaway)

	GD	VG	FN	VF	VF/NM	NM-
nn-Half comic, half text; Popeye, Olive Oyl, Henry, Mandrake, Little King, Katzenjammer Kids app.	8	16	24	46	58	70

DAISY COMICS (Daisy Air Rifles)
Eastern Color Printing Co.: Dec, 1936 (5-1/4x7-1/2")

	GD	VG	FN	VF	VF/NM	NM-
nn-Joe Palooka, Buck Rogers (2 pgs. from Famous Funnies No. 18, 1st full cover app.), Napoleon Flying to Fame, Butty & Fally	30	60	90	170	235	300

DAISY LOW OF THE GIRL SCOUTS
Girl Scouts of America: 1954, 1965 (16 pgs., paper-c)

	GD	VG	FN	VF	VF/NM	NM-
1954-Story of Juliette Gordon Low	5	10	14	20	24	28
1965	2	4	6	9	11	14

DAN CURTIS GIVEAWAYS
Western Publishing Co.:1974 (3x6", 24 pgs., reprints)

	GD	VG	FN	VF	VF/NM	NM-
1-Dark Shadows	3	6	9	16	20	25
2,6-Star Trek	3	6	9	16	20	25
3,4,7-9: 3-The Twilight Zone. 4-Ripley's Believe It or Not! 7-The Occult Files of Dr. Spektor. 8-Dagar the Invincible. 9-Grimm's Ghost Stories	2	4	6	10	12	15
5-Turok, Son of Stone (partial-r/Turok #78)	3	6	9	16	20	25

DANNY KAYE'S BAND FUN BOOK
H & A Selmer: 1959 (Giveaway)

	GD	VG	FN	VF	VF/NM	NM-
nn	6	12	18	31	38	45

DAREDEVIL
Marvel Comics Group: 1993

	GD	VG	FN	VF	VF/NM	NM-
...Vs. Vapora 1 (Engineering Show Giveaway, 16 pg.) - Intro Vapora						6.00

DAVY CROCKETT (TV)
Dell Publishing Co.

	GD	VG	FN	VF	VF/NM	NM-
...Christmas Book (no date, 16 pgs., paper-c)-Sears giveaway	6	12	18	31	38	45
...Safety Trails (1955, 16pgs, 3-1/4x7")-Cities Service giveaway	8	16	24	40	50	60

DAVY CROCKETT
Charlton Comics

	GD	VG	FN	VF	VF/NM	NM-
Hunting With... nn ('55, 16 pgs.)-Ben Franklin Store giveaway (Publ.-S. Rose)	5	10	15	24	30	35

DAVY CROCKETT
Walt Disney Prod.: (1955, 16 pgs., 5x7-1/4", slick, photo-c)

	GD	VG	FN	VF	VF/NM	NM-
...In the Raid at Piney Creek-American Motors giveaway	8	16	24	40	50	60

DC SAMPLER
DC Comics : nn (#1) 1983 - No. 3, 1984 (36 pgs.; 6 1/2" x 10", giveaway)

	GD	VG	FN	VF	VF/NM	NM-
nn(#1) -3: nn-Wraparound-c, previews upcoming issues. 3-Kirby-a						6.00

DC SPOTLIGHT
DC Comics : 1985 (50th anniversary special) (giveaway)

	GD	VG	FN	VF	VF/NM	NM-
1-Includes profiles on Batman:The Dark Knight & Watchmen						5.00

DENNIS THE MENACE
Hallden (Fawcett)

	GD	VG	FN	VF	VF/NM	NM-
...& Dirt ('59)-Soil Conservation giveaway; r-# 36; Wiseman-c/a	2	4	6	11	14	18
...& Dirt ('68)-reprints '59 edition	1	3	4	6	8	10
...Away We Go('70)-Caladryl giveaway	1	2	3	5	6	8
...Coping with Family Stress-giveaway	1	2	3	5	6	8
...Takes a Poke at Poison('61)-Food & Drug Admin. giveaway; Wiseman-c/a	1	3	4	6	8	10
...Takes a Poke at Poison-Revised 1/66, 11/70	1	2	3	4	5	7
...Takes a Poke at Poison-Revised 1972, 1974, 1977, 1981						6.00

DETECTIVE COMICS (Also see other Batman titles)
National Periodical Publications/DC Comics

	GD	VG	FN	VF	VF/NM	NM-
27 (1984)-Oreo Cookies giveaway (32 pgs., paper-c) r-/Det. #27,#38 & Batman #1 (1st Joker)	5	10	15	33	44	55
38 (1995) Blockbuster Video edition; reprints 1st Robin app.						3.00
38 (1997) Toys R Us edition						3.00
359 (1997) Toys R Us edition; reprints 1st Batgirl app.						3.00

DICK TRACY GIVEAWAYS
1939 - 1958; 1990

	GD	VG	FN	VF	VF/NM	NM-
Buster Brown Shoes Giveaway (1940s?, 36 pgs. in color); 1938-39-r by Gould	33	66	99	190	270	350
Gillmore Giveaway (See Superbook)						
...Hatful of Fun (No date, 1950-52, 32pgs.; 8-1/2x10")-Dick Tracy hat promotion; Dick Tracy games, magic tricks. Miller Bros. premium	17	34	51	98	134	170
Motorola Giveaway (1953)-Reprints Harvey Comics Library #2; "The Case of the Sparkle Plenty TV Mystery"	7	14	21	35	43	50
Original Dick Tracy by Chester Gould, The (Aug, 1990, 16 pgs., 5-1/2x8-1/2")-Gladstone Publ.; Bread Giveaway	1	3	4	6	8	10
Popped Wheat Giveaway (1947, 16 pgs. in color)-1940-r; Sig Feuchtwanger Publ.; Gould-a	4	8	11	16	19	22
...Presents the Family Fun Book; Tip Top Bread Giveaway, no date or number (1940, Fawcett Publ., 16 pgs. in color)-Spy Smasher, Ibis, Lance O'Casey app.	50	100	150	300	450	600
Same as above but without app. of heroes & Dick Tracy on cover only	15	30	45	84	115	145
Service Station Giveaway (1958, 16 pgs. in color)(regular size, slick cover)-Harvey Info. Press	4	8	12	18	22	25
Shoe Store Giveaway (Weatherbird)(1939, 16 pgs.)-Gould-a	14	28	42	79	107	135

DICK TRACY SHEDS LIGHT ON THE MOLE
Western Printing Co.: 1949 (16 pgs.) (Ray-O-Vac Flashlights giveaway)

	GD	VG	FN	VF	VF/NM	NM-
nn-Not by Gould	8	16	24	40	50	60

DICK WINGATE OF THE U.S. NAVY
Superior Publ./Toby Press: 1951; 1953 (no month)

	GD	VG	FN	VF	VF/NM	NM-
nn-U.S. Navy giveaway	5	10	15	23	28	32
1(1953, Toby)-Reprints nn issue? (same-c)	4	8	12	18	22	25

DIG 'EM
Kellogg's Sugar Smacks Giveaway: 1973 (2-3/8x6", 16 pgs.)

	GD	VG	FN	VF	VF/NM	NM-
nn-4 different issues	1	2	3	5	7	9

DOC CARTER VD COMICS
Health Publications Institute, Raleigh, N. C. (Giveaway): 1949 (16 pgs. in color) (Paper-c)

	GD	VG	FN	VF	VF/NM	NM-
nn	18	36	54	101	138	175

DONALD AND MICKEY MERRY CHRISTMAS (Formerly Famous Gang Book Of Comics)
K. K. Publ./Firestone Tire & Rubber Co.: 1943 - 1949 (Giveaway, 20 pgs.)
Put out each Christmas; 1943 issue titled "Firestone Presents Comics" (Disney)

	GD	VG	FN	VF	VF/NM	NM-
1943-Donald Duck-r/WDC&S #32 by Carl Barks	75	150	225	469	685	900
1944-Donald Duck-r/WDC&S #35 by Barks	70	140	210	438	644	850
1945- "Donald Duck's Best Christmas", 8 pgs. Carl Barks; intro. & 1st app. Grandma Duck in comic books	105	210	315	653	977	1300
1946-Donald Duck in "Santa's Stormy Visit", 8 pgs. Carl Barks	73	146	219	455	665	875
1947-Donald Duck in "Three Good Little Ducks", 8 pgs. Carl Barks	73	146	219	455	665	875
1948-Donald Duck in "Toyland", 8 pgs. Carl Barks	73	146	219	455	665	875
1949-Donald Duck in "New Toys", 8 pgs. Barks	66	132	198	412	606	800

Elsie the Cow Borden Giveaway © DS

Famous Comics nn © UFS

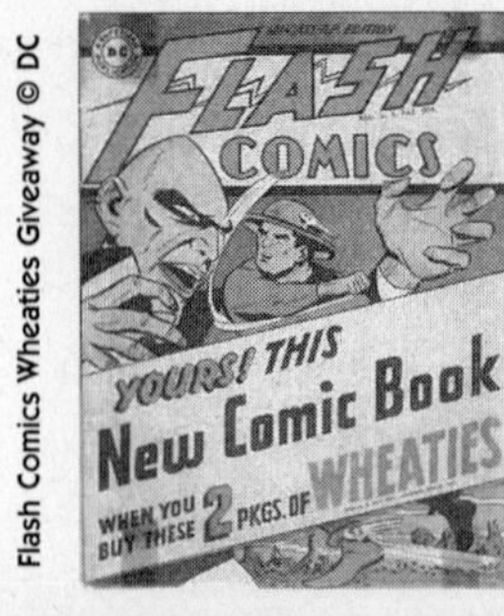

Flash Comics Wheaties Giveaway © DC

	GD 2.0	VG 4.0	FN 6.0	VF 8.0	VF/NM 9.0	NM- 9.2

DONALD DUCK
K. K. Publications: 1944 (Christmas giveaway, paper-c, 16 pgs.)(2 versions)

	GD	VG	FN	VF	VF/NM	NM-
nn-Kelly cover reprint	82	164	246	515	758	1000

DONALD DUCK AND THE RED FEATHER
Red Feather Giveaway: 1948 (8-1/2x11", 4 pgs., B&W)

	GD	VG	FN	VF	VF/NM	NM-
nn	19	38	57	106	146	185

DONALD DUCK IN "THE LITTERBUG"
Keep America Beautiful: 1963 (5x7-1/4", 16 pgs., soft-c) (Disney giveaway)

	GD	VG	FN	VF	VF/NM	NM-
nn	4	8	12	25	33	42

DONALD DUCK "PLOTTING PICNICKERS" (See Frito-Lay Giveaway)

DONALD DUCK'S SURPRISE PARTY
Walt Disney Productions: 1948 (16 pgs.) (Giveaway for Icy Frost Twins Ice Cream Bars)

	GD	VG	FN	VF	VF/NM	NM-
nn-(Rare)-Kelly-c/a	314	628	943	1600	2400	3200

DOT AND DASH AND THE LUCKY JINGLE PIGGIE
Sears Roebuck Co.: 1942 (Christmas giveaway, 12 pgs.)

	GD	VG	FN	VF	VF/NM	NM-
nn-Contains a war stamp album and a punch out Jingle Piggie bank	10	20	30	56	73	90

DOUBLE TALK (Also see Two-Faces)
Feature Publications: No date (1962?) (32 pgs., full color, slick-c)
Christian Anti-Communism Crusade (Giveaway)

	GD	VG	FN	VF	VF/NM	NM-
nn-Sickle with blood-c	10	20	30	70	100	130

DUMBO (Walt Disney's..., The Flying Elephant)
Weatherbird Shoes/Ernest Kern Co.(Detroit)/ Wieboldt's (Chicago): 1941
(K.K. Publ. Giveaway)

	GD	VG	FN	VF	VF/NM	NM-
nn-16 pgs., 9x10" (Rare)	48	96	144	288	432	575
nn-52 pgs., 5-1/2x8-1/2", slick cover in color; B&W interior; half text, half reprints 4-Color No. 17 (Dept. store)	27	54	81	155	218	280

DUMBO WEEKLY
Walt Disney Prod.: 1942 (Premium supplied by Diamond D-X Gas Stations)

	GD	VG	FN	VF	VF/NM	NM-
1	70	140	210	440	645	850
2-16	24	48	72	135	190	245
Binder only						475

NOTE: *A cover and binder came separate at gas stations. Came with membership card.*

EAT RIGHT TO WORK AND WIN
Swift & Company: 1942 (16 pgs.) (Giveaway)

	GD	VG	FN	VF	VF/NM	NM-
Blondie, Henry, Flash Gordon by Alex Raymond, Toots & Casper, Thimble Theatre(Popeye), Tillie the Toiler, The Phantom, The Little King, & Bringing up Father - original strips just for this book -(in daily strip form which shows what foods we should eat and why)	50	100	150	260	355	450

EDWARD'S SHOES GIVEAWAY
Edward's Shoe Store: 1954 (Has clown on cover)
Contains comic with new cover. Many combinations possible. Contents determines price, 50-60 percent of original. (Similar to Comics From Weatherbird & Free Comics to You)

ELSIE THE COW
D. S. Publishing Co.

	GD	VG	FN	VF	VF/NM	NM-
Borden's cheese comic picture bk ('40, giveaway)	21	42	63	118	164	210
Borden Milk Giveaway-(16 pgs., nn) (3 ishs, 1957)	14	28	42	79	107	135
Elsie's Fun Book(1950; Borden Milk)	14	28	42	79	107	135
Everyday Birthday Fun With... (1957; 20 pgs.)(100th Anniversary); Kubert-a	14	28	42	79	107	135

ESCAPE FROM FEAR
Planned Parenthood of America: 1956, 1962, 1969 (Giveaway, 8 pgs., color) (On birth control)

	GD	VG	FN	VF	VF/NM	NM-
1956 edition	10	20	30	56	73	90
1962 edition	4	8	12	29	40	50
1969 edition	3	6	9	16	20	25

EVEL KNIEVEL
Marvel Comics Group (Ideal Toy Corp.): 1974 (Giveaway, 20 pgs.)

	GD	VG	FN	VF	VF/NM	NM-
nn-Contains photo on inside back-c	4	8	12	27	36	45

FAMOUS COMICS (Also see Favorite Comics)
Zain-Eppy/United Features Syndicate: No date; Mid 1930's (24 pgs., paper-c)

	GD	VG	FN	VF	VF/NM	NM-
nn-Reprinted from 1933 & 1934 newspaper strips in color; Joe Palooka, Hairbreadth Harry, Napoleon, The Nebbs, etc. (Many different versions known)	50	100	150	300	425	550

FAMOUS FAIRY TALES
K. K. Publ. Co.: 1942; 1943 (32 pgs.); 1944 (16 pgs.) (Giveaway, soft-c)

	GD	VG	FN	VF	VF/NM	NM-
1942-Kelly-a	40	80	120	240	340	440
1943-r-/Fairy Tale Parade No. 2,3; Kelly-a	30	60	90	170	240	310
1944-Kelly-a	27	54	81	153	214	275

FAMOUS FUNNIES -A CARNIVAL OF COMICS
Eastern Color: 1933

	GD	VG	FN	VF	VF/NM	NM-
(Probably the second comic book), 36 pgs., no date given, no publisher, no number; contains strip reprints of The Bungle Family, Dixie Dugan, Hairbreadth Harry, Joe Palooka, Keeping Up With the Jones, Mutt & Jeff, Reg'lar Fellers, S'Matter Pop, Strange As It Seems, and others. This book was sold by M. C. Gaines to Wheatena, Milk-O-Malt, John Wanamaker, Kinney Shoe Stores, & others to be given away as premiums and radio giveaways (1933). Originally came with a mailing envelope.	913	1816	2740	5480	8740	12,000

FAMOUS GANG BOOK OF COMICS (Becomes Donald & Mickey Merry Christmas 1943 on)
Firestone Tire & Rubber Co.: Dec, 1942 (Christmas giveaway, 32 pgs., paper-c)

	GD	VG	FN	VF	VF/NM	NM-
nn-(Rare)-Porky Pig, Bugs Bunny, Mary Jane & Sniffles, Elmer Fudd; r/Looney Tunes	65	130	195	406	611	815

FANTASTIC FOUR
Marvel Comics

	GD	VG	FN	VF	VF/NM	NM-
nn (1981, 32 pgs.) Young Model Builders Club						8.00
Vol.2 #60 Baltimore Comic Book Show (10/02, newspaper supplement) 200,000 copies were distributed to Baltimore Sun home subscribers to promote Baltimore Comic Con						2.50

FATHER OF CHARITY
Catechetical Guild Giveaway: No date (32 pgs.; paper cover)

	GD	VG	FN	VF	VF/NM	NM-
nn	4	8	12	18	22	25

FAVORITE COMICS (Also see Famous Comics)
Grocery Store Giveaway (Diff. Corp.) (detergent): 1934 (36 pgs.)

	GD	VG	FN	VF	VF/NM	NM-
Book 1-The Nebbs, Strange As It Seems, Napoleon, Joe Palooka, Dixie Dugan, S'Matter Pop, Hairbreadth Harry, etc. reprints	84	168	252	525	788	1050
Book 2,3	55	110	165	340	508	675

FAWCETT MINIATURES (See Mighty Midget)
Fawcett Publications: 1946 (3-3/4x5", 12-24 pgs.) (Wheaties giveaways)

	GD	VG	FN	VF	VF/NM	NM-
Captain Marvel "And the Horn of Plenty"; Bulletman story	18	36	54	104	142	180
Captain Marvel "& the Raiders From Space"; Golden Arrow story	18	36	54	104	142	180
Captain Marvel Jr. "The Case of the Poison Press!" Bulletman story	18	36	54	104	142	180
Delecta of the Planets; C. C. Beck art; B&W inside; 12 pgs.; 3 printing variations (coloring) exist	25	50	75	144	198	255

FEARLESS FOSDICK
Capp Enterprises Inc.: 1951

	GD	VG	FN	VF	VF/NM	NM-
...& The Case of The Red Feather	5	10	15	24	30	35

FIGHT FOR FREEDOM
National Assoc. of Mfgrs./General Comics: 1949, 1951 (Giveaway, 16 pgs.)

	GD	VG	FN	VF	VF/NM	NM-
nn-Dan Barry-c/a; used in **POP**, pg. 102	6	12	18	31	38	45

FIRE AND BLAST
National Fire Protection Assoc.: 1952 (Giveaway, 16 pgs., paper-c)

	GD	VG	FN	VF	VF/NM	NM-
nn-Mart Baily A-Bomb-c; about fire prevention	15	30	45	84	115	145

FIRE CHIEF AND THE SAFE OL' FIREFLY, THE
National Board of Fire Underwriters: 1952 (16 pgs.) (Safety brochure given away at schools) (produced by American Visuals Corp.)(Eisner)

	GD	VG	FN	VF	VF/NM	NM-
nn-(Rare) Eisner-c/a	45	90	135	280	395	525

FLASH
DC Comics: 1990

	GD	VG	FN	VF	VF/NM	NM-
nn-Brochure for CBS TV series						4.00

FLASH COMICS (Also see Captain Marvel and Funny Stuff)
National Periodical Publications: 1946 (6-1/2x8-1/4", 32 pgs.)
(Wheaties Giveaway)

	GD	VG	FN	VF	VF/NM	NM-
nn-Johnny Thunder, Ghost Patrol, The Flash & Kubert Hawkman app.; Irwin Hasen-c/a	325	912	1500	-	-	-

NOTE: *All known copies were taped to Wheaties boxes and are never found in mint condition. Copies with light tape residue bring the listed prices in all grades*

FLASH FORCE 2000
DC Comics: 1984

	GD	VG	FN	VF	VF/NM	NM-
1-5						4.00

FLASH GORDON
Dell Publishing Co.: 1943 (20 pgs.)

	GD	VG	FN	VF	VF/NM	NM-
Macy's Giveaway-(Rare); not by Raymond	59	118	177	369	555	740

FLASH GORDON
Harvey Comics: 1951 (16 pgs. in color, regular size, paper-c) (Gordon Bread giveaway)

	GD	VG	FN	VF	VF/NM	NM-
1,2: 1-r/strips 10/24/37 - 2/6/38. 2-r/strips 7/14/40 - 10/6/40; Reprints by Raymond each....	2	4	6	10	12	15

NOTE: *Most copies have brittle edges.*

The Fork in the Road © U.S. Army

Freedom Train © S&S

Golden Arrow Well Known Comics © FAW

	GD 2.0	VG 4.0	FN 6.0	VF 8.0	VF/NM 9.0	NM- 9.2

FLOOD RELIEF
Malibu Comics (Ultraverse): Jan, 1994 (36 pgs.)(Ordered thru mail w/$5.00 to Red Cross)
1-Hardcase, Prime & Prototype app. 6.00

FOREST FIRE (Also see The Blazing Forest and Smokey Bear)
American Forestry Assn.(Commerical Comics): 1949 (dated-1950) (16 pgs., paper-c)
nn-Intro/1st app. Smokey The Forest Fire Preventing Bear; created by Rudy Wendelein; Wendelein/Sparling-a; 'Carter Oil Co.' on back-c of original 17 34 51 95 130 165

FOREST RANGER HANDBOOK
Wrather Corp.: 1967 (5x7", 20 pgs., slick-c)
nn-WIth Corey Stuart & Lassie photo-c 2 4 6 14 18 22

FORGOTTEN STORY BEHIND NORTH BEACH, THE
Catechetical Guild: No date (8 pgs., paper-c)
nn 4 8 12 17 21 24

FORK IN THE ROAD
U.S. Army Recruiting Service: 1961 (16 pgs., paper-c)
nn 4 8 10 14 17 20

48 FAMOUS AMERICANS
J. C. Penney Co. (Cpr. Edwin H. Stroh): 1947 (Giveaway) (Half-size in color)
nn - Simon & Kirby-a 12 24 36 69 92 115

FOXHOLE ON YOUR LAWN
No Publisher: No date
nn-Charles Biro art 4 7 10 14 17 20

FRANKIE LUER'S SPACE ADVENTURES
Luer Packing Co.: 1955 (5x7", 36 pgs., slick-c)
nn - With Davey Rocket 4 8 11 16 19 22

FREDDY
Charlton Comics
Schiff's Shoes Presents... #1 (1959)-Giveaway 4 7 9 14 16 18

FREE COMICS TO YOU FROM... (name of shoe store) (Has clown on cover & another with a rabbit) (Like comics from Weather Bird & Edward's Shoes)
Shoe Store Giveaway: Circa 1956, 1960-61
Contains a comic bound with new cover - several combinations possible; some Harvey titles known. Contents determine price.

FREEDOM TRAIN
Street & Smith Publications: 1948 (Giveaway)
nn-Powell-c w/mailer 20 40 60 112 156 200

FREIHOFER'S COMIC BOOK
All-American Comics: 1940s (7 1/2 x 10 1/4")
2nd edition-(Scarce) Cover features All-American Comics characters Ultra-Man, Hop Harrigan, Red, White and Blue and others 59 118 176 350 525 700

FRIENDLY GHOST, CASPER, THE (Becomes Casper... #254 on)
Harvey Publications
American Dental Assoc. giveaway-Small size (1967, 16 pgs.) 3 6 9 18 24 30

FRITO-LAY GIVEAWAY
Frito-Lay: 1962 (3-1/4x7", soft-c, 16 pgs.) (Disney)
nn-Donald Duck "Plotting Picnickers" 6 12 18 38 52 65
nn-Ludwig Von Drake "Fish Stampede" 4 8 12 22 30 38
nn- Mickey Mouse & Goofy "Bicep Bungle" 4 8 12 25 33 42

FRONTIER DAYS
Robin Hood Shoe Store (Brown Shoe): 1956 (Giveaway)
1 4 7 10 14 17 20

FUNNIES ON PARADE (Premium)(See Toy World Funnies)
Eastern Color Printing Co.: 1933 (Probably the 1st comic book) (36 pgs., slick cover)
No date or publisher listed
nn-Contains Sunday page reprints of Mutt & Jeff, Joe Palooka, Hairbreadth Harry, Reg'lar Fellers, Skippy, & others (10,000 print run). This book was printed for Proctor & Gamble to be given away & came out before Famous Funnies or Century of Comics. 1160 2320 3480 6960 10,730 14,500

FUNNY PICTURE STORIES (Comic Pages V3#4 on)
Comics Magazine Co./Centaur Publications
Laundry giveaway (16-20 pgs., 1930s)-slick-c 30 60 100 155 218 280

FUNNY STUFF (Also see Captain Marvel & Flash Comics)
National Periodical Publications (Wheaties Giveaway): 1946 (6-1/2x8-1/4")
nn-(Scarce)-Dodo & the Frog, Three Mouseketeers, etc.; came taped to Wheaties box; never found in better than fine 170 322 475 – – –

FUTURE COP: L.A.P.D. (Electronic Arts video game)
DC Comics (WildStorm): 1998
nn-Ron Lim-a/Dave Johnson-c 2.25

GABBY HAYES WESTERN (Movie star)
Fawcett Publications
Quaker Oats Giveaway nn's(#1-5, 1951, 2-1/2x7") (Kagran Corp.)-...In Tracks of Guilt, ...In the Fence Post Mystery, ...In the Accidental Sherlock, ...In the Frame-Up, ...In the Double Cross Brand known 10 20 30 56 73 90
Mailing Envelope (has illo of Gabby on front) 10 20 30 56 73 90

GARY GIBSON COMICS (Donut club membership)
National Dunking Association: 1950 (Included in donut box with pin and card)
1-Western soft-c, 16 pgs.; folded into the box 5 10 14 20 24 28

GENE AUTRY COMICS
Dell Publishing Co.
...Adventure Comics And Play-Fun Book ('47)-32 pgs., 8x6-1/2"; games, comics, magic (Pillsbury premium) 40 80 120 233 329 425
Quaker Oats Giveaway(1950)-2-1/2x6-3/4"; 5 different versions; "Death Card Gang", "Phantoms of the Cave", "Riddle of Laughing Mtn.", "Secret of Lost Valley", "Bond of the Broken Arrow" (came in wrapper) each... 15 30 45 84 115 145
Mailing Envelope (has illo. of Gene on front) 15 30 45 84 115 145
3-D Giveaway(1953)-Pocket-size; 5 different 15 30 45 84 115 145
Mailing Envelope (no art on front) 10 20 30 58 77 100

GENE AUTRY TIM (Formerly Tim) (Becomes Tim in Space)
Tim Stores: 1950 (Half-size) (B&W Giveaway)
nn-Several issues (All Scarce) 19 38 57 106 141 175

GENERAL FOODS SUPER-HEROES
DC Comics: 1979, 1980
1-4 (1979), 1-4 (1980) each... 10.00

G. I. COMICS (Also see Jeep & Overseas Comics)
Giveaways: 1945 - No. 73?, 1946 (Distributed to U. S. Armed Forces)
1-73-Contains Prince Valiant by Foster, Blondie, Smilin' Jack, Mickey Finn, Terry & the Pirates, Donald Duck, Alley Oop, Moon Mullins & Capt. Easy strip reprints (at least 73 issues known to exist) 8 16 24 43 54 65

GOLDEN ARROW
Fawcett Publications
...Well Known Comics (1944; 12 pgs.; 8-1/2x10-1/2"; paper-c; glued binding)- Bestmaid/ Samuel Lowe giveaway; printed in green 9 18 27 54 70 85

GOLDILOCKS & THE THREE BEARS
K. K. Publications: 1943 (Giveaway)
nn 10 20 30 58 77 95

GREAT PEOPLE OF GENESIS, THE
David C. Cook Publ. Co.: No date (Religious giveaway, 64 pgs.)
nn-Reprint/Sunday Pix Weekly 5 10 14 20 24 28

GREAT SACRAMENT, THE
Catechetical Guild: 1953 (Giveaway, 36 pgs.)
nn 4 9 13 18 22 26

GRIT (YOU'VE GOT TO HAVE...)
GRIT Publishing Co.: 1959
nn-GRIT newspaper sales recruitment comic; Schaffenberger-a. Later version has altered artwork 5 10 14 20 24 28

GULF FUNNY WEEKLY (Gulf Comic Weekly No. 1-4)(See Standard Oil Comics)
Gulf Oil Company (Giveaway): 1933 - No. 422, 5/23/41 (in full color; 4 pgs.; tabloid size to 2/3/39; 2/10/39 on, regular comic book size)(early issues undated)
1 75 150 300 475 612 750
2-5 30 60 90 165 212 260
6-30 19 38 56 98 129 160
31-100 13 26 39 69 90 110
101-196 8 16 24 45 55 65
197-Wings Winfair begins(1/29/37); by Fred Meagher beginning in 1938 28 56 83 144 192 240
198-300 (Last tabloid size) 14 28 42 75 98 120
301-350 (Regular size) 8 16 24 42 51 60
351-422 6 12 18 32 39 45

GULLIVER'S TRAVELS
Macy's Department Store: 1939, small size
nn-Christmas giveaway 14 28 42 79 107 135

Hopalong Cassidy Grape Nuts Flakes © FAW

If The Devil Could Talk © CG

The Iron Horse Goes to War © AAR

	GD 2.0	VG 4.0	FN 6.0	VF 8.0	VF/NM 9.0	NM- 9.2

GUN THAT WON THE WEST, THE
Winchester-Western Division & Olin Mathieson Chemical Corp.: 1956 (Giveaway, 24 pgs.)
nn-Painted-c 5 10 15 24 30 35

HAPPINESS AND HEALING FOR YOU (Also see Oral Roberts'...)
Commercial Comics: 1955 (36 pgs., slick cover) (Oral Roberts Giveaway)
nn 9 18 27 52 66 80
NOTE: *The success of this book prompted Oral Roberts to go into the publishing business himself to produce his own material.*

HAPPY TOOTH
DC Comics: 1996
1 3.00

HAWTHORN-MELODY FARMS DAIRY COMICS
Everybody's Publishing Co.: No date (1950's) (Giveaway)
nn-Cheerie Chick, Tuffy Turtle, Robin Koo Koo, Donald & Longhorn Legends 2 4 6 9 11 14

HENRY ALDRICH COMICS (TV)
Dell Publishing Co.
Giveaway (16 pgs., soft-c, 1951)-Capehart radio 3 6 9 18 24 30

HERE IS SANTA CLAUS
Goldsmith Publishing Co. (Kann's in Washington, D.C.): 1930s (16 pgs., 8 in color) (stiff paper covers)
nn 11 22 33 63 84 105

HERE'S HOW AMERICA'S CARTOONISTS HELP TO SELL U.S. SAVINGS BONDS
Harvey Comics: 1950? (16 pgs., giveaway, paper cover)
Contains: Joe Palooka, Donald Duck, Archie, Kerry Drake, Red Ryder, Blondie & Steve Canyon 19 38 57 106 146 185

HISTORY OF GAS
American Gas Assoc.: Mar, 1947 (Giveaway, 16 pgs.)
nn-Miss Flame narrates 6 12 18 28 34 40

HONEYBEE BIRDWHISTLE AND HER PET PEPI (Introducing...)
Newspaper Enterprise Assoc.: 1969 (Giveaway, 24 pgs., B&W, slick cover)
nn-Contains Freckles newspaper strips with a short biography of Henry Fornhals (artist) & Fred Fox (writer) of the strip 5 10 15 36 48 60

HOPALONG CASSIDY
Fawcett Publications
Grape Nuts Flakes giveaway (1950,9x6") 15 30 45 84 115 145
...& the Mad Barber (1951 Bond Bread giveaway)-7x5"; used in **SOTI**, pgs. 308,309 25 50 75 144 198 255
...Meets the Brend Brothers Bandits (1951 Bond Bread giveaway, color, paper-c, 16 pgs., 3-1/2x7")- Fawcett Publ. 12 24 36 69 92 115
...Strange Legacy (1951 Bond Bread giveaway) 12 24 36 69 92 115
White Tower Giveaway (1946, 16pgs., paper-c) 13 26 39 74 100 125

HOPELESS SAVAGES
Oni Press: May, 2002 (B&W)
Free Comic Book Day giveaway-Reprints #1 with "Free Comic Book Day" banner on-c 2.25

HOPPY THE MARVEL BUNNY (WELL KNOWN COMICS)
Fawcett Publications: 1944 (8-1/2x10-1/2", paper-c)
Bestmaid/Samuel Lowe (printed in red or blue) 10 20 30 56 73 90

HOT STUFF, THE LITTLE DEVIL
Harvey Publications (Illustrated Humor):1963
Shoestore Giveaway 4 8 12 24 32 40

HOW STALIN HOPES WE WILL DESTROY AMERICA
Joe Lowe Co. (Pictorial Media): 1951 (Giveaway, 16 pgs.)
nn 50 100 150 280 415 550

HURRICANE KIDS, THE (Also See Magic Morro, The Owl, Popular Comics #45)
R.S. Callender: 1941 (Giveaway, 7-1/2x5-1/4", soft-c)
nn-Will Ely-a. 10 20 30 56 73 90

IF THE DEVIL WOULD TALK
Roman Catholic Catechetical Guild/Impact Publ.: 1950; 1958 (32 pgs.; paper cover; in full color)
nn-(Scarce)-About secularism (20-30 copies known to exist); very low distribution 76 152 228 475 713 950
1958 Edition-(Impact Publ.); art & script changed to meet church criticism of earlier edition; 80 plus copies known to exist 24 48 72 138 194 250
Black & White version of nn edition; small size; only 4 known copies exist 31 62 93 178 252 325
NOTE: *The original edition of this book was printed and killed by the Guild's board of directors. It is believed that a very limited number of copies were distributed. The 1958 version was a complete bomb with very limited, if any, circulation. In 1979, 11 original, 4 1958 reprints, and 4 B&W's surfaced from the Guild's old files in St. Paul, Minnesota.*

IN LOVE WITH JESUS
Catechetical Educational Society: 1952 (Giveaway, 36 pgs.)
nn 5 10 15 24 30 35

INTERSTATE THEATRES' FUN CLUB COMICS
Interstate Theatres: Mid 1940's (10¢ on cover) (B&W cover) (Premium)
Cover features MLJ characters looking at a copy of Top-Notch Comics, but contains an early Detective Comic on inside; many combinations possible 9 18 27 54 70 85

IN THE GOOD HANDS OF THE ROCKEFELLER TEAM
Country Art Studios: No date (paper cover, 8 pgs.)
nn-Joe Simon-a 8 16 24 43 54 65

IRON GIANT
DC Comics: 1999 (4 pages, theater giveaway)
1-Previews movie 2.50

IRON HORSE GOES TO WAR, THE
Association of American Railroads: 1960 (Giveaway, 16 pgs.)
nn-Civil War & railroads 3 6 9 16 20 25

IS THIS TOMORROW?
Catechetical Guild: 1947 (One Shot) (3 editions) (52 pgs.)
1-Theme of communists taking over the USA; (no price on cover) Used in **POP**, pg. 102 17 34 51 95 130 165
1-(10¢ on cover) 22 44 66 124 172 220
1-Has blank circle with no price on cover 23 46 69 129 180 230
Black & White advance copy titled "Confidential" (52 pgs.)-Contains script and art edited out of the color edition, including one page of extreme violence showing mob nailing a Cardinal to a door; (only two known copies) 65 130 195 406 611 815
NOTE: *The original color version first sold for 10 cents. Since sales were good, it was later printed as a giveaway. Approximately four million in total were printed. The two black and white copies listed plus two other versions as well as a full color untrimmed version surfaced in 1979 from the Guild's old files in St. Paul, Minnesota.*

IT'S FUN TO STAY ALIVE
National Automobile Dealers Association: 1948 (Giveaway, 16 pgs., heavy stock paper)
Featuring: Bugs Bunny, The Berrys, Dixie Dugan, Elmer, Henry, Tim Tyler, Bruce Gentry, Abbie & Slats, Joe Jinks, The Toodles, & Cokey; all art copyright 1946-48 drawn especially for this book 17 34 51 95 130 165

JACK & JILL VISIT TOYTOWN WITH ELMER THE ELF
Butler Brothers (Toytown Stores): 1949 (Giveaway, 16 pgs., paper cover)
nn 5 10 15 22 26 30

JACK ARMSTRONG (Radio)(See True Comics)
Parents' Institute: 1949
12-Premium version(distr. in Chicago only); Free printed on upper right-c; no price (Rare) 18 36 54 104 142 180

JACKIE JOYNER KERSEE IN HIGH HURDLES (Kellogg's Tony's Sports Comics)
DC Comics: 1992 (Sports Illustrated)
nn 3.00

JACKPOT OF FUN COMIC BOOK
DCA Food Ind.: 1957, giveaway
nn-Features Howdy Doody 11 22 33 63 84 105

JEEP COMICS
R. B. Leffingwell & Co.: 1945 - 1946
1-46 (Giveaways)-Strip reprints in all; Tarzan, Flash Gordon, Blondie, The Nebbs, Little Iodine, Red Ryder, Don Winslow, The Phantom, Johnny Hazard, Katzenjammer Kids; distr. to U.S. Armed Forces from 1945-1946 6 12 18 31 38 45

JINGLE BELLS CHRISTMAS BOOK
Montgomery Ward (Giveaway): 1971 (20 pgs., B&W inside, slick-c)
nn 6.00

JOAN OF ARC
Catechetical Guild (Topix) (Giveaway): No date (28 pgs.)
nn 9 18 27 52 66 80
NOTE: *Unpublished version exists which came from the Guild's files.*

JOE PALOOKA (2nd Series)
Harvey Publications
...Body Building Instruction Book (1958 B&M Sports Toy giveaway, 16pgs., 5-1/4x7")-Origin 9 18 27 49 62 75
...Fights His Way Back (1945 Giveaway, 24 pgs.) Family Comics

Kasco Komics #2 © Kasko

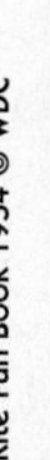
Kite Fun Book 1954 © WDC

Labor is a Partner © CG

	GD 2.0	VG 4.0	FN 6.0	VF 8.0	VF/NM 9.0	NM- 9.2
	16	32	48	89	122	155
...in Hi There! (1949 Red Cross giveaway, 12 pgs., 4-3/4x6")	9	18	27	49	62	75
...in It's All in the Family (1945 Red Cross giveaway, 16 pgs., regular size)	10	20	30	56	73	90

JOE THE GENIE OF STEEL
U.S. Steel Corp., Pittsburgh, PA: 1950 (16 pgs.)

	GD	VG	FN	VF	VF/NM	NM-
nn	5	10	14	20	24	28

JOHNNY JINGLE'S LUCKY DAY
American Dairy Assoc.: 1956 (16 pgs.; 7-1/4x5-1/8") (Giveaway) (Disney)

	GD	VG	FN	VF	VF/NM	NM-
nn	5	10	15	23	28	32

JO-JOY (The Adventures of...)
W. T. Grant Dept. Stores: 1945 - 1953 (Christmas gift comic, 16 pgs., 7-1/16x10-1/4")

	GD	VG	FN	VF	VF/NM	NM-
1945-53 issues	6	12	18	27	33	38

JOLLY CHRISTMAS BOOK (See Christmas Journey Through Space)
Promotional Publ. Co.: 1951; 1954; 1955 (36 pgs.; 24 pgs.)

	GD	VG	FN	VF	VF/NM	NM-
1951-(Woolworth giveaway)-slightly oversized; no slick cover; Marv Levy-c/a	7	14	21	37	46	55
1954-(Hot Shoppes giveaway)-regular size-reprints 1951 issue; slick cover added; 24 pgs.; no ads	6	12	18	31	38	45
1955-(J. M. McDonald Co. giveaway)-reg. size	6	12	18	28	34	40

JOURNEY OF DISCOVERY WITH MARK STEEL (See Mark Steel)

JUMPING JACKS PRESENTS THE WHIZ KIDS
Jumping Jacks Stores giveaway: 1978 (In 3-D) with glasses (4 pgs.)

	GD	VG	FN	VF	VF/NM	NM-
nn						6.00

JUNGLE BOOK FUN BOOK, THE (Disney)
Baskin Robbins: 1978

	GD	VG	FN	VF	VF/NM	NM-
nn-Ice Cream giveaway	2	4	6	10	12	15

JUSTICE LEAGUE ADVENTURES (Based on Cartoon Network series)
DC Comics: May, 2002

	GD	VG	FN	VF	VF/NM	NM-
Free Comic Book Day giveaway-Reprints #1 with "Free Comic Book Day" banner on-c						2.25

JUSTICE LEAGUE OF AMERICA
DC Comics: 1999 (included in Justice League of America Monopoly game)

	GD	VG	FN	VF	VF/NM	NM-
nn - Reprints 1st app. in Brave and the Bold #28						2.50

KASCO KOMICS
Kasko Grainfeed (Giveaway): 1945; No. 2, 1949 (Regular size, paper-c)

	GD	VG	FN	VF	VF/NM	NM-
1(1945)-Similar to Katy Keene; Bill Woggon-a; 28 pgs.; 6-7/8x9-7/8"	17	34	51	95	130	165
2(1949)-Woggon-c/a	13	26	39	74	100	125

KATY AND KEN VISIT SANTA WITH MISTER WISH
S. S. Kresge Co. : 1948 (Giveaway, 16 pgs., paper-c)

	GD	VG	FN	VF	VF/NM	NM-
nn	6	12	18	28	34	40

KELLOGG'S CINNAMON MINI-BUNS SUPER-HEROES
DC Comics: 1993 (4 1/4" x 2 3/4")

	GD	VG	FN	VF	VF/NM	NM-
4 editions: Flash, Justice League America, Superman, Wonder Woman and the Star Riders each.....						4.00

KERRY DRAKE DETECTIVE CASES
Publisher's Syndicate

	GD	VG	FN	VF	VF/NM	NM-
...in the Case of the Sleeping City-(1951)-16 pg. giveaway for armed forces; paper cover	6	12	18	28	34	40

KEY COMICS
Key Clothing Co./Peterson Clothing: 1951 - 1956 (32 pgs.) (Giveaway)
Contains a comic from different publishers bound with new cover. Cover changed each year. Many combinations possible. Distributed in Nebraska, Iowa, & Kansas. Contents would determine price, 40-60 percent of original.

KIRBY'S SHOES COMICS
Kirby's Shoes: 1959 (8 pgs., soft-c)

	GD	VG	FN	VF	VF/NM	NM-
nn-Features Kirby the Golden Bear	3	5	7	10	12	14

KITE FUN BOOK
Pacific, Gas & Electric/Sou. California Edison/Florida Power & Light/ Missouri Public Service Co.: 1953 - 1981 (16pgs, 5x7-1/4", soft-c)

	GD	VG	FN	VF	VF/NM	NM-
1953-Pinocchio Learns About Kites (Disney)	47	94	141	260	380	500
1954-Donald Duck Tells About Kites-Fla. Power, S.C.E. & version with label issues -Barks pencils-8 pgs.; inks-7 pgs. (Rare)	400	800	1200	2000	2700	3400
1954-Donald Duck Tells About Kites-P.G.&E. issue -7th page redrawn changing middle 3 panels to show P.G.&E. in story line; (All Barks-a) Scarce	247	494	741	1470	2085	2700
1955-Brer Rabbit in "A Kite Tail" (Disney)	34	68	103	173	236	300
1956-Woody Woodpecker (Lantz)	14	28	42	78	104	130
1957-?						
1958-Tom And Jerry (M.G.M.)	10	20	30	51	63	80
1960-Porky Pig (Warner Bros.)	6	12	18	38	52	65
1960-Bugs Bunny (Warner Bros.)	6	12	18	38	52	65
1961-Huckleberry Hound (Hanna-Barbera)	6	12	18	43	59	75
1962-Yogi Bear (Hanna-Barbera)	5	10	15	33	44	55
1963-Rocky and Bullwinkle (TV)(Jay Ward)	10	20	30	70	100	130
1963-Top Cat (TV)(Hanna-Barbera)	6	12	18	38	52	65
1964-Magilla Gorilla (TV)(Hanna-Barbera)	5	10	15	36	48	60
1965-Jinks, Pixie and Dixie (TV)(Hanna-Barbera)	4	8	12	25	33	42
1965-Tweety and Sylvester (Warner); S.C.E. version with Reddy Kilowatt app.	3	6	9	16	20	24
1966-Secret Squirrel (Hanna-Barbera); S.C.E. version with Reddy Kilowatt app.	7	14	21	51	71	90
1967-Beep! Beep! The Road Runner (TV)(Warner)	3	6	9	18	24	30
1968-Bugs Bunny (Warner Bros.)	3	6	9	19	25	32
1969-Dastardly and Muttley (TV)(Hanna-Barbera)	5	10	15	36	48	60
1970-Rocky and Bullwinkle (TV)(Jay Ward)	7	14	21	51	71	90
1971-Beep! Beep! The Road Runner (TV)(Warner)	3	6	9	18	23	28
1972-The Pink Panther (TV)	3	6	9	16	20	24
1973-Lassie (TV)	4	8	12	25	33	42
1974-Underdog (TV)	3	6	9	18	23	30
1975-Ben Franklin	2	4	6	10	13	16
1976-The Brady Bunch (TV)	4	8	12	27	36	45
1977-Ben Franklin	2	4	6	10	13	16
1977-Popeye	3	6	9	18	23	28
1978-Happy Days (TV)	3	6	9	19	25	32
1979-Eight is Enough (TV)	3	6	9	18	23	28
1980-The Waltons (TV, released in 1981)	3	6	9	18	23	28

KNOW YOUR MASS
Catechetical Guild: No. 303, 1958 (35¢, 100 Pg. Giant) (Square binding)

	GD	VG	FN	VF	VF/NM	NM-
303-In color	6	12	18	31	38	45

KOLYNOS PRESENTS THE WHITE GUARD
Whitehall Pharmacal Co.: 1949 (paper cover, 8 pgs.)

	GD	VG	FN	VF	VF/NM	NM-
nn	6	12	18	27	33	38

K. O. PUNCH, THE (Also see Lucky Fights It Through)
E. C. Comics: 1948 (Educational giveaway)

	GD	VG	FN	VF	VF/NM	NM-
nn-Feldstein-splash; Kamen-a	85	170	255	520	760	1000

KOREA MY HOME (Also see Yalta to Korea)
Johnstone and Cushing: nd (1950s)

	GD	VG	FN	VF	VF/NM	NM-
nn-Anti-communist; Korean War	22	44	66	127	176	225

KRIM-KO KOMICS
Krim-ko Chocolate Drink: 5/18/35 - No. 6, 6/22/35; 1936 - 1939 (weekly)

	GD	VG	FN	VF	VF/NM	NM-
1-(16 pgs., soft-c, Dairy giveaways)-Tom, Mary & Sparky Advs. by Russell Keaton, Jim Hawkins by Dick Moores, Mystery Island! by Rick Yager begin	14	28	42	79	107	135
2-6 (6/22/35)	10	20	30	56	73	90
Lola, Secret Agent; 184 issues, 4 pg. giveaways - all original stories each....	7	14	21	37	46	55

LABOR IS A PARTNER
Catechetical Guild Educational Society: 1949 (32 pgs., paper-c)

	GD	VG	FN	VF	VF/NM	NM-
nn-Anti-communism	19	38	57	106	146	185
Confidential Preview-(8-1/2x11", B&W, saddle stitched)-only one known copy; text varies from color version, advertises next book on secularism (If the Devil Would Talk)	22	44	66	124	172	220

LADY AND THE TRAMP IN "BUTTER LATE THAN NEVER"
American Dairy Assoc. (Premium): 1955 (16 pgs., 5x7-1/4", soft-c) (Disney)

	GD	VG	FN	VF	VF/NM	NM-
nn	10	20	30	56	73	90

LASSIE (TV)
Dell Publ. Co

	GD	VG	FN	VF	VF/NM	NM-
The Adventures of... nn-(Red Heart Dog Food giveaway, 1949)-16 pgs, soft-c; 1st app. Lassie in comics	34	68	102	193	274	355

LEAVE IT TO CHANCE
Image Comics: 2003

	GD	VG	FN	VF	VF/NM	NM-
Free Comic Book Day Edition - James Robinson-s/Paul Smith-a						2.25

LIFE OF THE BLESSED VIRGIN
Catechetical Guild (Giveaway): 1950 (68pgs.) (square binding)

	GD	VG	FN	VF	VF/NM	NM-
nn-Contains "The Woman of the Promise" & "Mother of Us All" rebound	6	12	18	29	36	42

Little Klinker © Montgomery Ward

Lone Ranger in Milk For Big Mike © DELL

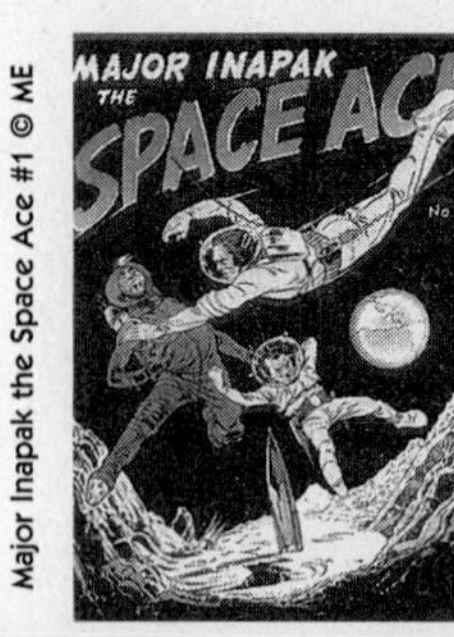

Major Inapak the Space Ace #1 © ME

	GD 2.0	VG 4.0	FN 6.0	VF 8.0	VF/NM 9.0	NM- 9.2

LIGHTNING RACERS
DC Comics: 1989
1 — 4.00

LI'L ABNER (Al Capp's) (Also see Natural Disasters!)
Harvey Publ./Toby Press
...& the Creatures from Drop-Outer Space-nn (Job Corps giveaway; 36 pgs., in color) (entire book by Frank Frazetta) — 25 50 75 147 202 260
...Joins the Navy (1950) (Toby Press Premium) — 11 22 33 63 84 105
Al Capp by Li'l Abner (Circa 1946, nd, giveaway) Al Capp bio and his life as an amputee — 11 22 33 63 84 105

LITTLE ALONZO
Macy's Dept. Store: 1938 (B&W, 5-1/2x8-1/2")(Christmas giveaway)
nn-By Ferdinand the Bull's Munro Leaf — 9 18 27 49 62 75

LITTLE DOT
Harvey Publications
Shoe store giveaway 2 — 4 8 12 28 38 48

LITTLE FIR TREE, THE
W. T. Grant Co. : nd (1942) (8-1/2x11") (12 pgs. with cover, color & B&W, heavy paper) (Christmas giveaway)
nn-Story by Hans Christian Anderson; 8 pg. Kelly-r/Santa Claus Funnies (not signed); X-Mas-c
(One copy in Mint sold for $1750.00 in 1986, another copy in VF sold for $1000.00 in 1991 and one copy in VG/FN sold for $1500 in 2002)

LITTLE KLINKER
Little Klinker Ventures: Nov, 1960 (20 pgs.) (slick cover) (Montgomery Ward Giveaway)
nn — 2 4 6 10 13 16

LITTLE MISS SUNBEAM COMICS
Magazine Enterprises/Quality Bakers of America
Bread Giveaway 1-4(Quality Bakers, 1949-50)-14 pgs. each — 6 12 18 31 38 45
Bread Giveaway (1957,61; 16pgs, reg. size) — 5 10 15 24 30 35

LITTLE ORPHAN ANNIE
David McKay Publ./Dell Publishing Co.
Junior Commandos Giveaway (same-c as 4-Color #18, K.K. Publ.)(Big Shoe Store); same back cover as '47 Popped Wheat giveaway; 16 pgs; flag-c; r/strips 9/7/42-10/10/42 — 31 62 93 175 248 320
Popped Wheat Giveaway ('47)-16 pgs. full color; reprints strips from 5/3/40 to 6/20/40 — 4 8 12 18 22 25
Quaker Sparkies Giveaway (1940) — 20 40 60 112 156 200
Quaker Sparkies Giveaway (1941, full color, 20 pgs.); "LOA and the Rescue"; r/strips 4/13/39-6/21/39 & 7/6/39-7/17/39. "LOA and the Kidnappers"; r/strips 11/28/38-1/28/39 — 18 36 54 101 138 165
Quaker Sparkies Giveaway (1942, full color, 20 pgs.); "LOA and Mr. Gudge"; r/strips 2/13/38-3/21/38 & 4/18/37-5/30/37. "LOA and the Great Am" — 17 34 51 95 130 165

LITTLE TREE THAT WASN'T WANTED, THE
W. T. Grant Co. (Giveaway): 1960, (Color, 28 pgs.)
nn-Christmas story, puzzles and games — 3 6 9 21 28 35

LOADED (Also see Re-Loaded)
DC Comics: 1995 (Interplay Productions)
1-Garth Ennis-s; promotes video game — 4.00

LONE RANGER, THE
Dell Publishing Co.
Cheerios Giveaways (1954, 16 pgs., 2-1/2x7", soft-c) #1- "The Lone Ranger, His Mask & How He Met Tonto". #2- "The Lone Ranger & the Story of Silver" each.... — 20 40 60 92 126 160
Doll Giveaways (Gabriel Ind.)(1973, 3-1/4x5")- "The Story of The Lone Ranger," "The Carson City Bank Robbery" & "The Apache Buffalo Hunt" — 2 4 6 11 14 18
How the Lone Ranger Captured Silver Book(1936)-Silvercup Bread giveaway — 90 180 270 400 575 750
...In Milk for Big Mike (1955, Dairy Association giveaway), soft-c; 5x7-1/4", 16 pgs. — 20 40 60 100 130 160
Legend of The Lone Ranger (1969, 16 pgs., giveaway)-Origin The Lone Ranger — 4 8 12 24 32 40
Merita Bread giveaway (1954, 16 pgs., 5x7-1/4")- "How to Be a Lone Ranger Health & Safety Scout" — 25 50 75 120 155 190

LONE RANGER COMICS, THE
Lone Ranger, Inc. : Book 1, 1939(inside) (shows 1938 on-c) (52 pgs. in color; regular size) (Ice cream mail order)
Book 1-(Scarce)-The first western comic devoted to a single character; not by Vallely — 923 1961 3000 6500 - -
2nd version w/large full color promo poster pasted over centerfold & a smaller poster pasted over back cover; includes new additional premiums not originally offered (Rare) — 1040 2120 3200 7000 - -

LOONEY TUNES
DC Comics: 1991, 1998
Claritan promotional issue (1998) — 2.50
Colgate mini-comic (1998) — 2.50
Tyson's 1-10 (1991) — 4.00

LUCKY FIGHTS IT THROUGH (Also see The K. O. Punch)
Educational Comics: 1949 (Giveaway, 16 pgs. in color, paper-c)
nn-(Very Rare)-1st Kurtzman work for E. C.; V.D. prevention — 125 250 375 700 950 1200
nn-Reprint in color (1977) — 6.00
NOTE: *Subtitled "The Story of That Ignorant, Ignorant Cowboy". Prepared for Communications Materials Center, Columbia University.*

LUDWIG VON DRAKE (See Frito-Lay Giveaway)

MACO TOYS COMIC
Maco Toys/Charlton Comics: 1959 (Giveaway, 36 pgs.)
1-All military stories featuring Maco Toys — 2 4 6 11 14 18

MAD MAGAZINE
DC Comics: 1997, 1999
Special Edition (1997, Tang giveaway) — 2.50
Stocking Stuffer (1999) — 2.50

MAGAZINELAND
DC Comics: 1977
nn — 3.00

MAGIC MORRO (Also see Super Comics #21, The Owl, & The Hurricane Kids)
K. K. Publications: 1941 (7-1/2x5-1/4, giveaway, soft-c)
nn-Ken Ernst-a. — 13 26 39 74 100 125

MAGIC OF CHRISTMAS AT NEWBERRYS, THE
E. S. London: 1967 (Giveaway) (B&W, slick-c, 20 pgs.)
nn — 1 3 4 6 8 10

MAJOR INAPAK THE SPACE ACE
Magazine Enterprises (Inapac Foods): 1951 (20 pgs.) (Giveaway)
1-Bob Powell-c/a — 6.00
NOTE: *Many warehouse copies surfaced in 1973.*

MAMMY YOKUM & THE GREAT DOGPATCH MYSTERY
Toby Press: 1951 (Giveaway)
nn-Li'l Abner — 17 34 51 95 130 165
nn-Reprint (1956) — 5 10 15 22 26 30

MAN NAMED STEVENSON, A
Democratic National Committee: 1952 (20 pgs., 5 1/4 x 7")
nn — 9 18 27 47 60 72

MAN OF PEACE, POPE PIUS XII
Catechetical Guild: 1950 (See Pope Pius XII... & To V2#8)
nn-All Powell-a — 6 12 18 28 34 40

MAN OF STEEL BEST WESTERN
DC Comics: 1997
nn-Best Western hotels — 3.00

MAN WHO WOULDN'T QUIT, THE
Harvey Publications Inc.: 1952 (16 pgs., paper cover)
nn-The value of voting — 4 8 12 18 22 25

MARCH OF COMICS (Boys' and Girls'...#3-353)
K. K. Publications/Western Publishing Co.: 1946 - No. 488, April, 1982 (#1-4 are not numbered) (K.K. Giveaway) (Founded by Sig Feuchtwanger)
Early issues were full size, 32 pages, and were printed with and without an extra cover of slick stock, just for the advertiser. The binding was stapled if the slick cover was added; otherwise, the pages were glued together at the spine. Most 1948 - 1951 issues were full size,24 pages, pulp covers. Starting in 1952 they were half-size (with a few exceptions) and 32 pages with slick covers.1959 and later issues had only 16 pages plus covers. 1952 -1959 issues read oblong; 1960 and later issues read upright. All have new stories except where noted.
nn (#1, 1946)-Goldilocks; Kelly back-c (16 pgs., stapled) — 31 62 93 171 235 300
nn (#2, 1946)-How Santa Got His Red Suit; Kelly-a (11 pgs., r/4-Color #61 from 1944) (16pgs., stapled) — 29 58 87 160 225 290
nn (#3, 1947)-Our Gang (Walt Kelly) — 40 80 120 220 310 400
nn (#4)-Donald Duck by Carl Barks, "Maharajah Donald", 28 pgs.; Kelly-c?

March of Comics #74 © WDC

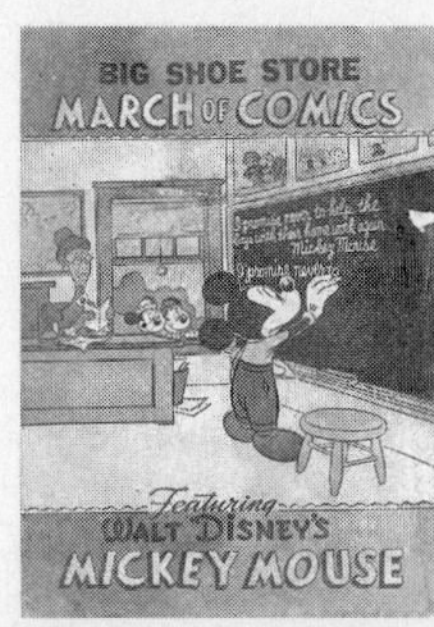

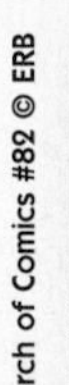
March of Comics #82 © ERB

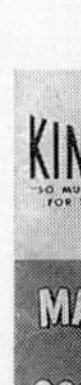
March of Comics #86 © Roy Rogers

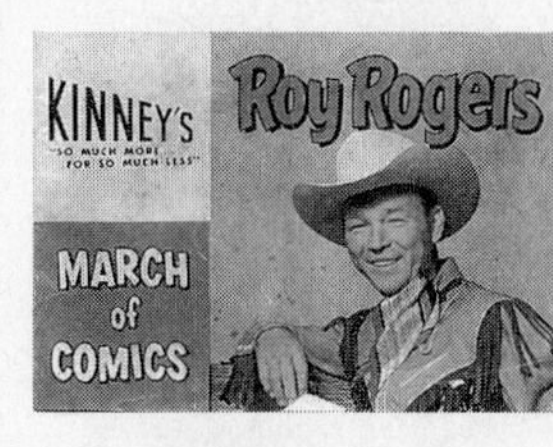

	GD 2.0	VG 4.0	FN 6.0	VF 8.0	VF/NM 9.0	NM- 9.2
(Disney)	825	1650	2475	4538	6019	7500
5-Andy Panda (Walter Lantz)	18	36	54	99	135	170
6-Popular Fairy Tales; Kelly-c; Noonan-a(2)	21	42	63	112	156	200
7-Oswald the Rabbit	19	38	57	106	146	185
8-Mickey Mouse, 32 pgs. (Disney)	59	118	177	325	442	560
9(nn)-The Story of the Gloomy Bunny	11	22	33	63	84	105
10-Out of Santa's Bag	10	20	30	58	77	95
11-Fun With Santa Claus	9	18	27	54	70	85
12-Santa's Toys	9	18	27	54	70	85
13-Santa's Surprise	9	18	27	54	70	85
14-Santa's Candy Kitchen	9	18	27	54	70	85
15-Hip-It-Ty Hop & the Big Bass Viol	9	18	27	49	62	75
16-Woody Woodpecker (1947)(Walter Lantz)	13	26	39	74	100	125
17-Roy Rogers (1948)	28	56	84	154	200	260
18-Popular Fairy Tales	11	22	33	63	84	105
19-Uncle Wiggily	10	20	30	56	73	90
20-Donald Duck by Carl Barks, "Darkest Africa", 22 pgs.; Kelly-c (Disney)	470	940	1410	2585	3492	4400
21-Tom and Jerry	11	22	33	63	84	105
22-Andy Panda (Lantz)	10	20	30	58	77	95
23-Raggedy Ann & Andy; Kerr-a	14	28	42	77	103	130
24-Felix the Cat, 1932 daily strip reprints by Otto Messmer	25	50	75	138	181	225
25-Gene Autry	25	50	75	138	181	225
26-Our Gang; Walt Kelly	22	44	66	121	160	200
27-Mickey Mouse; r/in M. M. #240 (Disney)	41	82	123	225	305	385
28-Gene Autry	24	48	72	132	176	220
29-Easter Bonnet Shop	7	14	21	35	43	50
30-Here Comes Santa	6	12	18	31	38	45
31-Santa's Busy Corner	6	12	18	31	38	45
32-No book produced						
33-A Christmas Carol (12/48)	7	14	21	35	43	50
34-Woody Woodpecker	10	20	30	58	77	95
35-Roy Rogers (1948)	24	48	72	138	194	250
36-Felix the Cat(1949); by Messmer; '34 strip-r	19	38	57	107	149	190
37-Popeye	14	28	42	81	111	140
38-Oswald the Rabbit	9	18	27	49	62	75
39-Gene Autry	22	44	66	124	172	220
40-Andy and Woody	9	18	27	49	62	75
41-Donald Duck by Carl Barks, "Race to the South Seas", 22 pgs.; Kelly-c	350	700	1050	2000	2950	3900
42-Porky Pig	9	18	27	52	66	80
43-Henry	8	16	24	46	58	70
44-Bugs Bunny	10	20	30	56	73	90
45-Mickey Mouse (Disney)	30	60	90	164	232	300
46-Tom and Jerry	10	20	30	56	73	90
47-Roy Rogers	21	42	63	121	168	215
48-Greetings from Santa	5	10	15	24	30	35
49-Santa Is Here	5	10	15	24	30	35
50-Santa Claus' Workshop (1949)	5	10	15	24	30	35
51-Felix the Cat (1950) by Messmer	17	34	51	95	130	165
52-Popeye	12	24	36	71	96	120
53-Oswald the Rabbit	8	16	24	46	58	70
54-Gene Autry	19	38	57	107	149	190
55-Andy and Woody	8	16	24	43	54	65
56-Donald Duck; not by Barks; Barks art on back-c (Disney)	27	54	81	155	218	280
57-Porky Pig	8	16	24	46	58	70
58-Henry	7	14	21	35	43	50
59-Bugs Bunny	9	18	27	52	66	80
60-Mickey Mouse (Disney)	26	52	78	150	210	270
61-Tom and Jerry	8	16	24	46	58	70
62-Roy Rogers	21	42	63	118	164	210
63-Welcome Santa (1/2-size, oblong)	5	10	15	24	30	35
64(nn)-Santa's Helpers (1/2-size, oblong)	5	10	15	24	30	35
65(nn)-Jingle Bells (1950) (1/2-size, oblong)	5	10	15	24	30	35
66-Popeye (1951)	11	22	33	63	84	105
67-Oswald the Rabbit	8	16	24	43	54	65
68-Roy Rogers	20	40	60	112	156	200
69-Donald Duck; Barks-a on back-c (Disney)	24	48	72	138	194	250
70-Tom and Jerry	8	16	24	40	50	60
71-Porky Pig	8	16	24	43	54	65
72-Krazy Kat	9	18	27	52	66	80
73-Roy Rogers	18	36	54	101	138	175
74-Mickey Mouse (1951)(Disney)	22	44	66	124	172	220
75-Bugs Bunny	8	16	24	43	54	65
76-Andy and Woody	8	16	24	40	50	60
77-Roy Rogers	17	34	51	95	130	165
78-Gene Autry (1951); last regular size issue	16	32	48	89	122	155

Note: All pre #79 issues came with or without a slick protective wrap-around cover over the regular cover which advertised Poll Parrot Shoes, Sears, etc. This outer cover protects the inside pages making them in nicer condition.
Issues with the outer cover are worth 15-25% more

	GD 2.0	VG 4.0	FN 6.0	VF 8.0	VF/NM 9.0	NM- 9.2
79-Andy Panda (1952, 5x7" size)	6	12	18	28	34	40
80-Popeye	10	20	30	56	73	90
81-Oswald the Rabbit	5	10	15	24	30	35
82-Tarzan; Lex Barker photo-c	17	34	51	98	134	170
83-Bugs Bunny	6	12	18	31	38	45
84-Henry	5	10	15	24	30	35
85-Woody Woodpecker	5	10	15	24	30	35
86-Roy Rogers	13	26	39	76	103	130
87-Krazy Kat	8	16	24	40	50	60
88-Tom and Jerry	6	12	18	28	34	40
89-Porky Pig	5	10	15	24	30	35
90-Gene Autry	12	24	36	69	92	115
91-Roy Rogers & Santa	13	26	39	74	100	125
92-Christmas with Santa	5	10	15	22	26	30
93-Woody Woodpecker (1953)	5	10	14	20	24	28
94-Indian Chief	9	18	27	52	66	80
95-Oswald the Rabbit	5	10	14	20	24	28
96-Popeye	9	18	27	52	66	80
97-Bugs Bunny	6	12	18	28	34	40
98-Tarzan; Lex Barker photo-c	16	32	48	92	126	160
99-Porky Pig	5	10	14	20	24	28
100-Roy Rogers	10	20	30	60	80	100
101-Henry	4	8	12	18	22	25
102-Tom Corbett (TV)('53, early app).; painted-c	13	26	39	74	100	125
103-Tom and Jerry	5	10	14	20	24	28
104-Gene Autry	10	20	30	58	77	95
105-Roy Rogers	10	20	30	58	77	95
106-Santa's Helpers	5	10	15	22	26	30
107-Santa's Christmas Book - not published						
108-Fun with Santa (1953)	5	10	15	22	26	30
109-Woody Woodpecker (1954)	5	10	15	22	26	30
110-Indian Chief	6	12	18	28	34	40
111-Oswald the Rabbit	4	8	12	18	22	25
112-Henry	4	8	11	16	19	22
113-Porky Pig	4	8	12	18	22	25
114-Tarzan; Russ Manning-a	16	32	48	92	126	160
115-Bugs Bunny	5	10	15	23	28	32
116-Roy Rogers	10	20	30	58	77	95
117-Popeye	9	18	27	52	66	80
118-Flash Gordon; painted-c	11	22	33	66	88	110
119-Tom and Jerry	4	8	12	18	22	25
120-Gene Autry	10	20	30	58	77	95
121-Roy Rogers	10	20	30	58	77	95
122-Santa's Surprise (1954)	4	8	12	18	22	25
123-Santa's Christmas Book	4	8	12	18	22	25
124-Woody Woodpecker (1955)	4	8	11	16	19	22
125-Tarzan; Lex Barker photo-c	15	30	45	86	118	150
126-Oswald the Rabbit	4	8	11	16	19	22
127-Indian Chief	6	12	18	31	38	45
128-Tom and Jerry	4	8	11	16	19	22
129-Henry	4	7	10	14	17	20
130-Porky Pig	4	8	11	16	19	22
131-Roy Rogers	10	20	30	58	77	95
132-Bugs Bunny	5	10	14	20	24	28
133-Flash Gordon; painted-c	10	20	30	58	77	95
134-Popeye	7	14	21	37	46	55
135-Gene Autry	9	18	27	54	70	85
136-Roy Rogers	9	18	27	54	70	85
137-Gifts from Santa	3	6	8	12	14	16
138-Fun at Christmas (1955)	3	6	8	12	14	16
139-Woody Woodpecker (1956)	4	8	11	16	19	22
140-Indian Chief	6	12	18	31	38	45
141-Oswald the Rabbit	4	8	11	16	19	22
142-Flash Gordon	10	20	30	58	77	95
143-Porky Pig	4	8	11	16	19	22
144-Tarzan; Russ Manning-a; painted-c	14	28	42	81	111	140
145-Tom and Jerry	4	8	11	16	19	22
146-Roy Rogers; photo-c	9	18	27	54	70	85
147-Henry	4	7	9	14	16	18
148-Popeye	7	14	21	37	46	55
149-Bugs Bunny	4	8	12	18	22	25

March of Comics #174 © Lone Ranger Inc.

March of Comics #192 © WB

March of Comics #285 © NBC, Inc.

	GD 2.0	VG 4.0	FN 6.0	VF 8.0	VF/NM 9.0	NM- 9.2
150-Gene Autry	9	18	27	54	70	85
151-Roy Rogers	9	18	27	54	70	85
152-The Night Before Christmas	4	7	9	14	16	18
153-Merry Christmas (1956)	4	8	11	16	19	22
154-Tom and Jerry (1957)	4	8	11	16	19	22
155-Tarzan; photo-c	14	28	42	79	107	135
156-Oswald the Rabbit	4	8	11	16	19	22
157-Popeye	6	12	18	31	38	45
158-Woody Woodpecker	4	8	11	16	19	22
159-Indian Chief	6	12	18	31	38	45
160-Bugs Bunny	4	8	12	18	22	25
161-Roy Rogers	9	18	27	49	62	75
162-Henry	4	7	9	14	16	18
163-Rin Tin Tin (TV)	7	14	21	37	46	55
164-Porky Pig	4	8	11	16	19	22
165-The Lone Ranger	9	18	27	52	66	80
166-Santa and His Reindeer	3	6	8	12	14	16
167-Roy Rogers and Santa	9	18	27	49	62	75
168-Santa Claus' Workshop (1957, full size)	4	7	9	14	16	18
169-Popeye (1958)	6	12	18	31	38	45
170-Indian Chief	6	12	18	31	38	45
171-Oswald the Rabbit	4	7	10	14	17	20
172-Tarzan	11	22	33	63	84	105
173-Tom and Jerry	4	7	10	14	17	20
174-The Lone Ranger	9	18	27	52	66	80
175-Porky Pig	4	7	10	14	17	20
176-Roy Rogers	8	16	24	43	54	65
177-Woody Woodpecker	4	7	10	14	17	20
178-Henry	4	7	9	14	16	18
179-Bugs Bunny	4	7	10	14	17	20
180-Rin Tin Tin (TV)	7	14	21	35	43	50
181-Happy Holiday	3	5	7	10	12	14
182-Happi Tim	4	7	9	14	16	18
183-Welcome Santa (1958, full size)	3	5	7	10	12	14
184-Woody Woodpecker (1959)	4	7	9	14	16	18
185-Tarzan; photo-c	10	20	30	60	80	100
186-Oswald the Rabbit	4	7	9	14	16	18
187-Indian Chief	5	10	15	24	30	35
188-Bugs Bunny	4	7	9	14	16	18
189-Henry	3	6	8	12	14	16
190-Tom and Jerry	4	7	9	14	16	18
191-Roy Rogers	8	16	24	40	50	60
192-Porky Pig	4	7	9	14	16	18
193-The Lone Ranger	9	18	27	49	62	75
194-Popeye	6	12	18	28	34	40
195-Rin Tin Tin (TV)	6	12	18	31	38	45
196-Sears Special - not published						
197-Santa Is Coming	3	6	8	12	14	16
198-Santa's Helpers (1959)	3	6	8	12	14	16
199-Huckleberry Hound (TV)(1960, early app.)	7	14	21	37	46	55
200-Fury (TV)	5	10	15	24	30	35
201-Bugs Bunny	4	7	9	14	16	18
202-Space Explorer	8	16	24	40	50	60
203-Woody Woodpecker	3	6	8	12	14	16
204-Tarzan	9	18	27	52	66	80
205-Mighty Mouse	6	12	18	29	36	42
206-Roy Rogers; photo-c	8	16	24	40	50	60
207-Tom and Jerry	3	6	8	12	14	16
208-The Lone Ranger; Clayton Moore photo-c	10	20	30	60	80	100
209-Porky Pig	3	6	8	12	14	16
210-Lassie (TV)	6	12	18	29	36	42
211-Sears Special - not published						
212-Christmas Eve	3	6	8	12	14	16
213-Here Comes Santa (1960)	3	6	8	12	14	16
214-Huckleberry Hound (TV)(1961)	6	12	18	31	38	45
215-Hi Yo Silver	7	14	21	35	43	50
216-Rocky & His Friends (TV)(1961); predates Rocky and His Fiendish Friends #1 (see Four Color #1128)	9	18	27	54	70	85
217-Lassie (TV)	6	12	18	28	34	40
218-Porky Pig	3	6	8	12	14	16
219-Journey to the Sun	5	10	15	24	30	35
220-Bugs Bunny	4	7	9	14	16	18
221-Roy and Dale; photo-c	7	14	21	37	46	55
222-Woody Woodpecker	3	6	8	12	14	16
223-Tarzan	9	18	27	52	66	80
224-Tom and Jerry	3	6	8	12	14	16
225-The Lone Ranger	7	14	21	37	46	55
226-Christmas Treasury (1961)	3	6	8	12	14	16
227-Letters to Santa (1961)	3	6	8	12	14	16
228-Sears Special - not published?						
229-The Flintstones (TV)(1962); early app.; predates 1st Flintstones Gold Key issue (#7)	10	20	30	58	77	95
230-Lassie (TV)	5	10	15	23	28	32
231-Bugs Bunny	4	7	9	14	16	18
232-The Three Stooges	9	18	27	52	66	80
233-Bullwinkle (TV) (1962, very early app.)	10	20	30	56	73	90
234-Smokey the Bear	5	10	14	20	24	28
235-Huckleberry Hound (TV)	6	12	18	31	38	45
236-Roy and Dale	6	12	18	31	38	45
237-Mighty Mouse	5	10	15	23	28	32
238-The Lone Ranger	7	14	21	37	46	55
239-Woody Woodpecker	3	6	8	12	14	16
240-Tarzan	8	16	24	43	54	65
241-Santa Claus Around the World	3	5	7	10	12	14
242-Santa's Toyland (1962)	3	5	7	10	12	14
243-The Flintstones (TV)(1963)	8	16	24	43	54	65
244-Mister Ed (TV); early app.; photo-c	6	12	18	31	38	45
245-Bugs Bunny	4	7	9	14	16	18
246-Popeye	5	10	15	23	28	32
247-Mighty Mouse	5	10	15	23	28	32
248-The Three Stooges	9	18	27	52	66	80
249-Woody Woodpecker	3	6	8	12	14	16
250-Roy and Dale	6	12	18	31	38	45
251-Little Lulu & Witch Hazel	11	22	33	66	88	110
252-Tarzan; painted-c	8	16	24	40	50	60
253-Yogi Bear (TV)	7	14	21	37	46	55
254-Lassie (TV)	5	10	15	24	30	35
255-Santa's Christmas List	3	6	8	12	14	16
256-Christmas Party (1963)	3	6	8	12	14	16
257-Mighty Mouse	5	10	15	23	28	32
258-The Sword in the Stone (Disney)	8	16	24	40	50	60
259-Bugs Bunny	4	7	9	14	16	18
260-Mister Ed (TV)	6	12	18	28	34	40
261-Woody Woodpecker	3	6	8	12	14	16
262-Tarzan	7	14	21	37	46	55
263-Donald Duck; not by Barks (Disney)	9	18	27	49	62	75
264-Popeye	5	10	15	23	28	32
265-Yogi Bear (TV)	6	12	18	28	34	40
266-Lassie (TV)	5	10	14	20	24	28
267-Little Lulu; Irving Tripp-a	10	20	30	56	73	90
268-The Three Stooges	8	16	24	43	54	65
269-A Jolly Christmas	2	4	6	8	10	12
270-Santa's Little Helpers	2	4	6	8	10	12
271-The Flintstones (TV)(1965)	9	18	27	49	62	75
272-Tarzan	7	14	21	37	46	55
273-Bugs Bunny	4	7	9	14	16	18
274-Popeye	5	10	15	23	28	32
275-Little Lulu; Irving Tripp-a	9	18	27	49	62	75
276-The Jetsons (TV)	13	26	39	76	103	130
277-Daffy Duck	4	7	9	14	16	18
278-Lassie (TV)	5	10	14	20	24	28
279-Yogi Bear (TV)	6	12	18	28	34	40
280-The Three Stooges; photo-c	8	16	24	43	54	65
281-Tom and Jerry	3	5	7	10	12	14
282-Mister Ed (TV)	6	12	18	28	34	40
283-Santa's Visit	3	6	8	12	14	16
284-Christmas Parade (1965)	3	6	8	12	14	16
285-Astro Boy (TV); 2nd app. Astro Boy	31	62	93	178	252	325
286-Tarzan	7	14	21	35	43	50
287-Bugs Bunny	4	7	9	14	16	18
288-Daffy Duck	3	6	8	12	14	16
289-The Flintstones (TV)	9	18	27	49	62	75
290-Mister Ed (TV); photo-c	5	10	15	23	28	32
291-Yogi Bear (TV)	5	10	15	24	30	35
292-The Three Stooges; photo-c	8	16	24	43	54	65
293-Little Lulu; Irving Tripp-a	8	16	24	40	50	60
294-Popeye	5	10	15	23	28	32
295-Tom and Jerry	3	5	7	10	12	14
296-Lassie (TV); photo-c	4	8	12	18	22	25
297-Christmas Bells	3	5	7	10	12	14
298-Santa's Sleigh (1966)	3	5	7	10	12	14
299-The Flintstones (TV)(1967)	9	18	27	49	62	75

March of Comics #324 © WEST

March of Comics #395 © WEST

March of Comics #468 © WEST

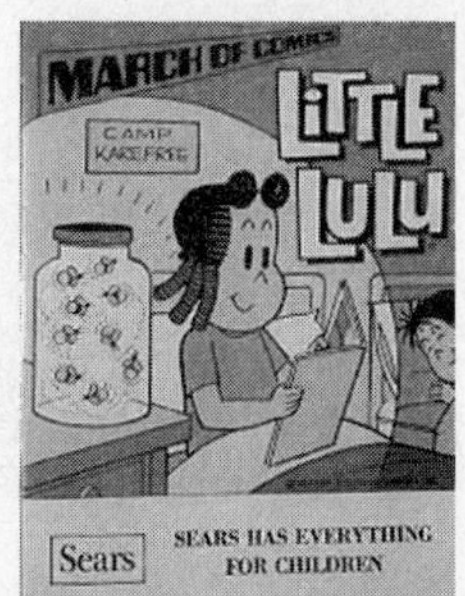

	GD 2.0	VG 4.0	FN 6.0	VF 8.0	VF/NM 9.0	NM- 9.2
300-Tarzan	7	14	21	35	43	50
301-Bugs Bunny	3	6	8	12	14	16
302-Laurel and Hardy (TV); photo-c	5	10	15	24	30	35
303-Daffy Duck	2	4	6	8	10	12
304-The Three Stooges; photo-c	8	16	24	40	50	60
305-Tom and Jerry	2	4	6	8	10	12
306-Daniel Boone (TV); Fess Parker photo-c	6	12	18	31	38	45
307-Little Lulu; Irving Tripp-a	7	14	21	35	43	50
308-Lassie (TV); photo-c	4	8	12	18	22	25
309-Yogi Bear (TV)	5	10	15	23	28	32
310-The Lone Ranger; Clayton Moore photo-c	10	20	30	60	80	100
311-Santa's Show	3	6	8	12	14	16
312-Christmas Album (1967)	3	6	8	12	14	16
313-Daffy Duck (1968)	2	4	6	8	10	12
314-Laurel and Hardy (TV)	5	10	15	23	28	32
315-Bugs Bunny	3	6	8	12	14	16
316-The Three Stooges	7	14	21	35	43	50
317-The Flintstones (TV)	8	16	24	40	50	60
318-Tarzan	6	12	18	31	38	45
319-Yogi Bear (TV)	5	10	15	23	28	32
320-Space Family Robinson (TV); Spiegle-a	12	24	36	71	96	120
321-Tom and Jerry	2	4	6	8	10	12
322-The Lone Ranger	7	14	21	35	43	50
323-Little Lulu; not by Stanley	5	10	15	23	28	32
324-Lassie (TV); photo-c	4	8	12	18	22	25
325-Fun with Santa	3	6	8	12	14	16
326-Christmas Story (1968)	3	6	8	12	14	16
327-The Flintstones (TV)(1969)	8	16	24	40	50	60
328-Space Family Robinson (TV); Spiegle-a	12	24	36	71	96	120
329-Bugs Bunny	3	6	8	12	14	16
330-The Jetsons (TV)	10	20	30	56	73	90
331-Daffy Duck	2	4	6	8	10	12
332-Tarzan	5	10	15	24	30	35
333-Tom and Jerry	2	4	6	8	10	12
334-Lassie (TV)	4	8	11	16	19	22
335-Little Lulu	5	10	15	23	28	32
336-The Three Stooges	7	14	21	35	43	50
337-Yogi Bear (TV)	5	10	15	23	28	32
338-The Lone Ranger	7	14	21	35	43	50
339-(Was not published)						
340-Here Comes Santa (1969)	3	5	7	10	12	14
341-The Flintstones (TV)	8	16	24	40	50	60
342-Tarzan	3	7	10	21	28	35
343-Bugs Bunny	2	4	6	9	11	14
344-Yogi Bear (TV)	3	6	9	18	23	28
345-Tom and Jerry	2	4	6	8	10	12
346-Lassie (TV)	2	4	6	14	18	22
347-Daffy Duck	2	4	6	8	10	12
348-The Jetsons (TV)	7	14	21	46	63	80
349-Little Lulu; not by Stanley	3	6	9	16	20	25
350-The Lone Ranger	3	6	9	19	25	32
351-Beep-Beep, the Road Runner (TV)	2	4	6	10	13	16
352-Space Family Robinson (TV); Spiegle-a	9	18	27	65	93	120
353-Beep-Beep, the Road Runner (1971) (TV)	2	4	6	10	13	16
354-Tarzan (1971)	3	6	9	19	25	32
355-Little Lulu; not by Stanley	3	6	9	16	20	25
356-Scooby Doo, Where Are You? (TV)	7	14	21	46	63	80
357-Daffy Duck & Porky Pig	2	4	6	8	10	12
358-Lassie (TV)	2	4	6	14	18	22
359-Baby Snoots	2	4	6	10	13	16
360-H. R. Pufnstuf (TV); photo-c	7	14	21	46	63	80
361-Tom and Jerry	2	4	6	8	10	12
362-Smokey Bear (TV)	2	4	6	8	10	12
363-Bugs Bunny & Yosemite Sam	2	4	6	9	11	14
364-The Banana Splits (TV); photo-c	6	12	18	38	52	65
365-Tom and Jerry (1972)	2	4	6	8	10	12
366-Tarzan	3	6	9	19	25	32
367-Bugs Bunny & Porky Pig	2	4	6	9	11	14
368-Scooby Doo (TV)(4/72)	6	12	18	38	52	65
369-Little Lulu; not by Stanley	2	4	6	12	16	20
370-Lassie (TV); photo-c	2	4	6	14	18	22
371-Baby Snoots	2	4	6	9	11	14
372-Smokey the Bear (TV)	2	4	6	8	10	12
373-The Three Stooges	4	8	12	27	36	45
374-Wacky Witch	2	4	6	8	10	12
375-Beep-Beep & Daffy Duck (TV)	2	4	6	8	10	12
376-The Pink Panther (1972) (TV)	2	4	6	10	13	16

	GD 2.0	VG 4.0	FN 6.0	VF 8.0	VF/NM 9.0	NM- 9.2
377-Baby Snoots (1973)	2	4	6	9	11	14
378-Turok, Son of Stone; new-a	10	20	30	67	96	125
379-Heckle & Jeckle New Terrytoons (TV)	2	4	6	8	10	12
380-Bugs Bunny & Yosemite Sam	2	4	6	8	10	12
381-Lassie (TV)	2	4	6	11	14	18
382-Scooby Doo, Where Are You? (TV)	5	10	15	33	44	55
383-Smokey the Bear (TV)	2	4	6	8	10	12
384-Pink Panther (TV)	2	4	6	8	10	12
385-Little Lulu	2	4	6	11	14	18
386-Wacky Witch	2	4	6	8	10	12
387-Beep-Beep & Daffy Duck (TV)	2	4	6	8	10	12
388-Tom and Jerry (1973)	2	4	6	8	10	12
389-Little Lulu; not by Stanley	2	4	6	11	14	18
390-Pink Panther (TV)	2	4	6	8	10	12
391-Scooby Doo (TV)	4	8	12	27	36	45
392-Bugs Bunny & Yosemite Sam	1	3	4	6	8	10
393-New Terrytoons (Heckle & Jeckle) (TV)	1	3	4	6	8	10
394-Lassie (TV)	2	4	6	9	11	14
395-Woodsy Owl	1	3	4	6	8	10
396-Baby Snoots	2	4	6	8	10	12
397-Beep-Beep & Daffy Duck (TV)	1	3	4	6	8	10
398-Wacky Witch	1	3	4	6	8	10
399-Turok, Son of Stone; new-a	9	18	27	60	85	110
400-Tom and Jerry	1	3	4	6	8	10
401-Baby Snoots (1975) (r/#371)	2	4	6	8	10	12
402-Daffy Duck (r/#313)	1	2	3	5	7	9
403-Bugs Bunny (r/#343)	1	3	4	6	8	10
404-Space Family Robinson (TV)(r/#328)	7	14	21	50	68	85
405-Cracky	1	2	3	5	7	9
406-Little Lulu (r/#355)	2	4	6	10	13	16
407-Smokey the Bear (TV)(r/#362)	1	3	4	6	8	10
408-Turok, Son of Stone; c-r/Turok #20 w/changes; new-a	7	14	21	46	63	80
409-Pink Panther (TV)	1	2	3	5	7	9
410-Wacky Witch	1	2	3	4	5	7
411-Lassie (TV)(r/#324)	2	4	6	9	11	14
412-New Terrytoons (1975) (TV)	1	2	3	4	5	7
413-Daffy Duck (1976)(r/#331)	1	2	3	4	5	7
414-Space Family Robinson (r/#328)	7	14	21	46	63	80
415-Bugs Bunny (r/#329)	1	2	3	4	5	7
416-Beep-Beep, the Road Runner (r/#353)(TV)	1	2	3	4	5	7
417-Little Lulu (r/#323)	2	4	6	10	13	16
418-Pink Panther (r/#384) (TV)	1	2	3	4	5	7
419-Baby Snoots (r/#377)	1	2	3	5	7	9
420-Woody Woodpecker	1	2	3	4	5	7
421-Tweety & Sylvester	1	2	3	4	5	7
422-Wacky Witch (r/#386)	1	2	3	4	5	7
423-Little Monsters	1	2	3	5	7	9
424-Cracky (12/76)	1	2	3	4	5	7
425-Daffy Duck	1	2	3	4	5	7
426-Underdog (TV)	4	8	12	22	30	38
427-Little Lulu (r/#335)	2	4	6	8	10	12
428-Bugs Bunny						6.00
429-The Pink Panther (TV)						6.00
430-Beep-Beep, the Road Runner (TV)						6.00
431-Baby Snoots	1	2	3	4	5	7
432-Lassie (TV)	1	3	4	6	8	10
433-437: 433-Tweety & Sylvester. 434-Wacky Witch. 435-New Terrytoons (TV). 436-Wacky Advs. of Cracky. 437-Daffy Duck						6.00
438-Underdog (TV)	3	6	9	19	25	32
439-Little Lulu (r/#349)	2	4	6	8	10	12
440-442,444-446: 440-Bugs Bunny. 441-The Pink Panther (TV). 442-Beep-Beep, the Road Runner (TV). 444-Tom and Jerry. 445-Tweety and Sylvester. 446-Wacky Witch	1	2	3	4	5	7
443-Baby Snoots	1	2	3	4	5	7
447-Mighty Mouse	1	3	4	6	8	10
448-455,457,458: 448-Cracky. 449-Pink Panther (TV). 450-Baby Snoots. 451-Tom and Jerry. 452-Bugs Bunny. 453-Popeye. 454-Woody Woodpecker. 455-Beep-Beep, the Road Runner (TV). 457-Tweety & Sylvester. 458-Wacky Witch	1	2	3	4	5	7
456-Little Lulu (r/#369)	1	3	4	6	8	10
459-Mighty Mouse	1	3	4	6	8	10
460-466: 460-Daffy Duck. 461-The Pink Panther (TV). 462-Baby Snoots. 463-Tom and Jerry. 464-Bugs Bunny. 465-Popeye. 466-Woody Woodpecker	1	2	3	4	5	7
467-Underdog (TV)	3	6	9	18	23	28
468-Little Lulu (r/#385)	1	2	3	4	5	7
469-Tweety & Sylvester	1	2	3	4	5	7

Marvel Comics Presents Spider-Man © MAR

The Matrix © WB

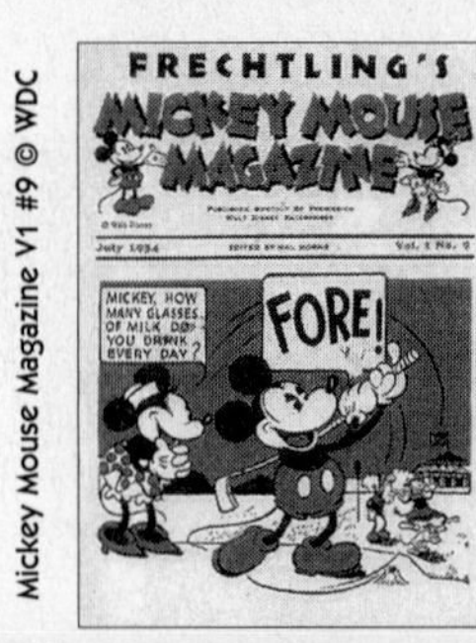

Mickey Mouse Magazine V1 #9 © WDC

	GD 2.0	VG 4.0	FN 6.0	VF 8.0	VF/NM 9.0	NM- 9.2
470-Wacky Witch	1	2	3	4	5	7
471-Mighty Mouse	1	2	3	5	7	9
472-474,476-478: 472-Heckle & Jeckle(12/80). 473-Pink Panther(1/81)(TV). 474-Baby Snoots. 476-Bugs Bunny. 477-Popeye. 478-Woody Woodpecker	1	2	3	4	5	7
475-Little Lulu (r/#323)	1	2	3	5	7	9
479-Underdog (TV)	2	4	6	14	18	22
480-482: 480-Tom and Jerry. 481-Tweety and Sylvester. 482-Wacky Witch	1	2	3	4	5	7
483-Mighty Mouse	1	2	3	5	7	9
484-487: 484-Heckle & Jeckle. 485-Baby Snoots. 486-The Pink Panther (TV). 487-Bugs Bunny	1	2	3	4	5	7
488-Little Lulu (4/82) (r/#335) (Last issue)	2	4	6	10	13	16

MARGARET O'BRIEN (See The Adventures of...)

MARK STEEL
American Iron & Steel Institute: 1967, 1968, 1972 (Giveaway) (24 pgs.)

	GD	VG	FN	VF	VF/NM	NM-
1967,1968- "Journey of Discovery with..."; Neal Adams art	4	8	12	24	32	40
1972- "...Fights Pollution"; N. Adams-a	3	6	9	16	20	25

MARVEL COLLECTOR'S EDITION: X-MEN
Marvel Comics: 1993 (3-3/4x6-1/2")

1-4-Pizza Hut giveaways 4.00

MARVEL COMICS PRESENTS
Marvel Comics: 1987, 1988 (4 1/4 x 6 1/4, 20 pgs.)
...Mini Comic Giveaway

	GD	VG	FN	VF	VF/NM	NM-
nn-(1988) Alf	1	2	3	5	6	8
nn-(1987) Captain America r/ #250	1	2	3	4	5	7
nn-(1987) Care Bears (Star Comics...)	1	2	3	4	5	7
nn-(1988) Flintstone Kids	1	2	3	5	6	8
nn-(1987) Heathcliffe (Star Comics...)	1	2	3	4	5	7
nn-(1987) Spider-Man-r/Spect. Spider-Man #21	1	2	3	4	5	7
nn-(1988) Spider-Man-r/Amazing Spider-Man #1	1	2	3	4	5	7
nn-(1988) X-Men-reprints X-Men #53; B. Smith-a	1	2	3	4	5	7

MARVEL GUIDE TO COLLECTING COMICS, THE
Marvel Comics: 1982 (16 pgs., newsprint pages and cover)

1-Simonson-c 6.00

MARVEL MINI-BOOKS
Marvel Comics Group: 1966 (50 pgs., B&W; 5/8x7/8") (6 different issues) (Smallest comics ever published) (Marvel Mania Giveaways)

	GD	VG	FN	VF	VF/NM	NM-
Captain America, Millie the Model, Sgt. Fury, Hulk, Thor each...	8	16	24	55	78	100
Spider-Man	9	18	27	60	85	110

NOTE: *Each came in six different color covers, usually one color: Pink, yellow, green, etc.*

MARVEL SUPER-HERO ISLAND ADVENTURES
Marvel Comics: 1999 (Sold at the park polybagged with Captain America V3 #19, one other comic, 5 trading cards and a cloisonne pin)

1-Promotes Universal Studios Islands of Adventures theme park 2.25

MARY'S GREATEST APOSTLE (St. Louis Grignion de Montfort)
Catechetical Guild (Topix) (Giveaway): No date (16 pgs.; paper cover)

	GD	VG	FN	VF	VF/NM	NM-
nn	4	9	13	18	22	26

MASK
DC Comics: 1985

1-3 4.00

MASKED PILOT, THE (See Popular Comics #43)
R.S. Callender: 1939 (7-1/2x5-1/4", 16 pgs., premium, non-slick-c)

	GD	VG	FN	VF	VF/NM	NM-
nn-Bob Jenney-a	10	20	30	56	73	90

MASTERS OF THE UNIVERSE (He-Man)
DC Comics: 1982

1-7 5.00

MATRIX, THE (1999 movie)
Warner Brothers: 1999 (Recalled by Warner Bros. over questionable content)

nn-Paul Chadwick-s/a (16 pgs.); Geof Darrow-c 6.00

McCRORY'S CHRISTMAS BOOK
Western Printing Co: 1955 (36 pgs., slick-c) (McCrory Stores Corp. giveaway)

	GD	VG	FN	VF	VF/NM	NM-
nn-Painted-c	4	8	12	18	22	25

McCRORY'S TOYLAND BRINGS YOU SANTA'S PRIVATE EYES
Promotional Publ. Co.: 1956 (16 pgs.) (Giveaway)

	GD	VG	FN	VF	VF/NM	NM-
nn-Has 9 pg. story plus 7 pgs. toy ads	4	8	11	16	19	22

McCRORY'S WONDERFUL CHRISTMAS
Promotional Publ. Co.: 1954 (20 pgs., slick-c) (Giveaway)

	GD	VG	FN	VF	VF/NM	NM-
nn	4	8	12	18	22	25

McDONALDS COMMANDRONS
DC Comics: 1985

nn-Four editions 3.50

MEET HIYA A FRIEND OF SANTA CLAUS
Julian J. Proskauer/Sundial Shoe Stores, etc.: 1949 (18 pgs.?, paper-c)(Giveaway)

	GD	VG	FN	VF	VF/NM	NM-
nn	6	12	18	31	38	45

MEET THE NEW POST GAZETTE SUNDAY FUNNIES
Pittsburgh Post Gazette: 3/12/49 (7-1/4x10-1/4", 16 pgs., paper-c)
Commercial Comics (insert in newspaper) (Rare)
Dick Tracy by Gould, Gasoline Alley, Terry & the Pirates, Brenda Starr, Buck Rogers by Yager, The Gumps, Peter Rabbit by Fago, Superman, Funnyman by Siegel & Shuster, The Saint, Archie, & others done especially for this book. A fine copy sold at auction in 1985 for $276.00.

GD	VG	FN	VF	VF/NM	NM-
550	1100	1650	4500	-	-

MEN OF COURAGE
Catechetical Guild: 1949

	GD	VG	FN	VF	VF/NM	NM-
Bound Topix comics-V7#2,4,6,8,10,16,18,20	6	12	18	29	36	42

MEN WHO MOVE THE NATION
Publisher unknown: (Giveaway) (B&W)

	GD	VG	FN	VF	VF/NM	NM-
nn-Neal Adams-a	6	12	18	29	36	42

MERRY CHRISTMAS, A
K. K. Publications (Child Life Shoes): 1948 (Giveaway)

	GD	VG	FN	VF	VF/NM	NM-
nn	6	12	18	32	39	46

MERRY CHRISTMAS
K. K. Publications (Blue Bird Shoes Giveaway): 1956 (7-1/4x5-1/4")

	GD	VG	FN	VF	VF/NM	NM-
nn	4	8	12	18	22	25

MERRY CHRISTMAS FROM MICKEY MOUSE
K. K. Publications: 1939 (16 pgs.) (Color & B&W) (Shoe store giveaway)

	GD	VG	FN	VF	VF/NM	NM-
nn-Donald Duck & Pluto app.; text with art (Rare); c-reprint/Mickey Mouse Mag. V3#3 (12/37)(Rare)	315	630	1260	1800	2400	3000

MERRY CHRISTMAS FROM SEARS TOYLAND (See Santa's Christmas Comic)
Sears Roebuck Giveaway: 1939 (16 pgs.) (Color)

	GD	VG	FN	VF	VF/NM	NM-
nn-Dick Tracy, Little Orphan Annie, The Gumps, Terry & the Pirates	109	218	436	682	991	1300

METALLIX
Future Comics: Apr, 2003

1-Free Comic Book Day Edition; Layton-c 2.25

MICKEY MOUSE (Also see Frito-Lay Giveaway)
Dell Publ. Co

	GD	VG	FN	VF	VF/NM	NM-
...& Goofy Explore Business(1978)	1	3	4	6	8	10
...& Goofy Explore Energy(1976-1978, 36 pgs.); Exxon giveaway in color; regular size	1	3	4	6	8	10
...& Goofy Explore Energy Conservation(1976-1978)-Exxon	1	3	4	6	8	10
...& Goofy Explore The Universe of Energy(1985, 20 pgs.); Exxon giveaway in color; regular size	1	2	3	4	5	7

The Perils of Mickey nn (1993, 5-1/4x7-1/4", 16 pgs.)-Nabisco giveaway w/ games, Nabisco coupons & 6 pgs. of stories; Phantom Blot app. 5.00

MICKEY MOUSE MAGAZINE
Walt Disney Productions: V1#1, Jan, 1933 - V1#9, Sept, 1933 (5-1/4x7-1/4")
No. 1-3 published by Kamen-Blair (Kay Kamen, Inc.)
(Scarce)-Distributed by dairies and leading stores through their local theatres. First few issues had 5¢ listed on cover, later ones had no price.

	GD	VG	FN	VF	VF/NM	NM-
V1#1	535	1070	2140	6000	-	-
2-4	220	440	880	1600	-	-
5-9	171	342	684	1200	-	-

MICKEY MOUSE MAGAZINE
Walt Disney Productions: V1#1, 11/33 - V2#12, 10/35 (Mills giveaways issued by different dairies)

	GD	VG	FN	VF	VF/NM	NM-
V1#1	240	600	960	1350	1875	2400
2-12: 2-X-Mas issue	80	200	320	475	638	800
V2#1-4,6-12: 2-X-Mas issue. 4-St. Valentine-c	55	124	192	310	430	550
V2#5 (3/35) 1st app. Donald Duck in sailor outfit on-c	96	192	288	600	900	1200

MICKEY MOUSE MAGAZINE
K.K. Publications: V4#1, Oct, 1938 (Giveaway)

	GD	VG	FN	VF	VF/NM	NM-
V4#1	55	124	192	310	430	550

New Adventures of Peter Pan © WDC

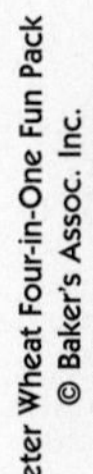

New Frontiers © HARV

Peter Wheat Four-in-One Fun Pack © Baker's Assoc. Inc.

	GD 2.0	VG 4.0	FN 6.0	VF 8.0	VF/NM 9.0	NM- 9.2

MIGHTY ATOM, THE
Whitman

Giveaway (1959, '63, Whitman)-Evans-a	3	6	9	16	20	24
Giveaway ('64r, '65r, '66r, '67r, '68r)-Evans-r?	2	4	6	9	11	14
Giveaway ('73r, '76r)	1	3	4	6	8	10

MILITARY COURTESY
Harvey Publications: (16 pgs.)

nn-Regulations and saluting instructions	5	10	14	20	24	28

MINUTE MAN
Sovereign Service Station giveaway: No date (16 pgs., B&W, paper-c blue & red)

nn-American history	3	6	8	12	14	16

MINUTE MAN ANSWERS THE CALL, THE
By M. C. Gaines: 1942,1943,1944,1945 (4 pgs.) (Giveaway inserted in Jr. JSA Membership Kit)

nn-Sheldon Moldoff-a	23	46	69	129	180	230

MIRACLE ON BROADWAY
Broadway Comics: Dec, 1995 (Giveaway)

1-Ernie Colon-c/a; Jim Shooter & Co. story; 1st known digitally printed comic book; 1st app. Spire & Knights on Broadway (1150 print run)						20.00

NOTE: Miracle on Broadway was a limited edition comic given to 1100 VIPs in the entertainment industry for the 1995 Holiday Season.

MISS SUNBEAM (See Little Miss Sunbeam Comics)

MR. BUG GOES TO TOWN (See Cinema Comics Herald)
K.K. Publications: 1941 (Giveaway, 52 pgs.)

nn-Cartoon movie (scarce)	75	150	300	500	700	900

MR. PEANUT, THE PERSONAL HISTORY OF
Planters Nut & Chocolate Co.: 1956

nn	4	8	12	25	33	42

MOTHER OF US ALL
Catechetical Guild Giveaway: 1950? (32 pgs.)

nn	5	10	14	20	24	28

MOTION PICTURE FUNNIES WEEKLY (Amazing Man #5 on?)
First Funnies, Inc.: 1939 (Giveaway)(B&W, 36 pgs.) No month given; last panel in Sub-Mariner story dated 4/39 (Also see Colossus, Green Giant & Invaders No. 20)

1-Origin & 1st printed app. Sub-Mariner by Bill Everett (8 pgs.); Fred Schwab-c; reprinted in Marvel Mystery #1 with color added over the craft tint which was used to shade the black & white version; Spy Ring, American Ace (reprinted in Marvel Mystery #3) app. (Rare)-only eight known copies, one near mint with white pages, the rest with brown pages.	4400	7700	11,000	16,500	22,250	28,000
Covers only to #2-4 (set)						1000

NOTE: The only eight known copies (with a ninth suspected) were discovered in 1974 in the estate of the deceased publisher. Covers only to issues No. 2-4 were also found which evidently were printed in advance along with #1. #1 was to be distributed only through motion picture movie houses. However, it is believed that only advanced copies were sent out and the motion picture houses not going for the idea. Possible distribution at local theaters in Boston suspected. The last panel of Sub-Mariner contains a rectangular box with "Continued Next Week" printed in it. When reprinted in Marvel Mystery, the box was left in with lettering omitted.

MY DOG TIGE (Buster Brown's Dog)
Buster Brown Shoes: 1957 (Giveaway)

nn	5	10	15	24	30	35

MY GREATEST THRILLS IN BASEBALL
Mission of California: Date? (16 pg. Giveaway)

nn-By Mickey Mantle	79	145	212	390	520	650

NATURAL DISASTERS!
Graphic Information Service/ Civil Defense: 1956 (16 pgs., soft-c)

nn-Al Capp Li'l Abner-c; Li'l Abner cameo (1 panel); narrated by Mr. Civil Defense	10	20	30	56	73	90

NAVY: HISTORY & TRADITION
Stokes Walesby Co./Dept. of Navy: 1958 - 1961 (nn) (Giveaway)

1772-1778, 1778-1782, 1782-1817, 1817-1865, 1865-1936, 1940-1945:

1772-1778-16 pg. in color	5	10	15	22	26	30
1861: Naval Actions of the Civil War: 1865-36 pg. in color; flag-c	5	10	15	22	26	30

NEW ADVENTURE OF WALT DISNEY'S SNOW WHITE AND THE SEVEN DWARFS, A (See Snow White Bendix Giveaway)

NEW ADVENTURES OF PETER PAN (Disney)
Western Publishing Co.: 1953 (5x7-1/4", 36 pgs.) (Admiral giveaway)

nn	14	28	42	79	107	135

NEW FRONTIERS
Harvey Information Press (United States Steel Corp.) : 1958 (16 pgs., paper-c)

nn-History of barbed wire	2	4	6	14	18	22

NEW TEEN TITANS, THE
DC Comics: Nov. 1983

nn(11/83-Keebler Co. Giveaway)-In cooperation with "The President's Drug Awareness Campaign"; came in Presidential envelope w/letter from White House (Nancy Reagan)						6.00
nn-(re-issue of above on Mando paper for direct sales market); American Soft Drink Industry version; I.B.M. Corp. version						5.00

NOLAN RYAN IN THE WINNING PITCH (Kellogg's Tony's Sports Comics)
DC Comics: 1992 (Sports Illustrated)

nn						3.00

OLD GLORY COMICS
Chesapeake & Ohio Railway: 1944 (Giveaway)

nn-Capt. Fearless reprint	7	14	21	35	43	50

ON THE AIR
NBC Network Comic: 1947 (Giveaway, paper-c)

nn-(Rare)	27	54	80	140	200	260

OUT OF THE PAST A CLUE TO THE FUTURE
E. C. Comics (Public Affairs Comm.): 1946? (16 pgs.) (paper cover)

nn-Based on public affairs pamphlet "What Foreign Trade Means to You"	24	48	71	127	174	220

OUTSTANDING AMERICAN WAR HEROES
The Parents' Institute: 1944 (16 pgs., paper-c)

nn-Reprints from True Comics	5	10	14	20	24	28

OVERSEAS COMICS (Also see G.I. Comics & Jeep Comics)
Giveaway (Distributed to U.S. Armed Forces): 1944 - No. 105?, 1946 (7-1/4x10-1/4"; 16 pgs. in color)

23-105-Bringing Up Father (by McManus), Popeye, Joe Palooka, Dick Tracy, Superman, Gasoline Alley, Buz Sawyer, Li'l Abner, Blondie, Terry & the Pirates, Out Our Way	7	14	21	35	43	50

OWL, THE (See Crackajack Funnies #25 & Popular Comics #72)(Also see The Hurricane Kids & Magic Morro)
Western Pub. Co./R.S. Callender: 1940 (Giveaway)(7-1/2x5-1/4")(Soft-c, color)

nn-Frank Thomas-a	22	44	66	112	156	200

OXYDOL-DREFT
Toby Press:1950 (Set of 6 pocket-size giveaways; distributed through the mail as a set) (Scarce)

1-3: 1-Li'l Abner. 2-Daisy Mae. 3-Shmoo	13	26	39	74	100	125
4-John Wayne; Williamson/Frazetta-c from John Wayne #3	17	34	51	95	130	165
5-Archie	16	32	48	89	122	155
6-Terrytoons Mighty Mouse	13	26	39	74	100	125
Mailing Envelope (has All Capp's Shmoo on front)	15	30	45	79	107	135

OZZIE SMITH IN THE KID WHO COULD (Kellogg's Tony's Sports Comics)
DC Comics: 1992 (Sports Illustrated)

nn-Ozzie Smith app.						4.00

PADRE OF THE POOR
Catechetical Guild: nd (Giveaway) (16 pgs., paper-c)

nn	5	10	14	20	24	28

PAUL TERRY'S HOW TO DRAW FUNNY CARTOONS
Terrytoons, Inc. (Giveaway): 1940's (14 pgs.) (Black & White)

nn-Heckle & Jeckle, Mighty Mouse, etc.	12	24	36	69	92	115

PETER PAN (See New Adventures of Peter Pan)

PETER PENNY AND HIS MAGIC DOLLAR
American Bankers Association, N. Y. (Giveaway): 1947 (16 pgs.; paper-c; regular size)

nn-(Scarce)-Used in **SOTI**, pg. 310, 311	17	34	51	95	130	165
Diff. version (7-1/4x11")-redrawn, 16 pgs., paper-c	10	20	30	56	73	90

PETER WHEAT (The Adventures of...)
Bakers Associates Giveaway: 1948 - 1956? (16 pgs. in color) (paper covers)

nn(No.1)-States on last page, end of 1st Adventure of...; Kelly-a	33	66	130	200	250	300
nn(4 issues)-Kelly-a	20	50	80	120	147	175
6-10-All Kelly-a	15	30	45	81	108	135
11-20-All Kelly-a	13	26	40	69	92	115
21-35-All Kelly-a	11	22	33	60	80	100
36-66	8	16	24	46	58	70
...Artist's Workbook ('54, digest size)	8	16	24	46	58	70
...Four-In-One Fun Pack (Vol. 2, '54), oblong, comics w/puzzles						

Poll Parrot #1 © K.K. Pub.

Popsicle Pete Fun Book © Joe Lowe

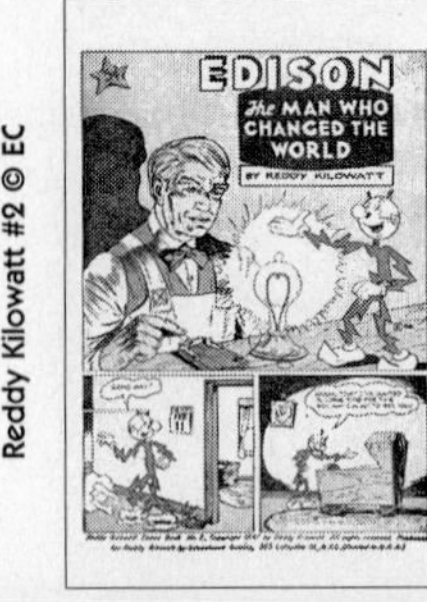

Reddy Kilowatt #2 © EC

	GD 2.0	VG 4.0	FN 6.0	VF 8.0	VF/NM 9.0	NM- 9.2
	10	20	30	54	69	85
...Fun Book ('52, 32 pgs., paper-c, B&W & color, 8-1/2x10-3/4")-Contains cut-outs, puzzles, games, magic & pages to color	12	24	36	66	88	110

NOTE: *Al Hubbard art #36 on; written by Del Connell.*

PETER WHEAT NEWS
Bakers Associates: 1948 - No. 30, 1950 (4 pgs. in color)

Vol. 1-All have 2 pgs. Peter Wheat by Kelly	27	54	110	160	210	260
2-10	18	36	54	92	126	160
11-20	11	22	33	60	80	100
21-30	8	16	24	46	58	70

NOTE: *Early issues have no date & **Kelly** art.*

PINOCCHIO
Cocomalt/Montgomery Ward Co.: 1940 (10 pgs.; giveaway, linen-like paper)

nn-Cocomalt edition	46	92	138	276	400	525
nn-store edition	40	80	120	230	325	420

PIUS XII MAN OF PEACE
Catechetical Guild: No date (12 pgs.; 5-1/2x8-1/2") (B&W)

nn-Catechetical Guild Giveaway	5	10	15	24	30	35

PLOT TO STEAL THE WORLD, THE
Work & Unity Group: 1948, 16pgs., paper-c

nn-Anti commumism	18	36	54	101	138	175

POCAHONTAS
Pocahontas Fuel Company (Coal): 1941 - No. 2, 1942

nn(#1), 2-Feat. life story of Indian princess Pocahontas & facts about Pocahontas coal, Pocahontas, VA.	16	32	48	89	122	155

POLL PARROT
Poll Parrot Shoe Store/International Shoe
K. K. Publications (Giveaway): 1950 - No. 4, 1951; No. 2, 1959 - No. 16, 1962

1 ('50)-Howdy Doody; small size	25	50	75	112	156	200
2-4('51)-Howdy Doody	20	40	60	92	126	160
2('59)-16('62): 2-The Secret of Crumbley Castle. 5-Bandit Busters. 7-The Make-Believe Mummy. 8-Mixed Up Mission('60). 10-The Frightful Flight. 11-Showdown at Sunup. 12-Maniac at Mubu Island. 13-...and the Runaway Genie. 14-Bully for You. 15-Trapped In Tall Timber. 16-...& the Rajah's Ruby('62)	3	6	9	17	22	26

POPEYE
Whitman

Bold Detergent giveaway (Same as regular issue #94)	2	4	6	8	10	12
Quaker Cereal premium (1989, 16pp, small size,4 diff.)(Popeye & the Time Machine, --On Safari, --& Big Foot, --vs. Bluto)	1	3	4	6	8	10

POPEYE
Charlton (King Features) (Giveaway): 1972 - 1974 (36 pgs. in color)

E-1 to E-15 (Educational comics)	2	4	6	8	10	12
nn-Popeye Gettin' Better Grades-4 pgs. used as intro. to above giveaways (in color)	2	4	6	8	10	12

POPSICLE PETE FUN BOOK (See All-American Comics #6)
Joe Lowe Corp.: 1947, 1948

nn-36 pgs. in color; Sammy 'n' Claras, The King Who Couldn't Sleep & Popsicle Pete stories, games, cut-outs	11	22	33	63	84	105
Adventure Book ('48)-Has Classics ad with checklist to HRN #343 (Great Expectations #43)	10	20	30	56	73	90

PORKY'S BOOK OF TRICKS
K. K. Publications (Giveaway): 1942 (8-1/2x5-1/2", 48 pgs.)

nn-7 pg. comic story, text stories, plus games & puzzles	50	125	200	340	457	575

POST GAZETTE (See Meet the New...)

POWER RECORD COMICS
Marvel Comics/Power Records: 1974 - 1978 ($1.49, 7x10" comics, 20 pgs. with 45 R.P.M. record) (Clipped corners - reduce value 20%) (Comic alone - 50%; record alone - 50%)

PR10-Spider-Man-r/from #124,125; Man-Wolf app. PR18-Planet of the Apes-r. PR19-Escape From the Planet of the Apes-r. PR20-Beneath the Planet of the Apes-r. PR21-Battle for the Planet of the Apes-r. PR24-Spider-Man II-New-a begins. PR27-Batman "Stacked Cards"; N. Adams-a(p). PR30-Batman; N. Adams-r/Det.(7 pgs.).

With record; each...	5	10	15	33	44	55

PR11-Hulk-r. PR12-Captain America-r/#168. PR13-Fantastic Four-r/#126. PR14-Frankenstein-Ploog-r/#1. PR15-Tomb of Dracula-Colan-r/#2. PR16-Man-Thing-Ploog-r/#5. PR17-Werewolf By Night-Ploog-r/Marvel Spotlight #2. PR28-Superman "Alien Creatures". PR29-Space: 1999 "Breakaway". PR31-Conan-N. Adams-a; reprinted in Conan #116. PR32-Space: 1999 "Return to the Beginning". PR33-Superman-G.A. origin, Buckler-a(p). PR34-Superman. PR35-Wonder Woman-Buckler-a(p)

With record; each...	4	8	12	27	36	45

PR25-Star Trek "Passage to Moauv". PR26-Star Trek "Crier in Emptiness." PR36-Holo-Man. PR37-Robin Hood. PR39-Huckleberry Finn. PR40-Davy Crockett. PR41-Robinson Crusoe. PR42-20,000 Leagues Under the Sea. PR46-Star Trek "The Robot Masters". PR47-Little Women

	GD 2.0	VG 4.0	FN 6.0	VF 8.0	VF/NM 9.0	NM- 9.2
With record; each...	4	8	12	22	30	38

PURE OIL COMICS (Also see Salerno Carnival of Comics, 24 Pages of Comics, & Vicks Comics)
Pure Oil Giveaway: Late 1930's (24 pgs., regular size, paper-c)

nn-Contains 1-2 pg. strips; i.e., Hairbreadth Harry, Skyroads, Buck Rogers by Calkins & Yager, Olly of the Movies, Napoleon, S'Matter Pop, etc. Also a 16 pg. 1938 giveaway with Buck Rogers	50	100	150	240	320	400

QUAKER OATS (Also see Cap'n Crunch)
Quaker Oats Co.: 1965 (Giveaway) (2-1/2x5-1/2") (16 pgs.)

"Plenty of Glutton", starring Quake & Quisp;	3	6	9	16	20	24
"Lava Come-Back", "Kite Tale"	1	3	4	6	8	10

QUEEN AND COUNTRY
Oni Press: May, 2002 (B&W)

Free Comic Book Day giveaway-Reprints #1 with "Free Comic Book Day" banner on-c 2.25

RAILROADS DELIVER THE GOODS!
Assoc. of American Railroads: Dec, 1954; Sept, 1957 (16 pgs.)

nn-The story of railway freight	6	12	18	28	34	40

RAILS ACROSS AMERICA!
Assoc. of American Railroads: nd (16 pgs.)

nn	6	12	18	28	34	40

REAL FUN OF DRIVING!!, THE
Chrysler Corp.: 1965, 1966, 1967 (Regular size, 16 pgs.)

nn-Schaffenberger-a (12 pgs.)	1	2	3	5	6	8

REAL HIT
Fox Features Publications: 1944 (Savings Bond premium)

1-Blue Beetle-r	18	36	54	101	138	175

NOTE: *Two versions exist, with and without covers. The coverless version has the title, No. 1 and price printed at top of splash page.*

RED BALL COMIC BOOK
Parents' Magazine Institute: 1947 (Red Ball Shoes giveaway)

nn-Reprints from True Comics	4	7	10	14	17	20

REDDY GOOSE
International Shoe Co. (Western Printing): No number, 1958?; No. 2, Jan, 1959 - No. 16, July, 1962 (Giveaway)

nn (#1)	5	10	15	36	48	60
2-16	3	7	10	21	28	35

REDDY KILOWATT (5¢) (Also see Story of Edison)
Educational Comics (E. C.): 1946 - No. 2, 1947; 1956 - 1965 (no month) (16 pgs., paper-c)

nn-Reddy Made Magic (1946, 5¢)	13	26	39	79	107	125
nn-Reddy Made Magic (1958)	9	18	27	49	62	75
2-Edison, the Man Who Changed the World (3/4" smaller than #1) (1947, 5¢)	13	26	39	79	107	125
...Comic Book 2 (1954)- "Light's Diamond Jubilee"	9	18	27	52	66	80
...Comic Book 2 (1958, 16 pgs.)- "Wizard of Light"	9	18	27	49	62	75
...Comic Book 2 (1965, 16 pgs.)- "Wizard of Light"	5	10	15	36	48	60
...Comic Book 3 (1956, 8 pgs.)- "The Space Kite"; Orlando story; regular size	9	18	27	49	62	75
...Comic Book 3 (1960, 8 pgs.)- "The Space Kite"; Orlando story; regular size	5	10	15	36	48	60

NOTE: *Several copies surfaced in 1979.*

REDDY MADE MAGIC
Educational Comics (E. C.): 1956, 1958 (16 pgs., paper-c)

1-Reddy Kilowatt-r (splash panel changed)	11	22	33	56	73	90
1 (1958 edition)	6	12	18	31	38	45

RED ICEBERG, THE
Impact Publ. (Catechetical Guild): 1960 (10¢, 16 pgs., Communist propaganda)

nn-(Rare)- "We The People" back-c	31	62	93	223	329	435
2nd version- "Impact Press" back-c	31	62	93	205	290	375
3rd version- "Explains comic" back-c	31	62	93	205	290	375
4th version- "Impact Press w/World Wide Secret Heart Program ad"	31	62	93	205	290	375
5th version- "Chicago Inter-Student Catholic Action" back-c	31	62	93	205	290	375

NOTE: *This book was the Guild's last anti-communist propaganda book and had very limited circulation. 3 - 4 copies surfaced in 1979 from the defunct publisher's files. Other copies do turn up.*

RED RYDER COMICS
Dell Publ. Co.

Buster Brown Shoes Giveaway (1941, color, soft-c, 32 pgs.)

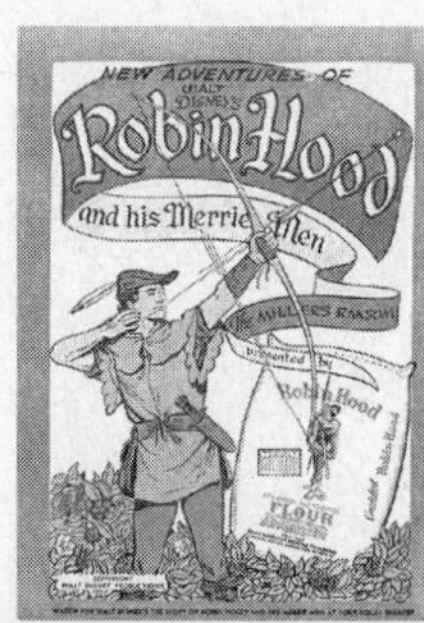

Robin Hood - The Miller's Ransom © WDC

Robocop Free Comic Book Day Ed. © Orion Pictures

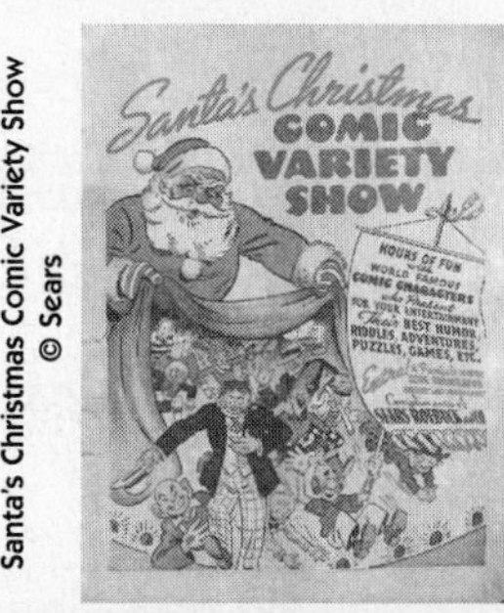

Santa's Christmas Comic Variety Show © Sears

GD VG FN VF VF/NM NM-
2.0 4.0 6.0 8.0 9.0 9.2

27 54 81 153 214 275

Red Ryder Super Book of Comics (1944, paper-c, 32 pgs.; blank back-c)
Magic Morro app. 29 58 87 164 232 300

Red Ryder Victory Patrol-nn(1942, 32 pgs.)(Langendorf bread; includes cut-out membership card and certificate, order blank and "Slide-Up" decoder, and a Super Book of Comics in color (same content as Super Book #4 w/diff. cover (Pan-Am)) (Rare) 463 1042 1621 3000 4000 5000

Red Ryder Victory Patrol-nn(1943, 32 pgs.)(Langendorf bread; includes cut-out "Rodeomatic" radio decoder, order coupon for "Magic V-Badge", cut-out membership card and certificate and a full color Super Book of comics comic book) (Rare) 421 948 1475 2700 3650 4600

Red Ryder Victory Patrol-nn(1944, 32 pgs.)-r-/#43,44; comic has a paper-c & is stapled inside a triple cardboard fold-out-c; contains membership card, decoder, map of R.R. home range, etc. Herky app. (Langendorf Bread giveaway; sub-titled 'Super Book of Comics') (Rare) 400 900 1400 2700 3650 4600

Wells Lamont Corp. giveaway (1950)-16 pgs. in color; regular size; paper-c; 1941-r 25 50 75 132 181 230

RELOADED (Also see Loaded)
DC Comics: 1996 (Interplay Productions, 16 pgs.)

1-Promotes video game; Alan Grrant-s/John Mueller-a 4.00

RICHIE RICH, CASPER & WENDY NATIONAL LEAGUE
Harvey Publications: June, 1976 (52 pgs.) (newsstand edition also exists)

1 (Released-3/76 with 6/76 date) 2 4 6 14 18 22
1 (6/76)-2nd version w/San Francisco Giants & KTVU 2 logos; has "Compliments of Giants and Straw Hat Pizza" on-c 2 4 6 14 18 22
1-Variants for other 11 NL teams, similar to Giants version but with different ad on inside front-c 2 4 6 14 18 22

RIDE THE HIGH IRON!
Assoc. of American Railroads: Jan, 1957 (16 pgs.)

nn-The Story of modern passenger trains 6 12 18 28 34 40

RIPLEY'S BELIEVE IT OR NOT!
Harvey Publications

J. C. Penney giveaway (1948) 9 18 27 49 62 75

ROBIN HOOD (New Adventures of...)
Walt Disney Productions: 1952 (Flour giveaways, 5x7-1/4", 36 pgs.)

"New Adventures of Robin Hood", "Ghosts of Waylea Castle", & "The Miller's Ransom" each.... 5 10 15 23 28 32

ROBIN HOOD'S FRONTIER DAYS (...Western Tales, Adventures of... #1)
Shoe Store Giveaway (Robin Hood Stores): 1956 (20 pgs., slick-c)(7 issues?)

nn 5 10 15 24 29 34
nn-Issues with Crandall-a 7 14 21 38 47 56

ROBOCOP (FRANK MILLER'S...)
Avatar Press: Apr, 2003

Free Comic Book Day Edition - Previews Robocop & Stargate SG•1; Busch-c 2.25

ROCKET COMICS: IGNITE
Dark Horse Comics: Apr, 2003 (Free Comic Book Day giveaway)

1-Previews Dark Horse series Syn, Lone, and Go Boy 7 2.25

ROCKETS AND RANGE RIDERS
Richfield Oil Corp.: May, 1957 (Giveaway, 16 pgs., soft-c)

nn-Toth-a 17 34 51 86 118 150

ROUND THE WORLD GIFT
National War Fund (Giveaway): No date (mid 1940's) (4 pgs.)

nn 12 24 36 66 88 110

ROY ROGERS COMICS
Dell Publishing Co.

...& the Man From Dodge City (Dodge giveaway, 16 pgs., 1954)-Frontier, Inc. (5x7-1/4") 14 28 42 81 111 140
Official Roy Rogers Riders Club Comics (1952; 16 pgs., reg. size, paper-c) 40 100 160 212 296 380

RUDOLPH, THE RED-NOSED REINDEER
Montgomery Ward: 1939 (2,400,000 copies printed); Dec, 1951 (Giveaway)

Paper cover-1st app. in print; written by Robert May; ill. by Denver Gillen 14 28 42 81 111 140
Hardcover version 20 40 60 109 150 190
1951 Edition (Has 1939 date)-36 pgs., slick-c printed in red & brown; pulp interior printed in four mixed-ink colors: red, green, blue & brown 10 20 30 58 77 90
1951 Edition with red-spiral promotional booklet printed on high quality stock, 8-1/2"x11", in red & brown, 25 pages composed of 4 fold outs, single sheets and the Rudolph comic book inserted (rare) 50 100 150 290 420 550

SAD CASE OF WAITING ROOM WILLIE, THE
American Visuals Corp. (For Baltimore Medical Society): (nd, 1950?) (14 pgs. in color; paper covers; regular size)

nn-By Will Eisner (Rare) 48 96 144 280 380 480

SAD SACK COMICS
Harvey Publications: 1957-1962

Armed Forces Complimentary copies, HD #1-40 (1957-1962) 2 4 6 12 16 20

SALERNO CARNIVAL OF COMICS (Also see Pure Oil Comics, 24 Pages of Comics, & Vicks Comics)
Salerno Cookie Co.: Late 1930s (Giveaway, 16 pgs, paper-c)

nn-Color reprints of Calkins' Buck Rogers & Skyroads, plus other strips from Famous Funnies 50 100 150 290 407 525

SALUTE TO THE BOY SCOUTS
Association of American Railroads: 1960 (16 pgs.)

nn-History of scouting and the railroad 3 6 9 16 20 24

SANTA AND POLLYANNA PLAY THE GLAD GAME
Sales Promotion: Aug, 1960 (16 pgs.) (Disney giveaway)

nn 2 4 6 14 18 22

SANTA & THE BUCCANEERS
Promotional Publ. Co.: 1959 (Giveaway)

nn-Reprints 1952 Santa & the Pirates 2 4 6 12 16 20

SANTA & THE CHRISTMAS CHICKADEE
Murphy's: 1974 (Giveaway, 20 pgs.)

nn 2 4 6 8 10 12

SANTA & THE PIRATES
Promotional Publ. Co.: 1952 (Giveaway)

nn-Marv Levy-c/a 4 8 11 16 19 22

SANTA CLAUS FUNNIES (Also see The Little Fir Tree)
W. T. Grant Co./Whitman Publishing: nd; 1940 (Giveaway, 8x10"; 12 pgs., color & B&W, heavy paper)

nn-(2 versions- no date and 1940) 14 28 42 79 107 135

SANTA ON THE JOLLY ROGER
Promotional Publ. Co. (Giveaway): 1965

nn-Marv Levy-c/a 2 4 6 8 10 12

SANTA! SANTA!
R. Jackson: 1974 (20 pgs.) (Montgomery Ward giveaway)

nn 1 3 4 6 8 10

SANTA'S BUNDLE OF FUN
Gimbels: 1969 (Giveaway, B&W, 20 pgs.)

nn-Coloring book & games 2 4 6 8 10 12

SANTA'S CHRISTMAS COMIC VARIETY SHOW (See Merry Christmas From Sears Toyland)
Sears Roebuck & Co.: 1943 (24 pgs.)

Contains puzzles & new comics of Dick Tracy, Little Orphan Annie, Moon Mullins, Terry & the Pirates, etc. 81 162 325 480 615 700

SANTA'S CHRISTMAS TIME STORIES
Premium Sales, Inc.: nd (Late 1940s) (16 pgs., paper-c) (Giveaway)

nn 6 12 18 31 38 45

SANTA'S CIRCUS
Promotional Publ. Co.: 1964 (Giveaway, half-size)

nn-Marv Levy-c/a 2 4 6 9 11 14

SANTA'S FUN BOOK
Promotional Publ. Co.: 1951, 1952 (Regular size, 16 pgs., paper-c) (Murphy's giveaway)

nn 5 10 15 23 28 32

SANTA'S GIFT BOOK
No Publisher: No date (16 pgs.)

nn-Puzzles, games only 4 8 11 16 19 22

SANTA'S NEW STORY BOOK
Wallace Hamilton Campbell: 1949 (16 pgs., paper-c) (Giveaway)

nn 6 12 18 31 38 45

SANTA'S REAL STORY BOOK
Wallace Hamilton Campbell/W. W. Orris: 1948, 1952 (Giveaway, 16 pgs.)

nn 6 12 18 31 38 45

SANTA'S RIDE

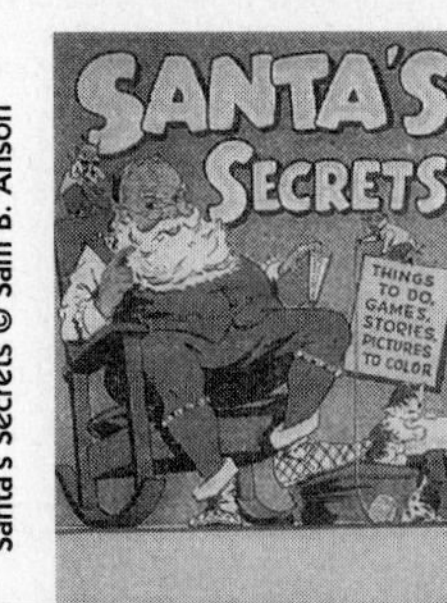

Santa's Secrets © Sam B. Anson

Sergeant Preston of the Yukon © DELL

Special Edition #6 © DC

	GD 2.0	VG 4.0	FN 6.0	VF 8.0	VF/NM 9.0	NM- 9.2
W. T. Grant Co.: 1959 (Giveaway)						
nn	3	6	9	16	20	24
SANTA'S RODEO						
Promotional Publ. Co.: 1964 (Giveaway, half-size)						
nn-Marv Levy-a	2	4	6	9	11	14
SANTA'S SECRET CAVE						
W.T. Grant Co.: 1960 (Giveaway, half-size)						
nn	2	4	6	12	16	20
SANTA'S SECRETS						
Sam B. Anson Christmas giveaway: 1951, 1952? (16 pgs., paper-c)						
nn-Has games, stories & pictures to color	4	8	12	17	21	24
SANTA'S STORIES						
K. K. Publications (Klines Dept. Store): 1953 (Regular size, paper-c)						
nn-Kelly-a	17	34	51	95	130	165
nn-Another version (1953, glossy-c, half-size, 7-1/4x5-1/4")-Kelly-a	11	22	33	63	84	105
SANTA'S SURPRISE						
K. K. Publications: 1947 (Giveaway, 36 pgs., slick-c)						
nn	7	14	21	38	47	56
SANTA'S TOYTOWN FUN BOOK						
Promotional Publ. Co.: 1953 (Giveaway)						
nn-Marv Levy-c	4	8	11	16	19	22
SANTA TAKES A TRIP TO MARS						
Bradshaw-Diehl Co., Huntington, W.VA.: 1950s (nd) (Giveaway, 16 pgs.)						
nn	4	8	11	16	19	22
SCIENCE FAIR STORY OF ELECTRONICS						
Radio Shack/Tandy Corp.: 1975 - 1987 (Giveaway)						
11 different issues (approx. 1 per year) each....						3.00
SERGEANT PRESTON OF THE YUKON						
Quaker Cereals: 1956 (4 comic booklets) (Soft-c, 16 pgs., 7x2-1/2" & 5x2-1/2") Giveaways						
"How He Found Yukon King", "The Case That Made Him A Sergeant", "How Yukon King Saved Him From The Wolves", "How He Became A Mountie" each...	10	20	30	56	73	90
SHAZAM! (Visits Portland Oregon in 1943)						
DC Comics: 1989 (69¢ cover)						
nn-Promotes Super-Heroes exhibit at Oregon Museum of Science and Industry; reprints Golden Age Captain Marvel story	2	4	6	8	10	12
SHERIFF OF COCHISE, THE (TV)						
Mobil: 1957 (16 pgs.) Giveaway						
nn-Schaffenberger-a	4	8	11	16	19	22
SILLY PUTTY MAN						
DC Comics: 1978						
1	1	3	4	6	8	10
SKATING SKILLS						
Custom Comics, Inc./Chicago Roller Skates: 1957 (36 & 12 pgs.; 5x7", two versions) (10¢)						
nn-Resembles old ACG cover plus interior art	4	7	10	14	17	20
SKINWALKER						
Oni Press: May, 2003 (Giveaway, B&W)						
1-Free Comic Book Day Edition						2.25
SKIPPY'S OWN BOOK OF COMICS (See Popular Comics)						
No publisher listed: 1934 (Giveaway, 52 pgs., strip reprints)						
nn-(Scarce)-By Percy Crosby	450	900	1350	2900	4150	5400
Published by Max C. Gaines for Phillip's Dental Magnesia to be advertised on the Skippy Radio Show and given away with the purchase of a tube of Phillip's Tooth Paste. This is the first four-color comic book of reprints about one character.						
SKY KING "RUNAWAY TRAIN" (TV)						
National Biscuit Co.: 1964 (Regular size, 16 pgs.)						
nn	10	20	30	40	62	85
SLAM BANG COMICS						
Post Cereal Giveaway: No. 9, No date						
9-Dynamic Man, Echo, Mr. E, Yankee Boy app.	9	18	27	49	62	75
SLAVE LABOR STORIES						
SLG Publishing: May, 2003 (Giveaway, B&W)						
1-Free Comic Book Day Edition; short stories by various; Dorkin Milk & Cheese-c						2.25

	GD 2.0	VG 4.0	FN 6.0	VF 8.0	VF/NM 9.0	NM- 9.2
SMILIN' JACK						
Dell Publishing Co.						
Popped Wheat Giveaway (1947)-1938 strip reprints; 16 pgs. in full color	2	4	6	8	10	12
Shoe Store Giveaway-1938 strip reprints; 16 pgs.	5	10	15	24	30	35
Sparked Wheat Giveaway (1942)-16 pgs. in full color	5	10	15	24	30	35
SMOKEY BEAR (See Forest Fire for 1st app.)						
Dell Publ. Co.: 1959,1960						
True Story of..., The -U.S. Forest Service giveaway-Publ. by Western Printing Co.; reprints 1st 16 pgs. of Four Color #932. Inside front-c differs slightly in 1959 & 1960 editions	5	10	14	20	24	28
1964,1969 reprints	2	4	6	12	16	20
SMOKEY STOVER						
Dell Publishing Co.						
General Motors giveaway (1953)	7	14	21	35	43	50
National Fire Protection giveaway(1953 & 1954)-16 pgs., paper-c	7	14	21	35	43	50
SNOW FOR CHRISTMAS						
W. T. Grant Co.: 1957 (16 pgs.) (Giveaway)						
nn	4	8	12	18	22	25
SNOW WHITE AND THE SEVEN DWARFS						
Bendix Washing Machines: 1952 (32 pgs., 5x7-1/4", soft-c) (Disney)						
nn	12	24	36	69	92	115
SNOW WHITE AND THE SEVEN DWARFS						
Promotional Publ. Co.: 1957 (Small size)						
nn	6	12	18	28	34	40
SNOW WHITE AND THE SEVEN DWARFS						
Western Printing Co.: 1958 (16 pgs, 5x7-1/4", soft-c) (Disney premium)						
nn- "Mystery of the Missing Magic"	8	16	24	43	54	65
SNOW WHITE AND THE 7 DWARFS IN "MILKY WAY"						
American Dairy Assoc.: 1955 (16 pgs., soft-c, 5x7-1/4") (Disney premium)						
nn	12	24	36	69	92	115
SPACE GHOST COAST TO COAST						
Cartoon Network: Apr, 1994 (giveaway to Turner Broadcasting employees)						
1-(8 pgs.); origin of Space Ghost						6.00
SPACE PATROL (TV)						
Ziff-Davis Publishing Co. (Approved Comics)						
...'s Special Mission (8 pgs., B&W, Giveaway)	60	120	180	360	480	600
SPECIAL AGENT						
Assoc. of American Railroads: Oct, 1959 (16 pgs.)						
nn-The Story of the railroad police	8	16	24	40	50	60
SPECIAL DELIVERY						
Post Hall Synd.: 1951 (32 pgs.; B&W) (Giveaway)						
nn-Origin of Pogo, Swamp, etc.; 2 pg. biog. on Walt Kelly (One copy sold in 1980 for $150.00)						
SPECIAL EDITION (U. S. Navy Giveaways)						
National Periodical Publications: 1944 - 1945 (Regular comic format with wording simplified, 52 pgs.)						
1-Action (1944)-Reprints Action #80	59	118	177	365	520	675
2-Action (1944)-Reprints Action #81	59	118	177	365	520	675
3-Superman (1944)-Reprints Superman #33	59	118	177	365	520	675
4-Detective (1944)-Reprints Detective #97	59	118	177	365	520	675
5-Superman (1945)-Reprints Superman #34	59	118	177	365	520	675
6-Action (1945)-Reprints Action #84	59	118	177	365	520	675
NOTE: ***Wayne Boring** c-1, 2, 6. **Dick Sprang** c-4.*						
SPIDER-MAN (See Amazing Spider-Man, The)						
SPIRIT, THE (Weekly Comic Book)						
Will Eisner: 6/2/40 - 10/5/52 (16 pgs.; 8 pgs.) (no cover) (in color) (Distributed through various newspapers and other sources)						
NOTE: **Eisner** script, pencils/inks for the most part from 6/2/40-4/26/42; a few stories assisted by Jack Cole, Fine, Powell and Kotsky.						
6/2/40(#1)-Origin/1st app. The Spirit; reprinted in Police #11; Lady Luck (Brenda Banks) (1st app.) by Chuck Mazoujian & Mr. Mystic (1st. app.) by S. R. (Bob) Powell begin	57	114	171	350	525	700
6/9/40(#2)	27	54	81	153	214	275
6/16/40(#3)-Black Queen app. in Spirit	17	34	51	98	134	170
6/23/40(#4)-Mr. Mystic receives magical necklace	14	28	42	81	111	140

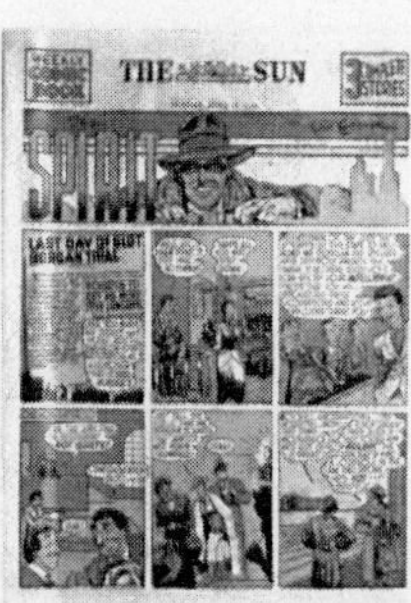
The Spirit 6/16/40 © Will Eisner

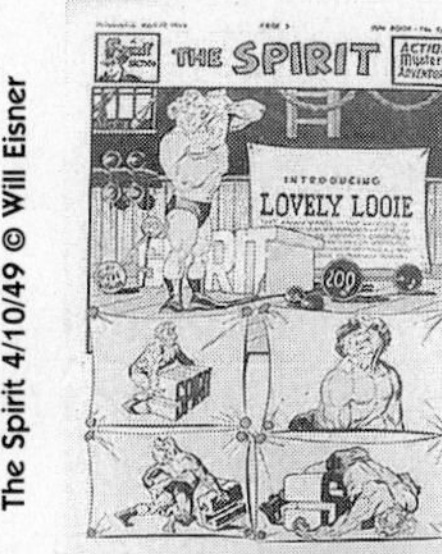
The Spirit 4/10/49 © Will Eisner

The Spirit 3/12/50 © Will Eisner

	GD 2.0	VG 4.0	FN 6.0	VF 8.0	VF/NM 9.0	NM- 9.2
6/30/40(#5)	14	28	42	81	111	140
7/7/40(#6)-1st app. Spirit carplane; Black Queen app. in Spirit	14	28	42	81	111	140
7/14/40(#7)-8/4/40(#10): 7/21/40-Spirit becomes fugitive wanted for murder	12	24	36	69	92	115
8/11/40-9/22/40	11	22	33	63	84	105
9/29/40-Ellen drops engagement with Homer Creep	10	20	30	56	73	90
10/6/40-11/3/40	10	20	30	56	73	90
11/10/40-The Black Queen app.	10	20	30	56	73	90
11/17/40, 11/24/40	10	20	30	56	73	90
12/1/40-Ellen spanking by Spirit on cover & inside; Eisner-1st 3 pgs., J. Cole rest	14	28	42	79	107	135
12/8/40-3/9/41	9	18	27	49	62	75
3/16/41-Intro. & 1st app. Silk Satin	12	24	36	69	92	115
3/23/41-6/1/41: 5/11/41-Last Lady Luck by Mazoujian; 5/18/41-Lady Luck by Nick Viscardi begins, ends 2/22/42	9	18	27	49	62	75
6/8/41-2nd app. Satin; Spirit learns Satin is also a British agent	10	20	30	58	77	95
6/15/41-1st app. Twilight	9	18	27	54	70	85
6/22/41-Hitler app. in Spirit	9	18	27	54	70	85
6/29/41-1/25/42,2/8/42	8	16	24	42	53	64
2/1/42-1st app. Duchess	9	18	27	54	70	85
2/15/42-4/26/42-Lady Luck by Klaus Nordling begins 3/1/42	8	16	24	46	58	70
5/3/42-8/16/42-Eisner/Fine/Quality staff assists on Spirit	6	12	18	35	43	50
8/23/42-Satin cover splash; Spirit by Eisner/Fine although signed by Fine	10	20	30	56	73	90
8/30/42,9/27/42-10/11/42,10/25/42-11/8/42-Eisner/Fine/Quality staff assists on Spirit	7	14	21	35	43	50
9/6/42-9/20/42,10/18/42-Fine/Belfi art on Spirit; scripts by Manly Wade Wellman	5	10	15	23	28	32
11/15/42-12/6/42,12/20/42,12/27/42,1/17/43-4/18/43,5/9/43-8/8/43-Wellman/Woolfolk scripts, Fine pencils, Quality staff inks	5	10	15	23	28	32
12/13/42,1/3/43,1/10/43,4/25/43,5/2/43-Eisner scripts/layouts; Fine pencils, Quality staff inks	6	12	18	28	34	40
8/15/43-Eisner script/layout; pencils/inks by Quality staff; Jack Cole-a	5	10	14	20	24	28
8/22/43-12/12/43-Wellman/Woolfolk scripts, Fine pencils, Quality staff inks; Mr. Mystic by Guardineer-10/10/43-10/24/43	5	10	14	20	24	28
12/19/43-8/13/44-Wellman/Woolfolk/Jack Cole scripts; Cole, Fine & Robin King-a; Last Mr. Mystic-5/14/44	4	9	13	18	22	26
8/20/44-12/16/45-Wellman/Woolfolk scripts; Fine art with unknown staff assists	4	9	13	18	22	26
NOTE: *Scripts/layouts by Eisner, or Eisner/Nordling, Eisner/Mercer or Spranger/Eisner; inks by Eisner or Eisner/Spranger in issues 12/23/45-2/2/47.*						
12/23/45-1/6/46: 12/23/45-Christmas-c	6	12	18	28	34	40
1/13/46-Origin Spirit retold	8	16	24	42	53	64
1/20/46-1st postwar Satin app.	7	14	21	35	43	50
1/27/46-3/10/46: 3/3/46-Last Lady Luck by Nordling	6	12	18	28	34	40
3/17/46-Intro. & 1st app. Nylon	7	14	21	35	43	50
3/24/46,3/31/46,4/14/46	6	12	18	28	34	40
4/7/46-2nd app. Nylon	6	12	18	31	38	45
4/21/46-Intro. & 1st app. Mr. Carrion & His Pet Buzzard Julia	8	16	24	40	50	60
4/28/46-5/12/46,5/26/46-6/30/46: Lady Luck by Fred Schwab in issues 5/5/46-11/3/46	6	12	18	28	34	40
5/19/46-2nd app. Mr. Carrion	6	12	18	31	38	45
7/7/46-Intro. & 1st app. Dulcet Tone & Skinny	7	14	21	35	43	50
7/14/46-9/29/46	6	12	18	28	34	40
10/6/46-Intro. & 1st app. P'Gell	8	16	24	40	50	60
10/13/46-11/3/46,11/16/46-11/24/46	6	12	18	28	34	40
11/10/46-2nd app. P'Gell	6	12	18	31	38	45
12/1/46-3rd app. P'Gell	6	12	18	29	36	42
12/8/46-2/2/47	5	10	15	24	30	35
NOTE: *Scripts, pencils/inks by Eisner except where noted in issues 2/9/47-12/19/48.*						
2/9/47-7/6/47: 6/8/47-Eisner self satire	5	10	15	24	30	35
7/13/47- "Hansel & Gretel" fairy tales	7	14	21	35	43	50
7/20/47-Li'L Abner, Daddy Warbucks, Dick Tracy, Fearless Fosdick parody; A-Bomb blast-c	8	16	24	40	50	60
7/27/47-9/14/47	5	10	15	24	30	35
9/21/47-Pearl Harbor flashback	6	12	18	28	34	40
9/28/47-1st mention of Flying Saucers in comics-3 months after 1st sighting in Idaho on 6/25/47	10	20	30	56	73	90
10/5/47- "Cinderella" fairy tales	7	14	21	35	43	50
10/12/47-11/30/47	5	10	15	24	30	35
12/7/47-Intro. & 1st app. Powder Pouf	8	16	24	40	50	60
12/14/47-12/28/47	5	10	15	24	30	35
1/4/48-2nd app. Powder Pouf	6	12	18	31	38	45
1/11/48-1st app. Sparrow Fallon; Powder Pouf app.	6	12	18	31	38	45
1/18/48-He-Man ad cover; satire issue	6	12	18	31	38	45
1/25/48-Intro. & 1st app. Castanet	8	16	24	40	50	60
2/1/48-2nd app. Castanet	6	12	18	28	34	40
2/8/48-3/7/48	5	10	15	24	30	35
3/14/48-Only app. Kretchma	6	12	18	28	34	40
3/21/48,3/28/48,4/11/48-4/25/48	5	10	15	24	30	35
4/4/48-Only app. Wild Rice	6	12	18	28	34	40
5/2/48-2nd app. Sparrow	5	10	15	24	30	35
5/9/48-6/27/48,7/11/48,7/18/48: 6/13/48-TV issue	5	10	15	24	30	35
7/4/48-Spirit by Andre Le Blanc	5	10	14	20	24	28
7/25/48-Ambrose Bierce's "The Thing" adaptation classic by Eisner/Grandenetti	10	20	30	56	73	90
8/1/48-8/15/48,8/29/48-9/12/48	5	10	15	24	30	35
8/22/48-Poe's "Fall of the House of Usher" classic by Eisner/Grandenetti	10	20	30	56	73	90
9/19/48-Only app. Lorelei	6	12	18	31	38	45
9/26/48-10/31/48	5	10	15	24	30	35
11/7/48-Only app. Plaster of Paris	7	14	21	35	43	50
11/14/48-12/19/48	5	10	15	24	30	35
NOTE: *Scripts by Eisner or Feiffer or Eisner/Feiffer or Nordling. Art by Eisner with backgrounds by Eisner, Grandenetti, Le Blanc, Stallman, Nordling, Dixon and/or others in issues 12/26/48-4/1/51 except where noted.*						
12/26/48-Reprints some covers of 1948 with flashbacks	5	10	15	24	30	35
1/2/49-1/16/49	5	10	15	24	30	35
1/23/49,1/30/49-1st & 2nd app. Thorne	6	12	18	31	38	45
2/6/49-8/14/49	5	10	15	24	30	35
8/21/49,8/28/49-1st & 2nd app. Monica Veto	6	12	18	31	38	45
9/4/49,9/11/49	5	10	15	24	30	35
9/18/49-Love comic cover; has gag love comic ads on inside	6	12	18	31	38	45
9/25/49-Only app. Ice	6	12	18	28	34	40
10/2/49,10/9/49-Autumn News appears & dies in 10/9 issue	6	12	18	31	34	40
10/16/49-11/27/49,12/18/49,12/25/49	5	10	15	24	30	35
12/4/49,12/11/49-1st & 2nd app. Flaxen	6	12	18	31	34	40
1/1/50-Flashbacks to all of the Spirit girls-Thorne, Ellen, Satin, & Monica	8	16	24	46	58	70
1/8/50-Intro. & 1st app. Sand Saref	9	18	27	54	70	85
1/15/50-2nd app. Saref	8	16	24	40	50	60
1/22/50-2/5/50	5	10	15	24	30	35
2/12/50-Roller Derby issue	6	12	18	31	38	45
2/19/50-Half Dead Mr. Lox - Classic horror	6	12	18	35	43	50
2/26/50-4/23/50,5/14/50,5/28/50,7/23/50-9/3/50	5	10	15	24	30	35
4/30/50-Script/art by Le Blanc with Eisner framing	4	8	12	17	21	24
5/7/50,6/4/50-7/16/50-Abe Kanegson-a	4	8	12	17	21	24
5/21/50-Script by Feiffer/Eisner, art by Blaisdell, Eisner framing	4	8	12	17	21	24
9/10/50-P'Gell returns	6	12	18	31	38	45
9/17/50-1/7/51	5	10	15	24	30	35
1/14/51-Life Magazine cover; brief biography of Comm. Dolan, Sand Saref, Silk Satin, P'Gell, Sammy & Willum, Darling O'Shea, & Mr. Carrion & His Pet Buzzard Julia, with pin-ups by Eisner	7	14	21	35	43	50
1/21/51,2/4/51-4/1/51	5	10	15	24	30	35
1/28/51- "The Meanest Man in the World" classic by Eisner	7	14	21	35	43	50
4/8/51-7/29/51,8/12/51-Last Eisner issue	5	10	15	24	30	35
8/5/51,8/19/51-7/20/52-Not Eisner	4	8	11	16	19	22
7/27/52-(Rare)-Denny Colt in Outer Space by Wally Wood; 7 pg. S/F story of E.C. vintage	30	60	90	161	223	285
8/3/52-(Rare)- "Mission...The Moon" by Wood	30	60	90	161	223	285
8/10/52-(Rare)- "A DP On The Moon" by Wood	30	60	90	161	223	285
8/17/52-(Rare)- "Heart" by Wood/Eisner	25	50	75	135	187	240
8/24/52-(Rare)- "Rescue" by Wood	30	60	90	161	223	285
8/31/52-(Rare)- "The Last Man" by Wood	30	60	90	161	223	285
9/7/52-(Rare)- "The Man in The Moon" by Wood	30	60	90	161	223	285
9/14/52-(Rare)-Eisner/Wenzel-a	10	20	30	56	73	90
9/21/52-(Rare)- "Denny Colt, Alias The Spirit/Space Report" by Eisner/Wenzel	11	22	33	63	84	105
9/28/52-(Rare)- "Return From The Moon" by Wood	30	60	90	161	223	285
10/5/52-(Rare)- "The Last Story" by Eisner	12	24	36	69	92	115

Large Tabloid pages from 1946 on (Eisner) - Price 200 percent over listed prices.

NOTE: *Spirit sections came out in both large and small format. Some newspapers went to the 8-pg. format months before others. Some printed the pages so they cannot be folded into a small comic book section; these are worth less. (Also see Three Comics & Spiritman).*

Steve Canyon's Secret Mission © HARV

Super Book of Comics #7 © News Syndicate

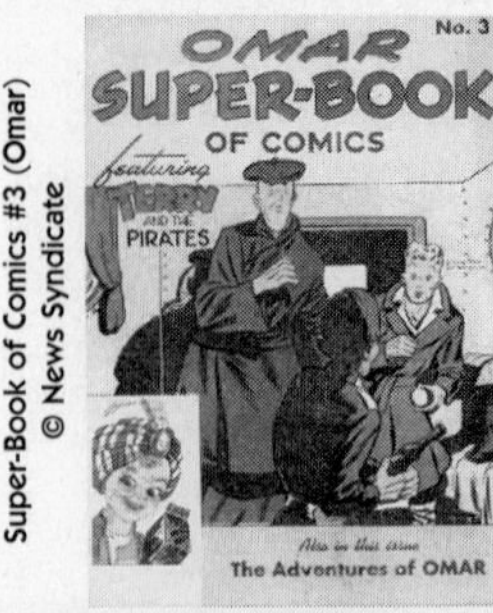

Super-Book of Comics #3 (Omar) © News Syndicate

SPY SMASHER
Fawcett Publications

	GD 2.0	VG 4.0	FN 6.0	VF 8.0	VF/NM 9.0	NM- 9.2
Well Known Comics (1944, 12 pgs., 8-1/2x10-1/2"), paper-c, glued binding, printed in green; Bestmaid/Samuel Lowe giveaway	16	32	48	89	122	155

STANDARD OIL COMICS (Also see Gulf Funny Weekly)
Standard Oil Co.: 1933 (Giveaway, tabloid size, 4 pgs. in color)

	GD 2.0	VG 4.0	FN 6.0	VF 8.0	VF/NM 9.0	NM- 9.2
1-Series has original art	55	110	165	315	457	600
2-5	25	50	75	132	186	240
6-14: 14-Fred Opper strip, 1 pg.	13	26	39	76	103	130

STAR TEAM
Marvel Comics Group: 1977 (6-1/2x5", 20 pgs.) (Ideal Toy Giveaway)

	GD 2.0	VG 4.0	FN 6.0	VF 8.0	VF/NM 9.0	NM- 9.2
nn	2	4	6	10	12	15

STAR WARS: TALES - A JEDI'S WEAPON
Dark Horse Comics: May, 2002 (Free Comic Book Day giveaway, 16 pgs.)

	GD 2.0	VG 4.0	FN 6.0	VF 8.0	VF/NM 9.0	NM- 9.2
nn-Anakin Skywalker Episode 2 photo-c						2.00

STEVE CANYON COMICS
Harvey Publications

	GD 2.0	VG 4.0	FN 6.0	VF 8.0	VF/NM 9.0	NM- 9.2
Dept. Store giveaway #3(6/48, 36pp)	10	20	30	56	73	90
...'s Secret Mission (1951, 16 pgs., Armed Forces giveaway); Caniff-a	9	18	27	54	70	85
Strictly for the Smart Birds (1951, 16 pgs.)-Information Comics Div. (Harvey) Premium	9	18	27	51	65	78

STORIES OF CHRISTMAS
K. K. Publications: 1942 (Giveaway, 32 pgs., paper cover)

	GD 2.0	VG 4.0	FN 6.0	VF 8.0	VF/NM 9.0	NM- 9.2
nn-Adaptation of "A Christmas Carol"; Kelly story "The Fir Tree"; Infinity-c	38	76	113	195	272	350

STORY HOUR SERIES (Disney)
Whitman Publ. Co.: 1948, 1949; 1951-1953 (36 pgs., paper-c) (4-3/4x6-1/2")
Given away with subscription to Walt Disney's Comics & Stories

	GD 2.0	VG 4.0	FN 6.0	VF 8.0	VF/NM 9.0	NM- 9.2
nn(1948)-Mickey Mouse and the Boy Thursday	12	24	36	66	88	110
nn(1948)-Mickey Mouse the Miracle Master	12	24	36	66	88	110
nn(1948)-Minnie Mouse and Antique Chair	12	24	36	66	88	110
nn(1949)-The Three Orphan Kittens(B&W & color)	8	16	24	42	53	64
nn(1949)-Danny-The Little Black Lamb	8	16	24	42	53	64
800(1948)-Donald Duck in "Bringing Up the Boys"	17	34	51	98	134	170
1953 edition	11	22	33	63	84	105
801(1948)-Mickey Mouse's Summer Vacation	9	18	27	54	70	85
1951, 1952 editions	6	12	18	29	36	42
802(1948)-Bugs Bunny's Adventures	8	16	24	45	58	70
803(1948)-Bongo	7	14	21	36	44	54
804(1948)-Mickey and the Beanstalk	8	16	24	45	57	68
805-15(1949)-Andy Panda and His Friends	7	14	21	38	47	56
806-15(1949)-Tom and Jerry	8	16	24	42	53	64
808-15(1949)-Johnny Appleseed	7	14	21	36	44	54

1948, 1949 Hard Cover Edition of each....30% - 40% more.

STORY OF EDISON, THE
Educational Comics: 1956 (16 pgs.) (Reddy Killowatt)

	GD 2.0	VG 4.0	FN 6.0	VF 8.0	VF/NM 9.0	NM- 9.2
nn-Reprint of Reddy Kilowatt #2(1947)	7	14	21	35	43	50

STORY OF HARRY S. TRUMAN, THE
Democratic National Committee: 1948 (Giveaway, regular size, soft-c, 16 pg.)

	GD 2.0	VG 4.0	FN 6.0	VF 8.0	VF/NM 9.0	NM- 9.2
nn-Gives biography on career of Truman; used in **SOTI**, pg. 311	14	28	42	79	107	135

STORY OF THE BALLET, THE
Selva and Sons, Inc.: 1954 (16 pgs., paper cover)

	GD 2.0	VG 4.0	FN 6.0	VF 8.0	VF/NM 9.0	NM- 9.2
nn	4	8	11	16	19	22

STRANGE AS IT SEEMS
McNaught Syndicate: 1936 (B&W, 5x7", 24 pgs.)

	GD 2.0	VG 4.0	FN 6.0	VF 8.0	VF/NM 9.0	NM- 9.2
nn-Ex-Lax giveaway	8	16	24	42	53	64

STRAY BULLETS
El Capitan Books: May, 2002 (48 pgs., B&W, flip book)

	GD 2.0	VG 4.0	FN 6.0	VF 8.0	VF/NM 9.0	NM- 9.2
Free Comic Book Day giveaway-Reprints #2 with "Free Comic Book Day" banner on-c; flip book with The Matrix (printing of internet comic)						2.25

SUGAR BEAR
Post Cereal Giveaway: No date, circa 1975? (2-1/2x4-1/2", 16 pgs.)

	GD 2.0	VG 4.0	FN 6.0	VF 8.0	VF/NM 9.0	NM- 9.2
"The Almost Take Over of the Post Office", "The Race Across the Atlantic", "The Zoo Goes Wild" each...	1	2	3	5	6	8

SUNDAY WORLD'S EASTER EGG FULL OF EASTER MEAT FOR LITTLE PEOPLE
Supplement to the New York World: 3/27/1898 (soft-c, 16pg, 4"x8" approx., opens at top, color & B&W)(Giveaway)(shaped like an Easter egg)

	GD 2.0	VG 4.0	FN 6.0	VF 8.0	VF/NM 9.0	NM- 9.2
nn-By R.F. Outcault	19	38	57	106	146	185

SUPER BOOK OF COMICS
Western Publishing Co.: nd (1942-1943?) (Soft-c, 32 pgs.) (Pan-Am/Gilmore Oil/Kelloggs premiums)

	GD 2.0	VG 4.0	FN 6.0	VF 8.0	VF/NM 9.0	NM- 9.2
nn-Dick Tracy (Gilmore)-Magic Morro app.	40	80	120	232	315	400
1-Dick Tracy & The Smuggling Ring; Stratosphere Jim app. (Rare) (Pan-Am)	40	80	120	232	315	400
1-Smilin' Jack, Magic Morro (Pan-Am)	15	30	45	83	109	135
2-Smilin' Jack, Stratosphere Jim (Pan-Am)	15	30	45	83	109	135
2-Smitty, Magic Morro (Pan-Am)	15	30	45	83	109	135
3-Captain Midnight, Magic Morro (Pan-Am)	31	62	93	173	232	290
3-Moon Mullins?	15	30	45	83	109	135
4-Red Ryder, Magic Morro (Pan-Am). Same content as Red Ryder Victory Patrol comic w/diff. cover	19	38	57	101	133	165
4-Smitty, Stratosphere Jim (Pan-Am)	15	30	45	83	109	135
5-Don Winslow, Magic Morro (Gilmore)	19	38	57	101	133	165
5-Don Winslow, Stratosphere Jim (Pan-Am)	19	38	57	101	133	165
5-Terry & the Pirates	22	44	66	121	161	200
6-Don Winslow, Stratosphere Jim (Pan-Am)-McWilliams-a	19	38	57	101	133	165
6-King of the Royal Mounted, Magic Morro (Pan-Am)	19	38	57	101	133	165
7-Dick Tracy, Magic Morro (Pan-Am)	25	50	75	138	184	230
7-Little Orphan Annie	13	26	39	72	94	115
8-Dick Tracy, Stratosphere Jim (Pan-Am)	22	44	66	121	161	200
8-Dan Dunn, Magic Morro (Pan-Am)	13	26	39	72	94	115
9-Terry & the Pirates, Magic Morro (Pan-Am)	22	44	66	121	161	200
10-Red Ryder, Magic Morro (Pan-Am)	19	38	57	101	133	165

SUPER-BOOK OF COMICS
Western Publishing Co.: (Omar Bread & Hancock Oil Co. giveaways) 1944 - No. 30, 1947 (Omar); 1947 - 1948 (Hancock) (16 pgs.)

NOTE: The Hancock issues are all exact reprints of the earlier Omar issues. The issue numbers were removed in some of the reprints.

	GD 2.0	VG 4.0	FN 6.0	VF 8.0	VF/NM 9.0	NM- 9.2
1-Dick Tracy (Omar, 1944)	22	44	66	118	157	195
1-Dick Tracy (Hancock, 1947)	16	32	48	89	117	145
2-Bugs Bunny (Omar, 1944)	8	16	24	42	51	60
2-Bugs Bunny (Hancock, 1947)	6	12	18	32	39	46
3-Terry & the Pirates (Omar, 1944)	12	24	36	66	86	105
3-Terry & the Pirates (Hancock, 1947)	11	22	33	58	74	90
4-Andy Panda (Omar, 1944)	8	16	24	42	51	60
4-Andy Panda (Hancock, 1947)	6	12	18	32	39	46
5-Smokey Stover (Omar, 1945)	6	12	18	32	39	46
5-Smokey Stover (Hancock, 1947)	5	10	15	25	30	35
6-Porky Pig (Omar, 1945)	8	16	24	42	51	60
6-Porky Pig (Hancock, 1947)	6	12	18	32	39	46
7-Smilin' Jack (Omar, 1945)	8	16	24	42	51	60
7-Smilin' Jack (Hancock, 1947)	6	12	18	32	39	46
8-Oswald the Rabbit (Omar, 1945)	6	12	18	32	39	46
8-Oswald the Rabbit (Hancock, 1947)	5	10	15	25	30	35
9-Alley Oop (Omar, 1945)	13	26	39	72	94	115
9-Alley Oop (Hancock, 1947)	12	24	36	66	86	105
10-Elmer Fudd (Omar, 1945)	6	12	18	32	39	46
10-Elmer Fudd (Hancock, 1947)	5	10	15	25	30	35
11-Little Orphan Annie (Omar, 1945)	8	16	24	44	54	64
11-Little Orphan Annie (Hancock, 1947)	7	14	21	37	46	54
12-Woody Woodpecker (Omar, 1945)	6	12	18	32	39	46
12-Woody Woodpecker (Hancock, 1947)	5	10	15	25	30	35
13-Dick Tracy (Omar, 1945)	13	26	39	72	94	115
13-Dick Tracy (Hancock, 1947)	12	24	36	66	86	105
14-Bugs Bunny (Omar, 1945)	6	12	18	32	39	46
14-Bugs Bunny (Hancock, 1947)	5	10	15	25	30	35
15-Andy Panda (Omar, 1945)	6	12	18	29	35	40
15-Andy Panda (Hancock, 1947)	5	10	15	25	30	35
16-Terry & the Pirates (Omar, 1945)	12	24	36	66	86	105
16-Terry & the Pirates (Hancock, 1947)	9	18	27	51	63	75
17-Smokey Stover (Omar, 1946)	6	12	18	32	39	46
17-Smokey Stover (Hancock, 1948?)	5	10	15	25	30	35
18-Porky Pig (Omar, 1946)	6	12	18	29	35	40
18-Porky Pig (Hancock, 1948?)	5	10	15	25	30	35
19-Smilin' Jack (Omar, 1946)	6	12	18	32	39	46
nn-Smilin' Jack (Hancock, 1948)	5	10	15	25	30	35
20-Oswald the Rabbit (Omar, 1946)	6	12	18	29	35	40
nn-Oswald the Rabbit (Hancock, 1948)	5	10	15	25	30	35

Super Circus #1 © Cross Pub.

Superman's Christmas Adventure © DC

Superman-Tim 5/46 © DC

	GD 2.0	VG 4.0	FN 6.0	VF 8.0	VF/NM 9.0	NM- 9.2
21-Gasoline Alley (Omar, 1946)	8	16	24	44	54	64
nn-Gasoline Alley (Hancock, 1948)	7	14	21	37	46	54
22-Elmer Fudd (Omar, 1946)	6	12	18	29	35	40
nn-Elmer Fudd (Hancock, 1948)	5	10	15	25	30	35
23-Little Orphan Annie (Omar, 1946)	8	16	24	42	51	60
nn-Little Orphan Annie (Hancock, 1948)	6	12	18	32	39	46
24-Woody Woodpecker (Omar, 1946)	6	12	18	29	35	40
nn-Woody Woodpecker (Hancock, 1948)	5	10	15	25	30	35
25-Dick Tracy (Omar, 1946)	12	24	36	66	86	105
nn-Dick Tracy (Hancock, 1948)	10	20	30	55	67	80
26-Bugs Bunny (Omar, 1946))	6	12	18	29	35	40
nn-Bugs Bunny (Hancock, 1948)	5	10	15	25	30	35
27-Andy Panda (Omar, 1946)	6	12	18	29	35	40
27-Andy Panda (Hancock, 1948)	5	10	15	25	30	35
28-Terry & the Pirates (Omar, 1946)	12	24	36	66	86	105
28-Terry & the Pirates (Hancock, 1948)	10	20	30	55	65	75
29-Smokey Stover (Omar, 1947)	6	12	18	29	35	40
29-Smokey Stover (Hancock, 1948)	5	10	15	25	30	35
30-Porky Pig (Omar, 1947)	6	12	18	29	35	40
30-Porky Pig (Hancock, 1948)	5	10	15	25	30	35
nn-Bugs Bunny (Hancock, 1948)-Does not match any Omar book	6	12	18	29	35	40

SUPER CIRCUS (TV)
Cross Publishing Co.

	GD	VG	FN	VF	VF/NM	NM-
1-(1951, Weather Bird Shoes giveaway)	7	14	21	38	47	56

SUPER FRIENDS
DC Comics: 1981 (Giveaway, no ads, no code or price)

	GD	VG	FN	VF	VF/NM	NM-
...Special 1 -r/Super Friends #19 & 36	1	3	4	6	8	10

SUPERGEAR COMICS
Jacobs Corp.: 1976 (Giveaway, 4 pgs. in color, slick paper)

	GD	VG	FN	VF	VF/NM	NM-
nn-(Rare)-Superman, Lois Lane; Steve Lombard app. (500 copies printed, over half destroyed?)	13	26	39	90	133	175

SUPERGIRL
DC Comics: 1984, 1986 (Giveaway, Baxter paper)

	GD	VG	FN	VF	VF/NM	NM-
nn-(American Honda/U.S. Dept. Transportation) Torres-c/a	1	2	3	5	6	8

SUPER HEROES PUZZLES AND GAMES
General Mills Giveaway (Marvel Comics Group): 1979 (32 pgs., regular size)

	GD	VG	FN	VF	VF/NM	NM-
nn-Four 2-pg. origin stories of Spider-Man, Captain America, The Hulk, & Spider-Woman	2	4	6	14	18	22

SUPERMAN
National Periodical Publ./DC Comics

	GD	VG	FN	VF	VF/NM	NM-
72-Giveaway(9-10/51)-(Rare)-Price blackened out; came with banner wrapped around book; without banner	74	148	221	450	650	850
72-Giveaway with banner	103	206	308	625	912	1200
Bradman birthday custom (1988)						4.00
... For the Animals (2000, Doris Day Animal Foundation, 30 pgs.) polybagged with Gotham Adventures #22, Hourman #12, Impulse #58, Looney Tunes #62, Stars and S.T.R.I.P.E. #8 and Superman Adventures #41						2.50
Kelloggs Giveaway-(2/3 normal size, 1954)-r-two stories/Superman #55	34	68	103	167	233	300
Kenner: Man of Steel (Doomsday is Coming) (1995, 16 pgs.) packaged with set of Superman and Doomsday action figures						3.50
...Meets the Quik Bunny (1987, Nestles Quik premium, 36 pgs.)	1	2	3	4	5	7
Pizza Hut Premiums (12/77)-Exact reprints of 1950s comics except for paid ads (set of 6 exist?); Vol. 1-r#97 (#113-r also known)	1	2	3	5	7	9
Radio Shack Giveaway-36 pgs. (7/80) "The Computers That Saved Metropolis", Starlin/ Giordano-a; advertising insert in Action #509, New Advs. of Superboy #7, Legion of Super-Heroes #265, & House of Mystery #282. (All comics were 68 pgs.) Cover of inserts printed on newsprint. Giveaway contains 4 extra pgs. of Radio Shack advertising that inserts do not have						6.00
Radio Shack Giveaway-(7/81) "Victory by Computer"						6.00
Radio Shack Giveaway-(7/82) "Computer Masters of Metropolis"						6.00

SUPERMAN ADVENTURES, THE (TV)
DC Comics: 1996 (Based on animated series)

	GD	VG	FN	VF	VF/NM	NM-
1-(1996) Preview issue distributed at Warner Bros. stores						4.00
Titus Game Edition (1998)						2.50

SUPERMAN AND THE GREAT CLEVELAND FIRE
National Periodical Publ.: 1948 (Giveaway, 4 pgs., no cover) (Hospital Fund)

	GD	VG	FN	VF	VF/NM	NM-
nn-In full color	90	195	300	450	575	700

SUPERMAN (Miniature)
National Periodical Publ.: 1942; 1955 - 1956 (3 issues, no #'s, 32 pgs.)
The pages are numbered in the 1st issue: 1-32; 2nd: 1A-32A, and 3rd: 1B-32B

	GD	VG	FN	VF	VF/NM	NM-
No date-Py-Co-Pay Tooth Powder giveaway (8 pgs.; circa 1942)	74	148	221	450	600	750
1-The Superman Time Capsule (Kellogg's Sugar Smacks)(1955)	48	96	144	300	390	480
1A-Duel in Space (1955)	45	90	135	270	348	425
1B-The Super Show of Metropolis (also #1-32, no B)(1955)	45	90	135	270	348	425

NOTE: *Numbering variations exist. Each title could have any combination-#1, 1A, or 1B.*

SUPERMAN RECORD COMIC
National Periodical Publications: 1966 (Golden Records)

	GD	VG	FN	VF	VF/NM	NM-
(With record)-Record reads origin of Superman from comic; came with iron-on patch, decoder, membership card & button; comic-r/Superman #125,146	22	44	66	116	168	220
Comic only	13	26	39	66	90	115

SUPERMAN'S BUDDY (Costume Comic)
National Periodical Publications: 1954 (4 pgs., slick paper-c; one-shot)
(Came in box w/costume)

	GD	VG	FN	VF	VF/NM	NM-
1-With box & costume	131	262	395	830	1215	1600
Comic only	63	126	189	390	545	700
1-(1958 edition)-Printed in 2 colors	20	40	60	105	145	185

SUPERMAN'S CHRISTMAS ADVENTURE
National Periodical Publications: 1940, 1944 (Giveaway, 16 pgs.)
Distributed by Nehi drinks, Bailey Store, Ivey-Keith Co., Kennedy's Boys Shop, Macy's Store, Boston Store

	GD	VG	FN	VF	VF/NM	NM-
1(1940)-Burnley-a; F. Ray-c/r from Superman #6 (Scarce)-Superman saves Santa Claus. Santa makes real Superman Toys offered in 1940. 1st merchandising story	625	1563	2500	3600	4650	5700
nn(1944) w/Santa Claus & X-mas tree-c	128	320	511	790	1050	1300
nn(1944) w/Candy cane & Superman-c	117	292	467	725	962	1200

SUPERMAN-TIM (Becomes Tim)
Superman-Tim Stores/National Periodical Publ.: Aug, 1942 - May, 1950 (Half size)
(B&W Giveaway w/2 color covers) (Publ. monthly 2/43 on)

	GD	VG	FN	VF	VF/NM	NM-
8/42 (#1)-All have Superman illos.	150	375	600	900	1150	1400
1/43 (#2)	44	88	133	260	367	475
2/43 (#3)	42	84	125	245	347	450
3/43 (#4)	42	84	125	245	347	450
4/43, 5/43, 6/43, 7/43, 8/43	40	80	120	221	305	390
9/43, 10/43, 11/43, 12/43	35	70	105	190	260	330
1/44-12/44	28	56	83	155	212	270
1/45-5/45, 10-12/45, 1/46-8/46	25	50	75	144	197	250
6/45-Classic Superman-c	28	56	84	155	212	270
7/45-Classic Superman flag-c	28	56	84	155	212	270
9/45-1st stamp album issue	60	120	180	370	505	640
9/46-2nd stamp album issue	48	96	144	290	407	525
10/46-1st Superman story	33	66	99	190	265	340
11/46, 12/46, 1/47-8/47 issues-Superman story in each; 2/47-Infinity-c. All 36 pgs.	35	70	105	190	265	340
9/47-Stamp album issue & Superman story	45	90	135	265	382	500
10/47, 11/47, 12/47-Superman stories (24 pgs.)	35	70	105	190	265	340
1/48-7/48,10/48, 11/48, 2/49, 4/49-11/49	28	56	83	155	212	270
8/48-Contains full page ad for Superman-Tim watch giveaway	28	56	83	155	212	270
9/48-Stamp album issue	36	72	108	207	288	370
1/49-Full page Superman bank cut-out	28	56	84	161	221	285
3/49-Full page Superman boxing game cut-out	28	56	84	161	221	285
12/49-3/50, 5/50-Superman stories	31	62	94	173	236	300
4/50-Superman story, baseball stories; photo-c without Superman	33	66	99	190	265	340

NOTE: *All issues have Superman illustrations throughout. The page count varies depending on whether a Superman-Tim comic story is inserted. If it is, the page count is either 36 or 24 pages. Otherwise all issues are 16 pages. Each issue has a special place for inserting a full color Superman stamp. The stamp album issues had spaces for the stamps given away the past year. The books were mailed as a subscription premium. The stamps were given away free (or when you made a purchase) only when you physically came into the store.*

SUPER SEAMAN SLOPPY
Allied Pristine Union Council, Buffalo, NY: 1940s, 8pg., reg. size (Soft-c)

	GD	VG	FN	VF	VF/NM	NM-
nn	4	8	12	17	21	24

SWAMP FOX, THE
Walt Disney Productions: 1960 (14 pgs, small size) (Canada Dry Premiums)
Titles: (A)-Tory Masquerade, (B)-Turnabout Tactics, (C)-Rindau Rampage; each came in paper sleeve, books 1,2 & 3;

Tastee-Freez Comics #3 © HARV

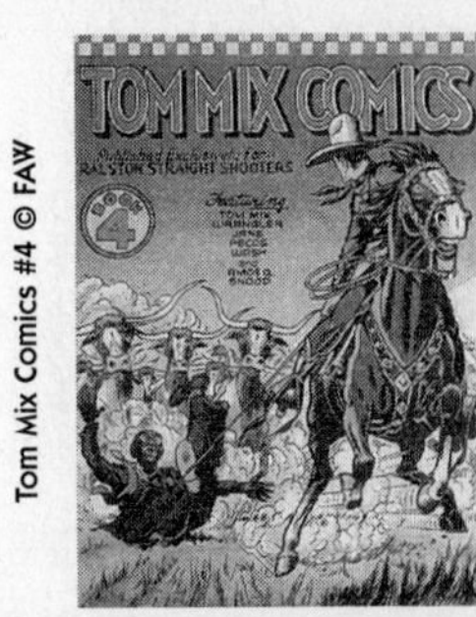

Tom Mix Comics #4 © FAW

Transformers Armada Free Comic Book Day Ed. © Hasbro

	GD 2.0	VG 4.0	FN 6.0	VF 8.0	VF/NM 9.0	NM- 9.2
Set with sleeves	6	12	18	40	55	70
Comic only	2	4	6	13	17	21

SWORDQUEST
DC Comics/Atari Pub.: 1982, 52pg., 5"x7" (Giveaway with video games)

	GD	VG	FN	VF	VF/NM	NM-
1,2-Roy Thomas & Gerry Conway-s; George Pérez & Dick Giordano-c/a in all	2	4	6	9	11	14
3-Low print	2	4	6	11	14	18

SYNDICATE FEATURES (Sci/fi)
Harry A. Chesler Syndicate: V1#3, 11/15/37 (Tabloid size, 3 colors, 4 pgs.) (Editors premium) (Came folded)

	GD	VG	FN	VF	VF/NM	NM-
V1#3-Dan Hastings daily strips-Guardineer-a	450	900	1350	1800	2400	3000

TASTEE-FREEZ COMICS
Harvey Comics: 1957 (10¢, 36 pgs.)(6 different issues given away)

	GD	VG	FN	VF	VF/NM	NM-
1-Little Dot	7	14	21	50	68	85
2,4,5: 2-Rags Rabbit. 4-Sad Sack. 5-Mazie	4	8	12	27	36	45
3-Casper	6	12	18	38	52	65
6-Dick Tracy	6	12	18	38	52	65

TAYLOR'S CHRISTMAS TABLOID
Dept. Store Giveaway: Mid 1930s, Cleveland, Ohio (Tabloid size; in color)

nn-(Very Rare)-Among the earliest pro work of Siegel & Shuster; one full color page called "The Battle in the Stratosphere", with a pre-Superman look; Shuster art thoughout. (Only 1 known copy) Estimated value... 4000.00

TAZ'S 40TH BIRTHDAY BLOWOUT
DC Comics: 1994 (K-Mart giveaway, 16 pgs.)

nn-Six pg. story, games and puzzles 3.00

TEE AND VEE CROSLEY IN TELEVISION LAND COMICS (Also see Crosley's House of Fun)
Crosley Division, Avco Mfg. Corp. : 1951 (52 pgs.; 8x11"; paper cover; in color) (Giveaway)

	GD	VG	FN	VF	VF/NM	NM-
Many stories, puzzles, cut-outs, games, etc.	6	12	18	31	38	45

TENNESSEE JED (Radio)
Fox Syndicate? (Wm. C. Popper & Co.): nd (1945) (16 pgs.; paper-c; regular size; giveaway)

	GD	VG	FN	VF	VF/NM	NM-
nn	22	44	66	127	176	225

TENNIS (...For Speed, Stamina, Strength, Skill)
Tennis Educational Foundation: 1956 (16 pgs.; soft cover; 10¢)

	GD	VG	FN	VF	VF/NM	NM-
Book 1-Endorsed by Gene Tunney, Ralph Kiner, etc. showing how tennis has helped them	6	12	18	27	33	38

TERRY AND THE PIRATES
Dell Publishing Co.: 1939 - 1953 (By Milton Caniff)

	GD	VG	FN	VF	VF/NM	NM-
Buster Brown Shoes giveaway(1938)-32 pgs.; in color	25	50	75	144	197	250
Canada Dry Premiums-Books #1-3(1953, 36 pgs.; 2x5")-Harvey; #1-Hot Shot Charlie Flies Again; 2-In Forced Landing; 3-Dragon Lady in Distress)	16	32	48	86	118	150
Gambles Giveaway (1938, 16 pgs.)	9	18	27	54	70	85
Gillmore Giveaway (1938, 24 pgs.)	10	20	30	56	73	90
Popped Wheat Giveaway(1938)-Strip reprints in full color; Caniff-a	2	4	6	8	10	12
Shoe Store giveaway (Weatherbird)(1938, 16 pgs., soft-c)(2-diff.)	10	20	30	56	73	90
Sparked Wheat Giveaway(1942, 16 pgs.)-In color	10	20	30	56	73	90

TERRY AND THE PIRATES
Libby's Radio Premium: 1941 (16 pgs.; reg. size)(shipped folded in the mail)

	GD	VG	FN	VF	VF/NM	NM-
"Adventure of the Ruby of Genghis Khan" - Each pg. is a puzzle that must be completed to read the story	400	875	1350	2600	-	-

THAT THE WORLD MAY BELIEVE
Catechetical Guild Giveaway: No date (16 pgs.) (Graymoor Friars distr.)

	GD	VG	FN	VF	VF/NM	NM-
nn	4	8	11	16	19	22

3-D COLOR CLASSICS (Wendy's Kid's Club)
Wendy's Int'l Inc.: 1995 (5 1/2" x 8", comes with 3-D glasses)

The Elephant's Child, Gulliver's Travels, Peter Pan, The Time Machine, 20,000 Leagues Under the Sea: Neal Adams-a in all each.... 3.50

350 YEARS OF AMERICAN DAIRY FOODS
American Dairy Assoc.: 1957 (5x7", 16 pgs.)

	GD	VG	FN	VF	VF/NM	NM-
nn-History of milk	3	6	8	12	14	16

THUMPER (Disney)
Grosset & Dunlap: 1942 (50¢, 32pgs., hardcover book, 7"x8-1/2" w/dust jacket)

	GD	VG	FN	VF	VF/NM	NM-
nn-Given away (along with a copy of Bambi) for a $2.00, 2-year subscription to WDC&S in 1942. (Xmas offer). Book only	17	34	51	98	134	170
Dust jacket only	9	18	27	54	70	85

TILLY AND TED-TINKERTOTLAND
W. T. Grant Co.: 1945 (Giveaway, 20 pgs.)

	GD	VG	FN	VF	VF/NM	NM-
nn-Christmas comic	7	14	21	36	45	53

TIM (Formerly Superman-Tim; becomes Gene Autry-Tim)
Tim Stores: June, 1950 - Oct, 1950 (B&W, half-size)

	GD	VG	FN	VF	VF/NM	NM-
4 issues; 6/50, 9/50, 10/50 known	17	34	51	98	134	170

TIM AND SALLY'S ADVENTURES AT MARINELAND
Marineland Restaurant & Bar, Marineland, CA: 1957 (5x7", 16 pgs., soft-c)

	GD	VG	FN	VF	VF/NM	NM-
nn-copyright Oceanarium, Inc.	2	4	6	8	10	12

TIME MACHINE, THE
DC Comics: 2002 (10 pgs.)

nn-Promotes the 2002 DreamWorks movie 5.00

TIME OF DECISION
Harvey Publications Inc.: (16 pgs., paper cover)

	GD	VG	FN	VF	VF/NM	NM-
nn-ROTC recruitment	4	7	10	14	17	20

TIM IN SPACE (Formerly Gene Autry Tim; becomes Tim Tomorrow)
Tim Stores: 1950 (1/2 size giveaway) (B&W)

	GD	VG	FN	VF	VF/NM	NM-
nn	12	24	36	71	96	120

TIM TOMORROW (Formerly Tim In Space)
Tim Stores: 8/51, 9/51, 10/51, Christmas, 1951 (5x7-3/4")

	GD	VG	FN	VF	VF/NM	NM-
nn-Prof. Fumble & Captain Kit Comet in all	12	24	36	71	96	120

TITANS BEAT (Teen Titans)
DC Comics: Aug, 1996 (16 pgs., paper-c)

1-Intro./preview new Teen Titans members; Pérez-a 3.00

TOMB RAIDER: THE SERIES (Also see Witchblade/Tomb Raider)
Image Comics (Top Cow Prod.): May, 2002

Free Comic Book Day giveaway-Reprints #1 with "Free Comic Book Day" banner on-c 2.25

TOM MIX (...Commandos Comics #10-12)
Ralston-Purina Co.: Sept, 1940 - No. 12, Nov, 1942 (36 pgs.); 1983 (one-shot)
Given away for two Ralston box-tops; 1983 came in cereal box

	GD	VG	FN	VF	VF/NM	NM-
1-Origin (life) Tom Mix; Fred Meagher-a	350	1050	1750	2500	3250	4000
2	106	213	319	650	875	1100
3-9	66	132	197	400	550	700
10-12: 10-Origin Tom Mix Commando Unit; Speed O'Dare begins; Japanese sub-c. 12-Sci/fi-c	55	110	165	325	475	625
1983- "Taking of Grizzly Grebb", Toth-a; 16 pg. miniature	2	4	6	10	12	15

TOM SAWYER COMICS
Giveaway: 1951? (Paper cover)

	GD	VG	FN	VF	VF/NM	NM-
nn-Contains a coverless Hopalong Cassidy from 1951; other combinations known	3	6	9	16	20	25

TOPPS COMICS PRESENTS
Topps Comics: No. 0, 1993 (Giveaway, B&W, 36 pgs.)

0-Dracula vs. Zorro, Teenagents, Silver Star, & Bill the Galactic Hero 2.50

TOWN THAT FORGOT SANTA, THE
W. T. Grant Co.: 1961 (Giveaway, 24 pgs.)

	GD	VG	FN	VF	VF/NM	NM-
nn	3	6	9	18	23	28

TOY LAND FUNNIES (See Funnies On Parade)
Eastern Color Printing Co.: 1934 (32 pgs., Hecht Co. store giveaway)

nn-Reprints Buck Rogers Sunday pages #199-201 from Famous Funnies #5. A rare variation of Funnies On Parade; same format, similar contents, same cover except for large Santa placed in center (value will be based on sale)

TOY WORLD FUNNIES (See Funnies On Parade)
Eastern Color Printing Co.: 1933 (36 pgs., slick cover, Golden Eagle and Wanamaker giveaway)

nn-Contains contents from Funnies On Parade/Century Of Comics. A rare variation of Funnies On Parade; same format, similar contents, same cover except for large Santa placed in center (value will be based on sale)

TRANSFORMERS ARMADA
Dreamwave Productions: May, 2003

Free Comic Book Day Edition 2.25

TRAPPED
Harvey Publications (Columbia Univ. Press): 1951 (Giveaway, soft-c, 16 pgs)

	GD	VG	FN	VF	VF/NM	NM-
nn-Drug education comic (30,000 printed?) distributed to schools.; mentioned in **SOTI**, pgs. 256,350	2	4	6	8	10	12

Ultimate X-Men #1 Free Comic Book Day Ed. © MAR

Walt Disney's Donald Duck Adventures Free Comic Book Day Ed. © WDC

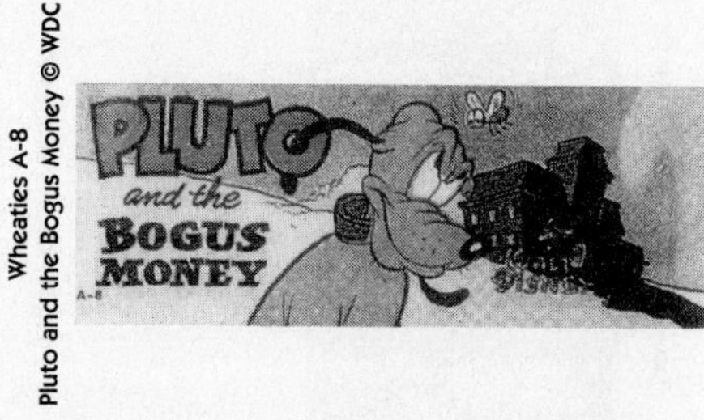

Wheaties A-8 Pluto and the Bogus Money © WDC

	GD 2.0	VG 4.0	FN 6.0	VF 8.0	VF/NM 9.0	NM- 9.2

NOTE: *Many copies surfaced in 1979 causing a setback in price; beware of trimmed edges, because many copies have a brittle edge.*

TRIP TO OUTER SPACE WITH SANTA
Sales Promotions, Inc/Peoria Dry Goods: 1950s (paper-c)

nn-Comics, games & puzzles 5 10 15 22 26 30

TRIP WITH SANTA ON CHRISTMAS EVE, A
Rockford Dry Goods Co.: No date (Early 1950s) (Giveaway, 16 pgs., paper-c)

nn 5 10 15 22 26 30

TRUTH BEHIND THE TRIAL OF CARDINAL MINDSZENTY, THE (See Cardinal Mindszenty)

24 PAGES OF COMICS (No title) (Also see Pure Oil Comics, Salerno Carnival of Comics, & Vicks Comics)
Giveaway by various outlets including Sears: Late 1930s

nn-Contains strip reprints-Buck Rogers, Napoleon, Sky Roads, War on Crime 50 100 150 250 315 380

TWISTED METAL (Video game)
DC Comics: 1996

nn 3.00

TWO FACES OF COMMUNISM (Also see Double Talk)
Christian Anti-Communism Crusade, Houston, Texas: 1961 (Giveaway, paper-c, 36 pgs.)

nn 13 26 39 76 103 130

2001, A SPACE ODYSSEY (Movie)
Marvel Comics Group

Howard Johnson giveaway (1968, 8pp); 6 pg. movie adaptation, 2 pg. games, puzzles; McWilliams-a 2 4 6 8 10 12

ULTIMATE SPIDER-MAN
Marvel Comics: May, 2002

Free Comic Book Day giveaway - reprints #1 with "Free Comic Book Day" banner on-c 2.25
1-Kay Bee Toys variant edition 2 4 6 10 12 15

ULTIMATE X-MEN
Marvel Comics: July, 2003

1-Free Comic Book Day Edition - reprints #1 with "Free Comic Book Day" banner on-c 2.25

UNCLE SAM'S CHRISTMAS STORY
Promotional Publ. Co.: 1958 (Giveaway)

nn-Reprints 1956 Christmas USA 2 4 6 10 13 16

UNKEPT PROMISE
Legion of Truth: 1949 (Giveaway, 24 pgs.)

nn-Anti-alcohol 9 18 27 51 65 78

UNTOLD LEGEND OF THE BATMAN, THE
DC Comics: 1989 (28 pgs., 6X9", limited series of cereal premiums)

1-1st & 2nd printings known; Byrne-a 1 2 3 5 6 8
2,3: 1st & 2nd printings known 6.00

UNTOUCHABLES, THE (TV)
Leaf Brands, Inc.

Topps Bubblegum premiums produced by Leaf Brands, Inc.-2-1/2x4-1/2", 8 pgs. (3 diff. issues) "The Organization, Jamaica Ginger, The Otto Frick Story (drug), 3000 Suspects, The Antidote, Mexican Stakeout, Little Egypt, Purple Gang, Bugs Moran Story, & Lily Dallas Story" 3 6 9 18 24 30

VICKS COMICS (See Pure Oil Comics, Salerno Carnival of Comics & 24 Pages of Comics)
Eastern Color Printing Co. (Vicks Chemical Co.): nd (circa 1938) (Giveaway, 68 pgs. in color)

nn-Famous Funnies-r (before #40); contains 5 pgs. Buck Rogers (4 pgs. from F.F. #15, & 1 pg. from #16) Joe Palooka, Napoleon, etc. app. 69 138 206 420 585 750
nn-16 loose, untrimmed page giveaway; paper-c; r/Famous Funnies #14; Buck Rogers, Joe Palooka app. Has either "Vicks Comics" printed on cover or only a local store name as the logo. 26 53 79 130 185 240

WALT DISNEY'S COMICS & STORIES
K.K. Publications: 1942-1963 known (7-1/3"x10-1/4", 4 pgs. in color, slick paper) (folded horizontally once or twice as mailers) (Xmas subscription offer)

1942 mailer-r/Kelly cover to WDC&S 25; 2-year subscription + two Grosset & Dunlap hardcover books (32-pages each), of Bambi and of Thumper, offered for $2.00; came in an illustrated C&S envelope with an enclosed postage paid envelope
(Rare) Mailer only 25 50 75 156 216 275
with envelopes 32 64 96 200 275 350
1947,1948 mailer 18 36 54 113 157 200
1949 mailer-A rare Barks item: Same WDC&S cover as 1942 mailer, but with art changed so that nephew is handing teacher Donald a comic book rather than an apple, as originally drawn by Kelly. The tiny, 7/8"x1-1/4" cover shown was a rejected cover by Barks that was intended for C&S 110, but was redrawn by Kelly for C&S 111. The original art has been lost and this is its only app. (Rare) 45 90 135 285 393 500
1950 mailer-P.1 r/Kelly cover to Dell Xmas Parade 1 (without title); p.2 r/Kelly cover to C&S 101 (w/o title), but with the art altered to show Donald reading C&S 122 (by Kelly); hardcover book, "Donald Duck in Bringing Up the Boys" given with a $1.00 one-year subscription; P.4 r/full Kelly Xmas cover to C&S 99 (Rare) 18 36 54 113 157 200
1952 mailer-P1 r/cover WDC&S #88 13 26 39 81 111 140
1953 mailer-P.1 r/cover Dell Xmas Parade 4 (w/o title); insides offer "Donald Duck Full Speed Ahead," a 28-page, color, 5-5/8"x6-5/8" book, not of the Story Hour series; P.4 r/full Barks C&S 148 cover (Rare) 13 26 39 81 111 140
1963 mailer-Pgs. 1,2 & 4 r/GK Xmas art; P.3 r/a 1963 C&S cover (Scarce) 9 18 27 56 76 95

NOTE: *It is assumed a different mailer was printed each Xmas for at least twenty years.*

WALT DISNEY'S COMICS & STORIES
Walt Disney Productions: 1943 (36 pgs.) (Dept. store Xmas giveaway)

nn-X-Mas-c with Donald & the Boys; Donald Duck by Jack Hannah; Thumper by Ken Hultgren 51 102 153 306 453 600

WALT DISNEY'S DONALD DUCK ADVENTURES
Gemstone Publishing: May, 2003 (giveaway promoting 2003 return of Disney Comics)

...Free Comic Book Day Edition - cover logo on red background; reprints "Maharajah Donald" & "The Peaceful Hills" from March of Comics #4; Barks-s/a; Kelly original-c on back-c 2.25
...San Diego Comic-Con 2003 Edition - cover logo on gold background 2.25
...ANA World's Fair of Money Baltimore Edition - cover logo on green background 2.25
...WizardWorld Chicago 2003 Edition - cover logo on blue background 2.25

WATCH OUT FOR BIG TALK
Giveaway: 1950

nn-Dan Barry-a; about crooked politicians 7 14 21 35 43 50

WAY OF THE RAT
CrossGeneration Comics: Jun, 2003

Free Comic Book Day Special; reprints #1 w/features, interviews, CrossGen info 2.25

WEATHER-BIRD (See Comics From..., Dick Tracy, Free Comics to You..., Super Circus & Terry and the Pirates)
International Shoe Co./Western Printing Co.: 1958 - No. 16, July, 1962 (Shoe store giveaway)

1 4 8 12 27 36 45
2-16 2 4 6 12 16 20

NOTE: *The numbers are located in the lower bottom panel, pg. 1. All feature a character called Weather-Bird.*

WEATHER BIRD COMICS (See Comics From Weather Bird)
Weather Bird Shoes: 1957 (Giveaway)

nn-Contains a comic bound with new cover. Several combinations possible; contents determine price (40 - 60 percent of contents).

WEEKLY COMIC MAGAZINE
Fox Publications: May 12, 1940 (16 pgs.) (Others exist w/o super-heroes)

(1st Version)-8 pg. Blue Beetle story, 7 pg. Patty O'Day story; two copies known to exist. Estimated value... $625.00
(2nd Version)-7 two-pg. adventures of Blue Beetle, Patty O'Day, Yarko, Dr. Fung, Green Mask, Spark Stevens, & Rex Dexter; one copy known to exist. Estimated value... $525.00
(3rd version)-Captain Valor (only one known copy) $315.00

Discovered with business papers, letters and exploitation material promoting **Weekly Comic Magazine** for use by newspapers in the same manner of **The Spirit** weeklies. Interesting note: these are dated three weeks before the first Spirit comic. Letters indicate that samples may have been sent to a few newspapers. These sections were actually 15-1/2x22" pages which will fold down to an approximate 8x10" comic booklet. Other various comic sections were found with the above, but were more like the Sunday comic sections in format.

WHAT DO YOU KNOW ABOUT THIS COMICS SEAL OF APPROVAL?
No publisher listed (DC Comics Giveaway): nd (1955) (4 pgs., slick paper-c)

nn-(Rare) 68 137 205 426 600 775

WHAT'S BEHIND THESE HEADLINES
William C. Popper Co.: 1948 (16 pgs.)

nn-Comic insert "The Plot to Steal the World" 6 12 18 32 39 45

WHAT'S IN IT FOR YOU?
Harvey Publications Inc.: (16 pgs., paper cover)

nn-National Guard recruitment 4 7 10 14 17 20

WHEATIES (Premiums)
Walt Disney Productions: 1950 & 1951 (32 titles, pocket-size, 32 pgs.)

Mailing Envelope (no art on front)(Designates sets A,B,C or D on front) 8 16 24 46 58 70

(Set A-1 to A-8, 1950)

A-1-Mickey Mouse & the Disappearing Island, A-5-Mickey Mouse, Roving Reporter each... 7 14 21 35 43 50
A-2-Grandma Duck, Homespun Detective, A-6-Li'l Bad Wolf, Forest Ranger, A-7-Goofy, Tightrope Acrobat, A-8-Pluto & the Bogus Money

Wisco/Klarer Comic Book - Jim Solar Conquers Outer Space © VITL

Wisco/Klarer Comic Book - Return of the Black Phantom © VITL

	GD 2.0	VG 4.0	FN 6.0	VF 8.0	VF/NM 9.0	NM- 9.2
each...	6	12	18	31	38	45
A-3-Donald Duck & the Haunted Jewels, A-4-Donald Duck & the Giant Ape each...	9	18	27	52	66	80
(Set B-1 to B-8, 1950)						
B-1-Mickey Mouse & the Pharoah's Curse, B-4-Mickey Mouse & the Mystery Sea Monster each...	7	14	21	37	46	55
B-2-Pluto, Canine Cowpoke, B-5-Li'l Bad Wolf in the Hollow Tree Hideout, B-7-Goofy & the Gangsters each...	6	12	18	31	38	45
B-3-Donald Duck & the Buccaneers, B-6-Donald Duck,Trail Blazer, B-8 Donald Duck, Klondike Kid each...	9	18	27	52	66	80
(Set C-1 to C-8, 1951)						
C-1-Donald Duck & the Inca Idol, C-5-Donald Duck in the Lost Lakes, C-8-Donald Duck Deep-Sea Diver each...	9	18	27	52	66	80
C-2-Mickey Mouse & the Magic Mountain, C-6-Mickey Mouse & the Stagecoach Bandits each...	7	14	21	37	46	55
C-3-Li'l Bad Wolf, Fire Fighter, C-4-Gus & Jaq Save the Ship, C-7-Goofy, Big Game Hunter each...	6	12	18	31	38	45
(Set D-1 to D-8, 1951)						
D-1-Donald Duck in Indian Country, D-5-Donald Duck, Mighty Mystic each...	9	18	27	52	66	80
D-2-Mickey Mouse and the Abandoned Mine, D-6-Mickey Mouse & the Medicine Man each...	7	14	21	37	46	55
D-3-Pluto & the Mysterious Package, D-4-Bre'r Rabbit's Sunken Treasure, D-7-Li'l Bad Wolf and the Secret of the Woods, D-8-Minnie Mouse, Girl Explorer each...	6	12	18	31	38	45

NOTE: *Some copies lack the Wheaties ad.*

WHIZ COMICS (Formerly Flash Comics & Thrill Comics #1)
Fawcett Publications

	GD	VG	FN	VF	VF/NM	NM-
Wheaties Giveaway(1946, Miniature, 6-1/2x8-1/4", 32 pgs.); all copies were taped at each corner to a box of Wheaties and are never found in very fine or mint condition; "Capt. Marvel & the Water Thieves", plus Golden Arrow, Ibis, Crime Smasher stories	150	375	600	–	–	–

WILD KINGDOM (TV) (Mutual of Omaha's...)
Western Printing Co.: 1965, 1966 (Giveaway, regular size, slick-c, 16 pgs.)

	GD	VG	FN	VF	VF/NM	NM-
nn-Front & back-c are different on 1966 edition	2	4	6	10	12	15

WISCO/KLARER COMIC BOOK (Miniature)
Marvel Comics/Vital Publ./Fawcett Publ.: 1948 - 1964 (3-1/2x6-3/4", 24 pgs.)

Given away by Wisco "99" Service Stations, Carnation Malted Milk, Klarer Health Wieners, Fleers Dubble Bubble Gum, Rodeo All-Meat Wieners, Perfect Potato Chips, & others; see ad in Tom Mix #21

	GD	VG	FN	VF	VF/NM	NM-
Blackstone & the Gold Medal Mystery (1948)	8	16	24	46	58	70
Blackstone "Solves the Sealed Vault Mystery" (1950)	8	16	24	46	58	70
Blaze Carson in "The Sheriff Shoots It Out" (1950)	8	16	24	46	58	70
Captain Marvel & Billy's Big Game (r/Capt. Marvel Adv. #76)	28	56	84	161	228	295
(Prices vary widely on this book)						
China Boy in "A Trip to the Zoo" #10 (1948)	6	12	18	27	33	38
Indoors-Outdoors Game Book	4	8	11	16	19	22
Jim Solar Space Sheriff in "Battle for Mars", "Between Two Worlds", "Conquers Outer Space", "The Creatures on the Comet", "Defeats the Moon Missile Men", "Encounter Creatures on Comet", "Meet the Jupiter Jumpers", "Meets the Man From Mars", "On Traffic Duty", "Outlaws of the Spaceways", "Pirates of the Planet X", "Protects Space Lanes", "Raiders From the Sun", "Ring Around Saturn", "Robots of Rhea", "The Sky Ruby", "Spacetts of the Sky", "Spidermen of Venus", "Trouble on Mercury"	8	16	24	40	50	60
Johnny Starboard & the Underseas Pirates (1948)	5	10	15	24	30	35
Kid Colt in "He Lived by His Guns" (1950)	9	18	27	52	66	80
Little Aspirin as "Crook Catcher" #2 (1950)	4	8	12	18	22	25
Little Aspirin in "Naughty But Nice" #6 (1950)	4	8	12	18	22	25
Return of the Black Phantom (not M.E. character)(Roy Dare)(1948)	7	14	21	35	43	50
Secrets of Magic	5	10	14	20	24	28
Slim Morgan "Brings Justice to Mesa City" #3	5	10	14	20	24	28
Super Rabbit(1950)-Cuts Red Tape, Stops Crime Wave!	10	20	30	58	77	95
Tex Farnum, Frontiersman (1948)	5	10	15	23	28	32
Tex Taylor in "Draw or Die, Cowpoke!" (1950)	7	14	21	37	46	55
Tex Taylor in "An Exciting Adventure at the Gold Mine" (1950)	7	14	21	35	43	50
Wacky Quacky in "All-Aboard"	4	7	9	14	16	18
When School Is Out	4	7	9	14	16	18
Willie in a "Comic-Comic Book Fall" #1	4	8	11	16	19	22
Wonder Duck "An Adventure at the Rodeo of the Fearless Quacker!" (1950)	9	18	27	52	66	80
Rare uncut version of three; includes Capt. Marvel, Tex Farnum, Black Phantom Estimated value...						420.00
Rare uncut version of three; includes China Boy, Blackstone, Johnny Starboard & the Underseas Pirates Estimated value...						135.00

WOLVERINE
Marvel Comics

	GD	VG	FN	VF	VF/NM	NM-
145-(1999 Nabisco mail-in offer) Sienkiewicz-c	10	20	30	70	98	125
...Son of Canada (4/01, ed. of 65,000) Spider-Man & The Hulk app.; Lim-a						3.00

WOMAN OF THE PROMISE, THE
Catechetical Guild: 1950 (General Distr.) (Paper cover, 32 pgs.)

	GD	VG	FN	VF	VF/NM	NM-
nn	5	10	15	25	31	36

WONDERFUL WORLD OF DUCKS (See Golden Picture Story Book)
Colgate Palmolive Co.: 1975

	GD	VG	FN	VF	VF/NM	NM-
1-Mostly-r	1	2	3	5	6	8

WONDER WOMAN
DC Comics: 1977

	GD	VG	FN	VF	VF/NM	NM-
Pizza Hut Giveaways (12/77)-Reprints #60,62	2	4	6	8	10	12

WONDER WORKER OF PERU
Catechetical Guild: No date (5x7", 16 pgs., B&W, giveaway)

	GD	VG	FN	VF	VF/NM	NM-
nn	5	10	15	23	28	32

WOODY WOODPECKER
Dell Publishing Co.

	GD	VG	FN	VF	VF/NM	NM-
Clover Stamp-Newspaper Boy Contest('56)-9 pg. story-(Giveaway)	6	12	18	33	41	48
In Chevrolet Wonderland(1954-Giveaway)(Western Publ.)-20 pgs., full story line; Chilly Willy app.	20	40	60	112	156	200
...Meets Scotty MacTape(1953-Scotch Tape giveaway)-16 pgs., full size	20	40	60	112	156	200

WOOLWORTH'S CHRISTMAS STORY BOOK
Promotional Publ. Co.(Western Printing Co.): 1952 - 1954 (16 pgs., paper-c) (See Jolly Christmas Book)

	GD	VG	FN	VF	VF/NM	NM-
nn	6	12	18	32	39	46

NOTE: *1952 issue-Marv Levy c/a.*

WOOLWORTH'S HAPPY TIME CHRISTMAS BOOK
F. W. Woolworth Co. (Western Printing Co.): 1952 (Christmas giveaway)

	GD	VG	FN	VF	VF/NM	NM-
nn-36 pgs.	6	12	18	29	36	42

WORLD'S FINEST COMICS
National Periodical Publ./DC Comics

	GD	VG	FN	VF	VF/NM	NM-
Giveaway (c. 1944-45, 8 pgs., in color, paper-c)-Johnny Everyman-r/World's Finest	25	50	75	130	185	240
Giveaway (c. 1949, 8 pgs., in color, paper-c)- "Make Way For Youth" r/World's Finest; based on film of same name	22	44	66	116	163	210
#176, #179- Best Western reprint edition (1997)						3.00

WORLD'S GREATEST SUPER HEROES
DC Comics (Nutra Comics) (Child Vitamins, Inc.): 1977 (Giveaway, 3-3/4x3-3/4", 24 pgs.)

	GD	VG	FN	VF	VF/NM	NM-
nn-Batman & Robin app.; health tips	2	4	6	9	11	14

XMAS FUNNIES
Kinney Shoes: No date (Giveaway, paper cover, 36 pgs.?)

	GD	VG	FN	VF	VF/NM	NM-
Contains 1933 color strip-r; Mutt & Jeff, etc.	50	125	200	260	310	360

X-MEN THE MOVIE
Marvel Comics/Toys R' Us: 2000

	GD	VG	FN	VF	VF/NM	NM-
Special Movie Prequel Edition						5.00

YALTA TO KOREA (Also see Korea My Home)
M. Phillip Corp. (Republican National Committee): 1952 (Giveaway, paper-c)

	GD	VG	FN	VF	VF/NM	NM-
nn-(8 pgs.)-Anti-communist propaganda book	20	40	60	112	156	200

YOGI BEAR (TV)
Dell Publishing Co.

	GD	VG	FN	VF	VF/NM	NM-
Giveaway ('84, '86)-City of Los Angeles, "Creative First Aid" & "Earthquake Preparedness for Children"						6.00

YOUR TRIP TO NEWSPAPERLAND
Philadelphia Evening Bulletin (Printed by Harvey Press): June, 1955 (14x11-1/2", 12 pgs.)

	GD	VG	FN	VF	VF/NM	NM-
nn-Joe Palooka takes kids on newspaper tour	5	10	15	24	30	35

YOUR VOTE IS VITAL!
Harvey Publications Inc.: 1952 (5" x 7", 16 pgs., paper cover)

	GD	VG	FN	VF	VF/NM	NM-
nn-The importance of voting	4	8	12	18	22	25

The Victorian Age

The American Comic Book: 1646-1890s

ORIGINS OF AMERICAN COMIC STRIPS BEFORE THE YELLOW KID

by Robert L. Beerbohm & Richard D. Olson, PhD ©2004

With special thanks to Richard Samuel West and Leonardo De Sá

(This article was originally created by Doug Wheeler, Robert Beerbohm and Richard D. Olson, PhD for OCBPG #32 2002 and continues to be revised annually by the current authors.)

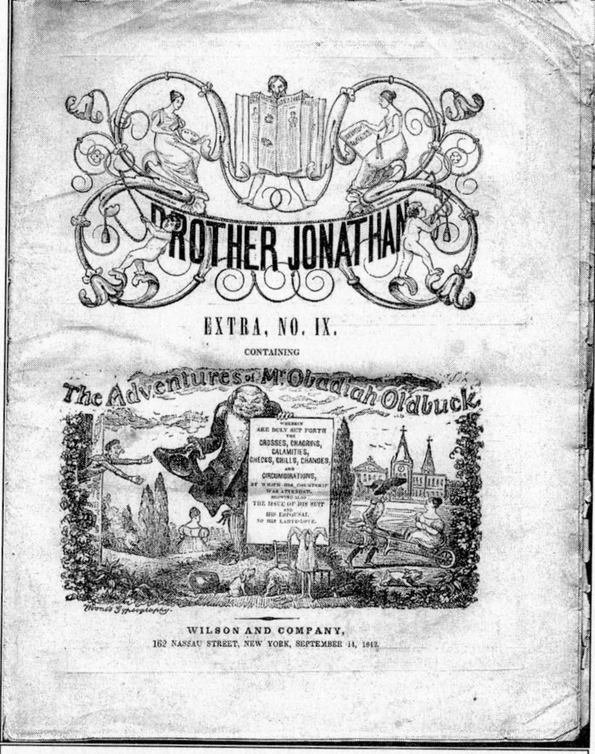

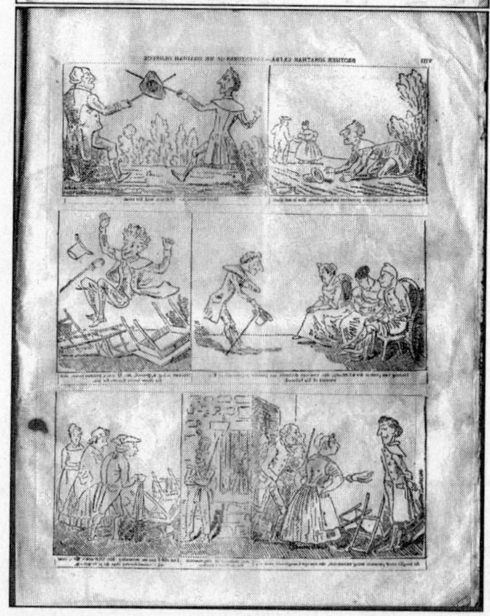

***ABOVE**: Cover to the subscriber version of the earliest known sequential comic book published in America,* ***The Adventures of Mr. Obadiah Oldbuck**, by Swiss comics creator, Rodolphe Töpffer, Sept. 1842, Wilson & Co. New York.*

***RIGHT**: Pages 8 and 28 from this 40-page 1842 graphic novel which launched the comic book business in America....the history books are being rewritten right here and once again we have more new information for you to learn of this medium which started over 160 years ago. We welcome any and all corrections and additions.*

"The Burning of Mr. John Rogers," *1646 is the earliest-known North American cartoon.*

The pamphlet ***Plain Truth*** *1747 contains Ben Franklin's earliest-known cartoon titled "Heaven Helps Only Those Who Help Themselves" depicting Hercules in the upper right corner.*

The Victorian Age section is devoted to comic strips and books published during the years the United States expanded across the North American continent, fought a Civil War, shifted from an agrarian to an industrial society, "welcomed" waves of immigrants, and struggled over race, class, religion, temperance, and suffrage - and all of it depicted and satirized by generations of mostly now long-forgotten cartoonists. The social attitudes, beliefs, and conventions of 19th century America, the good as well as the bad, are to be found in abundance. We can imagine the first question to pop into most readers' minds will be, "What, beyond the happenstance of publication date, are Victorian Age comics?"

The aspect we believe most distinguishes Victorian comics from those of later eras was the extremely rare use of word balloons within sequential (multi-picture) comic stories. When word balloons were used, it was nearly always within single-panel cartoons. On the occasions when they appeared inside a strip, with very few exceptions, the ballooned dialogue was non-essential to understanding the story. Nineteenth Century comics tended to place both narration and dialogue beneath comic panels rather than within the panel's borders. These comics are to the word balloon-strewn post-**Yellow Kid** comics of the 20th Century as silent movies are to the later "talkies." Just as sound changed how stories were structured on film, so too did comics change when the words were moved from beneath panels to inside them, and dialogue rather than narration was made to forward a story in conjunction with the pictures.

The Victorian Age of comic books began on different dates in different nations, depending on when the first publication

Following a wave of anti-Catholic violence, the Protestant D.C. Johnston drew a series of cartoons decrying Protestant fanaticism in his self-published ***Scraps*** *#6, 1835, and also converted to Catholicism himself. This pair of* ***Scraps*** *#6 cartoons contrasts nuns caring for Protestant cholera victims against a mob burning a Catholic church in Charlestown, Mass. Note use of word balloons, common to many pre-Civil War American cartoons.*

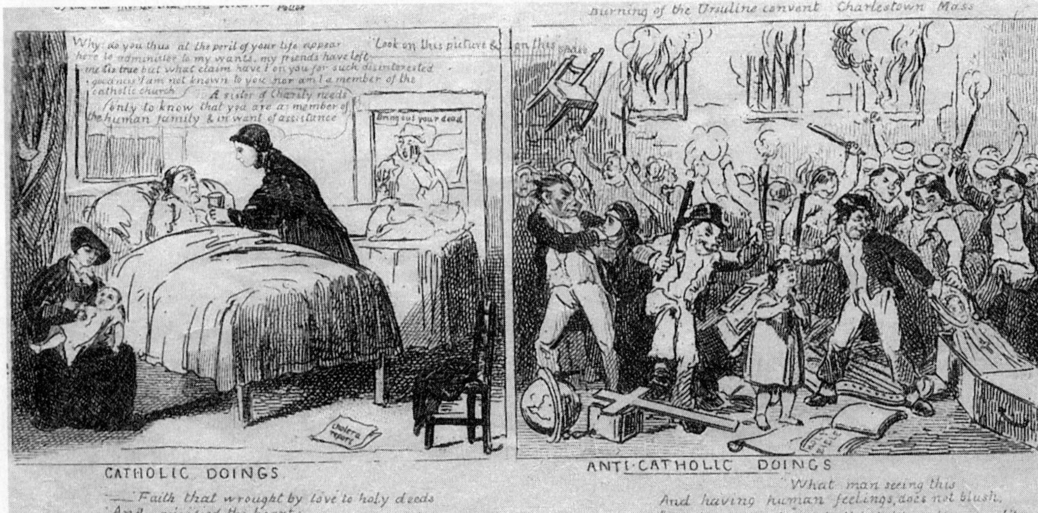

***"A Warm Place - Hell"**, one of two images known to be drawn and engraved by Paul Revere, 1768.*

of a sequential comic book on their soil is known to have occurred. For the U.S.A. this happened when the American humor periodical **Brother Jonathan** printed the 40-page, 195-panel graphic novel **The Adventures of Mr. Obadiah Oldbuck** as a special extra dated September 14, 1842. Almost six decades later, America's Victorian comics came to their end, replaced by the onslaught of Platinum Age books reprinting newspaper strips from Bennett, Hearst & Pulitzer Sunday comic sections, among many others.

There is a lot of overlap between Victorian Era and Platinum Age comic books and strips. There has been a long slow-motion evolution of the comic strip. Those publications which continued from one century into the next, such as **Puck**, **Judge**, and **Life**, have their pre-1900 issues listed within the Victorian Age section, while their post-1899 issues can be found inside the Platinum Age. Some non-sequential (i.e., single panel) American comic items existing prior to 1842 are also listed herein, going back at present to 1795. These belong to what could tentatively be called the **Age of Caricature** (1770s through 1830s), during which Gillray, Rowlandson, Cruikshank, Heath, and Seymour were England's top cartoonists.

The earliest known cartoon-like woodcut printed on paper in North America was in a Puritan children's book first published in 1646. Titled simply "The Burning of Mr. John Rogers," it showed in flaming graphic detail what happens to those who stray from the flock and have to be burned at the stake. Wertham would have had a field day with that one!

THE ADVENTURES OF MR. OBADIAH OLDBUCK. Wherein are duly set forth the Crosses, Chagrins, Calamities, Checks, Chills, Changes, and Circumgyrations, by which his Courtship was attended. Showing also the Issue of his Suit, and his Espousal to his Lady-Love. New York, Wilson & Company. (Jonathan Press.)

[illegible] has ever encountered such a variety of adventures as fell to [illegible] Mr. Oldbuck, and if the author has not drawn a little on his fancy for his facts in this relation, the eighth wonder of the world is at last revealed in this surprising history. The reader has undoubtedly heard graphic narrations spoken of, and will be compelled to acknowledge that this work comes entirely under that description, for a more exclusively as well as eloquently graphic production it was never any body's lot to see. In a word it is not a "story and picters to match" as Jack Downing says, but a story told entirely with the graver; being a series of over two hundred engravings of the most mirthmoving description. Their absurdity and grotesque wit—their depicture of the most ridiculous impossibilities challenge comparison.

The wildest fancy of the grotesque school could not conceive a series of adventures more laughably absurd than are here presented; and we can imagine no publication better devised to amuse children of all growths than Obadiah Oldbuck. Nor are the designs wanting in excellent keeping, and a whimsical regard for the rules of drawing. The canons are never departed from arbitrarily, or without an object; and we plead guilty to having lost more than one hour in mirth over this clever and bizarre performance. The price, like the other Jonathan extras, is only one shilling. Copies in any quantity are ready to answer orders—ten copies for one dollar.

***Brother Jonathan**, Sept 17, 1842, page 90 first known advertisement selling **The Adventures of Obadiah Oldbuck**, America's first comic book. Priced at one shilling each or ten for a dollar, the distribution systems were still being invented.*

Cartoon broadsheets and other single panel images, often using word balloons, appeared from Pre-Revolution days through the end of the 19th Century. The earliest known cartoon published by someone calling himself an "American" is generally credited as the Benjamin Franklin designed "Heaven Helps Only Those Who Help Themselves," which first appeared in his periodical **Plain Truth** in 1747.

The most popularly remembered 18th-Century American cartoons are likely Franklin's "Join or Die" in 1754, representing the American Colonies as severed snake parts, and "The Bloody Massacre Perpetrated in King Street" - Paul Revere's 1770 depiction of the Boston Massacre, whose

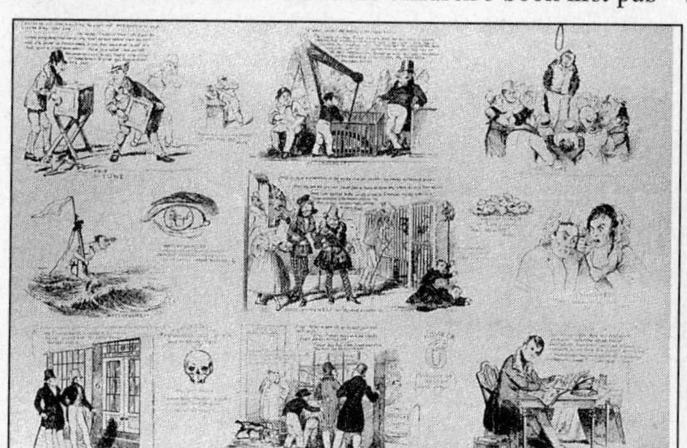

*Another page of D.C. Johnston's **Scraps**, 1830s.*

***Finn's Comic Sketch Book**, 1831 sample page.*

design he likely pirated from the earlier Henry Pelham broadsheet cartoon "The Fruits of Arbitrary Power."

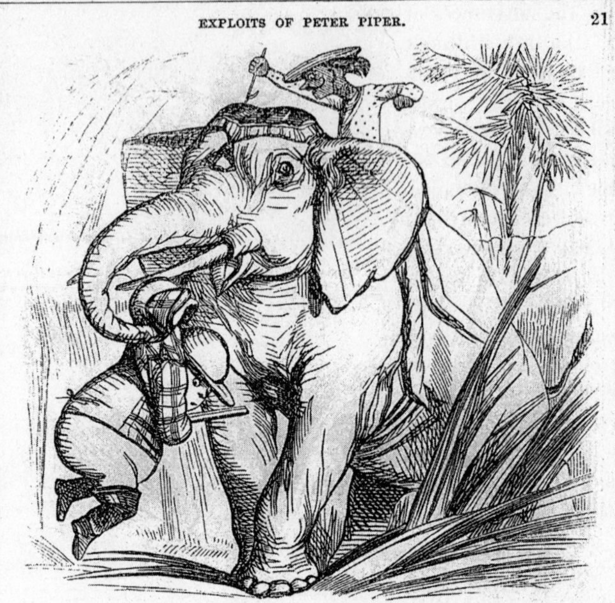

But is fortunately rescued from immediate peril by the faithful elephant.

LIST of BOOKS for sale at the Brother Jonathan Office.

THE ADVENTURES OF OBADIAH OLDBUCK.—A Book of Pictures, which set forth, in a laughable manner, the Curious, Comical, Cunning, Extraordinary, Extravagant, Funny, Farcical, Lively, Pathetic, Perplexing, Quizzical, and Wonderful Incidents which attended the Courtship and Marriage of that unfortunate and perplexed old gentleman—showing likewise how he attempted to commit suicide on five different occasions, and each time was saved by "invidious fate." The story of Mr. Oldbuck's Love, as set forth by these pictures, is one of the most admirable satires and caricatures of a love-sick old bachelor that can be imagined. It is full of genuine, original, sparkling wit—nothing old or borrowed. It will amuse the most refined person, and cannot fail to please everybody. This book comprises 80 pages of pictures, well printed on fine hot-pressed paper. It is one of the cheapest pictorial works ever published. We send it free of postage for 25 cents per copy.

A DAY'S SPORT—Or, Hunting Adventures of S. Winks Wattles, a shopkeeper, Thomas Titt. Esq., a "lega' gent.," and Major Nicholas Noggin, a jolly good fellow generally. This story is told by Pictures, and is really a witty and amusing book—the drawings by Henry L. Stevens of Philadelphia. It will make you laugh out loud to look over this book. It is handsomely printed, and put up in an illustrated cover, suitable for the centre table. We send it free of postage for 12½ cents per copy.

THE SEA-WITCH—A Story of Life and Adventure on board an African Slaver, and on the Coast. One of the best novels we have issued in a long time. Sent free of postage for 25 cents.

Send cash for the above books to B. H. Day, 48 Beekman-st., New York.

*B. H. Day's **Brother Jonathan Cheap Book Establishment** 1855 catalog with 32-panel comic strip "Peter Piper in Bengal'" by John Tenniel (later Alice of Wonderland fame) with two comic books for sale on the above page: **Obadiah Oldbuck** by Töpffer and **A Day's Sport** by Henry L. Stevens of Philadelphia, a scarce newly-rediscovered original American comic book.*

In September 1826, John Warner Barber, New Haven, Ct. (1798-1885) designed and self-published the broadside **The Drunkard's Progress, Or The Direct Road to Poverty, Wretchedness & Ruin** showing in four stages sequentially "The Morning Dram" which is "The Beginning of Sorrow, " "The Grog Shop" with its "Bad Company," "The Confirmed Drunkard" in a state of "Beastly Intoxication," and the "Concluding Scene" with the family being driven off to the alms house. It is an interesting set of cuts, faintly reminiscent of Hogarth. Barber began his cartooning career in 1819, age 21, engraving on wood. He worked on a multitude of varied art chores for books. As late as 1870 he was issuing **Barber's Temperance Tracts** which built upon his 1826 original plus four panels showing forward positive motion in living without alcohol.

The earliest-known American whose fame was based solely on his cartoons was David Claypool Johnston (1798-1865). Johnston provided illustrations for various almanacs, books, and periodicals, including the masthead for **Brother Jonathan**. This same masthead appears on the top half of the cover of the **Brother Jonathan** edition of **Obadiah Oldbuck**. Most notable of Johnston's comics work was his nine-issue series **Scraps**, which he self-published from 1828 to 1849, and his one-shot album **Outlines Illustrative of the Journal of F****** A*** K*******, which parodies passages from the Journal of Frances A. Kemble. Johnston was widely known in his day as "the American Cruikshank." His **Scraps** series was highly influenced by George Cruikshank's series **Scraps and Sketches**, which first appeared in 1827. Each issue of Johnston's **Scraps** consists of four large folio-sized pages, printed on one side, with 9 to 12 single-panel cartoons per page, and each page often organized around a theme.

In 1831 Peabody & Co, 233 Broadway, New York City published a collection by D.C. Johnston's friend, actor Henry J. Finn, titled simply **Finn's Comic Sketch Book**, running 12 pages with upwards of half a dozen single-panel cartoons per page. Peabody was in business from 1831-1843, also publishing **Knickerbocker Magazine.**

Johnston was also involved in the theater, and he began collaborating with Finn in 1825 on various projects, including the 1831 **(American) Comic Annual**, with Finn as editor and Johnston as artist, published by Richardson, Lord and Holbrook, Boston. It has an inscription dated Dec. 26, 1830 on the front end-paper on one of the known copies which has almost 30 full-page copper engravings and woodcuts Johnston designed. Their collaborations ended when Finn died tragically in a steamboat accident on January 13, 1840.

The next step forward in the development of comics in America occurred when the weekly humor periodical **Brother Jonathan** published a parallel "Extra" series which reprinted mainly prose European novels. For example their eighth "extra" was the first American printing of a Charles Dickens novel. Becoming adventurous, the editors chose

Rodolphe Töpffer's graphic novel, **The Adventures of Mr. Obadiah Oldbuck** for **Extra**, No. IX, reformatting it from its original small oblong strip shape to the side-stitched magazine shape in which the earlier Extras were published. This had the inadvertent prophetic effect of making this edition (alone) of **Obadiah Oldbuck** resemble a modern comic book. The arrival of this comic book on the shores of the New World would directly inspire a wave of American imitators, as happened earlier in European nations where Töpffer's comics had appeared. [This first Wilson printing of **Oldbuck** from 1842 was reprinted in same-size limited edition facsimile by the Naples Comicon in 2003.]

A translation by Leonardo De Sá of Töpffer's original draft is at leonardodesa.interdinamica.net/comics/lds/.

According to **The New York Times** (Sept. 3, 1904), the first American comic book was issued as a supplement to **Brother Jonathan** (New York, Sept. 14, 1842). Even so, by the beginning of the 20th century, this comics pioneer was largely forgotten in the New World. It is high time Töpffer received credit long overdue as the person who invented the modern comic strip, laying previously long-held myths to rest.

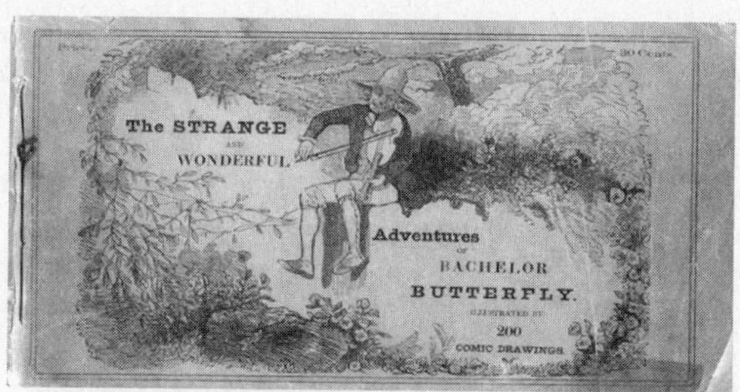

The Strange and Wonderful Adventures of Bachelor Butterfly *by Rodolphe Töpffer (New York, 1846) was Wilson & Company's second comic book, this time out staying with the original European format. Below: sample pages 8, 9, 15 & 16.*

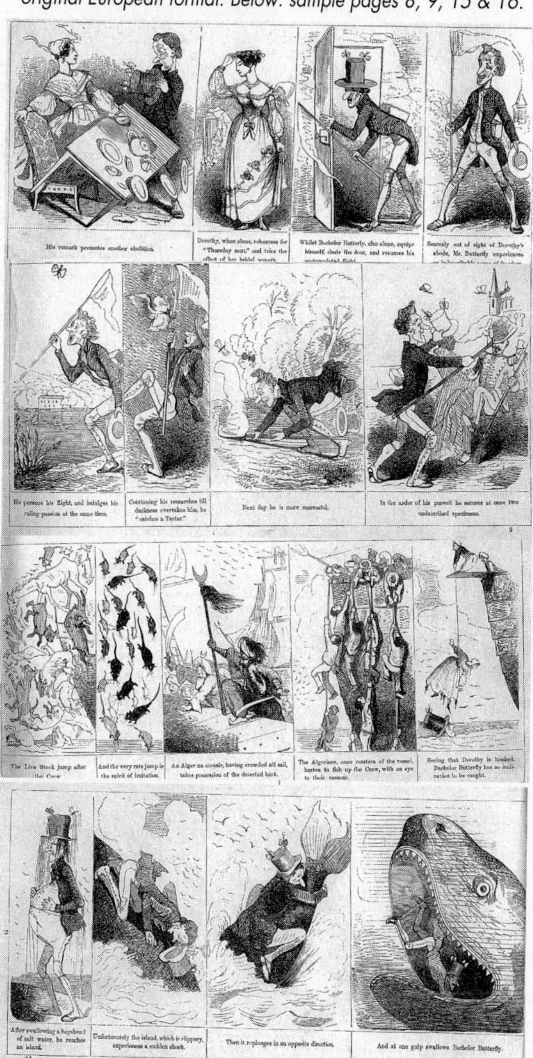

Töpffer (1799-1846) was a playwright, novelist, artist, and teacher from Geneva, Switzerland, who in 1827 had begun producing what he called "picture novels," sharing them with his friends and students. His earliest editions were published by him privately in Geneva via lithography on transfer paper as they use the word "autographie" in their imprints. The earliest printers were J. Freydig, Frutiger (1830s) and Schmidt (1840s). These first sequential comic books, scripted in Töpffer's native French language, found their way to Paris & became an instant hit. According to Gombrich in **Art and Illusion** (1960), "Töpffer recognized that he could rely on the reader to supplement from their own lives what was omitted between the panels. This is crucial in the development of the sequential comic strip."

The demand for his comic books soon outstripped the supply, and pirated editions, redrawn by others, were created by Parisian publisher Aubert to capitalize on this. In a world where international copyright conventions did not exist, this was perfectly legal, if morally questionable. London publisher Tilt & Bogue struck a deal with George Cruikshank, resulting in the 1841 English version of Aubert's piracy of **Les Amours de M. Vieux Bois**.

This English translation was co-financed by George Cruikshank himself, and sported a new cover page by George's brother Robert, based on a montage of Töpffer's scenes. Confirmation came when George Cruikshank's personal copy surfaced in auction recently with the inscription "Copied from a French book by my Brother Robert" above the title page with the same scene. A still-unknown scenario led to America's Wilson and Company reprinting this translation.

Tilt & Bogue followed up their success by translating into English two additional stories of Töpffer's seven published graphic novels: **Beau Ogleby**, circa 1843 (originally **Histoire de M. Jabot**), and **Bachelor Butterfly** two years later (from **Histoire de M. Cryptogame**). David Bogue also published picture-story strip books by John Leighton using the pseudonym Luke Limner. He wrote and drew beautiful looking comic books titled **London Out of Town or The Adventures of the Browns At The Seaside**; **Comic Art-Manufactures**; and **The Ancient Story of the Old Dame and Her Pig** starting in 1847, but none of these seem to have had American editions discovered to date. They follow a definite Töpffer influence. This growing body of comic book production was made easier by the spreading understanding of transfer paper lithography, otherwise the panels would have to be drawn and lettered mirror reverse. Gombrich referred to Töpffer's comic books as "the innocent ancestors of today's manufactured dreams...everywhere in these countless episodes of almost surrealist inconsequence we find a mastery of physiognomic characterization which sets the standard for such influential humorous draftsmen in the 19th century as Wilhelm Busch in Germany."

A Register of The New York City Book Trades 1821-1842 by Sidney F. & Elizabeth Stege Huttner (The Bibliographical Society of America, NYC, 1993) mentions Benjamin H. Day bought into **Brother Jonathan** in this year, becoming at some point some sort of equal partner with owner J. Gregg Wilson of Wilson & Company, who had been publishing since 1839. The **Register** lists them both at the address of 162 Nassau Street, and mentions them both as publishers with the same address as **Brother Jonathan**. Other historical artifacts state he eventually became sole-owner and publisher. Exactly when this happened remains open for debate.

This is the same Benjamin H. Day who in 1833 started the first successful penny newspaper, **The (New York) Sun**, transforming it in four short years into the largest circulation daily in the world, at the time. He sold out his ownership to his brother-in-law in that newspaper during the financial "panic" of 1837, a mistake he regretted his entire life. He re-emerged heavily involved in **Brother Jonathan** definitely by 1840 and as a partner by 1841. **Brother Jonathan** was right next door to Tamany Hall. (See the 2002 movie **Gangs of New York** to visualize the period atmosphere and their customer base.) According to **The Brothers Harper** by Eugene Exmen (Harper & Row, 1965), on page 125, "... **Brother Jonathan**... offered in its weekly edition and also in special supplements very cheap reprints of English novels. In effect, it began a price-cutting war against the older established 'pirates' among the book publishers..." This sounds perfect for Day to sink his teeth into and redeem himself.

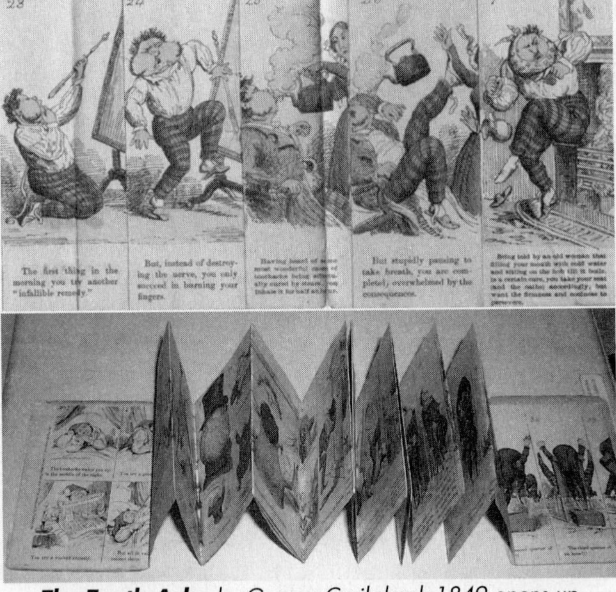

The Tooth-Ache *by George Cruikshank 1849 opens up accordion-like into a single strip 7 feet, 3 inches long!*

With his own words as documented proof, along with the previous reference to them both listed in the New York City directories as working and living at the same address beginning in 1841, Benjamin H. Day and J. Gregg Wilson became the earliest-known comic book publishers in America. They were printers first, then became publishers who joined forces, but the exact relationship between these individuals in still dimly known. What we do know is that Wilson & Company picked up on **Bachelor Butterfly** in the States in 1846. In 1849, Wilson & Company reformatted **Obadiah Oldbuck** back into its original British shape using lithography, dropping a handful of comic panels and altering the text to hide these deletions. And soon thereafter published other comic books for a steadily growing market.

Back in Europe, perhaps inspired by his involvement with Töpffer's **Obadiah Oldbuck**, George Cruikshank soon created several sequential comic books of his own. These too found their way to America. **The Bachelor's Own Book**, published first in Britain in 1844, became the second known U.S. published sequential comic book when reprinted by Burgess, Stringer & Company the following year. Next was Cruikshank's masterpiece **The Bottle**, the Hogarthian-style tale of a man whose addiction to alcohol brings himself and his family to ruin. After debuting in London in 1847, it was reprinted the same year in a British-American co-publication between David Bogue and Americans Wiley and Putnam. Both printings were in huge folio form, available in either black & white or professionally hand-tinted versions. In 1848, the story saw American print again, this time in smaller form, placed at the front of the otherwise prose volume **Temperance Tales; Or, Six Nights with the Washingtonians**. It continued to be reprinted by a variety of publishers into the early 20th Century. **The Bottle** was popular in Revival and Temperance circles, made more so by its use in lectures, where the story was reproduced onto painted glass slides then projected for audiences by a magic lantern. **The Drunkard's Children**, Cruikshank's sequel to **The Bottle**, was issued July 1, 1848 as a British-American-

Cover of 1849's ***Journey to the Gold Diggins By Jeremiah Saddlebags****, the earliest known sequential comic book by American creators, J.A. and D.F. Read Below: a couple sample pages - note similarity to Töpffer's comics especially* ***Bachelor Butterfly****.*

Australian co-publishing venture, but was less successful, and had not nearly as many reprints.

The most clearly sequential, as well as fun, of George Cruikshank's comic books was **The Tooth-Ache,** first issued in London in 1849. It was reprinted in the America later that same year by Philadelphia map maker J.L. Smith. An additional concurrent version was also issued from Boston.

When closed, this booklet appears an unassuming 5-1/4 inches tall by 3-1/4 inches wide. Its striking feature is that the book folds open accordian style, stretching the entire 43-panel story along one single strip of paper, which when fully extended is seven feet, three inches long! **The Tooth-Ache** was issued in both black & white and professionally hand-colored editions. Abridged editions of the story, printed in black & white and with a "normal" page-turning rather than fold-out presentation, appeared inside promotional give-away comics issued by American companies in the 1880s.

Between Töpffer and Cruikshank, 1842-1849 had seen six sequential European comic books reprinted in the U.S., not to mention additional comics imported directly without American reproduction. At that decade's end, this combined influence met with a national craze screaming for satirization - California's Gold Rush. The result was the earliest known American created sequential comic book.

Journey to the Gold Diggins by Jeremiah Saddlebags, by brothers James and Donald Read, was published in 1849, first in New York City by Stringer & Townsend, then soon after re-published in Cincinnati, Ohio, by U.P. James. This Töpffer-influenced comic book chronicles the adventures of its hero **Jeremiah Saddlebags** in his get-rich-quick quest for gold in California and is highly sought by collectors of Western Americana. Interestingly, the back cover of the Stringer & Townsend edition carries an advertisement for **Rose and Gertrude-a Genevese Story**, one of Rodolphe Töpffer's non-comics prose novels. Stringer was one of the 1845 participants in the American publication of **The Bachelor's Own Book**. One might speculate that his earlier involvement with Cruikshank's comic could have made Stringer more receptive to the Read brothers' **Jeremiah Saddlebags**.

Still other contemporary Gold Rush comics appeared. **The Adventures of Mr. Tom Plump** (a fat man who nearly starves to death in his failed attempt at California Gold riches) saw print in 1850. **The Adventures of Jeremiah Old-pot** was serialized across all twelve monthly issues of **Yankee Notions** in 1852. Gold Rush cartoons are found in the 1849 edition of David Claypool Johnston's **Scraps**, in comic almanacs, and in Currier & Ives broadsheets.

The circa 1850-51 booklet **The Clown, Or The Banquet of Wit**, includes a 13-page comic story "Moses Keyser the Bowery Bully's Trip to the California Gold Mines," reprinted from **Elton's Californian Comic All-My-Nack** for 1850. **The Clown** is also notable as the earliest known anthology of sequential comics, with the bonus that each multi-panel story is by a different artist. Many of the artists are as yet unidentified, and how much of it is original American material versus that reprinted from Europe is presently unknown. But verified are cartoons by George Cruikshank, Elton (American), the Read brothers, Grandville (French), and Richard Doyle (British). The Doyle contribution reprints the comics story "Brown, Jones and Robinson and How They Went to a Ball," which originally saw print in the August 24, 1850 issue of **Punch**. This is the first known American appearance of these Doyle characters, and was almost certainly pirated.

Richard Doyle's **The Foreign Tour of Messrs. Brown, Jones, and Robinson** is basically a travelogue in illustrated form, told via humorous episodes, part sequential cartoon sequences, and part snapshots of moments jumping forward

The Adventures of Tom Plump *story page 5, Huestis & Cozans, NYC c1850-51 which also has similarities to Töpffer's and the Read Bros' comics.*

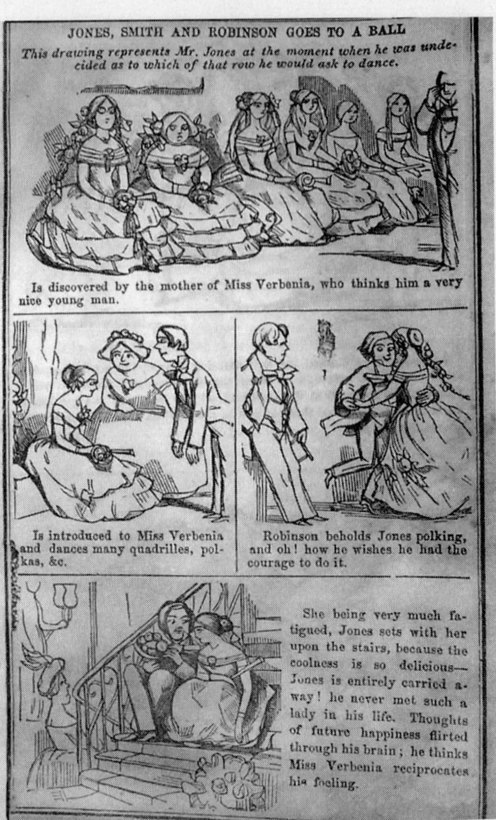

Richard Doyle's ***Foreign Tour****, as it first appeared in America within* ***The Clown, or The Banquet of Wit*** *1850-51 pirated from Punch.*

in time. This halfway sequential format was ideal for most 19th Century cartoonists, who, with rare exception, had not quite grasped how to maintain a single sequential story for much longer than two dozen successive panels. Doyle had simplified Töpffer's formula in a manner most artists could attempt to emulate. Episodes of "Brown, Jones, and Robinson" originally appeared in **Punch** in 1850, until a dispute between the Roman Catholic Doyle and **Punch's** editors over an anti-Papal joke ended with Doyle quitting in particular because of a cartoon by John Tenniel. Doyle redrew and expanded the story into a single album, first seeing print in 1854 from British publisher Bradbury & Evans.

New York publisher D. Appleton brought the album to America, where he reprinted it in 1860, 1871, and 1877. Next, Dick & Fitzgerald (NY) pirated Doyle's story sometime in the early 1870s. Doyle's format from **Foreign Tour** was emulated again and again. Examples include: the 1857 **Mr. Hardy Lee, His Yacht**, by Charles Stedman; the 1860s to 1870s Carleton published **Our Artist In...** series, set in various Latin American countries; the Augustus Hoppin 1870s sketch novels **On the Nile, Crossing the Atlantic,** and **Ups and Downs on Land and Water**; and **Life** founder John Ames Mitchell's 1881 (pre-**Life**) **The Summer School of Philosophy at Mt. Desert**. D. Appleton, the official, authorized American publisher of **Foreign Tour**, even commissioned an American artist - Toby - to create a sequel comic album involving Doyle's characters visiting the U.S. and Canada, published in 1872 as **The American Tour of Messrs Brown, Jones and Robinson**. In terms of influencing the development of mid-19th Century American comics, Doyle's **Foreign Tour** ranks with the works of Töpffer, Cruikshank, and Busch.

Doyle additionally produced a second, earlier cartoon series for **Punch**, the popularity of which likewise exerted influence decades beyond its publication. In **Manners and Customs of Ye Englyshe, Mr. Pips Hys Diary**, gathered from **Punch** & reprinted in 1849, Doyle told his story using a deliberately primitive almost stick-figure art style, combined with the Hogarthian structure of large single panel cartoons leaping forward in time with each picture.

Manners and Customs of Ye Harvard Studente, which ran in the **Harvard Lampoon**, shows the clearest influence. The series by then student Francis Gilbert Attwood was collected in 1877 by Houghton Mifflin. Attwood followed it up with **Manners and Customs of Ye Bostonians**, again in the pages of the **Harvard Lampoon**, but it is unknown whether that series was ever reprinted in book form. Attwood later became one of the regular artists in **Life**.

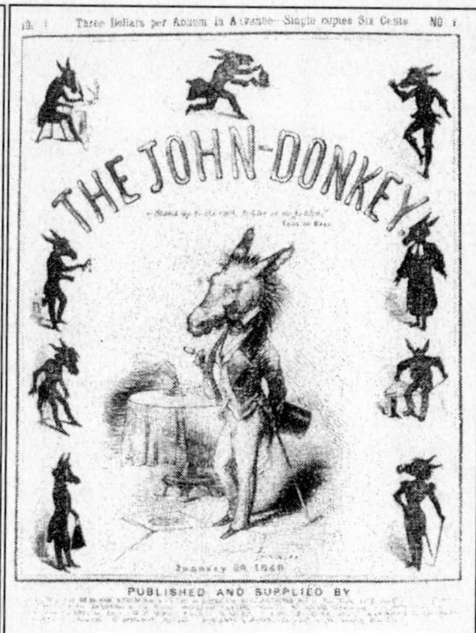

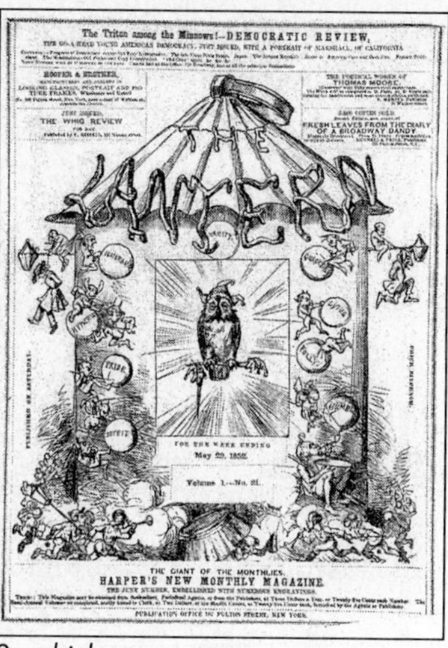

A few samples of the many humor magazines of the mid-1800s which ran cartoons. Wide-spread acceptance of the comic srtip slowly evolved over the decades. Left: ***Yankee Doodle*** *#30 title ran October 1846-October 1847; Middle:* ***The John-Donkey*** *#4 title ran January-October 1848; Right:* ***The Lantern*** *#21, May 29, 1851 title ran Jan. 10 1852-July 1853*

The British humor periodical **Punch** additionally influenced American comics beyond Richard Doyle's series. Consisting of humorous text interspersed with (mostly) single panel cartoons, it began its weekly run in July 1841, and continued uninterrupted well into the 20th Century. A large subset of **Punch**'s subscriber base was located in the U.S., to which thousands of copies were exported on an ongoing basis. The result was that when American humor periodicals emerged, they invariably imitated **Punch**'s format and style.

The earliest known of these American imitators, **Yankee Doodle**, debuted on October 10, 1846, and lasted one year. **Punch in Canada** likewise appeared in the late 1840s, kicking off a smaller parallel comics evolution just north of the U.S. (The earliest known "illustrated" American humor periodical, **The Humourist**, was published monthly in Baltimore from January 1829 to at least December of that same year, sans input from **Punch**. This monthly contained but one cartoon per issue, albeit hand-colored.)

Collections reprinting cartoons from **Punch** saw print in the U.S., such as **Merry Pictures by the Comic Hands**, imported for the 1859 Christmas Season, plus various John Leech, George Du Maurier, and Phil May books which appeared from the 1850s through 1910s. Finally, many American illustrated newspapers and periodicals, humorous and non-humorous, carried reprints of **Punch** cartoons. Such inclusions often became a prelude to switching to original material by American artists, should that publication's cartoon section become popular. Such was the case with **Harper's Monthly**. In the early 1850s, near the rear of each issue, it began to carry a few pages of single panel cartoons reprinted from **Punch**. This evolved into reprinting sequential comic pages from the British periodical **Town Talk**, and then, starting December 1853, original sequential comics by American artist Frank Bellew.

Bellew (1828-1888) could be regarded as the father of American sequential comics. Born in India, educated in France and England, he emigrated to America in 1850. His earliest work shows an influence from Doyle, but he rapidly developed his own unique art style. Bellew's comics, both sequential and single panel, graced numerous periodicals from the 1850s through the 1870s.

In the year prior to his **Harper's Monthly** appearances, in **The Lantern** volume one, Bellew had presented the 18-panel story "Mr. Blobb in Search of a Physician," serialized across six weekly issues. This was followed soon after by the 16-panel, three issue story "Mr. Bulbear's Dream", which concluded with the main character awakened from his dream by falling out of bed, in the exact same manner as would **Little Nemo** five decades later.

According to a 1923 article on famous cartoonists written by Charles Dana Gibson, it was Bellew's conception of **Uncle Sam** which "became the popular figure emblematic of the United States" starting with **The Lantern** issue published March 13, 1852. This was in a cartoon titled "Collins and

Recently rediscovered USA printing of ***The Laughable Adventures of Messrs. Brown, Jones and Robinson*** *by Richard Doyle published by Garrett, Dick & Fitzgerald, circa 1856.*

Cunard - Raising the Wind; Or Both Sides of the Story." Gibson went on, "Thomas Nast (later) added whiskers and put stars on the vest, retaining Bellew's hat, high collar, and striped trousers."

Frank Bellew's son, Frank Bellew Jr., also became a cartoonist of note, which has caused confusion amongst those trying to identify the work of 19th century cartoonists. Bellew Sr. often signed his work by placing his name or initials within a triangle, with Bellew Jr. most frequently signing his using the nickname "Chips."

The Extraordinary and Mirth-provoking Adventures by Sea & Land of Oscar Shanghai, inspired by **Bachelor Butterfly**, was issued around the same time circa 1853 by Garrett & Co., Publishers, No. 18 Ann Street, New York. **Oscar Shanghai** has many misadventures including being swallowed by a whale, making a trip in a flying machine which flies to Africa, where he is shot out of a huge bow by a "Black Prince" for not marrying a local princess of color. After more adventures, he makes it back home.

Oscar Shanghai's first publisher was confirmed this year with the discovery of a very rare 36-page catalog circa 1855 of books, pamphlets and prints handled by B.H. Day, owner & publisher of **Brother Jonathan** since the mid-1840s. The catalog has a few crossover advertisement pages from an associate publisher, Garrett. This newly rediscovered treasure, which sold for $750 in late 2002 itself, contains a sequential strip of one panel per page over 32 of those pages titled "Peter Piper in Bengal," by John Tenniel, reprinted from four 1853 issues of **Punch** to entice the reader to page through the entire booklet. Peter Piper tried his hand hunting all different kinds of wild game with many misadventures.

Amongst the many varied type of "Cheap Books" for sale in this rare catalog are the comic books **The Adventures of Obadiah Oldbuck**, **Bachelor Butterfly's Queer Love Adventures and Misfortunes** and **The Fortunes of Ferdinand Flipper** plus the aforementioned **Oscar Shanghai**. All priced at "25¢ per copy, postage free, refunds paid out in stamps."

There is also an advertisement for a comic book we have never heard of before titled **A Day's Sport - Or, Hunting Adventures of S. Winks Wattles, a Shopkeeper, Thomas Titt, a "legal gent," and Major Nicholas Noggin, a Jolly Good Fellow Generally** by Henry L. Stevens of Philadelphia. As we go to press again this year, we know of no existing complete copies and hope one still exists.

This catalog trumpets the concept that **Brother Jonathan** was for sale at the 1851 London World's Fair. Owner Benjamin H. Day was perhaps better known as the founder of **The New York Sun**, the very first successful "penny" newspaper in America begun in 1833, as well as having bought **Brother Jonathan** from Wilson sometime after selling out his interest in **The Sun**. Exactly when seems to be a matter open for debate amongst present-day historians.

Garrett & Co. was also responsible for the circa 1855 publication of **The Sad Tale of the Courtship of Chevalier Slyfox-Wikof, Showing His Heart-Rending Astounding & Most Wonderful Love Adventures with Fanny Elssler and Miss Gambol.** This book parodied the very public relationship between the then-famous wealthy American aristocrat Henry Wikoff, and the even more famous European actress/dancer Fanny Elssler. It is dated thusly because Wikoff's memoir is pictured in the comic book.

It appears circa 1855-56 Garrett & Co. formed a brief two-year partnership with Dick & Fitzgerald, becoming Garrett, Dick & Fitzgerald, while continuing to operate out of the same 18 Ann Street address in New York. During this time, they reprinted Richard Doyle's British published graphic novel **The Foreign Tour of Messrs. Brown, Jones, and Robinson**, reformatting it into the same oblong shape as Garrett's two prior comic books (which in turn were formatted in imitation of Töpffer's albums).

In 1858, Garrett appears to have dropped out, leaving Dick & Fitzgerald alone with the former's book stock, his place of business, and most importantly, the printing plates for his comic books. The Civil War was about to start, and for slightly more than a decade Dick & Fitzgerald steered away from reprinting his comic books. But in the 1870s they resumed publication - not only of the three albums published by Garrett, but also of **Obadiah Oldbuck** and **Bachelor Butterfly** from Wilson & Company, and **Ferdinand Flipper** from Brother Jonathan - all of them also making use of the original printing plates. The inclusion of books from Brother Jonathan, Wilson & Company, and Garrett & Co. all within the same promotional **Peter Piper** catalog from B.H. Day suggests (though not yet proven) that all these companies may have been part of Day's publishing empire, and that Dick & Fitzgerald became the inheritor/acquirer of all of it. Dick & Fitzgerald became simply Fitzgerald Publishing in 1889, and are believed to have dropped out of the comic book business. Dick & Fitzgerald also reprinted in the 1870s the earlier William T. Peter published **Ichabod Academicus** (how that title might have connected, if at all, with B.H. Day's business remains

***The Wonderful and Amusing Doings of Oscar Shanghai**, first published circa 1855 by Garrett & Co.; pictured here is a later Dick & Fitzgerald 1870's edition.*

unclear). We can now say, though, that an evolving group of a handful of publishers was responsible, over a span of 46 years, beginning with the very first graphic novel published in America in 1842, for keeping in print in America a cluster of slightly over half a dozen graphic novels.

While Bellew stood out for his sequential comics, Thomas Nast (1840-1902) brought a new style to American political cartoons, of which he is regarded the father. Even though he created several sequential strips early in his career, Nast made his name in the pages of the national news periodical **Harper's Weekly**, whose staff he joined a year into the Civil War. As Nast grew in prominence & success, American cartoonists increasingly emulated him. U.S. humor publications evolved towards an amalgamation of Nast and **Punch**, rather than sheer imitation of the latter.

While the northern **Vanity Fair** (December 31, 1859 - July 4, 1863) and the Confederate **Southern Punch** (August 15, 1863 - September, 1864) were both modeled after **Punch**, other Civil War era humor periodicals such as J.C. Haney's **Comic Monthly** and Frank Leslie's **Budget of Fun** were clearly absorbing lessons from Nast. These last two were issued in the same large folio size as **Harper's Weekly**, with a large front page cartoon, a larger double-page cartoon centerfold, and still more cartoons located on the back cover - a format approaching what eventually emerged in what **Puck** began doing.

The Sad Tale of the Courtship of Chevalier Slyfox-Wikof, *Garrett & Co, New York, c1855.*

(1.) THE ALARM
"On Thursday night Mr. Lincoln was aroused, and informed that a stranger desired to see him on a matter of life and death. * * * A conversation elicited the fact that an organized body of men had determined that Mr. Lincoln should never leave Baltimore alive. * * * Statesmen laid the plan and bankers indorsed it."

(2.) THE COUNCIL
"Mr. Lincoln did not want to yield, and his friends cried with indignation. But they insisted, and he left."

(3.) THE SPECIAL TRAIN
"He wore a Scotch plaid cap and a very long military cloak, so that he was entirely unrecognizable."
(4.) THE OLD COMPLAINT
"Mr. Lincoln, accompanied by Mr. Seward, paid his respects to President Buchanan."
THE FLIGHT OF ABRAHAM
(As Reported by a Modern Paper)

"The Flight of Abraham Lincoln," first appeared in ***Harper's Weekly****, March 9, 1861.*

Sample panels from Frank Bellew Sr's ***The Flying Machine; And Professor High's Adventure therein in a Trip across the Ocean, Merryman's Monthly*** *V3#5, May 1865.*

After the War, with Nast's style of cartoons more entrenched in American readers' minds, efforts to launch **Punch**-like American periodicals floundered quickly. **Mrs. Grundy**, ironically most famous for its cover design by Nast, died after a mere twelve issues (running July 8 to September 23, 1865). **Punchinello** (April 2 to December 24, 1870) struggled nine months before its backers gave up. **Punchinello** had been financed by Tammany Hall politicians Tweed and Sweeney, as counter-propaganda against Nast's ongoing assault upon their corruption. They attempted to buy and threaten Nast into silence, to no avail.

American comics were also being pulled away from their initial Anglo-Franco imitation by the infusion of a third major source of European influence. Numerous European humor periodicals besides **Punch** found significant subscriber bases in America. The large German immigrant population imported their favorite humor periodicals into the U.S., including the popular **Fliegende Blätter** ("Flying Leaves") and **Münchener Bilderbogen**. As high in quality as these were, one German comic artist in particular excelled beyond the rest, his stories breaking out and crossing over into English language translations, the demand for which resulted in numerous printings. This artist, of course, was Heinrich Christian Wilhelm Busch (1832-1908).

Busch's work appeared in English in the 1860s in both British and American periodicals, often uncredited. For example, four of Busch's strips appeared in English in the pages of **Merryman's Monthly** in 1864, while in 1879 his graphic story "Fipps der Affe" was serialized across a 10-issue run of **Puck** as "Troddledums the Simian." The earliest known English language appearance of Busch in book form was **The Flying Dutchman, or The Wrath of Herr von Stoppelnoze**, in 1862, from New York publisher Carleton. Carleton not only pirated Busch's strip, but went so far as to credit the story to American poet John G. Saxe, with Busch's cartoons mere illustrations accompanying Saxe's prose!

The next known English language Busch book was **A Bushel of Merry Thoughts**, an 1868 London-published anthology collecting various Busch strips. Some of these same stories later appeared in the U.S.-published **The Mischief Book** (1880), newly translated and with a few more Busch tales added. One of these additions was "Hans Huckebein." A tale of a mischievous pet raven who in the end gets drunk and accidentally hangs himself, it became, at least in the States, Busch's 2nd most popular sequential comic story. The unrepentant bird was promoted to title character in two later collections: **Jack Huckaback, the Scapegrace Raven**, circa 1888, and the rarer **Hookeybeak the Raven and Other Tales** in 1878. There were also at least 3 trade card series in the 1870s & 1880s which reprinted the ending sequence, as **Fritz Spindle-Shanks-The Raven Black**.

The most popular Busch tale, though, was easily **Max und Moritz**, which in the U.S. saw print as **Max and Maurice - A Juvenile History in Seven Tricks**. Published in Boston in 1871, this English language version saw at minimum 60 reprintings by the century's end, plus countless more printings later. A separate British translation debuted in 1874, under the title **Max & Mortiz**. It is well known that the later Rudolph Dirks comic strip series, **Katzenjammer Kids** beginning in late 1897 was based on **Max und Moritz**.

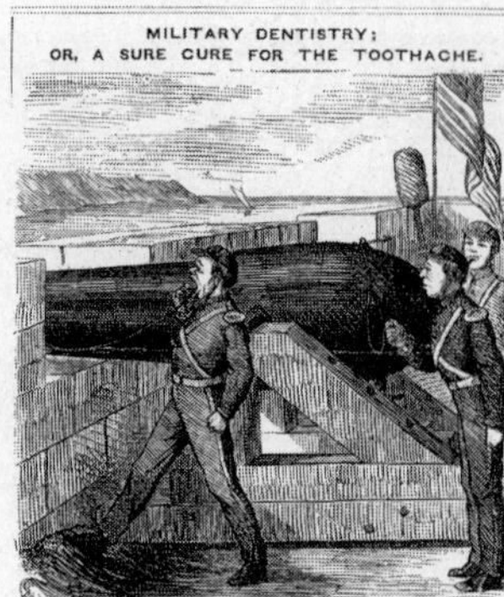

MRS. GRUNDY.
MILITARY DENTISTRY:
OR, A SURE CURE FOR THE TOOTHACHE.
One!
Two!!

THREE!!!

*Panels from **Mrs. Grundy**, Saturday, July 15, 1865.*

Sample comics panels by Wilhelm Busch circa 1870.

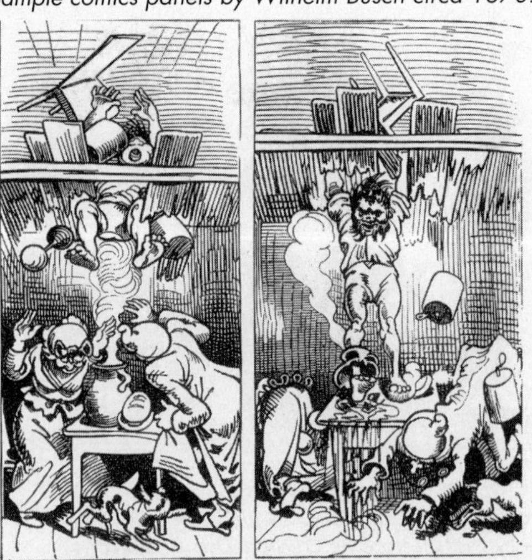

According to documents found by Alfredo Castelli, **Katzenjammer Kids** was not yet another rip-off of Busch. Rather, William R. Hearst may have licensed the characters. Hearst's paper was published in different language editions for New York City's immigrant communities. In the German edition, the strip was published under its original name, **Max und Moritz**. Numerous other translations of Busch were published in America - too many to name in this article. Several can be found in the Victorian Age Index. There were many prominent talented artists in the incredibly scarce, still legendary (but now largely forgotten but to a few) 1870s humor periodicals, **Wild Oats** and **Schnedereddeng**, the German language companion publication to **Wild Oats**. In terms of the quality of their cartoons and comics, these two New York City publications were in 1872 at an artistic level **Puck** would not achieve until 1880.

Published by Winchell & Small and distributed through the New York News Company, **Schnedereddeng** and **Wild Oats** carried a crossroads of old and next generation comic artists, from the more established W. M. Avery, Thomas Francis "Frank" Beard, Frank Henry Temple Bellew, E.S. Bisbee, Michael Angelo Woolf, and Thomas Worth (remembered more these days for his Currier & Ives cartoon sheets), and up-and-comers such as Livingston Hopkins, Frederick Burr Opper, Palmer Cox and Wales.

Wild Oats began carrying sequential comic strips as early as #26, dated March 14, 1872, with the Livingston Hopkins strip pictured below (we do not know anything yet about the first 25 issues). The very next issue has a Worth double-page spread titled "The Political Humpty Dumpty... Horace Greeley" told in 11 panels plus the sequential fictional "Graphic Account of the Assassination of Queen Victoria" and "Love As the Angels Love." "The Doings of the Japanese Embasey At Washington" related in 12 panels by W. M. Avery follows up in #28 April 11, 1872. An unknown hand drew "The Physiology of Moving" in 6 panels in #30. Hopkins returns with a beautiful intense 28-panel double-page spread in #31 May 23. Hopkins and Worth alternated for many issues with sequential comic strips on baseball, horse racing and other pertinent subjects of the day.

In #45 December 5, 1872, E.S. Bisbee contributed his first sequential in 17 panels and Worth showed up in "Humor & Pathos of a New England Thanksgiving" in 11 panels. Issue 47 expands the concept with a 12-panel job by Bisbee, 20-panel effort on one page by Hopkins and a 3-panel effort by Worth. And on it goes through 1873 as well - comic strip after comic strip. Issue 58 June 5, 1873, includes a particularly humorous 19-panel double-pager drawn by someone still unknown titled "The Terrible Adventures of Messrs. Buster & Stumps, with the Indians" which begins with two white men heading out west in an effort to exterminate Indians - and their misadventures of not quite getting the job done. It reads across both pages in a unique evolution similar to **Popeye** #2052 (found in the Platinum listings). Issue 65 contains two 9-panel Thomas Worth strips "Only a Mad Dog Scare - Another Lesson For Nervous People" and "Only a Cholera Scare - Something For Nervous People to Read and Ponder Over." Issue 66 Sept 18, 1873, has the very funny Hopkins 12-panel strip as well as two more 10-panel Worth strips on the delights of Hunting and Fishing plus one by Hopkins titled "The Adventures of Mr Old Party with Jersey Mosquitoes" in 12-panels. All told, four comic strips in this issue. They obviously liked what they were doing, judging from the exuberance of the work.

***Wild Oats** #26, 14 March 1872 Livingston Hopkins sequential comic strip. Hopkins later moved to Australia and became its premiere political cartoonist.*

The next issue has Worth's 9-panel report on "The Adventures of Young Muttonhead Among the Free Lovers" which was all about the "free sex" convention recently held in Chicago. Issue 68 has a 9-panel "An Adventure With a New Jersey Mosquito" which smacks of Winsor McCay in subject and even art style. Maybe McCay was inspired by this for his later animated cartoon as well as earlier **Rarebit Fiend**. We'll never know for sure. On through 1875, **Wild Oats** presented sequential comic strips issue after issue. With #148, October 27, 1875, Fredrick Opper has his very first **Wild Oats** cover, centering on inflation then rampant in the USA. He does covers through at least #161 before a short break and then comes right back with many more. By #158 January 5, 1876, Palmer Cox - some five years before inventing **The Brownies** - began a wonderful series of 24-panel double page spread comic strips, with a couple sample titles being "The Adventures of Mr & Mrs Sprowl And Their Christmas Turkey-A Crashing Chasing Tearful Tragedy But Happily Ending Well" and "Bachelor Broke & Widow Snuggi: A Pictorial Account of Their Sleigh Ride & What Became of It."

__Wild Oats__ #163, Feb 9 1876 last six panels by Palmer Cox who began doing sequential comic strips some years years before he created __The Brownies__.

Even though he had been contributing many covers and interior single panel jobs to **Wild Oats** for years, by-then elderly Frank Bellew Sr. does not show up with his first comic strip until $190, August 16, 1876, with a 9-panel effort he titled, "Rodger's Patent Mosquito Armour." By this time the USA's "Father of the sequential comic strip" had inspired many other cartoonists to try their hand telling stories with words & pictures. Bellew Sr. had been making sequential comic strips for over a quarter century.

The seemingly disparate influences of Thomas Nast and German comics came together in Austrian immigrant Joseph Keppler (1838-1894). Like many cartoonists in America, Keppler's desire was to rival Nast. Unlike most, he possessed the talent and drive to accomplish it. Keppler first settled in St. Louis, Missouri, where he took his first stab at starting a comic weekly, the German language **Die Vehme** (Aug 28, 1869 - Aug. 20, 1870). Seven months later, still in St. Louis, he tried again, launching another German language humor periodical, titled **Puck**. This German **Puck** began on

March 18, 1871, joined by an English language version one year later, but both soon folded and ended on Aug. 24, 1872.

Keppler moved to New York City, doing cartoons primarily for Frank Leslie publications (including a one-shot, English language publication - **Centennial Fun** - which capitalized on the July, 1876 Centennial Exposition in Philadelphia). Four years after the first **Puck** died, Keppler was ready to try again. He re-launched the German language edition of **Puck** in New York City on September 27, 1876.

It was a Presidential Election year, with Republican candidate Hayes versus the Democrat Tilden. Keppler lucked out with material to satirize, when the election ended so close that each candidate needed only the electoral college votes of a few states in question - most notably Florida and Louisiana - and both parties were claiming to have won. Keppler depicted the two candidates as two trains on the same track, steaming towards each other, with the stability of the nation in the balance. After months of dispute, the victory was handed to the loser of the popular vote, the Republican Hayes. (Much later, scholars showed that Tilden, in truth, was the electoral as well as popular winner.)

With his revamped **Puck** series, Keppler introduced a new element to American humor periodicals - color lithography. The color was initially limited, but it appeared, ambitiously, every week, and set **Puck** apart from anything else on American stands. The parallel English language edition of **Puck** was launched six months after the German version, on March 14, 1877. This English edition of **Puck** was a money-loser for several years, kept afloat by the German edition's profits and the determination of the English edition's literary editor,

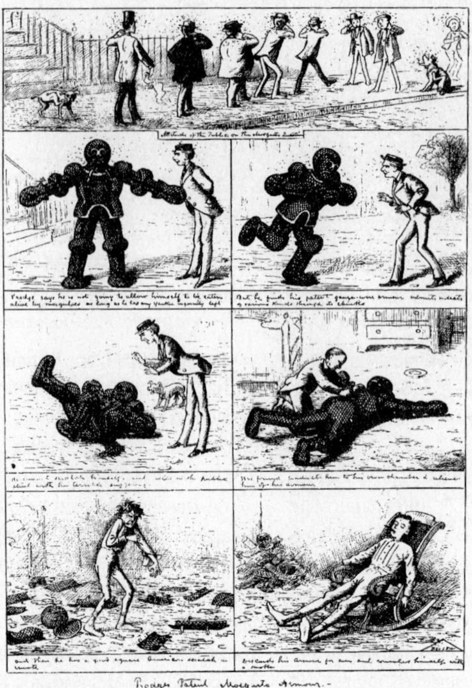

***Wild Oats** #190 August 16, 1876 by Frank Bellew Sr., Father of American Comic Strips This one titled "Rodger's Patent Mosquito Armor."*

***Puck** #1, March 14, 1877, NYC, was very important; but **Wild Oats** had been running sequential comic strips regularly for over six years.*

H.C. Bunner, not to give up. **Puck** became the new model for American humor publications. Keppler brought in other artists over time, most notably Opper, Zim and Howarth, and added black & white sequential comics and cartoons in the pages between the color front cover, back cover, and centerspread.

Puck was the model which William Randolph Hearst followed in 1895, adding a color comics section to his Sunday newspaper. He basically wanted to offer a "free" **Puck**-like supplement within his **New York Journal**. Further, **Puck** artist F.M. Howarth pointed the direction of those future newspaper comics pages, by creating full page sequential color comic strips on most **Puck** back covers starting in the early 1890s.

With the first issue dated October 29, 1881, **Puck's** chief rival, **Judge**, was born. Founded by **Puck** artist James A. Wales, **Judge** made several forays into **Puck's** talent pool over the years. Their best capture was Eugene Zimmerman (known popularly as "Zim"), who became for **Judge** the star artist that Frederick Burr Opper was for **Puck**

When Wales broke away to form **Judge**, it was from amongst his pre-**Puck** associates at the by-then defunct **Wild Oats** that he first recruited. One can speculate that having been a star artist in these earlier magazines may have driven Wales' desire to have more control of his cartoons rather than remain subordinate to Keppler, leading to Wales' creation of **Judge**.

Judge struggled financially for several years, and likely would have ceased publication if not for the Presidential Election of 1884, in which Republicans blamed Keppler and **Puck** for their loss. By 1884 Frank Beard was the editor.

Republican backers had attempted to create a **Puck** rival titled **Jingo** in the last few months of that election, but it lacked the creative talent of **Puck** & **Judge**, and its backers let it die once the election results were known. Soon after, Republican backers bought and poured money into **Judge**, hoping to make the until-then politically neutral **Judge** their counterweight against Keppler's **Puck**.

By this time, most of the ex-**Wild Oats** artists, save Wales, had moved elsewhere.

Numerous other **Puck** imitators emerged in the 1880s but quickly died. Note should be made of the **Puck**-like San Francisco **Wasp**, which debuted October 14, 1876 (too early for it to have been a mere **Puck** knockoff), and the black & white **Texas Siftings**, which debuted on May 9, 1881. Though neither approached **Puck** or **Judge** in circulation, both cut their own paths, managing to survive as cartoon humor magazines into the 1890s.

*Sample panels from **Quiddities of an Alaskan Trip**, 1873 - all about going to then-recently purchased Alaska.*

Published basically concurrent to **Wild Oats** during much of the latter's run was the New York City newspaper **The Daily Graphic** (March 4, 1873 to Sept 23, 1889), which has the claim to being the first regularly illustrated daily newspaper in the world. It was published every day except Sundays and holidays, with the vast majority of its illustrations being straight depictions of news events. (Not until the late 1890s could photographs be reproduced inexpensively enough for inclusion in mass publications, and so the norm was to send out photographers to record images of newsworthy events, but then have artists render those images into drawn engravings, which then were reproduced in newspapers.)

With so many artists needed for illustrated publications, the result was that virtually all 19th century periodicals which regularly featured illustrations, even if their primary aim was to provide realistic pictures, at some point in their runs included both single-panel cartoons, and sequential comics. At a publication rate of six days per week, unbroken over a 15-year run, **The Daily Graphic** had more than the usual hunger for illustrated material to fill its pages with.

Thus, **The Daily Graphic** became a rotating door for many circa 1870s and 1880s American cartoonists, usually those in the early parts of their careers (making one suspect that it was possibly not the best paying gig in town). Within its pages, like needles to be found in the haystack of its more than 4800 issues, is early work by Livingston Hopkins (who mysteriously appears, vanishes, reappears, etc., for months to whole years at a time, right up to his 1884 departure to Australia), pre-**Life** work by Kemble, pre-Harper's appearances by A.B. Frost and W.A. Rogers, pre-**Puck** C.J. Taylor, Hamilton, and Gillam. Old hats, too, appear at times, such as Michael Woolf and Frank Bellew, Sr. Opper appears also.

Further, **The Daily Graphic** regularly plundered British periodicals for its back and sometimes center pages, not only perpetrating the usual swipes of single panel Punch cartoons, but also stealing sequential strips from **Punch**'s two main rival publications, **Judy** and **Fun**. This included occasionally reprinting (albeit at random) episodes of continuing British strips "The British Workman" by James Sullivan, and "McNab of that Ilk" by James Brown. Though, strangely enough, no episodes of Marie Duval's **Ally Sloper**, despite the fact that **The Daily Graphic** did reprint some of Duval's non-"Sloper" strips ("**Ally Sloper**" was a continuing sequential strip character who debuted in 1867, lasting into the 1920s, and had very successful solo British book collections of his strips published as early as 1873 - more than two decades prior to **Yellow Kid in McFadden's Flats**).

Livingston Hopkins, whose art style changed like a chameleon from one year to the next, exhibited a definite Duval influence in his work within a year following the publication of the first **Ally Sloper** collection. Given that Hopkins worked for **The Daily Graphic** during the same period in which **The Daily Graphic** was stealing cartoons from Sloper's home publication, **Judy**, this can hardly be considered coincidental. By the time Hopkins was about to emigrate to Australia to become lead cartoonist for the **Melbourne Punch**, his art style was imitating Kemble, who was working at **The Daily Graphic** just prior to his **Life** covers.

Another highly desirable American graphic novel, sought especially by collectors of Western lore, is **Quiddities of an Alaskan Trip** by William H. Bell which debuted in 1873. Bell was Timothy O'Sullivan's assistant photographer on the 1871-74 expeditions of Lt. George Wheeler, surveying & mapping the western territories for the U.S. government. The story panels are laid out within ornate frames like those of stereograph cards, such as Bell was involved in creating on the expedition. It involves a parody of a trip from Washington, D.C. to survey the newly purchased territory of Alaska, which

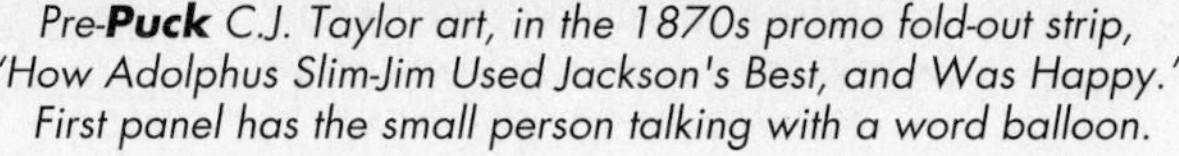

*Pre-**Puck** C.J. Taylor art, in the 1870s promo fold-out strip, "How Adolphus Slim-Jim Used Jackson's Best, and Was Happy." First panel has the small person talking with a word balloon.*

at the time was derisively referred to as "Seward's Folly." Bell published **Quiddities** in Portland, Oregon in 1873, a date which would have required that he drew it during the time he was on just such an expedition.

Life debuted on January 4, 1883, founded by J.A. Mitchell, and modeled after the **Harvard Lampoon**. It quickly rose to become the third main pillar of late 1800s American humor periodicals. Smaller in size, black & white, and priced the same as **Puck** and **Judge**, it nevertheless succeeded by appealing to the more genteel, romantic and apolitical notions of the white upper class. Its earliest artists included Kemble and Palmer Cox, but its foremost artist would be Charles Dana Gibson, becoming world renowned as the hand behind the graceful, aristocratic "Gibson Girls."

"Take charge of these, Hen-ery, and bring me a nice, tender rump steak, smoking hot."
Bump! . . . Bump!! . . . Bump!!!
"Something wrong with someone's hat, eh, Hen-ery?" "Yessir."
"Someone's hat down again—eh, Hen-ery?" "Yessir."
"Hen-ery, is that that fellow's blessed hat again, eh?" "Yessir."
"Well, thank God for a good dinner. And now, Hen-ery, my hat and stick, please . . . Why! Confound it!" . . .
M.D.
A HAT OFF A PEG.

The Daily Graphic *- In 1873 this newspaper began running comic strips for 15 years, and there are other places comic strips keep cropping up; sample comic strip might be by Marie Duval of* ***Alley Sloper*** *fame.*

Unlike **Judge**, which had to change format to survive in the next century, and **Puck**, which faded to a shadow of its former self, **Life** transitioned into the 20th century virtually unaltered, and thrived. By the mid-1880s, with **Puck**, **Judge**, and **Life** all solidly in place, American comics and cartoon humor had become very much their own, no longer looking first at Europe to take their cues.

Also very American in character were the country's promotional comics, which flourished throughout the latter half of the 19th century, starting first with comic almanacs in the mid-1850s. These free almanacs, usually created by medicine and farm product companies, initially killed off the more elaborate illustrated almanacs of the 1830s to early 1850s, which readers paid for. Competition amongst companies, whose goal was to get customers to read the almanacs and the advertisements contained therein again and again, meant that attention-getting humorous cartoons soon found their way back into these giveaway pamphlets. Initially their cartoons were done cheap, either poorly drawn or pirated from elsewhere, such as those found in the **Hostetter's** and **Wright's** almanac series. More elaborate promotional almanacs eventually did evolve, though, and amongst the best of these was **Barker's Illustrated Almanac**, first produced for the year 1878, and annually into the 1930s. Each **Barker's Almanac** contained ten to twelve full page cartoons, wonderful and bizarre in design, frequently racist, but also comically manic and crammed with details in a manner similar to Outcault's much later **Yellow Kid** pages. The cartoons in **Barker's Almanac** were so popular that in 1892, The Barker, Moore, and Mein Medicine Company published their first edition of **Barker's Komic Picture Souvenir**, reprinting nearly 150 pages of cartoons from their almanacs.

This first **Barker's Souvenir** features a wraparound color cover depicting people headed towards the Columbian World's Fair Exposition, which was to be held in Chicago the next year. It is the earliest confirmed "premium" comic book, sent to customers who mailed in a box label and outside wrapper from two different Barker's products. The **Souvenir** album was Barker's most in-demand premium. It was reprinted as a thick unnumbered booklet three more times in the 1890s, with the contents reorganized each time. Later, between 1901 and 1903, Barker's broke the album into three separate "Parts," each of which required still more box labels and wrappers to obtain. The 3-part series of reprint albums expanded to four parts circa 1906 or 1907. Both the 3 and 4-part album series had multiple printings.

The first promotional comics which did not double as almanacs began to appear in the 1870s.

Sequence by A.B. Frost, from the ***MidSummer Puck*** *1887.*

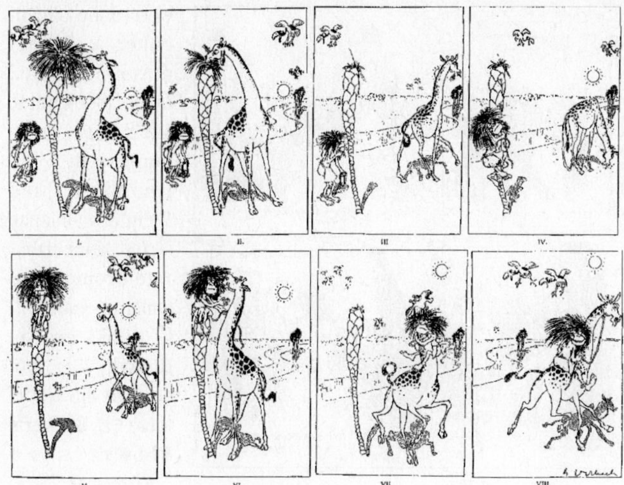

***Truth** #438, page 11, Sept 7, 1895, NYC "Girraffe Hunting Up to Date" by immigrant Gustave Verbeek who went on to do **The Incredible Upside Downs** by 1903.*

They included the aforementioned reprints of Cruikshank and Busch strips, reprints of strips lifted from American sources (A.B. Frost's strip "The Bull Calf" was a particular favorite), and original material placing the product being promoted as the focus of the story. These original short cartoon dramas were in many ways similar in storyline to those found in modern television advertisements, except that the clothing is Victorian, and the claims, pre-F.D.A. and F.C.C., were unabashedly wild, over-the-top, and blunt. Chewing tobacco and snuff saved romances, calmed crying babies, and made the sick well. Stove polish that propelled you to wealth and power. Corsets that brought you a husband. The objective, of course, in an era before TV or radio, was to make each comic handout so entertaining that customers would want to keep and read the advertisement again and again.

The more wonderful graphics and outrageous claims tended to come from tobacco companies, who were using comic books and strips to sell their products more than a century before cries against "Joe Camel." The most elaborate of these were printed full color, and unfolded into a single long strip, just like Cruikshank's **The Tooth-Ache** from the 1840s, though usually limited to just the cover plus seven panels.

Examples are the Jackson Chewing Tobacco comics **How Adolphus Slim-Jim Used Jackson's Best** and **Ye Veracious Chronicle of Gruff & Pompey**, and Durham Smoking Tobacco's **Home Made Happy - A Romance for Married Men**. The artists of these comics are mostly unidentified, but their level of skill was equal to anything in **Puck** and **Judge**. The **Home Made Happy** comic, in fact, was produced for Durham by The Graphic Company -- the publisher of **The Daily Graphic**, the aforementioned 1870s illustrated newspaper which included cartoons.

In addition to the debut of **Puck** and the spread of non-almanac promotional comics, the 1870s saw a third major development. It was at this time that an unusually high number of full-length sequential comic book stories, or graphic novels, began to appear. A sort of mini-boom occurred in the U.S. following the 1840s appearances of Töpffer's and Cruikshank's comic books, but then largely died down for an approximate twenty year span. With the 1870s, graphic novels were back in even greater numbers.

A large part of this revival was brought about by New York City publisher Dick & Fitzgerald, infamous for their piracies after they evolved from Garrett and B.H. Day, who issued seven such comic books. These included Doyle's **Foreign Tour**, the reprints of the two Wilson and Company-printed Töpffer booklets and **Oscar Shangai** from Garrett retitled as **The Wonderful And Amusing Doings By Sea And Land of Oscar Shanghai**, **Sad Tale of the Courtship of Chevalier Slyfox-Wikof**; and the Yale-derived **College Experiences of Ichabod Academicus**. (**Ichabod Academicus**' original publication was in New Haven, CT in 1850, placing it right after **Jeremiah Saddlebags**).

Other graphic novels also appeared during this period which have been mentioned earlier. The earliest known anthology devoted to collecting the comic strips of a single American artist was A.B. Frost's **Stuff and Nonsense** in 1884. The next known American collection came in 1888 -

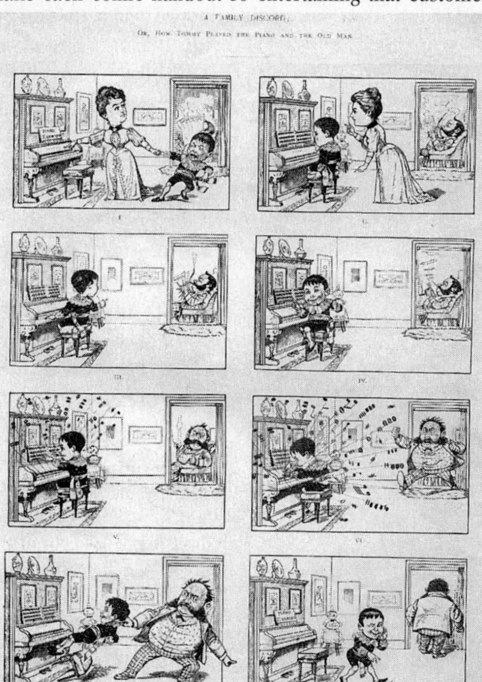

*"A Family Discord" - One of many F.M. Howarth **Puck** back covers, this one later reprinted in **Pickings From Puck** #18 Dec 1895.*

Judge *1896 Eugene "ZIM" Zimmerman*
"A Sagacious Animal" is but one of hundreds by Zim who went on to run an early cartoonist training school.

A SAGACIOUS ANIMAL.

the very rare Frederick Burr Opper anthology, **Puck's Opper Book**. Both proved popular, so more Frost and Opper collections followed, to be joined within a few years by reprints collecting the cartoons and strips of American artists Kemble, Zim, Keppler, Gibson, Mayer, Taylor, "Chips," Howarth, Woolf, etc.

Puck, **Judge**, and **Texas Siftings** all began monthly **Library** series - smaller 8-1/2" x 11" magazines, mostly black & white, which organized previously published material around one theme or one artist. For example, the first **Puck's Library** (July 1887) was titled "The National Game," and gathered beneath one cover **Puck** material poking fun at the game of baseball.

Life tended more towards hardcover collections, such as its annual ten-issue series **The Good Things of Life** (1884-1893), which included cartoons and strips by Palmer Cox, T.S. Sullivant, Hy Mayer, and others.

The Good Things of Life was published initially by the firm of White, Stokes, and Allen, but by the fourth book, the reprint series was published by Frederick A. Stokes alone. Stokes published a number of other cartoon books in the 1880s and 1890s, the majority of them reprint collections. The experience he gained at this time with these reprint albums placed Stokes in the perfect position to pick up the wealth of material about to be created for the comics supplements of William R. Hearst's newspapers, making Stokes the first major publisher of the coming Platinum Age.

In 1892, Charles Scribner's Sons published A. B. Frost's **Bull Calf and Other Tales**. It contains sequential comic strip art on quite a few pages as well as single panel cartoons. By 1898, Charles Scribner's Sons also issued Kemble's **The Billy Goat and Other Comicalities** as a 112-page hardcover, which also has sequential comic strips.

In the early 1890s, the slum children cartoons of artist Michael Woolf (many of which were reprinted in the 1899 collection titled **Sketches of Lowly Life in a Great City**) were popular. **Truth** magazine, which followed **Puck**'s format of color front cover, back cover and centerspread cartoons, but in style was more akin to the aristocratic **Life**, was initially unable to secure Woolf's services, creating an opportunity for the young cartoonist Richard F. Outcault, who desired to break into one of the weekly comic periodicals.

It was in his Woolf-inspired slum children cartoons for **Truth** that Outcault's prototype of the **Yellow Kid** first emerged. The bald, sack-clothed youngster made four appearances in **Truth**, starting with #372 on June 2, 1894, prior to his newspaper debut.

During the rise of **Yellow Kid**'s popularity, he appeared in American comic magazines in parodies drawn by others, with politicians, even Hearst and Pulitzer, dressed up as the **Yellow Kid**. Such cartoons are known to have appeared in **Judge**, **Life**, and **Vim** plus various newspapers across the country. More about the Yellow Kid's importance can be found in the Platinum Age section of this book.

While comics have their roots in Europe, and the earliest American comic books either reprinted or emulated those of Europe, the direction of influence was by no means one way.

TIME, ONE MINUTE.

Time, One Minute *by Hy Mayer,* ***Truth****, 1896*
"Our artist-draws-a picture-before the kinetscope"
The last panel says "Thoz. A. Edizon," inventor of movies.

Sample cartoon from the ***Barker's Illustrated Almanac for 1897*** *released in late 1896 reads "The Big Nose Club – Nosey People Telling What Each Knows About the Size of Some Other Fellow's Nose." Art by R.A. Williams.*

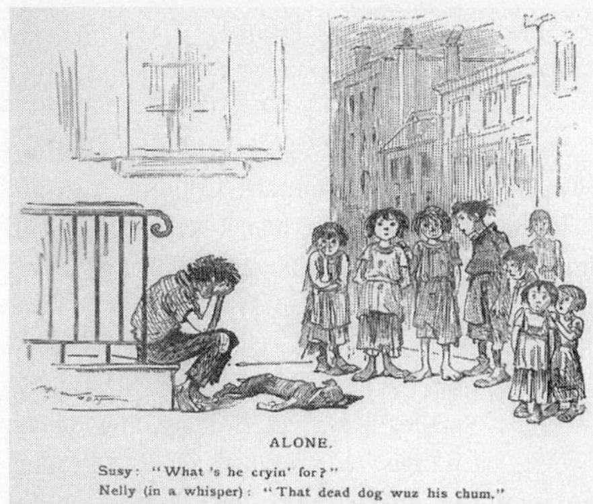

Michael Angelo Woolf cartoon ***Truth-r in 99 Truths From Woolf****. His many scenes from slum life in New York City was a major influence on Outcault's formulation of the Yellow Kid. Titled "Alone," caption reads Susy: "What's he cryin' for?" Nelly (in a whisper): "That dog was his chum."*

By at least the 1870s, American cartoons were being seen in the Old World, as evidenced by the arrest in Spain of the on-the-lamb corrupt Tammany Hall politician Boss Tweed by Spanish police who recognized Tweed from a Nast cartoon.

European piracy of American cartoons was just as lucrative as the American piracy of Europeans. In the 1880s and '90s, the comics of Zim, Chips Bellew, and Charles Dana Gibson all saw reprint in Europe. F.M. Howarth's domestic comedies from **Puck** were favorites in France. American Hy Mayer was commissioned to create original comics work for **Black and White** (Britain), **Le Rire** (France), and **Fliegende Blätter**. Michael Woolf's slum children cartoons saw print in the British periodical **Pick-Me-Up**, during the same years that top British artist Phil May's first published work debuted in that publication. May later became famous for his Woolf-inspired street children cartoons as well as his influence on the development of comics in Australia.

As the 19th Century ended, American comics were coming to the fore worldwide, soon to explode into a position of dominance with the Platinum Age revolution brought about by the emergence of the color comic supplement in America's newspapers and the arrival of Richard F. Outcault's **Yellow Kid.**

END NOTE: Victorian Era comics were issued in many relatively obscure formats compared to what most of us are used to today. The Victorian Era section can only grow as there are many more heretofore undiscovered comics from the 1800s which have fallen off the radar of history. Some may wonder why some of the earlier items listed contain as of yet no prices. The reason is simple. These books are part of a relatively "new" market which is still establishing itself. High-grade copies are almost unheard of in almost all instances. Some books may truly have only a handful left in existence. We are sure there are some known to have been published which no (as of yet) known copies have survived the ravages of time and neglect. Next year expect another quantum leap in our ever-expanding knowledge of the fascinating earliest origins of the comics as they relate to North America. Your input in helping this section of the Guide grow is most welcome.

Happy Hunting!

Judge *#791, Dec 12, 1896, depicting Tammany Hall politicians as RFO's Yellow Kid & Cox's Brownies. Art by Hamilton.*

Robert Beerbohm *sold comics through* ***RBCC*** *and set up at his first comicon beginning in 1967, helped found the Comics & Comix chain stores in August 1972, co-hosted Berkeleycon 1973 first UG creator-owned comix con; still buys & sells comics material for a living and also has been compiling a detailed history book of the business behind the comic book for some time now. You can contact him at this e-address:*

beerbohm@teknetwork.com

Richard Olson *is an Emeritus Research Professor at the University of New Orleans. He published the Richard Outcault Collector for years and may be reached directly at:*

redoak1@netdoor.com

Both are life-long collectors and students of all forms of the comics who welcome corrections and additions to this concise compilation of our earliest comics heritage dating back well over two centuries.

The Strange and Wonderful Adventures of Bachelor Butterfly by Rodolphe Töpffer 1870s © Dick & Fitzgerald, New York

Bachelor's Own Book by Cruikshank 1844 © D. Bougue, London

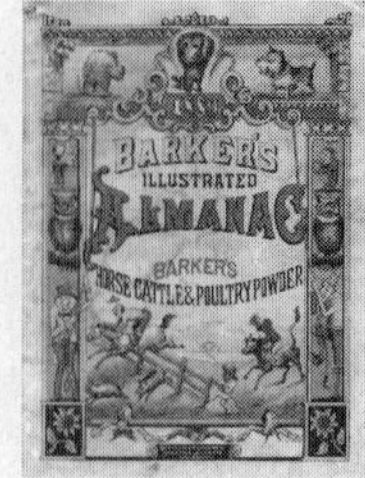

Barker's Illustrated Almanac 1889 © Barker, Moore & Mein Medicine Co.

FR1.0 GD2.0 FN6.0

COLLECTOR'S NOTE: Some of books listed in this section were published well over a century before organized comics fandom began archiving and helping to preserve these fragile popular culture artifacts. Consequently, copies of most all of these comics almost never surface in Fine+ or better shape. Most are in the Poor to VG range. If you want to collect these only in high grade, your collection will be extremely small. Each year we are filling in the price blanks on more items. The past few years we have been more concerned with simply establishing what is known to exist. The prices given for Fair, Good and Fine categories are for strictly graded editions. If you need help grading your item, we refer you to the grading section in this book or contact the authors of this essay. Items marked rare we are trying to figure out how many copies might still be in existence. We welcome help.

For ease ascertaining the contents of each item of this listing and the Platinum index list, we offer the following list of categories found immediately following most of the titles:

E - REPRINT OF EUROPEAN COMICS MATERIAL
G - GRAPHIC NOVEL (LONGER FORMAT COMIC TELLING A SINGLE STORY)
H - "HOW TO DRAW CARTOONS" BOOKS
I - ILLUSTRATED BOOKS NOTABLE FOR THE ARTIST, BUT NOT A COMIC.
M - REPRINT OF MAGAZINE / PERIODICAL COMICS MATERIAL
N - REPRINT OF NEWSPAPER COMICS MATERIAL
O - ORIGINAL COMIC MATERIAL NOT REPRINTED FROM ANOTHER SOURCE
P - PROMOTIONAL COMIC, EITHER GIVEN AWAY FOR FREE, OR A PREMIUM GIVEN IN CONJUNCTION WITH THE PURCHASE OF A PRODUCT.
S - SINGLE PANEL / NON-SEQUENTIAL CARTOONS (ENTIRELY OR PREDOMINANTLY)

Measurements are in inches. The first dimension given is Height and the second is Width. Some original British editions are included in the section, so as to better explain and differentiate their American counterparts. This section created, revised, and expanded by Robert Beerbohm, Doug Wheeler & Richard Olson with acknowledgment to Bill Blackbeard, Chris Brown, Alfredo Castelli, Darrell Coons, Leonardo De Sá, Scott Deschaine, Joe Evans, Ron Friggle, Tom Gordon, Michel Kempeneers, Andy Konkykru, Don Kurtz, Robert Quesinberry, Steve Rowe, Randy Scott, John Snyder, Art Spiegelman, Steve Thompson, Richard Samuel West and Richard Wright. Giant kudos to Gabriel Laderman.

ACROBATIC ANIMALS
R.H. Russell: 1899 (9x11-7/8", 72 pgs, B&W, hard-c)

nn 40.00 80.00 160.00
NOTE: *Animal strips by Gustave Verbeck, presented 1 panel per page.*

ALMY'S SANTA CLAUS (P,E)
Edward C. Almy & Co., Providence, R.I.: nd (1880's) (5-3/4x4-5/8", 20 pgs, B&W, paper cover)

nn - (Rare) 12.50 40.00 80.00
NOTE: *Department store Christmas giveaway containing an abbreviated 28-panel reprinting of George Cruikshank's* ***The Tooth-ache****. Santa Claus cover.*

AMERICANS (see **GIBSON'S PUBLISHED DRAWINGS**)

ATTWOOD'S PICTURES - AN ARTIST'S HISTORY OF THE LAST TEN YEARS OF THE NINETEENTH CENTURY (M,S)
Life Publishing Company, New York: 1900 (11-1/4x9-1/8", 156 pgs, B&W, gilted blue hard-c)

nn - By Attwood 40.00 80.00 160.00
NOTE: *Reprints monthly calendar cartoons which appeared in* ***LIFE****, for 1887 through 1899.*

BACHELOR BUTTERFLY, THE VERITABLE HISTORY OF MR. (E,G)
D. Bogue, London: 1845 (5-1/2x10-1/4", 74 pgs, B&W, gilted hardcover)

nn - By Rodolphe Töpffer (Scarce) 300.00 600.00 1200.00
nn - Hand colored edition (Very Rare) (no known sales)
NOTE: *This is the British Edition, translated from the re-engraved by Cham serialization found in* ***L'Illustration*** *- a periodical from Paris publisher Dubochet. Predates the first French collected edition. Third Töpffer comic book published in English. The first story page is numbered Page 3. Page 17 shows Bachelor Butterfly being swallowed by a whale.*

BACHELOR BUTTERFLY, THE STRANGE ADVENTURES OF (E,G)
Wilson & Co., New York: 1846 (5-3/8x10-1/8", 68 pgs, B&W, hardcover)

nn - By Rodolphe Töpffer (Very Rare) 300.00 600.00 1200.00
nn - At least one hand colored copy exists (Very Rare) (no known sales)
NOTE: *2nd Töpffer comic book printed in the U.S., 3rd earliest known sequential comic book in the USA. Reprinted from the British D. Bogue 1845 edition, itself from the earlier French language* ***Histoire de Mr. Cryptogame****. Released the same year as the French Dubochet edition. Two variations known, the earlier printing with Page number 17 placed on the inside (left) bottom corner in error, with slightly later printings corrected to place page number 17 on the outside (right) bottom corner of that page. For both printings: the first story page is numbered 2. Page 17 shows Bachelor Butterfly already in the whale. In most panels with 3 lines of text, the third line is indented further than the second, which is in turn indented further than the first.*

BACHELOR BUTTERFLY,THE STRANGE & WONDERFUL ADVENTURES OF
Dick & Fitzgerald, New York: 1870s-1888 (various printings 30 Cent cover price, 68 pgs, B&W, paper cover) (all versions Rare) (E,G)

nn - Black print on blue cover (5-1/2x10-1/2"); string bound 100.00 200.00 400.00
nn - Black print on green cover (5-1/2x10-1/2"); string bound 100.00 200.00 400.00
NOTE: *Reprints the earlier Wilson & Co. edition. Page 2 is the first story page. Page 17 shows Bachelor Butterfly already in the whale. In most panels with 3 lines of text, the second and third lines are equally indented in from the first. Unknown which cover (blue or green) is earlier.*

BACHELOR'S OWN BOOK. BEING THE PROGRESS OF MR. LAMBKIN, (GENT.) IN THE PURSUIT OF PLEASURE AND AMUSEMENT (E,O,G)
(See also PROGRESS OF MR. LAMBKIN)
D. Bogue, London: August 1, 1844 (5x8-1/4", 28 pgs printed one side only, cardboard cover & interior) (all versions Rare)

nn - First printing hand colored (no known sales)
nn - First printing black & white (no known sales)
NOTE: *First printing has misspellings in the title. "PURSUIT" is spelled "PERSUIT", and "AMUSEMENT" is spelled "AMUSEMEMT".*
nn - Second printing hand colored (no known sales)
nn - Second printing black & white (no known sales)
NOTE: Second printing. The misspelling of "PURSUIT" has been corrected, but "AMUSEMEMT" error is still present.
nn - Third printing hand colored No misspellings (no known sales)
nn - Third printing black & white (no known sales)
NOTE: *By George Cruikshank. This is the British Edition. Issued both in black & white, and professionally hand-colored editions. Hand-colored editions have survived in higher quantities than uncolored.*

BACHELOR'S OWN BOOK. BEING TWENTY-FOUR PASSAGES IN THE LIFE OF MR. LAMBKIN, GENT. (E,G)
Burgess, Stringer & Co., New York on cover; Carey & Hart, Philadelphia on title page: 1845 (31-1/4 cents, 7-1/2x4-5/8", 52 pgs, B&W, paper cover)

nn - By George Cruikshank (Very Rare) (no known sales)
NOTE: *This is the second known sequential comic book story published in America. Reprints the earlier British edition. Pages printed on one side only. New cover art by an unknown artist.*

BAD BOY'S FIRST READER (O,S)
G.W. Carleton & Co.: 1881 (5-3/4 x 4-1/8", 44 pgs, B&W, paper cover)

nn - By Frank Bellew (Senior) 50.00 100.00 200.00
NOTE: *Parody of a children's ABC primer, one cartoon illustration plus text per page. Includes one panel of Boss Tweed. Frank Bellew is considered the "Father of the American Sequential Comics."*

BARKER'S ILLUSTRATED ALMANAC (O,P,S)
Barker, Moore & Mein Medicine Co: 1878-1932+ (36 pgs, B&W, color paper-cr)

1878-1879 (Rare) 40.00 80.00 160.00
NOTE: *Not known what the cover art is.*
1880-1883 (Scarce, 7-3/4x6-1/8") 30.00 60.00 120.00
NOTE: *Cover art shows 4-mast ships & lighthouse.*
1884-1889 (8x6-1/4") 20.00 40.00 80.00
NOTE: *New cover art shows horse & rider jumping picket fence.*
1890-1897 (8-1/8x6-1/4") 20.00 40.00 80.00
1898-1899 (7-3/8x5-7/8") 20.00 40.00 80.00
1900+: see the Platinum Age Comics section (7x5-7/8")
NOTE: *Barker's Almanacs were actually issued in November of the year preceding the year which appears on the almanac. For example, the 1878 dated almanac was issued November 1877. They were given away to retailers of Barker's farm animal medicinal products, to in turn be given away to customers. Each Barker's almanac contains 10 full page cartoons. These frequently included racist stereotypes of blacks. Each cartoon contained advertisements for Barker's products. It is unknown whether the cartoons appeared only in the almanacs, or if they also ran as newspaper ads or flyers. Originally issued with a metal hook attached in the upper right hand corner, which could be used to hang the almanac.*

BARKER'S "KOMIC" PICTURE SOUVENIR (P,S)
Barker, Moore & Mein Medicine Co: nd (1892-94) (color cardboard cover, B&W interior) (all unnumbered editions Very Rare)

nn - (1892) (1st edition, 150 pgs) wraparound cover showing people headed towards Chicago for the 1893 World's Fair 80.00 160.00 320.00
nn - (1893) (2nd edition, ??? pgs) same cover as 1st edition 80.00 160.00 320.00
nn - (1894) (3rd edition, 180 pgs, 6-3/4x10-3/8") 80.00 160.00 320.00
NOTE: *New cover art showing crowd of people laughing with a copy of Barker's Almanac.The crowd picture is flanked on both sides by picture of a tall thin person.*
nn - (1894) (4th edition, 124 pgs, 6-3/8x9-3/8") same-c as 3rd edition 80.00 160.00 320.00
NOTE: *Essentially same-c as 3rd edition, except flanking picture on left edge is now gone. The 2nd through 4th editions state their printing on the first interior page, in the paragraph beneath the picture of the Barker's Building. These have been confirmed as premium comic books, predating the Buster Brown premiums. They reprint advertising cartoons from Barker's Illustrated Almanac. For the 50 page booklets by this same name, numbered as "Part"s, see the PLATINUM AGE SECTION. All "Editions in Parts", without exception, were published after 1900.*

BEAU OGLEBY, THE COMICAL ADVENTURES OF (E,G)
Tilt & Bogue: nd (c1843) (5-7/8x9-1/8", 72 pgs, printed one side only, green gilted hard-c, B&W)

nn - By Rodolphe Töpffer (Rare) 200.00 400.00 1000.00
nn - Hand coloured edition (Very Rare) (no known sales)
NOTE: *British Edition; no known American Edition. Second Töpffer comic book published in English. Translated from Paris publisher Aubert's unauthorized redrawn 1839 bootleg edition of Töpffer's* ***Histoire de Mr. Jabot****. The backmost interior page is an advertisement for* ***Obadiah Oldbuck****, showing the cover for that comic book.*

Barker's "Komic" Picture Souvenir, Third Edition
1894 © Barker. Moore & Klein Medicine Co.

The Bottle by George Cruickshank
1871 © Geo. Gebbie, Philadelphia

The Story of The Man of Humanity and The Bull Calf by A. B. Frost
1890 © C.H. Fargo & Co.

BEFORE AND AFTER. A LOCOFOCO CHRISTMAS PRESENT. (O, C)
D.C. Johnston, Boston: 1837 (4-3/4x3", 1 page, hand colored cardboard)

nn - (Very Rare) by David Claypool Johnston (sold at auction for $400 in GD)
NOTE: *Pull-tab cartoon envelope, parodying the 1836 New York City mayoral election, picturing the candidate of the Locofoco Party smiling "Before the N.York election", then, when the tab is pulled, picturing him with an angry sneer "After the N.York election".*

BILLY GOAT AND OTHER COMICALITIES, THE (M)
Charles Scribner's Sons: 1898 (6-3/4x8-1/2", 116 pgs., B&W, Hardcover)

nn - By E. W. Kemble 67.50 133.00 400.00

BLACKBERRIES, THE (N.S) (see Coontown's 400)
R. H. Russell: 1897 (9"x12", 76 pgs, hard-c, every other page in color, every other page in one color sepia tone)

nn - By E. W. Kemble 139.50 279.00 975.00
NOTE: *Tastefully done comics about Black Americana during the USA's Jim Crow days.*

BOOK OF BUBBLES, YE (S)
Endicott & Co., New York: March 1864 (6-1/4 x 9-7/8",152 pgs?, guilt-illus. hard-c, B&W

nn - By unknown 40.00 80.00 160.00
NOTE: *Subtitle: A contribution to the New York Fair in aid of the Sanitary Commission; 68 single-sided pages of B&W cartoons, each with an accompanying limerick. A few are sequential.*

BOOK OF DRAWINGS BY FRED RICHARDSON (N,S)
Lakeside Press, Chicago: 1899 (13-5/8x10-1/2", 116 pgs, B&W, hard-c)

nn - (Scarce) 80.00 160.00 320.00
NOTE: *Reprinted from the* ***Chicago Daily News****. Mostly single panel. Includes one* ***Yellow Kid*** *parody, some Spanish-American War cartoons.*

BOTTLE, THE (E,O) (see also THE DRUNKARD'S CHILDREN, and TEA GARDEN TO TEA POT, and TEMPERANCE TALES; OR, SIX NIGHTS WITH THE WASHINGTONIANS)
D. Bogue, London, with others in later editions: nd (1846) (11-1/2x16-1/2", 16 pgs, printed one side only, paper cover)

D. Bogue, London (nd; 1846): first edition:
nn - Black & white (Scarce) 200.00 400.00 900.00
nn - Hand colored (Rare) (no known sales)
D. Bogue, London, and Wiley and Putnam, New York (nd; 1847) : second edition, misspells American publisher "Putnam" as "Putman":
nn - Black & white (Scarce) 150.00 300.00 600.00
nn - Hand colored (Rare) (no known sales)
D. Bogue, London, and Wiley and Putnam, New York (nd; 1847) : third edition has "Putnam" spelled correctly.
nn - Black & white (Scarce) 150.00 300.00 600.00
nn - Hand colored (Rare) (no known sales)
D. Bogue, London, Wiley and Putnam, New York, and J. Sands, Sydney, New South Wales: (nd; 1847) : fourth edition with no misspellings
nn - Black & white (Scarce) 150.00 300.00 600.00
nn - Hand colored (Rare) (no known sales)
NOTE: *By George Cruikshank. Temperance/anti-alcohol story. All editions are in precisely identical format. The only difference is to be found on the cover, where it lists who published it. Cover is text only - no cover art.*

BOTTLE, THE HISTORY OF THE
J.C. Becket, 22 Grea St James St, Montreal, Canada: 1851 (9-1/8x6", B&W)

nn - From Engravings by Cruikshank 150.00 300.00 600.00
NOTE: *As published in The Canada Temperance Advocate.*

BOTTLE, THE (E)
W. Tweedie, London: nd (1862) (11-1/2x17-1/3", 16 pgs, printed one side only, paper cover)

nn - Black & white; By George Cruikshank (Scarce) 100.00 200.00 400.00
nn - Hand colored (Scarce) (no known sales)

BOTTLE, THE (E)
Geo. Gebbie, Philadelphia: nd (c.1871) (11-3/8x17-1/8", 42 pgs, tinted interior, hard-c)

nn - By George Cruikshank 100.00 200.00 400.00
NOTE: *New cover art (cover not by Cruikshank).*

BOTTLE, THE (E)
National Temperance, London: nd (1881) (11-1/2x16-1/2", 16 pgs, printed one side only, paper-c, color)

nn - By George Cruikshank 100.00 200.00 400.00
NOTE: *See Platinum Age section for 1900s printings.*

BOTTLE, THE (E) (for the later Gowans & Gray, and the Frederick A. Stokes printings, see PLATINUM AGE section).

BULL CALF, THE (P,M)
Creme Oatmeal Toilet Soap: nd (c1890's) (3-7/8x4-1/8", 16 pgs, B&W, paper-c)

nn - By A.B. Frost 25.00 50.00 100.00
NOTE: *Reprints the popular strip story by Frost, with the art modified to place a sign for Creme Oatmeal Soap within each panel. The back cover advertises the specific merchant who gave this booklet away - multiple variations exist.*

BULL CALF AND OTHER TALES, THE (M)
Charles Scribner's Sons: 1892 (120 pgs., 6-3/4x8-7/8", B&W, illus. hard cover)

nn - By Arthur Burdett Frost 50.00 100.00 450.00
NOTE: *Blue, grey, tan hard covers known to exist.*

BULL CALF, THE STORY OF THE MAN OF HUMANITY AND THE (P,M)
C.H. Fargo & Co.: 1890 (5-1/4x6-1/4", 24 pgs, B&W, color paper-c)

nn - By A.B. Frost 42.50 85.00 185.00
NOTE: *Fargo shoe company giveaway; pages alternate between shoe advertisements and the strip story.*

BUSHEL OF MERRY THOUGHTS, A (see Mischief Book, The) (E)
Sampson Low Son & Marsten: 1868 (68 pgs, handcolored hardcover, B&W)

nn - (6-1/4 x 9-7/8", 138 pgs) red binding, publisher's name on title page only 200.00 400.00 800.00
nn - (6-1/2 x 10", 134 pgs) green binding, publisher's name on cover & title page 200.00 400.00 800.00
NOTE: *Cover plus story title pages designed by Leighton Brothers, based on Busch art. Translated by Harry Rogers (who is credited instead of Busch). This is a British publication, notable as the earliest known English language anthology collection of Wilhelm Busch comic strips. Page 13 of second story missing from all editions (panel dropped). Unknown which of the two editions was published first. Had a modern reprint, by Dover in 1971.*

BUTTON BURSTER, THE (M) (says on cover "ten cents hard cash")
M.J. Ivers & Co., 86 Nassau St., New York: 1873 (11x8-1/8", soft paper, B&W)

By various cartoonists 100.00 200.00 400.00
NOTE: *Reprints from various 1873 issues of Wild Oats; has (5) different sequential comic strips: (3) by Livingston Hopkins, (1) by Thomas Worth, other one creator presently unknown; Bellew, Sr. single panel cartoons.*

BUZZ A BUZZ OR THE BEES (E)
Griffith & Farran, London: September 1872 (8-1/2x5-1/2", 168 pgs, printed one side only, orange, black & white hardcover, B&W interior)

nn - By Wilhelm Busch (Scarce) 100.00 200.00 400.00
NOTE: *Reprint published by Phillipson & Golder, Chester; text written by English to accompany Busch art.*

BUZZ A BUZZ OR THE BEES (E)
Henry Holt & Company, New York: 1873 (9x6", 96 pgs, gilted hardcover, hand colored)

nn - By Wilhelm Busch (Scarce) 100.00 200.00 400.00
NOTE: *Completely different translation than the Griffith & Farran version. Also, contains 28 additional illustrations by Park Benjamin. The lower page count is because the Henry Holt edition prints on both sides of each page, and the Griffith & Farran edition is printed one side only.*

CALENDAR FOR THE MONTH; YE PICTORIAL LYSTE OF YE MATTERS OF INTEREST FOR SUMMER READING (P,M)
S.E. Bridgman & Company, Northampton, Mass: nd (c. late 1880's-1890's) (5-5/8x7-1/4", 64 pgs, paper-c, B&W)

nn - (Very Rare) T.S. Sullivant-c/a 100.00 200.00 400.00
NOTE: *Book seller's catalog, with every other page reprinting cartoons and strips (from Life??). Art by: Chips Bellew, Gibson, Howarth, Kemble, Sullivant, Townsend, Woolf.*

CARICATURE AND OTHER COMIC ART
Harper & Brothers, NY: 1877 (9-5/16x7-1/8", 360 pgs, B&W, green hard-c)

nn - By James Parton (over 200 illustrations) 25.00 75.00 150.00
NOTE: *This is the earliest known serious history of comics & related genre from around the world produced by an American. Parton was a cousin of Thomas Nast's wife Sarah. A large portion of this book was first serialized in* ***Harper's Monthly*** *in 1875.*

CARICATURE HISTORY OF CANADIAN POLITICS (M,S)
Grip, Toronto: 1886; 1886 (12-3/4x10-3/8", 440 pgs, hard-c, B&W)

nn (Vol. 1) - (blue gilted-c) cartoon-r from 1849-1878 67.50 125.00 250.00
NOTE: *The pages of Volume 1 are heavily interlaced with advertising sheets for Toronto businesses (these are not part of the page count), including a smaller sized 96-pg machinery catalog, all bound into the volume.*

Vol. 2 - (brown gilted-c) cartoon-r from 1879-1884 67.50 125.00 250.00
NOTE: *Chronologically organized reprinting of single panel Canadian political cartoons, taken from a variety of Canadian publications. Each right-hand page is a full page cartoon, while each left-hand page is text describing the political situation which was being satirized.*

CARROT-POMADE (O.G)
James G. Gregory, Publisher, New York: 1864 (9x6-7/8", 36 pgs, B&W)

nn - By Augustus Hoppin 70.00 140.00 280.00
NOTE: *The story of a quack remedy for baldness, sequentially told in the format parodying ABC primers. Has protective tissue pages (not part of page count).*

CARTOONS BY HOMER C. DAVENPORT (M,N,S)
De Witt Publishing House: 1898 (16-1/8x12", 102 pgs, hard-c, B&W)

nn 70.00 140.00 280.00
NOTE: *Reprinted from Harper's Weekly and the New York Journal. Includes cartoons about the Spanish-American War. Title page reads "Davenport's Cartoons".*

A Bushel of Merry Thoughts by Wilhelm Busch
1868 © Samuel Low Son & Marston

The Button Burster from Wild Oats
1873 © M.J. Ivers & Co., NY

The Clown, or The Banquet of Wit
1851 © Fisher & Brother

FR1.0 GD2.0 FN6.0

CARTOONS BY WILL E. CHAPIN (P,N,S)
The Times-Mirror Printing and Binding House, Los Angeles: 1899 (15-1/4x12", 98 pgs, hard-c, B&W)

nn 70.00 140.00 280.00
NOTE: *Premium item for subscribing to the Los-Angeles Times-Mirror newspaper, from which these cartoons were reprinted. Includes cartoons about the Spanish-American War.*

CARTOONS OF OUR WAR WITH SPAIN (N,S)
Frederick A. Stokes Company: 1898 (11-1/2x10", 72 pgs, hardcover, B&W)

nn - By Charles Nelan (r-New York Herald) 40.00 80.00 160.00
nn - 2nd printing noted on copy right page 30.00 60.00 120.00

CARTOONS OF THE WAR OF 1898 (E,M,N,S)
Belford, Middlebrook & Co., Chicago: 1898 (7x10-3/8",190 pgs, B&W, hard-c)

nn 50.00 100.00 200.00
NOTE: *Reprints single panel editorial cartoons on the Spanish-American War, from American, Spanish, Latino, and European newspapers and magazines, at rate of 2 to 6 cartoons per page. Art by Bart, Berryman, Bowman, Bradley, Chapin, Gillam, Nelan, Tenniel, others.*

CENTENNIAL FUN (O,S) (Rare)
Frank Leslie, Philadelphia: (July) 1876 (25¢, 11x8", 32 pgs, paper cover, B&W)

nn - By Joseph Keppler-c/a;Thomas Worth-a 50.00 100.00 200.00
NOTE: *Issued for the 1876 Centennial Exposition in Philadelphia. Exists with both black & white, and orange, black & white covers. One copy of the latter had an embossed newstand label from Partland, Maine, implying that the orange cover version, at least, was distributed and sold outside of Philadelphia.*

CHILDREN'S CHRISTMAS BOOK, THE
The New York Sunday World: 1897 (10-1/4x8-3/4", 16 pgs, full color)

Dec 12, 1897 - By George Luks, G.H. Grant, Will Crawford, others) (Rare) 50.00 100.00 280.00

CHIP'S DOGS (M)
R.H. Russell and Son Publishers: 1895 hardcover, B&W)

nn - By Frank P. W. "Chip" Bellew 25.00 50.00 100.00
Early printing 80 pgs, 8-7/8x11-7/8"; dark green border of hardcover surrounds all four sides of pasted on cover image; pages arranged in error -- see NOTE below. (more scarce)
nn - By Frank P. W. "Chip" Bellew 12.50 25.00 50.00
Later printing 72 pgs, 8-7/8x11-3/4";green border only on the binding side (one side) of the cover image.
NOTE: *Both are strip reprints from **LIFE**. The difference in page count is due to more blank pages in the first printing -- all printings have the same comics contents, but with the pages in the first printing arranged differently. This is noticeable particularly in the 2-page strip "Getting a Pointer", which appears on the 2nd & 3rd to last pages of the later printings, but in the early printing the first half of this strip is near the middle of the book, while the last half appears on the 2nd to last story page.*

CHIP'S OLD WOOD CUTS (M,S)
R.H. Russell & Son: 1895 (8-7/8x11-3/4", 72 pgs, hardcover, B&W)

nn - By Frank P. W. ("Chip") Bellew 25.00 50.00 100.00

CHIP'S UN-NATURAL HISTORY (O,S)
Frederick A. Stokes & Brother: 1888 (7x5-1/4", 64 pgs, hardcover, B&W)

nn - By Frank P. W. ("Chip") Bellew 12.50 25.00 50.00
NOTE: *Title page lists publisher as "Successors to White, Stokes & Allen."*

CLOWN, OR THE BANQUET OF WIT, THE (E,M,O)
Fisher & Brother, Philadelphia, Baltimore, New York, Boston: nd (c.1851) (7-3/8x4-1/2", 88 pgs, paper cover, B&W)

nn - (Very Rare; 2 known copies) 300.00 600.00 900.00
NOTE: *Earliest known multi-artist anthology of sequential comics; contains multiple sequential comics, plus numerous single panel cartoons. A mixture of reprinted and original material, involving both European and American artists. "Jones, Smith, and Robinson Goes to a Ball" by Richard Doyle (1st app. of Doyle's "Foreign Tour" in America, reprinted from PUNCH, August 24, 1850); "Moses Keyser The Bowery Bully's Trip to the Californian Gold Mines", by John H. Manning; "The Adventures of Mr. Gulp" (by the Read brothers?); more comics by artists unknown; cartoons by George Cruikshank, Grandville, Elton.*

COLD CUTS AND PICKLED EELS' FEET; DONE BROWN BY JOHN BROWN
P.J. Cozans, New York: nd (c1855-60) (B&W)

nn 50.00 100.00 200.00
NOTE: *Mostly a children's book. But, pages 87 to 110, and 111 to 122, contain narrative sequential stories.*

COLLEGE SCENES (O,G)
N. Hayward, Boston: 1850 (5x6-3/4", 72 pgs, printed one side only, B&W lithography)

nn - (Rare) by Nathan Hayward 200.00 400.00 600.00
NOTE: *This is the 2nd such production for an American University; the first issued at Yale circa 1845, decent funny art of story about life of a Harvard student from his entrance thru graduation entirely in caricature. Has art on back cover as well.*

COLLEGE CUTS Chosen From The Columbia Spectator 1880-81-82 (S)
White & Stokes, NY: 1882 (8x9-5/8", B&W)

By F. Benedict Herzog,H. McVickar,W. Bard McVickar,others 20.00 40.00 80.00

COMICAL COONS (M)
R.H. Russell: 1898 (8-7/8 x 11-7/8", 68 pgs, hardcover, B&W)

FR1.0 GD2.0 FN6.0

nn - By E. W. Kemble 150.00 300.00 700.00
NOTE: *Black Americana collection of 2-panel stories.*

COMIC ANNUAL, AMERICAN (O,I)
Richardson, Lord, & Holbrook, Boston: 1831 (6-7/8x4-3/8", 268 pgs, B&W, hard-c)

nn - (Very Rare) (no known sales)
NOTE: *Mostly text; front & back cover illustrations, 13 full page, and scattered smaller illustrations by David Claypool Johnston; edited by Henry J. Finn.*

COMIC HISTORY OF THE UNITED STATES, (I)
Carleton & Co., NY: 1876 (6-7/8x5-1/8", 336 pgs, hardcover, B&W)

nn - By Livingston Hopkins. 12.50 25.00 50.00
2nd printing: Cassell, Petter, Galpin & Co.: 1880 (6-7/8x5-1/8", 336 pgs, hardcover, B&W)
nn - By Livingston Hopkins. 12.50 25.00 50.00
NOTE: *Text with many B&W illustrations; some are multi-panel comics. Not to beconfused with **Bill Nye's Comic History Of The U.S.** which contains Frederick Opper illustrations.*

COMICS FROM SCRIBNER'S MAGAZINE (M)
Scribner's: nd (1891) (10 cents, 9-1/2x6-5/8", 24 pgs, paper cover, side stapled, B&W)

nn - (Rare) F.M.Howarth C&A 75.00 150.00 300.00
NOTE: *Advertised in SCRIBNER'S MAGAZINE in the June 1891 issue, page 793, as available by mail order for 10 cents. Collects together comics material which ran in the back pages of Scribner's Magazine. Art by Attwood, "Chip" Bellew, Does, Frost, Gibson, Zim.*

COONTOWN'S 400 (M) (see **Blackberries**) (M)
The Life (Magazine) Co.: 1899 (10-15/16x8-7/8, 68 pgs, cloth light-brown hard-c, B&W

nn - By E.W. Kemble (scarce) 150.00 300.00 1000.00
NOTE: *Tastefully drawn depictions of Black Americana over one hundred years ago during Jim Crow days.*

CROSSING THE ATLANTIC (O,G)
James R. Osgood & Co., Boston: 1872 (68 pgs, hardcover, B&W); **Houghton, Osgood & Co., Boston:** 1880

1st printing - by Augustus Hoppin 45.00 90.00 180.00
2nd printing (1880; 66 pgs; 8-1/8x11-1/8") 32.50 65.00 150.00

CRUIKSHANK'S OMNIBUS: A VEHICLE FOR FUN AND FROLIC (E,S)
E. Ferrett & Co., Philadelphia: 1845 (25 cents, 7-1/2" x 4-5/8", 96 pgs, B&W, paper-c)

nn - By George Cruikshank c/a (Very Rare) 75.00 150.00 300.00
NOTE: *Mostly prose, with 10 plates of cartoons printed on one-side (about half the plates with multiple cartoons), plus illustrated cover, all by George Cruikshank. First (perhaps only) American printing of Cruikshank's Omnibus, which was published first in Britain. It is only a partial reprinting.*

CUBAN PICTURES (see OUR ARTIST IN CUBA) (O)

DAVENPORT'S CARTOONS (see CARTOONS BY HOMER C. DAVENPORT)

DAY'S SPORT - OR, HUNTING ADVENTURES OF S. WINKS WATTLES, A SHOPKEEPER, THOMAS TITT, A "LEGAL GENT," AND MAJOR NICHOLAS NOGGIN, A JOLLY GOOD FELLOW GENERALLY, A (O)
Brother Jonathan, NY: c1850s (???)

nn - By Henry L. Stevens, Philadelphia (no known sales)
NOTE: *Known only so far from a mid 1850s Brother Jonathan catalog - see Victorian Age essay. One partial copy turned by in late 2003 bound in with other 1800s material.*

DIE VEHME, ILLUSTRIRTES WOCHENBLATT FUR SCHERZ UND ERNEST (M,O)
Heinrich Binder, St. Louis: No.1 Aug 28, 1869 - No.?? Aug 20, 1870 (10 cents, 8 pgs, B&W, paper-c) (see also PUCK)

1-?? (Very Rare) by Joseph Keppler (no known sales)
NOTE: *Joseph Keppler's first attempt at a weekly American humor periodical. Entirely in German. The title translates into: **"The Star Chamber: An Illustrated Weekly Paper in Fun and Ernest"**.*

DRUNKARD'S CHILDREN, THE (see also THE BOTTLE) (E,O)
David Bogue, London; John Wiley and G.P. Putnam, New York; J. Sands, Sydney, New South Wales: July 1, 1848 (11x16", 16 pgs, printed on one side only, paper-c)

nn - Black & white edition (Rare) 300.00 600.00 900.00
nn - Hand colored edition (Rare) (no known sales)
NOTE: *Sequel story to THE BOTTLE, by George Cruikshank. Temperance/anti-alcohol story. British-American-Australian co-publication. Cover is text only - no cover art.*

DRUNKARD'S PROGRESS, OR THE DIRECT ROAD TO POVERTY, WRETCHEDNESS & RUIN, THE
J. W. Barber, New Haven, Conn.: Sept 1826 (single sheet)

nn - By John Warner Barber (no known sales)
NOTE: *Broadside designed and printed by barber contains four large wood engravings showing "The Morning Dram" which is "The Beginning of Sorrow"; "The Grog Shop" with its "Bad Company"; "The Confirmed Drunkard" in a state of "Beastly Intoxication"; and the "Concluding Scene" with the family being drive off to the alms house. It is an interesting set of cuts, faintly reminiscent of Hogarth.*

DUEL FOR LOVE, A (O,P)
E.C. DeWitt & Co., Chicago: nd (c1880's) (3-3/8" x 2-5/8", 12 pgs, B&W, paper-c)

nn - Art by F.M. Howarth 25.00 50.00 100.00
NOTE: *Advertising giveaway for DeWitt's Little Early Risers, featuring an 8-panel strip story, spread out 1 panel per page.*

Comics From Scribner's Magazine
1891 © Scribner's

Crossing the Atlantic by Augustus Heppin
1880 © Houghton, Osgood & Co., Boston

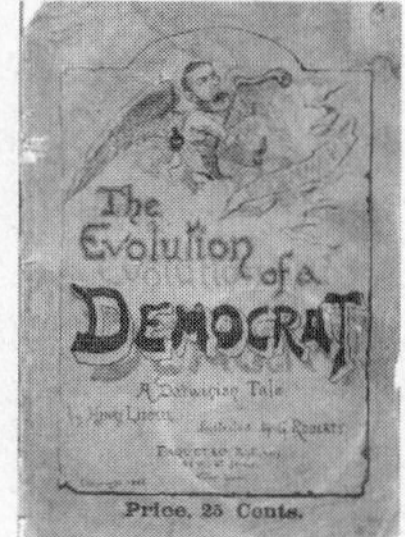

The Evolution of A Democrat
A Darwinian Tale
1888 © Paquet & Co., New York

EDUCATION OF MR. PIPP, THE (M) (see GIBSON'S PUBLISHED DRAWINGS)

ELTON'S COMIC ALL-MY-NACK (E,O.S)
Elton, Publisher, 18 Division & 90 Nassau St, NY: 1833-?? 1850s (7-1/2x4-1/2", 36 pgs, B&W)

1-15 - 99% single panel cartoons 60.00 120.00 240.00
16 - contains 6 panel "A Tales of A Tayl-or" 1848-49 200.00 400.00 600.00
17 - contains "Moses Keyser, The Bowery Bully's Trip To the California Gold Mines" 1850 By John H. Manning, early comics creator told in 15 panels 200.00 400.00 600.00
18-up presently unknown contents 60.00 120.00 240.00
NOTE: *Contains both original American, and pirated European, cartoons. All single panel material, except where noted. Almanacs are published near the end of the year prior to that for which they are printed -- like calendars today. Thus, the 1833 No. 1 issue was really published in the last months of 1832. #17 has Elton's Californian Comic-All-My-Nack on the cover.*

ENTER: THE COMICS (E,G)
University of Nebraska Press: 1965

nn - By Ellen Weisse 25.00 50.00 100.00
NOTE: *Contains overview of Töpffer's life and career plus only published English translation of Töpffer's Monsieur Crepin (1837); appears to have been re-drawn by Weisse in the days before xerox machines.*

EVOLUTION OF A DEMOCRAT - A DARWINIAN TALE, THE (O,G)
Paquet & Co., New York: 1888 (25 cents, 7-7/8x5-1/2", 100 pgs, printed one side only, orange paper cover, B&W) (Very Rare)

nn - Written by Henry Liddell, art by G. Roberty 50.00 100.00 200.00
NOTE: *Political parody about the rise of an Irishman through Tammany Hall. Grover Cleveland appears as linked with Tammany. Ireland becomes the next state in the USA.*

FABLES FOR OUR TIMES (S, I)
R.H. Russell & Son, New York: 1896 (52 pgs, yellow hard-c)

nn - By H.W. Phillips and T.S. Sullivant 25.00 50.00 100.00

FERDINAND FLIPPER, ESQ., THE FORTUNES OF (O,G)
Brother Jonathan, Publisher, NY: nd (1851) (80 pgs, B&W, printed both sides)

nn - By Various (scarce) 300.00 600.00 900.00
NOTE: *Extended title: "...Commencing With A Period of Four Months And Anterior To His Birth Going Thru The Various Stages of His Infancy, Childhood, Verdant Years, Manhood, Middle Life, and Green and Ripe Old Age, And Ending A Short Time Subsequent to His Sudden Decease With His Final Exit, Funeral And Burial." Extremely unique comic book, put together by gathering 145 independent single illustrations and cartoons, by various artists, and stringing them together into a sequential story. The majority of panels are by Grandville. Also included are at least 19 signed Charles Martin, reprinted from 1847 issues of Yankee Doodle, 5 panels from D.C. Johnston, plus other panels by F.O.C. Darley, T.H. Matheson, and others. Printed by E.A. Alverds. The 1851 date is derived from an advertisement found in the Oct-Dec 1851 issue of the Brother Jonathan newspaper. It ispossible, however, that it actually came out even earlier.*

FERDINAND FLIPPER, ESQ., THE FORTUNES OF (G)
Dick & Fitzgerald, New York: nd (1870's to 1888) (30 Cents, 80 pgs, B&W, paper cover)

nn - (scarce reprint - several editions possible) 100.00 200.00 300.00

FINN'S COMIC SKETCHBOOK (S)
Peabody & Co., 223 Broadway, NY: 1831 (10-1/2x16", 12 pgs, B&W)

nn - By Henry J. Finn (no known sales)
NOTE: *Designs on copper plates; etched by J. Harris, NY; should have tissue paper in front of each plate.*

50 GREAT CARTOONS (M,P,S)
Ram's Horn Press: 1899

nn - By Frank Beard 30.00 60.00 120.00
NOTE: *Premium in return for a subscription to **The Ram's Horn** magazine.*

F**** A*** K*****, OUTLINES ILLUSTRATIVE OF THE JOURNAL OF** (O,S)
D.C. Johnston, Boston: 1835 (9-5/16 x 6", 12 pgs, printed one side only, blue paper cover, B&W interior) (see also **SCRAPS**)

nn - (Rare) by David Claypool Johnston 200.00 400.00 600.00
NOTE: *This is a series of 8 plates parodying passages from the Journal of Fanny (Frances) A. Kemble, a British woman who wrote a highly negative book about American Culture after returning from the U.S. Though remembered now for her campaign against slavery, she was prejudiced against most everything American culture, thus inspiring Johnston's satire. Contains 4 protective sheets (not part of page count.)*

FLY-ING DUTCHMAN; OR, THE WRATH OF HERR VON STOPPELNOZE, THE (E)
Carleton Publishing, New York: 1862 (7-5/8x5-1/4", 84 pgs, printed on one side only, gilted hardcover, B&W)

nn - By Wilhelm Busch (Scarce) 35.00 70.00 140.00
NOTE: *This is the earliest known English language book publication of a Wilhelm Busch work. The story is plagiarized by American poet John G. Saxe, who is credited with the text, while the uncredited Busch cartoons are described merely as accompanying illustrations.*

FLYING LEAVES (E)
E.R. Herrick & Company, New York: nd (c1889/1890's) (8-1/4" x 11-1/2", 76 pgs, B&W interior, orange, b&w hard-c)

nn- (Scarce) 80.00 160.00 240.00
NOTE: *Reprints strips and single panel cartoons from 1888 Fliegende Blatter issues, translated into English. Various artists, including Bechstein, Adolf Hengeler, Lothar Meggendorfer, Emil Reinicke.*

FOOLS PARADISE WITH THE MANY ADVENTURES THERE AS SEEN IN THE STRANGE SURPRISING PEEP SHOW OF PROFESSOR WOLLEY COBBLE, THE (E)
(see also THE COMICAL PEEP SHOW)
John Camden Hotten, London: Nov 1871 (1 crown, 9-7/8x7-3/8", 172 pgs, printed one side only, gilted green hardcover, hand colored interior)

nn - By Wilhelm Busch (Rare) 400.00 800.00 1600.00
NOTE: *Title on cover is: **WALK IN! WALK IN!! JUST ABOUT TO BEGIN!!! the FOOLS PARADISE**; below the above title page. Anthology of Wilhelm Busch comics, translated into English.*

FOOLS PARADISE WITH THE MANY WONDERFUL SIGHTS AS SEEN IN THE STRANGE SURPRISING PEEP SHOW OF PROFESSOR WOLLEY COBBLE, FURTHER ADVENTURES IN (E)
Chatto & Windus, London: 1873 (10x7-3/8", 128 pgs, printed one side only, brown hardcover, hand colored interior)

nn - By Wilhelm Busch (Rare) 300.00 600.00 1200.00
NOTE: *Sequel to the 1871 **FOOLS PARADISE**, containing a completely different set of Busch stories, translated into English.*

FOOLS PARADISE MIRTH AND FUN FOR OLD & YOUNG (E)
Griffith & Farran, London: May 1883 (9-3/4x7-5/8", 78 pgs, color cover, color interior)

nn - By Wilhelm Busch (Rare) 100.00 200.00 400.00
NOTE: *Collection of selected stories reprinted from both the 1871 & 1873 **FOOLS PARADISE**.*

FOREIGN TOUR OFMESSRS. BROWN, JONES, AND ROBINSON, THE (see Messrs...,)

FUN BY RALL
Unknown: circa 1865 (11x7-7/8", 68 pgs, soft-c, B&W)

nn - By presently unknown 100.00 200.00 300.00
NOTE: *Wraparound soft cover like modern comic book; yellow paper cover with red & black ink.*

FUN FOR THE FAMILY IN PICTURES
D. Lothrop and Company: 1886 (3-3/4x6-3/4", 48 pgs, Silver & Red stiff-c; interior pages have various single color inks)

nn - By unknown hand 50.00 100.00 200.00
NOTE: *Single panel cartoons and sequential stories.*

FUNNY FOLK (M)
E. P. Dutton: 1899 (12x16-1/2", 90 pgs,14 strips in color-rest in b&w, hard-c)

nn - By Franklin Morris Howarth 162.50 325.00 1300.00
nn - London: J.M. Dent, 1899 embossed-c; same interior 100.00 300.00 600.00
NOTE: *Reprints many sequential strips & single panel cartoons from **Puck**. This is considered by many to be yet another "missing link" between Victorian & Platinum Age comic books. Most comic books 1900-1917 reprinting Sunday newspaper comic strips follow this size format, except using cardboard-c rather than hard-c.*

GIBSON BOOK, THE (M,S)
Charles Scribner's Sons & R.H. Russell, New York: 1906 (11-3/8x17-5/8", gilted red hard-c, B&W)

Book I 50.00 100.00 200.00
NOTE: *Reprints in whole the books: Drawings, Pictures of People, London,Sketches and Cartoons, Education of Mr. Pipp, Americans. 414 pgs. 1907 2nd editions exist same value.*
Book II 50.00 100.00 200.00
NOTE: *Reprints in whole the books: A Widow and Her Friends, The Weaker Sex, Everyday People, Our Neighbors. 314 pgs 1907 second edition for both also exists. Same value.*

GIBSON'S PUBLISHED DRAWINGS, MR. (M,S) (see Plat index for later issues post 1900)
R.H. Russell, New York: No.1 1894 - No. 9 1904 (11x17-3/4", hard-c, B&W)

nn (No.1; 1894) Drawings 96 pgs 30.00 60.00 120.00
nn (No.2; 1896) Pictures of People 92 pgs 30.00 60.00 120.00
nn (No.3; 1898) Sketches and Cartoons 94 pgs 30.00 60.00 120.00
nn (No.4; 1899) The Education of Mr. Pipp 88 pgs 30.00 60.00 120.00
nn (No.5; 1900) Americans 30.00 60.00 120.00
NOTE: *By Charles Dana Gibson cartoons, reprinted from magazines, primarily **LIFE**. The Education of Mr. Pipp tells a story. Series continues how long after 1904?*

GIRL WHO WOULDN'T MIND GETTING MARRIED, THE (O)
Frederick Warne & Co., London & New York: nd (c1870's) (9-1/2x11-1/2", 28 pgs, printed 1 side, paper-c, B&W)

nn - By Harry Parkes 62.50 125.00 250.00
NOTE: *Published simultaneously with its companion volume, **The Man Who Would Like to Marry**.*

GOBLIN SNOB, THE (O)
DeWitt & Davenport, New York: nd (c1853-56) (24 x 17 cm, 96 pgs, B&W, color hard-c)

nn - (Rare) by H.L. Stephens (no known sales)

GREAT LOCOFOCO JUGGERNAUT, THE (S)
Imprint Society: 1971 (reprint)

nn - By David Claypool Johnston - 12.00 25.00

HALF A CENTURY OF ENGLISH HISTORY (S. M)
G.P. Putnam's Sons - The Knickerbocker Press, New York and London: 1884 (7-3/4 x 5-3/4", 316 pgs., illustrated hard-c)

Flying Leaves
1880s © E.R. Herrick & Company, New York

The Fools Paradise Mirth and Fun
For Old and Young
1883 © Griffith & Farran, London

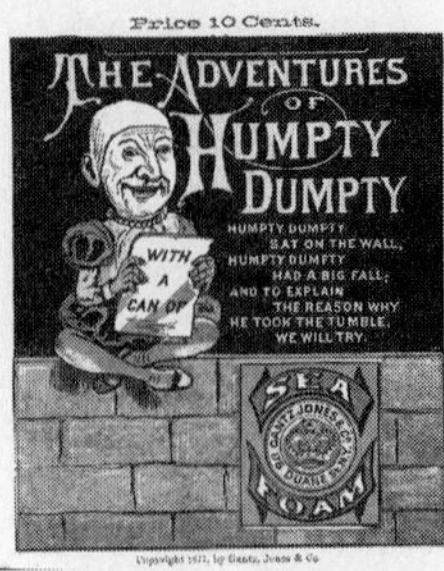

Humpty Dumpty, The Adventures of...
© Gantz, Jones and Co.

FR1.0 GD2.0 FN6.0

nn - By Various 25.00 50.00 175.00
NOTE: *Subtitle: Pictorially Presented in a Series of Cartoons from the Collection of Mr. Punch. Comprising 150 plates by Doyle, Leech, Tenniel, and others, in which are portrayed the political careers of Peel, Palmerston, Russell, Cobden, Bright, Beaconsfield, Derby, Salisbury, Gladstone and other English statesmen.*

HAIL COLUMBIA! HISTORICAL, COMICAL, AND CENTENNIAL (O,S)
The Graphic Co., New York & Walter F. Brown, Providence, RI: 1876 (10x11-3/8", 60 pgs, red gilted hard-c, B&W)

nn - (Rare) by Walter F. Brown 100.00 200.00 400.00

HEALTH GUYED (I)
Frederick A. Stokes Company: 1890 (5-3/8 x 8-3/8, 56 pgs, hardcover, B&W)

nn - By Frank P.W. ("Chip") Bellew (Junior) 25.00 50.00 175.00
NOTE: *Text & cartoon illustration parody of a health guide.*

HITS AT POLITICS (M,S)
R.H. Russell, New York: 1899 (15" x 12", 156 pgs, B&W, hard-c)

nn - W.A. Rogers c/a 100.00 200.00 300.00
NOTE: *Collection of W.A. Rogers cartoons, all reprinted from Harper's Weekly. Includes Spanish-American War cartoons.*

HOME MADE HAPPY. A ROMANCE FOR MARRIED MEN IN SEVEN CHAPTERS (O,P)
Genuine Durham Smoking Tobacco & The Graphic Co.: nd (c1870's) (5-1/4 tall x 3-3/8" wide folded, 27" wide unfolded, color cardboard)

nn - With all 8 panels attached (Scarce) 30.00 60.00 150.00
nn - Individual panels/cards 5.00 10.00 25.00
NOTE: *Consists of 8 attached cards, printed on one side, which unfold into a strip story of title card & 7 panels. Scrapbook hobbyists in the 19th Century tended to pull the panels apart to paste into their scrapbooks, making copies with all panels still attached scarce.*

HOME PICTURE BOOK FOR LITTLE CHILDREN (E,P)
Home Insurance Company, New York: July 1887 (8 x 6-1/8", 36 pgs, b&w, color paper-c)

nn 40.00 80.00 160.00
NOTE: *Contains an abbreviated 32-panel reprinting of "THE TOOTHACHE" by George Cruikshank. Remainder of booklet does not contain comics.*

HOOD'S COMICALITIES. COMICAL PICTURES FROM HIS WORKS (E,S)
Porter & Coates: nd (8-1/2x10-3/8", 104 pgs, printed one side, hard-c, B&W)

nn 20.00 40.00 80.00
NOTE: *Reprints 4 cartoon illustrations per page from the British Hood's Comic Annuals, which were poetry books by Thomas Hood.*

HOOKEYBEAK THE RAVEN, AND OTHER TALES (see also JACK HUCKABACK, THE SCAPEGRACE RAVEN) (E)
George Routledge and Sons, London & New York: nd (1878) (7-1/4x5-5/8", 104 pgs, hardcover, B&W)

nn - By Wilhelm Busch (Very Rare) 100.00 200.00 400.00

HOW ADOLPHUS SLIM-JIM USED JACKSON'S BEST, AND WAS HAPPY. A LENGTHY TALE IN 7 ACTS. (O,P)
Jackson's Best Chewing Tobacco & Donaldson Brothers: nd(c1870's) (5-1/8 tall x 3-3/8" wide folded, 27" wide unfolded, color cardboard)

nn - With all 8 panels attached (Scarce) 30.00 60.00 150.00
nn - Individual panels/cards 5.00 10.00 25.00
NOTE: *Consists of 8 attached cards, printed on one side, which unfold into a strip story of title card & 7 panels. Scrapbook hobbyists in the 19th Century tended to pull the panels apart topaste into their scrapbooks, making copies with all panels still attached scarce.*

HOW DAYS' DURHAM STANDARD OF THE WORLD SMOKING TOBACCO MADE TWO PAIRS OF TWINS HAPPY (O,P)
J.R. Day & Bro. Standard Durham Smoking Tobacco, Durham, NC: nd (c late 1870's/early 1880's) (3-5/8" x 5-1/2", folded, 21-3/4" tall unfolded, color cardboard)

nn- With all 6 panels attached (Scarce) 120.00 240.00 480.00
nn- Individual panels/cards 20.00 40.00 60.00
NOTE: *Highly sought by both Black Americana and Tobacciana collectors. Recurring mid-19th Century story about two African-American twin brothers who romance and marry a pair of African-American twin sisters. Although the text is racist at points, the art is not. Consists of 6 attached cards, printed on one side, which unfold downwards into a strip story of title card & 5 panels. Scrapbook hobbyists in the 19th Century tended to pull the panels apart and paste into their scrapbooks, making copies with all panels attached scarce. Note, there are numerous cartoon tellings of this same story, including several card series versions (with different art, and story variations, each time). But, the above is the only version which unfolds as a strip of attached cards. The cards from all the unattached versions are smaller sized, and thus distinguishable.*

HUGGINIANA; OR, HUGGINS' FANTASY, BEING A COLLECTION OF THE MOST ESTEEMED MODERN LITERARY PRODUCTIONS (I,S,P)
H.C. Southwick, New York: 1808 (18 pgs, printed one side, B&W)

nn - (Very Rare) (no known sales)
NOTE: *The earliest known surviving collected promotional cartoons in America. This is a booklet collecting 7 folded plus 1 full page flyer advertisements for barber John Richard Desborus Huggins, who hired American artists Elkanah Tisdale and William S. Leney to modify previously published illustrations into cartoons referring to his barber shop.*

FR1.0 GD2.0 FN6.0

HUMOROUS MASTERPIECES - PICTURES BY JOHN LEECH (E,M)
Frederick A. Stokes: nd (late 1900's - early 1910's) No.1-2 (5-5/8x3-7/8", 68 pgs, cardboard covers, B&W)

1- John Leech (single panel cartoon-r from **Punch**) 17.50 35.00 70.00
2- John Leech (single panel cartoon-r from **Punch**) 17.50 35.00 70.00

HUMOURIST, THE (E,I,S)
C.V. Nickerson and Lucas and Deaver, Baltimore: No.1 Jan 1829 - No.12 Dec 1829 (5-3/4x3-1/2", B&W text w/hand colored cartoon pg.)

Bound volume No.1-12 (Very Rare; 1 copy known; 270 pgs) (no known sales)
NOTE: *Earliest known American published periodical to contain a cartoon every issue. Surviving individual issues currently unknown -- all information comes from 1 surviving bound volume. Each issue is mostly text, with one full page hand-colored cartoon. Bound volume contains an additional hand-colored cartoons at front of each six month set (total of 14 cartoons in volume). Cartoons appear to be of British origin, possibly by George Cruikshank.*

HUMPTY DUMPTY, ADVENTURES OF...
1877 (Promotional chapbook from Gantz, Jones & Co, 10¢-c.)

nn-Promotes Gantz Sea Foam Baking Powder; early app. of a costumed character, dressed as Humpty Dumpty 50.00 100.00 300.00

HUSBAND AND WIFE, OR THE STORY OF A HAIR. (O,P)
Garland Stoves and Ranges, Michigan Stove Co.: 1883 (4-3/16 tall x 2-11/16" wide folded, 16" wide unfolded, color cardboard)

nn - With all 6 panels attached (Scarce) 25.00 50.00 125.00
nn - Individual panels/cards 5.00 10.00 25.00
NOTE: *Consists of 6 attached cards, printed on one side, which unfold into a strip story of title card & 5 panels. Scrapbook hobbyists in the 19th Century tended to pull the panels apart topaste into their scrapbooks, making copies with all panels still attached scarce.*

ICHABOD ACADEMICUS, THE COLLEGE EXPERIENCES OF (O,G)
William T. Peters, New Haven, CT: 1850 (5-1/2x9-3/4",108 pgs, B&W)

nn - By William T. Peters (Very Rare) 200.00 400.00 800.00
NOTE: *Pages are not uniform in size.*

ICHABOD ACADEMICUS, THE COLLEGE EXPERIENCES OF (O,G)
Dick & Fitzgerald, New York: nd (1870s-1888) (paper-c, B&W)

nn - By William T. Peters (Very Rare) 100.00 200.00 400.00
NOTE: *Pages are uniform in size.*

ILLUSTRATED SCRAP-BOOK OF HUMOR AND INTELLIGENCE (M)
John J. Dyer & Co.: nd (c1859-1860)

nn - Very Rare (no known sales)
NOTE: *A "printed scrapbook" of images culled from some unidentified periodical. About half of it is illustrations that would have accompanied prose pieces. There are pages of single panel cartoons (multiple per page). And there are roughly 8 to 12 pages of sequential comics (all different stories, but appears to all be by the same presently unidentified artist).*

IMAGERIE d'EPINAL (untrimmed individual sheets) (E)
Pellerin for Humoristic Publishing Co, Kansas City, Mo.: nd (1888) No.1-60 (15-7/8x11-3/4",single sheets, hand colored) (All are Rare)

1-14, 21, 22, 25-46, 49-60 - in the Album d'Images 25.00 50.00 100.00
15-20, 23,24, 47, 48 - not in the Album d'Images 40.00 80.00 160.00
NOTE: *Printed and hand colored in France expressly for the Humoristic Publishing Company . Printed on one side only. These are single sheets, sold separately. Reprints and translates the sheets from their original French.*

IMAGERIE d'EPINAL ALBUM d'IMAGES (E)
Pellerin for Humoristic Publishing Co., Kansas City. Mo: nd (1888) (15-1/2x11-1/2",108 pgs plus full color hard-c, hand colored interior)

nn - Various French artists (Rare) 300.00 600.00 1800.00
NOTE: *Printed and hand colored in France expressly for the Humoristic Publishing Company . Printed on one side only. This is supposedly a collection of sixty broadsheets, originally sold separately. All copies known only have fifty of the sixty known of these broadsheets (slightly bigger, before binding, trimming the margins in the process, down to 15-1/4x11-3/8".). Three slightly different covers known to exist, with or without the indication in French "Textes en Anglais" ("Texts in English), with or without the general title "Contes de FÉes" ("Fairy Tales"). All known copies were collected with sheets 15-20, 23,24, 47, and 48 missing.*

IN LAUGHLAND (M)
R.H. Russell, New York: 1899 (14-9/16x12", 72 pgs, hard-c)

nn - By Henry "Hy" Mayer (scarce) 100.00 200.00 400.00
NOTE: *Mostly strips plus single panel cartoon-r from various magazines. The majority are reprinted from Life, with the rest from: Truth, Dramatic Mirror, Black and White, Figaro Illustre, Le Rire, and Fliegende Blatter.*

IN THE "400" AND OUT (M,S) (see also **THE TAILOR-MADE GIRL**)
Keppler & Schwarzmann, New York: 1888 (8-1/4x12", 64 pgs, hardc, B&W)

nn - By C.J. Taylor 42.50 85.00 170.00
NOTE: *Cartoons reprinted from **Puck**. The "400" is a reference to New York City's aristocratic elite.*

IN VANITY FAIR (M,S)
R.H.Russell & Son, New York: 1896 (11-7/8x17-7/8", 80 pgs, hard-c, B&W)

Jingo No. 3, Sept 24
1884 © Art Newspaper Co, Boston & NYC

Judge, No. 1, October 29, 1881
1881 © Judge Publishing, NYC

Life And Adventures of Jeff Davis
1865 © J.C. Haney & Co.

nn - By A.B.Wenzell, r-LIFE and HARPER'S 45.00 90.00 180.00

JACK HUCKABACK, THE SCAPEGRACE RAVEN (see also HOOKEYBEAK THE RAVEN) (E)
Stroefer & Kirchner, New York: nd (c1888) (9-3/8x6-3/8", 56 pgs, printed one side only, hand colored hardcover, B&W interior)

nn - By Wilhelm Busch (Rare) 50.00 100.00 300.00
NOTE: *The 1888 date is derived from a gift signature on one known copy. The publication date might in truth be earlier.*

JINGO (M,O)
Art Newspaper Co., Boston & New York: No.1 Sept 10, 1884 - No.11 Nov 19, 1884 (10 cents, 13-7/8" x 10-1/4",16 pgs, color front/back-c and center, remainder B&W, paper-c)

1-11(Rare) 25.00 50.00 100.00
NOTE: *Satirical Republican propaganda magazine, modeled after **Puck** and **Judge**, which was published during the last couple months of the 1884 Presidential Election campaign. The Republicans lost, **Jingo** ceased publication, and Republican backers soon after purchased **Judge** magazine.*

JOURNEY TO THE GOLD DIGGINS BY JEREMIAH SADDLEBAGS (O,G)
Various publishers: 1849 (25 cents, 5-5/8 x 8-3/4", 68 pgs, green & black paper cover, B&W interior)

nn -- New York edition, Stringer & Townsend, Publishers
(Very Rare) 1000.00 2000.00 4000.00
nn -- Cincinnati, Ohio edition, published by U.P. James
(Very Rare) 1000.00 2000.00 4000.00
nn -- 1950 reprint, with introduction, published by William P. Wreden, Burlingame, California: 1950 (5-7/8 x 9", 92 pgs, hardcover, color interior)
(390 copies printed) 37.50 75.00 150.00
NOTE: *By J.A. and D.F. Read. Earliest known sequential comic book by an American creator; directly inspired by Töpffer's **Obadiah Oldbuck** and **Bachelor Butterfly**. The New York and Cincinnati editions were both published in 1849, one soon after the other. Antiquarian Book sources have traditionally cited that the Cincinnati edition preceded the New York, but without referencing their evidence. Conflicting with this, the Cincinnati edition lists the New York publishers' 1849 copyright, while the New York edition makes no reference to the Cincinnati publishers. Such would indicate that the New York edition was first. Both are very rare, and until resolved both will be regarded as published simultaneously. A New York copy with missing back cover, detached front cover, and G/VG interior sold for $2000 in 2000.*

JUDGE (M,O)
Judge Publishing, New York: No.1 Oct 29, 1881 - No. 950, Dec ??, 1899 (10 cents, color front/back c and centerspread, remainder B&W, paper-c)

1 (Scarce) (no known sales)
2-26 (Volume 1; Scarce) 20.00 40.00 80.00
27-790,792-950 12.50 25.00 50.00
791 (12/12/1896; Vol.31) - satirical-c depicting Tammany Hall politicians as the Yellow Kid & Brownies 25.00 50.00 100.00
Bound Volumes (six month, 26 issue run each):
Vol. 1 (Scarce) (no known sales)
Vol. 2-30,32-37 140.00 280.00 560.00
Vol. 31 - includes issue 791 **YK/Brownies** parody 165.00 230.00 660.00
NOTE: *Rival publication to Puck. Purchased by Republican Party backers, following their loss in the 1884 Presidential Election, to become a Republican propaganda satire magazine.*

JUDGE'S LIBRARY (M)
Judge Publishing, New York: No.1, April 1890 - No. 141, Dec 1899 (10 cents, 11x8-1/8", 36 pgs, color paper-c, B&W)

1 7.50 15.00 30.00
2-141 7.50 15.00 30.00
151-??? (post-1900 issues; see Platinum Age section)
NOTE: ***Judge's Library** was a monthly magazine reprinting cartoons & prose from **Judge**, with each issue's material organized around the same subject. The cover art was often original. All issues were kept in print for the duration of the series, so later issues are more scarce than earlier ones.*

JUDGE'S QUARTERLY (M)
Judge Publishing Company/Arkell Publishing Company, New York: No.1 April 1892 - 31 Oct 1899 (25¢, 13-3/4x10-1/4", 64 pgs, color paper-c, B&W)

1-31 15.00 30.00 60.00
NOTE: *Similar to **Judge's Library**, except larger in size, and issued quarterly. All reprint material, except for the cover art.*

JUVENILE GEM, THE (see also THE ADVENTURES OF MR. TOM PLUMP, and OLD MOTHER MITTEN) (O,I)
Huestis & Cozans: nd (1850-1852) (6x3-7/8", 64 pgs, hand colored paper-c, B&W) (all versions Very Rare)

nn - First printing(s) publisher's address is 104 Nassau Street (1850-1851)(no known sales)
nn - 2nd printing(s) publisher's address is 116 Nassau Street (1851-1852) (no known sales)
nn - 3rd printing(s) publisher's address is 107 Nassau Street (1852+) (no known sales)
NOTE: *The JUVENILE GEM is a gathering of multiple booklets under a single, hand colored cover (none of the interior booklets have the covers which they were given when sold separately). The publisher appears to have gathered whichever printings of each booklet were available when copies of THE JUVENILE GEM was assembled, so that the booklets within, and the conglomerate cover, may be from a mixture of printings. Contains two sequential comic booklets: THE ADVENTURES OF MR. TOM PLUMP, and OLD MOTHER MITTEN AND HER FUNNY KITTEN, plus five heavily illustrated children's booklets - **The Pretty Primer**, **The Funny Book**, **The Picture Book**, **The Two Sisters**, and **Story Of The Little Drummer**. Six of these -- including the two comic books -- were reprinted in the 1960's by Americana Review as a set of individual booklets, and included in a folder collectively titled "Six Children's Books of the 1850's".*

LATER PENCILLINGS FROM PUNCH (see also PICTURES OF LIFE AND CHARACTER) (M,S,E)
Bradbury and Evans, London: nd (13-1/4x11",272 pgs, red gilted hard-c, B&W)

nn - By John Leech; reprints from Punch 25.00 50.00 100.00

LIFE (miniature reprint of issue No.1) (M,P)
Mutual Life Insurance Company: falsely dated Jan 4, 1883 (actually published 1933) (3x2-1/2", 16 pgs, B&W, paper-c)

1 .25 2.00 5.00
NOTE: *Fiftieth Anniversary miniaturized reprint of **Life** No. 1, given away by the Mutual Life Insurance Company. This item is frequently misrepresented by sellers, knowingly or unknowingly, as the actual **Life** Number 1. It is an extremely common and near worthless item, listed here only to prevent further misrepresentation.*

LIFE (miniature reprint of issue No.1) (M,P)
Life Magazine: falsely dated Jan 4, 1883 (actually published 1958) (3x2-1/2", 16 pgs, B&W, paper-c) 1.25 2.00 5.00
NOTE: 1958 Life Magazine premium, sent to subscribers for renewing their subscriptions. Originally came in a small folder, along with a loose, folded flyer explaining what the booklet was. This item is frequently misrepresented by sellers, knowingly or unknowingly, as the actual Life Number 1. It is an extremely common and near worthless item, listed here only to prevent further misrepresentation.

LIFE (M,O) (continues with Vol.35 No. 894+ in the Platinum Age section)
J.A.Mitchell: Vol.1 No.1 Jan. 4, 1883 - Vol.1 No.26 June 29, 1883 (10-1/4x8", 16 pgs, B&W, paper cover); J.A. Mitchell: Vol. 2 No. 27, July 5, 1883 - Vol. 6 No.148, Oct 29, 1885 (10-1/4x8-1/4", 16 pgs., B&W, paper cover); Mitchell & Miller: Vol.6 No.149, Nov. 5, 1885 - Vol. 31, No. 796, March 17, 1898 (10-3/8x8-3/8", 16 pgs., B&W, paper cover); Life Publishing Company: Vol. 31 No. 797, March 24, 1898 - Vol. 34 No. 893, Dec 28, 1899 (10-3/8 x 8-1/2", 20 pgs., B&W, paper cover)

1-26 (Scarce) (no known sales)
27-799 5.00 10.00 20.00
800 (4/7/1898) parody Yellow Kid / Spanish-American War cover
(not by Outcault) 25.00 50.00 100.00
801-893 5.00 10.00 20.00
NOTE: *All covers for issues 1 - 26 are identical, apart from issue number & date.*
Hard bound collected volumes:
V. 1 (No.1-26) (Scarce) (no known sales)
V. 2-34 45.00 90.00 180.00
V. 31 YK #800 parody-c not by RFO 70.00 140.00 280.00
NOTE: *Because the covers of all issues in Volume 1 are identical, it was common practice to remove the covers before binding the issues together. This is not true of later volumes, though, in all volumes it was common to drop the advertising pages which appeared at the rear of each issue. Information on many more individual issues will expand next Guide.*

LIFE AND ADVENTURES OF JEFF DAVIS (I)
J.C. Haney & Co., NY: 1865 (10 cents, 7-1/2" x 4", 36 pgs, B&W, paper-c)

nn - By McArone 100.00 200.00 400.00
NOTE: *Humorous telling of the capture of Confederate President Jeff Davis in women's clothing, from the publisher of Merryman's Monthly. It contains an ad page for that publication; the material is perhaps reprinted from it. J.C. Haney licensed it to local printers, and so various publishers are found -- all printings currently regarded as simultaneous. (The Geo. H. Hees printing, Oswego, NY, contains an ad for the upcoming October 1865 issue of Merryman's Monthly, thus placing that printing in September 1865). Modern facsimile editions have been produced.*

LIFE IN PHILADELPHIA
W. Simpson, 66 Chestnut, Philadelphia; Siltart, No. 65 South Third St, Philadelphia: 1830 (7-3/4x6-7/8", 15 loose plates, hand colored copies exist, maybe B&W also)

nn - By Edward Williams Clay (1799-1857) (no known sales)
NOTE: *First 13 plates etched, with many word balloons; scenes of exaggerated Black Americana in Philadelphia viewed one by one as broadsides. Had several publishers over the years. Was also eventually collected into a book of same name but only with the first 13 plates used; the last two not used in book. Collected book not yet viewed to share info.*

LIFE'S BOOK OF ANIMALS (M,S)
Doubleday & McClure Co.: 1898 (7-1/4x10-1/8", 88 pgs, color hardcover, B&W)

nn 25.00 50.00 100.00
NOTE: *Reprints funny animal single panel and strip cartoons reprinted from LIFE. Art by Blaisdell, Chip Bellew, Kemble, Hy Mayer, Sullivant, Woolf.*

LIFE'S COMEDY (M,S)
Charles Scribner's Sons: Series 1 1897 - Series 3 1898 (12x9-3/8", hardcover, B&W)

1 (142 pgs). 2, 3 (138 pgs) 60.00 120.00 240.00
NOTE: *Gibson a-1-3; c-3. Hy Mayer a-1-3. Rose O'Neill a-2-3. Stanlaws a-2-3. Sullivant a-1-2. Verbeek a-2. Wenzell a-1-3; c(painted)-2.*

LIFE, THE GOOD THINGS OF (M,S)
White, Stokes, & Allen, NY: 1884 - No.3 1886 ; Frederick A. Stokes, NY: No.4

Max and Maurice by Wilhelm Busch
1871 © Roberts Brothers, Boston

Merryman's Monthly v3#5 with Bellew strip
May 1865 © J. C. Haney & Co., New York

Minneapolis Journal Cartoons Second Series
1895

FR1.0 GD2.0 FN6.0

1887; Frederick Stokes & Brother, NY: No.5 1888 - No.6 1889; Frederick A. Stokes Company, NY: No. 7 1890 - No.10 1893 (8-3/8x10-1/2", 74 pgs, gilted hardcover, B&W)

	FR1.0	GD2.0	FN6.0
nn - 1884 (most common issue)	32.50	65.00	130.00
2 - 1885	32.50	65.00	130.00
3 - 1886 (76 pgs)	32.50	65.00	130.00
4 - 1887 (76 pgs)	32.50	65.00	130.00
5 - 1888	32.50	65.00	130.00
6 - 1889	32.50	65.00	130.00
7 - 1890	32.50	65.00	130.00
8 - 1891	32.50	65.00	130.00
9 - 1892	32.50	65.00	130.00
10 - 1893	32.50	65.00	130.00

NOTE: Contains mostly single panel, and some sequential, comics reprinted from LIFE. Attwood a-1-4,10. Roswell Bacon a-5. Chip Bellew a-4-6. Frank Bellew a-4,6. Palmer Cox a-1. H. E. Dey a-5. C. D. Gibson a-4-10. F.M. Howarth a-5-6. Kemble a-1-3. Klapp a-5. Walt McDougall a-1-2. H. McVickar a-5; J. A. Mitchell a-5. Peter Newell a-2-3. Gray Parker a-4-5,7. J. Smith a-5. Albert E. Steiner a-5; T. S. Sullivant a-7-9. Wenzell a-8-10. Wilder a-3. Woolf a-3-6.

LIFE, MINIATURE (see also LIFE (miniature reprint of of issue No. 1)) (M,P,S)
Life Publishing Co.: No. 1 ??? - No.2 1913 (5-3/4x4-5/8", 20 pgs, color paper cover, mostly B&W interior)

1- Exist? (no known sales)
2- (Rare) (no known sales)

NOTE: Giveaway item from Life, to promote subscriptions. All reprint material. No.2: James Montgomery Flagg-c; a-Chip Bellew, Gus Dirks, Gibson, F.M.Howarth, Art Young.

LIFE, THE SPICE OF (see SPICE OF LIFE, THE)

LIFE'S PICTURE GALLERY (becomes LIFE'S PRINTS) (M,S,P)
Life Publishing Company, New York: nd (1898-1899) (paper cover, B&W) (all are scarce)

nn - (nd; 1898, 100 pgs, 5-1/4x8-1/2") Gibson-c of a woman with closed umbrella; 1st interior page announcing that after January 1, 1899 Gibson will draw exclusively for LIFE; the word "SPECIMEN" is printed in red, diagonally, across every print; a-Gibson, Rose O'Neill, Sullivant 25.00 50.00 100.00
nn - (nd; 1899, 128 pgs, 4-7/8x7-3/8") Gibson-c of a woman golfer; 1st interior page announcing that Gibson & Hanna, Jr. draw exclusively for LIFE; the word "SPECIMEN" is printed in red, horizontally, across every print. Includes prints from Gibson's **THE EDUCATION OF MR. PIPP**; a-Gibson, Sullivant 25.00 50.00 100.00

*NOTE: Catalog of prints reprinted from **LIFE** covers & centerspreads. The first catalog was given away free to anyone requesting it, but after many people got the catalog without ordering anything, subsequent catalogs were sold at 10 cents.*

LOVING BALLADS OF LORD BATEMAN, THE (E,I)
G.W. Carleton & Co., Publishers, Madison Square, NY: 1871 (9x5-7/8", 6 cents)

nn - By George Cruikshank 50.00 100.00 200.00

MANNERS AND CUSTOMS OF YE HARVARD STUDENTE (M,S)
Houghton Mifflin & Co., Boston & Moses King, Cambridge: 1877 (7-7/8x11", 72 pgs, printed one side, hardc, B&W)

nn - by F.G. Attwood 175.00 350.00 700.00

*NOTE: Collection of cartoons originally serialized in the **Harvard Lampoon**. Attwood later became a major cartoonist for **Life**.*

MAN WHO WOULD LIKE TO MARRY, THE (O)
Frederick Warne & Co., London & New York: nd (c 1880's) (9-1/2x11-1/2", 28 pgs, printed 1 side, paper-c, B&W)

nn - By Harry Parkes 62.50 125.00 250.00

*NOTE: Published simultaneously with its companion volume, **The Girl Who Wouldn't Mind Getting Married**.*

MAX AND MAURICE: A JUVENILE HISTORY IN SEVEN TRICKS (E)
(see also Teasing Tom and Naughty Ned)
Roberts Brothers, Boston: 1871 first edition (8-1/8 x 5-1/2", 76 pgs, hard & soft-c B&W)

nn - By Wilhelm Busch (green or brown cloth hardbound) 200.00 400.00 800.00
nn - exactly the same, but soft paper cover 150.00 300.00 600.00

NOTE: Page count includes 56 pgs of art, two blank endpapers at the front (one colored), 8 pgs of ads at the back, two blank endpapers at the end (one colored), and the covers. Green or brown illustrated hardcover. The name of the author is given on the title page as "William Busch." We assume this to be the 1st edition. Back side of title page states: Entered according to Act of Congress, in the year 1870, by Roberts Brothers, In the office of the Librarian of Congress at Washington.

nn - By Wilhelm Busch (1872 edition) 150.00 300.00 600.00
nn - 1875 reprint 100.00 200.00 400.00
nn - 1882 reprint (76 pgs, hand colored- c/a, 75¢) 100.00 200.00 400.00

NOTE: Each of the above contains 56 pages of art and text in a transitional format between a regular children's book and a comic book (the page count difference is ad pages in back). Seminal inspiration for William Randolph Hearst to acquire as a "new comic" (following the wild success of Outcault's Yellow Kid) to license M&M from Busch and hire Rudolph Dirks in late 1897 to create a New York American newspaper incarnation. In Hearst's English language newspapers it was called The Katzenjammer Kids and in his German language NYC newspaper it was titled Max & Moritz, Busch's original title. At least 50 other reprints versions are reputed to exist printed thru 1900. Translated from the 1865 German original. We are still sorting out the edition confusion.

FR1.0 GD2.0 FN6.0

MAX AND MAURICE: A JUVENILE HISTORY IN SEVEN TRICKS (E)
(see also Teasing Tom and Naughty Ned)
Little, Brown, and Company, Boston: 1899 first edition(?) (8-1/8 x 5-5/8", 72 pgs, hardcover, black ink on orange paper)

nn - 1899 By Wilhelm Busch 50.00 100.00 200.00
nn - 1902 (64 pages, B&W) 10.00 30.00 90.00

MERRY MAPLE LEAVES Or A Summer In The Country (S)
E.P. Dutton And Company, New York: 1872 (9-3/8x7-3/8", 90 & 86 pgs pgs, hard-c)

nn - By Abner Perk 25.00 50.00 150.00

NOTE: Each drawing contained in a maple leaf motif by Livingston Hopkins and others.

MERRYMAN'S MONTHLY A COMIC MAGAZINE FOR THE FAMILY (M,O,E)
J.C. Haney & Co, NY: 1863-1877 (10-7/8x7-13/16", 30 pgs average, B&W)

Certain issues with short sequential comics 25.00 50.00 150.00

NOTE: Sequential strips by Frank Bellew Sr, Wilhelm Busch found so far; others?

MESSRS. BROWN, JONES, AND ROBINSON, THE FOREIGN TOUR OF
(see also **THE CLOWN, OR THE BANQUET OF WIT**) (E,M,O,G)
Bradbury & Evans, London: 1854 (11-5/8x9-1/2", 196 pgs, gilted hard-c, B&W)

nn - By Richard Doyle 35.00 70.00 140.00
nn - Bradbury & Evans 1900 reprint 20.00 40.00 80.00

NOTE: Protective sheets between each page (not part of page count). Expanded and redrawn sequential comics story from the serialized episodes originally published in PUNCH. Also comes in a 174 pg 8-3/4x11" version.

MESSRS. BROWN, JONES, AND ROBINSON, THE LAUGHABLE ADVENTURES OF (E,M,G)
Garrett, Dick & Fitzgerald, NY: nd (1856 or 1857) (5-3/4x9-1/4", 100 pgs, printed one side only, paper-c, B&W)

nn - (Very Rare) by Richard Doyle c/a 200.00 400.00 700.00

NOTE: 1st American reprinting of the "Foreign Tour"; reformatted into a small oblong format. Links the earlier Garrett & Co. to the later Dick & Fitzgerald. Back cover reprints full size the Garrett & Co. version cover for Oscar Shanghai. Interior front cover reprints full size the Garrett & Co. version cover for Slyfox-Wikof. Issued without a title page.

MESSRS. BROWN, JONES, AND ROBINSON, THE FOREIGN TOUR OF (E,M,G)
D. Appleton & Co., New York: 1860 & 1877 (11-5/8x9-1/2", 196 pgs, gilted hard-c, B&W)

nn - (1860 printing) by Richard Doyle 30.00 60.00 120.00
nn - (1871 printing) by Richard Doyle 30.00 60.00 120.00
nn - (1877 printing) by Richard Doyle 30.00 60.00 120.00

NOTE: Protective sheets between each page (not part of page count). Reprints the Bradbury & Evans edition.

MESSRS BROWN JONES AND ROBINSON, THE AMERICAN TOUR OF (O,G)
D. Appleton & Co., New York: 1872 (11-5/8x9-1/2", 158 pgs, printed one side only, B&W, green gilted hard-c)

nn - By Toby 70.00 140.00 300.00

NOTE: Original American graphic novel sequel to Richard Doyle's Foreign Tour of Brown, Jones, and Robinson, with the same characters visiting New York, Canada, and Cuba. Protective sheets between each page (not part of page count).

MESSRS. BROWN, JONES, AND ROBINSON, THE LAUGHABLE ADVEN. OF (E,M,G)
Dick & Fitzgerald, NY: nd (late 1870's - 1888) (5-3/4x9-1/4", 100 pgs, printed one side only, green paper-c, B&W)

nn - (Scarce) by Richard Doyle 100.00 200.00 400.00

NOTE: Reprints the Garrett, Dick & Fitzgerald printing, with the following changes: Takes what had been page 12 in the Garrett, D&F printing (art by M.H. Henry), and makes it a title page, which is numbered page 1. The first story page, "Go to the Races", is numbered 2 (whereas it is numbered 1 in the Garrett, Dick & Fitzgerald version). Numbering stays ahead of the G,D&F edition by 1 page up through page 12, after which the page numbering becomes identical.

MINNEAPOLIS JOURNAL CARTOONS (N,S)
Minneapolis Journal: nn 1894 - No.2 1895 (7-3/4" x 10-7/8", 76 pgs, B&W, paper-c)

nn (1894) (Rare) 25.00 50.00 100.00
Second Series (1895) (Rare) 25.00 50.00 100.00
nn- "War Cartoons" Jan 1899 (9x8", 160 pgs, paperback, punched & string bound) 24.00 96.00 170.00

NOTE: Reprints single panel cartoons from the prior year, by Charles "Bart" L. Bartholomew.

MISCHIEF BOOK, THE (E)
R. Worthington, New York: 1880 (7-1/8 x 10-3/4", 176 pgs, hard-c, B&W)

nn - Green cloth binding; green on brown cover; cover art by R. Lewis based on Busch art by Wilhelm Busch 175.00 350.00 700.00
nn - Blue cloth binding; hand colored cover; completely different cover art based on Busch by Wilhelm Busch 175.00 350.00 700.00

NOTE: Translated by Abby Langdon Alger. American published anthology collection of Wilhelm Busch comic strips. Includes two of the strips found in the British "Bushel of Merry-Thoughts" collection, translated better, and with the dropped panel restored. Unknown which cover version was first.

MISSES BROWN, JONES AND ROBINSON, THE FOREIGN TOUR OF THE (E,O,G)

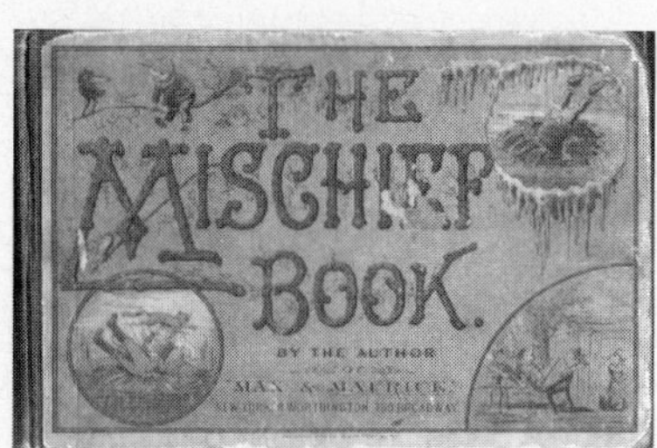

The Mischief Book by Wilhelm Busch
color cover art variation
1880 © R. Worthington, New York

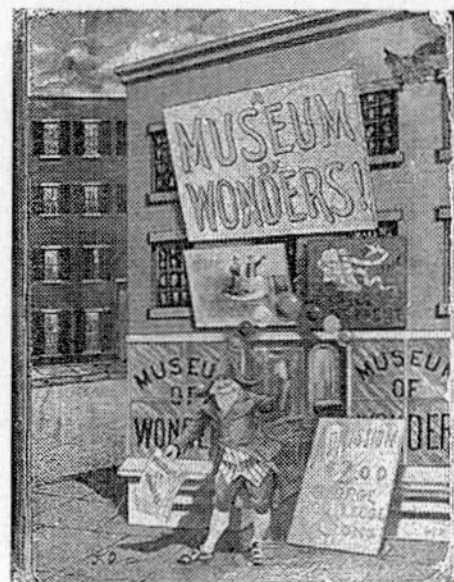

Museum of Wonders by Opper
1894 © Routledge & Sons

99 "Woolf's" from Truth
1896 © Truth Company

FR1.0 GD2.0 FN6.0

Bickers & Sons, London: nd (c1850's) (12-1/4" x 9-7/8", 108 pgs, printed on one side, B&W, hard-c)

nn- "by Miss Brown" (Rare) 35.00 70.00 140.00
NOTE: *A female take on Doyle's Foreign Tour, by an unknown woman artist, using the pseudonym "Miss Brown."*

MISS MILLY MILLEFLEUR'S CAREER (S)
Sheldon & Co., NY: 1869 (10-3/4x9-7/8", 74 pgs, purple hard-c)

nn - Artist unknown 25.00 50.00 150.00

MUSEUM OF WONDERS, A (O,I)
Routledge & Sons: 1894 (13x10", 64 pgs, color-c, color thru out)

nn - By Frederick Opper 100.00 200.00 400.00

MY FRIEND WRIGGLES, A (Laughter) Moving Panorama, of His Fortunes And Misfortunes, Illustrated With Over 200 Engravings, of Most Comic Catastrophes And Side-Splitting Merriment) (O,G)
Stearn & Co, 202 Williams St, NY: 1850s (5-7/8x9-3/4", 100 pgs, B&W)

nn - By S. P. Avery (also the engraver) 200.00 400.00 800.00

MY SKETCHBOOK (E,S)
Dana Estes & Charles E. Lauriat, Boston; J. Sabins & Sons, New York: circa 1880s (9-3/8x12", brown hard-c)

nn - By George Cruikshank 25.00 50.00 150.00
NOTE: *Reprints British editions 1834-36; extensive usage of word balloons.*

NEW BOOK OF NONSENSE, THE: A Contribution To The Great Central Fair In Aid of the Sanitary Commission (O,S)
Ashmead & Evans, No. 724 Chestnut St, Philadelphia: June 1864 (red hard-c)

nn - Artists unknown 50.00 150.00 300.00

99 "WOOLFS" FROM TRUTH (see Sketches of Lowly Life in a Great City, Truth)
Truth Company, NY: 1896 (9x5-1/2", varnished paper-like cloth hard-c, 25 cents)

nn - By Michael Angelo Woolf 100.00 200.00 400.00
NOTE: *Woolf's cartoons are regarded as a primary influence on R.F. Outcault in the later development of The Yellow Kid newspaper strip. Copy sold in 2002 on eBay for $800.00.*

OBADIAH OLDBUCK, THE ADVENTURES OF MR. (E,G)
Tilt & Bogue, London: nd (1840-41) (5-15/16x9-3/16", 176 pgs,B&W, gilted hard-c)

nn - By Rodolphe Töpffer (Scarce) 300.00 600.00 1000.00
nn - Hand coloured edition (Very Rare) (no known sales)
NOTE: *This is the British edition, translating the unauthorized redrawn 1839 edition from Parisian publisher Aubert, adapted from Töpffer's "Les Amours de Mr. Vieux Bois" (aka "Histoire de Mr. Vieux Bois"), originally published in French in Switzerland, in 1837 (2nd ed. 1839). Early 19th century books are often found rebound, with original cover and/or title page gone. To distinguish editions having no cover or title page: the British oblong editions (published by Tilt & Bogue) use Roman Numerals to number pages. American oblong shaped editions use Arabic Numerals. British are printed on one side only. This is the earliest known English language sequential comic book. Has a new title page with art by Robert Cruikshank.*

OBADIAH OLDBUCK, THE ADVENTURES OF MR. (E,G)
Wilson and Company, New York: September 14, 1842 (11-3/4x9", 44 pgs, B&W, yellow paper-c on bookstand editions, hemp paper interior)

Brother Jonathan Extra No. IX - Very Rare bookstand edition 700.00 1400.00 4000.00
Brother Jonathan Extra No. IX Very Rare subscriber/mailorder 700.00 1400.00 4000.00
NOTE: *By Rodolphe Töpffer. Earliest known sequential American comic book, reprinting the 1841 British edition. Pages are numbered via Roman numerals. States "BROTHER JONATHAN EXTRA - ADVENTURES OF MR. OBADIAH OLDBUCK." at the top of each page. Prints 2 to 3 tiers of panels on both sides of each page. Copies could be had for ten cents according to adverts in* ***Brother Jonathan***. *By Rodolphe Töpffer with cover masthead design by David Claypool Johnston, and cover art beneath the masthead reprinting Robert Cruikshank's title page art from the Tilt & Bogue edition. A special, additional cover was added for copies sold on stands (it was not issued with mail order or subscriber copies). Only 1 known copy possesses (partially) this very thin outer yellow cover. A decent (subscriber) copy sold on eBay in later October 2002 for over $3500.00.*

OBADIAH OLDBUCK, THE ADVENTURES OF MR. (E,G)
Wilson & Co, New York: nd (1849) (5-11/16x8-3/8", 92 pgs, B&W, hard-c)

nn - by Rodolphe Töpffer; title page by Robert Cruikshank (Very Rare) 300.00 700.00 1500.00
NOTE: *2nd Wilson & Co printing, reformatted into a small oblong format, with nine panels edited out, and text modified to smooth out this removal. Results in four less printed tiers/strips. Pages are numbered via Arabic numerals. Every panel on Pages 11, 14, 19, 21, 24, 34, 35 has one line of text. Reformatted to conform with British first edition.*

OBADIAH OLDBUCK, THE ADVENTURES OF MR. (E,G)
Dick & Fitzgerald, New York: nd (various printings; est. 1870s to 1888) (Thirty Cents, 84 pgs, B&W, paper-c) (all versions Rare)

nn - Black print on green cover(5-11/16x8-15/16"); string bound 200.00 400.00 600.00
nn - Black print on blue cover; same format as green-c 200.00 400.00 600.00
nn - Black print on white cover(5-13/16x9-3/16"); staple bound beneath cover); this is a later printing than the blue or green-c 200.00 400.00 600.00
NOTE: *Reprints the abbreviated 1849 Wilson & Co. 2nd printing. Pages are numbered via Arabic numerals. Many of the panels on Pages 11, 14, 19, 21, 24, 34, 35 take two lines to print the same words found in the Wilson & Co version, which used only one text line for the same panels. Unknown whether the blue or green cover is earlier. White cover version has "thirty cents" line blackened out on the two copies known to exist. Robert Cruikshank's title page has been made the cover in the D&F editions.*

FR1.0 GD2.0 FN6.0

OLD MOTHER MITTEN AND HER FUNNY KITTEN (see also **The Juvenile Gem**) (O)
Huestis & Cozans: nd(1850-1852) (6x3-7/8"12pgs, hand colored paper-c, B&W)

nn - first printing(s) publisher's address is 104 Nassau Street (1850-1851) (Very Rare) (no known sales)
NOTE: *A hand colored outer cover is highly rare, with only 1 recorded copy possessing it. Front cover image and text is repeated precisely on page 3 (albeit b&w), and only interior pages are numbered, together leading owners of coverless copies to believe they have the cover. The true back cover has ads for the publisher. Cover was issued only with copies which were sold separately - books which were bound together as part of THE JUVENILE GEM never had such covers.*

OLD MOTHER MITTEN AND HER FUNNY KITTEN (see JUVENILE GEM) (O)
Philip J. Cozans: nd (1850-1852) (6x3-7/8",12 pgs, hand colored paper-c, B&W)

nn - Second printing(s) publisher's address is 116 Nassau Street (1851-1852) (Very Rare) (no known sales)
nn - Third printing(s) publisher's address is 107 Nassau Street (1852+) (Very Rare) (no known sales)

OLD MOTHER MITTEN AND HER FUNNY KITTEN
Americana Review, Scotia, NY: nd (1960's) (6-1/4x4-1/8", 8 pgs, side-stapled, cardboard, B&W)

nn - Modern reprint 2.50 5.00 10.00
NOTE: *Issued within a folder titled SIX CHILDREN'S BOOKS OF THE 1850'S. States "Reprinted by American Review" at bottom of front cover. Reprints the 104 Nassau Street address.*

ON THE NILE (O,G)
James R. Osgood & Co., Boston: 1874 ; **Houghton, Osgood & Co., Boston:** 1880 (112 pgs, gilted green hardcover, B&W)

1st printing (1874; 10-3/4x16") - by Augustus Hoppin 45.00 90.00 180.00
2nd printing (1880; smaller sized) 32.50 65.00 130.00

OSCAR SHANGHAI, THE EXTRAORDINARY AND MIRTH-PROVKING ADVENTURES BY SEA & LAND OF (O, G)
Garrett & Co., Publishers, No. 18 Ann Street, New York: circa 1852-55 (5-3/4x9-1/4", 100 pgs, printed one side only, paper-c, 25¢, B&W)

nn - Samuel Avery-c; interior by ALC Very Rare) 400.00 800.00 1600.00
NOTE: *Not much is known of this first edition as the data comes from a recently rediscovered* ***Brother Jonathan*** *catalog issued circa 1853-55. No original known yet to exist.*

OSCAR SHANGHAI, THE WONDERFUL AND AMUSING DOINGS BY SEA AND LAND OF (G)
Dick & Fitzgerald, 10 Ann St, NY: nd (1870s-1888) (25 ¢, 5-3/4x9-1/4", 100 pgs, printed one side only, green paper c, B&W)

nn - Cover by Samuel Avery; interior by ALC (Rare) 200.00 300.00 600.00
NOTE: *Exact reprint of Garrett & Co original.*

OUR ARTIST IN CUBA (O)
Carleton, New York: 1865 (6-5/8x4-3/8", 120 pgs, printed one side only, gilted hard-c, B&W)

nn - By Geo. W. Carleton 37.50 75.00 150.00

OUR ARTIST IN CUBA, PERU, SPAIN, AND ALGIERS (O)
Carleton: 1877 (6-1/2x5-1/8", 156 pgs, hardcover, B&W)

nn - By Geo. W. Carleton 32.50 65.00 130.00
NOTE: *Reprints OUR ARTIST IN CUBA and OUR ARTIST IN PERU, then adds new section on Spain and Algiers.*

OUR ARTIST IN PERU (O)
Carleton, New York: 1866 (7-3/4x5-7/8", 68 pgs, gilted hardcover, B&W)

nn- By Geo. W. Carleton 37.50 75.00 150.00
NOTE: *Contains advertisement for the upcoming books* ***OUR ARTIST IN ITALY*** *and* ***OUR ARTIST IN FRANCE***, *but no such publications have been found to date.*

PEN AND INK SKETCHES OF YALE NOTABLES (O,S)
Soule, Thomas and Winsor, St. Louis: 1872 (12-1/4x9-3/4", B&W)

By Squills 25.00 50.00 100.00
NOTE: *Printed by Steamlith Press, The R.P. Studley Company, St Louis.*

PETER PIPER IN BENGAL
Bengamin H Day.Publisher, Brother Jonathan Cheap Book Establishment, 48 Beekman, NY: 1953-55 (6-5/8x4-1/4, 36 pgs, yellow paper-c, B&W, 3 cents - two dollars per hundred)

nn - By John Tenniel - 32 panel comic strip Punch-r 500.00 1000.00 1500.00
NOTE: *Actually also a catalog of inexpensive books, prints, maps and half a dozen comic books for sale on separate pages from publishers Day and Garrett - see full story of this brand new find in the Victorian Era essay. A complete copy with split spine sold in November 2002 for $750.00. Published date most likely 1855.*

PHIL MAY'S SKETCH BOOK (E,S,M)
Chatto & Windus, London: 1897 (14-1/2x9-3/4", 64 pgs, red hard-c, B&W)

nn - By Phil May 42.50 85.00 170.00

The Wonderful and Amusing Doings by Sea & Land of Oscar Shanghai
1870s © Dick & Fitzgerald, New York

PUCK
© Keppler & Schwarzman, NY

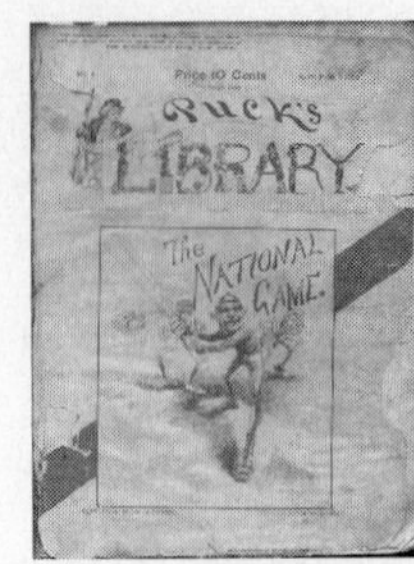

Puck's Library

FR1.0 GD2.0 FN6.0

PHIL MAY'S SKETCH BOOK (E,S,M)
R.H. Russell, New York: 1899 (14-5/8x10", 64 pgs, brown hard-c, B&W)

	FR1.0	GD2.0	FN6.0
nn - By Phil May	32.50	65.00	130.00

NOTE: *American reprint of the British edition.*

PICTURES OF ENGLISH SOCIETY (Parchment-Paper Series, No.4) (M,S,E)
D. Appleton & Co., New York: 1884 (5-5/8x4-3/8", 108 pgs, paper-c, B&W)

	FR1.0	GD2.0	FN6.0
4 - By George du Maurier; Punch-r	15.00	30.00	60.00

NOTE: *Every other page is a full page cartoon, with the opposite page containing the cartoon's caption.*

PICTURES OF LIFE AND CHARACTER (M,S,E)
Bradbury and Evans, London: No.1 1855 - No.5 c1864 (12-1/2x18", 100 pgs, illustrated hard-c, B&W)

	FR1.0	GD2.0	FN6.0
nn (No.1) (1855)	32.50	65.00	130.00
2 (1858), 3 (1860)	32.50	65.00	130.00
4 (nd; c1862) 5 (nd; c1864)	32.50	65.00	130.00
nn (nd (late 1860's)	32.50	65.00	130.00

NOTE: 2-1/2x18-1/4", 494 pgs, green gilted-c) reprints 1-5 in one book

	FR1.0	GD2.0	FN6.0
1-3 John Leech's... (nd; 12-3/8x10", ? pgs, red gilted-c).	25.00	50.00	100.00

NOTE: *Reprints John Leech cartoons from* ***Punch****. note that the Volume Number is mentioned only on the last page of these versions.*

PICTURES OF LIFE AND CHARACTER (E,M,S)
G.P. Putnam's Sons: 1880's (8-5/8x6-1/4", 218 pgs, hardcover, color-cr, B&W)

	FR1.0	GD2.0	FN6.0
nn - John Leech (single panel **Punch** cartoon-r)	20.00	40.00	160.00

NOTE: *Leech reprints which extend back to the 1850s.*

PICTURES OF LIFE AND CHARACTER (Parchment-Paper Series) (E,M,S)
(see also Humerous Masterpieces)
D. Appleton & Co., NY: 1884 (30¢, 5-3/4 x 4-1/2", 104 pgs, paper-c, B&W)

	FR1.0	GD2.0	FN6.0
nn - John Leech (single panel **Punch** cartoon-r)	20.00	40.00	160.00

NOTE: *An advertisment in the back refers to a cloth-bound edition for 50 cents.*

PICTURES OF PEOPLE (see Gibson's Published Drawings)

PIPPIN AMONG THE WIDE-AWAKES (O,S)
Werill & Chapin, 113 Nassau St, NYC, NY): 1860 (6x4-1/2", 36 pgs, 6 cents)

	FR1.0	GD2.0	FN6.0
nn - Artist unknown	100.00	200.00	400.00

PLISH AND PLUM (E.G)
Roberts Brothers, Boston: 1883 (8-1/8x5-3/4", 80 pgs, hardcover, B&W)

	FR1.0	GD2.0	FN6.0
nn - By Wilhelm Busch (Scarce)	40.00	80.00	160.00
nn - Reprint (Little, Brown & Co., 1899)	40.00	80.00	160.00

NOTE: *The adventures of two dogs.*

PROGRESS OF MR. LAMBKIN, (GENT) (E,G) (see also Bachelor's Own Book)
David Bryce and Son, Glasgow: 1884 (1 shilling, 7-7/8x5-3/4", 60 pgs, printed one side only, cardboard cover, B&W)

	FR1.0	GD2.0	FN6.0
nn	17.50	35.00	70.00

NOTE: *Reprint of George Cruikshank's* ***Bachelor's Own Book****.*

PUCK (German language edition, St. Louis) (M,O) (see also Die Vehme)
Publisher unknown, St. Louis: No.1, March 18, 1871 - No. ??, Aug. 24, 1872 (B&W, paper-c)

1-?? (Very Rare) by Joseph Keppler (no known sales)

NOTE: *Joseph Keppler's second attempt at a weekly humor periodical, following* ***Die Vehme*** *one year earlier. This was his first attempt to launch using the title* ***Puck****. This German language version ran for a full year before being joined by an English language version.*

PUCK (English language edition, St. Louis) (M,O)
Publisher unknown, St. Louis: No.1, March ?? 1872 - No. ??, Aug. 24, 1872 (B&W, paper c)

1-?? (Very Rare) by Joseph Keppler (no known sales)

NOTE: *Same material as in the German language edition, but in English.*

PUCK, ILLUSTRIRTES HUMORISTISCHES WOCHENBLATT (German language edition, NYC) (M,O)
Keppler & Schwarzmann, New York: No.1 Sept (27) 1876 - 1164 Dec ?? 1899 (10 cents, color front/back-c and centerspread, remainder B&W, paper-c)

	FR1.0	GD2.0	FN6.0
1-26 (Volume 1; Rare) by Joseph Keppler - these issues precede the English language version, and contain cartoons not found in them. Includes cartoons on the controversial Tilden-Hayes 1876 Presidential Election debacle.	(no known sales)		
27-52 (Volume 2; Rare) by Joseph Keppler - contains some cartoon material not found in the English language editions. Particularly in the earlier issues.	(no known sales)		
53-1164	7.50	15.00	30.00
Bound Volumes (six month, 26 issue run each):			
Vol. 1 (Rare)	(no known sales)		
Vol. 2-4 (Rare)	(no known sales)		
Vol. 5-47	62.50	125.00	250.00

NOTE: *Joseph Keppler's second, and successful, attempt to launch* ***Puck****. In German. The first six months precede the launch of the English language edition. Soon after (but not immediately after) the launch of the English edition, both editions began sharing the same cartoons, but, their prose material always remained different. The German language edition ceased publication at the end of 1899, while the English language edition continued into the early 20th Century. First American periodical to feature printed color every issue.*

PUCK (English language edition, NYC) (M,O)
Keppler & Schwarzmann, New York: No.1 March (14) 1877 - 1190 Dec ?? 1899 (10 cents, color front/back-c and centerspread, remainder B&W, paper-c)

	FR1.0	GD2.0	FN6.0
1 (Rare) by Joseph Keppler	(no known sales)		
2-26 (Rare) by Joseph Keppler	(no known sales)		
27-1190	12.50	25.00	50.00
(see Platinum Age section for year 1900+ issues)			
Bound volumes (six month, 26 issue run each):			
Vol. 1 (Rare)	(no known sales)		
Vol. 2 (Scarce)	(no known sales)		
Vol. 3-6 (pre-1880 issues)	175.00	350.00	700.00
Vol. 7-46	140.00	280.00	560.00

NOTE: *The English language editions began six months after the German editions, and so the English edition numbering is always one volume number, and 26 issue numbers, behind its parallel German language edition. Pre-1880 & post-1900 issues are more scarce than 1880's & 1890's.*

PUCK (miniature) (M,P,I)
Keppler & Schwarzmann, New York: nd (c1895) (7x5-1/8", 12 pgs, color front & back paper-c, B&W interior)

	FR1.0	GD2.0	FN6.0
nn - Scarce	25.00	50.00	100.00

NOTE: *C.J.Taylor-c; F.M.Howarth-a; F.Opper-a; giveaway item promoting* ***Puck's*** *various publications. Mostly text, with art reprinted from* ***Puck****.*

PUCK, CARTOONS FROM (M,S)
Keppler & Schwarzmann, New York: 1893 (14-1/4x11-1/2", 244 pgs, hard-c, mostly B&W)

	FR1.0	GD2.0	FN6.0
nn - (Scarce) by Joseph Keppler (S/N)	25.00	50.00	100.00

NOTE: *Reprints Keppler cartoons from 1877 to 1893, mostly in B&W, though a few in color, with a text opposite each cartoon explaining the situation then being satirized. Issued only in an edition of 300 numbered issues, signed by Keppler. Only 1/4 of the pages are cartoons.*

PUCK'S LIBRARY (M)
Keppler & Schwarzmann, New York: No.1, July, 1887 - No. 174, Dec, 1899 (10 cents, 11-1/2x8-1/4", 36 pgs, color paper-c, B&W)

	FR1.0	GD2.0	FN6.0
1- "The National Game" (Baseball)	25.00	50.00	100.00
2-149	7.50	15.00	30.00

NOTE: ***Puck's Library*** *was a monthly magazine reprinting cartoons & prose from* ***Puck****, with each issue's material organized around the same subject. The cover art was often original. All issues were kept in print for the duration of the series, so later issues are more scarce than earlier ones.*

PUCK'S OPPER BOOK (M)
Keppler & Schwarzmann, New York: 1888 (30 cents, color paper-c, B&W)

	FR1.0	GD2.0	FN6.0
nn - (Very Rare) by F. Opper	50.00	100.00	300.00

NOTE: *Solidly strip and cartoon material by Opper, all of it reprinted from* ***Puck****.*

PUCK, PICKINGS FROM (M)
Keppler & Schwarzmann, New York: No.1, Sept, 1891 - No. 34, Dec, 1899 (25 cents, 13-1/4x10-1/4", 68 pgs, color paper-c, B&W)

	FR1.0	GD2.0	FN6.0
1-34	15.00	30.00	60.00

NOTE: *Similar to* ***Puck's Library****, except larger in size, and issued quarterly. All reprint material, except for the cover art. There also exist variations with "RAILROAD EDITION 30 CENTS" printed on the cover in place of the standard 25 cent price.*

PUCK PROOFS (M,P,S)
Keppler & Schwarzmann, New York: nd (1906-1909) (76 pgs, paper cover; B&W) (all are Scarce)

	FR1.0	GD2.0	FN6.0
nn - (c.1906, no price, 4-1/8x5-1/4") B&W painted -c of couple kissing over a chess board; 1905 & 1906-r	25.00	50.00	100.00
nn- (c.1909, 10 cents, 4-3/8x5-3/8") plain green paper-c; 1905-1909-r	25.00	50.00	100.00

NOTE: *Catalog of prints available from* ***Puck****, reprinting mostly cover & centerspread art from* ***Puck****. There likely exist more as yet unreported* ***Puck Proofs*** *catalogs. Art by Rose O'Neill.*

PUCK, THE TARIFF ?, CARTOONS AND COMMENTS FROM (M,S)
Keppler & Schwarzmann, New York: 1888 (10 cents, 6-7/8x10-3/8", 36 pgs, paper-c, B&W)

	FR1.0	GD2.0	FN6.0
nn - (Scarce)	25.00	50.00	100.00

NOTE: *Reprints both cartoons and commentary from* ***Puck****, concerning the issue of tariffs which were then being debated in Congress. Art by Gillam, Keppler, Opper, Taylor.*

PUCK, WORLD'S FAIR
Keppler & Schwarzmann, PUCK BUILDING, World's Fair Grounds, Chicago: No.1 May 1, 1893 - No.26 Oct 30, 1893 (10 cents, 11-1/4x8-3/4, 14 pgs, paper-c, color front/back/center pages, rest B&W)(All issues Scarce to Rare)

	FR1.0	GD2.0	FN6.0
1-26	30.00	60.00	120.00
1-26 bound volume:	500.00	1000.00	2000.00

Rays of Light
1886 © Morse Bros., Canton, Mass.

Scraps, New Series #1 by D.C. Johnston
1849 © D.C. Johnston, Boston

Shakespeare Would Ride the Bicycle If Alive Today. "The Reasons Why" by Opper
1896 © H. A. Lozier & Co.

*NOTE: Art by Joseph Keppler, F. Opper, F.M. Howarth, C.J. Taylor, W.A. Rogers. This was a separate, parallel run of **Puck**, published during the 1893 Chicago World's Fair from within the fairgrounds, and containing all new and different material than the regular weekly **Puck**. Smaller sized and priced the same, this originally sold poorly, and had not as wide distribution as **Puck**, and so consequently issues are much more rare than regular **Puck** issues from the same period. Not to be confused with the larger sized regular **Puck** issues from 1893 which sometimes also contained World's Fair related material, and sometimes had the words "World's Fair" appear on the cover. Can also be distinguished by the fact that **Puck's** issue numbering was in the 800's in 1893, while these issue number 1 through 26.*

QUIDDITIES OF AN ALASKAN TRIP (O,G)
G.A. Steel & Co., Portland, OR: 1873 (6-3/4x10-1/2", 80 pgs, gilted blue hard-c, B&W)

nn - By William H. Bell (Very Rare) 300.00 600.00 900.00
NOTE: Highly sought Western Americana collectors. Parody of a trip from Washington DC to Alaska, by a member of the team which went to survey Alaska, purchase commonly known then as "Seward's Folly".

RARE CARTOONS OF CANADIAN HISTORY (see Caricature History of Canadian Politics)

"RAG TAGS" AND THEIR ADVENTURES, THE (N,S)
A. M. Robertson, San Francisco: 1899 (color hard-c, B&W interiors)

nn - By Arthur M. Lewis (SF Chronicle newspaper-r) 60.00 120.00 240.00

RAYS OF LIGHT (O,P)
Morse Bros., Canton, Mass.: No.1 1886 (7-1/8x5-1/8", 8 pgs, color paper-c, B&W)

1- (Rare) 50.00 100.00 200.00
NOTE: Giveaway pamphlet in guise of an educational publication, consisting entirely of a sequential story in which a teacher instructs her classroom of young girls in the use of Rising Sun Stove Polish. Color front & back covers.

RELIC OF THE ITALIAN REVOLUTION OF 1849, A
Gabici's Music Stores, New Orleans: 1849 (10-1/8x12-3/4", 144 pgs, hardcover)

nn - By G. Daelli 100.00 200.00 400.00
NOTE: From the title page: "Album of fifty line engravings, executed on copper, by the most eminent artists at Rome in 1849; secreted from the papal police after the 'Restoration of Order,' And just imported into America."

REMARKS ON THE JACOBINIAD (I,S)
Unknown, Boston: 1795 (8-1/4x5-1/8", 72 pgs, a number of B&W plates with text)

nn - Written by Rev. James Sylvester Gardner, artist unknown (no known sales)
NOTE: Early comics-type characters. Not sequential comics, but uses word balloons. Satire directed against "The Jacobin Club," supporters of the French Revolution and Radical Republicans. Gardner came to America from England in 1783, was minister of Trinity Church, Boston.

REV. MR. SOURBALL'S EUROPEAN TOUR, THE RECREATION OF A CITY, THE
Duffield Ashmead, Philadelphia: 1867 (7-5/8x6-1/4", 72 pgs, turquoise blue soft wrappers)

By Horace Cope 35.00 70.00 140.00

RHYMES OF NONSENSE TRUTH & FICTION (S)
G.W. Carleton & Co, Publishers, NY: 1874 (10x7-3/4", 44 pgs, hard-c, B&W)

nn - By Chaucer Jones and Michael Angelo Raphael Smith 25.00 50.00 100.00
NOTE: Creator names obviously pseudonyms; looks like weak A.B. Frost.

ROMANCE OF A HAMMOCK, THE - AS RECITED BY MR. GUS WILLIAMS IN "ONE OF THE FINEST" (O,P)
Unknown: 1880s (5-1/2x3-5/8" folded, 7 attached cardboard cards which fold out into a strip, color)

nn - By presently unknown 25.00 50.00 100.00
NOTE: 12-panel story, which one begins reading on one side of the folded-out strip, then flip to the other side to continue -- unlike the vast majority of folded strips, which are printed on only one side. This was a promotional handout, for a play titled "One of the Finest". The story pictured comes from a poem read in the play by then famous New York stage actor Gus Williams, who is pictured on the "cover"/title card."

SAD TALE OF THE COURTSHIP OF CHEVALIER SLYFOX-WIKOF, SHOWING HIS HEART-RENDING ASTOUNDING & MOST WONDERFUL LOVE ADVENTURES WITH FANNY ELSSLER AND MISS GAMBOL, THE (O,G)
Garrett & Co., NY: nd (c1852-55) (25 ¢, 5-3/4x9-1/4", 100 pages, paper-c, B&W)

nn - (Very Rare) By T.C. Bond ?? 300.00 600.00 900.00
NOTE: No surviving copies yet reported -- known via ads. Cover art by John McLenan and Samuel Avery. Graphic novel parodying the real-life romance between European actress/dancer Fanny Elssler and American aristocrat Henry Wikoff. The entire graphic novel is reprinted in the 1976 book "Fanny Elssler in America."

SAD TALE OF THE COURTSHIP OF CHEVALIER SLYFOX-WIKOF, SHOWING HIS HEART-RENDING ASTOUNDING & MOST WONDERFUL LOVE ADVENTURES WITH FANNY ELSSLER AND MISS GUMBEL, THE (G) (25 cents printed on cover)
Dick And Fitzgerald, NY: 1870s-1888 (5-3/4x9-1/4", ??? pages, soft paper-c, B&W)

nn - By T.C. Bond ?? 100.00 200.00 300.00
NOTE: Reprint of Garrett original printing before G,D&F partnership begins.

SCRAPS (O,S) (see also **F****** A*** K*******)
D.C. Johnston, Boston: 1828 - No.8 1840; New Series No.1 1849 (12 pgs, printed one side only, paper-c, B&W)

1 - 1828 (9-1/4 x 11-3/4") (Very Rare) (no known sales)
2 - 1830 (9-3/4 x 12-3/4") (Very Rare) (no known sales)
3 - 1832 (10-7/8 x 13-1/8") (Very Rare) (no known sales)
4 - 1833 (11 x 13-5/8") (Very Rare) (no known sales)
5- 1834 (10-3/8 x 13-3/8") (Very Rare) (no known sales)
6 - 1835 (10-3/8 x 13-1/4") red lettering in title SCRAPS (Very Rare) 200.00 400.00 800.00
6 - 1835 (10-3/8 x 13-1/4") no red lettering in title (Very Rare) 200.00 400.00 800.00
7 - 1837 (10-3/4 x 13-7/8") 1st Edition (Very Rare) 200.00 400.00 800.00
7 - 1837 (10-3/4 x 13-3/4") 2nd Edition (so stated) (Scarce) 75.00 125.00 250.00
NOTE: 20 pgs. of text (double-sided), 4 pgs. of art (single-sided), plus the covers. There are no protective sheets between the art pages.
8 - 1840 (10-1/2 x 13-7/8") (Very Rare) 200.00 400.00 800.00
New Series 1- 1849 (10-7/8 x 13-3/4") (Scarce) 75.00 125.00 250.00
NOTE: By David Claypool Johnston. All issues consist of four one-sided sheets with 9 to 12 single panel cartoons per sheet. The other pages are blank or text. Contains 4 protective sheets (not part of page count) Only the 1849 New Series Number 1 has cover art along with 4 art pgs. (single sided) with 4 protective sheets and no text pages.New Series Number 1, and the second printing of issue 7, have survived in higher numbers due to a 1940s warehouse discovery.

SHAKESPEARE WOULD RIDE THE BICYCLE IF ALIVE TODAY. "THE REASON WHY" (O,P,S)
Cleveland Bicycles H.A. Lozier & Co., Toledo, OH: 1896 (5-1/2x4",16 pgs, paper-c, color)

nn - By F. Opper (Rare) 70.00 140 .00 280.00
NOTE: Original cartoons of Shakespearian characters riding bicycles; also popular amongst collectors of bicycle ephemera.

SHAKINGS - ETCHINGS FROM THE NAVAL ACADEMY BY A MEMBER OF THE CLASS OF '67 (O.S)
Unknown: 1867 (7-7/8x10", 132 pages, blue hard-c)

By: Park Benjamin 35.00 70.00 140.00
NOTE: Park Benjamin later became editor of Harper's Bazaar magazine.

SHYS AT SHAKESPEARE
J.P. and T.C.P., Philadelphia: 1869 (9-1/4x6", 52 pgs)

nn - Artist unknown 35.00 70.00 140.00

SKETCHES AND CARTOONS (see Gibson's Published Drawings)

SKETCHES OF LOWLY LIFE IN A GREAT CITY (M,S) (See 99 "Woolfs" From Truth)
G. P. Puntam's Sons: 1899 (8-5/8x11-1/4", 200 pgs, hard-c, B&W)
(reprints from Life and Judge of Woolf's cartoons of NYC slum children)

nn - By Michael Angelo Woolf 75.00 150.00 300.00
NOTE: Woolf's cartoons are regarded as a primary influence on R.F. Outcault in the later development of The Yellow Kid newspaper strip.

SLOVENLY PETER; or, Cheerful Stories and Funny Pictures, For Good Little People. (E,I)
Porter & Coates, Philadelphia: 1880 (4to, 100 pgs, handcolored hard-c)

nn - By Heinrich Hoffman 50.00 100.00 400.00
NOTE: The John C. Winston Co. did a number of reprints from at least 1901-1940 which range in price from $95 to $350 plus The Limited Editions Club, New York, published 1500 copies of a Samuel ("Mark Twain") Clemons translated version done in 1891 in Berlin but not printed until 1935, ranges in price from $285 to $450.

SOCIAL LADDER, THE (see Gibson's Published Drawings)

SOCIETY PICTURES (M,S,E)
Charles H. Sergel Company, Chicago: 1895 (5-1/4x7-3/4", 168 pgs, printed 1 side, paper-c, B&W)

nn - By George du Maurier; reprints from **Punch**. 12.50 25.00 50.00

SOUVENIR OF SOHMER CARTOONS FROM PUCK, JUDGE, AND FRANK LESLIE'S (M,S,P)
Sohmer Piano Co.: nd(c.1893) (6x4-3/4", 16 pgs, paper-c, B&W)

nn 20.00 40.00 80.00
NOTE: Reprints painted "cartoon" Sohmer Piano advertisements which appeared in the above publications. Artists include Keppler, Gillam, others.

SPICE OF LIFE, THE (E,M,)
White and Allen: 1888 NY & London: 1888 (8-3/8x10-1/2",76 pgs, hard-c, B&W)

nn 50.00 100.00 200.00
*NOTE: Resembles **THE GOOD THINGS OF LIFE** in layout and format, and appears to be an attempt to compete with their former partner Frederick A. Stokes. However, the material is not from **LIFE**, but rather is reprinted and translated German sequential and single panel comics.*

STORY OF THE MAN OF HUMANITY AND THE BULL CALF, THE
(see Bull Calf, The Story of The Man Of Humanity And The)
NOTE: Reprints of two of A. B. Frost's mostfamous sequential comic strips.

STUFF AND NONSENSE (Harper's Monthly strip-r) (M)
Charles Scribner's Sons: 1884 (10-1/4x7-3/4", 100 pgs, hardcover, B&W)

nn - By Arthur Burdett Frost 60.00 120.00 240.00
nn - By A.B. Frost (1888 reprint, 104 pgs) 40.00 80.00 160.00
NOTE: Earliest known anthology devoted to collecting the comic strips of a single American artist.

SUMMER SCHOOL OF PHILOSOPHY AT MT. DESERT, THE
Henry Holt & Co.: 1881 (10-3/8x8-5/8", 60 pgs, illus. gilt hard-c, B&W)

nn - By J. A. Mitchell 60.00 120.00 240.00

Stuff and Nonsense by A.B. Frost
1884 © Charles Scribner's Sons

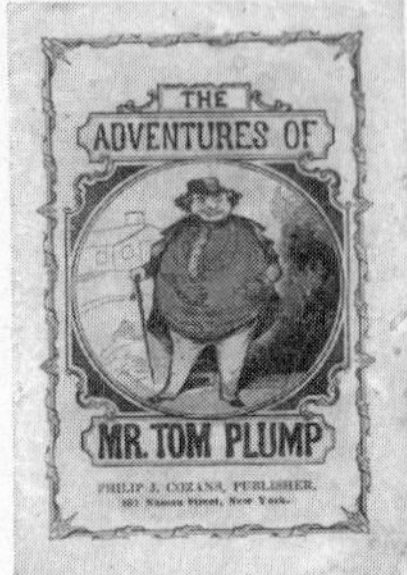

The Adventures of Mr. Tom Plump
1851 © Philip J. Cozans, New York

The Tooth-Ache by George Cruickshank
1849 © J. L. Smith, Philadelphia, PA

FR1.0 GD2.0 FN6.0

NOTE: *J.A.Mitchell went on to found* ***LIFE*** *two years later in 1883. Also, the long-running mascot for* ***LIFE*** *was Cupid - which you see multitudes of Cupids flying around in this story.*

TAILOR-MADE GIRL, HER FRIENDS, HER FASHIONS, AND HER FOLLIES, THE
(see also IN THE "400" AND OUT) (O,I)
Charles Scribner's Sons, New York: 1888 (8-3/8x10-1/2", 68 pgs, hard-c, B&W)

nn - Art by C.J. Taylor 17.50 35.00 70.00
NOTE: *Format is a full page cartoon on every other page, with a script style vignette, written by Philip H. Welch, on every page opposite the art.*

TALL STUDENT, THE
Roberts Brothers, Boston: 1873 (7x5", 48 pgs, printed one side only, gilted hard-c, B&W)

nn - By Wilhelm Busch (Scarce) 30.00 60.00 120.00

TARIFF ?, CARTOONS AND COMMENTS FROM PUCK, THE (see Puck, The Tariff...)

TEASING TOM AND NAUGHTY NED WITH A SPOOL OF CLARK'S COTTON, THE ADVENTURES OF (O,P)
Clark's O.N.T. Spool Cotton: nd (c1879-1880) (4-1/4x3", 12 pgs, B&W, paper-c)

nn 17.50 35.00 70.00
NOTE: *Knock-off of the "First Trick" in Wilhelm Busch's* ***Max and Maurice****, modified to involve Clark's Spool Cotton in the story, with similar but new art by an artist identified as "HB". The back cover advertises the specific merchant who gave this booklet away -- multiple variations of back cover suspected.*

TEMPERANCE TALES; OR, SIX NIGHTS WITH THE WASHINGTONIANS, VOL I & II
W.A. Leary & Co., Philadelphia: 1848 (50¢, 6-1/8x4", 328 pgs, B&W, hard-c)

nn (no known sales)
NOTE: *Mostly text. This edition gathers Volume I & II together. The first 8 pages reprints George Cruikshank's* ***THE BOTTLE****, re-drawn & re-engraved by Phil A. Pilliner. Later editions of this book do not include* ***THE BOTTLE*** *reprint and are therefore of little interest to comics collectors.*

THAT COMIC PRIMER (S)
G.W. Carleton & Co., Publishers: 1877 (6-5/8x5", 52 pgs, paper soft-c, B&W)

nn - By Frank Bellew Sr 35.00 70.00 140.00
NOTE: *Premium for the United States Life Insurance Company, New York.*

TOM PLUMP, THE ADVENTURES OF MR. (see also The Juvenile Gem) (O)
Huestis & Cozans, New York: nd (c1850-1851) (6x3-7/8", 12 pgs, hand colored paper-c, B&W)

nn- First printing(s) publisher's address is 104 Nassau Street (1850-1851)
(Very Rare) 200.00 400.00 700.00
NOTE: *California Gold Rush story. The hand colored outer cover is highly rare, with only 1 recorded copy possessing it. The front cover image and text is repeated precisely on page 3 (albeit b&w), and only interior pages are numbered, together leading owners of coverless copies to believe they have the cover. The true back cover contains ads for the publisher. The cover was issued only with copies which were sold separately - booklets which were bound together as part of* ***THE JUVENILE GEM*** *never had such covers.*

TOM PLUMP, THE ADVENTURES OF MR. (see also The Juvenile Gem) (O)
Philip J. Cozans: nd (1851-1852) (6x3-7/8", 12 pgs,hand colored paper-c, B&W)

nn- Second printing(s) publisher's address is 116 Nassau Street (1851-1852)
(Very Rare) 200.00 400.00 700.00
nn- Third printing(s) publisher's address is 107 Nassau Street (1852+)
(Very Rare) 200.00 400.00 700.00

TOM PLUMP, THE ADVENTURES OF MR.
Americana Review, Scotia, NY: nd(1960's) (6-1/4x4-1/8", 8 pgs, side-stapled, cardboard-c, B&W)

nn - Modern reprint - 12.00 24.00
NOTE: *Issued within a folder titled SIX CHILDREN'S BOOKS OF THE 1850'S. States "Reprinted by American Review" at bottom of front cover. Reprints the 104 Nassau Street address.*

TOM PLUMP, THE ADVENTURES OF MR.
Unknown: nd (1980's) (5-1/2x4-1/4", 8 pgs, side-stapled, black ink on colored paper)

nn - Modern reprint (Scarce) - 5.00 10.00
NOTE: *Photocopy reprint by a comix zine publisher, from an Americana Review copy, and available by mail order only.*

TOOTH-ACHE, THE (E,O)
D. Bogue, London: 1849 (???) --

nn - By Cruikshank, B&W (Very Rare) (no known sales)
nn - By Cruikshank, hand colored (Rare) (no known sales)
NOTE: *Scripted by Horace Mayhew, art by George Cruikshank. This is the British edition. Price 1/6 b&w, 3 hand colored. In British editions, the panels are not numbered. Publisher's name appears on cover. Booklet's "pages" unfold into a single, long, strip.*

TOOTH-ACHE, THE (E) (see also Almy's Santa Claus, and Home Picture Book for Little Children)
J.L. Smith, Philadelphia, PA: nd (1849) (15 cents, 5-1/8"x 3-3/4" folded, 86-7/8" wide unfolded, 26 pgs, cardboard-c, color)

nn - By Cruikshank, hand colored (Very Rare) (no known sales)
NOTE: *Reprints the D. Bogue edition. In American editions, the panels are numbered (43 panels, not counting front & back cover). Publisher's name stamped on inside front cover, plus printed along left-hand side of first interior page. Page 1 is pasted to inside back cover, and unfolds from there. Front cover not attached to back cover by design. Booklet's "pages" unfold into a single, long, strip (made from four individual strips pasted together on the blank back side).*

FR1.0 GD2.0 FN6.0

TOOTH-ACHE, THE (E)
Arts Council of Great Britain: nd (1974) (5-1/2x3-5/8", 28 pgs, B&W, cardboard-c, color interior)

nn - By Cruikshank, printed color - 15.00 30.00
NOTE: *Modern reprint of D. Bogue edition. 5000 copies printed, included in a catalogue issued with a show at the Victoria and Albert Museum, in London, 28 February-28 April 1974. Also included in the catalogue was a modern reprint of the Cruikshank booklet "A Comic Alphabet".*

TRUTH (See Platinum Age section for 1900-1906 issues)
Truth Company, NY: 1886-1906? (13-11/16x10-5/16", 16 pgs, process color-c & center-folds, rest B&W)

	FR1.0	GD2.0	FN6.0
1886-1887 issues	20.00	40.00	90.00
1888-1893 issues	15.00	30.00	70.00
1894-1895 non Outcault issues	10.00	20.00	50.00
Mar 10 1894 - precursor Yellow Kid RFO	50.00	150.00	300.00
#372 June 2 1894 - first app Yellow Kid RFO	150.00	450.00	900.00
June 23 1894 - precursor Yellow Kid R. F. Outcault	50.00	150.00	300.00
July 14 1894 -2nd app Yellow Kid RFO	100.00	300.00	600.00
Sept 15 1894 - (2) 3rd app YK RFO plus YK precursor	100.00	300.00	600.00
Feb 9 1895 - 4th app Yellow Kid RFO	100.00	300.00	600.00
1896-1899 issues	10.00	20.00	50.00

NOTE: *This magazine contains the earliest known appearances of* ***The Yellow Kid*** *by Richard Felton Outcault. Feb 9 1895 issue's YK cartoon was reprinted one week later in the* ***New York World*** *Feb 17 1895 edition. We are still sorting out further Outcault appearances. Truth also contained full color sequential strips by Hy Mayer on the back plus Woolf, Verbeek, etc.*

TWO HUNDRED SKETCHES, HUMOROUS AND GROTESQUE, BY GUSTAVE DORE (E)
Frederick Warne & Co, London: 1867 (13-3/4x11-3/8, 94 pgs, hard-c, B&W)

	FR1.0	GD2.0	FN6.0
nn - (1867) by Gustave Dore	100.00	200.00	400.00
nn - (Second Edition; 1871)- by Gustave Dore	50.00	100.00	200.00
nn - (Third Edition; 1870's)- by Gustave Dore	50.00	100.00	200.00
nn - (Fourth Edition; 1870's- by Gustave Dore	50.00	100.00	200.00

NOTE: *Contains sequential comics stories, single panel cartoons, and sketches. Reprints and translates material which originally appeared in the French publications "Le Journal pour Rire", circa 1848-49. Although dated 1867, it was likely published & available for the 1866 Christmas Season, as has been confirmed for the American edition. Printed by Dalziel. The American & first British editions were printed simultaneously, the American edition is not a reprint of the British.*

TWO HUNDRED SKETCHES, HUMOROUS AND GROTESQUE, BY GUSTAVE DORE (E)
Roberts Brothers, Boston: 1867 (13-3/4x11-3/8", 96 pgs, hard-c, B&W)

nn - By Gustave Dore 100.00 200.00 400.00
NOTE: *Although dated 1867, it was published & available for the 1866 Christmas Season. Printed by Dalziel, in England, and imported to the USA expressly for a USA publisher.*

UNCLE BANTAM'S FUNNY BOOKS, FOR THE AMUSEMENT OF HIS LITTLE NEPHEWS AND NIECES. WITH SEVENTY-FIVE ILLUSTRATIONS. (I)
Davis Porter & Co., Philadelphia : 1865 (Quarto, 54 pgs, col. ill. ; pictorial paper covered boards) (See also Slovenly Peter)

nn - By Heinrich Hoffman 250.00 500.00 1000.00
NOTE: *Translation of "Der Struwwelpeter", first published in Germany in 1844. Hand-colored illustrations with lines of verse. This is a complete collection of six of the "Uncle Bantam's Funny Books" in one volume, each with 8 pgs.*

UNTIDY TOM & OTHER STORIES. (I)
Davis Porter & Co., Philadelphia: 1865 (8 pgs., color illustrations, 24 cm.)

nn - By Henrich Hoffman (no known sales)
NOTE: *Uncle Bantam's funny books for the amusement of his little nephews and nieces. Pub lisher's advertisement on back cover.(Contents: Untidy Tom -- Story of Johnny Look-in-the-Air -- Story of Augustus who would not have any soup -- Story of Little Suck-a-Thumb -- Story of Flying Robert.*

UPS AND DOWNS ON LAND AND WATER (O,G)
James R. Osgood & Co., Boston: 1871 ; **Houghton, Osgood & Co., Boston:** 1880 (108 pgs, gilted hard-c, B&W)

1st printing (1871; 10-3/4x16") - By Augustus Hoppin 45.00 90.00 180.00
2nd printing (1880; smaller sized) 32.50 65.00 130.00
NOTE: *Exists as blue or orange hard covers.*

VERY VERY FUNNY (M,S)
Dick & Fitzgerald, New York: nd(c1880's) (10¢, 7-1/2x5", 68 pgs, paper-c, B&W)

nn 22.50 45.00 90.00
NOTE: *Unauthorized reprints of prose and cartoons extracted from Puck, Texas Siftings, and other publications. Includes art by Chips Bellew, Bisbee, Graetz, Opper, Wales, Zim.*

WAR IN THE MIDST OF AMERICA. FROM A NEW POINT OF VIEW. (E,O,G)
Ackermann & Co., London: 1864 (4-3/8" x 5-7/8", folded, 36 feet wide unfolded, 80 pgs, hard-c, B&W)

nn- by Charles Dryden (rare) (no known sales)
NOTE: *British graphic novel about the American Civil War, with a pro-Confederate bent. Adventures of a British artist who decides to visually summarize the American Civil War for his countrymen, from newspaper accounts. Reaching current events, he finds he can not finish the story until the War ends, and so he travels to America, to end it. Book unfolds into a single long strip (binding was issued split, to enable the unfolding).*

WHAT I KNOW OF FARMING: Founded On The Experience of Horace Greeley (S)

Truth #372 (first app. The Yellow Kid)
June 2 1894 © Truth Company, NY

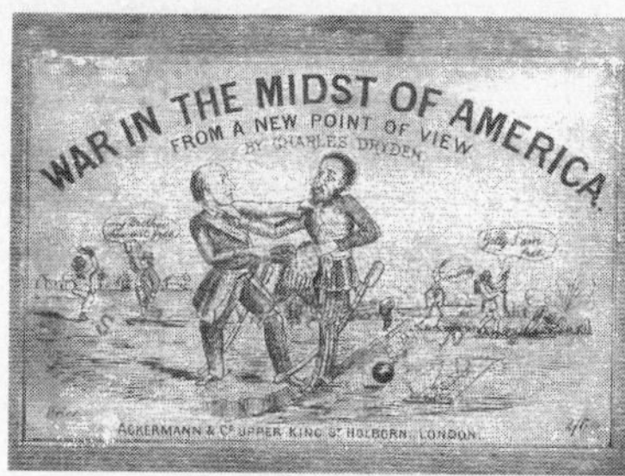

War in the Midst of America

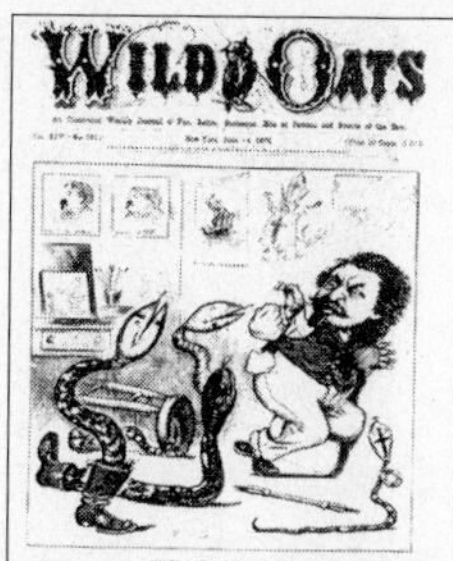

Wild Oats Vol. XIV #181330
June 14, 1876 © Winchell & Small

The American News Company, New York: 1871 (7-1/4x4-1/2", paper-c, B&W)

nn - By Joseph Hull 35.00 70.00 140.00

NOTE: *Pay & Cox, Printers & Engravers, NY; political tract regarding Presidential elections.*

WIDOW AND HER FRIENDS, A (see Gibson's Published Drawings)

WILD OATS, An Illustrated Weekly Journal of Fun, Satire, Burlesque, and Nits at Persons and Events of the Day (O) (does anybody have any loose issues?)
Winchell & Small, 113 Fulton St /48 Ann St, NYC: Feb 1870-1881 (16-1/4x11", generally 16 pages, B&W, began as monthly, then bi-weekly, then weekly) (all loose issues scarce)

1-25 scarce, contents currently unknown (no known sales)
26 (3/14/72) Hopkins 16 panel sequential (no known sales)
27 (3/28/72) Worth 11 panel double pg sequential; Hopkins-c (no known sales)
28 (4/11/72) Avery double pg sequential; Howard-c (no known sales)
29 Worth-c; no sequential strips (no known sales)
30 Howard sequential "Physiology of Moving"; Hopkins-c (no known sales)
31 (5/23/72) beautiful Hopkins 28 panel sequential (no known sales)
32 (6/6/72) unknown sequential 12 panel (no known sales)
33 (6/20/72) Bellew; Bisbee-c (no known sales)
34 (7/4/72) two Hopikns sequential comic strips (no known sales)
35 (7/18/72) Worth sequential; Bellew-c (no known sales)
36 (8/1/72) Worth 10 panel baseball sequential; Worth-c (no known sales)
37 no sequentials (no known sales)
38 (8/29/72) Hopkins 20 panel sequential (no known sales)
39 Worth 13 panel horse racing sequential; Bellew-c (no known sales)
40 (9/26/72) Worth 12 panel sequential (no known sales)
41 (10/11/72) unknown 11 panel sequenial; F.R.-c (no known sales)
42 no sequenials (no known sales)
43 Worth 6 panel sequential; Worth-c (no known sales)
44 Worth 13 panel double page spread; F.J.-c (no known sales)
45 Bisbee 17 panel, Worth 11 panel double page; Bellew-c (no known sales)
46 Worth & Beard full pagers semi-sequential (no known sales)
47 Bisbee 12 panel, Hopkins 20 panel, Worth 3 panel sequentials; Worth-c (no known sales)
48 (1/16/73) Worth 13 panel sequential; first Woolf-c (no known sales)
49 (1/30/73) Worth 17 panel double page sequentials; Sears-c (no known sales)
50 (2/13/73) Bellew; Frenzeny-c (no known sales)
51 (Worth 18 panel double page spread, Woolf 9 panel (no known sales)
52 (3/13/73) no sequentials; Worth-c (no known sales)
53 (3/27/73) Worth 6 panel sequential; Worth-c (no known sales)
54 Beard double page spread (no known sales)
55 Hopkins 22 panel double page spread;unk 6 panel;Bellew-c (no known sales)
56, 59, 63 no sequentials (no known sales)
57 intense unknown 6 panel "Two Relics of Barbarism, or A Few Contrasted Pictures, Showing the origin of the North American Indian; Worth Hopkins single panel cartoons (no known sales)
58 (6/5/73) unknown 19 panel double pager "The Terrible Adventures of Messrs Buster & Stumps, About Exterminating the Indians" reads across both pages like Popeye #2095 (1933); Woolf-c (no known sales)
60 (7/3/73) Worth 17 panel "Life on Wall Street", unknown 13 panel job; Kappes first-c (no known sales)
61 (7/17/73) unknown 9 panel "Uncle Bumberton's 4th of July Visit to New York City";A.K.-c (no known sales)
62 (7/31/73) Worth 15 panel sequential' Woolf-c (no known sales)
64 unk. 6 panel, Worth 12 panel, Bisbee 6 panel sequentials (no known sales)
65 (9/4/73) two Worth 9 panel sequential comic strips titled "Only a Mad Dog Scare-Anothe Lesson for Nervous People" and "Only a Cholera Scare-Something for Nervous People to Read & Ponder Over" (no known sales)
66 (9/18/73) two Worth 10 panel "Hunting" & "Fishing"; unknown 6 panel;Hopkins 12 panel "Adv of Mr Old Portly with New Jersey Mosquitoes"; Beard-c (no known sales)
67 Shelton full pager;Worth 9 panel "Adv of Young Muttonhead Among the Free Lovers about "free sex" - convention in Chicago (no known sales)
68 (10/16/73) unknown 9 panel "Adv of New jersey Mosquito" looks like Winsor McCay type style: early inspiration for McCay's animated cartoon? (no known sales)
69 (10/30/73) unknown 6 panel; Bellew-c (no known sales)
70 unknown 6 panel; Hopkins 6 panel "Hopkins novel: A Tale of True Love, with all the variations"; Bellew-c (no known sales)
71 no sequentials; Woolf-c (no known sales)
72 (12/11/73) Worth 11 panel; Wales President Grant war-c (no known sales)
73 Hopkins 12 panel sequential comic strip (no known sales)
74 Hopkins 10 panel; Davenport comic like double page spread (no known sales)
75 (1/22/74) Hopkins 3 panel job; Hopkins first cover? (no known sales)
76 unknown 12 panel; Worth-c (no known sales)
77 unknown 7 panel; Worth-c (no known sales)
78 Bellew 5 panel double pager (no known sales)
79-105 (March 1874-Dec 1874) contents presently unknown (no known sales)
106 107 111 no sequentials; Bellew-c #106 110; Wales-c #107 (no known sales)
108 (1/20/75) Wales 12 panel double pg spread; Bellew-c (no known sales)
109 (1/27/75) unknown 6 panel; Wales-c (no known sales)
111 Busch 13 panel "The Conundrum of the Day - Is Lager Beer Intoxicating?"; Bellew-c (no known sales)
112 Wales 11 panel sequential comic strip (no known sales)
113 114 115 no sequentials Worth-c #114 (no known sales)
116 Wales 6 panel; Bellew full pager' Howard-c (no known sales)
117 intense Wales 6 panel "One of the Oppresions of the Civil Rights Laws"' Bellew-c (no known sales)
118-137 (3/31/75-8/4/75) no sequential comic strips (no known sales)
138 (8/18/75) both Bellew Sr & Bellew "Chips" Jr singles appear (no known sales)
139-143 145-147 154-157 159 no sequentials (no known sales)
144 (9/29/75) Hopkins 8 panel sequential; Wales-c (no known sales)
148 (10/27/75) Fred Opper's first cover; Opper singles (no known sales)
149 150 151 152 153 all Opper-c and much interior work (no known sales)
158 (1/5/76) Palmer Cox 1rst comic strip 24 panel double page spread "The Adv of Mr & Mrs Sprowl And Their Christmas Turkey - A Crashing Chasing Tearful Tragedy But Happily Ending Well"; Opper-c (no known sales)
159 160 162 167 Opper-c 165 Bellew-c no sequentials (no known sales)
161 Palmer Cox 11 panel sequential; unk 6 panel; Opper-c (no known sales)
163 (2/9/76) Palmer Cox 24 panel double pager (no known sales)
164 (2/16/76) Palmer Cox 12 panel double pager; Bellew-c (no known sales)
166 (3/1/76) Cox 12 panel sequential comic strip (no known sales)
168 (3/15/76) Palmer Cox 24 panel double page opus "Bachelor Boke & Widow Snugg: A Pictorial Account of Their Sleigh Ride And What Became of It" (no known sales)
169-173 no sequentials; Bellew-c #170 Opper-c #172 (no known sales)
174 (4/26/76) Cox 24 panel double pager "The Tramp's Progress; A Story of the West And the Union Pacific Railroad" (no known sales)
175-178 no sequentials; first Mann singles #170 (no known sales)
179 (5/31/76) Cox 3 panel "Story of a Collision"' Opper-c (no known sales)
180 (6/7/76) Beard & Opper work together; Woolf, Bellew singles (no known sales)
181 more Mann two panel jobs; Opper-c (no known sales)
182 (6/21/76) Cox 12 panel; Opper full page single; Opper-c (no known sales)
183-189 no sequentials (no known sales)
190 (8/16/76) Bellew 9 panel "Rodger's Patent Mosquito Armour" (no known sales)
191-end contents currently unknown (no known sales)

NOTE: *There are no known loose issues. All issues are scarce. We present this index from the Library of Congress bound set. We would love to hear from any one who turns up loose copies. This scarce humor bi-weekly contains easily a couple hundred original first-time published sequential comic strips found in most issues plus innumerable single panel cartoons in every issue; distributed thru New York News Company, 8 Spruce St, NYC. Began as a monthly, at some point early on it became almost always bi-weekly (ie twice a month) till it died. Livingston Y. Hopkins, Thomas Worth, W.M. Avery, C.J. Howard, Frank Beard, Frank Bellew Sr & Jr, E.S. Bisbee, Michael Angelo Woolf, E. Sears, Paul Frenzeny, W.H. Shelton, Jae A. Wales, Kappes, Wilhelm Busch, Fredrick Opper and Palmer Cox are some of the cartoonists who graced its pages. Most of these cartoonists were doing sequentials and most likely interacting with each other as cartoonists were wont to do. Some cartoons carry double by-lines proving they were jamming together. Currently there is just one bound almost complete run (missing v1-2 (Feb 1870-Mar 1872, 7-8 (Mar 1874-Dec 1874) known to exist to the authors located at The Library of Congress. Any help locating further issues would be immensely appreciated. Please contact the authors of the Victorian & Platinum sections: Robert Beerbohm and Richard Olson whose e-mail addresses are at the end of each history essay.*

WOMAN IN SEARCH OF HER RIGHTS, THE ADVENTURES OF (G)
Lee & Shepard, Boston And New York: early 1850s (8-3/8x13", 40 pgs, hard-c)

By Florence Claxton (scarce) 300.00 600.00 900.00

NOTE: *Earliest known original comic book sequential story by a woman; contains "nearly 100 original drawings by the author, which have been reproduced in fac-simile by the graphotype process of engraving." Tinted two color lithography; orange tint printed first, thenprinted 2nd time with black ink; early women's sufferage.*

WORLD OVER, THE (I)
G. W. Dillingham Company, New York: 1897 (192 pgs, hardbound)

nn - By Joe Kerr; 80 illustrations by R.F. Outcault 30.00 90.00 300.00

WRECK-ELECTIONS OF BUSY LIFE (S)
Kellogg & Bulkeley: 1864? (9-1/4x11-3/4", ??? pages, soft-c)

nn - By J. Bowler 45.00 90.00 200.00

NOTE: *Says "Sold by American News Company, New York" on cover.*

YE VERACIOUS CHRONICLE OF GRUFF & POMPEY IN 7 TABLEAUX. (O,P)
Jackson's Best Chewing Tobacco & Donaldson Brothers: nd (c1870's) (5-1/8 tall x 3-3/8" wide folded, 27" wide unfolded, color cardboard)

nn - With all 8 panels attached (Scarce) 40.00 80.00 160.00
nn - Individual panels/cards 6.00 12.00 24.00

NOTE: *Black Americana interest. Consists of 8 attached cards, printed on one side, which unfold into a strip story of title card & 7 panels. Scrapbook hobbyists in the 19th Century tended to pull the panels apart and paste into their scrapbooks, making copies with all panels attached scarce.*

Read the introduction essays to learn more about the 160+ year history and origins of comics in America. For regular on-line discussions, go to:
PlatinumAgeComics@yahoogroups.com

The Platinum Age

The American Comic Book: 1883-1935

A MULTITUDE OF VARIED FORMATS FIGHT IT OUT IN THE MARKETPLACE

by Robert L. Beerbohm and Richard D. Olson, PhD ©2004

(This article series was originally created by Robert L. Beerbohm and Richard D. Olson beginning in OCBPG #27 1997 and is revised annually as new information comes to light.)

The story of the success of the modern comic strip as we know it today is tied closely to the companies who sponsored them and bought licenses from the copyright holder for the purpose of advertising products. What mainly keeps the Platinum Age from being collected as much as later era comics is simply a general lack of awareness of these important historical books as well as the scarcity of many of these volumes, especially in any type of higher-grade condition. Many Platinum Age books are much rarer than so-called Golden Age comic books, yet despite this scarcity, **Mutt & Jeff**, **Bringing Up Father**, **The Katzenjammer Kids**, and many more were as popular, if not more so, than **Superman** and **Batman** when they were introduced. Recent research has come up with some more amazing rediscoveries. There is much that can be learned and applied to today's comics market by a simple historical examination of the medium's evolution over more than 160 years.

It should be noted that "ages" are applied to historical periods in the history of comics for convenience. In fact, ages typically overlap and there is no discrete beginning or ending for any given "age." This is the case with the Platinum Age, which clearly began with Palmer Cox's creation of The Brownies in 1883 even though it overlaps with the Victorian Age which ran through the end of the 19th Century. Cox introduced a qualitative change to the field, not an incremental quantitative change. Specifically he produced art and verse for children in children's magazines and then merchandised those characters. He published work for children not only in books but in magazines and newspapers, and he merchandised his creations to an extent that had never been done previously.

Palmer Cox was born in 1840 near Granby, Quebec. He journeyed to Oakland, California in 1863, and began publishing cartoon, prose and poems in the local press and media outlets such as **The San Francisco Examiner** wherein by 1867 it has been reported he also began creating sequential comic strips.

His first book, **Squibs of California,** was published in 1874. He subsequently moved to New York in 1875 and almost immediately began working for the magazine **Wild Oats**, of which more is written about in the preceding Victorian Age history introduction. He drew dozens of sequential comic strips for **Wild Oats**, a humor magazine so scarce no single copies have been offered on eBay yet in the past five years. And we're still diligently looking.

Soon thereafter he became a major contributor to the Scribner publications, including **The St. Nicholas**, an illustrated magazine for young folk. His first cartoon for them was "The Wasp And The Bee," published in the March 1879 cover-date issue. While it is now clear that Cox used elves and brownie-like characters in his art for several different magazines as early as 1877 in **Harper's Young People** magazine as well as using Brownies-type characters beginning in the Feb

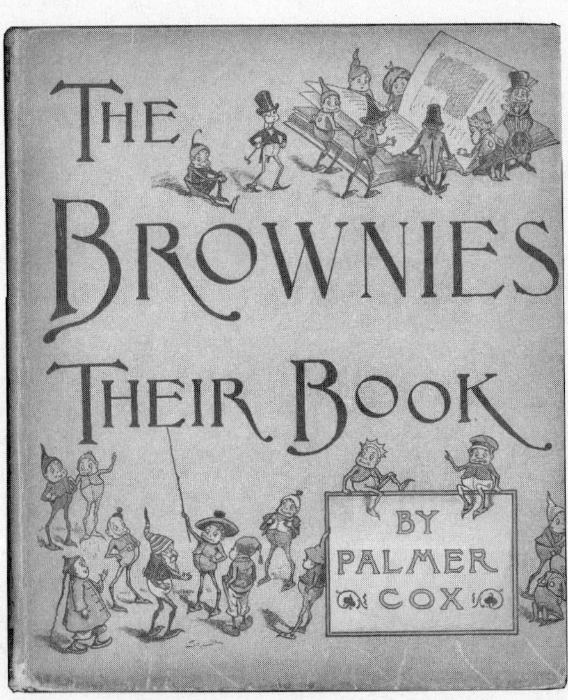

The Brownies' first book by Palmer Cox (from 1887) set the precedent for the Platinum Age by collecting and reprinting previously published material.

1881 issue of **Wide Awake**, the first true appearance of the Brownies in their own story using that title, a combination of art and verse was February, 1883, in **St. Nicholas.** Palmer Cox's **The Brownies** were the first North American comics-type characters to be internationally merchandised. Even though Cox was continuously doing sequential comic strips in magazines like **Wild Oats**, he left the medium of comics when he hit paydirt with The Brownies. For over a quarter of a century, Cox deftly combined the popular advertising motifs of animals and fairies into a wonderful, whimsical world of society at its best and worst.

The Brownies' first book was issued in 1887, titled **The Brownies: Their Book**; many more followed. Cox also added a run of his hugely popular characters in **Ladies Home Journal** from October 1891 through February 1895, as well as a special for December 1910. With the 1892-93 World's Fair, the merchandising exploded with a host of products, including pianos, paper dolls and other figurines, chairs, stoves, puzzles, cough drops, coffee, soap, boots, candy, and many more. **Brownies** material was being produced in Europe as well as the United States of America.

Cox tried out **The Brownies** as a newspaper strip in the **San Francisco Examiner** during 1898, where he had begun his newspaper career over 30 years before, and then in the **New York World** in 1900. It was syndicated from 1903 through 1907. He seems to have retired from regularly drawing **The Brownies** with the January 1914 issue of **St. Nicholas** when he was 74. A wealthy man, he lived to the ripe old age of 84, spending his last decade in his home he affectionately called Brownie Castle, back in Granby, Quebec.

By the mid-1890s, while keeping careful track of quickly rising circulations of magazines with graphic humor such as **Harper's**, **Puck**, **St. Nicholas**, **Judge**, **Life** and **Truth**, New York based newspaper publishers began to recognize that illustrated humor would sell extra papers. Thus was born the Sunday "comic supplement." Most of the regular favorites were under contract with these magazines. However, there was an artist working for **Truth** who wasn't. Roy L McCardell, then a staffer at **Puck**, informed Morrill Goddard, Sunday editor of **The New York World**, that he knew someone who could fit what was needed at the then-largest newspaper in America.

Richard F. Outcault (1863-1928) first introduced his street children strip in **Truth** #372, June 2, 1894, somewhat inspired by Michael Angelo Woolf's slum kids single panel cartoons in **Life** which had begun in the mid 1880s. The interested collector should seek out a copy of Woolf's **Sketches of Lowly Life In A Great City** (1899) listed in the Guide. It's also possible that Outcault's **Hogan's Alley** cast, including the Yellow Kid, was inspired by Charles W. Saalburg's **The Ting Ling Kids,** which began in the **Chicago Inter-Ocean** by May 1894. By 1895, Saalburg was Art Director in charge of coloring for the new color printing press at the **New York World**. Edward Harrigan's play "O'Reilly and the Four Hundred," which had a song beginning with the words "Down in Hogan's Alley..." likely provided direct inspiration.

By the November 18, 1894 issue of the **World**, Outcault was working for Goddard and Saalburg. Outcault produced a successful Sunday newspaper sequential comic strip in color with "The Origin of a New Species" on the back page in the World's first colored Sunday supplement. Long time pro Walt McDougall, a famous cartoonist reputed to have turned the 1884 Presidential race with a single cartoon that ran in the **World**, handled the cartoon art on the front page. Earlier, **The World** began running full page color single panels on May 21, 1893. McDougall did various other page panels during

The Brownies in the Philippines *by Palmer Cox - scarce original artwork from the chapter "The Brownies on Marinduque," page 142, Oct 1904. President Teddy Roosevelt is also pictured within these multitudes of Brownie madness which was a Cox "signature trademark." His stories are comic strip-oriented in nature of time sequence as he boldly took his Brownies around the world.*

1893, but it was Jan. 28, 1894 when the first sequence of comic pictures in a newspaper appeared in panels in the same format as our comic strips today. It was a full page cut up into nine panels. This historic sequence was drawn entirely in pantomime, with no words, by Mark Fenderson.

The second page to appear in panels was an eight panel strip from February 4, 1894, also lacking words except for the title. This page was a collaboration between Walt McDougall and Mark Fenderson titled "The Unfortunate Fate of a Well-Intentioned Dog." From then on, many full page color strips by McDougall and Fenderson appeared; they were the first cartoonists to draw for the Sunday newspaper comic section. It was Outcault, however, who soon became the most famous cartoonist featured. After first appearing in black and white in Pulitzer's **The New York World** on February 17, 1895 and again on March 10, 1895, **The Yellow Kid** was introduced to the public in color on May 5, 1895.

Some have erroneously reported in scholarly journals that perhaps it was Frank Ladendorf's "Uncle Reuben," first introduced May 26, 1895, which became the first regularly recurring comics character in newspapers. This is wrong, as even Outcault's "Yellow Kid" began in Pulitzer's paper a good three months before **Uncle Reuben**. Until firm evidence to the contrary comes to light, that honor will forever be enshrined with Jimmy Swinnerton's **Little Bears** cartoon characters, found all over inside Hearst's **San Francisco Examiner** as early as 1892. Though never actually a comic strip, they nonetheless were the earliest presently known recurring comics characters in American newspapers. There never was a strip titled **Little Bears and Tigers**, as the Tigers portion was strictly for New York consumption when Hearst ordered Swinnerton to move to the Big Apple to compete better in the brewing comic strip wars.

The Yellow Kid's importance is widely recognized today as the first newspaper comic strip to demonstrate without a doubt that the general public was ready for full color comics. **The Yellow Kid** was the first in the USA to show that (1), comics could increase newspaper sales, and that (2), comic characters could be merchandised. **The Yellow Kid** was the headlining spark of what was soon dubbed by Hearst as "eight pages of polychromatic effulgence that makes the rainbow look like a lead pipe."

Ongoing research suggests that Palmer Cox's fabulous success with **The Brownies** was a direct inspiration for Richard Outcault's future merchandising work. The ultimate proof lies in the fourth Yellow Kid cartoon, which appeared in the February 9, 1895 issue of **Truth**. It was reprinted in the **New York World** eight days later on February 17, 1895,

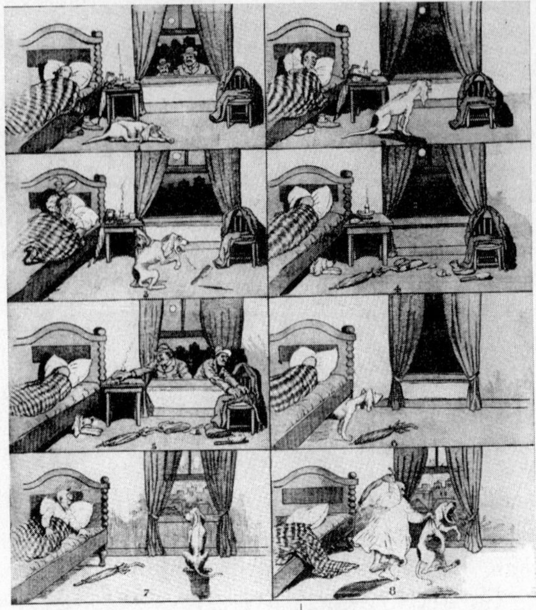

ORIGIN OF A NEW SPECIES, OR —
THE EVOLUTION OF THE CROCODILE EXPLAINED.

Top: ***Walt McDougall & Mark Fenderson****, the second American newspaper sequential comic strip,* ***New York World****, February 4, 1894, predates* ***Yellow Kid*** *in* ***The World*** *by over a year. Mark Fenderson drew the first real newspaper comic strip and we are still hunting down an example to display in future editions. Bottom:* ***New York World****, Nov. 18, 1894 predates YK "Origin of A New Species," Richard F. Outcault.*

"A Fair Champion" artwork by Richard F. Outcault, ***Truth****, July 14 1894 (2nd Yellow Kid app.) Many of RFO's comics were fully integrated down around the corner of Hogan's Alley and Ryan's Arcade*

"Fourth Ward Brownies," artwork by Richard F. Outcault, Feb. 17, 1895, the 4th Yellow Kid app. and 1st in Pulitzer's ***New York World****. Note the Kid, second from left. This panel first saw print in* ***Truth****, Feb 9, 1895.*

becoming the first Yellow Kid cartoon in the newspapers. The caption read "FOURTH WARD BROWNIES. MICKEY, THE ARTIST (adding a finishing touch) Dere, Chimmy! If Palmer Cox wuz t' see yer, he'd git yer copyrighted in a minute." The Yellow Kid was widely licensed in the greater New York area for all kinds of products, including gum and cigarette cards, toys, pinbacks, cookies, postcards, tobacco products, and appliances. There was also a short-lived humor magazine from Street & Smith named **The Yellow Kid**, featuring exquisite Outcault covers, plus a 196-page comic book from Dillingham & Co. known as **The Yellow Kid in McFadden's Flats**, dated to early 1897. In addition, there were several Yellow Kid plays produced, spawning other collectibles like show posters, programs and illustrated sheet music. (For those interested in more information regarding the Yellow Kid, it is available on the Internet at www.neponset.com/yellowkid.)

Mickey Dugan burned brightly for a few years as Outcault secured a copyright on the character with the United States Government by Sept. 1896. By the time he completed the necessary paperwork, however, hundreds of business people nationwide had pirated the image of The Yellow Kid and plas-

Left: ***The Yellow Kid*** *#5, May 22, 1897, Street & Smith as Howard Ainslee, NY cover by Richard F. Outcault; lasted six issues with RFO YK covers. Right:* ***Yellow Kids On Parade*** *1897 part of Gilmore & Leonard's Hogan's Alley Company; one of at least half a dozen Yellow Kid productions performed with collectible sheet music generated.*

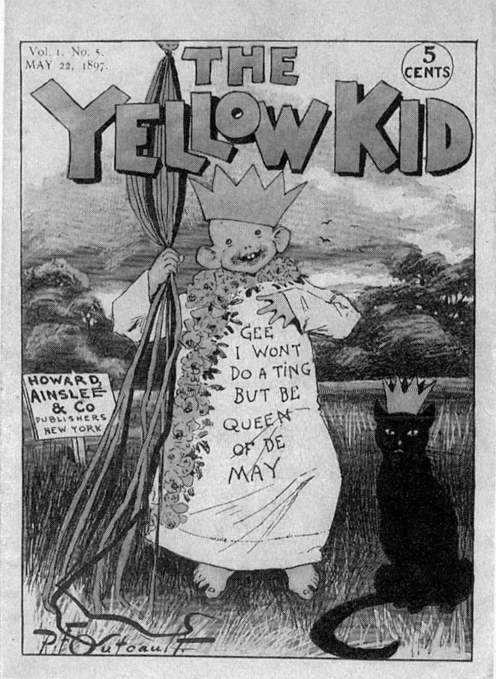

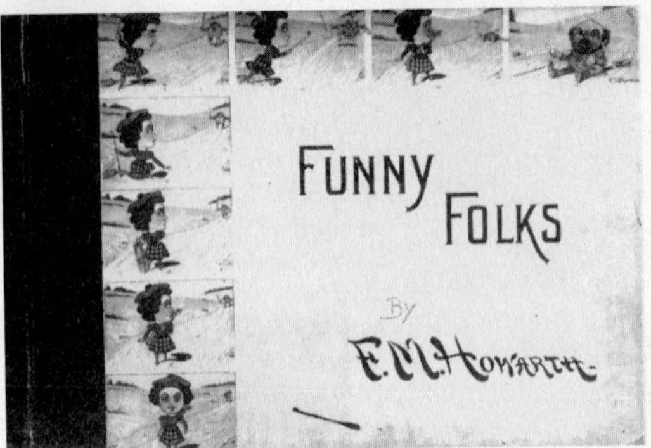

Funny Folks, *F. M. Howarth, 1899, collected many early sequential comics from Puck; one of the titles many consider bridges the Victorian & Platinum Ages of comics.*

The Adventures of Foxy Grandpa*, late 1900, newly re-discovered cover for the earliest known first edition of Carl "Bunny" Schultze's famous creation. He was one of the newspaper comics' first superstars.*

tered it all over every product imaginable; mothers were even dressing their newborns to look like Dugan. (Outcault, however, kept regularly utilizing images of **The Yellow Kid** in his comics style advertising work confirmed as late as 1915.) Outcault soon found himself in a maelstrom not of his choosing, which probably pushed him to eventually drop the character. Outcault's creation went back and forth between newspaper giants Pulitzer and Hearst until Bennett's New York Herald mercifully snatched the cartoonist away in 1900 to do what amounted to a few relatively short-run strips. Later, he did one particular strip for a year–a satire of rural Black America titled **Pore Li'l Mose**, and then his newer creation, **Buster Brown**, debuted May 4, 1902. Mose had a very rare comic book collection published in 1902 by Cupples & Leon, now highly sought after by today's savvy collectors. Outcault continued drawing him in the background of occasional **Buster Brown** strips for many years to come.

William Randolph Hearst loved the comic strip medium ever since he was a little boy growing up on **Max & Moritz** by Wilhelm Busch in American collected book editions translated from the original German (these collections were first published in book form in 1871, serving as the influence for **The Katzenjammer Kids**). One of the ways Hearst responded to losing Outcault in 1900 was by purchasing the highly successful 23-year-old humor magazine **Puck** from the heirs of founder Joseph Keppler. With **Puck** and its exclusive cartoonist contracts, he commanded, among others, the very popular F. M. Howarth and Frederick Burr Opper's undivided attention. Opper had first burst upon the comics scene in America back in 1880. Within a year Hearst had expanded this **National Lampoon** of its day into the colored Sunday comics section, **Puck-The Comic Weekly**. At first featuring Rudolph Dirk's **The Katzenjammer Kids** (1897), **Happy Hooligan** and other fine strips by the wildly popular Opper and a few others including Rudolph's brother Gus Dirks, the Hearst comic section steadily added more strips. For decades to come, there wasn't anything else that could compete with **Puck**. Hearst hired the best of the best and transformed **Puck** into the most popular comics section anywhere.

Outcault, meanwhile, followed in Palmer Cox's footprints a decade later by using the nexus of a World's Fair as a jumping off venue. **Buster Brown** was an instant sensation when he debuted as the new merchandising mascot of the Brown Shoe Company at the 1904 St. Louis World's Fair in a special Buster Brown Shoes pavilion. The character has the honor of being the first nationally licensed comic strip character in America. Many hundreds of different **Buster Brown** premiums have been issued. Comic books by Frederick A. Stokes Company featuring **Buster Brown & His Dog Tige** began as early as 1903 with **Buster Brown and His Resolutions**, simultaneously published in several different languages throughout the world.

After a few years, Buster and Outcault returned to Hearst in late 1905, joining what soon became the flagship of the comics world. Buster's popularity quickly spread all over the United States and then the world as he single-handedly spawned the first great comics licensing dynasty. For years, there were little people traveling from town to town performing as **Buster Brown** and selling shoes while accompanied by small dogs named Tige. Many other highly competitive licensed strips would soon follow. We suggest getting **Hake's Price Guide to Character Toys** for information on several hundred **Buster Brown** competitors, as well as several pages of the more fascinating **Buster Brown** material.

Soon there were many comic strip syndicates not only offering hundreds of various comic strips but also offering to license the characters for any company interested in paying the fee. The history of the comic strip with wide popularity

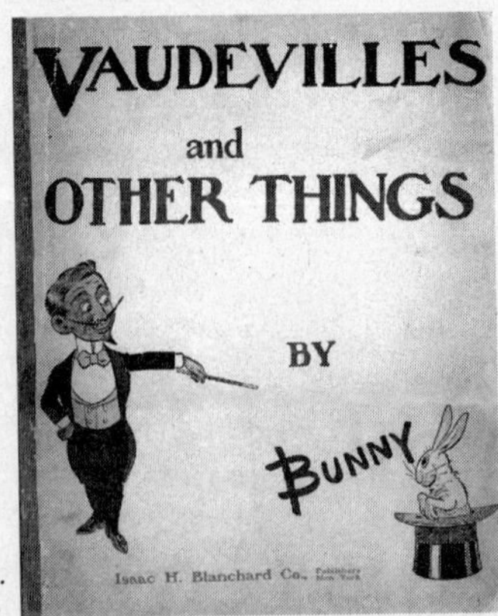

Vaudevilles And Other Things*, 1900, first printing. Carl Schultze became famous creating* ***Foxy Grandpa****.*

Beginning in late 1902, ***The Chicago Tribune*** *introduced a straight super hero with obvious super strength called "Hugo Hercules" by the unknown artist J. Koerner. This Sunday strip ran until early 1903 and ran only in this one paper. It is entirely possible a very young Chicago-resident named Philip Wylie read "Hugo" since that was the same name he gave his super-heroic main character in his much-later book* ***The Gladiator*** *(1930). Other appearances have Hugo running with almost super speed.*

since **The Yellow Kid** has been intertwined with giveaway premiums and character-based, store-bought merchandise of all kinds. Since its infancy as a profitable art form unto itself with **The Yellow Kid**, the comic strip world has profited from selling all sorts of "stuff" to the public featuring their favorite character or strip as its motif. American business gladly responded to the desire for comic character memorabilia with thousands of fun items to enjoy and collect. Most of the early comics were not aimed specifically at kids, though children understandably enjoyed them as well.

Comic books have generally been associated with almost all of the licensed merchandise in this century. In the Platinum Age section beginning right after this essay, you will find a great many comic books in varied formats and sizes published before the advent of the first successful monthly newsstand comic magazine, **Famous Funnies**. What drove each of these evolutionary format changes was the need by their producers to make money so more books could be issued.

A very significant format was F. M. Howarth's **Funny Folks**, published in 1899 by E. P. Dutton and drawn from color as well as black and white pages of **Puck**. This rather large hardcover volume measured 16 1/2" wide by 12" tall. It contains numerous sequential comic strip pages as well as single gag illustrations. Howarth's art was a joy to behold and deserves wider recognition.

By Oct. 1900, Hearst had already caused Opper's **Folks In Funnyville** to be collected by publisher R. H. Russell, NY in a 12x9 hard cover format from his **New York Journal American Humorist** section. At the end of 1900, Carl Shultze had a first edition of **Vaudevilles and Other Things**

Katzenjammer Kids *#1, 1902, by Rudolph Dirks was inspired by Wilhelm Busch.*

Happy Hooligan Book *#1, 1902, by Frederick Opper, was wildly popular.*

Katzenjammer Kids *#2 by Rudolph Dirks. These Katz Kids have the longest running strip in America.*

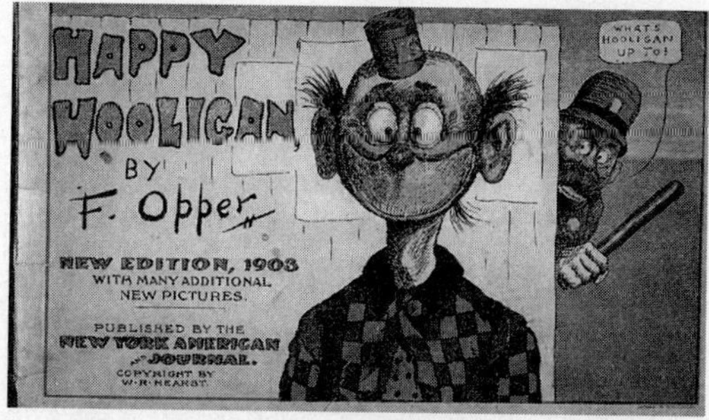

The second ***Happy Hooligan*** *comic book, 1903, by Frederick Opper set a high standard.*

Originally discovered listed for sale in a 1906 Lockwood Art School brochure, the existences of ***The Naughty Adventures of Vivacious Mr. Jack*** *and* ***Alphonse and Gaston New Edition 1903*** *were recently verified. So far only one copy of each is known to exist. We ask collectors who might have one of these to contact the authors.*

published by Isaac H. Blanchard Co., NY. It measures 10 1/2" wide by 13" tall with 22 pages including covers. Each interior page is a 2 to 7 panel comic strip with lots of color.

There were also recently unearthed format variation second and third printings of **Vaudevilles** with the inscription "From the Originator of the 'Foxy Grandpa' Series" at the bottom of its front cover of the third printing. This note is lacking on the earlier first two editions, and it also switches format size to 11" tall by 13" wide. Discovered last year was a heretofore undocumented **The Adventures of Foxy Grandpa** - also issued in 1900 - new to the Platinum listings. The second number dated 1901 drops the words "The Adventures of..." from the title.

E. W. Kemble's **The Blackberries** had a color collection by 1901, also published by R. H. Russell, NY, as well as a few other comic-related volumes by Kemble still to be unearthed and properly identified. An earlier one was titled **Coontown's 400** (1899) newly listed this year. While the title is definitely not "PC" by today's standards, Kemble's drawings are excellent slices of African-American life in the USA with some humor injected. Kemble did a good job documenting aspects of life.

Confirmed is the exact format of Hearst's 1902 **The Katzenjammer Kids** and **Happy Hooligan And His Brother Gloomy Gus**. They both measure 15 5/16" wide by 10" tall and contain 88 pages including covers. Confirmed also is the fact that there are two separate editions with different covers for the pictured 1902 first edition and a 1903 Frederick Stokes edition of **Katzenjammer Kids** and **Happy Hooligan** with differing contents. They both are two different books entirely, and what confuses many collectors is that they have identical indicia title pages, as does an entirely different **KK** from 1905.

Settling on a popular size of 17" wide by 11" tall, comic books were soon available that featured Charles "Bunny" Schultze's **Foxy Grandpa**, Rudolph Dirk's **The Katzenjammer Kids**, Winsor McCay's **Little Sammy Sneeze**, **Rarebit Fiend** and **Little Nemo**, and Fred Opper's **Happy Hooligan** and **Maud**, in addition to dozens of **Buster Brown** comic books. For well over a decade, these large-size, full-color volumes were the norm, retailing for 60¢. These collections offered full-size Sunday comics with the back side blank per page.

The very rare **Brainy Bowers and Drowsy Dugan** by R. W. Taylor is now crowned the first collection of strip reprints from daily newspapers published in America. There are now four different collections of Brainy Bower known to exist.

The Outbursts of Everett True by A. D. Condo and J. W. Raper was first published by Saalfield in 1907 in a 88-page hardcover collection. It qualifies as the second daily comic strip collection as it predates the first **Mutt & Jeff** collection from Ball by three years. Condo & Raper's creation began its regular run several times a week in 1905 daily newspapers and lasted until 1927, when Condo became too sick to continue. This same **Everett True** collection was later truncated a bit by Saalfield in

Little Sammy Sneeze*, 1905, by Winsor McCay is his best looking.*

The Three FunMakers*, 1908, the first anthology Platinum Age comic book.*

***Brainy Bowers** appears to be the earliest known daily strip compilation; sample comic strip, 1905.*

1921 to 56 strips in just 32 pages measuring the standard 10"x10" Cupples & Leon size.

By 1908 Stokes had a large backlist of full color comic books for sale at 60¢ each. Some of these titles date back to 1903 and were reprinted over and over as demand warranted. Note the number of titles in the advertisement pulled from the back of **The Three Fun Makers** shown below.

With the ever-increasing popularity of Bud Fisher's new daily strip sensation, **Mutt & Jeff**, a new format was created for reprinting daily strips in black and white, a hardcover book about 15" wide by 5" tall, published by Ball starting in 1910 for five volumes. In 1912, Ball also branched out with at least the now-obscure **Doings of the Van Loons** by Fred I. Leipziger, a rare comic book in the same format as the **Mutt & Jeffs.**

Cartoons Magazine also began in 1912 and ran through 1921 before undergoing a radical format change. It is notable as a wonderful source for information on early comics and their creators. See also the Platinum index.

The next significant evolutionary change occurred in 1919, when Cupples & Leon began issuing their black and white daily strip reprint books in a new aforementioned format, about 10" wide by 10" tall, with four panels reprinted per page in a two by two matrix. These books were 52 pages for 25¢. The first ones featured **Bringing Up Father** and **Mutt & Jeff**; there were about 100 others.

By 1921, the last of the oblong (11"x15") color comic books were issued, with Cupples & Leon's **Jimmie Dugan** and **The Reg'lar Fellers** by Gene Byrne and EmBee's **The Trouble Of Bringing Up Father** by self publisher George McManus. Of special historical interest, Embee issued the first 10¢ monthly comic book, **Comic Monthly**, with a first issue dated January 1922. A dozen 8-1/2"x9" issues were published, each featuring solo adventures of popular King Features strips. The monthly 10¢ comic book concept had finally arrived, though it would be more than a decade before it became truly successful.

Skippy by Percy Crosby debuted in the long-running humor magazine **Life** in the March 22, 1923 issue. By 1924 the first hard cover collection, **Life Presents Skippy,** was published. The newspaper comic strip debuted June 23, 1925 with the McClure syndicate. Hearst soon picked up a

CIRCULATION

"America's Circulation Wow"

SKIPPY!

A New Sunday Comic Page in Colors by PERCY CROSBY

The most lovable kid comic page ever drawn

KING FEATURES SYNDICATE

***Circulation** V5 #26 May 1926. The second Skippy solicitation ad from Hearst to sell this well-known strip by Percy L. Crosby to newspapers around the world via his King Feature Syndicate.*

*Left, **The Outbursts of Everett True**. This is the second daily strip collection, published 1907; reprinted in the '20s in the then-modern 10x10 format. Right: The earliest known display ad for comic books, found in the back of several 1908 Stokes comic books, with 27 titles then in print. Note cover prices are 60¢ for 80 pages of four color fun!*

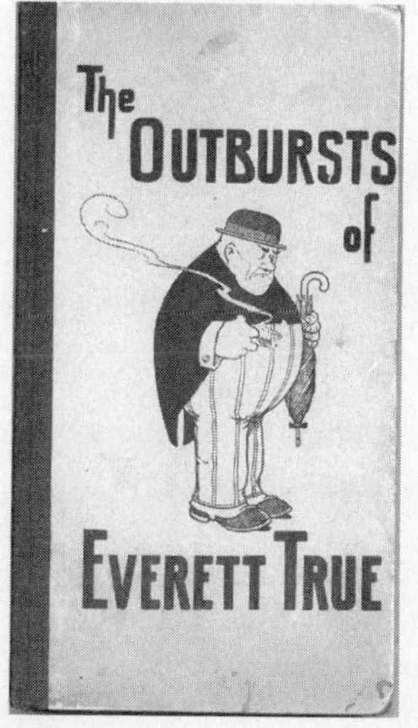

Sunday page a year later in mid-1926, then added a daily strip in 1929. By the 1930s it was red hot - think **Calvin & Hobbes** or **Peanuts** in popularity. In its day, it was one of the most popular comic strips ever created. Read the Modern era essay for more on **Skippy**'s immense popularity.

*Above, **Mutt & Jeff** #5 by Bud Fisher, 1916, is fairly scarce as there was only one printing. Below, **Regular Fellers** by Gene Byrne, 1921, one of the very last large oblong comics.*

In 1926, Cupples & Leon added a new 7" wide by 9" tall format with **Little Orphan Annie**, **Smitty**, and others. These were issued in both softcover and hardcover editions with dust jackets, and became extremely popular at 60¢ per copy.

Dell began publishing all original material in **The Funnies** in late 1929 in a larger tabloid format. At least three dozen issues were published before Delacorte threw in the towel. Even the extremely popular **Big Little Book**, introduced in 1932, can be viewed as a smaller version of the existing formats. The competition amongst publishers now included Dell, McKay, Sonnet, Saalfield and Whitman. The 1930s saw a definite shift in merchandising comic strip material from adults to children. This was the decade when Kellogg's placed **Buck Rogers** on the map, and when Ovaltine issued tons of **Little Orphan Annie** material. Merchandising from such pioneers as Sam Gold and Kay Kamen spearheaded this next re-transformation of the comics biz beginning in the early 1930s.

Upwards of a thousand of these **Funnies On Parade** precursors, in all formats, were published through 1935 and were very popular. Towards the end of this era of once-popular comic book formats, beautiful collections of **Popeye**, **Mickey Mouse**, **Dick Tracy**, and many others were published which today command ever higher prices on the open market as they are rediscovered by the advanced collector who appreciates and enjoys truly great classic comics.

END NOTE: We are continuing to add many of the 1930s variant formats such as the **Little Lulu** series by Marjorie Henderson Buell reprinted from her **Saturday Evening Post** run. Each year, this Platinum Age section has grown as advanced collectors continue to report in with new finds. We encourage interested collectors and scholars to help with this section of the book, as each new data entry is very important for recovering our history.

For corrections and additions to next year's Guide of some treasures you may have uncovered, please feel free to contact Robert at this e-mail address: **beerbohm@teknetwork.com** or Richard at **redoak1@netdoor.com**

For further information on this era of American comic books, read Robert L. Beerbohm's "The American Comic Book 1897-1932," originally printed in the 27th edition of **The Overstreet Comic Book Price Guide** and now available online at www.gemstonepub.com. Also see evolving comics history essays in Guides #29-#33.

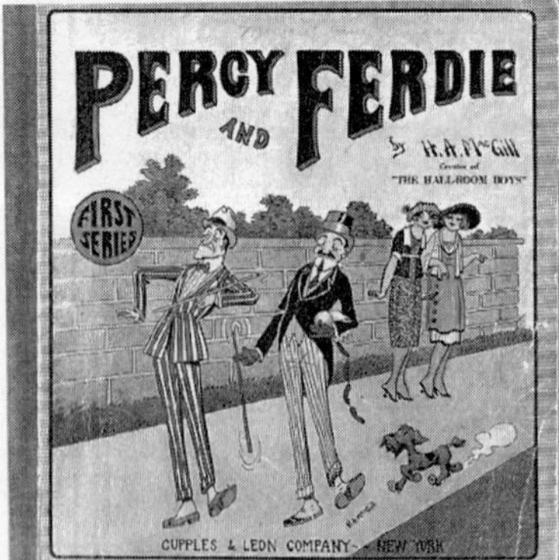

A 1921 example of Cupples & Leon's revolutionary new format.

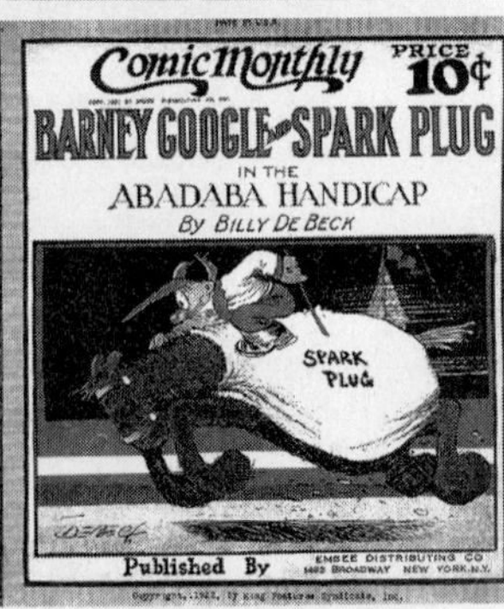

***Comic Monthly** #8 (top), #11 (bottom) 1922 the first 10¢ monthly newsstand comic book title.*

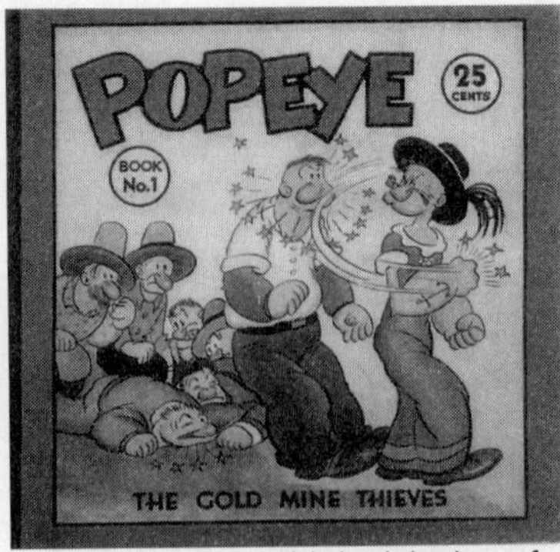

*David McKay published the last of the 10x10 comic books in 1935 as **Famous Funnies** grew.*

Alphonse and Gaston by Opper
1902 © Hearst's NY American & Journal

American-Journal-Examiner Joke Book
Special Supplement #2 - M&J by Bud Fisher
1911 © New York American

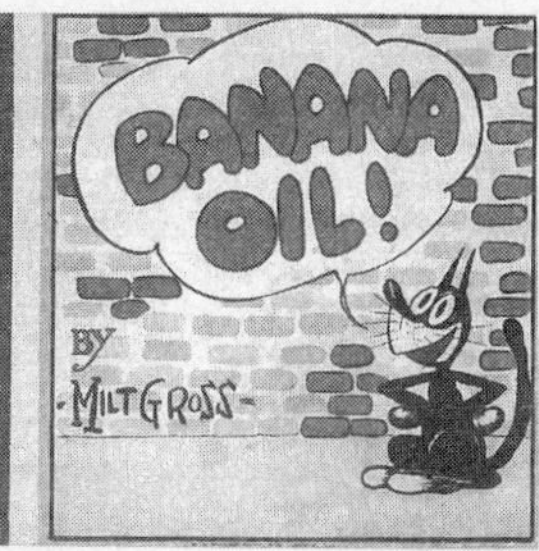

Banana Oil by Milt Gross
1924 © M.S. Publishing Company

GD2.0 FN6.0 VF8.0

COLLECTOR'S NOTE: The books listed in this section were published many decades before organized comics fandom began archiving and helping to preserve these fragile popular culture artifacts. Consequently, copies of most all of these comics do not often surface in Fine+ or better shape. eBay is proving that many items once considered rare actually are not, though they are in higher grades. Most Platinum Age comic books are in the Fair to VG range. If you want to collect these only in high grade, your collection will be extremely small. The prices given for Good, Fine and Very Fine categories are for strictly graded editions. If you need help grading your item, we refer you to the grading section in the front of book or contact the authors of the Platinum essay. Items marked scarce we are trying to ascertain how many copies might still be in existence. Your input is always welcome.

For ease of ascertaining the contents of each item of this listing, there is a code letter or two following most titles. A helpful list of categories pertaining to these codes can be found at the beginning of the Victorian Age pricing. Most measurements are in inches. A few measurements are in centimeters. The first dimension given is Height and the second is Width. This section created, revised, and expanded by Robert Beerbohm with Doug Wheeler & Richard Olson and able assistance from Ray Agricola, Bill Blackbeard, Roy Bonario, Ray Bottorff Jr., Chris Brown, Alfredo Castelli, Darrell Coons, Sol Davidson, Leonardo De Sá, Scott Deschaine, Mitchell Duval, Joe Evans, Tom Gordon, Bruce Hamilton, Andy Konkykru, Don Kurtz, Gabriel Laderman, Bruce Mason, Donald Puff, Robert Quesinberry, Steve Rowe, Randy Scott, John Snyder, Art Spiegelman, Steve Thompson, Joan Crosby Tibbets, Richard Samuel West, Richard Wright and Craig Yoe.

ADVENTURES OF EVA, PORA AND TED (M)
Evaporated Milk Association: 1932 (5x15", 16 pgs, B&W)
nn - By Steve 10.00 30.00 60.00
NOTE: *Appears to have had green, blue or white paper cover versions.*

ADVENTURES OF HAWKSHAW (N) (See Hawkshaw The Detective)
The Saalfield Publishing Co.: 1917 (9-3/4x13-1/2", 48 pgs., color & two-tone)
nn - By Gus Mager (only 24 pgs. of strips, reverse of each pg. is blank)
30.00 150.00 260.00
nn - 1927 Reprints 1917 issue 30.00 150.00 260.00
NOTE: *Started Feb 23, 1913-Sept 4, 1922, then begins again Dec 13, 1931-Feb 11, 1952.*

ADVENTURES OF SLIM AND SPUD, THE (M)
Prairie Farmer Publ. Co.: 1924 (3-3/4x 9-3/4", 104 pgs., B&W strip reprints)
nn 21.00 84.00 150.00
NOTE: *Illustrated mailing envelope exists postmarked out of Chicago, add 50%.*

ADVENTURES OF WILLIE WINTERS, THE (O,P)
Kelloggs Toasted Corn Flake Co.: 1912 (6-7/8x9-1/2", 20 pgs, full color)
nn - By Byron Williams & Dearborn Melvill 54.00 189.00 325.00

ADVENTURES OF WILLIE GREEN, THE (N) (see The Willie Green Comics)
Frank M. Acton Co.: 1915 (50¢, 52 pgs, 8-1/2X16", B&W, soft-c)
Book 1 - By Harris Brown; strip-r 54.00 189.00 325.00

A. E. F. IN CARTOONS BY WALLY, THE (N)
Don Sowers & Co.: 1933 (12x10-1/8", 88 pgs, hardcover B&W)
nn - By Wally Wallgren (WW One Stars & Stripes-r) 20.00 80.00 120.00

AFTER THE TOWN GOES DRY (I)
The Howell Publishing Co, Chicago: 1919 (48 pgs, 6-1/2x4", hardbound two color-c)
nn - By Henry C. Taylor; illus by Frank King 20.00 70.00 140.00

AIN'T IT A GRAND & GLORIOUS FEELING? (N) (Also see Mr. & Mrs.)
Whitman Publishing Co.: 1922 (9x9-3/4", 52 pgs., stiff cardboard-c)
nn - 1921 daily strip-r; B&W, color-c; Briggs-a 36.00 143.00 250.00
nn -(9x9-1/2", 28pgs., stiff cardboard-c)-Sunday strip-r in color (inside front-c says "More of the Married Life of Mr. & Mrs".) 36.00 143.00 250.00
NOTE: *Strip started in 1917; This is the 2nd Whitman comic book, after Brigg's MR. & MRS.*

ALL THE FUNNY FOLKS (I)
World Press Today, Inc.: 1926 (11-1/2x8-1/2", 112 pgs., color, hard-c)
nn-Barney Google, Spark Plug, Jiggs & Maggie, Tillie The Toiler, Happy Hooligan, Hans & Fritz, Toots & Casper, etc. 100.00 400.00 700.00
With Dust Jacket By Louis Biedermann 150.00 625.00 1200.00
NOTE: *Booklength race horse story masterfully enveloping all major King Features characters.*

ALPHONSE AND GASTON AND THEIR FRIEND LEON (N)
Hearst's New York American & Journal: 1902,1903 (10x15-1/4", Sunday strip reprints in color)
nn - (1902) - By Frederick Opper (scarce) 400.00 1400.00 -
nn - (1903) - By Frederick Opper (scarce) 400.00 1400.00 -
NOTE: *Strip ran Sept 22, 1901to at least July 17, 1904.*

ALWAYS BELITTLIN' (see Skippy; That Rookie From the 13th Squad; Between Shots)
Henry Holt & Co.: 1927 (6x8", hard-c with DJ,
nn -By Percy Crosby (text with cartoons) 43.00 172.00 300.00

ALWAYS BELITTLIN' (I) (see Skippy; That Rookie From the 13th Squad, Between Shots)
Percy Crosby, Publisher: 1933 (14 1/4 x 11", 72 pgs, hard-c, B&W)
nn - By Percy Crosby 43.00 172.00 300.00
NOTE: *Self-published; primarily political cartoons with text pages denouncing prohibition's gang warfare effects and cuts in the national defense budget as Crosby saw war looming in Europe and with Japan.*

GD2.0 FN6.0 VF8.0

AMERICAN-JOURNAL-EXAMINER JOKE BOOK SPECIAL SUPPLEMENT (O)
New York American: 1911-12 (12 x 9 3/4", 16 pgs) (known issues) (Very Rare)
1 Tom Powers Joke Book(12/10/11) 80.00 280.00 -
2 Mutt & Jeff Joke Book (Bud Fisher 12/17/11) 100.00 350.00 -
3 TAD's Joke Book (Thomas Dorgan 12/24/11) 80.00 280.00 -
4 F. Opper's Joke Book (Frederick Burr Opper 12/31/11) (contains Happy Hooligan) 100.00 350.00 -
5 not known to exist
6 Swinnerton's Joke Book (Jimmy Swinnerton 01/14/12) (contains Mr. Jack) 100.00 350.00 -
7 The Monkey's Joke Book (Gus Mager 01/21/12) (contains Sherlocko the Monk) 100.00 350.00 -
8 Joys And Glooms Joke Book (T. E. Powers 01/28/12) 80.00 280.00 -
9 The Dingbat Family's Joke Book (George Herriman 02/04/12) (contains early Krazy Kat & Ignatz) 200.00 700.00 -
10 Valentine Joke Book, A (Opper, Howarth, Mager, T. E. Powers 02/11/12) 80.00 280.00 -
11 Little Hatchet Joke Book (T. E. Powers 02/18/12) 80.00 280.00 -
12 Jungle Joke Book (Rudolph Dirks 02/25/12) 100.00 350.00 -
13 The Hayseeds Joke Book (03/03/12) 80.00 280.00 -
14 Married Life Joke Book (T.E. Powers 03/10/12) 80.00 280.00 -
NOTE: *These were insert newspaper supplements similar to Eisner's later Spirit sections. A Valentine Joke Book recently surfaced from Hearst's Boston Sunday American proving that other cities besides New York City had these special supplements. Each issue also contains work by other cartoonists besides the cover featured creator and those already listed above such as Sidney Smith, Winsor McCay, Hy Mayer, Grace Weiderseim (later Drayton), others.*

AMERICA'S BLACK & WHITE BOOK 100 Pictured Reasons Why We Are At War (N,S)
Cupples & Leon: 1917 (10 3/4 x 8", 216 pgs)
nn - W. A. Rogers (New York Herald-r) 32.00 114.00 195.00

AMONG THE FOLKS IN HISTORY
Rand McNally Print Guild: 1935 (192 pgs, 8-1/2x9-1/2", hard-c, B&W)
nn - By Gaar Williams 21.00 84.00 150.00

AMONG THE FOLKS IN HISTORY
The Book and Print Guild: 1935 (200 pgs, 8-1/2x9-1/2:,
nn - By Gaar Williams 21.00 84.00 150.00
NOTE: *Both the above are evidently different editions and contain largely full-page, single panel cartoons similar to Briggs' work of that sort. 8 or 10 pages are broken into panels, usually with a this is how it was in the old days, this is how it is today theme.*

ANGELIC ANGELINA (N)
Cupples & Leon Company: 1909 (11-1/2x17", 56 pgs., 2 colors)
nn - By Munson Paddock 67.00 233.00 400.00
NOTE: *Strip ran March 22, 1908-Feb 7, 1909.*

ANDY GUMP, HIS LIFE STORY (I)
The Reilly & Lee Co, Chicago: 1924 (192 pgs, hardbound)
nn - By Sidney Smith (over 100 illustrations) 20.00 80.00 140.00

ANIMAL CIRCUS, THE (from Puggery Wee)
Rand McNally + Company: 1908 (48 pgs, 11x8-1/2", color-c, 3-color insides)
nn - By unknown 20.00 80.00 140.00
NOTE: *Illustrated verse, many pages with multiple illustrations.*

ANIMAL SERIALS
T. Y. Crowell: 1906 (9x6-7/8", 214 pgs, hard-c, B&W)
nn - By E Warde Balisdell 20.00 80.00 140.00
NOTE: *Multi-page comic strip stories.*

A NOBODY'S SCRAP BOOK
Frederik A. Stokes Co., New York: 1900 (11" x 8-5/8", hard-c, color)
nn- (Scarce) 67.00 233.00 400.00
NOTE: *Designed in England, printed in Holland, on English paper -- which likely explains the mispelling of Frederick Stokes' name. Highly fragile paper. Strips and cartoons, all by the same unidentified artist, "A Nobody", almost certainly reprinted from somewhere, as they are very professional.*

AT THE BOTTOM OF THE LADDER (M)
J.P. Lippincott Company: 1926 (11x8-1/4", 296 pgs, hardcover, B&W)
nn - By Camillus Kessler 45.00 157.50 300.00
NOTE: *Hilarious single panel cartoons showing first jobs of then important "captains of industry."*

AUTO FUN, PICTURES AND COMMENTS FROM "LIFE"
Thomas Y. Crowell & Co.: 1905 (148 pgs, 9x7", hard-c, B&W)
nn -By various 45.00 157.00 300.00
NOTE: *The cover just has "Auto Fun" but the title page also has the subheading listed here. This is similar to other reprint books of Life cartoons printed in the guide. Largely single panel cartoons but also several sequential. One or more cartoons by Kemble, Levering, Dirks, Flagg, Sullivant. Sequential cartoons by Kemble, Levering, Sullivant, and the highpoint, a 2 pg 6 panel piece by Winsor McCay.*

BANANA OIL (N)
MS Publ. Co.: 1924 (9-7/8x10", 52 pgs., B&W)
nn - Milt Gross-a; not reprints 75.00 250.00 450.00

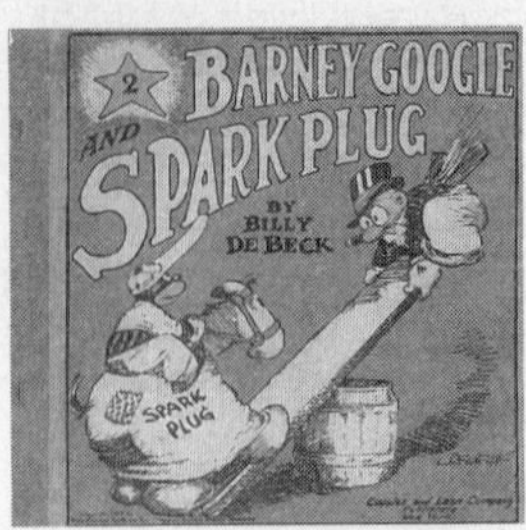

Barney Google & Spark Plug #2 by Billy DeBeck
1924 © Cupples & Leon

Bill the Boy Artist's Book by Ed Payne
1910 © C.M. Clark Publishing Co

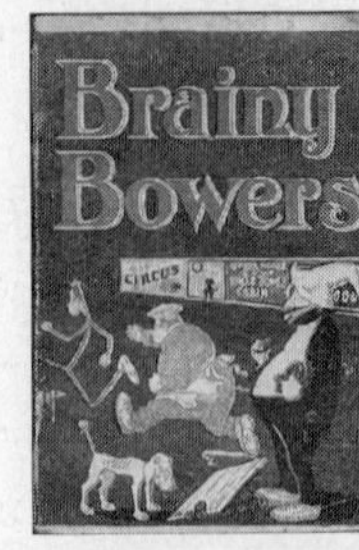

Brainy Bowers and Drowsy Duggan by R.W. Taylor
1905 © Star Publishing Co. - the first daily reprints

	GD2.0	FN6.0	VF8.0

BARKER'S ILLUSTRATED ALMANAC (O,P,S) (See Barkers in Victorian Era section)
Barker, Moore & Mein Medicine Co: 1900-1932+ (36 pgs, B&W, color paper-c)

1900-1932+ (7x5-7/8")	10.00	30.00	60.00

BARKER'S "KOMIC" PICTURE SOUVENIR (P,S) (see Barker's in Victorian)
Barker, Moore & Mein Medicine Co: nd (Parts 1-3, 1901-1903; Parts 1-4, 1906+) (color cardboard-c, B&W interior, 50 pages)

Parts 1-3 (Rare, earliest printing, nd (1901))	60.00	120.00	240.00

NOTE: Same cover as 4th edition in Victorian Age Section, except has "Part 1", "Part 2", or "Part 3" printed in the blank space beneath the crate on which central figure is sitting. States "Edition in 3 Parts" on the first interior page, beneath the picture of the Barker's Building.

Parts 1-3 (nd, c1901-1903)	30.00	60.00	120.00

NOTE: New cover art on all Parts. States "Edition in 3 Parts" on the first interior page.

Parts 1-4 (nd, c1906+)	25.00	50.00	75.00

NOTE: States "Edition in 4 Parts" on the first interior page. Various printings known. These have been confirmed as premium comic books, predating the Buster Brown premiums. They reprint advertising cartoons from Barker's Illustrated Almanac. For the 50 page booklets by this same name, numbered as "Part"s, without exception, were published after 1900. Some editions are found to have 54 pages.

BARNEY GOOGLE AND SPARK PLUG (N) (See **Comic Monthly**)
Cupples & Leon Co.: 1923 - No.6, 1928 (9-7/8x9-3/4"; 52 pgs., B&W, daily-r)

1 (nn)-By Billy DeBeck	57.00	229.00	400.00
2-4 (#5 & #6 do not exist)	46.00	186.00	325.00

NOTE: Started June 17, 1919 as newspaper strip; Spark Plug introduced July 17, 1922; strip still running making it one of the oldest still in existence.

BART'S CARTOONS FOR 1902 FROM THE MINNEAPOLIS JOURNAL (N,S)
Minneapolis Journal: 1903 (11x9", 102 pgs, paperback, B&W)

nn - By Charles L. Bartholomew	28.00	99.00	170.00

BELIEVE IT OR NOT! by Ripley (N,S)
Simon & Schuster: 1929 (8x 5-1/4", 68 pgs, red, B&W cover, B&W interior)

nn - By Robert Ripley (strip-r text & art)	40.00	120.00	240.00

NOTE: 1929 was the first printing of many reprintings . Strip began Dec 19, 1918 and is still running.

BEN WEBSTER (N)
Standard Printing Company: 1928-1931 (13-3/4x4-7/16", 768 pgs, soft-c)

1 - "Bound to Win"	40.00	120.00	240.00
2 - "...in old Mexico	40.00	120.00	240.00
3 - "...At Wilderness Lake	40.00	120.00	240.00
4 - "...in the Oil Fields	40.00	120.00	240.00

NOTE: Self Published by Edwin Alger, also contains fan's letter pages.

BIG SMOKER
W.T. Blackwell & Co.: 1908 (16 pgs, 5-1/2x3-1/2", color-c & interior)

nn - By unknown	12.00	48.00	80.00

NOTE: Stated reprint of 1878 version. no known copies of original printing.

BILLY BOUNCE (I)
Donohue & Co.: 1906 (288 pgs, hardbound)

nn - By W.W. Denslow & Dudley Bragdon	150.00	525.00	900.00

NOTE: Billy Bounce was created in 1901 as a comic strip by W. W. Denslow (strip ran from 1901 NOV 11 to 1905 DEC 3), but the series is best remembered in the C. W. Kahles version (from 1902 SEP 28). Denslow resumed his character in the above illustrated book.

BILLY HON'S FAMOUS CARTOON BOOK (H)
Wasley Publishing Co.: 1927 (7-1/2x10", 68 pgs, softbound wraparound)

nn - By Billy Hon	12.00	48.00	80.00

BILLY THE BOY ARTIST'S BOOK OF FUNNY PICTURES (N)
C.M.Clark Publishing Co.: 1910 (9x12", hardcover-c, Boston Globe strip-r)

nn - By Ed Payne	79.00	316.00	550.00

*NOTE: This long lived strip ran in **The Boston Globe** from Nov 5 1899-Jan 7 1955; one of the longer run strips.*

BILLY THE BOY ARTIST'S PAINTING BOOK OF FUNNY PICTURES

(we know it exists but need more data)	???	???	???

BIRD CENTER CARTOONS: A Chronicle of Social Happenings (N,S)
A. C. McClurg & Co.: 1904 (12-3/8x9-1/2", 216 pgs, hardcover, B&W)

nn - By John McCutcheon	40.00	140.00	240.00

*NOTE: Strip began in **The Chicago Tribune** in 1903. Satirical cartoons and text concerning a mythical town.*

BLASTS FROM THE RAM'S HORN
The Rams Horn Company: 1902 (330 pgs, 7x9", B&W)

nn - By various	20.00	70.00	120.00

NOTE: Cartoons reprinted from what was, apparently, a religious newspaper. Many cartoons by Frank Beard. Mostly single panel but occasionally sequential. Allegorical cartoons similar to the Christian Cartoons book. This book mixes cartoons and text sort of like the Caricature books. One or more cartoons on every page.

BOBBY THATCHER & TREASURE CAVE (N)
Altemus Co.: 1932 (9x7", 86 pgs., B&W, hard-c)

nn - Reprints; Storm-a	54.00	189.00	325.00

BOBBY THATCHER'S ROMANCE (N)
The Bell Syndicate/Henry Altemus Co.: 1931 (8-3/4x7", color cover, B&W)

nn - By Storm	54.00	189.00	325.00

BOOK OF CARTOONS, A (M,S)
Edward T. Miller: 1903 (12-1/4x9-1/4", 120 pgs, hardcover, B&W)

nn - By Harry J. Westerman (Ohio State Journal-r)	20.00	70.00	120.00

BOTTLE, THE (E) (see Victorian Age section for earlier printings)
Gowans & Gray, London & Glasgow: June 1905 (3-3/4x6", 72 pgs, printed one side only, paper cover, B&W)

nn - 1st printing (June 1905)	17.50	35.00	70.00
nn - 2nd printing (March 1906)	17.50	35.00	70.00
nn - 3rd printing (January 1911)	17.50	35.00	70.00

NOTE: By George Cruikshank. Reprints both THE BOTTLE and THE DRUNKARD'S CHILDREN. Cover is text only - no cover art.

BOTTLE, THE (E)
Frederick A. Stokes: nd (c1906) (3-3/4x6", 72 pgs, printed one side only, paper-c, B&W)

nn- by George Cruikshank	17.50	35.00	70.00

NOTE: Reprint of the Gowans & Gray edition. Reprints both THE BOTTLE and THE DRUNKARD'S CHILDREN. Cover is text only - no cover art.

BOYS AND FOLKS (N).
George H. Dornan Company: 1917 (10-1/4 x 8-1/4", 232 pgs. (single-sided), B&W strip-r.

nn - By Webster	21.00	64.00	150.00

NOTE: Four sections: Life's Darkest Moments, Mostly About Folks, The Thrill That Comes Once in a Lifetime, and Our Boyhood Ambitions. Most are single-panel cartoons, but there are some sequential comic strips.

BOY'S & GIRLS' BIG PAINTING BOOK OF INTERESTING COMIC PICTURES (N)
M. A. Donohue & Co.: 1914-16 (9x15, 70 pgs)

nn - By Carl "Bunny" Schultze (Foxy Grandpa-r)	81.00	284.00	-
#2 (1914)	81.00	284.00	-
#337 (1914) (sez "Big Painting & Drawing Book")	81.00	284.00	-
nn - (1916) (sez "Big Painting Book")(9-1/4x15")	81.00	284.00	-

*NOTE: These are all **Foxy Grandpa** items.*

BRAIN LEAKS: Dialogues of Mutt & Flea (N)
O. K. Printing Co. (Rochester Evening Times): 1911 (76 pgs, 6-5/8x4-5/8, hard-c, B&W)

nn - By Leo Edward O'Melia; newspaper strip-r	29.00	100.00	171.00

BRAINY BOWERS AND DROWSY DUGGAN (N)
Star Publishing: 1905 (7-1/4 x 4-9/16", 98 pgs., blue, brown & white color cover, B&W interior, 25¢) (daily strip-r 1902-04 Chicago Daily News)

#74 - By R. W. Taylor (Scarce)	400.00	1200.00	-

*NOTE: Part of a series of Atlantic Library Heart Series. Strip begins in 1901 and runs thru 1906. Taylor also created Yen the janitor for the **Chicago Daily News.***

BRAIN BOWERS AND DROWSY DUGAN (N)
Max Stein Pub. House, Chicago: 1905 (6-3/16x4-3/8", 64 pgs, B&W)

nn - By R.W. Taylor (Scarce)	400.00	1200.00	-

NOTE: A coverless copy of this surfaced on eBay in 2002 selling for $700.00.;

BRAINY BOWERS AND DROWSY DUGGAN GETTING ON IN THE WORLD WITH NO VISIBLE MEANS OF SUPPORT (STORIES TOLD IN PICTURES TO MAKE THEIR TELLING SHORT) (N)
Max Stein/Star Publishing: 1905 (7-3/8x5 1/8", 164 pgs, slick black, red & tan color cover, interior newsprint) (daily strip-r 1902-04 Chicago Daily News)

nn - By R. W. Taylor (Scarce)	400.00	1200.00	-
nn - Possible hard cover edition also?	???	???	???

NOTE: These Brainy Bowers editions are the earliest known daily newspaper strip reprint books.

BRINGING UP FATHER (N)
Star Co. (King Features): 1917 (5-1/2x16-1/2", 100 pgs., B&W, cardboard-c)

nn - (Scarcer)-Daily strip- by George McManus	158.00	553.00	950.00

BRINGING UP FATHER (N)
Cupples & Leon Co.: 1919 - No. 26, 1934 (10x10", 52 pgs., B&W, stiff cardboard-c) (No. 22 is 9-1/4x9-1/2")

1-Daily strip-r by George McManus in all	25.00	100.00	250.00
2-10	25.00	100.00	250.00
11-20	40.00	200.00	350.00
21-26 (Scarcer)	60.00	300.00	500.00

NOTE: Strip began Jan 2 1913-May 28 2000

The Big Book 1 (1926)-Thick book (hardcover; 10-1/4x10-1/4", 142 pgs.)	121.00	484.00	850.00
w/dust jacket (rare)	183.00	732.00	1275.00
The Big Book 2 (1929)	96.00	384.00	675.00
w/dust jacket (rare)	183.00	732.00	1275.00

NOTE: The Big Books contain 3 regular issues rebound.

BRINGING UP FATHER, THE TROUBLE OF (N)
Embee Publ. Co.: 1921 (9x15", 46 pgs, Sunday-r in color)

nn - (Rare)	75.00	300.00	525.00

NOTE: Ties with Mutt & Jeff (EmBee) and Jimmie Dugan And The Reg'lar Fellers (C&L) as the last of the oblong size era. This was self published by George McManus.

BRINGING UP FATHER (N) (see also SAGARA'S ENGLISH CARTOONS AND CARTOON STORIES)
Publisher unknown (actually, unreadable), Tokyo: October 1924 (9-7/8" x 7-1/2", 90

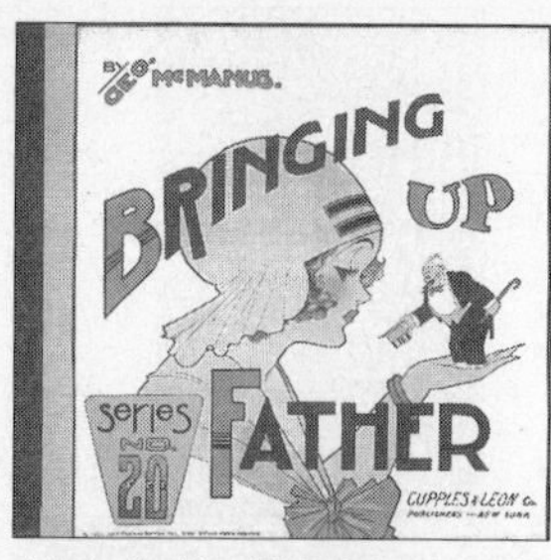

Bringing Up Father #20 by George McManus
1931 © Cupples & Leon

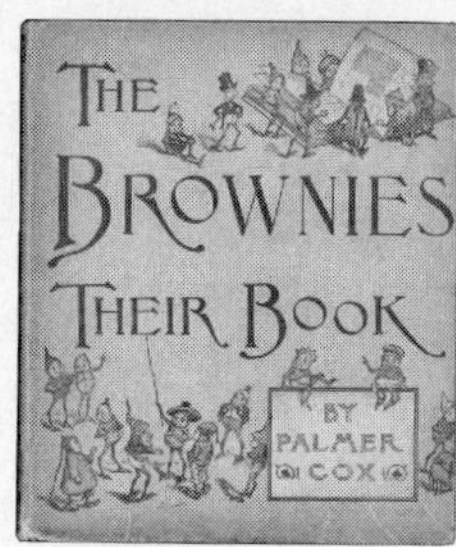

The Brownies: Their Book
1887 © The Century Co.

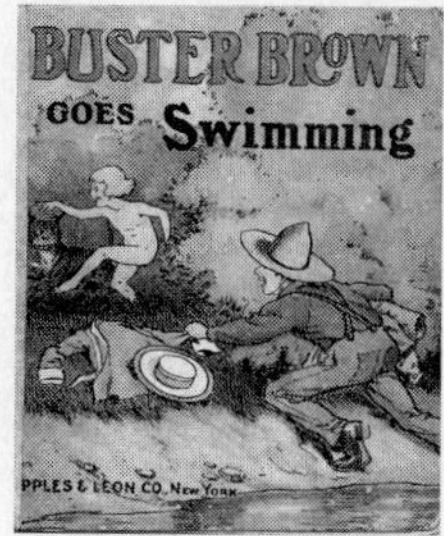

Buster Brown Nuggets - Goes Swimming
1907 © Cupples & Leon

GD2.0 FN6.0 VF8.0

pgs, color hard-c, B&W)
nn- (Scarce) by George McManus C&A ??? ??? ???
NOTE: *Published in Tokyo, Japan, with all strips in both English and Japanese, to facilitate learning English. Introduction by George McManus. Scarce in USA.*

BRONX BALLADS (I)
Simon & Schuster, NY: 1927 (9-1/2x7-1/4", hard-c, B&W)
nn - By Robert Simon and Harry Hershfield 36.00 143.00 250.00

BROWNIES, THE
The Century Co.: 1887 - 1914 (all came with dust jackets; add $100-150 to value if original dust jacket is included and intact)
Book 1 - The Brownies: Their Book (1887) 200.00 800.00 1200.00
Book 2 - Another Brownies Book (1890) 150.00 600.00 900.00
Book 3 - The Brownies at Home (1893) 125.00 500.00 750.00
Book 4 - The Brownies Around the World (1894) 100.00 400.00 600.00
Book 5 - The Brownies Through the Union (1895) 100.00 400.00 600.00
Book 6 - The Brownies Abroad (1899) 100.00 400.00 600.00
Book 7 - The Brownies in the Philippines (1904) 100.00 400.00 600.00
Book 8 - The Brownies' Latest Adventures (1910) 100.00 400.00 600.00
Book 9 - The Brownies Many More Nights (1914) 100.00 400.00 600.00

BROWNIE CLOWN OF BROWNIE TOWN (N)
The Century Co.: 1908 (6-7/8 x 9-3/8", 112 pgs, color hardcover & interior)
nn - By Palmer Cox (rare; 1907 newspaper strip-r) 250.00 750.00 1250.00
NOTE: *The Brownies created 1883 in* ***St Nicholas Magazine.***

BUDDY TUCKER & HIS FRIENDS (N) (Also see **Buster Brown Nuggets**)
Cupples & Leon Co.: 1906 (11-5/8 x17", 58 pgs, color)
nn - 1905 Sunday strip-r by R. F. Outcault 300.00 950.00 1500.00
NOTE: *Strip began Apr 30, 1905 thru at least Oct 1908.*

BUFFALO BILL'S PICTURE STORIES
Street & Smith Publications: 1909 (Soft cardboard cover)
nn - Very rare 67.00 233.00 400.00

BUGHOUSE FABLES (N) (see also **Comic Monthly**)
Embee Distributing Co. (King Features): 1921 (10¢, 4x4-1/2", 48 pgs.)
1-By Barney Google (Billy DeBeck) 43.00 172.00 300.00

BUG MOVIES (O) (Also see Clancy The Cop & Deadwood Gulch)
Dell Publishing Co.: 1931 (9-13/16x9-7/8", 52 pgs., B&W)
nn - Original material; Stookie Allen-a 43.00 172.00 300.00

BULL
Bull Publishing Company, New York: No.1, March, 1916 - No.12, Feb, 1917 (10 cents, 10-3/4x8-3/4", 24 pgs, color paper-c, B&W)
1-12 (Very Rare) ??? ??? ???
NOTE: *Pro-German, Anti-British cartoon/humor monthly, whose goal was to keep the U.S. neutral and out of World War I. We know of no copies which have sold in the past few years.*

BUNNY'S BLUE BOOK (see also Foxy Grandpa) (N)
Frederick A. Stokes Co.: 1911 (10x15, 60¢)
nn - By Carl "Bunny" Schultze strip-r 100.00 350.00 -

BUNNY'S RED BOOK (see also Foxy Grandpa) (N)
Frederick A. Stokes Co.: 1912 (10x15)
nn - By Carl "Bunny" Schultze strip-r 100.00 350.00 -

BUNNY'S GREEN BOOK (see also Foxy Grandpa) (N)
Frederick A. Stokes Co.: 1913 (10x15")
nn - By Carl "Bunny" Schultze 100.00 350.00 -

BUSTER BROWN (C) (Also see Brown's Blue Ribbon Book of Jokes and Jingles & Buddy Tucker & His Friends)
Frederick A. Stokes Co.: 1903 - 1916 (Daily strip-r in color)
1903...& His Resolutions (11-1/4x16", 66 pgs.) by R. F. Outcault (Rare)-1st nationally distributed comic. Distr. through Sears & Roebuck 1500.00 5000.00 -
1904...His Dog Tige & Their Troubles (11-1/4x16-1/4", 66 pgs.)(Rare) 600.00 1800.00 -
1905...Pranks (11-1/4x16-3/8", 66 pgs.) 400.00 1400.00 -
1906...Antics (11x16-3/8", 66 pgs.) 400.00 1400.00 -
1906...And Company (11x16-1/2", 66 pgs.) 300.00 1000.00 -
1906...Mary Jane & Tige (11-1/4x16, 66 pgs.) 300.00 1000.00 -
NOTE: ***Yellow Kid*** *pictured on two pages.*
1908 Collection of Buster Brown Comics 250.00 800.00 -
1909 Outcault's Real Buster and The Only Mary Jane (11x16, 66 pgs, Stokes) 250.00 800.00 -
1910...Up to Date (10-1/8x15-3/4", 66 pgs.) 208.00 729.00 1250.00
1911...Fun And Nonsense (10-1/8x15-3/4", 66 pgs.) 183.00 642.00 1100.00
1912...The Fun Maker (10-1/8x15-3/4", 66 pgs.) -Yellow Kid (4 pgs.) 183.00 642.00 1100.00
1913...At Home (10-1/8x15-3/4", 56 pgs.) 167.00 583.00 1000.00
1914...And Tige Here Again (10x16, 62 pgs, Stokes) 150.00 525.00 900.00
1915...And His Chum Tige (10x16, Stokes) 150.00 525.00 900.00
1916...The Little Rogue (10-1/8x15-3/4", 62 pgs.) 162.00 567.00 975.00
1917...And the Cat (5-1/2x 6-1/2, 26 pgs, Stokes) 112.00 392.00 675.00
1917...Disturbs the Family (5-1/2x 6 1/2, 26 pgs, Stokes
NOTE: *Story featuring statue of "the Chinese Yellow Kid"* 112.00 392.00 675.00
1917...The Real Buster Brown (5-1/2x 6 -/2, 26 pgs, Stokes 112.00 392.00 675.00

Frederick A. Stokes Co. Hard Cover Series (I)
...Abroad (1904, 10-1/4x8", 86 pgs., B&W, hard-c)-R. F. Outcault-a (Rare) 200.00 700.00 1200.00
...Abroad (1904, B&W, 67 pgs.)-R. F. Outcault-a 200.00 700.00 1200.00
NOTE: *Not an actual comic book, but prose with illustrations.*
..."Tige" His Story 1905 (10x8", 63 pgs., B&W) (63 illos.)
nn-By RF Outcault 143.00 500.00 -
...My Resolutions 1906 (10x8", B&W, 68 pgs.)-R.F. Outcault-a (Rare) 233.00 817.00 1400.00
...Autobiography 1907 (10x8", B&W, 71 pgs.) (16 color plates & 36 B&W illos) 67.00 233.00 400.00
...And Mary Jane's Painting Book 1907 (10x13-1/4", 60 pgs, both card & hardcover versions exist
nn-RFO (first printing blank on top of cover) 67.00 233.00 400.00
First Series- this is a reprint if it says First Series 67.00 233.00 400.00
Volume Two - By RFO 67.00 233.00 400.00
... My Resolutions by Buster Brown (1907, 68 pgs, small size, cardboard covers) scarce 43.00 150.00 260.00
NOTE: *Not actual comic book per se, but a compilation of the Resolutions found at the end of Outcault's Buster Brown newspaper strips.*

BUSTER BROWN (N)
Cupples & Leon Co./N. Y. Herald Co.: 1906 - 1917 (11x17", color, strip-r)
NOTE: *Early issues by R. F. Outcault; most C&L editions are not by Outcault.*
1906...His Dog Tige And Their Jolly Times (11-3/8x16-5/8", 68 pgs.) 300.00 1050.00 1800.00
1906...His Dog Tige & Their Jolly Times (11x16, 46 pgs.) 163.00 570.00 975.00
1907...Latest Frolics (11-3/8x16-5/8", 66 pgs., reprints 1905-06 strips) 163.00 570.00 975.00
1908...Amusing Capers (58 pgs.) 129.00 451.00 775.00
1909...The Busy Body (11-3/8x16-5/8", 62 pgs.) 129.00 451.00 775.00
1910...On His Travels (11x16", 58 pgs.) 112.00 392.00 675.00
1911...Happy Days (11-3/8x16-5/8", 58 pgs.) 112.00 392.00 675.00
1912...In Foreign Lands (10x16", 58 pgs) 112.00 392.00 675.00
1913...And His Pets (11x16", 58 pgs.) STOKES???? 112.00 392.00 675.00
1913...And His Pets (26 pg partial reprint) - - -
1914...Funny Tricks (11-3/8x16-5/8", 58 pgs.) 112.00 392.00 675.00
1916...At Play (10x16, 58 pgs) 112.00 392.00 675.00

BUSTER BROWN NUGGETS (N)
Cupples & Leon Co./N.Y.Herald Co.: 1907 (1905, 7-1/2x6-1/2", 36 pgs., color, strip-r, hard-c)(By R. F. Outcault) (NOTE: books are all unnumbered)
Buster Brown Goes Fishing 39.00 137.00 235.00
Buster Brown Goes Swimming 39.00 137.00 235.00
Buster Brown Plays Indian 39.00 137.00 235.00
Buster Brown Goes Shooting 39.00 137.00 235.00
Buster Brown Plays Cowboy 39.00 137.00 235.00
Buster Brown On Uncle Jack's Farm 39.00 137.00 235.00
Buster Brown Tige And The Bull 39.00 137.00 235.00
Buster Brown And Uncle Buster 39.00 137.00 235.00
Buddy Tucker Meets Alice in Wonderland 50.00 175.00 300.00
Buddy Tucker Visits The House That Jack Built 39.00 137.00 235.00

BUSTER BROWN MUSLIN SERIES (N)
Saalfield: 1907 (also contain copyright Cupples & Leon)
...Goes Fishing (1907, 6-7/8x6-1/8", 24 pgs., color)-r/1905 Sunday comics page by Outcault (Rare) 50.00 175.00 300.00
...Plays Indian (1907, 6-7/8x6-1/8", 24 pgs., color)-r/1905 Sunday comics page by Outcault (Rare) 42.00 146.00 250.00
...Plays Cowboy (1907, 6-3/4x6", 10 pgs., color)-r/1905 Sunday comics page by Outcault (Rare) 42.00 146.00 250.00
...And The Donkey (1907, 6-7/8x6-1/8", 24 pgs., color)-r/1905 Sunday comics page by Outcault (Rare) 42.00 146.00 250.00
NOTE: *These are muslin versions of the C&L BB Nugget series.*
NOTE: *Muslin books are all cloth books, made to be washable so as not easily stained/destroyed by very young children. The Muslin books contain one strip each (the title strip), to the more common NUGGET's three strips.*

BUSTER BROWN PREMIUMS (Advertising premium booklets)
Various Publishers: 1904 - 1912 (3x5" to 5x7"; sizes vary)
American Fruit Product Company, Rochester, NY
Buster Brown Duffy's 1842 Cider (1904, 7x5". 12 pgs, C.E. Sherin Co, NYC)
nn - By R. F. Outcault (scarce) 100.00 350.00 600.00

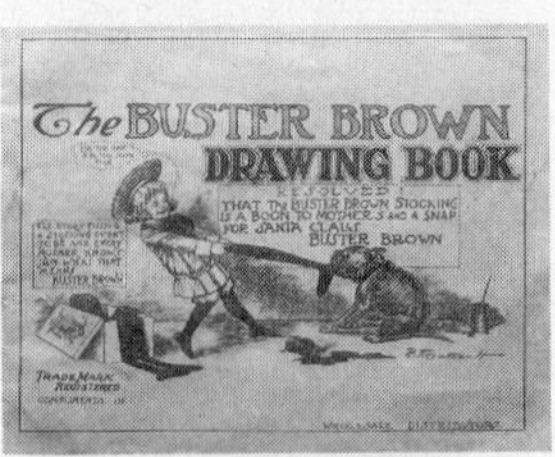

Buster Brown Drawing Book
1904 © Buster Brown Stocking Co

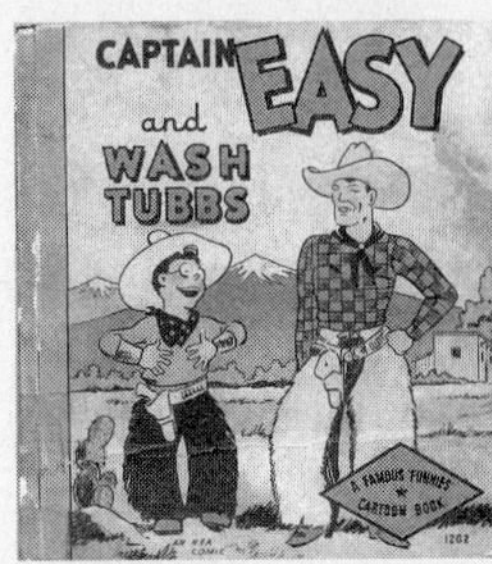

Captain Easy and Wash Tubbs by Roy Crane
1934 © Whitman Famous Comics Cartoon Book

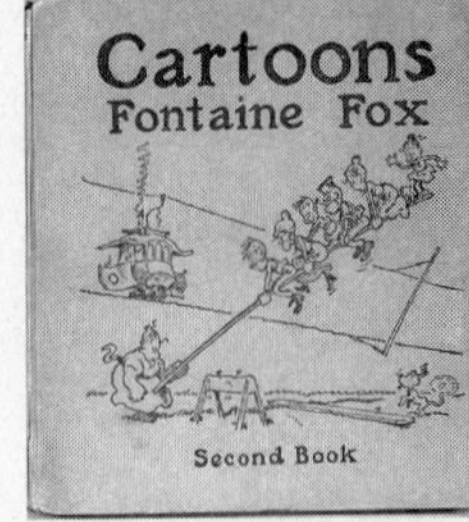

Cartoons Fontaine Fox Second Book
early 1920s © Harper & Bros, NY

GD2.0 FN6.0 VF8.0

The Brown Shoe Company, St. Louis, USA
Set of five books (5x7", 16 pgs., color)

Brown's Blue Ribbon Book of Jokes and Jingles Book 1 (nn, 1904)-By R. F. Outcault; Buster Brown & Tige, Little Tommy Tucker, Jack & Jill, Little Boy Blue, Dainty Jane; The Yellow Kid app. on back-c (1st BB comic book premium) 300.00 1050.00 1800.00

Buster Brown's Blue Ribbon Book of Jokes and Jingles Book 2 (1905)-Original color art by Outcault 200.00 600.00 1200.00

Buster's Book of Jokes & Jingles Book 3 (1909) not by R.F. Outcault 150.00 400.00 800.00

NOTE: *Reprinted from the Blue Ribbon post cards with advert jingles added.*

Buster's Book of Instructive Jokes and Jingles Book 4 (1910)-Original color art not by R.F. Outcault 150.00 585.00 1000.00

...Book of Travels nn (1912, 3x5")-Original color art not signed by Outcault 117.00 408.00 700.00

NOTE: *Estimated 5 or 6 known copies exist of books #1-4.*

The Buster Brown Bread Company

"Buster Brown" Bread Book of Rhymes, The (1904, 4x6", 12 pgs., half color, half B&W)- Original color art not signed by RFO 158.00 553.00 950.00

Buster Brown's Hosiery Mills

"How Buster Brown Got The Pie" nn (nd, 7x5-1/4". 16 pgs, color paper cover and color interior By R.F. Outcault 83.00 292.00 500.00

"The Autobiography of Buster Brown" nn (nd,9x6-1/8", 36 pgs, text story & art by R.F. Outcault 83.00 292.00 500.00

NOTE: *Similar to, but a distinctly different item than "Buster Brown's Autobiography."*

The Buster Brown Stocking Company

Buster Brown Drawing Book, The nn (nd, 5x6", 20 pgs.)-B&W reproductions of 1903 R.F. Outcault art to trace 50.00 150.00 300.00

NOTE: *Reprints a comic strip from Burr McIntosh Magazine, which includes Buster, Yellow Kid, and Pore Li'l Mose (only known story involving all three.)*

Buster Brown Stocking Magazine nn (Jan. 1906, 7-3/4x5-3/8", 36 pgs.) R.F. Outcault 35.00 70.00 125.00

NOTE: *This was actually a store bought item selling for 5 cents per copy.*

Collins Baking Company

Buster Brown Drawing Book nn (1904, 5x3", 12 pgs.)-Original B&W art to trace, not signed by R.F. Outcault 50.00 150.00 300.00

C. H. Morton, St. Albans, VT

Merry Antics of Buster Brown, Buddy Tucker & Tige nn (nd, 3-1/2x5-1/2", 16 pgs.) -Original B&W art by R.F. Outcault 83.00 292.00 500.00

Ivan Frank & Company

Buster Brown nn (1904, 3x5", 12 pgs.)-B&W repros of R. F. Outcault Sunday pages (First premium to actually reproduce Sunday comic pages – may be first premium comic strip-r book?) 125.00 438.00 750.00

Buster Brown's Pranks (1904, 3-1/2x5-1/8", 12 pgs.)-reprints intro of Buddy Tucker into the BB newspaper strip before he was spun off into his own short lived newspaper strip 125.00 438.00 750.00

Kaufmann & Strauss

Buster Brown Drawing Book (1906, 28 pages, 5x3-1/2") Color Cover, B+W original story signed by Outcault, tracing paper inserted as alternate pages. Back cover imprinted for Nox' Em All Shoes 50.00 150.00 300.00

Pond's Extract

Buster Brown's Experiences With Pond's Extract nn (1904, 6-3/4x4-1/2", 28 pgs.) Original color art by R.F. Outcault (may be the first BB premium comic book with original art) 100.00 250.00 500.00

C. A. Cross & Co.

Red Cross Drawing Book nn (1906, 4-7/8x3-1/2", color paper -c, B&W interior, 12 pgs.) 50.00 150.00 300.00

NOTE: *This is for Red Cross coffee; not the health organization.*

Ringen Stove Company

Quick Meal Steel Ranges nn (nd, 5x3", 16 pgs.)-Original B&W art not signed by R.F. Outcault 35.00 125.00 250.00

Steinwender Stoffregen Coffee Co.

"Buster Brown Coffee" (1905, 4-7/8x3", color paper cover, B&W interior, 12 printed pages, plus 1 tracing paper page above each interior image (total of 8 sheets) (Very Rare) 83.00 292.00 500.00

NOTE: *Part of a BB drawing contest. If instructions had been followed, most copies would have ended up destroyed.*

U. S. Playing Card Company

Buster Brown - My Own Playing Cards (1906, 2-1/2x1-3/4", full color)
nn - By R. F. Outcault 42.00 147.00 250.00

NOTE: *Series of full color panels tell stories, average about 5 cards per story.*

Publisher Unknown

The Drawing Book nn (1906, 3-9/16x5", 8 pgs.)-Original B&W art to trace not by R.F. Outcault 50.00 150.00 300.00

BUTLER BOOK A Series of Clever Cartoons of Yale Undergraduate Life
Yale Record: June 16, 1913 (10-3/4 x 17", 34 pgs, paper cover B&W)

nn - By Alban Bernard Butler 20.00 70.00 120.00

NOTE: *Cartoons and strips reprinted from The Yale Record student newspaper.*

BUTTONS & FATTY IN THE FUNNIES
Whitman Publishing Co.: nd 1927 (10-1/4x15-1/2", 28pg., color)

W936 - Signed "M.E.B.", probably Merrill Blosser; strips in color copyright The Brooklyn Daily Eagle; (very rare) 61.00 244.00 425.00

BY BRIGGS (M,N,P) (see also OLD GOLD THE SMOOTHER AND BETTER CIGARETTE)
Old Gold Cigarettes: nd (c1920's) (11" x 9-11/16", 44 pgs, cardboard-c, B&W)

nn- (Scarce) 20.00 70.00 120.00

NOTE: *Collection reprinting strip cartoons by Clare Briggs, advertising Old Gold Cigarettes. These strips originally appeared in various magazines, play program booklets, newspapers, etc. Some of the strips involve regular Briggs strip series. Contains all of the strips in the smaller, color "OLD GOLD" giveaways, plus more.*

CAMION CARTOONS
Marshall Jones Company: 1919 (7-1/2x5", 136 pgs, B&W)

nn - By Kirkland H. Day (W.W.One occupation) 20.00 70.00 120.00

CANYON COUNTRY KIDDIES (M)
Doubleday, Page & Co: 1923 (8x10-1/4", 88 pgs, hard-c, B&W)

nn - By James Swinnerton 39.00 137.00 235.00

CARLO (H)
Doubleday, Page & Co.: 1913 (8 x 9-5/8, 120 pgs, hardcover, B&W)

nn - By A.B. Frost 40.00 140.00 240.00

NOTE: *Original sequential strips about a dog. Became short lived newspaper comic strip in 1914. Originally published with a dust jacket which increases value 50%.*

CARTOON BOOK, THE
Bureau of Publicity, War Loan Organization, Treasury Department, Washington, D.C.: 1918 (6-1/2x4-7/8", 48 pgs, paper cover, B&W)

nn - By various artists 31.00 108.00 185.00

NOTE: *U.S. government issued booklet of WW I propaganda cartoons by 46 artists promoting the third sale of Liberty Loan bonds. The artists include: Berryman, Clare Briggs, Cesare, J. N. "Ding" Darling, Rube Goldberg, Kemble, McCutcheon, George McManus, F. Opper, T. E. Powers, Ripley, Satterfield, H. T. Webster, Gaar Williams.*

CARTOON CATALOGUE (S)
The Lockwood Art School, Kalamazoo, Mich.: 1919 (11-5/8x9, 52 pgs, B&W)

nn - Edited by Mr. Lockwood 20.00 60.00 100.00

NOTE: *Jammed with 100s of single panel cartoons and some sequential comics; Mr Lockwood began the very first cartoonist school back in 1892. Clare Briggs was one of his students.*

CARTOON COMICS
Lasco Publications, Detroit, Mich: #1, April 1930 - #2, May 1930 (8-3/6x5-1/5")

1 - By Lu Harris 20.00 60.00 100.00
2 - By Lu Harris 20.00 60.00 100.00

NOTE: *Contains recurring characters Hollywood Horace, Campus Charlie, Pair-A-Dice Alley and Jocko Monkey. Not much is presently known about the creator(s) or publisher.*

CARTOON HISTORY OF ROOSEVELT'S CAREER, A
The Review of Reviews Company: 1910 (276 pgs, 8-1/4x11",

nn - By various 40.00 120.00 240.00

NOTE: *Reprints editorial cartoons about Teddy Roosevelt from U.S. and international newspapers and cartoons from the humor magaines (Puck, Judge, etc.). A few cartoonists whose work is included are Dalrymple, Opper, McDougall, McCutcheon, Remington, Rogers, Kemble. Mostly single panel but 10 or so are sequential strips.*

CARTOON HUMOR
Collegian Press: 1938 (102 pgs, squarebound, B&W)

nn 20.00 70.00 120.00

NOTE: *Contains cartoons & strips by Otto Soglow, Syd Hoff, Peter Arno, Abner Dean, others.*

CARTOONIST'S PHILOSOPHY, A
Percy Crosby: 1931, HC, 252 pgs, 5-1/2x7-1/2", hard-c, celluloid dust wrapper

nn - By Percy Crosby (10 plates, 6 are of Skippy) 20.00 60.00 100.00

NOTE: *Crosby's partial autobiography regarding his return to France in 1929, and portrayals of Normandy, the "cliff dwellers" on Normandy cliffs (destroyed in WWII), his visit to London, comments on art, philosophy, several poems, and political dialogue. His description of his Cockney driver, " Harold" is amusing. Also describes his experience visiting Chicago to speak out against Capone, his concerns over the evils of Prohibition, and the economy prior to the 1929 crash. This book reveals he was aware of the dangers of his outspoken views, and is prophetic, re: his later years as political prisoner. Also reveals his religious beliefs.*

CARTOONS BY BRADLEY: CARTOONIST OF THE CHICAGO DAILY NEWS
Rand McNally & Company: 1917 (11-1/4x8-3/4", 112 pgs, hardcover, B&W)

nn - By Luther D. Bradley (editorial) 20.00 70.00 120.00

CARTOONS BY FONTAINE FOX (Toonerville Trolley) (S)
Harper & Brothers Publishers: nd early '20s (9x7-7/8",102 pgs., hard-c, B&W)

Second Book- By Fontaine Fox (Toonerville-r) 54.00 189.00 325.00

CARTOONS BY HALLADAY (N,S)
Providence Journal Co., Rhode Island: Dec 1914 (116 pgs, 10-1/2x 7-3/4", hard-c, B&W)

nn- (Scarce) 50.00 125.00 250.00

NOTE: *Cartoons on Rhode Island politics, plus some Teddy Roosevelt & WW I cartoons.*

CARTOONS BY McCUTCHEON (S)
A. C. McClurg & Co.: 1903 (12-3/8x9-3/4", 212 pgs., hardcover, B&W)

nn - By John McCutcheon 20.00 70.00 120.00

CARTOONS BY W. A. IRELAND (S)
The Columbus-Evening Dispatch: 1907 (13-3/4 x 10-1/2", 66 pgs, hardcover)

Cartoons Magazine v9 #5 by various creators
May 1916 © H. H. Windsor, Chicago

Charlie Chaplin in the Army by Segar
1917 © Essaney

Deadwood Gulch By Boody Rogers
1931 © Dell Publishing Company

GD2.0 FN6.0 VF8.0

nn - By W. A. Ireland (strip-r) 20.00 70.00 120.00

CARTOONS MAGAZINE (I,N,S)
H. H. Windsor, Publisher: Jan 1912-June 1921; July 1921-1923; 1923-1924; 1924-1927 (1912-July 1913 issues 12x9-1/4", 68-76 pgs; 1913-1921 issues 10x7", average 112 to 188 pgs, color covers)

1912-Jan-Dec 15.00 51.00 90.00
1913-1915 15.00 51.00 90.00
1916-1917 15.00 51.00 90.00
1917-(Apr) "How Comickers Regard Their Characters" 30.00 105.00 150.00
1917-(June) "A Genius of the Comic Page" - long article on George Herriman, Krazy Kat, etc with lots of Herriman art; "Cartoonists and Their Cars" 58.00 204.00 350.00
1918-1919 20.00 70.00 120.00
1920-June 1921 15.00 53.00 90.00
July 1921-1923 titled Wayside Tales & Cartoons Magazine 10.00 30.00 60.00
1923-1924 becomes Cartoons Magazine again 10.00 30.00 60.00
1924-1927 becomes Cartoons & Movie Magazine 10.00 30.00 60.00
NOTE: *Many issues contain a wealth of historical background on then current cartoonists of the day with an international slant; each issue profusely illustrated with many cartoons. We are unsure if this magazine continued after 1927.*

CARTOONS BY J. N. DARLING (S,N - some sequential strips)
The Register & Tribune Co., Des Moines, Iowa: 1909?-1920 (12x8-7/8",B&W)

Book 1 15.00 51.00 90.00
Book 2 Education of Alonzo Applegate (1910) 15.00 51.00 90.00
2nd printing 10.00 30.00 90.00
Book 3 Cartoons From The Files (1911) 15.00 51.00 90.00
Book 4 15.00 51.00 90.00
Book 5 In Peace And War (1916) 15.00 51.00 90.00
Book 6 Aces & Kings War Cartoons (Dec 1, 1918) 15.00 51.00 90.00
Book 7 The Jazz Era (Dec 1920) 15.00 51.00 90.00
Book 8 Our Own Outlines of History (1922) 15.00 51.00 90.00
NOTE: *Some of the most inspired hard hitting cartoons ever printed. Are there more?*

CARTOONS THAT MADE PRINCE HENRY FAMOUS, THE (N,S)
The Chicago Record-Herald: February 1902 (12-1/8" x 9", 32 pgs, paper-c, B&W)

nn- (Scarce) by McCutcheon 15.00 51.00 90.00
NOTE: *Cartoons about the visit of the British Prince Henry to the U.S.*

CAVALRY CARTOONS (O)
R. Montalboddi: nd (c1918) (14-1/4" x 11", 30 pgs, printed on one side, olive & black construction paper-c, B&W interior)

nn - By R.Montalboddi 15.00 51.00 90.00
NOTE: *Comics about life in the U.S.Cavalry during World War I, by a soldier who was in the 1st Cavalry.*

CHARLIE CHAPLIN (N)
Essanay/M. A. Donohue & Co.: 1917 (9x16", B&W, large size soft-c)

Series 1, #315-Comic Capers (9-3/4x15-3/4")-20 pgs. by Segar;
Series 1, #316-In the Movies 150.00 525.00 1200.00
#317-Up in the Air (20 pgs), #318-In the Army 150.00 525.00 1400.00
Funny Stunts-(12-1/2x16-3/8",16 color pgs) 150.00 525.00 1400.00
NOTE: *All contain pre-Thimble Theatre Segar art. The thin paper used makes high grade copies very scarce.*

CHASING THE BLUES
Doubleday Page: 1912 (7-1/2x10", 108 pgs., B&W, hard-c)

nn - By Rube Goldberg 150.00 525.00 900.00
NOTE: *Contains a dozen Foolish Questions, baseball, a few Goldberg poems and lots of sequential strips.*

CHRISTIAN CARTOONS (N,S)
The Sunday School Times Company: 1922 (7-1/4 x 6-1/8,104 pgs, brown hard-c, B&W)

nn - E.J. Pace 15.00 51.00 90.00
NOTE: *Religious cartoons reprinted from The Sunday School Times.*

CLANCY THE COP (O))
Dell Publishing Co.: 1930 - No. 2, 1931 (10x10", 52 pgs., B&W, cardboard-c)
(Also see Bug Movies & Deadwood Gulch)

1, 2-By Vep (original material; not reprints) 50.00 200.00 350.00

CLIFFORD MCBRIDE'S IMMORTAL NAPOLEON & UNCLE ELBY (N)
The Castle Press: 1932 (12x17"; soft-c cartoon book)

nn - Intro. by Don Herod 36.00 144.00 250.00

COLLECTED DRAWINGS OF BRUCE BAIRNSFATHER, THE
W. Colston Leigh: 1931 (11-1/4x8-1/4 ", 168 pages, hardcover, B&W)

nn - By Bruce Bairnsfather 24.00 96.00 165.00

COMICAL PEEP SHOW
McLoughlin Bros: 1902 (36 pgs, B&W)

nn 24.00 96.00 165.00
NOTE: *Comic stories of Wilhelm Busch redrawn; two versions with green or gold front cover logos; back covers different.*

COMIC ANIMALS (I)
Charles E. Graham & Co.: 1903 (9-3/4x7-1/4", 90 pgs, color cover)

nn - By Walt McDougall (not comic strips) 43.00 150.00 260.00

COMIC CUTS (O)
H. L. Baker Co., Inc.: 5/19/34-7/28/34 (Tabloid size 10-1/2x15-1/2", 24 pgs., 5¢) (full color, not reprints; published weekly; created for news stand sales)

V1#1 - V1#7(6/30/34), V1#8(7/14/34), V1#9(7/28/34)-Idle Jack strips 50.00 150.00 300.00
NOTE: *According to a 1958 Lloyd Jacquet interview, this short-lived comics mag was the direct inspiration for Major Malcolm Wheeler-Nicholson's* ***New Fun Comics****, not* ***Famous Funnies****.*

COMIC MONTHLY (N)
Embee Dist. Co.: Jan, 1922 - No. 12, Dec, 1922 (10¢, 8-1/2"x9", 28 pgs., 2-color covers) (1st monthly newsstand comic publication) (Reprints 1921 B&W dailies)

1-Polly & Her Pals by Cliff Sterrett 193.00 772.00 1350.00
2-Mike & Ike by Rube Goldberg 114.00 456.00 800.00
3-S'Matter, Pop? 114.00 456.00 800.00
4-Barney Google by Billy DeBeck 114.00 456.00 800.00
5-Tillie the Toiler by Russ Westover 114.00 456.00 800.00
6-Indoor Sports by Tad Dorgan 114.00 456.00 800.00
NOTE: *#6 contains more Judge Rummy than Indoor Sports.*
7-Little Jimmy by James Swinnerton 114.00 456.00 800.00
8-Toots and Casper by Jimmy Murphy 114.00 456.00 800.00
9-New Bughouse Fables by Barney Google 114.00 456.00 800.00
10-Foolish Questions by Rube Goldberg 114.00 456.00 800.00
11-Barney Google & Spark Plug by Billy DeBeck 114.00 456.00 800.00
12-Polly & Her Pals by Cliff Sterrett 193.00 772.00 1350.00
NOTE: *This series was published by George McManus (Bringing Up Father) as Em & Rudolph Block, Jr., son of Hearst's cartoon editor for many years, as "Bee." One would have thought this series would have done very well considering the tremendous amount of talent assembled. All issues are extremely hard to find these days and rarely show up in any type of higher grade.*

COMIC PAINTING AND CRAYONING BOOK (H)
Saalfield Publ. Co.: 1917 (13-1/2x10", 32 pgs.) (No price on-c)

nn - Tidy Teddy by F. M. Follett, Clarence the Cop, Mr. & Mrs. Butt-In; regular comic stories to read or color 50.00 175.00 300.00

COMPLETE TRIBUNE PRIMER, THE (I)
Mutual Book Company: 1901 (7 1/4 x 5", 152 pgs, red hard-c)

nn - By Frederick Opper; has 75 Opper cartoons 25.00 88.00 150.00

COURTSHIP OF TAGS, THE (N)
McCormick Press: pre-1910 (9x4", 88 pgs, red & B&W-c, B&W interior)

nn - By O. E. Wertz (strip-r Wichita Daily Beacon) 25.00 88.00 150.00

DAFFYDILS (N)
Cupples & Leon Co.: 1911 (5-3/4x7-7/8", 52 pgs., B&W, hard-c)

nn - By "Tad" Dorgan 58.00 204.00 350.00
NOTE: *Also exists in self-published TAD edition: The T.A. Dorgan Company; unknown which is first printing.*

DAN DUNN SECRET OPERATIVE 48 (Also See Detective Dan) (N)
Whitman Publishing: 1937 ((5 1/2 x 7 1/4", 68pgs., color cardboard-c, B&W)

1010 And The Gangsters' Frame-Up 36.00 144.00 250.00
NOTE: *There are two versions of the book the later printing has a 5 cent cover price. Dick Tracy look-alike character by Norman Marsh.*

DANGERS OF DOLLY DIMPLE, THE (N)
Penn Tobacco Co.: nd (1930's) (9-3/8x7-7/8", 28 pgs, red cardboard-c, B&W)

nn - (Rare) by Walter Enright 25.00 88.00 150.00
NOTE: *Reprints newspaper comic strip advertisements, in which in every episode, Dolly Dimple's life is saved by Penn's Smoking Tobacco. - how very un-P.C. by today's standards.*

DEADWOOD GULCH (O) (See The Funnies 1929)(also see Bug Movies & Clancy The Cop)
Dell Publishing Co.: 1931 (10x10", 52 pgs., B&W, color covers, B&W interior)

nn - By Charles "Boody" Rogers (original material) 50.00 200.00 350.00

DESTINY A Novel In Pictures (O)
Farrar & Rinehart: 1930 (8x7", 424 pgs, B&W, hard-c, dust jacket?)

nn - By Otto Nuckel (original graphic novel) 25.00 100.00 175.00

DICK TRACY & DICK TRACY JR. CAUGHT THE RACKETEERS, HOW
Cupples & Leon Co.: 1933 (8-1/2x7", 88 pgs., hard-c) (See Treasure Box of Famous Comics) (N)

2-(Numbered on pg. 84)-Continuation of Stooge Viller book (daily strip reprints from 8/3/33 thru 11/8/33)(Rarer than #1) 86.00 344.00 600.00
With dust jacket... 118.00 472.00 825.00

DICK TRACY & DICK TRACY JR. AND HOW THEY CAPTURED "STOOGE" VILLER (N)
Cupples & Leon Co.: 1933 (8-1/2x7", 100 pgs., hard-c, one-shot)
Reprints 1932 & 1933 Dick Tracy daily strips

nn(No.1)-1st app. of "Stooge" Viller 86.00 344.00 600.00
With dust jacket... 118.00 472.00 825.00

DIMPLES By Grace Drayton (N) (See Dolly Dimples)
Hearst's International Library Co.: 1915 (6 1/4 x 5 1/4, 12 pgs) (5 known)

nn-Puppy and Pussy; nn-She Goes For a Walk; nn-She Had A Sneeze; nn-She Has a Naughty Play Husband; nn-Wait Till Fido Comes Home 20.00 70.00 140.00

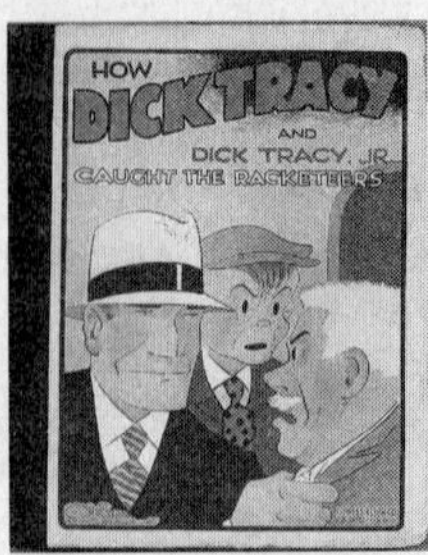

How Dick Tracy and Dick Tracy, Jr.
Caught the Racketeers by Chester Gould
1933 © Cupples & Leon

Felix the Cat Book 260 by Otto Messmer
1931 © McLoughlin Bros.

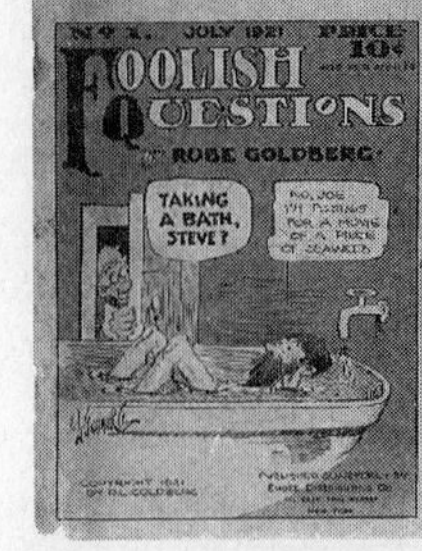

Foolish Questions by Rube Goldberg
1921 © EmBee Distributing Co., NY.

GD2.0 FN6.0 VF8.0

DOINGS OF THE DOO DADS, THE (N)
Detroit News (Universal Feat. & Specialty Co.): 1922 (50¢, 7-3/4x7-3/4", 34 pgs, B&W, red & white-c, square binding)
nn-Reprints 1921 newspaper strip "Text & Pictures" given away as prize in the Detroit News Doo Dads contest; by Arch Dale 43.00 173.00 300.00

DOINGS OF THE VAN-LOONS (N) (see Mutt & Jeff #1-#5)
Ball Publications: 1912 (5-3/4X15-1/2", 68pg., B&W, hard-c)
nn - By Fred I. Leipziger 88.00 306.00 525.00

DOLLY DIMPLES & BOBBY BOUNCE (See Dimples)
Cupples & Leon Co.: 1933 (8-3/4x7", color hardcover, B&W)
nn - Grace Drayton-a 24.00 96.00 165.00

DOO DADS, THE (Sleepy Sam and Tiny the Elephant)
Universal Feature * Specialty Co: 1922 (5-1/4x14", 36 pgs.,B&W, R&W-c,square binding)
nn - By Arch Dale 24.00 96.00 165.00

DREAMS OF THE RAREBIT FIEND (N)
Frederick A. Stokes Co.:1905 (10-1/4x7-1/2", 68 pgs, thin paper cover all B&W) newspaper reprints from the New York Evening Telegram printed on yellow paper
nn-By Winsor "Silas" McCay (Very Rare) (Four copies known to exist) Estimated value.... 571.00 2000.00 -

DRISCOLL'S BOOK OF PIRATES (O)
David McKay Publ.: 1934 (9x7", 124 pgs, B&W, hardcover)
nn - By Montford Amory (original material) 21.00 64.00 150.00

DUCKY DADDLES
Frederick A. Stokes Co: July 1911 (15x10")
nn - By Grace Weiderseim (later Drayton) strip-r 50.00 175.00 300.00

DUMBUNNIES AND THEIR FRIENDS IN RABBITBORO, THE (O)
Albertine Randall Wheelan: 1931 (8-3/4x7-1/8", 82 pgs, color hardcover, B&W)
nn - By Albertine Randall Wheelan (self-pub) 34.00 103.00 240.00

EDISON - INSPIRATION TO YOUTH (N)(Also see Life of Thomas---)
Thomas A. Edison, Incorporated: 1939 (9-1/2 x 6-1/2, paper cover, B&W)
nn - Photo-c 46.00 138.00 275.00
NOTE: *Reprints strip material found in the 1928 Life of Thomas A. Edison in Word and Picture.*

'ERBIE AND 'IS PLAYMATES
Democratic National Committee: 1932 (8x9-1/2, 16 pgs, B&W)
nn - By Frederick Opper (Rare) 34.00 103.00 240.00
NOTE: *Anti-Hoover/Pro-Roosevelt political comics.*

EXPANSION BEING BART'S BEST CARTOONS FOR 1899
Minneapolis Journal: 1900 (10-1/4x8-1/4", 124 pgs, paperback, B&W)
v2#1 - By Charles L. Bartholomew 24.00 84.00 145.00

FAMOUS COMICS (N)
King Features Synd. (Whitman Pub. Co.): 1934 (100 pgs., daily newspaper-r) (3-1/2x8-1/2"; paper cover)(came in an illustrated box)
684 (#1) - Little Jimmy, Katz Kids & Barney Google 34.00 103.00 240.00
684 (#2) - Polly, Little Jimmy, Katzenjammer Kids 34.00 103.00 240.00
684 (#3) - Little Annie Rooney, Polly and Her Pals, Katzenjammer Kids 34.00 103.00 240.00
Box price... 32.00 96.00 225.00

FAMOUS COMICS CARTOON BOOKS (N)
Whitman Publishing Co.: 1934 (8x7-1/4", 72 pgs, B&W hard-c, daily strip-r)
1200-The Captain & the Kids; Dirks reprints credited to Bernard Dibble 29.00 86.00 200.00
1202-Captain Easy & Wash Tubbs by Roy Crane; 2 slightly different versions of cover exist 34.00 103.00 240.00
1203-Ella Cinders By Conselman & Plumb 28.00 84.00 195.00
1204-Freckles & His Friends 25.00 75.00 175.00
NOTE: *Called Famous Funnies Cartoon Books inside back area sales advertisement.*

FANTASIES IN HA-HA (M)
Meyer Bros & Co.: 1900 (14 x 11-7/8", 64 pgs, color cover hardcover, B&W)
nn - By Hy Mayer 40.00 140.00 240.00

FELIX (N)
Henry Altemus Company: 1931 (6-1/2"x8-1/4", 52 pgs., color, hard-c w/dust jacket)
1-3-Sunday strip reprints of Felix the Cat by Otto Messmer. Book No. 2 r/1931 Sunday panels mostly two to a page in a continuity format oddly arranged so each tier of panels reads across two pages, then drops to the next tier. (Books 1 & 3 have not been documented.)(Rare)
Each 104.00 416.00 725.00
With dust jacket 150.00 600.00 1050.00

FELIX THE CAT BOOK (N)
McLoughlin Bros.: 1927 (8"x15-3/4", 52 pgs, half in color-half in B&W)
nn - Reprints 23 Sunday strips by Otto Messmer from 1926 & 1927, every other one in color, two pages per strip. (Rare) 200.00 800.00 1400.00
260-Reissued (1931), reformatted to 9-1/2"x10-1/4" (same color plates, but one strip per every three pages), retitled ("Book" dropped from title) and abridged (only eight strips repeated from first issue, 28 pgs.).(Rare) 79.00 316.00 550.00

F. FOX'S FUNNY FOLK (see Toonerville Trolley; Cartoons by Fontaine Fox) (C)
George H. Doran Company: 1917 (10-1/4x8-1/4", 228 pgs, red, B&W cover, B&W interior, hardcover; dust jacket?)
nn - By Fontaine Fox (Toonerville Trolley strip-r) 50.00 200.00 350.00

52 CAREY CARTOONS (O,S)
Carey Cartoon Service, NY: 1915 (25 cents, 6-3/4" x 10-1/2", 118 pgs, printed on one side, color cardboard-c, B&W)
nn - (1915) War ??? ??? ???
NOTE: *The Carey Cartoon Service supplied a weekly, hand-colored single panel cartoon broadsheet, on current news events, starting in 1906 or 1907, for window display in Carey Fountain Pen chain stores. These broadsheets were 22-1/2" x 33" in size. Starting circa 1915, Carey Fountain Pens began offering subscriptions for the broadsheets to other merchants, for window display in their stores as well. This collects, in B&W, the cartoons for 1915. An "Edition Deluxe" was also advertised, with all cartoons hand colored. It is currently unknown whether a reprint collection was only issued in 1915, or if other editions exist.*

52 LETTERS TO SALESMEN
Steven-Davis Company: 1927 (???)
nn - (Rare) 21.00 64.00 128.00
NOTE: *52 motivational letters to salesmen, with page of comics for each week, bound into embossed leather binder.*

FOLKS IN FUNNYVILLE (S)
R.H. Russell: 1900 (12"x9-1/4", 48 pgs.)(cardboard-c)
nn - By Frederick Opper 271.00 950.00 -
NOTE: *Reprinted from Hearst's NY Journal American Humorist supplements.*

FOOLISH QUESTIONS (S)
Small, Maynard & Co.: 1909 (6-7/8 x 5-1/2", 174 pgs, hardcover, B&W)
nn - By Rube Goldberg (first Goldberg item) 75.00 263.00 450.00
NOTE: *Comic strip began Oct 23, 1908 running thru 1941. Also drawn by George Frinkin in 1909.*

FOOLISH QUESTIONS THAT ARE ASKED BY ALL
Levi Strauss & Co./Small, Maynard & Co.: 1909 (5-1/2x5-3/4", 24 pgs, paper-c, B&W)
nn- (Rare) by Rube Goldberg 46.00 160.00 275.00

FOOLISH QUESTIONS (Boxed card set) (S)
Wallie Dorr Co., N.Y.: 1919 (5-1/4x3-3/4")(box & card backs are red)
nn - Boxed set w/52 B&W comics on cards; each a single panel gag complete set w/box 75.00 263.00 450.00
NOTE: *There are two diff sets put out simultaneously with the first set, by the same company. One set continues/picks up the numbering of the cards from the other set.*

FOOLISH QUESTIONS (S)
EmBee Distributing Co.: 1921 (10¢, 4x5 1/2; 52 pgs, 3 color covers; B&W)
1-By Rube Goldberg 46.00 160.00 275.00

FOXY GRANDPA
Foxy Grandpa Company, 33 Wall St, NY : 1900 (9x15", 84 pgs, full color, cardboard-c)
nn - By Carl Schultze (By Permission of New York Herald) 271.00 950.00 -
NOTE: *This seminal comic strip began Jan 7, 1900 and was collected later that same year.*

FOXY GRANDPA (Also see The Funnies, 1st series) (N)
N. Y. Herald/Frederick A. Stokes Co./M. A. Donahue & Co./Bunny Publ. (L. R. Hammersly Co.): 1901 - 1916 (Strip-r in color, hard-c)
1901- 9x15" in color-N. Y. Herald 271.00 950.00 -
1902- "Latest Larks of...", 32 pgs., 9-1/2x15-1/2" 164.00 575.00 -
1902- "The Many Advs. of...", 9x12", 148 pgs., Hammersly Co. 179.00 625.00 -
1903- "Latest Advs.", 9x15", 24 pgs., Hammersly Co. 164.00 575.00 -
1903- "...'s New Advs.", 11x15", 66 pgs., Stokes 164.00 575.00 -
1904- "Up to Date", 10x15", 66 pgs., Stokes 146.00 510.00 875.00
1904- "The Many Adventures of...", 9x15, 144pgs, Donohue 146.00 510.00 875.00
1905- "& Flip-Flaps", 9-1/2x15-1/2", 52 pgs. 146.00 510.00 875.00
1905- "The Latest Advs. of...", 9x15", 28, 52, & 68 pgs, M.A. Donohue Co.; re-issue of 1902 issue 104.00 365.00 625.00
1905- "Latest Larks of...", 9-1/2x15-1/2", 52 pgs., Donahue; re-issue of 1902 issue with more pages added 104.00 365.00 625.00
1905- "Latest Larks of...", 9-1/2x15-1/2", 24 pgs. edition, Donahue; re-issue of 1902 issue 104.00 365.00 625.00
1905- "Merry Pranks of...", 9-1/2x15-1/2", 28, 52 & 62 pgs., Donahue 104.00 365.00 625.00
1905-"...Surprises",10x15", color, 64 pg,Stokes, 60¢ 104.00 365.00 625.00
1906- "Frolics", 10x15", 30 pgs., Stokes 104.00 365.00 625.00
1907?-"...& His Boys",10x15", 64 color pgs, Stokes 104.00 365.00 625.00
1907- "Triumphs", 10x15", 62 pgs, Stokes 104.00 365.00 625.00
1908-"...Mother Goose", Stokes 104.00 365.00 625.00
1909- "...& Little Brother", 10x15, 58 pgs, Stokes 104.00 365.00 625.00
1911- "Latest Tricks", r-1910,1911 Sundays-Stokes Co. 104.00 365.00 625.00

Gasoline Alley by Frank King
1929 © Reilly & Lee

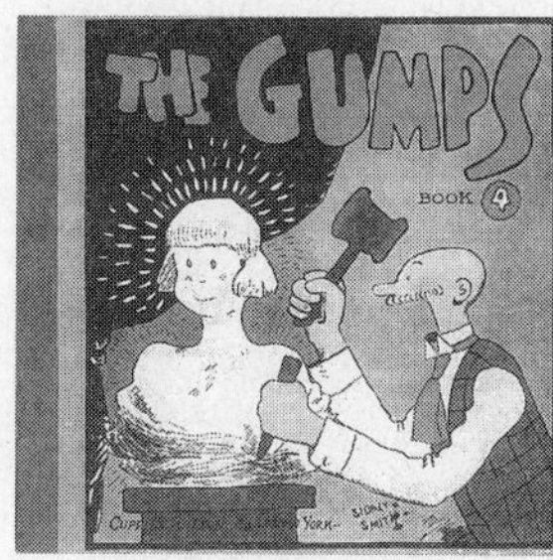

The Gumps by Sidney Smith
1927? © Cupples & Leon

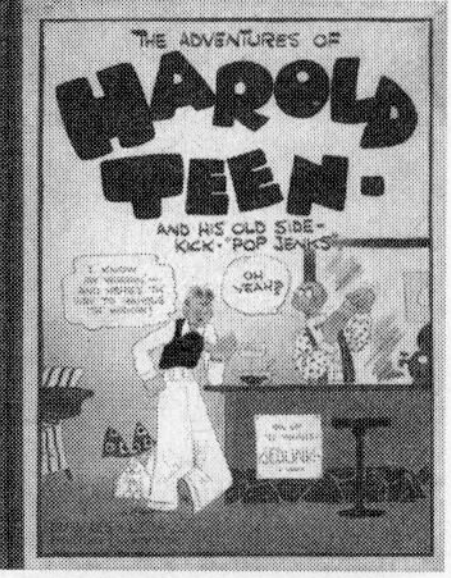

Harold Teen #2 by Carl Ed
1931 © Cupples & Leon

GD2.0 FN6.0 VF8.0

1914-(9-1/2x15-1/2", 24 pgs.)-6 color cartoons/page, Bunny Publ. Co. 88.00 306.00 525.00
1915 - ...Always Jolly (10x16, Stokes) 88.00 306.00 525.00
1916- "Merry Book", (10x15", 64 pgs, Stokes) 88.00 306.00 525.00
1917-"...Adventures (5 1/2 x 6 1/2, 26 pgs, Stokes) 52.00 184.00 315.00
1917-"...Frolics (5 1/2 x 6 1/2, 26 pgs, Stokes) 52.00 184.00 315.00
1917-"...Triumphs (5 1/2 x 6 1/2, 26 pgs, Stokes) 52.00 184.00 315.00

FOXY GRANDPA, FUNNY TRICKS OF (The Stump Books)
M.A. Donahue Co, Chicago: approx 1903 (1-7/8x6-3/8", 44 pgs, blue hardcover)
nn - By Carl Schultze 52.00 184.00 315.00
NOTE: *One of a series of ten "stump" books; the only comics one.*

FOXY GRANDPA'S MOTHER GOOSE (I)
Stokes: October 1903 (10-11/16x8-1/2", 86 pgs, hard-c)
nn - By Carl Schultze (not comics - illustrated book) 52.00 184.00 315.00

FOXY GRANDPA SPARKLETS SERIES (N)
M. A. Donahue & Co.: 1908 (7-3/4x6-1/2"; 24 pgs., color)
"... Rides the Goat", "...& His Boys", "...Playing Ball", "...Fun on the Farm", "...Fancy Shooting", "...Show His Boys Up-To-Date Sports", "...Plays Santa Claus" each.... 88.00 306.00 525.00
900- "Playing Ball"; Bunny illos; 8 pgs., linen like pgs., no date 73.00 254.00 435.00

FOXY GRANDPA VISITS RICHMOND (O,P)
Dietz Printing Co., Richmond, VA / Hotel Rueger: nd (c1920's) (5-7/8" x 4-1/2", 16 pgs, paper-c, B&W)
nn - (Scarce) By Bunny 25.00 88.00 150.00
NOTE: *Promotional comic given away to its guests by the Hotel Rueger, about Foxy Grandpa visiting and enjoying the Hotel. Originally came in an envelope, with the words "Foxy Grandpa Visits Richmond -- and Rueger's" printed on it.*

FOXY GRANDPA VISITS WASHINGTON, D.C. (P)
Dietz Printing Co., Richmond, VA / Hamilton Hotel: nd (c1920's) (5-7/8" x 4-1/2", 16 pgs, paper-c, B&W)
nn - (Scarce) By Bunny 25.00 88.00 150.00
NOTE: *Mostly reprints "... Visits Richmond", changing all references to Hotel Rueger, to Hamilton Hotel instead. Also, changes depictions of a waiter and a cook from black to white, plus incompletely erases the cover art on a book Foxy Grandpa falls asleep with (the latter is how we know that the Richmond version was first).*

FRAGMENTS FROM FRANCE (S)
G. P. Putnam & Sons: 1917 (9x6-1/4", 168 pgs, hardcover, $1.75)
nn - By Bruce Bairnsfather 25.00 88.00 150.00
NOTE: *WW1 trench warfare cartoons; color dust jacket.*

FUNNIES, THE (H) (See Clancy the Cop, Deadwood Gulch, Bug Movies)
Dell Publishing Co.: 1929 - No. 36, 10/18/30 (10¢; 5¢ No. 22 on) (16 pgs.)
Full tabloid size in color; not reprints; published every Saturday
1-My Big Brudder, Jonathan, Jazzbo & Jim, Foxy Grandpa, Sniffy, Jimmy Jams & other strips begin; first four-color comic newsstand publication; also contains magic, puzzles & stories 186.00 684.00 1300.00
2-21 (1930, 10¢) 54.00 214.00 375.00
22(nn-7/12/30-5¢) 43.00 171.00 300.00
23(nn-7/19/30-5¢), 24(nn-7/26/30-5¢), 25(nn-8/2/30), 26(nn-8/9/30), 27(nn-8/16/30), 28(nn-8/23/30), 29(nn-8/30/30), 30(nn-9/6/30), 31(nn-9/13/30), 32(nn-9/20/30), 33(nn-9/27/30), 34(nn-10/4/30), 35(nn-10/11/30), 36(nn, no date-10/18/30) each.... 43.00 171.00 300.00

GASOLINE ALLEY (Also see Popular Comics & Super Comics) (N)
Reilly & Lee Publishers: 1929 (8-3/4x7", B&W daily strip-r, hard-c)
nn - By King (96 pgs.) 57.00 228.00 400.00
Dust Wrapper - add 50% more
NOTE: *Of all the Frank King reprint books, this is the only one to reprint actual complete newspaper strips - all others are illustrated prose text stories.*

GIBSON'S PUBLISHED DRAWINGS, MR. (M,S) (see Victorian index for earlier issues)
R.H. Russell, New York: No.1 1894 - No. 9 1904 (11x17-3/4", hard-c, B&W)
nn (No.6; 1901) A Widow and her Friends (90 pgs.) 30.00 60.00 120.00
nn (No.7; 1902) The Social Ladder (88 pgs.) 30.00 60.00 120.00
8 - 1903 The Weaker Sex (88 pgs.) 30.00 60.00 120.00
9 - 1904 Everyday People (88 pgs.) 30.00 60.00 120.00
NOTE: *By Charles Dana Gibson cartoons, reprinted from magazines, primarily LIFE. The Education of Mr. Pipp tells a story. Series continues how long after 1904?*

GIGGLES
Pratt Food Co., Philadelphia, PA: 1908-09? (12x9", 8 pgs, color, 5 cents-c)
1-6: By Walt McDougall (#6 dated Jan 1909) 40.00 140.00 -
8 - Recently re-discovered dated March 1909 40.00 140.00 -
NOTE: *Appears to be monthly; almost tabloid size; yearly subscriptions was 25 cents.*

GOD'S MAN (H)
Jonathan Cape and Harrison Smith Inc.: 1929 (8-1/4x6", 298 pgs, B&W hardcover w/dust jacket) (original graphic novel in wood cuts)
nn - By Lynd Ward 43.00 171.00 300.00

GD2.0 FN6.0 VF8.0

GOLD DUST TWINS
N. K. Fairbank Co.: 1904 (4-5/8x6-3/4", 18 pgs, color and B&W)
nn - By E. W. Kemble (Rare) 30.00 60.00 120.00
NOTE: *Promo comic for Gold DustWashing Powder; includes page of watercolor paints.*

GOLF
Volland Co.: 1916 (9x12-3/4", 132 pgs, hard-c, B&W)
nn - By Clair Briggs 52.00 84.00 315.00

GUMPS, THE (N)
Landfield-Kupfer: No. 1, 1918 - No. 6, 1921; (B&W Daily strip-r)
Book No. 1(1918)(Rare)-cardboard-c, 5-1/4x13-1/3", 64 pgs., daily strip-r by Sidney Smith 67.00 233.00 400.00
Book No.2(1918)-(Rare); 5-1/4x13-1/3"; paper cover; 36 pgs. daily strip reprints by Sidney Smith 67.00 233.00 400.00
Book No. 3 121.00 423.00 725.00
Book No. 4 (1918) 5-3/8x13-7/8", 20 pgs. Color card-c 121.00 423.00 725.00
Book No. 5 10-1/4x13-1/2", 20 pgs. Color paper-c 121.00 423.00 725.00
Book No. 6 (Rare) 121.00 423.00 725.00

GUMPS, ANDY AND MIN, THE (N)
Landfield-Kupfer Printing Co., Chicago/Morrison Hotel: nd (1920s) (Giveaway, 5-1/2"x14", 20 pgs., B&W, soft-c)
nn - Strip-r by Sidney Smith; art & logo embossed on cover w/hotel restaurant menu on back-c or a hotel promo ad; 4 different contents of issues known 50.00 175.00 300.00

GUMPS, THE (N)
Cupples & Leon: 1924-1930 (10x10, 52 pgs, B&W)
nn (1924)-By Sidney Smith 61.00 244.00 425.00
2,3 39.00 154.00 270.00
4-7 33.00 131.00 230.00

GUMP'S CARTOON BOOK, THE (N)
The National Arts Company: 1931 (13-7/8x10", 36 pgs, color covers, B&W)
nn - By Sidney Smith 57.00 228.00 400.00

GUMPS PAINTING BOOK, THE (N)
The National Arts Company: 1931 (11 x 15 1/4", 20 pgs, half in full color)
nn - By Sidney Smith 57.00 228.00 400.00

HALT FRIENDS! (see also **HELLO BUDDY**)
???: 1918? (4-3/8x5-3/4", 36 pgs, color-c, B&W, no cover price listed)
nn - Unknown 10.00 30.00 70.00
NOTE: *Says on front cover: "Comics of War Facts of Service Sold on its merits by Unemployed or Disabled Ex-Service Men. Credentials Shown On Request. Price - Pay What You Please." These are very common; contents vary widely.*

HAMBONE'S MEDITATIONS
Jahl & Co.: no date 1920 (6-1/8 x 7-1/2, 108 pgs, paper cover, B&W)
nn - By J. P. Alley 33.00 132.00 230.00
NOTE: *Reprint of racist single panel newspaper series, 2 cartoons per page.*

HAN OLA OG PER (N)
Anundsen Publishing Co, Decorah, Iowa: 1927 (10-3/8 x 15-3/4", 54 pgs, paper cover, B&W)
nn - American origin Norwegian language strips-r 33.00 131.00 230.00
NOTE: *1940s and modern reprints exist.*

HANS UND FRITZ (N)
The Saalfield Publishing Co.: 1917, 1927-29 (10x13-1/2", 28 pgs., B&W)
nn - By R. Dirks (1917, r-1916 strips) 96.00 335.00 575.00
nn - By R. Dirks (1923 edition- reprint of 1917 edition) 58.00 204.00 350.00
nn - By R. Dirks (1926 edition- reprint of 1917 edition) 58.00 204.00 350.00
The Funny Larks Of... By R. Dirks (©1917 outside cover; ©1916 inside indicia) 96.00 335.00 575.00
The Funny Larks Of... (1927) reprints 1917 edition of 1916 strips Halloween-c 58.00 204.00 350.00
The Funny Larks Of... 2 (1929) 58.00 204.00 350.00
193 - By R. Dirks; contains 1916 Sunday strip reprints of Katzenjammer Kids & Hawkshaw the Detective - reprint of 1917 nn edition (1929) this edition is not rare 58.00 204.00 350.00

HAPPY DAYS (S)
Coward-McCann Inc.: 1929 (12-1/2x9-5/8", 110 pgs, hardcover B&W)
nn - By Alban Butler (WW 1 cartoons) 20.00 60.00 120.00

HAPPY HOOLIGAN (See Alphonse...) (N)
Hearst's New York American & Journal: 1902,1903
Book 1-(1902)-"And His Brother Gloomy Gus", By Fred Opper; has 1901-02-r; (yellow & black)(86 pgs.)(10x15-1/4") 400.00 1400.00 -
New Edition, 1903 -10x15" 82 pgs. in color 300.00 1100.00 -
NOTE: *Strip ran March 26, 1900-Aug 14, 1932 and is widely recognized as setting the format standard for all newspaper comic strips which came after it. Opper (1857-1937) was going blind towards the end.*

Jimmy By Jimmy Swinnerton
1905 © New York American & Journal

Highlights of History by J. Mansfield
The Winning of the Old Northwest
1934 © World Syndicate Publishing Co.

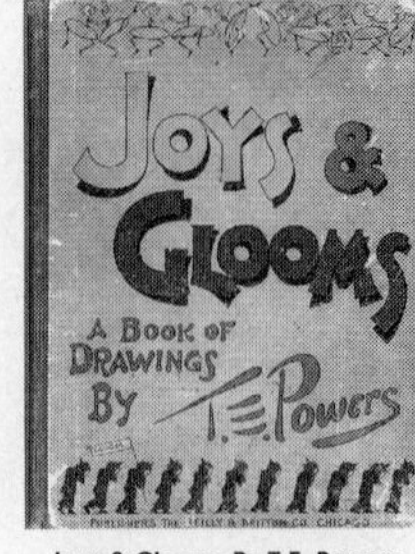

Joys & Glooms By T.E. Powers
1912 © Reilly & Britton Co.

GD2.0 FN6.0 VF8.0

HAPPY HOOLIGAN (N) (By Fredrick Opper)
Frederick A. Stokes Co.: 1906-08 (10-1/4x15-3/4", cardboard color-c)

1906 - :Travels of...), 32 pgs,10-1/4x15-3/4", 1905-r 200.00 700.00 -
1907 - "--Home Again", 68 pgs., 10x15-3/4", 60¢; full color-c 200.00 700.00 -
1908 - "Handy--", 68 pgs, color 200.00 700.00 -

HAPPY HOOLIGAN (Story of...) (G)
McLoughlin Bros.: No. 281, 1932 (12x9-1/2", 16 pgs., soft-c)

281-Three-color text, pictures on heavy paper 57.00 228.00 400.00
NOTE: *An homage to Opper's creation on its 30th Anniversary in 1932.*

HAROLD HARDHIKE'S REJUVENATION
O'Sullivan Rubber: 1917 (6-1/4x3-1/2, 16 pgs, B&W)

nn 25.00 100.00 175.00
NOTE: *Comic book to promote rubber shoe heels.*

HAROLD TEEN (N)
Cupples & Leon Co.: 1929 (9-7/8x9-7/8", 52 pgs, cardboard covers)

nn - By Carl Ed 41.00 164.00 290.00
nn - (1931, 8-11/16x6-7/8", 96 pgs, hardcover w/dj) 41.00 164.00 290.00
NOTE: *Title 2nd book:* ***HAROLD TEEN AND HIS OLD SIDE-KICK– POP JENKINS,*** *(Adv. of...). Precursor for Archie Andrews & crew; strip began May 4, 1919 running into 1959.*

HAROLD TEEN PAINT AND COLOR BOOK (N)
McLoughlin Bros Inc.: 1932 (13x9-3/4, 28 pgs, B&W and color)

#2054 25.00 100.00 175.00

HAWKSHAW THE DETECTIVE (See Advs. of..., Hans Und Fritz & Okay) (N)
The Saalfield Publishing Co.: 1917 (10-1/2x13-1/2", 24 pgs., B&W)

nn - By Gus Mager (Sunday strip-r) 54.00 190.00 325.00
nn - By Gus Mayer (1923 reprint of 1917 edition) 25.00 100.00 175.00
nn - By Gus Mager (1926 reprint of 1917 edition) 25.00 100.00 175.00
NOTE: *Runs Feb 23, 1913-Sept 4, 1922, starts again from Dec 13, 1931-Feb 11, 1952; Sherlock Holmes spoof.*

HEALTH IN PICTURES
American Public Health Association, NYC: 1930 (6-1/2" x 5-3/16", 76 pgs, green & black paper-c, B&W interior)

nn - By various 15.00 51.00 90.00
NOTE: *Collection of strips and cartoons put out by the Public Health Association, on topics ranging from boating and food safety, to small pox and typhoid prevention.*

HE DONE HER WRONG (O)
Doubleday, Doran & Company: 1930 (8-1/4x 7-1/4", 276pgs, hardcover with dust jacket, B&W interiors)

nn - By Milt Gross 50.00 200.00 350.00
NOTE: *A seminal original-material wordless graphic novel, not reprints. Several modern reprints.*

HELLO BUDDY (see also **HALT FRIENDS**)
???: 1919? (4-3/8x5-3/4", 36 pgs, color-c, B&W, 15¢)

nn - Unknown 10.00 30.00 70.00
NOTE: *Says on front cover: "Comics of War Facts of Service Sold on its merits by Unemployed or Disabled Ex-Service Men." These are very common; contents vary widely.*

HENRY (N)
David McKay Co.: 1935 (25¢, soft-c)

Book 1 - By Carl Anderson 50.00 200.00 350.00
NOTE: *Strip began March 19 1932; this book ties with Popeye (David McKay) and Little Annie Rooney (David McKay) as the last of the 10x10" Platinum Age comic books.*

HENRY (M)
Greenberg Publishers Inc.: 1935 (11-1/4x 8-5/8", 72 pgs, red & blue color hardcover, dust jacket, B&W interiors) (strip-r from Saturday Evening Post)

nn - By Carl Anderson 50.00 200.00 350.00

HIGH KICKING KELLYS, THE (M)
Vaudeville News Corporation, NY: 1926 (5x11", B&W, two color soft-c)

nn - By Jack A. Ward (scarce) 40.00 160.00 280.00

HIGHLIGHTS OF HISTORY (N)
World Syndicate Publishing Co.: 1933-34 (4-1/2x4", 288 pgs)

nn - 5 different unnumbered issues; daily strip-r 10.00 40.00 70.00
NOTE: *Titles include Buffalo Bill, Daniel Boone, Kit Carson, Pioneers of the Old West, Winning of the Old Northwest. There are line drawing color covers and embossed hardcover versions. It is unknown which came out first.*

HOMER HOLCOMB AND MAY (N)
no publisher listed: 1920s (4 x 9-1/2", 40 pgs, paper cover, B&W)

nn - By Doc Bird Finch (strip-r) 10.00 40.00 70.00

HOME, SWEET HOME (N)
M.S. Publishing Co.: 1925 (10-1/4x10")

nn - By Tuthill 33.00 134.00 235.00

HOW THEY DRAW PROHIBITION (S)
Association Against Prohibition: 1930 (10x9", 100 pgs.)

nn - Single panel and multi-panel comics (rare) 71.00 285.00 500.00
NOTE: *Contains art by J.N. "Ding" Darling, James Flagg, Rollin Kirby, Winsor McCay, T.E. Powers, H.T. Webster, others. Also comes with a loose sheet listing all the newspapers where the cartoons originally appeared.*

HOW TO BE A CARTOONIST (H)
Saalfield Pub. Co: 1936 (10-3/8x12-1/2", 16 pgs, color-c, B&W)

nn - By Chas. H. Kuhn 10.00 40.00 70.00

HOW TO DRAW: A PRACTICAL BOOK OF INSTRUCTION (H)
Harper & Brothers: 1904 (9-1/4x12-3/8", 128 pgs, hardcover, B&W)

nn - Edited By Leon Barritt 57.00 228.00 400.00
NOTE: *Strips reprinted include: "Buster Brown" by Outcault, "Foxy Grandpa" by Bunny, "Happy Hooligan" by Opper, "Katzenjammer Kids" by Dirks, "Lady Bountiful" by Gene Carr, "Mr. Jack" by Swinnerton, "Panhandle Pete" by George McManus, "Mr E.Z. Mark" by F.M. Howarth others; non-character strips by Hy Mayer, Winsor McCay, T.E. Powers, others; single panel cartoons by Davenport, Frost, McDougall, Nast, W.A. Rogers, Sullivant, others.*

HOW TO DRAW CARTOONS (H)
Garden City Publishing Co.: 1926, 1937 (10 1/4 x 7 1/2, 150 pgs)

1926 first edition By Clare Briggs 25.00 75.00 150.00
1937 2nd edition By Clare Briggs 20.00 60.00 120.00
NOTE: *Seminal "how to" break into the comics syndicates with art by Briggs, Fisher, Goldberg, King, Webster, Opper, Tad, Hershfield, McCay, Ding, others. Came with Dust Jacket -add 50%.*

HOW TO DRAW FUNNY PICTURES: A Complete Course in Cartooning (H)
Frederick J. Drake & Co., Chicago: 1936 (10-3/8x6-7/8", 168 pgs, hardcover, B&W)

nn - By E.C. Matthews (200 illus by Eugene Zimmerman) 20.00 60.00 120.00

HY MAYER (M)
Puck Publishing: 1915 (13-1/2 x 20-3/4", 52 pgs, hardcover cover, color & B&W interiors) (reprints from Puck)

nn - By Hy Mayer 40.00 140.00 240.00

HYSTERICAL HISTORY OF THE CIVILIAN CONSERVATION CORPS
Peerless Engraving: 1934 (10-3/4x7-1/2", 104 pgs, soft-c, B&W)

nn - By various 20.00 60.00 120.00
NOTE: *Comics about CCC life, includes two color insert postcards in back.*

INDOOR SPORTS (N,S)
National Specials Co., New York: nd circa 1912 (25 cents, 6 x 9", 68 pgs, B&W)

nn - Tad 40.00 120.00 200.00
NOTE: *Cartoons reprinted from Hearst papers.*

IT HAPPENS IN THE BEST FAMILIES (N)
Powers Photo Engraving Co.: 1920 (52 pgs.)(9-1/2x10-3/4")

nn - By Briggs; B&W Sunday strips-r 29.00 114.00 200.00
Special Railroad Edition (30¢)-r/strips from 1914-1920 26.00 103.00 180.00

JIMMIE DUGAN AND THE REG'LAR FELLERS (N)
Cupples & Leon: 1921, 46 pgs. (11"x16")

nn - By Gene Byrne 71.00 284.00 500.00
NOTE: *Ties with EmBee's Mutt & Jeff and Trouble of Bringing Up Father as the last of this size.*

JIMMY (N)
N. Y. American & Journal: 1905 (10x15", 40 pgs., color)

nn - By Jimmy Swinnerton 200.00 700.00 1200.00
NOTE: *James Swinnerton was one of the original first pioneers of the American newspaper comic strip.*

JIMMY AND HIS SCRAPES (N)
Frederick A. Stokes: 1906, (10-1/4x15-1/4", 66 pgs, cardboard-c, color)

nn - By Jimmy Swinnerton 64.00 256.00 450.00

JIMMY, STORY OF (I)
McLoughlin Bros.:1932 (9-1/2"X12", 16 pgs., soft cover)

nn - By Jimmy Swinnerton and Mary Kinnaird 57.00 228.00 400.00

JOE PALOOKA (N)
Cupples & Leon Co.: 1933 (9-13/16x10", 52 pgs., B&W daily strip-r)

nn - By Ham Fisher (scarce) 114.00 456.00 800.00

JOLLY POLLY'S BOOK OF ENGLISH AND ETIQUETTE (S)
Jos. J. Frisch: 1931 (60 cents, 8 x 5-1/8, 88 pgs, paper-c, B&W)

nn - By Jos. J. Frisch 20.00 60.00 120.00
NOTE: *Reprint of single panel newspaper series, 4 per page, of English and etiquette lessons taught by a flapper.*

JOHN, JONATHAN, AND MR. OPPER (N,S)
Grant Richards, London: 1903 (2 shillings, 9-5/8" x 8-1/8", 100 pgs, hard-c, B&W)

nn- (Scarce) by F. Opper 20.00 60.00 120.00
NOTE: *Collection of single panel cartoons involving Uncle Sam (also known as Brother Jonathan), and John Bull (symbolic character for Britain), all reprinted from the* ***New York American and Journal.***

JOYS AND GLOOMS (N)
Reilly & Britton Co.: 1912 (11x8", 72 pgs, hard-c, B&W interior)

nn - By T. E. Powers (newspaper strip-r) 39.00 156.00 275.00

JUDGE - yet to be indexed

The Katzenjammer Kids by Rudolph Dirks
1921 © EmBee Distributing Co.

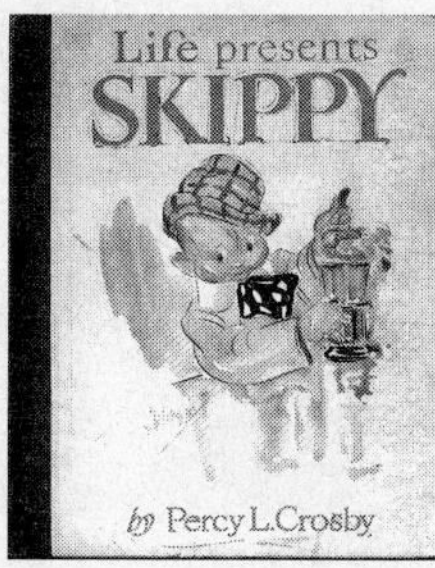

Life Presents Skippy by Percy L. Crosby
1924 © Life Publishing Company

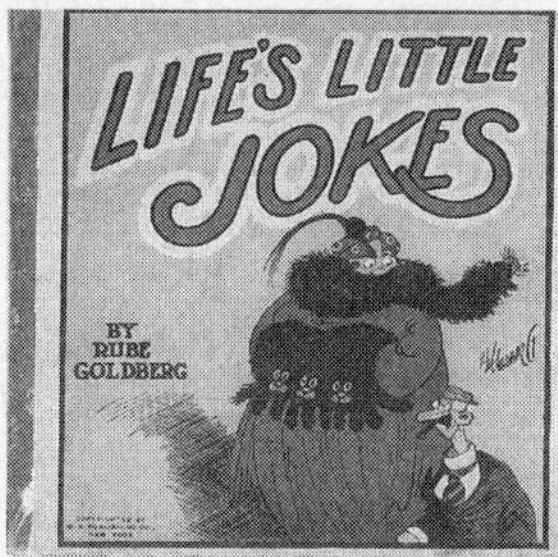

Life's Little Jokes by Rube Goldberg
1924 © M.S. Publishing Co., N.Y.

GD2.0 FN6.0 VF8.0

JUDGE'S LIBRARY - yet to be indexed

JUST KIDS COMICS FOR CRAYON COLORING
King Features. NYC: 1928 (11x8-1/2, 16 pgs, soft-c)
nn - By Ad Carter 25.00 75.00 150.00
NOTE: *Porous better grade paper; top pics printed in color; lower in b&w to color.*

JUST KIDS, THE STORY OF (I)
McLoughlin Bros.: 1932 (12x9-1/2", 16 pgs., paper-c)
283-Three-color text, pictures on heavy paper 39.00 156.00 275.00

KAPTAIN KIDDO AND PUPPO (N)
Frederick A. Stokes Co.: 1910-1913 (11x16-1/2", 62 pgs)
1910-By Grace Wiederseim (later Drayton) 40.00 140.00 240.00
1910-Turr-ble Tales of... By Grace Wiederseim (Edward Stern & Co., 11x16-1/2", 64 pgs.) 40.00 140.00 240.00
1913- ...'Speriences By Grace Drayton 40.00 140.00 240.00
NOTE: *Strip ran approx. 1909-1912.*

KATZENJAMMER KIDS, THE (Also see Hans Und Fritz) (N)
New York American & Journal: 1902,1903 (10x15-1/4", 86 pgs., color)
(By Rudolph Dirks; strip first appeared in 1897) © W.R. Hearst
NOTE: *All KK books 1902-1905 all have the same exact title page with a 1902 copyright by W.R. Hearst; almost always look instead on the front cover.*
1902 (Rare) (red & black); has 1901-02 strips 500.00 1700.00 -
1903- **A New Edition** (Rare), 86 pgs 450.00 1500.00 -
1904- 10x15", 84 pgs 250.00 750.00 -
1905?-The Cruise of the, 10x15", 60¢, in color 250.00 750.00 -
1905-A Series of Comic Pictures, 10x15", 84 pgs. in color, possible reprint of 1904 edition 250.00 750.00 -
1905-Tricks of... (10x15", 66 pgs, Stokes) 250.00 750.00 -
1906-Stokes (10x16", 32 pgs. in color) 186.00 650.00 -
1907- The Cruise of the, 10x15", 62 pgs 1905-r? 186.00 650.00 -
1910-The Komical...(10x15) 108.00 379.00 650.00
1921-Embee Dist. Co., 10x16", 20 pgs. in color 100.00 350.00 600.00

KATZENJAMMER KIDS MAGIC DRAWING AND COLORING BOOK (N)
Sam L Gabriel Sons And Company: 1931 (8 1/2 x 12", 36 pages, stiff-c
838-By Knerr 50.00 200.00 350.00

KEEPING UP WITH THE JONESES (N)
Cupples & Leon Co.: 1920 - No. 2, 1921 (9-1/4x9-1/4",52 pgs.,B&W daily strip-r)
1,2-By Pop Momand 39.00 154.00 270.00

KID KARTOONS (N,S)
The Century Co.: 1922 (232 pgs, printed 1 side, 9-3/4 x 7-3/4", hard-c, B&W)
nn - By Gene Carr 60.00 240.00 -

KING OF THE ROYAL MOUNTED (Also See Dan Dunn) (N)
Whitman Publishing: 1937 (5 1/2 x 7 1/4", 68 pgs., color cardboard-c, B&W)
1010 36.00 144.00 250.00

LADY BOUNTIFUL (N)
Saalfield Publ. Co./Press Publ. Co.: 1917 (13-3/8x10", 36 pgs, color cardboard-c, B&W interiors)
nn - By Gene Carr; 2 panels per page 50.00 175.00 300.00
193S - 2nd printing (13-1/8x10",28 pgs color-c, B&W) 33.00 117.00 200.00

LAUGHS YOU MIGHT HAVE HAD From The Comic Pages of Six Week Day Issues of the Post-Dispatch (N)
St. Louis Post-Dispatch: 1921 (9 x 10 1/2", 28 pgs, B&W, red ink cover)
nn - Various comic strips 39.00 154.00 270.00

LIFE, DOGS FROM (M)
Doubleday, Page & Company: nn 1920 - No.2 1926 (130 pgs, 11-1/4 x 9", color painted-c, hard-c, B&W)
nn (No.1) 120.00 360.00 -
Second Litter 80.00 320.00 -
NOTE: *Reprints strips & cartoons featuring dogs, from Life Magazine. Editted by Thomas L. Masson. Highly sought by collectors of dog ephemera. Art in both books is mostly by Robert L. Dickey. Other art: Carl Anderson-1,2; Barbes-1; Chip Bellew-1; Lang Campbell-1,2; Percy Crosby-1,2; Edwina-2; Frueh-2; R.B. Fuller-1; Gibson-1,2; Don Herold-2; Gus Mager-2; Orr-1; J.R. Shaver-1,2; T.S. Sullivant-2; Russ Westover-1,2; Crawford Young-1.*

LIFE OF DAVY CROCKETT IN PICTURE AND STORY, THE
Cupples & Leon: 1935 (8-3/4x7", 64 pgs, B&W hardcover, dust jacket?)
nn - By C. Richard Schaare 28.00 112.00 195.00

LIFE OF THOMAS A. EDISON IN WORD AND PICTURE, THE (N)(Also see Edison...)
Thomas A. Edison Industries: 1928 (10x8", 56 pgs, paper cover, B&W)
nn - Photo-c 50.00 200.00 350.00
NOTE: *Reprints newspaper strip which ran August to November 1927.*

LIFE'S LITTLE JOKES (S)
M.S. Publ. Co.: No date (1924)(10-1/16x10", 52 pgs., B&W)
nn - By Rube Goldberg 64.00 257.00 450.00

LIFE PRESENTS SKIPPY (see SKIPPY, LIFE PRESENTS)

LIFE'S PRINTS (was **LIFE'S PICTURE GALLERY** - See Victorian Age section) (M,S,P)
Life Publishing Company, New York: nd (c1907) (7x4-1/2", 132 pgs, paper cover, B&W) (all are Scarce)
nn - (nd; c1907) unillustrated black construction paper cover; reprints art from 1895-1907; art by J.M.Flagg, A.B.Frost, Gibson - - -
nn - (nd; c1908) b&w cardboard painted cover by Gibson, showing angel raising a champagne glass; reprints art from 1901-1908; art by J.M.Flagg, A.B.Frost, Gibson, Walt Kuhn, Art Young - - -
NOTE: *Catalog of prints reprinted from LIFE covers & centerspreads. There are likely more as yet unreported catalogs.*

LIFE, THE COMEDY OF LIFE
Life Publishing Company: 1907 (130 pgs, 11-3/4x9-1/4",embossed printed cloth covered board-c, B+W
nn - By various 20.00 80.00 120.00
NOTE: *Single cartoons and some sequential cartoons). Artists include Charles Dana Gibson, Harrison Cady, E.W. Kemble, James Montgomery Flagg.*

LILY OF THE ALLEY IN THE FUNNIES
Whitman Publishing Co.: No date (1927) (10-1/4x15-1/2"; 28 pgs., color)
W936 - By T. Burke (Rare) 57.00 228.00 400.00

LITTLE ANNIE ROONEY (N)
David McKay Co.: 1935 (25¢, soft-c)
Book 1 43.00 172.00 300.00
NOTE: *Ties with Henry & Popeye (David McKay) as the last of the 10x10" size Plat comic books.*

LITTLE ANNIE ROONEY WISHING BOOK (G) (See Happy Hooligan, Story of #281)
McLoughlin Bros.: 1932 (12x9-1/2", 16 pgs., soft-c, 3-color text, heavier paper)
282 - By Darrell McClure 38.00 134.00 230.00

LITTLE BIRD TOLD ME, A (E)
Life Publishing Co.: 1905? (96 pgs, hardbound)
nn - By Walt Kuhn (Life-r) 38.00 134.00 230.00

LITTLE FOLKS PAINTING BOOK (N)
The National Arts Company: 1931 (10-7/8 x 15-1/4", 20 pgs, half in full color)
nn - By "Tack" Knight (strip-r) 33.00 132.00 230.00

LITTLE JOHNNY & THE TEDDY BEARS (Judge-r) (M) (see Teddy Bear Books)
Reilly & Britton Co.: 1907 (10x14", 32 pgs.; green, red, black interior color)
nn - By J. R. Bray-a/Robert D. Towne-s 67.00 233.00 400.00

LITTLE JOURNEY TO THE HOME OF BRIGGS THE SKY-ROCKET, THE
Lockhart Art School: 1917 (10-3/4x7-7/8", 20 pgs, B&W) (I)
nn - About Clare Briggs (bio & lots of early art) 38.00 134.00 230.00

LITTLE KING, THE (see New Yorker Cartoon Albums for 1st appearance) (M)
Farrar & Reinhart, Inc: 1933 (10-1/4 x 8-3/4, 80 pgs, hardcover w/dust jacket
nn - By Otto Soglow (strip-r The New Yorker) 43.00 129.00 300.00
NOTE: *Copies with dust jacket are worth 50% more. Also exists in a 12x8-3/4 edition.*

LITTLE LULU BY MARGE (M)
Rand McNally & Company, Chicago: 1936 (6-9/16x6", 68 pgs, yellow hard-c, B&W)
nn - By Marjorie Henderson Buell 25.00 100.00 200.00
NOTE: *Begins reprinting single panel Little Lulu cartoons which began with Saturday Evening Post Feb. 23, 1935. This book was reprinted several times as late as 1940.*

LITTLE NAPOLEON
No publisher listed: 1924 , 50 pages, 10" by 10"; Color cardstock-c, B&W
nn - By Bud Counihan 25.00 100.00 200.00
NOTE: *Same format as Cupples and Leon books.*

LITTLE NEMO (...in Slumberland) (N)
Doffield & Co.(1906)/Cupples & Leon Co.(1909): 1906, 1909 (Sunday strip-r in color, cardboard covers)
1906-11x16-1/2" by Winsor McCay; 30 pgs. (scarce) 900.00 3200.00 -
1909-10x14" by Winsor McCay (scarce) 850.00 2600.00 -

LITTLE ORPHAN ANNIE (See Treasure Box of Famous Comics) (N)
Cupples & Leon Co.: 1926 - 1934 (8-3/4x7", 100 pgs., B&W daily strip-r, hard-c)
1 (1926)-Little Orphan Annie (softback see Treasure Box) 50.00 200.00 350.00
2 (1927)-In the Circus (softback see Wonder Box...) 36.00 144.00 250.00
3 (1928)-The Haunted House (softback see Wonder Box...) 36.00 144.00 250.00
4 (1929)-Bucking the World 36.00 144.00 250.00
5 (1930)-Never Say Die 30.00 120.00 210.00
6 (1931)-Shipwrecked 30.00 120.00 210.00
7 (1932)-A Willing Helper 24.00 96.00 170.00
8 (1933)-In Cosmic City 24.00 96.00 170.00
9 (1934)-Uncle Dan (not rare) 24.00 96.00 170.00
NOTE: *Each book reprints dailies from the previous year. Each hardcover came with a dust jacket. Books with out dust jackets are worth 50% less. Many of copies of #9 Uncle Dan have been turning up on eBay recently.*

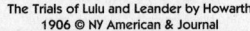

The Trials of Lulu and Leander by Howarth
1906 © NY American & Journal

Maud the Mirthful Mule by Opper
1908 © Frederick A. Stokes

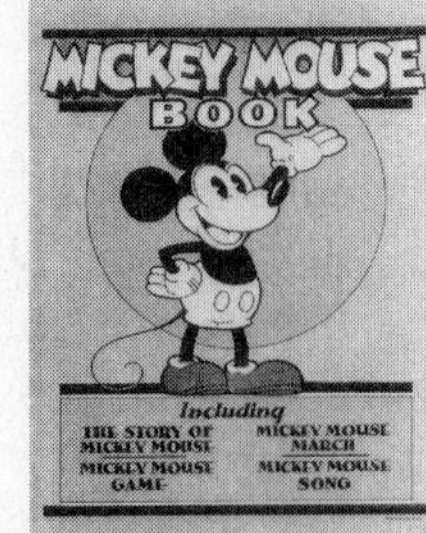

Mickey Mouse Book
1930 © Bibo & Lang

GD2.0 FN6.0 VF8.0

LITTLE ORPHAN ANNIE RUMMY CARDS (N)
Whitman Publishing Co., Racine: 1935 (box: 5 x 6 1/2" Cards: 3 1/2 x 2 1/4")

	GD2.0	FN6.0	VF8.0
nn-Harold Gray	20.00	60.00	120.00

NOTE: *36 cards, including 1 instruction card, 5 character cards and 30 cards forming 5 sequential stories (6 cards each).*

LITTLE SAMMY SNEEZE (N)
New York Herald Co.: Dec 1905 (11x16-1/2", 72 pgs., color)

	GD2.0	FN6.0	VF8.0
nn - By Winsor McCay (Very Rare)	1300.00	3900.00	-

NOTE: *Rarely found in fine to mint condition.*

LIVE AND LET LIVE
Travelers Insurance Co.: 1936 (5-3/4x7/3/4", 16 pgs. color and B&W)

	GD2.0	FN6.0	VF8.0
nn - Bill Holman, Carl Anderson, etc	20.00	60.00	120.00

LULU AND LEANDER (N)
New York American & Journal: 1904 (76 pgs); **William A Stokes & Co:** 1906

	GD2.0	FN6.0	VF8.0
nn - By F.M. Howarth	143.00	500.00	860.00
nn - The Trials of...(1906, 10x16", 68 pgs. in color)	143.00	500.00	860.00

NOTE: *F. M. Howarth helped pioneer the American comic strip in the pages of PUCK magazine in the early 1890s before the Yellow Kid.*

MADMAN'S DRUM (O)
Jonathan Cape and Harrison Smith Inc.: 1930 (8-1/4x6", 274 pgs, B&W hardcover w/dust jacket) (original graphic novel in wood cuts)

	GD2.0	FN6.0	VF8.0
nn - By Lynd Ward	50.00	175.00	300.00

MAMA'S ANGEL CHILD IN TOYLAND (I)
Rand McNally, Chicago: 1915 (128 pgs, hardbound)

	GD2.0	FN6.0	VF8.0
nn - By M.T. "Penny" Ross & Marie C, Sadler	40.00	140.00	240.00

NOTE: *Mamma's Angel Child published as a comic strip by the "Chicago Tribune" 1908 Mar 1 to 1920 Oct 17.This novel dedicated to Esther Starring Richartz, "the original Mamma's Angel Kid."*

MAUD (N) (see also **Happy Hooligan**)
Frederick A. Stokes Co.: 1906 - 1908? (10x15-1/2", cardboard-c)

	GD2.0	FN6.0	VF8.0
1906-By Fred Opper (Scarce), 66 pgs. color	257.00	900.00	-
1907-The Matchless, 10x15" 70 pgs in color	200.00	700.00	-
1908-The Mirthful Mule, 10x15", 64 pgs in color	200.00	700.00	-

NOTE: *First run of strip began July 24, 1904 to at least Oct 6, 1907, spun out of* ***Happy Hooligan.***

MEMORIAL EDITION The Drawings of Clare Briggs (S)
Wm H. Wise & Company: 1930 (7-1/2x8-3/4", 284 pgs, pebbled false black leather, B&W) (posthumous boxed set of 7 books by Clare Briggs)

nn - The Days of Real Sport; nn-Golf; nn-Real Folks at Home; nn-Ain't it a Grand and Glorious Feeling?; nn-That Guiltiest Feeling; nn-Somebody's Always Taking the Joy Out of Life; nn-When a Feller Needs a Friend

	GD2.0	FN6.0	VF8.0
Each book...	30.00	120.00	210.00

NOTE: *Also exists in a whitish cream colored paper back edition; first edition unknown presently.*

MENACE CARTOONS (M, S)
Menace Publishing Company, Aurora, Missouri: 1914 (10-3/8x8", 80 pgs, cardboard-c, B&W)

	GD2.0	FN6.0	VF8.0
nn - (Rare)	50.00	150.00	450.00

NOTE: *Reprints anti-Catholic cartoons from K.K.K. related publication* ***The Menace.***

MEN OF DARING (N)
Cupples & Leon Co.: 1933 (8-3/4x7", 100 pgs)

	GD2.0	FN6.0	VF8.0
nn - By Stookie Allen, intro by Lowell Thomas	30.00	90.00	180.00

MICKEY MOUSE BOOK
Bibo & Lang: 1930-1931 (12x9", stapled-c, 20 pgs., 4 printings)

nn - First Disney licensed publication (a magazine, not a book–see first book, Adventures of Mickey Mouse). Contains story of how Mickey met Walt and got his name; games, cartoons & song "Mickey Mouse (You Cute Little Feller)," written by Irving Bibo; Minnie, Clarabelle Cow, Horace Horsecollar & caricature of Walt shaking hands with Mickey. The changes made with the 2nd printing have been verified by billing affidavits in the Walt Disney Archives and include:Two Win Smith Mickey strips from 4/15/30 and 4/17/30 added to page 8 & back-c; "Printed in U.S.A." added to front cover; Bobette Bibo's age of 11 years added to title page; faulty type on the word "tail" corrected top of page 3; the word "start" added to bottom of page 7, removing the words "start 1 2 3 4" from the top of page 7; music and lyrics were rewritten on pages 12-14. A green ink border was added beginning with 2nd printing and some covers have inking variations. Art by Albert Barbelle, drawn in an Ub Iwerks style. Total circulation : 97,938 copies varying from 21,000 to 26,000 per printing.

	GD2.0	FN6.0	VF8.0
1st printing. Contains the song lyrics **censored** in later printings, "When little Minnie's pursued by a big bad villain we feel so bad then we're glad when you up and kill him." Attached to the Nov. 15, 1930 issue of the Official Bulletin of the Mickey Mouse Club notes: "Attached to this Bulletin is a new Mickey Mouse Book that has just been published." This is thought to be the reason why a slightly disproportionate larger number of copies of the first printing still exist	1200.00	5400.00	11,000.00
2nd printing with a theater/advertising. Christmas greeting added to inside front cover (1 copy known with Dec. 27, 1930 date)	–	12,000.00	–
2nd-4th printings	1100.00	5000.00	10,000.00

NOTE: *Theater/advertising copies do not qualify as separate printings. Most copies are missing pages 9 & 10 which had a puzzle to be cut out. Puzzle (pages 9 and 10) cut out or missing, subtract 60% to 75%.*

GD2.0 FN6.0 VF8.0

MICKEY MOUSE COLORING BOOK (S)
Saalfield Publishing Company:1931 (15-1/4x10-3/4", 32 pgs, color soft cover, half printed in full color interior, rest B&W, only Saalfield Mickey Mouse item known)

	GD2.0	FN6.0	VF8.0
871 - By Ub Iwerks & Floyd Gottfredson (rare)	400.00	1200.00	2400.00

NOTE: *Contains reprints of first MM daily strip ever, including the "missing" speck the chicken is after found only on the original daily strip art by Iwerks plus other very early MM art.*

MICKEY MOUSE, THE ADVENTURES OF (I)
David McKay Co., Inc.: Book I, 1931 - Book II, 1932 (5-1/2"x8-1/2", 32 pgs.)

Book I-First Disney book, by strict definition (1st printing-50,000 copies)(see Mickey Mouse Book by Bibo & Lang). Illustrated text refers to Clarabelle Cow as "Carolyn" and Horace Horsecollar as "Henry". The name "Donald Duck" appears with a non-costumed generic duck on back cover & inside, not in the context of the character that later debuted in the Wise Little Hen.

	GD2.0	FN6.0	VF8.0
Hardback w/characters on back-c	75.00	300.00	525.00
Softcover w/characters on back-c	38.00	151.00	265.00
Version without characters on back-c	45.00	180.00	315.00
Book II-Less common than Book I. Character development brought into conformity with the Mickey Mouse cartoon shorts and syndicated strips. Captain Church Mouse, Tanglefoot, Peg-Leg Pete and Pluto appear with Mickey & Minnie	46.00	186.00	325.00

MICKEY MOUSE COMIC (N)
David McKay Co.: 1931 - No. 4, 1934 (10"x9-3/4", 52 pgs., cardboard-c)
(Later reprints exist)

	GD2.0	FN6.0	VF8.0
1 (1931)-Reprints Floyd Gottfredson daily strips in black & white from 1930 & 1931, including the famous two week sequence in which Mickey tries to commit suicide	229.00	914.00	1600.00
2 (1932)-1st app. of Pluto reprinted from 7/8/31 daily. All pgs. from 1931	164.00	656.00	1150.00
3 (1933)-Reprints 1932 & 1933 Sunday pages in color, one strip per page, including the "Lair of Wolf Barker" continuity pencilled by Gottfredson and inked by Al Taliaferro & Ted Thwaites. First app. Mickey's nephews, Morty & Ferdie, one identified by name of Mortimer Fieldmouse, not to be confused with Uncle Mortimer Mouse who is introduced in the Wolf Barker story	214.00	856.00	1500.00
4 (1934)-1931 dailies, include the only known reprint of the infamous strip of 2/4/31 where the villainous Kat Nipp snips off the end of Mickey's tail with a pair of scissors	129.00	514.00	900.00

MICKEY MOUSE (N)
Whitman Publishing Co.: 1933-34 (10x8-3/4", 34 pgs, cardboard-c)

	GD2.0	FN6.0	VF8.0
948-1932 & 1933 Sunday strips in color, printed from the same plates as Mickey Mouse Book #3 by David McKay, but only pages 5-17 & 32-48 (including all of the "Wolf Barker" continuity)	157.00	629.00	1100.00

NOTE: *Some copies bound with back cover upside down. Variance doesn't affect value. Same art appears on front and back covers of all copies. Height of Whitman reissue trimmed 1/2 inch.*

MILITARY WILLIE
J. I. Austen Co.: 1907 (7x9-1/2", 12 pgs., every other page in color, stapled)

	GD2.0	FN6.0	VF8.0
nn - By F. R. Morgan	70.00	245.00	400.00

MINNEAPOLIS TRIBUNE CARTOON BOOK (S)
Minneapolis Tribune: 1899-1903 (11-3/8x9-3/8", B&W, paper cover)

	GD2.0	FN6.0	VF8.0
nn (#1) (1899)	28.00	99.00	170.00
nn (#2) (1900)	28.00	99.00	170.00
nn (#3) (1901) (published Jan 01, 1901)	28.00	99.00	170.00
nn (#4) (1902) (114 pgs)	28.00	99.00	170.00
nn (#5) (1903) (9x10-3/4",110 pgs, B&W; color-c)	28.00	99.00	170.00

NOTE: *All by Roland C. Bowman (editorial-r).*

MINUTE BIOGRAPHIES: INTIMATE GLIMPSES INTO THE LIVES OF 150 FAMOUS MEN AND WOMEN
Grossett & Dunlap: 1931, 1933 (10-1/4x7-3/4", 168 pgs, hardcover, B&W)

	GD2.0	FN6.0	VF8.0
nn - By Nisenson (art) & Parker(text)	20.00	60.00	120.00
More.... (1933)	20.00	60.00	120.00

MISCHIEVOUS MONKS OF CROCODILE ISLE, THE (N)
J. I. Austen Co., Chicago: 1908 (8-1/2x11-1/2", 12 pgs., 4 pgs. in color)

	GD2.0	FN6.0	VF8.0
nn - By F. R. Morgan; reads longwise	96.00	335.00	575.00

MR. & MRS. (Also see Ain't It A Grand and Glorious Feeling?) (N)
Whitman Publishing Co.: 1922 (9x9-1/2", 52 & 28 pgs., cardboard-c)

	GD2.0	FN6.0	VF8.0
nn - By Briggs (B&W, 52 pgs.)	37.00	149.00	260.00
nn - 28 pgs.-(9x9-1/2")-Sunday strips-r in color	41.00	163.00	285.00

NOTE: *The earliest presently-known Whitman comic books*

MR. BLOCK (N)
Industrial Workers of the World (IWW): 1913, 1919

	GD2.0	FN6.0	VF8.0
nn - By Ernest Riebe (C)	50.00	150.00	-
...And The Profiteers (original material) (H)	50.00	150.00	

NOTE: *Mr Block was a daily strip published from 1912 NOV 7 to 1913 SEP ? by the socialist newspaper "Industrial Worker"; Mr Block was a "square" guy (his head was in fact a block) who enthusiastically supported the same system that exploited him. The noted Joe Hill wrote a song about him (Mr Block,1913, on the air of*

Moon Mullins #5 by Frank Willard
1931 © Cupples & Leon

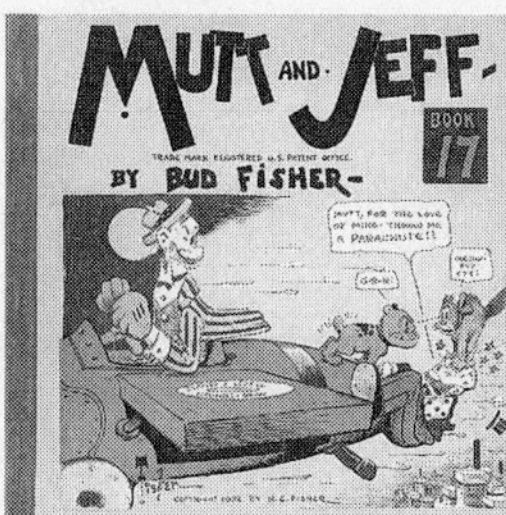

Mutt & Jeff #17 by Bud Fisher
1932 © Cupples & Leon

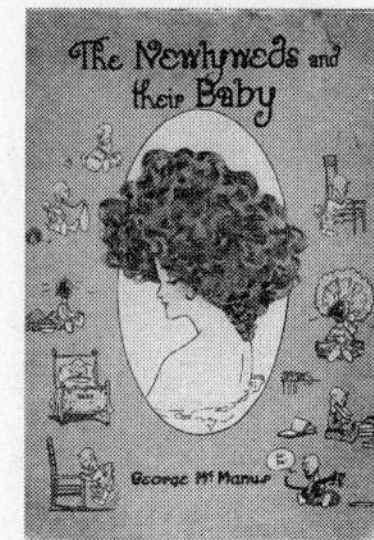

The Newlyweds by George McManus
1907 © Saalfield Publishing Co.

GD2.0 FN6.0 VF8.0

"It loooks me like a big time tonight") for the "Industrial Worker Songbook".

MR. TWEE-DEEDLE (N)
Cupples & Leon: 1913, 1917 (11-3/8 x 16-3/4" color strips-r from NY Herald)
nn - By John B. Gruelle (later of Raggedy Ann fame) 200.00 700.00 1300.00
nn - "Further Adventures of..." By Gruelle 200.00 700.00 1300.00
NOTE: *Strip ran Feb 5, 1911-March 10, 1918.*

MONKEY SHINES OF MARSELEEN AND SOME OF HIS ADVENTURES (C)
McLaughlin Bros. New York: 1906 (10 x 12-3/8", 36 pgs, full color hardcover)
nn - By Norman E. Jennett strip-r NY Evening Telegram 67.00 233.00 400.00
NOTE: *Strip began in 1906 until at least March 13, 1910.*

MONKEY SHINES OF MARSELEEN (N)
Cupples & Leon Co.: 1909 (11-1/2 x 17", 58 pgs. in two colors)
nn - By Norman E. Jennett (strip-r New York Herald) 63.00 219.00 375.00

MOON MULLINS (N)
Cupples & Leon Co.: 1927 - 1933 (52 pgs., B&W daily strip-r)
Series 1 ('27)-By Willard 57.00 228.00 400.00
Series 2 ('28), Series 3 ('29), Series 4 ('30) 39.00 156.00 275.00
Series 5 ('31), 6 ('32), 7 ('33) 36.00 144.00 250.00
Big Book 1 ('30)-B&W (scarce) 100.00 400.00 700.00
w/dust jacket (rare) 183.00 732.00 1275.00

MUTT & JEFF (...Cartoon, The) (N)
Ball Publications: 1911 - No. 5, 1916 (5-3/4 x 15-1/2", 68 pgs, B&W, hard-c)
1 (1910)(50¢) very common 71.00 286.00 500.00
2,3: 2 (1911)-Opium den panels; Jeff smokes opium (pipe dreams).
3 (1912) both very common 71.00 286.00 500.00
2-Reprint of 1913 edition with black ink cover 50.00 175.00 300.00
4 (1915) (50¢) (Scarce) 100.00 300.00 600.00
5 (1916) (Rare) -Photos of Fisher, 1st pg. (68 pages) 150.00 450.00 800.00
5-Scarce 84 page reprint edition 150.00 450.00 800.00
NOTE: *Mutt & Jeff first appeared in newspapers in 1907. Cover variations exist showing Mutt & Jeff reading various newspapers; i.e., The Oregon Journal, The American, and The Detroit News. Reprinting of each issue began soon after publication. No. 4 and 5 may not have been reprinted. Values listed include the reprints. Mutt & Jeff was the first successful American daily newspaper comic strip and as such remains one of the seminal strips of all time.*

MUTT & JEFF (N)
Cupples & Leon Co.: No. 6, 1919 - No. 22, 1934? (9-1/2x9-1/2", 52 pgs., B&W dailies, stiff-c)
6, 7 - By Bud Fisher (very common) 32.00 128.00 225.00
8-10 46.00 186.00 325.00
11-18 (Somewhat Scarcer) 60.00 240.00 420.00
19-22 (Rare) (do these #s even exist?) 71.00 286.00 500.00
nn (1920)-(Advs. of...) 11x16"; 44 pgs.; full color reprints of 1919 Sunday strips
93.00 372.00 650.00
Big Book nn (1926, 144 pgs., hardcovers) 114.00 456.00 800.00
w/dust jacket 193.00 772.00 1350.00
Big Book 1 (1928) - Thick book (hardcovers) 114.00 456.00 800.00
w/dust jacket (rare) 182.00 729.00 1275.00
Big Book 2 (1929) - Thick book (hardcovers) 114.00 456.00 800.00
w/dust jacket (rare) 182.00 729.00 1275.00
NOTE: *The Big Books contain three previous issues rebound.*

MUTT & JEFF (N)
Embee Publ. Co.: 1921 (9x15", color cardboard-c & interior)
nn - Sunday strips in color (Rare)- BY Bud Fisher 143.00 572.00 1000.00
NOTE: *Ties with The Trouble of Bringing Up Father (EmBee) and Jimmie Dugan & The Reg'lar Fellers (C&L) as the last of this size.*

MYSTERIOUS STRANGER AND OTHER CARTOONS, THE
McClure, Phillips & Co.: 1905 (12-3/8x9-3/4", 338 pgs, hardcover, B&W)
nn - By John McCutcheon 32.00 128.00 225.00

MY WAR - Szeged (Szuts)
Wm. Morrow Co.: 1932 (7x10-1/2", 210 pgs, hard-c, B&W)
nn - (All story panels, no words - powerful) 32.00 128.00 225.00

NAUGHTY ADVENTURES OF VIVACIOUS MR. JACK, THE
New York American & Journal: 1904 (15x10", color strips)
nn - By James Swinnerton (no known sales)

NEBBS, THE (N)
Cupples & Leon Co.: 1928 (52 pgs., B&W daily strip-r)
nn - By Sol Hess; Carlson-a 40.00 160.00 280.00

NERVY NAT'S ADVENTURES (E)
Leslie-Judge Co.: 1911 (90 pgs, 85¢, 1903 strip reprints from **Judge**)
nn - By James Montgomery Flagg 75.00 263.00 450.00

THE NEWLYWEDS AND THEIR BABY (N)
Saalfield Publ. Co.: 1907 (13x10", 52 pgs., hardcover)
...& Their Baby' by McManus; daily strips 50% color 200.00 700.00 -
NOTE: *Strip ran Apr 10, 1904 thru Jan 14, 1906 and then May 19, 1907-Dec 5, 1916; was a huge success with Baby Snookums long before McManus invented Bringing Up Father; Snookums brought back as a topper strip over BUF Nov 19, 1941-Dec 30, 1956.*

THE NEWLYWEDS AND THEIR BABY'S COMIC PICTURES FOR PAINTING AND CRAYONING (N)
Saalfield Publishign Company: 1916 (10-1/4x14-3/4", 52 pgs. Cardboard-c)
nn - 44 B&W pages, covers, and one color wrap glued to B&W title page.
Color wrap: color title pg. & 3 pgs of color strips 82.00 286.00 490.00
nn - (1917, 10x14", 20 pgs, oblong, cardboard-c) partial reprint of 1916 edition
30.00 120.00 240.00

THE NEWLYWEDS AND THEIR BABY (N)
Saalfield Publishing Company: 1917 (10-1/8x13-9/16 ", 52 pgs, full color cardstock-c, some pages full color, others two color (orange, blue))
nn 82.00 286.00 490.00

NEW YORKER CARTOON ALBUM, THE (M)
Doubleday, Doran & Company Inc.: (1928-1931); **Harper & Brothers.:** (1931-1933); **Random House** (1935-1937), 12x9", various pg counts, hardcovers w/dust jackets)
1928: nn-114 pgs Arno, Held, Soglow, Williams, etc 20.00 60.00 120.00
1928: SECOND-114 pgs Arno, Bairnsfather, Gross, Held, Soglow, Williams
10.00 30.00 60.00
1930: THIRD-172 pgs Arno, Bairnsfather, Held, Soglow, Art Young
10.00 30.00 60.00
1931: FOURTH-154 pgs Arno, Held, Soglow, Steig, Thurber, Williams, Art Young, "Little King" by Soglow begins 10.00 30.00 60.00
1932: FIFTH-156 pgs Arno, Bairnsfather, Held, Hoff, Soglow, Steig, Thurber, Williams 10.00 30.00 60.00
1933: SIXTH-156 pgs same as above 10.00 30.00 60.00
1935: SEVENTH-164 pgs 10.00 30.00 60.00
1937: 168 pgs; Charles Addams plus same as above but no Little King, two page "Gone With The Wind" parody strip 10.00 30.00 60.00
NOTE: *Some sequential strips but mostly single panel cartoons.*

NIPPY'S POP (N)
The Saalfield Publishing Co.: 1917 (10-1/2x13-1/2", 36 pgs., B&W, Sunday strip-r)
nn - 43.00 152.00 260.00

OH, MAN (A Bully Collection of Those Inimitable Humor Cartoons) (S)
P.F. Volland & Co.: 1919 (8-1/2x13"; 136 pgs.)
nn - By Briggs 43.00 152.00 260.00
NOTE: *Originally came in illustrated box with Briggs art (box is Rare - worth 50% more with box).*

OH SKIN-NAY! (S)
P.F. Volland & Co.: 1913 (8-1/2x13", 136 pgs.)
nn - The Days Of Real Sport by Briggs 43.00 152.00 260.00
NOTE: *Originally came in illustrated box with Briggs art (box is Rare - worth 50% more with box).*

OLD GOLD THE SMOOTHER AND BETTER CIGARETTE...NOT A COUGH IN A CARLOAD (M,N,P) (see also BY BRIGGS)
Old Gold Cigarettes: nd (c1920's) (16 pgs, paper-c, color) (both Scarce)
nn- (4-1/4" x 3-7/8") cover strip is "Oh, Man!"; also contains: "Real Folks at Home", "Ain't It a Grand and Glorious Feelin?", "It Happens in the Best Regulated Families", and "Mr. and Mrs." ??? ??? ???
1440- (5-9/16" x 5-1/4") cover strip is "Frank and Ernest"; also contains: "That Guiltiest Feeling", "Real Folks at Home", "Oh, Man!", "When a Feller Needs a Friend".
??? ??? ???
NOTE: *Collection reprinting strip cartoons by Clare Briggs, advertising Old Gold Cigarettes. These strips originally appeared in various magazines, play program booklets, newspapers, etc. Some of the strips involve regular Briggs strip series. The two booklets contain a completely different set of comics.*

ON AND OFF MOUNT ARARAT (also see **Tigers**) (N)
Hearst's New York American & Journal: 1902, 86pgs. 10x15-1/4"
nn - Noah's Ark satire by Jimmy Swinnerton (rare) 286.00 1000.00 -

ON THE LINKS (N)
Associated Feature Service: Dec, 1926 (9x10", 48 pgs.)
nn - Daily strip-r 25.00 100.00 175.00

ONE HUNDRED WAR CARTOONS (S)
Idaho Daily Statesman: 1918 (7-3/4x10", 102 pgs, paperback, B&W)
nn - By Villeneuve (WW I cartoons) 20.00 60.00 120.00

OUR ANTEDILUVIAN ANCESTORS (N,S)
New York Evening Journal, NY: 1903 (11-3/8x8-7/8", hardcover)
nn - By F Opper 25.00 100.00 175.00
NOTE: *There is a simultaneously published British edition, identical size and contents, from C. Arthur Pearson Ltd, London. A collection of single panel cartoons about cavemen. Similar to an earlier British cartoon book "Prehistoric Peeps from Punch", by E.T. Reed.*

OUTBURSTS OF EVERETT TRUE, THE (N)
Saalfield Publ. Co.(Werner Co.): 1907 (92 pgs, 9-7/16x5-1/4")
1907 (2-4 panel strips-r)-By Condo & Raper 75.00 300.00 525.00
1921-Full color-c; reprints 56 of 88 cartoons from 1907 ed. (10x10", 32 pgs B&W)

Oh Skin-nay! by Claire Briggs
1913 © P.F. Volland

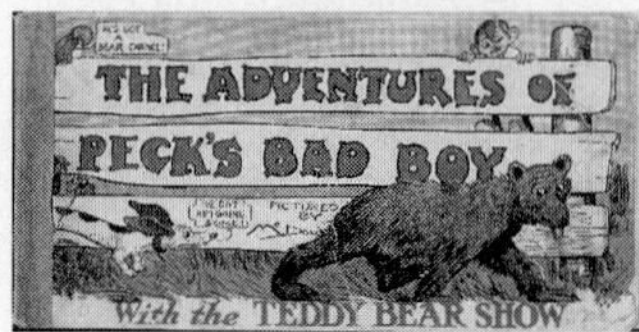

The Adventures of Peck's Bad Boy With the Teddy Bear Show by McDougall
1907 © Charles C. Thompson, Co.

Pore Li'l Mose by R. F. Outcault
1902 © New York Herald Co.

GD2.0 FN6.0 VF8.0

37.00 148.00 260.00

OVER THERE COMEDY FROM FRANCE
Observer House Printing: nd (WW 1 era) (6x14", 60 pgs, paper cover)
nn - Artist(s) unknown 15.00 53.00 90.00

OWN YOUR OWN HOME (I)
Bobbs-Merrill Company, Indianapolis: 1919 (7-7/16x5-1/4")
nn - By Fontaine Fox ??? ??? ???

PECKS BAD BOY (N)
Charles C. Thompson Co, Chicago (by Walt McDougal): 1906-1908 (strip-r)
...& His Country Cousin Cynthia (1907)-12x16-1/2," 34 pgs In color 100.00 400.00 700.00
Advs. of...And His Country Cousins (1907) 5-1/2x10 1/2", 18 pgs In color 50.00 175.00 300.00
...& Their Advs With The Teddy Bear (1907) 5-1/2x10-1/2", 18 pgs in color 50.00 175.00 300.00
...& Their Balloon Trip To the Country (1907) 5-1/2x 10-1/2, 18 pgs in color 50.00 175.00 300.00
...With the Teddy Bear Show (1907) 5-1/2x 10-1/2 50.00 175.00 300.00
...With The Billy Whiskers Goats (1907) 5-1/2 x 10-1/2, 18 pgs in color 50.00 175.00 300.00
...& His Chums (1908) - 11x16-3/8", 36 pgs. Stanton & Van Vliet Co 100.00 400.00 700.00
...& His Chums (1908)-Hardcover; full color;16 pgs. 100.00 350.00 600.00
Advs. of...in Pictures (1908) (11x17, 36 pgs)-In color; Stanton & Van V. Liet Co. 100.00 400.00 700.00

PERCY & FERDIE (N)
Cupples & Leon Co.: 1921 (10x10", 52 pgs., B&W dailies, cardboard-c)
nn - By H. A. MacGill (Rare) 61.00 244.00 425.00

PETER RABBIT (N)
John H. Eggers Co. The House of Little Books Publishers: 1922 - 1923
B1-B4-(Rare)-(Set of 4 books which came in a cardboard box)-Each book reprints half of a Sunday page per page and contains 8 B&W and 2 color pages; by Harrison Cady (9-1/4x6-1/4", paper-c) each.... 43.00 172.00 300.00
Box only 57.00 228.00 400.00

PHILATELIC CARTOONS (M)
Essex Publishing Company, Lynn, Mass.: 1916 (8-11/16" x 5-7/8", 40 pgs, light blue construction paper-c, B&W interior)
nn - By Leroy S. Bartlett 25.00 75.00 150.00
NOTE: *Comics reprinted from The New England Philatelist.*

PICTORIAL HISTORY OF THE DEPARTMENT OF COMMERCE UNDER HERBERT HOOVER (see Picture Life of a Great American) (O)
Hoover-Curtis Campaign Committee of New York State: no date, 1928 (3-1/4 x 5-1/4, 32 pgs, paper cover, B&W)
nn - By Satterfield (scarce) 40.00 120.00 240.00
NOTE: *1928 Presidential Campaign giveaway. Original material, contents completely different from Picture Life of a Great American.*

PICTURE LIFE OF A GREAT AMERICAN (see Pictorial History of the Department of Commerce under Herbert Hoover) (O)
Hoover-Curtis Campaign Committee of New York State: no date, 1928 (paper cover, B&W)
nn - (8-3/4 x 7, 20 pgs) Text cover, 2 page text introduction, 18 pgs of comics (scarcer first print) 40.00 120.00 240.00
nn - (9 x 6-3/4,24 pgs) Illustrated cover,5 page text introduction, 18 pgs of comics (scarce) 40.00 120.00 240.00
NOTE: *1928 Presidential Campaign giveaway. Unknown which above version was published first. Both contain the same original comics material by Satterfield.*

PINK LAFFIN (I)
Whitman Publishing Co.: 1922 (9x12")(Strip-r)
...the Lighter Side of Life, ...He Tells 'Em, ...and His Family, ...Knockouts; Ray Gleason-a (All rare) each... 26.00 104.00 185.00

POLLY (AND HER PALS) - (N)
Newspaper Feature Service: 1916 (3x2-1/2", color)
Altogether: Three Rahs and a Tiger! by Cliff Sterrett 20.00 60.00 120.00
There Is A Limit To Pa's Patience by Cliff Sterrett 20.00 60.00 120.00
NOTE: *Single sheet printed in full color on both sides, unfolds to show 12 panel story.*

POPEYE PAINT BOOK (N)
McLaughlin Bros, Inc., Springfield, Mass.: 1932 (9-7/8x13", 28 pgs, color-c)
2052 - By E. C. Segar 64.00 256.00 450.00
NOTE: *Contains a full color panel above and the exact same art in below panel n B&W which one was to color in; strip-r panels.*

POPEYE CARTOON BOOK (N)
The Saalfield Co.: 1934 (8-1/2x13", 40 pgs, cardboard-c)
2095-(scarce)-1933 strip reprints in color by Segar. Each page contains a vertical half of a Sunday strip, so the continuity reads row by row completely across each double page spread. If each page is read by itself, the continuity makes no sense. Each double page spread reprints one complete Sunday page from 1933 300.00 900.00 2400.00
12 Page Version 100.00 300.00 800.00

POPEYE (See Thimble Theatre for earlier Popeye-r from Sonnott) (N)
David McKay Publications: 1935 (25¢; 52 pgs, B&W) (By Segar)
1-Daily strip reprints- "The Gold Mine Thieves" 107.00 321.00 750.00
2-Daily strip-r (scarce) 100.00 300.00 700.00
NOTE: *Ties with Henry & Little Annie Rooney (David McKay) as the last of the 10x10" size books.*

PORE LI'L MOSE (N)
New York Herald Publ. by Grand Union Tea
Cupples & Leon Co.: 1902 (10-1/2x15", 78 pgs., color)
nn - By R. F. Outcault; Earliest known C&L comic book (scarce in high grade - very high demand) 1500.00 5250.00 -
NOTE: *Black Americana one page newspaper strips; falls in between Yellow Kid & Buster Brown. Complete copies have become scarce. Some have cut this book apart thinking that reselling individual pages will bring them more money.*

PRETTY PICTURES (M)
Farrar & Rinehart: 1931 (12 x 8-7/8", 104 pgs, color hardcover w/dust jacket, B&W; reprints from New Yorker, Judge, Life, Collier's Weekly)
nn - By Otto Soglow (contains "The Little King") 33.00 134.00 235.00

PUCK - to be indexed in next year's Guide

QUAINT OLD NEW ENGLAND (S)
Triton Syndicate: 1936 (5-1/4x6-1/4", 100 pgs, soft-c squarebound, B&W)
nn - By Jack Withycomb 36.00 144.00 250.00
NOTE: *Comics about weird doings in Old New England.*

RED CARTOONS (S)
Daily Worker Publishing Company: 1926 (12 x 9", 68 pgs,cardboard cover, B&W)
nn - By Various (scarce) 40.00 160.00 280.00
NOTE: *Reprint of American Communist Party editorial cartoons, from The Daily Worker, The Workers Monthly, and the Liberator. Art by Fred Ellis, William Gropper, Clive Weed, Art Young.*

REG'LAR FELLERS (See All-American Comics, Jimmie Dugan & The..., Popular Comics & Treasure Box of Famous Comics) (N)
Cupples & Leon Co./MS Publishing Co.: 1921-1929
1 (1921)-52 pgs. B&W dailies (Cupples & Leon, 10x10") 43.00 171.00 300.00
1925, 48 pgs. B&W dailies (MS Publ.) 39.00 157.00 275.00
Hardcover (1929, 8-3/4x7-1/2"; 96 pgs.)-B&W-r 54.00 214.00 375.00

REG'LAR FELLERS STORY PAINT BOOK
Whitman, Racine, Wisc.: 1932 (8-3/4x12-1/8", 132 pgs, red soft-c)
By Gene Byrnes 25.00 75.00 150.00

RIPLEY (See Believe It Or Not)

ROGER BEAN, R. G. (Regular Guy) (N)
The Indiana News Co, Distributers.: 1915 - No. 2, 1915 (5-3/8x17", 68 pgs., B&W, hardcovers); #3-#5 published by **Chas. B. Jackson:** 1916-1919
(No. 1 2 4 & 5 bound on side, No. 3 bound at top)
1-By Chas B. Jackson (68pgs.)(Scarce) 60.00 210.00 360.00
2- 5-5/8x17-1/8", 66 pgs (says 1913 inside - an obvious printing error) (red or green binding) 60.00 210.00 360.00
3-Along the Firing Line... (1916; 68 pgs, 6x17") 60.00 210.00 360.00
4-Into the Trenches and Out Again with... (1917, 68 pgs) 60.00 210.00 360.00
5 ...And The Reconstruction Period (1919, 5-3/8x15-1/2", 84 pgs) (Scarce) (has $1 printed on cover) 60.00 210.00 360.00
Baby Grand Editions 1-5 (10x10", cardboard-c) 60.00 210.00 360.00
NOTE: *No. 2 of the Twin Baby Grands (nd) 8-1/4x10-7/8", 52 pgs. Cardboard cover. B&W strip reprints. Cover also says "Politics Pickles People Police."*

ROGER BEAN PHILOSOPHER
Schnull & Co: 1917 (5-1/2x17", 36 pgs., B&W, brown & black paper-c, square binding)
nn - By Chic Jackson ??? ??? ???

ROUND THE WORLD WITH THE DOO-DADS (see Doings of the Doo-Dads, Doo Dads)
Universal Feature And Specialty Co, Chicago: 1922 (12x10-1/2", 52 pgs, B&W, red & light blue-c, square binding)
nn - By Arch Dale newspaper strip-r 43.00 173.00 300.00
NOTE: *Intermixed single panel and sequential comic strips with scenes from Scotland, Ireland, England, Holland, Italy, Spain, Egypt, Africa, and Lions & Elephants along the Nile River, China, Australia & back home.*

RUBAIYKT OF THE EGG
The John C Winston Co, Philadelphia: 1905 (7x5/12", 64 pgs, purple-c, B&W)
nn - By Clare Victor Dwiggins 20.00 60.00 120.00
NOTE: *Book is printed & cut into the shape of an egg.*

RULING CLAWSS, THE (N,S)
The Daily Worker: 1935 (192 pgs, 10-1/4 x 7-3/8", hard-c, B&W)
nn - By Redfield 60.00 240.00 -
NOTE: *Reprints cartoons from the American Communist Party newspaper The Daily Worker.*

Sam And His Laugh by Swinnerton
1906 © Frederick A. Stokes

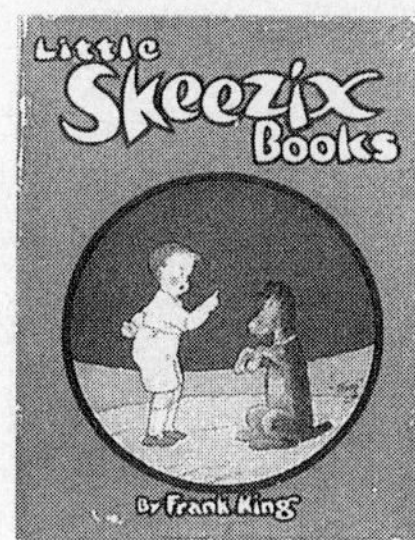

Little Skeezix Books by Frank King
1929 © Reilly & Lee

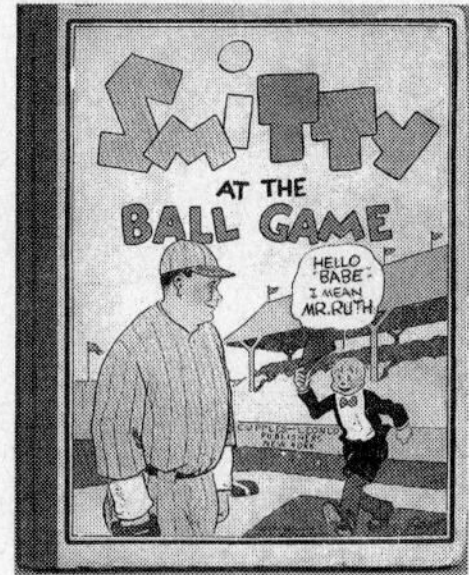

Smitty #2 By Walter Berndt
1929 © Cupples & Leon

GD2.0 FN6.0 VF8.0

SAGARA'S ENGLISH CARTOONS AND CARTOON STORIES (N)
Bunkosha, Tokyo: nd (c1925) (6-5/8" x 4-1/4", 272 pgs, hard-c, B&W)

nn- (Scarce) ??? ??? ???
NOTE: *Published in Tokyo, Japan, with all strips in both English and Japanese, to facilitate learning English. Majority of book is Bringing Up Father by George McManus. Also contains Japanese strip Father Takes it Easy, by T. Sagara, reprinted from the Kokusai News Agency.*

SAM AND HIS LAUGH (N)
Frederick A. Stokes: 1906 (10x15", cardboard-c, Sunday strip-r in color)

nn - By Jimmy Swinnerton (scarce) 250.00 750.00 1350.00
NOTE: *Strip ran July 24, 1904 into 1906; its ethnic humor might be considered racist by today's standards.*

SCHOOL DAYS (N)
Harper & Bros.: 1919 (9x8", 104 pgs.)

nn - By Clare Victor Dwiggins 42.00 144.00 250.00

SEAMAN SI - A Book of Cartoons About the Funniest "Gob" in the Navy (N)
Pierce Publishing Co.: 1916 (4x8-1/2, 200 pgs, hardcover, B&W); 1918 (4-1/8x8-1/4, 104 pgs, hardcover, B&W)

nn - By Perce Pearce (1916) 43.00 150.00 260.00
nn - 1918 - (Reilly & Britton Co.) 26.00 90.00 156.00
NOTE: *There exists two different covers for the 1918 reprints. The earlier edition was self published by the artist. The newspaper strip is sometimes also known as "The American Sailor."*

SECRET AGENT X-9 (N)
David McKay Pbll.: 1934 (Book 1: 84 pgs; Book 2: 124 pgs.) (8x7-1/2")

Book 1-Contains reprints of the first 13 weeks of the strip by Dashiell Hammett & Alex Raymond, complete except for 2 dailies 83.00 250.00 575.00
Book 2-Contains reprints immediately following contents of Book 1, for 20 weeks by Dashiell Hammett & Alex Raymond; complete except for two dailies. 83.00 250.00 575.00
NOTE: *Raymond misdated the last 5 strips from 6/34, and while the dating sequence is confusing, the continuity is correct.*

SILK HAT HARRY'S DIVORCE SUIT (N)
M. A. Donoghue & Co.: 1912 (5-3/4x15-1/2", B&W)

nn - Newspaper-r by Tad (Thomas A. Dorgan) 33.00 117.00 200.00

SINBAD A DOG'S LIFE (M)
Coward - McCann, Inc.: 1930 (11x 8-3/4", 104 pgs., single-sided, illustrated hard-c, B&W

nn - By Edwina 11.00 33.00 100.00
Sinbad...Again (1932, 10-15/16x 8-9/16", 104 pgs.) 11.00 33.00 100.00
NOTE: *Wordless comic strips from LIFE.*

SIS HOPKINS OWN BOOK AND MAGAZINE OF FUN
Leslie-Judge Co.: 1899-July 1911 (36 pgs, color-c, B&W) (merged into Judge's Library, later titled Film Fun)

any issue - By various 11.00 33.00 100.00
NOTE: *Zim, Flagg, Young, Newell, Adams, etc.*

SKEEZIX (Also see Gasoline Alley & Little Skeezix Books listed below) (I)
Reilly & Lee Co.: 1925 - 1928 (Strip-r, soft covers) (pictures & text)

...and Uncle Walt (1924)-Origin 26.00 104.00 180.00
...and Pal (1925) 21.00 84.00 150.00
...at the Circus (1926) 21.00 84.00 150.00
...& Uncle Walt (1927) (does this actually exist?) - - -
...Out West (1928) 21.00 84.00 150.00
Hardback Editions... 34.00 136.00 235.00

SKEEZIX BOOKS, LITTLE (Also see Skeezix, Gasoline Alley) (G)
Reilly & Lee Co.: No date (1928, 1929) (Boxed set of three Skeezix books)

nn - Box with 3 issues of Skeezix. Skeezix & Pal, Skeezix at the Circus, Skeezix & Uncle Walt known. 1928 Set... 60.00 180.00 360.00
nn - Box with 4 issues of (3) above Skeezix plus "Out West" 80.00 330.00 550.00

SKEEZIX COLOR BOOK (N)
McLaughlin Bros. Inc, Springfield, Mass: 1929 (9-1/2x10-1/4", 28 pgs, one third in full color, rest in B&W)

2023 - By Frank King; strip-r to color 20.00 75.00 135.00

SKIPPY (see also Life Presents Skippy, Always Belittlin', That Rookie From 13th Squad)
No publisher listed: Circa 1920s (10x8", 16 pgs., color/B&W cartoons)

nn - By Percy Crosby 20.00 84.00 150.00

SKIPPY, LIFE PRESENTS (M)
Life Publishing Company & Henry Holt, NY: nd 1924 (134 pgs, 10-13/16x8-3/4", color hard-c, B&W

nn - By Percy L Crosby ??? ??? ???
NOTE: *Many sequential & single panel reprints from Skippy's earliest appearances in Life Magazine.*

SKIPPY
Greenberg, Publisher, Inc, NY: 1925. (11-14x8-5/8, 72 pgs, hard-c, B&W and color

nn - By Percy L. Crosby ??? ??? ???
NOTE: *Some but not all of these comics were also in Life Presents Skippy; issued with dust wrapper.*

SKIPPY AND OTHER HUMOR

GD2.0 FN6.0 VF8.0

Greenberg: Publisher, NY: 1929 (11-1/4x8-1/2",72 pgs,tan hard-c, B&W and color)

nn - By Percy L. Crosby 50.00 175.00 300.00
NOTE: *Came with a dust jacket.*

SKIPPY (I)
Grossett & Dunlap: 1929 (7-3/8x6, 370 pgs, hardcover text with some art)

nn - By Percy Crosby (issued with a dust jacket) 21.00 84.00 150.00
NOTE: *This is worth very little without the dust wrapper; very common without athe dust jacket.*

SKIPPY
Greenberg Press: 1930 (soft cover, ca. 16 pp.,

nn - By Percy Crosby (scarce) 50.00 175.00 300.00
NOTE: *Reprints from LIFE cartoons, color, b/w. Crosby told Greenberg to withdraw from the market as it cheapened the hard cover prior editions. Greenberg then stopped publishing per agreement, and sent Crosby all the copper & zinc bookplates, which were in Crosby estate until 1996.*

SKIPPY CRAYON AND COLORING BOOK (N)
McLoughlin Bros, Inc., Springfield, MA: 1931 (13x9-3/4", 28 pgs, color-c, color & B&W)

2050 - By Percy Crosby 28.00 84.00 195.00
NOTE: *This item says on the front cover: "Licensed by Percy Crosby" because he owned his creation. About half the pages have one panel pre-printed in full color with same one b&w below for person to copy the colors.*

SKIPPY RAMBLES (I)
G.P. Putnam's Sons: 1932 (7 1/8 x 5 1/8, 202 pgs)

nn - By Percy Crosby 21.00 84.00 150.00
NOTE: *Issued with a dustjacket. Has Skippy plates by Crosby every 4 or 5 pages.*

SKUDDABUD STARRY STORY SERIES - FOLK FROM THE FUTURE (O,G)
no publisher listed: 1936 (9" x 11-7/8", 48 pgs, cardboard-c, B&W)

Book One (Rare) "Parachuting" 21.00 84.00 150.00
NOTE: *By Columba Krebs. Top half of each page is a continuing strip story, while bottom half are different stories, in prose, about the same characters -- a race of aliens who have migrated to Earth, from their dying world.*

S'MATTER POP? (N)
Saalfield Publ. Co.: 1917 (10x14", 44 pgs., B&W, cardboard-c,)

nn - By Charlie Payne; in full color; pages printed on one side 48.00 169.00 290.00

S'MATTER POP? (N) (25 ¢ cover price)
E.I. Company, New York: 1927 (8-15/16x7-1/8", 52 pgs, yellow soft-c perfect bound

nn - By C.M. Payne (scarce) 24.00 84.00 145.00
NOTE: *First comic book published by Hugo Gernsback, noted for inventing Amazing Stories among other memorable science fiction pulps. The World Science Fiction Convention Award, The Hugo, is named for him.*

SMITTY (See Treasure Box of Famous Comics) (N)
Cupples & Leon Co.: 1928 - 1933 (9x7", 96 pgs., B&W strip-r, hardcover)

1928-(96 pgs. 7x8-3/4") By Walter Berndt 41.00 166.00 290.00
1929-At the Ball Game (Babe Ruth on cover) 57.00 229.00 400.00
1930-The Flying Office Boy, 1931-The Jockey, 1932-In the North Woods each... 31.00 126.00 220.00
1933-At Military School 31.00 126.00 220.00
NOTE: *Each hardbound was published with a dust jacket; worth 50% more with dust jacket. The 1923 edition is very popular with baseball collectors. Strip debuted Nov 27, 1922.*

SMOKEY STOVER (See Dan Dunn & King of the Royal Mounted) (N)
Whitman Publishing: 1937 (5 1/2 x 7 1/4", 68pgs., color cardboard-c, B&W)

1010 36.00 144.00 250.00

SOCIAL HELL, THE (O)
Rich Hill: 1902

nn - By Ryan Walker 20.00 70.00 120.00
NOTE: *"The conditions of workers and the corruption of a political system beholden to corporate interests have been a major focus of human rights concerns since the 19th century. This early graphic novel depicts the social evils of unreformed capitalism. Ryan Walker was a syndicate cartoonist for many mainstream newspapers as well as for the communist Daily Worker." This description comes from <http://www.lib.uconn.edu/DoddCenter/ascexh3.html>, where you can find also a reproduction of the cover. I add that Ryan Walker was the editor of "The Saint Louis Republic" comic section since its inception in 1897; the supplement published "Alma and Oliver", George McManus's first series.*

SPORT AND THE KID (see The Umbrella Man) (N)
Lowman & Hanford Co.: 1913 (6-1/4x6-5/8",114 pgs, hardcover, B&W&orange)

nn - By J.R. "Dok" Hager 20.00 70.00 120.00

STORY OF CONNECTICUT (N)
The Hartford Times: Vol.1 1935 - Vol.3 1936 (10-1/2" x 7-3/8",304 pgs,color hard-c, B&W)

Vol.1 - 3 20.00 70.00 120.00
NOTE: *Collects a newspaper strip on Connecticut State history, which ran in the Hartford Times. Strip is in a similar format to "Texas History Movies". Also published in a plain, blue hardcover.*

STORY OF JAPAN IN CHINA, THE (N,S)
Trans-Pacific News Service, NYC: Vol. 3, No.1 March 10, 1938 (9" x 6", 36 pgs, construction paper-c, B&W)

Vol.3 No.1 21.00 64.00 150.00
NOTE: *Part of the "China Reference Series" of booklets, detailing the Japanese occupation and brutalization of China. Consists entirely of cartoons. The other booklets in the series have no cartoons. Art by: Ding, Fitzpatrick, Herblock, Herman, Rollin Kirby, Knox, Low, Manning, Orr, Shoemaker, Talburt.*

STRANGE AS IT SEEMS (S)

Thimble Theater #1 by E.C. Segar
1931 © Sonnet Publishing Co.

Tillie the Toiler #7 by Russ Westover
1932 © Cupples & Leon

Ton Sawyer and Huck Finn
1925 © Stoll & Edwards Co.

GD2.0 FN6.0 VF8.0

Blue-Star Publishing Co.: 1932 (64 pgs., B&W, square binding)

1-Newspaper-r 32.00 128.00 225.00

NOTE: *Published with and without No. 1 and price on cover.*

Ex-Lax giveaway (1936, B&W, 24 pgs., 5x7") - McNaught Synd. 13.00 52.00 90.00

SULLIVANT'S ABC ZOO (I)
The Old Wine Press: 1946 (11-3/4x9-3/8", hardcover)

nn - By T.S. Sullivant ??? ??? ???

NOTE: *Reprints Mitchell & Miller material 1895-1898 and Life Publishing 1898-1926.*

TAILSPIN TOMMY STORY & PICTURE BOOK (N)
McLoughlin Bros.: No. 266, 1931? (nd) (10x10-1/2", color strip-r)

266 - By Forrest 43.00 172.00 300.00

TAILSPIN TOMMY (Also see Famous Feature Stories & The Funnies)(N)
Cupples & Leon Co.: 1932 (100 pgs., hard-c)

nn - (Scarce)-B&W strip reprints from 1930 by Hal Forrest & Glenn Claffin 50.00 150.00 300.00

TALES OF DEMON DICK AND BUNKER BILL (O)
Whitman Publishing Co.: 1934 (5-1/4x10-1/2", 80 pgs, color hardcover, B&W)

793 - By Spencer 33.00 100.00 225.00

TARZAN BOOK (The Illustrated...) (N)
Grosset & Dunlap: 1929 (9x7", 80 pgs.)

1(Rare)-Contains 1st B&W Tarzan newspaper comics from 1929. By Hal Foster Cloth reinforced spine & dust jacket (50¢); Foster-c
- With dust jacket... 86.00 344.00 600.00
- Without dust jacket... 43.00 172.00 300.00

2nd Printing(1934, 25¢, 76 pgs.)-4 Foster pgs. dropped; paper spine, circle in lower right cover with 25¢ price. The 25¢ is barely visible on some copies 34.00 136.00 240.00

1967-House of Greystoke reprint-7x10", using the complete 300 illustrations/text from the 1929 edition minus the original indicia, foreword, etc. Initial version bound in gold paper & sold for $5.00. Officially titled **Burroughs Bibliophile #2.** A very few additional copies were bound in heavier blue paper.
- Gold binding... 2.25 6.75 18.00
- Blue binding... 2.50 7.50 24.00

TARZAN OF THE APES TO COLOR (N)
Saalfield Publishing Co.: No. 988, 1933 (15-1/4x10-3/4", 24 pgs)
(Coloring book)

988-(Very Rare)-Contains 1929 daily reprints with some new art by Hal Foster. Two panels blown up large on each page with one at the top of opposing pages on every other double-page spread. Believed to be the only time these panels appeared in color. Most color panels are reproduced a second time in B&W to be colored 271.00 1084.00 1900.00

TARZAN OF THE APES The Big Little Cartoon Book (N)
Whitman Publishing Company: 1933 (4-1/2x3 5/8", 320 pgs, color-c, B&W)

744 - By Hal Foster (comics on every page) 36.00 144.00 250.00

TECK HASKINS AT OHIO STATE (S)
Lea-Mar Press: 1908 (7-1/4x5-3/8", 84 pgs, B&W hardcover)

nn - By W.A. Ireland; football cartoons-r from Columbus Ohio Evening Dispatch 28.00 99.00 170.00

NOTE: *Small blue & white patch of cover art pasted atop a color cloth quilt patter; pasted patch can easily peel off some copies.*

TECK 1909 (S)
Lea-Mar Press: 1909 (8-5/8 x 8-1/8", 124 pgs., B&W hardcover, 25¢)

nn - By W.A. Ireland; Ohio State University baseball cartoons-r from Columbus Evening Dispatch 28.00 99.00 170.00

TEDDY BEAR BOOKS, THE (M) (see also LITTLE JOHNNY AND THE TEDDY BEARS)
Reilly & Britton Co., Chicago: 1907 (7-1/16" x 5-3/8", 24 pgs, hard-c, color

	GD2.0	FN6.0	VF8.0
The Teddy Bears Come to Life	20.00	60.00	120.00
The Teddy Bears at the Circus	20.00	60.00	120.00
The Teddy Bears in a Smashup	20.00	60.00	120.00
The Teddy Bears on a Lark	20.00	60.00	120.00
The Teddy Bears on a Toboggan	20.00	60.00	120.00
The Teddy Bears at School	20.00	60.00	120.00
The Teddy Bears Go Fishing	20.00	60.00	120.00
The Teddy Bears in Hot Water	20.00	60.00	120.00

NOTE: *Books are all unnumbered. C & A by J.R. Bray; s-Robert D. Towne. Reprints "Little Johnny & the Teddy Bears" strips, from Judge Magazine. Similar in format to the Buster Brown Nuggets series. All eight books debuted simultaneously.*

TEDDY BEARS IN FUN AND FROLIC (M) (see LITTLE JOHNNY & THE TEDDY BEARS)
Reilly & Britton Co., Chicago: 1908 (8-3/4" x 8-3/4", 50 pgs, cardboard-c, color)

nn - (Rare) by J.R. Bray-a; Robert D. Towne-s 100.00 400.00 700.00

NOTE: *Reprints "Little Johnny & the Teddy Bears" strips, from Judge Magazine. Unknown if there were any other "Teddy Bear" titles published in this format.*

THE TEENIE WEENIES
Reilly & Britton, Chicago: 1916 (16-3/8x10-1/2", 52 pgs, cardboard-c, full color)

nn - By Wm. Donahey (Chicago Tribune-r) 100.00 400.00 700.00

TEXAS HISTORY MOVIES (N)
Various editions, 1928 to 1986 (B&W)

Book I -1928 Southwest Press (7-1/4 x 5-3/8, 56 pgs, cardboard cover) for the Magnolia Petroleum Company 30.00 90.00 180.00

nn - 1928 Southwest Press (12-3/8 x 9-1/4, 232 pgs, hardcover) 50.00 150.00 300.00

nn - 1935 Magnolia Petroleum Company (6 x 9, 132 pgs, paper cover) 20.00 60.00 120.00

NOTE: *Exists with either Wagon Train or Texas Flag & Lafitte/pirate covers.*

nn - 1943 Magnolia Petroleum Company (132 pgs, paper cover) 15.00 45.00 90.00

nn - 1963 Graphic Ideas Inc (11 x 8-1/2, softcover) 10.00 30.00 60.00

NOTE: *Reprints daily newspaper strips from the Dallas News, on Texas history. 1935 editions onward distributed within the Texas Public School System. Prior to that they appear to be giveaway comic books for the Magnolia Petroleum Company. There are many more editions than the ones pointed out above.*

THAT ROOKIE FROM THE 13TH SQUAD (N) (also Between Shots; Always Belittlin'; Skippy)
Harper & Brothers Publishers: Feb. 1918 (8x9-1/4", 72 pgs, hardcover, B&W)

nn - By Lieut. P(ercy) L. Crosby 58.00 204.00 350.00

NOTE: *Strip began in 1917 at an Army base during basic training.*

THAT SON-IN-LAW OF PA'S! (N)
Newspaper Feature Service: 1914 (2-1/2 by 3", color)

nn ??? ??? ???

NOTE: *Single sheet printed in full color on both sides, unfolds to show 12 panel story. Imprinted on back for THE LESTER SHOE STORE.*

THIMBLE THEATRE STARRING POPEYE (See also Popeye) (N)
Sonnet Publishing Co.: 1931 - No. 2, 1932 (25¢, B&W, 52 pgs.)(Rare)

1-Daily strip serial-r in both by Segar 157.00 628.00 1100.00
2 136.00 544.00 950.00

NOTE: *The very first Popeye reprint book. The first Thimble Theatre Sunday page appeared Dec 19, 1919. Popeye first entered Thimble Theatre on Jan 17, 1929.*

THREE FUN MAKERS, THE (N)
Stokes and Company: 1908 (10x15", 64 pgs., color) (1904-06 Sunday strip-r)

nn - Maud, Katzenjammer Kids, Happy Hooligan 314.00 1100.00 -

NOTE: *This is the first comic book to compile more than one newspaper strip together.*

TIGERS (Also see On and Off Mount Ararat) (N)
Hearst's New York American & Journal: 1902, 86 pgs. 10x15-1/4"

nn - Funny animal strip-r by Jimmy Swinnerton 286.00 1000.00 -

NOTE: *The strip began as The Journal Tigers in The New York Journal Dec 12, 1897-1902.*

TILLIE THE TOILER (N)
Cupples & Leon Co.: 1925 - No. 8, 1933 (52 pgs., B&W, daily strip-r)

nn (#1) By Russ Westover 54.00 216.00 375.00
2-8 50.00 175.00 300.00

NOTE: *First newspaper strip appearance was in January, 1921.*

TILLIE THE TOILER MAGIC DRAWING AND COLORING BOOK
Sam L Gabriel Sons And Company: 1931 (8-1/2 x 12", 36 pages, stiff-c)

838-By Russ Westover 39.00 156.00 275.00

TIMID SOUL, THE (N)
Simon & Schuster: 1931 (12-1/4x9", 136 pgs, B&W hardcover, dust jacket?)

nn - By H. T. Webster (newspaper strip-r) 40.00 120.00 240.00

TIM McCOY, POLICE CAR 17 (O)
Whitman Publishing Co.: 1934 (14-3/4x11", 32 pgs, stiff color covers)

674-1933 movie illustrated; first movie adaptation in comic books original material? 50.00 200.00 350.00

TOAST BOOK
John C. Winston Co: 1905 (7-1/4 x 6,104 pgs, skull-shaped book, feltcover, B&W)

nn - By Clare Dwiggins 50.00 175.00 300.00

NOTE: *Cartoon illustrations accompanying toasts/poems, most involving alcohol.*

TOM SAWYER & HUCK FINN (N)
Stoll & Edwards Co.:1925 (10x10-3/4", 52 pgs, stiff covers)

nn - By "Dwig" Dwiggins; 1923, 1924-r color Sunday strips 39.00 156.00 275.00

NOTE: *By Permission of the Estate of Samuel L. Clemons and the Mark Twain Company.*

TOONERVILLE TROLLEY AND OTHER CARTOONS (N) (See Cartoons by Fontaine Fox)
Cupples & Leon Co.: 1921 (10 x10", 52 pgs., B&W, daily strip-r)

1 - By Fontaine Fox 68.00 272.00 475.00

TRAINING FOR THE TRENCHES (M)
Palmer Publishing Company: 1917 (5-3/8 x 7", 20 pgs., paper-c, 10¢)

nn - By Lieut. Alban B. Butler, Jr. 21.00 84.00 150.00

NOTE: *Subtitle: "A book of humorous cartoons on a serious subject." Single-panels about military training.*

TREASURE BOX OF FAMOUS COMICS (N) (see Wonder Chest of Famous Comics)
Cupples & Leon Co.: 1934 8-1/2x(6-7/8", 36 pgs, soft covers) (Boxed set of 5 books)

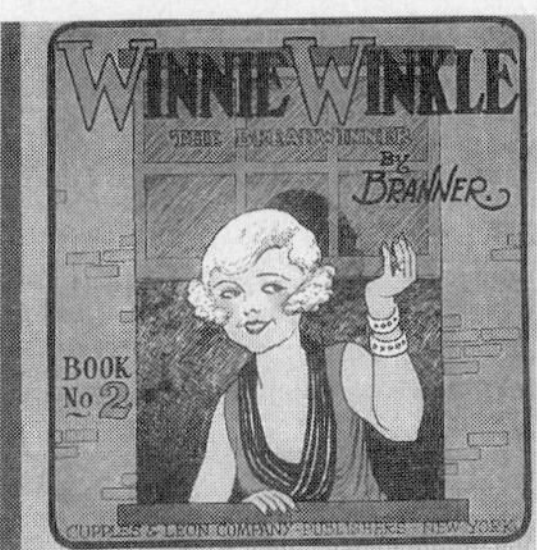

Winnie Winkle #2 by Branner
1931 © Cupples & Leon, NY

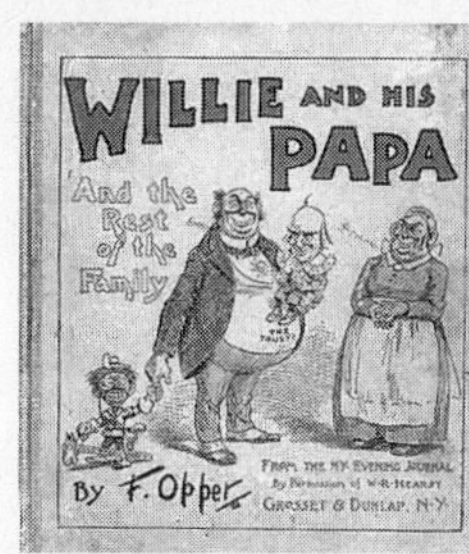

Willie and His Papa & the Rest of the Family by Opper
1901 © Grossett & Dunlap

The Yellow Kid #4 cover by Outcault
1897 © Howard Ainslee & Co.

	GD2.0	FN6.0	VF8.0
Little Orphan Annie (1926)	21.00	84.00	150.00
Reg'lar Fellers (1928)	19.00	76.00	130.00
Smitty (1928)	19.00	76.00	130.00
Harold Teen (1931)	19.00	76.00	130.00
How Dick Tracy & Dick Tracy Jr. Caught The Racketeers (1933)	26.00	104.00	185.00
Softcover set of five books in box	160.00	640.00	1125.00
Box only	57.00	228.00	400.00

NOTE: *Dates shown are copyright dates; all books actually came out in 1934 or later. The softcovers are abbreviated versions of the hardcover editions listed under each character.*

T.R. IN CARTOONS (N)
A.C. McClurg & Co., Chicago: June 13, 1910 (10-5/8" x 8", 104? pgs, paper-c, B&W)
nn - By McCutcheon ??? ??? ???
NOTE: *Strips and cartoons about Teddy Roosevelt, all by McCutcheon.*

TRUTH (See Victorian section for earlier issues)
Truth Company, NY: 1886-1906? (13-11/16x10-5/16", 16 pgs, process color-c & center-folds, rest B&W)
1900-1906 issues 10.00 20.00 50.00

TRUTH SAVE IT FROM ABUSE & OVERWORK BEING THE EPISODE OF THE HIRED HAND & MRS. STIX PLASTER, CONCERTIST (N)
Radio Truth Society of WBAP: no date, 1924 (6-3/8 x 4-7/8, 40 pgs, paper cover, B&W)
nn - By V.T. Hamlin (Very Rare) 100.00 400.00 700.00
NOTE: *Radio station WBAP giveaway reprints strips from the Ft. Worth Texas Star-Telegram set at local radio station. 1st collected work by V.T. Hamlin, pre-Alley Oop.*

TWENTY FIVE YEARS AGO (see At The Bottom Of The Ladder) (M,S)
Coward-McCann: 1931 (5-3/4x8-1/4, 328 pgs, hardcover, B&W)
nn - By Camillus Kessler 32.00 128.00 225.00
NOTE: *Multi-image panel cartoons showing historical events for dates during the year.*

UMBRELLA MAN, THE (N) (See Sport And The Kid)
Lowman & Hanford Co.: 1911 (8-7/8x5-1/8",112 pgs, paperback, B&W&orange)
nn - By J.R. "Dok" Hager (Seattle Times-r) 20.00 70.00 120.00

UNCLE REMUS AND BRER RABBIT (N)
Frederick A. Stokes Co.: 1907 (64 pgs, hardbound, color)
nn - By Joel C Harris & J.M. Conde 50.00 175.00 300.00

UPSIDE DOWNS OF LITTLE LADY LOVEKINS AND OLD MAN MUFFAROO
New York Herald: 1905 (?) (N)
nn - By Gustav Verbeck 100.00 350.00 650.00

VAUDEVILLES AND OTHER THINGS (N)
Isaac H. Blandiard Co.: 1900 (13x10-1/2", 22 pgs., color) plus two reprints
nn - By Bunny (Scarce) 229.00 800.00 -
nn - 2nd print "By the Creator of Foxy Grandpa" on-c but only has copyright info of 1900 (10-1/2x15 1/2, 28 pgs, color) 171.00 600.00
nn - 3rd print. "By the creator of Foxy Grandpa" on-c; has both 1900 and 1901 copyright info (11x13") 171.00 600.00 -

WALLY - HIS CARTOONS OF THE A.E.F. (N)
Stars & Stripes: 1917 (96 and 108 pgs, B&W)
nn - By Abian A "Wally" Wallgren (7x18; 96 pgs) 20.00 70.00 120.00
nn - another edition (108 pgs, 7x17-1/2) 20.00 70.00 120.00
NOTE: *World War One cartoons reprints from Stars & Stripes; sold to U.S. servicemen with profits to go to French War Orphans Fund. various editions from 1917-1920; there might be more than what we list here.*

WAR CARTOONS (S)
Dallas News: 1918 (11x9", 112 pgs, hardcover, B&W)
nn - By John Knott (WWOne cartoons) 20.00 70.00 120.00

WAR CARTOONS FROM THE CHICAGO DAILY NEWS (N,S)
Chicago Daily News: 1914 (10 cents, 7-3/4x10-3/4", 68 pgs, paper-c, B&W)
nn - By L.D. Bradley 20.00 70.00 120.00

WEBER & FIELD'S FUNNYISMS (S,M,O)
Arkell Comoany, NY: 1904 (10-7/8x8", 112 pgs, color-c, B&W)
1 - By various (later issues?) 20.00 70.00 120.00
NOTE: *Contains some sequential & many single panel strips by Outcault, George Luks, CA David, Houston, L Smith, Hy Mayer, Verbeck, Woolf, Sydney Adams, Frank "Chip" Bellew, Eugene "ZIM" Zimmerman, Phil May, FT Richards, Billy Marriner, Grosvenor and many others.*

WE'RE NOT HEROES (O,S)
E.C. Wells and J.W. Moss: 1933 (8-11/16" x 5-7/8", 52 pgs, red & black paper-c, B&W interior)
nn - By Eddie Wells 10.00 30.00 60.00
NOTE: *Amateurish cartoons about World War I vets in the Walter Reed Veteran's Hospital.*

WHEN A FELLER NEEDS A FRIEND (S)
P. F. Volland & Co.: 1914 (11-11/16x8-7/8)
nn - By Clare Briggs 37.00 131.00 225.00
NOTE: *Originally came in box with Briggs art (box is Rare - worth more with box. There are also numerous more modern reprints)*

WILD PILGRIMAGE (O)
Harrison Smith & Robert Haas: 1932 (9-7/8x7", 210 pgs, B&W hardcover w/dust jacket)
(original wordless graphic novel in woodcuts)
nn - By Lynd Ward 50.00 175.00 300.00

WILLIE AND HIS PAPA AND THE REST OF THE FAMILY (I)
Grossett & Dunlap: 1901 (9-1/2x8", 200 pgs, hardcover from N.Y. Evening Journal by Permission of W. R. Hearst) (pictures & text)
nn - By Frederick Opper 50.00 200.00 340.00
NOTE: *Political satire series of single panel cartoons, involving whiny child Willie (President William McKinley), his rambunctious and uncontrollable cousin Teddy (Vice President Roosevelt), and Willie's Papa (trusts/monopolies) and their Maid (Senator) Hanna.*

WILLIE GREEN COMICS, THE (N) (see Adventures of Willie Green)
Frank M. Acton Co./Harris Brown: 1915 (8x15, 36 pgs); 1921 (6x10-1/8", 52 pgs, color paper cover, B&W interior, 25¢)
Book No. 1 By Harris Brown 45.00 158.00 270.00
Book 2 (#2 sold via mail order directly from the artist)(very rare) 45.00 172.00 300.00
NOTE: *Book No. 1 possible reprint of Adv. of Willie Green; definitely two different editions.*

WILLIE WESTINGHOUSE EDISON SMITH THE BOY INVENTOR (N)
William A. Stokes Co.: 1906 (10x16", 36 pgs. in color)
nn - By Frank Crane (Scarce) 214.00 750.00 -
NOTE: *Comic strip began May 27, 1900 and ran thru 1914. Parody of inventors Westinghouse and Edison.*

WINNIE WINKLE (N)
Cupples & Leon Co.: 1930 - No. 4, 1933 (52 pgs., B&W daily strip-r)
1 43.00 172.00 300.00
2-4 29.00 116.00 200.00
NOTE: *Strip began as a daily Sept 20, 1920.*

WISDOM OF CHING CHOW, THE (see also The Gumps)
R. J. Jefferson Printing Co.: 1928 (4x3", 100 pgs, red & B&W cardboard cover) (newspaper strip-r The Chicago Tribune)
nn - By Sidney Smith (scarce) 20.00 80.00 120.00

WONDER CHEST OF FAMOUS COMICS (N) see Treasure Chest of Famous Comics)
Cupples & Leon Co.: 1935? 8-1/2x(6-7/8", 36 pgs, soft covers) (Boxed set of 5 books)

	GD2.0	FN6.0	VF8.0
Little Orphan Annie #2 (1927) (Haunted House)	21.00	84.00	130.00
Little Orphan Annie #3 (1928) (in the Circus)	19.00	76.00	130.00
Smitty #2 (1929) (Babe Ruth app.)	19.00	76.00	130.00
Dolly Dimples and Bobby Bounce (1933) by Grace Drayton	19.00	76.00	130.00
How Dick Tracy & Dick Tracy Jr. Caught The Racketeers (1933)	26.00	104.00	185.00
Softcover set of five books in box	160.00	640.00	1125.00
Box only	57.00	228.00	400.00

NOTE: *Dates shown are original copyright dates of the first printings; all books actually came out in 1934 or later. The softcovers are extremely abbreviated versions of the hardcover editions listed under each character. It is suspected this new listing came out the Christmas season following the Teasure Chest of Famous Comics. which contains earlier editions of mainly the same poplulat titles.*

WORLD OF TROUBLE, A (S)
Minneapolis Journal: 1901 (10x8-3/4", 100 pgs, 40 pgs full color)
v3#1 - By Charles L. Bartholomew (editorial-r) 28.00 99.00 170.00

WORLD OVER, THE (I)
G. W. Dillingham Company, New York: 1897 (192 pgs, hardbound)
nn - By Joe Kerr; 80 illus by R.F. Outcault 200.00 700.00 ???

WRIGLEY'S "MOTHER GOOSE"
Wm. Wrigley Jr. Company, Chicago: 1915 (6" x 4", 28 pgs, full color)
nn 20.00 70.00 120.00
NOTE: *Promotional comics for Wrigley's gum. Introduces Wrigley's "Spearmen."*

THE WRIGLEY SPEARMEN AT WORK AND PLAY - BOOK No. 2
Wm. Wrigley Jr. Company, Chicago: 1915 (6" x 4", 24 pgs, full color)
nn 20.00 70.00 120.00
NOTE: *Promotional comics for Wrigley's gum.*

YELLOW KID, THE (Magazine)(I) (becomes **The Yellow Book** #10 on)
Howard Ainslee & Co., N.Y.: Mar. 20, 1897 - #9, July 17, 1897
(5¢, B&W w/color covers, 52p., stapled) (not a comic book)
1-R.F. Outcault Yellow kid on-c only #1-6. The same Yellow Kid color ad app. on back-c #1-6 (advertising the New York Sunday Journal) 857.00 3000.00 -
2-6 (#2 4/3/97, #5 5/22/97, #6, 6/5/97) 743.00 2600.00 -
7-9 (Yellow Kid not on-c) 121.00 425.00 -
NOTE: *Richard Outcault's Yellow Kid from the Hearst New York American represents the very first successful newspaper comic strip in America. Listed here due to historical importance.*

YELLOW KID IN MCFADDEN'S FLATS, THE (N)
G. W. Dillingham Co., New York: 1897 (50¢, 7-1/2x5-1/2", 196 pgs., B&W, squarebound)
nn - The first "comic" book featuring The Yellow Kid; E. W. Townsend narrative w/R. F. Outcault Sunday comic page art-r & some original drawings 5000.00 8700.00 ???

For a free, lively e-mail discussion group of Platinum Age comics collectors, fans, dealers, enthusiasts, and scholars you can join to look, listen, learn, and share by going to PlatinumAgeComics@Yahoogroups.com. Also go to The Grand Comics Database at www.comics.org. and www.bugpowder.com/andy/early for more resources always building. Any addititions or corrections to this section are always welcome.

The American Comic Book: 1929-Present

THE MODERN COMIC BOOKS SUPPLANT THE EARLIER FORMATS

by Robert L. Beerbohm & Richard D. Olson, PhD ©2004

(This article series was originally created by Robert Beerbohm and Richard Olson for OCBPG #27 1997 and is revised annually.)

Although somewhat similar in appearance to comic books of the Golden Age of the superhero, the varied formats that comic publishing pioneer Cupples & Leon popularized beginning in 1919 are quite different in appearance from today's comics. Even so, the books and those formats were consistently successful until the early 1930s, when they had to compete against The Great Depression; the Depression eventually won. One major reason for a format change was that at a cost of 25¢ per book for the 10" x 10" cardboard style and 60¢ for the 7" x 8 1/2" dustjacketed hardcovers, the price became increasingly prohibitive for most consumers already stifled by the crushed economy. As a result, all Cupples & Leon style books published between 1929-1935 are much rarer than their earlier counterparts because most Americans had little money to spend after paying for necessities like food and shelter.

By the early 1930s, the era of the Prestige Format black & white reprint comic book was over. In 1932-33 a lot of format variations arose, collecting such newspaper strips as **Bobby Thatcher, Bringing Up Father, Buck Rogers, Dick Tracy, Happy Hooligan, Joe Palooka, The Little King, Little Orphan Annie, Mickey Mouse, Moon Mullins, Mutt & Jeff, Smitty, Tailspin Tommy, Tarzan, Thimble Theater starring Popeye, Tillie the Toiler, Winnie Winkle,** and the **Highlights of History** series.

There had been Embee's **Comic Monthly**'s dozen issues in 1922, and several dozen of Dell & Eastern's **The Funnies** tabloid in 1929-30. It contained only original material and still failed.

It has been recently discovered that Eastern Color and Dell were also copartners in **The Funnies**. It is possible that Eastern came up with the idea and Delecorte agreed to publish it for general standalone distribution. Similar format Sunday sections of the same material have been discovered by comics historian Ken Barker to be published at the same time in the **Montreal Standard**, a Canadian newspaper; it appears to have been an effort to get a new comics syndicate off the ground. The effort was not too successful as **The Standard** dropped the sections after just a few months. Allan Holtz went through the **E&P** yearbooks and found that this section (presumably a preprint) was advertised from 1930-34 by Eastern Color Printing out of New York City. This is a rediscovery of important magnitude as it pushes back the time known for Eastern Color Printing Company and Dell Publishing Company to be partners by four years into late 1928. They had almost discovered the winning formula which has ruled the format of comic books in America for the last 70 years. Unfortunately, it would be another four years before they successfully figured it out.

The Funnies *#1, early 1929, Dell Publishing Company and Eastern Color. This was the very first original material newsstand comic book!*

With the 1933 newsstand appearance of Humor's **Detective Dan, Adventures of Detective Ace King, Bob Scully, Two Fisted Hick Detective**, and possibly the still unrediscovered but definitely advertised **Happy Mulligan**, these little understood original-material comic books were the direct inspiration for Jerry Siegel and Joe Shuster to transform their fanzine's evil character The Superman from **Science Fiction** #3 (January 1933) into a comic strip that would stand as a watershed heroic mark in American pop culture. The stage was set for a new frontier. With another format change including four colors, page counts beginning at 32 (soon hitting a whopping 68), and a hefty price reduction (starting for free as promotional premiums due to the nationwide numbing effects of worldwide deflation), the birthing pangs of the modern American comic book occurred in late 1932. Created out of desperation, to keep the printing presses rolling, the modern American comic book was born when a 45-year-old sales manager for Eastern Color Printing Company of New York reinvented the format from the failed tabloid **The Funnies**.

Harry I. Wildenberg's job was to come up with ideas that would sell color printing for Eastern, a company which also printed the comic sections for a score of newspapers along the eastern seaboard, including the **Boston Globe**, the **Brooklyn Times**, the **Providence Journal**, and the **Newark Ledger**. Downtime meant less take-home pay, so Wildenberg was always racking his brains for something to fit the color presses. He was fascinated by the miles of funny sheets which rolled off Eastern's presses each week, and he constantly sought new ways to exploit their commercial possibilities. If the funny papers were this popular, he reasoned, they should prove a good advertising medium. He decided to suggest a comics tabloid to a client.

Gulf Oil Company liked the idea and hired a few artists to create an original comic called **Gulf Comic Weekly**. The comic was dated April 1933 and was 10 1/2" x 15". It was the first comic to be advertised nationally on the radio beginning April 30th. Its first artists were Stan Schendel doing **The Uncovered Wagon**, Victor doing **Curly and the Kids**, and Svess on a strip named **Smileage**. All were full page, full color comic strips. Wildenberg promptly had Eastern print this four page comic, making it probably the first tabloid newsprint comic published for American distribution outside of a newspaper in the 20th Century. Wildenberg and Gulf were astonished when the tabloids were grabbed up as fast as Gulf service stations could offer them. Distribution shot up to 3,000,000 copies a week after Gulf changed the name to **Gulf Funny Weekly** with its 5th issue. The series remained a tabloid until early 1939 & ran for 422 issues until May 23, 1941.

Recent research has also turned up "new" rediscovered comics material from other oil companies from this same time span of 1933-34. Perhaps spurred by the runaway success of **Gulf Funny Weekly**, these other oil companies found they had to compete with licensed comic strip material of their own in order to remain profitable. The authors of this essay are actively soliciting help in uncovering more information regarding the following: There are at least 14 issues each of at least an A and a B series of a four page tabloid-size full color comics giveaway titled **Standard Oil Comics**, dating from 1933. The issues seen so far contain Fred Opper's **Si & Mirandi**, an older couple who interact with perennial favorites, **Happy Hooligan** & **Maud the Mule**, drawn by the grand old master himself, Frederick Opper, who had been a professional cartoonist for over 60 years by this time.

Other strips include **Pesty And His Pop** & **Smiling Slim** by Sid Hicks. Considering the concept of **Gulf Funny Weekly** has been well known for decades while **Standard Oil Comics** remains virtually unknown, our guess is **Gulf Comic Weekly** began first and ran many years longer than Rockefeller's version.

Beginning with the March-April 1934 issue of **Shell Globe** (V4 #2), characters from Bud Fisher (**Mutt & Jeff**) and Fontaine Fox (**Toonerville Folks**) were licensed to sell gas & oil for this company. 52,000 eight foot standees were made for Fisher's **Mutt and Jeff** and Fox's **Powerful Katrinka** and **The Skipper** for placement around 13,000 Shell gas stations. Augmenting them was an army of 250,000 miniature figures of the same characters. In addition, more than 1,000,000 play masks were given away to children along with more than 285,000 window stickers. If that wasn't enough, hundreds of thousands of 3x5 foot posters featuring these characters were released in conjunction with twenty-four sheet outdoor billboards. Radio announcements of this promotion began running April 7th, 1934. It is presently unknown if Shell had a comics tabloid created to give away to customers.

The idea for creating an actual comic book as we know it today, however, did not occur to Wildenberg until later in 1933, when he said he was idly folding a newspaper in halves, then in quarters. As he looked at the twice-folded paper, it occurred to him that it was a convenient book size (actually it was late stage "Dime Novel" size, which companies like Street & Smith were pumping out). The format had its heyday from the 1880s through the 1910s, having been invented by the firm of Beadle and Adam in 1860 in more of a digest format. According to a 1942 article by Max Gaines (née Ginzberg), another contributing factor in the development of the format was an

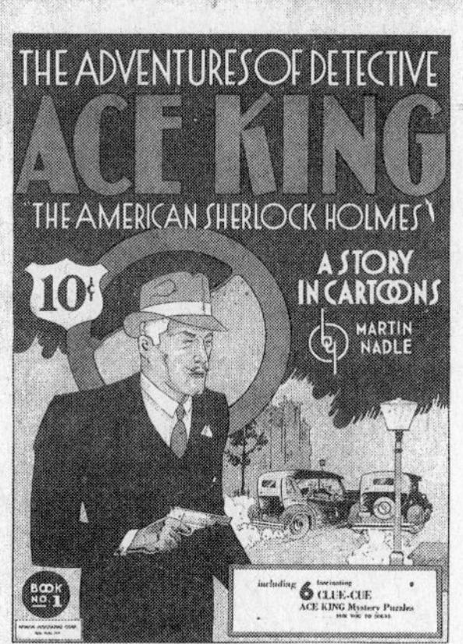

Detective Dan Secret Op. #48*, *Bob Scully The Two Fisted Hick Detective & The Adventures of Detective Ace King *, early 1933, Humor Publishing Co. Very rare from the 2nd original newsstand comic book publisher & the direct inspiration for Jerry Siegel & Joe Shuster's 1933 conversion of* ***The Superman*** *into a comic book due to a promise of publication. This earliest Superman was never published.*

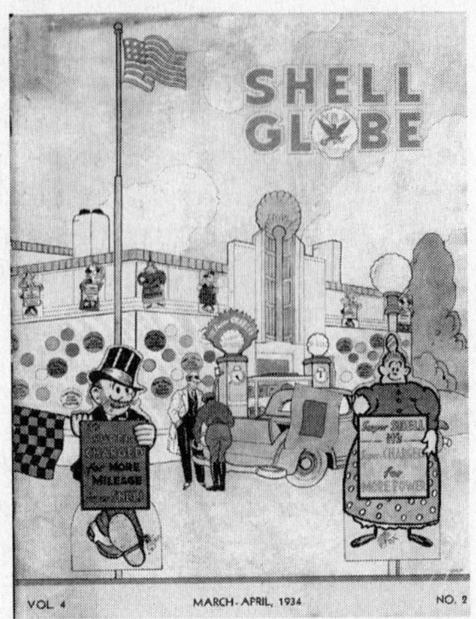

*Left, **Gulf Funny Weekly** #5, early 1933, Wildenberg's very first successful comics experiment. Middle, **Standard Oil Comics Weekly** #14, 1933. A recently discovered comics tabloid the same size as **Gulf Funny Weekly**. The oil companies recognized the power of comics early on!. Right, Not to be outdone, Shell Oil began a huge comics promotion in March 1934 to compete with Gulf and Standard Oil.*

inspection of a promotional folder published by the Ledger Syndicate, in which four-color Sunday comic pages were printed in 7"x9".

According to a 1949 interview with Wildenberg, he thought "why not a comic book? It would have 32 or 64 pages and make a fine item for concerns which distribute premiums." All they did at Eastern Color that one fateful day is fold a tabloid newspaper format down to "dime novel" size running full color throughout on most of the comic strips, then staple it, and they hit upon their winning formula.

But they did not yet know this...as we will find out.

Working for Eastern Color at this same time were quite a few future legends of the comics business, such as Max Gaines, Lev Gleason and a fellow named Harold Moore (all sales staff directly underneath the supervision of Wildenberg), Sol Harrison as a color separator, and George Dougherty Sr. as a printer.

Janosik, Wildenberg, Gaines, Gleason and crew obtained publishing rights to certain Associated, Bell, Fisher, McNaught and Public Ledger Syndicate comics, had an artist make up a few dummies by hand. The sales staff then walked them around to their biggest prospects. Wildenberg received a telegram from Proctor & Gamble for an order of a million copies for a 32-page color comic magazine called **Funnies on Parade**. The entire print run was given away in just a few weeks in the Spring of 1933. Most copies no longer exist and it is now hard to find. All of them worked on the **Funnies on Parade** project. Morris Margolis was brought in from Charlton in Derby, Connecticut to solve binding problems centered on getting the pages in proper numerical sequence on that last fold to "modern" comic book size. Most of them were infected with the comics bug for most of the rest of their lives.

The success of **Funnies on Parade** quickly led to Eastern publishing additional giveaway books in the same format by late 1933, including the 32-page **Famous Funnies A Carnival of Comics**, the 100-page **A Century of Comics** and the 52-page **Skippy's Own Book of Comics**.

The latter became the first "new" format comic book about a single character. Out of all the comic strips on the market in 1933, Eastern Color's growing comics market as devised by Harry Wildenberg, M.C. Gaines and Lev Gleason chose the Percy Crosby creation in **Skippy's Own Book of Comics** to be its first standalone title. This first solo effort in their new 52-page newsprint **Funnies On Parade** format had an initial print run of half a million, as did their 100-pager.

The idea that anyone would pay for them seemed fantastic to Wildenberg, so Max Gaines stickered ten cents on several dozen of the latest premium, **Famous Funnies A Carnival of Comics**, as a test, and talked a couple newsstands into participating in this experiment. The copies sold out over the weekend and newsies asked for more.

Eastern sales staffers then approached Woolworth's. The late Oscar Fitz-Alan Douglas, sales brains of Woolworth, showed some interest, but after several months of deliberation decided the book would not give enough value for ten cents. Kress, Kresge, McCrory, and several other dime stores turned them down even more abruptly. Wildenberg next went to George Hecht, editor of **Parents Magazine**, and tried to persuade him to run a comic supplement or publish a "higher level" comic magazine. Hecht also frowned on the idea.

In Wildenberg's 1949 interview, he noted that "even the comic syndicates couldn't see it. 'Who's going to read old comics?' they asked." With the failures of EmBee's **Comic Monthly** (1922) and Dell's **The Funnies** (1929) still fresh in some minds, no one could see why children would pay ten cents for a comic magazine when they could get all they wanted for free in a Sunday newspaper. But Wildenberg had become convinced that children as well as grown-ups were not getting all the comics they wanted in the Sunday papers; otherwise, the **Gulf Comic Weekly** and the premium comics would not have met with such success. Wildenberg said, "I decided that if boys and girls were willing to work for premium coupons to obtain comic books, they might be willing to pay ten cents on the newsstands." This conviction was also strengthened by Max Gaines' ten cent sticker experiment.

George Janosik, the president of Eastern Color, then called on George Delacorte to form another 50-50 joint venture to publish and market a comic book "magazine" for retail sales as they did with **The Funnies** just a few years previously, but this time American News turned them down cold. The magazine monopoly remembered the abortive **The Funnies** from just a few years before. After much discussion on how to proceed, Delacorte finally agreed to publish it and a partnership was formed. Feeling cautious, they printed 40,000 copies for distribution to a few chain stores who agreed to try it out. Known today as **Famous Funnies Series One**, it clocks in at 68 pages, with half its pages coming from reprints of the reprints in **Funnies on Parade** and half from **Famous Funnies A Carnival of Comics**. It is the scarcest issue.

With 68 full-color pages at only ten cents a piece, it sold out in thirty days with not a single returned copy. Delacorte refused to print a second edition. "Advertisers won't use it," he complained. "They say it's not dignified enough." The profit, however, was approximately $2,000. This particular edition is the rarest of all these early Eastern comic book experiments.

In early 1934, while riding the train, another Eastern Color employee named Harold A. Moore read an account from a prominent New York newspaper that indicated they owed much of their circulation success to their comics section. Mr. Moore went back to Harry Gold, President of American News, with the article in hand. He succeeded in acquiring a print order for 250,000 copies for a proposed monthly comics magazine. In May 1934, **Famous Funnies** #1 (with a July cover date) hit the newsstands with Steven O. Douglass as its only editor (even though Harold Moore was listed as such in #1) until it ceased publication some twenty years later. It was a 64-page version of the 32-page giveaways, and more importantly, it still sold for a dime! The first issue lost $4,150.60. Ninety percent of the copies sold out and a second issue dated September debuted in July. From then on, the comic book was published monthly. **Famous Funnies** also began carrying original material, apparently as early as the second issue. With #3, Buck Rogers took center stage and stayed there for the next twenty years, with covers by Frank Frazetta towards the end of the run–some of his best comics work ever.

***Funnies on Parade**, 1933 - what we recognize today as the first "modern" comic book.*

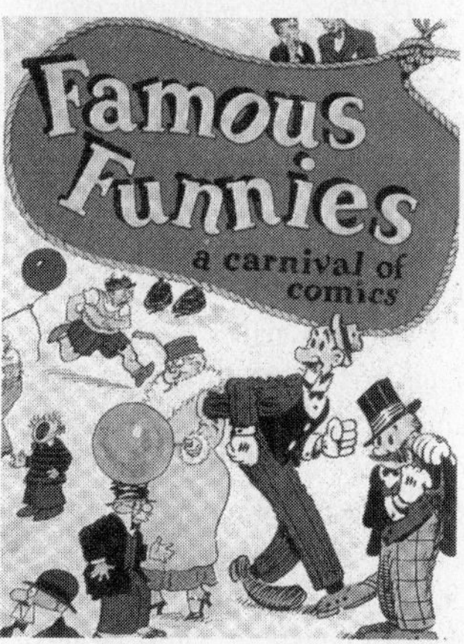

The fateful version Charlie Gaines stickered 10¢ a copy one weekend in late 1933.

***Famous Funnies Series One** is the rare one, as only 40,000 copies were printed.*

Delacorte got cold feet and sold back his interest to Eastern, even though the seventh issue cleared a profit of $2,664.25. Wildenberg emphasized that Eastern could make a manufacturer's profit by printing its own books as well as the publishing profits once it was distributed. Every issue showed greater sales than the preceding one, until within a year, close to a million 64-page books were being sold monthly at ten cents apiece; Eastern received the lion's share of the receipts, and soon found it was netting $30,000 per issue. The comic syndicates received $640 ($10 a page) for publishing rights. Original material could be obtained from budding professionals for just $5 a page. According to Will Eisner in R. C. Harvey's **The Art of the Comic Book**, the prices then paid for original material had a long range effect of keeping creator wages low for years.

Initially, Eastern's experiment was eyed with skepticism by the publishing world, but within a year or so after **Famous Funnies** was nonchalantly placed on sale alongside slicker magazines like **Atlantic Monthly** or **Harper's**, at least five other competitors tried this brand new format.

However, one other abortive periodical comics experiment was launched cover dated a full two months before the highly successful newsstand **Famous Funnies** format would have an important influence on a chain of events which led ultimately to **Superman** being published.

Comic Cuts #1, May 19, 1934, debuted published by H.L. Baker Co., Inc., 195 Main St, Buffalo, New York with editorial and executive offices at 381 Fourth St, NYC, same address as ULTEM (Centaur) would use just a couple years later - this address housed a number of publishers fighting to exist during the Great Depression. Indica says H. L. Baker was President &

Famous Funnies *#1, July 1934, was the first successful newsstand comic book, lasting until 1955.*

Treasurer and J. D. Geller was Vice President and Secretary. It lasted nine issues with the final one cover-dated July 28. It appears Jake Geller, Windsor, Ontario, Canada, acquired American rights to a number of comic strips from the publisher Amalgamated Press, publisher of **Comic Cuts** in England. He partnered in the publishing with H. L. Baker and they acquired the backing of S-M News Co., Inc. as their distributor. Most distributors back then functioned on many important levels. It was common practice for the distributor back then to front the funds to pay the paper company and the printer, collecting the revenue from the 900 I.D. distributors located around the country after months of on-sale time, then paying the publisher.

In late 1934, army officer/diplomat turned pulp writer turned publisher Major Wheeler-Nicholson (1890-1968) formed the under-funded National Allied Publishing which introduced **New Fun #1** (Feb 1935) at almost tabloid-size. **New Fun** was also distributed by S-M News. It is entirely possible Wheeler-Nicholson somehow convinced them he could produce a superior "home-grown" package as the imported strips were not selling well. **New Fun** was basically the same as **Comic Cuts** while also containing all original USA material such as carried in **The Funnies** (1929-30) from Dell/Eastern. With **New Fun,** what S-M News offered was more familiar American home grown. Coulton Waugh speculated in his 1947 history book **The Comics** on page 342: "...The Major had gone back to the 1929 idea of **The Funnies**, for the contents of **New Fun** were original material. (It should be recorded here that original art work had appeared in a one-color book called **Detective Dan**..."

Comic Cuts *#8, July 14, 1934, issued weekly by H.L. Baker Co. Inc., Buffalo, New York; editorial offices at 381 Fourth Ave, NYC; co-owner Jake .D. Geller was Canadian. Title provided inspiration for* ***New Fun****.*

However, Lloyd Jacquet, a person definitely in a position to know better, wrote as Chapter One of a proposed "History of the Comic Book" in 1957, "When Major Malcolm Wheeler-Nicholson set up his card table and chair in an eleventh floor office of the Hathaway Building in New York that Fall of 1934, these most modest beginnings sparked off what can rightly be called the 'comic book era.' When he came back to the U.S. after his last stay abroad, he looked over the American newsstand, and thought that the European juvenile weekly papers, with their picture-story continuities, their colorful illustrations, and their low price would appeal to the American boys and girls in the same way. He knew that those European publications were made up of new material, specially drawn and produced for each little magazine. He also knew that the American presentation of such material would have to be different, and merely importing, or translating European produced features for republication here was not the answer. This was about the time I joined with him in his project. It was still embryonic, but beginning to take form under Nicholson's direction. We were in the depression then, & it was not too difficult to secure writers and artists - but it was a task to instruct them as to exactly what was wanted. We finally rounded up a small but gifted group of creative people, and we produced our first issue of a monthly magazine composed of original features and material, and which was called, simply, "**FUN**."

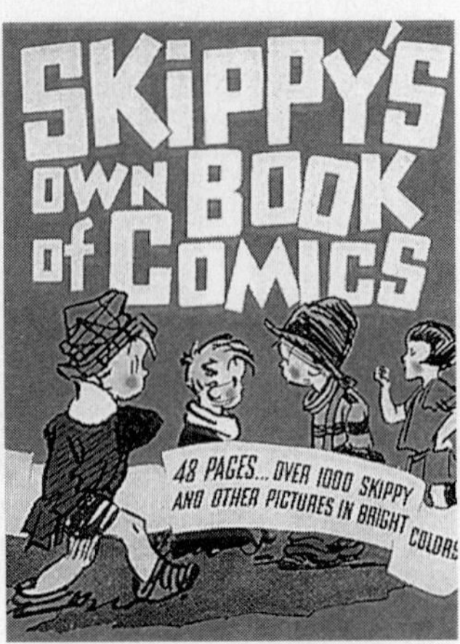

Skippy's Own Book of Comics*, 1934, had half a million issues printed and was the very first single character comic book in this "new" format.*

Around this same time in late 1934, M.C. Gaines left Eastern Color moving over to the McClure Newspaper Syndicate to become their manager of their Color Printing Department He immediately went to work convincing clients to

New Fun *#1, Feb 1935. According to first-employee Lloyd Jacquet, the format Major Malcolm Wheeler-Nicholson used was directly inspired by* ***Comic Cuts****. Many of the non-comics features were the same.*

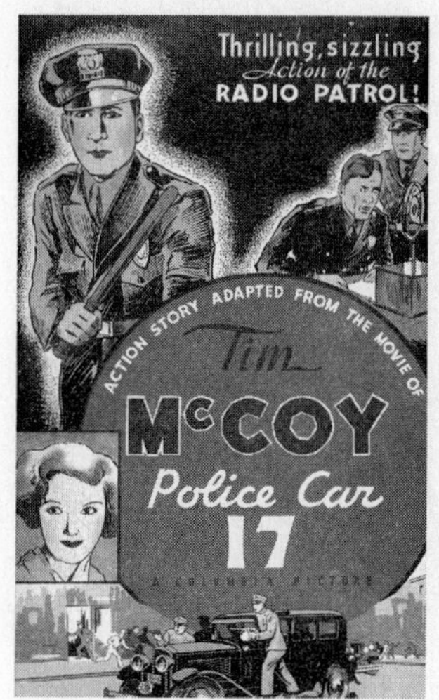

***Tim McCoy Police Car #17**, Whitman's first 1930s comic book (1934); the first movie adaptation*

issue promotional comics. Also, long-time comics publisher Whitman brought out the first original material movie adaptation, **Tim McCoy Police Car 17**, in the tabloid **New Fun** format with stiff card covers. A few years before, they had introduced the new comics formats known as the **Big Little Book** and the **Big Big Book**. The BLB and BBB formats would go toe-to-toe with Eastern's creation throughout the 1930s, but Eastern would win out with their new comics magazine format.

The very last 10" x 10" comic books pioneered by Cupples & Leon were published by the David McKay Publishing Company around mid-1935. Around this same time the Major published his 2nd comic book in which the editorial mentions amongst other exciting stories they were going to be showcasing the adventures of "hero supermen of the days to come."

By late 1935, Max Gaines (with his youthful assistant Sheldon Mayer) reached a business agreement with George Delacorte (who was re-entering the comic book business a third time) and McClure Syndicate (a growing newspaper comic strip enterprise) to be come editor of reprint newspaper comic strips in **Popular Comics**.

Also by late '35, Lev Gleason, another pioneer who participated in mercantiling **Funnies on Parade** and the early

***New Comics** #1, Dec. 1935, was the Major's second entry into comic books, re-emphasizing the concept of "New!"*

Famous Funnies, had become the first editor of United Feature's own **Tip Top Comics** with its first issue cover dated April 1936. In 1939 he would begin publishing his own titles starting with **Silver Streak**, created by the comics genius, Jack Cole, best known for Plastic Man. Gleason later created the crime comic book as a separate popular genre by 1942 with **Crime Does Not Pay** with a long run until 1955.

Wheeler-Nicholson introduced the concept of "the annual" into this new format with **Big Book of Fun Comics** #1 cover dated March 1936. It featured reprints from his earlier efforts in **New Fun** #1-5 as he struggled to make a go of it.

Industry giant King Features introduced **King Comics** #1 cover dated April 1936 through publisher David McKay, with Ruth Plumly Thompson as editor. McKay had already been issuing various format comic books with King Feature characters for a few years, including Mickey Mouse, Henry, Popeye and Secret Agent X-9, wherein Dashiell Hammett received cover billing and Alex Raymond was listed inside simply as "illustrator." McKay readily adapted to trying several formats. Soon many young comic book illustrators were copying Raymond.

The next month, William Cook & John Mahon, former disgruntled employees of Major Wheeler-Nicholson, issued their first issue of **Comics Magazine** #1 in May 1936.

This was followed by Henle Publishing issuing **Wow What**

*Left, Charlie Gaines & Sheldon Mayer packaged **Popular Comics** #1, Feb. 1936, for George Delecorte in late 1935 after the former left Eastern Color. Middle, **King Comics** #1, April 1936, marked King Features Syndicate's entry into the new 64-page color comic market with their new heavyweights, **Flash Gordon** and **Popeye**. By this point, Hearst had been involved in publishing comic books for close to 40 years. Right, Lev Gleason left Eastern & Wildenberg about the same time as Gaines to edit **Tip Top Comics** #1, April 1936, for United Features.*

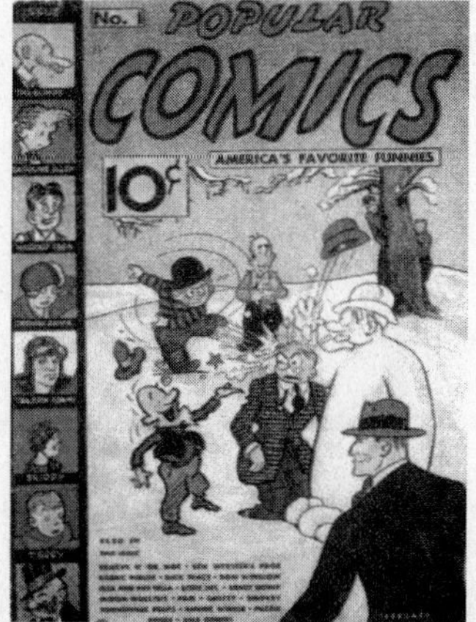

Left, ***The Comics Magazine*** *#2, June 1936, was the first title of what later became Centaur. Soon it had a name change and quickly made history. Middle,* ***Wow What A Magazine*** *is a rare title which ran four issues beginning in June 1936 with the first published work by youthful, eager Bernard Baily, Dick Briefer, Will Eisner & Bob Kane. Painted cover by Will Eisner.* ***Western Picture Stories*** *#1, Feb. 1937 has more art by Eisner, ties with* ***Star Ranger Funnies*** *#1 as first western comic book. Centaur also introduced the earliest crime comic book,* ***Detective Picture Stories #1*** *dated December 1936.*

A Magazine, which contained the earliest comic work of Will Eisner, Bob Kane, Dick Briefer & others. By the end of 1936, Cook and Mahon pioneered the first single theme comic books: **Funny Picture Stories** #1 in Nov. 1936 (adventure), **Detective Picture Stories** #1 in Feb. 1937 (crime), as well as **Western Picture Stories** #1 in Feb. 1937 (the Western). The company would eventually be known historically as Centaur Comics, and serve as the subject of endless debate among fan historians regarding their earliest origins as to who the owners were, where they came from and where they went.

Dell issued the second western genre comic book titled **Western Action Thrillers** #1 in April 1937. It was ten cents for one hundred pages as well as **100 Pages of Comics** 101, containing Big Little Book art reworked back into sequential comics.

Harry 'A' Chesler jumped ship from the Major, issuing his first comic books with **Star Comics** and **Star Ranger Funnies**, dated Feb 1937. Later that year, he sold these two titles to Ultem while remaining editor, and his newly set up art shop supplied contents. He then began **Feature Funnies** #1 in Oct. 1937, headlining Joe Palooka, at one time the #1 newspaper comic strip in America. Issue #2 sported a Rube Goldberg cover while #3 contains "Hawk of the Sea," Will Eisner's first work for what would soon become the Quality Comics Group when Everett "Busy" Arnold bought the company. **Feature Funnies** #3 also contains the first appearance of The Clock by George Brenner - the first costumed comic book hero.

Almost forty years after the first newspaper strip comic book compilations were issued at the dawn of international popularity for American comic strips, the race was on to get

Left, ***Feature Funnies #3****, Dec. 1937, contains George Brenner's The Clock, the first comic book costumed hero plus Eisner's first work for Quality Comics, when still owned by Chesler.* ***Circus the Comic Riot*** *#1, June 1938, contains Basil Wolverton's earliest professional comic book work plus more Will Eisner and Bob Kane. Right,* ***Action Comics*** *#1, June 1938, began revolutionizing the industry when Superman by Jerome Siegel & Joseph Shuster debuted. The publishers did not understand what they had at first as Superman does not appear on a cover again until #7. Nobody knew at first, it seemed, except book-keeper Victor Fox counting copies sold, who quit and formed his own comic book company.*

Left, ***Jumbo Comics*** *#1, Sept. 1938, debuts pulp publisher Fiction House's entry into the growing comic book industry. Middle,* ***Detective Comics*** *#27 introduced Batman created by Bob Kane and Bill Finger - need we say more? Right,* ***Wonder Comics*** *#1, May 1939, became Victor Fox's first entry into the comics biz when he fast-talked a youthful Will Eisner into creating a near-exact clone of the creation of Siegel & Shuster's brainchild, Superman. There was a quick lawsuit and #2 featured Yarko The Great instead. Bob Kane was busy that May as he is also in* ***Wonder*** *#1.*

titles out of the starting block. In late 1937 the Major began stumbling when he couldn't pay his printing bill to Harry Donenfeld. In recent interviews, Harry's son, Irwin, who as a 12-year old read the original art to the first issue of **Action Comics** #1 and **Detective Comics** #27 said "in 1932 my father and Paul Sampliner started Independent News with Liebowitz as the accountant. The company was begun with Paul Sampliner's mother's money. If it hadn't been for her investments into building the distribution as well as purchasing color printing presses, there might never have been a DC Comics....My father took over Wheeler-Nicholson's company with the Major's books literally on the printing presses. Harry had to absorb debt that could not otherwise be paid." Irwin told this writer " my dad did not originally willingly enter the comics business..."

Soon after the Major lost control of his company, **Action Comics** #1 was published with a cover date of June 1938, and the first Golden Age of superhero comics had begun. Early in 1938 at McClure Syndicate, Max Gaines and Shelly Mayer showed editor Vin Sullivan a many times rejected sample strip. Sullivan then talked Donenfeld, Paul Sampliner and Jack Liebowitz into publishing Jerry Siegel & Joe Shuster's creation of "The Last Son of Krypton." This was followed in 1939 by a lucrative partnership for Gaines beginning with Harry Donenfeld as the All-American Comics Group.

While there's a great deal of controversy surrounding such labeling, the "Golden Age" is viewed by many these days as beginning with **Action Comics** #1 and continuing through the end of World War II. There was a time not that long ago that the newspaper reprint comic book was collected with more fervor than the heroic comics of the '40s. **Prince Valiant FB** #26, **Flash Gordon 4C** #10 and **Tarzan SS** #20

Left, ***Marvel Comics*** *#1, Oct. 1939, was the first Martin Goodman comic book, introducing Human Torch by Carl Burgos and Sub-Mariner by Bill Everett. Middle,* ***Silver Streak*** *#1, Dec. 1939, Lev Gleason's first published comic book, introduced Jack Cole's classic, The Claw, running until #24, when the title changed to* ***Crime Does Not Pay****. Right,* ***Whiz Comics*** *#2 (#1), Feb. 1940, ushered Fawcett onto the comic book scene with yet another Superman clone - Captain Marvel, who was successful from the get-go. At one time his main title was issued every three weeks.*

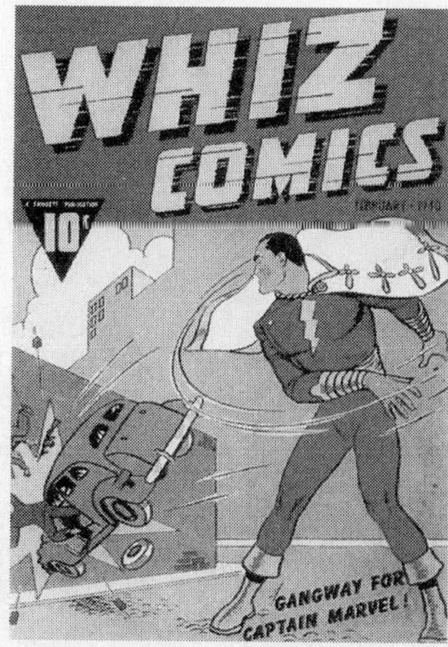

Left, ***Crime Does Not Pay*** *#43, Nov. 1945. Lev Gleason instigated a popular new genre which brought the industry unfairly under heavy fire from church and state. Middle,* ***My Date*** *#1, July 1947. Joe Simon and Jack Kirby created the romance genre when they developed the older female audience which lasted into the '70s. Right,* ***Atomic War*** *#1, Nov. 1952. Nuclear obliteration was heavy on the minds of most Americans. Due to the Korean War, there was a plethora of war titles and the genre survived well into the 1970s before being eventually marginalized by the super hero revival.*

were some of the highest Holy Grails of collecting, but no more even though they contain fantastic art & story.

Today's marketplace dictates super heroes command the highest prices and are seemingly the most desirable. Maybe one day that pendulum will swing once again as there have been many years since they were introduced when super heroes almost disappeared completely from the racks.

The **Atomic/Romance** Age debuted with a bang by early 1946, revamping the industry once again as circulations soon hit their all-time highs with well over 1.3 billion periodical issues sold a year by the consignment honor system. By the early 1950s one in three periodicals sold in the USA was a comic book. 90% of all children admitted they read and enjoyed comics. There were dozens of genres being published. There were comic books for every taste and style. Hundreds of titles were being issued every month.

For many readers, the pinnacle was reached with the "New Trend" Entertaining Comics (E.C.) began delivering to the newsstands in 1950. The company still has a large following even today - a testament to its emphasis on quality art & story.

Comic book publishers glutted the market place by 1952-53. The attacks on comics begun the late 1940s came back anew in 1954 brought on by over-zealous church people and district attorneys with an agenda.

This continued until the advent of the self-censoring, industry-stifling Comics Code, created in response to a public outcry spearheaded by Dr. Frederic Wertham's tirade against the American comics industry, published as a book titled

Left, ***Crime Detective*** *#9, July 1948. Some say the tied-up figure represents Dr. Fredric Wertham following his earliest attacks on the crime comic book. Hillman joined the first Code. Middle,* ***Justice Traps the Guilty*** *#56, Nov. 1953. The S&K studio placed themselves in the spotlight, with a pretty mother pointing out Joe Simon as the tall, dastardly ringleader. Jack Kirby is on the right end. Right,* ***Thing*** *#15, Apr. 1954. Ditko wreaks havoc on a world rising against comics as a giant worm eats Brooklyn in one of the most gruesome titles created. His early work is intense.*

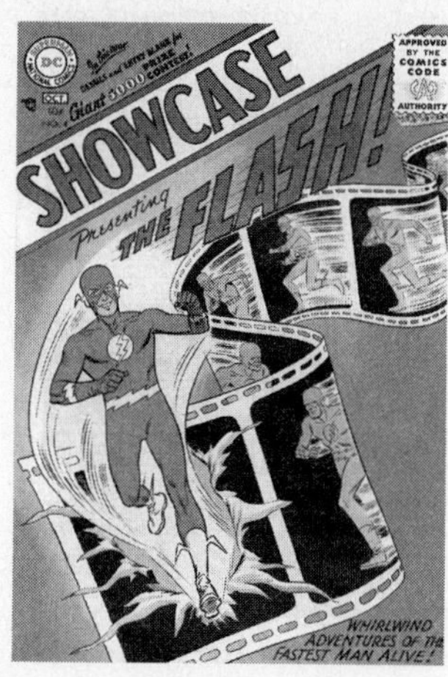

Left, By the early 1950s, Carl Barks increased the circulation of ***Walt Disney's C&S*** *to over 4 million per issue & in 1952 his creation, Uncle Scrooge, got his own book, selling over a million an issue through the '50s while superheroes slumbered. Middle, Harvey Kurtzman created* ***Mad Comics*** *#1, 1952, and soon sent the comics industry in an entirely "New" Direction and has directly inspired countless comics creators for years. Right,* ***Showcase #4****, Sept. 1956, the superhero revival starts a year after the Code, though it was three years before the Flash earned his own title once again.*

Seduction of the Innocent, which removed crime and horror comic books from the marketplace. Some of them were quite gruesome; however in his last book, **The World of Fanzines**, Wertham exhonerated comics fans for misinterpreting his data more than 20 years previous.

It took a year or two to recover from that moralistic assault, with many historians speculating the Silver Age of Superheroes began with the publication of **Showcase** #4 in 1956. Others point to the 1952 successful releases of Kurtzman's **MAD** #1 and Bark's **Uncle Scrooge** 4C 386 as true Silver, since those titles soon broke the "million sold per issue" mark when the rest of the comic book industry was reeling from the effects of the public uproar fueled by Wertham. Within the Silver Era the term Bronze Age has been stated by some to begin when the Code approved newsstand comic book industry raised its standard cover price from 12 to 15 cents and Jack Kirby left Marvel for DC. As circulations plummeted after the Batman TV craze wore off by 1968 and the ensuing superhero glut withered on the stands, out in the Bay Area cartoonist Robert Crumb's creator-owned **Zap Comics** #1 appeared in Feb 1968, printed by Charles Plymell & Don Donahue on a small printing press. Soon after in Chicago, Jay Lynch and Skip Williamson brought out **Bijou Funnies**, Gilbert Shelton self-published **Feds 'N' Heads** while still in Austin, Texas, with Print Mint reprinting it almost immediately & Crumb let S. Clay Wilson, Victor Moscoso & Rick Griffin into **Zap #2.**

As originally published by the Print Mint beginning with #2 in 1968, **Zap Comics** almost single-handedly spawned an industry with tremendous growth in alternative comix running through the 1970s. During this decade the San

Left, ***Brave & Bold*** *#28, Feb/Mar. 1960, gathered together the revived DC heroes, further expanding the resurging super hero market DC Comics ushered in. Middle,* ***Fantastic Four*** *#1, Nov. 1962, began the revitalization of Martin Goodman's moribund Marvel Comics Group, directly inspired by the success of the JLA's own regular series begun 2 years earlier in late 1960. Right,* ***Amazing Fantasy*** *#15, Aug. 1962, introduced the Amazing Spider-Man, created almost completely by Steve Ditko with some assists from Stan Lee and Jack Kirby, which revolutionized the way comic book stories could be told.*

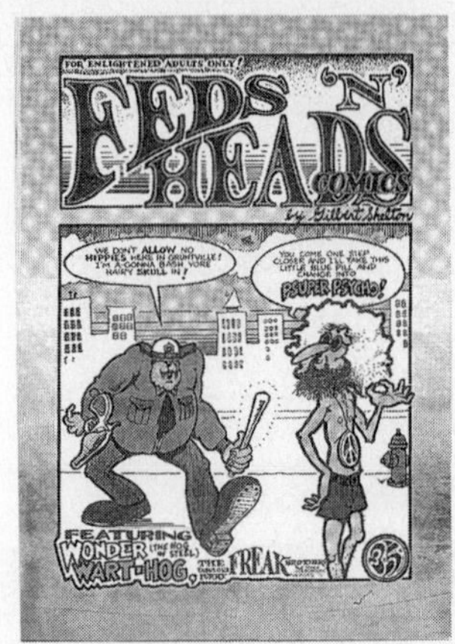

Left, ***Zap Comics*** *#1, Plymell first printing, Feb. 1968, was the "direct" inspiration for the earliest successful origins of the Direct Market and has sold over a million copies. Most issues have been continuously in print for over 30 years. First printings have sold for over $3500. Middle, soon afterwards Gilbert Shelton brought* ***Feds 'N' Heads*** *to Print Mint and later joined* ***Zap****. It has sold for $800. Right, famed poster artist Rick Griffin edited his own comic book,* ***Tales From the Tube****, in 1973, with most of the* ***Zap*** *crew joining him. It currently brings over $150 in NM high grade.*

Francisco Bay Area was an intense hotbed of comix being issued without a comics code "seal of approval" from companies such as Rip Off Press, Last Gasp, San Francisco Comic Book Company, Company & Sons, Weirdom Publications, Star*Reach, and Comics & Comix. Kitchen Sink prospered for many years in Wisconsin and many small press comix publishers scattered across the USA and Canada - all of whom created the Direct Sales Market. There were hundreds of people involved with an independent mind producing & distributing alternative underground comix, creating the direct market. Phil Seuling introduced DC, Marvel and Warren to this already developed for five years, San Francisco Bay Area-based, comix business system as a "new" way of selling comics in late 1973, acknowedged by Phil himself in his last interview in **Will Eisner's Quarterly** #3, Summer 1984.

After DC and Marvel joined the DM in a serious way in 1979, the last 20 years have generally been called the "Modern Age", although there are hints of a new age emerging since the mid-'90s. The jury is still out on naming it.

The comic book store as an industry came into its own in the 1980s. Thousands of fans & entrepreneurs opened stores, fulfilling a life's dream for many of them - fueled by a vibrant speculator's market which lasted until the early 1990s, its last hurrah being when DC "killed" Superman in 1992. The comic book marketplace has been rebuilding ever since. Much of that growth has been outside the super hero genre.

In each of the preceding eras, however, the secret for collectors has remained the same: buy what you enjoy. We did, and we are still collectors today!

Portions excerpted from **Comics Archeology 101** *© 2004 Robert L. Beerbohm, a detailed, heavily researched book in progress covering the more than 160 year history of the comic book business. His E-mail is:* **beerbohm@teknetwork.com**

Left, ***Conan*** *#1, Oct. 1970, by Roy Thomas and Barry Windsor-Smith introduced the sword & sorcery genre. Middle,* ***StarReach*** *#1, April 1974, published by Mike Friedrich, was the first comic book directed specifically at comic book stores. Right,* ***Giant-Size X-Men*** *#1, Summer, 1975, introduced the new X-team, which later on revolutionized the comic book store system with its phenomenal sales once Chris Claremont and John Byrne teamed up on the title.*

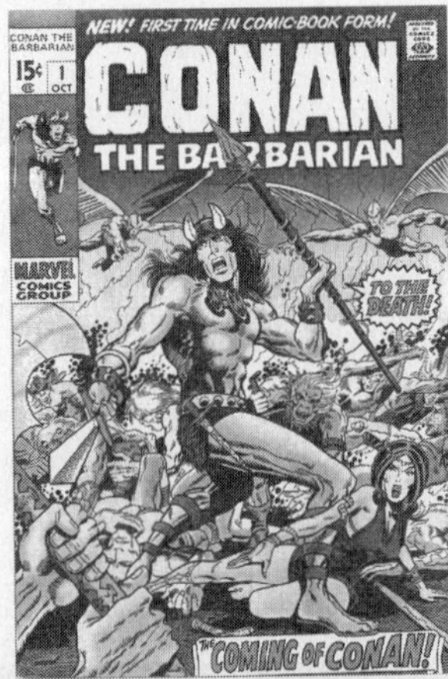

Abbott and Costello #3 © STJ

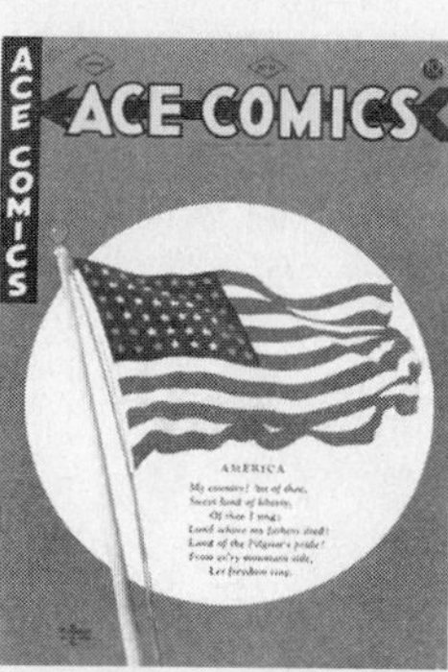

Ace Comics #65 © DMP

Acme Novelty Library #1 Vol. 5 © Chris Ware

	GD 2.0	VG 4.0	FN 6.0	VF 8.0	VF/NM 9.0	NM- 9.2

The correct title listing for each comic book can be determined by consulting the indicia (publication data) on the beginning interior pages of the comic. The official title is determined by those words of the title in capital letters only, and not by what is on the cover. Titles are listed in this book as if they were one word, ignoring spaces, hyphens, and apostrophes, to make finding titles easier. Exceptions are made in rare cases. Comic books listed should be assumed to be in color unless noted "B&W".

Comic publishers are invited to send us sample copies for possible inclusion in future guides.

PRICING IN THIS GUIDE: Prices for **GD 2.0** (Good), **VG 4.0** (Very Good), **FN 6.0** (Fine), **VF 8.0** (Very Fine), **VF/NM 9.0** (Very Fine/Near Mint),and **NM– 9.2** (Near Mint-) are listed in whole U.S. dollars except for prices below $7 which show dollars and cents. **The minimum price listed is $2.25**, the cover price for current new comics. Many books listed at this price can be found in $1.00 boxes at conventions and dealers stores.

A-1 (See A-One)

ABBIE AN' SLATS (...With Becky No. 1-4) (See Comics On Parade, Fight for Love, Giant Comics Edition 2, Giant Comics Editions #1, Sparkler Comics, Tip Topper, Treasury of Comics, & United Comics)
United Features Syndicate: 1940; March, 1948 - No. 4, Aug, 1948 (Reprints)

	GD	VG	FN	VF	VF/NM	NM-
Single Series 25 ('40)	39	78	117	230	325	420
Single Series 28	33	66	99	190	270	350
1 (1948)	19	38	57	107	149	190
2-4: 3-r/Sparkler #68-72	10	20	30	58	77	95

ABBOTT AND COSTELLO (...Comics)(See Giant Comics Editions #1 & Treasury of Comics)
St. John Publishing Co.: Feb, 1948 - No. 40, Sept, 1956 (Mort Drucker-a in most issues)

	GD	VG	FN	VF	VF/NM	NM-
1	57	114	171	356	538	720
2	33	66	99	190	270	350
3-9 (#8, 8/49; #9, 2/50)	21	42	63	118	164	210
10-Son of Sinbad story by Kubert (new)	24	48	72	138	194	250
11,13-20 (#11, 10/50; #13, 8/51; #15, 12/52)	16	32	48	92	126	160
12-Movie issue	17	34	51	98	134	170
21-30: 28-r/#8. 30-Painted-c	11	22	33	66	88	110
31-40: 33,38-Reprints	9	18	27	54	70	85
3-D #1 (11/53, 25¢)-Infinity-c	35	70	105	201	288	370

ABBOTT AND COSTELLO (TV)
Charlton Comics: Feb, 1968 - No. 22, Aug, 1971 (Hanna-Barbera)

	GD	VG	FN	VF	VF/NM	NM-
1	9	18	27	60	85	110
2	5	10	15	33	44	55
3-10	4	8	12	25	33	42
11-22	3	6	9	19	25	32

ABC (See America's Best TV Comics)

ABE SAPIEN: DRUMS OF THE DEAD
Dark Horse Comics: Mar, 1998 ($2.95, one-shot)

1-McDonald-s/Thompson-a. Hellboy back-up; Mignola-s/a/c 3.00

A. BIZARRO
DC Comics: Jul, 1999 - No. 4, Oct, 1999 (2.50, limited series)

1-4-Gerber-s/Bright-a 2.50

ABOMINATIONS (See Hulk)
Marvel Comics: Dec, 1996 - No. 3, Feb, 1997 (1.50, limited series)

1-3-Future Hulk storyline 2.25

ABRAHAM LINCOLN LIFE STORY (See Dell Giants)

ABRAHAM STONE
Marvel Comics (Epic): July, 1995 - No. 2, Aug, 1995 ($6.95, limited series)

1,2-Joe Kubert-s/a 7.00

ABSENT-MINDED PROFESSOR, THE
Dell Publishing Co.: Apr, 1961 (Disney)

	GD	VG	FN	VF	VF/NM	NM-
Four Color #1199-Movie, photo-c	9	18	27	60	85	110

ABSOLUTE VERTIGO
DC Comics (Vertigo): Winter, 1995 (99¢, mature)

	GD	VG	FN	VF	VF/NM	NM-
nn-1st app. Preacher. Previews upcoming titles including Jonah Hex: Riders of the Worm, The Invisibles (King Mob), The Eaters, Ghostdancing & Preacher	1	2	3	5	6	8

ABYSS, THE (Movie)
Dark Horse Comics: June, 1989 - No. 2, July, 1989 ($2.25, limited series)

1,2-Adaptation of film; Kaluta & Moebius-a 3.00

ACCELERATE
DC Comics (Vertigo): Aug, 2000 - No. 4, Nov, 2000 ($2.95, limited series)

1-4-Pander Bros.-a/Kadrey-s 3.00

ACCLAIM ADVENTURE ZONE
Acclaim Books: 1997 ($4.50, digest size)

1-Short stories of Turok, Troublemakers, Ninjak and others 4.50

ACE COMICS
David McKay Publications: Apr, 1937 - No. 151, Oct-Nov, 1949 (All contain some newspaper strip reprints)

	GD	VG	FN	VF	VF/NM	NM-
1-Jungle Jim by Alex Raymond, Blondie, Ripley's Believe It Or Not, Krazy Kat begin (1st app. of each)	311	622	933	2022	3111	4200
2	92	184	276	575	862	1150
3-5	63	126	189	394	590	785
6-10	46	92	138	276	413	550
11-The Phantom begins (1st app., 2/38) (in brown costume)	76	152	228	475	713	950
12-20	39	78	117	233	329	425
21-25,27-30	36	72	108	204	290	375
26-Origin & 1st app. Prince Valiant (5/39); begins series?	100	200	300	625	937	1250
31-40: 37-Krazy Kat ends	26	52	78	147	206	265
41-60	19	38	57	107	149	190
61-64,66-76-(7/43; last 68 pgs.)	17	34	51	98	134	170
65-(8/42)-Flag-c	19	38	57	106	146	185
77-84 (3/44; all 60 pgs.)	14	28	42	79	107	135
85-99 (52 pgs.)	12	24	36	69	92	115
100 (7/45; last 52 pgs.)	14	28	42	81	111	140
101-134: 128-(11/47)-Brick Bradford begins. 134-Last Prince Valiant (all 36 pgs.)	10	20	30	56	73	90
135-151: 135-(6/48)-Lone Ranger begins	9	18	27	51	66	80

ACE KELLY (See Tops Comics & Tops In Humor)

ACE KING (See Adventures of Detective...)

ACES
Acme Press (Eclipse): Apr, 1988 - No. 5, Dec, 1988 ($2.95, B&W, magazine)

1-5 3.00

ACES HIGH
E.C. Comics: Mar-Apr, 1955 - No. 5, Nov-Dec, 1955

	GD	VG	FN	VF	VF/NM	NM-
1-Not approved by code	21	42	63	157	223	290
2	12	24	36	90	125	160
3-5	11	22	33	82	116	150

NOTE: *All have stories by* ***Davis, Evans, Krigstein,*** *and* ***Wood. Evans*** *c-1-5.*

ACES HIGH
Gemstone Publishing: Apr, 1999 - No. 5, Aug, 1999 ($2.50)

1-5-Reprints E.C. issues 2.50
Annual 1 ($13.50) r/#1-5 13.50

ACME NOVELTY LIBRARY, THE
Fantagraphics Books: Winter 1993-94 - Present (quarterly, various sizes)

1-Introduces Jimmy Corrigan; Chris Ware-s/a in all 7.00
1-2nd and later printings 4.00
2,3: 2-Quimby 5.00
4-Sparky's Best Comics & Stories 6.00
5-12: Jimmy Corrigan in all 5.00
13,15-($10.95-c) 11.00
14-($12.95-c) Concludes Jimmy Corrigan saga 13.00
Jimmy Corrigan, The Smartest Kid on Earth (2000, Pantheon Books, Hardcover, $27.50, 380 pgs.) Collects Jimmy Corrigan stories; folded dust jacket 27.50
Jimmy Corrigan, The Smartest Kid on Earth (2003, Softcover, $17.95) 18.00
NOTE: *Multiple printings exist for most issues.*

ACROSS THE UNIVERSE: THE DC UNIVERSE STORIES OF ALAN MOORE
DC Comics: 2003 ($19.95, TPB)

nn-Reprints selected Moore stories from '85-'87; Superman, Batman, Swamp Thing app. 20.00

ACTION ADVENTURE (War) (Formerly Real Adventure)
Gillmor Magazines: V1#2, June, 1955 - No. 4, Oct, 1955

	GD	VG	FN	VF	VF/NM	NM-
V1#2-4	6	12	18	27	33	38

ACTION COMICS (...Weekly #601-642) (Also see The Comics Magazine #1, More Fun #14-17 & Special Edition) (Also see Promotional Comics section)
National Periodical Publ./Detective Comics/DC Comics: 6/38 - No. 583, 9/86; No. 584, 1/87 - Present

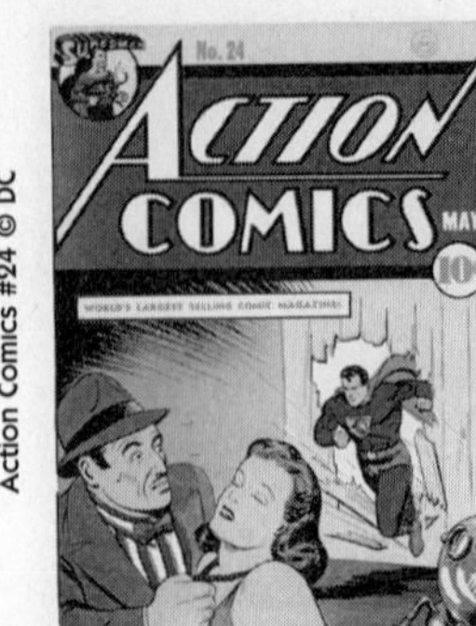

Action Comics #24 © DC

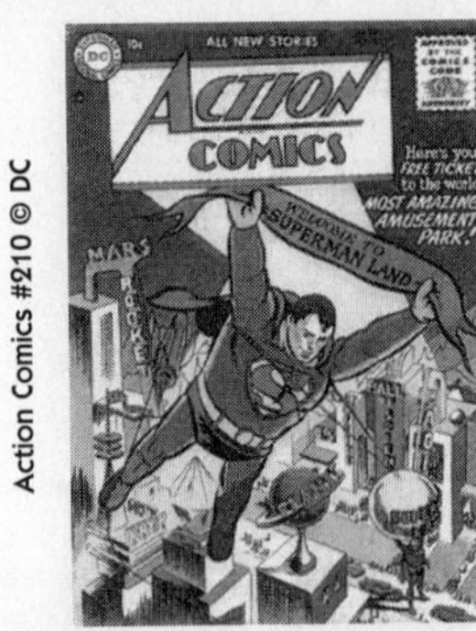

Action Comics #210 © DC

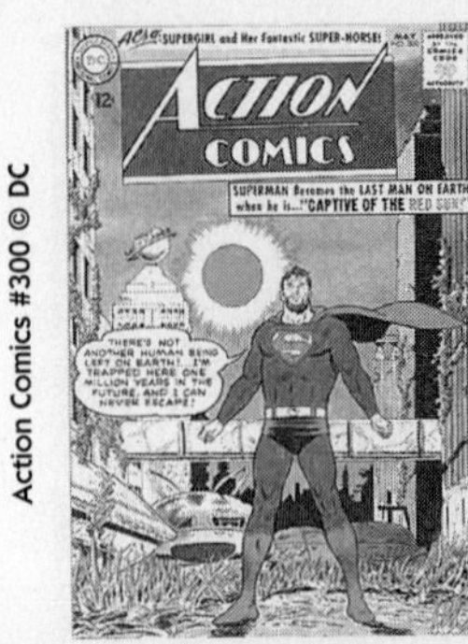

Action Comics #300 © DC

GD 2.0 | VG 4.0 | FN 6.0 | VF 8.0 | VF/NM 9.0 | NM- 9.2

1-Origin & 1st app. Superman by Siegel & Shuster, Marco Polo, Tex Thompson, Pep Morgan, Chuck Dawson & Scoop Scanlon; 1st app. Zatara & Lois Lane; Superman story missing 4 pgs. which were included when reprinted in Superman #1; Clark Kent works for Daily Star; story continued in #2 38,250 76,500 114,750 220,000 330,000 440,000
1-Reprint, Oversize 13-1/2x10". **WARNING:** This comic is an exact reprint of the original except for its size. DC published it in 1974 with a second cover titling it as a Famous First Edition. There have been many reported cases of the outer cover being removed and the interior sold as the original edition. The reprint with the new outer cover removed is practically worthless. See Famous First Edition for value.
2-O'Mealia non-Superman covers thru #6 3538 7076 10,615 24,765 35,383 46,000
3 (Scarce)-Superman apps. in costume in only one panel 2154 4308 6462 15,078 21,539 28,000
4-6: 6-1st Jimmy Olsen (called office boy) 1346 2692 4038 9422 13,461 17,500
7-2nd Superman cover 2692 5384 8076 18,844 26,922 35,000
8,9 885 1770 2655 6195 8848 11,500
10-3rd Superman cover by Siegel & Shuster 1692 3384 5076 11,844 16,922 22,000
11,14: 14-Clip Carson begins, ends #41; Zatara-c 428 856 1284 2996 4598 6200
12-Has 1 pg. Batman ad for Det. #27 (5/39); Zatara sci-fi cover 462 924 1386 3234 4967 6700
13-Shuster Superman-c; last Scoop Scanlon 793 1586 2379 5551 8526 11,500
15-Guardineer Superman-c; Detective Comics ad 621 1242 1863 4347 6674 9000
16 318 636 954 2067 3184 4300
17-Superman cover; last Marco Polo 483 966 1449 3381 5191 7000
18-Origin 3 Aces; 1st X-Ray Vision? 318 636 954 2067 3184 4300
19-Superman covers begin; has full pg. ad for New York World's Fair 1939 462 924 1386 3234 4967 6700
20-The 'S' left off Superman's chest; Clark Kent works at 'Daily Star' 441 882 1323 3087 4744 6400
21-Has 2 ads for More Fun #52 (1st Spectre) 300 600 900 1875 2838 3800
22,24,25: 24-Kent at Daily Planet. 25-Last app. Gargantua T. Potts, Tex Thompson's sidekick 296 592 888 1850 2775 3700
23-1st app. Luthor (w/red hair) & Black Pirate; Black Pirate by Moldoff; 1st mention of The Daily Planet (4/40)-Has 1 panel ad for Spectre in More Fun 676 1352 2028 4732 7266 9800
26-28,30 248 496 744 1550 2325 3100
29-1st Lois Lane-c (10/40) 288 576 864 1800 2700 3600
31,32: 32-Intro/1st app. Krypto Ray Gun in Superman story by Burnley 160 320 480 1000 1500 2000
33-Origin Mr. America; Superman by Burnley; has half page ad for All Star Comics #3 176 352 528 1100 1650 2200
34,35,38,39 152 304 456 950 1425 1900
36,37: 36-Classic robot-c. 37-Origin Congo Bill 160 320 480 1000 1500 2000
40-(9/41)-Intro/1st app. Star Spangled Kid & Stripesy; Jerry Siegel photo 164 328 492 1025 1538 2050
41 128 256 384 800 1200 1600
42-1st app./origin Vigilante; Bob Daley becomes Fat Man; origin Mr. America's magic flying carpet; The Queen Bee & Luthor app; Black Pirate ends; not in #41 172 344 546 1075 1613 2150
43-46,48-50: 44-Fat Man's i.d. revealed to Mr. America. 45-1st app. Stuff (Vigilante's oriental sidekick) 128 256 384 800 1200 1600
47-1st Luthor cover in comics (4/42) 196 392 588 1225 1838 2450
51-1st app. The Prankster 140 280 420 875 1313 1750
52-Fat Man & Mr. America become the Ameri-commandos; origin Vigilante retold; classic Superman and back-ups-c 152 304 456 950 1425 1900
53-56,59,60: 56-Last Fat Man. 59-Kubert Vigilante begins?, ends #70. 60-First app. Lois Lane as Super-woman 112 224 336 700 1050 1400
57-2nd Lois Lane-c in Action (3rd anywhere, 2/43) 120 240 360 750 1125 1500
58-"Slap a Jap-c" 124 248 372 775 1163 1550
61-Historic Atomic Radiation-c (6/43) 116 232 348 725 1088 1450
62,63-Japan war-c: 63-Last 3 Aces 112 224 336 700 1050 1400
64-Intro Toyman 116 232 348 725 1088 1450
65-70 92 184 276 575 863 1150
71-79: 74-Last Mr. America 78 156 234 488 732 975
80-2nd app. & 1st Mr. Mxyztplk-c (1/45) 108 216 324 675 1013 1350
81-88,90: 83-Intro Hocus & Pocus 74 148 222 463 694 925
89-Classic rainbow cover 78 156 234 488 732 975
91-99: 93-X-Mas-c. 99-1st small logo (8/46) 70 140 210 438 657 875
100 72 144 216 450 675 900
101-Nuclear explosion-c (10/46) 132 264 396 825 1238 1650
102-107,109-120: 102-Mxyztplk-c. 105,117-X-Mas-c 62 124 186 388 582 775
108-Classic molten metal-c 70 140 210 438 657 875
121,122,124-126,128-140: 135,136,138-Zatara by Kubert 57 114 171 356 538 720
123-(8/48) 1st time Superman flies rather than leaps 59 118 177 369 555 740
127-Vigilante by Kubert; Tommy Tomorrow begins (12/48, see Real Fact #6) 61 122 183 381 573 765
141-157,159,160: 151-Luthor/Mr. Mxyztplk/Prankster team-up. 156-Lois as Super Woman. 160- Last 52 pgs. 55 110 165 330 495 660
158-Origin Superman retold 122 244 366 763 1144 1525
161-180: 168,176-Used in **POP**, pg. 90. 173-Robot-c 48 96 144 288 432 575
181-201: 191-Intro. Janu in Congo Bill. 198-Last Vigilante. 201-Last pre-code issue 46 92 138 276 413 550
202-220,232: 212-(1/56)-Includes 1956 Superman calendar that is part of story. 232-1st Curt Swan-c in Action 40 80 120 240 363 485
221-231,233-240: 221-1st S.A. issue. 224-1st Golden Gorilla story. 228-(5/57)-Kongorilla in Congo Bill story (Congorilla try-out) 38 76 114 219 310 400
241,243-251: 241-Batman x-over. 248-Origin/1st app. Congorilla; Congo Bill renamed Congorilla. 251-Last Tommy Tomorrow 32 64 96 182 259 335
242-Origin & 1st app. Brainiac (7/58); 1st mention of Shrunken City of Kandor 137 274 411 1165 1783 2400
252-Origin & 1st app. Supergirl (5/59); intro new Metallo 143 286 429 1216 1858 2500
253-2nd app. Supergirl 50 100 150 300 450 600
254-1st meeting of Bizarro & Superman-c/story 40 80 120 240 345 450
255-1st Bizarro Lois Lane-c/story & both Bizarros leave Earth to make Bizarro World 34 68 102 196 278 360
256-260: 259-Red Kryptonite used 22 44 66 127 176 225
261-1st X-Kryptonite which gave Streaky his powers; last Congorilla in Action; origin & 1st app. Streaky The Super Cat 23 46 69 132 186 240
262,264-266,268-270 19 38 57 109 152 195
263-Origin Bizarro World 24 48 72 138 194 250
267(8/60)-3rd Legion app; 1st app. Chameleon Boy, Colossal Boy, & Invisible Kid, 1st app. of Supergirl as Superwoman. 48 96 144 288 432 575
271-275,277-282: 274-Lois Lane as Superwoman; 282-Last 10¢ issue 16 32 48 92 126 160
276(5/61)-6th Legion app; 1st app. Brainiac 5, Phantom Girl, Triplicate Girl, Bouncing Boy, Sun Boy, & Shrinking Violet; Supergirl joins Legion 27 54 81 155 218 280
283(12/61)-Legion of Super-Villains app. 1st 12¢ 12 24 36 84 125 165
284(1/62)-Mon-el app. 12 24 36 84 125 165
285(2/62)-12th Legion app; Brainiac 5 cameo; Supergirl's existence revealed to world; JFK & Jackie cameos 14 28 42 102 149 195
286-287,289-292,294-299: 286(3/62)-Legion of Super Villains app. 287(4/62)-15th Legion app. (cameo). 289(6/62)-16th Legion app. (Adult); Lightning Man & Saturn Woman's marriage 1st revealed. 290(7/62)-Legion app. (cameo); Phantom Girl app. 1st Supergirl emergency squad. 291-1st meeting Supergirl & Mr. Mxyzptlk. 292-2nd app. Superhorse (see Adv.#293). 297-Mon-el app. 298-Legion cameo 10 20 30 67 96 125
288-Mon-el app.; r-origin Supergirl 10 20 30 72 104 135
293-Origin Comet (Superhorse) 12 24 36 84 125 165
300-(5/63) 11 22 33 77 114 150
301-303,305,307,308,310-312,315-320: 307-Saturn Girl app. 317-Death of Nor-Kan of Kandor. 319-Shrinking Violet app. 7 14 21 46 63 80
304,306,313: 304-Origin/1st app. Black Flame (9/63). 306-Brainiac 5, Mon-el app. 313-Batman app. 7 14 21 50 68 85
309-(2/64)-Legion app.; Batman & Robin-c & cameo; JFK app. (he died 11/22/63; on stands last week of Dec, 1963) 7 14 21 50 68 85
314-Retells origin Supergirl; J.L.A. x-over 7 14 21 50 68 85
321-333,335-339: 336-Origin Akvar (Flamebird) 6 12 18 38 52 65
334-Giant G-20; origin Supergirl, Streaky, Superhorse & Legion (all-r) 10 20 30 72 104 135
340-Origin, 1st app. of the Parasite 6 12 18 43 59 75
341,344,350,358: 341-Batman app. in Supergirl back-up story. 344-Batman x-over. 350-Batman, Green Arrow & Green Lantern app. in Supergirl back-up story. 358-Superboy meets Supergirl 4 8 12 29 40 50
342,343,345,346,348,349,351-357,359: 342-UFO story. 345-Allen Funt/Candid Camera story. 4 8 12 27 36 45
347,360-Giant Supergirl G-33,G-45; 347-Origin Comet-r plus Bizarro story. 360-Legion-r; r/origin Supergirl 7 14 21 50 68 85
361-364,367-372,374-378: 361-2nd app. Parasite. 363-366-Leper/Death story. 370-New facts about Superman's origin. 376-Last Supergirl in Action. 377-Legion begins (thru #392). 378-Last 12¢ issue 4 8 12 24 32 40
365,366: 365-JLA & Legion app. 366-JLA app. 4 8 12 24 32 40
373-Giant Supergirl G-57; Legion-r 6 12 18 43 59 75
379-399,401: 388-Sgt. Rock app. 392-Batman-c/app.; last Legion in Action; Saturn Girl gets new costume. 393-401-All Superman issues 3 6 9 18 23 28
400 4 8 12 24 32 40
402-Last 15¢ issue; Superman vs. Supergirl duel 3 6 9 19 25 32
403-413: All 52 pg. issues. 411-Origin Eclipso-(r). 413-Metamorpho begins, ends #418 3 7 10 21 28 35

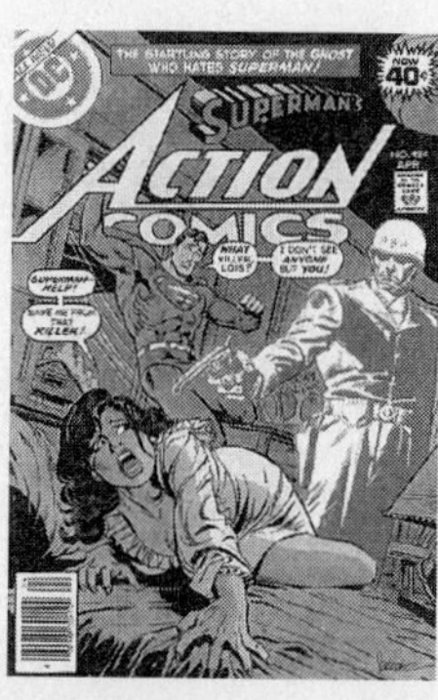
Action Comics #494 © DC

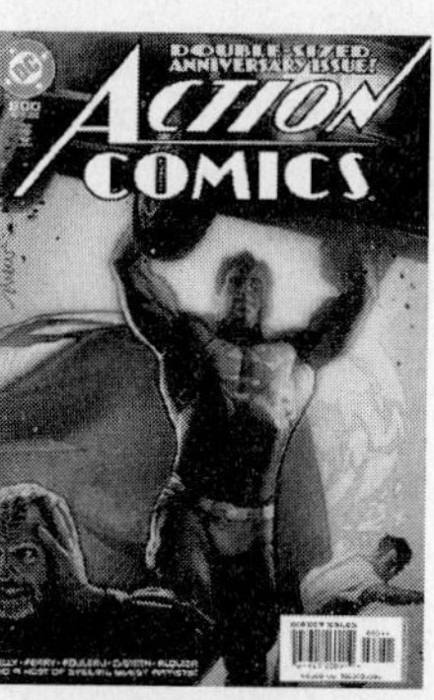
Action Comics #800 © DC

Adam Strange Book 2 © DC

	GD 2.0	VG 4.0	FN 6.0	VF 8.0	VF/NM 9.0	NM- 9.2
414-424: 419-Intro. Human Target. 421-Intro Capt. Strong; Green Arrow begins. 422,423-Origin Human Target	2	4	6	10	12	15
425-Neal Adams-a(p); The Atom begins	2	4	6	14	18	22
426-431,433-436,438,439	2	4	6	8	10	12
432-1st S.A. Toyman app (2/74).	2	4	6	14	18	22
437,443-(100 pg. Giants)	4	8	12	27	36	45
440-1st Grell-a on Green Arrow	2	4	6	10	13	16
441,442,444-448: 441-Grell-a on Green Arrow continues	1	3	4	6	8	10
449-(68 pgs.)	2	4	6	10	13	16
450-465,467-483,486,489-499: 454-Last Atom. 456-Grell Jaws-c. 458-Last Green Arrow.	1	2	3	4	5	7
466,485,487,488: 466-Batman, Flash app. 485-Adams-c. 487,488-(44 pgs.). 487-Origin & 1st app. Microwave Man; origin Atom retold	1	2	3	5	7	9
481-483,485-492,495-498,501-508-Whitman variants (low print run; none show issue # on cover)	1	2	3	4	5	7
484-Earth II Superman & Lois Lane wed; 40th anniversary issue(6/78)	1	3	4	6	8	10
484-Variant includes 3-D Superman punchout doll in cello. pack; 4 different inserts; Canadian promo?)	2	4	6	10	12	15
500-($1.00, 68 pgs.)-Infinity-c; Superman life story; shows Legion statues in museum	1	3	4	6	8	10
501-543,545,547-551: 511-514-Airwave II solo stories. 513-The Atom begins. 517-Aquaman begins; ends #541. 521-1st app. The Vixen. 532,536-New Teen Titans cameo. 535,536-Omega Men app. 551-Starfire becomes Red-Star						3.00
504,505,507,508-Whitman variants (no cover price)						6.00
544-(6/83, Mando paper, 68 pgs.)-45th Anniversary issue; origins new Luthor & Brainiac; Omega Men cameo; Shuster-a (pin-up); article by Siegel	1	2	3	4	5	7
546-J.L.A., New Teen Titans app.	1	2	3	5	6	8
552,553-Animal Man-c & app. (2/84 & 3/84)						6.00
554-582						4.00
583-Alan Moore scripts; last Earth 1 Superman story (cont'd from Superman #423)	1	3	4	6	8	10
584-Byrne-a begins; New Teen Titans app.						6.00
585-599: 586-Legends x-over. 596-Millennium x-over; Spectre app. 598-1st Checkmate						3.00
600-($2.50, 84 pgs., 5/88)						6.00
601-610,619-642: (#601-642 are weekly issues) ($1.50, 52 pgs.) 601-Re-intro The Secret Six; death of Katma Tui						3.00
611-618: 611-614-Catwoman stories (new costume in #611). 613-618-Nightwing stories						3.00
643-Superman & monthly issues begin again; Perez-c/a/scripts begin; swipes cover to Superman #1						4.00
644-649,651-661,663-673,675-683: 645-1st app. Maxima. 654-Part 3 of Batman storyline. 655-Free extra 8 pgs. 660-Death of Lex Luthor. 661-Begin $1.00-c. 667-($1.75, 52 pgs.). 675-Deathstroke cameo. 679-Last $1.00 issue. 683-Doomsday cameo						2.50
650-($1.50, 52 pgs.)-Lobo cameo (last panel)						3.00
662-Clark Kent reveals i.d. to Lois Lane; story cont'd in Superman #53						4.00
674-Supergirl logo & c/story (reintro)						5.00
683-685-2nd & 3rd printings						2.25
684-Doomsday battle issue						3.00
685,686-Funeral for a Friend issues; Supergirl app.						2.50
687-($1.95)-Collector's Ed.w/die-cut-c						2.50
687-($1.50)-Newsstand Edition with mini-poster						2.25
688-699,701-703-($1.50): 688-Guy Gardner-c/story. 697-Bizarro-c/story. 703-(9/94)-Zero Hour						2.25
695-($2.50)-Collector's Edition w/embossed foil-c						2.50
700-($2.95, 68 pgs.)-Fall of Metropolis Pt 1, Guice-a; Pete Ross marries Lana Lang and Smallville flashbacks with Curt Swan art & Murphy Anderson inks						3.00
700-Platinum						15.00
700-Gold						10.00
0(10/94), 704(11/94)-710-719,721-731: 710-Begin $1.95-c. 714-Joker app. 719-Batman-c/app. 721-Mr. Mxyzptlk app. 723-Dave Johnson-c. 727-Final Night x-over.						2.25
720-Lois breaks off engagement w/Clark						3.00
720-2nd print.						2.25
732-749,751-767: 732-New powers. 733-New costume, Ray app. 738-Immonen-s/a(p) begins. 741-Legion app. 744-Millennium Giants x-over. 745-747-70's-style Superman vs. Prankster. 753-JLA-c/app. 757-Hawkman-c. 760-1st Encantadora. 761-Wonder Woman app. 765-Joker & Harley-c/app. 766-Batman-c/app.						2.25
750-($2.95)						3.00
768,769,771-774: 768-Begin $2.25-c; Marvel Family-c/app. 771-Nightwing-c/app. 772,773-Ra's al Ghul app. 774-Martian Manhunter-c/app.						2.25
770-($3.50) Conclusion of Emperor Joker x-over						3.50
775-($3.75) Bradstreet-c; intro. The Elite						3.75
776-799: 776-Farewell to Krypton; Rivoche-c. 780-782-Our Worlds at War x-over. 781-Hippolyta and Maj. Lane killed. 782-War ends. 784-Joker: Last Laugh; Batman & Green Lantern app. 793-Return to Krypton. 795-The Elite app. 798-Van Fleet-c						2.25
800-(4/03, $3.95) Struzan painted-c; guest artists include Ross, Jim Lee, Jurgens, Sale						4.00
801-811: 801-Raney-a. 809-The Creeper app.						2.25
#1,000,000 (11/98) Gene Ha-c; 853rd Century x-over						2.25
Annual 1-6('87-'94, $2.95)-1-Art Adams-c/a(p); Batman app. 2-Perez-c/a(i). 3-Armageddon 2001. 4-Eclipso vs. Shazam. 5-Bloodlines; 1st app. Loose Cannon. 6-Elseworlds story						3.00
Annual 7,9 ('95, '97, $3.95)-7-Year One story. 9-Pulp Heroes sty						4.00
Annual 8 (1996, $2.95)-Legends of the Dead Earth story						3.00

NOTE: ***Supergirl's*** *origin in 262, 280, 285, 291, 305, 309.* ***N. Adams*** *c-356, 358, 359, 361-364, 366, 367, 370-374, 377-379i, 398-400, 402, 404,405, 419p, 466, 468, 469, 473i, 485.* ***Aparo*** *a-642.* ***Austin*** *c/a-682i.* ***Baily*** *a-24, 25.* ***Boring*** *a-164, 194, 211, 223, 233, 241, 250, 261, 266-268, 346, 348, 352, 356, 357.* ***Burnley*** *a-28-33; c-48?, 53-55, 58, 59?, 60-63, 65, 66p, 67p, 70p, 71p, 79p, 82p, 84-86p, 90-92p, 93p?, 94p, 107p, 108p.* ***Byrne*** *a-584-598p, 599i, 600p; c-584-591, 596-600.* ***Ditko*** *a-642.* ***Giffen*** *a-560, 563, 565, 577, 579; c-539, 560, 563, 565, 577, 579.* ***Grell*** *a-440-442, 444-446, 450-452, 456-458; c-456.* ***Guardineer*** *a-24, 25; c-8, 11, 12, 14-16, 18. 25.* ***Guice*** *a(p)-676-681, 683-698, 700; c-683, 685, 686, 687(direct), 688-693i, 694-696, 697i, 698-700.* ***Infantino*** *a-642.* ***Kaluta*** *c-613.* ***Bob Kane's*** *Clip Carson-14-41.* ***Gil Kane*** *a-443r, 493r, 539-541, 544-546, 551-554, 601-605, 642; c-535p, 540, 541, 544p, 545-549, 551-554, 580, 627.* ***Kirby*** *c-638.* ***Meskin*** *a-42-121(most).* ***Mignola*** *a-600, Annual 2; c-c-614.* ***Moldoff*** *a-23-25, 443r.* ***Mooney*** *a-667p.* ***Mortimer*** *c-153, 154, 159-172, 174, 178-181, 184, 186-189, 191-193, 196, 200, 206.* ***Orlando*** *a-617p; c-621.* ***Perez*** *a-600i, 643-652p, Annual 2p; c-529p, 602, 643-651, Annual 2p.* ***Quesada*** *c-Annual 4p.* ***Fred Ray*** *c-34, 36-46, 50-52.* ***Siegel & Shuster*** *a-1-27.* ***Paul Smith*** *c-608.* ***Starlin*** *a-509; c-631.* ***Leonard Starr*** *a-597i(part),* ***Staton*** *a-525p, 526p, 531p, 535p, 536p.* ***Swan/Moldoff*** *c-281, 286, 287, 293, 298, 334.* ***Thibert*** *c-676, 677p, 678-681, 684.* ***Toth*** *a-406, 407, 413, 431; c-616.* ***Tuska*** *a-486p, 550.* ***Williamson*** *a-568i.* ***Zeck*** *c-Annual 5*

ACTION FORCE (Also see G.I. Joe European Missions)
Marvel Comics Ltd. (British): Mar, 1987 - No. 50, 1988 ($1.00, weekly, magazine)

	GD	VG	FN	VF	VF/NM	NM-
1,3: British G.I. Joe series. 3-w/poster insert						6.00
2,4						4.00
5-10						3.00
11-50						2.50
...Special 1 (7/87) Summer holiday special; Snake Eyes-c/app.						6.00
...Special 2 (10/87) Winter special;						4.00

ACTION GIRL
Slave Labor Graphics: Oct, 1994 - Present ($2.50/$2.75/$2.95, B&W)

	GD	VG	FN	VF	VF/NM	NM-
1-19: 4-Begin $2.75-c. 19-Begin $2.95-c						3.00
1-6 ($2.75, 2nd printings): All read 2nd Print in indicia. 1-(2/96). 2-(10/95). 3-(2/96). 4-(7/96). 5-(2/97). 6-(9/97)						2.75
1-4 ($2.75, 3rd printings): All read 3rd Print in indicia.						2.75

ACTION PLANET COMICS
Action Planet: 1996 - No. 3, Sept, 1997 ($3.95, B&W, 44 pgs.)

	GD	VG	FN	VF	VF/NM	NM-
1-3: 1-Intro Monster Man by Mike Manley & other stories						4.00
Giant Size Action Planet Halloween Special (1998, $5.95, oversized)						6.00

ACTUAL CONFESSIONS (Formerly Love Adventures)
Atlas Comics (MPI): No. 13, Oct, 1952 - No. 14, Dec, 1952

	GD	VG	FN	VF	VF/NM	NM-
13,14	7	14	21	37	46	55

ACTUAL ROMANCES (Becomes True Secrets #3 on?)
Marvel Comics (IPS): Oct, 1949 - No. 2, Jan, 1950 (52 pgs.)

	GD	VG	FN	VF	VF/NM	NM-
1	11	22	33	66	88	110
2-Photo-c	8	16	24	43	54	65

ADAM AND EVE
Spire Christian Comics (Fleming H. Revell Co.): 1975,1978 (35¢/49¢)

	GD	VG	FN	VF	VF/NM	NM-
nn-By Al Hartley	2	4	6	8	10	12

ADAM STRANGE (Also see Green Lantern #132, Mystery In Space #53 & Showcase #17)
DC Comics: 1990 - No. 3, 1990 ($3.95, 52 pgs, limited series, squarebound)

	GD	VG	FN	VF	VF/NM	NM-
Book One - Three: Andy & Adam Kubert-c/a						4.00
...: The Man of Two Worlds (2003, $19.95, TPB) r/#1-3; sketch pages by Andy Kubert						20.00

ADAM-12 (TV)
Gold Key: Dec, 1973 - No. 10, Feb, 1976 (Photo-c)

	GD	VG	FN	VF	VF/NM	NM-
1	7	14	21	51	71	90
2-10	4	8	12	24	32	40

ADDAM OMEGA
Antarctic Press: Feb, 1997 - No. 4, Aug, 1997 ($2.95, B&W)

	GD	VG	FN	VF	VF/NM	NM-
1-4						3.00

ADDAMS FAMILY (TV cartoon)
Gold Key: Oct, 1974 - No. 3, Apr, 1975 (Hanna-Barbera)

	GD	VG	FN	VF	VF/NM	NM-
1	10	20	30	70	100	130
2,3	7	14	21	46	63	80

ADLAI STEVENSON
Dell Publishing Co.: Dec, 1966

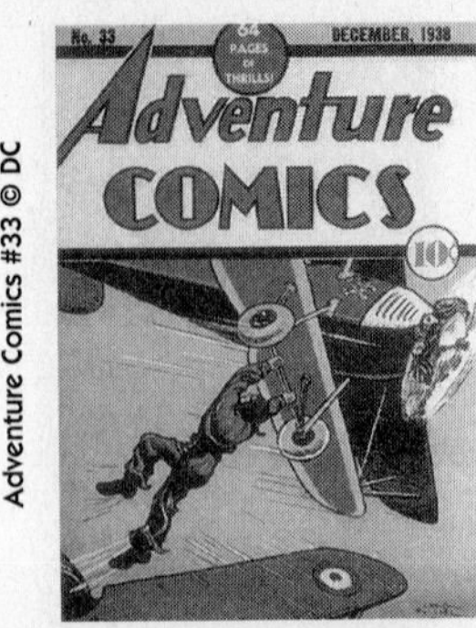

Adventure Comics #33 © DC

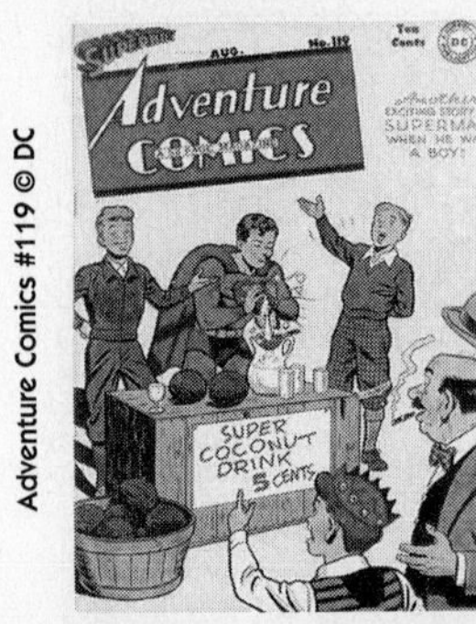

Adventure Comics #119 © DC

Adventure Comics #143 © DC

GD 2.0 | VG 4.0 | FN 6.0 | VF 8.0 | VF/NM 9.0 | NM- 9.2

12-007-612-Life story; photo-c 4 8 12 24 32 40

ADOLESCENT RADIOACTIVE BLACK BELT HAMSTERS (See Clint)
Comic Castle/Eclipse Comics: 1986 - No. 9, Jan, 1988 ($1.50, B&W)
1-9: 1st & 2nd printings exist 2.25
1-Limited Edition 3.00
1-In 3-D (7/86), 2-4 ($2.50) 2.50
Massacre The Japanese Invasion #1 (8/89, $2.00) 2.25

ADRENALYNN (See The Tenth)
Image Comics: Aug, 1999 - No. 4, Feb, 2000 ($2.50)
1-4-Tony Daniel-s/Marty Egeland-a; origin of Adrenalynn 2.50

ADULT TALES OF TERROR ILLUSTRATED (See Terror Illustrated)

ADVANCED DUNGEONS & DRAGONS (Also see TSR Worlds)
DC Comics: Dec, 1988 - No. 36, Dec, 1991 (Newsstand #1 is Holiday, 1988-89) ($1.25-$1.75)
1-Based on TSR role playing game 4.00
2-36: 25-$1.75-c begins 2.25
Annual 1 (1990, $3.95, 68 pgs.) 4.00

ADVENTURE BOUND
Dell Publishing Co.: Aug, 1949
Four Color 239 6 12 18 40 55 70

ADVENTURE COMICS (Formerly New Adventure)(...Presents Dial H For Hero #479-490)
National Periodical Publications/DC Comics: No. 32, 11/38 - No. 490, 2/82; No. 491, 9/82 - No. 503, 9/83
32-Anchors Aweigh (ends #52), Barry O'Neil (ends #60, not in #33), Captain Desmo (ends #47), Dale Daring (ends #47), Federal Men (ends #70), The Golden Dragon (ends #36), Rusty & His Pals (ends #52) by Bob Kane, Todd Hunter (ends #38) and Tom Brent (ends #39) begin 422 844 1266 2321 3061 3900
33-38: 37-Cover used on Double Action #2 200 400 600 1100 1450 1850
39(6/39)- Jack Wood begins, ends #42; 1st mention of Marijuana in comics 200 400 600 1100 1450 1850
40-(Rare, 7/39, on stands 6/10/39)-The Sandman begins by Bert Christman (who died in WWII); believed to be 1st conceived story (see N.Y. World's Fair for 1st published app.); Socko Strong begins, ends #54 4267 8534 12,800 30,000 47,000 64,000
41-O'Mealia shark-c 531 1062 1593 3717 5709 7700
42,44-Sandman-c by Flessel. 44-Opium story 676 1352 2028 4732 7266 9800
43,45 307 614 921 1996 3073 4150
46,47-Sandman covers by Flessel. 47-Steve Conrad Adventurer begins, ends #76 470 940 1410 3290 5045 6800
48-Intro & 1st app. The Hourman by Bernard Baily; Baily-c (Hourman c-48,50,52-59) 2188 4376 6564 16,400 25,700 35,000
49,50: 50-Cotton Carver by Jack Lehti begins, ends #64 248 496 744 1550 2325 3100
51,60-Sandman-c: 51-Sandman-c by Flessel. 333 666 999 2165 3333 4500
52-59: 53-1st app. Jimmy "Minuteman" Martin & the Minutemen of America in Hourman; ends #78. 58-Paul Kirk Manhunter begins (1st app.), ends #72 220 440 660 1375 2063 2750
61-1st app. Starman by Jack Burnley (4/41); Starman c-61-72; Starman by Burnley in #61-80 1063 2126 3189 7973 12,487 17,000
62-65,67,68,70: 67-Origin & 1st app. The Mist; classic Burnley-c. 70-Last Federal Men 188 376 564 1175 1763 2350
66-Origin/1st app. Shining Knight (9/41) 228 456 684 1425 2138 2850
69-1st app. Sandy the Golden Boy (Sandman's sidekick) by Paul Norris (in a Bob Kane style); Sandman dons new costume 196 392 588 1225 1838 2450
71-Jimmy Martin becomes costumed aide to the Hourman; 1st app. Hourman's Miracle Ray machine 180 360 540 1125 1688 2250
72-1st Simon & Kirby Sandman (3/42, 1st DC work) 1000 2000 3000 7500 11,750 16,000
73-Origin Manhunter by Simon & Kirby; begin new series; Manhunter-c (scarce) 1094 2188 3282 8205 12,853 17,500
74-78,80: 74-Thorndyke replaces Jimmy, Hourman's assistant; new Sandman-c begin by S&K. 75-Thor app. by Kirby; 1st Kirby Thor (see Tales of the Unexpected #16). 77-Origin Genius Jones; Mist story. 80-Last S&K Manhunter & Burnley Starman 184 368 552 1150 1725 2300
79-Classic Manhunter-c 232 464 696 1450 2175 2900
81-90: 83-Last Hourman. 84-Mike Gibbs begins, ends #102 118 236 354 738 1107 1475
91-Last Simon & Kirby Sandman 107 214 321 669 1005 1340
92-99,101,102: 92-Last Manhunter. 101-Shining Knight origin retold. 102-Last Starman, Sandman, & Genius Jones; most-S&K-c (Genius Jones cont'd in More Fun #108) 96 192 288 600 900 1200
100-S&K-c 128 256 384 800 1200 1600
103-Aquaman, Green Arrow, Johnny Quick & Superboy all move over from More Fun Comics #107; 8th app. Superboy; Superboy-c begin; 1st small logo (4/46) 312 624 936 1950 2925 3900
104 109 218 327 681 1021 1360
105-110 80 160 240 500 750 1000
111-120: 113-X-Mas-c 68 136 204 425 638 850
121,122-126,128-130: 128-1st meeting Superboy & Lois Lane 59 118 177 369 555 740
127-Brief origin Shining Knight retold 61 122 183 381 573 765
131-141,143-149: 132-Shining Knight 1st return to King Arthur time; origin aide Sir Butch 51 102 153 306 463 620
142-Origin Shining Knight & Johnny Quick retold 55 110 165 330 495 660
150,151,153,155,157,159,161,163-All have 6 pg. Shining Knight stories by Frank Frazetta. 159-Origin Johnny Quick 66 132 198 413 619 825
152,154,156,158,160,162,164-169: 166-Last Shining Knight. 168-Last 52 pg. issue 44 88 132 264 395 525
170-180 42 84 126 252 376 500
181-199: 189-B&W and color illo in **POP** 40 80 120 240 354 470
200 (5/54) 55 110 165 330 495 660
201-208: 207-Last Johnny Quick (not in 205) 39 78 117 230 325 420
209-Last pre-code issue; origin Speedy 40 80 120 240 340 440
210-1st app. Krypto (Superdog)-c/story (3/55) 294 588 882 2352 3676 5000
211-213,215-219 37 74 111 212 301 390
214-2nd app. Krypto 56 112 168 336 506 675
220-Krypto-c/sty 40 80 120 230 345 450
221-246: 229-1st S.A. issue. 237-1st Intergalactic Vigilante Squadron (6/57). 239-Krypto-c 32 64 96 182 259 335
247(4/58)-1st Legion of Super Heroes app.; 1st app. Cosmic Boy, Saturn Girl & Lightning Boy (later Lightning Lad in #267) (origin) 357 714 1071 3213 5357 7500
248-252,254,255-Green Arrow in all: 255-Intro. Red Kryptonite in Superboy (used in #252 but with no effect) 26 52 78 150 210 270
253-1st meeting of Superboy & Robin; Green Arrow by Kirby in #250-255 (also see World's Finest #96-99) 32 64 96 182 259 335
256-Origin Green Arrow by Kirby 65 130 195 406 613 820
257-259: 258-Green Arrow x-over in Superboy 22 44 66 127 176 225
260-1st Silver-Age origin Aquaman (5/59) 74 148 222 463 694 925
261-265,268,270: 262-Origin Speedy in Green Arrow. 270-Congorilla begins, ends #281,283 18 36 54 104 142 180
266-(11/59)-Origin & 1st app. Aquagirl (tryout, not same as later character) 19 38 57 107 149 190
267(12/59)-2nd Legion of Super Heroes; Lightning Boy now called Lightning Lad; new costumes for Legion 88 176 264 550 825 1100
269-Intro. Aqualad (2/60); last Green Arrow (not in #206) 31 62 93 178 252 325
271-Origin Luthor retold 34 68 102 196 278 360
272-274,277-280: 279-Intro White Kryptonite in Superboy. 280-1st meeting Superboy & Lori Lemaris 16 32 48 92 126 160
275-Origin Superman-Batman team retold (see World's Finest #94) 26 52 78 147 206 265
276-(9/60) Robinson Crusoe-like story 17 34 51 98 134 170
281,284,287-289: 281-Last Congorilla. 284-Last Aquaman in Adv.; Mooney-a. 287,288-Intro Dev-Em, the Knave from Krypton. 287-1st Bizarro Perry White & Jimmy Olsen. 288-Bizarro-c. 289-Legion cameo (statues) 15 30 45 84 115 145
282(3/61)-5th Legion app; intro/origin Star Boy 27 54 81 155 218 280
283-Intro. The Phantom Zone 25 50 75 144 198 255
285-1st Tales of the Bizarro World-c/story (ends #299) in Adv. (see Action #255) 21 42 63 118 164 210
286-1st Bizarro Mxyzptlk; Bizarro-c 19 38 57 109 152 195
290(11/61)-9th Legion app; origin Sunboy in Legion (last 10¢ issue) 25 50 75 147 202 260
291,292,295-298: 291-1st 12¢ ish, (12/61). 292-1st Bizarro Lana Lang & Lucy Lane. 295-Bizarro-c; 1st Bizarro Titano 10 20 30 72 104 135
293(2/62)-13th Legion app; Mon-el & Legion of Super Pets (1st app./origin) app. (1st Superhorse). 1st Bizarro Luthor & Kandor 16 32 48 113 167 220
294-1st Bizarro Marilyn Monroe, Pres. Kennedy. 12 24 36 87 129 170
299-1st Gold Kryptonite (8/62) 10 20 30 73 107 140
300-Tales of the Legion of Super-Heroes series begins (9/62); Mon-el leaves Phantom Zone (temporarily), joins Legion 37 74 111 278 414 550
301-Origin Bouncing Boy 15 30 45 104 152 200
302-305: 303-1st app. Matter-Eater Lad. 304-Death of Lightning Lad in Legion 11 22 33 75 110 145
306-310: 306-Intro. Legion of Substitute Heroes. 307-1st app. Element Lad in Legion. 308-1st app. Lightning Lass in Legion 10 20 30 72 104 135
311-320: 312-Lightning Lad back in Legion. 315-Last new Superboy story; Colossal Boy app. 316-Origins & powers of Legion given. 317-Intro. Dream Girl in Legion; Lightning Lass

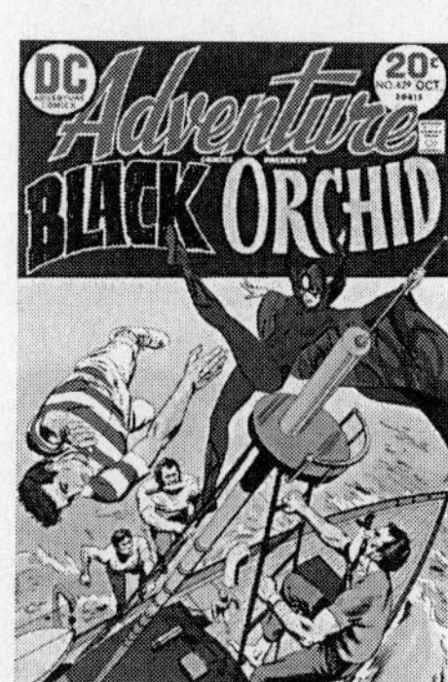

Adventure Comics #429 © DC

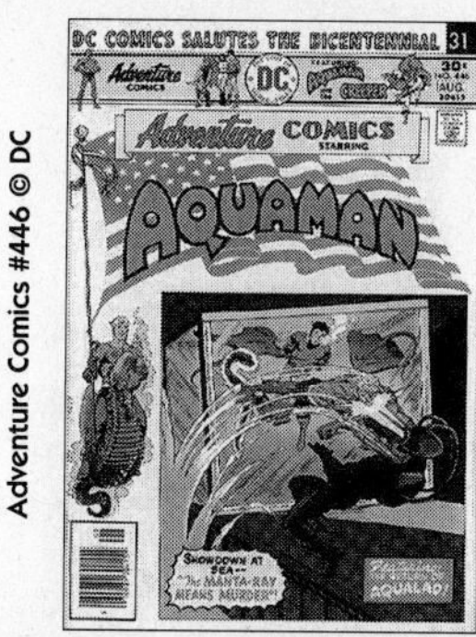

Adventure Comics #446 © DC

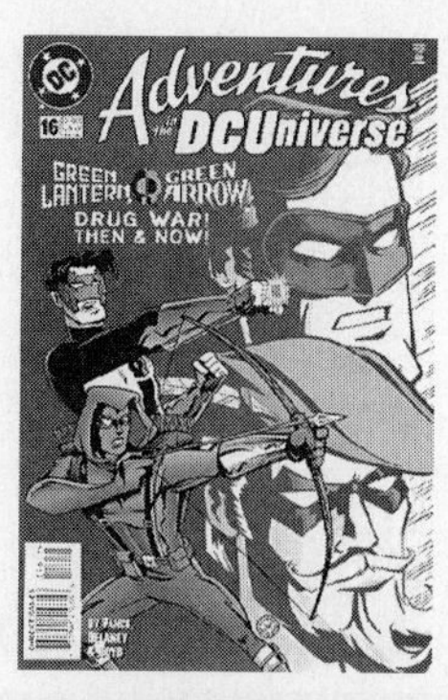

Adventures in the DC Universe #16 © DC

becomes Light Lass; Hall of Fame series begins. 320-Dev-Em 2nd app. 9 18 27 60 85 110
321-Intro. Time Trapper 8 16 24 53 74 95
322-330: 327-Intro/1st app. Lone Wolf in Legion. 329-Intro The Bizarro Legionnaires; intro. Legion flight rings 7 14 21 50 68 85
331-340: 337-Chlorophyll Kid & Night Girl app. 340-Intro Computo in Legion 6 12 18 43 59 75
341-Triplicate Girl becomes Duo Damsel 6 12 18 38 52 65
342-345,347-351: 345-Last Hall of Fame; returns in 356,371. 348-Origin Sunboy; intro Dr. Regulus in Legion. 349-Intro Universo & Rond Vidar. 351-1st app. White Witch 5 10 15 36 48 60
346-1st app. Karate Kid, Princess Projectra, Ferro Lad, & Nemesis Kid. 7 14 21 50 68 85
352,354-360: 354,355-Superman meets the Adult Legion. 355-Insect Queen joins Legion (4/67) 5 10 15 33 44 55
353-Death of Ferro Lad in Legion 6 12 18 40 55 70
361-364,366,368-370: 369-Intro Mordru in Legion 4 8 12 28 38 48
365,367: 365-Intro Shadow Lass (memorial to Shadow Woman app. in #354's Adult Legion-s); lists origins & powers of L.S.H. 367-New Legion headquarters 4 8 12 29 40 50
371,372: 371-Intro. Chemical King (mentioned in #354's Adult Legion-s). 372-Timber Wolf & Chemical King join 4 8 12 29 40 50
373,374,376-380: 373-Intro. Tornado Twins (Barry Allen Flash descendants). 374-Article on comics fandom. 380-Last Legion in Adventure; last 12¢-c 4 8 12 27 36 45
375-Intro Quantum Queen & The Wanderers 4 8 12 29 40 50
381-Supergirl begins; 1st full length Supergirl story & her 1st solo book (6/69) 9 18 27 65 93 120
382-389 4 8 12 24 32 40
390-Giant Supergirl G-69 6 12 18 40 55 70
391-396,398 3 6 9 19 25 32
397-1st app. new Supergirl 4 8 12 27 36 45
399-Unpubbed G.A. Black Canary story 4 8 12 22 30 38
400-New costume for Supergirl (12/70) 4 8 12 27 36 45
401,402,404-408-(15¢-c) 3 6 9 16 20 25
403-68 pg. Giant G-81; Legion-r/#304,305,308,312 6 12 18 40 55 70
409-411,413-415,417-420-(52 pgs.): 413-Hawkman by Kubert r/B&B #44; G.A. Robotman-r/Det. #178; Zatanna by Morrow. 414-r-2nd Animal Man/Str. Advs. #184. 415-Animal Man-r/Str. Adv.#190 (origin recap). 417-Morrow Vigilante; Frazetta Shining Knight-r/Adv. #161; origin The Enchantress; no Zatanna. 418-Prev. unpub. Dr. Mid-Nite story from 1948; no Zatanna. 420-Animal Man-r/Str. Adv. #195 3 6 9 19 25 32
412-(52 pgs.) Reprints origin & 1st app. of Animal Man from Strange Adventures #180 3 6 9 19 25 32
416-Also listed as DC 100 Pg. Super Spectacular #10; Golden Age-r; r/1st app. Black Canary from Flash #86; no Zatanna
(see DC 100 Pg. Super Spectacular #10 for price)
421-424,427: 424-Last Supergirl in Adventure. 427-Last Vigilante 2 4 6 10 12 15
425-New look, content change to adventure; Kaluta-c; Toth-a, origin Capt. Fear 3 6 9 18 24 30
426-1st Adventurers Club. 2 4 6 10 12 15
428-Origin/1st app. Black Orchid (c/story, 6-7/73) 6 12 18 38 52 65
429,430-Black Orchid-c/stories 3 6 9 19 25 32
431-Spectre by Aparo begins, ends #440. 6 12 18 40 55 70
432-439-Spectre app. 433-437-Cover title is Weird Adventure Comics. 436-Last 20¢ issue 3 7 10 21 28 35
440-New Spectre origin. 4 8 12 28 38 48
441-458: 441-452-Aquaman app. 443-Fisherman app. 445-447-The Creeper app. 446-Flag-c. 449-451-Martian Manhunter app. 450-Weather Wizard app. in Aquaman story. 453-458-Superboy app. 453-Intro. Mighty Girl. 457,458-Eclipso app. 1 2 3 5 7 9
459,460 (68 pgs.): 459-New Gods/Darkseid storyline concludes from New Gods #19 (#459 is dated 9-10/78) without missing a month. 459-Flash (ends #466), Deadman (ends #466), Wonder Woman (ends #464), Green Lantern (ends #460). 460-Aquaman (ends #478) 3 6 9 16 20 24
461,462 ($1.00, 68 pgs.): 461-Justice Society begins; ends 466. 461,462-Death Earth II Batman 3 6 9 19 25 32
463-466 ($1.00 size, 68 pgs.) 2 4 6 10 13 16
467-Starman by Ditko & Plastic Man begins; 1st app. Prince Gavyn (Starman). 2 4 6 8 10 12
468-490: 470-Origin Starman. 479-Dial 'H' For Hero begins, ends #490. 478-Last Starman & Plastic Man. 480-490: Dial 'H' For Hero 5.00
491-503: 491-100pg. Digest size begins; r/Legion of Super Heroes/Adv. #247, 267; Spectre, Aquaman, Superboy, S&K Sandman, Black Canary-r & new Shazam by Newton begin. 492,495,496,499-S&K Sandman-r/Adventure in all. 493-Challengers of the Unknown begins by Tuska w/brief origin. 493-495,497-499-G.A. Captain Marvel-r. 494-499-Spectre-r/Spectre 1-3, 5-7. 496-Capt. Marvel Jr. new-s, Cockrum-a. 498-Mary Marvel new-s; Plastic Man-r begin; origin Bouncing Boy-r/ #301. 500-Legion-r (Digest size, 148 pgs.).
501-503: G.A.-r 2 4 6 10 13 16
... 80 Page Giant (10/98, $4.95) Wonder Woman, Shazam, Superboy, Supergirl, Green Arrow, Legion, Bizarro World stories 5.00

NOTE: *Bizarro covers-285, 286, 288, 294, 295, 329. Vigilante app.-420, 426, 427.* **N. Adams** *a(r)-495i-498i; c-365-369, 371-373, 375-379, 381-383.* **Aparo** *a-431-433, 434i, 435, 436, 437i, 438i, 439-452, 503r; c-431-452.* **Austin** *a-449i 451i.* **Bernard Baily** *c-48, 50, 52-59.* **Bolland** *c-475.* **Burnley** *c-61-72, 116-120p.* **Chaykin** *a-438.* **Ditko** *a-467-478p; c-467p.* **Creig Flessel** *c-32, 33, 40, 42, 44, 46, 47, 51, 60.* **Giffen** *c-491p-494p, 500p.* **Grell** *a-435-437, 440.* **Guardineer** *c-34, 35, 45.* **Infantino** *a-416r.* **Kaluta** *c-425.* **Bob Kane** *a-38.* **G. Kane** *a-414r, 425; c-496-499, 537.* **Kirby** *a-250-256.* **Kubert** *a-413.* **Meskin** *a-81,127.* **Moldoff** *a-494i; c-49.* **Morrow** *a-413-415, 417, 422, 502r, 503r.* **Netzer/Nasser** *a-449-451.* **Newton** *a-459-461, 464-466, 491p, 492p.* **Paul Norris** *a-69.* **Orlando** *a-457p, 458p.* **Perez** *c-484-486, 490p.* **Simon/Kirby** *a-503r; c-73-97, 100-102.* **Starlin** *c-471.* **Staton** *a-445-447i, 456-458p, 459, 460, 461p-465p, 466,467p-478p, 502p(r); c-458, 461(back).* **Toth** *a-418, 419, 425, 431, 495p-497p.* **Tuska** *a-494p.*

ADVENTURE COMICS (Also see All Star Comics 1999 crossover titles)
DC Comics: May, 1999 ($1.99, one-shot)

1-Golden Age Starman and the Atom; Snejbjerg-a 2.25

ADVENTURE INTO MYSTERY
Atlas Comics (BFP No. 1/OPI No. 2-8): May, 1956 - No. 8, July, 1957

1-Powell s/f-a; Forte-a; Everett-c 39 78 117 230 325 420
2-Flying Saucer story 22 44 66 124 172 220
3,6-Everett-c 19 38 57 107 149 190
4-7: 4-Williamson-a, 4 pgs; Powell-a. 5-Everett-c/a, Orlando-a. 7-Torres-a; Everett-c 21 42 63 118 164 210
8-Moriera, Sale, Torres, Woodbridge-a, Severin-c 19 38 57 107 149 190

ADVENTURE IS MY CAREER
U.S. Coast Guard Academy/Street & Smith: 1945 (44 pgs.)

nn-Simon, Milt Gross-a 21 42 63 118 164 210

ADVENTURERS, THE
Aircel Comics/Adventure Publ.: Aug, 1986 - No. 10, 1987? ($1.50, B&W)
V2#1, 1987 - V2#9, 1988; V3#1, Oct, 1989 - V3#6, 1990

1-Peter Hsu-a 1 2 3 5 6 7
1-Cover variant, limited ed. 1 3 4 6 8 10
1-2nd print (1986); 1st app. Elf Warrior 3.00
2,3, 0 (#4, 12/86)-Origin, 5-10, Book II, reg. & Limited Ed. #1 3.50
Book II, #2,3,0,4-7 2.25
Book III, #1 (10/89, $2.25)-Reg. & limited-c, Book III, #2-6 2.25

ADVENTURES (No. 2 Spectacular... on cover)
St. John Publishing Co.: Nov, 1949 - No. 2, Feb, 1950 (No. 1 ...in Romance on cover) (Slightly larger size)

1(Scarce); Bolle, Starr-a(2) 28 56 84 159 225 290
2(Scarce)-Slave Girl; China Bombshell app.; Bolle, L. Starr-a 40 80 120 240 350 460

ADVENTURES FOR BOYS
Bailey Enterprises: Dec, 1954

nn-Comics, text, & photos 7 14 21 37 46 55

ADVENTURES IN PARADISE (TV)
Dell Publishing Co.: Feb-Apr, 1962

Four Color#1301 6 12 18 43 59 75

ADVENTURES IN ROMANCE (See Adventures)

ADVENTURES IN SCIENCE (See Classics Illustrated Special Issue)

ADVENTURES IN THE DC UNIVERSE
DC Comics: Apr, 1997 - No. 19, Oct, 1998 ($1.75/$1.95/$1.99)

1-Animated style in all: JLA-c/app 5.00
2-11,13-17,19: 2-Flash app. 3-Wonder Woman. 4-Green Lantern. 6-Aquaman. 7-Shazam Family. 8-Blue Beetle & Booster Gold. 9-Flash. 10-Legion. 11-Green Lantern & Wonder Woman. 13-Impulse & Martian Manhunter. 14-Superboy/Flash race 3.50
12,18-JLA-c/app 3.50
Annual 1(1997, $3.95)-Dr. Fate, Impulse, Rose & Thorn, Superboy, Mister Miracle app. 4.50

ADVENTURES IN THE RIFLE BRIGADE
DC Comics (Vertigo): Oct, 2000 - No. 3, Dec, 2000 ($2.50, limited series)

1-3-Ennis-s/Ezquerra-a/Bolland-c 2.50

ADVENTURES IN THE RIFLE BRIGADE: OPERATION BOLLOCK
DC Comics (Vertigo): Oct, 2001 - No. 3, Jan, 2002 ($2.50, limited series)

1-3-Ennis-s/Ezquerra-a/Fabry-c 2.50

ADVENTURES IN 3-D (With glasses)

Adventures Into Terror #31 © MAR

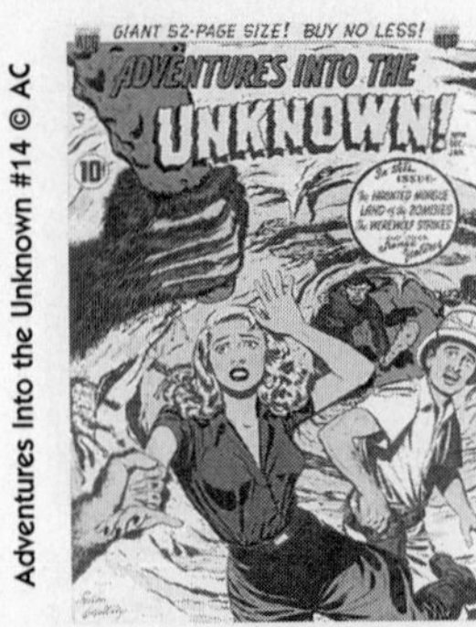

Adventures Into the Unknown #14 © AC

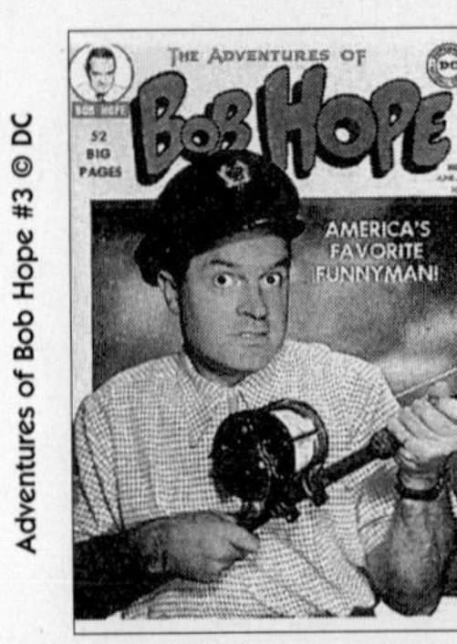

Adventures of Bob Hope #3 © DC

Harvey Publications: Nov, 1953 - No. 2, Jan, 1954 (25¢)

	GD 2.0	VG 4.0	FN 6.0	VF 8.0	VF/NM 9.0	NM- 9.2
1-Nostrand, Powell-a, 2-Powell-a	19	38	57	106	146	185

ADVENTURES INTO DARKNESS (See Seduction of the Innocent 3-D)
Better-Standard Publications/Visual Editions: No. 5, Aug, 1952- No. 14, 1954

	GD 2.0	VG 4.0	FN 6.0	VF 8.0	VF/NM 9.0	NM- 9.2
5-Katz-c/a; Toth-a(p)	40	80	120	240	350	460
6-Tuska, Katz-a	28	56	84	159	225	290
7-9: 7-Katz-c/a. 8,9-Toth-a(p)	28	56	84	159	225	290
10-12: 10,11-Jack Katz-a. 12-Toth-a; lingerie panel	25	50	75	144	198	255
13-Toth-a(p); Cannibalism story cited by T. E. Murphy articles	30	60	90	173	244	315
14	19	38	57	106	146	185

NOTE: *Fawcette a-13. Moriera a-5. Sekowsky a-10, 11, 13(2).*

ADVENTURES INTO TERROR (Formerly Joker Comics)
Marvel/Atlas Comics (CDS): No. 43, Nov, 1950 - No. 31, May, 1954

	GD 2.0	VG 4.0	FN 6.0	VF 8.0	VF/NM 9.0	NM- 9.2
43(#1)	66	132	198	413	617	820
44(#2, 2/51)-Sol Brodsky-c	43	86	129	258	389	520
3(4/51), 4	30	60	90	173	244	315
5-Wolverton-c panel/Mystic #6; Rico-c panel also; Atom Bomb story	34	68	102	196	278	360
6,8: 8-Wolverton text illo r-/Marvel Tales #104	28	56	84	161	228	295
7-Wolverton-a "Where Monsters Dwell", 6 pgs.; Tuska-c; Maneely-c panels	58	116	174	363	544	725
9,10,12-Krigstein-a. 9-Decapitation panels	24	48	72	138	194	250
11,13-20	22	44	66	124	172	220
21-24,26-31	19	38	57	109	152	195
25-Matt Fox-a	25	50	75	147	202	260

NOTE: *Ayers a-21. Colan a-3, 5, 14, 21, 24, 25, 28, 29; c-27. Colletta a-30. Everett c-13, 21, 25. Fass a-28, 29. Forte a-28. Heath a-43, 44, 4-6, 22, 24, 26; c-43, 9, 11. Lazarus a-7. Maneely a-7(3 pg.), 10, 11, 21., 22 c-15, 29. Don Rico a-4, 5(3 pg.). Sekowsky a-43, 3, 4. Sinnott a-8, 9, 11, 28. Tuska a-14; c-7.*

ADVENTURES INTO THE UNKNOWN
American Comics Group: Fall, 1948 - No. 174, Aug, 1967 (No. 1-33: 52 pgs.)
(1st continuous series Supernatural comic; see Eerie #1)

	GD 2.0	VG 4.0	FN 6.0	VF 8.0	VF/NM 9.0	NM- 9.2
1-Guardineer-a; adapt. of 'Castle of Otranto' by Horace Walpole	212	424	636	1325	1988	2650
2,3: 3-Feldstein-a (9 pgs)	76	152	228	475	713	950
4,5: 5- 'Spirit Of Frankenstein' series begins, ends #12 (except #11)	40	80	120	240	358	475
6-10	34	68	102	193	274	365
11-16,18-20: 13-Starr-a	28	56	84	161	228	295
17-Story similar to movie 'The Thing'	34	68	102	193	274	355
21-26,28-30	24	48	72	138	194	250
27-Williamson/Krenkel-a (8 pgs.)	32	64	96	180	255	330
31-50: 38-Atom bomb panels	19	38	57	109	152	195
51-(1/54)-(3-D effect-c/story)-Only white cover	38	76	114	219	310	400
52-58: (3-D effect-c/stories with black covers). 52-E.C. swipe/Haunt Of Fear #14	36	72	108	204	290	375
59-3-D effect story only; new logo	29	58	87	164	232	300
60-Wood*esque*-a by Landau	14	28	42	81	111	140
61-Last pre-code issue (1-2/55)	14	28	42	81	111	140
62-70	8	16	24	55	78	100
71-90	7	14	21	46	63	80
91,96(#95 on inside),107,116-All have Williamson-a	8	16	24	53	74	95
92-95,97-99,101-106,108-115,117-128: 109-113,118-Whitney painted-c. 128-Williamson/Krenkel/Torres-a(r)/Forbidden Worlds #63; last 10¢ issue	5	10	15	36	48	60
100	6	12	18	38	52	65
129-153,157: 153,157-Magic Agent app.	4	8	12	28	38	48
154-Nemesis series begins (origin), ends #170	5	10	15	36	48	60
155,156,158-167,170-174	4	8	12	27	36	45
168-Ditko-a(p)	5	10	15	33	44	55
169-Nemesis battles Hitler	5	10	15	33	44	55

NOTE: *"Spirit of Frankenstein" series in 5, 6, 8-10, 12, 16. Buscema a-100, 106, 108-110, 158r, 165r. Cameron a-34. Craig a-152, 160. Goode a-45, 47, 60. Landau a-51, 59-63. Lazarus a-34, 48, 51, 52, 56, 58, 79, 87; c-31-56, 58. Reinman a-102, 111, 112, 115-118, 124, 130, 137, 141, 145, 164. Whitney c-12-30, 57, 59-on (most.) Torres/Williamson a-116.*

ADVENTURES INTO WEIRD WORLDS
Marvel/Atlas Comics (ACI): Jan, 1952 - No. 30, June, 1954

	GD 2.0	VG 4.0	FN 6.0	VF 8.0	VF/NM 9.0	NM- 9.2
1-Atom bomb panels	59	118	177	369	555	740
2-Sci/fic stories (2); one by Maneely	39	78	117	230	325	420
3-10: 7-Tongue ripped out. 10-Krigstein, Everett-a	28	56	84	159	225	290
11-20	23	46	69	130	183	235
21-Hitler in Hell story	26	52	78	150	210	270
22-26: 24-Man holds hypo & splits in two	20	40	60	112	156	200
27-Matt Fox end of world story-a; severed head-c	38	76	114	219	310	400
28-Atom bomb story; decapitation panels	23	46	69	130	183	235
29,30	17	34	51	95	130	165

NOTE: *Ayers a-8, 26. Everett a-4, 5; c-6, 8, 10-13, 18, 19, 22, 24, 25; a-4, 25. Fass a-7. Forte a-21, 24. Al Hartley a-2. Heath a-1, 4, 17, 22; c-7, 9, 20. Maneely a-2, 3, 11, 20, 22, 23, 25; c-1, 3, 22, 25-27, 29. Reinman a-24, 28. Rico a-13. Robinson a-13. Sinnott a-25, 30. Tuska a-1, 2, 12, 15. Whitney a-7. Wildey a-28. Bondage c-22.*

ADVENTURES IN WONDERLAND
Lev Gleason Publications: April, 1955 - No. 5, Feb, 1956 (Jr. Readers Guild)

	GD 2.0	VG 4.0	FN 6.0	VF 8.0	VF/NM 9.0	NM- 9.2
1-Maurer-a	11	22	33	63	84	105
2-4	7	14	21	37	46	55
5-Christmas issue	8	16	24	40	50	60

ADVENTURES OF AARON
Image Comics: Mar, 1997 - No. 3, Sept, 1997 (2.95, B&W)

	GD 2.0	VG 4.0	FN 6.0	VF 8.0	VF/NM 9.0	NM- 9.2
1,2,100(#3),3(#4)						3.00

ADVENTURES OF ALAN LADD, THE
National Periodical Publ.: Oct-Nov, 1949 - No. 9, Feb-Mar, 1951 (All 52 pgs.)

	GD 2.0	VG 4.0	FN 6.0	VF 8.0	VF/NM 9.0	NM- 9.2
1-Photo-c	92	184	276	575	863	1150
2-Photo-c	48	96	144	288	432	575
3-6: Last photo-c	39	78	117	230	325	420
7-9	33	66	99	190	270	350

NOTE: *Dan Barry a-1. Moreira a-3-7.*

ADVENTURES OF ALICE (Also see Alice in Wonderland & ...at Monkey Island)
Civil Service Publ./Pentagon Publishing Co.: 1945

	GD 2.0	VG 4.0	FN 6.0	VF 8.0	VF/NM 9.0	NM- 9.2
1	14	28	42	79	107	135
2-Through the Magic Looking Glass	10	20	30	60	80	100

ADVENTURES OF BARON MUNCHAUSEN, THE
Now Comics: July, 1989 - No. 4, Oct, 1989 ($1.75, limited series)

	GD 2.0	VG 4.0	FN 6.0	VF 8.0	VF/NM 9.0	NM- 9.2
1-4: Movie adaptation						2.25

ADVENTURES OF BARRY WEEN, BOY GENIUS, THE
Image Comics: Mar, 1999 - No. 3, May, 1999 ($2.95, B&W, limited series)

	GD 2.0	VG 4.0	FN 6.0	VF 8.0	VF/NM 9.0	NM- 9.2
1-3-Judd Winick-s/a						3.00
TPB (Oni Press, 11/99, $8.95)						9.00

ADVENTURES OF BARRY WEEN, BOY GENIUS 2.0, THE
Oni Press: Feb, 2000 - No. 3, Apr, 2000 ($2.95, B&W, limited series)

	GD 2.0	VG 4.0	FN 6.0	VF 8.0	VF/NM 9.0	NM- 9.2
1-3-Judd Winick-s/a						3.00
TPB (2000, $8.95)						9.00

ADVENTURES OF BARRY WEEN, BOY GENIUS 3, THE : MONKEY TALES
Oni Press: Feb, 2001 - No. 6, Feb, 2002 ($2.95, B&W, limited series)

	GD 2.0	VG 4.0	FN 6.0	VF 8.0	VF/NM 9.0	NM- 9.2
1-6-Judd Winick-s/a						3.00
TPB (2001, $8.95) r/#1-3; intro. by Peter David						9.00
...4 TPB (5/02, $8.95) r/#4-6						9.00

ADVENTURES OF BAYOU BILLY, THE
Archie Comics: Sept, 1989 - No. 5, June, 1990 ($1.00)

	GD 2.0	VG 4.0	FN 6.0	VF 8.0	VF/NM 9.0	NM- 9.2
1-5: Esposito-c/a(i). 5-Kelley Jones-c						3.00

ADVENTURES OF BOB HOPE, THE (Also see True Comics #59)
National Per. Publ.: Feb-Mar, 1950 - No. 109, Feb-Mar, 1968 (#1-10: 52pgs.)

	GD 2.0	VG 4.0	FN 6.0	VF 8.0	VF/NM 9.0	NM- 9.2
1-Photo-c	184	369	552	1150	1725	2300
2-Photo-c	80	160	240	500	750	1000
3,4-Photo-c	50	100	150	300	450	600
5-10	40	80	120	240	358	475
11-20	27	54	81	155	218	280
21-31 (2-3/55; last precode)	19	38	57	106	146	185
32-40	10	20	30	73	107	140
41-50	9	18	27	60	85	110
51-70	7	14	21	46	63	80
71-93	5	10	15	33	44	55
94-Aquaman cameo	5	10	15	36	48	60
95-1st app. Super-Hip & 1st monster issue (11/65)	7	14	21	46	63	80
96-105: Super-Hip and monster stories in all. 103-Batman, Robin, Ringo Starr cameos	5	10	15	33	44	55
106-109-All monster-c/stories by N. Adams-c/a	7	14	21	50	68	85

NOTE: *Buzzy in #34. Kitty Karr of Hollywood in #15, 17-20, 23, 28. Liz in #26, 109. Miss Beverly Hills of Hollywood in #7, 8, 10, 13, 14. Miss Melody Lane of Broadway in #15. Rusty in #23, 25. Tommy in #24. No 2nd feature in #2-4, 6, 8, 11, 12, 28-108.*

ADVENTURES OF CAPTAIN AMERICA
Marvel Comics: Sept, 1991 - No. 4, Jan, 1992 ($4.95, 52 pgs., squarebound, limited series)

1-4: 1-Origin in WW2; embossed-c; Nicieza scripts; Maguire-c/a(p) begins, ends #3.

Adventures of Dean Martin and Jerry Lewis #3 © DC

Adventures of Mighty Mouse #3 © STJ

Adventures of Rex the Wonder Dog #5 © DC

	GD 2.0	VG 4.0	FN 6.0	VF 8.0	VF/NM 9.0	NM- 9.2
2-4-Austin-c/a(i). 3,4-Red Skull app.						5.00

ADVENTURES OF CYCLOPS AND PHOENIX (Also See Askani'son & The Further Adventures of Cyclops And Phoenix)
Marvel Comics: May, 1994 - No. 4, Aug, 1994 ($2.95, limited series)

	GD 2.0	VG 4.0	FN 6.0	VF 8.0	VF/NM 9.0	NM- 9.2
1-4-Characters from X-Men; origin of Cable						4.00
Trade paperback ($14.95)-reprints #1-4						15.00

ADVENTURES OF DEAN MARTIN AND JERRY LEWIS, THE
(The Adventures of Jerry Lewis #41 on) (See Movie Love #12)
National Periodical Publications: July-Aug, 1952 - No. 40, Oct, 1957

	GD 2.0	VG 4.0	FN 6.0	VF 8.0	VF/NM 9.0	NM- 9.2
1	100	200	300	625	938	1250
2-3 pg origin on how they became a team	50	100	150	300	450	600
3-10: 3- I Love Lucy text featurette	31	62	93	175	248	320
11-19: Last precode (2/55)	20	40	60	112	156	200
20-30	15	30	45	86	118	150
31-40	12	24	36	71	96	120

ADVENTURES OF DETECTIVE ACE KING, THE (Also see Bob Scully-- & Detective Dan)
Humor Publ. Corp.: No date (1933) (36 pgs., 9-1/2x12") (10¢, B&W, one-shot) (paper-c)

	GD 2.0	VG 4.0	FN 6.0	VF 8.0	VF/NM 9.0	NM- 9.2
Book 1-Along with Bob Scully & Detective Dan, the first comic w/original art & the first of a single theme.; Not reprints; Ace King by Martin Nadle (The American Sherlock Holmes). A Dick Tracy look-alike	350	700	1050	2800	-	-

ADVENTURES OF EVIL AND MALICE, THE
Image Comics: June, 1999 - No. 3, Nov, 1999 ($3.50/$3.95, limited series)

	GD 2.0	VG 4.0	FN 6.0	VF 8.0	VF/NM 9.0	NM- 9.2
1,2-Jimmie Robinson-s/a						3.50
3-(3.95)						4.00

ADVENTURES OF FELIX THE CAT, THE
Harvey Comics: May, 1992 ($1.25)

	GD 2.0	VG 4.0	FN 6.0	VF 8.0	VF/NM 9.0	NM- 9.2
1-Messmer-r						4.00

ADVENTURES OF FORD FAIRLANE, THE
DC Comics: May, 1990 - No. 4, Aug, 1990 ($1.50, limited series, mature)

	GD 2.0	VG 4.0	FN 6.0	VF 8.0	VF/NM 9.0	NM- 9.2
1-4: Andrew Dice Clay movie tie-in; Don Heck inks						3.00

ADVENTURES OF HOMER COBB, THE
Say/Bart Prod. : Sept, 1947 (Oversized) (Published in the U.S., but printed in Canada)

	GD 2.0	VG 4.0	FN 6.0	VF 8.0	VF/NM 9.0	NM- 9.2
1-(Scarce)-Feldstein-c/a	31	62	93	175	248	320

ADVENTURES OF HOMER GHOST (See Homer The Happy Ghost)
Atlas Comics: June, 1957 - No. 2, Aug, 1957

	GD 2.0	VG 4.0	FN 6.0	VF 8.0	VF/NM 9.0	NM- 9.2
V1#1,2: 2-Robot-c	9	18	27	52	66	80

ADVENTURES OF JERRY LEWIS, THE (Adventures of Dean Martin & Jerry Lewis No. 1-40) (See Super DC Giant)
National Periodical Publ.: No. 41, Nov, 1957 - No. 124, May-June, 1971

	GD 2.0	VG 4.0	FN 6.0	VF 8.0	VF/NM 9.0	NM- 9.2
41	9	18	27	60	85	110
42-60	7	14	21	50	68	85
61-67,69-73,75-80	6	12	18	40	55	70
68,74-Photo-c (movie)	7	14	21	51	71	90
81,82,85-87,90,91,94,96,98,99	5	10	15	33	44	55
83,84,88: 83-1st Monsters-c/s. 84-Jerry as a Super-hero-c/s. 88-1st Witch, Miss Kraft	5	10	15	36	48	60
89-Bob Hope app.; Wizard of Oz & Alfred E. Neuman in MAD parody	6	12	18	40	55	70
92-Superman cameo	6	12	18	40	55	70
93-Beatles parody as babies	5	10	15	36	48	60
95-1st Uncle Hal Wack-A-Boy Camp-c/s	5	10	15	36	48	60
97-Batman/Robin/Joker-c/story; Riddler & Penguin app; Dick Sprang-c.	9	18	27	65	93	120
100	6	12	18	38	52	65
101,103,104-Neal Adams-c/a	7	14	21	50	68	85
102-Beatles app.; Neal Adams c/a	9	18	27	60	85	110
105-Superman x-over	6	12	18	43	59	75
106-111,113-116	4	8	12	27	36	45
112,117: 112-Flash x-over. 117-W. Woman x-over	6	12	18	43	59	75
118-124	4	8	12	24	32	40

NOTE: *Monster-c/s-90,93,96,98,101. Wack-A-Buy Camp-c/s-96,99,102,107,108.*

ADVENTURES OF JO-JOY, THE (See Jo-Joy)

ADVENTURES OF LASSIE, THE (See Lassie)

ADVENTURES OF LUTHER ARKWRIGHT, THE
Valkyrie Press/Dark Horse Comics: Oct, 1987 - No. 9, Jan, 1989 ($2.00, B&W) V2, #1, Mar, 1990 - V2#9, 1990 ($1.95, B&W)

	GD 2.0	VG 4.0	FN 6.0	VF 8.0	VF/NM 9.0	NM- 9.2
1-9: 1-Alan Moore intro., V2#1-9 (Dark Horse): r-1st series; new-c						4.00
TPB (1997, $14.95) r/#1-9 w/Michael Moorcock intro.						15.00

ADVENTURES OF MIGHTY MOUSE (Mighty Mouse Adventures No. 1)
St. John Publishing Co.: No. 2, Jan, 1952 - No. 18, May, 1955

	GD 2.0	VG 4.0	FN 6.0	VF 8.0	VF/NM 9.0	NM- 9.2
2	25	50	75	147	202	260
3-5	14	28	42	81	111	140
6-18	10	20	30	58	77	95

ADVENTURES OF MIGHTY MOUSE (2nd Series) (Becomes Mighty Mouse #161 on)
(Two No. 144's; formerly Paul Terry's Comics; No. 129-137 have nn's)
St. John/Pines/Dell/Gold Key: No. 126, Aug, 1955 - No. 160, Oct, 1963

	GD 2.0	VG 4.0	FN 6.0	VF 8.0	VF/NM 9.0	NM- 9.2
126(8/55), 127(10/55), 128(11/55)-St. John	9	18	27	49	62	75
nn(129, 4/56)-144(8/59)-Pines	5	10	15	36	48	60
144(10-12/59)-155(7-9/62) Dell	4	8	12	29	40	50
156(10/62)-160(10/63) Gold Key	4	8	12	29	40	50

NOTE: *Early issues titled "Paul Terry's Adventures of ...."*

ADVENTURES OF MIGHTY MOUSE (Formerly Mighty Mouse)
Gold Key: No. 166, Mar, 1979 - No. 172, Jan, 1980

	GD 2.0	VG 4.0	FN 6.0	VF 8.0	VF/NM 9.0	NM- 9.2
166-172	1	2	3	5	6	8

ADVS. OF MR. FROG & MISS MOUSE (See Dell Junior Treasury No. 4)

ADVENTURES OF OZZIE & HARRIET, THE (See Ozzie & Harriet)

ADVENTURES OF PATORUZU
Green Publishing Co.: Aug, 1946 - Winter, 1946

	GD 2.0	VG 4.0	FN 6.0	VF 8.0	VF/NM 9.0	NM- 9.2
nn's-Contains Animal Crackers reprints	6	12	18	28	34	40

ADVENTURES OF PINKY LEE, THE (TV)
Atlas Comics: July, 1955 - No. 5, Dec, 1955

	GD 2.0	VG 4.0	FN 6.0	VF 8.0	VF/NM 9.0	NM- 9.2
1	28	56	84	157	221	285
2-5	17	34	51	98	134	170

ADVENTURES OF PIPSQUEAK, THE (Formerly Pat the Brat)
Archie Publications (Radio Comics): No. 34, Sept, 1959 - No. 39, July, 1960

	GD 2.0	VG 4.0	FN 6.0	VF 8.0	VF/NM 9.0	NM- 9.2
34	4	8	12	24	32	40
35-39	3	6	9	18	24	30

ADVENTURES OF QUAKE & QUISP, THE (See Quaker Oats "Plenty of Glutton")

ADVENTURES OF REX THE WONDER DOG, THE (Rex...No. 1)
National Periodical Publ.: Jan-Feb, 1952 - No. 45, May-June, 1959; No. 46, Nov-Dec, 1959

	GD 2.0	VG 4.0	FN 6.0	VF 8.0	VF/NM 9.0	NM- 9.2
1-(Scarce)-Toth-c/a	124	248	372	775	1163	1550
2-(Scarce)-Toth-c/a	57	114	171	356	538	720
3-(Scarce)-Toth-a	46	92	138	276	413	550
4,5	39	78	117	230	325	420
6-10	31	62	93	175	248	320
11-Atom bomb-c/story; dinosaur-c/sty	36	72	108	204	290	375
12-19: 19-Last precode (1-2/55)	19	38	57	106	146	185
20-46	14	28	42	79	107	135

NOTE: ***Infantino, Gil Kane** art in 5-19 (most)*

ADVENTURES OF RHEUMY PEEPERS AND CHUNKY HIGHLIGHTS, THE
Oni Press: Feb, 1999 ($2.95, B&W, one-shot)

	GD 2.0	VG 4.0	FN 6.0	VF 8.0	VF/NM 9.0	NM- 9.2
nn-Penn Jillette-s/Renée French-a						3.00

ADVENTURES OF ROBIN HOOD, THE (Formerly Robin Hood)
Magazine Enterprises (Sussex Publ. Co.): No. 7, 9/57 - No. 8, 11/57
(Based on Richard Greene TV Show)

	GD 2.0	VG 4.0	FN 6.0	VF 8.0	VF/NM 9.0	NM- 9.2
7,8-Richard Greene photo-c. 7-Powell-a	16	32	48	89	122	155

ADVENTURES OF ROBIN HOOD, THE
Gold Key: Mar, 1974 - No. 7, Jan, 1975 (Disney cartoon) (36 pgs.)

	GD 2.0	VG 4.0	FN 6.0	VF 8.0	VF/NM 9.0	NM- 9.2
1(90291-403)-Part-r of $1.50 editions	2	4	6	12	16	20
2-7: 1-7 are part-r	2	4	6	8	10	12

ADVENTURES OF SNAKE PLISSKEN
Marvel Comics: Jan, 1997 ($2.50, one-shot)

	GD 2.0	VG 4.0	FN 6.0	VF 8.0	VF/NM 9.0	NM- 9.2
1-Based on Escape From L.A. movie; Brereton-c						3.50

ADVENTURES OF SPIDER-MAN, THE (Based on animated TV series)
Marvel Comics: Apr, 1996 - No. 12, Mar, 1997 (99¢)

	GD 2.0	VG 4.0	FN 6.0	VF 8.0	VF/NM 9.0	NM- 9.2
1-12: 1-Punisher app. 2-Venom cameo. 3-X-Men. 6-Fantastic Four						3.00

ADVENTURES OF SUPERBOY, THE (See Superboy, 2nd Series)

ADVENTURES OF SUPERMAN (Formerly Superman)
DC Comics: No. 424, Jan, 1987 - No. 499, Feb, 1993; No. 500, Early June, 1993 - Present

	GD 2.0	VG 4.0	FN 6.0	VF 8.0	VF/NM 9.0	NM- 9.2
424-Ordway-c/a/Wolfman-s begin following Byrne's Superman revamp						3.00
425-435,437-462: 426-Legends x-over. 432-1st app. Jose Delgado who becomes Gangbuster						

Adventures of Superman #612 © DC

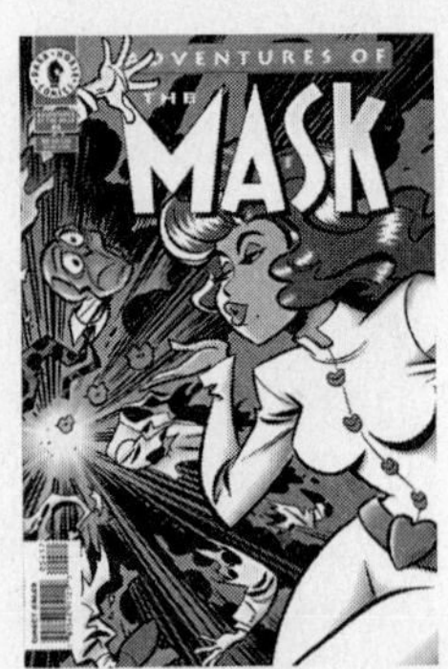

Adventures of the Mask #4 © DH

The Agency #4 © TCOW & Paul Jenkins & Kyle Hotz

GD 2.0 | VG 4.0 | FN 6.0 | VF 8.0 | VF/NM 9.0 | NM- 9.2

in #434. 437-Millennium x-over. 438-New Brainiac app. 440-Batman app. 449-Invasion 3.00
436-Byrne scripts begin; Millennium x-over 3.50
463-Superman/Flash race; cover swipe/Superman #199 5.00
464-Lobo-c & app. (pre-dates Lobo #1) 4.00
465-495: 467-Part 2 of Batman story. 473-Hal Jordan, Guy Gardner x-over. 477-Legion app. 491-Last $1.00-c. 480-($1.75, 52 pgs.). 495-Forever People-c/story; Darkseid app. 2.50
496,497: 496-Doomsday cameo. 497-Doomsday battle issue 3.00
496,497-2nd printings 2.25
498,499-Funeral for a Friend; Supergirl app. 2.50
498-2nd & 3rd printings 2.25
500-($2.95, 68 pgs.)-Collector's edition w/card 3.50
500-($2.50, 68 pgs.)-Regular edition w/different-c 2.50
500-Platinum edition 30.00
501-($1.95)-Collector's edition with die-cut-c 2.25
501-($1.50)-Regular edition w/mini-poster & diff.-c 2.25
502-516: 502-Supergirl-c/story. 508-Challengers of the Unknown app. 510-Bizarro-c/story. 516-(9/94)-Zero Hour 2.25
505-($2.50)-Holo-grafx foil-c edition 2.50
0,517-523: 0-(10/94). 517-(11/94) 2.25
524-549,551-580: 524-Begin $1.95-c. 527-Return of Alpha Centurion (Zero Hour). 533-Impulse-c/app. 535-Luthor-c/app. 536-Brainiac app. 537-Parasite app. 540-Final Night x-over. 541-Superboy-c/app.; Lois & Clark honeymoon. 545-New powers. 546-New costume. 551-Cyborg app. 555-Red & Blue Supermen battle. 557-Millennium Giants x-over. 558-560: Superman Silver Age-style story; Krypto app. 561-Begin $1.99-c. 565-JLA app. 2.25
550-($3.50)-Double sized 3.50
581-588: 581-Begin $2.25-c. 583-Emperor Joker. 588-Casey-s 2.25
589-595: 589-Return to Krypton; Rivoche-c. 591-Wolfman-s. 593-595-Our Worlds at War x-over. 593-New Suicide Squad formed. 594-Doomsday-c/app. 2.25
596-Aftermath of "War" x-over has panel showing damaged World Trade Center buildings; issue went on sale the day after the Sept. 11 attack 5.00
597-599,601-623: 597-Joker: Last Laugh. 604,605-Ultraman, Owlman,Superwoman app. 606-Return to Krypton. 612-616,619-623-Nowlan-c 2.25
600-($3.95) Wieringo-a; painted-c by Adel; pin-ups by various 4.00
#1,000,000 (11/98) Gene Ha-c; 853rd Century x-over 3.00
Annual 1 (1987, $1.25, 52 pgs.)-Starlin-c & scripts 4.00
Annual 2,3 (1990, 1991, $2.00, 68 pgs.): 2-Byrne-c/a(i); Legion '90 (Lobo) app. 3-Armageddon 2001 x-over 3.00
Annual 4-6 ('92-'94, $2.50, 68 pgs.): 4-Guy Gardner/Lobo-c/story; Eclipso storyline; Quesada-c(p). 5-Bloodlines storyline. 6-Elseworlds sty. 3.00
Annual 7,9('95, '97, $3.95)-7-Year One story. 9-Pulp Heroes sty 4.00
Annual 8 (1996, $2.95)-Legends of the Dead Earth story 3.00
NOTE: **Erik Larsen** *a-431.*

ADVENTURES OF THE DOVER BOYS
Archie Comics (Close-up): September, 1950 - No. 2, 1950 (No month given)
1,2 9 18 27 52 66 80

ADVENTURES OF THE FLY (The Fly #1-6; Fly Man No. 32-39; See The Double Life of Private Strong, The Fly, Laugh Comics & Mighty Crusaders)
Archie Publications/Radio Comics: Aug, 1959 - No. 30, Oct, 1964; No. 31, May, 1965
1-Shield app.; origin The Fly; S&K-c/a 48 96 144 386 581 775
2-Williamson, S&K-a 29 58 87 210 305 400
3-Origin retold; Davis, Powell-a 24 48 72 169 247 325
4-Neal Adams-a(p)(1 panel); S&K-c; Powell-a; 2 pg. Shield story 14 28 42 97 141 185
5,6,9,10: 9-Shield app. 9-1st app. Cat Girl. 10-Black Hood app. 9 18 27 65 93 120
7,8: 7-1st S.A. app. Black Hood (7/60). 8-1st S.A. app. Shield (9/60) 11 22 33 75 110 145
11-13,15-20: 13-1st app. Fly Girl w/o costume. 16-Last 10¢ issue. 20-Origin Fly Girl retold 6 12 18 43 59 75
14-Origin & 1st app. Fly Girl in costume 8 16 24 53 74 95
21-30: 23-Jaguar cameo. 27-29-Black Hood 1 pg. strips. 30-Comet x-over (1st S.A. app.) in Fly Girl 4 8 12 29 40 50
31-Black Hood, Shield, Comet app. 5 10 15 33 44 55
NOTE: **Simon** *c-2-4.* **Tuska** *a-1. Cover title to #31 is Flyman; Advs. of the Fly inside.*

ADVENTURES OF THE JAGUAR, THE (See Blue Ribbon Comics, Laugh Comics & Mighty Crusaders)
Archie Publications (Radio Comics): Sept, 1961 - No. 15, Nov, 1963
1-Origin Jaguar (1st app?) by J. Rosenberger 20 40 60 140 205 270
2,3: 3-Last 10¢ issue 10 20 30 72 104 135
4-6-Catgirl app. (#4's-c is same as splash pg.) 8 16 24 55 78 100
7-10 6 12 18 43 59 75
11-15:13,14-Catgirl, Black Hood app. in both 5 10 15 36 48 60

ADVENTURES OF THE MASK (TV cartoon)
Dark Horse Comics: Jan, 1996 - No. 12, Dec, 1996 ($2.50)
1-12: Based on animated series 2.50

ADVENTURES OF THE NEW MEN (Formerly Newmen #1-21)
Maximum Press: No. 22, Nov, 1996; No. 23, March, 1997 ($2.50)
22,23-Sprouse-c/a 2.50

ADVENTURES OF THE OUTSIDERS, THE (Formerly Batman & The Outsiders; also see The Outsiders)
DC Comics: No. 33, May, 1986 - No. 46, June, 1987
33-46: 39-45-r/Outsiders #1-7 by Aparo 2.25

ADVENTURES OF THE SUPER MARIO BROTHERS (See Super Mario Bros.)
Valiant: 1990 - No. 9, Oct, 1991 ($1.50)
V2#1-9 5.00

ADVENTURES OF THE THING, THE (Also see The Thing)
Marvel Comics: Apr, 1992 - No. 4, July, 1992, ($1.25, limited series)
1-4: 1-r/Marvel Two-In-One #50 by Byrne; Kieth-c. 2-4-r/Marvel Two-In-One #80,51 & 77; 2-Ghost Rider-c/story; Quesada-c. 3-Miller-r/Quesada-c; new Perez-a (4 pgs.) 2.25

ADVENTURES OF THE X-MEN, THE (Based on animated TV series)
Marvel Comics: Apr, 1996 - No. 12, Mar, 1997 (99¢)
1-12: 1-Wolverine/Hulk battle. 3-Spider-Man-c. 5,6-Magneto-c/app. 3.00

ADVENTURES OF TINKER BELL (See Tinker Bell, 4-Color No. 896 & 982)

ADVENTURES OF TOM SAWYER (See Dell Junior Treasury No. 10)

ADVENTURES OF YOUNG DR. MASTERS, THE
Archie Comics (Radio Comics): Aug, 1964 - No. 2, Nov, 1964
1 3 6 9 19 25 32
2 2 4 6 14 18 22

ADVENTURES ON OTHER WORLDS (See Showcase #17 & 18)

ADVENTURES ON THE PLANET OF THE APES (Also see Planet of the Apes)
Marvel Comics Group: Oct, 1975 - No. 11, Dec, 1976
1-Planet of the Apes magazine-r in color; Starlin-c; adapts movie thru #6 3 6 9 18 23 28
2-5: 5-(25¢-c edition) 2 4 6 9 11 14
5-7-(30¢-c variants, limited distribution) 3 6 9 18 23 28
6-10: 6,7-(25¢-c edition). 7-Adapts 2nd movie (thru #11) 2 4 6 10 13 16
11-Last issue; concludes 2nd movie adaptation 2 4 6 12 16 20
NOTE: **Alcala** *a-6-11r.* **Buckler** *c-2p.* **Nasser** *c-7.* **Ploog** *a-1-9.* **Starlin** *c-6.* **Tuska** *a-1-5r.*

AFRICA
Magazine Enterprises: 1955
1(A-1#137)-Cave Girl, Thun'da;Powell-c/a(4) 27 54 81 155 218 280

AFRICAN LION (Disney movie)
Dell Publishing Co.: Nov, 1955
Four Color #665 6 12 18 43 59 75

AFTER DARK
Sterling Comics: No. 6, May, 1955 - No. 8, Sept, 1955
6-8-Sekowsky-a in all 9 18 27 52 66 80

AFTERMATH (Leads into Lady Death: Dark Millennium)
Chaos! Comics: Feb, 2000 ($2.95, one-shot)
1-Pulido & Kaminski-s/Luke Ross-a; Reis-c 3.00
1-($6.95) DF Edition; Brereton painted-c 7.00

AGAINST BLACKSHARD 3-D (Also see SoulQuest)
Sirius Comics: August, 1986 ($2.25)
1 3.50

AGENCY, THE
Image Comics (Top Cow): August, 2001 - No. 6, Mar, 2002 ($2.50/$2.95/$4.95)
1,2: 1-Jenkins-s/Hotz-a; three covers by Hotz, Turner, Silvestri 2.50
3-5 ($2.95) 3.00
6-($4.95) Flip-c preview of Jeremiah TV series 5.00
Preview (2001, 16 pgs.) B&W pages, cover previews, sketch pages 2.25

AGENT LIBERTY SPECIAL (See Superman, 2nd Series)
DC Comics: 1992 ($2.00, 52 pgs, one-shot)
1-1st solo adventure; Guice-c/a(i) 2.50

AGENTS, THE

Agent X #1 © MAR

Airboy Comics #110 © HILL

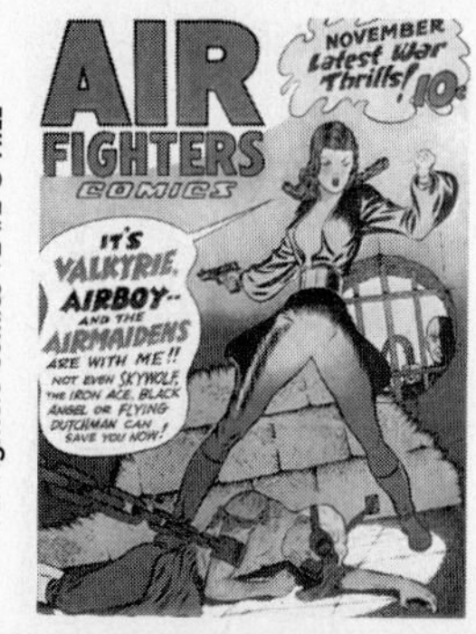

Air Fighters Comics V2 #2 © HILL

	GD 2.0	VG 4.0	FN 6.0	VF 8.0	VF/NM 9.0	NM- 9.2

Image Comics: Apr, 2003 - No. 6, Sept, 2003 ($2.95, B&W)

1-6-Ben Dunn-c/a 3.00

AGENTS OF LAW (Also see Comic's Greatest World)
Dark Horse Comics: Mar, 1995 - No. 6, Sept, 1995 ($2.50)

1-6: 5-Predator app. 6-Predator app.; death of Law 2.50

AGENT X (Continued from Deadpool)
Marvel Comics: Sept. 2002 - No. 15, Dec, 2003 ($2.99/$2.25)

1-($2.99) Simone-s/Udon Studios-a; Taskmaster app. 3.00
2-9-($2.25) 2-Punisher app. 2.25
10-15-($2.99) 10,11-Evan Dorkin-s. 12-Hotz-a 3.00

AGE OF APOCALYPSE: THE CHOSEN
Marvel Comics: Apr, 1995 ($2.50, one-shot)

1-Wraparound-c 3.00

AGE OF BRONZE
Image Comics: Nov, 1998 - Present ($2.95/$3.50, B&W, limited series)

1-6-Eric Shanower-c/s/a 3.00
7-18-($3.50) 3.50
...Behind the Scenes (5/02, $3.50) background info and creative process 3.50
...Special (6/99, $2.95) Story of Agamemnon and Menelaus 3.00
A Thousand Ships (7/01, $19.95, TPB) r/#1-9 20.00

AGE OF HEROES, THE
Halloween Comics/Image Comics #3 on: 1996 - No. 5, 1999 ($2.95, B&W)

1-5: James Hudnall scripts; John Ridgway-c/a 3.00
...Special ($4.95) r/#1,2 5.00
...Special 2 ($6.95) r/#3,4 7.00
...Wex 1 ('98, $2.95) Hudnall-s/Angel Fernandez-a 3.00

AGE OF INNOCENCE: THE REBIRTH OF IRON MAN
Marvel Comics: Feb, 1996 ($2.50, one-shot)

1-New origin of Tony Stark 3.00

AGE OF REPTILES
Dark Horse Comics: Nov, 1993 - No. 4, Feb, 1994 ($2.50, limited series)

1-4: Delgado-c/a/scripts in all 3.00

AGE OF REPTILES: THE HUNT
Dark Horse Comics: May, 1996 - No. 5, Sept, 1996 ($2.95, limited series)

1-5: Delgado-c/a/scripts in all; wraparound-c 3.00

AGGIE MACK
Four Star Comics Corp./Superior Comics Ltd.: Jan, 1948 - No. 8, Aug, 1949

	GD	VG	FN	VF	VF/NM	NM-
1-Feldstein-a, "Johnny Prep"	38	76	114	219	310	400
2,3-Kamen-c	20	40	60	112	156	200
4-Feldstein "Johnny Prep"; Kamen-c	27	54	81	155	218	280
5-8-Kamen-c/a	21	42	63	118	164	210

AGGIE MACK
Dell Publishing Co.: Apr - Jun, 1962

	GD	VG	FN	VF	VF/NM	NM-
Four Color #1335	4	8	12	28	38	48

AIR ACE (Formerly Bill Barnes No. 1-12)
Street & Smith Publications: V2#1, Jan, 1944 - V3#8(No. 20), Feb-Mar, 1947

	GD	VG	FN	VF	VF/NM	NM-
V2#1-Nazi concentration camp-c	40	80	120	240	345	450
V2#2-Classic-c	39	78	117	233	329	425
V2#3-12: 7-Powell-a	17	34	51	98	134	170
V3#1-6	14	28	42	79	107	135
V3#7-Powell bondage-c/a; all atomic issue	25	50	75	147	202	260
V3#8 (V5#8 on-c)-Powell-c/a	15	30	45	86	118	150

AIRBOY (Also see Airmaidens, Skywolf, Target: Airboy & Valkyrie)
Eclipse Comics: July, 1986 - No. 50, Oct, 1989 (#1-8, 50¢, 20 pgs., bi-weekly; #9-on, 36pgs.; #34-on monthly)

1-4: 2-1st Marisa; Skywolf gets new costume. 3-The Heap begins 4.00
5-Valkyrie returns; Dave Stevens-c 6.00
6-49: 9-Begin $1.25-c; Skywolf begins. 11-Origin of G.A. Airboy & his plane Birdie. 28-Mr. Monster vs. The Heap. 33-Begin $1.75-c. 38-40-The Heap by Infantino. 41-r/1st app. Valkyrie from Air Fighters. 42-Begin $1.95-c. 46,47-part-r/Air Fighters. 48-Black Angel-r/A.F 3.00
50 ($4.95, 52 pgs.)-Kubert-c 5.00

NOTE: ***Evans*** *c-21.* ***Gulacy*** *c-7, 20.* ***Spiegle*** *a-34, 35, 37.* ***Ken Steacy*** *painted c-17, 33.*

AIRBOY COMICS (Air Fighters Comics No. 1-22)
Hillman Periodicals: V2#11, Dec, 1945 - V10#4, May, 1953 (No V3#3)

	GD	VG	FN	VF	VF/NM	NM-
V2#11	72	144	216	450	675	900
12-Valkyrie-c/app.	49	98	147	294	442	590
V3#1,2(no #3)	40	80	120	234	332	430
4-The Heap app. in Skywolf	37	74	111	212	301	390
5,7,8,10,11	32	64	96	182	259	335
6-Valkyrie-c/app.	34	68	102	196	278	360
9-Origin The Heap	37	74	111	212	301	390
12-Skywolf & Airboy x-over; Valkyrie-c/app.	40	80	120	234	332	430
V4#1-Iron Lady app.	35	70	105	201	288	370
2,3,12: 2-Rackman begins	25	50	75	147	202	260
4-Simon & Kirby-c	28	56	84	161	228	295
5-9,11-All S&K-a	28	56	84	157	221	285
10-Valkyrie-c/app.	29	58	87	164	232	300
V5#1-4,6-11: 4-Infantino Heap. 10-Origin The Heap	19	38	57	109	152	195
5-Skull-c.	22	44	66	127	176	225
12-Krigstein-a(p)	21	42	63	118	164	210
V6#1-3,5-12: 6,8-Origin The Heap	18	36	54	104	142	180
4-Origin retold	23	46	69	130	183	235
V7#1-12: 7,8,10-Origin The Heap	18	36	54	104	142	180
V8#1-3,5-12	17	34	51	98	134	170
4-Krigstein-a	18	36	54	104	142	180
V9#1,3,4,6-12: 7-One pg. Frazetta ad	14	28	42	81	111	140
2-Valkyrie app.	15	30	45	86	118	150
5(#100)	15	30	45	86	118	150
V10#1-4	13	26	39	74	100	125

NOTE: ***Barry*** *a-V2#3, 7.* ***Bolle*** *a-V4#12.* ***McWilliams*** *a-V3#7, 9.* ***Powell*** *a-V7#2, 3, V8#1, 6.* ***Starr*** *a-V5#1, 12.* ***Dick Wood*** *a-V4#12. Bondage-c V5#8.*

AIRBOY MEETS THE PROWLER
Eclipse Comics: Aug, 1987 ($1.95, one-shot)

1-John Snyder, III-c/a 3.00

AIRBOY-MR. MONSTER SPECIAL
Eclipse Comics: Aug, 1987 ($1.75, one-shot)

1 3.00

AIRBOY VERSUS THE AIR MAIDENS
Eclipse Comics: July, 1988 ($1.95)

1 3.00

AIR FIGHTERS CLASSICS
Eclipse Comics: Nov, 1987 - No. 6, May, 1989 ($3.95, 68 pgs., B&W)

1-6: Reprints G.A. Air Fighters #2-7. 1-Origin Airboy 4.00

AIR FIGHTERS COMICS (Airboy Comics #23 (V2#11) on)
Hillman Periodicals: Nov, 1941; No. 2, Nov, 1942 - V2#10, Fall, 1945

	GD	VG	FN	VF	VF/NM	NM-
V1#1-(Produced by Funnies, Inc.); Black Commander only app.	220	440	660	1375	2063	2750
2(11/42)-(Produced by Quality artists & Biro for Hillman); Origin & 1st app. Airboy & Iron Ace; Black Angel (1st app.), Flying Dutchman & Skywolf (1st app.) begin; Fuje-a; Biro-c/a	341	682	1023	2217	3409	4600
3-Origin/1st app. The Heap; origin Skywolf; 2nd Airboy app./c	180	360	540	1125	1688	2250
4-Japan war-c	128	256	384	800	1200	1600
5-Japanese octopus War-c	109	218	327	681	1021	1360
6-Japanese soldiers as rats-c	124	248	372	775	1163	1550
7-Classic Nazi swastika-c	116	232	348	725	1088	1450
8-12: 8,10,11-War covers	80	160	240	500	750	1000
V2#1-Classic Nazi War-c	82	164	246	513	769	1025
2-Skywolf by Giunta; Flying Dutchman by Fuje; 1st meeting Valkyrie & Airboy (she worked for the Nazis in beginning); 1st app. Valkyrie (11/43); Valkyrie-c	106	212	318	663	994	1325
3,4,6,8,9	63	126	189	394	590	785
5,7: 5-Flag-c; Fuje-a. 7-Valkyrie app.	67	134	201	419	627	835
10-Origin The Heap & Skywolf	72	144	216	450	675	900

NOTE: ***Fuje*** *a-V1#2, 5, 7, V2#2, 3, 5, 7-9.* ***Giunta*** *a-V2#2, 3, 7, 9.*

AIRFIGHTERS MEET SGT. STRIKE SPECIAL, THE
Eclipse Comics: Jan, 1988 ($1.95, one-shot, stiff-c)

1-Airboy, Valkyrie, Skywolf app. 3.00

AIR FORCES (See American Air Forces)

AIRMAIDENS SPECIAL
Eclipse Comics: August, 1987 ($1.75, one-shot, Baxter paper)

1-Marisa becomes La Lupina (origin) 3.00

AIR RAIDERS

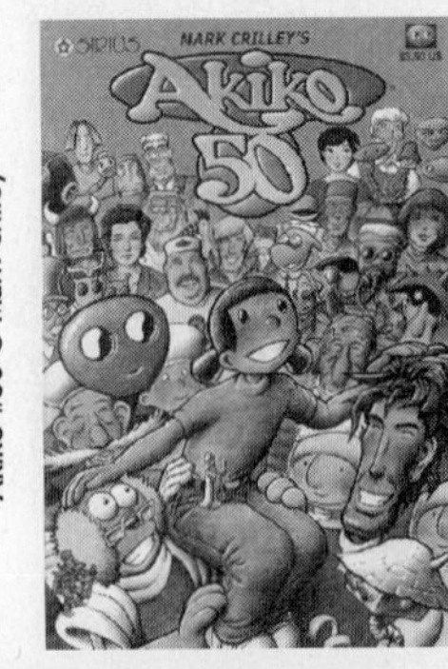

Akiko #50 © Mark Crilley

Akira #31 © Kodansha, Ltd.

Alan Moore's Songbook © Alan Moore

Marvel Comics (Star Comics)/Marvel #3 on: Nov, 1987- No. 5, Mar, 1988 ($1.00)

	GD 2.0	VG 4.0	FN 6.0	VF 8.0	VF/NM 9.0	NM- 9.2
1,5: Kelley Jones-a in all						3.50
2-4: 2-Thunderhammer app.						2.50

AIRTIGHT GARAGE, THE (Also see Elsewhere Prince)
Marvel Comics (Epic Comics): July, 1993 - No. 4, Oct, 1993 ($2.50, lim. series, Baxter paper)

	GD 2.0	VG 4.0	FN 6.0	VF 8.0	VF/NM 9.0	NM- 9.2
1-4: Moebius-c/a/scripts						4.00

AIR WAR STORIES
Dell Publishing Co.: Sept-Nov, 1964 - No. 8, Aug, 1966

	GD 2.0	VG 4.0	FN 6.0	VF 8.0	VF/NM 9.0	NM- 9.2
1-Painted-c; Glanzman-c/a begins	4	8	12	29	40	50
2-8: 2-Painted-c (all painted?)	3	6	9	18	24	30

A.K.A. GOLDFISH
Caliber Comics: 1994 - 1995 (B&W, $3.50/$3.95)

	GD 2.0	VG 4.0	FN 6.0	VF 8.0	VF/NM 9.0	NM- 9.2
...:Ace; ...:Jack; ...:Queen; ...:Joker; ...:King -Brian Michael Bendis-s/a						4.00
TPB (1996, $17.95)						20.00
Goldfish: The Definitive Collection (Image, 2001, $19.95) r/series plus promo art and new prose story; intro. by Matt Wagner						20.00
10th Anniversary HC (Image, 2002, $49.95)						50.00

AKIKO
Sirius: Mar, 1996 - Present ($2.50/$2.95, B&W)

	GD 2.0	VG 4.0	FN 6.0	VF 8.0	VF/NM 9.0	NM- 9.2
1-Crilley-c/a/scripts in all						5.00
2						4.00
3-39: 25-($2.95, 32 pgs.)-w/Asala back-up pages						3.00
40-49: 40-Begin $2.95-c						3.00
50-($3.50)						3.50
Flights of Fancy TPB (5/02, $12.95) r/various features, pin-ups and gags						13.00
TPB Volume 1,4 ('97, 2/00, $14.95) 1-r/#1-7. 4-r/#19-25						15.00
TPB Volume 2,3 ('98, '99, $11.95) 2-r/#8-13. 3- r/#14-18						12.00
TPB Volume 5 (12/01, $12.95) r/#26-31						13.00
TPB Volume 6 (6/03, $14.95) r/#32-38						15.00

AKIKO ON THE PLANET SMOO
Sirius: Dec, 1995 ($3.95, B&W)

	GD 2.0	VG 4.0	FN 6.0	VF 8.0	VF/NM 9.0	NM- 9.2
V1#1-($3.95)-Crilley-c/a/scripts; gatefold-c						5.00
Ashcan ('95, mail offer)						3.00
Hardcover V1#1 (12/95, $19.95, B&W, 40 pgs.)						20.00
The Color Edition(2/00,$4.95)						5.00

AKIRA
Marvel Comics (Epic): Sept, 1988 - No. 38, Dec, 1995 ($3.50/$3.95/$6.95, deluxe, 68 pgs.)

	GD 2.0	VG 4.0	FN 6.0	VF 8.0	VF/NM 9.0	NM- 9.2
1-Manga by Katsuhiro Otomo	3	6	9	18	24	30
1,2-2nd printings (1989, $3.95)						5.00
2	2	4	6	10	12	15
3-5	2	4	6	8	10	12
6-16	1	2	3	5	7	9
17-33: 17-$3.95-c begins						6.00
34-38: 34-(1994)-$6.95-c begins. 35-37: 35-(1995). 37-Texeira back-up, Gibbons, Williams pin-ups. 38-Moebius, Allred, Pratt, Toth, Romita, Van Fleet, O'Neill, Madureira pin-ups	2	4	6	8	10	12

ALADDIN & HIS WONDERFUL LAMP (See Dell Jr Treasury #2)

ALAN LADD (See The Adventures of...)

ALAN MOORE'S AWESOME UNIVERSE HANDBOOK (Also see Across the Universe:...)
Awesome Entertainment: Apr, 1999 ($2.95, B&W)

	GD 2.0	VG 4.0	FN 6.0	VF 8.0	VF/NM 9.0	NM- 9.2
1-Alan Moore-text/ Alex Ross-sketch pages and 2 covers						5.00

ALAN MOORE'S SONGBOOK
Caliber Comics: 1998 ($5.95, B&W)

	GD 2.0	VG 4.0	FN 6.0	VF 8.0	VF/NM 9.0	NM- 9.2
1-Alan Moore song lyrics w/illust. by various	1	2	3	4	5	7

ALARMING ADVENTURES
Harvey Publications: Oct, 1962 - No. 3, Feb, 1963

	GD 2.0	VG 4.0	FN 6.0	VF 8.0	VF/NM 9.0	NM- 9.2
1-Crandall/Williamson-a	9	18	27	65	93	120
2-Williamson/Crandall-a	6	12	18	40	55	70
3	5	10	15	36	48	60

NOTE: ***Bailey** a-1, 3.* ***Crandall** a-1p, 2i.* ***Powell** a-2(2).* ***Severin** c-1-3.* ***Torres** a-2?* ***Tuska** a-1.* ***Williamson** a-1i, 2p.*

ALARMING TALES
Harvey Publications (Western Tales): Sept, 1957 - No. 6, Nov, 1958

	GD 2.0	VG 4.0	FN 6.0	VF 8.0	VF/NM 9.0	NM- 9.2
1-Kirby-c/a(4); Kamandi prototype story by Kirby	27	54	81	155	218	280
2-Kirby-a(4)	20	40	60	112	156	200
3,4-Kirby-a. 4-Powell, Wildey-a	15	30	45	86	118	150
5-Kirby/Williamson-a; Wildey-a; Severin-c	16	32	48	92	126	160
6-Williamson-a?; Severin-c	13	26	39	74	100	125

ALBEDO
Thoughts And Images: Apr, 1985 - No. 14, Spring, 1989 (B&W)
Antarctic Press: (Vol. 2) Jun, 1991 - No. 10 ($2.50)

	GD 2.0	VG 4.0	FN 6.0	VF 8.0	VF/NM 9.0	NM- 9.2
0-Yellow cover; 50 copies	8	16	24	55	78	100
0-White cover, 450 copies	4	8	12	29	40	50
0-Blue, 1st printing, 500 copies	4	8	12	24	32	40
0-Blue, 2nd printing, 1000 copies	2	4	6	12	16	20
0-3rd & 4th printing	1	2	3	4	5	7
1-Dark red - low print run	3	7	10	21	28	35
1-Bright red - low print run	3	6	9	16	20	25
2 -1st app. Usagi Yojimbo by Stan Sakai; 2000 copies - no 2nd printing	15	30	45	104	152	200
3	2	4	6	11	14	18
4-Usagi Yojimbo-c	3	6	9	16	20	24
5-14						5.00
(Vol. 2) 1-10, Color Special						4.00

ALBEDO ANTHROPOMORPHICS
Antarctic Press: (Vol. 3) Spring, 1994 - No. 4, Jan, 1996 ($2.95, color); (Vol. 4) Dec, 1999 - No. 2, Jan, 1999 ($2.95/$2.99, B&W)

	GD 2.0	VG 4.0	FN 6.0	VF 8.0	VF/NM 9.0	NM- 9.2
V3#1-4-Steve Gallacci-c/a. V4#1,2						3.00

ALBERTO (See The Crusaders)

ALBERT THE ALLIGATOR & POGO POSSUM (See Pogo Possum)

ALBUM OF CRIME (See Fox Giants)

ALBUM OF LOVE (See Fox Giants)

AL CAPP'S DOGPATCH (Also see Mammy Yokum)
Toby Press: No. 71, June, 1949 - No. 4, Dec, 1949

	GD 2.0	VG 4.0	FN 6.0	VF 8.0	VF/NM 9.0	NM- 9.2
71(#1)-Reprints from Tip Top #112-114	24	48	72	138	194	250
2-4: 4-Reprints from Li'l Abner #73	17	34	51	95	130	165

AL CAPP'S SHMOO (Also see Oxydol-Dreft & Washable Jones & Shmoo)
Toby Press: July, 1949 - No. 5, Apr, 1950 (None by Al Capp)

	GD 2.0	VG 4.0	FN 6.0	VF 8.0	VF/NM 9.0	NM- 9.2
1	39	78	117	233	329	425
2-5: 3-Sci-fi trip to moon. 4-X-Mas-c; origin/1st app. Super-Shmoo	28	56	84	159	225	290

AL CAPP'S WOLF GAL
Toby Press: 1951 - No. 2, 1952

	GD 2.0	VG 4.0	FN 6.0	VF 8.0	VF/NM 9.0	NM- 9.2
1,2-Edited-r from Li'l Abner #63,64	34	68	102	196	278	360

ALEXANDER THE GREAT (Movie)
Dell Publishing Co.: No. 688, May, 1956

	GD 2.0	VG 4.0	FN 6.0	VF 8.0	VF/NM 9.0	NM- 9.2
Four Color 688-Buscema-a; photo-c	8	16	24	55	78	100

ALF (TV) (See Star Comics Digest)
Marvel Comics: Mar, 1988 - No. 50, Feb, 1992 ($1.00)

	GD 2.0	VG 4.0	FN 6.0	VF 8.0	VF/NM 9.0	NM- 9.2
1-Photo-c						4.00
1-2nd printing						2.50
2-19: 6-Photo-c						2.50
20-22: 20-Conan parody. 21-Marx Brothers. 22-X-Men parody						3.00
23-30: 24-Rhonda-c/app. 29-3-D cover						2.50
31-43,46-49						3.00
44,45: 44-X-Men parody. 45-Wolverine, Punisher, Capt. America-c						4.00
50-($1.75, 52 pgs.)-Final issue; photo-c						4.00
Annual 1-3: 1-Rocky & Bullwinkle app. 2-Sienkiewicz-c. 3-TMNT parody						3.00
...Comics Digest 1,2: 1-(1988)-Reprints Alf #1,2	1	2	3	5	6	8
Holiday Special 1,2 ('88, Wint. '89, 68 pgs.): 2-X-Men parody-c						3.00
Spring Special 1 (Spr/89, $1.75, 68 pgs.) Invisible Man parody						3.00
TPB (68 pgs.) r/#1-3; photo-c						5.00

ALFRED HARVEY'S BLACK CAT
Lorne-Harvey Productions: 1995 ($3.50, B&W/color)

	GD 2.0	VG 4.0	FN 6.0	VF 8.0	VF/NM 9.0	NM- 9.2
1-Origin by Mark Evanier & Murphy Anderson; contains history of Alfred Harvey & Harvey Publications; 5 pg. B&W Sad Sack story; Hildebrandts-c						5.00

ALGIE (LITTLE...)
Timor Publ. Co.: Dec, 1953 - No. 3, 1954

	GD 2.0	VG 4.0	FN 6.0	VF 8.0	VF/NM 9.0	NM- 9.2
1-Teenage	7	14	21	35	43	50
1-Misprint exists w/Secret Mysteries #19 inside	8	16	24	46	58	70
2,3	5	10	15	23	28	32
Accepted Reprint #2(nd)	3	6	8	12	14	16
Super Reprint #15	2	4	6	10	12	14

ALIAS:
Now Comics: July, 1990 - No. 5, Nov, 1990 ($1.75)

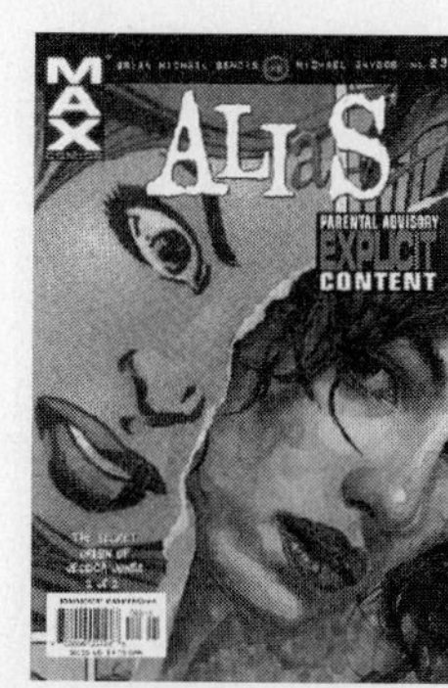

Alias #23 © MAR

Alice #10 © Z-D

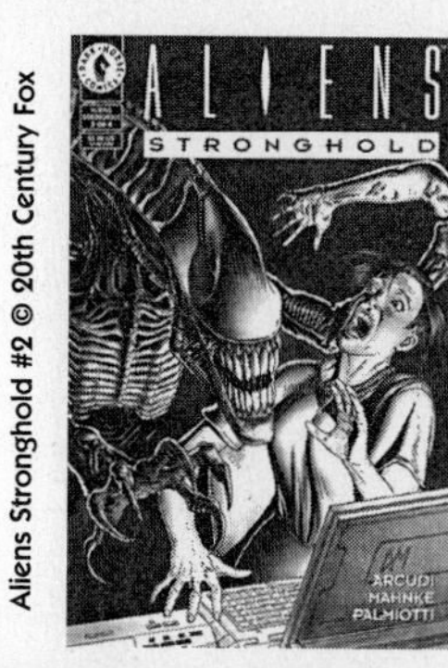

Aliens Stronghold #2 © 20th Century Fox

GD 2.0 | VG 4.0 | FN 6.0 | VF 8.0 | VF/NM 9.0 | NM- 9.2

1-5: 1-Sienkiewicz-c 2.25

ALIAS
Marvel Comics (MAX Comics): Nov, 2001 - No. 28, Jan, 2004 ($2.99)
1-Bendis-s/Gaydos-a/Mack-c; intro Jessica Jones; Luke Cage app. 1 2 3 5 6 8
2-4 5.00
5-28: 7,8-Sienkiewicz-a (2 pgs.) 16-21-Spider-Woman app. 22,23-Jessica's origin. 24-28-Purple; Avengers app.; flashback-a by Bagley 3.00
HC (2002, $29.99) r/#1-9; intro. by Jeph Loeb 30.00
Vol. 1: TPB (2003, $19.99) r/#1-9 20.00
Vol. 2: Come Home TPB (2003, $13.99) r/#11-15 14.00
Vol. 3: The Underneath TPB (2003, $16.99) r/#10,16-21 17.00

ALICE (New Adventures in Wonderland)
Ziff-Davis Publ. Co.: No. 10, 7-8/51 - No. 11(#2), 11-12/51
10-Painted-c; Berg-a 24 48 72 138 194 250
11-(#2 on inside) Dave Berg-a 14 28 42 81 111 140

ALICE AT MONKEY ISLAND (See The Adventures of Alice)
Pentagon Publ. Co. (Civil Service): No. 3, 1946
3 9 18 27 52 66 80

ALICE IN WONDERLAND (Disney; see Advs. of Alice, Dell Jr. Treasury #1, The Dreamery, Movie Comics, Walt Disney Showcase #22, and World's Greatest Stories)
Dell Publishing Co.: No. 24, 1940; No. 331, 1951; No. 341, July, 1951
Single Series 24 (#1)(1940) 44 88 132 264 395 525
Four Color 331, 341-"Unbirthday Party w/..." 16 32 48 111 163 215
1-(Whitman; 3/84)-r/4-Color #331 6.00

ALIEN ENCOUNTERS (Replaces Alien Worlds)
Eclipse Comics: June, 1985 - No. 14, Aug, 1987 ($1.75, Baxter paper, mature)
1-10: Nudity, strong language in all. 9-Snyder-a 4.00
11-14-Low print run 5.00

ALIEN LEGION (See Epic & Marvel Graphic Novel #25)
Marvel Comics (Epic Comics): Apr, 1984 - No. 20, Sept, 1987
nn-With bound-in trading card; Austin-i 4.00
2-20: 2-$1.50-c. 7,8-Portacio-i 3.00

ALIEN LEGION (2nd Series)
Marvel Comics (Epic): Aug, 1987(indicia)(10/87 on-c) - No. 18, Aug, 1990
V2#1-18-Stroman-a in all. 7-18-Farmer-i 2.25
...: Force Nomad TPB (Checker Book Pub. Group, 2001, $24.95) r/#1-11 25.00
...: Piecemaker TPB (Checker Book Pub. Group, 2002, $19.95) r/#12-18 20.00

ALIEN LEGION: (Series of titles; all Marvel/Epic Comics)
--BINARY DEEP, 1993 ($3.50, one-shot, 52 pgs.), nn-With bound-in trading card 3.50
--JUGGER GRIMROD, 8/92 ($5.95, one-shot, 52 pgs.) Book 1 6.00
--ONE PLANET AT A TIME, 5/93 - Book 3, 7/93 ($4.95, squarebound, 52 pgs.)
Book 1-3: Hoang Nguyen-a 5.00
--ON THE EDGE (The... #2 & 3), 11/90 - No. 3, 1/91 ($4.50, 52 pgs.)
1-3-Stroman & Farmer-a 4.50
--TENANTS OF HELL, '91 - No. 2, '1 ($4.50, squarebound, 52 pgs.)
Book 1,2-Stroman-c/a(p) 4.50

ALIEN NATION (Movie)
DC Comics: Dec, 1988 ($2.50; 68 pgs.)
1-Adaptation of film; painted-c 4.00

ALIEN RESURRECTION (Movie)
Dark Horse Comics: Oct, 1997 - No. 2, Nov, 1997 ($2.50; limited series)
1,2-Adaptation of film; Dave McKean-c 3.00

ALIENS, THE (Captain Johner and...)(Also see Magnus Robot Fighter...)
Gold Key: Sept-Dec, 1967; No. 2, May, 1982
1-Reprints from Magnus #1,3,4,6-10; Russ Manning-a in all 4 8 12 22 30 38
2-(Whitman) Same contents as #1 1 2 3 5 6 8

ALIENS (Movie) (See Alien: The Illustrated..., Dark Horse Comics & Dark Horse Presents #24)
Dark Horse Comics: May, 1988 - No. 6, July, 1989 ($1.95, B&W, limited series)
1-Based on movie sequel;1st app. Aliens in comics 2 4 6 12 16 20
1-2nd - 6th printings; 4th w/new inside front-c 3.00
2 1 2 3 5 7 9
2-2nd & 3rd printing, 3-6-2nd printings 3.00
3 1 2 3 4 5 7
4-6 5.00
Mini Comic #1 (2/89, 4x6")-Was included with Aliens Portfolio 4.00
Collection 1 ($10.95,)-r/#1-6 plus Dark Horse Presents #24 plus new-a 12.00
Collection 1-2nd printing (1991, $11.95)-On higher quality paper than 1st print; Dorman painted-c 12.00
Hardcover ('90, $24.95, B&W)-r/1-6, DHP #24 30.00
Platinum Edition - (See Dark Horse Presents: Aliens Platinum Edition) -

ALIENS
Dark Horse Comics: V2#1, Aug, 1989 - No. 4, 1990 ($2.25, limited series)
V2#1-Painted art by Denis Beauvais 5.00
1-2nd printing (1990), 2-4 3.00

ALIENS: (Series of titles, all Dark Horse)
--ALCHEMY, 10/97 - No. 3, 11/97 ($2.95),1-3-Corben-c/a, Arcudi-s 3.00
--APOCALYPSE - THE DESTROYING ANGELS, 1/99 - No. 4, 4/99 ($2.95)
1-4-Doug Wheatly-a/Schultz-s 3.00
--BERSERKERS, 1/95 - No. 4, 4/95 ($2.50) 1-4 3.00
--COLONIAL MARINES, 1/93 - No. 10, 7/94 ($2.50) 1-10 3.00
--EARTH ANGEL. 8/94 ($2.95) 1-Byrne-a/story; wraparound-c 3.00
--EARTH WAR, 6/90 - No. 4, 10/90 ($2.50) 1-All have Sam Kieth-a & Bolton painted-c 5.00
1-2nd printing, 3,4 3.00
2 4.00
--GENOCIDE, 11/91 - No. 4, 2/92 ($2.50) 1-4-Suydam painted-c. 4-Wraparound-c, poster 3.00
--GLASS CORRIDOR, 6/98 ($2.95) 1-David Lloyd-s/a 3.00
--HARVEST (See Aliens: Hive)
--HAVOC, 6/97 - No. 2, 7/97 ($2.95) 1,2: Schultz-s, Kent Williams-c, 40 artists including Art Adams, Kelley Jones, Duncan Fegredo, Kevin Nowlan 3.00
--HIVE, 2/92 - No. 4,5/92 ($2.50) 1-4: Kelley Jones-c/a in all 3.00
...Harvest TPB ('98, $16.95) r/series; Bolton-c 17.00
--KIDNAPPED, 12/97 - No. 3, 2/98 ($2.50) 1-3 3.00
--LABYRINTH, 9/93 - No. 4, 1/94 ($2.50)1-4: 1-Painted-c 3.00
--LOVESICK, 12/96 ($2.95) 1 3.00
--MONDO HEAT, 2/96 ($2.50) nn-Sequel to Mondo Pest 3.00
--MONDO PEST, 4/95 ($2.95, 44 pgs.)nn-r/Dark Horse Comics #22-24 3.00
--MUSIC OF THE SPEARS, 1/94 - No. 4, 4/94 ($2.50) 1-4 3.00
--NEWT'S TALE, 6/92 - No. 2, 7/92 ($4.95) 1,2-Bolton-c 5.00
--PIG, 3/97 ($2.95)1 3.00
--PREDATOR: THE DEADLIEST OF SPECIES, 7/93 - No. 12,8/95 ($2.50)
1-Bolton painted-c; Guice-a(p) 5.00
1-Embossed foil platinum edition 10.00
2-12: Bolton painted-c. 2,3-Guice-a(p) 3.00
--PURGE, 8/97 ($2.95) nn-Hester-a 3.00
--ROGUE, 4/993 - No. 4, 7/93 ($2.50)1-4: Painted-c 3.00
--SACRIFICE, 5/93 ($4.95, 52 pgs.) nn-P. Milligan scripts; painted-c/a 5.00
--SALVATION, 11/93 ($4.95, 52 pgs.) nn-Mignola-c/a(p); Gibbons script 5.00
--SPECIAL, 6/97 ($2.50) 1 3.00
--STALKER, 6/98 ($2.50)1-David Wenzel-s/a 3.00
--STRONGHOLD, 5/94 - No. 4, 9/94 ($2.50) 1-4 3.00
--SURVIVAL, 2/98 - No. 3, 4/98 ($2.95)1-3-Tony Harris-c 3.00

ALIENS VS. PREDATOR (See Dark Horse Presents #36)
Dark Horse Comics: June, 1990 - No. 4, Dec, 1990 ($2.50, limited series)
1-Painted-c 1 2 3 5 6 8
1-2nd printing 3.00
0-(7/90, $1.95, B&W)-r/Dark Horse Pres. #34-36 1 2 3 5 7 9
2,3 5.00
4-Dave Dorman painted-c 4.00
Annual (7/99, $4.95) Jae Lee-c 5.00
--VS. PREDATOR: BOOTY, 1/96 ($2.50) nn-painted-c 3.00
--VS. PREDATOR: DUEL, 3/95 - No. 2, 4/95 ($2.50) 1,2 3.00
--VS. PREDATOR: ETERNAL, 6/98 - No. 4, 9/98 ($2.50)1-4: Edginton-s/Maleev-a; Fabry-c 3.00
--VS. PREDATOR VS. THE TERMINATOR, 4/00 - No. 4, 7/00 ($2.95) 1-4: Ripley app. 3.00
--VS. PREDATOR: WAR, No. 0, 5/95 - No. 4, 8/95 ($2.50) 0-4: Corben painted-c 3.00

All-American Comics #16 © DC

All-American Men of War #8 © DC

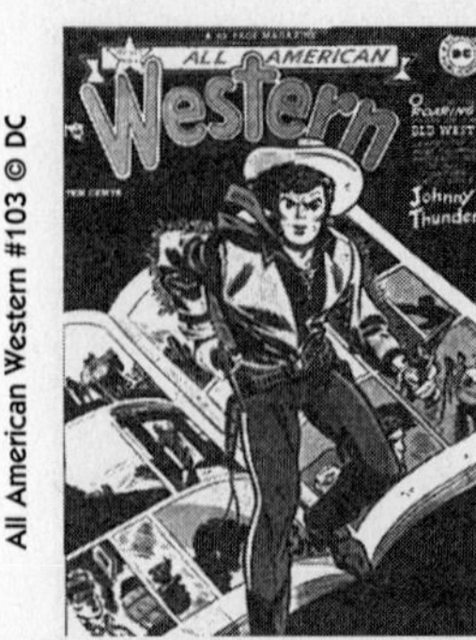

All American Western #103 © DC

GD 2.0 | VG 4.0 | FN 6.0 | VF 8.0 | VF/NM 9.0 | NM- 9.2

--VS. PREDATOR: XENOGENESIS, 12/99 - No. 4, 3/00 ($2.95) 1-4: Watson-s/Mel Rubi-a 3.00
--WRAITH, 7/98 ($2.95)1-Jay Stephens-s 3.00
--XENOGENESIS, 8/99 - No. 4, 11/99 ($2.95) 1-4: T&M Bierbaum-s 3.00

ALIEN TERROR (See 3-D Alien Terror)

ALIEN: THE ILLUSTRATED STORY (Also see Aliens)
Heavy Metal Books: 1980 ($3.95, soft-c, 8x11")
nn-Movie adaptation; Simonson-a 3 6 9 16 20 24

ALIEN 3 (Movie)
Dark Horse Comics: June, 1992 - No. 3, July, 1992 ($2.50, limited series)
1-3: Adapts 3rd movie; Suydam painted-c 3.00

ALIEN WORLDS (Also see Eclipse Graphic Album #22)
Pacific Comics/Eclipse: Dec, 1982 - No. 9, Jan, 1985
1,2,4: 2,4-Dave Stevens-c/a 6.00
3,5-7 4.00
8,9 1 2 3 4 5 7
3-D No. 1-Art Adams 1st published art 1 2 3 4 5 7

ALISON DARE, LITTLE MISS ADVENTURES (Also see Return of ...)
Oni Press: Sept, 2000 ($4.50, B&W, one-shot)
1-J. Torres-s/J.Bone-c/a 4.50

ALISON DARE & THE HEART OF THE MAIDEN
Oni Press: Jan, 2002 - No. 2, Feb, 2002 ($2.95, B&W, limited series)
1,2-J. Torres-s/J.Bone-c/a 3.00

ALISTER THE SLAYER
Midnight Press: Oct, 1995 ($2.50)
1-Boris-c 2.50

ALL-AMERICAN COMICS (...Western #103-126, ...Men of War #127 on; also see The Big All-American Comic Book)
All-American/National Periodical Publ.: April, 1939 - No. 102, Oct, 1948
1-Hop Harrigan (1st app.), Scribbly by Mayer (1st DC app.), Toonerville Folks, Ben Webster, Spot Savage, Mutt & Jeff, Red White & Blue (1st app.), Adventures in the Unknown, Tippie, Reg'lar Fellers, Skippy, Bobby Thatcher, Mystery Men of Mars, Daiseybelle, Wiley of West Point begin 700 1400 2100 4200 5600 7200
2-Ripley's Believe It or Not begins, ends #24 200 400 600 1200 1600 2100
3-5: 5-The American Way begins, ends #10 155 310 465 930 1240 1600
6,7: 6-Last Spot Savage; Popsicle Pete begins, ends #26, 28. 7-Last Bobby Thatcher 130 260 390 780 1040 1325
8-The Ultra Man begins & 1st-c app. 260 520 780 1560 2180 2800
9,10: 10-X-Mas-c 120 240 360 720 960 1225
11,15: 11-Ultra Man-c. 15-Last Tippie & Reg'lar Fellars; Ultra Man-c 130 260 390 780 1040 1350
12-14: 12-Last Toonerville Folks 110 220 330 660 880 1125
16-(Rare)-Origin/1st app. Green Lantern by Sheldon Moldoff (c/a)(7/40) & begin series; appears in costume on-c & only one panel inside; created by Martin Nodell. Inspired in 1940 by a switchman's green lantern that would give trains the go ahead to proceed 9143 18,286 27,429 72,500 116,250 160,000
17-2nd Green Lantern 1281 2562 3843 9608 15,054 20,500
18-N.Y. World's Fair-c/story 966 1932 2898 6762 10,381 14,000
19-Origin/1st app. The Atom (10/40); last Ultra Man 1375 2750 4125 10,313 16,157 22,000
20-Atom dons costume; Ma Hunkle becomes Red Tornado (1st app.)(1st DC costumed heroine, before Wonder Woman, 11/40); Rescue on Mars begins, ends #25; 1 pg. origin Green Lantern 441 882 1323 3087 4744 6400
21-23: 21-Last Wiley of West Point & Skippy. 23-Last Daiseybelle; 3 Idiots begin, end #82 280 560 840 1750 2625 3500
24-Sisty & Dinky become the Cyclone Kids; Ben Webster ends; origin Dr. Mid-Nite & Sargon, The Sorcerer in text with app. 304 608 912 1976 3038 4100
25-Origin & 1st story app. Dr. Mid-Nite by Stan Asch; Hop Harrigan becomes Guardian Angel; last Adventure in the Unknown 862 1724 2586 6034 9267 12,500
26-Origin/1st story app. Sargon, the Sorcerer 352 704 1056 2288 3519 4750
27: #27-32 are misnumbered in indicia with correct No. appearing on-c. Intro. Doiby Dickles, Green Lantern's sidekick 370 740 1110 2405 3703 5000
28-Hop Harrigan gives up costumed i.d. 176 352 528 1100 1650 2200
29,30 176 352 528 1100 1650 2200
31-40: 35-Doiby learns Green Lantern's i.d. 132 264 396 825 1238 1650
41-50: 50-Sargon ends 107 214 321 669 1005 1340
51-60: 59-Scribbly & the Red Tornado ends 92 184 276 575 863 1150
61-Origin/1st app. Solomon Grundy (11/44) 496 992 1488 3472 5336 7200
62-70: 70-Kubert Sargon; intro Sargon's helper, Maximillian O'Leary 83 166 249 519 780 1040
71-88: 71-Last Red White & Blue. 72-Black Pirate begins (not in #74-82); last Atom. 73-Winky, Blinky & Noddy begins, ends #82. 79,83-Mutt & Jeff-c. 68 136 204 425 638 850
89-Origin & 1st app. Harlequin 107 214 321 669 1005 1340
90-99: 90-Origin/1st app. Icicle. 99-Last Hop Harrigan 102 204 306 638 957 1275
100-1st app. Johnny Thunder by Alex Toth (8/48); western theme begins (Scarce) 192 384 576 1200 1800 2400
101-Last Mutt & Jeff (Scarce) 128 256 384 800 1200 1600
102-Last Green Lantern, Black Pirate & Dr. Mid-Nite (Scarce) 278 556 834 1738 2607 3475

NOTE: *No Atom in 47, 62-69.* **Kinstler** *Black Pirate-89.* **Stan Aschmeier** *a (Dr. Mid-Nite) 25-84; c-7.* **Mayer** *c-1, 2(part), 6, 10.* **Moldoff** *c-16-23.* **Nodell** *c-31.* **Paul Reinman** *a (Green Lantern)-53-55p, 56-84, 87; (Black Pirate)-83-88, 90; c-52, 55-76, 78, 80, 81, 87.* **Toth** *a-88, 92, 96, 98-102; c(p)-92, 96-102. Scribbly by* **Mayer** *in #1-59. Ultra Man by* **Mayer** *in #8-19.*

ALL-AMERICAN COMICS (Also see All Star Comics 1999 crossover titles)
DC Comics: May, 1999 ($1.99, one-shot)
1-Golden Age Green Lantern and Johnny Thunder; Barreto-a 2.25

ALL-AMERICAN MEN OF WAR (Previously All-American Western)
National Periodical Publ.: No. 127, Aug-Sept, 1952 - No. 117, Sept-Oct, 1966
127 (#1, 1952) 71 142 213 604 1027 1450
128 (1952) 51 102 153 408 592 825
2(12-1/'52-53)-5 44 88 132 352 526 700
6-Devil Dog story; Ghost Squadron story 35 70 105 263 392 520
7-10: 8-Sgt. Storm Cloud-s 35 70 105 263 392 520
11-16,18: 18-Last precode (2/55) 31 62 93 223 329 435
17-1st Frogman-s in this title 31 62 93 230 328 460
19,20,22-27 22 44 66 160 235 310
21-Easy Co. prototype 25 50 75 181 266 350
28 (12/55)-1st Sgt. Rock prototype; Kubert-a 32 64 96 240 358 475
29,30,32-Wood-a 24 48 72 169 247 325
31,33-38,40: 34-Gunner prototype-s. 35-Greytone-c. 36-Little Sure Shot prototype-s. 38-1st S.A. issue 19 38 57 133 194 255
39 (11/56)-2nd Sgt. Rock prototype; 1st Easy Co.? 29 58 87 210 305 400
41,43-47,49,50: 46-Tankbusters-c/s 15 30 45 109 160 210
42-Pre-Sgt. Rock Easy Co.-c/s 19 38 57 136 198 260
48-Easy Co.-c/s; Nick app.; Kubert-a 19 38 57 136 198 260
51-56,58-62,65,66: 61-Gunner-c/s 12 24 36 84 125 165
57(5/58),63,64 -Pre-Sgt. Rock Easy Co.-c/s 17 34 51 118 174 230
67-1st Gunner & Sarge by Andru & Esposito 32 64 96 240 360 480
68,69: 68-2nd app. Gunner & Sarge. 69-1st Tank Killer-c/s 15 30 45 109 160 210
70 11 22 33 80 118 155
71-80: 71,72,76-Tank Killer-c/s. 74-Minute Commandos-c/s 9 18 27 65 93 120
81,84-88: 88-Last 10¢ issue 8 16 24 53 74 95
82-Johnny Cloud begins(1st app.), ends #117 14 28 42 97 141 185
83-2nd Johnny Cloud 9 18 27 65 93 120
89-100: 89-Battle Aces of 3 Wars begins, ends #98 6 12 18 40 55 70
101-111,113-116: 111,114,115-Johnny Cloud 4 8 12 29 40 50
112-Balloon Buster series begins, ends #114,116 5 10 15 33 44 55
117-Johnny Cloud-c & 3-part story 5 10 15 33 44 55

NOTE: *Frogman stories in 17, 38, 44, 45, 50, 51, 53, 55-58, 63, 65, 66, 72, 76, 77.* **Colan** *a-112.* **Drucker** *a-47, 58, 61, 63, 65, 69, 71, 74, 77.* **Grandenetti** *c(p)-127, 128, 2-17(most).* **Heath** *a-14, 27, 32, 38, 41, 45, 47, 50, 51, 55-58, 62, 64, 71, 75, 76, 78, 95, 111-117; c-85, 91, 94-96, 100, 101, 110-112, others?* **Infantino** *a-8.* **Kirby** *a-29.* **Krigstein** *a-128('52), 2, 3, 5.* **Kubert** *a-22, 24, 28, 29, 33, 34, 36, 38, 39, 41-43, 47-50, 52, 53, 55, 56, 59, 60, 63-65, 69, 71-73, 76, 102, 103, 105, 106, 108, 114; c-41, 44, 52, 54, 55, 58, 64, 69, 76, 77, 79, 102-106, 108, 113-117, others? Tank Killer in 69, 71, 76 by* **Kubert**. **P. Reinman** *c-55, 57, 61, 62, 71, 72, 74-76, 80.* **J. Severin** *a-58.*

ALL-AMERICAN SPORTS
Charlton Comics: Oct, 1967
1 3 6 9 19 25 32

ALL-AMERICAN WESTERN (Formerly All-American Comics; Becomes All-American Men of War)
National Periodical Publ.: No. 103, Nov, 1948 - No. 126, June-July, 1952 (103-121: 52 pgs.)
103-Johnny Thunder & his horse Black Lightning continues by Toth, ends #126; Foley of The Fighting 5th, Minstrel Maverick, & Overland Coach begin; Captain Tootsie by Beck; mentioned in Love and Death 50 100 150 300 450 600
104-Kubert-a 39 78 117 224 317 410
105,107-Kubert-a 32 64 96 184 262 340
106,108-110,112: 112-Kurtzman's "Pot-Shot Pete" (1 pg.) 27 54 81 153 214 275
111,114-116-Kubert-a 28 56 84 159 225 290
113-Intro. Swift Deer, J. Thunder's new sidekick (4-5/50); classic Toth-c;

Allegra #3 © IM

All-Flash Quarterly #5 © DC

COMICS 50¢ 256 PAGES ALL GOOD

All Good © STJ

	GD 2.0	VG 4.0	FN 6.0	VF 8.0	VF/NM 9.0	NM- 9.2
Kubert-a	30	60	90	170	240	310
117-126: 121-Kubert-a; bondage-c	19	38	57	109	152	195

NOTE: ***G. Kane*** *c(p)-112, 119, 120, 123.* ***Kubert*** *a-103-105, 107, 111, 112(1 pg.), 113-116, 121.* ***Toth*** *a 103-125; c(p)-103-111,113-116, 121, 122, 124-126. Some copies of #125 have #12 on-c.*

ALL COMICS
Chicago Nite Life News: 1945

1 — 15 30 45 84 115 145

ALLEGRA
Image Comics (WildStorm): Aug, 1996 - No. 4, Dec, 1996 ($2.50)

1-4 — 2.50

ALLEY CAT (Alley Baggett)
Image Comics: July, 1999 - No. 6, Mar, 2000 ($2.50/$2.95)

Preview Edition — 6.00
Prelude — 5.00
Prelude w/variant-c — 6.00
1-Photo-c — 2.50
1-Painted-c by Dorian — 3.50
1-Another Universe Edition, 1-Wizard World Edition — 7.00
2-4: 4-Twin towers on-c — 2.50
5,6-($2.95) — 3.00
Lingerie Edition (10/99, $4.95) Photos, pin-ups, cover gallery — 5.00
...Vs. Lady Pendragon ('99, $3.00) Stinsman-c — 3.00

ALLEY OOP (See The Comics, The Funnies, Red Ryder and Super Book #9)
Dell Publishing Co.: No. 3, 1942

Four Color 3 (#1) — 46 92 138 368 554 740

ALLEY OOP
Argo Publ.: Nov, 1955 - No. 3, Mar, 1956 (Newspaper reprints)

1 — 18 36 54 104 142 180
2,3 — 12 24 36 71 96 120

ALLEY OOP
Dell Publishing Co.: 12-2/62-63 - No. 2, 9-11/63

1 — 7 14 21 50 68 85
2 — 6 12 18 40 55 70

ALLEY OOP
Standard Comics: No. 10, Sept, 1947 - No. 18, Oct, 1949

10 — 24 48 72 138 194 250
11-18: 17,18-Schomburg-c — 19 38 57 109 152 195

ALLEY OOP ADVENTURES
Antarctic Press: Aug, 1998 - No. 3, Dec, 1998 ($2.95)

1-3-Jack Bender-s/a — 3.00

ALLEY OOP ADVENTURES (Alley Oop Quarterly in indicia)
Antarctic Press: Sept, 1999 - No. 3, Mar, 2000 ($2.50/$2.99, B&W)

1-3-Jack Bender-s/a — 3.00

ALL-FAMOUS CRIME (2nd series - Formerly Law Against Crime #1-3; becomes All-Famous Police Cases #6 on)
Star Publications: No. 8, 5/51 - No. 10, 11/51; No. 4, 2/52 - No. 5, 5/52;

8 (#1-1st series) — 22 44 66 127 176 225
9 (#2)-Used in **SOTI**, illo- "The wish to hurt or kill couples in lovers' lanes is a not uncommon perversion;" L.B. Cole-c/a(r)/Law-Crime #3 — 36 72 108 204 290 375
10 (#3) — 19 38 57 109 152 195
4 (#4-2nd series)-Formerly Law-Crime — 19 38 57 106 146 185
5 (#5) Becomes All-Famous Police Cases #6 — 19 38 57 106 146 185

NOTE: *All have* ***L.B. Cole*** *covers.*

ALL FAMOUS CRIME STORIES (See Fox Giants)

ALL-FAMOUS POLICE CASES (Formerly All Famous Crime #5)
Star Publications: No. 6, Feb, 1952 - No. 16, Sept, 1954

6 — 19 38 57 109 152 195
7,8: 7-Baker story. 8-Marijuana story — 19 38 57 106 146 185
9-16 — 16 32 48 92 126 160

NOTE: ***L. B. Cole*** *c-all; a-15, 1pg.* ***Hollingsworth*** *a-15.*

ALL-FLASH (...Quarterly No. 1-5)
National Per. Publ./All-American: Summer, 1941 - No. 32, Dec-Jan, 1947-48

1-Origin The Flash retold by E. E. Hibbard; Hibbard c-1-10,12-14,16,31p. — 1375 2750 4125 10,313 16,157 22,000
2-Origin recap — 333 666 999 2165 3333 4500
3,4 — 172 344 516 1075 1613 2150
5-Winky, Blinky & Noddy begins (1st app.), ends #32 — 128 256 384 800 1200 1600
6-10 — 104 208 312 650 975 1300
11-13: 12-Origin/1st The Thinker. 13-The King app. — 90 180 270 563 844 1125
14-Green Lantern cameo — 104 208 312 650 975 1300
15-20: 18-Mutt & Jeff begins, ends #22 — 74 148 222 463 694 925
21-31 — 60 120 180 375 563 750
32-Origin/1st app. The Fiddler; 1st Star Sapphire — 112 224 336 700 1050 1400

NOTE: *Book length stories in 2-13, 16. Bondage c-31, 32.* ***Martin Nodell*** *c-15, 17-28.*

ALL FOR LOVE (Young Love V3#5-on)
Prize Publications: Apr-May, 1957 - V3#4, Dec-Jan, 1959-60

V1#1 — 8 16 24 53 74 95
2-6: 5-Orlando-c — 5 10 14 31 42 52
V2#1-5(1/59), 5(3/59) — 3 7 10 21 28 36
V3#1(5/59), 1(7/59)-4: 2-Powell-a — 3 6 9 16 20 25

ALL FUNNY COMICS
Tilsam Publ./National Periodical Publications (Detective): Winter, 1943-44 - No. 23, May-June, 1948

1-Genius Jones (1st app.), Buzzy (1st app., ends #4), Dover & Clover (see More Fun #93) begin; Bailey-a — 48 96 144 288 432 575
2 — 24 48 72 135 190 245
3-10 — 15 30 45 86 118 150
11-13,15,18,19-Genius Jones app. — 14 28 42 81 111 140
14,17,20-23 — 10 20 30 56 73 90
16-DC Super Heroes app. — 33 66 99 190 270 350

ALL GOOD
St. John Publishing Co.: Oct, 1949 (50¢, 260 pgs.)

nn-(8 St. John comics bound together) — 66 132 198 413 619 825

NOTE: *Also see Li'l Audrey Yearbook & Treasury of Comics.*

ALL GOOD COMICS (See Fox Giants)
Fox Features Syndicate: No.1, Spring, 1946 (36 pgs.)

1-Joy Family, Dick Transom, Rick Evans, One Round Hogan — 27 54 81 155 218 280

ALL GREAT (See Fox Giants)
Fox Feature Syndicate: 1946 (36 pgs.)

1-Crazy House, Bertie Benson Boy Detective, Gussie the Gob — 27 54 81 155 218 280

ALL GREAT
William H. Wise & Co.: nd (1945?) (132 pgs.)

nn-Capt. Jack Terry, Joan Mason, Girl Reporter, Baron Doomsday; Torture scenes — 40 80 120 240 358 475

ALL GREAT COMICS (Formerly Phantom Lady #13? Dagar, Desert Hawk No. 14 on)
Fox Features Syndicate: No. 14, Oct, 1947 - No. 13, Dec, 1947 (Newspaper strip reprints)

14(#12)-Brenda Starr & Texas Slim-r (Scarce) — 56 112 168 350 525 700
13-Origin Dagar, Desert Hawk; Brenda Starr (all-r); Kamen-c; Dagar covers begin — 60 120 180 375 563 750

ALL-GREAT CONFESSIONS (See Fox Giants)

ALL GREAT CRIME STORIES (See Fox Giants)

ALL GREAT JUNGLE ADVENTURES (See Fox Giants)

ALL HALLOW'S EVE
Innovation Publishing: 1991 ($4.95, 52 pgs.)

1-Painted-c/a — 1 2 3 4 5 7

ALL HERO COMICS
Fawcett Publications: Mar, 1943 (100 pgs., cardboard-c)

1-Capt. Marvel Jr., Capt. Midnight, Golden Arrow, Ibis the Invincible, Spy Smasher, Lance O'Casey; 1st Banshee O'Brien; Raboy-c — 168 336 504 1050 1575 2100

ALL HUMOR COMICS
Quality Comics Group: Spring, 1946 - No. 17, December, 1949

1 — 21 42 63 118 164 210
2-Atomic Tot story; Gustavson-a — 11 22 33 63 84 105
3-9: 3-Intro Kelly Poole who is cover feature #3 on. 5-1st app. Hickory? 8-Gustavson-a — 7 14 21 37 46 55
10-17 — 6 12 18 31 38 45

ALLIANCE, THE
Image Comics (Shadowline Ink): Aug, 1995 - No. 3, Nov, 1995 ($2.50)

1-3: 2-(9/95) — 2.50

All-New Collectors' Edition C-56 © DC

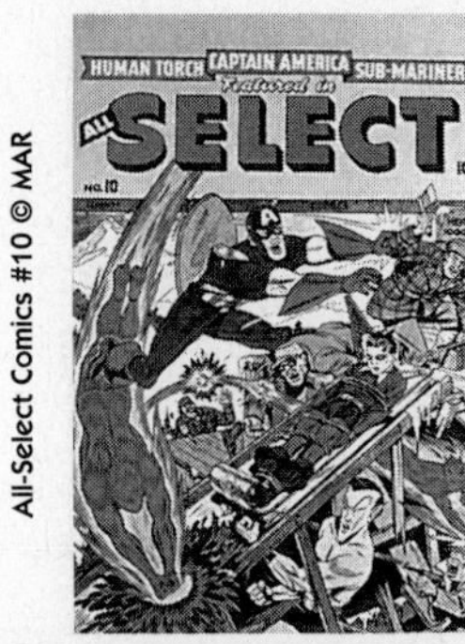

All-Select Comics #10 © MAR

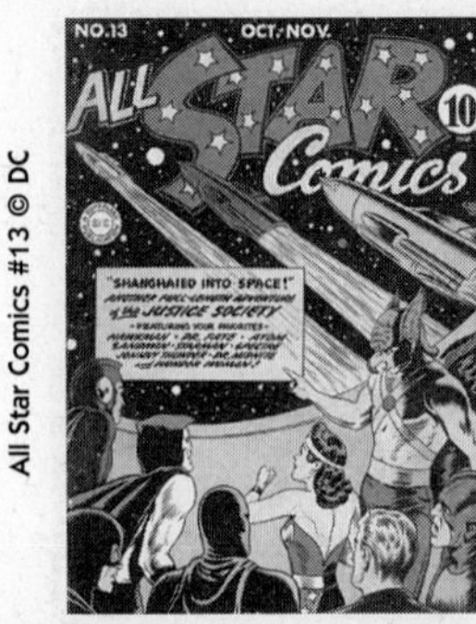

All Star Comics #13 © DC

ALL LOVE (...Romances No. 26)(Formerly Ernie Comics)
Ace Periodicals (Current Books): No. 26, May, 1949 - No. 32, May, 1950

	GD 2.0	VG 4.0	FN 6.0	VF 8.0	VF/NM 9.0	NM- 9.2
26 (No. 1)-Ernie, Lily Belle app.	9	18	27	52	66	80
27-L. B. Cole-a	14	28	42	79	107	135
28-32	6	12	18	33	41	48

ALL-NEGRO COMICS
All-Negro Comics: June, 1947 (15¢)

	GD 2.0	VG 4.0	FN 6.0	VF 8.0	VF/NM 9.0	NM- 9.2
1 (Rare)	667	1334	2000	3669	4835	6000

NOTE: *Seldom found in fine or mint condition; many copies have brown pages.*

ALL-NEW COLLECTORS' EDITION (Formerly Limited ...)
DC Comics, Inc.: Jan, 1978 - Vol. 8, No. C-62, 1979 (No. 54-58: 76 pgs.)

	GD 2.0	VG 4.0	FN 6.0	VF 8.0	VF/NM 9.0	NM- 9.2
C-53-Rudolph the Red-Nosed Reindeer	5	10	14	31	42	52
C-54-Superman Vs. Wonder Woman	4	8	12	25	33	42
C-55-Superboy & the Legion of Super-Heroes; Wedding of Lightning Lad & Saturn Girl; Grell-c/a	4	8	12	25	33	42
C-56-Superman Vs. Muhammad Ali: story & wraparound N. Adams-c/a	6	12	18	40	55	70
C-56-Superman Vs. Muhammad Ali (Whitman variant)-low print	7	14	21	50	68	85
C-58-Superman Vs. Shazam	4	8	12	24	32	40
C-60-Rudolph's Summer Fun(8/78)	4	8	12	28	38	48
C-61-(See Famous First Edition-Superman #1)						
C-62-Superman the Movie (68 pgs.; 1979)-Photo-c from movie plus photos inside (also see DC Special Series #25)	3	6	9	16	20	24

NOTE: ***Buckler** a-C-58; c-C-58*

ALL-NEW COMICS (...Short Story Comics No. 1-3)
Family Comics (Harvey Publications): Jan, 1943 - No. 14, Nov, 1946; No. 15, Mar-Apr, 1947 (10 x 13-1/2")

	GD 2.0	VG 4.0	FN 6.0	VF 8.0	VF/NM 9.0	NM- 9.2
1-Steve Case, Crime Rover, Johnny Rebel, Kayo Kane, The Echo, Night Hawk, Ray O'Light, Detective Shane begin (all 1st app.?); Red Blazer on cover only; Sultan-a	300	600	900	1900	2850	3800
2-Origin Scarlet Phantom by Kubert	109	218	327	681	1021	1360
3-Nazi war-c	84	168	252	525	788	1050
4	66	132	198	413	619	825
5-11: 5-Schomburg-c thru #11. 6-The Boy Heroes & Red Blazer (text story) begin, end #12; Black Cat app.; intro. Sparky in Red Blazer. 7-Kubert, Powell-a; Black Cat & Zebra app. 8,9: 8-Shock Gibson app.; Kubert, Powell-a; Schomburg-c. 9-Black Cat app.; Kubert-a. 10-The Zebra app. (from Green Hornet Comics); Kubert-a(3). 11-Girl Commandos, Man In Black app.	80	160	240	500	750	1000
12,13: 12-Kubert-a. 13-Stuntman by Simon & Kirby; Green Hornet, Joe Palooka, Flying Fool app.; Green Hornet-c	62	124	186	388	582	775
14-The Green Hornet & The Man in Black Called Fate by Powell, Joe Flying Fool app.; Flying Fool app.; J. Palooka-c by Ham Fisher	58	116	174	363	542	720
15-(Rare)-Small size (5-1/2x8-1/2"; B&W; 32 pgs.). Distributed to mail subscribers only. Black Cat and Joe Palooka app.	96	192	288	600	900	1200

NOTE: *Also see Boy Explorers No. 2, Flash Gordon No. 5, and Stuntman No. 3.* ***Powell** a-11.* ***Schomburg** c-5-11. Captain Red Blazer & Spark on c-5-11 (w/Boy Heroes #12).*

ALL-OUT WAR
DC Comics: Sept-Oct, 1979 - No. 6, Aug, 1980 ($1.00, 68 pgs.)

	GD 2.0	VG 4.0	FN 6.0	VF 8.0	VF/NM 9.0	NM- 9.2
1-The Viking Commando(origin), Force Three(origin), & Black Eagle Squadron begin	2	4	6	8	10	12
2-6	1	2	3	4	5	7

NOTE: ***Ayers** a(p)-1-6.* ***Elias** r-2.* ***Evans** a-1-6.* ***Kubert** c-16.*

ALL PICTURE ADVENTURE MAGAZINE
St. John Publishing Co.: Oct, 1952 - No. 2, Nov, 1952 (100 pg. Giants, 25¢, squarebound)

	GD 2.0	VG 4.0	FN 6.0	VF 8.0	VF/NM 9.0	NM- 9.2
1-War comics	31	62	93	175	248	320
2-Horror-crime comics	44	88	132	264	395	525

NOTE: *Above books contain three St. John comics rebound; variations possible.* ***Baker** art known in both.*

ALL PICTURE ALL TRUE LOVE STORY
St. John Publishing Co.: Oct., 1952 - No. 2, Nov., 1952 (100 pgs., 25¢)

	GD 2.0	VG 4.0	FN 6.0	VF 8.0	VF/NM 9.0	NM- 9.2
1-Canteen Kate by Matt Baker	48	96	144	288	432	575
2-Baker-c/a	33	66	99	190	270	350

ALL-PICTURE COMEDY CARNIVAL
St. John Publishing Co.: October, 1952 (100 pgs., 25¢)(Contains 4 rebound comics)

	GD 2.0	VG 4.0	FN 6.0	VF 8.0	VF/NM 9.0	NM- 9.2
1-Contents can vary; Baker-a	43	86	129	258	364	470

ALL REAL CONFESSION MAGAZINE (See Fox Giants)

ALL ROMANCES (Mr. Risk No. 7 on)
A. A. Wyn (Ace Periodicals): Aug, 1949 - No. 6, June, 1950

	GD 2.0	VG 4.0	FN 6.0	VF 8.0	VF/NM 9.0	NM- 9.2
1	10	20	30	58	77	95
2	6	12	18	29	36	42
3-6	6	12	18	27	33	38

ALL-SELECT COMICS (Blonde Phantom No. 12 on)
Timely Comics (Daring Comics): Fall, 1943 - No. 11, Fall, 1946

	GD 2.0	VG 4.0	FN 6.0	VF 8.0	VF/NM 9.0	NM- 9.2
1-Capt. America (by Rico #1), Human Torch, Sub-Mariner begin; Black Widow story (4 pgs.); Classic Schomburg-c	1063	2126	3189	7973	12,487	17,000
2-Red Skull app.	370	740	1110	2405	3703	5000
3-The Whizzer begins	240	480	720	1500	2250	3000
4,5-Last Sub-Mariner	172	344	516	1075	1613	2150
6-9: 6-The Destroyer app. 8-No Whizzer	136	272	408	850	1275	1700
10-The Destroyer & Sub-Mariner app.; last Capt. America & Human Torch issue	136	272	408	850	1275	1700
11-1st app. Blonde Phantom; Miss America app.; all Blonde Phantom-c by Shores	264	528	792	1650	2475	3300

NOTE: ***Schomburg** c-1-10.* ***Sekowsky** a-7. #7 & 8 show 1944 in indicia, but should be 1945.*

ALL SPORTS COMICS (Formerly Real Sports Comics; becomes All Time Sports Comics No. 4 on)
Hillman Periodicals: No. 2, Dec-Jan, 1948-49; No. 3, Feb-Mar, 1949

	GD 2.0	VG 4.0	FN 6.0	VF 8.0	VF/NM 9.0	NM- 9.2
2-Krigstein-a(p), Powell, Starr-a	37	74	111	212	301	390
3-Mort Lawrence-a	25	50	75	147	202	260

ALL STAR COMICS (All Star Western No. 58 on)
National Periodical Publ./All-American/DC Comics: Sum, '40 - No. 57, Feb-Mar, '51; No. 58, Jan-Feb, '76 -No. 74, Sept-Oct, '78

	GD 2.0	VG 4.0	FN 6.0	VF 8.0	VF/NM 9.0	NM- 9.2
1-The Flash (#1 by E.E. Hibbard), Hawkman (by Shelly), Hourman (by Bernard Baily), The Sandman(by Creig Flessel), The Spectre(by Baily), Biff Bronson, Red White & Blue (ends #2) begin; Ultra Man's only app. (#1-3 are quarterly; #4 begins bi-monthly issues)	1125	2250	3375	8438	13,219	18,000
2-Green Lantern (by Martin Nodell), Johnny Thunder begin; Green Lantern figure swipe from the cover of All-American Comics #16; Flash figure swipe from cover of Flash Comics #8; Moldoff/Bailey-c (cut & paste-c.)	497	994	1491	3479	5340	7200
3-Origin & 1st app. The Justice Society of America (Win/40); Dr. Fate & The Atom begin, Red Tornado cameo	3438	6876	10,314	26,000	40,500	55,000
3-Reprint, Oversize 13-1/2x10". **WARNING:** This comic is an exact reprint of the original except for its size. DC published it in 1974 with a second cover titling it as a Famous First Edition. There have been many reported cases of the outer cover being removed and the interior sold as the original edition. The reprint with the new outer cover removed is practically worthless. See Famous First Edition for value.						
4-1st adventure for J.S.A.	517	1034	1551	3619	5560	7500
5-1st app. Shiera Sanders as Hawkgirl (1st costumed super-heroine, 6-7/41)	434	868	1302	3038	4669	6300
6-Johnny Thunder joins JSA	300	600	900	1900	2850	3800
7-Batman, Superman, Flash cameo; last Hourman; Doiby Dickles app.	326	652	978	2119	3260	4400
8-Origin & 1st app. Wonder Woman (12-1/41-42)(added as 9 pgs. making book 76 pgs.; origin cont'd in Sensation #1; see W.W. #1 for more detailed origin); Dr. Fate dons new helmet; Hop Harrigan text stories & Starman begin; Shiera app.; Hop Harrigan JSA guest; Starman & Dr. Mid-Nite become members	2750	5500	8250	21,000	32,500	44,000
9-11: 9-JSA's girlfriends cameo; Shiera app.; J. Edgar Hoover of FBI made associate member of JSA. 10-Flash, Green Lantern cameo; Sandman new costume. 11-Wonder Woman begins; Spectre cameo; Shiera app.; Moldoff Hawkman-c	288	576	864	1800	2700	3600
12-Wonder Woman becomes JSA Secretary	256	512	768	1600	2400	3200
13,15: Sandman w/Sandy in #14 & 15. 15-Origin & 1st app. Brain Wave; Shiera app.	240	480	720	1500	2250	3000
14-(12/42) Junior JSA Club begins; w/membership offer & premiums	244	488	732	1525	2288	3050
16-20: 19-Sandman w/Sandy. 20-Dr. Fate & Sandman cameo	176	352	528	1100	1650	2200
21-23: 21-Spectre & Atom cameo; Dr. Fate by Kubert; Dr. Fate, Sandman end. 22-Last Hop Harrigan; Flag-c. 23-Origin/1st app. Psycho Pirate; last Spectre & Starman	154	308	462	963	1444	1925
24-Flash & Green Lantern cameo; Mr. Terrific only app.; Wildcat, JSA guest; Kubert Hawkman begins; Hitler-c	154	308	462	963	1444	1925
25-27: 25-Flash & Green Lantern start again. 26-Robot-c. 27-Wildcat, JSA guest (#24-26: only All-American imprint)	132	264	396	825	1238	1650
28-32	120	240	360	750	1125	1500
33-Solomon Grundy & Doiby Dickles app; classic Solomon Grundy cover & last G.A. app.	333	666	999	2165	3333	4500
34,35-Johnny Thunder cameo in both	116	232	348	725	1088	1450
36-Batman & Superman JSA guests	272	544	816	1700	2550	3400
37-Johnny Thunder cameo; origin & 1st app. Injustice Society; last Kubert Hawkman	152	304	456	950	1425	1900
38-Black Canary begins; JSA Death issue	176	352	528	1100	1650	2200
39,40: 39-Last Johnny Thunder	112	224	336	700	1050	1400

All Star Comics #58 © DC

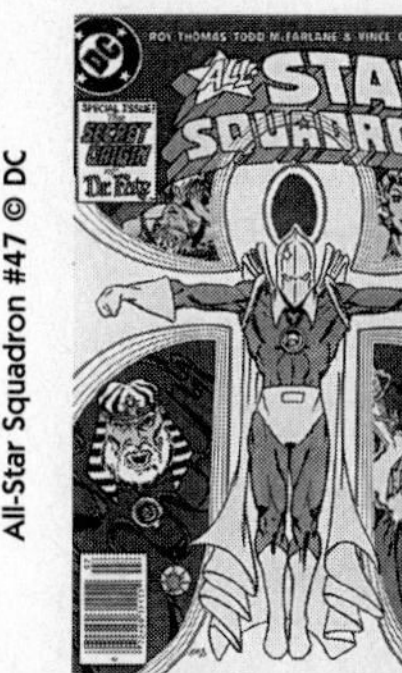

All-Star Squadron #47 © DC

All Top Comics #16 © FOX

	GD 2.0	VG 4.0	FN 6.0	VF 8.0	VF/NM 9.0	NM- 9.2
41-Black Canary joins JSA; Injustice Society app. (2nd app.?)	112	224	336	700	1050	1400
42-Atom & the Hawkman don new costumes	112	224	336	700	1050	1400
43-49,51-56: 43-New logo; Robot-c. 55-Sci/Fi story. 56-Robot-c	112	224	336	700	1050	1400
50-Frazetta art, 3 pgs.	120	240	360	750	1125	1500
57-Kubert-a, 6 pgs. (Scarce); last app. G.A. Green Lantern, Flash & Dr. Mid-Nite	160	320	480	1000	1500	2000
V12 #58-(1976) JSA (Flash, Hawkman, Dr. Mid-Nite, Wildcat, Dr. Fate, Green Lantern, Robin & Star Spangled Kid) app.; intro. Power Girl	4	8	12	24	32	40
V12 #59,60: 59-Estrada & Wood-a	2	4	6	11	14	18
V12 #61-68: 62-65-Superman app. 64,65-Wood-c/a; Vandal Savage app. 66-Injustice Society app. 68-Psycho Pirate app.	2	4	6	11	14	18
V12 #69-1st Earth-2 Huntress (Helena Wayne)	3	6	9	18	24	30
V12 #70-73: 70-Full intro. of Huntress	2	4	6	11	14	18
V12 #74-(44 pgs.) Last issue, story continues in Adventure Comics #461 & 462 (death of Earth-2 Batman; Staton-c/a	3	6	9	16	20	24

NOTE: *No Atom-27, 36; no Dr. Fate-13; no Flash-8, 9, 11-23; no Green Lantern-8, 9,11-23; Hawkman in 1-57 (only one to app. in all 57 issues); no Johnny Thunder-5, 36; no Wonder Woman-9, 10, 23. Book length stories in 4-9, 11-14, 18-22, 25, 26, 29, 30, 32-36, 40, 42, 43. Johnny Peril in #42-46, 48, 49, 51, 52,54-57.* ***Baily*** *a-1-10, 12, 13, 14i, 15-20.* ***Burnley*** *Starman-8-13; c-12, 13.* ***Grell*** *c-58.* ***E.E. Hibbard*** *c-3, 4, 6-10.* ***Infantino*** *c-40.* ***Kubert*** *Hawkman-24-30, 33-37.* ***Lampert/Baily/Flessel*** *c-1, 2.* ***Moldoff*** *Hawkman-3-23; c-11.* ***Mart Nodell*** *c-25i, 26i, 27-32.* ***Purcell*** *c-5.* ***Simon & Kirby*** *Sandman 14-17, 19.* ***Staton*** *a-66-74p. c-74p.* ***Toth*** *a-37(2), 38(2), 40, 41; c-38, 41.* ***Wood*** *a-58i-63i, 64, 65; c-63i, 64, 65. Issues 1-7, 9-16 are 68 pgs.; #8 is 76 pgs.; #17-19 are 60 pgs.; #20-57 are 52 pgs.*

ALL STAR COMICS (Also see crossover 1999 editions of Adventure, All-American, National, Sensation, Smash, Star Spangled and Thrilling Comics)
DC Comics: May, 1999 - No. 2, May, 1999 ($2.95, bookends for JSA x-over)

	GD 2.0	VG 4.0	FN 6.0	VF 8.0	VF/NM 9.0	NM- 9.2
1,2-Justice Society in World War 2; Robinson-s/Johnson-c						3.00
...80-Page Giant (9/99, $4.95) Phantom Lady app.						5.00

ALL STAR INDEX, THE
Independent Comics Group (Eclipse): Feb, 1987 ($2.00, Baxter paper)

	GD 2.0	VG 4.0	FN 6.0	VF 8.0	VF/NM 9.0	NM- 9.2
1	1	2	3	5	6	8

ALL-STAR SQUADRON (See Justice League of America #193)
DC Comics: Sept, 1981 - No. 67, Mar, 1987

	GD 2.0	VG 4.0	FN 6.0	VF 8.0	VF/NM 9.0	NM- 9.2
1-Original Atom, Hawkman, Dr. Mid-Nite, Robotman (origin), Plastic Man, Johnny Quick, Liberty Belle, Shining Knight begin	1	2	3	4	5	7
2-10: 4, 7-Spectre app. 5-Danette Reilly becomes new Firebrand. 8-Re-intro Steel, the Indestructable Man						5.00
11-46,48,49: 12-Origin G.A. Hawkman retold. 23-Origin/1st app. The Amazing Man. 24-Batman app. 25-1st app. Infinity, Inc. (9/83), 26-Origin Infinity, Inc.(2nd app.); Robin app. 27-Dr. Fate vs. The Spectre. 30-35-Spectre app. 33-Origin Freedom Fighters of Earth-X. 36,37-Superman vs. Capt. Marvel; Ordway-c. 41-Origin Starman						4.00
47-Origin Dr. Fate; McFarlane-a (1st full story)/part-c (7/85)	1	3	4	6	8	10
50-Double size; Crisis x-over						6.00
51-67: 51-56-Crisis x-over. 61-Origin Liberty Belle. 62-Origin The Shining Knight. 63-Origin Robotman. 65-Origin Johnny Quick. 66-Origin Tarantula						4.50
Annual 1-3: 1(11/82)-Retells origin of G.A. Atom, Guardian & Wildcat; Jerry Ordway's 1st pencils for DC.(1st work was inking Carmine Infantino in House of Mystery #94). 2(11/83)-Infinity, Inc. app. 3(9/84)						4.50

NOTE: ***Buckler*** *a-1-5; c-1, 3-5, 51.* ***Kubert*** *c-2, 7-18. JLA app. in 14, 15. JSA app. in 4, 14, 15, 19, 27, 28.*

ALL-STAR STORY OF THE DODGERS, THE
Stadium Communications: Apr, 1979 ($1.00)

	GD 2.0	VG 4.0	FN 6.0	VF 8.0	VF/NM 9.0	NM- 9.2
1	2	4	6	10	12	15

ALL STAR WESTERN (Formerly All Star Comics No. 1-57)
National Periodical Publ.: No. 58, Apr-May, 1951 - No. 119, June-July, 1961

	GD 2.0	VG 4.0	FN 6.0	VF 8.0	VF/NM 9.0	NM- 9.2
58-Trigger Twins (ends #116), Strong Bow, The Roving Ranger & Don Caballero begin	44	88	132	264	395	525
59,60: Last 52 pgs.	27	54	81	153	214	275
61-66: 61-64-Toth-a	22	44	66	124	172	220
67-Johnny Thunder begins; Gil Kane-a	27	54	81	153	214	275
68-81: Last precode (2-3/55)	12	24	36	71	96	120
82-98: 97-1st S.A. issue	11	22	33	63	84	105
99-Frazetta-r/Jimmy Wakely #4	11	22	33	66	88	110
100	11	22	33	66	88	110
101-107,109-116,118,119	9	18	27	54	70	85
108-Origin J. Thunder; J. Thunder logo begins	22	44	66	124	172	220
117-Origin Super Chief	13	26	39	74	100	125

NOTE: ***Gil Kane*** *c(p)-58, 59, 61, 63, 64, 68, 69, 70-95(most), 97-199(most).* ***Infantino*** *art in most issues. Madame .44 app.-#117-119.*

ALL-STAR WESTERN (Weird Western Tales No. 12 on)
National Periodical Publications: Aug-Sept, 1970 - No. 11, Apr-May, 1972

	GD 2.0	VG 4.0	FN 6.0	VF 8.0	VF/NM 9.0	NM- 9.2
1-Pow-Wow Smith-r; Infantino-a	5	10	15	33	44	55
2-Outlaw begins; El Diablo by Morrow begins; has cameos by Williamson, Torres, Kane, Giordano & Phil Seuling	4	8	12	27	36	45
3-Origin El Diablo	4	8	12	27	36	45
4-6: 5-Last Outlaw issue. 6-Billy the Kid begins, ends #8	3	6	9	19	25	32
7-9-(52 pgs.) 9-Frazetta-a, 3pgs.(r)	4	8	12	24	32	40
10-(52 pgs.) Jonah Hex begins (1st app., 2-3/72)	37	74	111	278	419	560
11-(52 pgs.) 2nd app. Jonah Hex; 1st cover	17	34	51	118	174	230

NOTE: ***Neal Adams*** *c-2-5;* ***Aparo*** *a-5.* ***G. Kane a****-3, 4, 6, 8.* ***Kubert*** *a-4r, 7-9r.* ***Morrow*** *a-2-4, 10, 11. No. 7-11 have 52 pgs..*

ALL SURPRISE (Becomes Jeanie #13 on) (Funny animal)
Timely/Marvel (CPC): Fall, 1943 - No. 12, Winter, 1946-47

	GD 2.0	VG 4.0	FN 6.0	VF 8.0	VF/NM 9.0	NM- 9.2
1-Super Rabbit, Gandy & Sourpuss begin	34	68	102	196	278	360
2	17	34	51	98	134	170
3-10,12	13	26	39	74	100	125
11-Kurtzman "Pigtales" art	14	28	42	79	107	135

ALL TEEN (Formerly All Winners; All Winners & Teen Comics No. 21 on)
Marvel Comics (WFP): No. 20, January, 1947

	GD 2.0	VG 4.0	FN 6.0	VF 8.0	VF/NM 9.0	NM- 9.2
20-Georgie, Mitzi, Patsy Walker, Willie app.; Syd Shores-c	13	26	39	76	103	130

ALL-TIME SPORTS COMICS (Formerly All Sports Comics)
Hillman Per.: V2No. 4, Apr-May, 1949 - V2No. 7, Oct-Nov, 1949 (All 52 pgs.)

	GD 2.0	VG 4.0	FN 6.0	VF 8.0	VF/NM 9.0	NM- 9.2
V2#4	24	48	72	135	190	245
5-7: 5-(V1#5 inside)-Powell-a; Ty Cobb sty. 7-Krigstein-p; Walter Johnson & Knute Rockne sty	18	36	54	104	142	180

ALL TOP
William H. Wise Co.: 1944 (132 pgs.)

	GD 2.0	VG 4.0	FN 6.0	VF 8.0	VF/NM 9.0	NM- 9.2
nn-Capt. V, Merciless the Sorceress, Red Robbins, One Round Hogan, Mike the M.P., Snooky, Pussy Katnip app.	32	64	96	182	259	335

ALL TOP COMICS (My Experience No. 19 on)
Fox Features Synd./Green Publ./Norlen Mag.: 1945; No. 2, Sum, 1946 - No. 18, Mar, 1949; 1957 - 1959

	GD 2.0	VG 4.0	FN 6.0	VF 8.0	VF/NM 9.0	NM- 9.2
1-Cosmo Cat & Flash Rabbit begin (1st app.)	25	50	75	147	202	260
2 (#1-7 are funny animal)	12	24	36	71	96	120
3-7	9	18	27	52	66	80
8-Blue Beetle, Phantom Lady, & Rulah, Jungle Goddess begin (11/47); Kamen-c	252	504	756	1575	2363	3150
9-Kamen-c	130	260	390	813	1219	1625
10-Kamen bondage-c	139	278	417	869	1305	1740
11-13,15-17: 11-Rulah-c. 15-No Blue Beetle	112	224	336	700	1050	1400
14-No Blue Beetle; used in **SOTI**, illo- "Corpses of colored people strung up by their wrists"	144	288	432	900	1350	1800
18-Dagar, Jo-Jo app; no Phantom Lady or Blue Beetle	70	140	210	438	657	875
6(1957-Green Publ.)-Patoruzu the Indian; Cosmo Cat on cover only. 6(1958-Literary Ent.)-Muggy Doo; Cosmo Cat on cover only. 6(1959-Norlen)-Atomic Mouse; Cosmo Cat on-c only. 6(1959)-Little Eva. 6(Cornell)-Supermouse on-c	5	10	15	24	30	35

NOTE: *Jo-Jo by* ***Kamen****-12,18.*

ALL TRUE ALL PICTURE POLICE CASES
St. John Publishing Co.: Oct, 1952 - No. 2, Nov, 1952 (100 pgs.)

	GD 2.0	VG 4.0	FN 6.0	VF 8.0	VF/NM 9.0	NM- 9.2
1-Three rebound St. John crime comics	43	86	129	258	364	470
2-Three comics rebound	32	64	96	182	259	335

NOTE: *Contents may vary.*

ALL-TRUE CRIME (...Cases No. 26-35; formerly Official True Crime Cases)
Marvel/Atlas Comics: No. 26, Feb, 1948 - No. 52, Sept, 1952
(OFI #26,27/CFI #28,29/LCC #30-46/LMC #47-52)

	GD 2.0	VG 4.0	FN 6.0	VF 8.0	VF/NM 9.0	NM- 9.2
26(#1)-Syd Shores-c	35	70	105	201	283	365
27(4/48)-Electric chair-c	27	54	81	153	214	275
28-41,43-48,50-52: 35-37-Photo-c	11	22	33	66	88	110
42,49-Krigstein-a. 49-Used in **POP**, Pg 79	12	24	36	71	96	120

NOTE: ***Robinson*** *a-47, 50.* ***Shores*** *c-26.* ***Tuska*** *a-48(3).*

ALL-TRUE DETECTIVE CASES (Kit Carson No. 5 on)
Avon Periodicals: #2, Apr-May, 1954 - No. 4, Aug-Sept, 1954

	GD 2.0	VG 4.0	FN 6.0	VF 8.0	VF/NM 9.0	NM- 9.2
2(#1)-Wood-a	24	48	72	138	194	250
3-Kinstler-c	13	26	39	74	100	125
4-r/Gangsters And Gun Molls #2; Kamen-a	19	38	57	109	152	195
nn(100 pgs.)-7 pg. Kubert-a, Kinstler back-c	39	78	117	230	325	420

ALL TRUE ROMANCE (...Illustrated No. 3)

All True Romance #6 © Harwell

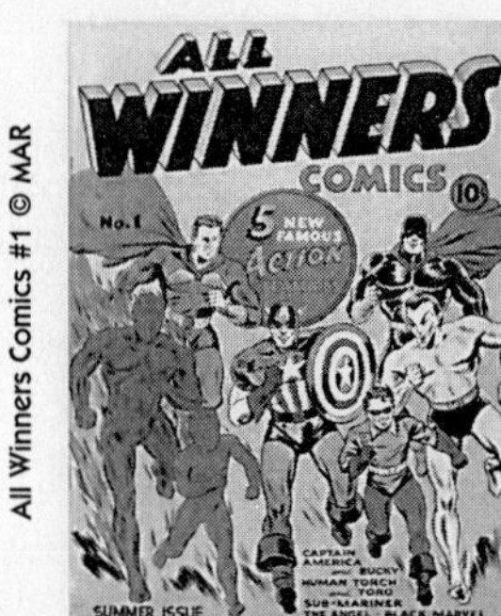

All Winners Comics #1 © MAR

Alpha Flight #97 © MAR

Artful Publ. #1-3/Harwell(Comic Media) #4-20?/Ajax-Farrell(Excellent Publ.) No. 22 on/Four Star Comic Corp.: 3/51 - No. 20, 12/54; No. 22, 3/55 - No. 30?, 7/57; No. 3(#31), 9/57;No. 4(#32), 11/57; No. 33, 2/58 - No. 34, 6/58

	GD 2.0	VG 4.0	FN 6.0	VF 8.0	VF/NM 9.0	NM- 9.2
1 (3/51)	17	34	51	95	130	165
2 (10/51; 11/51 on-c)	9	18	27	52	66	80
3(12/51) - #5(5/52)	8	16	24	40	50	60
6-Wood-a, 9 pgs. (exceptional)	17	34	51	95	130	165
7-10 [two #7s: #7(11/52, 9/52 inside), #7(11/52, 11/52 inside)]	7	14	21	35	43	50
11-13,16-19(9/54),20(12/54) (no #21)	6	12	18	27	33	38
14-Marijuana story	6	12	18	29	36	42
22: Last precode issue (1st Ajax, 3/55)	6	12	18	27	33	38
23-27,29,30(7/57)	5	10	15	22	26	30
28 (9/56)-L. B. Cole, Disbrow-a	10	20	30	58	77	95
3(#31, 9/57),4(#32, 11/57),33,34 (Farrell, '57- '58)	5	10	14	20	24	28

ALL WESTERN WINNERS (Formerly All Winners; becomes Western Winners with No. 5; see Two-Gun Kid No. 5)
Marvel Comics(CDS): No. 2, Winter, 1948-49 - No. 4, April, 1949

	GD 2.0	VG 4.0	FN 6.0	VF 8.0	VF/NM 9.0	NM- 9.2
2-Black Rider (origin/1st app.) & his horse Satan, Kid Colt & his horse Steel, & Two-Gun Kid & his horse Cyclone begin; Shores c-2-4	78	156	234	449	712	975
3-Anti-Wertham editorial	39	78	117	233	329	425
4-Black Rider i.d. revealed; Heath, Shores-a	39	78	117	233	329	425

ALL WINNERS COMICS (All Teen #20) (Also see Timely Presents: ...)
USA No. 1-7/WFP No. 10-19/YAI No. 21: Summer, 1941 - No. 19, Fall, 1946; No. 21, Winter, 1946-47; (No #20) (No. 21 continued from Young Allies No. 20)

	GD 2.0	VG 4.0	FN 6.0	VF 8.0	VF/NM 9.0	NM- 9.2
1-The Angel & Black Marvel only app.; Capt. America by Simon & Kirby, Human Torch & Sub-Mariner begin (#1 was advertised as All Aces); 1st app. All-Winners Squad in text story by Stan Lee	1875	3750	5625	14,000	22,000	30,000
2-The Destroyer & The Whizzer begin; Simon & Kirby Captain America	483	966	1449	3381	5191	7000
3	311	622	933	2022	3111	4200
4-Classic War-c by Al Avison	341	682	1023	2217	3409	4600
5	220	440	660	1375	2063	2750
6-The Black Avenger only app.; no Whizzer story; Hitler, Hirohito & Mussolini-c	264	528	792	1650	2475	3300
7-10	184	368	552	1150	1725	2300
11,13-18: 11-1st Atlas globe on-c (Winter, 1943-44; also see Human Torch #14). 14-16-No Human Torch	136	272	408	850	1275	1700
12-Red Skull story; last Destroyer; no Whizzer story	168	336	504	1050	1575	2100
19-(Scarce)-1st story app. & origin All Winners Squad (Capt. America & Bucky, Human Torch & Toro, Sub-Mariner, Whizzer, & Miss America; r-in Fantasy Masterpieces #10	428	856	1284	2996	4598	6200
21-(Scarce)-All Winners Squad; bondage-c	385	770	1155	2503	3852	5200

NOTE: ***Everett** Sub-Mariner-1, 3, 4; **Burgos** Torch-1, 3, 4. **Schomburg** c-1, 7-18. **Shores** c-19p, 21.*

(2nd Series - August, 1948, Marvel Comics (CDS))
(Becomes All Western Winners with No. 2)

	GD 2.0	VG 4.0	FN 6.0	VF 8.0	VF/NM 9.0	NM- 9.2
1-The Blonde Phantom, Capt. America, Human Torch, & Sub-Mariner app.	288	576	864	1800	2700	3600

ALL YOUR COMICS (See Fox Giants)
Fox Feature Syndicate (R. W. Voight): Spring, 1946 (36 pgs.)

	GD 2.0	VG 4.0	FN 6.0	VF 8.0	VF/NM 9.0	NM- 9.2
1-Red Robbins, Merciless the Sorceress app.	22	44	66	124	172	220

ALMANAC OF CRIME (See Fox Giants)

AL OF FBI (See Little Al of the FBI)

ALONE IN THE DARK (Based on video game)
Image Comics: Feb, 2003 ($4.95)

	NM- 9.2
1-Matt Haley-c/a; Jean-Marc & Randy Lofficier-s	5.00

ALPHA AND OMEGA
Spire Christian Comics (Fleming H. Revell): 1978 (49¢)

	GD 2.0	VG 4.0	FN 6.0	VF 8.0	VF/NM 9.0	NM- 9.2
nn	1	3	4	6	8	10

ALPHA CENTURION (See Superman, 2nd Series & Zero Hour)
DC Comics: 1996 ($2.95, one-shot)

	NM- 9.2
1	3.00

ALPHA FLIGHT (See X-Men #120,121 & X-Men/Alpha Flight)
Marvel Comics: Aug, 1983 - No. 130, Mar, 1994 (#52-on are direct sales only)

	NM- 9.2
1-(52 pgs.) Byrne-a begins (thru #28) -Wolverine & Nightcrawler cameo	4.00
2-28: 2-Vindicator becomes Guardian; origin Marrina & Alpha Flight. 3-Concludes origin Alpha Flight. 6-Origin Shaman. 7-Origin Snowbird. 10,11-Origin Sasquatch. 12-(52 pgs.)-Death of Guardian. 13-Wolverine app. 16,17-Wolverine cameo. 17-X-Men x-over (mostly r-/X-Men #109); 20-New headquarters. 25-Return of Guardian. 28-Last Byrne issue	3.00
29-32,35-50: 39-47,49-Portacio-a(i). 50-Double size; Portacio-a(i)	2.50
33,34: 33-1st app. Lady Deathstrike; Wolverine app. 34-Origin Wolverine	3.00
51-Jim Lee's 1st work at Marvel (10/87); Wolverine cameo; 1st Lee Wolverine; Portacio-a(i)	5.00
52,53-Wolverine app.; Lee-a on Wolverine; Portacio-a(i); 53-Lee/Portacio-a	3.00
54-73,76-86,91-99,101-105: 54,63,64-No Jim Lee-a. 54-Portacio-a(i). 55-62-Jim Lee-a(p). 71-Intro The Sorcerer (villain). 91-Dr. Doom app. 94-F.F. x-over. 99-Galactus, Avengers app. 102-Intro Weapon Omega	2.25
74,75,87-90,100: 74-Wolverine, Spider-Man & The Avengers app. 75-Double size ($1.95, 52 pgs.). 87-90-Wolverine. 4 part story w/Jim Lee-c. 89-Original Guardian returns. 100-($2.00, 52 pgs.)-Avengers & Galactus app.	3.00
106-Northstar revelation issue	2.50
106-2nd printing (direct sale only)	2.25
107-109,112-119,121-129: 107-X-Factor x-over. 112-Infinity War x-overs	2.25
110,111: Infinity War x-overs, Wolverine app. (brief). 111-Thanos cameo	3.00
120-($2.25)-Polybagged w/Paranormal Registration Act poster	2.50
130-($2.25, 52 pgs.)	3.00
Annual 1,2 (9/86, 12/87)	3.00
Special V2#1(6/92, $2.50, 52 pgs.)-Wolverine-c/story	2.50

NOTE: ***Austin** c-1i, 2i, 53i. **Byrne** c-81, 82. **Guice** c-85, 91-99. **Jim Lee** a(p)-51, 53, 55-62, 64; c-53, 87-90. **Mignola** a-29-31p. **Whilce Portacio** a(i)-39-47, 49-54.*

ALPHA FLIGHT (2nd Series)
Marvel Comics: Aug, 1997 - No. 20, Mar, 1999 ($2.99/$1.99)

	NM- 9.2
1-($2.99)-Wraparound cover	6.00
2,3: 2-Variant-c	4.00
4-11: 8,9-Wolverine-c/app.	3.00
12-($2.99) Death of Sasquatch; wraparound-c	4.00
13-20	3.00
.../Inhumans '98 Annual ($3.50) Raney-a	3.50

ALPHA FLIGHT: IN THE BEGINNING
Marvel Comics: July, 1997 ($1.95, one-shot)

	NM- 9.2
(-1)-Flashback w/Wolverine	2.25

ALPHA FLIGHT SPECIAL
Marvel Comics: July, 1991 - No. 4, Oct, 1991 ($1.50, limited series)

	NM- 9.2
1-4: 1-3-r-A. Flight #97-99 w/covers. 4-r-A.Flight #100	2.25

ALPHA KORPS
Diversity Comics: Sept, 1996 ($2.50)

	NM- 9.2
1-Origin/1st app. Alpha Korps	2.50

ALPHA WAVE
Darkline Comics: Mar, 1987 ($1.75, 36 pgs.)

	NM- 9.2
1	2.25

ALTERED IMAGE
Image Comics: Apr, 1998 - No. 3, Sept, 1998 ($2.50, limited series)

	NM- 9.2
1-3-Spawn, Witchblade, Savage Dragon; Valentino-s/a	3.00

ALTER EGO
First Comics: May, 1986 - No. 4, Nov, 1986 (Mini-series)

	NM- 9.2
1-4	2.25

ALVIN (TV) (See Four Color Comics No. 1042 or Three Chipmunks #1)
Dell Publishing Co.: Oct-Dec, 1962 - No. 28, Oct, 1973

	GD 2.0	VG 4.0	FN 6.0	VF 8.0	VF/NM 9.0	NM- 9.2
12-021-212 (#1)	10	20	30	67	96	125
2	6	12	18	40	55	70
3-10	5	10	15	36	48	60
11-28: 11-"Chipmunks sing the Beatles Hits"	4	8	12	27	36	45
Alvin For President (10/64)	5	10	15	33	44	55
...& His Pals in Merry Christmas with Clyde Crashcup & Leonardo 1 (02-120-402)-(12-2/64)	8	16	24	58	82	105
Reprinted in 1966 (12-023-604)	6	12	18	40	55	70

ALVIN & THE CHIPMUNKS
Harvey Comics: July, 1992 - No. 5, May, 1994

	NM- 9.2
1-5: 1-Richie Rich app.	4.00

AMALGAM AGE OF COMICS, THE: THE DC COMICS COLLECTION
DC Comics: 1996 ($12.95, trade paperback)

	NM- 9.2
nn-r/Amazon, Assassins, Doctor Strangefate, JLX, Legends of the Dark Claw, & Super Soldier	13.00

AMANDA AND GUNN
Image Comics: Apr, 1997 - No. 4, Oct, 1997 ($2.95, B&W, limited series)

	NM- 9.2
1-4	3.00

Amazing Adult Fantasy #9 © MAR

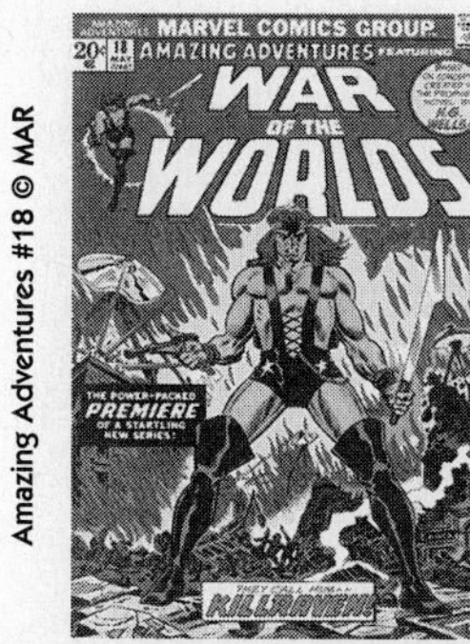

Amazing Adventures #18 © MAR

Amazing-Man Comics #16 © CEN

AMAZING ADULT FANTASY (Formerly Amazing Adventures #1-6; becomes Amazing Fantasy #15)
Marvel Comics Group (AMI): No. 7, Dec, 1961 - No. 14, July, 1962

	GD 2.0	VG 4.0	FN 6.0	VF 8.0	VF/NM 9.0	NM- 9.2
7-Ditko-c/a begins, ends #14	50	100	150	400	600	800
8-Last 10¢ issue	41	82	123	308	464	620
9-13: 12-1st app. Mailbag. 13-Anti-communist sty	39	78	117	293	442	590
13-2nd printing (1994)	2	4	6	8	10	12
14-Prototype issue (Professor X)	42	84	126	315	475	635

AMAZING ADVENTURE FUNNIES (Fantoman No. 2 on)
Centaur Publications: June, 1940 - No. 2, Sept. 1940

	GD 2.0	VG 4.0	FN 6.0	VF 8.0	VF/NM 9.0	NM- 9.2
1-The Fantom of the Fair by Gustavson (r/Amaz. Mystery Funnies V2#7,V2#8), The Arrow, Skyrocket Steele From the Year X by Everett (r/AMF #2); Burgos-a	184	368	552	1150	1725	2300
2-Reprints; Published after Fantoman #2	118	236	354	738	1107	1475

NOTE: *Burgos a-1(2). Everett a-1(3). Gustavson a-1(5), 2(3). Pinajian a-2.*

AMAZING ADVENTURES (Also see Boy Cowboy & Science Comics)
Ziff-Davis Publ. Co.: 1950; No. 1, Nov, 1950 - No. 6, Fall, 1952 (Painted covers)

	GD 2.0	VG 4.0	FN 6.0	VF 8.0	VF/NM 9.0	NM- 9.2
1950 (no month given) (8-1/2x11) (8 pgs.) Has the front & back cover plus Schomburg story used in Amazing Advs. #1 (Sent to subscribers of Z-D s/f magazines & ordered through mail for 10¢. Used to test market)	50	100	150	300	450	600
1-Wood, Schomburg, Anderson, Whitney-a	76	152	228	475	713	950
2-5: 2-Schomburg-a. 2,4,5-Anderson-a. 3,5-Starr-a	39	78	117	233	329	425
6-Krigstein-a	41	82	123	236	336	435

AMAZING ADVENTURES (Becomes Amazing Adult Fantasy #7 on)
Atlas Comics (AMI)/Marvel Comics No. 3 on: June, 1961 - No. 6, Nov, 1961

	GD 2.0	VG 4.0	FN 6.0	VF 8.0	VF/NM 9.0	NM- 9.2
1-Origin Dr. Droom (1st Marvel-Age Superhero) by Kirby; Kirby/Ditko-a (5 pgs.) Ditko & Kirby-a in all; Kirby monster c-1-6	109	218	327	927	1414	1900
2	48	96	144	384	580	775
3-6: 6-Last Dr. Droom	41	82	123	324	487	650

AMAZING ADVENTURES
Marvel Comics Group: Aug, 1970 - No. 39, Nov, 1976

	GD 2.0	VG 4.0	FN 6.0	VF 8.0	VF/NM 9.0	NM- 9.2
1-Inhumans by Kirby(p) & Black Widow (1st app. in Tales of Suspense #52) double feature begins	6	12	18	38	52	65
2-4: 2-F.F. brief app. 4-Last Inhumans by Kirby	3	6	9	18	24	30
5-8: Adams-a(p); 8-Last Black Widow; last 15¢-c	4	8	12	27	36	45
9,10: Magneto app. 10-Last Inhumans (origin-r by Kirby)	3	6	9	18	23	28
11-New Beast begins(1st app. in mutated form; origin in flashback); X-Men cameo in flashback (#11-17 are X-Men tie-ins)	12	24	36	84	125	165
12-17: 12-Beast battles Iron Man. 13-Brotherhood of Evil Mutants x-over from X-Men. 15-X-Men app. 16-Rutland Vermont - Bald Mountain Halloween x-over; Juggernaut app. 17-Last Beast (origin); X-Men app.	4	8	12	28	38	48
18-War of the Worlds begins (5/73); 1st app. Killraven; Neal Adams-a(p)	3	6	9	18	23	28
19-35,38,39: 19-Chaykin-a. 25-Buckler-a. 35-Giffen's first published story (art), along with Deadly Hands of Kung-Fu #22 (3/76)	1	3	4	6	8	10
36,37-(Regular 25¢ edition)(7-8/76)	1	3	4	6	8	10
36,37-(30¢-c variants, limited distribution)	3	6	9	16	20	25

NOTE: *N. Adams c-6-8. Buscema a-1p, 2p. Colan a-3-5p, 26p. Ditko a-24r. Everett a(i)3-5, 7-9. Giffen a-35i, 38p. G. Kane c-11, 25p, 29p. Ploog a-12i. Russell a-27-32, 34-37, 39; c-28, 30-32, 33i, 34, 35, 37, 39i. Starlling a-17. Starlin c-15p, 16, 17, 27. Sutton a-11-15p.*

AMAZING ADVENTURES
Marvel Comics Group: Dec, 1979 - No. 14, Jan, 1981

	GD 2.0	VG 4.0	FN 6.0	VF 8.0	VF/NM 9.0	NM- 9.2
V2#1-Reprints story/X-Men #1 & 38 (origins)	1	2	3	5	6	8
2-14: 2-6-Early X-Men-r. 7,8-Origin Iceman						6.00

NOTE: *Byrne c-6p, 9p. Kirby a-1-14r; c-7, 9. Steranko a-12r. Tuska a-7-9.*

AMAZING ADVENTURES
Marvel Comics: July, 1988 ($4.95, squarebound, one-shot, 80 pgs.)

	GD 2.0	VG 4.0	FN 6.0	VF 8.0	VF/NM 9.0	NM- 9.2
1-Anthology; Austin, Golden-a						5.00

AMAZING ADVENTURES OF CAPTAIN CARVEL AND HIS CARVEL CRUSADERS, THE
(See Carvel Comics in the Promotional Comics section)

AMAZING CHAN & THE CHAN CLAN, THE (TV)
Gold Key: May, 1973 - No. 4, Feb, 1974 (Hanna-Barbera)

	GD 2.0	VG 4.0	FN 6.0	VF 8.0	VF/NM 9.0	NM- 9.2
1-Warren Tufts-a in all	3	7	10	21	28	35
2-4	3	6	9	16	20	24

AMAZING COMICS (Complete Comics No. 2)
Timely Comics (EPC): Fall, 1944

	GD 2.0	VG 4.0	FN 6.0	VF 8.0	VF/NM 9.0	NM- 9.2
1-The Destroyer, The Whizzer, The Young Allies (by Sekowsky), Sergeant Dix; Schomburg-c	212	424	636	1325	1988	2650

AMAZING DETECTIVE CASES (Formerly Suspense No. 2?)
Marvel/Atlas Comics (CCC): No. 3, Nov, 1950 - No. 14, Sept, 1952

	GD 2.0	VG 4.0	FN 6.0	VF 8.0	VF/NM 9.0	NM- 9.2
3	29	58	87	164	232	300
4-6	17	34	51	95	130	165
7-10	15	30	45	86	118	150
11,12,14: 11-(3/52)-Horror format. 12-Krigstein-a	29	58	87	164	232	300
13-(Scarce)-Everett-a; electrocution-c/story	33	66	99	190	270	350

NOTE: *Colan a-9. Maneely c-13. Sekowsky a-12. Sinnott a-13. Tuska a-10.*

AMAZING FANTASY (Formerly Amazing Adult Fantasy #7-14)
Atlas Magazines/Marvel: #15, Aug, 1962 (Sept, 1962 shown in indicia); #16, Dec, 1995 - #18, Feb, 1996

	GD 2.0	VG 4.0	FN 6.0	VF 8.0	VF/NM 9.0	NM- 9.2
15-Origin/1st app. of Spider-Man by Steve Ditko (11 pgs.); 1st app. Aunt May & Uncle Ben; Kirby/Ditko-c	1300	2600	3900	13,000	32,500	42,500
16-18 ('95-'96, $3.95): Kurt Busiek scripts; painted-c/a by Paul Lee						4.00

AMAZING GHOST STORIES (Formerly Nightmare)
St. John Publishing Co.: No. 14, Oct, 1954 - No. 16, Feb, 1955

	GD 2.0	VG 4.0	FN 6.0	VF 8.0	VF/NM 9.0	NM- 9.2
14-Pit & the Pendulum story by Kinstler; Baker-c	34	68	102	196	278	360
15-r/Weird Thrillers #5; Baker-c, Powell-a	25	50	75	144	198	255
16-Kubert reprints of Weird Thrillers #4; Baker-c; Roussos, Tuska-a; Kinstler-a (1 pg.)	25	50	75	147	202	260

AMAZING HIGH ADVENTURE
Marvel Comics: 8/84; No. 2, 10/85; No. 3, 10/86 - No. 5, 1986 ($2.00)

	GD 2.0	VG 4.0	FN 6.0	VF 8.0	VF/NM 9.0	NM- 9.2
1-5: Painted-c on all. 3,4-Baxter paper. 4-Bolton-c/a. 5-Bolton-a						3.50

NOTE: *Bissette a-4. Severin a-1, 3. Sienkiewicz a-1,2. Paul Smith a-2. Williamson a-2i.*

AMAZING-MAN COMICS (Formerly Motion Picture Funnies Weekly?)
(Also see Stars And Stripes Comics)
Centaur Publications: No. 5, Sept, 1939 - No. 26, Jan, 1942

	GD 2.0	VG 4.0	FN 6.0	VF 8.0	VF/NM 9.0	NM- 9.2
5(#1)(Rare)-Origin/1st app. A-Man the Amazing Man by Bill Everett; The Cat-Man by Tarpe Mills (also #8), Mighty Man by Filchock, Minimidget & sidekick Ritty, & The Iron Skull by Burgos begins	1375	2750	4125	10,313	16,157	22,000
6-Origin The Amazing Man retold; The Shark begins; Ivy Menace by Tarpe Mills app.	311	622	933	2022	3111	4200
7-Magician From Mars begins; ends #11	228	456	684	1425	2138	2850
8-Cat-Man dresses as woman	176	352	528	1100	1650	2200
9-Magician From Mars battles the 'Elemental Monster,' swiped into The Spectre in More Fun #54 & 55. Ties w/Marvel Mystery #4 for 1st Nazi War-c on a comic (2/40)	180	360	540	1125	1688	2250
10,11: 11-Zardi, the Eternal Man begins; ends #16; Amazing Man dons costume; last Everett issue	132	264	396	825	1238	1650
12,13	112	224	336	700	1050	1400
14-Reef Kinkaid, Rocke Wayburn (ends #20), & Dr. Hypno (ends #21) begin; no Zardi or Chuck Hardy	92	184	276	575	863	1150
15,17-20: 15-Zardi returns; no Rocke Wayburn. 17-Dr. Hypno returns; no Zardi	80	160	240	500	750	1000
16-Mighty Man's powers of super strength & ability to shrink & grow explained; Rocke Wayburn returns; no Dr. Hypno; Al Avison (a character) begins, ends #18 (a tribute to the famed artist)	85	170	255	531	796	1060
21-Origin Dash Dartwell (drug-use story); origin & only app. T.N.T.	85	170	255	531	796	1060
22-Dash Dartwell, the Human Meteor & The Voice app; last Iron Skull & The Shark; Silver Streak app. (classic-c)	112	224	336	700	1050	1400
23-Two Amazing Man stories; intro/origin Tommy the Amazing Kid; The Marksman only app.	76	152	228	475	713	950
24-King of Darkness, Nightshade, & Blue Lady begin; end #26; 1st app. Super-Ann	76	152	228	475	713	950
25,26 (Scarce): Meteor Martin by Wolverton in both; 26-Electric Ray app.	116	232	348	725	1088	1450

NOTE: *Everett a-5-11; c-5-11. Gilman a-14-20. Giunta/Mirando a-7-10. Sam Glanzman a-14-16, 18-21, 23. Louis Glanzman a-6, 9-11, 14-21; c-13-19, 21. Robert Golden a-9. Gustavson a-6; c-22, 23. Lubbers a-14-21. Simon a-10. Frank Thomas a-6, 9-11, 14, 15, 17-21.*

AMAZING MYSTERIES (Formerly Sub-Mariner Comics No. 31)
Marvel Comics (CCC): No. 32, May, 1949 - No. 35, Jan, 1950 (1st Marvel Horror Comic)

	GD 2.0	VG 4.0	FN 6.0	VF 8.0	VF/NM 9.0	NM- 9.2
32-The Witness app.	80	160	240	500	750	1000
33-Horror format	39	78	117	233	329	425
34,35: Changes to Crime. 34,35-Photo-c	21	42	63	118	164	210

AMAZING MYSTERY FUNNIES
Centaur Publications: Aug, 1938 - No. 24, Sept, 1940 (All 52 pgs.)

	GD 2.0	VG 4.0	FN 6.0	VF 8.0	VF/NM 9.0	NM- 9.2
V1#1-Everett-c(1st); Dick Kent Adv. story; Skyrocket Steele in the Year X on cover only	348	696	1044	2262	3481	4700
2-Everett 1st-a (Skyrocket Steele)	184	368	552	1150	1725	2300
3	92	184	276	575	863	1150

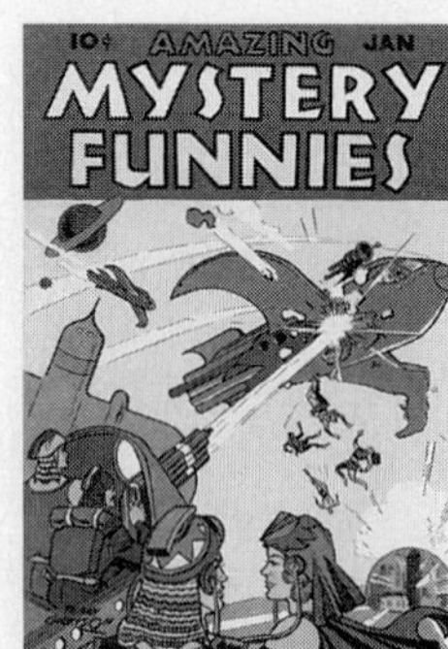

Amazing Mystery Funnies V2 #1 © CEN

Amazing Spider-Man #51 © MAR

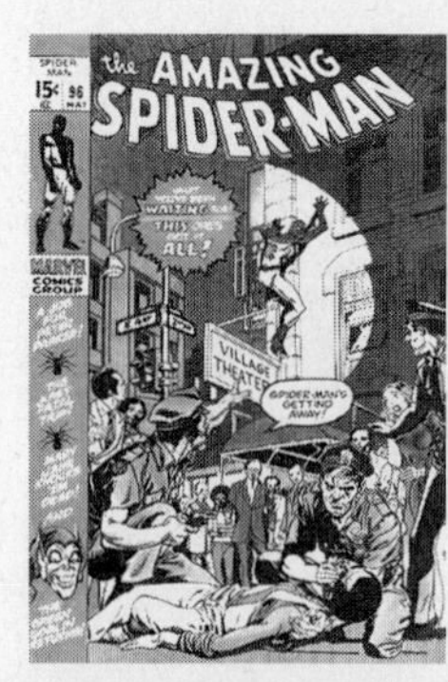

Amazing Spider-Man #96 © MAR

	GD 2.0	VG 4.0	FN 6.0	VF 8.0	VF/NM 9.0	NM- 9.2
3(#4, 12/38)-nn on cover, #3 on inside; bondage-c	83	166	249	519	780	1040
V2#1-4,6: 2-Drug use story. 3-Air-Sub DX begins by Burgos. 4-Dan Hastings, Sand Hog begins (ends #5). 6-Last Skyrocket Steele	76	152	228	475	713	950
5-Classic Everett-c	128	256	384	800	1200	1600
7 (Scarce)-Intro. The Fantom of the Fair & begins; Everett, Gustavson, Burgos-a	341	682	1023	2217	3409	4600
8-Origin & 1st app. Speed Centaur	132	264	396	825	1238	1650
9-11: 11-Self portrait and biog. of Everett; Jon Linton begins; early Robot cover (11/39)	76	152	228	475	713	950
12 (Scarce)-1st Space Patrol; Wolverton-a (12/39); new costume Phantom of the Fair	192	384	576	1200	1800	2400
V3#1(#17, 1/40)-Intro. Bullet; Tippy Taylor serial begins, ends #24 (continued in The Arrow #2)	76	152	228	475	713	950
18,20: 18-Fantom of the Fair by Gustavson	74	148	222	463	694	925
19,21-24: Space Patrol by Wolverton in all	92	184	276	575	863	1150

NOTE: ***Burgos** a-V2#3-9. **Eisner** a-V1#2, 3(2). **Everett** a-V1#2-4, V2#1, 3-6; c-V1#1-4,V2#3, 5, 18. **Filchock** a-V2#9. **Flessel** a-V2#6. **Guardineer** a-V1#4, V2#4-6; **Gustavson** a-V2#4, 5, 9-12, V3#1, 18, 19; c-V2#7, 9, 12, V3#1, 21, 22; **McWilliams** a-V2#9, 10. **TarpeMills** a-V2#2, 4-6, 9-12, V3#1. **Leo Morey**(Pulp artist) c-V2#10; text illo-V2#11. **FrankThomas** a-6-V2#11. **Webster** a-V2#4.*

AMAZING SAINTS
Logos International: 1974 (39¢)

	GD	VG	FN	VF	VF/NM	NM-
nn-True story of Phil Saint	1	3	4	6	8	10

AMAZING SCARLET SPIDER
Marvel Comics: Nov, 1995 - No. 2, Dec, 1995 ($1.95, limited series)

1,2: Replaces "Amazing Spider-Man" for two issues. 1-Venom/Carnage cameos. 2-Green Goblin & Joystick-c/app. 2.25

AMAZING SCREW-ON HEAD, THE
Dark Horse Comics (Maverick): May, 2002 ($2.99, one-shot)

1-Mike Mignola-s/a/c 3.00

AMAZING SPIDER-MAN, THE (See All Detergent Comics, Amazing Fantasy, America's Best TV Comics, Aurora, Deadly Foes of Spider-Man, Fireside Book Series, Giant-Size Spider-Man, Giant Size Super-Heroes Featuring..., Marvel Collectors Item Classics, Marvel Fanfare, Marvel Graphic Novel, Marvel Spec. Ed., Marvel Tales, Marvel Team-Up, Marvel Treasury Ed., Nothing Can Stop the Juggernaut, Official Marvel Index To..., Peter Parker..., Power Record Comics, Spectacular..., Spider-Man, Spider-Man Digest, Spider-Man Saga, Spider-Man 2099, Spider-Man Vs. Wolverine, Spidey Super Stories, Strange Tales Annual #2, Superman Vs. ..., Try-Out Winner Book, Ultimate Marvel Team-Up, Ultimate Spider-Man, Web of Spider- Man & Within Our Reach)

AMAZING SPIDER-MAN, THE
Marvel Comics Group: March, 1963 - No. 441, Nov, 1998

	GD	VG	FN	VF	VF/NM	NM-
1-Retells origin by Steve Ditko; 1st Fantastic Four x-over (ties with F.F. #12 as first Marvel x-over); intro. John Jameson & The Chameleon; Spider-Man's 2nd app.; Kirby/Ditko-c; Ditko-c/a #1-38	850	1700	2550	8750	20,375	32,000
1-Reprint from the Golden Record Comic set	14	28	42	97	141	185
With record (1966)	20	40	60	145	213	280
2-1st app. the Vulture & the Terrible Tinkerer	300	600	900	2685	4343	6000
3-1st full-length story; Human Torch cameo; intro. & 1st app. Doc Octopus; Spider-Man pin-up by Ditko	215	430	645	1881	3041	4200
4-Origin & 1st app. The Sandman (see Strange Tales #115 for 2nd app.); Intro. Betty Brant & Liz Allen	189	378	567	1654	2577	3500
5-Dr. Doom app.	157	314	471	1374	2137	2900
6-1st app. Lizard	153	306	459	1308	2004	2700
7,8,10: 7-Vs. The Vulture; 1st monthly issue. 8-Fantastic Four app. in back-up story by Kirby & Ditko. 10-1st app. Big Man & The Enforcers	100	200	300	850	1300	1750
9-Origin & 1st app. Electro (2/64)	106	212	318	901	1376	1850
11,12: 11-1st app. Bennett Brant. 12-Doc Octopus unmasks Spider-Man-c/story	60	120	180	480	840	1200
13-1st app. Mysterio	77	154	231	616	1083	1550
14-(7/64)-1st app. The Green Goblin (c/story)(Norman Osborn); Hulk x-over	165	330	495	1320	2310	3300
15-1st app. Kraven the Hunter; 1st mention of Mary Jane Watson (not shown)	65	130	195	520	910	1300
16-Spider-Man battles Daredevil (1st x-over 9/64); still in old yellow costume	54	108	162	405	702	1000
17-2nd app. Green Goblin (c/story); Human Torch x-over (also in #18 & #21)	65	130	195	552	926	1300
18-1st app. Ned Leeds who later becomes Hobgoblin; Fantastic Four cameo; 3rd app. Sandman	44	88	132	319	535	750
19-Sandman app.	37	74	111	268	447	625
20-Origin & 1st app. The Scorpion	53	106	159	398	649	900
21-2nd app. The Beetle (see Strange Tales #123)	34	68	102	247	411	575
22-1st app. Princess Python	29	58	87	210	355	500
23-3rd app. The Green Goblin-c/story; Norman Osborn app.	43	86	129	312	519	725

	GD 2.0	VG 4.0	FN 6.0	VF 8.0	VF/NM 9.0	NM- 9.2
24	27	54	81	196	323	450
25-(6/65)-1st app. Mary Jane Watson (cameo; face not shown); 1st app. Spencer Smythe; Norman Osborn app.	32	64	96	232	389	545
26-4th app. The Green Goblin-c/story; 1st app. Crime Master; dies in #27	34	68	102	247	411	575
27-5th app. The Green Goblin-c/story; Norman Osborn app.	32	64	96	232	389	545
28-Origin & 1st app. Molten Man (9/65, scarcer in high grade)	54	108	162	459	730	1000
29,30	21	42	63	152	251	350
31-1st app. Harry Osborn who later becomes 2nd Green Goblin, Gwen Stacy & Prof. Warren.	23	46	69	167	279	390
32-38: 34-4th app. Kraven the Hunter. 36-1st app. Looter. 37-Intro. Norman Osborn. 38-(7/66)-2nd app. Mary Jane Watson (cameo; face not shown); last Ditko issue	19	38	57	138	234	330
39-The Green Goblin-c/story; Green Goblin's i.d. revealed as Norman Osborn; Romita-a begins (8/66; see Daredevil #16 for 1st Romita-a on Spider-Man)	27	54	81	196	323	450
40-1st told origin The Green Goblin-c/story	35	70	105	254	427	600
41-1st app. Rhino	25	50	75	181	300	420
42-(11/66)-3rd app. Mary Jane Watson (cameo in last 2 panels); 1st time face is shown	17	34	51	123	201	280
43-49: 44,45-2nd & 3rd app. The Lizard. 46-Intro. Shocker. 47-M. J. Watson & Peter Parker 1st date. 47-Green Goblin cameo; Harry & Norman Osborn app. 47,49-5th & 6th app. Kraven the Hunter	15	30	45	109	160	210
50-1st app. Kingpin (7/67)	49	98	147	416	658	900
51-2nd app. Kingpin	22	44	66	156	228	300
52-58,60: 52-1st app. Joe Robertson & 3rd app. Kingpin. 56-1st app. Capt. George Stacy. 57,58-Ka-Zar app.	11	22	33	77	114	150
59-1st app. Brainwasher (alias Kingpin); 1st-c app. M. J. Watson	12	24	36	82	121	160
61-74: 67-1st app. Randy Robertson. 69-Kingpin-c. 69,70-Kingpin app. 73-1st app. Silvermane. 74-Last 12¢ issue	9	18	27	63	89	115
75-83,87-89,91,92,95,99: 78,79-1st app. The Prowler. 83-1st app. Schemer & Vanessa (Kingpin's wife)	8	16	24	53	74	95
84-86,93: 84,85-Kingpin-c/story. 86-Re-intro & origin Black Widow in new costume. 93-1st app. Arthur Stacy	8	16	24	53	74	95
90-Death of Capt. Stacy	9	18	27	65	93	120
94-Origin retold	10	20	30	73	107	140
96-98-Green Goblin app. (97,98-Green Goblin-c); drug books not approved by CCA	11	22	33	77	114	150
100-Anniversary issue (9/71); Green Goblin cameo (2 pgs.)	18	36	54	130	215	300
101-1st app. Morbius the Living Vampire; Wizard cameo; last 15¢ issue (10/71)	17	34	51	118	174	230
101-Silver ink 2nd printing (9/92, $1.75)						2.25
102-Origin & 2nd app. Morbius (25¢, 52 pgs.)	12	24	36	84	125	165
103-118: 104,111-Kraven the Hunter-c/stories. 108-1st app. Sha-Shan. 109-Dr. Strange-c/story (6/72). 110-1st app. Gibbon. 113-1st app. Hammerhead. 116-118-reprints story from Spectacular Spider-Man Mag. in color with some changes	6	12	18	38	52	65
119,120-Spider-Man vs. Hulk (4 & 5/73)	8	16	24	55	78	100
121-Death of Gwen Stacy (6/73) (killed by Green Goblin) (reprinted in Marvel Tales #98 & 192)	18	36	54	131	191	250
122-Death of The Green Goblin-c/story (7/73) (reprinted in Marvel Tales #99 & 192)	19	38	57	138	202	265
123,126-128: 123-Cage app. 127-1st mention of Harry Osborn becoming Green Goblin	5	10	15	33	44	55
124-1st app. Man-Wolf (9/73)	6	12	18	43	59	75
125-Man-Wolf origin	5	10	15	36	48	60
129-1st app. The Punisher (2/74); 1st app. Jackal	24	48	72	174	287	400
130-133: 131-Last 20¢ issue	4	8	12	27	36	45
134-(7/74); 1st app. Tarantula; Harry Osborn discovers Spider-Man's ID; Punisher cameo	5	10	15	33	44	55
135-2nd full Punisher app. (8/74)	7	14	21	51	71	90
136-Reappearance of The Green Goblin (Harry Osborn; Norman Osborn's son)	7	14	21	50	68	85
137-Green Goblin-c/story (2nd Harry Osborn)	6	12	18	43	59	75
138-141: 139-1st Grizzly. 140-1st app. Glory Grant	3	7	10	21	28	35
142,143-Gwen Stacy clone cameos: 143-1st app. Cyclone	4	8	12	24	32	40
144-147: 144-Full app. of Gwen Stacy clone. 145,146-Gwen Stacy clone storyline continues. 147-Spider-Man learns Gwen Stacy is clone	4	8	12	24	32	40
148-Jackal revealed	4	8	12	27	36	45

Amazing Spider-Man #185 © MAR

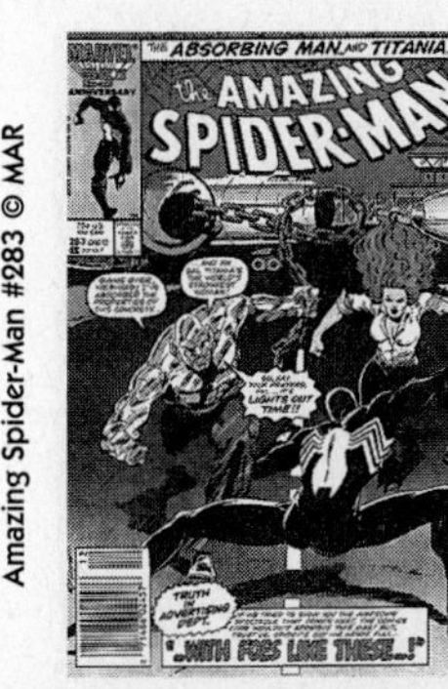

Amazing Spider-Man #283 © MAR

Amazing Spider-Man #368 © MAR

	GD 2.0	VG 4.0	FN 6.0	VF 8.0	VF/NM 9.0	NM- 9.2
149-Spider-Man clone story begins, clone dies (?); origin of Jackal	7	14	21	46	63	80
150-Spider-Man decides he is not the clone	4	8	12	24	32	40
151-Spider-Man disposes of clone body	4	8	12	24	32	40
152-160-(Regular 25¢ editions). 159-Last 25¢ issue(8/76)	3	6	9	16	20	25
155-159-(30¢-c variants, limited distribution)	4	8	12	24	32	40
161-Nightcrawler app. from X-Men; Punisher cameo; Wolverine & Colossus app.	3	7	10	21	28	35
162-Punisher, Nightcrawler app.; 1st Jigsaw	3	7	10	21	28	35
163-168,181-188: 167-1st app. Will O' The Wisp. 181-Origin retold; gives life history of Spidey; Punisher cameo in flashback (1 panel). 182-(7/78)-Peter's first proposal to Mary Jane, but she declines	2	4	6	10	13	16
169-173-(Regular 30¢ edition). 169-Clone story recapped. 171-Nova app.	2	4	6	10	13	16
169-173-(35¢-c variants, limited dist.)(6-10/77)	3	6	9	16	20	24
174,175-Punisher app.	2	4	6	12	16	20
176-180-Green Goblin app.	3	6	9	18	23	28
189,190-Byrne-a	2	4	6	11	14	18
191-193,195-199,203-205,207,208,210-219: 193-Peter & Mary Jane break up. 196-Faked death of Aunt May. 203-3rd app. Dazzler (4/80). 210-1st app. Madame Web. 212-1st app. Hydro Man; origin Sandman	2	4	6	8	10	12
NOTE: *Whitman 3-packs containing #192-194 exist.*						
194-1st app. Black Cat	3	6	9	19	25	32
200-Giant origin issue (1/80)	4	8	12	22	30	38
201,202-Punisher app.	2	4	6	10	12	15
206-Byrne-a	2	4	6	9	11	14
209-Origin & 1st app. Calypso (10/80)	2	4	6	11	14	18
220-237: 225-(2/82)-Foolkiller-c/story. 226,227-Black Cat returns. 236-Tarantula dies. 234-Free 16 pg. insert "Marvel Guide to Collecting Comics". 235-Origin Will-'O-The-Wisp	1	3	4	6	8	10
238-(3/83)-1st app. Hobgoblin (Ned Leeds); came with skin "Tattooz" decal. **NOTE:** The same decal appears in the more common Fantastic Four #252 which is being removed & placed in this issue as incentive to increase value (Value listed is with or without tattooz)	7	14	21	51	71	90
239-2nd app. Hobgoblin & 1st battle w/Spidey	4	8	12	29	40	50
240-243,246-248: 241-Origin The Vulture. 243-Reintro Mary Jane Watson after 4 year absence	1	2	3	5	6	8
244-3rd app. Hobgoblin (cameo)	2	4	6	10	12	15
245-(10/83)-4th app. Hobgoblin (cameo); Lefty Donovan gains powers of Hobgoblin & battles Spider-Man	2	4	6	10	12	15
249-251: 3 part Hobgoblin/Spider-Man battle. 249-Retells origin & death of 1st Green Goblin. 251-Last old costume	2	4	6	10	13	16
252-Spider-Man dons new black costume (5/84); ties with Marvel Team-Up #141 & Spectacular Spider-Man #90 for 1st new costume in regular title (See Marvel Super-Heroes Secret Wars #8 for debut)	4	8	12	22	30	38
253-1st app. The Rose	1	3	4	6	8	10
254-258: 256-1st app. Puma. 257-Hobgoblin cameo; 2nd app. Puma; M.J. Watson reveals she knows Spidey's i.d. 258-Hobgoblin app.	1	2	3	5	6	8
259-Full Hobgoblin app.; Spidey back to old costume; origin Mary Jane Watson	2	4	6	8	10	12
260-Hobgoblin app.	1	3	4	6	8	10
261-Hobgoblin-c/story; painted-c by Vess	1	3	4	6	8	11
262-Spider-Man unmasked; photo-c	1	2	3	5	7	9
263,264,266-274,277-280,282,283: 274-Zarathos (The Spirit of Vengeance) app. 277-Vess back-up art. 279-Jack O'Lantern-c/story. 282-X-Factor x-over	1	2	3	4	5	7
265-1st app. Silver Sable (6/85)	2	4	6	9	11	14
265-Silver ink 2nd printing ($1.25)						2.25
275-($1.25, 52 pgs.)-Hobgoblin-c/story; origin-r by Ditko	2	4	6	11	14	18
276-Hobgoblin app.	1	3	4	6	8	10
281-Hobgoblin battles Jack O'Lantern	1	3	4	6	8	10
284,285: 284-Punisher cameo; Gang War story begins; Hobgoblin-c/story. 285-Punisher app.; minor Hobgoblin app.	1	3	4	6	8	10
286-288: 286-Hobgoblin-c & app. (minor). 287-Hobgoblin app. (minor). 288-Full Hobgoblin app.; last Gang War	1	3	4	6	8	10
289-(6/87, $1.25, 52 pgs.)-Hobgoblin's i.d. revealed as Ned Leeds; death of Ned Leeds; Macendale (Jack O'Lantern) becomes new Hobgoblin (1st app.)	2	4	6	14	18	22
290-292,295-297: 290-Peter proposes to Mary Jane. 292-She accepts; leads into wedding in Amazing Spider-Man Annual #21	1	2	3	4	5	7
293,294-Part 2 & 5 of Kraven story from Web of Spider-Man. 294-Death of Kraven	1	3	4	6	8	10

	GD 2.0	VG 4.0	FN 6.0	VF 8.0	VF/NM 9.0	NM- 9.2
298-Todd McFarlane-c/a begins (3/88); 1st app. Eddie Brock who becomes Venom; (cameo on last pg.)	4	8	12	27	36	45
299-1st app. Venom with costume (cameo)	3	6	9	18	23	28
300 ($1.50, 52 pgs.; 25th Anniversary)-1st full Venom app.; last black costume (5/88)	7	14	21	51	71	90
301-305: 301 ($1.00 issues begin). 304-1st bi-weekly issue	2	4	6	10	12	15
306-311,313,314: 306-Swipes-c from Action #1	2	4	6	8	10	12
312-Hobgoblin battles Green Goblin	2	4	6	11	14	18
315-317-Venom app.	2	4	6	11	14	18
318-323,325: 319-Bi-weekly begins again	1	2	3	5	7	9
324-Sabretooth app.; McFarlane cover only	1	2	3	5	7	9
326,327,329: 327-Cosmic Spidey continues from Spectacular Spider-Man (no McFarlane-c/a)						5.00
328-Hulk x-over; last McFarlane issue	1	3	4	6	8	10
330,331-Punisher app. 331-Minor Venom app.						4.00
332,333-Venom-c/story	1	2	3	4	5	7
334-336,338-343: 341-Tarantula app.						4.00
337-Hobgoblin app.						4.00
344-1st app. Cletus Kasady (Carnage)	2	4	6	8	10	12
345-1st full app. Cletus Kasady; Venom cameo on last pg.	2	4	6	8	10	12
346,347-Venom app.	1	2	3	4	5	7
348,349,351-359: 348-Avengers x-over. 351,352-Nova of New Warriors app. 353-Darkhawk app.; brief Punisher app. 354-Punisher cameo & Nova, Night Thrasher (New Warriors), Darkhawk & Moon Knight app. 357,358-Punisher, Darkhawk, Moon Knight, Night Thrasher, Nova x-over. 358-3 part gatefold-c; last $1.00-c. 360-Carnage cameo						3.00
350-($1.50, 52pgs.)-Origin retold; Spidey vs. Dr. Doom; pin-ups; Uncle Ben app.						5.00
360-Carnage cameo						4.00
361-Intro Carnage (the Spawn of Venom); begin 3 part story; recap of how Spidey's alien costume became Venom	2	4	6	8	10	12
361-($1.25)-2nd printing; silver-c						2.50
362,363-Carnage & Venom-c/story	1	2	3	4	5	7
362-2nd printing						2.25
364,366-374,376-387: 364-The Shocker app. (old villain). 366-Peter's parents-c/story. 369-Harry Osborn back-up (Gr. Goblin II). 373-Venom back-up. 374-Venom-c/story. 376-Cardiac app. 378-Maximum Carnage part 3. 381,382-Hulk app. 383-The Jury app. 384-Venom/carnage app. 387-New costume Vulture						2.50
365-($3.95, 84 pgs.)-30th anniversary issue w/silver hologram on-c; Spidey/Venom/Carnage pull-out poster; contains 5 pg. preview of Spider-Man 2099 (1st app.); Spidey's origin retold; Lizard app.; reintro Peter's parents in Stan Lee 3 pg. text w/illo (story continues thru #370)						5.00
375-($3.95, 68 pgs.)-Holo-grafx foil-c; vs. Venom story; ties into Venom: Lethal Protector #1; Pat Olliffe-a.						5.00
388-($2.25, 68 pgs.)-Newsstand edition; Venom back-up & Cardiac & chance back-up						2.25
388-($2.95, 68 pgs.)-Collector's edition w/foil-c						3.00
389-396,398,399,401-420: 389-$1.50-c begins; bound-in trading card sheet; Green Goblin app. 394-Power & Responsibility Pt. 2. 396-Daredevil-c & app. 403-Carnage app. 406-1st New Doc Octopus. 407-Human Torch, Silver Sable, Sandman app. 409-Kaine, Rhino app. 410-Carnage app. 414-The Rose app. 415-Onslaught story; Spidey vs. Sentinels. 416-Epilogue to Onslaught; Garney-a(p); Williamson-a(i)						2.25
390-($2.95)-Collector's edition polybagged w/16 pg. insert of new animated Spidey TV show plus animation cel						3.00
394-($2.95, 48 pgs.)-Deluxe edition; flip book w/Birth of a Spider-Man Pt. 2; silver foil both-c; Power & Responsibility Pt. 2						3.00
397-($2.25)-Flip book w/Ultimate Spider-Man						2.25
400-($2.95)-Death of Aunt May						3.00
400-($3.95)-Death of Aunt May; embossed double-c						5.00
400-Collector's Edition; white-c	1	2	3	5	7	9
408-($2.95) Polybagged version with TV theme song cassette						8.00
421-424,426,428-433: 426-Begin $1.99-c. 432-Spiderhunt pt. 2						2.25
425-($2.99)-48 pgs., wraparound-c						3.00
427-($2.25) Return of Dr. Octopus; double gatefold-c						2.50
434-440: 434-Double-c with "Amazing Ricochet #1". 438-Daredevil app. 439-Avengers-c/app. 440-Byrne-s						2.25
441-Final issue; Byrne-s						4.00
#500-up (See Amazing Spider-Man Vol. 3; series resumed original numbering after Vol. 3 #58)						
#(-1) Flashback issue (7/97, $1.95-c)						2.25
Annual 1 (1964, 72 pgs.)-Origin Spider-Man; 1st app. Sinister Six (Dr. Octopus, Electro, Kraven the Hunter, Mysterio, Sandman, Vulture) (new 41 pg. story); plus gallery of Spidey foes; early X-Men app.	80	160	240	680	1040	1400
Annual 2 (1965, 25¢, 72 pgs.)-Reprints from #1,2,5 plus new Doctor Strange story	33	66	99	248	374	500
Special 3 (11/66, 25¢, 72 pgs.)-New Avengers story & Hulk x-over; Doctor Octopus-r						

Amazing Spider-Man #500 © MAR

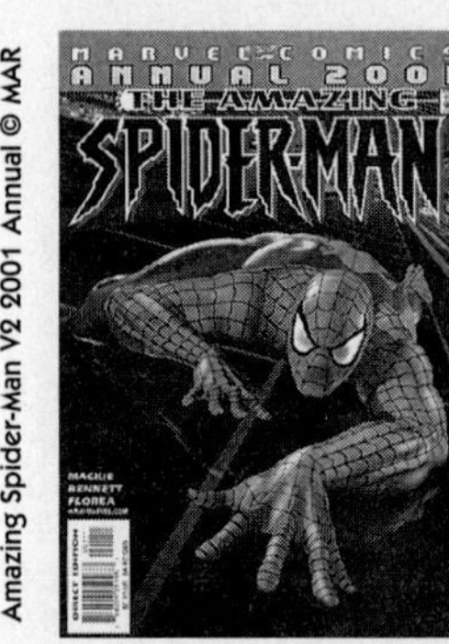

Amazing Spider-Man V2 2001 Annual © MAR

Amazing World of DC Comics #9 © DC

GD VG FN VF VF/NM NM-
2.0 4.0 6.0 8.0 9.0 9.2

from #11,12; Romita-a 15 30 45 109 160 210
Special 4 (11/67, 25¢, 68 pgs.)-Spidey battles Human Torch (new 41 pg. story) 13 26 39 90 133 175
Special 5 (11/68, 25¢, 68 pgs.)-New 40 pg. Red Skull story; 1st app. Peter Parker's parents; last annual with new-a 12 24 36 84 125 165
Special 5-2nd printing (1994) 2 4 6 8 10 12
Special 6 (11/69, 25¢, 68 pgs.)-Reprints 41 pg. Sinister Six story from annual #1 plus 2 Kirby/Ditko stories (r) 5 10 15 36 48 60
Special 7 (12/70, 25¢, 68 pgs.)-All-r(#1,2) new Vulture-c 5 10 15 36 48 60
Special 8 (12/71)-All-r 5 10 15 36 48 60
King Size 9 ('73)-Reprints Spectacular Spider-Man (mag.) #2; 40 pg. Green Goblin-c/story (re-edited from 58 pgs.) 5 10 15 36 48 60
Annual 10 (1976)-Origin Human Fly (vs. Spidey); new-a begins 3 6 9 16 20 25
Annual 11-13 ('77-'79):12-Spidey vs. Hulk-r/#119,120. 13-New Byrne/Austin-a; Dr. Octopus x-over w/Spectacular S-M Ann. #1 2 4 6 10 12 15
Annual 14 (1980)-Miller-c/a(p); Dr. Strange app. 2 4 6 11 14 18
Annual 15 (1981)-Miller-c/a(p); Punisher app. 2 4 6 11 14 18
Annual 16-20:16 ('82)-Origin/1st app. new Capt. Marvel (female heroine). 17 ('83)-Kingpin app. 18 ('84)-Scorpion app.; JJJ weds. 19 ('85). 20 ('86)-Origin Iron Man of 2020 1 2 3 4 5 7
Annual 21 (1987)-Special wedding issue; newsstand & direct sale versions exist & are worth same 2 4 6 8 10 12
Annual 22 (1988, $1.75, 68 pgs.)-1st app. Speedball; Evolutionary War x-over; Daredevil app. 6.00
Annual 23 (1989, $2.00, 68 pgs.)-Atlantis Attacks; origin Spider-Man retold; She-Hulk app.; Byrne-c; Liefeld-a(p), 23 pgs. 4.00
Annual 24 (1990, $2.00, 68 pgs.)-Ant-Man app. 3.00
Annual 25 (1991, $2.00, 68 pgs.)-3 pg. origin recap; Iron Man app.; 1st Venom solo story; Ditko-a (6 pgs.) 5.00
Annual 26 (1992, $2.25, 68 pgs.)-New Warriors-c/story; Venom solo story cont'd in Spectacular Spider-Man Annual #12 4.00
Annual 27,28 ('93, '94, $2.95, 68 pgs.)-27-Bagged w/card; 1st app. Annex. 28-Carnage-c/story; Rhino & Cloak and Dagger back-ups 3.00
'96 Special-($2.95, 64 pgs.)-"Blast From The Past" 3.00
'97 Special-($2.99)-Wraparound-c,Sundown app. 3.00
Marvel Graphic Novel - Parallel Lives (3/89, $8.95) 2 4 6 8 10 12
Marvel Graphic Novel - Spirits of the Earth (1990, $18.95, HC) 3 6 9 18 23 28
Super Special 1 (4/95, $3.95)-Flip Book 4.00
...: Skating on Thin Ice 1(1990, $1.25, Canadian)-McFarlane-c; anti-drug issue; Electro app. 1 2 3 5 7 9
...: Skating on Thin Ice 1 (2/93, $1.50, American) 4.00
...: Double Trouble 2 (1990, $1.25, Canadian) 6.00
...: Double Trouble 2 (2/93, $1.50, American) 3.00
...: Hit and Run 3 (1990, $1.25, Canadian)-Ghost Rider-c/story 1 2 3 5 7 9
...: Hit and Run 3 (2/93. $1.50, American) 3.00
... : Carnage (6/93, $6.95)-r/ASM #344,345,359-363 1 2 3 4 5 7
...: Chaos in Calgary 4 (Canadian; part of 5 part series)-Turbine,Night Rider, Frightful app. 2 4 6 9 11 14
...: Chaos in Calgary 4 (2/93, $1.50, American) 3.00
...: Deadball 5 (1993, $1.60, Canadian)-Green Goblin-c/story; features Montreal Expos 2 4 6 11 14 18
Note: Prices listed above are for English Canadian editions. French editions are worth double.
...: Soul of the Hunter nn (8/92, $5.95, 52 pgs.)-Zeck-c/a(p) 6.00
Wizard #1 Ace Edition ($13.99) r/#1 w/ new Ramos acetate-c 14.00
Wizard #129 Ace Edition ($13.99) r/#129 w/ new Ramos acetate-c 14.00

NOTE: ***Austin*** *a(i)-248, 335, 337, Annual 13; c(i)-188, 241, 242, 248, 331, 334, 343, Annual 25.* ***J. Buscema*** *a(p)-72, 73, 76-81, 84, 85.* ***Byrne*** *a-189p, 190p, 206p, Annual 3r, 6r, 7r, 13p; c-189p, 268, 296, Annual 12.* ***Ditko*** *a-1-38, Annual 1, Special 3(r), 2, 24(2); c-1i, 2-38.* ***Guice*** *c/a-Annual 18i.* ***Gil Kane*** *a(p)-89-105, 120-124, 150, Annual 10, 12i, 24p; c-90p, 96, 98, 99, 101-105p, 129p, 131p, 132p, 137-140p, 143p, 148p, 149p, 151p, 153p, 160p, 161p, Annual 10p, 24.* ***Kirby*** *a-8.* ***Erik Larsen*** *a-324, 327, 329-350; c-327, 329-350, 354i, Annual 25.* ***McFarlane*** *a-298p, 299p, 300-303, 304-323p, 325p, 328; c-298-325, 328.* ***Miller*** *c-218, 219.* ***Mooney*** *a-65i, 67-82i, 84-88i, 173i, 178i, 189i, 190i, 192i, 193i, 196-202i, 207i, 211-219i, 221i, 222i, 226i, 227i, 229-233i, Annual 11i, 17i.* ***Nasser*** *c-228p.* ***Nebres*** *a-Annual 24i.* ***Russell*** *c-357i.* ***Simonson*** *c-222, 337i.* ***Starlin*** *a-113i, 114i, 187p.* ***Williamson*** *a-365i.*

AMAZING SPIDER-MAN (Volume 2)
Marvel Comics: Jan, 1999 - Present ($2.99/$1.99/$2.25)

1-($2.99)-Byrne-a 6.00
1-($6.95) Dynamic Forces variant-c by the Romitas 1 3 4 6 8 10
2-($1.99) Two covers -by John Byrne and Andy Kubert 4.00
3-11: 4-Fantastic Four app. 5-Spider-Woman-c 2.25
12-($2.99) Sinister Six return (cont. in Peter Parker #12) 3.00
13-17: 13-Mary Jane's plane explodes 2.25

GD VG FN VF VF/NM NM-
2.0 4.0 6.0 8.0 9.0 9.2

18,19,21-24,26-28: 18-Begin $2.25-c. 19-Venom-c. 24-Maximum Security 2.25
20-($2.99, 100 pgs.) Spider-Slayer issue; new story and reprints 3.00
25-($2.99) Regular cover; Peter Parker becomes the Green Goblin 3.00
25-($3.99) Holo-foil enhanced cover 4.00
29-Peter is reunited with Mary Jane 2.25
30-Straczynski-s/Campbell-c begin; intro. Ezekiel 6.00
31-35: Battles Morlun 4.00
36-Black cover; aftermath of the Sept. 11 tragedy in New York 6.00
37-49: 39-'Nuff Said issue 42-Dr. Strange app. 43-45-Doctor Octopus app. 46-48-Cho-c 2.25
50-Peter and MJ reunite; Captain America & Dr. Doom app.; Campbell-c 2.50
51-58: 51,52-Campbell-c. 55,56-Avery scripts. 57,58-Avengers, FF, Cyclops app. 2.25
(After #58 [Nov, 2003] numbering reverted back to original Vol. 1 with #500, Dec, 2003)
500-($3.50) J. Scott Campbell-c; Romita Jr. & Sr.-a; Uncle Ben app. 3.50
501,502: 501-Harris-c. 502-Pearson-c 2.25
1999, 2000 Annual (6/99, '00, $3.50) 1999-Buscema-a 3.50
2001 Annual ($2.99) Follows Peter Parker: S-M #29; last Mackie-s 3.00
Collected Edition #30-32 ($3.95) reprints #30-32 w/cover #30 4.00
...Vol. 1: Coming Home (2001, $15.95) r/#30-35; J. Scott Campbell-c 16.00
...Vol. 2: Revelations (2002, $8.99) r/#36-39; Kaare Andrews-c 9.00
...Vol. 3: Until the Stars Turn Cold (2002, $12.99) r/#40-45; Romita Jr.-c 13.00
...Vol. 4: The Life and Death of Spiders (2003, $11.99) r/#46-50; Campbell-c 12.00
...Vol. 5: Unintended Consequences (2003, $12.99) r/#51-56; Dodson-c 13.00

AMAZING WILLIE MAYS, THE
Famous Funnies Publ.: No date (Sept, 1954)

nn 74 148 222 463 694 925

AMAZING WORLD OF DC COMICS
DC Comics: Jul, 1974 - No. 17, 1978 ($1.50, B&W, mail-order DC Pro-zine)

1-Kubert interview; unpublished Kirby-a; Infantino-c 6 12 18 43 59 75
2-4: 3-Julie Schwartz profile. 4-Batman; Robinson-c 4 8 12 29 40 50
5-Sheldon Mayer 4 8 12 25 33 42
6,8,13: 6-Joe Orlando; EC-r; Wrightson pin-up. 8-Infantino; Batman-r from Pop Tart giveaway. 13-Humor; Aragonés-c; Wood/Ditko-a; photos from serials of Superman, Batman, Captain Marvel 3 6 9 18 23 28
7,10-12: 7-Superman; r/1955 Pep comic giveaway. 10-Behind the scenes at DC; Showcase article. 11-Super-Villains; unpubl. Secret Society of S.V. story. 12-Legion; Grell-c/interview; 3 6 9 19 25 32
9-Legion of Super-Heroes; lengthy bios and history; Cockrum-c 7 14 21 51 71 90
14-Justice League 3 7 10 21 28 35
15-Wonder Woman; Nasser-c 4 8 12 27 36 45
16-Golden Age heroes 4 8 12 24 32 40
17-Shazam; G.A., 70s, TV and Fawcett heroes 3 7 10 21 28 35
Special 1 (Digest size) 3 6 9 18 24 30

AMAZING WORLD OF SUPERMAN (See Superman)

AMAZING X-MEN
Marvel Comics: Mar, 1995 - No. 4, July, 1995 ($1.95, limited series)

1-Age of Apocalypse; Andy Kubert-c/a 3.50
2-4 2.50

AMAZON
Comico: Mar, 1989 - No. 3, May, 1989 ($1.95, limited series)

1-3: Ecological theme 2.25

AMAZON (Also see Marvel Versus DC #3 & DC Versus Marvel #4)
DC Comics (Amalgam): Apr, 1996 ($1.95, one-shot)

1-John Byrne-c/a/scripts 2.25

AMAZON ATTACK 3-D
The 3-D Zone: Sept, 1990 ($3.95, 28 pgs.)

1-Chaykin-a 6.00

AMAZON WOMAN (1st Series)
FantaCo: Summer, 1994 - No. 2, Fall, 1994 ($2.95, B&W, limited series, mature)

1,2: Tom Simonton-c/a/scripts 3.00

AMAZON WOMAN (2nd Series)
FantaCo: Feb, 1996 - No. 4, May, 1996 ($2.95, B&W, limited series, mature)

1-4: Tom Simonton-a/scripts 3.00
...: Invaders of Terror ('96, $5.95) Simonton-a/s 6.00

AMBUSH (See Zane Grey, Four Color 314)

AMBUSH BUG (Also see Son of...)
DC Comics: June, 1985 - No. 4, Sept, 1985 (75¢, limited series)

1-4: Giffen-c/a in all 3.00

American Splendor - Music Comics © Harvey Pekar

America's Best Comics #24 © Nedor

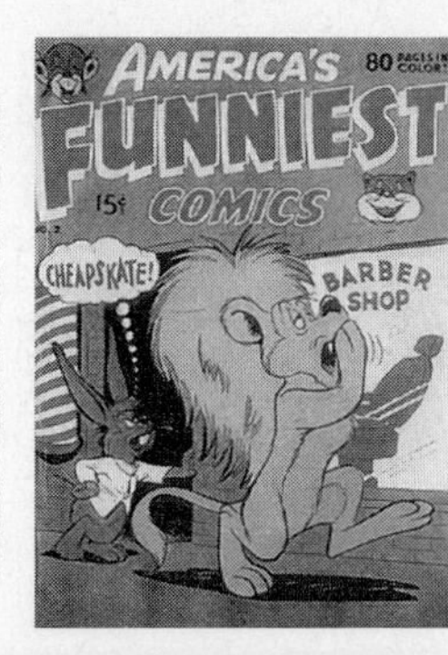

America's Funniest Comics #2 © WHW

	GD	VG	FN	VF	VF/NM	NM-
	2.0	4.0	6.0	8.0	9.0	9.2

Nothing Special 1 (9/92, $2.50, 68pg.)-Giffen-c/a 3.00
Stocking Stuffer (2/86, $1.25)-Giffen-c/a 3.00

AMERICA AT WAR - THE BEST OF DC WAR COMICS (See Fireside Book Series)

AMERICA IN ACTION
Dell(Imp. Publ. Co.)/Mayflower House Publ.: 1942; Winter, 1945 (36 pgs.)
1942-Dell-(68 pgs.) 18 36 54 104 142 180
1-(1945)-Has 3 adaptations from American history; Kiefer, Schrotter & Webb-a
12 24 36 71 96 120

AMERICAN, THE
Dark Horse Comics: July, 1987 - No. 8, 1989 ($1.50/$1.75, B&W)
1-8: ($1.50) 2.25
Collection ($5.95, B&W)-Reprints 6.00
Special 1 (1990, $2.25, B&W) 2.25

AMERICAN AIR FORCES, THE (See A-1 Comics)
William H. Wise(Flying Cadet Publ. Co./Hasan(No.1)/Life's Romances/ Magazine Ent. No. 5 on): Sept-Oct, 1944-No. 4, 1945; No. 5, 1951-No. 12, 1954
1-Article by Zack Mosley, creator of Smilin' Jack; Jap war-c
19 38 57 107 149 190
2-Classic-Jap war-c 25 50 75 147 202 260
3,4-Jap war-c 10 20 30 60 80 100
NOTE: *All part comic, part magazine. Art by* ***Whitney, Chas. Quinlan, H. C. Kiefer,*** *and* ***Tony Dipreta.***
5(A-1 45)(Formerly Jet Powers), 6(A-1 54), 7(A-1 58), 8(A-1 65), 9(A-1 67), 10(A-1 74),
11(A-1 79), 12(A-1 91) 8 16 24 40 50 60
NOTE: ***Powell*** *c/a-5-12.*

AMERICAN CENTURY
DC Comics (Vertigo): May, 2001 - No. 27, Oct, 2003 ($2.50/$2.75)
1-Chaykin-s/painted-c; Tischman-a 4.00
2-27: 5-New story arc begins. 10-16,22-27-Orbik-c. 17-21-Silke-c. 18-$2.75-c begins 2.75
Hollywood Babylon (2002, $12.95, TPB) r/#5-9; w/sketch-to-art pages 13.00
Scars & Stripes (2001, $8.95, TPB) r/#1-4; Tischman intro. 9.00

AMERICAN FLAGG! (See First Comics Graphic Novel 3,9,12,21 & Howard Chaykin's..)
First Comics: Oct, 1983 - No. 50, Mar, 1988
1,21-27: 1-Chaykin-c/a begins. 21-27-Alan Moore scripts 4.00
2-20,28-49: 31-Origin Bob Violence 3.00
50-Last issue 4.00
Special 1 (11/86)-Introduces Chaykin's Time² 4.00

AMERICAN FREAK: A TALE OF THE UN-MEN
DC Comics (Vertigo): Feb, 1994 - No. 5, Jun, 1994 ($1.95, mini-series, mature)
1-5 2.25

AMERICAN GRAPHICS
Henry Stewart: No. 1, 1954; No. 2, 1957 (25¢)
1-The Maid of the Mist, The Last of the Eries (Indian Legends of Niagara)
(sold at Niagara Falls) 10 20 30 60 80 100
2-Victory at Niagara & Laura Secord (Heroine of the War of 1812)
8 16 24 40 50 60

AMERICAN INDIAN, THE (See Picture Progress)

AMERICAN LIBRARY
David McKay Publ.: 1943 - No. 6, 1944 (15¢, 68 pgs., B&W, text & pictures)
nn (#1)-Thirty Seconds Over Tokyo (movie) 38 76 114 219 310 400
nn (#2)-Guadalcanal Diary; painted-c (only 10¢) 28 56 84 159 225 290
3-6: 3-Look to the Mountain. 4-Case of the Crooked Candle (Perry Mason).
5-Duel in the Sun. 6-Wingate's Raiders 14 28 42 81 111 140

AMERICAN: LOST IN AMERICA, THE
Dark Horse Comics: July, 1992 - No. 4, Oct, 1992 ($2.50, limited series)
1-4: 1-Dorman painted-c. 2-Phillips painted-c. 3-Mignola-c. 4-Jim Lee-c 2.50

AMERICAN SPLENDOR: (Series of titles)
Dark Horse Comics: Aug, 1996 - Present (B&W, all one-shots)
--**COMIC-CON COMICS** (8/96) 1-H. Pekar script. --**MUSIC COMICS** (11/97) nn-H. Pekar-s/ Sacco-a; r/Village Voice jazz strips. --**ODDS AND ENDS** (12/97) 1-Pekar-s. --**ON THE JOB** (5/97) 1-Pekar-s. --**A STEP OUT OF THE NEST** (8/94) 1-Pekar-s. --**TERMINAL** (9/99) 1-Pekar-s. --**TRANSATLANTIC** (7/98) 1-"American Splendour" on cover; Pekar-s 3.00
--**A PORTRAIT OF THE AUTHOR IN HIS DECLINING YEARS** (4/01, $3.99) 1-Photo-c. --**BEDTIME STORIES** (6/00, $3.95) 4.00

AMERICAN SPLENDOR: UNSUNG HERO
Dark Horse Comics: Aug, 2002 - No. 3, Oct, 2002 ($3.99, B&W, limited series)
1-3-Pekar script/Collier-a; biography of Robert McNeill 4.00
TPB (8/03, $11.95) r/#1-3 12.00

AMERICAN SPLENDOR: WINDFALL
Dark Horse Comics: Sept, 1995 - No. 2, Oct,1995 ($3.95, B&W, limited series)
1,2-Pekar script 4.00

AMERICAN TAIL: FIEVEL GOES WEST, AN
Marvel Comics: Early Jan, 1992 - No. 3, Early Feb, 1992 ($1.00, limited series)
1-3-Adapts Universal animated movie; Wildman-a 3.00
1-($2.95-c, 69 pgs.) Deluxe squarebound edition 5.00

AMERICA'S BEST COMICS
Nedor/Better/Standard Publications: Feb, 1942; No. 2, Sept, 1942 - No. 31, July, 1949 (New logo with #9)
1-The Woman in Red, Black Terror, Captain Future, Doc Strange, The Liberator,
& Don Davis, Secret Ace begin 256 512 768 1600 2400 3200
2-Origin The American Eagle; The Woman in Red ends
100 200 300 625 938 1250
3-Pyroman begins (11/42, 1st app.; also see Startling Comics #18, 12/42)
74 148 222 463 694 925
4-6: 5-Last Capt. Future (not in #4); Lone Eagle app. 6-American Crusader app.
57 114 171 356 538 720
7-Hitler, Mussolini & Hirohito-c 96 192 288 600 900 1200
8-Last Liberator 56 112 168 350 525 700
9-The Fighting Yank begins; The Ghost app. 64 128 192 400 600 800
10,12-17,19-21: 10-Flag-c. 14-American Eagle ends. 21-Infinity-c.
51 102 153 306 463 620
11-Hirohito & Tojo-c. (10/44) 64 128 192 400 600 800
18-Classic-c 60 120 180 375 563 750
22-Capt. Future app. 46 92 138 276 413 550
23-Miss Masque begins; last Doc Strange 55 110 165 330 495 660
24-Miss Masque bondage-c 53 106 159 318 477 635
25-Last Fighting Yank; Sea Eagle app. 40 80 120 240 350 460
26-31: 26-The Phantom Detective & The Silver Knight app.; Frazetta text illo & some panels in Miss Masque. 27,28-Commando Cubs. 27-Doc Strange. 28-Tuska Black Terror.
29-Last Pyroman 40 80 120 240 340 440
NOTE: *American Eagle not in 3, 8, 9, 13. Fighting Yank not in 10, 12. Liberator not in 2, 6, 7. Pyroman not in 9, 11, 14-16, 23, 25-27.* ***Schomburg (Xela)*** *c-5, 7-31. Bondage c-18, 24.*

AMERICA'S BEST COMICS PREVIEW
Wizard: 1999 (Magazine supplement)
1-Previews Tom Strong, Top Ten, Promethea, Tomorrow Stories 2.25

AMERICA'S BEST COMICS SKETCHBOOK
America's Best Comics: 2002 ($5.95, square-bound)
1-Design sketches by Sprouse, Ross, Adams, Nowlan, Ha and others 6.00

AMERICA'S BEST COMICS SPECIAL
America's Best Comics: Feb, 2001 ($6.95, square-bound)
1-Short stories of Alan Moore's characters; art by various; Ross-c 7.00

AMERICA'S BEST TV COMICS (TV)
American Broadcasting Co. (Prod. by Marvel Comics): 1967 (25¢, 68 pgs.)
1-Spider-Man, Fantastic Four (by Kirby/Ayers), Casper, King Kong, George of the Jungle, Journey to the Center of the Earth stories (promotes new TV cartoon show)
15 30 45 104 152 200

AMERICA'S BIGGEST COMICS BOOK
William H. Wise: 1944 (196 pgs., one-shot)
1-The Grim Reaper, The Silver Knight, Zudo, the Jungle Boy, Commando Cubs,
Thunderhoof app. 40 80 120 240 350 460

AMERICA'S FUNNIEST COMICS
William H. Wise: 1944 - No. 2, 1944 (15¢, 80 pgs.)
nn(#1), 2 31 62 93 175 248 320

AMERICA'S GREATEST COMICS
Fawcett Publications: May?, 1941 - No. 8, Summer, 1943 (15¢, 100 pgs., soft cardboard-c)
1-Bulletman, Spy Smasher, Capt. Marvel, Minute Man & Mr. Scarlet begin; Classic Mac Raboy-c. 1st time that Fawcett's major super-heroes appear together as a group on a cover. Fawcett's 1st squarebound comic 326 652 978 2119 3260 4400
2 144 288 432 900 1350 1800
3 104 208 312 650 975 1300
4,5: 4-Commando Yank begins; Golden Arrow, Ibis the Invincible & Spy Smasher cameo in Captain Marvel 76 152 228 475 713 950
6,7: 7-Balbo the Boy Magician app.; Captain Marvel, Bulletman cameo in Mr. Scarlet
70 140 210 438 657 875
8-Capt. Marvel Jr. & Golden Arrow app.; Spy Smasher x-over in Capt. Midnight; no Minute Man or Commando Yank 70 140 210 438 657 875

Anarky #8 © DC

Angel and the Ape #2 © DC

Animal Adventures #2 © Timor

	GD 2.0	VG 4.0	FN 6.0	VF 8.0	VF/NM 9.0	NM- 9.2
AMERICA'S SWEETHEART SUNNY (See Sunny, ...)						
AMERICA VS. THE JUSTICE SOCIETY						
DC Comics: Jan, 1985 - No. 4, Apr, 1985 ($1.00, limited series)						
1-Double size; Alcala-a(i) in all	1	2	3	5	7	9
2-4: 3,4-Spectre cameo	1	2	3	4	5	7
AMERICOMICS						
Americomics: April, 1983 - No. 6, Mar, 1984 ($2.00, Baxter paper/slick paper)						
1-Intro/origin The Shade; Intro. The Slayer, Captain Freedom and The Liberty Corps; Perez-c						5.00
1,2-2nd printings ($2.00)						2.25
2-6: 2-Messenger app. & 1st app. Tara on Jungle Island. 3-New & old Blue Beetle battle. 4-Origin Dragonfly & Shade. 5-Origin Commando D. 6-Origin the Scarlet Scorpion						3.00
Special 1 (8/83, $2.00)-Sentinels of Justice (Blue Beetle, Captain Atom, Nightshade & The Question)						4.50
AMETHYST						
DC Comics: Jan, 1985 - No. 16, Aug, 1986 (75¢)						
1-16: 8-Fire Jade's i.d. revealed						2.25
Special 1 (10/86, $1.25), 1-4 (11/87 - 2/88)(Limited series)						2.25
AMETHYST, PRINCESS OF GEMWORLD (See Legion of Super-Heroes #298)						
DC Comics: May, 1983 - No. 12, Apr, 1984 (Maxi-series)						
1-(60¢)						2.25
1,2-(75¢): tested in Austin & Kansas City	2	4	6	12	16	20
2-12, Annual 1(9/84): 5-11-Pérez-c(p)						2.25
AMY RACECAR COLOR SPECIAL (See Stray Bullets)						
El Capitán Books: July, 1997; Oct, 1999 ($2.95/$3.50)						
1,2-David Lapham-a/scripts. 2-($3.50)						3.50
ANARCHO DICTATOR OF DEATH (See Comics Novel)						
ANARKY (See Batman titles)						
DC Comics: May, 1997 - No. 4, Aug, 1997 ($2.50, limited series)						
1						3.50
2-4						2.50
ANARKY (See Batman titles)						
DC Comics: May, 1999 - No. 8, Dec, 1999 ($2.50)						
1-8: 1-JLA app.; Grant-s/Breyfogle-a. 3-Green Lantern app. 7-Day of Judgment; Haunted Tank app. 8-Joker-c/app.						2.50
ANCHORS ANDREWS (The Saltwater Daffy)						
St. John Publishing Co.: Jan, 1953 - No. 4, July, 1953 (Anchors the Saltwater... No. 4)						
1-Canteen Kate by Matt Baker (9 pgs.)	21	42	63	118	164	210
2-4	8	16	24	40	50	60
ANCIENT JOE						
Dark Horse Comics: Oct, 2001 - No. 3, Dec, 2001 ($3.50, B&W, limited series)						
1-3-C. Scott Morse-s/a						3.50
ANDY & WOODY (See March of Comics No. 40, 55, 76)						
ANDY BURNETT (TV, Disney)						
Dell Publishing Co.: Dec, 1957						
Four Color 865-Photo-c	10	20	30	70	100	130
ANDY COMICS (Formerly Scream Comics; becomes Ernie Comics)						
Current Publications (Ace Magazines): No. 20, June, 1948-No. 21, Aug, 1948						
20,21: Archie-type comic	8	16	24	40	50	60
ANDY DEVINE WESTERN						
Fawcett Publications: Dec, 1950 - No. 2, 1951						
1	59	118	177	369	555	740
2	42	84	126	252	376	525
ANDY GRIFFITH SHOW, THE (TV)(1st show aired 10/3/60)						
Dell Publishing Co.: #1252, Jan-Mar, 1962; #1341, Apr-Jun, 1962						
Four Color 1252(#1)	38	76	114	285	430	575
Four Color 1341-Photo-c	35	70	105	263	394	525
ANDY HARDY COMICS (See Movie Comics #3 by Fiction House)						
Dell Publishing Co.: April, 1952 - No. 6, Sept-Nov, 1954						
Four Color 389(#1)	5	10	15	33	44	55
Four Color 447,480,515, #5,#6	4	8	12	22	30	38
ANDY PANDA (Also see Crackajack Funnies #39, The Funnies, New Funnies & Walter Lantz...)						
Dell Publishing Co.: 1943 - No. 56, Nov-Jan, 1961-62 (Walter Lantz)						
Four Color 25(#1, 1943)	54	108	162	405	603	800

	GD 2.0	VG 4.0	FN 6.0	VF 8.0	VF/NM 9.0	NM- 9.2
Four Color 54(1944)	31	62	93	228	339	450
Four Color 85(1945)	17	34	51	123	182	240
Four Color 130(1946),154,198	12	24	36	82	121	160
Four Color 216,240,258,280,297	9	18	27	60	85	110
Four Color 326,345,358	6	12	18	43	59	75
Four Color 383,409	5	10	15	33	44	55
16(11-1/52-53) - 30	3	7	10	21	28	35
31-56	3	6	9	16	20	24
(See March of Comics #5, 22, 79, & Super Book #4, 15, 27.)						
A-NEXT (See Avengers)						
Marvel Comics: Oct, 1998 - No. 12, Sept, 1999 ($1.99)						
1-Next generation of Avengers; Frenz-a						3.00
2-12: 2-Two covers. 3-Defenders app.						2.25
ANGEL						
Dell Publishing Co.: Aug, 1954 - No. 16, Nov-Jan, 1958-59						
Four Color 576(#1, 8/54)	3	7	10	21	28	35
2(5-7/55) - 16	2	4	6	14	18	22
ANGEL (TV) (Also see Buffy the Vampire Slayer)						
Dark Horse Comics: Nov, 1999 - No. 17, Apr, 2001 ($2.95/$2.99)						
1-17: 1-3,5-7,10-14-Zanier-a. 1-4,7,10-Matsuda & photo-c. 16-Buffy-c/app.						3.00
...: Earthly Possessions TPB (4/01, $9.95) r/#5-7, photo-c						10.00
...: Surrogates TPB (12/00, $9.95) r/#1-3; photo-c						10.00
ANGEL (Buffy the Vampire Slayer)						
Dark Horse Comics: Sept, 2001 - No. 4, May, 2002 ($2.99, limited series)						
1-4-Joss Whedon & Matthews-s/Rubi-a; photo-c and Rubi-c on each						3.00
ANGELA						
Image Comics (Todd McFarlane Prod.): Dec, 1994 - No. 3, Feb, 1995 ($2.95, lim. series)						
1-Gaiman scripts & Capullo-c/a in all; Spawn app.	1	2	3	5	6	8
2						6.00
3						5.00
Special Edition (1995)-Pirate Spawn-c	3	6	9	16	20	25
Special Edition (1995)-Angela-c	3	6	9	16	20	25
TPB ($9.95, 1995) reprints #1-3 & Special Ed. w/additional pin-ups						10.00
ANGELA/GLORY: RAGE OF ANGELS (See Glory/Angela: Rage of Angels)						
Image Comics (Todd McFarlane Productions): Mar, 1996 ($2.50, one-shot)						
1-Liefeld-c/Cruz-a(p); Darkchylde preview flip book						4.00
1-Variant-c						4.00
ANGEL AND THE APE (Meet Angel No. 7) (See Limited Collector's Edition C-34 & Showcase No. 77)						
National Periodical Publications: Nov-Dec, 1968 - No. 6, Sept-Oct, 1969						
1-(11-12/68)-Not Wood-a	5	10	15	33	44	55
2-5-Wood inks in all. 4-Last 12¢ issue	3	7	10	21	28	35
6-Wood inks	4	8	12	25	33	42
ANGEL AND THE APE (2nd Series)						
DC Comics: Mar, 1991 - No. 4, June, 1991 ($1.00, limited series)						
1-4						3.00
ANGEL AND THE APE (3rd Series)						
DC Comics(Vertigo): Oct, 2001 - No. 4, Jan 2002 ($2.95, limited series)						
1-4-Chaykin & Tischman-s/Bond-a/Art Adams-c						3.00
ANGEL FIRE						
Crusade Comics: June, 1997 - No. 3, Oct, 1997 ($2.95, limited series)						
1-3: 1-(3 variant covers). 3-B&W						3.00
ANGEL LOVE						
DC Comics: Aug, 1986 - No. 8, Mar, 1987 (75¢, limited series)						
1-8, Special 1 (1987, $1.25, 52 pgs.)						2.25
ANGEL OF LIGHT, THE (See The Crusaders)						
ANGRY CHRIST COMIX (See Cry For Dawn)						
ANIMA						
DC Comics: Mar, 1994 - No. 15, July, 1995 ($1.75/$1.95/$2.25)						
1-7,0,8-15: 7-(9/94)-Begin $1.95-c; Zero Hour x-over						2.50
ANIMAL ADVENTURES						
Timor Publications/Accepted Publ. (reprints): Dec, 1953 - No. 3, May?, 1954						
1-Funny animal	7	14	21	37	46	55
2,3: 2-Featuring Soopermutt (2/54)	5	10	15	24	30	35
1-3 (reprints, nd)	3	6	8	11	13	15

Animal Man: Deus Ex Machina TPB © DC

Animaniacs #23 © WB

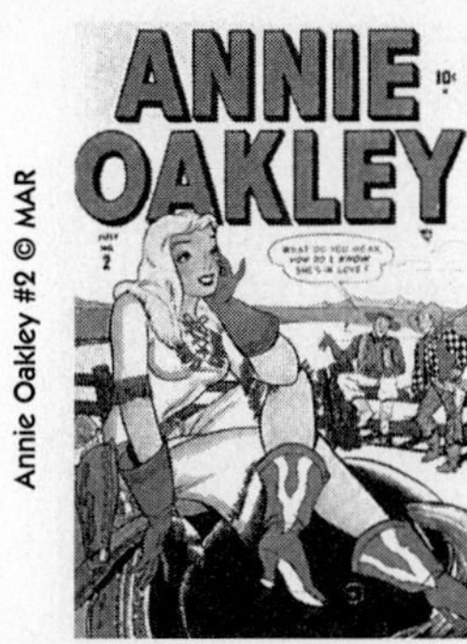

Annie Oakley #2 © MAR

	GD 2.0	VG 4.0	FN 6.0	VF 8.0	VF/NM 9.0	NM- 9.2
ANIMAL ANTICS (Movietown... No. 24 on)						
National Periodical Publ: Mar-Apr, 1946 - No. 23, Nov-Dec, 1949 (All 52 pgs.?)						
1-Raccoon Kids begins by Otto Feur; some-c by Grossman; Seaman Sy Wheeler by Kelly in some issues	44	88	132	264	395	525
2	26	52	78	147	206	265
3-10: 10-Post-c/a	16	32	48	92	126	160
11-23: 14,15,18,19-Post-a	11	22	33	63	84	105
ANIMAL COMICS						
Dell Publishing Co.: Dec-Jan, 1941-42 - No. 30, Dec-Jan, 1947-48						
1-1st Pogo app. by Walt Kelly (Dan Noonan art in most issues)	90	180	270	630	915	1200
2-Uncle Wiggily begins	45	90	135	315	458	600
3,5	33	66	99	231	336	440
4,6,7-No Pogo	18	36	54	131	191	250
8-10	23	46	69	164	240	315
11-15	14	28	42	99	145	190
16-20	10	20	30	67	96	125
21-30: 24-30- "Jigger" by John Stanley	8	16	24	55	78	100
NOTE: ***Dan Noonan*** *a-18-30.* ***Gollub*** *art in most later issues; c-29, 30.* ***Kelly*** *c-7-26, part #27-30.*						
ANIMAL CRACKERS (Also see Adventures of Patoruzu)						
Green Publ. Co./Norlen/Fox Feat.(Hero Books): 1946; No. 31, July, 1950; No. 9, 1959						
1-Super Cat begins (1st app.)	19	38	57	107	149	190
2	10	20	30	56	73	90
31(Fox)-Formerly My Love Secret	7	14	21	37	46	55
9(1959-Norlen)-Infinity-c	5	10	14	20	24	28
nn, nd ('50s), no publ.; infinity-c	5	10	14	20	24	28
ANIMAL FABLES						
E. C. Comics (Fables Publ. Co.): July-Aug, 1946 - No. 7, Nov-Dec, 1947						
1-Freddy Firefly (clone of Human Torch), Korky Kangaroo, Petey Pig, Danny Demon begin	47	94	141	282	421	560
2-Aesop Fables begin	30	60	90	170	240	310
3-6	24	48	72	138	194	250
7-Origin Moon Girl	62	124	186	388	582	775
ANIMAL FAIR (Fawcett's...)						
Fawcett Publications: Mar, 1946 - No. 11, Feb, 1947						
1	28	56	84	159	225	290
2	14	28	42	79	107	135
3-6	10	20	30	60	80	100
7-11	9	18	27	49	62	75
ANIMAL FUN						
Premier Magazines: 1953 (25¢, came w/glasses)						
1-(3-D)-Ziggy Pig, Silly Seal, Billy & Buggy Bear	36	72	108	207	294	380
ANIMAL MAN (See Action Comics #552, 553, DC Comics Presents #77, 78, Secret Origins #39, Strange Adventures #180 & Wonder Woman #267, 268)						
DC Comics (Vertigo imprint #57 on): Sept, 1988 - No. 89, Nov, 1995 ($1.25/$1.50/$1.75/$1.95/$2.25, mature)						
1-Grant Morrison scripts begin, ends #26	1	3	4	6	8	10
2-10: 2-Superman cameo. 6-Invasion tie-in. 9-Manhunter-c/story						6.00
11-49,51-55,57-89: 24-Arkham Asylum story; Bizarro Superman app. 25-Inferior Five app. 26-Morrison apps. in story; part photo-c (of Morrison?)						3.00
50-($2.95, 52 pgs.)-Last issue w/Veitch scripts						5.00
56-($3.50, 68 pgs.)						5.00
Annual 1 (1993, $3.95, 68 pgs.)-Bolland-c; Children's Crusade Pt. 3						6.00
...: Deus Ex Machina TPB (2003, $19.95) r/#18-26; Morrison-a; new Bolland-c						20.00
...: Origin of the Species TPB (2002, $19.95) r/#10-17 & Secret Origins #39						20.00
NOTE: ***Bolland*** *c-1-63. 71-**Sutton**-a(i)*						
ANIMAL MYSTIC (See Dark One...)						
Cry For Dawn/Sirius: 1993 - No. 4, 1995 ($2.95?/$3.50, B&W)						
1	3	6	9	16	20	24
1-Alternate	4	8	12	27	36	45
1-2nd printing						5.00
2	2	4	6	11	14	18
2,3-2nd prints (Sirius)						3.50
3 ,4: 4-Color poster insert, Linsner-s	1	2	3	5	7	9
TPB ($14.95) r/series						18.00
ANIMAL MYSTIC WATER WARS						
Sirius: 1996 - Present ($2.95, limited series)						
1-6-Dark One-c/a/scripts						5.00

	GD 2.0	VG 4.0	FN 6.0	VF 8.0	VF/NM 9.0	NM- 9.2
ANIMAL WORLD, THE (Movie)						
Dell Publishing Co.: No. 713, Aug, 1956						
Four Color 713	4	8	12	25	33	42
ANIMANIACS (TV)						
DC Comics: May, 1995 - No. 59, Apr, 2000 ($1.50/$1.75/$1.95/$1.99)						
1	1	2	3	4	5	7
2-20: 13-Manga issue. 19-X-Files parody; Miran Kim-c; Adlard-a (4 pgs.)						4.00
21-59: 26-E.C. parody-c. 34-Xena parody. 43-Pinky & the Brain take over						3.00
A Christmas Special (12/94, $1.50, "1" on-c)						3.00
ANIMATED COMICS						
E. C. Comics: No date given (Summer, 1947?)						
1 (Rare)	76	152	228	475	713	950
ANIMATED FUNNY COMIC TUNES (See Funny Tunes)						
ANIMATED MOVIE-TUNES (Movie Tunes No. 3)						
Margood Publishing Corp. (Timely): Fall, 1945 - No. 2, Sum, 1946						
1,2-Super Rabbit, Ziggy Pig & Silly Seal	27	54	81	155	218	280
ANIMAX						
Marvel Comics (Star Comics): Dec, 1986 - No. 4, June, 1987						
1-4: Based on toys; Simonson-a						3.00
ANNE RICE'S INTERVIEW WITH THE VAMPIRE						
Innovation Books: 1991 - No. 12, Jan, 1994 ($2.50, limited series)						
1-12: Adapts novel; Moeller-a						3.00
ANNE RICE'S THE MASTER OF RAMPLING GATE						
Innovation Books: 1991 ($6.95, one-shot)						
1-Bolton painted-c; Colleen Doran painted-a						7.00
ANNE RICE'S THE MUMMY OR RAMSES THE DAMNED						
Millennium Publications: Oct, 1990 - No. 12, Feb, 1992 ($2.50, limited series)						
1-12: Adapts novel; Mooney-p in all						3.00
ANNE RICE'S THE WITCHING HOUR						
Millennium Publ./Comico: 1992 - No. 13, Jan, 1993 ($2.50, limited series)						
1-13						3.00
ANNETTE (Disney, TV)						
Dell Publishing Co.: No. 905, May, 1958; No. 1100, May, 1960 (Mickey Mouse Club)						
Four Color 905-Annette Funicello photo-c	31	62	93	223	329	435
Four Color 1100-...'s Life Story (Movie); A. Funicello photo-c	25	50	75	181	266	350
ANNEX (See Amazing Spider-Man Annual #27 for 1st app.)						
Marvel Comics: Aug, 1994 - No. 4, Nov, 1994 ($1.75)						
1-4: 1,4-Spider-Man app.						2.25
ANNIE						
Marvel Comics Group: Oct, 1982 - No. 2, Nov, 1982 (60¢)						
1,2-Movie adaptation						4.00
Treasury Edition ($2.00, tabloid size)	3	6	9	17	21	26
ANNIE OAKLEY (See Tessie The Typist #19, Two-Gun Kid & Wild Western)						
Marvel/Atlas Comics(MPI No. 1-4/CDS No. 5 on): Spring, 1948 - No. 4, 11/48; No. 5, 6/55 - No. 11, 6/56						
1 (1st Series, 1948)-Hedy Devine app.	42	84	126	252	376	500
2 (7/48, 52 pgs.)-Kurtzman-a, "Hey Look", 1 pg; Intro. Lana; Hedy Devine app; Captain Tootsie by Beck	27	54	81	153	214	275
3,4	23	46	69	130	183	235
5 (2nd Series, 1955)-Reinman-a ; Maneely-c	17	34	51	98	134	170
6-9: 6,8-Woodbridge-a. 9-Williamson-a (4 pgs.)	13	26	39	76	103	130
10,11: 11-Severin-c	12	24	36	71	96	120
ANNIE OAKLEY AND TAGG (TV)						
Dell Publishing Co./Gold Key: 1953 - No. 18, Jan-Mar, 1959; July, 1965 (Gail Davis photo-c #3 on)						
Four Color 438 (#1)	16	32	48	113	167	220
Four Color 481,575 (#2,3)	10	20	30	70	100	130
4(7-9/55)-10	9	18	27	63	89	115
11-18(1-3/59)	8	16	24	53	74	95
1(7/65-Gold Key)-Photo-c (c-r/#6)	6	12	18	40	55	70
NOTE: ***Manning*** *a-13. Photo back c-4, 9, 11.*						
ANOTHER WORLD (See Strange Stories From...)						

Anti-Hitler Comics #1 © NEC

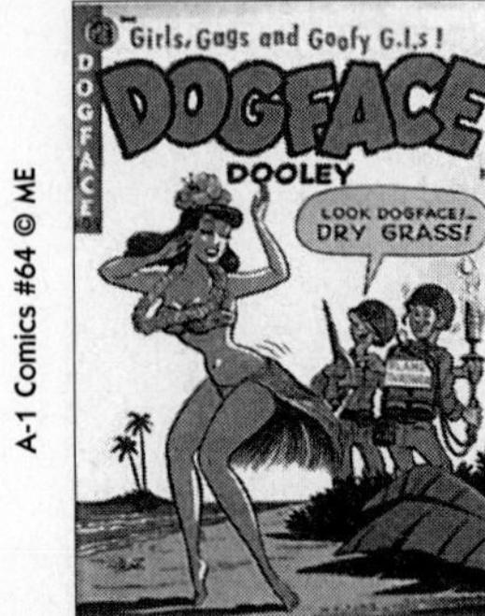

A-1 Comics #64 © ME

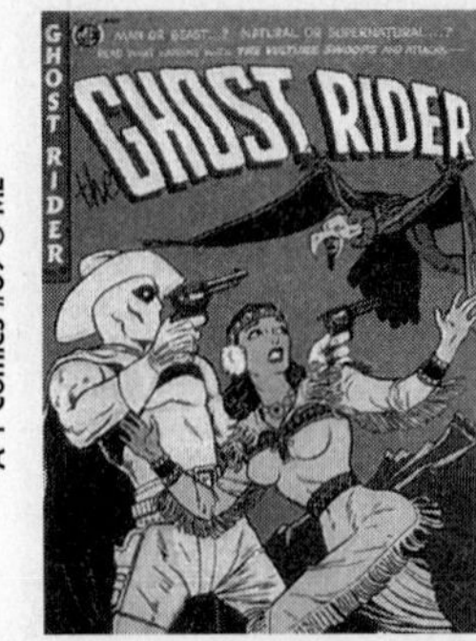

A-1 Comics #69 © ME

	GD	VG	FN	VF	VF/NM	NM-
	2.0	4.0	6.0	8.0	9.0	9.2

ANTHRO (See Showcase #74)
National Periodical Publications: July-Aug, 1968 - No. 6, July-Aug, 1969

1-(7-8/68)-Howie Post-a in all	6	12	18	40	55	70
2-5: 5-Last 12¢ issue	4	8	12	24	32	40
6-Wood-c/a (inks)	4	8	12	27	36	45

ANTI-HITLER COMICS
New England Comics Press: Summer, 1992 ($2.75, B&W, one-shot)

1-Reprints Hitler as Devil stories from wartime comics 5.00

ANT-MAN'S BIG CHRISTMAS
Marvel Comics: Feb, 2000 ($5.95, square-bound, one-shot)

1-Bob Gale-s/Phil Winslade-a; Avengers app. 6.00

ANTONY AND CLEOPATRA (See Ideal, a Classical Comic)

ANYTHING GOES
Fantagraphics Books: Oct, 1986 - No. 6, 1987 ($2.00, #1-5 color & B&W/#6 B&W, lim. series)

1-6: 1-Flaming Carrot app. (1st in color?); G. Kane-c. 2-6: 2-Miller-c(p); Alan Moore scripts; Kirby-a; early Sam Kieth-a (2 pgs.). 3-Capt. Jack, Cerebus app.; Cerebus-c by N. Adams. 4-Perez-c. 5-3rd color Teenage Mutant Ninja Turtles app. 3.50

A-1
Marvel Comics (Epic Comics): 1992 - No. 4, 1993 ($5.95, limited series, mature)

1-4: 1-Fabry-c/a, Russell-a, S. Hampton-a. 3-Bisley-c; Kent Williams-a. 4-McKean-a; Dorman-s/a	1	2	3	4	5	7

A-1 COMICS (A-1 appears on covers No. 1-17 only)(See individual title listings for #11-139) (1st two issues not numbered.)
Life's Romances Publ.-No. 1/Compix/Magazine Ent.: 1944 - No. 139, Sept-Oct, 1955 (No #2)

nn-(1944) (See Kerry Drake Detective Cases)

1-Dotty Dripple (1 pg.), Mr. Ex, Bush Berry, Rocky, Lew Loyal (20 pgs.)	12	24	36	71	96	120
3-8,10: Texas Slim & Dirty Dalton, The Corsair, Teddy Rich, Dotty Dripple, Inca Dinca, Tommy Tinker, Little Mexico & Tugboat Tim, The Masquerader & others. 7-Corsair-c/s. 8-Intro Rodeo Ryan	8	16	24	46	58	70
9-All Texas Slim	9	18	27	49	62	75

(See Individual Alphabetical listings for prices)

11-Teena; Ogden Whitney-c
12,15-Teena
13-Guns of Fact & Fiction (1948). Used in **SOTI**, pg. 19; Ingels & Johnny Craig-a
14-Tim Holt Western Adventures #1
16-Vacation Comics; The Pixies, Tom Tom, Flying Fredd, & Koko & Kola
17-Tim Holt #2; photo-c; last issue to carry A-1 on cover (9-10/48)
18,20-Jimmy Durante; photo covers on both
19-Tim Holt #3; photo-c
21-Joan of Arc (1949)-Movie adaptation; Ingrid Bergman photo-covers & interior photos; Whitney-a
22-Dick Powell (1949)-Photo-c
23-Cowboys and Indians #6; Doc Holiday-c/story
24-Trail Colt #1-Frazetta-r in-Manhunt #13; Ingels-c; L. B. Cole-a
25-Fibber McGee & Molly (1949) (Radio)
26-Trail Colt #2-Ingels-c
27-Ghost Rider #1(1950)-Origin
28-Christmas-(Koko & Kola #6) ("50)
29-Ghost Rider #2-Frazetta-c (1950)
30-Jet Powers #1-Powell-a
31-Ghost Rider #3-Frazetta-c & origin ('51)
32-Jet Powers #2
33-Muggsy Mouse #1('51)
34-Ghost Rider #4-Frazetta-c (1951)
35-Jet Powers #3-Williamson/Evans-a
36-Muggsy Mouse #2; Racist-c
37-Ghost Rider #5-Frazetta-c (1951)
38-Jet Powers #4-Williamson/Wood-a
39-Muggsy Mouse #3
40-Dogface Dooley #1('51)
41-Cowboys 'N' Indians #7 (1951)
42-Best of the West #1-Powell-a
43-Dogface Dooley #2
44-Ghost Rider #6
45-American Air Forces #5-Powell-c/a
46-Best of the West #2
47-Thun'da, King of the Congo #1-Frazetta-c/a('52)
48-Cowboys 'N' Indians #8
49-Dogface Dooley #3
50-Danger Is Their Business #11 ('52)-Powell-a
51-Ghost Rider #7 ('52)
52-Best of the West #3
53-Dogface Dooley #4
54-American Air Forces #6(8/52)-Powell-a
55-U.S. Marines #5-Powell-a
56-Thun'da #2-Powell-c/a
57-Ghost Rider #8
58-American Air Forces #7-Powell-a
59-Best of the West #4
60-The U.S. Marines #6-Powell-a
61-Space Ace #5('53)-Guardineer-a
62-Starr Flagg, Undercover Girl #5 (#1) reprinted from A-1 #24
63-Manhunt #13-Frazetta
64-Dogface Dooley #5
65-American Air Forces #8-Powell-a
66-Best of the West #5
67-American Air Forces #9-Powell-a
68-U.S. Marines #7-Powell-a
69-Ghost Rider #9(10/52)
70-Best of the West #6
71-Ghost Rider #10(12/52)-Vs. Frankenstein
72-U.S. Marines #8-Powell-a(3)
73-Thun'da #3-Powell-c/a
74-American Air Forces #10-Powell-a
75-Ghost Rider #11(3/52)
76-Best of the West #7
77-Manhunt #14
78-Thun'da #4-Powell-c/a
79-American Air Forces #11-Powell-a
80-Ghost Rider #12(6/52)-One-eyed Devil-c
81-Best of the West #8
82-Cave Girl #11(1953)-Powell-c/a; origin (#1)
83-Thun'da #5-Powell-c/a
84-Ghost Rider #13(7-8/53)
85-Best of the West #9
86-Thun'da #6-Powell-c/a
87-Best of the West #10(9-10/53)
88-Bobby Benson's B-Bar-B Riders #20
89-Home Run #3-Powell-a; Stan Musial photo-c
90-Red Hawk #11(1953)-Powell-c/a
91-American Air Forces #12-Powell-a
92-Dream Book of Romance #5-Photo-c; Guardineer-a
93-Great Western #8('54)-Origin The Ghost Rider; Powell-a
94-White Indian #11-Frazetta-a(r); Powell-c
95-Muggsy Mouse #4
96-Cave Girl #12, with Thun'da; Powell-c/a
97-Best of the West #11
98-Undercover Girl #6-Powell-c
99-Muggsy Mouse #5
100-Badmen of the West #1-Meskin-a(?)
101-White Indian #12-Frazetta-a(r)
101-Dream Book of Romance #6 (4-6/54); Marlon Brando photo-c; Powell, Bolle, Guardineer-a
103-Best of the West #12-Powell-a
104-White Indian #13-Frazetta-a(r) ('54)
105-Great Western #9-Ghost Rider app.; Powell-a, 6 pgs.; Bolle-c
106-Dream Book of Love #1 (6-7/54) -Powell, Bolle-a; Montgomery Clift, Donna Reed photo-c
107-Hot Dog #1
108-Red Fox #15 (1954)-L.B. Cole-c/a; Powell-a
109-Dream Book of Romance #7 (7-8/54). Powell-a; movie photo-c
110-Dream Book of Romance #8 (10/54)-Movie photo-c
111-I'm a Cop #1 ('54); drug mention story; Powell-a
112-Ghost Rider #14 ('54)
113-Great Western #10; Powell-a
114-Dream Book of Love #2- Guardineer, Bolle-a; Piper Laurie, Victor Mature photo-c
115-Hot Dog #3
116-Cave Girl #13-Powell-c/a
117-White Indian #14
118-Undercover Girl #7-Powell-c
119-Straight Arrow's Fury #1 (origin); Fred Meagher-c/a
120-Badmen of the West #2
121-Mysteries of Scotland Yard #1; reprinted from Manhunt (5 stories)
122-Black Phantom #1 (11/54)
123-Dream Book of Love #3 (10-11/54)-Movie photo-c
124-Dream Book of Romance #8 (10-11/54)
125-Cave Girl #14-Powell-c/a
126-I'm a Cop #2-Powell-a
127-Great Western #11('54)-Powell-a
128-I'm a Cop #3-Powell-a
129-The Avenger #1('55)-Powell-c
130-Strongman #1-Powell-a (2-3/55)
131-The Avenger #2('55)-Powell-c/a
132-Strongman #2
133-The Avenger #3-Powell-c/a
134-Strongman #3
135-White Indian #15
136-Hot Dog #4
137-Africa #1-Powell-c/a(4)
138-The Avenger #4-Powell-c/a
139-Strongman #4-Powell-a

NOTE: *Bolle a-110. Photo-c-17-22, 89, 92, 101, 106, 109, 110, 114, 123, 124.*

APACHE
Fiction House Magazines: 1951

1	23	46	69	132	186	240
I.W. Reprint No. 1-r/#1 above	3	7	10	21	28	35

APACHE KID (Formerly Reno Browne; Western Gunfighters #20 on) (Also see Two-Gun Western & Wild Western)
Marvel/Atlas Comics(MPC No. 53-10/CPS No. 11 on): No. 53, 12/50 - No. 10, 1/52; No. 11, 12/54 - No. 19, 4/56

53(#1)-Apache Kid & his horse Nightwind (origin), Red Hawkins by Syd Shores begins	36	72	108	207	294	380
2(2/51)	18	36	54	104	142	180
3-5	12	24	36	71	96	120
6-10 (1951-52): 7-Russ Heath-a	10	20	30	58	77	95
11-19 (1954-56)	9	18	27	49	62	75

NOTE: *Heath a-7. c-11, 13. **Maneely** a-53; c-53(#1), 12, 14-16. **Powell** a-14. **Severin** c-17.*

APACHE MASSACRE (See Chief Victorio's...)

APACHE SKIES
Marvel Comics: Sept, 2002 - No. 4, Dec, 2002 ($2.99, limited series)

1-4-Apache Kid app.; Ostrander-s/Manco-c/a 3.00
TPB (2003, $12.99) r/#1-4 13.00

APACHE TRAIL
Steinway/America's Best: Sept, 1957 - No. 4, June, 1958

1	11	22	33	66	88	110
2-4: 2-Tuska-a	8	16	24	40	50	60

APE (Magazine)

Approved Comics #11 © STJ

Aquaman (3rd series) #73 © DC

Arcanum #2 © Brandon Peterson

	GD	VG	FN	VF	VF/NM	NM-
	2.0	4.0	6.0	8.0	9.0	9.2

GD VG FN VF VF/NM NM- 2.0 4.0 6.0 8.0 9.0 9.2

Dell Publishing Co.: 1961 (52 pgs., B&W)
1-Comics and humor 4 8 12 24 32 40

APHRODITE IX
Image Comics (Top Cow): Sept, 2000 - No. 4, Mar, 2002 ($2.50)
1-3: 1-Four covers by Finch, Turner, Silvestri, Benitez 4.00
1-Tower Record Ed.; Finch-c 3.00
1-DF Chrome ($14.99) 15.00
4-($4.95) Double-sized issue; Finch-c 5.00
Convention Preview 10.00
Wizard #0 (4/00, bagged w/Tomb Raider magazine) Preview & sketchbook 5.00
#0-(6/01, $2.95) r/Wizard #0 with cover gallery 3.00

APOLLO SMILE
Eagle Wing Press: July, 1998 - No. 2 ($2.95)
1,2-Manga 3.00

APPARITION
Caliber Comics: 1995 ($3.95, 52 pgs., B&W)
1 ($3.95) 4.00
V2#1-6 ($2.95) 3.00
Visitations 4.00

APPLESEED
Eclipse Comics: Sept, 1988 - Book 4, Vol. 4, Aug, 1991 ($2.50/$2.75/$3.50, 52/68 pgs, B&W)
Book One, Vol. 1-5: 5-(1/89), Book Two, Vol. 1(2/89) -5(7/89): Art Adams-c, Book Three, Vol. 1(8/89) -4 ($2.75), Book Three, Vol. 5 ($3.50), Book Four, Vol. 1 (1/91) - 4 (8/91) ($3.50, 68 pgs.) 6.00

APPLESEED DATABOOK
Dark Horse Comics: Apr, 1994 - No. 2, May, 1994 ($3.50, B&W, limited series)
1,2: 1-Flip book format 3.50

APPROVED COMICS (Also see Blue Ribbon Comics)
St. John Publishing Co. (Most have no c-price): March, 1954 - No. 12, Aug, 1954 (Painted-c on #1-5,7,8,10)
1-The Hawk #5-r 10 20 30 58 77 95
2-Invisible Boy (3/54)-Origin; Saunders-c 18 36 54 101 138 175
3-Wild Boy of the Congo #11-r (4/54) 10 20 30 58 77 95
4,5: 4-Kid Cowboy-r. 5-Fly Boy-r 10 20 30 58 77 95
6-Daring Adv.-r (5/54); Krigstein-a(2); Baker-c 13 26 39 74 100 125
7-The Hawk #6-r 10 20 30 58 77 95
8-Crime on the Run (6/54); Powell-a; Saunders-c 10 20 30 58 77 95
9-Western Bandit Trails #3-r, with new-c; Baker-c/a 13 26 39 76 103 130
10-Dinky Duck (Terrytoons) 6 12 18 28 34 40
11-Fightin' Marines #3-r (8/54); Canteen Kate app; Baker-c/a 14 28 42 79 107 135
12-Northwest Mounties #4-r(8/54); new Baker-c 14 28 42 79 107 135

AQUAMAN (See Adventure Comics #260, Brave & the Bold, DC Comics Presents #5, DC Special #28, DC Special Series #1, DC Super Stars #7, Detective Comics, JLA, Justice League of America, More Fun #73, Showcase #30-33, Super DC Giant, Super Friends, and World's Finest Comics)

AQUAMAN (1st Series)
National Periodical Publications/DC Comics: Jan-Feb, 1962 - #56, Mar-Apr, 1971; #57, Aug-Sept,1977 - #63, Aug-Sept, 1978
1-(1-2/62)-Intro. Quisp 71 142 213 604 927 1250
2 31 62 93 228 339 450
3-5 18 36 54 131 191 250
6-10 13 26 39 90 133 175
11,18: 11-1st app. Mera. 18-Aquaman weds Mera; JLA cameo 10 20 30 72 104 135
12-17,19,20 10 20 30 67 96 125
21-32: 23-Birth of Aquababy. 26-Huntress app.(3-4/66). 29-1st app. Ocean Master, Aquaman's step-brother. 30-Batman & Superman-c & cameo 6 12 18 43 59 75
33-1st app. Aqua-Girl (see Adventure #266) 7 14 21 50 68 85
34-40: 40-Jim Aparo's 1st DC work (8/68) 5 10 15 33 44 55
41-46,47,49: 45-Last 12¢-c 4 8 12 27 36 45
48-Origin reprinted 4 8 12 29 40 50
50-52-Deadman by Neal Adams 7 14 21 50 68 85
53-56('71): 56-1st app. Crusader; last 15¢-c 2 4 6 10 13 16
57('77)-63: 58-Origin retold 1 2 3 5 7 9
NOTE: *Aparo a-40-45, 46p, 47-59; c-58-63.* ***Nick Cardy*** *c-1-40.* ***Newton*** *a-60-63.*

AQUAMAN (1st limited series)
DC Comics: Feb, 1986 - No. 4, May, 1986 (75¢, limited series)
1-New costume; 1st app. Nuada of Thierna Na Oge. 5.50
2-4: 3-Retelling of Aquaman & Ocean Master's origins. 4.00
Special 1 (1988, $1.50, 52 pgs.) 3.75
NOTE: ***Craig Hamilton*** *c/a-1-4p.* ***Russell*** *c-2-4i.*

AQUAMAN (2nd limited series)
DC Comics: June, 1989 - No. 5, Oct, 1989 ($1.00, limited series)
1-5: Giffen plots/breakdowns; Swan-a(p). 3.00
Special 1 (Legend of..., $2.00, 1989, 52 pgs.)-Giffen plots/breakdowns; Swan-a(p) 3.00

AQUAMAN (2nd Series)
DC Comics: Dec, 1991 - No. 13, Dec, 1992 ($1.00/$1.25)
1-5 2.50
6-13: 6-Begin $1.25-c. 9-Sea Devils app. 2.50

AQUAMAN (3rd Series)(Also see Atlantis Chronicles)
DC Comics: Aug, 1994 - No. 75, Jan, 2001 ($1.50/$1.75/$1.95/$1.99/$2.50)
1-(8/94)-Peter David scripts begin; reintro Dolphin 6.00
2-(9/94)-Aquaman loses hand 6.50
0-(10/94)-Aquaman replaces lost hand with hook. 6.50
3-8: 3-(11/94)-Superboy-c/app. 4-Lobo app. 6-Deep Six app. 3.50
9-69: 9-Begin $1.75-c. 10-Green Lantern app. 11-Reintro Mera. 15-Re-intro Kordax. 16-vs. JLA. 18-Reintro Ocean Master & Atlan (Aquaman's father). 19-Reintro Garth (Aqualad). 23-1st app. Deep Blue (Neptune Perkins & Tsunami's daughter). 23,24-Neptune Perkins, Nuada, Tsunami, Arion, Power Girl, & The Sea Devils app. 26-Final Night. 28-Martian Manhunter-c/app. 29-Black Manta-c/app. 32-Swamp Thing-c/app. 37-Genesis x-over. 41-Maxima-c/app. 43-Millennium Giants x-over; Superman-c/app. 44-G.A. Flash & Sentinel app. 50-Larsen-s begins. 53-Superman app. 60-Tempest marries Dolphin; Teen Titans app. 63-Kaluta covers begin. 66-JLA app. 2.50
70-75: 70-Begin $2.50-c. 71-73-Warlord-c/app. 75-Final issue 2.50
#1,000,000 (11/98) 853rd Century x-over 3.00
Annual 1 (1995, $3.50)-Year One story 3.50
Annual 2 (1996, $2.95)-Legends of the Dead Earth story 3.00
Annual 3 (1997, $3.95)-Pulp Heroes story 4.00
Annual 4,5 ('98, '99, $2.95)-4-Ghosts; Wrightson-c. 5-JLApe 3.00
...Secret Files 1 (12/98, $4.95) Origin-s and pin-ups 5.00
NOTE: ***Art Adams****-c, Annual 5.* ***Mignola*** *c-6.* ***Simonson*** *c-15.*

AQUAMAN (4th Series)(Also see JLA #69-75)
DC Comics: Feb, 2003 - Present ($2.50)
1-Veitch-s/Guichet-a/Maleev-c 3.00
2-14: 2-Martian Manhunter app. 8-11-Black Manta app. 2.50
...Secret Files 2003 (5/03, $4.95) background on Aquaman's new powers; pin-ups 5.00
: The Waterbearer TPB (2003, $12.95) r/#1-4, stories from Aquaman Secret Files and JLA/JSA Secret Files #1; JG Jones-c 13.00

AQUAMAN: TIME & TIDE (3rd limited series) (Also see Atlantis Chronicles)
DC Comics: Dec, 1993 - No. 4, Mar, 1994 ($1.50, limited series)
1-4: Peter David scripts; origin retold. 3.00
Trade paperback ($9.95) 10.00

AQUANAUTS (TV)
Dell Publishing Co.: May - July, 1961
Four Color 1197-Photo-c 8 16 24 55 78 100

ARABIAN NIGHTS (See Cinema Comics Herald)

ARACHNOPHOBIA (Movie)
Hollywood Comics (Disney Comics): 1990 ($5.95, 68 pg. graphic novel)
nn-Adaptation of film; Spiegle-a 6.00
Comic edition ($2.95, 68 pgs.) 3.00

ARAK/SON OF THUNDER (See Warlord #48)
DC Comics: Sept, 1981 - No. 50, Nov, 1985
1,24,50: 1-1st app. Angelica, Princess of White Cathay. 24,50-(52 pgs.) 3.00
2-23,25-49: 3-Intro Valda. 12-Origin Valda. 20-Origin Angelica 2.25
Annual 1(10/84) 3.00

ARCANA (Also see Books of Magic limited & ongoing series and Mister E)
DC Comics (Vertigo): 1994 ($3.95, 68 pgs., annual)
1-Bolton painted-c; Children's Crusade/Tim Hunter story 4.00

ARCANUM
Image Comics (Top Cow Productions): Apr, 1997 - No. 8, Feb, 1998 ($2.50)
1/2 Gold Edition 12.00
1-Brandon Peterson-s/a(p), 1-Variant-c, 4-American Ent. Ed. 3.00
2-8 2.50
3-Variant-c 4.00

ARCHANGEL (See Uncanny X-Men, X-Factor & X-Men)
Marvel Comics: Feb, 1996 ($2.50, B&W, one-shot)

Archard's Agents #1 © CRO

Archie & Friends #79 © AP

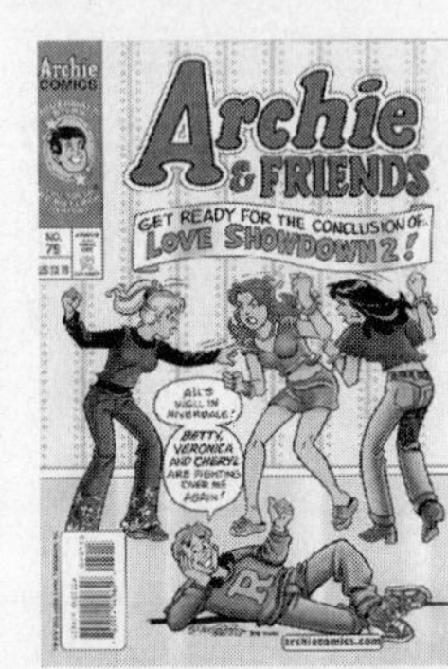

Archie Comics #56 © AP

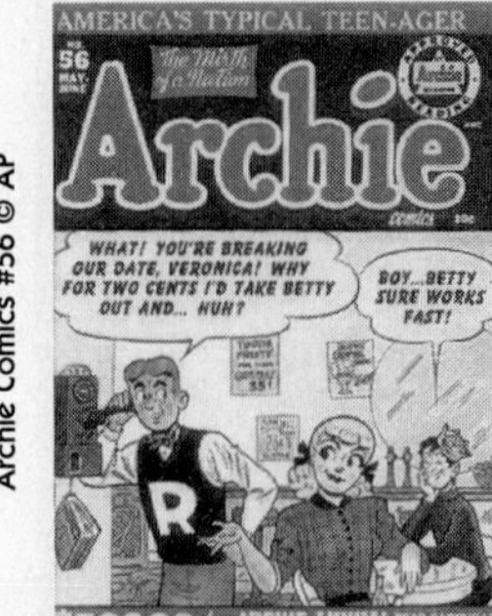

GD VG FN VF VF/NM NM-
2.0 4.0 6.0 8.0 9.0 9.2

1-Milligan story 2.50

ARCHARD'S AGENTS (See Ruse)
CrossGeneration Comics: Jan, 2003; Nov, 2003 ($2.95)

1-Dixon-s/Perkins-a 3.00
...: The Case of the Puzzled Pugilist (11/03) Dixon-s/Perkins-a 3.00

ARCHER & ARMSTRONG
Valiant: July (June inside), 1992 - No. 26, Oct, 1994 ($2.50)

0-(7/92)-B. Smith-c/a; Reese-i assists 3.00
0-(Gold Logo) 6.00
1-7,9-26: 1-(8/92)-Origin & 1st app. Archer; Miller-c; B. Smith/Layton-a. 2-2nd app. Turok (c/story); Smith/Layton-a; Simonson-c. 3,4-Smith-c&a(p) & scripts. 10-2nd app. Ivar. 10,11-B. Smith-c. 21,22-Shadowman app. 22-w/bound-in trading card. 25-Eternal Warrior app. 26-Flip book w/Eternal Warrior #26 2.50
8-($4.50, 52 pgs.)-Combined with Eternal Warrior #8; B. Smith-c/a & scripts; 1st app. Ivar the Time Walker 4.50

ARCHIE (See Archie Comics) (Also see Christmas & Archie, Everything's..., Explorers of the Unknown, Jackpot, Little..., Oxydol-Dreft, Pep, Riverdale High, Teenage Mutant Ninja Turtles Adventures & To Riverdale and Back Again)

ARCHIE AMERICANA SERIES, BEST OF THE FORTIES
Archie Publications: 1991,2002 ($10.95, trade paperback)

Vol. 1,2-r/early strips from 1940's 1-Intro. by Steven King. 2-Intro. by Paul Castiglia 11.00

ARCHIE AMERICANA SERIES, BEST OF THE FIFTIES
Archie Publications: 1991 ($8.95, trade paperback)

V2-r/strips from 1950's; 9.00
2nd printing (1998, $9.95) 10.00
Book 2 (2003, $10.95) 11.00

ARCHIE AMERICANA SERIES, BEST OF THE SIXTIES
Archie Publications: 1995 ($9.95, trade paperback)

V3-r/strips from 1960's; intro. by Frankie Avalon. 10.00

ARCHIE AMERICANA SERIES, BEST OF THE SEVENTIES
Archie Publications: 1997 ($9.95, trade paperback)

V4-r/strips from 1970's 10.00

ARCHIE AMERICANA SERIES, BEST OF THE EIGHTIES
Archie Publications: 2001 ($10.95, trade paperback)

V5-r/strips from 1980's; foreward by Steve Geppi 11.00

ARCHIE AND BIG ETHEL
Spire Christian Comics (Fleming H. Revell Co.): 1982 (69¢)

nn-(Low print run) 2 4 6 10 13 16

ARCHIE & FRIENDS
Archie Comics: Dec, 1992 - Present ($1.25/$1.50/$1.75/$1.79/$1.99/$2.19, bi-monthly)

1 5.00
2,4,10-14,17,18,20-Sabrina app. 20-Archie's Band-c 4.00
3,5-9,16 2.50
15-Babewatch-s with Sabrina app. 6.00
19-Josie and the Pussycats app.; E.T. parody-c/s 5.00
21-46 2.25
47-All Josie and the Pussycats issue; movie and actress profiles/photos 2.25
48-79: 48-56,58,60-Josie and the Pussycats-c/s. 79-Cheryl Blossom returns 2.25

ARCHIE AND ME (See Archie Giant Series Mag. #578, 591, 603, 616, 626)
Archie Publications: Oct, 1964 - No. 161, Feb, 1987

1 17 34 51 118 174 230
2 9 18 27 63 89 115
3-5 6 12 18 38 52 65
6-10 4 8 12 24 32 40
11-20 3 6 9 18 23 28
21(6/68)-26,28-30: 21-UFO story. 26-X-Mas-c 2 4 6 14 18 22
27-Groovyman & Knowman superhero-s; UFO-sty 3 6 9 18 23 28
31-42: 37-Japan Expo '70-c/s 2 4 6 10 12 15
43-48,50-63-(All Giants): 43-(8/71) Mummy-s. 44-Mermaid-s. 62-Elvis cameo-c. 63-(2/74) 2 4 6 14 18 22
49-(Giant) Josie & the Pussycats-c/app. 3 6 9 18 24 30
64-66,68-99-(Regular size): 85-Bicentennial-s. 98-Collectors Comics 1 3 4 6 8 10
67-Sabrina app.(8/74) 2 4 6 10 13 16
100-(4/78) 2 4 6 8 10 12
101-120: 107-UFO-s 6.00
121(8/80)-159: 134-Riverdale 2001 5.00
160,161: 160-Origin Mr. Weatherbee. 161-Last issue 6.00

GD VG FN VF VF/NM NM-
2.0 4.0 6.0 8.0 9.0 9.2

ARCHIE AND MR. WEATHERBEE
Spire Christian Comics (Fleming H. Revell Co.): 1980 (59¢)

nn - (Low print run) 2 4 6 8 10 12

ARCHIE...ARCHIE ANDREWS, WHERE ARE YOU? (...Comics Digest #9, 10; ...Comics Digest Mag. No. 11 on)
Archie Publications: Feb, 1977 - Present (Digest size, 160-128 pgs., quarterly)

1 3 6 9 18 24 30
2,3,5,7-9-N. Adams-a; 8-r-/origin The Fly by S&K. 9-Steel Sterling-r 2 4 6 10 13 16
4,6,10 ($1.00/$1.50) 2 4 6 8 10 12
11-20: 17-Katy Keene story 1 2 3 5 7 9
21-50,100 1 2 3 4 5 7
51-70 4.00
71-117: 113-Begin $1.95-c 3.00

ARCHIE AS PUREHEART THE POWERFUL (Also see Archie Giant Series #142, Jughead as Captain Hero, Life With Archie & Little Archie)
Archie Publications (Radio Comics): Sept, 1966 - No. 6, Nov, 1967

1-Super hero parody 10 20 30 70 100 130
2 6 12 18 40 55 70
3-6 5 10 15 33 44 55

NOTE: *Evilheart cameos in all. Title: Archie As Pureheart the Powerful #1-3; ...As Capt. Pureheart-#4-6.*

ARCHIE AT RIVERDALE HIGH (See Archie Giant Series Magazine #573, 586, 604 & Riverdale High)
Archie Publications: Aug, 1972 - No. 113, Feb, 1987

1 7 14 21 46 63 80
2 4 8 12 24 32 40
3-5 3 6 9 18 23 28
6-10 2 4 6 12 16 20
11-30 2 4 6 8 10 12
31(12/75)-46,48-50(12/77) 1 2 3 5 7 9
47-Archie in drag-s; Betty mud wrestling-s 2 4 6 9 11 14
51-80,100 (12/84) 6.00
81(8/81)-88, 91,93-95,97,98: 96-Anti-smoking issue 5.00
89,90-Early Cheryl Blossom app. 90-Archies Band app. 2 4 6 9 11 14
92,96,99-Cheryl Blossom app. 1 3 4 6 8 10
101,102,104-109,111,112: 102-Ghost-c 4.00
103-Archie dates Cheryl Blossom-s 1 3 4 6 8 10
110,113: 110-Godzilla-s. 113-Last issue 6.00

ARCHIE COMICS (Archie #114 on; 1st Teen-age comic; Radio show aired 6/2/45 by NBC)
MLJ Magazines No. 1-19/Archie Publ. No. 20 on: Winter, 1942-43 - No. 19, 3-4/46; No. 20, 5-6/46 - Present

1 (Scarce)-Jughead, Veronica app.; 1st app. Mrs. Andrews 1281 2562 3843 9608 15,054 20,500
2 311 622 933 2022 3111 4200
3 (60 pgs.)(scarce) 248 496 744 1550 2325 3100
4,5: 4-Article about Archie radio series 132 264 396 825 1238 1650
6,8-10: 6-X-Mas-c. 9-1st Miss Grundy cover 92 184 276 575 863 1150
7-1st definitive love triangle story 96 192 288 600 900 1200
11-20: 15,17,18-Dotty & Ditto by Woggon. 16-Woggon-a 62 124 186 388 582 775
21-30: 23-Betty & Veronica by Woggon. 25-Woggon-a. 30-Coach Piffle app., a Coach Kleets prototype. 34-Pre-Dilton try-out (named Dilbert) 40 80 120 240 358 475
31-40 28 56 84 159 225 290
41-50 19 38 57 109 152 195
51-60 10 20 30 72 104 135
61-70 (1954): 65-70, Katy Keene app. 9 18 27 60 85 110
71-80: 72-74-Katy Keene app. 7 14 21 46 63 80
81-99: 94-1st Coach Kleets 6 12 18 38 52 65
100 7 14 21 46 63 80
101-122,126,128-130 (1962) 4 8 12 27 36 45
123-125,127-Horror/SF covers. 123-UFO-c/s 4 8 12 29 40 50
131,132,134-157,159,160 3 6 9 18 23 28
133 (12/62)-1st app. Cricket O'Dell 4 8 12 24 32 40
158-Archie in drag story 3 6 9 19 25 32
161(2/66)-182,184,186-195,197-199: 168-Superhero gag-c. 176,178-Twiggy-c 2 4 6 12 16 20
183-1st Caveman Archie gang story 3 6 9 17 21 26
185-1st "The Archies" Band story 3 6 9 19 27 34
196 (12/69)-Early Cricket O'Dell app. 3 6 9 18 24 30
200 (6/70) 2 4 6 14 18 22

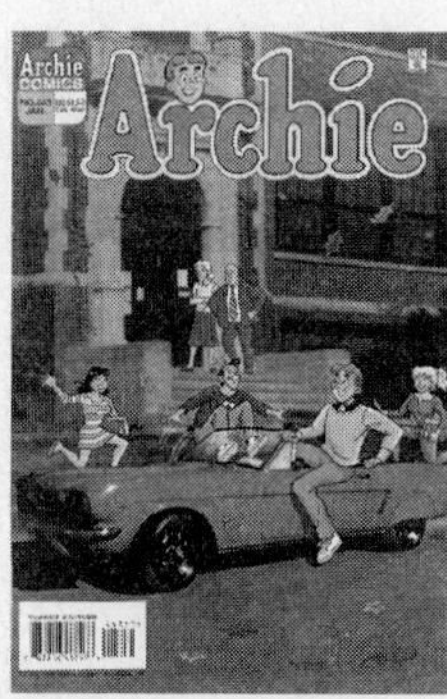

Archie Comics #443 © AP

Archie Giant Series #18 © AP

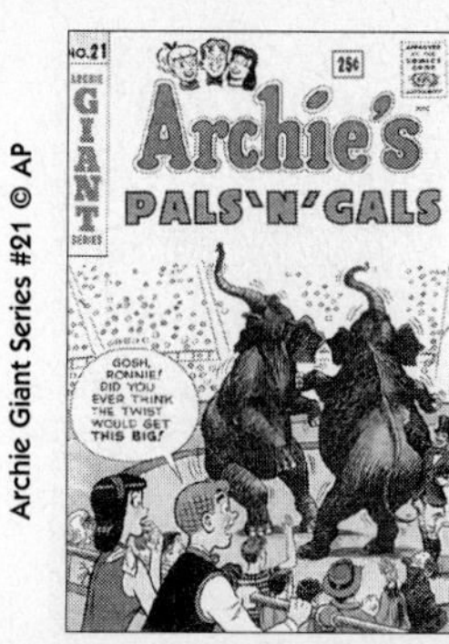

Archie Giant Series #21 © AP

	GD 2.0	VG 4.0	FN 6.0	VF 8.0	VF/NM 9.0	NM- 9.2

201-230(11/73): 213-Sabrina/Josie-c cameos. 229-Lost Child issue 2 4 6 8 10 12
231-260(3/77): 253-Tarzan parody 1 2 3 5 7 9
261-282, 284-299 1 2 3 4 5 7
283(8/79)-Cover/story plugs "International Children's Appeal" which was a fraudulent charity, according to TV's 20/20 news program broadcast July 20, 1979 1 2 3 5 6 8
300(1/81)-Anniversary issue 1 2 3 5 7 9
301-321,323-325,327-335,337-350: 323-Cheryl Blossom pin-up 5.00
322-E.T. story 6.00
326-Early Cheryl Blossom story 2 4 6 10 13 16
336-Michael Jackson/Boy George parody 6.00
351-399: 356-Calgary Olympics Special. 393-Infinity-c; 1st comic book printed on recycled paper 4.00
400 (6/92)-Shows 1st meeting of Little Archie and Veronica 6.00
401-428 3.00
429-Love Showdown part 1 5.00
430-544: 467- "A Storm Over Uniforms" x-over parts 3,4. 538-Comic-Con issue 2.25
Annual 1 ('50)-116 pgs. (Scarce) 168 336 504 1050 1575 2100
Annual 2 ('51) 84 168 252 525 788 1050
Annual 3 ('52) 50 100 150 300 450 600
Annual 4,5 (1953-54) 39 78 117 230 325 420
Annual 6-10 (1955-59): 8,9-(100 pgs.). 10-(84 pgs.) Elvis record on-c 15 30 45 104 152 200
Annual 11-15 (1960-65): 12,13-(84 pgs.) 14,15-(68 pgs.) 8 16 24 55 78 100
Annual 16-20 (1966-70)(all 68 pgs.): 20-Archie's band-c 4 8 12 29 40 50
Annual 21,22,24-26 (1971-75): 21,22-(68 pgs.). 22-Archie's band-s. 24-26-(52 pgs.). 25-Cavemen-s 3 6 9 16 20 25
Annual 23-Archie's band-c/s; Josie/Sabrina-c 3 6 9 18 24 30
Annual Digest 27 ('75) 4 8 12 22 30 38
...28-30 2 4 6 14 18 22
...31-34 2 4 6 10 13 16
...35-40 (...Magazine #35 on) 1 3 4 6 8 10
...41-65 ('94) 5.00
...66-69 3.00
...All-Star Specials(Winter '75, $1.25)-6 remaindered Archie comics rebound in each; titles: "The World of Giant Comics", "Giant Grab Bag of Comics", "Triple Giant Comics" & "Giant Spec. Comics 4 8 12 27 36 45
Special Edition-Christmas With Archie 1(1/75)-Treasury (rare) 6 12 18 38 52 65

NOTE: *Archies Band-s-185, 188-192, 197, 198, 201, 204, 205, 208, 209, 215, 329, 330; Band-c-191, 330. Cavemen Archie Gang-s-183, 192, 197, 208, 210, 220, 223, 282, 333, 335, 338, 340.* ***Al Fagly*** *c-17-35.* ***Bob Montana*** *c-38, 41-50, 58, Annual 1-4.* ***Bill Woggon*** *c-53, 54.*

ARCHIE COMICS DIGEST (...Magazine No. 37-95)
Archie Publications: Aug, 1973 - Present (Small size, 160-128 pgs.)

1-1st Archie digest 10 20 30 67 96 125
2 5 10 15 36 48 60
3-5 4 8 12 25 33 42
6-10 3 6 9 16 20 24
11-33: 32,33-The Fly-r by S&K 2 4 6 10 12 15
34-60 1 3 4 6 8 10
61-80,100 1 2 3 5 6 8
81-99 5.00
101-140: 36-Katy Keene story 4.00
141-165 3.00
166-204: 194-Begin $2.39-c 2.50

NOTE: ***Neal Adams*** *a-1, 2, 4, 5, 19-21, 24, 25, 27, 29, 31, 33. X-mas c-88, 94, 100, 106.*

ARCHIE COMICS PRESENTS: THE LOVE SHOWDOWN COLLECTION
Archie Publications: 1994 ($4.95, squarebound)

nn-r/Archie #429, Betty #19, Betty & Veronica #82, & Veronica #39 1 2 3 4 5 7

ARCHIE GETS A JOB
Spire Christian Comics (Fleming H. Revell Co.): 1977

nn 2 4 6 8 10 12

ARCHIE GIANT SERIES MAGAZINE
Archie Publications: 1954 - No. 632, July, 1992 (No #36-135, no #252-451)
(#1 not code approved) (#1-233 are Giants; #12-184 are 68 pgs.,#185-194,197-233 are 52 pgs.; #195,196 are 84 pgs.; #234-up are 36 pgs.)

1-Archie's Christmas Stocking 124 248 372 775 1163 1550
2-Archie's Christmas Stocking('55) 70 140 210 438 657 875
3-6-Archie's Christmas Stocking('56- '59) 48 96 144 288 432 575
7-10: 7-Katy Keene Holiday Fun(9/60); Bill Woggon-c. 8-Betty & Veronica Summer Fun (10/60); baseball story w/Babe Ruth & Lou Gehrig. 9-The World of Jughead (12/60). 10-Archie's Christmas Stocking(1/61) 38 76 114 219 310 400
11,13,16,18: 11-Betty & Veronica Spectacular (6/61). 13-Betty & Veronica Summer Fun (10/61). 16-Betty & Veronica Spectacular (6/62). 18-Betty & Veronica Summer Fun (10/62) 25 50 75 147 202 260
12,14,15,17,19,20: 12-Katy Keene Holiday Fun (9/61). 14-The World of Jughead (12/61); Vampire-s. 15-Archie's Christmas Stocking (1/62). 17-Archie's Jokes (9/62); Katy Keene app. 19-The World of Jughead (12/62). 20-Archie's Christmas Stocking (1/63) 18 36 54 104 142 180
21,23,28: 21-Betty & Veronica Spectacular (6/63). 23-Betty & Veronica Summer Fun (10/63). 28-Betty & Veronica Summer Fun (9/64) 10 20 30 70 100 130
22,24,25,27,29,30: 22-Archie's Jokes (9/63). 24-The World of Jughead (12/63). 25-Archie's Christmas Stocking (1/64). 27-Archie's Jokes (8/64). 29-Around the World with Archie (10/64); Doris Day-s. 30-The World of Jughead (12/64) 9 18 27 60 85 110
26-Betty & Veronica Spectacular (6/64); all pin-ups; DeCarlo-c/a 10 20 30 73 107 140
31,33-35: 31-Archie's Christmas Stocking (1/65). 33-Archie's Jokes (8/65). 34-Betty & Veronica Summer Fun (9/65). 35-Around the World with Archie (10/65). 7 14 21 50 68 85
32-Betty & Veronica Spectacular (6/65); all pin-ups; DeCarlo-c/a 8 16 24 55 78 100
36-135-**Do not exist**
136-141: 136-The World of Jughead (12/65). 137-Archie's Christmas Stocking (1/66). 138-Betty & Veronica Spectacular (6/66). 139-Archie's Jokes (6/66). 140-Betty & Veronica Summer Fun (8/66). 141-Around the World with Archie (9/66) 7 14 21 50 68 85
142-Archie's Super-Hero Special (10/66)-Origin Capt. Pureheart, Capt. Hero, and Evilheart 7 14 21 51 71 90
143-The World of Jughead(12/66); Capt. Hero-c/s; Man From R.I.V.E.R.D.A.L.E., Pureheart, Superteen app. 6 12 18 40 55 70
144-160: 144-Archie's Christmas Stocking (1/67). 145-Betty & Veronica Spectacular (6/67). 146-Archie's Jokes (6/67). 147-Betty & Veronica Summer Fun (8/67) 148-World of Archie (9/67). 149-World of Jughead (10/67). 150-Archie's Christmas Stocking (1/68). 151-World of Archie (2/68). 152-World of Jughead (2/68). 153-Betty & Veronica Spectacular (6/68). 154-Archie Jokes (6/68). 155-Betty & Veronica Summer Fun (8/68). 156-World of Archie (10/68). 157-World of Jughead (12/68). 158-Archie's Christmas Stocking (1/69). 159-Betty & Veronica Christmas Spectacular (1/69). 160-World of Archie (2/69); Frankenstein-s each... 4 8 12 24 32 40
161-World of Jughead (2/69); Super-Jughead-s; 11 pg.early Cricket O'Dell-s 4 8 12 25 33 42
162-183: 162-Betty & Veronica Spectacular (6/69). 163-Archie's Jokes(8/69). 164-Betty & Veronica Summer Fun (9/69). 165-World of Archie (9/69). 166-World of Jughead (9/69). 167-Archie's Christmas Stocking (1/70). 168-Betty & Veronica Christmas Spect. (1/70). 169-Archie's Christmas Love-In (1/70). 170-Jughead's Eat-Out Comic Book Mag. (12/69). 171-World of Archie (2/70). 172-World of Jughead (2/70). 173-Betty & Veronica Spectacular (6/70). 174-Archie's Jokes (8/70). 175-Betty & Veronica Summer Fun (9/70). 176-Li'l Jinx Giant Laugh-Out (8/70). 177-World of Archie (9/70). 178-World of Jughead (9/70). 179-Archie's Christmas Stocking(1/71). 180-Betty & Veronica Christmas Spect. (1/71). 181-Archie's Christmas Love-In (1/71). 182-World of Archie (2/71). 183-World of Jughead (2/71)-Last squarebound each... 3 6 9 18 23 28
184-189,193,194,197-199 (52 pgs.): 184-Betty & Veronica Spectacular (6/71). 185-Li'l Jinx Giant Laugh-Out (6/71). 186-Archie's Jokes (8/71). 187-Betty & Veronica Summer Fun (9/71). 188-World of Archie (9/71). 189-World of Jughead (9/71). 193-World of Archie (3/72).194-World of Jughead (4/72). 197-Betty & Veronica Spectacular (6/72). 198-Archie's Jokes (8/72). 199-Betty & Veronica Summer Fun (9/72) each... 3 6 9 16 20 24
190-192: 190-Archie's Christmas Stocking (12/71); Sabrina on-c. 191-Betty & Veronica Christmas Spect.(2/72); Sabrina app.. 192-Archie's Christmas Love-In (1/72); Archie Band-c/s 3 7 10 21 28 35
195-(84 pgs.)-Li'l Jinx Christmas Bag (1/72). 4 8 12 24 32 40
196-(84 pgs.)-Sabrina's Christmas Magic (1/72) 6 12 18 40 55 70
200-(52 pgs.)-World of Archie (10/72) 3 7 10 21 28 35
201-206,208-219,221-230,232,233 (All 52 pgs.): 201-Betty & Veronica Spectacular (10/72). 202-World of Jughead (11/72). 203-Archie's Christmas Stocking (12/72). 204-Betty & Veronica Christmas Spectacular (2/73). 205-Archie's Christmas Love-In (1/73). 206-Li'l Jinx Christmas Bag (12/72). 208-World of Archie (3/73). 209-World of Jughead (4/73). 210-Betty & Veronica Spectacular (6/73). 211-Archie's Jokes (8/73). 212-Betty & Veronica Summer Fun (9/73). 213-World of Archie (10/73). 214-Betty & Veronica Spectacular (10/73). 215-World of Jughead (11/73). 216-Archie's Christmas Stocking (12/73). 217-Betty & Veronica Christmas Spectacular (2/74). 218-Archie's Christmas Love-In (1/74). 219-Li'l Jinx Christmas Bag (12/73). 221-Betty & Veronica Spectacular (Advertised as World of Archie) (6/74). 222-Archie's Jokes (advertised as World of Jughead) (8/74). 223-Li'l Jinx (8/74). 224-Betty & Veronica Summer Fun (9/74). 225-World of Archie (9/74). 226-Betty & Veronica

Archie Giant Series #457 © AP

Archie Meets the Punisher © AP & MAR

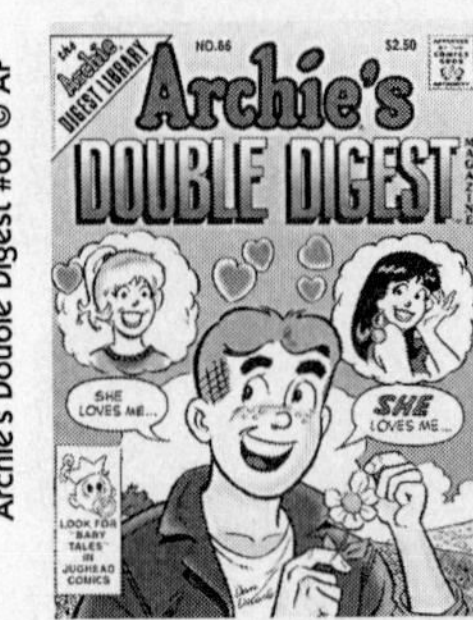

Archie's Double Digest #66 © AP

GD 2.0 | VG 4.0 | FN 6.0 | VF 8.0 | VF/NM 9.0 | NM- 9.2

Spectacular (10/74). 227-World of Jughead (10/74). 228-Archie's Christmas Stocking (12/74). 229-Betty & Veronica Christmas Spectacular (12/74). 230-Archie's Christmas Love-In (1/75). 232-World of Archie (3/75). 233-World of Jughead (4/75)
each... 2 4 6 10 12 15
207,220,231,243: Sabrina's Christmas Magic. 207-(12/72). 220-(12/73). 231-(1/75). 243-(1/76)
each... 3 6 9 16 20 24
234-242,244-251 (36 pgs.): 234-Betty & Veronica Spectacular (6/75). 235-Archie's Jokes (8/75). 236-Betty & Veronica Summer Fun (9/75). 237-World of Archie (9/75) 238-Betty & Veronica Spectacular (10/75). 239-World of Jughead (10/75). 240-Archie's Christmas Stocking (12/75). 241-Betty & Veronica Christmas Spectacular (12/75). 242-Archie's Christmas Love-In (1/76). 244-World of Archie (3/76). 245-World of Jughead (4/76). 246-Betty & Veronica Spectacular (6/76). 247-Archie's Jokes (8/76). 248-Betty & Veronica Summer Fun (9/76). 249-World of Archie (9/76). 250-Betty & Veronica Spectacular (10/76). 251-World of Jughead each.... 2 4 6 8 10 12
252-451-Do not exist
452-454,456-466,468-478, 480-490,492-499: 452-Archie's Christmas Stocking (12/76). 453-Betty & Veronica Christmas Spectacular (12/76). 454-Archie's Christmas Love-In (1/77). 456-World of Archie (3/77). 457-World of Jughead (4/77). 458-Betty & Veronica Spectacular (6/77). 459-Archie's Jokes (8/77)-Shows 8/76 in error. 460-Betty & Veronica Summer Fun (9/77). 461-World of Archie (9/77). 462-Betty & Veronica Spectacular (10/77). 463-World of Jughead (10/77). 464-Archie's Christmas Stocking (12/77). 465-Betty & Veronica Christmas Spectacular (12/77). 466-Archie's Christmas Love-In (1/78). 468-World of Archie (2/78). 469-World of Jughead (2/78). 470-Betty & Veronica Spectacular(6/78). 471-Archie's Jokes (8/78). 472-Betty & Veronica Summer Fun (9/78). 473-World of Archie (9/78). 474-Betty & Veronica Spectacular (10/78). 475-World of Jughead (10/78). 476-Archie's Christmas Stocking (12/78). 477-Betty & Veronica Christmas Spectacular (12/78). 478-Archie's Christmas Love-In (1/79). 480-The World of Archie (3/79). 481-World of Jughead (4/79). 482-Betty & Veronica Spectacular (6/79). 483-Archie's Jokes (8/79). 484-Betty & Veronica Summer Fun(9/79). 485-The World of Archie (9/79). 486-Betty & Veronica Spectacular (10/79). 487-The World of Jughead (10/79). 488-Archie's Christmas Stocking (12/79). 489-Betty & Veronica Christmas Spectacular (1/80). 490-Archie's Christmas Love-in (1/80). 492-The World of Archie (2/80). 493-The World of Jughead (4/80). 494-Betty & Veronica Spectacular (6/80). 495-Archie's Jokes (8/80). 496-Betty & Veronica Summer Fun (9/80). 497-The World of Archie (9/80). 498-Betty & Veronica Spectacular (10/80). 499-The World of Jughead (10/80) each... 1 3 4 6 8 10
455,467,479,491,503-Sabrina's Christmas Magic: 455-(1/77). 467-(1/78). 479-(1/79) Dracula/ Werewolf-s. 491-(1/80), 503(1/81) 2 4 6 11 14 18
500-Archie's Christmas Stocking (12/80) 2 4 6 8 10 12
501-514,516-527,529-532,534-539,541-543,545-550: 501-Betty & Veronica Christmas Spectacular (12/80). 502-Archie's Christmas Love-in (1/81). 504-The World of Archie (3/81). 505-The World of Jughead (4/81). 506-Betty & Veronica Spectacular (6/81). 507-Archie's Jokes (8/81). 508-Betty & Veronica Summer Fun (9/81). 509-The World of Archie (9/81). 510-Betty & Vernonica Spectacular (9/81). 511-The World of Jughead (10/81). 512-Archie's Christmas Stocking (12/81). 513-Betty & Veronica Christmas Spectacular (12/81). 514-Archie's Christmas Love-in (1/82). 516-The World of Archie(3/82). 517-The World of Jughead (4/82). 518-Betty & Veronica Spectacular (6/82). 519-Archie's Jokes (8/82). 520-Betty & Veronica Summer Fun (9/82). 521-The World of Archie (9/82). 522-Betty & Veronica Spectacular (10/82). 523-The World of Jughead (10/82).524-Archie's Christmas Stocking (1/83). 525-Betty and Veronica Christmas Spectacular (1/83). 526-Betty and Veronica Spectacular (5/83). 527-Little Archie (8/83). 529-Betty and Veronica Summer Fun (8/83). 530-Betty and Veronica Spectacular (9/83). 531-The World of Jughead (9/83). 532-The World of Archie (10/83). 534-Little Archie (1/84). 535-Archie's Christmas Stocking (1/84). 536-Betty and Veronica Christmas Spectacular (1/84). 537-Betty and Veronica Spectacular (6/84). 538-Little Archie (8/84). 539-Betty and Veronica Summer Fun (8/84). 541-Betty and Veronica Spectacular (9/84). 542-The World of Jughead (9/84). 543-The World of Archie (10/84). 545-Little Archie (12/84). 546-Archie's Christmas Stocking (12/84). 547-Betty and Veronica Christmas Spectacular (12/84). 548-?. 549-Little Archie. 550-Betty and Veronica Summer Fun each... 1 2 3 5 6 8
515,528,533,540,544: 515-Sabrina's Christmas Magic (1/82). 528-Josie and the Pussycats (8/83). 533-Sabrina; Space Pirates by Frank Bolling (10/83). 540-Josie and the Pussycats (8/84). 544-Sabrina the Teen-Age Witch (10/84).
each... 2 4 6 10 13 16
551,562,571,584,597-Josie and the Pussycats 1 3 4 6 8 10
552-561,563-570,572-583,585-596,598-600: 552-Betty & Veronica Spectacular. 553-The World of Jughead. 554-The World of Archie. 555-Betty's Diary. 556-Little Archie (1/86). 557-Archie's Christmas Stocking (1/86). 558-Betty & Veronica Christmas Spectacular (1/86). 559-Betty & Veronica Spectacular. 560-Little Archie. 561-Betty & Veronica Summer Fun. 563-Betty & Veronica Spectacular. 564-World of Jughead. 565-World of Archie. 566-Little Archie. 567-Archie's Christmas Stocking. 568-Betty & Veronica Christmas Spectacular. 569-Betty & Veronica Spring Spectacular. 570-Little Archie. 571-Dracula-c/s. 572-Betty & Veronica Summer Fun. 573-Archie At Riverdale High. 574-World of Archie. 575-Betty & Veronica Spectacular. 576-Pep. 577-World of Jughead. 578-Archie And Me. 579-Archie's Christmas Stocking. 580-Betty and Veronica Christmas Spectacular. 581-Little Archie Christmas Special. 582-Betty & Veronica Spring Spectacular. 583-Little Archie. 585-Betty & Veronica Summer Fun. 586-Archie At Riverdale High. 587-The World of Archie (10/88); 1st app. Explorers of the Unknown. 588-Betty & Veronica Spectacular. 589-Pep (10/88). 590-The World of Jughead. 591-Archie & Me. 592-Archie's Christmas Stocking. 593-Betty & Veronica Christmas Spectacular. 594-Little Archie. 595-Betty & Veronica Spring Spectacular. 596-Little Archie. 598-Betty & Veronica Summer Fun. 599-The World of Archie (10/89); 2nd app. Explorers of the Unknown. 600-Betty and Veronica Spectacular
each.... 6.00
601,602,604-609,611-629: 601-Pep. 602-The World of Jughead. 604-Archie at Riverdale High. 605-Archie's Christmas Stocking. 606-Betty and Veronica Christmas Spectacular. 607-Little Archie. 608-Betty and Veronica Spectacular. 609-Little Archie. 611-Betty and Veronica Summer Fun. 612-The World of Archie. 613-Betty and Veronica Spectacular. 614-Pep (10/90). 615-Veronica's Summer Special. 616-Archie and Me. 617-Archie's Christmas Stocking. 618-Betty & Veronica Christmas Spectacular. 619-Little Archie. 620-Betty and Veronica Spectacular. 621-Betty and Veronica Summer Fun. 622-Josie & the Pussycats; not published. 623-Betty and Veronica Spectacular. 624-Pep Comics. 625-Veronica's Summer Special. 626-Archie and Me. 627-World of Archie. 628-Archie's Pals 'n' Gals Holiday Special. 629-Betty & Veronica Christmas Spectacular.
each.... 4.00
603-Archie and Me; Titanic app. 5.00
610-Josie and the Pussycats 1 2 3 4 5 7
630-631: 630-Archie's Christmas Stocking. 631-Archie's Pals 'n' Gals 4.00
632-Last issue; Betty & Veronica Spectacular 5.00
NOTE: *Archies Band-c-173,180,192; s-189,192. Archie Cavemen-165,225,232,244,249. Little Sabrina-527,534, 538,545,556,566. UFO-s-178,487,594.*

ARCHIE MEETS THE PUNISHER (Same contents as The Punisher Meets Archie)
Marvel Comics & Archie Comics Publ.: Aug, 1994 ($2.95, 52 pgs., one-shot)
1-Batton Lash story, J. Buscema-a on Punisher, S. Goldberg-a on Archie 6.00

ARCHIE'S ACTIVITY COMICS DIGEST MAGAZINE
Archie Enterprises: 1985 - No. 4 (Annual, 128 pgs., digest size)
1 2 4 6 9 11 14
2-4 1 2 3 5 6 8

ARCHIE'S CAR
Spire Christian Comics (Fleming H. Revell co.): 1979 (49¢)
nn 1 3 4 6 8 10

ARCHIE'S CHRISTMAS LOVE-IN (See Archie Giant Series Mag. No. 169, 181,192, 205, 218, 230, 242, 454, 466, 478, 490, 502, 514)

ARCHIE'S CHRISTMAS STOCKING (See Archie Giant Series Mag. No. 1-6,10, 15, 20, 25, 31, 137, 144, 150, 158, 167, 179, 190, 203, 216, 228, 240, 452, 464, 476, 488, 500, 512, 524, 535, 546, 557, 567, 579, 592, 605, 617, 630)

ARCHIE'S CHRISTMAS STOCKING
Archie Comics: 1993 - Present ($2.00, 52 pgs.)(Bound-in calendar poster in all)
1-Dan DeCarlo-c/a 5.00
2-5 4.00
6,7: 6-(1998, $2.25). 7-(1999, $2.29) 3.00

ARCHIE'S CLASSIC CHRISTMAS STORIES
Archie Comics: 2002 ($10.95, TPB)
Volume 1 - Reprints stories from 1955-1964 Archie's Christmas Stocking issues 11.00

ARCHIE'S CLEAN SLATE
Spire Christian Comics (Fleming H. Revell Co.): 1973 (35/49¢)
1-(35¢-c edition)(Some issues have nn) 2 4 6 9 11 14
1-(49¢-c edition) 2 4 6 8 10 12

ARCHIE'S DATE BOOK
Spire Christian comics (Fleming H. Revell Co.): 1981
nn 2 4 6 8 10 12

ARCHIE'S DOUBLE DIGEST QUARTERLY MAGAZINE
Archie Comics: 1981 - Present ($1.95/$2.75/$2.95/$3.19, 256 pgs.) (Archie's Double Digest Magazine No. 10 on)
1 3 6 9 18 23 28
2-10; 6-Katy Keene story. 2 4 6 10 13 16
11-30: 29-Pureheart story 2 4 6 8 10 12
31-50 1 2 3 4 5 7
51-70,100 5.00
71-99 4.00
101-148: 115-Begin $3.19-c. 123-Begin $3.29-c. 139-Begin $3.59-c 3.60

ARCHIE'S FAMILY ALBUM
Spire Christian Comics (Fleming H. Revell Co.): 1978 (39¢, 36 pgs.)
nn 1 3 4 6 8 10

ARCHIE'S FESTIVAL

Archie's Girls, Betty and Veronica Annual #3 © AP

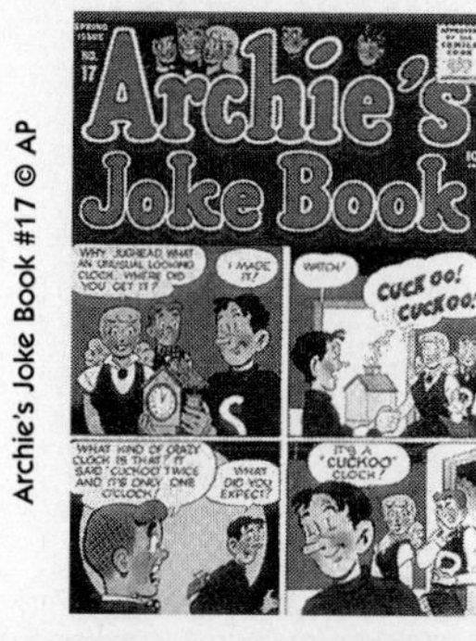

Archie's Joke Book #17 © AP

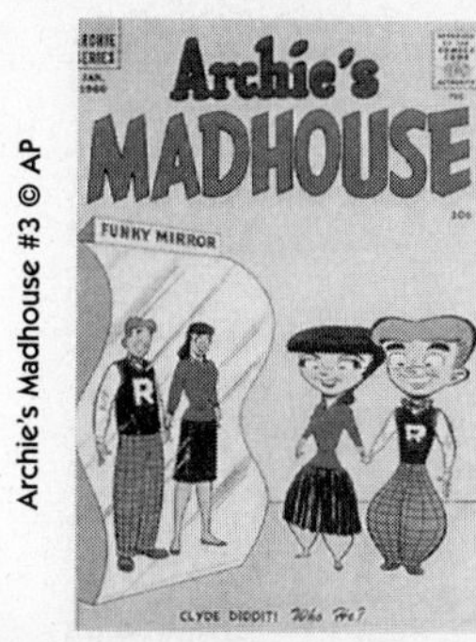

Archie's Madhouse #3 © AP

	GD 2.0	VG 4.0	FN 6.0	VF 8.0	VF/NM 9.0	NM- 9.2
Spire Christian Comics (Fleming H. Revell Co.): 1980 (49¢)						
nn	1	3	4	6	8	10

ARCHIE'S GIRLS, BETTY AND VERONICA (Becomes Betty & Veronica)(Also see Veronica)
Archie Publications (Close-Up): 1950 - No. 347, Apr, 1987

	GD 2.0	VG 4.0	FN 6.0	VF 8.0	VF/NM 9.0	NM- 9.2
1	176	352	528	1100	1650	2200
2	76	152	228	475	713	950
3-5: 3-Betty's 1st ponytail. 4-Dan DeCarlo's 1st Archie work	46	92	138	276	413	550
6-10: 10-Katy Keene app. (2 pgs.)	40	80	120	240	340	440
11-20: 11,13,14,17-19-Katy Keene app. 17-Last pre-code issue (3/55). 20-Debbie's Diary (2 pgs.)	31	62	93	175	248	320
21-30: 27,30-Katy Keene app. 29-Tarzan	22	44	66	127	176	225
31-43,45-50: 41-Marilyn Monroe and Brigitte Bardot mentioned. 45-Fabian 1 pg. photo & bio. 46-Bobby Darin 1 pg. photo & bio	15	30	45	86	118	150
44-Elvis Presley 1 pg. photo & bio	17	34	51	98	134	170
51-55,57-74: 67-Jackie Kennedy homage. 73-Sci-fi-c	8	16	24	53	74	95
56-Elvis and Bobby Darin records parody	9	18	27	63	89	115
75-Betty & Veronica sell souls to Devil	15	30	45	109	160	210
76-99: 82-Bobby Rydell 1 pg. illustrated bio; Elvis mentioned on-c. 84-Connie Francis 1 pg. illustrated bio	6	12	18	38	52	65
100	6	12	18	43	59	75
101-104, 106-117,120 (12/65): 113-Monsters-s	4	8	12	27	36	45
105-Beatles wig parody (5 pg. story)(9/64)	4	8	12	29	40	50
118-(10/65) 1st app./origin Superteen (also see Betty & Me #3)	6	12	18	40	55	70
119-2nd app./last Superteen story	4	8	12	29	40	50
121,122,124-126,128-140 (8/67): 135,140-Mod-c. 136-Slave Girl-s	3	6	9	18	23	28
123-"Jingo"-Ringo parody-c	3	6	9	19	25	32
127-Beatles Fan Club-s	4	8	12	27	36	45
141-156,158-163,165-180 (12/70)	2	4	6	12	16	20
157,164-Archies Band	3	6	9	18	23	28
181-193,195-199	2	4	6	9	11	14
194-Sabrina-c/s	3	6	9	18	23	28
200-(8/72)	2	4	6	10	13	16
201-205,207,209,211-215,217-240	1	3	4	6	8	10
206,208,216-Sabrina c/app. 206-Josie-c. 210-Sabrina app.	2	4	6	12	16	20
241 (1/76)-270 (6/78)	1	2	3	5	7	9
271-299: 281-UFO-s	1	2	3	5	6	8
300 (12/80)-Anniversary issue	1	2	3	5	7	9
301-309						6.00
310-John Travolta parody story	1	2	3	5	6	8
311-319						6.00
320 (10/82)-Intro. of Cheryl Blossom on cover and inside story (she also appears, but not on the cover, in Jughead #325 with same 10/82 publication date)	4	8	12	27	36	45
321,322-Cheryl Blossom app.	2	4	6	12	16	20
323,326,327,330,331,333-347: 333-Monsters-s						5.00
324,325-Crickett O'Dell app.						7.00
328-Cheryl Blossom app.	2	4	6	9	11	14
329,332: 329-Betty dressed as Madonna. 332-Superhero costume party	1	2	3	5	6	8
Annual 1 (1953)	86	172	258	538	807	1075
Annual 2 (1954)	40	80	120	240	358	475
Annual 3-5 (1955-1957)	36	72	108	204	290	375
Annual 6-8 (1958-1960)	24	48	72	138	194	250

ARCHIE'S HOLIDAY FUN DIGEST
Archie Comics: 1997 - Present ($1.75/$1.95/$1.99/$2.19/$2.39, annual)

	GD 2.0	VG 4.0	FN 6.0	VF 8.0	VF/NM 9.0	NM- 9.2
1-8-Christmas stories						2.50

ARCHIE'S JOKEBOOK COMICS DIGEST ANNUAL (See Jokebook...)

ARCHIE'S JOKE BOOK MAGAZINE (See Joke Book ...)
Archie Publ: 1953 - No. 3, Sum, 1954; No. 15, Fall, 1954 - No. 288, 11/82 (subtitled...Laugh-In #127-140; ...Laugh-Out #141-194)

	GD 2.0	VG 4.0	FN 6.0	VF 8.0	VF/NM 9.0	NM- 9.2
1953-One Shot (#1)	88	176	264	550	825	1100
2	46	92	138	276	413	550
3 (no #4-14)	39	78	117	233	329	425
15-20: 15-Formerly Archie's Rival Reggie #14; last pre-code issue (Fall/54). 15-17-Katy Keene app.	24	48	72	138	194	250
21-30	15	30	45	84	115	145
31-40,42,43: 42-Bio of Ed "Kookie" Byrnes. 43-story about guitarist Duane Eddy	10	20	30	58	77	95
41-1st professional comic work by Neal Adams (9/59), 1 pg.	24	48	72	138	194	250
44-47-N. Adams-a in all, 1-3 pgs.	14	28	42	79	107	135
48-Four pgs. N. Adams-a	15	30	45	84	115	145
49,50	5	10	15	36	48	60
51-56,58-60 (1962)	4	8	12	27	36	45
57-Elvis mentioned; Marilyn Monroe cameo	5	10	15	33	44	55
61-80 (8/64): 66-(12¢ cover)	3	6	9	18	23	28
66-(15¢ cover variant)	3	6	9	19	25	32
81-89,91,92,94-99	2	4	6	12	16	20
90,93: 90-Beatles gag. 93-Beatles cameo	3	6	9	18	23	28
100 (5/66)	3	6	9	16	20	24
101,103-117,119-123,127,129,131-140 (9/69): 105-Superhero gag-c. 108-110-Archies Archers Band-s. 116-Beatles/Monkees/Bob Dylan cameos (posters)	2	4	6	10	13	16
102 (7/66) Archie Band prototype-c; Elvis parody panel, Rolling Stones mention	3	6	9	18	24	30
118,124,125,126,128,130: 118-Archie Band-c; Veronica & Groovers band-s. 124-Archies Band-c/app. 125-Beatles cameo (poster). 126,130-Monkees cameo. 128-Veronica/Archies Band app.	3	6	9	16	20	25
141-173,175-181,183-199	2	4	6	8	10	12
174-Sabrina-c. 182-Sabrina cameo	2	4	6	10	12	15
200 (9/74)	2	4	6	10	12	15
201-230 (3/77)	1	2	3	5	6	8
231-239,241-287						6.00
240-Elvis record-c	1	2	3	5	6	8
288-Last issue	1	2	3	4	5	7

NOTE: *Archies Band-c-118,124,147,172; 1 pg.-s-127,128,138,140,143,147,167; 2 pg.-s-124,131, 155. Sabrina app.-247,248,252-259,261,262,264,266-270,274,277,284-286.*

ARCHIE'S JOKES (See Archie Giant Series Mag. No. 17, 22, 27, 33, 139, 146, 154, 163, 174, 186, 198, 211, 222, 235, 247, 459, 471, 483, 495, 519)

ARCHIE'S LOVE SCENE
Spire Christian Comics (Fleming H. Revell Co.): 1973 (35¢/49¢/no price)

	GD 2.0	VG 4.0	FN 6.0	VF 8.0	VF/NM 9.0	NM- 9.2
1-(35¢ Edition)	2	4	6	10	12	15
1-(49¢ Edition/no price) (Some copies have nn)	2	4	6	8	10	12

ARCHIE'S LOVE SHOWDOWN SPECIAL
Archie Publications: 1994 ($2.00, one-shot)

	GD 2.0	VG 4.0	FN 6.0	VF 8.0	VF/NM 9.0	NM- 9.2
1-Concludes x-over from Archie #429, Betty #19, B&V #82, Veronica #39						3.00

ARCHIE'S MADHOUSE (Madhouse Ma-ad No. 67 on)
Archie Publications: Sept, 1959 - No. 66, Feb, 1969

	GD 2.0	VG 4.0	FN 6.0	VF 8.0	VF/NM 9.0	NM- 9.2
1-Archie begins	24	48	72	169	247	325
2	12	24	36	84	125	165
3-5	9	18	27	60	85	110
6-10	6	12	18	43	59	75
11-17 (Last w/regular characters)	5	10	15	36	48	60
18-21,23,29: 18-New format begins. 23-No Sabrina	4	8	12	27	36	45
22-1st app. Sabrina, the Teen-age Witch (10/62)	24	48	72	169	247	325
24-2nd app.Sabrina a	9	18	27	60	85	110
25,26,28-Sabrina app. 25-1st app. Captain Sprocket (4/63)	7	14	21	46	63	80
27-Sabrina-c; no story	6	12	18	38	52	65
30,34,38-40: No Sabrina. 34-Bordered-c begin.	3	6	9	18	23	28
31,32-Sabrina app.?	3	6	9	18	23	28
33,37-Sabrina app.	5	10	15	36	48	60
35-Beatles cameo. No Sabrina	3	6	9	19	25	32
36-1st Salem the Cat w/Sabrina story	7	14	21	50	68	85
41-48,51-57,60-62,64-66; No Sabrina 43-Mighty Crusaders cameo. 44-Swipes Mad #4 (Super-Duperman) in "Bird Monsters From Outer Space"	2	4	6	14	18	22
49,50,58,59,63-Sabrina stories	4	8	12	27	36	45
Annual 1 (1962-63) no Sabrina	8	16	24	53	74	95
Annual 2 (1964) no Sabrina	5	10	15	36	48	60
Annual 3 (1965)-Origin Sabrina the Teen-Age Witch	9	18	27	65	93	120
Annual 4,5('66-68)(Becomes Madhouse Ma-ad Annual #7 on); no Sabrina	3	6	9	18	24	30
Annual 6 (1969)-Sabrina the Teen-Age Witch-sty	6	12	18	38	52	65

NOTE: *Cover title to #61-65 is "Madhouse" and to #66 is "Madhouse Ma-ad Jokes".*

ARCHIE'S MECHANICS
Archie Publications: Sept, 1954 - No. 3, 1955

	GD 2.0	VG 4.0	FN 6.0	VF 8.0	VF/NM 9.0	NM- 9.2
1-(15¢; 52 pgs.)	78	156	234	488	732	975
2-(10¢)-Last pre-code issue	48	96	144	288	432	575
3-(10¢)	40	80	120	240	350	460

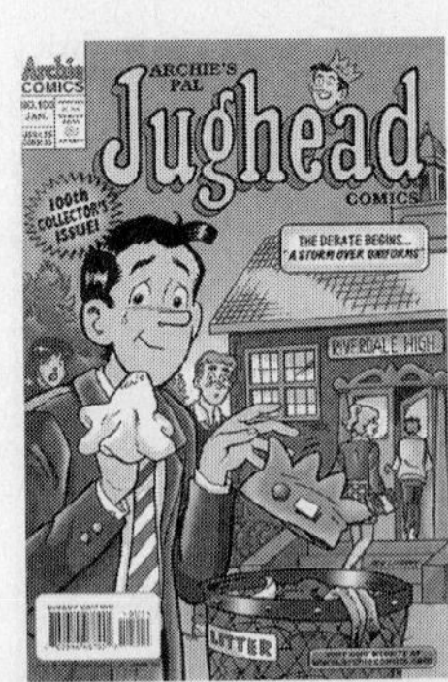

Archie's Pal Jughead #100 © AP

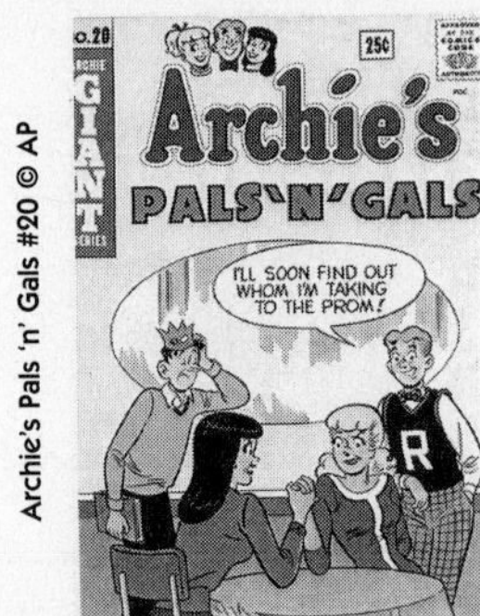

Archie's Pals 'n' Gals #20 © AP

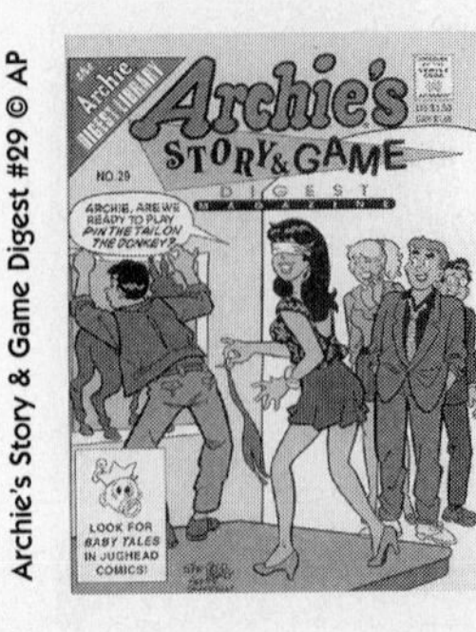

Archie's Story & Game Digest #29 © AP

ARCHIE'S MYSTERIES (Continued from Archie's Weird Mysteries)
Archie Comics: No. 25, Feb, 2003 - Present ($2.19)

	GD 2.0	VG 4.0	FN 6.0	VF 8.0	VF/NM 9.0	NM- 9.2
25-32- Archie and gang as "Teen Scene Investigators"						2.25

ARCHIE'S ONE WAY
Spire Christian Comics (Fleming H. Revell Co.): 1972 (35¢/39¢/49¢, 36 pgs.)

	GD 2.0	VG 4.0	FN 6.0	VF 8.0	VF/NM 9.0	NM- 9.2
nn-(35¢ Edition)	2	4	6	9	11	14
nn-(39¢, 49¢, no price editions)	2	4	6	8	10	12

ARCHIE'S PAL, JUGHEAD (Jughead No. 127 on)
Archie Publications: 1949 - No. 126, Nov, 1965

	GD 2.0	VG 4.0	FN 6.0	VF 8.0	VF/NM 9.0	NM- 9.2
1 (1949)-1st app. Moose (see Pep #33)	140	280	420	875	1313	1750
2 (1950)	66	132	198	413	617	820
3-5	40	80	120	240	358	475
6-10: 7-Suzie app.	31	62	93	175	248	320
11-20: 20-Jughead as Sherlock Holmes parody	19	38	57	109	152	195
21-30: 23-25,28-30-Katy Keene app. 23-Early Dilton-s. 28-Debbie's Diary app.	14	28	42	79	107	135
31-50: 49-Archies Rock 'N' Rollers band-c	7	14	21	50	68	85
51-70: 59- Bio of Will Hutchins of TV's Sugarfoot. 67-Betty seducing Jughead-c. 68-Early Archie Gang Cavemen-s	5	10	15	33	44	55
71-76,81-84,89-99: 72-Jughead dates Betty & Veronica.	3	6	9	19	25	32
77,78,80,85,86,88-Horror/Sci-Fi-c	4	8	12	27	36	45
79-Creature From the Black Lagoon-c	5	10	15	36	48	60
87-Early Big Ethel app.; UGAJ (United Girls Against Jughead)-s	4	8	12	27	36	45
100	4	8	12	24	32	40
101-Return of Big Ethyl	4	8	12	24	32	40
102-126	3	6	9	18	23	28
Annual 1 (1953, 25¢)	55	110	165	330	495	660
Annual 2 (1954, 25¢)-Last pre-code issue	39	78	117	230	325	420
Annual 3-5 (1955-57, 25¢)	28	56	84	159	225	290
Annual 6-8 (1958-60, 25¢)	18	36	54	104	142	180

ARCHIE'S PAL JUGHEAD COMICS (Formerly Jughead #1-45)
Archie Comic Publ.: No. 46, June, 1993 - Present ($1.25/$1.50/$1.75/$1.79/$1.99/$2.19)

	GD 2.0	VG 4.0	FN 6.0	VF 8.0	VF/NM 9.0	NM- 9.2
46-60						3.00
61-155: 100-"A Storm Over Uniforms" x-over part 1,2						2.25

ARCHIE'S PALS 'N' GALS (Also see Archie Giant Series Magazine #628)
Archie Publ: 1952-53 - No. 6, 1957-58; No. 7, 1958 - No. 224, Sept, 1991
(...All News Stories on-c #49-59)

	GD 2.0	VG 4.0	FN 6.0	VF 8.0	VF/NM 9.0	NM- 9.2
1-(116 pgs., 25¢)	74	148	222	463	694	925
2(Annual)('54, 25¢)	40	80	120	240	350	460
3-5(Annual, '55-57, 25¢): 3-Last pre-code issue	31	62	93	175	248	320
6-10('58-'60)	19	38	57	107	149	190
11-18,20 (84 pgs.): 12-Harry Belafonte 2 pg. photos & bio. 17-B&V paper dolls	10	20	30	60	80	100
19-Marilyn Monroe app.	14	28	42	81	111	140
21,22,24-28,30 (68 pgs.)	6	12	18	38	52	65
23-(Wint./62) 6 pg. Josie-s with Pepper and Melody (1st app.?); Betty in towel pin-up	10	20	30	73	107	140
29-Beatles satire (68 pgs.)	9	18	27	60	85	110
31(Wint. 64/65)-39 -(68 pgs.)	5	10	15	33	44	55
40-Early Superteen-s; with Pureheart	6	12	18	40	55	70
41(8/67)-43,45-50(2/69) (68 pgs.)	4	8	12	22	30	38
44-Archies Band-s; WEB cameo	4	8	12	29	40	50
51(4/69),52,55-64(6/71): 62-Last squarebound	3	6	9	18	24	30
53-Archies Band-c/s	4	8	12	22	30	38
54-Satan meets Veronica-s	4	8	12	29	40	50
65(8/70),67-70,73-81,83(6/74) (52 pgs.)	2	4	6	12	16	20
66,82-Sabrina-c	3	6	9	19	25	32
71,72-Two part drug story (8/72,9/72)	3	6	9	18	24	30
75-Archies Band-s	3	6	9	18	23	28
84-99	1	3	4	6	8	10
100 (12/75)	2	4	6	10	12	15
101-130(3/79): 125,126-Riverdale 2001-s	1	2	3	5	6	8
131-160,162-170 (7/84)						6.00
161 (11/82) 3rd app./1st solo Cheryl Blossom-s and pin-up; 2nd Jason Blossom	3	6	9	18	23	28
171-173,175,177-197,199: 197-G. Colan-a						4.00
174,176,198: 174-New Archies Band-s. 176-Cyndi Lauper-c. 198-Archie gang on strike at Archie Ent. offices						6.00
200(9/88)-Illiteracy-s						6.00
201,203-223: Later issues $1.00 cover						3.00
202-Explains end of Archie's jalopy; Dezerland-c/s; James Dean cameo						6.00
224-Last issue						5.00

NOTE: *Archies Band-c-45,47,49,53,56; s-44,53,75,174. UFO-s-50,63,209,220.*

ARCHIE'S PALS 'N' GALS DOUBLE DIGEST MAGAZINE
Archie Comic Publications: Nov, 1992 - Present ($2.50-$3.59)

	GD 2.0	VG 4.0	FN 6.0	VF 8.0	VF/NM 9.0	NM- 9.2
1-Capt. Hero story; Pureheart app.	1	3	4	6	8	10
2,3: 2-Superduck story; Little Jinx in all						6.00
4-29: 4-Begin $2.75-c.						4.00
30-81: 40-Begin $2.99-c. 48-Begin $3.19-c. 56-Begin $3.29-c. 72-Begin $3.59-c						3.60

ARCHIE'S PARABLES
Spire Christian Comics (Fleming H. Revell Co.): 1973,1975 (39/49¢, 36 pgs.)

	GD 2.0	VG 4.0	FN 6.0	VF 8.0	VF/NM 9.0	NM- 9.2
nn-By Al Hartley; 39¢ Edition	2	4	6	9	11	14
49¢, no price editions	2	4	6	8	10	12

ARCHIE'S R/C RACERS (Radio controlled cars)
Archie Comics: Sept, 1989 - No. 10, Mar, 1991 (95¢/$1)

	GD 2.0	VG 4.0	FN 6.0	VF 8.0	VF/NM 9.0	NM- 9.2
1						6.00
2,5-7,10: 5-Elvis parody. 7-Supervillain-c/s. 10-UFO-c/s						4.00
3,4,8,9						3.00

ARCHIE'S RIVAL REGGIE (Reggie & Archie's Joke Book #15 on)
Archie Publications: 1950 - No. 14, Aug, 1954

	GD 2.0	VG 4.0	FN 6.0	VF 8.0	VF/NM 9.0	NM- 9.2
1-Reggie 1st app. in Jackpot Comics #5	76	152	228	475	713	950
2	40	80	120	240	340	440
3-5	31	62	93	175	248	320
6-10	22	44	66	127	176	225
11-14: Katy Keene in No. 10-14, 1-2 pgs.	16	32	48	89	122	155

ARCHIE'S RIVERDALE HIGH (See Riverdale High)

ARCHIE'S ROLLER COASTER
Spire Christian Comics (Fleming H. Revell Co.): 1981 (69¢)

	GD 2.0	VG 4.0	FN 6.0	VF 8.0	VF/NM 9.0	NM- 9.2
nn	2	4	6	8	10	12

ARCHIE'S SOMETHING ELSE
Spire Christian Comics (Fleming H. Revell Co.): 1975 (39/49¢, 36 pgs.)

	GD 2.0	VG 4.0	FN 6.0	VF 8.0	VF/NM 9.0	NM- 9.2
nn-(39¢-c) Hell's Angels Biker on motorcycle-c	2	4	6	10	12	15
nn-(49¢-c)	1	3	4	6	8	10
Barbour Christian Comics Edition ('86, no price listed)	1	2	3	5	6	8

ARCHIE'S SONSHINE
Spire Christian Comics (Fleming H. Revell Co.): 1973, 1974 (39/49¢, 36 pgs.)

	GD 2.0	VG 4.0	FN 6.0	VF 8.0	VF/NM 9.0	NM- 9.2
39¢ Edition	2	4	6	9	11	14
49¢, no price editions	1	3	4	6	8	10

ARCHIE'S SPORTS SCENE
Spire Christian Comics (Fleming H. Revell Co.): 1983 (no cover price)

	GD 2.0	VG 4.0	FN 6.0	VF 8.0	VF/NM 9.0	NM- 9.2
nn	2	4	6	9	11	14

ARCHIE'S SPRING BREAK
Archie Comics: 1996 - Present ($2.00, 48 pgs., annual)

	GD 2.0	VG 4.0	FN 6.0	VF 8.0	VF/NM 9.0	NM- 9.2
1-Dan DeCarlo-c						3.00
2-4: 2-Dan DeCarlo-c						2.50

ARCHIE'S STORY & GAME COMICS DIGEST MAGAZINE
Archie Enterprises: Nov, 1986 - No. 42 ($1.25/$1.35/$1.50/$1.95, 128 pgs., digest-size)

	GD 2.0	VG 4.0	FN 6.0	VF 8.0	VF/NM 9.0	NM- 9.2
1: Marked-up copies are common	2	4	6	10	13	16
2-10	1	3	4	6	8	10
11-20						6.00
21-38						3.00
39-42-($1.95)						2.50

ARCHIE'S SUPER HERO SPECIAL (See Archie Giant Series Mag. No. 142)

ARCHIE'S SUPER HERO SPECIAL (...Comics Digest Mag. 2)
Archie Publications (Red Circle): Jan, 1979 - No. 2, Aug, 1979 (95¢, 148 pgs.)

	GD 2.0	VG 4.0	FN 6.0	VF 8.0	VF/NM 9.0	NM- 9.2
1-Simon & Kirby r-/Double Life of Pvt. Strong #1,2; Black Hood, The Fly, Jaguar, The Web app.	2	4	6	11	14	18
2-Contains contents to the never published Black Hood #1; origin Black Hood; N. Adams, Wood, McWilliams, Morrow, S&K-a(r); N. Adams-c. The Shield, The Fly, Jaguar, Hangman, Steel Sterling, The Web, The Fox-r	2	4	6	12	16	20

ARCHIE'S SUPER TEENS
Archie Comic Publications, Inc.: 1994 - No. 4, 1996 ($2.00, 52 pgs.)

	GD 2.0	VG 4.0	FN 6.0	VF 8.0	VF/NM 9.0	NM- 9.2
1-Staton/Esposito-c/a; pull-out poster						3.00
2-4: 2-Fred Hembeck script; Bret Blevins/Terry Austin-a						2.50

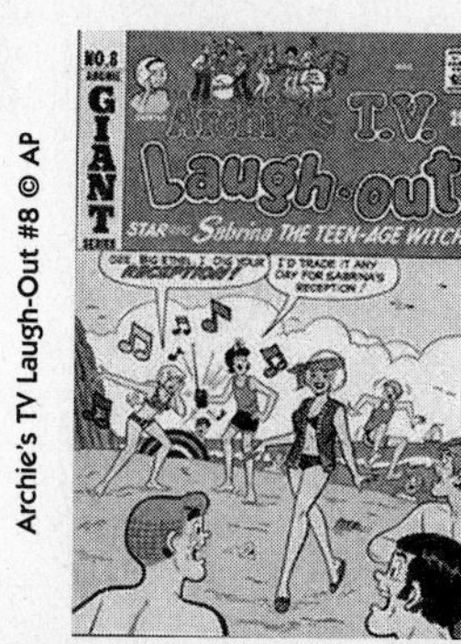

Archie's TV Laugh-Out #8 © AP

Aria: The Soul Market #2 © Haberlin & Holguin

Arkanium #1 © Dreamwave

	GD 2.0	VG 4.0	FN 6.0	VF 8.0	VF/NM 9.0	NM- 9.2
ARCHIE'S TV LAUGH-OUT ("...Starring Sabrina" on-c #1-50)						
Archie Publications: Dec, 1969 - No. 106, Apr, 1986 (#1-7: 68 pgs.)						
1-Sabrina begins, thru #106	10	20	30	70	100	130
2 (68 pgs.)	6	12	18	38	52	65
3-6 (68 pgs.)	4	8	12	27	36	45
7-Josie begins, thru #105; Archie's & Josie's Bands cover logos begin	7	14	21	50	68	85
8-23 (52 pgs.): 10-1st Josie on-c. 12-1st Josie and Pussycats on-c. 14-Beatles cameo on poster	4	8	12	24	32	40
24-40: 37,39,40-Bicenntennial-c	2	4	6	14	18	22
41,47,56: 41-Alexandra rejoins J&P band. 47-Fonz cameo; voodoo-s. 56-Fonz parody; B&V with Farrah hair-c	3	6	9	16	20	24
42-46,48-55,57-60	2	4	6	9	11	14
61-68,70-80: 63-UFO-s. 79-Mummy-s	1	3	4	6	8	10
69-Sherlock Holmes parody	1	3	4	6	8	10
81-90,94,95,97-99: 84 Voodoo-s	1	2	3	5	6	8
91-Early Cheryl Blossom-s; Sabrina/Archies Band-c	2	4	6	11	14	18
92-A-Team parody	1	2	3	5	7	9
93-(2/84) Archie in drag-s; Hill Street Blues-s; Groucho Marx parody; cameo parody app. of Batman, Spider-Man, Wonder Woman and others	2	4	6	8	10	12
96-MASH parody-s; Jughead in drag; Archies Band-c	1	2	3	5	7	9
100-(4/85) Michael Jackson parody-c/s; J&P band and Archie band on-c	2	4	6	10	12	15
101-104-Lower print run. 104-Miami Vice parody-c	1	2	3	5	7	9
105-Wrestling/Hulk Hogan parody-c; J&P band-s	2	4	6	8	10	12
106-Last issue; low print run	2	4	6	8	10	12

NOTE: ***Dan DeCarlo-a*** *78-up(most),* ***c****-89-up(most).* ***Archies Band-s*** *2,7,9-11,15,20,25,37,64,65,67,68,70,73, 76,78,79,83,84,86,90,96,100,101;* ***Archies Band-c*** *2,17,20,91,94,96,99-103.* ***Josie-s*** *12,21,26,35,52,78,80,90.* ***Josie-c*** *10,91,94.* ***Josie and the Pussycats (as a band in costume)-s*** *7,9,10,37,38,41,42,66,84,99-101,105.* ***Josie w/Pussycats member Valerie &/or Melody-s*** *17,20,22,25,27-29,31,33,36,39,40,43-51,53-65,67-77,79,81-83,85-89,92-94,102-104.* ***Josie w/Pussycats band-c*** *12,14,17,18,22,24.* ***Sabrina-s*** *1-9,11-86,88-106.* ***Sabrina-c*** *1-18,21,23,27,49,91,94.*

	GD 2.0	VG 4.0	FN 6.0	VF 8.0	VF/NM 9.0	NM- 9.2
ARCHIE'S VACATION SPECIAL						
Archie Publications: Winter, 1994 - Present ($2.00/$2.25/$2.29/$2.49, annual)						
1						4.00
2-8: 8-(2000, $2.49)						3.00
ARCHIE'S WEIRD MYSTERIES (Continues as Archie's Mysteries)						
Archie Comics: Feb, 2000 - No. 24, Dec, 2002 ($1.79/$1.99)						
1						3.50
2-10: 3-Mighty Crusaders app.						3.00
11-24: 14-Super Teens-c/app.; Mighty Crusaders app.						2.50
ARCHIE'S WORLD						
Spire Christian Comics (Fleming H. Revell Co.): 1973, 1976 (39/49¢)						
39¢ Edition	2	4	6	9	11	14
49¢ Edition, no price editions	1	3	4	6	8	10
ARCHIE 3000						
Archie Comics: May, 1989 - No. 16, July, 1991 (75¢/95¢/$1.00)						
1,16: 16-Aliens-c/s						4.00
2-15: 6-Begin $1.00-c; X-Mas-c						3.00
ARCOMICS PREMIERE						
Arcomics: July, 1993 ($2.95)						
1-1st lenticular-c on a comic (flicker-c)						3.00
AREA 52						
Image Comics: Jan, 2001 - No. 4, June, 2001 ($2.95)						
1-4-Haberlin-s/Henry-a						3.00
AREA 88						
Eclipse Comics/VIZ Comics #37 on: May 26, 1987 - No. 42, 1989 ($1.50/$1.75, B&W)						
1-42: 1,2-2nd printings exist						2.25
AREALA: ANGEL OF WAR (See Warrior Nun titles)						
Antarctic Press: Sept, 1998 - No. 4, June, 1999 ($2.95/$2.99, color/B&W)						
1-4: 3,4-B&W. 4-($2.99-c)						3.00
ARENA						
Alchemy Studios: Jan, 1990 ($1.50, 7x10-1/8", 20 pgs.)						
1-Science fiction						2.25
1-Signed & numbered ed. (500 copies)						3.00
ARGUS (See Flash, 2nd Series) (Also see Showcase '95 #1,2)						
DC Comics: Apr, 1995 - No. 6, Oct, 1995 ($1.50, limited series)						
1-6: 4-Begin $1.75-c						2.25

	GD 2.0	VG 4.0	FN 6.0	VF 8.0	VF/NM 9.0	NM- 9.2
ARIA						
Image Comics (Avalon Studios): Jan, 1999 - Present ($2.50)						
Preview (11/98, $2.95)						5.00
1-Anacleto-c/a	1	2	3	5	6	8
1-Variant-c by Michael Turner	1	2	3	5	6	8
1-($10.00) Alternate-c by Turner	1	3	4	6	8	10
1,2-(Blanc & Noir) Black and white printing of pencil art						3.00
1-(Blanc & Noir) DF Edition						5.00
2-4: 2,4-Anacleto-c/a. 3-Martinez-a						3.00
4-($6.95) Glow in the Dark-c	1	3	4	6	8	10
Aria Angela 1 (2/00, $2.95) Anacleto-a; 4 covers by Anacleto, JG Jones, Portacio and Quesada						3.00
Aria Angela Blanc & Noir 1 (4/00, $2.95) Anacleto-c						3.00
Aria Angela European Ashcan						10.00
Aria Angela 2 (10/00, $2.95) Anacleto-a/c						3.00
...: A Midwinter's Dream 1 (1/02, $4.95, 7"x7") text-s w/Anacleto panels						5.00
ARIA: SUMMER'S SPELL						
Image Comics (Avalon Studios): Mar, 2002 - No. 2, Jun, 2002 ($2.95)						
1,2-Anacleto-c/Holguin-s/Pajarillo & Medina-a						3.00
ARIA: THE SOUL MARKET						
Image Comics (Avalon Studios): Mar, 2001 - No. 6, Dec, 2001 ($2.95)						
1-6-Anacleto-c/Holguin-s						3.00
HC (2002, $26.95, 8.25" x 12.25") oversized r/#1-6						27.00
ARIA: THE USES OF ENCHANTMENT						
Image Comics (Avalon Studios): Feb, 2003 - No. 4, Sept, 2003 ($2.95)						
1-4-Anacleto-c/Holguin-s/Medina-a						3.00
ARIANE AND BLUEBEARD (See Night Music #8)						
ARIEL & SEBASTIAN (See Cartoon Tales & The Little Mermaid)						
ARION, LORD OF ATLANTIS (Also see Warlord #55)						
DC Comics: Nov, 1982 - No. 35, Sept, 1985						
1-Story cont'd from Warlord #62						3.00
2-35, Special #1 (11/85)						2.25
ARION THE IMMORTAL (Also see Showcase '95 #7)						
DC Comics: July, 1992 - No. 6, Dec, 1992 ($1.50, limited series)						
1						3.00
2-6: 4-Gustovich-a(i)						2.25
ARISTOCATS (See Movie Comics & Walt Disney Showcase No. 16)						
ARISTOKITTENS, THE (...Meet Jiminy Cricket No. 1)(Disney)						
Gold Key: Oct, 1971 - No. 9, Oct, 1975						
1	3	7	10	21	28	35
2-5,7-9	2	4	6	14	18	22
6-(52 pgs.)	3	6	9	16	20	24
ARIZONA KID, THE (Also see The Comics & Wild Western)						
Marvel/Atlas Comics(CSI): Mar, 1951 - No. 6, Jan, 1952						
1	24	48	72	138	194	250
2-4: 2-Heath-a(3)	12	24	36	71	96	120
5,6	10	20	30	58	77	95

NOTE: ***Heath*** *a-1-3; c-1-3.* ***Maneely*** *c-4-6.* ***Morisi*** *a-4-6.* ***Sinnott*** *a-6.*

	GD 2.0	VG 4.0	FN 6.0	VF 8.0	VF/NM 9.0	NM- 9.2
ARK, THE (See The Crusaders)						
ARKAGA						
Image Comics: Sept, 1997 ($2.95, one-shot)						
1-Jorgensen-s/a						3.00
ARKANIUM						
Dreamwave Productions: Sept, 2002 - Present ($2.95)						
1-5: 1-Gatefold wraparound-c						3.00
ARKHAM ASYLUM: LIVING HELL						
DC Comics: July, 2003 - No. 6, Dec, 2003 ($2.50, limited series)						
1-6-Ryan Sook-a; Batman app. 3-Batgirl-c/app.						2.50
ARMAGEDDON						
Chaos! Comics: Oct, 1999 - No. 4, Jan, 2000 ($2.95, limited series)						
Preview						5.00
1-4-Lady Death, Evil Ernie, Purgatori app.						3.00
ARMAGEDDON: ALIEN AGENDA						
DC Comics: Nov, 1991 - No. 4, Feb, 1992 ($1.00, limited series)						
1-4						2.25

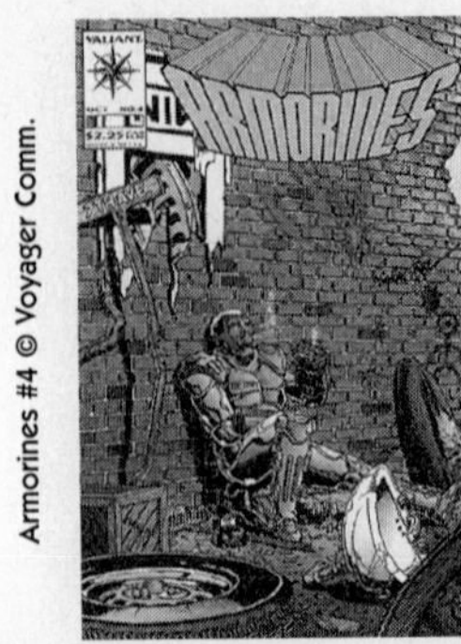

Armorines #4 © Voyager Comm.

Army of Darkness #1 © DH

Arrowsmith #1 © Busiek & Pacheco

GD VG FN VF VF/NM NM-
2.0 4.0 6.0 8.0 9.0 9.2

ARMAGEDDON FACTOR, THE
AC Comics: 1987 - No. 2, 1987; No. 3, 1990 ($1.95)
1,2: Sentinels of Justice, Dragonfly, Femforce 2.25
3-($3.95, color)-Almost all AC characters app. 4.00

ARMAGEDDON: INFERNO
DC Comics: Apr, 1992 - No. 4, July, 1992 ($1.00, limited series)
1-4: Many DC heroes app. 3-A. Adams/Austin-a 2.50

ARMAGEDDON 2001
DC Comics: May, 1991 - No. 2, Oct, 1991 ($2.00, squarebound, 68 pgs.)
1-Features many DC heroes; intro Waverider 4.00
1-2nd & 3rd printings; 3rd has silver ink-c 2.25
2 3.00

ARMATURE
Olyoptics: Nov, 1996 - No. 2, ($2.95, limited series)
1,2-Steve Oliff-c/s/a; Maxx app. 3.00

ARMED & DANGEROUS
Acclaim Comics (Armada): Apr, 1996 - No.4, July, 1996 ($2.95, B&W)
1-4-Bob Hall-c/a & scripts 3.00
Special 1 (8/96, $2.95, B&W)-Hall-c/a & scripts. 3.00

ARMED & DANGEROUS HELL'S SLAUGHTERHOUSE
Acclaim Comics (Armada): Oct, 1996 - No. 4, Jan, 1997 ($2.95, B&W)
1-4: Hall-c/a/scripts. 3.00

ARMOR (AND THE SILVER STREAK) (Revengers Featuring... in indicia for #1-3)
Continuity Comics: Sept, 1985 - No.13, Apr, 1992 ($2.00)
1-13: 1-Intro/origin Armor & the Silver Streak; Neal Adams-c/a. 7-Origin Armor; Nebres-i 3.50

ARMOR (DEATHWATCH 2000)
Continuity Comics: Apr, 1993 - No. 6, Nov, 1993 ($2.50)
1-6: 1-3-Deathwatch 2000 x-over 3.00

ARMORED TROOPER VOTOMS (Manga)
CPM Comics: July, 1996 ($2.95)
1 3.00

ARMORINES (See X-O Manowar #25 for 16 pg. bound-in Armorines #0)
Valiant: June, 1994 - No. 12, June, 1995 ($2.25)
0-Stand-alone edition with cardstock-c 25.00
0-Gold 10.00
1-12: 7-Wraparound-c. 12-Byrne-c/swipe (X-Men, 1st Series #138) 2.50

ARMORINES (Volume 2)
Acclaim Comics: Oct, 1999 - No. 4 ($3.95/$2.50, limited series)
1-($3.95) Calafiore & P. Palmiotti-a 4.00
2,3-($2.50) 2.50

ARMY AND NAVY COMICS (Supersnipe No. 6 on)
Street & Smith Publications: May, 1941 - No. 5, July, 1942
1-Cap Fury & Nick Carter 53 106 159 318 479 640
2-Cap Fury & Nick Carter 32 64 96 182 259 335
3,4: 4-Jack Farr-c/a 23 46 69 130 183 235
5-Supersnipe app.; see Shadow V2#3 for 1st app.; Story of Douglas MacArthur; George Marcoux-c/a 53 106 159 318 479 640

ARMY ATTACK
Charlton Comics: July, 1964 - No. 4, Feb, 1965; V2#38, July, 1965 - No. 47, Feb, 1967
V1#1 4 8 12 29 40 50
2-4(2/65) 3 6 9 18 24 30
V2#38(7/65)-47 (formerly U.S. Air Force #1-37) 3 6 9 16 20 24
NOTE: *Glanzman a-1-3. Montes/Bache a-44.*

ARMY AT WAR (Also see Our Army at War & Cancelled Comic Cavalcade)
DC Comics: Oct-Nov, 1978
1-Kubert-c; all new story and art 2 4 6 8 10 12

ARMY OF DARKNESS (Movie)
Dark Horse Comics: Nov, 1992 - No. 2, Dec, 1992; No. 3, Oct, 1993 ($2.50, limited series)
1-3-Bolton painted-c/a 5.00

ARMY SURPLUS KOMIKZ FEATURING CUTEY BUNNY
Army Surplus Komikz/Eclipse Comics: 1982 - No. 5, 1985 ($1.50, B&W)
1-Cutey Bunny begins 1 2 3 5 7 9
2-5: 5-(Eclipse)-JLA/X-Men/Batman parody 4.50

ARMY WAR HEROES (Also see Iron Corporal)
Charlton Comics: Dec, 1963 - No. 38, June, 1970
1 5 10 15 33 44 55
2-10 3 6 9 19 25 32
11-21,23-30: 24-Intro. Archer & Corp. Jack series 3 6 9 16 20 24
22-Origin/1st app. Iron Corporal series by Glanzman 4 8 12 24 32 40
31-38 2 4 6 10 13 16
Modern Comics Reprint 36 ('78) 4.00
NOTE: *Montes/Bache a-1, 16, 17, 21, 23-25, 27-30.*

AROUND THE BLOCK WITH DUNC & LOO (See Dunc and Loo)

AROUND THE WORLD IN 80 DAYS (Movie) (See A Golden Picture Classic)
Dell Publishing Co.: Feb, 1957
Four Color 784-Photo-c 7 14 21 51 71 90

AROUND THE WORLD UNDER THE SEA (See Movie Classics)

AROUND THE WORLD WITH ARCHIE (See Archie Giant Series Mag. #29, 35, 141)

AROUND THE WORLD WITH HUCKLEBERRY & HIS FRIENDS (See Dell Giant No. 44)

ARRGH! (Satire)
Marvel Comics Group: Dec, 1974 - No. 5, Sept, 1975 (25¢)
1-Dracula story; Sekowsky-a(p) 3 6 9 16 20 25
2-5: 2-Frankenstein. 3-Mummy. 4-Nightstalker(TV); Dracula-c/app., Hunchback. 5-Invisible Man, Dracula 2 4 6 10 13 16
NOTE *Alcala a-2; c-3. Everett a-1r, 2r. Grandenetti a-4. Maneely a-4r. Sutton a-1-3.*

ARROW (See Protectors)
Malibu Comics: Oct, 1992 ($1.95, one-shot)
1-Moder-a(p) 2.25

ARROW, THE (See Funny Pages)
Centaur Publications: Oct, 1940 - No. 2, Nov, 1940; No. 3, Oct, 1941
1-The Arrow begins(r/Funny Pages) 300 600 900 1925 2963 4000
2,3: 2-Tippy Taylor serial continues from Amazing Mystery Funnies #24. 3-Origin Dash Dartwell, the Human Meteor; origin The Rainbow-r; bondage-c 132 264 396 825 1238 1650
NOTE: *Gustavson a-1, 2; c-3.*

ARROWHEAD (See Black Rider and Wild Western)
Atlas Comics (CPS): April, 1954 - No. 4, Nov, 1954
1-Arrowhead & his horse Eagle begin 17 34 51 98 129 180
2-4: 4-Forte-a 10 20 30 56 71 90
NOTE: *Heath c-3. Jack Katz a-3. Maneely c-2. Pakula a-2. Sinnott a-1-4; c-1.*

ARROWSMITH
DC Comics (Cliffhanger): Sept, 2003 - Present ($2.95)
1-4-Pacheco-a/Busiek-s 3.00

ARSENAL (Teen Titans' Speedy)
DC Comics: Oct, 1998 - No. 4, Jan, 1999 ($2.50, limited series)
1-4: Grayson-s. 1-Black Canary app. 2-Green Arrow app. 2.50

ARSENAL SPECIAL (See New Titans, Showcase '94 #7 & Showcase '95 #8)
DC Comics: 1996 ($2.95, one-shot)
1 3.00

ARTBABE
Fantagraphics Books: May, 1996 - Apr, 1999 ($2.50/$2.95/$3.50, B&W)
V1 #5, V2 #1-3 3.00
#4-($3.50) 3.50

ARTEMIS: REQUIEM (Also see Wonder Woman, 2nd Series #90)
DC Comics: June, 1996 - No. 6, Nov, 1996 ($1.75, limited series)
1-6: Messner-Loebs scripts & Benes-c/a in all. 1,2-Wonder Woman app. 3.00

ARTESIA
Sirius Entertainment: Jan, 1999 - No. 6, June, 1999 ($2.95, limited series)
1-6-Mark Smylie-s/a 3.00
Annual 1 (1999, $3.50) 3.50
Annual 2 (2001, $3.95) Crilley back-c 4.00

ARTESIA AFIELD
Sirius Entertainment: Jul, 2000 - No. 6, Feb, 2001 ($2.95, limited series)
1-6-Mark Smylie-s/a 3.00

ARTESIA AFIRE
Archaia Studios Press: June, 2003 - No. 6 ($3.95, limited series)
1-5-Mark Smylie-s/a 4.00

ART OF ZEN INTERGALACTIC NINJA, THE

Ascension #16 © TCOW

Aspen (Michael Turner's...) #1 © AspenMLT

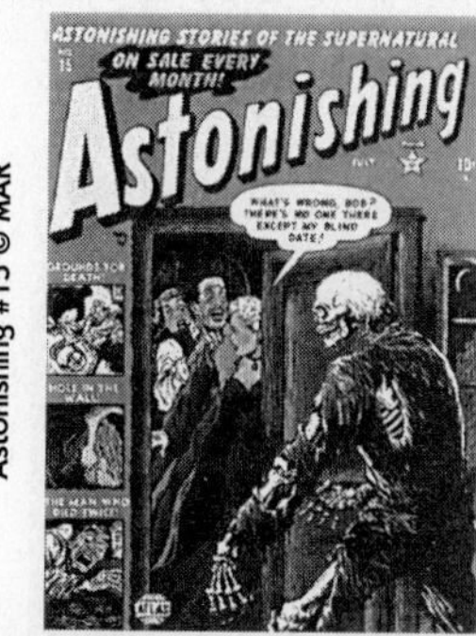

Astonishing #15 © MAR

GD 2.0 | VG 4.0 | FN 6.0 | VF 8.0 | VF/NM 9.0 | NM- 9.2

Entity Comics: 1994 - No. 2, 1994 ($2.95)
1,2 — 3.00

ARZACH (See Moebius...)
Dark Horse Comics: 1996 ($6.95, one-shot)
nn-Moebius-c/a/scripts 1 2 3 4 5 7

ASCENSION
Image Comics (Top Cow Productions): Oct, 1997 - No. 22, Mar, 2000 ($2.50)
Preview 5.00
Preview Gold Edition 8.00
Preview San Diego Edition 2 4 6 8 10 12
0 4.00
1/2 6.00
1-David Finch-s/a(p)/Batt-s/a(i) 4.00
1-Variant-c w/Image logo at lower right 6.00
2-6 3.00
7-22 2.50
Fan Club Edition 5.00

...COLLECTED EDITION
1998 - No. 2 ($4.95, squarebound) 1,2: 1-r/#1,2. 2-r/#3,4 5.00

ASH
Event Comics: Nov, 1994 - No. 6, Dec, 1995; No. 0, May, 1996 ($2.50/$3.00)
0-Present & Future (Both 5/96, $3.00, foil logo-c)-w/pin-ups 3.00
0-Blue Foil logo-c (Present and Future) (1000 each) 4.00
0-Silver Prism logo-c (Present and Future) (500 each) 10.00
0-Red Prism logo-c (Present and Future) (250 each) 20.00
0-Gold Hologram logo-c (Present and Future) (1000 each) 8.00
1-Quesada-p/story; Palmiotti-i/story: Barry Windsor-Smith pin-up 2 4 6 8 10 12
2-Mignola Hellboy pin-up 1 2 3 4 5 7
3,4: 3-Big Guy pin-up by Geoff Darrow. 4-Jim Lee pin-up 4.00
4-Fahrenheit Gold 7.00
4-6-Fahrenheit Red (5,6-1000) 8.00
4-6-Fahrenheit White 12.00
5, 6-Double-c w/Hildebrandt Bros.-a, Quesada & Palmiotti. 6-Texeira-c 3.00
5,6-Fahrenheit Gold (2000) 4.00
6-Fahrenheit White (500)-Texeira-c 12.00
Volume 1 (1996, $14.95, TPB)-r/#1-5, intro by James Robinson 15.00
Wizard Mini-Comic (1996, magazine supplement) 2.25
Wizard #1/2 (1997, mail order) 4.00

ASH: CINDER & SMOKE
Event Comics: May, 1997 - No. 6, Oct, 1997 ($2.95, limited series)
1-6: Ramos-a/Waid, Augustyn-s in all. 2-6-variant covers by Ramos and Quesada 3.00

ASH: FILES
Event Comics: Mar, 1997 ($2.95, one-shot)
1-Comics w/text 3.00

ASH: FIRE AND CROSSFIRE
Event Comics: Jan, 1999 - No. 5 ($2.95, limited series)
1,2-Robinson-s/Quesada & Palmiotti-c/a 3.00

ASH: FIRE WITHIN, THE
Event Comics: Sept, 1996 - No. 2, Jan, 1997 ($2.95, unfinished limited series)
1,2: Quesada & Palmiotti-c/s/a 3.00

ASH/ 22 BRIDES
Event Comics: Dec, 1996 - No. 2, Apr, 1997 ($2.95, limited series)
1,2: Nicieza-s/Ramos-c/a 3.00

ASKANI'SON (See Adventures of Cyclops & Phoenix limited series)
Marvel Comics: Jan, 1996 - No. 4, May, 1996 ($2.95, limited series)
1-4: Story cont'd from Advs. of Cyclops & Phoenix; Lobdell/Loeb story; Gene Ha-c/a(p) 3.00
TPB (1997, $12.99) r/#1-4; Gene Ha painted-c 13.00

ASPEN (MICHAEL TURNER PRESENTS:...) (Also see Fathom)
Aspen MLT, Inc.: July, 2003 - Present ($2.99)
1-Fathom story; Turner-a/Johns-s; interviews w/Turner & Johns; two covers by Turner 3.00
2,3:2-Fathom story; Turner-a/Johns-s; two covers by Turner; pin-ups and interviews 3.00

ASSASSINETTE
Pocket Change Comics: 1994 - No. 7, 1995? ($2.50, B&W)
1-7: 1-Silver foil-c 2.50

ASSASSINETTE HARDCORE
Pocket Change Comics: 1995 - No. 2, 1995 ($2.50, B&W, limited series)
1,2 2.50

ASSASSINS
DC Comics (Amalgam): Apr, 1996 ($1.95)
1 2.25

ASSASSINS, INC.
Silverline Comics: 1987 - No. 2, 1987 ($1.95)
1,2 2.25

ASTER
Entity Comics: Oct, 1994 - No. 4, 1995 ($2.95)
0-4: 1,3,4-Foil Logo. 2-Foil-c. 3-Variant-c exists. 3.00

ASTER: THE LAST CELESTIAL KNIGHT
Entity Comics: 1995 - No. 3, 1996 ($2.50)
1-3 2.50

ASTONISHING (Formerly Marvel Boy No. 1, 2)
Marvel/Atlas Comics(20CC): No. 3, Apr, 1951 - No. 63, Aug, 1957
3-Marvel Boy continues; 3-5-Marvel Boy-c 92 184 276 575 863 1150
4-6-Last Marvel Boy; 4-Stan Lee app. 64 128 192 400 600 800
7-10: 7-Maneely s/f story. 10-Sinnott s/f story 33 66 99 190 270 350
11,12,15,17,20 30 60 90 173 244 315
13,14,16,18,19-Krigstein-a. 18-Jack The Ripper sty 31 62 93 175 248 320
21,22,24 26 52 78 147 206 265
23-E.C. swipe "The Hole In The Wall" from Vault Of Horror #16 26 52 78 150 210 270
25,29: 25-Crandall-a. 29-Decapitation-c 24 48 72 138 194 250
26-28 22 44 66 124 172 220
30-Tentacled eyeball-c/story; classic-c 32 64 96 184 262 340
31-37-Last pre-code issue 19 38 57 109 152 195
38-43,46,48-52,56,58,59,61 15 30 45 84 115 145
44,45,47,53-55,57,60: 44-Crandall swipe/Weird Fantasy #22. 45,47-Krigstein-a. 53-Ditko-a. 54-Torres-a, 55-Crandall, Torres-a. 57-Williamson/Krenkel-a (4 pgs.). 60-Williamson/Mayo-a (4 pgs.) 16 32 48 92 126 160
62,63: 62-Torres, Powell-a. 63-Woodbridge-a 16 32 48 89 122 155

NOTE: ***Ayers** a-16. **Berg** a-36, 53, 56. **Cameron** a-50. **Gene Colan** a-12, 20, 29, 56. **Ditko** a-53. **Drucker** a-41, 62. **Everett** a-3-6(3), 6, 10, 12, 37, 47, 48, 58; c-3-5, 13,15, 16, 18, 29, 47, 49, 51, 53-55, 57, 59-63. **Fass** a-11, 34. **Forte** a-53, 58, 60. **Fuje** a-11. **Heath** a-8, 29; c-8, 9, 19, 22, 25, 26. **Kirby** a-56. **Lawrence** a-28, 37, 38, 42. **Maneely** a-7(2); c-7, 31, 33, 34, 56. **Moldoff** a-33. **Morisi** a-10, 60. **Morrow** a-52, 61. **Orlando** a-47, 58, 61. **Pakula** a-10. **Powell** a-43, 44, 48. **Ravielli** a-28. **Reinman** a-32, 34, 38. **Robinson** a-20. **J. Romita** a-7, 18, 24, 43, 57,61. **Roussos** a-55. **Sale** a-28, 38, 59; c-32. **Sekowsky** a-13. **Severin** c-46. **Shores** a-16, 60. **Sinnott** a-11, 30. **Whitney** a-13. **Ed Win** a-20. Canadian reprints exist.*

ASTONISHING TALES (See Ka-Zar)
Marvel Comics Group: Aug, 1970 - No. 36, July, 1976 (#1-7: 15¢; #8: 25¢)
1-Ka-Zar (by Kirby(p) #1,2; by B. Smith #3-6) & Dr. Doom (by Wood #1-4; by Tuska #5,6; by Colan #7,8; 1st Marvel villain solo series) double feature begins; Kraven the Hunter-c/story; Nixon cameo 6 12 18 38 52 65
2-Kraven the Hunter-c/story; Kirby, Wood-a 3 6 9 19 25 32
3-6: B. Smith-p; Wood-a-#3,4. 5,6-Red Skull 2-part story 4 8 12 24 32 40
7-Last 15¢ issue; Black Panther app. 2 4 6 14 18 22
8-(25¢, 52 pgs.)-Last Dr. Doom of series 3 7 10 21 28 35
9-All Ka-Zar issues begin; Lorna-r/Lorna #14 2 4 6 11 14 18
10-B. Smith/Sal Buscema-a. 3 6 9 16 20 24
11-Origin Ka-Zar & Zabu; death of Ka-Zar's father 2 4 6 12 16 20
12-2nd app.Man-Thing; by Neal Adams (see Savage Tales #1 for 1st app.) 4 8 12 22 30 38
13-3rd app.Man-Thing 3 6 9 18 23 28
14-20: 14-Jann of the Jungle-r (1950s); reprints censored Ka-Zar-s from Savage Tales #1. 17-S.H.I.E.L.D. begins. 19-Starlin-a(p). 20-Last Ka-Zar (continues into 1974 Ka-Zar series) 1 3 4 6 8 10
21-(12/73)-It! the Living Colossus begins, ends #24 (see Supernatural Thrillers #1) 3 6 9 18 24 30
22-24: 23,24-IT vs. Fin Fang Foom 2 4 6 12 16 20
25-1st app. Deathlok the Demolisher; full length stories begin, end #36; Perez's 1st work, 2 pgs. (8/74) 4 8 12 29 40 50
26-28,30 2 4 6 10 12 15
29-r/origin/1st app. Guardians of the Galaxy from Marvel Super-Heroes #18 plus-c w/4 pgs. omitted; no Deathlok story 1 2 3 5 7 9
31-34: 31-Watcher-r/Silver Surfer #3 2 4 6 8 10 12
35,36-(Regular 25¢ edition)(5,7/76) 2 4 6 8 10 12
35,36-(30¢-c, low distribution) 2 4 6 14 18 22

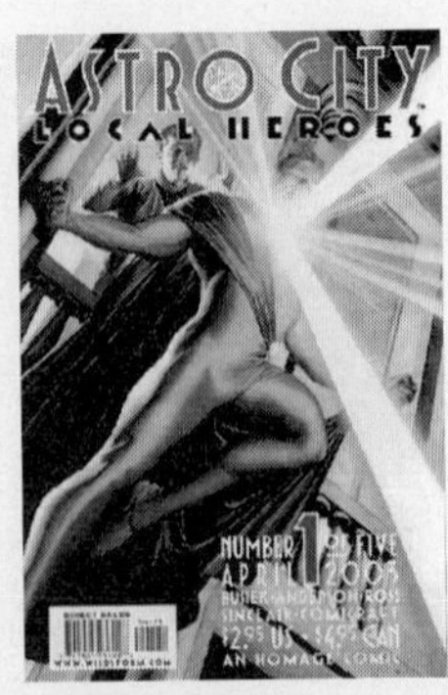

Astro City: Local Heroes #1 © Jukebox Prod.

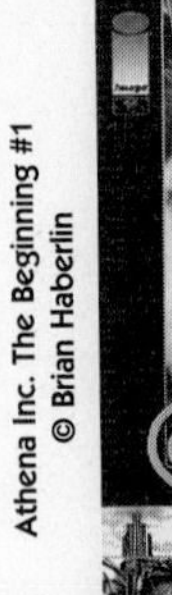

Athena Inc. The Beginning #1 © Brian Haberlin

The Atom #19 © DC

GD 2.0 | VG 4.0 | FN 6.0 | VF 8.0 | VF/NM 9.0 | NM- 9.2

NOTE: **Buckler** a-13i, 16p, 25, 26p, 27p, 28, 29p-36p; c-13, 25p, 26-30, 32-35p, 36. **John Buscema** a-9, 12p-14p, 16p; c-4-6p, 12p. **Colan** a-7p, 8p. **Ditko** a-21r. **Everett** a-6i. **G. Kane** a-11p, 15p; c-9, 10p, 11p, 14, 15p, 21p. **McWilliams** a-30i. **Starlin** a-19p; c-16p. **Sutton & Trimpe** a-8. **Tuska** a-5p, 6p, 8p. **Wood** a-1-4. **Wrightson** c-31i.

ASTONISHING X-MEN
Marvel Comics: Mar, 1995 - No.4, July, 1995 ($1.95, limited series)
1-Age of Apocalypse; Magneto-c 4.00
2-4 3.00

ASTONISHING X-MEN
Marvel Comics: Sept, 1999 - No.3, Nov, 1999 ($2.50, limited series)
1-3-New team, Cable & X-Man app.; Peterson-a 2.50
TPB (11/00, $15.95) r/#1-3, X-Men #92 & #95, Uncanny X-Men #375 16.00

ASTOUNDING SPACE THRILLS: THE COMIC BOOK
Image Comics: Apr, 2000 - No. 4, Dec, 2000 ($2.95, limited series)
1-4-Steve Conley-s/a. 2,3-Flip book w/Crater Kid 3.00
Galaxy-Sized Astounding Space Thrills 1 (10/01, $4.95) 5.00

ASTRA
CPM Manga: 2001 - No. 8 ($2.95, B&W, limited series)
1-4: Created by Jerry Robinson; Tanaka-a. 1-Balent variant-c 3.00
TPB (2002, $15.95) r/#1-8; JH Williams III-c from #3 16.00

ASTRO BOY (TV) (See March of Comics #285 & The Original...)
Gold Key: August, 1965 (12¢)
1(10151-508)-Scarce;1st app. Astro Boy in comics 44 88 132 324 487 650

ASTRO CITY: LOCAL HEROES (Also see Kurt Busiek's Astro City)
DC Comics (WildStorm Productions): Apr, 2003 - No. 5, Feb, 2004 ($2.95, limited series)
1-5-Busiek-s/Anderson-a/Ross-c 3.00

ASYLUM
Millennium Publications: 1993 ($2.50)
1-3: 1-Bolton-c/a; Russell 2-pg. illos 2.50

ASYLUM
Maximum Press: Dec, 1995 - No. 11, Jan, 1997 ($2.95/$2.99, anthology)
(#1-6 are flip books)
1-11: 1-Warchild by Art Adams, Beanworld, Avengelyne, Battlestar Galactica. 2-Intro Mike Deodato's Deathkiss; Cybrid story begins, ends #5. 4-1st app.Christian; painted Battlestar Galactica story begins. 5-Intro Black Seed (formerly Black Flag) by Dan Fraga; B&W Christian story. 6-Intro Bionix (Six Million Dollar Man & the Bionic Woman). 7-Begin $2.99-c; Don Simpson's Megaton Man; Black Seed pinup. 8-B&W-a. 9- Foot Soldiers & Kid Supreme 10-Lady Supreme by Terry Moore-c/app. 4.00

ATARI FORCE (Also see Promotional comics section)
DC Comics: Jan, 1984 - No. 20, Aug, 1985 (Mando paper)
1-(1/84)-Intro Tempest, Packrat, Babe, Morphea, & Dart 4.00
2-20 3.00
Special 1 (4/86) 3.00
NOTE: **Byrne** c-Special 1i. **Giffen** a-12p, 13i. **Rogers** a-18p, Special 1p.

A-TEAM, THE (TV) (Also see Marvel Graphic Novel)
Marvel Comics Group: Mar, 1984 - No. 3, May, 1984 (limited series)
1-3 5.00
1,2-(Whitman bagged set) w/75¢-c 1 3 4 6 8 10
3-(Whitman, no bag) w/75¢-c 1 2 3 5 6 8

ATHENA INC. THE MANHUNTER PROJECT
Image Comics: Dec, 2001; Apr, 2002 - Present ($2.95/$4.95/$5.95)
...The Beginning (12/01, $5.95) Anacleto-c/a; Haberlin-s 6.00
1-5: 1-(4/02, $2.95) two covers by Anacleto 3.00
6-($4.95) 5.00
...: Agents Roster #1 (11/02, $5.95, 8 1/2 x 11") bios and sketch pages by Anacleto 6.00
Vol. 1 TPB (4/03, $19.95) r/#1-6 & Agents Roster; cover gallery 20.00

ATLANTIS CHRONICLES, THE (Also see Aquaman, 3rd Series & Aquaman: Time & Tide)
DC Comics: Mar, 1990 - No. 7, Sept, 1990 ($2.95, limited series, 52 pgs.)
1-7: 1-Peter David scripts. 7-True origin of Aquaman; nudity panels 3.25

ATLANTIS, THE LOST CONTINENT
Dell Publishing Co.: May, 1961
Four Color #1188-Movie, photo-c 12 24 36 82 121 150

ATLAS (See 1st Issue Special)

ATLAS
Dark Horse Comics: Feb, 1994 - No. 4, 1994 ($2.50, limited series)
1-4 2.50

GD 2.0 | VG 4.0 | FN 6.0 | VF 8.0 | VF/NM 9.0 | NM- 9.2

ATMOSPHERICS
Avatar Press: June, 2002 ($5.95, B&W, one-shot graphic novel)
1-Warren Ellis-s/Ken Meyer Jr.-painted-a/c 6.00

ATOM, THE (See Action #425, All-American #19, Brave & the Bold, D.C. Special Series #1, Detective Comics, Flash Comics #80, Hawkman, JLA, Power Of The Atom, Showcase #34 -36, Super Friends, Sword of The Atom, Teen Titans & World's Finest)

ATOM, THE (...& the Hawkman No. 39 on)
National Periodical Publ.: June-July, 1962 - No. 38, Aug-Sept, 1968
1-(6-7/62)-Intro Plant-Master; 1st app. Maya 73 146 219 621 948 1275
2 31 62 93 231 346 460
3-1st Time Pool story; 1st app. Chronos (origin) 22 44 66 160 235 310
4,5: 4-Snapper Carr x-over 17 34 51 123 182 240
6,9,10 12 24 36 87 129 170
7-Hawkman x-over (6-7/63; 1st Atom & Hawkman team-up); 1st app. Hawkman since Brave & the Bold tryouts 30 60 90 218 319 420
8-Justice League, Dr. Light app. 13 26 39 94 137 180
11-15: 13-Chronos-c/story 9 18 27 63 89 115
16-20: 19-Zatanna x-over 7 14 21 51 71 90
21-28,30: 28-Chronos-c/story 6 12 18 43 59 75
29-1st solo Golden Age Atom x-over in S.A. 15 30 45 109 160 210
31-35,37,38: 31-Hawkman x-over. 37-Intro. Major Mynah; Hawkman cameo 6 12 18 38 52 65
36-G.A. Atom x-over 7 14 21 50 68 85
NOTE: **Anderson** a-1-11i, 13i; c-inks-1-25, 31-35, 37. **Sid Greene** a-8i-37i. **Gil Kane** a-1p-37p; c-1p-28p, 29, 33p, 34. **George Roussos** 38i **Mike Sekowsky** 38p Time Pool stories also in 6, 9,12, 17, 21, 27, 35.

ATOM, THE (See Tangent Comics/ The Atom)

ATOM AGE (See Classics Illustrated Special Issue)

ATOM-AGE COMBAT
St. John Publishing Co.: June, 1952 - No. 5, Apr, 1953; Feb, 1958
1-Buck Vinson in all 46 92 138 276 413 550
2-Flying saucer story 30 60 90 170 240 310
3,5: 3-Mayo-a (6 pgs.). 5-Flying saucer-c/story 25 50 75 147 202 260
4 (Scarce) 30 60 90 170 240 310
1(2/58-St. John) 21 42 63 118 164 210

ATOM-AGE COMBAT
Fago Magazines: No. 2, Jan, 1959 - No. 3, Mar, 1959
2-A-Bomb explosion-c; 27 54 81 155 218 280
3 21 42 63 118 164 210

ATOMAN
Spark Publications: Feb, 1946 - No. 2, April, 1946
1-Origin & 1st app. Atoman; Robinson/Meskin-a; Kidcrusaders, Wild Bill Hickok, Marvin the Great app. 66 132 198 413 619 825
2-Robinson/Meskin-a; Robinson c-1,2 43 86 129 258 389 520

ATOM & HAWKMAN, THE (Formerly The Atom)
National Periodical Publ: No. 39, Oct-Nov, 1968 - No. 45, Oct-Nov, 1969
39-43: 40-41-Kubert/Anderson-a. 43-(7/69)-Last 12¢ issue; 1st app. Gentleman Ghost 5 10 15 36 48 60
44,45: 44-(9/69)-1st 15¢-c; origin Gentleman Ghost 5 10 15 36 48 60
NOTE: **M. Anderson** a-39, 40i, 41i, 43, 44. **Sid Greene** a-40i-45i. **Kubert** a-40p, 41p; c-39-45.

ATOM ANT (TV) (See Golden Comics Digest #2) (Hanna-Barbera)
Gold Key: January, 1966 (12¢)
1(10170-601)-1st app. Atom Ant, Precious Pup, and Hillbilly Bears 31 62 93 231 346 460

ATOM ANT & SECRET SQUIRREL (See Hanna-Barbera Presents)

ATOMIC AGE
Marvel Comics (Epic Comics): Nov, 1990 - No. 4, Feb, 1991 ($4.50, limited series, squarebound, 52 pgs.)
1-4: Williamson-a(i); sci-fi story set in 1957 4.50

ATOMIC ATTACK (True War Stories; formerly Attack, first series)
Youthful Magazines: No. 5, Jan, 1953 - No. 8, Oct, 1953 (1st story is sci/fi in all issues)
5-Atomic bomb-c; science fiction stories in all 40 80 120 240 340 440
6-8 27 54 81 153 214 275

ATOMIC BOMB
Jay Burtis Publications: 1945 (36 pgs.)
1-Airmale & Stampy (scarce) 68 136 204 425 638 850

ATOMIC BUNNY (Formerly Atomic Rabbit)
Charlton Comics: No. 12, Aug, 1958 - No. 19, Dec, 1959

Atomic Rabbit #6 © CC

The Atomics #1 © Mike Allred

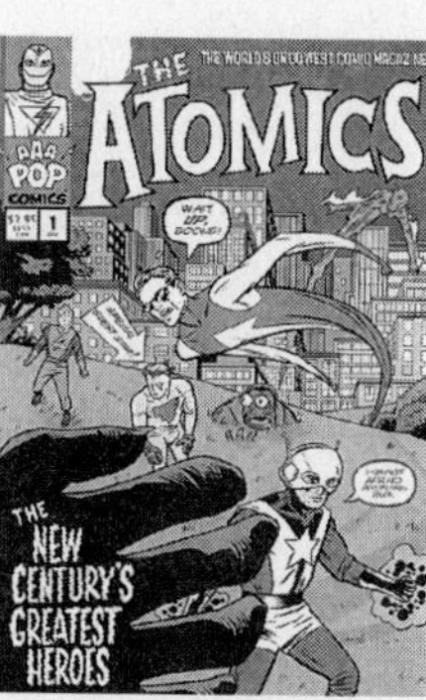

Authentic Police Cases #5 © STJ

	GD 2.0	VG 4.0	FN 6.0	VF 8.0	VF/NM 9.0	NM- 9.2
12	12	24	36	71	96	120
13-19	8	16	24	43	54	65
ATOMIC COMICS						
Daniels Publications (Canadian): Jan, 1946 (Reprints, one-shot)						
1-Rocketman, Yankee Boy, Master Key app.	39	78	117	230	325	420
ATOMIC COMICS						
Green Publishing Co.: Jan, 1946 - No. 4, July-Aug, 1946 (#1-4 were printed w/o cover gloss)						
1-Radio Squad by Siegel & Shuster; Barry O'Neal app.; Fang Gow cover-r/ Detective Comics (Classic-c)	130	260	390	813	1219	1625
2-Inspector Dayton; Kid Kane by Matt Baker; Lucky Wings, Congo King, Prop Powers (only app.) begin	61	122	183	381	571	760
3,4: 3-Zero Ghost Detective app.; Baker-a(2) each; 4-Baker-c	42	84	126	252	376	500
ATOMIC KNIGHTS (See Strange Adventures #117)						
ATOMIC MOUSE (TV, Movies) (See Blue Bird, Funny Animals, Giant Comics Edition & Wotalife Comics)						
Capitol Stories/Charlton Comics: 3/53 - No. 54, 6/63; No. 1, 12/84; V2#10, 19/85 - No. 12, 1/86						
1-Origin & 1st app.; Al Fago-c/a in all?	34	68	102	196	278	360
2	14	28	42	81	111	140
3-10: 5-Timmy The Timid Ghost app.; see Zoo Funnies	10	20	30	58	77	95
11-13,16-25	7	14	21	37	46	55
14,15-Hoppy The Marvel Bunny app.	9	18	27	49	62	75
26-(68 pgs.)	11	22	33	66	88	110
27-40: 36,37-Atom The Cat app.	6	12	18	28	34	40
41-54	5	10	14	20	24	28
1 (1984)-Low print run	2	4	6	8	10	12
V2#10 (9/85) -12(1/86)-Low print run	1	3	4	6	8	10
ATOMIC RABBIT (Atomic Bunny #12 on; see Giant Comics #3 & Wotalife)						
Charlton Comics: Aug, 1955 - No. 11, Mar, 1958						
1-Origin & 1st app.; Al Fago-c/a in all?	31	62	93	175	248	320
2	14	28	42	79	107	135
3-10	9	18	27	54	70	85
11-(68 pgs.)	14	28	42	79	107	135
ATOMICS, THE						
AAA Pop Comics: Jan, 2000 - No. 15, Nov, 2001 ($2.95)						
1-11-Mike Allred-s/a; 1-Madman-c/app.						3.00
12-15-($3.50): 13-15-Savage Dragon-c/app. 15-Afterword by Alex Ross; colored reprint of 1st Frank Einstein story						3.50
...King-Size Giant Spectacular: Jigsaw (2000, $10.00) r/#1-4						10.00
...King-Size Giant Spectacular: Lessons in Light, Lava, & Lasers (2000, $8.95) r/#5-8						9.00
...King-Size Giant Spectacular: Running With the Dragon ('02, $8.95) r/#13-15 and r/1st Frank Einstein app. in color						9.00
...King-Size Giant Spectacular: Worlds Within Worlds ('01, $8.95) r/#9-12						9.00
...: Spaced Out & Grounded in Snap City TPB (10/03, $12.95) r/one-shots - It Girl, Mr. Gum, Spaceman and Crash Metro & the Star Squad; sketch pages						13.00
ATOMIC SPY CASES						
Avon Periodicals: Mar-Apr, 1950 (Painted-c)						
1-No Wood-a; A-bomb blast panels; Fass-a	34	68	102	196	278	360
ATOMIC THUNDERBOLT, THE						
Regor Company: Feb, 1946 (one-shot) (scarce)						
1-Intro. Atomic Thunderbolt & Mr. Murdo	66	132	198	413	619	825
ATOMIC TOYBOX						
Image Comics: Dec, 1999 ($2.95)						
1- Aaron Lopresti-c/s/a						3.00
ATOMIC WAR!						
Ace Periodicals (Junior Books): Nov, 1952 - No. 4, Apr, 1953						
1-Atomic bomb-c	92	184	276	575	863	1150
2,3: 3-Atomic bomb-c	59	118	177	369	552	735
4-Used in **POP**, pg. 96 & illo.	59	118	177	369	552	735
ATOMIK ANGELS						
Crusade Comics: May, 1996 - No. 4, Nov. 1996 ($2.50)						
1-4: 1-Freefall from Gen 13 app.						3.00
1-Variant-c						4.00
Intrep-Edition (2/96, B&W, giveaway at launch party)-Previews Atomik Angels #1; includes Billy Tucci interview.						4.00
ATOM SPECIAL (See Atom & Justice League of America)						

	GD 2.0	VG 4.0	FN 6.0	VF 8.0	VF/NM 9.0	NM- 9.2
DC Comics: 1993/1995 ($2.50/$2.95)(68pgs.)						
1,2: 1-Dillon-c/a. 2-McDonnell-a/Bolland-c/Peyer-s						3.00
ATOM THE CAT (Formerly Tom Cat; see Giant Comics #3)						
Charlton Comics: No. 9, Oct, 1957 - No. 17, Aug, 1959						
9	9	18	27	54	70	85
10,13-17	6	12	18	33	41	48
11,12: 11(64 pgs)-Atomic Mouse app. 12(100 pgs.)	11	22	33	63	84	105
ATTACK						
Youthful Mag./Trojan No. 5 on: May, 1952 - No. 4, Nov, 1952; No. 5, Jan, 1953 - No. 5, Sept, 1953						
1-(1st series)-Extreme violence	32	64	96	180	255	330
2,3-Both Harrison-c/a; bondage, whipping	17	34	51	95	130	165
4-Krenkel-a (7 pgs.); Harrison-a (becomes Atomic Attack #5 on)	17	34	51	95	130	165
5-(#1, Trojan, 2nd series)	14	28	42	79	107	135
6-8 (#2-4), 5	10	20	30	58	77	95
ATTACK						
Charlton Comics: No. 54, 1958 - No. 60, Nov, 1959						
54 (25¢, 100 pgs.)	11	22	33	66	88	110
55-60	6	12	18	28	34	40
ATTACK!						
Charlton Comics: 1962 - No. 15, 3/75; No. 16, 8/79 - No. 48, 10/84						
nn(#1)-('62) Special Edition	5	10	15	33	44	55
2('63), 3(Fall, '64)	3	7	10	21	28	35
V4#3(10/66), 4(10/67)-(Formerly Special War Series #2; becomes Attack At Sea V4#5)	3	6	9	16	20	25
1(9/71)	3	6	9	16	20	25
2-5: 4-American Eagle app.	2	4	6	10	12	15
6-15(3/75):	1	3	4	6	8	10
16(8/79) - 40						5.00
41-47 Low print run						7.00
48(10/84)-Wood-r; S&K-c (low print)	1	3	4	6	8	10
Modern Comics 13('78)-r						4.00
NOTE: ***Sutton*** *a-9,10,13.*						
ATTACK!						
Spire Christian Comics (Fleming H. Revell Co.): 1975 (39¢/49¢, 36 pgs.)						
nn	1	2	3	5	7	9
ATTACK AT SEA (Formerly Attack!, 1967)						
Charlton Comics: V4#5, Oct, 1968 (one-shot)						
V4#5	3	6	9	16	20	25
ATTACK ON PLANET MARS (See Strange Worlds #18)						
Avon Periodicals: 1951						
nn-Infantino, Fawcette, Kubert & Wood-a; adaptation of Tarrano the Conqueror by Ray Cummings	76	152	228	475	713	950
ATTITUDE LAD						
Slave Labor Graphics: Apr, 1994 - No. 3, Nov, 1994 ($2.95, B&W)						
1-3						3.00
AUDREY & MELVIN (Formerly Little...)(See Little Audrey & Melvin)						
Harvey Publications: No. 62, Sept, 1974						
62	2	4	6	8	10	12
AUGIE DOGGIE (TV) (See Hanna-Barbera Band Wagon, Quick-Draw McGraw, Spotlight #2, Top Cat & Whitman Comic Books)						
Gold Key: October, 1963 (12¢)						
1-Hanna-Barbera character	20	40	60	140	205	270
AUTHENTIC POLICE CASES						
St. John Publishing Co.: 2/48 - No. 6, 11/48; No. 7, 5/50 - No. 38, 3/55						
1-Hale the Magician by Tuska begins	43	86	129	258	389	520
2-Lady Satan, Johnny Rebel app.	28	56	84	159	225	290
3-Veiled Avenger app.; blood drainage story plus 2 Lucky Coyne stories; used in **SOTI**, illo. from Red Seal #16	46	92	138	276	413	550
4,5: 4-Masked Black Jack app. 5-Late 1930s Jack Cole-a(r); transvestism story	28	56	84	159	225	290
6-Matt Baker-c; used in **SOTI**, illo- "An invitation to learning", r-in Fugitives From Justice #3; Jack Cole-a; also used by the N.Y. Legis. Comm.	48	96	144	288	432	575
7,8,10-14: 7-Jack Cole-a; Matt Baker-a begins #8, ends #?; Vic Flint in #10-14. 10-12-Baker-a(2 each)	24	48	72	135	190	245
9-No Vic Flint	19	38	57	109	152	195

The Authority #14 © WSP

Automatic Kafka #7 © WSP

Automation #2 © Flypaper Press

GD 2.0 | VG 4.0 | FN 6.0 | VF 8.0 | VF/NM 9.0 | NM- 9.2

15-Drug-c/story; Vic Flint app.; Baker-c 24 48 72 135 190 245
16,18,20,21,23: Baker-a(i) 15 30 45 84 115 145
17,19,22-Baker-c 17 34 50 95 130 165
24-28 (All 100 pgs.): 26-Transvestism 32 64 96 184 262 340
29,31,32-Baker-c 11 22 33 66 88 110
30 10 20 30 58 77 95
33-38: 33-Transvestism; Baker-c. 34-Baker-c; r/#9. 35-Baker-c/a(2); r/#10. 36-r/#11; Vic Flint strip-r; Baker-c/a(2) unsigned. 37-Baker-c; r/#17. 38- Baker-c/a; r/#18 14 28 42 79 107 135

NOTE: ***Matt Baker** c-6-16, 17, 19, 22, 27, 29, 31-38; a-13, 16. Bondage c-1, 3.*

AUTHORITY, THE (See Stormwatch and Jenny Sparks: The Secret History of...)
DC Comics (WildStorm): May, 1999 - No. 29, Jul, 2002 ($2.50)

1-Wraparound-c; Warren Ellis-s/Bryan Hitch and Paul Neary-a 2 4 6 9 11 14
2-4 1 3 4 6 8 10
5-12: 12-Death of Jenny Sparks; last Ellis-s 1 2 3 5 6 8
13-Mark Millar-s/Frank Quitely-c/a begins 2 4 6 8 10 12
14-16-Authority vs. Marvel-esque villains 1 2 3 4 5 7
17-22: 17,18-Weston-a. 19,20,22-Quitely-a. 21-McCrea-a 5.00
23-29: 23-26-Peyer-s/Nguyen-a; new Authority. 24-Preview of "The Establishment." 25,26-Jenny Sparks app. 27,28-Millar-s/Adams-a/c 4.00
Annual 2000 ($3.50) Devil's Night x-over; Hamner-a/Bermejo-c 1 2 3 4 5 7
Absolute Authority Slipcased Hardcover (2002, $49.95) oversized r/#1-12 plus script pages by Ellis and sketch pages by Hitch 50.00
...: Earth Inferno and Other Stories TPB (2002, $14.95) r/#17-20, Annual 2000, and Wildstorm Summer Special; new Quitely-c 15.00
...: Kev (10/02, $4.95) Ennis-s/Fabry-c/a 5.00
...: Relentless TPB (2000, $17.95) r/#1-8 18.00
...: Scorched Earth (2/03, $4.95) Robbie Morrison-s/Frazer Irving-a/Ashley Wood-c 5.00
...: Transfer of Power TPB (2002, $17.95) r/#22-29 18.00
...: Under New Management TPB (2000, $17.95) r/#9-16; new Quitely-c 18.00

AUTHORITY, THE (See previews in Sleeper, Stormwatch: Team Achilles and Wildcats Version 3.0)
DC Comics (WildStorm): Jul, 2003 - Present ($2.95)

1-9: 1-Robbie Morrison-s/Dwayne Turner-a. 5-Huat-a 3.00
#0 (10/03, $2.95) r/preview back-up-s listed above; Turner sketch pages 3.00
.../Lobo: Jingle Hell (2/04, $4.95) Bisley-c/a; Giffen & Grant-s 5.00

AUTOMATIC KAFKA
DC Comics (WildStorm): Sept, 2002 - No. 9, Jul, 2003 ($2.95)

1-9-Ashley Wood-c/a; Joe Casey-s 3.00

AUTOMATON
Image Comics (Flypaper Press): Sept, 1998 - No. 3, 1998 ($2.95, lim. series)

1-3-R.A. Jones-s/Peter Vale-a 3.00

AUTUMN
Caliber Comics: 1995 - No. 3, 1995 ($2.95, B&W)

1-3 3.00

AUTUMN ADVENTURES (Walt Disney's...)
Disney Comics: Autumn, 1990; No. 2, Autumn, 1991 ($2.95, 68 pgs.)

1-Donald Duck-r(2) by Barks, Pluto-r, & new-a 4.00
2-D. Duck-r by Barks; new Super Goof story 4.00

AVATAARS: COVENANT OF THE SHIELD
Marvel Comics: Sept, 2000 - No. 3, Nov, 2000 ($2.99, limited series)

1-3-Kaminski-s/Oscar Jimenez-a 3.00

AVATAR
DC Comics: Feb, 1991 - No. 3, Apr, 1991 ($5.95, limited series, 100 pgs.)

1-3: Based on TSR's Forgotten Realms 6.00

AVENGEBLADE
Maximum Press: July, 1996 - No. 2, Aug, 1996 ($2.99, limited series)

1,2: Bad Girls parody 3.00

AVENGELYNE
Maximum Press: May, 1995 - No. 3, July, 1995 ($2.50/$3.50, limited series)

1/2 2 4 6 8 10 12
1/2 Platinum 15.00
1-Newstand ($2.50)-Photo-c; poster insert 6.00
1-Direct Market ($3.50)-Chromium-c; poster 1 2 3 4 5 7
1-Glossy edition 2 4 6 12 16 20
1-Gold 12.00
2-3: 2-Polybagged w/card 3.00
3-Variant-c; Deodato pin-up 5.00
.../Glory Swimsuit Special (6/96, $2.95) photo and illos. covers 3.00
...Swimsuit (8/95, $2.95)-Pin-ups/photos. 3-Variant-c exist (2 photo, 1 Liefeld-a) 4.00
...Swimsuit (1/96, $3.50, 2nd printing)-photo-c 4.00
Trade paperback (12/95, $9.95) 10.00

AVENGELYNE
Maximum Press: V2#1, Apr, 1996 - No. 14, Apr, 1997 ($2.95/$2.50)

V2#1-Four covers exist (2 photo-c). 4.00
V2#2-Three covers exist (1 photo-c); flip book w/Darkchylde 2 4 6 10 12 15
V2#0, 3-14: 0-(10/96).3-Flip book w/Priest preview. 4-Cybrid app; w/Darkchylde/Avengelyne poster. 5-Flip book w/Blindside 3.00
...Bible (10/96, $3.50) 4.00

AVENGELYNE (Volume 3)
Awesome Comics: Mar, 1999 ($2.50)

1-Fraga & Liefeld-a 3.00

AVENGELYNE: ARMAGEDDON
Maximum Press: Dec, 1996 - No. 3, Feb, 1997 ($2.99, limited series)

1-3-Scott Clark-a(p) 3.00

AVENGELYNE: DEADLY SINS
Maximum Press: Feb, 1996 - No. 2, Mar, 1996 ($2.95, limited series)

1,2: 1-Two-c exist (1 photo, 1 Liefeld-a). 2-Liefeld-c; Pop Mhan-a(p). 3.00

AVENGELYNE/GLORY
Maximum Press: Sept, 1995 ($3.95, one-shot)

1-Chromium-c 4.00
1-Variant-c 5.00

AVENGELYNE/GLORY: GODYSSEY, THE (See Glory/...)
Maximum Press: Sept, 1996 ($2.99, one-shot)

1-Two covers (1 photo) 3.00

AVENGELYNE/POWER
Maximum Press: Nov, 1995 - No.3, Jan, 1996 ($2.95, limited series)

1-3: 1,2-Liefeld-c. 3-Three variant-c. exist (1 photo-c) 3.00

AVENGELYNE • PROPHET
Maximum Press: May, 1996; No. 2, Feb. 1997 ($2.95, unfinished lim. series)

1,2-Liefeld-c/a(p) 3.00

AVENGELYNE: REVELATION ONE
Avatar Press: Jan, 2001 ($3.50, one-shot)

1-Three regular covers by Haley, Rio, Shaw; Shaw-a 3.50

AVENGELYNE/SHI
Avatar Press: Nov, 2001 ($3.50, one-shot)

1-Eight covers; Waller-a 3.50

AVENGELYNE/ WARRIOR NUN AREALA (See Warrior Nun/...)
Maximum Press: Nov, 1996 ($2.99, one-shot)

1 4.00

AVENGER, THE (See A-1 Comics)
Magazine Enterprises: Feb-Mar, 1955 - No. 4, Aug-Sept, 1955

1(A-1 #129)-Origin 40 80 120 240 340 440
2(A-1 #131), 3(A-1 #133) Robot-c, 4(A-1 #138) 28 56 84 159 225 290
IW Reprint #9('64)-Reprints #1 (new cover) 4 8 12 22 30 38

NOTE: ***Powell** a-2-4; c-1-4.*

AVENGERS, THE (TV)(Also see Steed and Mrs. Peel)
Gold Key: Nov, 1968 ("John Steed & Emma Peel" cover title) (15¢)

1-Photo-c 25 50 75 181 266 350
1-(Variant with photo back-c) 31 62 93 223 329 435

AVENGERS, THE (See Essential..., Giant-Size..., JLA/..., Kree/Skrull War Starring..., Marvel Graphic Novel #27, Marvel Super Action, Marvel Super Heroes('66), Marvel Treasury Ed., Marvel Triple Action, Solo Avengers, Tales Of Suspense #49, West Coast Avengers & X-Men Vs....)

AVENGERS, THE (The Mighty Avengers on cover only #63-69)
Marvel Comics Group: Sept, 1963 - No. 402, Sept, 1996

1-Origin & 1st app. The Avengers (Thor, Iron Man, Hulk, Ant-Man, Wasp); Loki app. 241 482 723 2109 3405 4700
2-Hulk leaves Avengers 60 120 180 510 780 1050
3-2nd Sub-Mariner x-over outside the F.F. (see Strange Tales #107 for 1st); Sub-Mariner & Hulk team-up & battle Avengers; Spider-Man cameo (1/64) 41 82 123 324 487 650

Avengers #9 © MAR

Avengers #141 © MAR

Avengers #396 © MAR

GD VG FN VF VF/NM NM-
2.0 4.0 6.0 8.0 9.0 9.2

4-Revival of Captain America who joins the Avengers; 1st Silver Age app.
of Captain America & Bucky (3/64) 143 286 429 1216 1858 2500
4-Reprint from the Golden Record Comic set 11 22 33 75 110 145
With Record (1966) 16 32 48 113 167 220
5-Hulk app. 29 58 87 210 305 400
6,8: 6-Intro/1st app. original Zemo & his Masters of Evil. 8-Intro Kang
22 44 66 160 235 310
7-Rick Jones app. in Bucky costume 30 60 90 218 322 425
9-Intro Wonder Man who dies in same story 29 58 87 210 305 400
10-Intro/1st app. Immortus; early Hercules app. (11/64)
20 40 60 145 213 280
11-Spider-Man-c & x-over (12/64) 26 52 78 189 275 360
12-15: 15-Death of original Zemo 15 30 45 109 160 210
16-New Avengers line-up (Hawkeye, Quicksilver, Scarlet Witch join; Thor, Iron Man, Giant-Man, Wasp leave) 20 40 60 142 209 275
17,18 12 24 36 82 121 160
19-1st app. Swordsman; origin Hawkeye (8/65) 13 26 39 90 133 175
20-22: Wood inks 8 16 24 55 78 100
23-30: 23-Romita Sr. inks (1st Silver Age Marvel work). 25-Dr. Doom-c/story. 28-Giant-Man becomes Goliath (5/66) 7 14 21 46 63 80
31-40 6 12 18 38 52 65
41-46,49-52,54-56: 43,44-1st app. Red Guardian. 46-Ant-Man returns (re-intro, 11/67). 52-Black Panther joins; 1st app. The Grim Reaper. 54-1st app. new Masters of Evil. 56-Zemo app; story explains how Capt. America became imprisoned in ice during WWII, only to be rescued in Avengers #4 5 10 15 33 44 55
47-Magneto-c/story 5 10 15 36 48 60
48-Origin/1st app. new Black Knight (1/68) 5 10 15 36 48 60
53-X-Men app. 6 12 18 43 59 75
57-1st app. S.A. Vision (10/68) 12 24 36 87 129 170
58-Origin The Vision 7 14 21 50 68 85
59-65: 59-Intro. Yellowjacket. 60-Wasp & Yellowjacket wed. 63-Goliath becomes Yellowjacket; Hawkeye becomes the new Goliath. 65-Last 12¢ issue
4 8 12 29 40 50
66,67-B. Smith-a 5 10 15 33 44 55
68-70: 70-Nighthawk on cover 4 8 12 27 36 45
71-1st app. The Invaders (12/69); 1st app. Nighthawk; Black Knight joins
6 12 18 40 55 70
72-79,81,82,84-86,89-91: 82-Daredevil app 4 8 12 24 32 40
80-Intro. Red Wolf (9/70) 4 8 12 27 36 45
83-Intro. The Liberators (Wasp, Valkyrie, Scarlet Witch, Medusa & the Black Widow)
4 8 12 28 38 48
87-Origin The Black Panther 4 8 12 29 40 50
88-Written by Harlan Ellison 4 8 12 25 33 42
88-2nd printing (1994) 2 4 6 8 10 12
92-Last 15¢ issue; Neal Adams-c 4 8 12 27 36 45
93-(52 pgs.)-Neal Adams-c/a 8 16 24 55 78 100
94-96-Neal Adams-c/a 6 12 18 38 52 65
97-G.A. Capt. America, Sub-Mariner, Human Torch, Patriot, Vision, Blazing Skull, Fin, Angel, & new Capt. Marvel x-over 4 8 12 27 36 45
98,99: 98-Goliath becomes Hawkeye; Smith c/a(i). 99-Smith-c, Smith/Sutton-a 4 8 12 25 33 42
100-(6/72)-Smith-c/a; featuring everyone who was an Avenger
9 18 27 65 93 120
101-Harlan Ellison scripts 3 6 9 18 24 30
102-106,108,109 3 6 9 16 20 25
107-Starlin-a(p) 3 6 9 18 24 30
110,111-X-Men app. 4 8 12 24 32 40
112-1st app. Mantis 3 7 10 21 28 35
113-115,119-124,126-130: 123-Origin Mantis 2 4 6 12 16 20
116-118-Defenders/Silver Surfer app. 3 7 10 21 28 35
125-Thanos-c & brief app. 3 6 9 16 20 25
131-133,136-140: 136-Ploog-r/Amazing Advs. #12 2 4 6 9 11 14
134,135-Origin of the Vision revised (also see Avengers Forever mini-series)
2 4 6 12 16 20
141-143,145,152-163 1 3 4 6 8 10
144-Origin & 1st app. Hellcat 2 4 6 11 14 18
146-149-(Reg.25¢ editions)(4-7/76) 1 3 4 6 8 10
146-149-(30¢-c variants, limited distribution) 3 6 9 16 20 25
150-Kirby-a(r); new line-up: Capt. America, Scarlet Witch, Iron Man, Wasp, Yellowjacket, Vision & The Beast 2 4 6 8 10 12
150-(30¢-c variant, limited distribution) 3 6 9 16 20 25
151-Wonder Man returns w/new costume 1 3 4 6 8 11
160-164-(35¢-c variants, limited dist.)(6-10/77) 2 4 6 12 16 20
164-166: Byrne-a 2 4 6 8 10 12

GD VG FN VF VF/NM NM-
2.0 4.0 6.0 8.0 9.0 9.2

167-180: 168-Guardians of the Galaxy app. 174-Thanos cameo. 176-Starhawk app.
1 2 3 4 5 7
181-191-Byrne-a: 181-New line-up: Capt. America, Scarlet Witch, Iron Man, Wasp, Vision, Beast & The Falcon. 183-Ms. Marvel joins. 185-Origin Quicksilver & Scarlet Witch
1 2 3 5 7 9
192-199: 195-1st Taskmaster 6.00
200-(10/80, 52 pgs.)-Ms. Marvel leaves. 1 2 3 5 7 9
201-213,217-238,241-249, 251-262: 211-New line-up: Capt. America, Iron Man, Tigra, Thor, Wasp & Yellowjacket. 213-Yellowjacket leaves. 217-Yellowjacket & Wasp return. 221-Hawkeye & She-Hulk join. 227-Capt. Marvel (female) joins; origins of Ant-Man, Wasp, Giant-Man, Goliath, Yellowjacket, & Avengers. 230-Yellowjacket quits. 231-Iron Man leaves. 232-Starfox (Eros) joins. 234-Origin Quicksilver, Scarlet Witch. 238-Origin Blackout 3.50
214-Ghost Rider-c/story 6.00
215,216,239,240,250: 215,216-Silver Surfer app. 216-Tigra leaves. 239-(1/84) Avengers app. on David Letterman show. 240-Spider-Woman revived. 250-($1.00, 52 pgs.) 4.00
263-1st app. X-Factor (1/86)(story continues in Fant. Four #286) 6.00
264-299: 272-Alpha Flight app. 291-$1.00 issues begin. 297-Black Knight, She-Hulk & Thor resign. 298-Inferno tie-in 3.00
300 (2/89, $1.75, 68 pgs.)-Thor joins; Simonson-a 4.00
301-304,306-313,319-325,327,329-343: 302-Re-intro Quasar. 320-324-Alpha Flight app. (320-cameo). 327-2nd app. Rage. 341,342-New Warriors app. 343-Last $1.00-c 3.00
305,314-318: 305-Byrne scripts begin. 314-318-Spider-Man x-over 3.50
326-1st app. Rage (11/90) 4.00
328,344-349,351-359,361,362,364,365,367: 328-Origin Rage. 365-Contains coupon for Hunt for Magneto contest 3.00
350-($2.50, 68 pgs.)-Double gatefold-c showing-c to #1; r/#53 w/cover in flip book format; vs. The Starjammers 3.50
360-($2.95, 52 pgs.)-Embossed all-foil-c; 30th ann. 4.00
363-($2.95, 52 pgs.)-All silver foil-c 4.00
366-($3.95, 68 pgs.)-Embossed all gold foil-c 4.00
368,370-374,376-399: 368-Bloodties part 1; Avengers/X-Men x-over. 374-bound-in trading card sheet. 380-Deodato-a. 390,391-"The Crossing." 395-Death of "old" Tony Stark; wraparound-c. 3.00
369-($2.95)-Foil embossed-c; Bloodties part 5 4.00
375-($2.00, 52 pgs.)-Regular ed.; Thunderstrike returns; leads into Malibu Comics' Black September. 3.00
375-($2.50, 52 pgs.)-Collector's ed. w/bound-in poster; leads into Malibu Comics' Black September. 3.50
400-402: Waid-s; 402-Deodato breakdowns; cont'd in X-Men #56 & Onslaught: Marvel Universe. 4.00
Special 1 (9/67, 25¢, 68 pgs.)-New-a; original & new Avengers team-up
9 18 27 63 89 115
Special 2 (9/68, 25¢, 68 pgs.)-New-a; original vs. new Avengers
5 10 15 36 48 60
Special 3 (9/69, 25¢, 68 pgs.)-r/Avengers #4 plus 3 Capt. America stories by Kirby (art); origin Red Skull 4 8 12 24 32 40
Special 4 (1/71, 25¢, 68 pgs.)-Kirby-r/Avengers #5,6 3 6 9 16 20 24
Special 5 (1/72, 52 pgs.)-Spider-Man x-over 3 6 9 16 20 24
Annual 6 (11/76) 2 4 6 10 12 15
Annual 7 (11/77)-Starlin-c/a; Warlock dies; Thanos app.
4 8 12 24 32 40
Annual 8 (1978)-Dr. Strange, Ms. Marvel app. 1 3 4 6 8 10
Annual 9 (1979)-Newton-a(p) 1 2 3 5 6 8
Annual 10 (1981)-Golden-p; X-Men cameo; 1st app. Rogue & Madelyne Pryor
4 8 12 24 32 40
Annual 11-13: 11(1982)-Vs. The Defenders. 12('83), 13('84) 4.00
Annual 14-18: 14('85),15('86),16('87),17('88)-Evolutionary War x-over, 18('89)-Atlantis Attacks
4.00
Annual 19-23 ('90-'94, 68 pgs.): 22-Bagged/card 3.00
...Kree-Skrull War ('00, $24.95, TPB) new Neal Adams-c 25.00
...: Legends Vol. 3: George Perez ('03, $16.99)-r/#161,162,194-196,201, Ann. #6&8 17.00
Marvel Double Feature...Avengers/Giant-Man #379 ($2.50, 52 pgs.)-Same as Avengers #379 w/Giant-Man flip book 2.50
Marvel Graphic Novel - Deathtrap: The Vault (1991, $9.95) Venom-c/app.
2 4 6 8 10 12
The Korvac Saga TPB (2003, $19.95)-r/#167,168,170-177; Perez-c 20.00
The Yesterday Quest ($6.95)-r/#181,182,185-187 1 2 3 4 5 7
Under Siege ('98, $16.95, TPB) r/#270,271,273-277 17.00
...: Visionaries ('99, $16.95)-r/early George Perez art 17.00

NOTE: ***Austin*** *c(i)-157, 167, 168, 170-177, 181, 183-188, 198-201, Annual 8.* ***John Buscema*** *a-41-44p, 46p, 47p, 49, 50, 51-62p, 74-77, 79-85, 87-91, 97, 105p, 121p, 124p,125p, 152, 153p, 255-279p, 281-302p; c-41-66, 68-71, 73-91, 97-99, 178, 256-259p, 261-279p, 281-302p.* ***Byrne*** *a-164-166p, 181-191p, 233p, Annual 13i, 14p; c-186-190p, 233p, 260, 305p; scripts-305-312.* ***Colan*** *a(p)-63-65, 111, 206-208, 210, 211; c(p)-65, 206-208, 210, 211.* ***Ditko*** *a-Annual 13.* ***Guice*** *a-Annual 12p.* ***Don Heck*** *a-9-15, 17-40, 157.* ***Kane*** *c-37p, 159p.* ***Kane/Everett*** *c-97.* ***Kirby*** *a-1-8p, Special 3r, 4r(p); c-1-30, 148, 151-158; layouts-14-16.* ***Ron Lim*** *c(p)-335-341.* ***Miller*** *c-193p.* ***Mooney*** *a-86i,*

Avengers Vol. 3 #65 © MAR

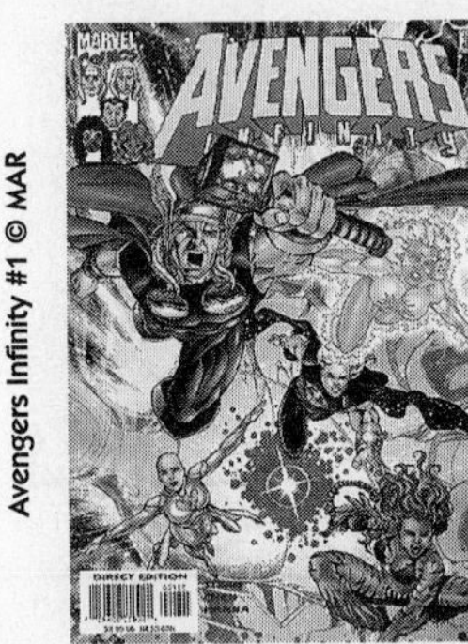

Avengers Infinity #1 © MAR

Avengers/JLA #2 © MAR & DC

GD 2.0 | VG 4.0 | FN 6.0 | VF 8.0 | VF/NM 9.0 | NM- 9.2

179p, 180p. ***Nebres*** *a-178i; c-179i.* ***Newton*** *a-204p, Annual 9p.* ***Perez*** *a(p)-141, 143, 144, 148, 150, 154, 155, 160, 161, 162, 167,168, 170, 171, 194-196, 198-202, Annual 6, 8; c(p)-160-162, 164-166, 170-174, 181,183-185, 191, 192, 194-201, 379-382, Annual 8.* ***Starlin*** *c-121, 135.* ***Staton*** *a-127-134i.* ***Tuska*** *a-47i,48i, 51i, 53i, 54i, 106p, 107p, 135p, 137-140p, 163p. Guardians of the Galaxy app. in #167, 168, 170, 173, 175, 181.*

AVENGERS, THE (Volume Two)
Marvel Comics: V2#1, Nov, 1996 - No. 13, Nov, 1997 ($2.95/$1.95/$1.99) (Produced by Extreme Studios)

1-($2.95)-Heroes Reborn begins; intro new team (Captain America, Swordsman, Scarlet Witch, Vision, Thor, Hellcat & Hawkeye); 1st app. Avengers Island; Loki & Enchantress app.; Rob Liefeld-p & plot; Chap Yaep-p; Jim Valentino scripts; variant-c exists 5.00
1-($1.95)-Variant-c 6.00
2-13: 2,3-Jeph Loeb scripts begin, Kang app. 4-Hulk-c/app. 5-Thor/Hulk battle; 2 covers. 10,11,13-"World War 3"-pt. 2, x-over w/Image characters. 12-($2.99) "Heroes Reunited"-pt. 2 4.00

AVENGERS, THE (Volume Three)
Marvel Comics: Feb, 1998 - Present ($2.99/$1.99/$2.25)

1-($2.99, 48 pgs.) Busiek-s/Perez-a/wraparound-c; Avengers reassemble after Heroes Return 5.00
1-Variant Heroes Return cover 1 2 3 4 5 7
1-Rough Cut-Features original script and pencil pages 3.00
2-($1.99)Perez-c, 2-Lago painted-c 4.00
3,4: 3-Wonder Man-c/app. 4-Final roster chosen; Perez poster 3.00
5-11: 5,6-Squadron Supreme-c/app. 8-Triathlon-c/app. 2.50
12-($2.99) Thunderbolts app. 3.00
12-Alternate-c of Avengers w/white background; no logo 15.00
13-24,26,28: 13-New Warriors app. 16-18-Ordway-s/a. 19-Ultron returns. 26-Immonen-a 2.25
16-Variant-c with purple background 5.00
25,27-($2.99) 25-vs. the Exemplars; Spider-Man app. 27-100 pgs. 3.00
29-33,35-47: 29-Begin $2.25-c. 35-Maximum Security x-over; Romita Jr.-a. 36-Epting-a; poster by Alan Davis. 38-Davis-a begins ($1.99-c) 2.25
34-($2.99) Last Pérez-a; Thunderbirds app. 3.00
48-($3.50, 100 pgs.) new story w/Dwyer-a & r/#98-100 3.50
49,51-59: 49-'Nuff Said story. 51-Anderson-a. 52-Reis-a. 57-Johns-s begin 2.25
50,60-($3.50): 50 Dwyer-a; Quasar app. 3.50
61-77: 61,62-Frank-a; new line-up. 63-Davis-a. 64-Reis-a. 65-70-Coipel-a. 75-Hulk app. 76-Jack of Hearts dies; Jae Lee-c. 77-(50¢-c) Coipel-a/Cassaday-c 2.25
#11/2 (12/99, $2.50) Timm-c/a/Stern-s; 1963-style issue 2.50
.../ Squadron Supreme '98 Annual ($2.99) 3.00
1999, 2000 Annual (7/99, '00, $3.50) 1999-Manco-a. 2000-Breyfogle-a 3.50
2001 Annual ($2.99) Reis-a; back-up-s art by Churchill 3.00
...: Clear and Present Dangers TPB ('01, $19.95) r/#8-15 20.00
...Supreme Justice TPB (4/01, $17.95) r/Squadron Supreme appearances in Avengers #5-7, '98 Annual, Iron Man #7, Capt. America #8, Quicksilver #10; Pérez-c 18.00
The Kang Dynasty TPB ('02, $29.99) r/#41-55 & 2001 Annual 30.00
The Morgan Conquest TPB ('00, $14.95) r/#1-4 15.00
Ultron Unleashed TPB (8/99, $3.50) reprints early app. 3.50
Ultron Unlimited TPB (4/01, $14.95) r/#19-22 & #0 prelude 15.00
Wizard #0-Ultron Unlimited prelude 2.50
World Trust TPB ('03, $14.99) r/#57-62 & Marvel Double-Shot #2 15.00

AVENGERS: CELESTIAL QUEST
Marvel Comics: Nov, 2001 - No. 8, June, 2002 ($2.50/$3.50, limited series)

1-7-Englehart-s/Santamaría-a; Thanos app. 2.50
8-($3.50) 3.50

AVENGERS COLLECTOR'S EDITION, THE
Marvel Comics: 1993 (Ordered through mail w/candy wrapper, 20 pgs.)

1-Contains 4 bound-in trading cards 5.00

AVENGERS FOREVER
Marvel Comics: Dec, 1998 - No. 12, Feb, 2000 ($2.99)

1-Busiek-s/Pacheco-a in all 4.00
2-12: 4-Four covers. 6-Two covers. 8-Vision origin revised. 12-Rick Jones becomes Capt. Marvel 3.00
TPB (1/01, $24.95) r/#1-12; Busiek intro.; new Pacheco-c 25.00

AVENGERS INFINITY
Marvel Comics: Sept, 2000 - No. 4, Dec, 2000 ($2.99, limited series)

1-4-Stern-s/Chen-a 3.00

AVENGERS/ JLA (See JLA/Avengers for #1 & #3)
DC Comics: No, 2, 2003; No. 4, 2004 ($5.95, limited series)

2-Busiek-s/Pérez-a; wraparound-c; Krona, Galactus app. 6.00

AVENGERS LOG, THE
Marvel Comics: Feb, 1994 ($1.95)

GD 2.0 | VG 4.0 | FN 6.0 | VF 8.0 | VF/NM 9.0 | NM- 9.2

1-Gives history of all members; Perez-c 2.25

AVENGERS SPOTLIGHT (Formerly Solo Avengers #1-20)
Marvel Comics: No. 21, Aug, 1989 - No. 40, Jan, 1991 (75¢/$1.00)

21-Byrne-c/a 3.00
22-40: 26-Acts of Vengeance story. 31-34-U.S. Agent series. 36-Heck-i. 37-Mortimer-i. 40-The Black Knight app. 2.25

AVENGERS STRIKEFILE
Marvel Comics: Jan, 1994 ($1.75, one-shot)

1 2.25

AVENGERS: THE CROSSING
Marvel Comics: July, 1995 ($4.95, one-shot)

1-Deodato-c/a; 1st app. Thor's new costume 5.00

AVENGERS: THE TERMINATRIX OBJECTIVE
Marvel Comics: Sept, 1993 - No. 4, Dec, 1993 ($1.25, limited series)

1 ($2.50)-Holo-grafx foil-c 3.00
2-4-Old vs. current Avengers 2.25

AVENGERS: THE ULTRON IMPERATIVE
Marvel Comics: Nov, 2001 ($5.99, one-shot)

1-Follow-up to the Ultron Unlimited ending in Avengers #42; BWS-c 6.00

AVENGERS: TIMESLIDE
Marvel Comics: Feb, 1996 ($4.95, one-shot)

1-Foil-c 5.00

AVENGERS TWO: WONDER MAN & BEAST
Marvel Comics: May, 2000 - No. 3, July, 2000 ($2.99, limited series)

1-3: Stern-s/Bagley-c/a 3.00

AVENGERS/ULTRAFORCE (See Ultraforce/Avengers)
Marvel Comics: Oct, 1995 ($3.95, one-shot)

1-Wraparound foil-c by Perez 4.00

AVENGERS UNITED THEY STAND
Marvel Comics: Nov, 1999 - No. 7, June, 2000 ($2.99/$1.99)

1-Based on the animated series 3.00
2-6-($1.99) 2-Avengers battle Hydra 2.25
7-($2.99) Devil Dinosaur-c/app.; reprints Avengers Action Figure Comic 3.00

AVENGERS UNIVERSE
Marvel Comics: Jun, 2000 - No. 3, Oct, 2000 ($3.99)

1-3-Reprints recent stories 4.00

AVENGERS UNPLUGGED
Marvel Comics: Oct, 1995 - No. 6, Aug, 1996 (99¢, bi-monthly)

1-6 2.25

AVENGERS WEST COAST (Formerly West Coast Avengers)
Marvel Comics: No. 48, Sept, 1989 - No. 102, Jan, 1994 ($1.00/$1.25)

48,49: 48-Byrne-c/a & scripts continue thru #57 3.00
50-Re-intro original Human Torch 4.00
51-69,71-74,76-83,85,86,89-99: 54-Cover swipe/F.F. #1. 78-Last $1.00-c. 79-Dr. Strange x-over. 93-95-Darkhawk app. 2.25
70,75,84,87,88: 70-Spider-Woman app. 75 (52 pgs.)-Fantastic Four x-over. 84-Origin Spider-Woman retold; Spider-Man app. (also in #85,86). 87,88-Wolverine-c/story 3.00
100-($3.95, 68 pgs.)-Embossed all red foil-c 4.00
101,102: 101-X-Men x-over 4.00
Annual 5-8 ('90- '93, 68 pgs.)-5,6-West Coast Avengers in indicia. 7-Darkhawk app. 8-Polybagged w/card 3.00

AVIATION ADVENTURES AND MODEL BUILDING (True Aviation Advs. ...No. 15)
Parents' Magazine Institute: No. 16, Dec, 1946 - No. 17, Feb, 1947

16,17-Half comics and half pictures 8 16 24 43 54 65

AVIATION CADETS
Street & Smith Publications: 1943

nn 19 37 57 106 146 185

A-V IN 3-D
Aardvark-Vanaheim: Dec, 1984 ($2.00, 28 pgs. w/glasses)

1-Cerebus, Flaming Carrot, Normalman & Ms. Tree 4.00

AWAKENING, THE
Image Comics: Oct, 1997 - No. 4, Apr, 1998 ($2.95, B&W, limited series)

1-4-Stephen Blue-s/c/a 3.00

Azrael #99 © DC

Babe #7 © PRIZE

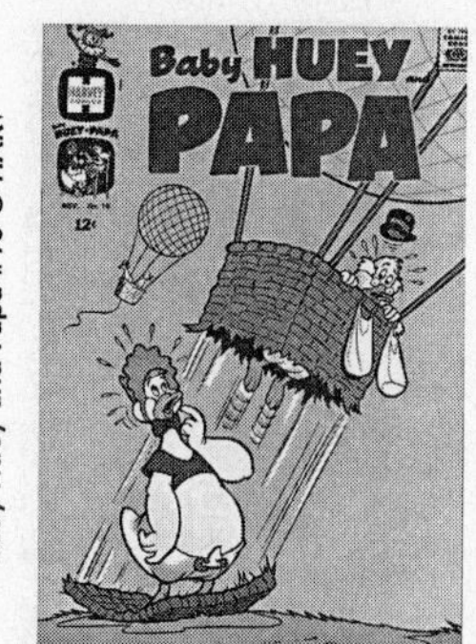

Baby Huey and Papa #10 © HARV

AWESOME ADVENTURES
Awesome Entertainment: Aug, 1999 ($2.50)

	GD 2.0	VG 4.0	FN 6.0	VF 8.0	VF/NM 9.0	NM- 9.2
1-Alan Moore-s/ Steve Skroce-a; Youngblood story						3.00

AWESOME HOLIDAY SPECIAL
Awesome Entertainment: Dec, 1997 ($2.50, one-shot)

	GD 2.0	VG 4.0	FN 6.0	VF 8.0	VF/NM 9.0	NM- 9.2
1-Flip book w/covers of Fighting American & Coven. Holiday stories also featuring Kaboom and Shaft by regular creators.						3.00
1-Gold Edition						5.00

AWFUL OSCAR (Formerly & becomes Oscar Comics with No. 13)
Marvel Comics: No. 11, June, 1949 - No. 12, Aug, 1949

	GD 2.0	VG 4.0	FN 6.0	VF 8.0	VF/NM 9.0	NM- 9.2
11,12	11	22	33	63	84	105

AWKWARD UNIVERSE
Slave Labor Graphics: 12/95 ($9.95, graphic novel)

	GD 2.0	VG 4.0	FN 6.0	VF 8.0	VF/NM 9.0	NM- 9.2
nn						10.00

AXA
Eclipse Comics: Apr, 1987 - No. 2, Aug, 1987 ($1.75)

	GD 2.0	VG 4.0	FN 6.0	VF 8.0	VF/NM 9.0	NM- 9.2
1,2						2.25

AXEL PRESSBUTTON (Pressbutton No. 5; see Laser Eraser &...)
Eclipse Comics: Nov, 1984 - No. 6, July, 1985 ($1.50/$1.75, Baxter paper)

	GD 2.0	VG 4.0	FN 6.0	VF 8.0	VF/NM 9.0	NM- 9.2
1-6: Reprints Warrior (British mag.). 1-Bolland-c; origin Laser Eraser & Pressbutton						3.00

AXIS ALPHA
Axis Comics: Feb, 1994 ($2.50, one-shot)

	GD 2.0	VG 4.0	FN 6.0	VF 8.0	VF/NM 9.0	NM- 9.2
V1-Previews Axis titles including, Tribe, Dethgrip, B.E.A.S.T.I.E.S. & more; Pitt app. in Tribe story.						3.00

AZRAEL (...Agent of the Bat #47 on)(Also see Batman: Sword of Azrael)
DC Comics: Feb, 1995 - No. 100, May, 2003 ($1.95/$2.25/$2.50/$2.95)

	GD 2.0	VG 4.0	FN 6.0	VF 8.0	VF/NM 9.0	NM- 9.2
1-Dennis O'Neil scripts begin						5.00
2,3						3.00
4-46,48-62: 5,6-Ras Al Ghul app. 13-Nightwing-c/app. 15-Contagion Pt. 5 (Pt. 4 on-c). 16-Contagion Pt. 10. 22-Batman-c/app. 23,27-Batman app. 27,28-Joker app. 35-Hitman app. 36-39-Batman, Bane app. 50-New costume. 53-Joker-c/app. 56,57,60-New Batgirl app.						2.50
47-($3.95) Flip book with Batman: Shadow of the Bat #80						4.00
63-74,76-92: 63-Huntress-c/app.; Azrael returns to old costume. 67-Begin $2.50-c. 70-79-Harris-c. 83-Joker x-over. 91-Bruce Wayne: Fugitive pt. 15						2.50
75-($3.95) New costume; Harris-c						4.00
93-100: 93-Begin $2.95-c. 95,96-Two-Face app. 100-Last issue; Zeck-c						3.00
#1,000,000 (11/98) Giarrano-a						2.50
Annual 1 (1995, $3.95)-Year One story						4.00
Annual 2 (1996, $2.95)-Legends of the Dead Earth story						3.00
Annual 3 (1997, $3.95)-Pulp Heroes story; Orbik-c						4.00
Plus (12/96, $2.95)-Question-c/app.						3.00

AZRAEL/ ASH
DC Comics: 1997 ($4.95, one-shot)

	GD 2.0	VG 4.0	FN 6.0	VF 8.0	VF/NM 9.0	NM- 9.2
1-O'Neil-s/Quesada, Palmiotti-a						5.00

AZTEC ACE
Eclipse Comics: Mar, 1984 - No. 15, Sept, 1985 ($2.25/$1.50/$1.75, Baxter paper)

	GD 2.0	VG 4.0	FN 6.0	VF 8.0	VF/NM 9.0	NM- 9.2
1-$2.25-c (52 pgs.)						3.00
2-15: 2-Begin 36 pgs.						2.25

NOTE: *N. Redondo a-1i-8i, 10i. c-6-8i.*

AZTEK: THE ULTIMATE MAN
DC Comics: Aug, 1996 - No. 10, May 1997 ($1.75)

	GD 2.0	VG 4.0	FN 6.0	VF 8.0	VF/NM 9.0	NM- 9.2
1-1st app. Aztek & Synth; Grant Morrison & Mark Millar scripts in all						6.00
2-9: 2-Green Lantern app. 3-1st app. Death-Doll. 4-Intro The Lizard King. 5-Origin. 6-Joker app.; Batman cameo. 7-Batman app. 8-Luthor app. 9-vs. Parasite-c/app.						4.00
10-JLA-c/app.	1	2	4	6	8	10

NOTE: *Breyfogle c-5p. N. Steven Harris a-1-5p. Porter c-1p. Wieringo c-2p.*

BABE (...Darling of the Hills, later issues)(See Big Shot and Sparky Watts)
Prize/Headline/Feature: June-July, 1948 - No. 11, Apr-May, 1950

	GD 2.0	VG 4.0	FN 6.0	VF 8.0	VF/NM 9.0	NM- 9.2
1-Boody Rogers-a	25	50	75	147	202	260
2-Boody Rogers-a	15	30	45	86	118	150
3-11-All by Boody Rogers	13	26	39	74	100	125

BABE
Dark Horse Comics (Legend): July, 1994 - No. 4, Jan, 1994 ($2.50, lim. series)

	GD 2.0	VG 4.0	FN 6.0	VF 8.0	VF/NM 9.0	NM- 9.2
1-4: John Byrne-c/a/scripts; ProtoTykes back-up story						2.50

BABE RUTH SPORTS COMICS (Becomes Rags Rabbit #11 on?)
Harvey Publications: April, 1949 - No. 11, Feb, 1951

	GD 2.0	VG 4.0	FN 6.0	VF 8.0	VF/NM 9.0	NM- 9.2
1-Powell-a	40	80	120	240	358	475
2-Powell-a	30	60	90	170	240	310
3-11: Powell-a in most	24	48	72	138	194	250

NOTE: *Baseball c-2-4, 9. Basketball c-1, 6. Football c-5. Yogi Berra c/story-8. Joe DiMaggio c/story-3. Bob Feller c/story-4. Stan Musial c-9.*

BABES IN TOYLAND (Disney, Movie) (See Golden Pix Story Book ST-3)
Dell Publishing Co.: No. 1282, Feb-Apr, 1962

	GD 2.0	VG 4.0	FN 6.0	VF 8.0	VF/NM 9.0	NM- 9.2
Four Color 1282-Annette Funicello photo-c	15	30	45	104	152	200

BABES OF BROADWAY
Broadway Comics: May, 1996 ($2.95, one-shot)

	GD 2.0	VG 4.0	FN 6.0	VF 8.0	VF/NM 9.0	NM- 9.2
1-Pin-ups of Broadway Comics' female characters; Alan Davis, Michael Kaluta, J. G. Jones, Alan Weiss, Guy Davis & others-a; Giordano-c.						3.00

BABE 2
Dark Horse Comics (Legend): Mar, 1995 - No. 2, May, 1995 ($2.50, lim. series)

	GD 2.0	VG 4.0	FN 6.0	VF 8.0	VF/NM 9.0	NM- 9.2
1,2: John Byrne-c/a/scripts						2.50

BABY HUEY
Harvey Comics: No. 1, Oct, 1991 - No. 9, June, 1994 ($1.00/$1.25/$1.50, quarterly)

	GD 2.0	VG 4.0	FN 6.0	VF 8.0	VF/NM 9.0	NM- 9.2
1 ($1.00): 1-Cover says "Big Baby Huey"						5.00
2-9 ($1.25-$1.50)						3.00

BABY HUEY AND PAPA (See Paramount Animated...)
Harvey Publications: May, 1962 - No. 33, Jan, 1968 (Also see Casper The Friendly Ghost)

	GD 2.0	VG 4.0	FN 6.0	VF 8.0	VF/NM 9.0	NM- 9.2
1	18	36	54	131	191	250
2	9	18	27	65	93	120
3-5	6	12	18	40	55	70
6-10	4	8	12	24	32	40
11-20	3	6	9	18	23	28
21-33	2	4	6	14	18	22

BABY HUEY DIGEST
Harvey Publications: June, 1992 (Digest-size, one-shot)

	GD 2.0	VG 4.0	FN 6.0	VF 8.0	VF/NM 9.0	NM- 9.2
1-Reprints	1	2	3	4	5	7

BABY HUEY DUCKLAND
Harvey Publications: Nov, 1962 - No. 15, Nov, 1966 (25¢ Giants, 68 pgs.)

	GD 2.0	VG 4.0	FN 6.0	VF 8.0	VF/NM 9.0	NM- 9.2
1	13	26	39	94	137	180
2-5	6	12	18	43	59	75
6-15	4	8	12	24	32	40

BABY HUEY, THE BABY GIANT (Also see Big Baby Huey, Casper, Harvey Hits #22, Harvey Comics Hits #60, & Paramount Animated Comics)
Harvey Publ: 9/56 - #97, 10/71; #98, 10/72; #99, 10/80; #100, 10/90; #101, 11/90

	GD 2.0	VG 4.0	FN 6.0	VF 8.0	VF/NM 9.0	NM- 9.2
1-Infinity-c	47	94	141	376	563	750
2	24	48	72	169	247	325
3-Baby Huey takes anti-pep pills	15	30	45	109	160	210
4,5	10	20	30	73	107	140
6-10	7	14	21	50	68	85
11-20	6	12	18	38	52	65
21-40	4	8	12	27	36	45
41-60	3	6	9	18	23	28
61-79 (12/67)	2	4	6	14	18	22
80(12/68) - 95-All 68 pg. Giants	3	6	9	19	25	32
96,97-Both 52 pg. Giants	3	6	9	16	20	24
98-Regular size	2	4	6	10	12	15
99-Regular size	1	2	3	5	6	8
100,101 ($1.00)						4.00

BABYLON 5 (TV)
DC Comics: Jan, 1995 - No. 11, Dec, 1995 ($1.95/$2.50)

	GD 2.0	VG 4.0	FN 6.0	VF 8.0	VF/NM 9.0	NM- 9.2
1	2	4	6	9	11	14
2-5	1	2	3	5	7	9
6-11: 7-Begin $2.50-c	1	2	3	4	5	7
... The Price of Peace (1998, $9.95, TPB) r/#1-4,11						10.00

BABYLON 5: IN VALEN'S NAME
DC Comics: Mar, 1998 - No. 3, May, 1998 ($2.50, limited series)

	GD 2.0	VG 4.0	FN 6.0	VF 8.0	VF/NM 9.0	NM- 9.2
1-3						4.00

BABY SNOOTS (Also see March of Comics #359,371,396,401,419,431,443,450,462,474,485)
Gold Key: Aug, 1970 - No. 22, Nov, 1975

	GD 2.0	VG 4.0	FN 6.0	VF 8.0	VF/NM 9.0	NM- 9.2
1	3	6	9	19	25	32
2-11	2	4	6	10	13	16
12-22: 22-Titled Snoots, the Forgetful Elefink	1	3	4	6	8	10

Backlash #3 © IM

The Badger #14 © FC

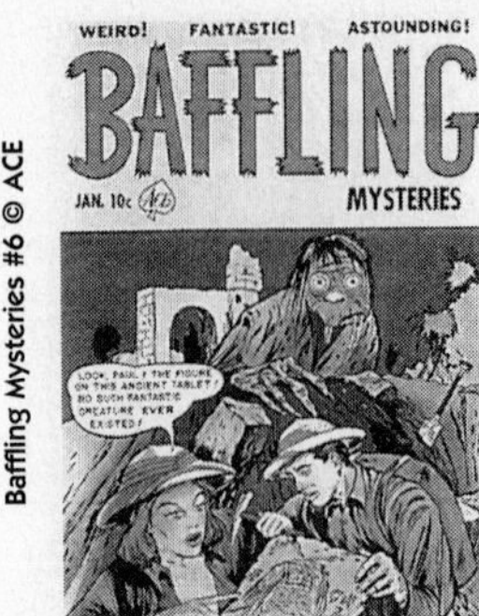

Baffling Mysteries #6 © ACE

GD	VG	FN	VF	VF/NM	NM-
2.0	4.0	6.0	8.0	9.0	9.2

BACCHUS (Also see Eddie Campbell's ...)
Harrier Comics (New Wave): 1988 - No. 2, Aug, 1988 ($1.95, B&W)

1,2: Eddie Campbell-c/a/scripts. 2.25

BACHELOR FATHER (TV)
Dell Publishing Co.: No. 1332, 4-6/62 - No. 2, Sept.-Nov., 1962

Four Color 1332 (#1), 2-Written by Stanley 9 18 27 60 85 110

BACHELOR'S DIARY
Avon Periodicals: 1949 (15¢)

1(Scarce)-King Features panel cartoons & text-r; pin-up, girl wrestling photos; similar to Sideshow 42 84 126 252 359 465

BACKPACK MARVELS (B&W backpack-sized reprint collections)
Marvel Comics: Nov, 2000 - Present ($6.95, B&W, digest-size)

Avengers 1 -r/Avengers #181-189; profile pages 7.00
Spider-Man 1-r/ASM #234-240 7.00
X-Men 1-r/Uncanny X-Men #167-173 7.00
X-Men 2-r/Uncanny X-Men #174-179; new painted-c by Greg Horn 7.00

BACK DOWN THE LINE
Eclipse Books: 1991 (Mature adults, 8-1/2 x 11", 52 pgs.)

nn (Soft-c, $8.95)-Bolton-c/a 9.00
nn (Limited Hard-c, $29.95) 30.00

BACKLASH (Also see The Kindred)
Image Comics (WildStorm Prod.): Nov,1994 - No. 32, May, 1997 ($1.95/$2.50)

1-Double-c; variant-double-c 3.00
2-7,9-32: 5-Intro Mindscape; 2 pinups. 19-Fire From Heaven Pt 2. 20-Fire From Heaven Pt 10. 31-WildC.A.T.S app. 2.50
8-($1.95, newsstand)-Wildstorm Rising Pt. 8 2.50
8-($2.50, direct market)-Wildstorm Rising Pt. 8 2.50
25-($3.95)-Double-size 4.00
...& Taboo's African Holiday (9/99, $5.95) Booth-s/a(p) 6.00

BACKLASH/SPIDER-MAN
Image Comics (WildStorm Productions): Aug, 1996 - No. 2, Sept, 1996 ($2.50, lim. series)

1,2: Pike (villain from WildC.A.T.S) & Venom app. 3.00

BACK TO THE FUTURE (Movie, TV cartoon)
Harvey Comics: Nov, 1991 - No. 4, June, 1992 ($1.25)

1-4: 1,2-Gil Kane-c; based on animated cartoon 3.00

BACK TO THE FUTURE: FORWARD TO THE FUTURE
Harvey Comics: Oct, 1992 - No. 3, Feb, 1993 ($1.50, limited series)

1-3 3.00

BAD BOY
Oni Press: Dec, 1997 ($4.95, one-shot)

1-Frank Miller-s/Simon Bisley-a/painted-c 5.00

BAD COMPANY
Quality Comics/Fleetway Quality #15 on: Aug, 1988 - No. 19?, 1990 ($1.50/$1.75, high quality paper)

1-19: 5,6-Guice-c 2.25

BADGE OF JUSTICE (Formerly Crime And Justice #21)
Charlton Comics: No. 22, 1/55 - No. 2, 4/55 - No. 4, 10/55

22(#1)(1/55) 10 20 30 58 77 95
2-4 6 12 18 33 41 48

BADGER, THE
Capital Comics(#1-4)/First Comics: Dec, 1983 - No. 70, Apr, 1991; V2#1, Spring, 1991

1 5.00
2-70: 52-54-Tim Vigil-c/a 3.00
50-($3.95, 52 pgs.) 4.00
V2#1 (Spring, 1991, $4.95) 5.00

BADGER, THE
Image Comics: V3#78, May, 1997 - V3#88 ($2.95, B&W)

78-Cover lists #1, Baron-s 3.00
79/#2, 80/#3, 81(indicia lists #80)/#4,82-88/#5-11 3.00

BADGER GOES BERSERK
First Comics: Sept, 1989 - No. 4, Dec, 1989 ($1.95, lim. series, Baxter paper)

1-4: 2-Paul Chadwick-c/a(2pgs.) 3.00

BADGER: SHATTERED MIRROR
Dark Horse Comics: July, 1994 - No. Oct, 1994 ($2.50, limited series)

1-4 3.00

BADGER: ZEN POP FUNNY-ANIMAL VERSION
Dark Horse Comics: July, 1994 - No. 2, Aug, 1994 ($2.50, limited series)

1,2 3.00

BAD GIRLS
DC Comics: Oct, 2003 - No. 5, Feb, 2004 ($2.50, limited series)

1-5-Vance-s/Graves-a/Cook-c 2.50

BAD KITTY
Chaos! Comics: Feb, 2001 - No. 3, Apr, 2001 ($2.99, limited series)

1-3-Pulido-s/Batista-a 3.00
1-Premium Edition ($9.99) Scott Lewis-c 10.00
...Mischief Night 1 (11/01, one-shot) Mota-a 3.00
...Reloaded 1-4 (10/01- No. 4, 2/02) Batista-a; Chastity app. 3.00

BADLANDS
Vortex Comics: May, 1990 ($3.00, glossy stock, mature)

1-Chaykin-c 3.00

BADLANDS
Dark Horse Comics: July, 1991 - No. 6, Dec, 1991 ($2.25, B&W, limited series)

1-6: 1-John F. Kennedy-c; reprints Vortex Comics issue 2.25

BADMEN OF THE WEST
Avon Periodicals: 1951 (Giant) (132 pgs., painted-c)

1-Contains rebound copies of Jesse James, King of the Bad Men of Deadwood, Badmen of Tombstone; other combinations possible. Issues with Kubert-a... 40 80 120 240 340 440

BADMEN OF THE WEST! (See A-1 Comics)
Magazine Enterprises: 1953 - No. 3, 1954

1(A-1 100)-Meskin-a? 26 52 78 147 206 265
2(A-1 120), 3: 2-Larsen-a 16 32 48 92 126 160

BADMEN OF TOMBSTONE
Avon Periodicals: 1950

nn 17 34 51 95 130 165

BADROCK (Also see Youngblood)
Image Comics (Extreme Studios): Mar, 1995 - No. 2, Jan, 1996 ($1.75/$2.50)

1-Variant-c (3) 3.00
2-Liefeld-c/a & story; Savage Dragon app, flipbook w/Grifter/Badrock #2; variant-c exist 2.50
Annual 1(1995,$2.95)-Arthur Adams-c 3.00
Annual 1 Commemorative ($9.95)-3,000 printed 10.00
.../Wolverine (6/96, $4.95, squarebound)-Sauron app; pin-ups; variant-c exists 5.00
.../Wolverine (6/96)-Special Comicon Edition 5.00

BADROCK AND COMPANY (Also see Youngblood)
Image Comics (Extreme Studios): Sept, 1994 - No.6, Feb, 1995 ($2.50)

1-6 : 6-Indicia reads "October 1994"; story cont'd in Shadowhawk #17 2.50

BAFFLING MYSTERIES (Formerly Indian Braves No. 1-4; Heroes of the Wild Frontier No. 26-on)
Periodical House (Ace Magazines): No. 5, Nov, 1951 - No. 26, Oct, 1955

5 39 78 117 233 329 425
6-19,21-24: 8-Woodish-a by Cameron. 10-E.C. Crypt Keeper swipe on-c. 24-Last pre-code issue 25 50 75 144 198 255
20-Classic-c 32 64 96 182 259 335
25-Reprints; surrealistic-c 19 38 57 109 152 195
26-Reprints 17 34 51 95 130 165

NOTE: ***Cameron*** *a-8, 10, 16-18, 20-22.* ***Colan*** *a-5, 11, 25r/5.* ***Sekowsky*** *a-5, 6, 22. Bondage c-20, 23. Reprints in 18(1), 19(1), 24(3).*

BALBO (See Master Comics #33 & Mighty Midget Comics)

BALDER THE BRAVE
Marvel Comics Group: Nov, 1985 - No. 4, 1986 (Limited series)

1-4: Simonson-c/a; character from Thor 3.00

BALLAD OF HALO JONES, THE
Quality Comics: Sept, 1987 - No. 12, Aug, 1988 ($1.25/$1.50)

1-12: Alan Moore scripts in all 2.25

BALL AND CHAIN
DC Comics (Homage): Nov, 1999 - No. 4, Feb, 2000 ($2.50, limited series)

1-4-Lobdell-s/Garza-a 2.50

BALLISTIC (Also See Cyberforce)
Image Comics (Top Cow Productions): Sept, 1995 - No. 3, Dec, 1995 ($2.50, limited series)

Ballistic Imagery #1 © TCOW

Mattel #32 © Mattel, Inc.

The Barker #2 © QUA

	GD 2.0	VG 4.0	FN 6.0	VF 8.0	VF/NM 9.0	NM- 9.2
1-3: Wetworks app, Turner-c/a						3.00
BALLISTIC ACTION						
Image Comics (Top Cow Productions): May, 1996 ($2.95, one-shot)						
1-Pin-ups of Top Cow characters participating in outdoor sports						3.00
BALLISTIC IMAGERY						
Image Comics (Top Cow Productions): Jan, 1996 ($2.50, anthology, one-shot)						
1-Cyberforce app.						2.50
BALLISTIC/ WOLVERINE						
Image Comics (Top Cow Productions): Feb, 1997 ($2.95, one-shot)						
1-Devil's Reign pt. 4; Witchblade cameo (1 page)						4.00
BALOO & LITTLE BRITCHES (Disney)						
Gold Key: Apr, 1968						
1-From the Jungle Book	4	8	12	25	33	42
BAMBI (Disney) (See Movie Classics, Movie Comics, and Walt Disney Showcase No. 31)						
Dell Publishing Co.: No. 12, 1942; No. 30, 1943; No. 186, Apr, 1948; 1984						
Four Color 12-Walt Disney's...	59	158	177	417	639	860
Four Color 30-Bambi's Children (1943)	56	112	168	400	605	810
Four Color 186-Walt Disney's...; reprinted as Movie Classic Bambi #3 (1956)	18	36	54	127	186	245
1-(Whitman, 1984; 60¢)-r/Four Color #186 (3-pack)	1	2	3	6	8	10
BAMBI (Disney)						
Grosset & Dunlap: 1942 (50¢, 7"x8-1/2", 32pg, hard-c w/dust jacket)						
nn-Given away w/a copy of Thumper for a $2.00, 2-yr. subscription to WDC&S in 1942 (Xmas offer). Book only	22	44	66	127	176	225
w/dust jacket	39	78	117	233	329	425
BAMM BAMM & PEBBLES FLINTSTONE (TV)						
Gold Key: Oct, 1964 (Hanna-Barbera)						
1	10	20	30	70	100	130
BANANA SPLITS, THE (TV) (See Golden Comics Digest & March of Comics No. 364)						
Gold Key: June, 1969 - No. 8, Oct, 1971 (Hanna-Barbera)						
1-Photo-c on all	12	24	36	87	129	170
2-8	8	16	24	55	78	100
BAND WAGON (See Hanna-Barbera Band Wagon)						
BANDY MAN, THE						
Caliber: 1996 - No. 3, ($2.95, B&W, limited series)						
1-3-Stephan Petrucha scripts; 1-Jill Thompson-a; Miran Kim-c						3.00
BANG-UP COMICS						
Progressive Publishers: Dec, 1941 - No. 3, June, 1942						
1-Cosmo Mann & Lady Fairplay begin; Buzz Balmer by Rick Yager in all (origin #1)	100	200	300	625	938	1250
2,3	50	100	150	300	450	600
BANISHED KNIGHTS (See Warlands)						
Image Comics: Dec, 2001 - No. 4, June, 2002 ($2.95)						
1-4-Two covers (Alvin Lee, Pat Lee)						3.00
BANNER COMICS (Becomes Captain Courageous No. 6)						
Ace Magazines: No. 3, Sept, 1941 - No. 5, Jan, 1942						
3-Captain Courageous (1st app.) & Lone Warrior & Sidekick Dicky begin; Jim Mooney-c	107	214	321	669	1005	1340
4,5: 4-Flag-c	66	132	198	413	617	820
BANZAI GIRL						
Sirius Entertainment Inc.: 2002 - Present ($2.95)						
1-3-Tortosa-a						3.00
BARABBAS						
Slave Labor Graphics: Aug, 1986 - No. 2, Nov, 1986 ($1.50, B&W, lim. series)						
1,2						2.25
BARBARIANS, THE						
Atlas Comics/Seaboard Periodicals: June, 1975						
1-Origin, only app. Andrax; Iron Jaw app.; Marcos-a	1	2	3	5	6	8
BARBIE						
Marvel Comics: Jan, 1991 - No. 66, Apr, 1996 ($1.00/$1.25/$1.50)						
1-Polybagged w/Barbie Pink Card; Romita-c	2	4	6	10	12	15
2-49,51-66	1	2	3	5	7	9
50-(Giant)	2	4	6	8	10	12

	GD 2.0	VG 4.0	FN 6.0	VF 8.0	VF/NM 9.0	NM- 9.2
BARBIE & KEN						
Dell Publishing Co.: May-July, 1962 - No. 5, Nov-Jan, 1963-64						
01-053-207(#1)-Based on Mattel toy dolls	40	80	120	300	450	600
2-4	33	66	99	239	350	460
5 (Rare)	33	66	99	248	374	500
BARBIE FASHION						
Marvel Comics: Jan, 1991 - No. 63, Jan, 1996 ($1.00/$1.25/$1.50)						
1-Polybagged w/doorknob hanger	2	4	6	10	12	15
2-49,51-63: 4-Contains preview to Sweet XVI. 14-Begin $1.25-c	1	2	3	5	7	9
50-(Giant)	2	4	6	8	10	12
BARBI TWINS, THE						
Topps Comics: 1995 ($2.50/$5.00)						
1-Razor app.						2.50
Swimsuit Art Calendar ($5.00)-art by Linsner, Bradstreet, Hughes; Julie Bell-c						5.00
BARB WIRE (See Comics' Greatest World)						
Dark Horse Comics: Apr, 1994 - No. 9, Feb, 1995 ($2.00/$2.50)						
1-9: 1-Foil logo						3.00
Trade paperback (1996, $8.95)-r/#2,3,5,6 w/Pamela Anderson bio						9.00
BARB WIRE: ACE OF SPADES						
Dark Horse Comics: May, 1996 - No. 4, Sept, 1996 ($2.95, limited series)						
1-4: Chris Warner-c/a(p)/scripts; Tim Bradstreet-c/a(i) in all						3.00
BARB WIRE COMICS MAGAZINE SPECIAL						
Dark Horse Comics: May, 1996 ($3.50, B&W, magazine, one-shot)						
nn-Adaptation of film; photo-c; poster insert.						3.50
BARB WIRE MOVIE SPECIAL						
Dark Horse Comics: May, 1996 ($3.95, one-shot)						
nn-Adaptation of film; photo-c; 1st app. new look						4.00
BARKER, THE (Also see National Comics #42)						
Quality Comics Group/Comic Magazine: Autumn, 1946 - No. 15, Dec, 1949						
1	22	44	66	124	172	220
2	11	22	33	66	88	110
3-10	9	18	27	49	62	75
11-14	7	14	21	35	43	50
15-Jack Cole-a(p)	7	14	21	37	46	55
NOTE: ***Jack Cole** art in some issues.*						
BARNABY						
Civil Service Publications Inc.: 1945 (25¢,102 pgs., digest size)						
V1#1-r/Crocket Johnson strips from 1942	5	10	14	20	24	28
BARNEY AND BETTY RUBBLE (TV) (Flintstones' Neighbors)						
Charlton Comics: Jan, 1973 - No. 23, Dec, 1976 (Hanna-Barbera)						
1	4	8	12	29	40	50
2-11: 11(2/75)-1st Mike Zeck-a (illos)	3	6	9	16	20	25
12-23	2	4	6	11	14	18
Digest Annual (1972, B&W, 100 pgs.) (scarce)	3	7	10	21	28	35
BARNEY BAXTER (Also see Magic Comics)						
David McKay/Dell Publishing Co./Argo: 1938 - No. 2, 1956						
Feature Books 15(McKay-1938)	40	80	120	240	340	440
Four Color 20(1942)	29	58	87	209	300	390
1,2 (1956-Argo)	9	18	27	49	62	75
BARNEY BEAR ...						
Spire Christian Comics (Fleming H. Revell Co.): 1977-1981						
...Home Plate nn-(1979, 49¢), ...Lost and Found nn-(1979, 49¢), Out of The Woods nn-(1980, 49¢), Sunday School Picnic nn-(1981, 69¢, The Swamp Gang!-(1977, 39¢)	1	3	4	6	8	10
BARNEY GOOGLE & SNUFFY SMITH						
Dell Publishing Co./Gold Key: 1942 - 1943; April, 1964						
Four Color 19(1942)	38	76	115	285	418	550
Four Color 40(1944)	24	48	72	169	247	325
Large Feature Comic 11(1943)	37	74	111	212	301	390
1(10113-404)-Gold Key (4/64)	4	8	12	29	40	50
BARNEY GOOGLE & SNUFFY SMITH						
Toby Press: June, 1951 - No. 4, Feb, 1952 (Reprints)						
1	14	28	42	79	107	135
2,3	8	16	24	46	58	70

Barney Google and Snuffy Smith #4 © TOBY

Bastard Samurai TPB © Oeming & Shannon

Batgirl: Year One #9 © DC

	GD 2.0	VG 4.0	FN 6.0	VF 8.0	VF/NM 9.0	NM- 9.2
4-Kurtzman-a "Pot Shot Pete", 5 pgs.; reprints John Wayne #5	13	26	39	74	100	125

BARNEY GOOGLE AND SNUFFY SMITH
Charlton Comics: Mar, 1970 - No. 6, Jan, 1971

	GD	VG	FN	VF	VF/NM	NM-
1	3	6	9	18	24	30
2-6	2	4	6	11	14	18

BARNUM!
DC Comics (Vertigo): 2003 ($29.95, hardcover with dust jacket)

	GD	VG	FN	VF	VF/NM	NM-
Hardcover-Chaykin & Tischman-s/Henrichon-a						30.00

BARNYARD COMICS (Dizzy Duck No. 32 on)
Nedor/Polo Mag./Standard(Animated Cartoons): June, 1944 - No. 31, Sept, 1950; No. 10, 1957

	GD	VG	FN	VF	VF/NM	NM-
1 (nn, 52 pgs.)-Funny animal	21	42	63	118	164	210
2 (52 pgs.)	11	22	33	63	84	105
3-5	8	16	24	43	54	65
6-12,16	7	14	21	37	46	55
13-15,17,21,23,26,27,29-All contain Frazetta text illos	9	18	27	49	62	75
18-20,22,24,25-All contain Frazetta-a & text illos	11	22	33	66	88	110
28,30,31	6	12	18	28	34	40
10 (1957)(Exist?)	4	7	10	14	17	20

BARRY M. GOLDWATER
Dell Publishing Co.: Mar, 1965 (Complete life story)

	GD	VG	FN	VF	VF/NM	NM-
12-055-503-Photo-c	4	8	12	27	36	45

BARRY WINDSOR-SMITH: STORYTELLER
Dark Horse Comics: Oct, 1996 - No. 9, July, 1997 ($4.95, oversize)

	GD	VG	FN	VF	VF/NM	NM-
1-9: 1-Intro Young Gods, Paradox Man & the Freebooters; Barry Smith-c/a/scripts						5.00
Preview						4.00

BAR SINISTER (Also see Shaman's Tears)
Acclaim Comics (Windjammer): Jun, 1995 - No. 4, Sept, 1995 ($2.50, lim. series)

	GD	VG	FN	VF	VF/NM	NM-
1-4: Mike Grell-c/a/scripts						2.50

BARTMAN (Also see Simpson's Comics & Radioactive Man)
Bongo Comics: 1993 - No. 6, 1994 ($1.95/$2.25)

	GD	VG	FN	VF	VF/NM	NM-
1-($2.95)-Foil-c; bound-in jumbo Bartman poster						6.00
2-6: 3-w/trading card						4.00

BART SIMPSON (See Simpsons Comics Presents Bart Simpson)

BASEBALL COMICS
Will Eisner Productions: Spring, 1949 (Reprinted later as a Spirit section)

	GD	VG	FN	VF	VF/NM	NM-
1-Will Eisner-c/a	70	140	210	438	657	875

BASEBALL COMICS
Kitchen Sink Press: 1991 ($3.95, coated stock)

	GD	VG	FN	VF	VF/NM	NM-
1-r/1949 ish. by Eisner; contains trading cards						6.00

BASEBALL HEROES
Fawcett Publications: 1952 (one-shot)

	GD	VG	FN	VF	VF/NM	NM-
nn (Scarce)-Babe Ruth photo-c; baseball's Hall of Fame biographies	78	156	234	488	732	975

BASEBALL'S GREATEST HEROES
Magnum Comics: Dec, 1991 - No. 2, May, 1992 ($1.75)

	GD	VG	FN	VF	VF/NM	NM-
1-Mickey Mantle #1; photo-c; Sinnott-a(p)						5.00
2-Brooks Robinson #1; photo-c; Sinnott-a(i)						4.00

BASEBALL THRILLS
Ziff-Davis Publ. Co.: No. 10, Sum, 1951 - No. 3, Sum, 1952 (Saunders painted-c No.1,2)

	GD	VG	FN	VF	VF/NM	NM-
10(#1)-Bob Feller, Musial, Newcombe & Boudreau stories	41	82	123	246	371	495
2-Powell-a(2)(Late Sum, '51); Feller, Berra & Mathewson stories	32	64	96	182	259	335
3-Kinstler-c/a; Joe DiMaggio story	32	64	96	182	259	335

BASEBALL THRILLS 3-D
The 3-D Zone: May, 1990 ($2.95, w/glasses)

	GD	VG	FN	VF	VF/NM	NM-
1-New L.B. Cole-c; life stories of Ty Cobb & Ted Williams						6.00

BASICALLY STRANGE (Magazine)
John C. Comics (Archie Comics Group): Dec, 1982 ($1.95, B&W)

	GD	VG	FN	VF	VF/NM	NM-
1-(21,000 printed; all but 1,000 destroyed; pgs. out of sequence)	2	4	6	14	18	22
1-Wood, Toth-a; Corben-c; reprints & new art	2	4	6	11	14	18

BASIC HISTORY OF AMERICA ILLUSTRATED
Pendulum Press: 1976 (B&W) (Soft-c $1.50; Hard-c $4.50)

07-1999-America Becomes a World Power 1890-1920. 07-2251-The Industrial Era 1865-1915. 07-226x-Before the Civil War 1830-1860. 07-2278-Americans Move Westward 1800-1850. 07-2286-The Civil War 1850-1876; Redondo-a. 07-2294-The Fight for Freedom 1750-1783. 07-2308-The New World 1500-1750. 07-2316-Problems of the New Nation 1800-1830. 07-2324-Roaring Twenties and the Great Depression 1920-1940. 07-2332-The United States Emerges 1783-1800. 07-2340-America Today 1945-1976. 07-2359-World War II 1940-1945

	GD	VG	FN	VF	VF/NM	NM-
Softcover editions each						5.00
Hardcover editions each						10.00

BASIL (...the Royal Cat)
St. John Publishing Co.: Jan, 1953 - No. 4, Sept, 1953

	GD	VG	FN	VF	VF/NM	NM-
1-Funny animal	7	14	21	37	46	55
2-4	5	10	15	22	26	30
I.W. Reprint 1	2	4	6	10	12	15

BASIL WOLVERTON'S FANTASTIC FABLES
Dark Horse Comics: Oct, 1993 - No. 2, Dec, 1993 ($2.50, B&W, limited series)

	GD	VG	FN	VF	VF/NM	NM-
1,2-Wolverton-c/a(r)						6.00

BASIL WOLVERTON'S GATEWAY TO HORROR
Dark Horse Comics: June, 1988 ($1.75, B&W, one-shot)

	GD	VG	FN	VF	VF/NM	NM-
1-Wolverton-r						6.00

BASIL WOLVERTON'S PLANET OF TERROR
Dark Horse Comics: Oct, 1987 ($1.75, B&W, one-shot)

	GD	VG	FN	VF	VF/NM	NM-
1-Wolverton-r; Alan Moore-c						6.00

BASTARD SAMURAI
Image Comics: Apr, 2002 - No. 3, Aug, 2002 ($2.95)

	GD	VG	FN	VF	VF/NM	NM-
1-3-Oeming & Gunter-s; Shannon-a/Oeming-i						3.00
TPB (2003, $12.95) r/#1-3; plus sketch pages and pin-ups						13.00

BATGIRL (See Batman: No Man's Land stories)
DC Comics: Apr, 2000 - Present ($2.50)

	GD	VG	FN	VF	VF/NM	NM-
1-Scott & Campanella-a						6.00
1-(2nd printing)						2.50
2-10: 8-Lady Shiva app.						4.50
11-24: 12-"Officer Down" x-over. 15-Joker-c/app. 24-Bruce Wayne: Murderer pt. 2.						4.00
25-($3.25) Batgirl vs Lady Shiva						3.50
26-29: 27- Bruce Wayne: Fugitive pt. 5; Noto-a. 29-B.W.:F. pt. 13						3.50
30-46: 30-32-Connor Hawke app. 39-Intro. Black Wind. 41-Superboy-c/app.						3.00
Annual 1 ('00, $3.50) Planet DC; intro. Aruna						5.00
...: A Knight Alone (2001, $12.95, TPB) r/#7-11,13,14						13.00
...: Death Wish (2003, $14.95, TPB) r/#17-20,22,23,25 & Secret Files and Origins #1						15.00
... Secret Files and Origins (8/02, $4.95) origin-s Noto-a; profile pages and pin-ups						5.00
...: Silent Running (2001, $12.95, TPB) r/#1-6						13.00

BATGIRL ADVENTURES (See Batman Adventures, The)
DC Comics: Feb, 1998 ($2.95, one-shot) (Based on animated series)

	GD	VG	FN	VF	VF/NM	NM-
1-Harley Quinn and Poison Ivy app.; Timm-c						5.00

BATGIRL SPECIAL
DC Comics: 1988 ($1.50, one-shot, 52 pgs)

	GD	VG	FN	VF	VF/NM	NM-
1-Kitson-a/Mignola-c	1	2	3	5	7	9

BATGIRL: YEAR ONE
DC Comics: Feb, 2003 - No. 9, Oct, 2003 ($2.95, limited series)

	GD	VG	FN	VF	VF/NM	NM-
1-9-Barbara Gordon becomes Batgirl; Killer Moth app.; Beatty & Dixon-s						3.00
TPB (2003, $17.95) r/#1-9						18.00

BAT LASH (See DC Special Series #16, Showcase #76, Weird Western Tales)
National Periodical Publications: Oct-Nov, 1968 - No. 7, Oct-Nov, 1969
(All 12¢ issues)

	GD	VG	FN	VF	VF/NM	NM-
1-(10-11/68)-2nd app. Bat Lash	5	10	15	33	44	55
2-7	3	6	9	19	25	32

BATMAN (See Anarky, Aurora [in Promo. Comics section], Azrael, The Best of DC #2, Blind Justice, The Brave & the Bold, Cosmic Odyssey, DC 100-Page Super Spec. #14,20, DC Special, DC Special Series, Detective, Dynamic Classics, 80-Page Giants, Gotham By Gaslight, Gotham Nights, Greatest Batman Stories Ever Told, Greatest Joker Stories Ever Told, Heroes Against Hunger, JLA,The Joker, Justice League of America, Justice League Int., Legends of the Dark Knight, Limited Coll. Ed., Man-Bat, Nightwing, Power Record Comics, Real Fact #5, Robin, Saga of Ra's Al Ghul, Shadow of the..., Star Spangled, Super Friends, 3-D Batman, Untold Legend of..., Wanted... & World's Finest Comics)

BATMAN
National Per. Publ./Detective Comics/DC Comics: Spring, 1940 - Present
(#1-5 were quarterly)

1-Origin The Batman reprinted (2 pgs.) from Det. #33 w/splash from #34 by Bob Kane; see Detective #33 for 1st origin; 1st app. Joker (2 stories intended for 2 separate issues of

Batman #9 © DC

Batman #49 © DC

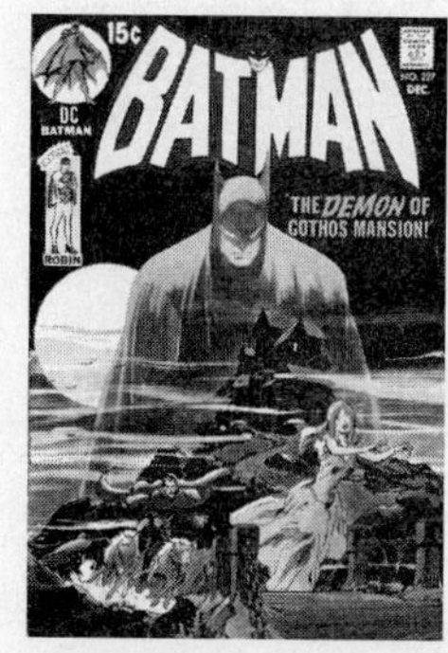

Batman #237 © DC

GD VG FN VF VF/NM NM-
2.0 4.0 6.0 8.0 9.0 9.2

Det. Comics which would have been 1st & 2nd app.); splash pg. to 2nd Joker story is similar to cover of Det. #40 (story intended for #40); 1st app. The Cat (Catwoman) (1st villainess in comics); has Batman story (w/Hugo Strange) without Robin originally planned for Det. #38; mentions location (Manhattan) where Batman lives (see Det. #31). This book was created entirely from the inventory of Det. Comics; 1st Batman/Robin pin-up on back-c; has text piece & photo of Bob Kane
6944 13,888 20,832 49,200 87,100 125,000

1-Reprint, oversize 13-1/2x10". **WARNING**: This comic is an exact duplicate reprint of the original except for its size. DC published it in 1974 with a second cover titling it as a Famous First Edition. There have been many reported cases of the outer cover being removed and the interior sold as the original edition. The reprint with the new outer cover removed is practically worthless. See Famous First Edition for value.

2-2nd app. The Joker; 2nd app. Catwoman (out of costume) in Joker story; 1st time called Catwoman (NOTE: A 15¢-c for Canadian distr. exists.)
1219 2438 3657 9143 14,322 19,500

3-3rd app Catwoman (1st in costume & 1st costumed villainess); 1st Puppet Master app.; classic Kane & Moldoff-c 828 1655 2485 5800 8900 12,000

4-3rd app. The Joker (see Det. #45 for 4th); 1st mention of Gotham City in a Batman comic (on newspaper)(Win/40) 665 1310 1965 4585 7043 9500

5-1st app. the Batmobile with its bat-head front 470 940 1410 3290 5045 6800

6,7: 7-Bullseye-c 423 846 1269 2856 4428 6000

8-Infinity-c. 356 712 1068 2314 3557 4800

9-10:9-1st Batman x-mas story; Burnley-c. 10-Catwoman story (gets new costume)
341 682 1023 2217 3409 4600

11-Classic Joker-c by Ray/Robinson (3rd Joker-c, 6-7/42); Joker & Penguin app.
655 1310 1965 4585 7043 9500

12,15: 15-New costume Catwoman 296 592 888 1850 2775 3700

13-Jerry Siegel (Superman's co-creator) appears in a Batman story.
300 600 900 1900 2850 3800

14-2nd Penguin-c; Penguin app. (12-1/42-43) 312 624 936 1950 2925 3900

16-Intro/origin Alfred (4-5/43); cover is a reverse of #9 cover by Burnley; 1st small logo
497 994 1491 3479 5340 7200

17,20: 17-Classic war-c; Penguin app. 20-1st Batmobile-c (12-1/43-44); Joker app.
216 432 648 1350 2025 2700

18-Hitler, Hirohito, Mussolini-c. 280 560 840 1750 2625 3500

19-Joker app. 192 384 576 1200 1800 2400

21,22,24,26,28-30: 21-1st skinny Alfred in Batman (2-3/44). 21,30-Penguin app. 22-1st Alfred solo-c/story (Alfred solo stories in 22-32,36); Catwoman & The Cavalier app. 28-Joker story
152 304 456 950 1425 1900

23-Joker-c/story; classic black-c 240 480 720 1500 2250 3000

25-Only Joker/Penguin team-up; 1st team-up between two major villains
224 448 672 1400 2100 2800

27-Classic Burnley Christmas-c; Penguin app. 200 400 600 1250 1875 2500

31,32,34-36,39: 32-Origin Robin retold; Joker app. 35-Catwoman story (in new costume w/o cat head mask). 36-Penguin app. 112 224 336 700 1050 1400

33-Christmas-c 120 240 360 750 1125 1500

37,40,44-Joker-c/stories 152 304 456 950 1425 1900

38-Penguin-c/story 128 256 384 800 1200 1600

41,45,46: 41-1st Sci-fi cover/story in Batman; Penguin app.(6-7/47). 45-Christmas-c/story; Catwoman story 82 164 246 513 769 1025

42-2nd Catwoman-c (1st in Batman)(8-9/47); Catwoman story also.
128 256 384 800 1200 1600

43-Penguin-c/story 109 218 327 681 1021 1360

47-1st detailed origin The Batman (6-7/48); 1st Bat-signal-c this title (see Detective #108); Batman tracks down his parent's killer and reveals i.d. to him
311 622 933 2022 3111 4200

48-1000 Secrets of the Batcave; r-in #203; Penguin story
108 216 324 675 1013 1350

49-Joker-c/story; 1st app. Mad Hatter; 1st app. Vicki Vale
172 344 516 1075 1613 2150

50-Two-Face impostor app. 92 184 276 575 863 1150

51,54,56,57,59,60: 57-Centerfold is a 1950 calendar. 59-1st app. Deadshot; Batman in the future-c/story 78 156 234 488 732 975

52,55-Joker-c/stories 104 208 312 650 975 1300

53-Joker story 83 116 249 519 780 1040

58,61: 58-Penguin-c. 61-Origin Batman Plane II 85 170 255 531 796 1060

62-Origin Catwoman; Catwoman-c 120 240 360 750 1125 1500

63,80-Joker stories. 63-1st app. Killer Moth; flying saucer story(2-3/51)
74 148 222 463 694 925

64,67,70-72,74-77,79: 67-Joker story. 70-Robot-c. 72-Last 52 pg. issue. 74-Used in **POP**, Pg. 90. 76-Penguin story. 79-Vicki Vale in "The Bride of Batman"
61 122 183 381 573 765

65,69,84-Catwoman-c/stories. 84-Two-Face app. 74 148 222 463 694 925

66,73-Joker-c/stories. 66-Pre-2nd Batman & Robin team try-out. 73-Vicki Vale story
84 168 252 525 788 1050

GD VG FN VF VF/NM NM-
2.0 4.0 6.0 8.0 9.0 9.2

68,81-Two-Face-c/stories 66 132 198 413 617 820

78-(8-9/53)-Roh Kar, The Man Hunter from Mars story-the 1st lawman of Mars to come to Earth (green skinned) 76 152 228 475 713 950

82,83,85-89: 85,87-Joker story. 86-Intro Batmarine (Batman's submarine). 89-Last pre-code issue 58 116 174 363 542 720

90,91,93-99: 97-2nd app. Bat-Hound-c/story; Joker story. 99-(4/56)-Last G.A. Penguin app.
50 100 150 300 450 600

92-1st app. Bat-Hound-c/story 66 132 198 413 617 820

100-(6/56) 252 504 756 1575 2363 3150

101-(8/56)-Clark Kent x-over who protects Batman's i.d. (3rd story)
51 102 153 306 458 610

102-104,106-109: 103-1st S.A. issue; 3rd Bat-Hound-c/story
44 88 132 264 395 525

105-1st Batwoman in Batman (2nd anywhere) 56 112 168 350 525 700

110-Joker story 45 90 135 270 403 535

111-120: 112-1st app. Signalman (super villain). 113-1st app. Fatman; Batman meets his counterpart on Planet X w/a chest plate similar to S.A. Batman's design (yellow oval w/black design inside). 39 78 117 230 325 420

121- Origin/1st app. of Mr. Zero (Mr. Freeze). 46 92 138 276 413 550

122,124-126,128,130: 122,126-Batwoman-c/story. 124-2nd app. Signal Man. 128-Batwoman cameo. 130-Lex Luthor app. 29 58 87 164 232 300

123,127: 123-Joker story; Bat-Hound app. 127-(10/59)-Batman vs. Thor the Thunder God c/story; Joker story; Superman cameo 31 62 93 178 252 325

129-Origin Robin retold; bondage-c; Batwoman-c/story (reprinted in Batman Family #8)
32 64 96 184 262 340

131-135,137-139,141-143: 131-Intro 2nd Batman & Robin series (see #66; also in #135,145, 154,159,163). 133-1st Bat-Mite in Batman (3rd app. anywhere). 134-Origin The Dummy (not Vigilante's villain). 139-Intro 1st original Bat-Girl; only app. Signalman as the Blue Bowman. 141-2nd app. original Bat-Girl. 143-(10/61)-Last 10¢ issue
22 44 66 127 176 225

136-Joker-c/story 26 52 78 150 210 270

140-Joker story, Batwoman-c/s; Superman cameo 23 46 69 132 186 240

144-(12/61)-1st 12¢ issue; Joker story 17 34 51 121 178 235

145,148-Joker-c/stories 19 38 57 138 202 265

146,147,149,150 13 26 39 90 133 175

151-154,156-158,160-162,164-168,170: 152-Joker story. 156-Ant-Man/Robin team-up(6/63). 164-New Batmobile(6/64) new look & Mystery Analysts series begins
10 20 30 73 107 140

155-1st S.A. app. The Penguin (5/63) 31 62 93 228 339 450

159,163-Joker-c/stories. 159-Bat-Girl app. 13 26 39 90 133 175

169-2nd SA Penguin app. 14 28 42 99 145 190

171-1st Riddler app.(5/65) since Dec. 1948 38 76 114 285 430 575

172-175,177,178,180,184 8 16 24 58 82 105

176-(80-Pg. Giant G-17); Joker-c/story; Penguin app. in strip-r; Catwoman reprint
10 20 30 73 107 140

179-2nd app. Silver Age Riddler 15 30 45 109 160 210

181-Batman & Robin poster insert; intro. Poison Ivy 18 36 54 131 191 250

182,187-(80 Pg. Giants G-24, G-30); Joker-c/stories 9 18 27 63 89 115

183-2nd app. Poison Ivy 10 20 30 73 107 140

185-(80 Pg. Giant G-27) 9 18 27 60 85 110

186-Joker-c/story 9 18 27 60 85 110

188,191,192,194-196,199 6 12 18 40 55 70

189-1st S.A. app. Scarecrow; retells origin of G.A. Scarecrow from World's Finest #3(1st app.)
10 20 30 73 107 140

190-Penguin-c/app. 7 14 21 51 71 90

193-(80-Pg. Giant G-37) 8 16 24 55 78 100

197-4th S.A. Catwoman app. cont'd from Det. #369; 1st new Batgirl app. in Batman (5th anywhere) 8 16 24 55 78 100

198-(80-Pg. Giant G-43); Joker-c/story-r/World's Finest #61; Catwoman-r/Det. #211; Penguin-r; origin-r/#47 9 18 27 60 85 110

200-(3/68)-Joker cameo; retells origin of Batman & Robin; 1st Neal Adams work this title (cover only) 15 30 45 104 152 200

201-Joker story 6 12 18 38 52 65

202,204-207,209-212: 210-Catwoman-c/app. 212-Last 12¢ issue
5 10 15 33 44 55

203-(80 Pg. Giant G-49); r/#48, 61, & Det. 185; Batcave Blueprints
7 14 21 46 63 80

208-(80 Pg. Giant G-55); New origin Batman by Gil Kane plus 3 G.A. Batman reprints w/Catwoman, Vicki Vale & Batwoman 7 14 21 46 63 80

213-(80-Pg. Giant G-61); 30th anniversary issue (7-8/69); origin Alfred (r/Batman #16), Joker(r/Det. #168), Clayface; new origin Robin with new facts
9 18 27 60 85 110

214-217: 214-Alfred given a new last name- "Pennyworth" (see Detective #96)
4 8 12 27 36 45

Batman #393 © DC

Batman #504 © DC

Batman #612 © DC

	GD 2.0	VG 4.0	FN 6.0	VF 8.0	VF/NM 9.0	NM- 9.2
218-(80-Pg. Giant G-67)	6	12	18	40	55	70
219-Neal Adams-a	6	12	18	38	52	65
220,221,224-226,229-231	4	8	12	24	32	40
222-Beatles take-off; art lesson by Joe Kubert	5	10	15	36	48	60
223,228,233: 223,228-(80-Pg. Giants G-73,G-79). 233-G-85-(68 pgs., "64 pgs." on-c)	6	12	18	38	52	65
227-Neal Adams cover swipe of Detective #31	5	10	15	33	44	55
232-N. Adams-a. Intro/1st app. Ra's al Ghul; origin Batman & Robin retold; last 15¢ issue	12	24	36	82	121	160
234-(9/71)-1st modern app. of Harvey Dent/Two-Face; (see World's Finest #173 for Batman as Two-Face; only S.A. mention of character); N. Adams-a; 52 pg. issues begin, end #242	15	30	45	104	152	200
235,236,239-242: 239-XMas-c. 241-Reprint/#5	4	8	12	27	36	45
237-N. Adams-a. 1st Rutland Vermont - Bald Mountain Halloween x-over. G.A. Batman-r/ Det. #37; 1st app. The Reaper; Wrightson/Ellison plots	8	16	24	53	74	95
238-Also listed as DC 100 Page Super Spectacular #8; Batman, Legion, Aquaman-r; G.A. Atom, Sargon (r/Sensation #57), Plastic Man (r/Police #14) stories; Doom Patrol origin-r; N. Adams wraparound-c (see DC 100 Pg. Super Spectacular #8 for price)						
243-245-Neal Adams-a	6	12	18	38	52	65
246-250,252,253: 246-Scarecrow app. 253-Shadow-c & app.	3	7	10	21	28	35
251-(9/73)-N. Adams-c/a; Joker-c/story	8	16	24	53	74	95
254,256-259,261-All 100 pg. editions; part-r: 254-(2/74)-Man-Bat-c & app. 256-Catwoman app. 257-Joker & Penguin app. 258-The Cavalier-r. 259-Shadow-c/app.	6	12	18	38	52	65
255-(100 pgs.)-N. Adams-c/a; tells of Bruce Wayne's father who wore bat costume & fought crime (r/Det. #235); r/story Batman #22	7	14	21	46	63	80
260-Joker-c/story (100 pgs.)	7	14	21	46	63	80
262 (68pgs.)	4	8	12	24	32	40
263,264,266-285,287-290,292,293,295-299: 266-Catwoman back to old costume	2	4	6	10	13	16
265-Wrightson-a(i)	2	4	6	11	14	18
286,291,294: 294-Joker-c/stories	3	6	9	16	20	24
300-Double-size	3	6	9	16	20	25
301-(7/78)-310,312-315,317-320,325-331,333-352: 304-(44 pgs.). 306-3rd app. Black Spider. 308-Mr. Freeze app. 310-1st modern app. The Gentleman Ghost in Batman; Kubert-c. 312,314,346-Two-Face-c/stories. 313-2nd app. Calendar Man. 318-Intro Firebug. 319-2nd modern age app. The Gentleman Ghost; Kubert-c. 344-Poison Ivy app. 345-1st app. new Dr. Death. 345,346,351-Catwoman back-ups	2	4	6	8	10	12
306,307,312-315,320,323,324,326-(Whitman variants; low print run; none show issue # on cover)	2	4	6	10	12	15
311,316,322-324: 311-Batgirl-c/story; Batgirl reteams w/Batman. 316-Robin returns. 322-324-Catwoman (Selina Kyle) app. 322,323-Cat-Man cameos (1st in Batman, 1 panel each). 323-1st meeting Catwoman & Cat-Man. 324-1st full app. Cat-Man this title	2	4	6	10	12	15
321,353,359-Joker-c/stories.	2	4	6	11	14	18
332-Catwoman's 1st solo.	2	4	6	11	14	18
354-356,358,360-365,369,370: 361-1st app Harvey Bullock	1	2	3	5	7	9
357-1st app. Jason Todd (3/83); see Det. #524; 1st app. Croc (cameo)	2	4	6	10	12	15
366-Jason Todd 1st in Robin costume; Joker-c/story	2	4	6	11	14	18
367-Jason in red & green costume (not as Robin)	2	4	6	8	10	12
368-1st new Robin in costume (Jason Todd)	2	4	6	10	12	15
371-399,401-403: 371-Cat-Man-c/story; brief origin Cat-Man (cont'd in Det. #538). 386,387-Intro Black Mask (villain). 380-391-Catwoman app. 398-Catwoman & Two-Face app. 401-2nd app. Magpie (see Man of Steel #3 for 1st). 403-Joker cameo						6.00

NOTE: *Most issues between 397 & 432 were reprinted in 1989 and sold in multi-packs. Some are not identified as reprints but have newer ads copyrighted after cover dates. 2nd and 3rd printings exist.*

	GD 2.0	VG 4.0	FN 6.0	VF 8.0	VF/NM 9.0	NM- 9.2
400 ($1.50, 68pgs.)-Dark Knight special; intro by Stephen King; Art Adams/Austin-a	3	6	9	16	20	24
404-Miller scripts begin (end 407); Year 1; 1st modern app. Catwoman (2/87)	2	4	6	12	16	20
405-407: 407-Year 1 ends (See Detective Comics #575-578 for Year 2)	2	4	6	10	12	15
408-410: New Origin Jason Todd (Robin)	1	2	3	5	6	8
411-416,421-425: 411-Two-face app. 412-Origin/1st app. Mime. 414-Starlin scripts begin, end #429. 416-Nightwing-c/story. 423-McFarlane-c						5.00
417-420: "Ten Nights of the Beast" storyline	1	3	4	6	8	10
426-($1.50, 52 pgs.)- "A Death In The Family" storyline begins, ends #429	2	4	6	11	14	18
427- "A Death In The Family" part 2.	2	4	6	10	12	15
428-Death of Robin (Jason Todd)	2	4	6	11	14	18
429-Joker-c/story; Superman app.	2	4	6	8	10	12
430-432						3.00
433-435-Many Deaths of the Batman story by John Byrne-c/scripts						3.00
436-Year 3 begins (ends #439); origin original Robin retold by Nightwing (Dick Grayson); 1st app. Timothy Drake (8/89)						4.00
436-441: 436-2nd printing. 437-Origin Robin cont. 440,441: "A Lonely Place of Dying" Parts 1 & 3						3.00
442-1st app. Timothy Drake in Robin costume						4.00
443-456,458,459,462-464: 445-447-Batman goes to Russia. 448,449-The Penguin Affair Pts 1 & 3. 450-Origin Joker. 450,451-Joker-c/stories. 452-454-Dark Knight Dark City storyline; Riddler app. 455-Alan Grant scripts begin, ends #466, 470. 464-Last solo Batman story; free 16 pg. preview of Impact Comics line						3.00
457-Timothy Drake officially becomes Robin & dons new costume						5.00
457-Direct sale edition (has #000 in indicia)						5.00
460,461,465-487: 460,461-Two part Catwoman story. 465-Robin returns to action with Batman. 470-War of the Gods x-over. 475,476-Return of Scarface-c/story. 476-Last $1.00-c. 477,478-Photo-c						3.00
488-Cont'd from Batman: Sword of Azrael #4; Azrael-c & app.	1	2	3	5	6	8
489-Bane-c/story; 1st app. Azrael in Bat-costume						5.00
490-Riddler-c/story; Azrael & Bane app.						6.00
491,492: 491-Knightfall lead-in; Joker-c/story; Azrael & Bane app.; Kelley Jones-c begin. 492-Knightfall part 1; Bane app.						4.00
492-Platinum edition (promo copy)						10.00
493-496: 493-Knightfall Pt. 3. 494-Knightfall Pt. 5; Joker-c & app. 495-Knightfall Pt. 7; brief Bane & Joker apps. 496-Knightfall Pt. 9, Joker-c/story; Bane cameo						3.00
497-(Late 7/93)-Knightfall Pt. 11; Bane breaks Batman's back; B&W outer-c; Aparo-a(p); Giordano-a(i)						5.00
497-499: 497-2nd printing. 497-Newsstand edition w/o outer cover. 498-Knightfall part 15; Bane & Catwoman-c & app. (see Showcase 93 #7 & 8) 499-Knightfall Pt. 17; Bane app.						3.00
500-($2.50, 68 pgs.)-Knightfall Pt. 19; Azrael in new Bat-costume; Bane-c/story						3.00
500-($3.95, 68 pgs.)-Collector's Edition w/die-cut double-c w/foil by Joe Quesada & 2 bound-in post cards						5.00
501-508,510,511: 501-Begin $1.50-c. 501-508-Knightquest. 503,504-Catwoman app. 507-Ballistic app.; Jim Balent-a(p). 510-KnightsEnd Pt. 7. 511-(9/94)-Zero Hour; Batgirl-c/story						2.50
509-($2.50, 52 pgs.)-KnightsEnd Pt. 1						3.00
512-514,516-518: 512-(11/94)-Dick Grayson assumes Batman role						2.50
515-Special Ed.($2.50)-Kelley Jones-a begins; all black embossed-c; Troika Pt. 1						3.00
515-Regular Edition						2.50
519-534,536-549: 519-Begin $1.95-c. 521-Return of Alfred, 522-Swamp Thing app. 525-Mr. Freeze app. 527,528-Two Face app. 529-Contagion Pt. 6. 530-532-Deadman app. 533-Legacy prelude. 534-Legacy Pt. 5. 536-Final Night x-over; Man-Bat-c/app. 540,541-Spectre-c-app. 544-546-Joker & The Demon. 548,549-Penguin-c/app.						2.50
530-532 ($2.50)-Enhanced edition; glow-in-the-dark-c.						3.00
535-(10/96, $2.95)-1st app. The Ogre						3.00
535-(10/96, $3.95)-1st app. The Ogre; variant, cardboard, foldout-c						4.00
550-($3.50)-Collector's Ed., includes 4 collector cards; intro. Chase, return of Clayface; Kelley Jones-c						3.50
550-($2.95)-Standard Ed.; Williams & Gray-c						3.00
551,552,554-562: 551,552-Ragman c/app. 554-Cataclysm pt. 12.						2.50
553-Cataclysm pt.3						4.00
563-No Man's Land; Joker-c by Campbell; Bob Gale-s						5.00
564-574: 569-New Batgirl-c/app. 572-Joker and Harley app.						2.50
575-579: 575-New look Batman begins; McDaniel-a						2.50
580-598: 580-Begin $2.25-c. 587-Gordon shot. 591,592-Deadshot-c/app.						2.50
599-Bruce Wayne: Murderer pt. 7						2.50
600-($3.95) Bruce Wayne: Fugitive pt. 1; back-up homage stories in '50s, 60's, & 70s styles; by Aragonés, Gaudiano, Shanower and others						5.00
600-(2nd printing)						4.00
601-604, 606,607: 601,603-Bruce Wayne: Fugitive pt.3,13. 606,607-Deadshot-c/app.						2.50
605-($2.95) Conclusion to Bruce Wayne: Fugitive x-over; Noto-c						3.00
608-(12/02) Jim Lee-a/c & Jeph Loeb-s begin; Poison Ivy & Catwoman app.						8.00
608-2nd printing; has different cover with Batman standing on gargoyle						12.00
608-Special Edition; has different cover; 200 printed; used for promotional purposes (one copy sold for $930 in Sept. 2003, and a CGC graded 9.8 copy sold for $2,425)						
609-Huntress app.						9.00
610,611: 610-Killer Croc-c/app.; Batman & Catwoman kiss						8.00
612-Batman vs. Superman; 1st printing with full color cover						9.00
612-2nd printing with B&W sketch cover						15.00
613,614: 614-Joker-c/app.						7.00
615-617: 615-Reveals ID to Catwoman. 616-Ra's al Ghul app. 617-Scarecrow app.						5.00
618- Batman vs. "Jason Todd"						4.00

Batman #619 (2nd printing) © DC

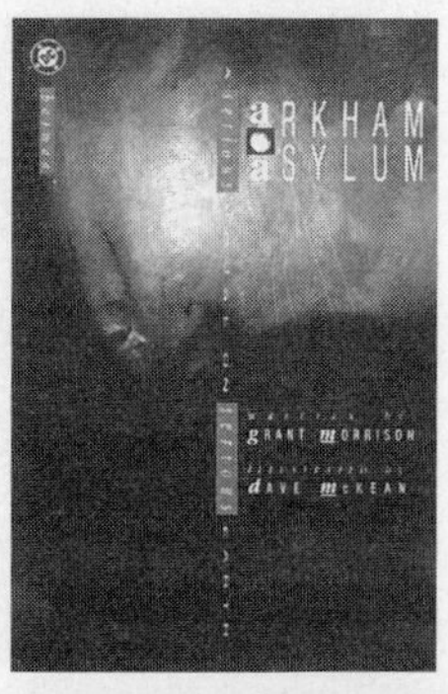

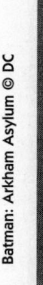

Batman: Arkham Asylum © DC

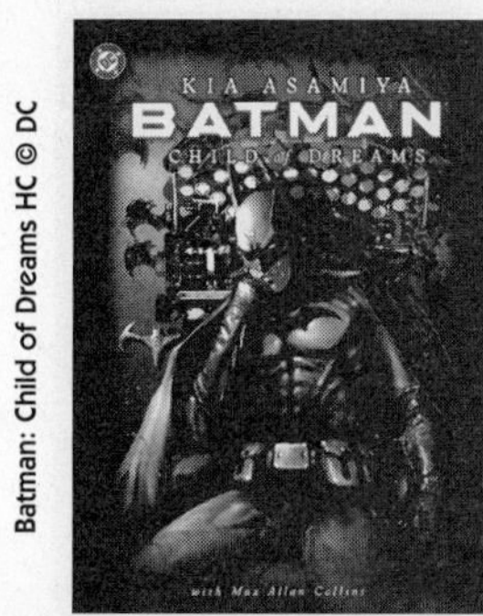

Batman: Child of Dreams HC © DC

	GD 2.0	VG 4.0	FN 6.0	VF 8.0	VF/NM 9.0	NM- 9.2
619-Newsstand cover; Hush story concludes; Riddler app.						5.00
619-Two variant tri-fold covers; one Heroes group , one Villains group						5.00
619-2nd printing with Riddler chess cover						5.00
620-Azzarello-s/Risso-a/c begin; Killer Croc app.						3.00
621,622-Azzarello-s/Risso-a/c						3.00
#0 (10/94)-Zero Hour issue released between #511 & #512; Origin retold						2.50
#1,000,000 (11/98) 853rd Century x-over						2.50
Annual 1 (8-10/61)-Swan-c	57	114	171	485	743	1000
Annual 2	30	60	90	218	319	420
Annual 3 (Summer, '62)-Joker-c/story	31	62	93	222	326	430
Annual 4,5	14	28	42	99	145	190
Annual 6,7 (7/64, 25¢, 80 pgs.)	11	22	33	77	114	150
Annual V5#8 (1982)-Painted-c	1	2	3	5	6	8
Annual 9,10,12: 9(7/85). 10(1986). 12(1988, $1.50)						6.00
Annual 11 (1987, $1.25)-Penguin-c/story; Moore-s	1	2	3	5	6	8
Annual 13 (1989, $1.75, 68 pgs.)-Gives history of Bruce Wayne, Dick Grayson, Jason Todd, Alfred, Comm. Gordon, Barbara Gordon (Batgirl) & Vicki Vale; Morrow-i						5.00
Annual 14-17 ('90-'93, 68 pgs.)-14-Origin Two-Face. 15-Armageddon 2001 x-over; Joker app. 15 (2nd printing). 16-Joker-c/s; Kieth-c. 17 (1993, $2.50, 68 pgs.)-Azrael in Bat-costume; intro Ballistic						4.00
Annual 18 (1994, $2.95)						3.00
Annual 19 (1995, $3.95)-Year One story; retells Scarecrow's origin						4.00
Annual 20 (1996, $2.95)-Legends of the Dead Earth story; Giarrano-a						3.00
Annual 21 (1997, $3.95)-Pulp Heroes story						4.00
Annual 22,23 ('98, '99, $2.95)-22-Ghosts; Wrightson-c. 23-JLApe; Art Adams-c						3.00
Annual 24 ('00, $3.50) Planet DC; intro. The Boggart; Aparo-a						3.50
Special 1 (4/84)-Mike W. Barr story; Golden-c/a	1	2	3	5	6	8

NOTE: ***Art Adams*** *a-400p.* ***Neal Adams*** *c-200, 203, 210, 217, 219-222, 224-227, 229, 230, 232, 234, 236-241, 243-246, 251, 255, Annual 14.* ***Aparo*** *a-414-420, 426-435, 440-448, 450, 451, 480-483, 486-491, 494-500; c-414-416, 481, 482, 463i, 486, 487i.* ***Bolland*** *a-400; c-445-447.* ***Burnley*** *a-10, 12-18, 20, 22, 25, 27; c-9, 15, 16, 27, 28p, 40p, 42p.* ***Byrne*** *c-401, 433-435, 533-535, Annual 11.* ***Travis Charest*** *c-488-490p.* ***Colan*** *a-340p, 343-345p, 348-351p, 373p, 383p; c-343p, 345p, 350p.* ***J. Cole*** *a-238r.* ***Cowan*** *a-Annual 10p.* ***Golden*** *a-295p, 303p, 484, 485.* ***Alan Grant*** *scripts-455-466, 470, 474-476, 479, 480, Annual 16(part).* ***Grell*** *a-287, 288p, 289p, 290; c-287-290.* ***Infantino/Anderson*** *c-167, 173, 175, 181, 186, 191, 192, 194, 195, 198, 199.* ***Kelley Jones*** *a-513-519, 521-525, 527; c-491-499, 500(newsstand), 501-510, 513.* ***Kaluta*** *c-242, 248, 253, Annual 12.* ***G. Kane/Anderson*** *c-178-180.* ***Bob Kane*** *a-1, 2, 5; c-1-5, 7, 17.* ***G. Kane*** *a-(r)-254, 255, 259, 261, 353i.* ***Kubert*** *a-238r, 400; c-310, 319p, 327, 328, 344.* ***McFarlane*** *c-423.* ***Mignola*** *c-426-429, 452-454, Annual 18.* ***Moldoff*** *c-101-140.* ***Moldoff/Giella*** *a-164-175, 177-181, 183, 184, 186.* ***Moldoff/Greene*** *a-169, 172-174, 177-179, 181, 184.* ***Mooney*** *a-255r.* ***Morrow*** *a-Annual 13i.* ***Newton*** *a-305, 306, 328p, 331p, 332p, 337p, 338p, 346p, 352-357p, 360-372p, 374-378p; c-374p, 378p.* ***Nino*** *a-Annual 9.* ***Irv Novick*** *c-201, 202.* ***Perez*** *a-400; c-436-442.* ***Fred Ray*** *c-8, 10; w/****Robinson****-11.* ***Robinson/Roussos*** *a-12-17, 20, 22, 24, 25, 27, 28, 31, 33, 37.* ***Robinson*** *a-12, 14, 18, 22-32,34, 36, 37, 255r, 260r, 261r; c-6, 8, 10, 12-15, 18, 21, 24, 26, 30, 37, 39.* ***Simonson*** *a-300p, 312p, 321p; c-300p, 312p, 366, 413i.* ***P. Smith*** *a-Annual 9.* ***Dick Sprang*** *c-19, 20, 22, 23, 25, 29, 31-36, 38, 51, 55, 66, 73, 76.* ***Starlin*** *c/a-402.* ***Staton*** *a-334.* ***Sutton*** *a-400.* ***Wrightson*** *a-265i, 400; c-320r. Bat-Hound app. in 92, 97, 103, 123, 125, 133, 156, 158. Bat-Mite app. in 133, 136, 144, 146, 158, 161. Batwoman app. in 105, 116, 122, 125, 128, 129, 131, 133, 139, 140, 141, 144, 145, 150, 151, 153, 154, 157, 159, 162, 163.* ***Zeck*** *c-417-420. Catwoman back-ups in 332, 345, 346, 348-351. Joker app. in 1, 2, 4, 5, 7-9, 11-13, 19, 20, 23, 25, 28, 32 & many more. Robin solo back-up stories in 337-339, 341-343.*

BATMAN (Hardcover books and trade paperbacks)

	GD 2.0	VG 4.0	FN 6.0	VF 8.0	VF/NM 9.0	NM- 9.2
...: ABSOLUTION (2002, $24.95)-Hard-c.; DeMatteis-s/Ashmore painted-a						25.00
...: ABSOLUTION (2003, $17.95)-Soft-c.; DeMatteis-s/Ashmore painted-a						18.00
...: A LONELY PLACE OF DYING (1990, $3.95, 132 pgs.)-r/Batman #440-442 & New Titans #60,61; Perez-c						4.00
...: ANARKY TPB (1999, $12.95) r/early appearances						13.00
...AND DRACULA: RED RAIN nn (1991, $24.95)-Hard-c.; Elseworlds storyline						32.00
...AND DRACULA: Red Rain nn (1992, $9.95)-SC						12.00
ARKHAM ASYLUM Hard-c (1989, $24.95)						30.00
ARKHAM ASYLUM Soft-c ($14.95)						15.00
BIRTH OF THE DEMON Hard-c (1992, $24.95)-Origin of Ra's al Ghul						25.00
BIRTH OF THE DEMON Soft-c (1993, $12.95)						13.00
BLIND JUSTICE nn (1992, $7.50)-r/Det. #598-600						7.50
BLOODSTORM (1994, $24.95,HC) Kelley Jones-c/a						28.00
BRIDE OF THE DEMON Hard-c (1990, $19.95)						20.00
BRIDE OF THE DEMON Soft-c ($12.95)						13.00
...: BRUCE WAYNE: FUGITIVE Vol. 1 ('02, $12.95)-r/ story arc						13.00
...: BRUCE WAYNE: FUGITIVE Vol. 2 ('03, $12.95)-r/ story arc						13.00
...: BRUCE WAYNE: FUGITIVE Vol. 3 ('03, $12.95)-r/ story arc						13.00
...: BRUCE WAYNE-MURDERER? ('02, $19.95)-r/ story arc						20.00
...: CASTLE OF THE BAT ($5.95)-Elseworlds story						6.00
...: CATACLYSM ('99, $17.95)-r/ story arc						18.00
...: CHILD OF DREAMS (2003, $24.95, B&W, HC) Reprint of Japanese manga with Kia Asamiya-s/a/c; English adaptation by Max Allan Collins; Asamiya interview						25.00
...: CHILD OF DREAMS (2003, $19.95, B&W, SC)						20.00
...: COLLECTED LEGENDS OF THE DARK KNIGHT nn (1994, $12.95)-r/Legends of the Dark Knight #32-34,38,42,43						13.00
...: CRIMSON MIST (1999, $24.95,HC)-Vampire Batman Elseworlds story Doug Moench-s/Kelley Jones-c/a						25.00
...: CRIMSON MIST (2001, $14.95,SC)						25.00
...: DARK JOKER-THE WILD (1993, $24.95,HC)-Elseworlds story; Moench-s/Jones-c/a						25.00
...: DARK JOKER-THE WILD (1993, $9.95,SC)						10.00
...DARK KNIGHT DYNASTY nn (1997, $24.95)-Hard-c.; 3 Elseworlds stories; Barr-s/ S. Hampton painted-a, Gary Frank, McDaniel-a(p)						25.00
...DARK KNIGHT DYNASTY Softcover (2000, $14.95) Hampton-c						15.00
...DEADMAN: DEATH AND GLORY nn (1996, $24.95)-Hard-c.; Robinson-s/ Estes-c/a						25.00
...DEADMAN: DEATH AND GLORY ($12.95)-SC						13.00
DEATH IN THE FAMILY (1988, $3.95, trade paperback)-r/Batman #426-429 by Aparo						5.00
DEATH IN THE FAMILY: (2nd - 5th printings)						4.00
...: DETECTIVE #27 HC (2003, $19.95)-Elseworlds; Uslan-s/Snejbjerg-a						20.00
DIGITAL JUSTICE nn (1990, $24.95, Hard-c.)-Computer generated art						25.00
... :EVOLUTION (2001, $12.95, SC)-r/Detective Comics #743-750						13.00
... FACES (1995, $9.95, TPB)						10.00
...: FORTUNATE SON HC (1999, $24.95) Gene Ha-a						25.00
...: FORTUNATE SON SC (2000, $14.95) Gene Ha-a						15.00
FOUR OF A KIND TPB (1998, $14.95)-r/1995 Year One Annuals featuring Poison Ivy, Riddler, Scarecrow, & Man-Bat						15.00
...GOTHIC (1992, $12.95, TPB)-r/Legends of the Dark Knight #6-10						13.00
...: HARVEST BREED-(2000, $24.95) George Pratt-s/painted-a						25.00
...: HARVEST BREED-(2003, $17.95) George Pratt-s/painted-a						18.00
...: HAUNTED KNIGHT-(1997, $12.95) r/ Halloween specials						13.00
...: HONG KONG-(2003, $24.95, with dustjacket) Doug Moench-s/Tony Wong-a						25.00
...: HUSH DOUBLE FEATURE-(2003, $3.95) r/#608,609(1st 2 Jim Lee-a issues)						4.00
...: HUSH VOLUME 1 HC-(2003, $19.95) r/#608-612; & new 2 pg. origin w/Lee-a						20.00
...: HUSH VOLUME 2 HC-(2003, $19.95) r/#613-619; Lee intro & sketchpages						20.00
... IN THE FIFTIES TPB ($19.95) Intro. by Michael Uslan						20.00
... IN THE SEVENTIES TPB ($19.95) Intro. by Dennis O'Neil						20.00
... IN THE SIXTIES TPB ($19.95) Intro. by Adam West						20.00
... LEGACY-(1996,17.95) reprints Legacy						18.00
...: THE MANY DEATHS OF THE BATMAN (1992, $3.95, 84 pgs.)-r/Batman #433-435 w/new Byrne-c						4.00
...: THE MOVIES (1997, $19.95)-r/movie adaptations of Batman, Batman Returns, Batman Forever, Batman and Robin						20.00
...: NINE LIVES HC (2002, $24.95, sideways format) Motter-s/Lark-a						25.00
...: NINE LIVES SC (2003, $17.95, sideways format) Motter-s/Lark-a						18.00
...: OFFICER DOWN (2001, $12.95)-r/Commissioner shot x-over; Talon-c						13.00
...: PREY (1992, $12.95)-Gulacy/Austin-a						13.00
...: PRODIGAL (1997, $14.95)-Gulacy/Austin-a						15.00
SHAMAN (1993, $12.95)-r/Legends/D.K. #1-5						13.00
...: SON OF THE DEMON Hard-c (9/87, $14.95)						30.00
...: SON OF THE DEMON limited signed & numbered Hard-c (1,700)						45.00
...: SON OF THE DEMON Soft-c w/new-c ($8.95)						10.00
...: SON OF THE DEMON Soft-c (1989, $9.95, 2nd printing - 5th printing)						10.00
... : STRANGE APPARITIONS ($12.95) r/'77-'78 Englehart/Rogers stories from Detective #469-479; also Simonson-a						13.00
...: TALES OF THE DEMON (1991, $17.95, 212 pgs.)-Intro by Sam Hamm; reprints by Neal Adams(3) & Golden; contains Saga of Ra's al Ghul #1						18.00
...: TEN NIGHTS OF THE BEAST (1994, $5.95)-r/Batman #417-420						6.00
...: TERROR (2003, $12.95, TPB)-r/Legends of the Dark Knight #137-141; Gulacy-c						13.00
...: THE CHALICE (HC, '99, $24.95) Van Fleet painted-a						25.00
...: THE CHALICE (SC, '00, $14.95) Van Fleet painted-a						15.00
...: THE LAST ANGEL (1994, $12.95, TPB) Lustbader-s						13.00
...: THE RING, THE ARROW AND THE BAT (2003, $19.95, TPB) r/Legends of the DCU #7-9 & Batman: Legends of the Dark Knight #127-131; Green Lantern & Green Arrow app.						20.00
...: THRILLKILLER (1998, $12.95, TPB)-r/series & Thrillkiller '62						13.00
...: VENOM (1993, $9.95, TPB)-r/Legends of the Dark Knight #16-20; embossed-c						10.00
YEAR ONE Hard-c (1988, $12.95)						18.00
YEAR ONE (1988, $9.95, TPB)-r/Batman #404-407 by Miller; intro by Miller						10.00
YEAR ONE (TPB, 2nd & 3rd printings)						10.00
YEAR TWO (1990, $9.95, TPB)-r/Det. 575-578 by McFarlane; wraparound-c						10.00

BATMAN (one-shots)

	GD 2.0	VG 4.0	FN 6.0	VF 8.0	VF/NM 9.0	NM- 9.2
... ABDUCTION, THE (1998, $5.95)						6.00
... & ROBIN (1997, $5.95)-Movie adaptation						6.00
...: ARKHAM ASYLUM - TALES OF MADNESS (5/98, $2.95) Cataclysm x-over pt. 16						3.00
... : BANE (1997, $4.95)-Dixon-s/Burchett-a; Stelfreeze-c; cover art interlocks w/Batman:(Batgirl, Mr. Freeze, Poison Ivy)						5.00
... : BATGIRL (1997, $4.95)-Puckett-s/Haley,Kesel-a; Stelfreeze-c; cover art interlocks w/Batman:(Bane, Mr. Freeze, Poison Ivy)						5.00
... : BATGIRL (6/98, $1.95)-Girlfrenzy; Balent-a						2.50
... : BLACKGATE (1/97, $3.95) Dixon-s						4.00
... : BLACKGATE - ISLE OF MEN (4/98, $2.95) Cataclysm x-over pt. 8; Moench-s/Aparo-a						3.00
... BOOK OF SHADOWS, THE (1999, $5.95)						6.00
BROTHERHOOD OF THE BAT (1995, $5.95)-Elseworlds-s						6.00
... BULLOCK'S LAW (8/99, $4.95) Dixon-s						5.00

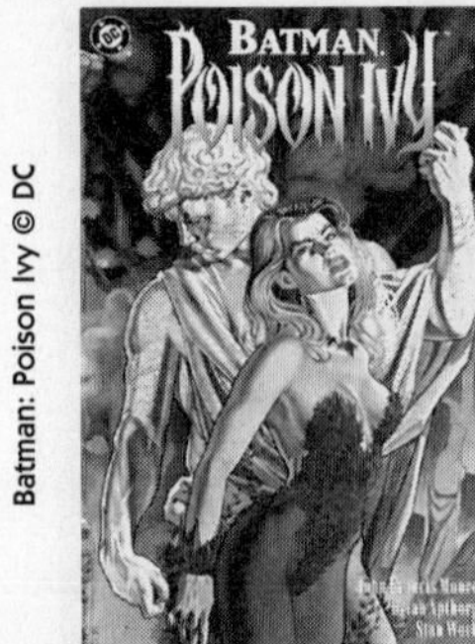
Batman: Poison Ivy © DC

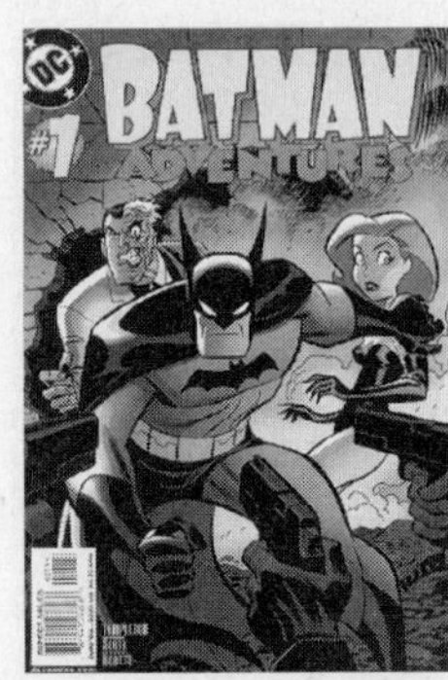
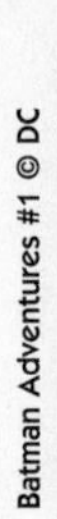
Batman Adventures #1 © DC

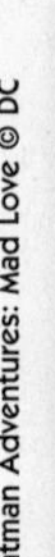
Batman Adventures: Mad Love © DC

GD	VG	FN	VF	VF/NM	NM-
2.0	4.0	6.0	8.0	9.0	9.2

.../CAPTAIN AMERICA (1996, $5.95, DC/Marvel) Elseworlds story; Byrne-c/s/a 6.00
... : CATWOMAN DEFIANT nn (1992, $4.95, prestige format)-Milligan scripts; cover art interlocks w/Batman: Penguin Triumphant; special foil logo 5.00
... /DAREDEVIL (2000, $5.95)-Barreto-a 6.00
...: DARK ALLEGIANCES (1996, $5.95)-Elseworlds story, Chaykin-c/a 6.00
...: DARK KNIGHT GALLERY (1/96, $3.50)-Pin-ups by Pratt, Balent, & others 3.50
...:DAY OF JUDGMENT (11/99, $3.95) 4.00
...:DEATH OF INNOCENTS (12/96, $3.95)-O'Neil-s/ Staton-a(p) 4.00
.../DEMON (1996, $4.95)-Alan Grant scripts 5.00
.../DEMON: A TRAGEDY (2000, $5.95)-Grant-s/Murray painted-a 6.00
...:D.O.A. (1999, $6.95)-Bob Hall-s/a 7.00
...:DREAMLAND (2000, $5.95)-Grant-s/Breyfogle-a 6.00
... : EGO (2000, $6.95)-Darwyn Cooke-s/a 7.00
... 80-PAGE GIANT (8/98, $4.95) Stelfreeze-c 6.00
... 80-PAGE GIANT 2 (10/99, $4.95) Luck of the Draw 6.00
... 80-PAGE GIANT 3 (7/00, $5.95) Calendar Man 6.00
... FOREVER (1995, $5.95, direct market) 6.00
... FOREVER (1995, $3.95, newsstand) 4.00
FULL CIRCLE nn (1991, $5.95, 68 pgs.)-Sequel to Batman: Year Two 6.00
...GALLERY, The 1 (1992, $2.95)-Pin-ups by Miller, N. Adams & others 3.00
...GOLDEN STREETS OF GOTHAM (2003, $6.95) Elseworlds in early 1900s 7.00
...GOTHAM BY GASLIGHT (1989, $3.95) 4.00
...GOTHAM CITY SECRET FILES 1 (4/00, $4.95) Batgirl app. 5.00
...: GOTHAM NOIR (2001, $6.95)-Elseworlds; Brubaker-s/Phillips-c/a 7.00
.../GREEN ARROW: THE POISON TOMORROW nn (1992, $5.95, square-bound, 68 pgs.) Netzer-c/a 6.00
HOLY TERROR nn (1991, $4.95, 52 pgs.)-Elseworlds story 5.00
.../HOUDINI: THE DEVIL'S WORKSHOP (1993, $5.95) 6.00
... :HUNTRESS/SPOILER - BLUNT TRAUMA (5/98, $2.95) Cataclysm pt. 13; Dixon-s/Barreto & Sienkiewicz-a 3.00
...: I, JOKER nn (1998, $4.95)-Elseworlds story; Bob Hall-s/a 5.00
...: IN DARKEST KNIGHT nn (1994, $4.95, 52 pgs.)-Elseworlds story; Batman w/Green Lantern's ring. 5.00
...:JOKER'S APPRENTICE (5/99, $3.95) Von Eeden-a 4.00
.../ JOKER: SWITCH (2003, $6.95)-Bolton-a/Grayson-s 7.00
...:JUDGE DREDD: JUDGEMENT ON GOTHAM nn (1991, $5.95, 68 pgs.) Simon Bisley-c/a; Grant/Wagner scripts 6.00
...:JUDGE DREDD: JUDGEMENT ON GOTHAM nn (2nd printing) 6.00
...:JUDGE DREDD: THE ULTIMATE RIDDLE (1995, $4.95) 5.00
...:JUDGE DREDD: VENDETTA IN GOTHAM (1993, $5.95) 6.00
...: KNIGHTGALLERY (1995, $3.50)-Elseworlds sketchbook. 3.50
.../ LOBO (2000, $5.95)-Elseworlds; Joker app.; Bisley-a 6.00
...: MASK OF THE PHANTASM (1994, $2.95)-Movie adapt. 3.00
...: MASK OF THE PHANTASM (1994, $4.95)-Movie adapt. 5.00
...: MASQUE (1997, $6.95)-Elseworlds; Grell-c/s/a 7.00
...: MASTER OF THE FUTURE nn (1991, $5.95, 68 pgs.)-Elseworlds storyline; sequel to Gotham By Gaslight; embossed-c 6.00
...: MITEFALL (1995, $4.95)-Alan Grant script, Kevin O'Neill-a 5.00
... : MR. FREEZE (1997, $4.95)-Dini-s/Buckingham-a; Stelfreeze-c; cover art interlocks w/Batman:(Bane, Batgirl, Poison Ivy) 5.00
... /NIGHTWING: BLOODBORNE (2002, $5.95) Cypress-a; McKeever-c 6.00
...: NOSFERATU (1999, $5.95) McKeever-a 6.00
...: OF ARKHAM (2000, $5.95)-Elseworlds; Grant-s/Alcatena-a 6.00
...: OUR WORLDS AT WAR (8/01, $2.95)-Jae Lee-c 3.00
...: PENGUIN TRIUMPHANT nn (1992, $4.95)-Staton-a(p); foil logo 5.00
...•PHANTOM STRANGER nn (1997, $4.95) nn-Grant-s/Ransom-a 5.00
... : PLUS (2/97, $2.95) Arsenal-c/app. 3.00
... : POISON IVY (1997, $4.95)-J.F. Moore-s/Apthorp-a; Stelfreeze-c; cover art interlocks w/Batman:(Bane, Batgirl, Mr. Freeze) 5.00
.../PUNISHER: LAKE OF FIRE (1994, $4.95, DC/Marvel) 5.00
... :REIGN OF TERROR ('99, $4.95) Elseworlds 5.00
...RETURNS MOVIE SPECIAL (1992, $3.95) 4.00
...RETURNS MOVIE PRESTIGE (1992, $5.95, squarebound)-Dorman painted-c 6.00
...:RIDDLER-THE RIDDLE FACTORY (1995, $4.95)-Wagner script 5.00
...: SCARECROW 3-D (12/98, $3.95) w/glasses 4.00
.../ SCARFACE: A PSYCHODRAMA (2001, $5.95)-Adlard-a/Sienkiewicz-c 6.00
...: SCAR OF THE BAT nn (1996, $4.95)-Elseworlds; Max Allan Collins script; Barreto-a 5.00
... :SCOTTISH CONNECTION (1998, $5.95) Quitely-a 6.00
... :SEDUCTION OF THE GUN nn (1992, $2.50, 68 pgs.) 3.00
.../SPAWN: WAR DEVIL nn (1994, $4.95, 52 pgs.) 5.00
.../SPIDER-MAN (1997, $4.95) Dematteis-s/Nolan & Kesel-a 5.00
... : THE ABDUCTION ('98, $5.95) 6.00
... :THE BLUE, THE GREY, & THE BAT (1992, $5.95)-Weiss/Lopez-a 6.00
... :THE HILL (5/00, $2.95)-Priest-s/Martinbrough-a 3.00

GD	VG	FN	VF	VF/NM	NM-
2.0	4.0	6.0	8.0	9.0	9.2

... :THE KILLING JOKE (1988, deluxe 52 pgs., mature readers)-Bolland-c/a; Alan Moore scripts; Joker cripples Barbara Gordon 2 4 6 10 12 15
...: THE KILLING JOKE (2nd thru 10th printings) 4.00
...: THE OFFICIAL COMIC ADAPTATION OF THE WARNER BROS. MOTION PICTURE (1989, $2.50, regular format, 68 pgs.)-Ordway-c 3.00
...: THE OFFICIAL COMIC ADAPTATION OF THE WARNER BROS. MOTION PICTURE (1989, $4.95, prestige format, 68 pgs.)-same interiors but different-c 5.00
...: THE 10-CENT ADVENTURE (3/02, 10¢) intro. to the "Bruce Wayne: Murderer" x-over; Rucka-s/Burchett & Janson-a/Dave Johnson-c 2.25

NOTE: (Also see Promotional Comics section for alternate copies with special outer half-covers promoting local comic shops)

...: TWO-FACE-CRIME AND PUNISHMENT-(1995, $4.95)-McDaniel-a 5.00
... : TWO FACES (11/98, $4.95) Elseworlds 5.00
...: VENGEANCE OF BANE SPECIAL 1 (1992, $2.50, 68 pgs.)-Origin & 1st app. Bane (see Batman #491) 2 4 6 8 10 12
...: VENGEANCE OF BANE SPECIAL 1 (2nd printing) 3.00
....:VENGEANCE OF BANE II nn (1995, $3.95)-sequel 4.00
...Vs. THE INCREDIBLE HULK (1995, $3.95)-r/DC Special Series #27 4.00
...: VILLAINS SECRET FILES (10/98, $4.95) Origin-s 5.00

BATMAN ADVENTURES, THE (Based on animated series)
DC Comics: Oct, 1992 - No. 36, Oct, 1995 ($1.25/$1.50)

1-Penguin-c/story 4.00
1 ($1.95, Silver Edition)-2nd printing 2.25
2-6,8-19: 2,12-Catwoman-c/story. 3-Joker-c/story. 5-Scarecrow-c/story. 10-Riddler-c/story. 11-Man-Bat-c/story. 12-Batgirl & Catwoman-c/story. 16-Joker-c/story; begin $1.50-c. 18-Batgirl-c/story. 19-Scarecrow-c/story. 3.00
7-Special edition polybagged with Man-Bat trading card 5.00
20-24,26-32: 26-Batgirl app. 2.50
25-($2.50, 52 pgs.)-Superman app. 3.00
33-36: 33-Begin $1.75-c 2.25
Annual 1,2 ('94, '95): 2-Demon-c/story; Ra's al Ghul app. 3.50
...: Dangerous Dames & Demons (2003, $14.95, TPB) r/Annual 1,2, Mad Love & Adventures in the DC Universe #3; Bruce Timm painted-c 15.00
Holiday Special 1 (1995, $2.95) 4.00
The Collected Adventures Vol. 1,2 ('93, '95, $5.95) 6.00
TPB ('98, $7.95) r/#1-6; painted wraparound-c 8.00

BATMAN ADVENTURES (Based on animated series)
DC Comics: Jun, 2003 - Present ($2.25)

1-Timm-c (2003 Free Comic Book Day edition is listed in Promotional Comics section) 2.25
2-9: 3-Joker-c/app. 4-Ra's al Ghul app. 6-8-Phantasm app. 2.25

BATMAN ADVENTURES, THE: MAD LOVE
DC Comics: Feb, 1994 ($3.95/$4.95)

1-Origin of Harley Quinn; Dini-s/Timm-c/a 2 4 6 8 10 12
1-($4.95, Prestige format) new Timm painted-c 1 2 3 5 6 8

BATMAN ADVENTURES, THE: THE LOST YEARS (TV)
DC Comics: Jan, 1998 - No. 5, May, 1998 ($1.95) (Based on animated series)

1-5-Leads into Fall '97's new animated episodes. 4-Tim Drake becomes Robin. 5-Dick becomes Nightwing 2.25
TPB-(1999, $9.95) r/series 10.00

BATMAN/ALIENS
DC Comics/Dark Horse: Mar, 1997 - No. 2, Apr, 1997 ($4.95, limited series)

1,2: Wrightson-c/a. 5.00
TPB-(1997, $14.95) w/prequel from DHP #101,102 15.00

BATMAN/ALIENS II
DC Comics/Dark Horse: 2003 - No. 3, 2003 ($5.95, limited series)

1-3-Edginton-s/Staz Johnson-a 6.00
TPB-(2003, $14.95) r/#1-3 15.00

BATMAN AND ROBIN ADVENTURES (TV)
DC Comics: Nov, 1995 - No. 25, Dec, 1997 ($1.75) (Based on animated series)

1-Dini-s. 3.00
2-24: 2-4-Dini script. 4-Penguin-c/story. 5-Joker-c/story; Poison Ivy, Harley Quinn-c/app. 9-Batgirl & Talia-c/story. 10-Ra's al Ghul-c/story. 11-Man-Bat app. 12-Bane-c/app. 13-Scarecrow-c/app. 15 Deadman-c/app. 16-Catwoman-c/app. 18-Joker-c/app. 24-Poison Ivy app. 2.25
25-($2.95, 48 pgs.) 3.00
Annual 1,2 (11/96, 11/97): 1-Phantasm-c/app. 2-Zatara & Zatanna-c/app. 4.00
...: Sub-Zero(1998, $3.95) Adaptation of animated video 4.00

BATMAN AND SUPERMAN ADVENTURES: WORLD'S FINEST
DC Comics: 1997 ($6.95, square-bound, one-shot) (Based on animated series)

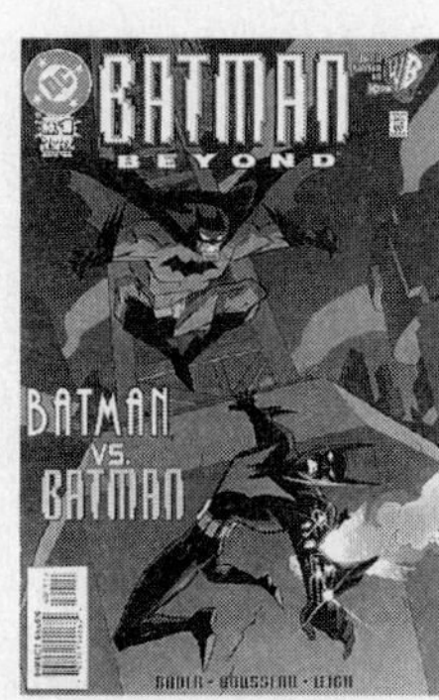

Batman Beyond #1 © DC

Batman: Death and the Maidens #1 © DC

Batman: Gotham Knights #15 © DC

	GD	VG	FN	VF	VF/NM	NM-
	2.0	4.0	6.0	8.0	9.0	9.2

1-Adaptation of animated crossover episode; Dini-s/Timm-c. 7.00

BATMAN AND SUPERMAN: WORLD'S FINEST
DC Comics: Apr, 1999 - No. 10, Jan, 2000 ($4.95/$1.99, limited series)

1,10-($4.95, squarebound) Taylor-a 5.00
2-9-($1.99) 5-Batgirl app. 8-Catwoman-c/app. 2.25
TPB (2003, $19.95) r/#1-10

BATMAN AND THE OUTSIDERS (The Adventures of the Outsiders #33 on)
(Also see Brave & The Bold #200 & The Outsiders) (Replaces The Brave and the Bold)
DC Comics: Aug, 1983 - No. 32, Apr, 1986 (Mando paper #5 on)

1-Batman, Halo, Geo-Force, Katana, Metamorpho & Black Lightning begin 4.00
2-32: 5-New Teen Titans x-over. 9-Halo begins. 11,12-Origin Katana. 18-More info on Metamorpho's origin. 28-31-Lookers origin. 32-Team disbands 2.50
Annual 1,2 (9/84, 9/85): 2-Metamorpho & Sapphire Stagg wed 3.00
NOTE: ***Aparo*** *a-1-9, 11-13p, 16-20; c-1-4, 5i, 6-21, Annual 1, 2.* ***B. Kane*** *a-3r.* ***Layton*** *a-19i, 20i.* ***Lopez*** *a-3p.* ***Miller*** *c-Annual 1.* ***Perez*** *c-5p.* ***B. Willingham*** *a-14p.*

BATMAN: BANE OF THE DEMON
DC Comics: Mar, 1998 - No. 4, June, 1998 ($1.95, limited series)

1-4-Dixon-s/Nolan-a; prelude to Legacy x-over 2.50

BATMAN BEYOND (Based on animated series)(Mini-series)
DC Comics: Mar, 1999 - No. 6, Aug, 1999 ($1.99)

1-6: 1,2-Adaptation of pilot episode, Timm-c 2.25
TPB (1999, $9.95) r/#1-6 10.00

BATMAN BEYOND (Based on animated series)(Continuing series)
DC Comics: Nov, 1999 - No. 24, Oct, 2001 ($1.99)

1-24: 1-Rousseau-a; Batman vs. Batman. 14-Demon-c/app. 21,22-Justice League Unlimited-c/app. 2.25
...: Return of the Joker (2/01, $2.95) adaptation of video release 3.00

BATMAN: BLACK & WHITE
DC Comics: June, 1996 - No. 4, Sept, 1996 ($2.95, B&W, limited series)

1-Stories by McKeever, Timm, Kubert, Chaykin, Goodwin; Jim Lee-c; Allred inside front-c; Moebius inside back-c 4.00
2-4: 2-Stories by Simonson, Corben, Bisley & Gaiman; Miller-c. 3-Stories by M. Wagner, Janson, Sienkiewicz, O'Neil & Kristiansen; B. Smith-c; Russell inside front-c; Silvestri inside back-c. 4-Stories by Bolland, Goodwin & Gianni, Strnad & Nowlan, O'Neil & Stelfreeze; Toth-c; pin-ups by Neal Adams & Alex Ross 3.00
Hardcover ('97, $39.95) r/series w/new art & cover plate 40.00
Softcover ('00, $19.95) r/series 20.00
Volume 2 HC ('02, $39.95, 7 3/4"x12") r/B&W back-up-s from Batman: Gotham Knights #1-16; stories and art by various incl. Ross, Buscema, Byrne, Ellison, Sale; Mignola-c 40.00
Volume 2 SC ('03, $19.95, 7 3/4"x12") same contents as HC 20.00

BATMAN: BOOK OF THE DEAD
DC Comics: Jun, 1999 - No. 2, July, 1999 ($4.95, limited series, prestige format)

1,2-Elseworlds; Kitson-a 5.00

BATMAN: CATWOMAN DEFIANT (See Batman one-shots)

BATMAN CHRONICLES, THE
DC Comics: Summer, 1995 - No. 23, Winter, 2001 ($2.95, quarterly)

1-3,5-19: 1-Dixon/Grant/Moench script. 3-Bolland-c. 5-Oracle Year One story, Richard Dragon app.,Chaykin-c. 6-Kaluta-c; Ra's al Ghul story. 7-Superman-c/app.11-Paul Pope-s/a. 12-Cataclysm pt. 10. 18-No Man's Land 3.50
4-Hitman story by Ennis, Contagion tie-in; Balent-c 2 4 6 8 10 12
20-23: 20-Catwoman and Relative Heroes-c/app. 21-Pander Bros.-a 3.00
...Gallery (3/97, $3.50) Pin-ups 3.50
...Gauntlet, The (1997, $4.95, one-shot) 5.00

BATMAN: CITY OF LIGHT
DC Comics: Dec, 2003 - No. 8 ($2.95, limited series)

1-4-Pander Brothers-a/s; Paniccia-s 3.00

BATMAN: DARK KNIGHT OF THE ROUND TABLE
DC Comics: 1999 - No. 2, 1999 ($4.95, limited series, prestige format)

1,2-Elseworlds; Giordano-a 5.00

BATMAN: DARK VICTORY
DC Comics: 1999 - No. 13, 2000 ($4.95/$2.95, limited series)

Wizard #0 Preview 2.25
1-($4.95) Loeb-s/Sale-c/a 5.00
2-12-($2.95) 3.00
13-($4.95) 5.00
Hardcover (2001, $29.95) with dust jacket; r/#0,1-13 30.00
Softcover (2002, $19.95) r/#0,1-13 20.00

	GD	VG	FN	VF	VF/NM	NM-
	2.0	4.0	6.0	8.0	9.0	9.2

BATMAN: DEATH AND THE MAIDENS
DC Comics: Oct, 2003 - No. 9 ($2.95, limited series)

1-Ra's al Ghul app.; Rucka-s/Janson-a 4.00
2-6 3.00

BATMAN/ DEATHBLOW: AFTER THE FIRE
DC Comics/WildStorm: 2002 - No. 3, 2002 ($5.95, limited series)

1-3-Azzarello-s/Bermejo & Bradstreet-a 6.00
TPB (2003, $12.95) r/#1-3; plus concept art 13.00

BATMAN FAMILY, THE
National Periodical Pub./DC Comics: Sept-Oct, 1975 - No. 20, Oct-Nov, 1978
(#1-4, 17-on: 68 pgs.) (Combined with Detective Comics with No. 481)

1-Origin/2nd app. Batgirl-Robin team-up (The Dynamite Duo); reprints plus one new story begins; N. Adams-a(r); r/1st app. Man-Bat from Det. #400
3 6 9 18 24 30
2-5: 2-r/Det. #369. 3-Batgirl & Robin learn each's i.d.; r/Batwoman app. from Batman #105. 4-r/1st Fatman app. from Batman #113. 5-r/1st Bat-Hound app. from Batman #92
2 4 6 11 14 18
6,9-Joker's daughter on cover (1st app?) 2 4 6 14 18 22
7,8,14-16: 8-r/Batwoman app.14-Batwoman app. 15-3rd app. Killer Moth. 16-Bat-Girl cameo (last app. in costume until New Teen Titans #47) 2 4 6 10 12 15
10-1st revival Batwoman; Cavalier app.; Killer Moth app.
3 6 9 16 20 24
11-13,17-20: 11-13-Rogers-a(p): 11-New stories begin; Man-Bat begins. 13-Batwoman cameo. 17-($1.00 size)-Batman, Huntress begin; Batwoman & Catwoman 1st meet. 18-20: Huntress by Staton in all. 20-Origin Ragman retold
2 4 6 14 18 22
NOTE: ***Aparo*** *a-17; c-11-16.* ***Austin*** *a-12i.* ***Chaykin*** *a-14p.* ***Michael Golden*** *a-15-17,18-20p.* ***Grell*** *a-1; c-1.* ***Gil Kane*** *a-2r.* ***Kaluta*** *c-17, 19.* ***Newton*** *a-13.* ***Robinson*** *a-1r, 3i(r), 9r.* ***Russell*** *a-18i, 19i.* ***Starlin*** *a-17; c-18, 20.*

BATMAN: FAMILY
DC Comics: Dec, 2002 - No. 8, Feb, 2003 ($2.95/$2.25, weekly limited series)

1,8-($2.95). John Francis Moore-s/Hoberg & Gaudiano-a 3.00
2-7-($2.25). 3-Orpheus & Black Canary app. 2.25

BATMAN: GCPD
DC Comics: Aug, 1996 - No. 4, Nov, 1996 ($2.25, limited series)

1-4: Features Jim Gordon; Aparo/Sienkiewicz-a 2.50

BATMAN: GORDON OF GOTHAM
DC Comics: June, 1998 - No. 4, Sept, 1998 ($1.95, limited series)

1-4: Gordon's early days in Chicago 2.50

BATMAN: GORDON'S LAW
DC Comics: Dec, 1996 - No. 3, Feb, 1997 ($1.95, limited series)

1-3: Dixon-s/Janson-c/a 2.50

BATMAN: GOTHAM ADVENTURES (TV)
DC Comics: June, 1998 - No. 60, May, 2003 ($2.95/$1.95/$1.99/$2.25)

1-($2.95) Based on Kids WB Batman animated series 3.00
2-3-($1.95): 2-Two-Face-c/app. 2.50
4-22: 4-Begin $1.99-c. 5-Deadman-c. 13-MAD #1 cover swipe 2.50
23-60: 31,60-Joker-c/app. 50-Catwoman-c/app. 53-Begin $2.25-c. 58-Creeper-c/app. 2.25
TPB (2000, $9.95) r/#1-6 10.00

BATMAN: GOTHAM KNIGHTS
DC Comics: Mar, 2000 - Present ($2.50/$2.75)

1-Grayson-s; B&W back-up by Warren Ellis & Jim Lee 4.00
2-10-Grayson-s; B&W back-ups by various 2.75
11-($3.25) Bolland-c; Kyle Baker back-up story 3.25
12-24: 13-Officer Down x-over; Ellison back-up-s. 15-Colan back-up. 20-Superman-c/app. 2.75
25,26-Bruce Wayne: Murderer pt. 4,10 3.00
27-31: 28,30,31-Bruce Wayne: Fugitive pt. 7,14,17 2.75
32-48: 32-Begin $2.75-c; Kaluta-a back-up. 33,34-Bane-c/app. 35-Mahfood-a back-up. 38-Bolton-a back-up. 43-Jason Todd & Batgirl app. 44-Jason Todd flashback 2.75

BATMAN: GOTHAM NIGHTS II (First series listed under Gotham Nights)
DC Comics: Mar, 1995 - No. 4, June, 1995 ($1.95, limited series)

1-4 2.50

BATMAN/GRENDEL (1st limited series)
DC Comics: 1993 - No. 2, 1993 ($4.95, limited series, squarebound; 52 pgs.)

1,2: Batman vs. Hunter Rose. 1-Devil's Riddle; Matt Wagner-c/a/scripts. 2-Devil's Masque; Matt Wagner-c/a/scripts 6.00

BATMAN/GRENDEL (2nd limited series)
DC Comics: June, 1996 - No. 2, July, 1996 ($4.95, limited series, squarebound)

Batman/Hellboy/Starman #1
© DC & Mike Mignola

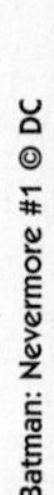

Batman: Nevermore #1 © DC

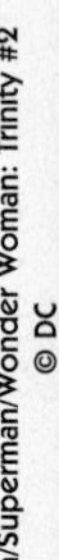

Batman/Superman/Wonder Woman: Trinity #2
© DC

GD VG FN VF VF/NM NM-
2.0 4.0 6.0 8.0 9.0 9.2

1,2: Batman vs. Grendel Prime. 1-Devil's Bones. 2-Devil's Dance; Wagner-c/a/s 5.00

BATMAN: HARLEY QUINN
DC Comics: 1999 ($5.95, prestige format)

1-Intro. of Harley Quinn into regular DC continuity; Dini-s/Alex Ross-c 9.00
1-(2nd printing) 6.00

BATMAN: HAUNTED GOTHAM
DC Comics: 2000 - No. 4, 2000 ($4.95, limited series, squarebound)

1-4-Moench-s/Kelley Jones-c/a 5.00

BATMAN/ HELLBOY/STARMAN
DC Comics/Dark Horse: Jan, 1999 - No. 2, Feb, 1999 ($2.50, limited series)

1,2: Robinson-s/Mignola-a. 2-Harris-c 2.50

BATMAN: HOLLYWOOD KNIGHT
DC Comics: Apr, 2001 - No. 3, Jun, 2001 ($2.50, limited series)

1-3-Elseworlds Batman as a 1940's movie star; Giordano-a/Layton-s 2.50

BATMAN/ HUNTRESS: CRY FOR BLOOD
DC Comics: Jun, 2000 - No. 6, Nov, 2000 ($2.50, limited series)

1-6: Rucka-s/Burchett-a; The Question app. 2.50
TPB (2002, $12.95) r/#1-6 13.00

BATMAN: JOKER TIME (...: It's Joker Time! on cover)
DC Comics: 2000 - No. 3 ($4.95, limited series, squarebound)

1-3-Bob Hall-s/a 5.00

BATMAN/ JUDGE DREDD "DIE LAUGHING"
DC Comics: 1998 - No. 2, 1999 ($4.95, limited series, squarebound)

1,2: 1-Fabry-c/a. 2-Jim Murray-c/a 5.00

BATMAN: KNIGHTGALLERY (See Batman one-shots)

BATMAN: LEAGUE OF BATMEN
DC Comics: 2001 - No. 2, 2001 ($5.95, limited series, squarebound)

1,2-Elseworlds; Moench-s/Bright & Tanghal-a/Van Fleet-c 6.00

BATMAN: LEGENDS OF THE DARK KNIGHT (Legends of the Dark...#1-36)
DC Comics: Nov, 1989 - Present ($1.50/$1.75/$1.95/$1.99/$2.25/$2.50)

1- "Shaman" begins, ends #5; outer cover has four different color variations, all worth same 4.00
2-10: 6-10- "Gothic" by Grant Morrison (scripts) 3.00
11-15: 11-15-Gulacy/Austin-a. 13-Catwoman app. 3.00
16-Intro drug Bane uses; begin Venom story 5.00
17-20 4.00
21-49,51-63: 38-Bat-Mite-c/story. 46-49-Catwoman app. w/Heath-c/a. 51-Ragman app.; Joe Kubert-c. 59,60,61-Knightquest x-over. 62,63-KnightsEnd Pt. 4 & 10 3.00
50-($3.95, 68 pgs.)-Bolland embossed gold foil-c; Joker-c/story; pin-ups by Chaykin, Simonson, Williamson, Kaluta, Russell, others 5.00
64-99: 64-(9/94)-Begin $1.95-c. 71-73-James Robinson-s,Watkiss-c/a. 74,75-McKeever-c/a/s. 76-78-Scott Hampton-c/a/s. 81-Card insert. 83,84-Ellis-s. 85-Robinson-s. 91-93-Ennis-s. 94-Michael T. Gilbert-s/a. 3.00
100-($3.95) Alex Ross painted-c; gallery by various 5.00
101-115: 101-Ezquerra-a. 102-104-Robinson-s 2.50
116-No Man's Land stories begin; Huntress-c 4.00
117-119,121-126: 122-Harris-c 2.50
120-ID of new Batgirl revealed 4.00
127-131: Return to Legends stories; Green Arrow app. 2.50
132-175: 132-136 ($2.25-c) Archie Goodwin-s/Rogers-a. 137-141-Gulacy-a. 142-145-Joker and Ra's al Ghul app. 146-148-Kitson-a. 158-Begin $2.50-c 169-171-Tony Harris-c/a 2.50
#0-(10/94)-Zero Hour; Quesada/Palmiotti-c; released between #64&65 3.00
Annual 1-7 ('91-'97, $3.50-$3.95, 68 pgs.): 1-Joker app. 2-Netzer-c/a. 3-New Batman (Azrael) app. 4-Elseworlds story. 5-Year One; Man-Bat app. 6-Legend of the Dead Earth story. 7-Pulp Heroes story 4.00
Halloween Special 1 (12/93, $6.95, 84 pgs.)-Embossed & foil stamped-c
1 2 3 4 5 7
Batman Madness-...Halloween Special (1994, $4.95) 5.00
Batman Ghosts-...Halloween Special (1995, $4.95) 5.00

NOTE: *Aparo a-Annual 1. **Chaykin** scripts-24-26. **Giffen** a-Annual 1. **Golden** a-Annual 1. **Alan Grant** scripts-38, 52, 53. **Gil Kane** c/a-24-26. **Mignola** a-54; c-54, 62. **Morrow** a-Annual 3i. **Quesada** a-Annual 1. **James Robinson** scripts- 71-73. **Russell** c/a-42, 43. **Sears** a-21, 23; c-21, 23. **Zeck** a-69, 70; c-69, 70.*

BATMAN-LEGENDS OF THE DARK KNIGHT: JAZZ
DC Comics: Apr, 1995 - No. 3, June, 1995 ($2.50, limited series)

1-3 2.50

BATMAN: MANBAT
DC Comics: Oct, 1995 - No. 3, Dec, 1995 ($4.95, limited series)

GD VG FN VF VF/NM NM-
2.0 4.0 6.0 8.0 9.0 9.2

1-3-Elseworlds-Delano-script; Bolton-a. 5.00
TPB-(1997, $14.95) r/#1-3 15.00

BATMAN: MITEFALL (See Batman one-shots)

BATMAN MINIATURE (See Batman Kellogg's)

BATMAN: NEVERMORE
DC Comics: June, 2003 - No. 5, Oct, 2003 ($2.50, limited series)

1-5-Elseworlds Batman & Edgar Allan Poe; Wrightson-c/Guy Davis-a/Len Wein-s 2.50

BATMAN: NO MAN'S LAND (Also see 1999 Batman titles)
DC Comics: (one shots)

nn (3/99, $2.95) Alex Ross-c; Bob Gale-s; begins year-long story arc 3.00
Collector's Ed. (3/99, $3.95) Ross lenticular-c 5.00
#0 (: Ground Zero on cover) (12/99, $4.95) Orbik-c 5.00
...: Gallery (7/99, $3.95) Jim Lee-c 4.00
...: Secret Files (12/99, $4.95) Maleev-c 5.00
TPB ('99, $12.95) r/early No Man's Land stories; new Batgirl early app. 13.00
No Law and a New Order TPB(1999, $5.95) Ross-c 6.00
Volume 2 ('00, $12.95) r/later No Man's Land stories; Batgirl(Huntress) app.; Deodato-c 13.00
Volume 3-5 ('00,'01 $12.95) 3-Intro. new Batgirl. 4-('00). 5-('01) Land-c 13.00

BATMAN: ORPHEUS RISING
DC Comics: Oct, 2001 - No. 5, Feb, 2002 ($2.50, limited series)

1-5-Intro. Orpheus; Simmons-s/Turner & Miki-a 2.50

BATMAN: OUTLAWS
DC Comics: 2000 - No. 3, 2000 ($4.95, limited series)

1-3-Moench-s/Gulacy-a 5.00

BATMAN: PENGUIN TRIUMPHANT (See Batman one-shots)

BATMAN/PREDATOR III: BLOOD TIES
DC Comics/Dark Horse Comics: Nov, 1997 - No. 4, Feb, 1998 ($1.95, lim. series)

1-4: Dixon-s/Damaggio-c/a 2.50
TPB-(1998, $7.95) r/#1-4 8.00

BATMAN RETURNS MOVIE SPECIAL (See Batman one-shots)

BATMAN: RIDDLER-THE RIDDLE FACTORY (See Batman one-shots)

BATMAN: RUN, RIDDLER, RUN
DC Comics: 1992 - Book 3, 1992 ($4.95, limited series)

Book 1-3: Mark Badger-a & plot 5.00

BATMAN: SECRET FILES
DC Comics: Oct, 1997 ($4.95)

1-New origin-s and profiles 5.00

BATMAN: SHADOW OF THE BAT
DC Comics: June, 1992 - No. 94, Feb, 2000 ($1.50/$1.75/$1.95/$1.99)

1-The Last Arkham-c/story begins; Alan Grant scripts in all 4.00
1-($2.50)-Deluxe edition polybagged w/poster, pop-up & book mark 5.00
2-7: 4-The Last Arkham ends. 7-Last $1.50-c 3.00
8-28: 14,15-Staton-a(p). 16-18-Knightfall tie-ins. 19-28-Knightquest tie-ins w/Azrael as Batman. 25-Silver ink-c; anniversary issue 2.50
29-($2.95, 52 pgs.)-KnightsEnd Pt. 2 3.00
30-72: 30-KnightsEnd Pt. 8. 31-(9.94)-Begin $1.95-c; Zero Hour. 32-(11/94). 33-Robin-c. 35-Troika-Pt.2. 43,44-Cat-Man & Catwoman-c. 48-Contagion Pt. 1; card insert. 49-Contagion Pt.7. 56,57,58-Poison Ivy-c/app. 62-Two-Face app. 69,70-Fate app. 2.50
35-($2.95)-Variant embossed-c 3.00
73,74,76-78: Cataclysm x-over pts. 1,9. 76-78-Orbik-c 2.50
75-($2.95) Mr. Freeze & Clayface app.; Orbik-c 3.00
79,81,82: 79-Begin $1.99-c; Orbik-c 2.50
80-($3.95) Flip book with Azrael #47 4.00
83-No Man's Land; intro. new Batgirl (Huntress) 12.00
84,85-No Man's Land 4.00
86-94: 87-Deodato-a. 90-Harris-c. 92-Superman app. 93-Joker and Harley app. 94-No Man's Land ends 3.00
#0 (10/94) Zero Hour; released between #31&32 3.00
#1,000,000 (11/98) 853rd Century x-over; Orbik-c 2.50
Annual 1-5 ('93-'97 $2.95-$3.95, 68 pgs.): 3-Year One story; Poison Ivy app. 4-Legends of the Dead Earth story; Starman cameo. 5-Pulp Heroes story; Poison Ivy app. 4.00

BATMAN-SPAWN: WAR DEVIL (See Batman one-shots)

BATMAN SPECTACULAR (See DC Special Series No. 15)

BATMAN/ SUPERMAN/WONDER WOMAN: TRINITY
DC Comics: 2003 - No. 3, 2003 ($6.95, limited series, squarebound)

1-3-Matt Wagner-s/a/c. 1-Ra's al Ghul & Bizarro app. 7.00

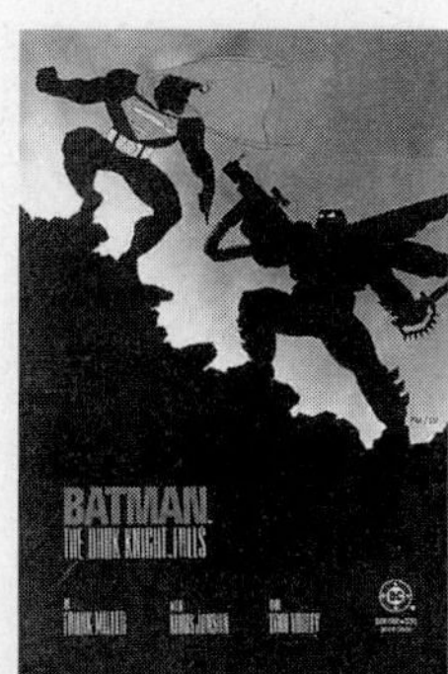
Batman: The Dark Knight Returns #4 © DC

Batman/Wildcat #3 © DC

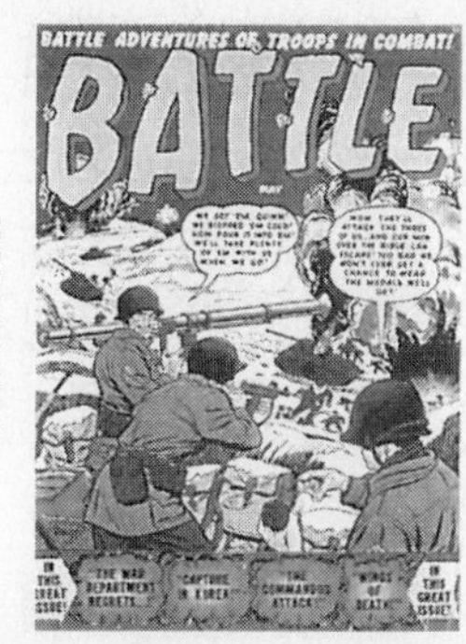

Battle #2 © MAR

GD VG FN VF VF/NM NM-
2.0 4.0 6.0 8.0 9.0 9.2

BATMAN: SWORD OF AZRAEL (Also see Azrael & Batman #488,489)
DC Comics: Oct, 1992 - No. 4, Jan, 1993 ($1.75, limited series)

1-Wraparound gatefold-c; Quesada-c/a(p) in all; 1st app. Azrael
2 4 6 8 10 12
2-4: 4-Cont'd in Batman #488 1 2 3 5 6 8
Silver Edition 1-4 (1993, $1.95)-Reprints #1-4 2.25
Trade Paperback (1993, $9.95)-Reprints #1-4 10.00
Trade Paperback Gold Edition 15.00

BATMAN/ TARZAN: CLAWS OF THE CAT-WOMAN
Dark Horse Comics/DC Comics: Sept, 1999 - No. 4, Dec, 1999 ($2.95, limited series)

1-4: Marz-s/Kordey-a 3.00

BATMAN: TENSES
DC Comics: 2003 - No. 2, 2003 ($6.95, limited series)

1,2-Joe Casey-s/Cully Hamner-a; Bruce Wayne's first year back in Gotham 7.00

BATMAN: THE ANKH
DC Comics: 2002 - No. 2, 2002 ($5.95, limited series)

1,2-Dixon-s/Van Fleet-a 6.00

BATMAN: THE CULT
DC Comics: 1988 - No. 4, Nov, 1988 ($3.50, deluxe limited series)

1-Wrightson-a/painted-c in all 6.00
2-4 5.00
Trade Paperback ('91, $14.95)-New Wrightson-c 15.00

BATMAN: THE DARK KNIGHT RETURNS (Also see Dark Knight Strikes Again)
DC Comics: Mar, 1986 - No. 4, 1986 ($2.95, squarebound, limited series)

1-Miller story & c/a(p); set in the future 4 8 12 29 40 50
1,2-2nd & 3rd printings, 3-2nd printing 6.00
2-Carrie Kelly becomes 1st female Robin 3 6 9 16 20 25
3-Death of Joker; Superman app. 2 4 6 12 16 20
4-Death of Alfred; Superman app. 2 4 6 10 13 16
Hardcover, signed & numbered edition ($40.00)(4000 copies) 250.00
Hardcover, trade edition 50.00
Softcover, trade edition (1st printing only) 2 4 6 11 14 18
Softcover, trade edition (2nd thru 8th printings) 1 2 3 5 7 9
10th Anniv. Slipcase set ('96, $100.00): Signed & numbered hard-c edition (10,000 copies), sketchbook, copy of script for #1, 2 color prints 100.00
10th Anniv. Hardcover ('96, $45.00) 45.00
10th Anniv. Softcover ('97, $14.95) 15.00
Hardcover 2nd printing ('02, $24.95) with 3 1/4" tall partial dustjacket 25.00
NOTE: *The #2 second printings can be identified by matching the grey background colors on the inside front cover and facing page. The inside front cover of the second printing has a dark grey background which does not match the lighter grey of the facing page. On the true 1st printings, the backgrounds are both light grey. All other issues are clearly marked.*

BATMAN: THE DOOM THAT CAME TO GOTHAM
DC Comics: 2000 - No. 3, 2001 ($4.95, limited series)

1-3-Elseworlds; Mignola-c/s; Nixey-a; Etrigan app. 5.00

BATMAN: THE KILLING JOKE (See Batman one-shots)

BATMAN: THE LONG HALLOWEEN
DC Comics: Oct, 1996 - No. 13, Oct, 1997 ($2.95/$4.95, limited series)

1-($4.95)-Loeb-s/Sale-c/a in all 1 2 3 5 6 8
2-5($2.95): 2-Solomon Grundy-c/app. 3-Joker-c/app., Catwoman, Poison Ivy app. 6.00
6-10: 6-Poison Ivy-c. 7-Riddler-c/app. 5.00
11,12 4.00
13-($4.95, 48 pgs.)-Killer revelations 5.00
HC-($29.95) r/series 30.00
SC-($19.95) 20.00

BATMAN: THE OFFICIAL COMIC ADAPTATION OF THE WARNER BROS. MOTION PICTURE
(See Batman one-shots)

BATMAN: THE ULTIMATE EVIL
DC Comics: 1995 ($5.95, limited series, prestige format)

1,2-Barrett, Jr. adaptation of Vachss novel. 6.00

BATMAN 3-D (Also see 3-D Batman)
DC Comics: 1990 ($9.95, w/glasses, 8-1/8x10-3/4")

nn-Byrne-a/scripts; Riddler, Joker, Penguin & Two-Face app. plus r/1953 3-D Batman; pin-ups by many artists 2 4 6 8 10 12

BATMAN: TOYMAN
DC Comics: Nov, 1998 - No. 4, Feb, 1999 ($2.25, limited series)

1-4-Hama-s 2.50

BATMAN: TURNING POINTS
DC Comics: Jan, 2001 - No. 5, Jan, 2001 ($2.50, weekly limited series)

1-5: 2-Giella-a. 3-Kubert-c/Giordano-a. 4-Chaykin-c. 5-Pope-c/a 2.50

BATMAN: TWO-FACE-CRIME AND PUNISHMENT (See Batman one-shots)

BATMAN: TWO-FACE STRIKES TWICE
DC Comics: 1993 - No. 2, 1993 ($4.95, 52 pgs.)

1,2-Flip book format w/Staton-a (G.A. side) 5.00

BATMAN VERSUS PREDATOR
DC Comics/Dark Horse Comics: 1991 - No. 3, 1992 ($4.95/$1.95, limited series) (1st DC/Dark Horse x-over)

1 (Prestige format, $4.95)-1 & 3 contain 8 Batman/Predator trading cards; Andy & Adam Kubert-a; Suydam painted-c 6.00
1-3 (Regular format, $1.95)-No trading cards 3.00
2,3-(Prestige)-2-Extra pin-ups inside; Suydam-c 5.00
TPB (1993, $5.95, 132 pgs.)-r/#1-3 w/new introductions & forward plus new wraparound-c by Dave Gibbons 6.00

BATMAN VERSUS PREDATOR II: BLOODMATCH
DC Comics: Late 1994 - No. 4, 1995 ($2.50, limited series)

1-4-Huntress app.; Moench scripts; Gulacy-a 3.00
TPB (1995, $6.95)-r/#1-4 7.00

BATMAN VS. THE INCREDIBLE HULK (See DC Special Series No. 27)

BATMAN: WAR ON CRIME
DC Comics: Nov, 1999 ($9.95, treasury size, one-shot)

nn-Painted art by Alex Ross; story by Alex Ross and Paul Dini 10.00

BATMAN/ WILDCAT
DC Comics: Apr, 1997 - No.3, June, 1997 ($2.25, mini-series)

1-3: Dixon/Smith-s: 1-Killer Croc app. 2.50

BAT MASTERSON (TV) (Also see Tim Holt #28)
Dell Publishing Co.: Aug-Oct, 1959; Feb-Apr, 1960 - No. 9, Nov-Jan, 1961-62

Four Color 1013 (#1) (8-10/59) 13 26 39 94 137 180
2-9: Gene Barry photo-c on all. 2-Two different back-c exist
7 14 21 51 71 90

BATS (See Tales Calculated to Drive You Bats)

BATS, CATS & CADILLACS
Now Comics: Oct, 1990 - No. 2, Nov, 1990 ($1.75)

1,2: 1-Gustovich-a(i); Snyder-c 2.25

BAT-THING
DC Comics (Amalgam): June, 1997 ($1.95, one-shot)

1-Hama-s/Damaggio & Sienkiewicz-a 2.25

BATTLE
Marvel/Atlas Comics(FPI #1-62/ Male #63 on): Mar, 1951 - No. 70, Jun, 1960

1 32 64 96 180 255 330
2 16 32 48 89 122 155
3-10: 4-1st Buck Pvt. O'Toole. 10-Pakula-a 11 22 33 66 88 110
11-20: 11-Check-a 9 18 27 52 66 80
21,23-Krigstein-a 10 20 30 56 73 90
22,24-36: 32-Tuska-a. 36-Everett-a 8 16 24 43 54 65
37-Kubert-a (Last precode, 2/55) 9 18 27 49 62 75
38-40,42-48 8 16 24 40 50 60
41,49: 41-Kubert/Moskowitz-a. 49-Davis-a 8 16 24 46 58 70
50-54,56-58 7 14 21 37 46 55
55-Williamson-a (5 pgs.) 8 16 24 46 58 70
59-Torres-a 8 16 24 40 50 60
60-62: 60,62-Combat Kelly app. 61-Combat Casey app.
7 14 21 37 46 55
63-Ditko-a 11 22 33 63 84 105
64-66-Kirby-a. 66-Davis-a; has story of Fidel Castro in pre-Communism days (an admiring profile) 14 28 42 79 107 135
67,68: 67-Williamson/Crandall-a (4 pgs.); Kirby, Davis-a. 68-Kirby/Williamson-a (4 pgs.); Kirby/Ditko-a 14 28 42 81 111 140
69,70: 69-Kirby-a. 70-Kirby/Ditko-a 14 28 42 79 107 135
NOTE: ***Andru** a-37. **Berg** a-38, 14, 60-62. **Colan** a-33, 55. **Everett** a-36, 50, 70; c-56, 57. **Heath** a-6, 9, 13, 31, 69; c-6, 9, 12, 26, 35, 37. **Kirby** c-64-69. **Maneely** a-4, 6, 31, 61; c-4, 33, 59, 61. **Orlando** a-47. **Powell** a-53, 55. **Reinman** a-8, 9, 26, 32. **Robinson** a-9, 39. **Romita** a-26. **Severin** a-28, 32-34, 66-69; c-36, 55. **Sinnott** a-33, 37. **Woodbridge** a-52, 55.*

BATTLE ACTION

Battleaxes #4 © Terry Laban

Battlefield #4 © ATLAS

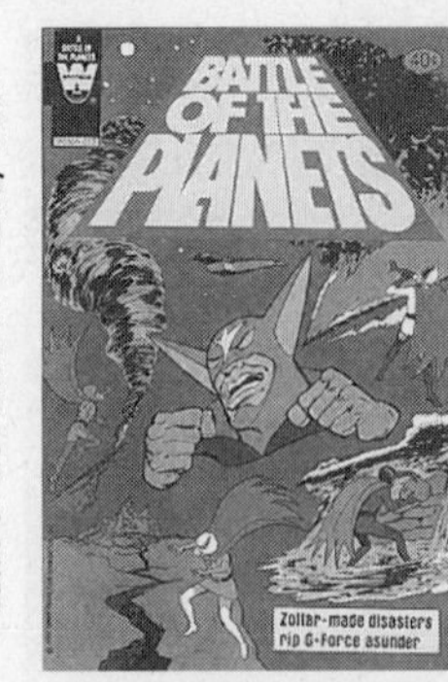

Battle of the Planets #9 © Sandy Frank

	GD 2.0	VG 4.0	FN 6.0	VF 8.0	VF/NM 9.0	NM- 9.2

GD VG FN VF VF/NM NM-
2.0 4.0 6.0 8.0 9.0 9.2

Atlas Comics (NPI): Feb, 1952 - No. 12, 5/53; No. 13, 11/54 - No. 30, 8/57

	GD 2.0	VG 4.0	FN 6.0	VF 8.0	VF/NM 9.0	NM- 9.2
1-Pakula-a	26	52	78	150	210	270
2	14	28	42	79	107	135
3,4,6,7,9,10: 6-Robinson-c/a. 7-Partial nudity	8	16	24	46	58	70
5-Used in **POP**, pg. 93,94	9	18	27	49	62	75
8-Krigstein-a	9	18	27	52	66	80
11-15 (Last precode, 2/55)	8	16	24	46	58	70
16-30: 27,30-Torres-a	8	16	24	43	54	65

NOTE: *Battle Brady app. 5-7, 10-12.* ***Berg*** *a-3.* ***Check*** *a-11.* ***Everett*** *a-7; c-13, 25.* ***Heath*** *a-3, 8, 18; c-3,15, 18, 21.* ***Maneely*** *a-1; c-5.* ***Reinman*** *a-1.* ***Robinson*** *a-6, 7; c-6.* ***Shores*** *a-7(2).* ***Sinnott*** *a-3.* ***Woodbridge*** *a-28, 30.*

BATTLE ATTACK
Stanmor Publications: Oct, 1952 - No. 8, Dec, 1955

	GD 2.0	VG 4.0	FN 6.0	VF 8.0	VF/NM 9.0	NM- 9.2
1	11	22	33	63	84	105
2	7	14	21	37	46	55
3-8: 3-Hollingsworth-a	6	12	18	31	38	45

BATTLEAXES
DC Comics (Vertigo): May, 2000 - No. 4, Aug, 2000 ($2.50, limited series)

	GD 2.0	VG 4.0	FN 6.0	VF 8.0	VF/NM 9.0	NM- 9.2
1-4: Terry LaBan-s/Alex Horley-a						2.50

BATTLE BEASTS
Blackthorne Publishing: Feb, 1988 - No. 4, 1988 ($1.50/$1.75, B&W/color)

	GD 2.0	VG 4.0	FN 6.0	VF 8.0	VF/NM 9.0	NM- 9.2
1-4: 1-3- (B&W)-Based on Hasbro toys. 4-Color						2.50

BATTLE BRADY (Formerly Men in Action No. 1-9; see 3-D Action)
Atlas Comics (IPC): No. 10, Jan, 1953 - No. 14, June, 1953

	GD 2.0	VG 4.0	FN 6.0	VF 8.0	VF/NM 9.0	NM- 9.2
10: 10-12-Syd Shores-c	16	32	48	89	122	155
11-Used in **POP**, pg. 95 plus B&W & color illos	10	20	30	56	73	90
12-14	9	18	27	49	62	75

BATTLE CHASERS
Image Comics (Cliffhanger): Apr, 1998 - No. 4, Dec, 1998;
DC Comics (Cliffhanger): No. 5, May, 1999 - No. 8, May, 2001 ($2.50)
Image Comics: No. 9, Sept, 2001 ($3.50)

	GD 2.0	VG 4.0	FN 6.0	VF 8.0	VF/NM 9.0	NM- 9.2
Prelude (2/98)	1	3	4	6	8	10
Prelude Gold Ed.	1	3	4	6	8	10
1-Madureira & Sharrieff-s/Madureira-a(p)/Charest-c	1	2	3	5	7	9
1-American Ent. Ed. w/"racy" cover	1	3	4	6	8	10
1-Gold Edition						9.00
1-Chromium cover						40.00
1-2nd printing						3.00
2						5.00
2-Dynamic Forces BattleChrome cover	2	4	6	8	10	12
3-Red Monika cover by Madureira						4.00
4-8: 4-Four covers. 6-Back-up by Warren-s/a. 7-3 covers (Madureira, Ramos, Campbell)						3.00
9-($3.50, Image) Flip cover/story by Adam Warren						3.50
...: A Gathering of Heroes HC ('99, $24.95) r/#1-5, Prelude, Frank Frazetta Fantasy Ill.; cover gallery						25.00
...: A Gathering of Heroes SC ('99, $14.95)						15.00
...Collected Edition 1,2 (11/98, 5/99, $5.95) 1-r/#1,2. 2-r/#3,4						6.00

BATTLE CLASSICS (See Cancelled Comic Cavalcade)
DC Comics: Sept-Oct, 1978 (44 pgs.)

	GD 2.0	VG 4.0	FN 6.0	VF 8.0	VF/NM 9.0	NM- 9.2
1-Kubert-r; new Kubert-c	1	2	3	5	7	9

BATTLE CRY
Stanmor Publications: 1952 (May) - No. 20, Sept, 1955

	GD 2.0	VG 4.0	FN 6.0	VF 8.0	VF/NM 9.0	NM- 9.2
1	14	28	42	81	111	140
2	8	16	24	46	58	70
3,5-10: 8-Pvt. Ike begins, ends #13,17	6	12	18	31	38	45
4-Classic E.C. swipe	8	16	24	40	50	60
11-20	6	12	18	27	33	38

NOTE: ***Hollingsworth*** *a-9; c-20.*

BATTLEFIELD (War Adventures on the...)
Atlas Comics (ACI): April, 1952 - No. 11, May, 1953

	GD 2.0	VG 4.0	FN 6.0	VF 8.0	VF/NM 9.0	NM- 9.2
1-Pakula, Reinman-a	22	44	66	124	172	220
2-5: 2-Heath, Maneely, Pakula, Reinman-a	11	22	33	66	88	110
6-11	9	18	27	49	62	75

NOTE: ***Colan*** *a-11.* ***Everett*** *a-8.* ***Heath*** *a-1, 2, 5p; c-2, 8, 9, 11.* ***Ravielli*** *a-11.*

BATTLEFIELD ACTION (Formerly Foreign Intrigues)
Charlton Comics: No. 16, Nov, 1957 - No. 62, 2-3/66; No. 63, 7/80 - No. 89, 11/84

	GD 2.0	VG 4.0	FN 6.0	VF 8.0	VF/NM 9.0	NM- 9.2
V2#16	7	14	21	37	46	55
17,20-30	5	10	15	22	26	30
18,19-Check-a (2 stories in #18)	3	7	10	21	28	35
31-62(1966)	2	4	6	14	18	22
63-80(1983-84)						5.00
81-83,85-89 (Low print run)	1	2	3	4	5	7
84-Kirby reprints; 3 stories	1	3	4	6	8	10

NOTE: ***Montes/Bache*** *a-43, 55, 62.* ***Glanzman*** *a-87r.*

BATTLE FIRE
Aragon Magazine/Stanmor Publications: Apr, 1955 - No. 7, 1955

	GD 2.0	VG 4.0	FN 6.0	VF 8.0	VF/NM 9.0	NM- 9.2
1	10	20	30	56	73	90
2	6	12	18	31	38	45
3-7	5	10	15	23	28	32

BATTLE FOR A THREE DIMENSIONAL WORLD
3D Cosmic Publications: May, 1983 (20 pgs., slick paper w/stiff-c, $3.00)

	GD 2.0	VG 4.0	FN 6.0	VF 8.0	VF/NM 9.0	NM- 9.2
nn-Kirby c/a in 3-D; shows history of 3-D	2	4	6	8	10	12

BATTLEFORCE
Blackthorne Publishing: Nov, 1987 - No. 2, 1988 ($1.75, color/B&W)

	GD 2.0	VG 4.0	FN 6.0	VF 8.0	VF/NM 9.0	NM- 9.2
1,2: Based on game. 1-In color. 2-B&W						2.50

BATTLE FOR INDEPENDENTS, THE (Also See Cyblade/Shi & Shi/Cyblade: The Battle For Independents)
Image Comics (Top Cow Productions)/Crusade Comics: 1995 ($29.95)

	GD 2.0	VG 4.0	FN 6.0	VF 8.0	VF/NM 9.0	NM- 9.2
nn-boxed set of all editions of Shi/Cyblade & Cyblade/Shi plus new variant.	4	8	12	24	32	40

BATTLE FOR THE PLANET OF THE APES (See Power Record Comics)

BATTLEFRONT
Atlas Comics (PPI): June, 1952 - No. 48, Aug, 1957

	GD 2.0	VG 4.0	FN 6.0	VF 8.0	VF/NM 9.0	NM- 9.2
1-Heath-c	30	60	90	170	240	310
2-Robinson-a(4)	15	30	45	86	118	150
3-5	12	24	36	71	96	120
6-10: Combat Kelly in No. 6-10	10	20	30	58	77	95
11-22,24-28: 14,16-Battle Brady app. 22-Teddy Roosevelt & His Rough Riders story. 28-Last pre-code (2/55)	8	16	24	46	58	70
23,43-Check-a	9	18	27	49	62	75
29-39,41,44-47	8	16	24	40	50	60
40,42-Williamson-a	9	18	27	52	66	80
48-Crandall-a	8	16	24	46	58	70

NOTE: ***Ayers*** *a-19, 32.* ***Berg*** *a-44.* ***Colan*** *a-21, 22, 32, 33, 40.* ***Drucker*** *a-28, 29.* ***Everett*** *a-44.* ***Heath*** *c-23, 26, 27, 29, 32.* ***Maneely*** *a-22, 23; c-2, 13, 22, 35.* ***Morisi*** *a-42.* ***Morrow*** *a-41.****Orlando*** *a-47.* ***Powell*** *a-19, 21, 25, 29, 32, 40, 47.* ***Robinson*** *a-1-4, 5(4); c-4, 5.* ***Robert Sale*** *a-19.* ***Severin*** *a-32; c-40.* ***Woodbridge*** *a-45, 46.*

BATTLEFRONT
Standard Comics: No. 5, June, 1952

	GD 2.0	VG 4.0	FN 6.0	VF 8.0	VF/NM 9.0	NM- 9.2
5-Toth-a	15	30	45	86	118	150

BATTLE GODS: WARRIORS OF THE CHAAK
Dark Horse Comics: Apr, 2000 - No. 4, July, 2000 ($2.95)

	GD 2.0	VG 4.0	FN 6.0	VF 8.0	VF/NM 9.0	NM- 9.2
1-4-Francisco Ruiz Velasco-s/a						3.00

BATTLE GROUND
Atlas Comics (OMC): Sept, 1954 - No. 20, Aug, 1957

	GD 2.0	VG 4.0	FN 6.0	VF 8.0	VF/NM 9.0	NM- 9.2
1	22	44	66	124	172	220
2-Jack Katz-a	11	22	33	66	88	110
3,4-Last precode (3/55)	9	18	27	52	66	80
5-8,10	8	16	24	46	58	70
9,11,13,18: 9-Krigstein-a. 11,13,18-Williamson-a in each	10	20	30	56	73	90
12,15-17,19,20	8	16	24	43	54	65
14-Kirby-a	11	22	33	63	84	105

NOTE: ***Ayers*** *a-13.* ***Colan*** *a-11, 13.* ***Drucker*** *a-7, 12, 13, 20.* ***Heath*** *c-2, 5, 13.* ***Maneely*** *a-19; c-1, 19.* ***Orlando*** *a-17.****Pakula*** *a-11.* ***Severin*** *a-5, 12, 19. c-20.* ***Tuska*** *a-11.*

BATTLE HEROES
Stanley Publications: Sept, 1966 - No. 2, Nov, 1966 (25¢, squarebound giants)

	GD 2.0	VG 4.0	FN 6.0	VF 8.0	VF/NM 9.0	NM- 9.2
1	4	8	12	24	32	40
2	3	6	9	18	23	28

BATTLE OF THE BULGE (See Movie Classics)

BATTLE OF THE PLANETS (Based on syndicated cartoon by Sandy Frank)
Gold Key/Whitman No. 6 on: 6/79 - No. 10, 12/80

	GD 2.0	VG 4.0	FN 6.0	VF 8.0	VF/NM 9.0	NM- 9.2
1: Mortimer a-1-4,7-10	3	6	9	18	24	30
2-6,10	2	4	6	12	16	20
7-Low print run	4	8	12	24	32	40
8,9-Low print run: 8(11/80). 9-(3-pack only?)	3	7	10	21	28	35

BATTLE OF THE PLANETS (Also see Thundercats/...)
Image Comics (Top Cow): Aug, 2002 - No. 12, Sept, 2003 ($2.95/$2.99)

Battle of the Planets #4 © Sandy Frank

Battlestar Galactica #15 © MAR

Battle Stories #6 © FAW

	GD 2.0	VG 4.0	FN 6.0	VF 8.0	VF/NM 9.0	NM- 9.2
1-($2.95) Alex Ross-c & art director; Tortosa-a(p); re-intro. G-Force						3.00
1-($5.95) Holofoil-c by Ross						6.00
2-11-($2.99) Ross-c on all						3.00
12-($4.99)						5.00
#1/2 (7/03, $2.99) Benitez-c; Alex Ross sketch pages						3.00
... Battle Book 1 (5/03, $4.99) background info on characters, equipment, stories						5.00
... : Jason 1 (7/03, $4.99) Ross-c; Erwin David-a; preview of Tomb Raider: Epiphany						5.00
... : Mark 1 (5/03, $4.99) Ross-c; Erwin David-a; preview of BotP: Jason						5.00
.../Thundercats 1 (Image/WildStorm, 5/03, $4.99) 2 covers by Ross & Campbell						5.00
.../Witchblade 1 (2/03, $5.95) Ross-c; Christina and Jo Chen-a						6.00
Vol.1: Trial By Fire (2003, $7.99) r/#1-3						8.00
Vol.1: Digest (1/04, $9.99, 7-3/8x5", B&W) r/#1-9 & ...: Mark						10.00
Vol.2: Blood Red Sky (9/03, $16.95) r/#4-9						17.00
Vol.3: Destroy All Monsters (11/03, $19.95) r/#10-12, ...: Jason, ...: Mark, .../Witchblade						20.00
BATTLE OF THE PLANETS: MANGA						
Image Comics (Top Cow): Nov, 2003 - No. 3, jan, 2004 ($2.99, B&W)						
1-3-Edwin David-a/David Wohl-s; previews for Wanted & Tomb Raider #35						3.00
BATTLE REPORT						
Ajax/Farrell Publications: Aug, 1952 - No. 6, June, 1953						
1	10	20	30	56	73	90
2-6	7	14	21	35	43	50
BATTLE SQUADRON						
Stanmor Publications: April, 1955 - No. 5, Dec, 1955						
1	9	18	27	52	66	80
2-5: 3-Iwo Jima & flag-c	6	12	18	28	34	40
BATTLESTAR GALACTICA (TV) (Also see Marvel Comics Super Special #8)						
Marvel Comics Group: Mar, 1979 - No. 23, Jan, 1981						
1: 1-5 adapt TV episodes	1	3	4	6	8	10
2-23: 1-3-Partial-r	1	2	3	4	5	7
NOTE: ***Austin** c-9i, 10i. **Golden** c-18. **Simonson** a(p)-4, 5, 11-13, 15-20, 22, 23; c(p)-4, 5,11-17, 19, 20, 22, 23.*						
BATTLESTAR GALACTICA (TV) (Also see Asylum)						
Maximum Press: July, 1995 - No.4, Nov, 1995 ($2.50, limited series)						
1-4: Continuation of TV series						4.00
Trade paperback (12/95, $12.95)-reprints series						13.00
BATTLESTAR GALACTICA (TV)						
Realm Press: Dec, 1997 - No. 5, July, 1998 ($2.99)						
1-5-Chris Scalf-s/painted-a/c						3.00
...Search For Sanctuary (9/98, $2.99) Scalf & Kuhoric-s						3.00
...Search For Sanctuary Special (4/00, $3.99) Kuhoric-s/Scalf & Scott-a						4.00
BATTLESTAR GALACTICA: APOLLO'S JOURNEY (TV)						
Maximum Press: Apr, 1996 - No. 3, June, 1996 ($2.95, limited series)						
1-3: Richard Hatch scripts						4.00
BATTLESTAR GALACTICA: JOURNEY'S END (TV)						
Maximum Press: Aug, 1996 - No. 4, Nov, 1996 ($2.99, limited series)						
1-4-Continuation of the T.V. series						4.00
BATTLESTAR GALACTICA: SEASON III						
Realm Press: June/July, 1999 - No. 3, Sept, 1999 ($2.99)						
1-3: 1-Kuhoric-s/Scalf & Scott-a; two covers by Scalf & Jae Lee. 2,3-Two covers						3.00
Gallery (4/00, $3.99) short story and pin-ups						4.00
1999 Tour Book (5/99, $2.99)						3.00
1999 Tour Book Convention Edition (6.99)						7.00
...Special: Centurion Prime (12/99, $3.99) Kuhoric-s						4.00
BATTLESTAR GALACTICA: SPECIAL EDITION (TV)						
Maximum Press: Jan, 1997 ($2.99, one-shot)						
1-Fully painted; Scalf-c/s/a; r/Asylum						3.00
BATTLESTAR GALACTICA: STARBUCK (TV)						
Maximum Press: Dec, 1995 - No. 3, Mar, 1996 ($2.50, limited series)						
1-3						4.00
BATTLESTAR GALACTICA: THE COMPENDIUM (TV)						
Maximum Press: Feb, 1997 ($2.99, one-shot)						
1						3.00
BATTLESTAR GALACTICA: THE ENEMY WITHIN (TV)						
Maximum Press: Nov, 1995 - No. 3, Feb, 1996 ($2.50, limited series)						
1-3: 3-Indicia reads Feb, 1995 in error.						4.00
BATTLESTONE (Also see Brigade & Youngblood)						
Image Comics (Extreme): Nov, 1994 - No. 2, Dec, 1994 ($2.50, limited series)						
1,2-Liefeld plots						2.50
BATTLE STORIES (See XMas Comics)						
Fawcett Publications: Jan, 1952 - No. 11, Sept, 1953						
1-Evans-a	16	32	48	89	122	155
2	9	18	27	49	62	75
3-11	8	16	24	40	50	60
BATTLE STORIES						
Super Comics: 1963 - 1964						
Reprints #10-12,15-18: 10-r/U.S Tank Commandos #? 11-r/? 11, 12,17-r/Monty Hall #?; 13-Kintsler-a (1pg).15-r/American Air Forces #7 by Powell; Bolle-r. 18-U.S. Fighting Air Force #?	2	4	6	10	13	16
BATTLETECH (See Blackthorne 3-D Series #41 for 3-D issue)						
Blackthorne Publishing: Oct, 1987 - No. 6, 1988 ($1.75/$2.00)						
1-6: Based on game. 1-Color. 2-Begin B&W						3.00
Annual 1 ($4.50, B&W)						5.00
BATTLETECH						
Malibu Comics: Feb, 1995 ($2.95)						
0						3.00
BATTLETECH FALLOUT						
Malibu Comics: Dec, 1994 - No. 4, Mar, 1995 ($2.95)						
1-4-Two edi. exist #1; normal logo						3.00
1-Gold version w/foil logo stamped "Gold Limited Edition						8.00
1-Full-c holographic limited edition						6.00
BATTLETIDE (Death's Head II & Killpower...)						
Marvel Comics UK, Ltd.: Dec, 1992 - No. 4, Mar, 1993 ($1.75, mini-series)						
1-4: Wolverine, Psylocke, Dark Angel app.						2.25
BATTLETIDE II (Death's Head II & Killpower...)						
Marvel Comics UK, Ltd.: Aug, 1993 - No. 4, Nov, 1993 ($1.75, mini-series)						
1-($2.95)-Foil embossed logo						3.00
2-4: 2-Hulk-c/story						2.25
BATTLEZONES: DREAM TEAM 2 (See Dream Team)						
Malibu Comics (Ultraverse): Mar, 1996 ($3.95)						
1-Pin-ups of Marvel & Malibu characters by Mike Wieringo, Phil Jimenez, Mike McKone, Cully Hamner, Gary Frank & others						4.00
BAY CITY JIVE						
DC Comics (WildStorm): Jul, 2001 - No. 3, Sept, 2001 ($2.95, limited series)						
1-3: Intro Sugah Rollins in 1970s San Francisco; Layman-s/Johnson-a						3.00
BAYWATCH COMIC STORIES (TV) (Magazine)						
Acclaim Comics (Armada): May, 1996 - No. 4, 1997 ($4.95) (Photo-c on all)						
1-4: Photo comics based on TV show						5.00
BEACH BLANKET BINGO (See Movie Classics)						
BEAGLE BOYS, THE (Walt Disney)(See The Phantom Blot)						
Gold Key: 11/64; No. 2, 11/65; No. 3, 8/66 - No. 47, 2/79 (See WDC&S #134)						
1	5	10	15	36	48	60
2-5	3	6	9	18	24	30
6-10	3	6	9	16	20	24
11-20: 11,14,19-r	2	4	6	11	14	18
21-30: 27-r	2	4	6	8	10	12
31-47	1	2	3	5	7	9
BEAGLE BOYS VERSUS UNCLE SCROOGE						
Gold Key: Mar, 1979 - No. 12, Feb, 1980						
1	2	4	6	10	13	16
2-12: 9-r	1	2	3	5	6	8
BEANBAGS						
Ziff-Davis Publ. Co. (Approved Comics): Winter, 1951 - No. 2, Spring, 1952						
1,2	11	22	33	63	84	105
BEANIE THE MEANIE						
Fago Publications: No. 3, May, 1959						
3	5	10	15	24	30	35
BEANY AND CECIL (TV) (Bob Clampett's...)						
Dell Publishing Co.: Jan, 1952 - 1955; July-Sept, 1962 - No. 5, July-Sept, 1963						
Four Color 368	29	58	87	210	305	400
Four Color 414,448,477,530,570,635(1/55)	17	34	51	123	182	240

The Beast #1 © MAR

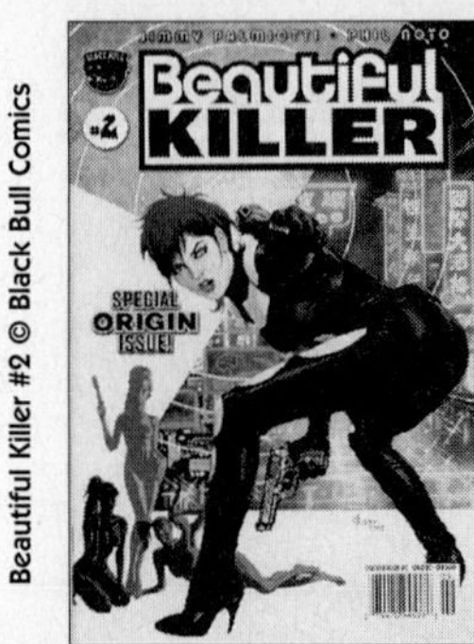

Beautiful Killer #2 © Black Bull Comics

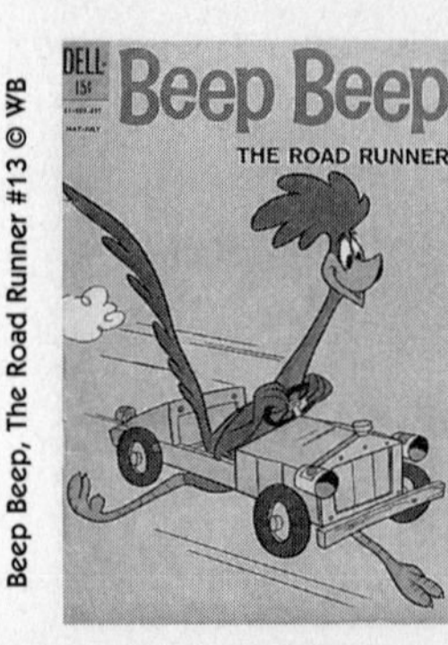

Beep Beep, The Road Runner #13 © WB

	GD 2.0	VG 4.0	FN 6.0	VF 8.0	VF/NM 9.0	NM- 9.2

01-057-209 (#1) 16 32 48 113 167 220
2-5 11 22 33 75 110 145

BEAR COUNTRY (Disney)
Dell Publishing Co.: No. 758, Dec, 1956
Four Color 758-Movie 6 12 18 40 55 70

BEAST (See X-Men)
Marvel Comics: May, 1997 - No. 3, 1997 ($2.50, mini-series)
1-3-Giffen-s/Nocon-a 3.00

BEAST BOY (See Titans)
DC Comics: Jan, 2000 - No. 4, Apr, 2000 ($2.95, mini-series)
1-4-Justiano-c/a; Raab & Johns-s 3.00

B.E.A.S.T.I.E.S. (Also see Axis Alpha)
Axis Comics: Apr, 1994 ($1.95)
1-Javier Saltares-c/a/scripts 2.25

BEATLES, THE (See Girls' Romances #109, Go-Go, Heart Throbs #101, Herbie #5, Howard the Duck Mag. #4, Laugh #166, Marvel Comics Super Special #4, My Little Margie #54, Not Brand Echh, Strange Tales #130, Summer Love, Superman's Pal Jimmy Olsen #79, Teen Confessions #37, Tippy's Friends & Tippy Teen)

BEATLES, THE (Life Story)
Dell Publishing Co.: Sept-Nov, 1964 (35¢)
1-(Scarce)-Stories with color photo pin-ups; Paul S. Newman-s
42 84 126 336 506 675

BEATLES EXPERIENCE, THE
Revolutionary Comics: Mar, 1991 - No. 8, 1991 ($2.50, B&W, limited series)
1-8: 1-Gold logo 5.00

BEATLES YELLOW SUBMARINE (See Movie Comics under Yellow...)

BEAUTIFUL KILLER
Black Bull Comics: Sept., 2002 - No. 3, Jan, 2003 ($2.99, limited series)
...Limited Preview Edition (5/02, $5.00) preview pgs. & creator interviews 5.00
1-Noto-a/Palmiotti-s; Hughes-c; intro Brigit Cole 3.00
2,3: 2-Jusko-c. 3-Noto-c 3.00
TPB (5/03, $9.99) r/#1-3; cover gallery and Adam Hughes sketch pages 10.00

BEAUTIFUL PEOPLE
Slave Labor Graphics: Apr, 1994 ($4.95, 8-1/2x11", one-shot)
nn 5.00

BEAUTIFUL STORIES FOR UGLY CHILDREN
DC Comics (Piranha Press): 1989 - No. 30, 1991 ($2.00/$2.50, B&W, mature)
Vol. 1-20: 12-$2.50-c begins 3.50
21-30 4.50
A Cotton Candy Autopsy ($12.95, B&W)-Reprints 1st two volumes 13.00

BEAUTY AND THE BEAST, THE
Marvel Comics Group: Jan, 1985 - No. 4, Apr, 1985 (limited series)
1-4: Dazzler & the Beast from X-Men; Sienkiewicz-c on all 3.00

BEAUTY AND THE BEAST (Graphic novel)(Also see Cartoon Tales & Disney's New Adventures of...)
Disney Comics: 1992
nn-($4.95, prestige edition)-Adapts animated film 7.00
nn-($2.50, newsstand edition) 3.00

BEAUTY AND THE BEAST
Disney Comics: Sept., 1992 - No. 2, 1992 ($1.50, limited series)
1,2 3.00

BEAUTY AND THE BEAST: PORTRAIT OF LOVE (TV)
First Comics: May, 1989 - No. 2, Mar, 1990 ($5.95, 60 pgs., squarebound)
1,2: 1-Based on TV show, Wendy Pini-a/scripts. 2-...: Night of Beauty; by Wendy Pini 6.00

BEAVER VALLEY (Movie)(Disney)
Dell Publishing Co.: No. 625, Apr, 1955
Four Color 625 7 14 21 50 68 85

BEAVIS AND BUTTHEAD (MTV's...)(TV cartoon)
Marvel Comics: Mar, 1994 - No. 28, June, 1996 ($1.95)
1-Silver ink-c. 1, 2-Punisher & Devil Dinosaur app. 4.00
1-2nd printing 2.25
2,3: 2-Wolverine app. 3-Man-Thing, Spider-Man, Venom, Carnage, Mary Jane & Stan Lee cameos; John Romita, Sr. art (2 pgs.) 2.50
4-28: 5-War Machine, Thor, Loki, Hulk, Captain America & Rhino cameos. 6-Psylocke, Polaris, Daredevil & Bullseye app. 7-Ghost Rider & Sub-Mariner app. 8-Quasar & Eon app. 9-Prowler & Nightwatch app. 11-Black Widow app. 12-Thunderstrike & Bloodaxe app. 13-Night Thrasher app. 14-Spider-Man 2099 app. 15-Warlock app. 16-X-Factor app. 25-Juggernaut app. 2.50

BECK & CAUL INVESTIGATIONS
Gauntlet Comics (Caliber): Jan, 1994 - No. 5, 1995? ($2.95, B&W)
1-5 3.00
Special 1 ($4.95) 5.00

BEDKNOBS AND BROOMSTICKS (See Walt Disney Showcase No. 6 & 50)

BEDLAM
Chaos! Comics: Sept, 2000 ($2.95, one-shot)
1-Steven Grant-s/David Brewer-a 3.00

BEDLAM!
Eclipse Comics: Sept, 1985 - No. 2, Sept, 1985 (B&W-r in color)
1,2: Bissette-a 3.00

BEDTIME STORY (See Cinema Comics Herald)

BEELZELVIS
Slave Labor Graphics: Feb, 1994 ($2.95, B&W, one-shot)
1 3.00

BEEP BEEP, THE ROAD RUNNER (TV)(See Daffy & Kite Fun Book)
Dell Publishing Co./Gold Key No. 1-88/Whitman No. 89 on: July, 1958 - No. 14, Aug-Oct, 1962; Oct, 1966 - No. 105, 1984
Four Color 918 (#1, 7/58) 11 22 33 77 114 150
Four Color 1008,1046 (11-1/59-60) 6 12 18 43 59 75
4(2-4/60)-14(Dell) 6 12 18 38 52 65
1(10/66, Gold Key) 6 12 18 40 55 70
2-5 4 8 12 25 33 42
6-14 3 6 9 18 24 30
15-18,20-40 2 4 6 14 18 22
19-With pull-out poster 4 8 12 24 32 40
41-50 2 4 6 10 13 16
51-70 1 3 4 6 8 10
71-88 1 2 3 4 5 7
89,90,94-101: 100(3/82), 101(4/82) 1 2 3 5 6 8
91(8/80), 92(9/80), 93 (3-pack?) (low printing) 2 4 6 12 16 20
102-105 (All #90189 on-c; nd or date code; pre-pack) 102(6/83), 103(7/83), 104(5/84), 105(6/84) 2 4 6 10 12 15
NOTE: *See March of Comics #351, 353, 375, 387, 397, 416, 430, 442, 455. #5, 8-10, 35, 53, 59-62, 68-r; 96-102, 104 are 1/3-r.*

BEETLE BAILEY (See Giant Comic Album, Sarge Snorkel; also Comics Reading Libraries in the Promotional Comics section)
Dell Publishing Co./Gold Key #39-53/King #54-66/Charlton #67-119/Gold Key #120-131/ Whitman #132: #459, 5/53 - #38, 5-7/62; #39, 11/62 - #53, 5/66; #54, 8/66 - #65, 12/67;#67, 2/69 - #119, 11/76; #120, 4/78 - #132, 4/80
Four Color 469 (#1)-By Mort Walker 11 22 33 77 114 150
Four Color 521,552,622 6 12 18 43 59 75
5(2-4/56)-10(5-7/57) 5 10 15 36 48 60
11-20(4-5/59) 4 8 12 25 33 42
21-38(5-7/62) 3 6 9 18 24 30
39-53(5/66) 3 6 9 16 20 24
54-65 (No. 66 publ. overseas only?) 2 4 6 12 16 20
67-69: 69-Last 12¢ issue 2 4 6 11 14 18
70-99 2 4 6 9 11 14
100 2 4 6 11 14 18
101-119 1 3 4 6 8 10
120-132 6.00

BEETLE BAILEY
Harvey Comics: V2#1, Sept, 1992 - V2#9, Aug, 1994 ($1.25/$1.50)
V2#1 4.00
2-9-($1.50) 3.00
Big Book 1(11/92),2(5/93)(Both $1.95, 52 pgs.) 3.50
Giant Size V2#1(10/92),2(3/93)(Both $2.25,68 pgs.) 3.50

BEETLEJUICE (TV)
Harvey Comics: Oct, 1991 ($1.25)
1 3.00

BEETLEJUICE CRIMEBUSTERS ON THE HAUNT
Harvey Comics: Sept, 1992 - No. 3, Jan, 1993 ($1.50, limited series)
1-3 3.00

BEE 29, THE BOMBARDIER

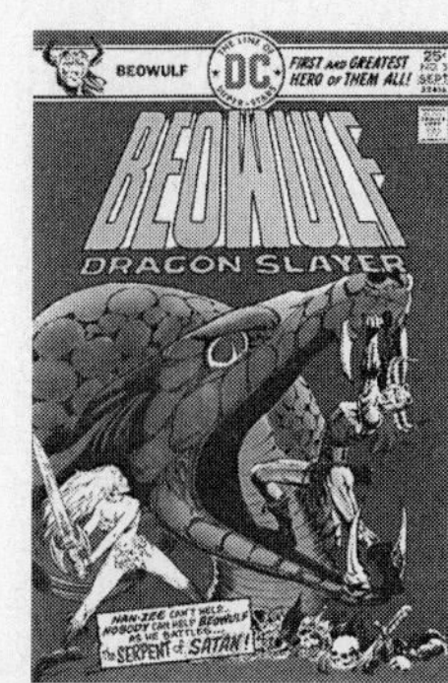

Beowulf #3 © DC

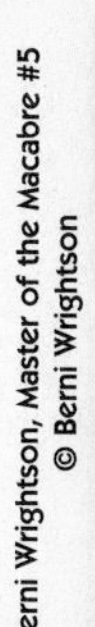

Berni Wrightson, Master of the Macabre #5 © Berni Wrightson

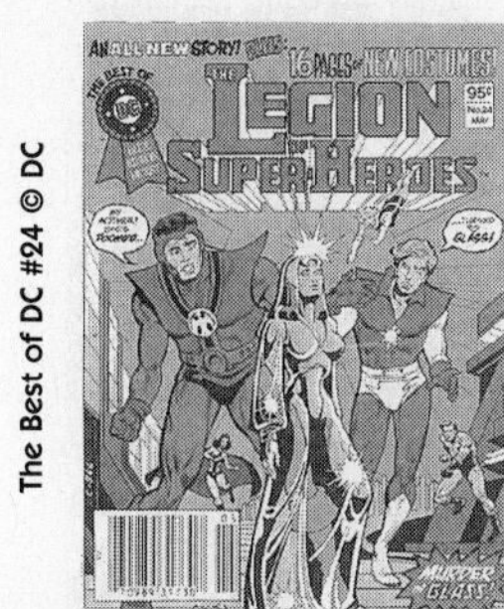

The Best of DC #24 © DC

	GD 2.0	VG 4.0	FN 6.0	VF 8.0	VF/NM 9.0	NM- 9.2

Neal Publications: Feb, 1945
1-(Funny animal) 31 62 93 175 248 320

BEFORE THE FANTASTIC FOUR: BEN GRIMM AND LOGAN
Marvel Comics: July, 2000 - No. 3, Sept, 2000 ($2.99, limited series)
1-3-The Thing and Wolverine app.; Hama-s 3.00

BEFORE THE FANTASTIC FOUR: REED RICHARDS
Marvel Comics: Sept, 2000 - No. 3, Dec, 2000 ($2.99, limited series)
1-3-Peter David-s/Duncan Fegredo-c/a 3.00

BEFORE THE FANTASTIC FOUR: THE STORMS
Marvel Comics: Dec, 2000 - No. 3, Feb, 2001 ($2.99, limited series)
1-3-Adlard-a 3.00

BEHIND PRISON BARS
Realistic Comics (Avon): 1952
1-Kinstler-c 32 64 96 182 259 335

BEHOLD THE HANDMAID
George Pflaum: 1954 (Religious) (25¢ with a 20¢ sticker price)
nn 5 10 15 23 28 32

BELIEVE IT OR NOT (See Ripley's...)

BEN AND ME (Disney)
Dell Publishing Co.: No. 539, Mar, 1954
Four Color 539 4 8 12 28 38 48

BEN BOWIE AND HIS MOUNTAIN MEN
Dell Publishing Co.: 1952 - No. 17, Nov-Jan, 1958-59
Four Color 443 (#1) 8 16 24 55 78 100
Four Color 513,557,599,626,657 4 8 12 29 40 50
7(5-7/56)-11: 11-Intro/origin Yellow Hair 4 8 12 27 36 45
12-17 4 8 12 22 30 38

BEN CASEY (TV)
Dell Publishing Co.: June-July, 1962 - No. 10, June-Aug, 1965 (Photo-c)
12-063-207 (#1) 7 14 21 46 63 80
2(10/62),3,5-10 4 8 12 29 40 50
4-Marijuana & heroin use story 5 10 15 36 48 60

BEN CASEY FILM STORY (TV)
Gold Key: Nov, 1962 (25¢) (Photo-c)
30009-211-All photos 9 18 27 60 85 110

BENEATH THE PLANET OF THE APES (See Movie Comics & Power Record Comics)

BEN FRANKLIN (See Kite Fun Book)

BEN HUR
Dell Publishing Co.: No. 1052, Nov, 1959
Four Color 1052-Movie, Manning-a 10 20 30 73 107 140

BEN ISRAEL
Logos International: 1974 (39¢)
nn-Christian religious 2 4 6 8 10 12

BEOWULF (Also see First Comics Graphic Novel #1)
National Periodical Publications: Apr-May, 1975 - No. 6, Feb-Mar, 1976
1 2 4 6 9 11 14
2,3,5,6: 5-Flying saucer-c/story 1 2 3 5 6 8
4-Dracula-c/s 1 2 3 5 7 9

BERLIN
Black Eye Productions: Apr, 1996 - Present ($2.50/$2.95/$3.50, B&W)
1-8: Jason Lutes-c/a/scripts. 5-7-($2.95) 3.00
9,10-($3.50) 3.50
City of Stones TPB (2001, $15.95) r/#1-8 16.00

BERNI WRIGHTSON, MASTER OF THE MACABRE
Pacific Comics/Eclipse Comics No. 5: July, 1983 - No. 5, Nov, 1984 ($1.50, Baxter paper)
1-5: Wrightson-c/a(r). 4-Jeff Jones-r (11 pgs.) 5.00

BERRYS, THE (Also see Funny World)
Argo Publ.: May, 1956
1-Reprints daily & Sunday strips & daily Animal Antics by Ed Nofziger
6 12 18 29 36 42

BERZERKERS (See Youngblood V1#2)
Image Comics (Extreme Studios): Aug, 1995 - No. 3, Oct, 1995 ($2.50, limited series)
1-3: Beau Smith scripts, Fraga-a 2.50

BEST COMICS
Better Publications: Nov, 1939 - No. 4, Feb, 1940(Large size, reads sideways)
1-(Scarce)-Red Mask begins(1st app.) & c/s-all. Contains 6 pg. Boston Celtics photo story
85 170 255 531 796 1060
2-4: 4-Cannibalism story 50 100 150 300 450 600

BEST FROM BOY'S LIFE, THE
Gilberton Company: Oct, 1957 - No. 5, Oct, 1958 (35¢)
1-Space Conquerors & Kam of the Ancient Ones begin, end #5; Bob Cousy photo/story
12 24 36 71 96 120
2,3,5 8 16 24 40 50 60
4-L.B. Cole-a 8 16 24 46 58 70

BEST LOVE (Formerly Sub-Mariner Comics No. 32)
Marvel Comics (MPI): No. 33, Aug, 1949 - No. 36, April, 1950 (Photo-c 33-36)
33-Kubert-a 12 24 36 71 96 120
34 8 16 24 40 50 60
35,36-Everett-a 9 18 27 52 66 80

BEST OF BUGS BUNNY, THE
Gold Key: Oct, 1966 - No. 2, Oct, 1968
1,2-Giants 6 12 18 38 52 65

BEST OF DC, THE (Blue Ribbon Digest) (See Limited Coll. Ed. C-52)
DC Comics: Sept-Oct, 1979 - No. 71, Apr, 1986 (100-148 pgs; mostly reprints)
1-Superman, w/"Death of Superman"-r 2 4 6 12 16 20
2,5-9: 2-Batman 40th Ann. Special. 5-Best of 1979. 6,8-Superman. 7-Superboy. 9-Batman, Creeper app. 2 4 6 8 10 12
3-Superfriends 2 4 6 10 12 15
4-Rudolph the Red Nosed Reindeer 2 4 6 10 13 16
10-Secret Origins of Super Villains; 1st ever Penguin origin-s
3 6 9 18 23 28
11-16,18-20: 11-The Year's Best Stories. 12-Superman Time and Space Stories.13-Best of DC Comics Presents. 14-New origin stories of Batman villains. 15-Superboy. 16-Superman Anniv. 18-Teen Titans new-s., Adams, Kane-a; Perez-c. 19-Superman. 20-World's Finest
1 2 3 5 7 9
17-Supergirl 2 4 6 8 10 12
21,22: 21-Justice Society. 22-Christmas; unpublished Sandman story w/Kirby-a
2 4 6 11 14 18
23-27: 23-(148 pgs.)-Best of 1981. 24 Legion, new story and 16 pgs. new costumes. 25-Superman. 26-Brave & Bold. 27-Superman vs. Luthor
2 4 6 10 12 15
28,29: 28-Binky, Sugar & Spike app. 29-Sugar & Spike, 3 new stories; new Stanley & his Monster story 2 4 6 9 11 14
30,32-36,38,40: 30-Detective Comics. 32-Superman. 33-Secret origins of Legion Heroes and Villains. 34-Metal Men; has #497 on-c from Adv. Comics. 35-The Year's Best Comics Stories (148 pgs.). 36-Superman vs. Kryptonite. 38-Superman. 40-World of Krypton
2 4 6 10 12 15
31-JLA 2 4 6 11 14 18
37,39: 37-"Funny Stuff", Mayer-a. 39-Binky 2 4 6 11 14 18
41,43,45,47,49,53,55,58,60,63,65,68,70: 41-Sugar & Spike new stories with Mayer-a. 43,49,55-Funny Stuff. 45,53,70-Binky. 47,58,65,68-Sugar & Spike. 60-Plop!; Wood-c(r) & Aragonés-r (5/85). 63-Plop!; Wrightson-a(r) 2 4 6 14 18 22
42,44,46,48,50-52,54,56,57,59,61,62,64,66,67,69,71: 42,56-Superman vs. Aliens. 44,57,67-Superboy & LSH. 46-Jimmy Olsen. 48-Superman Team-ups. 50-Year's best Superman. 51-Batman Family. 52 Best of 1984. 54,56,59-Superman. 61-(148 pgs.)Year's best. 62-Best of Batman 1985. 69-Year's best Team stories. 71-Year's best
2 4 6 10 13 16

NOTE: ***N. Adams** a-2r, 14r, 18r, 26, 51. **Aparo** a-9, 14, 26, 30; c-9, 14, 26. **Austin** a-51i. **Buckler** a-40p; c-16, 22. **Giffen** a-50, 52; c-33p. **Grell** a-33p. **Grossman** a-37. **Heath** a-26. **Infantino** a-10r, 18. **Kaluta** a-40. **G. Kane** a-10r, 18r; c-40, 44. **Kubert** a-10r, 21, 26. **Layton** a-21. **S. Mayer** c-29, 37, 41, 43, 47; a-28, 29, 37, 41, 43, 47, 58, 65, 68. **Moldoff** c-64p. **Morrow** a-40; c-40. **W. Mortimer** a-39p. **Newton** a-5, 51. **Perez** a-24, 50p; c-18, 21, 23. **Rogers** a-14, 51p. **Simonson** a-11r. **Spiegle** a-52. **Starlin** a-51. **Staton** a-5, 21. **Tuska** a-24. **Wolverton** a-60. **Wood** a-60, 63; c-60, 63. **Wrightson** a-60. New art in #14, 18, 24.*

BEST OF DENNIS THE MENACE, THE
Hallden/Fawcett Publications: Summer, 1959 - No. 5, Spring, 1961 (100 pgs.)
1-All reprints; Wiseman-a 8 16 24 53 74 95
2-5 5 10 15 36 48 60

BEST OF DONALD DUCK, THE
Gold Key: Nov, 1965 (12¢, 36 pgs.)(Lists 2nd printing in indicia)
1-Reprints Four Color #223 by Barks 8 16 24 58 82 105

BEST OF DONALD DUCK & UNCLE SCROOGE, THE
Gold Key: Nov, 1964 - No. 2, Sept, 1967 (25¢ Giants)

Best of the Brave and the Bold #1 © DC

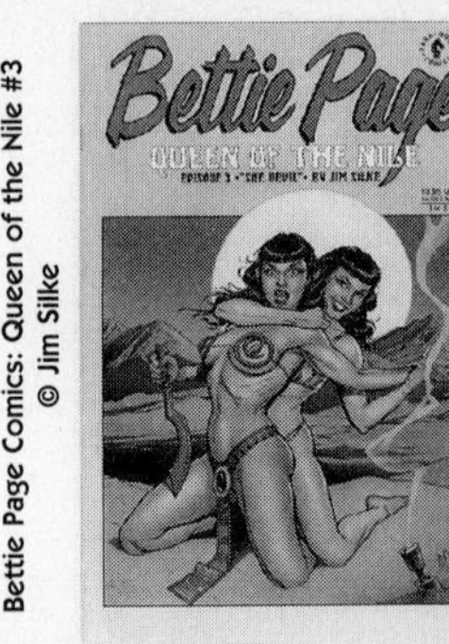

Bettie Page Comics: Queen of the Nile #3 © Jim Silke

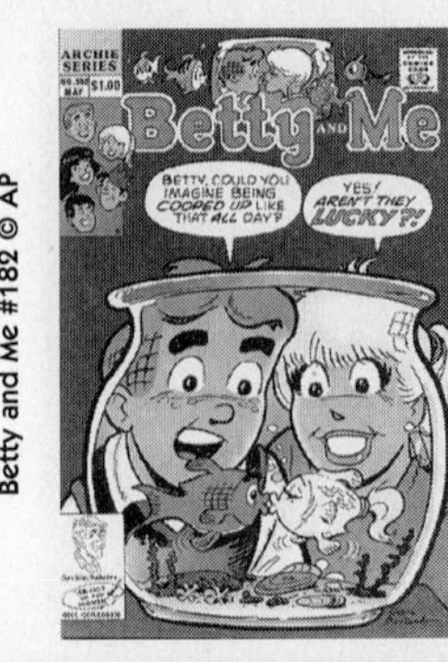

Betty and Me #182 © AP

GD VG FN VF VF/NM NM-
2.0 4.0 6.0 8.0 9.0 9.2

GD VG FN VF VF/NM NM-
2.0 4.0 6.0 8.0 9.0 9.2

1(30022-411)('64)-Reprints 4-Color #189 & 408 by Carl Barks; cover of F.C. #189 redrawn by Barks 9 18 27 63 89 115
2(30022-709)('67)-Reprints 4-Color #256 & "Seven Cities of Cibola" & U.S. #8 by Barks 8 16 24 58 82 105

BEST OF HORROR AND SCIENCE FICTION COMICS
Bruce Webster: 1987 ($2.00)

1-Wolverton, Frazetta, Powell, Ditko-r 5.00

BEST OF JOSIE AND THE PUSSYCATS
Archie Comics: 2001 ($10.95, TPB)

1-Reprints 1st app. and noteworthy stories 11.00

BEST OF MARMADUKE, THE
Charlton Comics: 1960

1-Brad Anderson's strip reprints 3 7 10 21 28 35

BEST OF MS. TREE, THE
Pyramid Comics: 1987 - No. 4, 1988 ($2.00, B&W, limited series)

1-4 2.50

BEST OF RAY BRADBURY, THE
ibooks: 2003 ($18.95, TPB)

The Graphic Novel - Reprints from Ray Bradbury Comics; adaptations by various 19.00

BEST OF THE BRAVE AND THE BOLD, THE (See Super DC Giant)
DC Comics: Oct, 1988 - No. 6, Jan, 1989 ($2.50, limited series)

1-6: Neal Adams-r, Kubert-r & Heath-r in all 4.00

BEST OF THE WEST (See A-1 Comics)
Magazine Enterprises: 1951 - No. 12, April-June, 1954

1(A-1 42)-Ghost Rider, Durango Kid, Straight Arrow, Bobby Benson begin 40 80 120 240 360 480
2(A-1 46) 23 46 69 132 186 240
3(A-1 52), 4(A-1 59), 5(A-1 66) 19 38 57 109 152 195
6(A-1 70), 7(A-1 76), 8(A-1 81), 9(A-1 85), 10(A-1 87), 11(A-1 97), 12(A-1 103) 14 28 42 81 111 140

NOTE: *Bolle a-9. Borth a-12. Guardineer a-5, 12. Powell a-1, 12.*

BEST OF UNCLE SCROOGE & DONALD DUCK, THE
Gold Key: Nov, 1966 (25¢)

1(30030-611)-Reprints part 4-Color #159 & 456 & Uncle Scrooge #6,7 by Carl Barks 8 16 24 58 82 105

BEST OF WALT DISNEY COMICS, THE
Western Publishing Co.: 1974 ($1.50, 52 pgs.) (Walt Disney)
(8-1/2x11" cardboard covers; 32,000 printed of each)

96170-Reprints 1st two stories less 1 pg. each from 4-Color #62 4 8 12 28 38 48
96171-Reprints Mickey Mouse and the Bat Bandit of Inferno Gulch from 1934 (strips) by Gottfredson 4 8 12 28 38 48
96172-r/Uncle Scrooge #386 & two other stories 4 8 12 28 38 48
96173-Reprints "Ghost of the Grotto" (from 4-Color #159) & "Christmas on Bear Mountain" (from 4-Color #178) 4 8 12 28 38 48

BEST ROMANCE
Standard Comics (Visual Editions): No. 5, Feb-Mar, 1952 - No. 7, Aug, 1952

5-Toth-a; photo-c 13 26 39 74 100 125
6,7-Photo-c 7 14 21 35 43 50

BEST SELLER COMICS (See Tailspin Tommy)

BEST WESTERN (Formerly Terry Toons? or Miss America Magazine
Marvel Comics (IPC): V7#24(#57)?; Western Outlaws & Sheriffs No. 60 on)
No. 58, June, 1949 - No. 59, Aug, 1949

58,59-Black Rider, Kid Colt, Two-Gun Kid app.; both have Syd Shores-c 22 44 66 127 176 225

BETTIE PAGE COMICS
Dark Horse Comics: Mar, 1996 ($3.95)

1-Dave Stevens-c; Blevins & Heath-a; Jaime Hernandez pin-up 1 2 3 4 5 7

BETTIE PAGE COMICS: QUEEN OF THE NILE
Dark Horse Comics: Dec, 1999 - No. 3, Apr, 2000 ($2.95, limited series)

1-3-Silke-s/a; Stevens-c 3.00

BETTIE PAGE COMICS: SPICY ADVENTURE
Dark Horse Comics: Jan, 1997 ($2.95, one-shot, mature)

nn-Silke-c/s/a 4.00

BETTY (See Pep Comics #22 for 1st app.)
Archie Comics: Sept, 1992 - Present ($1.25/$1.50/$1.75/$1.79/$1.99/$2.19)

1 5.00
2-18,20-24: 20-1st Super Sleuther-s 3.00
19-Love Showdown part 2 5.00
25-Pin-up page of Betty as Marilyn Monroe, Madonna, Lady Di 5.00
26-50 3.00
51-134: 57- "A Storm Over Uniforms" x-over part 5,6 2.25

BETTY AND HER STEADY (Going Steady with Betty No. 1)
Avon Periodicals: No. 2, Mar-Apr, 1950

2 10 20 30 56 73 90

BETTY AND ME
Archie Publications: Aug, 1965 - No. 200, Aug, 1992

1 10 20 30 70 100 130
2,3: 3-Origin Superteen 6 12 18 38 52 65
4-8: Superteen in new costume #4-7; dons new helmet in #5, ends #8. 4 8 12 27 36 45
9,10: Girl from R.I.V.E.R.D.A.L.E. 9-UFO-s 3 7 10 21 28 35
11-15,17-20(4/69) 3 6 9 18 23 28
16-Classic cover; w/risqué cover dialogue 4 8 12 22 30 38
21,24-35: 33-Paper doll page 2 4 6 12 16 20
22-Archies Band-s 3 6 9 16 20 24
23-I Dream of Jeannie parody 3 6 9 18 23 28
36(8/71),37,41-55 (52 pgs.): 42-Betty as vamp-s 2 4 6 14 18 22
38-Sabrina app. 3 7 10 21 28 35
39-Josie and Sabrina cover cameos 3 6 9 18 24 30
40-Archie & Betty share a cabin 3 6 9 16 20 24
56(4/71)-80(12/76): 79 Betty Cooper mysteries thru #86. 79-81-Drago the Vampire-s 2 4 6 8 10 12
81-99: 83-Harem-c. 84-Jekyll & Hyde-c/s 1 2 3 5 7 9
100(3/79) 2 4 6 8 10 12
101,118: 101-Elvis mentioned. 118-Tarzan mentioned 1 2 3 4 5 7
102-117,119-130(9/82): 103,104-Space-s. 124-DeCarlo-c begins 6.00
131-138,140,142-147,149-154,156-158: 135,136-Jason Blossom app. 136-Cheryl Blossom cameo. 137-Space-s. 138-Tarzan parody 4.00
139,141,148: 139-Katy Keene collecting-s; Archie in drag-s. 141-Tarzan parody-s. 148-Cyndi Lauper parody-s 5.00
155,159,160(8/87): 155-Archie in drag-s. 159-Superhero gag-c. 160-Wheel of Fortune parody 5.00
161-169,171-199 3.00
170,200: 170-New Archie Superhero-s 5.00

BETTY AND VERONICA (Also see Archie's Girls...)
Archie Enterprises: June, 1987 - Present (75¢ /$1.25/$1.50/$1.75/$1.79/$1.99/$2.19)

1 1 2 3 5 7 9
2-10 5.50
11-30 4.00
31-50 3.00
51-81 2.50
82-Love Showdown part 3 5.00
83-158 2.50
159-196 2.25
Summer Fun 1 (1994, $2.00, 52 pgs. plus poster) 3.00

BETTY & VERONICA ANNUAL DIGEST (...Digest Magazine #1-4, 44 on; ...Comics Digest Mag. #5-43)
Archie Publications: Nov, 1980 - Present ($1.00/$1.50/$1.75/$1.95/$1.99/$2.39, digest size)

1 3 6 9 18 23 28
2-10: 2(11/81-Katy Keene story), 3(8/82) 2 4 6 10 13 16
11-30 1 3 4 6 8 10
31-50 1 2 3 4 5 7
51-70 4.00
71-144: 110-Begin $2.19-c. 135-Begin $2.39-c 2.40

BETTY & VERONICA ANNUAL DIGEST MAGAZINE
Archie Comics: Sept, 1989 - Present ($1.50/$1.75/$1.79, 128 pgs.)

1 1 2 3 5 7 9
2-10: 9-Neon ink logo 5.00
11-17: 16-Begin $1.79-c 3.00

BETTY & VERONICA CHRISTMAS SPECTACULAR (See Archie Giant Series Magazine #159, 168, 180, 191, 204, 217, 229, 241, 453, 465, 477, 489, 501, 513, 525, 536, 547, 558, 568, 580, 593, 606, 618)

BETTY & VERONICA DOUBLE DIGEST MAGAZINE
Archie Enterprises: 1987 - Present ($2.25-$2.99, digest size, 256 pgs.)(...Digest #12 on)

Beware #16 (#4) © TM

Beware the Creeper #5 © DC

Big Bang Comics V2 #18 © Gary Carlson

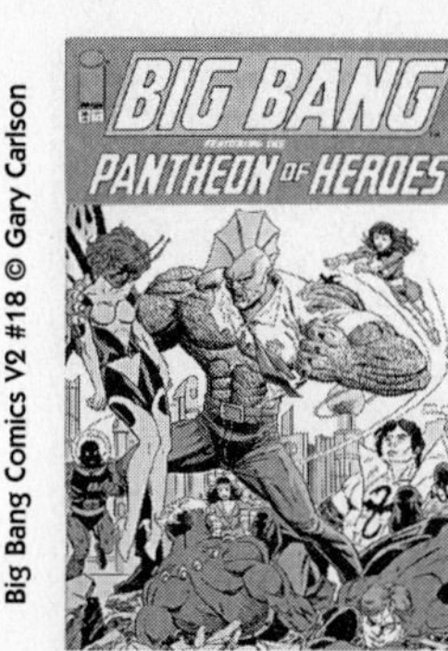

	GD 2.0	VG 4.0	FN 6.0	VF 8.0	VF/NM 9.0	NM- 9.2
1	2	4	6	8	10	12
2-10	1	2	3	4	5	7
11-25: 5,17-Xmas-c. 16-Capt. Hero story						5.00
26-50						4.00
51-121: 87-Begin $3.19-c. 95-Begin $3.29-c. 114-Begin $3.59-c						3.60

BETTY & VERONICA SPECTACULAR (See Archie Giant Series Mag. #11, 16, 21, 26, 32, 138, 145, 153, 162, 173, 184, 197, 201, 210, 214, 221, 226, 234, 238, 246, 250, 458, 462, 470, 482, 486, 494, 498, 506, 510, 518, 522, 526, 530, 537, 552, 559, 563, 569, 575, 582, 588, 600, 608, 613, 620, 623, and Betty & Veronica)

BETTY AND VERONICA SPECTACULAR
Archie Comics: Oct, 1992 - Present ($1.25/$1.50/$1.75/$1.99/$2.19)

1-Dan DeCarlo-c/a 5.00
2-20 3.00
21-64: 48-Cheryl Blossom leaves Riverdale. 64-Cheryl Blossom returns 2.25

BETTY & VERONICA SPRING SPECTACULAR (See Archie Giant Series Magazine #569, 582, 595)

BETTY & VERONICA SUMMER FUN (See Archie Giant Series Mag. #8, 13, 18, 23, 28, 34, 140, 147, 155, 164, 175, 187, 199, 212, 224, 236, 248, 460, 484, 496, 508, 520, 529, 539, 550, 561, 572, 585, 598, 611, 621)
Archie Comics: 1994 - Present ($2.00/$2.25/$2.29)

1-6: 5-($2.25-c). 6-($2.29-c) 2.50
Vol. 1 (2003, $10.95) reprints stories from Archie Giant Series editions 11.00

BETTY BOOP'S BIG BREAK
First Publishing: 1990 ($5.95, 52 pgs.)

nn-By Joshua Quagmire; 60th anniversary ish. 6.00

BETTY PAGE 3-D COMICS
The 3-D Zone: 1991 ($3.95, "7-1/2x10-1/4," 28 pgs., no glasses)

1-Photo inside covers; back-c nudity 1 2 3 5 6 8

BETTY'S DIARY (See Archie Giant Series Magazine No. 555)
Archie Enterprises: April, 1986 - No. 40, Apr, 1991 (#1:65¢; 75¢/95¢)

1 6.00
2-10 4.00
11-40 2.50

BETTY'S DIGEST
Archie Enterprises: Nov, 1996 - No. 2 ($1.75/$1.79)

1,2 3.00

BEVERLY HILLBILLIES (TV)
Dell Publishing Co.: 4-6/63 - No. 18, 8/67; No. 19, 10/69; No. 20, 10/70; No. 21, Oct, 1971

	GD	VG	FN	VF	VF/NM	NM-
1-Photo-c	18	36	54	131	191	250
2-Photo-c	10	20	30	67	96	125
3-9: All have photo covers	8	16	24	53	74	95
10: No photo cover	5	10	15	36	48	60
11-21: All have photo covers. 18-Last 12¢ issue. 19-21-Reprint #1-3 (covers and insides)	6	12	18	40	55	70

NOTE: *#1-9, 11-21 are photo covers.*

BEWARE (Formerly Fantastic; Chilling Tales No. 13 on)
Youthful Magazines: No. 10, June, 1952 - No. 12, Oct, 1952

	GD	VG	FN	VF	VF/NM	NM-
10-E.A. Poe's Pit & the Pendulum adaptation by Wildey; Harrison/Bache-a; atom bomb and shrunken head-c	55	110	165	338	507	675
11-Harrison-a; Ambrose Bierce adapt.	38	76	114	219	310	400
12-Used in **SOTI**, pg. 388; Harrison-a	38	76	114	219	310	400

BEWARE
Trojan Magazines/Merit Publ. No. ?: No. 13, 1/53 - No. 16, 7/53; No. 5, 9/53 - No. 15, 5/55

	GD	VG	FN	VF	VF/NM	NM-
13(#1)-Harrison-a	55	110	165	338	507	675
14(#2, 3/53)-Krenkel/Harrison-c; dismemberment, severed head panels	38	76	114	219	310	400
15,16(#3, 5/53; #4, 7/53)-Harrison-a	32	64	96	184	262	340
5,9,12,13	32	64	96	180	255	330
6-Ill. in **SOTI**- "Children are first shocked and then desensitized by all this brutality." Corpse on cover swipe/V.O.H. #26; girl on cover swipe/Advs. Into Darkness #10	58	116	174	363	544	725
7,8-Check-a	32	64	96	184	262	340
10-Frazetta/Check-c; Disbrow, Check-a	66	132	198	413	619	825
11-Disbrow-a; heart torn out, blood drainage	38	76	114	219	310	400
14,15: 14-Myron Fass-c. 15-Harrison-a	27	54	81	155	218	280

NOTE: ***Fass** a-5, 6, 8; c-6, 11, 14. **Forte** a-8. **Hollingsworth** a-15(#3), 16(#4), 9; c-16(#4), 8, 9. **Kiefer** a-16(#4), 5, 6, 10.*

BEWARE (Becomes Tomb of Darkness No. 9 on)
Marvel Comics Group: Mar, 1973 - No. 8, May, 1974 (All reprints)

	GD	VG	FN	VF	VF/NM	NM-
1-Everett-c; Kirby & Sinnott-r ('54)	3	6	9	16	20	24
2-8: 2-Forte, Colan-r. 6-Tuska-a. 7-Torres-r/Mystical Tales #7	2	4	6	10	12	15

NOTE: ***Infantino** a-4r. **Gil Kane** c-4. **Wildey** a-7r.*

BEWARE TERROR TALES
Fawcett Publications: May, 1952 - No. 8, July, 1953

	GD	VG	FN	VF	VF/NM	NM-
1-E.C. art swipe/Haunt of Fear #5 & Vault of Horror #26	46	92	138	276	413	550
2	32	64	96	180	255	330
3-7	23	52	78	147	206	265
8-Tothish-a; people being cooked-c	30	60	90	173	244	315

NOTE: ***Andru** a-2. **Bernard Bailey** a-1; c-1-5. **Powell** a-1, 2, 8. **Sekowsky** a-2.*

BEWARE THE CREEPER (See Adventure, Best of the Brave & the Bold, Brave & the Bold, 1st Issue Special, Flash #318-323, Showcase #73, World's Finest Comics #249)
National Periodical Publications: May-June, 1968 - No. 6, Mar-Apr, 1969 (All 12¢ issues)

	GD	VG	FN	VF	VF/NM	NM-
1-(5-6/68)-Classic Ditko-c; Ditko-a in all	10	20	30	73	107	140
2-6: 2-5-Ditko-c. 2-Intro. Proteus. 6-Gil Kane-c	6	12	18	40	55	70

BEWARE THE CREEPER
DC Comics (Vertigo): June, 2003 - No. 5, Oct, 2003 ($2.95, limited series)

1-5-Female vigilante in 1920s Paris; Jason Hall-s/Cliff Chiang-a 3.00

BEWITCHED (TV)
Dell Publishing Co.: 4-6/65 - No. 11, 10/67; No. 12, 10/68 - No. 13, 1/69; No. 14, 10/69

	GD	VG	FN	VF	VF/NM	NM-
1-Photo-c	17	34	51	123	182	240
2-No photo-c	9	18	27	60	85	110
3-13-All have photo-c. 12-Rep. #1. 13-Last 12¢-c	7	14	21	50	68	85
14-No photo-c; reprints #2	5	10	15	36	48	60

BEYOND, THE
Ace Magazines: Nov, 1950 - No. 30, Jan, 1955

	GD	VG	FN	VF	VF/NM	NM-
1-Bakerish-a(p)	42	84	126	252	376	500
2-Bakerish-a(p)	29	58	87	164	232	300
3-10: 10-Woodish-a by Cameron	20	40	60	112	156	200
11-20: 18-Used in **POP**, pgs. 81,82	16	32	48	89	122	155
21-26,28-30	15	30	45	86	118	150
27-Used in **SOTI**, pg. 111	16	32	48	89	122	155

NOTE: ***Cameron** a-10, 11p, 12p, 15, 16, 21-27, 30; c-20. **Colan** a-6, 13, 17. **Sekowsky** a-2, 3, 5, 7, 11, 14, 27r. No. 1 was to appear as Challenge of the Unknown No. 7.*

BEYOND THE GRAVE
Charlton Comics: July, 1975 - No. 6, June, 1976; No. 7, Jan, 1983 - No. 17, Oct, 1984

	GD	VG	FN	VF	VF/NM	NM-
1-Ditko-a (6 pgs.); Sutton painted-c	3	6	9	18	24	30
2-6: 2-5-Ditko-a; Ditko c-2,3,6	2	4	6	10	13	16
7-17: ('83-'84) Reprints. 13-Aparo-c(r). 15-Sutton-c (low print run)						6.00
Modern Comics Reprint 2('78)						3.50

NOTE: ***Howard** a-4. **Kim** a-1. **Larson** a-4, 6.*

BIBLE TALES FOR YOUNG FOLK (...Young People No. 3-5)
Atlas Comics (OMC): Aug, 1953 - No. 5, Mar, 1954

	GD	VG	FN	VF	VF/NM	NM-
1	27	54	81	155	218	280
2-Everett, Krigstein-a	19	38	57	109	152	195
3-5: 4-Robinson-c	16	32	48	89	122	155

BIG (Movie)
Hit Comics (Dark Horse Comics): Mar, 1989 ($2.00)

1-Adaptation of film; Paul Chadwick-c 2.50

BIG ALL-AMERICAN COMIC BOOK, THE (See All-American Comics)
All-American/National Per. Publ.: 1944 (132 pgs., one-shot) (Early DC Annual)

	GD	VG	FN	VF	VF/NM	NM-
1-Wonder Woman, Green Lantern, Flash, The Atom, Wildcat, Scribbly, The Whip, Ghost Patrol, Hawkman by Kubert (1st on Hawkman), Hop Harrigan, Johnny Thunder, Little Boy Blue, Mr. Terrific, Mutt & Jeff app.; Sargon on cover only; cover by Kubert/Hibbard/Mayer and others	931	1862	2793	6517	10,000	13,500

BIG BABY HUEY (See Baby Huey)

BIG BANG COMICS (Becomes Big Bang #4)
Caliber Press: Spring, 1994 - No. 4, Feb, 1995; No. 0, May, 1995 ($1.95, lim. series)

1-4-($1.95-c) 2.25
0-(5/95, $2.95) Alex Ross-c; color and B&W pages 3.00
Your Big Book of Big Bang Comics TPB ('98, $11.00) r/#0-2 11.00

BIG BANG COMICS (Volume 2)
Image Comics (Highbrow Entertainment): V2#1, May, 1996 - Present ($1.95/$2.50/$2.95/$3.95)

1-23,26: 1-Mighty Man app. 2-4-S.A. Shadowhawk app. 5-Begin $2.95-c. 6-Curt Swan/Murphy Anderson-c. 7-Begin B&W. 12-Savage Dragon-c/app. 15-Bissette-c. 16,17,21-Shadow Lady 3.00

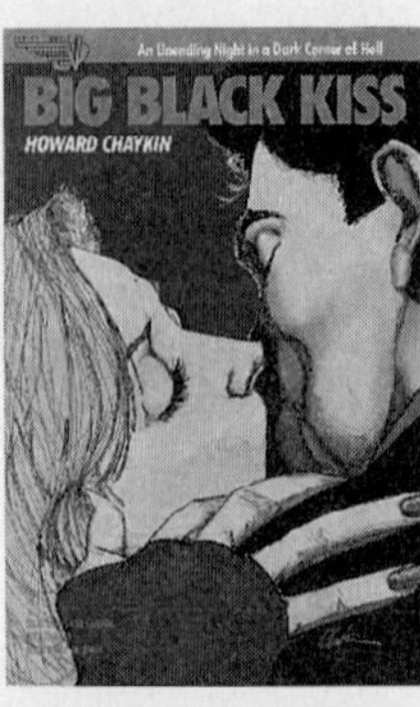

Big Black Kiss #3 © Howard Chaykin

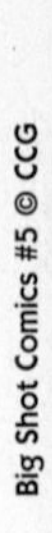
Big Shot Comics #5 © CCG

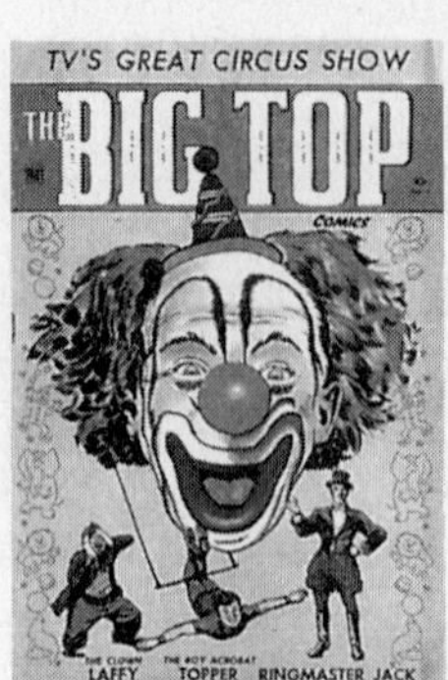

Big Top #1 © TOBY

GD 2.0 | VG 4.0 | FN 6.0 | VF 8.0 | VF/NM 9.0 | NM- 9.2

24,25,27-35-($3.95): 24,27-History of Big Bang Comics Vol. 1,2. 35-Big Bang vs. Alan Moore's "1963" characters 4.00
...Summer Special (8/03, $4.95) World's Nastiest Nazis app. 5.00

BIG BLACK KISS
Vortex Comics: Sep, 1989 - No, 3, Nov, 1989 ($3.75, B&W, lim. series, mature)
1-3-Chaykin-s/a 4.00

BIG BLOWN BABY (Also see Dark Horse Presents)
Dark Horse Comics: Aug, 1996 - No. 4, Nov, 1996 ($2.95, lim. series, mature)
1-4: Bill Wray-c/a/scripts 3.00

BIG BOOK OF ..., THE
DC Comics (Paradox Press): 1994 - Present (B&W)($12.95 - $14.95)
nn-...**BAD**,1998 ($14.95),...**CONSPIRACIES**, 1995 ($12.95), ...**DEATH**,1994 ($12.95), ...**FREAKS**, 1996 ($14.95), ...**GRIMM**, 1999 ($14.95), ...**HOAXES**, 1996 ($14.95), ...**LITTLE CRIMINALS**, 1996 ($14.95), ...**LOSERS**,1997 ($14.95), **MARTYRS**, 1997 ($14.95), ...**SCANDAL**,1997 ($14.95), ...**THE WEIRD WILD WEST**,1998 ($14.95), ...**THUGS**, 1997 ($14.95), ...**UNEXPLAINED**, 1997 ($14.95), ...**URBAN LEGENDS**, 1994 ($12.95), ...**VICE**, 1999 ($14.95), ...**WEIRDOS**, 1995 ($12.95) cover price

BIG BOOK OF FUN COMICS (See New Book of Comics)
National Periodical Publications: Spring, 1936 (Large size, 52 pgs.)
(1st comic book annual & DC annual)
1 (Very rare)-r/New Fun #1-5 2250 4500 6750 14,000 - -

BIG BOOK ROMANCES
Fawcett Publications: Feb, 1950 (no date given) (148 pgs.)
1-Contains remaindered Fawcett romance comics - several combinations possible
40 80 120 240 345 450

BIG BRUISERS
Image Comics (WildStorm Productions): July, 1996 ($3.50, one-shot)
1-Features Maul from WildC.A.T.S, Impact from Cyberforce & Badrock from Youngblood 3.50

BIG CHIEF WAHOO
Eastern Color Printing/George Dougherty (distr. by Fawcett): July, 1942 - No. 7, Wint., 1943/44?(no year given)(Quarterly)
1-Newspaper-r (on sale 6/15/42) 40 80 120 240 345 450
2-Steve Roper app. 23 46 69 132 186 240
3-5: 4-Chief is holding a Katy Keene comic 18 36 54 101 138 175
6-7 13 26 39 76 103 130
NOTE: *Kerry Drake in some issues.*

BIG CIRCUS, THE (Movie)
Dell Publishing Co.: No. 1036, Sept-Nov, 1959
Four Color 1036-Photo-c 7 14 21 51 71 90

BIG COUNTRY, THE (Movie)
Dell Publishing Co.: No. 946, Oct, 1958
Four Color 946-Photo-c 8 16 24 55 78 100

BIG DADDY DANGER
DC Comics: Oct, 2002 - No. 9, June, 2003 ($2.95, limited series)
1-9-Adam Pollina-s/a/c 3.00

BIG DADDY ROTH (Magazine)
Millar Publications: Oct-Nov, 1964 - No. 4, Apr-May, 1965 (35¢)
1-Toth-a 18 36 54 131 191 250
2-4-Toth-a 12 24 36 84 125 165

BIGG TIME
DC Comics (Vertigo): 2002 ($14.95, B&W, graphic novel)
nn-Ty Templeton-s/c/a 15.00

BIG GUY AND RUSTY THE BOY ROBOT, THE (Also See Madman Comics #6,7 & Martha Washington Stranded In Space)
Dark Horse (Legend): July, 1995 - No. 2, Aug, 1995 ($4.95, oversize, limited series)
1,2-Frank Miller scripts & Geoff Darrow-c/a 1 2 3 4 5 7
Trade paperback (10/96, $14.95)-r/1,2 w/cover gallery 15.00

BIG HERO ADVENTURES (See Jigsaw)

BIG HAIR PRODUCTIONS
Image Comics: Feb, 2000 - No. 2, Mar, 2000 ($3.50, B&W)
1,2 3.50

BIG JON & SPARKIE (Radio)(Formerly Sparkie, Radio Pixie)
Ziff-Davis Publ. Co.: No. 4, Sept-Oct, 1952 (Painted-c)
4-Based on children's radio program 21 42 63 118 164 210

BIG LAND, THE (Movie)
Dell Publishing Co.: No. 812, July, 1957
Four Color 812-Alan Ladd photo-c 10 20 30 72 104 135

BIG RED (See Movie Comics)

BIG SHOT COMICS
Columbia Comics Group: May, 1940 - No. 104, Aug, 1949
1-Intro. Skyman; The Face (1st app.; Tony Trent), The Cloak (Spy Master), Marvelo, Monarch of Magicians, Joe Palooka, Charlie Chan, Tom Kerry, Dixie Dugan, Rocky Ryan begin; Charlie Chan moves over from Feature Comics #31 (4/40)
232 464 696 1450 2175 2900
2 84 168 252 525 788 1050
3-The Cloak called Spy Chief; Skyman-c 76 152 228 475 713 950
4,5 55 110 165 344 512 680
6-10: 8-Christmas-c 44 88 132 264 395 525
11-13 40 80 120 240 353 465
14-Origin & 1st app. Sparky Watts (6/41) 43 86 129 258 389 520
15-Origin The Cloak 44 88 132 264 395 525
16-20 34 68 102 196 278 360
21-23,26,27,29,30: 29-Intro. Capt. Yank; Bo (a dog) newspaper strip-r by Frank Beck begin, ends #104. 30-X-Mas-c 29 58 87 164 232 300
24-Classic Tojo-c. 40 80 120 240 358 475
25-Hitler-c 34 68 102 196 278 360
28-Hitler, Tojo & Mussolini-c 46 92 138 276 413 550
31,33-40 22 44 66 127 176 225
32-Vic Jordan newspaper strip reprints begin, ends #52; Hitler, Tojo & Mussolini-c
39 78 117 233 329 425
41,42,44,45,47-50: 42-No Skyman. 50-Origin The Face retold
19 38 57 106 146 185
43-Hitler-c 32 64 96 182 259 335
46-Hitler, Tojo-c (6/44) 30 60 90 170 240 310
51-56,58-60 16 32 48 89 122 155
57-Hitler, Tojo Halloween mask-c 22 44 66 127 176 225
61-70: 63 on-Tony Trent, the Face 13 26 39 76 103 130
71-80: 73-The Face cameo. 74-(2/47)-Mickey Finn begins. 74,80-The Face app. in Tony Trent. 78-Last Charlie Chan strip-r 12 24 36 71 96 120
81-90: 85-Tony Trent marries Babs Walsh. 86-Valentines-c
10 20 30 56 73 90
91-99,101-104: 69-94-Skyman in Outer Space. 96-Xmas-c
9 18 27 49 62 75
100 10 20 30 58 77 95
NOTE: ***Mart Bailey** art on "The Face" No. 1-104. **Guardineer** a-5. Sparky Watts by **Boody Rogers**-No. 14-42, 77-104, (by others No. 43-76). Others than Tony Trent wear "The Face" mask in No. 46-63, 93. Skyman by **Ogden Whitney**-No. 1, 2, 4, 12-37, 49, 70-101. Skyman covers-No. 1, 3, 7-12, 14, 16, 20, 27, 89, 95, 100.*

BIG SMASH BARGAIN COMICS
No publisher listed: Early 1950s (25¢, 160pgs., Canadian reprints)
1-4: Contains 4 comics from various companies bundled with new cover
22 44 66 124 172 220

BIG TEX
Toby Press: June, 1953
1-Contains (3) John Wayne stories-r with name changed to Big Tex
10 20 30 56 73 90

BIG-3
Fox Features Syndicate: Fall, 1940 - No. 7, Jan, 1942
1-Blue Beetle, The Flame, & Samson begin 220 440 660 1375 2063 2750
2 88 176 264 550 825 1100
3-5 63 126 189 394 590 785
6,7: 6-Last Samson. 7-V-Man app. 50 100 150 300 450 600

BIG TOP COMICS, THE (TV's Great Circus Show)
Toby Press: 1951 - No. 2, 1951 (No month)
1 10 20 30 58 77 95
2 9 18 27 49 62 75

BIG TOWN (Radio/TV) (Also see Movie Comics, 1946)
National Periodical Publ: Jan, 1951 - No. 50, Mar-Apr, 1958 (No. 1-9: 52pgs.)
1-Dan Barry-a begins 66 132 198 413 617 820
2 37 74 111 210 298 385
3-10 22 44 66 124 172 220
11-20 16 32 48 89 122 155
21-31: Last pre-code (1-2/55) 12 24 36 71 96 120
32-50 9 18 27 54 70 85

BIG VALLEY, THE (TV)

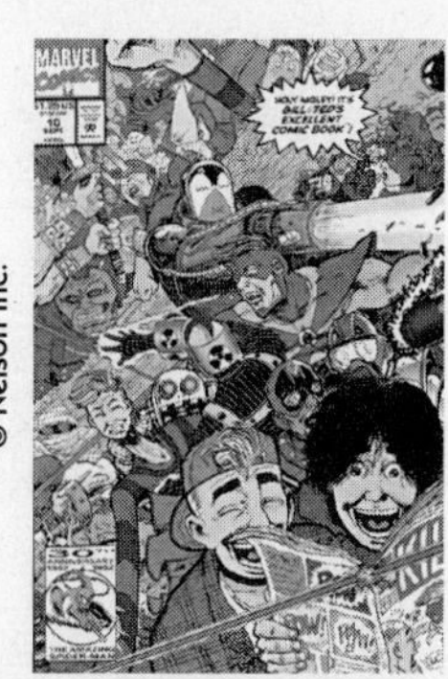

Bill & Ted's Excellent Comic Book #10 © Nelson Inc.

Bill Boyd Western #1 © FAW

Billy the Kid #8 © TOBY

	GD 2.0	VG 4.0	FN 6.0	VF 8.0	VF/NM 9.0	NM- 9.2

Dell Publishing Co.: June, 1966 - No. 5, Oct, 1967; No. 6, Oct, 1969

	GD	VG	FN	VF	VF/NM	NM-
1: Photo-c #1-5	6	12	18	40	55	70
2-6: 6-Reprints #1	4	8	12	24	32	40

BIKER MICE FROM MARS (TV)
Marvel Comics: Nov, 1993 - No. 3, Jan, 1994 ($1.50, limited series)

1-3: 1-Intro Vinnie, Modo & Throttle. 2-Origin 3.50

BILL & TED'S BOGUS JOURNEY
Marvel Comics: Sept, 1991 ($2.95, squarebound, 84 pgs.)

1-Adapts movie sequel 3.00

BILL & TED'S EXCELLENT COMIC BOOK (Movie)
Marvel Comics: Dec, 1991 - No. 12, 1992 ($1.00/$1.25)

1-12: 3-Begin $1.25-c 2.50

BILL BARNES COMICS (...America's Air Ace Comics No. 2 on) (Becomes Air Ace V2#1 on; also see Shadow Comics)
Street & Smith Publications: Oct, 1940(No. month given) - No. 12, Oct, 1943

	GD	VG	FN	VF	VF/NM	NM-
1-23 pgs.-comics; Rocket Rooney begins	83	166	249	519	780	1040
2-Barnes as The Phantom Flyer app.; Tuska-a	43	86	129	258	389	520
3-5	39	78	117	230	325	420
6-12	34	68	102	196	278	360

BILL BATTLE, THE ONE MAN ARMY (Also see Master Comics No. 133)
Fawcett Publications: Oct, 1952 - No. 4, Apr, 1953 (All photo-c)

	GD	VG	FN	VF	VF/NM	NM-
1	14	28	42	79	107	135
2	8	16	24	46	58	70
3,4	8	16	24	40	50	60

BILL BLACK'S FUN COMICS
Paragon #1-3/Americomics #4: Dec, 1982 - No. 4, Mar, 1983 ($1.75/$2.00, Baxter paper) (1st AC comic)

	GD	VG	FN	VF	VF/NM	NM-
1-(B&W fanzine; 7x8-1/2"; low print) Intro. Capt. Paragon, Phantom Lady & Commando D	2	4	6	12	16	20
2-4: 2,3-(B&W fanzines; 8-1/2x11"). 3-Kirby-c. 4-($2.00, color)-Origin Nightfall (formerly Phantom Lady); Nightveil app.; Kirby-a	1	2	3	5	7	9

BILL BOYD WESTERN (Movie star; see Hopalong Cassidy & Western Hero)
Fawcett Publ: Feb, 1950 - No. 23, June, 1952 (1-3,7,11,14-on: 36 pgs.)

	GD	VG	FN	VF	VF/NM	NM-
1-Bill Boyd & his horse Midnite begin; photo front/back-c	48	96	144	288	432	575
2-Painted-c	28	56	84	159	225	290
3-Photo-c begin, end #23; last photo back-c	21	42	63	118	164	210
4-6(52 pgs.)	17	34	51	98	134	170
7,11(36 pgs.)	14	28	42	79	107	135
8-10,12,13(52 pgs.)	14	28	42	81	111	140
14-22	13	26	39	74	100	125
23-Last issue	14	28	42	79	107	135

BILL BUMLIN (See Treasury of Comics No. 3)

BILL ELLIOTT (See Wild Bill Elliott)

BILLI 99
Dark Horse Comics: Sept, 1991 - No. 4, 1991 ($3.50, B&W, lim. series, 52 pgs.)

1-4: Tim Sale-c/a 3.50

BILL STERN'S SPORTS BOOK
Ziff-Davis Publ. Co.(Approved Comics): Spring-Sum, 1951 - V2#2, Win, 1952

	GD	VG	FN	VF	VF/NM	NM-
V1#10-(1951)	22	44	66	124	172	220
2-(Sum/52; reg. size)	17	34	51	95	130	165
V2#2-(1952, 96 pgs.)-Krigstein, Kinstler-a	23	46	69	129	180	230

BILL THE BULL: ONE SHOT, ONE BOURBON, ONE BEER
Boneyard Press: Dec, 1994 ($2.95, B&W, mature)

1 3.00

BILL THE CLOWN
Slave Labor Graphics: Feb, 1992 ($2.50, one-shot)

1 ,1-(2nd printing, 4/93, $2.95) 3.00
Comedy Isn't Pretty 1 (11/92, $2.50) 3.00
Death & Clown White 1 (9/93, $2.95) 3.00

BILLY AND BUGGY BEAR (See Animal Fun)
I.W. Enterprises/Super: 1958; 1964

	GD	VG	FN	VF	VF/NM	NM-
I.W. Reprint #1, #7('58)-All Surprise Comics #?(Same issue-r for both)	2	4	6	11	14	18
Super Reprint #10(1964)	2	4	6	9	11	14

BILLY BUCKSKIN WESTERN (2-Gun Western No. 4)
Atlas Comics (IMC No. 1/MgPC No. 2,3): Nov, 1955 - No. 3, Mar, 1956

	GD	VG	FN	VF	VF/NM	NM-
1-Mort Drucker-a; Maneely-c/a	16	32	48	92	126	160
2-Mort Drucker-a	10	20	30	58	77	95
3-Williamson, Drucker-a	12	24	36	69	92	115

BILLY BUNNY (Black Cobra No. 6 on)
Excellent Publications: Feb-Mar, 1954 - No. 5, Oct-Nov, 1954

	GD	VG	FN	VF	VF/NM	NM-
1	8	16	24	46	58	70
2	5	10	15	24	30	35
3-5	5	10	15	22	26	30

BILLY BUNNY'S CHRISTMAS FROLICS
Farrell Publications: 1952 (25¢ Giant, 100 pgs.)

	GD	VG	FN	VF	VF/NM	NM-
1	20	40	60	115	160	205

BILLY COLE
Cult Press: May, 1994 - No. 4, Aug, 1994 ($2.75, B&W, limited series)

1-4 2.75

BILLY MAKE BELIEVE
United Features Syndicate: No. 14, 1939

	GD	VG	FN	VF	VF/NM	NM-
Single Series 14	32	64	96	180	255	330

BILLY NGUYEN, PRIVATE EYE
Caliber Press: V2#1, 1990 ($2.50)

V2#1 2.50

BILLY THE KID (Formerly The Masked Raider; also see Doc Savage Comics & Return of the Outlaw)
No. 9, Nov, 1957 - No. 121, Dec, 1976; No. 122, Sept, 1977 - No. 123,
Charlton Publ. Co.: Oct, 1977; No. 124, Feb, 1978 - No. 153, Mar, 1983

	GD	VG	FN	VF	VF/NM	NM-
9	10	20	30	58	77	95
10,12,14,17-19: 12-2 pg Check-sty	7	14	21	37	46	55
11-(68 pgs.)-Origin & 1st app. The Ghost Train	9	18	27	49	62	75
13-Williamson/Torres-a	8	16	24	43	54	65
15-Origin; 2 pgs. Williamson-a	8	16	24	43	54	65
16-Williamson-a, 2 pgs.	8	16	24	40	50	60
20-26-Severin-a(3-4 each)	8	16	24	43	54	65
27-30: 30-Masked Rider app.	3	7	10	21	28	35
31-40	3	6	9	16	20	25
41-60	2	4	6	12	16	20
61-65	2	4	6	10	12	15
66-Bounty Hunter series begins.	2	4	6	11	14	18
67-80: Bounty Hunter series; not in #79,82,84-86	2	4	6	9	11	14
81-90: 87-Last Bounty Hunter	1	2	3	5	7	9
91-123: 110-Dr. Young of Boothill app. 111-Origin The Ghost Train. 117-Gunsmith & Co., The Cheyenne Kid app.						6.00
124(2/78)-153						4.00
Modern Comics 109 (1977 reprint)						4.00

NOTE: *Boyette a-91-110.* ***Kim*** *a-73.* ***Morsi*** *a-12,14.* ***Sattler*** *a-118-123.* ***Severin*** *a(r)-121-129, 134; c-23, 25.* ***Sutton*** *a-111.*

BILLY THE KID ADVENTURE MAGAZINE
Toby Press: Oct, 1950 - No. 29, 1955

	GD	VG	FN	VF	VF/NM	NM-
1-Williamson/Frazetta-a (2 pgs) r/from John Wayne Adventure Comics #2; photo-c	31	62	93	175	248	320
2-Photo-c	10	20	30	60	80	100
3-Williamson/Frazetta "The Claws of Death", 4 pgs. plus Williamson art	34	68	102	196	278	360
4,5,7,8,10: 4,7-Photo-c	9	18	27	49	62	75
6-Frazetta assist on "Nightmare"; photo-c	15	30	45	86	118	150
9-Kurtzman Pot-Shot Pete; photo-c	11	22	33	66	88	110
11,12,15-20: 11-Photo-c	8	16	24	40	50	60
13-Kurtzman-r/John Wayne #12 (Genius)	8	16	24	46	58	70
14-Williamson/Frazetta; r-of #1 (2 pgs.)	10	20	30	56	73	90
21,23-29	7	14	21	35	43	50
22-Williamson/Frazetta-r(1pg.)/#1; photo-c	8	16	24	40	50	60

BILLY THE KID AND OSCAR (Also see Fawcett's Funny Animals)
Fawcett Publications: Winter, 1945 - No. 3, Summer, 1946 (Funny animal)

	GD	VG	FN	VF	VF/NM	NM-
1	15	30	45	86	118	150
2,3	10	20	30	56	73	90

BILLY WEST (Bill West No. 9,10)
Standard Comics (Visual Editions): 1949-No. 9, Feb, 1951; No. 10, Feb, 1952

	GD	VG	FN	VF	VF/NM	NM-
1	12	24	36	71	96	120

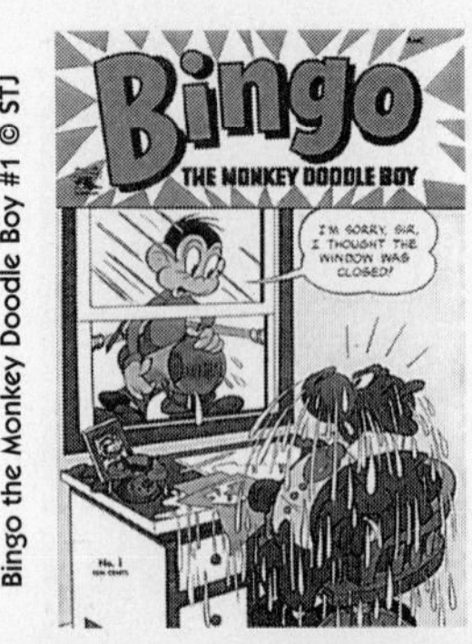

Bingo the Monkey Doodle Boy #1 © STJ

Birds of Prey #47 © DC

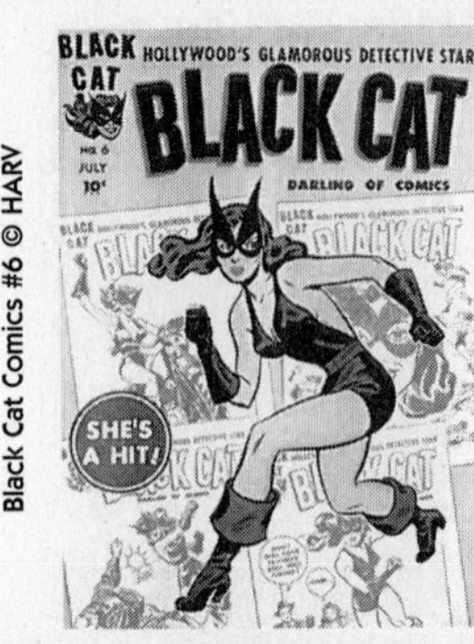

Black Cat Comics #6 © HARV

GD VG FN VF VF/NM NM-
2.0 4.0 6.0 8.0 9.0 9.2

2 8 16 24 40 50 60
3-6,9,10 6 12 18 31 38 45
7,8-Schomburg-c 7 14 21 37 46 55
NOTE: ***Celardo*** *a-1-6, 9; c-1-3.* ***Moreira*** *a-3.* ***Roussos*** *a-2.*

BING CROSBY (See Feature Films)

BINGO (...Comics) (H. C. Blackerby)
Howard Publ.: 1945 (Reprints National material)
1-L. B. Cole opium-c 37 74 111 212 299 385

BINGO, THE MONKEY DOODLE BOY
St. John Publishing Co.: Aug, 1951; Oct, 1953
1(8/51)-By Eric Peters 7 14 21 37 46 55
1(10/53) 6 12 18 27 33 38

BINKY (Formerly Leave It to...)
National Periodical Publ./DC Comics: No. 72, 4-5/70 - No. 81, 10-11/71; No. 82, Summer/77
72-76 3 6 9 18 23 28
77-79: (68pgs.). 77-Bobby Sherman 1pg. story w/photo. 78-1 pg. sty on Barry Williams of Brady Bunch. 79-Osmonds 1pg. story 4 8 12 29 40 50
80,81 (52pgs.)-Sweat Pain story 4 8 12 24 32 40
82 (1977, one-shot) 3 7 10 21 28 35

BINKY'S BUDDIES
National Periodical Publications: Jan-Feb, 1969 - No. 12, Nov-Dec, 1970
1 5 10 15 36 48 60
2-12: 3-Last 12¢ issue 3 6 9 18 24 30

BIONEERS
Mirage Publishing: Aug, 1994 ($2.75)
1-w/bound-in trading card 2.75

BIONIC WOMAN, THE (TV)
Charlton Publications: Oct, 1977 - No. 5, June, 1978
1 3 6 9 16 20 25
2-5 2 4 6 10 12 15

BIRDS OF PREY (Also see Black Canary/Oracle: Birds of Prey)
DC Comics: Jan, 1999 - Present ($1.99/$2.50)
1-Dixon-s/Land-c/a 1 3 4 6 8 10
2-4 6.00
6,7,9-15: 15-Guice-a begins. 4.00
8-Nightwing-c/app.; Barbara & Dick's circus date 2 4 6 10 12 15
16-38: 23-Grodd-c/app. 26-Bane app. 32-Noto-c begin 2.50
39,40-Bruce Wayne: Murderer pt. 5,12 3.00
41-Bruce Wayne: Fugitive pt. 2 4.00
42-46: 42-Fabry-a. 45-Deathstroke-c/app. 2.50
47-62: 47-49-Terry Moore-s/Conner & Palmiotti-a; Noto-c. 50-Gilbert Hernandez-s begin. 52,54-Metamorpho app. 56-Simone-s/Benes-a begin 2.50
TPB (1999, $17.95) r/ previous series and one-shots 18.00
...: Batgirl 1 (2/98, $2.95) Dixon-s/Frank-c 5.00
...: Batgirl/Catwoman 1 ('03, $5.95) Robertson-a; cont'd in BOP: Catwoman/Oracle 1 6.00
...: Catwoman/Oracle 1 ('03, $5.95) Cont'd from BOP: Batgirl/Catwoman 1; David Ross-a 6.00
...: Old Friends, New Enemies TPB (2003, $17.95) r/#1-6, ...: Batgirl, ...: Wolves 18.00
...: Revolution 1 (1997, $2.95) Frank-c/Dixon-s 5.00
... Secret Files 2003 (8/03, $4.95) Short stories, pin-ups and profile pages; Noto-c 5.00
...: The Ravens 1 (6/98, $1.95)-Dixon-s; Girlfrenzy issue 4.00
...: Wolves 1 (10/97, $2.95) Dixon-s/Giordano & Faucher-a 5.00

BIRDS OF PREY: MANHUNT
DC Comics: Sept, 1996 - No. 4, Dec, 1996 ($1.95, limited series)
1-Features Black Canary, Oracle, Huntress, & Catwoman; Chuck Dixon scripts; Gary Frank-c on all. 1-Catwoman cameo only 1 2 3 5 6 8
2-4 6.00
NOTE: ***Gary Frank*** *c-1-4.* ***Matt Haley*** *a-1-4p.* ***Wade Von Grawbadger*** *a-1i.*

BIRTH CAUL, THE
Eddie Campbell Comics: 1999 ($5.95, B&W, one-shot)
1-Alan Moore-s/Eddie Campbell-a 6.00

BIRTH OF THE DEFIANT UNIVERSE, THE
Defiant Comics: May, 1993
nn-Contains promotional artwork & text; limited print run of 1000 copies. 2 4 6 8 10 12

BISHOP (See Uncanny X-Men & X-Men)
Marvel Comics: Dec, 1994 - No.4, Mar, 1995 ($2.95, limited series)
1-4: Foil-c; Shard & Mountjoy in all. 1-Storm app. 3.00

BISHOP THE LAST X-MAN
Marvel Comics: Oct, 1999 - No. 16, Jan, 2001 ($2.99/$1.99/$2.25)
1-($2.99)-Jeanty-a 3.50
2-8-($1.99): 2-Two covers 2.50
9-11,13-16: 9-Begin $2.25-c. 15-Maximum Security x-over; Xavier app. 2.50
12-($2.99) 3.00

BISHOP: XAVIER SECURITY ENFORCER
Marvel Comics: Jan, 1998 - No.3, Mar, 1998 ($2.50, limited series)
1-3: Ostrander-s 3.00

BIZARRE ADVENTURES (Formerly Marvel Preview)
Marvel Comics Group: No. 25, 3/81 - No. 34, 2/83 (#25-33: Magazine-$1.50)
25,26: 25-Lethal Ladies. 26-King Kull; Bolton-c/a 1 3 4 6 8 10
27,28: 27-Phoenix, Iceman & Nightcrawler app. 28-The Unlikely Heroes; Elektra by Miller; Neal Adams-a 2 4 6 9 11 14
29,30,32,33: 29-Stephen King's Lawnmower Man. 30-Tomorrow; 1st app. Silhouette. 32-Gods; Thor-c/s. 33-Horror; Dracula app.; photo-c 1 2 3 5 7 9
31-After The Violence Stops; new Hangman story; Miller-a 1 3 4 6 8 10
34 ($2.00, Baxter paper, comic size)-Son of Santa; Christmas special; Howard the Duck by Paul Smith 1 2 3 5 6 8
NOTE: ***Alcala*** *a-27i.* ***Austin*** *a-25i, 28i.* ***Bolton*** *a-26, 32.* ***J. Buscema*** *a-27p, 29, 30p; c-26.* ***Byrne*** *a-31 (2 pg.).* ***Golden*** *a-25p, 28p.* ***Perez*** *a-27p.* ***Rogers*** *a-25p.* ***Simonson*** *a-29; c-29.* ***Paul Smith*** *a-34.*

BIZARRO COMICS!
DC Comics: 2001 ($29.95, hardcover, one-shot)
HC-Short stories by various alternative cartoonists including Dorkin, Pope, Fingerman, Abel Haspiel, Kidd, Kochalka, Millionaire, Stephens, Wray; includes "Superman's Babysitter" by Kyle Baker from Elseworlds 80-Page Giant recalled by DC; Groening-c 30.00
Softcover (2003, $19.95) 20.00

BLACK AND WHITE (See Large Feature Comic, Series I)

BLACK & WHITE (Also see Codename: Black & White)
Image Comics (Extreme): Oct,1994 - No. 3, Jan,1995 ($1.95, limited series)
1-3: Thibert-c/story 2.25

BLACK & WHITE MAGIC
Innovation Publishing: 1991 ($2.95, 98 pgs., B&W w/30 pgs. color, squarebound)
1-Contains rebound comics w/covers removed; contents may vary 3.00

BLACK AXE
Marvel Comics (UK): Apr, 1993 - No. 7, Oct, 1993 ($1.75)
1-4: 1-Romita Jr.-c. 2-Sunfire-c/s 3.00
5-7: 5-Janson-c; Black Panther app. 6,7-Black Panther-c/s 3.00

BLACKBALL COMICS
Blackball Comics: Mar, 1994 ($3.00)
1-Trencher-c/story by Giffen; John Pain by O'Neill 3.00

BLACKBEARD'S GHOST (See Movie Comics)

BLACK BEAUTY (See Son of Black Beauty)
Dell Publishing Co.: No. 440, Dec, 1952
Four Color 440 4 8 12 27 36 45

BLACKBURNE COVENANT, THE
Dark Horse Comics: Apr, 2003 - No. 4, July, 2003 ($2.99, limited series)
1-4-Nicieza-s/Raffaele-a 3.00
TPB (2003, $12.95) r/#1-4 13.00

BLACK CANARY (See All Star Comics #38, Flash Comics #86, Justice League of America #75 & World's Finest #244)
DC Comics: Nov, 1991 - No. 4, Feb, 1992 ($1.75, limited series)
1-4 2.50

BLACK CANARY
DC Comics: Jan, 1993 - No. 12, Dec, 1993 ($1.75)
1-7 2.50
8-12: 8-The Ray-c/story. 9,10-Huntress-c/story 3.00

BLACK CANARY/ORACLE: BIRDS OF PREY (Also see Showcase '96 #3)
DC Comics: 1996 ($3.95, one-shot)
1-Chuck Dixon scripts & Gary Frank-c/a. 1 2 3 5 7 9

BLACK CAT COMICS (...Western #16-19; ...Mystery #30 on)
(See All-New #7,9, The Original Black Cat, Pocket & Speed Comics)
Harvey Publications (Home Comics): June-July, 1946 - No. 29, June, 1951
1-Kubert-a; Joe Simon c-1-3 70 140 210 438 657 875

Black Cobra #6(#2) © Farrell

Black Condor #12 © DC

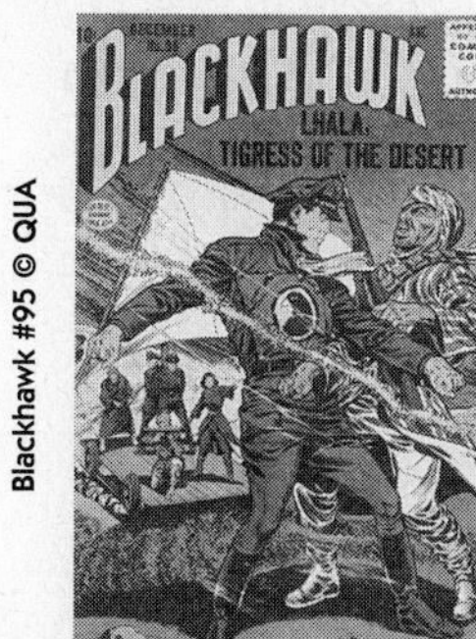

Blackhawk #95 © QUA

	GD 2.0	VG 4.0	FN 6.0	VF 8.0	VF/NM 9.0	NM- 9.2
2-Kubert-a	39	78	117	233	329	425
3,4: 4-The Red Demons begin (The Demon #4 & 5)	32	64	96	182	259	335
5,6,7: 5,6-The Scarlet Arrow app. in ea. by Powell; S&K-a in both. 6-Origin Red Demon. 7-Vagabond Prince by S&K plus 1 more story	39	78	117	230	325	420
8-S&K-a; Kerry Drake begins, ends #13	35	70	105	201	283	365
9-Origin Stuntman (r/Stuntman #1)	39	78	117	224	320	415
10-20: 14,15,17-Mary Worth app. plus Invisible Scarlet O'Neil-#15,20,24	27	54	81	155	218	280
21-26	22	44	66	127	176	225
27,28: 27-Used in **SOTI**, pg. 193; X-Mas-c; 2 pg. John Wayne story. 28-Intro. Kit, Black Cat's new sidekick	23	46	69	132	186	240
29-Black Cat bondage-c; Black Cat stories	23	46	69	130	183	235

BLACK CAT MYSTERY (Formerly Black Cat; ...Western Mystery #54; ...Western #55,56; ...Mystery #57; ...Mystic #58-62; Black Cat #63-65)
Harvey Publications: No. 30, Aug, 1951 - No. 65, Apr, 1963

	GD 2.0	VG 4.0	FN 6.0	VF 8.0	VF/NM 9.0	NM- 9.2
30-Black Cat on cover only	31	62	93	175	248	320
31,32,34,37,38,40	24	48	72	135	190	245
33-Used in **POP**, pg. 89; electrocution-c	27	54	81	153	214	275
35-Atomic disaster cover/story	30	60	90	170	240	310
36,39-Used in **SOTI**: #36-Pgs. 270,271; #39-Pgs. 386-388	29	58	87	164	232	300
41-43	24	48	72	135	190	245
44-Eyes, ears, tongue cut out; Nostrand-a	25	50	75	147	202	260
45-Classic "Colorama" by Powell; Nostrand-a	40	80	120	240	345	450
46-49,51-Nostrand-a in all	25	50	75	144	198	255
50-Check-a; classic Warren Kremer-c showing a man's face & hands burning away	72	144	216	450	675	900
52,53 (r/#34 & 35)	16	32	48	89	122	155
54-Two Black Cat stories (2/55, last pre-code)	19	38	57	109	152	195
55,56-Black Cat app.	16	32	48	89	122	155
57(7/56)-Kirby-c	16	32	48	89	122	155
58-60-Kirby-a(4). 58,59-Kirby-c. 60,61-Simon-c	20	40	60	115	160	205
61-Nostrand-a; "Colorama" r/#45	19	38	57	109	152	195
62 (3/58)-E.C. story swipe	15	30	45	84	115	145
63-65: Giants(10/62,1/63, 4/63); Reprints; Black Cat app. 63-origin Black Kitten. 65-1 pg. Powell-a	19	38	57	107	149	190

NOTE: ***Kremer** a-37, 39, 43; c-36, 37, 47. **Meskin** a-51. **Palais** a-30, 31(2), 32(2), 33-35, 37-40. **Powell** a-32-35, 36(2), 40, 41, 43-53, 57. **Simon** c-63-65. **Sparling** a-44. Bondage c-32, 34, 43.*

BLACK COBRA (Bride's Diary No. 4 on) (See Captain Flight #8)
Ajax/Farrell Publications(Excellent Publ.): No. 1, 10-11/54; No. 6(No. 2), 12-1/54-55; No. 3, 2-3/55

	GD 2.0	VG 4.0	FN 6.0	VF 8.0	VF/NM 9.0	NM- 9.2
1-Re-intro Black Cobra & The Cobra Kid (costumed heroes)	34	68	102	196	278	360
6(#2)-Formerly Billy Bunny	19	38	57	109	152	195
3-(Pre-code)-Torpedoman app.	18	36	54	104	142	180

BLACK CONDOR (Also see Crack Comics, Freedom Fighters & Showcase '94 #10,11)
DC Comics: June, 1992 - No. 12, May, 1993 ($1.25)

	NM- 9.2
1-8-Heath-c	2.50
9-12: 9,10,12-Heath-c. 9,10-The Ray app. 12-Batman-c/app.	3.00

BLACK CROSS SPECIAL (See Dark Horse Presents)
Dark Horse Comics: Jan, 1988 ($1.75, B&W, one-shot)(Reprints & new-a)

	NM- 9.2
1-1st printing	3.00
1-(2nd printing) has 2 pgs. new-a	2.50

BLACK CROSS: DIRTY WORK (See Dark Horse Presents)
Dark Horse Comics: Apr, 1997 ($2.95, one-shot)

	NM- 9.2
1-Chris Warner-c/s/a	3.00

BLACK DIAMOND
Americomics: May, 1983 - No. 5, 1984 (no month)($2.00-$1.75, Baxter paper)

	NM- 9.2
1-3-Movie adapt.; 1-Colt back-up begins	4.00
4,5	3.00

NOTE: ***Bill Black** a-1i; c-1. **Gulacy** c-2-5. Sybil Danning photo back-c-1.*

BLACK DIAMOND WESTERN (Formerly Desperado No. 1-8)
Lev Gleason Publ: No. 9, Mar, 1949 - No. 60, Feb, 1956 (No. 9-28: 52 pgs.)

	GD 2.0	VG 4.0	FN 6.0	VF 8.0	VF/NM 9.0	NM- 9.2
9-Black Diamond & his horse Reliapon begin; origin & 1st app. Black Diamond	22	44	66	124	172	220
10	11	22	33	63	84	105
11-15	9	18	27	49	62	75
16-28(11/49-11/51)-Wolverton's Bing Bang Buster	12	24	36	69	92	115
29-40: 31-One pg. Frazetta anti-drug ad	7	14	21	37	46	55
41-50,53-59	6	12	18	31	38	45
51-3-D effect-c/story	15	30	45	86	118	150
52-3-D effect story	14	28	42	79	107	135
60-Last issue	7	14	21	37	46	55

NOTE: ***Biro** c-9-35?. **Fass** a-58, c-54-56, 58. **Guardineer** a-9, 15, 18. **Kida** a-9. **Maurer** a-10. **Ed Moore** a-16. **Morisi** a-55. **Tuska** a-10, 48.*

BLACK DRAGON, THE
Marvel Comics (Epic Comics): 5/85 - No. 6, 10/85 (Baxter paper, mature)

	NM- 9.2
1-6: 1-Chris Claremont story & John Bolton painted-c/a in all	3.00

BLACK DRAGON, THE
Dark Horse Comics: Apr, 1996 ($17.95, B&W, trade paperback)

	NM- 9.2
nn-Reprints Epic Comics limited series; intro by Anne McCaffrey	18.00

BLACK FLAG (See Asylum #5)
Maximum Press: Jan, 1995 - No.4, 1995; No. 0, July, 1995 ($2.50, B&W) (No. 0 in color)

	NM- 9.2
Preview Edition (6/94, $1.95, B&W)-Fraga/McFarlane-c.	3.00
0-4: 0-(7/95)-Liefeld/Fraga-c. 1-(1/95).	3.00
1-Variant cover	5.00
2,4-Variant covers	3.00

NOTE: ***Fraga** a-0-4, Preview Edition; c-1-4. **Liefeld/Fraga** c-0. **McFarlane/Fraga** c-Preview Edition.*

BLACK FURY (Becomes Wild West No. 58) (See Blue Bird)
Charlton Comics Group: May, 1955 - No. 57, Mar-Apr, 1966 (Horse stories)

	GD 2.0	VG 4.0	FN 6.0	VF 8.0	VF/NM 9.0	NM- 9.2
1	8	16	24	43	54	65
2	5	10	15	23	28	32
3-10	4	8	12	18	22	25
11-15,19,20	3	6	8	12	14	16
16-18-Ditko-a	8	16	24	43	54	65
21-30	2	4	6	9	11	14
31-57	1	3	4	6	8	10

BLACK GOLIATH (See Avengers #32-35,41,54)
Marvel Comics Group: Feb, 1976 - No. 5, Nov, 1976

	GD 2.0	VG 4.0	FN 6.0	VF 8.0	VF/NM 9.0	NM- 9.2
1-Tuska-a(p) thru #3	2	4	6	8	10	12
2-5: 2-4-(Regular 25¢ editions). 4-Kirby-c/Buckler-a	1	2	3	5	6	8
2-4-(30¢-c variants, limited distribution)(4,6,8/76)	2	4	6	8	10	12

BLACKHAWK (Formerly Uncle Sam #1-8; see Military & Modern Comics)
Comic Magazines(Quality)No. 9-107(12/56); National Periodical Publications No. 108 (1/57) -250; DC Comics No. 251 on: No. 9, Winter, 1944 - No. 243, 10-11/68; No. 244, 1-2/76 - No. 250, 1-2/77; No. 251, 10/82 - No. 273, 11/84

	GD 2.0	VG 4.0	FN 6.0	VF 8.0	VF/NM 9.0	NM- 9.2
9 (1944)	370	740	1110	2405	3703	5000
10 (1946)	124	248	372	775	1163	1550
11-15: 14-Ward-a; 13,14-Fear app.	84	168	252	525	788	1050
16-20: 20-Ward Blackhawk	67	134	201	419	630	840
21-30 (1950)	46	92	138	276	413	550
31-40: 31-Chop Chop by Jack Cole	39	78	117	224	317	410
41-49,51-60: 42-Robot-c	32	64	96	180	255	330
50-1st Killer Shark; origin in text	34	68	102	196	278	360
61,62: 61-Used in **POP**, pg. 91. 62-Used in **POP**, pg. 92 & color illo	28	56	84	157	221	285
63-70,72-80: 65-H-Bomb explosion panel. 66-B&W & color illos **POP**. 70-Return of Killer Shark; atomic explosion panel. 75-Intro. Blackie the Hawk	26	52	78	147	206	265
71-Origin retold; flying saucer-c; A-Bomb panels	30	60	90	170	240	310
81-86: Last precode (3/55)	23	46	69	132	186	240
87-92,94-99,101-107: 91-Robot-c. 105-1st S.A.	19	38	57	107	149	190
93-Origin in text	19	38	57	109	152	195
100	23	46	69	132	186	240
108-1st DC issue (1/57); re-intro. Blackie, the Hawk, their mascot; not in #115	41	82	123	324	487	650
109-117: 117-(10/57)-Mr. Freeze app.	16	32	48	116	171	225
118-(11/57)-Frazetta-r/Jimmy Wakely #4 (3 pgs.)	17	34	51	121	178	235
119-130 (11/58): 120-Robot-c	11	22	33	80	118	155
131-140 (9/59): 133-Intro. Lady Blackhawk	10	20	30	67	96	125
141-150,152-163,165,166: 141-Cat-Man returns-c/s. 143-Kurtzman-r/Jimmy Wakely #4. 150-(7/60)-King Condor returns. 166-Last 10¢ issue	7	14	21	51	71	90
151-Lady Blackhawk receives & loses super powers	8	16	24	53	74	95
164-Origin retold	8	16	24	55	78	100
167-180	5	10	15	33	44	55
181-190	4	8	12	24	32	40
191-196,199,201,202,204-210: 196-Combat Diary series begins.	3	6	9	19	25	32
197,198,200: 197-New look for Blackhawks. 198-Origin retold						

Blackhawk #261 © DC

Black Knight #4 © MAR

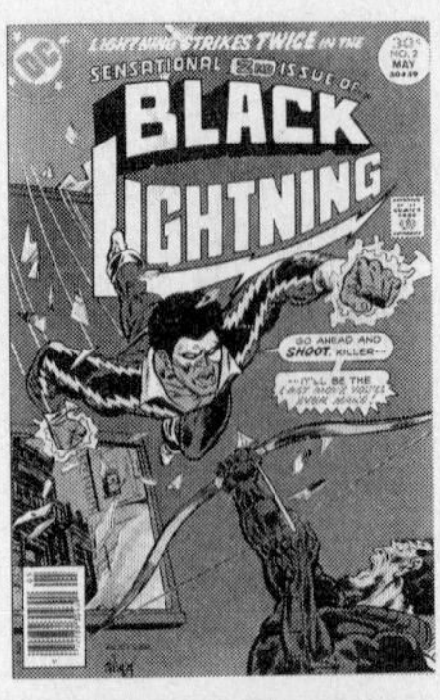

Black Lightning #2 © DC

GD 2.0 | VG 4.0 | FN 6.0 | VF 8.0 | VF/NM 9.0 | NM- 9.2

4 8 12 22 30 38
203-Origin Chop Chop (12/64) 4 8 12 25 33 42
211-227,229-243(1968): 230-Blackhawks become superheroes; JLA cameo
242-Return to old costumes 3 6 9 18 23 28
228-Batman, Green Lantern, Superman, The Flash cameos.
3 6 9 19 25 32
244 ('76) -250: 250-Chuck dies 1 2 3 4 5 7
251-273: 251-Origin retold; Black Knights return. 252-Intro Domino. 253-Part origin Hendrickson. 258-Blackhawk's Island destroyed. 259-Part origin Chop-Chop. 265-273 (75¢ cover price) 3.00

NOTE: ***Chaykin** a-260; c-257-260, 262. **Crandall** a-10, 11, 13, 16?, 18-20, 22-26, 30-33, 35p, 36(2), 37, 38?, 39-44, 46-50, 52-58, 60, 63, 64, 66, 67; c-14-20, 22-63(most except #28-33, 36, 37, 39). **Evans** a-244, 245,246i, 248-250i. **G. Kane** c-263, 264. **Kubert** c-244, 245. **Newton** a-266p. **Severin** a-257.**Spiegle** a-261-267, 269-273; c-265-272. **Toth** a-260p. **Ward** a-16-27(Chop Chop, 8pgs. ea.); pencilled stories-No. 17-63(approx.). **Wildey** a-268. Chop Chop solo stories in #10-95?*

BLACKHAWK
DC Comics: Mar, 1988 - No. 3, May, 1988 ($2.95, limited series, mature)

1-3: Chaykin painted-c/a/scripts 4.00

BLACKHAWK (Also see Action Comics #601)
DC Comics: Mar, 1989 - No. 16, Aug, 1990 ($1.50, mature)

1 3.50
2-6,8-16: 16-Crandall-c swipe 2.50
7-($2.50, 52 pgs.)-Story-r/Military #1 3.00
Annual 1 (1989, $2.95, 68 pgs.)-Recaps origin of Blackhawk, Lady Blackhawk, and others 3.50
Special 1 (1992, $3.50, 68 pgs.)-Mature readers 3.50

BLACKHAWK INDIAN TOMAHAWK WAR, THE
Avon Periodicals: 1951 (Also see Fighting Indians of the Wild West)

nn-Kinstler-c; Kit West story 20 40 60 115 160 205

BLACK HEART ASSASSIN
Iguana Comics: Jan, 1994 ($2.95)

1 3.00

BLACK HOLE (See Walt Disney Showcase #54) (Disney, movie)
Whitman Publishing Co.: Mar, 1980 - No. 4, Sept, 1980

11295(#1) (1979, Golden, $1.50-c, 52 pgs., graphic novel; 8 1/2x11") Photo-c; Spiegle-a. 2 4 6 12 16 20
1-4: 1,2-Movie adaptation. 2-4-Spiegle-a. 3-McWilliams-a; photo-c.
3,4-New stories 1 3 4 6 8 10

BLACK HOOD, THE (See Blue Ribbon, Flyman & Mighty Comics)
Red Circle Comics (Archie): June, 1983 - No. 3, Oct, 1983 (Mandell paper)

1-Morrow, McWilliams, Wildey-a; Toth-c 6.00
2,3: The Fox by Toth-c/a; Boyette-a. 3-Morrow-a; Toth wraparound-c 4.00
(Also see Archie's Super-Hero Special Digest #2)

BLACK HOOD
DC Comics (Impact Comics): Dec, 1991 - No. 12, Dec, 1992 ($1.00)

1 3.50
2-12: 11-Intro The Fox. 12-Origin Black Hood 2.50
Annual 1 (1992, $2.50, 68 pgs.)-w/Trading card 3.00

BLACK HOOD COMICS (Formerly Hangman #2-8; Laugh Comics #20 on; also see Black Swan, Jackpot, Roly Poly & Top-Notch #9)
MLJ Magazines: No. 9, Wint., 1943-44 - No. 19, Sum., 1946 (on radio in 1943)

9-The Hangman & The Boy Buddies cont'd 107 214 321 669 1005 1340
10-Hangman & Dusty, the Boy Detective app. 61 122 183 381 573 765
11-Dusty app.; no Hangman 48 96 144 288 432 575
12-18: 14-Kinstler blood-c. 17-Hal Foster swipe from Prince Valiant; 1st issue with "An Archie Magazine" on-c 41 82 123 246 368 490
19-I.D. exposed; last issue 52 104 157 312 469 625
NOTE: *Hangman by **Fuje** in 9, 10. **Kinstler** a-15, c-14-16.*

BLACK JACK (Rocky Lane's...; formerly Jim Bowie)
Charlton Comics: No. 20, Nov, 1957 - No. 30, Nov, 1959

20 9 18 27 52 66 80
21,27,29,30 6 12 18 31 38 45
22,23: 22-(68 pgs.). 23-Williamson/Torres-a 8 16 24 43 54 65
24-26,28-Ditko-a 10 20 30 56 73 90

BLACK KNIGHT, THE
Toby Press: May, 1953; 1963

1-Bondage-c 26 52 78 147 206 265
Super Reprint No. 11 (1963)-Reprints 1953 issue 3 6 9 19 25 32

BLACK KNIGHT, THE
Atlas Comics (MgPC): May, 1955 - No. 5, April, 1956

1-Origin Crusader; Maneely-c/a 84 168 252 525 788 1050
2-Maneely-c/a(4) 59 118 177 369 552 735
3-5: 4-Maneely-c/a. 5-Maneely-c, Shores-a 46 92 138 276 413 550

BLACK KNIGHT (See The Avengers #48, Marvel Super Heroes & Tales To Astonish #52)
Marvel Comics: June, 1990 - No. 4, Sept, 1990 ($1.50, limited series)

1-4: 1-Original Black Knight returns. 3,4-Dr. Strange app. 2.50
NOTE: ***Buckler** c-1-4p*

BLACK KNIGHT: EXODUS
Marvel Comics: Dec, 1996 ($2.50, one-shot)

1-Raab-s; Apocalypse-c/app. 2.50

BLACK LAMB, THE
DC Comics (Helix): Nov, 1996 - No, 6, Apr, 1997 ($2.50, limited series)

1-6: Tim Truman-c/a/scripts 2.50

BLACK LIGHTNING (See The Brave & The Bold, Cancelled Comic Cavalcade, DC Comics Presents #16, Detective #490 and World's Finest #257)
National Periodical Publ./DC Comics: Apr, 1977 - No. 11, Sept-Oct, 1978

1-Origin Black Lightning 2 4 6 8 10 12
2,3,6-10 6.00
4,5-Superman-c/s. 4-Intro Cyclotronic Man 1 2 3 4 5 7
11-The Ray new solo story 1 2 3 5 7 9
NOTE: ***Buckler** c-1-3p, 6-11p. #11 is 44 pgs.*

BLACK LIGHTNING (2nd Series)
DC Comics: Feb, 1995 - No. 13, Feb, 1996 ($1.95/$2.25)

1-5-Tony Isabella scripts begin, ends #8 3.00
6-13: 6-Begin $2.25-c. 13-Batman-c/app. 3.00

BLACK MAGIC (...Magazine) (Becomes Cool Cat V8#6 on)
Crestwood Publ. V1#1-4,V6#1-V7#5/Headline V1#5-V5#3,V7#6-V8#5: 10-11/50 - V4#1, 6-7/53: V4#2, 9-10/53 - V5#3, 11-12/54; V6#1, 9-10/57 - V7#2, 11-12/58: V7#3, 7-8/60 - V8#5, 11-12/61 (V1#1-5, 52pgs.; V1#6-V3#3, 44pgs.)

V1#1-S&K-a, 10 pgs.; Meskin-a(2) 128 256 384 800 1200 1600
2-S&K-a, 17 pgs.; Meskin-a 56 112 168 350 525 700
3-6(8-9/51)-S&K, Roussos, Meskin-a 50 100 150 300 450 600
V2#1(10-11/51),4,5,7(#13),9(#15),12(#18)-S&K-a 36 72 108 204 290 375
2,3,6,8,10,11(#17) 28 56 84 157 221 285
V3#1(#19, 12/52) - 6(#24, 5/53)-S&K-a 29 58 87 164 232 300
V4#1(#25, 6-7/53), 2(#26, 9-10/53)-S&K-a(3-4) 30 60 90 170 240 310
3(#27, 11-12/53)-S&K-a; Ditko-a (2nd published-a); also see Captain 3-D, Daring Love #1, Strange Fantasy #9, & Fantastic Fears #5 (Fant. Fears was 1st drawn, but not 1st publ.) 48 96 144 288 432 575
4(#28)-Eyes ripped out/story-S&K, Ditko-a 40 80 120 240 340 440
5(#29, 3-4/54)-S&K, Ditko-a 31 62 93 178 252 325
6(#30, 5-6/54)-S&K, Powell?-a 23 46 69 132 186 240
V5#1(#31, 7-8/54 - 3(#33, 11-12/54)-S&K-a 18 36 54 104 142 180
V6#1(#34, 9-10/57), 2(#35, 11-12/57) 10 20 30 58 77 95
3(1-2/58) - 6(7-8/58) 10 20 30 58 77 95
V7#1(9-10/58) - 3(7-8/60) 9 18 27 54 70 85
4(9-10/60) 10 20 30 58 77 95
5(11-12/60)-Hitler-c; Torres-a 12 24 36 71 96 120
6(1-2/61)-Powell-a(2) 9 18 27 54 70 85
V8#1(3-4/61)-Powell-c/a 9 18 27 54 70 85
2(5-6/61)-E.C. story swipe/W.F. #22; Ditko, Powell-a
10 20 30 58 77 95
3(7-8/61)-E.C. story swipe/W.F. #22; Powell-a(2) 10 20 30 58 77 95
4(9-10/61)-Powell-a(5) 9 18 27 54 70 85
5-E.C. story swipe/W.S.F. #28; Powell-a(3) 10 20 30 58 77 95

NOTE: ***Bernard Baily** a-V4#6?, V5#3(2). **Grandenetti** a-V2#3, 11. **Kirby** c-V1#1-6, V2#1-12, V3#1-6, V4#1, 2, 4-6, V5#1-3. **McWilliams** a-V3#2i. **Meskin** a-V1#1(2), 2, 3, 4(2), 5(2), 6, V2/1, 2, 3(2), 4(3), 5, 6(2), 7-9, 11, 12i, V3#1(2), 5, 6, V5#1(2), 2. **Orlando** a-V6#1, 4, V7#2; c-V6/1-6. **Powell** a-V5#1?. **Roussos** a-V1#3-5, 6(2), V2#3(2), 4, 5(2), 6, 8, 9, 10(2), 11, 12p, V3#1(2), 2i, 5, V5#2. **Simon** a-V2#12, V3#2, V7#5? c-V4#3?, V7#3?, 4, 5?, 6?, V8#1-5. **Simon & Kirby** a-V1#1, 2(2), 3-6, V2#1, 4, 5, 7, 9, 12, V3#1-6, V4#1(3), 2(4), 3(2), 4(2), 5, 6, V5#1-3; c-V2#1. **Leonard Starr** a-V1#1. **Tuska** a-V6#3, 4. **Woodbridge** a-V7#4.*

BLACK MAGIC
National Periodical Publications: Oct-Nov, 1973 - No. 9, Apr-May, 1975

1-S&K reprints 3 6 9 18 24 30
2-8-S&K reprints 2 4 6 10 13 16
9-S&K reprints 2 4 6 11 14 18

BLACK MAGIC
Eclipse International: Apr, 1990 - No. 4, Oct, 1990 ($2.75, B&W, mini-series)

1-($3.50, 68pgs.)-Japanese manga 4.00

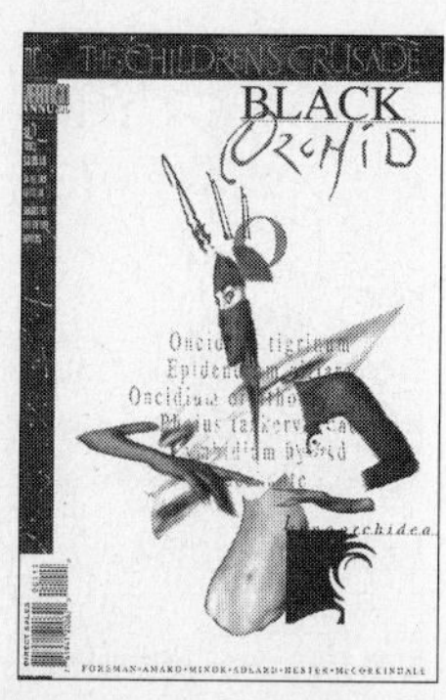

Black Orchid Annual #1 © DC

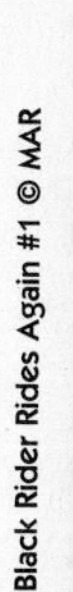

Black Rider Rides Again #1 © MAR

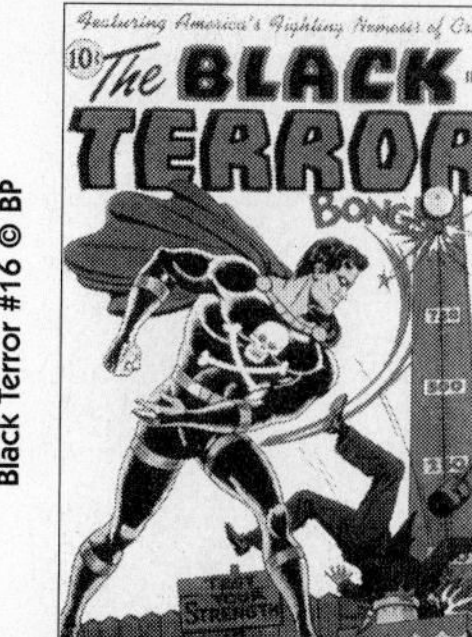

Black Terror #16 © BP

	GD 2.0	VG 4.0	FN 6.0	VF 8.0	VF/NM 9.0	NM- 9.2

2-4 ($2.75, 52 pgs.) 3.00

BLACKMAIL TERROR (See Harvey Comics Library)

BLACK MASK
DC Comics: 1993 - No. 3, 1994 ($4.95, limited series, 52 pgs.)

1-3 5.00

BLACK OPS
Image Comics (WildStorm): Jan, 1996 - No. 5, May, 1996 ($2.50, lim. series)

1-5 2.50

BLACK ORCHID (See Adventure Comics #428 & Phantom Stranger)
DC Comics: Holiday, 1988-89 - No. 3, 1989 ($3.50, lim. series, prestige format)

Book 1,3: Gaiman scripts & McKean painted-a in all 6.00
Book 2-Arkham Asylum story; Batman app. 1 2 3 5 6 8
TPB (1991, $19.95) r/#1-3; new McKean-c 20.00

BLACK ORCHID
DC Comics: Sept, 1993 - No. 22, June, 1995 ($1.95/$2.25)

1-22: Dave McKean-c all issues 2.50
1-Platinum Edition 12.00
Annual 1 (1993, $3.95, 68 pgs.)-Children's Crusade 4.00

BLACKOUTS (See Broadway Hollywood...)

BLACK PANTHER, THE (Also see Avengers #52, Fantastic Four #52, Jungle Action & Marvel Premiere #51-53)
Marvel Comics Group: Jan, 1977 - No. 15, May, 1979

1 3 6 9 18 23 28
2-13: 4,5-(Regular 30¢ editions). 8-Origin 2 4 6 8 10 12
4,5-(35¢-c variants, limited dist.)(7,9/77) 3 6 9 18 23 28
14,15-Avengers x-over. 14-Origin 2 4 6 10 12 15
NOTE: ***J. Buscema** c-15p. **Kirby** c/a & scripts-1-12. **Layton** c-13i.*

BLACK PANTHER
Marvel Comics Group: July, 1988 - No. 4, Oct, 1988 ($1.25)

1-4-Gillis-s/Cowan & Delarosa-a 2.50

BLACK PANTHER (Marvel Knights)
Marvel Comics: Nov, 1998 - Present ($2.50)

1-Texeira-a/c; Priest-s 6.00
1-($6.95) DF edition w/Quesada & Palmiotti-c 1 2 3 5 6 8
2-4: 2-Two covers by Texeira and Timm. 3-Fantastic Four app. 3.50
5-35,37-40: 5-Evans-a. 6-8-Jusko-a. 8-Avengers-c/app. 15-Hulk app. 22-Moon Knight app. 23-Avengers app. 25-Maximum Security x-over. 26-Storm-c/app. 28-Magneto & Sub-Mariner-c/app. 29-WWII flashback meeting w/Captain America. 35-Defenders-c/app. 37-Luke Cage and Falcon-c/app. 2.50
36-($3.50, 100 pgs.) 35th Anniversary issue incl. r/1st app. in FF #52 3.50
41-56: 41-44-Wolverine app. 47-Thor app. 48,49-Magneto app. 2.50
57-62: 57-Begin $2.99-c. 59-Falcon app. 3.00
...: The Client (6/01, $14.95, TPB) r/#1-5 15.00

BLACK PANTHER: PANTHER'S PREY
Marvel Comics: May, 1991 - No. 4, Oct, 1991 ($4.95, squarebound, lim. series, 52 pgs.)

1-4: McGregor-s/Turner-a 5.00

BLACK PEARL, THE
Dark Horse Comics: Sept, 1996 - No. 5, Jan, 1997 ($2.95, limited series)

1-5: Mark Hamill scripts 3.00

BLACK PHANTOM (See Tim Holt #25, 38)
Magazine Enterprises: Nov, 1954 (one-shot) (Female outlaw)

1 (A-1 #122)-The Ghost Rider story plus 3 Black Phantom stories; Headlight-c/a 39 78 117 230 325 420

BLACK PHANTOM
AC Comics: 1989 - No. 3, 1990 ($2.50, B&W; #2 color)(Reprints & new-a)

1-3: 1-Ayers-r, Bolle-r/B.P. #1-3-Redmask-r 2.75

BLACK PHANTOM, RETURN OF THE (See Wisco)

BLACK RIDER (Western Winners #1-7; Western Tales of Black Rider #28-31; Gunsmoke Western #32 on)(See All Western Winners, Best Western, Kid Colt, Outlaw Kid, Rex Hart, Two-Gun Kid, Two-Gun Western, Western Gunfighters, Western Winners, & Wild Western)
Marvel/Atlas Comics(CDS No. 8-17/CPS No. 19 on): No. 8, 3/50 - No. 18, 1/52; No. 19, 11/53 - No. 27, 3/55

8 (#1)-Black Rider & his horse Satan begin; 36 pgs; Stan Lee photo-c as Black Rider) 42 84 126 252 376 500
9-52 pgs. begin, end #14 24 48 72 135 190 245
10-Origin Black Rider 28 56 84 161 228 295
11-14: 14-Last 52pgs. 18 36 54 104 142 180
15-19: 19-Two-Gun Kid app. 15 30 45 86 118 150
20-Classic-c; Two-Gun Kid app. 17 34 51 98 134 170
21-27: 21-23-Two-Gun Kid app. 24,25-Arrowhead app. 26-Kid Colt app. 27-Last issue; last precode. Kid Colt app. The Spider (a villain) burns to death 14 28 42 79 107 135
NOTE: *Ayers c-22. **Jack Keller** a-15, 26, 27. **Maneely** a-14; c-16, 17, 25, 27. **Syd Shores** a-19, 21, 22, 23(3), 24(3), 25-27; c-19, 21, 23. **Sinnott** a-24, 25. **Tuska** a-12, 19-21.*

BLACK RIDER RIDES AGAIN!, THE
Atlas Comics (CPS): Sept, 1957

1-Kirby-a(3); Powell-a; Severin-c 26 52 78 147 206 265

BLACK SEPTEMBER (Also see Avengers/Ultraforce, Ultraforce (1st series) #10 & Ultraforce/Avengers)
Malibu Comics (Ultraverse): 1995 ($1.50, one-shot)

Infinity-Intro to the newUltraverse; variant-c exists. 2.25

BLACKSTONE (See Super Magician Comics & Wisco Giveaways)

BLACKSTONE, MASTER MAGICIAN COMICS
Vital Publ./Street & Smith Publ.: Mar-Apr, 1946 - No. 3, July-Aug, 1946

1 31 62 93 175 248 320
2,3 19 38 57 109 152 195

BLACKSTONE, THE MAGICIAN (...Detective on cover only #3 & 4)
Marvel Comics (CnPC): No. 2, May, 1948 - No. 4, Sept, 1948 (No #1) (Cont'd from E.C. #1?)

2-The Blonde Phantom begins, ends #4 61 122 183 381 571 760
3,4: 3-Blonde Phantom by Sekowsky 40 80 120 240 340 440

BLACKSTONE, THE MAGICIAN DETECTIVE FIGHTS CRIME
E. C. Comics: Fall, 1947

1-1st app. Happy Houlihans 50 100 150 300 450 600

BLACK SUN (X-Men Black Sun on cover)
Marvel Comics: Nov, 2000 - No. 5, Nov, 2000 ($2.99, weekly limited series)

1-(...: X-Men), 2-(...: Storm), 3-(...: Banshee and Sunfire), 4-(...: Colossus and Nightcrawler), 5-(...: Wolverine and Thunderbird); Claremont-s in all; Evans interlocking painted covers; Magik returns 3.00

BLACK SUN
DC Comics (WildStorm): Nov, 2002 - No. 6, Jun, 2003 ($2.95, limited series)

1-6-Andreyko-s/Scott-a 3.00

BLACK SWAN COMICS
MLJ Magazines (Pershing Square Publ. Co.): 1945

1-The Black Hood reprints from Black Hood No. 14; Bill Woggon-a; Suzie app. 23 46 69 132 186 240

BLACK TARANTULA (See Feature Presentations No. 5)

BLACK TERROR (See America's Best Comics & Exciting Comics)
Better Publications/Standard: Winter, 1942-43 - No. 27, June, 1949

1-Black Terror, Crime Crusader begin 300 600 900 1900 2850 3800
2 112 224 336 700 1050 1400
3 77 154 231 481 721 960
4,5 66 132 198 413 619 825
6-10: 7-The Ghost app. 56 112 168 350 525 700
11-20: 20-The Scarab app. 49 98 147 294 440 585
21-Miss Masque app. 53 106 159 318 474 630
22-Part Frazetta-a on one Black Terror story 49 98 147 294 440 585
23,25-27 43 86 130 258 389 520
24-Frazetta-a (1/4 pg.) 44 88 132 264 397 530
NOTE: ***Schomburg (Xela)** c-2-27; bondage c-2, 17, 24. **Meskin** a-27. **Moreira** a-27. **Robinson/Meskin** a-23, 24(3), 25, 26. **Roussos/Mayo** a-24. **Tuska** a-26, 27.*

BLACK TERROR, THE (Also see Total Eclipse)
Eclipse Comics: Oct, 1989 - No. 3, June, 1990 ($4.95, 52 pgs., squarebound, limited series)

1-3: Beau Smith & Chuck Dixon scripts; Dan Brereton painted-c/a 5.00

BLACKTHORNE 3-D SERIES
Blackthorne Publishing Co.: May, 1985 - No. 80, 1989 ($2.25/$2.50)

1-Sheena in 3-D #1. D. Stevens-c/retouched-a 1 2 3 5 6 8
2-10: 2-MerlinRealm in 3-D #1. 3-3-D Heroes #1. Goldyn in 3-D #1. 5-Bizarre 3-D Zone #1. 6-Salimba in 3-D #1. 7-Twisted Tales in 3-D #1. 8-Dick Tracy in 3-D #1. 9-Salimba in 3-D #2. 10-Gumby in 3-D #1 6.00
11-19: 11-Betty Boop in 3-D #1. 12-Hamster Vice in 3-D #1. 13-Little Nemo in 3-D #1. 14-Gumby in 3-D #2. 15-Hamster Vice #6 in 3-D. 16-Laffin' Gas #6 in 3-D. 17-Gumby in 3-D #3. 18-Bullwinkle and Rocky in 3-D #1. 19-The Flintstones in 3-D #1 6.00

Black Widow: Pale Little Spider #1 © MAR

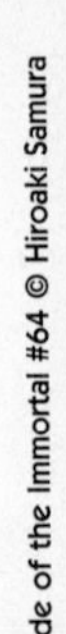
Blade of the Immortal #64 © Hiroaki Samura

Blade: Vampire Hunter #1 © MAR

GD 2.0 | VG 4.0 | FN 6.0 | VF 8.0 | VF/NM 9.0 | NM- 9.2

20(#1),26(#2),35(#3),39(#4),52(#5),62,71(#6)-G.I. Joe in 3-D. 62-G.I. Joe Annual 2 4 6 8 10 12
21-24,27-28: 21-Gumby in 3-D #4. 22-The Flintstones in 3-D #2. 23-Laurel & Hardy In 3-D #1. 24-Bozo the Clown in 3-D #1. 27-Bravestarr in 3-D #1. 28- Gumby in 3-D #5 6.00
25,29,37-The Transformers in 3-D 2 4 6 8 10 12
30-Star Wars in 3-D #1 2 4 6 14 18 22
31-34,36,38,40: 31-The California Raisins in 3-D #1. 32-Richie Rich & Casper in 3-D #1. 33-Gumby in 3-D #6. 34-Laurel & Hardy in 3-D #2. 36-The Flintstones in 3-D #3. 38-Gumby in 3-D #7. 40-Bravestarr in 3-D #2 6.00
41-46,49,50: 41-Battletech in 3-D #1. 42-The Flintstones in 3-D #4. 43-Underdog in 3-D #1 44-The California Raisins in 3-D #2. 45-Red Heat in 3-D #1 (movie adapt.). 46-The California Raisins in 3-D #3. 49-Rambo in 3-D #1. 49-Sad Sack in 3-D #1. 50-Bullwinkle For President in 3-D #1 6.00
47,48-Star Wars in 3-D #2,3 2 4 6 10 13 16
51,53-60: 51-Kull in 3-D #1. 53-Red Sonja in 3-D #1. 54-Bozo in 3-D #2. 55-Waxwork in 3-D #1 (movie adapt.). 57-Casper in 3-D #1. 58-Baby Huey in 3-D #1. 59-Little Dot in 3-D #1. 60-Solomon Kane in 3-D #1 6.00
61,63-70,72-80: 61-Werewolf in 3-D #1. 63-The California Raisins in 3-D #4. 64-To Die For in 3-D #1. 65-Capt. Holo in 3-D #1. 66-Playful Little Audrey in 3-D #1. 67-Kull in 3-D #2. 69-The California Raisins in 3-D #5. 70-Wendy in 3-D #1. 72-Sports Hall of Shame #1. 74-The Noid in 3-D #1. 75-Moonwalker in 3-D #1 (Michael Jackson movie adapt.). 76-79. 80-The Noid in 3-D #2 6.00

BLACK TIDE
Image Comics: Nov, 2001 - No. 4, May, 2002 ($2.95)
1-4-Bishop-s; Mike Miller-a. 1-Three covers by Miller, Park & Bachalo 3.00

BLACK TIDE (Volume 2)
Avatar Press/Angel Gate: July, 2002 - Present ($3.50/$2.95)
1-4: 1-Bishop-s; Mike Miller-a. 1-Three covers by Miller, Park & Pajarillo 3.50
5-8-($2.95) Breyfogle-a/c 3.00

BLACK WIDOW (Marvel Knights) (Also see Marvel Graphic Novel)
Marvel Comics: May, 1999 - No. 3, Aug, 1999 ($2.99, limited series)
1-(June on-c) Devin Grayson-s/J.G. Jones-c/a; Daredevil app. 5.00
1-Variant-c by J.G. Jones 6.00
2,3 4.00
...Web of Intrigue (6/99, $3.50) r/origin & early appearances 3.50
TPB (7/01, $15.95) r/Vol. 1 & 2; Jones-c 16.00

BLACK WIDOW (Marvel Knights) (Volume 2)
Marvel Comics: Jan, 2001 - No. 3, May, 2001 ($2.99, limited series)
1-3-Grayson & Rucka-s/Scott Hampton-c/a; Daredevil app. 3.00

BLACK WIDOW: PALE LITTLE SPIDER (Marvel Knights) (Volume 3)
Marvel Comics: Jun, 2002 - No. 3, Aug, 2002 ($2.99, limited series)
1-3-Rucka-s/Kordey-a/Horn-c 3.00

BLACKWULF
Marvel Comics: June, 1994 - No. 10, Mar, 1995 ($1.50)
1-($2.50)-Embossed-c; Angel Medina-a 3.00
2-10 2.25

BLADE (The Vampire Hunter)
Marvel Comics: Mar, 1998 ($3.50, one-shot)
1-Colan-a(p)/Christopher Golden-s 3.50

BLADE (The Vampire Hunter)
Marvel Comics: Nov, 1998 - No. 3, Jan, 1999 ($3.50/$2.99)
1-($3.50) Contains Movie insider pages; McKean-a 3.50
2,3-($2.99): 2-Two covers 3.00
...Sins of the Father (10/98, $5.99) Sears-a; movie adaption 6.00
Blade 2: Movie Adaptation (5/02, $5.95) Ponticelli-a/Bradstreet-c 6.00

BLADE (Volume 2)
Marvel Comics (MAX): May, 2002 -No. 6, Oct, 2002 (/$2.99)
1-6-Bradstreet-c/Hinz-s. 1-5-Pugh-a. 6-Homs-a 3.00

BLADE OF THE IMMORTAL (Manga)
Dark Horse Comics: June, 1996 - Present ($2.95/$2.99/$3.95, B&W)
1-Hiroaki Samura-s/a in all 1 3 4 6 8 10
2-5: 2-#1 on cover in error 6.00
6-10 5.00
11,19,20,34-($3.95, 48 pgs.): 34-Food one-shot 4.00
12-18,21-33,35-41,43-82: 12-20-Dreamsong. 21-28-On Silent Wings. 29-33-Dark Shadow. 35-42-Heart of Darkness. 43-57-The Gathering 3.00
42-($3.50) Ends Heart of Darkness 3.50

BLADE RUNNER (Movie)
Marvel Comics Group: Oct, 1982 - No. 2, Nov, 1982
1,2-r/Marvel Super Special #22; 1-Williamson-c/a. 2-Williamson-a 3.50

BLADESMEN UNDERSEA
Blue Comet Press: 1994 ($3.50, B&W)
1-Polybagged w/trading card 3.50

BLADE: THE VAMPIRE-HUNTER
Marvel Comics: July, 1994 - No. 10, Apr, 1995 ($1.95)
1-($2.95)-Foil-c; Dracula returns; Wheatley-c/a 3.50
2-10: 2,3,10-Dracula-c/app. 8-Morbius app. 2.50

BLADE: VAMPIRE-HUNTER
Marvel Comics: Dec, 1999 - No. 6, May, 2000 ($3.50/$2.50)
1-($3.50)-Bart Sears-s; Sears and Smith-a 3.50
2-6-($2.50): 2-Regular & Wesley Snipes photo-c 2.50

BLAIR WITCH CHRONICLES, THE
Oni Press: Mar, 2000 - No. 4, July, 2000 ($2.95, B&W, limited series)
1-4-Van Meter-s.1-Guy Davis-a. 2-Mireault-a 3.00
1-DF Alternate-c by John Estes 7.00
TPB (9/00, $15.95) r/#1-4 & Blair Witch Project one-shot 16.00

BLAIR WITCH: DARK TESTAMENTS
Image Comics: Oct, 2000 ($2.95, one-shot)
1-Edington-s/Adlard-a; story of murderer Rustin Parr 3.00

BLAIR WITCH PROJECT, THE (Movie companion, not adaption)
Oni Press: July, 1999 ($2.95, B&W, one-shot)
1-(1st printing) History of the Blair Witch, art by Edwards, Mireault, and Davis; Van Meter-s; only the stick figure is red on the cover 12.00
1-(2nd printing) Stick figure and title lettering are red on cover 4.00
1-(3rd printing) Stick figure, title, and creator credits are red on cover 3.00
DF Glow in the Dark variant-c ($10.00) 10.00

BLAST (Satire Magazine)
G & D Publications: Feb, 1971 - No. 2, May, 1971
1-Wrightson & Kaluta-a/Everette-c 7 14 21 46 63 80
2-Kaluta-c/a 5 10 15 36 48 60

BLAST CORPS
Dark Horse Comics: Oct, 1998 ($2.50, one-shot, based on Nintendo game)
1-Reprints from Nintendo Power magazine; Mahn-a 2.50

BLASTERS SPECIAL
DC Comics: 1989 ($2.00, one-shot)
1-Peter David scripts; Invasion spin-off 2.50

BLAST-OFF (Three Rocketeers)
Harvey Publications (Fun Day Funnies): Oct, 1965 (12¢)
1-Kirby/Williamson-a(2); Williamson/Crandall-a; Williamson/Torres/Krenkel-a; Kirby/Simon-c 6 12 18 43 59 75

BLAZE
Marvel Comics: Aug, 1994 - No. 12, July, 1995 ($1.95)
1-($2.95)-Foil embossed-c 3.50
2-12: 2-Man-Thing-c/story. 11,12-Punisher app. 2.50

BLAZE CARSON (Rex Hart #6 on)(See Kid Colt, Tex Taylor, Wild Western, Wisco)
Marvel Comics (USA): Sept, 1948 - No. 5, June, 1949
1: 1,2-Shores-c 28 56 84 157 221 285
2,4,5: 4-Two-Gun Kid app. 5-Tex Taylor app. 19 38 57 109 152 195
3-Used by N.Y. State Legis. Comm. (injury to eye splash); Tex Morgan app. 20 40 60 115 160 205

BLAZE: LEGACY OF BLOOD (See Ghost Rider & Ghost Rider/Blaze)
Marvel Comics (Midnight Sons imprint): Dec, 1993 - No. 4, Mar, 1994 ($1.75, limited series)
1-4 2.50

BLAZE OF GLORY
Marvel Comics: Feb, 2000 - No. 4, Mar, 2000 ($2.99, limited series)
1-4-Ostrander-s/Manco-a; Two-Gun Kid, Rawhide Kid, Red Wolf and Ghost Rider app. 3.00
TPB (7/02, $9.99) r/#1-4 10.00

BLAZE THE WONDER COLLIE (Formerly Molly Manton's Romances #1?)
Marvel Comics(SePI): No. 2, Oct, 1949 - No. 3, Feb, 1950 (Both have photo-c)
2(#1), 3-(Scarce) 24 48 72 138 194 250

BLAZING BATTLE TALES

Blazing Comics #1 © Enwil

Blitzkrieg #4 © DC

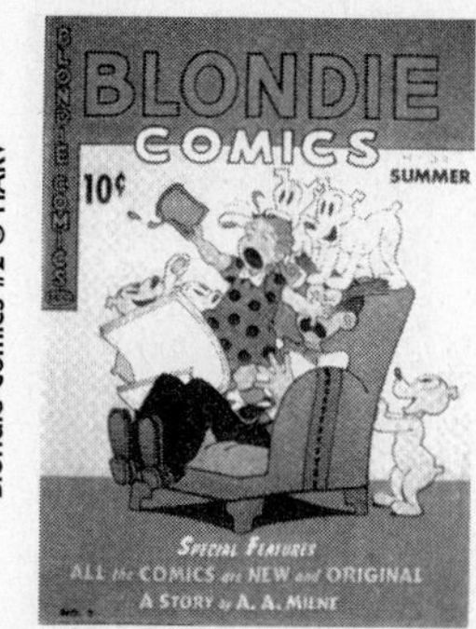

Blondie Comics #2 © HARV

Seaboard Periodicals (Atlas): July, 1975
1-Intro. Sgt. Hawk & the Sky Demon; Severin, McWilliams, Sparling-a; Nazi-c by Thorne
2 4 6 9 11 14

BLAZING COMBAT (Magazine)
Warren Publishing Co.: Oct, 1965 - No. 4, July, 1966 (35¢, B&W)
1-Frazetta painted-c on all 17 34 51 118 174 230
2 6 12 18 38 52 65
3,4: 4-Frazetta half pg. ad 5 10 15 33 44 55
nn-Anthology (reprints from No. 1-4) (low print) 6 12 18 38 52 65
NOTE: ***Adkins** a-4. **Colan** a-3,4,nn. **Crandall** a-all. **Evans** a-1,4. **Heath** a-4,nn. **Morrow** a-1-3,nn. **Orlando** a-1-3,nn. **J. Severin** a-all. **Torres** a-1-4. **Toth** a-all. **Williamson** a-2. and **Wood** a-3,4,nn.*

BLAZING COMBAT: WORLD WAR I AND WORLD WAR II
Apple Press: Mar, 1994 ($3.75, B&W)
1,2: 1-r/Colan, Toth, Goodwin, Severin, Wood-a. 2-r/Crandall, Evans, Severin, Torres, Williamson-a 4.00

BLAZING COMICS (Also see Blue Circle Comics and Red Circle Comics)
Enwil Associates/Rural Home: 6/44 - #3, 9/44; #4, 2/45; #5, 3/45; #5(V2#2), 3/55 - #6(V2#3), 1955?
1-The Green Turtle, Red Hawk, Black Buccaneer begin; origin Jun-Gal
50 100 150 300 450 600
2-5: 3-Briefer-a. 5-(V2#2 inside) 34 68 102 196 278 360
5(3/55, V2#2-inside)-Black Buccaneer-c, 6(V2#3-inside, 1955)-Indian/Japanese-c; cover is from Apr. 1945 18 36 54 104 142 180
NOTE: No. 5 & 6 contain remaindered comics rebound and the contents can vary. Cloak & Daggar, Will Rogers, Superman 64, Star Spangled 130, Kaanga known. Value would be half of contents.

BLAZING SIXGUNS
Avon Periodicals: Dec, 1952
1-Kinstler-c/a; Larsen/Alascia-a(2), Tuska?-a; Jesse James, Kit Carson, Wild Bill Hickok app. 17 34 51 95 130 165

BLAZING SIXGUNS
I.W./Super Comics: 1964
I.W. Reprint #1,8,9: 1-r/Wild Bill Hickok #26, Western True Crime #? & Blazing Sixguns #1 by Avon; Kinstler-c. 8-r/Blazing Western #?; Kinstler-c. 9-r/Blazing Western #1; Ditko-r; Kintsler-c reprinted from Dalton Boys #1 2 4 6 11 14 18
Super Reprint #10,11,15,16: 10,11-r/The Rider #2,1. 15-r/Silver Kid Western #?. 16-r/Buffalo Bill #?; Wildey-r; Severin-c. 17(1964)-r/Western True Crime #?
2 4 6 11 14 18
12-Reprints Bullseye #3; S&K-a 4 8 12 22 30 38
18-r/Straight Arrow #? by Powell; Severin-c 2 4 6 11 14 18

BLAZING SIX-GUNS (Also see Sundance Kid)
Skywald Comics: Feb, 1971 - No. 2, Apr, 1971 (52 pgs.)
1-The Red Mask, Sundance Kid begin, Avon's Geronimo reprint by Kinstler; Wyatt Earp app. 2 4 6 14 18 22
2-Wild Bill Hickok, Jesse James, Kit Carson-r plus M.E. Red Mask-r
2 4 6 10 12 15

BLAZING WEST (The Hooded Horseman #21 on)
American Comics Group (B&I Publ./Michel Publ.): Fall, 1948 - No. 20, Nov-Dec, 1951
1-Origin & 1st app. Injun Jones, Tenderfoot & Buffalo Belle; Texas Tim & Ranger begins, ends #13 21 42 63 118 164 210
2,3 (1-2/49) 10 20 30 58 77 95
4-Origin & 1st app. Little Lobo; Starr-a (3-4/49) 9 18 27 52 66 80
5-10: 5-Starr-a 8 16 24 43 54 65
11-13 7 14 21 35 43 50
14(11-12/50)-Origin/1st app. The Hooded Horseman 12 24 36 69 92 115
15-20: 15,16,18,19-Starr-a 8 16 24 46 58 70

BLAZING WESTERN
Timor Publications: Jan, 1954 - No. 5, Sept, 1954
1-Ditko-a (1st Western-a?); text story by Bruce Hamilton
17 34 51 98 134 170
2-4 8 16 24 43 54 65
5-Disbrow-a 8 16 24 46 58 70

BLEAT
Slave Labor Graphics: Aug, 1995 ($2.95)
1 3.00

BLINDSIDE
Image Comics (Extreme Studios): Aug, 1996 ($2.50)
1-Variant-c exists 2.50

BLINK (See X-Men Age of Apocalypse storyline)
Marvel Comics: March, 2001 - No. 4, June, 2001 ($2.99, limited series)
1-4-Adam Kubert-c/Lobdell-s/Winick-script; leads into Exiles #1 3.00

BLIP
Marvel Comics Group: 2/1983 - 1983 (Video game mag. in comic format)
1-1st app. Donkey Kong & Mario Bros. in comics, 6pgs. comics; photo-c
1 2 3 5 6 8
2-Spider-Man photo-c; 6pgs. Spider-Man comics w/Green Goblin
1 2 3 5 7 9
3,4,6 5.00
5-E.T., Indiana Jones; Rocky-c 6.00
7-6pgs. Hulk comics; Pac-Man & Donkey Kong Jr. Hints 1 2 3 4 5 7

BLISS ALLEY
Image Comics: July, 1997 - No. 2, Sept, 1997 ($2.95, B&W)
1,2-Messner-Loebs-s/a 3.00

BLITZKRIEG
National Periodical Publications: Jan-Feb, 1976 - No. 5, Sept-Oct, 1976
1-Kubert-c on all 4 8 12 27 36 45
2-5 3 6 9 16 20 25

BLONDE PHANTOM (Formerly All-Select #1-11; Lovers #23 on)(Also see Blackstone, Marvel Mystery, Millie The Model #2, Sub-Mariner Comics #25 & Sun Girl)
Marvel Comics (MPC): No. 12, Winter, 1946-47 - No. 22, Mar, 1949
12-Miss America begins, ends #14 160 320 480 1000 1500 2000
13-Sub-Mariner begins (not in #16) 96 192 288 600 900 1200
14,15: 15-Kurtzman's "Hey Look" 88 176 264 550 825 1100
16-Captain America with Bucky story by Rico(p), 6 pgs.; Kurtzman's "Hey Look" (1 pg.)
120 240 360 750 1125 1500
17-22: 22-Anti Wertham editorial 76 152 228 475 713 950
*NOTE: **Shores** c-12-18.*

BLONDIE (See Ace Comics, Comics Reading Libraries (Promotional Comics section), Dagwood, Daisy & Her Pups, Eat Right to Work..., King & Magic Comics)
David McKay Publications: 1942 - 1946
Feature Books 12 (Rare) 78 156 238 488 732 975
Feature Books 27-29,31,34(1940) 22 44 66 124 172 220
Feature Books 36,38,40,42,43,45,47 20 40 60 115 160 205
...1944 (Hard-c, 1938, B&W, 128 pgs.)-1944 daily strip-r
17 34 51 95 130 165

BLONDIE & DAGWOOD FAMILY
Harvey Publ. (King Features Synd.): Oct, 1963 - No. 4, Dec, 1965 (68 pgs.)
1 4 8 12 27 36 45
2-4 3 6 9 18 23 28

BLONDIE COMICS (...Monthly No. 16-141)
David McKay #1-15/Harvey #16-163/King #164-175/Charlton #177 on:
Spring, 1947 - No. 163, Nov, 1965; No. 164, Aug, 1966 - No. 175, Dec, 1967; No. 177, Feb, 1969 - No. 222, Nov, 1976
1 27 54 81 153 214 275
2 14 28 42 81 111 140
3-5 11 22 33 63 84 105
6-10 9 18 27 52 66 80
11-15 8 16 24 40 50 60
16-(3/50; 1st Harvey issue) 9 18 27 52 66 80
17-20: 20-(3/51)-Becomes Daisy & Her Pups #21 & Chamber of Chills #21
5 10 15 33 44 55
21-30 4 8 12 27 36 45
31-50 3 7 10 21 28 35
51-80 3 6 9 18 24 30
81-99 3 6 9 18 23 28
100 3 7 10 21 28 35
101-124,126-130 3 6 9 16 20 24
125 (80 pgs.) 4 8 12 27 36 45
131-136,138,139 2 4 6 12 16 20
137,140-(80 pgs.) 4 8 12 25 33 42
141-147,149-154,156,160,164-167 2 4 6 12 16 20
148,155,157-159,161-163 are 68 pgs. 3 6 9 19 25 32
168-175 2 4 6 10 13 16
177-199 (no #176) 2 4 6 8 10 12
200 2 4 6 9 11 14
201-210,213-222 1 2 3 5 7 9
211,212-1st & 2nd app. Super Dagwood 2 4 6 8 10 12

BLOOD

Blood and Water #1 © Judd Winick & Tomm Coker

Blood Legacy: The Story of Ryan #1 © TCOW

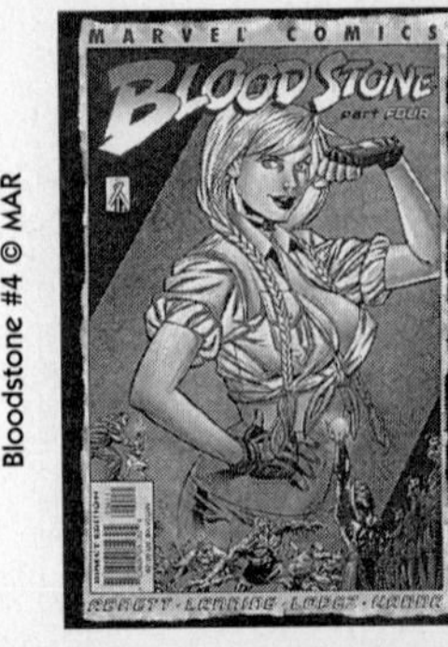

Bloodstone #4 © MAR

GD	VG	FN	VF	VF/NM	NM-
2.0	4.0	6.0	8.0	9.0	9.2

Marvel Comics (Epic Comics): Feb, 1988 - No. 4, Apr, 1988 ($3.25, mature)
1-4: DeMatteis scripts & Kent Williams c/a 3.50

BLOOD AND GLORY (Punisher & Captain America)
Marvel Comics: Oct, 1992 - No. 3, Dec, 1992 ($5.95, limited series)
1-3: 1-Embossed wraparound-c by Janson; Chichester & Clarke-s 6.00

BLOOD & ROSES: FUTURE PAST TENSE (Bob Hickey's...)
Sky Comics: Dec, 1993 ($2.25)
1-Silver ink logo 2.50

BLOOD & ROSES: SEARCH FOR THE TIME-STONE (Bob Hickey's...)
Sky Comics: Apr, 1994 ($2.50)
1 2.50

BLOOD AND SHADOWS
DC Comics (Vertigo): 1996 - Book 4, 1996 ($5.95, squarebound, mature)
Books 1-4: Joe R. Lansdale scripts; Mark A. Nelson-c/a. 6.00

BLOOD AND WATER
DC Comics (Vertigo): May, 2003 - No. 5, Sept, 2003 ($2.95, limited series)
1-5-Judd Winick-s/Tomm Coker-a/Brian Bolland-c 3.00

BLOOD: A TALE
DC Comics (Vertigo): Nov, 1996 - No. 4, Feb, 1997 ($2.95, limited series)
1-4: Reprints Epic series w/new-c; DeMatteis scripts; Kent Williams-c/a 3.00

BLOODBATH
DC Comics: Early Dec, 1993 - No. 2, Late Dec, 1993 ($3.50, 68 pgs.)
1-Neon ink-c; Superman app.; new Batman-c /app. 3.50
2-Hitman 2nd app. 1 2 3 4 5 7

BLOODFIRE
Lightning Comics: June, 1993 - No. 12, May, 1994 ($2.95)
1-($3.50)-Foil-c; 1st app. Bloodfire 3.50
2-12: 2-Origin; contracts HIV virus via transfusion. 5-Polybagged w/card & collectors warning on bag. 12-(5/94) 3.00
0-(Indicia reads June 1994, May on-c, $3.50) 3.50
.../Hellina 1 (7/95, $3.00) 3.00
.../Hellina 1 (7/95, $9.95)-Nude edition; Deodato-c 10.00
.../Hellina (8/95, $9.95)-Commemorative edition 10.00

BLOOD LEGACY
Image Comics (Top Cow): May, 2000 - No. 4, Nov, 2000; Apr, 2003 ($2.50/$4.99)
...: The Story of Ryan 1-4-Kerri Hawkins-s. 1-Andy Park-a(p); 3 covers 2.50
...: The Young Ones 1 (4/03, $4.99, one-shot) Basaldua-c/a 5.00
Preview Special ('00, $4.95) B&W flip-book w/The Magdalena Preview 5.00

BLOODLINES: A TALE FROM THE HEART OF AFRICA (See Tales From the Heart of Africa)
Marvel Comics (Epic Comics): 1992 ($5.95, 52 pgs.)
1-Story cont'd from Tales From... 6.00

BLOOD OF DRACULA
Apple Comics: Nov, 1987 - No. 20?, 1990 ($1.75/$1.95, B&W)($2.25 #14,16 on)
1-3,5-14,20: 1-10-Chadwick-c 3.00
4,16-19-Lost Frankenstein pgs. by Wrightson 5.00
15-Contains stereo flexidisc ($3.75) 4.00

BLOOD OF THE INNOCENT (See Warp Graphics Annual)
WaRP Graphics: 1/7/86 - No. 4, 1/28/86 (Weekly mini-series, mature)
1-4 2.50

BLOODPACK
DC Comics: Mar, 1995 - No. 4, June,1995 ($1.50, limited series)
1-4 2.25

BLOODPOOL
Image Comics (Extreme): Aug, 1995 - No. 4, Nov, 1995 ($2.50, limited series)
1-4: Jo Duffy scripts in all 2.50
Special (3/96, $2.50)-Jo Duffy scripts 2.50
Trade Paperback (1996, $12.95)-r/#1-4 13.00

BLOODSCENT
Comico: Oct, 1988 ($2.00, one-shot, Baxter paper)
1-Colan-p 2.50

BLOODSEED
Marvel Comics (Frontier Comics): Oct, 1993 - No. 2, Nov, 1993 ($1.95)
1,2: Sharp/Cam Smith-a 3.00

GD	VG	FN	VF	VF/NM	NM-
2.0	4.0	6.0	8.0	9.0	9.2

BLOODSHOT (See Eternal Warrior #4 & Rai #0)
Valiant/Acclaim Comics (Valiant): Feb, 1993 - No. 51, Aug, 1996 ($2.25/$2.50)
0-(3/94, $3.50)-Wraparound chromium-c by Quesada(p); origin 3.50
0-Gold variant; no cover price 5.00
Note: There is a "Platinum variant" ; press run error of Gold ed. (25 copies exist)
1-($3.50)-Chromium embossed-c by B. Smith w/poster 3.50
2-5,8-14: 3-$2.25-c begins; cont'd in Hard Corps #5. 4-Eternal Warrior-c/story. 5-Rai & Eternal Warrior app. 14-(3/94)-Reese-c(i) 2.25
6,7: 6-1st app. Ninjak (out of costume). 7-In costume 2.25
15(4/94)-51: 16-w/bound-in trading card. 51-Bloodshot dies? 2.25
Yearbook 1 (1994, $3.95) 4.00
Special 1 (3/94, $5.95)-Zeck-c/a(p); Last Stand 6.00

BLOODSHOT (Volume Two)
Acclaim Comics (Valiant): July, 1997 - No. 16, Oct, 1998 ($2.50)
1-16: 1-Two covers. 5-Copycat-c. X-O Manowar-c/app 2.50

BLOODSTONE
Marvel Comics: Dec, 2001 - No. 4, Mar, 2002 ($2.99)
1-4-Intro. Elsa Bloodstone; Abnett & Lanning-s/Lopez-a 3.00

BLOODSTREAM
Image Comics: Jan, 2004 - Present ($2.95)
1-Adam Shaw painted-a 3.00

BLOODSTRIKE (See Supreme V2#3)
Image Comics (Extreme Studios): 1993 - No. 22, May, 1995; No. 25, May, 1994 ($1.95/$2.50)
1-22, 25: Liefeld layouts in early issues. 1-Blood Brothers prelude. 2-1st app. Lethal. 5-1st app. Noble. 9-Black and White part 6 by Art Thibert; Liefeld pin-up. 9,10-Have coupon #3 & 7 for Extreme Prejudice #0. 10-(4/94). 11-(7/94). 16:Platt-c; Prophet app. 17-19-polybagged w/card . 25-(5/94)-Liefeld/Fraga-c 3.00
NOTE: *Giffen story/layouts-4-6.* ***Jae Lee*** *c-7, 8.* ***Rob Liefeld*** *layouts-1-3.* ***Art Thibert*** *c-6i.*

BLOODSTRIKE ASSASSIN
Image Comics (Extreme Studios): June, 1995 - No. 3, Aug, 1995; No. 0, Oct, 1995 ($2.50, limited series)
0-3: 3-(8/95)-Quesada-c. 0-(10/95)-Battlestone app. 3.00

BLOOD SWORD, THE
Jademan Comics: Aug, 1988 - No. 53, Dec, 1992 ($1.50/$1.95, 68 pgs.)
1-Kung Fu stories in all 3.00
2-53 3.00

BLOOD SWORD DYNASTY
Jademan Comics: 1989 -No. 41, Jan, 1993 ($1.25, 36 pgs.)
1-Ties into Blood Sword 2.50
2-41: Ties into Blood Sword 2.50

BLOOD SYNDICATE
DC Comics (Milestone): Apr, 1993 - No. 35, Feb, 1996 ($1.50/-$3.50)
1-($2.95)-Collector's Edition; polybagged with poster, trading card, & acid-free backing board (direct sale only) 3.50
1-9,11-24,26,27,29,33-34: 8-Intro Kwai. 15-Byrne-c. 16-Worlds Collide Pt. 6; Superman-c/app. 17-Worlds Collide Pt. 13. 29-(99¢); Long Hot Summer x-over 2.25
10,28,30-32: 10-Simonson-c. 30-Long Hot Summer x-over 2.50
25-($2.95, 52 pgs.) 3.00
35-Kwai disappears; last issue 3.50

BLOODWULF
Image Comics (Extreme): Feb, 1995 - No. 4, May, 1995 ($2.50, limited series)
1-4: 1-Liefeld-c w/4 diferent captions & alternate-c. 2.50
Summer Special (8/95, $2.50)-Jeff Johnson-c/a; Supreme app; story takes place between Legend of Supreme #3 & Supreme #23. 2.50

BLOODY MARY
DC Comics (Helix): Oct, 1996 - No. 4, Jan, 1997 ($2.25, limited series)
1-4: Garth Ennis scripts; Ezquerra-c/a in all 3.50

BLOODY MARY: LADY LIBERTY
DC Comics (Helix): Sept, 1997 - No. 4, Dec, 1997 ($2.50, limited series)
1-4: Garth Ennis scripts; Ezquerra-c/a in all 3.00

BLUE
Image Comics (Action Toys): Aug, 1999 - No. 2, Apr, 2000 ($2.50)
1,2-Aronowitz-s/Struzan-c 2.50

BLUEBEARD
Slave Labor Graphics: Nov, 1993 - No. 3, Mar, 1994 ($2.95, B&W, lim. series)

Blue Beetle #18 © FOX

Blue Beetle #12 © DC

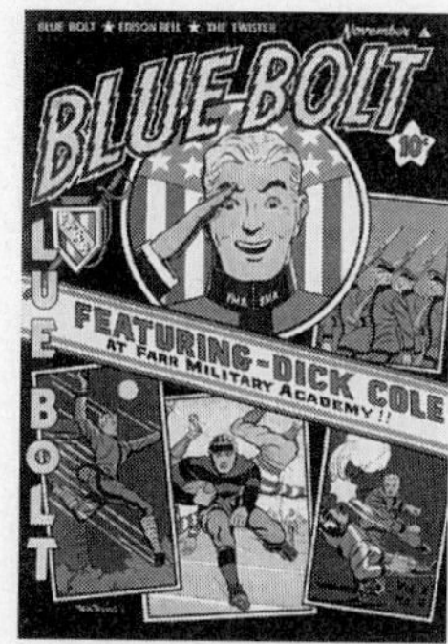

Blue Bolt V2#6 © NOVP

GD 2.0 VG 4.0 FN 6.0 VF 8.0 VF/NM 9.0 NM- 9.2

1-3: James Robinson scripts. 2-(12/93) 3.00
Trade paperback (6/94, $9.95) 13.00
Trade paperback (2nd printing, 7/96, $12.95)-New-c 13.00

BLUE BEETLE, THE (Also see All Top, Big-3, Mystery Men & Weekly Comic Magazine)
Fox Publ. No. 1-11, 31-60; Holyoke No. 12-30: Winter, 1939-40 - No. 57, 7/48; No. 58, 4/50 - No. 60, 8/50

1-Reprints from Mystery Men #1-5; Blue Beetle origin; Yarko the Great-r/from Wonder Comics /Wonderworld #2-5 all by Eisner; Master Magician app.; (Blue Beetle in 4 different costumes) 448 896 1344 3136 4818 6500
2-K-51-r by Powell/Wonderworld #8,9 152 304 456 950 1425 1900
3-Simon-c 112 224 336 700 1050 1400
4-Marijuana drug mention story 74 148 222 463 694 925
5-Zanzibar The Magician by Tuska 66 132 198 413 617 820
6-Dynamite Thor begins (1st); origin Blue Beetle 61 122 183 381 571 760
7,8-Dynamo app. in both. 8-Last Thor 55 110 165 340 510 680
9-12: 9,10-The Blackbird & The Gorilla app. in both. 10-Bondage/hypo-c. 11(2/42)-The Gladiator app. 12(6/42)-The Black Fury app. 50 100 150 300 450 600
13-V-Man begins (1st app.), ends #18; Kubert-a; centerfold spread 60 120 180 375 563 750
14,15-Kubert-a in both. 14-Intro. side-kick (c/text only), Sparky (called Spunky #17-19) 52 104 156 312 469 625
16-18: 17-Brodsky-c 42 84 126 252 376 500
19-Kubert-a 43 86 129 258 384 510
20-Origin/1st app. Tiger Squadron; Arabian Nights begin 46 92 138 276 413 550
21-26: 24-Intro. & only app. The Halo. 26-General Patton story & photo 35 70 105 201 288 370
27-Tamaa, Jungle Prince app. 33 66 99 190 270 350
28-30(2/44) 29 58 87 164 232 300
31(6/44), 33,34,36-40: 34-38-"The Threat from Saturn" serial. 27 54 81 155 218 280
32-Hitler-c 42 84 126 252 359 465
35-Extreme violence 33 66 99 190 270 350
41-45 (#43 exist?) 25 50 75 147 202 260
46-The Puppeteer app. 29 58 87 164 232 300
47-Kamen & Baker-a begin 120 240 360 750 1125 1500
48-50 96 192 288 600 900 1200
51,53 80 160 240 500 750 1000
52-Kamen bondage-c; true crime stories begin 120 240 360 750 1125 1500
54-Used in **SOTI**. Illo, "Children call these 'headlights' comics" 128 256 384 800 1200 1600
55-57: 56-Used in **SOTI**, pg. 145. 57(7/48)-Last Kamen issue; becomes Western Killers? 78 156 234 488 732 975
58(4/50)-60-No Kamen-a 17 34 51 98 134 170
NOTE: ***Kamen** a-47-51, 53, 55-57; c-47, 49-52. **Powell** a-4(2). Bondage-c 9-12, 46, 52.*

BLUE BEETLE (Formerly The Thing; becomes Mr. Muscles No. 22 on) (See Charlton Bullseye & Space Adventures)
Charlton Comics: No. 18, Feb, 1955 - No. 21, Aug, 1955

18,19-(Pre-1944-r). 18-Last pre-code issue. 19-Bouncer, Rocket Kelly-r 21 42 63 121 168 215
20-Joan Mason by Kamen 26 52 78 150 210 270
21-New material 19 38 57 109 152 195

BLUE BEETLE (Unusual Tales #1-49; Ghostly Tales #55 on)(See Captain Atom #83 & Charlton Bullseye)
Charlton Comics: V2#1, June, 1964 - V2#5, Mar-Apr, 1965; V3#50, July, 1965 - V3#54, Feb-Mar, 1966; #1, June, 1967 - #5, Nov, 1968

V2#1-Origin/1st S.A. app. Dan Garrett-Blue Beetle 9 18 27 65 93 120
2-5: 5-Weiss illo; 1st published-a? 6 12 18 40 55 70
V3#50-54-Formerly Unusual Tales 6 12 18 38 52 65
1(1967)-Question series begins by Ditko 11 22 33 75 110 145
2-Origin Ted Kord-Blue Beetle (see Capt. Atom #83 for 1st Ted Kord Blue Beetle); Dan Garrett x-over 6 12 18 40 55 70
3-5 (All Ditko-c/a in #1-5) 5 10 15 36 48 60
1,3(Modern Comics-1977)-Reprints 1 2 3 4 5 7
NOTE: *#6 only appeared in the fanzine 'The Charlton Portfolio.'*

BLUE BEETLE (Also see Americomics, Crisis On Infinite Earths, Justice League & Showcase '94 #2-4)
DC Comics: June, 1986 - No. 24, May, 1988

1-Origin retold; intro. Firefist 4.00
2-10,15-19,21-24: 2-Origin Firefist. 5-7-The Question app. 21-Millennium tie-in 2.25
11-14-New Teen Titans x-over 3.00
20-Justice League app.; Millennium tie-in 3.00

GD 2.0 VG 4.0 FN 6.0 VF 8.0 VF/NM 9.0 NM- 9.2

BLUEBERRY (See Lt. Blueberry & Marshal Blueberry)
Marvel Comics (Epic Comics): 1989 - No. 5, 1990 ($12.95/$14.95, graphic novel)

1,3,4,5-($12.95)-Moebius-a in all 15.00
2-($14.95) 17.00

BLUE BOLT
Funnies, Inc. No. 1/Novelty Press/Premium Group of Comics: June, 1940 - No. 101 (V10#2), Sept-Oct, 1949

V1#1-Origin Blue Bolt by Joe Simon, Sub-Zero Man, White Rider & Super Horse, Dick Cole, Wonder Boy & Sgt. Spook (1st app. of each) 304 608 912 1976 3038 4100
2-Simon & Kirby's 1st art & 1st super-hero (Blue Bolt) 166 332 498 1038 1557 2075
3-1 pg. Space Hawk by Wolverton; 2nd S&K-a on Blue Bolt (same cover date as Red Raven #1); 1st time S&K names app. in a comic; Simon-c 139 278 417 869 1305 1740
4,5-S&K-a in each; 5-Everett-a begins on Sub-Zero 126 252 378 788 1182 1575
6,8-10-S&K-a 118 236 354 738 1107 1475
7-S&K-c/a 130 260 390 813 1219 1625
11,12: 11-Robot-c 112 224 336 700 1050 1400
V2#1-Origin Dick Cole & The Twister; Twister x-over in Dick Cole, Sub-Zero, & Blue Bolt; origin Simba Karno who battles Dick Cole thru V2#5 & becomes main supporting character V2#6 on; battle-c 40 80 120 240 340 440
2-Origin The Twister retold in text 32 64 96 184 262 340
3-5: 5-Intro. Freezum 30 60 90 173 244 315
6-Origin Sgt. Spook retold 25 50 75 147 202 260
7-12: 7-Lois Blake becomes Blue Bolt's costume aide; last Twister. 12-Text-sty by Mickey Spillaine 22 44 66 124 172 220
V3#1-3 18 36 54 101 138 175
4-12: 4-Blue Bolt abandons costume 14 28 42 78 111 140
V4#1-Hitler, Tojo, Mussolini-c 34 68 102 196 278 360
V4#2-12: 3-Shows V4#3 on-c, V4#4 inside (9-10/43). 5-Infinity-c. 8-Last Sub-Zero 11 22 33 66 88 110
V5#1-8, V6#1-3,5-10, V7#1-12 11 22 33 63 84 105
V6#4-Racist cover 17 34 51 95 130 165
V8#1-6,8-12, V9#1-4,7,8, V10#1(#100),V10#2(#101)-Last Dick Cole, Blue Bolt 10 20 30 58 77 95
V8#7,V9#6,9-L. B. Cole-c 22 44 66 124 172 220
V9#5-Classic fish in the face-c 20 40 60 112 156 200
NOTE: ***Everett** c-V1#4, 11, V2#1, 2. **Gustavson** a-V1#1-12, V2#1-7. **Kiefer** c-V3#1. **Rico** a-V6#10, V7#4. Blue Bolt not in V9#8.*

BLUE BOLT (Becomes Ghostly Weird Stories #120 on; continuation of Novelty Blue Bolt) (...Weird Tales of Terror #111,112,...Weird Tales #113-119)
Star Publications: No. 102, Nov-Dec, 1949 - No. 119, May-June, 1953

102-The Chameleon, & Target app. 37 74 111 213 299 385
103,104-The Chameleon app. 104-Last Target 35 70 105 201 283 365
105-Origin Blue Bolt (from #1) retold by Simon; Chameleon & Target app.; opium den story 52 104 156 312 469 625
106-Blue Bolt by S&K begins; Spacehawk reprints from Target by Wolverton begin, ends #110; Sub-Zero begins; ends #109 50 100 150 300 450 600
107-110: 108-Last S&K Blue Bolt reprint. 109-Wolverton-c(r)/inside Spacehawk splash. 110-Target app. 48 96 144 288 432 575
111,112: 111-Red Rocket & The Mask-r; last Blue Bolt; 1pg. L. B. Cole-a. 112-Last Torpedo Man app. 44 88 132 264 395 525
113-Wolverton's Spacehawk-r/Target V3#7 46 92 138 276 413 550
114,116: 116-Jungle Jo-r 44 88 132 264 395 525
115-Sgt. Spook app. 46 92 138 276 413 550
117-Jo-Jo & Blue Bolt-r 45 90 135 270 403 535
118-"White Spirit" by Wood 46 92 138 276 413 550
119-Disbrow/Cole-c; Jungle Jo-r 45 90 135 270 403 535
Accepted Reprint #103(1957?, nd) 12 24 36 71 96 120
NOTE: ***L. B. Cole** c-102-108, 110 on. **Disbrow** a-112(2), 113(3), 114(2), 115(2), 116-118. **Hollingsworth** a-117. **Palais** a-112r. Sci/Fi c-105-110. Horror c-111.*

BLUE BULLETEER, THE (Also see Femforce Special)
AC Comics: 1989 ($2.25, B&W, one-shot)

1-Origin by Bill Black; Bill Ward-a 4.00

BLUE BULLETEER (Also see Femforce Special)
AC Comics: 1996 ($5.95, B&W, one-shot)

1-Photo-c 6.00

BLUE CIRCLE COMICS (Also see Red Circle Comics, Blazing Comics & Roly Poly Comic Book)
Enwil Associates/Rural Home: June, 1944 - No. 6, Apr, 1945

Blue Devil #3 © DC

Blue Monday: Nobody's Fool © Chynna Clugston-Major

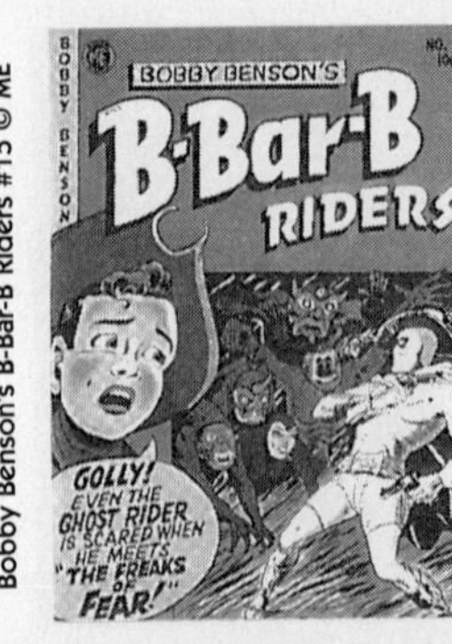

Bobby Benson's B-Bar-B Riders #15 © ME

GD VG FN VF VF/NM NM-
2.0 4.0 6.0 8.0 9.0 9.2

1-The Blue Circle begins (1st app.); origin & 1st app. Steel Fist 31 62 93 178 252 325
2 20 40 60 112 156 200
3-Hitler parody-c 26 52 78 150 210 270
4-6: 5-Last Steel Fist. 16 32 48 92 126 160
6-(Dated 4/45, Vol. 2#3 inside)-Leftover covers to #6 were later restapled over early 1950's coverless comics; variations of the coverless comics exist. Colossal Features known. 16 32 48 92 126 160

BLUE DEVIL (See Fury of Firestorm #24, Underworld Unleashed, Starman (2nd) #38)
DC Comics: June, 1984 - No. 31, Dec, 1986 (75¢/$1.25)

1 4.00
2-16,19-31: 4-Origin Nebiros. 7-Gil Kane-a. 8-Giffen-a 2.50
17,18-Crisis x-over 3.00
Annual 1 (11/85)-Team-ups w/Black Orchid, Creeper, Demon, Madame Xanadu, Man-Bat & Phantom Stranger 3.00

BLUE MONDAY: ... (one-shots)
Oni Press: Feb, 2002 - Present (B&W, Chynna Clugston-Major-s/a/c in all)

Dead Man's Party (10/02, $2.95) Dan Brereton painted back-c 3.00
Inbetween Days (9/03, $9.95, 8" x 5-1/2") r/Dead Man's Party, Lovecats, & Nobody's Fool 10.00
Lovecats (2/02, $2.95) Valentine's Day themed 3.00
Nobody's Fool (2/03, $2.95) April Fool's Day themed 3.00

BLUE MONDAY: ABSOLUTE BEGINNERS
Oni Press: Feb, 2001 - No. 4, Sept, 2001 ($2.95, B&W)

1-4-Chynna Clugston-Major-s/a/c 3.00
TPB (12/01, $11.95, 8" x 6") r/series 12.00

BLUE MONDAY: THE KIDS ARE ALRIGHT
Oni Press: Feb, 2000 - No. 3, May, 2000 ($2.95, B&W)

1-3-Chynna Clugston-Major-s/a/c. 1-Variant-c by Warren. 2-Dorkin-c 3.00
3-Variant cover by J. Scott Campbell 4.00
TPB (12/00, $10.95, digest-sized) r/#1-3 & earlier short stories 11.00

BLUE PHANTOM, THE
Dell Publishing Co.: June-Aug, 1962

1(01-066-208)-by Fred Fredericks 4 8 12 24 32 40

BLUE RIBBON COMICS (...Mystery Comics No. 9-18)
MLJ Magazines: Nov, 1939 - No. 22, Mar, 1942 (1st MLJ series)

1-Dan Hastings, Richy the Amazing Boy, Rang-A-Tang the Wonder Dog begin (1st app. of each); Little Nemo app. (not by W. McCay); Jack Cole-a(3) (1st MLJ comic) 370 740 1110 2405 3703 5000
2-Bob Phantom, Silver Fox (both in #3), Rang-A-Tang Club & Cpl. Collins begin (1st app. of each); Jack Cole-a 136 272 408 850 1275 1700
3-J. Cole-a 86 172 258 538 807 1075
4-Doc Strong, The Green Falcon, & Hercules begin (1st app. each); origin & 1st app. The Fox & Ty-Gor, Son of the Tiger 96 192 288 600 900 1200
5-8: 8-Last Hercules; 6,7-Biro, Meskin-a. 7-Fox app. on-c 64 128 192 400 600 800
9-(Scarce)-Origin & 1st app. Mr. Justice (2/41) 296 592 888 1850 2775 3700
10-13: 12-Last Doc Strong. 13-Inferno, the Flame Breather begins, ends #19; Devil-c 102 204 306 638 957 1275
14,15,17,18: 15-Last Green Falcon 85 170 255 531 796 1060
16-Origin & 1st app. Captain Flag (9/41) 165 330 495 1031 1546 2060
19-22: 20-Last Ty-Gor. 22-Origin Mr. Justice retold 85 170 255 531 796 1060
NOTE: *Biro c-3-5; a-2 (Cpl. Collins & Scoop Cody).* ***S. Cooper*** *c-9-17. 20-22 contain "Tales From the Witch's Cauldron" (same strip as "Stories of the Black Witch" in Zip Comics). Mr. Justice c-9-18. Captain Flag c-16(w/Mr. Justice), 19-22.*

BLUE RIBBON COMICS (Becomes Teen-Age Diary Secrets #4)
(Also see Approved Comics, Blue Ribbon Comics and Heckle &Jeckle)
Blue Ribbon (St. John): Feb, 1949 - No. 6, Aug, 1949

1,3-Heckle & Jeckle (Terrytoons) 10 20 30 56 73 90
2(4/49)-Diary Secrets; Baker-c 23 46 69 130 183 235
4(6/49)-Teen-Age Diary Secrets; Baker c/a(2) 23 46 69 130 183 235
5(8/49)-Teen-Age Diary Secrets; Oversize; photo-c; Baker-a(2)- Continues as Teen-Age Diary Secrets 29 58 87 164 232 300
6-Dinky Duck(8/49)(Terrytoons) 7 14 21 35 43 50

BLUE RIBBON COMICS
Red Circle Prod./Archie Ent. No. 5 on: Nov, 1983 - No. 14, Dec, 1984

1-S&K-r/Advs. of the Fly #1,2; Williamson/Torres-r/Fly #2; Ditko-c 6.00
2-7,9,10: 3-Origin Steel Sterling. 5-S&K Shield-r; new Kirby-c. 6,7-The Fox app. 5.00
8-Toth centerspread; Black Hood app.; Neal Adams-a(r) 6.00
11,13,14: 11-Black Hood. 13-Thunder Bunny. 14-Web & Jaguar 5.00
12-Thunder Agents; Noman new Ditko-a 6.00
NOTE: ***N. Adams*** *a(r)-8.* ***Buckler*** *a-4i.* ***Nino*** *a-2i.* ***McWilliams*** *a-8.* ***Morrow*** *a-8.*

BLUE STREAK (See Holyoke One-Shot No. 8)

BLUNTMAN AND CHRONIC TPB(Also see Jay and Silent Bob, Clerks, and Oni Double Feature)
Image Comics: Dec, 2001 ($14.95, TPB)

nn-Tie-in for "Jay & Silent Bob Strike Back" movie; new Kevin Smith-s/Michael Oeming-a; r/app. from Oni Double Feature #12 in color; Ben Affleck & Jason Lee afterwords 15.00

BLYTHE (Marge's)
Dell Publishing Co.: No. 1072, Jan-Mar, 1960

Four Color 1072 6 12 18 40 55 70

B-MAN (See Double-Dare Adventures)

BO (Tom Cat #4 on) (Also see Big Shot #29 & Dixie Dugan)
Charlton Comics Group: June, 1955 - No. 3, Oct, 1955 (A dog)

1-3: Newspaper reprints by Frank Beck 8 16 24 43 54 65

BOATNIKS, THE (See Walt Disney Showcase No. 1)

BOB BURDEN'S ORIGINAL MYSTERYMEN PRESENTS
Dark Horse Comics: 1999 - No. 4 ($2.95/$3.50)

1-3-Bob Burden-s/Sadowski-a(p) 3.50
4-($3.50) All Villain issue 3.50

BOBBY BENSON'S B-BAR-B RIDERS (Radio) (See Best of The West, The Lemonade Kid & Model Fun)
Magazine Enterprises/AC Comics: May-June, 1950 - No. 20, May-June, 1953

1-The Lemonade Kid begins; Powell-a (Scarce) 42 84 126 252 376 500
2 18 36 54 101 138 175
3-5: 4,5-Lemonade Kid-c (#4-Spider-c) 14 28 42 79 107 135
6-8,10 13 26 39 72 100 125
9,11,13-Frazetta-c; Ghost Rider in #13-15 by Ayers-a. 13-Ghost Rider-c 34 68 102 196 278 360
12,17-20: 20-(A-1 #88) 11 22 33 66 88 110
14-Decapitation/Bondage-c & story; classic horror-c 26 52 78 147 206 265
15-Ghost Rider-c 20 40 60 112 156 200
16-Photo-c 14 28 42 79 107 135
1 (1990, $2.75, B&W)-Reprints; photo-c & inside covers 3.00
NOTE: ***Ayers*** *a-13-15, 20.* ***Powell*** *a-1-12(4 ea.), 13(3), 14-16(Red Hawk only); c-1-8,1 0, 12. Lemonade Kid in most 1-13.*

BOBBY COMICS
Universal Phoenix Features: May, 1946

1-By S. M. Iger 8 16 24 46 58 70

BOBBY SHERMAN (TV)
Charlton Comics: Feb, 1972 - No. 7, Oct, 1972

1-Based on TV show "Getting Together" 5 10 15 33 44 55
2-7: 2,4-Photo-c 3 7 10 21 28 35

BOB COLT (Movie star)(See XMas Comics)
Fawcett Publications: Nov, 1950 - No. 10, May, 1952

1-Bob Colt, his horse Buckskin & sidekick Pablo begin; photo front/back-c begin 41 82 123 246 348 450
2 25 50 75 147 202 260
3-5 20 40 60 115 160 205
6-Flying Saucer story 18 36 54 101 138 175
7-10: 9-Last photo back-c 16 32 48 92 126 160

BOB HOPE (See Adventures of... & Calling All Boys #12)

BOB MARLEY, TALE OF THE TUFF GONG (Music star)
Marvel Comics: Aug, 1994 - No, 3, Nov, 1994 ($5.95, limited series)

1-3 6.00

BOB POWELL'S TIMELESS TALES
Eclipse Comics: March, 1989 ($2.00, B&W)

1-Powell-r/Black Cat #5 (Scarlet Arrow), 9 & Race for the Moon #1 3.00

BOB SCULLY, THE TWO-FISTED HICK DETECTIVE (Also see Advs. of Detective Ace King and Detective Dan)
Humor Publ. Co.: No date (1933) (36 pgs., 9-1/2x11", B&W, paper-c; 10¢-c)

nn-By Howard Dell; not reprints; along with Advs. of Det. Ace King and Detective Dan, the first comic w/original art & the first of a single theme; has a blue 2-tone cover 350 700 1050 2800 - -

BOB SON OF BATTLE
Dell Publishing Co.: No. 729, Nov, 1956

Bodycount #1 © MS

Bonanza #21 © GK

Bone #52 © Jeff Smith

	GD 2.0	VG 4.0	FN 6.0	VF 8.0	VF/NM 9.0	NM- 9.2
Four Color 729	4	8	12	27	36	45

BOB STEELE WESTERN (Movie star)
Fawcett Publications/AC Comics: Dec, 1950 - No. 10, June, 1952; 1990

	GD	VG	FN	VF	VF/NM	NM-
1-Bob Steele & his horse Bullet begin; photo front/back-c begin	56	112	168	350	525	700
2	32	64	96	182	259	335
3-5: 4-Last photo back-c	23	46	69	132	186	240
6-10: 10-Last photo-c	19	38	57	107	149	190
1 (1990, $2.75, B&W)-Bob Steele & Rocky Lane reprints; photo-c & inside covers						3.00

BOB SWIFT (Boy Sportsman)
Fawcett Publications: May, 1951 - No. 5, Jan, 1952

	GD	VG	FN	VF	VF/NM	NM-
1	10	20	30	56	73	90
2-5: Saunders painted-c #1-5	6	12	18	31	38	45

BOB, THE GALACTIC BUM
DC Comics: Feb, 1995 - No. 4, June, 1995 ($1.95, limited series)

1-4: 1-Lobo app. 2.50

BODY BAGS
Dark Horse Comics (Blanc Noir): Sept, 1996 - No. 4, Jan, 1997 ($2.95, mini-series, mature) (1st Blanc Noir series)

	GD	VG	FN	VF	VF/NM	NM-
1-Jason Pearson-c/a/scripts in all. 1-Intro Clownface & Panda.	1	2	3	5	6	8
2	1	3	4	6	8	10
3,4						6.00

BODYCOUNT (Also see Casey Jones & Raphael)
Image Comics (Highbrow Entertainment): Mar, 1996 - No. 4, July, 1996 ($2.50, lim. series)

1-4: Kevin Eastman-a(p)/scripts; Simon Bisley-c/a(i); Turtles app. 2.50

BODY DOUBLES (See Resurrection Man)
DC Comics: Oct, 1999 - No. 4, Jan, 2000 ($2.50, limited series)

1-4-Lanning & Abnett-s. 2-Black Canary app. 4-Wonder Woman app. 2.50
...(Villains) (2/98, $1.95, one-shot) 1-Pearson-c; Deadshot app. 2.50

BOFFO LAFFS
Paragraphics: 1986 - No. 5 ($2.50/$1.95)

1-($2.50) First comic cover with hologram 3.00
2-5 2.25

BOHOS
Image Comics (Flypaper Press): June, 1998 - No. 3 ($2.95)

1-3-Whorf-s/Penaranda-a 3.00

BOLD ADVENTURES
Pacific Comics: Oct, 1983 - No. 3, June, 1984 ($1.50)

1-Time Force, Anaconda, & The Weirdling begin 3.00
2,3: 2-Soldiers of Fortune begins. 3-Spitfire 3.00
NOTE: *Kaluta c-3.* ***Nebres*** *a-1-3.* ***Nino*** *a-2, 3.* ***Severin*** *a-3.*

BOLD STORIES (Also see Candid Tales & It Rhymes With Lust)
Kirby Publishing Co.: Mar, 1950 - July, 1950 (Digest size, 144 pgs.)

	GD	VG	FN	VF	VF/NM	NM-
March issue (Very Rare) - Contains "The Ogre of Paris" by Wood	128	256	384	800	1200	1600
May issue (Very Rare) - Contains "The Cobra's Kiss" by Graham Ingels (21 pgs.)	110	220	330	688	1032	1375
July issue (Very Rare) - Contains "The Ogre of Paris" by Wood	96	192	288	600	900	1200

BOLT AND STAR FORCE SIX
Americomics: 1984 ($1.75)

1-Origin Bolt & Star Force Six 3.00
Special 1 (1984, $2.00, 52pgs., B&W) 3.00

BOMBARDIER (See Bee 29, the Bombardier & Cinema Comics Herald)

BOMBAST
Topps Comics: 1993 ($2.95, one-shot) (Created by Jack Kirby)

1-Polybagged w/Kirbychrome trading card; Savage Dragon app.; Kirby-c; has coupon for Amberchrome Secret City Saga #0 3.00

BOMBA THE JUNGLE BOY (TV)
National Periodical Publ.: Sept-Oct, 1967 - No. 7, Sept-Oct, 1968 (12¢)

	GD	VG	FN	VF	VF/NM	NM-
1-Intro. Bomba; Infantino/Anderson-c	4	8	12	25	33	42
2-7	3	6	9	16	20	25

BOMBER COMICS
Elliot Publ. Co./Melverne Herald/Farrell/Sunrise Times: Mar, 1944 - No. 4, Winter, 1944-45

	GD 2.0	VG 4.0	FN 6.0	VF 8.0	VF/NM 9.0	NM- 9.2
1-Wonder Boy, & Kismet, Man of Fate begin	70	140	210	438	657	875
2-Hitler-c	55	110	165	338	507	675
3: 2-4-Have Classics Comics ad to HRN 20	42	84	126	252	359	465
4-Hitler, Tojo & Mussolini-c; Sensation Comics #13-c/swipe; has Classics Comics ad to HRN 20.	61	122	183	381	573	765

BONANZA (TV)
Dell/Gold Key: June-Aug, 1960 - No. 37, Aug, 1970 (All Photo-c)

	GD	VG	FN	VF	VF/NM	NM-
Four Color 1110 (6-8/60)	36	72	108	270	405	540
Four Color 1221,1283, & #01070-207, 01070-210	20	40	60	140	205	270
1(12/62-Gold Key)	21	42	63	147	216	285
2	11	22	33	77	114	150
3-10	9	18	27	65	93	120
11-20	7	14	21	51	71	90
21-37: 29-Reprints	6	12	18	43	59	75

BONE
Cartoon Books #1-20, 28 on/Image Comics #21-27: July, 1991 - Present ($2.95, B&W)

	GD	VG	FN	VF	VF/NM	NM-
1-Jeff Smith-c/a in all	7	14	21	51	71	90
1-2nd printing	2	4	6	8	10	12
1-3rd thru 5th printings						4.00
2-1st printing	4	8	12	27	36	45
2-2nd & 3rd printings						4.00
3-1st printing	3	7	10	21	28	35
3-2nd thru 4th printings						4.00
4,5	2	4	6	11	14	18
6-10	1	2	3	5	7	9
11-37: 21-1st Image issue						4.00
13 1/2 (1/95, Wizard)	1	3	4	6	8	10
13 1/2 (Gold)	2	4	6	8	10	12
38-($4.95) Three covers by Miller, Ross, Smith						5.00
39-53-($2.95)						3.00
1-27-($2.95): 1-Image reprints begin w/new-c. 2-Allred pin-up.						3.00
... Holiday Special (1993, giveaway)						3.00
... Reader -($9.95) Behind the scenes info						10.00
... Sourcebook-San Diego Edition						3.00
...10th Anniversary Edition (8/01, $5.95) r/#1 in color; came with figure						6.00
Complete Bone Adventures Vol 1,2 ('93, '94, $12.95, r/#1-6 & #7-12)						13.00
Volume 1-($19.95, hard-c)-"Out From Boneville"						20.00
Volume 1-($12.95, soft-c)						13.00
Volume 2,5-($22.95, hard-c)-"The Great Cow Race" & "Rock Jaw"						23.00
Volume 2,5-($14.95, soft-c)						15.00
Volume 3,4-($24.95, hard-c)-"Eyes of the Storm" & "The Dragonslayer"						25.00
Volume 3,4,7-($16.95, soft-c)						17.00
Volume 6-($15.95, soft-c)-"Old Man's Cave"						16.00
Volume 7-($24.95, hard-c)-"Ghost Circles"						25.00
Volume 8-($23.95, hard-c)-"Treasure Hunters"						24.00

NOTE: *Printings not listed sell for cover price.*

BONGO (See Story Hour Series)

BONGO & LUMPJAW (Disney, see Walt Disney Showcase #3)
Dell Publishing Co.: No. 706, June, 1956; No. 886, Mar, 1958

	GD	VG	FN	VF	VF/NM	NM-
Four Color 706 (#1)	6	12	18	43	59	75
Four Color 886	5	10	15	36	48	60

BONGO COMICS PRESENTS RADIOACTIVE MAN (See Radioactive Man)

BON VOYAGE (See Movie Classics)

BOOF
Image Comics (Todd McFarlane Prod.): July, 1994 - No. 6, Dec, 1994 ($1.95)

1-6 2.25

BOOF AND THE BRUISE CREW
Image Comics (Todd McFarlane Prod.): July, 1994 - No. 6, Dec, 1994 ($1.95)

1-6 2.25

BOOK AND RECORD SET (See Power Record Comics)

BOOK OF ALL COMICS
William H. Wise: 1945 (196 pgs.)(Inside f/c has Green Publ. blacked out)

	GD	VG	FN	VF	VF/NM	NM-
nn-Green Mask, Puppeteer & The Bouncer	42	84	126	252	359	465

BOOK OF ANTS, THE
Artisan Entertainment: 1998 ($2.95, B&W)

1-Based on the movie Pi; Aronofsky-s 3.00

BOOK OF BALLADS AND SAGAS, THE
Green Man Press: Oct, 1995 - No. 4 ($2.95/$3.50/$3.25, B&W)

Book of Fate #4 © DC

Books of Magic #8 © DC

Born #1 © MAR

	GD 2.0	VG 4.0	FN 6.0	VF 8.0	VF/NM 9.0	NM- 9.2
1-4: 1-Vess-c/a; Gaiman story.						3.50

BOOK OF COMICS, THE
William H. Wise: No date (1944) (25¢, 132 pgs.)

	GD 2.0	VG 4.0	FN 6.0	VF 8.0	VF/NM 9.0	NM- 9.2
nn-Captain V app.	40	80	120	240	340	440

BOOK OF FATE, THE (See Fate)
DC Comics: Feb, 1997 - No. 12, Jan, 1998 ($2.25/$2.50)

	GD 2.0	VG 4.0	FN 6.0	VF 8.0	VF/NM 9.0	NM- 9.2
1-12: 4-Two-Face-c/app. 6-Convergence. 11-Sentinel app.						3.00

BOOK OF LOVE (See Fox Giants)

BOOK OF NIGHT, THE
Dark Horse Comics: July, 1987 - No. 3, 1987 ($1.75, B&W)

	GD 2.0	VG 4.0	FN 6.0	VF 8.0	VF/NM 9.0	NM- 9.2
1-3: Reprints from Epic Illustrated; Vess-a						2.25
TPB-r/#1-3						15.00
Hardcover-Black-c with red crest						100.00
Hardcover w/slipcase (1991) signed and numbered						50.00

BOOK OF THE DEAD
Marvel Comics: Dec, 1993 - No. 4, Mar, 1994 ($1.75, limited series, 52 pgs.)

	GD 2.0	VG 4.0	FN 6.0	VF 8.0	VF/NM 9.0	NM- 9.2
1-4: 1-Ploog Frankenstein & Morrow Man-Thing-r begin; Wrightson-r/Chamber of Darkness #7. 2-Morrow new painted-c; Chaykin/Morrow Man-Thing; Krigstein-r/Uncanny Tales #54; r/Fear #10. 3-r/Astonishing Tales #10 & Starlin Man-Thing. 3,4-Painted-c						5.00

BOOKS OF FAERIE, THE
DC Comics (Vertigo): Mar, 1997 - No. 3, May,1997 ($2.50, limited series)

	GD 2.0	VG 4.0	FN 6.0	VF 8.0	VF/NM 9.0	NM- 9.2
1-3-Gross-a						3.00
TPB (1998, $14.95) r/#1-3 & Arcana Annual #1						15.00

BOOKS OF FAERIE, THE : AUBERON'S TALE
DC Comics (Vertigo): Aug, 1998 - No. 3, Oct,1998 ($2.50, limited series)

	GD 2.0	VG 4.0	FN 6.0	VF 8.0	VF/NM 9.0	NM- 9.2
1-3-Gross-a						3.00

BOOKS OF FAERIE, THE : MOLLY'S STORY
DC Comics (Vertigo): Sept, 1999 - No. 4, Dec,1999 ($2.50, limited series)

	GD 2.0	VG 4.0	FN 6.0	VF 8.0	VF/NM 9.0	NM- 9.2
1-4-Ney Rieber-s/Mejia-a						3.00

BOOKS OF MAGIC
DC Comics: 1990 - No. 4, 1991 ($3.95, 52 pgs., limited series, mature)

	GD 2.0	VG 4.0	FN 6.0	VF 8.0	VF/NM 9.0	NM- 9.2
1-Bolton painted-c/a; Phantom Stranger app.; Gaiman scripts in all	1	3	4	6	8	10
2,3: 2-John Constantine, Dr. Fate, Spectre, Deadman app. 3-Dr. Occult app.; minor Sandman app.	1	2	3	4	5	7
4-Early Death-c/app. (early 1991)	1	2	3	5	6	8
Trade paperback-($19.95)-Reprints limited series						20.00

BOOKS OF MAGIC (Also see Hunter: The Age of Magic and Names of Magic)
DC Comics (Vertigo): May, 1994 - No. 75, Aug, 2000 ($1.95/$2.50, mature)

	GD 2.0	VG 4.0	FN 6.0	VF 8.0	VF/NM 9.0	NM- 9.2
1-Charles Vess-c	2	4	6	8	10	12
1-Platinum	2	4	6	14	18	22
2-4: 4-Death app.	1	2	3	4	5	7
5-14; Charles Vess-c						4.00
15-50: 15-$2.50-c begins. 22-Kaluta-c. 25-Death-c/app; Bachalo-c						3.00
51-75: 51-Peter Gross-s/a begins. 55-Medley-a						2.50
Annual 1,2 (2/97, 2/98, $3.95)						4.00
Bindings (1995, $12.95, TPB)-r/#1-4						13.00
Death After Death (2001, $19.95, TPB)-r/#42-50						20.00
Girl in the Box (1999, $14.95, TPB)-r/#26-32						15.00
Reckonings (1997, $12.95, TPB)-r/#14-20						13.00
Summonings (1996, $17.50, TPB)-r/#5-13, Vertigo Rave #1						17.50
The Burning Girl (2000, $17.95, TPB)-r/#33-41						18.00
Transformations (1998, $12.95, TPB)-r/#21-25						13.00

BOONDOGGLE
Knight Press: Mar, 1995 - No. 4 ($2.95, B&W)

	GD 2.0	VG 4.0	FN 6.0	VF 8.0	VF/NM 9.0	NM- 9.2
1-4: Stegelin-c/a/scripts						3.00

BOONDOGGLE
Caliber Press: Jan, 1997 - No. 2 ($2.95, B&W)

	GD 2.0	VG 4.0	FN 6.0	VF 8.0	VF/NM 9.0	NM- 9.2
1,2: Stegelin-c/a/scripts						3.00

BOOSTER GOLD (See Justice League #4)
DC Comics: Feb, 1986 - No. 25, Feb, 1988 (75¢)

	GD 2.0	VG 4.0	FN 6.0	VF 8.0	VF/NM 9.0	NM- 9.2
1-Dan Jurgens-s/a(p)						3.00
2-25: 4-Rose & Thorn app. 6-Origin. 6,7,23-Superman app. 8,9-LSH app. 22-JLI app. 24,25-Millennium tie-ins						2.50

NOTE: *Austin c-22i. Byrne c-23i.*

BOOTS AND HER BUDDIES
Standard Comics/Visual Editions/Argo (NEA Service):
No. 5, 0/48 - No. 9, 9/49; 12/55 - No. 3, 1956

	GD 2.0	VG 4.0	FN 6.0	VF 8.0	VF/NM 9.0	NM- 9.2
5-Strip-r	17	34	51	95	130	165
6,8	11	22	33	63	84	105
7-(Scarce)	13	26	39	76	103	130
9-(Scarce)-Frazetta-a (2 pgs.)	26	52	78	150	210	270
1-3(Argo-1955-56)-Reprints	6	12	18	31	38	45

BOOTS & SADDLES (TV)
Dell Publ. Co.: No. 919, July, 1958; No. 1029, Sept, 1959; No. 1116, Aug, 1960

	GD 2.0	VG 4.0	FN 6.0	VF 8.0	VF/NM 9.0	NM- 9.2
Four Color 919 (#1)-Photo-c	9	18	27	60	85	110
Four Color 1029, 1116-Photo-c	6	12	18	40	55	70

BORDERLINE
Friction Press: June, 1992 ($2.25, B&W)

	GD 2.0	VG 4.0	FN 6.0	VF 8.0	VF/NM 9.0	NM- 9.2
0-Ashcan edition; 1st app. of Cliff Broadway						2.25
1-Painted-c						3.00
1-Special Edition (bagged w/ photo, S&N)						4.00

BORDER PATROL
P. L. Publishing Co.: May-June, 1951 - No. 3, Sept-Oct, 1951

	GD 2.0	VG 4.0	FN 6.0	VF 8.0	VF/NM 9.0	NM- 9.2
1	13	26	39	76	103	130
2,3	9	18	27	52	66	80

BORDER WORLDS (Also see Megaton Man)
Kitchen Sink Press: 7/86 - No. 7, 1987; V2#1, 1990 - No. 4, 1990 ($1.95-$2.00, B&W, mature)

	GD 2.0	VG 4.0	FN 6.0	VF 8.0	VF/NM 9.0	NM- 9.2
1-7, V2#1-4: Donald Simpson-c/a/scripts						3.00

BORIS KARLOFF TALES OF MYSTERY (TV) (...Thriller No. 1,2)
Gold Key: No. 3, April, 1963 - No. 97, Feb, 1980

	GD 2.0	VG 4.0	FN 6.0	VF 8.0	VF/NM 9.0	NM- 9.2
3-5-(Two #5's, 10/63,11/63): 5-(10/63)-11 pgs. Toth-a.	4	8	12	29	40	50
6-8,10: 10-Orlando-a	4	8	12	22	30	38
9-Wood-a	4	8	12	24	32	40
11-Williamson-a, 8 pgs.; Orlando-a, 5 pgs.	4	8	12	24	32	40
12-Torres, McWilliams-a; Orlando-a(2)	3	6	9	19	25	32
13,14,16-20	3	6	9	18	23	28
15-Crandall	3	6	9	18	24	30
21-Jeff Jones-a(3 pgs.) "The Screaming Skull"	3	6	9	18	24	30
22-Last 12¢ issue	2	4	6	14	18	22
23-30: 23-Reprint; photo-c	2	4	6	12	16	20
31-50: 36-Weiss-a	2	4	6	10	13	16
51-74: 74-Origin & 1st app. Taurus	2	4	6	8	10	12
75-79,87-97: 90-r/Torres, McWilliams-a/#12; Morrow-c	1	2	3	5	7	9
80-86-(52 pgs.)	2	4	6	8	10	12
Story Digest 1(7/70-Gold Key)-All text/illos.; 148pp.	5	10	15	33	44	55

(See Mystery Comics Digest No. 2, 5, 8, 11, 14, 17, 20, 23, 26)
NOTE: ***Bolle** a-51-54, 56, 58, 59. **McWilliams** a-12, 14, 18, 19, 72, 80, 81, 93. **Orlando** a-11-15, 21. Reprints: 78, 81-86, 88, 90, 92, 95, 97.*

BORIS KARLOFF THRILLER (TV) (Becomes Boris Karloff Tales...)
Gold Key: Oct, 1962 - No. 2, Jan, 1963 (84 pgs.)

	GD 2.0	VG 4.0	FN 6.0	VF 8.0	VF/NM 9.0	NM- 9.2
1-Photo-c	10	20	30	67	96	125
2	6	12	18	43	59	75

BORIS THE BEAR
Dark Horse Comics/Nicotat Comics #13 on: Aug, 1986 - No. 34, 1990 ($1.50/$1.75/$1.95, B&W)

	GD 2.0	VG 4.0	FN 6.0	VF 8.0	VF/NM 9.0	NM- 9.2
1 , Annual 1 (1988, $2.50)						3.00
1 (2nd printing),2,3,4A,4B,5-12, 14-34: 8-(44 pgs.)						2.25
13-1st Nicotat Comics issue						3.00

BORIS THE BEAR INSTANT COLOR CLASSICS
Dark Horse Comics: July, 1987 - No. 3, 1987 ($1.75/$1.95)

	GD 2.0	VG 4.0	FN 6.0	VF 8.0	VF/NM 9.0	NM- 9.2
1-3						2.25

BORN
Marvel Comics: 2003 - No. 4, 2003 ($3.50, limited series)

	GD 2.0	VG 4.0	FN 6.0	VF 8.0	VF/NM 9.0	NM- 9.2
1-4-Frank Castle (the Punisher) in 1971 Vietnam; Ennis-s/Robertson-a						3.50

BORN AGAIN
Spire Christian Comics (Fleming H. Revell Co.): 1978 (39¢)

	GD 2.0	VG 4.0	FN 6.0	VF 8.0	VF/NM 9.0	NM- 9.2
nn-Watergate, Nixon, etc.	1	2	3	5	7	9

BOUNCER, THE (Formerly Green Mask #9)
Fox Features Syndicate: 1944 - No. 14, Jan, 1945

	GD 2.0	VG 4.0	FN 6.0	VF 8.0	VF/NM 9.0	NM- 9.2
nn(1944, #10?)	31	62	93	175	248	320

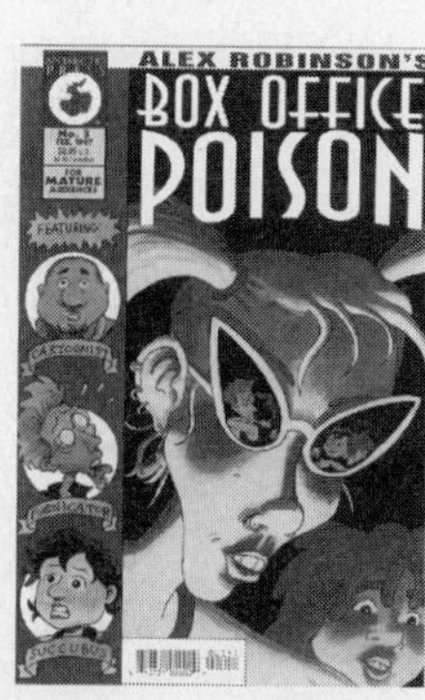

Box Office Poison #3 © Alex Robinson

Boy Commandos #24 © DC

Bozo Four Color #464 © Capitol Records

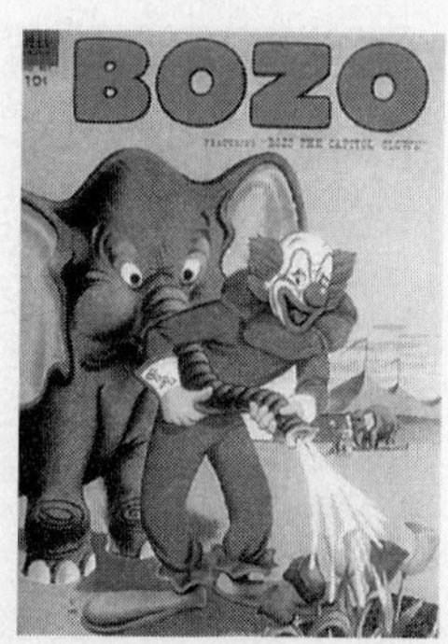

GD VG FN VF VF/NM NM-
2.0 4.0 6.0 8.0 9.0 9.2

11 (9/44)-Origin; Rocket Kelly, One Round Hogan app.
23 46 69 132 186 240
12-14: 14-Reprints no # issue 19 38 57 106 146 185

BOUNTY GUNS (See Luke Short's..., Four Color 739)

BOX OFFICE POISON
Antarctic Press: 1996 - No. 21, Sept, 2000 ($2.95, B&W)
1-Alex Robinson-s/a in all 1 2 3 4 5 7
2-5 4.00
6-21, ...Kolor Karnival 1 (5/99, $2.99) 3.00
...Super Special 0 (5/97, $4.95) 5.00
Sherman's March: Collected BOP Vol. 1 (9/98, $14.95) r/#0-4 15.00
TPB (2002, $29.95, 608 pgs.) r/entire series 30.00

BOY AND HIS 'BOT, A
Now Comics: Jan, 1987 ($1.95)
1-A Holiday Special 3.00

BOY AND THE PIRATES, THE (Movie)
Dell Publishing Co.: No. 1117, Aug, 1960
Four Color 1117-Photo-c 7 14 21 51 71 90

BOY COMICS (Captain Battle No. 1 & 2; Boy Illustories No. 43-108) (Stories by Charles Biro) (Also see Squeeks)
Lev Gleason Publ. (Comic House): No. 3, Apr, 1942 - No. 119, Mar, 1956
3(No.1)-Origin Crimebuster, Bombshell & Young Robin Hood; Yankee Longago, Case 1001-1008, Swoop Storm, & Boy Movies begin; 1st app. Iron Jaw; Crimebuster's pet monkey Squeeks begins 300 600 900 1925 2963 4000
4-Hitler, Tojo, Mussolini-c 126 252 378 788 1182 1575
5 88 176 264 550 825 1100
6-Origin Iron Jaw; origin & death of Iron Jaw's son; Little Dynamite begins, ends #39; 1st Iron Jaw-c 288 576 864 1800 2700 3600
7-Flag & Hitler, Tojo, Mussolini-c 90 180 270 563 844 1125
8-Death of Iron Jaw; Iron Jaw-c 90 180 270 563 844 1125
9-Iron Jaw-c 78 156 234 488 732 975
10-Return of Iron Jaw; classic Biro-c; Iron Jaw-c 120 240 360 750 1125 1500
11-Classic Iron Jaw-c 80 160 240 500 750 1000
12,13 55 110 165 330 495 660
14-Iron Jaw-c 63 126 189 394 590 785
15-Death of Iron Jaw 72 144 216 450 675 900
16,18-20 39 78 117 233 329 425
17-Flag-c 40 80 120 240 345 450
21-29,31,32-(All 68 pgs.). 28-Yankee Longago ends. 32-Swoop Storm & Young Robin Hood end 26 52 78 147 206 265
30-(68 pgs.)-Origin Crimebuster retold 36 72 108 207 294 380
33-40: 34-Crimebuster story(2); suicide-c/story 20 40 60 112 156 200
41-50 17 34 51 98 134 170
51-59: 57-Dilly Duncan begins, ends #71 15 30 45 84 115 145
60-Iron Jaw returns 16 32 48 92 126 160
61-Origin Crimebuster & Iron Jaw retold 18 36 54 104 142 180
62-Death of Iron Jaw explained 17 34 51 98 134 170
63-73: 63-McWilliams-a. 73-Frazetta 1-pg. ad 12 24 36 69 92 115
74-88: 80-1st app. Rocky X of the Rocketeers; becomes "Rocky X" #101; Iron Jaw, Sniffer & the Deadly Dozen in 80-118 9 18 27 54 70 85
89-92-The Claw serial app. in all 10 20 30 56 73 90
93-Claw cameo; Rocky X by Sid Check 9 18 27 54 70 85
94-97,99 9 18 27 52 66 80
98,100: 98-Rocky X by Sid Check 9 18 27 54 70 85
101-107,109,111,119: 101-Rocky X becomes spy strip. 106-RobinHood app. 119-Last Crimebuster. 111-Crimebuster becomes Chuck Chandler.
8 16 24 46 58 70
108,110,112-118-Kubert-a; 108-Ditko-a 9 18 27 52 66 80
(See Giant Boy Book of Comics)
NOTE: *Boy Movies in 3-5,40,41. Iron Jaw app.-3, 4, 6, 8, 10, 11, 13-15; returns-60-62, 68, 69, 72-79, 81-118.* ***Biro*** *c-all.* ***Briefer*** *a-5, 13, 14, 16-20 among others.* ***Fuje*** *a-14, 16, 17, 19, 20 among others.*

BOY COMMANDOS (See Detective #64 & World's Finest Comics #8)
National Periodical Publications: Winter, 1942-43 - No. 36, Nov-Dec, 1949
1-Origin Liberty Belle; The Sandman & The Newsboy Legion x-over in Boy Commandos; S&K-a, 48 pgs.; S&K cameo? (classic WWII-c) 517 1034 1551 3619 5560 7500
2-Last Liberty Belle; Hitler-c; S&K-a, 46 pgs.; WWII-c
200 400 600 1250 1875 2500
3-S&K-a, 45 pgs.; WWII-c 110 220 330 688 1032 1375
4-6: All WWII-c. 6-S&K-a 80 160 240 500 750 1000
7-10: All WWII-c 53 106 159 318 479 640
11-13: All WWII-c. 11-Infinity-c 39 78 117 233 329 425
14,16,18-19-All have S&K-a. 18-2nd Crazy Quilt-c 31 62 93 175 248 320
15-1st app. Crazy Quilt, their arch nemesis 40 80 120 235 343 450
17,20-Sci/fi-c/stories 35 70 105 201 283 365
21,22,25: 22-3rd Crazy Quilt-c; Judy Canova x-over 24 48 72 135 190 245
23-S&K-c/a(all) 32 64 96 184 262 340
24-1st costumed superhero satire-c (11-12/47). 29 58 87 164 232 300
26-Flying Saucer story (3-4/48)-4th of this theme; see The Spirit 9/28/47(1st), Shadow Comics V7#10 (2nd, 1/48) & Captain Midnight #60 (3rd, 2/48)
28 56 84 157 221 285
27,28,30: 30-Cleveland Indians story 23 46 69 130 183 235
29-S&K story (1) 25 50 75 144 198 255
31-35: 32-Dale Evans app. on-c & in story. 33-Last Crazy Quilt-c. 34-Intro. Wolf, their mascot 22 44 66 124 172 220
36-Intro The Atomobile c/sci-fi story (Scarce) 39 78 117 230 325 420
NOTE: *Most issues signed by* ***Simon & Kirby*** *are not by them.* ***S&K*** *c-1-9, 13, 14, 17, 21, 23, 24, 30-32.* ***Feller*** *c-30.*

BOY COMMANDOS
National Per. Publ.: Sept-Oct, 1973 - No. 2, Nov-Dec, 1973 (G.A. S&K reprints)
1,2: 1-Reprints story from Boy Commandos #1 plus-c & Detective #66 by S&K. 2-Infantino/Orlando-c 2 4 6 9 11 14

BOY COWBOY (Also see Amazing Adventures & Science Comics)
Ziff-Davis Publ. Co.: 1950 (8 pgs. in color)
nn-Sent to subscribers of Ziff-Davis mags. & ordered through mail for 10¢; used to test market for Kid Cowboy 26 52 78 150 210 270

BOY DETECTIVE
Avon Periodicals: May-June, 1951 - No. 4, May, 1952
1 20 40 60 112 156 200
2-4: 3,4-Kinstler-c 13 26 39 74 100 125

BOY EXPLORERS COMICS (Terry and The Pirates No. 3 on)
Family Comics (Harvey Publ.): May-June, 1946 - No. 2, Sept-Oct, 1946
1-Intro The Explorers, Duke of Broadway, Calamity Jane & Danny Dixon...Cadet; S&K-c/a, 24 pgs. 63 126 189 394 590 785
2-(Scarce)-Small size (5-1/2x8-1/2"; B&W; 32 pgs.) Distributed to mail subscribers only; S&K-a 96 192 288 600 900 1200
(Also see All New No. 15, Flash Gordon No. 5, and Stuntman No. 3)

BOY ILLUSTORIES (See Boy Comics)

BOY LOVES GIRL (Boy Meets Girl No. 1-24)
Lev Gleason Publications: No. 25, July, 1952 - No. 57, June, 1956
25(#1) 8 16 24 43 54 65
26,27,29-33: 30-33-Serial, 'Loves of My Life 6 12 18 27 33 38
34-42: 39-Lingerie panels 5 10 15 23 28 32
28-Drug propaganda story 6 12 18 29 36 42
43-Toth-a 7 14 21 35 43 50
44-50: 50-Last pre-code (2/55) 5 10 14 20 24 28
51-57: 57-Ann Brewster-a 4 8 11 16 19 22

BOY MEETS GIRL (Boy Loves Girl No. 25 on)
Lev Gleason Publications: Feb, 1950 - No. 24, June, 1952 (No. 1-17: 52 pgs.)
1-Guardineer-a 11 22 33 66 88 110
2 8 16 24 40 50 60
3-10 7 14 21 35 43 50
11-24 6 12 18 31 38 45
NOTE: ***Briefer*** *a-24.* ***Fuje*** *c-3,7. Painted-c 1-17. Photo-c 19-21, 23.*

BOYS' AND GIRLS' MARCH OF COMICS (See March of Comics)

BOYS' RANCH (Also see Western Tales & Witches' Western Tales)
Harvey Publ.: Oct, 1950 - No. 6, Aug, 1951 (No.1-3, 52 pgs.; No. 4-6, 36 pgs.)
1-S&K-c/a(3) 61 122 183 381 571 760
2-S&K-c/a(3) 42 84 126 252 376 500
3-S&K-c/a(2); Meskin-a 40 80 120 240 340 440
4-S&K-c/a, 5 pgs. 36 72 108 207 294 380
5,6-S&K-c, splashes & centerspread only; Meskin-a
21 42 63 118 164 210

BOZO (Larry Harmon's Bozo, the World's Most Famous Clown)
Innovation Publishing: 1992 ($6.95, 68 pgs.)
1-Reprints Four Color #285(#1) 1 2 3 4 5 7

BOZO THE CLOWN (TV) (Bozo No. 7 on)
Dell Publishing Co.: July, 1950 - No. 4, Oct-Dec, 1963
Four Color 285(#1) 21 42 63 149 220 290
2(7-9/51)-7(10-12/52) 12 24 36 82 121 160

Brainbanx #3 © Elaine Lee & Jason Temujin Minor

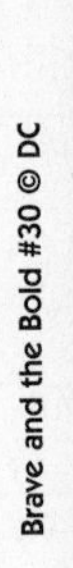
Brave and the Bold #30 © DC

Brave and the Bold #62 © DC

	GD 2.0	VG 4.0	FN 6.0	VF 8.0	VF/NM 9.0	NM- 9.2
Four Color 464,508,551,594(10/54)	10	20	30	70	100	130
1(nn, 5-7/62)	8	16	24	53	74	95
2 - 4(1963)	6	12	18	40	55	70
BOZZ CHRONICLES, THE						
Marvel Comics (Epic Comics): Dec, 1985 - No. 6, 1986 (Lim. series, mature)						
1-6-Logan/Wolverine look alike in 19th century. 1,3,5- Blevins-a						3.00
B.P.R.D.: HOLLOW EARTH (Mike Mignola's...)						
Dark Horse Comics: Jan, 2002 - No. 3, June, 2002 ($2.99, limited series)						
1-3-Mignola, Golden & Sniegoski-s/Sook-a/Mignola-c; Hellboy and Abe Sapien app.						3.00
... and Other Stories TPB (1/03, $17.95) r/#1-3, Hellboy: Box Full of Evil, Abe Sapien: Drums of the Dead, and Dark Horse Extra; plus sketch pages						18.00
B.P.R.D Dark Waters (7/03, $2.99) Guy Davis-c/a; Augustyn-s						3.00
B.P.R.D Night Train (9/03, $2.99) Johns & Kolins-s; Kolins & Stewart-a						3.00
B.P.R.D The Soul of Venice (5/03, $2.99) Oeming-a/c; Gunter & Oeming-s						3.00
BRADLEYS, THE (Also see Hate)						
Fantagraphics Books: Apr, 1999 - No. 6, Jan, 2000 ($2.95, B&W, limited series)						
1-6-Reprints Peter Bagge's-s/a						3.00
BRADY BUNCH, THE (TV)(See Kite Fun Book and Binky #78)						
Dell Publishing Co.: Feb, 1970 - No. 2, May, 1970						
1	12	24	36	84	125	165
2	9	18	27	60	85	110
BRAIN, THE						
Sussex Publ. Co./Magazine Enterprises: Sept, 1956 - No. 7, 1958						
1-Dan DeCarlo-a in all including reprints	10	20	30	58	77	95
2,3	7	14	21	35	43	50
4-7	4	8	12	24	32	40
I.W. Reprints #1-4,8-10('63),14: 2-Reprints Sussex #2 with new cover added	2	4	6	10	13	16
Super Reprint #17,18(nd)	2	4	6	10	13	16
BRAINBANX						
DC Comics (Helix): Mar, 1997 - No. 6, Aug, 1997 ($2.50, limited series)						
1-6: Elaine Lee-s/Temujin-a						2.50
BRAIN BOY						
Dell Publishing Co.: Apr-June, 1962 - No. 6, Sept-Nov, 1963 (Painted c-#1-6)						
Four Color 1330(#1)-Gil Kane-a; origin	14	28	42	99	145	190
2(7-9/62),3-6: 4-Origin retold	8	16	24	58	82	105
BRAM STOKER'S BURIAL OF THE RATS (Movie)						
Roger Corman's Cosmic Comics: Apr, 1995 - No.3, June, 1995 ($2.50)						
1-3: Adaptation of film; Jerry Prosser scripts						2.50
BRAM STOKER'S DRACULA (Movie)(Also see Dracula: Vlad the Impaler)						
Topps Comics: Oct, 1992 - No. 4, Jan, 1993 ($2.95, limited series, polybagged)						
1-(1st & 2nd printing)-Adaptation of film begins; Mignola-c/a in all; 4 trading cards & poster; photo scenes of movie						3.00
1-Crimson foil edition (limited to 500)						8.00
2-4: 2-Bound-in poster & cards. 4 trading cards in both. 3-Contains coupon to win 1 of 500 crimson foil-c edition of #1. 4-Contains coupon to win 1 of 500 uncut sheets of all 16 trading cards						3.00
BRAND ECHH (See Not Brand Echh)						
BRAND NEW YORK: WHAT JUSTICE						
Comic Box Inc.: July, 1997 ($3.95, B&W&Red)						
1-Zoltan-s/a, Peter Avanti-s						4.00
BRAND OF EMPIRE (See Luke Short's...Four Color 771)						
BRASS						
Image Comics (WildStorm Productions): Aug, 1996 - No. 3, May, 1997 ($2.50, limited series)						
1-($4.50) Folio Ed.; oversized						4.50
1-3: Wiesenfeld-s/Bennett-a. 3-Grunge & Roxy(Gen 13) cameo						2.50
BRASS						
DC Comics (WildStorm): Aug, 2000 - No. 6 ($2.50, limited series)						
1-5-Arcudi-s						2.50
BRATH						
CrossGeneration Comics: Feb, 2003 - Present ($2.95)						
Prequel-Dixon-s/Di Vito-a						3.00
1-12: 1-(3/03)-Dixon-s/Di Vito-a						3.00
Vol. 1: Hammer of Vengeance (2003, $9.95) Digest-sized reprint of Prequel & #1-6						10.00

	GD 2.0	VG 4.0	FN 6.0	VF 8.0	VF/NM 9.0	NM- 9.2
BRATPACK/MAXIMORTAL SUPER SPECIAL						
King Hell Press: 1996 ($2.95, B&W, limited series)						
1,2: Veitch-s/a						3.00
BRATS BIZARRE						
Marvel Comics (Epic/Heavy Hitters): 1994 - No. 4, 1994 ($2.50, limited series)						
1-4: All w/bound-in trading cards						2.50
BRAVADOS, THE (See Wild Western Action)						
Skywald Publ. Corp.: Aug, 1971 (52 pgs., one-shot)						
1-Red Mask, The Durango Kid, Billy Nevada-r; Bolle-a; 3-D effect story	2	4	6	12	16	20
BRAVE AND THE BOLD, THE (See Best Of... & Super DC Giant) (Replaced by Batman & The Outsiders)						
National Periodical Publ./DC Comics: Aug-Sept, 1955 - No. 200, July, 1983						
1-Viking Prince by Kubert, Silent Knight, Golden Gladiator begin; part Kubert-c	231	462	693	2021	3261	4500
2	103	206	309	876	1338	1800
3,4	57	114	171	485	743	1000
5-Robin Hood begins (4-5/56, 1st DC app.), ends #15; see Robin Hood Tales #7	60	120	180	510	780	1050
6-10: 6-Robin Hood by Kubert; last Golden Gladiator app.; Silent Knight; no Viking Prince. 8-1st S.A. issue	44	88	132	352	526	700
11-22,24: 12,14-Robin Hood-c. 18,21-23-Grey tone-c. 22-Last Silent Knight. 24-Last Viking Prince by Kubert (2nd solo book)	35	70	105	263	394	525
23-Viking Prince origin by Kubert; 1st B&B single theme issue & 1st Viking Prince solo book	44	88	132	352	526	700
25-1st app. Suicide Squad (8-9/59)	41	82	123	324	487	650
26,27-Suicide Squad	31	62	93	223	329	435
28-(2-3/60)-Justice League intro./1st app.; origin/1st app. Snapper Carr	390	780	1170	3569	5785	8000
29-Justice League (4-5/60)-2nd app. battle the Weapons Master; robot-c	173	346	519	1514	2357	3200
30-Justice League (6-7/60)-3rd app.; vs. Amazo	140	280	420	1190	1820	2450
31-1st app. Cave Carson (8-9/60); scarce in high grade; 1st try-out series	38	76	114	285	430	575
32,33-Cave Carson	24	48	72	169	247	325
34-Origin/1st app. Silver-Age Hawkman, Hawkgirl & Byth (2-3/61); Gardner Fox story, Kubert-c/a ; 1st S.A. Hawkman tryout series; 2nd in #42-44; both series predate Hawkman #1 (4-5/64)	184	368	552	1610	250	3400
35-Hawkman by Kubert (4-5/61)-2nd app.	47	94	141	376	563	750
36-Hawkman by Kubert; origin & 1st app. Shadow Thief (6-7/61)-3rd app.	41	82	123	324	487	650
37-Suicide Squad (2nd tryout series)	24	48	72	169	247	325
38,39-Suicide Squad. 38-Last 10¢ issue	20	40	60	145	213	280
40,41-Cave Carson Inside Earth (2nd try-out series). 40-Kubert-a. 41-Meskin-a	15	30	45	107	156	205
42-Hawkman by Kubert (2nd tryout series); Hawkman earns helmet wings; Byth app.	30	60	90	218	319	420
43-Hawkman by Kubert; more detailed origin	35	70	105	263	392	520
44-Hawkman by Kubert; grey-tone-c	28	56	84	203	294	385
45-49-Strange Sports Stories by Infantino	9	18	27	60	85	110
50-The Green Arrow & Manhunter From Mars (10-11/63); 1st Manhunter x-over outside of Detective Comics (pre-dates House of Mystery #143); team-ups begin	19	38	57	136	198	260
51-Aquaman & Hawkman (12-1/63-64); pre-dates Hawkman #1	24	48	72	169	247	325
52-(2-3/64)-3 Battle Stars; Sgt. Rock, Haunted Tank, Johnny Cloud, & Mlle. Marie team-up for 1st time by Kubert (c/a)	19	38	57	136	198	260
53-Atom & The Flash by Toth	9	18	27	60	85	110
54-Kid Flash, Robin & Aqualad; 1st app./origin Teen Titans (6-7/64)	30	60	90	218	319	420
55-Metal Men & The Atom	7	14	21	51	71	90
56-The Flash & Manhunter From Mars	7	14	21	51	71	90
57-Origin & 1st app. Metamorpho (12-1/64-65)	18	36	54	131	191	250
58-2nd app. Metamorpho by Fradon	9	18	27	65	93	120
59-Batman & Green Lantern; 1st Batman team-up in Brave and the Bold	11	22	33	77	114	150
60-Teen Titans (2nd app.)-1st app. new Wonder Girl (Donna Troy), who joins Titans (6-7/65)	11	22	33	80	118	155
61-Origin Starman & Black Canary by Anderson	13	26	39	94	137	180
62-Origin Starman & Black Canary cont'd. 62-1st S.A. app. Wildcat (10-11/65); 1st S.A. app. of G.A. Huntress (W.W. villain)	11	22	33	77	114	150
63-Supergirl & Wonder Woman	7	14	21	51	71	90

Brave and the Bold #76 © DC

Brave and the Bold #130 © DC

Brave and the Bold #198 © DC

	GD 2.0	VG 4.0	FN 6.0	VF 8.0	VF/NM 9.0	NM- 9.2
64-Batman Versus Eclipso (see H.O.S. #61)	8	16	24	53	74	95
65-Flash & Doom Patrol (4-5/66)	5	10	15	36	48	60
66-Metamorpho & Metal Men (6-7/66)	5	10	15	36	48	60
67-Batman & The Flash by Infantino; Batman team-ups begin, end #200 (8-9/66)	7	14	21	46	63	80
68-Batman/Metamorpho/Joker/Riddler/Penguin-c/story; Batman as Bat-Hulk (Hulk parody)	9	18	27	60	85	110
69-Batman & Green Lantern	6	12	18	38	52	65
70-Batman & Hawkman; Craig-a(p)	6	12	18	38	52	65
71-Batman & Green Arrow	6	12	18	38	52	65
72-Spectre & Flash (6-7/67); 4th app. The Spectre; predates Spectre #1	6	12	18	40	55	70
73-Aquaman & The Atom	5	10	15	36	48	60
74-Batman & Metal Men	5	10	15	36	48	60
75-Batman & The Spectre (12-1/67-68); 6th app. Spectre; came out between Spectre #1 & #2	6	12	18	38	52	65
76-Batman & Plastic Man (2-3/68); came out between Plastic Man #8 & #9	5	10	15	36	48	60
77-Batman & The Atom	5	10	15	36	48	60
78-Batman, Wonder Woman & Batgirl	5	10	15	36	48	60
79-Batman & Deadman by Neal Adams (8-9/68); early Deadman app.	8	16	24	55	78	100
80-Batman & Creeper (10-11/68); N. Adams-a; early app. The Creeper; came out between Creeper #3 & #4	7	14	21	46	63	80
81-Batman & Flash; N. Adams-a	7	14	21	46	63	80
82-Batman & Aquaman; N. Adams-a; origin Ocean Master retold (2-3/69)	7	14	21	46	63	80
83-Batman & Teen Titans; N. Adams-a (4-5/69)	7	14	21	46	63	80
84-Batman (G.A., 1st S.A. app.) & Sgt. Rock; N. Adams-a; last 12¢ issue (6-7/69)	7	14	21	46	63	80
85-Batman & Green Arrow; 1st new costume for Green Arrow by Neal Adams (8-9/69)	7	14	21	50	68	85
86-Batman & Deadman (10-11/69); N. Adams-a; story concludes from Strange Adventures #216 (1-2/69)	7	14	21	46	63	80
87-Batman & Wonder Woman	4	8	12	27	36	45
88-Batman & Wildcat	4	8	12	27	36	45
89-Batman & Phantom Stranger (4-5/70); early Phantom Stranger app. (came out between Phantom Stranger #6 & 7	4	8	12	24	32	40
90-Batman & Adam Strange	4	8	12	24	32	40
91-Batman & Black Canary (8-9/70)	4	8	12	24	32	40
92-Batman; intro the Bat Squad	4	8	12	24	32	40
93-Batman-House of Mystery; N. Adams-a	6	12	18	40	55	70
94-Batman-Teen Titans	3	6	9	19	25	32
95-Batman & Plastic Man	3	6	9	19	25	32
96-Batman & Sgt. Rock; last 15¢ issue	3	7	10	21	28	35
97-Batman & Wildcat; 52 pg. issues begin, end #102; reprints origin & 1st app. Deadman from Strange Advs. #205	3	7	10	21	28	35
98-Batman & Phantom Stranger; 1st Jim Aparo Batman-a?	3	7	10	21	28	35
99-Batman & Flash	3	7	10	21	28	35
100-(2-3/72, 25¢, 52 pgs.)-Batman-Green Lantern-Green Arrow-Black Canary-Robin; Deadman-r by Adams/Str. Advs. #210	6	12	18	40	55	70
101-Batman & Metamorpho; Kubert Viking Prince	3	6	9	19	25	32
102-Batman-Teen Titans; N. Adams-a(p)	4	8	12	27	36	45
103-107,109,110: Batman team-ups: 103-Metal Men. 104-Deadman. 105-Wonder Woman. 106-Green Arrow. 107-Black Canary. 109-Demon. 110-Wildcat	2	4	6	12	16	20
108-Sgt. Rock	2	4	6	14	18	22
111-Batman/Joker-c/story	3	6	9	16	20	25
112-117: All 100 pgs.; Batman team-ups: 112-Mr. Miracle. 113-Metal Men; reprints origin/1st Hawkman from Brave and the Bold #34; r/origin Multi-Man/Challengers #14. 114-Aquaman. 115-Atom; r/origin Viking Prince from #23; r/Dr. Fate/Hourman/Solomon Grundy/Green Lantern from Showcase #55. 116-Spectre. 117-Sgt. Rock; last 100 pg. issue	4	8	12	27	36	45
118-Batman/Wildcat/Joker-c/story	3	6	9	16	20	25
119,121-123,125-128,132-140: Batman team-ups: 119-Man-Bat. 121-Metal Men. 122-Swamp Thing. 123-Plastic Man/Metamorpho. 125-Flash. 126-Aquaman. 127-Wildcat. 128-Mr. Miracle. 132-Kung-Fu Fighter. 133-Deadman. 134-Green Lantern. 135-Metal Men. 136-Metal Men/Green Arrow. 137-Demon. 138-Mr. Miracle. 139-Hawkman. 140-Wonder Woman	2	4	6	8	10	12
120-Kamandi (68 pgs.)	2	4	6	14	18	22
124-Sgt. Rock	2	4	6	10	12	15
129,130-Batman/Green Arrow/Atom parts 1 & 2; Joker & Two Face-c/stories	2	4	6	12	16	20

	GD 2.0	VG 4.0	FN 6.0	VF 8.0	VF/NM 9.0	NM- 9.2
131-Batman & Wonder Woman vs. Catwoman-c/sty	2	4	6	10	12	15
141-Batman/Black Canary vs. Joker-c/story	2	4	6	12	16	20
142-160: Batman team-ups: 142-Aquaman. 143-Creeper; origin Human Target (44 pgs.). 144-Green Arrow; origin Human Target part 2 (44 pgs.). 145-Phantom Stranger. 146-G.A. Batman/Unknown Soldier. 147-Supergirl. 148-Plastic Man; X-Mas-c. 149-Teen Titans. 150-Anniversary issue; Superman. 151-Flash. 152-Atom. 153-Red Tornado. 154-Metamorpho. 155-Green Lantern. 156-Dr. Fate. 157-Batman vs. Kamandi (ties into Kamandi #59). 158-Wonder Woman. 159-Ra's Al Ghul. 160-Supergirl.	1	2	3	5	7	9
145(11/79),146,150-155,157,159,165(8/80)-(Whitman variants; low print run; none show issue # on cover)	2	4	6	8	10	12
161-181,183-190,192-195,198,199: Batman team-ups: 161-Adam Strange. 162-G.A. Batman/ Sgt. Rock. 163-Black Lightning. 164-Hawkman. 165-Man-Bat. 166-Black Canary; Nemesis (intro) back-up story begins, ends #192; Penguin-c/story. 167-G.A. Batman/Blackhawk; origin Nemesis. 168-Green Arrow. 169-Zatanna. 170-Nemesis. 171-Scalphunter. 172-Firestorm. 173-Guardians of the Universe. 174-Green Lantern. 175-Lois Lane. 176-Swamp Thing. 177-Elongated Man. 178-Creeper. 179-Legion. 180-Spectre. 181-Hawk & Dove. 183-Riddler. 184-Huntress. 185-Green Arrow. 186-Hawkman. 187-Metal Men. 188,189-Rose & the Thorn. 190-Adam Strange. 192-Superboy vs. Mr. I.Q. 193-Nemesis. 194-Flash. 195-I...Vampire. 198-Karate Kid. 199-Batman vs. The Spectre						6.00
182-G.A. Robin; G.A. Starman app.; 1st modern app. G.A. Batwoman	1	2	3	4	5	7
191-Batman/Joker-c/story; Nemesis app.	2	4	6	8	10	12
196-Ragman; origin Ragman retold.	1	2	3	5	6	8
197-Catwoman; Earth II Batman & Catwoman marry; 2nd modern app. of G.A. Batwoman	2	4	6	8	10	12
200-Double-sized (64 pgs.); printed on Mando paper; Earth One & Earth Two Batman app. in separate stories; intro/1st app. Batman & The Outsiders	1	3	4	6	8	10

NOTE: ***Neal Adams** a-79-86, 93, 100r, 102; c-75, 76, 79-86, 88-90, 93, 95, 99, 100r. **M. Anderson** a-115r; c-72i, 96i. **Andru/Esposito** c-25-27. **Aparo** a-98, 100-102, 104-125, 126i, 127-136, 138-145, 147, 148i, 149-152, 154, 155, 157-162, 168-170, 173-178, 180-182, 184, 186i-189i, 191i-193i, 195, 196, 200; c-105-109, 111-136, 137i, 138-175, 177, 180-184, 186-200. **Austin** a-166i. **Bernard Baily** c-32, 33, 58. **Buckler** a-185, 186p; c-137, 178p, 185p, 186p. **Giordano** a-143, 144. **Infantino** a-67p, 72p, 97r, 98r, 115r, 172p, 183p, 190p, 194p; c-45-49, 67p, 69p, 70p, 72p, 96p, 98r. **Kaluta** c-176. **Kane** a-115r; c-59, 64. **Kubert** &/or **Heath** a-1-24; reprints-101, 113, 115, 117. **Kubert** a-99r; c-22-24, 34-36, 40, 42-44, 52. **Mooney** a-114r. **Mortimer** a-64, 69. **Newton** a-153p, 156p, 165p. **Irv Novick** c-1(part), 2-21. **Fred Ray** a-78r. **Roussos** a-50, 76i, 114r. **Staton** 148p. 52 pgs.-97, 100; 68 pgs.-120; 100 pgs.-112-117.*

BRAVE AND THE BOLD, THE
DC Comics: Dec, 1991 - No. 6, June, 1992 ($1.75, limited series)

1-6: Green Arrow, The Butcher, The Question in all; Grell scripts in all — 2.50
NOTE: ***Grell** c-3, 4-6.*

BRAVE AND THE BOLD ANNUAL NO. 1 1969 ISSUE, THE
DC Comics: 2001 ($5.95, one-shot)

1-Reprints silver age team-ups in 1960s-style 80 pg. Giant format — 6.00

BRAVE AND THE BOLD SPECIAL, THE (See DC Special Series No. 8)

BRAVE EAGLE (TV)
Dell Publishing Co.: No. 705, June, 1956 - No. 929, July, 1958

	GD	VG	FN	VF	VF/NM	NM-
Four Color 705 (#1)-Photo-c	7	14	21	51	71	90
Four Color 770, 816, 879 (2/58), 929-All photo-c	4	8	12	28	38	48

BRAVE OLD WORLD (V2K)
DC Comics (Vertigo): Feb, 2000 - No. 4, May, 2000 ($2.50, mini-series)

1-4-Messner-Loeb-s/Guy Davis & Phil Hester-a — 2.50

BRAVE ONE, THE (Movie)
Dell Publishing Co.: No. 773, Mar, 1957

	GD	VG	FN	VF	VF/NM	NM-
Four Color 773-Photo-c	6	12	18	40	55	70

BRAVURA
Malibu Comics (Bravura): 1995 (mail-in offer)

0-wraparound holographic-c; short stories and promo pin-ups of Chaykin's Power & Glory, Gil Kane's & Steven Grant's Edge, Starlin's Breed, & Simonson's Star Slammers — 5.00
1 1/2 — 7.00

BREAKFAST AFTER NOON
Oni Press: May, 2000 - No. 6, Jan, 2001($2.95, B&W, limited series)

1-6-Andi Watson-s/a — 3.00
TPB (2001, $19.95) r/series — 20.00

BREAKNECK BLVD.
MotioN Comics/Slave Labor Graphics Vol. 2: No. 0, Feb, 1994 - No. 2, Nov, 1994; Vol. 2#1, Jul, 1995 - #6, Dec., 1996 ($2.50/$2.95, B&W)

0-2, V2#1-6: 0-Perez/Giordano-c — 3.00

BREAK-THRU (Also see Exiles V1#4)

Brenda Starr #3 © SUPR

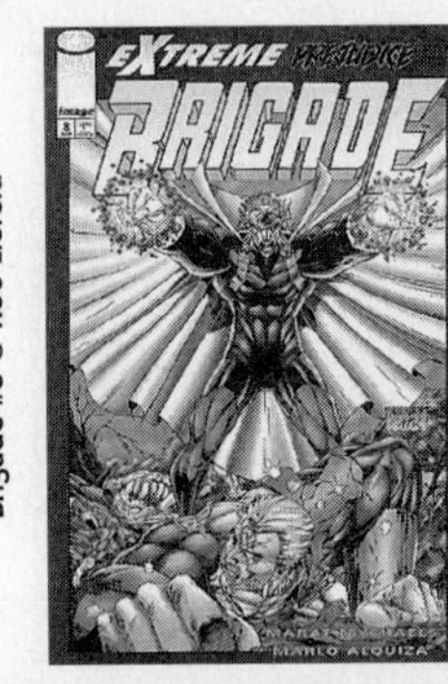

Brigade #8 © Rob Liefeld

Brit #1 © Robert Kirkman

	GD 2.0	VG 4.0	FN 6.0	VF 8.0	VF/NM 9.0	NM- 9.2

Malibu Comics (Ultraverse): Dec, 1993 - No. 2, Jan, 1994 ($2.50, 44 pgs.)

Issue	GD	VG	FN	VF	VF/NM	NM-
1,2-Perez-c/a(p); has x-overs in Ultraverse titles						2.50

BREATHTAKER
DC Comics: 1990 - No. 4, 1990 ($4.95, 52 pgs., prestige format, mature)

Issue	GD	VG	FN	VF	VF/NM	NM-
Book 1-4: Mark Wheatley-painted-c/a & scripts; Marc Hempel-a						5.00
TPB (1994, $14.95) r/#1-4; intro by Neil Gaiman						15.00

'BREED
Malibu Comics (Bravura): Jan, 1994 - No. 6, 1994 ($2.50, limited series)

Issue	GD	VG	FN	VF	VF/NM	NM-
1-6: 1-(48 pgs.)-Origin/1st app. of 'Breed by Starlin; contains Bravura stamps; spot varnish-c. 2-5-contains Bravura stamps. 6-Death of Rachel						3.00
...:Book of Genesis (1994, $12.95)-reprints #1-6						13.00

'BREED II
Malibu Comics (Bravura): Nov, 1994 - No. 6, Apr, 1995 ($2.95, limited series)

Issue	GD	VG	FN	VF	VF/NM	NM-
1-6: Starlin-c/a/scripts in all. 1-Gold edition						3.00

BREEZE LAWSON, SKY SHERIFF (See Sky Sheriff)

BRENDA LEE'S LIFE STORY
Dell Publishing Co.: July-Sept., 1962

Issue	GD	VG	FN	VF	VF/NM	NM-
01-078-209	9	18	27	63	89	115

BRENDA STARR (Also see All Great)
Four Star Comics Corp./Superior Comics Ltd.: No. 13, 9/47; No. 14, 3/48; V2#3, 6/48 - V2#12, 12/49

Issue	GD	VG	FN	VF	VF/NM	NM-
V1#13-By Dale Messick	80	160	240	500	750	1000
14-Kamen bondage-c	84	168	252	525	788	1050
V2#3-Baker-a?	67	134	201	419	630	840
4-Used in **SOTI**, pg. 21; Kamen bondage-c	80	160	240	500	750	1000
5-10	65	130	195	406	608	810
11,12 (Scarce)	66	132	198	413	619	825

NOTE: *Newspaper reprints plus original material through #6. All original #7 on.*

BRENDA STARR (...Reporter)(Young Lovers No. 16 on?)
Charlton Comics: No. 13, June, 1955 - No. 15, Oct, 1955

Issue	GD	VG	FN	VF	VF/NM	NM-
13-15-Newspaper-r	39	78	117	230	325	420

BRENDA STARR REPORTER
Dell Publishing Co.: Oct, 1963

Issue	GD	VG	FN	VF	VF/NM	NM-
1	17	34	51	118	174	230

BRER RABBIT (See Kite Fun Book, Walt Disney Showcase #28 and Wheaties)
Dell Publishing Co.: No. 129, 1946; No. 208, Jan, 1949; No. 693, 1956 (Disney)

Issue	GD	VG	FN	VF	VF/NM	NM-
Four Color 129 (#1)-Adapted from Disney movie "Song of the South"	29	58	87	210	305	400
Four Color 208 (1/49)	12	24	36	84	125	165
Four Color 693-Part-r 129	10	20	30	67	96	125

BRIAN BOLLAND'S BLACK BOOK
Eclipse Comics: July, 1985 (one-shot)

Issue	GD	VG	FN	VF	VF/NM	NM-
1-British B&W-r in color						3.00

BRIAN PULIDO'S LADY DEATH... (See Lady Death)

BRICK BRADFORD (Also see Ace Comics & King Comics)
King Features Syndicate/Standard: No. 5, July, 1948 - No. 8, July, 1949 (Ritt & Grey reprints)

Issue	GD	VG	FN	VF	VF/NM	NM-
5	20	40	60	112	156	200
6-Robot-c (by Schomburg?).	32	64	96	184	262	340
7-Schomburg-c. 8-Says #7 inside, #8 on-c	17	34	51	95	130	165

BRIDE'S DIARY (Formerly Black Cobra No. 3)
Ajax/Farrell Publ.: No. 4, May, 1955 - No. 10, Aug, 1956

Issue	GD	VG	FN	VF	VF/NM	NM-
4 (#1)	8	16	24	43	54	65
5-8	6	12	18	27	33	38
9,10-Disbrow-a	7	14	21	37	46	55

BRIDES IN LOVE (Hollywood Romances & Summer Love No. 46 on)
Charlton Comics: Aug, 1956 - No. 45, Feb, 1965

Issue	GD	VG	FN	VF	VF/NM	NM-
1	10	20	30	58	77	95
2	6	12	18	33	41	48
3-6,8-10	3	7	10	21	28	35
7-(68 pgs.)	4	8	12	28	38	48
11-20	3	6	9	16	20	24
21-45	2	4	6	10	12	15

BRIDES ROMANCES
Quality Comics Group: Nov, 1953 - No. 23, Dec, 1956

Issue	GD	VG	FN	VF	VF/NM	NM-
1	12	24	36	71	96	120
2	7	14	21	37	38	45
3-10: Last precode (3/55)	6	12	18	31	38	45
11-17,19-22: 15-Baker-a(p)?; Colan-a	6	12	18	27	33	38
18-Baker-a	6	12	18	33	41	48
23-Baker-c/a	9	18	27	54	70	85

BRIDE'S SECRETS
Ajax/Farrell(Excellent Publ.)/Four-Star: Apr-May, 1954 - No. 19, May, 1958

Issue	GD	VG	FN	VF	VF/NM	NM-
1	10	20	30	58	77	95
2	6	12	18	33	41	48
3-6: Last precode (3/55)	6	12	18	27	33	38
7-11,13-19: 18-Hollingsworth-a	5	10	15	23	28	32
12-Disbrow-a	6	12	18	28	34	40

BRIDE-TO-BE ROMANCES (See True...)

BRIGADE
Image Comics (Extreme Studios): Aug, 1992 - No. 4, 1993 ($1.95, lim. series)

Issue	GD	VG	FN	VF	VF/NM	NM-
1-Liefeld part plots/scripts in all, Liefeld-c(p); contains 2 Brigade trading cards						3.00
1-Gold foil stamped logo edition						8.00
2-Contains coupon for Image Comics #0 & 2 trading cards						3.00
2-With coupon missing						2.25
3,4: 3-Contains 2 trading cards; 1st Birds of Prey. 4-Flip book featuring Youngblood #5						2.50

BRIGADE
Image Comics (Extreme): V2#1, May, 1993 - V2#22, July, 1995, V2#25, May, 1996 ($1.95/$2.50)

Issue	GD	VG	FN	VF	VF/NM	NM-
V2#1-22,25: 1-Gatefold-c; Liefeld co-plots; Blood Brothers part 1; Bloodstrike app.; 1st app. Boone & Hacker. 2-(6/93, V2#1 on inside)-Foil merricote-c (newsstand ed. w/out foil-c exists). 3-1st app. Roman; Perez-c(i); Liefeld scripts. 6-8-Thibert-c(i). 8-Liefeld scripts; Black and White part 5 by Art Thibert. 8,9-Coupons #2 & 6 for Extreme Prejudice #0 bound-in. 11-(8/94, $2.50) WildC.A.T.S app. 16-Polybagged w/ trading card. 19-Glory app. 20-(Regular-c.)-Troll, Supreme, Shadowhawk, Glory, Vanguard, & Roman form new team. 22-"Supreme Apocalypse" Pt. 4; w/ trading card. 25-Images of Tomorrow						2.50
0-(9/93)-Liefeld scripts; 1st app. Warcry; Youngblood & Wildcats app.;						2.50
20-Variant-c. by Quesada & Palmiotti						2.50
Sourcebook 1 (8/94, $2.95)						3.00

BRIGADE
Awesome Entertainment: July, 2000 ($2.99)

Issue	GD	VG	FN	VF	VF/NM	NM-
1-Flip book w/Century preview						3.00

BRIGAND, THE (See Fawcett Movie Comics No. 18)

BRINGING UP FATHER
Dell Publishing Co.: No. 9, 1942 - No. 37, 1944

Issue	GD	VG	FN	VF	VF/NM	NM-
Large Feature Comic 9	29	58	87	164	232	300
Four Color 37	20	40	60	145	213	280

BRING BACK THE BAD GUYS
Marvel Comics: 1998($24.95, TPB)

Issue	GD	VG	FN	VF	VF/NM	NM-
1-Reprints stories of Marvel villains' secrets						25.00

BRING ON THE BAD GUYS (See Fireside Book Series)

BRINKE OF DESTRUCTION
High-Top and Brinke Stevens: Dec, 1995 - Jan, 1997($2.95)

Issue	GD	VG	FN	VF	VF/NM	NM-
1-3: 1-Boris-c. 2-Julie Bell-c. 3-Garris-c						3.00
Holiday Special ($6.99)-Comic w/audio tape	1	2	3	4	5	7

BRINKE OF DISASTER
Revenge Entertainment Group: 1996 ($2.25, B&W, one-shot)

Issue	GD	VG	FN	VF	VF/NM	NM-
nn-Photo-c						2.25

BRINKE OF ETERNITY
Chaos! Comics: Apr, 1994 ($2.75, one-shot)

Issue	GD	VG	FN	VF	VF/NM	NM-
1						3.00
1-Signed Edition						4.00

BRIT
Image Comics: July, 2003 ($4.95, B&W)

Issue	GD	VG	FN	VF	VF/NM	NM-
1-Robert Kirkman-s/Tony Moore-a						5.00
...Vol. 2 Cold Death						5.00

BROADWAY HOLLYWOOD BLACKOUTS
Stanhall: Mar-Apr, 1954 - No. 3, July-Aug, 1954

Issue	GD	VG	FN	VF	VF/NM	NM-
1	12	24	36	71	96	120
2,3	8	16	24	46	58	70

BROADWAY ROMANCES
Quality Comics Group: January, 1950 - No. 5, Sept, 1950

Broadway Romances #1 © STD

Brotherhood #5 © MAR

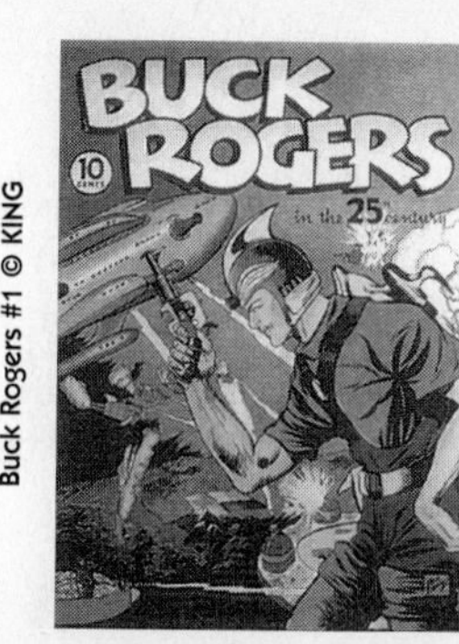

Buck Rogers #1 © KING

	GD 2.0	VG 4.0	FN 6.0	VF 8.0	VF/NM 9.0	NM- 9.2
1-Ward-c/a (9 pgs.); Gustavson-a	37	74	111	213	299	385
2-Ward-a (9 pgs.); photo-c	26	52	78	147	206	265
3-5: All-Photo-c	13	26	39	76	103	130

BROKEN ARROW (TV)
Dell Publishing Co.: No. 855, Oct, 1957 - No. 947, Nov, 1958

	GD 2.0	VG 4.0	FN 6.0	VF 8.0	VF/NM 9.0	NM- 9.2
Four Color 855 (#1)-Photo-c	6	12	18	43	59	75
Four Color 947-Photo-c	6	12	18	38	52	65

BROKEN CROSS, THE (See The Crusaders)

BRONCHO BILL (See Comics On Parade, Sparkler & Tip Top Comics)
United Features Syndicate/Standard(Visual Editions) No. 5-on: 1939 - 1940; No. 5, 1?/48 - No. 16, 8?/50

	GD 2.0	VG 4.0	FN 6.0	VF 8.0	VF/NM 9.0	NM- 9.2
Single Series 2 ('39)	51	102	153	306	458	610
Single Series 19 ('40)(#2 on cvr)	42	84	126	252	376	500
5	14	28	42	81	111	140
6(4/48)-10(4/49)	8	16	24	46	58	70
11(6/49)-16	7	14	21	37	46	55

NOTE: *Schomburg c-6, 7, 9-13, 16.*

BROOKLYN DREAMS
DC Comics (Paradox Press): 1994 ($4.95, B&W, limited series, mature)

	GD 2.0	VG 4.0	FN 6.0	VF 8.0	VF/NM 9.0	NM- 9.2
1-4						5.00

BROOKS ROBINSON (See Baseball's Greatest Heroes #2)

BROTHER BILLY THE PAIN FROM PLAINS
Marvel Comics Group: 1979 (68pgs.)

	GD 2.0	VG 4.0	FN 6.0	VF 8.0	VF/NM 9.0	NM- 9.2
1-B&W comics, satire, Jimmy Carter-c & x-over w/Brother Billy peanut jokes. Joey Adams-a (scarce)	3	6	9	18	24	30

BROTHERHOOD, THE (Also see X-Men titles)
Marvel Comics: July, 2001 - No. 9, Mar, 2002 ($2.25)

	GD 2.0	VG 4.0	FN 6.0	VF 8.0	VF/NM 9.0	NM- 9.2
1-Intro. Orwell & the Brotherhood; Ribic-a/X-s/Sienkiewicz-c						2.25
2-9: 2-Two covers (JG Jones & Sienkiewicz). 4-6-Fabry-c. 7-9-Phillips-c/a						2.25

BROTHER POWER, THE GEEK (See Saga of Swamp Thing Annual & Vertigo Visions)
National Periodical Publications: Sept-Oct, 1968 - No. 2, Nov-Dec, 1968

	GD 2.0	VG 4.0	FN 6.0	VF 8.0	VF/NM 9.0	NM- 9.2
1-Origin; Simon-c(i?)	6	12	18	40	55	70
2	3	7	10	21	28	35

BROTHERS, HANG IN THERE, THE
Spire Christian Comics (Fleming H. Revell Co.): 1979 (49¢)

	GD 2.0	VG 4.0	FN 6.0	VF 8.0	VF/NM 9.0	NM- 9.2
nn	1	3	4	6	8	10

BROTHERS OF THE SPEAR (Also see Tarzan)
Gold Key/Whitman No. 18: June, 1972 - No. 17, Feb, 1976; No. 18, May, 1982

	GD 2.0	VG 4.0	FN 6.0	VF 8.0	VF/NM 9.0	NM- 9.2
1	4	8	12	29	40	50
2-Painted-c begin, end #17	3	6	9	16	20	25
3-10	2	4	6	11	14	18
11-18: 12-Line drawn-c. 13-17-Spiegle-a. 18(5/82)-r/#2; Leopard Girl-r	2	4	6	8	10	12

BROTHERS, THE CULT ESCAPE, THE
Spire Christian Comics (Fleming H. Revell Co.): 1980 (49¢)

	GD 2.0	VG 4.0	FN 6.0	VF 8.0	VF/NM 9.0	NM- 9.2
nn	1	2	3	5	7	9

BROWNIES (See New Funnies)
Dell Publishing Co.: No. 192, July, 1948 - No. 605, Dec, 1954

	GD 2.0	VG 4.0	FN 6.0	VF 8.0	VF/NM 9.0	NM- 9.2
Four Color 192(#1)-Kelly-a	15	30	45	107	156	205
Four Color 244(9/49), 293 (9/50)-Last Kelly c/a	11	22	33	75	110	145
Four Color 337(7-8/51), 365(12-1/51-52), 398(5/52)	5	10	15	33	44	55
Four Color 436(11/52), 482(7/53), 522(12/53), 605	4	8	12	29	40	50

BRUCE GENTRY
Better/Standard/Four Star Publ./Superior No. 3: Jan, 1948 - No. 8, Jul, 1949

	GD 2.0	VG 4.0	FN 6.0	VF 8.0	VF/NM 9.0	NM- 9.2
1-Ray Bailey strip reprints begin, end #3; E. C. emblem appears as a monogram on stationery in story; negligee panels	50	100	150	300	450	600
2,3	37	74	111	213	299	385
4-8	26	52	78	147	206	265

NOTE: *Kamenish a-2-7; c-1-8.*

BRUCE LEE (Also see Deadly Hands of Kung Fu)
Malibu Comics: July, 1994 - No. 6, Dec, 1994 ($2.95, 36 pgs.)

	GD 2.0	VG 4.0	FN 6.0	VF 8.0	VF/NM 9.0	NM- 9.2
1-6: 1-(44 pgs.)-Mortal Kombat prev., 1st app. in comics. 2,6-(36 pgs.)						5.00

BRUCE JONES' OUTER EDGE
Innovation: 1993 ($2.50, B&W, one-shot)

	GD 2.0	VG 4.0	FN 6.0	VF 8.0	VF/NM 9.0	NM- 9.2
1-Bruce Jones-c/a/script						2.50

BRUCE WAYNE: AGENT OF S.H.I.E.L.D. (Also see Marvel Vs. DC #3 & DC Vs. Marvel #4)
Marvel Comics (Amalgam): Apr, 1996 ($1.95, one-shot)

	GD 2.0	VG 4.0	FN 6.0	VF 8.0	VF/NM 9.0	NM- 9.2
1-Chuck Dixon scripts & Cary Nord-c/a.						2.50

BRUISER
Anthem Publications: Feb, 1994 ($2.45)

	GD 2.0	VG 4.0	FN 6.0	VF 8.0	VF/NM 9.0	NM- 9.2
1						2.50

BRUTE, THE
Seaboard Publ. (Atlas): Feb, 1975 - No. 3, July, 1975

	GD 2.0	VG 4.0	FN 6.0	VF 8.0	VF/NM 9.0	NM- 9.2
1-Origin & 1st app; Sekowsky-a(p)	1	3	4	6	8	10
2-Sekowsky-a(p); Fleisher-s	1	2	3	4	5	7
3-Brunner/Starlin/Weiss-a(p)	1	2	3	5	6	8

BRUTE & BABE
Ominous Press: July, 1994 - No. 2, Aug, 1994

	GD 2.0	VG 4.0	FN 6.0	VF 8.0	VF/NM 9.0	NM- 9.2
1-($3.95, 8 tablets plus-c)-"...It Begins..."; tablet format						4.00
2-($2.50, 36 pgs.)-"Mael's Rage", 2-(40 pgs.)-Stiff additional variant-c						2.50

BRUTE FORCE
Marvel Comics: Aug, 1990 - No. 4, Nov, 1990 ($1.00, limited series)

	GD 2.0	VG 4.0	FN 6.0	VF 8.0	VF/NM 9.0	NM- 9.2
1-4: Animal super-heroes; Delbo & DeCarlo-a						2.50

B-SIDES (The Craptacular...)
Marvel Comics: Nov, 2002 - No. 3, Jan, 2003 ($2.99, limited series)

	GD 2.0	VG 4.0	FN 6.0	VF 8.0	VF/NM 9.0	NM- 9.2
1-3-Kieth-c/Weldele-a. 2-Dorkin-a (1 pg.) 2-FF cameo. 3-FF app.						3.00

BUBBLEGUM CRISIS: GRAND MAL
Dark Horse Comics: Mar, 1994 - No. 4, June, 1994 ($2.50, limited series)

	GD 2.0	VG 4.0	FN 6.0	VF 8.0	VF/NM 9.0	NM- 9.2
1-4-Japanese manga						2.50

BUCCANEER
I. W. Enterprises: No date (1963)

	GD 2.0	VG 4.0	FN 6.0	VF 8.0	VF/NM 9.0	NM- 9.2
I.W. Reprint #1(r-/Quality #20), #8(r-/#23): Crandall-a in each	3	6	9	19	25	32

BUCCANEERS (Formerly Kid Eternity)
Quality Comics: No. 19, Jan, 1950 - No. 27, May, 1951 (No. 24-27: 52 pgs.)

	GD 2.0	VG 4.0	FN 6.0	VF 8.0	VF/NM 9.0	NM- 9.2
19-Captain Daring, Black Roger, Eric Falcon & Spanish Main begin; Crandall-a	52	104	156	312	469	625
20,23-Crandall-a	39	78	117	230	325	420
21-Crandall-c/a	40	80	120	240	360	480
22-Bondage-c	32	64	96	180	255	330
24-26: 24-Adam Peril, U.S.N. begins. 25-Origin & 1st app. Corsair Queen. 26-last Spanish Main	28	56	84	157	221	285
27-Crandall-c/a	39	78	117	230	325	420
Super Reprint #12 (1964)-Crandall-r/#21	4	8	12	22	30	38

BUCCANEERS, THE (TV)
Dell Publishing Co.: No. 800, 1957

	GD 2.0	VG 4.0	FN 6.0	VF 8.0	VF/NM 9.0	NM- 9.2
Four Color 800-Photo-c	8	16	24	55	78	100

BUCKAROO BANZAI (Movie)
Marvel Comics Group: Dec, 1984 - No. 2, Feb, 1985

	GD 2.0	VG 4.0	FN 6.0	VF 8.0	VF/NM 9.0	NM- 9.2
1,2-Movie adaptation; r/Marvel Super Special #33; Texiera-c/a						3.00

BUCK DUCK
Atlas Comics (ANC): June, 1953 - No. 4, Dec, 1953

	GD 2.0	VG 4.0	FN 6.0	VF 8.0	VF/NM 9.0	NM- 9.2
1-Funny animal stories in all	14	28	42	81	111	140
2-4: 2-Ed Win-a(5)	8	16	24	43	54	65

BUCK JONES (Also see Crackajack Funnies, Famous Feature Stories, Master Comics #7 & Wow Comics #1, 1936)
Dell Publishing Co.: No. 299, Oct, 1950 - No. 850, Oct, 1957 (All Painted-c)

	GD 2.0	VG 4.0	FN 6.0	VF 8.0	VF/NM 9.0	NM- 9.2
Four Color 299(#1)-Buck Jones & his horse Silver-B begin; painted back-c begins, ends #5	14	28	42	99	145	190
2(4-6/51)	8	16	24	53	74	95
3-8(10-12/52)	6	12	18	43	59	75
Four Color 460,500,546,589	6	12	18	40	55	70
Four Color 652,733,850	4	8	12	29	40	50

BUCK ROGERS (Also see Famous Funnies, Pure Oil Comics, Salerno Carnival of Comics, 24 Pages of Comics, & Vicks Comics)
Famous Funnies: Winter, 1940-41 - No. 6, Sept, 1943
NOTE: Buck Rogers first appeared in the pulp magazine Amazing Stories Vol. 3 #5 in Aug, 1928.

	GD 2.0	VG 4.0	FN 6.0	VF 8.0	VF/NM 9.0	NM- 9.2
1-Sunday strip reprints by Rick Yager; begins with strip #190; Calkins-c	304	608	912	1976	3038	4100
2 (7/41)-Calkins-c	130	260	390	813	1219	1625

Buffalo Bill #3 © YM

Buffy the Vampire Slayer #46 © 20th Century Fox

Buffy the Vampire Slayer: Angel #1 © 20th Century Fox

	GD	VG	FN	VF	VF/NM	NM-
	2.0	4.0	6.0	8.0	9.0	9.2

3 (12/41), 4 (7/42) 112 224 336 700 1050 1400
5,6: 5-Story continues with Famous Funnies No. 80; Buck Rogers, Sky Roads. 6-Reprints of 1939 dailies; contains B.R. story "Crater of Doom" (2 pgs.) by Calkins not-r from Famous Funnies 96 192 288 600 900 1200

BUCK ROGERS
Toby Press: No. 100, Jan, 1951 - No. 9, May-June, 1951

100(#7)-All strip-r begin 31 62 93 175 248 320
101(#8), 9-All Anderson-a(1947-49-r/dailies) 24 48 72 138 194 250

BUCK ROGERS (...in the 25th Century No. 5 on) (TV)
Gold Key/Whitman No. 7 on: Oct, 1964; No. 2, July, 1979 - No. 16, May, 1982 (No #10; story was written but never released. #17 exists only as a press proof without covers and was never published)

1(10128-410, 12¢)-1st S.A. app. Buck Rogers & 1st new B. R. in comics since 1933 giveaway; painted-c; back-c pin-up 9 18 27 65 93 120
2(7/79)-6: 3,4,6-Movie adaptation; painted-c 2 4 6 8 10 12
7,11 (Whitman) 2 4 6 10 12 15
8,9 (prepack)(scarce) 3 6 9 16 20 25
12-16: 14(2/82), 15(3/82), 16(5/82) 1 2 3 5 7 9
Giant Movie Edition 11296(64pp, Whitman, $1.50), reprints GK #2-4 minus cover; tabloid size; photo-c (See Marvel Treasury) 3 6 9 18 23 28
Giant Movie Edition 02489(Western/Marvel, $1.50), reprints GK #2-4 minus cover 3 6 9 16 20 25

NOTE: ***Bolle** a-2p,3p, Movie Ed.(p). **McWilliams** a-2i,3i, 5-11, Movie Ed.(i). Painted c-1-9,11-13.*

BUCK ROGERS (Comics Module)
TSR, Inc.: 1990 - No. 10, 1991 ($2.95, 44 pgs.)

1-10 (1990): 1-Begin origin in 3 parts. 2-Indicia says #1. 2,3-Black Barney back-up story. 4-All Black Barney issue; B. B.-c. 5-Indicia says #6; Black Barney-c & lead story; Buck Rogers back-up story. 10-Flip book (72pgs.) 3.00

BUCKSKIN (TV)
Dell Publishing Co.: No. 1011, July, 1959 - No. 1107, June-Aug, 1960

Four Color 1011 (#1)-Photo-c 8 16 24 55 78 100
Four Color 1107-Photo-c 7 14 21 51 71 90

BUCKY O'HARE (Funny Animal)
Continuity Comics: 1988 ($5.95, graphic novel)

1-Golden-c/a(r); r/serial-Echo of Futurepast #1-6 1 2 3 4 5 7
Deluxe Hardcover ($40, 52pg, 8x11") 40.00

BUCKY O'HARE
Continuity Comics: Jan, 1991 - No. 5, 1991 ($2.00)

1-6: 1-Michael Golden-c/a 2.50

BUDDIES IN THE U.S. ARMY
Avon Periodicals: Nov, 1952 - No. 2, 1953

1-Lawrence-c 13 26 39 76 103 130
2-Mort Lawrence-c/a 9 18 27 52 66 80

BUFFALO BEE (TV)
Dell Publishing Co.: No. 957, Nov, 1958 - No. 1061, Dec-Feb, 1959-60

Four Color 957 (#1) 10 20 30 70 100 130
Four Color 1002 (8-10/59), 1061 8 16 24 53 74 95

BUFFALO BILL (See Frontier Fighters, Super Western Comics & Western Action Thrillers)
Youthful Magazines: No. 2, Oct, 1950 - No. 9, Dec, 1951

2-Annie Oakley story 13 26 39 76 103 130
3-9: 2-4-Walter Johnson-c/a. 9-Wildey-a 9 18 27 52 66 80

BUFFALO BILL CODY (See Cody of the Pony Express)

BUFFALO BILL, JR. (TV) (See Western Roundup)
Dell/Gold Key: Jan, 1956 - No. 13, Aug-Oct, 1959; 1965 (All photo-c)

Four Color 673 (#1) 8 16 24 58 82 105
Four Color 742,766,798,828,856(11/57) 6 12 18 38 52 65
7(2-4/58)-13 5 10 15 33 44 55
1(6/65, Gold Key)-Photo-c(r/F.C. #798); photo-b/c 4 8 12 29 40 50

BUFFALO BILL PICTURE STORIES
Street & Smith Publications: June-July, 1949 - No. 2, Aug-Sept, 1949

1,2-Wildey, Powell-a in each 14 28 42 79 107 135

BUFFY THE VAMPIRE SLAYER (Based on the TV series)
Dark Horse Comics: 1998 - No. 63, Nov, 2003 ($2.95/$2.99)

1-Bennett-a/Watson-s; Art Adams-c 1 2 3 5 7 9
1-Variant photo-c 1 2 3 5 7 9
1-Gold foil logo Art Adams-c 15.00
1-Gold foil logo photo-c 20.00
2-15-Regular and photo-c. 4-7-Gomez-a. 5,8-Green-c 5.00
16-48: 29,30-Angel x-over. 43-45-Death of Buffy. 47-Lobdell-s begin. 48-Pike returns 3.00
50-($3.50) Scooby gang battles Adam; back-up story by Watson 3.50
51-62: 51-54-Viva Las Buffy; pre-Sunnydale Buffy & Pike in Vegas 3.00
Annual '99 ($4.95)-Two stories and pin-ups 1 2 3 4 5 7
...: Chaos Bleeds (6/03, $2.99) Based on the video game; photo & Campbell-c 3.00
...: Creatures of Habit (3/02, $17.95) text with Horton & Paul Lee-a 18.00
...: Jonathan 1 (1/01, $2.99) two covers; Richards-a 3.00
...: Lost and Found 1 (3/02, $2.99) aftermath of Buffy's death; Richards-a 3.00
... Lovers Walk (2/01, $2.99) short stories by various; Richards & photo-c 3.00
...: Note From the Underground (3/03, $12.95) r/#47-50 13.00
...: Reunion (6/02, $3.50) Buffy & Angel's; Espenson-s; art by various 3.50
...: Slayer Interrupted TPB (2003, $14.95) r/#56-59 15.00
...: Tales of the Slayers (10/02, $3.50) art by Matsuda and Colan; art & photo-c 3.50
...: The Death of Buffy TPB (8/02, $15.95) r/#43-46 16.00
...: Viva Las Buffy TPB (7/03, $12.95) r/#51-54 13.00
Wizard #1/2 1 2 3 6 8 9

BUFFY THE VAMPIRE SLAYER: ANGEL
Dark Horse Comics: May, 1999 - No. 3, July, 1999 ($2.95, limited series)

1-3-Gomez-a; Matsuda-c & photo-c for each 3.00

BUFFY THE VAMPIRE SLAYER: GILES
Dark Horse Comics: Oct, 2000 ($2.95, one-shot)

1-Eric Powell-a; Powell & photo-c 3.00

BUFFY THE VAMPIRE SLAYER: HAUNTED
Dark Horse Comics: Dec, 2001 - No. 4, Mar, 2002 ($2.99, limited series)

1-4-Faith and the Mayor app.; Espenson-s/Richards-a 3.00
TPB (9/02, $12.95) r/series; photo-c 13.00

BUFFY THE VAMPIRE SLAYER: OZ
Dark Horse Comics: July, 2001 - No. 3, Sept, 2001 ($2.99, limited series)

1-3-Totleben & photo-c; Golden-s 3.00

BUFFY THE VAMPIRE SLAYER: SPIKE AND DRU
Dark Horse Comics: Apr, 1999; No. 2, Oct, 1999; No. 3, Dec, 2000 ($2.95)

1-3: 1,2-Photo-c. 3-Two covers (photo & Sook) 3.00

BUFFY THE VAMPIRE SLAYER: THE ORIGIN (Adapts movie screenplay)
Dark Horse Comics: Jan, 1999 - No. 3, Mar, 1999 ($2.95, limited series)

1-3-Brereton-s/Bennett-a; reg & photo-c for each 3.00

BUFFY THE VAMPIRE SLAYER: WILLOW & TARA
Dark Horse Comics: Apr, 2001 ($2.99, one-shot)

1-Terry Moore-a/Chris Golden & Amber Benson-s; Moore-c & photo-c 3.00
TPB (4/03, $9.95) r/#1 & W&T - Wilderness; photo-c 10.00

BUFFY THE VAMPIRE SLAYER: WILLOW & TARA - WILDERNESS
Dark Horse Comics: Jul, 2002 - No. 2, Sept, 2002 ($2.99, limited series)

1,2-Chris Golden & Amber Benson-s; Jothikaumar-c & photo-c 3.00

BUG
Marvel Comics: Mar, 1997 ($2.99, one-shot)

1-Micronauts character 3.00

BUGALOOS (TV)
Charlton Comics: Sept, 1971 - No. 4, Feb, 1972

1 4 8 12 29 40 50
2-4 3 6 9 18 24 30

NOTE: *No. 3(1/72) went on sale late in 1972 (after No. 4) with the 1/73 issues.*

BUGBOY
Image Comics: June, 1998 ($3.95, B&W, one-shot)

1-Mark Lewis-s/a 4.00

BUGHOUSE (Satire)
Ajax/Farrell (Excellent Publ.): Mar-Apr, 1954 - No. 4, Sept-Oct, 1954

V1#1 21 42 63 118 164 210
2-4 12 24 36 71 96 120

BUGS BUNNY (See The Best of..., Camp Comics, Comic Album #2, 6, 10, 14, Dell Giant #28, 32, 46, Dynabrite, Golden Comics Digest #1, 3, 5, 6, 8, 10, 14, 15, 17, 21, 26, 30, 34, 39, 42, 47, Kite Fun Book, Large Feature Comic #8, Looney Tunes and Merry Melodies, March of Comics #44, 59, 75, 83, 97, 115, 132, 149, 160, 179, 188, 201, 220, 231, 245, 259, 273, 287, 301, 315, 329, 343, 363, 367, 380, 392, 403, 415, 428, 440, 452, 464, 476, 487, Porky Pig, Puffed Wheat, Story Hour Series #802, Super Book #14, 26 and Whitman Comic Books)

BUGS BUNNY (See Dell Giants for annuals)
Dell Publishing Co./Gold Key No. 86-218/Whitman No. 219 on: 1942 - No. 245, April, 1984

Bugs Bunny #88 © WB

Bulletman #5 © FAW

Bullets and Bracelets #1 © DC & MAR

	GD 2.0	VG 4.0	FN 6.0	VF 8.0	VF/NM 9.0	NM- 9.2
Large Feature Comic 8(1942)-(Rarely found in fine-mint condition)	128	256	384	896	1423	1950
Four Color 33 ('43)	115	230	345	805	1240	1675
Four Color 51	35	70	105	263	394	525
Four Color 88	23	46	69	167	244	320
Four Color 123('46),142,164	17	34	51	121	178	235
Four Color 187,200,217,233	12	24	36	87	129	170
Four Color 250-Used in **SOTI**, pg. 309	13	26	39	94	137	180
Four Color 266,274,281,289,298('50)	10	20	30	70	100	130
Four Color 307,317(#1),327(#2),338,347,355,366,376,393	9	18	27	63	89	115
Four Color 407,420,432(10/52)	8	16	24	53	74	95
Four Color 498(9/53),585(9/54), 647(9/55)	6	12	18	40	55	70
Four Color 724(9/56),838(9/57),1064(12/59)	5	10	15	36	48	60
28(12-1/52-53)-30	6	12	18	40	55	70
31-50	4	8	12	29	40	50
51-85(7-9/62)	3	7	10	21	28	35
86(10/62)-88-Bugs Bunny's Showtime-(25¢, 80pgs.)	7	14	21	50	68	85
89-99	3	6	9	18	23	28
100	3	6	9	18	24	30
101-118: 118-Last 12¢ issue	2	4	6	12	16	20
119-140	2	4	6	10	13	16
141-170	2	4	6	8	10	12
171-218	1	2	3	5	7	9
219,220,225-237(5/82): 229-Swipe of Barks story/WDC&S #223. 233(2/82)	1	3	4	6	8	10
221(9/80),222(11/80)-Pre-pack? (Scarce)	2	4	6	12	16	20
223 (1/81),224 (3/81)-Low distr.	2	4	6	10	13	16
238-245 (#90070 on-c, nd, nd code; pre-pack): 238(5/83), 239(6/83), 240(7/83), 241(7/83), 242(8/83), 243(8/83), 244(3/84), 245(4/84)	2	4	6	11	14	18

NOTE: *Reprints-100,102-104,110,115,123,143,144,147,167,173,175-177,179-185,187,190.*

	GD 2.0	VG 4.0	FN 6.0	VF 8.0	VF/NM 9.0	NM- 9.2
...Comic-Go-Round 11196-(224 pgs.)($1.95)(Golden Press, 1979)	4	8	12	24	32	40
...Winter Fun 1(12/67-Gold Key)-Giant	5	10	15	36	48	60

BUGS BUNNY
DC Comics: June, 1990 - No. 3, Aug, 1990 ($1.00, limited series)

	GD 2.0	VG 4.0	FN 6.0	VF 8.0	VF/NM 9.0	NM- 9.2
1-3: Daffy Duck, Elmer Fudd, others app.						4.00

BUGS BUNNY (...Monthly on-c)
DC Comics: 1993 - No. 3, 1994? ($1.95)

	GD 2.0	VG 4.0	FN 6.0	VF 8.0	VF/NM 9.0	NM- 9.2
1-3-Bugs, Porky Pig, Daffy, Road Runner						3.50

BUGS BUNNY & PORKY PIG
Gold Key: Sept, 1965 (Paper-c, giant, 100 pgs.)

	GD 2.0	VG 4.0	FN 6.0	VF 8.0	VF/NM 9.0	NM- 9.2
1(30025-509)	9	18	27	63	89	115

BUGS BUNNY'S ALBUM (See Bugs Bunny, Four Color No. 498,585,647,724)

BUGS BUNNY LIFE STORY ALBUM (See Bugs Bunny, Four Color No. 838)

BUGS BUNNY MERRY CHRISTMAS (See Bugs Bunny, Four Color No. 1064)

BUILDING, THE
Kitchen Sink Press: 1987; 2000 (8 1/2" x 11" sepia toned graphic novel)

	GD 2.0	VG 4.0	FN 6.0	VF 8.0	VF/NM 9.0	NM- 9.2
nn-Will Eisner-s/c/a						10.00
nn-(DC Comics, 9/00, $9.95) reprints 1987 edition						10.00

BULLET CROW, FOWL OF FORTUNE
Eclipse Comics: Mar, 1987 - No. 2, Apr, 1987 ($2.00, B&W, limited series)

	GD 2.0	VG 4.0	FN 6.0	VF 8.0	VF/NM 9.0	NM- 9.2
1,2-The Comic Reader-r & new-a						2.50

BULLETMAN (See Fawcett Miniatures, Master Comics, Mighty Midget Comics, Nickel Comics & XMas Comics)
Fawcett Publications: Sum, 1941 - #12, 2/12/43; #14, Spr, 1946 - #16, Fall, 1946 (No #13)

	GD 2.0	VG 4.0	FN 6.0	VF 8.0	VF/NM 9.0	NM- 9.2
1-Silver metallic-c	370	740	1110	2405	3703	5000
2-Raboy-c	160	320	480	1000	1500	2000
3,5-Raboy-c each	109	218	327	681	1021	1360
4	96	192	288	600	900	1200
6-10: 7-Ghost Stories told by night watchman of cemetery begins; Eisnerish-a; hidden message "Chic Stone is a jerk"	80	160	240	500	750	1000
11,12,14-16 (nn 13): 12-Robot-c	61	122	183	381	571	760

NOTE: ***Mac Raboy** c-1-3, 5, 6, 10. "Bulletman the Flying Detective" on cover #8 on.*

BULLETPROOF MONK (Inspired the 2003 film)
Image Comics (Flypaper Press): 1998 - No. 3, 1999 ($2.95, limited series)

	GD 2.0	VG 4.0	FN 6.0	VF 8.0	VF/NM 9.0	NM- 9.2
1-3-Oeming-a						3.00
...: Tales of the BPM (3/03, $2.95) Flip book; 2 covers by Sale; art by Sale, Oeming, Dave Johnson; Seann William Scott afterword						3.00
TPB (2002, $9.95) r/#1-3; foreword by John Woo						10.00

BULLETS AND BRACELETS (Also see Marvel Versus DC #3 & DC Versus Marvel #4)
Marvel Comics (Amalgam): Apr, 1996 ($1.95)

	GD 2.0	VG 4.0	FN 6.0	VF 8.0	VF/NM 9.0	NM- 9.2
1-John Ostrander script & Gary Frank-c/a						2.50

BULLS-EYE (Cody of The Pony Express No. 8 on)
Mainline No. 1-5/Charlton No. 6,7: 7-8/54-No. 5, 3-4/55; No. 6, 6/55; No. 7, 8/55

	GD 2.0	VG 4.0	FN 6.0	VF 8.0	VF/NM 9.0	NM- 9.2
1-S&K-c, 2 pgs.-a	55	110	165	330	495	660
2-S&K-c/a	46	92	138	276	413	550
3-5-S&K-c/a(2 each). 4-Last pre-code issue (1-2/55). 5-Censored issue with tomahawks removed in battle scene	40	80	120	240	340	440
6-S&K-c/a	34	68	102	193	274	355
7-S&K-c/a(3)	40	80	120	240	340	440

BULLS-EYE COMICS (Formerly Komik Pages #10; becomes Kayo #12)
Harry 'A' Chesler: No. 11, 1944

	GD 2.0	VG 4.0	FN 6.0	VF 8.0	VF/NM 9.0	NM- 9.2
11-Origin K-9, Green Knight's sidekick, Lance; The Green Knight, Lady Satan, Yankee Doodle Jones app.	42	84	126	252	376	500

BULLWHIP GRIFFIN (See Movie Comics)

BULLWINKLE (...and Rocky No. 22 on; See March of Comics #233 and Rocky & Bullwinkle) (TV) (Jay Ward)
Dell/Gold Key: 3-5/62 - #11, 4/74; #12, 6/76 - #19, 3/78; #20, 4/79 - #25, 2/80

	GD 2.0	VG 4.0	FN 6.0	VF 8.0	VF/NM 9.0	NM- 9.2
Four Color 1270 (3-5/62)	21	42	63	149	220	290
01-090-209 (Dell, 7-9/62)	17	34	51	118	174	230
1(11/62, Gold Key)	15	30	45	104	152	200
2(2/63)	10	20	30	67	96	125
3(4/72)-11(4/74-Gold Key)	6	12	18	38	52	65
12-14: 12(6/76)-Reprints. 13(9/76), 14-New stories	3	6	9	18	23	28
15-25	2	4	6	10	13	16
Mother Moose Nursery Pomes 01-530-207 (5-7/62, Dell)	19	38	57	136	198	260

NOTE: *Reprints: 6, 7, 20-24.*

BULLWINKLE (...& Rocky No. 2 on)(TV)
Charlton Comics: July, 1970 - No. 7, July, 1971

	GD 2.0	VG 4.0	FN 6.0	VF 8.0	VF/NM 9.0	NM- 9.2
1	6	12	18	43	59	75
2-7	4	8	12	29	40	50

BULLWINKLE AND ROCKY
Star Comics/Marvel Comics No. 3 on: Nov, 1987 - No. 9, Mar, 1989

	GD 2.0	VG 4.0	FN 6.0	VF 8.0	VF/NM 9.0	NM- 9.2
1-9: Boris & Natasha in all. 3,5,8-Dudley Do-Right app. 4-Reagan-c						4.00
Marvel Moosterworks (1/92, $4.95)	1	3	4	6	8	10

BUMMER
Fantagraphics Books: June, 1995 ($3.50, B&W, mature)

	GD 2.0	VG 4.0	FN 6.0	VF 8.0	VF/NM 9.0	NM- 9.2
1						3.50

BUNNY (Also see Harvey Pop Comics)
Harvey Publications: Dec, 1966 - No. 20, Dec, 1971; No. 21, Nov, 1976

	GD 2.0	VG 4.0	FN 6.0	VF 8.0	VF/NM 9.0	NM- 9.2
1-68 pg. Giants begin	8	16	24	53	74	95
2-10	4	8	12	29	40	50
11-18: 18-Last 68 pg. Giant	4	8	12	27	36	45
19-21-52 pg. Giants: 21-Fruitman app.	4	8	12	24	32	40

BURKE'S LAW (TV)
Dell Publ.: 1-3/64; No. 2, 5-7/64; No. 3, 3-5/65 (All have Gene Barry photo-c)

	GD 2.0	VG 4.0	FN 6.0	VF 8.0	VF/NM 9.0	NM- 9.2
1-Photo-c	6	12	18	38	52	65
2,3-Photo-c	4	8	12	28	38	48

BURNING ROMANCES (See Fox Giants)

BUSTER BEAR
Quality Comics Group (Arnold Publ.): Dec, 1953 - No. 10, June, 1955

	GD 2.0	VG 4.0	FN 6.0	VF 8.0	VF/NM 9.0	NM- 9.2
1-Funny animal	10	20	30	58	77	95
2	6	12	18	33	41	48
3-10	6	12	18	27	33	38
I.W. Reprint #9,10 (Super on inside)	2	4	6	10	13	16

BUSTER BROWN COMICS (See Promotional Comics section)

BUSTER BUNNY
Standard Comics(Animated Cartoons)/Pines: Nov, 1949 - No. 16, Oct, 1953

	GD 2.0	VG 4.0	FN 6.0	VF 8.0	VF/NM 9.0	NM- 9.2
1-Frazetta 1 pg. text illo.	10	20	30	58	77	95
2	6	12	18	33	41	48
3-14,16	5	10	15	24	30	35
15-Racist-c	6	12	18	31	38	45

BUSTER CRABBE (TV)

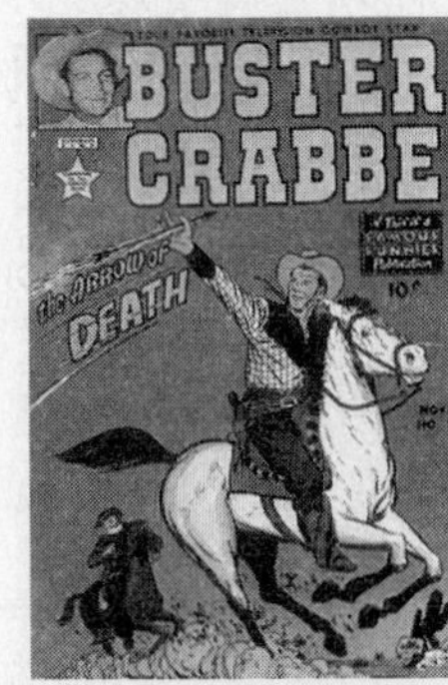

Buster Crabbe #1 © FF

The Buzz #3 © MAR

Cable #99 © MAR

	GD 2.0	VG 4.0	FN 6.0	VF 8.0	VF/NM 9.0	NM- 9.2

Famous Funnies Publ.: Nov, 1951 - No. 12, 1953

	GD	VG	FN	VF	VF/NM	NM-
1-1st app.(?) Frazetta anti-drug ad; text story about Buster Crabbe & Billy the Kid	39	78	117	233	329	425
2-Williamson/Evans-c; text story about Wild Bill Hickok & Pecos Bill	38	76	114	219	310	400
3-Williamson/Evans-c/a	39	78	117	233	329	425
4-Frazetta-c/a, 1pg.; bondage-c	48	96	144	288	432	575
5-Frazetta-c; Williamson/Krenkel/Orlando-a, 11pgs. (per Mr. Williamson)	118	236	354	738	1107	1475
6,8	19	38	57	109	152	195
7-Frazetta one pg. ad	20	40	60	112	156	200
9-One pg. Frazetta Boy Scouts ad (1st?)	17	34	51	98	134	170
10-12	12	24	36	69	92	115

NOTE: Eastern Color sold 3 dozen each NM file copies of #s 9-12 a few years ago.

BUSTER CRABBE (The Amazing Adventures of...)(Movie star)
Lev Gleason Publications: Dec, 1953 - No. 4, June, 1954

	GD	VG	FN	VF	VF/NM	NM-
1,4: 1-Photo-c. 4-Flash Gordon-c	23	46	69	129	180	230
2,3-Toth-a	21	42	63	118	164	210

BUTCH CASSIDY
Skywald Comics: June, 1971 - No. 3, Oct, 1971 (52 pgs.)

	GD	VG	FN	VF	VF/NM	NM-
1-Red Mask reprint, retitled Maverick; Bolle-a; Sutton-a	2	4	6	14	18	22
2,3: 2-Whip Wilson-r. 3-Dead Canyon Days reprint/Crack Western No. 63; Sundance Kid app.; Crandall-a	2	4	6	10	13	16

BUTCH CASSIDY (...& the Wild Bunch)
Avon Periodicals: 1951

	GD	VG	FN	VF	VF/NM	NM-
1-Kinstler-c/a	19	38	57	107	149	190

NOTE: *Reinman story; Issue number on inside spine.*

BUTCH CASSIDY (See Fun-In No. 11 & Western Adventure Comics)

BUTCHER, THE (Also see Brave and the Bold, 2nd Series))
DC Comics: May, 1990 - No. 5, Sept, 1990 ($1.50, mature)

1-5: 1-No indicia inside 2.50

BUTCHER KNIGHT
Image Comics (Top Cow): Jan, 2001 - No. 4, June, 2001 ($2.95, limited series)

Preview (B&W, 16 pgs.) Dwayne Turner-c/a 2.25
1-4-Dwayne Turner-c/a 3.00

BUZ SAWYER (Sweeney No. 4 on)
Standard Comics: June, 1948 - No. 3, 1949

	GD	VG	FN	VF	VF/NM	NM-
1-Roy Crane-a	23	46	69	132	186	240
2-Intro his pal Sweeney	14	28	42	79	107	135
3	11	22	33	63	84	105

BUZ SAWYER'S PAL, ROSCOE SWEENEY (See Sweeney)

BUZZ, THE (Also see Spider-Girl)
Marvel Comics: July, 2000 - No. 3, Sept, 2000 ($2.99, limited series)

1-3-Buscema-a/DeFalco & Frenz-s 3.00

BUZZ BUZZ COMICS MAGAZINE
Horse Press: May, 1996 ($4.95, B&W, over-sized magazine)

1-Paul Pope-c/a/scripts; Moebius-a 5.00

BUZZY (See All Funny Comics)
National Periodical Publications/Detective Comics: Winter, 1944-45 - No. 75, 1-2/57; No. 76, 10/57; No. 77, 10/58

	GD	VG	FN	VF	VF/NM	NM-
1 (52 pgs. begin); "America's favorite teenster"	32	64	96	180	255	330
2 (Spr, 1945)	16	32	48	89	122	155
3-5	11	22	33	63	84	105
6-10	9	18	27	49	62	75
11-20	8	16	24	40	50	60
21-30	7	14	21	35	43	50
31,35-38	6	12	18	31	38	45
32-34,39-Last 52 pgs. Scribbly story by Mayer in each (these four stories were done for Scribbly #14 which was delayed for a year)	7	14	21	37	46	55
40-77: 62-Last precode (2/55)	6	12	18	28	34	40

BUZZY THE CROW (See Harvey Comics Hits #60 & 62, Harvey Hits #18 & Paramount Animated Comics #1)

BY BIZARRE HANDS
Dark Horse Comics: Apr, 1994 - No. 3, June, 1994 ($2.50, B&W, mature)

1-3: Lansdale stories 2.50

CABBOT: BLOODHUNTER (Also see Bloodstrike & Bloodstrike: Assassin)
Maximum Press: Jan, 1997 ($2.50, one-shot)

1-Rick Veitch-a/script; Platt-c; Thor, Chapel & Prophet cameos 2.50

CABLE (See Ghost Rider &..., & New Mutants #87) (Title becomes Soldier X)
Marvel Comics: May, 1993 - No. 107, Sept, 2002 ($3.50/$1.95/$1.50-$2.25)

1-($3.50, 52 pgs.)-Gold foil & embossed-c; Thibert a-1-4p; c-1-3 5.00
2-15: 3-Extra 16 pg. X-Men/Avengers ann. preview. 4-Liefeld-a assist; last Thibert-a(p). 6-8-Reveals that Baby Nathan is Cable; gives background on Stryfe. 9-Omega Red-c/story. 11-Bound-in trading card sheet 3.50
16-Newsstand edition 2.50
16-Enhanced edition 5.00
17-20-($1.95)-Deluxe edition, 20-w/bound in '95 Fleer Ultra cards 3.00
17-20-($1.50)-Standard edition 2.50
21-24, 26-44, -1(7/97): 21-Begin $1.95-c; return from Age of Apocalyse. 24-Grizzly dies. 28-vs. Sugarman; Mr. Sinister app. 30-X-Man-c/app.; Exodus app. 31-vs. X-Man. 32-Post app. 33-Post-c/app; Mandarin app (flashback); includes "Onslaught Update". 34-Onslaught x-over; Hulk-c/app; Apocalypse app. (cont'd in Hulk #444). 35-Onslaught x-over; Apocalypse vs. Cable. 36-w/card insert. 38-Weapon X-c/app; Psycho Man & Micronauts app. 40-Scott Clark-a(p). 41-Bishop-c/app. 3.00
25 ($3.95)-Foil gatefold-c 4.00
45-49,51-74: 45-Operation Zero Tolerance. 51-1st Casey-s. 54-Black Panther. 55-Domino-c/app. 62-Nick Fury-c/app.63-Stryfe-c/app. 67,68-Avengers-c/app. 71,73-Liefeld-a 2.50
50-($2.99) Double sized w/wraparound-c 3.00
75 -($2.99) Liefeld-c/a; Apocalypse: The Twelve x-over 3.00
76-79: 76-Apocalypse: The Twelve x-over 2.50
80-96: 80-Begin $2.25-c. 87-Mystique-c/app. 2.50
97-99,101-107: 97-Tischman-s/Kordey-a/c begin 2.25
100($3.99) Dialogue-free 'Nuff Said back-up story 4.00
.../Machine Man '98 Annual ($2.99) Wraparound-c 3.00
.../X-Force '96 Annual ($2.95) Wraparound-c 3.00
...'99 Annual ($3.50) vs. Sinister; computer photo-c 3.50
...Second Genesis 1 (9/99, $3.99) r/New Mutants #99, 100 and X-Force #1; Liefeld-c 4.00
...: The End (2002, $14.99, TPB) r/#101-107 15.00

CABLE - BLOOD AND METAL (Also see New Mutants #87 & X-Force #8)
Marvel Comics: Oct, 1992 - No. 2, Nov, 1992 ($2.50, limited series, 52 pgs.)

1-Fabian Nicieza scripts; John Romita, Jr.-c/a in both; Cable vs. Stryfe; 2nd app. of The Wild Pack (becomes The Six Pack); wraparound-c 4.00
2-Prelude to X-Cutioner's Song 3.00

CADET GRAY OF WEST POINT (See Dell Giants)

CADILLACS & DINOSAURS (TV)
Marvel Comics (Epic Comics): Nov, 1990 - No. 6, Apr, 1991 ($2.50, limited series)

1-6: r/Xenozoic Tales in color w/new-c 3.00
...In 3-D #1 (7/92, $3.95, Kitchen Sink)-With glasses 6.00

CADILLACS AND DINOSAURS (TV)
Topps Comics: V2#1, Feb, 1994 - V2#9, 1995 ($2.50, limited series)

V2#1-($2.95)-Collector's edition w/Stout-c & bound-in poster; Buckler-a; foil stamped logo; Giordano-a in all 6.00
V2#1-9: 1-Newsstand edition w/Giordano-c. 2,3-Collector's editions w/Stout-c & posters. 2,3-Newsstand ed. w/Giordano-c; w/o posters. 4-6-Collectors & Newsstand editions; Kieth-c. 7-9-Linsner-c 3.00

CAFFEINE
Slave Labor Graphics: Jan, 1996 - No. 10, 1999 ($2.95/$3.95, B&W)

1-9 3.00
10-($3.95) 4.00

CAGE (Also see Hero for Hire, Power Man & Punisher)
Marvel Comics: Apr, 1992 - No. 20, Nov, 1993 ($1.25)

1,3,10,12: 3-Punisher-c & minor app. 10-Rhino & Hulk-c/app. 12-(52 pgs.)-Iron Fist app. 3.00
2,4-9,11,13-20: 9-Rhino-c/story; Hulk cameo 2.50

CAGE (Volume 3)
Marvel Comics (MAX): Mar, 2002 - No. 5, Sept, 2002 ($2.99, mature)

1-5-Corben-c/a; Azzarello-s 3.00
HC (2002, $19.99, with dustjacket) r/#1-5; intro. by Darius James; sketch pages 20.00
SC (2003, $13.99) r/#1-5; intro. by Darius James 14.00

CAGED HEAT 3000 (Movie)
Roger Corman's Cosmic Comics: Nov, 1995 - No. 3, Jan, 1996 ($2.50)

1-3: Adaptation of film 2.50

CAGES
Tundra Publ.: 1991 - No. 10, May, 1996 ($3.50/$3.95/$4.95, limited series)

	GD	VG	FN	VF	VF/NM	NM-
1-Dave McKean-c/a in all	2	4	6	8	10	12

The Call #1 © MAR

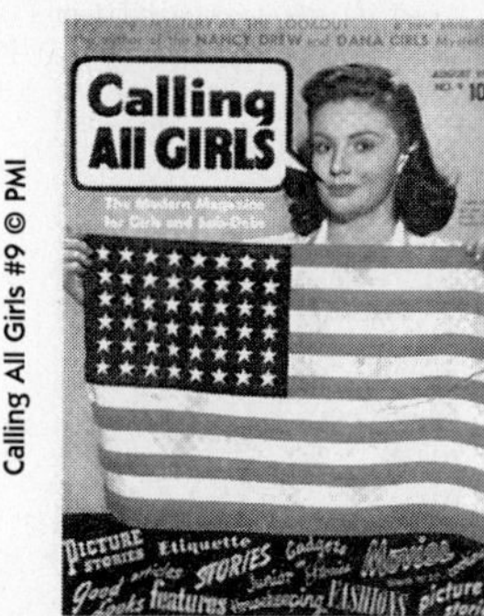

Calling All Girls #9 © PMI

Camp Candy #2 © DIC

	GD 2.0	VG 4.0	FN 6.0	VF 8.0	VF/NM 9.0	NM- 9.2
2-Misprint exists	1	2	3	5	6	8
3-9: 5-$3.95-c begins						4.00
10-($4.95)						5.00

CAIN'S HUNDRED (TV)
Dell Publishing Co.: May-July, 1962 - No. 2, Sept-Nov, 1962

	GD	VG	FN	VF	VF/NM	NM-
nn(01-094-207)	4	8	12	22	30	38
2	3	6	9	16	20	24

CAIN/VAMPIRELLA FLIP BOOK
Harris Comics: Oct, 1994 ($6.95, one-shot, squarebound)

	GD	VG	FN	VF	VF/NM	NM-
nn-contains Cain #3 & #4; flip book is r/Vampirella story from 1993 Creepy Fearbook	1	2	3	5	7	9

CALIBER PRESENTS
Caliber Press: Jan, 1989 - No. 24, 1991 ($1.95/$2.50, B&W, 52 pgs.)

	GD	VG	FN	VF	VF/NM	NM-
1-Anthology; 1st app. The Crow; Tim Vigil-c/a	6	12	18	40	55	70
2-Deadworld story; Tim Vigil-a	2	4	6	9	11	14
3-24: 15-24 ($3.50, 68 pgs.)						3.50

CALIBER PRESENTS: CINDERELLA ON FIRE
Caliber Press: 1994 ($2.95, B&W, mature)

	GD	VG	FN	VF	VF/NM	NM-
1						3.00

CALIBER SPOTLIGHT
Caliber Press: May, 1995 ($2.95, B&W)

	GD	VG	FN	VF	VF/NM	NM-
1-Kabuki app						3.50

CALIBRATIONS
Caliber: 1996 - No. 5 (99¢, anthology)

	GD	VG	FN	VF	VF/NM	NM-
1-5: 1-Jill Thompson-c/a. 1,2-Atmospherics by Warren Ellis						2.50

CALIFORNIA GIRLS
Eclipse Comics: June, 1987 - No. 8, May, 1988 ($2.00, 40 pgs, B&W)

	GD	VG	FN	VF	VF/NM	NM-
1-8: All contain color paper dolls						3.00

CALL, THE
Marvel Comics: June, 2003 - No. 4, Sept, 2003 ($2.25)

	GD	VG	FN	VF	VF/NM	NM-
1-4-Austen-s/Olliffe-a						2.25

CALLING ALL BOYS (Tex Granger No. 18 on)
Parents' Magazine Institute: Jan, 1946 - No. 17, May, 1948 (Photo c-1-5,7,8)

	GD	VG	FN	VF	VF/NM	NM-
1	12	24	36	69	92	120
2-Contains Roy Rogers article	7	14	21	37	46	55
3-7,9,11,14-17: 6-Painted-c. 11-Rin Tin Tin photo on-c; Tex Granger begins. 14-J. Edgar Hoover photo on-c. 15-Tex Granger-c begin	6	12	18	27	33	38
8-Milton Caniff story	8	16	24	43	54	65
10-Gary Cooper photo on-c	8	16	24	40	50	60
12-Bob Hope photo on-c	12	24	36	71	96	120
13-Bing Crosby photo on-c	10	20	30	60	80	100

CALLING ALL GIRLS
Parents' Magazine Institute: Sept, 1941 - No. 89, Sept, 1949 (Part magazine, part comic)

	GD	VG	FN	VF	VF/NM	NM-
1	17	34	51	95	130	165
2-Photo-c	9	18	27	52	66	80
3-Shirley Temple photo-c	11	22	33	66	88	110
4-10: 4,5,7,9-Photo-c. 9-Flag-c	7	14	21	37	46	55
11-Tina Thayer photo-c; Mickey Rooney photo-b/c; B&W photo inside of Gary Cooper as Lou Gehrig in "Pride of Yankees"	8	16	24	43	54	65
12-20	6	12	18	31	38	45
21-39,41-43(10-11/45)-Last issue with comics	6	12	18	27	33	38
40-Liz Taylor photo-c	16	32	48	92	126	160
44-51(7/46)-Last comic book size issue	5	10	15	23	28	32
52-89	5	10	14	20	24	28

NOTE: ***Jack Sparling** art in many issues; becomes a girls' magazine "Senior Prom" with #90.*

CALLING ALL KIDS (Also see True Comics)
Parents' Magazine Institute: Dec-Jan, 1945-46 - No. 26, Aug, 1949

	GD	VG	FN	VF	VF/NM	NM-
1-Funny animal	12	24	36	71	96	120
2	7	14	21	37	46	55
3-10	6	12	18	28	34	40
11-26	5	10	15	24	30	35

CALL OF DUTY, THE : THE BROTHERHOOD
Marvel Comics: Aug, 2002 - No. 6, Jan, 2003 ($2.25)

	GD	VG	FN	VF	VF/NM	NM-
1-Exploits of NYC Fire Dept.; Finch-c/a; Austen & Bruce Jones-s						4.00
2-6-Austen-s						2.50
...Vol 1: The Brotherhood & The Wagon TPB (2002, $14.99) r/#1-6 & ...The Wagon #1-4						15.00

CALL OF DUTY, THE : THE PRECINCT
Marvel Comics: Sept, 2002 - No. 5, Jan, 2003 ($2.25, limited series)

	GD	VG	FN	VF	VF/NM	NM-
1-Exploits of NYC Police Dept.; Finch-c; Bruce Jones-s/Mandrake-a						3.00
2-4						2.25
...Vol 2: The Precinct TPB (2003, $9.99) r/#1-4						10.00

CALL OF DUTY, THE : THE WAGON
Marvel Comics: Oct, 2002 - No. 4, Jan, 2003 ($2.25, limited series)

	GD	VG	FN	VF	VF/NM	NM-
1-4-Exploits of NYC EMS Dept.; Finch-c; Austen-s/Zelzej-a						2.25

CALVIN (See Li'l Kids)

CALVIN & THE COLONEL (TV)
Dell Publishing Co.: No. 1354, Apr-June, 1962 - No. 2, July-Sept, 1962

	GD	VG	FN	VF	VF/NM	NM-
Four Color 1354(#1)	10	20	30	67	96	125
2	7	14	21	46	63	80

CAMBION
Slave Labor Graphics: Dec, 1995 - No. 2, Feb, 1996 ($2.95, B&W)

	GD	VG	FN	VF	VF/NM	NM-
1,2						3.00

CAMELOT 3000
DC Comics: Dec, 1982 - No. 11, July, 1984; No. 12, Apr, 1985 (Direct sales, maxi series, Mando paper)

	GD	VG	FN	VF	VF/NM	NM-
1-12: 1-Mike Barr scripts & Brian Bolland-c/a begin. 5-Intro Knights of New Camelot						3.00
TPB (1988, $12.95) r/#1-12						13.00

NOTE: ***Austin** a-7i-12i. **Bolland** a-1-12p; c-1-12.*

CAMERA COMICS
U.S. Camera Publishing Corp./ME: July, 1944 - No. 9, Summer, 1946

	GD	VG	FN	VF	VF/NM	NM-
nn (7/44)	25	50	75	147	202	260
nn (9/44)	19	38	57	109	152	195
1(10/44)-The Grey Comet	19	38	57	109	152	195
2	14	28	42	79	107	135
3-Nazi WW II-c; photos	13	26	39	76	103	130
4-9: All half photos	11	22	33	66	88	110

CAMP CANDY (TV)
Marvel Comics: May, 1990 - No. 6, Oct, 1990 ($1.00, limited series)

	GD	VG	FN	VF	VF/NM	NM-
1-6: Post-c/a(p); featuring John Candy						4.00

CAMP COMICS
Dell Publishing Co.: Feb, 1942 - No. 3, April, 1942 (All have photo-c)

	GD	VG	FN	VF	VF/NM	NM-
1- "Seaman Sy Wheeler" by Kelly, 7 pgs.; Bugs Bunny app.; Mark Twain adaptation	72	144	216	450	675	900
2-Kelly-a, 12 pgs.; Bugs Bunny app.; classic-c	72	144	216	450	675	900
3-(Scarce)-Dave Berg & Walt Kelly-a	59	118	177	369	555	740

CAMP RUNAMUCK (TV)
Dell Publishing Co.: Apr, 1966

	GD	VG	FN	VF	VF/NM	NM-
1-Photo-c	4	8	12	24	32	40

CAMPUS LOVES
Quality Comics Group (Comic Magazines): Dec, 1949 - No. 5, Aug, 1950

	GD	VG	FN	VF	VF/NM	NM-
1-Ward-c/a (9 pgs.)	33	66	99	190	270	350
2-Ward-c/a	26	52	78	147	206	265
3-5	13	26	39	76	103	130

NOTE: ***Gustavson** a-1-5. Photo c-3-5.*

CAMPUS ROMANCE (...Romances on cover)
Avon Periodicals/Realistic: Sept-Oct, 1949 - No. 3, Feb-Mar, 1950

	GD	VG	FN	VF	VF/NM	NM-
1-Walter Johnson-a; c-/Avon paperback #348	24	48	72	138	194	250
2-Grandenetti-a; c-/Avon paperback #151	18	36	54	101	138	175
3-c-/Avon paperback #201	18	36	54	101	138	175
Realistic reprint	8	16	24	46	58	70

CANADA DRY PREMIUMS (See Swamp Fox, The & Terry & The Pirates in the Promotional Comics section)

CANCELLED COMIC CAVALCADE (See the Promotional Comics section)

CANDID TALES (Also see Bold Stories & It Rhymes With Lust)
Kirby Publ. Co.: April, 1950; June, 1950 (Digest size) (144 pgs.) (Full color)

	GD	VG	FN	VF	VF/NM	NM-
nn-(Scarce) Contains Wood female pirate story, 15 pgs., and 14 pgs. in June issue; Powell-a	96	192	288	600	900	1200

NOTE: *Another version exists with Dr. Kilmore by Wood; no female pirate story.*

CANDY
William H. Wise & Co.: Fall, 1944 - No. 3, Spring, 1945

	GD	VG	FN	VF	VF/NM	NM-
1-Two Scoop Scuttle stories by Wolverton	40	80	120	240	340	440
2,3-Scoop Scuttle by Wolverton, 2-4 pgs.	29	58	87	164	232	300

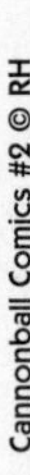
Cannonball Comics #2 © RH

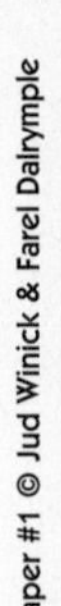
Caper #1 © Jud Winick & Farel Dalrymple

Captain America #225 © MAR

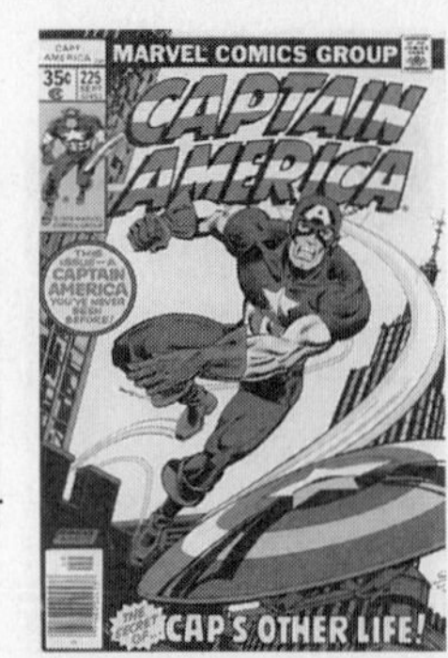

	GD 2.0	VG 4.0	FN 6.0	VF 8.0	VF/NM 9.0	NM- 9.2
CANDY (Teen-age)(Also see Police Comics #37)						
Quality Comics Group (Comic Magazines): Autumn, 1947 - No. 64, Jul, 1956						
1-Gustavson-a	24	48	72	138	194	250
2-Gustavson-a	13	26	39	74	100	125
3-10	9	18	27	49	62	75
11-30	7	14	21	35	43	50
31-64: 64-Ward-c(p)?	6	12	18	31	38	45
Super Reprint No. 2,10,12,16,17,18('63- '64):17-Candy #12	2	4	6	11	14	18
NOTE: ***Jack Cole** 1-2 pg. art in many issues.*						
CANNON (See Heroes, Inc. Presents Cannon)						
CANNONBALL COMICS						
Rural Home Publishing Co.: Feb, 1945 - No. 2, Mar, 1945						
1-The Crash Kid, Thunderbrand, The Captive Prince & Crime Crusader begin; skull-c	85	170	255	531	796	1060
2-Devil-c	66	132	198	413	617	820
CANNON GOD EXAXXION (Manga)						
Dark Horse Comics: Nov, 2001 - Present ($2.99, B&W, limited series)						
1-8,16,17: 1-Kenichi Sonoda-s/a in all						3.00
9,12-($3.99, 48 pages)						4.00
10-18-($3.50)						3.50
CANTEEN KATE (See All Picture All True Love Story & Fightin' Marines)						
St. John Publishing Co.: June, 1952 - No. 3, Nov, 1952						
1-Matt Baker-c/a	59	118	177	369	555	740
2-Matt Baker-c/a	42	84	126	252	376	500
3-(Rare)-Used in **POP**, pg. 75; Baker-c/a	50	100	150	300	450	600
CAPER						
DC Comics: Dec, 2003 - No. 12 ($2.95, limited series)						
1-3-Judd Winick-s/Farel Dalrymple-a						3.00
CAPES						
Image Comics: Sept, 2003 - No. 3, Nov, 2003 ($3.50)						
1-3-Robert Kirkman-s/Mark Englert-a/c						3.50
CAP'N QUICK & A FOOZLE (Also see Eclipse Mag. & Monthly)						
Eclipse Comics: July, 1984 - No. 3, Nov, 1985 ($1.50, color, Baxter paper)						
1-3-Rogers-c/a						3.00
CAPTAIN ACTION (Toy)						
National Periodical Publications: Oct-Nov, 1968 - No. 5, June-July, 1969 (Based on Ideal toy)						
1-Origin; Wood-a; Superman-c app.	10	20	30	70	100	130
2,3,5-Kane/Wood-a	7	14	21	51	71	90
4	6	12	18	40	55	70
CAPTAIN AERO COMICS (Samson No. 1-6; also see Veri Best Sure Fire & Veri Best Sure Shot Comics)						
Holyoke Publishing Co.: V1#7(#1), Dec, 1941 - V2#4(#10), Jan, 1943; V3#9(#11), Sept, 1943 -V4#3(#17), Oct, 1944; #21, Dec, 1944 - #26, Aug, 1946 (No #18-20)						
V1#7(#1)-Flag-Man & Solar, Master of Magic, Captain Aero, Cap Stone, Adventurer begin	164	328	492	1025	1538	2050
8-10: 8(#2)-Pals of Freedom app. 9(#3)-Alias X begins; Pals of Freedom app.						
10(#4)-Origin The Gargoyle; Kubert-a	78	156	234	488	732	975
11,12(#5,6)-Kubert-a; Miss Victory in #6	64	128	192	400	600	800
V2#1,2(#7,8): 8-Origin The Red Cross; Miss Victory app.; Brodsky-c(i)	40	80	120	240	350	460
3(#9)-Miss Victory app.	38	76	114	219	310	400
4(#10)-Miss Victory app.	30	60	90	173	244	315
V3#9 - V3#13(#11-15): 11,15-Miss Victory app.	25	50	75	147	202	260
V4#2(#16)	24	48	72	138	194	250
V4#3(#17), 21-25-L. B. Cole covers. 22-Intro/origin Mighty Mite.	44	88	132	264	395	525
26-L. B. Cole S/F-c; Palais-a(2) (scarce)	88	176	264	550	825	1100
NOTE: ***L.B. Cole** c-17. **Hollingsworth** a-23. **Infantino** a-23, 26. **Schomburg** c-15, 16.*						
CAPTAIN AMERICA (See Adventures of..., All-Select, All Winners, Aurora, Avengers #4, Blood and Glory, Captain Britain 16-20, Giant-Size..., The Invaders, Marvel Double Feature, Marvel Fanfare, Marvel Mystery, Marvel Super-Action, Marvel Super Heroes V2#3, Marvel Team-Up, Marvel Treasury Special, Power Record Comics, Ultimates, USA Comics, Young Allies & Young Men)						
CAPTAIN AMERICA (Formerly Tales of Suspense #1-99) (Captain America and the Falcon #134-223 & Steve Rogers: Captain America #444-454 appears on cover only)						
Marvel Comics Group: No. 100, Apr, 1968 - No. 454, Aug, 1996						
100-Flashback on Cap's revival with Avengers & Sub-Mariner; story continued from Tales of Suspense #99; Kirby-c/a begins	31	62	93	228	339	450
101-The Sleeper-c/story; Red Skull app.	9	18	27	60	85	110
102-104: 102-Sleeper-c/s. 103,104-Red Skull-c/sty	7	14	21	46	63	80
105-108	6	12	18	38	52	65
109-Origin Capt. America retold	8	16	24	55	78	100
109-2nd printing (1994)	2	4	6	8	10	12
110-Rick becomes Cap's partner; Hulk x-over	11	22	33	75	110	145
111,113-Classic Steranko-c/a: 111-Death of Steve Rogers. 113-Cap's funeral	8	16	24	55	78	100
112-Origin retold; last Kirby-c/a	4	8	12	29	40	50
114,115: 115-Last 12¢ issue	3	7	10	21	28	35
116,118-120	3	6	9	18	23	28
117-1st app. The Falcon (9/69)	7	14	21	50	68	85
121-136,139,140: 121-Retells origin. 133-The Falcon becomes Cap's partner; origin Modok. 140-Origin Grey Gargoyle retold	2	4	6	12	16	20
137,138-Spider-Man x-over	3	6	9	16	20	25
141,142: 142-Last 15¢ issue	2	4	6	11	14	18
143-(52 pgs).	3	6	9	16	20	25
144-153: 144-New costume Falcon. 153-1st app. (cameo) Jack Monroe	2	4	6	10	12	15
154-1st full app. Jack Monroe (Nomad)(10/72)	2	4	6	11	14	18
155-Origin; redrawn w/Falcon added; origin Jack Monroe	2	4	6	11	14	18
156-171,176-179: 155-158-Cap's strength increased. 160-1st app. Solarr. 164-1st app. Nightshade. 176-End of Capt. America.	1	3	4	6	8	10
172-175: X-Men x-over	2	4	6	11	14	18
180-Intro/origin of Nomad (Steve Rogers)	2	4	6	11	14	18
181-Intro/origin new Cap.	2	4	6	10	12	15
182,184-192: 186-True origin The Falcon	1	2	3	5	6	8
183-Death of new Cap; Nomad becomes Cap	2	4	6	8	10	12
193-Kirby-c/a begins	2	4	6	12	16	20
194-199-(Regular 25¢ edition)(4-7/76)	2	4	6	10	12	15
196-199-(30¢-c variants, limited distribution)	2	4	6	14	18	22
200-(Regular 25¢ edition)(8/76)	2	4	6	11	14	18
200-(30¢-c variant, limited distribution)	3	6	9	16	20	25
201-214-Kirby-c/a	2	4	6	8	10	12
210-214-(35¢-c variants, limited dist.)(6-10/77)	2	4	6	11	14	18
215,216,218-229,231-234,236-240,242-246: 215-Retells Cap's origin. 216-r/story from Strange Tales #114. 229-Marvel Man app. 233-Death of Sharon Carter. 234-Daredevil x-over. 244,245-Miller-c						5.00
217,230,235: 217-1st app. Marvel Man (later Quasar). 230-Battles Hulk-c/story cont'd in Hulk #232. 235-(7/79) Daredevil x-over; Miller-a(p)	1	2	3	4	5	7
241-Punisher app.; Miller-c.	3	6	9	16	20	25
241-2nd print						3.00
247-255-Byrne-a. 255-Origin; Miller-c.	1	2	3	5	6	8
256-281,284,285,289-322,324-326,328-331: 264-Old X-Men cameo in flashback. 265,266-Nick Fury & Spider-Man app. 267-1st app. Everyman. 269-1st Team America. 279-(3/83)-Contains Tattooz skin decals. 281-1950s Bucky returns. 284-Patriot (Jack Mace) app. 285-Death of Patriot. 298-Origin Red Skull. 328-Origin & 1st app. D-Man						3.00
282-Bucky becomes new Nomad (Jack Monroe)						5.00
282-Silver ink 2nd print ($1.75) w/original date (6/83)						2.25
283,327,333-340: 283-2nd app. Nomad. 327-Capt. Amer. battles Super Patriot. 333-Intro & origin new Captain (Super Patriot). 339-Fall of the Mutants tie-in						4.00
286-288-Deathlok app.						4.00
323-1st app. new Super Patriot (see Nick Fury)						4.00
332-Old Cap resigns						6.00
341-343,345-349						3.00
344-($1.50, 52 pgs.)-Ronald Reagan cameo						4.00
350-($1.75, 68 pgs.)-Return of Steve Rogers (original Cap) to original costume						4.00
351-382,384-396: 351-Nick Fury app. 354-1st app. U.S. Agent (6/89, see Avengers West Coast). 373-Bullseye app. 375-Daredevil app. 386-U.S. Agent app. 387-389-Red Skull back-up stories. 396-Last $1.00-c. 396,397-1st app. all new Jack O'Lantern						2.50
383-($2.00, 68 pgs.)-50th anniversary issue; Red Skull story; Jim Lee-c(i)						4.00
397-399,401-424,425: 402-Begin 6 part Man-Wolf story w/Wolverine in #403-407. 405-410-New Jack O'Lantern app. in back-up story. 406-Cable & Shatterstar cameo. 407-Capwolf vs. Cable-c/story. 408-Infinity War x-over; Falcon solo back-up. 423-Vs. Namor-c/story						2.25
400-($2.25, 84 pgs.)-Flip book format w/double gatefold-c; r/Avengers #4 plus-c; contains cover pin-ups.						3.00
425-($2.95, 52 pgs.)-Embossed Foil-c ed.n; Fighting Chance Pt. 1						3.00
426-443,446,447,449-453: 427-Begin $1.50-c; bound-in trading card sheet. 449-Thor app. 450-"Man Without A Country" storyline begins, ends #453; Bill Clinton app; variant-c exists. 451-1st app.Cap's new costume. 453-Cap gets old costume back; Bill Clinton app.						2.25
444-Mark Waid scripts & Ron Garney-c/a(p) begins, ends #454; Avengers app.						5.00
445,454: 445-Sharon Carter & Red Skull return.						3.00

Captain America (3rd series) #1 © MAR

Captain America (4th series) #4 © MAR

Captain America Comics #3 © MAR

GD 2.0 | VG 4.0 | FN 6.0 | VF 8.0 | VF/NM 9.0 | NM- 9.2

448-($2.95, double-sized issue)-Waid script & Garney-c/a; Red Skull "dies" 4.00
Special 1(1/71)-Origin retold 4 8 12 29 40 50
Special 2(1/72, 52 pgs.)-Colan-r/Not Brand Echh; all-r 3 6 9 18 23 28
Annual 3('76, 52 pgs.)-Kirby-c/a(new) 2 4 6 12 16 20
Annual 4('77, 34 pgs.)-Magneto-c/story 2 4 6 12 16 20
Annual 5-7: (52 pgs.)('81-'83) 5.00
Annual 8(9/86)-Wolverine-c/story 3 6 9 18 24 30
Annual 9-13('90-'94, 68 pgs.)-9-Nomad back-up. 10-Origin retold (2 pgs.). 11-Falcon solo story. 12-Bagged w/card. 13-Red Skull-c/story 3.00
...Ashcan Edition ('95, 75¢) 3.00
...: Deathlok Lives! nn(10/93, $4.95)-r/#286-288 5.00
...Drug War 1-(1994, $2.00, 52 pgs.)-New Warriors app. 3.00
...Man Without a Country(1998, $12.99, TPB)-r/#450-453 13.00
...Medusa Effect 1 (1994, $2.95, 68 pgs.)-Origin Baron Zemo 3.00
...Operation Rebirth (1996, $9.95)-r/#445-448 10.00
...Streets of Poison ($15.95)-r/#372-378 16.00
...: The Movie Special nn (5/92, $3.50, 52 pgs.)-Adapts movie; printed on coated stock; The Red Skull app. 3.50

NOTE: ***Austin*** *c-225i, 239i, 246i.* ***Buscema*** *a-115p, 217p; c-136p, 217, 297.* ***Byrne*** *c-223(part), 238, 239, 247p-254p, 290, 291, 313p; a-247-254p, 255, 313p, 350.* ***Colan*** *a(p)-116-137, 256, Annual 5; c(p)-116-123, 126, 129.* ***Everett*** *a-136i, 137i; c-126i.* ***Garney*** *a(p)-444-454.* ***Gil Kane*** *a-145p; c-147p, 149p, 150p, 170p, 172-174, 180, 181p, 183-190p, 215, 216, 220, 221.* ***Kirby*** *a(p)-100-109, 112, 193-214, 216, Special 1, 2(layouts), Annual 3, 4; c-100-109, 112, 126p, 193-214.* ***Ron Lim*** *a(p)-366, 368-378, 380-386; c-366p, 368-378p, 379, 380-393p.* ***Miller*** *c-241p, 244p, 245p, 255p, Annual 5.* ***Mooney*** *a-149i.* ***Morrow*** *a-144.* ***Perez*** *c-243p, 246p.* ***Robbins*** *c(p)-183-187, 189-192, 225.* ***Roussos*** *a-140i, 168i.* ***Starlin/Sinnott*** *c-162.* ***Sutton*** *a-244i.* ***Tuska*** *a-112i, 215p, Special 2.* ***Waid*** *scripts-444-454.* ***Williamson*** *a-313i.* ***Wood*** *a-127i.* ***Zeck*** *a-263-289; c-300.*

CAPTAIN AMERICA (Volume Two)
Marvel Comics: V2#1, Nov, 1996 - No. 13, Nov, 1997($2.95/$1.95/$1.99)
(Produced by Extreme Studios)

1-($2.95)-Heroes Reborn begins; Rob Liefeld-c/a; Jeph Loeb scripts; reintro Nick Fury 6.00
1-($2.95)-(Variant-c)-Liefeld-c/a 6.00
1-(7/96, $2.95)-(Exclusive Comicon Ed.)-Liefeld-c/a. 1 2 3 5 6 8
2-11,13: 5-Two-c. 6-Cable-c/app. 13-"World War 3"-pt. 4, x-over w/Image 3.00
12-($2.99) "Heroes Reunited"-pt. 4 4.00

CAPTAIN AMERICA (Vol. Three) (Also see Capt. America: Sentinel of Liberty)
Marvel Comics: Jan, 1998 - No. 50, Feb, 2002 ($2.99/$1.99/$2.25)

1-($2.99) Mark Waid-s/Ron Garney-a 4.00
1-Variant cover 6.00
2-($1.99): 2-Two covers 3.00
3-11: 3-Returns to old shield. 4-Hawkeye app. 5-Thor-c/app. 7-Andy Kubert-c/a begin. 9-New shield 2.50
12-($2.99) Battles Nightmare; Red Skull back-up story 3.50
13-17,19-Red Skull returns 2.25
18-($2.99) Cap vs. Korvac in the Future 3.00
20-24,26-29: 20,21-Sgt. Fury back-up story painted by Evans 2.25
25-($2.99) Cap & Falcon vs. Hatemonger 3.00
30-49: 30-Begin $2.25-c. 32-Ordway-a. 33-Jurgens-s/a begins; U.S. Agent app. 36-Maximum Security x-over. 41,46-Red Skull app. 2.25
.../Citizen V '98 Annual ($3.50) Busiek & Kesel-s 3.50
50-($5.95) Stories by various incl. Jurgens, Quitely, Immonen; Ha-c 6.00
1999 Annual ($3.50) Flag Smasher app. 3.50
2000 Annual ($3.50) Continued from #35 vs. Protocide; Jurgens-s 3.50
2001 Annual ($2.99) Golden Age flashback; Invaders app. 3.00
...: To Serve and Protect TPB (2/02, $17.95) r/Vol. 3 #1-7 18.00

CAPTAIN AMERICA (Volume 4)
Marvel Comics: Jun, 2002 - Present ($3.99/$2.99)

1-Ney Rieber-s/Cassaday-c/a 4.00
2-9-($2.99) 3-Cap reveals Steve Rogers ID. 7-9-Hairsine-a 3.00
10-22: 10-16-Jae Lee-a. 17-20-Gibbons-s/Weeks-a. 21,22-Bachalo-a 3.00
...Vol. 1: The New Deal HC (2003, $22.99) r/#1-6; foreward by Max Allan Collins 23.00
...Vol. 2: The Extremists TPB (2003, $13.99) r/#7-11; Cassaday-c 14.00
...Vol. 3: Ice TPB (2003, $12.99) r/#12-16; Jae Lee-a; Cassaday-c 13.00
...Vol. 4: Cap Lives TPB (2004, $12.99) r/#17-22 & Tales of Suspense #66 13.00

CAPTAIN AMERICA COMICS
Timely/Marvel Comics (TCI 1-20/CmPS 21-68/MjMC 69-75/Atlas Comics (PrPI 76-78): Mar, 1941 - No. 75, Feb, 1950; No. 76, 5/54 - No. 78, 9/54
(No. 74 & 75 titled Capt. America's Weird Tales)

1-Origin & 1st app. Captain America & Bucky by S&K; Hurricane, Tuk the Caveboy begin by S&K; 1st app. Red Skull; Hitler-c (by Simon?); intro of the "Capt. America Sentinels of Liberty Club" (advertised on inside front-c.); indicia reads Vol. 2, Number 1
6944 13,888 20,832 49,200 87,100 125,000
2-S&K Hurricane; Tuk by Avison (Kirby splash); classic Hitler-c
1188 2376 3563 8910 13,955 19,000
3-Classic Red Skull-c & app; Stan Lee's 1st text (1st work for Marvel)
1069 2138 3207 7483 11,492 15,500
4-Early use of full pg. panel in comic 690 1380 2070 4830 7415 10,000
5 621 1242 1863 4347 6674 9000
6-Origin Father Time; Tuk the Caveboy ends 538 1076 1614 3766 5783 7800
7-Red Skull app.; classic-c 607 1214 1821 4249 6525 8800
8-10-Last S&K issue, (S&K centerfold #6-10) 428 856 1284 2996 4598 6200
11-Last Hurricane, Headline Hunter; Al Avison Captain America begins, ends #20; Avison-c(p) 378 756 1134 2457 3779 5100
12-The Imp begins, ends #16; last Father Time 359 718 1077 2334 3592 4850
13-Origin The Secret Stamp; classic-c 393 786 1179 2555 3928 5300
14,15 359 718 1077 2334 3592 4850
16-Red Skull unmasks Cap; Red Skull-c 423 846 1269 2856 4428 6000
17-The Fighting Fool only app. 304 608 912 1976 3038 4100
18-Classic-c 304 608 912 1976 3038 4100
19-Human Torch begins #19 264 528 792 1650 2475 3300
20-Sub-Mariner app.; no H. Torch 264 528 792 1650 2475 3300
21-25: 25-Cap drinks liquid opium 248 496 744 1550 2325 3100
26-30: 27-Last Secret Stamp; last 68 pg. issue. 28-60 pg. issues begin.
232 464 696 1450 2175 2900
31-35,38-40: 34-Centerfold poster of Cap 200 400 600 1250 1875 2500
36-Classic Hitler-c 300 600 900 1875 2813 3750
37-Red Skull app. 248 496 744 1550 2325 3100
41-45,47: 41-Last Jap War-c. 47-Last German War-c
172 344 516 1075 1613 2150
46-German Holocaust-c; classic 224 448 672 1400 2100 2800
48-58,60 132 264 396 825 1238 1650
59-Origin retold 300 600 900 1925 2963 4000
61-Red Skull-c/story 264 528 792 1650 2475 3300
62,64,65: 65-Kurtzman's "Hey Look" 172 344 516 1075 1613 2150
63-Intro/origin Asbestos Lady 176 352 528 1100 1650 2200
66-Bucky is shot; Golden Girl teams up with Captain America & learns his i.d; origin Golden Girl 194 388 582 1213 1819 2425
67-73: 67-Captain America/Golden Girl team-up; Mxyztplk swipe; last Toro in Human Torch. 68,70-Sub-Mariner/Namora, and Captain America/Golden Girl team-up in each. 69-Human Torch/Sun Girl team-up. 70-Science fiction-c/story. 71-Anti Wertham editorial; The Witness, Bucky app. 184 368 552 1150 1725 2300
74-(Scarce)(10/49)-Titled "Captain America's Weird Tales"; Red Skull-c & app.; classic-c 517 1034 1551 3619 5560 7500
75(2/50)-Titled "C.A.'s Weird Tales"; no C.A. app.; horror cover/stories
184 368 552 1150 1725 2300
76-78(1954): Human Torch/Toro stories; all have communist-c/stories
100 200 300 625 938 1250
132-Pg. Issue (B&W-1942)(Canadian)-Very rare. Has blank inside-c and back-c; contains Marvel Mystery #33 & Captain America #18 w/cover from Captain America #22; same contents as one version of the Marvel Mystery annuals
3200 6400 9600 21,000 - -

NOTE: ***Crandall*** *a-2i, 3i, 9i, 10i.* ***Kirby*** *c-1, 2, 5-8p.* ***Rico*** *c-69-71.* ***Romita*** *c-77, 78.* ***Schomburg*** *c-3, 4, 26-29, 31, 33, 37-39, 41, 42, 45-54, 58.* ***Sekowsky*** *c-55, 56.* ***Shores*** *c-1i, 2i, 5-7i, 11i, 20-25, 30, 32, 34, 35, 40, 57, 59-67.* ***S&K*** *c-9, 10. Bondage c-3, 7, 15, 16, 34, 38.*

CAPTAIN AMERICA: DEAD MEN RUNNING
Marvel Comics: Mar, 2002 - No. 3, May, 2002 ($2.99, limited series)

1-3-Macan-s/Zezelj-a 3.00

CAPTAIN AMERICA/NICK FURY: BLOOD TRUCE
Marvel Comics: Feb, 1995 ($5.95, one-shot, squarebound)

nn-Chaykin story 6.00

CAPTAIN AMERICA/NICK FURY: THE OTHERWORLD WAR
Marvel Comics: Oct, 2001 ($6.95, one-shot, squarebound)

nn-Manco-a; Bucky and Red Skull app. 7.00

CAPTAIN AMERICA: RED, WHITE & BLUE
Marvel Comics: Sept, 2002 ($29.99, one-shot, hardcover with dustjacket)

nn-Reprints from Lee & Kirby, Steranko, Miller and others; and new short stories and pin-ups by various incl. Ross, Dini, Timm, Waid, Dorkin, Sienkiewicz, Miller, Bruce Jones, Collins, Piers-Rayner, Pope, Deodato, Quitely, Nino; Stelfreeze-c 30.00

CAPTAIN AMERICA, SENTINEL OF LIBERTY (See Fireside Book Series)

CAPTAIN AMERICA: SENTINEL OF LIBERTY
Marvel Comics: Sept, 1998 - No. 12, Aug, 1999 ($1.99)

1-Waid-s/Garney-a 3.00
1-Rough Cut ($2.99) Features original script and pencil pages 3.00
2-5: 2-Two-c; Invaders WW2 story 2.25

Captain America: What Price Glory #4 © MAR

Captain Atom #2 © DC

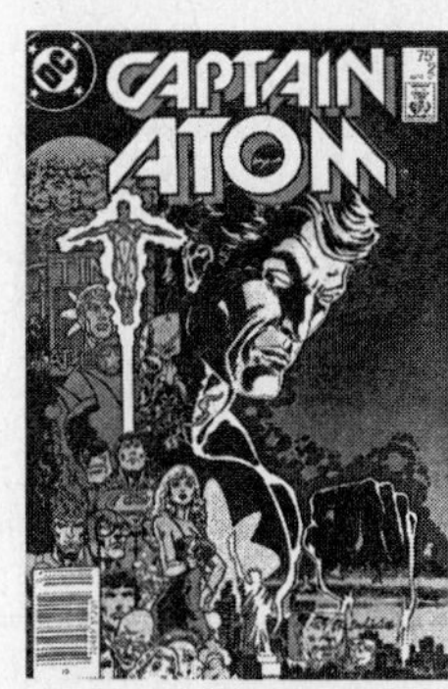

Captain Britain #2 © MAR

	GD 2.0	VG 4.0	FN 6.0	VF 8.0	VF/NM 9.0	NM- 9.2

6-($2.99) Iron Man-c/app. 3.00

7-11: 8-Falcon-c/app. 9-Falcon poses as Cap 2.25

12-($2.99) Final issue; Bucky-c/app. 3.00

CAPTAIN AMERICA SPECIAL EDITION
Marvel Comics Group: Feb, 1984 - No. 2, Mar, 1984 ($2.00, Baxter paper)

1-Steranko-c/a(r) in both; r/ Captain America #110,111 6.00

2-Reprints the scarce Our Love Story #5, and C.A. #113 1 2 3 5 6 8

CAPTAIN AMERICA: THE CLASSIC YEARS
Marvel Comics: Jun, 1998 -No. 2 (trade paperbacks)

1-($19.95) Reprints Captain America Comics #1-5 25.00

2-($24.95) Reprints Captain America Comics #6-10 25.00

CAPTAIN AMERICA: THE LEGEND
Marvel Comics: Sept, 1996 ($3.95, one-shot)

1-Tribute issue; wraparound-c 4.00

CAPTAIN AMERICA: WHAT PRICE GLORY
Marvel Comics: May, 2003 - No. 4, May, 2003 ($2.99, weekly limited series)

1-4-Bruce Jones-s/Steve Rude & Mike Royer-a 3.00

CAPTAIN AND THE KIDS, THE (See Famous Comics Cartoon Books)

CAPTAIN AND THE KIDS, THE (See Comics on Parade, Katzenjammer Kids, Okay Comics & Sparkler Comics)
United Features Syndicate/Dell Publ. Co.: 1938 -12/39; Sum, 1947 - No. 32, 1955; Four Color No. 881, Feb, 1958

Single Series 1(1938) 88 176 264 550 825 1100

Single Series 1(Reprint)(12/39- "Reprint" on-c) 46 92 138 276 413 550

1(Summer, 1947-UFS)-Katzenjammer Kids 16 32 48 92 126 160

2 9 18 27 52 66 80

3-10 8 16 24 40 50 60

11-20 6 12 18 28 34 40

21-32 (1955) 5 10 15 24 30 35

50th Anniversary issue-(1948)-Contains a 2 pg. history of the strip, including an account of the famous Supreme Court decision allowing both Pulitzer & Hearst to run the same strip under different names 10 20 30 56 73 90

Special Summer issue, Fall issue (1948) 8 16 24 40 50 60

Four Color 881 (Dell) 4 8 12 27 36 45

CAPTAIN ATOM
Nationwide Publishers: 1950 - No. 7, 1951 (5¢, 5x7-1/4", 52 pgs.)

1-Science fiction 40 80 120 240 350 460

2-7 23 46 69 129 180 230

CAPTAIN ATOM (Formerly Strange Suspense Stories #77)(Also see Space Adventures)
Charlton Comics: V2#78, Dec, 1965 - V2#89, Dec, 1967

V2#78-Origin retold; Bache-a (3 pgs.) 9 18 27 65 93 120

79-82: 79-1st app. Dr. Spectro; 3 pg. Ditko cut & paste /Space Adventures #24. 82-Intro. Nightshade (9/66) 6 12 18 40 55 70

83-86: Ted Kord Blue Beetle in all. 83-(11/66)-1st app. Ted Kord. 84-1st app. new Captain Atom 6 12 18 38 52 65

87-89: Nightshade by Aparo in all 6 12 18 38 52 65

83-85(Modern Comics-1977)-reprints 1 2 3 4 5 7

NOTE: **Aparo** *a-87-89.* **Ditko** *c/a(p) 78-89. #90 only published in fanzine 'The Charlton Bullseye' #1, 2.*

CAPTAIN ATOM (Also see Americomics & Crisis On Infinite Earths)
DC Comics: Mar, 1987 - No. 57, Sept, 1991 (Direct sales only #35 on)

1-(44 pgs.)-Origin/1st app. with new costume 4.00

2-49: 5-Firestorm x-over. 6-Intro. new Dr. Spectro. 11-Millennium tie-in. 14-Nightshade app. 16-Justice League app. 17-$1.00-c begins; Swamp Thing app. 20-Blue Beetle x-over. 24,25-Invasion tie-in 2.50

51-57: 50-($2.00, 52 pgs.). 57-War of the Gods x-over 2.50

Annual 1,2 ('88, '89)-1-Intro Major Force 3.00

CAPTAIN BATTLE (Boy Comics #3 on) (See Silver Streak Comics)
New Friday Publ./Comic House: Summer, 1941 - No. 2, Fall, 1941

1-Origin Blackout by Rico; Captain Battle begins (1st appeared in Silver Streak #10, 5/41) 136 272 408 850 1275 1700

2 80 160 240 500 750 1000

CAPTAIN BATTLE (2nd Series)
Magazine Press/Picture Scoop No. 5: No. 3, Wint, 1942-43; No. 5, Sum, 1943 (No #4)

3-Origin Silver Streak-r/SS#3; origin Lance Hale-r/Silver Streak; Simon-a(r) (52 pgs., nd) 70 140 210 438 657 875

5-Origin Blackout retold (68 pgs.) 50 100 150 300 450 600

CAPTAIN BATTLE, JR.
Comic House (Lev Gleason): Fall, 1943 - No. 2, Winter, 1943-44

1-The Claw vs. The Ghost 122 256 384 800 1200 1600

2-Wolverton's Scoop Scuttle; Don Rico-c/a; The Green Claw story is reprinted from Silver Streak #6; bondage/torture-c 80 160 240 500 750 1000

CAPTAIN BEN DIX (See Promotional Comics section)

CAPTAIN BRITAIN (Also see Marvel Team-Up No. 65, 66)
Marvel Comics International: Oct. 13, 1976 - No. 39, July 6, 1977 (Weekly)

1-Origin; with Capt. Britain's face mask inside 2 4 6 10 13 16

2-Origin, part II; Capt. Britain's Boomerang inside 1 3 4 6 8 10

3-11: 3,8-Vs. Bank Robbers. 4-7-Vs. Hurricane. 9-11: Vs. Dr. Synne 5.00

12-23,25-27: (scarce)-12,13-Vs. Dr. Synne. 14,15-Vs. Mastermind. 16-23,25,26-With Captain America. 17 misprinted & color section reprinted in #18. 27-Origin retold 2 4 6 8 10 12

24-With C.B.'s Jet Plane inside 2 4 6 10 13 16

28-32,36-39: 28-32-Vs. Lord Hawk. 37-39-Vs. Highwayman & Munipulator 3.50

33-35-More on origin 4.00

Annual (1978, Hardback, 64 pgs.)-Reprints #1-7 with pin-ups of Marvel characters 2 4 6 9 11 14

Summer Special (1980, 52 pgs.)-Reprints 5.00

NOTE: *No. 1, 2, & 24 are rarer in mint due to inserts. Distributed in Great Britain only. Nick Fury-r by* **Steranko** *in 1-20, 24-31, 35-37. Fantastic Four-r by* **J. Buscema** *in all. New* **Buscema**-*a in 24-30. Story from No. 39 continues in Super Spider-Man (British weekly) No. 231-247. Following cancellation of his series, new Captain Britain stories appeared in "Super Spider-Man" (British weekly) No. 231-247. Captain Britain stories which appear in Super-Spider-Man No 248-253 are reprints of Marvel Team-Up No. 65&66. Capt. Britain strips also appeared in Hulk Comic (weekly) 1, 3-30, 42-55, 57-60, in Marvel Superheroes (monthly) 377-388, in Daredevils (monthly) 1-11, Mighty World of Marvel (monthly) 7-16 & Captain Britain (monthly) 1-14. Issues 1-23 have B&W & color, paper-c, & are 32 pgs. Issues 24 on are all B&W w/glossy-c & are 36 pgs.*

CAPTAIN CANUCK
Comely Comix (Canada) (All distr. in U. S.): 7/75 - No. 4, 7/77; No. 4, 7-8/79 - No. 14, 3-4/81

1-1st app. Bluefox 5.00

2,3(5-7/76)-2-1st app. Dr. Walker, Redcoat & Kebec. 3-1st app. Heather 4.00

4(1st printing-2/77)-10x14-1/2"; (5.00); B&W; 300 copies serially numbered and signed with one certificate of authenticity 8 16 24 53 74 95

4(2nd printing-7/77)-11x17", B&W; only 15 copies printed; signed by creator Richard Comely, serially #'d and two certificates of authenticity inserted; orange cardboard covers (Very Rare) 10 20 30 67 96 125

4-14: 4(7-8/79)-1st app. Tom Evans & Mr. Gold; origin The Catman. 5-Origin Capt. Canuck's powers; 1st app. Earth Patrol & Chaos Corps. 8-Jonn 'The Final Chapter'. 9-1st World Beyond. 11-1st 'Chariots of Fire' story 3.00

Special Collectors Pack (polybagged) 1 2 3 5 7 9

Summer Special 1(7-9/80, 95¢, 64 pgs.) 3.00

NOTE: *30,000 copies of No. 2 were destroyed in Winnipeg.*

CAPTAIN CARROT AND HIS AMAZING ZOO CREW (Also see New Teen Titans & Oz-Wonderland War)
DC Comics: Mar, 1982 - No. 20, Nov, 1983

1-20: 1-Superman app. 3-Re-intro Dodo & The Frog. 9-Re-intro Three Mouseketeers, the Terrific Whatzit. 10,11- Pig Iron reverts back to Peter Porkchops. 20-Changeling app. 3.00

CAPTAIN CARVEL AND HIS CARVEL CRUSADERS (See Carvel Comics)

CAPTAIN CONFEDERACY
Marvel Comics (Epic Comics): Nov, 1991 - No. 4, Feb, 1992 ($1.95)

1-4: All new stories 2.25

CAPTAIN COURAGEOUS COMICS (Banner #3-5; see Four Favorites #5)
Periodical House (Ace Magazines): No. 6, March, 1942

6-Origin & 1st app. The Sword; Lone Warrior, Capt. Courageous app.; Capt. moves to Four Favorites #5 in May 75 150 225 469 705 940

CAPT'N CRUNCH COMICS (See Cap'n...)

CAPTAIN DAVY JONES
Dell Publishing Co.: No. 598, Nov, 1954

Four Color 598 5 10 15 36 48 60

CAPTAIN EASY (See The Funnies & Red Ryder #3-32)
Hawley/Dell Publ./Standard(Visual Editions)/Argo: 1939 - No. 17, Sept, 1949; April, 1956

nn-Hawley(1939)-Contains reprints from The Funnies & 1938 Sunday strips by Roy Crane 88 176 264 550 825 1100

Four Color 24 (1943) 40 80 120 300 450 600

Four Color 111(6/46) 15 30 45 107 156 205

10(Standard-10/47) 12 24 36 69 92 115

11,12,14,15,17: 11-17 all contain 1930s & '40s strip-r 10 20 30 56 73 90

13,16: Schomburg-c 10 20 30 60 80 100

Argo 1(4/56)-Reprints 7 14 21 37 46 55

Captain Flash #4 © Sterling Comics

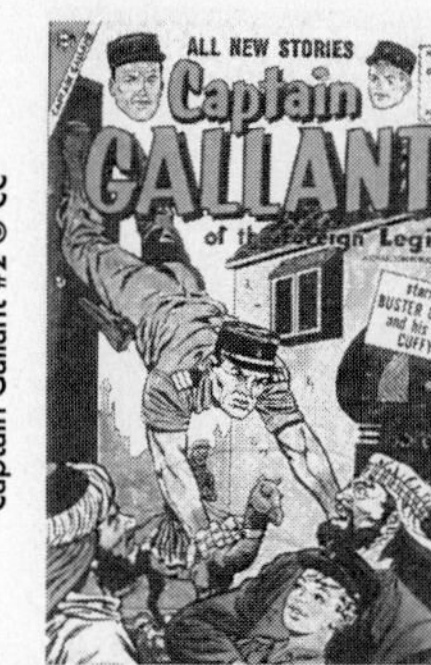

Captain Gallant #2 © CC

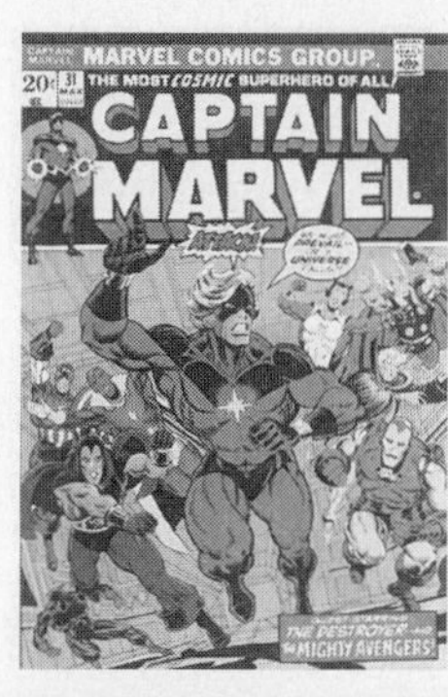

Captain Marvel #31 © MAR

	GD 2.0	VG 4.0	FN 6.0	VF 8.0	VF/NM 9.0	NM- 9.2

CAPTAIN EASY & WASH TUBBS (See Famous Comics Cartoon Books)

CAPTAIN ELECTRON
Brick Computer Science Institute: Aug, 1986 ($2.25)

Issue	GD	VG	FN	VF	VF/NM	NM-
1-Disbrow-a						2.50

CAPTAIN EO 3-D (Disney)
Eclipse Comics: July, 1987 (Eclipse 3-D Special #18, $3.50, Baxter)

Issue	GD	VG	FN	VF	VF/NM	NM-
1-Adapts 3-D movie						4.00
1-2-D limited edition						6.00
1-Large size (11x17", 8/87)-Sold only at Disney Theme parks ($6.95)	2	4	6	10	13	16

CAPTAIN FEARLESS COMICS (Also see Holyoke One-Shot #6, Old Glory Comics & Silver Streak #1)
Helnit Publishing Co. (Holyoke Publ. Co.): Aug, 1941 - No. 2, Sept, 1941

Issue	GD	VG	FN	VF	VF/NM	NM-
1-Origin Mr. Miracle, Alias X, Captain Fearless, Citizen Smith Son of the Unknown Soldier; Miss Victory (1st app.) begins (1st patriotic heroine? before Wonder Woman)	84	168	252	525	788	1050
2-Grit Grady, Captain Stone app.	52	104	156	312	469	625

CAPTAIN FLAG (See Blue Ribbon Comics #16)

CAPTAIN FLASH
Sterling Comics: Nov, 1954 - No. 4, July, 1955

Issue	GD	VG	FN	VF	VF/NM	NM-
1-Origin; Sekowsky-a; Tomboy (female super hero) begins; only pre-code issue; atomic rocket-c	40	80	120	240	358	475
2-4: 4-Flying saucer invasion-c	24	48	72	138	194	250

CAPTAIN FLEET (Action Packed Tales of the Sea)
Ziff-Davis Publishing Co.: Fall, 1952

Issue	GD	VG	FN	VF	VF/NM	NM-
1-Painted-c	16	32	48	92	126	160

CAPTAIN FLIGHT COMICS
Four Star Publications: Mar, 1944 - No. 10, Dec, 1945; No. 11, Feb-Mar, 1947

Issue	GD	VG	FN	VF	VF/NM	NM-
nn	42	84	126	252	376	500
2-4: 4-Rock Raymond begins, ends #7	25	50	75	147	202	260
5-Bondage, classic torture-c; Red Rocket begins; the Grenade app. (scarce)	107	214	321	669	1005	1340
6	24	48	72	138	194	250
7-10: 7-L. B. Cole covers begin, end #11. 8-Yankee Girl begins; intro. Black Cobra & Cobra Kid & begins. 9-Torpedoman app.; last Yankee Girl; Kinstler-a. 10-Deep Sea Dawson, Zoom of the Jungle, Rock Raymond, Red Rocket, & Black Cobra app; bondage-c	51	102	153	306	458	610
11-Torpedoman, Blue Flame (Human Torch clone) app.; last Black Cobra, Red Rocket; classic L. B. Cole robot-c (scarce)	112	224	336	700	1050	1400

CAPTAIN GALLANT (...of the Foreign Legion) (TV) (Texas Rangers in Action No. 5 on?)
Charlton Comics: 1955; No. 2, Jan, 1956 - No. 4, Sept, 1956

Issue	GD	VG	FN	VF	VF/NM	NM-
Non-Heinz version (#1)-Buster Crabbe photo on-c; full page Buster Crabbe photo inside front-c	9	18	27	54	70	85
(Heinz version is listed in the Promotional Comics section)						
2-4: Buster Crabbe in all	9	18	27	49	62	75

CAPTAIN GLORY
Topps Comics: Apr, 1993 ($2.95) (Created by Jack Kirby)

Issue	GD	VG	FN	VF	VF/NM	NM-
1-Polybagged w/Kirbychrome trading card; Ditko-a & Kirby-c; has coupon for Amberchrome Secret City Saga #0						3.00

CAPTAIN HERO (See Jughead as...)

CAPTAIN HERO COMICS DIGEST MAGAZINE
Archie Publications: Sept, 1981

Issue	GD	VG	FN	VF	VF/NM	NM-
1-Reprints of Jughead as Super-Guy	2	4	6	10	13	16

CAPTAIN HOBBY COMICS
Export Publication Ent. Ltd. (Dist. in U.S. by Kable News Co.): Feb, 1948 (Canadian)

Issue	GD	VG	FN	VF	VF/NM	NM-
1	8	16	24	40	50	60

CAPT. HOLO IN 3-D (See Blackthorne 3-D Series #65)

CAPTAIN HOOK & PETER PAN (Movie)(Disney)
Dell Publishing Co.: No. 446, Jan, 1953

Issue	GD	VG	FN	VF	VF/NM	NM-
Four Color 446	10	20	30	70	100	130

CAPTAIN JET (Fantastic Fears No. 7 on)
Four Star Publ./Farrell/Comic Media: May, 1952 - No. 5, Jan, 1953

Issue	GD	VG	FN	VF	VF/NM	NM-
1-Bakerish-a	23	46	69	129	180	230
2	12	24	36	71	96	120
3-5,6(?)	10	20	30	58	77	95

CAPTAIN JOHNER & THE ALIENS
Valiant: May, 1995 - No. 2, May, 1995 ($2.95, shipped in same month)

Issue	GD	VG	FN	VF	VF/NM	NM-
1,2: Reprints Magnus Robot Fighter 4000 A.D. back-up stories; new Paul Smith-c						3.00

CAPTAIN JUSTICE (TV)
Marvel Comics: Mar, 1988 - No. 2, Apr, 1988 (limited series)

Issue	GD	VG	FN	VF	VF/NM	NM-
1,2-Based on the 1987 "Once a Hero" television series						2.25

CAPTAIN KANGAROO (TV)
Dell Publishing Co.: No. 721, Aug, 1956 - No. 872, Jan, 1958

Issue	GD	VG	FN	VF	VF/NM	NM-
Four Color 721 (#1)-Photo-c	18	36	54	131	191	250
Four Color 780, 872-Photo-c	15	30	45	104	152	200

CAPTAIN KIDD (Formerly Dagar; My Secret Story #26 on)(Also see Comic Comics & Fantastic Comics)
Fox Feature Syndicate: No. 24, June, 1949 - No. 25, Aug, 1949

Issue	GD	VG	FN	VF	VF/NM	NM-
24,25: 24-Features Blackbeard the Pirate	15	30	45	86	118	150

CAPTAIN MARVEL (See All Hero, All-New Collectors' Ed., America's Greatest, Fawcett Miniature, Gift, JSA, Kingdom Come, Legends, Limited Collectors' Ed., Marvel Family, Master No. 21, Mighty Midget Comics, Power of Shazam!, Shazam, Special Edition Comics, Whiz, Wisco (in Promotional Comics section), World's Finest #253 and XMas Comics)

CAPTAIN MARVEL (Becomes ...Presents the Terrible 5 No. 5)
M. F. Enterprises: April, 1966 - No. 4, Nov, 1966 (25¢ Giants)

Issue	GD	VG	FN	VF	VF/NM	NM-
nn-(#1 on pg. 5)-Origin; created by Carl Burgos	4	8	12	29	40	50
2-4: 3-(#3 on pg. 4)-Fights the Bat	3	6	9	18	24	30

CAPTAIN MARVEL (Marvel's Space-Born Super-Hero! Captain Marvel #1-6; see Giant-Size..., Life Of..., Marvel Graphic Novel #1, Marvel Spotlight V2#1 & Marvel Super-Heroes #12)
Marvel Comics Group: May, 1968 - No. 19, Dec, 1969; No. 20, June, 1970 - No. 21, Aug, 1970; No. 22, Sept, 1972 - No. 62, May, 1979

Issue	GD	VG	FN	VF	VF/NM	NM-
1	13	26	39	94	137	180
2-Super Skrull-c/story	5	10	15	36	48	60
3-5: 4-Captain Marvel battles Sub-Mariner	4	8	12	24	32	40
6-11: 11-Capt. Marvel given great power by Zo the Ruler; Smith/Trimpe-c; Death of Una	3	6	9	16	20	25
12,13,15-20: 16,17-New costume	2	4	6	11	14	18
14,21: 14-Capt. Marvel vs. Iron Man; last 12¢ issue. 21-Capt. Marvel battles Hulk; last 15¢ issue	3	6	9	18	23	28
22-24	2	4	6	10	12	15
25,26: 25-Starlin-c/a begins; Starlin's 1st Thanos saga begins (3/73), ends #34; Thanos cameo (5 panels). 26-Minor Thanos app. (see Iron Man #55); 1st Thanos-c	3	6	9	18	24	30
27,28-1st & 2nd full app. Thanos. 28-Thanos-c/s	3	6	9	16	20	25
29,30-Thanos cameos. 29-C.M. gains more powers	2	4	6	11	14	18
31,32: Thanos app. 31-Last 20¢ issue. 32-Thanos-c	2	4	6	12	16	20
33-Thanos-c & app.; Capt. Marvel battles Thanos; 1st origin Thanos	3	6	9	16	20	25
34-1st app. Nitro; C.M. contracts cancer which eventually kills him; last Starlin-c/a	2	4	6	11	14	18
35,37-40,42,46-48,50,53-56,58-62: 39-Origin Watcher. 58-Thanos cameo	1	2	3	4	5	7
36,41,43,49: 36-R-origin/1st app. Capt. Marvel from Marvel Super-Heroes #12. 41,43-Wrightson part inks; #43-c(i). 49-Starlin & Weiss-p assists	1	2	3	5	6	8
44,45-(Regular 25¢ editions)(5,7/76)	1	2	3	4	5	7
44,45-(30¢-c variants, limited distribution)	1	3	4	6	8	10
51,52-(Regular 30¢ editions)(7,9/77)	1	2	3	4	5	7
51,52-(35¢-c variants, limited distribution)	1	3	4	6	8	10
57-Thanos appears in flashback	1	3	4	6	8	10

NOTE: *Alcala a-35. Austin a-46i, 49-53i; c-52i. Buscema a-18p-21p. Colan a(p)-1-4; c(p)-1-4, 8, 9. Heck a-5-10p, 16p. Gil Kane a-17-21p; c-17-24p, 37p, 53. Starlin a-36. McWilliams a-40i. #25-34 were reprinted in The Life of Captain Marvel.*

CAPTAIN MARVEL
Marvel Comics: Nov, 1989 ($1.50, one-shot, 52 pgs.)

Issue	GD	VG	FN	VF	VF/NM	NM-
1-Super-hero from Avengers; new powers						3.00

CAPTAIN MARVEL
Marvel Comics: Feb, 1994 ($1.75, 52 pgs.)

Issue	GD	VG	FN	VF	VF/NM	NM-
1-(Indicia reads Vol 2 #2)-Minor Captain America app.						2.50

CAPTAIN MARVEL
Marvel Comics: Dec, 1995 - No. 6, May, 1996 ($2.95/$1.95)

Issue	GD	VG	FN	VF	VF/NM	NM-
1 ($2.95)-Advs. of Mar-Vell's son begins; Fabian Nicieza scripts; foil-c						3.50
2-6: 2-Begin $1.95-c						2.50

CAPTAIN MARVEL (Vol. 3) (See Avengers Forever)

Captain Marvel V4#15 © MAR

Captain Marvel Adventures #16 © FAW

Captain Marvel, Jr. #7 © FAW

GD VG FN VF VF/NM NM-
2.0 4.0 6.0 8.0 9.0 9.2

Marvel Comics: Jan, 2000 - No. 35, Oct, 2002 ($2.50)
1-Peter David-s in all 4.00
2-10: 2-Two covers; Hulk app. 9-Silver Surfer app. 3.00
11-35: 12-Maximum Security x-over. 17,18-Starlin-a. 27-30-Spider-Man 2099 app. 2.50
Wizard #0-Preview and history of Rick Jones 4.00
...: First Contact (8/01, $16.95, TPB) r/#0,1-6 17.00

CAPTAIN MARVEL (Vol. 4) (See Avengers Forever)
Marvel Comics: Nov, 2002 - Present ($2.25)
1-Peter David-s/Chriscross-a ; 3 covers by Ross, Jusko & Chriscross 3.00
2-7: 2,3-Punisher app. 3-Alex Ross-c; new costume debuts. 4-Noto-c. 7-Thor app. 2.25
3-Sketchbook Edition-($3.50) includes Ross' concept design pages for new costume 3.50
8-18: 8-Begin $2.99-c; Thor app.; Manco-c. 10-Spider-Man-c/app. 15-Neal Adams-c 3.00

CAPTAIN MARVEL ADVENTURES (See Special Edition Comics for pre #1)
Fawcett Publications: 1941 (March) - No. 150, Nov, 1953 (#1 on stands 1/16/41)
nn(#1)-Captain Marvel & Sivana by Jack Kirby. The cover was printed on unstable paper stock and is rarely found in Fine or Mint condition; blank back inside-c
2625 5250 7875 19,700 30,850 42,000
2-(Advertised as #3, which was counting Special Edition Comics as the real #1); Tuska-a 415 830 1245 2698 4149 5600
3-Metallic silver-c 278 556 834 1738 2094 3475
4-Three Lt. Marvels app. 196 392 588 1225 1838 2450
5 152 304 456 950 1425 1900
6-10: 9-1st Otto Binder scripts on Capt. Marvel 115 230 345 719 1080 1440
11-15: 12-Capt. Marvel joins the Army. 13-Two pg. Capt. Marvel pin-up. 15-Comic cards on back-c begin, end #26 90 180 270 563 844 1125
16,17: 17-Painted-c 85 170 255 531 796 1060
18-Origin & 1st app. Mary Marvel & Marvel Family (12/11/42); painted-c; Mary Marvel by Marcus Swayze 220 440 660 1375 2063 2750
19-Mary Marvel x-over; Christmas-c 72 144 216 450 675 900
20,21-Attached to the cover, each has a miniature comic just like the Mighty Midget Comics #11, except that each has a full color promo ad on the back cover. Most copies were circulated without the miniature comic. These issues with miniatures attached are very rare, and should not be mistaken for copies with the similar Mighty Midget glued in its place. The Mighty Midgets had blank back covers except for a small victory stamp seal. Only the Capt. Marvel, Captain Marvel Jr. and Golden Arrow No. 11 miniatures have been positively documented as having been affixed to these covers. Each miniature was only partially glued by its back cover to the Captain Marvel comic making it easy to see if it's the genuine miniature rather than a Mighty Midget.
with comic attached.... 352 704 1056 2288 3519 4750
20-Without miniature 67 134 201 419 630 840
21-Without miniature; Hitler-c 88 176 264 550 825 1100
22-Mr. Mind serial begins; 1st app. Mr. Mind 94 188 282 588 882 1175
23-25 66 132 198 413 619 825
26-28,30: 26-Flag-c. 27-1st Mr. Mind app. (his voice was heard over the radio before now) (9/43) 55 110 165 344 515 685
29-1st Mr. Mind-c (11/43) 58 116 174 363 542 720
31-35: 35-Origin Radar (5/44, see Master #50) 50 100 150 300 450 600
36-40: 37-Mary Marvel x-over 46 92 138 276 413 550
41-46: 42-Christmas-c. 43-Capt. Marvel 1st meets Uncle Marvel; Mary Batson cameo. 46-Mr. Mind serial ends 40 80 120 240 340 440
47-50 38 76 114 219 310 400
51-53,55-60: 51-63-Bi-weekly issues. 52-Origin & 1st app. Sivana Jr.; Capt. Marvel Jr. x-over
32 64 96 184 262 340
54-Special oversize 68 pg. issue 33 66 99 190 270 350
61-The Cult of the Curse serial begins 37 74 111 209 297 385
62-65-Serial cont.; Mary Marvel x-over in #65 32 64 96 184 262 340
66-Serial ends; Atomic War-c 37 74 111 209 297 385
67-77,79: 69-Billy Batson's Christmas; Uncle Marvel, Mary Marvel, Capt. Marvel Jr. x-over. 71-Three Lt. Marvels app. 79-Origin Mr. Tawny 28 56 84 159 225 290
78-Origin Mr. Atom 32 64 96 180 255 330
80-Origin Capt. Marvel retold 61 122 183 381 571 760
81-84,86-90: 81,90-Mr. Atom app. 82-Infinity-c. 82,86,88,90-Mr. Tawny app.
27 54 81 153 214 275
85-Freedom Train issue 32 64 96 180 255 330
91-99: 92-Mr. Tawny app. 96-Gets 1st name "Tawky" 26 52 78 147 206 265
100-Origin retold; silver metallic-c 46 92 138 276 413 550
101-115,117-120 25 50 75 144 198 255
116-Flying Saucer issue (1/51) 28 56 84 159 225 290
121-Origin retold 33 66 99 190 270 350
122-137,139-149: 141-Pre-code horror story "The Hideous Head-Hunter". 142-used in **POP**, pgs. 92,96 24 48 72 135 190 245
138-Flying Saucer issue (11/52) 28 56 84 159 225 290
150-(Low distribution) 42 84 126 252 359 465
NOTE: *Swayze a-12, 14, 15, 18, 19, 40; c-12, 15, 19.*

CAPTAIN MARVEL AND THE GOOD HUMOR MAN (Movie)
Fawcett Publications: 1950
nn-Partial photo-c w/Jack Carson & the Captain Marvel Club Boys
48 96 144 288 407 525

CAPTAIN MARVEL COMIC STORY PAINT BOOK (See Comic Story...)

CAPTAIN MARVEL, JR. (See Fawcett Miniatures, Marvel Family, Master Comics, Mighty Midget Comics, Shazam & Whiz Comics)

CAPTAIN MARVEL, JR.
Fawcett Publications: Nov, 1942 - No. 119, June, 1953 (No #34)
1-Origin Capt. Marvel Jr. retold (Whiz #25); Capt. Nazi app. Classic Raboy-c
524 1048 1572 3668 5634 7600
2-Vs. Capt. Nazi; origin Capt. Nippon 200 400 600 1250 1875 2500
3 112 224 336 700 1050 1400
4-Classic Raboy-c 118 236 354 738 1107 1475
5-Vs. Capt. Nazi 96 192 288 600 900 1200
6-8: 8-Vs. Capt. Nazi 78 156 234 488 732 975
9-Classic flag-c 83 166 249 519 780 1040
10-Hitler-c 96 192 288 600 900 1200
11,12,15-Capt. Nazi app. 68 136 204 425 638 850
13-Classic Hitler, Tojo and Mussolini football-c 94 188 282 588 882 1175
14,16-20: 14-X-Mas-c. 16-Capt. Marvel & Sivana x-over. 19-Capt. Nazi & Capt. Nippon app.
56 112 168 350 525 700
21-30: 25-Flag-c 46 92 138 276 413 550
31-33,36-40: 37-Infinity-c 33 66 99 190 270 350
35-#34 on inside; cover shows origin of Sivana Jr. which is not on inside. Evidently the cover to #35 was printed out of sequence and bound with contents to #34
33 66 99 190 270 350
41-70: 42-Robot-c. 53-Atomic Bomb-c/story 27 54 81 153 214 275
71-99,101-104: 87-Robot-c. 104-Used in **POP**, pg. 89
19 38 57 109 152 195
100 23 46 69 129 180 230
105-114,116-118: 116-Vampira, Queen of Terror app.
18 36 54 101 138 175
115-Injury to eye-c; Eyeball story w/injury-to-eye panels
38 76 114 219 310 400
119-Electric chair-c (scarce) 41 82 123 246 348 450
NOTE: *Mac Raboy c-1-28, 30-32, 57, 59 among others.*

CAPTAIN MARVEL PRESENTS THE TERRIBLE FIVE
M. F. Enterprises: Aug, 1966; V2#5, Sept, 1967 (No #2-4) (25¢)
1 4 8 12 29 40 50
V2#5-(Formerly Captain Marvel) 3 6 9 18 24 30

CAPTAIN MARVEL'S FUN BOOK
Samuel Lowe Co.: 1944 (1/2" thick) (cardboard covers)(25¢)
nn-Puzzles, games, magic, etc.; infinity-c 37 74 111 209 297 385

CAPTAIN MARVEL SPECIAL EDITION (See Special Edition)

CAPTAIN MARVEL STORY BOOK
Fawcett Publications: Summer, 1946 - No. 4, Summer?, 1948
1-Half text 54 108 162 324 487 650
2-4 39 78 117 230 325 420

CAPTAIN MARVEL THRILL BOOK (Large-Size)
Fawcett Publications: 1941 (B&W w/color-c)
1-Reprints from Whiz #8,10, & Special Edition #1 (Rare)
290 580 870 2900 - -
NOTE: *Rarely found in Fine or Mint condition.*

CAPTAIN MIDNIGHT (TV, radio, films) (See The Funnies, Popular Comics & Super Book of Comics)(Becomes Sweethearts No. 68 on)
Fawcett Publications: Sept, 1942 - No. 67, Fall, 1948 (#1-14: 68 pgs.)
1-Origin Captain Midnight, star of radio and movies; Captain Marvel cameo on cover
304 608 912 1976 3038 4100
2-Smashes the Jap Juggarnaut 144 288 432 900 1350 1800
3-Classic Nazi war-c 128 256 384 800 1200 1600
4,5: 4-Grapples the Gremlins 112 224 336 700 1050 1400
6-8 76 152 228 475 713 950
9-Raboy-c 78 156 234 488 732 975
10-Raboy Flag-c 80 160 240 500 750 1000
11-20: 11,17,18-Raboy-c. 16 (1/44) 55 110 165 344 515 685
21-23,25-30: 22-War savings stamp-c 44 88 132 264 395 525
24-Japan flag sunburst-c 46 92 138 276 413 550
31-40 33 66 99 190 270 350
41-59,61-67: 50-Sci/fi theme begins? 28 56 84 161 228 295

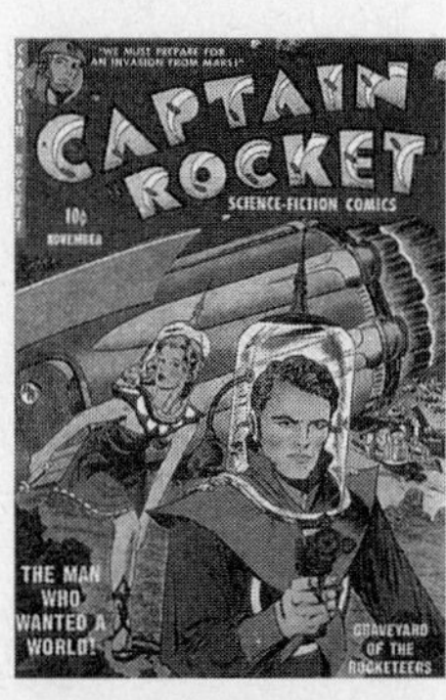

Captain Rocket #1 © P.L. Publ.

Capt. Storm #15 © DC

Captain Video #5 © FAW

	GD	VG	FN	VF	VF/NM	NM-
	2.0	4.0	6.0	8.0	9.0	9.2

60-Flying Saucer issue (2/48)-3rd of this theme; see The Spirit 9/28/47(1st), Shadow Comics V7#10 (2nd, 1/48) & Boy Commandos #26 (4th, 3-4/48) 36 72 108 204 290 375

CAPTAIN NICE (TV)
Gold Key: Nov, 1967 (one-shot)

1(10211-711)-Photo-c 8 16 24 53 74 95

CAPTAIN N: THE GAME MASTER (TV)
Valiant Comics: 1990 - No. 6? ($1.95, thick stock, coated-c)

1-6: 4-6-Layton-c 3.00

CAPTAIN PARAGON (See Bill Black's Fun Comics)
Americomics: Dec, 1983 - No. 4, 1985

1-Intro/1st app. Ms. Victory 4.00
2-4 3.00

CAPTAIN PARAGON AND THE SENTINELS OF JUSTICE
AC Comics: April, 1985 - No. 6, 1986 ($1.75)

1-6: 1-Capt. Paragon, Commando D., Nightveil, Scarlet Scorpion, Stardust & Atoman 3.00

CAPTAIN PLANET AND THE PLANETEERS (TV cartoon)
Marvel Comics: Oct, 1991 - No. 12, Oct, 1992 ($1.00/$1.25)

1-N. Adams painted-c 4.00
2-12: 3-Romita-c 3.00

CAPTAIN POWER AND THE SOLDIERS OF THE FUTURE (TV)
Continuity Comics: Aug, 1988 - No. 2, 1988 ($2.00)

1,2: 1-Neal Adams-c/layouts/inks; variant-c exists. 3.00

CAPTAIN PUREHEART (See Archie as...)

CAPTAIN ROCKET
P. L. Publ. (Canada): Nov, 1951

1 43 86 129 258 389 520

CAPT. SAVAGE AND HIS LEATHERNECK RAIDERS (...And His Battlefield Raiders #9 on)
Marvel Comics Group (Animated Timely Features): Jan, 1968 - No. 19, Mar, 1970
(See Sgt. Fury No. 10)

1-Sgt. Fury & Howlers cameo 4 8 12 29 40 50
2,7,11: 2-Origin Hydra. 1-5,7-Ayers/Shores-a. 7-Pre-"Thing" Ben Grimm story. 11-Sgt. Fury app. 3 6 9 16 20 25
3-6,8-10,12-14: 14-Last 12¢ issue 2 4 6 14 18 22
15-19 2 4 6 12 16 20

CAPTAIN SCIENCE (Fantastic No. 8 on)
Youthful Magazines: Nov, 1950 - No. 7, Dec, 1951

1-Wood-a; origin; 2 pg. text w/ photos of George Pal's "Destination Moon." 85 170 255 531 796 1060
2 44 88 132 264 395 525
3,6,7; 3,6-Bondage c-swipes/Wings #94,91 42 84 126 252 359 465
4,5-Wood/Orlando-c/a(2) each 80 160 240 500 750 1000
NOTE: *Fass a-4. Bondage c-3, 6, 7.*

CAPTAIN SILVER'S LOG OF SEA HOUND (See Sea Hound)

CAPTAIN SINBAD (Movie Adaptation) (See Fantastic Voyages of... & Movie Comics)

CAPTAIN STERNN: RUNNING OUT OF TIME
Kitchen Sink Press: Sept, 1993 - No. 5, 1994 ($4.95, limited series, coated stock, 52 pgs.)

1-5: Berni Wrightson-c/a/scripts 6.00
1-Gold ink variant 10.00

CAPTAIN STEVE SAVAGE (...& His Jet Fighters, No. 2-13)
Avon Periodicals: 1950 - No. 8, 1/53; No. 5, 9-10/54 - No. 13, 5-6/56

nn(1st series)-Wood art, 22 pgs. (titled "...Over Korea") 39 78 117 230 325 420
1(4/51)-Reprints nn issue (Canadian) 17 34 51 95 130 165
2-Kamen-a 11 22 33 66 88 110
3-11 (#6, 9-10/54, last precode) 8 16 24 46 58 70
12-Wood-a (6 pgs.) 12 24 36 69 92 115
13-Check, Lawrence-a 9 18 27 49 62 75
NOTE: ***Kinstler** c-2-5, 7-9, 11. **Lawrence** a-8. **Ravielli** a-5, 9.*
5(9-10/54-2nd series)(Formerly Sensational Police Cases) 8 16 24 46 58 70
6-Reprints nn issue; Wood-a 10 20 30 56 73 90
7-13: 9,10-Kinstler-c. 10-r/cover #2 (1st series). 13-r/cover #8 (1st series) 7 14 21 35 43 50

CAPTAIN STONE (See Holyoke One-Shot No. 10)

CAPT. STORM (Also see G. I. Combat #138)

	GD	VG	FN	VF	VF/NM	NM-
	2.0	4.0	6.0	8.0	9.0	9.2

National Periodical Publications: May-June, 1964 - No. 18, Mar-Apr, 1967

1-Origin 7 14 21 46 63 80
2-7,9-18: 3,6,13-Kubert-a. 4-Colan-a. 12-Kubert-c 4 8 12 29 40 50
8-Grey-tone-c 5 10 15 33 44 55

CAPTAIN 3-D (Super hero)
Harvey Publications: December, 1953 (25¢, came with 2 pairs of glasses)

1-Kirby/Ditko-a (Ditko's 3rd published work tied with Strange Fantasy #9, see also Daring Love #1 & Black Magic V4 #3); shows cover in 3-D on inside; Kirby/Meskin-c 12 24 36 71 96 120
NOTE: *Half price without glasses*

CAPTAIN THUNDER AND BLUE BOLT
Hero Comics: Sept, 1987 - No. 10, 1988 ($1.95)

1-10: 1-Origin Blue Bolt. 3-Origin Capt. Thunder. 6-1st app. Wicket. 8-Champions x-over 2.25

CAPTAIN TOOTSIE & THE SECRET LEGION (Advs. of...)(Also see Monte Hale #30,39 & Real Western Hero)
Toby Press: Oct, 1950 - No. 2, Dec, 1950

1-Not Beck-a; both have sci/fi covers 33 66 99 190 270 350
2-The Rocketeer Patrol app.; not Beck-a 21 42 63 118 164 210

CAPTAIN TRIUMPH (See Crack Comics #27)

CAPTAIN VENTURE & THE LAND BENEATH THE SEA (See Space Family Robinson)
Gold Key: Oct, 1968 - No. 2, Oct, 1969

1-r/Space Family Robinson serial; Spiegle-a 5 10 15 36 48 60
2-Spiegle-a 4 8 12 29 40 50

CAPTAIN VICTORY AND THE GALACTIC RANGERS
Pacific Comics: Nov, 1981 - No. 13, Jan, 1984 ($1.00, direct sales, 36-48 pgs.)
(Created by Jack Kirby)

1-1st app. Mr. Mind 4.00
2-13: 3-N. Adams-a 3.00
Special 1-(10/83)-Kirby c/a(p) 4.00
NOTE: ***Conrad** a-10, 11. **Ditko** a-6. **Kirby** a-1-3p; c-1-13.*

CAPTAIN VICTORY AND THE GALACTIC RANGERS
Jack Kirby Comics: July, 2000 - No. 2, Sept, 2000 ($2.95, B&W)

1,2-New Jeremy Kirby-s with reprinted Jack Kirby-a; Liefeld pin-up art 3.00

CAPTAIN VIDEO (TV) (See XMas Comics)
Fawcett Publications: Feb, 1951 - No. 6, Dec, 1951 (No. 1,5,6-36pgs.; 2-4, 52pgs.) (All photo-c)

1-George Evans-a(2); 1st TV hero comic 116 232 348 725 1088 1450
2-Used in **SOTI**, pg. 382 76 152 228 475 713 950
3-6-All Evans-a except #5 mostly Evans 64 128 192 400 600 800
NOTE: *Minor **Williamson** assists on most issues. Photo c-1, 5, 6; painted c-2-4.*

CAPTAIN WILLIE SCHULTZ (Also see Fightin' Army)
Charlton Comics: No. 76, Oct, 1985 - No. 77, Jan, 1986

76,77-Low print run 1 2 3 4 5 7

CAPTAIN WIZARD COMICS (See Meteor, Red Band & Three Ring Comics)
Rural Home: 1946

1-Capt. Wizard dons new costume; Impossible Man, Race Wilkins app. 33 66 99 190 270 350

CARE BEARS (TV, Movie)(See Star Comics Magazine)
Star Comics/Marvel Comics No. 15 on: Nov, 1985 - No. 20, Jan, 1989

1-20: Post-a begins. 11-$1.00-c begins. 13-Madballs app. 4.00

CAREER GIRL ROMANCES (Formerly Three Nurses)
Charlton Comics: June, 1964 - No. 78, Dec, 1973

V4#24-31 3 6 9 16 20 24
32-Elvis Presley, Herman's Hermits, Johnny Rivers line drawn-c 11 22 33 77 114 150
33-50 2 4 6 12 16 20
51-78 2 4 6 10 12 15

CAR 54, WHERE ARE YOU? (TV)
Dell Publishing Co.: Mar-May, 1962 - No. 7, Sept-Nov, 1963; 1964 - 1965 (All photo-c)

Four Color 1257(#1, 3-5/62) 9 18 27 65 93 120
2(6-8/62)-7 6 12 18 38 52 65
2,3(10-12/64), 4(1-3/65)-Reprints #2,3,&4 of 1st series 4 8 12 22 30 38

CARL BARKS LIBRARY OF WALT DISNEY'S GYRO GEARLOOSE COMICS AND FILLERS IN COLOR, THE
Gladstone: 1993 ($7.95, 8-1/2x11", limited series, 52 pgs.)

The Carneys #1 © AP

Cartoon Cartoons #6 © Cartoon Network

Casey - Crime Photographer #4 © MAR

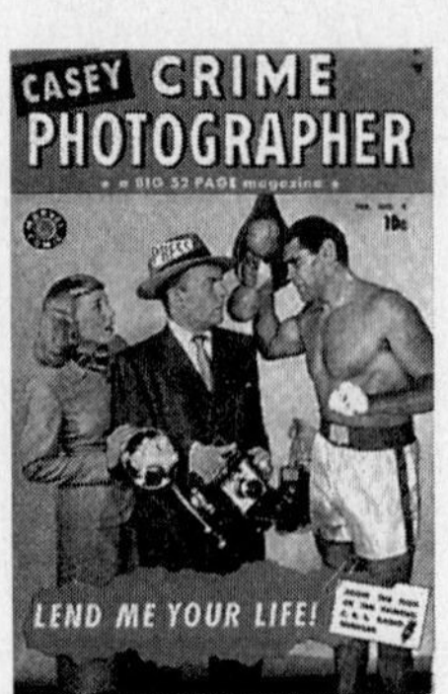

GD VG FN VF VF/NM NM-
2.0 4.0 6.0 8.0 9.0 9.2

1-6: Carl Barks reprints 1 3 4 6 8 10

CARL BARKS LIBRARY OF WALT DISNEY'S COMICS AND STORIES IN COLOR, THE
Gladstone: Jan, 1992 - No. 51, Mar, 1996 ($8.95, 8-1/2x11", 60 pgs.)

1,2,6,8-51: 1-Barks Donald Duck-r/WDC&S #31-35; 2-r/#36,38-41; 6-r/#57-61; 8-r/#67-71; 9-r/#72-76; 10-r/#77-81; 11-r/#82-86; 12-r/#87-91; 13-r/#92-96; 14-r/#97-101; 15-r/#102-106; 16-r/#107-111; 17-r/#112,114,117,124,125; 18-r/#126-130; 19-r/#131,132(2),133,134; 20-r/#135-139; 21-r/#140-144; 22-r/#145-149; 23-r/#150-154; 24-r/#155-159; 25-r/#160-164; 26-r/#165-169; 27-r/#170-174;28-r/#175-179; 29-r/#180-184; 30-r/#185-189; 31-r/#190-194; 32-r/#195-199;33-r/#200-204; 34-r/#205-209; 35-r/#210-214; 36-r/#215-219; 37-r/#220-224; 38-r/#225-229; 39-r/#230-234; 40-r/#235-239; 41-r/#240-244; 42r/#245-249; 43-r/#250-254; 44-50; All contain one Heroes & Villains trading card each
1 3 4 6 8 10
3,4,7: 3-r/#42-46. 4-r/#47-51. 7-r/#62-66. 2 4 6 10 12 15
5-r/#52-56 2 4 6 12 16 20

CARL BARKS LIBRARY OF WALT DISNEY'S DONALD DUCK ADVENTURES IN COLOR, THE
Gladstone: Jan, 1994 - No. 25, Jan, 1996 ($7.95-$9.95, 44-68 pgs., 8-1/2"x11")
(all contain one Donald Duck trading card each)

1-5,7-25-Carl Barks-r: 1-r/FC #9; 2-r/FC #29; 3-r/FC #62; 4-r/FC #108; 5-r/FC #147 & #79(Mickey Mouse); 7-r/FC #159. 8-r/FC #178 & 189. 9-r/FC #199 & 203; 10-r/FC 223 & 238; 11-r/Christmas Parade #1 & 2; 12-r/FC #296; 13-r/FC #263; 14-r/MOC #20 & 41; 15-r/FC 275 & 282; 16-r/FC #291&300; 17-r/FC #308 & 318; 18-r/Vac. Parade #1 & Summer Fun #2; 19-r/FC #328 & 367 2 4 6 8 10 12
6-r/MOC #4, Cheerios "Atom Bomb," D.D. Tells About Kites
2 4 6 12 16 20

CARL BARKS LIBRARY OF WALT DISNEY'S DONALD DUCK CHRISTMAS STORIES IN COLOR, THE
Gladstone: 1992 ($7.95, 44pgs., one-shot)

nn-Reprints Firestone giveaways 1945-1949 2 4 6 10 12 15

CARL BARKS LIBRARY OF WALT DISNEY'S UNCLE SCROOGE COMICS ONE PAGERS IN COLOR, THE
Gladstone: 1992 - No. 2, 1993 ($8.95, limited series, 60 pgs., 8-1/2x11")

1-Carl Barks one pg. reprints 3 6 9 16 20 25
2-Carl Barks one pg. reprints 2 4 6 10 12 15

CARNAGE: IT'S A WONDERFUL LIFE
Marvel Comics: Oct, 1996 ($1.95, one-shot)

1-David Quinn scripts 3.00

CARNAGE: MIND BOMB
Marvel Comics: Feb, 1996 ($2.95, one-shot)

1-Warren Ellis script; Kyle Hotz-a 3.00

CARNATION MALTED MILK GIVEAWAYS (See Wisco)

CARNEYS, THE
Archie Comics: Summer, 1994 ($2.00, 52 pgs)

1-Bound-in pull-out poster 2.50

CARNIVAL COMICS (Formerly Kayo #12; becomes Red Seal Comics #14)
Harry 'A' Chesler/Pershing Square Publ. Co.: 1945

nn (#13)-Guardineer-a 18 36 54 101 138 175

CAROLINE KENNEDY
Charlton Comics: 1961 (one-shot)

nn-Interior photo covers of Kennedy family 9 18 27 65 93 120

CAROUSEL COMICS
F. E. Howard, Toronto: V1#8, April, 1948

V1#8 7 14 21 35 43 50

CARTOON CARTOONS (Anthology)
DC Comics: Mar, 2001 - Present ($1.99/ $2.25)

1-25-Short stories of Cartoon Network characters. 3,6,10,13,15-Space Ghost. 13-Begin $2.25-c. 17-Dexter's Laboratory begins 2.25

CARTOON KIDS
Atlas Comics (CPS): 1957 (no month)

1-Maneely-c/a; Dexter The Demon, Willie The Wise-Guy, Little Zelda app.
10 20 30 58 77 95

CARTOON NETWORK PRESENTS
DC Comics: Aug, 1997 - No. 24, Aug, 1999 ($1.75-$1.99, anthology)

1-Dexter's Lab 5.00
1-Platinum Edition 1 2 3 5 7 9
2-10: 2-Space Ghost 3.50
11-24: 12-Bizarro World 2.25

CARTOON NETWORK PRESENTS SPACE GHOST
Archie Comics: Mar, 1997 ($1.50)

1-Scott Rosema-p 5.00

CARTOON NETWORK STARRING... (Anthology)
DC Comics: Sept, 1999 - No. 18, Feb, 2001 ($1.99)

1-Powerpuff Girls 5.00
2-18: 2,8,11,14,17-Johnny Bravo. 12,15,18-Space Ghost 3.00

CARTOON TALES (Disney's...)
W.D. Publications (Disney): nd, nn (1992) ($2.95, 6-5/8x9-1/2", 52 pgs.)

nn-Ariel & Sebastian-Serpent Teen; Beauty and the Beast; A Tale of Enchantment; Darkwing Duck - Just Us Justice Ducks; 101 Dalmatians - Canine Classics; Tale Spin - Surprise in the Skies; Uncle Scrooge - Blast to the Past 4.00

CARVERS
Image Comics (Flypaper Press): 1998 - No. 3, 1999 ($2.95)

1-3-Pander Bros.-a/Fleming-s 3.00

CAR WARRIORS
Marvel Comics (Epic): June, 1991 - No. 4, Sept, 1991 ($2.25, lim. series)

1-4: 1-Says April in indicia 2.25

CASE FILES: SAM & TWITCH (Also see the Spawn titles)
Image Comics: May, 2003 - Present ($2.50)

1-5-Scott Morse-a/Marc Andreyko-s 2.50

CASE OF THE SHOPLIFTER'S SHOE (See Perry Mason, Feature Book No.50)

CASE OF THE WINKING BUDDHA, THE
St. John Publ. Co.: 1950 (132 pgs.; 25¢; B&W; 5-1/2x7-5-1/2x8")

nn-Charles Raab-a; reprinted in Authentic Police Cases No. 25
29 58 87 164 232 300

CASEY-CRIME PHOTOGRAPHER (Two-Gun Western No. 5 on)(Radio)
Marvel Comics (BFP): Aug, 1949 - No. 4, Feb, 1950

1-Photo-c; 52 pgs. 25 50 75 144 198 255
2-4: Photo-c 17 34 51 98 134 170

CASEY JONES (TV)
Dell Publishing Co.: No. 915, July, 1958

Four Color 915-Alan Hale photo-c 6 12 18 40 55 70

CASEY JONES & RAPHAEL (See Bodycount)
Mirage Studios: Oct, 1994 ($2.75, unfinished limited series)

1-Bisley-c; Eastman story & pencils 2.75

CASEY JONES: NORTH BY DOWNEAST
Mirage Studios: May, 1994 - No. 2, July, 1994 ($2.75, limited series)

1,2-Rick Veitch script & pencils; Kevin Eastman story & inks 2.75

CASPER ADVENTURE DIGEST
Harvey Comics: V2#1, Oct, 1992 - V2#8, Apr, 1994 ($1.75/$1.95, digest-size)

V2#1: Casper, Richie Rich, Spooky, Wendy 5.00
2-8 3.50

CASPER AND...
Harvey Comics: Nov, 1987 - No. 12, June, 1990 (.75/$1.00, all reprints)

1-Ghostly Trio 5.00
2-12: 2-Spooky; begin $1.00-c. 3-Wendy. 4-Nightmare. 5-Ghostly Trio. 6-Spooky. 7-Wendy. 8-Hot Stuff. 9-Baby Huey. 10-Wendy.11-Ghostly Trio. 12-Spooky 3.00

CASPER AND FRIENDS
Harvey Comics: Oct, 1991 - No. 5, July, 1992 ($1.00/$1.25)

1-Nightmare, Ghostly Trio, Wendy, Spooky 4.00
2-5 3.00

CASPER AND FRIENDS MAGAZINE: Mar, 1997 - No. 3, July, 1997 ($3.99)

1-3 4.00

CASPER AND NIGHTMARE (See Harvey Hits# 37, 45, 52, 56, 59, 62, 65, 68,71, 75)

CASPER AND NIGHTMARE (Nightmare & Casper No. 1-5)
Harvey Publications: No. 6, 11/64 - No. 44, 10/73; No. 45, 6/74 - No. 46, 8/74 (25¢)

6: 68 pg. Giants begin, ends #32 5 10 15 33 44 55
7-10 4 8 12 22 30 38
11-20 3 6 9 18 23 28
21-37: 33-37-(52 pg. Giants) 2 4 6 14 18 22
38-46 2 4 6 9 11 14

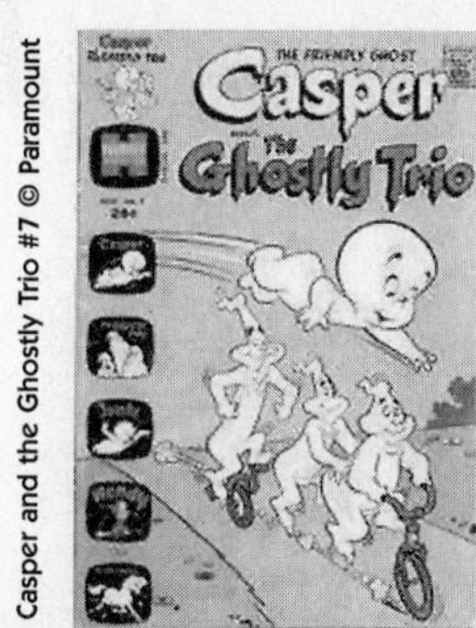

Casper and the Ghostly Trio #7 © Paramount

Casper, The Friendly Ghost #69 © Paramount

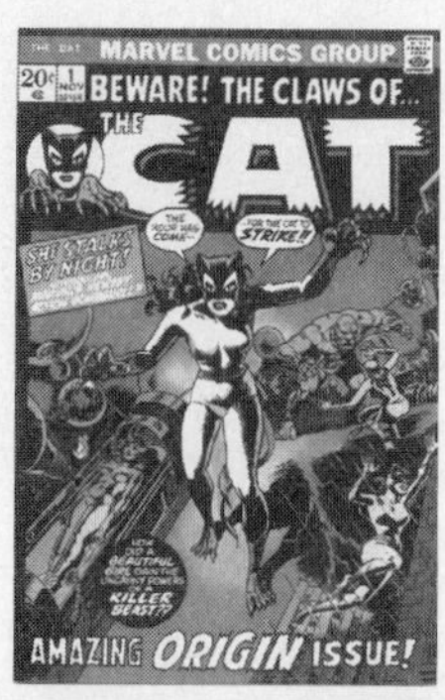

The Cat #1 © MAR

NOTE: *Many issues contain reprints.*

CASPER AND SPOOKY (See Harvey Hits No. 20)
Harvey Publications: Oct, 1972 - No. 7, Oct, 1973

	GD 2.0	VG 4.0	FN 6.0	VF 8.0	VF/NM 9.0	NM- 9.2
1	3	6	9	19	25	32
2-7	2	4	6	10	13	16

CASPER AND THE GHOSTLY TRIO
Harvey Pub.: Nov, 1972 - No. 7, Nov, 1973; No. 8, Aug, 1990 - No. 10, Dec, 1990

	GD 2.0	VG 4.0	FN 6.0	VF 8.0	VF/NM 9.0	NM- 9.2
1	3	6	9	19	25	32
2-7	2	4	6	10	13	16
8-10						5.00

CASPER AND WENDY
Harvey Publications: Sept, 1972 - No. 8, Nov, 1973

	GD 2.0	VG 4.0	FN 6.0	VF 8.0	VF/NM 9.0	NM- 9.2
1: 52 pg. Giant	3	6	9	19	25	32
2-8	2	4	6	10	13	16

CASPER BIG BOOK
Harvey Comics: V2#1, Aug, 1992 - No. 3, May, 1993 ($1.95, 52 pgs.)

	GD 2.0	VG 4.0	FN 6.0	VF 8.0	VF/NM 9.0	NM- 9.2
V2#1-Spooky app.						4.00
2,3						3.00

CASPER CAT (See Dopey Duck)
I. W. Enterprises/Super: 1958; 1963

	GD 2.0	VG 4.0	FN 6.0	VF 8.0	VF/NM 9.0	NM- 9.2
1,7:1-Wacky Duck #?.7-Reprint, Super No. 14('63)	2	4	6	10	13	16

CASPER DIGEST (...Magazine #?; ...Halloween Digest #8, 10)
Harvey Publications: Oct, 1986 - No. 18, Jan, 1991 ($1.25/$1.75, digest-size)

	GD 2.0	VG 4.0	FN 6.0	VF 8.0	VF/NM 9.0	NM- 9.2
1	1	3	4	6	8	10
2-18: 11-Valentine-c. 18-Halloween-c						6.00

CASPER DIGEST (...Magazine #? on)
Harvey Comics: V2#1, Sept, 1991 - V2#14, Nov, 1994 ($1.75/$1.95, digest-size)

	GD 2.0	VG 4.0	FN 6.0	VF 8.0	VF/NM 9.0	NM- 9.2
V2#1						5.00
2-14						3.50

CASPER DIGEST STORIES
Harvey Publications: Feb, 1980 - No. 4, Nov, 1980 (95¢, 132 pgs., digest size)

	GD 2.0	VG 4.0	FN 6.0	VF 8.0	VF/NM 9.0	NM- 9.2
1	2	4	6	10	13	16
2-4	1	2	3	5	7	9

CASPER DIGEST WINNERS
Harvey Publications: Apr, 1980 - No. 3, Sept, 1980 (95¢, 132 pgs., digest size)

	GD 2.0	VG 4.0	FN 6.0	VF 8.0	VF/NM 9.0	NM- 9.2
1	2	4	6	10	13	16
2,3	1	2	3	5	7	9

CASPER ENCHANTED TALES DIGEST
Harvey Comics: May, 1992 - No. 10, Oct, 1994 ($1.75, digest-size, 98 pgs.)

	GD 2.0	VG 4.0	FN 6.0	VF 8.0	VF/NM 9.0	NM- 9.2
1-Casper, Spooky, Wendy stories						5.00
2-10						3.50

CASPER GHOSTLAND
Harvey Comics: May, 1992 ($1.25)

	GD 2.0	VG 4.0	FN 6.0	VF 8.0	VF/NM 9.0	NM- 9.2
1						3.00

CASPER GIANT SIZE
Harvey Comics: Oct, 1992 - No. 4, Nov, 1993 ($2.25, 68 pgs.)

	GD 2.0	VG 4.0	FN 6.0	VF 8.0	VF/NM 9.0	NM- 9.2
V2#1-Casper, Wendy, Spooky stories						5.00
2-4						4.00

CASPER HALLOWEEN TRICK OR TREAT
Harvey Publications: Jan, 1976 (52 pgs.)

	GD 2.0	VG 4.0	FN 6.0	VF 8.0	VF/NM 9.0	NM- 9.2
1	3	6	9	19	25	32

CASPER IN SPACE (Formerly Casper Spaceship)
Harvey Publications: No. 6, June, 1973 - No. 8, Oct, 1973

	GD 2.0	VG 4.0	FN 6.0	VF 8.0	VF/NM 9.0	NM- 9.2
6-8	2	4	6	10	13	16

CASPER'S GHOSTLAND
Harvey Publications: Winter, 1958-59 - No. 97, 12/77; No. 98, 12/79 (25¢)

	GD 2.0	VG 4.0	FN 6.0	VF 8.0	VF/NM 9.0	NM- 9.2
1-84 pgs. begin, ends #10	20	40	60	140	205	270
2	10	20	30	72	104	135
3-10	8	16	24	55	78	100
11-20: 11-68 pgs. begin, ends #61. 13-X-Mas-c	6	12	18	43	59	75
21-40	4	8	12	29	40	50
41-61	3	6	9	18	24	30
62-77: 62-52 pgs. begin	2	4	6	10	13	16
78-98: 94-X-Mas-c	2	4	6	8	10	12

NOTE: *Most issues contain reprints w/new stories.*

CASPER SPACESHIP (Casper in Space No. 6 on)
Harvey Publications: Aug, 1972 - No. 5, April, 1973

	GD 2.0	VG 4.0	FN 6.0	VF 8.0	VF/NM 9.0	NM- 9.2
1: 52 pg. Giant	3	7	10	21	28	35
2-5	2	4	6	11	14	18

CASPER STRANGE GHOST STORIES
Harvey Publications: October, 1974 - No. 14, Jan, 1977 (All 52 pgs.)

	GD 2.0	VG 4.0	FN 6.0	VF 8.0	VF/NM 9.0	NM- 9.2
1	3	7	10	21	28	35
2-14	2	4	6	11	14	18

CASPER, THE FRIENDLY GHOST (See America's Best TV Comics, Famous TV Funday Funnies, The Friendly Ghost..., Nightmare &..., Richie Rich and..., Tastee-Freez, Treasury of Comics, Wendy the Good Little Witch & Wendy Witch World)

CASPER, THE FRIENDLY GHOST (Becomes Harvey Comics Hits No. 61 (No. 6), and then continued with Harvey issue No. 7)(1st Series)
St. John Publishing Co.: Sept, 1949 - No. 5, Aug, 1951

	GD 2.0	VG 4.0	FN 6.0	VF 8.0	VF/NM 9.0	NM- 9.2
1(1949)-Origin & 1st app. Baby Huey & Herman the Mouse (1st time the name Casper app. in any media, even films)	184	368	552	1150	1725	2300
2,3 (2/50 & 8/50)	72	144	216	450	675	900
4,5 (3/51 & 8/51)	56	112	168	336	506	675

CASPER, THE FRIENDLY GHOST (Paramount Picture Star...)(2nd Series)
Harvey Publications (Family Comics): No. 7, Dec, 1952 - No. 70, July, 1958
Note: No. 6 is Harvey Comics Hits No. 61 (10/52)

	GD 2.0	VG 4.0	FN 6.0	VF 8.0	VF/NM 9.0	NM- 9.2
7-Baby Huey begins, ends #9	33	66	99	248	374	500
8,9	20	40	60	142	209	275
10-Spooky begins (1st app., 6/53), ends #70?	24	48	72	169	247	325
11-18: Alfred Harvey app. in story	12	24	36	87	129	170
19-1st app. Nightmare (4/54)	19	38	57	136	198	260
20-Wendy the Witch begins (1st app., 5/54)	25	50	75	181	266	350
21-30: 24-Infinity-c	10	20	30	72	104	135
31-40	8	16	24	53	74	95
41-50	6	12	18	43	59	75
51-70 (Continues as Friendly Ghost... 8/58)	5	10	15	36	48	60

CASPER THE FRIENDLY GHOST (Formerly The Friendly Ghost...)(3rd Series)
Harvey Comics: No. 254, July, 1990 - No. 260, Jan, 1991 ($1.00)

	GD 2.0	VG 4.0	FN 6.0	VF 8.0	VF/NM 9.0	NM- 9.2
254-260						3.00

CASPER THE FRIENDLY GHOST (4th Series)
Harvey Comics: Mar, 1991 - No. 28, Nov, 1994 ($1.00/$1.25/$1.50)

	GD 2.0	VG 4.0	FN 6.0	VF 8.0	VF/NM 9.0	NM- 9.2
1-Casper becomes Mighty Ghost; Spooky & Wendy app.						5.00
2-10: 7,8-Post-a						3.00
11-28-($1.50)						2.50

CASPER T.V. SHOWTIME
Harvey Comics: Jan, 1980 - No. 5, Oct, 1980

	GD 2.0	VG 4.0	FN 6.0	VF 8.0	VF/NM 9.0	NM- 9.2
1	2	4	6	9	11	14
2-5	1	2	3	4	5	7

CASSETTE BOOKS (Classics Illustrated)
Cassette Book Co./I.P.S. Publ.: 1984 (48 pgs, b&w comic with cassette tape)
NOTE: *This series was illegal. The artwork was illegally obtained, and the Classics Illustrated copyright owner, Twin Circle Publ. sued to get an injunction to prevent the continued sale of this series. Many C.I. collectors obtained copies before the 1987 injunction, but now they are already scarce. Here again the market is just developing, but sealed mint copies of com ic and tape should be worth at least $25.*

1001 (CI#1-A2)New-PC 1002(CI#3-A2)CI-PC 1003(CI#13-A2)CI-PC
1004(CI#25)CI-LDC 1005(CI#10-A2)New-PC 1006(CI#64)CI-LDC

CASTILIAN (See Movie Classics)

CASTLE WAITING
Olio: 1997 - No. 7, 1999 ($2.95, B&W)
Cartoon Books: Vol. 2, Aug, 2000 - Present ($2.95, B&W)

	GD 2.0	VG 4.0	FN 6.0	VF 8.0	VF/NM 9.0	NM- 9.2
1-Linda Medley-s/a in all	1	2	3	5	6	8
2						4.00
3-7						3.00
The Lucky Road TPB r/#1-7						17.00
Hiatus Issue (1999) Crilley-c; short stories and previews						3.00
Vol. 2 #1-6,14-16 (#5&6 also have #12&13 on cover, for series numbering)						3.00

CASUAL HEROES
Image Comics (Motown Machineworks): Apr, 1996 ($2.25, unfinished lim. series)

	GD 2.0	VG 4.0	FN 6.0	VF 8.0	VF/NM 9.0	NM- 9.2
1-Steve Rude-c						2.25

CAT, T.H.E. (TV) (See T.H.E. Cat)

CAT, THE (See Movie Classics)

CAT, THE (Female hero)
Marvel Comics Group: Nov, 1972 - No. 4, June, 1973

Catman Comics #3 © HOKE

Catwoman #12 © DC

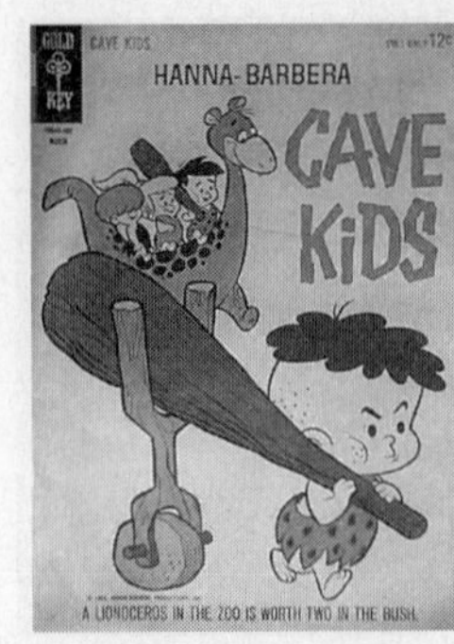

Cave Kids #4 © H-B

GD 2.0 | VG 4.0 | FN 6.0 | VF 8.0 | VF/NM 9.0 | NM- 9.2

1-Origin & 1st app. The Cat (who later becomes Tigra); Mooney-a(i); Wood-c(i)/a(i) 4 8 12 24 32 40
2,3: 2-Marie Severin/Mooney-a. 3-Everett inks 2 4 6 12 16 20
4-Starlin/Weiss-a(p) 2 4 6 14 18 22

CATALYST: AGENTS OF CHANGE (Also see Comics' Greatest World)
Dark Horse Comics: Feb, 1994 - No.7, Nov, 1994 ($2.00, limited series)

1-7: 1-Foil stamped logo 2.50

CAT & MOUSE
EF Graphics (Silverline): Dec, 1988 ($1.75, color w/part B&W)

1-1st printing (12/88, 32 pgs.), 1-2nd printing (5/89, 36 pgs.) 2.25

CAT FROM OUTER SPACE (See Walt Disney Showcase #46)

CATHOLIC COMICS (See Heroes All Catholic...)
Catholic Publications: June, 1946 - V3#10, July, 1949

1 31 62 93 178 252 325
2 16 32 48 92 126 160
3-13(7/47) 14 28 42 81 111 140
V2#1-10 10 20 30 58 77 95
V3#1-10: Reprints 10-part Treasure Island serial from Target V2#2-11 (see Key Comics #5) 10 20 30 60 80 100

CATHOLIC PICTORIAL
Catholic Guild: 1947

1-Toth-a(2) (Rare) 40 80 120 240 350 460

CATMAN COMICS (Formerly Crash Comics No. 1-5)
Holyoke Publishing Co./Continental Magazines V2#12, 7/44 on:
5/41 - No. 17, 1/43; No. 18, 7/43 - No. 22, 12/43; No. 23, 3/44 - No. 26, 11/44; No. 27, 4/45 - No. 30, 12/45; No. 31, 6/46 - No. 32, 8/46

1(V1#6)-Origin The Deacon & Sidekick Mickey, Dr. Diamond & Rag-Man; The Black Widow app.; The Catman by Chas. Quinlan & Blaze Baylor begin 370 740 1110 2405 3703 5000
2(V1#7) 132 264 396 825 1238 1650
3(V1#8)-The Pied Piper begins; classic Hitler, Stalin & Mussolini-c 114 228 342 713 1069 1425
4(V1#9) 94 188 282 588 882 1175
5(V2#10)-1st app. Kitten; The Hood begins (c-redated), 6,7(V2#11,12) 78 156 234 488 732 975
8(V2#13,3/42)-Origin Little Leaders; Volton by Kubert begins (his 1st comic book work) 94 188 282 588 882 1175
9,10(V2#14,15): 10-Origin Blackout; Phantom Falcon begins 66 132 198 413 617 820
11 (V3#1)-Kubert-a 66 132 198 413 617 820
12 (V3#2), 14, 15, 17, 18(V3#8, 7/43). 12-Volton by Brodsky, not Kubert. 14-Brodsky-a 55 110 165 330 495 660
13-(scarce) 85 170 255 531 796 1060
16 (V3#5)-Hitler, Tojo, Mussolini, Goehring-c 76 152 228 475 713 950
19,20: 19 (V2#6)-Hitler, Tojo, Mussolini-c. 20 (V2#7): Classic Hitler-c 80 160 240 500 750 1000
21-23 (V2#10, 3/44) 50 100 150 300 450 600
nn(V3#13, 5/44)-Rico-a; Schomburg bondage-c 50 100 150 300 450 600
nn(V2#12, 7/44, nn(V3#1, 9/44)-Origin The Golden Archer; Leatherface app. 46 92 138 276 413 550
nn(V3#2, 11/44)-L. B. Cole-c 78 156 234 488 732 975
27-Origins Catman & Kitten retold; L. B. Cole Flag-c; Infantino-a 90 180 270 563 844 1125
28-Dr. Macabre app.; L. B. Cole-c/a 96 192 288 600 900 1200
29-32-L. B. Cole-c; bondage-#30 83 166 249 519 780 1040

NOTE: *Fuje* a-11, 27, 28(2), 29(3), 30. *Palais* a-11, 16, 27, 28, 29(2), 30(2), 32; c-25(7/44). *Rico* a-11(2), 23, 27, 28.

CATSEYE
Hyperwerks Comics: Dec, 1998 - No. 4, June, 1999 ($2.95)

1-4-Altstaetter-s/a 3.00

CAT TALES (3-D)
Eternity Comics: Apr, 1989 ($2.95)

1-Felix the Cat-r in 3-D 5.00

CATWOMAN (Also see Action Comics Weekly #611, Batman #404-407, Detective Comics, & Superman's Girlfriend Lois Lane #70, 71)
DC Comics: Feb, 1989 - No. 4, May, 1989 ($1.50, limited series, mature)

1 1 3 4 6 8 10
2-4: 3-Batman cameo. 4-Batman app. 1 2 3 5 7 9
Her Sister's Keeper (1991, $9.95, trade paperback)-r/#1-4 10.00

CATWOMAN (Also see Showcase '93, Showcase '95 #4, & Batman #404-407)
DC Comics: Aug, 1993 - No. 94, Jul, 2001 ($1.50-$2.25)

0-(10/94)-Zero Hour; origin retold. Released between #14&15 3.00
1-($1.95)-Embossed-c; Bane app.; Balent c-1-10; a-1-10p 4.00
2-20: 3-Bane flashback cameo. 4-Brief Bane app. 6,7-Knightquest tie-ins; Batman (Azrael) app. 8-1st app. Zephyr. 12-KnightsEnd pt. 6. 13-new Knights End Aftermath. 14-(9/94)-Zero Hour 3.00
21-24, 26-30, 33-49: 21-$1.95-c begins. 28,29-Penguin cameo app. 36-Legacy pt. 2. 38-40-Year Two; Batman, Joker, Penguin & Two-Face app. 46-Two-Face app. 2.50
25,31,32: 25-($2.95)-Robin app. 31,32-Contagion pt. 4 (Reads pt. 5 on-c) & pt. 9. 3.00
50-($2.95, 48 pgs.)-New armored costume 3.00
50-($2.95, 48 pgs.)-Collector's Ed.w/metallic ink-c 3.00
51-77: 51-Huntress-c/app. 54-Grayson-s begins. 56-Cataclysm pt.6. 57-Poison Ivy-c/app. 63-65-Joker-c/app. 72-No Man's Land; Ostrander-s begins 2.50
78-82: 80-Catwoman goes to jail 2.25
83-94: 83-Begin $2.25-c. 83,84,89-Harley Quinn-c/app. 2.25
#1,000,000 (11/98) 853rd Century x-over 2.25
Annual 1 (1994, $2.95, 68 pgs.)-Elseworlds story; Batman app.; no Balent-a 3.00
Annual 2,4 ('95, '97, $3.95) 2-Year One story. 4-Pulp Heroes 4.00
Annual 3 (1996, $2.95)-Legends of the Dead Earth story 3.00
...Plus 1 (11/97, $2.95) Screamqueen (Scare Tactics) app. 3.00
TPB ($9.95) r/#15-19, Balent-c 10.00

CATWOMAN (Also see Detective Comics #759-762)
DC Comics: Jan, 2002 - Present ($2.50)

1-Darwyn Cooke & Mike Allred-a; Ed Brubaker-s 6.00
2-4 3.00
5-26: 5-9-Rader-a/Paul Pope-c. 10-Morse-c. 16-JG Jones-c. 22-Batman-c/app. 2.50
...: Crooked Little Town TPB (2003, $14.95) r/#5-10 & Secret Files; Oeming-c 15.00
... Secret Files and Origins (10/02, $4.95) origin-s Oeming-a; profiles and pin-ups 5.00
...Selina's Big Score HC (2002, $24.95) Cooke-s/a; pin-ups by various 25.00
...Selina's Big Score SC (2003, $17.95) Cooke-s/a; pin-ups by various 18.00
...: The Dark End of the Street TPB (2002, $12.95) r/#1-4 & Slam Bradley back-up stories from Detective Comics #759-762 13.00

CATWOMAN/ GUARDIAN OF GOTHAM
DC Comics: 1999 - No. 2, 1999 ($5.95, limited series)

1,2-Elseworlds; Moench-s/Balent-a 6.00

CATWOMAN/VAMPIRELLA: THE FURIES
DC Comics/Harris Publ.: Feb, 1997 ($4.95, squarebound, 46 pgs.) (1st DC/Harris x-over)

nn-Reintro Pantha; Chuck Dixon scripts; Jim Balent-c/a 5.00

CATWOMAN/WILDCAT
DC Comics: Aug, 1998 - No. 4, Nov, 1998 ($2.50, limited series)

1-4-Chuck Dixon & Beau Smith-s; Stelfreeze-c 3.00

CAUGHT
Atlas Comics (VPI): Aug, 1956 - No. 5, Apr, 1957

1 23 46 69 132 186 240
2-4: 3-Maneely, Pakula, Torres-a. 4-Maneely-a 12 24 36 71 96 120
5-Crandall, Krigstein-a 13 26 39 76 103 130

NOTE: *Drucker* a-2. *Heck* a-4. *Severin* c-1, 2, 4, 5. *Shores* a-4.

CAVALIER COMICS
A. W. Nugent Publ. Co.: 1945; 1952 (Early DC reprints)

2(1945)-Speed Saunders, Fang Gow 22 44 66 124 172 220
2(1952) 11 22 33 66 88 110

CAVE GIRL (Also see Africa)
Magazine Enterprises: No. 11, 1953 - No. 14, 1954

11(A-1 82)-Origin; all Cave Girl stories 46 92 138 276 413 550
12(A-1 96), 13(A-1 116), 14(A-1 125)-Thunda by Powell in each 37 74 111 210 298 385

NOTE: *Powell* c/a in all.

CAVE GIRL
AC Comics: 1988 ($2.95, 44 pgs.) (16 pgs. of color, rest B&W)

1-Powell-r/Cave Girl #11; Nyoka photo back-c from movie; Powell/Bill Black-c; Special Limited Edition on-c 4.00

CAVE KIDS (TV) (See Comic Album #16)
Gold Key: Feb, 1963 - No. 16, Mar, 1967 (Hanna-Barbera)

1 8 16 24 53 74 95
2-5 4 8 12 27 36 45
6-16: 7,12-Pebbles & Bamm Bamm app. 16-1st Space Kidettes 3 7 10 21 28 35

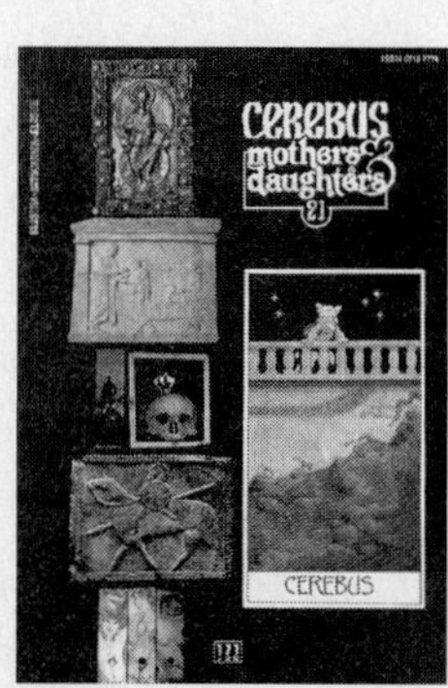
Cerebus #171 © Dave Sim & Gerhard

Challenge of the Unknown #6 © ACE

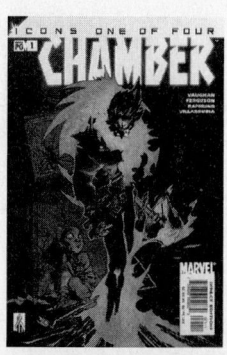

Chamber #1 © MAR

	GD 2.0	VG 4.0	FN 6.0	VF 8.0	VF/NM 9.0	NM- 9.2

CAVEWOMAN
Basement Comics: Jan, 1994 - No. 6, 1995 ($2.95)
1 3 6 9 18 24 30
2 2 4 6 10 12 15
3-6 1 2 3 5 6 8
...: Meets Explorers ('97, $2.95) 3.00
...: One-Shot Special (7/00, $2.95) Massey-s/a 3.00

CELESTINE (See Violator Vs. Badrock #1)
Image Comics (Extreme): May, 1996 - No. 2, June, 1996 ($2.50, limited series)
1,2: Warren Ellis scripts 2.50

CENTURION OF ANCIENT ROME, THE
Zondervan Publishing House: 1958 (no month listed) (B&W, 36 pgs.)
(Rare) All by Jay Disbrow 42 84 126 252 376 500

CENTURIONS (TV)
DC Comics: June, 1987 - No. 4, Sept, 1987 (75¢, limited series)
1-4 2.50

CENTURY: DISTANT SONS
Marvel Comics: Feb, 1996 ($2.95, one-shot)
1-Wraparound-c 3.00

CENTURY OF COMICS (See Promotional Comics section)

CEREBUS BI-WEEKLY
Aardvark-Vanaheim: Dec. 2, 1988 - No. 26, Nov. 11, 1989 ($1.25, B&W)
Reprints Cerebus The Aardvark#1-26
1-16, 18, 19, 21-26: 3.00
17-Hepcats app. 2 4 6 8 10 12
20-Milk & Cheese app. 2 4 6 10 12 15

CEREBUS: CHURCH & STATE
Aardvark-Vanaheim: Feb, 1991 - No. 30, Apr, 1992 ($2.00, B&W, bi-weekly)
1-30: r/Cerebus #51-80 3.00

CEREBUS: HIGH SOCIETY
Aardvark-Vanaheim: Feb, 1990 - No. 25, 1991 ($1.70, B&W)
1-25: r/Cerebus #26-50 3.00

CEREBUS JAM
Aardvark-Vanaheim: Apr, 1985
1-Eisner, Austin, Dave Sim-a (Cerebus vs. Spirit) 6.00

CEREBUS THE AARDVARK (See A-V in 3-D, Nucleus, Power Comics)
Aardvark-Vanaheim: Dec, 1977 - No. 300, March, 2004 ($1.70/$2.00/$2.25, B&W)
0 3.00
0-Gold 20.00
1-1st app. Cerebus; 2000 print run; most copies poorly printed
33 66 99 248 374 500
Note: *There is a counterfeit version known to exist. It can be distinguished from the original in the following ways: inside cover is glossy instead of flat, black background on the front cover is blotted or spotty. Reports show that a counterfeit #2 also exists.*
2-Dave Sim art in all 10 20 30 67 96 125
3-Origin Red Sophia 9 18 27 63 89 115
4-Origin Elrod the Albino 7 14 21 46 63 80
5,6 6 12 18 40 55 70
7-10 4 8 12 29 40 50
11,12: 11-Origin The Cockroach 3 6 9 19 25 32
13-15: 14-Origin Lord Julius 3 6 9 16 20 24
16-20 2 4 6 10 12 15
21-B. Smith letter in letter column 4 8 12 29 40 50
22-Low distribution; no cover price 3 6 9 16 20 25
23-30: 23-Preview of Wandering Star by Teri S. Wood. 26-High Society begins, ends #50
1 3 4 6 8 10
31-Origin Moonroach 2 4 6 9 11 14
32-40, 53-Intro. Wolveroach (cameo) 1 2 3 5 6 8
41-50,52: 52-Church & State begins, ends #111; Cutey Bunny app.
1 2 3 4 5 7
51,54: 51-Cutey Bunny app. 54-1st full Wolveroach story
1 3 4 6 8 10
55,56-Wolveroach app.; Normalman back-ups by Valentino
1 2 3 5 6 8
57-100: 61,62: Flaming Carrot app. 65-Gerhard begins 4.00
101-160: 104-Flaming Carrot app. 112/113-Double issue. 114-Jaka's Story begins, ends #136. 139-Melmoth begins, ends #150. 151-Mothers & Daughters begins, ends #200 3.00
161-Bone app. 1 3 4 6 8 10
162-231: 175-($2.25, 44 pgs). 186-Strangers on Paradise cameo. 201-Guys storyline begins; Eddie Campbell's Bacchus app. 220-231-Rick's Story 2.50
232-265-Going Home 2.25
266-288,291-298-Latter Days: 267-Five-Bar Gate. 276-Spore (Spawn spoof) 2.25
289&290 ($4.50) Two issues combined 4.50
Free Cerebus (Giveaway, 1991-92?, 36 pgs.)-All-r 4.00

CHAIN GANG WAR
DC Comics: July, 1993 - No. 12, June, 1994 ($1.75)
1-($2.50)-Embossed silver foil-c, Dave Johnson-c/a 3.00
2-4,6-12: 3-Deathstroke app. 4-Brief Deathstroke app. 6-New Batman (Azrael) cameo. 11-New Batman-c/story. 12-New Batman app. 2.25
5-($2.50)-Foil-c; Deathstroke app; new Batman cameo (1 panel) 3.00

CHAINS OF CHAOS
Harris Comics: Nov, 1994 - No. 3, Jan, 1995 ($2.95, limited series)
1-3-Re-Intro of The Rook w/ Vampirella 3.00

CHALLENGE OF THE UNKNOWN (Formerly Love Experiences)
Ace Magazines: No. 6, Sept, 1950 (See Web Of Mystery No. 19)
6- "Villa of the Vampire" used in N.Y. Joint Legislative Comm. Publ; Sekowsky-a
33 66 99 190 270 350

CHALLENGER, THE
Interfaith Publications/T.C. Comics: 1945 - No. 4, Oct-Dec, 1946
nn; nd; 32 pgs.; Origin the Challenger Club; Anti-Fascist with funny animal filler
44 88 132 264 395 525
2-4: Kubert-a; 4-Fuje-a 36 72 108 204 290 375

CHALLENGERS OF THE FANTASTIC
Marvel Comics (Amalgam): June 1997 ($1.95, one-shot)
1-Karl Kesel-s/Tom Grummett-a 2.50

CHALLENGERS OF THE UNKNOWN (See Showcase #6, 7, 11, 12, Super DC Giant, and Super Team Family)
National Per. Publ./DC Comics: 4-5/58 - No. 77, 12-1/70-71; No. 78, 2/73 - No. 80, 6-7/73; No. 81, 6-7/77 - No. 87, 6-7/78
1-(4-5/58)-Kirby/Stein-a(2); Kirby-c 189 378 567 1654 2577 3500
2-Kirby/Stein-a(2) 67 134 201 570 873 1175
3-Kirby/Stein-a(2) 57 114 171 485 743 1000
4-8-Kirby/Wood-a plus cover to #8 45 90 135 360 543 725
9,10 29 58 87 210 305 400
11-15: 11-Grey tone-c. 14-Origin/1st app. Multi-Man (villain)
19 38 57 136 198 260
16-22: 18-Intro. Cosmo, the Challengers Spacepet. 22-Last 10¢ issue
13 26 39 94 137 180
23-30 8 16 24 53 74 95
31-Retells origin of the Challengers 8 16 24 55 78 100
32-40 5 10 15 33 44 55
41-47,49,50,52-60: 43-New look begins. 49-Intro. Challenger Corps. 55-Death of Red Ryan. 60-Red Ryan returns 4 8 12 24 32 40
48,51: 48-Doom Patrol app. 51-Sea Devils app. 4 8 12 27 36 45
61-68: 64,65-Kirby origin-r, parts 1 & 2. 66-New logo. 68-Last 12¢ issue.
3 6 9 16 20 25
69-73,75-80: 69-1st app. Corinna. 77-Last 15¢ issue 2 4 6 10 12 15
74-Deadman by Tuska/Adams; 1 pg. Wrightson-a 4 8 12 27 36 45
81,83-87: 81-(6-7/77). 83-87-Swamp Thing app. 1 3 4 6 8 10
82-Swamp Thing begins, c/s 2 4 6 9 11 14
NOTE: ***N. Adams** c-67, 68, 70, 72, 74i, 81i. **Buckler** c-83-86p. **Giffen** a-83-87p. **Kirby** a-75-80r; c-75, 77, 78. **Kubert** c-64, 66, 69, 76, 79. **Nasser** c/a-81p, 82p. **Tuska** a-73. **Wood** r-76.*

CHALLENGERS OF THE UNKNOWN
DC Comics: Mar, 1991 - No. 8, Oct, 1991 ($1.75, limited series)
1-Jeph Loeb scripts & Tim Sale-a in all (1st work together); Bolland-c 3.00
2-8: 2-Superman app. 3-Dr. Fate app. 6-G. Kane-c(p). 7-Steranko-c/swipe by Art Adams 2.50
NOTE: ***Art Adams** c-7. **Hempel** c-5. **Gil Kane** c-6p. **Sale** a-1-8; c-3, 8. **Wagner** c-4.*

CHALLENGERS OF THE UNKNOWN
DC Comics: Feb, 1997 - No. 18, July, 1998 ($2.25)
1-18: 1-Intro new team; Leon-c/a(p) begins. 4-Origin of new team. 11,12-Batman app. 15-Millennium Giants x-over; Superman-c/app. 2.50

CHALLENGE TO THE WORLD
Catechetical Guild: 1951 (10¢, 36 pgs.)
nn 5 10 15 23 28 32

CHAMBER (See Generation X and Uncanny X-Men)
Marvel Comics: Oct, 2002 - No. 4, Jan, 2003 ($2.99, limited series)

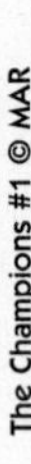

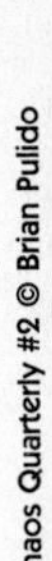

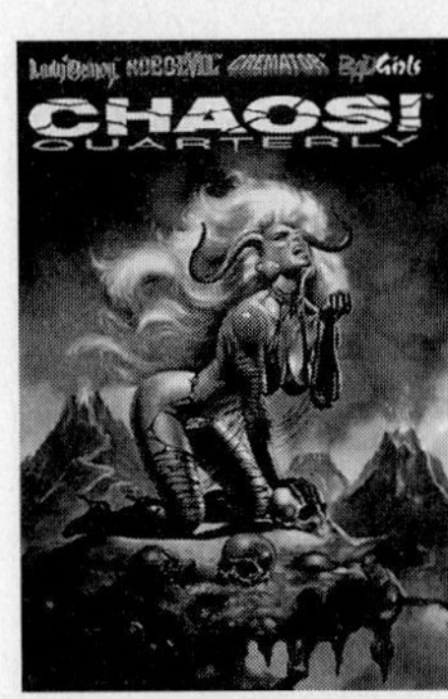

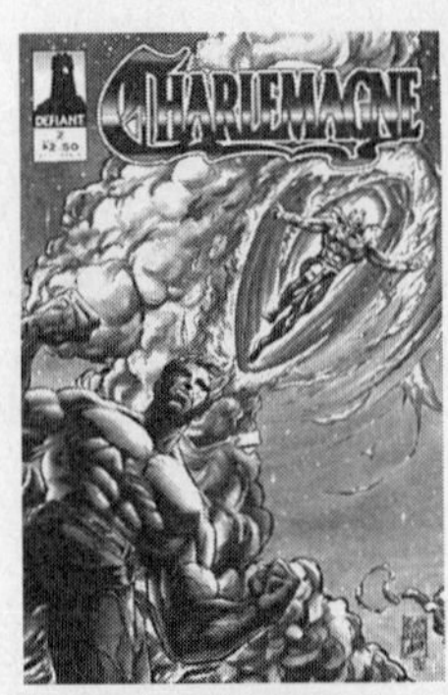

Charlemagne #2 © Defiant

	GD 2.0	VG 4.0	FN 6.0	VF 8.0	VF/NM 9.0	NM- 9.2
1-4-Bachalo-c/Vaughan-s/Ferguson-a. 1-Cyclops app.						3.00

CHAMBER OF CHILLS (Formerly Blondie Comics #20, ...of Clues No. 27 on)
Harvey Publications/Witches Tales: No. 21, June, 1951 - No. 26, Dec, 1954

	GD 2.0	VG 4.0	FN 6.0	VF 8.0	VF/NM 9.0	NM- 9.2
21 (#1)	46	92	138	276	413	550
22,24 (#2,4)	32	64	96	180	255	330
23 (#3)-Excessive violence; eyes torn out	35	70	105	201	283	365
5(2/52)-Decapitation, acid in face scene	35	70	105	201	283	365
6-Woman melted alive	33	66	99	190	270	350
7-Used in **SOTI**, pg. 389; decapitation/severed head panels	32	64	96	180	255	330
8-10: 8-Decapitation panels	27	54	81	153	214	275
11,12,14	21	42	63	118	164	210
13,15-24-Nostrand-a in all. 13,21-Decapitation panels. 18-Atom bomb panels. 20-Nostrand-c	27	54	81	153	214	275
25,26	17	34	51	95	130	165

NOTE: *About half the issues contain bondage, torture, sadism, perversion, gore, cannabalism, eyes ripped out, acid in face, etc.* ***Elias*** *c-4-11, 14-19, 21-26.* ***Kremer*** *a-12, 17.* ***Palais*** *a-21(1), 23.* ***Nostrand/Powell*** *a-13, 15, 16.* ***Powell*** *a-21, 23, 24('51), 5-8, 11, 13, 18-21, 23-25. Bondage-c-21, 24('51), 7. 25-r/#5; 26-r/#9.*

CHAMBER OF CHILLS
Marvel Comics Group: Nov, 1972 - No. 25, Nov, 1976

	GD 2.0	VG 4.0	FN 6.0	VF 8.0	VF/NM 9.0	NM- 9.2
1-Harlan Ellison adaptation	3	6	9	18	24	30
2-5: 2-1st app. John Jakes (Brak the Barbarian)	2	4	6	10	13	16
6-25: 22,23-(Regular 25¢ editions)	2	4	6	8	10	12
22,23-(30¢-c variants, limited distribution)(5,7/76)	2	4	6	11	14	18

NOTE: ***Adkins*** *a-1i, 2i.* ***Brunner*** *a-2-4; c-4.* ***Chaykin*** *a-4.* ***Ditko*** *r-14, 16, 19, 23, 24.* ***Everett*** *a-3i, 11r,21r.* ***Heath*** *a-1r.* ***Gil Kane*** *c-2p.* ***Kirby*** *r-11, 18, 19, 22.* ***Powell*** *a-13r.* ***Russell*** *a-1p, 2p.* ***Williamson/Mayo*** *a-13r.* ***Robert E. Howard*** *horror story adaptation-2, 3.*

CHAMBER OF CLUES (Formerly Chamber of Chills)
Harvey Publications: No. 27, Feb, 1955 - No. 28, April, 1955

	GD 2.0	VG 4.0	FN 6.0	VF 8.0	VF/NM 9.0	NM- 9.2
27-Kerry Drake-r/#19; Powell-a; last pre-code	7	14	21	37	46	55
28-Kerry Drake	6	12	18	31	38	45

CHAMBER OF DARKNESS (Monsters on the Prowl #9 on)
Marvel Comics Group: Oct, 1969 - No. 8, Dec, 1970

	GD 2.0	VG 4.0	FN 6.0	VF 8.0	VF/NM 9.0	NM- 9.2
1-Buscema-a(p)	6	12	18	40	55	70
2,3: 2-Neal Adams scripts. 3-Smith, Buscema-a	3	7	10	21	28	35
4-A Conan-esque tryout by Smith (4/70); reprinted in Conan #16; Marie Severin/Everett-c	7	14	21	46	63	80
5,8: 5-H.P. Lovecraft adaptation. 8-Wrightson-c	3	6	9	18	23	28
6	3	6	9	16	20	24
7-Wrightson-c/a, 7pgs. (his 1st work at Marvel); Wrightson draws himself in 1st & last panels; Kirby/Ditko-r; last 15¢-c	4	8	12	27	36	45
1-(1/72; 25¢ Special, 52 pgs.)	3	7	10	21	28	35

NOTE: ***Adkins/Everett*** *a-8.* ***Buscema*** *a-Special 1r.* ***Craig*** *a-5.* ***Ditko*** *a-6-8r.* ***Heck*** *a-1, 2, 8, Special 1r.* ***Kirby*** *a(p)-4, 5, 7r.* ***Kirby/Everett*** *c-5.* ***Severin/Everett*** *c-6.* ***Shores*** *a-2, 3i, Special 1r.* ***Sutton*** *a-1, 2i, 4, 7, Special 1r.* ***Wrightson*** *c-7, 8.*

CHAMP COMICS (Formerly Champion No. 1-10)
Worth Publ. Co./Champ Publ./Family Comics(Harvey Publ.): No. 11, Oct, 1940 - No. 24, Dec, 1942; No. 25, April, 1943

	GD 2.0	VG 4.0	FN 6.0	VF 8.0	VF/NM 9.0	NM- 9.2
11-Human Meteor cont'd. from Champion	88	176	264	550	825	1100
12-17,20: 14,15-Crandall-c. 20-The Green Ghost app.	68	136	204	425	638	850
18,19-Simon-c. 19-The Wasp app.	83	166	249	519	780	1040
21-23,25: 22-The White Mask app. 23-Flag-c	52	104	156	312	469	625
24-Hitler, Tojo & Mussolini-c	58	116	174	363	544	725

CHAMPION (See Gene Autry's...)

CHAMPION COMICS (Formerly Speed Comics #1?; Champ Comics No. 11 on)
Worth Publ. Co.(Harvey Publications): No. 2, Dec, 1939 - No. 10, Aug, 1940 (no No.1)

	GD 2.0	VG 4.0	FN 6.0	VF 8.0	VF/NM 9.0	NM- 9.2
2-The Champ, The Blazing Scarab, Neptina, Liberty Lads, Jungleman, Bill Handy, Swingtime Sweetie begin	174	348	522	1088	1632	2175
3-7: 7-The Human Meteor begins?	78	156	234	488	732	975
8-10: 8-Simon-c. 9-1st S&K-c (1st collaboration together). 10-Bondage-c by Kirby	140	280	420	875	1313	1750

CHAMPIONS, THE
Marvel Comics Group: Oct, 1975 - No. 17, Jan, 1978

	GD 2.0	VG 4.0	FN 6.0	VF 8.0	VF/NM 9.0	NM- 9.2
1-Origin & 1st app. The Champions (The Angel, Black Widow, Ghost Rider, Hercules, Iceman); Venus x-over	3	6	9	18	24	30
2-4,8-10,16: 2,3-Venus x-over	1	3	4	6	8	10
5-7-(Regular 25¢ edition)(4-8/76) 6-Kirby-c	2	4	6	9	11	14
5-7-(30¢-c variants, limited distribution)	2	4	6	12	16	20
11-14,17-Byrne-a. 14-(Regular 30¢ edition)	2	4	6	9	11	14
14,15-(35¢-c variant, limited distribution)	2	4	6	12	16	20
15-(Regular 30¢ edition)(9/77)-Byrne-a	2	4	6	9	11	14

NOTE: ***Buckler/Adkins*** *c-3.* ***Byrne*** *a-11-15, 17.* ***Kane/Adkins*** *c-1.* ***Kane/Layton*** *c-11.* ***Tuska*** *a-3p, 4p, 6p, 7p. Ghost Rider c-1-4, 7, 8, 10, 14, 16, 17 (4, 10, 14 are more prominent).*

CHAMPIONS (Game)
Eclipse Comics: June, 1986 - No. 6, Feb, 1987 (limited series)

	GD 2.0	VG 4.0	FN 6.0	VF 8.0	VF/NM 9.0	NM- 9.2
1-6: 1-Intro Flare; based on game. 5-Origin Flare						2.50

CHAMPIONS (Also see The League of Champions)
Hero Comics: Sept, 1987 - No. 12, 1989 ($1.95)

	GD 2.0	VG 4.0	FN 6.0	VF 8.0	VF/NM 9.0	NM- 9.2
1-12: 1-Intro The Marksman & The Rose. 14-Origin Malice						2.25
Annual 1(1988, $2.75, 52pgs.)-Origin of Giant						2.75

CHAMPION SPORTS
National Periodical Publications: Oct-Nov, 1973 - No. 3, Feb-Mar, 1974

	GD 2.0	VG 4.0	FN 6.0	VF 8.0	VF/NM 9.0	NM- 9.2
1	3	6	9	18	23	28
2,3	2	4	6	9	11	14

CHANNEL ZERO
Image Comics: Feb, 1998 - No. 5 ($2.95, B&W, limited series)

	GD 2.0	VG 4.0	FN 6.0	VF 8.0	VF/NM 9.0	NM- 9.2
1-5, ...Dupe (1/99) -Brian Wood-s/a						3.00

CHAOS (See The Crusaders)

CHAOS! BIBLE
Chaos! Comics: Nov, 1995 ($3.30, one-shot)

	GD 2.0	VG 4.0	FN 6.0	VF 8.0	VF/NM 9.0	NM- 9.2
1-Profiles of characters & creators						3.50

CHAOS! CHRONICLES
Chaos! Comics: Feb, 2000 ($3.50, one-shot)

	GD 2.0	VG 4.0	FN 6.0	VF 8.0	VF/NM 9.0	NM- 9.2
1-Profiles of characters, checklist of Chaos! comics and products						3.50

CHAOS EFFECT, THE
Valiant: 1994

	GD 2.0	VG 4.0	FN 6.0	VF 8.0	VF/NM 9.0	NM- 9.2
Alpha (Giveaway w/trading card checklist)						2.25
Alpha-Gold variant, Alpha-Red variant, Omega-Gold variant						5.00
Omega (11/94, $2.25); Epilogue Pt. 1, 2 (12/94, 1/95; $2.95)						3.00

CHAOS! GALLERY
Chaos! Comics: Aug, 1997 ($2.95, one-shot)

	GD 2.0	VG 4.0	FN 6.0	VF 8.0	VF/NM 9.0	NM- 9.2
1-Pin-ups of characters						3.00

CHAOS! QUARTERLY
Chaos! Comics: Oct, 1995 -No. 3, May, 1996 ($4.95, quarterly)

	GD 2.0	VG 4.0	FN 6.0	VF 8.0	VF/NM 9.0	NM- 9.2
1-3: 1-anthology; Lady Death-c by Julie Bell. 2-Boris "Lady Demon"-c						5.00
1-Premium Edition (7,500)						25.00

CHAPEL (Also see Youngblood & Youngblood Strikefile #1-3)
Image Comics (Extreme Studios): No. 1 Feb, 1995 - No. 2, Mar, 1995 ($2.50, limited series)

	GD 2.0	VG 4.0	FN 6.0	VF 8.0	VF/NM 9.0	NM- 9.2
1,2						2.50

CHAPEL (Also see Youngblood & Youngblood Strikefile #1-3)
Image Comics (Extreme Studios): V2 #1, Aug, 1995 - No. 7, Apr, 1996 ($2.50)

	GD 2.0	VG 4.0	FN 6.0	VF 8.0	VF/NM 9.0	NM- 9.2
V2#1-7: 4-Babewatch x-over. 5-vs. Spawn. 7-Shadowhawk-c/app; Shadowhunt x-over						2.50
#1-Quesada & Palmiotti variant-c						2.50

CHAPEL (Also see Youngblood & Youngblood Strikefile #1-3)
Awesome Entertainment: Sept, 1997 ($2.99, one-shot)

	GD 2.0	VG 4.0	FN 6.0	VF 8.0	VF/NM 9.0	NM- 9.2
1 (Reg. & alternate covers)						3.00

CHARLEMAGNE (Also see War Dancer)
Defiant Comics: Mar, 1994 - No. 5, July, 1994 ($2.50)

	GD 2.0	VG 4.0	FN 6.0	VF 8.0	VF/NM 9.0	NM- 9.2
1/2 (Hero Illustrated giveaway)-Adam Pollina-c/a.						
1-(3/94, $3.50, 52 pgs.)-Adam Pollina-c/a.						3.50
2,3,5: Adam Pollina-c/a. 2-War Dancer app. 5-Pre-Schism issue.						2.50
4-($3.25, 52 pgs.)						3.25

CHARLIE CHAN (See Big Shot Comics, Columbia Comics, Feature Comics & The New Advs. of...)

CHARLIE CHAN (The Adventures of...) (Zaza The Mystic No. 10 on) (TV)
Crestwood(Prize) No. 1-5; Charlton No. 6(6/55) on: 6-7/48 - No. 5, 2-3/49; No.6, 6/55 - No. 9, 3/56

	GD 2.0	VG 4.0	FN 6.0	VF 8.0	VF/NM 9.0	NM- 9.2
1-S&K-c, 2 pgs.; Infantino-a	78	156	234	488	732	975
2-5-S&K-c: 3-S&K-c/a	50	100	150	300	450	600
6 (6/55-Charlton)-S&K-c	38	76	114	219	310	400
7-9	20	40	60	112	156	200

CHARLIE CHAN
Dell Publishing Co.: Oct-Dec, 1965 - No. 2, Mar, 1966

	GD 2.0	VG 4.0	FN 6.0	VF 8.0	VF/NM 9.0	NM- 9.2
1-Springer-a	6	12	18	38	52	65
2	4	8	12	22	30	38

Charlton Bullseye #3 © CC

Chastity: Crazytown #2 © Chaos!

Cheval Noir #13 © DH

	GD 2.0	VG 4.0	FN 6.0	VF 8.0	VF/NM 9.0	NM- 9.2

CHARLIE McCARTHY (See Edgar Bergen Presents...)
Dell Publishing Co.: No. 171, Nov, 1947 - No. 571, July, 1954 (See True Comics #14)

Four Color 171	28	56	84	203	294	385
Four Color 196-Part photo-c; photo back-c	18	36	54	131	191	250
1(3-5/49)-Part photo-c; photo back-c	16	32	48	111	163	215
2-9(7/52; #5,6-52 pgs.)	9	18	27	60	85	110
Four Color 445,478,527,571	6	12	18	40	55	70

CHARLTON BULLSEYE
CPL/Gang Publications: 1975 - No. 5, 1976 ($1.50, B&W, bi-monthly, magazine format)

1: 1 & 2 are last Capt. Atom by Ditko/Byrne intended for the never published Capt. Atom #90; Nightshade app.; Jeff Jones-a	5	10	15	36	48	60
2-Part 2 Capt. Atom story by Ditko/Byrne	4	8	12	24	32	40
3-Wrong Country by Sanho Kim	2	4	6	12	16	20
4-Doomsday + 1 by John Byrne	3	6	9	18	24	30
5-Doomsday + 1 by Byrne, The Question by Toth; Neal Adams back-c; Toth-c	4	8	12	27	36	45

CHARLTON BULLSEYE
Charlton Publications: June, 1981 - No. 10, Dec, 1982; Nov, 1986

1-Blue Beetle, The Question app.; 1st app. Rocket Rabbit	1	2	3	5	6	8
2-5: 2-1st app. Neil The Horse; Rocket Rabbit app. 4-Vanguards						6.00
6-10: Low print run. 6-Origin & 1st app. Thunderbunny	1	2	3	5	6	8
Special 1,2: 1(11/86) (Half in B&W). 2-Atomic Mouse app. (1987)(exist?)						6.00

CHARLTON CLASSICS
Charlton Comics: Apr, 1980 - No. 9, Aug, 1981

1-Hercules-r by Glanzman in all						6.00
2-9						5.00

CHARLTON CLASSICS LIBRARY (1776)
Charlton Comics: V10 No.1, Mar, 1973 (one-shot)

1776 (title) - Adaptation of the film musical "1776"; given away at movie theatres	2	4	6	12	16	20

CHARLTON PREMIERE (Formerly Marine War Heroes)
Charlton Comics: V1#19, July, 1967; V2#1, Sept, 1967 - No. 4, May, 1968

V1#19, V2#1,2,4: V1#19-Marine War Heroes. V2#1-Trio; intro. Shape, Tyro Team & Spookman. 2-Children of Doom; Boyette classic-a. 4-Unlikely Tales; Aparo, Ditko-a	3	6	9	17	22	26
V2#3-Sinistro Boy Fiend; Blue Beetle & Peacemaker x-over	3	6	9	19	25	32

CHARLTON SPORT LIBRARY - PROFESSIONAL FOOTBALL
Charlton Comics: Winter, 1969-70 (Jan. on cover) (68 pgs.)

1	4	8	12	22	30	38

CHARM SCHOOL (See Action Girl Comics #13)
Slave Labor Graphics: Apr, 2000 - Present ($2.95, B&W)

1-6-Elizabeth Watasin-s/a						3.00

CHASE (See Batman #550 for 1st app.)
DC Comics: Feb, 1998 - No. 9, Oct, 1998; #1,000,000 Nov, 1998 ($2.50)

1-9: Williams III & Gray-a. 1-Includes 4 Chase cards. 4-Teen Titans app. 7,8-Batman app. 9-GL Hal Jordan-c/app.						2.50
#1,000,000 (11/98) Final issue; 853rd Century x-over						2.50

CHASING DOGMA (See Jay and Silent Bob)

CHASSIS
Millenium Publications: 1996 - No. 3 ($2.95)

1-3: 1-Adam Hughes-c. 2-Conner var-c.						3.00

CHASSIS
Hurricane Entertainment: 1998 - No. 3 ($2.95)

0,1-3: 1-Adam Hughes-c. 0-Green var-c.						3.00

CHASSIS (Vol. 3)
Image Comics: Nov, 1999 - No. 4 ($2.95, limited series)

1-4: 1-Two covers by O'Neil and Green. 2-Busch var-c.						3.00
1-($6.95) DF Edition alternate-c by Wieringo						7.00

CHASTITY
Chaos! Comics: (one-shots)

#1/2 (1/01, $2.95) Batista-a						3.00
Heartbreaker (3/02, $2.99) Adrian-a/Molenaar-c						3.00
Love Bites (3/01, $2.99) Vale-a/Romano-c						3.00
Reign of Terror 1 (10/00, $2.95) Grant-s/Ross-a/Rio-c						3.00
Re-Imagined 1 (7/02, $2.99) Conner-c; Toledo-a						3.00

CHASTITY: CRAZYTOWN
Chaos! Comics: Apr, 2002 - No. 3, June, 2002 ($2.99, limited series)

1-3-Nicieza-s/Batista-c/a						3.00

CHASTITY: LUST FOR LIFE
Chaos! Comics: May, 1999 - No. 3, July, 1999 ($2.95, limited series)

1-3-Nutman-s/Benes-c/a						3.00

CHASTITY: ROCKED
Chaos! Comics: Nov, 1998 - No. 4, Feb, 1999 ($2.95, limited series)

1-4-Nutman-s/Justiniano-c/a						3.00

CHASTITY: SHATTERED
Chaos! Comics: Jun, 2001 - No. 3, Sept, 2001 ($2.99, limited series)

1-3-Kaminski & Pulido-s/Batista-c/a						3.00

CHASTITY: THEATER OF PAIN
Chaos! Comics: Feb, 1997 - No. 3, June, 1997 ($2.95, limited series)

1-3-Pulido-s/Justiniano-c/a						3.00
TPB (1997, $9.95) r/#1-3						10.00

CHECKMATE (TV)
Gold Key: Oct, 1962 - No. 2, Dec, 1962

1-Photo-c on both	6	12	18	43	59	75
2	6	12	18	38	52	65

CHECKMATE! (See Action Comics #598)
DC Comics: Apr, 1988 - No. 33, Jan, 1991 ($1.25)

1-33: 13: New format begins						2.50

NOTE: ***Gil Kane** c-2, 4, 7, 8, 10, 11, 15-19.*

CHERYL BLOSSOM (See Archie's Girls, Betty and Veronica #320 for 1st app.)
Archie Publications: Sept, 1995 - No. 3, Nov, 1995 ($1.50, limited series)

1-3						6.00
Special 1-4 ('95, '96, $2.00)						6.00

CHERYL BLOSSOM (Cheryl's Summer Job)
Archie Publications: July, 1996 - No. 3, Sept, 1996 ($1.50, limited series)

1-3						4.50

CHERYL BLOSSOM (...Goes Hollywood)
Archie Publications: Dec, 1996 - No. 3, Feb, 1997 ($1.50, limited series)

1-3						4.00

CHERYL BLOSSOM
Archie Publications: Apr, 1997 - No. 37, Mar, 2001 ($1.50/$1.75/$1.79/$1.99)

1-Dan DeCarlo-c/a						6.00
2-10: 2-7-Dan DeCarlo-c/a						3.50
11-37: 32-Begin $1.99-c. 34-Sabrina app.						2.25

CHESTY SANCHEZ
Antarctic Press: Nov, 1995 - No. 2, Mar, 1996 ($2.95, B&W)

1,2						3.00
...Super Special (2/99, $5.99)						6.00

CHEVAL NOIR
Dark Horse Comics: 1989 - No. 48, Nov, 1993 ($3.50, B&W, 68 pgs.)

1-8,10 ($3.50): 6-Moebius poster insert						3.50
9,11,13,15,17,20,22 ($4.50, 84 pgs.)						4.50
12,18,19,21,23,25,26 ($3.95): 12-Geary-a; Mignola-c. 26-Moebius-a begins						4.00
14 ($4.95, 76 pgs.)(7 pgs. color)						5.00
16,24 ($3.75): 16-19-Contain trading cards						3.75
27-48 ($2.95): 33-Snyder III-c						3.00

NOTE: ***Bolland** a-2, 6, 7, 13, 14. **Bolton** a-2, 4, 45; c-4, 20. **Chadwick** c-13. **Dorman** painted c-16. **Geary** a-13, 14. **Kelley Jones** c-27. **Kaluta** a-6; c-6, 18. **Moebius** c-5, 9, 26. **Dave Stevens** c-1, 7. **Sutton** painted c-36.*

CHEYENNE (TV)
Dell Publishing Co.: No. 734, Oct, 1956 - No. 25, Dec-Jan, 1961-62

Four Color 734(#1)-Clint Walker photo-c	18	36	54	131	191	250
Four Color 772,803: Clint Walker photo-c	9	18	27	65	93	120
4(8-10/57) - 20: 4-9,13-20-Clint Walker photo-c. 10-12-Ty Hardin photo-c	6	12	18	43	59	75
21-25-Clint Walker photo-c on all	7	14	21	46	63	80

CHEYENNE AUTUMN (See Movie Classics)

CHEYENNE KID (Formerly Wild Frontier No. 1-7)
Charlton Comics: No. 8, July, 1957 - No. 99, Nov, 1973

Cheyenne #15 © DELL

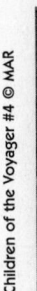

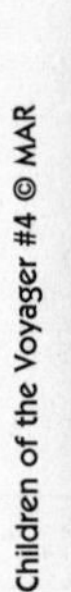
Children of the Voyager #4 © MAR

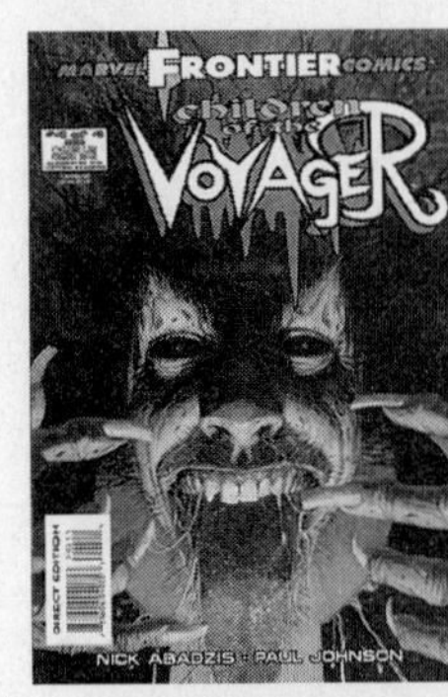

Chilling Tales of Horror V2#2 © Stanley Publ.

	GD 2.0	VG 4.0	FN 6.0	VF 8.0	VF/NM 9.0	NM- 9.2
8 (#1)	8	16	24	40	50	60
9,15-19	6	12	18	28	34	40
10-Williamson/Torres-a(3); Ditko-c	10	20	30	60	80	100
11-(68 pgs.)-Cheyenne Kid meets Geronimo	10	20	30	58	77	95
12-Williamson/Torres-a(2)	10	20	30	58	77	95
13-Williamson/Torres-a (5 pgs.)	8	16	24	43	54	65
14-Williamson-a (5 pgs.?)	8	16	24	40	50	60
20-22,24,25-Severin c/a(3) each	4	8	12	24	32	40
23,27-29	3	6	9	16	20	24
26,30-Severin-a	3	6	9	18	24	30
31-59	2	4	6	10	13	16
60-65,67-80	2	4	6	8	10	12
66-Wander by Aparo begins, ends #87	2	4	6	9	11	14
81-99: Apache Red begins #88, origin in #89	1	2	3	5	7	9
Modern Comics Reprint 87,89(1978)						4.00
CHIAROSCURO (THE PRIVATE LIVES OF LEONARDO DA VINCI)						
DC Comics (Vertigo): July, 1995 - No. 10, Apr, 1996 ($2.50/$2.95, limited series, mature)						
1-9						2.50
10-($2.95)						3.00
CHICAGO MAIL ORDER (See C-M-O Comics)						
CHI-CHIAN						
Sirius Entertainment: 1997 - No. 6, 1998 ($2.95, limited series)						
1-6-Voltaire-s/a						3.00
CHIEF, THE (Indian Chief No. 3 on)						
Dell Publishing Co.: No. 290, Aug, 1950 - No. 2, Apr-June, 1951						
Four Color 290(#1)	7	14	21	50	68	85
2	6	12	18	40	55	70
CHIEF CRAZY HORSE (See Wild Bill Hickok #21)						
Avon Periodicals: 1950 (Also see Fighting Indians of the Wild West!)						
nn-Fawcette-c	21	42	63	118	164	210
CHIEF VICTORIO'S APACHE MASSACRE (See Fight Indians of/Wild West!)						
Avon Periodicals: 1951						
nn-Williamson/Frazetta-a (7 pgs.); Larsen-a; Kinstler-c	44	88	132	264	395	525
CHILDHOOD'S END						
Image Comics: Oct, 1997 ($2.95, B&W)						
1-Bourne-s/Calafiore-a						3.00
CHILDREN OF FIRE						
Fantagor Press: Nov, 1987 - No. 3, 1988 ($2.00, limited series)						
1-3: by Richard Corben						4.00
CHILDREN OF THE VOYAGER (See Marvel Frontier Comics Unlimited)						
Marvel Frontier Comics: Sept, 1993 - No. 4, Dec, 1993 ($1.95, limited series)						
1-($2.95)-Embossed glow-in-the-dark-c; Paul Johnson-c/a						3.00
2-4						2.25
CHILDREN'S BIG BOOK						
Dorene Publ. Co.: 1945 (25¢, stiff-c, 68 pgs.)						
nn-Comics & fairy tales; David Icove-a	12	24	36	71	96	120
CHILDREN'S CRUSADE, THE						
DC Comics (Vertigo): Dec, 1993 - No. 2, Jan, 1994 ($3.95, limited series)						
1,2-Neil Gaiman scripts & Chris Bachalo-a; framing issues for Children's Crusade x-over						4.00
CHILD'S PLAY: THE SERIES (Movie)						
Innovation Publishing: May, 1991 - #3, 1991 ($2.50, 28pgs.)						
1-3						2.50
CHILD'S PLAY 2 THE OFFICIAL MOVIE ADAPTATION (Movie)						
Innovation Publishing: 1990 - No. 3, 1990 ($2.50, bi-weekly limited series)						
1-3: Adapts movie sequel						2.50
CHILI (Millie's Rival)						
Marvel Comics Group: 5/69 - No. 17, 9/70; No. 18, 8/72 - No. 26, 12/73						
1	7	14	21	46	63	80
2-5	4	8	12	24	32	40
6-17	3	6	9	18	23	28
18-26	2	4	6	14	18	22
Special 1(12/71, 52 pgs.)	4	8	12	27	36	45
CHILLER						

	GD 2.0	VG 4.0	FN 6.0	VF 8.0	VF/NM 9.0	NM- 9.2
Marvel Comics (Epic): Nov, 1993 - No. 2, Dec, 1993 ($7.95, lim. series)						
1,2-(68 pgs.)	1	2	3	5	6	8
CHILLING ADVENTURES IN SORCERY (...as Told by Sabrina #1, 2) (Red Circle Sorcery No. 6 on)						
Archie Publications (Red Circle Productions): 9/72 - No. 2, 10/72; No. 3, 10/73 - No. 5, 2/74						
1-Sabrina cameo as narrator	4	8	12	29	40	50
2-Sabrina cameo as narrator	3	6	9	16	20	25
3-5: Morrow-c/a, all. 4,5-Alcazar-a	2	4	6	10	12	15
CHILLING TALES (Formerly Beware)						
Youthful Magazines: No. 13, Dec, 1952 - No. 17, Oct, 1953						
13(No.1)-Harrison-a; Matt Fox-c/a	58	116	174	363	544	725
14-Harrison-a	40	80	120	240	350	460
15-Has #14 on-c; Matt Fox-c; Harrison-a	48	96	144	288	432	575
16-Poe adapt.-`Metzengerstein'; Rudyard Kipling adapt.- 'Mark of the Beast,' by Kiefer; bondage-c	37	74	111	210	298	385
17-Matt Fox-c; Sir Walter Scott & Poe adapt.	40	80	120	240	360	480
CHILLING TALES OF HORROR (Magazine)						
Stanley Publications: V1#1, 6/69 - V1#7, 12/70; V2#2, 2/71 - V2#6, 10/71(50¢, B&W, 52 pgs.)						
V1#1	6	12	18	38	52	65
2-7: 7-Cameron-a	4	8	12	25	33	42
V2#2-6: 2-Two different #2 issues exist (2/71 & 4/71). 2-(2/71) Spirit of Frankenstein -r/Adventures into the Unknown #16. 4-(8/71) different from other V2#4(6/71)	4	8	12	22	30	38
V2#4-(6/71) r/9 pg. Feldstein-a from Adventures into the Unknown #3	4	8	12	25	33	42
NOTE: *Two issues of V2#2 exist, Feb, 1971 and April, 1971. Two issues of V2#4 exist, Jun, 1971 and Aug, 1971.*						
CHILLY WILLY (Also see New Funnies #211)						
Dell Publ. Co.: No. 740, Oct, 1956 - No. 1281, Apr-June, 1962 (Walter Lantz)						
Four Color 740 (#1)	6	12	18	43	59	75
Four Color 852 (2/58),967 (2/59),1017 (9/59),1074 (2-4/60),1122 (8/60), 1177 (4-6/61), 1212 (7-9/61), 1281	4	8	12	29	40	50
CHIMERA						
CrossGeneration Comics: Mar, 2003 - No. 4, July, 2003 ($2.95, limited series)						
1-4-Marz-s/Peterson-c/a						3.00
Vol. 1 TPB (2003, $15.95) r/#1-4 plus sketch pages, 3-D models, how-to guides						16.00
CHINA BOY (See Wisco in the Promotional Comics section)						
CHIP 'N' DALE (Walt Disney)(See Walt Disney's C&S #204)						
Dell Publishing Co./Gold Key/Whitman No. 65 on: Nov, 1953 - No. 30, June-Aug, 1962; Sept, 1967 - No. 83, July, 1984						
Four Color 517(#1)	11	22	33	77	114	150
Four Color 581,636	6	12	18	43	59	75
4(12/55-2/56)-10	6	12	18	38	52	65
11-30	4	8	12	29	40	50
1(Gold Key, 1967)-Reprints	3	6	9	19	25	32
2-10	2	4	6	10	13	16
11-20	1	3	4	6	8	10
21-40	1	2	3	5	6	8
41-64,70-77: 75(2/82), 76(2-3/82), 77(3/82)	1	2	3	4	5	7
65,66 (Whitman)	1	3	4	6	8	10
67-69 (3-pack? 1980): 67(8/80), 68(10/80) (scarce)	2	4	6	14	18	22
78-83 (All #90214; 3-pack, nd, nd code): 78(4/83), 79(5/83), 80(7/83), 81(8/83), 82(5/84), 83(7/84)	2	4	6	9	11	14
NOTE: *All Gold Key/Whitman issues have reprints except No. 32-35, 38-41, 45-47. No. 23-28, 30-42, 45-47, 49 have new covers.*						
CHIP 'N DALE RESCUE RANGERS						
Disney Comics: June, 1990 - No. 19, Dec, 1991 ($1.50)						
1-New stories; origin begins						3.00
2-19: 2-Origin continued						2.50
CHITTY CHITTY BANG BANG (See Movie Comics)						
C.H.I.X.						
Image Comics (Studiosaurus): Jan, 1998 ($2.50)						
1-Dodson, Haley, Lopresti, Randall, and Warren-s/c/a						3.00
1-($5.00) "X-Ray Variant" cover						5.00
C.H.I.X. That Time Forgot 1 (8/98, $2.95)						3.00
CHOICE COMICS						
Great Publications: Dec, 1941 - No. 3, Feb, 1942						
1-Origin Secret Circle; Atlas the Mighty app.; Zomba, Jungle Fight, Kangaroo Man, & Fire Eater begin	160	320	480	1000	1500	2000

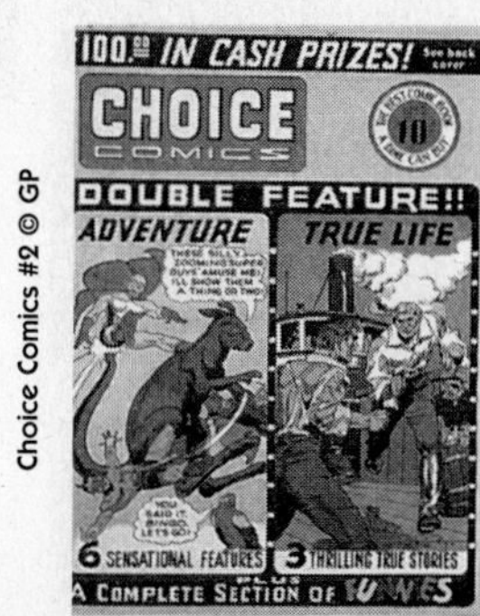

Choice Comics #2 © GP

Chroma-Tick #8 © NEC

Chronos #6 © DC

	GD 2.0	VG 4.0	FN 6.0	VF 8.0	VF/NM 9.0	NM- 9.2
2	84	168	252	525	788	1050
3-Double feature; Features movie "The Lost City" (classic cover); continued from Great Comics #3	120	240	360	750	1125	1500

CHOO CHOO CHARLIE
Gold Key: Dec, 1969

1-John Stanley-a 10 20 30 72 104 135

CHRISTIAN (See Asylum)
Maximum Press: Jan, 1996 ($2.99, one-shot)

1-Pop Mhan-a 3.00

CHRISTIAN HEROES OF TODAY
David C. Cook: 1964 (36 pgs.)

nn 2 4 6 14 18 22

CHRISTMAS (Also see A-1 Comics)
Magazine Enterprises: No. 28, 1950

A-1 28 6 12 18 33 41 48

CHRISTMAS ADVENTURE, A (See Classics Comics Giveaways, 12/69)

CHRISTMAS ALBUM (See March of Comics No. 312)

CHRISTMAS ANNUAL
Golden Special: 1975 ($1.95, 100 pgs., stiff-c)

nn-Reprints Mother Goose stories with Walt Kelly-a 4 8 12 24 32 42

CHRISTMAS & ARCHIE
Archie Comics: Jan, 1975 ($1.00, 68 pgs., 10-1/4x13-1/4" treasury-sized)

1-(scarce) 6 12 18 38 52 65

CHRISTMAS BELLS (See March of Comics No. 297)

CHRISTMAS CARNIVAL
Ziff-Davis Publ. Co./St. John Publ. Co. No. 2: 1952 (25¢, one-shot, 100 pgs.)

nn 34 68 102 196 278 360
2-Reprints Ziff-Davis issue plus-c 18 36 54 104 142 180

CHRISTMAS CAROL, A (See March of Comics No. 33)

CHRISTMAS EVE, A (See March of Comics No. 212)

CHRISTMAS IN DISNEYLAND (See Dell Giants)

CHRISTMAS PARADE (See Dell Giant No. 26, Dell Giants, March of Comics No. 284, Walt Disney Christmas Parade & Walt Disney's...)

CHRISTMAS PARADE (Walt Disney's)
Gold Key: 1962 (no month listed) - No. 9, Jan, 1972 (#1,5: 80 pgs.; #2-4,7-9: 36 pgs.)

1 (30018-301)-Giant 10 20 30 67 96 125
2-6: 2-r/F.C. #367 by Barks. 3-r/F.C. #178 by Barks. 4-r/F.C. #203 by Barks. 5-r/Christmas Parade #1 (Dell) by Barks; giant. 6-r/Christmas Parade #2 (Dell) by Barks (64 pgs.); giant 7 14 21 51 71 90
7-Pull-out poster (half price w/o poster) 6 12 18 38 52 65
8-r/F.C. #367 by Barks; pull-out poster 7 14 21 51 71 90
9 4 8 12 29 40 50

CHRISTMAS PARTY (See March of Comics No. 256)

CHRISTMAS STORIES (See Little People No. 959, 1062)

CHRISTMAS STORY (See March of Comics No. 326 in the Promotional Comics section)

CHRISTMAS STORY BOOK (See Woolworth's Christmas Story Book)

CHRISTMAS TREASURY, A (See Dell Giants & March of Comics No. 227)

CHRISTMAS WITH ARCHIE
Spire Christian Comics (Fleming H. Revell Co.): 1973, 1974 (49¢, 52 pgs.)

nn-Low print run 2 4 6 10 13 16

CHRISTMAS WITH MOTHER GOOSE
Dell Publishing Co.: No. 90, Nov, 1945 - No. 253, Nov, 1949

Four Color 90 (#1)-Kelly-a 19 38 57 136 198 260
Four Color 126 ('46), 172 (11/47)-By Walt Kelly 14 28 42 102 149 195
Four Color 201 (10/48), 253-By Walt Kelly 13 26 39 90 133 175

CHRISTMAS WITH SANTA (See March of Comics No. 92)

CHRISTMAS WITH THE SUPER-HEROES (See Limited Collectors' Edition)
DC Comics: 1988; No. 2, 1989 ($2.95)

1,2: 1-(100 pgs.)-All reprints; N. Adams-r, Byrne-c; Batman, Superman, JLA, LSH Christmas stories; r-Miller's 1st Batman/DC Special Series #21. 2-(68 pgs.)-Superman by Chadwick; Batman, Wonder Woman, Deadman, Green Lantern, Flash app.; Morrow-a; Enemy Ace by Byrne; all new-a 5.00

CHROMA-TICK, THE (...Special Edition, #1,2) (Also see The Tick)
New England Comics Press: Feb, 1992 - No. 8, Nov, 1993 ($3.95/$3.50, 44 pgs.)

1,2-Includes serially numbered trading card set 5.00
3-8 ($3.50, 36 pgs.): 6-Bound-in card 4.00

CHROME
Hot Comics: 1986 - No. 3, 1986 ($1.50, limited series)

1-3 2.25

CHROMIUM MAN, THE
Triumphant Comics: Aug, 1993 - No.10, May, 1994 ($2.50)

1-1st app. Mr. Death; all serially numbered 2.50
2-10: 2-1st app. Prince Vandal. 3-1st app. Candi, Breaker & Coil. 4,5-Triumphant Unleashed x-over. 8,9-(3/94). 10-(5/94) 2.50
0-(4/94)-Four color-c 2.50
0-All pink-c & all blue-c; no cover price 2.50

CHROMIUM MAN: VIOLENT PAST, THE
Triumphant Comics: Jan, 1994 - No. 2, Jan, 1994 ($2.50, limited series)

1,2-Serially numbered to 22,000 each 2.50

CHRONICLES OF CORUM, THE (Also see Corum...)
First Comics: Jan, 1987 - No. 12, Nov, 1988 ($1.75/$1.95, deluxe series)

1-12: Adapts Michael Moorcock's novel 2.50

CHRONOS
DC Comics: Mar, 1998 - No. 11, Feb. 1999 ($2.50)

1-11-J.F. Moore-s/Guinan-a 2.50
#1,000,000 (11/98) 853rd Century x-over 2.50

CHRONOWAR (Manga)
Dark Horse Comics: Aug, 1996 - No. 9, Apr, 1997 ($2.95, limited series)

1-9 3.00

CHUCKLE, THE GIGGLY BOOK OF COMIC ANIMALS
R. B. Leffingwell Co.: 1945 (132 pgs., one-shot)

1-Funny animal 22 44 66 124 172 220

CHUCK NORRIS (TV)
Marvel Comics (Star Comics): Jan, 1987 - No. 4, July, 1987

1-3: Ditko-a 3.50
4-No Ditko-a (low print run) 5.00

CHUCK WAGON (See Sheriff Bob Dixon's...)

CHYNA (WWF Wrestling)
Chaos! Comics: Sept, 2000; July, 2001 ($2.95/$2.99, one-shots)

1-Grant-s/Barrows-a; photo-c 3.00
1-($9.95) Premium Edition; Cleavenger-c 10.00
II -(7/01, $2.99) Deodato-a; photo-c 3.00

CICERO'S CAT
Dell Publishing Co.: July-Aug, 1959 - No. 2, Sept-Oct, 1959

1-Cat from Mutt & Jeff 5 10 15 36 48 60
2 4 8 12 29 40 50

CIMARRON STRIP (TV)
Dell Publishing Co.: Jan, 1968

1-Stuart Whitman photo-c 4 8 12 28 38 48

CINDER AND ASHE
DC Comics: May, 1988 - No. 4, Aug, 1988 ($1.75, limited series)

1-4: Mature readers 2.25

CINDERELLA (Disney) (See Movie Comics)
Dell Publishing Co.: No. 272, Apr, 1950 - No. 786, Apr, 1957

Four Color 272 13 26 39 90 133 175
Four Color 786-Partial-r 272 8 16 24 53 74 95

CINDERELLA
Whitman Publishing Co.: Apr, 1982

nn-Reprints 4-Color #272 1 2 3 4 5 7

CINDERELLA LOVE
Ziff-Davis/St. John Publ. Co. No. 12 on: No. 10, 1950; No. 11, 4-5/51; No. 12, 9/51; No. 4, 10-11/51 - No. 11, Fall, 1952; No. 12, 10/53 - No. 15, 8/54; No. 25, 12/54 - No. 29, 10/55 (No #16-24)

10(#1)(1st Series, 1950)-Painted-c 15 30 45 86 118 150
11(#2, 4-5/51)-Crandall-a; Saunders painted-c 10 20 30 56 73 90

Cinderella Love #25 © STJ

City of Heroes #1 © NCsoft Corp.

Clandestine #7 © MAR

	GD 2.0	VG 4.0	FN 6.0	VF 8.0	VF/NM 9.0	NM- 9.2
12(#3, 9/51)-Photo-c	8	16	24	46	58	70
4-8: 4,6,7-Photo-c	8	16	24	40	50	60
9-Kinstler-a; photo-c	9	18	27	49	62	75
10,11(Fall/'52), 14: 10,11-Photo-c. 14-Baker-a	8	16	24	46	58	70
12(St. John-10/53)-#13:13-Painted-c.	7	14	21	37	46	55
15(8/54)-Matt Baker-c	9	18	27	52	66	80
25(2nd Series)(Formerly Romantic Marriage) Baker-c	7	14	21	37	46	55
26-Baker-c; last precode (2/55)	9	18	27	52	66	80
27,29: Both Matt Baker-c	9	18	27	52	66	80
28	6	12	18	31	38	45

CINDY COMICS (...Smith No. 39, 40; Crime Can't Win No. 41 on)(Formerly Krazy Komics) (See Junior Miss & Teen Comics)
Timely Comics: No. 27, Fall, 1947 - No. 40, July, 1950

	GD 2.0	VG 4.0	FN 6.0	VF 8.0	VF/NM 9.0	NM- 9.2
27-Kurtzman-a, 3 pgs: Margie, Oscar begin	22	44	66	124	172	220
28-31-Kurtzman-a	13	26	39	76	103	130
32-40: 33-Georgie story; anti-Wertham editorial	9	18	27	54	70	85

NOTE: *Kurtzman's "Hey Look"-#27(3), 29(2), 30(2), 31; "Giggles 'n' Grins"-28.*

CINNAMON: EL CICLO
DC Comics: Oct, 2003 - No. 5, Feb, 2004 ($2.50, limited series)

	GD 2.0	VG 4.0	FN 6.0	VF 8.0	VF/NM 9.0	NM- 9.2
1-5-Van Meter-s/Chaykin-c/Paronzini-a						2.50

CIRCUS (...the Comic Riot)
Globe Syndicate: June, 1938 - No. 3, Aug, 1938

	GD 2.0	VG 4.0	FN 6.0	VF 8.0	VF/NM 9.0	NM- 9.2
1-(Scarce)-Spacehawks (2 pgs.), & Disk Eyes by Wolverton (2 pgs.), Pewee Throttle by Cole (2nd comic book work; see Star Comics V1#11), Beau Gus, Ken Craig & The Lords of Crillon, Jack Hinton by Eisner, Van Bragger by Kane	800	1600	2400	4800	6600	8400
2,3-(Scarce)-Eisner, Cole, Wolverton, Bob Kane-a in each	400	800	1200	2400	3300	4200

CIRCUS BOY (TV) (See Movie Classics)
Dell Publishing Co.: No. 759, Dec, 1956 - No. 813, July, 1957

	GD 2.0	VG 4.0	FN 6.0	VF 8.0	VF/NM 9.0	NM- 9.2
Four Color 759 (#1)-The Monkees' Mickey Dolenz photo-c	14	28	42	102	149	195
Four Color 785 (4/57),813-Mickey Dolenz photo-c	12	24	36	82	121	160

CIRCUS COMICS
Farm Women's Pub. Co./D. S. Publ.: 1945 - No. 2, Jun, 1945; Wint., 1948-49

	GD 2.0	VG 4.0	FN 6.0	VF 8.0	VF/NM 9.0	NM- 9.2
1-Funny animal	13	26	39	76	103	130
2	9	18	27	52	66	80
1(1948)-D.S. Publ.; 2 pgs. Frazetta	25	50	75	147	202	260

CIRCUS OF FUN COMICS
A. W. Nugent Publ. Co.: 1945 - No. 3, Dec, 1947 (A book of games & puzzles)

	GD 2.0	VG 4.0	FN 6.0	VF 8.0	VF/NM 9.0	NM- 9.2
1	14	28	42	81	111	140
2,3	9	18	27	52	66	80

CISCO KID, THE (TV)
Dell Publishing Co.: July, 1950 - No. 41, Oct-Dec, 1958

	GD 2.0	VG 4.0	FN 6.0	VF 8.0	VF/NM 9.0	NM- 9.2
Four Color 292(#1)-Cisco Kid, his horse Diablo, & sidekick Pancho & his horse Loco begin; painted-c begin	26	52	78	189	277	365
2(1/51)	12	24	36	87	129	170
3-5	11	22	33	77	114	150
6-10	9	18	27	65	93	120
11-20	8	16	24	58	82	105
21-36-Last painted-c	7	14	21	50	68	85
37-41: All photo-c	10	20	30	72	104	135

NOTE: ***Buscema** a-40. **Ernest Nordli** painted c-5-16, 20, 35.*

CISCO KID COMICS
Bernard Bailey/Swappers Quarterly: Winter, 1944 (one-shot)

	GD 2.0	VG 4.0	FN 6.0	VF 8.0	VF/NM 9.0	NM- 9.2
1-Illustrated Stories of the Operas: Faust; Funnyman by Giunta; Cisco Kid (1st app.) & Superbaby begin; Giunta-c	42	84	126	252	376	500

CITIZEN SMITH (See Holyoke One-Shot No. 9)

CITIZEN V AND THE V-BATTALION (See Thunderbolts)
Marvel Comics: June, 2001 - No. 3, Aug, 2001 ($2.99, limited series)

	GD 2.0	VG 4.0	FN 6.0	VF 8.0	VF/NM 9.0	NM- 9.2
1-3-Nicieza-a; Michael Ryan-c/a						3.00
...: The Everlasting 1-4 (3/02 - No. 4, 7/02) Nicieza-s/LaRosa-a(p)						3.00

CITY OF HEROES (Online game)
Dark Horse Comics: Sept, 2002 (no cover price)

	GD 2.0	VG 4.0	FN 6.0	VF 8.0	VF/NM 9.0	NM- 9.2
1-Dakan-s/Zombo-a						2.25

CITY OF SILENCE
Image Comics: May, 2000 - No. 3, July, 2000 ($2.50)

	GD 2.0	VG 4.0	FN 6.0	VF 8.0	VF/NM 9.0	NM- 9.2
1-3-Ellis-s/Erskine-a						2.50

CITY OF THE LIVING DEAD (See Fantastic Tales No. 1)
Avon Periodicals: 1952

	GD 2.0	VG 4.0	FN 6.0	VF 8.0	VF/NM 9.0	NM- 9.2
nn-Hollingsworth-c/a	46	92	138	276	413	550

CITY PEOPLE NOTEBOOK
Kitchen Sink Press: 1989 ($9.95, B&W, magazine sized)

	GD 2.0	VG 4.0	FN 6.0	VF 8.0	VF/NM 9.0	NM- 9.2
nn-Will Eisner-s/a						10.00
nn-(DC Comics, 2000) Reprint						10.00

CITY SURGEON (Blake Harper...)
Gold Key: August, 1963

	GD 2.0	VG 4.0	FN 6.0	VF 8.0	VF/NM 9.0	NM- 9.2
1(10075-308)-Painted-c	4	8	12	28	38	45

CIVIL WAR MUSKET, THE (Kadets of America Handbook)
Custom Comics, Inc.: 1960 (25¢, half-size, 36 pgs.)

	GD 2.0	VG 4.0	FN 6.0	VF 8.0	VF/NM 9.0	NM- 9.2
nn	3	6	9	18	23	28

CLAIRE VOYANT (Also see Keen Teens)
Leader Publ./Standard/Pentagon Publ.: 1946 - No. 4, 1947 (Sparling strip reprints)

	GD 2.0	VG 4.0	FN 6.0	VF 8.0	VF/NM 9.0	NM- 9.2
nn	61	122	183	381	571	760
2,4: 2-Kamen-c. 4-Kamen bondage-c	48	96	144	288	432	575
3-Kamen bridal-c; contents mentioned in Love and Death, a book by Gershom Legman(1949) referenced by Dr. Wertham in **SOTI**	55	110	165	342	511	680

CLANDESTINE (Also see Marvel Comics Presents & X-Men: ClanDestine)
Marvel Comics: Oct, 1994 - No.12, Sept, 1995 ($2.95/$2.50)

	GD 2.0	VG 4.0	FN 6.0	VF 8.0	VF/NM 9.0	NM- 9.2
1-($2.95)-Alan Davis-c/a(p)/scripts & Mark Farmer-c/a(i) begin, ends #8; Modok app.; Silver Surfer cameo; gold foil-c						3.00
2-12: 2-Wraparound-c. 2,3-Silver Surfer app. 5-Origin of ClanDestine. 6-Capt. America, Hulk, Spider-Man, Thing & Thor-c; Spider-Man cameo. 7-Spider-Man-c/app; Punisher cameo. 8-Invaders & Dr. Strange app. 10-Captain Britain-c/app. 11-Sub-Mariner app.						2.50
Preview (10/94, $1.50)						2.50

CLASH
DC Comics: 1991 - No. 3, 1991 ($4.95, limited series, 52 pgs.)

	GD 2.0	VG 4.0	FN 6.0	VF 8.0	VF/NM 9.0	NM- 9.2
Book One - Three: Adam Kubert-c/a						5.00

CLASSIC COMICS/ILLUSTRATED - INTRODUCTION
by Dan Malan

Further revisions have been made to help in understanding the **Classics** section. **Classics** reprint editions prior to 1963 had either incorrect dates or no dates listed. Those reprint editions should be identified only by the highest number on the reorder list (HRN). Past price guides listed what were calculated to be approximately correct dates, but many people found it confusing for the price guide to list a date not listed in the comic itself.

We have also attempted to clear up confusion about edition variations, such as color, printer, etc. Such variations will be identified by letters. Editions will now be determined by three categories. Original edition variations will be Edition 1A, 1B, etc. All reprint editions prior to 1963 will be identified by HRN only. All reprint editions from 9/63 on will be identified by the correct date listed in the comic.

We have also included new information on four recent reprintings of **Classics** not previously listed. From 1968-1976 Twin Circle, the Catholic newspaper, serialized over 100 **Classics** titles. That list can be found under non-series items at the end of this section. In 1972 twelve **Classics** were reissued as **Now Age Books Illustrated**. They are listed under **Pendulum Illustrated Classics**. In 1982, 20 **Classics** were reissued, adapted for teaching English as a second language. They are listed under **Regents Illustrated Classics**. Then in 1984, six **Classics** were reissued with cassette tapes. See the listing under **Cassette Books**.

UNDERSTANDING CLASSICS ILLUSTRATED
by Dan Malan

Since **Classics Illustrated** is the most complicated comic book series, with all its reprint editions and variations, with changes in covers and artwork, with a variety of means of identifying editions, and with the most extensive worldwide distribution of any comic-book series; therefore this introductory section is provided to assist you in gaining expertise about this series.

THE HISTORY OF CLASSICS

The **Classics** series was the brain child of Albert L. Kanter, who saw in the new comic-book medium a means of introducing children to the great classics of literature. In October of 1941 his Gilberton Co. began the **Classic Comics** series with **The Three Musketeers**, with 64 pages of storyline. In those early years, the struggling series saw irregular schedules and numerous printers, not to mention variable art quality and liberal story adaptations. With No.13 the page total was reduced to 56 (except for No. 33, originally scheduled to be No. 9), and with No. 15 the coming-next ad on the outside back cover moved inside. In 1945 the Jerry Iger Shop began producing all new CC titles, beginning with No. 23. In 1947 the search for a classier logo resulted in **Classics Illustrated**, beginning with No. 35, **Last Days of Pompeii**. With No. 45 the page total dropped again to 48, which was to become the standard.

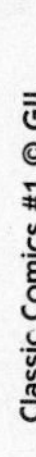

Classic Comics #1 © GIL

Classic Comics #2 © GIL

Classic Comics #3 © GIL

Two new developments in 1951 had a profound effect upon the success of the series. One was the introduction of painted covers, instead of the old line drawn covers, beginning with No. 81, **The Odyssey**. The second was the switch to the major national distributor Curtis. They raised the cover price from 10 to 15 cents, making it the highest priced comic-book, but it did not slow the growth of the series, because they were marketed as books, not comics. Because of this higher quality image, **Classics** flourished during the fifties while other comic series were reeling from outside attacks. They diversified with their new **Juniors**, **Specials**, and **World Around Us** series.

Classics artwork can be divided into three distinct periods. The pre-Iger era (1941-44) was mentioned above for its variable art quality. The Iger era (1945-53) was a major improvement in art quality and adaptations. It came to be dominated by artists Henry Kiefer and Alex Blum, together accounting for some 50 titles. Their styles gave the first real personality to the series. The EC era (1954-62) resulted from the demise of the EC horror series, when many of their artists made the major switch to classical art.

But several factors brought the production of new CI titles to a complete halt in 1962. Gilberton lost its 2nd class mailing permit. External factors like television, cheap paperback books, and Cliff Notes were all eating away at their market. Production halted with No.167, **Faust**, even though many more titles were already in the works. Many of those found their way into foreign series, and are very desirable to collectors. In 1967, **Classics Illustrated** was sold to Patrick Frawley and his Catholic publication, Twin Circle. They issued two new titles in 1969 as part of an attempted revival, but succumbed to major distribution problems in 1971. In 1988, the trio: First Publishing, Berkley Press, and Classics Media Group acquired the use rights for the old CI series art, logo, and name from the Frawley Group. So far they have used only the name in the new series, but do have plans to reprint the old CI.

One of the unique aspects of the **Classics Illustrated** (CI) series was the proliferation of reprint variations. Some titles had as many as 25 editions. Reprinting began in 1943. Some **Classic Comics** (CC) reprints (r) had the logo format revised to a banner logo, and added a motto under the banner. In 1947 CC titles changed to the CI logo, but kept their line drawn covers (LDC). In 1948, Nos. 13, 18, 29 and 41 received second covers (LDC2), replacing covers considered too violent, and reprints of Nos. 13-44 had pages reduced to 48, except for No. 26, which had 48 pages to begin with.

Starting in the mid-1950s, 70 of the 80 LDC titles were reissued with new painted covers (PC). Thirty of them also received new interior artwork (A2). The new artwork was generally higher quality with larger art panels and more faithful but abbreviated storylines. Later on, there were 29 second painted covers (PC2), mostly by Twin Circle. Altogether there were 199 interior art variations (169 (O)s and 30 A2 editions) and 272 different covers (169 (O)s, four LDC2s, 70 new PCs of LDC (O)s, and 29 PC2s). It is mildly astounding to realize that there are nearly 1400 different editions in the U.S. CI series.

FOREIGN CLASSICS ILLUSTRATED

If U.S. Classics variations are mildly astounding, the veritable plethora of foreign CI variations will boggle your imagination. While we still anticipate additional discoveries, we presently know about series in 25 languages and 27 countries. There were 250 new CI titles in foreign series, and nearly 400 new foreign covers of U.S. titles. The 1400 U.S. CI editions pale in comparison to the 4000 plus foreign editions. The very nature of CI lent itself to flourishing as an international series. Worldwide, they published over one billion copies! The first foreign CI series consisted of six Canadian Classic Comic reprints in 1946.

The following chart shows when CI series first began in each country:
1946: Canada. 1947: Australia. 1948: Brazil/The Netherlands. 1950: Italy. 1951: Greece/Japan/Hong Kong(?)/England/Argentina/Mexico. 1952: West Germany. 1954: Norway. 1955: New Zealand/South Africa. 1956: Denmark/Sweden/Iceland. 1957: Finland/France. 1962: Singapore(?). 1964: India (8 languages). 1971: Ireland (Gaelic). 1973: Belgium(?)/Philippines(?) & Malaysia(?).

Significant among the early series were Brazil and Greece. In 1950, Brazil was the first country to begin doing its own new titles. They issued nearly 80 new CI titles by Brazilian authors. In Greece in 1951 they actually had debates in parliament about the effects of Classics Illustrated on Greek culture, leading to the inclusion of 88 new Greek History & Mythology titles in the CI series.

But by far the most important foreign CI development was the joint European series which began in 1956 in 10 countries simultaneously. By 1960, CI had the largest European distribution of any American publication, not just comics! So when all the problems came up with U.S. distribution, they literally moved the CI operation to Europe in 1962, and continued producing new titles in all four CI series. Many of them were adapted and drawn in the U.S., the most famous of which was the British CI #158A. Dr. No, drawn by Norman Nodel. Unfortunately, the British CI series ended in late 1963, which limited the European CI titles available in English to 15. Altogether there were 82 new CI art titles in the joint European series, which ran until 1976.

IDENTIFYING CLASSICS EDITIONS

HRN: This is the highest number on the reorder list. It should be listed in ( ) after the title number. It is crucial to understanding various CI editions.

ORIGINALS (O): This is the all-important First Edition. To determine (O)s, there is one primary rule and two secondary rules (with exceptions):

Rule No. 1: All (O)s and only (O)s have coming-next ads for the next number. **Exceptions**: No. 14(15) (reprint) has an ad on the last inside text page only. No. 14(0) also has a full-page outside back cover ad (also rule 2). Nos.55(75) and 57(75) have coming-next ads. (Rules 2 and 3 apply here). Nos. 168(0) and 169(0) do not have coming-next ads. No.168 was never reprinted; No. 169(0) has HRN (166). No. 169(169) is the only reprint.

Rule No. 2: On nos.1-80, all (O)s and only (O)s list 10c on the front cover. **Exceptions**: Reprint variations of Nos. 37(62), 39(71), and 46(62) list 10c on the front cover. (Rules 1 and 3 apply here.)

Rule No. 3: All (O)s have HRN close to that title No. **Exceptions**: Some reprints also have HRNs close to that title number: a few CC(r)s, 58(62), 60(62), 149(149), 152(149) 153(149), and title nos. in the 160's. (Rules 1 and 2 apply here.)

DATES: Many reprint editions list either an incorrect date or no date. Since Gilberton apparently kept track of CI editions by HRN, they often left the (O) date on reprints. Often, someone with a CI collection for sale will swear that all their copies are originals. That is why we are so detailed in pointing out how to identify original editions. Except for original editions, which should have a coming-next ad, etc., all CI dates prior to 1963 are incorrect! So you want to go by HRN only if it is (165) or below, and go by listed date if it is 1963 or later. There are a few (167) editions with incorrect dates. They could be listed either as (167) or (62/3), which is meant to indicate that they were issued sometime between late 1962 and early 1963.

COVERS: A change from CC to LDC indicates a logo change, not a cover change; while a change from LDC to LDC2, LDC to PC, or from PC to PC2 does indicate a new cover. New PCs can be identified by HRN, and PC2s can be identified by HRN and date. Several covers had color changes, particularly from purple to blue.

Notes: If you see 15 cents in Canada on a front cover, it does not necessarily indicate a Canadian edition. Editions with an HRN between 44 and 75, with 15 cents on the cover are Canadian. Check the publisher's address. An HRN listing two numbers with a / between them indicates that there are two different reorder lists in the front and back covers. Official Twin Circle editions have a full-page back cover ad for their TC magazine, with no CI reorder list. Any CI with just a Twin Circle sticker on the front is not an official TC edition.

TIPS ON LISTING CLASSICS FOR SALE

It may be easy to just list Edition 17, but Classics collectors keep track of CI editions in terms of HRN and/or date, (O) or (r), CC or LDC, PC or PC2, A1 or A2, soft or stiff cover, etc. Try to help them out. For originals, just list (0), unless there are variations such as color (Nos. 10 and 61), printer (Nos. 18-22), HRN (Nos. 95, 108, 160), etc. For reprints, just list HRN if it's (165) or below. Above that, list HRN and date. Also, please list type of logo/cover/art for the convenience of buyers. They will appreciate it.

CLASSIC COMICS (Also see Best from Boys Life, Cassette Books, Famous Stories, Fast Fiction, Golden Picture Classics, King Classics, Marvel Classics Comics, Pendulum Illustrated Classics, Picture Parade, Picture Progress, Regents Ill. Classics, Spitfire, Stories by Famous Authors, Superior Stories, and World Around Us.)

CLASSIC COMICS (Classics Illustrated No. 35 on)
Elliot Publishing #1-3 (1941-1942)/Gilberton Publications #4-167 (1942-1967) /Twin Circle Pub. (Frawley) #168-169 (1968-1971):
10/41 - No. 34, 2/47; No. 35, 3/47 - No. 169, Spring 1969
(Reprint Editions of almost all titles 5/43 - Spring 1971)
(Painted Covers (0)s No. 81 on, and (r)s of most Nos. 1-80)

Abbreviations:
A–Art; C or c–Cover; CC–Classic Comics; CI–Classics Ill.; Ed–Edition; LDC–Line Drawn Cover; PC–Painted Cover; r–Reprint

GD VG FN VF VF/NM NM-
2.0 4.0 6.0 8.0 9.0 9.2

1. The Three Musketeers

Ed	HRN	Date	Details	A	C	GD 2.0	VG 4.0	FN 6.0	VF 8.0	VF/NM 9.0	NM- 9.2
1	–	10/41	Date listed-1941; Elliot Pub; 68 pgs.	1	1	448	896	1344	3136	4818	6500
2	10	–	10¢ price removed on all (r)s; Elliot Pub; CC-r	1	1	37	74	111	212	301	390
3	15	–	Long Isl. Ind. Ed.; CC-r	1	1	27	54	81	153	214	275
4	18/20	–	Sunrise Times Ed.; CC-r	1	1	19	38	57	106	146	185
5	21	–	Richmond Courier Ed.; CC-r	1	1	17	34	51	95	130	165
6	28	1946	CC-r	1	1	14	28	42	79	107	135
7	36	–	LDC-r	1	1	8	16	24	43	54	65
8	60	–	LDC-r	1	1	6	12	18	27	33	38
9	64	–	LDC-r	1	1	5	10	15	22	26	30
10	78	–	C-price 15¢;LDC-r	1	1	4	9	13	18	22	26
11	93	–	LDC-r	1	1	4	9	13	18	22	26
12	114	–	Last LDC-r	1	1	4	8	11	16	19	22
13	134	–	New-c; old-a; 64 pg. PC-r	1	2	3	6	9	18	23	28
14	143	–	Old-a; PC-r; 64 pg.	1	2	2	4	6	12	16	20
15	150	–	New-a; PC-r;	2	2	3	6	9	17	21	26

Classic Comics #4 © GIL

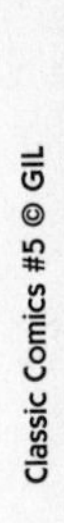

Classic Comics #5 © GIL

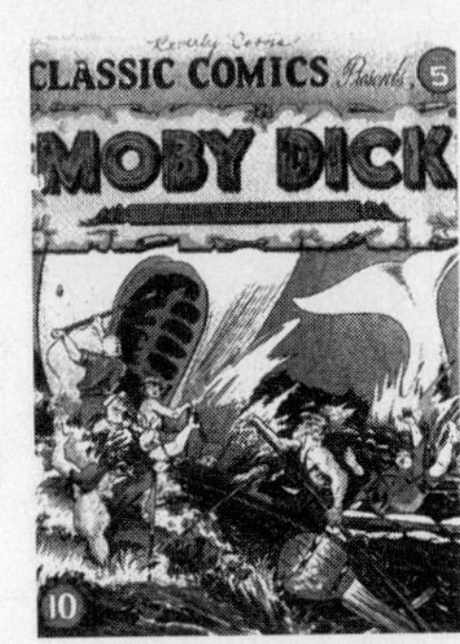

Classic Comics #6 © GIL

Ed	HRN	Date	Details	A	C	GD 2.0	VG 4.0	FN 6.0	VF 8.0	VF/NM 9.0	NM- 9.2
			Evans/Crandall-a								
16	149	–	PC-r	2	2	2	4	6	8	10	12
17	167	–	PC-r	2	2	2	4	0	0	10	12
18	167	4/64	PC-r	2	2	2	4	6	8	10	12
19	167	1/65	PC-r	2	2	2	4	6	8	10	12
20	167	3/66	PC-r	2	2	2	4	6	8	10	12
21	166	11/67	PC-r	2	2	2	4	6	8	10	12
22	166	Spr/69	C-price 25¢ ; stiff-c; PC-r	2	2	2	4	6	8	10	12
23	169	Spr/71	PC-r; stiff-c	2	2	2	4	6	8	10	12

2. Ivanhoe

Ed	HRN	Date	Details	A	C	GD 2.0	VG 4.0	FN 6.0	VF 8.0	VF/NM 9.0	NM- 9.2
1	(O)	12/41?	Date listed-1941; Elliot Pub; 68 pgs.	1	1	224	448	672	1400	2100	2800
2	10	–	Price & 'Presents' removed; Elliot Pub; CC-r	1	1	33	60	99	190	270	350
3	15	–	Long Isl. Ind. ed.; CC-r	1	1	21	42	63	121	168	215
4	18/20	–	Sunrise Times ed.; CC-r	1	1	19	38	57	106	146	185
5	21	–	Richmond Courier ed.; CC-r	1	1	17	34	51	95	130	165
6	28	1946	Last 'Comics'-r	1	1	14	28	42	79	107	135
7	36	–	1st LDC-r	1	1	9	18	27	49	62	75
8	60	–	LDC-r	1	1	6	12	18	27	33	38
9	64	–	LDC-r	1	1	5	10	15	22	26	30
10	78	–	C-price 15¢; LDC-r	1	1	4	9	13	18	22	26
11	89	–	LDC-r	1	1	4	8	12	17	21	24
12	106	–	LDC-r	1	1	4	7	10	14	17	20
13	121	–	Last LDC-r	1	1	4	7	10	14	17	20
14	136	–	New-c&a; PC-r	2	2	5	10	15	22	26	30
15	142	–	PC-r	2	2	2	4	6	9	11	14
16	153	–	PC-r	2	2	2	4	6	9	11	14
17	149	–	PC-r	2	2	2	4	6	9	11	14
18	167	–	PC-r	2	2	2	4	6	8	10	12
19	167	5/64	PC-r	2	2	2	4	6	8	10	12
20	167	1/65	PC-r	2	2	2	4	6	8	10	12
21	167	3/66	PC-r	2	2	2	4	6	8	10	12
22A	166	9/67	PC-r	2	2	2	4	6	8	10	12
22B	166	–	Center ad for Children's Digest & Young Miss; rare; PC-r	2	2	11	22	33	63	84	105
23	166	R/68	C-Price 25¢; PC-r	2	2	2	4	6	8	10	12
24	169	Win/69	Stiff-c	2	2	2	4	6	8	10	12
25	169	Win/71	PC-r; stiff-c	2	2	2	4	6	8	10	12

3. The Count of Monte Cristo

Ed	HRN	Date	Details	A	C	GD 2.0	VG 4.0	FN 6.0	VF 8.0	VF/NM 9.0	NM- 9.2
1	(O)	3/42	Elliot Pub; 68 pgs.	1	1	142	284	426	888	1332	1775
2	10	–	Conray Prods; CC-r	1	1	28	56	84	157	221	285
3	15	–	Long Isl. Ind. ed.; CC-r	1	1	22	44	66	124	172	220
4	18/20	–	Sunrise Times ed.; CC-r	1	1	20	40	60	112	156	200
5	20	–	Sunrise Times ed.; CC-r	1	1	18	36	54	101	138	175
6	21	–	Richmond Courier ed.; CC-r	1	1	17	34	51	95	130	165
7	28	1946	CC-r; new Banner logo	1	1	14	28	42	79	107	135
8	36	–	1st LDC-r	1	1	9	18	27	49	62	75
9	60	–	LDC-r	1	1	6	12	18	27	33	38
10	62	–	LDC-r	1	1	6	12	18	29	36	42
11	71	–	LDC-r	1	1	5	10	14	20	24	28
12	87	–	C-price 15¢; LDC-r	1	1	4	9	13	18	22	26
13	113	–	LDC-r	1	1	4	7	10	14	17	20
14	135	–	New-c&a; PC-r; Cameron-a	2	2	3	6	9	18	23	28
15	143	–	PC-r	2	2	2	4	6	9	11	14
16	153	–	PC-r	2	2	2	4	6	9	11	14
17	161	–	PC-r	2	2	2	4	6	9	11	14
18	167	–	PC-r	2	2	2	4	6	8	10	12
19	167	7/64	PC-r	2	2	2	4	6	8	10	12
20	167	7/65	PC-r	2	2	2	4	6	8	10	12
21	167	7/66	PC-r	2	2	2	4	6	8	10	12
22	166	R/68	C-price 25¢; PC-r	2	2	2	4	6	8	10	12
23	169	–	Win/69 Stiff-c; PC-r	2	2	2	4	6	8	10	12

4. The Last of the Mohicans

Ed	HRN	Date	Details	A	C	GD 2.0	VG 4.0	FN 6.0	VF 8.0	VF/NM 9.0	NM- 9.2
1	(O)	8/42	Date listed-1942; Gilberton #4(0) on; 68 pgs.	1	1	118	236	354	738	1107	1475
2	12	–	Elliot Pub; CC-r	1	1	28	56	84	157	221	285
3	15	–	Long Isl. Ind. ed.; CC-r	1	1	22	44	66	124	172	220
4	20	–	Long Isl. Ind. ed.; CC-r; banner logo	1	1	19	38	57	106	146	185
5	21	–	Queens Home News ed.; CC-r	1	1	17	34	51	95	130	165
6	28	1946	Last CC-r; new	1	1	14	28	42	79	107	135
7	36	–	1st LDC-r	1	1	9	18	27	49	62	75
8	60	–	LDC-r	1	1	6	12	18	27	33	38
9	64	–	LDC-r	1	1	5	10	14	20	24	28
10	78	–	C-price 15¢; LDC-r	1	1	4	9	13	18	22	26
11	89	–	LDC-r	1	1	4	8	12	17	21	24
12	117	–	Last LDC-r	1	1	4	7	10	14	17	20
13	135	–	New-c; PC-r	1	2	5	10	14	20	24	28
14	141	–	PC-r	1	2	3	6	8	12	14	16
15	150	–	New-a; PC-r; Severin, L.B. Cole-a	2	2	5	10	15	22	26	30
16	161	–	PC-r	2	2	2	4	6	8	10	12
17	167	–	PC-r	2	2	2	4	6	8	10	12
18	167	6/64	PC-r	2	2	2	4	6	8	10	12
19	167	8/65	PC-r	2	2	2	4	6	8	10	12
20	167	8/66	PC-r	2	2	2	4	6	8	10	12
21	166	R/67	C-price 25¢; PC-r	2	2	2	4	6	8	10	12
22	169	Spr/69	Stiff-c; PC-r	2	2	2	4	6	8	10	12

5. Moby Dick

Ed	HRN	Date	Details	A	C	GD 2.0	VG 4.0	FN 6.0	VF 8.0	VF/NM 9.0	NM- 9.2
1A	(O)	9/42	Date listed-1942; Gilberton; 68 pgs.	1	1	150	300	450	938	1407	1875
1B			inside-c, rare free promo			228	456	684	1425	2138	2850
2	10	–	Conray Prods; Pg. 64 changed from 105 title list to letter from Editor; CC-r	1	1	30	60	90	170	240	310
3	15	–	Long Isl. Ind. ed.; Pg. 64 changed from Letter to the Editor to Ill. poem-Concord Hymn; CC-r	1	1	25	50	75	144	198	255
4	18/20	–	Sunrise Times ed.; CC-r	1	1	20	40	60	112	156	200
5	20	–	Sunrise Times ed.; CC-r	1	1	19	38	57	106	146	185
6	21	–	Sunrise Times ed.; CC-r	1	1	17	34	51	95	130	165
7	28	1946	CC-r; new banner logo	1	1	15	30	45	84	115	145
8	36	–	1st LDC-r	1	1	9	18	27	49	62	75
9	60	–	LDC-r	1	1	6	12	18	27	33	38
10	62	–	LDC-r	1	1	6	12	18	29	36	42
11	71	–	LDC-r	1	1	5	10	15	22	26	30
12	87	–	C-price 15¢; LDC-r	1	1	5	10	14	20	24	28
13	118	–	LDC-r	1	1	4	8	12	17	21	24
14	131	–	New c&a; PC-r	2	2	5	10	15	22	26	30
15	138	–	PC-r	2	2	2	4	6	9	11	14
16	148	–	PC-r	2	2	2	4	6	9	11	14
17	158	–	PC-r	2	2	2	4	6	9	11	14
18	167	–	PC-r	2	2	2	4	6	8	10	12
19	167	6/64	PC-r	2	2	2	4	6	8	10	12
20	167	7/65	PC-r	2	2	2	4	6	8	10	12
21	167	3/66	PC-r	2	2	2	4	6	8	10	12
22	166	9/67	PC-r	2	2	2	4	6	8	10	12
23	166	Win/69	New-c & c-price	2	3	3	6	9	16	20	24

Classic Comics #7 © GIL

Classic Comics #9 © GIL

Classic Comics #11 © GIL

Ed	HRN	Date	Details	A	C	GD 2.0	VG 4.0	FN 6.0	VF 8.0	VF/NM 9.0	NM- 9.2
			25¢; Stiff-c; PC-r								
24	169	Win/71	PC-r	2	3	2	4	6	12	16	20

6. A Tale of Two Cities

Ed	HRN	Date	Details	A	C	GD 2.0	VG 4.0	FN 6.0	VF 8.0	VF/NM 9.0	NM- 9.2
1	(O)	10/42	Date listed-1942; 68 pgs. Zeckerberg c/a	1	1	118	236	354	738	1107	1475
2	14	–	Elliot Pub; CC-r	1	1	27	54	81	153	214	275
3	18	–	Long Isl. Ind. ed.; CC-r	1	1	21	42	63	118	164	210
4	20	–	Sunrise Times ed.; CC-r	1	1	19	38	57	106	146	185
5	28	1946	Last CC-r; new banner logo	1	1	14	28	42	79	107	135
6	51	–	1st LDC-r	1	1	8	16	24	43	54	65
7	64	–	LDC-r	1	1	5	10	15	23	28	32
8	78	–	C-price 15¢; LDC-r	1	1	5	10	14	20	24	28
9	89	–	LDC-r	1	1	4	7	10	14	17	20
10	117	–	LDC-r	1	1	4	7	10	14	17	20
11	132	–	New-c&a; PC-r; Joe Orlando-a	2	2	5	10	15	22	26	30
12	140	–	PC-r	2	2	2	4	6	8	10	12
13	147	–	PC-r	2	2	2	4	6	8	10	12
14	152	–	PC-r; very rare	2	2	19	38	57	106	146	185
15	153	–	PC-r	2	2	2	4	6	9	11	14
16	149	–	PC-r	2	2	2	4	6	9	11	14
17	167	–	PC-r	2	2	2	4	6	8	10	12
18	167	6/64	PC-r	2	2	2	4	6	8	10	12
19	167	8/65	PC-r	2	2	2	4	6	8	10	12
20	166	5/67	PC-r	2	2	2	4	6	8	10	12
21	166	Fall/68	New-c & 25¢; PC-r	2	3	3	6	9	17	21	26
22	169	Sum/70	Stiff-c; PC-r	2	3	2	4	6	12	16	20

7. Robin Hood

Ed	HRN	Date	Details	A	C	GD 2.0	VG 4.0	FN 6.0	VF 8.0	VF/NM 9.0	NM- 9.2
1	(O)	12/42	Date listed-1942; first Gift Box ad-bc; 68 pgs.	1	1	85	170	255	531	796	1060
2	12	–	Elliot Pub; CC-r	1	1	26	52	78	147	206	265
3	18	–	Long Isl. Ind. ed.; CC-r	1	1	20	40	60	112	156	200
4	20	–	Nassau Bulletin ed.; CC-r	1	1	19	38	57	106	146	185
5	22	–	Queens Cty. Times ed.; CC-r	1	1	17	34	51	95	130	165
6	28	–	CC-r	1	1	15	30	45	84	115	145
7	51	–	LDC-r	1	1	8	16	24	43	54	65
8	64	–	LDC-r	1	1	5	10	15	24	30	35
9	78	–	LDC-r	1	1	4	9	13	18	22	26
10	97	–	LDC-r	1	1	4	8	12	17	21	24
11	106	–	LDC-r	1	1	4	7	10	14	17	20
12	121	–	LDC-r	1	1	4	7	10	14	17	20
13	129	–	New-c; PC-r	1	2	5	10	15	22	26	30
14	136	–	New-a; PC-r	2	2	5	10	14	20	24	28
15	143	–	PC-r	2	2	2	4	6	9	11	14
16	153	–	PC-r	2	2	2	4	6	9	11	14
17	164	–	PC-r	2	2	2	4	6	8	10	12
18	167	–	PC-r	2	2	2	4	6	8	10	12
19	167	6/64	PC-r	2	2	2	4	6	8	10	12
20	167	5/65	PC-r	2	2	2	4	6	8	10	12
21	167	7/66	PC-r	2	2	2	4	6	8	10	12
22	166	12/67	PC-r	2	2	2	4	6	8	10	12
23	169	Sum/69	Stiff-c; c-price 25¢; PC-r	2	2	2	4	6	8	10	12

8. Arabian Nights

Ed	HRN	Date	Details	A	C	GD 2.0	VG 4.0	FN 6.0	VF 8.0	VF/NM 9.0	NM- 9.2
1	(O)	2/43	Original; 68 pgs. Lilian Chestney-c/a	1	1	147	294	441	919	1397	1875
2	17	–	Long Isl. ed.; pg. 64 changed from Gift Box ad to Letter from British Medical Worker; CC-r	1	1	55	110	165	330	495	660
3	20	–	Nassau Bulletin; Pg. 64 changed from letter to article-Three Men Named Smith; CC-r	1	1	44	88	132	264	395	525
4A	28	1946	CC-r; new banner logo, slick-c	1	1	34	68	102	193	274	355
4B	28	1946	Same, but w/stiff-c	1	1	34	68	102	193	227	355
5	51	–	LDC-r	1	1	24	48	72	135	190	245
6	64	–	LDC-r	1	1	20	40	60	112	156	200
7	78	–	LDC-r	1	1	19	38	57	106	146	185
8	164	–	New-c&a; PC-r	2	2	16	32	48	89	122	155

9. Les Miserables

Ed	HRN	Date	Details	A	C	GD 2.0	VG 4.0	FN 6.0	VF 8.0	VF/NM 9.0	NM- 9.2
1A	(O)	3/43	Original; slick paper cover; 68 pgs.	1	1	85	170	255	531	796	1060
1B	(O)	3/43	Original; rough, pulp type-c; 68 pgs.	1	1	107	214	321	669	1005	1340
2	14	–	Elliot Pub; CC-r	1	1	28	56	84	157	221	285
3	18	3/44	Nassau Bul. Pg. 64 changed from Gift Box ad to Bill of Rights article; CC-r	1	1	24	48	72	135	190	245
4	20	–	Richmond Courier ed.; CC-r	1	1	20	40	60	112	156	200
5	28	1946	Gilberton; pgs. 60-64 rearranged/ illos added; CC-r	1	1	15	30	45	84	115	145
6	51	–	LDC-r	1	1	9	18	27	49	62	75
7	71	–	LDC-r	1	1	6	12	18	29	36	42
8	87	–	C-price 15¢; LDC-r	1	1	6	12	18	27	33	38
9	161	–	New-c&a; PC-r	2	2	6	12	18	31	38	45
10	167	9/63	PC-r	2	2	2	4	6	12	16	20
11	167	12/65	PC-r	2	2	2	4	6	12	16	20
12	166	R/1968	New-c & price 25¢; PC-r	2	3	3	6	9	18	23	28

10. Robinson Crusoe (Used in **SOTI**, pg. 142)

Ed	HRN	Date	Details	A	C	GD 2.0	VG 4.0	FN 6.0	VF 8.0	VF/NM 9.0	NM- 9.2
1A	(O)	4/43	Original; Violet-c; 68 pgs; Zuckerberg c/a	1	1	74	148	222	463	692	920
1B	(O)	4/43	Original; blue-grey-c, 68 pgs.	1	1	83	166	249	519	780	1040
2A	14	–	Elliot Pub; violet-c; 68 pgs; CC-r	1	1	30	60	90	170	240	310
2B	14	–	Elliot Pub; blue-grey-c; CC-r	1	1	27	54	81	153	214	275
3	18	–	Nassau Bul. Pg. 64 changed from Gift Box ad to Bill of Rights article; CC-r	1	1	20	40	60	112	156	200
4	20	–	Queens Home News ed.; CC-r	1	1	17	34	51	95	130	165
5	28	1946	Gilberton; pg. 64 changes from Bill of Rights to WWII article-One Leg Shot Away; last CC-r	1	1	14	28	42	79	107	135
6	51	–	LDC-r	1	1	8	16	24	43	54	65
7	64	–	LDC-r	1	1	6	12	18	27	33	38
8	78	–	C-price 15¢; LDC-r	1	1	5	10	14	20	24	28
9	97	–	LDC-r	1	1	4	9	13	18	22	26
10	114	–	LDC-r	1	1	4	7	10	14	17	20
11	130	–	New-c; PC-r	1	2	5	10	15	22	26	30
12	140	–	New-a; PC-r	2	2	5	10	14	20	24	28
13	153	–	PC-r	2	2	2	4	6	8	10	12
14	164	–	PC-r	2	2	2	4	6	8	10	12
15	167	–	PC-r	2	2	2	4	6	8	10	12
16	167	7/64	PC-r	2	2	2	4	6	10	13	16
17	167	5/65	PC-r	2	2	2	4	6	10	13	16
18	167	6/66	PC-r	2	2	2	4	6	8	10	12
19	166	Fall/68	C-price 25¢; PC-r	2	2	2	4	6	8	10	12
20	166	R/68	(No Twin Circle ad)	2	2	2	4	6	9	11	14
21	169	Sm/70	Stiff-c; PC-r	2	2	2	4	6	9	11	14

11. Don Quixote

Ed	HRN	Date	Details	A	C

Classic Comics #13 © GIL

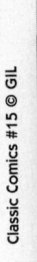

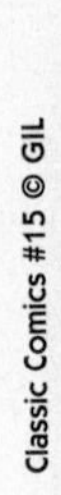
Classic Comics #15 © GIL

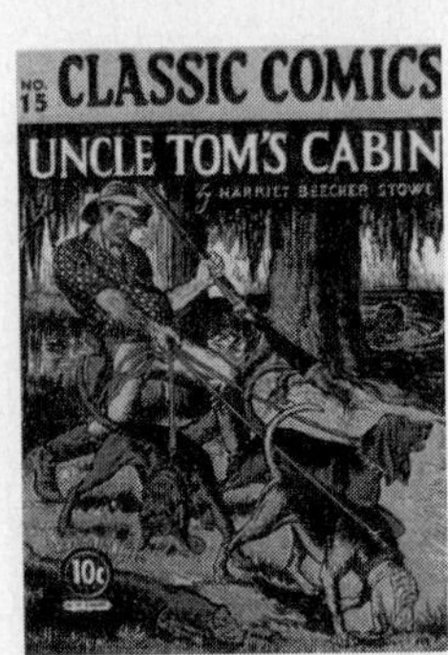

Classic Comics #17 © GIL

Ed	HRN	Date	Details	A	C	GD 2.0	VG 4.0	FN 6.0	VF 8.0	VF/NM 9.0	NM- 9.2
1	10	5/43	First (O) with HRN list; 68 pgs.	1	1	80	160	240	500	750	1000
2	18	–	Nassau Bulletin ed.; CC-r	1	1	25	50	75	144	108	255
3	21	–	Queens Home News ed.; CC-r	1	1	20	40	60	112	156	200
4	28	–	CC-r	1	1	15	30	45	84	115	145
5	110	–	New-PC; PC-r	1	2	6	12	18	29	36	42
6	156	–	Pgs. reduced 68 to 52; PC-r	1	2	4	7	10	14	17	20
7	165	–	PC-r	1	2	2	4	6	9	11	14
8	167	1/64	PC-r	1	2	2	4	6	9	11	14
9	167	11/65	PC-r	1	2	2	4	6	9	11	14
10	166	R/1968	New-c & price 25¢; PC-r	1	3	3	6	9	18	24	30

12. Rip Van Winkle and the Headless Horseman

Ed	HRN	Date	Details	A	C	GD 2.0	VG 4.0	FN 6.0	VF 8.0	VF/NM 9.0	NM- 9.2
1	11	6/43	Original; 68 pgs.	1	1	80	160	240	500	750	1000
2	15	–	Long Isl. Ind. ed.; CC-r	1	1	25	50	75	144	198	255
3	20	–	Long Isl. Ind. ed.;	1	1	20	40	60	112	156	200
4	22	–	Queens Cty. Times ed.; CC-r	1	1	17	34	51	95	130	165
5	28	–	CC-r	1	1	14	28	42	79	107	135
6	60	–	1st LDC-r	1	1	8	16	24	40	50	60
7	62	–	LDC-r	1	1	5	10	15	23	28	32
8	71	–	LDC-r	1	1	4	9	13	18	22	26
9	89	–	C-price 15¢; LDC-r	1	1	4	8	12	17	21	24
10	118	–	LDC-r	1	1	4	7	10	14	17	20
11	132	–	New-c; PC-r	1	2	5	10	15	22	26	30
12	150	–	New-a; PC-r	2	2	5	10	14	20	24	28
13	158	–	PC-r	2	2	2	4	6	9	11	14
14	167	–	PC-r	2	2	2	4	6	9	11	14
15	167	12/63	PC-r	2	2	2	4	6	8	10	12
16	167	4/65	PC-r	2	2	2	4	6	8	10	12
17	167	4/66	PC-r	2	2	2	4	6	8	10	12
18	166	R/1968	New-c&price 25¢; PC-r; stiff-c	2	3	2	4	6	14	18	22
19	169	Sm/70	PC-r; stiff-c	2	3	2	4	6	10	13	16

13. Dr. Jekyll and Mr. Hyde (Used in **SOTI**, pg. 143)(1st horror comic?)

Ed	HRN	Date	Details	A	C	GD 2.0	VG 4.0	FN 6.0	VF 8.0	VF/NM 9.0	NM- 9.2
1	12	8/43	Original 60 pgs.	1	1	122	244	366	763	1144	1525
2	15	–	Long Isl. Ind. ed.; CC-r	1	1	35	70	105	201	288	370
3	20	–	Long Isl. Ind. ed.; CC-r	1	1	25	50	75	144	198	255
4	28	–	No c-price; CC-r	1	1	19	38	57	106	146	185
5	60	–	New-c; Pgs. reduced from 60 to 52; H.C. Kiefer-c; LDC-r	1	2	8	16	24	43	54	65
6	62	–	LDC-r	1	2	6	12	18	28	34	40
7	71	–	LDC-r	1	2	5	10	15	23	28	32
8	87	–	Date returns (erroneous); LDC-r	1	2	5	10	15	22	26	30
9	112	–	New-c&a; PC-r; Cameron-a	2	3	6	12	18	29	36	42
10	153	–	PC-r	2	3	2	4	6	10	12	15
11	161	–	PC-r	2	3	2	4	6	10	12	15
12	167	–	PC-r	2	3	2	4	6	8	10	12
13	167	8/64	PC-r	2	3	2	4	6	8	10	12
14	167	11/65	PC-r	2	3	2	4	6	8	10	12
15	166	R/68	C-price 25¢; PC-r	2	3	2	4	6	8	10	12
16	169	Wn/69	PC-r; stiff-c	2	3	2	4	6	8	10	12

14. Westward Ho!

Ed	HRN	Date	Details	A	C	GD 2.0	VG 4.0	FN 6.0	VF 8.0	VF/NM 9.0	NM- 9.2
1	13	9/43	Original; last outside bc coming-next ad; 60 pgs.	1	1	192	384	576	1200	1800	2400
2	15	–	Long Isl. Ind. ed.; CC-r	1	1	55	110	165	330	495	660
3	21	–	Queens Home News; Pg. 56 changed from coming-next ad to Three Men Named Smith; CC-r	1	1	44	88	132	264	395	525
4	28	1946	Gilberton; Pg. 56 changed again to WWII article-Speaking for America; last CC-r	1	1	39	78	117	230	325	420
5	53	–	Pgs. reduced from 60 to 52; LDC-r	1	1	35	70	105	201	288	370

15. Uncle Tom's Cabin (Used in **SOTI**, pgs. 102, 103)

Ed	HRN	Date	Details	A	C	GD 2.0	VG 4.0	FN 6.0	VF 8.0	VF/NM 9.0	NM- 9.2
1	14	11/43	Original; Outside-bc ad: 2 Gift Boxes; 60 pgs.; color var. on-c; green trunk,root on left & brown trunk, root on left	1	1	66	132	198	413	619	825
2	15	–	Long Isl. Ind. listed- bottom inside-fc; also Gilberton listed bottom-pg. 1; CC-r; green root vs. brown root var. occurs again	1	1	27	54	81	153	214	275
3	21	–	Nassau Bulletin ed.; CC-r	1	1	21	42	63	118	164	210
4	28	–	No c-price; CC-r	1	1	15	30	45	84	115	145
5	53	–	Pgs. reduced 60 to 52; LDC-r	1	1	8	16	24	43	54	65
6	71	–	LDC-r	1	1	6	12	18	27	33	38
7	89	–	C-price 15¢; LDC-r	1	1	5	10	15	24	30	35
8	117	–	New-c/lettering changes; PC-r	1	2	5	10	15	22	26	30
9	128	–	'Picture Progress' promo; PC-r	1	2	2	4	6	10	13	16
10	137	–	PC-r	1	2	2	4	6	9	11	14
11	146	–	PC-r	1	2	2	4	6	9	11	14
12	154	–	PC-r	1	2	2	4	6	9	11	14
13	161	–	PC-r	1	2	2	4	6	8	10	12
14	167	–	PC-r	1	2	2	4	6	8	10	12
15	167	6/64	PC-r	1	2	2	4	6	8	10	12
16	167	5/65	PC-r	1	2	2	4	6	8	10	12
17	166	5/67	PC-r	1	2	2	4	6	8	10	12
18	166	Wn/69	New-stiff-c; PC-r	1	3	2	4	6	14	18	22
19	169	Sm/70	PC-r; stiff-c	1	3	2	4	6	10	13	16

16. Gullivers Travels

Ed	HRN	Date	Details	A	C	GD 2.0	VG 4.0	FN 6.0	VF 8.0	VF/NM 9.0	NM- 9.2
1	15	12/43	Original-Lilian Chestney c/a; 60 pgs.	1	1	69	138	207	431	646	860
2	18/20	–	Price deleted; Queens Home News ed; CC-r	1	1	24	48	72	135	190	245
3	22	–	Queens Cty. Times ed.; CC-r	1	1	19	38	57	106	146	185
4	28	–	CC-r	1	1	14	28	42	79	107	135
5	60	–	Pgs. reduced to 48; LDC-r	1	1	6	12	18	31	38	45
6	62	–	LDC-r	1	1	5	10	15	23	28	32
7	78	–	C-price 15¢; LDC-r	1	1	5	10	14	20	24	28
8	89	–	LDC-r	1	1	4	8	12	17	21	24
9	155	–	New-c; PC-r	1	2	5	10	15	22	26	30
10	165	–	PC-r	1	2	2	4	6	8	10	12
11	167	5/64	PC-r	1	2	2	4	6	8	10	12
12	167	11/65	PC-r	1	2	2	4	6	8	10	12
13	166	R/1968	C-price 25¢; PC-r	1	2	2	4	6	8	10	12
14	169	Wn/69	PC-r; stiff-c	1	2	2	4	6	8	10	12

17. The Deerslayer

Ed	HRN	Date	Details	A	C	GD 2.0	VG 4.0	FN 6.0	VF 8.0	VF/NM 9.0	NM- 9.2
1	16	1/44	Original; Outside-bc ad: 3 Gift Boxes; 60 pgs.	1	1	59	118	177	369	555	740
2A	18	–	Queens Cty Times (inside-fc); CC-r	1	1	25	50	75	144	198	255
2B	18	–	Gilberton (bottom-pg. 1); CC-r; Scarce	1	1	35	70	105	201	288	370

Classic Comics #18 © GIL

Classic Comics #21 © GIL

Classic Comics #22 © GIL

Ed	HRN	Date	Details	A	C	GD 2.0	VG 4.0	FN 6.0	VF 8.0	VF/NM 9.0	NM- 9.2
3	22	–	Queens Cty. Times ed.; CC-r	1	1	20	40	60	112	156	200
4	28	–	CC-r	1	1	15	30	45	84	115	145
5	60	–	Pgs.reduced to 52; LDC-r	1	1	7	14	21	37	46	55
6	64	–	LDC-r	1	1	5	10	15	22	26	30
7	85	–	C-price 15¢; LDC-r	1	1	4	8	12	17	21	24
8	118	–	LDC-r	1	1	4	7	10	14	17	20
9	132	–	LDC-r	1	1	4	7	10	14	17	20
10	167	11/66	Last LDC-r	1	1	2	4	6	12	16	20
11	166	R/1968	New-c & price 25¢; PC-r	1	2	3	6	9	18	23	28
12	169	Spr/71	Stiff-c; letters from parents & educators; PC-r	1	2	2	4	6	11	14	18

18. The Hunchback of Notre Dame

Ed	HRN	Date	Details	A	C	GD 2.0	VG 4.0	FN 6.0	VF 8.0	VF/NM 9.0	NM- 9.2
1A	17	3/44	Orig.; Gilberton ed; 60 pgs.	1	1	78	156	234	488	732	975
1B	17	3/44	Orig.; Island Pub. Ed.; 60 pgs.	1	1	69	138	207	431	646	860
2	18/20	–	Queens Home News ed.; CC-r	1	1	27	54	81	153	214	275
3	22	–	Queens Cty. Times ed.; CC-r	1	1	20	40	60	112	156	200
4	28	–	CC-r	1	1	17	34	51	95	130	165
5	60	–	New-c; 8pgs. deleted; Kiefer-c; LDC-r	1	2	8	16	24	43	54	65
6	62	–	LDC-r	1	2	5	10	15	22	26	30
7	78	–	C-price 15¢; LDC-r	1	2	5	10	14	20	24	28
8A	89	–	H.C.Kiefer on bottom right-fc; LDC-r	1	2	4	9	13	18	22	26
8B	89	–	Name omitted; LDC-r	1	2	5	10	15	24	30	35
9	118	–	LDC-r	1	2	4	8	12	17	21	24
10	140	–	New-c; PC-r	1	3	6	12	18	28	34	40
11	146	–	PC-r	1	3	4	9	13	18	22	26
12	158	–	New-c&a; PC-r; Evans/Crandall-a	2	4	5	10	15	22	26	30
13	165	–	PC-r	2	4	2	4	6	9	11	14
14	167	9/63	PC-r	2	4	2	4	6	9	11	14
15	167	10/64	PC-r	2	4	2	4	6	9	11	14
16	167	4/66	PC-r	2	4	2	4	6	8	10	12
17	166	R/1968	New price 25¢; PC-r	2	4	2	4	6	8	10	12
18	169	Sp/70	Stiff-c; PC-r	2	4	2	4	6	8	10	12

19. Huckleberry Finn

Ed	HRN	Date	Details	A	C	GD 2.0	VG 4.0	FN 6.0	VF 8.0	VF/NM 9.0	NM- 9.2
1A	18	4/44	Orig.; Gilberton ed.; 60 pgs.	1	1	50	100	150	300	450	600
1B	18	4/44	Orig.; Island Pub.; 60 pgs.	1	1	55	110	165	330	495	660
2	18	–	Nassau Bulletin ed.; fc-price 15¢-Canada; no coming-next ad; CC-r	1	1	25	50	75	144	198	255
3	22	–	Queens City Times ed.; CC-r	1	1	20	40	60	112	156	200
4	28	–	CC-r	1	1	14	28	42	79	107	135
5	60	–	Pgs. reduced to 48; LDC-r	1	1	6	12	18	31	38	45
6	62	–	LDC-r	1	1	5	10	15	23	28	32
7	78	–	LDC-r	1	1	4	9	13	18	22	26
8	89	–	LDC-r	1	1	4	8	12	17	21	24
9	117	–	LDC-r	1	1	4	7	10	14	17	20
10	131	–	New-c&a; PC-r	2	2	5	10	14	20	24	28
11	140	–	PC-r	2	2	2	4	6	9	11	14
12	150	–	PC-r	2	2	2	4	6	9	11	14
13	158	–	PC-r	2	2	2	4	6	9	11	14
14	165	–	PC-r (scarce)	2	2	3	6	9	16	20	24
15	167	–	PC-r	2	2	2	4	6	8	10	12
16	167	6/64	PC-r	2	2	2	4	6	8	10	12
17	167	6/65	PC-r	2	2	2	4	6	8	10	12
18	167	10/65	PC-r	2	2	2	4	6	8	10	12
19	166	9/67	PC-r	2	2	2	4	6	8	10	12
20	166	Win/69	C-price 25¢; PC-r; stiff-c	2	2	2	4	6	8	10	12
21	169	Sm/70	PC-r; stiff-c	2	2	2	4	6	9	11	12

20. The Corsican Brothers

Ed	HRN	Date	Details	A	C	GD 2.0	VG 4.0	FN 6.0	VF 8.0	VF/NM 9.0	NM- 9.2
1A	20	6/44	Orig.; Gilberton ed.; bc-ad: 4 Gift Boxes; 60 pgs.	1	1	43	86	129	258	389	520
1B	20	6/44	Orig.; Courier ed.; 60 pgs.	1	1	39	78	117	230	325	420
1C	20	6/44	Orig.; Long Island Ind. ed.; 60 pgs.	1	1	39	78	117	230	325	420
2	22	–	Queens Cty. Times ed.; white logo banner; CC-r	1	1	21	42	63	118	164	210
3	28	–	CC-r	1	1	20	40	60	112	156	200
4	60	–	CI logo; no price; 48 pgs.; LDC-r	1	1	17	34	51	95	130	165
5A	62	–	LDC-r; Classics Ill. logo at top of pgs.	1	1	15	30	45	84	115	145
5B	62	–	w/o logo at top of pg. (scarcer)	1	1	16	32	48	89	122	155
6	78	–	C-price 15¢; LDC-r	1	1	14	28	42	79	107	135
7	97	–	LDC-r	1	1	13	26	39	74	100	125

21. 3 Famous Mysteries ("The Sign of the 4", "The Murders in the Rue Morgue", "The Flayed Hand")

Ed	HRN	Date	Details	A	C	GD 2.0	VG 4.0	FN 6.0	VF 8.0	VF/NM 9.0	NM- 9.2
1A	21	7/44	Orig.; Gilberton ed.; 60 pgs.	1	1	90	180	270	563	844	1125
1B	21	7/44	Orig. Island Pub. Co.; 60 pgs.	1	1	94	188	282	588	882	1175
1C	21	7/44	Original; Courier Ed.; 60 pgs.	1	1	78	156	234	488	732	975
2	22	–	Nassau Bulletin ed.; CC-r	1	1	39	78	117	230	325	420
3	30	–	CC-r	1	1	30	60	90	170	240	310
4	62	–	LDC-r; 8 pgs. deleted; LDC-r	1	1	24	48	72	135	190	245
5	70	–	LDC-r	1	1	22	44	66	124	172	220
6	85	–	C-price 15¢; LDC-r	1	1	19	38	57	106	146	185
7	114	–	New-c; PC-r	1	2	19	38	57	106	146	185

22. The Pathfinder

Ed	HRN	Date	Details	A	C	GD 2.0	VG 4.0	FN 6.0	VF 8.0	VF/NM 9.0	NM- 9.2
1A	22	10/44	Orig.; No printer listed; ownership statement inside fc lists Gilberton & date; 60 pgs.	1	1	43	86	129	258	389	520
1B	22	10/44	Orig.; Island Pub. ed.; 60 pgs.	1	1	40	80	120	240	340	440
1C	22	10/44	Orig.; Queens Cty Times ed. 60 pgs.	1	1	40	80	120	240	340	440
2	30	–	C-price removed; CC-r	1	1	15	30	45	84	115	145
3	60	–	Pgs. reduced to 52; LDC-r	1	1	6	12	18	27	33	38
4	70	–	LDC-r	1	1	5	10	15	22	26	30
5	85	–	C-price 15¢; LDC-r	1	1	4	9	13	18	22	26
6	118	–	LDC-r	1	1	4	8	12	17	21	24
7	132	–	LDC-r	1	1	4	7	10	14	17	20
8	146	–	LDC-r	1	1	4	7	10	14	17	20
9	167	11/63	New-c; PC-r	1	2	4	8	12	24	32	40
10	167	12/65	PC-r	1	2	2	4	6	12	16	20
11	166	8/67	PC-r	1	2	2	4	6	12	16	20

23. Oliver Twist (1st Classic produced by the Iger Shop)

Ed	HRN	Date	Details	A	C	GD 2.0	VG 4.0	FN 6.0	VF 8.0	VF/NM 9.0	NM- 9.2
1	23	7/45	Original; 60 pgs.	1	1	42	84	126	252	376	500
2A	30	–	Printers Union logo on bottom left-fc same as 23(Orig.) (very rare); CC-r	1	1	33	66	99	190	270	350

Classic Comics #25 © GIL

Classic Comics #27 © GIL

Classic Comics #29 © GIL

Ed	HRN	Date	Details	A	C	GD 2.0	VG 4.0	FN 6.0	VF 8.0	VF/NM 9.0	NM- 9.2
2B	30	–	Union logo omitted; CC-r	1	1	14	28	42	79	107	135
3	60	–	Pgs. reduced to 48; LDC-r	1	1	6	12	10	20	36	42
4	62	–	LDC-r	1	1	5	10	15	23	28	32
5	71	–	LDC-r	1	1	5	10	14	20	24	28
6	85	–	C-price 15¢; LDC-r	1	1	4	9	13	18	22	26
7	94	–	LDC-r	1	1	4	7	10	14	17	20
8	118	–	LDC-r	1	1	4	7	10	14	17	20
9	136	–	New-PC, old-a; PC-r	1	2	5	10	14	20	24	28
10	150	–	Old-a; PC-r	1	2	4	7	10	14	17	20
11	164	–	Old-a; PC-r	1	2	4	8	11	16	19	22
12	164	–	New-a; PC-r; Evans/Crandall-a	2	2	4	8	12	24	32	40
13	167	–	PC-r	2	2	2	4	6	12	16	20
14	167	8/64	PC-r	2	2	2	4	6	8	10	12
15	167	12/65	PC-r	2	2	2	4	6	8	10	12
16	166	R/1968	New 25¢; PC-r	2	2	2	4	6	8	10	12
17	169	Win/69	Stiff-c; PC-r	2	2	2	4	6	8	10	12

24. A Connecticut Yankee in King Arthur's Court

Ed	HRN	Date	Details	A	C	GD 2.0	VG 4.0	FN 6.0	VF 8.0	VF/NM 9.0	NM- 9.2
1	–	9/45	Original	1	1	40	80	120	240	340	440
2	30	–	No price circle; CC-r	1	1	14	28	42	79	107	135
3	60	–	8 pgs. deleted; LDC-r	1	1	6	12	18	27	33	38
4	62	–	LDC-r	1	1	5	10	15	23	28	32
5	71	–	LDC-r	1	1	5	10	15	22	26	30
6	87	–	C-price 15¢; LDC-r	1	1	4	9	13	18	22	26
7	121	–	LDC-r	1	1	4	8	12	17	21	24
8	140	–	New-c&a; PC-r	2	2	5	10	15	22	26	30
9	153	–	PC-r	2	2	2	4	6	9	11	14
10	164	–	PC-r	2	2	2	4	6	8	10	12
11	167	–	PC-r	2	2	2	4	6	8	10	12
12	167	7/64	PC-r	2	2	2	4	6	8	10	12
13	167	6/66	PC-r	2	2	2	4	6	8	10	12
14	166	R/1968	C-price 25¢; PC-r	2	2	2	4	6	8	10	12
15	169	Spr/71	PC-r; stiff-c	2	2	2	4	6	8	10	12

25. Two Years Before the Mast

Ed	HRN	Date	Details	A	C	GD 2.0	VG 4.0	FN 6.0	VF 8.0	VF/NM 9.0	NM- 9.2
1	–	10/45	Original; Webb/Heames-a&c	1	1	40	80	120	240	340	440
2	30	–	Price circle blank; CC-r	1	1	14	28	42	79	107	135
3	60	–	8 pgs. deleted; LDC-r	1	1	6	12	18	27	33	38
4	62	–	LDC-r	1	1	5	10	15	23	28	32
5	71	–	LDC-r	1	1	4	9	13	18	22	26
6	85	–	C-price 15¢; LDC-r	1	1	4	8	12	17	21	24
7	114	–	LDC-r	1	1	4	7	10	14	17	20
8	156	–	3 pgs. replaced by fillers; new-c; PC-r	1	2	5	10	15	22	26	30
9	167	12/63	PC-r	1	2	2	4	6	8	10	12
10	167	12/65	PC-r	1	2	2	4	6	8	10	12
11	166	9/67	PC-r	1	2	2	4	6	8	10	12
12	169	Win/69	C-price 25¢; stiff-c PC-r	1	2	2	4	6	8	10	12

26. Frankenstein (2nd horror comic?)

Ed	HRN	Date	Details	A	C	GD 2.0	VG 4.0	FN 6.0	VF 8.0	VF/NM 9.0	NM- 9.2
1	26	12/45	Orig.; Webb/Brewster a&c; 52 pgs.	1	1	96	192	288	600	900	1200
2A	30	–	Price circle blank; no indicia; CC-r	1	1	31	62	93	175	248	320
2B	30	–	With indicia; scarce; CC-r	1	1	36	72	108	204	290	375
3	60	–	LDC-r	1	1	17	34	51	95	130	165
4	62	–	LDC-r	1	1	15	30	45	84	115	145
5	71	–	LDC-r	1	1	7	14	21	35	43	50
6A	82	–	C-price 15¢; soft-c LDC-r	1	1	6	12	18	28	34	40
6B	82	–	Stiff-c; LDC-r	1	1	7	14	21	35	43	50
7	117	–	LDC-r	1	1	4	8	12	18	22	25
8	146	–	New Saunders-c; PC-r	1	2	5	10	15	24	30	35
9	152	–	Scarce; PC-r	1	2	7	14	21	37	46	55
10	153	–	PC-r	1	2	2	4	6	9	11	14
11	160	–	PC-r	1	2	2	4	6	9	11	14
12	165	–	PC-r	1	2	2	4	6	8	10	12
13	167	–	PC-r	1	2	2	4	6	8	10	12
14	167	6/64	PC-r	1	2	2	4	6	8	10	12
15	167	6/65	PC-r	1	2	2	4	6	8	10	12
16	167	10/65	PC-r	1	2	2	4	6	8	10	12
17	166	9/67	PC-r	1	2	2	4	6	8	10	12
18	169	Fall/69	C-price 25¢; stiff-c PC-r	1	2	2	4	6	8	10	12
19	169	Spr/71	PC-r; stiff-c	1	2	2	4	6	8	10	12

27. The Adventures of Marco Polo

Ed	HRN	Date	Details	A	C	GD 2.0	VG 4.0	FN 6.0	VF 8.0	VF/NM 9.0	NM- 9.2
1	–	4/46	Original	1	1	40	80	120	240	340	440
2	30	–	Last 'Comics' reprint; CC-r	1	1	14	28	42	79	107	135
3	70	–	8 pgs. deleted; no c-price; LDC-r	1	1	5	10	15	24	30	35
4	87	–	C-price 15¢; LDC-r	1	1	4	9	13	18	22	26
5	117	–	LDC-r	1	1	4	7	10	14	17	20
6	154	–	New-c; PC-r	1	2	5	10	14	20	24	28
7	165	–	PC-r	1	2	2	4	6	8	10	12
8	167	4/64	PC-r	1	2	2	4	6	8	10	12
9	167	6/66	PC-r	1	2	2	4	6	8	10	12
10	169	Spr/69	New price 25¢; stiff-c; PC-r	1	2	2	4	6	8	10	12

28. Michael Strogoff

Ed	HRN	Date	Details	A	C	GD 2.0	VG 4.0	FN 6.0	VF 8.0	VF/NM 9.0	NM- 9.2
1	–	6/46	Original	1	1	40	80	120	240	340	440
2	51	–	8 pgs. cut; LDC-r	1	1	14	28	42	79	107	135
3	115	–	New-c; PC-r	1	2	6	12	18	27	33	38
4	155	–	PC-r	1	2	4	7	10	14	17	20
5	167	11/63	PC-r	1	2	2	4	6	10	13	16
6	167	7/66	PC-r	1	2	2	4	6	10	13	16
7	169	Sm/69	C-price 25¢; stiff-c PC-r	1	3	3	6	9	16	20	24

29. The Prince and the Pauper

Ed	HRN	Date	Details	A	C	GD 2.0	VG 4.0	FN 6.0	VF 8.0	VF/NM 9.0	NM- 9.2
1	–	7/46	Orig.; "Horror"-c	1	1	55	110	165	337	506	675
2	60	–	8 pgs. cut; new-c by Kiefer; LDC-r	1	2	8	16	24	43	54	65
3	62	–	LDC-r	1	2	5	10	15	24	30	35
4	71	–	LDC-r	1	2	4	9	13	18	22	26
5	93	–	LDC-r	1	2	4	8	12	17	21	24
6	114	–	LDC-r	1	2	4	7	10	14	17	20
7	128	–	New-c; PC-r	1	3	5	10	14	20	24	28
8	138	–	PC-r	1	3	2	4	6	9	11	14
9	150	–	PC-r	1	3	2	4	6	9	11	14
10	164	–	PC-r	1	3	2	4	6	8	10	12
11	167	–	PC-r	1	3	2	4	6	8	10	12
12	167	7/64	PC-r	1	3	2	4	6	8	10	12
13	167	11/65	PC-r	1	3	2	4	6	8	10	12
14	166	R/68	C-price 25¢; PC-r	1	3	2	4	6	8	10	12
15	169	Sm/70	PC-r; stiff-c	1	3	2	4	6	8	10	12

30. The Moonstone

Ed	HRN	Date	Details	A	C	GD 2.0	VG 4.0	FN 6.0	VF 8.0	VF/NM 9.0	NM- 9.2
1	–	9/46	Original; Rico-c/a	1	1	40	80	120	240	340	440
2	60	–	LDC-r; 8pgs. cut	1	1	8	16	24	40	50	60
3	70	–	LDC-r	1	1	7	14	21	37	46	55
4	155	–	New L.B. Cole-c; PC-r	1	2	4	8	12	29	40	50
5	165	–	PC-r; L.B. Cole-c	1	2	3	6	9	18	24	30
6	167	1/64	PC-r; L.B. Cole-c	1	2	2	4	6	11	14	18
7	167	9/65	PC-r; L.B. Cole-c	1	2	2	4	6	10	13	16
8	166	R/1968	C-price 25¢; PC-r	1	2	2	4	6	9	11	14

31. The Black Arrow

Ed	HRN	Date	Details	A	C	GD 2.0	VG 4.0	FN 6.0	VF 8.0	VF/NM 9.0	NM- 9.2
1	30	10/46	Original	1	1	34	68	102	193	274	355
2	51	–	CI logo; LDC-r 8pgs. deleted	1	1	6	12	18	29	36	42

Classic Comics #33 © GIL

Classics Illustrated #35 © GIL

Classics Illustrated #40 © GIL

Ed	HRN	Date	Details	A	C	GD 2.0	VG 4.0	FN 6.0	VF 8.0	VF/NM 9.0	NM- 9.2
3	64	–	LDC-r	1	1	4	9	13	18	22	26
4	87	–	C-price 15¢; LDC-r	1	1	4	8	12	17	21	24
5	108	–	LDC-r	1	1	4	7	10	14	17	20
6	125	–	LDC-r	1	1	4	7	10	14	17	20
7	131	–	New-c; PC-r	1	2	5	10	14	20	24	28
8	140	–	PC-r	1	2	2	4	6	9	11	14
9	148	–	PC-r	1	2	2	4	6	9	11	14
10	161	–	PC-r	1	2	2	4	6	8	10	12
11	167	–	PC-r	1	2	2	4	6	8	10	12
12	167	7/64	PC-r	1	2	2	4	6	8	10	12
13	167	11/65	PC-r	1	2	2	4	6	8	10	12
14	166	R/1968	C-price 25¢; PC-r	1	2	2	4	6	8	10	12

32. Lorna Doone

Ed	HRN	Date	Details	A	C	GD 2.0	VG 4.0	FN 6.0	VF 8.0	VF/NM 9.0	NM- 9.2
1	–	12/46	Original; Matt Baker c&a	1	1	40	80	120	240	340	440
2	53/64	–	8 pgs. deleted; LDC-r	1	1	8	16	24	43	54	65
3	85	1951	C-price 15¢; LDC-r; Baker c&a	1	1	6	12	18	31	38	45
4	118	–	LDC-r	1	1	4	9	13	18	22	26
5	138	–	New-c; old-c becomes new title pg.; PC-r	1	2	5	10	15	23	28	32
6	150	–	PC-r	1	2	2	4	6	8	10	12
7	165	–	PC-r	1	2	2	4	6	8	10	12
8	167	1/64	PC-r	1	2	2	4	6	9	11	14
9	167	11/65	PC-r	1	2	2	4	6	9	11	14
10	166	R/1968	New-c; PC-r	1	3	3	6	9	18	24	30

33. The Adventures of Sherlock Holmes

Ed	HRN	Date	Details	A	C	GD 2.0	VG 4.0	FN 6.0	VF 8.0	VF/NM 9.0	NM- 9.2
1	33	1/47	Original; Kiefer-c; contains Study in Scarlet & Hound of the Baskervilles; 68 pgs.	1	1	118	236	354	738	1107	1475
2	53	–	"A Study in Scarlet" (17 pgs.) deleted; LDC-r	1	1	44	88	132	264	395	525
3	71	–	LDC-r	1	1	37	74	111	212	301	390
4A	89	–	C-price 15¢; LDC-r	1	1	30	60	90	170	240	310
4B	89	–	Kiefer's name omitted from-c	1	1	31	62	93	175	248	320

34. Mysterious Island (Last "Classic Comic")

Ed	HRN	Date	Details	A	C	GD 2.0	VG 4.0	FN 6.0	VF 8.0	VF/NM 9.0	NM- 9.2
1	35	2/47	Original; Webb/Heames-c/a	1	1	40	80	120	240	340	440
2	60	–	8 pgs. deleted; LDC-r	1	1	6	12	18	31	38	45
3	62	–	LDC-r	1	1	5	10	15	23	28	32
4	71	–	LDC-r	1	1	6	12	18	31	38	45
5	78	–	C-price 15¢ in circle; LDC-r	1	1	5	10	14	20	24	28
6	92	–	LDC-r	1	1	4	9	13	18	22	26
7	117	–	LDC-r	1	1	4	7	10	14	17	20
8	140	–	New-c; PC-r	1	2	5	10	14	20	24	28
9	156	–	PC-r	1	2	2	4	6	9	11	14
10	167	10/63	PC-r	1	2	2	4	6	8	10	12
11	167	5/64	PC-r	1	2	2	4	6	8	10	12
12	167	6/66	PC-r	1	2	2	4	6	8	10	12
13	166	R/1968	C-price 25¢; PC-r	1	2	2	4	6	8	10	12

35. Last Days of Pompeii (First "Classics Illustrated")

Ed	HRN	Date	Details	A	C	GD 2.0	VG 4.0	FN 6.0	VF 8.0	VF/NM 9.0	NM- 9.2
1	35	3/47	Original; LDC; Kiefer-c/a	1	1	40	80	120	240	340	440
2	161	–	New c&a; 15¢; PC-r; Kirby/Ayers-a	2	2	4	8	12	29	40	50
3	167	1/64	PC-r	2	2	3	6	9	16	20	24
4	167	7/66	PC-r	2	2	3	6	9	16	20	24
5	169	Spr/70	New price 25¢; stiff-c; PC-r	2	2	3	6	9	16	20	24

36. Typee

Ed	HRN	Date	Details	A	C	GD 2.0	VG 4.0	FN 6.0	VF 8.0	VF/NM 9.0	NM- 9.2
1	36	4/47	Original	1	1	24	48	72	135	190	245
2	64	–	No c-price; 8 pg. ed.; LDC-r	1	1	6	12	18	31	38	45
3	155	–	New-c; PC-r	1	2	5	10	14	20	24	28
4	167	9/63	PC-r	1	2	2	4	6	10	12	15
5	167	7/65	PC-r	1	2	2	4	6	10	12	15
6	169	Sm/69	C-price 25¢; stiff-c PC-r	1	2	2	4	6	10	12	15

37. The Pioneers

Ed	HRN	Date	Details	A	C	GD 2.0	VG 4.0	FN 6.0	VF 8.0	VF/NM 9.0	NM- 9.2
1	37	5/47	Original; Palais-c/a	1	1	22	44	66	124	172	220
2A	62	–	8 pgs. cut; LDC-r; price circle blank	1	1	5	10	15	23	28	32
2B	62	–	10¢; LDC-r;	1	1	26	52	78	147	206	265
3	70	–	LDC-r	1	1	4	8	12	17	21	24
4	92	–	15¢; LDC-r	1	1	4	8	11	16	19	22
5	118	–	LDC-r	1	1	4	7	10	14	17	20
6	131	–	LDC-r	1	1	4	7	10	14	17	20
7	132	–	LDC-r	1	1	4	7	10	14	17	20
8	153	–	LDC-r	1	1	4	7	10	14	17	20
9	167	5/64	LDC-r	1	1	2	4	6	9	11	14
10	167	6/66	LDC-r	1	1	2	4	6	9	11	14
11	166	R/1968	New-c; 25¢; PC-r	1	2	3	6	9	18	24	30

38. Adventures of Cellini

Ed	HRN	Date	Details	A	C	GD 2.0	VG 4.0	FN 6.0	VF 8.0	VF/NM 9.0	NM- 9.2
1	–	6/47	Original; Froehlich c/a	1	1	30	60	90	170	240	310
2	164	–	New-c&a; PC-r	2	2	3	6	9	18	24	30
3	167	12/63	PC-r	2	2	2	4	6	10	12	15
4	167	7/66	PC-r	2	2	2	4	6	10	12	15
5	169	Spr/70	Stiff-c; new price 25¢; PC-r	2	2	2	4	6	10	13	16

39. Jane Eyre

Ed	HRN	Date	Details	A	C	GD 2.0	VG 4.0	FN 6.0	VF 8.0	VF/NM 9.0	NM- 9.2
1	–	7/47	Original	1	1	29	58	87	164	232	300
2	60	–	No c-price; 8 pgs. cut; LDC-r	1	1	6	12	18	28	34	40
3	62	–	LDC-r	1	1	5	10	15	24	30	35
4	71	–	LDC-r; c-price 10¢	1	1	5	10	15	22	26	30
5	92	–	C-price 15¢; LDC-r	1	1	4	9	13	18	22	26
6	118	–	LDC-r	1	1	4	8	12	17	21	24
7	142	–	New-c; old-a; PC-r	1	2	5	10	15	23	28	32
8	154	–	Old-a; PC-r	1	2	4	8	12	17	21	24
9	165	–	New-a; PC-r	2	2	3	6	9	18	23	28
10	167	12/63	PC-r	2	2	3	6	9	16	20	24
11	167	4/65	PC-r	2	2	2	4	6	14	18	22
12	167	8/66	PC-r	2	2	2	4	6	14	18	22
13	166	R/1968	New-c; PC-r	2	3	6	12	18	38	52	65

40. Mysteries ("The Pit and the Pendulum", "The Advs. of Hans Pfall" & "The Fall of the House of Usher")

Ed	HRN	Date	Details	A	C	GD 2.0	VG 4.0	FN 6.0	VF 8.0	VF/NM 9.0	NM- 9.2
1	40	8/47	Original; Kiefer-c/a, Froehlich, Griffiths-a	1	1	60	120	180	375	563	750
2	62	–	LDC-r; 8pgs. cut	1	1	26	52	78	147	206	265
3	75	–	LDC-r	1	1	22	44	66	124	172	220
4	92	–	C-price 15¢; LDC-r	1	1	19	38	57	106	146	185

41. Twenty Years After

Ed	HRN	Date	Details	A	C	GD 2.0	VG 4.0	FN 6.0	VF 8.0	VF/NM 9.0	NM- 9.2
1	–	9/47	Original; 'horror'-c	1	1	39	78	117	230	325	420
2	62	–	New-c; no c-price 8 pgs. cut; LDC-r; Kiefer-c	1	2	6	12	18	33	41	48
3	78	–	C-price 15¢; LDC-r	1	2	5	10	15	23	28	32
4	156	–	New-c; PC-r	1	3	5	10	14	20	24	28
5	167	12/63	PC-r	1	3	2	4	6	8	10	12
6	167	11/66	PC-r	1	3	2	4	6	8	10	12
7	169	Spr/70	New price 25¢; stiff-c; PC-r	1	3	2	4	6	8	10	12

42. Swiss Family Robinson

Ed	HRN	Date	Details	A	C	GD 2.0	VG 4.0	FN 6.0	VF 8.0	VF/NM 9.0	NM- 9.2
1	42	10/47	Orig.; Kiefer-c&a;	1	1	22	44	66	124	172	220

Classics Illustrated #45 © GIL

Classics Illustrated #47 © GIL

Classics Illustrated #48 © GIL

Ed	HRN	Date	Details	A	C	GD 2.0	VG 4.0	FN 6.0	VF 8.0	VF/NM 9.0	NM- 9.2
2A	62	–	8 pgs. cut; outside bc: Gift Box ad; LDC-r	1	1	6	12	18	29	36	42
2B	62	–	8 pgs. cut; outside-bc: Reorder list; scarce; LDC-r	1	1	10	20	30	56	73	90
3	75	–	LDC-r	1	1	5	10	14	20	24	28
4	93	–	LDC-r	1	1	4	9	13	18	22	26
5	117	–	LDC-r	1	1	3	6	9	16	20	24
6	131	–	New-c; old-a; PC-r	1	2	3	6	9	17	21	26
7	137	–	Old-a; PC-r	1	2	2	4	6	11	14	18
8	141	–	Old-a; PC-r	1	2	2	4	6	11	14	18
9	152	–	New-a; PC-r	2	2	3	6	9	17	21	26
10	158	–	PC-r	2	2	2	4	6	8	10	12
11	165	–	PC-r	2	2	3	6	9	17	21	26
12	167	12/63	PC-r	2	2	2	4	6	9	11	14
13	167	4/65	PC-r	2	2	2	4	6	8	10	12
14	167	5/66	PC-r	2	2	2	4	6	8	10	12
15	166	11/67	PC-r	2	2	2	4	6	8	10	12
16	169	Spr/69	PC-r; stiff-c	2	2	2	4	6	8	10	12

43. Great Expectations (Used in **SOTI**, pg. 311)

Ed	HRN	Date	Details	A	C	GD 2.0	VG 4.0	FN 6.0	VF 8.0	VF/NM 9.0	NM- 9.2
1	42	11/47	Original; Kiefer-a/c	1	1	88	176	264	550	825	1100
2	62	–	No c-price; 8 pgs. cut; LDC-r	1	1	58	116	174	363	542	720

44. Mysteries of Paris (Used in **SOTI**, pg. 323)

Ed	HRN	Date	Details	A	C	GD 2.0	VG 4.0	FN 6.0	VF 8.0	VF/NM 9.0	NM- 9.2
1A	44	12/47	Original; 56 pgs.; Kiefer-c/a	1	1	64	128	192	400	600	800
1B	44	12/47	Orig.; printed on white/heavier paper; (rare)	1	1	74	148	222	463	692	920
2A	62	–	8 pgs. cut; outside-bc: Gift Box ad; LDC-r	1	1	30	60	90	170	240	310
2B	62	–	8 pgs. cut; outside-bc: reorder list; LDC-r	1	1	30	60	90	170	240	310
3	78	–	C-price 15¢; LDC-r	1	1	25	50	75	144	198	255

45. Tom Brown's School Days

Ed	HRN	Date	Details	A	C	GD 2.0	VG 4.0	FN 6.0	VF 8.0	VF/NM 9.0	NM- 9.2
1	44	1/48	Original; 1st 48pg. issue	1	1	16	32	48	89	122	155
2	64	–	No c-price; LDC-r	1	1	6	12	18	31	38	45
3	161	–	New-c&a; PC-r	2	2	3	6	9	17	21	26
4	167	2/64	PC-r	2	2	2	4	6	9	11	14
5	167	8/66	PC-r	2	2	2	4	6	9	11	14
6	166	R/1968	C-price 25¢; PC-r	2	2	2	4	6	9	11	14

46. Kidnapped

Ed	HRN	Date	Details	A	C	GD 2.0	VG 4.0	FN 6.0	VF 8.0	VF/NM 9.0	NM- 9.2
1	47	4/48	Original; Webb-c/a	1	1	16	32	48	89	122	155
2A	62	–	Price circle blank; LDC-r	1	1	5	10	15	24	30	35
2B	62	–	C-price 10¢; rare; LDC-r	1	1	30	60	90	170	240	310
3	78	–	C-price 15¢; LDC-r	1	1	5	10	14	20	24	28
4	87	–	LDC-r	1	1	4	9	13	18	22	26
5	118	–	LDC-r	1	1	4	7	10	14	17	20
6	131	–	New-c; PC-r	1	2	4	9	13	18	22	26
7	140	–	PC-r	1	2	2	4	6	9	11	14
8	150	–	PC-r	1	2	2	4	6	9	11	14
9	164	–	Reduced pg.width; PC-r	1	2	2	4	6	8	10	12
10	167	–	PC-r	1	2	2	4	6	8	10	12
11	167	3/64	PC-r	1	2	2	4	6	8	10	12
12	167	6/65	PC-r	1	2	2	4	6	8	10	12
13	167	12/65	PC-r	1	2	2	4	6	8	10	12
14	166	9/67	PC-r	1	2	2	4	6	8	10	12
15	166	Win/69	New price 25¢; PC-r; stiff-c	1	2	2	4	6	8	10	12
16	169	Sm/70	PC-r; stiff-c	1	2	2	4	6	8	10	12

47. Twenty Thousand Leagues Under the Sea

Ed	HRN	Date	Details	A	C	GD 2.0	VG 4.0	FN 6.0	VF 8.0	VF/NM 9.0	NM- 9.2
1	47	5/48	Orig.; Kiefer-a&c;	1	1	17	34	51	95	130	165
2	64	–	No c-price; LDC-r	1	1	5	10	15	24	30	35
3	78	–	C price 15¢; LDC-r	1	1	4	9	13	18	22	26
4	94	–	LDC-r	1	1	4	8	12	17	21	24
5	118	–	LDC-r	1	1	4	7	10	14	17	20
6	128	–	New-c; PC-r	1	2	5	10	14	20	24	28
7	133	–	PC-r	1	2	2	4	6	10	13	16
8	140	–	PC-r	1	2	2	4	6	9	11	14
9	148	–	PC-r	1	2	2	4	6	9	11	14
10	156	–	PC-r	1	2	2	4	6	9	11	14
11	165	–	PC-r	1	2	2	4	6	9	11	14
12	167	–	PC-r	1	2	2	4	6	9	11	14
13	167	3/64	PC-r	1	2	2	4	6	9	11	14
14	167	8/65	PC-r	1	2	2	4	6	9	11	14
15	167	10/66	PC-r	1	2	2	4	6	9	11	14
16	166	R/1968	C-price 25¢; new-c PC-r	1	3	2	4	6	11	14	18
17	169	Spr/70	Stiff-c; PC-r	1	3	2	4	6	12	16	20

48. David Copperfield

Ed	HRN	Date	Details	A	C	GD 2.0	VG 4.0	FN 6.0	VF 8.0	VF/NM 9.0	NM- 9.2
1	47	6/48	Original; Kiefer-c/a	1	1	16	32	48	89	122	155
2	64	–	Price circle replaced by motif of boy reading; LDC-r	1	1	5	10	15	24	30	35
3	87	–	C-price 15¢; LDC-r	1	1	4	8	12	17	21	24
4	121	–	New-c; PC-r	1	2	4	8	12	17	21	24
5	130	–	PC-r	1	2	2	4	6	9	11	14
6	140	–	PC-r	1	2	2	4	6	9	11	14
7	148	–	PC-r	1	2	2	4	6	9	11	14
8	156	–	PC-r	1	2	2	4	6	9	11	14
9	167	–	PC-r	1	2	2	4	6	8	10	12
10	167	4/64	PC-r	1	2	2	4	6	8	10	12
11	167	6/65	PC-r	1	2	2	4	6	8	10	12
12	166	5/67	PC-r	1	2	2	4	6	8	10	12
13	166	R/67	PC-r; C-price 25¢	1	2	2	4	6	10	13	16
14	166	Spr/69	C-price 25¢; stiff-c PC-r	1	2	2	4	6	8	10	12
15	169	Win/69	Stiff-c; PC-r	1	2	2	4	6	8	10	12

49. Alice in Wonderland

Ed	HRN	Date	Details	A	C	GD 2.0	VG 4.0	FN 6.0	VF 8.0	VF/NM 9.0	NM- 9.2
1	47	7/48	Original; 1st Blum a & c	1	1	20	40	60	112	156	200
2	64	–	No c-price; LDC-r	1	1	7	14	21	35	43	50
3A	85	–	C-price 15¢; soft-c LDC-r	1	1	6	12	18	28	34	40
3B	85	–	Stiff-c; LDC-r	1	1	6	12	18	31	38	45
4	155	–	New PC, similar to orig.; PC-r	1	2	4	8	12	25	33	42
5	165	–	PC-r	1	2	3	6	9	18	23	28
6	167	3/64	PC-r	1	2	3	6	9	16	20	24
7	167	6/66	PC-r	1	2	3	6	9	16	20	24
8A	166	Fall/68	New-c; soft-c; 25¢ c-price; PC-r	1	3	4	8	12	25	33	42
8B	166	Fall/68	New-c; stiff-c; 25¢ c-price; PC-r	1	3	7	14	21	51	71	90

50. Adventures of Tom Sawyer (Used in **SOTI**, pg. 37)

Ed	HRN	Date	Details	A	C	GD 2.0	VG 4.0	FN 6.0	VF 8.0	VF/NM 9.0	NM- 9.2
1A	51	8/48	Orig.; Aldo Rubano a&c	1	1	16	32	48	89	122	155
1B	51	9/48	Orig.; Rubano c&a	1	1	16	32	48	89	122	155
1C	51	9/48	Orig.; outside-bc: blue & yellow only; rare	1	1	22	44	66	124	172	220
2	64	–	No c-price; LDC-r	1	1	5	10	15	22	26	30
3	78	–	C-price 15¢; LDC-r	1	1	4	8	12	17	21	24
4	94	–	LDC-r	1	1	4	7	10	14	17	20
5	117	–	LDC-r	1	1	2	4	6	11	14	18
6	132	–	LDC-r	1	1	2	4	6	11	14	18
7	140	–	New-c; PC-r	1	2	3	6	9	18	23	28
8	150	–	PC-r	1	2	2	4	6	9	11	14
9	164	–	New-a; PC-r	2	2	3	6	9	18	23	28
10	167	–	PC-r	2	2	2	4	6	9	11	14
11	167	1/65	PC-r	2	2	2	4	6	8	10	12

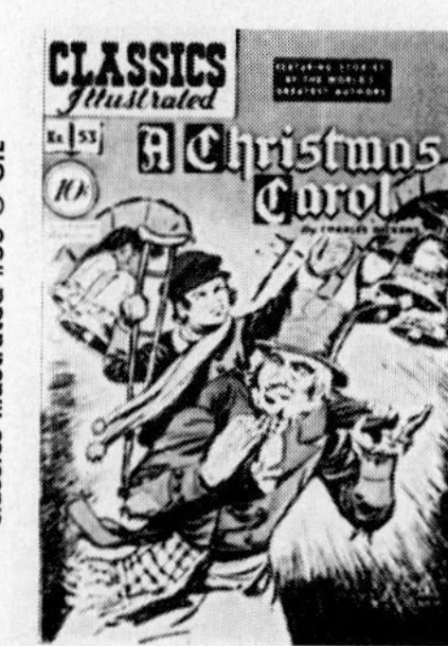

Classics Illustrated #53 © GIL

Classics Illustrated #57 © GIL

Classics Illustrated #58 © GIL

Ed	HRN	Date	Details	A	C	GD 2.0	VG 4.0	FN 6.0	VF 8.0	VF/NM 9.0	NM- 9.2
12	167	5/66	PC-r	2	2	2	4	6	8	10	12
13	166	12/67	PC-r	2	2	2	4	6	8	10	12
14	169	Fall/69	C-price 25¢; stiff-c; PC-r	2	2	2	4	6	8	10	12
15	169	Win/71	PC-r	2	2	2	4	6	8	10	12

51. The Spy

Ed	HRN	Date	Details	A	C	GD 2.0	VG 4.0	FN 6.0	VF 8.0	VF/NM 9.0	NM- 9.2
1A	51	9/48	Original; inside-bc illo: Christmas Carol	1	1	15	30	45	84	115	145
1B	51	9/48	Original; inside-bc illo: Man in Iron Mask	1	1	15	30	45	84	115	145
1C	51	8/48	Original; outside-bc: full color	1	1	15	30	45	84	115	145
1D	51	8/48	Original; outside-bc: blue & yellow only; scarce	1	1	17	34	51	95	130	165
2	89	–	C-price 15¢; LDC-r	1	1	5	10	14	20	24	28
3	121	–	LDC-r	1	1	4	8	12	17	21	24
4	139	–	New-c; PC-r	1	2	3	6	9	18	23	28
5	156	–	PC-r	1	2	2	4	6	9	11	14
6	167	11/63	PC-r	1	2	2	4	6	8	10	12
7	167	7/66	PC-r	1	2	2	4	6	8	10	12
8A	166	Win/69	C-price 25¢; soft-c; scarce; PC-r	1	2	3	6	9	17	21	26
8B	166	Win/69	C-price 25¢; stiff-c; PC-r	1	2	2	4	6	8	10	12

52. The House of the Seven Gables

Ed	HRN	Date	Details	A	C	GD 2.0	VG 4.0	FN 6.0	VF 8.0	VF/NM 9.0	NM- 9.2
1	53	10/48	Orig.; Griffiths a&c	1	1	15	30	45	84	115	145
2	89	–	C-price 15¢; LDC-r	1	1	5	10	14	20	24	28
3	121	–	LDC-r	1	1	4	8	12	17	21	24
4	142	–	New-c&a; PC-r; Woodbridge-a	2	2	5	10	15	22	26	30
5	156	–	PC-r	2	2	2	4	6	9	11	14
6	165	–	PC-r	2	2	2	4	6	8	10	12
7	167	5/64	PC-r	2	2	2	4	6	9	11	14
8	167	3/66	PC-r	2	2	2	4	6	8	10	12
9	166	R/1968	C-price 25¢; PC-r	2	2	2	4	6	8	10	12
10	169	Spr/70	Stiff-c; PC-r	2	2	2	4	6	8	10	12

53. A Christmas Carol

Ed	HRN	Date	Details	A	C	GD 2.0	VG 4.0	FN 6.0	VF 8.0	VF/NM 9.0	NM- 9.2
1	53	11/48	Original & only ed; Kiefer-c/a	1	1	20	40	60	112	156	200

54. Man in the Iron Mask

Ed	HRN	Date	Details	A	C	GD 2.0	VG 4.0	FN 6.0	VF 8.0	VF/NM 9.0	NM- 9.2
1	55	12/48	Original; Froehlich-a, Kiefer-c	1	1	15	30	45	84	115	145
2	93	–	C-price 15¢; LDC-r	1	1	5	10	15	23	28	32
3A	111	–	(O) logo lettering; scarce; LDC-r	1	1	6	12	18	31	38	45
3B	111	–	New logo as PC; LDC-r	1	1	5	10	15	22	26	30
4	142	–	New-c&a; PC-r	2	2	5	10	15	22	26	30
5	154	–	PC-r	2	2	2	4	6	9	11	14
6	165	–	PC-r	2	2	2	4	6	8	10	12
7	167	5/64	PC-r	2	2	2	4	6	8	10	12
8	167	4/66	PC-r	2	2	2	4	6	8	10	12
9A	166	Win/69	C-price 25¢; soft-c PC-r	2	2	3	6	9	17	21	26
9B	166	Win/69	Stiff-c	2	2	2	4	6	8	10	12

55. Silas Marner (Used in **SOTI**, pgs. 311, 312)

Ed	HRN	Date	Details	A	C	GD 2.0	VG 4.0	FN 6.0	VF 8.0	VF/NM 9.0	NM- 9.2
1	55	1/49	Original-Kiefer-c	1	1	15	30	45	84	115	145
2	75	–	Price circle blank; 'Coming Next' ad; LDC-r	1	1	5	10	15	24	30	35
3	97	–	LDC-r	1	1	3	6	9	16	20	24
4	121	–	New-c; PC-r	1	2	3	6	9	18	23	28
5	130	–	PC-r	1	2	2	4	6	9	11	14
6	140	–	PC-r	1	2	2	4	6	9	11	14
7	154	–	PC-r	1	2	2	4	6	9	11	14
8	165	–	PC-r	1	2	2	4	6	8	10	12
9	167	2/64	PC-r	1	2	2	4	6	8	10	12
10	167	6/65	PC-r	1	2	2	4	6	8	10	12
11	166	5/67	PC-r	1	2	2	4	6	8	10	12
12A	166	Win/69	C-price 25¢; soft-c PC-r	1	2	3	6	9	18	21	26
12B	166	Win/69	C-price 25¢; stiff-c PC-r	1	2	2	4	6	8	10	12

56. The Toilers of the Sea

Ed	HRN	Date	Details	A	C	GD 2.0	VG 4.0	FN 6.0	VF 8.0	VF/NM 9.0	NM- 9.2
1	55	2/49	Original; A.M. Froehlich-c/a	1	1	24	48	72	135	190	245
2	165	–	New-c&a; PC-r; Angelo Torres-a	2	2	6	12	18	33	41	48
3	167	3/64	PC-r	2	2	3	6	9	17	21	26
4	167	10/66	PC-r	2	2	3	6	9	17	21	26

57. The Song of Hiawatha

Ed	HRN	Date	Details	A	C	GD 2.0	VG 4.0	FN 6.0	VF 8.0	VF/NM 9.0	NM- 9.2
1	55	3/49	Original; Alex Blum-c/a	1	1	14	28	42	79	107	135
2	75	–	No c-price w/15¢ sticker; 'Coming Next' ad; LDC-r	1	1	5	10	15	24	30	35
3	94	–	C-price 15¢; LDC-r	1	1	5	10	14	20	24	28
4	118	–	LDC-r	1	1	3	6	9	16	20	24
5	134	–	New-c; PC-r	1	2	3	6	9	18	23	28
6	139	–	PC-r	1	2	2	4	6	9	11	14
7	154	–	PC-r	1	2	2	4	6	9	11	14
8	167	–	Has orig.date; PC-r	1	2	2	4	6	8	10	12
9	167	9/64	PC-r	1	2	2	4	6	8	10	12
10	167	10/65	PC-r	1	2	2	4	6	8	10	12
11	166	F/1968	C-price 25¢; PC-r	1	2	2	4	6	8	10	12

58. The Prairie

Ed	HRN	Date	Details	A	C	GD 2.0	VG 4.0	FN 6.0	VF 8.0	VF/NM 9.0	NM- 9.2
1	60	4/49	Original; Palais c/a	1	1	14	28	42	79	107	135
2A	62	–	No c-price; no coming-next ad; LDC-r	1	1	8	16	24	43	55	65
2B	62		10¢ (rare)	1	1	17	34	51	95	130	165
3	78	–	C-price 15¢ in dbl. circle; LDC-r	1	1	5	10	14	20	24	28
4	114	–	LDC-r	1	1	4	8	12	17	21	24
5	131	–	LDC-r	1	1	4	7	10	14	17	20
6	132	–	LDC-r	1	1	4	7	10	14	17	20
7	146	–	New-c; PC-r	1	2	5	10	14	20	24	28
8	155	–	PC-r	1	2	2	4	6	9	11	14
9	167	5/64	PC-r	1	2	2	4	6	8	10	12
10	167	4/66	PC-r	1	2	2	4	6	8	10	12
11	169	Sm/69	New price 25¢; stiff-c; PC-r	1	2	2	4	6	8	10	12

59. Wuthering Heights

Ed	HRN	Date	Details	A	C	GD 2.0	VG 4.0	FN 6.0	VF 8.0	VF/NM 9.0	NM- 9.2
1	60	5/49	Original; Kiefer-c/a	1	1	15	30	45	84	115	145
2	85	–	C-price 15¢; LDC-r	1	1	6	12	18	28	34	40
3	156	–	New-c; PC-r	1	2	5	10	15	22	26	30
4	167	1/64	PC-r	1	2	2	4	6	9	11	14
5	167	10/66	PC-r	1	2	2	4	6	9	11	14
6	169	Sm/69	C-price 25¢; stiff-c; PC-r	1	2	2	4	6	9	11	14

60. Black Beauty

Ed	HRN	Date	Details	A	C	GD 2.0	VG 4.0	FN 6.0	VF 8.0	VF/NM 9.0	NM- 9.2
1	62	6/49	Original; Froehlich-c/a	1	1	14	28	42	79	107	135
2	62	–	No c-price; no coming-next ad; LDC-r (rare)	1	1	16	32	48	92	126	160
3	85	–	C-price 15¢; LDC-r	1	1	5	10	15	23	28	32
4	158	–	New L.B. Cole-c/a; PC-r	2	2	6	12	18	28	34	40
5	167	2/64	PC-r	2	2	2	4	6	12	16	20
6	167	3/66	PC-r	2	2	2	4	6	12	16	20
7	166	R/1968	New-c&price, 25¢; PC-r	2	3	5	10	15	36	48	60

Classics Illustrated #64 © GIL

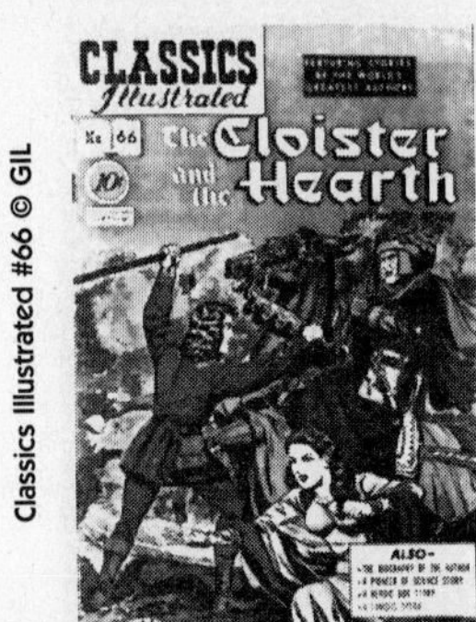

Classics Illustrated #66 © GIL

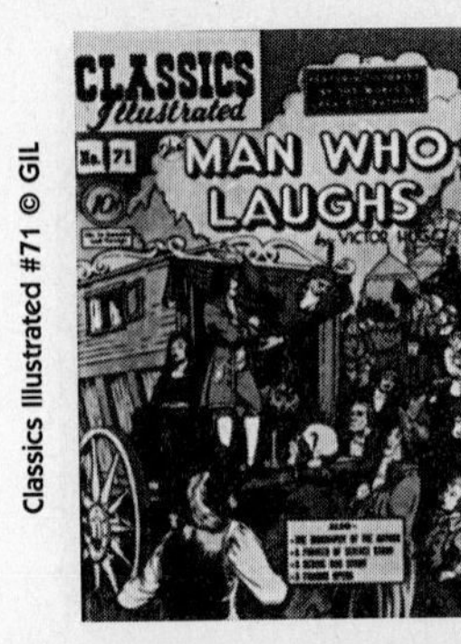

Classics Illustrated #71 © GIL

61. The Woman in White

Ed	HRN	Date	Details	A	C	GD 2.0	VG 4.0	FN 6.0	VF 8.0	VF/NM 9.0	NM- 9.2
1A	62	7/49	Original; Blum-c/a fc-purple; bc: top illos light blue	1	1	15	30	45	84	115	145
1B	62	7/49	Original; Blum-c/a fc-pink; bc: top illos light violet	1	1	15	30	45	84	115	145
2	156	–	New-c; PC-r	1	2	5	10	15	23	28	32
3	167	1/64	PC-r	1	2	2	4	6	12	16	20
4	166	R/1968	C-price 25¢; PC-r	1	2	2	4	6	12	16	20

62. Western Stories ("The Luck of Roaring Camp" and "The Outcasts of Poker Flat")

Ed	HRN	Date	Details	A	C	GD 2.0	VG 4.0	FN 6.0	VF 8.0	VF/NM 9.0	NM- 9.2
1	62	8/49	Original; Kiefer-c/a	1	1	13	26	39	74	100	125
2	89	–	C-price 15¢; LDC-r	1	1	5	10	15	23	28	32
3	121	–	LDC-r	1	1	3	6	9	17	21	26
4	137	–	New-c; PC-r	1	2	3	6	9	18	23	28
5	152	–	PC-r	1	2	2	4	6	8	10	12
6	167	10/63	PC-r	1	2	2	4	6	8	10	12
7	167	6/64	PC-r	1	2	2	4	6	8	10	12
8	167	11/66	PC-r	1	2	2	4	6	8	10	12
9	166	R/1968	New-c&price 25¢; PC-r	1	3	3	6	9	17	21	26

63. The Man Without a Country

Ed	HRN	Date	Details	A	C	GD 2.0	VG 4.0	FN 6.0	VF 8.0	VF/NM 9.0	NM- 9.2
1	62	9/49	Original; Kiefer-c/a	1	1	14	28	42	79	107	135
2	78	–	C-price 15¢ in double circle; LDC-r	1	1	5	10	15	23	28	32
3	156	–	New-c, old-a; PC-r	1	2	5	10	15	23	28	32
4	165	–	New-a & text pgs.; PC-r; A. Torres-a	2	2	5	10	14	20	24	28
5	167	3/64	PC-r	2	2	2	4	6	8	10	12
6	167	8/66	PC-r	2	2	2	4	6	8	10	12
7	169	Sm/69	New price 25¢; stiff-c; PC-r	2	2	2	4	6	8	10	12

64. Treasure Island

Ed	HRN	Date	Details	A	C	GD 2.0	VG 4.0	FN 6.0	VF 8.0	VF/NM 9.0	NM- 9.2
1	62	10/49	Original; Blum-c/a	1	1	15	30	45	84	115	145
2A	82	–	C-price 15¢; soft-c LDC-r	1	1	5	10	15	22	26	30
2B	82	–	Stiff-c; LDC-r	1	1	5	10	15	23	28	32
3	117	–	LDC-r	1	1	3	6	9	17	21	26
4	131	–	New-c; PC-r	1	2	3	6	9	18	23	28
5	138	–	PC-r	1	2	2	4	6	9	11	14
6	146	–	PC-r	1	2	2	4	6	9	11	14
7	158	–	PC-r	1	2	2	4	6	9	11	14
8	165	–	PC-r	1	2	2	4	6	8	10	12
9	167	–	PC-r	1	2	2	4	6	8	10	12
10	167	6/64	PC-r	1	2	2	4	6	8	10	12
11	167	12/65	PC-r	1	2	2	4	6	8	10	12
12A	166	10/67	PC-r	1	2	2	4	6	8	10	12
12B	166	10/67	w/Grit ad stapled in book	1	2	14	28	42	79	107	135
13	169	Spr/69	New price 25¢; stiff-c; PC-r	1	2	2	4	6	9	11	14
14	–	1989	Long John Silver's Seafood Shoppes; $1.95, First/Berkley Publ.; Blum-r	1	2						5.00

65. Benjamin Franklin

Ed	HRN	Date	Details	A	C	GD 2.0	VG 4.0	FN 6.0	VF 8.0	VF/NM 9.0	NM- 9.2
1	64	11/49	Original; Kiefer-c; Iger Shop-a	1	1	14	28	42	79	107	135
2	131	–	New-c; PC-r	1	2	5	10	15	22	26	30
3	154	–	PC-r	1	2	2	4	6	10	12	15
4	167	2/64	PC-r	1	2	2	4	6	9	11	14
5	167	4/66	PC-r	1	2	2	4	6	9	11	14
6	169	Fall/69	New price 25¢; stiff-c; PC-r	1	2	2	4	6	9	11	14

66. The Cloister and the Hearth

Ed	HRN	Date	Details	A	C	GD 2.0	VG 4.0	FN 6.0	VF 8.0	VF/NM 9.0	NM- 9.2
1	67	12/49	Original & only ed; Kiefer-a & c	1	1	29	58	87	164	232	300

67. The Scottish Chiefs

Ed	HRN	Date	Details	A	C	GD 2.0	VG 4.0	FN 6.0	VF 8.0	VF/NM 9.0	NM- 9.2
1	67	1/50	Original; Blum-a&c	1	1	12	24	36	69	92	115
2	85	–	C-price 15¢; LDC-r	1	1	5	10	15	23	28	32
3	118	–	LDC-r	1	1	3	6	9	17	21	26
4	136	–	New-c; PC-r	1	2	3	6	9	18	24	30
5	154	–	PC-r	1	2	2	4	6	9	11	14
6	167	11/63	PC-r	1	2	2	4	6	10	13	16
7	167	8/65	PC-r	1	2	2	4	6	9	11	14

68. Julius Caesar (Used in SOTI, pgs. 36, 37)

Ed	HRN	Date	Details	A	C	GD 2.0	VG 4.0	FN 6.0	VF 8.0	VF/NM 9.0	NM- 9.2
1	70	2/50	Original; Kiefer-c/a	1	1	12	24	36	69	92	115
2	85	–	C-price 15¢; LDC-r	1	1	5	10	15	22	26	30
3	108	–	LDC-r	1	1	4	9	13	18	22	26
4	156	–	New L.B. Cole-c; PC-r	1	2	5	10	15	23	28	32
5	165	–	New-a by Evans, Crandall; PC-r	2	2	5	10	15	22	26	30
6	167	2/64	PC-r	2	2	2	4	6	8	10	12
7	167	10/65	Tarzan books inside cover; PC-r	2	2	2	4	6	8	10	12
8	166	R/1967	PC-r	2	2	2	4	6	8	10	12
9	169	Win/69	PC-r; stiff-c	2	2	2	4	6	8	10	12

69. Around the World in 80 Days

Ed	HRN	Date	Details	A	C	GD 2.0	VG 4.0	FN 6.0	VF 8.0	VF/NM 9.0	NM- 9.2
1	70	3/50	Original; Kiefer-c/a	1	1	12	24	36	69	92	115
2	87	–	C-price 15¢; LDC-r	1	1	5	10	15	22	26	30
3	125	–	LDC-r	1	1	4	9	13	18	22	26
4	136	–	New-c; PC-r	1	2	5	10	15	22	26	30
5	146	–	PC-r	1	2	2	4	6	9	11	14
6	152	–	PC-r	1	2	2	4	6	9	11	14
7	164	–	PC-r	1	2	2	4	6	8	10	12
8	167	–	PC-r	1	2	2	4	6	8	10	12
9	167	7/64	PC-r	1	2	2	4	6	8	10	12
10	167	11/65	PC-r	1	2	2	4	6	8	10	12
11	166	7/67	PC-r	1	2	2	4	6	8	10	12
12	169	Spr/69	C-price 25¢; stiff-c; PC-r	1	2	2	4	6	8	10	12

70. The Pilot

Ed	HRN	Date	Details	A	C	GD 2.0	VG 4.0	FN 6.0	VF 8.0	VF/NM 9.0	NM- 9.2
1	71	4/50	Original; Blum-c/a	1	1	10	20	30	56	73	90
2	92	–	C-price 15¢; LDC-r	1	1	5	10	15	23	28	32
3	125	–	LDC-r	1	1	4	9	13	18	22	26
4	156	–	New-c; PC-r	1	2	5	10	15	23	28	32
5	167	2/64	PC-r	1	2	2	4	6	12	16	20
6	167	5/66	PC-r	1	2	2	4	6	10	13	16

71. The Man Who Laughs

Ed	HRN	Date	Details	A	C	GD 2.0	VG 4.0	FN 6.0	VF 8.0	VF/NM 9.0	NM- 9.2
1	71	5/50	Original; Blum-c/a	1	1	17	34	51	95	130	165
2	165	–	New-c&a; PC-r	2	2	11	22	33	63	84	105
3	167	4/64	PC-r	2	2	10	20	30	56	73	90

72. The Oregon Trail

Ed	HRN	Date	Details	A	C	GD 2.0	VG 4.0	FN 6.0	VF 8.0	VF/NM 9.0	NM- 9.2
1	73	6/50	Original; Kiefer-c/a	1	1	10	20	30	56	73	90
2	89	–	C-price 15¢; LDC-r	1	1	5	10	15	23	28	32
3	121	–	LDC-r	1	1	4	9	13	18	22	26
4	131	–	New-c; PC-r	1	2	5	10	15	22	26	30
5	140	–	PC-r	1	2	2	4	6	9	11	14
6	150	–	PC-r	1	2	2	4	6	9	11	14
7	164	–	PC-r	1	2	2	4	6	8	10	12
8	167	–	PC-r	1	2	2	4	6	8	10	12
9	167	8/64	PC-r	1	2	2	4	6	8	10	12
10	167	10/65	PC-r	1	2	2	4	6	8	10	12
11	166	R/1968	C-price 25¢; PC-r	1	2	2	4	6	8	10	12

73. The Black Tulip

Ed	HRN	Date	Details	A	C	GD 2.0	VG 4.0	FN 6.0	VF 8.0	VF/NM 9.0	NM- 9.2
1	75	7/50	1st & only ed.; Alex Blum-c/a	1	1	36	72	108	204	290	375

74. Mr. Midshipman Easy

Ed	HRN	Date	Details	A	C

Classics Illustrated #76 © GIL

Classics Illustrated #78 © GIL

Classics Illustrated #84 © GIL

Ed	HRN	Date	Details	A	C	GD 2.0	VG 4.0	FN 6.0	VF 8.0	VF/NM 9.0	NM- 9.2
1	75	8/50	1st & only edition	1	1	36	72	108	204	290	375

75. The Lady of the Lake

Ed	HRN	Date	Details	A	C	GD 2.0	VG 4.0	FN 6.0	VF 8.0	VF/NM 9.0	NM- 9.2
1	75	9/50	Original; Kiefer-c/a	1	1	10	20	30	56	73	90
2	85	–	C-price 15¢; LDC-r	1	1	5	10	15	24	30	35
3	118	–	LDC-r	1	1	5	10	14	20	24	28
4	139	–	New-c; PC-r	1	2	5	10	15	22	26	30
5	154	–	PC-r	1	2	2	4	6	9	11	14
6	165	–	PC-r	1	2	2	4	6	8	10	12
7	167	4/64	PC-r	1	2	2	4	6	8	10	12
8	167	5/66	PC-r	1	2	2	4	6	8	10	12
9	169	Spr/69	New price 25¢; stiff-c; PC-r	1	2	2	4	6	8	10	12

76. The Prisoner of Zenda

Ed	HRN	Date	Details	A	C	GD 2.0	VG 4.0	FN 6.0	VF 8.0	VF/NM 9.0	NM- 9.2
1	75	10/50	Original; Kiefer-c/a	1	1	10	20	30	56	73	90
2	85	–	C-price 15¢; LDC-r	1	1	5	10	15	23	28	32
3	111	–	LDC-r	1	1	3	6	9	17	21	26
4	128	–	New-c; PC-r	1	2	3	6	9	18	23	28
5	152	–	PC-r	1	2	2	4	6	9	11	14
6	165	–	PC-r	1	2	2	4	6	8	10	12
7	167	4/64	PC-r	1	2	2	4	6	8	10	12
8	167	9/66	PC-r	1	2	2	4	6	8	10	12
9	169	Fall/69	New price 25¢; stiff-c; PC-r	1	2	2	4	6	8	10	12

77. The Iliad

Ed	HRN	Date	Details	A	C	GD 2.0	VG 4.0	FN 6.0	VF 8.0	VF/NM 9.0	NM- 9.2
1	78	11/50	Original; Blum-c/a	1	1	10	20	30	56	73	90
2	87	–	C-price 15¢; LDC-r	1	1	5	10	15	24	30	35
3	121	–	LDC-r	1	1	3	6	9	18	21	26
4	139	–	New-c; PC-r	1	2	3	6	9	18	22	26
5	150	–	PC-r	1	2	2	4	6	9	11	14
6	165	–	PC-r	1	2	2	4	6	8	10	12
7	167	10/63	PC-r	1	2	2	4	6	8	10	12
8	167	7/64	PC-r	1	2	2	4	6	8	10	12
9	167	5/66	PC-r	1	2	2	4	6	8	10	12
10	166	R/1968	C-price 25¢; PC-r	1	2	2	4	6	8	10	12

78. Joan of Arc

Ed	HRN	Date	Details	A	C	GD 2.0	VG 4.0	FN 6.0	VF 8.0	VF/NM 9.0	NM- 9.2
1	78	12/50	Original; Kiefer-c/a	1	1	10	20	30	56	73	90
2	87	–	C-price 15¢; LDC-r	1	1	5	10	15	23	28	32
3	113	–	LDC-r	1	1	3	6	9	17	22	26
4	128	–	New-c; PC-r	1	2	3	6	9	18	23	28
5	140	–	PC-r	1	2	2	4	6	9	11	14
6	150	–	PC-r	1	2	2	4	6	9	11	14
7	159	–	PC-r	1	2	2	4	6	9	11	14
8	167	–	PC-r	1	2	2	4	6	8	10	12
9	167	12/63	PC-r	1	2	2	4	6	8	10	12
10	167	6/65	PC-r	1	2	2	4	6	8	10	12
11	166	6/67	PC-r	1	2	2	4	6	8	10	12
12	166	Win/69	New-c&price, 25¢; PC-r; stiff-c	1	3	3	6	9	18	23	28

79. Cyrano de Bergerac

Ed	HRN	Date	Details	A	C	GD 2.0	VG 4.0	FN 6.0	VF 8.0	VF/NM 9.0	NM- 9.2
1	78	1/51	Orig.; movie promo inside front-c; Blum-c/a	1	1	10	20	30	56	73	90
2	85	–	C-price 15¢; LDC-r	1	1	5	10	15	23	28	32
3	118	–	LDC-r	1	1	3	6	9	18	23	28
4	133	–	New-c; PC-r	1	2	3	6	9	17	21	26
5	156	–	PC-r	1	2	2	4	6	12	16	20
6	167	8/64	PC-r	1	2	2	4	6	12	16	20

80. White Fang (Last line drawn cover)

Ed	HRN	Date	Details	A	C	GD 2.0	VG 4.0	FN 6.0	VF 8.0	VF/NM 9.0	NM- 9.2
1	79	2/51	Orig.; Blum-c/a	1	1	10	20	30	56	73	90
2	87	–	C-price 15¢; LDC-r	1	1	5	10	15	24	30	35
3	125	–	LDC-r	1	1	3	6	9	17	22	26
4	132	–	New-c; PC-r	1	2	3	6	9	17	21	26
5	140	–	PC-r	1	2	2	4	6	9	11	14
6	153	–	PC-r	1	2	2	4	6	9	11	14
7	167	–	PC-r	1	2	2	4	6	8	10	12
8	167	9/64	PC-r	1	2	2	4	6	8	10	12
9	167	7/65	PC-r	1	2	2	4	6	8	10	12
10	166	6/67	PC-r	1	2	2	4	6	8	10	12
11	169	Fall/69	New price 25¢; PC-r; stiff-c	1	2	2	4	6	8	10	12

81. The Odyssey (1st painted cover)

Ed	HRN	Date	Details	A	C	GD 2.0	VG 4.0	FN 6.0	VF 8.0	VF/NM 9.0	NM- 9.2
1	82	3/51	First 15¢ Original; Blum-c	1	1	10	20	30	56	73	90
2	167	8/64	PC-r	1	1	2	4	6	12	16	20
3	167	10/66	PC-r	1	1	2	4	6	12	16	20
4	169	Spr/69	New, stiff-c; PC-r	1	2	3	6	9	18	24	30

82. The Master of Ballantrae

Ed	HRN	Date	Details	A	C	GD 2.0	VG 4.0	FN 6.0	VF 8.0	VF/NM 9.0	NM- 9.2
1	82	4/51	Original; Blum-c	1	1	8	16	24	46	58	70
2	167	8/64	PC-r	1	1	3	6	9	16	20	24
3	166	Fall/68	New, stiff-c; PC-r	1	2	3	6	9	18	24	30

83. The Jungle Book

Ed	HRN	Date	Details	A	C	GD 2.0	VG 4.0	FN 6.0	VF 8.0	VF/NM 9.0	NM- 9.2
1	85	5/51	Original; Blum-c Bossert/Blum-a	1	1	8	16	24	46	58	70
2	110	–	PC-r	1	1	2	4	6	10	13	16
3	125	–	PC-r	1	1	2	4	6	9	11	14
4	134	–	PC-r	1	1	2	4	6	9	11	14
5	142	–	PC-r	1	1	2	4	6	9	11	14
6	150	–	PC-r	1	1	2	4	6	9	11	14
7	159	–	PC-r	1	1	2	4	6	9	11	14
8	167	–	PC-r	1	1	2	4	6	8	10	12
9	167	3/65	PC-r	1	1	2	4	6	8	10	12
10	167	11/65	PC-r	1	1	2	4	6	8	10	12
11	167	5/66	PC-r	1	1	2	4	6	8	10	12
12	166	R/1968	New c&a; stiff-c; PC-r	2	2	3	6	9	18	24	30

84. The Gold Bug and Other Stories ("The Gold Bug", "The Tell-Tale Heart", "The Cask of Amontillado")

Ed	HRN	Date	Details	A	C	GD 2.0	VG 4.0	FN 6.0	VF 8.0	VF/NM 9.0	NM- 9.2
1	85	6/51	Original; Blum-c/a; Palais, Laverly-a	1	1	12	24	36	69	92	115
2	167	7/64	PC-r	1	1	10	20	30	56	73	90

85. The Sea Wolf

Ed	HRN	Date	Details	A	C	GD 2.0	VG 4.0	FN 6.0	VF 8.0	VF/NM 9.0	NM- 9.2
1	85	7/51	Original; Blum-c/a	1	1	8	16	24	40	50	60
2	121	–	PC-r	1	1	2	4	6	9	11	14
3	132	–	PC-r	1	1	2	4	6	9	11	14
4	141	–	PC-r	1	1	2	4	6	9	11	14
5	161	–	PC-r	1	1	2	4	6	8	10	12
6	167	2/64	PC-r	1	1	2	4	6	8	10	12
7	167	11/65	PC-r	1	1	2	4	6	8	10	12
8	169	Fall/69	New price 25¢; stiff-c; PC-r	1	1	2	4	6	8	10	12

86. Under Two Flags

Ed	HRN	Date	Details	A	C	GD 2.0	VG 4.0	FN 6.0	VF 8.0	VF/NM 9.0	NM- 9.2
1	87	8/51	Original; first delBourgo-a	1	1	7	14	21	37	46	55
2	117	–	PC-r	1	1	2	4	6	10	13	16
3	139	–	PC-r	1	1	2	4	6	9	11	14
4	158	–	PC-r	1	1	2	4	6	9	11	14
5	167	2/64	PC-r	1	1	2	4	6	8	10	12
6	167	8/66	PC-r	1	1	2	4	6	8	10	12
7	169	Sm/69	New price 25¢; stiff-c; PC-r	1	1	2	4	6	8	10	12

87. A Midsummer Nights Dream

Ed	HRN	Date	Details	A	C	GD 2.0	VG 4.0	FN 6.0	VF 8.0	VF/NM 9.0	NM- 9.2
1	87	9/51	Original; Blum c/a	1	1	8	16	24	40	50	60
2	161	–	PC-r	1	1	2	4	6	9	11	14
3	167	4/64	PC-r	1	1	2	4	6	8	10	12
4	167	5/66	PC-r	1	1	2	4	6	8	10	12
5	169	Sm/69	New price 25¢; stiff-c; PC-r	1	1	2	4	6	8	10	12

88. Men of Iron

Ed	HRN	Date	Details	A	C	GD 2.0	VG 4.0	FN 6.0	VF 8.0	VF/NM 9.0	NM- 9.2
1	89	10/51	Original	1	1	8	16	24	40	50	60
2	154	–	PC-r	1	1	2	4	6	9	11	14

Classics Illustrated #91 © GIL

Classics Illustrated #95 © GIL

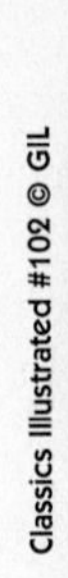
Classics Illustrated #102 © GIL

Ed	HRN	Date	Details	A	C	GD 2.0	VG 4.0	FN 6.0	VF 8.0	VF/NM 9.0	NM- 9.2
3	167	1/64	PC-r	1	1	2	4	6	8	10	12
4	166	R/1968	C-price 25¢; PC-r	1	1	2	4	6	8	10	12

89. Crime and Punishment (Cover illo. in **POP**)

Ed	HRN	Date	Details	A	C	GD 2.0	VG 4.0	FN 6.0	VF 8.0	VF/NM 9.0	NM- 9.2
1	89	11/51	Original; Palais-a	1	1	8	16	24	40	50	60
2	152	–	PC-r	1	1	2	4	6	9	11	14
3	167	4/64	PC-r	1	1	2	4	6	8	10	12
4	167	5/66	PC-r	1	1	2	4	6	8	10	12
5	169	Fall/69	New price 25¢ stiff-c; PC-r	1	1	2	4	6	8	10	12

90. Green Mansions

Ed	HRN	Date	Details	A	C	GD 2.0	VG 4.0	FN 6.0	VF 8.0	VF/NM 9.0	NM- 9.2
1	89	12/51	Original; Blum-c/a	1	1	8	16	24	40	50	60
2	148	–	New L.B. Cole-c; PC-r	1	2	4	8	12	17	21	24
3	165	–	PC-r	1	2	2	4	6	8	10	12
4	167	4/64	PC-r	1	2	2	4	6	8	10	12
5	167	9/66	PC-r	1	2	2	4	6	8	10	12
6	169	Sm/69	New price 25¢; stiff-c; PC-r	1	2	2	4	6	8	10	12

91. The Call of the Wild

Ed	HRN	Date	Details	A	C	GD 2.0	VG 4.0	FN 6.0	VF 8.0	VF/NM 9.0	NM- 9.2
1	92	1/52	Orig.; delBourgo-a	1	1	8	16	24	40	50	60
2	112	–	PC-r	1	1	2	4	6	9	11	14
3	125	–	'Picture Progress' on back-c; PC-r	1	1	2	4	6	9	11	14
4	134	–	PC-r	1	1	2	4	6	9	11	14
5	143	–	PC-r	1	1	2	4	6	9	11	14
6	165	–	PC-r	1	1	2	4	6	9	11	14
7	167	–	PC-r	1	1	2	4	6	8	10	12
8	167	4/65	PC-r	1	1	2	4	6	8	10	12
9	167	3/66	PC-r	1	1	2	4	6	8	10	12
10	166	11/67	PC-r	1	1	2	4	6	8	10	12
11	169	Spr/70	New price 25¢; stiff-c; PC-r	1	1	2	4	6	8	10	12

92. The Courtship of Miles Standish

Ed	HRN	Date	Details	A	C	GD 2.0	VG 4.0	FN 6.0	VF 8.0	VF/NM 9.0	NM- 9.2
1	92	2/52	Original; Blum-c/a	1	1	7	14	21	37	46	55
2	165	–	PC-r	1	1	2	4	6	9	11	14
3	167	3/64	PC-r	1	1	2	4	6	9	11	14
4	166	5/67	PC-r	1	1	2	4	6	9	11	14
5	169	Win/69	New price 25¢ stiff-c; PC-r	1	1	2	4	6	9	11	14

93. Pudd'nhead Wilson

Ed	HRN	Date	Details	A	C	GD 2.0	VG 4.0	FN 6.0	VF 8.0	VF/NM 9.0	NM- 9.2
1	94	3/52	Orig.; Kiefer-c/a;	1	1	8	16	24	40	50	60
2	165	–	New-c; PC-r	1	2	2	4	6	12	16	20
3	167	3/64	PC-r	1	2	2	4	6	9	11	14
4	166	R/1968	New price 25¢; soft-c; PC-r	1	2	2	4	6	10	12	15

94. David Balfour

Ed	HRN	Date	Details	A	C	GD 2.0	VG 4.0	FN 6.0	VF 8.0	VF/NM 9.0	NM- 9.2
1	94	4/52	Original; Palais-a	1	1	8	16	24	40	50	60
2	167	5/64	PC-r	1	1	2	4	6	12	16	20
3	166	R/1968	C-price 25¢; PC-r	1	1	2	4	6	14	18	22

95. All Quiet on the Western Front

Ed	HRN	Date	Details	A	C	GD 2.0	VG 4.0	FN 6.0	VF 8.0	VF/NM 9.0	NM- 9.2
1A	96	5/52	Orig.; del Bourgo-a	1	1	11	22	33	63	84	105
1B	99	5/52	Orig.; del Bourgo-a	1	1	9	18	27	54	70	85
2	167	10/64	PC-r	1	1	3	6	9	17	22	26
3	167	11/66	PC-r	1	1	3	6	9	17	22	26

96. Daniel Boone

Ed	HRN	Date	Details	A	C	GD 2.0	VG 4.0	FN 6.0	VF 8.0	VF/NM 9.0	NM- 9.2
1	97	6/52	Original; Blum-a	1	1	7	14	21	37	46	55
2	117	–	PC-r	1	1	2	4	6	9	11	14
3	128	–	PC-r	1	1	2	4	6	9	11	14
4	132	–	PC-r	1	1	2	4	6	9	11	14
5	134	–	"Story of Jesus" on back-c; PC-r	1	1	2	4	6	9	11	14
6	158	–	PC-r	1	1	2	4	6	9	11	14
7	167	1/64	PC-r	1	1	2	4	6	8	10	12
8	167	5/65	PC-r	1	1	2	4	6	8	10	12
9	167	11/66	PC-r	1	1	2	4	6	8	10	12
10	166	Win/69	New-c; price 25¢; PC r; stiff-c	1	2	3	6	9	16	20	24

97. King Solomon's Mines

Ed	HRN	Date	Details	A	C	GD 2.0	VG 4.0	FN 6.0	VF 8.0	VF/NM 9.0	NM- 9.2
1	96	7/52	Orig.; Kiefer-a	1	1	7	14	21	37	46	55
2	118	–	PC-r	1	1	2	4	6	9	11	14
3	131	–	PC-r	1	1	2	4	6	9	11	14
4	141	–	PC-r	1	1	2	4	6	9	11	14
5	158	–	PC-r	1	1	2	4	6	9	11	14
6	167	2/64	PC-r	1	1	2	4	6	8	10	12
7	167	9/65	PC-r	1	1	2	4	6	8	10	12
8	169	Sm/69	New price 25¢; stiff-c; PC-r	1	1	2	4	6	8	10	12

98. The Red Badge of Courage

Ed	HRN	Date	Details	A	C	GD 2.0	VG 4.0	FN 6.0	VF 8.0	VF/NM 9.0	NM- 9.2
1	98	8/52	Original	1	1	7	14	21	37	46	55
2	118	–	PC-r	1	1	2	4	6	9	11	14
3	132	–	PC-r	1	1	2	4	6	9	11	14
4	142	–	PC-r	1	1	2	4	6	9	11	14
5	152	–	PC-r	1	1	2	4	6	9	11	14
6	161	–	PC-r	1	1	2	4	6	9	11	14
7	167	–	Has orig.date; PC-r	1	1	2	4	6	9	11	14
8	167	9/64	PC-r	1	1	2	4	6	9	11	14
9	167	10/65	PC-r	1	1	2	4	6	9	11	14
10	166	R/1968	New-c&price 25¢; PC-r; stiff-c	1	2	3	6	9	17	21	26

99. Hamlet (Used in **POP**, pg. 102)

Ed	HRN	Date	Details	A	C	GD 2.0	VG 4.0	FN 6.0	VF 8.0	VF/NM 9.0	NM- 9.2
1	98	9/52	Original; Blum-a	1	1	8	16	24	40	50	60
2	121	–	PC-r	1	1	2	4	6	9	11	14
3	141	–	PC-r	1	1	2	4	6	9	11	14
4	158	–	PC-r	1	1	2	4	6	9	11	14
5	167	–	Has orig.date; PC-r	1	1	2	4	6	8	10	12
6	167	7/65	PC-r	1	1	2	4	6	8	10	12
7	166	4/67	PC-r	1	1	2	4	6	8	10	12
8	169	Spr/69	New-c&price 25¢; PC-r; stiff-c	1	2	3	6	9	17	21	26

100. Mutiny on the Bounty

Ed	HRN	Date	Details	A	C	GD 2.0	VG 4.0	FN 6.0	VF 8.0	VF/NM 9.0	NM- 9.2
1	100	10/52	Original	1	1	7	14	21	37	46	55
2	117	–	PC-r	1	1	2	4	6	9	11	14
3	132	–	PC-r	1	1	2	4	6	9	11	14
4	142	–	PC-r	1	1	2	4	6	9	11	14
5	155	–	PC-r	1	1	2	4	6	9	11	14
6	167	–	Has orig. date;PC-r	1	1	2	4	6	8	10	12
7	167	5/64	PC-r	1	1	2	4	6	8	10	12
8	167	3/66	PC-r	1	1	2	4	6	8	10	12
9	169	Spr/70	PC-r; stiff-c	1	1	2	4	6	8	10	12

101. William Tell

Ed	HRN	Date	Details	A	C	GD 2.0	VG 4.0	FN 6.0	VF 8.0	VF/NM 9.0	NM- 9.2
1	101	11/52	Original; Kiefer-c delBourgo-a	1	1	7	14	21	37	46	55
2	118	–	PC-r	1	1	2	4	6	9	11	14
3	141	–	PC-r	1	1	2	4	6	9	11	14
4	158	–	PC-r	1	1	2	4	6	9	11	14
5	167	–	Has orig.date; PC-r	1	1	2	4	6	8	10	12
6	167	11/64	PC-r	1	1	2	4	6	8	10	12
7	166	4/67	PC-r	1	1	2	4	6	8	10	12
8	169	Win/69	New price 25¢; stiff-c; PC-r	1	1	2	4	6	8	10	12

102. The White Company

Ed	HRN	Date	Details	A	C	GD 2.0	VG 4.0	FN 6.0	VF 8.0	VF/NM 9.0	NM- 9.2
1	101	12/52	Original; Blum-a	1	1	10	20	30	56	73	90
2	165	–	PC-r	1	1	3	6	9	18	23	28
3	167	4/64	PC-r	1	1	3	6	9	18	23	28

103. Men Against the Sea

Ed	HRN	Date	Details	A	C	GD 2.0	VG 4.0	FN 6.0	VF 8.0	VF/NM 9.0	NM- 9.2
1	104	1/53	Original; Kiefer-c; Palais-a	1	1	8	16	24	40	50	60
2	114	–	PC-r	1	1	4	8	11	16	19	22
3	131	–	New-c; PC-r	1	2	5	10	15	22	26	30

Classics Illustrated #108 © GIL

Classics Illustrated #111 © GIL

Classics Illustrated #118 © GIL

Ed	HRN	Date	Details	A	C	GD 2.0	VG 4.0	FN 6.0	VF 8.0	VF/NM 9.0	NM- 9.2
4	158	–	PC-r	1	2	4	7	10	14	17	20
5	149	–	White reorder list; came after HRN-158; PC-r	1	2	5	10	15	22	26	30
6	167	3/64	PC-r	1	2	2	4	6	9	11	14

104. Bring 'Em Back Alive

Ed	HRN	Date	Details	A	C	GD 2.0	VG 4.0	FN 6.0	VF 8.0	VF/NM 9.0	NM- 9.2
1	105	2/53	Original; Kiefer-c/a	1	1	7	14	21	37	46	55
2	118	–	PC-r	1	1	2	4	6	9	11	14
3	133	–	PC-r	1	1	2	4	6	9	11	14
4	150	–	PC-r	1	1	2	4	6	9	11	14
5	158	–	PC-r	1	1	2	4	6	9	11	14
6	167	10/63	PC-r	1	1	2	4	6	8	10	12
7	167	9/65	PC-r	1	1	2	4	6	8	10	12
8	169	Win/69	New price 25¢; stiff-c; PC-r	1	1	2	4	6	8	10	12

105. From the Earth to the Moon

Ed	HRN	Date	Details	A	C	GD 2.0	VG 4.0	FN 6.0	VF 8.0	VF/NM 9.0	NM- 9.2
1	106	3/53	Original; Blum-a	1	1	7	14	21	37	46	55
2	118	–	PC-r	1	1	2	4	6	9	11	14
3	132	–	PC-r	1	1	2	4	6	9	11	14
4	141	–	PC-r	1	1	2	4	6	9	11	14
5	146	–	PC-r	1	1	2	4	6	9	11	14
6	156	–	PC-r	1	1	2	4	6	9	11	14
7	167	–	Has orig. date; PC-r	1	1	2	4	6	8	10	12
8	167	5/64	PC-r	1	1	2	4	6	8	10	12
9	167	5/65	PC-r	1	1	2	4	6	8	10	12
10A	166	10/67	PC-r	1	1	2	4	6	8	10	12
10B	166	10/67	w/Grit ad stapled in book	1	1	9	18	27	60	85	110
11	169	Sm/69	New price 25¢; stiff-c; PC-r	1	1	2	4	6	8	10	12
12	169	Spr/71	PC-r	1	1	2	4	6	8	10	12

106. Buffalo Bill

Ed	HRN	Date	Details	A	C	GD 2.0	VG 4.0	FN 6.0	VF 8.0	VF/NM 9.0	NM- 9.2
1	107	4/53	Orig.; delBourgo-a	1	1	7	14	21	35	43	50
2	118	–	PC-r	1	1	2	4	6	9	11	14
3	132	–	PC-r	1	1	2	4	6	9	11	14
4	142	–	PC-r	1	1	2	4	6	9	11	14
5	161	–	PC-r	1	1	2	4	6	8	10	12
6	167	3/64	PC-r	1	1	2	4	6	8	10	12
7	166	7/67	PC-r	1	1	2	4	6	8	10	12
8	169	Fall/69	PC-r; stiff-c	1	1	2	4	6	8	10	12

107. King of the Khyber Rifles

Ed	HRN	Date	Details	A	C	GD 2.0	VG 4.0	FN 6.0	VF 8.0	VF/NM 9.0	NM- 9.2
1	108	5/53	Original	1	1	7	14	21	35	43	50
2	118	–	PC-r	1	1	2	4	6	9	11	14
3	146	–	PC-r	1	1	2	4	6	9	11	14
4	158	–	PC-r	1	1	2	4	6	9	11	14
5	167	–	Has orig.date; PC-r	1	1	2	4	6	8	10	12
6	167	–	PC-r	1	1	2	4	6	8	10	12
7	167	10/66	PC-r	1	1	2	4	6	8	10	12

108. Knights of the Round Table

Ed	HRN	Date	Details	A	C	GD 2.0	VG 4.0	FN 6.0	VF 8.0	VF/NM 9.0	NM- 9.2
1A	108	6/53	Original; Blum-a	1	1	8	16	24	40	50	60
1B	109	6/53	Original; scarce	1	1	8	16	24	43	54	65
2	117	–	PC-r	1	1	2	4	6	9	11	14
3	165	–	PC-r	1	1	2	4	6	8	10	12
4	167	4/64	PC-r	1	1	2	4	6	8	10	12
5	166	4/67	PC-r	1	1	2	4	6	8	10	12
6	169	Sm/69	New price 25¢; stiff-c; PC-r	1	1	2	4	6	8	10	12

109. Pitcairn's Island

Ed	HRN	Date	Details	A	C	GD 2.0	VG 4.0	FN 6.0	VF 8.0	VF/NM 9.0	NM- 9.2
1	110	7/53	Original; Palais-a	1	1	8	16	24	40	50	60
2	165	–	PC-r	1	1	2	4	6	9	11	14
3	167	3/64	PC-r	1	1	2	4	6	9	11	14
4	166	6/67	PC-r	1	1	2	4	6	9	11	14

110. A Study in Scarlet

Ed	HRN	Date	Details	A	C	GD 2.0	VG 4.0	FN 6.0	VF 8.0	VF/NM 9.0	NM- 9.2
1	111	8/53	Original	1	1	12	24	36	69	92	115
2	165	–	PC-r	1	1	10	20	30	56	73	90

111. The Talisman

Ed	HRN	Date	Details	A	C	GD 2.0	VG 4.0	FN 6.0	VF 8.0	VF/NM 9.0	NM- 9.2
1	112	9/53	Original; last H.C. Kiefer-a	1	1	8	16	24	40	50	60
2	165	–	PC-r	1	1	2	4	6	9	11	14
3	167	5/64	PC-r	1	1	2	4	6	9	11	14
4	166	Fall/68	C-price 25¢; PC-r	1	1	2	4	6	9	11	14

112. Adventures of Kit Carson

Ed	HRN	Date	Details	A	C	GD 2.0	VG 4.0	FN 6.0	VF 8.0	VF/NM 9.0	NM- 9.2
1	113	10/53	Original; Palais-a	1	1	7	14	21	37	46	55
2	129	–	PC-r	1	1	2	4	6	9	11	14
3	141	–	PC-r	1	1	2	4	6	9	11	14
4	152	–	PC-r	1	1	2	4	6	9	11	14
5	161	–	PC-r	1	1	2	4	6	8	10	12
6	167	–	PC-r	1	1	2	4	6	8	10	12
7	167	2/65	PC-r	1	1	2	4	6	8	10	12
8	167	5/66	PC-r	1	1	2	4	6	8	10	12
9	166	Win/69	New-c&price 25¢; PC-r; stiff-c	1	2	2	4	6	12	16	20

113. The Forty-Five Guardsmen

Ed	HRN	Date	Details	A	C	GD 2.0	VG 4.0	FN 6.0	VF 8.0	VF/NM 9.0	NM- 9.2
1	114	11/53	Orig.; delBourgo-a	1	1	9	18	27	52	66	80
2	166	7/67	PC-r	1	1	3	6	9	19	25	32

114. The Red Rover

Ed	HRN	Date	Details	A	C	GD 2.0	VG 4.0	FN 6.0	VF 8.0	VF/NM 9.0	NM- 9.2
1	115	12/53	Original	1	1	9	18	27	52	66	80
2	166	7/67	PC-r	1	1	3	6	9	19	25	32

115. How I Found Livingstone

Ed	HRN	Date	Details	A	C	GD 2.0	VG 4.0	FN 6.0	VF 8.0	VF/NM 9.0	NM- 9.2
1	116	1/54	Original	1	1	10	20	30	56	73	90
2	167	1/67	PC-r	1	1	4	8	12	27	36	45

116. The Bottle Imp

Ed	HRN	Date	Details	A	C	GD 2.0	VG 4.0	FN 6.0	VF 8.0	VF/NM 9.0	NM- 9.2
1	117	2/54	Orig.; Cameron-a	1	1	10	20	30	56	73	90
2	167	1/67	PC-r	1	1	4	8	12	27	36	45

117. Captains Courageous

Ed	HRN	Date	Details	A	C	GD 2.0	VG 4.0	FN 6.0	VF 8.0	VF/NM 9.0	NM- 9.2
1	118	3/54	Orig.; Costanza-a	1	1	9	18	27	52	66	80
2	167	2/67	PC-r	1	1	3	6	9	16	20	24
3	169	Fall/69	New price 25¢; stiff-c; PC-r	1	1	3	6	9	16	20	24

118. Rob Roy

Ed	HRN	Date	Details	A	C	GD 2.0	VG 4.0	FN 6.0	VF 8.0	VF/NM 9.0	NM- 9.2
1	119	4/54	Original; Rudy & Walter Palais-a	1	1	10	20	30	56	73	90
2	167	2/67	PC-r	1	1	4	8	12	27	36	45

119. Soldiers of Fortune

Ed	HRN	Date	Details	A	C	GD 2.0	VG 4.0	FN 6.0	VF 8.0	VF/NM 9.0	NM- 9.2
1	120	5/54	Schaffenberger-a	1	1	8	16	24	46	58	70
2	166	3/67	PC-r	1	1	3	6	9	16	20	24
3	169	Spr/70	New price 25¢; stiff-c; PC-r	1	1	3	6	9	16	20	24

120. The Hurricane

Ed	HRN	Date	Details	A	C	GD 2.0	VG 4.0	FN 6.0	VF 8.0	VF/NM 9.0	NM- 9.2
1	121	6/54	Orig.; Cameron-a	1	1	8	16	24	46	58	70
2	166	3/67	PC-r	1	1	3	6	9	19	25	32

121. Wild Bill Hickok

Ed	HRN	Date	Details	A	C	GD 2.0	VG 4.0	FN 6.0	VF 8.0	VF/NM 9.0	NM- 9.2
1	122	7/54	Original	1	1	7	14	21	35	43	50
2	132	–	PC-r	1	1	2	4	6	9	11	14
3	141	–	PC-r	1	1	2	4	6	9	11	14
4	154	–	PC-r	1	1	2	4	6	9	11	14
5	167	–	PC-r	1	1	2	4	6	8	10	12
6	167	8/64	PC-r	1	1	2	4	6	8	10	12
7	166	4/67	PC-r	1	1	2	4	6	8	10	12
8	169	Win/69	PC-r; stiff-c	1	1	2	4	6	8	10	12

122. The Mutineers

Ed	HRN	Date	Details	A	C

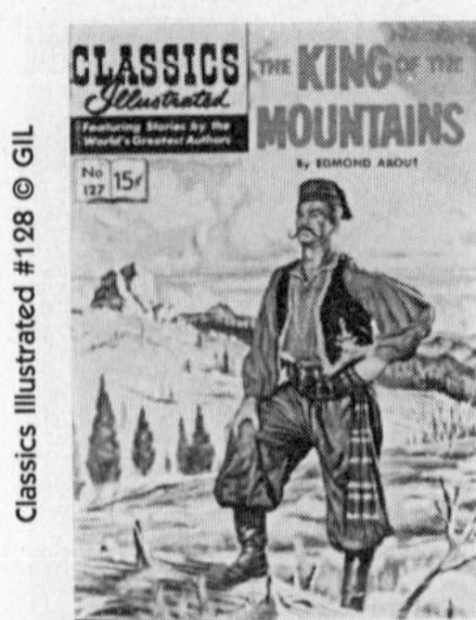

Classics Illustrated #128 © GIL

Classics Illustrated #130 © GIL

Classics Illustrated #138 © GIL

Ed	HRN	Date	Details	A	C	GD 2.0	VG 4.0	FN 6.0	VF 8.0	VF/NM 9.0	NM- 9.2
1	123	9/54	Original	1	1	8	16	24	40	50	60
2	136	–	PC-r	1	1	2	4	6	9	11	14
3	146	–	PC-r	1	1	2	4	6	9	11	14
4	158	–	PC-r	1	1	2	4	6	9	11	14
5	167	11/63	PC-r	1	1	2	4	6	8	10	12
6	167	3/65	PC-r	1	1	2	4	6	8	10	12
7	166	8/67	PC-r	1	1	2	4	6	8	10	12

123. Fang and Claw

Ed	HRN	Date	Details	A	C	GD 2.0	VG 4.0	FN 6.0	VF 8.0	VF/NM 9.0	NM- 9.2
1	124	11/54	Original	1	1	8	16	24	40	50	60
2	133	–	PC-r	1	1	2	4	6	9	11	14
3	143	–	PC-r	1	1	2	4	6	9	11	14
4	154	–	PC-r	1	1	2	4	6	9	11	14
5	167	–	Has orig.date; PC-r	1	1	2	4	6	8	10	12
6	167	9/65	PC-r	1	1	2	4	6	8	10	12

124. The War of the Worlds

Ed	HRN	Date	Details	A	C	GD 2.0	VG 4.0	FN 6.0	VF 8.0	VF/NM 9.0	NM- 9.2
1	125	1/55	Original; Cameron-c/a	1	1	9	18	27	54	70	85
2	131	–	PC-r	1	1	2	4	6	10	13	16
3	141	–	PC-r	1	1	2	4	6	10	13	16
4	148	–	PC-r	1	1	2	4	6	10	13	16
5	156	–	PC-r	1	1	2	4	6	10	13	16
6	165	–	PC-r	1	1	2	4	6	12	16	20
7	167	–	PC-r	1	1	2	4	6	9	11	14
8	167	11/64	PC-r	1	1	2	4	6	10	13	16
9	167	11/65	PC-r	1	1	2	4	6	9	11	14
10	166	R/1968	C-price 25¢; PC-r	1	1	2	4	6	9	11	14
11	169	Sm/70	PC-r; stiff-c	1	1	2	4	6	9	11	14

125. The Ox Bow Incident

Ed	HRN	Date	Details	A	C	GD 2.0	VG 4.0	FN 6.0	VF 8.0	VF/NM 9.0	NM- 9.2
1	–	3/55	Original; Picture Progress replaces reorder list	1	1	7	14	21	35	43	50
2	143	–	PC-r	1	1	2	4	6	9	11	14
3	152	–	PC-r	1	1	2	4	6	9	11	14
4	149	–	PC-r	1	1	2	4	6	9	11	14
5	167	–	PC-r	1	1	2	4	6	8	10	12
6	167	11/64	PC-r	1	1	2	4	6	8	10	12
7	166	4/67	PC-r	1	1	2	4	6	8	10	12
8	169	Win/69	New price 25¢; stiff-c; PC-r	1	1	2	4	6	8	10	12

126. The Downfall

Ed	HRN	Date	Details	A	C	GD 2.0	VG 4.0	FN 6.0	VF 8.0	VF/NM 9.0	NM- 9.2
1	5/55	–	Orig.; 'Picture Progress' replaces reorder list; Cameron-c/a	1	1	8	16	24	40	50	60
2	167	8/64	PC-r	1	1	2	4	6	12	16	20
3	166	R/1968	C-price 25¢; PC-r	1	1	2	4	6	12	16	20

127. The King of the Mountains

Ed	HRN	Date	Details	A	C	GD 2.0	VG 4.0	FN 6.0	VF 8.0	VF/NM 9.0	NM- 9.2
1	128	7/55	Original	1	1	8	16	24	40	50	60
2	167	6/64	PC-r	1	1	2	4	6	10	13	16
3	166	F/1968	C-price 25¢; PC-r	1	1	2	4	6	10	13	16

128. Macbeth (Used in **POP**, pg. 102)

Ed	HRN	Date	Details	A	C	GD 2.0	VG 4.0	FN 6.0	VF 8.0	VF/NM 9.0	NM- 9.2
1	128	9/55	Orig.; last Blum-a	1	1	8	16	24	40	50	60
2	143	–	PC-r	1	1	2	4	6	9	11	14
3	158	–	PC-r	1	1	2	4	6	9	11	14
4	167	–	PC-r	1	1	2	4	6	8	10	12
5	167	6/64	PC-r	1	1	2	4	6	8	10	12
6	166	4/67	PC-r	1	1	2	4	6	8	10	12
7	166	R/1968	C-Price 25¢; PC-r	1	1	2	4	6	8	10	12
8	169	Spr/70	Stiff-c; PC-r	1	1	2	4	6	8	10	12

129. Davy Crockett

Ed	HRN	Date	Details	A	C	GD 2.0	VG 4.0	FN 6.0	VF 8.0	VF/NM 9.0	NM- 9.2
1	129	11/55	Orig.; Cameron-a	1	1	12	24	36	69	92	115
2	167	9/66	PC-r	1	1	10	20	30	56	73	90

130. Caesar's Conquests

Ed	HRN	Date	Details	A	C	GD 2.0	VG 4.0	FN 6.0	VF 8.0	VF/NM 9.0	NM- 9.2
1	130	1/56	Original; Orlando-a	1	1	8	16	24	40	50	60
2	142	–	PC-r	1	1	2	4	6	9	11	14
3	152	–	PC-r	1	1	2	4	6	9	11	14
4	149	–	PC-r	1	1	2	4	6	9	11	14
5	167	–	PC-r	1	1	2	4	6	8	10	12
6	167	10/64	PC-r	1	1	2	4	6	8	10	12
7	167	4/66	PC-r	1	1	2	4	6	8	10	12

131. The Covered Wagon

Ed	HRN	Date	Details	A	C	GD 2.0	VG 4.0	FN 6.0	VF 8.0	VF/NM 9.0	NM- 9.2
1	131	3/56	Original	1	1	4	8	12	29	40	50
2	143	–	PC-r	1	1	2	4	6	9	11	14
3	152	–	PC-r	1	1	2	4	6	9	11	14
4	158	–	PC-r	1	1	2	4	6	9	11	14
5	167	–	PC-r	1	1	2	4	6	8	10	12
6	167	11/64	PC-r	1	1	2	4	6	8	10	12
7	167	4/66	PC-r	1	1	2	4	6	8	10	12
8	169	Win/69	New price 25¢; stiff-c; PC-r	1	1	2	4	6	8	10	12

132. The Dark Frigate

Ed	HRN	Date	Details	A	C	GD 2.0	VG 4.0	FN 6.0	VF 8.0	VF/NM 9.0	NM- 9.2
1	132	5/56	Original	1	1	5	10	15	36	48	60
2	150	–	PC-r	1	1	2	4	6	10	12	15
3	167	1/64	PC-r	1	1	2	4	6	9	11	14
4	166	5/67	PC-r	1	1	2	4	6	9	11	14

133. The Time Machine

Ed	HRN	Date	Details	A	C	GD 2.0	VG 4.0	FN 6.0	VF 8.0	VF/NM 9.0	NM- 9.2
1	132	7/56	Orig.; Cameron-a	1	1	6	12	18	40	55	70
2	142	–	PC-r	1	1	2	4	6	10	13	16
3	152	–	PC-r	1	1	2	4	6	10	13	16
4	158	–	PC-r	1	1	2	4	6	10	13	16
5	167	–	PC-r	1	1	2	4	6	9	11	14
6	167	6/64	PC-r	1	1	2	4	6	10	13	16
7	167	3/66	PC-r	1	1	2	4	6	9	11	14
8	166	12/67	PC-r	1	1	2	4	6	9	11	14
9	169	Win/71	New price 25¢; stiff-c; PC-r	1	1	2	4	6	9	11	14

134. Romeo and Juliet

Ed	HRN	Date	Details	A	C	GD 2.0	VG 4.0	FN 6.0	VF 8.0	VF/NM 9.0	NM- 9.2
1	134	9/56	Original; Evans-a	1	1	5	10	15	36	48	60
2	161	–	PC-r	1	1	2	4	6	9	11	14
3	167	9/63	PC-r	1	1	2	4	6	8	10	12
4	167	5/65	PC-r	1	1	2	4	6	8	10	12
5	166	6/67	PC-r	1	1	2	4	6	8	10	12
6	166	Win/69	New c&price 25¢; stiff-c; PC-r	1	2	3	6	9	18	23	28

135. Waterloo

Ed	HRN	Date	Details	A	C	GD 2.0	VG 4.0	FN 6.0	VF 8.0	VF/NM 9.0	NM- 9.2
1	135	11/56	Orig.; G. Ingels-a	1	1	5	10	15	36	48	60
2	153	–	PC-r	1	1	2	4	6	9	11	14
3	167	–	PC-r	1	1	2	4	6	8	10	12
4	167	9/64	PC-r	1	1	2	4	6	8	10	12
5	166	R/1968	C-price 25¢; PC-r	1	1	2	4	6	8	10	12

136. Lord Jim

Ed	HRN	Date	Details	A	C	GD 2.0	VG 4.0	FN 6.0	VF 8.0	VF/NM 9.0	NM- 9.2
1	136	1/57	Original; Evans-a	1	1	5	10	15	36	48	60
2	165	–	PC-r	1	1	2	4	6	8	10	12
3	167	3/64	PC-r	1	1	2	4	6	8	10	12
4	167	9/66	PC-r	1	1	2	4	6	8	10	12
5	169	Sm/69	New price 25 ¢; stiff-c; PC-r	1	1	2	4	6	8	10	12

137. The Little Savage

Ed	HRN	Date	Details	A	C	GD 2.0	VG 4.0	FN 6.0	VF 8.0	VF/NM 9.0	NM- 9.2
1	136	3/57	Original; Evans-a	1	1	5	10	15	36	48	60
2	148	–	PC-r	1	1	2	4	6	9	11	14
3	156	–	PC-r	1	1	2	4	6	9	11	14
4	167	–	PC-r	1	1	2	4	6	8	10	12
5	167	10/64	PC-r	1	1	2	4	6	8	10	12
6	166	8/67	PC-r	1	1	2	4	6	8	10	12
7	169	Spr/70	New price 25¢; stiff-c; PC-r	1	1	2	4	6	8	10	12

138. A Journey to the Center of the Earth

Ed	HRN	Date	Details	A	C	GD 2.0	VG 4.0	FN 6.0	VF 8.0	VF/NM 9.0	NM- 9.2
1	136	5/57	Original	1	1	7	14	21	50	68	85

Classics Illustrated #140 © GIL

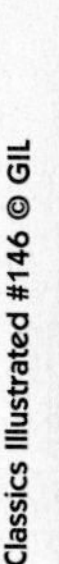

Classics Illustrated #146 © GIL

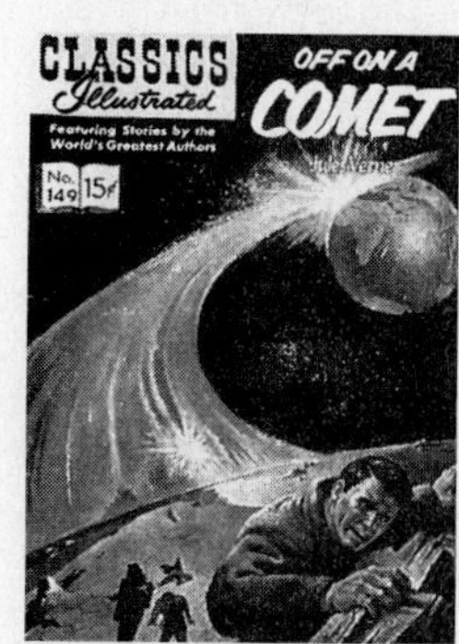

Classics Illustrated #149 © GIL

Ed	HRN	Date	Details	A	C	GD 2.0	VG 4.0	FN 6.0	VF 8.0	VF/NM 9.0	NM- 9.2
2	146	–	PC-r	1	1	2	4	6	11	14	18
3	156	–	PC-r	1	1	2	4	6	11	14	18
4	158	–	PC-r	1	1	2	4	6	11	14	18
5	167	–	PC-r	1	1	2	4	6	11	14	14
6	167	6/64	PC-r	1	1	2	4	6	12	16	20
7	167	4/66	PC-r	1	1	2	4	6	12	16	20
8	166	R/68	C-price 25¢; PC-r	1	1	2	4	6	10	13	16

139. In the Reign of Terror

Ed	HRN	Date	Details	A	C	GD 2.0	VG 4.0	FN 6.0	VF 8.0	VF/NM 9.0	NM- 9.2
1	139	7/57	Original; Evans-a	1	1	4	8	12	29	40	50
2	154	–	PC-r	1	1	2	4	6	9	11	14
3	167	–	Has orig.date; PC-r	1	1	2	4	6	8	10	12
4	167	7/64	PC-r	1	1	2	4	6	8	10	12
5	166	R/1968	C-price 25¢; PC-r	1	1	2	4	6	8	10	12

140. On Jungle Trails

Ed	HRN	Date	Details	A	C	GD 2.0	VG 4.0	FN 6.0	VF 8.0	VF/NM 9.0	NM- 9.2
1	140	9/57	Original	1	1	4	8	12	29	40	50
2	150	–	PC-r	1	1	2	4	6	9	11	14
3	160	–	PC-r	1	1	2	4	6	9	11	14
4	167	9/63	PC-r	1	1	2	4	6	8	10	12
5	167	9/65	PC-r	1	1	2	4	6	8	10	12

141. Castle Dangerous

Ed	HRN	Date	Details	A	C	GD 2.0	VG 4.0	FN 6.0	VF 8.0	VF/NM 9.0	NM- 9.2
1	141	11/57	Original	1	1	6	12	18	38	52	65
2	152	–	PC-r	1	1	2	4	6	9	11	14
3	167	–	PC-r	1	1	2	4	6	9	11	14
4	166	7/67	PC-r	1	1	2	4	6	9	11	14

142. Abraham Lincoln

Ed	HRN	Date	Details	A	C	GD 2.0	VG 4.0	FN 6.0	VF 8.0	VF/NM 9.0	NM- 9.2
1	142	1/58	Original	1	1	5	10	15	36	48	60
2	154	–	PC-r	1	1	2	4	6	9	11	14
3	158	–	PC-r	1	1	2	4	6	9	11	14
4	167	10/63	PC-r	1	1	2	4	6	8	10	12
5	167	7/65	PC-r	1	1	2	4	6	8	10	12
6	166	11/67	PC-r	1	1	2	4	6	8	10	12
7	169	Fall/69	New price 25¢; stiff-c; PC-r	1	1	2	4	6	8	10	12

143. Kim

Ed	HRN	Date	Details	A	C	GD 2.0	VG 4.0	FN 6.0	VF 8.0	VF/NM 9.0	NM- 9.2
1	143	3/58	Original; Orlando-a	1	1	4	8	12	29	40	50
2	165	–	PC-r	1	1	2	4	6	8	10	12
3	167	11/63	PC-r	1	1	2	4	6	8	10	12
4	167	8/65	PC-r	1	1	2	4	6	8	10	12
5	169	Win/69	New price 25¢; stiff-c; PC-r	1	1	2	4	6	8	10	12

144. The First Men in the Moon

Ed	HRN	Date	Details	A	C	GD 2.0	VG 4.0	FN 6.0	VF 8.0	VF/NM 9.0	NM- 9.2
1	143	5/58	Original; Woodbridge/Williamson/Torres-a	1	1	6	12	18	40	55	70
2	152	–	(Rare)-PC-r	1	1	7	14	21	50	68	85
3	153	–	PC-r	1	1	2	4	6	9	11	14
4	161	–	PC-r	1	1	2	4	6	8	10	12
5	167	–	PC-r	1	1	2	4	6	8	10	12
6	167	12/65	PC-r	1	1	2	4	6	8	10	12
7	166	Fall/68	New-c&price 25¢; PC-r; stiff-c	1	2	3	6	9	16	20	24
8	169	Win/69	Stiff-c; PC-r	1	2	2	4	6	11	14	18

145. The Crisis

Ed	HRN	Date	Details	A	C	GD 2.0	VG 4.0	FN 6.0	VF 8.0	VF/NM 9.0	NM- 9.2
1	143	7/58	Original; Evans-a	1	1	5	10	15	36	48	60
2	156	–	PC-r	1	1	2	4	6	9	11	14
3	167	10/63	PC-r	1	1	2	4	6	8	10	12
4	167	3/65	PC-r	1	1	2	4	6	8	10	12
5	166	R/68	C-price 25¢; PC-r	1	1	2	4	6	8	10	12

146. With Fire and Sword

Ed	HRN	Date	Details	A	C	GD 2.0	VG 4.0	FN 6.0	VF 8.0	VF/NM 9.0	NM- 9.2
1	143	9/58	Original; Woodbridge-a	1	1	5	10	15	36	48	60
2	156	–	PC-r	1	1	2	4	6	10	13	16
3	167	11/63	PC-r	1	1	2	4	6	9	11	14
4	167	3/65	PC-r	1	1	2	4	6	9	11	14

147. Ben-Hur

Ed	HRN	Date	Details	A	C	GD 2.0	VG 4.0	FN 6.0	VF 8.0	VF/NM 9.0	NM- 9.2
1	147	11/58	Original; Orlando-a	1	1	5	10	15	33	44	55
2	152	–	Scarce; PC-r	1	1	5	10	15	36	48	60
3	153	–	PC-r	1	1	2	4	6	9	11	14
4	158	–	PC-r	1	1	2	4	6	9	11	14
5	167	–	Orig.date; but PC-r	1	1	2	4	6	8	10	12
6	167	2/65	PC-r	1	1	2	4	6	8	10	12
7	167	9/66	PC-r	1	1	2	4	6	8	10	12
8A	166	Fall/68	New-c&price 25¢; PC-r; soft-c	1	2	3	6	9	18	23	28
8B	166	Fall/68	New-c&price 25¢; PC-r; stiff-c; scarce	1	2	4	8	12	27	36	45

148. The Buccaneer

Ed	HRN	Date	Details	A	C	GD 2.0	VG 4.0	FN 6.0	VF 8.0	VF/NM 9.0	NM- 9.2
1	148	1/59	Orig.; Evans/Jenny-a; Saunders-c	1	1	4	8	12	29	40	50
2	568	–	Juniors list only PC-r	1	1	2	4	6	9	11	14
3	167	–	PC-r	1	1	2	4	6	8	10	12
4	167	9/65	PC-r	1	1	2	4	6	8	10	12
5	169	Sm/69	New price 25¢; PC-r; stiff-c	1	1	2	4	6	8	10	12

149. Off on a Comet

Ed	HRN	Date	Details	A	C	GD 2.0	VG 4.0	FN 6.0	VF 8.0	VF/NM 9.0	NM- 9.2
1	149	3/59	Orig.;G.McCann-a; blue reorder list	1	1	5	10	15	36	48	60
2	155	–	PC-r	1	1	2	4	6	9	11	14
3	149	–	PC-r; white reorder list; no coming-next ad	1	1	2	4	6	9	11	14
4	167	12/63	PC-r	1	1	2	4	6	8	10	12
5	167	2/65	PC-r	1	1	2	4	6	8	10	12
6	167	10/66	PC-r	1	1	2	4	6	8	10	12
7	166	Fall/68	New-c & price 25¢; PC-r	1	2	3	6	9	17	21	26

150. The Virginian

Ed	HRN	Date	Details	A	C	GD 2.0	VG 4.0	FN 6.0	VF 8.0	VF/NM 9.0	NM- 9.2
1	150	5/59	Original	1	1	6	12	18	38	52	65
2	164	–	PC-r	1	1	2	4	6	12	16	20
3	167	10/63	PC-r	1	1	3	6	9	17	21	26
4	167	12/65	PC-r	1	1	2	4	6	12	16	20

151. Won By the Sword

Ed	HRN	Date	Details	A	C	GD 2.0	VG 4.0	FN 6.0	VF 8.0	VF/NM 9.0	NM- 9.2
1	150	7/59	Original	1	1	5	10	15	36	48	60
2	164	–	PC-r	1	1	2	4	6	10	13	16
3	167	10/63	PC-r	1	1	2	4	6	10	13	16
4	166	7/67	PC-r	1	1	2	4	6	10	13	16

152. Wild Animals I Have Known

Ed	HRN	Date	Details	A	C	GD 2.0	VG 4.0	FN 6.0	VF 8.0	VF/NM 9.0	NM- 9.2
1	152	9/59	Orig.; L.B. Cole c/a	1	1	6	12	18	40	55	70
2A	149	–	PC-r; white reorder list; no coming-next ad; IBC: Jr. list #572	1	1	2	4	6	9	11	14
2B	149	–	PC-r; inside-bc: Jr. list to #555	1	1	2	4	6	10	12	15
2C	149	–	PC-r; inside-bc: has World Around Us ad; scarce	1	1	3	6	9	17	21	26
3	167	9/63	PC-r	1	1	2	4	6	8	10	12
4	167	8/65	PC-r	1	1	2	4	6	8	10	12
5	169	Fall/69	New price 25¢; stiff-c; PC-r	1	1	2	4	6	8	10	12

153. The Invisible Man

Ed	HRN	Date	Details	A	C	GD 2.0	VG 4.0	FN 6.0	VF 8.0	VF/NM 9.0	NM- 9.2
1	153	11/59	Original	1	1	7	14	21	46	63	80
2A	149	–	PC-r; white reorder list; no coming-next ad; inside-bc: Jr. list to #572	1	1	2	4	6	11	14	18
2B	149	–	PC-r; inside-bc: Jr. list to #555	1	1	2	4	6	12	16	20

Classics Illustrated #160 © GIL

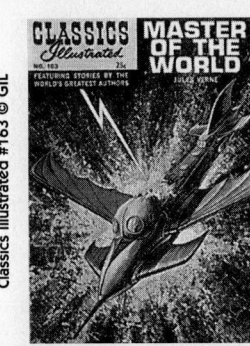

Classics Illustrated #163 © GIL

Classics Illustrated #164 © GIL

Ed	HRN	Date	Details	A	C	GD 2.0	VG 4.0	FN 6.0	VF 8.0	VF/NM 9.0	NM- 9.2
3	167	–	PC-r	1	1	2	4	6	10	12	15
4	167	2/65	PC r	1	1	2	4	6	10	12	15
5	167	9/66	PC-r	1	1	2	4	6	10	12	15
6	166	Win/69	New price 25¢; PC-r; stiff-c	1	1	2	4	6	10	12	15
7	169	Spr/71	Stiff-c; letters spelling 'Invisible Man' are 'solid' not 'invisible;' PC-r	1	1	2	4	6	10	12	15

154. The Conspiracy of Pontiac

Ed	HRN	Date	Details	A	C	GD 2.0	VG 4.0	FN 6.0	VF 8.0	VF/NM 9.0	NM- 9.2
1	154	1/60	Original	1	1	6	12	18	38	52	65
2	167	11/63	PC-r	1	1	2	4	6	12	16	20
3	167	7/64	PC-r	1	1	2	4	6	12	16	20
4	166	12/67	PC-r	1	1	2	4	6	12	16	20

155. The Lion of the North

Ed	HRN	Date	Details	A	C	GD 2.0	VG 4.0	FN 6.0	VF 8.0	VF/NM 9.0	NM- 9.2
1	154	3/60	Original	1	1	5	10	15	36	48	60
2	167	1/64	PC-r	1	1	2	4	6	11	14	18
3	166	R/1967	C-price 25¢; PC-r	1	1	2	4	6	10	12	15

156. The Conquest of Mexico

Ed	HRN	Date	Details	A	C	GD 2.0	VG 4.0	FN 6.0	VF 8.0	VF/NM 9.0	NM- 9.2
1	156	5/60	Orig.; Bruno Premiani-c/a	1	1	5	10	15	36	48	60
2	167	1/64	PC-r	1	1	2	4	6	10	12	15
3	166	8/67	PC-r	1	1	2	4	6	10	12	15
4	169	Spr/70	New price 25¢; stiff-c; PC-r	1	1	2	4	6	8	10	12

157. Lives of the Hunted

Ed	HRN	Date	Details	A	C	GD 2.0	VG 4.0	FN 6.0	VF 8.0	VF/NM 9.0	NM- 9.2
1	156	7/60	Orig.; L.B. Cole-c	1	1	6	12	18	38	52	65
2	167	2/64	PC-r	1	1	2	4	6	12	16	20
3	166	10/67	PC-r	1	1	2	4	6	12	16	20

158. The Conspirators

Ed	HRN	Date	Details	A	C	GD 2.0	VG 4.0	FN 6.0	VF 8.0	VF/NM 9.0	NM- 9.2
1	156	9/60	Original	1	1	6	12	18	38	52	65
2	167	7/64	PC-r	1	1	2	4	6	12	16	20
3	166	10/67	PC-r	1	1	2	4	6	12	16	20

159. The Octopus

Ed	HRN	Date	Details	A	C	GD 2.0	VG 4.0	FN 6.0	VF 8.0	VF/NM 9.0	NM- 9.2
1	159	11/60	Orig.; Gray Morrow-a; L.B. Cole-c	1	1	6	12	18	38	52	65
2	167	2/64	PC-r	1	1	2	4	6	12	16	20
3	166	R/1967	C-price 25¢; PC-r	1	1	2	4	6	12	16	20

160. The Food of the Gods

Ed	HRN	Date	Details	A	C	GD 2.0	VG 4.0	FN 6.0	VF 8.0	VF/NM 9.0	NM- 9.2
1A	159	1/61	Original	1	1	6	12	18	40	55	70
1B	160	1/61	Original; same, except for HRN	1	1	6	12	18	38	52	65
2	167	1/64	PC-r	1	1	2	4	6	12	16	20
3	166	6/67	PC-r	1	1	2	4	6	12	16	20

161. Cleopatra

Ed	HRN	Date	Details	A	C	GD 2.0	VG 4.0	FN 6.0	VF 8.0	VF/NM 9.0	NM- 9.2
1	161	3/61	Original	1	1	6	12	18	38	52	65
2	167	1/64	PC-r	1	1	2	4	6	14	18	22
3	166	8/67	PC-r	1	1	2	4	6	14	18	22

162. Robur the Conqueror

Ed	HRN	Date	Details	A	C	GD 2.0	VG 4.0	FN 6.0	VF 8.0	VF/NM 9.0	NM- 9.2
1	162	5/61	Original	1	1	6	12	18	38	52	65
2	167	7/64	PC-r	1	1	2	4	6	12	16	20
3	166	8/67	PC-r	1	1	2	4	6	12	16	20

163. Master of the World

Ed	HRN	Date	Details	A	C	GD 2.0	VG 4.0	FN 6.0	VF 8.0	VF/NM 9.0	NM- 9.2
1	163	7/61	Original; Gray Morrow-a	1	1	6	12	18	38	52	65
2	167	1/65	PC-r	1	1	2	4	6	12	16	20
3	166	R/1968	C-price 25¢; PC-r	1	1	2	4	6	12	16	20

164. The Cossack Chief

Ed	HRN	Date	Details	A	C	GD 2.0	VG 4.0	FN 6.0	VF 8.0	VF/NM 9.0	NM- 9.2
1	164	(1961)	Orig.; nd(10/61?)	1	1	6	12	18	38	52	65
2	167	4/65	PC-r	1	1	2	4	6	12	16	20
3	166	Fall/68	C-price 25¢; PC-r	1	1	2	4	6	12	16	20

165. The Queen's Necklace

Ed	HRN	Date	Details	A	C	GD 2.0	VG 4.0	FN 6.0	VF 8.0	VF/NM 9.0	NM- 9.2
1	164	1/62	Original; Morrow-a	1	1	6	12	18	38	52	65
2	167	4/65	PC-r	1	1	2	4	6	12	16	20
3	166	Fall/68	C-price 25¢; PC-r	1	1	2	4	6	12	16	20

166. Tigers and Traitors

Ed	HRN	Date	Details	A	C	GD 2.0	VG 4.0	FN 6.0	VF 8.0	VF/NM 9.0	NM- 9.2
1	165	5/62	Original	1	1	8	16	24	55	78	100
2	167	2/64	PC-r	1	1	3	7	10	21	28	35
3	167	11/66	PC-r	1	1	3	7	10	21	28	35

167. Faust

Ed	HRN	Date	Details	A	C	GD 2.0	VG 4.0	FN 6.0	VF 8.0	VF/NM 9.0	NM- 9.2
1	165	8/62	Original	1	1	13	26	39	90	133	175
2	167	2/64	PC-r	1	1	6	12	18	38	52	65
3	166	6/67	PC-r	1	1	6	12	18	38	52	65

168. In Freedom's Cause

Ed	HRN	Date	Details	A	C	GD 2.0	VG 4.0	FN 6.0	VF 8.0	VF/NM 9.0	NM- 9.2
1	169	Win/69	Original; Evans/Crandall-a; stiff-c; 25¢; no coming-next ad;	1	1	14	28	42	102	149	195

169. Negro Americans The Early Years

Ed	HRN	Date	Details	A	C	GD 2.0	VG 4.0	FN 6.0	VF 8.0	VF/NM 9.0	NM- 9.2
1	166	Spr/69	Orig. & last issue; 25¢; Stiff-c; no coming-next ad; other sources indicate publication date of 5/69	1	1	13	26	39	90	133	175
2	169	Spr/69	Stiff-c	1	1	7	14	21	46	63	80

NOTE: *Many other titles were prepared or planned but were only issued in British/European series.*

CLASSIC PUNISHER (Also see Punisher)
Marvel Comics: Dec, 1989 ($4.95, B&W, deluxe format, 68 pgs.)

1-Reprints Marvel Super Action #1 & Marvel Preview #2 plus new story 5.00

CLASSICS ILLUSTRATED
First Publishing/Berkley Publishing: Feb, 1990 - No. 27, July, 1991 ($3.75/$3.95, 52 pgs.)

1-27: 1-Gahan Wilson-c/a. 4-Sienkiewicz painted-c/a. 6-Russell scripts/layouts. 7-Spiegle-a. 9-Ploog-c/a. 16-Staton-a. 18-Gahan Wilson-c/a; 20-Geary-a. 26-Aesop's Fables (6/91). 26,27-Direct sale only 5.00

CLASSICS ILLUSTRATED
Acclaim Books/Twin Circle PublishingCo.: Feb, 1997 - Present ($4.99, digest-size) (Each book contains study notes)

A Christmas Carol-(12/97), A Connecticut Yankee in King Arthur's Court-(5/97), All Quiet on the Western Front-(1/98), A Midsummer's Night Dream-(4/97) Around the World in 80 Days-(1/98), A Tale of Two Cities-(2/97)Joe Orlando-r, Captains Courageous-(11/97), Crime and Punishment-(3/97), Dr. Jekyll and Mr. Hyde-(10/97), Don Quixote-(12/97), Frankenstein-(10/97), Great Expectations-(4/97), Hamlet-(3/97), Huckleberry Finn-(3/97), Jane Eyre-(2/97), Kidnapped-(1/98), Les Miserables-(5/97), Lord Jim-(9/97),Macbeth-(5/97), Moby Dick-(4/97), Oliver Twist-(5/97), Robinson Crusoe-(9/97), Romeo & Juliet-(2/97), Silas Marner-(11/97), The Call of the Wild-(9/97), The Count of Monte Cristo-(1/98), The House of the Seven Gables-(9/97), The Iliad-(12/97), The Invisible Man-(10/97), The Last of the Mohicans-(12/97), The Master of Ballantrae-(11/97), The Odyssey-(3/97), The Prince and the Pauper-(4/97), The Red Badge Of Courage-(9/97), Tom Sawyer-(2/97) Wuthering Heights-(11/97) 5.00

NOTE: *Stories reprinted from the original Gilberton Classic Comics and Classics Illustrated.*

CLASSICS ILLUSTRATED GIANTS
Gilberton Publications: Oct, 1949 (One-Shots - "OS")

These Giant Editions, all with new front and back covers, were advertised from 10/49 to 2/52. They were 50¢ on the newsstand and 60¢ by mail. They are actually four Classics in one volume. All the stories are reprints of the Classics Illustrated Series.

NOTE: There were also British hardback Adventure & Indian Giants in 1952, with the same covers but different contents: Adventure - 2, 7, 10; Indian - 17, 22, 37, 58. They are also rare.

	GD 2.0	VG 4.0	FN 6.0	VF 8.0	VF/NM 9.0	NM- 9.2
"An Illustrated Library of Great Adventure Stories" - reprints of No. 6,7,8,10 (Rare); Kiefer-c	139	278	417	869	1305	1740
"An Illustrated Library of Exciting Mystery Stories" - reprints of No. 30,21,40, 13 (Rare); Blum-c	152	304	456	950	1425	1900
"An Illustrated Library of Great Indian Stories" - reprints of No. 4,17,22,37 (Rare); Blum-c	139	278	417	869	1305	1740

Classics Illustrated Junior #502 © GIL

Classics Illustrated Special #144A © GIL

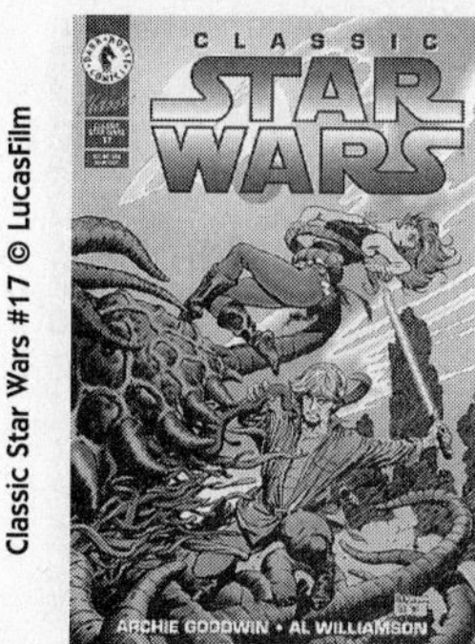

Classic Star Wars #17 © LucasFilm

GD 2.0 VG 4.0 FN 6.0 VF 8.0 VF/NM 9.0 NM- 9.2

INTRODUCTION TO CLASSICS ILLUSTRATED JUNIOR

Collectors of Juniors can be put into one of two categories: those who want any copy of each title, and those who want all the originals. Those seeking every original and reprint edition are a limited group, primarily because Juniors have no changes in art or covers to spark interest, and because reprints are so low in value it is difficult to get dealers to look for specific reprint editions.

In recent years it has become apparent that most serious Classics collectors seek Junior originals. Those seeking reprints seek them for low cost. This has made the previous note about the comparative market value of reprints inadequate. Three particular reprint editions are worth even more. For the 535-Twin Circle edition, see Giveaways. There are also reprint editions of 501 and 503 which have a full-page bc ad for the very rare Junior record. Those may sell as high as $10-$15 in mint. Original editions of 557 and 558 also have that ad.

There are no reprint editions of 577. The only edition, from 1969, is a 25 cent stiff-cover edition with no ad for the next issue. All other original editions have coming-next ad. But 577, like C.I. #168, was prepared in 1962 but not issued. Copies of 577 can be found in 1963 British/European series, which then continued with dozens of additional new Junior titles.

PRICES LISTED BELOW ARE FOR ORIGINAL EDITIONS, WHICH HAVE AN AD FOR THE NEXT ISSUE.

NOTE: *Non HRN 576 copies- many are written on or colored . Reprints with 576 HRN are worth about 1/3 original prices. All other HRN #'s are 1/2 original price*

CLASSICS ILLUSTRATED JUNIOR
Famous Authors Ltd. (Gilberton Publications): Oct, 1953 - Spring, 1971

501-Snow White & the Seven Dwarfs; Alex Blum-a 11 22 33 60 80 105
502-The Ugly Duckling 8 16 24 43 54 65
503-Cinderella 6 12 18 31 38 45
504-512: 504-The Pied Piper. 505-The Sleeping Beauty. 506-The Three Little Pigs. 507-Jack & the Beanstalk. 508-Goldilocks & the Three Bears. 509-Beauty and the Beast. 510-Little Red Riding Hood. 511-Puss-N Boots. 512-Rumpelstiltskin
5 10 15 23 28 32
513-Pinocchio 6 12 18 31 38 45
514-The Steadfast Tin Soldier 8 16 24 43 54 65
515-Johnny Appleseed 5 10 15 23 28 32
516-Aladdin and His Lamp 6 12 18 27 33 38
517-519: 517-The Emperor's New Clothes. 518-The Golden Goose. 519-Paul Bunyan
5 10 15 23 28 32
520-Thumbelina 6 12 18 28 34 40
521-King of the Golden River 5 10 15 23 28 32
522,523,530: 522-The Nightingale. 523-The Gallant Tailor. 530-The Golden Bird
5 10 15 22 26 30
524-The Wild Swans 6 12 18 27 33 38
525,526: 525-The Little Mermaid. 526-The Frog Prince 6 12 18 27 33 38
527-The Golden-Haired Giant 5 10 15 23 28 32
528-The Penny Prince 5 10 15 23 28 32
529-The Magic Servants 5 10 15 23 28 32
531-Rapunzel 5 10 15 23 28 32
532-534: 532-The Dancing Princesses. 533-The Magic Fountain. 534-The Golden Touch
5 10 14 20 24 28
535-The Wizard of Oz 8 16 24 40 50 60
536-The Chimney Sweep 5 10 15 23 28 32
537-The Three Fairies 5 10 15 24 30 35
538-Silly Hans 5 10 14 20 24 28
539-The Enchanted Fish 6 12 18 28 34 40
540-The Tinder-Box 6 12 18 28 34 40
541-Snow White & Rose Red 5 10 15 22 26 30
542-The Donkey's Tale 5 10 15 22 26 30
543-The House in the Woods 5 10 15 23 28 32
544-The Golden Fleece 6 12 18 29 36 42
545-The Glass Mountain 5 10 15 22 26 30
546-The Elves & the Shoemaker 5 10 15 22 26 30
547-The Wishing Table 5 10 15 23 28 32
548-551: 548-The Magic Pitcher. 549-Simple Kate. 550-The Singing Donkey. 551-The Queen Bee 5 10 14 20 24 28
552-The Three Little Dwarfs 5 10 15 23 28 32
553,556: 553-King Thrushbeard. 556-The Elf Mound 5 10 14 20 24 28
554-The Enchanted Deer 6 12 18 27 33 38
555-The Three Golden Apples 5 10 15 22 26 30
557-Silly Willy 5 10 15 24 30 35
558-The Magic Dish; L.B. Cole-c; soft and stiff-c exist on original
7 14 21 35 43 50
559-The Japanese Lantern; 1 pg. Ingels-a; L.B. Cole-c
7 14 21 35 43 50
560-The Doll Princess; L.B. Cole-c 7 14 21 35 43 50
561-Hans Humdrum; L.B. Cole-c 6 12 18 27 33 38
562-The Enchanted Pony; L.B. Cole-c 7 14 21 35 43 50
563,565-567,570: 563-The Wishing Well; L.B. Cole-c. 565-The Silly Princess; L.B. Cole-c. 566-Clumsy Hans; L.B. Cole-c. 567-The Bearskin Soldier; L.B. Cole-c. 570-The Pearl Princess 5 10 15 23 28 32
564-The Salt Mountain; L.B.Cole-c. 568-The Happy Hedgehog; L.B. Cole-c.
5 10 15 24 30 35
569,573: 569-The Three Giants.573-The Crystal Ball 5 10 15 22 26 30
571,572: 571-How Fire Came to the Indians. 572-The Drummer Boy
6 12 18 28 34 40
574-Brightboots 5 10 15 22 26 30
575-The Fearless Prince 5 10 15 24 30 35
576-The Princess Who Saw Everything 6 12 18 31 38 45
577-The Runaway Dumpling 8 16 24 40 50 60

NOTE: *Prices are for original editions. Last reprint - Spring, 1971.* ***Costanza*** *&* ***Schaffenberger*** *art in many issues.*

CLASSICS ILLUSTRATED SPECIAL ISSUE
Gilberton Co.: (Came out semi-annually) Dec, 1955 - Jul, 1962 (35¢, 100 pgs.)

129-The Story of Jesus (titled ...Special Edition) "Jesus on Mountain" cover
10 20 30 58 77 95
"Three Camels" cover (12/58) 12 24 36 69 92 115
"Mountain" cover (no date)-Has checklist on inside b/c to HRN #161 & different testimonial on back-c 9 18 27 49 62 75
"Mountain" cover (1968 re-issue; has white 50¢ circle) 8 16 24 40 50 60
132A-The Story of America (6/56); Cameron-a 9 18 27 49 62 75
135A-The Ten Commandments(12/56) 8 16 24 43 54 65
138A-Adventures in Science(6/57); HRN to 137 8 16 24 40 50 60
138A-(6/57)-2nd version w/HRN to 149 6 12 18 28 34 40
138A-(12/61)-3rd version w/HRN to 149 7 14 21 35 43 50
141A-The Rough Rider (Teddy Roosevelt)(12/57); Evans-a
8 16 24 43 54 65
144A-Blazing the Trails West(6/58)- 73 pgs. of Crandall/Evans plus Severin-a 8 16 24 46 58 70
147A-Crossing the Rockies(12/58)-Crandall/Evans-a 8 16 24 43 54 65
150A-Royal Canadian Police(6/59)-Ingels, Sid Check-a
8 16 24 43 54 65
153A-Men, Guns & Cattle(12/59)-Evans-a (26 pgs.); Kinstler-a
8 16 24 43 54 65
156A-The Atomic Age(6/60)-Crandall/Evans, Torres-a
8 16 24 43 54 65
159A-Rockets, Jets and Missiles(12/60)-Evans, Morrow-a
8 16 24 43 54 65
162A-War Between the States(6/61)-Kirby & Crandall/Evans-a; Ingels-a
15 30 45 84 115 145
165A-To the Stars(12/61)-Torres, Crandall/Evans, Kirby-a
9 18 27 52 66 80
166A-World War II('62)-Torres, Crandall/Evans, Kirby-a
11 22 33 63 84 105
167A-Prehistoric World(7/62)-Torres & Crandall/Evans-a; two versions exist (HRN to 165 & HRN to 167) 11 22 33 63 84 105
nn Special Issue-The United Nations (1964; 50¢; scarce); this is actually part of the European Special Series, which cont'd on after the U.S. series stopped issuing new titles in 1962. This English edition was prepared specifically for sale at the U.N. It was printed in Norway
34 68 102 193 274 355

NOTE: *There was another U.S. Special Issue prepared in 1962 with artwork by* ***Torres*** *entitled World War I. Unfortunately, it was never issued in any English-language edition. It was issued in 1964 in West Germany, The Netherlands, and some Scandanavian countries, with another edition in 1974 with a new cover.*

CLASSICS LIBRARY (See King Classics)

CLASSIC STAR WARS (Also see Star Wars)
Dark Horse Comics: Aug, 1992 - No. 20, June, 1994 ($2.50)

1-Begin Star Wars strip-r by Williamson; Williamson redrew portions of the panels to fit comic book format 6.00
2-10: 8-Polybagged w/Star Wars Galaxy trading card. 8-M. Schultz-c 4.00
11-19: 13-Yeates-c. 17-M. Schultz-c. 19-Evans-c 3.00
20-($3.50, 52 pgs.)-Polybagged w/trading card 3.50
Escape To Hoth TPB ($16.95) r/#15-20 17.00
The Rebel Storm TPB - r/#8-14 17.00
Trade paperback ($29.95, slip-cased)-Reprints all movie adaptations 30.00

NOTE: *Williamson c-1-5,7,9,10,14,15,20.*

CLASSIC STAR WARS: (Title series). **Dark Horse Comics**

--A NEW HOPE, 6/94 - No. 2, 7/94 ($3.95)
1,2: 1-r/Star Wars #1-3, 7-9 publ; 2-r/Star Wars #4-6, 10-12 publ. by Marvel Comics 4.00

--DEVILWORLDS, 8/96 - No.2, 9/96 ($2.50s)1,2: r/Alan Moore-s 2.50

--HAN SOLO AT STARS' END, 3/97 - No. 3, 5/97 ($2.95)
1-3: r/strips by Alfredo Alcala 3.00

--RETURN OF THE JEDI, 10/94 - No.2, 11/94 ($3.50)

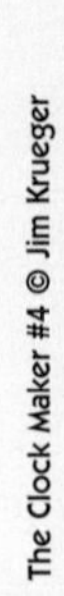
Clive Barker's Hellraiser #7 © MAR

The Clock Maker #4 © Jim Krueger

Cloudfall #1 © Robert Kirkman & EJ Su

	GD 2.0	VG 4.0	FN 6.0	VF 8.0	VF/NM 9.0	NM- 9.2

1,2: 1-r/1983-84 Marvel series; polybagged with w/trading card 3.50

--THE EARLY ADVENTURES, 8/94 - No. 9, 4/95 ($2.50)1-9 2.50

--THE EMPIRE STRIKES BACK, 8/94 - No. 2, 9/94 ($3.95)
1-r/Star Wars #39-44 published by Marvel Comics 4.00

CLASSIC X-MEN (Becomes X-Men Classic #46 on)
Marvel Comics Group: Sept, 1986 - No. 45, Mar, 1990
1-Begins-r of New X-Men 5.00
2-10: 10-Sabretooth app. 4.00
11-45: 11-1st origin of Magneto in back-up story. 17-Wolverine-c. 27-r/X-Men #121. 26-r/X-Men #120; Wolverine-c/app. 35-r/X-Men #129. 39-New Jim Lee back-up story (2nd-a on X-Men). 43-Byrne-c/a(r); $1.75, double-size 3.00
NOTE: ***Art Adams*** *c(p)-1-10, 12-16, 18-23.* ***Austin*** *c-10,15-21,24-28i.* ***Bolton*** *back up stories in 1-28,30-35.* ***Williamson*** *c-12-14i.*

CLAW (See Capt. Battle, Jr., Daredevil Comics & Silver Streak Comics)

CLAW THE UNCONQUERED (See Cancelled Comic Cavalcade)
National Periodical Publications/DC Comics: 5-6/75 - No. 9, 9-10/76; No. 10, 4-5/78 - No. 12, 8-9/78
1-1st app. Claw 1 3 4 6 8 10
2-12: 3-Nudity panel. 9-Origin 6.00
NOTE: ***Giffen*** *a-8-12p.* ***Kubert*** *c-10-12.* ***Layton*** *a-9i, 12i.*

CLAY CODY, GUNSLINGER
Pines Comics: Fall, 1957
1-Painted-c 6 12 18 31 38 45

CLEAN FUN, STARRING "SHOOGAFOOTS JONES"
Specialty Book Co.: 1944 (10¢, B&W, oversized covers, 24 pgs.)
nn-Humorous situations involving Negroes in the Deep South
White cover issue... 10 20 30 60 80 100
Dark grey cover issue... 11 22 33 66 88 110

CLEMENTINA THE FLYING PIG (See Dell Jr. Treasury)

CLEOPATRA (See Ideal, a Classical Comic No. 1)

CLERKS: THE COMIC BOOK (Also see Oni Double Feature #1)
Oni Press: Feb, 1998 ($2.95, B&W, one-shot)
1-Kevin Smith-s 2 4 6 8 10 12
1-Second printing 4.00
...Holiday Special (12/98, $2.95) Smith-s 5.00
...The Lost Scene (12/99, $2.95) Smith-s/Hester-a 5.00

CLIFFHANGER (See Battle Chasers, Crimson, and Danger Girl)
WildStorm Prod./Wizard Press: 1997 (Wizard supplement)
0-Sketchbook preview of Cliffhanger titles 6.00

CLIMAX! (Mystery)
Gillmor Magazines: July, 1955 - No. 2, Sept, 1955
1 17 34 51 95 130 165
2 14 28 42 79 107 135

CLINT (Also see Adolescent Radioactive Black Belt Hamsters)
Eclipse Comics: Sept, 1986 - No. 2, Jan, 1987 ($1.50, B&W)
1,2 2.25

CLINT & MAC (TV, Disney)
Dell Publishing Co.: No. 889, Mar, 1958
Four Color 889-Alex Toth-a, photo-c 14 28 42 97 141 185

CLIVE BARKER'S BOOK OF THE DAMNED: A HELLRAISER COMPANION
Marvel Comics (Epic): Oct, 1991 - No. 3, Nov, 1992 ($4.95, semi-annual)
Volume 1-3-(52 pgs.): 1-Simon Bisley-c. 2-(4/92). 3-(11/92)-McKean-a (1 pg.) 5.00

CLIVE BARKER'S HELLRAISER (Also see Epic, Hellraiser Nightbreed –Jihad, Revelations, Son of Celluloid, Tapping the Vein & Weaveworld)
Marvel Comics (Epic Comics): 1989 - No. 20, 1993 ($4.50-6.95, mature, quarterly, 68 pgs.)
Book 1-4,10-16,18,19: Based on Hellraiser & Hellbound movies; Bolton-c/a; Spiegle & Wrightson-a (graphic album). 10-Foil-c. 12-Sam Kieth-a 6.00
Book 5-9 ($5.95): 7-Bolton-a. 8-Morrow-a 6.00
Book 17-Alex Ross-a, 34 pgs. 2 4 6 8 10 12
Book 20-By Gaiman/McKean 1 2 3 5 6 8
...Collected Best ('02, $21.95)-r/by various incl. Ross, Gaiman, Mignola 22.00
...Collected Best II ('03, $19.95)-r/by various incl. Bolton, L. Wachowski, Dorman 20.00
...Dark Holiday Special ('92, $4.95)-Conrad-a 6.00
...Spring Slaughter 1 ('94, $6.95, 52 pgs.)-Painted-c 7.00
...Summer Special 1 ('92, $5.95, 68 pgs.) 6.00

CLIVE BARKER'S NIGHTBREED (Also see Epic)
Marvel Comics (Epic Comics): Apr, 1990 - No. 25, Mar, 1993 ($1.95/$2.25/$2.50, mature readers)
1-25: 1-4-Adapt horror movie. 5-New stories; Guice-a(p) 2.50

CLIVE BARKER'S THE HARROWERS
Marvel Comics (Epic Comics): Dec, 1993 - No. 6, May, 1994 ($2.50)
1-($2.95)-Glow-in-the-dark-c; Colan-c/a in all 3.00
2-6 2.50
NOTE: ***Colan*** *a(p)-1-6; c-1-3, 4p, 5p.* ***Williamson*** *a(i)-2, 4, 5(part).*

CLOAK AND DAGGER
Ziff-Davis Publishing Co.: Fall, 1952
1-Saunders painted-c 28 56 84 157 221 285

CLOAK AND DAGGER (Also see Marvel Fanfare)
Marvel Comics Group: Oct, 1983 - No. 4, Jan, 1984 (Mini-series) (See Spectacular Spider-Man #64)
1-4-Austin-c/a(i) in all. 4-Origin 3.00

CLOAK AND DAGGER (2nd Series)(Also see Marvel Graphic Novel #34 & Strange Tales)
Marvel Comics Group: July, 1985 - No. 11, Jan, 1987
1-11: 9-Art Adams-p 2.50
...And Power Pack (1990, $7.95, 68 pgs.) 8.00
NOTE: ***Mignola*** *c-7, 8.*

CLOAK AND DAGGER (3rd Series listed as Mutant Misadventures Of...)

CLOBBERIN' TIME
Marvel Comics: Sept, 1995 ($1.95) (Based on card game)
nn-Overpower game guide; Ben Grimm story 2.25

CLOCK MAKER, THE
Image Comics: Jan, 2003 - Present ($2.50, comic unfolds to 10"x13" pages)
1-4-Krueger-s 2.50

CLONEZONE SPECIAL
Dark Horse Comics/First Comics: 1989 ($2.00, B&W)
1-Back-up series from Badger & Nexus 2.25

CLOSE ENCOUNTERS (See Marvel Comics Super Special & Marvel Special Edition)

CLOSE SHAVES OF PAULINE PERIL, THE (TV cartoon)
Gold Key: June, 1970 - No. 4, March, 1971
1 4 8 12 22 30 38
2-4 3 6 9 16 20 24

CLOWN COMICS (No. 1 titled Clown Comic Book)
Clown Comics/Home Comics/Harvey Publ.: 1945 - No. 3, Win, 1946
nn (#1) 12 24 36 71 96 120
2,3 8 16 24 46 58 70

CLOUDFALL
Image Comics: Nov, 2003 - Present ($4.95, B&W, squarebound)
1-Kirkman-s/Su-a/c 5.00

CLOWNS, THE (I Pagliacci)
Dark Horse Comics: 1998 ($2.95, B&W, one-shot)
1-Adaption of the opera; P. Craig Russell-script 3.00

CLUBHOUSE RASCALS (#1 titled ...Presents?) (Also see Three Rascals)
Sussex Publ. Co. (Magazine Enterprises): June, 1956 - No. 2, Oct, 1956
1-The Brain app. in both; DeCarlo-a 8 16 24 43 54 65
2 7 14 21 36 43 50

CLUB "16"
Famous Funnies: June, 1948 - No. 4, Dec, 1948
1-Teen-age humor 12 24 36 71 96 120
2-4 8 16 24 43 54 65

CLUE COMICS (Real Clue Crime V2#4 on)
Hillman Periodicals: Jan, 1943 - No. 15(V2#3), May, 1947
1-Origin The Boy King, Nightmare, Micro-Face, Twilight, & Zippo
124 248 372 775 1163 1550
2 (scarce) 68 136 204 425 638 850
3-5 (9/43) 42 84 126 252 359 465
6,8,9: 8-Palais-c/a(2) 31 62 93 178 252 325
7-Classic torture-c (3/44) 46 92 138 276 413 550
10-Origin/1st app. The Gun Master & begin series; content changes to crime (10/46) 31 62 93 178 252 325

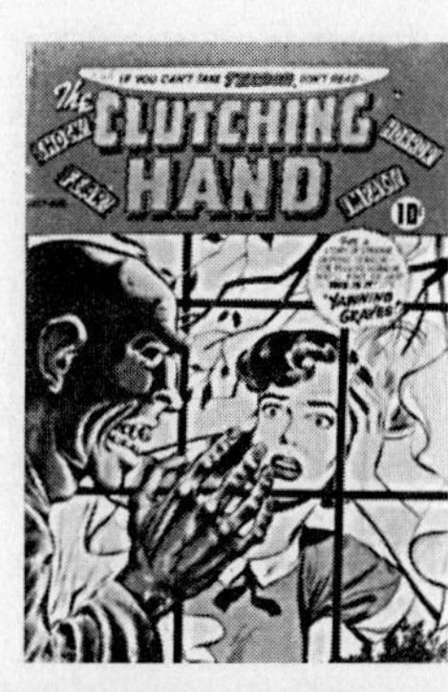

Clutching Hand #1 © ACG

Code of Honor #4 © MAR

Colossus Comics #1 © Sun Publ.

	GD 2.0	VG 4.0	FN 6.0	VF 8.0	VF/NM 9.0	NM- 9.2
11(12/46)	23	46	69	132	186	240
12-Origin Rackman; McWilliams-a, Guardineer-a(2)	29	58	87	164	232	300
V2#1-Nightmare new origin; Iron Lady app.; Simon & Kirby-a (3/47)	48	96	144	288	432	575
V2#2-S&K-a(2)-Bondage/torture-c; man attacks & kills people with electric iron. Infantino-a	66	132	198	413	617	820
V2#3-S&K-a(3)	50	100	150	300	450	600

CLUELESS SPRING SPECIAL (TV)
Marvel Comics: May, 1997 ($3.99, magazine sized, one-shot)

1-Photo-c from TV show 4.00

CLUTCHING HAND, THE
American Comics Group: July-Aug, 1954

1 39 78 117 230 325 420

CLYDE BEATTY COMICS (Also see Crackajack Funnies)
Commodore Productions & Artists, Inc.: October, 1953 (84 pgs.)

1-Photo front/back-c; movie scenes and comics 27 54 81 153 214 275

CLYDE CRASHCUP (TV)
Dell Publishing Co.: Aug-Oct, 1963 - No. 5, Sept-Nov, 1964

1-All written by John Stanley 14 28 42 99 145 190
2-5 12 24 36 84 125 165

COBALT BLUE (Also see Power Comics)
Innovation Publishing: Sept, 1989 - No. 2, Oct, 1989 ($1.95, 28 pgs.)

1,2-Gustovich-c/a/scripts 2.25
The Graphic Novel ($6.95, color, 52 pgs.)-r/1,2 7.00

CODE BLUE
Image Comics (Jet-Black): Apr, 1998 ($2.95, B&W)

1-Jimmie Robinson-s/a 3.00

CODE NAME: ASSASSIN (See 1st Issue Special)

CODENAME: DANGER
Lodestone Publishing: Aug, 1985 - No. 4, May, 1986 ($1.50)

1-4 2.25

CODENAME: FIREARM (Also see Firearm)
Malibu Comics (Ultraverse): June, 1995 - No. 5, Sept, 1995 ($2.95, bimonthly limited series)

0-5: 0-2-Alec Swan back-up story by James Robinson 3.00
NOTE: *Perez c-0.*

CODENAME: GENETIX
Marvel Comics UK: Jan, 1993 - No. 4, May, 1993 ($1.75, limited series)

1-4: Wolverine in all 3.00

CODENAME: KNOCKOUT
DC Comics (Vertigo): No. 0, Jun, 2001 - No. 23, June, 2003 ($2.50/$2.75)

0-15: Rodi-s in all. 0-6-Small Jr. -a. 1-Two covers by Chiodo & Cho. 7,8,10,11,12-Paquette-a. 9,13,14-Conner-a 2.50
16-23: 16-Begin $2.75-c. 23-Last issue; JG Jones-c 2.75

CODENAME SPITFIRE (Formerly Spitfire And The Troubleshooters)
Marvel Comics Group: No. 10, July, 1987 - No. 13, Oct, 1987

10-13: 10-Rogers-c/a (low printing) 3.50

CODENAME: STRYKE FORCE (Also See Cyberforce V1#4 & Cyberforce/Stryke Force: Opposing Forces
Image Comics (Top Cow Productions): Jan, 1994 - No. 14, Sept, 1995 ($1.95-$2.25)

0,1-14: 1-12-Silvestri stories, Peterson-a. 4-Stormwatch app. 14-Story continues in Cyberforce/Stryke Force: Opposing Forces; Turner-a 2.25
1-Gold, 1-Blue 4.00

CODE NAME: TOMAHAWK
Fantasy General Comics: Sept, 1986 ($1.75, high quality paper)

1-Sci/fi 2.25

CODE OF HONOR
Marvel Comics: Feb, 1997 - No. 4, May, 1997 ($5.95, limited series)

1-4-Fully painted by various; Dixon-s 6.00

CODY OF THE PONY EXPRESS (See Colossal Features Magazine)
Fox Features Syndicate: Sept, 1950 (See Women Outlaws)(One shot)

1-Painted-c 14 28 42 81 111 140

CODY OF THE PONY EXPRESS (Buffalo Bill...) (Outlaws of the West #11 on; Formerly Bullseye)
Charlton Comics: No. 8, Oct, 1955; No. 9, Jan, 1956; No. 10, June, 1956

	GD 2.0	VG 4.0	FN 6.0	VF 8.0	VF/NM 9.0	NM- 9.2
8-Bullseye on splash pg; not S&K-a	8	16	24	43	54	65
9,10: Buffalo Bill app. in all	6	12	18	28	34	40

CODY STARBUCK (1st app. in Star Reach #1)
Star Reach Productions: July, 1978

nn-Howard Chaykin-c/a 1 3 4 6 8 10
2nd printing 7.00
NOTE: *Both printings say First Printing. True first printing is on lower-grade paper, somewhat off-register, and snow in snow sequence has green tint.*

CO-ED ROMANCES
P. L. Publishing Co.: November, 1951

1 8 16 24 40 50 60

COFFEE WORLD
World Comics: Oct, 1995 ($1.50, B&W, anthology)

1-Shannon Wheeler's Too Much Coffee Man story 3.00

COFFIN, THE
Oni Press: Sept, 2000 - No. 4, May, 2001 ($2.95, B&W, limited series)

1-4-Hester-s/Huddleston-a 3.00
TPB (8/01, $11.95, TPB) r/#1-4 12.00

COLLECTORS DRACULA, THE
Millennium Publications: 1994 - No. 2, 1994 ($3.95, color/B&W, 52 pgs., limited series)

1,2-Bolton-a (7 pgs.) 4.00

COLLECTORS ITEM CLASSICS (See Marvel Collectors Item Classics)

COLONIA
Colonia Press: 1998 ($2.95, B&W)

1-5-Jeff Nicholson-s/a 3.00

COLORS IN BLACK
Dark Horse Comics: Mar, 1995 - No. 4, June, 1995 ($2.95, limited series)

1-4 3.00

COLOSSAL FEATURES MAGAZINE (Formerly I Loved) (See Cody of the Pony Express)
Fox Features Syndicate: No. 33, 5/50 - No. 34, 7/50; No. 3, 9/50 (Based on Columbia serial)

33,34: Cody of the Pony Express begins. 33-Painted-c. 34-Photo-c 14 28 42 81 111 140
3-Authentic criminal cases 14 28 42 81 111 140

COLOSSAL SHOW, THE (TV)
Gold Key: Oct, 1969

1 6 12 18 38 52 65

COLOSSUS (See X-Men)
Marvel Comics: Oct, 1997 ($2.99, 48 pgs., one-shot)

1-Raab-s/Hitch & Neary-a, wraparound-c 3.00

COLOSSUS COMICS (See Green Giant & Motion Picture Funnies Weekly)
Sun Publications (Funnies, Inc.?): March, 1940

1-(Scarce)-Tulpa of Tsang(hero); Colossus app. 517 1034 1551 3619 5560 7500
NOTE: *Cover by artist that drew Colossus in Green Giant Comics.*

COLOUR OF MAGIC, THE (Terry Pratchett's...)
Innovation Publishing: 1991 - No. 4, 1991 ($2.50, limited series)

1-4: Adapts 1st novel of the Discworld series 3.00

COLT .45 (TV)
Dell Publishing Co.: No. 924, 8/58 - No. 1058, 11-1/59-60; No. 4, 2-4/60 - No. 9, 5-7/61

Four Color 924(#1)-Wayde Preston photo-c on all 11 22 33 77 114 150
Four Color 1004,1058, #4,5,7-9: 1004-Photo-b/c 9 18 27 63 89 115
6-Toth-a 10 20 30 67 96 125

COLUMBIA COMICS
William H. Wise Co.: 1943

1-Joe Palooka, Charlie Chan, Capt. Yank, Sparky Watts, Dixie Dugan app. 29 58 87 164 232 300

COLUMBUS
Dark Horse Comics: Sept, 1992 ($2.50, B&W, one-shot)

1-Yeates painted-c 2.50

COMANCHE (See Four Color No. 1350)

COMANCHEROS, THE
Dell Publishing Co.: No. 1300, Mar-May, 1962

Four Color 1300-Movie, John Wayne photo-c 17 34 51 123 182 240

Combat Kelly and the Deadly Dozen #4 © MAR

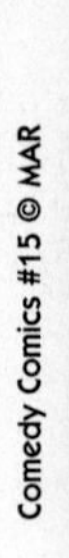

Comedy Comics #15 © MAR

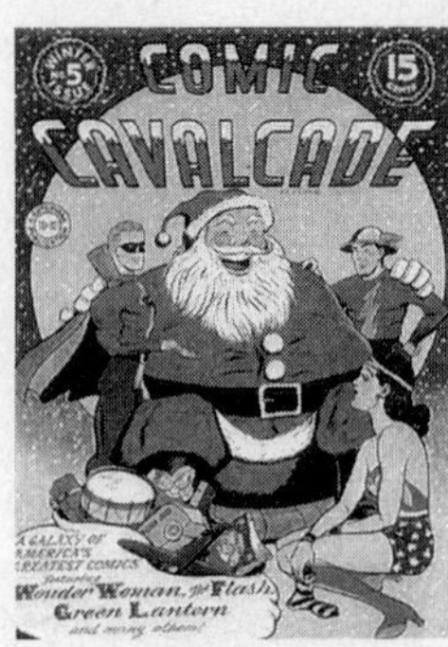

Comic Cavalcade #5 © DC

COMBAT
Atlas Comics (ANC): June, 1952 - No. 11, April, 1953

	GD 2.0	VG 4.0	FN 6.0	VF 8.0	VF/NM 9.0	NM- 9.2
1	25	50	75	147	202	260
2-Heath-c/a	13	26	39	76	103	130
3,5-9,11: 9-Robert Q. Sale-a	10	20	30	56	73	905
4-Krigstein-a	10	20	30	58	77	95
10-B&W and color illos. in **POP**	10	20	30	56	73	90

NOTE: *Combat Casey in 7-11.* ***Heath*** *c-1, 2, 9.* ***Maneely*** *a-1; c-3.* ***Pakula*** *a-1.* ***Reinman*** *a-1.*

COMBAT
Dell Publishing Co.: Oct-Nov, 1961 - No. 40, Oct, 1973 (No #9)

	GD 2.0	VG 4.0	FN 6.0	VF 8.0	VF/NM 9.0	NM- 9.2
1	6	12	18	38	52	65
2,3,5:	4	8	12	22	30	38
4-John F. Kennedy c/story (P.T. 109)	4	8	12	29	40	50
6,7,8(4-6/63), 8(7-9/63)	3	7	10	21	28	35
10-26: 26-Last 12¢ issue	3	6	9	16	20	24
27-40(reprints #1-14). 30-r/#4	2	4	6	12	16	20

COMBAT CASEY (Formerly War Combat)
Atlas Comics (SAI): No. 6, Jan, 1953 - No. 34, July, 1957

	GD 2.0	VG 4.0	FN 6.0	VF 8.0	VF/NM 9.0	NM- 9.2
6 (Indicia shows 1/52 in error)	15	30	45	86	118	150
7	9	18	27	52	66	80
8-Used in **POP**, pg. 94	8	16	24	46	58	70
9	8	16	24	43	54	65
10,13-19-Violent art by R. Q. Sale; Battle Brady x-over #10	11	22	33	63	84	105
11,12,20-Last Precode (2/55)	8	16	24	43	54	65
21-34	8	16	24	40	50	60

NOTE: ***Everett*** *a-6.* ***Heath*** *c-10, 17, 19, 30.* ***Maneely*** *c-6, 8.* ***Powell*** *a-29(5), 30(5), 34.* ***Severin*** *c-26, 33.*

COMBAT KELLY
Atlas Comics (SPI): Nov, 1951 - No. 44, Aug, 1957

	GD 2.0	VG 4.0	FN 6.0	VF 8.0	VF/NM 9.0	NM- 9.2
1-1st app. Combat Kelly; Heath-a	30	60	90	170	240	310
2	15	30	45	86	118	150
3-10	11	22	33	63	84	105
11-Used in **POP**, pgs. 94,95 plus color illo.	9	18	27	52	66	80
12-Color illo. in **POP**	9	18	27	52	66	80
13-16	8	16	24	46	58	70
17-Violent art by R. Q. Sale; Combat Casey app.	11	22	33	63	84	105
18-20,22-44: 18-Battle Brady app. 28-Last precode (1/55). 38-Green Berets story (8/56)	8	16	24	40	50	60
21-Transvestism-c	8	16	24	43	54	65

NOTE: ***Berg*** *a-8, 12-14, 16, 17, 19-23, 25, 26, 28, 31-36, 42-44; c-2.* ***Colan*** *a-42.* ***Heath*** *a-4; c-31.* ***Lawrence*** *a-23.* ***Maneely*** *a-4(2), 6, 7(3), 8; c-4, 5, 7, 8, 10, 25.* ***R.Q. Sale*** *a-17, 25.* ***Severin*** *c-41, 42.* ***Whitney*** *a-5.*

COMBAT KELLY (...and the Deadly Dozen)
Marvel Comics Group: June, 1972 - No. 9, Oct, 1973

	GD 2.0	VG 4.0	FN 6.0	VF 8.0	VF/NM 9.0	NM- 9.2
1-Intro & origin new Combat Kelly; Ayers/Mooney-a; Severin-c (20¢)	3	6	9	16	20	25
2,5-8	2	4	6	9	11	14
3,4: 3-Origin. 4-Sgt. Fury-c/s	2	4	6	11	14	18
9-Death of the Deadly Dozen	2	4	6	12	16	20

COMBINED OPERATIONS (See The Story of the Commandos)

COMEBACK (See Zane Grey 4-Color 357)

COMEDY CARNIVAL
St. John Publishing Co.: no date (1950's) (100 pgs.)

	GD 2.0	VG 4.0	FN 6.0	VF 8.0	VF/NM 9.0	NM- 9.2
nn-Contains rebound St. John comics	36	72	108	204	290	375

COMEDY COMICS (1st Series) (Daring Mystery #1-8) (Becomes Margie Comics #35 on)
Timely Comics (TCI 9,10): No. 9, April, 1942 - No. 34, Fall, 1946

	GD 2.0	VG 4.0	FN 6.0	VF 8.0	VF/NM 9.0	NM- 9.2
9-(Scarce)-The Fin by Everett, Capt. Dash, Citizen V, & The Silver Scorpion app.; Wolverton-a; 1st app. Comedy Kid; satire on Hitler & Stalin; The Fin, Citizen V & Silver Scorpion cont. from Daring Mystery	272	544	816	1700	2550	3400
10-(Scarce)-Origin The Fourth Musketeer, Victory Boys; Monstro, the Mighty app.	208	416	624	1300	1950	2600
11-Vagabond, Stuporman app.	52	104	157	312	469	625
12,13	15	30	45	86	118	150
14-Origin/1st app. Super Rabbit (3/43) plus-c	52	104	157	312	469	625
15-20	14	28	42	79	107	135
21-32	10	20	30	58	77	95
33-Kurtzman-a (5 pgs.)	13	26	39	74	100	125
34-Intro Margie; Wolverton-a (5 pgs.)	20	40	60	112	156	200

COMEDY COMICS (2nd Series)
Marvel Comics (ACI): May, 1948 - No. 10, Jan, 1950

	GD 2.0	VG 4.0	FN 6.0	VF 8.0	VF/NM 9.0	NM- 9.2
1-Hedy, Tessie, Millie begin; Kurtzman's "Hey Look" (he draws himself)	34	68	102	196	278	360
2	14	28	42	81	111	140
3,4-Kurtzman's "Hey Look" (?&3)	15	30	45	84	115	145
5-10	9	18	27	49	62	75

COMET, THE (See The Mighty Crusaders & Pep Comics #1)
Red Circle Comics (Archie): Oct, 1983 - No. 2, Dec, 1983

	GD 2.0	VG 4.0	FN 6.0	VF 8.0	VF/NM 9.0	NM- 9.2
1-Re-intro & origin The Comet; The American Shield begins. Nino & Infantino art in both. Hangman in both						5.00
2-Origin continues.						4.00

COMET, THE
DC Comics (Impact Comics): July, 1991 - No. 18, Dec, 1992 ($1.00/$1.25)

	GD 2.0	VG 4.0	FN 6.0	VF 8.0	VF/NM 9.0	NM- 9.2
1						3.00
2-18: 4-Black Hood app. 6-Re-intro Hangman. 8-Web x-over. 10-Contains Crusaders trading card. 4-Origin. Netzer(Nasser) c(p)-11,14-17						2.50
Annual 1 (1992, $2.50, 68 pgs.)-Contains Impact trading card; Shield back-up story						2.50

COMET MAN, THE (Movie)
Marvel Comics Group: Feb, 1987 - No. 6, July, 1987 (limited series)

	GD 2.0	VG 4.0	FN 6.0	VF 8.0	VF/NM 9.0	NM- 9.2
1-6: 3-Hulk app. 4-She-Hulk shower scene c/s. Fantastic 4 app. 5-Fantastic 4 app.						2.50

NOTE: ***Kelley Jones*** *a-1-6p.*

COMIC ALBUM (Also see Disney Comic Album)
Dell Publishing Co.: Mar-May, 1958 - No. 18, June-Aug, 1962

	GD 2.0	VG 4.0	FN 6.0	VF 8.0	VF/NM 9.0	NM- 9.2
1-Donald Duck	9	18	27	65	93	120
2-Bugs Bunny	5	10	15	36	48	60
3-Donald Duck	8	16	24	53	74	95
4-6,8-10: 4-Tom & Jerry. 5-Woody Woodpecker. 6,10-Bugs Bunny. 8-Tom & Jerry. 9-Woody Woodpecker	4	8	12	29	40	50
7,11,15: Popeye. 11-(9-11/60)	5	10	15	36	48	60
12-14: 12-Tom & Jerry. 13-Woody Woodpecker. 14-Bugs Bunny	4	8	12	29	40	50
16-Flintstones (12-2/61-62)-3rd app. Early Cave Kids app.	9	18	27	60	85	110
17-Space Mouse (3rd app.)	5	10	15	36	48	60
18-Three Stooges; photo-c	9	18	27	60	85	110

COMIC BOOK
Marvel Comics-#1/Dark Horse Comics-#2: 1995 ($5.95, oversize)

	GD 2.0	VG 4.0	FN 6.0	VF 8.0	VF/NM 9.0	NM- 9.2
1-Spumco characters by John K.	1	2	3	4	5	7
2-(Dark Horse)						6.00

COMIC CAPERS
Red Circle Mag./Marvel Comics: Fall, 1944 - No. 6, Summer, 1946

	GD 2.0	VG 4.0	FN 6.0	VF 8.0	VF/NM 9.0	NM- 9.2
1-Super Rabbit, The Creeper, Silly Seal, Ziggy Pig, Sharpy Fox begin	27	54	81	153	214	275
2	14	28	42	81	111	140
3-6	11	22	33	66	88	110

COMIC CAVALCADE
All-American/National Periodical Publications: Winter, 1942-43 - No. 63, June-July, 1954
(Contents change with No. 30, Dec-Jan, 1948-49 on)

	GD 2.0	VG 4.0	FN 6.0	VF 8.0	VF/NM 9.0	NM- 9.2
1-The Flash, Green Lantern, Wonder Woman, Wildcat, The Black Pirate by Moldoff (also #2), Ghost Patrol, and Red White & Blue begin; Scribbly app.; Minute Movie	931	1862	2793	6517	10,009	13,500
2-Mutt & Jeff begin; last Ghost Patrol & Black Pirate; Minute Movies	244	488	732	1525	2288	3050
3-Hop Harrigan & Sargon, the Sorcerer begin; The King app.	166	332	498	1038	1557	2075
4,5: 4-The Gay Ghost, The King, Scribbly, & Red Tornado app. 5-Christmas-c. 5-Prints ad for Jr. JSA membership kit that includes "The Minute Man Answers The Call"	150	300	450	938	1407	1875
6-10: 7-Red Tornado & Black Pirate app.; last Scribbly. 9-Fat & Slat app.; X-Mas-c	116	232	348	725	1088	1450
11,12,14: 12-Last Red White & Blue	96	192	288	600	900	1200
13-Solomon Grundy app.; X-Mas-c	152	304	456	950	1425	1900
15-Just a Story begins	102	204	306	638	957	1275
16-20: 19-Christmas-c	91	182	273	569	855	1140
21-23: 22-Johnny Peril begins. 23-Harry Lampert-c (Toth swipes)	85	170	255	531	796	1060
24-Solomon Grundy x-over in Green Lantern	112	224	336	700	1050	1400
25-28: 25-Black Canary app.; X-Mas-c. 26-28-Johnny Peril app. 28-Last Mutt & Jeff	76	152	228	475	713	950

29-(10-11/48)-Last Flash, Wonder Woman, Green Lantern & Johnny Peril; Wonder Woman invents "Thinking Machine"; 2nd computer in comics (after Flash Comics #52);

The Comics #3 © DELL

Comics and Stories #1 © DH

Comics on Parade #23 © UFS

	GD 2.0	VG 4.0	FN 6.0	VF 8.0	VF/NM 9.0	NM- 9.2

Leave It to Binky story (early app.) 85 170 255 531 796 1060
30-(12-1/48-49)-The Fox & the Crow, Dodo & the Frog & Nutsy Squirrel begin
40 80 120 240 345 450
31-35 24 48 72 138 194 250
36-49: 41-Last squarebound issue 18 36 54 101 138 175
50-62(Scarce) 22 44 66 124 172 220
63(Rare) 34 68 102 196 278 360

NOTE: ***Grossman** a-30-63. **E.E. Hibbard** c-(Flash only)-1-4, 7-14, 16-19, 21. **Sheldon Mayer** a(2-3)-40-63. **Moulson** c(G.L.)-7, 15. **Nodell** c(G.L.)-9. **H.G. Peter** c(W. Woman only)-1, 3-21, 24. **Post** a-31, 36. **Purcell** c(G.L.)-2-5, 10. **Reinman** a(Green Lantern)-4-6, 8, 9, 13, 15-21; c(Gr. Lantern)-6, 8, 19. **Toth** a(Green Lantern)-26-28; c-27. Atom app.-22, 23.*

COMIC COMICS
Fawcett Publications: Apr, 1946 - No. 10, Feb, 1947

1-Captain Kid; Nutty Comics #1 in indicia 14 28 42 81 111 140
2-10-Wolverton-a, 4 pgs. each. 5-Captain Kidd app. Mystic Moot by Wolverton in #2-10? 15 30 45 86 118 150

COMIC LAND
Fact and Fiction Publ.: March, 1946

1-Sandusky & the Senator, Sam Stupor, Sleuth, Marvin the Great, Sir Passer, Phineas Gruff app.; Irv Tirman & Perry Williams art 15 30 45 86 118 150

COMICO CHRISTMAS SPECIAL
Comico: Dec, 1988 ($2.50, 44pgs.)

1-Rude/Williamson-a; Dave Stevens-c 4.00

COMICO COLLECTION (Also see Grendel)
Comico: 1987 ($9.95, slipcased collection)

nn-Contains exclusive Grendel: Devil's Vagary, 9 random Comico comics, a poster and newsletter in black slipcase w/silver ink 25.00

COMICO PRIMER (See Primer)

COMIC PAGES (Formerly Funny Picture Stories)
Centaur Publications: V3#4, July, 1939 - V3#6, Dec, 1939

V3#4-Bob Wood-a 54 108 162 324 487 650
5,6: 6-Schwab-c 42 84 126 252 376 500

COMICS (See All Good)

COMICS, THE
Dell Publ. Co.: Mar, 1937 - No. 11, Nov, 1938 (Newspaper strip-r; bi-monthly)

1-1st app. Tom Mix in comics; Wash Tubbs, Tom Beatty, Myra North, Arizona Kid, Erik Noble & International Spy w/Doctor Doom begin 176 352 528 1100 1650 2200
2 80 160 240 500 750 1000
3-11: 3-Alley Oop begins 66 132 198 413 617 820

COMICS AND STORIES (See Walt Disney's Comics and Stories)

COMICS & STORIES (Also see Wolf & Red)
Dark Horse Comics: Apr, 1996 - No. 4, July, 1996 ($2.95, lim. series) (Created by Tex Avery)

1-4: Wolf & Red app; reads Comics and Stories on-c. 1-Terry Moore-a. 2-Reed Waller-a 3.00

COMICS CALENDAR, THE (The 1946...)
True Comics Press (ordered through the mail): 1946 (25¢, 116 pgs.) (Stapled at top)

nn-(Rare) Has a "strip" story for every day of the year in color
40 80 120 240 345 450

COMICS DIGEST (Pocket size)
Parents' Magazine Institute: Winter, 1942-43 (B&W, 100 pgs)

1-Reprints from True Comics (non-fiction World War II stories)
9 18 27 54 70 85

COMICS EXPRESS
Eclipse Comics: Nov, 1989 - No. 2, Jan, 1990 ($2.95, B&W, 68pgs.)

1,2: Collection of strip-r; 2(12/89-c, 1/90 inside) 3.00

COMICS FOR KIDS
London Publ. Co./Timely: 1945 (no month); No. 2, Sum, 1945 (Funny animal)

1,2-Puffy Pig, Sharpy Fox 15 30 45 86 118 150

COMICS' GREATEST WORLD
Dark Horse Comics: Jun, 1993 - V4#4, Sept, 1993 ($1.00, weekly, lim. series)

Arcadia (Wk 1): V1#1,2,4: 1-X: Frank Miller-c. 2-Pit Bulls. 4-Monster. 2.25
1-B&W Press Proof Edition (1500 copies) 1 3 4 6 8 10
1-Silver-c; distr. retailer bonus w/print & cards 1 2 3 5 6 8
3-Ghost, Dorman-c; Hughes-a 4.00
Retailer's Prem. Emb. Silver Foil Logo-r/V1#1-4 1 3 4 6 8 10
Golden City (Wk 2: V2#1-4: 1-Rebel; Ordway-c. 2-Mecha; Dave Johnson-c. 3-Titan; Walt Simonson-c. 4-Catalyst; Perez-c. 2.25
1-Gold-c; distr. retailer bonus w/print & cards. 6.00
Retailer's Prem. Embos. Gold Foil Logo-r/V2#1-4 1 2 3 5 6 8
Steel Harbor (Week 3): V3#1-Barb Wire; Dorman-c; Gulacy-a(p) 4.00
2-4: 2-The Machine. 3-Wolfgang. 4-Motorhead 2.25
1-Silver-c; distr. retailer bonus w/print & cards 1 2 3 5 6 8
Retailer's Prem. Emb. Red Foil Logo-r/V3#1-4. 1 3 4 6 8 10
Vortex (Week 4): V4#1-4: 1-Division 13; Dorman-c. 2-Hero Zero; Art Adams-c. 3-King Tiger; Chadwick-a(p); Darrow-c. 4-Vortex; Miller-c. 2.25
1-Gold-c; distr. retailer bonus w/print & cards. 6.00
Retailer's Prem. Emb. Blue Foil Logo-r/V4#1-4. 1 2 3 5 6 8

COMICS' GREATEST WORLD: OUT OF THE VORTEX (See Out of The Vortex)

COMICS HITS (See Harvey Comics Hits)

COMICS MAGAZINE, THE (...Funny Pages #3)(Funny Pages #6 on)
Comics Magazine Co. (1st Comics Mag./Centaur Publ.): May, 1936 - No. 5, Sept, 1936 (Paper covers)

1-1st app. Dr. Mystic (a.k.a. Dr. Occult) by Siegel & Shuster (the 1st app. of a Superman prototype in comics). Dr. Mystic is not in costume but later appears in costume as a more pronounced prototype in More Fun #14-17. (1st episode of "The Koth and the Seven"; continues in More Fun #14; originally scheduled for publication at DC). 1 pg. Kelly-a; Sheldon Mayer-a 1500 3000 4500 12,000 - -
2-Federal Agent (a.k.a. Federal Men) by Siegel & Shuster; 1 pg. Kelly-a
275 550 825 1550 2075 2600
3-5 225 450 675 1250 1725 2200

COMICS NOVEL (Anarcho, Dictator of Death)
Fawcett Publications: 1947

1-All Radar; 51 pg anti-fascism story 31 62 93 178 252 325

COMICS ON PARADE (No. 30 on are a continuation of Single Series)
United Features Syndicate: Apr, 1938 - No. 104, Feb, 1955

1-Tarzan by Foster; Captain & the Kids, Little Mary Mixup, Abbie & Slats, Ella Cinders, Broncho Bill, Li'l Abner begin 348 696 1044 2262 3481 4700
2 (Tarzan & others app. on-c of #1-3,17) 123 246 369 769 1155 1540
3 96 192 288 600 900 1200
4,5 74 148 222 463 694 925
6-10 52 104 156 312 469 625
11-16,18-20 42 84 126 252 376 500
17-Tarzan-c 48 96 144 288 432 575
21-29: 22-Son of Tarzan begins. 22,24,28-Tailspin Tommy-c. 29-Last Tarzan issue
38 76 114 219 310 400
30-Li'l Abner 23 46 69 130 183 235
31-The Captain & the Kids 17 34 51 98 134 170
32-Nancy & Fritzi Ritz 14 28 42 81 111 140
33,36,39,42-Li'l Abner 19 38 57 109 152 195
34,37,40-The Captain & the Kids (10/41,6/42,3/43) 16 32 48 92 126 160
35,38-Nancy & Fritzi Ritz. 38-Infinity-c 14 28 42 79 107 135
41-Nancy & Fritzi Ritz 10 20 30 60 80 100
43-The Captain & the Kids 16 32 48 92 126 160
44 (3/44),47,50: Nancy & Fritzi Ritz 10 20 30 60 80 100
45-Li'l Abner 16 32 48 92 126 160
46,49-The Captain & the Kids 13 26 39 76 103 130
48-Li'l Abner (3/45) 16 32 48 92 126 160
51,54-Li'l Abner 13 26 39 76 103 130
52-The Captain & the Kids (3/46) 10 20 30 56 73 90
53,55,57-Nancy & Fritzi Ritz 10 20 30 56 73 90
56-The Captain & the Kids (r/Sparkler) 10 20 30 56 73 90
58-Li'l Abner; continues as Li'l Abner #61? 13 26 39 76 103 130
59-The Captain & the Kids 8 16 24 46 58 70
60-70-Nancy & Fritzi Ritz 8 16 24 43 54 65
71-99,101-104-Nancy & Sluggo: 71-76-Nancy only 7 14 21 37 46 55
100-Nancy & Sluggo 13 26 39 76 103 130
Special Issue, 7/46; Summer, 1948 - The Captain & the Kids app.
8 16 24 43 54 65

NOTE: Bound Volume (Very Rare) includes No. 1-12; bound by publisher in pictorial comic boards & distributed at the 1939 World's Fair and through mail order from ads in comic books (also see Tip Top)
256 512 768 1600 2400 3200

NOTE: *Li'l Abner reprinted from Tip Top.*

COMICS READING LIBRARIES (See the Promotional Comics section)

COMICS REVUE
St. John Publ. Co. (United Features Synd.): June, 1947 - No. 5, Jan, 1948

1-Ella Cinders & Blackie 11 22 33 63 84 105
2,4: 2-Hap Hopper (7/47). 4-Ella Cinders (9/47) 8 16 24 46 58 70
3,5: 3-Iron Vic (8/47). 5-Gordo No. 1 (1/48) 8 16 24 43 54 65

Commander Battle and the Atomic Sub #1 © ACG

Common Grounds #1 © TCOW

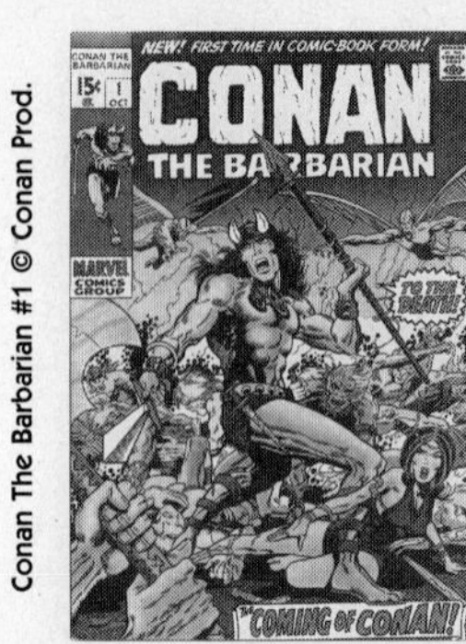

Conan The Barbarian #1 © Conan Prod.

	GD	VG	FN	VF	VF/NM	NM-
	2.0	4.0	6.0	8.0	9.0	9.2

COMIC STORY PAINT BOOK
Samuel Lowe Co.: 1943 (Large size, 68 pgs.)
1055-Captain Marvel & a Captain Marvel Jr. story to read & color; 3 panels in color per pg. (reprints) 76 152 228 475 713 950

COMIX BOOK
Marvel Comics Group/Krupp Comics Works No. 4,5: 1974 - No. 5, 1976 ($1.00, B&W, magazine)
1-Underground comic artists; 2 pgs. Wolverton-a 3 6 9 16 20 25
2,3: 2-Wolverton-a (1 pg.) 2 4 6 14 18 22
4(2/76), 4(5/76), 5 (Low distribution) 3 6 9 16 20 24
NOTE: *Print run No. 1-3: 200-250M; No. 4&5: 10M each.*

COMIX INTERNATIONAL
Warren Magazines: Jul, 1974 - No. 5, Spring, 1977 (Full color, stiff-c, mail only)
1-Low distribution; all Corben story remainders from Warren; Corben-c on all 8 16 24 55 78 100
2,4: 2-Two Dracula stories; Wood, Wrightson-r; Crandall-a; Maroto-a. 4-Printing w/ 3 Corben sty 4 8 12 27 36 45
3-5: 3-Dax story. 4-(printing without Corben story). 4-Crandall-a. 4,5-Vampirella stories. 5-Spirit story; Eisner-a 4 8 12 22 30 38
NOTE: *No. 4 had two printings with extra **Corben** story in one. No. 3 may also have a variation. No. 3 has two Jeff Jones reprints from Vampirella.*

COMMANDER BATTLE AND THE ATOMIC SUB
Amer. Comics Group (Titan Publ. Co.): Jul-Aug, 1954 - No. 7, Aug-Sep, 1955
1 (3-D effect)-Moldoff flying saucer-c 48 96 144 288 432 575
2,4-7: 2-Moldoff-c. 4-(1-2/55)-Last pre-code; Landau-a. 5-3-D effect story (2 pgs.). 6,7-Landau-a. 7-Flying saucer-c 33 66 99 190 270 350
3-H-Bomb-c; Atomic Sub becomes Atomic Spaceship 35 70 105 201 283 365

COMMANDO ADVENTURES
Atlas Comics (MMC): June, 1957 - No. 2, Aug, 1957
1-Severin-c 12 24 36 71 96 120
2-Severin-c; Drucker-a? 10 20 30 56 73 90

COMMANDO YANK (See The Mighty Midget Comics & Wow Comics)

COMMON GROUNDS
Image Comics (Top Cow): Feb, 2004 - Present ($2.99)
1-Two covers; art by Jurgens and Oeming 3.00

COMPLETE BOOK OF COMICS AND FUNNIES
William H. Wise & Co.: 1944 (25¢, one-shot, 196 pgs.)
1-Origin Brad Spencer, Wonderman; The Magnet, The Silver Knight by Kinstler, & Zudo the Jungle Boy app. 42 84 126 252 359 465

COMPLETE BOOK OF TRUE CRIME COMICS
William H. Wise & Co.: No date (Mid 1940's) (25¢, 132 pgs.)
nn-Contains Crime Does Not Pay rebound (includes #22) 112 224 336 700 1050 1400

COMPLETE COMICS (Formerly Amazing Comics No. 1)
Timely Comics (EPC): No. 2, Winter, 1944-45
2-The Destroyer, The Whizzer, The Young Allies & Sergeant Dix; Schomburg-c 152 304 456 950 1425 1900

COMPLETE GUIDE TO THE DEADLY ARTS OF KUNG FU AND KARATE
Marvel Comics: 1974 (68 pgs., B&W magazine)
V1#1-Bruce Lee-c and 5 pg. story (scarce) 4 8 12 29 40 50

COMPLETE LOVE MAGAZINE (Formerly a pulp with same title)
Ace Periodicals (Periodical House): V26#2, May-June, 1951 - V32#4(#191), Sept, 1956
V26#2-Painted-c (52 pgs.) 8 16 24 40 50 60
V26#3-6(2/52), V27#1(4/52)-6(1/53) 6 12 18 31 38 45
V28#1(3/53), V28#2(5/53), V29#3(7/53)-6(12/53) 6 12 18 28 34 40
V30#1(2/54), V30#1(#176, 4/54),2,4-6(#181, 1/55) 5 10 15 24 30 40
V30#3(#178)-Rock Hudson photo-c 6 12 18 31 38 45
V31#1(#182, 3/55)-Last precode 5 10 15 24 30 35
V31#2(5/55)-6(#187, 1/56) 5 10 15 22 26 30
V32#1(#188, 3/56)-4(#191, 9/56) 5 10 15 22 26 30
NOTE: *(34 total issues). Photo-c V27#5-on. Painted-c V26#3.*

COMPLETE MYSTERY (True Complete Mystery No. 5 on)
Marvel Comics (PrPI): Aug, 1948 - No. 4, Feb, 1949 (Full length stories)
1-Seven Dead Men 44 88 132 264 395 525
2-4: 2-Jigsaw of Doom! 3-Fear in the Night; Burgos-c/a (28 pgs.). 4-A Squealer Dies Fast 39 78 117 230 325 420

COMPLETE ROMANCE
Avon Periodicals: 1949
1-(Scarce)-Reprinted as Women to Love 40 80 120 240 340 440

CONAN (See Chamber of Darkness #4, Giant-Size..., Handbook of..., King Conan, Marvel Graphic Novel #19, 28, Marvel Treasury Ed., Power Record Comics, Robert E. Howard's.., Savage Sword of Conan, and Savage Tales)

CONAN: (Title Series): Marvel Comics

CONAN, 8/95 - No. 11, 6/96 ($2.95), 1-11: 4-Malibu Comic's Rune app. 3.00

...CLASSIC, 6/94 - No. 11, 4/95 ($1.50), 1-11: 1-r/Conan #1 by B. Smith, r/covers w/changes. 2-11-r/Conan #2-11 by Smith. 2-Bound w/cover to Conan The Adventurer #2 by mistake 2.25

...DEATH COVERED IN GOLD, 9/99 - No. 3, 11/99 ($2.99), 1-3-Roy Thomas-s/ John Buscema-a 3.00

...FLAME AND THE FIEND, 8/00 - No. 3, 10/00 ($2.99), 1-3-Thomas-s 3.00

...RETURN OF STYRM, 9/98 - No. 3, 11/98 ($2.99), 1-3-Parente & Soresina-a; painted-c 3.00

...RIVER OF BLOOD, 6/98 - No. 3, 8/98 ($2.50), 1-3 2.50

...SCARLET SWORD, 12/98 - No. 3, 2/99 ($2.99), 1-3-Thomas-s/Raffaele-a 3.00

CONAN SAGA, THE
Marvel Comics: June, 1987 - No. 97, Apr, 1995 ($2.00/$2.25, B&W, magazine)
1-Barry Smith-r; new Smith-c 6.00
2-27: 2-9,11-new Barry Smith-c. 13,15-Boris-c. 17-Adams-r.18,25-Chaykin-r. 22-r/Giant-Size Conan 1,2 4.00
28-90: 28-Begin $2.25-c. 31-Red Sonja-r by N. Adams/SSOC #1; 1 pg. Jeff Jones-r. 32-Newspaper strip-r begin by Buscema. 33-Smith/Conrad-a. 39-r/Kull #1('71) by Andru & Wood. 44-Swipes-c/Savage Tales #1. 57-Brunner-r/SSOC #30. 66-r/Conan Annual #2 by Buscema. 79-r/Conan #43-45 w/Red Sonja. 85-Based on Conan #57-63 3.00
91-97 4.00
NOTE: ***J. Buscema** r-32-on; c-86. **Chaykin** r-34. **Chiodo** painted c-63, 65, 66, 82. **G. Colan** a-47p. **Jusko** painted c-64, 83. **Kaluta** c-84. **Nino** a-37. **Ploog** a-50. **N. Redondo** painted c-48, 50, 51, 53, 57, 62. **Simonson** r-50-54, 56. **B. Smith** r-51. **Starlin** c-34. **Williamson** r-50i.*

CONAN THE ADVENTURER
Marvel Comics: June, 1994 - No. 14, July, 1995 ($1.50)
1-($2.50)-Embossed foil-c; Kayaran-a 3.00
2-14 2.50
2-Contents are Conan Classics #2 by mistake 2.50

CONAN THE BARBARIAN
Marvel Comics: Oct, 1970 - No. 275, Dec, 1993
1-Origin/1st app. Conan (in comics) by Barry Smith; 1st app. Kull (cameo); #1-9 are 15¢ issues 22 44 66 156 228 300
2 9 18 27 65 93 120
3-(Low distribution in some areas) 15 30 45 109 160 210
4,5 7 14 21 50 68 85
6-9: 8-Hidden panel message, pg. 14. 9-Last 15¢-c 6 12 18 38 52 65
10,11 (25¢ 52 pg. giants): 10-Black Knight-r; Kull story by Severin 7 14 21 46 63 80
12,13: 12-Wrightson-c(i) 5 10 15 33 44 55
14,15-Elric app. 6 12 18 38 52 65
16,19,20: 16-Conan-r/Savage Tales #1 4 8 12 29 40 50
17,18-No Barry Smith-a 3 6 9 18 24 30
21,22: 22-Has reprint from #1 4 8 12 24 32 40
23-1st app. Red Sonja (2/73) 5 10 15 36 48 60
24-1st full Red Sonja story; last Smith-a 5 10 15 33 44 55
25-John Buscema-c/a begins 2 4 6 12 16 20
26-30 2 4 6 10 12 15
31-36,38-40 1 3 4 6 8 10
37-Neal Adams-c/a; last 20¢ issue; contains pull-out subscription form 2 4 6 11 14 18
41-43,46-50: 48-Origin retold 1 2 3 5 6 8
44,45-N. Adams-i(Crusty Bunkers). 45-Adams-c 2 4 6 8 10 12
51-57,59,60: 59-Origin Belit 6.00
58-2nd Belit app. (see Giant-Size Conan #1) 1 2 3 5 6 8
61-65-(Regular 25¢ editions)(4-8/76) 5.00
61-65-(30¢-c variants, limited distribution) 1 2 3 4 5 7
66-99: 68-Red Sonja story cont'd from Marvel Feature #7. 75-79-(Reg. 30¢-c). 84-Intro. Zula. 85-Origin Zula. 87-r/Savage Sword of Conan #3 in color 4.00
75-79-(35¢-c variants, limited distribution) 6.00
100-(52 pg. Giant)-Death of Belit 6.00
101-114 2.25
115-Double size 3.00
116-199,201-231,233-249: 116-r/Power Record Comic PR31. 244-Zula returns 2.25

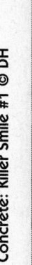

Conan The Barbarian Annual #2 © Conan Prod.

Concrete: Killer Smile #1 © DH

Confessions of Romance #9 © STAR

	GD 2.0	VG 4.0	FN 6.0	VF 8.0	VF/NM 9.0	NM- 9.2
200,232: 200-(52 pgs.). 232-Young Conan storyline begins; Conan is born						4.00
250-(60 pgs.)						3.00
251-270: 262-Adapted from R.E. Howard story						3.00
271-274						5.00
275-($2.50, 68 pgs.)-Final issue; painted-c						4.00
King Size 1(1973, 35¢)-Smith-r/#2,4; Smith-c	2	4	6	14	18	22
Annual 2(1976, 50¢)-New full length story	1	3	4	6	8	10
Annual 3,4: 3('78)-Chaykin/N. Adams-r/SSOC #2. 4('78)-New full length story	1	2	3	4	5	7
Annual 5,6: 5(1979)-New full length Buscema story & part-c, 6(1981)-Kane-c/a						4.00
Annual 7-12: 7('82)-Based on novel "Conan of the Isles" (new-a). 8(1984). 9(1984). 10(1986). 11(1986). 12(1987)						3.00
Special Edition 1 (Red Nails)						4.00
The Chronicles of Conan: Tower of the Elephant and Other Stories (Dark Horse, 2003, $15.95) r/#1-8; afterword by Roy Thomas						16.00

NOTE: ***Arthur Adams** c-248, 249. **Neal Adams** a-116r(i); c-49i. **Austin** a-125, 126; c-125i, 126i. **Brunner** c-17i. c-40. **Buscema** a-25-36p, 38, 39, 41-56p, 58-63p, 65-67p, 68, 70-78p, 84-86p, 88-91p, 93-126p, 136p, 140, 141-144p, 146-158p, 159, 161, 162, 163p, 165-185p, 187-190p, Annual 2(3pgs.). 3-5p, 7p; c(p)-26, 36, 44, 46, 52, 56, 58, 59, 64, 65, 72, 78-80, 83-91, 93-103, 105-126, 136-151, 155-159, 161, 162, 168, 169, 171, 172, 174, 175, 178-185, 188, 189, Annual 4, 5, 7. **Chaykin** a-79-83. **Golden** c-152. **Kaluta** c-167. **Gil Kane** a-12p, 17p, 18p, 127-130, 131-134p; c-12p, 17p, 18p, 23, 25, 27-32, 34, 35, 38, 39, 41-43, 45-51, 53-55, 57, 60-63, 65-71, 73p, 76p, 127-134. **Jim Lee** c-242. **McFarlane** c-241p. **Ploog** a-57. **Russell** a-21; c-251i. **Simonson** c-135. **B. Smith** a-1-11p, 12, 13-15p, 16, 19-21, 23, 24; c-1-11, 13-16, 19-24p. **Starlin** a-64. **Wood** a-47r. Issue Nos. 3-5, 7-9, 11, 16-18, 21, 23, 25, 27-30, 35, 37, 38, 42, 45, 52, 57, 58, 65, 69-71, 73, 79-83, 99, 100, 104, 114, Annual 2 have original Robert E. Howard stories adapted. Issues #32-34 adapted from Norvell Page's novel **Flame Winds**.*

CONAN THE BARBARIAN (Volume 2)
Marvel Comics: July, 1997 - No. 3, Oct, 1997 ($2.50, limited series)

	GD 2.0	VG 4.0	FN 6.0	VF 8.0	VF/NM 9.0	NM- 9.2
1-3-Castellini-a						2.50

CONAN THE BARBARIAN MOVIE SPECIAL (Movie)
Marvel Comics Group: Oct, 1982 - No. 2, Nov, 1982

	GD 2.0	VG 4.0	FN 6.0	VF 8.0	VF/NM 9.0	NM- 9.2
1,2-Movie adaptation; Buscema-a						3.00

CONAN THE BARBARIAN: THE USURPER
Marvel Comics: Dec, 1997 - No. 3, Feb, 1998 ($2.50, limited series)

	GD 2.0	VG 4.0	FN 6.0	VF 8.0	VF/NM 9.0	NM- 9.2
1-3-Dixon-s						2.50

CONAN THE DESTROYER (Movie)
Marvel Comics Group: Jan, 1985 - No. 2, Mar, 1985

	GD 2.0	VG 4.0	FN 6.0	VF 8.0	VF/NM 9.0	NM- 9.2
1,2-r/Marvel Super Special						2.50

CONAN THE KING (Formerly King Conan)
Marvel Comics Group: No. 20, Jan, 1984 - No. 55, Nov, 1989

	GD 2.0	VG 4.0	FN 6.0	VF 8.0	VF/NM 9.0	NM- 9.2
20-49						3.00
50-54						4.00
55-Last issue						6.00

NOTE: ***Kaluta** c-20-23, 24i, 26, 27, 30, 50, 52. **Williamson** a-37i; c-37i, 38i.*

CONAN: THE LEGEND
Dark Horse Comics: No. 0, Nov, 2003 - Present (25¢/$2.99)

	GD 2.0	VG 4.0	FN 6.0	VF 8.0	VF/NM 9.0	NM- 9.2
0-(25¢-c) Busiek-s/Nord-a						2.25
1-($2.99) Busiek-s/Nord-a/Linsner-c						3.00

CONAN: THE LORD OF THE SPIDERS
Marvel Comics: Mar, 1998 - No. 3, May, 1998 ($2.50, limited series)

	GD 2.0	VG 4.0	FN 6.0	VF 8.0	VF/NM 9.0	NM- 9.2
1-3-Roy Thomas-s/Raffaele-a						2.50

CONAN THE SAVAGE
Marvel Comics: Aug, 1995 - No. 10, May, 1996 ($2.95, B&W, Magazine)

	GD 2.0	VG 4.0	FN 6.0	VF 8.0	VF/NM 9.0	NM- 9.2
1-10: 1-Bisley-c. 4-vs. Malibu Comic's Rune. 5,10-Brereton-c						3.00

CONAN VS. RUNE (Also See Conan #4)
Marvel Comics: Nov, 1995 ($2.95, one-shot)

	GD 2.0	VG 4.0	FN 6.0	VF 8.0	VF/NM 9.0	NM- 9.2
1-Barry Smith-c/a/scripts						3.00

CONCRETE (Also see Dark Horse Presents & Within Our Reach)
Dark Horse Comics: March, 1987 - No. 10, Nov, 1988 ($1.50, B&W)

	GD 2.0	VG 4.0	FN 6.0	VF 8.0	VF/NM 9.0	NM- 9.2
1-Paul Chadwick-c/a in all	1	3	4	6	8	10
1-2nd print						3.00
2						6.00
3-Origin						5.00
4-10						4.00
A New Life 1 (1989, $2.95, B&W)-r/#3,4 plus new-a (11 pgs.)						3.00
Celebrates Earth Day 1990 ($3.50, 52 pgs.)						6.00
Color Special 1 (2/89, $2.95, 44 pgs.)-r/1st two Concrete apps. from Dark Horse Presents #1,2 plus new-a						6.00
Land And Sea 1 (2/89, $2.95, B&W)-r/#1,2						6.00
Odd Jobs 1 (7/90, $3.50)-r/5,6 plus new-a						3.50

CONCRETE: (Title series), **Dark Horse Comics**

	GD 2.0	VG 4.0	FN 6.0	VF 8.0	VF/NM 9.0	NM- 9.2
--ECLECTICA, 4/93 - No. 2, 5/93 ($2.95) 1,2						3.00
--FRAGILE CREATURE, 6/91 - No. 4, 2/92 ($2.50) 1-4						3.00
--KILLER SMILE, (Legend), 7/94 - No. 4, 10/94 ($2.9) 1-4						3.00
--STRANGE ARMOR, 12/97 - No. 5, 5/98 ($2.95, color) 1-5-Chadwick-s/c/a; retells origin						3.00
--THINK LIKE A MOUNTAIN, (Legend), 3/96 - No. 6, 8/96 ($2.95) 1-6: Chadwick-a/scripts & Darrow-c in all						3.00

CONDORMAN (Walt Disney)
Whitman Publishing: Oct, 1981 - No. 3, Jan, 1982

	GD 2.0	VG 4.0	FN 6.0	VF 8.0	VF/NM 9.0	NM- 9.2
1-3: 1,2-Movie adaptation; photo-c	1	3	4	6	8	10

CONEHEADS
Marvel Comics: June, 1994 - No. 4, 1994 ($1.75, limited series)

	GD 2.0	VG 4.0	FN 6.0	VF 8.0	VF/NM 9.0	NM- 9.2
1-4						2.50

CONFESSIONS ILLUSTRATED (Magazine)
E. C. Comics: Jan-Feb, 1956 - No. 2, Spring, 1956

	GD 2.0	VG 4.0	FN 6.0	VF 8.0	VF/NM 9.0	NM- 9.2
1-Craig, Kamen, Wood, Orlando-a	20	4	060	112	156	200
2-Craig, Crandall, Kamen, Orlando-a	15	30	45	89	122	150

CONFESSIONS OF LOVE
Artful Publ.: Apr, 1950 - No. 2, July, 1950 (25¢, 7-1/4x5-1/4", 132 pgs.)

	GD 2.0	VG 4.0	FN 6.0	VF 8.0	VF/NM 9.0	NM- 9.2
1-Bakerish-a	28	56	84	157	221	285
2-Art & text; Bakerish-a	16	32	48	92	126	160

CONFESSIONS OF LOVE (Formerly Startling Terror Tales #10; becomes Confessions of Romance No. 7 on)
Star Publications: No. 11, 7/52 - No. 14, 1/53; No. 4, 3/53- No. 6, 8/53

	GD 2.0	VG 4.0	FN 6.0	VF 8.0	VF/NM 9.0	NM- 9.2
11-13: 12,13-Disbrow-a	16	32	48	92	126	160
14,5,6	12	24	36	71	96	120
4-Disbrow-a	13	26	39	76	103	130

NOTE: *All have **L. B. Cole** covers.*

CONFESSIONS OF ROMANCE (Formerly Confessions of Love)
Star Publications: No. 7, Nov, 1953 - No. 11, Nov, 1954

	GD 2.0	VG 4.0	FN 6.0	VF 8.0	VF/NM 9.0	NM- 9.2
7	16	32	48	92	126	160
8	12	24	36	71	96	120
9-Wood-a	14	28	42	81	111	140
10,11-Disbrow-a	13	26	39	76	103	130

NOTE: *All have **L. B. Cole** covers.*

CONFESSIONS OF THE LOVELORN (Formerly Lovelorn)
American Comics Group (Regis Publ./Best Synd. Features): No. 52, Aug, 1954 - No. 114, June-July, 1960

	GD 2.0	VG 4.0	FN 6.0	VF 8.0	VF/NM 9.0	NM- 9.2
52 (3-D effect)	29	58	87	164	232	300
53,55	9	18	27	52	66	80
54 (3-D effect)	29	58	87	164	232	300
56-Anti-communist propaganda story, 10 pgs; last pre-code (2/55)	11	22	33	66	88	110
57-90,100	7	14	21	35	43	50
91-Williamson-a	9	18	27	52	66	80
92-99,101-114	6	12	18	28	34	40

NOTE: ***Whitney** a-most issues; c-52, 53. Painted c-106, 107.*

CONFIDENTIAL DIARY (Formerly High School Confidential Diary; Three Nurses #18 on)
Charlton Comics: No. 12, May, 1962 - No. 17, Mar, 1963

	GD 2.0	VG 4.0	FN 6.0	VF 8.0	VF/NM 9.0	NM- 9.2
12-17	3	6	9	16	20	24

CONGO BILL (See Action Comics & More Fun Comics #56)
National Periodical Publication: Aug-Sept, 1954 - No. 7, Aug-Sept, 1955

	GD 2.0	VG 4.0	FN 6.0	VF 8.0	VF/NM 9.0	NM- 9.2
1 (Scarce)	131	262	393	1050	-	-
2,7 (Scarce)	103	206	309	825	-	-
3-6 (Scarce). 4-Last pre-code issue	78	156	234	625	-	-

NOTE: *(Rarely found in fine to mint condition.)* ***Nick Cardy** c-1-7.*

CONGO BILL
DC Comics (Vertigo): Oct, 1999 - No. 4, Jan, 2000 ($2.95, limited series)

	GD 2.0	VG 4.0	FN 6.0	VF 8.0	VF/NM 9.0	NM- 9.2
1-4-Corben-c						3.00

CONGORILLA (Also see Actions Comics #224)
DC Comics: Nov, 1992 - No. 4, Feb, 1993 ($1.75, limited series)

	GD 2.0	VG 4.0	FN 6.0	VF 8.0	VF/NM 9.0	NM- 9.2
1-4: 1,2-Brian Bolland-c						3.00

CONJURORS
DC Comics: Apr, 1999 - No. 3, Jun, 1999 ($2.95, limited series)

	GD 2.0	VG 4.0	FN 6.0	VF 8.0	VF/NM 9.0	NM- 9.2
1-3-Elseworlds; Phantom Stranger app.; Barreto-c/a						3.00

Contact Comics #12 © Aviation Press

Cookie #6 © ACG

Cosmic Boy #4 © DC

GD 2.0 | VG 4.0 | FN 6.0 | VF 8.0 | VF/NM 9.0 | NM- 9.2

CONNECTICUT YANKEE, A (See King Classics)

CONQUEROR, THE
Dell Publishing Co.: No., 690, Mar, 1956
Four Color 690-Movie, John Wayne photo-c 18 36 54 131 191 250

CONQUEROR COMICS
Albrecht Publishing Co.: Winter, 1945
nn 21 42 63 118 164 210

CONQUEROR OF THE BARREN EARTH (See The Warlord #63)
DC Comics: Feb, 1985 - No. 4, May, 1985 (Limited series)
1-4: Back-up series from Warlord 2.50

CONQUEST
Store Comics: 1953 (6¢)
1-Richard the Lion Hearted, Beowulf, Swamp Fox 6 12 18 33 41 48

CONQUEST
Famous Funnies: Spring, 1955
1-Crandall-a, 1 pg.; contains contents of 1953 ish. 5 10 14 20 24 28

CONSPIRACY
Marvel Comics: Feb, 1998 - No. 2, Mar, 1998 ($2.99, limited series)
1,2-Painted art by Korday/Abnett-s 3.00

CONSTRUCT
Caliber (New Worlds): 1996 - No. 6, 1997 ($2.95, B&W, limited series)
1-6: Paul Jenkins scripts 3.00

CONTACT COMICS
Aviation Press: July, 1944 - No. 12, May, 1946
nn-Black Venus, Flamingo, Golden Eagle, Tommy Tomahawk begin
52 104 156 312 469 625
2-5: 3-Last Flamingo. 3,4-Black Venus by L. B. Cole. 5-The Phantom Flyer app.
40 80 120 240 350 460
6,11-Kurtzman's Black Venus; 11-Last Golden Eagle, last Tommy Tomahawk; Feldstein-a 46 92 138 276 413 550
7-10 40 80 120 240 340 440
12-Sky Rangers, Air Kids, Ace Diamond app.; L.B. Cole sci-fi cover
78 156 234 488 732 975
NOTE: ***L. B. Cole** a-3, 9; c-1-12. **Giunta** a-3. **Hollingsworth** a-5, 7, 10. **Palais** a-11, 12.*

CONTEMPORARY MOTIVATORS
Pendelum Press: 1977 - 1978 ($1.45, 5-3/8x8", 31 pgs., B&W)
14-3002 The Caine Mutiny; 14-3010 Banner in the Sky; 14-3029 God Is My Co-Pilot; 14-3037 Guadalcanal Diary; 14-3045 Hiroshima; 14-3053 Hot Rod; 14-3061 Just Dial a Number; 14-3088 The Diary of Anne Frank; 14-3096 Lost Horizon
1 2 3 5 7 9
NOTE: *Also see Pendulum Illustrated Classics. Above may have been distributed the same.*

CONTEST OF CHAMPIONS (See Marvel Super-Hero...)

CONTEST OF CHAMPIONS II
Marvel Comics: Sept, 1999 - No. 5 ($2.50, limited series)
1-5-Claremont-s/Jimenez-a 2.50

CONTRACTORS
Eclipse Comics: June, 1987 ($2.00, B&W, one-shot)
1-Funny animal 2.25

CONTRACT WITH GOD, A
Baronet Publishing Co./Kitchen Sink Press: 1978 ($7.95, B&W, graphic novel)
nn-Will Eisner-s/a 2 4 6 12 16 20
Reprint (DC Comics, 2000, $12.95) 13.00

CONVOCATIONS: A MAGIC THE GATHERING GALLERY
Acclaim Comics (Armada): Jan, 1996 ($2.50, one-shot)
1-pin-ups by various artists including Kaluta, Vess, and Dringenberg 2.50

COO COO COMICS (...the Bird Brain No. 57 on)
Nedor Publ. Co./Standard (Animated Cartoons): Oct, 1942 - No. 62, Apr, 1952
1-Origin/1st app. Super Mouse & begin series (cloned from Superman); the first funny animal super hero series (see Looney Tunes #5 for 1st funny animal super hero)
31 62 93 175 248 320
2 14 28 42 81 111 140
3-10: 10-(3/44) 9 18 27 52 66 80
11-33: 33-1 pg. Ingels-a 8 16 24 40 50 60
34-40,43-46,48-Text illos by Frazetta in all. 36-Super Mouse covers begin
10 20 30 58 77 95
41-Frazetta-a (6-pg. story & 3 text illos) 20 40 60 112 156 200
42,47-Frazetta-a & text illos. 14 28 42 81 111 140
49-(1/50)-3-D effect story; Frazetta text illo 11 22 33 63 84 105
50,51-3-D effect-c only. 50-Frazetta text illo 10 20 30 58 77 95
52-62: 56-Last Supermouse? 7 14 21 35 43 50

"COOKIE" (Also see Topsy-Turvy)
Michel Publ./American Comics Group(Regis Publ.): Apr, 1946 - No. 55, Aug-Sept, 1955
1-Teen-age humor 21 42 63 118 164 210
2 11 22 33 63 84 105
3-10 8 16 24 46 58 70
11-20 8 16 24 40 50 60
21-23,26,28-30 6 12 18 29 36 42
24,25,27-Starlett O'Hara stories 6 12 18 33 41 48
31-34,37-50,52-55 6 12 18 27 33 38
35,36-Starlett O'Hara stories 6 12 18 29 36 42
51-(10-11/54) 8pg. TrueVision 3-D effect story 9 18 27 54 70 85

COOL CAT (Formerly Black Magic)
Prize Publications: V8#6, Mar-Apr, 1962 - V9#2, July-Aug, 1962
V8#6, nn(V9#1, 5-6/62), V9#2 3 6 9 18 24 30

COOL WORLD (Movie by Ralph Bakshi)
DC Comics: Apr, 1992 - No. 4, Sept, 1992 ($1.75, limited series)
1-4: Prequel to animated/live action movie. 1-Bakshi-c. Bill Wray inks in all 2.25
Movie Adaptation nn ('92, $3.50, 68pg.)-Bakshi-c 3.50

COPPER CANYON (See Fawcett Movie Comics)

COPS (TV)
DC Comics: Aug, 1988 - No. 15, Aug, 1989 ($1.00)
1 ($1.50, 52 pgs.)-Based on Hasbro Toys 3.00
2-15: 14-Orlando-c(p) 2.25

COPS: THE JOB
Marvel Comics: June, 1992 - No. 4, Sept, 1992 ($1.25, limited series)
1-4: All have Jusko scripts & Golden-c 2.25

CORBEN SPECIAL, A
Pacific Comics: May, 1984 (one-shot)
1-Corben-c/a; E.A. Poe adaptation 5.00

CORKY & WHITE SHADOW (Disney, TV)
Dell Publishing Co.: No. 707, May, 1956 (Mickey Mouse Club)
Four Color 707-Photo-c 8 16 24 55 78 100

CORLISS ARCHER (See Meet Corliss Archer)

CORMAC MAC ART (Robert E. Howard's...)
Dark Horse Comics: 1990 - No. 4, 1990 ($1.95, B&W, mini-series)
1-4: All have Bolton painted-c; Howard adapts. 3.00

CORNY'S FETISH
Dark Horse Comics: Apr, 1998 ($4.95, B&W, one-shot)
1-Renée French-s/a; Bolland-c 5.00

CORPORAL RUSTY DUGAN (See Holyoke One-Shot #2)

CORPSES OF DR. SACOTTI, THE (See Ideal a Classical Comic)

CORSAIR, THE (See A-1 Comics No. 5, 7, 10 under Texas Slim)

CORTEZ AND THE FALL OF THE AZTECS
Tome Press: 1993 ($2.95, B&W, limited series)
1,2 3.00

CORUM: THE BULL AND THE SPEAR (See Chronicles Of Corum)
First Comics: Jan, 1989 - No. 4, July, 1989 ($1.95)
1-4: Adapts Michael Moorcock's novel 2.50

COSMIC BOOK, THE
Ace Comics: Dec, 1986 - No. 1, 1987 ($1.95)
1,2: 1-(44pgs.)-Wood, Toth-a. 2-(B&W) 2.25

COSMIC BOY (Also see The Legion of Super-Heroes)
DC Comics: Dec, 1986 - No. 4, Mar, 1987 (limited series)
1-4: Legends tie-ins all issues 2.50

COSMIC HEROES
Eternity/Malibu Graphics: Oct, 1988 - No. 11, Dec, 1989 ($1.95, B&W)
1-11: Reprints 1934-1936's Buck Rogers newspaper strips #1-728 2.25

COSMIC ODYSSEY

Cosmo Cat #3 © FOX

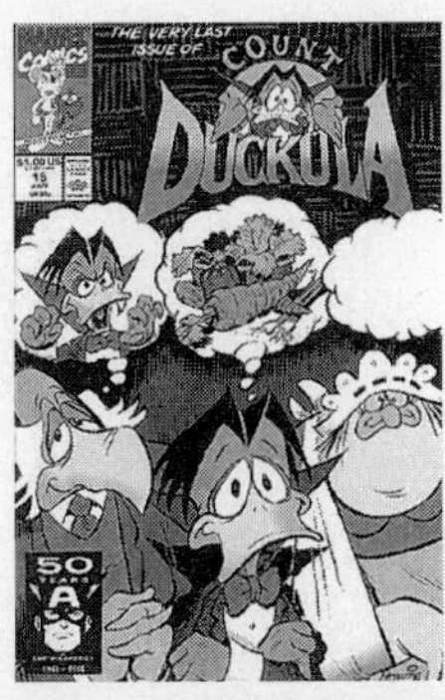

Count Duckula #15 © Cosgrove-Hall

Cowboy Love #3 © FAW

	GD 2.0	VG 4.0	FN 6.0	VF 8.0	VF/NM 9.0	NM- 9.2

DC Comics: 1988 - No. 4, 1988 ($3.50, limited series, squarebound)

	GD 2.0	VG 4.0	FN 6.0	VF 8.0	VF/NM 9.0	NM- 9.2
1-4: Reintro. New Gods into DC continuity; Superman, Batman, Green Lantern (John Stewart) app; Starlin scripts, Mignola-c/a in all. 2-Darkseid merges Demon & Jason Blood (separated in Demon limited series #4); John Stewart responsible for the death of a star system						5.00
Trade paperback-r/#1-4.						20.00

COSMIC POWERS
Marvel Comics: Mar, 1994 - No. 6, Aug, 1994 ($2.50, limited series)

	GD 2.0	VG 4.0	FN 6.0	VF 8.0	VF/NM 9.0	NM- 9.2
1-6: 1-Ron Lim-c/a(p). 1,2-Thanos app. 2-Terrax. 3-Ganymede & Jack of Hearts app.						2.50

COSMIC POWERS UNLIMITED
Marvel Comics: May, 1995 - No. 5, May, 1996 ($3.95, quarterly)

	GD 2.0	VG 4.0	FN 6.0	VF 8.0	VF/NM 9.0	NM- 9.2
1-5						4.00

COSMIC RAY
Image Comics: June, 1999 - No. 2 ($2.95, B&W)

	GD 2.0	VG 4.0	FN 6.0	VF 8.0	VF/NM 9.0	NM- 9.2
1,2-Steven Blue-s/a						3.00

COSMIC SLAM
Ultimate Sports Entertainment: 1999 ($3.95, one-shot)

	GD 2.0	VG 4.0	FN 6.0	VF 8.0	VF/NM 9.0	NM- 9.2
1-McGwire, Sosa, Bagwell, Justice battle aliens; Sienkiewicz-c						4.00

COSMO CAT (Becomes Sunny #11 on; also see All Top & Wotalife Comics)
Fox Publications/Green Publ. Co./Norlen Mag.: July-Aug, 1946 - No. 10, Oct, 1947; 1957; 1959

	GD 2.0	VG 4.0	FN 6.0	VF 8.0	VF/NM 9.0	NM- 9.2
1	28	56	84	159	225	290
2	15	30	45	84	115	145
3-Origin (11-12/46)	19	38	57	109	152	195
4-Robot-c	11	22	33	66	88	110
5-10	10	20	30	56	73	90
2-4(1957-Green Publ. Co.)	6	12	18	27	33	38
2-4(1959-Norlen Mag.)	5	10	15	23	28	32
I.W. Reprint #1	2	4	6	12	16	20

COSMO THE MERRY MARTIAN
Archie Publications (Radio Comics): Sept, 1958 - No. 6, Oct, 1959

	GD 2.0	VG 4.0	FN 6.0	VF 8.0	VF/NM 9.0	NM- 9.2
1-Bob White-a in all	15	30	45	86	118	150
2-6	10	20	30	58	77	95

COTTON WOODS
Dell Publishing Co.: No. 837, Sept, 1957

	GD 2.0	VG 4.0	FN 6.0	VF 8.0	VF/NM 9.0	NM- 9.2
Four Color 837	4	8	12	25	33	42

COUGAR, THE (Cougar No. 2)
Seaboard Periodicals (Atlas): April, 1975 - No. 2, July, 1975

	GD 2.0	VG 4.0	FN 6.0	VF 8.0	VF/NM 9.0	NM- 9.2
1,2: 1-Vampire; Adkins-a(p). 2-Cougar origin; werewolf-s; Buckler-c(p)	1	2	3	5	6	8

COUNTDOWN (See Movie Classics)

COUNTDOWN
DC Comics (WildStorm): June, 2000 - No. 8, Jan, 2001 ($2.95)

	GD 2.0	VG 4.0	FN 6.0	VF 8.0	VF/NM 9.0	NM- 9.2
1-8-Mariotte-s/Lopresti-a						3.00

COUNT DUCKULA (TV)
Marvel Comics: Nov, 1988 - No. 15, Jan, 1991 ($1.00)

	GD 2.0	VG 4.0	FN 6.0	VF 8.0	VF/NM 9.0	NM- 9.2
1,8: 1-Dangermouse back-up. 8-Geraldo Rivera photo-c/& app.; Sienkiewicz-a(i)						5.00
2-7,9-15: Dangermouse back-ups in all						4.00

COUNT OF MONTE CRISTO, THE
Dell Publishing Co.: No. 794, May, 1957

	GD 2.0	VG 4.0	FN 6.0	VF 8.0	VF/NM 9.0	NM- 9.2
Four Color 794-Movie, Buscema-a	10	20	30	67	96	125

COURAGE COMICS
J. Edward Slavin: 1945

	GD 2.0	VG 4.0	FN 6.0	VF 8.0	VF/NM 9.0	NM- 9.2
1,2,77	13	26	39	74	100	125

COURTNEY CRUMRIN & THE COVEN OF MYSTICS
Oni Press: Dec, 2002 - No. 4, March, 2003 ($2.95, B&W, limited series)

	GD 2.0	VG 4.0	FN 6.0	VF 8.0	VF/NM 9.0	NM- 9.2
1-4-Ted Naifeh-s/a						3.00
TPB (9/03, $11.95, 8" x 5-1/2") r/#1-4						12.00

COURTNEY CRUMRIN & THE NIGHT THINGS (Also see Promotional Section for FCBD Ed.)
Oni Press: Mar, 2002 - No. 4, June, 2002 ($2.95, B&W, limited series)

	GD 2.0	VG 4.0	FN 6.0	VF 8.0	VF/NM 9.0	NM- 9.2
1-4-Ted Naifeh-s/a						3.00
TPB (12/02, $11.95) r/#1-4						12.00

COURTNEY CRUMRIN IN THE TWILIGHT KINGDOM
Oni Press: Dec, 2003 - No. 4, ($2.99, B&W, limited series)

	GD 2.0	VG 4.0	FN 6.0	VF 8.0	VF/NM 9.0	NM- 9.2
1-Ted Naifeh-s/a						3.00

COURTSHIP OF EDDIE'S FATHER (TV)
Dell Publishing Co.: Jan, 1970 - No. 2, May, 1970

	GD 2.0	VG 4.0	FN 6.0	VF 8.0	VF/NM 9.0	NM- 9.2
1-Bill Bixby photo-c on both	5	10	15	36	48	60
2	4	8	12	27	36	45

COVEN
Awesome Entertainment: Aug, 1997 - No. 5, Mar, 1998 ($2.50)

	GD 2.0	VG 4.0	FN 6.0	VF 8.0	VF/NM 9.0	NM- 9.2
Preview	1	2	3	5	6	8
1-Loeb-s/Churchill-a; three covers by Churchill, Liefeld, Pollina	1	2	3	5	6	8
1-Fan Appreciation Ed.(3/98); new Churchill-c						3.00
1+ :Includes B&W art from Kaboom	1	3	4	6	8	10
2-Regular-c w/leaping Fantom						6.00
2-Variant-c w/circle of candles	1	2	3	5	6	8
3-6-Contains flip book preview of ReGex						3.00
3-White variant-c	1	2	3	4	5	7
3,4: 3-Halloween wraparound-c. 4-Purple variant-c						3.00
...Black & White (9/98) Short stories						3.00
...Fantom Special (2/98) w/sketch pages						5.00

COVEN
Awesome Entertainment: Jan, 1999 - No. 3, June, 1999 ($2.50)

	GD 2.0	VG 4.0	FN 6.0	VF 8.0	VF/NM 9.0	NM- 9.2
1-3: 1-Loeb-s/Churchill-a; 6 covers by various. 2-Supreme-c/app. 3-Flip book w/Kaboom preview						2.50
... Dark Origins (7/99, 2.50) w/Lionheart gallery						2.50

COVERED WAGONS, HO (Disney, TV)
Dell Publishing Co.: No. 814, June, 1957 (Donald Duck)

	GD 2.0	VG 4.0	FN 6.0	VF 8.0	VF/NM 9.0	NM- 9.2
Four Color 814-Mickey Mouse app.	6	12	18	40	55	70

COWBOY ACTION (Formerly Western Thrillers No. 1-4; Becomes Quick-Trigger Western No. 12 on)
Atlas Comics (ACI): No. 5, March, 1955 - No. 11, March, 1956

	GD 2.0	VG 4.0	FN 6.0	VF 8.0	VF/NM 9.0	NM- 9.2
5	14	28	42	81	111	140
6-10: 6-8-Heath-c	10	20	30	56	73	90
11-Williamson-a (4 pgs.); Baker-a	11	22	33	63	84	105

NOTE: *Ayers a-8. Drucker a-6. Maneely c/a-5, 6. Severin c-10. Shores a-7.*

COWBOY COMICS (Star Ranger #12, Stories #14)(Star Ranger Funnies #15)
Centaur Publishing Co.: No. 13, July, 1938 - No. 14, Aug, 1938

	GD 2.0	VG 4.0	FN 6.0	VF 8.0	VF/NM 9.0	NM- 9.2
13-(Rare)-Ace and Deuce, Lyin Lou, Air Patrol, Aces High, Lee Trent, Trouble Hunters begin	124	248	372	775	1163	1550
14-Filchock-c	85	170	255	531	796	1060

NOTE: *Guardineer a-13, 14. Gustavson a-13, 14.*

COWBOY IN AFRICA (TV)
Gold Key: Mar, 1968

	GD 2.0	VG 4.0	FN 6.0	VF 8.0	VF/NM 9.0	NM- 9.2
1(10219-803)-Chuck Connors photo-c	5	10	15	36	48	60

COWBOY LOVE (Becomes Range Busters?)
Fawcett Publications/Charlton Comics No. 28 on: 7/49 - V2#10, 6/50; No. 11, 1951; No. 28, 2/55 - No. 31, 8/55

	GD 2.0	VG 4.0	FN 6.0	VF 8.0	VF/NM 9.0	NM- 9.2
V1#1-Rocky Lane photo back-c	20	40	60	112	156	200
2	8	16	24	46	58	70
V1#3,4,6 (12/49)	8	16	24	40	50	60
5-Bill Boyd photo back-c (11/49)	9	18	27	49	62	75
V2#7-Williamson/Evans-a	10	20	30	58	77	95
V2#8-11	7	14	21	35	43	50
V1#28 (Charlton)-Last precode (2/55) (Formerly Romantic Story?)	6	12	18	31	38	45
V1#29-31 (Charlton; becomes Sweetheart Diary #32 on)	6	12	18	28	34	40

NOTE: *Powell a-10. Marcus Swayze a-2, 3. Photo c-1-11. No. 1-3, 5-7, 9, 10 are 52 pgs.*

COWBOY ROMANCES (Young Men No. 4 on)
Marvel Comics (IPC): Oct, 1949 - No. 3, Mar, 1950 (All photo-c & 52 pgs.)

	GD 2.0	VG 4.0	FN 6.0	VF 8.0	VF/NM 9.0	NM- 9.2
1-Photo-c	24	48	72	138	194	250
2-William Holden, Mona Freeman "Streets of Laredo" photo-c	17	34	51	95	130	165
3-Photo-c	14	28	42	81	111	140

COWBOYS 'N' INJUNS (...and Indians No. 6 on)
Com No. 1-5/Magazine Enterprises No. 6 on: 1946 - No. 5, 1947; No. 6, 1949 - No. 8, 1952

	GD 2.0	VG 4.0	FN 6.0	VF 8.0	VF/NM 9.0	NM- 9.2
1	13	26	39	76	103	130
2-5-All funny animal western	9	18	27	52	66	80
6(A-1 23)-Half violent, half funny; Ayers-a	11	22	33	66	88	110

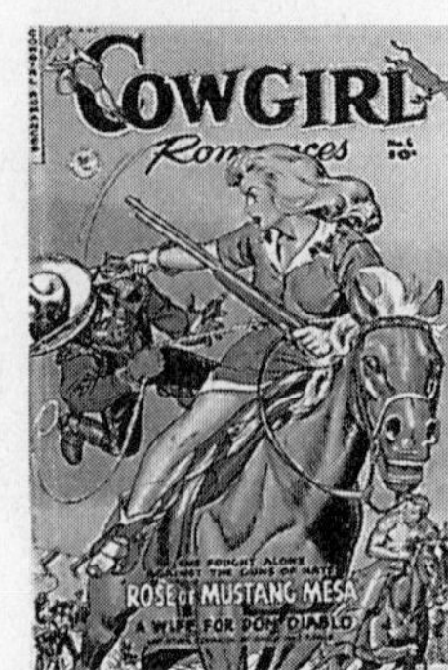

Cowgirl Romances #6 © FH

Crackajack Funnies #24 © DELL

Crack Comics #34 © QUA

	GD 2.0	VG 4.0	FN 6.0	VF 8.0	VF/NM 9.0	NM- 9.2
7(A-1 41, 1950), 8(A-1 48)-All funny	8	16	24	46	58	70
I.W. Reprint No. 1,7 (Reprinted in Canada by Superior, No. 7)	2	4	6	12	16	20
Super Reprint #10 (1963)	2	4	6	12	16	20

COWBOY WESTERN COMICS (TV)(Formerly Jack In The Box; Becomes Space Western No. 40-45 & Wild Bill Hickok & Jingles No. 68 on; title:Cowboy Western Heroes No. 47 & 48; Cowboy Western No. 49 on)
Charlton (Capitol Stories): No. 17, 7/48 - No. 39, 8/52; No. 46, 10/53; No. 47, 12/53; No. 48, Spr, '54; No. 49, 5-6/54 - No. 67, 3/58 (nn 40-45)

	GD	VG	FN	VF	VF/NM	NM-
17-Jesse James, Annie Oakley, Wild Bill Hickok begin; Texas Rangers app.	22	44	66	124	172	220
18,19-Orlando-c/a. 18-Paul Bunyan begins. 19-Wyatt Earp story	13	26	39	74	100	125
20-25: 21-Buffalo Bill story. 22-Texas Rangers-c/story. 24-Joel McCrea photo-c & adaptation from movie "Three Faces West". 25-James Craig photo-c & adaptation from movie "Northwest Stampede"	10	20	30	60	80	100
26-George Montgomery photo-c and adaptation from movie "Indian Scout"; 1 pg. bio on Will Rogers	13	26	39	74	100	125
27-Sunset Carson photo-c & adapts movie "Sunset Carson Rides Again" plus 1 other Sunset Carson story	58	116	174	363	547	730
28-Sunset Carson line drawn-c; adapts movies "Battling Marshal" & "Fighting Mustangs" starring Sunset Carson	32	64	96	184	262	340
29-Sunset Carson line drawn-c; adapts movies "Rio Grande" with Sunset Carson & "Winchester '73" w/James Stewart plus 5 pg. life history of Sunset Carson featuring Tom Mix	32	64	96	184	262	340
30-Sunset Carson photo-c; adapts movie "Deadline" starring Sunset Carson plus 1 other Sunset Carson story	57	114	171	356	533	710
31-34,38,39,47-50 (no #40-45): 50-Golden Arrow, Rocky Lane & Blackjack (r?) stories	9	18	27	54	70	85
35,36-Sunset Carson-c/stories (2 in each). 35-Inside front-c photo of Sunset Carson plus photo on-c	32	64	96	184	262	340
37-Sunset Carson stories (2)	22	44	66	124	172	220
46-(Formerly Space Western)-Space western story	22	44	66	124	172	220
51-57,59-66: 51-Golden Arrow(r?) & Monte Hale-r renamed Rusty Hall. 53,54-Tom Mix-r. 55-Monte Hale story(r?). 66-Young Eagle story. 67-Wild Bill Hickok and Jingles-c/story	8	16	24	40	50	60
58-(1/56, 15¢, 68 pgs.)-Wild Bill Hickok, Annie Oakley & Jesse James stories; Forgione-a	9	18	27	52	66	80
67-(15¢, 68 pgs.)-Williamson/Torres-a, 5 pgs.	10	20	30	58	77	95

NOTE: *Many issues trimmed 1" shorter.* ***Maneely*** *a-67(5). Inside front/back photo c-29.*

COWGIRL ROMANCES
Marvel Comics (CCC): No. 28, Jan, 1950 (52 pgs.)

	GD	VG	FN	VF	VF/NM	NM-
28(#1)-Photo-c	22	44	66	124	172	220

COWGIRL ROMANCES
Fiction House Magazines: 1950 - No. 12, Winter, 1952-53 (No. 1-3: 52 pgs.)

	GD	VG	FN	VF	VF/NM	NM-
1-Kamen-a	37	74	111	212	301	390
2	19	38	57	109	152	195
3-5: 5-12-Whitman-c (most)	17	34	51	95	130	165
6-9,11,12	16	32	48	89	122	155
10-Frazetta?/Williamson?-a; Kamen?/Baker-a; r/Mitzi story from Movie Comics #4 w/all new dialogue	32	64	96	184	262	340

COW PUNCHER (...Comics)
Avon Periodicals: Jan, 1947; No. 2, Sept, 1947 - No. 7, 1949

	GD	VG	FN	VF	VF/NM	NM-
1-Clint Cortland, Texas Ranger, Kit West, Pioneer Queen begin; Kubert-a; Alabam stories begin	42	84	126	252	359	465
2-Kubert, Kamen/Feldstein-a; Kamen-c	37	74	111	213	299	385
3-5,7: 3-Kiefer story	27	54	81	153	214	275
6-Opium drug mention story; bondage, headlight-c; Reinman-a	33	66	99	190	270	350

COWPUNCHER
Realistic Publications: 1953 (nn) (Reprints Avon's No. 2)

	GD	VG	FN	VF	VF/NM	NM-
nn-Kubert-a	11	22	33	63	84	105

COWSILLS, THE (See Harvey Pop Comics)

COW SPECIAL, THE
Image Comics (Top Cow): Spring-Summer 2000; 2001 ($2.95)

	GD	VG	FN	VF	VF/NM	NM-
1-Previews upcoming Top Cow projects; Yancy Butler photo-c						3.00
Vol. 2 #1-Witchblade-c; previews and interviews						3.00

COYOTE
Marvel Comics (Epic Comics): June, 1983 - No. 16, Mar, 1986

	GD	VG	FN	VF	VF/NM	NM-
1-10,15: 7-10-Ditko-a						2.50
11-1st McFarlane-a						6.00
12-14,16: 12-14-McFarlane-a. 14-Badger x-over. 16-Reagan c/app.						4.00

CRACKAJACK FUNNIES (Also see The Owl)
Dell Publishing Co.: June, 1938 - No. 43, Jan, 1942

	GD	VG	FN	VF	VF/NM	NM-
1-Dan Dunn, Freckles, Myra North, Wash Tubbs, Apple Mary, The Nebbs, Don Winslow, Tom Mix, Buck Jones, Major Hoople, Clyde Beatty, Boots begin	240	480	720	1500	2250	3000
2	96	192	288	600	900	1200
3	70	140	210	438	659	880
4	53	106	159	318	477	635
5-Nude woman on cover	55	110	165	330	495	660
6-8,10: 8-Speed Bolton begins (1st app.)	42	84	126	252	376	500
9-(3/39)-Red Ryder strip-r begin by Harman; 1st app. in comics & 1st cover app.	168	336	504	1050	1575	2100
11-14	40	80	120	240	350	460
15-Tarzan text feature begins by Burroughs (9/39); not in #26,35	43	86	129	258	384	510
16-24: 18-Stratosphere Jim begins (1st app., 12/39). 23-Ellery Queen begins plus-c (1st comic book app., 5/40)	34	68	102	196	278	360
25-The Owl begins (1st app., 7/40); in new costume #26 by Frank Thomas (also see Popular Comics #72)	76	152	228	475	713	950
26-30: 28-Part Owl-c	53	106	159	318	477	635
31-Owl covers begin, end #42	55	110	165	330	495	660
32-Origin Owl Girl	58	116	174	363	542	720
33-38: 36-Last Tarzan issue. 37-Cyclone & Midge begin (1st app.)	51	102	153	306	458	610
39-Andy Panda begins (intro/1st app., 9/41)	56	112	168	350	525	700
40-42: 42-Last Owl-c.	40	80	120	240	340	440
43-Terry & the Pirates-r	36	72	108	207	294	380

NOTE: ***McWilliams*** *art in most issues.*

CRACK COMICS (Crack Western No. 63 on)
Quality Comics Group: May, 1940 - No. 62, Sept, 1949

	GD	VG	FN	VF	VF/NM	NM-
1-Origin & 1st app. The Black Condor by Lou Fine, Madame Fatal, Red Torpedo, Rock Bradden & The Space Legion; The Clock, Alias the Spider (by Gustavson), Wizard Wells, & Ned Brant begin; Powell-a; Note: Madame Fatal is a man dressed as a woman	470	940	1410	3290	5045	6800
2	232	464	696	1450	2175	2900
3	160	320	480	1000	1500	2000
4	132	264	396	825	1238	1650
5-10: 5-Molly The Model begins. 10-Tor, the Magic Master begins	102	204	306	638	957	1275
11-20: 13-1 pg. J. Cole-a. 15-1st app. Spitfire	88	176	264	550	825	1100
21-24: 23-Pen Miller begins; continued from National Comics #22. 24-Last Fine Black Condor	66	132	198	413	619	825
25,26: 26-Flag-c	55	110	165	330	495	660
27-(1/43)-Intro & origin Captain Triumph by Alfred Andriola (Kerry Drake artist) & begin series	102	204	306	638	957	1275
28-30	46	92	138	276	413	550
31-39: 31-Last Black Condor	30	60	90	170	240	310
40-46	22	44	66	127	176	225
47-57,59,60-Capt. Triumph by Crandall	23	46	69	132	186	240
58,61,62-Last Captain Triumph	16	32	48	92	126	160

NOTE: *Black Condor by* ***Fine****: No. 1, 2, 4-6, 8, 10-24; by* ***Sultan****: No. 3, 7; by* ***Fugitani****: No. 9.* ***Cole*** *a-34.* ***Crandall*** *a-61(unsigned); c-48, 49, 51-61.* ***Guardineer*** *a-17.* ***Gustavson*** *a-1, 2, 7, 13, 17, 23.* ***McWilliams*** *a-15-27. Black Condor c-2, 4, 6, 8, 10, 12, 14, 16, 18, 20-26. Capt. Triumph c-27-62. The Clock c-1, 3, 5, 7, 9, 11, 13, 15, 17, 19.*

CRACKED (Magazine) (Satire) (Also see The 3-D Zone #19)
Major Magazines(#1-212)/Globe Communications(#213-346/American Media #347 on): Feb-Mar, 1958 - Present

	GD	VG	FN	VF	VF/NM	NM-
1-One pg. Williamson-a; Everett-c; Gunsmoke-s	15	30	45	109	160	210
2-1st Shut-Ups & Bonus Cut-Outs; Superman parody-c by Severin (his 1st cover on the title) Frankenstein-s	8	16	24	55	78	100
3-5	6	12	18	43	59	75
6-10: 7-Reprints 1st 6 covers on-c. 8-Frankenstein-c. 10-Wolverton-a	5	10	15	36	48	60
11-12, 13(nn,3/60),	4	8	12	29	40	50
14-Kirby-a	5	10	15	36	48	60
15-17, 18(nn,2/61), 19,20	4	8	12	27	36	45
21-27(11/62), 27(No.28, 2/63; mis-#d), 29(5/63)	4	8	12	24	32	40
30-40(11/64): 37-Beatles and Superman cameos	4	8	12	22	30	38
41-45,47-56,59,60: 47,49,52-Munsters. 51-Beatles inside-c. 59-Laurel and Hardy photos	3	6	9	19	25	32
46,57,58: 46,58-Man From U.N.C.L.E. 46-Beatles. 57-Rolling Stones						

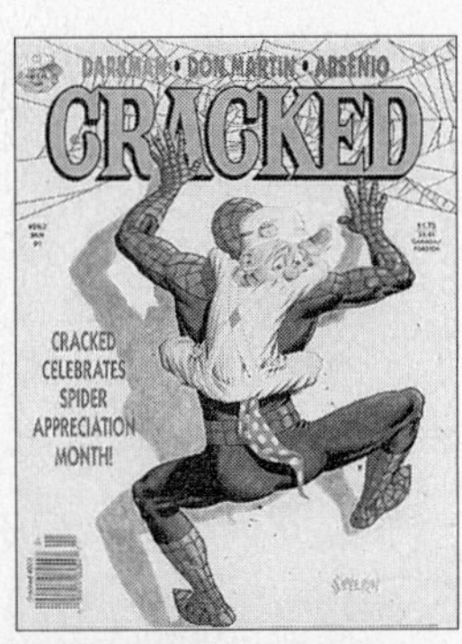

Cracked #260 © Globe Comm. Corp.

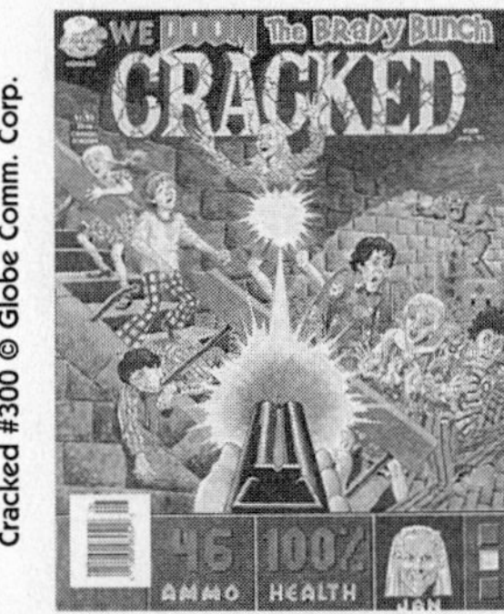

Cracked #300 © Globe Comm. Corp.

Crack Western #69 © QUA

	GD	VG	FN	VF	VF/NM	NM-
	2.0	4.0	6.0	8.0	9.0	9.2

3 7 10 21 28 35
61-80: 62-Beatles cameo. 69-Batman, Superman app. 70-(8/68) Elvis cameo.
71-Garrison's Gorillas; W.C. Fields photos 3 6 9 16 20 24
81-99: 99-Alfred E. Neuman on-c 2 4 6 12 16 20
100 3 6 9 18 24 30
101-119: 104-Godfather-c/s. 108-Archie Bunker-s. 112,119-Kung Fu (TV). 113-Tarzan-s.
115-MASH. 117-Cannon. 118-The Sting-c/s 2 4 6 9 11 14
120(12/74) Six Million Dollar Man-c/s; Ward-a 2 4 6 11 14 18
121,122,124-126,128-133,136-140: 121-American Graffiti. 122-Korak-c/s.
124,131-Godfather-c/s. 128-Capone-c. 129,131-Jaws. 132-Baretta-c/s. 133-Space 1999.
136-Laverne and Shirley/Fonz-c. 137-Travolta/Kotter-c/s. 138-Travolta/Laverne and Shirley/
Fonz-c. 139-Barney Miller-c/s. 140-King Kong-c/s; Fonz-s
2 4 6 9 11 14
123-Planet of the Apes-c/s; Six Million Dollar Man 2 4 6 11 14 18
127,134,135: 127-Star Trek-c/s; Ward-a. 134-Fonz-c/s; Starsky and Hutch. 135-Bionic Woman-
c/s; Ward-a 2 4 6 10 13 16
141,151-Charlie's Angels-c/s. 151-Frankenstein 2 4 6 10 13 16
142,143,150,152-155,157: 142-MASH-c/s. 143-Rocky-c/s; King Kong-s. 150-(5/78) Close
Encounters-c/s. 152-Close Enc./Star Wars-c/s. 153-Close Enc./Fonz-c/s. 154-Jaws II-c/s;
Star Wars-s. 155-Star Wars/Fonz-c 2 4 6 9 11 14
144,149,156,158-160: 144-Fonz/Happy Days-c. 149-Star Wars/Six Mil.$ Man-c/s.
156-Grease/Travolta-c. 158-Mork & Mindy. 159-Battlestar Galactica-c/s; MASH-s.
160-Superman-c/s 2 4 6 10 13 16
145,147-Both have insert postcards: 145-Fonz/Rocky/L&S-c/s. 147-Star Wars-s;
Farrah photo page (missing postcards-1/2 price) 2 4 6 14 18 22
146,148: 46-Star Wars-c/s with stickers insert (missing stickers-1/2 price). 148-Star Wars-c/s
with inside-c color poster 3 6 9 17 21 26
161,170-Ward-a: 161-Mork & Mindy-c/s. 170-Dukes of Hazzard-c/s
1 3 4 6 8 10
162,165-168,171,172,175-178,180-Ward-a: 162-Sherlock Holmes-s. 165-Dracula-c/s.
167-Mork-c/s. 168,175-MASH-c/s. 168-Mork-s. 172-Dukes of Hazzard/CHiPs-c/s.
176-Barney Miller-c/s 1 2 3 5 7 9
163,179:163-Postcard insert; Mork & Mindy-c/s. 179-Insult cards insert; Popeye,
Dukes of Hazzard-c/s 2 4 6 12 16 20
164,169,173,174: 164-Alien movie-c/s; Mork & Mindy-s. 169-Star Trek. 173,174-Star Wars-
Empire Strikes Back. 173-SW poster 2 4 6 9 11 14
181,182,185-191,193,194,196-198-most Ward-a: 182-MASH-c/s. 185-Dukes of Hazzard-c/s;
Jefferson-s. 187-Love Boat. 188-Fall Guy-s. 189-Fonz/Happy Days-c. 190,194-MASH-c/s.
191-Magnum P.I./Rocky-c; Magnum-s. 193-Knight Rider-s. 196-Dukes of Hazzard/Knight
Rider-c/s. 198-Jaws III-c/s; Fall Guy-s 1 2 3 5 6 8
183,184,192,195,199,200-Ward-a in all: 183-Superman-c/s. 184-Star Trek-c/s. 192-E.T.-c/s;
Rocky-s. 195-E.T.-c/s. 199-Jabba-c; Star Wars-s. 200-(12/83)
1 2 3 5 7 9
201,203,210-A-Team-c/s 6.00
202,204-206,211-224,226,227,230-233: 202-Knight Rider-s. 204-Magnum P.I.; A-Team-s.
206-Michael Jackson/Mr. T-c/s. 212-Prince-s; Cosby-s. 213-Monsters issue-c/s. 215-Hulk
Hogan/Mr. T-c/s. 216-Miami Vice-s; James Bond-s. 217-Rambo-s; Cosby-s; A-Team-s.
218-Rocky-c/s. 219-Arnold/Commando-c/s; Rocky-s; Godzilla. 220-Rocky-c/s.
221-Stephen King app. 223-Miami Vice-s. 224-Cosby-s. 226-29th Anniv.; Tarzan-s; Aliens-s;
Family Ties-s. 227-Cosby, Family Ties, Miami Vice-s. 230-Monkees-c/s; Elvis on-c; Gumby-s.
232-Alf, Cheers, StarTrek-s. 233-Superman/James Bond-c/s; Robocop, Predator-s 5.00
207-209,225,234: 207-Michael Jackson-c/s. 208-Indiana Jones-c/s. 209-MichaelJackson/
Gremlins-c/s; Star Trek III-s. 225-Schwarzenegger/Stallone/G.I. Joe-c/s. 234-Don Martin-a
begins; Batman/Robocop/Clint Eastwood-c/s 6.00
228,229: 228-Star Trek-c/s; Alf, Pee Wee Herman-s. 229-Monsters issue-c/s; centerfold
with many superheroes 6.00
235,239,243,249: 235-1st Martin-c; Star Trek:TNG-s; Alf-s. 239-Beetlejuice-c/s; Mike Tyson-s.
243-X-Men and other heroes app. 249-Batman/Indiana Jones/Ghostbusters-c/s 6.00
236,244,246,248: 236 Madonna/Stallone c/s; Twilight Zone s. 244 Elvis c/s; Martin c.
245-Roger Rabbit-c/s. 248-Batman issue 6.00
237,238,240-242,246,247,250: 237-Robocop-s. 238-Rambo-c/s; Star Trek-s. 242-Dirty Harry-s,
Ward-a. 246-Alf-s; Star Trek-s., Ward-a. 247-Star Trek-s. 250-Batman/Ghostbusters-s 4.00
251-253,255,256,259,261-265,275-278,281,284,286-297,299: 252-Star Trek-s. 253-Back to
the Future-c/s. 255-TMNT-c/s. 256-TMNT-c/s; Batman, Bart Simpson on-c. 259-Die Hard II,
Robocop-s. 261-TMNT, Twin Peaks-s. 262-Rocky-c/s; Rocky Horror-s. 265-TMNT-s.
276-Aliens III, Batman-s. 277-Clinton-c. 284-Bart Simpson-c; 90210-s. 297-Van Damme-
s/photo-c. 299-Dumb & Dumber-c/s 4.00
254,257,266,267,272,280,282,285,298,300: 254-Back to the Future, Punisher-s; Wolverton-a,
Batman-s, Ward-a. 257-Batman, Simpsons-s; Spider-Man and other heroes app.
266-Terminator-c/s. 267-Toons-c/s. 272-Star Trek VI-s. 280-Swimsuit issue. 282-Cheers-c/s.
285-Jurassic Park-c/s. 298-Swimsuit issue; Martin-c. 300-(8/95) Brady Bunch-c/s 5.00
258,260,274,279,283: 258-Simpsons-c/s; Back to the Future-s. 260-Spider-Man-c/s;
Simpsons-s. 274-Batman-c/s. 279-Madonna-c/s. 283-Jurassic Park-c/s;
Wolverine app. inside back-c 5.00

	GD	VG	FN	VF	VF/NM	NM-
	2.0	4.0	6.0	8.0	9.0	9.2

301-305,307-348 2.50
306-Toy Story-c/s 4.00
Biggest... (Winter, 1977) 2 4 6 11 14 18
Biggest, Greatest... nn('65) 4 8 12 29 40 50
Biggest, Greatest... 2('66) - #5('69) 3 6 9 18 24 30
Biggest, Greatest... 6('70) - #12('76) 2 4 6 12 16 20
Biggest, Greatest...13('77) - #21(Wint. '86) 1 3 4 6 8 10
...Blockbuster 1(Sum '87), 2('88) 1 2 3 5 6 8
...Digest 1(Fall, '86, 148 pgs.) - #5 1 2 3 5 6 8
...Collectors' Edition 4 ('73; formerly ...Special) 2 4 6 11 14 18
5-10 2 4 6 10 13 16
11-30: 23-Ward-a 1 3 4 6 8 10
31-50 1 2 3 5 6 8
51-70 6.00
71-84: 83-Elvis, Batman parodies 4.00
...Party Pack 1,2('88) 4.00
...Shut-Ups (2/72-'72; Cracked Spec. #3) 1 3 6 9 18 24 30
2 2 4 6 12 16 20
...Special 3('73; formerly Cracked Shut-Ups; ...Collectors' Edition#4 on)
2 4 6 11 14 18
Extra Special... 1('76) 2 4 6 10 13 16
Extra Special... 2('76) 2 4 6 9 11 14
Giant... nn('65) 5 10 15 33 44 55
Giant... 2('66)-5('69) 3 6 9 19 25 32
Giant...6('70)-12('76) 3 6 9 16 20 25
Giant...nn(9/77)-24 2 4 6 10 13 16
Giant...25-35 2 4 6 8 10 12
Giant...36-48('87) 1 2 3 5 6 8
King Sized... 1('67) 4 8 12 27 36 45
King Sized... 2('68)-5('71) 3 6 9 18 24 30
King Sized... 6('72)-11('77) 2 4 6 14 18 22
King Sized... 12-17 2 4 6 8 10 12
King Sized... 18-22 (Sum/'86) 1 2 3 5 6 8
Super... 1('68) 4 8 12 25 33 42
Super... 2('69)-5 3 6 9 18 24 30
Super... 6-10 3 6 9 16 20 24
Super... 11-16 2 4 6 10 13 16
Super... 17-24('84): #23 mis-numbered as #24 2 4 6 8 10 12
Super... 1('87, 100 pgs.)-Severin & Elder-a 1 2 3 5 6 8
NOTE: ***Burgos** a-1-10. **Colan** a-257. **Davis** a-5, 11-17, 24, 40, 80; c-12-14, 16. **Elder** a-5, 6, 10-13; c-10. **Everett** a-1-10, 23-25, 61; c-1. **Heath** a-1-3, 6, 13, 14, 17, 110; c-6. **Jaffee** a-5, 6. **Don Martin** c-235, 244, 247, 259, 261, 264. **Morrow** a-8-10. **Reinman** a-1-4. **Severin** c/a-in most all issues. **Shores** a-3-7. **Torres** a-7-10. **Ward** a-22-24, 27, 35, 40, 120-193, 195, 197-205, 242, 244, 246, 247, 250, 252-257. **Williamson** a-1 (1 pg.). **Wolverton** a-10 (2 pgs.), Giant nn('65). **Wood** a-27, 35, 40. Alfred E. Neuman c-177, 200, 202. Batman c-234, 248, 249, 256, 274. Captain America c-256. Christmas c-234, 243. Spider-Man c-260. Star Trek c-127, 169, 207, 228. Star Wars c-145, 146, 148, 149, 152, 155, 173, 174, 199. Superman c-183, 233. #144, 146 have free full-color pre-glued stickers. #145, 147, 155, 163 have free full-color postcards. #123, 137, 154, 157 have free iron-ons.*

CRACKED MONSTER PARTY
Globe Communications: July, 1988 - No. 26, 1990?

1 2 4 6 9 11 14
2-10 1 2 3 5 7 9
11-26 5.00

CRACKED'S FOR MONSTERS ONLY
Major Magazines: Sept, 1969 - No. 9, Sept, 1969

1 4 8 12 27 36 45
2-9 2 4 6 14 18 22

CRACKED SPACED OUT
Globe Communications: Fall, 1993 - No. 4, 1994?

1-4 3.00

CRACK WESTERN (Formerly Crack Comics; Jonesy No. 85 on)
Quality Comics Group: No. 63, Nov, 1949 - No. 84, May, 1953 (36 pgs., 63-68,74-on)

63(#1)-Ward-c; Two-Gun Lil (origin & 1st app.)(ends #84), Arizona Ames, his horse Thunder
(with sidekick Spurs & his horse Calico), Frontier Marshal (ends #70), & Dead Canyon
Days (ends #69) begin; Crandall-a 23 46 69 132 186 240
64,65: 64-Ward-c. Crandall-a in both. 18 36 54 104 142 180
66,68-Photo-c. 66-Arizona Ames becomes A. Raines (ends #84)
15 30 45 86 118 150
67-Randolph Scott photo-c; Crandall-a 17 34 51 98 134 170
69(52pgs.)-Crandall-a 15 30 45 86 118 150
70(52pgs.)-The Whip (origin & 1st app.) & his horse Diablo begin (ends #84);
Crandall-a 15 30 45 86 118 150
71(52pgs.)-Frontier Marshal becomes Bob Allen F. Marshal (ends #84);
Crandall-c/a 17 34 51 98 134 170

Crash Comics #2 © Tem Publ.

Crazy #3 © MAR

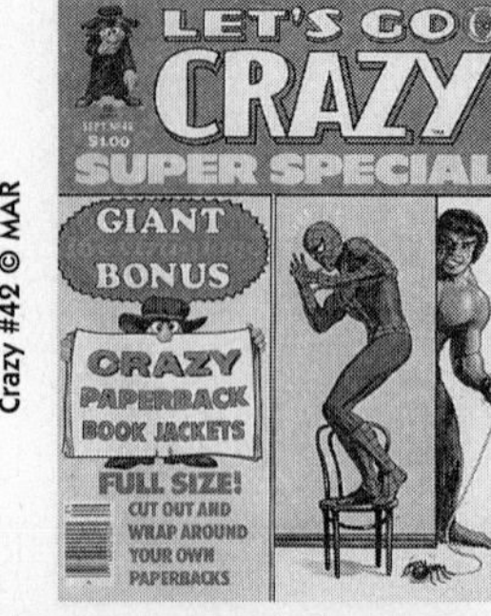

Crazy #42 © MAR

	GD 2.0	VG 4.0	FN 6.0	VF 8.0	VF/NM 9.0	NM- 9.2
72(52pgs.)-Tim Holt photo-c	14	28	42	81	111	140
73(52pgs.)-Photo-c	10	20	30	58	77	95
74-76,78,79,81,83-Crandall-c. 83-Crandall-a(p)	13	26	39	76	103	130
77,80,82	9	18	27	52	66	80
84-Crandall-c/a	14	28	42	81	111	140

NOTE: ***Crandall** c-71p, 74-81, 83p(w/**Cuidera**-i).*

CRASH COMICS (Catman Comics No. 6 on)
Tem Publishing Co.: May, 1940 - No. 5, Nov, 1940

	GD	VG	FN	VF	VF/NM	NM-
1-The Blue Streak, Strongman (origin), The Perfect Human, Shangra begin (1st app. of each); Kirby-a	304	608	912	1976	3038	4100
2-Simon & Kirby-a	152	304	456	950	1425	1900
3,5-Simon & Kirby-a	128	256	384	800	1200	1600
4-Origin & 1st app. The Catman; S&K-a	304	608	912	1976	3038	4100

NOTE: *Solar Legion by **Kirby** No. 1-5 (5 pgs. each). Strongman c-1-4. Catman c-5.*

CRASH DIVE (See Cinema Comics Herald)

CRASH METRO AND THE STAR SQUAD
Oni Press: May, 1999 ($2.95, B&W, one-shot)

1-Allred-s/Ontiveros-a 3.00

CRASH RYAN (Also see Dark Horse Presents #44)
Marvel Comics (Epic): Oct, 1984 - No. 4, Jan, 1985 (Baxter paper, lim. series)

1-4 2.25

CRAZY (Also see This Magazine is Crazy)
Atlas Comics (CSI): Dec, 1953 - No. 7, July, 1954

	GD	VG	FN	VF	VF/NM	NM-
1-Everett-c/a	29	58	87	164	232	300
2	20	40	60	112	156	200
3-7: 4-I Love Lucy satire. 5-Satire on censorship	16	32	48	92	126	160

NOTE: ***Ayers** a-5. **Berg** a-1, 2. **Burgos** c-5, 6. **Drucker** a-6. **Everett** a-1-4. **Al Hartley** a-4. **Heath** a-3, 7; c-7. **Maneely** a-1-7, c-3, 4. **Post** a-3-6. Funny monster c-1-4.*

CRAZY (Satire)
Marvel Comics Group: Feb, 1973 - No. 3, June, 1973

	GD	VG	FN	VF	VF/NM	NM-
1-Not Brand Echh-r; Beatles cameo (r)	3	6	9	16	20	24
2,3-Not Brand Echh-r; Kirby-a	2	4	6	10	13	16

CRAZY MAGAZINE (Satire)
Oct, 1973 - No. 94, Apr, 1983 (40-90¢, B&W magazine)
Marvel Comics: (#1, 44 pgs; #2-90, reg. issues, 52 pgs; #92-95, 68 pgs)'

	GD	VG	FN	VF	VF/NM	NM-
1-Wolverton(1 pg.), Bode-a; 3 pg. photo story of Neal Adams & Dick Giordano; Harlan Ellison story; TV Kung Fu sty.	4	8	12	24	32	40
2-"Live & Let Die" c/s; 8pgs; Adams/Buscema-a; McCloud w5 pgs. Adams-a; Kurtzman's "Hey Look" 2 pg.-r	3	6	9	17	23	28
3-5: 3-"High Plains Drifter" w/Clint Eastwood c/s; Waltons app; Drucker, Reese-a. 4-Shaft-c/s; Ploog-a; Nixon 3 pg. app; Freas-a. 5-Michael Crichton's "Westworld" c/s; Nixon app.	3	6	9	16	20	24
6,7,18: 6-Exorcist c/s; Nixon app. 7-TV's Kung Fu c/s; Nixon app.; Ploog & Freas-a. 18-Six Million Dollar Man/Bionic Woman c/s; Welcome Back Kotter story	2	4	6	12	16	20
8-10: 8-Serpico c/s; Casper parody; TV's Police Story. 9-Joker cameo; Chinatown story; Eisner s/a begins; Has 1st 8 covers on-c. 10-Playboy Bunny-c; M. Severin-a; Lee Marrs-a begins; "Deathwish" story	2	4	6	11	14	18
11-17,19: 11-Towering Inferno. 12-Rhoda. 13-"Tommy" the Who Rock Opera. 14-Mandingo. 15-Jaws story. 16-Santa/Xmas-c; "Good Times" TV story; Jaws. 17-Bicentennial issue; Baretta; Woody Allen. 19-King Kong c/s; Reagan, J. Carter, Howard the Duck cameos, "Laverne & Shirley"	2	4	6	9	11	14
20,24,27: 20-Bicentennial-c; Space 1999 sty; Superheroes song sheet, 4pgs. 24-Charlie's Angels. 27-Charlie's Angels/Travolta/Fonz-c; Bionic Woman sty	2	4	6	11	14	18
21-23,25,26,28-30: 21-Starsky & Hutch. 22-Mount Rushmore/J. Carter-c; TV's Barney Miller; Superheroes spoof. 23-Santa/Xmas-c; "Happy Days" sty; "Omen" sty. 25-J. Carter-c/s; Grandenetti-a begins; TV's Alice; Logan's Run. 26-TV Stars-c; Mary Hartman, King Kong. 28-Donny & Marie Osmond-c/s; Marathon Man. 29-Travolta/Kotter-c; "One Day at a Time", Gong Show. 30-1977, 84 pgs. w/bonus; Jaws, Baretta, King Kong, Happy Days	2	4	6	8	10	12
31,33-35,38,40: 31-"Rocky"-c/s; TV game shows. 33-Peter Benchley's "Deep". 34-J. Carter-c; TV's "Fish". 35-Xmas-c with Fonz/Six Million Dollar Man/Wonder Woman/Darth Vader/ Travolta, TV's "Mash" & "Family Matters". 38-Close Encounters of the Third Kind-c/s. 40-"Three's Company-c/s	1	2	3	5	7	9
32-Star Wars/Darth Vader-c/s; "Black Sunday"	2	4	6	12	16	20
36,42,47,49: 36-Farrah Fawcett/Six Million Dollar Man-c; TV's Nancy Drew & Hardy Boys; 1st app. Howard The Duck in Crazy, 2 pgs. 42-84 pgs. w/bonus; TV Hulk/Spider-Man-c; Mash, Gong Show, One Day at a Time, Disco, Alice. 47-Battlestar Galactica xmas-c; movie "Foul Play". 49-1979, 84 pgs. w/bonus; Mork & Mindy-c; Jaws, Saturday Night Fever, Three's Company	2	4	6	8	10	12
37-1978, 84 pgs. w/bonus. Darth Vader-c; Barney Miller, Laverne & Shirley, Good Times, Rocky, Donny & Marie Osmond, Bionic Woman	2	4	6	11	14	18
39,44: 39-Saturday Night Fever-c/s. 44-"Grease"-c w/Travolta/O. Newton-John	2	4	6	10	13	16
41-Kiss-c & 1pg. photos; Disaster movies, TV's "Family", Annie Hall	4	8	12	24	32	40
43,45,46,48,51: 43-Jaws-c; Saturday Night Fever. 43-E.C. swipe from Mad #131. 45-Travolta/O. Newton-John/J. Carter-c; Eight is Enough. 46-TV Hulk-c/s; Punk Rock. 48-"Wiz"-c, Battlestar Galactica-s. 51-Grease/Mork & Mindy/D&M Osmond-c, Mork & Mindy-sty. "Boys from Brazil"	1	2	3	5	7	9
50,58: 50-Superman movie-c/sty, Playboy Mag., TV Hulk, Fonz; Howard the Duck, 1 pg. 58-1980, 84 pgs. w/32 pg. color comic bonus insert-Full reprint of Crazy Comic #1, Battlestar Galactica, Charlie's Angels, Starsky & Hutch	2	4	6	10	13	16
52,59,60,64: 52-1979, 84 pgs. w/bonus. Marlon Brando-c; TV Hulk, Grease. Kiss, 1 pg. photos. 59-Santa Ptd-c by Larkin; "Alien", "Moonraker", Rocky-2, Howard the Duck, 1 pg. 60-Star Trek w/Muppets-c; Star Trek sty; 1st app/origin Teen Hulk; Severin-a. 64-84 pgs. w/bonus Monopoly game satire. "Empire Strikes Back", 8 pgs., One Day at a Time	2	4	6	10	13	16
53,54,65,67-70: 53-"Animal House"-c/sty; TV's "Vegas", Howard the Duck, 1 pg. 54-Love at First Bite-c/sty, Fantasy Island sty, Howard the Duck 1 pg. 65-(Has #66 on-c, Aug/'80). "Black Hole" w/Janson-a; Kirby,Wood/Severin-a(r), 5 pgs. Howard the Duck, 3 pgs.; Broderick-a; Buck Rogers, Mr. Rogers. 67-84 pgs. w/bonus; TV's Kung Fu, Exorcist; Ploog-a(r). 68-American Gigolo, Dukes of Hazzard, Teen Hulk; Howard the Duck, 3 pgs. Broderick-a; Monster sty/5 pg. Ditko-a(r). 69-Obnoxio the Clown-c/sty; Stephen King's "Shining", Teen Hulk, Richie Rich, Howard the Duck, 3pgs; Broderick-a. 70-84 pgs. Towering Inferno, Daytime TV; Trina Robbins-a	1	2	3	5	6	8
55-57,61,63: 55-84 pgs. w/bonus; Love Boat, Mork & Mindy, Fonz, TV Hulk. 56-Mork/Rocky/ J. Carter-c; China Syndrome. 57-TV Hulk with Miss Piggy-c, Dracula, Taxi, Muppets. 61-1980, 84 pgs. Adams-a(r), McCloud, Pro wrestling, Casper, TV's Police Story. 63-Apocalypse Now-Coppola's cult movie; 3rd app. Teen Hulk, Howard the Duck, 3 pgs.	1	3	4	6	8	10
62-Kiss-c & 2 pg. app; Quincy, 2nd app. Teen Hulk	3	6	9	19	25	32
66-Sept/'80, Empire Strikes Back-c/sty; Teen Hulk by Severin, Howard the Duck, 3pgs. by Broderick	2	4	6	9	11	14
71,72,75-77,79: 71-Blues Brothers parody, Teen Hulk, Superheroes parody, WKRP in Cincinnati, Howard the Duck, 3pgs. by Broderick. 72-Jackie Gleason/Smokey & the Bandit II-c/sty, Shogun, Teen Hulk. Howard the Duck, 3pgs. by Broderick. 75-Flash Gordon movie c/sty; Teen Hulk, Cat in the Hat, Howard the Duck 3pgs. by Broderick. 76-84 pgs. w/bonus; Monster-sty w/ Crandall-a(r), Monster-stys(2) w/Kirby-a(r), 5pgs. ea; Mash, TV Hulk, Chinatown. 77-Popeye movie/R. Williams-c/sty; Teen Hulk, Love Boat, Howard the Duck 3 pgs. 79-84 pgs. w/bonus color stickers; has new material; "9 to 5" w/Dolly Parton, Teen Hulk, Magnum P.I., Monster-sty w/5pgs, Ditko-a(r), "Rat" w/Sutton-a(r), Everett-a, 4 pgs.(r)	1	2	3	5	6	8
73,74,78,80: 73-84 pgs. w/bonus Hulk/Spiderman Finger Puppets-c & bonus; "Live & Let Die, Jaws, Fantasy Island. 74-Dallas/"Who Shot J.R."-c/sty; Elephant Man, Howard the Duck 3pgs. by Broderick. 78-Clint Eastwood-c/sty; Teen Hulk, Superheroes parody, Lou Grant. 80-Star Wars, 2 pg. app; "Howling", TV's "Greatest American Hero"	1	3	4	6	8	10
81,84,86,87,89: 81-.Superman Movie II-c/sty; Wolverine cameo, Mash, Teen Hulk. 84-American Werewolf in London, Johnny Carson app; Teen Hulk. 86-Time Bandits-c/sty; Private Benjamin. 87-Rubix Cube-c; Hill Street Blues, "Ragtime", Origin Obnoxio the Clown; Teen Hulk. 89-Burt Reynolds "Sharkey's Machine", Teen Hulk	1	2	3	5	6	8
82-X-Men-c w/new Byrne-a, 84 pgs. w/new material; Fantasy Island, Teen Hulk, "For Your Eyes Only", Spiderman/Human Torch-r by Kirby/Ditko; Sutton-a(r); Rogers-a; Hunchback of Notre Dame, 5 pgs.	2	4	6	10	13	16
83-Raiders of the Lost Ark-c/sty; Hart to Hart; Reese-a; Teen Hulk	2	4	6	8	10	12
85,88: 85-84 pgs; Escape from New York, Teen Hulk; Kirby-a(r), 5 pgs, Posiedon Adventure, Flintstones, Sesame Street. 88-84 pgs. w/bonus Dr. Strange Game; some new material; Jeffersons, X-Men/Wolverine, 10 pgs.; Byrne-a; Apocalypse Now, Teen Hulk	1	2	3	5	7	9
90-94: 90-Conan-c/sty; M. Severin-a; Teen Hulk. 91-84 pgs, some new material; Bladerunner-c/sty, "Deathwish-II, Teen Hulk, Black Knight, 10 pgs.-'50s-r w/Maneely-a. 92-Wrath of Khan Star Trek-c/sty; Joanie & Chachi, Teen Hulk. 93-"E.T."-c/sty, Teen Hulk, Archie Bunkers Place, Dr. Doom Game. 94-Poltergeist, Smurfs, Teen Hulk, Casper, Avengers parody-8pgs. Adams-a	2	4	6	9	11	14
Crazy Summer Special #1 (Sum, '75, 100 pgs.)-Nixon, TV Kung Fu, Babe Ruth, Joe Namath, Waltons, McCloud, Chariots of the Gods	2	4	6	12	16	20

NOTE: ***N. Adams** a-2, 61r, 94p. **Austin** a-82i. **Buscema** a-2, 82. **Byrne** c-82p. **Nick Cardy** c-7, 8, 10, 12-16, Super Special 1. **Crandall** a-76r. **Ditko** a-68r, 79r, 82r. **Drucker** a-3. **Eisner** a-9-16. **Kelly Freas** c-1-6, 9, 11; a-7. **Kirby/Wood** a-65r. **Ploog** a-1, 4, 7, 67r, 73r. **Rogers** a-82. **Sparling** a-92. **Wood** a-65r. Howard the Duck in 36, 50, 51, 53, 54, 59, 63, 65, 66, 68, 69, 71, 72, 74, 75, 77. Hulk in 46, c-42, 46, 57, 73. Star Wars in 32, 66; c-37.*

CRAZYMAN

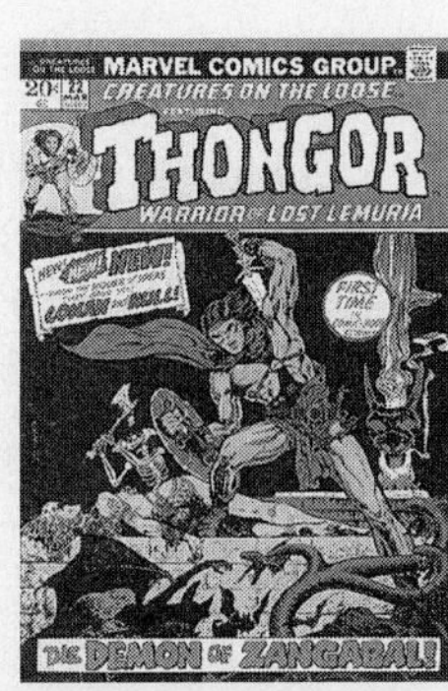

Creatures on the Loose #22 © MAR

Creech #1 © Greg Capullo

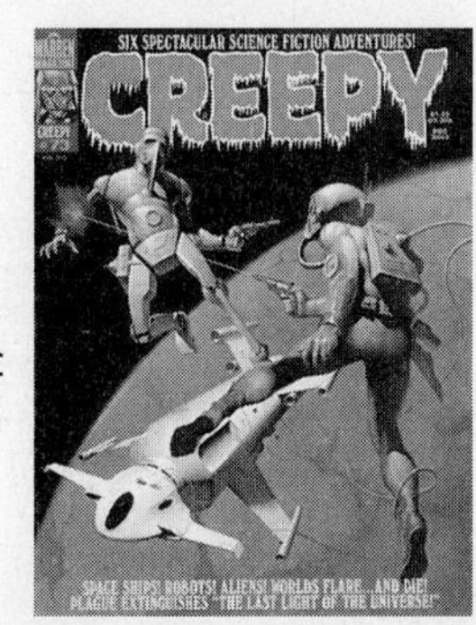

Creepy #73 © WP

GD 2.0 | VG 4.0 | FN 6.0 | VF 8.0 | VF/NM 9.0 | NM- 9.2

Continuity Comics: Apr, 1992 - No. 3, 1992 ($2.50, high quality paper)
1-($3.95, 52 pgs.)-Embossed-c; N. Adams part-i 4.00
2,3 ($2.50): 2-N. Adams/Bolland-c 2.50

CRAZYMAN
Continuity Comics: V2#1, 5/93 - No. 4, 1/94 ($2.50, high quality paper)
V2#1-4: 1-Entire book is die-cut. 2-(12/93)-Adams-c(p) & part scripts. 3-(12/93). 4-Indicia says #3, Jan. 1993 2.50

CRAZY, MAN, CRAZY (Magazine) (Becomes This Magazine is...?) (Formerly From Here to Insanity)
Humor Magazines (Charlton): V2#1, Dec, 1955 - V2#2, June, 1956
V2#1,V2#2-Satire; Wolverton-a, 3 pgs. 14 28 42 81 111 140

CREATURE, THE (See Movie Classics)

CREATURE
Antarctic Press: Oct, 1997 - No. 2 ($2.95, B&W)
1,2-Don Walker-s/a 3.00

CREATURE COMMANDOS
DC Comics: May, 2000 - No. 8, Dec, 2000 ($2.50, limited series)
1-8: Truman-s/Eaton-a 2.50

CREATURES OF THE ID
Caliber Press: 1990 ($2.95, B&W)
1-Frank Einstein (Madman) app.; Allred-a 3 6 9 18 24 30

CREATURES ON THE LOOSE (Formerly Tower of Shadows No. 1-9)(See Kull)
Marvel Comics: No. 10, March, 1971 - No. 37, Sept, 1975 (New-a & reprints)
10-(15¢)-1st full app. King Kull; see Kull the Conqueror; Wrightson-a 6 12 18 40 55 70
11-15: 15-Last 15¢ issue 2 4 6 14 18 22
16-Origin Warrior of Mars (begins, ends #21) 2 4 6 10 13 16
17-20 1 3 4 6 8 10
21-Steranko-c 2 4 6 10 13 16
22-Steranko-c; Thongor stories begin 2 4 6 11 14 18
23-29-Thongor-c/stories 1 2 3 5 6 8
30-Manwolf begins 2 4 6 14 18 22
31-33 2 4 6 8 10 12
34-37 1 3 4 6 8 10
NOTE: *Crandall a-13.* ***Ditko*** *r-15, 17, 18, 20, 22, 24, 27, 28.* ***Everett*** *a-16i(new).* ***Matt Fox*** *r-21i.* ***Howard*** *a-26i.* ***Gil Kane*** *a-16p, 17p, 19i; c-16, 17, 19, 20, 25, 29, 33p, 35p, 36p.* ***Kirby*** *a-10-15r, 16(2)r, 17r, 19r.* ***Morrow*** *a-20, 21.* ***Perez*** *a-33-37; c-34p.* ***Shores*** *a-11.* ***innott*** *r-21.* ***Sutton*** *c-10.* ***Tuska*** *a-31p, 32p.*

CREECH, THE
Image Comics: Oct, 1997 - No. 3, Dec, 1997 ($1.95/$2.50, limited series)
1-3: 1-Capullo-s/c/a(p) 2.50
TPB (1999, $9.95) r/#1-3, McFarlane intro. 10.00
Out for Blood 1-3 (7/01 - No. 3, 11/01; $4.95) Capullo-s/c/a 5.00

CREED
Hall of Heroes Comics: Dec, 1994 - No. 2, Jan, 1995 ($2.50, B&W)
1 2 4 6 10 12 15
2 2 4 6 8 10 12

CREED
Lightning Comics: June, 1995 - Present ($2.75/$3.00, B&W/color)
1-($2.75) 4.00
1-($3.00, color) 5.00
1-($9.95)-Commemorative Edition 10.00
1-TwinVariant Edition (1250? print run) 10.00
1-Special Edition; polybagged w/certificate 4.00
1 Gold Collectors Edition; polybagged w/certificate 3.00
2,3-($3.00, color)-Butt Naked Edition & regular-c 3.00
3-($9.95)-Commemorative Edition; polybagged w/certificate & card 10.00

CREED: APPLE TREE
Gearbox Press: Dec, 2000 - No. 2 ($2.95, B&W)
1,2-Kaniuga-s/c/a 3.00

CREED: CRANIAL DISORDER
Lightning Comics: Oct, 1996 ($3.00, limited series)
1-3-Two covers 3.00
1-($5.95)-Platinum Edition 6.00
2,3-($9.95)Ltd.l Edition 10.00

CREED: MECHANICAL EVOLUTION
Gearbox Press: Sept, 2000 - No. 2, Oct, 2000 ($2.95, B&W)
1,2-Kaniuga-s/c/a 3.00

CREED/TEENAGE MUTANT NINJA TURTLES
Lightning Comics: May, 1996 ($3.00, one-shot)
1-Kaniuga-a(p)/scripts; Laird-c; variant-c exists 3.00
1-($9.95)-Platinum Edition 10.00
1-Special Edition; polybagged w/certificate 5.00

CREED: USE YOUR DELUSION
Avatar Press: Jan, 1998 - No. 2, Feb, 1998 ($3.00, B&W)
1,2-Kaniuga-s/c/a 3.00
1,2-($4.95) Foil cover 5.00

CREED: UTOPIATE
Image Comics: Feb, 2002 - No. 3, Aug, 2002 ($2.95/$4.95, color)
1,2-Kaniuga-c/a/Christina Z-s 3.00
3-($4.95) 5.00

CREEPER, THE (See Beware... , Showcase #73 & 1st Issue Special #7)
DC Comics: Dec, 1997 - No. 11; #1,000,000 Nov, 1998 ($2.50)
1-11-Kaminski-s/Martinbrough-a(p). 7,8-Joker-c/app. 3.00
#1,000,000 (11/98) 853rd Century x-over 3.00

CREEPS
Image Comics: Oct, 2001 - No. 4, May, 2002 ($2.95)
1-4-Mandrake-a/Mishkin-s 3.00

CREEPSHOW
Plume/New American Library Pub.: July, 1982 (softcover graphic novel)
1st edition-nn-(68 pgs.) Kamen-c/Wrightson-a; screenplay by Stephen King for the George Romero movie 3 6 9 19 25 32
2nd-7th printings 2 4 6 12 16 20

CREEPSVILLE
Laughing Reindeer Press: V2#1, Winter, 1995 ($4.95)
V2#1-Comics w/text 5.00

CREEPY (See Warren Presents)
Warren Publishing Co./Harris Publ. #146: 1964 - No. 145, Feb, 1983; No. 146, 1985 (B&W, magazine)
1-Frazetta-a (his last story in comics?); Jack Davis-c; 1st Warren all comics magazine; 1st app. Uncle Creepy 10 20 30 72 104 135
2-Frazetta-c & 1 pg. strip 6 12 18 43 59 75
3-8,11-13,15-17: 3-7,9-11,15-17-Frazetta-c. 7-Frazetta 1 pg. strip. 15,16-Adams-a. 16-Jeff Jones-a 3 7 10 21 28 35
9-Creepy fan club sketch by Wrightson (1st published-a); has 1/2 pg. anti-smoking strip by Frazetta; Frazetta-c; 1st Wood and Ditko art on this title; Toth-a (low print) 6 12 18 40 55 70
10-Brunner fan club sketch (1st published work) 4 8 12 25 33 42
14-Neal Adams 1st Warren work 4 8 12 25 33 42
18-28,30,31: 27-Frazetta-c 3 6 9 18 24 30
29,34: 29-Jones-a 3 6 9 19 25 32
32-(scarce) Frazetta-c; Harlan Ellison sty 5 10 15 33 44 55
33,35,37,39,40,42-47,49: 35-Hitler/Nazi-s. 39-1st Uncle Creepy solo-s, Cousin Eerie app.; early Brunner-a. 42-1st San Julian-c. 44-1st Ploog-a. 46-Corben-a 3 6 9 16 20 25
36-(11/70)1st Corben art at Warren 3 7 10 21 28 35
38,41-(scarce): 38-1st Kelly-c. 41-Corben-a 4 8 12 24 32 40
48,55,65-(1972, 1973, 1974 Annuals) #55 & 65 contain an 8 pg. slick comic insert. 48-(84 pgs.). 55-Color poster bonus (1/2 price if missing). 65-(100 pgs.) Summer Giant 3 7 10 21 28 35
50-Vampirella/Eerie/Creepy-c 4 8 12 24 32 40
51,54,56-61,64: All contain an 8 pg. slick comic insert in middle. 59-Xmas horror. 54,64-Chaykin-a 3 6 9 18 24 30
52,53,66,71,72,75,76,78-80: 71-All Bermejo-a; Space & Time issue. 72-Gual-a. 78-Fantasy issue. 79,80-Monsters issue 2 4 6 11 14 18
62,63-1st & 2nd full Wrightson story art; Corben-a; 8 pg. color comic insert 3 6 9 18 24 30
67,68,73 2 4 6 14 18 22
69,70-Edgar Allan Poe issues; Corben-a 2 4 6 12 16 20
74,77: 74-All Crandell-a. 77-Xmas Horror issue; Corben-a,Wrightson-a 3 6 9 16 20 25
81,84,85,88-90,92-94,96-99,102,104-112,114-118,120,122-130: 84,93-Sports issue. 85,97,102-Monster issue. 89-All war issue; Nino-a. 94-Weird Children issue. 96,109-Aliens issue. 99-Disasters. 103-Corben-a. 104-Robots issue. 106-Sword & Sorcery.107-Sci-fi. 116-End of Man. 125-Xmas Horror 1 2 3 5 7 9
82,100,101: 82-All Maroto issue. 100-(8/78) Anniversary. 101-Corben-a

Creepy #120 © WP

The Crew #7 © MAR

Crime and Punishment #10 © LEV

	GD 2.0	VG 4.0	FN 6.0	VF 8.0	VF/NM 9.0	NM- 9.2
	2	4	6	10	13	16
83,85 Wrightson-a. 83-Corben-a. 85-Gorilla/Apes.	2	4	6	8	10	12
86,87,91,103-Wrightson-a. 86-Xmas Horror	2	4	6	8	10	12
113-All Wrightson-r issue	2	4	6	14	18	22
119,121: 119-All Nino issue.121-All Severin-r issue	2	4	6	8	10	12
131,133-136,138,140: 135-Xmas issue	2	4	6	8	10	12
132,137,139: 132-Corben. 137-All Williamson-r issue. 139-All Toth-r issue	2	4	6	10	12	15
141,143,144 (low dist.): 144-Giant, $2.25; Frazetta-c	2	4	6	12	16	20
142,145 (low dist.): 142-(10/82, 100 pgs.) All Torres issue. 145-(2/83) last Warren issue	2	4	6	12	16	20
146 ($2.95)-1st from Harris; resurrection issue	7	14	21	46	63	80
Year Book '68-'70: '70-Neal Adams, Ditko-a(r)	4	8	12	24	32	40
Annual 1971,1972	3	7	10	21	28	35
1993 Fearbook ($3.95)-Harris Publ.; Brereton-c; Vampirella by Busiek-s/Art Adams-a; David-s; Paquette-a	3	7	10	21	28	35
...:The Classic Years TPB (Harris/Dark Horse,'91, $12.95) Kaluta-c; art by Frazetta,Torres, Crandall, Ditko, Morrow, Williamson, Wrightson						25.00

NOTE: *All issues contain many good artists works:* ***Neal Adams, Brunner, Corben, Craig (Taycee), Crandall, Ditko, Evans, Frazetta, Heath, Jeff Jones, Krenkel, McWilliams, Morrow, Nino, Orlando, Ploog, Severin, Torres, Toth, Williamson, Wood, & Wrightson****; covers by* ***Crandall, Davis, Frazetta, Morrow, San Julian, Todd/Bode****; Otto Binder's "Adam Link" stories in No. 2, 4, 6, 8, 9, 12, 13, 15 with* ***Orlando*** *art.* ***Frazetta*** *c-2-7, 9-11, 15-17, 27, 32, 83r, 89r, 91r.* ***E.A. Poe*** *adaptations in 66, 69, 70.*

CREEPY (Mini-series)
Harris Comics/Dark Horse: 1992 - Book 4, 1992 (48 pgs, B&W, squarebound)

	GD	VG	FN	VF	VF/NM	NM-
Book 1-4: Brereton painted-c on all. Stories and art by various incl. David (all), Busiek(2), Infantino(2), Guice(3), Colan(1)	2	4	6	8	10	12

CREEPY THINGS
Charlton Comics: July, 1975 - No. 6, June, 1976

	GD	VG	FN	VF	VF/NM	NM-
1	2	4	6	12	16	20
2-6: Ditko-a in 3,5. Sutton c-3,4	1	3	4	6	8	10
Modern Comics Reprint 2-6(1977)						4.00

NOTE: ***Larson*** *a-2,6.* ***Sutton*** *a-1,2,4,6.* ***Zeck*** *a-2.*

CREMATOR
Chaos! Comics: Dec, 1998 - No. 5, May, 1999 ($2.95, limited series)

	GD	VG	FN	VF	VF/NM	NM-
1-5-Leonardo Jimenez-s/a						3.00

CREW, THE
Marvel Comics: July, 2003 - No. 7, Jan, 2004 ($2.50)

	GD	VG	FN	VF	VF/NM	NM-
1-7-Priest-s/Bennett-a; James Rhodes(War Machine) app.						2.50

CRIME AND JUSTICE (Badge Of Justice #22 on; Rookie Cop? No. 27 on)
Capitol Stories/Charlton Comics: March, 1951 - No. 21; No. 23 - No. 26, Sept, 1955 (No #22)

	GD	VG	FN	VF	VF/NM	NM-
1	33	66	99	190	270	350
2	13	26	39	74	100	125
3-8,10-13: 6-Negligee panels	10	20	30	58	77	95
9-Classic story "Comics Vs. Crime"	24	48	72	138	194	250
14-Color illos in **POP**; gory story of man who beheads women	19	38	57	109	152	195
15-17,19-21,23-26; 15-Negligee panels. 23-26 (exist?)	8	16	24	43	54	65
18-Ditko-a	25	50	75	147	202	260

NOTE: ***Alascia*** *c-20.* ***Ayers*** *a-17.* ***Shuster*** *a-19-21; c-19. Bondage c-11, 12.*

CRIME AND PUNISHMENT (Title inspired by 1935 film)
Lev Gleason Publications: April, 1948 - No. 74, Aug, 1955

	GD	VG	FN	VF	VF/NM	NM-
1-Mr. Crime app. on-c	33	66	99	190	270	350
2	18	36	54	101	138	175
3-Used in **SOTI**, pg. 112; injury-to-eye panel; Fuje-a	20	40	60	112	156	200
4,5	13	26	39	76	103	130
6-10	11	22	33	63	84	105
11-20	10	20	30	56	73	90
21-30	8	16	24	46	58	70
31-38,40-44,46: 46-One pg. Frazetta-a	8	16	24	40	50	60
39-Drug mention story "The 5 Dopes"	10	20	30	58	77	95
45- "Hophead Killer" drug story	10	20	30	58	77	95
47-57,60-65,70-74:	7	14	21	37	46	55
58-Used in **POP**, pg. 79	8	16	24	40	50	60
59-Used in **SOTI**, illo "What comic-book America stands for"	29	58	87	164	232	300
66-Toth-c/a(4); 3-D effect issue (3/54); 1st "Deep Dimension" process	39	78	117	230	325	420
67- "Monkey on His Back" heroin story; 3-D effect issue	34	68	102	196	278	360
68-3-D effect issue; Toth-c (7/54)	29	58	87	164	232	300
69- "The Hot Rod Gang" dope crazy kids	10	20	30	58	77	95

NOTE: ***Biro*** *c-most.* ***Everett*** *a-31.* ***Fuje*** *a-3, 4, 12, 13, 17, 18, 20, 26, 27.* ***Guardineer*** *a-2-4, 10, 14, 17, 18, 20, 26-28, 32, 38-44,54.* ***Kinstler*** *c-69.* ***McWilliams*** *a-41, 48, 49.* ***Tuska*** *a-28, 30, 51, 64, 70.*

CRIME AND PUNISHMENT: MARSHALL LAW TAKES MANHATTAN
Marvel Comics (Epic Comics): 1989 ($4.95, 52 pgs., direct sales only, mature)

	GD	VG	FN	VF	VF/NM	NM-
nn-Graphic album featuring Marshall Law						5.00

CRIME CAN'T WIN (Formerly Cindy Smith)
Marvel/Atlas Comics (TCI 41/CCC 42,43,4-12): No. 41, 9/50 - No. 43, 2/51; No. 4, 4/51 - No. 12, 9/53

	GD	VG	FN	VF	VF/NM	NM-
41(#1)	26	52	78	150	210	270
42(#2)	15	30	45	86	118	150
43(#3)-Horror story	18	36	54	104	142	180
4(4/51),5-12: 10-Possible use in **SOTI**, pg. 161	12	24	36	71	96	120

NOTE: ***Robinson*** *a-9-11.* ***Tuska*** *a-43.*

CRIME CASES COMICS (Formerly Willie Comics)
Marvel/Atlas Comics(CnPC No.24-8/MJMC No.9-12): No. 24, 8/50 - No. 27, 3/51; No. 5, 5/51 - No. 12, 7/52

	GD	VG	FN	VF	VF/NM	NM-
24 (#1, 52 pgs.)-True police cases	18	36	54	104	142	180
25-27(#2-4): 27-Morisi-a	12	24	36	71	96	120
5-12: 11-Robinson-a. 12-Tuska-a	10	20	30	60	80	100

CRIME CLINIC
Ziff-Davis Publishing Co.: No. 10, July-Aug, 1951 - No. 5, Summer, 1952

	GD	VG	FN	VF	VF/NM	NM-
10(#1)-Painted-c; origin Dr. Tom Rogers	29	58	87	164	232	300
11(#2),4,5: 4,5-Painted-c	20	40	60	112	156	200
3-Used in **SOTI**, pg. 18	21	42	63	118	164	210

NOTE: *All have painted covers by* ***Saunders. Starr*** *a-10.*

CRIME CLINIC
Slave Labor Graphics: May, 1995 - No. 2, Oct, 1995 ($2.95, B&W, limited series)

	GD	VG	FN	VF	VF/NM	NM-
1,2						3.00

CRIME DETECTIVE COMICS
Hillman Periodicals: Mar-Apr, 1948 - V3#8, May-June, 1953

	GD	VG	FN	VF	VF/NM	NM-
V1#1-The Invisible 6, costumed villains app; Fuje-c/a, 15 pgs.	29	58	87	164	232	300
2,5: 5-Krigstein-a	13	26	39	74	100	125
3,4,6,7,10-12: 6-McWilliams-a	10	20	30	58	77	95
8-Kirbyish-a by McCann	10	20	30	58	77	95
9-Used in **SOTI**, pg. 16 & "Caricature of the author in a position comic book publishers wish he were in permanently" illo.	37	74	111	213	299	385
V2#1,4,7-Krigstein-a: 1-Tuska-a	10	20	30	58	77	95
2,3,5,6,8-12 (1-2/52)	8	16	24	46	58	70
V3#1-Drug use-c	9	18	27	49	62	75
2-8	7	14	21	37	46	55

NOTE: ***Briefer*** *a-11, V3#1.* ***Kinstlerish****-a by* ***McCann****-V2#7, V3#2.* ***Powell*** *a-10, 11.* ***Starr*** *a-10.*

CRIME DETECTOR
Timor Publications: Jan, 1954 - No. 5, Sept, 1954

	GD	VG	FN	VF	VF/NM	NM-
1	21	42	63	118	164	210
2	11	22	33	63	84	105
3,4	10	20	30	56	73	90
5-Disbrow-a (classic)	22	44	66	127	176	225

CRIME DOES NOT PAY (Formerly Silver Streak Comics No. 1-21)
Comic House/Lev Gleason/Golfing: No. 22, June, 1942 - No. 147, July, 1955 (1st crime comic)(Title inspired by film)

	GD	VG	FN	VF	VF/NM	NM-
22 (23 on cover, 22 on indicia)-Origin The War Eagle & only app.; Chip Gardner begins; #22 was rebound in Complete Book of True Crime (Scarce)	248	496	744	1550	2325	3100
23 (Scarce)	132	264	396	825	1238	1650
24-Intro. & 1st app. Mr. Crime (Scarce).	104	208	312	650	975	1300
25,26,28-30: 30-Wood and Biro app.	58	116	174	363	544	725
27-Classic Biro-c	66	132	198	413	619	825
31,32,34-40	41	82	123	246	348	450
33-Classic Biro Hanging & hatchet-c	44	88	132	264	395	525
41-Origin & 1st app. Officer Common Sense	31	62	93	178	252	325
42-Electrocution-c	36	72	108	204	290	375
43-46,48-50: 44,45,50 are 68 pg. issues; 44-"legs" diamond story	20	40	60	112	156	200
47-Electric chair-c	34	68	102	196	278	360
51-70: 63,64-Possible use in **SOTI**, pg. 306. 63-Contains Biro & Gleason's self censorship code of 12 listed restrictions (5/48)	17	34	51	98	134	170

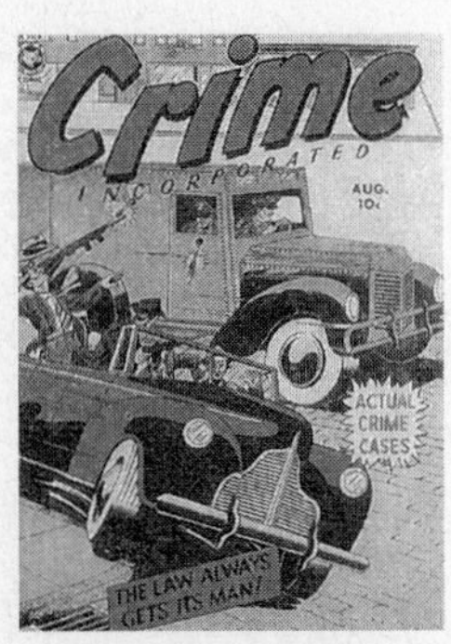

Crime Incorporated #3 © FOX

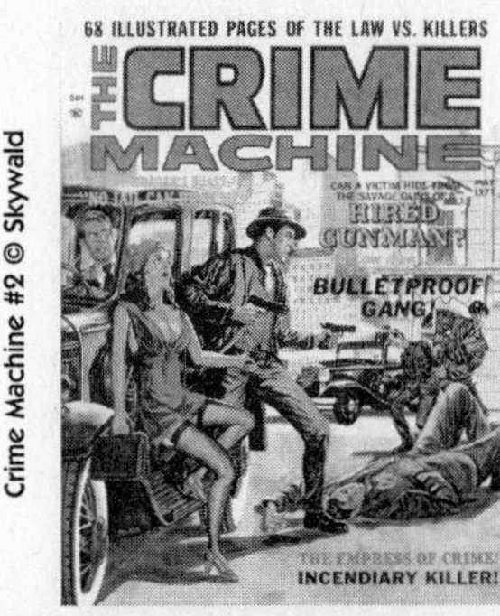

Crime Machine #2 © Skywald

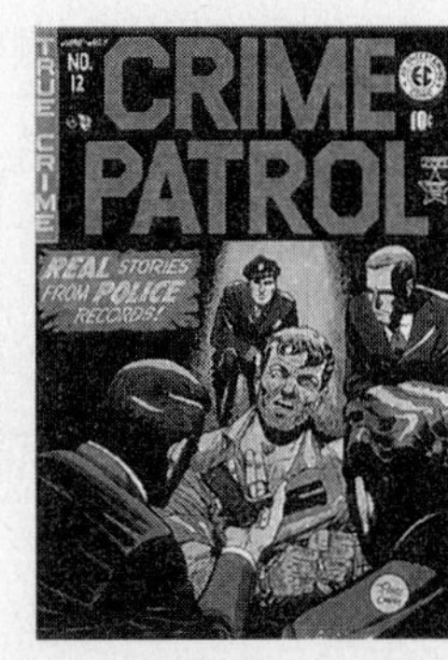

Crime Patrol #12 © WMG

	GD 2.0	VG 4.0	FN 6.0	VF 8.0	VF/NM 9.0	NM- 9.2
71-99: 87-Chip Gardner begins, ends #100	15	30	45	84	115	145
100	16	32	48	92	126	160
101-104,107-110: 102-Chip Gardner app	11	22	33	63	84	105
105-Used in **POP**, pg. 84	12	24	36	69	92	115
106,114-Frazetta-a, 1 pg.	11	22	33	63	84	105
111-Used in **POP**, pgs. 80 & 81; injury-to-eye sty illo	12	24	36	69	92	115
112,113,115-130	9	18	27	49	62	75
131-140	8	16	24	40	50	60
141,142-Last pre-code issue; Kubert-a(1)	10	20	30	56	73	90
143-Kubert-a in one story	10	20	30	56	73	90
144-146	8	16	24	40	50	60
147-Last issue (scarce); Kubert-a	14	28	42	79	107	135
1(Golfing-1945)	8	16	24	40	50	60
The Best of...(1944, 128 pgs.)-Series contains 4 rebound issues	78	156	234	488	732	975
...1945 issue	59	118	177	369	555	740
...1946-48 issues	44	88	132	264	395	525
...1949-50 issues	41	82	123	246	348	450
...1951-53 issues	34	68	102	196	278	360

NOTE: *Many issues contain violent covers and stories. Who Dunnit by* **Guardineer**-*39-42, 44-105, 108-110; Chip Gardner by* **Bob Fujitani (Fuje)**-*88-103.* **Alderman** *a-29, 41-44, 49.* **Dan Barry** *a-67, 75.* **Biro** *c-1-76, 122, 142.* **Briefer** *a-29(2), 30, 31, 33, 37, 39.* **G. Colan** *a-105.* **Fuje** *c-88, 89, 91-94, 96, 98, 99, 102, 103.* **Guardineer** *a-57, 67, 68, 71, 74.* **Kubert** *c-143.* **Landau** *a-118.* **Maurer** *a-29, 39, 41, 42.* **McWilliams** *a-91, 93, 95, 100-103.* **Palais** *a-30, 33, 37, 39, 41-43, 44(2), 46, 49.* **Powell** *a-146, 147.* **Tuska** *a-48, 50(2), 51, 52, 56, 57(2), 60-64, 66, 67, 68, 71, 74. Painted c-87-102. Bondage c-43, 62, 98.*

CRIME EXPOSED
Marvel Comics (PPI)/Marvel Atlas Comics (PrPI): June, 1948; Dec, 1950 - No. 14, June, 1952

	GD 2.0	VG 4.0	FN 6.0	VF 8.0	VF/NM 9.0	NM- 9.2
1(6/48)	34	68	102	193	274	355
1(12/50)	20	40	60	112	156	200
2	14	28	42	79	107	135
3-9,11,14	11	22	33	63	84	105
10-Used in **POP**, pg. 81	12	24	36	69	92	115
12-Krigstein & Robinson-a	12	24	36	69	92	115
13-Used in **POP**, pg. 81; Krigstein-a	12	24	36	71	96	120

NOTE: **Maneely** *c-8.* **Robinson** *a-11, 12.* **Tuska** *a-3, 4.*

CRIMEFIGHTERS
Marvel Comics (CmPS 1-3/CCC 4-10): Apr, 1948 - No. 10, Nov, 1949

	GD 2.0	VG 4.0	FN 6.0	VF 8.0	VF/NM 9.0	NM- 9.2
1-Some copies are undated & could be reprints	25	50	75	147	202	260
2,3: 3-Morphine addict story	14	28	42	79	107	135
4-10: 6-Anti-Wertham editorial. 9,10-Photo-c	12	24	36	69	92	115

CRIME FIGHTERS (...Always Win)
Atlas Comics (CnPC): No. 11, Sept, 1954 - No. 13, Jan, 1955

	GD 2.0	VG 4.0	FN 6.0	VF 8.0	VF/NM 9.0	NM- 9.2
11-13: 11-Maneely-a,13-Pakula, Reinman, Severin-a	12	24	36	69	92	115

CRIME-FIGHTING DETECTIVE (Shock Detective Cases No. 20 on; formerly Criminals on the Run)
Star Publications: No. 11, Apr-May, 1950 - No. 19, June, 1952 (Based on true crime cases)

	GD 2.0	VG 4.0	FN 6.0	VF 8.0	VF/NM 9.0	NM- 9.2
11-L. B. Cole-c/a (2 pgs.); L. B. Cole-c on all	20	40	60	112	156	200
12,13,15-19: 17-Young King Cole & Dr. Doom app.	15	30	45	84	115	145
14-L. B. Cole-c/a, r/Law-Crime #2	17	34	51	95	130	165

CRIME FILES
Standard Comics: No. 5, Sept, 1952 - No. 6, Nov, 1952

	GD 2.0	VG 4.0	FN 6.0	VF 8.0	VF/NM 9.0	NM- 9.2
5-1pg. Alex Toth-a; used in **SOTI**, pg. 4 (text)	25	50	75	144	198	255
6-Sekowsky-a	13	26	39	74	100	125

CRIME ILLUSTRATED (Magazine)
E. C. Comics: Nov-Dec, 1955 - No. 2, Spring, 1956 (25¢, Adult Suspense Stories on-c)

	GD 2.0	VG 4.0	FN 6.0	VF 8.0	VF/NM 9.0	NM- 9.2
1-Ingels & Crandall-a	16	32	48	92	126	160
2-Ingels & Crandall-a	13	26	39	74	100	125

NOTE: **Craig** *a-2.* **Crandall** *a-1, 2; c-2.* **Evans** *a-1.* **Davis** *a-2.* **Ingels** *a-1, 2.* **Krigstein/Crandall** *a-1.* **Orlando** *a-1, 2; c-1.*

CRIME INCORPORATED (Formerly Crimes Incorporated)
Fox Features Syndicate: No. 2, Aug, 1950; No. 3, Aug, 1951

	GD 2.0	VG 4.0	FN 6.0	VF 8.0	VF/NM 9.0	NM- 9.2
2	27	54	81	153	214	275
3(1951)-Hollingsworth-a	19	38	57	109	152	195

CRIME MACHINE (Magazine reprints pre-code crime and gangster comics)
Skywald Publications: Feb, 1971 - No. 2, May, 1971 (B&W, 68 pgs., roundbound)

	GD 2.0	VG 4.0	FN 6.0	VF 8.0	VF/NM 9.0	NM- 9.2
1-Kubert-a(2)(r)(Avon); bikini girl in cake-c	6	12	18	40	55	70
2-Torres, Wildey-a; violent-c/a	4	8	12	24	32	40

CRIME MUST LOSE! (Formerly Sports Action?)
Sports Action (Atlas Comics): No. 4, Oct, 1950 - No. 12, April, 1952

	GD 2.0	VG 4.0	FN 6.0	VF 8.0	VF/NM 9.0	NM- 9.2
4-Ann Brewster-a in all; c-used in N.Y. Legis. Comm. documents	19	38	57	106	146	185
5-12: 9-Robinson-a. 11-Used in **POP**, pg. 89	13	26	39	74	100	125

CRIME MUST PAY THE PENALTY (Formerly Four Favorites; Penalty #47, 48)
Ace Magazines (Current Books): No. 33, Feb, 1948; No. 2, Jun, 1948 - No. 48, Jan, 1956

	GD 2.0	VG 4.0	FN 6.0	VF 8.0	VF/NM 9.0	NM- 9.2
33(#1, 2/48)-Becomes Four Teeners #34?	34	68	102	196	278	360
2(6/48)-Extreme violence; Palais-a?	22	44	66	124	172	220
3,4,8: 3- "Frisco Mary" story used in Senate Investigation report, pg. 7. 4,8-Transvestism stories	16	32	48	89	122	155
5-7,9,10	11	22	33	63	84	105
11-19	10	20	30	58	77	95
20-Drug story "Dealers in White Death"	13	26	39	76	103	130
21-32,34-40,42-48	8	16	24	40	50	60
33(7/53)- "Dell Fabry-Junk King" drug story; mentioned in Love and Death	10	20	30	58	77	95
41-reprints "Dealers in White Death"	8	16	24	46	58	70

NOTE: **Cameron** *a-29-31, 34, 35, 39-41.* **Colan** *a-20, 31.* **Kremer** *a-3, 37r.* **Larsen** *a-32.* **Palais** *a-5?,37.*

CRIME MUST STOP
Hillman Periodicals: October, 1952 (52 pgs.)

	GD 2.0	VG 4.0	FN 6.0	VF 8.0	VF/NM 9.0	NM- 9.2
V1#1(Scarce)-Similar to Monster Crime; Mort Lawrence, Krigstein-a	66	132	198	413	619	825

CRIME MYSTERIES (Secret Mysteries #16 on; combined with Crime Smashers #7 on)
Ribage Publ. Corp. (Trojan Magazines): May, 1952 - No. 15, Sept, 1954

	GD 2.0	VG 4.0	FN 6.0	VF 8.0	VF/NM 9.0	NM- 9.2
1-Transvestism story; crime & terror stories begin	55	110	165	330	495	660
2-Marijuana story (7/52)	40	80	120	240	340	440
3-One pg. Frazetta-a	37	74	111	213	299	385
4-Cover shows girl in bondage having her blood drained; 1 pg. Frazetta-a	55	110	165	330	495	660
5-10	31	62	93	175	248	320
11,12,14	29	58	87	164	232	300
13-(5/54)-Angelo Torres 1st comic work (inks over Check's pencils); Check-a	34	68	102	196	278	360
15-Acid in face-c	40	80	120	240	350	460

NOTE: **Fass** *a-13; c-4, 10.* **Hollingsworth** *a-10-13, 15; c-2, 12, 13, 15.* **Kiefer** *a-4.* **Woodbridge** *a-13? Bondage-c-1, 8, 12.*

CRIME ON THE RUN (See Approved Comics #8)

CRIME ON THE WATERFRONT (Formerly Famous Gangsters)
Realistic Publications: No. 4, May, 1952 (Painted cover)

	GD 2.0	VG 4.0	FN 6.0	VF 8.0	VF/NM 9.0	NM- 9.2
4	30	60	90	170	240	310

CRIME PATROL (Formerly International #1-5; International Crime Patrol #6; becomes Crypt of Terror #17 on)
E. C. Comics: No. 7, Summer, 1948 - No. 16, Feb-Mar, 1950

	GD 2.0	VG 4.0	FN 6.0	VF 8.0	VF/NM 9.0	NM- 9.2
7-Intro. Captain Crime	66	132	198	413	619	825
8-14: 12-Ingels-a	58	116	174	363	542	720
15-Intro. of Crypt Keeper (inspired by Witches Tales radio show) & Crypt of Terror (see Tales From the Crypt #33 for origin); used by N.Y. Legis. Comm.; last pg. Feldstein-a	250	500	750	1875	2688	3500
16-2nd Crypt Keeper app.; Roussos-a	164	328	492	1230	1765	2300

NOTE: **Craig** *c/a in most issues.* **Feldstein** *a-9-16.* **Kiefer** *a-8, 10, 11.* **Moldoff** *a-7.*

CRIME PATROL
Gemstone Publishing: Apr, 2000 - No. 10, Jan, 2001 ($2.50)

	GD 2.0	VG 4.0	FN 6.0	VF 8.0	VF/NM 9.0	NM- 9.2
1-10: E.C. reprints						2.50
Volume 1,2 (2000, $13.50) 1-r/#1-5. 2-r/#6-10						14.00

CRIME PHOTOGRAPHER (See Casey...)

CRIME REPORTER
St. John Publ. Co.: Aug, 1948 - No. 3, Dec, 1948 (Indicia shows Oct.)

	GD 2.0	VG 4.0	FN 6.0	VF 8.0	VF/NM 9.0	NM- 9.2
1-Drug club story	50	100	150	300	450	600
2-Used in **SOTI**: illo- "Children told me what the man was going to do with the red-hot poker;" r/Dynamic #17 with editing; Baker-c; Tuska-a	70	140	210	438	657	875
3-Baker-c; Tuska-a	40	80	120	240	350	460

CRIMES BY WOMEN
Fox Features Syndicate: June, 1948 - No. 15, Aug, 1951; 1954 (True crime cases)

	GD 2.0	VG 4.0	FN 6.0	VF 8.0	VF/NM 9.0	NM- 9.2
1-True story of Bonnie Parker	123	246	369	769	1155	1540
2,3: 3-Used in **SOTI**, pg. 234	64	128	192	400	600	800
4,5,7-9,11-15: 8-Used in **POP**	58	116	174	363	542	720
6-Classic girl fight-c; acid-in-face panel	63	126	189	394	592	790
10-Used in **SOTI**, pg. 72; girl fight-c	59	118	177	369	555	740
54(M.S. Publ.-'54)-Reprint; (formerly My Love Secret)						

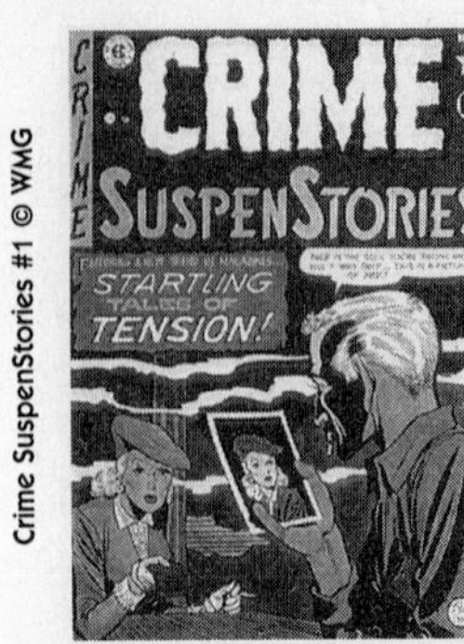

Crime SuspenStories #1 © WMG

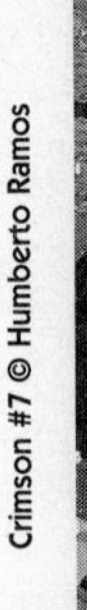
Crimson #7 © Humberto Ramos

Crisis on Multiple Earths TPB © DC

GD VG FN VF VF/NM NM-
2.0 4.0 6.0 8.0 9.0 9.2

27 54 81 153 214 275

CRIMES INCORPORATED (Formerly My Past)
Fox Features Syndicate: No. 12, June, 1950 (Crime Incorporated No. 2 on)

12 — 15 30 45 84 115 145

CRIMES INCORPORATED (See Fox Giants)

CRIME SMASHER (See Whiz #76)
Fawcett Publications: Summer, 1948 (one-shot)

1-Formerly Spy Smasher — 44 88 132 264 395 525

CRIME SMASHERS (Becomes Secret Mysteries No. 16 on)
Ribage Publishing Corp.(Trojan Magazines): Oct, 1950 - No. 15, Mar, 1953

1-Used in **SOTI**, pg. 19,20, & illo "A girl raped and murdered;" Sally the Sleuth begins
85 170 255 531 796 1060
2-Kubert-c — 46 92 138 276 413 550
3,4 — 38 76 114 219 310 400
5-Wood-a — 44 88 132 264 395 525
6,8-11: 8-Lingerie panel — 29 58 87 164 232 300
7-Female heroin junkie story — 32 64 96 180 255 330
12-Injury to eye panel; 1 pg. Frazetta-a — 32 64 96 180 255 330
13-Used in **POP**, pgs. 79,80; 1 pg. Frazetta-a — 32 64 96 180 255 330
14,15 — 25 50 75 147 202 260

NOTE: ***Hollingsworth** a-14. **Kiefer** a-15. Bondage c-7, 9.*

CRIME SUSPENSTORIES (Formerly Vault of Horror No. 12-14)
E. C. Comics: No. 15, Oct-Nov, 1950 - No. 27, Feb-Mar, 1955

15-Identical to #1 in content; #1 printed on outside front cover. #15 (formerly "The Vault of Horror") printed and blackened out on inside front cover with Vol. 1, No. 1 printed over it. Evidently, several of No. 15 were printed before a decision was made not to drop the Vault of Horror and Haunt of Fear series. The print run was stopped on No. 15 and continued on No. 1. All of the No. 15 issues were changed as described above.
143 286 429 1073 1537 2000
1 — 105 210 315 788 1132 1475
2 — 57 114 171 428 614 800
3-5: 3-Poe adaptation. 3-Old Witch stories begin — 39 78 117 293 422 550
6-10 — 33 64 96 240 353 465
11,12,14,15: 15-The Old Witch guest stars — 25 50 75 188 269 350
13,16-Williamson-a — 27 54 81 203 292 380
17-Williamson/Frazetta-a (6 pgs.) — 32 64 96 240 345 450
18,19: 19-Used in **SOTI**, pg. 235 — 22 44 66 165 233 300
20-Cover used in **SOTI**, illo "Cover of a children's comic book"
27 54 81 203 292 380
21,24-26: 24- "Food For Thought" similar to "Cave In" in Amazing Detective Cases #13 (1952)
16 32 48 120 170 220
22,23-Used in Senate investigation on juvenile delinquency. 22-Ax decapitation-c
22 44 66 165 233 300
27-Last issue (Low distribution) — 19 38 57 143 207 270

NOTE: ***Craig** a-1-21; c-1-18, 20-22. **Crandall** a-18-26. **Davis** a-4, 5, 7, 9-12, 20. **Elder** a-17,18. **Evans** a-15, 19, 21, 23, 25, 27; c-23, 24. **Feldstein** c-19. **Ingels** a-1-12, 14, 15, 27. **Kamen** a-2, 4-18, 20-27; c-25-27. **Krigstein** a-22, 24, 25, 27. **Kurtzman** a-1, 3. **Orlando** a-16, 22, 24, 26. **Wood** a-1, 3. Issues No. 1-3 were printed in Canada as "Weird Suspenstories." Issues No. 11-15 have E. C. "quickie" stories. No. 25 contains the famous "Are You a Red Dupe?" editorial. Ray Bradbury adaptations-15, 17.*

CRIME SUSPENSTORIES
Russ Cochran/Gemstone Publ.: Nov, 1992 - No. 24 ($1.50/$2.00/$2.50)

1-24: Reprints Crime SuspenStories series — 3.00

CRIMINALS ON THE RUN (Formerly Young King Cole) (Crime Fighting Detective No. 11 on)
Premium Group (Novelty Press): V4#1, Aug-Sep, 1948-#10, Dec-Jan, 1949-50

V4#1-Young King Cole continues — 31 62 93 175 248 320
2-6: 6-Dr. Doom app. — 27 54 81 153 214 275
7-Classic "Fish in the Face" c by L. B. Cole — 55 110 165 330 495 660
V5#1,2 (#8,9),10: 9,10-L. B. Cole-c — 25 50 75 144 198 255

NOTE: *Most issues have **L. B. Cole** covers. **McWilliams** a-V4#6, 7, V5#2; c-V4#5.*

CRIMINAL MACABRE: A CAL MCDONALD MYSTERY
Dark Horse Comics: May, 2003 - No. 5, Sept, 2003 ($2.99)

1-5-Niles-s/Templesmith-a — 3.00

CRIMSON (Also see Cliffhanger #0)
Image Comics (Cliffhanger Productions): May, 1998 - No. 7, Dec, 1998;
DC Comics (Cliffhanger Prod.): No. 8, Mar, 1999 - No. 24, Apr, 2001 ($2.50)

1-Humberto Ramos-a/Augustyn-s — 5.00
1-Variant-c by Warren — 8.00
1-Chromium-c — 20.00
2-Ramos-c with street crowd, 2-Variant-c by Art Adams — 3.00
2-Dynamic Forces CrimsonChrome cover — 15.00
3-7: 3-Ramos Moon background-c. 7-3 covers by Ramos, Madureira, & Campbell — 3.50
8-23: 8-First DC issue — 2.50
24-($3.50) Final issue; wraparound-c — 3.50
DF Premiere Ed. 1998 ($6.95) covers by Ramos and Jae Lee — 7.00
Crimson: Scarlet X Blood on the Moon (10/99, $3.95) — 4.00
Crimson Sourcebook (11/99, $2.95) Pin-ups and info — 3.00
Earth Angel TPB (2001, $14.95) r/#13-18 — 15.00
Heaven and Earth TPB (1/00, $14.95) r/#7-12 — 15.00
Loyalty and Loss TPB ('99, $12.95) r/#1-6 — 13.00
Redemption TPB ('01, $14.95) r/#19-24 — 15.00

CRIMSON AVENGER, THE (See Detective Comics #20 for 1st app.)(Also see Leading Comics #1 & World's Best/Finest Comics)
DC Comics: June, 1988 - No. 4, Sept, 1988 ($1.00, limited series)

1-4 — 2.50

CRIMSON DYNAMO
Marvel Comics (Epic): Oct, 2003 - Present ($2.50)

1-4-John Jackson Miller-s/Steve Ellis-a/c — 2.50

CRIMSON NUN
Antarctic Press: May, 1997 - No. 4, Nov, 1997 ($2.95, limited series)

1-4 — 3.00

CRIMSON PLAGUE
Event Comics: June, 1997 ($2.95, unfinished mini-series)

1-George Perez-a — 3.00

CRIMSON PLAGUE (George Pérez's...)
Image Comics (Gorilla): June, 2000 - No. 2, Aug, 2000 ($2.95, mini-series)

1-George Perez-a; reprints 6/97 issue with 16 new pages — 3.00
2-($2.50) — 2.50

CRIMSON SKIES
Image Comics (Top Cow): Winter, 2000

Preview-Comic and Microsoft video game preview — 3.00

CRISIS ON INFINITE EARTHS (Also see Official... Index and Legends of the DC Universe)
DC Comics: Apr, 1985 - No. 12, Mar, 1986 (maxi-series)

1-1st DC app. Blue Beetle & Detective Karp from Charlton; Pérez-c on all
2 4 6 10 13 16
2-6: 6-Intro Charlton's Capt. Atom, Nightshade, Question, Judomaster, Peacemaker & Thunderbolt into DC Universe — 1 3 4 6 8 10
7-Double size; death of Supergirl — 2 4 6 14 18 22
8-Death of the Flash (Barry Allen) — 2 4 6 12 16 20
9-11: 9-Intro. Charlton's Ghost into DC Universe. 10-Intro. Charlton's Banshee, Dr. Spectro, Image, Punch & Jewellee into DC Universe; Starman (Prince Gavyn) dies
1 3 4 6 8 10
12-(52 pgs.)-Deaths of Dove, Kole, Lori Lemaris, Sunburst, G.A. Robin &Huntress; Kid Flash becomes new Flash; 3rd & final DC app. of the 3 Lt. Marvels; Green Fury gets new look (becomes Green Flame in Infinity, Inc. #32) — 2 4 6 9 11 14
Slipcased Hardcover (1998, $99.95) Wraparound dust-jacket cover by Pérez and Alex Ross; sketch pages by Pérez; intro by Wolfman — 125.00
TPB (2000, $29.95) Wraparound-c by Pérez and Ross — 30.00

NOTE: *Crossover issues: All Star Squadron 50-56,60; Amethyst 13; Blue Devil 17,18; DC Comics Presents 78,86-88,95; Detective Comics 558; Fury of Firestorm 41,42; G.I. Combat 274; Green Lantern 194-196,198; Infinity, Inc. 18-25 & Annual 1, Justice League of America 244,245 & Annual 3; Legion of Super-Heroes 16,18; Losers Special 1; New Teen Titans 13,14; Omega Men 31,33; Superman 413-415; Swamp Thing 44,46; Wonder Woman 327-329.*

CRISIS ON MULTIPLE EARTHS
DC Comics: 2002, 2003 ($14.95, trade paperback)

TPB-(2003) Reprints 1st 4 Silver Age JLA/JSA crossovers from J.L.ofA. #21,22; 29,30; 37,38; 46,47; new painted-c by Alex Ross; intro. by Mark Waid — 15.00
Volume 2 (2003, $14.95) r/J.L.ofA. #55,56; 64,65; 73,74; 82,83; new Ordway-c — 15.00

CRITICAL MASS (See A Shadowline Saga: Critical Mass)

CRITTERS (Also see Usagi Yojimbo Summer Special)
Fantagraphics Books: 1986 - No. 50, 1990 ($1.70/$2.00, B&W)

1-Cutey Bunny, Usagi Yojimbo app. — 1 2 3 5 6 8
2,4,5,8,9 — 5.00
3,6,7,10-Usagi Yojimbo app. — 6.00
11-22,24-37,39-49: 11,14-Usagi Yojimbo app. 11-Christmas Special (68 pgs.); Usagi Yojimbo. 22-Watchmen parody; two diff. covers exist — 2.50
23-With Alan Moore Flexi-disc ($3.95) — 5.00
38-($2.75-c) Usagi Yojimbo app. — 3.00
50 ($4.95, 84 pgs.)-Neil the Horse, Capt. Jack, Sam & Max & Usagi Yojimbo app.; Quagmire, Shaw-a — 6.00
Special 1 (1/88, $2.00) — 2.50

The Crow: Wild Justice #2 © James O'Barr

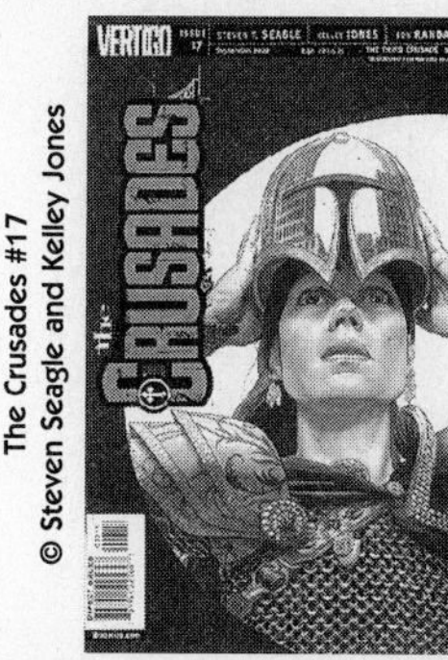

The Crusades #17 © Steven Seagle and Kelley Jones

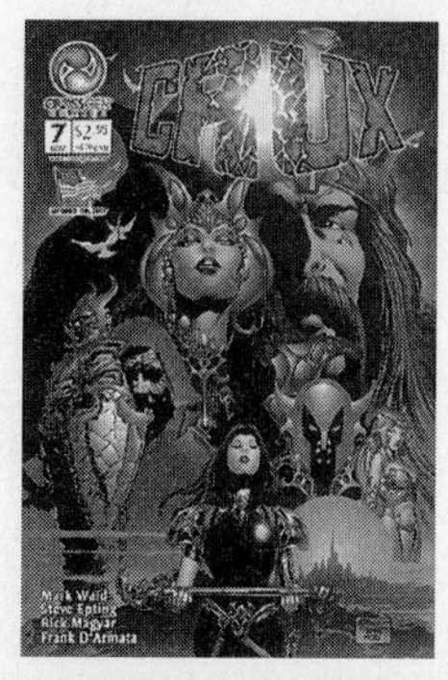

Crux #7 © CRO

	GD 2.0	VG 4.0	FN 6.0	VF 8.0	VF/NM 9.0	NM- 9.2

CROSS
Dark Horse Comics: No. 0, Oct, 1995 - No. 6, Apr, 1995 ($2.95, limited series, mature)
0-6: Darrow-c & Vachss scripts in all 3.00

CROSS AND THE SWITCHBLADE, THE
Spire Christian Comics (Fleming H. Revell Co.): 1972 (35-49¢)
1-Some issues have nn 1 3 4 6 8 10

CROSSFIRE
Spire Christian Comics (Fleming H. Revell Co.): 1973 (39/49¢)
nn 1 3 4 6 8 10

CROSSFIRE (Also see DNAgents)
Eclipse Comics: 5/84 - No. 17, 3/86; No. 18, 1/87 - No. 26, 2/88 ($1.50, Baxter paper) (#18-26 are B&W)
1-11,14-26: 1-DNAgents x-over; Spiegle-c/a begins 2.50
12,13-Death of Marilyn Monroe. 12-Dave Stevens-c 4.00

CROSSFIRE AND RAINBOW (Also see DNAgents)
Eclipse Comics: June, 1986 - No. 4, Sept, 1986 ($1.25, deluxe format)
1-3: Spiegle-a. 4-Dave Stevens-c 2.25

CROSSGEN...
CrossGeneration Comics
CrossGenesis (1/00) Previews CrossGen universe; cover gallery 3.00
...Primer (1/00) Wizard supplement; intro. to the CrossGen universe 2.25
...Sampler (2/00) Retailer preview book 3.00

CROSSGEN CHRONICLES
CrossGeneration Comics: June, 2000 - Present ($3.95)
1-Intro. to CrossGen characters & company 4.00
1-(no cover price) same contents, customer preview 4.00
2-(3/01) George Pérez-c/a 10.00
3-8: 3-5-Pérez-a/Waid-s. 6,7-Nebres-c/a 4.00

CROSSING THE ROCKIES (See Classics Illustrated Special Issue)

CROSSOVERS, THE
CrossGeneration Comics: Feb, 2003 - Present ($2.95)
1-12-Robert Rodi-s. 1-6-Mauricet & Ernie Colon-a. 7-Staton-a begins 3.00
Vol. 1: Cross Currents (2003, $9.95) digest-sized reprints #1-6 10.00

CROSSROADS
First Comics: July, 1988 - No. 5, Nov, 1988 ($3.25, lim. series, deluxe format)
1-5 3.25

CROW, THE (Also see Caliber Presents)
Caliber Press: Feb, 1989 - No. 4, 1989 ($1.95, B&W, limited series)
1-James O'Barr-c/a/scripts 5 10 15 33 44 55
1-3-2nd printing 6.00
2-4 3 6 9 18 24 30
2-3rd printing 4.00

CROW, THE
Tundra Publishing, Ltd.: Jan, 1992 - No. 3, 1992 ($4.95, B&W, 68 pgs.)
1-3: 1-r/#1,2 of Caliber series. 2-r/#3 of Caliber series w/new material. 3-All new material
1 2 3 5 6 8

CROW, THE
Kitchen Sink Press: 1/96 - No. 3, 3/96 ($2.95, B&W)
1-3: James O'Barr-c/scripts 5.00
#0-A Cycle of Shattered Lives (12/98, $3.50) new story by O'Barr 4.00

CROW, THE
Image Comics (Todd McFarlane Prod.): Feb, 1999 - No. 10, Nov, 1999 ($2.50)
1-10: 1-Two covers by McFarlane and Kent Williams; Muth-s in all. 2-6,10-Paul Lee-a 3.00
Book 1 - Vengeance (2000, $10.95, TPB) r/#1-3,5,6 11.00
Book 2 - Evil Beyond Reach (2000, $10.95, TPB) r/#4,7-10 11.00
Todd McFarlane Presents The Crow Magazine 1 (3/00, $4.95) 5.00

CROW, THE: CITY OF ANGELS (Movie)
Kitchen Sink Press: July, 1996 - No. 3, Sept, 1996 ($2.95, limited series)
1-3: Adaptation of film; two-c (photo & illos.). 1-Vincent Perez interview 3.00

CROW, THE: FLESH AND BLOOD
Kitchen Sink Press: May, 1996 - No. 3, July, 1996 ($2.95, limited series)
1-3: O'Barr-c 3.00

CROW, THE: RAZOR - KILL THE PAIN
London Night Studios: Apr, 1998 - No. 3, July, 1998 ($2.95, B&W, lim. series)
1-3-Hartsoe-s/O'Barr-painted-c 3.00
0(10/98) Dorien painted-c, Finale (2/99) 3.00
The Lost Chapter (2/99, $4.95), Tour Book-(12/97) pin-ups; 4 diff.-c 5.00

CROW, THE: WAKING NIGHTMARES
Kitchen Sink Press: Jan, 1997 - No. 4, 1998 ($2.95, B&W, limited series)
1-4-Miran Kim-c 5.00

CROW, THE: WILD JUSTICE
Kitchen Sink Press: Oct, 1996 - No. 3, Dec, 1996 ($2.95, B&W, limited series)
1-3-Prosser-s/Adlard-a 3.00

CROWN COMICS
Golfing/McCombs Publ.: Wint, 1944-45; No. 2, Sum, 1945 - No. 19, July, 1949
1- "The Oblong Box" E.A. Poe adaptation 38 76 114 219 310 400
2,3-Baker-a; 3-Voodah by Baker 26 52 78 147 206 265
4-6-Baker-c/a; Voodah app. #4,5 29 58 87 164 232 300
7-Feldstein, Baker, Kamen-a; Baker-c 29 58 87 167 236 305
8-Baker-a; Voodah app. 24 48 72 138 194 250
9-11,13-19: Voodah in #10-19. 13-New logo 16 32 48 89 122 155
12-Master Marvin by Feldstein, Starr-a; Voodah-c 17 34 51 95 130 165
NOTE: *Bolle a-11, 13-16, 18, 19; c-11p, 15.* **Powell** *a-19.* **Starr** *a-11-13; c-11i.*

CRUCIBLE
DC Comics (Impact): Feb, 1993 - No. 6, July, 1993 ($1.25, limited series)
1-6: 1-(99¢)-Neon ink-c. 1,2-Quesada-c(p). 1-4-Quesada layouts 2.50

CRUEL AND UNUSUAL
DC Comics (Vertigo): June, 1999 - No. 4, Sept, 1999 ($2.95, limited series)
1-4-Delano & Peyer-s/McCrea-c/a 3.00

CRUSADER FROM MARS (See Tops in Adventure)
Ziff-Davis Publ. Co.: Jan-Mar, 1952 - No. 2, Fall, 1952 (Painted-c)
1-Cover is dated Spring 74 148 222 463 694 925
2-Bondage-c 55 110 165 342 511 680

CRUSADER RABBIT (TV)
Dell Publishing Co.: No. 735, Oct, 1956 - No. 805, May, 1957
Four Color 735 (#1) 31 62 93 233 352 470
Four Color 805 26 52 78 185 270 355

CRUSADERS, THE (Religious)
Chick Publications: 1974 - Vol. 17, 1988 (39/69¢, 36 pgs.)
Vol.1-Operation Bucharest ('74). Vol.2-The Broken Cross ('74). Vol.3-Scarface ('74). Vol.4-Exorcists ('75). Vol.5-Chaos ('75) 1 3 4 6 8 10
Vol.6-Primal Man? ('76)-(Disputes evolution theory). Vol.7-The Ark-(claims proof of existence, destroyed by Bolsheviks). Vol.8-The Gift-(Life story of Christ). Vol.9-Angel of Light-(Story of the Devil). Vol.10-Spellbound?-(Tells how rock music is Satanic & produced by witches). 11-Sabotage?. 12-Alberto. 13-Double Cross. 14-The Godfathers. (No. 6-14 low in distribution; loaded with religious propaganda.). 15-The Force. 16-The Four Horsemen
1 3 4 6 8 10
Vol. 17-The Prophet (low print run) 2 4 6 8 10 12

CRUSADERS (Southern Knights No. 2 on)
Guild Publications: 1982 (B&W, magazine size)
1-1st app. Southern Knights 1 2 3 5 7 9

CRUSADERS, THE (Also see Black Hood, The Jaguar, The Comet, The Fly, Legend of the Shield, The Mighty... & The Web)
DC Comics (Impact): May, 1992 - No. 8, Dec, 1992 ($1.00/$1.25)
1-8-Contains 3 Impact trading cards 2.50

CRUSADES, THE
DC Comics (Vertigo): 2001 - No. 20, Dec, 2002 ($3.95/$2.50)
...: Urban Decree ('01, $3.95) Intro. the Knight; Seagle-s/Kelley Jones-c/a 4.00
1-(5/01, $2.50) Sienkiewicz-c 3.00
2-20: 2-Moeller-c. 18-Begin $2.95-c 3.00

CRUSH
Dark Horse Comics: Oct, 2003 - Present ($2.99)
1-Jason Hall-s/Sean Murphy-a 3.00

CRUSH, THE
Image Comics (Motown Machineworks): Jan, 1996 - No. 5, July, 1996 ($2.25, limited series)
1-5: Baron scripts 3.00

CRUX
CrossGeneration Comics: May, 2001 - Present ($2.95)
1-23: 1-Waid-s/Epting & Magyar-a/c. 6-Pelletier-a. 13-Dixon-s begin. 25-Cover has fake

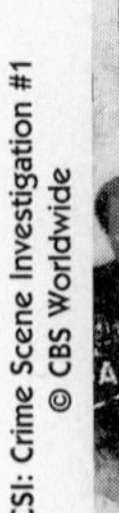
CSI: Crime Scene Investigation #1 © CBS Worldwide

Cursed #1 © TCOW

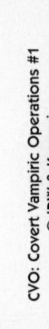

CVO: Covert Vampiric Operations #1 © IDW & Konami

	GD 2.0	VG 4.0	FN 6.0	VF 8.0	VF/NM 9.0	NM- 9.2
creases and other aging						3.00
Atlantis Rising Vol. 1 TPB (2002, $15.95) r/#1-6						16.00
Test of Time Vol. 2 TPB (12/02, $15.95) r/#7-12						16.00
Vol. 3: Strangers in Atlantis (2003, $15.95) r/#13-18						16.00
Vol. 4: Chaos Reborn (2003, $15.95) r/#19-24						16.00

CRY FOR DAWN
Cry For Dawn Pub.: 1989 - No. 9 ($2.25, B&W, mature)

	GD	VG	FN	VF	VF/NM	NM-
1	8	16	24	55	78	100
1-2nd printing	3	7	10	21	28	35
1-3rd printing	3	6	9	16	20	25
2	5	10	15	36	48	60
2-2nd printing	2	4	6	12	16	20
3	4	8	12	24	32	40
3a-HorrorCon Edition (1990, less than 400 printed, signed inside-c)						200.00
4-6	2	4	6	12	16	20
5-2nd printing	1	2	3	5	6	8
7-9	2	4	6	9	11	14
4-9-Signed & numbered editions	3	6	9	16	20	25
Angry Christ Comix HC (4/03, $29.99) reprints various stories; and 30pgs. new material						30.00
...Calendar (1993)						35.00

CRYIN' LION COMICS
William H. Wise Co.: Fall, 1944 - No. 3, Spring, 1945

	GD	VG	FN	VF	VF/NM	NM-
1-Funny animal	15	30	45	86	118	150
2-Hitler app.	13	26	39	74	100	125
3	10	20	30	56	73	90

CRYPT
Image Comics (Extreme): Aug, 1995 - No.2, Oct. 1995 ($2.50, limited series)

1,2-Prophet app. 2.50

CRYPTIC WRITINGS OF MEGADETH
Chaos! Comics: Sept, 1997 - No. 4, Jun, 1998 ($2.95, quarterly)

1-4-Stories based on song lyrics by Dave Mustaine 3.00

CRYPT OF DAWN (see Dawn)
Sirius: 1996 ($2.95, B&W, limited series)

	NM-
1-Linsner-c/s; anthology.	5.00
2, 3 (2/98)	4.00
4,5: 4- (6/98), 5-(11/98)	3.00
Ltd. Edition	20.00

CRYPT OF SHADOWS
Marvel Comics Group: Jan, 1973 - No. 21, Nov, 1975 (#1-9 are 20¢)

	GD	VG	FN	VF	VF/NM	NM-
1-Wolverton-r/Advs. Into Terror #7	3	6	9	16	20	24
2-10: 2-Starlin/Everett-c	2	4	6	10	12	15
11-21: 18,20-Kirby-a	2	4	6	8	10	12

NOTE: ***Briefer*** *a-2r.* ***Ditko*** *a-13r, 18-20r.* ***Everett*** *a-6, 14r; c-2i.* ***Heath*** *a-1r.* ***Gil Kane*** *c-1, 6.* ***Mort Lawrence*** *a-1r, 8r.* ***Maneely*** *a-2r.* ***Moldoff*** *a-8.* ***Powell*** *a-12r, 14r.* ***Tuska*** *a-2r.*

CRYPT OF TERROR (Formerly Crime Patrol; Tales From the Crypt No. 20 on)
E. C. Comics: No. 17, Apr-May, 1950 - No. 19, Aug-Sept, 1950

	GD	VG	FN	VF	VF/NM	NM-
17-1st New Trend to hit stands	271	542	813	2033	2917	3800
18,19	157	314	471	1178	1689	2200

NOTE: ***Craig*** *c/a-17-19.* ***Feldstein*** *a-17-19.* ***Ingels*** *a-19.* ***Kurtzman*** *a-18.* ***Wood*** *a-18. Canadian reprints known; see Table of Contents.*

CSI: CRIME SCENE INVESTIGATION (Based on TV series)
IDW Publishing: Jan, 2003 - No. 5, May, 2003 ($3.99, limited series)

	NM-
1-Two covers (photo & Ashley Wood); Max Allan Collins-s	4.00
2-5	4.00
...: Serial TPB (2003, $19.99) r/#1-5; bonus short story by Collins/Wood	20.00
...: Thicker Than Blood (7/03, $6.99) Mariotte-s/Rodriguez-a	7.00

CSI: CRIME SCENE INVESTIGATION - BAD RAP
IDW Publishing: Aug, 2003 - No. 5, Dec, 2003 ($3.99, limited series)

1-5-Two photo covers; Max Allan Collins-s/Rodriguez-a 4.00

CSI: MIAMI - SMOKING GUN
IDW Publishing: Oct, 2003 ($6.99, one-shot)

nn-Mariotte-s/Avilés & Wood-a 7.00

C•23 (Jim Lee's...) (Based on Wizards of the Coast card game)
Image Comics: Apr, 1998 - No. 8, Nov, 1998 ($2.50)

1-8: 1,2-Choi & Mariotte-s/ Charest-c. 2-Variant-c by Jim Lee. 4-Ryan Benjamin-c. 5,8-Corben var-c. 6-Flip book with Planetary preview; Corben-c 3.00

CUD
Fantagraphics Books: 8/92 - No. 8, 12/94 ($2.25-$2.75, B&W, mature)

1-8: Terry LaBan scripts & art in all. 6-1st Eno & Plum 3.00

CUD COMICS
Dark Horse Comics: Jan, 1995 - No. 8, Sept, 1997 ($2.95, B&W)

	NM-
1-8: Terry LaBan-c/a/scripts. 5-Nudity; marijuana story	3.00
Eno and Plum TPB (1997, $12.95) r/#1-4, DHP #93-95	13.00

CUPID
Marvel Comics (U.S.A.): Dec, 1949 - No. 2, Mar, 1950

	GD	VG	FN	VF	VF/NM	NM-
1-Photo-c	15	30	45	86	118	150
2-Bettie Page ('50s pin-up queen) photo-c; Powell-a (see My Love #4)	34	68	102	196	278	360

CURIO
Harry 'A' Chesler: 1930's(?) (Tabloid size, 16-20 pgs.)

	GD	VG	FN	VF	VF/NM	NM-
nn	21	42	63	118	164	210

CURLY KAYOE COMICS (Boxing)
United Features Syndicate/Dell Publ. Co.: 1946 - No. 8, 1950; Jan, 1958

	GD	VG	FN	VF	VF/NM	NM-
1 (1946)-Strip-r (Fritzi Ritz); biography of Sam Leff, Kayoe's artist	19	38	57	107	149	190
2	10	20	30	58	77	95
3-8	9	18	27	49	62	75
United Presents...(Fall, 1948)	9	18	27	49	62	75
Four Color 871 (Dell, 1/58)	4	8	12	24	32	40

CURSED
Image Comics (Top Cow): Oct, 2003 - No. 4, Feb, 2004 ($2.99)

1-4-Avery & Blevins-s/Molenaar-a 3.00

CURSE OF DRACULA, THE
Dark Horse Comics: July, 1998 - No. 3, Sept, 1998 ($2.95, limited series)

1-3-Wolfman-s/Colan-a 3.00

CURSE OF DREADWOLF
Lightning Comics: Sept, 1994 ($2.75, B&W)

1 2.75

CURSE OF RUNE (Becomes Rune, 2nd Series)
Malibu Comics (Ultraverse): May, 1995 - No. 4, Aug, 1995 ($2.50, lim. series)

1-4: 1-Two covers form one image 2.50

CURSE OF THE SPAWN
Image Comics (Todd McFarlane Prod.): Sept, 1996 - No. 29, Mar, 1999 ($1.95)

	GD	VG	FN	VF	VF/NM	NM-
1-Dwayne Turner-a(p)						6.00
1-B&W Edition	2	4	6	10	13	16
2-3						4.00
4-29: 12-Movie photo-c of Melinda Clarke (Priest)						2.50
Blood and Sutures ('99, $9.95, TPB) r/#5-8						10.00
Lost Values ('00, $10.95, TPB) r/#12-14,22; Ashley Wood-c						11.00
Sacrifice of the Soul ('99, $9.95, TPB) r/#1-4						10.00
Shades of Gray ('00, $9.95, TPB) r/#9-11,29						10.00

CURSE OF THE WEIRD
Marvel Comics: Dec, 1993 - No. 4, Mar, 1994 ($1.25, limited series)
(Pre-code horror-r)

1-4: 1,3,4-Wolverton-r(1-Eye of Doom; 3-Where Monsters Dwell; 4-The End of the World). 2-Orlando-r. 4-Zombie-r by Everett; painted-c 4.00

NOTE: ***Briefer*** *r-2.* ***Jack Davis*** *a-4r.* ***Ditko*** *a-1r, 2r, 4r; c-1r.* ***Everett*** *r-1.* ***Heath*** *r-1-3.* ***Kubert*** *r-3.* ***Wolverton*** *a-1r, 3r, 4r.*

CUSTER'S LAST FIGHT
Avon Periodicals: 1950

	GD	VG	FN	VF	VF/NM	NM-
nn-Partial reprint of Cowpuncher #1	18	36	54	101	138	175

CUTEY BUNNY (See Army Surplus Komikz Featuring...)

CUTIE PIE
Junior Reader's Guild (Lev Gleason): May, 1955 - No. 3, Dec, 1955; No. 4, Feb, 1956; No. 5, Aug, 1956

	GD	VG	FN	VF	VF/NM	NM-
1	8	16	24	40	50	60
2-5: 4-Misdated 2/55	5	10	15	24	30	35

CUTTING EDGE
Marvel Comics: Dec, 1995 ($2.95)

1-Hulk-c/story; Messner-Loebs scripts 3.00

CVO: COVERT VAMPIRIC OPERATIONS
IDW Publishing: June, 2003 ($5.99, one-shot)

Cyberforce V2#23 © TCOW

Cybernary #2 © WSP

Daffy Duck #22 © WB

	GD 2.0	VG 4.0	FN 6.0	VF 8.0	VF/NM 9.0	NM- 9.2

1-Alex Garner-s/Mindy Lee-a(p) 6.00

CVO: COVERT VAMPIRIC OPERATIONS - ARTIFACT
IDW Publishing: Oct, 2003 - No. 3, Dec, 2003 ($3.99, limited series)

1-3-Jeff Mariotte-s/Gabriel Hernandez-a/Alex Garner-c 4.00

CYBERELLA
DC Comics (Helix): Sept, 1996 - No. 12, Aug, 1997 ($2.25/$2.50)(1st Helix series)

1-12: 1-5-Chaykin & Cameron-a. 1,2-Chaykin-c. 3-5-Cameron-c 2.50

CYBERFORCE
Image Comics (Top Cow Productions): Oct, 1992 - No. 4, 1993; No. 0, Sept, 1993 ($1.95, limited series)

1-Silvestri-c/a in all; coupon for Image Comics #0; 1st Top Cow Productions title 6.00
1-With coupon missing 2.25
2-4,0: 2-(3/93). 3-Pitt-c/story. 4-Codename: Stryke Force back-up (1st app.); foil-c. 0-(9/93)-Walt Simonson-c/a/scripts 3.00

CYBERFORCE
Image Comics (Top Cow Productions)/Top Cow Comics No. 28 on:
V2#1, Nov, 1993 - No. 35, Sept. 1997 ($1.95)

V2#1-24: 1-7-Marc Silvestri/Keith Williams-c/a. 8-McFarlane-c/a. 10-Painted variant-c exists. 18-Variant-c exists. 23-Velocity-c. 2.50
1-3: 1-Gold Logo-c. 2-Silver embossed-c. 3-Gold embossed-c 10.00
1-(99¢, 3/96, 2nd printing) 2.25
25-($3.95)-Wraparound, foil-c 4.00
26-35: 28-(11/96)-1st Top Cow Comics iss. Quesada & Palmiotti's Gabriel app. 27-Quesada & Palmiotti's Ash app. 2.50
Annual 1,2 (3/95, 8/96, $2.50, $2.95) 3.00
NOTE: *Annuals read Volume One in the indica.*

CYBERFORCE ORIGINS
Image Comics (Top Cow Productions): Jan, 1995 - No. 3, Nov, 1995 ($2.50)

1-Cyblade (1/95) 5.00
1-Cyblade (3/96, 99¢, 2nd printing) 2.25
1A-Exclusive Ed.; Tucci-c 4.00
2,3: 2-Stryker (2/95)-1st Mike Turner-a. 3-Impact 2.50
(#4) Misery (12/95, $2.95) 3.00

CYBERFORCE/STRYKEFORCE: OPPOSING FORCES (See Codename: Stryke Force #15)
Image Comics (Top Cow Productions): Sept, 1995 - No.2, Oct, 1995 ($2.50, limited series)

1,2: 2-Stryker disbands Strykeforce. 2.50

CYBERFORCE UNIVERSE SOURCEBOOK
Image Comics (Top Cow Productions): Aug, 1994/Feb, 1995 ($2.50)

1,2-Silvestri-c 2.50

CYBERFROG
Hall of Heroes: June, 1994 - No. 2, Dec, 1994 ($2.50, B&W, limited series)

1,2 3.00

CYBERFROG
Harris Comics: Feb, 1996 - No. 3, Apr, 1996 ($2.95)

0-3: Van Sciver-c/a/scripts. 2-Variant-c exists 5.00

CYBERFROG: (Title series), **Harris Comics**

--RESERVOIR FROG, 9/96 - No. 2, 10/96 ($2.95) 1,2: Van Sciver-c/a/scripts; wraparound-c 3.00

--3RD ANNIVERSARY SPECIAL, 1/97 - #2, ($2.50, B&W) 1,2 3.00

--VS. CREED, 7/97 ($2.95, B&W)1 3.00

CYBERNARY (See Deathblow #1)
Image Comics (WildStorm Productions): Nov, 1995 - No.5, Mar, 1996 ($2.50)

1-5 2.50

CYBERNARY 2.0
DC Comics (WildStorm): Sept, 2001 - No. 6, Apr, 2002 ($2.95, limited series)

1-6: Joe Harris-s/Eric Canete-a. 6-The Authority app. 3.00

CYBERPUNK
Innovation Publishing: Sept, 1989 - No. 2, Oct, 1989 ($1.95, 28 pgs.) Book 2, #1, May, 1990 - No. 2, 1990 ($2.25, 28 pgs.)

1,2, Book 2 #1,2:1,2-Ken Steacy painted-covers (Adults) 2.25

CYBERPUNK: THE SERAPHIM FILES
Innovation Publishing: Nov, 1990 - No. 2, Dec, 1990 ($2.50, 28 pgs., mature)

1,2: 1-Painted-c; story cont'd from Seraphim 2.50

CYBERPUNX
Image Comics (Extreme Studios): Mar, 1996 ($2.50)

1 3.00

CYBERRAD
Continuity Comics: 1991 - No. 7, 1992 ($2.00)(Direct sale & newsstand-c variations) V2#1, 1993 ($2.50)

1-7: 5-Glow-in-the-dark-c by N. Adams (direct sale only). 6-Contains 4 pg. fold-out poster; N. Adams layouts 2.50
V2#1-($2.95, direct sale ed.)-Die-cut-c w/B&W hologram on-c; Neal Adams sketches 3.00
V2#1-($2.50, newsstand ed.)-Without sketches 2.50

CYBERRAD DEATHWATCH 2000 (Becomes CyberRad w/#2, 7/93)
Continuity Comics: Apr, 1993 - No. 2, 1993 ($2.50)

1,2: 1-Bagged w/2 cards; Adams-c & layouts & plots. 2-Bagged w/card; Adams scripts 2.50

CYBER 7
Eclipse Comics: Mar, 1989 - #7, Sept, 1989; V2#1, Oct, 1989 - #10, 1990 ($2.00, B&W)

1-7, Book 2 #1-10: Stories translated from Japanese 2.50

CYBLADE/ GHOST RIDER
Marvel Comics /Top Cow Productions: Jan 1997 ($2.95, one-shot)

1-Devil's Reign pt. 2 4.00

CYBLADE/SHI (Also see Battle For The Independents & Shi/Cyblade: The Battle For The Independents)
Image Comics (Top Cow Productions): 1995 ($2.95, one-shot)

	GD	VG	FN	VF	VF/NM	NM-
San Diego Preview	3	6	9	16	20	25
1-($2.95)-1st app. Witchblade	2	4	6	12	16	20
1-($2.95)-variant-c; Tucci-a	2	4	6	10	12	15

CYBRID
Maximum Press: July, 1995; No. 0, Jan, 1997 ($2.95/$3.50)

1-(7/95) 3.50
0-(1/97)-Liefeld-a/script; story cont'd in Avengelyne #4 3.50

CYCLONE COMICS (Also see Whirlwind Comics)
Bilbara Publishing Co.: June, 1940 - No. 5, Nov, 1940

	GD	VG	FN	VF	VF/NM	NM-
1-Origin Tornado Tom; Volton (the human generator), Tornado Tom, Kingdom of the Moon, Mister Q begin (1st app. of each)	152	304	456	950	1425	1900
2	76	152	228	475	713	950
3-Classic-c (scarce)	104	208	312	650	975	1300
4	60	120	180	375	563	750
5-(Scarce)	78	156	234	488	732	975

CYCLOPS (X-Men)
Marvel Comics: Oct, 2001 - No. 4, Jan, 2002 ($2.50, limited series)

1-4-Texeira-c/a. 1,2-Black Tom and Juggernaut app. 2.50

CYCLOPS: RETRIBUTION
Marvel Comics: 1994 ($5.95, trade paperback)

nn-r/Marvel Comics Presents #17-24 6.00

CY-GOR (See Spawn #38 for 1st app.)
Image Comics (Todd McFarlane Prod.): July, 1999 - No. 6, Dec, 1999 ($2.50)

1-6-Veitch-s 2.50

CYNTHIA DOYLE, NURSE IN LOVE (Formerly Sweetheart Diary)
Charlton Publications: No. 66, Oct, 1962 - No. 74, Feb, 1964

	GD	VG	FN	VF	VF/NM	NM-
66-74	2	4	6	14	18	22

DAEMONSTORM
Caliber Comics: 1997 ($3.95, one-shot)

1-McFarlane-c 4.00

DAEMONSTORM: STORMWALKER
Caliber Comics: 1997 ($3.95, B&W, one-shot)

nn 4.00

DAFFY (Daffy Duck No. 18 on)(See Looney Tunes)
Dell Publishing Co./Gold Key No. 31-127/Whitman No. 128 on: #457, 3/53 - #30, 7-9/62; #31, 10-12/62 - #145, 6/84 (No #132,133)

	GD	VG	FN	VF	VF/NM	NM-
Four Color 457(#1)-Elmer Fudd x-overs begin	10	20	30	70	100	130
Four Color 536,615('55)	6	12	18	38	52	65
4(1-3/56)-11('57)	4	8	12	29	40	50
12-19(1958-59)	3	7	10	21	28	35
20-40(1960-64)	3	6	9	16	20	25
41-60(1964-68)	2	4	6	12	16	20
61-90(1969-74)-Road Runner in most	2	4	6	9	11	14
91-110	1	3	4	6	8	10

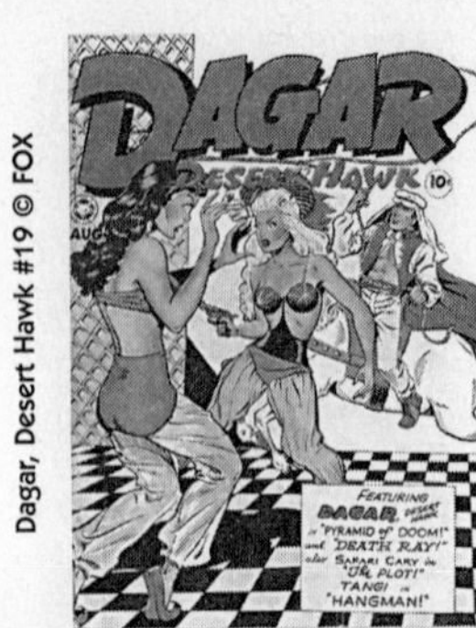

Dagar, Desert Hawk #19 © FOX

Dale Evans Comics #20 © DC

Damage #18 © DC

	GD 2.0	VG 4.0	FN 6.0	VF 8.0	VF/NM 9.0	NM- 9.2
111-127	1	2	3	5	6	8
128,134-141: 139(2/82), 140(2-3/82), 141(4/82)	1	2	3	5	7	9
129(8/80),130,131 (pre-pack?) (scarce). 129-Sherlock Holmes parody-s	2	4	6	12	16	20
142-145(#90029 on-c; nd, nd code, pre-pack): 142(6/83), 143(8/83), 144(3/84), 145(6/84)	2	4	6	10	13	16
Mini-Comic 1 (1976; 3-1/4x6-1/2")						6.00

NOTE: *Reprint issues-No.41-46, 48, 50, 53-55, 58, 59, 65, 67, 69, 73, 81, 96, 103-108; 136-142, 144, 145(1/3-2/3-r). (See March of Comics No. 277, 288, 303, 313, 331, 347, 357,375, 387, 397, 402, 413, 425, 437, 460).*

DAFFY TUNES COMICS
Four-Star Publications: June, 1947; No. 12, Aug, 1947

	GD	VG	FN	VF	VF/NM	NM-
nn	9	18	27	49	62	75
12-Al Fago-c/a; funny animal	8	16	24	42	54	65

DAGAR, DESERT HAWK (Captain Kidd No. 24 on; formerly All Great)
Fox Features Syndicate: No. 14, Feb, 1948 - No. 23, Apr, 1949 (No #17,18)

	GD	VG	FN	VF	VF/NM	NM-
14-Tangi & Safari Cary begin; Good bondage-c/a	75	150	225	469	705	940
15,16-E. Good-a; 15-Bondage-c	46	92	138	276	413	550
19,20,22: 19-Used in **SOTI**, pg. 180 (Tangi)	40	80	120	240	350	460
21,23: 21- "Bombs & Bums Away" panel in "Flood of Death" story used in **SOTI.** 23-Bondage-c	44	88	132	264	395	525

NOTE: *Tangi by **Kamen**-14-16, 19, 20; c-20, 21.*

DAGAR THE INVINCIBLE (Tales of Sword & Sorcery...) (Also see Dan Curtis Giveaways & Gold Key Spotlight)
Gold Key: Oct, 1972 - No. 18, Dec, 1976; No. 19, Apr, 1982

	GD	VG	FN	VF	VF/NM	NM-
1-Origin; intro. Villains Olstellon & Scor	3	7	10	21	28	35
2-5: 3-Intro. Graylin, Dagar's woman; Jarn x-over	2	4	6	10	13	16
6-1st Dark Gods story	2	4	6	8	10	12
7-10: 9-Intro. Torgus. 10-1st Three Witches story	2	4	6	8	10	12
11-18: 13-Durak & Torgus x-over; story continues in Dr. Spektor #15. 14-Dagar's origin retold. 18-Origin retold	1	2	3	5	7	9
19(4/82)-Origin-r/#18						6.00

NOTE: *Durak app. in 7, 12, 13. Tragg app. in 5, 11.*

DAGWOOD (Chic Young's) (Also see Blondie Comics)
Harvey Publications: Sept, 1950 - No. 140, Nov, 1965

	GD	VG	FN	VF	VF/NM	NM-
1	15	30	45	104	152	200
2	8	16	24	55	78	100
3-10	6	12	18	43	59	75
11-20	5	10	15	36	48	60
21-30	5	10	15	33	44	55
31-50	4	8	12	27	36	45
51-70	3	6	9	19	25	32
71-100	3	6	9	16	20	24
101-128,130,135	2	4	6	12	16	20
129,131-134,136-140-All are 68-pg. issues	3	6	9	19	25	32

NOTE: *Popeye and other one page strips appeared in early issues.*

DAI KAMIKAZE!
Now Comics: June, 1987 - No. 12, Aug, 1988 ($1.75)

	GD	VG	FN	VF	VF/NM	NM-
1-1st app. Speed Racer; 2nd print exists						3.50
2-12						2.50

DAILY BUGLE (See Spider-Man)
Marvel Comics: Dec, 1996 - No. 3, Feb, 1997 ($2.50, B&W, limited series)

	GD	VG	FN	VF	VF/NM	NM-
1-3-Paul Grist-s						2.50

DAISY AND DONALD (See Walt Disney Showcase No. 8)
Gold Key/Whitman No. 42 on: May, 1973 - No. 59, July, 1984 (no No. 48)

	GD	VG	FN	VF	VF/NM	NM-
1-Barks-r/WDC&S #280,308	3	7	10	21	28	35
2-5: 4-Barks-r/WDC&S #224	2	4	6	11	14	18
6-10	2	4	6	9	11	14
11-20	1	3	4	6	8	10
21-41: 32-r/WDC&S #308	1	2	3	5	6	8
42-44 (Whitman)	2	4	6	8	10	12
45 (8/80),46-(pre-pack?)(scarce)	3	6	9	19	25	32
47-(12/80)-Only distr. in Whitman 3-pack (scarce)	5	10	15	36	48	60
48(3/81)-50(8/81): 50-r/#3	2	4	6	10	13	16
51-54: 51-Barks-r/4-Color #1150. 52-r/#2. 53(2/82), 54(4/82)	2	4	6	9	11	14
55-59-(all #90284 on-c, nd, nd code, pre-pack): 55(5/83), 56(7/83), 57(8/83), 58(8/83), 59(7/84)	2	4	6	12	16	20

DAISY & HER PUPS (Dagwood & Blondie's Dogs)(Formerly Blondie Comics #20)
Harvey Publications: No. 21, 7/51 - No. 27, 7/52; No. 8, 9/52 - No. 18, 5/54

	GD	VG	FN	VF	VF/NM	NM-
21 (#1)-Blondie's dog Daisy and her 5 pups led by Elmer begin. Rags Rabbit app.	6	12	18	40	55	70
22-27 (#2-7): 26 has No. 6 on cover but No. 26 on inside. 23,25-The Little King app. 24-Bringing Up Father by McManus app. 25-27-Rags Rabbit app.	4	8	12	25	33	42
8-18: 8,9-Rags Rabbit app. 8,17-The Little King app. 11-The Flop Family Swan begins. 22-Cookie app. 11-Felix The Cat app. by 17,18-Popeye app.	4	8	12	22	30	38

DAISY DUCK & UNCLE SCROOGE PICNIC TIME (See Dell Giant #33)

DAISY DUCK & UNCLE SCROOGE SHOW BOAT (See Dell Giant #55)

DAISY DUCK'S DIARY (See Dynabrite Comics, & Walt Disney's C&S #298)
Dell Publishing Co.: No. 600, Nov, 1954 - No. 1247, Dec-Fef, 1961-62 (Disney)

	GD	VG	FN	VF	VF/NM	NM-
Four Color 600 (#1)	8	16	24	53	74	95
Four Color 659, 743 (11/56)	6	12	18	43	59	75
Four Color 858 (11/57), 948 (11/58), 1247 (12-2/61-62)	6	12	18	38	52	65
Four Color 1055 (11-1/59-60), 1150 (12-1/60-61)-By Carl Barks)	10	20	30	70	100	130

DAISY HANDBOOK
Daisy Manufacturing Co.: 1946; No. 2, 1948 (10¢, pocket-size, 132 pgs.)

	GD	VG	FN	VF	VF/NM	NM-
1-Buck Rogers, Red Ryder; Wolverton-a (2 pgs.)	39	78	117	230	325	420
2-Captain Marvel & Ibis the Invincible, Red Ryder, Boy Commandos & Robotman; Wolverton-a (2 pgs.); contains 8 pg. color catalog	39	78	117	230	325	420

DAISY MAE (See Oxydol-Dreft)

DAISY'S RED RYDER GUN BOOK
Daisy Manufacturing Co.: 1955 (25¢, pocket-size, 132 pgs.)

	GD	VG	FN	VF	VF/NM	NM-
nn-Boy Commandos, Red Ryder; 1pg. Wolverton-a	27	54	81	153	214	275

DAKKON BLACKBLADE ON THE WORLD OF MAGIC: THE GATHERING
Acclaim Comics (Armada): June, 1996 ($5.95, one-shot)

	GD	VG	FN	VF	VF/NM	NM-
1-Jerry Prosser scripts; Rags Morales-c/a.						6.00

DAKOTA LIL (See Fawcett Movie Comics)

DAKOTA NORTH
Marvel Comics Group: June, 1986 - No. 5, Feb, 1987

	GD	VG	FN	VF	VF/NM	NM-
1-5						2.25

DAKTARI (Ivan Tors) (TV)
Dell Publishing Co.: July, 1967 - No. 3, Oct, 1968; No. 4, Oct, 1969

	GD	VG	FN	VF	VF/NM	NM-
1-Marshall Thompson photo-c on all	4	8	12	28	38	48
2-4	3	6	9	19	25	32

DALE EVANS COMICS (Also see Queen of the West...)(See Boy Commandos #32)
National Periodical Publications: Sept-Oct, 1948 - No. 24, Jul-Aug, 1952 (No. 1-19: 52 pgs.)

	GD	VG	FN	VF	VF/NM	NM-
1-Dale Evans & her horse Buttermilk begin; Sierra Smith begins by Alex Toth	96	192	288	600	900	1200
2-Alex Toth-a	46	92	138	276	413	550
3-11-Alex Toth-a	32	64	96	184	262	340
12-20: 12-Target-c	18	36	54	104	142	180
21-24	19	38	57	107	149	190

NOTE: *Photo-c-1, 2, 4-14.*

DALGODA
Fantagraphics Books: Aug, 1984 - No. 8, Feb, 1986 (High quality paper)

	GD	VG	FN	VF	VF/NM	NM-
1,8: 1- Fujitake-c/a in all. 8-Alan Moore story						3.00
2-7: 2,3-Debut Grimwood's Daughter.						2.25

DALTON BOYS, THE
Avon Periodicals: 1951

	GD	VG	FN	VF	VF/NM	NM-
1-(Number on spine)-Kinstler-c	18	36	54	101	138	175

DAMAGE
DC Comics: Apr, 1994 - No. 20, Jan, 1996 ($1.75/$1.95/$2.25)

	GD	VG	FN	VF	VF/NM	NM-
1-20: 6-(9/94)-Zero Hour. 0-(10/94). 7-(11/94). 14-Ray app.						3.00

DAMAGE CONTROL (See Marvel Comics Presents #19)
Marvel Comics: 5/89 - No. 4, 8/89; V2#1, 12/89 - No. 4, 2/90 ($1.00)
V3#1, 6/91 - No. 4, 9/91 ($1.25, all are limited series)

	GD	VG	FN	VF	VF/NM	NM-
V1#1-4,V2#1-4,V3#1-4: V1#4-Wolverine app. V2#2,4-Punisher app. 1-Spider-Man app. 2-New Warriors app. 3,4-Silver Surfer app. 4-Infinity Gauntlet parody						2.50

DAMNED
Image Comics (Homage Comics): June, 1997 - No. 4, Sept, 1997 ($2.50, limited series)

	GD	VG	FN	VF	VF/NM	NM-
1-4-Steven Grant-s/Mike Zeck-c/a in all						2.50

DANCES WITH DEMONS (See Marvel Frontier Comics Unlimited)

Dandy Comics #5 © WMG

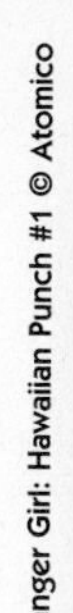

Danger Girl: Hawaiian Punch #1 © Atomico

Danger Trail #2 © DC

	GD 2.0	VG 4.0	FN 6.0	VF 8.0	VF/NM 9.0	NM- 9.2

Marvel Frontier Comics: Sept, 1993 - No. 4, Dec, 1993 ($1.95, limited series)

1-($2.95)-Foil embossed-c; Charlie Adlard & Rod Ramos-a 3.00
2-4 2.25

DANDEE: Four Star Publications: 1947 (Advertised, not published)

DAN DUNN (See Crackajack Funnies, Detective Dan, Famous Feature Stories & Red Ryder)

DANDY COMICS (Also see Happy Jack Howard)
E. C. Comics: Spring, 1947 - No. 7, Spring, 1948

1-Funny animal; Vince Fago-a in all; Dandy in all 38 76 114 219 310 400
2 27 54 81 153 214 275
3-7: 3-Intro Handy Andy who is c-feature #3 on 21 42 63 118 164 210

DANGER
Comic Media/Allen Hardy Assoc.: Jan, 1953 - No. 11, Aug, 1954

1-Heck-c/a 23 46 69 129 180 230
2,3,5,7,9-11: 12 24 36 69 92 115
4-Marijuana cover/story 16 32 48 89 122 155
6- "Narcotics" story; begin spy theme 14 28 42 79 107 135
8-Bondage/torture/headlights panels 17 34 51 98 134 170
NOTE: *Morisi a-2, 5, 6(3), 10; c-2. Contains some reprints from Danger & Dynamite.*

DANGER (Formerly Comic Media title)
Charlton Comics Group: No. 12, June, 1955 - No. 14, Oct, 1955

12(#1) 10 20 30 60 80 100
13,14: 14-r/#12 9 18 27 49 62 75

DANGER
Super Comics: 1964

Super Reprint #10-12 (Black Dwarf; #10-r/Great Comics #1 by Novack. #11-r/Johnny Danger #1. #12-r/Red Seal #14), #15-r/Spy Cases #26. #16-Unpublished Chesler material (Yankee Girl), #17-r/Scoop #8 (Capt. Courage & Enchanted Dagger), #18(nd)-r/Guns Against Gangsters #5 (Gun-Master, Annie Oakley, The Chameleon; L.B. Cole-r) 2 4 6 12 16 20

DANGER AND ADVENTURE (Formerly This Magazine Is Haunted; Robin Hood and His Merry Men No. 28 on)
Charlton Comics: No. 22, Feb, 1955 - No. 27, Feb, 1956

22-Ibis the Invincible-c/story; Nyoka app.; last pre-code issue
11 22 33 63 84 105
23-Lance O'Casey-c/sty; Nyoka app.; Ditko-a thru #27
13 26 39 74 100 125
24-27: 24-Mike Danger & Johnny Adventure begin 9 18 27 49 62 75

DANGER GIRL (Also see Cliffhanger #0)
Image Comics (Cliffhanger Productions): Mar, 1998 - No. 4, Dec, 1998;
DC Comics (Cliffhanger Prod.): No. 5, July, 1999 - No. 7, Feb, 2001

Preview-Bagged in DV8 #14 Voyager Pack 4.00
Preview Gold Edition 8.00
1-($2.95) Hartnell & Campbell-s/Campbell/Garner-a 1 2 3 5 6 8
1-($4.95) Chromium cover 45.00
1-American Entertainment Ed. 8.00
1-American Entertainment Gold Ed., 1-Tourbook edition 10.00
1-"Danger-sized" ed.; over-sized format 3 6 9 18 24 30
2-($2.50) 4.00
2-Smoking Gun variant cover, 2-Platinum Ed., 2-Dynamic Forces Omnichrome variant-c 2 4 6 10 13 16
2-Gold foil cover 9.00
2-Ruby red foil cover 90.00
3,4: 3-c by Campbell, Charest and Adam Hughes. 4-Big knife variant-c 3.00
3,5: 3-Gold foil cover. 5-DF Bikini variant-c 5.00
4-6 3.00
7-($5.95) Wraparound gatefold-c; Last issue 6.00
...: Hawaiian Punch (5/03, $4.95) Campbell-c; Phil Noto-a 5.00
San Diego Preview (8/98, B&W) flip book w/Wildcats preview 5.00
Sketchbook (2001, $6.95) Campbell-a; sketches for comics, toys, games 7.00
...Special (2/00, $3.50) art by Campbell, Chiodo, and Art Adams 3.50
... 3-D #1 (4/03, $4.95, bagged with 3-D glasses) r/ Preview & #1 in 3-D 5.00
...: Viva Las Danger (1/04, $4.95) Noto-a/Campbell-c 5.00
... :The Dangerous Collection nn(8/98; r-#1) 6.00
... :The Dangerous Collection 2,3: 2-(11/98, $5.95) r/#2,3. 3-('99) r/#4,5 6.00
... :The Dangerous Collection nn, 2-($10.00) Gold foil logo 10.00
... :The Ultimate Collection HC ($29.95) r/#1-7; intro by Bruce Campbell 30.00
... :The Ultimate Collection SC ($19.95) r/#1-7; intro by Bruce Campbell 20.00

DANGER GIRL KAMIKAZE
DC Comics (Cliffhanger): Nov, 2001 - No. 2, Dec., 2001 ($2.95, lim. series)

1,2-Tommy Yune-s/a 3.00

DANGER IS OUR BUSINESS!
Toby Press: 1953(Dec.) - No. 10, June, 1955

1-Captain Comet by Williamson/Frazetta-a, 6 pgs. (science fiction)
44 88 132 264 395 525
2 13 26 39 76 103 130
3-10 11 22 33 63 84 105
I.W. Reprint #9('64)-Williamson/Frazetta-r/#1; Kinstler-c
9 18 27 65 93 120

DANGER IS THEIR BUSINESS (Also see A-1 Comic)
Magazine Enterprises: No. 50, 1952

A-1 50-Powell-a 14 28 42 79 107 135

DANGER MAN (TV)
Dell Publishing Co.: No. 1231, Sept-Nov, 1961

Four Color 1231-Patrick McGoohan photo-c 12 24 36 84 125 165

DANGER TRAIL (Also see Showcase #50, 51)
National Periodical Publ.: July-Aug, 1950 - No. 5, Mar-Apr, 1951 (52 pgs.)

1-King Faraday begins, ends #4; Toth-a in all 120 240 360 750 1125 1500
2 85 170 255 531 796 1060
3-(Rare) one of the rarest early '50s DCs 120 240 360 750 1125 1500
4,5: 5-Johnny Peril-c/story (moves to Sensation Comics #107); new logo (also see Comic Cavalcade #15-29) 69 138 207 431 646 860

DANGER TRAIL
DC Comics: Apr, 1993 - No. 4, July, 1993 ($1.50, limited series)

1-4: Gulacy-c on all 2.25

DANGER UNLIMITED (See San Diego Comic Con Comics #2 & Torch of Liberty Special)
Dark Horse (Legend): Feb, 1994 - No. 4, May, 1994 ($2.00, limited series)

1-4: Byrne-c/a/scripts in all; origin stories of both original team (Doc Danger, Thermal, Miss Mirage, & Hunk) & future team (Thermal, Belebet, & Caucus). 1-Intro Torch of Liberty & Golgotha (cameo) in back-up story. 4-Hellboy & Torch of Liberty cameo in lead story 2.50
TPB (1995, $14.95)-r/#1-4; includes last pg. originally cut from #4 15.00

DAN HASTINGS (See Syndicate Features)

DANIEL BOONE (See The Exploits of..., Fighting... Frontier Scout...,The Legends of... & March of Comics No. 306)
Dell Publishing Co.: No. 1163, Mar-May, 1961

Four Color 1163-Marsh-a 6 12 18 40 55 70

DANIEL BOONE (TV) (See March of Comics No. 306)
Gold Key: Jan, 1965 - No. 15, Apr, 1969 (All have Fess Parker photo-c)

1 10 20 30 67 96 125
2 6 12 18 38 52 65
3-5 4 8 12 29 40 50
6-15 3 7 10 21 28 35

DAN'L BOONE
Sussex Publ. Co.: Sept, 1955 - No. 8, Sept, 1957

1 15 30 45 86 118 150
2 10 20 30 56 73 90
3-8 8 16 24 40 50 60

DANNY BLAZE (...Firefighter) (Nature Boy No. 3 on)
Charlton Comics: Aug, 1955 - No. 2, Oct, 1955

1 11 22 33 66 88 110
2 9 18 27 49 62 75

DANNY DINGLE (See Sparkler Comics)
United Features Syndicate: No. 17, 1940

Single Series 17 27 54 81 153 214 275

DANNY THOMAS SHOW, THE (TV)
Dell Publishing Co.: No. 1180, Apr-June, 1961 - No. 1249, Dec-Feb, 1961-62

Four Color 1180-Toth-a, photo-c 18 36 54 131 191 250
Four Color 1249-Manning-a, photo-c 17 34 51 121 178 235

DARBY O'GILL & THE LITTLE PEOPLE (Movie)(See Movie Comics)
Dell Publishing Co.: 1959 (Disney)

Four Color 1024-Toth-a; photo-c. 11 22 33 77 114 150

DAREDEVIL (...& the Black Widow #92-107 on-c only; see Giant-Size...,Marvel Advs., Marvel Graphic Novel #24, Marvel Super Heroes, '66 & Spider-Man &...)
Marvel Comics Group: Apr, 1964 - No. 380, Oct, 1998

Daredevil #4 © MAR

Daredevil #94 © MAR

Daredevil #200 © MAR

	GD 2.0	VG 4.0	FN 6.0	VF 8.0	VF/NM 9.0	NM- 9.2
1-Origin/1st app. Daredevil; intro Foggy Nelson & Karen Page; death of Battling Murdock; Bill Everett-c/a; reprinted in Marvel Super Heroes #1 (1966)	205	410	615	1794	2797	3800
2-Fantastic Four cameo; 2nd app. Electro (Spidey villain); Thing guest star	54	108	162	405	703	1000
3-Origin & 1st app. The Owl (villain)	38	76	114	275	462	650
4-The Purple Man app.	33	66	99	239	370	500
5-Minor costume change; Wood-a begins	27	54	81	196	285	375
6-Mr. Fear app.	17	34	51	123	182	240
7-Daredevil battles Sub-Mariner & dons red costume for 1st time (4/65)	44	88	132	330	565	800
8-10: 8-Origin/1st app. Stilt-Man	15	30	45	109	160	210
11-15: 12-1st app. Plunderer; Ka-Zar app. 13-Facts about Ka-Zar's origin; Kirby-a	9	18	27	65	93	120
16,17-Spider-Man x-over. 16-1st Romita-a on Spider-Man (5/66)	12	24	36	87	129	170
18-Origin & 1st app. Gladiator	9	18	27	60	85	110
19,20	7	14	21	50	68	85
21-26,28-30: 24-Ka-Zar app.	6	12	18	38	52	65
27-Spider-Man x-over	7	14	21	46	63	80
31-40: 38-Fantastic Four x-over; cont'd in F.F. #73. 39-1st Exterminator (later becomes Death-Stalker)	4	8	12	29	40	50
41,42,44-49: 41-Death Mike Murdock. 42-1st app. Jester. 45-Statue of Liberty photo-c	4	8	12	27	36	45
43-Daredevil battles Captain America; origin partially retold	5	10	15	36	48	60
50-53: 50-52-B. Smith-a. 53-Origin retold; last 12¢ issue	4	8	12	29	40	50
54-56,58-60: 54-Spider-Man cameo. 56-1st app. Death's Head (9/69); story cont'd in #57 (not same as new Death's Head)	3	6	9	18	24	30
57-Reveals i.d. to Karen Page; Death's Head app.	3	6	9	19	25	32
61-76,78-80: 79-Stan Lee cameo. 80-Last 15¢ issue	3	6	9	16	20	25
77-Spider-Man x-over	3	7	10	21	28	35
81-(52 pgs.) Black Widow begins (11/71).	3	7	10	21	28	35
82,84-99: 87-Electro-c/story	2	4	6	12	16	20
83-B. Smith layouts/Weiss-p	2	4	6	14	18	22
100-Origin retold	3	6	9	19	25	32
101-104,106-120: 107-Starlin-c; Thanos cameo. 113-1st app. Deathstalker (cameo). 114-1st full app. Deathstalker	2	4	6	10	13	16
105-Origin Moondragon by Starlin (12/73); Thanos cameo in flashback (early app.)	2	4	6	12	16	20
121-130,137: 124-1st app. Copperhead; Black Widow leaves. 126-1st new Torpedo	2	4	6	8	10	12
131-Origin/1st app. new Bullseye (see Nick Fury #15)	4	8	12	29	40	50
132-2nd app. new Bullseye (Regular 25¢ edition)	3	6	9	18	24	30
132-(30¢-c variant, limited distribution)(4/76)	4	8	12	27	36	45
133-136-(Regular 25¢ editions)	1	3	4	6	8	10
133-136-(30¢-c variants, limited distribution)(5-8/76)	2	4	6	10	12	15
138-Ghost Rider-c/story; Death's Head is reincarnated; Byrne-a	2	4	6	10	12	15
139,140,142-145,147-157: 142-Nova cameo. 147,148-(Reg. 30¢-c). 150-1st app. Paladin. 151-Reveals i.d. to Heather Glenn. 155-Black Widow returns. 156-The '60s Daredevil app.	1	3	4	6	8	10
141,146-Bullseye app.	2	4	6	12	16	20
146-(35¢-c variant, limited distribution)	3	6	9	18	24	30
147,148-(35¢-c variants, limited distribution)	2	4	6	10	12	15
158-Frank Miller art begins (5/79); origin/death of Deathstalker (see Captain America #235 & Spectacular Spider-Man #27	6	12	18	43	59	75
159	4	8	12	22	30	38
160,161-Bullseye app.	3	6	9	18	24	30
162-Ditko-a; no Miller-a	1	2	3	5	7	9
163,164: 163-Hulk cameo. 164-Origin retold	2	4	6	14	18	22
165-167,170	2	4	6	11	14	18
168-Origin/1st app. Elektra; 1st Miller scripts	8	16	24	55	78	100
169-2nd Electra app.	3	7	10	21	28	35
171-173	2	4	6	10	12	15
174,175-Elektra app.	2	4	6	11	14	18
176-180-Elektra app. 178-Cage app. 179-Anti-smoking issue mentioned in the Congressional Record	2	4	6	10	12	15
181-(52 pgs.)-Death of Elektra; Punisher cameo out of costume	3	6	9	18	23	28
182-184-Punisher app. by Miller (drug issues)	2	4	6	8	10	12
185-191: 187-New Black Widow. 189-Death of Stick. 190-($1.00, 52 pgs.)-Elektra returns, part origin. 191-Last Miller Daredevil	1	2	3	5	7	9

	GD 2.0	VG 4.0	FN 6.0	VF 8.0	VF/NM 9.0	NM- 9.2
192-195,198,199,201-207,209-218,220-226,234-237: 226-Frank Miller plots begin						3.50
196-Wolverine-c/app.	2	4	6	9	11	14
197-Bullseye-c/app.						5.00
200,238: 200-Bullseye app. 238-Mutant Massacre; Sabretooth app.						6.00
208,219,228-233: 208-Harlan Ellison scripts borrowed from Avengers TV episode "House that Jack Built". 219-Miller-c/script. 228-233-Last Miller scripts						4.00
227-Miller scripts begin						6.00
239,240,242-247						3.00
241-Todd McFarlane-a(p)						5.00
248,249-Wolverine app.						6.00
250,251,253,258: 250-1st app. Bullet. 258-Intro The Bengal (a villain)						3.00
252,260 (52 pgs.): 252-Fall of the Mutants. 260-Typhoid Mary app.						5.00
254-Origin & 1st app. Typhoid Mary (5/88)	1	2	3	4	5	8
255,256,258: 255,256-2nd/3rd app. Typhoid Mary. 259-Typhoid Mary app.						5.00
257-Punisher app. (x-over w/Punisher #10)	1	3	4	6	8	10
261-281,283-294,296-299,301-304,307-318: 270-1st app. Black Heart. 272-Intro Shotgun (villain). 281-Silver Surfer cameo. 283-Capt. America app. 297-Typhoid Mary app.; Kingpin storyline begins. 292-D.G. Chichester scripts begin. 293-Punisher app. 303-Re-intro the Owl. 304-Garney-c/a. 309-Punisher-c.; Terror app. 310-Calypso-c						2.50
282,295,300,305,306: 282-Silver Surfer app. 295-Ghost Rider app. 300-($2.00, 52 pgs.) Kingpin story ends. 305,306-Spider-Man-c						3.00
319-Prologue to Fall From Grace; Elektra returns						6.00
319-2nd printing w/black-c						2.50
320-Fall From Grace Pt 1						5.00
321-Fall From Grace regular ed.; Pt 2; new costume; Venom app.						3.00
321-($2.00)-Wraparound Glow-in-the-dark-c ed.						5.00
322-Fall From Grace Pt 3; Eddie Brock app.						4.00
323,324-Fall From Grace Pt. 4 & 5: 323-Vs. Venom-c/story. 324-Morbius-c/story						4.00
325-($2.50, 52 pgs.)-Fall From Grace ends; contains bound-in poster						4.00
326-349,351-353: 326-New logo. 328-Bound-in trading card sheet. 330-Gambit app. 348-1st Cary Nord art in DD (1/96);"Dec" on-c. 353-Karl Kesel scripts; Nord-c/a begins; Mr. Hyde-c/app.						2.50
350-($2.95)-Double-sized						3.00
350-($3.50)-Double-sized; gold ink-c						3.50
354-374,376-379: Kesel scripts, Nord-c/a in all. 354-$1.50-c begins. 355-Larry Hama layouts; Pyro app. 358-Mysterio-c/app. 359-Absorbing Man cameo. 360-Absorbing Man-c/app. 361-Black Widow-c/app. 363-Gene Colan-a(p) begins. 368-Omega Red-c/app. 372-Ghost Rider-c/app. 376-379-"Flying Blind", DD goes undercover for S.H.I.E.L.D.						2.50
375-($2.99) Wraparound-c; Mr. Fear-c/app.						3.00
380-($2.99) Final issue; flashback story						4.00
Special 1(9/67, 25¢, 68 pgs.)-New art/story	5	10	15	36	48	60
Special 2,3: 2(2/71, 25¢, 52 pgs.)-Entire book has Powell/Wood-r; Wood-c. 3(1/72, 52 pgs.)-Reprints	2	4	6	14	18	22
Annual 4(10/76)	1	2	3	5	7	9
Annual 4(#5)-10: ('89-94 68 pgs.)-5-Atlantis Attacks. 6-Sutton-a. 7-Guice-a (7 pgs.). 8-Deathlok-c/story. 9-Polybagged w/card						3.00
... :Born Again TPB ($17.95)-r/#227-233; Miller-s/Mazzucchelli-a & new-c						20.00
.../Deadpool- (Annual '97, $2.99)-Wraparound-c						3.00
...:Fall From Grace TPB ($19.95)-r/#319-325						20.00
... :Gang War TPB ($15.95)-r/#169-172,180; Miller-s/a(p)						16.00
...Legends: (Vol. 4) Typhoid Mary TPB (2003, $19.95) r/#254-257,259-263						20.00
... :Love's Labors Lost TPB ($19.99)-r/#215-217,219-222,225,226; Mazzucchelli-c						20.00
.../Punisher TPB (1988, $4.95)-r/D.D. #182-184 (all printings)						5.00
...Visionaries: Frank Miller Vol. 1 TPB ($17.95) r/#158-161,163-167						18.00
...Visionaries: Frank Miller Vol. 2 TPB ($24.95) r/#168-182; new Miller-c						25.00
...Visionaries: Frank Miller Vol. 3 TPB ($24.95) r/#183-191, What If? #28,35 & Bizarre Adventures #28; new Miller-c						25.00
Wizard Ace Edition: Daredevil (Vol. 1) #1 (4/03, $13.99) Acetate Campbell-c						14.00

NOTE: **Art Adams** *c-238p, 239.* **Austin** *a-191i; c-151i, 200i.* **John Buscema** *a-136, 137p, 234p, 235p; c-86p, 136i, 137p, 142, 219.* **Byrne** *c-200p, 201, 203, 223.* **Capullo** *a-286p.* **Colan** *a(p)-20-49, 53-82, 84-98, 100, 110, 112, 124, 153, 154, 156, 157, Spec. 1p; c(p)-20-42, 44-49, 53-60, 71, 92, 98, 138, 153, 154, 156, 157, Annual 1.* **Craig** *a-50i, 52i.* **Ditko** *a-162, 234p, 235p, 264p; c-162.* **Everett** *c/a-1; inks-21, 83.* **Garney** *c/a-304.* **Gil Kane** *a-141p, 146-148p, 151p; c(p)-85, 90, 91, 93, 94, 115, 116, 119, 120, 125-128, 133, 139, 147, 152.* **Kirby** *c-2-4, 5p, 12p, 13p, 43, 136p.* **Layton** *c-202.* **Miller** *scripts-168-182, 183(part), 184-191, 219, 227-233; a-158-161p, 163-184p, 191p; c-158-161p, 163-184p, 185-189, 190p, 191.* **Orlando** *a-2-4p.* **Powell** *a-9p, 11p, Special 1r, 2r.* **Simonson** *c-199, 236p.* **B. Smith** *a-236p; c-51p, 52p, 217.* **Starlin** *a-105p.* **Steranko** *c-44i.* **Tuska** *a-39i, 145p.* **Williamson** *a(i)-237, 239, 240, 243, 248-257, 259-282, 283(part), 284, 285, 287, 288(part), 289(part), 293-300; c(i)-237, 243, 244, 248-257, 259-263, 265-278, 280-289, Annual 8.* **Wood** *a-5-8, 9i, 10, 11i, Spec. 2i; c-5i, 6-11, 164i.*

DAREDEVIL (Volume 2) (Marvel Knights)
Marvel Comics: Nov, 1998 - Present ($2.50)

	NM- 9.2
1-Kevin Smith-s/Quesada & Palmiotti-a	12.00
1-($6.95) DF Edition w/Quesada & Palmiotti var.-c	15.00
1-($6.00) DF Sketch Ed. w/B&W-c	10.00
2-Two covers by Campbell and Quesada/Palmiotti	9.00
3-8: 4,5-Bullseye app. 8-Spider-Man-c/app.; last Smith-s	6.00

Daredevil V2#46 © MAR

Daredevil: Yellow #6 © MAR

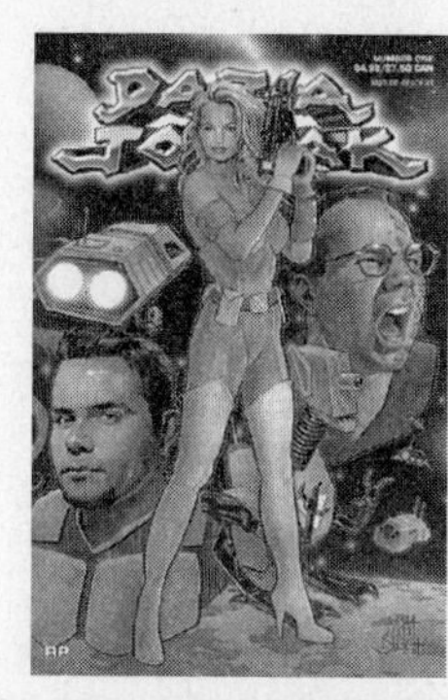
Daria Jontak #1 © Planet Matt Ent.

GD 2.0 | VG 4.0 | FN 6.0 | VF 8.0 | VF/NM 9.0 | NM- 9.2

9-15: 9-11-David Mack-s; intro Echo. 12-Begin $2.99-c; Haynes-a. 13,14-Quesada-a 3.00
16-19-Direct editions; Bendis-s/Mack-c/painted-a 3.00
18,19,21,22-Newsstand editions with variant cover logo "Marvel Unlimited Featuring..." 3.00
20-($3.50) Gale-s/Winslade-a; back-up by Stan Lee-s/Colan-a; Mack-c 3.50
21-40: 21-25-Gale-s. 26-38-Bendis-s/Maleev-a. 32-Daredevil's ID revealed. 35-Spider-Man-c/app. 38-Iron Fist & Luke Cage app. 40-Dodson-a 3.50
41-(25¢-c) Begins "Lowlife" arc; Maleev-a; intro Milla Donovan 2.25
41-(Newsstand edition with 2.99¢-c) 4.00
42-45-"Lowlife" arc; Maleev-a 2.25
46-50-($2.99). 46-Typhoid Mary returns. 49-Bullseye app. 50-Art panels by various incl. Romita, Colan, Mack, Janson, Oeming, Quesada 3.00
51-55-Mack-s/a; Echo app. 54-Wolverine-c/app. 3.00
TPB ($9.95) r/#1-3 10.00
...Vol. 1 HC (2001, $29.99, with dustjacket) r/#1-11,13-15 30.00
...Vol. 1 HC (2003, $29.99, with dustjacket) r/#1-11,13-15; larger page size 30.00
...Vol. 2 HC (2002, $29.99, with dustjacket) r/#26-37; afterword by Bendis 30.00
(Vol. 1) Visionaries TPB ($19.95) r/#1-8; Ben Affleck intro. 20.00
(Vol. 2) Parts of a Hole TPB (1/02, $17.95) r/#9-15; David Mack intro. 18.00
(Vol. 3) Wake Up TPB (7/02, $9.99) r/#16-19 10.00
...Vol. 4: Underboss TPB (8/02, $14.99) r/#26-31 15.00
...Vol. 5: Out TPB (2003, $19.99) r/#32-40 20.00
...Vol. 6: Lowlife TPB (2003, $13.99) r/#41-45 14.00
...Vol. 7: Hardcore TPB (2003, $13.99) r/#46-50 14.00

DAREDEVIL/ BATMAN (Also see Batman/Daredevil)
Marvel Comics/ DC Comics: 1997 ($5.99, one-shot)
nn-McDaniel-c/a 6.00

DAREDEVIL/ ELEKTRA: LOVE AND WAR
Marvel Comics: 2003 ($29.99, hardcover with dust jacket)
HC-Larger-size reprints of Daredevil: Love and War (Marvel Graphic Novel #24) & Elektra: Assassin; Frank Miller-s; Bill Sienkiewicz-a 30.00

DAREDEVIL: NINJA
Marvel Comics: Dec, 2000 - No. 3, Feb, 2001 ($2.99, limited series)
1-3: Bendis-s/Haynes-a 3.00
1-Dynamic Forces foil-c 10.00
TPB (7/01, $12.95) r/#1-3 with cover and sketch gallery 13.00

DAREDEVIL/ SHI (See Shi/ Daredevil)
Marvel Comics/ Crusade Comics: Feb,1997 ($2.95, limited series)
1 3.00

DAREDEVIL/ SPIDER-MAN
Marvel Comics: Jan, 2001 - No. 4, Apr, 2001 ($2.99, limited series)
1-4-Jenkins-s/Winslade-a/Alex Ross-c; Stilt Man app. 3.00
TPB (8/01, $12.95) r/#1-4; Ross-c 13.00

DAREDEVIL THE MAN WITHOUT FEAR
Marvel Comics: Oct, 1993 - No. 5, Feb, 1994 ($2.95, limited series) (foil embossed covers)
1-Miller scripts; Romita, Jr./Williamson-c/a 6.00
2-5 5.00
Hardcover 100.00
Trade paperback 20.00

DAREDEVIL: THE MOVIE (2003 movie adaptation)
Marvel Comics: March, 2003 ($3.50/$12.95, one-shot)
1-Photo-c of Ben Affleck; Bruce Jones-s/Manuel Garcia-a 3.50
TPB ($12.95) r/movie adaptation; Daredevil #32; Ultimate Daredevil & Elektra #1 and Spider-Man's Tangled Web #4; photo-c of Ben Affleck 13.00

DAREDEVIL: THE TARGET (Daredevil Bullseye on cover)
Marvel Comics: Jan, 2003 - No. 4, ($3.50, limited series)
1-Kevin Smith-s/Glenn Fabry-c/a 3.50

DAREDEVIL: YELLOW
Marvel Comics: Aug, 2001 - No. 6, Jan, 2002 ($3.50, limited series)
1-6-Jeph Loeb-s/Tim Sale-a/c; origin & yellow costume days retold 3.50
HC (5/02, $29.95) r/#1-6 with dustjacket; intro by Stan Lee; sketch pages 30.00
Daredevil Legends Vol. 1: Daredevil Yellow (2002, $14.99, TPB) r/#1-6 15.00

DAREDEVIL COMICS (See Silver Streak Comics)
Lev Gleason Publications (Funnies, Inc. No. 1): July, 1941 - No. 134, Sept, 1956 (Charles Biro stories)
1-No. 1 titled "Daredevil Battles Hitler"; The Silver Streak, Lance Hale, Cloud Curtis, Dickey Dean, Pirate Prince team up w/Daredevil and battle Hitler; Daredevil battles the Claw; Origin of Hitler feature story. Hitler photo app. on-c
1125 2250 3375 8438 13,219 18,000
2-London, Pat Patriot (by Reed Crandall), Nightro, Real American No. 1 (by Briefer #2-11), Dickie Dean, Pirate Prince, & Times Square begin; intro. & only app. The Pioneer, Champion of America 300 600 900 1925 2963 4000
3-Origin of 13 192 384 576 1200 1800 2400
4 166 332 498 1038 1557 2075
5-Intro. Sniffer & Jinx; Ghost vs. Claw begins by Bob Wood, ends #20
128 256 384 800 1200 1600
6-(#7 in indicia) 110 220 330 688 1032 1375
7-10: 8-Nightro ends 91 182 273 569 855 1140
11-London, Pat Patriot end; classic bondage/torture-c
122 244 366 763 1144 1525
12-Origin of The Claw; Scoop Scuttle by Wolverton begins (2-4 pgs.), ends #22, not in #21 142 284 426 888 1332 1775
13-Intro. of Little Wise Guys (10/42) 118 236 354 738 1107 1475
14 64 128 192 400 600 800
15-Death of Meatball 94 188 282 588 882 1175
16,17 60 120 180 375 563 750
18-New origin of Daredevil (not same as Silver Streak #6). Hitler, Mussolini Tojo and Mickey Mouse app. on-c 128 256 384 800 1200 1600
19,20 50 100 150 300 450 600
21-Reprints cover of Silver Streak #6 (on inside) plus intro. of The Claw from Silver Streak #1 90 180 270 563 844 1125
22-30: 27-Bondage/torture-c 42 84 126 252 359 465
31-Death of The Claw 80 160 240 500 750 1000
32-37,39-41: 35-Two Daredevil stories begin, end #68 (35-41 are 64 pgs.)
31 62 93 178 252 325
38-Origin Daredevil retold from #18 44 88 132 264 395 525
42-50: 42-Intro. Kilroy in Daredevil 25 50 75 147 202 260
51-69-Last Daredevil issue (12/50) 18 36 54 104 142 180
70-Little Wise Guys take over book; McWilliams-a; Hot Rock Flanagan begins, ends #80
11 22 33 66 88 110
71-78,81 9 18 27 49 62 75
79,80: 79-Daredevil returns. 80-Daredevil x-over 9 18 27 52 66 80
82,90,100: 82,90-One pg. Frazetta ad in both 9 18 27 49 62 75
83-89,91-99,101-134 8 16 24 43 54 65
NOTE: ***Biro** c/a-all?* ***Bolle** a-125.* ***Maurer** a-75.* ***McWilliams** a-73, 75, 79, 80.*

DARIA JONTAK
JMJ Media Group: Jan, 2001 ($4.99)
1-Matt Busch-s/a 5.00

DARING ADVENTURES (Also see Approved Comics)
St. John Publishing Co.: Nov, 1953 (25¢, 3-D, came w/glasses)
1 (3-D)-Reprints lead story from Son of Sinbad #1 by Kubert
35 70 105 201 288 370

DARING ADVENTURES
I.W. Enterprises/Super Comics: 1963 - 1964
I. W. Reprint #8-r/Fight Comics #53; Matt Baker-a 6 12 18 38 52 65
I.W. Reprint #9-r/Blue Bolt #115; Disbrow-a(3) 6 12 18 40 55 70
Super Reprint #10,11('63)-r/Dynamic #24,16; 11-Marijuana story; Yankee Boy app.; Mac Raboy-a 4 8 12 27 36 45
Super Reprint #12('64)-Phantom Lady from Fox (r/#14 only? w/splash pg. omitted); Matt Baker-a 12 24 36 84 125 165
Super Reprint #15('64)-r/Hooded Menace #1 8 16 24 53 74 95
Super Reprint #16('64)-r/Dynamic #12 4 8 12 24 32 40
Super Reprint #17('64)-r/Green Lama #3 by Raboy 5 10 15 33 44 55
Super Reprint #18-Origin Atlas from unpublished Atlas Comics #1
4 8 12 29 40 50

DARING COMICS (Formerly Daring Mystery) (Jeanie Comics No. 13 on)
Timely Comics (HPC): No. 9, Fall, 1944 - No. 12, Fall, 1945
9-Human Torch, Toro & Sub-Mariner begin 122 244 366 763 1144 1525
10-12: 10-The Angel only app. 11,12-The Destroyer app.
100 200 300 625 938 1250
NOTE: ***Schomburg** c-9-11.* ***Sekowsky** c-12? Human Torch, Toro & Sub-Mariner c-9-12.*

DARING CONFESSIONS (Formerly Youthful Hearts)
Youthful Magazines: No. 4, 11/52 - No. 7, 5/53; No. 8, 10/53
4-Doug Wildey-a; Tony Curtis story 16 32 48 92 126 160
5-8: 5-Ray Anthony photo on-c. 6,8-Wildey-a 12 24 36 69 92 115

DARING ESCAPES
Image Comics: Sept, 1998 - No. 4, Mar, 1999 ($2.95/$2.50, mini-series)
1-Houdini; following app. in Spawn #19,20 3.00
2-4-($2.50) 2.50

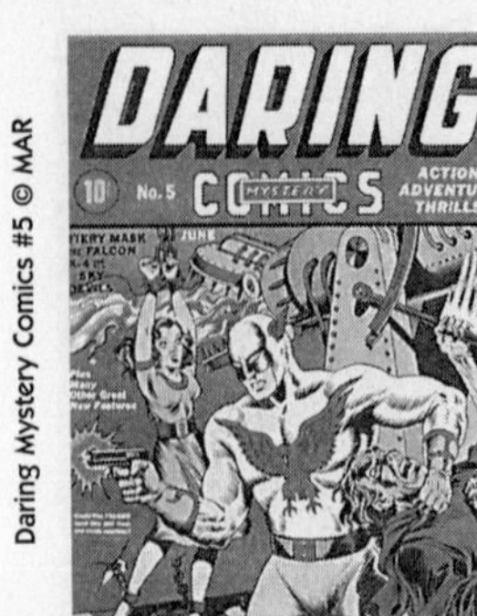

Daring Mystery Comics #5 © MAR

Dark Days #1 © Niles & Templesmith

Darkchylde #4 © Randy Queen

GD VG FN VF VF/NM NM-
2.0 4.0 6.0 8.0 9.0 9.2

GD VG FN VF VF/NM NM-
2.0 4.0 6.0 8.0 9.0 9.2

DARING LOVE (Radiant Love No. 2 on)
Gilmor Magazines: Sept-Oct, 1953

1-Steve Ditko's 1st published work (1st drawn was Fantastic Fears #5)(Also see Black Magic #27)(scarce) 50 100 150 300 450 600

DARING LOVE (Formerly Youthful Romances)
Ribage/Pix: No. 15, 12/52; No. 16, 2/53-c, 4/53-Indicia; No. 17-4/53-c & indicia

15 11 22 33 63 84 105
16,17: 17-Photo-c 10 20 30 56 73 90
NOTE: ***Colletta** a-15. **Wildey** a-17.*

DARING LOVE STORIES (See Fox Giants)

DARING MYSTERY COMICS (Comedy Comics No. 9 on; title changed to Daring Comics with No. 9)
Timely Comics (TPI 1-6/TCI 7,8): 1/40 - No. 5, 6/40; No. 6, 9/40; No. 7, 4/41 - No. 8, 1/42

1-Origin The Fiery Mask (1st app.) by Joe Simon; Monako, Prince of Magic (1st app.), John Steele, Soldier of Fortune (1st app.), Doc Denton (1st app.) begin; Flash Foster & Barney Mullen, Sea Rover only app; bondage-c 1812 3624 5436 13,590 21,295 29,000
2-(Rare)-Origin The Phantom Bullet (1st & only app.); The Laughing Mask & Mr. E only app.; Trojak the Tiger Man begins, ends #6; Zephyr Jones & K-4 & His Sky Devils app., also #4 966 1932 2898 6762 10,381 14,000
3-The Phantom Reporter, Dale of FBI, Captain Strong only app.; Breeze Barton, Marvex the Super-Robot, The Purple Mask begin 483 966 1449 3381 5191 7000
4,5: 4-Last Purple Mask; Whirlwind Carter begins; Dan Gorman, G-Man app. 5-The Falcon begins (1st app.); The Fiery Mask, Little Hercules app. by Sagendorf in the Segar style; bondage-c 326 652 978 2119 3260 4400
6-Origin & only app. Marvel Boy by S&K; Flying Flame, Dynaman, & Stuporman only app.; The Fiery Mask by S&K; S&K-c 423 846 1269 2751 4226 5700
7-Origin The Blue Diamond, Captain Daring by S&K, The Fin by Everett, The Challenger, The Silver Scorpion & The Thunderer by Burgos; Mr. Millions app 341 682 1023 2217 3409 4600
8-Origin Citizen V; Last Fin, Silver Scorpion, Capt. Daring by Borth, Blue Diamond & The Thunderer; Kirby & part solo Simon-c; Rudy the Robot only app.; Citizen V, Fin & Silver Scorpion continue in Comedy #9 288 576 864 1800 2700 3600
NOTE: ***Schomburg** c-1-4, 7. **Simon** a-2, 3, 5. Cover features: 1-Fiery Mask; 2-Phantom Bullet; 3-Purple Mask; 4-G-Man; 5-The Falcon; 6-Marvel Boy; 7, 8-Multiple characters.*

DARING NEW ADVENTURES OF SUPERGIRL, THE
DC Comics: Nov, 1982 - No. 13, Nov, 1983 (Supergirl No. 14 on)

1-Origin retold; Lois Lane back-ups in #2-12 1 2 3 5 6 8
2-13: 8,9-Doom Patrol app. 13-New costume; flag-c 4.00
NOTE: ***Buckler** c-1p, 2p. **Giffen** c-3p, 4p. **Gil Kane** c-6, ,8, 9, 11-13.*

DARK, THE
Continum Comics: Nov, 1990 - No. 4, Feb, 1993; V2#1, May, 1993 - V2#7, Apr?, 1994 ($1.95)

1-4: 1-Bright-p; Panosian, Hanna-i; Stroman-c. 2-(1/92)-Stroman-c/a(p). 4-Perez-c & part-i 3.00
V2#1,V2#2-6: V2#1-Red foil Bart Sears-c. V2#1-Red non-foil variant-c. V2#1-2nd printing w/blue foil Bart Sears-c. V2#2-Stroman/Bryant-a. 3-Perez-c(i). 3-6-Foil-c. 4-Perez-c & part-i; bound-in trading cards. 5,6-(2,3/94)-Perez-c(i). 7-(B&W)-Perez-c(i) 2.25
Convention Book 1 ,2(Fall/94, 10/94)-Perez-c 2.25

DARK ANGEL (Formerly Hell's Angel)
Marvel Comics UK, Ltd.: No. 6, Dec, 1992 - No. 16, Dec, 1993 ($1.75)

6-8,13-16: 6-Excalibur-c/story. 8-Psylocke app. 2.25
9-12-Wolverine/X-Men app. 3.00

DARK ANGEL: PHOENIX RESURRECTION (Kia Asamiya's...)
Image Comics: May, 2000 - No. 4, Oct, 2001 ($2.95)

1-4-Kia Asamiya-s/a. 3-Van Fleet variant-c 3.00

DARKCHYLDE (Also see Dreams of the Darkchylde)
Maximum Press #1-3/ Image Comics #4 on: June, 1996 - No. 5, Sept, 1997 ($2.95/ $2.50)

1-Randy Queen-c/a/scripts; "Roses" cover 6.00
1-American Entertainment Edition-wraparound-c 6.00
1-"Fashion magazine-style" variant-c 1 2 3 4 5 7
1-Special Comicon Edition (contents of #1) Winged devil variant-c 5.00
1-($2.50)-Remastered Ed.-wraparound-c 4.00
2(Reg-c),2-Spiderweb and Moon variant-c 6.00
3(Reg-c),3-"Kalvin Clein" variant-c by Drew 3.00
4(Reg-c), 4-Variant-c 4.00
5 4.00
5-B&W Edition, 5-Dynamic Forces Gold Ed. 8.00
0-(3/98, $2.50) 2.50
0-Remastered (1/01, $2.95) includes Darkchylde: Redemption preview 3.00
1/2-WIzard offer 4.00
1/2 Variant-c 6.00
... The Descent TPB ('98, $19.95) r/#1-5; bagged with Darkchylde The Legacy Preview Special 1998; listed price is for TPB only 20.00

DARKCHYLDE LAST ISSUE SPECIAL
Darkchylde Entertainment: June, 2002 ($3.95)

1-Wraparound-c; cover gallery 4.00

DARKCHYLDE REDEMPTION
Darkchylde Entertainment: Feb, 2001 - No. 2, Dec, 2001 ($2.95)

1,2: 1-Wraparound-c 3.00
1-Dynamic Forces alternate-c 6.00
1-Dynamic Forces chrome-c 16.00

DARKCHYLDE SKETCH BOOK
Image Comics (Dynamic Forces): 1998

1-Regular-c 8.00
1-DarkChrome cover 16.00

DARKCHYLDE SUMMER SWIMSUIT SPECTACULAR
DC Comics (WildStorm): Aug, 1999 ($3.95, one-shot)

1-Pin-up art by various 4.00

DARKCHYLDE SWIMSUIT ILLUSTRATED
Image Comics: 1998 ($2.50, one-shot)

1-Pin-up art by various 2.50
1-(6.95) Variant cover 7.00
1-Chromium cover 15.00

DARKCHYLDE THE DIARY
Image Comics: June, 1997 ($2.50, one-shot)

1-Queen-c/s/ art by various 2.50
1-Variant-c 5.00
1-Holochrome variant-c 8.00

DARKCHYLDE THE LEGACY
Image Comics/DC (WildStorm) #3 on: Aug, 1998 - No. 3, June, 1999 ($2.50)

1-3: 1-Queen-c. 2-Two covers by Queen and Art Adams 2.50

DARK CLAW ADVENTURES
DC Comics (Amalgam): June, 1997 ($1.95, one-shot)

1-Templeton-c/s/a & Burchett-a 2.50

DARK CROSSINGS: DARK CLOUDS RISING
Image Comics (Top Cow): June, 2000; Oct, 2000 ($5.95, limited series)

1-Witchblade, Darkness, Tomb Raider crossover; Dwayne Turner-a 6.00
1-(Dark Clouds Overhead) 6.00

DARK CRYSTAL, THE (Movie)
Marvel Comics Group: April, 1983 - No. 2, May, 1983

1,2-Adaptation of film 3.00

DARK DAYS (See 30 Days of Night)
IDW Publishing: June, 2003 - No. 6, Dec, 2003 ($3.99, limited series)

1-6-Sequel to 30 Days of Night; Niles-s/Templesmith-a 4.00
1-Retailer variant (Diamond/Alliance Fort Wayne 5/03 summit) 15.00

DARKDEVIL (See Spider-Girl)
Marvel Comics: Nov, 2000 - No. 3, Jan, 2001 ($2.99, limited series)

1-3: 1-Origin of Darkdevil; Kingpin-c/app. 3.00

DARK DOMINION
Defiant: Oct, 1993 - No. 10, July, 1994 ($2.50)

1-10-Len Wein scripts begin. 4-Free extra 16 pgs. 7-9-J.G. Jones-c/a. 10-Pre-Schism issue; Shooter/Wein script; John Ridgway-a 2.50

DARKER IMAGE (Also see Deathblow, The Maxx, & Bloodwulf)
Image Comics: Mar, 1993 ($1.95, one-shot)

1-The Maxx by Sam Kieth begins; Bloodwulf by Rob Liefeld & Deathblow by Jim Lee begin (both 1st app.); polybagged w/1 of 3 cards by Kieth, Lee or Liefeld 2.50
1-B&W interior pgs. w/silver foil logo 6.00

DARKEWOOD
Aircel Publishing: 1987 - No. 5, 1988 ($2.00, 28pgs, limited series)

1-5 2.25

DARK FANTASIES
Dark Fantasy: 1994 - No. 8, 1995 ($2.95)

1-Test print Run (3,000)-Linsner-c 1 2 3 5 6 8
1-Linsner-c 5.00

Darkhawk #1 © MAR

Dark Horse Comics #22 © DH

Dark Horse Presents #89 © DH

GD VG FN VF VF/NM NM-
2.0 4.0 6.0 8.0 9.0 9.2

2-8: 2-4 (Deluxe), 2-4 (Regular), 5-8 (Deluxe; $3.95) 4.00
5-8 (Regular; $3.50) 3.50

DARK GUARD
Marvel Comics UK: Oct, 1993 - No. 4, Jan, 1994 ($1.75)

1-($2.95)-Foil stamped-c 3.00
2-4 2.25

DARKHAWK
Marvel Comics: Mar, 1991 - No. 50, Apr, 1995 ($1.00/$1.25/$1.50)

1-Origin/1st app. Darkhawk; Hobgoblin cameo 4.00
2,3,13,14: 2-Spider-Man & Hobgoblin app. 3-Spider-Man & Hobgoblin app. 13,14-Venom-c/story 3.00
4-12,15-24,26-49: 6-Capt. America & Daredevil x-over. 9-Punisher app. 11,12-Tombstone app. 19-Spider-Man & Brotherhood of Evil Mutants-c/story. 20-Spider-Man app. 22-Ghost Rider-c/story. 23-Origin begins, ends #25. 27-New Warriors-c/story. 35-Begin 3 part Venom story. 39-Bound-in trading card sheet 2.25
25,50: (52 pgs.)-Red holo-grafx foil-c w/double gatefold poster; origin of Darkhawk armor 3.00
Annual 1-3 ('92-'94,68 pgs.)-1-Vs. Iron Man. 2 -Polybagged w/card 3.00

DARKHOLD: PAGES FROM THE BOOK OF SINS (See Midnight Sons Unlimited)
Marvel Comics (Midnight Sons imprint #15 on): Oct, 1992 - No. 16, Jan, 1994

1-($2.75, 52 pgs.)-Polybagged w/poster by Andy & Adam Kubert; part 4 of Rise of the Midnight Sons storyline 3.00
2-10,12-16: 3-Reintro Modred the Mystic (see Marvel Chillers #1). 4-Sabertooth-c/sty. 5-Punisher & Ghost Rider app. 15-Spot varnish-c. 15,16-Siege of Darkness pt. 4&12 2.25
11-($2.25)-Outer-c is a Darkhold envelope made of black parchment w/gold ink 2.50

DARK HORSE BOOK OF HAUNTINGS, THE
Dark Horse Comics: Aug, 2003 ($14.95, hardcover, 9 1/4" x 6 1/4")

nn-Short stories by various incl. Mignola (Hellboy), Thompson, Dorkin, Russell; Gianni-c 15.00

DARK HORSE CLASSICS (Title series), **Dark Horse Comics**
1992 ($3.95, B&W, 52 pgs. nn's): The Last of the Mohicans. 20,000 Leagues Under the Sea 4.00

DARK HORSE CLASSICS, 5/96 ($2.95) 1-r/Predator: Jungle Tales 3.00
--ALIENS VERSUS PREDATOR, 2/97 - No. 6, 7/97 ($2.95,) 1-6: r/Aliens Versus Predator 3.00
--GODZILLA: KING OF THE MONSTERS, 4/98 ($2.95) 1-6: 1-r/Godzilla: Color Special; Art Adams-a 3.00
--STAR WARS: DARK EMPIRE, 3/97 - No. 6, 8/97 ($2.95) 1-6: r/Star Wars: Dark Empire 3.00
--TERROR OF GODZILLA, 8/98 - No. 6, 1/99 ($2.95) 1-6-r/manga Godzilla in color; Art Adams-c 3.00

DARK HORSE COMICS
Dark Horse Comics: Aug, 1992 - No. 25, Sept, 1994 ($2.50)

1-Dorman double gategold painted-c; Predator, Robocop, Timecop (3-part) & Renegade stories begin 3.00
2-6,11-25: 2-Mignola-c. 3-Begin 3-part Aliens story; Aliens-c. 4-Predator-c. 6-Begin 4 part Robocop story. 12-Begin 2-part Aliens & 3-part Predator stories. 13-Thing From Another World begins w/Nino-a(i). 15-Begin 2-part Aliens: Cargo story. 16-Begin 3-part Predator story. 17-Begin 3-part StarWars: Droids story & 3-part Aliens: Alien story; Droids-c. 19-Begin 2-part X story; X cover 2.50
7-Begin Star Wars: Tales of the Jedi 3-part story 1 2 3 4 5 7
8-1st app. X and begins; begin 4-part James Bond 6.00
9,10: 9-Star Wars ends. 10-X ends; Begin 3-part Predator & Godzilla stories 4.00
NOTE: *Art Adams c-11.*

DARK HORSE DOWN UNDER
Dark Horse Comics: June, 1994 - No. 3, Oct, 1994 ($2.50, B&W, limited series)

1-3 2.50

DARK HORSE MAVERICK
Dark Horse Comics: July, 2000; July, 2001; Sept, 2002 (B&W, annual)

2000-($3.95) Short stories by Miller, Chadwick, Sakai, Pearson 4.00
2001-($4.99) Short stories by Sakai, Wagner and others; Miller-c 5.00
...: Happy Endings (9/02, $9.95) Short stories by Bendis, Oeming, Mahfood, Mignola, Miller, Kieth and others; Miller-c 10.00

DARK HORSE MONSTERS
Dark Horse Comics: Feb, 1997 ($2.95, one-shot)

1-reprints 3.00

DARK HORSE PRESENTS
Dark Horse Comics: July, 1986 - No. 157, Sept, 2000 ($1.50-$2.95, B&W)

1-1st app. Concrete by Paul Chadwick 2 4 6 9 11 14
1-2nd printing (1988, $1.50) 2.25
1-Silver ink 3rd printing (1992, $2.25)-Says 2nd printing inside 2.25
2-9: 2-6,9-Concrete app. 6.00
10-1st app. The Mask; Concrete app. 2 4 6 10 12 15
11-19,21-23: 11-19,21-Mask stories. 12,14,16,18,22-Concrete app. 15(2/88). 17-All Roachmill issue 6.00
20-(68 pgs.)-Concrete, Flaming Carrot, Mask 1 3 4 6 8 10
24-Origin Aliens-c/story (11/88); Mr. Monster app. 2 4 6 11 14 18
25-31,33,37-41,44,45,47-49: 28-(52 pgs.)-Concrete app.; Mr. Monster story (homage to Graham Ingels). 33-(44 pgs.). 38-Concrete. 40-(52 pgs.)-1st Argosy story. 44-Crash Ryan. 48,49-Contain 2 trading cards 3.00
32,34,35: 32-(68 pgs.)-Annual; Concrete, American. 34-Aliens-c/story. 35-Predator-c/app. 4.00
36-1st Aliens Vs. Predator story; painted-c, 36-Variant line drawn-c 5.00
42,43,46: 42,43-Aliens-c/stories. 46-Prequel to new Predator II mini-series 3.00
50-S/F story by Perez; contains 2 trading cards 4.00
51-53-Sin City by Frank Miller, parts 2-4; 51,53-Miller-c (see D.H.P. Fifth Anniversary Special for pt. 1) 4.00
54-62: 54-(9/91) The Next Men begins (1st app.) by Byrne; Miller-a/Morrow-c. Homocide by Morrow (also in #55). 55-2nd app. The Next Men; parts 5 & 6 of Sin City by Miller; Miller-c. 56-(68 pg. annual)-part 7 of Sin City by Miller; part prologue to Aliens: Genocide; Next Men by Byrne. 57-(52 pgs.)-Part 8 of Sin City by Miller; Next Men by Byrne; Byrne & Miller-c; Alien Fire story; swipes cover to Daredevil #1. 58,59-Alien Fire stories.58-61- Part 9-12 Sin City by Miller. 62-Last Sin City (entire book by Miller, c/a; 52 pgs.) 5.00
63-66,68-79,81-84-($2.25): 64-Dr. Giggles begins (1st app.), ends #66; Boris the Bear story. 66-New Concrete-c/story by Chadwick. 71-Begin 3 part Dominque story by Jim Balent; Balent-c. 72-(3/93)-Begin 3-part Eudaemon (1st app.) story by Nelson 3.00
67-($3.95, 68 pgs.)-Begin 3-part prelude to Predator: Race War mini-series; Oscar Wilde adapt. by Russell 4.00
80-Art Adams-c/a (Monkeyman & O'Brien) 4.00
85-87,92-99: 85-Begin $2.50-c. 92, 93, 95-Too Much Coffee Man 3.00
88-91-Hellboy by Mignola. 4.00
NOTE: *There are 5 different Dark Horse Presents #100 issues*
100-1-Intro Lance Blastoff by Miller; Milk & Cheese by Evan Dorkin 4.00
100-2-100-5: 100-2-Hellboy-c by Wrightson; Hellboy story by Mignola; includes Roberta Gregory & Paul Pope stories. 100-3-Darrow-c, Concrete by Chadwick; Pekar story. 100-4-Gibbons-c: Miller story, Geary story/a. 100-5-Allred-c, Adams, Dorkin, Pope 3.00
101-125: 101-Aliens c/a by Wrightson, story by Paul Pope. 103-Kirby gatefold-c. 106-Big Blown Baby by Bill Wray. 107-Mignola-c/a. 109-Begin $2.95-c; Paul Pope-c. 110-Ed Brubaker-a/s. 114-Flip books begin; Lance Blastoff by Miller; Star Slammers by Simonson. 115-Miller-c. 117-Aliens-c/app. 118-Evan Dorkin-c/a. 119-Monkeyman & O'Brien. 124-Predator. 125-Nocturnals 3.00
126-($3.95, 48 pgs.)-Flip book: Nocturnals, Starship Troopers 4.00
127-134,136-140: 127-Nocturnals. 129-The Hammer. 132-134-Warren-a 3.00
135-($3.50) The Mark 3.50
141-All Buffy the Vampire Slayer issue 4.00
142-149: 142-Mignola-c. 143-Tarzan. 146,147-Aliens vs. Predator. 148-Xena 3.00
150-($4.50) Buffy-c by Green; Buffy, Concrete, Fish Police app. 4.50
151-157: 151-Hellboy-c/app. 153-155-Angel flip-c. 156,157-Witch's Son 3.00
Annual 1997 ($4.95, 64 pgs.)-Flip book; Body Bags, Aliens. Pearson-c; stories by Allred & Stephens, Pope, Smith & Morrow 1 2 3 5 6 8
Annual 1998 ($4.95, 64 pgs.) 1st Buffy the Vampire Slayer comic app.; Hellboy story and cover by Mignola 1 2 3 4 5 7
Annual 1999 (7/99, $4.95) Stories of Xena, Hellboy, Ghost, Luke Skywalker, Groo, Concrete, the Mask and Usagi Yojimbo in their youth. 5.00
Annual 2000 ($4.95) Girl sidekicks; Chiodo-c and flip photo Buffy-c 5.00
...Aliens Platinum Edition (1992)-r/DHP #24,43,43,56 & Special 11.00
...Fifth Anniversary Special nn (4/91, $9.95)-Part 1 of Sin City by Frank Miller (c/a); Aliens, Aliens vs. Predator, Concrete, Roachmill, Give Me Liberty & The American stories 10.00
The One Trick Rip-off (1997, $12.95, TPB)-r/stories from #101-112 13.00
NOTE: ***Geary** a-59, 60. **Miller** a-Special, 51-53, 55-62; c-59-62, 100-1; c-51, 53, 55, 59-62, 100-1. **Moebius** a-63; c-63, 70. **Vess** a-78; c-75, 78.*

DARK KNIGHT (See Batman: The Dark Knight Returns & Legends of the...)

DARK KNIGHT STRIKES AGAIN, THE (Also see Batman: The Dark Knight Returns)
DC Comics: 2001 - No. 3, 2002 ($7.95, prestige format, limited series)

1-Frank Miller-s/a/c; sequel 3 years after Dark Knight Returns; 2 covers 8.00
2,3 8.00
HC (2002, $29.95) intro. by Miller; sketch pages and exclusive artwork; cover has 3 1/4" tall partial dustjacket 30.00
SC (2002, $19.95) intro. by Miller; sketch pages 20.00

DARKLON THE MYSTIC (Also see Eerie Magazine #79,80)
Pacific Comics: Oct, 1983 (one-shot)

1-Starlin-c/a(r) 4.00

DARKMAN (Movie)
Marvel Comics: Sept, 1990; Oct, 1990 - No. 3, Dec, 1990 ($1.50)

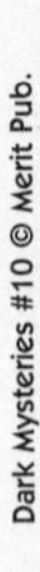
Dark Mysteries #10 © Merit Pub.

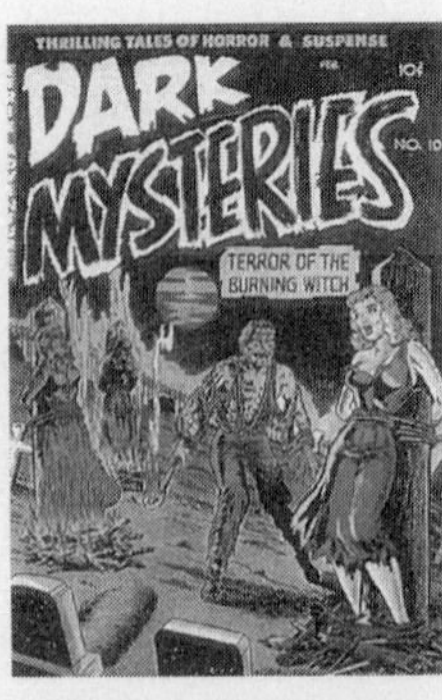

The Darkness V2#1 © TCOW

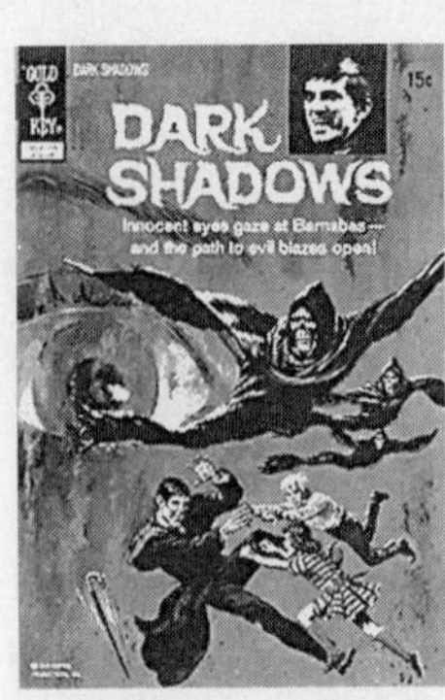

Dark Shadows #15 © Dan Curtis Prod.

GD VG FN VF VF/NM NM-
2.0 4.0 6.0 8.0 9.0 9.2

1 (9/90, $2.25, B&W mag., 68 pgs.)-Adaptation of film 3.00
1-3: Reprints B&W magazine 2.25

DARKMAN
Marvel Comics: V2#1, Apr, 1993 -No. 6, Sept, 1993 ($2.95, limited series)

V2#1 ($3.95, 52 pgs.) 4.00
2-6 3.00

DARK MANSION OF FORBIDDEN LOVE, THE (Becomes Forbidden Tales of Dark Mansion No. 5 on)
National Periodical Publ.: Sept-Oct, 1971 - No. 4, Mar-Apr, 1972 (52 pgs.)

1 16 32 48 116 171 225
2-4: 2-Adams-c. 3-Jeff Jones-c 7 14 21 51 71 90

DARKMINDS
Image Comics (Dreamwave Prod.): July, 1998 - No. 8, Apr, 1999 ($2.50)

1-Manga; Pat Lee-s/a; 2 covers 1 3 4 6 8 10
1-2nd printing 2.50
2, 0-(1/99, $5.00) Story and sketch pages 5.00
3-8, 1/2-(5/99, $2.50) Story and sketch pages 2.50
... Collected 1,2 (1/99,3/99; $7.95) 1-r/#1-3. 2-r/#4-6 8.00
... Collected 3 (5/99; $5.95) r/#7,8 6.00

DARKMINDS (Volume 2)
Image Comics (Dreamwave Prod.): Feb, 2000 - No. 10, Apr, 2001 ($2.50)

1-10-Pat Lee-c 2.50
0-(7/00) Origin of Mai Murasaki; sketchbook 2.50

DARKMINDS: MACROPOLIS
Image Comics (Dreamwave Prod.): Jan, 2002 - No. 4, Dec, 2002 ($2.95)

Preview (8/01) Flip book w/Banished Knights preview 2.25
1-4-Jo Chen-a 3.00

DARKMINDS: MACROPOLIS (Volume 2)
Dreamwave Prod.: Sept, 2003 - Present ($2.95)

1-3-Chris Sarracini-s/Kwang Mook Lim-a 3.00

DARKMINDS / WITCHBLADE
Image Comics (Top Cow/Dreamwave Prod.): Aug, 2000 ($5.95, one-shot)

1-Wohl-s/Pat Lee-a; two covers by Silvestri and Lee 6.00

DARK MYSTERIES (Thrilling Tales of Horror & Suspense)
"Master" - "Merit" Publications: June-July, 1951 - No. 24, July, 1955

1-Wood-c/a (8 pgs.) 110 220 330 688 1032 1375
2-Wood/Harrison-c/a (8 pgs.) 76 152 228 475 713 950
3-9: 7-Dismemberment, hypo blood drainage stys 42 84 126 252 376 500
10-Cannibalism story; witch burning-c 46 92 138 276 413 550
11-13,15-18: 11-Severed head panels. 13-Dismemberment-c/story. 17-The Old Gravedigger host 38 76 114 219 310 400
14-Several E.C. Craig swipes 39 78 117 224 317 410
19-Injury-to-eye panel; E.C. swipe; torture-c 44 88 132 264 395 525
20-Female bondage, blood drainage story 40 80 120 240 353 465
21,22: 21-Devil-c. 22-Last pre-code issue, misdated 3/54 instead of 3/55 27 54 81 153 214 275
23,24 21 42 63 118 164 210

NOTE: ***Cameron*** *a-1, 2.* ***Myron Fass*** *c/a-21.* ***Harrison*** *a-3, 7; c-3.* ***Hollingsworth*** *a-7-17, 20, 21, 23.* ***Wildey*** *a-5. Woodish art by* ***Fleishman****-9; c-10, 14-17. Bondage c-10, 18, 19.*

DARK NEMESIS (VILLAINS) (See Teen Titans)
DC Comics: Feb, 1998 ($1.95, one-shot)

1-Jurgens-s/Pearson-c 2.25

DARKNESS, THE (See Witchblade #10)
Image Comics (Top Cow Productions): Dec, 1996 - No. 40, Aug, 2001 ($2.50)

Special Preview Edition-(7/96, B&W)-Ennis script; Silvestri-a(p) 2 4 6 10 13 16
0 2 4 6 8 10 12
0-Gold Edition 16.00
1/2 1 3 4 6 8 10
1/2-Christmas-c 3 6 9 16 20 24
1/2-(3/01, $2.95) r/#1/2 w/new 6 pg. story & Silvestri-c 3.00
1-Ennis-s/Silvestri-a, 1-Black variant-c 2 4 6 10 12 15
1-Platinum variant-c 20.00
1-DF Green variant-c 12.00
1,2: 1-Fan Club Ed. 1 3 4 6 8 10
3-5 6.00
6-10: 9,10-Witchblade "Family Ties" x-over pt. 2,3 4.00
7-Variant-c w/concubine 1 2 3 5 7 9
8-American Entertainment 6.00
8-10-American Entertainment Gold Ed. 7.00
11-Regular Ed.; Ennis-s/Silverstri & D-Tron-c 3.00
11-Nine (non-chromium) variant-c (Benitez, Cabrera, the Hildebrandts, Finch, Keown, Peterson, Portacio, Tan, Turner 4.50
11-Chromium-c by Silvestri & Batt 20.00
12-19: 13-Begin Benitez-a(p) 3.00
20-24,26-40: 34-Ripclaw app. 2.50
25-($3.99) Two covers (Benitez, Silvestri) 4.00
25-Chromium-c variant by Silvestri 8.00
Holiday Pin-up-American Entertainment 5.00
Holiday Pin-up Gold Ed.-American Entertainment 7.00
Infinity #1 (8/99, $3.50) Lobdell-s 3.50
Prelude-American Entertainment 4.00
Prelude Gold Ed.-American Entertainment 9.00
Wizard ACE Ed.- Reprints #1 2 4 6 8 10 12
...Collected Editions #1-4 ($4.95,TPB) 1-r/#1,2. 2-r/#3,4. 3- r/#5,6. 4- r/#7,8 6.00
...Collected Editions #5,6 ($5.95, TPB)5- r/#11,12. 6-r/#13,14 6.00
Deluxe Collected Editions #1 (12/98, $14.95, TPB) r/#1-6 & Preview 15.00
...: Heart of Darkness (2001, $14.95, TPB) r/ #7,8, 11-14 15.00
...: Wanted Dead 1 (8/03, $2.99) Texiera-a/Tieri-s 3.00

DARKNESS (Volume 2)
Image Comics (Top Cow Productions): Dec, 2002 - Present ($2.99)

1-6-Jenkins-s/Keown-a 3.00

DARKNESS/ BATMAN
Image Comics (Top Cow Productions): Aug, 1999 ($5.95, one-shot)

1-Silvestri, Finch, Lansing-a(p) 6.00

DARKNESS FALLS, THE TRAGIC LIFE OF MATILDA DIXON
Dark Horse Comics: 2003 ($2.99, one-shot)

1-Based on the 2003 movie "Darkness Falls"; Adlard-a 3.00

DARK ONE'S THIRD EYE
Sirius Entertainment: 1996; Dec, 1998 ($4.95, B&W)

nn-Dark One-a; squarebound; pinups, Vol. 2-(12/98) 5.00

DARK OZ
Arrow Comics: 1997 - No. 5 ($2.75, B&W, limited series)

1-5-Bill Bryan-a 2.75

DARK REALM
Image Comics: Oct, 2000 - No. 4, June, 2001 ($2.95, limited series)

1-4-Taeson Chang-a. 3-Flip book w/Mech Destroyer prequel 3.00

DARKSEID (VILLAINS) (See Jack Kirby's New Gods and New Gods)
DC Comics: Feb, 1998 ($1.95, one-shot)

1-Byrne-s/Pearson-c 2.25

DARKSEID VS. GALACTUS: THE HUNGER
DC Comics: 1995 ($4.95, one-shot) (1st DC/Marvel x-over by John Byrne)

nn-John Byrne-c/a/script 5.00

DARK SHADOWS
Steinway Comic Publ. (Ajax)(America's Best): Oct, 1957 - No. 3, May, 1958

1 24 48 72 138 194 250
2,3 19 38 57 106 146 185

DARK SHADOWS (TV) (See Dan Curtis Giveaways)
Gold Key: Mar, 1969 - No. 35, Feb, 1976 (Photo-c: 1-7)

1(30039-903)-With pull-out poster (25¢) 28 56 84 203 297 390
1-With poster missing 10 20 30 73 107 140
2 9 18 27 63 89 115
3-With pull-out poster 14 28 42 102 149 195
3-With poster missing 7 14 21 51 71 90
4-7: 7-Last photo-c 8 16 24 55 78 100
8-10 6 12 18 43 59 75
11-20 6 12 18 38 52 65
21-35: 30-Last painted-c 5 10 15 33 44 55
Story Digest 1 (6/70, 148pp.)-Photo-c (low print) 9 18 27 65 93 120

DARK SHADOWS (TV) (See Nightmare on Elm Street)
Innovation Publishing: June, 1992 - No. 4, Spring, 1993 ($2.50, limited series, coated stock)

1-Based on 1991 NBC TV mini-series; painted-c 5.00
2-4 4.00

DARK SHADOWS: BOOK TWO
Innovation Publishing: 1993 - No. 4, July, 1993 ($2.50, limited series)

Darkstars #12 © DC

Davy Crockett #3 © CC

Dawn: Three Tiers #1 © J.M. Linsner

	GD 2.0	VG 4.0	FN 6.0	VF 8.0	VF/NM 9.0	NM- 9.2

1-4-Painted-c. 4-Maggie Thompson scripts 4.00

DARK SHADOWS: BOOK THREE
Innovation Publishing: Nov, 1993 ($2.50)
1-(Whole #9) 4.00

DARKSIDE
Maximum Press: Oct, 1996 ($2.99, one-shot)
1-Avengelyne-c/app. 3.00

DARKSTARS, THE
DC Comics: Oct, 1992 - No. 38, Jan, 1996 ($1.75/$1.95)
1-1st app. The Darkstars 3.00
2-24,0,25-38: 5-Hawkman & Hawkwoman app. 18-20-Flash app. 24-(9/94)-Zero Hour. 0-(10/94). 25-(11/94). 30-Green Lantern app. 31-...vs. Darkseid. 32-Green Lantern app. 2.50
NOTE: *Travis Charest a(p)-4-7; c(p)-2-5; c-6-11. Stroman a-1-3; c-1.*

DARK TOWN
Mad Monkey Press: 1995 ($3.95, magazine-size, quarterly)
1-Kaja Blackley scripts; Vanessa Chong-a 4.00

DARKWING DUCK (TV cartoon) (Also see Cartoon Tales)
Disney Comics: Nov, 1991 - No. 4, Feb, 1992 ($1.50, limited series)
1-4: Adapts hour-long premiere TV episode 3.00

DARLING LOVE
Close Up/Archie Publ. (A Darling Magazine): Oct-Nov, 1949 - No. 11, 1952 (no month) (52 pgs.)(Most photo-c)

	GD	VG	FN	VF	VF/NM	NM-
1-Photo-c	18	36	54	101	138	175
2-Photo-c	11	22	33	63	84	105
3-8,10,11: 3-6-photo-c	9	18	27	52	66	80
9-Krigstein-a	10	20	30	56	73	90

DARLING ROMANCE
Close Up (MLJ Publications): Sept-Oct, 1949 - No. 7, 1951 (All photo-c)

	GD	VG	FN	VF	VF/NM	NM-
1-(52 pgs.)-Photo-c	24	48	72	135	190	245
2	11	22	33	63	84	105
3-7	10	20	30	56	73	90

DARQUE PASSAGES (See Master Darque)
Acclaim (Valiant): April, 1998 ($2.50)
1-Christina Z.-s/Manco-c/a 2.50

DART (Also see Freak Force & Savage Dragon)
Image Comics (Highbrow Entertainment): Feb, 1996 - No. 3, May, 1996 ($2.50, lim. series)
1-3 3.00

DASTARDLY & MUTTLEY (See Fun-In No. 1-4, 6 and Kite Fun Book)

DATE WITH DANGER
Standard Comics: No. 5, Dec, 1952 - No. 6, Feb, 1953

	GD	VG	FN	VF	VF/NM	NM-
5,6-Secret agent stories: 6-Atom bomb story	9	18	27	52	66	80

DATE WITH DEBBI (Also see Debbi's Dates)
National Periodical Publ.: Jan-Feb, 1969 - No. 17, Sept-Oct, 1971; No. 18, Oct-Nov, 1972

	GD	VG	FN	VF	VF/NM	NM-
1-Teenage	5	10	15	36	48	60
2-5,17-(52 pgs) James Taylor sty.	3	6	9	18	24	30
6-12,18-Last issue	3	6	9	18	23	28
13-16-(68 pgs.): 14-1 pg. story on Jack Wild. 15-Marlo Thomas/"That Girl" story	3	7	10	21	28	35

DATE WITH JUDY, A (Radio/TV, and 1948 movie)
National Periodical Publications: Oct-Nov, 1947 - No. 79, Oct-Nov, 1960 (No. 1-25: 52 pgs.)

	GD	VG	FN	VF	VF/NM	NM-
1-Teenage	30	60	90	170	240	310
2	14	28	42	81	111	140
3-10	11	22	33	63	84	105
11-20	8	16	24	46	58	70
21-40	8	16	24	40	50	60
41-45: 45-Last pre-code (2-3/55)	7	14	21	35	43	50
46-79: 79-Drucker-c/a	6	12	18	31	38	45

DATE WITH MILLIE, A (Life With Millie No. 8 on)(Teenage)
Atlas/Marvel Comics (MPC): Oct, 1956 - No. 7, Aug, 1957; Oct, 1959 - No. 7, Oct, 1960

	GD	VG	FN	VF	VF/NM	NM-
1(10/56)-(1st Series)-Dan DeCarlo-a in #1-7	27	54	81	155	218	280
2	14	28	42	81	111	140
3-7	10	20	30	58	77	95
1(10/59)-(2nd Series)	14	28	42	81	111	140
2-7	10	20	30	56	73	90

DATE WITH PATSY, A (Also see Patsy Walker)
Atlas Comics: Sept, 1957 (One-shot)

	GD	VG	FN	VF	VF/NM	NM-
1-Starring Patsy Walker	11	22	33	66	88	110

DAVID AND GOLIATH (Movie)
Dell Publishing Co.: No. 1205, July, 1961

	GD	VG	FN	VF	VF/NM	NM-
Four Color 1205-Photo-c	7	14	21	51	71	90

DAVID AND GOLIATH
Image Comics: Sept, 2003 - Present ($2.95)
1,2-Jay Ju-s/Leonel Castellani-a 3.00

DAVID BORING (See Eightball)
Pantheon Books: 2000 ($24.95, hardcover w/dust jacket)
Hardcover - reprints David Boring stories from Eightball; Clowes-s/a 25.00

DAVID CASSIDY (TV)(See Partridge Family, Swing With Scooter #33 & Time For Love #30)
Charlton Comics: Feb, 1972 - No. 14, Sept, 1973

	GD	VG	FN	VF	VF/NM	NM-
1-Most have photo covers	6	12	18	43	59	75
2-5	4	8	12	27	36	45
6-14	4	8	12	24	32	40

DAVID LADD'S LIFE STORY (See Movie Classics)

DAVY CROCKETT (See Dell Giants, Fightin..., Frontier Fighters, It's Game Time, Power Record Comics, Western Tales & Wild Frontier)

DAVY CROCKETT (Frontier Fighter...)
Avon Periodicals: 1951

	GD	VG	FN	VF	VF/NM	NM-
nn-Tuska?, Reinman-a; Fawcette-c	19	38	57	106	146	185

DAVY CROCKETT (...King of the Wild Frontier No. 1,2)(TV)
Dell Publishing Co./Gold Key: 5/55 - No. 671, 12/55; No. 1, 12/63; No. 2, 11/69 (Walt Disney)

	GD	VG	FN	VF	VF/NM	NM-
Four Color 631(#1)-Fess Parker photo-c	21	42	63	147	216	285
Four Color 639-Photo-c	17	34	51	118	174	230
Four Color 664,671(Marsh-a)-Photo-c	16	32	48	113	167	220
1(12/63-Gold Key)-Fess Parker photo-c; reprints	16	32	48	113	167	220
2(11/69)-Fess Parker photo-c; reprints	6	12	18	38	52	65

DAVY CROCKETT (...Frontier Fighter #1,2; Kid Montana #9 on)
Charlton Comics: Aug, 1955 - No. 8, Jan, 1957

	GD	VG	FN	VF	VF/NM	NM-
1	10	20	30	56	73	90
2	7	14	21	35	43	50
3-8	5	10	15	24	30	35

DAWN
Sirius Entertainment/Image Comics: June, 1995 - No. 6, 1996 ($2.95)

	GD	VG	FN	VF	VF/NM	NM-
1/2-w/certificate	1	2	3	5	6	8
1/2-Variant-c	2	4	6	11	14	18
1-Linsner-c/a	1	2	3	5	6	8
1-Black Light Edition	2	4	6	10	13	16
1-White Trash Edition	3	6	9	18	24	30
1-Look Sharp Edition	4	8	12	22	30	38
2-4: Linsner-c/a						4.50
2-Variant-c, 3-Limited Edition	2	4	6	14	18	22
4-6-Vibrato-c						3.50
4, 5-Limited Edition	2	4	6	8	10	12
6-Limited Edition	2	4	6	8	10	12

...Convention Sketchbook (Image Comics, 2002, $2.95) pin-ups 3.00
...2003 Convention Sketchbook (Image Comics, 3/03, $2.95) pin-ups 3.00
Genesis Edition ('99, Wizard supplement) previews Return of the Goddess 2.25
Lucifer's Halo TPB (11/97, $19.95) r/Drama, Dawn #1-6 plus 12 pages of new artwork 20.00
...: Tenth Anniversary Special(9/99, $2.95) Interviews 3.00
The Portable Dawn ($9.95, 5"x4", 64 pgs.) Pocket-sized cover gallery 10.00

DAWN: THE RETURN OF THE GODDESS
Sirius Entertainment: Apr, 1999 - No. 4, July, 2000 ($2.95, limited series)
1-4-Linsner-s/a 3.00
TPB (4/02, $12.95) r/#1-4; intro. by Linsner 13.00

DAWN: THREE TIERS
Image Comics: Jun, 2003 - No. 6 ($2.95, limited series)
1,2-Linsner-s/a. 2-Preview of Vampire's Christmas 3.00

DAYDREAMERS (See Generation X)
Marvel Comics: Aug, 1997 - No. 3, Oct, 1997 ($2.50, limited series)
1-3-Franklin Richards, Howard the Duck, Man-Thing app. 2.50

DAY OF JUDGMENT
DC Comics: Nov, 1999 - No. 5, Nov, 1999 ($2.95/$2.50, limited series)

The Dazzler #26 © MAR

DC Comics Presents #32 © DC

DC 100 Page Super Spectacular #22 © DC

GD VG FN VF VF/NM NM-
2.0 4.0 6.0 8.0 9.0 9.2

1-($2.95) Spectre possessed; Matt Smith-a 3.00
2-5: Parallax returns. 5-Hal Jordan becomes the Spectre 3.00
...Secret Files 1 (11/99, $4.95) Harris-c 5.00

DAYS OF THE DEFENDERS (See Defenders, The)
Marvel Comics: Mar, 2001 ($3.50, one-shot)

1-Reprints early team-ups of members, incl. Marvel Feature #1; Larsen-c 3.50

DAYS OF THE MOB (See In the Days of the Mob)

DAZEY'S DIARY
Dell Publishing Co.: June-Aug, 1962

01-174-208: Bill Woggon-c/a 4 8 12 29 40 50

DAZZLER, THE (Also see Marvel Graphic Novel & X-Men #130)
Marvel Comics Group: Mar, 1981 - No. 42, Mar, 1986

1,22,24,27,28,38,42: 1-X-Men app. 22 (12/82)-vs. Rogue Battle-c/sty. 24-Full app. Rogue w/Powerman (Iron Fist). 27-Rogue app. 28-Full app. Rogue; Mystique app. 38-Wolverine-c/app.; X-Men app. 42-Beast-c/app. 4.00
2-21,23,25,26,29-37,39-41: 2-X-Men app. 10,11-Galactus app. 21-Double size; photo-c. 23-Rogue/Mystique 1 pg. app. 26-Jusko-c. 33-Michael Jackson thriller swipe-c/sty. 40-Secret Wars II 3.00

NOTE: *No. 1 distributed only through comic shops.* **Alcala** *a-1i, 2i.* **Chadwick** *a-38-42p; c(p)-39, 41, 42.* **Guice** *a-38i, 42i; c-38, 40.*

DC CHALLENGE (Most DC superheroes appear)
DC Comics: Nov, 1985 - No. 12, Oct, 1986 ($1.25/$2.00, maxi-series)

1-11: 1-Colan-a. 2,8-Batman-c/app. 4-Gil Kane-c/a 2.50
12-($2.00-c) Giant; low print 3.00

NOTE: *Batman app. in 1-4, 6-12. Joker app. in 7.* **nfantino** *a-3.* **Ordway** *c-12.* **Swan/Austin** *c-10.*

DC COMICS PRESENTS
DC Comics: July-Aug, 1978 - No. 97, Sept, 1986 (Superman team-ups in all)

1-4th Superman/Flash race 2 4 6 12 16 20
1-(Whitman variant) 2 4 6 14 18 22
2-Part 2 of Superman/Flash race 2 4 6 9 11 14
2-4,10-12,14,15,19,21,22-(Whitman variants, low print run, none have issue # on cover) 2 4 6 9 11 14
3-10: 4-Metal Men. 6-Green Lantern. 8-Swamp Thing. 9-Wonder Woman 1 2 3 4 5 7
11-25,27-40: 13-Legion of Super-Heroes. 19-Batgirl. 31-Robin. 35-Man-Bat 6.00
26-(10/80)-Green Lantern; intro Cyborg, Starfire, Raven (1st app. New Teen Titans in 16 pg. preview); Starlin-c/a; Sargon the Sorcerer back-up 3 6 9 16 20 25
41,72,77,78,97: 41-Superman/Joker-c/story. 72-Joker/Phantom Stranger-c/story. 77,78-Animal Man app. (77-c also). 97-Phantom Zone 5.00
42-46,48-50,52-71,73-76,79-83: 42-Sandman. 43,80-Legion of Super-Heroes. 52-Doom Patrol. 58-Robin. 82-Adam Strange. 83-Batman & Outsiders 4.00
47-He-Man-c/s (1st app. in comics) 2 4 6 9 11 14
51,84,85: 51-Preview insert (16 pgs.) of He-Man (2nd app.). 84-Challengers of the Unknown; Kirby-c/s. 85-Swamp Thing; Alan Moore scripts 6.00
86-96: 86-88-Crisis x-over. 88-Creeper 4.00
Annual 1,4: 1(9/82)-G.A. Superman. 4(10/85)-Superwoman 4.00
Annual 2,3: 2(7/83)-Intro/origin Superwoman. 3(9/84)-Shazam 4.00

NOTE: **Adkins** *a-2, 54; c-2.* **Buckler** *a-33, 34; c-30, 33, 34.* **Giffen** *a-39; c-59.* **Gil Kane** *a-28, 35, Annual 3; c-48p, 56, 58, 60, 62, 64, 68, Annual 2, 3.* **Kirby** *c/a-84.* **Kubert** *c/a-66.* **Morrow** *c/a-65.* **Newton** *c/a-54p.* **Orlando** *c-53i.* **Perez** *a-26p, 61p; c-38, 61, 94.* **Starlin** *a-26-29p, 36p, 37p; c-26-29, 36, 37, 93.* **Toth** *a-84.* **Williamson** *i-79, 85, 87.*

DC FIRST: ...(series of one-shots)
DC Comics: July, 2002 ($3.50)

Batgirl/Joker 1-Sienkiewicz & Terry Moore-a; Nowlan-c 3.50
Green Lantern/Green Lantern 1-Alan Scott & Hal Jordan vs. Krona 3.50
Flash/Superman 1-Superman races Jay Garrick; Abra Kadabra app. 3.50
Superman/Lobo 1-Giffen-s; Nowlan-c 3.50

DC GRAPHIC NOVEL (Also see DC Science Fiction...)
DC Comics: Nov, 1983 - No. 7, 1986 ($5.95, 68 pgs.)

1-3,5,7: 1-Star Raiders. 2-Warlords; not from regular Warlord series. 3-The Medusa Chain; Ernie Colon story/a. 5-Me and Joe Priest; Chaykin-c. 7-Space Clusters; Nino-c/a 2 4 6 10 12 15
4-The Hunger Dogs by Kirby; Darkseid kills Himon from Mister Miracle & destroys New Genesis 4 8 12 27 36 45
6-Metalzoic; Sienkiewicz-c ($6.95) 2 4 6 10 12 15

DC/MARVEL: ALL ACCESS (Also see DC Versus Marvel & Marvel Versus DC)
DC Comics: 1996 - No. 4, 1997 ($2.95, limited series)

1-4: 1-Superman & Spider-Man app. 2-Robin & Jubilee app. 3-Dr. Strange & Batman-c/app., X-Men, JLA app. 4-X-Men vs. JLA-c/app. rebirth of Amalgam 3.00

DC/MARVEL: CROSSOVER CLASSICS

GD VG FN VF VF/NM NM-
2.0 4.0 6.0 8.0 9.0 9.2

DC Comics: 1998; 2003 ($14.95, TPB)

Vol. II-Reprints Batman/Punisher: Lake of Fire, Punisher/Batman: Deadly Knights, Silver Surfer/Superman, Batman & Capt. America 15.00
Vol. 4 (2003, $14.95) Reprints Green Lantern/Silver Surfer: Unholy Alliances, Darkseid/ Galactus: The Hunger, Batman & Spider-Man, and Superman/Fantastic Four 15.00

DC 100 PAGE SUPER SPECTACULAR
(Title is 100 Page... No. 14 on)(Square bound) (Reprints, 50¢)
National Periodical Publications: No. 4, Summer, 1971 - No. 13, 6/72; No. 14, 2/73 - No. 22, 11/73 (No #1-3)

4-Weird Mystery Tales; Johnny Peril & Phantom Stranger; cover & splashes by Wrightson; origin Jungle Boy of Jupiter 17 34 51 123 182 240
5-Love Stories; Wood inks (7 pgs.)(scarcer) 44 88 132 352 526 700
6- "World's Greatest Super-Heroes"; JLA, JSA, Spectre, Johnny Quick, Vigilante & Hawkman; contains unpublished Wildcat story; N. Adams wrap-around-c; r/JLA #21,22 17 34 51 123 182 240
7-(Also listed as Superman #245) Air Wave, Kid Eternity, Hawkman-r; Atom-r/Atom #3 8 16 24 58 82 105
8-(Also listed as Batman #238) Batman, Legion, Aquaman-r; G.A. Atom, Sargon (r/Sensation #57), Plastic Man (r/Police #14) stories; Doom Patrol origin-r; Neal Adams wraparound-c 10 20 30 73 107 140
9-(Also listed as Our Army at War #242) Kubert-c 9 18 27 60 85 110
10-(Also listed as Adventure Comics #416) Golden Age-reprints; r/1st app. Black Canary from Flash #86; no Zatanna 10 20 30 72 104 135
11-(Also listed as Flash #214) origin Metal Men-r/Showcase #37; never before published G.A. Flash story. 8 16 24 53 74 95
12,14: 12-(Also listed as Superboy #185) Legion-c/story; Teen Titans, Kid Eternity (r/Hit #46), Star Spangled Kid-r(S.S. #55). 14-Batman-r/Detective #31,32,156; Atom-r/Showcase #34 7 14 21 50 68 85
13-(Also listed as Superman #252) Ray(r/Smash #17), Black Condor, (r/Crack #18), Hawkman(r/Flash #24); Starman-r/Adv. #67; Dr. Fate & Spectre-r/More Fun #57; Neal Adams-c 9 18 27 60 85 110
15,16,18,19,21,22: 15-r/2nd Boy Commandos/Det. #64. 21-Superboy; r/Brave & the Bold #54. 22-r/All-Flash #13. 5 10 15 33 44 55
17,20: 17-JSA-r/All Star #37 (10-11/47, 38 pgs.), Sandman-r/Adv. #65 (8/41), JLA #23 (11/63) & JLA #43 (3/66). 20-Batman-r/Det. #66,68, Spectre; origin Two-Face 5 10 15 36 48 60
... : Love Stories Replica Edition (2000, $6.95) reprints #5 7.00

NOTE: **Anderson** *r-11, 14, 18i, 22.* **B. Baily** *r-18, 20.* **Burnley** *r-18, 20.* **Crandall** *r-14p, 20.* **Drucker** *r-4.* **Grandenetti** *a-22(2)r.* **Heath** *a-22r.* **Infantino** *r-17, 20, 22.* **G. Kane** *r-18.* **Kirby** *r-15.* **Kubert** *r-6, 7, 16, 17; c-16, 19.* **Manning** *a-19r.* **Meskin** *r-4, 22.* **Mooney** *r-15, 21.* **Toth** *r-17, 20.*

DC ONE MILLION (Also see crossover #1,000,000 issues)
DC Comics: Nov, 1998 - No. 4, Nov, 1998 ($2.95/$1.99, weekly lim. series)

1-($2.95) JLA travels to the 853rd century; Morrison-s 3.00
2-4-($1.99) 2.25
... Eighty-Page Giant (8/99, $4.95) 5.00
TPB ('99, $14.95) r/#1-4 and several x-over stories 15.00

DC SCIENCE FICTION GRAPHIC NOVEL
DC Comics: 1985 - No. 7, 1987 ($5.95)

SF1-SF7: SF1-Hell on Earth by Robert Bloch; Giffen-p. SF2-Nightwings by Robert Silverberg; G. Colan-p. SF3-Frost & Fire by Bradbury. SF4-Merchants of Venus. SF5-Demon With A Glass Hand by Ellison; M. Rogers-a. SF6-The Magic Goes Away by Niven. SF7-Sandkings by George R.R. Martin 2 4 6 9 11 14

DC SILVER AGE CLASSICS
DC Comics: 1992 ($1.00, all reprints)

...Action Comics #252-r/1st Supergirl. Adventure Comics #247-r/1st Legion of Super-Heroes. The Brave and the Bold #28-r/1st JLA. Detective Comics #225-r/1st Martian Manhunter. Detective Comics #327-r/1st new look Batman. Green Lantern #76-r/1st Green Lantern/ Green Arrow. House of Secrets #92-r/1st Swamp Thing. Showcase #4-r/1st S.A. Flash. Showcase #22-r/1st S.A. Green Lantern 2.50
...Sugar and Spike #99; includes 2 unpublished stories 4.00

DC SPECIAL (Also see Super DC Giant)
National Per. Publ.: 10-12/68 - No. 15, 11-12/71; No. 16, Spr/75 - No. 29, 8-9/77

1-All Infantino issue; Flash, Batman, Adam Strange-r; begin 68 pg. issues, end #21 7 14 21 51 71 90
2-Teen humor; Binky, Buzzy, Harvey app. 10 20 30 67 96 125
3-All-Girl issue; unpubl. GA Wonder Woman story 8 16 24 55 78 100
4-15: 4-Horror (1st Abel cameo). 5-All Kubert issue; Viking Prince, Sgt. Rock-r. 6-Western. 7,9,13-Strangest Sports. 11-Monsters. 12-Viking Prince; Kubert-c/a (r/B&B almost entirely). 15-G.A. Plastic Man origin-r/Police #1; origin Woozy by Cole; 14,15-(52 pgs.) 4 8 12 27 36 45
16-27: 16-Super Heroes Battle Super Gorillas; r/Capt. Storm #1, 1st Johnny Cloud/All-Amer.

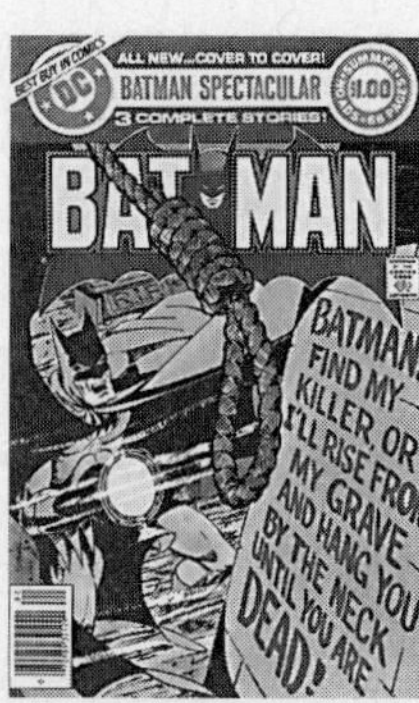

DC Special Series #15 © DC

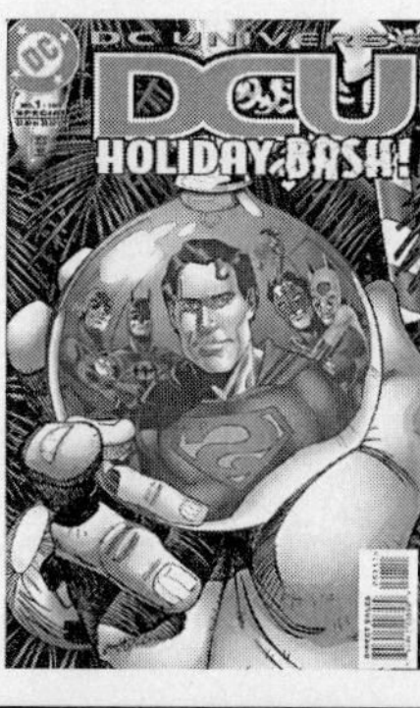

DCU Holiday Bash #1 © DC

Dead Corpse #2 © Hinz & Pugh

	GD 2.0	VG 4.0	FN 6.0	VF 8.0	VF/NM 9.0	NM- 9.2

Men of War #82. 17-Early S.A. Green Lantern-r. 22-Origin Robin Hood. 26-Enemy Ace on-c only. 27-Captain Comet story 2 4 6 14 18 22
28,29: 28-Earth Shattering Disaster Stories; Legion of Super-Heroes story. 29-New "The Untold Origin of the Justice Society"; Staton-a 3 6 9 17 21 26

NOTE: ***N. Adams** c-3, 4, 6, 11, 29. **Grell** a-20; c-17, 20. **Heath** a-12r. **G. Kane** a-6p, 13r, 17r, 19-21r. **Kirby** a-4,11. **Kubert** a-6r, 12r, 22. **Meskin** a-10. **Moreira** a-10. **Staton** a-29p. **Toth** a-13, 20r. #1-15: 25¢; 16-27: 50¢; 28, 29: 60¢. #1-13, 16-21: 68 pgs.; 14, 15: 52 pgs.; 25-27: oversized.*

DC SPECIAL BLUE RIBBON DIGEST
DC Comics: Mar-Apr, 1980 - No. 24, Aug, 1982

1,2,4,5: 1-Legion reprints. 2-Flash. 4-Green Lantern. 5-Secret Origins; new Zatara and Zatanna 2 4 6 8 10 12
3-Justice Society 2 4 6 10 13 16
6,8-10: 6-Ghosts. 8-Legion. 9-Secret Origins. 10-Warlord-"The Deimos Saga"-Grell-s/c/a 2 4 6 8 10 12
7-Sgt. Rock's Prize Battle Tales 2 4 6 12 16 20
11,16: 11-Justice League. 16-Green Lantern/Green Arrow-r; all Adams-a 2 4 6 11 14 18
12-Haunted Tank; reprints 1st app. 2 4 6 12 16 20
13-15,17-19: 13-Strange Sports Stories. 14-UFO Invaders; Adam Strange app. 15-Secret Origins of Super Villains; JLA app. 17-Ghosts. 18-Sgt. Rock; Kubert front & back-c. 19-Doom Patrol; new Perez-c 2 4 6 10 12 15
20-Dark Mansion of Forbidden Love (scarce) 4 8 12 29 40 50
21-Our Army at War 3 6 9 16 20 25
22-24: 22-Secret Origins. 23-Green Arrow, w/new 7 pg. story. 24-House of Mystery; new Kubert wraparound-c 2 4 6 12 16 20

NOTE: ***N. Adams** a-16(6)r, 17r, 23r; c-16. **Aparo** a-6r, 24r; c-23. **Grell** a-8, 10; c-10. **Heath** a-14. **Infantino** a-15r. **Kaluta** a-17r. **Gil Kane** a-15r, 22r. **Kirby** a-5, 9, 23r. **Kubert** a-3, 18r, 21r; c-7, 12, 14, 17, 18, 21, 24. **Morrow** a-24r. **Orlando** a-17r, 22r; c-1, 20. **Toth** a-21r, 24r. **Wood** a-3, 17r, 24r. **Wrightson** a-16r, 17r, 24r.*

DC SPECIAL SERIES
National Periodical Publications/DC Comics: 9/77 - No. 16, Fall, 1978; No. 17, 8/79 - No. 27, Fall, 1981 (No. 18, 19, 23, 24 - digest size, 100 pgs.; No. 25-27 - Treasury sized)

1-"5-Star Super-Hero Spectacular 1977"; Batman, Atom, Flash, Green Lantern, Aquaman, in solo stories, Kobra app.; N. Adams-c 3 6 9 18 23 28
2(#1)-"The Original Swamp Thing Saga 1977"-r/Swamp Thing #1&2 by Wrightson; new Wrightson wraparound-c. 2 4 6 8 10 12
3,4,6-8: 3-Sgt Rock. 4-Unexpected. 6-Secret Society of Super Villains, Jones-a. 7-Ghosts Special. 8-Brave and Bold w/ new Batman, Deadman & Sgt Rock team-up 2 4 6 10 12 15
5-"Superman Spectacular 1977"-(84 pg, $1.00)-Superman vs. Brainiac & Lex Luthor, new 63 pg. story 2 4 6 12 16 20
9-Wonder Woman; Ditko-a (11 pgs.) 2 4 6 12 16 20
10-"Secret Origins of Superheroes Special 1978"-(52 pgs.)-Dr. Fate, Lightray & Black Canary on-c/new origin stories; Staton, Newton-a 2 4 6 11 14 18
11-"Flash Spectacular 1978"-(84 pgs.) Flash, Kid Flash, GA Flash & Johnny Quick vs. Grodd; Wood-i on Kid Flash chapter 2 4 6 10 12 15
12-"Secrets of Haunted House Special Spring 1978" 2 4 6 10 13 16
13-"Sgt. Rock Special Spring 1978", 50 pg new story 2 4 6 10 13 16
14,17,20-"Original Swamp Thing Saga", Wrightson-a: 14-Sum '78, r/#3,4. 17-Sum '79 r/#5-7. 20-Jan/Feb '80, r/#8-10 1 3 4 6 8 10
15-"Batman Spectacular Summer 1978", Ra's Al Ghul-app.; Golden-a. Rogers-a/front & back-c 2 4 6 14 18 22
16-"Jonah Hex Spectacular Fall 1978"; death of Jonah Hex, Heath-a; Bat Lash and Scalphunter stories 6 12 18 38 52 65
18,19-Digest size: 18-"Sgt. Rock's Prize Battle Tales Fall 1979". 19-"Secret Origins of Super-Heroes Fall 1979"; origins Wonder Woman (new-a),r/Robin, Batman-Superman team, Aquaman, Hawkman and others 2 4 6 10 13 16
21-"Super-Star Holiday Special Spring 1980", Frank Miller-a in "Batman--Wanted Dead or Alive" (1st Batman story); Jonah Hex, Sgt. Rock, Superboy &LSH and House of Mystery/ Witching Hour-c/stories 3 6 9 18 24 30
22-"G.I. Combat Sept. 1980", Kubert-c. Haunted Tank-s 2 4 6 10 13 16
23,24-Digest size: 23-World's Finest-r. 24-Flash 2 4 6 10 13 16
V5#25-($2.95)-"Superman II, the Adventure Continues Summer 1981"; photos from movie & photo-c (see All-New Coll. Ed. C-62) 2 4 6 11 14 18
26-($2.50)-"Superman and His Incredible Fortress of Solitude Summer 1981" 2 4 6 11 14 18
27-($2.50)-"Batman vs. The Incredible Hulk Fall 1981" 3 6 9 19 25 32

NOTE: ***Aparo** c-8. **Heath** a-12i, 16. **Infantino** a-19r. **Kirby** a-23, 19r. **Kubert** c-13, 19r. **Nasser/Netzer** a-1, 10i, 15. **Newton** a-10. **Nino** a-4, 7. **Starlin** c-12. **Staton** a-1. **Tuska** a-19r. #25 & 26. were advertised as All-New Collectors' Edition C-63, C-64. #26 was originally planned as All-New Collectors' Ed. C-30?; has C-630 & A.N.C.E. on cover.*

DC SUPER-STARS
National Periodical Publications/DC Comics: March, 1976 - No. 18, Winter, 1978 (No.3-18: 52 pgs.)

1-(68 pgs.)-Re-intro Teen Titans (predates T. T. #44 (11/76); tryout iss.) plus r/Teen Titans; W.W. as girl was original Wonder Girl 2 4 6 12 16 20
2-7,9,11,12,16: 2,4,6,8-Adam Strange; 2-(68 pgs.)-r/1st Adam Strange/Hawkman team-up from Mystery in Space #90 plus Atomic Knights origin-r. 3-Legion issue. 4-r/Tales/Unexpected #45 1 3 4 6 8 10
8-r/1st Space Ranger from Showcase #15, Adam Strange-r/Mystery in Space #89 & Star Rovers-r/M.I.S. #80 2 4 6 8 10 12
10-Strange Sports Stories; Batman/Joker-c/story 2 4 6 8 10 12
13-Sergio Aragonés Special 2 4 6 12 16 20
14,15,18: 15-Sgt. Rock 2 4 6 8 10 12
17-Secret Origins of Super-Heroes (origin of The Huntress); origin Green Arrow by Grell; Legion app.; Earth II Batman & Catwoman marry (1st revealed; also see B&B #197 & Superman Family #211) 4 8 12 26 33 45

NOTE: ***M. Anderson** r-2, 4, 6. **Aparo** c-7, 14, 18. **Austin** a-11i. **Buckler** a-14p; c-10. **Grell** a-17. **G. Kane** a-1r, 10r. **Kubert** c-15. **Layton** c/a-16i, 17i. **Mooney** a-4r, 6r. **Morrow** c/a-11r. **Nasser** a-11. **Newton** c/a-16p. **Staton** a-17; c-17. No. 10, 12-18 contain all new material; the rest are reprints. #1 contains new and reprint material.*

DC 2000
DC Comics: 2000 - No. 2, 2000 ($6.95, limited series)

1,2-JLA visit 1941 JSA; Semeiks-a 7.00

DCU HEROES SECRET FILES
DC Comics: Feb, 1999 ($4.95, one-shot)

1-Origin-s and pin-ups; new Star Spangled Kid app. 5.00

DC UNIVERSE CHRISTMAS, A
DC Comics: 2000 ($19.95)

TPB-Reprints DC Christmas stories by various 20.00

DC UNIVERSE HOLIDAY BASH
DC Comics: 1997- 1999 ($3.95)

I,II-(X-mas '96,'97) Christmas stories by various 5.00
III (1999, for Christmas '98, $4.95) 5.00

DC UNIVERSE: TRINITY
DC Comics: Aug, 1993 - No. 2, Sept, 1993 ($2.95, 52 pgs, limited series)

1,2-Foil-c; Green Lantern, Darkstars, Legion app. 3.50

DCU VILLAINS SECRET FILES
DC Comics: Apr, 1999 ($4.95, one-shot)

1-Origin-s and profile pages 5.00

DC VERSUS MARVEL (See Marvel Versus DC) (Also see Amazon, Assassins, Bruce Wayne: Agent of S.H.I. E. L.D., Bullets & Bracelets, Doctor Strangefate, JLX, Legend of the Dark Claw, Magneto & The Magnetic Men, Speed Demon, Spider-Boy, Super Soldier, X-Patrol)
DC Comics: No. 1, 1996, No. 4, 1996 ($3.95, limited series)

1,4: 1-Marz script, Jurgens-a(p); 1st app. of Access. 4.00
.../Marvel Versus DC ($12.95, trade paperback) r/1-4 13.00

D-DAY (Also see Special War Series)
Charlton Comics (no No. 3): Sum/63; No. 2, Fall/64; No. 4, 9/66; No. 5, 10/67; No. 6, 11/68

1,2: 1(1963)-Montes/Bache-c. 2(Fall '64)-Wood-a(4) 4 8 12 27 36 45
4-6('66-'68)-Montes/Bache-a #5 3 6 9 16 20 25

DEAD AIR
Slave Labor Graphics: July, 1989 ($5.95, graphic novel)

nn-Mike Allred's 1st published work 6.00

DEAD CORPSE
DC Comics (Helix): Sept, 1998 - No. 4, Dec, 1998 ($2.50, limited series)

1-4-Pugh-a/Hinz-s 2.50

DEAD END CRIME STORIES
Kirby Publishing Co.: April, 1949 (52 pgs.)

nn-(Scarce)-Powell, Roussos-a; painted-c 50 100 150 300 450 600

DEAD ENDERS
DC Comics (Vertigo): Mar, 2000 - No. 16, June, 2001 ($2.50)

1-16-Brubaker-s/Pleece & Case-a 2.50
Stealing the Sun (2000, $9.95, TPB) r/#1-4, Vertigo Winter's Edge #3 10.00

DEAD-EYE WESTERN COMICS
Hillman Periodicals: Nov-Dec, 1948 - V3#1, Apr-May, 1953

V1#1-(52 pgs.)-Krigstein, Roussos-a 20 40 60 112 156 200
V1#2,3-(52 pgs.) 10 20 30 60 80 100
V1#4-12-(52 pgs.) 8 16 24 43 54 65
V2#1,2,5-8,10-12: 1-7-(52 pgs.) 7 14 21 35 43 50
3,4-Krigstein-a 8 16 24 40 50 60
9-One pg. Frazetta ad 7 14 21 35 43 50
V3#1 7 14 21 35 43 50

Deadline #2 © MAR

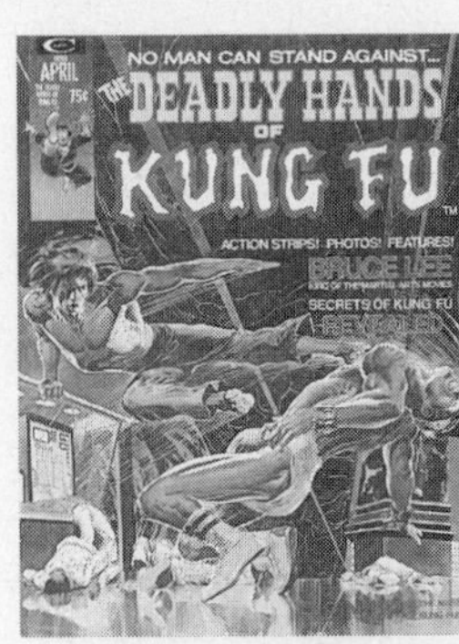

Deadly Hands of Kung Fu #1 © MAR

Deadman: Dead Again #5 © DC

GD VG FN VF VF/NM NM- 2.0 4.0 6.0 8.0 9.0 9.2

NOTE: ***Briefer** a-V1#8. Kinstleresque stories by **McCann**-12, V2#1, 2, V3#1. **McWilliams** a-V1#5. **Ed Moore** a-V1#4.*

DEADFACE: DOING THE ISLANDS WITH BACCHUS
Dark Horse Comics: July, 1991 - No. 3, Sept, 1991 ($2.95, B&W, lim. series)

1-3: By Eddie Campbell 3.00

DEADFACE: EARTH, WATER, AIR, AND FIRE
Dark Horse Comics: July, 1992 - No. 4, Oct, 1992 ($2.50, B&W, limited series; British-r)

1-4: By Eddie Campbell 3.00

DEAD IN THE WEST
Dark Horse Comics: Oct, 1993 - No. 2, Mar, 1994 ($3.95, B&W, 52 pgs.)

1,2-Timothy Truman-c 4.00

DEAD KING (See Evil Ernie)
Chaos! Comics: May, 1998 - No. 4, Aug, 1998, ($2.95, limited series)

1-4-Fisher-s 3.00

DEADLIEST HEROES OF KUNG FU (Magazine)
Marvel Comics Group: Summer, 1975 (B&W)(76 pgs.)

1-Bruce Lee vs. Carradine painted-c; TV Kung Fu, 4pgs. photos/article; Enter the Dragon, 24 pgs. photos/article w/ Bruce Lee; Bruce Lee photo pinup
3 6 9 18 23 28

DEADLINE
Marvel Comics: June, 2002 - No. 4, Sept, 2002 ($2.99, limited series)

1-4: 1-Intro. Kat Farrell; Bill Rosemann-s/Guy Davis-a; Horn painted-c 3.00
TPB (2002. $9.99) r/#1-4 10.00

DEADLINE USA
Dark Horse Comics: Apr, 1992 - No. 8, Nov, 1992 ($3.95, B&W, 52 pgs.)

1-8: Johnny Nemo w/Milligan scripts in all 4.00

DEADLY DUO, THE
Image Comics (Highbrow Entertainment): Nov, 1994 - No. 3, Jan, 1995 ($2.50, lim. series)

1-3: 1-1st app. of Kill Cat 2.50

DEADLY DUO, THE
Image Comics (Highbrow Entertainment): June, 1995 - No. 4, Oct, 1995 ($2.50, lim. series)

1-4: 1-Spawn app. 2-Savage Dragon app. 3-Gen 13 app. 2.50

DEADLY FOES OF SPIDER-MAN (See Lethal Foes of...)
Marvel Comics: May, 1991 - No. 4, Aug, 1991 ($1.00, limited series)

1-4: 1-Punisher, Kingpin, Rhino app. 2.50

DEADLY HANDS OF KUNG FU, THE (See Master of Kung Fu)
Marvel Comics Group: April, 1974 - No. 33, Feb, 1977 (75¢) (B&W, magazine)

1(V1#4 listed in error)-Origin Sons of the Tiger; Shang-Chi, Master of Kung Fu begins (ties w/Master of Kung Fu #17 as 3rd app. Shang-Chi); Bruce Lee painted-c by Neal Adams; 2pg. memorial photo pinup w/8 pgs. photos/articles; TV Kung Fu, 9 pgs. photos/articles; 15 pgs. Starlin-a 4 8 12 27 36 45
2-Adams painted-c; 1st time origin of Shang-Chi, 34 pgs. by Starlin. TV Kung Fu, 6 pgs. photos & article w/2 pg. pinup. Bruce Lee, 11 pgs. ph/a
3 7 10 21 28 35
3,4,7,10: 3-Adams painted-c; Gulacy-a. Enter the Dragon, photos/articles, 8 pgs. 4-TV Kung Fu painted-c by Neal Adams; TV Kung Fu 7 pg. article/art; Fu Manchu; Enter the Dragon, 10 pg. photos/article w/Bruce Lee. 7-Bruce Lee painted-c & 9 pgs. photos/articles-Return of Dragon plus 1 pg. photo pinup. 10-(3/75)-Iron Fist painted-c & 34 pg. sty-Early app.
3 6 9 16 20 24
5,6: 5-1st app. Manchurian, 6 pgs. Gulacy-a. TV Kung Fu, 4 pg. article; reprints books w/Barry Smith-a. Capt. America-sty, 10 pgs. Kirby-a(r). 6-Bruce Lee photos/article, 6 pgs.; 15 pgs. early Perez-a 2 4 6 14 18 22
8,9,11: 9-Iron Fist, 2 pg. Preview pinup; Nebres-a. 11-Billy Jack painted-c by Adams; 17 pgs. photos/article 2 4 6 12 16 20
12,13: 12-James Bond painted-c by Adams; 14 pg. photos/article. 13-16 pgs. early Perez-a; Piers Anthony, 7 pgs. photos/article 2 4 6 11 14 18
14-Classic Bruce Lee painted-c by Adams. Lee pinup by Chaykin. Lee 16 pg. photos/article w/2 pgs. Green Hornet TV 5 10 15 33 44 55
15,19: 15-Sum, '75 Giant Annual #1. 20pgs. Starlin-a. Bruce Lee photo pinup & 3 pg. photos/ article re book; Man-Thing app. Iron Fist-c/sty; Gulacy-a 18pgs. 19-Iron Fist painted-c & series begins; 1st White Tiger 2 4 6 12 16 20
16,18,20: 16-1st app. Corpse Rider, a Samurai w/Sanho Kim-a. 20-Chuck Norris painted-c & 16 pgs. interview w/photos/article; Bruce Lee vs. C. Norris pinup by Ken Barr. Origin The White Tiger, Perez-a 2 4 6 10 13 16
17-Bruce Lee painted-c by Adams; interview w/R. Clouse, director Enter Dragon 7 pgs. w/B. Lee app. 1st Giffen-a (1pg. 11/75) 3 6 9 19 25 32
21-Bruce Lee 1pg. photos/article 2 4 6 10 12 15
22,30-32: 22-1st app. Jack of Hearts (cameo). 1st Giffen sty-a (along w/Amazing Adv. #35, 3/76). 30-Swordquest-c/sty & conclusion; Jack of Hearts app. 31-Jack of Hearts app; Staton-a. 32-1st Daughters of the Dragon-c/sty, 21 pgs. M. Rogers-a/Claremont-sty; Iron Fist pinup 2 4 6 10 13 16
23-26,29: 23-1st full app. Jack of Hearts. 24-Iron Fist-c & centerfold pinup. early Zeck-a; Shang Chi pinup; 6 pgs. Piers Anthony text sty w/Perez/Austin-a; Jack of Hearts app. early Giffen-a. 25-1st app. Shimuru, "Samurai", 20 pgs. Mantlo-sty/Broderick-a; "Swordquest"-c & begins 17 pg. sty by Sanho Kim; 11 pg. photos/article; partly Bruce Lee. 26-Bruce Lee painted-c & pinup; 16 pgs. interviews w/Kwon & Clouse; talk about Bruce Lee re-filming of Lee legend. 29-Ironfist vs. Shang Chi battle-c/sty; Jack of Hearts app.
2 4 6 14 18 22
27 2 4 6 10 12 15
28-All Bruce Lee Special Issue; (1st time in comics). Bruce Lee painted-c by Ken Barr & pinup. 36 pgs. comics chronicaling Bruce Lee's life; 15 pgs. B. Lee photos/article (Rare in high grade) 6 12 18 40 55 70
33-Shang Chi-c/sty; Classic Daughters of the Dragon, 21 pgs. M. Rogers-a/Claremont-story with nudity; Bob Wall interview, photos/article, 14 pgs.
2 4 6 14 18 22
...Special Album Edition 1(Summer, '74)-Iron Fist-c/story (early app., 3rd?); 10 pgs. Adams-i; Shang Chi/Fu Manchu, 10 pgs.; Sons of Tiger, 11 pgs.; TV Kung Fu, 6 pgs. photos/article
3 6 9 16 20 25

NOTE: ***Bruce Lee:** 1-7, 14, 15, 17, 25, 26, 28. **Kung Fu (TV):** 1, 2, 4. **Jack of Hearts**: 22, 23, 29-33. **Shang Chi Master of Kung Fu**: 1-9, 11-18, 29, 31, 33. **Sons of Tiger:** 1, 3, 4, 6-14, 16-19. **Swordquest:** 25-27, 29-33. **White Tiger:** 19-24, 26, 27, 29-33. **N. Adams** a-1i(part), 27i; c-1, 2-4, 11, 12, 14, 17. **Giffen** a-22p, 24p. **G. Kane** a-23p. **Kirby** a-5r. **Nasser** a-27p, 28. **Perez** a(p)-6-14, 16, 17, 19, 21. **Rogers** a-26, 32, 33. **Starlin** a-1, 2r, 15r. **Staton** a-28p, 31, 32.*

DEADMAN (See The Brave and the Bold & Phantom Stranger #39)
DC Comics: May, 1985 - No. 7, Nov, 1985 ($1.75, Baxter paper)

1-7: 1-Deadman-r by Infantino, N. Adams in all. 5-Batman-c/story-r/Strange Adventures. 7-Batman-r 3.00

DEADMAN
DC Comics: Mar, 1986 - No. 4, June, 1986 (75¢, limited series)

1-4: Lopez-c/a. 4-Byrne-c(p) 3.00

DEADMAN
DC Comics: Feb, 2002 - No. 9, Oct, 2002 ($2.50)

1-9: 1-4-Vance-s/Beroy-a. 3,4-Mignola-c. 5,6-Garcia-Lopez-a 2.50

DEADMAN: DEAD AGAIN (Leads into 2002 series)
DC Comics: Oct, 2001 - No. 5, Oct, 2001 ($2.50, weekly limited series)

1-5: Deadman at the deaths of the Flash, Robin, Superman, Hal Jordan 2.50

DEADMAN: EXORCISM
DC Comics: 1992 - No. 2, 1992 ($4.95, limited series, 52 pgs.)

1,2: Kelley Jones-c/a in both 5.00

DEADMAN: LOVE AFTER DEATH
DC Comics: 1989 - No. 2, 1990 ($3.95, 52 pgs., limited series, mature)

Book One, Two: Kelley Jones-c/a in both. 1-contains nudity 4.00

DEAD OF NIGHT
Marvel Comics Group: Dec, 1973 - No. 11, Aug, 1975

1-Horror reprints 3 6 9 16 20 24
2-10: 10-Kirby-a 2 4 6 9 11 14
11-Intro Scarecrow; Kane/Wrightson-c 3 6 9 18 24 30

NOTE: ***Ditko** r-7, 10. **Everett** c-2. **Sinnott** r-1.*

DEAD OR ALIVE - A CYBERPUNK WESTERN
Image Comics (Shok Studio): Apr, 1998 - No. 4, July, 1998 ($2.50, lim. series)

1-4 3.00

DEADPOOL (See New Mutants #98)
Marvel Comics: Aug, 1994 - No. 4, Nov, 1994 ($2.50, limited series)

1-4: Mark Waid's 1st Marvel work; Ian Churchill-c/a 4.00

DEADPOOL (... : Agent of Weapon X on cover #57-60) (title becomes Agent X)
Marvel Comics: Jan, 1997 - No. 69, Sept, 2002 ($2.95/$1.95/$1.99)

1-($2.95)-Wraparound-c 1 2 3 4 5 7
2-Begin-$1.95-c. 5.00
3-10,12-22,24: 4-Hulk-c/app. 12-Variant-c. 14-Begin McDaniel-a. 22-Cable app. 5.00
11-($3.99)-Deadpool replaces Spider-Man from Amazing Spider-Man #47; Kraven, Gwen Stacy app. 6.00
23,25-($2.99); 23-Dead Reckoning pt. 1; wraparound-c 4.00
26-40: 27-Wolverine-c/app. 37-Thor app. 3.00
41-53,56-60: 41-Begin $2.25-c. 44-Black Panther-c/app. 46-49-Chadwick-a 51-Cover swipe of Detective #38. 57-60-BWS-c 3.00
54,55-Punisher-c/app. 54-Dillon-c. 55-Bradstreet-c 3.00

Deadpool #69 © MAR

Deadshot #2 © DC

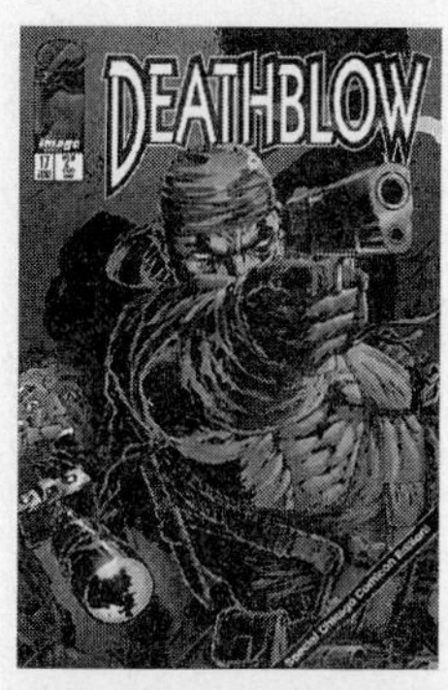

Deathblow #17 © WSP

	GD 2.0	VG 4.0	FN 6.0	VF 8.0	VF/NM 9.0	NM- 9.2

61-69: 61-64-Funeral For a Freak on cover. 65-69-Udon Studios-a. 67-Dazzler-c/app. 2.50
#(-1) Flashback (7/97) Lopresti-a; Wade Wilson's early days 3.00
.../Death '98 Annual ($2.99) Kelly-s, ... Team-Up (12/98, $2.99) Widdle Wade-c/app., Baby's First Deadpool Book (12/98, $2.99), Encyclopædia Deadpoolica (12/98, $2.99) Synopses 3.00
Mission Improbable TPB (9/98, $14.95) r/#1-5 15.00
Wizard #0 ('98, bagged with Wizard #87) 2.25

DEADPOOL: THE CIRCLE CHASE (See New Mutants #98)
Marvel Comics: Aug, 1993 - No. 4, Nov, 1993 ($2.00, limited series)

1-($2.50)-Embossed-c 4.00
2-4 3.00

DEADSHOT (See Batman #59, Detective Comics #474, & Showcase '93 #8)
DC Comics: Nov, 1988 - No. 4, Feb, 1989 ($1.00, limited series)

1-4 2.50

DEADSIDE (See Shadowman)
Acclaim Comics: Feb, 1999 - No. 4, ($2.50, limited series)

1-3-Jenkins-s/Haselden-Wood-a 2.50

DEAD WHO WALK, THE (See Strange Mysteries, Super Reprint #15, 16)
Realistic Comics: 1952 (one-shot)

	GD	VG	FN	VF	VF/NM	NM-
nn	52	104	156	312	469	625

DEADWORLD (Also see The Realm)
Arrow Comics/Caliber Comics: Dec, 1986 - No. 26 ($1.50/$1.95/#15-28: $2.50, B&W)

1-4 4.00
5-26-Each issue has both a Graphic cover and a Tame cover 3.00
...Archives 1-3 (1992, $2.50) 3.00

DEAN MARTIN & JERRY LEWIS (See Adventures of...)

DEAR BEATRICE FAIRFAX
Best/Standard Comics (King Features): No. 5, Nov, 1950 - No. 9, Sept, 1951 (Vern Greene art)

	GD	VG	FN	VF	VF/NM	NM-
5-All have Schomburg air brush-c	10	20	30	60	80	100
6-9	7	14	21	37	46	55

DEAR HEART (Formerly Lonely Heart)
Ajax: No. 15, July, 1956 - No. 16, Sept, 1956

	GD	VG	FN	VF	VF/NM	NM-
15,16	6	12	18	31	38	45

DEAR LONELY HEART (...Illustrated No. 1-6)
Artful Publications: Mar, 1951; No. 2, Oct, 1951 - No. 8, Oct, 1952

	GD	VG	FN	VF	VF/NM	NM-
1	17	34	51	98	134	170
2	9	18	27	49	62	75
3-Matt Baker Jungle Girl story	20	40	60	112	156	200
4-8	8	16	24	43	54	65

DEAR LONELY HEARTS (Lonely Heart #9 on)
Harwell Publ./Mystery Publ. Co. (Comic Media): Aug, 1953 -No. 8, Oct, 1954

	GD	VG	FN	VF	VF/NM	NM-
1	10	20	30	60	80	100
2-8	8	16	24	40	50	60

DEARLY BELOVED
Ziff-Davis Publishing Co.: Fall, 1952

	GD	VG	FN	VF	VF/NM	NM-
1-Photo-c	17	34	51	95	130	165

DEAR NANCY PARKER
Gold Key: June, 1963 - No. 2, Sept, 1963

	GD	VG	FN	VF	VF/NM	NM-
1-Painted-c on both	4	8	12	27	36	45
2	3	6	9	18	24	30

DEATH: AT DEATH'S DOOR (See Sandman: The Season of Mists)
DC Comics: 2003 ($9.95, graphic novel one-shot, B&W, 7-1/2" x 5")

1-Jill Thompson-s/a/c; manga-style; Morpheus and the Endless app. 10.00

DEATHBLOW (Also see Batman/Deathblow and Darker Image)
Image Comics (WildStorm Productions): May (Apr. inside), 1993 - No. 29, Aug, 1996 ($1.75/$1.95/$2.50)

0-(8/96, $2.95, 32 pgs.)-r/Darker Image w/new story & art; Jim Lee & Trevor Scott-a; new Jim Lee-c 3.00
1-($2.50)-Red foil stamped logo on black varnish-c; Jim Lee-c/a; flip-book side has Cybernary -c/story (#2 also) 3.00
1-($1.95)-Newsstand version w/o foil-c & varnish 2.25
2-29: 2-(8/93)-Lee-a; with bound-in poster. 2-($1.75)-Newsstand version w/o poster. 4-Jim Lee-c/Tim Sale-a begin. 13-W/pinup poster by Tim Sale & Jim Lee. 16-($1.95 Newsstand & $2.50 Direct Market editions)-Wildstorm Rising Pt. 6. 17-Variant "Chicago Comicon" edition exists. 20,21-Gen 13 app. 23-Backlash-c/app. 24,25-Grifter-c/app; Gen 13 & Dane from Wetworks app. 28-Deathblow dies. 29-Memorial issue 2.50
5-Alternate Portacio-c (Forms larger picture when combined with alternate-c for Gen 13 #5, Kindred #3, Stormwatch #10, Team 7 #1, Union #0, Wetworks #2 & WildC.A.T.S #11) 6.00
...:Sinners and Saints TPB ('99, $19.95) r/#1-12; Sale-c 20.00

DEATHBLOW BY BLOWS
DC Comics (WildStorm): Nov, 1999 - No. 3, Jan, 2000 ($2.95, limited series)

1-3-Alan Moore-s/Jim Baikie-a 3.00

DEATHBLOW/WOLVERINE
Image Comics (WildStorm Productions)/ Marvel Comics: Sept, 1996 - No. 2, Feb, 1997 ($2.50, limited series)

1,2: Wiesenfeld-s/Bennett-a 2.50
TPB (1997, $8.95) r/#1,2 9.00

DEATHDEALER
Verotik: July, 1995 - No. 4, July, 1997 ($5.95)

	GD	VG	FN	VF	VF/NM	NM-
1-Frazetta-c; Bisley-a	1	2	3	5	6	8
1-2nd print, 2-4-($6.95)-Frazetta-c; embossed logo	1	2	3	4	5	7

DEATHLOK (Also see Astonishing Tales #25)
Marvel Comics: July, 1990 - No. 4, Oct, 1990 ($3.95, limited series, 52 pgs.)

1-4: 1,2-Guice-a(p). 3,4-Denys Cowan-a, c-4 4.00

DEATHLOK
Marvel Comics: July, 1991 - No. 34, Apr, 1994 ($1.75)

1-Silver ink cover; Denys Cowan-c/a(p) begins 3.00
2-18,20-24,26-34: 2-Forge (X-Men) app. 3-Vs. Dr. Doom. 5-X-Men & F.F. x-over. 6,7-Punisher x-over. 9,10-Ghost Rider-c/story. 16-Infinity War x-over. 17-Jae Lee-c. 22-Black Panther app. 27-Siege app. 2.25
19-($2.25)-Foil-c 2.50
25-($2.95, 52 pgs.)-Holo-grafx foil-c 3.00
Annual 1 (1992, $2.25, 68 pgs.)-Guice-p; Quesada-c(p) 3.00
Annual 2 (1993, $2.95, 68 pgs.)-Bagged w/card; intro Tracer 3.00
NOTE: ***Denys Cowan** a(p)-9-13, 15, Annual 1; c-9-12, 13p, 14. **Guice/Cowan** c-8.*

DEATHLOK
Marvel Comics: Sept, 1999 - No. 11, June, 2000 ($1.99)

1-11: 1-Casey-s/Manco-a. 2-Two covers. 4-Canete-a 2.25

DEATHLOK SPECIAL
Marvel Comics: May, 1991 - No. 4, June, 1991 ($2.00, bi-weekly lim. series)

1-4: r/1-4(1990) w/new Guice-c #1,2; Cowan c-3,4 2.50
1-2nd printing w/white-c 2.25

DEATHMASK
Future Comics: Mar, 2003 - No. 3, June, 2003 ($2.99)

1-3-Giordano-a(p)/Michelinie & Layton-s 3.00

DEATHMATE
Valiant (Prologue/Yellow/Blue)/Image Comics (Black/Red/Epilogue):
Sept, 1993 - Epilogue (#6), Feb, 1994 ($2.95/$4.95, limited series)

Preview-(7/93, 8 pgs.) 2.25
Prologue (#1)–Silver foil; Jim Lee/Layton-c; B. Smith/Lee-a; Liefeld-a(p) 3.00
Prologue–Special gold foil ed. of silver ed. 4.00
Black (#2)-(9/93, $4.95, 52 pgs.)-Silvestri/Jim Lee-c; pencils by Peterson/Silvestri/Capullo/Jim Lee/Portacio; 1st story app. Gen 13 telling their rebellion against the Troika (see WildC.A.T.S. Trilogy) 6.00
Black-Special gold foil edition 7.00
Yellow (#3)-(10/93, $4.95, 52 pgs)-Yellow foil-c; Indicia says Prologue Sept 1993 by mistake; 3rd app. Ninjak; Thibert-c(i) 5.00
Yellow-Special gold foil edition 6.00
Blue (#4)-(10/93, $4.95, 52 pgs.)-Thibert blue foil-c(i); Reese-a(i) 5.00
Blue-Special gold foil edition 6.00
Red (#5), Epilogue (#6)-(2/94, $2.95)-Silver foil Quesada/Silvestri-c; Silvestri-a(p) 3.00

DEATH METAL
Marvel Comics UK: Jan, 1994 - No. 4, Apr, 1994 ($1.95, limited series)

1-4: 1-Silver ink-c. Alpha Flight app. 2.25

DEATH METAL VS. GENETIX
Marvel Comics UK: Dec, 1993 - No. 2, Jan, 1994 (Limited series)

1-($2.95)-Polybagged w/2 trading cards 3.00
2-($2.50)-Polybagged w/2 trading cards 2.50

DEATH OF CAPTAIN MARVEL (See Marvel Graphic Novel #1)

Deathstroke: The Terminator #4 © DC

Deathwish #3 © Milestone Media

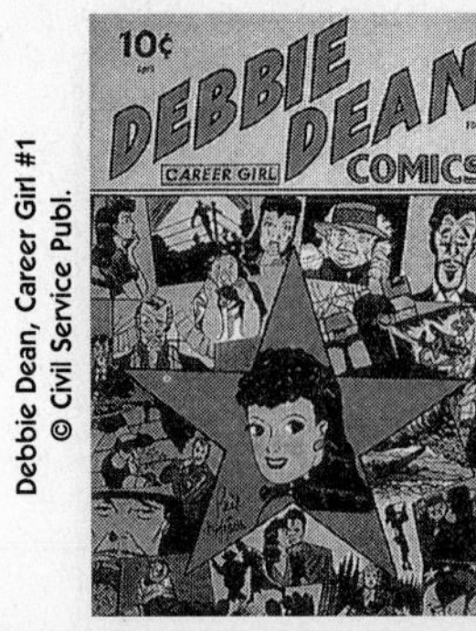

Debbie Dean, Career Girl #1 © Civil Service Publ.

GD 2.0 | VG 4.0 | FN 6.0 | VF 8.0 | VF/NM 9.0 | NM- 9.2

DEATH OF MR. MONSTER, THE (See Mr. Monster #8)

DEATH OF SUPERMAN (See Superman, 2nd Series)

DEATH RACE 2020
Roger Corman's Cosmic Comics: Apr, 1995 - No. 8, Nov, 1995 ($2.50)

1-8: Sequel to the Movie 2.50

DEATH RATTLE (Formerly an Underground)
Kitchen Sink Press: V2#1, 10/85 - No. 18, 1988, 1994 ($1.95, Baxter paper, mature); V3#1, 11/95 - No. 5, 6/96 ($2.95, B&W)

V2#1-7,9-18: 1-Corben-c. 2-Unpubbed Spirit story by Eisner. 5-Robot Woman-r by Wolverton. 6-B&W issues begin. 10-Savage World-r by by Williamson/Torres/ Krenkel/Frazetta from Witzend #1. 16-Wolverton Spacehawk-r 4.00
8-(12/86)-1st app. Mark Schultz's Xenozoic Tales/Cadillacs & Dinosaurs 1 3 4 6 8 10
8-(1994)-r plus interview w/Mark Schultz 3.00
V3#1-5 ($2.95-c) 3.00

DEATH'S HEAD (See Daredevil #56, Dragon's Claws #5 & Incomplete...)
Marvel Comics: Dec, 1988 - No. 10, Sept, 1989 ($1.75)

1-Dragon's Claws spin-off 3.00
2-Fantastic Four app.; Dragon's Claws x-over 2.50
3-10: 8-Dr. Who app. 9-F. F. x-over; Simonson-c(p) 2.25

DEATH'S HEAD II (Also see Battletide)
Marvel Comics UK, Ltd.: Mar, 1992 - No. 4, June (May inside), 1992 ($1.75, color, lim. series)

1-4: 2-Fantastic Four app. 4-Punisher, Spider-Man, Daredevil, Dr. Strange, Capt. America & Wolverine in the year 2020 2.25
1,2-Silver ink 2nd printiings 2.25

DEATH'S HEAD II (Also see Battletide)
Marvel Comics UK, Ltd.: Dec, 1992 - No. 16, Mar, 1994 ($1.75/$1.95)

V2#1-13,15,16: 1-Gatefold-c. 1-4-X-Men app.15-Capt. America & Wolverine app. 2.25
14-($2.95)-Foil flip-c w/Death's Head II Gold #0 3.00
...Gold 1 (1/94, $3.95, 68 pgs.)-Gold foil-c 4.00

DEATH'S HEAD II & THE ORIGIN OF DIE CUT
Marvel Comics UK, Ltd.: Aug, 1993 - No. 2, Sept, 1993 (limited series)

1-($2.95)-Embossed-c 3.00
2 ($1.75) 2.25

DEATHSTROKE: THE TERMINATOR (Deathstroke: The Hunted #0-47; Deathstroke #48-60) (Also see Marvel & DC Present, New Teen Titans #2, New Titans, Showcase '93 #7,9 & Tales of the Teen Titans #42-44)
DC Comics: Aug, 1991 - No. 60, June, 1996 ($1.75-$2.25)

1-New Titans spin-off; Mike Zeck c-1-28 4.00
1-Gold ink 2nd printing ($1.75) 2.25
2 3.00
3-40,0(10/94),41(11/94)-49,51-60: 6,8-Batman cameo. 7,9-Batman-c/story. 9-1st new Vigilante (female) in cameo. 10-1st full app. new Vigilante; Perez-i. 13-Vs. Justice League; Team Titans cameo on last pg. 14-Total Chaos, part 1; TeamTitans-c/story cont'd in New Titans #90. 15-Total Chaos, part 4. 40-(9/94). 0-(10/94)-Begin Deathstroke, The Hunted, ends #47. 2.50
50 ($3.50) 3.50
Annual 1-4 ('92-'95, 68 pgs.): 1-Nightwing & Vigilante app.; minor Eclipso app. 2-Bloodlines Deathstorm; 1st app. Gunfire. 3-Elseworlds story. 4-Year One story 4.00
NOTE: ***Golden** a-12. **Perez** a-11i. **Zeck** c-Annual 1, 2.*

DEATH: THE HIGH COST OF LIVING (See Sandman #8) (Also see the Books of Magic limited & ongoing series)
DC Comics (Vertigo): Mar, 1993 - No. 3, May, 1993 ($1.95, limited series)

1-Bachalo/Buckingham-a; Dave McKean-c; Neil Gaiman scripts in all 6.00
1-Platinum edition 40.00
2 3.50
3-Pgs. 19 & 20 had wrong placement 3.00
3-Corrected version w/pgs. 19 & 20 facing each other; has no-c & ads for Sebastion O & The Geek added 4.00
Death Talks About Life-giveaway about AIDS prevention 5.00
Hardcover (1994, $19.95)-r/#1-3 & Death Talks About Life; intro. by Tori Amos 20.00
Trade paperback (6/94, $12.95, Titan Books)-r/#1-3 & Death Talks About Life; prism-c 13.00

DEATH: THE TIME OF YOUR LIFE (See Sandman #8)
DC Comics (Vertigo): Apr, 1996 - No. 3, July, 1996 ($2.95, limited series)

1-3: Neil Gaiman story & Bachalo/Buckingham-a; Dave McKean-c. 2-(5/96) 3.00
Hardcover (1997, $19.95)-r/#1-3 w/3 new pages & gallery art by various 20.00
TPB (1997, $12.95)-r/#1-3 & Visions of Death gallery; Intro. by Claire Danes 13.00

DEATH 3
Marvel Comics UK: Sept, 1993 - No. 4, Dec, 1993 ($1.75, limited series)

1-($2.95)-Embossed-c 3.00
2-4 2.25

DEATH VALLEY (Cowboys and Indians)
Comic Media: Oct, 1953 - No. 6, Aug, 1954

1-Billy the Kid; Morisi-a; Andru/Esposito-c/a 13 26 39 76 103 130
2-Don Heck-c 8 16 24 46 58 70
3-6: 3,5-Morisi-a. 5-Discount-a 8 16 24 43 54 65

DEATH VALLEY (Becomes Frontier Scout, Daniel Boone No.10-13)
Charlton Comics: No. 7, 6/55 - No. 9, 10/55 (Cont'd from Comic Media series)

7-9: 8-Wolverton-a (half pg.) 7 14 21 37 46 55

DEATHWISH
DC Comics (Milestone Media): Dec, 1994 - No. 4, Mar, 1995 (2.50, lim. series)

1-4 2.50

DEATH WRECK
Marvel Comics UK: Jan, 1994 - No. 4, Apr, 1994 ($1.95, limited series)

1-4: 1-Metallic ink logo; Death's Head II app. 2.25

DEBBIE DEAN, CAREER GIRL
Civil Service Publ.: April, 1945 - No. 2, July, 1945

1,2-Newspaper reprints by Bert Whitman 14 28 42 79 107 135

DEBBI'S DATES (Also see Date With Debbi)
National Periodical Publications: Apr-May, 1969 - No. 11, Dec-Jan, 1970-71

1 5 10 15 36 48 60
2,3,5,7-11: 2-Last 12¢ issue 3 6 9 18 23 28
4-Neal Adams text illo 4 8 12 22 30 38
6-Superman cameo 5 10 15 36 48 60

DECADE OF DARK HORSE, A
Dark Horse Comics: Jul, 1996 - No. 4, Oct, 1996 ($2.95, B&W/color, lim. series)

1-4: 1-Sin City-c/story by Miller; Grendel by Wagner; Predator. 2-Star Wars wraparound-c. 3-Aliens-c/story; Nexus, Mask stories 3.00

DECAPITATOR (Randy Bowen's...)
Dark Horse Comics: Jun, 1998 - No. 4, ($2.95)

1-4-Bowen-s/art by various. 1-Mahnke-c. 3-Jones-c 4.00

DECEPTION, THE
Image Comics (Flypaper Press): 1999 - No. 3, 1999 ($2.95, B&W, mini-series)

1-3-Horley painted-c 3.00

DEEP, THE (Movie)
Marvel Comics Group: Nov, 1977 (Giant)

1-Infantino-c/a 1 2 3 5 6 8

DEEP DARK FANTASIES
Dark Fantasy Productions: Oct, 1995 ($4.50/$4.95, B&W)

1-($4.50)-Clive Barker-c, anthology 4.50
1-($4.95)-Red foil logo-c 5.00

DEFCON 4
Image Comics (WildStorm Productions): Feb, 1996 - No. 4, Sept, 1996 ($2.50, lim. series)

1/2 1 2 3 5 7 9
1/2 Gold-(1000 printed) 14.00
1-Main Cover by Mat Broome & Edwin Rosell 3.00
1-Hordes of Cymulants variant-c by Michael Golden 5.00
1-Backs to the Wall variant-c by Humberto Ramos & Alex Garner 5.00
1-Defcon 4-Way variant-c by Jim Lee 1 2 3 4 5 7
2-4 2.50

DEFENDERS, THE (TV)
Dell Publishing Co.: Sept-Nov, 1962 - No. 2, Feb-Apr, 1963

12-176-211(#1) 4 8 12 29 40 50
12-176-304(#2) 4 8 12 24 32 40

DEFENDERS, THE (Also see Giant-Size..., Marvel Feature, Marvel Treasury Edition, Secret Defenders & Sub-Mariner #34, 35; The New...#140-on)
Marvel Comics Group: Aug, 1972 - No. 152, Feb, 1986

1-The Hulk, Doctor Strange, Sub-Mariner begin 10 20 30 72 104 135
2-Silver Surfer x-over 5 10 15 36 48 60
3-5: 3-Silver Surfer x-over. 4-Valkyrie joins 4 8 12 24 32 40
6,7: 6-Silver Surfer x-over 3 6 9 18 24 30
8,9,11: 8-11-Defenders vs. the Avengers (Crossover with Avengers #115-118)
8,11-Silver Surfer x-over 4 8 12 24 32 40

The Defenders #55 © MAR

Dell Giant - Bugs Bunny's Halloween Parade #1 © WB

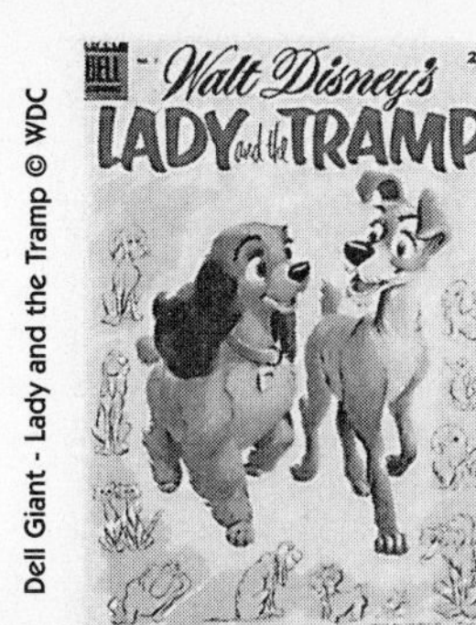

DELL
25¢
Walt Disney's
LADY and the TRAMP

Dell Giant - Lady and the Tramp © WDC

	GD 2.0	VG 4.0	FN 6.0	VF 8.0	VF/NM 9.0	NM- 9.2
10-Hulk vs. Thor battle	4	8	12	29	40	50
12-14: 12-Last 20¢ issue	2	4	6	11	14	18
15,16-Magneto & Brotherhood of Evil Mutants app. from X-Men	2	4	6	12	16	20
17-20: 17-Power Man x-over (11/74)	1	3	4	6	8	10
21-25: 24,25-Son of Satan app.						6.00
26-29-Guardians of the Galaxy app. (#26 is 8/75; pre-dates Marvel Presents #3): 28-1st full app. Starhawk (cameo #27). 29-Starhawk joins Guardians	1	2	3	5	6	8
30-33,39-50: 31,32-Origin Nighthawk. 44-Hellcat joins. 45-Dr. Strange leaves. 47-49-Early Moon Knight app. (5/77). 48-50-(Reg. 30¢-c)						5.00
34-38-(Regular 25¢ editions): 35-Intro New Red Guardian						5.00
34-38-(30¢-c variants, limited distribution)(4-8/76)	1	2	3	4	5	7
48-52-(35¢-c variants, limited distribution)(6-10/77)	1	2	3	4	5	7
51-60: 51,52-(Reg. 30¢-c). 53-1st app. Lunatik (cameo, Lobo lookalike). 55-Origin Red Guardian; Lunatik cameo. 56-1st full Lunatik story						4.00
61-75: 61-Lunatik & Spider-Man app. 70-73-Lunatik (origin #71). 73-75-Foolkiller II app. (Greg Salinger). 74-Nighthawk resigns						3.00
76-93,95,97-99,102-119,123,124,126-149,151: 77-Origin Omega. 78-Original Defenders return thru #101. 104-The Beast joins. 105-Son of Satan joins. 106-Death of Nighthawk. 129-New Mutants cameo (3/84, early x-over)						2.50
94,101,120-122: 94-1st Gargoyle. 101-Silver Surfer-c & app. 120,121-Son of Satan-c/stories. 122-Final app. Son of Satan (2 pgs.)						4.00
96-Ghost Rider app.						4.00
100-(52 pgs.)-Hellcat (Patsy Walker) revealed as Satan's daughter						5.00
125,150: 125-(52 pgs.)-Intro new Defenders. 150-(52 pgs.)-Origin Cloud						4.00
152-(52 pgs.)-Ties in with X-Factor & Secret Wars II						4.00
Annual 1 (1976, 52 pgs.)-New book-length story	2	4	6	14	18	22

NOTE: ***Art Adams** c-142p. **Austin** a-53i; c-65i, 119i, 145i. **Frank Bolle** a-7i, 10i, 11i. **Buckler** c(p)-34, 38, 76, 77, 79-86, 90, 91. **J. Buscema** c-66. **Giffen** a-42-49p, 50, 51-54p. **Golden** a-53p, 54p; c-94, 96. **Guice** c-129. **G. Kane** c(p)-13, 16, 18, 19, 21-26, 31-33, 35-37, 40, 41, 52, 55. **Kirby** c-42-45. **Mooney** a-3i, 31-34i, 62i, 63i, 85i. **Nasser** c-88p. **Perez** c(p)-51, 53, 54. **Rogers** c-98. **Starlin** c-110. **Tuska** a-57p. Silver Surfer in No. 2, 3, 6, 8-11, 92, 98-101, 107, 112-115, 122-125.*

DEFENDERS, THE (Volume 2) (Continues in The Order)
Marvel Comics: Mar, 2001 - No. 12, Feb, 2002 ($2.99/$2.25)

	GD	VG	FN	VF	VF/NM	NM-
1-Busiek & Larsen-s/Larsen & Janson-a/c						3.00
2-11: 2-Two covers by Larsen & Art Adams; Valkyrie app. 4-Frenz-a						2.25
12-($3.50) 'Nuff Said issue; back-up-s Reis-a						3.50

DEFENDERS OF DYNATRON CITY
Marvel Comics: Feb, 1992 - No. 6, July, 1992 ($1.25, limited series)

	GD	VG	FN	VF	VF/NM	NM-
1-6-Lucasarts characters. 2-Origin						3.00

DEFENDERS OF THE EARTH (TV)
Marvel Comics (Star Comics): Jan, 1987 - No. 4, July, 1987

	GD	VG	FN	VF	VF/NM	NM-
1-4: The Phantom, Mandrake The Magician, Flash Gordon begin. 3-Origin Phantom. 4-Origin Mandrake						4.00

DEFIANCE
Image Comics: Feb, 2002 - Present ($2.95)

	GD	VG	FN	VF	VF/NM	NM-
Preview Edition (12/01)						2.25
1-8-Barré-s/Kang & Suh-a						3.00

DEFINITIVE DIRECTORY OF THE DC UNIVERSE, THE (See Who's Who...)

DEITY (Also see Kosmic Kat)
Hyperwerks Comics: Sept, 1997 - No. 6, Apr, 1998, ($2.95, limited series)

	GD	VG	FN	VF	VF/NM	NM-
1-6, 0(5/98)						4.00
1-Variant-c						5.00
2-6,0-Variant covers						4.00
0-NDC Edition						4.00
0-NDC Silver Ed.						8.00
0-NDC Gold Ed.						12.00

DEITY (Volume 2)
Hyperwerks Comics: Sept, 1998 - No. 5 ($2.95)

	GD	VG	FN	VF	VF/NM	NM-
Preview (6/98) Flip book with Lady Pendragon preview						3.00
1-5: 1-Flip book w/Catseye preview						3.00

DEITY:REVELATIONS (Volume 3)
Hyperwerks Comics: July, 1999 - No. 4, Dec, 1999 ($2.95)

	GD	VG	FN	VF	VF/NM	NM-
1-4-Alstaetter and Napton-s/a						3.00

DELECTA OF THE PLANETS (See Don Fortune & Fawcett Miniatures)

DELICATE CREATURES
Image Comics (Top Cow): 2001 ($16.95, hardcover with dust jacket)

	GD	VG	FN	VF	VF/NM	NM-
nn-Fairy tale storybook; J. Michael Straczynski-s; Michael Zulli-a						17.00

DELLA VISION (...The Television Queen) (Patty Powers #4 on)
Atlas Comics: April, 1955 - No. 3, Aug, 1955

	GD 2.0	VG 4.0	FN 6.0	VF 8.0	VF/NM 9.0	NM- 9.2
1-Al Hartley-c	16	32	48	92	126	160
2,3	11	22	33	63	84	105

DELL GIANT COMICS

Dell Publishing began to release square bound comics in 1949 with a 132-page issue called Christmas Parade #1. The covers were of a heavier stock to accommodate the increased number of pages. The books proved profitable at 25 cents, but the average number of pages was quickly reduced to 100. Ten years later they were converted to a numbering system similar to the Four Color Comics, for greater ease in distribution and the page counts cut back to mostly 84 pages. The label "Dell Giant" began to appear on the covers in 1954. Because of the size of the books and the heavier, less pliant cover stock, they are rarely found in high grade condition, and with the exception of a small quantity of copies released from Western Publishing's warehouse–are almost never found in near mint.

	GD	VG	FN	VF	VF/NM	NM-
Abraham Lincoln Life Story 1(3/58)	6	12	18	48	87	125
Bugs Bunny Christmas Funnies 1(11/50, 116pp)	16	32	48	128	224	320
...Christmas Funnies 2(11/51, 116pp)	10	20	30	80	140	200
...Christmas Funnies 3-5(11/52-11/54,)-Becomes Christmas Party #6	9	18	27	72	124	175
...Christmas Funnies 7-9(12/56-12/58)	8	16	24	64	110	155
...Christmas Party 6(11/55)-Formerly Bugs Bunny Christmas Funnies	8	16	24	64	110	155
...County Fair 1(9/57)	9	18	27	72	126	180
...Halloween Parade 1(10/53)	10	20	30	80	140	200
...Halloween Parade 2(10/54)-Trick 'N' Treat Halloween Fun #3 on	8	16	24	64	115	165
...Trick 'N' Treat Halloween Fun 3,4(10/55-10/56)-Formerly Halloween Parade #2	8	16	24	64	115	165
...Vacation Funnies 1(7/51, 112pp)	16	32	48	128	219	310
...Vacation Funnies 2('52)	11	22	33	88	157	225
...Vacation Funnies 3-5('53-'55)	9	18	27	72	124	175
...Vacation Funnies 6-9('56-'59)	8	16	24	64	110	155
Cadet Gray of West Point 1(4/58)-Williamson-a, 10pgs.; Buscema-a; photo-c	6	12	18	48	87	125
Christmas In Disneyland 1(12/57)-Barks-a, 18 pgs.	23	46	69	184	317	450
Christmas Parade 1(11/49)(132 pgs.)(1st Dell Giant)-Donald Duck (25pgs. by Barks, r-in G.K. Christmas Parade #5); Mickey Mouse & other film oriented stories; Cinderella (prior to movie), 7 Dwarfs, Bambi & Thumper, So Dear To My Heart, Flying Mouse, Dumbo, Cookieland & others	53	106	159	424	737	1050
Christmas Parade 2('50)-Donald Duck (132 pgs.)(25 pgs. by Barks, r-in Gold Key's Christmas Parade #6). Mickey, Pluto, Chip & Dale, etc. Contents shift to a holiday expansion of W.D. C&S type format	39	78	117	312	544	775
Christmas Parade 3-7('51-'55, #3-116pgs; #4-7, 100 pgs.)	12	24	36	96	168	240
Christmas Parade 8(12/56)-Barks-a, 8 pgs.	19	38	57	152	269	385
Christmas Parade 9(12/58)-Barks-a, 20 pgs.	23	46	69	184	317	450
Christmas Treasury, A 1(11/54)	8	16	24	64	110	155
Davy Crockett, King Of The Wild Frontier 1(9/55)-Fess Parker photo-c; Marsh-a	18	36	54	144	247	350
Disneyland Birthday Party 1(10/58)-Barks-a, 16 pgs. r-by Gladstone	23	46	69	184	317	450
Donald and Mickey In Disneyland 1(5/58)	10	20	30	80	140	200
Donald Duck Beach Party 1(7/54)-Has an Uncle Scrooge story (not by Barks) that prefigures the later rivalry with Flintheart Glomgold and tells of Scrooge's wild rivalry with another millionaire	14	28	42	112	196	280
...Beach Party 2(1955)-Lady & Tramp	10	20	30	80	140	200
...Beach Party 3-5(1956-58)	9	18	27	72	131	190
...Beach Party 6(8/59, 84pp)-Stapled	7	14	21	56	98	140
Donald Duck Fun Book 1,2(1953 & 10/54)-Games, puzzles, comics & cut-outs (very rare in unused condition)(most copies commonly have defaced interior pgs.)	50	10	150	400	700	1000
Donald Duck In Disneyland 1(9/55)-1st Disneyland Dell Giant	13	26	39	104	182	260
Golden West Rodeo Treasury 1(10/57)	8	16	24	64	115	165
Huey, Dewey and Louie Back To School 1(9/58)	8	16	24	64	110	155
Lady and The Tramp 1(6/55)	15	30	45	120	210	300
Life Stories of American Presidents 1(11/57)-Buscema-a	6	12	18	48	84	120
Lone Ranger Golden West 3(8/55)-Formerly Lone Ranger Western Treasury	16	32	48	128	227	325
Lone Ranger Movie Story nn(3/56)-Origin Lone Ranger in text; Clayton Moore photo-c	33	66	99	264	457	650
...Western Treasury 1(9/53)-Origin Lone Ranger, Silver, & Tonto; painted cover						

Dell Giant - Marge's Lulu and Tubby Halloween Fun #6 © Marjorie H. Buell

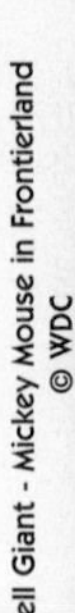
Dell Giant - Mickey Mouse in Frontierland © WDC

Dell Giant #33 © WDC

	GD 2.0	VG 4.0	FN 6.0	VF 8.0	VF/NM 9.0	NM- 9.2
	21	42	63	168	297	425
...Western Treasury 2(8/54)-Becomes Lone Ranger Golden West #3	16	32	48	128	227	325
Marge's Little Lulu & Alvin Story Telling Time 1(3/59)-r/#2,5,3,11,30,10,21,17,8, 14,16; Stanley-a	12	24	36	96	168	240
...& Her Friends 4(3/56)-Tripp-a	12	24	36	96	163	230
...& Her Special Friends 3(3/55)-Tripp-a	13	26	39	104	182	260
...& Tubby At Summer Camp 5,2: 5(10/57)-Tripp-a. 2(10/58)-Tripp-a	11	22	33	88	154	220
...& Tubby Halloween Fun 6,2: 6(10/57)-Tripp-a. 2(10/58)-Tripp-a	11	22	33	88	154	220
...& Tubby In Alaska 1(7/59)-Tripp-a	10	20	30	80	145	210
...On Vacation 1(7/54)-r/4C-110,14,4C-146,5,4C-97,4,4C-158,3,1;Stanley-a	23	46	69	184	317	450
...& Tubby Annual 1(3/53)-r/4C-165,4C-74,4C-146,4C-97,4C-158, 4C-139, 4C-131; Stanley-a (1st Lulu Dell Giant)	27	54	81	216	378	540
...& Tubby Annual 2('54)-r/4C-139,6,4C-115,4C-74,5,4C-97,3,4C-146,18; Stanley-a	23	46	69	184	317	450
Marge's Tubby & His Clubhouse Pals 1(10/56)-1st app. Gran'pa Feeb;1st app. Janie; written by Stanley; Tripp-a	13	26	39	104	182	260
Mickey Mouse Almanac 1(12/57)-Barks-a, 8pgs.	24	48	72	192	331	470
...Birthday Party 1(9/53)-r/entire 48pgs. of Gottfredson's "Mickey Mouse in Love Trouble" from WDC&S 36-39. Quality equal to original. Also reprints one story each from Four Color 27, 79, & 181 plus 6 panels of highlights in the career of Mickey Mouse	28	56	84	224	387	550
...Club Parade 1(12/55)-r/4-Color 16 with some death trap scenes redrawn by Paul Murry & recolored with night turned into day; quality less than original	20	40	60	160	280	400
...In Fantasy Land 1(5/57)	12	24	36	96	163	230
...In Frontier Land 1(5/56)-Mickey Mouse Club iss.	12	24	36	96	163	230
...Summer Fun 1(8/58)-Mobile cut-outs on back-c; becomes Summer Fun with #2	12	24	36	96	163	230
Moses & The Ten Commandments 1(8/57)-Not based on movie; Dell's adaptation; Sekowsky-a	6	12	18	48	79	110
Nancy & Sluggo Travel Time 1(9/58)	7	14	21	56	98	140
Peter Pan Treasure Chest 1(1/53, 212pp)-Disney; contains 54-page movie adaptation & other Peter Pan stories; plus Donald & Mickey stories w/P. Pan; a 32-page retelling of "D. Duck Finds Pirate Gold" with yellow beak, called "Capt. Hook & the Buried Treasure"	98	196	294	784	1367	1950
Picnic Party 6,7(7/55-6/56)(Formerly Vacation Parade)-Uncle Scrooge, Mickey & Donald	10	20	30	80	145	210
Picnic Party 8(7/57)-Barks-a, 6pgs	20	40	60	160	275	390
Pogo Parade 1(9/53)-Kelly-a(r-/Pogo from Animal Comics in this order: #11,13,21,14,27,16,23,9,18,15,17)	24	48	72	192	336	480
Raggedy Ann & Andy 1(2/55)	14	28	42	112	191	270
Santa Claus Funnies 1(11/52)-Dan Noonan -A Christmas Carol adaptation	8	16	24	64	110	155
Silly Symphonies 1(9/52)-Redrawing of Gotfredson's Mickey Mouse strip of "The Brave Little Tailor;" 2 Good Housekeeping pages (from 1943); Lady and the Two Siamese Cats, three years before "Lady & the Tramp;" a retelling of Donald Duck's first app. in "The Wise Little Hen" & other stories based on 1930's Silly Symphony cartoons	26	52	78	208	364	520
Silly Symphonies 2(9/53)-M. Mouse in "The Sorcerer's Apprentice", 2 Good Housekeeping pages (from 1944); The Pelican & the Snipe, Elmer Elephant, Peculiar Penguins, Little Hiawatha, & others	22	44	66	176	308	440
Silly Symphonies 3(2/54)-r/Mickey & The Beanstalk (4-Color #157, 39pgs.), Little Minnehaha, Pablo, The Flying Gauchito, Pluto, & Bongo, & 2 Good Housekeeping pages (1944)	18	36	54	144	252	360
Silly Symphonies 4(8/54)-r/Dumbo (4-Color 234), Morris The Midget Moose, The Country Cousin, Bongo, & Clara Cluck	18	36	54	144	252	360
Silly Symphonies 5-8: 5(2/55)-r/Cinderella (4-Color 272), Bucky Bug, Pluto, Little Hiawatha, The 7 Dwarfs & Dumbo, Pinocchio. 6(8/55)-r/Pinocchio (WDC&S 63), The 7 Dwarfs & Thumper (WDC&S 45), M. Mouse "Adventures With Robin Hood" (40 pgs.), Johnny Appleseed, Pluto & Peter Pan, & Bucky Bug; Cut-out on back-c. 7(2/57)-r/Reluctant Dragon, Ugly Duckling, M. Mouse & Peter Pan, Jiminy Cricket, Peter & The Wolf, Brer Rabbit, Bucky Bug; Cut-out on back-c. 8(2/58)-r/Thumper Meets The 7 Dwarfs (4-Color #19), Jiminy Cricket, Niok, Brer Rabbit; Cut-out on back-c	15	30	45	120	210	300
Silly Symphonies 9(2/59)-r/Paul Bunyan, Humphrey Bear, Jiminy Cricket, The Social Lion, Goliath II; cut-out on back-c	14	28	42	112	196	280
Sleeping Beauty 1(4/59)	24	48	72	192	336	480
Summer Fun 2(8/59, 84pp, stapled binding)(Formerly Mickey Mouse...)-Barks-a(2), 24 pgs.	23	46	69	184	317	450
Tarzan's Jungle Annual 1(8/52)-Lex Barker photo on-c of #1,2	13	26	39	104	177	250

	GD 2.0	VG 4.0	FN 6.0	VF 8.0	VF/NM 9.0	NM- 9.2
...Annual 2(8/53)	9	18	27	72	129	185
...Annual 3-7('54-9/58)(two No. 5s)-Manning-a-No. 3,5-7; Marsh-a in No. 1-7 plus painted-c 1-7	8	16	24	64	110	155
Tom And Jerry Back To School 1(9/56)	11	22	33	88	154	220
...Picnic Time 1(7/58)	8	16	24	64	117	170
...Summer Fun 1(7/54)-Droopy written by Barks	14	28	42	112	191	270
...Summer Fun 2-4(7/55-7/57)	7	14	21	56	96	135
...Toy Fair 1(6/58)	8	16	24	64	112	160
...Winter Carnival 1(12/52)-Droopy written by Barks	18	36	54	144	252	360
...Winter Carnival 2(12/53)-Droopy written by Barks	15	30	45	120	210	300
...Winter Fun 3(12/54)	8	16	24	64	107	150
...Winter Fun 4-7(12/55-11/58)	6	12	18	48	87	125
Treasury of Dogs, A 1(10/56)	6	12	18	48	84	120
Treasury of Horses, A (9/55)	6	12	18	48	84	120
Uncle Scrooge Goes To Disneyland 1(8/57p)-Barks-a, 20pgs.r-by Gladstone	23	46	69	184	317	450
Vacation In Disneyland 1(8/58)	10	20	30	80	140	200
Vacation Parade 1(7/50, 132pp)-Donald Duck & Mickey Mouse; Barks-a, 55 pgs.	78	156	234	624	1087	1550
Vacation Parade 2(7/51,116pp)	23	46	69	184	317	450
Vacation Parade 3-5(7/52-7/54)-Becomes Picnic Party No. 6 on. #4-Robin Hood Advs.	13	26	39	104	177	250
Western Roundup 1(6/52)-Photo-c; Gene Autry, Roy Rogers, Johnny Mack Brown, Rex Allen, & Bill Elliott begin; photo back-c begin, end No. 14,16,18	22	44	66	176	308	440
Western Roundup 2(2/53)-Photo-c	13	26	39	104	177	250
Western Roundup 3-5(7-9/53 - 1-3/54)-Photo-c	10	20	30	80	140	200
Western Roundup 6-10(4-6/54 - 4-6/55)-Photo-c	9	18	27	72	126	180
Western Roundup 11-17,25-Photo-c; 11-13,16,17-Manning-a. 11-Flying A's Range Rider, Dale Evans begin	8	16	24	64	112	160
Western Roundup 18-Toth-a; last photo-c; Gene Autry ends	9	18	27	72	126	180
Western Roundup 19-24-Manning-a. 19-Buffalo Bill Jr. begins (7-9/57; early app.). 19,20,22-Toth-a. 21-Rex Allen, Johnny Mack Brown end. 22-Jace Pearson's Texas Rangers, Rin Tin Tin, Tales of Wells Fargo (2nd app., 4-6/58) & Wagon Train (2nd app.) begin	8	16	24	64	112	160
Woody Woodpecker Back To School 1(10/52)	9	18	27	72	126	180
...Back To School 2-4,6('53-10/57)-County Fair No. 5	7	14	21	56	98	140
...County Fair 5(9/56)-Formerly Back To School	7	14	21	56	98	140
...County Fair 2(11/58)	6	12	18	48	84	120

DELL GIANTS (Consecutive numbering)
Dell Publishing Co.: No. 21, Sept, 1959 - No. 55, Sept, 1961 (Most 84 pgs., 25¢)

	GD 2.0	VG 4.0	FN 6.0	VF 8.0	VF/NM 9.0	NM- 9.2
21-(#1)-M.G.M.'s Tom & Jerry Picnic Time (84pp, stapled binding)-Painted-c	9	18	27	72	129	185
22-Huey, Dewey & Louie Back to School (Disney; 10/59, 84pp, square binding begins)	8	16	24	64	110	155
23-Marge's Little Lulu & Tubby Halloween Fun (10/59)-Tripp-a	10	20	30	80	140	200
24-Woody Woodpecker's Family Fun (11/59)(Walter Lantz)	7	14	21	56	100	145
25-Tarzan's Jungle World(11/59)-Marsh-a; painted-c	9	18	27	72	129	185
26-Christmas Parade(Disney; 12/59)-Barks-a, 16pgs.; Barks draws himself on wanted poster on pg. 13	18	36	54	144	252	360
27-Walt Disney's Man in Space (10/59) r-/4-Color 716,866, & 954 (100 pgs., 35¢)(TV)	8	16	24	64	115	165
28-Bugs Bunny's Winter Fun (2/60)	8	16	24	64	115	165
29-Marge's Little Lulu & Tubby in Hawaii (4/60)-Tripp-a	10	20	30	80	140	200
30-Disneyland USA(Disney; 6/60)	8	16	24	64	110	155
31-Huckleberry Hound Summer Fun (7/60)(TV)(HannaBarbera)-Yogi Bear & Pixie & Dixie app.	11	22	33	88	157	225
32-Bugs Bunny Beach Party	6	12	18	48	87	125
33-Daisy Duck & Uncle Scrooge Picnic Time (Disney; 9/60)	8	16	24	64	110	155
34-Nancy & Sluggo Summer Camp (8/60)	6	12	18	48	87	125
35-Huey, Dewey & Louie Back to School (Disney; 10/60)-1st app. Daisy Duck's Nieces, April, May & June	10	20	30	80	140	200
36-Marge's Little Lulu & Witch Hazel Halloween Fun (10/60)-Tripp-a	9	18	27	72	129	185
37-Tarzan, King of the Jungle (11/60)-Marsh-a; painted-c	8	16	24	64	115	165
38-Uncle Donald & His Nephews Family Fun (Disney; 11/60)-Cover painting based on a pencil sketch by Barks	11	22	33	88	157	225
39-Walt Disney's Merry Christmas (Disney; 12/60)-Cover painting based on a pencil sketch						

Dell Junior Treasury #5 © MGM

The Demon #5 © DC

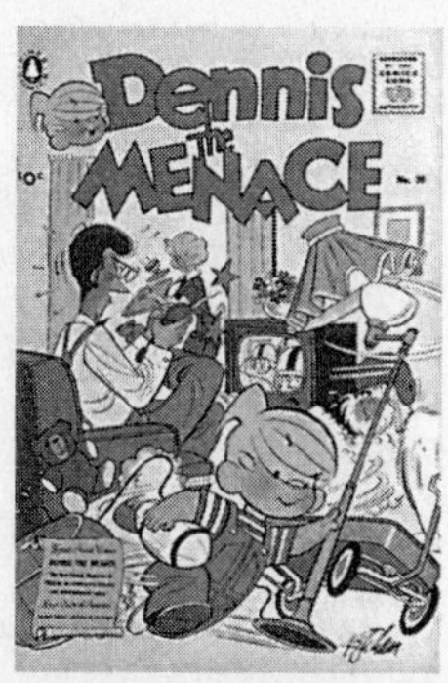

Dennis the Menace #20 © KFS

	GD 2.0	VG 4.0	FN 6.0	VF 8.0	VF/NM 9.0	NM- 9.2
by Barks	11	22	33	88	157	225
40-Woody Woodpecker Christmas Parade (12/60)(Walter Lantz)	5	10	15	40	73	105
41-Yogi Bear's Winter Sports (12/60)(TV)(Hanna-Barbera)-Huckleberry Hound, Pixie & Dixie, Augie Doggie app.	11	22	33	88	157	225
42-Marge's Little Lulu & Tubby in Australia (4/61)	10	20	30	80	140	200
43-Mighty Mouse in Outer Space (5/61)	17	34	51	136	238	340
44-Around the World with Huckleberry and His Friends (7/61)(TV)(Hanna-Barbera)-Yogi Bear, Pixie & Dixie, Quick Draw McGraw, Augie Doggie app.; 1st app. Yakky Doodle	12	24	36	96	166	235
45-Nancy & Sluggo Summer Camp (8/61)	6	12	18	48	82	115
46-Bugs Bunny Beach Party (8/61)	6	12	18	48	82	115
47-Mickey & Donald in Vacationland (Disney; 8/61)	7	14	21	56	100	145
48-The Flintstones (No. 1)(Bedrock Bedlam)(7/61)(TV)(Hanna-Barbera) 1st app. in comics	18	36	54	144	247	350
49-Huey, Dewey & Louie Back to School (Disney; 9/61)	8	16	24	64	110	155
50-Marge's Little Lulu & Witch Hazel Trick 'N' Treat (10/61)	9	18	27	72	129	185
51-Tarzan, King of the Jungle by Jesse Marsh (11/61)-Painted-c	7	14	21	56	96	135
52-Uncle Donald & His Nephews Dude Ranch (Disney; 11/61)	7	14	21	56	96	135
53-Donald Duck Merry Christmas (Disney; 12/61)	7	14	21	56	96	135
54-Woody Woodpecker's Christmas Party (12/61)-Issued after No. 55	6	12	18	48	87	125
55-Daisy Duck & Uncle Scrooge Showboat (Disney; 9/61)	8	16	224	64	110	155

NOTE: All issues printed with & without ad on back cover.

DELL JUNIOR TREASURY
Dell Publishing Co.: June, 1955 - No. 10, Oct, 1957 (15¢) (All painted-c)

	GD	VG	FN	VF	VF/NM	NM-
1-Alice in Wonderland; r/4-Color #331 (52 pgs.)	10	20	30	72	104	135
2-Aladdin & the Wonderful Lamp	8	16	24	55	78	100
3-Gulliver's Travels (1/56)	7	14	21	51	71	90
4-Adventures of Mr. Frog & Miss Mouse	8	16	24	53	74	95
5-The Wizard of Oz (7/56)	8	16	24	55	78	100
6-10: 6-Heidi (10/56). 7-Santa and the Angel. 8-Raggedy Ann and the Came with the Wrinkled Knees. 9-Clementina the Flying Pig. 10-Adventures of Tom Sawyer	7	14	21	51	71	90

DEMOLITION MAN
DC Comics: Nov, 1993 - No. 4, Feb, 1994 ($1.75, color, limited series)

1-4-Movie adaptation 2.25

DEMON, THE (See Detective Comics No. 482-485)
National Periodical Publications: Aug-Sept, 1972 - V3#16, Jan, 1974

	GD	VG	FN	VF	VF/NM	NM-
1-Origin; Kirby-c/a in all	5	10	15	33	44	55
2-5	3	6	9	18	23	28
6-16	2	4	6	11	14	18

DEMON, THE (1st limited series)(Also see Cosmic Odyssey #2)
DC Comics: Nov, 1986 - No. 4, Feb, 1987 (75¢, limited series)(#2 has #4 of 4 on-c)

1-4: Matt Wagner-a(p) & scripts in all. 4-Demon & Jason Blood become separate entities. 3.00

DEMON, THE (2nd Series)
DC Comics: July, 1990 - No. 57, May, 1995 ($1.50/$1.75/$1.95)

1-Grant scripts begin, ends #39: 1-4-Painted-c 4.00
2-18,20-27,29-39,41,42,46,47: 3,8-Batman app. (cameo #4). 12-Bisley painted-c. 12-15,21-Lobo app. (1 pg. cameo #11). 23-Robin app. 29-Superman app. 31,33-39-Lobo app. 2.50
19,28,40: 19-($2.50, 44 pgs.)-Lobo poster stapled inside. 28-Superman-c/story; begin $1.75-c. 40-Garth Ennis scripts begin 4.00

	GD	VG	FN	VF	VF/NM	NM-
43-45-Hitman app.	1	2	3	5	6	8
46-48 Return of The Haunted Tank-c/s. 48-Begin $1.95-c.						5.00
49,51,0-(10/94),55-57: 51-(9/94)						2.50
50 ($2.95, 52 pgs.)						3.00
52-54-Hitman-s						5.00
Annual 1 (1992, $3.00, 68 pgs.)-Eclipso-c/story						3.00
Annual 2 (1993, $3.50, 68 pgs.)-1st app. of Hitman	2	4	6	10	13	16

NOTE: *Alan Grant scripts in #1-16, 20, 21, 23-25, 30-39, Annual 1.* ***Wagner*** *a/scripts-22.*

DEMON DREAMS
Pacific Comics: Feb, 1984 - No. 2, May, 1984

1,2-Mostly r-/Heavy Metal 2.25

DEMON: DRIVEN OUT
DC Comics: Nov, 2003 - No. 6 ($2.50, limited series)

1-5-Dysart-s/Mhan-a 2.50

DEMONGATE
Sirius Entertainment: May, 1996 - No. 10 ($2.50, B&W)

1-10-Bao Lin Hum/Steve Blevins-s/a 2.50

DEMON GUN
Crusade Ent.: June, 1996 - No. 3, Jan, 1997 ($2.95, B&W, limited series)

1-3: Gary Cohn scripts in all. 2-(10/96) 3.00

DEMON-HUNTER
Seaboard Periodicals (Atlas): Sept, 1975

	GD	VG	FN	VF	VF/NM	NM-
1-Origin/1st app. Demon-Hunter; Buckler-c/a	1	2	3	4	5	7

DEMON KNIGHT: A GRIMJACK GRAPHIC NOVEL
First Publishing: 1990 ($8.95, 52 pgs.)

nn-Flint Henry-a 9.00

DEMONSLAYER
Image Comics: Nov, 1999 - No. 3, Jan, 2000 ($2.95)

1-3-Story & art by Mychaels & Mendoza 3.00

DEMONSLAYER: INTO HELL (Volume 2)
Image Comics: Apr, 2000 - No. 3, Aug, 2000 ($2.95)

1-3-Story & art by Mychaels 3.00
1-3 ($5.00) Variant cover editions 5.00

DEMONWARS: EYE FOR AN EYE (R.A. Salvatore's...)
CrossGeneration Comics (Code 6 Comics): Jun, 2003 - No. 5, Nov, 2003 ($2.95, lim. series)

1-5-Ciencin-s/Tocchini-a 3.00

DEMONWARS: TRIAL BY FIRE (R.A. Salvatore's...)
CrossGeneration Comics (Code 6 Comics): Jan, 2003 - No. 5, May, 2003 ($2.95, lim. series)

1-5-Ciencin-s/Wagner-a 3.00
TPB (2003, $9.95) r/#1-5; new short story by Salvatore 10.00

DENNIS THE MENACE (TV with 1959 issues) (Becomes ...Fun Fest Series; See The Best of... & The Very Best of...)(...Fun Fest on-c only to #156-166)
Standard Comics/Pines No.15-31/Hallden (Fawcett) No.32 on: 8/53 - #14, 1/56; #15, 3/56 - #31, 11/58; #32, 1/59 - #166, 11/79

	GD	VG	FN	VF	VF/NM	NM-
1-1st app. Dennis, Mr. & Mrs. Wilson, Ruff & Dennis' mom & dad; Wiseman-a, written by Fred Toole-most issues	58	116	174	363	544	725
2	29	58	87	164	232	300
3-10: 8-Last pre-code issue	16	32	48	92	126	160
11-20	12	24	36	71	96	120
21,23-30	9	18	27	54	70	85
22-1st app. Margaret w/blonde hair	10	20	30	60	80	100
31-1st app. Joey	10	20	30	60	80	100
32-38,40(1/60): 37-A-Bomb blast panel	7	14	21	35	43	50
39-1st app. Gina (11/59)	7	14	21	37	46	55
41-60(7/62)	3	7	10	21	28	35
61-80(9/65),100(1/69)	2	4	6	14	18	22
81-99	2	4	6	11	14	18
101-117: 102-Last 12¢ issue	2	4	6	9	11	14
118(1/72)-131 (All 52 pages)	2	4	6	10	13	16
132(1/74)-142,144-160	1	2	3	5	6	8
143(3/76) Olympic-c/s; low print	2	4	6	10	13	16
161-166	1	2	3	5	7	9

NOTE: ***Wiseman*** *c/a-1-46, 53, 68, 69.*

DENNIS THE MENACE (Giants) (No. 1 titled Giant Vacation Special; becomes Dennis the Menace Bonus Magazine No. 76 on)
(#1-8,18,23,25,30,38: 100 pgs.; rest to #41: 84 pgs.; #42-75: 68 pgs.)
Standard/Pines/Hallden(Fawcett): Summer, 1955 - No. 75, Dec, 1969

	GD	VG	FN	VF	VF/NM	NM-
nn-Giant Vacation Special(Summ/55-Standard)	18	36	54	104	142	180
nn-Christmas issue (Winter '55)	16	32	48	92	126	160
2-Giant Vacation Special (Summer '56-Pines)	14	28	42	79	107	135
3-Giant Christmas issue (Winter '56-Pines)	13	26	39	74	100	125
4-Giant Vacation Special (Summer '57-Pines)	12	24	36	69	92	115
5-Giant Christmas issue (Winter '57-Pines)	12	24	36	69	92	115
6-In Hawaii (Giant Vacation Special)(Summer '58-Pines)	11	22	33	63	84	105
6-In Hawaii (Summer '59-Hallden)-2nd printing; says 3rd large printing on-c						
6-In Hawaii (Summer '60)-3rd printing; says 4th large printing on-c						
6-In Hawaii (Summer '62)-4th printing; says 5th large printing on-c each....	8	16	24	43	54	65

Dennis the Menace #7 © KFS

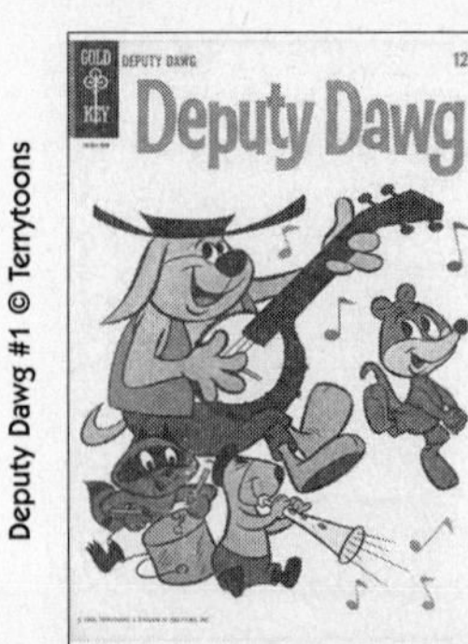

Deputy Dawg #1 © Terrytoons

Desperado #4 © LEV

	GD 2.0	VG 4.0	FN 6.0	VF 8.0	VF/NM 9.0	NM- 9.2
6-Giant Christmas issue (Winter '58)	11	22	33	63	84	105
7-In Hollywood (Winter '59-Hallden)	6	12	18	38	52	65
7-In Hollywood (Summer '61)-2nd printing	4	8	12	25	33	42
8-In Mexico (Winter '60, 100 pgs.-Hallden/Fawcett)	6	12	18	38	52	65
8-In Mexico (Summer '62, 2nd printing)	4	8	12	24	32	40
9-Goes to Camp (Summer '61, 84 pgs.)-1st CCA approved issue	6	12	18	38	52	65
9-Goes to Camp (Summer '62)-2nd printing	4	8	12	24	32	40
10-12: 10-X-Mas issue (Winter '61), 11-Giant Christmas issue (Winter '62), 12-Triple Feature (Winter '62)	6	12	18	40	55	70
13-17: 13-Best of Dennis the Menace (Spring '63)-Reprints, 14-And His Dog Ruff (Summer '63), 15-In Washington, D.C. (Summer '63), 16-Goes to Camp (Summer '63)-Reprints No. 9, 17-& His Pal Joey (Winter '63)	4	8	12	25	33	42
18-In Hawaii (Reprints No. 6)	3	6	9	19	25	32
19-Giant Christmas issue (Winter '63)	4	8	12	25	33	42
20-Spring Special (Spring '64)	4	8	12	25	33	42
21-40 (Summer '66): 30-r/#6. #35-Xmas spec.Wint,'65	3	6	9	18	24	30
41-60 (Fall '68)	2	4	6	12	16	20
61-75 (12/69): 68-Partial-r/#6	2	4	6	10	13	16

NOTE: ***Wiseman*** *c/a-1-8, 12, 14, 15, 17, 20, 22, 27, 28, 31, 35, 36, 41, 49.*

DENNIS THE MENACE
Marvel Comics Group: Nov, 1981 - No. 13, Nov, 1982

	GD	VG	FN	VF	VF/NM	NM-
1-New-a	1	3	4	6	8	10
2-13: 2-New art. 3-Part-r. 4,5-r. 5-X-Mas-c & issue, 7-Spider Kid-c/sty						6.00

NOTE: ***Hank Ketcham*** *c-most; a-3, 12.* ***Wiseman*** *a-4, 5.*

DENNIS THE MENACE AND HIS DOG RUFF
Hallden/Fawcett: Summer, 1961

	GD	VG	FN	VF	VF/NM	NM-
1-Wiseman-c/a	6	12	18	38	52	65

DENNIS THE MENACE AND HIS FRIENDS
Fawcett Publ.: 1969; No. 5, Jan, 1970 - No. 46, April, 1980 (All reprints)

	GD	VG	FN	VF	VF/NM	NM-
Dennis the Menace & Joey No. 2 (7/69)	2	4	6	12	16	20
Dennis the Menace & Ruff No. 2 (9/69)	2	4	6	12	16	20
Dennis the Menace & Mr. Wilson No. 1 (10/69)	3	6	9	17	21	26
Dennis & Margaret No. 1 (Winter '69)	3	6	9	17	21	26
5-12: 5-Dennis the Menace & Margaret. 6-...& Joey. 7-...& Ruff. 8-...& Mr. Wilson	2	4	6	8	10	12
13-21-(52 pg Giants): 13-(1/72). 21-(1/74)	2	4	6	10	13	16
22-37	1	2	3	5	7	9
38-46 (Digest size, 148 pgs., 4/78, 95¢)	2	4	6	8	10	12

NOTE: *Titles rotate every four issues, beginning with No. 5. Joey issues: #2(7/69),6,10,14,18,22,26,30,34. Ruff issues: #2(9/69), 7,11,15,19,23,27,31,35. Mr. Wilson issues: #1(10/69),8,12,16,20,24,28,32,36. Margaret issues: #1(Wint./69),5,9,13,17,21,25,29,33,37.*

DENNIS THE MENACE AND HIS PAL JOEY
Fawcett Publ.: Summer, 1961 (10¢) (See Dennis the Menace Giants No. 45)

	GD	VG	FN	VF	VF/NM	NM-
1-Wiseman-c/a	6	12	18	38	52	65

DENNIS THE MENACE AND THE BIBLE KIDS
Word Books: 1977 (36 pgs.)

	GD	VG	FN	VF	VF/NM	NM-
1-6: 1-Jesus. 2-Joseph. 3-David. 4-The Bible Girls. 5-Moses. 6-More About Jesus	1	3	4	6	8	10
7-9-Low print run: 7-The Lord's Prayer. 8-Stories Jesus told. 9-Paul, God's Traveller	2	4	6	10	13	16
10-Low print run; In the Beginning	2	4	6	12	16	20

NOTE: ***Ketcham*** *c/a in all.*

DENNIS THE MENACE BIG BONUS SERIES
Fawcett Publications: No. 10, Feb, 1980 - No. 11, Apr, 1980

	GD	VG	FN	VF	VF/NM	NM-
10,11	1	2	3	4	5	7

DENNIS THE MENACE BONUS MAGAZINE (Formerly Dennis the Menace Giants Nos. 1-75) (...Big Bonus Series on-c for #174-194)
Fawcett Publications: No. 76, 1/70 - No. 95, 7/71; No. 95, 7/71; No. 97, '71; No. 194, 10/79; (No. 76-124: 68 pgs.; No. 125-163: 52 pgs.; No. 164 on: 36 pgs.)

	GD	VG	FN	VF	VF/NM	NM-
76-90(3/71)	2	4	6	10	13	16
91-95, 97-110(10/72): Two #95's with same date(7/71) A-Summer Games, and B-That's Our Boy. No #96	2	4	6	9	11	14
111-124	1	3	4	6	8	10
125-163-(52 pgs.)	1	3	4	6	8	10
164-194: 166-Indicia printed backwards						6.00

DENNIS THE MENACE COMICS DIGEST
Marvel Comics Group: April, 1982 - No. 3, Aug, 1982 ($1.25, digest-size)

	GD	VG	FN	VF	VF/NM	NM-
1-3-Reprints	1	2	3	5	7	9
1-Mistakenly printed with DC emblem on cover	2	4	6	9	11	14

NOTE: ***Ketcham*** *c-all.* ***Wiseman*** *a-all. A few thousand #1's were published with a DC emblem on cover.*

DENNIS THE MENACE FUN BOOK
Fawcett Publications/Standard Comics: 1960 (100 pgs.)

	GD	VG	FN	VF	VF/NM	NM-
1-Part Wiseman-a	7	14	21	46	63	80

DENNIS THE MENACE FUN FEST SERIES (Formerly Dennis the Menace #166)
Hallden (Fawcett): No. 16, Jan, 1980 - No. 17, Mar, 1980 (40¢)

	GD	VG	FN	VF	VF/NM	NM-
16,17-By Hank Ketcham						6.00

DENNIS THE MENACE POCKET FULL OF FUN!
Fawcett Publications (Hallden): Spring, 1969 - No. 50, March, 1980 (196 pgs.) (Digest size)

	GD	VG	FN	VF	VF/NM	NM-
1-Reprints in all issues	6	12	18	38	52	65
2-10	4	8	12	24	32	40
11-20	2	4	6	14	18	22
21-28	2	4	6	10	13	16
29-50: 35,40,46-Sunday strip-r	1	2	3	6	8	10

NOTE: *No. 1-28 are 196 pgs.; No. 29-36: 164 pgs.; No. 37: 148 pgs.; No. 38 on: 132 pgs. No. 8, 11, 15, 21, 25, 29 all contain strip reprints.*

DENNIS THE MENACE TELEVISION SPECIAL
Fawcett Publ. (Hallden Div.): Summer, 1961 - No. 2, Spring, 1962 (Giant)

	GD	VG	FN	VF	VF/NM	NM-
1	6	12	18	43	59	75
2	4	8	12	24	32	40

DENNIS THE MENACE TRIPLE FEATURE
Fawcett Publications: Winter, 1961 (Giant)

	GD	VG	FN	VF	VF/NM	NM-
1-Wiseman-c/a	6	12	18	43	59	75

DEPUTY, THE (TV)
Dell Publishing Co.: No. 1077, Feb-Apr, 1960 - No. 1225, Oct-Dec, 1961 (all-Henry Fonda photo-c)

	GD	VG	FN	VF	VF/NM	NM-
Four Color 1077 (#1)-Buscema-a	14	28	42	99	145	190
Four Color 1130 (9-11/60)-Buscema-a,1225	10	20	30	73	107	140

DEPUTY DAWG (TV) (Also see New Terrytoons)
Dell Publishing Co./Gold Key: Oct-Dec, 1961 - No. 1299, 1962; No. 1, Aug, 1965

	GD	VG	FN	VF	VF/NM	NM-
Four Color 1238,1299	12	24	36	87	129	170
1(10164-508)(8/65)-Gold Key	12	24	36	87	129	170

DEPUTY DAWG PRESENTS DINKY DUCK AND HASHIMOTO-SAN (TV)
Gold Key: August, 1965

	GD	VG	FN	VF	VF/NM	NM-
1(10159-508)	10	20	30	73	107	140

DESERT GOLD (See Zane Grey 4-Color 467)

DESIGN FOR SURVIVAL (Gen. Thomas S. Power's...)
American Security Council Press: 1968 (36 pgs. in color) (25¢)

	GD	VG	FN	VF	VF/NM	NM-
nn-Propaganda against the Threat of Communism-Aircraft cover; H-Bomb panel	3	6	9	18	24	30
Twin Circle Edition-Cover shows panels from inside	2	4	6	11	14	18

DESPERADO (Becomes Black Diamond Western No. 9 on)
Lev Gleason Publications: June, 1948 - No. 8, Feb, 1949 (All 52 pgs.)

	GD	VG	FN	VF	VF/NM	NM-
1-Biro-c on all; contains inside photo-c of Charles Biro, Lev Gleason & Bob Wood	15	30	45	86	118	150
2	9	18	27	49	62	75
3-Story with over 20 killings	9	18	27	52	66	80
4-8	7	14	21	35	43	50

NOTE: ***Barry*** *a-2.* ***Fuje*** *a-4, 8.* ***Guardineer*** *a-5-7.* ***Kida*** *a-3-7.* ***Ed Moore*** *a-4, 6.*

DESPERADOES
Image Comics (Homage): Sept, 1997 - No. 5, June, 1998 ($2.50/$2.95)

	GD	VG	FN	VF	VF/NM	NM-
1-5-Mariotte-s/Cassaday-c/a: 1-($2.50-c). 2-5-($2.95)						3.00
...: A Moment's Sunlight TPB ('98, $16.95) r/#1-5						17.00
...: Epidemic! (11/99, $5.95) Mariotte-s						6.00

DESPERADOES: QUIET OF THE GRAVE
DC Comics (Homage): Jul, 2001 - No. 5, Nov, 2001 ($2.95)

	GD	VG	FN	VF	VF/NM	NM-
1-5-Jeff Mariotte-s/John Severin-c/a						3.00
TPB (2002, $14.95) r/#1-5; intro. by Brian Keene						15.00

DESPERATE TIMES (See Savage Dragon)
Image Comics: Jun, 1998 - No. 4, Dec, 1998; Nov, 2000 - No. 4, July, 2001 ($2.95, B&W)

	GD	VG	FN	VF	VF/NM	NM-
1-4-Chris Eliopoulos-s/a						3.00
(Vol. 2) 1-4						3.00

DESTINATION MOON (See Fawcett Movie Comics, Space Adventures #20, 23, & Strange Adventures #1)

DESTINY: A CHRONICLE OF DEATHS FORETOLD (See Sandman)

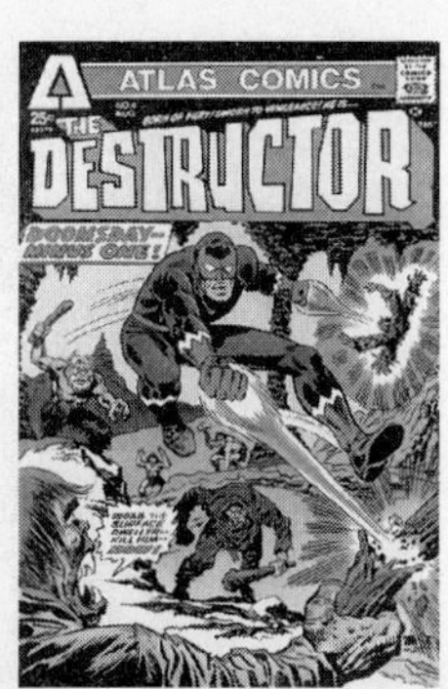

The Destructor #4 © Seaboard

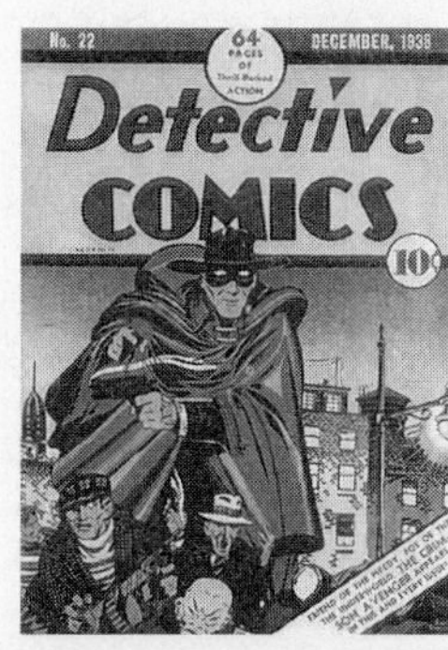

Detective Comics #22 © DC

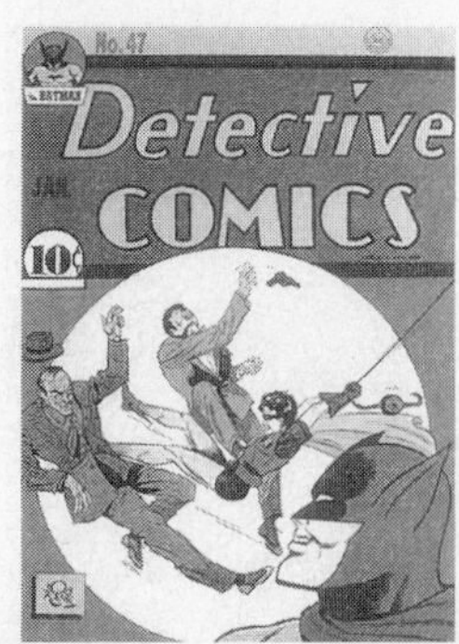

Detective Comics #47 © DC

GD VG FN VF VF/NM NM-
2.0 4.0 6.0 8.0 9.0 9.2

DC Comics (Vertigo): 1997 - No.3, 1998 ($5.95, limited series)
1-3-Alisa Kwitney-s in all: 1-Kent Williams & Michael Zulli-a, Williams painted-c. 2-Williams & Scott Hampton-painted-c/a. 3-Williams & Guay-a 6.00
TPB (2000, $14.95) r/series 15.00

DESTROY!!
Eclipse Comics: 1986 ($4.95, B&W, magazine-size, one-shot)
1 5.00
3-D Special 1-r-/#1 ($2.50) 5.00

DESTROYER, THE
Marvel Comics: Nov, 1989 - No. 9, Jun, 1990 ($2.25, B&W, magazine, 52 pgs.)
1-Based on Remo Williams movie, paperbacks 4.00
2-9: 2-Williamson part inks. 4-Ditko-a 3.00

DESTROYER, THE
Marvel Comics: V2#1, March, 1991 ($1.95, 52 pgs.)
V3#1, Dec, 1991 - No. 4, Mar, 1992 ($1.95, mini-series)
V2#1,V3#1-4: Based on Remo Williams paperbacks. V3#1-4-Simonson-c. 3-Morrow-a 2.50

DESTROYER, THE (Also see Solar, Man of the Atom)
Valiant: Apr, 1995 ($2.95, color, one-shot)
0-Indicia indicates #1 3.00

DESTROYER DUCK
Eclipse Comics: Feb, 1982 - No. 7, May, 1984 (#2-7: Baxter paper) ($1.50)
1-Origin Destroyer Duck; 1st app. Groo; Kirby-c/a(p) 1 3 4 6 8 10
2-5: 2-Starling back-up begins; Kirby-c/a(p) thru #5 5.00
6,7 4.00
NOTE: ***Neal Adams** c-1i. **Kirby** c/a-1-5p. **Miller** c-7.*

DESTRUCTOR, THE
Atlas/Seaboard: February, 1975 - No. 4, Aug, 1975
1-Origin/1st app.; Ditko/Wood-a; Wood-c(i) 1 2 3 5 7 9
2-4: 2-Ditko/Wood-a. 3,4-Ditko-a(p) 1 2 3 4 5 7

DETECTIVE COMICS (Also see other Batman titles)
National Periodical Publications/DC Comics: Mar, 1937 - Present
1-(Scarce)-Slam Bradley & Spy by Siegel & Shuster, Speed Saunders by Guardineer, Flat Foot Flannigan by Gustavson, Cosmo, the Phantom of Disguise, Buck Marshall, Bruce Nelson begin; Chin Lung in 'Claws of the Red Dragon' serial begins; Vincent Sullivan-c
8,333 16,000 25,000 58,000 - -
2 (Rare)-Creig Flessel-c begin; new logo 2333 4666 7000 16,300 - -
3 (Rare) 1666 3332 5000 11,500 - -
4,5: 5-Larry Steele begins 950 1900 2850 4750 6275 7800
6,7,9,10 688 1376 2064 3440 4520 5600
8-Mister Chang-c; classic-c 1025 2050 3075 5125 6763 8400
11-17,19: 17-1st app. Fu Manchu in Det. 525 1050 1575 2625 3438 4250
18-Fu Manchu-c; last Flessel-c 850 1700 2550 4250 5575 6900
20-The Crimson Avenger begins (1st app.) 788 1576 2364 3940 5170 6400
21,23-25 412 824 1236 2060 2705 3350
22-1st Crimson Avenger-c by Chambers (12/38) 538 1076 1614 2690 3520 4350
26 375 750 1125 1875 2488 3100
27-The Bat-Man & Commissioner Gordon begin (1st app.), created by Bill Finger & Bob Kane (5/39); Batman-c (1st)(by Kane). Bat-Man's secret identity revealed as Bruce Wayne in 6pg. sty. Signed Rob't Kane (also see Det. Plcture Stories #5 & Funny Pages V3#1)
31,250 62,500 93,750 187,500 281,250 375,000
27-Reprint, Oversize 13-1/2x10". WARNING: This comic is an exact duplicate reprint of the original except for its size. DC published it in 1974 with a second cover titling it as Famous First Edition. There have been many reported cases of the outer cover being removed and the interior sold as the original edition. The reprint with the new outer cover removed is practically worthless; see Famous First Edition for value.
28-2nd app. The Batman (6 pg. story); non-Bat-Man-c; signed Rob't Kane
1688 3376 5064 12,660 19,830 27,000
29-1st app. Doctor Death-c/story, Batman's 1st name villain. 1st 2 part story (10 pgs.). 2nd Batman-c by Kane 2815 5636 8445 21,100 33,050 45,000
30-Dr. Death app. Story concludes from issue #29. Classic Batman splash panel by Kane.
690 1380 2070 4830 7415 10,000
31-Classic Batman over castle cover; 1st app. The Monk & 1st Julie Madison (Bruce Wayne's 1st love interest); 1st Batplane (Bat-Gyro) and Batarang; 2nd 2-part Batman adventure. Gardner Fox takes over script from Bill Finger. 1st mention of locale (New York City) where Batman lives 2815 5636 8445 21,100 33,050 45,000
32-Batman story concludes from issue #31. 1st app. Dala (Monk's assistant). Batman uses gun for 1st time to slay The Monk and Dala. This was the 1st time a costumed hero used a gun in comic books. 1st Batman head logo on cover
607 1214 1821 4249 6525 8800
33-Origin The Batman (2 pgs.)(1st told origin); Batman gun holster-c; Batman w/smoking gun panel at end of story. Batman story now 12 pgs. Classic Batman-c
3750 7500 11,250 28,150 44,075 60,000
34-2nd Crimson Avenger-c by Creig Flessel and last non Batman-c. Story from issue #32 x-over as Bruce Wayne sees Julie Madison off to America from Paris. Classic Batman splash panel used later in Batman #1 for origin story. Steve Malone begins
470 940 1410 3290 5045 6800
35-Classic Batman hypodermic needle-c that reflects story in issue #34. Classic Batman with smoking .45 automatic splash panel. Batman-c begin
1000 2000 3000 7500 11,750 16,000
36-Batman-c that reflects adventure in issue #35. Origin/1st app. of Dr. Hugo Strange (1st major villain, 2/40). 1st finned-gloves worn by Batman
724 1448 2172 5068 7784 10,500
37-Last solo Golden-Age Batman adventure in Detective Comics. Panel at end of story reflects solo Batman adventure in Batman #1 that was originally planned for Detective #38. Cliff Crosby begins 655 1310 1965 4585 7043 9500
38-Origin/1st app. Robin the Boy Wonder (4/40); Batman and Robin-c begin; cover by Kane & Robinson taken from splash page 3438 6876 10,314 25,800 40,400 55,000
39-Opium story 566 1132 1698 3962 6081 8200
40-Origin & 1st app. Clay Face (Basil Karlo); 1st Joker cover app. (6/40); Joker story intended for this issue was used in Batman #1 instead; cover is similar to splash page in 2nd Joker story in Batman #1 655 1310 1965 4585 7043 9500
41-Robin's 1st solo 341 682 1023 2217 3409 4600
42-44: 44-Crimson Avenger-new costume 240 480 720 1500 2250 3000
45-1st Joker story in Det. (3rd book app. & 4th story app. over all, 11/40)
341 682 1023 2217 3409 4600
46-50: 46-Death of Hugo Strange. 48-1st time car called Batmobile (2/41); Gotham City 1st mention in Detective (1st mentioned in Wow #1; also see Batman #4).
49-Last Clay Face 224 448 672 1400 2100 2800
51-57 148 296 444 925 1388 1850
58-1st Penguin app. (12/41); last Speed Saunders; Fred Ray-c
423 846 1269 2751 4226 5700
59,60: 59-Last Steve Malone; 2nd Penguin; Wing becomes Crimson Avenger's aide.
60-Intro. Air Wave; Joker app. (2nd in Det.) 166 332 498 1038 1557 2075
61,63: 63-Last Cliff Crosby; 1st app. Mr. Baffle 146 292 438 913 1369 1825
62-Joker-c/story (2nd Joker-c, 4/42) 248 496 744 1550 2325 3100
64-Origin & 1st app. Boy Commandos by Simon & Kirby (6/42); Joker app.
385 770 1155 2503 3852 5200
65-1st Boy Commandos-c (S&K-a on Boy Commandos & Ray/Robinson-a on Batman & Robin on-c; 4 artists on one-c) 300 600 900 1900 2850 3800
66-Origin & 1st app. Two-Face 370 740 1110 2405 3703 5000
67-1st Penguin-c (9/42) 236 472 708 1475 2213 2950
68-Two-Face-c/story; 1st Two-Face-c 166 332 498 1038 1557 2075
69-Joker-c/story 166 332 498 1038 1557 2075
70 120 240 360 750 1125 1500
71-Joker-c/story 142 284 426 888 1332 1775
72,74,75: 74-1st Tweedledum & Tweedledee plus-c; S&K-a
107 214 321 669 1005 1340
73-Scarecrow-c/story (1st Scarecrow-c) 132 264 396 825 1238 1650
76-Newsboy Legion & The Sandman x-over in Boy Commandos; S&K-a; Joker-c/story 166 332 498 1038 1557 2075
77-79: All S&K-a 114 228 342 713 1069 1425
80-Two-Face app.; S&K-a 124 248 372 775 1163 1550
81,82,84,86-90: 81-1st Cavalier-c & app. 89-Last Crimson Avenger; 2nd Cavalier-c & app.
91 182 273 569 855 1140
83-1st "skinny" Alfred (1/44)(see Batman #21; last S&K Boy Commandos (also #92,128); most issues #84 on signed S&K are not by them
100 200 300 625 938 1250
85-Joker-c/story; last Spy; Kirby/Klech Boy Commandos
120 240 360 750 1125 1500
91,102-Joker-c/story 114 228 342 713 1069 1425
92-98: 96-Alfred's last name 'Beagle' revealed, later changed to 'Pennyworth' in #214
76 152 228 475 713 950
99-Penguin-c 114 228 342 713 1069 1425
100 (6/45) 124 248 372 775 1163 1550
101,103-108,110-113,115-117,119: 108-1st Bat-signal-c (2/46). 114-1st small logo (8/46) 72 144 216 450 675 900
109,114,118-Joker-c/stories 98 196 294 613 919 1225
120-Penguin-c (white-c, rare above fine) 166 332 498 1038 1557 2075
121,123,125,127,129,130 68 136 204 425 638 850
122-1st Catwoman-c (4/47) 140 280 420 875 1313 1750
124,128-Joker-c/stories 94 188 282 588 882 1175
126-Penguin-c 94 188 282 588 882 1175
131-134,136,139 60 120 180 375 563 750
135-Frankenstein-c/story 76 152 228 475 713 950
137-Joker-c/story; last Air Wave 78 156 234 488 732 975

Detective Comics #168 © DC

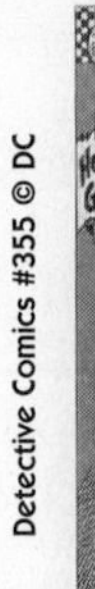

Detective Comics #355 © DC

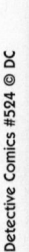

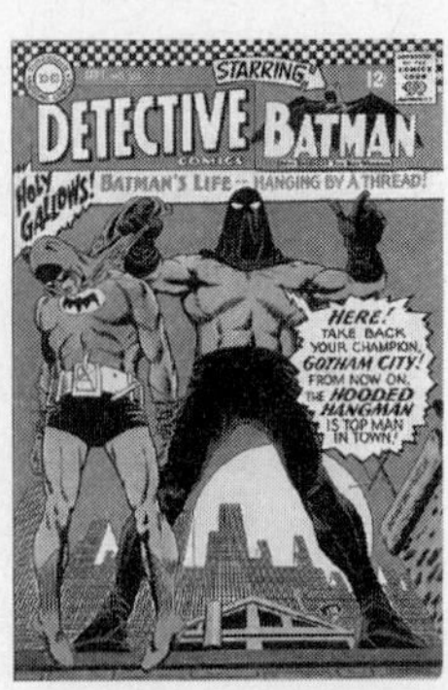

Detective Comics #524 © DC

	GD 2.0	VG 4.0	FN 6.0	VF 8.0	VF/NM 9.0	NM- 9.2
138-Origin Robotman (see Star Spangled #7 for 1st app.); series ends #202	112	224	336	700	1050	1400
140-The Riddler-c/story (1st app., 10/48)	434	868	1302	3038	4669	6300
141,143-148,150: 150-Last Boy Commandos	60	120	180	375	563	750
142-2nd Riddler-c/story	118	236	354	738	1107	1475
149-Joker-c/story	80	160	240	500	750	1000
151-Origin & 1st app. Pow Wow Smith, Indian lawman (9/49) & begins series	74	148	222	463	692	920
152,154,155,157-160: 152-Last Slam Bradley	60	120	180	375	563	750
153-1st app. Roy Raymond TV Detective (11/49) ; origin The Human Fly	68	136	204	425	638	850
156(2/50)-The new classic Batmobile	85	170	255	531	796	1060
161-167,169,170,172-176: Last 52 pg. issue	55	110	165	342	511	680
168-Origin the Joker	341	682	1023	2217	3409	4600
171-Penguin-c	87	174	261	544	815	1085
177-179,181-186,188,189,191,192,194-199,201,202,204,206-210,212,214-216: 184-1st app. Fire Fly. 185-Secret of Batman's utility belt. 187-Two-Face app. 202-Last Robotman & Pow Wow Smith. 215-1st app. of Batmen of all Nations. 216-Last precode (2/55)	51	102	153	306	458	610
180,193-Joker-c/story	56	112	168	350	525	700
187-Two-Face-c/story	55	110	165	330	495	660
190-Origin Batman retold	74	148	222	463	692	920
200(10/53), 205: 205-Origin Batcave	68	136	204	425	638	850
203,211-Catwoman-c/stories	56	112	168	350	525	700
213-Origin & 1st app. Mirror Man	60	120	180	375	563	750
217-224: 218-Batman Jr. & Robin Sr. app.	44	88	132	264	395	525
225-(11/55)-1st app. Martian Manhunter, John Jones; later changed to J'onn J'onzz; origin begins; also see Batman #78	361	722	1083	3303	5352	7400
226-Origin Martian Manhunter cont'd (2nd app.)	138	276	414	863	1294	1725
227-229: Martian Manhunter stories in all	55	110	165	330	495	660
230-1st app. Mad Hatter; brief recap origin of Martian Manhunter	55	110	165	344	515	685
231-Brief origin recap Martian Manhunter	40	80	120	240	350	460
232,234,237-240: 239-Early DC grey tone-c	40	80	120	240	340	440
233-Origin & 1st app. Batwoman (7/56)	132	264	396	825	1238	1650
235-Origin Batman & his costume; tells how Bruce Wayne's father (Thomas Wayne) wore Bat costume & fought crime (reprinted in Batman #255)	64	128	192	400	600	800
236-1st S.A. issue; J'onn J'onzz talks to parents and Mars-1st since being stranded on Earth; 1st app. Bat-Tank?	42	84	126	252	376	500
241-260: 246-Intro. Diane Meade, John Jones' girl. 249-Batwoman-c/app. 253-1st app. The Terrible Trio. 254-Bat-Hound-c/story. 257-Intro. & 1st app. Whirly Bats. 259-1st app. The Calendar Man	33	66	99	190	270	350
261-264,266,268-271: 261-J. Jones tie-in to sci/fi movie "Incredible Shrinking Man"; 1st app. Dr. Double X. 262-Origin Jackal. 268,271-Manhunter origin recap	27	54	81	153	214	275
265-Batman's origin retold with new facts	39	78	117	230	325	420
267-Origin & 1st app. Bat-Mite (5/59)	40	80	120	240	345	450
272,274,275,277-280	22	44	66	127	176	225
273-J'onn J'onzz i.d. revealed for 1st time	23	46	69	130	183	235
276-2nd app. Bat-Mite	24	48	72	138	194	250
281-292, 294-297: 285,286,292-Batwoman-c/app. 287-Origin J'onn J'onzz retold. 289-Bat-Mite-c/story. 292-Last Roy Raymond. 297-Last 10¢ issue (11/61)	18	36	54	101	138	175
293-(7/61)-Aquaman begins (pre #1); ends #300	19	38	57	106	146	185
298-(12/61)-1st modern Clayface (Matt Hagen)	25	50	75	181	266	350
299, 300-(2/62)-Aquaman ends	11	22	33	77	114	150
301-(3/62)-J'onn J'onzz returns to Mars (1st time since stranded on Earth six years before)	10	20	30	70	100	130
302-317,319-321,323,324,326,329,330: 302,307,311,321-Batwoman-c/app. 311-Intro. Zook in John Jones; 1st app. Cat-Man. 321-2nd Terrible Trio. 326-Last J'onn J'onzz, story cont'd in House of Mystery #143; intro. Idol-Head of Diabolu	8	16	24	58	82	105
318,322,325: 318,325-Cat-Man-c/story (2nd & 3rd app.); also 1st & 2nd app. Batwoman as the Cat-Woman. 322-Bat-Girl's 1st/only app. in Det. (6th in all); Batman cameo in J'onn J'onzz (only hero to app. in series)	8	16	24	58	82	105
327-(5/64)-Elongated Man begins, ends #383; 1st new look Batman with new costume; Infantino/Giella new look-a begins; Batman with gun	12	24	36	84	125	165
328-Death of Alfred; Bob Kane biog, 2 pgs.	11	22	33	77	114	150
331,333-340: 334-1st app. The Outsider	7	14	21	46	63	80
342-358,360,361,366-368: 345-Intro Block Buster. 347-"What If" theme story (1/66). 351-Elongated Man new costume. 355-Zatanna x-over in Elongated Man. 356-Alfred brought back in Batman, 1st SA app.?	6	12	18	40	55	70

	GD 2.0	VG 4.0	FN 6.0	VF 8.0	VF/NM 9.0	NM- 9.2
332,341,365-Joker-c/stories	8	16	24	53	74	95
359-Intro/origin Batgirl (Barbara Gordon)-c/story (1/67); 1st Silver Age app. Killer Moth	13	26	39	90	133	175
362-364: 362,364-S.A. Riddler app. (early). 363-2nd app. new Batgirl	6	12	18	43	59	75
369(11/67)-N. Adams-a (Elongated Man); 3rd app. S.A. Catwoman (cameo; leads into Batman #197); 4th app. new Batgirl	8	16	24	53	74	95
370-1st Neal Adams-a on Batman (cover only, 12/67)	6	12	18	43	59	75
371-(1/68) 1st new Batmobile from TV show; classic Batgirl-c	7	14	21	51	71	90
372-376,378-386,389,390: 375-New Batmobile-c	5	10	15	36	48	60
377-S.A. Riddler-c/sty	6	12	18	38	52	65
387-r/1st Batman story from #27 (30th anniversary, 5/69); Joker-c;	7	14	21	46	63	80
388-Joker-c/story; last 12¢ issue	6	12	18	43	59	75
391-394,396,398,399,401,403,405,406,409: 392-1st app. Jason Bard. 401-2nd Batgirl/Robin team-up	4	8	12	27	36	45
395,397,402,404,407,408,410-Neal Adams-a. 404-Tribute to Enemy Ace	6	12	18	38	52	65
400-(6/70)-Origin & 1st app. Man-Bat; 1st Batgirl/Robin team-up (cont'd in #401); Neal Adams-a	10	20	30	67	96	125
411-413: 413-Last 15¢ issue	3	7	10	21	28	35
414-424: All-25¢, 52 pgs. 418-Creeper x-over. 424-Last Batgirl.	4	8	12	24	32	40
425-436: 426,430,436-Elongated Man app. 428,434-Hawkman begins, ends #467	3	6	9	16	20	24
437-New Manhunter begins (10-11/73, 1st app.) by Simonson, ends #443	4	8	12	27	36	45
438-445 (All 100 Page Super Spectaculars): 438-Kubert Hawkman-r. 439-Origin Manhunter. 440-G.A. Manhunter(Adv. #79) by S&K, Hawkman, Dollman, Green Lantern; Toth-a. 441-G.A. Plastic Man, Batman, Ibis-r. 442-G.A. Newsboy Legion, Black Canary, Elongated Man, Dr. Fate-r. 443-Origin The Creeper-r; death of Manhunter; G.A. Green Lantern, Spectre-r; Batman-r/Batman #18. 444-G.A. Kid Eternity-r. 445-G.A. Dr. Midnite-r	6	12	18	38	52	65
446-460: 457-Origin retold & updated	2	4	6	11	14	18
461-465,470,480: 480-(44 pgs.). 463-1st app. Black Spider. 464-2nd app. Black Spider	2	4	6	10	12	15
466-468,471-474,478,479-Rogers-a in all: 466-1st app. Signalman since Batman #139. 470,471-1st modern app. Hugo Strange. 474-1st app. new Deadshot. 478-1st app. 3rd Clayface (Preston Payne). 479-(44 pgs.)-Clayface app.	3	6	9	19	25	32
469-Intro/origin Dr. Phosphorous; Simonson-a	3	6	9	18	24	30
475,476-Joker-c/stories; Rogers-a	6	12	18	38	52	65
477-Neal Adams-a(r); Rogers-a (3 pgs.)	3	6	9	18	24	30
481-(Combined with Batman Family, 12-1/78-79, begin $1.00, 68 pg. issues, ends #495); 481-495-Batgirl, Robin solo stories	2	4	6	12	16	20
482-Starlin/Russell, Golden-a; The Demon begins (origin-r), ends #485 (by Ditko #483-485)	2	4	6	10	13	16
483-40th Anniversary issue; origin retold; Newton Batman begins	2	4	6	12	16	20
484-495 (68 pgs): 484-Origin Robin. 485-Death of Batwoman. 487-The Odd Man by Ditko. 489-Robin/Batgirl team-up. 490-Black Lightning begins. 491-(#492 on inside)	2	4	6	8	10	12
496-499	1	2	3	5	6	8
500-($1.50, 52 pgs.)-Batman/Deadman team-up; new Hawkman story by Joe Kubert; incorrectly says 500th anniv. of Det.	2	4	6	10	13	16
501-503,505-523: 512-2nd app. new Dr. Death. 519-Last Batgirl. 521-Green Arrow series begins. 523-Solomon Grundy app.						6.00
504-Joker-c/story	1	3	4	6	8	10
524-2nd app. Jason Todd (cameo)(3/83)	1	2	3	5	6	8
525-3rd app. Jason Todd (See Batman #357)	1	2	3	5	6	8
526-Batman's 500th app. in Detective Comics ($1.50, 68 pgs.); Death of Jason Todd's parents, Joker-c/story (55 pgs.); Bob Kane pin-up	2	4	6	11	14	18
527-531,533,534,536-568,571,573: 538-Cat-Man-c/story cont'd from Batman #371. 542-Jason Todd quits as Robin (becomes Robin again #547). 549,550-Alan Moore scripts (Green Arrow). 554-1st new Black Canary (9/85). 566-Batman villains profiled. 567-Harlan Ellison scripts.						5.00
532,569,570-Joker-c/stories	1	2	3	5	7	9
535-Intro new Robin (JasonTodd)-1st appeared in Batman.						6.00
572-(3/87, $1.25, 60 pgs.)-50th Anniv. of Det. Comics						6.00
574-Origin Batman & Jason Todd retold						6.00
575-Year 2 begins, ends #578	2	4	6	11	14	18
576-578: McFarlane-c/a. 578-Clay Face app.	2	4	6	11	14	18
579-597,599,601-610: 579-New bat wing logo. 583-1st app. villains Scarface & Ventriloquist.						

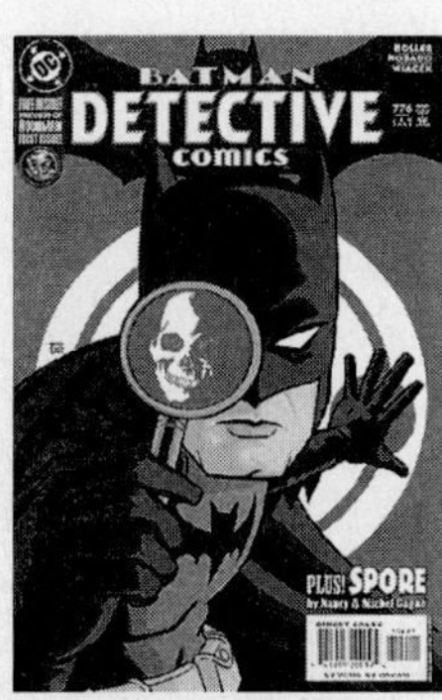

Detective Comics #776 © DC

Detective Eye #1 © CEN

Devil-Dog Dugan #2 © MAR

GD VG FN VF VF/NM NM-
2.0 4.0 6.0 8.0 9.0 9.2

589-595-(52 pgs.)-Each contain free 16 pg. Batman stories. 604-607-Mudpack storyline; 604,607-Contain Batman mini-posters. 610-Faked death of Penguin; artists names app. on tombstone on-c 3.00
598-($2.95, 84 pgs.)- "Blind Justice" storyline begins by Batman movie writer Sam Hamm, ends #600 4.00
600-(5/89, $2.95, 84 pgs.)-50th Anniv. of Batman in Det.; 1 pg. Neal Adams pin-up, among other artists 4.00
611-626,628-658: 612-1st new look Cat-Man; Catwoman app. 615- "The Penguin Affair" part 2 (See Batman #448,449). 617-Joker-c/story. 624-1st new Catwoman (w/death) & 1st new Batwoman. 626-Batman's 600th app. in Detective. 642-Return of Scarface, part 2. 644-Last $1.00-c. 652,653-Huntress-c/story w/new costume plus Charest-c on both 3.00
627-($2.95, 84 pgs.)-Batman's 601st app. in Det.; reprints 1st story/#27 plus 3 versions (2 new) of same story 4.00
659-664: 659-Knightfall part 2; Kelley Jones-c. 660-Knightfall part 4; Bane-c by Sam Kieth. 661-Knightfall part 6; brief Joker & Riddler app. 662-Knightfall part 8; Riddler app.; Sam Kieth-c. 663-Knightfall part 10; Kelley Jones-c. 664-Knightfall part 12; Bane-c/story; Joker app.; continued in Showcase 93 #7 & 8; Jones-c 3.00
665-675: 665,666-Knightfall parts 16 & 18; 666-Bane-c/story. 667-Knightquest: The Crusade & new Batman begins (1st app. in Batman #500). 669-Begin $1.50-c; Knightquest, cont'd in Robin #1. 671,673-Joker app. 2.75
675-($2.95)-Collectors edition w/foil-c 3.50
676-($2.50, 52 pgs.)-KnightsEnd pt. 3 3.00
677,678: 677-KnightsEnd pt. 9. 678-(9/94)-Zero Hour tie-in. 2.75
679-685: 679-(11/94). 682-Troika pt. 3 2.75
682-($2.50) Embossed-c Troika pt. 3 3.00
686-699,701-719: 686-Begin $1.95-c. 693,694-Poison Ivy-c/app. 695-Contagion pt. 2; Catwoman, Penguin app. 696-Contagion pt. 8. 698-Two-Face-c/app. 701-Legacy pt. 6; Batman vs. Bane-c/app. 702-Legacy Epilogue. 703-Final Night x-over. 705-707-Riddler-app. 714,715-Martian Manhunter-app. 2.75
700-($4.95, Collectors Edition)-Legacy pt. 1; Ra's Al Ghul-c/app; Talia & Bane app; book displayed at shops in envelope 5.00
700-($2.95, Regular Edition)-Different-c 3.00
720-740: 720,721-Cataclysm pts. 5,14. 723-Green Arrow app. 730-740-No Man's Land stories 2.75
741-($2.50) Endgame; Joker-c/app. 3.00
742-749,751-765: 742-New look Batman begins. 751,752-Poison Ivy app. 756-Superman-c/app. 759-762-Catwoman back-up; Cooke-a 2.75
750-($4.95, 64 pgs.) Ra's al Ghul-c 5.00
766-772: 766,767-Bruce Wayne: Murderer pt. 1,8. 769-772-Bruce Wayne: Fugitive pts. 4,8,12,16 2.75
773,774,776-790: 773-Begin $2.75-c; Sienkiewicz-c. 777-784-Sale-c. 784-786-Alan Scott app. 787-Mad Hatter app. 2.75
775-($3.50) Sienkiewicz-c 3.50
#0-(10/94) Zero Hour tie-in 2.75
#1,000,000 (11/98) 853rd Century x-over 2.75
Annual 1 (1988, $1.50) 5.00
Annual 2-7,9 ('89-'94, '96, 68 pgs.)-4-Painted-c. 5-Joker-c/story (54 pgs.) continued in Robin Annual #1; Sam Kieth-c; Eclipso app. 6-Azrael as Batman in new costume; intro Geist the Twilight Man; Bloodlines storyline. 7-Elseworlds story. 9-Legends of the Dead Earth story 3.00
Annual 8 (1995, $3.95, 68 pgs.)-Year One story 4.00
Annual 10 (1997, $3.95)-Pulp Heroes story 4.00

NOTE: **Neal Adams** *c-370, 372, 385, 389, 391, 392, 394-422, 439.* **Aparo** *a-437, 438, 444-446, 500, 625-632p, 638-643p; c-430, 437, 440-446, 448, 468-470, 480, 484(back), 492-502,508, 509, 515, 518-522, 641, 716, 719, 722, 724.* **Austin** *a(i)-450, 451, 463-468, 471-476; c(i)-474-476, 478.* **Baily** *a-443r.* **Buckler** *a-434, 446p, 479p; c(p)-467, 482, 505-507, 511, 513-516, 518.* **Burnley** *a(Batman)-65, 75, 78, 83, 100, 103, 125; c-62i, 63i, 64, 73i, 78, 83p, 96p, 103p, 105p, 106, 108, 121p, 123p, 125p.* **Chaykin** *a-441.* **Colan** *a(p)-510, 512, 517, 523, 528-538, 540-546, 555-567; c(p)-510, 512, 528, 530-535, 537, 538, 540, 541, 543-545, 556-558, 560-564.* **J. Craig** *a-488.* **Ditko** *a-443r, 483-485, 487.* **Golden** *a-482p; c-625, 626, 628-631, 633, 644-646.* **Alan Grant** *scripts-584-597, 601-621, 641, 642, Annual 5.* **Grell** *a-445, 455, 463p, 464p; c-455.* **Guardineer** *c-23, 24, 26, 28, 30, 32.* **Gustavson** *a-441r.* **Infantino** *a-442(2)r, 500, 572.* **Infantino/Anderson** *c-333, 337-340, 343, 344, 347, 351, 352, 359, 361-368, 371.* **Kelley Jones** *c-651, 657i, 658i, 659, 661, 663-675.* **Kaluta** *c-423, 424, 426-428, 431, 434, 438, 484, 486, 572.* **Bob Kane** *a-Most early issues #27 on, 297r, 356r, 438-440r, 442r, 443r.* **Kane/Robinson** *c-33.* **Gil Kane** *a(p)-368, 370-374, 384, 385, 388-407, 438r, 439r, 520.* **Kane/Anderson** *c-369.* **Sam Kieth** *c-654-656 (657, 658 w/***Kelley Jones***), 660, 662, Annual #5.* **Kubert** *a-438r, 439r, 500; c-348, 350.* **McFarlane** *c/a(p)-576-578.* **Meskin** *a-420r.* **Mignola** *c-583.* **Moldoff** *c-233-354, 259, 266, 267, 275, 287, 289, 290, 297, 300.* **Moldoff/Giella** *a-328, 330, 332, 334, 336, 338, 340, 342, 344, 346, 348, 350, 352, 354, 356.* **Mooney** *a-444r.* **Moreira** *a-153-300, 419r, 444r, 445r.* **Nasser/Netzer** *a-654, 655, 657, 658.* **Newton** *a(p)-480, 481, 483-499, 501-509, 511, 513-516, 518-520, 524, 526, 539; c-526p.* **Irv Novick** *c-375-377, 383.* **Robbins** *a-426p, 429p.* **Robinson** *a-part: 66, 68, 71-73; all: 74-76, 79, 80; c-62, 64, 66, 68-74, 76, 79, 82, 86, 88, 442r, 443r.* **Rogers** *a-466-468, 471-479p, 481p; c-471p, 472p, 473, 474-479p.* **Roussos** *Airwave-76-105(most); c(i)-71, 72, 74-76, 79, 107.* **Russell** *a-481i, 482i.* **Simon/Kirby** *a-440r, 442r.* **Simonson** *a-437-443, 450, 469, 470, 500.* **Dick Sprang** *c-77, 82, 84, 85, 87, 89-93, 95-100, 102, 103i, 104i, 106, 108, 114, 117, 118, 122, 123, 128, 129, 131, 133, 135, 141, 148, 149, 168, 622-624.* **Starlin** *a-481p, 482p; c-503, 504, 567p.* **Starr** *a-444r.* **Toth** *a-442; r-414, 416, 418, 424, 440-441, 443, 444.* **Tuska** *a-486p, 490p.* **Matt Wagner** *c-647-649.* **Wrightson** *c-425.*

DETECTIVE DAN, SECRET OP. 48 (Also see Adventures of Detective Ace King and Bob Scully, The Two-Fisted Hick Detective)
Humor Publ. Co. (Norman Marsh): 1933 (10¢, 10x13", 36 pgs., B&W, one-shot) (3 color, cardboard-c)

	GD 2.0	VG 4.0	FN 6.0	VF 8.0	VF/NM 9.0	NM- 9.2
nn-By Norman Marsh, 1st comic w/ original-a; 1st newsstand-c; Dick Tracy look-alike; forerunner of Dan Dunn. (Title and Wu Fang character inspired Detective Comics #1 four years later.) (1st comic of a single theme)	1500	3000	4500	8500	-	-

DETECTIVE EYE (See Keen Detective Funnies)
Centaur Publications: Nov, 1940 - No. 2, Dec, 1940

	GD 2.0	VG 4.0	FN 6.0	VF 8.0	VF/NM 9.0	NM- 9.2
1-Air Man (see Keen Detective) & The Eye Sees begins; The Masked Marvel & Dean Denton app.	212	424	636	1325	1988	2650
2-Origin Don Rance and the Mysticape; Binder-a; Frank Thomas-c	120	240	360	750	1125	1500

DETECTIVE PICTURE STORIES (Keen Detective Funnies No. 8 on?)
Comics Magazine Company: Dec, 1936 - No. 5, Apr, 1937
(1st comic of a single theme)

	GD 2.0	VG 4.0	FN 6.0	VF 8.0	VF/NM 9.0	NM- 9.2
1 (all issues are very scarce)	550	1100	1650	2800	3700	4600
2-The Clock app. (1/37, early app.)	233	466	699	1200	1600	2000
3,4: 4-Eisner-a	150	300	450	800	1038	1275
5-The Clock-c/story (4/37); 1st detective/adventure art by Bob Kane; Bruce Wayne prototype app.(see Funny Pages V3/1)	166	332	500	900	1200	1500

DETECTIVES, THE (TV)
Dell Publishing Co.: No. 1168, Mar-May, 1961 - No. 1240, Oct-Dec, 1961

	GD 2.0	VG 4.0	FN 6.0	VF 8.0	VF/NM 9.0	NM- 9.2
Four Color 1168 (#1)-Robert Taylor photo-c	11	22	33	77	114	150
Four Color 1219-Robert Taylor, Adam West photo-c	10	20	30	67	96	125
Four Color 1240-Tufts-a; Robert Taylor photo-c	10	20	30	67	96	125

DETECTIVES, INC. (See Eclipse Graphic Album Series)
Eclipse Comics: Apr, 1985 - No. 2, Apr, 1985 ($1.75, both w/April dates)

1,2: 2-Nudity 2.25

DETECTIVES, INC.: A TERROR OF DYING DREAMS
Eclipse Comics: Jun, 1987 - No. 3, Dec, 1987 ($1.75, B&W& sepia)

1-3: Colan-a 2.25
TPB ('99, $19.95) r/series 20.00

DETENTION COMICS
DC Comics: Oct, 1996 ($3.50, 56 pgs., one-shot)

1-Robin story by Dennis O'Neil & Norm Breyfogle; Superboy story by Ron Marz & Ron Lim; Warrior story by Ruben Diaz & Joe Phillips; Phillips-c 5.00

DETONATOR
Chaos! Comics: Dec, 1994 - No. 2, 1995 ($2.95, limited series)

1,2-Brian Pulido scripts; Steven Hughes-a 3.00

DEVASTATOR
Image Comics/Halloween: 1998 - No. 3 ($2.95, B&W, limited series)

1,2-Hudnall-s/Horn-c/a 3.00

DEVIL CHEF
Dark Horse Comics: July, 1994 ($2.50, B&W, one-shot)

nn 2.50

DEVIL DINOSAUR
Marvel Comics Group: Apr, 1978 - No. 9, Dec, 1978

	GD 2.0	VG 4.0	FN 6.0	VF 8.0	VF/NM 9.0	NM- 9.2
1-Kirby/Royer-a in all; all have Kirby-c	2	4	6	10	13	16
2-9: 4-7-UFO/sci. fic. 8-Dinoriders-c/sty	1	2	3	5	6	8

DEVIL DINOSAUR SPRING FLING
Marvel Comics: June, 1997 ($2.99. one-shot)

1-(48pgs.) Moon-Boy-c/app. 3.00

DEVIL-DOG DUGAN (Tales of the Marines No. 4 on)
Atlas Comics (OPI): July, 1956 - No. 3, Nov, 1956

	GD 2.0	VG 4.0	FN 6.0	VF 8.0	VF/NM 9.0	NM- 9.2
1-Severin-c	13	26	39	74	100	125
2-Iron Mike McGraw x-over; Severin-c	8	16	24	43	54	65
3	7	14	21	37	46	55

DEVIL DOGS
Street & Smith Publishers: 1942

	GD 2.0	VG 4.0	FN 6.0	VF 8.0	VF/NM 9.0	NM- 9.2
1-Boy Rangers, U.S. Marines	29	58	87	164	232	300

DEVILINA (Magazine)
Atlas/Seaboard: Feb, 1975 - No. 2, May, 1975 (B&W)

	GD 2.0	VG 4.0	FN 6.0	VF 8.0	VF/NM 9.0	NM- 9.2
1-Art by Reese, Marcos; "The Tempest" adapt.	2	4	6	14	18	22
2 (Low printing)	3	6	9	18	23	28

DEVIL KIDS STARRING HOT STUFF
Harvey Publications (Illustrated Humor): July, 1962 - No. 107, Oct, 1981 (Giant-Size #41-55)

The Devil's Footprints #1 © Allie, Lee & Horton

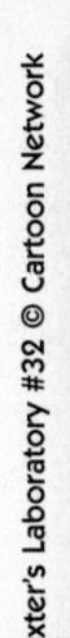

Dexter's Laboratory #32 © Cartoon Network

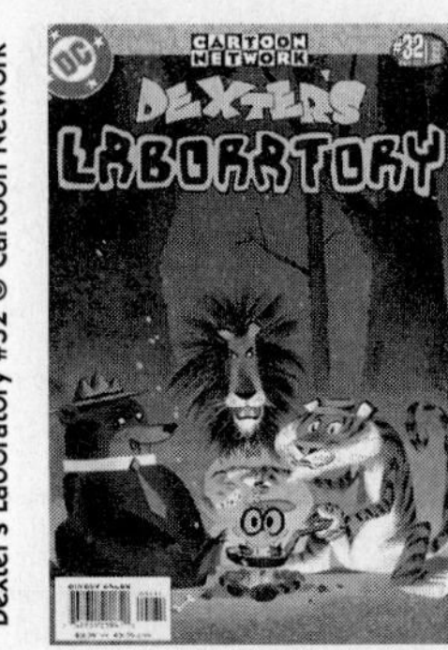

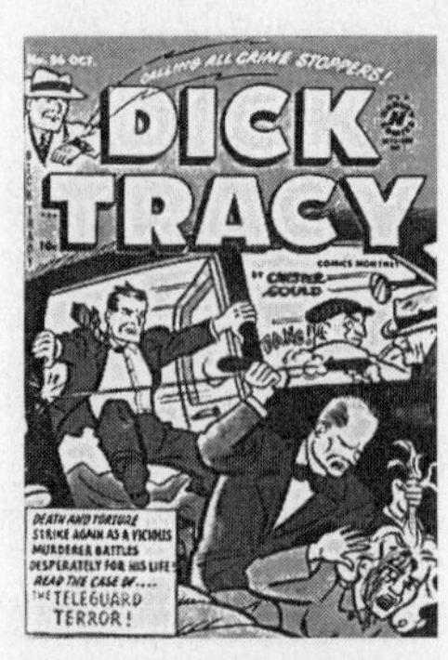

Dick Tracy #56 © NYNS

	GD 2.0	VG 4.0	FN 6.0	VF 8.0	VF/NM 9.0	NM- 9.2
1 (12¢ cover price #1-#41-9/69)	17	34	51	123	182	240
2	9	18	27	63	89	115
3-10 (1/64)	7	14	21	46	63	80
11-20	4	8	12	29	40	50
21-30	3	7	10	21	28	35
31-40: 40-(6/69)	3	6	9	16	20	25
41-50: All 68 pg. Giants	3	6	9	18	24	30
51-55: All 52 pg. Giants	3	6	9	16	20	25
56-70	2	4	6	10	12	15
71-90	1	2	3	5	7	9
91-107						6.00
DEVIL'S DUE STUDIOS MIX TAPE						
Image Comics(Devil's Due): March, 2003 ($1.00)						
1-Previews of upcoming titles like Voltron, Micronauts, G.I. Joe						2.00
DEVIL'S FOOTPRINTS, THE						
Dark Horse Comics: March, 2003 - No. 4, June, 2003 ($2.99, limited series)						
1-4-Paul Lee-c/a; Scott Allie-s						3.00
DEXTER COMICS						
Dearfield Publ.: Summer, 1948 - No. 5, July, 1949						
1-Teen-age humor	10	20	30	56	73	90
2-Junie Prom app.	8	16	24	40	50	60
3-5	6	12	18	31	38	45
DEXTER'S LABORATORY (Cartoon Network)						
DC Comics: Sept, 1999 - Present ($1.99/$2.25)						
1						4.00
2-10: 2-McCracken-s						3.00
11-24						2.25
25-(50¢-c) Tartakovsky-s/a; Action Hank-c/app.						.50
26-34: 31-Begin $2.25-c. 32-34-Wray-c						2.25
DEXTER THE DEMON (Formerly Melvin The Monster)(See Cartoon Kids & Peter the Little Pest)						
Atlas Comics (HPC): No. 7, Sept, 1957						
7	7	14	21	37	46	55
DHAMPIRE: STILLBORN						
DC Comics (Vertigo): 1996 ($5.95, one-shot, mature)						
1-Nancy Collins script; Paul Lee-c/a						6.00
DIABLO: TALES OF SANCTUARY (From the computer game)						
Dark Horse Comics (Blizzard): Nov, 2001 ($5.95, 6.5 x 9", one-shot)						
1-Francisco Ruiz-c/a						6.00
DIARY CONFESSIONS (Formerly Ideal Romance)						
Stanmor/Key Publ.(Medal Comics): No. 9, May, 1955 - No. 14, Apr, 1955						
9	8	16	24	40	50	60
10-14	6	12	18	28	34	40
DIARY LOVES (Formerly Love Diary #1; G. I. Sweethearts #32 on)						
Quality Comics Group: No. 2, Nov, 1949 - No. 31, April, 1953						
2-Ward-c/a, 9 pgs.	17	34	51	98	134	170
3 (1/50)-Photo-c begin, end #27?	8	16	24	43	54	65
4-Crandall-a	9	18	27	52	66	80
5-7,10	7	14	21	35	43	50
8,9-Ward-a 6,8 pgs. 8-Gustavson-a; Esther Williams photo-c	11	22	33	66	88	110
11,13,14,17-20	6	12	18	31	38	45
12,15,16-Ward-a 9,7,8 pgs.	10	20	30	58	77	95
21-Ward-a, 7 pgs.	9	18	27	52	66	80
22-31: 31-Whitney-a	6	12	18	28	34	40
NOTE: *Photo c-3-10, 12-27.*						
DIARY OF HORROR						
Avon Periodicals: December, 1952						
1-Hollingsworth-c/a; bondage-c	42	84	126	252	359	465
DIARY SECRETS (Formerly Teen-Age Diary Secrets)(See Giant Comics Ed.)						
St. John Publishing Co.: No. 10, Feb, 1952 - No. 30, Sept, 1955						
10-Baker-c/a most issues	19	38	57	106	146	185
11-16,18,19	14	28	42	79	107	135
17,20: Kubert-r/Hollywood Confessions #1. 17-r/Teen Age Romances #9	14	28	42	79	107	135
21-30: 22,27-Signed stories by Estrada. 28-Last precode (3/55)	10	20	30	56	73	90
nn-(25¢ giant, nd (1950?)-Baker-c & rebound St. John comics						

	GD 2.0	VG 4.0	FN 6.0	VF 8.0	VF/NM 9.0	NM- 9.2
	48	96	144	288	432	575
DICK COLE (Sport Thrills No. 11 on)(See Blue Bolt & Four Most #1)						
Curtis Publ./Star Publications: Dec-Jan, 1948-49 - No. 10, June-July, 1950						
1-Sgt. Spook; L. B. Cole-c; McWilliams-a; Curt Swan's 1st work	34	68	102	196	278	360
2,5	16	32	48	92	126	160
3,4,6-10: All-L.B. Cole-c. 10-Joe Louis story	24	48	72	135	190	245
Accepted Reprint #7(V1#6 on-c)(1950's)-Reprints #7; L.B. Cole-c	8	16	24	40	50	60
Accepted Reprint #9(nd)-(Reprints #9 & #8-c)	8	16	24	40	50	60
NOTE: ***L. B. Cole*** *c-1, 3, 4, 6-10.* ***Al McWilliams*** *a-6. Dick Cole in 1-9. Baseball c-10. Basketball c-9. Football c-8.*						
DICKIE DARE						
Eastern Color Printing Co.: 1941 - No. 4, 1942 (#3 on sale 6/15/42)						
1-Caniff-a, bondage-c by Everett	58	116	174	363	544	725
2	30	60	90	170	240	310
3,4-Half Scorchy Smith by Noel Sickles who was very influential in Milton Caniff's development	34	68	102	196	278	360
DICK POWELL (Also see A-1 Comics)						
Magazine Enterprises: No. 22, 1949 (one shot)						
A-1 22-Photo-c	26	52	78	147	206	265
DICK QUICK, ACE REPORTER (See Picture News #10)						
DICKS						
Caliber Comics: 1997 - No. 4, 1998 ($2.95, B&W)						
1-4-Ennis-s/McCrea-c/a; r/Fleetway						3.00
TPB ('98, $12.95) r/series						13.00
DICK'S ADVENTURES						
Dell Publishing Co.: No. 245, Sept, 1949						
Four Color 245	6	12	18	43	59	75
DICK TRACY (See Famous Feature Stories, Harvey Comics Library, Limited Collectors' Ed., Mammoth Comics, Merry Christmas, The Original..., Popular Comics, Super Book No. 1, 7, 13, 25, Super Comics & Tastee-Freez)						
DICK TRACY						
David McKay Publications: May, 1937 - Jan, 1938						
Feature Books nn - 100 pgs., partially reprinted as 4-Color No. 1 (appeared before Large Feature Comics, 1st Dick Tracy comic book) (Very Rare-five known copies; two incomplete)	641	1282	1923	4487	6894	9300
Feature Books 4 - Reprints nn issue w/new-c	120	240	360	750	1125	1500
Feature Books 6,9	88	176	264	550	825	1100
DICK TRACY (...Monthly #1-24)						
Dell Publishing Co.: 1939 - No. 24, Dec, 1949						
Large Feature Comic 1 (1939) -Dick Tracy Meets The Blank	160	320	480	1000	1500	2000
Large Feature Comic 4,8	88	176	264	550	825	1100
Large Feature Comic 11,13,15	78	156	234	488	732	975
Four Color 1(1939)('35-r)	628	1256	1884	4396	6748	9100
Four Color 6(1940)('37-r)-(Scarce)	146	292	438	1046	1598	2150
Four Color 8(1940)('38-'39-r)	73	146	219	519	797	1075
Large Feature Comic 3(1941, Series II)	76	152	228	475	713	950
Four Color 21('41)('38-r)	61	122	183	435	667	900
Four Color 34('43)('39-'40-r)	41	82	123	315	470	625
Four Color 56('44)('40-r)	35	70	105	263	394	525
Four Color 96('46)('40-r)	28	56	84	203	294	385
Four Color 133('47)('40-'41-r)	22	44	66	160	235	310
Four Color 163('47)('41-r)	19	38	57	138	202	265
Four Color 215('48)-Titled "Sparkle Plenty", Dick Tracy-r	12	24	36	84	125	165
1(1/48)('34-r)	40	80	120	300	450	600
2,3	24	48	72	174	255	335
4-10	22	44	66	156	228	300
11-18: 13-Bondage-c	16	32	48	116	171	225
19-1st app. Sparkle Plenty, B.O. Plenty & Gravel Gertie in a 3-pg. strip not by Gould	17	34	51	123	182	240
20-1st app. Sam Catchem; c/a not by Gould	16	32	48	111	163	215
21-24-Only 2 pg. Gould-a in each	15	30	45	107	156	205
NOTE: *No. 19-24 have a 2 pg. biography of a famous villain illustrated by* ***Gould****: 19-Little Face; 20-Flattop; 21-Breathless Mahoney; 22-Measles; 23-Itchy; 24-The Brow.*						
DICK TRACY (Continued from Dell series)(...Comics Monthly #25-140)						
Harvey Publications: No. 25, Mar, 1950 - No. 145, April, 1961						
25-Flat Top-c/story (also #26,27)	18	36	54	131	191	250
26-28,30: 28-Bondage-c. 28,29-The Brow-c/stories	14	28	42	97	141	185

Dick Tracy - Book One © WDC

Ding Dong #3 © ME

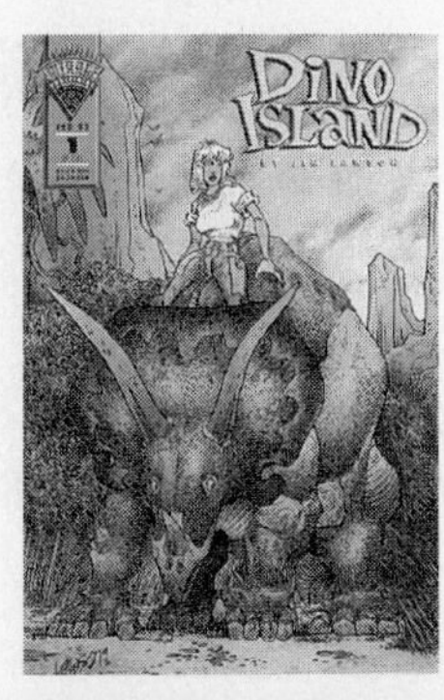

Dino Island #1 © Jim Lawson

	GD 2.0	VG 4.0	FN 6.0	VF 8.0	VF/NM 9.0	NM- 9.2
29-1st app. Gravel Gertie in a Gould-r	17	34	51	118	174	230
31,32,34,35,37-40: 40-Intro/origin 2-way wrist radio (6/51)	12	24	36	84	125	165
33- "Measles the Teen-Age Dope Pusher"	14	28	42	97	141	185
36-1st app. B.O. Plenty in a Gould-r	14	28	42	97	141	185
41-50	10	20	30	73	107	140
51-56,58-80: 51-2pgs Powell-a	10	20	30	67	96	125
57-1st app. Sam Catchem in a Gould-r	11	22	33	75	110	145
81-99,101-140	9	18	27	63	89	115
100, 141-145 (25¢)(titled "Dick Tracy")	10	20	30	67	96	125

NOTE: *Powell a(1-2pgs.)-43, 44, 104, 108, 109, 145. No. 110-120, 141-145 are all reprints from earlier issues.*

DICK TRACY
Blackthorne Publishing: 12/84 - No. 24, 6/89 (1-12: $5.95; 13-24: $6.95, B&W, 76 pgs.)

	GD 2.0	VG 4.0	FN 6.0	VF 8.0	VF/NM 9.0	NM- 9.2
1-8-1st printings; hard-c ed. ($14.95)						15.00
1-3-2nd printings, 1986; hard-c ed.						15.00
1-12-1st & 2nd printings; squarebound. thick-c						7.00
13-24 ($6.95): 21,22-Regular-c & stapled						7.00

NOTE: **Gould** daily & Sunday strip-r in all. 1-12 r-12/31/45-4/5/49; 13-24 r-7/13/41-2/20/44.

DICK TRACY (Disney)
WD Publications: 1990 - No. 3, 1990 (color) (Book 3 adapts 1990 movie)

	GD 2.0	VG 4.0	FN 6.0	VF 8.0	VF/NM 9.0	NM- 9.2
Book One ($3.95, 52pgs.)-Kyle Baker-c/a						6.00
Book Two, Three ($5.95, 68pgs.)-Direct sale						6.00
Book Two, Three ($2.95, 68pgs.)-Newsstand						3.00

DICK TRACY ADVENTURES
Gladstone Publishing: May, 1991 ($4.95, 76 pgs.)

	GD 2.0	VG 4.0	FN 6.0	VF 8.0	VF/NM 9.0	NM- 9.2
1-Reprints strips 2/1/42-4/18/42						5.00

DICK TRACY, EXPLOITS OF
Rosdon Books, Inc.: 1946 ($1.00, hard-c strip reprints)

	GD 2.0	VG 4.0	FN 6.0	VF 8.0	VF/NM 9.0	NM- 9.2
1-Reprints the near complete case of "The Brow" from 6/12/44 to 9/24/44 (story starts a few weeks late)	26	52	78	150	210	270
with dust jacket...	40	80	120	240	345	450

DICK TRACY MONTHLY/WEEKLY
Blackthorne Publishing: May, 1986 - No. 99, 1989 ($2.00, B&W)
(Becomes Weekly #26 on)

	GD 2.0	VG 4.0	FN 6.0	VF 8.0	VF/NM 9.0	NM- 9.2
1-60: Gould-r. 30,31-Mr. Crime app.						3.00
61-90						4.00
91-95						6.00
96-99-Low print	1	2	3	5	6	8

NOTE: *#1-10 reprint strips 3/10/40-7/13/41; #10(pg.8)-51 reprint strips 4/6/49-12/31/55; #52-99 reprint strips 12/26/56-4/26/64.*

DICK TRACY SPECIAL
Blackthorne Publ.: Jan, 1988 - No. 3, Aug. (no month), 1989 ($2.95, B&W)

	GD 2.0	VG 4.0	FN 6.0	VF 8.0	VF/NM 9.0	NM- 9.2
1-3: 1-Origin D. Tracy; 4/strips 10/12/31-3/30/32						3.00

DICK TRACY: THE EARLY YEARS
Blackthorne Publishing: Aug, 1987 - No. 4, Aug (no month) 1989 ($6.95, B&W, 76 pgs.)

	GD 2.0	VG 4.0	FN 6.0	VF 8.0	VF/NM 9.0	NM- 9.2
1-3: 1-4-r/strips 10/12/31(1st daily)-8/31/32 & Sunday strips 6/12/32-8/28/32; Big Boy apps. in #1-3	1	2	3	4	5	7
4 ($2.95, 52pgs.)						3.00

DICK TRACY UNPRINTED STORIES
Blackthorne Publishing: Sept, 1987 - No. 4, June, 1988 ($2.95, B&W)

	GD 2.0	VG 4.0	FN 6.0	VF 8.0	VF/NM 9.0	NM- 9.2
1-4: Reprints strips 1/1/56-12/25/56						3.00

DICK TURPIN (See Legend of Young...)

DIE-CUT
Marvel Comics UK, Ltd: Nov, 1993 - No. 4, Feb, 1994 ($1.75, limited series)

	GD 2.0	VG 4.0	FN 6.0	VF 8.0	VF/NM 9.0	NM- 9.2
1-4: 1-Die-cut-c; The Beast app.						2.25

DIE-CUT VS. G-FORCE
Marvel Comics UK, Ltd: Nov, 1993 - No. 2, Dec, 1993 ($2.75, limited series)

	GD 2.0	VG 4.0	FN 6.0	VF 8.0	VF/NM 9.0	NM- 9.2
1,2-($2.75)-Gold foil-c on both						2.75

DIE, MONSTER, DIE (See Movie Classics)

DIGIMON DIGITAL MONSTERS (TV)
Dark Horse Comics: May, 2000 - No. 12, Nov, 2000 ($2.95/$2.99)

	GD 2.0	VG 4.0	FN 6.0	VF 8.0	VF/NM 9.0	NM- 9.2
1-12						3.00

DIGITEK
Marvel UK, Ltd: Dec, 1992 - No. 4, Mar, 1993 ($1.95/$2.25, mini-series)

	GD 2.0	VG 4.0	FN 6.0	VF 8.0	VF/NM 9.0	NM- 9.2
1-4: 3-Deathlock-c/story						2.25

DILLY (Dilly Duncan from Daredevil Comics; see Boy Comics #57)
Lev Gleason Publications: May, 1953 - No. 3, Sept, 1953

	GD 2.0	VG 4.0	FN 6.0	VF 8.0	VF/NM 9.0	NM- 9.2
1-Teenage; Biro-c	6	12	18	33	41	48
2,3-Biro-c	5	10	15	22	26	30

DILTON'S STRANGE SCIENCE (See Pep Comics #78)
Archie Comics: May, 1989 - No. 5, May, 1990 (75¢/$1.00)

	GD 2.0	VG 4.0	FN 6.0	VF 8.0	VF/NM 9.0	NM- 9.2
1-5						3.00

DIME COMICS
Newsbook Publ. Corp.: 1945; 1951

	GD 2.0	VG 4.0	FN 6.0	VF 8.0	VF/NM 9.0	NM- 9.2
1-Silver Streak-c/story; L. B. Cole-c	66	132	198	413	619	825
1(1951)	8	16	24	46	58	70

DINGBATS (See 1st Issue Special)

DING DONG
Compix/Magazine Enterprises: Summer?, 1946 - No. 5, 1947 (52 pgs.)

	GD 2.0	VG 4.0	FN 6.0	VF 8.0	VF/NM 9.0	NM- 9.2
1-Funny animal	27	54	81	153	214	275
2 (9/46)	13	26	39	74	100	125
3 (Wint '46-'47) - 5	10	20	30	56	73	90

DINKY DUCK (Paul Terry's...) (See Approved Comics, Blue Ribbon, Giant Comics Edition #5A & New Terrytoons)
St. John Publishing Co./Pines No. 16 on: Nov, 1951 - No. 16, Sept, 1955; No. 16, Fall, 1956; No. 17, May, 1957 - No. 19, Summer, 1958

	GD 2.0	VG 4.0	FN 6.0	VF 8.0	VF/NM 9.0	NM- 9.2
1-Funny animal	12	24	36	71	96	120
2	8	16	24	40	50	60
3-10	6	12	18	27	33	38
11-16(9/55)	5	10	15	23	28	32
16(Fall,'56) - 19	4	8	12	18	22	25

DINKY DUCK & HASHIMOTO-SAN (See Deputy Dawg Presents...)

DINO (TV)(The Flintstones)
Charlton Publications: Aug, 1973 - No. 20, Jan, 1977 (Hanna-Barbera)

	GD 2.0	VG 4.0	FN 6.0	VF 8.0	VF/NM 9.0	NM- 9.2
1	3	7	10	21	28	35
2-10	2	4	6	11	14	18
11-20	2	4	6	8	10	12

DINO ISLAND
Mirage Studios: Feb, 1994 - No. 2, Mar, 1994 ($2.75, limited series)

	GD 2.0	VG 4.0	FN 6.0	VF 8.0	VF/NM 9.0	NM- 9.2
1,2-By Jim Lawson						2.75

DINO RIDERS
Marvel Comics: Feb, 1989 - No. 3, 1989 ($1.00)

	GD 2.0	VG 4.0	FN 6.0	VF 8.0	VF/NM 9.0	NM- 9.2
1-3: Based on toys						3.00

DINOSAUR REX
Upshot Graphics (Fantagraphics): 1986 - No. 3, 1986 ($2.00, limited series)

	GD 2.0	VG 4.0	FN 6.0	VF 8.0	VF/NM 9.0	NM- 9.2
1-3						2.25

DINOSAURS, A CELEBRATION
Marvel Comics (Epic): Oct, 1992 - No. 4, Oct, 1992 ($4.95, lim. series, 52 pgs.)

	GD 2.0	VG 4.0	FN 6.0	VF 8.0	VF/NM 9.0	NM- 9.2
1-4: 2-Bolton painted-c						5.00

DINOSAURS ATTACK! THE GRAPHIC NOVEL
Eclipse Comics: 1991 ($3.95, coated stock, stiff-c)

	GD 2.0	VG 4.0	FN 6.0	VF 8.0	VF/NM 9.0	NM- 9.2
Book One- Based on Topps trading cards						4.00

DINOSAURS FOR HIRE
Malibu Comics: Feb, 1993 - No. 12, Feb, 1994 ($1.95/$2.50)

	GD 2.0	VG 4.0	FN 6.0	VF 8.0	VF/NM 9.0	NM- 9.2
1-12: 1,10-Flip bk. 8-Bagged w/Skycap; Staton-c. 10-Flip book						2.50

DINOSAURS GRAPHIC NOVEL (TV)
Disney Comics: 1992 - No. 2, 1993 ($2.95, 52 pgs.)

	GD 2.0	VG 4.0	FN 6.0	VF 8.0	VF/NM 9.0	NM- 9.2
1,2-Staton-a; based on Dinosaurs TV show						3.00

DINOSAURUS
Dell Publishing Co.: No. 1120, Aug, 1960

	GD 2.0	VG 4.0	FN 6.0	VF 8.0	VF/NM 9.0	NM- 9.2
Four Color 1120-Movie, painted-c	9	18	27	60	85	110

DIPPY DUCK
Atlas Comics (OPI): October, 1957

	GD 2.0	VG 4.0	FN 6.0	VF 8.0	VF/NM 9.0	NM- 9.2
1-Maneely-a; code approved	9	18	27	52	66	80

DIRECTORY TO A NONEXISTENT UNIVERSE
Eclipse Comics: Dec, 1987 ($2.00, B&W)

	GD 2.0	VG 4.0	FN 6.0	VF 8.0	VF/NM 9.0	NM- 9.2
1						2.25

DIRTY DOZEN (See Movie Classics)

Dirty Pair: Sim Hell Remastered #3 © Haraka Takachiho

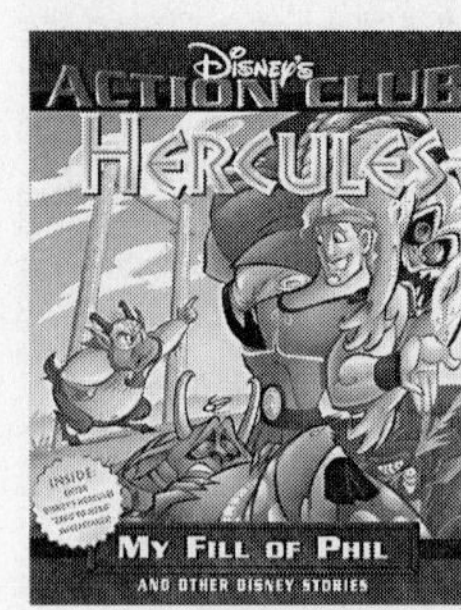

Disney's Action Club #1 © WDC

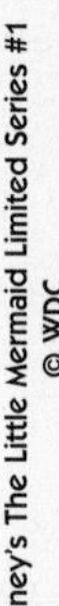

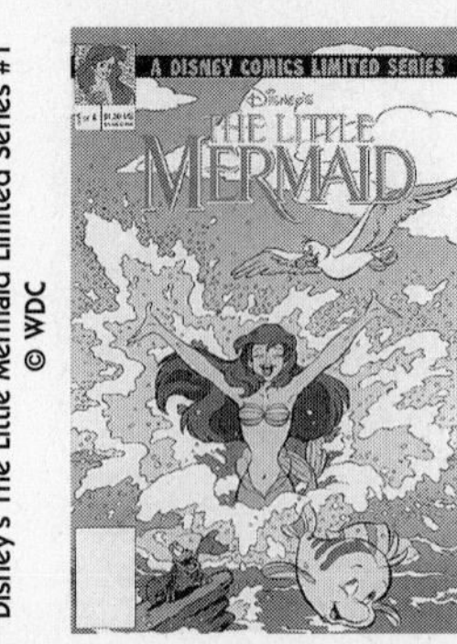

Disney's The Little Mermaid Limited Series #1 © WDC

GD 2.0 | VG 4.0 | FN 6.0 | VF 8.0 | VF/NM 9.0 | NM- 9.2

GD 2.0 | VG 4.0 | FN 6.0 | VF 8.0 | VF/NM 9.0 | NM- 9.2

DIRTY PAIR (Manga)
Eclipse Comics: Dec, 1988 - No. 4, Apr, 1989 ($2.00, B&W, limited series)
1-4: Japanese manga with original stories 3.00
...: Start the Violence (Dark Horse, 9/99, $2.95) r/B&W stories in color from Dark Horse Presents #132-134; covers by Warren & Pearson 3.00

DIRTY PAIR: FATAL BUT NOT SERIOUS (Manga)
Dark Horse Comics: July, 1995 - No. 5, Nov, 1995 ($2.95, limited series)
1-5 3.00

DIRTY PAIR: RUN FROM THE FUTURE (Manga)
Dark Horse Comics: Jan, 2000 - No. 4, Mar, 2000 ($2.95, limited series)
1-4-Warren-s/c/a. Var.-c by Hughes(1), Stelfreeze(2), Timm(3), Ramos(4) 3.00

DIRTY PAIR: SIM HELL (Manga)
Dark Horse Comics: May, 1993 - No. 4, Aug, 1993 ($2.50, B&W, limited series)
1-4 3.00
...Remastered #1-4 (5/01 - 8/01) reprints in color, with pin-up gallery 3.00

DIRTY PAIR II (Manga)
Eclipse Comics: June, 1989 - No. 5, Mar, 1990 ($2.00, B&W, limited series)
1-5: 3-Cover is misnumbered as #1 3.00

DIRTY PAIR III, THE (A Plague of Angels) (Manga)
Eclipse Comics: Aug, 1990 - No. 5, Aug, 1991 ($2.00/$2.25, B&W, lim. series)
1-5 3.00

DISAVOWED
DC Comics (Homage): Mar, 2000 - No. 6, Sept, 2000 ($2.50)
1-6: 1-3-Choi & Heisler-s/Edwards-a. 4,5-Lucas-a 2.50

DISCIPLES
Image Comics: Apr, 2001 - Present ($2.95)
1,2: 1-Wraparound-c 3.00
...: Wheel of Fortune (12/01, $4.95) 5.00

DISHMAN
Eclipse Comics: Sept, 1988 ($2.50, B&W, 52 pgs.)
1 2.50

DISNEY AFTERNOON, THE (TV)
Marvel Comics: Nov, 1994 - No. 10?, Aug, 1995 ($1.50)
1-10: 3-w/bound-in Power Ranger Barcode Card 3.00

DISNEY COMIC ALBUM
Disney Comics: 1990(no month, year) - No. 8, 1991 ($6.95/$7.95)
1,2 ($6.95): 1-Donald Duck and Gyro Gearloose by Barks(r). 2-Uncle Scrooge by Barks(r); Jr. Woodchucks app. 9.00
3-8: 3-Donald Duck-r/F.C. 308 by Barks; begin $7.95-c. 4-Mickey Mouse Meets the Phantom Blot; r/M.M Club Parade (censored 1956 version of story). 5-Chip 'n' Dale Rescue Rangers; new-a. 6-Uncle Scrooge. 7-Donald Duck in Too Many Pets; Barks-r(4) including F.C. #29. 8-Super Goof; r/S.G. #1, D.D. #102 9.00

DISNEY COMIC HITS
Marvel Comics: Oct, 1995 - No. 16, Jan, 1997 ($1.50/$2.50)
1-16: 4-Toy Story. 6-Aladdin. 7-Pocahontas. 10-The Hunchback of Notre Dame (Same story in Disney's The Hunchback of Notre Dame). 13-Aladdin and the Forty Thieves 4.00

DISNEY COMICS
Disney Comics: June, 1990
Boxed set of #1 issues includes Donald Duck Advs., Ducktales, Chip 'n Dale Rescue Rangers, Roger Rabbit, Mickey Mouse Advs. & Goofy Advs.; limited to 10,000 sets 2 4 6 10 12 15

DISNEYLAND BIRTHDAY PARTY (Also see Dell Giants)
Gladstone Publishing Co.: Aug, 1985 ($2.50)
1-Reprints Dell Giant with new-photo-c 2 4 6 8 10 12
...Comics Digest #1-(Digest) 2 4 6 9 11 14

DISNEYLAND MAGAZINE
Fawcett Publications: Feb. 15, 1972 - ? (10-1/4"x12-5/8", 20 pgs, weekly)
1-One or two page painted art features on Dumbo, Snow White, Lady & the Tramp, the Aristocats, Brer Rabbit, Peter Pan, Cinderella, Jungle Book, Alice & Pinocchio. Most standard characters app. 3 6 9 18 24 30

DISNEYLAND, USA (See Dell Giant No. 30)

DISNEY MOVIE BOOK
Walt Disney Productions (Gladstone): 1990 ($7.95, 8-1/2"x11", 52 pgs.) (w/pull-out poster)
1-Roger Rabbit in Tummy Trouble; from the cartoon film strips adapted to the comic format. Ron Dias-c 2 4 6 8 10 12

DISNEY'S ACTION CLUB
Acclaim Books: 1997 - No. 4 ($4.50, digest size)
1-4: 1-Hercules. 4-Mighty Ducks 4.50

DISNEY'S ALADDIN (Movie)
Marvel Comics: Oct, 1994 - No. 11, 1995 ($1.50)
1-11 3.00

DISNEY'S BEAUTY AND THE BEAST (Movie)
Marvel Comics: Sept, 1994 - No. 13, 1995 ($1.50)
1-13 3.00

DISNEY'S BEAUTY AND THE BEAST HOLIDAY SPECIAL
Acclaim Books: 1997 ($4.50, digest size, one-shot)
1-Based on The Enchanted Christmas video 4.50

DISNEY'S COLOSSAL COMICS COLLECTION
Disney Comics: 1991 - No. 10, 1993 ($1.95, digest-size, 96/132 pgs.)
1-10: Ducktales, Talespin, Chip 'n Dale's Rescue Rangers. 4-r/Darkwing Duck #1-4. 6-Goofy begins. 8-Little Mermaid 5.00

DISNEY'S COMICS IN 3-D
Disney Comics: 1992 ($2.95, w/glasses, polybagged)
1-Infinity-c; Barks, Rosa, Gottfredson-r 5.00

DISNEY'S ENCHANTING STORIES
Acclaim Books: 1997 - No. 5 ($4.50, digest size)
1-5: 1-Hercules. 2-Pocahontas 4.50

DISNEY'S NEW ADVENTURES OF BEAUTY AND THE BEAST (Also see Beauty and the Beast & Disney's Beauty and the Beast)
Disney Comics: 1992 - No. 2, 1992 ($1.50, limited series)
1,2-New stories based on movie 3.00

DISNEY'S POCAHONTAS (Movie)
Marvel Comics: 1995 ($4.95, one-shot)
1-Movie adaptation 1 2 3 4 5 7

DISNEY'S TALESPIN LIMITED SERIES: "TAKE OFF" (TV) (See Talespin)
W. D. Publications (Disney Comics): Jan, 1991 - No. 4, Apr, 1991 ($1.50, lim. series, 52 pgs.)
1-4: Based on animated series; 4 part origin 2.50

DISNEY'S TARZAN (Movie)
Dark Horse Comics: June, 1999 - No. 2, July, 1999 ($2.95, limited series)
1,2: Movie adaptation 3.00

DISNEY'S THE LION KING (Movie)
Marvel Comics: July, 1994 - No. 2, July, 1994 ($1.50, limited series)
1,2: 2-part movie adaptation 3.00
1-($2.50, 52 pgs.)-Complete story 5.00

DISNEY'S THE LITTLE MERMAID (Movie)
Marvel Comics: Sept, 1994 - No. 12, 1995 ($1.50)
1-12 4.00

DISNEY'S THE LITTLE MERMAID LIMITED SERIES (Movie)
Disney Comics: Feb, 1992 - No. 4, May, 1992 ($1.50, limited series)
1-4: Peter David scripts 3.00

DISNEY'S THE LITTLE MERMAID: UNDERWATER ENGAGEMENTS
Acclaim Books: 1997 ($4.50, digest size)
1-Flip book 4.50

DISNEY'S THE HUNCHBACK OF NOTRE DAME (Movie)(See Disney's Comic Hits #10)
Marvel Comics: July, 1996 ($4.95, squarebound, one-shot)
1-Movie adaptation. 1 2 3 4 5 7
NOTE: *A different edition of this series was sold at Wal-Mart stores with new covers depicting scenes from the 1989 feature film. Inside contents and price were identical.*

DISNEY'S THE THREE MUSKETEERS (Movie)
Marvel Comics: Jan, 1994 - No. 2, Feb, 1994 ($1.50, limited series)
1,2-Morrow-c; Spiegle-a; Movie adaptation 2.25

DISNEY'S TOY STORY (Movie)
Marvel Comics: Dec, 1995 ($4.95, one-shot)
nn-Adaptation of film 1 2 3 4 5 7

DISTANT SOIL, A (1st Series)
WaRP Graphics: Dec, 1983 - No. 9, Mar 1986 ($1.50, B&W)

A Distant Soil #13 © Colleen Doran

Divine Right #2 © DC

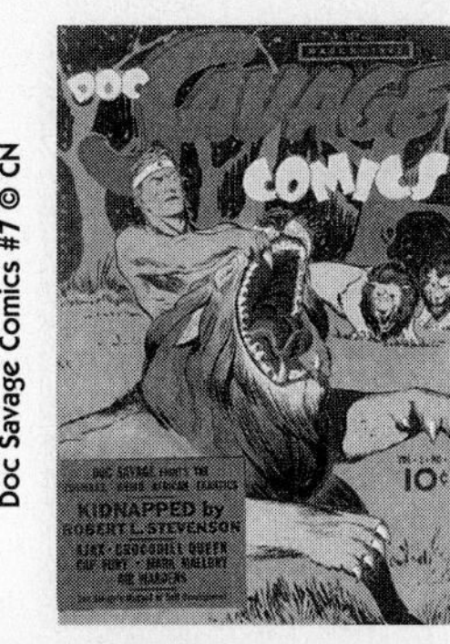

Doc Savage Comics #7 © CN

GD VG FN VF VF/NM NM-
2.0 4.0 6.0 8.0 9.0 9.2

1-Magazine size 4.00
2-9: 2-4 are magazine size 3.00
NOTE: Second printings exist of #1, 2, 3 & 6.

DISTANT SOIL, A
Donning (Star Blaze): Mar, 1989 ($12.95, trade paperback)
nn-new material 13.00

DISTANT SOIL, A (2nd Series)
Aria Press/Image Comics (Highbrow Entertainment) #15 on:
June, 1991 - Present ($1.75/$2.50/$2.95/$3.95, B&W)
1-27: 13-$2.95-c begins. 14-Sketchbook. 15-(8/96)-1st Image issue 3.00
29-33,35-($3.95) 4.00
34-($4.95, 64 pages) includes sketchbook pages 5.00
36-($4.50) Back-up story by Darnall & Doran 5.00
The Aria ('01, $16.95,TPB) r/#26-31 17.00
The Ascendant ('98, $18.95,TPB) r/#13-25 19.00
The Gathering ('97, $18.95,TPB) r/#1-13; intro. Neil Gaiman 19.00
NOTE: Four separate printings exist for #1 and are clearly marked. Second printings exist of #2-4 and are also clearly marked.

DISTANT SOIL, A: IMMIGRANT SONG
Donning (Star Blaze): Aug, 1987 ($6.95, trade paperback)
nn-new material 7.00

DIVER DAN (TV)
Dell Publishing Co.: Feb-Apr, 1962 - No. 2, June-Aug, 1962
Four Color 1254(#1), 2 6 12 18 40 55 70

DIVINE RIGHT
Image Comics (WildStorm Prod.): Sept, 1997 - No. 12, Nov, 1999 ($2.50)
Preview 5.00
1,2: 1-Jim Lee-s/a(p)/c, 1-Variant-c by Charest 4.00
1-($3.50)-Voyager Pack w/Stormwatch preview 3.50
1-American Entertainment Ed. 6.00
2-Variant-c of Exotica & Blaze 5.00
3-Chromium-c by Jim Lee 5.00
3-12: 3-5-Fairchild & Lynch app. 4-American Entertainment Ed. 8-Two covers. 9-1st DC issue. 11,12-Divine Intervention pt. 1,4 3.00
5-Pacific Comicon Ed. 6.00
6-Glow in the dark variant-c, European Tour Edition 20.00
...Book One TPB (2002, $17.95) r/#1-7 18.00
...Book Two TPB (2002, $17.95) r/#8-12 & Divine Intervention Gen13, ...Wildcats 18.00
...Collected Edition #1-3 ($5.95, TPB) 1-r/#1,2. 2-r/#3,4. 3-r/#5,6 6.00
Divine Intervention/Gen 13 (11/99, $2.50) Part 3; D'Anda-a 2.50
Divine Intervention/Wildcats (11/99, $2.50) Part 2; D'Anda-a 2.50

DIVISION 13 (See Comic's Greatest World)
Dark Horse Comics: Sept, 1994 - Jan, 1995 ($2.50, color)
1-4: Giffen story in all. 1-Art Adams-c 2.50

DIXIE DUGAN (See Big Shot, Columbia Comics & Feature Funnies)
McNaught Syndicate/Columbia/Publication Ent.: July, 1942 - No. 13, 1949
(Strip reprints in all)
1-Joe Palooka x-over by Ham Fisher 29 58 87 164 232 300
2 16 32 48 92 126 160
3 12 24 36 69 92 115
4,5(1945-46)-Bo strip-r 9 18 27 52 66 80
6-13(1/47-49): 6-Paperdoll cut-outs 8 16 24 43 54 65

DIXIE DUGAN
Prize Publications (Headline): V3#1, Nov, 1951 - V4#4, Feb, 1954
V3#1 9 18 27 52 66 80
2-4 7 14 21 35 43 50
V4#1-4(#5-8) 6 12 18 28 34 40

DIZZY DAMES
American Comics Group (B&M Distr. Co.): Sept-Oct, 1952 - No. 6, Jul-Aug, 1953
1-Whitney-c 15 30 45 86 118 150
2 9 18 27 52 66 80
3-6 8 16 24 40 50 60

DIZZY DON COMICS
F. E. Howard Publications/Dizzy Don Ent. Ltd (Canada): 1942 - No. 22, Oct, 1946; No. 3, Apr, 1947 (Most B&W)
1 (B&W) 13 26 39 74 100 125
2 (B&W) 8 16 24 40 50 60
4-21 (B&W) 7 14 21 37 46 55
22-Full color, 52 pgs. 15 30 45 86 118 150
3 (4/47)-Full color, 52 pgs. 15 30 45 86 118 150

GD VG FN VF VF/NM NM-
2.0 4.0 6.0 8.0 9.0 9.2

DIZZY DUCK (Formerly Barnyard Comics)
Standard Comics: No. 32, Nov, 1950 - No. 39, Mar, 1952
32-Funny animal 10 20 30 56 73 90
33-39 6 12 18 28 34 40

DNAGENTS (The New DNAgents V2/1 on)(Also see Surge)
Eclipse Comics: March, 1983 - No. 24, July, 1985 ($1.50, Baxter paper)
1,24: 1-Origin. 4-Amber app. 24-Dave Stevens-c 3.00
2-23: 8-Infinity-c 2.25

DOBERMAN (See Sgt. Bilko's Private...)

DOBIE GILLIS (See The Many Loves of...)

DOC CHAOS: THE STRANGE ATTRACTOR
Vortex Comics: Apr, 1990 - No. 3, 1990 ($3.00, 32 pgs.)
1-3: The Lust For Order 3.00

DOC SAMSON (Also see Incredible Hulk)
Marvel Comics: Jan, 1996 - No. 4, Apr, 1996 ($1.95, limited series)
1-4: 1-Hulk c/app. 2-She-Hulk-c/app. 3-Punisher-c/app. 4-Polaris-c/app. 2.25

DOC SAVAGE
Gold Key: Nov, 1966
1-Adaptation of the Thousand-Headed Man; James Bama c-r/1964 Doc Savage paperback 11 22 33 75 110 145

DOC SAVAGE (Also see Giant-Size...)
Marvel Comics Group: Oct, 1972 - No. 8, Jan, 1974
1 3 6 9 16 20 24
2,3-Steranko-c 2 4 6 10 12 15
4-8 1 3 4 6 8 10
NOTE: ***Gil Kane*** *c-5, 6.* ***Mooney*** *a-1i. No. 1, 2 adapts pulp story "The Man of Bronze"; No. 3, 4 adapts "Death in Silver"; No. 5, 6 adapts "The Monsters"; No. 7, 8 adapts "The Brand of The Werewolf".*

DOC SAVAGE (Magazine)
Marvel Comics Group: Aug, 1975 - No. 8, Spring, 1977 ($1.00, B&W)
1-Cover from movie poster; Ron Ely photo-c 2 4 6 10 13 16
2-5: 3-Buscema-a. 5-Adams-a(1 pg.), Rogers-a(1 pg) 1 2 3 5 7 9
6-8 1 3 4 6 8 10

DOC SAVAGE
DC Comics: Nov, 1987 - No. 4, Feb, 1988 ($1.75, limited series)
1-4 3.00

DOC SAVAGE
DC Comics: Nov, 1988 - No. 24, Oct, 1990 ($1.75/$2.00: #13-24)
1-16,19-24 3.00
17,18-Shadow x-over 4.00
Annual 1 (1989, $3.50, 68 pgs.) 4.00

DOC SAVAGE COMICS (Also see Shadow Comics)
Street & Smith Publ.: May, 1940 - No. 20, Oct, 1943 (1st app. in Doc Savage pulp, 3/33)
1-Doc Savage, Cap Fury, Danny Garrett, Mark Mallory, The Whisperer, Captain Death, Billy the Kid, Sheriff Pete & Treasure Island begin; Norgil, the Magician app. 483 966 1449 3381 5191 7000
2-Origin & 1st app. Ajax, the Sun Man; Danny Garrett, The Whisperer end; classic sci-fi cover 176 352 528 1100 1650 2200
3 124 248 372 775 1163 1550
4-Treasure Island ends; Tuska-a 100 200 300 625 938 1250
5-Origin & 1st app. Astron, the Crocodile Queen, not in #9 & 11; Norgi the Magician app. 76 152 228 475 713 950
6-10: 6-Cap Fury ends; origin & only app. Red Falcon in Astron story. 8-Mark Mallory ends; Charlie McCarthy app. on-c plus true life story. 9-Supersnipe app. 10-Origin & only app. The Thunderbolt 59 118 177 369 552 735
11,12 52 104 156 312 466 620
V2#1-8(#13-20): 15-Origin of Ajax the Sun Man; Jack Benny on-c; Hitler app. 16-The Pulp Hero, The Avenger app.; Fanny Brice story. 17-Sun Man ends; Nick Carter begins; Duffy's Tavern part photo-c & story. 18-Huckleberry Finn part-c/story. 19-Henny Youngman part photo-c & life story. 20-Only all funny-c w/Huckleberry Finn 51 102 153 306 458 610

DOC SAVAGE: CURSE OF THE FIRE GOD
Dark Horse Comics: Sept, 1995 - No, 4, Dec, 1995 ($2.95, limited series)
1-4 3.00

DOC SAVAGE: THE MAN OF BRONZE

Doctor Fate #1 © DC

Doctor Octopus: Negative Exposure #1 © MAR

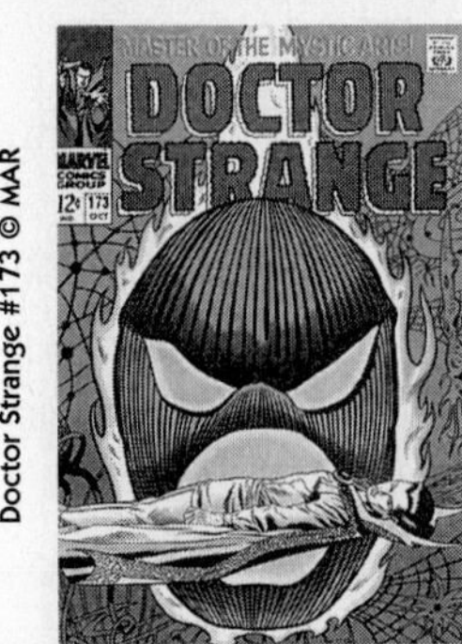

Doctor Strange #173 © MAR

GD VG FN VF VF/NM NM-
2.0 4.0 6.0 8.0 9.0 9.2

GD VG FN VF VF/NM NM-
2.0 4.0 6.0 8.0 9.0 9.2

Skylark Pub: Mar, 1979, 68pgs. (B&W comic digest, 5-1/4x7-5/8")(low print)
15406-0: Whitman-a, 60 pgs., new comics 3 7 10 21 28 35

DOC SAVAGE: THE MAN OF BRONZE
Millennium Publications: 1991 - No. 4, 1991 ($2.50, limited series)
1-4: 1-Bronze logo 3.00
...: The Manual of Bronze 1 ($2.50, B&W, color, one-shot)-Unpublished proposed Doc Savage strip in color, B&W strip-r 3.00

DOC SAVAGE: THE MAN OF BRONZE, DOOM DYNASTY
Millennium Publ.: 1992 (Says 1991) - No. 2, 1992 ($2.50, limited series)
1,2 3.00

DOC SAVAGE: THE MAN OF BRONZE - REPEL
Innovation Publishing: 1992 ($2.50)
1-Dave Dorman painted-c 3.00

DOC SAVAGE: THE MAN OF BRONZE THE DEVIL'S THOUGHTS
Millennium Publ.: 1992 (Says 1991) - No. 3, 1992 ($2.50, limited series)
1-3 3.00

DOC STEARN...MR. MONSTER (See Mr. Monster)

DR. ANTHONY KING, HOLLYWOOD LOVE DOCTOR
Minoan Publishing Corp./Harvey Publications No. 4: 1952(Jan) - No. 3, May, 1953; No. 4, May, 1954
1 13 26 39 76 103 130
2-4: 4-Powell-a 8 16 24 46 58 70

DR. ANTHONY'S LOVE CLINIC (See Mr. Anthony's...)

DR. BOBBS
Dell Publishing Co.: No. 212, Jan, 1949
Four Color 212 5 10 15 36 48 60

DOCTOR BOOGIE
Media Arts Publishing: 1987 ($1.75)
1-Airbrush wraparound-c; Nick Cuti-i 2.25

DOCTOR CHAOS
Triumphant Comics: Nov, 1993 - No. 6, Mar, 1994 ($2.50)
1-6: 1,2-Triumphant Unleashed x-over. 2-1st app. War Dancer in pin-up. 3-Intro The Cry 2.50

DOCTOR CYBORG
Attention! Publishing: 1996 - No. 5 ($2.95, B&W)
1-5 3.00
The Clone Conspiracy TPB (1998, $14.95) r/#1-5 15.00

DR. DOOM'S REVENGE
Marvel Comics: 1989 (Came w/computer game from Paragon Software)
V1#1-Spider-Man & Captain America fight Dr. Doom 3.00

DR. FATE (See 1st Issue Special, The Immortal..., Justice League, More Fun #55, & Showcase)

DOCTOR FATE
DC Comics: July, 1987 - No. 4, Oct, 1987 ($1.50, limited series, Baxter paper)
1-4: Giffen-c/a in all 3.00

DOCTOR FATE
DC Comics: Winter, 1988-'89 - No. 41, June, 1992 ($1.25/$1.50 #5 on)
1,15: 15-Justice League app. 3.50
2-14 3.00
16-41: 25-1st new Dr. Fate. 36-Original Dr. Fate returns 2.50
Annual 1(1989, $2.95, 68 pgs.)-Sutton-a 3.50

DOCTOR FATE
DC Comics: Oct, 2003 - No. 5, Feb, 2004 ($2.50, limited series)
1-5-Golden-s/Kramer-a 2.50

DR. FU MANCHU (See The Mask of...)
I.W. Enterprises: 1964
1-r/Avon's "Mask of Dr. Fu Manchu"; Wood-a 9 18 27 60 85 110

DR. GIGGLES (See Dark Horse Presents #64-66)
Dark Horse Comics: Oct, 1992 - No. 2, Oct, 1992 ($2.50, limited series)
1,2-Based on movie 2.50

DOCTOR GRAVES (Formerly The Many Ghosts of...)
Charlton Comics: No. 73, Sept, 1985 - No. 75, Jan, 1986
73-75-Low print run 6.00

DR. JEKYLL AND MR. HYDE (See A Star Presentation & Supernatural Thrillers #4)

DR. KILDARE (TV)
Dell Publishing Co.: No. 1337, 4-6/62 - No. 9, 4-6/65 (All Richard Chamberlain photo-c)
Four Color 1337(#1, 1962) 10 20 30 67 96 125
2-9 7 14 21 51 71 90

DR. MASTERS (See The Adventures of Young...)

DOCTOR MID-NITE (Also see All-American #25)
DC Comics: 1999 - No. 3, 1999 ($5.95, square-bound, limited series)
1-3-Matt Wagner-s/John K. Snyder III-painted art 6.00
TPB (2000, $19.95) r/series 20.00

DOCTOR OCTOPUS: NEGATIVE EXPOSURE
Marvel Comics: Dec, 2003 - No. 5 ($2.99, limited series)
1-4-Vaughan-s/Staz Johnson-a; Spider-Man app. 3.00

DR. ROBOT SPECIAL
Dark Horse Comics: Apr, 2000 ($2.95, one-shot)
1-Bernie Mireault-s/a; some reprints from Madman Comics #12-15 3.00

DOCTOR SOLAR, MAN OF THE ATOM (See The Occult Files of Dr. Spektor #14 & Solar)
Gold Key/Whitman No. 28 on: 10/62 - No. 27, 4/69; No. 28, 4/81 - No. 31, 3/82 (1-27 have painted-c)
1-(#10000-210)-Origin/1st app. Dr. Solar (1st original Gold Key character)
21 42 63 147 216 285
2-Prof. Harbinger begins 9 18 27 65 93 120
3,4 6 12 18 43 59 75
5-Intro. Man of the Atom in costume 7 14 21 46 63 80
6-10 5 10 15 33 44 55
11-14,16-20 4 8 12 24 32 40
15-Origin retold 4 8 12 27 36 45
21-23: 23-Last 12¢ issue 3 6 9 19 25 32
24-27 3 6 9 18 24 30
28-31: 29-Magnus Robot Fighter begins. 31-(3/82)The Sentinel app.
2 4 6 11 14 18

NOTE: ***Frank Bolle*** *a-6-19, 29-31; c-29i, 30i.* ***Bob Fugitani*** *a-1-5.* ***Spiegle*** *a-29-31.* ***Al McWilliams*** *a-20-23.*

DOCTOR SOLAR, MAN OF THE ATOM
Valiant Comics: 1990 - No. 2, 1991 ($7.95, card stock-c, high quality, 96 pgs.)
1,2: Reprints Gold Key series 1 2 3 5 7 9

DOCTOR SPEKTOR (See The Occult Files of..., & Spine-Tingling Tales)

DOCTOR STRANGE (Formerly Strange Tales #1-168) (Also see The Defenders, Giant-Size..., Marvel Fanfare, Marvel Graphic Novel, Marvel Premiere, Marvel Treasury Edition & Strange Tales, 2nd Series)
Marvel Comics Group: No. 169, 6/68 - No. 183, 11/69; 6/74 - No. 81, 2/87
169(#1)-Origin retold; panel swipe/M.D. #1-c 15 30 45 104 152 200
170-177: 177-New costume 4 8 12 29 40 50
178-183: 178-Black Knight app. 179-Spider-Man story-r. 180-Photo montage-c. 181-Brunner-c(part-i), last 12¢ issue 4 8 12 29 37 45
1(6/74, 2nd series)-Brunner-c/a 6 12 18 43 59 75
2 3 6 9 19 25 32
3-5 2 4 6 12 16 20
6-10 2 4 6 8 10 12
11-13,15-20: 13,15-17-(Regular 25¢ editions) 1 2 3 4 5 7
13-17-(30¢-c variants, limited distribution) 1 3 4 6 8 10
14-(5/76) Dracula app.; (regular 25¢ edition) 1 3 4 6 8 10
21-40: 21-Origin-r/Doctor Strange #169. 23-25-(Regular 30¢ editions). 31-Sub-Mariner-c/story 4.00
23-25-(35¢-c variants, limited distribution)(6,8,10/77) 1 2 3 5 6 8
41-57,63-77,79-81: 56-Origin retold 3.50
58-62: 58-Re-intro Hannibal King (cameo). 59-Hannibal King full app. 59-62-Dracula app. (Darkhold storyline). 61,62-Doctor Strange, Blade, Hannibal King & Frank Drake team-up to battle. Dracula. 62-Death of Dracula & Lilith 5.00
78-New costume 3.00
Annual 1(1976, 52 pgs.)-New Russell-a (35 pgs.) 2 4 6 9 11 14
.../Silver Dagger Special Edition 1 (3/83, $2.50)-r/#1,2,4,5; Wrightson-c 3.00
...What Is It That Disturbs You, Stephen? #1 (10/97, $5.99, 48 pgs.) Russell-a/Andreyko & Russell-s, retelling of Annual #1 story 6.00

NOTE: ***Adkins*** *a-169, 170, 171i; c-169-171, 172i, 173.* ***Adams*** *a-4i.* ***Austin*** *a(i)-48-60, 66, 68, 70, 73; c(i)-38, 47-53, 55, 58-60, 70.* ***Brunner*** *a-1-5p; c-1-6, 22, 28-30, 33.* ***Colan*** *a(p)-172-178, 180-183, 6-18, 36-45, 47; c(p)-172, 174-183, 11-21, 23, 27, 35, 36, 47.* ***Ditko*** *a-179r, 3r.* ***Everett*** *c-183i.* ***Golden*** *a-46p, 55p; c-42-44, 46, 55p.* ***G. Kane*** *c(p)-8-10.* ***Miller*** *c-46p.* ***Nebres*** *a-20, 22, 23, 24i, 26i, 32i; c-32i, 34.* ***Rogers*** *a-48-53p; c-47p-53p.* ***Russell*** *a-34i, 46i, Annual 1.* ***B. Smith*** *c-179.* ***Paul Smith*** *a-54p, 56p, 65, 66p, 68p, 69, 71-73; c-56, 65, 66, 68, 71.* ***Starlin*** *a-23p, 26; c-25, 26.* ***Sutton*** *a-27-29p, 31i, 33, 34p. Painted c-62, 63.*

DOCTOR STRANGE (Volume 2)

Doctor Tomorrow #9 © Acclaim/Valiant

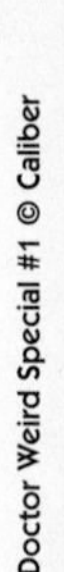

Doctor Weird Special #1 © Caliber

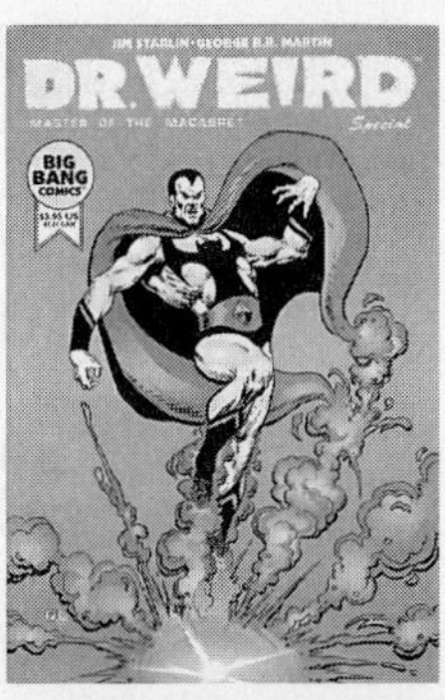

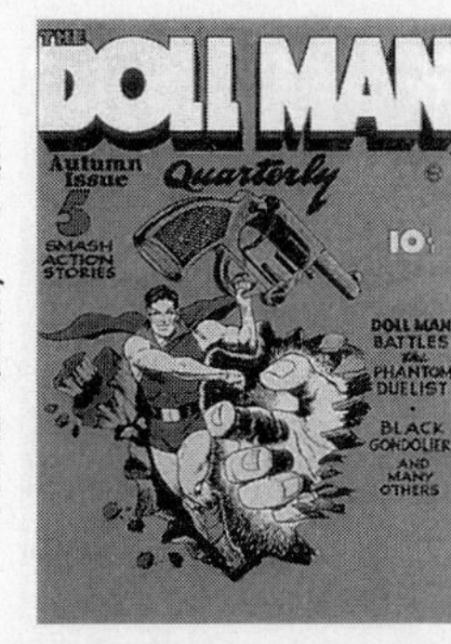

Doll Man Quarterly #1 © QUA

GD VG FN VF VF/NM NM-
2.0 4.0 6.0 8.0 9.0 9.2

Marvel Comics: Feb, 1999 - No. 4, May, 1999 ($2.99, limited series)

1-4: 1,2-Tony Harris-a/painted cover. 3,4-Chadwick-a 3.00

DOCTOR STRANGE CLASSICS
Marvel Comics Group: Mar, 1984 - No. 4, June, 1984 ($1.50, Baxter paper)

1-4: Ditko-r; Byrne-c. 4-New Golden pin-up 3.00
NOTE: ***Byrne*** *c-1i, 2-4.*

DOCTOR STRANGEFATE (See Marvel Versus DC #3 & DC Versus Marvel #4)
DC Comics (Amalgam): Apr, 1996 ($1.95)

1-Ron Marz script w/Jose Garcia-Lopez-(p) & Kevin Nowlan-(i). Access & Charles Xavier app. 2.50

DOCTOR STRANGE MASTER OF THE MYSTIC ARTS (See Fireside Book Series)

DOCTOR STRANGE, SORCERER SUPREME
Marvel Comics (Midnight Sons imprint #60 on): Nov, 1988 - No. 90, June, 1996 ($1.25/$1.50/$1.75/$1.95, direct sales only, Mando paper)

1 ($1.25) 4.00
2-9,12-14,16-25,27,29-40,42-49,51-64: 3-New Defenders app. 5-Guice-c/a begins. 14-18-Morbius story line. 31-36-Infinity Gauntlet x-overs. 31-Silver Surfer app. 33-Thanos-c & cameo. 36-Warlock app. 37-Silver Surfer app. 40-Daredevil x-over. 41-Wolverine-c/story. 42-47-Infinity War x-overs. 47-Gamora app. 52,53-Morbius-c/stories. 60,61-Siege of Darkness pt. 7 & 15. 60-Spot varnish-c. 61-New Doctor Strange begins (cameo, 1st app.). 62-Dr. Doom & Morbius app. 2.50
10,11,26,28,41: 10-Re-intro Morbius w/new costume (11/89). 11-Hobgoblin app. 26-Werewolf by Night app. 28-Ghost Rider-s cont'd from G.R. #12; published at same time as Doctor Strange/Ghost Rider Special #1(4/91) 3.00
15-Unauthorized Amy Grant photo-c 4.00
50-($2.95, 52 pgs.)-Holo-grafx foil-c; Hulk, Ghost Rider & Silver Surfer app.; leads into new Secret Defenders series 3.00
65-74, 76-90: 65-Begin $1.95-c; bound-in card sheet. 72-Silver ink-c. 80-82- Ellis-s. 84-DeMatteis story begins. 87-Death of Baron Mordo 2.50
75 ($2.50) 3.00
75 ($3.50)-Foil-c 4.00
Annual 2-4 ('92-'94, 68 pgs.)-2-Defenders app. 3-Polybagged w/card 3.00
Ashcan (1995, 75¢) 2.25
.../Ghost Rider Special 1 (4/91, $1.50)-Same book as D.S.S.S. #28 2.50
...Vs. Dracula 1 (3/94, $1.75, 52 pgs.)-r/Tomb of Dracula #44 & Dr. Strange #14 2.50
NOTE: ***Colan*** *c/a-19.* ***Golden*** *c-28.* ***Guice*** *a-5-16, 18, 20-24; c-5-12, 20-24. See 1st series for Annual #1.*

DR. TOM BRENT, YOUNG INTERN
Charlton Publications: Feb, 1963 - No. 5, Oct, 1963

	GD	VG	FN	VF	VF/NM	NM-
1	3	6	9	16	20	24
2-5	2	4	6	9	11	14

DR. TOMORROW
Acclaim Comics (Valiant): Sept, 1997 - No. 12 ($2.50)

1-12: 1-Mignola-c 2.50

DR. VOLTZ (See Mighty Midget Comics)

DR. WEIRD
Big Bang Comics: Oct, 1994 - No. 2, May, 1995 ($2.95, B&W)

1,2: 1-Frank Brunner-c 4.00

DR. WEIRD SPECIAL
Big Bang Comics: Feb, 1994 ($3.95, B&W, 68 pgs.)

1-Origin-r by Starlin; Starlin-c. 4.00

DOCTOR WHO (Also see Marvel Premiere #57-60)
Marvel Comics Group: Oct, 1984 - No. 23, Aug, 1986 ($1.50, direct sales, Baxter paper)

1-15-British-r 4.00
16-23 5.00
Graphic Novel Voyager (1985, $8.95) color reprints of B&W comic pages from Doctor Who Magazine #88-99; Colin Baker afterword 12.00

DR. WHO & THE DALEKS (See Movie Classics)

DR. WONDER
Old Town Publishing: June, 1996 - No. 5 ($2.95, B&W)

1-5: 1-Intro & origin of Dr. Wonder; Dick Ayers-c/a; Irwin Hasen-a 3.00

DOCTOR ZERO
Marvel Comics (Epic Comics): Apr, 1988 - No. 8, Aug, 1989 ($1.25/$1.50)

1-8: 1-Sienkiewicz-c. 6,7-Spiegle-a 2.25
NOTE: ***Sienkiewicz*** *a-3i, 4i; c-1.* ***Spiegle*** *a-6, 7.*

DO-DO (Funny Animal Circus Stories)
Nation-Wide Publishers: 1950 - No. 7, 1951 (5¢, 5x7-1/4" Miniature)

	GD	VG	FN	VF	VF/NM	NM-
1 (52 pgs.)	27	54	81	153	214	275
2-7	14	28	42	79	107	135

DODO & THE FROG, THE (Formerly Funny Stuff; also see It's Game Time #2)
National Periodical Publications: No. 80, 9-10/54 - No. 88, 1-2/56; No. 89, 8-9/56; No. 90, 10-11/56; No. 91, 9/57; No. 92, 11/57 (See Comic Cavalcade)

	GD	VG	FN	VF	VF/NM	NM-
80-1st app. Doodles Duck by Sheldon Mayer	21	42	63	118	164	210
81-91: Doodles Duck by Mayer in #81,83-90	13	26	39	76	103	130
92-(Scarce)-Doodles Duck by S. Mayer	19	38	57	106	146	185

DOGFACE DOOLEY
Magazine Enterprises: 1951 - No. 5, 1953

	GD	VG	FN	VF	VF/NM	NM-
1(A-1 40)	7	14	21	37	46	55
2(A-1 43), 3(A-1 49), 4(A-1 53), 5(A-1 64)	6	12	18	27	33	38
I.W. Reprint #1('64), Super Reprint #17	2	4	6	10	13	16

DOG MOON
DC Comics (Vertigo): 1996 ($6.95, one-shot)

1-Robert Hunter-scripts; Tim Truman-c/a. 7.00

DOG OF FLANDERS, A
Dell Publishing Co.: No. 1088, Mar, 1960

	GD	VG	FN	VF	VF/NM	NM-
Four Color 1088-Movie, photo-c	5	10	15	36	48	60

DOGPATCH (See Al Capp's... & Mammy Yokum)

DOGS OF WAR (Also see Warriors of Plasm)
Defiant: Apr, 1994 - No. 5, Aug, 1994 ($2.50)

1-5 2.50

DOGS-O-WAR
Crusade Comics: June, 1996 - No. 3, Jan, 1997 ($2.95, B&W, limited series)

1-3: 1,2-Photo-c 3.00

DOLLFACE & HER GANG (Betty Betz'...)
Dell Publishing Co.: No. 309, Jan, 1951

	GD	VG	FN	VF	VF/NM	NM-
Four Color 309	6	12	18	40	55	70

DOLLMAN (Movie)
Eternity Comics: Sept, 1991 - No. 4, Dec, 1991 ($2.50, limited series)

1-4: Adaptation of film 2.50

DOLL MAN QUARTERLY, THE (Doll Man #17 on; also see Feature Comics #27 & Freedom Fighters)
Quality Comics: Fall, 1941 - No. 7, Fall, '43; No. 8, Spr, '46 - No. 47, Oct, 1953

	GD	VG	FN	VF	VF/NM	NM-
1-Dollman (by Cassone), Justin Wright begin	311	622	933	2022	3111	4200
2-The Dragon begins; Crandall-a(5)	132	264	396	825	1238	1650
3,4	88	176	264	550	825	1100
5-Crandall-a	76	152	228	475	713	950
6,7(1943)	55	110	165	330	495	660
8(1946)-1st app. Torchy by Bill Ward	160	320	480	1000	1500	2000
9	55	110	165	330	495	660
10-20	42	84	126	252	376	500
21-30: 28-Vs. The Flame	38	76	114	219	310	400
31-36,38,40: 31-(12/50)-Intro Elmo, the wonder dog (Dollman's faithful dog). 32-34-Jeb Rivers app.; 34 by Crandall(p)	32	64	96	184	262	340
37-Origin & 1st app. Dollgirl; Dollgirl bondage-c	42	84	126	252	376	500
39- "Narcotics...the Death Drug" c-/story	34	68	102	196	278	360
41-47	23	43	69	130	183	235
Super Reprint #11('64, r/#20),15(r/#23),17(r/#28): 15,17-Torchy app.; Andru/Esposito-c	4	8	12	22	30	38

NOTE: ***Ward*** *Torchy in 8, 9, 11, 12, 14-24, 26, 27; by Fox-#30, 35-47.* ***Crandall*** *a-2, 5, 10, 13 & Super #11, 17, 18.* ***Crandall/Cuidera*** *c-40-42.* ***Guardineer*** *a-3. Bondage c-27, 37, 38, 39.*

DOLLS
Sirius: June, 1996 ($2.95, B&W, one-shot)

1 3.00

DOLLY
Ziff-Davis Publ. Co.: No. 10, July-Aug, 1951 (Funny animal)

	GD	VG	FN	VF	VF/NM	NM-
10-Painted-c	7	14	21	37	46	55

DOLLY DILL
Marvel Comics/Newsstand Publ.: 1945

	GD	VG	FN	VF	VF/NM	NM-
1	16	32	48	89	122	155

DOLLZ, THE
Image Comics: Apr, 2001 - No. 2, June, 2001 ($2.95)

1,2: 1-Four covers; Sniegoski & Green-s/Green-a 3.00

Dominion #5 © Masamune Shirow

Domino #1 © MAR

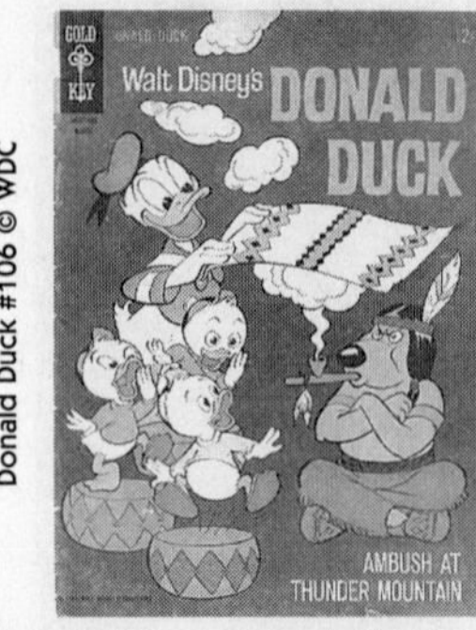

Donald Duck #106 © WDC

GD VG FN VF VF/NM NM-
2.0 4.0 6.0 8.0 9.0 9.2

DOMINATION FACTOR
Marvel Comics: Nov, 1999 - 4.8, Feb, 2000 ($2.50, interconnected mini- series)
1.1, 2.3, 3.5, 4.7-Fantastic Four; Jurgens-s/a 2.50
1.2, 2.4, 3.6, 4.8-Avengers; Ordway-s/a 2.50

DOMINION
Image Comics: Jan, 2003 - Present ($2.95)
1,2-Keith Giffen-s/a 3.00

DOMINION (Manga)
Eclipse Comics: Dec, 1990 - No. 6., July, 1990 ($2.00, B&W, limited series)
1-6 3.00

DOMINION: CONFLICT 1 (Manga)
Dark Horse Comics: Mar, 1996 - No. 6, Aug, 1996 ($2.95, B&W, limited series)
1-6: Shirow-c/a/scripts 3.00

DOMINIQUE: KILLZONE
Caliber Comics: May, 1995 ($2.95, B&W)
1 3.00

DOMINO (See X-Force)
Marvel Comics: Jan, 1997 - No. 3, Mar, 1997 ($1.95, limited series)
1-3: 2-Deathstrike-c/app. 2.25

DOMINO (See X-Force)
Marvel Comics: June, 2003 - No. 4, Aug, 2003 ($2.50, limited series)
1-4-Stelfreeze-c/a; Pruett-s. 2.50

DOMINO CHANCE
Chance Enterprises: May-June, 1982 - No. 9, May, 1985 (B&W)
1-9: 7-1st app. Gizmo, 2 pgs. 8-1st full Gizmo story. 1-Reprint, May, 1985 2.50

DONALD AND MICKEY IN DISNEYLAND (See Dell Giants)

DONALD AND SCROOGE
Disney Comics: 1992 ($8.95, squarebound, 100 pgs.)
nn-Don Rosa reprint special; r/U.S., D.D. Advs. 1 3 4 6 8 10
1-3 (1992, $1.50)-r/D.D. Advs. (Disney) #1,22,24 & U.S. #261-263,269 3.00

DONALD AND THE WHEEL (Disney)
Dell Publishing Co.: No. 1190, Nov, 1961
Four Color 1190-Movie, Barks-c 8 16 24 55 78 100

DONALD DUCK (See Adventures of Mickey Mouse, Cheerios, Donald & Mickey, Ducktales, Dynabrite Comics, Gladstone Comic Album, Mickey & Donald, Mickey Mouse Mag., Story Hour Series, Uncle Scrooge, Walt Disney's Comics & Stories, W. D.'s Donald Duck, Wheaties & Whitman Comic Books, Wise Little Hen, The)

DONALD DUCK
Whitman Publishing Co./Grosset & Dunlap/K.K.: 1935, 1936 (All pages on heavy linen-like finish cover stock in color;1st book ever devoted to Donald Duck; see Advs. of Mickey Mouse for 1st app.) (9-1/2x13")
978(1935)-16 pgs.; Illustrated text story book 380 760 1140 2090 2995 3900
nn(1936)-36 pgs.plus hard cover & dust jacket. Story completely rewritten with B&W illos added. Mickey appears and his nephews are named Morty & Monty
Book only 360 720 1080 1980 2840 3700
Dust jacket only.... 90 180 270 495 710 925

DONALD DUCK (Walt Disney's) (10¢)
Whitman/K.K. Publications: 1938 (8-1/2x11-1/2", B&W, cardboard-c)
(Has D. Duck with bubble pipe on-c)
nn-The first Donald Duck & Walt Disney comic book; 1936 & 1937 Sunday strip-r(in B&W); same format as the Feature Books; 1st strips with Huey, Dewey & Louie from 10/17/37
360 720 1080 1980 2840 3700

DONALD DUCK (Walt Disney's...#262 on; see 4-Color listings for titles & Four Color No. 1109 for origin story)
Dell Publ. Co./Gold Key #85-216/Whitman #217-245/Gladstone #246 on: 1940 - No. 84, Sept-Nov, 1962; No. 85, Dec, 1962 - No. 245, July, 1984; No. 246, Oct, 1986 - No. 279, May, 1990; No. 280, Sept, 1993 - No. 307, Mar,1998
Four Color 4(1940)-Daily 1939 strip-r by Al Taliaferro
875 1750 2625 6563 11,032 15,500
Large Feature Comic 16(1/41?)-1940 Sunday strips-r in B&W
400 800 1200 3000 5000 7000
Large Feature Comic 20('41)-Comic Paint Book, r-single panels from Large Feature #16 at top of each pg. to color; daily strip-r across bottom of each pg.
447 894 1341 3353 5527 7700
Four Color 9('42)- "Finds Pirate Gold"; 64 pgs. by Carl Barks & Jack Hannah (pgs. 1,2,5,12-40 are by Barks, his 1st Donald Duck comic book art work; © 8/17/42)
750 1500 2250 5625 9313 13,000
Four Color 29(9/43)- "Mummy's Ring" by Barks; reprinted in Uncle Scrooge & Donald Duck #1('65), W. D. Comics Digest #44('73) & Donald Duck Advs. #14
513 1026 1539 3848 6324 8800
Four Color 62(1/45)- "Frozen Gold"; 52 pgs. by Barks, reprinted in The Best of W.D. Comics & Donald Duck Advs. #4 162 332 498 1245 2048 2850
Four Color 108(1946)- "Terror of the River"; 52 pgs. by Carl Barks; reprinted in Gladstone Comic Album #2 125 250 375 938 1544 2150
Four Color 147(5/47)-in "Volcano Valley" by Barks 84 168 252 630 1040 1450
Four Color 159(8/47)-in "The Ghost of the Grotto";52 pgs. by Carl Barks; reprinted in Best of Uncle Scrooge & Donald Duck #1 ('66) & The Best of W.D. Comics & D.D. Advs. #9; two Barks stories 72 144 216 540 895 1250
Four Color 178(12/47)-1st app. Uncle Scrooge by Carl Barks; reprinted in Gold Key Christmas Parade #3 & The Best of Walt Disney Comics 100 200 300 750 1250 1750
Four Color 189(6/48)-by Carl Barks; reprinted in Best of Donald Duck & Uncle Scrooge #1('64) & D.D. Advs. #19 61 122 183 458 754 1050
Four Color 199(10/48)-by Carl Barks; mentioned in Love and Death; r/in Gladstone Comic Album #5 67 134 201 503 827 1150
Four Color 203(12/48)-by Barks; reprinted as Gold Key Christmas Parade #4
46 92 138 345 573 800
Four Color 223(4/49)-by Barks; reprinted as Best of Donald Duck #1 & Donald Duck Advs. #3
64 128 192 480 790 1100
Four Color 238(8/49)-in "Voodoo Hoodoo" by Barks 46 92 138 345 573 800
Four Color 256(12/49)-by Barks; reprinted in Best of Donald Duck & Uncle Scrooge #2('67), Gladstone Comic Album #16 & W.D. Comics Digest 44('73)
34 68 102 255 428 600
Four Color 263(2/50)-Two Barks stories; r-in D.D. #278
33 66 100 248 412 575
Four Color 275(5/50), 282(7/50), 291(9/50), 300(11/50)-All by Carl Barks; 275, 282 reprinted in W.D. Comics Digest #44('73). #275 r/in Gladstone Comic Album #10. #291 r/in D. Duck Advs. #16 31 62 93 233 392 550
Four Color 308(1/51), 318(3/51)-by Barks; #318-reprinted in W.D. Comics Digest #34 & D.D. Advs. #2,19 27 54 81 203 342 480
Four Color 328(5/51)-by Carl Barks 28 56 84 210 350 490
Four Color 339(7-8/51), 379-2nd Uncle Scrooge-c; art not by Barks.
9 18 27 65 93 120
Four Color 348(9-10/51), 356,394-Barks-c only 17 34 51 123 182 240
Four Color 367(1-2/52)-by Barks; reprinted as Gold Key Christmas Parade #2 & #8
25 50 75 188 314 440
Four Color 408(7-8/52), 422(9-10/52)-All by Carl Barks. #408-r-in Best of Donald Duck & Uncle Scrooge #1('64) & Gladstone Comic Album #13
25 50 75 188 314 440
26(11-12/52)-In "Trick or Treat" (Barks-a, 36pgs.) 1st story r-in Walt Disney Digest #16 & Gladstone C.A. #23 25 50 75 188 314 440
27-30-Barks-c only 12 24 36 82 121 160
31-44,47-50 6 12 18 43 59 75
45-Barks-a (6 pgs.) 13 26 39 94 137 180
46- "Secret of Hondorica" by Barks, 24 pgs.; reprinted in Donald Duck #98 & 154
20 40 60 140 205 270
51-Barks-a,1/2 pg. 7 14 21 46 63 80
52- "Lost Peg-Leg Mine" by Barks, 10 pgs. 14 28 42 99 145 190
53,55-59 6 12 18 38 52 65
54- "Forbidden Valley" by Barks, 26 pgs. (10¢ & 15¢ versions exist)
17 34 51 121 178 235
60- "Donald Duck & the Titanic Ants" by Barks, 20 pgs. plus 6 more pgs.
17 34 51 121 178 235
61-67,69,70 5 10 15 33 44 55
68-Barks-a, 5 pgs. 10 20 30 73 107 140
71-Barks-r, 1/2 pg. 5 10 15 36 48 60
72-78,80,82-97,99,100: 96-Donald Duck Album 5 10 15 33 44 55
79,81-Barks-a, 1pg. 5 10 15 36 48 60
98-Reprints #46 (Barks) 5 10 15 36 48 60
101,103-111,113-135: 120-Last 12¢ issue. 134-Barks-r/#52 & WDC&S 194. 135-Barks-r/WDC&S 198, 19 pgs. 4 8 12 22 30 38
102-Super Goof. 112-1st Moby Duck 4 8 12 24 32 40
136-153,155,156,158: 149-20¢-c begin 2 4 6 14 18 22
154-Barks-r(#46) 3 6 9 18 23 28
157,159,160,164: 157-Barks-r(#45); 25¢-c begin. 159-Reprints/WDC&S #192 (10 pgs.). 160-Barks-r(#26). 164-Barks-r(#79) 2 4 6 14 18 22
161-163,165-173,175-187,189-191: 175-30¢-c begin. 187-Barks r/#68.
2 4 6 11 14 18
174,188: 174-r/4-Color #394. 2 4 6 12 16 20
192-Barks-r(40 pgs.) from Donald Duck #60 & WDC&S #226,234 (52 pgs.)
3 6 9 16 20 24

Donald Duck #269 © WDC

Don Fortune Magazine #3 © Don Fortune Publ. Co.

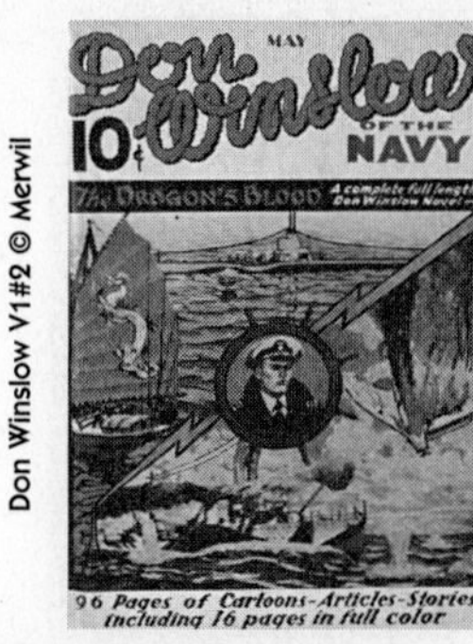

Don Winslow V1#2 © Merwil

	GD 2.0	VG 4.0	FN 6.0	VF 8.0	VF/NM 9.0	NM- 9.2
193-200,202-207,209-211,213-216	2	4	6	9	11	14
201,208,212: 201-Barks-r/Christmas Parade #26, 16pgs. 208-Barks-r/#60 (6 pgs.). 212-Barks-r/WDC&S #130	2	4	6	9	11	14
217-219: 217 has 216 on-c. 219-Barks-r/WDC&S #106,107, 10 pgs. ea.	2	4	6	10	13	16
220,225-228: 228-Barks-r/F.C. #275	2	4	6	12	16	20
221,223,224: Scarce; only sold in pre-packs. 221(8/80), 223(11/80), 224(12/80)	4	8	12	27	36	45
222-(9-10/80)-(Very low distribution)	17	34	51	123	182	240
229-240: 229-Barks-r/F.C. #282. 230-Barks-r/ #52 & WDC&S #194. 236(2/82), 237(2-3/82), 238(3/82), 239(4/82), 240(5/82)	2	4	6	9	11	14
241-245: 241(4/83), 242(5/83), 243(3/84), 244(4/84), 245(7/84)(low print)	2	4	6	14	18	22
246-(1st Gladstone issue)-Barks-r/FC #422	3	6	9	16	20	24
247-249,251: 248,249-Barks-r/DD #54 & 26. 251-Barks-r/1945 Firestone	2	4	6	10	13	16
250-($1.50, 68 pgs.)-Barks-r/4-Color #9	2	4	6	11	14	18
252-277,280: 254-Barks-r/FC #328. 256-Barks-r/FC #147. 257-($1.50, 52 pgs.)-Barks-r/ Vacation Parade #1. 261-Barks-r/FC #300. 275-Kelly-r/FC #92. 280 (#1, 2nd Series)	1	2	3	5	6	8
278,279,286: 278,279 ($1.95, 68 pgs.): 278-Rosa-a; Barks-r/FC #263. 279-Rosa-c; Barks-r/MOC #4. 286-Rosa-a	1	2	3	5	7	9
281,282,284	1	2	3	4	5	7
283-Don Rosa-a, part-c & scripts	1	2	3	5	6	8
285,287-307						5.00
286 ($2.95, 68 pgs.)-Happy Birthday, Donald						6.00
Mini-Comic #1(1976)-(3-1/4x6-1/2"); r/D.D. #150	2	4	6	8	10	12

NOTE: *Carl* ***Barks*** *wrote all issues he illustrated, but #117, 126, 138 contain his script only. Issues 4-Color #189, 199, 203, 223, 238, 256, 263, 275, 282, 308, 348, 356, 367, 394, 408, 422, 26-30, 35, 44, 46, 52, 55, 57, 60, 65, 70-73, 77-80, 83, 101, 103, 105, 106, 111, 126, 246r, 266r, 268r, 271r, 275r, 278r(F.C. 263) all have* ***Barks*** *covers.* ***Barks*** *r-263-267, 269-278-282, 284, 285. #96 titled "Comic Album", #99-"Christmas Album". New art issues (not reprints)-106-46, 148-63, 167, 169, 170, 172, 173, 175, 178, 179, 196, 209, 223, 225, 236.* ***Taliaferro*** *daily newspaper strips #258-260, 264, 284, 285; Sunday strips #247, 280-283.*

DONALD DUCK ADVENTURES (See Walt Disney's Donald Duck Adventures)

DONALD DUCK ALBUM (See Comic Album No. 1,3 & Duck Album)
Dell Publishing Co./Gold Key: 5-7/59 - F.C. No. 1239, 10-12/61; 1962; 8/63 - No. 2, Oct, 1963

	GD	VG	FN	VF	VF/NM	NM-
Four Color 995 (#1)	7	14	21	46	63	80
Four Color 1182, 01204-207 (1962-Dell)	5	10	15	36	48	60
Four Color 1099,1140,1239-Barks-c	7	14	21	51	71	90
1(8/63-Gold Key)-Barks-c	6	12	18	43	59	75
2(10/63)	5	10	15	36	48	60

DONALD DUCK AND THE BOYS (Also see Story Hour Series)
Whitman Publishing Co.: 1948 (5-1/4x5-1/2", 100pgs., hard-c; art & text)

	GD	VG	FN	VF	VF/NM	NM-
845-(49) new illos by Barks based on his Donald Duck 10-pager in WDC&S #74, Expanded text not written by Barks; Cover not by Barks	50	100	150	350	550	750

(Prices vary widely on this book)

DONALD DUCK AND THE CHRISTMAS CAROL
Whitman Publishing Co.: 1960 (A Little Golden Book, 6-3/8"x7-5/8", 28 pgs.)

	GD	VG	FN	VF	VF/NM	NM-
nn-Story book pencilled by Carl Barks with the intended title "Uncle Scrooge's Christmas Carol." Finished art adapted by Norman McGary. (Rare)-Reprinted in Uncle Scrooge in Color.	30	60	90	150	200	250

DONALD DUCK BEACH PARTY (Also see Dell Giants)
Gold Key: Sept, 1965 (12¢)

	GD	VG	FN	VF	VF/NM	NM-
1(#10158-509)-Barks-r/WDC&S #45; painted-c	7	14	21	51	71	90

DONALD DUCK BOOK (See Story Hour Series)

DONALD DUCK COMICS DIGEST
Gladstone Publishing: Nov, 1986 - No. 5, July, 1987 ($1.25/$1.50, 96 pgs.)

	GD	VG	FN	VF	VF/NM	NM-
1,3: 1-Barks-c/a-r	1	2	3	5	7	9
2,4,5: 4,5-$1.50-c						6.00

DONALD DUCK FUN BOOK (See Dell Giants)

DONALD DUCK IN DISNEYLAND (See Dell Giants)

DONALD DUCK MARCH OF COMICS (See March of Comics #4,20,41,56,69,263)

DONALD DUCK MERRY CHRISTMAS (See Dell Giant No. 53)

DONALD DUCK PICNIC PARTY (See Picnic Party listed under Dell Giants)

DONALD DUCK TELLS ABOUT KITES (See Kite Fun Book)

DONALD DUCK, THIS IS YOUR LIFE (Disney, TV)
Dell Publishing Co.: No. 1109, Aug-Oct, 1960

	GD 2.0	VG 4.0	FN 6.0	VF 8.0	VF/NM 9.0	NM- 9.2
Four Color 1109-Gyro flashback to WDC&S #141; origin Donald Duck (1st told)	15	30	45	104	152	200

DONALD DUCK XMAS ALBUM (See regular Donald Duck No. 99)

DONALD IN MATHMAGIC LAND (Disney)
Dell Publishing Co.: No. 1051, Oct-Dec, 1959 - No. 1198, May-July, 1961

	GD	VG	FN	VF	VF/NM	NM-
Four Color 1051 (#1)-Movie	10	20	30	67	96	125
Four Color 1198-Reprint of above	7	14	21	51	71	90

DONATELLO, TEENAGE MUTANT NINJA TURTLE
Mirage Studios: Aug, 1986 ($1.50, B&W, one-shot, 44 pgs.)

	GD	VG	FN	VF	VF/NM	NM-
1	1	2	3	5	6	8

DONDI
Dell Publishing Co.: No. 1176, Mar-May, 1961 - No. 1276, Dec, 1961

	GD	VG	FN	VF	VF/NM	NM-
Four Color 1176 (#1)-Movie; origin, photo-c	5	10	15	36	48	60
Four Color 1276	3	7	10	21	28	35

DON FORTUNE MAGAZINE
Don Fortune Publishing Co.: Aug, 1946 - No. 6, Feb, 1947

	GD	VG	FN	VF	VF/NM	NM-
1-Delecta of the Planets by C. C. Beck in all	25	50	75	147	202	260
2	14	28	42	81	111	140
3-6: 3-Bondage-c	12	24	36	71	96	120

DONKEY KONG (See Blip #1)

DONNA MATRIX
Reactor, Inc.: Aug, 1993 ($2.95, 52 pgs.)

	GD	VG	FN	VF	VF/NM	NM-
1-Computer generated-c/a by Mike Saenz; 3-D effects						3.00

DON NEWCOMBE
Fawcett Publications: 1950 (Baseball)

	GD	VG	FN	VF	VF/NM	NM-
nn-Photo-c	42	84	126	252	359	465

DON ROSA'S COMICS AND STORIES
Fantagraphics Books (CX Comics): 1983 ($2.95)

	GD	VG	FN	VF	VF/NM	NM-
1,2: 1-(68 pgs.) Reprints Rosa's The Pertwillaby Papers episodes #128-133. 2-(60 pgs.) Reprints episodes #134-138	2	4	6	10	13	16

DON SIMPSON'S BIZARRE HEROES (Also see Megaton Man)
Fiasco Comics: May, 1990 - No. 17, Sept, 1996 ($2.50/$2.95, B&W)

	GD	VG	FN	VF	VF/NM	NM-
1-10,0,11-17: 0-Begin $2.95-c; r/Bizarre Heroes #1. 17-(9/96)-Indicia also reads Megaton Man #0; intro Megaton Man and the Fiascoverse to new readers						3.00

DON'T GIVE UP THE SHIP
Dell Publishing Co.: No. 1049, Aug, 1959

	GD	VG	FN	VF	VF/NM	NM-
Four Color 1049-Movie, Jerry Lewis photo-c	9	18	27	65	93	120

DON WINSLOW OF THE NAVY
Merwil Publishing Co.: Apr, 1937 - No. 2, May, 1937 (96 pgs.)(A pulp/comic book cross; stapled spine)

	GD	VG	FN	VF	VF/NM	NM-
V1#1-Has 16 pgs. comics in color. Captain Colorful & Jupiter Jones by Sheldon Mayer; complete Don Winslow novel	629	1258	1887	4500	-	-
2-Sheldon Mayer-a	171	342	513	1225	-	-

DON WINSLOW OF THE NAVY (See Crackajack Funnies, Famous Feature Stories, Popular Comics & Super Book #5,6)
Dell Publishing Co.: No. 2, Nov, 1939 - No. 22, 1941

	GD	VG	FN	VF	VF/NM	NM-
Four Color 2 (#1)-Rare	138	276	414	1035	1518	2000
Four Color 22	32	64	96	240	358	475

DON WINSLOW OF THE NAVY (See TV Teens; Movie, Radio, TV) (Fightin' Navy No. 74 on)
Fawcett Publications/Charlton No. 70 on: 2/43 - #64, 12/48; #65, 1/51 - #69, 9/51; #70, 3/55 - #73, 9/55

	GD	VG	FN	VF	VF/NM	NM-
1-(68 pgs.)-Captain Marvel on cover	112	224	336	700	1050	1400
2	52	104	156	312	469	625
3	41	82	123	246	348	450
4-6: 6-Flag-c	34	68	102	196	278	360
7-10: 8-Last 68 pg. issue?	25	50	75	147	202	260
11-20	20	40	60	112	156	200
21-40	13	26	39	76	103	130
41-43,45-64: 51,60-Singapore Sal (villain) app. 64-(12/48)	11	22	33	63	84	105
44-Classic spider-c	15	30	45	84	115	145
65(1/51)-Flying Saucer attack; photo-c	15	30	45	86	118	150
66 - 69(9/51): All photo-c. 66-sci-fi story	14	28	42	79	107	135
70(3/55)-73: 70-73 r-/#26,58 & 59	10	20	30	56	73	90

DOOM

Doom Patrol #109 © DC

Dorothy Lamour #2 © Fox

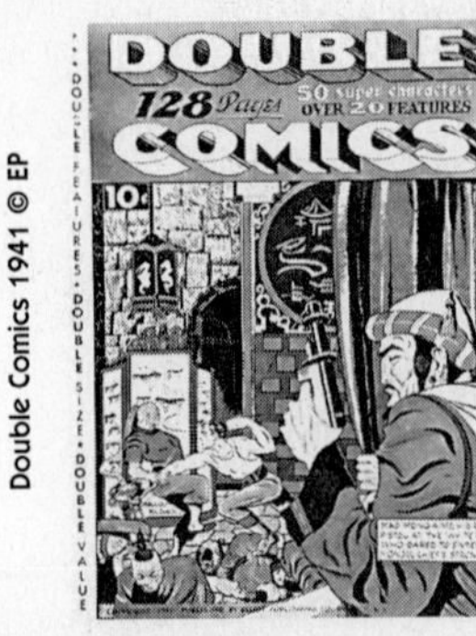

Double Comics 1941 © EP

	GD 2.0	VG 4.0	FN 6.0	VF 8.0	VF/NM 9.0	NM- 9.2

Marvel Comics: Oct, 2000 - No. 3, Dec, 2000 ($2.99, limited series)
1-3-Dr. Doom; Dixon-s/Manco-a 3.00

DOOM FORCE SPECIAL
DC Comics: July, 1992 ($2.95, 68 pgs., one-shot, mature) (X-Force parody)
1-Morrison scripts; Simonson, Steacy, & others-a; Giffen/Mignola-c 3.00

DOOM PATROL, THE (Formerly My Greatest Adventure No. 1-85; see Brave and the Bold, DC Special Blue Ribbon Digest 19, Official... Index & ShowcaseNo. 94-96)
National Periodical Publ.: No. 86, 3/64 - No. 121, 9-10/68; No. 122, 2/73 - No. 124, 6-7/73
86-1 pg. origin (#86-121 are 12¢ issues) 10 20 30 73 107 140
87-98: 88-Origin The Chief. 91-Intro. Mento 8 16 24 53 74 95
99-Intro. Beast Boy (later becomes the Changeling in New Teen Titans
8 16 24 58 82 105
100-Origin Beast Boy; Robot-Maniac series begins (12/65)
8 16 24 58 82 105
101-110: 102-Challengers of the Unknown app. 105-Robot-Maniac series ends. 106-Negative Man begins (origin) 5 10 15 36 48 60
111-120 4 8 12 29 40 50
121-Death of Doom Patrol; Orlando-c. 10 20 30 70 100 130
122-124: All reprints 1 3 4 6 8 10

DOOM PATROL
DC Comics (Vertigo imprint #64 on): Oct, 1987 - No, 87, Feb, 1995 (75¢-$1.95, new format)
1-Wraparound-c; Lightle-a 5.00
2-18: 3-1st app. Lodestone. 4-1st app. Karma. 8,15,16-Art Adams-c(i). 18-Invasion tie-in 3.00
19-(2/89)-Grant Morrison scripts begin, ends #63; 1st app Crazy Jane; $1.50-c & new format begins. 1 2 3 5 6 8
20-30: 29-Superman app. 30-Night Breed fold-out 5.00
31-49,51-56,58-60: 35-1st app. of Flex Mentallo (cameo). 36-1st full app. of Flex Mentallo. 39-World Without End preview.42-Origin of Flex Mentallo 2.50
50,57 ($2.50, 52 pgs.) 2.50
61-87: 61,70-Photo-c. 73-Death cameo (2 panels) 3.00
...And Suicide Squad 1 (3/88, $1.50, 52 pgs.)-Wraparound-c 2.50
Annual 1 (1988, $1.50, 52 pgs.) 2.50
Annual 2 (1994, $3.95, 68 pgs.)-Children's Crusade tie-in. 4.00
NOTE: *Bisley painted c-26-48, 55-58. Bolland c-64, 75. Dringenberg a-42(p). Steacy a-53.*

DOOM PATROL
DC Comics: Dec, 2001 - No. 22, Sept, 2003 ($2.50)
1-Intro. new team with Robotman; Tan Eng Huat-c/a; John Arcudi-s 3.00
2-22: 4,5-Metamorpho & Elongated Man app. 13,14-Fisher-a. 20-Geary-a 2.50

DOOM PATROL (See Tangent Comics/ Doom Patrol)

DOOMSDAY
DC Comics: 1995 ($3.95, one-shot)
1-Year One story by Jurgens, L. Simonson, Ordway, and Gil Kane; Superman app. 4.00

DOOMSDAY + 1 (Also see Charlton Bullseye)
Charlton Comics: July, 1975 - No. 6, June, 1976; No. 7, June, 1978 - No. 12, May, 1979
1: #1-5 are 25¢ issues 2 4 6 14 18 22
2-6: 4-Intro Lor. 5-Ditko-a(1 pg.) 6-Begin 30¢-c 2 4 6 9 11 14
V3#7-12 (reprints #1-6) 6.00
5 (Modern Comics reprint, 1977) 4.00
NOTE: *Byrne c/a-1-12; Painted covers-2-7.*

DOOMSDAY SQUAD, THE
Fantagraphics Books: Aug, 1986 - No. 7, 1987 ($2.00)
1-7: Byrne-a in all. 1-3-New Byrne-c. 3-Usagi Yojimbo app. (1st in color).4-Neal Adams-c. 5-7-Gil Kane-c 3.00

DOOM'S IV
Image Comics (Extreme): July, 1994 - No.4, Oct, 1994 ($2.50, limited series)
1-4-Liefeld story 2.50
1,2-Two alternate Liefeld-c each, 4 covers form 1 picture 5.00

DOOM: THE EMPEROR RETURNS
Marvel Comics: Jan, 2002 - No. 3, Mar, 2002 ($2.50, limited series)
1-3-Dixon-s/Manco-a; Franklin Richards app. 2.50

DOOM 2099 (See Marvel Comics Presents #118 & 2099: World of Tomorrow)
Marvel Comics: Jan, 1993 - No. 44, Aug, 1996 ($1.25/$1.50/$1.95)
1-24,26-44: 1-Metallic foil stamped-c. 4-Ron Lim-c(p). 17-bound-in trading card sheet. 40-Namor & Doctor Strange app. 41-Daredevil app., Namor-c/app. 44-Intro The Emissary; story contin'd in 2099: World of Tomorrow 2.25
1-2nd printing 2.25
18-Variant polybagged with Sega Sub-Terrania poster 4.00
25 ($2.25, 52 pgs.) 2.50
25 ($2.95, 52pgs.) Foil embossed cover 3.00
29 ($3.50)-acetate-c. 3.50

DOORWAY TO NIGHTMARE (See Cancelled Comic Cavalcade)
DC Comics: Jan-Feb, 1978 - No. 5, Sept-Oct, 1978
1-Madame Xanadu in all 2 4 6 9 11 14
2-5: 4-Craig-a 1 2 3 5 7 9
NOTE: *Kaluta covers on all. Merged into The Unexpected with No. 190.*

DOPEY DUCK COMICS (Wacky Duck No. 3) (See Super Funnies)
Timely Comics (NPP): Fall, 1945 - No. 2, Apr, 1946
1,2-Casper Cat, Krazy Krow 22 44 66 124 172 220

DORK
Slave Labor: June, 1993 - Present ($2.50-$2.95, B&W, mature)
1-7,9,10: Evan Dorkin-c/a/scripts in all. 1(8/95),2(1/96)-(2nd printings). 1(3/97) (3rd printing). 1-Milk & Cheese app. 3-Eltingville Club starts. 6-Reprints 1st Eltingville Club app. from Instant Piano #1 3.00
8-($3.50) 3.50
Who's Laughing Now? TPB (2001, $11.95) reprints most of #1-5 12.00
The Collected Dork, Vol. 2: Circling the Drain (6/03, $13.95) r/most of #7-10 & other-s 14.00

DOROTHY LAMOUR (Formerly Jungle Lil)(Stage, screen, radio)
Fox Features Syndicate: No. 2, June, 1950 - No. 3, Aug, 1950
2,3-Wood-a(3) each, photo-c 28 56 84 157 221 285

DOT DOTLAND (Formerly Little Dot Dotland)
Harvey Publications: No. 62, Sept, 1974 - No. 63, Nov, 1974
62,63 2 4 6 9 11 14

DOTTY (...& Her Boy Friends)(Formerly Four Teeners; Glamorous Romances No. 41 on)
Ace Magazines (A. A. Wyn): No. 35, June, 1948 - No. 40, May, 1949
35-Teen-age 8 16 24 40 50 60
36-40: 37-Transvestism story 5 10 15 24 30 35

DOTTY DRIPPLE (Horace & Dotty Dripple No. 25 on)
Magazine Ent.(Life's Romances)/Harvey No. 3 on: 1946 - No. 24, June, 1952 (Also see A-1 No. 1, 3-8, 10)
1 (nd) (10¢) 9 18 27 52 66 80
2 6 12 18 28 34 40
3-10: 3,4-Powell-a 5 10 15 22 26 30
11-24 4 8 11 16 19 22

DOTTY DRIPPLE AND TAFFY
Dell Publishing Co.: No. 646, Sept, 1955 - No. 903, May, 1958
Four Color 646 (#1) 4 8 12 29 40 50
Four Color 691,718,746,801,903 3 7 10 21 28 35

DOUBLE ACTION COMICS
National Periodical Publications: No. 2, Jan, 1940 (68 pgs., B&W)
2-Contains original stories(?); pre-hero DC contents; same cover as Adventure No. 37. (seven known copies, five in high grade) (not an ashcan)
1445 2890 4335 9000 13,000 17,000
NOTE: *The cover to this book was probably reprinted from Adventure #37. #1 exists as an ash can copy with B&W cover; contains a coverless comic on inside with 1st & last page missing. Two copies exist in fair & fine condition proving at least limited newsstand distribution.*

DOUBLE COMICS
Elliot Publications: 1940 - 1944 (132 pgs.)
1940 issues; Masked Marvel-c & The Mad Mong vs. The White Flash covers known
232 464 696 1450 2175 2900
1941 issues; Tornado Tim-c, Nordac-c, & Green Light covers known
157 314 471 981 1471 1960
1942 issues 115 230 345 719 1080 1440
1943,1944 issues 94 188 282 588 882 1175
NOTE: *Double Comics consisted of an almost endless combination of pairs of remaindered, unsold issues of comics representing most publishers and usually mixed publishers in the same book; e.g., a Captain America with a Silver Streak, or a Feature with a Detective, etc., could appear inside the same cover. The actual contents would have to determine its price. Prices listed are for average contents. Any containing rare origin or first issues are worth much more. Covers also vary in same year. Value would be approximately 50 percent of contents.*

DOUBLE-CROSS (See The Crusaders)

DOUBLE-DARE ADVENTURES
Harvey Publications: Dec, 1966 - No. 2, Mar, 1967 (35¢/25¢, 68 pgs.)
1-Origin Bee-Man, Glowing Gladiator, & Magic-Master; Simon/Kirby-a (last S&K art as a team?) 7 14 21 50 68 85
2-Williamson/Crandall-a; r/Alarming Adv. #3('63) 5 10 15 36 48 60
NOTE: *Powell a-1. Simon/Sparling c-1, 2.*

Double Image #3 © IM

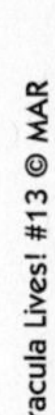
Dracula Lives! #13 © MAR

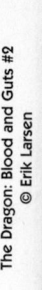

The Dragon: Blood and Guts #2 © Erik Larsen

	GD 2.0	VG 4.0	FN 6.0	VF 8.0	VF/NM 9.0	NM- 9.2

DOUBLE DRAGON
Marvel Comics: July, 1991 - No. 6, Dec, 1991 ($1.00, limited series)
1-6: Based on video game. 2-Art Adams-c 2.50

DOUBLE EDGE
Marvel Comics: Alpha, 1995; Omega, 1995 ($4.95, limited series)
Alpha ($4.95)- Punisher story, Nick Fury app. 5.00
Omega ($4.95)-Punisher, Daredevil, Ghost Rider app. Death of Nick Fury 5.00

DOUBLE IMAGE
Image Comics: Feb, 2001 - No. 5, July, 2001 ($2.95)
1-5: 1-Flip covers of Codeflesh (Casey-s/Adlard-a) and The Bod (Young-s). 2-Two covers. 5-"Trust in Me" begins; Chaudhary-a 3.00

DOUBLE LIFE OF PRIVATE STRONG, THE
Archie Publications/Radio Comics: June, 1959 - No. 2, Aug, 1959
1-Origin & re-intro The Shield; Simon & Kirby-c/a, their re-entry into the super-hero genre; intro./1st app. The Fly; 1st S.A. super-hero for Archie Publ. 52 104 156 416 621 825
2-S&K-c/a; Tuska-a; The Fly app. (2nd or 3rd?) 33 66 99 248 374 500

DOUBLE TROUBLE
St. John Publishing Co.: Nov, 1957 - No. 2, Jan-Feb, 1958
1,2: Tuffy & Snuffy by Frank Johnson; dubbed "World's Funniest Kids" 6 12 18 31 38 45

DOUBLE TROUBLE WITH GOOBER
Dell Publishing Co.: No. 417, Aug, 1952 - No. 556, May, 1954
Four Color 417 4 8 12 27 36 45
Four Color 471,516,556 3 6 9 18 23 28

DOUBLE UP
Elliott Publications: 1941 (Pocket size, 200 pgs.)
1-Contains rebound copies of digest sized issues of Pocket Comics, Speed Comics, & Spitfire Comics 76 152 228 475 713 950

DOVER & CLOVER (See All Funny & More Fun Comics #93)

DOVER BOYS (See Adventures of the...)

DOVER THE BIRD
Famous Funnies Publishing Co.: Spring, 1955
1-Funny animal; code approved 7 14 21 35 43 50

DOWN WITH CRIME
Fawcett Publications: Nov, 1952 - No. 7, Nov, 1953
1 33 66 99 190 270 350
2,4,5: 2,4-Powell-a in each. 5-Bondage-c 17 34 51 98 134 170
3-Used in **POP**, pg. 106; "H is for Heroin" drug story 19 38 57 107 149 190
6,7: 6-Used in **POP**, pg. 80 14 28 42 79 107 135

DO YOU BELIEVE IN NIGHTMARES?
St. John Publishing Co.: Nov, 1957 - No. 2, Jan, 1958
1-Mostly Ditko-c/a 50 100 150 300 450 600
2-Ayers-a 30 60 90 170 240 310

D.P. 7
Marvel Comics Group (New Universe): Nov, 1986 - No. 32, June, 1989
1-20, Annual #1 (11/87)-Intro. The Witness 2.25
21-32-Low print 3.00
NOTE: *Williamson a-9i, 11i; c-9i.*

DRACULA (See Bram Stoker's Dracula, Giant-Size..., Little Dracula, Marvel Graphic Novel, Requiem for Dracula, Spider-Man Vs...., Tomb of... & Wedding of...; also see Movie Classics under Universal Presents as well as Dracula)

DRACULA (See Movie Classics for #1)(Also see Frankenstein & Werewolf)
Dell Publ. Co.: No. 2, 11/66 - No. 4, 3/67; No. 6, 7/72 - No. 8, 7/73 (No #5)
2-Origin & 1st app. Dracula (11/66) (super hero) 4 8 12 28 38 48
3,4: 4-Intro. Fleeta ('67) 3 6 9 18 24 30
6-('72)-r/#2 w/origin 3 6 9 16 20 24
7,8-r/#3, #4 2 4 6 11 14 18

DRACULA (Magazine)
Warren Publishing Co.: 1979 (120 pgs., full color)
Book 1-Maroto art; Spanish material translated into English (mail order only) 6 12 18 38 52 65

DRACULA CHRONICLES
Topps Comics: Apr, 1995 - No. 3, June, 1995 ($2.50, limited series)
1-3-Linsner-c 3.00

DRACULA LIVES! (Magazine)(Also see Tomb of Dracula)
Marvel Comics Group: 1973(no month) - No. 13, July, 1975 (75¢, B&W) (76 pgs.)
1-Boris painted-c 5 10 15 36 48 60
2 (7/73)-1st time origin Dracula; Adams, Starlin-a 4 8 12 24 32 40
3-1st app. Robert E. Howard's Soloman Kane; Adams-c/a 4 8 12 24 32 40
4,5: 4-Ploog-a. 5(V2#1)-Bram Stoker's Classic Dracula adapt. begins 3 6 9 18 23 28
6-9: 6-8-Bram Stoker adapt. 9-Bondage-c 3 6 9 18 23 28
10 (1/75)-16 pg. Lilith solo (1st?) 4 8 12 22 30 38
11-13: 11-21 pg. Lilith solo sty. 12-31 pg. Dracula sty 3 6 9 18 24 30
Annual 1(Summer, 1975, $1.25, 92 pgs.)-Morrow painted-c; 6 Dracula stys. 25 pgs. Adams-a(r) 3 6 9 19 25 32
NOTE: ***N. Adams** a-2, 3i, 10i, Annual 1r(2, 3i). **Alcala** a-9. **Buscema** a-3p, 6p, Annual 1p. **Colan** a(p)-1, 2, 5, 6, 8. **Evans** a-7. **Gulacy** a-9. **Heath** a-1r, 13. **Pakula** a-6r. Sutton a-13.**Weiss** r-Annual 1p. 4 **Dracula** stories each in 1, 609; 3 **Dracula** stories each in 2, 4, 5,, 13.*

DRACULA: LORD OF THE UNDEAD
Marvel Comics: Dec, 1998 - No. 3, Dec, 1998 ($2.99, limited series)
1-3-Olliffe & Palmer-a 3.00

DRACULA: RETURN OF THE IMPALER
Slave Labor Graphics: July, 1993 - No. 4, Oct, 1994 ($2.95, limited series)
1-4 3.00

DRACULA VERSUS ZORRO
Topps Comics: Oct, 1993 - No. 2, Nov, 1993 ($2.95, limited series)
1,2: 1-Spot varnish & red foil-c. 2-Polybagged w/16 pg. Zorro #0 3.00

DRACULA VERSUS ZORRO
Dark Horse Comics: Sept, 1998 - No. 2, Oct, 1998 ($2.95, limited series)
1,2 3.00

DRACULA: VLAD THE IMPALER (Also see Bram Stoker's Dracula)
Topps Comics: Feb, 1993 - No. 3, Apr, 1993 ($2.95, limited series)
1-3-Polybagged with 3 trading cards each; Maroto-c/a 3.00

DRAFT, THE
Marvel Comics: 1988 ($3.50, one-shot, squarebound)
1-Sequel to "The Pitt" 3.50

DRAG 'N' WHEELS (Formerly Top Eliminator)
Charlton Comics: No. 30, Sept, 1968 - No. 59, May, 1973
30 5 10 15 33 44 55
31-40-Scot Jackson begins 3 7 10 21 28 35
41-50 3 6 9 18 24 30
51-59: Scot Jackson 2 4 6 12 16 20
Modern Comics Reprint 58('78) 5.00

DRAGON, THE (Also see The Savage Dragon)
Image Comics (Highbrow Ent.): Mar, 1996 - No. 5, July, 1996 (99¢, lim. series)
1-5: Reprints Savage Dragon limited series w/new story & art. 5-Youngblood app; includes 5 pg. Savage Dragon story from 1984 2.25

DRAGON ARCHIVES, THE (Also see The Savage Dragon)
Image Comics: Jun, 1998 - No. 4, Jan, 1999 ($2.95, B&W)
1-4: Reprints early Savage Dragon app. 3.00

DRAGON, THE: BLOOD & GUTS (Also see The Savage Dragon)
Image Comics (Highbrow Entertainment): Mar, 1995 - No. 3, May, 1995 ($2.50, lim. series)
1-3: Jason Pearson-c/a/scripts 2.50

DRAGON BALL
Viz Comics: 1998 - Present ($2.95, B&W, Manga reprints read right to left)
Part 1: 1-Akira Toriyama-s/a 1 2 3 5 6 8
2-12 5.00
1-12 (2nd & 3rd printings) 3.00
Part 2: 1-15: 15-($3.50-c) 4.00
Part 3: 1-14 3.00
Part 4: 1-10 3.00
Part 5: 1-7 3.00

DRAGON BALL Z
Viz Comics: 1998 - Present ($2.95, B&W, Manga reprints read right to left)
Part 1: 1-Akira Toriyama-s/a 2 4 6 8 10 12
2-9 5.00

Dragonflight © ECL

Drakuun #4 © Johji Manabe

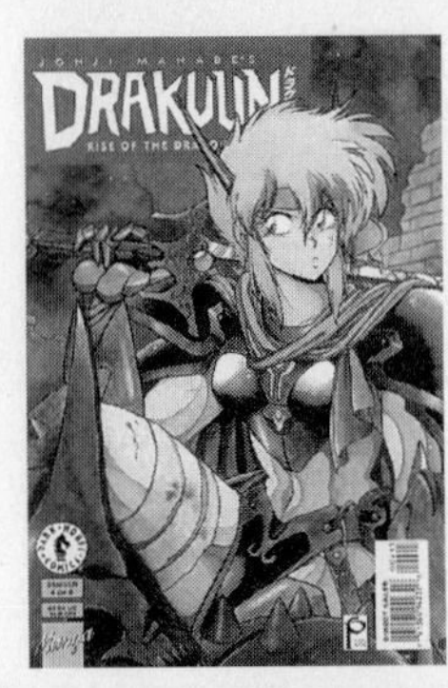

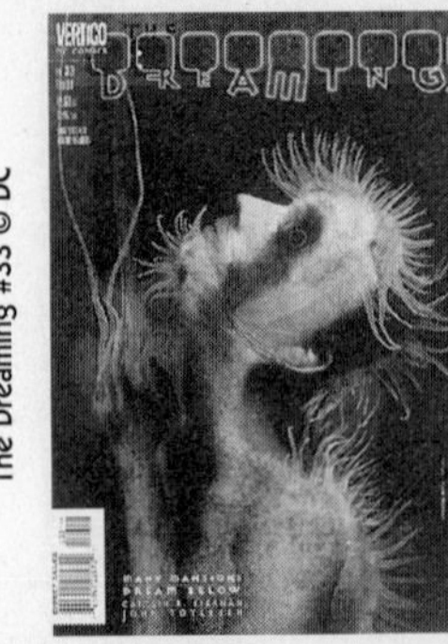

The Dreaming #33 © DC

GD 2.0 | VG 4.0 | FN 6.0 | VF 8.0 | VF/NM 9.0 | NM- 9.2

1-9 (2nd & 3rd printings) 3.00
Part 2: 1-14 4.00
Part 3: 1-10 3.00
Part 4: 1-15 3.00
Part 5: 1-12 3.00

DRAGON CHIANG
Eclipse Books: 1991 ($3.95, B&W, squarebound, 52 pgs.)
nn-Timothy Truman-c/a(p) 4.00

DRAGONFLIGHT
Eclipse Books: Feb, 1991 - No. 3, 1991 ($4.95, 52 pgs.)
Book One - Three: Adapts 1968 novel 5.00

DRAGONFLY (See Americomics #4)
Americomics: Sum, 1985 - No. 8, 1986 ($1.75/$1.95)
1 3.50
2-8 2.50

DRAGONFORCE
Aircel Publishing: 1988 - No. 13, 1989 ($2.00)
1-Dale Keown-c/a/scripts in #1-12 3.00
2-13: 13-No Keown-a 2.25
...Chronicles Book 1-5 ($2.95, B&W, 60 pgs.): Dale Keown-r/Dragonring & Dragonforce 3.00

DRAGONHEART (Movie)
Topps Comics: May, 1996 - No. 2, June, 1996 ($2.95/$4.95, limited series)
1-($2.95, 24 pgs.)-Adaptation of the film; Hildebrandt Bros-c; Lim-a. 3.00
2-($4.95, 64 pgs.) 5.00

DRAGONLANCE (Also see TSR Worlds)
DC Comics: Dec, 1988 - No. 34, Sept, 1991 ($1.25/$1.50, Mando paper)
1-Based on TSR game 4.00
2-34: Based on TSR game. 30-32-Kaluta-c 3.00

DRAGON LINES
Marvel Comics (Epic Comics/Heavy Hitters): May, 1993 - No. 4, Aug, 1993 ($1.95, limited series)
1-($2.50)-Embossed-c; Ron Lim-c/a in all 3.00
2-4 2.25

DRAGON LINES: WAY OF THE WARRIOR
Marvel Comics (Epic Comics/ Heavy Hitters): Nov, 1993 - No. 2, Jan, 1994 ($2.25, limited series)
1,2-Ron Lim-c/a(p) 2.25

DRAGONQUEST
Silverwolf Comics: Dec, 1986 - No. 2, 1987 ($1.50, B&W, 28 pgs.)
1,2-Tim Vigil-c/a in all 5.00

DRAGONRING
Aircel Publishing: 1986 - V2#15, 1988 ($1.70/$2.00, B&W/color)
1-6: 6-Last B&W issue, V2#1-15($2.00, color) 2.25

DRAGON'S CLAWS
Marvel UK, Ltd.: July, 1988 - No. 10, Apr, 1989 ($1.25/$1.50/$1.75, British)
1-10: 3-Death's Head 1 pg. strip on back-c (1st app.). 4-Silhouette of Death's Head on last pg. 5-1st full app. new Death's Head 2.25

DRAGON'S LAIR: SINGE'S REVENGE (Based on the Don Bluth video game)
CrossGen Comics: Sept, 2003 - No. 6 ($2.95, limited series)
1-3-Mangels-s/Laguna-a 3.00

DRAGONSLAYER (Movie)
Marvel Comics Group: October, 1981 - No. 2, Nov, 1981
1,2-Paramount Disney movie adaptation 3.00

DRAGON'S STAR 2
Caliber Press: 1994 ($2.95, B&W)
1 3.00

DRAGON STRIKE
Marvel Comics: Feb, 1994 ($1.25)
1-Based on TSR role playing game 2.25

DRAGOON WELLS MASSACRE
Dell Publishing Co.: No. 815, June, 1957
Four Color 815-Movie, photo-c 9 18 27 60 85 110

DRAGSTRIP HOTRODDERS (World of Wheels No. 17 on)
Charlton Comics: Sum, 1963; No. 2, Jan, 1965 - No. 16, Aug, 1967
1 7 14 21 51 71 90
2-5 4 8 12 29 40 50
6-16 4 8 12 24 32 40

DRAKUUN
Dark Horse Comics: Feb, 1997 - No. 25, Mar, 1999 ($2.95, B&W, manga)
1-25; 1-6- Johji Manabe-s/a in all. Rise of the Dragon Princess series. 7-12-Revenge of Gustav. 13-18-Shadow of the Warlock. 19-25-The Hidden War 3.00

DRAMA
Sirius: June, 1994 ($2.95, mature)
1-1st full color Dawn app. in comics 2 4 6 12 16 20
1-Limited edition (1400 copies); signed & numbered; fingerprint authenticity 4 8 12 29 40 50
NOTE: *Dawn's 1st full color app. was a pin-up in Amazing Heroes' Swimsuit Special #5.*

DRAMA OF AMERICA, THE
Action Text: 1973 ($1.95, 224 pgs.)
1- "Students' Supplement to History" 5.00

DRAWING ON YOUR NIGHTMARES
Dark Horse Comics: Oct, 2003 ($2.99, one-shot)
1-Short stories; The Goon, Criminal Macabre, Tales of the Vampires; Templesmith-c 3.00

DREADLANDS (Also see Epic)
Marvel Comics (Epic Comics): 1992 - No. 4, 1992 ($3.95, lim. series, 52 pgs.)
1-4: Stiff-c 4.00

DREADSTAR
Marvel Comics (Epic Comics)/First Comics No. 27 on: Nov, 1982 - No. 64, Mar, 1991
1 4.00
2-5,8-49 3.00
6,7,51-64: 6,7-1st app. Interstellar Toybox; 8pgs. ea.; Wrightson-a 4.00
50 5.00
Annual 1 (12/83)-r/The Price 4.00

DREADSTAR
Malibu Comics (Bravura): Apr, 1994 - No.6, Jan, 1995 ($2.50, limited series)
1-6-Peter David scripts: 1,2-Starlin-c 2.50
NOTE: *Issues 1-6 contain Bravura stamps.*

DREADSTAR AND COMPANY
Marvel Comics (Epic Comics): July, 1985 - No. 6, Dec, 1985
1-6: 1,3,6-New Starlin-a: 2-New Wrightson-c; reprints of Dreadstar series 2.25

DREAM BOOK OF LOVE (Also see A-1 Comics)
Magazine Enterprises: No. 106, June-July, 1954 - No. 123, Oct-Nov, 1954
A-1 106 (#1)-Powell, Bolle-a; Montgomery Clift, Donna Reed photo-c 12 24 36 71 96 120
A-1-114 (#2)-Guardineer, Bolle-a; Piper Laurie, Victor Mature photo-c 10 20 30 56 73 90
A-1 123 (#3)-Movie photo-c 9 18 27 52 66 80

DREAM BOOK OF ROMANCE (Also see A-1 Comics)
Magazine Enterprises: No. 92, 1954 - No. 124, Oct-Nov, 1954
A-1 92 (#5)-Guardineer-a; photo-c 11 22 33 66 88 110
A-1 101 (#6)(4-6/54)-Marlon Brando photo-c; Powell, Bolle, Guardineer-a 19 38 57 107 149 190
A-1 109,110,124: 109 (#7)(7-8/54)-Powell-a; movie photo-c. 110 (#8)(1/54)-Movie photo-c. 124 (#8)(10-11/54) 9 18 27 52 66 80

DREAMER, THE
Kitchen Sink Press: 1986 ($6.95, B&W, graphic novel)
nn-Will Eisner-s/a 12.00
DC Comics Reprint ($7.95, 6/00) 8.00

DREAMERY, THE
Eclipse Comics: Dec, 1986 - No. 14, Feb, 1989 ($2.00, B&W, Baxter paper)
1-14: 2-7-Alice In Wonderland adapt. 2.25

DREAMING, THE (See Sandman, 2nd Series)
DC Comics (Vertigo): June, 1996 - No. 60, May, 2001 ($2.50)
1-McKean-c on all.; LaBan scripts & Snejbjerg-a 4.00
2-30,32-60: 2,3-LaBan scripts & Snejbjerg-a. 4-7-Hogan scripts; Parkhouse-a. 8-Zulli-a. 9-11-Talbot-s/Taylor-a(p). 41-Previews Sandman: The Dream Hunters. 50-Hempel, Fegredo, McManus, Totleben-a 2.50
31-($3.95) Art by various 4.00

Dreamwalker #5 © Jenni Gregory

Droopy #1 © Turner Entertainment

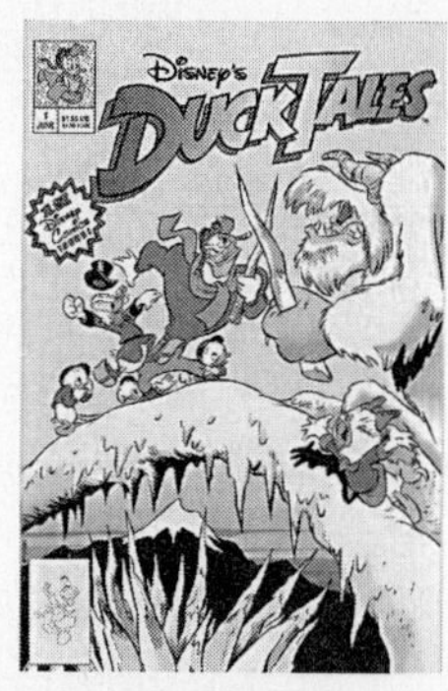

Ducktales #1 © WDC

	GD	VG	FN	VF	VF/NM	NM-
	2.0	4.0	6.0	8.0	9.0	9.2

...Beyond The Shores of Night TPB ('97, $19.95) r/#1-8 20.00
...Special (7/98, $5.95, one-shot) Trial of Cain 6.00
...Through The Gates of Horn and Ivory TPB ('99, $19.95) r/#15-19,22-25 20.00

DREAM OF LOVE
I. W. Enterprises: 1958 (Reprints)

1,2,8: 1-r/Dream Book of Love #1; Bob Powell-a. 2-r/Great Lover's Romances #10. 8-Great Lover's Romances #1; also contains 2 Jon Juan stories by Siegel & Schomburg; Kinstler-c. 2 4 6 11 14 18
9-Kinstler-c; 1pg. John Wayne interview & Frazetta illo from John Wayne Adv. Comics #2 2 4 6 11 14 18

DREAMS OF THE DARKCHYLDE
Darkchylde Entertainment: Oct, 2000 - No. 6, Sept, 2001 ($2.95)

1-6-Randy Queen-s in all. 1-Brandon Peterson-c/a 3.00

DREAM TEAM (See Battlezones: Dream Team 2)
Malibu Comics (Ultraverse): July, 1995 ($4.95, one-shot)

1-Pin-ups teaming up Marvel & Ultraverse characters by various artists including Allred, Romita, Darrow, Balent, Quesada & Palmiotti 5.00

DREAMWALKER
Dreamwalker Press: 1996 - No. 5, 1996 ($2.95, B&W)

1-5-Jenni Gregory-c/s/a 3.00

DREAMWALKER (Volume 2)
Caliber Comics (Tapestry): Dec, 1996 - No. 6, Jul, 1998 ($2.95, B&W)

1-6-Jenni Gregory-c/s/a 3.00

DREAMWALKER
Avatar Press: Jenni Gregory-c/s/a in all

#0 (11/98, $3.00) 3.00
--AUTUMN LEAVES, 9/99 - No. 2, 10/99 ($3.00) 1,2-wraparound-c 3.00
--CAROUSEL, 3/99 - No. 2, 4/99 ($3.00) 1,2 3.00
--SUMMER RAIN, 7/99 ($3.00, one-shot) 1 3.00

DREAMWAVE PRODUCTIONS PREVIEW
Dreamwave Productions: May, 2002 ($1.00, one-shot)

nn-Previews Arkanium, Transformers: The War Within and other series 2.25

DRIFT FENCE (See Zane Grey 4-Color 270)

DRIFT MARLO
Dell Publishing Co.: May-July, 1962 - No. 2, Oct-Dec, 1962

01-232-207 (#1) 5 10 15 36 48 60
2 (12-232-212) 5 10 15 33 44 55

DRISCOLL'S BOOK OF PIRATES
David McKay Publ. (Not reprints): 1934 (B&W, hardcover; 124 pgs, 7x9")

nn-By Montford Amory 25 50 75 150 200 250

DROIDS (Based on Saturday morning cartoon) (Also see Dark Horse Comics)
Marvel Comics (Star Comics): April, 1986 - No. 8, June, 1987

1-R2D2 & C-3PO from Star Wars app. in all 2 4 6 12 16 20
2-8: 2,5,7,8-Williamson-a(i) 2 4 6 8 10 12
NOTE: ***Romita** a-3p. **Sinnott** a-3i.*

DROOPY (see Tom & Jerry #60)

DROOPY (Tex Avery's...)
Dark Horse Comics: Oct, 1995 - No. 3, Dec, 1995 ($2.50, limited series)

1-3: Characters created by Tex Avery; painted-c 2.50

DROPSIE AVENUE: THE NEIGHBORHOOD
Kitchen Sink Press: June, 1995 ($15.95/$24.95, B&W)

nn-Will Eisner (softcover) 16.00
nn-Will Eisner (hardcover) 25.00

DROWNED GIRL, THE
DC Comics (Piranha Press): 1990 ($5.95, 52 pgs, mature)

nn 6.00

DRUG WARS
Pioneer Comics: 1989 ($1.95)

1-Grell-c 2.25

DRUID
Marvel Comics: May, 1995 - No. 4, Aug, 1995 ($2.50, limited series)

1-4: Warren Ellis scripts. 3.00

DRUM BEAT
Dell Publishing Co.: No. 610, Jan, 1955

Four Color 610-Movie, Alan Ladd photo-c 10 20 30 67 96 125

DRUMS OF DOOM
United Features Syndicate: 1937 (25¢)(Indian)(Text w/color illos.)

nn-By Lt. F.A. Methot; Golden Thunder app.; Tip Top Comics ad in comic; nice-c 35 70 105 210 280 350

DRUNKEN FIST
Jademan Comics: Aug, 1988 - No. 54, Jan, 1993 ($1.50/$1.95, 68 pgs.)

1 4.00
2-50 3.00
51-54 2.50

DUCK ALBUM (See Donald Duck Album)
Dell Publishing Co.: No. 353, Oct, 1951 - No. 840, Sept, 1957

Four Color 353 (#1)-Barks-c; 1st Uncle Scrooge-c (also appears on back-c). 10 20 30 67 96 125
Four Color 450-Barks-c 8 16 24 53 74 95
Four Color 492,531,560,586,611,649,686, 6 12 18 40 55 70
Four Color 726,782,840 6 12 18 40 55 70

DUCKMAN
Dark Horse Comics: Sept, 1990 ($1.95, B&W, one-shot)

1-Story & art by Everett Peck 4.00

DUCKMAN
Topps Comics: Nov, 1994 - No. 5, May, 1995; No. 0, Feb, 1996 ($2.50)

0 (2/96, $2.95, B&W)-r/Duckman #1 from Dark Horse Comics 4.00
1-5: 1-w/ coupon #A for Duckman trading card. 2-w/Duckman 1st season episode guide 3.00

DUCKMAN: THE MOB FROG SAGA
Topps Comics: Nov, 1994 - No. 3, Feb, 1995 ($2.50, limited series)

1-3: 1-w/coupon #B for Duckman tradiing card, S. Shaw!-c 2.50

DUCKTALES
Gladstone Publ.: Oct, 1988 - No. 13, May, 1990 (1,2,9-11: $1.50; 3-8: 95¢)

1-Barks-r 6.00
2-11: 2-7,9-11-Barks-r 4.00
12,13 ($1.95, 68 pgs.)-Barks-r; 12-r/F.C. #495 5.00

DUCKTALES (TV)
Disney Comics: June, 1990 - No. 18, Nov, 1991 ($1.50)

1-All new stories 3.00
2-18 2.50
The Movie nn (1990, $7.95, 68 pgs.)-Graphic novel adapting animated movie 9.00

DUDLEY (Teen-age)
Feature/Prize Publications: Nov-Dec, 1949 - No. 3, Mar-Apr, 1950

1-By Boody Rogers 15 30 45 86 118 150
2,3 10 20 30 56 73 90

DUDLEY DO-RIGHT (TV)
Charlton Comics: Aug, 1970 - No. 7, Aug, 1971 (Jay Ward)

1 10 20 30 67 96 125
2-7 7 14 21 50 68 85

DUEL MASTERS (Based on a trading card game)
Dreamwave Productions: Nov, 2003 - Present ($2.95)

1,2: 1-Bagged with card; Augustyn-s 3.00

DUKE OF THE K-9 PATROL
Gold Key: Apr, 1963

1 (10052-304) 4 8 12 28 38 48

DUMBO (Disney; see Movie Comics, & Walt Disney Showcase #12)
Dell Publishing Co.: No. 17, 1941 - No. 668, Jan, 1958

Four Color 17 (#1)-Mickey Mouse, Donald Duck, Pluto app. 185 370 555 1388 2094 2800
Large Feature Comic 19 ('41)-Part-r 4-Color 17 254 508 762 1905 2703 3500
Four Color 234 ('49) 13 26 39 90 133 175
Four Color 668 (12/55)-1st of two printings. Dumbo on-c with starry sky. Same-c as #234 10 20 30 73 107 140
Four Color 668 (1/58)-2nd printing. Same cover altered with Timothy Mouse added. Same contents 8 16 24 53 74 95

DUMBO COMIC PAINT BOOK (See Dumbo, Large Feature Comic No. 19)

DUMPED
Oni Press: 2002 ($5.95, B&W, 9"x 6", one-shot)

Durango Kid #28 © ME

DV8 #24 © WSP

Dynamo #2 © TC

GD VG FN VF VF/NM NM-
2.0 4.0 6.0 8.0 9.0 9.2

nn-Andi Watson-s/a 6.00

DUNC AND LOO (#1-3 titled "Around the Block with Dunc and Loo")
Dell Publishing Co.: Oct-Dec, 1961 - No. 8, Oct-Dec, 1963

1 10 20 30 70 100 130
2 7 14 21 51 71 90
3-8 6 12 18 40 55 70

NOTE: *Written by* ***John Stanley; Bill Williams*** *art.*

DUNCAN'S KINGDOM
Image Comics: 1999 - No. 2, 1999 ($2.95, B&W, limited series)

1,2-Gene Yang-s/Derek Kirk-a 3.00

DUNE (Movie)
Marvel Comics: Apr, 1985 - No. 3, June, 1985

1-3-r/Marvel Super Special; movie adaptation 3.00

DUNG BOYS, THE
Kitchen Sink Press: 1996 - No. 3, 1996 ($2.95, B&W, limited series)

1-3 3.00

DURANGO KID, THE (Also see Best of the West, Great Western & White Indian)
(Charles Starrett starred in Columbia's Durango Kid movies)
Magazine Enterprises: Oct-Nov, 1949 - No. 41, Oct-Nov, 1955 (All 36 pgs.)

1-Charles Starrett photo-c; Durango Kid & his horse Raider begin; Dan Brand & Tipi (origin) begin by Frazetta & continue through #16 72 144 216 450 675 900
2-Starrett photo-c. 38 76 114 219 310 400
3-5-All have Starrett photo-c. 35 70 105 201 288 370
6-10: 7-Atomic weapon-c/story 20 40 60 112 156 200
11-16-Last Frazetta issue 14 28 42 81 111 140
17-Origin Durango Kid 19 38 57 109 152 195
18-30: 18-Fred Meagher-a on Dan Brand begins.19-Guardineer-c/a(3) begins, end #41. 23-Intro. The Red Scorpion 10 20 30 60 80 100
31-Red Scorpion returns 10 20 30 58 77 95
32-41-Bolle/Frazetta*ish*-a (Dan Brand; true in later issues?) 10 20 30 58 77 95

NOTE: *#6, 8, 14, 15 contain* ***Frazetta*** *art not reprinted in White Indian.* ***Ayers*** *c-18.* ***Guardineer*** *a(3)-19-41; c-19-41.* ***Fred Meagher*** *a-18-29 at least.*

DURANGO KID, THE
AC Comics: 1990 - #2, 1990 ($2.50,$2.75, half-color)

1,2: 1-Starrett photo front/back-c; Guardineer-r. 2-B&W)-Starrett photo-c; White Indian-r by Frazetta; Guardineer-r (50th anniversary of films) 3.00

DUSTCOVERS: THE COLLECTED SANDMAN COVERS 1989-1997
DC Comics (Vertigo): 1997 ($39.95, Hardcover)

Reprints Dave McKean's Sandman covers with Gaiman text 40.00
Softcover (1998, $24.95) 25.00

DUSTY STAR
Image Comics (Desperado Studios): Apr, 1997 - No. 1 ($2.95, B&W)

0,1-Pruett-s/Robinson-a 3.00

DV8 (See Gen 13)
Image Comics (WildStorm Productions): Aug, 1996 - No. 25, Dec, 1998;
DC Comics (WildStorm Prod.): No. 0, Apr, 1999 - No. 32, Nov, 1999 ($2.50)

1/2 6.00
1-Warren Ellis scripts & Humberto Ramos-c/a(p) 4.00
1-(7-variant covers, w/1 by Jim Lee) ...each 4.00
2-4: 3-No Ramos-a 3.00
5-32: 14-Regular-c, 14-Variant-c by Charest. 26-(5/99)-McGuinness-c 2.50
14-($3.50) Voyager Pack w/Danger Girl preview 5.00
0-(4/99, $2.95) Two covers (Rio and McGuinness) 3.00
Annual 1 (1/98, $2.95) 3.00
Annual 1999 ($3.50) Slipstream x-over with Gen13 3.50
Rave-(7/96, $1.75)-Ramos-c; pinups & interviews 3.00
...: Neighborhood Threat TPB (2002, $14.95) r/#1-6 & #1/2; Ellis intro.; Ramos-c 15.00

DV8 VS. BLACK OPS
Image Comics (WildStorm): Oct, 1997 - No. 3, Dec, 1997 ($2.50, lim. series)

1-3-Bury-s/Norton-a 3.00

DWIGHT D. EISENHOWER
Dell Publishing Co.: December, 1969

01-237-912 - Life story 5 10 15 36 48 60

DYLAN DOG
Dark Horse (Bonelli Comics): Mar, 1999 - No. 6, Aug, 1999 ($4.95, B&W, digest size)

1-6-Reprints Italian series in English; Mignola-c 5.00

GD VG FN VF VF/NM NM-
2.0 4.0 6.0 8.0 9.0 9.2

DYNABRITE COMICS
Whitman Publishing Co.: 1978 - 1979 (69¢, 10x7-1/8", 48 pgs., cardboard-c)
(Blank inside covers)
11350 - Walt Disney's Mickey Mouse & the Beanstalk (4-C 157). 11350-1 - Mickey Mouse Album (4-C 1057, 1151,1246). 11351 - Mickey Mouse & His Sky Adventure (4-C 214, 343). 11354 - Goofy: A Gaggle of Giggles. 11354-1 - Super Goof Meets Super Thief. 11356 - (?). 11359 - Bugs Bunny-r. 11360 - Winnie the Pooh Fun and Fantasy (Disney-r).

each.... 1 3 4 6 8 10

11352 - Donald Duck (4-C 408, Donald Duck 45,52)-Barks-a. 11352-1 - Donald Duck (4-C 318, 10 pg. Barks/WDC&S 125,128)-Barks-c(r). 11353 - Daisy Duck's Diary (4-C 1055,1150) Barks-a. 11355 - Uncle Scrooge (Barks-a/U.S. 12,33). 11355-1 - Uncle Scrooge (Barks-a/U.S. 13,16) - Barks-c(r). 11357 - Star Trek (r/-Star Trek 33,41). 11358 - Star Trek (r/-Star Trek 34,36). 11361 - Gyro Gearloose & the Disney Ducks (r/4-C 1047,1184)-Barks-c(r)

each.... 2 4 6 8 10 12

DYNAMIC ADVENTURES
I. W. Enterprises: No. 8, 1964 - No. 9, 1964

8-Kayo Kirby-r by Baker?/Fight Comics 53. 3 6 9 16 20 25
9-Reprints Avon's "Escape From Devil's Island"; Kinstler-c 3 6 9 18 23 28
nn (no date)-Reprints Risks Unlimited with Rip Carson, Senorita Rio; r/Fight #53 3 6 9 18 23 28

DYNAMIC CLASSICS (See Cancelled Comic Cavalcade)
DC Comics: Sept-Oct, 1978 (44 pgs.)

1-Neal Adams Batman, Simonson Manhunter-r 1 3 4 6 8 10

DYNAMIC COMICS (No #4-7)
Harry 'A' Chesler: Oct, 1941 - No. 3, Feb, 1942; No. 8, Mar, 1944 - No. 25, May, 1948

1-Origin Major Victory by Charles Sultan (reprinted in Major Victory #1), Dynamic Man & Hale the Magician; The Black Cobra only app.; Major Victory & Dynamic Man begin 176 352 528 1100 1650 2200
2-Origin Dynamic Boy & Lady Satan; intro. The Green Knight & sidekick Lance Cooper 80 160 240 500 750 1000
3-1st small logo, resumes with #10 70 140 210 438 657 875
8-Classic-c; Dan Hastings, The Echo, The Master Key, Yankee Boy begin; Yankee Doodle Jones app.; hypo story 78 156 234 488 732 975
9-Mr. E begins; Mac Raboy-c 70 140 210 438 657 875
10-Small logo begins 55 110 165 330 495 660
11-16: 15-The Sky Chief app. 16-Marijuana story 46 92 138 276 413 550
17(1/46)-Illustrated in **SOTI**, "The children told me what the man was going to do with the hot poker," but Wertham saw this in Crime Reporter #2 64 128 192 400 600 800
18,19,21,22,25: 21-Dinosaur-c; new logo 40 80 120 240 340 440
20-Bare-breasted woman-c 68 136 204 425 638 850
23,24-(68 pgs.): 23-Yankee Girl app. 42 84 126 252 359 465
I.W. Reprint #1,8('64): 1-r/#23. 8-Exist? 3 7 10 21 28 35

NOTE: ***Kinstler*** *c-IW #1.* ***Tuska*** *art in many issues, #3, 9, 11, 12, 16, 19. Bondage c-16.*

DYNAMITE (Becomes Johnny Dynamite No. 10 on)
Comic Media/Allen Hardy Publ.: May, 1953 - No. 9, Sept, 1954

1-Pete Morisi-a; Don Heck-c; r-as Danger #6 27 54 81 155 218 280
2 14 28 42 81 111 140
3-Marijuana story; Johnny Dynamite (1st app.) begins by Pete Morisi(c/a); Heck text-a; man shot in face at close range 19 38 57 106 146 185
4-Injury-to-eye, prostitution; Morisi-c/a 18 36 54 104 142 180
5-9-Morisi-c/a in all. 7-Prostitute story & reprints 13 26 39 74 100 125

DYNAMO (Also see Tales of Thunder & T.H.U.N.D.E.R. Agents)
Tower Comics: Aug, 1966 - No. 4, June, 1967 (25¢)

1-Crandall/Wood, Ditko/Wood-a; Weed series begins; NoMan & Lightning cameos; Wood-c/a 9 18 27 65 93 120
2-4: Wood-c/a in all 6 12 18 40 55 70

NOTE: ***Adkins/Wood*** *a-2.* ***Ditko*** *a-4?.* ***Tuska*** *a-2, 3.*

DYNAMO JOE (Also see First Adventures & Mars)
First Comics: May, 1986 - No. 15, Jan, 1988 (#12-15: $1.75)

1-15: 4-Cargonauts begin, Special 1(1/87)-Mostly-r/Mars 2.25

DYNOMUTT (TV)(See Scooby-Doo (3rd series))
Marvel Comics Group: Nov, 1977 - No. 6, Sept, 1978 (Hanna-Barbera)

1-The Blue Falcon, Scooby Doo in all 4 8 12 24 32 40
2-6-All newsstand only 3 6 9 16 20 25

EAGLE, THE (1st Series) (See Science Comics & Weird Comics #8)
Fox Features Syndicate: July, 1941 - No. 4, Jan, 1942

1-The Eagle begins; Rex Dexter of Mars app. by Briefer; all issues feature German war covers 176 352 528 1100 1650 2200

Earth 4 #4 © Continuity Publications

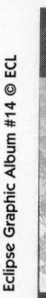

Eclipse Graphic Album #14 © ECL

Eclipso #4 © DC

GD 2.0 | VG 4.0 | FN 6.0 | VF 8.0 | VF/NM 9.0 | NM- 9.2

2-The Spider Queen begins (origin) 82 164 246 513 769 1025
3,4: 3-Joe Spook begins (origin) 66 132 198 413 619 825

EAGLE (2nd Series)
Rural Home Publ.: Feb-Mar, 1945 - No. 2, Apr-May, 1945

1-Aviation stories 46 92 138 276 413 550
2-Lucky Aces 27 54 81 153 214 275
NOTE: ***L. B. Cole*** *c/a in each.*

EAGLE
Crystal Comics/Apple Comics #17 on: Sept, 1986 - No. 23, 1989 ($1.50/1.75/1.95, B&W)

1-23: 12-Double size origin issue ($2.50) 2.50
1-Signed and limited 4.00

EARTH 4 (Also see Urth 4)
Continuity Comics: Dec, 1993 - No. 4, Jan, 1994 ($2.50)

1-4: 1-3 all listed as Dec, 1993 in indicia 2.50

EARTH 4 DEATHWATCH 2000
Continuity Comics: Apr, 1993 - No. 3, Aug, 1993 ($2.50)

1-3 2.50

EARTH MAN ON VENUS (An...) (Also see Strange Planets)
Avon Periodicals: 1951

nn-Wood-a (26 pgs.); Fawcette-c 128 256 384 800 1200 1600

EARTHWORM JIM (TV, cartoon)
Marvel Comics: Dec, 1995 - No. 3, Feb, 1996 ($2.25)

1-3: Based on video game and toys 3.00

EARTH X
Marvel Comics: No. 0, Mar, 1999 - No. 12, Apr, 2000 ($3.99/$2.99, lim. series)

nn- (Wizard supplement) Alex Ross sketchbook; painted-c
1 3 4 6 8 10
Sketchbook (2/99) New sketches and previews 6.00
0-(3/99)-Prelude; Leon-a(p)/Ross-c 1 2 3 4 5 7
1-(4/99)-Leon-a(p)/Ross-c 1 2 3 4 5 7
1-2nd printing 3.00
2-12 3.50
#X (6/00, $3.99) 4.00
TPB (12/00, $24.95) r/#0,1-12, X; foreward by Joss Whedon 25.00

EASTER BONNET SHOP (See March of Comics No. 29)

EASTER WITH MOTHER GOOSE
Dell Publishing Co.: No. 103, 1946 - No. 220, Mar, 1949

Four Color 103 (#1)-Walt Kelly-a 19 38 57 136 198 260
Four Color 140 ('47)-Kelly-a 15 30 45 109 160 210
Four Color 185 ('48),220-Kelly-a 14 28 42 97 141 185

EAST MEETS WEST
Innovation Publishing: Apr, 1990 - No. 2, 1990 ($2.50, limited series, mature)

1,2: 1-Stevens part-i; Redondo-c(i). 2-Stevens-c(i); 1st app. Cheech & Chong in comics 2.50

E. C. CLASSIC REPRINTS
East Coast Comix Co.: May, 1973 - No. 12, 1976 (E. C. Comics reprinted in color minus ads)

1-The Crypt of Terror #1 (Tales from the Crypt #46) 2 4 6 11 14 18
2-12: 2-Weird Science #15('52). 3-Shock SuspenStories #12. 4-Haunt of Fear #12. 5-Weird Fantasy #13('52). 6-Crime SuspenStories #25. 7-Vault of Horror #26. 8-Shock SuspenStories #6. 9-Two-Fisted Tales #34. 10-Haunt of Fear #23. 11-Weird Science 12(#1). 12-Shock SuspenStories #2 2 4 6 8 10 12

EC CLASSICS
Russ Cochran: Aug, 1985 - No. 12, 1986? (High quality paper; each-r 8 stories in color) (#2-12 were resolicited in 1990)($4.95, 56 pgs., 8x11")

1-12: 1-Tales From the Crypt. 2-Weird Science. 3-Two-Fisted Tales (r/31); Frontline Combat (r/9). 4-Shock SuspenStories. 5-Weird Fantasy. 6-Vault of Horror. 7-Weird Science-Fantasy (r/23,24). 8-Crime SuspenStories (r/17,18). 9-Haunt of Fear (r/14,15). 10-Panic (r/1,2). 11-Tales From the Crypt (r/23,24). 12-Weird Science (r/20,22) 6.00

ECHO
Image Comics (Dreamwave Prod.): Mar, 2000 - No. 5, Sept, 2000 ($2.50)

1-5: 1-3-Pat Lee-c 2.50
0-(7/00) 2.50

ECHO OF FUTUREPAST
Pacific Comics/Continuity Com.: May, 1984 - No. 9, Jan, 1986 ($2.95, 52 pgs.)

1-9: Neal Adams-c/a in all? 6.00
NOTE: ***N. Adams*** *a-1-6,7i,9i; c-1-3, 5p,7i,8,9i.* ***Golden*** *a-1-6 (Bucky O'Hare); c-6.* ***Toth*** *a-6,7.*

ECLIPSE GRAPHIC ALBUM SERIES
Eclipse Comics: Oct, 1978 - 1989 (8-1/2x11") (B&W #1-5)

1-Sabre (10/78, B&W, 1st print.); Gulacy-a; 1st direct sale graphic novel 16.00
1-Sabre (2nd printing, 1/79) 8.00
1-Sabre (3rd printing, $5.95) 6.00
3,4: 3-Detectives, Inc. (5/80, B&W, $6.95)-Rogers-a. 4-Stewart The Rat (1980, B&W) -G. Colan-a 10.00
5-The Price (10/81, B&W)-Starlin-a 16.00
2,6,7,13: 2-Night Music (11/79, B&W)-Russell-a. 6-I Am Coyote (11/84, color)-Rogers-c/a. 7-The Rocketeer (2nd print, $7.95). 7-The Rocketeer (3rd print, 1991, $8.95). 13-The Sisterhood of Steel ('87, $8.95, color) 10.00
7-The Rocketeer (9/85, color)-Dave Stevens-a (r/chapters 1-5)(see Pacific Presents & Starslayer); has 7 pgs. new-a 14.00
7-The Rocketeer, signed & limited HC 60.00
7-The Rocketeer, hardcover (1986, $19.95) 20.00
7-The Rocketeer, unsigned HC (3rd, $32.95) 33.00
8-Zorro In Old California ('86, color) 14.00
8,12-Hardcover 18.00
9,10: 9-Sacred And The Profane ('86)-Steacy-a. 10-Somerset Holmes ('86, $15.95)-Adults, soft-c 16.00
9,10,12-Hardcover ($24.95). 12-signed & #'d 25.00
11,14,16,18,20,23,24: 11-Floyd Farland, Citizen of the Future ('87, $3.95, B&W). 14-Samurai, Son of Death ('87, $4.95, B&W). 16,18,20,23-See Airfighters Classics #1-4. 24-Heartbreak ($4.95, B&W) 7.00
12,28,31,35: 12-Silverheels ('87, $7.95, color). 28-Miracleman Book I ($5.95). 31-Pigeons From Hell by R. E. Howard (11/88). 35-Rael: Into The Shadow of the Sun ('88, $7.95) 10.00
14,17,21,14-Samurai, Son of Death ($3.95, 2nd printing). 17-Valkyrie, Prisoner of the Past SC ('88, $3.95, color). 21-XYR-Multiple ending comic ('88, $3.95, B&W) 6.00
15,22,27: 15-Twisted Tales (11/87, color)-Dave Stevens-c. 22-Alien Worlds #1 (5/88, $3.95, 52 pgs.)-Nudity. 27-Fast Fiction (She) ($5.95, B&W) 8.00
17-Valkyrie, Prisoner of the Past S&N Hardcover ('88, $19.95) 20.00
19-Scout: The Four Monsters ('88, $14.95, color)-r/Scout #1-7; soft-c 15.00
25,30,32-34: 25-Alex Toth's Zorro Vol. 1 ,2($10.95, B&W). 30-Brought To Light; Alan Moore scripts ('89). 32-Teenaged Dope Slaves and Reform School Girls. 33-Bogie. 34-Air Fighters Classics #5 12.00
29-Real Love: Best of Simon & Kirby Romance Comics(10/88, $12.95) 15.00
30,31: Limited hardcover ed. ($29.95). 31-signed 30.00
36-Dr. Watchstop: Adventures in Time and Space ('89, $8.95) 10.00

ECLIPSE MAGAZINE (Becomes Eclipse Monthly)
Eclipse Publishing: May, 1981 - No. 8, Jan, 1983 ($2.95, B&W, magazine)

1-8: 1-1st app. Cap'n Quick and a Foozle by Rogers, Ms. Tree by Beatty, and Dope by Trina Robbins. 2-1st app. I Am Coyote by Rogers. 7-1st app. Masked Man by Boyer 3.00
NOTE: ***Colan*** *a-3, 5, 8.* ***Golden*** *c/a-2.* ***Gulacy*** *a-6, c-1, 6.* ***Kaluta*** *c/a-5.* ***Mayerik*** *a-2, 3.* ***Rogers*** *a-1-8.* ***Starlin*** *a-1.* ***Sutton*** *a-6.*

ECLIPSE MONTHLY
Eclipse Comics: Aug, 1983 - No. 10, Jul, 1984 (Baxter paper, $2.00/$1.50/$1.75)

1-10: ($2.00, 52 pgs.)-Cap'n Quick and a Foozle by Rogers, Static by Ditko, Dope by Trina Robbins, Rio by Wildey, The Masked Man by Boyer begin. 3-Ragamuffins begins 2.25
NOTE: ***Boyer*** *c-6.* ***Ditko*** *a-1-3.* ***Rogers*** *a-1-4; c-2, 4, 7.* ***Wildey*** *a-1, 2, 5, 9, 10; c-5, 10.*

ECLIPSO (See Brave and the Bold #64, House of Secrets #61 & Phantom Stranger, 1987)
DC Comics: Nov, 1992 - No. 18, Apr, 1994 ($1.25)

1-18: 1-Giffen plots/breakdowns begin. 10-Darkseid app. Creeper in #3-6,9,11-13. 18-Spectre-c/s 2.25
Annual 1 (1993, $2.50, 68 pgs.)-Intro Prism 2.50

ECLIPSO: THE DARKNESS WITHIN
DC Comics: July, 1992 - No. 2, Oct, 1992 ($2.50, 68 pgs.)

1,2: 1-With purple gem attached to-c, 1-Without gem; Superman, Creeper app., 2-Concludes Eclipso storyline from annuals 2.50

E. C. 3-D CLASSICS (See Three Dimensional...)

ECTOKID (See Razorline)
Marvel Comics: Sept, 1993 - No. 9, May, 1994 ($1.75/$1.95)

1-($2.50)-Foil embossed-c; created by C. Barker 3.00
2-9: 2-Origin. 5-Saint Sinner x-over 2.25
...: Unleashed! 1 (10/94, $2.95, 52 pgs.) 3.00

ED "BIG DADDY" ROTH'S RATFINK COMIX (Also see Ratfink)
World of Fandom/ Ed Roth: 1991 - No. 3, 1991 ($2.50)

1-3: Regular Ed., 1-Limited double cover 1 3 4 6 8 10

EDDIE CAMPBELL'S BACCHUS
Eddie Campbell Comics: May, 1995 - Present ($2.95, B&W)

Eden Matrix #2 © Aubrey McAuley

The Edge #1 © Steven Grant & Gil Kane

Eerie #21 © WP

GD VG FN VF VF/NM NM-
2.0 4.0 6.0 8.0 9.0 9.2

1-Cerebus app. 1 2 3 5 6 8
1-2nd printing (5/97) 3.00
2-10: 9-Alex Ross back-c 5.00
11-60 3.00
Doing The Islands With Bacchus ('97, $17.95) 18.00
Earth, Water, Air & Fire ('98, $9.95) 10.00
King Bacchus ('99, $12.95) 13.00
The Eyeball Kid ('98, $8.50) 8.50

EDDIE STANKY (Baseball Hero)
Fawcett Publications: 1951 (New York Giants)

nn-Photo-c 36 72 108 204 290 375

EDEN MATRIX, THE
Adhesive Comics: 1994 ($2.95)

1,2-Two variant-c; alternate-c on inside back-c 3.00

EDEN'S TRAIL
Marvel Comics: Jan, 2003 - No. 6 ($2.99, limited series, Marvelscope-printed sideways)

1-5-Chuck Austen-s/Steve Uy-a 3.00

EDGAR ALLAN POE'S - THE FALL OF THE HOUSE OF USHER AND OTHER TALES OF HORROR
Catlan Communications Pub.: Sept. 1985 (hardcover graphic novel)

nn-Reprints of Poe story issues from Warren comic mags; all Richard Corben-a; numbered edition of 350 signed by Corben 100.00

EDGAR BERGEN PRESENTS CHARLIE McCARTHY
Whitman Publishing Co. (Charlie McCarthy Co.): No. 764, 1938 (36 pgs.; 15x10-1/2"; color)

764 74 148 222 463 694 925

EDGAR RICE BURROUGHS' TARZAN: A TALE OF MUGAMBI
Dark Horse Comics: 1995 ($2.95, one-shot)

1 3.00

EDGAR RICE BURROUGHS' TARZAN: IN THE LAND THAT TIME FORGOT AND THE POOL OF TIME
Dark Horse Comics: 1996 ($12.95, trade paperback)

nn-r/Russ Manning-a 13.00

EDGAR RICE BURROUGHS' TARZAN OF THE APES
Dark Horse Comics: May, 1999 ($12.95, trade paperback)

nn-reprints 13.00

EDGAR RICE BURROUGHS' TARZAN: THE LOST ADVENTURE
Dark Horse Comics: Jan, 1995 - No. 4, Apr, 1995 ($2.95, B&W, limited series)

1-4: ERB's last Tarzan story, adapted by Joe Lansdale 3.00
Hardcover (12/95, $19.95) 20.00
Limited Edition Hardcover ($99.95)-signed & numbered 100.00

EDGAR RICE BURROUGHS' TARZAN: THE RETURN OF TARZAN
Dark Horse Comics: May, 1997 - No. 3, July, 1997 ($2.95, limited series)

1-3 3.00

EDGAR RICE BURROUGHS' TARZAN: THE RIVERS OF BLOOD
Dark Horse Comics: Nov, 1999 - No. 4, Feb, 2000 ($2.95, limited series)

1-4-Kordey-c/a 3.00

EDGE
Malibu Comics (Bravura): July, 1994 - No. 3, Apr, 1995 ($2.50/$2.95, unfinished lim.series)

1,2-S. Grant-story & Gil Kane-c/a; w/Bravura stamp 2.50
3-($2.95-c) 3.00

EDGE (Re-titled as Vector starting with #13)
CrossGeneration Comics: May, 2002 - No. 12, Apr, 2003 ($9.95/$11.95/$7.95, TPB)

1-3: Reprints from various CrossGen titles 10.00
4-8-($11.95) 12.00
9-12-($7.95, 8-1/4" x 5-1/2") digest-sized reprints 8.00

EDGE OF CHAOS
Pacific Comics: July, 1983 - No. 3, Jan, 1984 (Limited series)

1-3-Morrow c/a; all contain nudity 2.25

ED WHEELAN'S JOKE BOOK STARRING FAT & SLAT (See Fat & Slat)

EERIE (Strange Worlds No. 18 on)
Avon Per.: No. 1, Jan, 1947; No. 1, May-June, 1951 - No. 17, Aug-Sept, 1954

1(1947)-1st supernatural comic; Kubert, Fugitani-a; bondage-c (scarce)
370 740 1110 2405 3703 5000
1(1951)-Reprints story from 1947 #1 64 128 192 400 600 800
2-Wood-c/a; bondage-c 68 136 204 425 638 850
3-Wood-c; Kubert, Wood/Orlando-a 68 136 204 425 638 850
4,5-Wood-c 56 112 168 350 525 700
6,8,13,14: 8-Kinstler-a; bondage-c; Phantom Witch Doctor story
33 66 99 190 270 350
7-Wood/Orlando-c; Kubert-a 44 88 132 264 395 525
9-Kubert-a; Check-c 37 74 111 212 301 390
10,11: 10-Kinstler-a. 11-Kinstlerish-a by McCann 33 66 99 190 270 350
12-Dracula story from novel, 25 pgs. 39 78 117 224 317 410
15-Reprints No. 1('51) minus-c(bondage) 24 48 72 138 194 250
16-Wood-a r-/No. 2 24 48 72 138 194 250
17-Wood/Orlando & Kubert-a; reprints #3 minus inside & outside Wood-c
24 48 72 138 194 250

NOTE: ***Hollingsworth** a-9-11; c-10, 11.*

EERIE
I. W. Enterprises: 1964

I.W. Reprint #1('64)-Wood-c(r); r-story/Spook #1 4 8 12 27 36 45
I.W. Reprint #2,6,8: 8-Dr. Drew by Grandenetti from Ghost #9
4 8 12 24 32 40
I.W. Reprint #9-r/Tales of Terror #1(Toby); Wood-c 4 8 12 29 40 50

EERIE (Magazine)(See Warren Presents)
Warren Publ. Co.: No. 1, Sept, 1965; No. 2, Mar, 1966 - No. 139, Feb, 1983

1-24 pgs., black & white, small size (5-1/4x7-1/4"), low distribution; cover from inside back cover of Creepy No. 2; stories reprinted from Creepy No. 7, 8. At least three different versions exist.
First Printing - B&W, 5-1/4" wide x 7-1/4" high, evenly trimmed. On page 18, panel 5, in the upper left-hand corner, the large rear view of a bald headed man blends into solid black and is unrecognizable. Overall printing quality is poor. 29 58 87 210 305 400

Second Printing - B&W, 5-1/4x7-1/4", with uneven, untrimmed edges (if one of these were trimmed evenly, the size would be less than as indicated). The figure of the bald headed man on page 18, panel 5 is clear and discernible. The staples have a 1/4" blue stripe. 13 26 39 90 133 175

Other unauthorized reproductions for comparison's sake would be practically worthless. One known version was probably shot off a first printing copy with some loss of detail; the finer lines tend to disappear in this version which can be determined by looking at the lower right-hand corner of page one, first story. The roof of the house is shaded with straight lines. These lines are sharp and distinct on original, but broken on this version.

NOTE: ***The Overstreet Comic Book Price Guide** recommends that, before buying a 1st issue, you consult an expert.*

2-Frazetta-c; Toth-a; 1st app. host Cousin Eerie 8 16 24 58 82 105
3-Frazetta-c & half pg. ad (rerun in #4); Toth, Williamson, Ditko-a
6 12 18 43 59 75
4-7: 4-Frazetta-a (1/2 pg. ad). 5,7-Frazetta-c. Ditko-a in all.
4 8 12 27 36 45
8-Frazetta-c; Ditko-a 5 10 15 33 44 55
9-11,25: 9,10-Neal Adams-a, Ditko-a. 11-Karloff Mummy adapt.-Wood-s/a. 25-Steranko-c
4 8 12 28 38 48
12-16,18-22,24,32-35,40,45: 12,13,20-Poe-s. 12-Bloch-s. 12,15-Jones-a. 13-Lovecraft-s. 14,16-Toth-a. 16,19,24-Stoker-s. 16,32,33,43-Corben-a. 34-Early Boris-c. 35-Early Brunner-a. 35,40-Early Ploog-a. 40-Frankestein; Ploog-a (6/72, 6 months before Marvel's series) 3 6 9 19 25 32
17-(low distribution) 9 18 27 63 89 115
23-Frazetta-c; Adams-a(reprint) 5 10 15 33 44 55
26-31,36-38,43,44 3 6 9 18 23 28
39,41: 39-1st Dax the Warrior; Maroto-a. 41-(low distribution)
4 8 12 24 32 40
42,51: 42-('73 Annual, 84 pgs.) Spooktacular; Williamson-a. 51-('74 Annual, 76 pgs.) Color poster insert; Toth-a 4 8 12 22 30 38
46,48: 46-Dracula series by Sutton begins; 2pgs. Vampirella. 48-Begin "Mummy Walks" and "Curse of the Werewolf" series (both continue in #49,50,52,53)
3 6 9 18 24 30
47,49,50,52,53: 47-Lilith. 49-Marvin the Dead Thing. 50-Satanna, Daughter of Satan. 52-Hunter by Neary begins. 53-Adams-a 3 6 9 18 23 28
54,55-Color insert Spirit story by Eisner, reprints sections 12/21/47 & 6/16/46
54-Dr. Archaeus series begins 3 6 9 16 20 24
56,57,59,63,69,77,78: All have 8 pg. slick color insert. 56,57,77-Corben-a. 59-(100 pgs.) Summer Special, all Dax issue. 69-Summer Special, all Hunter issue, Neary-a.
78-All Mummy issue 3 6 9 16 20 24
58,60,62,68,72,: 8 pg. slick color insert & Wrightson-a in all. 58,60,62-Corben-a. 60-Summer Giant (9/74, $1.25) 1st Exterminator One; Wood-a. 62-Mummies Walk. 68-Summer Special (84 pgs.) 3 6 9 18 24 30
61,64-67,71: 61-Mummies Walk-s, Wood-a. 64-Corben-a. 64,65,67-Toth-a. 65,66-El Cid. 67-Hunter II. 71-Goblin-c/1st app. 2 4 6 14 18 22
70,73-75 2 4 6 10 13 16
76-1st app. Darklon the Mystic by Starlin-s/a 3 6 9 18 24 30
79,80-Origin Darklon the Mystic by Starlin 3 6 9 16 20 24

Egbert #12 © QUA

Eight Legged Freaks © WB

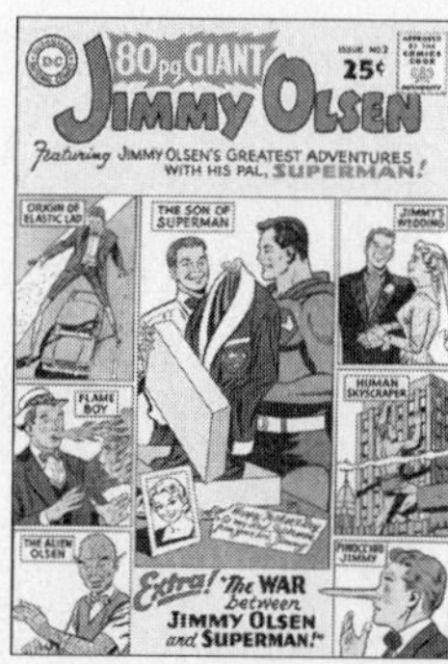

80 Page Giant #2 © DC

GD VG FN VF VF/NM NM-
2.0 4.0 6.0 8.0 9.0 9.2

81,86,97: 81-Frazetta-c, King Kong; Corben-a. 86-(92 pgs.) All Corben issue. 97-Time Travel/ Dinosaur issue; Corben,Adams-a 2 4 6 14 18 22

82-Origin/1st app. The Rook 3 6 9 18 23 28

83,85,88,89,91-93,98,99: 98-Rook (31 pgs.). 99-1st Horizon Seekers. 2 4 6 8 10 12

84,87,90,96,100: 84,100-Starlin-a. 87-Hunter 3; Nino-a. 87,90-Corben-a. 96-Summer Special (92 pgs.). 100-(92 pgs.) Anniverary issue; Rook (30 pgs.) 2 4 6 10 13 16

94,95-The Rook & Vampirella team-up. 95-Vampirella-c; 1st MacTavish 3 6 9 16 20 25

101,106,112,115,118,120,121,128: 101-Return of Hunter II, Starlin-a. 106-Hard John Nuclear Hit Parade Special, Corben-a. 112-All Maroto issue, Luana-s. 115-All José Ortiz issues. 118-1st Haggarth. 120-1st Zud Kamish. 121-Hunter/Darklon. 128-Starlin-a, Hsu-a 2 4 6 9 11 14

102-105,107-111,113,114,116,117,119,122-124,126,127,129: 104-Beast World. 103-105,109-111-Gulacy-a 2 4 6 8 10 12

125-(10/81, 84 pgs.) all Neal Adams issue 2 4 6 12 16 20

130-(76 pgs.) Vampirella-c/sty (54 pgs.); Pantha, Van Helsing, Huntress, Dax, Schreck, Hunter, Exterminator One, Rook app. 3 6 9 16 20 25

131-(Lower distr.); all Wood issue 2 4 6 14 18 22

132-134,136: 132-Rook returns. 133-All Ramon Torrents-a issue. 134,136-Color comic insert 2 4 6 9 11 14

135-(Lower distr., 10/82, 100 pgs.) All Ditko issue 2 4 6 14 18 22

137-139 (lower distr.):137-All Super-Hero issue. 138-Sherlock Holmes. 138,139-Color comic insert 2 4 6 11 14 18

Yearbook '70-Frazetta-c 5 10 15 33 44 55

Annual '71, '72-Reprints in both 4 8 12 24 32 40

NOTE: *The above books contain art by many good artists:* **N. Adams, Brunner, Corben, Craig (Taycee), Crandall, Ditko, Eisner, Evans, Jeff Jones, Krenkel, McWilliams, Morrow, Orlando, Ploog, Severin, Starlin, Torres, Toth, Williamson, Wood,** *and* **Wrightson**; *covers by* **Bode', Corben, Davis, Frazetta, Morrow**, *and* **Orlando**. **Frazetta** *c-2, 3, 7, 8, 23. Annuals from 1973-on are included in regular numbering. 1970-74 Annuals are complete reprints. Annuals from 1975-on are in the format of the regular issues.*

EERIE ADVENTURES (Also see Weird Adventures)
Ziff-Davis Publ. Co.: Winter, 1951 (Painted-c)

1-Powell-a(2), McCann-a; used in **SOTI;** bondage-c; Krigstein back-c 40 80 120 240 340 440

NOTE: *Title dropped due to similarity to Avon's Eerie & legal action.*

EERIE TALES (Magazine)
Hastings Associates: 1959 (Black & White)

1-Williamson, Torres, Tuska-a, Powell(2), & Morrow(2)-a 12 24 36 69 92 115

EERIE TALES
Super Comics: 1963-1964

Super Reprint No. 10,11,12,18: 10('63)-r/Spook #27. Purple Claw in #11,12 ('63); #12-r/Avon's Eerie #1('51)-Kida-r 3 6 9 19 25 32

15-Wolverton-a, Spacehawk-r/Blue Bolt Weird Tales #113; Disbrow-a 6 12 18 38 52 65

EGBERT
Arnold Publications/Quality Comics Group: Spring, 1946 - No. 20, 1950

1-Funny animal; intro Egbert & The Count 20 40 60 112 156 200
2 10 20 30 58 77 95
3-10 8 16 24 40 50 60
11-20 6 12 18 28 34 40

EGON
Dark Horse Comics: Jan, 1998 - No.2, Feb, 1998 ($2.95, limited series)

1,2-Horley-painted-c 3.00

EGYPT
DC Comics (Vertigo): Aug, 1995 - No.7, Feb, 1996 ($2.50, lim. series, mature)

1-7: Milligan scripts in all. 3.00

EH! (...Dig This Crazy Comic) (From Here to Insanity No. 8 on)
Charlton Comics: Dec, 1953 - No. 7, Nov-Dec, 1954 (Satire)

1-Davis-*ish*-c/a by Ayers, Wood-*ish*-a by Giordano; Atomic Mouse app. 36 72 108 204 290 375
2-Ayers-c/a 21 42 63 118 164 210
3,5,7 19 38 57 106 146 185
4,6: Sexual innuendo-c. 6-Ayers-a 20 40 60 112 156 200

EIGHTBALL (Also see David Boring)
Fantagraphics Books: Oct, 1989 - Present ($2.75/$2.95/$3.95, semi-annually, mature)

1 (1st printing) Daniel Clowes-s/a in all 2 4 6 8 10 12
2,3 1 2 3 5 6 8
4-8 6.00
9-19: 17-(8/96) 4.00
20-($4.50) 4.50
21-($4.95) Concludes David Boring 3-parter 5.00
22-($5.95) 29 short stories 6.00
Twentieth Century Eightball (2002, $19.00) r/Clowes strips 19.00

EIGHTH WONDER, THE
Dark Horse Comics: Nov, 1997 ($2.95, one-shot)

nn-Reprints stories from Dark Horse Presents #85-87 3.00

EIGHT IS ENOUGH KITE FUN BOOK (See Kite Fun Book)

EIGHT LEGGED FREAKS
DC Comics (WildStorm): 2002 ($6.95, one-shot, squarebound)

nn-Adaptation of 2002 mutant spider movie; Joe Phillips-a; intro by Dean Devlin 7.00

80 PAGE GIANT (...Magazine No. 2-15)
National Periodical Publications: 8/64 - No. 15, 10/65; No. 16, 11/65 - No. 89, 7/71 (25¢) (All reprints) (#1-56: 84 pgs.; #57-89: 68 pgs.)

1-Superman Annual; originally planned as Superman Annual #9 (8/64) 41 82 123 324 487 650
2-Jimmy Olsen 25 50 75 181 266 350
3,4: 3-Lois Lane. 4-Flash-G.A.-r; Infantino-a 20 40 60 142 209 275
5-Batman; has Sunday newspaper strip; Catwoman-r; Batman's Life Story-r (25th anniversary special) 20 40 60 142 209 275
6-Superman 17 34 51 123 182 240
7-Sgt. Rock's Prize Battle Tales; Kubert-c/a 23 46 69 167 244 320
8-More Secret Origins-origins of JLA, Aquaman, Robin, Atom, & Superman; Infantino-a 35 70 105 263 394 525
9-15: 9-Flash (r/Flash #106,117,123 & Showcase #14); Infantino-a. 10-Superboy. 11-Superman; all Luthor issue. 12-Batman; has Sunday newspaper strip. 13-Jimmy Olsen. 14-Lois Lane. 15-Superman and Batman; Joker-c/story 17 34 51 118 174 230

Continued as part of regular series under each title in which that particular book came out, a Giant being published instead of the regular size. Issues No. 16 to No. 89 are listed for your information. See individual titles for prices. 16-JLA #39 (11/65), 17-Batman #176, 18-Superman #183, 19-Our Army at War #164, 20-Action #334, 21-Flash #160, 22-Superboy #129, 23-Superman #187, 24-Batman #182, 25-Jimmy Olsen #95, 26-Lois Lane #68, 27-Batman #185, 28-World's Finest #161, 29-JLA #48, 30-Batman #187, 31-Superman #193, 32-Our Army at War #177, 33-Action #347, 34-Flash #169, 35-Superboy #138, 36-Superman #197, 37-Batman #193, 38-Jimmy Olsen #104, 39-Lois Lane #77, 40-World's Finest #170, 41-JLA #58, 42-Superman #202, 43-Batman #198, 44-Our Army at War #190, 45-Action #360, 46-Flash #178, 47-Superboy #147, 48-Superman #207, 49-Batman #203, 50-Jimmy Olsen #113, 51-Lois Lane #86, 52-World's Finest #179, 53-JLA #67, 54-Superman #212, 55-Batman #208, 56-Our Army at War #203, 57-Action #373, 58-Flash #187, 59-Superboy #156, 60-Superman #217, 61-Batman #213, 62-Jimmy Olsen #122, 63-Lois Lane #95, 64-World's Finest #188, 65-JLA #76, 66-Superman #222, 67-Batman #218, 68-Our Army at War #216, 69-Adventure #390, 70-Flash #196, 71-Superboy #165, 72-Superman #227, 73-Batman #223, 74-Jimmy Olsen #131, 75-Lois Lane #104, 76-World's Finest #197, 77-JLA #85, 78-Superman #232, 79-Batman #228, 80-Our Army at War #229, 81-Adventure #403, 82-Flash #205, 83-Superboy #174, 84-Superman #239, 85-Batman #233, 86-Jimmy Olsen #140, 87-Lois Lane #113, 88-World's Finest #206, 89-JLA #93.

87TH PRECINCT (TV) (Based on the Ed McBain novels)
Dell Publishing Co.: Apr-June, 1962 - No. 2, July-Sept, 1962

Four Color 1309(#1)-Krigstein-a 11 22 33 77 114 150
2 10 20 30 67 96 125

EL BOMBO COMICS
Standard Comics/Frances M. McQueeny: 1946

nn(1946), 1(no date) 11 22 33 63 84 105

EL CAZADOR
CrossGen Comics: Oct, 2003 - Present ($2.95)

1-Dixon-s/Epting-a 5.00
2-4 3.00
Collected Edition (2003, $5.95) r/#1-3 6.00

EL CID
Dell Publishing Co.: No. 1259, 1961

Four Color 1259-Movie, photo-c 8 16 24 55 78 100

EL DIABLO (See All-Star Western #2 & Weird Western Tales #12)
DC Comics: Aug, 1989 - No. 16, Jan, 1991 ($1.50-$1.75, color)

1 ($2.50, 52pgs.)-Masked hero 3.00
2-16 2.50

EL DIABLO
DC Comics (Vertigo): Mar, 2001 - No. 4, Jun, 2001 ($2.50, limited series)

1-4-Azzarello-s/Zezelj-a/Sale-c 2.50

EL DORADO (See Movie Classics)

Elektra V2#4 © MAR

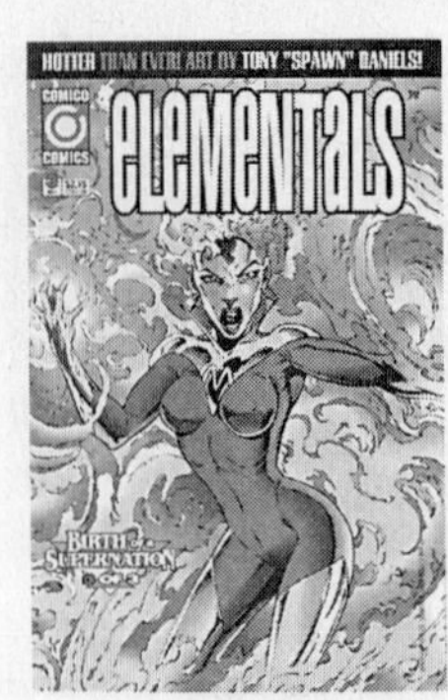

Elementals #3 © Bill Willingham

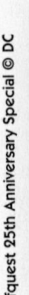

Elfquest 25th Anniversary Special © DC

GD VG FN VF VF/NM NM-
2.0 4.0 6.0 8.0 9.0 9.2

ELECTRIC UNDERTOW (See Strikeforce Morituri: Electric Undertow)

ELECTRIC WARRIOR
DC Comics: May, 1986 - No. 18, Oct, 1987 ($1.50, Baxter paper)
1-18 2.25

ELECTROPOLIS
Image Comics: May, 2001 - Present ($2.95/$5.95)
1-3-Dean Motter-s/a. 3-(12/01) 3.00
4-(1/03, $5.95, 72 pages) The Infernal Machine pts. 4-6 6.00

ELEKTRA (Also see Daredevil #319-325)
Marvel Comics: Mar, 1995 - No. 4, June, 1995 ($2.95, limited series)
1-4-Embossed-c; Scott McDaniel-a 3.00

ELEKTRA (Also see Daredevil)
Marvel Comics: Nov, 1996 - No. 19, Jun, 1998 ($1.95)
1-Peter Milligan scripts; Deodato-c/a 3.00
1-Variant-c 5.00
2-19: 4-Dr. Strange-c/app. 10-Logan-c/app. 2.50
#(-1) Flashback (7/97) Matt Murdock-c/app.; Deodato-c/a 2.50
.../Cyblade (Image, 3/97,$2.95) Devil's Reign pt. 7 3.00

ELEKTRA (Vol. 2) (Marvel Knights)
Marvel Comics: Sept, 2001 - Present ($3.50/$2.99)
1-Bendis-s/Austen-a/Horn-c 4.00
2-6: 2-Two covers (Sienkiewicz and Horn) 3,4-Silver Samurai app. 3.00
3-Initial printing with panel of nudity; most copies pulped 18.00
7-31: 7-Rucka-s begin. 9,10,17-Bennett-a. 19-Meglia-a. 23-25-Chen-a; Sienkiewicz-c 3.00
...Vol. 1: Introspect TPB (2002, $16.99) r/#10-15; Marvel Knights: Double Shot #3 17.00
...Vol. 2: Everything Old is New Again TPB (2003, $16.99) r/#16-22 17.00
...Vol. 3: Relentless TPB (2004, $14.99) r/#23-28 15.00

ELEKTRA & WOLVERINE: THE REDEEMER
Marvel Comics: Jan, 2002 - No. 3, Mar, 2002 ($5.95, square-bound, lim. series)
1-3-Greg Rucka-s/Yoshitaka Amano-a/c 6.00
HC (5/02, $29.95, with dustjacket) r/#1-3, interview with Greg Rucka 30.00

ELEKTRA: ASSASSIN (Also see Daredevil)
Marvel Comics (Epic Comics): Aug, 1986 - No. 8, June, 1987 (Limited series, mature)
1,8-Miller scripts in all; Sienkiewicz-c/a. 6.00
2-7 5.00
Signed & numbered hardcover (Graphitti Designs, $39.95, 2000 print run)- reprints 1-8 50.00
TPB (2000, $24.95) 25.00

ELEKTRA: GLIMPSE & ECHO
Marvel Comics: Sept, 2002 - No. 4, Dec, 2002 ($2.99, limited series)
1-4-Scott Morse-s/painted-a 3.00

ELEKTRA LIVES AGAIN (Also see Daredevil)
Marvel Comics (Epic Comics): 1990 ($24.95, oversize, hardcover, 76 pgs.)
(Produced by Graphitti Designs)
nn-Frank Miller-c/a/scripts; Lynn Varley painted-a; Matt Murdock & Bullseye app. 35.00
2nd printing (9/02, $24.99) 25.00

ELEKTRA MEGAZINE
Marvel Comics: Nov, 1996 - No. 2, Dec, 1996 ($3.95, 96 pgs., reprints, limited series)
1,2: Reprints Frank Miller's Elektra stories in Daredevil 4.00

ELEKTRA SAGA, THE
Marvel Comics Group: Feb, 1984 - No. 4, June, 1984 ($2.00, limited series, Baxter paper)
1-4-r/Daredevil 168-190; Miller-c/a 4.00

ELEMENTALS, THE (See The Justice Machine & Morningstar Spec.)
Comico The Comic Co. : June, 1984 - No. 29, Sept, 1988; V2#1, Mar, 1989 - No. 28, 1994?
($1.50/$2.50, Baxter paper); V3#1, Dec, 1995 - No. 3 ($2.95)
1-Willingham-c/a, 1-8 5.00
2-29, V2#1-28: 9-Bissette-a(p). 10-Photo-c. V2#6-1st app. Strike Force America. 18-Prelude to Avalon mini-series. 27-Prequel to Strike Force America series 3.00
V3#1-3: 1-Daniel-a(p), bagged w/gaming card 3.00
Lingerie (5/96, $2.95) 3.00
Special 1,2 (3/86, 1/89)-1-Willingham-a(p) 3.00

ELEMENTALS: (Title series), **Comico**
--GHOST OF A CHANCE, 12/95 ($5.95)-graphic novel, nn-Ross-c. 6.00
--HOW THE WAR WAS WON, 6/96 - No. 2, 8/96 ($2.95) 1,2-Tony Daniel-a, & 1-Variant-c; no logo 3.00
--SEX SPECIAL, 1991 - No. 4, Feb, 1993 ($2.95, color) 2 covers for each 3.00

GD VG FN VF VF/NM NM-
2.0 4.0 6.0 8.0 9.0 9.2

--SEX SPECIAL, 5/97 - No. 2, 6/97 ($2.95, B&W) 1-Tony Daniel, Jeff Moy-a, 2-Robb Phipps, Adam McDaniel-a 3.00
--SWIMSUIT SPECTACULAR 1996, 6/96 ($2.95), 1-pin-ups, 1-Variant-c; no logo 3.00
--THE VAMPIRE'S REVENGE, 6/96 - No. 2 8/96 ($2.95) 1,2-Willingham-s, 1-Variant-c; no logo 3.00

1111 (ELEVEN ELEVEN)
Crusade Entertainment: Oct, 1996 ($2.95, B&W, one-shot)
1-Wrightson-c/a 4.00

ELEVEN OR ONE
Sirius: Apr, 1995 ($2.95)
1-Linsner-c/a 1 3 4 6 8 10
1-(6/96) 2nd printing 3.50

ELFLORD
Aircel Publ.: 1986 - No. 6, Oct, 1989 ($1.70, B&W); V2#1- V2#31, 1995 ($2.00)
1 3.00
2-4,V2#1-20,22-30: 4-6: Last B&W issue. V2#1-Color-a begin. 22-New cast. 25-Begin B&W 2.50
1,2-2nd printings 2.50
21-Double size ($4.95) 5.00

ELFLORD
Warp Graphics: Jan, 1997-No.4, Apr, 1997 ($2.95, B&W, mini-series)
1-4 3.00

ELFLORD (CUTS LOOSE) (Vol. 2)
Warp Graphics: Sept, 1997 - No. 7, Apr, 1998 ($2.95, B&W, mini-series)
1-7 3.00

ELFLORD: DRAGON'S EYE
Night Wynd Enterprises: 1993 ($2.50, B&W)
1 2.50

ELFLORD: THE RETURN
Mad Monkey Press: 1996 ($6.95, magazine size)
1 7.00

ELFQUEST (Also see Fantasy Quarterly & Warp Graphics Annual)
Warp Graphics, Inc.: No. 2, Aug, 1978 - No. 21, Feb, 1985 (All magazine size)
No. 1, Apr, 1979
NOTE: ***Elfquest*** was originally published as one of the stories in **Fantasy Quarterly** #1. When the publisher went out of business, the creative team, Wendy and Richard Pini, formed WaRP Graphics and continued the series, beginning with **Elfquest** #2. **Elfquest** #1, which reprinted the story from **Fantasy Quarterly**, was published about the same time **Elfquest** #4 was released. Thereafter, most issues were reprinted as demand warranted, until Marvel announced it would reprint the entire series under its Epic imprint (Aug., 1985).

1(4/79)-Reprints Elfquest story from Fantasy Quarterly No. 1
1st printing ($1.00-c) 3 6 9 18 24 30
2nd printing ($1.25-c) 1 2 3 5 7 9
3rd printings ($1.50-c) 3.00
4th printing; different-c ($1.50-c) 2.50
2(8/78)-5: 1st printings ($1.00-c) 2 4 6 11 14 18
2nd printings ($1.25-c) 4.00
3rd & 4th printings ($1.50-c)(all 4th prints 1989) 2.50
6-9: 1st printings ($1.25-c) 1 2 3 5 7 9
2nd printings ($1.50-c) 3.00
3rd printings ($1.50-c) 2.50
10-21: ($1.50-c); 16-8pg. preview of A Distant Soil 6.00
10-14: 2nd printings ($1.50) 2.50

ELFQUEST
Marvel Comics (Epic Comics): Aug, 1985 - No. 32, Mar, 1988
1-Reprints in color the Elfquest epic by Warp Graphics 3.00
2-32 2.50

ELFQUEST
DC Comics: 2003 - Present
Archives Vol. 1 (2003, $49.95, HC) r/#1-5 50.00
25th Anniversary Special (2003, $2.95) r/Elfquest #1 (Apr, 1979); interview w/Pinis 3.00

ELFQUEST (Title series), Warp Graphics
'89 - No. 4, '89 ($1.50, B&W) 1-4: R-original Elfquest series 2.50

ELFQUEST (Volume 2),**Warp Graphics:** V2#1, 5/96 - No. 33, 2/99 ($4.95/$2.95, B&W)
V2#1-31: 1,3,5,8,10,12,13,18,21,23,25-Wendy Pini-c 5.00
32,33-($2.95-c) 3.00
--BLOOD OF TEN CHIEFS, 7/93 - No. 20, 9/95 ($2.00/$2.50) 1-20-By Richard & Wendy Pini 3.00

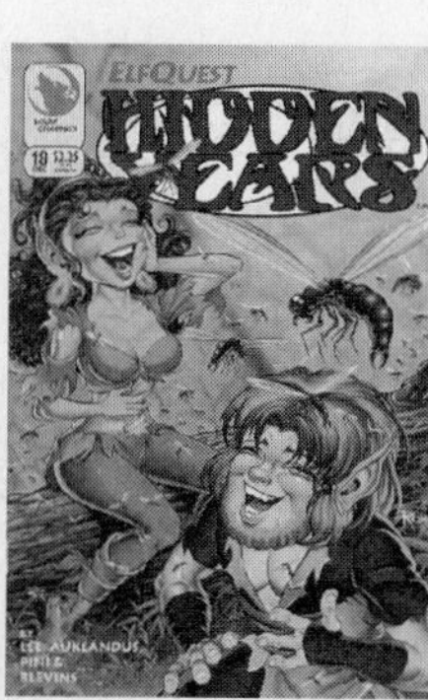

Elfquest: Hidden Years #18 © Warp Graphics

Ellery Queen #1 © Z-D

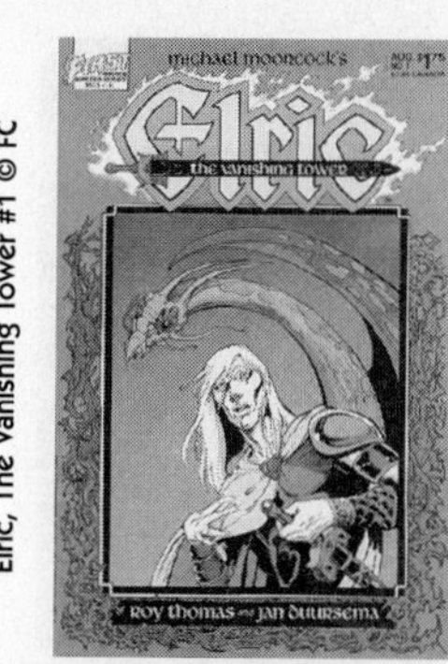

Elric, The Vanishing Tower #1 © FC

	GD 2.0	VG 4.0	FN 6.0	VF 8.0	VF/NM 9.0	NM- 9.2

--HIDDEN YEARS, 5/92 - No. 29, 3/96 ($2.00/$2.25)1-9,9 1/2, 10-29 — 3.00

--JINK, 11/94 - No. 12, 2/6 ($2.25/$2.50) 1-12-W. Pini/John Byrne-back-c — 3.00

--KAHVI, 10/95 - No. 6,3/96 ($2.25, B&W) 1-6 — 3.00

--KINGS CROSS, 11/97 - No. 2, 12/97 ($2.95, B&W) 1,2 — 3.00

--KINGS OF THE BROKEN WHEEL, 6/90 - No. 9, 2/92 ($2.00, B&W) (3rd Elfquest saga) 1-9: By R. & W. Pini; 1-Color insert — 3.00
1-2nd printing — 2.50

--METAMORPHOSIS, 4/96 ($2.95, B&W) 1 — 3.00

--NEW BLOOD (...Summer Special on-c #1 only), 8/92 - No. 35, 1/96 ($2.00-$2.50, color/ B&W) 1-($3.95, 68 pgs.,...Summer Special on-c)-Byrne-a/scripts (16 pgs.) — 4.00
2-35: Barry Blair-a in all — 3.00
1993 Summer Special ($3.95) Byrne-a/scripts — 4.00

--SHARDS, 8/94 - No. 16, 3/96 ($2.25/$2.50) 1-16 — 3.00

--SIEGE AT BLUE MOUNTAIN, WaRP Graphics/Apple 3/87 - No. 8, 12/88 (1.75/ $1.95, B&W) 1-Staton-a(i) in all; 2nd Elfquest saga — 4.00
1-3-2nd printing, 3-8 — 2.50
2 — 3.00

--THE REBELS, 11/94 - No. 12, 3/96 ($2.25/$2.50, B&W/color) 1-12 — 3.00

--TWO-SPEAR, 10/95 - No. 5, 2/96 ($2.25, B&W) 1-5 — 3.00

--WAVE DANCERS, 12/93 - No. 6, 3/96, 1-6: 1-Foil-c & poster — 3.00
Special 1 ($2.95) — 3.00

--WORLDPOOL, 7/97 ($2.95, B&W) 1-Richard Pini-s/Barry Blair-a — 3.00

ELFQUEST: THE GRAND QUEST
DC Comics: 2004 - Present

Volume 1 ('04, $9.95, B&W, digest-size) r/Elfquest #1-5; new W. Pini-c — 10.00

ELFQUEST: WOLFRIDER
DC Comics: 2003 - Present

Volume 1 ('03, $9.95, digest-size) r/Elfquest V2#19,21,23,25,27,29,31; Blood of Ten Chiefs #2; Hidden Years #5; New Blood Special #1; New Blood 1993 Special #1; new W. Pini-c — 10.00
Volume 2 ('03, $9.95, digest-size) r/Elfquest V2#33; Blood of Ten Chiefs #10,11,19; Warp Graphics Annual #1 — 10.00

ELF-THING
Eclipse Comics: March, 1987 ($1.50, B&W, one-shot)

1 — 2.25

ELIMINATOR (Also see The Solution #16 & The Night Man #16)
Malibu Comics (Ultraverse): Apr, 1995 - No. 3, Jul, 1995 ($2.95/$2.50, lim. series)

0-Mike Zeck-a in all — 3.00
1-3-($2.50): 1-1st app. Siren — 2.50
1-($3.95)-Black cover edition — 4.00

ELIMINATOR FULL COLOR SPECIAL
Eternity Comics: Oct, 1991 ($2.95, one-shot)

1-Dave Dorman painted-c — 3.00

ELLA CINDERS (See Comics On Parade, Comics Revue #1,4, Famous Comics Cartoon Book, Giant Comics Editions, Sparkler Comics, Tip Top & Treasury of Comics)

ELLA CINDERS
United Features Syndicate: 1938 - 1940

	GD	VG	FN	VF	VF/NM	NM-
Single Series 3(1938)	41	82	123	246	348	450
Single Series 21(#2 on-c, #21 on inside), 28('40)	36	72	108	204	290	375

ELLA CINDERS
United Features Syndicate: Mar, 1948 - No. 5, Mar, 1949

	GD	VG	FN	VF	VF/NM	NM-
1-(#2 on cover)	14	28	42	79	107	135
2	9	18	27	52	66	80
3-5	7	14	21	37	46	55

ELLERY QUEEN
Superior Comics Ltd.: May, 1949 - No. 4, Nov, 1949

	GD	VG	FN	VF	VF/NM	NM-
1-Kamen-c; L.B. Cole-a; r-in Haunted Thrills	52	104	156	312	469	625
2-4: 3-Drug use stories(2)	40	80	120	240	340	440

NOTE: *Iger shop art in all issues.*

ELLERY QUEEN (TV)
Ziff-Davis Publishing Co.: 1-3/52 (Spring on-c) - No. 2, Summer/52 (Saunders painted-c)

	GD	VG	FN	VF	VF/NM	NM-
1-Saunders-c	46	92	138	276	413	550
2-Saunders bondage, torture-c	40	80	120	240	340	440

ELLERY QUEEN (Also see Crackajack Funnies No. 23)
Dell Publishing Co.: No. 1165, Mar-May, 1961 - No.1289, Apr, 1962

	GD	VG	FN	VF	VF/NM	NM-
Four Color 1165 (#1)	12	24	36	84	125	165
Four Color 1243 (11-1/61-61), 1289	10	20	30	67	96	125

ELMER FUDD (Also see Camp Comics, Daffy, Looney Tunes #1 & Super Book #10, 22)
Dell Publishing Co.: No. 470, May, 1953 - No. 1293, Mar-May, 1962

	GD	VG	FN	VF	VF/NM	NM-
Four Color 470 (#1)	7	14	21	46	63	80
Four Color 558,628,689('56)	4	8	12	29	40	50
Four Color 725,783,841,888,938,977,1032,1081,1131,1171,1222,1293('62)	4	8	12	24	32	40

ELMO COMICS
St. John Publishing Co.: Jan, 1948 (Daily strip-r)

	GD	VG	FN	VF	VF/NM	NM-
1-By Cecil Jensen	10	20	30	56	73	90

ELONGATED MAN (See Flash #112 & Justice League of America #105)
DC Comics: Jan, 1992 - No. 4, Apr, 1992 ($1.00, limited series)

1-4: 3-The Flash app. — 2.25

ELRIC (Of Melnibone)(See First Comics Graphic Novel #6 & Marvel Graphic Novel #2)
Pacific Comics: Apr, 1983 - No. 6, Apr, 1984 ($1.50, Baxter paper)

1-6: Russell-c/a(i) in all — 3.00

ELRIC
Topps Comics: 1996 ($2.95, one-shot)

0--One Life: Russell-c/a; adapts Neil Gaiman's short story "One Life--Furnished in Early Moorcock." — 3.00

ELRIC, SAILOR ON THE SEAS OF FATE
First Comics: June, 1985 - No. 7, June, 1986 ($1.75, limited series)

1-7: Adapts Michael Moorcock's novel — 3.00

ELRIC, STORMBRINGER
Dark Horse Comics/Topps Comics: 1997 - No. 7, 1997($2.95, limited series)

1-7: Russell-c/s/a; adapts Michael Moorcock's novel — 3.00

ELRIC: THE BANE OF THE BLACK SWORD
First Comics: Aug, 1988 - No. 6, June, 1989 ($1.75/$1.95, limited series)

1-6: Adapts Michael Moorcock's novel — 3.00

ELRIC: THE VANISHING TOWER
First Comics: Aug, 1987 - No. 6, June, 1988 ($1.75, limited series)

1-6: Adapts Michael Moorcock's novel — 3.00

ELRIC: WEIRD OF THE WHITE WOLF
First Comics: Oct, 1986 - No. 5, June, 1987 ($1.75, limited series)

1-5: Adapts Michael Moorcock's novel — 3.00

EL SALVADOR - A HOUSE DIVIDED
Eclipse Comics: March, 1989 ($2.50, B&W, Baxter paper, stiff-c, 52 pgs.)

1-Gives history of El Salvador — 2.50

ELSEWHERE PRINCE, THE (Moebius' Airtight Garage)
Marvel Comics (Epic): May, 1990 - No. 6, Oct, 1990 ($1.95, limited series)

1-6: Moebius scripts & back-up-a in all — 3.00

ELSEWORLDS 80-PAGE GIANT
DC Comics: Aug, 1999 ($5.95, one-shot)

1-Most copies destroyed by DC over content of the "Superman's Babysitter" story; some UK shipments sold before recall — 175.00

ELSEWORLD'S FINEST
DC Comics: 1997 - No. 2, 1997 ($4.95, limited series)

1,2: Elseworld's story-Superman & Batman in the 1920's — 5.00

ELSEWORLD'S FINEST: SUPERGIRL & BATGIRL
DC Comics: 1998 ($5.95, one-shot)

1-Haley-a — 6.00

ELSIE THE COW
D. S. Publishing Co.: Oct-Nov, 1949 - No. 3, July-Aug, 1950

	GD	VG	FN	VF	VF/NM	NM-
1-(36 pgs.)	25	50	75	147	202	260
2,3	19	38	57	106	146	185

ELSON'S PRESENTS
DC Comics: 1981 (100 pgs., no cover price)

Series 1-6: Repackaged 1981 DC comics; 1-DC Comics Presents #29, Flash #303, Batman #331. 2-Superman #335, Ghosts #96, Justice League of America #186. 3-New Teen Titans #3, Secrets of Haunted House #32, Wonder Woman #275. 4-Secrets of the LSH #1, Brave & the Bold #170, New Adv. of Superboy #13. 5-LSH #271, Green Lantern #136, Super Friends #40. 6-Action #515, Mystery in Space #115, Detective #498

Elvira's House of Mystery #7 © DC

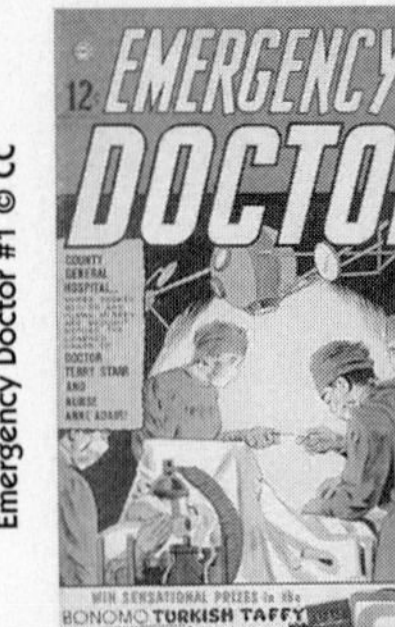

Emergency Doctor #1 © CC

Empire #0 © Mark Waid and Barry Kitson

GD VG FN VF VF/NM NM-
2.0 4.0 6.0 8.0 9.0 9.2

2 4 6 10 13 16

ELVEN (Also see Prime)
Malibu Comics (Ultraverse): Oct, 1994 - No. 4, Feb, 1995 ($2.50, lim. series)
0 ($2.95)-Prime app. 3.00
1-4: 2,4-Prime app. 3-Primevil app. 2.50
1-Limited Foil Edition- no price on cover 3.00

ELVIRA MISTRESS OF THE DARK
Marvel Comics: Oct, 1988 ($2.00, B&W, magazine size)
1-Movie adaptation 5.00

ELVIRA MISTRESS OF THE DARK
Claypool Comics (Eclipse): May, 1993 - Present ($2.50, B&W)
1-Austin-a(i). Spiegle-a 6.00
2-6: Spiegle-a 4.00
7-99,101-121-Photo-c: 2.50
100-(8/01) Kurt Busiek back-up-s; art by DeCarlo and others 2.50
TPB ($12.95) 13.00

ELVIRA'S HOUSE OF MYSTERY
DC Comics: Jan, 1986 - No. 11, Jan, 1987
1,11: 11-Dave Stevens-c 6.00
2-10: 9-Photo-c, Special 1 (3/87, $1.25) 4.00

ELVIS MANDIBLE, THE
DC Comics (Piranha Press): 1990 ($3.50, 52 pgs., B&W, mature)
nn 3.50

ELVIS PRESLEY (See Career Girl Romances #32, Go-Go, Howard Chaykin's American Flagg #10, Humbug #8, I Love You #60 & Young Lovers #18)

E-MAN
Charlton Comics: Oct, 1973 - No. 10, Sept, 1975 (Painted-c No. 7-10)
1-Origin & 1st app. E-Man; Staton c/a in all 3 6 9 16 20 24
2-4: 2,4-Ditko-a. 3-Howard-a 2 4 6 8 10 12
5-Miss Liberty Belle app. by Ditko 1 3 4 6 8 10
6-10: 6,7,9,10-Early Byrne-a (#6 is 1/75). 6-Disney parody. 8-Full-length story; Nova begins as E-Man's partner 2 4 6 10 12 15
1-4,9,10 (Modern Comics reprints, '77) 4.00
NOTE: *Killjoy app.-No. 2, 4. Liberty Belle app.-No. 5. Rog 2000 app.-No. 6, 7, 9, 10. Travis app.-No. 3.* ***Tom Sutton*** *a-1.*

E-MAN
Comico: Sept, 1989 ($2.75, one-shot, no ads, high quality paper)
1-Staton-c/a; Michael Mauser story 2.75

E-MAN
Comico: V4#1, Jan, 1990 - No. 3, Mar, 1990 ($2.50, limited series)
1-3: Staton-c/a 2.50

E-MAN
Alpha Productions: Oct, 1993 ($2.75)
V5#1-Staton-c/a; 20th anniversary issue 2.75

E-MAN COMICS (Also see Michael Mauser & The Original E-Man)
First Comics: Apr, 1983 - No. 25, Aug, 1985 ($1.00/$1.25, direct sales only)
1-25: 2-X-Men satire. 3-X-Men/Phoenix satire. 6-Origin retold. 8-Cutey Bunny app. 10-Origin Nova Kane. 24-Origin Michael Mauser 2.50
NOTE: ***Staton*** *a-1-5, 6-25p; c-1-25.*

E-MAN RETURNS
Alpha Productions: 1994 ($2.75, B&W)
1-Joe Staton-c/a(p) 2.75

EMERALD DAWN
DC Comics: 1991 ($4.95, trade paperback)
nn-Reprints Green Lantern: Emerald Dawn #1-6 5.00

EMERALD DAWN II (See Green Lantern...)

EMERGENCY (Magazine)
Charlton Comics: June, 1976 - No. 4, Jan, 1977 (B&W)
1-Neal Adams-c/a; Heath, Austin-a 4 8 12 22 30 38
2,3: 2-N. Adams-c. 3-N. Adams-a. 3 6 9 19 25 32
4-Alcala-a 3 6 9 16 20 24

EMERGENCY (TV)
Charlton Comics: June, 1976 - No. 4, Dec, 1976
1-Staton-c; early Byrne-a (22 pages) 3 6 9 19 25 32
2-4: 2-Staton-c. 2,3-Byrne text illos. 2 4 6 14 18 22

GD VG FN VF VF/NM NM-
2.0 4.0 6.0 8.0 9.0 9.2

EMERGENCY DOCTOR
Charlton Comics: Summer, 1963 (one-shot)
1 3 7 10 21 28 35

EMIL & THE DETECTIVES (See Movie Comics)

EMMA FROST
Marvel Comics: Aug, 2003 - Present ($2.50)
1-6-Emma in high school; Bollers-s/Green-a/Horn-c 2.50

EMMA PEEL & JOHN STEED (See The Avengers)

EMPEROR'S NEW CLOTHES, THE
Dell Publishing Co.: 1950 (10¢, 68 pgs., 1/2 size, oblong)
nn - (Surprise Books series) 5 10 15 24 30 35

EMPIRE
Image Comics (Gorilla): May, 2000 - No. 2, Sept, 2000 ($2.50)
DC Comics: No. 0, Aug, 2003; Sept, 2003 - No. 6, Feb, 2004 ($4.95/$2.50, limited series)
1,2: 1 (5/00)-Waid-s/Kitson-a; w/Crimson Plague prologue 2.50
0-(8/03) reprints #1,2 5.00
1-6: 1-(9/03) new Waid-s/Kitson-a/c 2.50

EMPIRE STRIKES BACK, THE (See Marvel Comics Super Special #16 & Marvel Special Edition)

EMPTY LOVE STORIES
Slave Labor #1 & 2/Funny Valentine Press: Nov, 1994 - Present ($2.95, B&W)
1,2: Steve Darnall scripts in all. 1-Alex Ross-c. 2-(8/96)-Mike Allred-c 4.00
1,2-2nd printing (Funny Valentine Press) 3.00
... 1999-Jeff Smith-c; Doran-a 3.00
..."Special" (2.95) Ty Templeton-c 3.00

ENCHANTED
Sirius Entertainment: 1997 - No. 3 ($2.50, B&W, limited series)
1-3-Robert Chang-s/a 2.50

ENCHANTED (Volume 2)
Sirius Entertainment: 1998 - No. 3 ($2.95, limited series)
1-Robert Chang-s/a 3.00

ENCHANTED APPLES OF OZ, THE (See First Comics Graphic Novel #5)

ENCHANTER
Eclipse Comics: Apr, 1987 - No. 3, Aug. 1987 ($2.00, B&W, limited series)
1-3 2.25

ENCHANTING LOVE
Kirby Publishing Co.: Oct, 1949 - No. 6, July, 1950 (All 52 pgs.)
1-Photo-c 14 28 42 81 111 140
2-Photo-c; Powell-a 8 16 24 46 58 70
3,4,6: 3-Jimmy Stewart photo-c 8 16 24 43 54 65
5-Ingels-a, 9 pgs.; photo-c 15 30 45 86 118 150

ENCHANTMENT VISUALETTES (Magazine)
World Editions: Dec, 1949 - No. 5, Apr, 1950 (Painted c-1)
1-Contains two romance comic strips each 15 30 45 86 118 150
2 11 22 33 63 84 105
3-5 10 20 30 56 73 90

ENEMY
Dark Horse Comics: May, 1994 - No. 5, Sept, 1994 ($2.50, limited series)
1-5 2.50

ENEMY ACE SPECIAL (Also see Our Army at War #151, Showcase #57, 58 & Star Spangled War Stories #138)
DC Comics: 1990 ($1.00, one-shot)
1-Kubert-r/Our Army #151,153; c-r/Showcase 57 5.00

ENEMY ACE: WAR IDYLL
DC Comics: 1990 (Graphic novel)
Hardcover-George Pratt-s/painted-a/c 30.00
Softcover (1991, $14.95) 15.00

ENEMY ACE: WAR IN HEAVEN
DC Comics: 2001 - No. 2, 2001 ($5.95, squarebound, limited series)
1,2-Ennis-s; Von Hammer in WW2. 1-Weston & Alamy-a. 2-Heath-a 6.00
TPB (2003, $14.95) r/#1,2 & Star Spangled War Stories #139; Jim Dietz-painted-c 15.00

ENIGMA
DC Comics (Vertigo): Mar, 1993 - No. 8, Oct, 1993 ($2.50, limited series)
1-8: Milligan scripts 2.50

Epic Illustrated #17 © MAR

Espers V3#3 © James D. Hudnall

The Establishment #8 © DC

GD 2.0 | VG 4.0 | FN 6.0 | VF 8.0 | VF/NM 9.0 | NM- 9.2

Trade paperback ($19.95)-reprints 20.00

ENO AND PLUM (Also see Cud Comics)
Oni Press: Mar, 1998 ($2.95, B&W)

1-Terry LaBan-s/c/a 3.00

ENSIGN O'TOOLE (TV)
Dell Publishing Co.: Aug-Oct, 1963 - No. 2, 1964

1 3 7 10 21 28 35
2 3 6 9 18 23 28

ENSIGN PULVER (See Movie Classics)

EPIC
Marvel Comics (Epic Comics): 1992 - Book 4, 1992 ($4.95, lim. series, 52 pgs.)

Book One-Four: 2-Dorman painted-c 5.00
NOTE: *Alien Legion in #3. Cholly & Flytrap by* ***Burden****(scripts) &* ***Suydam****(art) in 3, 4. Dinosaurs in #4. Dreadlands in #1. Hellraiser in #1. Nightbreed in #2. Sleeze Brothers in #2. Stalkers in #1-4. Wild Cards in #1-4.*

EPIC ILLUSTRATED (Magazine)
Marvel Comics Group: Spring, 1980 - No. 34, Feb, 1986 ($2.00/$2.50, B&W/color, mature)

1-Frazetta-c; Silver Surfer/Galactus-sty; Wendy Pini-s/a; Suydam-s/a; Metamorphosis Odyssey begins (thru #9) Starlin-a 2 4 6 8 10 12
2-10: 2-Bissette/Veitch-a; Goodwin-s. 3-Goodwin-s. 4-Ellison 15 pg. story w/art by Steacy; Hempel-s/a; Veitch-s/a. 5-Hildebrandts-c/interview; Jusko-a; Vess-s/a. 6-Ellison-s (26 pgs). 7-Adams-s/a(16 pgs.); BWS interview. 8-Suydam-s/a; Vess-s/a. 9-Conrad-c. 10-Marada the She-Wolf-c/sty(21 pgs.) by Claremont/Bolton 1 2 3 4 5 7
11-20: 11-Wood-a; Jusko-a. 12-Wolverton Spacehawk-r edited & recolored w/article on him; Muth-a. 13-Blade Runner preview by Williamson. 14-Elric of Melnibone by Russell; Revenge of the Jedi preview. 15-Vallejo-c & interview; 1st Dreadstar story (cont'd in Dreadstar #1). 16-B. Smith-c/a(2); Sim-s/a. 17-Starslammers preview. 18-Go Nagai; Williams-a. 19-Jabberwocky w/Hampton-a; Cheech Wizard-s. 20-The Sacred & the Profane begins by Ken Steacy; Elric by Gould; Williams-a 1 2 3 5 6 8
21-30: 21-Vess-s/a. 22-Frankenstein w/Wrightson-a. 26-Galactus series begins (thru #34); Cerebus the Aardvark story by Dave Sim. 27-Groo. 28-Cerebus. 29-1st Sheeva. 30-Cerebus; History of Dreadstar, Starlin-s/a; Williams-a; Vess-a 1 3 4 6 8 10
31-33: 31-Bolton-c/a. 32-Cerebus portfolio. 2 4 6 8 10 12
34-R.E.Howard tribute by Thomas-s/Plunkett-a; Moore-s/Veitch-a; Cerebus; Cholly & Flytrap w/Suydam-a; BWS-a 2 4 6 11 14 18
NOTE: ***N. Adams*** *a-7; c-6.* ***Austin*** *a-15-20i.* ***Bode*** *a-19, 23, 27r.* ***Bolton*** *a-7, 10-12, 15, 18, 22-25; c-10, 18, 22, 23.* ***Boris*** *c/a-15.* ***Brunner*** *c-12.* ***Buscema*** *a-1p, 9p, 11-13p.* ***Byrne/Austin*** *a-26-34.* ***Chaykin*** *a-2; c-8.* ***Conrad*** *a-2-5, 7-9, 25-34; c-17.* ***Corben*** *a-15; c-2.* ***Frazetta*** *c-1.* ***Golden*** *a-3r.* ***Gulacy*** *c/a-3.* ***Jeff Jones*** *c-25.* ***Kaluta*** *a-17r, 21, 24r, 26; c-4, 28.* ***Nebres*** *a-1.* ***Reese*** *a-12.* ***Russell*** *a-2-4, 9, 14, 33; c-14.* ***Simonson*** *a-17.* ***B. Smith*** *c/a-7, 16.* ***Starlin*** *a-1-9, 14, 15, 34.* ***Steranko*** *c-19.* ***Williamson*** *a-13, 27, 34.* ***Wrightson*** *a-13p, 22, 25, 27, 34; c-30.*

EPIC LITE
Marvel Comics (Epic Comics): Sept, 1991 ($3.95, 52 pgs., one-shot)

1-Bob the Alien, Normalman by Valentino 4.00

EPICURUS THE SAGE
DC Comics (Piranha Press): Vol. 1, 1991 - Vol. 2, 1991 ($9.95, 8-1/8x10-7/8")

Volume 1,2-Sam Kieth-c/a; Messner-Loebs-s 10.00
TPB (2003, $19.95) r/ #1,2, Fast Forward Rising the Sun; new story 20.00

EPSILON WAVE
Independent Comics/Elite Comics No. 5 on: Oct, 1985 - V2#2, 1987 ($1.50/$1.25/$1.75)

1-8,V2#1,2: 1-3,6-Seadragon app. V2 (B&W) 2.25

ERADICATOR
DC Comics: Aug, 1996 - No. 3, Oct, 1996 ($1.75, limited series)

1-3: Superman app. 3.00

ERNIE COMICS (Formerly Andy Comics #21; All Love Romances #26 on)
Current Books/Ace Periodicals: No. 22, Sept, 1948 - No. 25, Mar, 1949

nn (9/48,11/48; #22,23)-Teenage humor 7 14 21 37 46 55
24,25 5 10 15 27 33 38

ESCAPADE IN FLORENCE (See Movie Comics)

ESCAPE FROM DEVIL'S ISLAND
Avon Periodicals: 1952

1-Kinstler-c; r/as Dynamic Adventures #9 39 78 117 230 325 420

ESCAPE FROM THE PLANET OF THE APES (See Power Record Comics)

ESCAPE TO WITCH MOUNTAIN (See Walt Disney Showcase No. 29)

ESPERS (Also see Interface)
Eclipse Comics: July, 1986 - No. 5, Apr, 1987 ($1.25/$1.75, Mando paper)

1-5-James Hudnall story & David Lloyd-a. 3.00

ESPERS
Halloween Comics: V2#1, 1996 - No. 6, 1997 ($2.95, B&W)
(1st Halloween Comics series)

V2#1-6: James D. Hudnall scripts 3.00
Undertow TPB ('98, $14.95) r/#1-6 15.00

ESPERS
Image Comics: V3#1, 1997 - Present ($2.95, B&W, limited series)

V3#1-7: James D. Hudnall scripts 3.00
Black Magic TPB ('98, $14.95) r/#1-4 15.00

ESPIONAGE (TV)
Dell Publishing Co.: May-July, 1964 - No. 2, Aug-Oct, 1964

1,2 4 8 12 22 30 38

ESSENTIAL (Title series), **Marvel Comics**

--ANT-MAN, '02 (B&W- r) V1-Reprints app. from Tales To Astonish #27, #35-69; Kirby-c 15.00
--AVENGERS, '98 (B&W- r) V1-R-Avengers #1-24; new Immonen-c 15.00
V2(6/00)-Reprints Avengers #25-46, King-Size Special #1; Immonen-c 15.00
V3(3/01)-Reprints Avengers #47-68, Annual #2; Immonen-c 15.00
--CAPTAIN AMERICA, '00 (B&W- r) V1-Reprints stories from Tales of Suspense #59-99, Captain America #100-102; new Romita & Milgrom-c 15.00
V2(1/02)-Reprints #103-126; Steranko-c 15.00
--CONAN, '00 (B&W- r) V1-R-Conan the Barbarian#1-25; new Buscema-c 15.00
--FANTASTIC FOUR, '98 - Present (B&W-r)
V1-Reprints FF #1-20, Annual #1; new Alan Davis-c 15.00
V2-Reprints FF #21-40, Annual #2; Davis and Farmer-c 15.00
V3-Reprints FF #41-63, Annual #3,4; Davis-c 15.00
--HOWARD THE DUCK, '02 (B&W- r) V1-Reprints #1-27, Annual #1; plus stories from Marvel Treasury Ed. #12, Man-Thing #1, Giant-Size Man-Thing #4,5, Fear #19; Bolland-c 15.00
--HULK, '99 (B&W-r) V1-R-Incred. Hulk #1-6, Tales To Astonish stories; new Timm-c 15.00
V2-Reprints Tales To Astonish #102-117, Annual #1 15.00
--HUMAN TORCH, '03 (B&W-r) V1-Strange Tales #101-134 & Ann. 2; Kirby-c 15.00
--IRON MAN, '00 (B&W-r) V1-Tales Of Suspense #39-72; new Timm-c and back-c 15.00
--MARVEL TEAM-UP, '02 (B&W-r) V1-R/#1-24 15.00
--SILVER SURFER, '98 (B&W-r) V1-R-material from SS#1-18 and Fantastic Four Ann. #5 15.00
--SPIDER-MAN, '96 - Present (B&W-r)
V1-R-AF #15, Amaz. S-M #1-20, Ann. #1 (2 printings) 15.00
V2-R-Amaz. Spider-Man #21-43, Annual #2,3 15.00
V3-R-Amaz. Spider-Man #44-68 15.00
V4-R-Amaz. Spider-Man #69-89; Annual #4,5; new Timm-f&b-c 15.00
V5-R-Amaz. Spider-Man #90-113; new Romita-c 15.00
--THOR, '01 (B&W-r) V1-R-Journey Into Mystery #83-112 15.00
--UNCANNY X-MEN, '99 - Present (B&W reprints)
V1-Reprints X-Men (1st series) #1-24; Timm-c 15.00

ESSENTIAL VERTIGO: THE SANDMAN
DC Comics (Vertigo): Aug, 1996 - No. 32, Mar, 1999 ($1.95/$2.25, reprints)

1-13,15-31: Reprints Sandman, 2nd series 3.00
14-($2.95) 3.50
32-($4.50) Reprints Sandman Special #1 4.50

ESSENTIAL VERTIGO: SWAMP THING
DC Comics: Nov, 1996 - No. 24, Oct, 1998 ($1.95/$2.25,B&W, reprints)

1-11,13-24: 1-9-Reprints Alan Moore's Swamp Thing stories 3.00
12-($3.50) r/Annual #2 3.50

ESSENTIAL WOLVERINE
Marvel Comics: 1999 - Present (B&W reprints)

V1-r/#1-23, V2-r/#24-47, V3-R/#48-69 15.00

ESSENTIAL X-MEN
Marvel Comics: 1996 - Present (B&W reprints)

V1, V2-Reprints, V3--R-Uncanny X-Men #145-161, Ann. #3-5 15.00
V4-Uncanny X-Men #162-179, Ann. #6 15.00

ESTABLISHMENT, THE (Also see The Authority and The Monarchy)
DC Comics (WildStorm): Nov, 2001 - No. 13, Nov, 2002 ($2.50)

1-13-Edginton-s/Adlard-a 2.50

ETC
DC Comics (Piranha Press): 1989 - No. 5, 1990 ($4.50, 60 pgs., mature)

The Eternal #1 © MAR

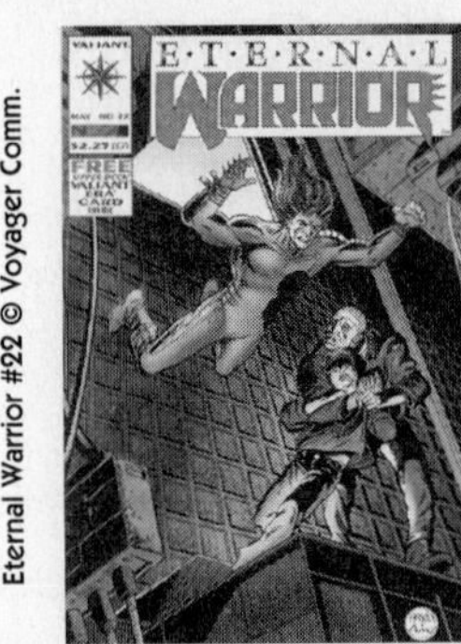

Eternal Warrior #22 © Voyager Comm.

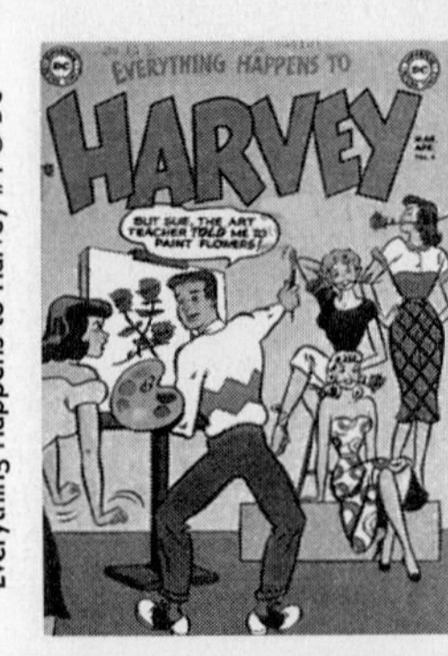

Everything Happens to Harvey #4 © DC

	GD 2.0	VG 4.0	FN 6.0	VF 8.0	VF/NM 9.0	NM- 9.2

Book 1-5: Conrad scripts/layouts in all 4.50

ETERNAL, THE
Marvel Comics (MAX): Aug, 2003 - No. 6, Jan, 2004 ($2.99, mature)
1-6-Austen-s/Walker-a 3.00

ETERNAL BIBLE, THE
Authentic Publications: 1946 (Large size) (16 pgs. in color)
1 15 30 45 86 118 150

ETERNALS, THE
Marvel Comics Group: July, 1976 - No. 19, Jan, 1978
1-(Regular 25¢ edition)-Origin & 1st app. Eternals 2 4 6 12 16 20
1-(30¢-c variant, limited distribution) 3 6 9 18 24 30
2-(Reg. 25¢ edition)-1st app. Ajak & The Celestials 1 2 3 5 7 9
2-(30¢-c variant, limited distribution) 2 4 6 9 11 14
3-19: 14,15-Cosmic powered Hulk-c/story 1 2 3 5 6 8
12-16-(35¢-c variants, limited distribution) 2 4 6 8 10 12
Annual 1(10/77) 1 2 3 5 6 8
NOTE: *Kirby c/a(p) in all.*

ETERNALS, THE
Marvel Comics: Oct, 1985 - No. 12, Sept, 1986 (Maxi-series, mando paper)
1,12 (52 pgs.): 12-Williamson-a(i) 3.00
2-11 2.50

ETERNALS: THE HEROD FACTOR
Marvel Comics: Nov, 1991 ($2.50, 68 pgs.)
1 2.50

ETERNAL WARRIOR (See Solar #10 & 11)
Valiant/Acclaim Comics (Valiant): Aug, 1992 - No. 50, Mar, 1996 ($2.25/$2.50)
1-Unity x-over; Miller-c; origin Eternal Warrior & Aram (Armstrong) 4.00
1-($2.25-c) Gold logo 5.00
1-Gold foil logo on embossed cover; no cover price 6.00
2-8: 2-Unity x-over; Simonson-c. 3-Archer & Armstrong x-over. 4-1st app. Bloodshot (last pg. cameo); see Rai #0 for 1st full app.; Cowan-c. 5-2nd full app. Bloodshot (12/92; see Rai #0). 6,7: 6-2nd app. Master Darque. 8-Flip book w/Archer & Armstrong #8 3.00
9-25,27-34: 9-1st Book of Geomancer. 14-16-Bloodshot app. 18-Doctor Mirage cameo. 19-Doctor Mirage app. 22-W/bound-in trading card. 25-Archer & Armstrong app.; cont'd from A&A #25 2.50
26-($2.75, 44 pgs.)-Flip book w/Archer & Armstrong 2.75
35-50: 35-Double-c; $2.50-c begins. 50-Geomancer app. 2.50
Special 1 (2/96, $2.50)-Wings of Justice; Art Holcomb script 2.50
Yearbook 1 (1993, $3.95), 2(1994, $3.95) 4.00

ETERNAL WARRIORS: BLACKWORKS
Acclaim Comics (Valiant Heroes): Mar, 1998 ($3.50, one-shot)
1 3.50

ETERNAL WARRIORS: DIGITAL ALCHEMY
Acclaim Comics (Valiant Heroes): Vol. 2, Sep, 1997 ($3.95, one-shot, 64 pgs.)
Vol. 2-Holcomb-s/Eaglesham-a(p) 4.00

ETERNAL WARRIORS: FIST AND STEEL
Acclaim Comics (Valiant): May, 1996 - No. 2, June, 1996 ($2.50, lim. series)
1,2: Geomancer app. in both. 1-Indicia reads "June." 2-Bo Hampton-a 2.50

ETERNAL WARRIORS: TIME AND TREACHERY
Acclaim Comics (Valiant Heroes): Vol. 1, Jun, 1997 ($3.95, one-shot, 48 pgs.)
Vol. 1-Reintro Aram, Archer, Ivar the Timewalker, & Gilad the Warmaster; 1st app. Shalla Redburn; Art Holcomb script 4.00

ETERNITY SMITH
Renegade Press: Sept, 1986 - No. 5, May, 1987 ($1.25/$1.50, 36 pgs.)
1-5: 1st app. Eternity Smith. 5-Death of Jasmine 2.25

ETERNITY SMITH
Hero Comics: Sept, 1987 - No. 9, 1988 ($1.95)
V2#1-9: 8-Indigo begins 2.25

ETTA KETT
King Features Syndicate/Standard: No. 11, Dec, 1948 - No. 14, Sept, 1949
11-Teenage 9 18 27 52 66 80
12-14 7 14 21 35 43 50

EUDAEMON, THE (See Dark Horse Presents #72-74)
Dark Horse Comics: Aug, 1993 - No. 3, Nov, 1993 ($2.50, limited series)
1-3: Nelson-a, painted-c & scripts 2.50

EUROPA AND THE PIRATE TWINS
Powder Monkey Productions: Oct, 1996 - No. 2, ($2.50, B&W, limited series)
1,2: Two covers 2.50

EVANGELINE (Also see Primer)
Comico/First Comics V2#1 on/Lodestone Publ.: 1984 - #2, 6/84; V2#1, 5/87 - V2#12, Mar, 1989 (Baxter paper)
1,2, V2#1 (5/87) - 12, Special #1 (1986, $2.00)-Lodestone Publ. 2.25

EVA THE IMP
Red Top Comic/Decker: 1957 - No. 2, Nov, 1957
1,2 5 10 14 20 24 28

E.V.E. PROTOMECHA
Image Comics (Top Cow): Mar, 2000 - No. 6, Sept, 2000 ($2.50)
Preview ($5.95) Flip book w/Soul Saga preview 2 4 6 8 10 12
1-6: 1-Covers by Finch, Madureira, Garza. 2-Turner var-c 3.00
1-Another Universe variant-c 5.00
TPB (5/01, $17.95) r/#1-6 plus cover galley and sketch pages 18.00

EVERQUEST: ... (Based on online role-playing game)
DC Comics (WildStorm): 2002 ($5.95, one-shots)
The Ruins of Kunark - Jim Lee & Dan Norton-a; McQuaid & Lee-s; Lee-c 6.00
Transformations - Philip Tan-a; Devin Grayson-s; Portacio-c 6.00

EVERYBODY'S COMICS (See Fox Giants)

EVERYMAN, THE
Marvel Comics (Epic Comics): Nov, 1991 ($4.50, one-shot, 52 pgs.)
1-Mike Allred-a 1 2 3 4 5 7

EVERYTHING HAPPENS TO HARVEY
National Periodical Publications: Sept-Oct, 1953 - No. 7, Sept-Oct, 1954
1 27 54 81 155 218 280
2 15 30 45 86 118 150
3-7 12 24 36 69 92 115

EVERYTHING'S ARCHIE
Archie Publications: May, 1969 - No. 157, Sept, 1991 (Giant issues No. 1-20)
1-(68 pages) 9 18 27 60 85 110
2-(68 pages) 6 12 18 38 52 65
3-5-(68 pages) 4 8 12 29 40 50
6-13-(68 pages) 3 6 9 19 25 32
14-31-(52 pages) 2 4 6 12 16 20
32 (7/74)-50 (8/76) 1 3 4 6 8 10
51-80 (12/79),100 (4/82) 1 2 3 5 6 8
81-99 6.00
101-120 5.00
121-156: 142,148-Gene Colan-a 4.00
157-Last issue 5.00

EVERYTHING'S DUCKY (Movie)
Dell Publishing Co.: No. 1251, 1961
Four Color 1251 5 10 15 36 48 60

EVIL ERNIE
Eternity Comics: Dec, 1991 - No. 5, 1992 ($2.50, B&W, limited series)
1-1st app. Lady Death by Steven Hughes (12,000 print run); Lady Death app. in all issues 4 8 12 29 40 50
2,3: 2-1st Lady Death-c. 2,3-(7,000 print run) 3 6 9 16 20 25
4-(8,000 print run) 2 4 6 12 16 20
5 2 4 6 10 13 16
Special Edition 1 3 6 9 16 20 25
Youth Gone Wild! ($9.95, trade paperback)-r/#1-5 1 3 4 6 8 10
Youth Gone Wild! Director's Cut ($4.95)-Limited to 15,000, shows the making of the comic 5.00

EVIL ERNIE (Monthly series)
Chaos! Comics: July, 1998 - No. 10, Apr, 1999 ($2.95)
1-10-Pulido & Nutman-s/Brewer-a 3.00
1-($10.00) Premium Ed. 10.00

EVIL ERNIE: BADDEST BATTLES
Chaos! Comics: Jan, 1997 ($1.50, one-shot)
1-Pin-ups, 1-Variant-c 3.00

EVIL ERNIE: DEPRAVED
Chaos! Comics: Jul, 1999 - No. 3, Sept, 1999 ($2.95, limited series)
1-3-Pulido-s/Brewer-a 3.00

Evo #1 © TCOW

Excalibur #116 © DC

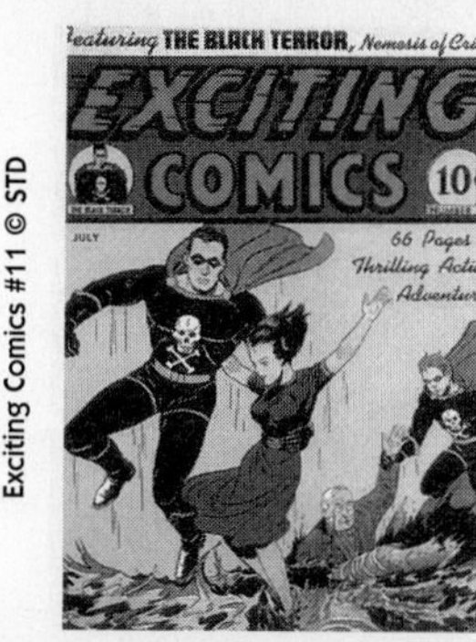

Exciting Comics #11 © STD

	GD 2.0	VG 4.0	FN 6.0	VF 8.0	VF/NM 9.0	NM- 9.2
EVIL ERNIE: DESTROYER						
Chaos! Comics: Oct, 1997 - No. 9, Jun, 1998 ($2.95, limited series)						
Preview ($2.50), 1-9-Flip cover						3.00
EVIL ERNIE: PIECES OF ME						
Chaos! Comics: Nov, 2000 ($2.95, B&W, one-shot)						
1-Flashback story; Pulido-s/Beck-a						3.00
EVIL ERNIE: RELENTLESS						
Chaos! Comics (Black Label Graphics): May, 2002 ($4.99, B&W, one-shot)						
1-Pulido-s/Beck, Bonk, & Brewer-a						5.00
EVIL ERNIE: RETURNS						
Chaos! Comics (Black Label Graphics): Oct, 2001 ($3.99, B&W, one-shot)						
1-Pulido-s/Beck-a						4.00
EVIL ERNIE: REVENGE						
Chaos! Comics: Oct, 1994 - No.4, Feb, 1995 ($2.95, limited series)						
1-Glow-in-the-dark-c; Lady Death app. 1-3-flip book w. Kilzone Preview (series of 3)						5.00
1-Commemorative-(4000 print run)	1	3	4	6	8	10
2-4						4.00
Trade paperback (10/95, $12.95)						13.00
EVIL ERNIE: STRAIGHT TO HELL						
Chaos! Comics: Oct, 1995 - No. 5, May, 1996 ($2.95, limited series)						
1-5: 1-fold-out-c						3.00
1,3:1-($19.95) Chromium Ed. 3-Chastity Chase-c-(4000 printed)						20.00
Special Edition (10,000)						20.00
EVIL ERNIE: THE RESURRECTION						
Chaos! Comics: 1993 - No. 4, 1994 (Limited series)						
0						5.00
1	2	4	6	8	10	12
1A-Gold	3	6	9	18	24	30
2-4	1	2	3	5	6	8
EVIL ERNIE VS. THE MOVIE MONSTERS						
Chaos! Comics: Mar, 1997 ($2.95, one-shot)						
1						3.00
1-Variant-"Chaos-Scope•Terror Vision" card stock-c						5.00
EVIL ERNIE VS. THE SUPER HEROES						
Chaos! Comics: Aug, 1995; Sept, 1998 ($2.95)						
1-Lady Death poster						3.00
1-Foil-c variant (limited to 10,000)	2	4	6	12	16	20
1-Limited Edition (1000)	2	4	6	12	16	20
2-(9/98) Ernie vs. JLA and Marvel parodies						3.00
EVIL ERNIE: WAR OF THE DEAD						
Chaos! Comics: Nov, 1999 - No. 3, Jan, 2000 ($2.95, limited series)						
1-3-Pulido & Kaminski-s/Brewer-a. 3-End of Evil Ernie						3.00
EVIL EYE						
Fantagraphics Books: June, 1998 - Present ($2.95/$3.50/$3.95, B&W)						
1-7-Richard Sala-s/a						3.00
8-10-($3.50)						3.50
11-($3.95)						4.00
EVO (Crossover from Tomb Raider #25 & Witchblade #60)						
Image Comics (Top Cow): Feb, 2003 ($2.99, one-shot)						
1-Silvestri-c/a(p); Endgame x-over pt. 3; Sara Pezzini & Lara Croft app.						3.00
EWOKS (Star Wars) (TV) (See Star Comics Magazine)						
Marvel Comics (Star Comics): June, 1985 - No. 14, Jul, 1987 (75¢/$1.00)						
1,10: 10-Williamson-a (From Star Wars)	2	4	6	10	12	15
2-9	2	4	6	8	10	12
11-14: 14-($1.00-c)	2	4	6	9	11	14
EXCALIBUR (Also see Marvel Comics Presents #31)						
Marvel Comics: Apr, 1988; Oct, 1988 - No. 125, Oct, 1998 ($1.50/$1.75/$1.99)						
Special Edition nn (The Sword is Drawn)(4/88, $3.25)-1st Excalibur comic						6.00
Special Edition nn (4/88)-no price on-c	1	3	4	6	8	10
Special Edition nn (2nd & print, 10/88, 12/89)						3.00
...The Sword is Drawn (Apr, 1992, $4.95)						5.00
1($1.50, 10/88)-X-Men spin-off; Nightcrawler, Shadowcat(Kitty Pryde), Capt. Britain, Phoenix & Meggan begin						5.00
2-4						4.00
5-10						3.00
11-49,51-70,72-74,76: 10,11-Rogers/Austin-a. 21-Intro Crusader X. 22-Iron Man x-over. 24-John Byrne app. in story. 26-Ron Lim-c/a. 27-B. Smith-a(p). 37-Dr. Doom & Iron Man app. 41-X-Men (Wolverine) app.; Cable cameo. 49-Neal Adams c-swipe. 52,57-X-Men (Cyclops, Wolverine) app. 53-Spider-Man-c/story. 58-X-Men (Wolverine, Gambit, Cyclops, etc.)-c/story. 61-Phoenix returns. 68-Starjammers-c/story						2.50
50-($2.75, 56 pgs.)-New logo						3.00
71-($3.95, 52 pgs.)-Hologram on-c; 30th anniversary						5.00
75-($3.50, 52 pgs.)-Holo-grafx foil-c						4.00
75-($2.25, 52 pgs.)-Regular edition						2.50
77-81,83-86: 77-Begin $1.95-c; bound-in trading card sheet. 83-86-Deluxe Editions and Standard Editions. 86-1st app. Pete Wisdom						2.50
82-($2.50)-Newsstand edition						3.00
82-($3.50)-Enhanced edition						4.00
87-89,91-99,101-110: 87-Return from Age of Apocalypse. 92-Colossus-c/app. 94-Days of Future Tense 95-X-Man-c/app. 96-Sebastian Shaw & the Hellfire Club app. 99-Onslaught app. 101-Onslaught tie-in. 102-w/card insert. 103-Last Warren Ellis scripts; Belasco app. 104,105-Hitch & Neary-c/a. 109-Spiral-c/app.						2.50
90,100-($2.95)-double-sized. 100-Onslaught tie-in; wraparound-c						4.00
111-124: 111-Begin $1.99-c, wraparound-c. 119-Calafiore-a						2.50
125-($2.99) Wedding of Capt. Britain and Meggan						4.00
Annual 1,2 ('93, '94, 68 pgs.)-1st app. Khaos. 2-X-Men & Psylocke app.						3.00
#(-1) Flashback (7/97)						2.50
...Air Apparent nn (12/91, $4.95)-Simonson-c						5.00
...Mojo Mayhem nn (12/89, $4.50)-Art Adams/Austin-c/a						5.00
...: The Possession nn (7/91, $2.95, 52 pgs.)						3.00
...: XX Crossing (7/92, 5/92-inside, $2.50)-vs. The X-Men						2.50
EXCALIBUR						
Marvel Comics: Feb, 2001 - No. 4, May, 2001 ($2.99)						
1-4-Return of Captain Britain; Raimondi-a						3.00
EXCITING COMICS						
Nedor/Better Publications/Standard Comics: Apr, 1940 - No. 69, Sept, 1949						
1-Origin & 1st app. The Mask, Jim Hatfield, Sgt. Bill King, Dan Williams begin; early Robot-c (see Smash #1)	385	770	1155	2503	3852	5200
2-The Sphinx begins; The Masked Rider app.; Son of the Gods begins, ends #8	166	332	498	1038	1557	2075
3-Robot-c	112	224	336	700	1050	1400
4-6	74	148	222	463	694	925
7,8	59	118	177	369	555	740
9-Origin/1st app. of The Black Terror & sidekick Tim, begin series (5/41) (Black Terror c-9-21,23-52,54,55)	897	1794	2691	6279	9640	13,000
10-2nd app. Black Terror	278	556	834	1738	2608	3475
11	140	280	420	875	1313	1750
12,13	91	182	273	569	855	1140
14-Last Sphinx, Dan Williams	63	126	189	394	592	790
15-The Liberator begins (origin)	65	130	195	406	613	820
16-20: 20-The Mask ends	55	110	165	330	495	660
21,23-25: 25-Robot-c	46	92	138	276	413	550
22-Origin The Eaglet; The American Eagle begins	55	110	165	330	495	660
26-Schomburg-c begin	62	124	186	388	582	775
27,29,30	58	116	174	363	542	720
28-(Scarce) Crime Crusader begins, ends #58	88	176	264	550	825	1100
31-38: 35-Liberator ends, not in 31-33	52	104	156	312	469	625
39-Origin Kara, Jungle Princess	63	126	189	394	592	790
40-50: 42-The Scarab begins. 45-Schomburg Robot-c. 49-Last Kara, Jungle Princess. 50-Last American Eagle	57	114	171	356	538	720
51-Miss Masque begins (1st app.)	61	122	183	381	573	765
52-54: Miss Masque ends. 53-Miss Masque-c	55	110	165	330	495	660
55-58: 55-Judy of the Jungle begins (origin), ends #60; 1 pg. Ingels-a; Judy of the Jungle c-56-66. 57,58-Airbrush-c	55	110	165	330	495	660
59-Frazetta art in Caniff style; signed Frank Frazeta (one t), 9 pgs.	55	110	165	340	510	680
60-66: 60-Rick Howard, the Mystery Rider begins. 66-Robinson/Meskin-a	50	100	150	300	450	600
67-69-All western covers	22	44	66	124	172	220

NOTE: ***Schomburg (Xela)*** *c-26-68; airbrush c-57-66. Black Terror by* ***R. Moreira****-#65.* ***Roussos*** *a-62. Bondage-c 9, 12, 13, 20, 23, 25, 30, 59.*

	GD 2.0	VG 4.0	FN 6.0	VF 8.0	VF/NM 9.0	NM- 9.2
EXCITING ROMANCES						
Fawcett Publications: 1949 (nd); No. 2, Spring, 1950 - No. 5, 10/50; No. 6 (1951, nd); No. 7, 9/51 -No. 12, 1/53						
1,3: 1(1949). 3-Wood-a	14	28	42	79	107	135
2,4,5-(1950)	9	18	27	52	66	80
6-12	8	16	24	43	54	65

NOTE: ***Powell*** *a-8-10.* ***Marcus Swayze*** *a-5, 6, 9. Photo c-1-7, 10-12.*

Exiles #28 © MAR

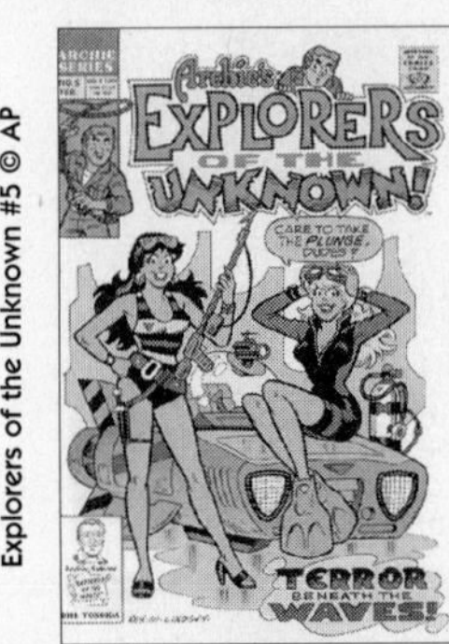

Explorers of the Unknown #5 © AP

Extreme Justice #10 © DC

	GD	VG	FN	VF	VF/NM	NM-
	2.0	4.0	6.0	8.0	9.0	9.2

EXCITING ROMANCE STORIES (See Fox Giants)

EXCITING WAR (Korean War)
Standard Comics (Better Publ.): No. 5, Sept, 1952 - No. 8, May, 1953; No. 9, Nov, 1953

5	9	18	27	52	66	80
6,7,9	6	12	18	33	41	48
8-Toth-a	8	16	24	43	54	65

EXCITING X-PATROL
Marvel Comics (Amalgam): June, 1997 ($1.95, one-shot)

1-Barbara Kesel-s/ Bryan Hitch-a 2.50

EXILES (Also see Break-Thru)
Malibu Comics (Ultraverse): Aug, 1993 - No. 4, Nov, 1993 ($1.95)

1,2,4: 1,2-Bagged copies of each exist. 2-Gustovich-c. 4-Team dies; story cont'd in Break-Thru #1 2.25
3-($2.50, 40 pgs.)-Rune flip-c/story by B. Smith (3 pgs.) 2.50
1-Holographic-c edition 1 2 3 5 6 8

EXILES (All New, The) (2nd Series) (Also see Black September)
Malibu Comics (Ultraverse): Sept, 1995 - V2#11, Aug, 1996 ($1.50)

Infinity (9/95, $1.50)-Intro new team including Marvel's Juggernaut & Reaper 2.25
Infinity (2000 signed), V2#1 (2000 signed) 1 3 4 6 8 10
V2#1-4,6-11: 1-(10/95, 64 pgs.)-Reprint of Ultraforce V2#1 follows lead story. 2-1st app. Hellblade. 8-Intro Maxis. 11-Vs. Maxis; Ripfire app.; cont'd in Ultraforce #12 2.25
V2#5-($2.50) Juggernaut returns to the Marvel Universe. 2.50

EXILES (Also see X-Men titles)
Marvel Comics: Aug, 2001 - Present ($2.99/$2.25)

1-($2.99) Blink and parallel world X-Men; Winick-s/McKone & McKenna-a 1 2 3 4 5 7
2-10-($2.25) 2-Two covers (McKone & JH Williams III). 5-Alpha Flight app. 3.00
11-24: 22-Blink leaves; Magik joins. 23,24-Walker-a; alternate Weapon-X app. 2.25
25-40: 25-Begin $2.99-c; Inhumans app.; Walker-a. 26-30-Austen-s. 33-Wolverine app. 35-37-Fantastic Four app. 37-Sunfire dies, Blink returns. 38-40-Hyperion app. 3.00
TPB (3/02, $12.95) r/#1-4 13.00
...: A World Apart TPB (7/02, $14.99) r/#5-11 15.00
...: Vol. 3: Out of Time TPB (2003, $17.99) r/#12-19 18.00
...: Vol. 4: Legacy TPB (2003, $12.99) r/#20-25 13.00

EXILES VS. THE X-MEN
Malibu Comics (Ultraverse): Oct, 1995 (one-shot)

0-Limited Super Premium Edition; signed w/certificate; gold foil logo,
0-Limited Premium Edition 1 3 4 6 8 10

EX-MUTANTS
Malibu Comics: Nov, 1992 - No. 18, Apr, 1994 ($1.95/$2.25/$2.50)

1-18: 1-Polybagged w/Skycap; prismatic cover 2.50

EXORCISTS (See The Crusaders)

EXOSQUAD (TV)
Topps Comics: No. 0, Jan, 1994 ($1.25)

0-($1.00, 20 pgs.)-1st app.; Staton-a(p); wraparound-c 2.25

EXOTIC ROMANCES (Formerly True War Romances)
Quality Comics Group (Comic Magazines): No. 22, Oct, 1955-No. 31, Nov, 1956

22	10	20	30	60	80	100
23-26,29	7	14	21	35	43	50
27,31-Baker-c/a	14	28	42	79	107	135
28,30-Baker-a	11	22	33	63	84	105

EXPLOITS OF DANIEL BOONE
Quality Comics Group: Nov, 1955 - No. 6, Oct, 1956

1-All have Cuidera-c(i)	28	56	84	161	228	295
2	19	38	57	106	146	185
3-6	16	32	48	92	126	160

EXPLOITS OF DICK TRACY (See Dick Tracy)

EXPLORER JOE
Ziff-Davis Comic Group (Approved Comics): Win, 1951 - No. 2, Oct-Nov, 1952

1-2: Saunders painted covers; 2-Krigstein-a 14 28 42 79 107 135

EXPLORERS OF THE UNKNOWN (See Archie Giant Series #587, 599)
Archie Comics: June, 1990 - No. 6, Apr, 1991 ($1.00)

1-6: Featuring Archie and the gang 3.00

EXPOSED (...True Crime Cases; ...Cases in the Crusade Against Crime #5-9)
D. S. Publishing Co.: Mar-Apr, 1948 - No. 9, July-Aug, 1949

1	24	48	72	135	190	245
2-Giggling killer story with excessive blood; two injury-to-eye panels; electrocution panel	29	58	87	164	232	300
3,8,9	12	24	36	69	92	115
4-Orlando-a	13	26	39	74	100	125
5-Breeze Lawson, Sky Sheriff by E. Good	13	26	39	74	100	125
6,7: 6-Ingels-a; used in **SOTI**, illo. "How to prepare an alibi" 7-Illo. in **SOTI**, "Diagram for housebreakers;" used by N.Y. Legis. Committee	37	74	111	212	301	390

EXPOSURE
Image Comics: 1999 - No. 4, 2000 ($2.50)

1-4: Al Rio-a/David Campiti-s. 1-Wraparound & photo covers 2.50
1-Variant-c 10.00
Prelude ($5.00) 5.00

EXPOSURE SECOND COMING
Avatar Press: Sept, 2000 ($3.50)

1-Al Rio-a/David Campiti-s; wraparound & photo covers 3.50

EXTINCT!
New England Comics Press: Wint, 1991-92 - No. 2, Fall, 1992 ($3.50, B&W)

1,2-Reprints and background info of "perfectly awful" Golden Age stories 3.50

EXTINCTION EVENT
DC Comics (WildStorm): Sept, 2003 - No. 5, Jan, 2004 ($2.50, limited series)

1-5-Booth-a/Weinberg-s 2.50

EXTRA!
E. C. Comics: Mar-Apr, 1955 - No. 5, Nov-Dec, 1955

1-Not code approved	19	38	57	143	207	270
2-5	12	24	36	90	133	175

NOTE: *Craig, Crandall, Severin art in all.*

EXTRA!
Gemstone Publishing: Jan, 2000 - No. 5, May, 2000 ($2.50)

1-5-Reprints E.C. series 2.50

EXTRA COMICS
Magazine Enterprises: 1948 (25¢, 3 comics in one)

1-Giant; consisting of rebound ME comics. Two versions known; (1)-Funnyman by Siegel & Shuster, Space Ace, Undercover Girl, Red Fox by L.B. Cole, Trail Colt & (2)-All Funnyman 55 110 165 330 495 660

EXTREME
Image Comics (Extreme Studios): Aug, 1993 (Giveaway)

0 3.00

EXTREME DESTROYER
Image Comics (Extreme Studios): Jan, 1996 ($2.50)

Prologue 1-Polybagged w/card; Liefeld-c, Epilogue 1-Liefeld-c 2.50

EXTREME JUSTICE
DC Comics: No. 0, Jan, 1995 - No. 18, July, 1996 ($1.50/$1.75)

0-18 3.00

EXTREMELY YOUNGBLOOD
Image Comics (Extreme Studios): Sept, 1996 ($3.50, one-shot)

1 3.50

EXTREME SACRIFICE
Image Comics (Extreme Studios): Jan, 1995 ($2.50, limited series)

Prelude (#1)-Liefeld wraparound-c; polybagged w/ trading card 2.50
Epilogue (#2)-Liefeld wraparound-c; polybagged w/trading card 2.50
Trade paperback (6/95, $16.95)-Platt-a 17.00

EXTREME SUPER CHRISTMAS SPECIAL
Image Comics (Extreme Studios): Dec, 1994 ($2.95, one-shot)

1 3.00

EXTREMIST, THE
DC Comics (Vertigo): Sept, 1993 - No. 4, Dec, 1993 ($1.95, limited series)

1-4-Peter Milligan scripts; McKeever-c/a 2.25
1-Platinum Edition 5.00

EYE OF THE STORM
Rival Productions: Dec, 1994 - No. 7, June, 1995? ($2.95)

1-7: Computer generated comic 3.00

EYE OF THE STORM
DC Comics (WildStorm): Sept, 2003 ($4.95)

Fables #6 Special Edition © Bill Willingham & DC

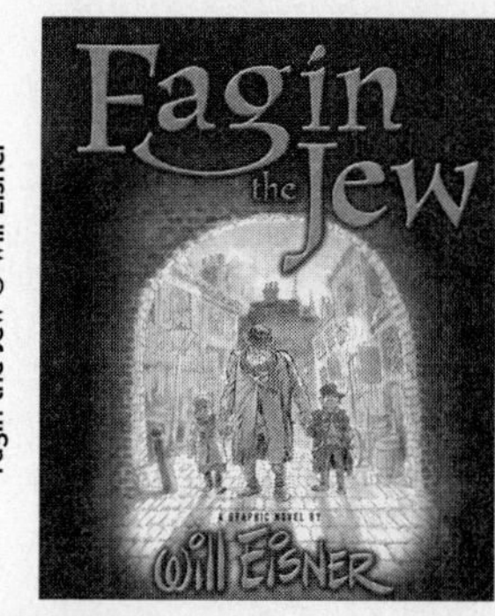

Fagin the Jew © Will Eisner

	GD 2.0	VG 4.0	FN 6.0	VF 8.0	VF/NM 9.0	NM- 9.2
Annual 1-Short stories by various incl. Portacio, Johns, Coker, Pearson, Arcudi						5.00

FABLES
DC Comics (Vertigo): July, 2002 - Present ($2.50)

	GD 2.0	VG 4.0	FN 6.0	VF 8.0	VF/NM 9.0	NM- 9.2
1-Willingham-s/Medina-a; two covers by Maleev & Jean						8.00
2-Medina-a						5.00
3-5						4.00
6-21: 6-10-Buckingham-a. 11-Talbot-a. 18-Medley-a						2.50
6-Special Edition wraparound variant-c; promotional giveaway for retailers (200 printed)						50.00
Animal Farm (2003, $12.95, TPB) r/#6-10; sketch pages by Buckingham & Jean						13.00
Legends in Exile (2002, $9.95, TPB) r/#1-5; new short story Willingham-s/a						10.00
...: The Last Castle (2003, $5.95) Hamilton-a/Willingham-s; prequel to title						6.00

FACE
DC Comics (Vertigo): Jan, 1995 ($4.95, one-shot)

	GD 2.0	VG 4.0	FN 6.0	VF 8.0	VF/NM 9.0	NM- 9.2
1						5.00

FACE, THE (Tony Trent, the Face No. 3 on) (See Big Shot Comics)
Columbia Comics Group: 1941 - No. 2, 1943

	GD 2.0	VG 4.0	FN 6.0	VF 8.0	VF/NM 9.0	NM- 9.2
1-The Face; Mart Bailey-c	88	176	264	550	825	1100
2-Bailey-c	52	104	156	312	469	625

FACTION PARADOX
Image Comics: Aug, 2003 - Present ($2.95)

	GD 2.0	VG 4.0	FN 6.0	VF 8.0	VF/NM 9.0	NM- 9.2
1,2-Calafiore-a						3.00

FACTOR X
Marvel Comics: Mar, 1995 - No. 4, July, 1995 ($1.95, limited series)

	GD 2.0	VG 4.0	FN 6.0	VF 8.0	VF/NM 9.0	NM- 9.2
1-Age of Apocalypse						3.00
2-4						2.50

FACULTY FUNNIES
Archie Comics: June, 1989 - No. 5, May, 1990 (75¢/95¢ #2 on)

	GD 2.0	VG 4.0	FN 6.0	VF 8.0	VF/NM 9.0	NM- 9.2
1-5: 1,2-The Awesome Four app.						3.00

FAFHRD AND THE GREY MOUSER (Also see Sword of Sorcery & Wonder Woman #202)
Marvel Comics: Oct, 1990 - No. 4, 1991 ($4.50, 52 pgs., squarebound)

	GD 2.0	VG 4.0	FN 6.0	VF 8.0	VF/NM 9.0	NM- 9.2
1-4: Mignola/Williamson-a; Chaykin scripts						4.50

FAGIN THE JAW
Doubleday: Oct, 2003 ($15.95, softcover graphic novel)

	GD 2.0	VG 4.0	FN 6.0	VF 8.0	VF/NM 9.0	NM- 9.2
nn-Will Eisner-s/a; story of Fagin from Dickens' Oliver Twist						16.00

FAIRY TALE PARADE (See Famous Fairy Tales)
Dell Publishing Co.: June-July, 1942 - No. 121, Oct, 1946 (Most by Walt Kelly)

	GD 2.0	VG 4.0	FN 6.0	VF 8.0	VF/NM 9.0	NM- 9.2
1-Kelly-a begins	123	246	369	876	1326	1775
2(8-9/42)	50	100	150	376	551	725
3-5 (10-11/42 - 2-4/43)	35	70	105	263	392	520
6-9 (5-7/43 - 11-1/43-44)	28	56	84	203	297	390
Four Color 50('44),69('45), 87('45)	26	52	78	189	277	365
Four Color 104,114('46)-Last Kelly issue	20	40	60	140	205	270
Four Color 121('46)-Not by Kelly	12	24	36	87	129	170

NOTE: *#1-9, 4-Color #50, 69 have **Kelly** c/a; 4-Color #87, 104, 114-**Kelly** art only. #9 has a redrawn version of The Reluctant Dragon. This series contains all the classic fairy tales from Jack In The Beanstalk to Cinderella.*

FAIRY TALES
Ziff-Davis Publ. Co. (Approved Comics): No. 10, Apr-May, 1951 - No. 11, June-July, 1951

	GD 2.0	VG 4.0	FN 6.0	VF 8.0	VF/NM 9.0	NM- 9.2
10,11-Painted-c	20	40	60	112	156	200

FAITH
DC Comics (Vertigo): Nov, 1999 - No. 5, Mar, 2000 ($2.50, limited series)

	GD 2.0	VG 4.0	FN 6.0	VF 8.0	VF/NM 9.0	NM- 9.2
1-5-Ted McKeever-s/c/a						2.50

FAITHFUL
Marvel Comics/Lovers' Magazine: Nov, 1949 - No. 2, Feb, 1950 (52 pgs.)

	GD 2.0	VG 4.0	FN 6.0	VF 8.0	VF/NM 9.0	NM- 9.2
1,2-Photo-c	10	20	30	56	73	90

FALCON (See Marvel Premiere #49, Avengers #181 & Captain America #117 & 133)
Marvel Comics Group: Nov, 1983 - No. 4, Feb, 1984 (Mini-series)

	GD 2.0	VG 4.0	FN 6.0	VF 8.0	VF/NM 9.0	NM- 9.2
1-4: 1-Paul Smith-c/a(p). 2-Paul Smith-c/Mark Bright-a. 3-Kupperberg-c						3.00

FALLEN ANGEL
DC Comics: Sept, 2003 - Present ($2.50)

	GD 2.0	VG 4.0	FN 6.0	VF 8.0	VF/NM 9.0	NM- 9.2
1-7-Peter David-s/David Lopez-a/Stelfreeze-c; intro. Lee						2.50

FALLEN ANGEL ON THE WORLD OF MAGIC: THE GATHERING
Acclaim (Armada): May, 1996 ($5.95, one-shot)

	GD 2.0	VG 4.0	FN 6.0	VF 8.0	VF/NM 9.0	NM- 9.2
1-Nancy Collins story						6.00

FALLEN ANGELS
Marvel Comics Group: April, 1987 - No. 8, Nov, 1987 (Limited series)

	GD 2.0	VG 4.0	FN 6.0	VF 8.0	VF/NM 9.0	NM- 9.2
1-8						2.50

FALLING IN LOVE
Arleigh Pub. Co./National Per. Pub.: Sept-Oct, 1955 - No. 143, Oct-Nov, 1973

	GD 2.0	VG 4.0	FN 6.0	VF 8.0	VF/NM 9.0	NM- 9.2
1	39	78	117	230	325	420
2	21	42	63	118	164	210
3-10	12	24	36	71	96	120
11-20	10	20	30	58	77	95
21-40	8	16	24	43	54	65
41-47: 47-Last 10¢ issue?	7	14	21	35	43	50
48-70	3	7	10	21	28	35
71-99,108: 108-Wood-a (4 pgs., 7/69)	3	6	9	16	20	25
100	4	8	12	24	32	40
101-107,109-124	2	4	6	12	16	20
134-143	2	4	6	10	13	16
125-133: 52 pgs.	3	6	9	19	25	32

NOTE: ***Colan** c/a-75, 81. 52 pgs.-#125-133.*

FALLING MAN, THE
Image Comics: Feb, 1998 ($2.95)

	GD 2.0	VG 4.0	FN 6.0	VF 8.0	VF/NM 9.0	NM- 9.2
1-McCorkindale-s/Hester-a						3.00

FALL OF THE HOUSE OF USHER, THE (See A Corben Special & Spirit section 8/22/48)

FALL OF THE ROMAN EMPIRE (See Movie Comics)

FAMILY AFFAIR (TV)
Gold Key: Feb, 1970 - No. 4, Oct, 1970 (25¢)

	GD 2.0	VG 4.0	FN 6.0	VF 8.0	VF/NM 9.0	NM- 9.2
1-With pull-out poster; photo-c	7	14	21	46	63	80
1-With poster missing	3	6	9	19	25	32
2-4: 3,4-Photo-c	4	8	12	24	32	40

FAMILY FUNNIES
Parents' Magazine Institute: No. 9, Aug-Sept, 1946

	GD 2.0	VG 4.0	FN 6.0	VF 8.0	VF/NM 9.0	NM- 9.2
9	5	10	15	24	30	35

FAMILY FUNNIES (Tiny Tot Funnies No. 9)
Harvey Publications: Sept, 1950 - No. 8, Apr, 1951

	GD 2.0	VG 4.0	FN 6.0	VF 8.0	VF/NM 9.0	NM- 9.2
1-Mandrake (has over 30 King Feature strips)	10	20	30	58	77	95
2-Flash Gordon, 1 pg.	7	14	21	37	46	55
3-8: 4,5,7-Flash Gordon, 1 pg.	6	12	18	31	38	45

FAMILY MAN
DC Comics (Paradox Press): 1995 - No. 3, 1995 ($4.95, B&W, digest-size, limited series)

	GD 2.0	VG 4.0	FN 6.0	VF 8.0	VF/NM 9.0	NM- 9.2
1-3						5.00

FAMILY MATTER
Kitchen Sink Press: 1998 ($24.95/$15.95, graphic novel)

	GD 2.0	VG 4.0	FN 6.0	VF 8.0	VF/NM 9.0	NM- 9.2
Hardcover ($24.95) Will Eisner-s/a						25.00
Softcover ($15.95)						16.00

FAMOUS AUTHORS ILLUSTRATED (See Stories by...)

FAMOUS CRIMES
Fox Features Syndicate/M.S. Dist. No. 51,52: June, 1948 - No. 19, Sept, 1950; No. 20, Aug, 1951; No. 51, 52, 1953

	GD 2.0	VG 4.0	FN 6.0	VF 8.0	VF/NM 9.0	NM- 9.2
1-Blue Beetle app. & crime story-r/Phantom Lady #16	50	100	150	300	450	600
2-Has woman dissolved in acid; lingerie-c/panels	40	80	120	240	340	440
3-Injury-to-eye story used in **SOTI**, pg. 112; has two electrocution stories	48	96	144	288	432	575
4-6	24	48	72	135	190	245
7- "Tarzan, the Wyoming Killer" used in **SOTI**, pg. 44; drug trial/ possession story	40	80	120	240	340	440
8-20: 17-Morisi-a. 20-Same cover as #15	18	36	54	101	138	175
51 (nd, 1953)	16	32	48	92	126	160
52 (Exist?)	10	20	30	60	80	100

FAMOUS FEATURE STORIES
Dell Publishing Co.: 1938 (7-1/2x11", 68 pgs.)

	GD 2.0	VG 4.0	FN 6.0	VF 8.0	VF/NM 9.0	NM- 9.2
1-Tarzan, Terry & the Pirates, King of the Royal Mtd., Buck Jones, Dick Tracy, Smilin' Jack, Dan Dunn, Don Winslow, G-Man, Tailspin Tommy, Mutt & Jeff, Little Orphan Annie reprints - all illustrated text	75	140	210	455	648	840

FAMOUS FIRST EDITION (See Limited Collectors' Edition)
National Periodical Publications/DC Comics: ($1.00, 10x13-1/2", 72 pgs.) (No.6-8, 68 pgs.) 1974 - No. 8, Aug-Sept, 1975; C-61, 1979
(Hardbound editions with dust jackets are from Lyle Stuart, Inc.)

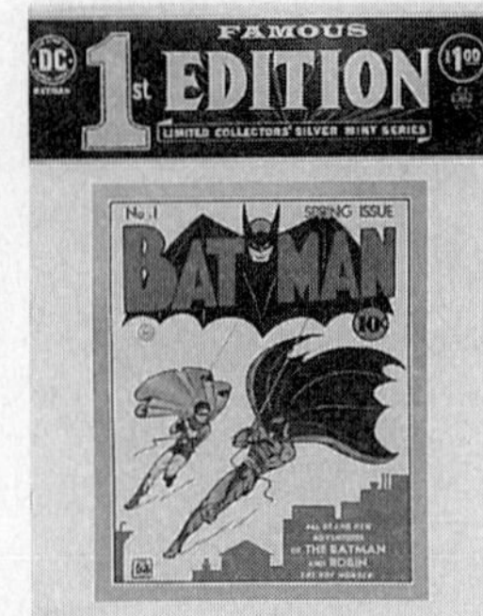

Famous First Edition F-5 © DC

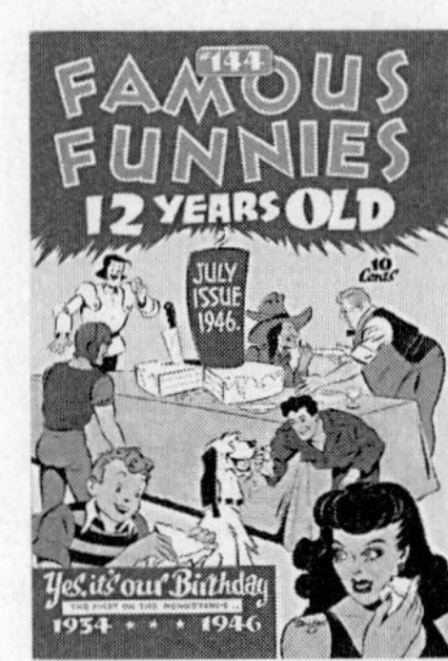

Famous Funnies #144 © EAS

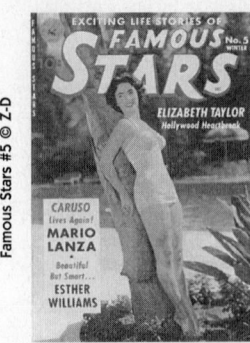

Famous Stars #5 © Z-D

	GD 2.0	VG 4.0	FN 6.0	VF 8.0	VF/NM 9.0	NM- 9.2
C-26-Action Comics #1; gold ink outer-c	4	8	12	29	40	50
C-26-Hardbound edition w/dust jacket	17	34	51	118	174	230
C-28-Detective #27; silver ink outer-c	6	12	18	43	59	75
C-28-Hardbound edition w/dust jacket	22	44	66	156	228	300
C-30-Sensation #1(1974); bronze ink outer-c	4	8	12	29	40	50
C-30-Hardbound edition w/dust jacket	17	34	51	118	174	230
F-4-Whiz Comics #2(#1)(10-11/74)-Cover not identical to original (dropped "Gangway for Captain Marvel" from cover); gold ink on outer-c	4	8	12	29	40	50
F-4-Hardbound edition w/dust jacket	17	34	51	118	174	230
F-5-Batman #1(F-6 inside); silver ink on outer-c	6	12	18	38	52	65
F-5-Hardbound edition w/dust jacket	17	34	51	118	174	230
V2#F-6-Wonder Woman #1	4	8	12	29	40	50
F-6-Wonder Woman #1 Hardbound w/dust jacket	17	34	51	118	174	230
F-7-All-Star Comics #3	4	8	12	29	40	50
F-8-Flash Comics #1(8-9/75)	4	8	12	29	40	50
V8#C-61-Superman #1(1979, $2.00)	4	8	12	24	32	40

Warning: The above books are almost **exact** reprints of the originals that they represent except for the Giant-Size format. None of the originals are Giant-Size. The first five issues and C-61 were printed with two covers. Reprint information can be found on the outside cover, but not on the inside cover which was reprinted exactly like the original (inside and out).

FAMOUS FUNNIES
Eastern Color: 1934; July, 1934 - No. 218, July, 1955

A Carnival of Comics (See Promotional Comics section)

Series 1-(Very rare)(nd-early 1934)(68 pgs.) No publisher given (Eastern Color PrintingCo.); sold in chain stores for 10¢. 35,000 print run. Contains Sunday strip reprints of Mutt & Jeff, Reg'lar Fellers, Nipper, Hairbreadth Harry, Strange As It Seems, Joe Palooka, Dixie Dugan, The Nebbs, Keeping Up With the Jones, and others. Inside front and back covers and pages 1-16 of Famous Funnies Series 1, #s 49-64 reprinted from **Famous Funnies, A Carnival of Comics**, and most of pages 17-48 reprinted from **Funnies on Parade**. This was the first comic book sold.

	GD	VG	FN	VF	VF/NM	NM-
	4000	8000	12,000	27,000	-	-

No. 1 (Rare)(7/34-on stands 5/34) - Eastern Color Printing Co. First monthly newsstand comic book. Contains Sunday strip reprints of Toonerville Folks, Mutt & Jeff, Hairbreadth Harry, S'Matter Pop, Nipper, Dixie Dugan, The Bungle Family, Connie, Ben Webster, Tailspin Tommy, The Nebbs, Joe Palooka, & others.

	GD	VG	FN	VF	VF/NM	NM-
	3000	6000	9000	20,000	-	-
2 (Rare, 9/34)	543	1086	2815	4000	-	-
3-Buck Rogers Sunday strip-r by Rick Yager begins, ends #218; not in #191-208; 1st comic book app. of Buck Rogers; the number of the 1st strip reprinted is pg. 190, Series No. 1	714	1428	3671	5200	-	-
4	229	458	1174	1660	-	-
5-1st Christmas-c on a newsstand comic	214	428	1101	1560	-	-
6-10	143	286	740	1050	-	-
11,12,18-Four pgs. of Buck Rogers in each issue, completes stories in Buck Rogers #1 which lacks these pages. 18-Two pgs. of Buck Rogers reprinted in Daisy Comics #1	100	200	300	600	825	1050
13-17,19,20: 14-Has two Buck Rogers panels missing. 17-2nd Christmas-c on a newsstand comic (12/35)	77	154	231	462	636	810
21,23-30: 27-(10/36)-War on Crime begins (4 pgs.); 1st true crime in comics (reprints); part photo-c. 29-X-Mas-c (12/36)	57	114	171	342	471	600
22-Four pgs. of Buck Rogers needed to complete stories in Buck Rogers #1	60	120	180	360	495	630
31,33,34,36,37,39,40: 33-Careers of Baby Face Nelson & John Dillinger traced	40	80	120	240	330	420
32-(3/37) 1st app. the Phantom Magician (costume hero) in Advs. of Patsy	44	88	132	264	365	465
35-Two pgs. Buck Rogers omitted in Buck Rogers #2	44	88	132	264	365	465
38-Full color portrait of Buck Rogers	42	84	126	252	349	445
41-60: 41,53-X-Mas-c. 55-Last bottom panel, pg. 4 in Buck Rogers redrawn in Buck Rogers #3	29	58	87	164	232	300
61,63,64,66,67,69,70	24	48	72	135	190	245
62,65,68,73-78-Two pgs. Kirby-a "Lightnin' & the Lone Rider". 65,77-X-Mas-c	26	52	78	150	210	270
71,79,80: 80-(3/41)-Buck Rogers story continues from Buck Rogers #5	18	36	54	101	138	175
72-Speed Spaulding begins by Marvin Bradley (artist), ends #88. This series was written by Edwin Balmer & Philip Wylie (later appeared as film & book "When Worlds Collide")	20	40	60	112	156	200
81-Origin & 1st app. Invisible Scarlet O'Neil (4/41); strip begins #82, ends #167; 1st non-funny-c (Scarlet O'Neil)	20	40	60	112	156	200
82-Buck Rogers-c	20	40	60	112	156	200
83-87,90: 86-Connie vs. Monsters on the Moon-c (sci/fi). 87 has last Buck Rogers full page-r. 90-Bondage-c	15	30	45	86	118	150
88,89: 88-Buck Rogers in "Moon's End" by Calkins, 2 pgs.(not reprints). Beginning with #88, all Buck Rogers pgs. have rearranged panels. 89-Origin & 1st app. Fearless Flint, the Flint Man	16	32	48	92	126	160
91-93,95,96,98-99,101,103-110: 105-Series 2 begins (Strip Page #1)	13	26	39	76	103	130
94-Buck Rogers in "Solar Holocaust" by Calkins, 3 pgs.(not reprints)	15	30	45	84	115	145
97-War Bond promotion, Buck Rogers by Calkins, 2 pgs.(not reprints)	15	30	45	84	115	145
100-1st comic to reach #100; 100th Anniversary cover features 11 major Famous Funnies characters, including Buck Rogers	16	32	48	92	126	160
102-Chief Wahoo vs. Hitler,Tojo & Mussolini-c (1/43)	48	96	144	288	432	575
111-130 (5/45): 113-X-Mas-c	10	20	30	58	77	95
131-150 (1/47): 137-Strip page No. 110 omitted	9	18	27	52	66	80
151-162,164-168	8	16	24	46	58	70
163-St. Valentine's Day-c	9	18	27	49	62	75
169,170-Two text illos. by Williamson, his 1st comic book work	11	22	33	63	84	105
171-190: 171-Strip pgs. 227,229,230, Series 2 omitted. 172-Strip Pg. 232 omitted. 190-Buck Rogers ends with start of strip pg. 302, Series 2; Oaky Doaks-c/story	8	16	24	40	50	60
191-197,199,201,203,206-208: No Buck Rogers. 191-Barney Carr, Space detective begins, ends #192.	7	14	21	37	46	55
198,200,202,205-One pg. Frazetta ads; no B. Rogers	8	16	24	40	50	60
204-Used in **POP**, pg. 79,99; war-c begin, end #208	8	16	24	43	54	65
209-216: Frazetta-c. 209-Buck Rogers begins (12/53) with strip pg. 480, Series 2; 211-Buck Rogers ads by Anderson begins, ends #217. #215-Contains B. Rogers strip pg. 515-518, series 2 followed by pgs.179-181, Series 3	122	244	366	763	1144	1525
1400						
217,218-B. Rogers ends with pg. 199, Series 3. 218-Wee Three-c/story	8	16	24	43	54	65

NOTE: ***Rick Yager*** *did the Buck Rogers Sunday strips reprinted in Famous Funnies. The Sundays were formerly done by Russ Keaton and Lt. Dick Calkins did the dailies, but would sometimes assist Yager on a panel or two from time to time. Strip No. 169 is Yager's first full Buck Rogers page. Yager did the strip until 1958 when* ***Murphy Anderson*** *took over.* ***Tuska*** *art from 4/26/59 - 1965. Virtually every panel was rewritten for Famous Funnies. Not identical to the original Sunday page. The Buck Rogers reprints run continuously through Famous Funnies issue No. 190 (Strip No. 302) with no break in story line. The story line has no continuity after No. 190. The Buck Rogers newspaper strips came out in four series: Series 1, 3/30/30 - 9/21/41 (No. 1 - 600); Series 2, 9/28/41 -10/21/51 (No. 1 - 525)(Strip No. 110-1/2 (1/2 pg.) published in only a few newspapers); Series 3, 10/28/51 -2/9/58 (No. 100-428)(No No.1-99); Series 4, 2/16/58 - 6/13/65 (No numbers, dates only).* ***Everett*** *c-85, 86.* ***Moulton*** *a-100. Chief Wahoo c-93, 97, 102, 116, 136, 139, 151. Dickie Dare c-83, 88. Fearless Flint c-89. Invisible Scarlet O'Neil c-81, 87, 95, 121(part), 132. Scorchy Smith c-84, 90.*

FAMOUS FUNNIES
Super Comics: 1964

	GD	VG	FN	VF	VF/NM	NM-
Super Reprint Nos. 15-18:17-r/Double Trouble #1. 18-Space Comics #?	2	4	6	11	14	18

FAMOUS GANGSTERS (Crime on the Waterfront No. 4)
Avon Periodicals/Realistic No. 3: Apr, 1951 - No. 3, Feb, 1952

	GD	VG	FN	VF	VF/NM	NM-
1-3: 1-Capone, Dillinger; c-/Avon paperback #329. 2-Dillinger Machine Gun Killer; Wood-c/a (1 pg.); r/Saint #7 & retitled "Mike Strong". 3-Lucky Luciano & Murder, Inc; c-/Avon paperback #66	39	78	117	230	325	420

FAMOUS INDIAN TRIBES
Dell Publishing Co.: July-Sept, 1962; No. 2, July, 1972

	GD	VG	FN	VF	VF/NM	NM-
12-264-209(#1) (The Sioux)	3	6	9	16	20	24
2(7/72)-Reprints above	1	2	3	5	7	9

FAMOUS STARS
Ziff-Davis Publ. Co.: Nov-Dec, 1950 - No. 6, Spring, 1952 (All have photo-c)

	GD	VG	FN	VF	VF/NM	NM-
1-Shelley Winters, Susan Peters, Ava Gardner, Shirley Temple; Jimmy Stewart & Shelley Winters photo-c; Whitney-a	34	68	102	196	278	360
2-Betty Hutton, Bing Crosby, Colleen Townsend, Gloria Swanson; Betty Hutton photo-c; Everett-a(2)	23	46	69	130	183	235
3-Farley Granger, Judy Garland's ordeal (life story; she died 6/22/69 at the age of 47), Alan Ladd; Farley Granger photo-c; Whitney-a	27	54	81	153	214	275
4-Al Jolson, Bob Mitchum, Ella Raines, Richard Conte, Vic Damone; Bob Mitchum photo-c; Crandall-a, 6pgs.	20	40	60	112	156	200
5-Liz Taylor, Betty Grable, Esther Williams, George Brent, Mario Lanza; Liz Taylor photo-c; Krigstein-a	36	72	108	204	290	375
6-Gene Kelly, Hedy Lamarr, June Allyson, William Boyd, Janet Leigh, Gary Cooper; Gene Kelly photo-c	17	34	51	98	134	170

FAMOUS STORIES (...Book No. 2)
Dell Publishing Co.: 1942 - No. 2, 1942

	GD	VG	FN	VF	VF/NM	NM-
1,2: 1-Treasure Island. 2-Tom Sawyer	32	64	96	180	255	330

FAMOUS TV FUNDAY FUNNIES
Harvey Publications: Sept, 1961 (25¢ Giant)

	GD	VG	FN	VF	VF/NM	NM-
1-Casper the Ghost, Baby Huey, Little Audrey	6	12	18	40	55	70

FAMOUS WESTERN BADMEN (Formerly Redskin)

Fanboy #1 © Horse Feathers Inc.

Fantastic Fears #3 © AJAX

Fantastic Four #48 © MAR

GD VG FN VF VF/NM NM-
2.0 4.0 6.0 8.0 9.0 9.2

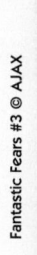

Youthful Magazines: No. 13, Dec, 1952 - No. 15, Apr, 1953
13-Redskin story 13 26 39 74 100 125
14,15: 15-The Dalton Boys story 10 20 30 56 73 90

FAN BOY
DC Comics: Mar, 1999 - No. 6, Aug, 1999 ($2.50, limited series)
1-6: 1-Art by Aragonés and various in all. 2-Green Lantern-c/a by Gil Kane. 3-JLA. 4-Sgt. Rock art by Heath, Marie Severin. 5-Batman art by Sprang, Adams, Miller, Timm. 6-Wonder Woman; art by Rude, Grell 2.50
TPB (2001, $12.95) r/#1-6 13.00

FANTASTIC (Formerly Captain Science; Beware No. 10 on)
Youthful Magazines: No. 8, Feb, 1952 - No. 9, Apr, 1952
8-Capt. Science by Harrison; decapitation, shrunken head panels 42 84 126 252 359 465
9-Harrison-a 33 66 99 190 270 350

FANTASTIC ADVENTURES
Super Comics: 1963 - 1964 (Reprints)
9,10,12,15,16,18: 9-r/? 10-r/He-Man #2(Toby). 11-Disbrow-a. 12-Unpublished Chesler material? 15-r/Spook #23. 16-r/Dark Shadows #2(Steinway); Briefer-a.18-r/Superior Stories #1 3 7 10 21 28 35
11-Wood-a; r/Blue Bolt #118 4 8 12 29 40 50
17-Baker-a(2) r/Seven Seas #6 4 8 12 29 40 50

FANTASTIC COMICS
Fox Features Syndicate: Dec, 1939 - No. 23, Nov, 1941
1-Intro/origin Samson; Stardust, The Super Wizard, Sub Saunders (by Kiefer), Space Smith, Capt. Kidd begin 448 896 1344 3136 4818 6500
2-Powell text illos 236 472 708 1475 2213 2950
3-Classic Lou Fine Robot-c; Powell text illos 1015 2030 3045 5200 6600 8000
4,5: Last Lou Fine-c 176 352 528 1100 1650 2200
6,7-Simon-c 132 264 396 825 1238 1650
8-10: 10-Intro/origin David, Samson's aide 92 184 276 575 863 1150
11-17,19,20: 16-Stardust ends 75 150 225 469 705 940
18,23: 18-1st app. Black Fury & sidekick Chuck; ends #23. 23-Origin The Gladiator 77 154 231 481 723 965
21-The Banshee begins(origin); ends #23; Hitler-c 82 164 246 513 769 1025
22-Hitler-c (likeness of Hitler as furnace on cover) 90 180 270 563 844 1125
NOTE: *Lou Fine c-1-5. Tuska a-3-5, 8. Bondage c-6, 8, 9. Issue #11 has indicia to Mystery Men Comics #15. All issues feature Samson covers.*

FANTASTIC COMICS (Fantastic Fears #1-9; Becomes Samson #12)
Ajax/Farrell Publ.: No. 10, Nov-Dec, 1954 - No. 11, Jan-Feb, 1955
10 (#1) 21 42 63 118 164 210
11-Robot-c 24 48 72 138 194 250

FANTASTIC FABLES
Silverwolf Comics: Feb, 1987 - No. 2, 1987 ($1.50, 28 pgs., B&W)
1,2: 1-Tim Vigil-a (6 pgs.). 2-Tim Vigil-a (7 pgs.) 4.00

FANTASTIC FEARS (Formerly Captain Jet) (Fantastic Comics #10 on)
Ajax/Farrell Publ.: No. 7, May, 1953 - No. 9, Sept-Oct, 1954
7(#1, 5/53)-Tales of Stalking Terror 46 92 138 276 413 550
8(#2, 7/53) 34 68 102 196 278 360
3,4 27 54 81 153 214 275
5-(1-2/54)-Ditko story (1st drawn) is written by Bruce Hamilton; r-in Weird V2#8 (1st pro work for Ditko but Daring Love #1 was published 1st) 80 160 240 500 750 1000
6-Decapitation-girl's head w/paper cutter (classic) 55 110 165 330 495 660
7(5-6/54), 9(9-10/54) 27 54 81 153 214 275
8(7-8/54)-Contains story intended for Jo-Jo; name changed to Kaza; decapitation story 30 60 90 170 240 310

FANTASTIC FIVE
Marvel Comics: Oct, 1999 - No. 5, Feb, 2000 ($1.99)
1-5: 1-M2 Universe; recaps origin; Ryan-a. 2-Two covers 2.25

FANTASTIC FORCE
Marvel Comics: Nov, 1994 - No. 18, Apr, 1996 ($1.75)
1-($2.50)-Foil wraparound-c; intro Fantastic Force w/Huntara, Delvor, Psi-Lord & Vibraxas 3.00
2-18: 13-She-Hulk app. 2.25

FANTASTIC FOUR (See America's Best TV..., Fireside Book Series, Giant-Size..., Giant Size Super-Stars, Marvel Collectors Item Classics, Marvel Milestone Edition, Marvel's Greatest, Marvel Treasury Edition, Marvel Triple Action, Official Marvel Index to... & Power Record Comics)

FANTASTIC FOUR
Marvel Comics Group: Nov, 1961 - No. 416, Sept, 1996 (Created by Stan Lee & Jack Kirby)
1-Origin & 1st app. The Fantastic Four (Reed Richards: Mr. Fantastic, Johnny Storm: The Human Torch, Sue Storm: The Invisible Girl, & Ben Grimm: The Thing–Marvel's 1st super-hero group since the G.A.; 1st app. S.A. Human Torch); origin/1st app. The Mole Man. 850 1700 2550 8925 21,463 34,000
1-Golden Record Comic Set Reprint (1966)-cover not identical to original 16 32 48 113 167 220
with Golden Record 24 48 72 171 251 330
2-Vs. The Skrulls (last 10¢ issue) 298 604 906 2533 4391 6250
3-Fantastic Four don costumes & establish Headquarters; brief 1pg. origin; intro. The Fantasti-Car; Human Torch drawn w/two left hands on-c 205 410 615 1742 3021 4300
4-1st S. A. Sub-Mariner app. (5/62) 229 458 687 1946 3373 4800
5-Origin & 1st app. Doctor Doom 309 618 927 2626 4563 6500
6-Sub-Mariner, Dr. Doom team up; 1st Marvel villain team-up (2nd S.A. Sub-Mariner app. 128 256 384 1024 1787 2550
7-10: 7-1st app. Kurrgo. 8-1st app. Puppet-Master & Alicia Masters. 9-3rd Sub-Mariner app. 10-Stan Lee & Jack Kirby app. in story 85 170 255 680 1190 1700
11-Origin/1st app. The Impossible Man (2/63) 70 140 210 560 980 1400
12-Fantastic Four Vs. The Hulk (1st meeting); 1st Hulk x-over & ties w/Amazing Spider-Man #1 as 1st Marvel x-over; (3/63) 143 286 429 1215 2107 3000
13-Intro. The Watcher; 1st app. The Red Ghost 47 94 141 400 625 850
14-19: 14-Sub-Mariner x-over. 15-1st app. Mad Thinker. 16-1st Ant-Man x-over (7/63); Wasp cameo. 18-Origin/1st app. The Super Skrull. 19-Intro. Rama-Tut; Stan Lee & Jack Kirby cameo 35 70 105 254 427 600
20-Origin/1st app. The Molecule Man 38 76 114 275 463 650
21-Intro. The Hate Monger; 1st Sgt. Fury x-over (12/63) 29 58 87 210 355 500
22-24: 22-Sue Storm gains more powers 19 38 57 138 219 300
25,26-The Hulk vs. The Thing (their 1st battle). 25-3rd Avengers x-over (1st time w/Captain America)(cameo, 4/64); 2nd S.A. app. Cap (takes place between Avengers #4 & 5. 26-4th Avengers x-over 44 88 132 330 565 800
27-1st Doctor Strange x-over (6/64) 23 46 69 167 284 400
28-Early X-Men x-over (7/64); same date as X-Men #6 32 64 96 232 391 550
29,30: 30-Intro. Diablo 19 38 57 138 219 300
31-40: 31-Early Avengers x-over (10/64). 33-1st app. Attuma; part photo-c. 35-Intro/1st app. Dragon Man. 36-Intro/1st app. Madam Medusa & the Frightful Four (Sandman, Wizard, Paste Pot Pete). 39-Wood inks on Daredevil (early x-over) 16 32 48 116 183 250
41-44,47: 41-43-Frightful Four app. 44-Intro. Gorgon 9 18 27 65 100 135
45-Intro/1st app. The Inhumans (c/story, 12/65); also see Incredible Hulk Special #1 & Thor #146, & 147 16 32 48 116 183 250
46-1st Black Bolt-c (Kirby) & 1st full app. 10 20 30 72 116 160
48-Partial origin/1st app. The Silver Surfer & Galactus (3/66) by Lee & Kirby; Galactus cameo in last panel; 1st of 3 part story 68 136 204 544 947 1350
49-2nd app./1st cover Silver Surfer & Galactus 29 58 87 210 355 500
50-Silver Surfer battles Galactus; full S.S.-c 35 70 105 262 431 600
51-Classic "This Man...This Monster" story 9 18 27 65 107 150
52-1st app. The Black Panther (7/66) 22 44 66 160 255 350
53-Origin & 2nd app. The Black Panther 11 22 33 80 130 180
54-Inhumans cameo 8 16 24 58 86 115
55-Thing battles Silver Surfer; 4th app. Silver Surfer 13 26 39 94 147 200
56-Silver Surfer cameo 9 18 27 65 93 120
57-60: Dr. Doom steals Silver Surfer's powers (See Silver Surfer: Loftier Than Mortals). 59,60-Inhumans cameos 9 18 27 60 85 110
61-65,68-71: 61-Silver Surfer cameo; Sandman-c/s 7 14 21 46 63 80
66-Begin 2 part origin of Him (Warlock); does not app. (9/67) 13 26 39 90 133 175
66,67-2nd printings (1994) 2 4 6 8 10 12
67-Origin/1st app. Him (Warlock); 1 pg. cameo; see Thor #165,166 for 1st full app. 13 26 39 90 133 175
72-Silver Surfer-c/story (pre-dates Silver Surfer #1) 10 20 30 67 96 125
73-Spider-Man, D.D., Thor x-over; cont'd from Daredevil #38 9 18 27 60 85 110
74-77: Silver Surfer app.(#77 is same date/S.S. #1) 7 14 21 51 71 90
78-80 6 12 18 40 55 70
81-88: 81-Crystal joins & dons costume. 82,83-Inhumans app. 84-87-Dr. Doom app. 88-Last 12¢ issue 5 10 15 36 48 60
89-99,101: 94-Intro. Agatha Harkness. 4 8 12 27 36 45
100 (7/70) F.F. vs Thinker and Puppet-Master 10 20 30 73 107 140
102-104: F.F. vs. Sub-Mariner. 104-Magneto-c/story 4 8 12 29 40 50
105-109,111: 108-Last Kirby issue (not in #103-107) 3 7 10 21 28 35
110-Initial version w/green Thing and blue faces and pink uniforms on-c 4 8 12 29 40 50
110-Corrected-c w/accurately colored faces and uniforms and orange Thing

Fantastic Four #249 © MAR

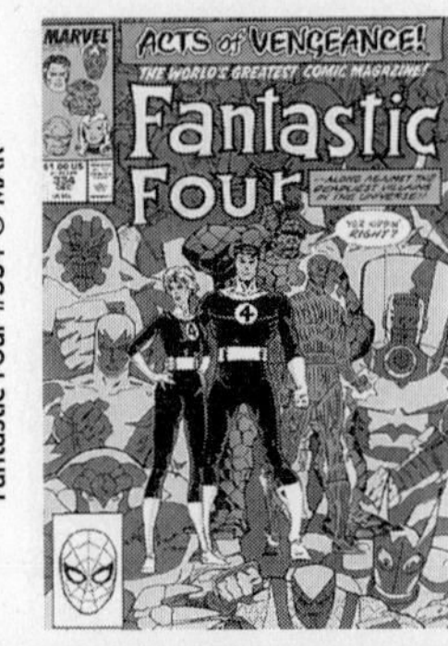

Fantastic Four #334 © MAR

Fantastic Four V3#60 © MAR

GD VG FN VF VF/NM NM-
2.0 4.0 6.0 8.0 9.0 9.2

4 8 12 27 36 45

112-Hulk Vs. Thing (7/71) 10 20 30 73 107 140

113-115: 115-Last 15¢ issue 3 6 9 19 25 32

116 (52 pgs.) 4 8 12 27 36 45

117-120 3 6 9 18 24 30

121-123-Silver Surfer-c/stories. 122,123-Galactus 3 7 10 21 28 35

124,125,127,129-149: 129-Intro. Thundra. 130-Sue leaves F.F. 131-Quicksilver app. 132-Medusa joins. 133-Thundra Vs. Thing. 142-Kirbyish-a by Buckler begins. 143-Dr. Doom-c/story. 147-Sub-Mariner 2 4 6 12 16 20

126-Origin F.F. retold; cover swipe of F.F. #1 3 6 9 16 20 24

128-Four pg. insert of F.F. Friends & Foes 3 6 9 16 20 24

150-Crystal & Quicksilver's wedding 3 6 9 18 23 28

151-154,158-160: 151-Origin Thundra. 159-Medusa leaves; Sue rejoins 2 4 6 8 10 12

155-157: Silver Surfer in all 2 4 6 11 14 18

161-165,168,174-180: 164-The Crusader (old Marvel Boy) revived (origin #165); 1st app. Frankie Raye. 168-170-Cage app. 176-Re-intro Impossible Man; Marvel artists app. 180-r/#101 by Kirby 1 2 3 5 6 8

166,167-vs. Hulk 2 4 6 10 12 15

169-173-(Regular 25¢ edition)(4-8/75) 1 2 3 5 6 8

169-173-(30¢-c, limited distribution) 2 4 6 8 10 12

181-199: 189-G.A. Human Torch app. & origin retold. 190,191-Fantastic Four break up 1 2 3 4 5 7

183-187-(35¢-c variants, limited dist.)(6-10/77) 1 3 4 6 8 10

200-(11/78, 52 pgs.)-F.F. re-united vs. Dr. Doom 2 4 6 8 10 12

201-208,219,222-231: 207-Human Torch vs. Spider-Man-c/story. 211-1st app. Terrax. 224-Contains unused alternate-c for FF #3 and pin-ups 5.00

209-216,218,220,221-Byrne-a. 209-1st Herbie the Robot. 220-Brief origin 6.00

217-Early app. Dazzler (4/80); by Byrne 6.00

232-Byrne-a begins 6.00

233-235,237-249,251-260: All Byrne-a. 238-Origin Frankie Raye. 244-Frankie Raye becomes Nova, Herald of Galactus. 252-Reads sideways; Annihilus app.; contains skin "Tattooz" decals 5.00

236-20th Anniversary issue(11/81, 68 pgs., $1.00)-Brief origin F.F.; Byrne-c/a(p); new Kirby-a(p) 6.00

250-(52 pgs)-Spider-Man x-over; Byrne-a; Skrulls impersonate New X-Men 6.00

261-285: 261-Silver Surfer. 262-Origin Galactus; Byrne writes & draws himself into story. 264-Swipes-c of F.F. #1. 274-Spider-Man's alien costume app. (4th app., 1/85, 2 pgs.) 4.00

286-2nd app. X-Factor continued from Avengers #263; story continues in X-Factor #1 5.00

287-295: 291-Action Comcis #1 cover swipe. 292-Nick Fury app. 293-Last Byrne-a 3.00

296-($1.50)-Barry Smith-c/a; Thing rejoins 4.00

297-318,321-330: 300-Johnny Storm & Alicia Masters wed. 306-New team begins (9/87). 311-Re-intro The Black Panther. 327-Mr. Fantastic & Invisible Girl return 3.00

319,320: 319-Double size. 320-Thing vs. Hulk 4.00

331-346,351-357,359,360: 334-Simonson-c/scripts begin. 337-Simonson-a begins. 342-Spider-Man cameo. 356-F.F. vs. The New Warriors; Paul Ryan-c/a begins. 360-Last $1.00-c 2.50

347-Ghost Rider, Wolverine, Spider-Man, Hulk-c/stories thru #349; Arthur Adams-c/a(p) in each 4.00

347,348-Gold 2nd printing 2.50

348-350: 350-($1.50, 52 pgs.)-Dr. Doom app. 3.00

358-(11/91, $2.25, 88 pgs.)-30th anniversary issue; gives history of F.F.; die cut-c; Art Adams back-up story-a 3.00

361-368,370,372-374,376-380,382-386: 362-Spider-Man app. 367-Wolverine app. (brief). 370-Infinity War x-over; Thanos & Magus app. 374-Secret Defenders (Ghost Rider, Hulk, Wolverine) x-over 2.25

369-Infinity War x-over; Thanos app. 2.50

371-All white embossed-c ($2.00) 4.00

371-All red 2nd printing ($2.00) 2.50

375-($2.95, 52 pgs.)-Holo-grafx foil-c; ann. issue 3.00

376-($2.95)-Variant polybagged w/Dirt Magazine #4 and music tape 5.00

381-Death of Reed Richards (Mister Fantastic) & Dr. Doom 4.00

387-Newsstand ed. ($1.25) 2.25

387-($2.95)-Collector's Ed. w/Die-cut foil-c 3.00

388-393,395-397: 388-bound-in trading card sheet. 394-($1.50-c) 2.25

394,398,399: 394 ($2.95)-Collector's Edition-polybagged w/16 pg. Marvel Action Hour book and acetate print; pink logo. 398,399-Rainbow Foil-c 3.00

400-Rainbow-Foil-c 4.00

401-415: 401,402-Atlantis Rising. 407,408-Return of Reed Richards. 411-Inhumans app. 414-Galactus vs. Hyperstorm. 415-Onslaught tie-in; X-Men app. 2.25

416-($2.50)-Onslaught tie-in; Dr. Doom app.; wraparound-c 3.00

#500-up (See Fantastic Four Vol. 3; series resumed original numbering after Vol. 3 #70)

Annual 1('63)-Origin F.F.; Ditko-i; early Spidey app. 66 132 198 561 856 1150

Annual 2('64)-Dr. Doom origin & c/story 37 74 111 278 414 550

GD VG FN VF VF/NM NM-
2.0 4.0 6.0 8.0 9.0 9.2

Annual 3('65)-Reed & Sue wed; r/#6,11 16 32 48 116 171 225

Special 4(11/66)-G.A. Torch x-over (1st S.A. app.) & origin retold; r/#25,26 (Hulk vs. Thing); Torch vs. Torch battle 11 22 33 77 114 150

Special 5(11/67)-New art; Intro. Psycho-Man; early Black Panther, Inhumans & Silver Surfer (1st solo story) app. 11 22 33 80 118 155

Special 6(11/68)-Intro. Annihilus; birth of Franklin Richards; new 48 pg. movie length epic; last non-reprint annual 7 14 21 51 71 90

Special 7(11/69)-r/F.F. #1,2; Marvel staff photos 4 8 12 24 32 40

Special 8-10: All reprints. 8(12/70)-F.F. vs. Sub-Mariner plus gallery of F.F. foes. 9(12/71). 10('73) 3 6 9 16 20 25

Annual 11-14: 11(1976)-New art begins again. 12(1978). 13(1978). 14(1979) 1 2 3 5 7 9

Annual 15-17: 15('80-'94, 68 pgs.).17(1983)-Byrne-c/a 5.00

Annual 18-27: 21(1988)-Evolutionary War x-over. 22-Atlantis Attacks x-over; Sub-Mariner & The Avengers app.; Buckler-a. 23-Byrne-c; Guice-p. 24-2 pg. origin recap of Fantastic Four; Guardians of the Galaxy x-over. 25-Moondragon story. 26-Bagged w/card 3.00

Special Edition 1(5/84)-r/Annual #1; Byrne-c/a 3.00

...: Monsters Unleashed nn (1992, $5.95)-r/F.F. #347-349 w/new Arthur Adams-c 6.00

...: Nobody Gets Out Alive (1994, $15.95) TPB r/ #387-392 16.00

... Visionaries (11/01, $19.95) r/#232-240 by John Byrne 20.00

NOTE: ***Arthur Adams*** *c/a-347-349p.* ***Austin*** *c(i)-232-236, 238, 240-242, 250i, 286i.* ***Buckler*** *c-151, 168.* ***John Buscema*** *a(p)-107, 108(w/**Kirby, Sinnott** & **Romita**),109-130, 132, 134-141, 160, 173-175, 202, 296-309p, Annual 11, 13; c(p)-107-122, 124-129, 133-139, 202, Annual 12p, Special 10.* ***Byrne*** *a-209-218p, 220p, 221p, 232-265, 266i, 267-273, 274-293p, Annual 17, 19; c-211-214p, 220p, 232-236p, 237, 238p, 239, 240-242p, 243-249, 250p, 251-267, 269-277, 278-281p, 283p, 284, 285, 286p, 288-293, Annual 17, 18.* ***Ditko*** *a-13i, 14i(w/**Kirby**-p), Annual 16.* ***G. Kane*** *c-145p, 146p, 150p, 160p.* ***Kirby*** *a-1-102p, 108p, 180r, 189r, 236p, Special 1-10; c-1-101, 164, 167, 171-177, 180, 181, 190, 200, Annual 11, Special 1-7, 9.* ***Marcos*** *a-Annual 14i.* ***Mooney*** *a-118i, 152i.* ***Perez*** *a(p)-164-167, 170-172, 176-178, 184-188, 191p, 192p. Annual 14p, 15p; c(p)-183-188, 191, 192, 194-197.* ***Simonson*** *a-337-341, 343, 344p, 345p, 346, 350p, 352-354; c-212, 334-341, 342p, 343-346, 350, 353, 354.* ***Steranko*** *c-130-132p.* ***Williamson*** *c-357i.*

FANTASTIC FOUR (Volume Two)
Marvel Comics: V2#1, Nov, 1996 - No. 13, Nov, 1997 ($2.95/$1.95/$1.99) (Produced by WildStorm Productions)

1-($2.95)-Reintro Fantastic Four; Jim Lee-c/a; Brandon Choi scripts; Mole Man app. 5.00

1-($2.95)-Variant-c 1 2 3 4 5 7

2-9: 2-Namor-c/app. 3-Avengers-c/app. 4-Two covers; Dr. Doom cameo 3.00

10,11,13: All $1.99-c. 13-"World War 3"-pt. 1, x-over w/Image 3.00

12-($2.99) "Heroes Reunited"-pt. 1 4.00

...: Heroes Reborn (7/00, $17.95, TPB) r/#1-6 18.00

FANTASTIC FOUR (Volume Three)
Marvel Comics: V3#1, Jan, 1998 - Present ($2.99/$1.99/$2.25)

1-($2.99)-Heroes Return; Lobdell-s/Davis & Farmer-a 5.00

1-Alternate Heroes Return-c 1 2 3 4 5 7

2-4,12: 2-2-covers. 4-Claremont-s/Larroca-a begin; Silver Surfer c/app. 12-($2.99) Wraparound-c by Larroca 4.00

5-11: 6-Heroes For Hire app. 9-Spider-Man-c/app. 3.00

13-24: 13,14-Ronan-c/app. 2.50

25-($2.99) Dr. Doom returns 3.00

26-49: 27-Dr. Doom marries Sue. 30-Begin $2.25-c. 32,42-Namor-c/app. 35-Regular cover; Pacheco-s/a begins. 37-Super-Skrull-c/app. 38-New Baxter Building 2.25

35-($3.25) Variant foil enhanced-c; Pacheco-s/a begins 3.25

50-($3.99, 64 pgs.) BWS-c; Grummett, Pacheco, Rude, Udon-a 4.00

51-53,55-59: 51-53-Bagley-a(p)/Wieringo-c; Inhumans app. 55,56-Immonen-a 57-59-Warren-s/Grant-a 2.25

54-($3.50, 100 pgs.) Birth of Valeria; r/Annual #6 birth of Franklin 3.50

60-(9¢-c) Waid-s/Wieringo-a begin 2.25

60-($2.25 newsstand edition)(also see Promotional Comics section) 2.25

61-70: 62-64-FF vs. Modulus. 65,66-Buckingham-a. 68-70-Dr. Doom app. 2.25

(After #70 [Aug, 2003] numbering reverted back to original Vol. 1 with #500, Sept, 2003)

500-($3.50) Regular edition; concludes Dr. Doom app.; Dr. Strange app.; Rivera painted-c 3.50

500-($4.99) Director's Cut Edition; chromium-c by Wieringo; sketch and script pages 8.00

501-508: 501,502-Casey Jones-a. 503-508-Porter-a 2.25

...'98 Annual ($3.50) Immonen-a 3.50

...'99 Annual ($3.50) Ladronn-a 3.50

...'00 Annual ($3.50) Larocca-a; Marvel Girl back-up story 3.50

...'01 Annual ($2.99) Maguire-a; Thing back-up w/Yu-a 3.00

Fantastic 4th Voyage of Sinbad (9/01, $5.95) Claremont-s/Ferry-a 6.00

Flesh and Stone (8/01, $12.95, TPB) r/#35-39 13.00

... Vol. 1: Imaginauts (2003, $17.99, TPB) r/#56,60-66; Mark Waid's series proposal 18.00

... Vol. 2: Unthinkable (2003, $17.99, TPB) r/#67-70,500-502; #500 Director's Cut extras 18.00

Wizard #1/2 -Lim-a 10.00

FANTASTIC FOUR: ATLANTIS RISING
Marvel Comics: June, 1995 - No. 2, July, 1995 ($3.95, limited series)

1,2: Acetate-c 5.00

Fantastic Four: World's Greatest Comics Magazine #10 © MAR

Fantoman #2 © CEN

Fast Fiction #2 © Seaboard

GD 2.0 | VG 4.0 | FN 6.0 | VF 8.0 | VF/NM 9.0 | NM- 9.2

Collector's Preview (5/95, $2.25, 52 pgs.) 2.50

FANTASTIC FOUR: BIG TOWN
Marvel Comics: Jan, 2001 - No. 4, Apr, 2001 ($2.99, limited series)
1-4:"What If?" story; McKone-a/Englehart-s 3.00

FANTASTIC FOUR: FIREWORKS
Marvel Comics: Jan, 1999 - No. 3, Mar, 1999 ($2.99, limited series)
1-3-Remix; Jeff Johnson-a 3.00

FANTASTIC FOUR INDEX (See Official...)

FANTASTIC FOUR: 1 2 3 4
Marvel Comics: Oct, 2001 - No. 4, Jan, 2002 ($2.99, limited series)
1-4-Morrison-s/Jae Lee-a. 2-4-Namor-c/app. 3.00
TPB (2002, $9.99) r/#1-4 10.00

FANTASTIC FOUR ROAST
Marvel Comics Group: May, 1982 (75¢, one-shot, direct sales)
1-Celebrates 20th anniversary of F.F.#1; X-Men, Ghost Rider & many others cameo; Golden, Miller, Buscema, Rogers, Byrne, Anderson art; Hembeck/Austin-c 4.00

FANTASTIC FOUR: THE LEGEND
Marvel Comics: Oct, 1996 ($3.95, one-shot)
1-Tribute issue 4.00

FANTASTIC FOUR 2099
Marvel Comics: Jan, 1996 - No. 8, Aug, 1996 ($3.95/$1.95)
1-($3.95)-Chromium-c; X-Nation preview 4.00
2-8: 4-Spider-Man 2099-c/app. 5-Doctor Strange app. 7-Thibert-c 2.25
NOTE: ***Williamson*** *a-1i; c-1i.*

FANTASTIC FOUR UNLIMITED
Marvel Comics: Mar, 1993 - No. 12, Dec, 1995 ($3.95, 68 pgs.)
1-12: 1-Black Panther app. 4-Thing vs. Hulk. 5-Vs. The Frightful Four. 6-Vs. Namor. 7, 9-12-Wraparound-c 4.00

FANTASTIC FOUR UNPLUGGED
Marvel Comics: Sept, 1995 - No. 6, Aug 1996 (99¢, bi-monthly)
1-6 2.25

FANTASTIC FOUR - UNSTABLE MOLECULES
(Indicia for #1 reads STARTLING STORIES: ... ; #2 reads UNSTABLE MOLECULES)
Marvel Comics: Mar, 2003 - No. 4, June, 2003 ($2.99, limited series)
1-4-Guy Davis-c/a 3.00
Fantastic Four Legends Vol. 1 TPB (2003, $13.99) r/#1-4, origin from FF #1 (1963) 14.00

FANTASTIC FOUR VS. X-MEN
Marvel Comics: Feb, 1987 - No. 4, June, 1987 (Limited series)
1-4: 4-Austin-a(i) 4.00

FANTASTIC FOUR: WORLD'S GREATEST COMICS MAGAZINE
Marvel Comics: Feb, 2001 - No. 12 (Limited series)
1-12: Homage to Lee & Kirby era of F.F.; s/a by Larsen & various. 5-Hulk-c/app. 10-Thor app. 3.00

FANTASTIC GIANTS (Formerly Konga #1-23)
Charlton Comics: V2#24, Sept, 1966 (25¢, 68 pgs.)
V2#24-Special Ditko issue; origin Konga & Gorgo reprinted plus two new Ditko stories 7 14 21 51 71 90

FANTASTIC TALES
I. W. Enterprises: 1958 (no date) (Reprint, one-shot)
1-Reprints Avon's "City of the Living Dead" 4 8 12 24 32 40

FANTASTIC VOYAGE (See Movie Comics)
Gold Key: Aug, 1969 - No. 2, Dec, 1969
1 (TV) 6 12 18 40 55 70
2 4 8 12 29 40 50

FANTASTIC VOYAGES OF SINDBAD, THE
Gold Key: Oct, 1965 - No. 2, June, 1967
1-Painted-c on both 7 14 21 50 68 85
2 6 12 18 38 52 65

FANTASTIC WORLDS
Standard Comics: No. 5, Sept, 1952 - No. 7, Jan, 1953
5-Toth, Anderson-a 36 72 108 204 290 375
6-Toth-c/a 31 62 93 175 248 320
7 20 40 60 112 156 200

FANTASY FEATURES
Americomics: 1987 - No. 2, 1987 ($1.75)
1,2 3.00

FANTASY ILLUSTRATED
New Media Publ.: Spring 1982 ($2.95, B&W magazine)
1-P. Craig Russell-c/a; art by Ditko, Sekowsky, Sutton; Englehart-s 1 2 3 4 5 7

FANTASY MASTERPIECES (Marvel Super Heroes No. 12 on)
Marvel Comics Group: Feb, 1966 - No. 11, Oct, 1967; V2#1, Dec, 1979 - No. 14, Jan, 1981
1-Photo of Stan Lee (12¢-c #1,2) 7 14 21 46 63 80
2-r/1st Fin Fang Foom from Strange Tales #89 4 8 12 27 36 45
3-8: 3-G.A. Capt. America-r begin, end #11; 1st 25¢ Giant; Colan-r. 3-6-Kirby-c(p). 4-Kirby-c(p)(i). 7-Begin G.A. Sub-Mariner, Torch-r/M. Mystery. 8-Torch battles the Sub-Mariner-r/Marvel Mystery #9 5 10 15 33 44 55
9-Origin Human Torch-r/Marvel Comics #1 5 10 15 36 48 60
10,11: 10-r/origin & 1st app. All Winners Squad from All Winners #19. 11-r/origin of Toro (H.T. #1) & Black Knight #1 4 8 12 29 40 50
V2#1(12/79, 75¢, 52 pgs.)-r/origin Silver Surfer from Silver Surfer #1 with editing plus reprints cover; J. Buscema-a 5.00
2-14-Reprints Silver Surfer #2-14 w/covers 3.00
NOTE: ***Buscema*** *c-V2#7-9(in part).* ***Ditko*** *r-1-3, 7, 9.* ***Everett*** *r-1,7-9.* ***Matt Fox*** *r-9i.* ***Kirby*** *r-1-11; c(p)-3, 4i, 5, 6.* ***Starlin*** *r-8-13. Some direct sale V2#14's had a 50¢ cover price. #3-11 contain Capt. America-r/Capt. America #3-10. #7-11 contain G.A.Human Torch & Sub-Mariner-r.*

FANTASY QUARTERLY (Also see Elfquest)
Independent Publishers Syndicate: Spring, 1978 (B&W)
1-1st app. Elfquest; Dave Sim-a (6 pgs.) 6 12 18 43 59 75

FANTOMAN (Formerly Amazing Adventure Funnies)
Centaur Publications: No. 2, Aug, 1940 - No. 4, Dec, 1940
2-The Fantom of the Fair, The Arrow, Little Dynamite-r begin; origin The Ermine by Filchock; Fantoman app. in 2-4; Burgos, J. Cole, Ernst, Gustavson-a 120 240 360 750 1125 1500
3,4: Gustavson-r. 4-Red Blaze story 96 192 288 600 900 1200

FAREWELL MOONSHADOW (See Moonshadow)
DC Comics (Vertigo): Jan, 1997 ($7.95, one-shot)
nn-DeMatteis-s/Muth-c/a 8.00

FARGO KID (Formerly Justice Traps the Guilty)(See Feature Comics #47)
Prize Publications: V11#3(#1), June-July, 1958 - V11#5, Oct-Nov, 1958
V11#3(#1)-Origin Fargo Kid, Severin-c/a; Williamson-a(2); Heath-a 19 38 57 109 152 195
V11#4,5-Severin-c/a 13 26 39 74 100 125

FARMER'S DAUGHTER, THE
Stanhall Publ./Trojan Magazines: Feb-Mar, 1954 - No. 3, June-July, 1954; No. 4, Oct, 1954
1-Lingerie, nudity panel 23 46 69 132 186 240
2-4(Stanhall) 14 28 42 81 111 140

FARSCAPE: WAR TORN (Based on TV series)
DC Comics (WildStorm): Apr, 2002 - No. 2, May, 2002 ($4.95, limited series)
1,2-Teranishi-a/Wolfman-s; photo-c 5.00

FASHION IN ACTION
Eclipse Comics: Aug, 1986 - Feb, 1987 (Baxter paper)
Summer Special 1 , Winter Special 1, each Snyder III-c/a 2.25

FASTBALL EXPRESS (Major League Baseball)
Ultimate Sports Force: 2000 ($3.95, one-shot)
1-Polybagged with poster; Johnson, Maddux, Park, Nomo, Clemens app. 4.00

FASTEST GUN ALIVE, THE (Movie)
Dell Publishing Co.: No. 741, Sept, 1956 (one-shot)
Four Color 741-Photo-c 8 16 24 55 78 100

FAST FICTION (...Action) (Stories by Famous Authors Illustrated #6 on)
Seaboard Publ./Famous Authors Ill.: Oct, 1949 - No. 5, Mar, 1950
(All have Kiefer-c)(48 pgs.)
1-Scarlet Pimpernel; Jim Lavery-c/a 38 76 114 219 310 400
2-Captain Blood; H. C. Kiefer-c/a 34 68 102 196 278 360
3-She, by Rider Haggard; Vincent Napoli-a 40 80 120 240 340 440
4-(1/50, 52 pgs.)-The 39 Steps; Lavery-c/a 27 54 81 153 214 275
5-Beau Geste; Kiefer-c/a 27 54 81 153 214 275
NOTE: ***Kiefer*** *a-2, 5; c-2, 3,5.* ***Lavery*** *c/a-1, 4.* ***Napoli*** *a-3.*

FAST FORWARD

Fate #22 © DC

Fate of the Blade #2 © Dreamwave

Fawcett Movie Comics #9 © FAW

GD 2.0 | VG 4.0 | FN 6.0 | VF 8.0 | VF/NM 9.0 | NM- 9.2

DC Comics (Piranha Press): 1992 - No. 3, 1993 ($4.95, 68 pgs.)
1-3: 1-Morrison scripts; McKean-c/a. 3-Sam Kieth-a 5.00

FAST WILLIE JACKSON
Fitzgerald Periodicals, Inc.: Oct, 1976 - No. 7, 1977
1 2 4 6 11 14 18
2-7 1 3 4 6 8 10

FAT ALBERT (...& the Cosby Kids) (TV)
Gold Key: Mar, 1974 - No. 29, Feb, 1979
1 4 8 12 22 30 38
2-10 2 4 6 12 16 20
11-29 2 4 6 10 12 15

FATALE (Also see Powers That Be #1 & Shadow State #1,2)
Broadway Comics: Jan, 1996 - No. 6, Aug, 1996 ($2.50)
1-6: J.G. Jones-c/a in all, Preview Edition 1 (11/95, B&W) 2.50

FAT AND SLAT (Ed Wheelan) (Becomes Gunfighter No. 5 on)
E. C. Comics: Summer, 1947 - No. 4, Spring, 1948
1-Intro/origin Voltage, Man of Lightning; "Comics" McCormick, the World's No. 1 Comic Book Fan begins, ends #4 36 72 108 204 290 375
2-4: 4-Comics McCormick-c feature 24 48 72 138 194 250

FAT AND SLAT JOKE BOOK
All-American Comics (William H. Wise): Summer, 1944 (52 pgs., one-shot)
nn-by Ed Wheelan 27 54 81 153 214 275

FATE (See Hand of Fate & Thrill-O-Rama)

FATE
DC Comics: Oct, 1994 - No. 22, Sept, 1996 ($1.95/$2.25)
0,1-22: 8-Begin $2.25-c. 11-14-Alan Scott (Sentinel) app. 10,14-Zatanna app. 21-Phantom Stranger app. 22-Spectre app. 2.25

FATE OF THE BLADE
Dreamwave Productions: Aug, 2002 - Present ($2.95)
1-5: 1-Sarracini-s/Yamen-a; gatefold wraparound--c 3.00

FATHOM
Comico: May, 1987 - No. 3, July, 1987 ($1.50, limited series)
1-3 2.25

FATHOM
Image Comics (Top Cow Prod.): Aug, 1998 - Present ($2.50)
Preview 12.00
0-Wizard supplement 7.00
0-($6.95) DF Alternate 7.00
1/2 (Wizard) origin of Cannon; Turner-a 6.00
1/2 (3/03, $2.99) origin of Cannon 3.00
1-Turner-s/a; three covers; alternate story pages 6.00
1-Wizard World Ed. 9.00
2-14: 12-14-Witchblade app. 13,14-Tomb Raider app. 3.00
9-Green foil-c edition 15.00
9,12-Holofoil editions 18.00
12,13-DFE alternate-c 6.00
13,14-DFE Gold edition 8.00
14-DFE Blue 15.00
... Collected Edition 1 (3/99, $5.95) r/Preview & all three #1's 6.00
... Collected Edition 2-4 (3-12/99, $5.95) 2-r/#2,3. 3-r/#4,5. 4-r/#6,7 6.00
... Collected Edition 5 (4/00, $5.95) 5-r/#8,9 6.00
... Swimsuit Special (5/99, $2.95) Pin-ups by various 3.00
... Swimsuit Special 2000 (12/00, $2.95) Pin-ups by various; Turner-c 3.00
Michael Turner's Fathom HC ('01, $39.95) r/#1-9, black-c w/silver foil 40.00
Michael Turner's Fathom SC ('01, $24.95) r/#1-9, new Turner-c 25.00

FATHOM: KILLIAN'S TIDE
Image Comics (Top Cow Prod.): Apr, 2001 - No. 4, Nov, 2001 ($2.95)
1-4-Caldwell-a(p); two covers by Caldwell and Turner. 2-Flip-book preview of Universe 3.00
1-DFE Blue, 1-Holographic logo 12.00
4-Foil-c 12.00

FATIMA...CHALLENGE TO THE WORLD
Catechetical Guild: 1951, 36 pgs. (15¢)
nn (not same as 'Challenge to the World') 4 8 12 18 22 25

FATMAN, THE HUMAN FLYING SAUCER
Lightning Comics(Milson Publ. Co.): April, 1967 - No. 3, Aug-Sept, 1967 (68 pgs.) (Written by Otto Binder)
1-Origin/1st app. Fatman & Tinman by Beck 7 14 21 46 63 80
2-C. C. Beck-a 4 8 12 29 40 50
3-(Scarce)-Beck-a 7 14 21 51 71 90

FAULTLINES
DC Comics (Vertigo): May, 1997 - No. 6, Oct, 1997 ($2.50, limited series)
1-6-Lee Marrs-s/Bill Koeb-a in all 2.50

FAUNTLEROY COMICS (Super Duck Presents...)
Close-Up/Archie Publications: 1950; No. 2, 1951; No. 3, 1952
1-Super Duck-c/stories by Al Fagaly in all 9 18 27 52 66 80
2,3 6 12 18 31 38 45

FAUST
Northstar Publishing/Rebel Studios #7 on: 1989 - No 11, 1997 ($2.00/$2.25, B&W, mature themes)
1-Decapitation-c; Tim Vigil-c/a in all 3 6 9 16 20 24
1-2nd - 4th printings 3.00
2 2 4 6 8 10 12
2-2nd & 3rd printings, 3,5-2nd printing 3.00
3 1 3 4 6 8 10
4-10: 7-Begin Rebel Studios series 5.00
11-($2.25) 3.00

FAWCETT MOTION PICTURE COMICS (See Motion Picture Comics)

FAWCETT MOVIE COMIC
Fawcett Publications: 1949 - No. 20, Dec, 1952 (All photo-c)
nn- "Dakota Lil"; George Montgomery & Rod Cameron (1949) 32 64 96 184 262 340
nn- "Copper Canyon"; Ray Milland & Hedy Lamarr (1950) 25 50 75 144 198 255
nn- "Destination Moon" (1950) 78 156 234 488 732 975
nn- "Montana"; Errol Flynn & Alexis Smith (1950) 25 50 75 144 198 255
nn- "Pioneer Marshal"; Monte Hale (1950) 25 50 75 144 198 255
nn- "Powder River Rustlers"; Rocky Lane (1950) 36 72 108 207 294 380
nn- "Singing Guns"; Vaughn Monroe, Ella Raines & Walter Brennan (1950) 22 44 66 124 172 220
7- "Gunmen of Abilene"; Rocky Lane; Bob Powell-a (1950) 27 54 81 153 214 275
8- "King of the Bullwhip"; Lash LaRue; Bob Powell-a (1950) 39 78 117 230 325 420
9- "The Old Frontier"; Monte Hale; Bob Powell-a (2/51; mis-dated 2/50) 26 52 78 147 206 265
10- "The Missourians"; Monte Hale (4/51) 26 52 78 147 206 265
11- "The Thundering Trail"; Lash LaRue (6/51) 32 64 96 184 262 340
12- "Rustlers on Horseback"; Rocky Lane (8/51) 27 54 81 153 214 275
13- "Warpath"; Edmond O'Brien & Forrest Tucker (10/51) 19 38 57 106 146 185
14- "Last Outpost"; Ronald Reagan (12/51) 42 84 126 252 359 465
15-(Scarce)- "The Man From Planet X"; Robert Clark; Schaffenberger-a (2/52) 228 456 684 1425 2138 2850
16- "10 Tall Men"; Burt Lancaster 15 30 45 86 118 150
17- "Rose of Cimarron"; Jack Buetel & Mala Powers 12 24 36 69 92 115
18- "The Brigand"; Anthony Dexter & Anthony Quinn; Schaffenberger-a 12 24 36 69 92 115
19- "Carbine Williams"; James Stewart; Costanza-a; James Stewart photo-c 13 26 39 76 103 130
20- "Ivanhoe"; Robert Taylor & Liz Taylor photo-c 23 46 69 132 186 240

FAWCETT'S FUNNY ANIMALS (No. 1-26, 80-on titled "Funny Animals"; becomes Li'l Tomboy No. 92 on?)
Fawcett Publications/Charlton Comics No. 84 on: 12/42 - #79, 4/53; #80, 6/53 - #83, 12?/53; #84, 4/54 - #91, 2/56
1-Capt. Marvel on cover; intro. Hoppy The Captain Marvel Bunny, cloned from Capt. Marvel; Billy the Kid & Willie the Worm begin 55 110 165 340 508 675
2-Xmas-c 33 66 99 190 270 350
3-5: 3(2/43)-Spirit of '43-c 20 40 60 112 156 200
6,7,9,10 14 28 42 81 111 140
8-Flag-c 15 30 45 86 118 150
11-20: 14-Cover is a 1944 calendar 11 22 33 63 84 105
21-40: 25-Xmas-c. 26-St. Valentines Day-c 8 16 24 46 58 70
41-86,90,91 7 14 21 37 46 55
87-89(10-54-2/55)-Merry Mailman ish (TV/Radio)-part photo-c 8 16 24 46 58 70

NOTE: *Marvel Bunny in all issues to at least No. 68 (not in 49-54).*

The F.B.I. #1 © DELL

Feature Comics #38 © QUA

Feature Films #2 © DC

GD VG FN VF VF/NM NM-
2.0 4.0 6.0 8.0 9.0 9.2

GD VG FN VF VF/NM NM-
2.0 4.0 6.0 8.0 9.0 9.2

FAZE ONE FAZERS
AC Comics: 1986 - No. 4, Sept, 1986 (Limited series)

1-4 2.25

F.B.I., THE
Dell Publishing Co.: Apr-June, 1965

1-Sinnott-a 3 6 9 19 25 32

F.B.I. STORY, THE (Movie)
Dell Publishing Co.: No. 1069, Jan-Mar, 1960

Four Color 1069-Toth-a; James Stewart photo-c 10 20 30 73 107 140

FEAR (Adventure into...)
Marvel Comics Group: Nov, 1970 - No. 31, Dec, 1975

1-Fantasy & Sci-Fi-r in early issues; 68 pg. Giant size; Kirby-a(r)
4 8 12 29 40 50
2-6: 2-4-(68 pgs.). 5,6-(52 pgs.) Kirby-a(r) 3 6 9 18 24 30
7-9-Kirby-a(r) 2 4 6 11 14 18
10-Man-Thing begins (10/72, 4th app.), ends #19; see Savage Tales #1 for 1st app.; 1st solo series; Chaykin/Morrow-c/a; 4 8 12 24 32 40
11,12: 11-N. Adams-c. 12-Starlin/Buckler-a 2 4 6 11 14 18
13,14,16-18: 17-Origin/1st app. Wundarr 2 4 6 10 12 15
15-1st full-length Man-Thing story (8/73) 2 4 6 11 14 18
19-Intro. Howard the Duck; Val Mayerik-a (12/73) 4 8 12 24 32 40
20-Morbius, the Living Vampire begins, ends #31; has history recap of Morbius with X-Men & Spider-Man 4 8 12 24 32 40
21-23,25 2 4 6 10 12 15
24-Blade-c/sty 3 6 9 18 23 28
26-31 2 4 6 8 10 12

NOTE: ***Bolle** a-13i. **Brunner** c-15-17. **Buckler** a-11p, 12i. **Chaykin** a-10i. **Colan** a-23r. **Craig** a-10p. **Ditko** a-6-8r. **Evans** a-30. **Everett** a-9, 10i, 21r. **Gulacy** a-20p. **Heath** a-12r. **Heck** a-8r, 13r. **Gil Kane** a-21p; c(p)-20, 21, 23-28, 31. **Kirby** a-1-9r. **Maneely** a-24r. **Mooney** a-11i, 26r. **Morrow** a-11i. **Paul Reinman** a-14r. **Robbins** a(p)-25-27, 31. **Russell** a-23p, 24p. **Severin** c-8. **Starlin** c-12p.*

FEARBOOK
Eclipse Comics: April, 1986 ($1.75, one-shot, mature)

1-Scholastic Mag- r; Bissette-a 2.25

FEAR EFFECT (Based on the video game)
Image Comics (Top Cow): May, 2000; March, 2001 ($2.95)

Retro Helix 1 (3/01), Special 1 (5/00) 3.00

FEAR IN THE NIGHT (See Complete Mystery No. 3)

FEARLESS FAGAN
Dell Publishing Co.: No. 441, Dec, 1952 (one-shot)

Four Color 441 4 8 12 28 38 48

FEATHER
Image Comics: Aug, 2003 - Present ($2.95)

1-3-Steve Uy-s/a 3.00

FEATURE BOOK (Dell) (See Large Feature Comic)

FEATURE BOOKS (Newspaper-r, early issues)
David McKay Publications: May, 1937 - No. 57, 1948 (B&W)
(Full color, 68 pgs. begin #26 on)

Note: See individual alphabetical listings for prices

nn-Popeye & the Jeep (#1, 100 pgs.); reprinted as Feature Books #3(Very Rare; only 3 known copies, 1-VF, 2-in low grade)
nn-Dick Tracy (#1)-Reprinted as Feature Book #4 (100 pgs.) & in part as 4-Color #1 (Rare, less than 10 known copies)

NOTE: *Above books were advertised together with different covers from Feat. Books #3 & 4.*

1-King of the Royal Mtd. (#1)
3-Popeye (7/37) by Segar;
4-Dick Tracy (8/37)-Same as nn issue but a new cover added
6-Dick Tracy (10/37)
8-Secret Agent X-9 (12/37) -Not by Raymond
9-Dick Tracy (1/38)
11-Little Annie Rooney (#1, 3/38)
13-Inspector Wade (5/38)
15-Barney Baxter (#1) (7/38)
17-Gangbusters (#1, 9/38) (1st app.)
20-Phantom (#1, 12/38)
22-Phantom
24-Lone Ranger (1941)
26-Prince Valiant (1941)-Hal Foster -c/a; newspaper strips reprinted, pgs. 1-28,30-63; color & 68 pg. issues begin; Foster cover is only original comic book artwork by him
2-Popeye (6/37) by Segar same as nn issue but a new cover added
5-Popeye (9/37) by Segar
7-Little Orphan Annie (#1, 11/37) (Rare)-Reprints strips from 12/31/34 to 7/17/35
10-Popeye (2/38)
12-Blondie (#1) (4/38) (Rare)
14-Popeye (6/38) by Segar
16-Red Eagle (8/38)
18,19-Mandrake
21-Lone Ranger
23-Mandrake
25-Flash Gordon (#1)-Reprints not by Raymond
36('43),38,40('44),42,43, 45,47-Blondie
39-Phantom
46-Mandrake in the Fire World-(58 pgs.)
48-Maltese Falcon by Dashiell Hammett('46)
51,54-Rip Kirby; Raymond-c/s; origin-#51
53,56,57-Phantom
27-29,31,34-Blondie
30-Katzenjammer Kids (#1, 1942)
32,35,41,44-Katzenjammer Kids
33(nn)-Romance of Flying; World War II photos
37-Katzenjammer Kids; has photo & biog. of Harold H.Knerr(1883-1949) who took over strip from Rudolph Dirks in 1914
49,50-Perry Mason; based on Gardner novels
52,55-Mandrake

NOTE: *All Feature Books through #25 are over-sized 8-1/2x11-3/8" comics with color covers and black and white interiors. The covers are rough, heavy stock. The page counts, including covers, are as follows: nn, #3, 4-100 pgs.; #1, 2-52 pgs.; #5-25 are all 76 pgs. #33 was found in bound set from publisher.*

FEATURE COMICS (Formerly Feature Funnies)
Quality Comics Group: No. 21, June, 1939 - No. 144, May, 1950

21-The Clock, Jane Arden & Mickey Finn continue from Feature Funnies
68 136 204 391 536 680
22-26: 23-Charlie Chan begins (8/39, 1st app.) 47 94 141 270 373 475
26-(nn, nd)-Cover in one color, (10¢, 36 pgs.; issue No. blanked out. Two variations exist, each contain half of the regular #26) 47 94 141 270 373 475
27-(Rare)-Origin/1st app. Doll Man by Eisner (scripts) & Lou Fine (art); Doll Man begins, ends #139 423 846 1269 2750 4375 6000
28-2nd app. Doll Man by Lou Fine 168 336 504 1050 1575 2100
29 96 192 288 600 900 1200
30-1st Doll Man-c 124 248 372 775 1163 1550
31-Last Clock & Charlie Chan issue (4/40); Charlie Chan moves to Big Shot #1 following month (5/40) 74 148 222 463 694 925
32,34,36: Dollman covers. 32-Rusty Ryan & Samar begin. 34-Captain Fortune app.
59 118 177 369 555 740
33,35,37: 37-Last Fine Doll Man 53 106 159 318 474 630

Note: *A 15¢ Canadian version of Feature Comics #37, made in the US, exists.*

38,40-Dollman covers. 38-Origin the Ace of Space. 40-Bruce Blackburn in costume
48 96 144 288 432 575
39,41: 39-Origin The Destroying Demon, ends #40; X-Mas-c.
42 84 126 252 376 500
42,46,48,50-Dollman covers. 42-USA, the Spirit of Old Glory begins. 46-Intro. Boyville Brigadiers in Rusty Ryan. 48-USA ends 39 78 117 230 325 420
43,45,47,49: 47-Fargo Kid begins 33 66 99 190 270 350
44-Doll Man by Crandall begins, ends #63; Crandall-a(2)
48 96 144 288 432 575
51,53,55,57,59: 57-Spider Widow begins 26 52 78 147 206 265
52,54,56,58,60-Dollman covers. 56-Marijuana story in Swing Sisson strip. 60-Raven begins, ends #71 30 60 90 170 240 310
61,63,65,67 23 46 69 132 186 240
62,64,66,68-Dollman covers. 68-(5/43) 27 54 81 153 214 275
69,71-Phantom Lady x-over in Spider Widow 26 52 78 147 206 265
70-Dollman-c; Phantom Lady x-over 29 58 87 164 232 300
72,74,77-80,100-Dollman covers. 72-Spider Widow ends
22 44 66 124 172 220
73,75,76 19 38 57 106 146 185
81-99-All Dollman covers 17 34 51 95 130 165
101-144: 139-Last Doll Man & last Doll Man cover. 140-Intro. Stuntman Stetson (Stuntman Stetson c-140-144) 13 26 39 74 100 125

NOTE: ***Celardo** a-37-43. **Crandall** a-44-60, 62, 63-on(most). **Gustavson** a-(Rusty Ryan)- 32-134. **Powell** a-34, 64-73. The Clock c-25, 28, 29. Doll Man c-30, 32, 34, 36, 38, 40, 42, 44, 46, 48, 50, 52, 54, 56, 58, 60, 62, 64, 66, 68, 70, 72, 74, 77-139. Joe Palooka c-21, 24, 27.*

FEATURE FILMS
National Periodical Publ.: Mar-Apr, 1950 - No. 4, Sept-Oct, 1950 (All photo-c)

1- "Captain China" with John Payne, Gail Russell, Lon Chaney & Edgar Bergen
66 132 198 413 619 825
2- "Riding High" with Bing Crosby 70 140 210 438 657 875
3- "The Eagle & the Hawk" with John Payne, Rhonda Fleming & D. O'Keefe
66 132 198 413 619 825
4- "Fancy Pants"; Bob Hope & Lucille Ball 74 148 222 463 694 925

FEATURE FUNNIES (Feature Comics No. 21 on)
Harry 'A' Chesler: Oct, 1937 - No. 20, May, 1939

1(V9#1-indicia)-Joe Palooka, Mickey Finn (1st app.), The Bungles, Jane Arden, Dixie Dugan (1st app.), Big Top, Ned Brant, Strange As It Seems, & Off the Record strip reprints begin
322 644 966 1770 2385 3000
2-The Hawk app. (11/37); Goldberg-c 150 300 450 825 1113 1400

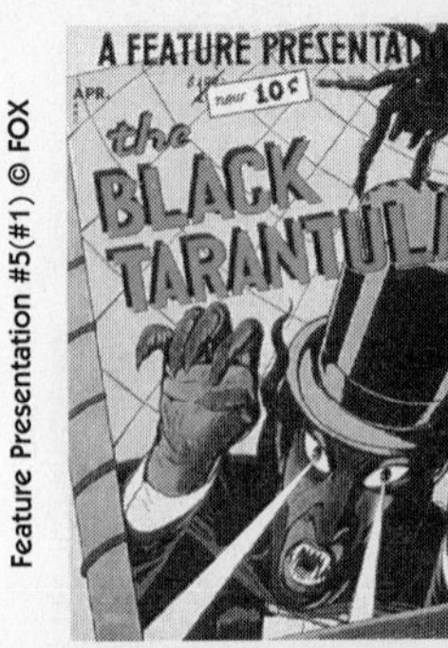

Feature Presentation #5(#1) © FOX

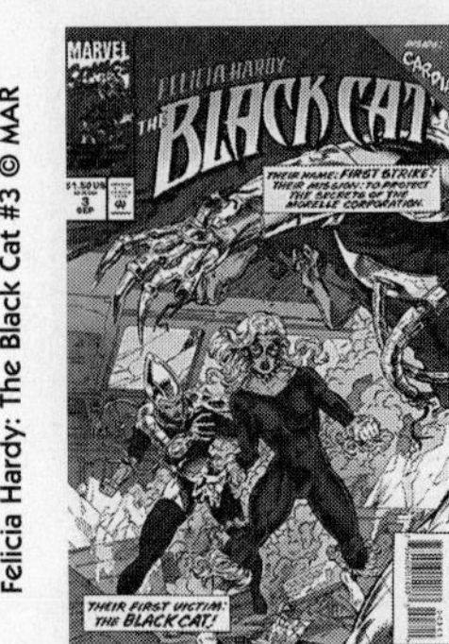

Felicia Hardy: The Black Cat #3 © MAR

Femforce #89 © AC

3-Hawks of Seas begins by Eisner, ends #12; The Clock begins; Christmas-c
117 234 351 644 872 1100
4,5 86 172 258 473 649 825
6-12: 11-Archie O'Toole by Bud Thomas begins, ends #22
67 134 201 369 505 640
13-Espionage, Starring Black X begins by Eisner, ends #20
71 142 213 391 533 675
14-20 50 100 150 275 380 485
NOTE: *Joe Palooka covers 1, 6, 9, 12, 15, 18.*

FEATURE PRESENTATION, A (Feature Presentations Magazine #6) (Formerly Women in Love) (Also see Startling Terror Tales #11)
Fox Features Syndicate: No. 5, April, 1950
5(#1)-Black Tarantula 40 80 120 240 340 440

FEATURE PRESENTATIONS MAGAZINE (Formerly A Feature Presentation #5; becomes Feature Stories Magazine #3 on)
Fox Features Syndicate: No. 6, July, 1950
6(#2)-Moby Dick; Wood-c 33 66 99 190 270 350

FEATURE STORIES MAGAZINE (Formerly Feature Presentations Mag. #6)
Fox Features Syndicate: No. 3, Aug, 1950
3-Jungle Lil, Zegra stories; bondage-c 35 70 105 201 288 370

FEDERAL MEN COMICS (See Adventure Comics #32, The Comics Magazine, New Adventure Comics, New Book of Comics, New Comics & Star Spangled Comics #91)
Gerard Publ. Co.: No. 2, 1945 (DC reprints from 1930's)
2-Siegel/Shuster-a; cover redrawn from Det. #9 40 80 120 240 340 440

FEEDERS
Dark Horse Comics: Oct, 1999 ($2.95, one-shot)
1-Mike Allred-c/a/Shane Hawks-s 3.00

FELICIA HARDY: THE BLACK CAT
Marvel Comics: July, 1994 - No. 4, Oct, 1994 ($1.50, limited series)
1-4: 1,4-Spider-Man app. 2.25

FELIX'S NEPHEWS INKY & DINKY
Harvey Publications: Sept, 1957 - No. 7, Oct, 1958
1-Cover shows Inky's left eye with 2 pupils 10 20 30 56 73 90
2-7 6 12 18 31 38 45
NOTE: ***Messmer** art in 1-6. **Oriolo** a-1-7.*

FELIX THE CAT (See Cat Tales 3-D, The Funnies, March of Comics #24,36,51, New Funnies & Popular Comics)
Dell Publ. No. 1-19/Toby No. 20-61/Harvey No. 62-118/Dell No. 1-12:
1943 - No. 118, Nov, 1961; Sept-Nov, 1962 - No. 12, July-Sept, 1965
Four Color 15 73 146 219 544 822 1100
Four Color 46('44) 40 80 120 300 450 600
Four Color 77('45) 37 74 111 278 419 560
Four Color 119('46)-All new stories begin 35 70 105 263 392 520
Four Color 135('46) 27 54 81 196 281 365
Four Color 162(9/47) 21 42 63 147 216 285
1(2-3/48)(Dell) 28 56 84 203 297 390
2 15 30 45 109 160 210
3-5 12 24 36 84 125 165
6-19(2-3/51-Dell) 10 20 30 67 96 125
20-30,32,33,36,38-61(6/55)-All Messmer issues.(Toby): 28-(2/52)-Some copies have #29 on cover, #28 on inside (Rare in high grade) 22 44 66 160 235 310
31,34,35-No Messmer-a; Messmer-c only 31,34 10 20 30 72 104 135
37-(100 pgs., 25 ¢, 1/15/53, X-Mas-c, Toby; daily & Sunday-r (rare)
44 88 132 330 490 650
62(8/55)-80,100 (Harvey) 6 12 18 38 52 65
81-99 5 10 15 33 44 55
101-118(11/61): 101-117-Reprints. 118-All new-a 4 8 12 24 32 40
12-269-211(#1, 9-11/62)(Dell)-No Messmer 5 10 15 34 45 60
2-12(7-9/65)(Dell, TV)-No Messmer 4 8 12 24 36 48
3-D Comic Book 1(1953-One Shot, 25¢)-w/glasses 35 70 105 218 319 420
Summer Annual nn ('53, 25¢, 100 pgs., Toby)-Daily & Sunday-r
37 74 111 278 414 550
Winter Annual 2 ('54, 25¢, 100 pgs., Toby)-Daily & Sunday-r
35 70 105 263 392 520
(Special note: Despite the covers on Toby 37 and the Summer Annual above proclaiming "all new stories," they were actually reformatted newspaper strips)
NOTE: ***Otto Messmer** went to work for Universal Film as an animator in 1915 and then worked for the Pat Sullivan animation studio in 1916. He created a black cat in the cartoon short, Feline Follies in 1919 that became known as Felix in the early 1920s. The Felix Sunday strip began Aug. 14, 1923 and continued until Sept. 19, 1943 whjen **Messmer** took the character to Dell (Western Publishing) and began doing Felix comic books, first adapting strips to the comic format. The first all new Felix comic was Four Color #119 in 1946 (#4 in the Dell run). The daily Felix was begun on May 9, 1927 by another artist, but by the following year, **Messmer** did it too. King Features took the daily away from **Messmer** in 1954 and he began to do some of his most dynamic art for Toby Press. The daily was continued by **Joe Oriolo** who drew it until it was discontinued Jan. 9, 1967. **Oriolo** was **Messmer's** assistant for many years and inked some of **Messmer's** pencils through the Toby run, as well as doing some of the stories by himself. Though **Messmer** continued to work for Harvey, his contirubitons were limited, and no all **Messmer** stories appeared after the Toby run until some early Toby reprints were published in the 1990s Harvey revival of the title. 4-Color No. 15, 46, 77 and the Toby Annuals are all daily or Sunday newspaper reprints from the 1930's-1940's drawn by **Otto Messmer**. #101-r/#64; 102-r/#65; 103-r/#67; 104-117-r/#68-81. **Messmer**-a in all Dell/Toby/Harvey issues except #31, 34, 35, 97, 98, 100, 118. **Oriolo** a-20, 31-on.*

FELIX THE CAT (Also see The Nine Lives of...)
Harvey Comics/Gladstone: Sept, 1991 - No. 7, Jan, 1993 ($1.25/$1.50, bi-monthly)
1: 1950s-r/Toby issues by Messmer begins. 1-Inky and Dinky back-up story (produced by Gladstone) 4.00
2-7, Big Book , V2#1 (9/92, $1.95, 52 pgs.) 3.00

FELIX THE CAT AND FRIENDS
Felix Comics: 1992 - No. 5, 1993 ($1.95)
1-5: 1-Contains Felix trading cards 3.00

FELIX THE CAT & HIS FRIENDS (Pat Sullivan's...)
Toby Press: Dec, 1953 - No. 3, 1954 (Indicia title for #2&3 as listed)
1 (Indicia title, "Felix and His Friends," #1 only) 31 62 93 175 248 320
2-3 19 38 57 109 152 195

FELIX THE CAT DIGEST MAGAZINE
Harvey Comics: July, 1992 ($1.75, digest-size, 98 pgs.)
1-Felix, Richie Rich stories 5.00

FELIX THE CAT KEEPS ON WALKIN'
Hamilton Comics: 1991 ($15.95, 8-1/2"x11", 132 pgs.)
nn-Reprints 15 Toby Press Felix the Cat and Felix and His Friends stories in new color 16.00

FELON
Image Comics (Minotaur Press): Nov, 2001 - No. 4, Apr, 2002 ($2.95, B&W)
1-4-Rucka-s/Clark-a/c 3.00

FEM FANTASTIQUE
AC Comics: Aug, 1988 ($1.95, B&W)
V2#1-By Bill Black; Betty Page pin-up 4.00

FEMFORCE (Also see Untold Origin of the Femforce)
Americomics: Apr, 1985 - No. 109 (1.75-/2.95, B&W #16-56)
1-Black-a in most; Nightveil, Ms. Victory begin 1 3 4 6 8 10
2-10 4.00
11-43: 25-Origin/1st app. new Ms. Victory. 28-Colt leaves. 29,30-Camilla-r by Mayo from Jungle Comics. 36-(2.95, 52 pgs.) 4.00
44,64: 44-W/mini-comic, Catman & Kitten #0. 64-Re-intro Black Phantom 5.00
45-63,65-99: 50 (2.95, 52 pgs.)-Contains flexi-disc; origin retold; most AC characters app. 51-Photo-c from movie. 57-Begin color issues. 95-Photo-c 3.00
100-($3.95) 5.00
100-($6.90)-Polybagged 1 2 3 5 6 8
101-109-($4.95) 5.00
Special 1 (Fall, '84)(B&W, 52pgs.)-1st app. Ms. Victory, She-Cat, Blue Bulleteer, Rio Rita & Lady Luger 4.00
Bad Girl Backlash-(12/95, $5.00) 5.00
Frightbook 1 ('92, $2.95, B&W)-Halloween special, In the House of Horror 1 ('89, 2.50, B&W), Night of the Demon 1 ('90, 2.75, B&W), Out of the Asylum Special 1 ('87, B&W, $1.95), Pin-Up Portfolio 3.50
Pin-Up Portfolio (5 issues) 4.00

FEMFORCE UP CLOSE
AC Comics: Apr, 1992 - No. 11, 1995 ($2.75, quarterly)
1-11: 1-Stars Nightveil; inside f/c photo from Femforce movie. 2-Stars Stardust. 3-Stars Dragonfly. 4-Stars She-Cat 3.50

FERDINAND THE BULL (See Mickey Mouse Magazine V4#3)
Dell Publishing Co.: 1938 (10¢, large size, some color w/rest B&W)
nn 20 40 60 112 156 200

FERRET
Malibu Comics: Sept, 1992; May, 1993 - No. 10, Feb, 1994 ($1.95)
1-(1992, one-shot) 3.00
1-10: 1-Die-cut-c. 2-4-Collector's Ed. w/poster. 5-Polybagged w/Skycap 2.50
2-4-($1.95)-Newsstand Edition w/different-c 2.25

FEUD
Marvel Comics (Epic Comics/Heavy Hitters): July, 1993 - No. 4, Oct, 1993 ($1.95, limited series)

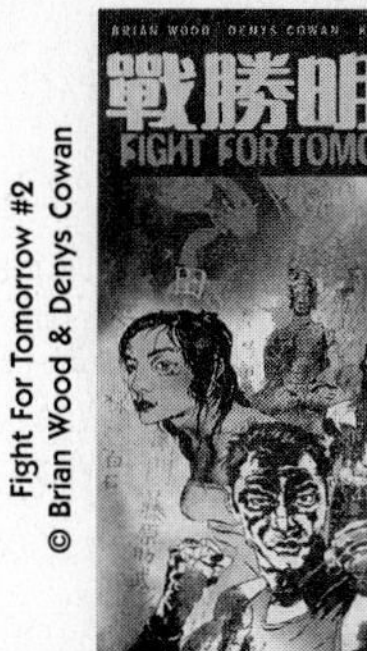

Fight Comics #74 © FH

Fight For Tomorrow #2 © Brian Wood & Denys Cowan

Fighting American: Dogs of War #1 © Awesome Ent.

	GD 2.0	VG 4.0	FN 6.0	VF 8.0	VF/NM 9.0	NM- 9.2
1-($2.50)-Embossed-c						3.00
2-4						2.25

F5
Image Comics/Dark Horse: Jan, 2000 - No. 4, Oct, 2000 ($2.50/$2.95)

	GD 2.0	VG 4.0	FN 6.0	VF 8.0	VF/NM 9.0	NM- 9.2
Preview (1/00, $2.50) Character bios and b&w pages; Daniel-s/a						2.50
1-($2.95, 48 pages) Tony Daniel-s/a						3.00
1-($20.00) Variant bikini-c						20.00
2-4-($2.50)						2.50
F5 Origin (Dark Horse Comics, 11/01, $2.99) w/cove gallery & sketches						3.00

FIBBER McGEE & MOLLY (Radio)(Also see A-1 Comics)
Magazine Enterprises: No. 25, 1949 (one-shot)

	GD 2.0	VG 4.0	FN 6.0	VF 8.0	VF/NM 9.0	NM- 9.2
A-1 25	10	20	30	58	77	95

55 DAYS AT PEKING (See Movie Comics)

FICTION ILLUSTRATED
Byron Preiss Visual Publ./Pyramid: No. 1, Jan, 1975 - No. 4, Jan, 1977 ($1.00, #1,2 are digest size, 132 pgs.; #3,4 are graphic novels for mail order and specialty bookstores only)

	GD 2.0	VG 4.0	FN 6.0	VF 8.0	VF/NM 9.0	NM- 9.2
1,2: 1-Schlomo Raven; Sutton-a. 2-Starfawn; Stephen Fabian-a.	2	4	6	12	16	20
3-($1.00-c, 4 3/4 x 6 1/2" digest size) Chandler; new Steranko-a	3	6	9	16	20	24
3-($4.95-c, 8 1/2 x 11" graphic novel; low print) same contents and indicia, but "Chandler" is the cover feature title	6	12	18	40	55	70
4-($4.95-c, 8 1/2 x 11" graphic novel; low print) Son of Sherlock Holmes; Reese-a	5	10	15	33	44	55

FIGHT AGAINST CRIME (Fight Against the Guilty #22, 23)
Story Comics: May, 1951 - No. 21, Sept, 1954

	GD 2.0	VG 4.0	FN 6.0	VF 8.0	VF/NM 9.0	NM- 9.2
1-True crime stories #1-4	39	78	117	230	325	420
2	20	40	60	112	156	200
3,5: 5-Frazetta-a, 1 pg.; content change to horror & suspense	18	36	54	101	138	175
4-Drug story "Hopped Up Killers"	19	38	57	106	146	185
6,7: 6-Used in **POP**, pgs. 83,84	15	30	45	86	118	150
8-Last crime format issue	14	28	42	79	107	135

NOTE: *No. 9-21 contain violent, gruesome stories with blood, dismemberment, decapitation, E.C. style plot twists and several E.C. swipes. Bondage c-4, 6, 18, 19.*

	GD 2.0	VG 4.0	FN 6.0	VF 8.0	VF/NM 9.0	NM- 9.2
9-11,13	38	76	114	219	310	400
12-Morphine drug story "The Big Dope"	40	80	120	240	340	440
14-Tothish art by Ross Andru; electrocution-c	39	78	117	233	329	425
15-B&W & color illos in **POP**	38	76	114	219	310	400
16-E.C. story swipe/Haunt of Fear #19; Tothish-a by Ross Andru; bondage-c	40	80	120	240	340	440
17-Wildey E.C. swipe/Shock SuspenStories #9; knife through neck-c (1/54)	39	78	117	233	329	425
18,19: 19-Bondage/torture-c	36	72	108	204	290	375
20-Decapitation cover; contains hanging, ax murder, blood & violence	58	116	174	363	544	725
21-E.C. swipe	31	62	93	178	252	325

NOTE: *Cameron a-4, 5, 8. **Hollingsworth** a-3-7, 9, 10, 13. **Wildey** a-6, 15, 16.*

FIGHT AGAINST THE GUILTY (Formerly Fight Against Crime)
Story Comics: No. 22, Dec, 1954 - No. 23, Mar, 1955

	GD 2.0	VG 4.0	FN 6.0	VF 8.0	VF/NM 9.0	NM- 9.2
22-Tothish-a by Ross Andru; Ditko-a; E.C. story swipe; electrocution-c (Last pre-code)	31	62	93	175	248	320
23-Hollingsworth-a	21	42	63	118	164	210

FIGHT COMICS
Fiction House Magazines: Jan, 1940 - No. 83, 11/52; No. 84, Wint, 1952-53; No. 85, Spring, 1953; No. 86, Summer, 1954

	GD 2.0	VG 4.0	FN 6.0	VF 8.0	VF/NM 9.0	NM- 9.2
1-Origin Spy Fighter, Starring Saber; Jack Dempsey life story; Shark Brodie & Chip Collins begin; Fine-c; Eisner-a	333	666	1000	2165	3333	4500
2-Joe Louis life story; Fine/Eisner-c	118	236	354	738	1107	1475
3-Rip Regan, the Power Man begins (3/40)	92	184	276	575	863	1150
4,5: 4-Fine-c	66	132	198	413	619	825
6-10: 6,7-Powell-c	50	100	150	300	450	600
11-14: Rip Regan ends	46	92	138	276	413	550
15-1st app. Super American plus-c (10/41)	60	120	180	375	563	750
16-Captain Fight begins (12/41); Spy Fighter ends	60	120	180	375	563	750
17,18: Super American ends	46	92	138	276	413	550
19-Captain Fight ends; Senorita Rio begins (6/42, origin & 1st app.); Rip Carson, Chute Trooper begins	48	96	144	288	432	575
20	41	82	123	246	348	450
21-30	33	66	99	190	270	350
31-Decapitation-c	36	72	108	204	290	375
32-Tiger Girl begins (6/44, 1st app.?)	40	80	120	240	340	440
33-50: 44-Capt. Fight returns. 48-Used in Love and Death by Legman. 49-Jungle-c begin, end #81	25	50	75	144	198	255
51-Origin Tiger Girl; Patsy Pin-Up app.	39	78	117	230	325	420
52-60,62-64-Last Baker issue	22	44	66	124	172	220
61-Origin Tiger Girl retold	24	48	72	135	190	245
65-78: 78-Used in **POP**, pg. 99	19	38	57	106	146	185
79-The Space Rangers app.	19	38	57	107	149	190
80-85: 81-Last jungle-c. 82-85-War-c/stories	16	32	48	92	126	160
86-Two Tigerman stories by Evans-r/Rangers Comics #40,41; Moreira-r/Rangers Comics #45	16	32	48	92	126	160

NOTE: *Bondage covers, Lingerie, headlights panels are common. Captain Fight by **Kamen**-51-66. Kayo Kirby by **Baker**-#43-64, 67(not by Baker). Senorita Rio by **Kamen**-#57-64; by **Grandenetti**-#65, 66. Tiger Girl by **Baker**-#36-60, 62-64; **Eisner** c-1-3, 5, 10, 11. **Kamen** a-54?, 57? **Tuska** a-1, 5, 8, 10, 21, 29, 34. **Whitman** c-73-84. **Zolnerwich** c-16, 17, 22. Power Man c-5, 6, 9. Super American c-15-17. Tiger Girl c-49-81.*

FIGHT FOR LOVE
United Features Syndicate: 1952 (no month)

	GD 2.0	VG 4.0	FN 6.0	VF 8.0	VF/NM 9.0	NM- 9.2
nn-Abbie & Slats newspaper-r	9	18	27	54	70	85

FIGHT FOR TOMORROW
DC Comics (Vertigo): Nov, 2002 - No. 6, Apr, 2003 ($2.50, limited series)

	GD 2.0	VG 4.0	FN 6.0	VF 8.0	VF/NM 9.0	NM- 9.2
1-6-Denys Cowan-a/Brian Wood-s. 1-Jim Lee-c						2.50

FIGHTING AIR FORCE (See United States Fighting Air Force)

FIGHTIN' AIR FORCE (Formerly Sherlock Holmes?; Never Again? War and Attack #54 on)
Charlton Comics: No. 3, Feb, 1956 - No. 53, Feb-Mar, 1966

	GD 2.0	VG 4.0	FN 6.0	VF 8.0	VF/NM 9.0	NM- 9.2
V1#3	8	16	24	46	58	70
4-10	6	12	18	28	34	40
11(3/58, 68 pgs.)	8	16	24	40	50	60
12 (100 pgs.)-U.S. Nukes Russia	11	22	33	63	84	105
13-30: 13,24-Glanzman-a. 24-Glanzman-c	3	6	9	19	25	32
31-50: 50-American Eagle begins	2	4	6	14	18	22
51-53	2	4	6	11	14	18

FIGHTING AMERICAN
Headline Publ./Prize (Crestwood): Apr-May, 1954 - No. 7, Apr-May, 1955

	GD 2.0	VG 4.0	FN 6.0	VF 8.0	VF/NM 9.0	NM- 9.2
1-Origin & 1st app. Fighting American & Speedboy (Capt. America & Bucky clones); S&K-c/a(3); 1st super hero satire series	168	336	504	1050	1575	2100
2-S&K-a(3)	77	154	231	481	723	965
3-5: 3,4-S&K-a(3). 5-S&K-a(2); Kirby/?-a	62	124	186	388	582	775
6-Origin-r (4 pgs.) plus 2 pgs. by S&K	59	118	177	369	552	735
7-Kirby-a	53	106	159	318	474	630

NOTE: ***Simon** & **Kirby** covers on all. 6 is last pre-code issue.*

FIGHTING AMERICAN
Harvey Publications: Oct, 1966 (25¢)

	GD 2.0	VG 4.0	FN 6.0	VF 8.0	VF/NM 9.0	NM- 9.2
1-Origin Fighting American & Speedboy by S&K-r; S&K-c/a(3); 1 pg. Neal Adams ad	6	12	18	40	55	70

FIGHTING AMERICAN
DC Comics: Feb, 1994 - No. 6, 1994 ($1.50, limited series)

	GD 2.0	VG 4.0	FN 6.0	VF 8.0	VF/NM 9.0	NM- 9.2
1-6						2.50

FIGHTING AMERICAN (Vol. 3)
Awesome Entertainment: Aug, 1997 - No. 2, Oct, 1997 ($2.50)

	GD 2.0	VG 4.0	FN 6.0	VF 8.0	VF/NM 9.0	NM- 9.2
Preview-Agent America (pre-lawsuit)	1	2	3	5	6	7
1-Four covers by Liefeld, Churchill, Platt, McGuinness						2.50
1-Platinum Edition, 1-Gold foil Edition						10.00
1-Comic Cavalcade Edition, 2-American Ent. Spice Ed.						4.00
2-Platt-c, 2-Liefeld variant-c						2.50

FIGHTING AMERICAN: DOGS OF WAR
Awesome-Hyperwerks: Sept, 1998 - No. 3, May, 1999 ($2.50)

	GD 2.0	VG 4.0	FN 6.0	VF 8.0	VF/NM 9.0	NM- 9.2
Limited Convention Special (7/98, B&W) Platt-a						2.50
1-3-Starlin-s/Platt-a/c						2.50

FIGHTING AMERICAN: RULES OF THE GAME
Awesome Entertainment: Nov, 1997 - No. 3, Mar, 1998 ($2.50, lim. series)

	GD 2.0	VG 4.0	FN 6.0	VF 8.0	VF/NM 9.0	NM- 9.2
1-3: 1-Loeb-s/McGuinness-a/c. 2-Flip book with Swat! preview						2.50
1-Liefeld SPICE variant-c, 1-Dynamic Forces Ed.; McGuinness-c						2.50
1-Liefeld Fighting American & cast variant-c						2.50

FIGHTIN' ARMY (Formerly Soldier and Marine Comics) (See Captain Willy Schultz)
Charlton Comics: No. 16, 1/56 - No. 127, 12/76; No. 128, 9/77 - No. 172, 11/84

	GD 2.0	VG 4.0	FN 6.0	VF 8.0	VF/NM 9.0	NM- 9.2
16	8	16	24	46	58	70
17-19,21-23,25-30	6	12	18	28	34	40

Fighting Underseas Commandos #4 © AVON

Fighting War Stories #1 © Men's Publ.

Fighting Yank #13 © Nedor

	GD 2.0	VG 4.0	FN 6.0	VF 8.0	VF/NM 9.0	NM- 9.2
20-Ditko-a	8	16	24	46	58	70
24 (3/58, 68 pgs.)	7	14	21	37	46	55
31-45	3	6	9	18	24	30
46-60	3	6	9	16	20	24
61-74	2	4	6	11	14	18
75-1st The Lonely War of Willy Schultz	3	6	9	18	23	28
76-80: 76-92-The Lonely War of Willy Schultz. 79-Devil Brigade	2	4	6	12	16	20
81-88,91,93-99: 82,83-Devil Brigade	2	4	6	10	12	15
89,90,92-Ditko-a	2	4	6	14	18	22
100	2	4	6	11	14	18
101-127	2	4	6	8	10	12
128-140	1	2	3	5	6	8
141-165						6.00
166-172-Low print run	1	2	3	5	6	8
108(Modern Comics-1977)-Reprint						4.00

NOTE: *Aparo c-154.* ***Glanzman*** *a-77-88.* ***Montes/Bache*** *a-48, 49, 51, 69, 75, 76, 170r.*

FIGHTING CARAVANS (See Zane Grey 4-Color 632)

FIGHTING DANIEL BOONE
Avon Periodicals: 1953

	GD 2.0	VG 4.0	FN 6.0	VF 8.0	VF/NM 9.0	NM- 9.2
nn-Kinstler-c/a, 22 pgs.	20	40	60	112	156	200
I.W. Reprint #1-Reprints #1 above; Kinstler-c/a; Lawrence/Alascia-a	3	6	9	16	20	24

FIGHTING DAVY CROCKETT (Formerly Kit Carson)
Avon Periodicals: No. 9, Oct-Nov, 1955

	GD 2.0	VG 4.0	FN 6.0	VF 8.0	VF/NM 9.0	NM- 9.2
9-Kinstler-c	9	18	27	54	70	85

FIGHTIN' FIVE, THE (Formerly Space War) (Also see The Peacemaker)
Charlton Comics: July, 1964 - No. 41, Jan, 1967; No. 42, Oct, 1981 - No. 49, Dec, 1982

	GD 2.0	VG 4.0	FN 6.0	VF 8.0	VF/NM 9.0	NM- 9.2
V2#28-Origin/1st app. Fightin' Five; Montes/Bache-a	6	12	18	40	55	70
29-39,41-Montes/Bache-a in all	3	7	10	21	28	35
40-Peacemaker begins (1st app.)	6	12	18	43	59	75
41-Peacemaker (2nd app.)	4	8	12	29	40	50
42-49: Reprints						5.00

FIGHTING FRONTS!
Harvey Publications: Aug, 1952 - No. 5, Jan, 1953

	GD 2.0	VG 4.0	FN 6.0	VF 8.0	VF/NM 9.0	NM- 9.2
1	9	18	27	52	66	80
2-Extreme violence; Nostrand/Powell-a	10	20	30	58	77	95
3-5: 3-Powell-a	7	14	21	35	43	50

FIGHTING INDIAN STORIES (See Midget Comics)

FIGHTING INDIANS OF THE WILD WEST!
Avon Periodicals: Mar, 1952 - No. 2, Nov, 1952

	GD 2.0	VG 4.0	FN 6.0	VF 8.0	VF/NM 9.0	NM- 9.2
1-Geronimo, Chief Crazy Horse, Chief Victorio, Black Hawk begin; Larsen-a; McCann-a(2)	17	34	51	98	134	170
2-Kinstler-c & inside-c only; Larsen, McCann-a	11	22	33	63	84	105
100 Pg. Annual (1952, 25¢)-Contains three comics rebound; Geronimo, Chief Crazy Horse, Chief Victorio; Kinstler-c	33	66	99	190	270	350

FIGHTING LEATHERNECKS
Toby Press: Feb, 1952 - No. 6, Dec, 1952

	GD 2.0	VG 4.0	FN 6.0	VF 8.0	VF/NM 9.0	NM- 9.2
1- "Duke's Diary"; full pg. pin-ups by Sparling	14	28	42	79	107	135
2-5: 2- "Duke's Diary". 3-5- "Gil's Gals"; full pg. pin-ups	10	20	30	56	73	90
6-(Same as No. 3-5?)	10	20	30	56	73	90

FIGHTING MAN, THE (War)
Ajax/Farrell Publications(Excellent Publ.): May, 1952 - No. 8, July, 1953

	GD 2.0	VG 4.0	FN 6.0	VF 8.0	VF/NM 9.0	NM- 9.2
1	14	28	42	79	107	135
2	8	16	24	40	50	60
3-8	7	14	21	35	43	50
Annual 1 (1952, 25¢, 100 pgs.)	24	48	72	138	194	250

FIGHTIN' MARINES (Formerly The Texan; also see Approved Comics)
St. John(Approved Comics)/Charlton Comics No. 14 on:
No. 15, 8/51 - No. 12, 3/53; No. 14, 5/55 - No. 132, 11/76; No. 133, 10/77 - No. 176, 9/84 (No #13?) (Korean War #1-3)

	GD 2.0	VG 4.0	FN 6.0	VF 8.0	VF/NM 9.0	NM- 9.2
15(#1)-Matt Baker c/a "Leatherneck Jack"; slightly large size; Fightin' Texan No. 16 & 17?	40	80	120	240	340	440
2-1st Canteen Kate by Baker; slightly large size; partial Baker-c	44	88	132	264	395	525
3-9,11-Canteen Kate by Baker; Baker c-#2,3,5-11; 4-Partial Baker-c	25	50	75	144	198	255
10-Matt Baker-c	10	20	30	58	77	95
12-No Baker-a; Last St. John issue?	7	14	21	35	43	50
14 (5/55; 1st Charlton issue; formerly?)-Canteen Kate by Baker; all stories reprinted from #2	19	38	57	106	146	185
15-Baker-c	9	18	27	52	66	80
16,18-20-Not Baker-c	6	12	18	28	34	40
17-Canteen Kate by Baker	14	28	42	79	107	135
21-24	5	10	15	24	30	35
25-(68 pgs.)(3/58)-Check-a?	9	18	27	49	62	75
26-(100 pgs.)(8/58)-Check-a(5)	13	26	39	74	100	125
27-50	3	6	9	18	24	30
51-81: 78-Shotgun Harker & the Chicken series begin	2	4	6	14	18	22
82-(100 pgs.)	4	8	12	29	40	50
83-85: 85-Last 12¢ issue	2	4	6	12	16	20
86-94: 94-Last 15¢ issue	2	4	6	10	13	16
95-100,122: 122-(1975) Pilot issue for "War" title (Fightin' Marines Presents War)	2	4	6	9	11	14
101-121	1	3	4	6	8	10
123-140	1	2	3	5	6	8
141-170						6.00
171-176-Low print run	1	2	3	5	6	8
120(Modern Comics reprint, 1977)						4.00

NOTE: *No. 14 & 16 (CC) reprint St. John issues; No. 16 reprints St. John insignia on cover.* ***Colan*** *a-3, 7.* ***Glanzman*** *c/a-92, 94.* ***Montes/Bache*** *a-48, 53, 55, 64, 65, 72-74, 77-83, 176r.*

FIGHTING MARSHAL OF THE WILD WEST (See The Hawk)

FIGHTIN' NAVY (Formerly Don Winslow)
Charlton Comics: No. 74, 1/56 - No. 125, 4-5/66; No. 126, 8/83 - No. 133, 10/84

	GD 2.0	VG 4.0	FN 6.0	VF 8.0	VF/NM 9.0	NM- 9.2
74	6	12	18	40	55	70
75-81	4	8	12	24	32	40
82-Sam Glanzman-a	4	8	12	25	33	42
83-(100 pgs.)	7	14	21	46	63	80
84-99,101: 101-UFO story	3	6	9	18	24	30
100	3	6	9	19	25	32
102-105,106-125('66)	2	4	6	14	18	22
126-133 (1984)-Low print run	1	2	3	5	6	8

NOTE: ***Montes/Bache*** *a-109.* ***Glanzman*** *a-82, 92, 96, 98, 100, 131r.*

FIGHTING PRINCE OF DONEGAL, THE (See Movie Comics)

FIGHTIN' TEXAN (Formerly The Texan & Fightin' Marines?)
St. John Publishing Co.: No. 16, Sept, 1952 - No. 17, Dec, 1952

	GD 2.0	VG 4.0	FN 6.0	VF 8.0	VF/NM 9.0	NM- 9.2
16,17: Tuska-a each. 17-Cameron-c/a	8	16	24	43	54	65

FIGHTING UNDERSEA COMMANDOS (See Undersea Fighting...)
Avon Periodicals: May, 1952 - No. 5, April, 1953 (U.S. Navy frogmen)

	GD 2.0	VG 4.0	FN 6.0	VF 8.0	VF/NM 9.0	NM- 9.2
1-Cover title is Undersea Fighting... #1 only	15	30	45	86	118	150
2	10	20	30	58	77	95
3-5: 1,3-Ravielli-c. 4-Kinstler-c	9	18	27	52	66	80

FIGHTING WAR STORIES
Men's Publications/Story Comics: Aug, 1952 - No. 5, 1953

	GD 2.0	VG 4.0	FN 6.0	VF 8.0	VF/NM 9.0	NM- 9.2
1	10	20	30	56	73	90
2-5	6	12	18	31	38	45

FIGHTING YANK (See America's Best Comics & Startling Comics)
Nedor/Better Publ./Standard: Sept, 1942 - No. 29, Aug, 1949

	GD 2.0	VG 4.0	FN 6.0	VF 8.0	VF/NM 9.0	NM- 9.2
1-The Fighting Yank begins; Mystico, the Wonder Man app; bondage-c	264	528	792	1650	2475	3300
2	109	218	327	681	1021	1360
3,4: 4-Schomburg-c begin	78	156	234	488	732	975
5-10: 7-Grim Reaper app. 8,10-Bondage/torture-c	61	122	183	381	571	760
11,13-20: 11-The Oracle app. 15-Bondage/torture-c. 18-The American Eagle app.	51	102	153	306	458	610
12-Hirohito bondage-c	58	116	174	363	544	725
21,24: 21-Kara, Jungle Princess app.; lingerie-c. 24-Miss Masque app.	46	92	138	276	413	550
22-Miss Masque-c/story	53	106	159	318	479	640
23-Classic Schomburg hooded vigilante-c	64	128	192	400	600	800
25-Robinson/Meskin-a; strangulation, lingerie panel; The Cavalier app.	53	106	159	318	479	640
26-29: All-Robinson/Meskin-a. 28-One pg. Williamson-a	44	88	132	264	395	525

NOTE: ***Schomburg (Xela)*** *c-4-29; airbrush-c 28, 29. Bondage c-1, 4, 8, 10, 11, 12, 15, 17.*

FIGHTMAN
Marvel Comics: June, 1993 ($2.00, one-shot, 52 pgs.)

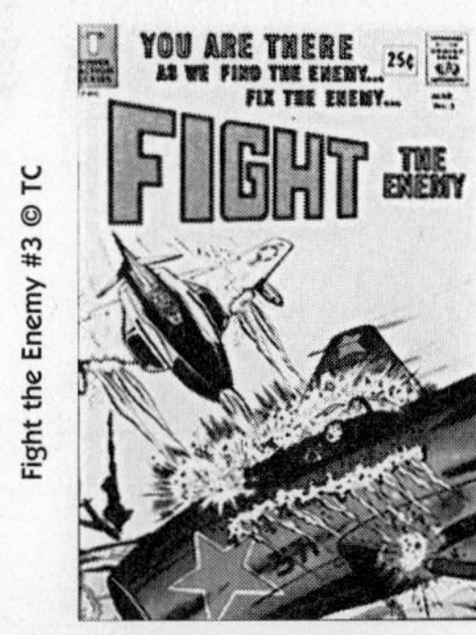

Fight the Enemy #3 © TC

Firebreather #1
© Phil Hester and Andy Kuhn

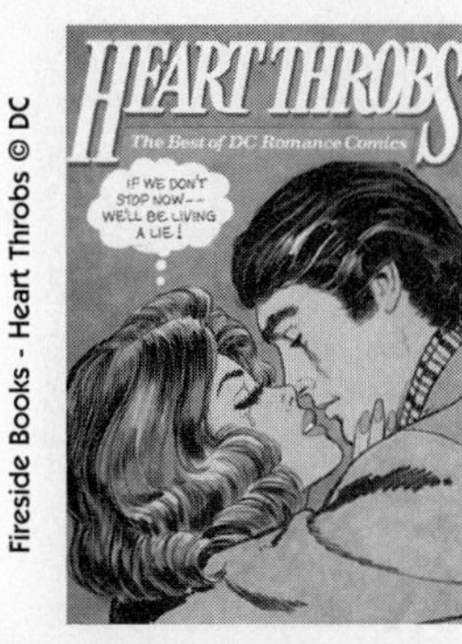

Fireside Books - Heart Throbs © DC

	GD	VG	FN	VF	VF/NM	NM-
	2.0	4.0	6.0	8.0	9.0	9.2

GD VG FN VF VF/NM NM- 2.0 4.0 6.0 8.0 9.0 9.2

1 — 2.25

FIGHT THE ENEMY
Tower Comics: Aug, 1966 - No. 3, Mar, 1967 (25¢, 68 pgs.)

1-Lucky 7 & Mike Manly begin	4	8	12	29	40	50
2-Boris Vallejo, McWilliams-a	4	8	12	22	30	38
3-Wood-a (1/2 pg.); McWilliams, Bolle-a	4	8	12	22	30	38

FILM FUNNIES
Marvel Comics (CPC): Nov, 1949 - No. 2, Feb, 1950 (52 pgs.)

1-Krazy Krow, Wacky Duck	19	38	57	106	146	185
2-Wacky Duck	14	28	42	79	107	135

FILM STARS ROMANCES
Star Publications: Jan-Feb, 1950 - No. 3, May-June, 1950 (True life stories of movie stars)

1-Rudy Valentino & Gregory Peck stories; L. B. Cole-c; lingerie panels	44	88	132	264	395	525
2-Liz Taylor/Robert Taylor photo-c & true life story	48	96	144	288	432	575
3-Douglas Fairbanks story; photo-c	27	54	81	153	214	275

FILTH, THE
DC Comics (Vertigo): Aug, 2002 - No. 13, Oct, 2003 ($2.95, limited series)

1-13-Morrison-s/Weston & Erskine-a — 3.00

FINAL CYCLE, THE
Dragon's Teeth Productions: July, 1987 - No. 4, 1988 (Limited series)

1-4 — 2.25

FINAL NIGHT, THE (See DC related titles and Parallax: Emerald Night)
DC Comics: Nov, 1996 - No. 4, Nov, 1996 ($1.95, weekly limited series)

1-4: Kesel-s/Immonen-a(p) in all. 4-Parallax's final acts — 3.50
Preview — 2.25
TPB-(1998, $12.95) r/#1-4, Parallax: Emerald Night #1, and preview — 13.00

FINALS
DC Comics (Vertigo): Sept, 1999 - No. 4, Dec, 1999 ($2.95, limited series)

1-4-Will Pfeifer-s/Jill Thompson-a — 3.00

FIRE
Caliber Press: 1993 - No. 2, 1993 ($2.95, B&W, limited series, 52 pgs.)

1,2-Brian Michael Bendis-s/a — 3.00
TPB (1999, 2001, $9.95) Restored reprints of series — 10.00

FIREARM (Also see Codename: Firearm, Freex #15, Night Man #4 & Prime #10)
Malibu Comics (Ultraverse): Sept, 1993 - No. 18, Mar, 1995 ($1.95/$2.50)

0 ($14.95)-Came w/ video containing 1st half of story (comic contains 2nd half); 1st app. Duet — 15.00
1,3-6: 1-James Robinson scripts begin; Cully Hamner-a; Chaykin-c; 1st app. Alec Swan. 3-Intro The Sportsmen; Chaykin-c. 4-Break-Thru x-over; Chaykin-c. 5-1st app. Ellen (Swan's girlfriend);2 pg. origin of Prime. 6-Prime app. (story cont'd in Prime #10); Brereton-c — 2.50
1-($2.50)-Newsstand edition polybagged w/card — 3.00
1-Ultra Limited silver foil-c — 5.00
2 ($2.50, 44 pgs.)-Hardcase app.;Chaykin-c; Rune flip-c/story by B. Smith (3 pgs.) — 3.00
7-10,12-17: 12-The Rafferty Saga begins, ends #18; 1st app. Rafferty. 15-Night Man & Freex app. 17-Swan marries Ellen — 2.50
11-($3.50, 68 pgs.)-Flip book w/Ultraverse Premiere #5 — 3.50
18-Death of Rafferty; Chaykin-c — 3.00

NOTE: ***Brereton** c-6. **Chaykin** c-1-4, 14, 16, 18. **Hamner** a-1-4. **Herrera** a-12. **James Robinson** scripts-0-18.*

FIRE BALL XL5 (See Steve Zodiac & The ...)

FIREBRAND (Also see Showcase '96 #4)
DC Comics: Feb, 1996 - No. 9, Oct, 1996 ($1.75)

1-9: Brian Augustyn scripts; Velluto-c/a in all. 9-Daredevil #319-c/swipe — 2.25

FIREBREATHER
Image Comics: Jan, 2003 - Present ($2.95)

1-4-Hester-s/Kuhn-a — 3.00

FIRE FROM HEAVEN
Image Comics (WildStorm Productions): Mar, 1996 ($2.50)

1,2-Moore-s — 2.50

FIREHAIR COMICS (Formerly Pioneer West Romances #3-6; also see Rangers Comics)
Fiction House Magazines (Flying Stories): Winter/48-49; No. 2, Wint/49-50; No. 7, Spr/51 - No. 11, Spr/52

1-Origin Firehair	53	106	159	318	474	630
2-Continues as Pioneer West Romances for #3-6	28	56	84	159	225	290
7-11	19	38	57	109	152	195
I.W. Reprint 8-(nd)-Kinstler-c; reprints Rangers #57; Dr. Drew story by Grandenetti	3	6	9	18	24	30

FIRESIDE BOOK SERIES (Hard and soft cover editions)
Simon and Schuster: 1974 - 1980 (130-260 pgs.), Square bound, color

Amazing Spider-Man, The, 1979,	HC	9	18	27	65	93	120
130 pgs., $3.95, Bob Larkin-c	SC	6	12	18	43	59	75
America At War–The Best of DC War	HC	13	26	39	90	133	175
Comics, 1979, $6.95, 260 pgs, Kubert-c	SC	8	16	24	58	82	105
Best of Spidey Super Stories (Electric Company) 1978, $3.95,	SC	7	14	21	50	68	85
Bring On The Bad Guys (Origins of the	HC	9	18	27	63	89	115
Marvel Comics Villains) 1976, $6.95, 260 pgs.; Romita-c	SC	6	12	18	38	52	65
Captain America, Sentinel of Liberty,1979,	HC	9	18	27	65	93	120
130 pgs., $12.95, Cockrum-c	SC	6	12	18	40	55	70
Doctor Strange Master of the Mystic	HC	9	18	27	64	87	120
Arts, 1980, 130 pgs.	SC	6	12	18	40	55	70
Fantastic Four, The, 1979, 130 pgs.	HC	9	18	27	63	89	115
	SC	6	12	18	38	52	65
Heart Throbs–The Best of DC Romance	HC	18	36	54	131	191	250
Comics, 1979, 260 pgs., $6.,95	SC	11	22	33	75	110	145
Incredible Hulk, The, 1978, 260 pgs.	HC	9	18	27	63	89	115
(8 1/4" x 11")	SC	6	12	18	38	52	65
Marvel's Greatest Superhero Battles,	HC	11	22	33	77	114	150
1978, 260 pgs., $6.95, Romita-c	SC	7	14	21	50	68	85
Mysteries in Space, 1980, $7,95,	HC	10	20	30	72	104	135
Anderson-c. r-DC sci/fi stories	SC	7	14	21	46	63	80
Origins of Marvel Comics, 1974, 260 pgs., $5.95. r-covers & origins of Fantastic Four, Hulk, Spider-Man, Thor,	HC	9	18	27	63	89	115
& Doctor Strange	SC	6	12	18	38	52	65
Silver Surfer, The, 1978, 130 pgs.,	HC	9	18	27	65	93	120
$4.95, Norem-c	SC	7	14	21	46	63	80
Son of Origins of Marvel Comics, 1975, 260 pgs., $6.95, Romita-c. Reprints covers & origins of X-Men, Iron Man,	HC	9	18	27	63	89	115
Avengers, Daredevil, Silver Surfer	SC	6	12	18	38	52	65
Superhero Women, The–Featuring the	HC	11	22	33	77	114	150
Fabulous Females of Marvel Comics, 1977, 260 pgs., $6.95, Romita-c	SC	7	14	21	50	68	85

Note: Prices listed are for 1st printings. Later printings have lesser value.

FIRESTAR
Marvel Comics Group: Mar, 1986 - No. 4, June, 1986 (75¢)(From Spider-Man TV series)

1,2: 1-X-Men & New Mutants app. 2-Wolverine-c (not real Wolverine?); Art Adams-a(p) — 5.00
3,4: 3-Art Adams/Sienkiewicz-c. 4-B. Smith-c — 3.00

FIRESTONE (See Donald And Mickey Merry Christmas)

FIRESTORM (See Cancelled Comic Cavalcade, DC Comics Presents, Flash #289, The Fury of... & Justice League of America #179)
DC Comics: March, 1978 - No. 5, Oct-Nov, 1978

1,5: 1-Origin & 1st app.	1	3	4	6	8	10
2-4: 2-Origin Multiplex. 3-Origin & 1st app. Killer Frost. 4-1st app. Hyena						6.00

FIRESTORM, THE NUCLEAR MAN (Formerly Fury of Firestorm)
DC Comics: No. 65, Nov, 1987 - No. 100, Aug, 1990

65-99: 66-1st app. Zuggernaut; Firestorm vs. Green Lantern. 71-Death of Capt. X. 67,68-Millennium tie-ins. 83-1st new look — 2.50
100-($2.95, 68 pgs.) — 4.00
Annual 5 (10/87)-1st app. new Firestorm — 3.00

FIRST, THE
CrossGeneration Comics: Jan, 2001 - No. 37, Jan, 2004 ($2.95)

1-3: 1-Barbara Kesel-s/Bart Sears & Andy Smith-a — 5.00
4-10 — 4.00
11-37 — 3.00
Preview (11/00, free) 8 pg. intro — 2.25
Two Houses Divided Vol. 1 TPB (11/01, $19.95) r/#1-7; new Moeller-c — 20.00
Magnificent Tension Vol. 2 TPB (2002, $19.95) r/#8-13 — 20.00
Sinister Motives Vol. 3 TPB (2003, $15.95) r/#14-19 — 16.00
Vol. 4 Futile Endeavors (2003, $15.95) r/#20-25 — 16.00
Vol. 5 Liquid Alliances (2003, $15.95) r/#26-31 — 16.00

The First #18 © CRO

First Issue Special #4 © DC

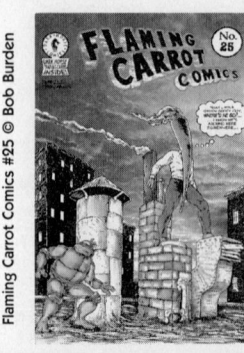

Flaming Carrot Comics #25 © Bob Burden

GD 2.0 | VG 4.0 | FN 6.0 | VF 8.0 | VF/NM 9.0 | NM- 9.2

Vol. 6 Ragnarok (2004, $15.95) r/#32-37 16.00

FIRST ADVENTURES
First Comics: Dec, 1985 - No. 5, Apr, 1986 ($1.25)
1-5: Blaze Barlow, Whisper & Dynamo Joe in all 2.25

FIRST AMERICANS, THE
Dell Publishing Co.: No. 843, Sept, 1957
Four Color 843-Marsh-a 10 20 30 67 96 125

FIRST CHRISTMAS, THE (3-D)
Fiction House Magazines (Real Adv. Publ. Co.): 1953 (25¢, 8-1/4x10-1/4", oversize)(Came w/glasses)
nn-(Scarce)-Kelly Freas painted-c; Biblical theme, birth of Christ; Nativity-c
33 66 99 190 270 350

FIRST COMICS GRAPHIC NOVEL
First Comics: Jan, 1984 - No. 21? (52pgs./176 pgs., high quality paper)
1,2: 1-Beowulf ($5.95)(both printings). 2-Time Beavers 9.00
3($11.95, 100 pgs.)-American Flagg! Hard Times (2nd printing exists) 15.00
4-Nexus ($6.95)-r/B&W 1-3 12.00
5,7: 5-The Enchanted Apples of Oz ($7.95, 52 pgs.)-Intro by Harlan Ellison (1986). 7-The Secret Island Of Oz ($7.95) 10.00
6-Elric of Melnibone ($14.95, 176 pgs.)-Reprints with new color 18.00
8,10,14,18: Teenage Mutant Ninja Turtles Book I -IV ($9.95, 132 pgs.)-8-r/TMNT #1-3 in color w/12 pgs. new-a; origin. 10-r/TMNT #4-6 in color. 14-r/TMNT #7,8 in color plus new 12 pg. story. 18-r/TMNT #10,11 plus 3 pg. fold-out 11.00
9-Time 2: The Epiphany by Chaykin (11/86, $7.95, 52pgs. - indicia says #8) 10.00
11-Sailor On The Sea of Fate ($14.95) 16.00
nn-Time 2: The Satisfaction of Black Mariah (9/87) 10.00
12-American Flagg! Southern Comfort (10/87, $11.95) 14.00
13,15-17,19,21: 13-The Ice King Of Oz. 15-Hex Breaker: Badger ($7.95). 16-The Forgotten Forest of Oz ($8.95). 17-Mazinger (68 pgs., $8.95).19-The Original Nexus Graphic Novel ($7.95, 104 pgs.)-Reprints First Comics Graphic Novel #4 ($7.95). 21-Elric, The Weird of the White Wolf; r/#1-5 10.00
20-American Flagg!: State of the Union ($11.95, 96 pgs.); r/A.F. #7-9 15.00
NOTE: *Most or all issues have been reprinted.*

1ST FOLIO (The Joe Kubert School Presents...)
Pacific Comics: Mar, 1984 ($1.50, one-shot)
1-Joe Kubert-c/a(2 pgs.); Adam & Andy Kubert-a 3.00

1ST ISSUE SPECIAL
National Periodical Publications: Apr, 1975 - No. 13, Apr, 1976 (Tryout series)
1,6: 1-Intro. Atlas; Kirby-c/a/script. 6-Dingbats 2 4 6 9 11 14
2,12: 2-Green Team (see Cancelled Comic Cavalcade). 12-Origin/1st app. "Blue" Starman (2nd app. in Starman, 2nd Series #3); Kubert-c 1 3 4 6 8 10
3-Metamorpho by Ramona Fradon 1 3 4 6 8 10
4,10,11: 4-Lady Cop. 10-The Outsiders. 11-Code Name: Assassin; Grell-c
1 2 3 5 7 9
5-Manhunter; Kirby-c/a/script 2 4 6 10 13 16
7,9: 7-The Creeper by Ditko (c/a). 9-Dr. Fate; Kubert-c/Simonson-a.
2 4 6 9 11 14
8,13: 8-Origin/1st app. The Warlord; Grell-c/a (11/75). 13-Return of the New Gods; Darkseid app.; 1st new costume Orion; predates New Gods #12 by more than a year
3 6 9 16 20 24

FIRST KISS
Charlton Comics: Dec, 1957 - No. 40, Jan, 1965
V1#1 5 10 15 33 44 55
V1#2-10 3 6 9 19 25 32
11-40 2 4 6 12 16 20

FIRST LOVE ILLUSTRATED
Harvey Publications(Home Comics)(True Love): 2/49 - No. 9, 6/50; No. 10, 1/51 - No. 86, 3/58; No. 87, 9/58 - No. 88, 11/58; No. 89, 11/62, No. 90, 2/63
1-Powell-a(2) 19 38 57 107 149 190
2-Powell-a 10 20 30 58 77 95
3-"Was I Too Fat To Be Loved" story 10 20 30 58 77 95
4-10 8 16 24 40 50 60
11-30: 13-"I Joined a Teen-age Sex Club" story. 30-Lingerie panel
6 12 18 31 38 45
31-34,37,39-49: 49-Last pre-code (2/55) 6 12 18 28 34 40
35-Used in **SOTI**, illo "The title of this comic book is First Love"
20 40 60 112 156 200
36-Communism story, "Love Slaves" 9 18 27 49 62 75
38-Nostrand-a 8 16 24 40 50 60
50-66,71-90 5 10 15 22 26 30
67-70-Kirby-c 6 12 18 31 38 45
NOTE: ***Disbrow** a-13. **Orlando** c-87. **Powell** a-1, 3-5, 7, 10, 11, 13-17, 19-24, 26-29, 33,35-41, 43, 45, 46, 50, 54, 55, 57, 58, 61-63, 65, 71-73, 76, 79r, 82, 84, 88.*

FIRSTMAN
Image Comics: June, 1997 ($2.50)
1 Snyder-s/ Andy Smith-a 2.50

FIRST MEN IN THE MOON (See Movie Comics)

FIRST ROMANCE MAGAZINE
Home Comics(Harvey Publ.)/True Love: 8/49 - #6, 6/50; #7, 6/51 - #50, 2/58; #51, 9/58 - #52, 11/58
1 16 32 48 92 126 160
2 9 18 27 52 66 80
3-5 8 16 24 43 54 65
6-10,28: 28-Nostrand-a(Powell swipe) 8 16 24 33 44 55
11-20 6 12 18 31 38 45
21-27,29-32: 32-Last pre-code issue (2/55) 6 12 18 28 34 40
33-40,44-52 5 10 15 24 30 35
41-43-Kirby-c 6 12 18 31 38 45
NOTE: ***Powell** a-1-5, 8-10, 14, 18, 20-22, 24, 25, 28, 36, 46, 48, 51.*

FIRST TRIP TO THE MOON (See Space Adventures No. 20)

FIRST WAVE (Based on Sci-Fi Channel TV series)
Andromeda Entertainment: Dec, 2000 - No. 4, Jun, 2001 ($2.99)
1-4-Kuhoric-s/Parsons-a/Busch-c 3.00

FISH POLICE (Inspector Gill of the...#2, 3)
Fishwrap Productions/Comico V2#5-17/Apple Comics #18 on:
Dec, 1985 - No. 11, Nov, 1987 ($1.50, B&W); V2#5, April, 1988 - V2#17, May, 1989 ($1.75, color) No. 18, Aug, 1989 - No. 26, Dec, 1990 ($2.25, B&W)
1-11, 1(5/86),2-2nd print, V2#5-17-(Color): V2#5-11. 12-17, new-a, 18-26 ($2.25-c, B&W). 18-Origin Inspector Gill 2.50
Special 1($2.50, 7/87, Comico) 2.50
Graphic Novel: Hairballs (1987, $9.95, TPB) r/#1-4 in color 10.00

FISH POLICE
Marvel Comics: V2#1, Oct, 1992 - No. 6, Mar, 1993 ($1.25)
V2#1-6: 1-Hairballs Saga begins; r/#1 (1985) 2.50

5 CENT COMICS (Also see Whiz Comics)
Fawcett Publ.: Feb, 1940 (8 pgs., reg. size, B&W)
1-(nn-on c) 1st app. Dan Dare 552 1104 1656 3864 5932 8000
NOTE: Only 2 known copies, in GD and NM condition. A promo comic, same as ***Flash** & **Thrill Comics**.*

5-STAR SUPER-HERO SPECTACULAR (See DC Special Series No. 1)

FLAME, THE (See Big 3 & Wonderworld Comics)
Fox Features Synd.: Sum, 1940 - No. 8, Jan, 1942 (#1,2: 68 pgs; #3-8: 44 pgs.)
1-Flame stories reprinted from Wonderworld #5-9; origin The Flame; Lou Fine-a (36 pgs.),
311 622 933 2022 3111 4200
2-Fine-a(2); Wing Turner by Tuska; r/Wonderworld #3,10
134 268 402 838 1257 1675
3-8: 3-Powell-a 88 176 264 550 825 1100

FLAME, THE (Formerly Lone Eagle)
Ajax/Farrell Publications (Excellent Publ.): No. 5, Dec-Jan, 1954-55 - No. 3, April-May, 1955
5(#1)-1st app. new Flame 46 92 138 276 413 550
2,3 31 62 93 175 248 320

FLAMING CARROT (...Comics #6? on; see Anything Goes, Cerebus, Teenage Mutant Ninja Turtles/Flaming Carrot Crossover & Visions)
Aardvark-Vanaheim/Renegade Press #6-17/Dark Horse #18 on:
5/84 - No. 5, 1/85; No. 6, 3/85 - Present? ($1.70/$2.00, B&W)
1-Bob Burden story/art 4 8 12 29 40 50
2 3 6 9 16 20 25
3 2 4 6 10 13 16
4-6 2 4 6 8 10 12
7-9 1 2 3 5 7 9
10-12 6.00
13-15 4.00
15-Variant without cover price 6.00
16-(6/87) 1st app. Mystery Men 1 2 3 5 6 8
17-20: 18-1st Dark Horse issue 4.00
21-23,25: 25-Contains trading cards; TMNT app. 3.00
24-(2.50, 52 pgs.)-10th anniversary issue 4.00
26-28: 26-Begin $2.25-c. 26,27-Teenage Mutant Ninja Turtles x-over. 27-McFarlane-c 3.00

GD 2.0 | VG 4.0 | FN 6.0 | VF 8.0 | VF/NM 9.0 | NM- 9.2

The Flash #129 © DC

The Flash #159 © DC

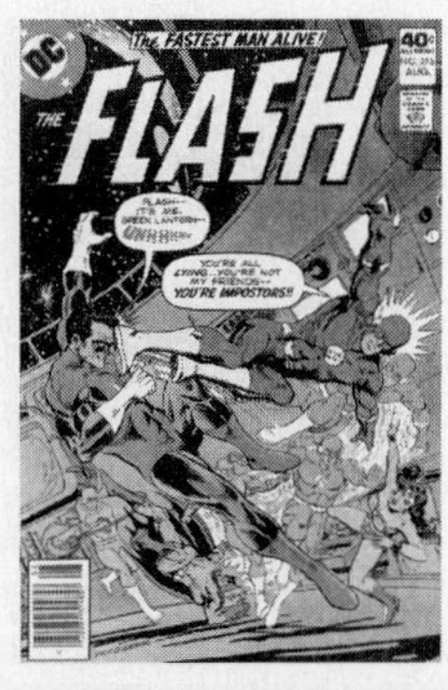

The Flash #276 © DC

	GD	VG	FN	VF	VF/NM	NM-
	2.0	4.0	6.0	8.0	9.0	9.2

29-31-(2.50-c) 3.00
Annual 1(1/97, $5.00) 5.00
... & Reid Fleming, World's Toughest Milkman (12/02, $3.99) listed as #32 in indicia 4.00
... :Fortune Favors the Bold (1998, $16.95, TPB) r/#19-24 17.00
... :Men of Mystery (7/97, $12.95, TPB) r/#1-3, + new material 13.00
... 's Greatest Hits (4/98, $17.95, TPB) r/#12-18, + new material 18.00
... :The Wild Shall Wild Remain (1997, $17.95, TPB) r/#4-11, + new s/a 18.00

FLAMING CARROT COMICS (Also see Junior Carrot Patrol)
Killian Barracks Press: Summer-Fall, 1981 ($1.95, one shot) (Lg size, 8-1/2x11")
1-Bob Burden-c/a/scripts; serially #'ed to 6500 6 12 18 38 52 65

FLAMING LOVE
Quality Comics Group (Comic Magazines): Dec, 1949 - No. 6, Oct, 1950 (Photo covers #2-6) (52 pgs.)
1-Ward-c/a (9 pgs.) 39 78 117 230 325 420
2 18 36 54 101 138 175
3-Ward-a (9 pgs.); Crandall-a 27 54 81 153 214 275
4-6: 4-Gustavson-a 15 30 45 86 118 150

FLAMING WESTERN ROMANCES (Formerly Target Western Romances)
Star Publications: No. 3, Mar-Apr, 1950
3-Robert Taylor, Arlene Dahl photo on-c with biographies inside; L. B. Cole-c
40 80 120 240 340 440

FLARE (Also see Champions for 1st app. & League of Champions)
Hero Comics/Hero Graphics Vol. 2 on: Nov, 1988 - No. 3, Jan, 1989 ($2.75, color, 52 pgs); V2#1, Nov, 1990 - No. 7, Nov, 1991 ($2.95/$3.50, color, mature, 52 pgs.);V2#8, Oct, 1992 - No. 16, Feb, 1994 ($3.50/$3.95, B&W, 36 pgs.)
V1#1-3, V2#1-16: 5-Eternity Smith returns. 6-Intro The Tigress 4.00
Annual 1(1992, $4.50, B&W, 52 pgs.)-Champions-r 4.50

FLARE ADVENTURES
Hero Graphics: Feb, 1992 - No. 12, 1993? ($3.50/$3.95)
1 (90¢, color, 20 pgs.) 2.50
2-12-Flip books w/Champions Classics 4.00

FLASH, THE (See Adventure Comics, The Brave and the Bold, Crisis On Infinite Earths, DC Comics Presents, DC Special, DC Special Series, DC Super-Stars, The Greatest Flash Stories Ever Told, Green Lantern, Impulse, JLA, Justice League of America, Showcase, Speed Force, Super Team Family, Titans & World's Finest)

FLASH, THE (1st Series)(Formerly Flash Comics)(See Showcase #4,8,13,14)
National Periodical Publ./DC: No. 105, Feb-Mar, 1959 - No. 350, Oct, 1985
105-(2-3/59)-Origin Flash(retold), & Mirror Master (1st app.)
415 830 1245 3797 6149 8500
106-Origin Grodd & Pied Piper; Flash's 1st visit to Gorilla City; begin Grodd the Super Gorilla trilogy (Scarce) 143 286 429 1216 1858 2500
107-Grodd trilogy, part 2 74 148 222 629 965 1300
108-Grodd trilogy ends 63 126 189 536 818 1100
109-2nd app. Mirror Master 50 100 150 400 600 800
110-Intro/origin Kid Flash who later becomes Flash in Crisis On Infinite Earths #12; begin Kid Flash trilogy, ends #112 (also in #114,116,118); 1st app. & origin of The Weather Wizard
120 240 360 1020 1560 2100
111-2nd Kid Flash tryout; Cloud Creatures 40 80 120 300 450 600
112-Origin & 1st app. Elongated Man (4-5/60); also apps. in #115,119,130
44 88 132 352 526 700
113-Origin & 1st app. Trickster 40 80 120 300 450 600
114-Captain Cold app. (see Showcase #8) 31 62 93 228 339 450
115,116,118-120: 119-Elongated Man marries Sue Dearborn. 120-Flash & Kid Flash team-up for 1st time 25 50 75 176 258 340
117-Origin & 1st app. Capt. Boomerang; 1st & only S.A. app. Winky Blinky & Noddy
30 60 90 218 322 425
121,122: 122-Origin & 1st app. The Top 19 38 57 136 198 260
123-(9/61)-Re-intro. Golden Age Flash; origins of both Flashes; 1st mention of an Earth II where DC G. A. heroes live 114 228 342 969 1485 2000
124-Last 10¢ issue 15 30 45 109 160 210
125-128,130: 127-Return of Grodd-c/story. 128-Origin & 1st app. Abra Kadabra. 130-(7/62)-1st Gauntlet of Super-Villains (Mirror Master, Capt. Cold, The Top, Capt. Boomerang & Trickster) 15 30 45 104 152 200
129-2nd G.A. Flash x-over; J.S.A. cameo in flashback (1st S.A. app. G.A. Green Lantern, Hawkman, Atom, Black Canary & Dr. Mid-Nite. Wonder Woman (1st S.A. app.?) appears)
29 58 87 210 305 400
131-136,138,140: 131-Early Green Lantern x-over (9/62). 135-1st app. of Kid Flash's yellow costume (3/63). 136-1st Dexter Miles. 140-Origin & 1st app. Heat Wave
13 26 39 90 133 175
137-G.A. Flash x-over; J.S.A. cameo (1st S.A. app.)(1st real app. since 2-3/51); 1st S.A. app. Vandal Savage & Johnny Thunder; JSA team decides to re-form
42 84 126 315 470 625
139-Origin & 1st app. Prof. Zoom 14 28 42 97 141 185
141-150: 142-Trickster app. 10 20 30 73 107 140
151-Engagement of Barry Allen & Iris West; G.A. Flash vs. The Shade.
14 28 42 97 141 185
152-159 9 18 27 65 93 120
160-(80-Pg. Giant G-21); G.A. Flash & Johnny Quick-r
13 26 39 90 133 175
161-164,166,167: 167-New facts about Flash's origin 8 16 24 58 82 105
165-Barry Allen weds Iris West 9 18 27 65 93 120
168,170: 168-Green Lantern-c/app. 170-Dr. Mid-Nite, Dr. Fate, G.A. Flash x-over
9 18 27 60 85 110
169-(80-Pg. Giant G-34)-New facts about origin 10 20 30 73 107 140
171,172,174,176,177,179,180: 171-JLA, Green Lantern, Atom flashbacks. 174-Barry Allen reveals I.D. to wife. 179-(5/68)-Flash travels to Earth-Prime and meets DC editor Julie Schwartz; 1st unnamed app. Earth-Prime (See Justice League of America #123 for 1st named app. & 3rd app. overall) 8 16 24 53 74 95
173-G.A. Flash x-over 8 16 24 58 82 105
175-2nd Superman/Flash race (12/67) (See Superman #199 & World's Finest #198,199); JLA cameo; gold kryptonite used (on J'onn J'onzz impersonating Superman)
18 36 54 131 191 250
178-(80-Pg. Giant G-46) 10 20 30 67 96 125
181-186,188,189: 186-Re-intro. Sargon. 189-Last 12¢-c
6 12 18 43 59 75
187,196: (68-Pg. Giants G-58, G-70) 7 14 21 51 71 90
190-195,197-199 5 10 15 33 44 55
200 6 12 18 38 52 65
201-204,206,207: 201-New G.A. Flash story. 206-Elongated Man begins
207-Last 15¢ issue 4 8 12 24 32 40
205-(68-Pg. Giant G-82) 6 12 18 40 55 70
208-213-(52 pg.): 211-G.A. Flash origin-r/#104. 213-Reprints #137
4 8 12 27 36 45
214-DC 100 Page Super Spectacular DC-11; origin Metal Men-r/Showcase #37; never before published G.A. Flash story.
(see DC 100 pg. Super Spec. #11 for price)
215 (52 pgs.)-Flash-r/Showcase #4; G.A. Flash x-over, continued in #216
4 8 12 29 40 50
216,220: 220-1st app. Turtle since Showcase #4 3 6 9 18 24 30
217-219: Neal Adams-a in all. 217-Green Lantern/Green Arrow series begins (9/72); 2nd G.L. & G.A. team-up series (see Green Lantern #76). 219-Last Green Arrow
4 8 12 29 40 50
221-225,227,228,230,231,233: 222-G. Lantern x-over. 228-(7-8/74)-Flash writer Cary Bates travels to Earth-One & meets Flash, Iris Allen & Trickster; 2nd unnamed app. Earth-Prime (See Justice League of America #123 for 1st named app. & 3rd app. overall)
2 4 6 12 16 20
226-Neal Adams-p 3 6 9 18 23 28
229,232-(100 pg. issues)-G.A. Flash-r & new-a 5 10 15 33 44 55
234-250: 235-Green Lantern x-over. 243-Death of The Top. 245-Origin The Floronic Man in Green Lantern back-up, ends #246. 246-Last Green Lantern. 250-Intro Golden Glider
2 4 6 10 12 15
251-274: 256-Death of The Top retold. 265-267-(44 pgs.). 267-Origin of Flash's uniform. 270-Intro The Clown 1 3 4 6 8 10
268,273-276,278,283,286-(Whitman variants; low print run; no issue #s shown on covers
2 4 6 8 10 12
275,276-Iris Allen dies 2 4 6 8 10 12
277-288,290: 286-Intro/origin Rainbow Raider 1 2 3 4 5 7
289-1st Perez DC art (Firestorm); new Firestorm back-up series begins (9/80), ends #304
1 2 3 5 7 9
291-299,301-305: 291-1st app. Saber-Tooth (villain). 295-Gorilla Grodd-c/story. 298-Intro/origin new Shade. 301-Atomic bomb-c. 303-The Top returns. 304-Intro/origin Colonel Computron; 305-G.A. Flash x-over 5.00
300-(52 pgs.)-Origin Flash retold; 25th ann. issue 1 2 3 4 5 7
306-313-Dr. Fate by Giffen. 309-Origin Flash retold 5.00
314-340: 318-323-Creeper back-ups. 323,324-Two part Flash vs. Flash story. 324-Death of Reverse Flash (Professor Zoom). 328-Iris West Allen's death retold 4.00
341-349: 344-Origin Kid Flash 5.00
350-Double size ($1.25) Final issue 6.00
Annual 1 (10-12/63, 84 pgs.)-Origin Elongated Man & Kid Flash-r; origin Grodd; G.A. Flash-r
38 76 114 285 430 575
Annual 1 Replica Edition (2001, $6.95)-Reprints the entire 1963 Annual 7.00
The Flash Spectacular (See DC Special Series No. 11)
The Life Story of the Flash (1997, $19.95, Hardcover) "Iris Allen's" chronicle of Barry Allen's life; comic panels w/additional text; Waid & Augustyn-s/ Kane & Staton-a/Orbik painted-c
20.00

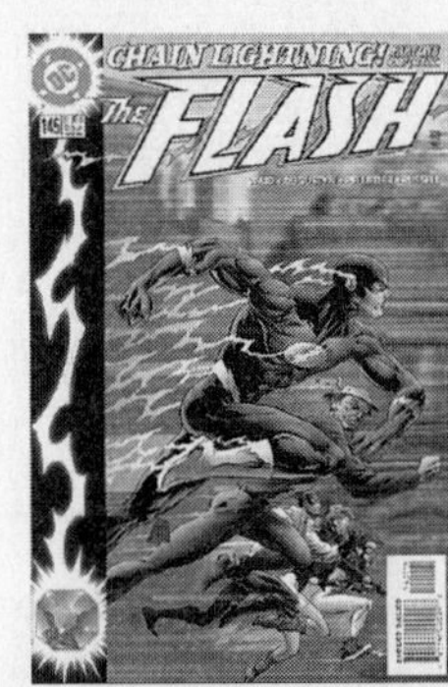

The Flash (2nd series) #145 © DC

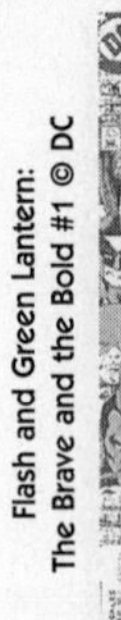

Flash and Green Lantern: The Brave and the Bold #1 © DC

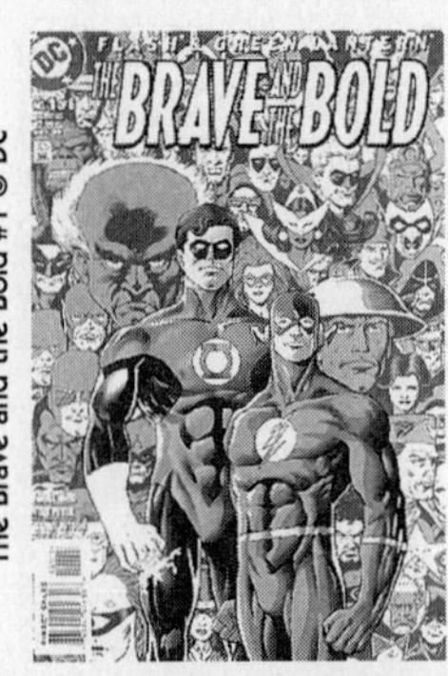

Flash Comics #26 © DC

	GD	VG	FN	VF	VF/NM	NM-
	2.0	4.0	6.0	8.0	9.0	9.2

The Life Story of the Flash (1998, $12.95, Softcover) New Orbik-c 13.00

NOTE: ***N. Adams*** *c-194, 195, 203, 204, 206-208, 211, 213, 215, 226p, 246.* ***M. Anderson*** *c-165, a(i)-195, 200-204, 206-208.* ***Austin*** *a-233i, 234i, 246i.* ***Buckler*** *a-271p, 272p; c(p)-247-250, 252, 253p, 255, 256p, 258, 262, 265-267, 269-271.* ***Giffen*** *a-306-313p; c-310p, 315.* ***Giordano*** *a-226i.* ***Sid Greene*** *a-167-174i, 229i(r).* ***Grell*** *a-237p, 238p, 240-243p; c-236.* ***Heck*** *a-198p.* ***Infantino/Anderson*** *a-135. c-135, 170-174, 192, 200, 201, 328-330.* ***Infantino/Giella*** *c-105-112, 163, 164, 166-168.* ***G. Kane*** *a-195p, 197-199p, 229r, 232r; c-197-199, 312p.* ***Kubert*** *a-108p, 215i(r); c-189-191.* ***Lopez*** *c-272.* ***Meskin*** *a-229r, 232r.* ***Perez*** *a-289-293p; c-293.* ***Starlin*** *a-294-296p.* ***Staton*** *c-263p, 264p. Green Lantern x-over-131, 143, 168, 171, 191.*

FLASH (2nd Series)(See Crisis on Infinite Earths #12 and Justice League Europe)
DC Comics: June, 1987 - Present (75¢-$2.25)

1-Guice-c/a begins; New Teen Titans app. 1 3 4 6 8 10
2-10: 3-Intro. Kilgore. 5-Intro. Speed McGee. 7-1st app. Blue Trinity. 8,9-Millennium tie-ins. 9-1st app. The Chunk 4.00
11-61: 12-Free extra 16 pg. Dr. Light story. 19-Free extra 16 pg. Flash story. 28-Capt. Cold app. 29-New Phantom Lady app. 40-Dr. Alchemy app. 50-($1.75, 52 pgs.) 3.00
62-78,80: 62-Flash: Year One begins, ends #65. 65-Last $1.00-c. 66-Aquaman app. 69,70-Green Lantern app. 70-Gorilla Grodd story ends. 73-Re-intro Barry Allen & begin saga ("Barry Allen's" true ID revealed in #78). 76-Re-intro of Max Mercury (Quality Comics' Quicksilver), not in uniform until #77. 80-($1.25-c) Regular Edition 4.00
79,80 ($2.50): 79-(68 pgs.) Barry Allen saga ends. 80-Foil-c 5.00
81-91,93,94,0,95-99,101: 81,82-Nightwing & Starfire app. 84-Razer app. 94-Zero Hour. 0-(10/94). 95-"Terminal Velocity" begins, ends #100. 96,98,99-Kobra app. 97-Origin Max Mercury; Chillblaine app. 4.00
92-1st Impulse 1 3 4 6 8 10
100 ($2.50)-Newstand edition; Kobra & JLA app. 4.00
100 ($3.50)-Foil-c edition; Kobra & JLA app. 5.00
102-131: 102-Mongul app.; begin-$1.75-c. 105-Mirror Master app. 107-Shazam app. 108-"Dead Heat" begins; 1st app. Savitar. 109-"Dead Heat" Pt. 2 (cont'd in Impulse #10). 110-"Dead Heat" Pt. 4 (cont'd in Impulse #11). 111-"Dead Heat" finale; Savitar disappears into the Speed Force; John Fox cameo (2nd app.). 112-"Race Against Time" begins, ends #118; re-intro John Fox. 113-Tornado Twins app. 119-Final Night x-over. 127-129-Rogue's Gallery & Neron. 128,129-JLA-app.130-Morrison & Millar-s begin 3.00
132-150: 135-GL & GA app. 142-Wally almost marries Linda; Waid-s return. 144-Cobalt Blue origin. 145-Chain Lightning begins.147-Professor Zoom app. 149-Barry Allen app. 150-($2.95) Final showdown with Cobalt Blue 3.00
151-162: 151-Casey-s. 152-New Flash-c. 154-New Flash ID revealed. 159-Wally marries Linda. 162-Last Waid-s. 2.50
163-187,189-196,198,199,201-205: 163-Begin $2.25-c. 164-186-Bolland-c. 183-New Trickster. 196-Winslade-a. 201-Dose-a begins. 205-Batman-c/app. 2.25
188-($2.95) Mirror Master, Weather Wizard, Trickster app. 3.00
197-Origin of Zoom (6/03) 6.00
200-($3.50) Flash vs. Zoom; Barry Allen & Hal Jordan app.; wraparound-c 3.50
#1,000,000 (11/98) 853rd Century x-over 2.50
Annual 1-7,9: 2-('87-'94,'96, 68 pgs), 3-Gives history of G.A.,S.A., & Modern Age Flash in text. 4-Armaggedon 2001. 5-Eclipso-c/story. 7-Elseworlds story. 9-Legends of the Dead Earth story; J.H. Williams-a(p); Mick Gray-a(i) 3.00
Annual 8 (1995, $3.50)-Year One story 3.50
Annual 10 (1997, $3.95)-Pulp Heroes stories 4.00
Annual 11,12 ('98, '99)-11-Ghosts; Wrightson-c. 12-JLApe; Art Adams-c 3.00
Annual 13 ('00, $3.50) Planet DC; Alcatena-c/a 3.50
...: Blood Will Run (2002, $17.95, TPB)-r/#170-176, Secret Files #3 18.00
Dead Heat (2000, $14.95, TPB)-r/#108-111, Impulse #10,11 15.00
...80-Page Giant (8/98, $4.95) Flash family stories by Waid, Millar and others; Mhan-c 5.00
...80-Page Giant 2 (4/99, $4.95) Stories of Flash family, future Kid Flash, original Teen Titans and XS 5.00
...: Iron Heights (2001, $5.95)-Van Sciver-c/a; intro. Murmur 6.00
...: Our Worlds at War 1 (10/01, $2.95)-Jae Lee-c; Black Racer app. 3.00
...Plus 1 (1/1997, $2.95)-Nightwing-c/app. 3.00
Race Against Time (2001, $14.95, TPB)-r/#112-118 15.00
...: Rogues (2003, $14.95, TPB)-r/#177-182 15.00
...Secret Files 1 (11/97, $4.95) Origin-s & pin-ups 5.00
...Secret Files 2 (11/99, $4.95) Origin of Replicant 5.00
...Secret Files 3 (11/01; $4.95) Intro. Hunter Zolomon (who later becomes Zoom) 5.00
Special 1 (1990, $2.95, 84 pgs.)-50th anniversary issue; Kubert-c; 1st Flash story by Mark Waid; 1st app. John Fox (27th Century Flash) 3.00
Terminal Velocity (1996, $12.95, TPB)-r/#95-100. 13.00
The Return of Barry Allen (1996, $12.95, TPB)-r/#74-79. 13.00
...: Time Flies (2002, $5.95)-Seth Fisher-c/a; Rozum-s 6.00
TV Special 1 (1991, $3.95, 76 pgs.)-Photo-c plus behind the scenes photos of TV show; Saltares-a, Byrne scripts 4.00

NOTE: ***Guice*** *a-1-9p, 11p, Annual 1p; c-1-9p, Annual 1p.* ***Perez*** *c-15-17, Annual 2i.* ***Charest*** *c/a-Annual 5p.*

FLASH, THE (See Tangent Comics/ The Flash)

FLASH AND GREEN LANTERN: THE BRAVE AND THE BOLD
DC Comics: Oct, 1999 - No. 6, Mar, 2000 ($2.50, limited series)

1-6-Waid & Peyer-s/Kitson-a. 4-Green Arrow app.; Grindberg-a(p) 2.50
TPB (2001, $12.95) r/#1-6 13.00

FLASH/ GREEN LANTERN: FASTER FRIENDS (See Green Lantern/Flash...)
DC Comics: No. 2, 1997 ($4.95, continuation of Green Lantern/Flash: Faster Friends #1)

2-Waid/Augustyn-s 5.00

FLASH COMICS (Whiz Comics No. 2 on)
Fawcett Publications: Jan, 1940 (12 pgs., B&W, regular size)
(Not distributed to newsstands; printed for in-house use)

NOTE: ***Whiz Comics*** *#2 was preceded by two books,* ***Flash Comics*** *and* ***Thrill Comics****, both dated Jan, 1940, (12 pgs, B&W, regular size) and were not distributed. These two books are identical except for the title, and were sent out to major distributors as ad copies to promote sales. It is believed that the complete 68 page issue of Fawcett's* ***Flash*** *and* ***Thrill Comics*** *#1 was finished and ready for publication with the January date. Since DC Comics was also about to publish a book with the same date and title, Fawcett hurriedly printed up the black and white version of* ***Flash Comics*** *to secure copyright before DC. The inside covers are blank, with the covers and inside pages printed on a high quality uncoated paper stock.The eight page origin story of Captain Thunder is composed of pages 1-7 and 13 of the Captain Marvel story essentially as they appeared in the first issue of* ***Whiz Comics****. The balloon dialogue on page thirteen was relettered to tie the story into the end of page seven in* ***Flash*** *and* ***Thrill Comics*** *to produce a shorter version of the origin story for copyright purposes. Obviously, DC acquired the copyright and Fawcett dropped* ***Flash*** *as well as* ***Thrill*** *and came out with* ***Whiz Comics*** *a month later. Fawcett never used the cover to* ***Flash*** *and* ***Thrill*** *#1, designing a new cover for* ***Whiz Comics****. Fawcett also must have discovered that Captain Thunder had already been used by another publisher (Captain Terry Thunder by Fiction House). All references to Captain Thunder were relettered to Captain Marvel before appearing in* ***Whiz****.*

1 (nn on-c, #1 on inside)-Origin & 1st app. Captain Thunder. Cover by C.C. Beck. Eight copies of Flash and three copies of Thrill exist. All 3 copies of Thrill sold in 1986 for between $4,000-$10,000 each. A NM copy of Thrill sold in 1987 for $12,000. A VG copy of Thrill sold in 1987 for $9000 cash. A VF(8.0) copy of Thrill sold in 2003 for $11,400.

FLASH COMICS (The Flash No. 105 on) (Also see All-Flash)
National Periodical Publ./All-American: Jan, 1940 - No. 104, Feb, 1949

1-The Flash (origin/1st app.) by Harry Lampert, Hawkman (origin/1st app.) by Gardner Fox, The Whip, & Johnny Thunder (origin/1st app.) by Stan Asch; Cliff Cornwall by Moldoff, Flash Picture Novelets (later Minute Movies w/#12) begin; Moldoff (Shelly) cover; 1st app. Shiera Sanders who later becomes Hawkgirl, #24; reprinted in Famous First Edition (on sale 11/10/39); The Flash-c 6200 12,400 18,600 46,500 71,750 97,000

1-Reprint, Oversize 13-1/2x10". **WARNING:** This comic is an exact reprint of the original except for its size. DC published it in 1974 with a second cover titling it as a Famous First Edition. There have been many reported cases of the outer cover being removed and the interior sold as the original edition. The reprint with the new outer cover removed is practically worthless. See Famous First Edition for value.

2-Rod Rian begins, ends #11; Hawkman-c 724 1448 2172 5068 7784 10,500
3-King Standish begins (1st app.), ends #41 (called The King #16-37,39-41); E.E. Hibbard-a begins on Flash 504 1008 1512 3528 5414 7300
4-Moldoff (Shelly) Hawkman begins; The Whip-c 423 846 1269 2751 4226 5700
5-The King-c 341 682 1023 2217 3409 4600
6-2nd Flash-c (alternates w/Hawkman #6 on) 470 940 1410 3290 5045 6800
7-2nd Hawkman-c; 1st Moldoff Hawkman-c 434 868 1302 3038 4669 6300
8-New logo begins; classic Moldoff Flash-c 300 600 900 1900 2850 3800
9,10: 9-Moldoff Hawkman-c; 10-Classic Moldoff Flash-c 311 622 933 2022 3111 4200
11-13,15-20: 12-Les Watts begins; "Sparks" #16 on. 17-Last Cliff Cornwall 200 400 600 1250 1875 2500
14-World War II cover 240 480 720 1500 2250 3000
21-Classic Hawkman-c 192 384 576 1200 1800 2400
22,23 172 344 516 1075 1613 2150
24-Shiera becomes Hawkgirl (12/41); see All-Star Comics #5 for 1st app. 210 420 630 1313 1969 2625
25-28,30: 28-Last Les Sparks. 116 232 348 725 1088 1450
29-Ghost Patrol begins (origin/1st app.), ends #104 130 260 390 813 1219 1625
31,33-Classic Hawkman-c. 33-Origin Shade 116 232 348 725 1085 1450
32,34-40: 36-1st app. Rag Doll 107 214 321 669 1005 1340
41-50 94 188 282 588 882 1175
51-61: 52-1st computer in comics, c/s (4/44). 59-Last Minute Movies. 61-Last Moldoff Hawkman 85 170 255 531 796 1060
62-Hawkman by Kubert begins 112 224 336 700 1050 1400
63-85: 66-68-Hop Harrigan in all. 70-Mutt & Jeff app. 80-Atom begins, ends #104 76 152 228 475 713 950
86-Intro. The Black Canary in Johnny Thunder (8/47); see All-Star #38. 280 560 840 1750 2625 3500
87,88,90: 87-Intro. The Foil. 88-Origin Ghost. 116 232 348 725 1088 1450
89-Intro villain The Thorn 168 336 504 1050 1575 2100
91,93-99: 98-Atom & Hawkman don new costumes 130 260 390 813 1219 1625
92-1st solo Black Canary plus-c; rare in Mint due to black ink smearing on white-c 341 682 1023 2217 3409 4600
100 (10/48),103(Scarce)-52 pgs. each 300 600 900 1900 2850 3800

Flash Gordon #5 © KING

Flex Mentallo #1 © DC

The Flintsones #7 © H-B

GD VG FN VF VF/NM NM-
2.0 4.0 6.0 8.0 9.0 9.2

101,102(Scarce) 248 496 744 1550 2325 3100
104-Origin The Flash retold (Scarce) 641 1282 1923 4487 6894 9300
NOTE: ***Irwin Hasen*** *a-Wheaties Giveaway. c-97, Wheaties Giveaway.* ***E.E. Hibbard*** *c-6, 12, 20, 24, 26, 28, 30, 44, 46, 48, 50, 62, 66, 68, 69, 72, 74, 76, 78, 80, 82.* ***Infantino*** *a-86p, 90, 93-95, 99-104; c-90, 92, 93, 97, 99, 101, 103.* ***Kinstler*** *a-87, 89(Hawkman); c-87.* ***Chet Kozlak*** *c-77, 79, 81.* ***Krigstein*** *a-94.* ***Kubert*** *a-62-76, 83, 85, 86, 88-104; c-63, 65, 67, 70, 71, 73, 75, 83, 85, 86, 88, 89, 91, 94, 96, 98, 100, 104.* ***Moldoff*** *a-3; c-3, 7-11, 13-17, plus odd #'s 19-61.* ***Martin Naydell*** *c-52, 54, 56, 58, 60, 64, 84.*

FLASH DIGEST, THE (See DC Special Series #24)

FLASH GORDON (See Defenders Of The Earth, Eat Right to Work..., Giant Comic Album, King Classics, King Comics, March of Comics #118, 133, 142, The Phantom #18, Street Comix & Wow Comics, 1st series)

FLASH GORDON
Dell Publishing Co.: No. 25, 1941; No. 10, 1943 - No. 512, Nov, 1953

Feature Books 25 (#1)(1941))-r-not by Raymond 90 180 270 646 998 1350
Four Color 10(1943)-by Alex Raymond; reprints "The Ice Kingdom"
96 192 288 680 1053 1425
Four Color 84(1945)-by Alex Raymond; reprints "The Fiery Desert"
41 82 123 324 487 650
Four Color 173 18 36 54 131 191 250
Four Color 190-Bondage-c; "The Adventures of the Flying Saucers"; 5th Flying Saucer story (6/48)- see The Spirit 9/28/47(1st), Shadow Comics V7#10 (2nd, 1/48), Captain Midnight #60 (3rd, 2/48) & Boy Commandos #26 (4th, 3-4/48)
21 42 63 147 216 285
Four Color 204,247 15 30 45 104 152 200
Four Color 424-Painted-c 11 22 33 77 114 150
2(5-7/53-Dell)-Painted-c; Evans-a? 8 16 24 55 78 100
Four Color 512-Painted-c 8 16 24 55 78 100

FLASH GORDON (See Tiny Tot Funnies)
Harvey Publications: Oct, 1950 - No. 4, April, 1951

1-Alex Raymond-a; bondage-c; reprints strips from 7/14/40 to 12/8/40
36 72 108 204 290 375
2-Alex Raymond-a; r/strips 12/15/40-4/27/41 24 48 72 138 194 250
3,4-Alex Raymond-a; 3-bondage-c; r/strips 5/4/41-9/21/41. 4-r/strips 10/24/37-3/27/38 22 44 66 127 176 225
5-(Rare)-Small size-5-1/2x8-1/2"; B&W; 32 pgs.; Distributed to some mail subscribers only 55 110 165 330 495 660
(Also see All-New No. 15, Boy Explorers No. 2, and Stuntman No. 3)

FLASH GORDON
Gold Key: June, 1965

1 (1947 reprint)-Painted-c 6 12 18 40 55 70

FLASH GORDON (Also see Comics Reading Libraries in the Promotional Comics section)
King #1-11/Charlton #12-18/Gold Key #19-23/Whitman #28 on:
9/66 - #11, 12/67; #12, 2/69 - #18, 1/70; #19, 9/78 - #37, 3/82 (Painted covers No. 19-30, 34)

1-1st S.A. app Flash Gordon; Williamson c/a(2); E.C. swipe/Incredible S.F. #32; Mandrake story 7 14 21 46 63 80
1-Army giveaway(1968)("Complimentary" on cover)(Same as regular #1 minus Mandrake story & back-c) 4 8 12 28 38 48
2-8: 2-Bolle, Gil Kane-c; Mandrake story. 3-Williamson-c. 4-Secret Agent X-9 begins, Williamson-c/a(3). 5-Williamson-c/a(2). 6,8-Crandall-a. 7-Raboy-a (last in comics?). 8-Secret Agent X-9-r 4 8 12 25 33 42
9-13: 9,10-Raymond-r. 10-Buckler's 1st pro work (11/67). 11-Crandall-a. 12-Crandall-c/a. 13-Jeff Jones-a (15 pgs.) 4 8 12 22 30 38
14,15: 15-Last 12¢ issue 3 6 9 18 23 28
16,17: 17-Brick Bradford story 2 4 6 14 18 22
18-Kaluta-a (3rd pro work?)(see Teen Confessions) 3 6 9 18 24 30
19(9/78, G.K.), 20-26 1 3 4 6 8 10
27-29.34-37: 34-37-Movie adaptation 2 4 6 8 10 12
30 (10/80) (scarce) 3 6 9 16 20 25
30 (7/81; re-issue), 31-33-single issues 1 3 4 6 8 10
31-33 (Bagged 3-pack): Movie adaptation; Williamson-a. 30.00
NOTE: ***Aparo*** *a-8.* ***Bolle*** *a-21, 22.* ***Boyette*** *a-14-18.* ***Briggs*** *c-10.* ***Buckler*** *a-10.* ***Crandall*** *c-6.* ***Estrada*** *a-3.* ***Gene Fawcette*** *a-29, 30, 34, 37.* ***McWilliams*** *a-31-33, 36.*

FLASH GORDON
DC Comics: June, 1988 - No. 9, Holiday, 1988-'89 ($1.25, mini-series)

1-9: 1,5-Painted-c 3.00

FLASH GORDON
Marvel Comics: June, 1995 - No. 2, July, 1995 ($2.95, limited series)

1,2: Schultz scripts; Williamson-a 3.00

FLASH GORDON THE MOVIE
Western Publishing Co.: 1980 (8-1/4 x 11", $1.95, 68 pgs.)

11294-Williamson-c/a; adapts movie 2 4 6 10 13 16

GD VG FN VF VF/NM NM-
2.0 4.0 6.0 8.0 9.0 9.2

13743-Hardback edition 2 4 6 14 18 22

FLASHPOINT (Elseworlds Flash)
DC Comics: Dec, 1999 - No. 3, Feb, 2000 ($2.95, limited series)

1-3-Paralyzed Barry Allen; Breyfogle-a/McGreal-s 3.00

FLAT-TOP
Mazie Comics/Harvey Publ.(Magazine Publ.) No. 4 on: 11/53 - No. 3, 5/54; No. 4, 3/55 - No. 7, 9/55

1-Teenage; Flat-Top, Mazie, Mortie & Stevie begin 8 16 24 43 54 65
2,3 5 10 15 23 28 32
4-7 5 10 14 20 24 28

FLESH & BLOOD
Brainstorm Comics: Dec, 1995 ($2.95, B&W, mature)

1-Balent-c; foil-c. 3.00

FLESH AND BONES
Upshot Graphics (Fantagraphics Books): June, 1986 - No. 4, Dec, 1986 (Limited series)

1-4: Alan Moore scripts (r) & Dalgoda by Fujitake 3.00

FLESH CRAWLERS
Kitchen Sink Press: Aug, 1993 - No. 3, 1995 ($2.50, B&W, limited series, mature)

1-3 2.50

FLEX MENTALLO (Man of Muscle Mystery) (See Doom Patrol, 2nd Series)
DC Comics (Vertigo): Jun, 1996 - No. 4, Sept, 1996 ($2.50, lim. series, mature)

1-4: Grant Morrison scripts & Frank Quitely-c/a in all 3.00

FLINCH (Horror anthology)
DC Comics (Vertigo): Jun, 1999 - No. 16, Jan, 2001 ($2.50)

1-16: 1-Art by Jim Lee, Quitely, and Corben. 5-Sale-c. 11-Timm-a 2.50

FLINTSTONE KIDS, THE (TV) (See Star Comics Digest)
Star Comics/Marvel Comics #5 on: Aug, 1987 - No. 11, Apr, 1989

1-11 4.50

FLINTSTONES, THE (TV)(See Dell Giant #48 for No. 1)
Dell Publ. Co./Gold Key No. 7 (10/62) on: No. 2, Nov-Dec, 1961 - No. 60, Sept, 1970 (Hanna-Barbera)

2-2nd app. (TV show debuted on 9/30/60); 1st app. of Cave Kids; 15¢-c thru #5
12 24 36 82 121 160
3-6(7-8/62): 3-Perry Gunnite begins. 6-1st 12¢-c 8 16 24 53 74 95
7 (10/62; 1st GK) 8 16 24 53 74 95
8-10 6 12 18 43 59 75
11-1st app. Pebbles (6/63) 10 20 30 67 96 125
12-15,17-20 5 10 15 36 48 60
16-1st app. Bamm-Bamm (1/64) 9 18 27 63 89 115
21-23,25-30,33: 33-Meet Frankenstein & Dracula 5 10 15 33 44 55
24-1st app. The Grusomes 7 14 21 46 63 80
31,32,35-40: 31-Xmas-c. 39-Reprints 4 8 12 28 38 48
34-1st app. The Great Gazoo 7 14 21 46 63 80
41-60: 45-Last 12¢ issue 4 8 12 24 32 40
At N. Y. World's Fair ('64)-J.W. Books (25¢)-1st printing; no date on-c (29¢ version exists, 2nd print?) Most H-B characters app.; including Yogi Bear, Top Cat, Snagglepuss and the Jetsons 6 12 18 40 55 70
At N. Y. World's Fair (1965 on-c; re-issue; Warren Pub.)
NOTE: Warehouse find in 1984 2 4 6 10 13 16
Bigger & Boulder 1(#30013-211) (Gold Key Giant, 11/62, 25¢, 84 pgs.)
9 18 27 65 93 120
Bigger & Boulder 2-(1966, 25¢)-Reprints B&B No. 1 6 12 18 38 52 65
...On the Rocks (9/61, $1.00, 6-1/4x9", cardboard-c, high quality paper,116 pgs.)
B&W new material 10 20 30 70 100 130
...With Pebbles & Bamm Bamm (100 pgs., G.K.)-30028-511 (paper-c, 25¢) (11/65)
9 18 27 65 93 120
NOTE: *(See Comic Album #16, Bamm-Bamm & Pebbles Flintstone, Dell Giant 48, Golden Comics Digest, March of Comics #229, 243, 271, 289, 299, 317, 327, 341, Pebbles Flintstone, Top Comics #2-4, and Whitman Comic Book.)*

FLINTSTONES, THE (TV)(...& Pebbles)
Charlton Comics: Nov, 1970 - No. 50, Feb, 1977 (Hanna-Barbera)

1 9 18 27 60 85 110
2 5 10 15 33 44 55
3-7,9,10 4 8 12 22 30 38
8- "Flintstones Summer Vacation" (Summer, 1971, 52 pgs.)
6 12 18 43 59 75
11-20,36: 36-Mike Zeck illos (early work) 3 6 9 18 24 30
21-35,38-41,43-45 3 6 9 16 20 24
37-Byrne text illos (early work; see Nightmare #20) 3 6 9 18 24 30

Flippity and Flop #8 © DC

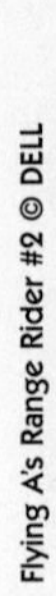

Flying A's Range Rider #2 © DELL

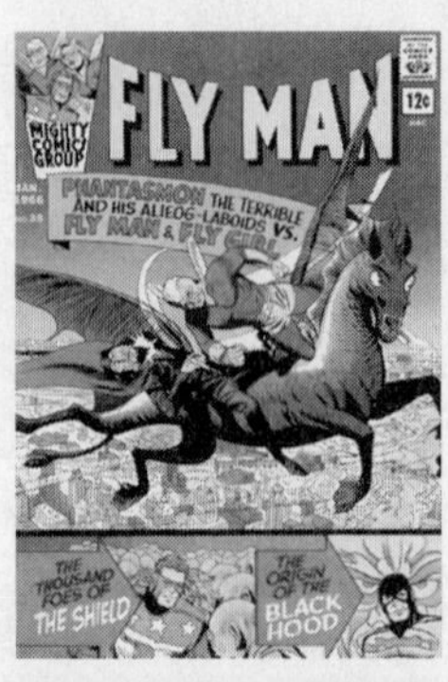

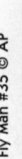

Fly Man #35 © AP

	GD 2.0	VG 4.0	FN 6.0	VF 8.0	VF/NM 9.0	NM- 9.2
42-Byrne-a (2 pgs.)	3	6	9	18	24	30
46-50	2	4	6	14	18	22
Digest nn (1972, B&W, 100 pgs.) (low print run)	4	8	12	22	30	38

(Also see Barney & Betty Rubble, Dino, The Great Gazoo, & Pebbles & Bamm-Bamm)

FLINTSTONES, THE (TV)(See Yogi Bear, 3rd series) (Newsstand sales only)
Marvel Comics Group: October, 1977 - No. 9, Feb, 1979 (Hanna-Barbera)

	GD	VG	FN	VF	VF/NM	NM-
1,7-9: 1-(30¢-c). 7-9-Yogi Bear app.	3	7	10	21	28	35
1-(35¢-c variant, limited distribution)	4	8	12	27	36	45
2,3,5,6: Yogi Bear app.	3	6	9	16	20	25
4-The Jetsons app.	3	6	9	18	24	30

FLINTSTONES, THE (TV)
Harvey Comics: Sept, 1992 - No. 13, Jun, 1994 ($1.25/$1.50) (Hanna-Barbera)

	GD	VG	FN	VF	VF/NM	NM-
V2#1-13						3.00
...Big Book 1,2 (11/92, 3/93; both $1.95, 52 pgs.)						3.50
...Giant Size 1-3 (10/92, 4/93, 11/93; $2.25, 68 pgs.)						3.50

FLINTSTONES, THE (TV)
Archie Publications: Sept, 1995 - No. 22, June, 1997 ($1.50)

	GD	VG	FN	VF	VF/NM	NM-
1-22						3.00

FLINTSTONES AND THE JETSONS, THE (TV)
DC Comics: Aug, 1997 - No. 21, May, 1999 ($1.75/$1.95/$1.99)

	GD	VG	FN	VF	VF/NM	NM-
1						6.00
2-21: 19-Bizarro Elroy-c						3.00

FLINTSTONES CHRISTMAS PARTY, THE (See The Funtastic World of Hanna-Barbera No. 1)

FLIP
Harvey Publications: April, 1954 - No. 2, June, 1954 (Satire)

	GD	VG	FN	VF	VF/NM	NM-
1,2-Nostrand-a each. 2-Powell-a	23	46	69	129	180	230

FLIPPER (TV)
Gold Key: Apr, 1966 - No. 3, Nov, 1967 (All have photo-c)

	GD	VG	FN	VF	VF/NM	NM-
1	7	14	21	51	71	90
2,3	5	10	15	36	48	60

FLIPPITY & FLOP
National Per. Publ. (Signal Publ. Co.): 12-1/51-52 - No. 46, 8-10/59; No. 47, 9-11/60

	GD	VG	FN	VF	VF/NM	NM-
1-Sam dog & his pets Flippity The Bird and Flop The Cat begin; Twiddle and Twaddle begin	28	56	84	159	225	290
2	15	30	45	84	115	145
3-5	13	26	39	74	100	125
6-10	11	22	33	63	84	105
11-20: 20-Last precode (3/55)	10	20	30	56	73	90
21-47	9	18	27	49	62	75

FLOATERS
Dark Horse Comics: Sept, 1993 - No. 5, Jan, 1994 ($2.50, B&W, lim. series)

	GD	VG	FN	VF	VF/NM	NM-
1-5						2.50

FLOYD FARLAND (See Eclipse Graphic Album Series #11)

FLY, THE (Also see Adventures of..., Blue Ribbon Comics & Flyman)
Archie Enterprises, Inc.: May, 1983 - No. 9, Oct, 1984

	GD	VG	FN	VF	VF/NM	NM-
1,2: 1-Mr. Justice app; origin Shield; Kirby-a; Steranko-c. 2-Ditko-a; Flygirl app.						5.00
3-9: Ditko-a in all. 4-8-Ditko-c(p)						4.00

NOTE: *Ayers c-9. Buckler a-1, 2. Kirby a-1. Nebres c-3, 4, 5i, 6, 7i. Steranko c-1, 2.*

FLY, THE
Impact Comics (DC): Aug, 1991 - No. 17, Dec, 1992 ($1.00)

	GD	VG	FN	VF	VF/NM	NM-
1						3.00
2-17: 4-Vs. The Black Hood. 9-Trading card inside						2.50
Annual 1 ('92, $2.50, 68 pgs.)-Impact trading card						3.00

FLYBOY (Flying Cadets)(Also see Approved Comics #5)
Ziff-Davis Publ. Co. (Approved): Spring, 1952 - No. 2, Oct-Nov, 1952

	GD	VG	FN	VF	VF/NM	NM-
1-Saunders painted-c	20	40	60	112	156	200
2-(10-11/52)-Saunders painted-c	14	28	42	79	107	135

FLYING ACES (Aviation stories)
Key Publications: July, 1955 - No. 5, Mar, 1956

	GD	VG	FN	VF	VF/NM	NM-
1	8	16	24	40	50	60
2-5: 2-Trapani-a	5	10	15	22	26	30

FLYING A'S RANGE RIDER, THE (TV)(See Western Roundup under Dell Giants)
Dell Publishing Co.: #404, 6-7/52; #2, June-Aug, 1953 - #24, Aug, 1959 (All photo-c)

	GD	VG	FN	VF	VF/NM	NM-
Four Color 404(#1)-Titled "The Range Rider"	12	24	36	82	121	160
2	8	16	24	53	74	95
3-10	6	12	18	43	59	75
11-16,18-24	6	12	18	38	52	65
17-Toth-a	7	14	21	46	63	80

FLYING CADET (WW II Plane Photos)
Flying Cadet Publ. Co.; Jan, 1943 - V2#8, 1947 (Half photos, half comics)

	GD	VG	FN	VF	VF/NM	NM-
V1#1-Painted-c	15	30	45	86	118	150
2	9	18	27	49	62	75
3-9 (Two #6's, Sept. & Oct.): 5,6a,6b-Photo-c	8	16	24	43	54	65
V2#1-7(#10-16)	7	14	21	37	46	55
8(#17)-Bare-breasted woman-c	19	38	57	106	146	185

FLYING COLORS 10th ANNIVERSARY SPECIAL
Flying Colors Comics: Fall 1998 ($2.95, one-shot)

	GD	VG	FN	VF	VF/NM	NM-
1-Dan Brereton-c; pin-ups by Jim Lee and Jeff Johnson						3.00

FLYIN' JENNY
Pentagon Publ. Co./Leader Enterprises #2: 1946 - No. 2, 1947 (1945 strip-r)

	GD	VG	FN	VF	VF/NM	NM-
nn-Marcus Swayze strip-r (entire insides)	14	28	42	79	107	135
2-Baker-c; Swayze strip reprints	16	32	48	89	122	155

FLYING MODELS
H-K Publ. (Health-Knowledge Publs.): V61#3, May, 1954 (5¢, 16 pgs.)

	GD	VG	FN	VF	VF/NM	NM-
V61#3 (Rare)	9	18	27	52	66	80

FLYING NUN (TV)
Dell Publishing Co.: Feb, 1968 - No. 4, Nov, 1968

	GD	VG	FN	VF	VF/NM	NM-
1-Sally Field photo-c	6	12	18	43	59	75
2-4: 2-Sally Field photo-c	4	8	12	27	36	45

FLYING NURSES (See Sue & Sally Smith...)

FLYING SAUCERS (See The Spirit 9/28/47(1st app.), Shadow Comics V7#10 (2nd, 1/48), Captain Midnight #60 (3rd, 2/48), Boy Commandos #26 (4th, 3-4/48) & Flash Gordon Four Color 190 (5th, 6/48))

FLYING SAUCERS
Avon Periodicals/Realistic: 1950; 1952; 1953

	GD	VG	FN	VF	VF/NM	NM-
1(1950)-Wood-a, 21 pgs.; Fawcette-c	78	156	234	488	732	975
nn(1952)-Cover altered plus 2 pgs. of Wood-a not in original	46	92	138	276	413	550
nn(1953)-Reprints above	36	72	108	207	296	385

FLYING SAUCERS (Comics)
Dell Publishing Co.: April, 1967 - No. 4, Nov, 1967; No. 5, Oct, 1969

	GD	VG	FN	VF	VF/NM	NM-
1	4	8	12	28	38	48
2-5	3	6	9	19	25	32

FLY MAN (Formerly Adventures of The Fly; Mighty Comics #40 on)
Mighty Comics Group (Radio Comics) (Archie): No. 32, July, 1965 - No. 39, Sept, 1966 (Also see Mighty Crusaders)

	GD	VG	FN	VF	VF/NM	NM-
32,33-Comet, Shield, Black Hood, The Fly & Flygirl x-over. 33-Re-intro Wizard, Hangman (1st S.A. appearances)	5	10	15	36	48	60
34-39: 34-Shield begins. 35-Origin Black Hood. 36-Hangman x-over in Shield; re-intro. & origin of Web (1st S.A. app.). 37-Hangman, Wizard x-over in Flyman; last Shield issue. 38-Web story. 39-Steel Sterling (1st S.A. app.)	4	8	12	24	32	40

FOES
Ram Comics: 1989 - No. 3, 1989 ($1.95, limited series)

	GD	VG	FN	VF	VF/NM	NM-
1-3						2.25

FOLLOW THE SUN (TV)
Dell Publishing Co.: May-July, 1962 - No. 2, Sept-Nov, 1962 (Photo-c)

	GD	VG	FN	VF	VF/NM	NM-
01-280-207(No.1)	5	10	15	36	48	60
12-280-211(No.2)	4	8	12	29	40	50

FOODANG
Continum Comics: July, 1994 ($1.95, B&W, bi-monthly)

	GD	VG	FN	VF	VF/NM	NM-
1						2.25

FOODINI (TV)(The Great...; see Jingle Dingle & Pinhead &...)
Continental Publ. (Holyoke): March, 1950 - No. 4, Aug, 1950 (All have 52 pgs.)

	GD	VG	FN	VF	VF/NM	NM-
1-Based on TV puppet show (very early TV comic)	23	46	69	129	180	230
2-Jingle Dingle begins	12	24	36	69	92	115
3,4	10	20	30	56	73	90

FOOEY (Magazine) (Satire)
Scoff Publishing Co.: Feb, 1961 - No. 4, May, 1961

	GD	VG	FN	VF	VF/NM	NM-
1	5	10	15	33	44	55
2-4	3	7	10	21	28	35

FOOFUR (TV)

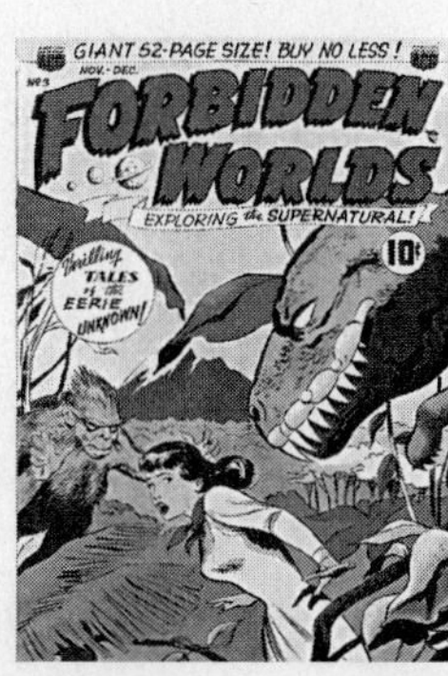

Forbidden Worlds #3 © ACG

Force Works #13 © MAR

Forever People #8 © DC

GD 2.0 | VG 4.0 | FN 6.0 | VF 8.0 | VF/NM 9.0 | NM- 9.2

Marvel Comics (Star Comics)/Marvel No. 5 on: Aug, 1987 - No. 6, Jun, 1988
1-6 3.00

FOOLKILLER (Also see The Amazing Spider-Man #225, The Defenders #73, Man-Thing #3 & Omega the Unknown #8)
Marvel Comics: Oct, 1990 - No. 10, Oct, 1991 ($1.75, limited series)
1-10: 1-Origin 3rd Foolkiller; Greg Salinger app; DeZuniga-a(i) in 1-4. 8-Spider-Man x-over 2.25

FOOM (Friends Of Ol' Marvel)
Marvel Comics: 1973 - No. 22, 1979 (Marvel fan magazine)
1 5 10 15 36 48 60
2-Hulk-c by Steranko 4 8 12 24 32 40
3,4 3 7 10 21 28 35
5-11: 11-Kirby-a and interview 3 6 9 18 24 30
12-15: 12-Vision-c. 13-Daredevil-c. 14-Conan. 15-Howard the Duck
3 6 9 16 20 25
16-20: 16-Marvel bullpen. 17-Stan Lee issue. 19-Defenders
2 4 6 12 16 20
21-Star Wars 3 6 9 16 20 25
22-Spider-Man-c; low print run final issue 4 8 12 29 40 50

FOOTBALL THRILLS (See Tops In Adventure)
Ziff-Davis Publ. Co.: Fall-Winter, 1951-52 - No. 2, Fall, 1952 (Edited by "Red" Grange)
1-Powell a(2); Saunders painted-c; Red Grange, Jim Thorpe stories
30 60 90 170 240 310
2-Saunders painted-c 20 40 60 112 156 200

FOOT SOLDIERS, THE
Dark Horse Comics: Jan, 1996 - No. 4, Apr, 1996 ($2.95, limited series)
1-4: Krueger story & Avon Oeming-a. in all. 1-Alex Ross-c. 4-John K. Snyder, III-c 3.00

FOOT SOLDIERS, THE (Volume Two)
Image Comics: Sept, 1997 - No. 5, May, 1998 ($2.95, limited series)
1-5: 1-Yeowell-a. 2-McDaniel, Hester, Sienkiewicz, Giffen-a 3.00

FOR A NIGHT OF LOVE
Avon Periodicals: 1951
nn-Two stories adapted from the works of Emile Zola; Astarita, Ravielli-a; Kinstler-c
31 62 93 175 248 320

FORBIDDEN KNOWLEDGE: ADVENTURE BEYOND THE DOORWAY TO SOULS WITH RADICAL DREAMER (Also see Radical Dreamer)
Mark's Giant Economy Size Comics: 1996 ($3.50, B&W, one-shot, 48 pgs.)
nn-Max Wrighter app.; Wheatley-c/a/script; painted infinity-c 3.50

FORBIDDEN LOVE
Quality Comics Group: Mar, 1950 - No. 4, Sept, 1950 (52 pgs.)
1-(Scarce)-Classic photo-c; Crandall-a 74 148 222 463 694 925
2-(Scarce)-Classic photo-c 62 124 186 388 582 775
3-(Scarce)-Photo-c 40 80 120 240 340 440
4-(Scarce)-Ward/Cuidera-a; photo-c 40 80 120 240 350 460

FORBIDDEN LOVE (See Dark Mansion of...)

FORBIDDEN PLANET
Innovation Publishing: May, 1992 - No. 4, 1992 ($2.50, limited series)
1-4: Adapts movie; painted-c 2.50

FORBIDDEN TALES OF DARK MANSION (Formerly Dark Mansion of Forbidden Love #1-4)
National Periodical Publ.: No. 5, May-June, 1972 - No. 15, Feb-Mar, 1974
5-(52 pgs.) 5 10 15 33 44 55
6-15: 13-Kane/Howard-a 2 4 6 14 18 22
NOTE: ***N. Adams*** *c-9.* ***Alcala*** *a-9-11, 13.* ***Chaykin*** *a-7,15.* ***Evans*** *a-14.* ***Heck*** *a-5.* ***Kaluta*** *a-7i, 8-12; c-7, 8, 13.* ***G. Kane*** *a-13.* ***Kirby*** *a-6.* ***Nino*** *a-8, 12, 15.* ***Redondo*** *a-14.*

FORBIDDEN WORLDS
American Comics Group: 7-8/51 - No. 34, 10-11/54; No. 35, 8/55 - No. 145, 8/67 (No. 1-5: 52 pgs.; No. 6-8: 44 pgs.)
1-Williamson/Frazetta-a (10 pgs.) 152 304 456 950 1425 1900
2 66 132 198 413 619 825
3-Williamson/Orlando-a (7 pgs.); Wood (2 panels); Frazetta (1 panel)
68 136 204 425 638 850
4 42 84 126 252 376 500
5-Krenkel/Williamson-a (8 pgs.) 55 110 165 330 495 660
6-Harrison/Williamson-a (8 pgs.) 48 96 144 288 432 575
7,8,10: 7-1st monthly issue 31 62 93 178 252 325
9-A-Bomb explosion story 34 68 102 196 278 360
11-20 22 44 66 127 176 225
21-33: 24-E.C. swipe by Landau 16 32 48 92 126 160
34(10-11/54)(Scarce)(becomes Young Heroes #35 on)-Last pre-code issue;
A-Bomb explosion story 19 38 57 106 146 185
35(8/55)-Scarce 17 34 51 98 134 170
36-62 11 22 33 66 88 110
63,69,76,78-Williamson-a in all; w/Krenkel #69 12 24 36 69 92 115
64,66-68,70-72,74,75,77,79-85,87-90 9 18 27 52 66 80
65- "There's a New Moon Tonight" listed in #114 as holding 1st record fan mail response
12 24 36 69 92 115
73-1st app. Herbie by Ogden Whitney 39 78 117 233 329 425
86-Flying saucer-c by Schaffenberger 10 20 30 58 77 95
91-93,95-100 6 12 18 38 52 65
94-Herbie (2nd app.) 9 18 27 65 93 120
101-109,111-113,115,117-120 4 8 12 29 40 50
110,116-Herbie app. 116-Herbie goes to Hell 7 14 21 46 63 80
114-1st Herbie-c; contains list of editor's top 20 ACG stories
8 16 24 55 78 100
121-123 4 8 12 27 36 45
124,126-130: 124-Magic Agent app. 4 8 12 29 40 50
125-Magic Agent app.; intro. & origin Magicman series, ends #141
6 12 18 43 59 75
131-139: 133-Origin/1st app. Dragonia in Magicman (1-2/66); returns in #138.
136-Nemesis x-over in Magicman 4 8 12 27 36 45
140-Mark Midnight app. by Ditko 4 8 12 29 40 50
141-145 4 8 12 24 32 40
NOTE: ***Buscema*** *a-75, 79, 81, 82, 140r.* ***Cameron*** *a-5.* ***Disbrow*** *a-10.* ***Ditko*** *a-137p, 138, 140.* ***Landau*** *a-24, 27-29, 31-34, 48, 86r, 96, 143-45.* ***Lazarus*** *a-18, 23, 24, 57.* ***Moldoff*** *a-27, 31, 139r.* ***Reinman*** *a-93.* ***Whitney*** *a-115, 116, 137; c-40, 46, 57, 60, 68, 78, 79, 90, 93, 94, 100, 102, 103, 106-108, 114, 129.*

FORCE, THE (See The Crusaders)

FORCE MAJEURE: PRAIRIE BAY (Also see Wild Stars)
Little Rocket Publications: May, 2002 ($2.95, B&W)
1-Tierney-s/Gil-c/a 3.00

FORCE OF BUDDHA'S PALM THE
Jademan Comics: Aug, 1988 - No. 55, Feb, 1993 ($1.50/$1.95, 68 pgs.)
1,55-Kung Fu stories in all 3.00
2-54 2.50

FORCE WORKS
Marvel Comics: July, 1994 - No. 22, Apr, 1996 ($1.50)
1-($3.95)-Fold-out pop-up-c; Iron Man, Wonder Man, Spider-Woman, U.S. Agent & Scarlet Witch (new costume) 4.00
2-11, 13-22: 5-Blue logo & pink logo versions. 9-Intro Dreamguard. 13-Avengers app. 2.25
5-Pink logo ($2.95)-polybagged w/ 16pg. Marvel Action Hour Preview & acetate print 3.00
12 ($2.50)-Flip book w/War Machine. 2.50

FORD ROTUNDA CHRISTMAS BOOK (See Christmas at the Rotunda)

FOREIGN INTRIGUES (Formerly Johnny Dynamite; becomes Battlefield Action #16 on)
Charlton Comics: No. 14, 1956 - No. 15, Aug, 1956
14,15-Johnny Dynamite continues 7 14 21 37 46 55

FOREMOST BOYS (See 4Most)

FOR ETERNITY
Antarctic Press: July, 1997 - No. 4, Jan, 1998 ($2.95, B&W)
1-4 3.00

FOREVER AMBER
Image Comics: July, 1999 - Oct, 1999 ($2.95, B&W)
1-4-Don Hudson-s/a 3.00

FOREVER DARLING (Movie)
Dell Publishing Co.: No. 681, Feb, 1956
Four Color 681-w/Lucille Ball & Desi Arnaz; photo-c 12 24 36 84 125 165

FOREVER MAELSTROM
DC Comics: Jan, 2003 - No. 6, Jun, 2003 ($2.95, limited series)
1-6-Chaykin & Tischman-s/Lucas & Barreto-a 3.00

FOREVER PEOPLE, THE
National Periodical Publications: Feb-Mar, 1971 - No. 11, Oct-Nov, 1972 (Fourth World) (#1-3, 10-11 are 36 pgs; #4-9 are 52 pgs.)
1-1st app. Forever People; Superman x-over; Kirby-c/a begins; 1st full app. Darkseid (3rd anywhere, 3 weeks before New Gods #1); Darkseid storyline begins, ends #8 (app. in 1-4,6,8; cameos in 5,11) 7 14 21 51 71 90
2-9: 4-G.A. reprints thru #9. 9,10-Deadman app. 4 8 12 27 36 45
10,11 3 6 9 18 24 30
Jack Kirby's Forever People TPB ('99, $14.95, B&W&Grey) r/#1-11 plus cover gallery 15.00

Formerly Known as the Justice League #1 © DC

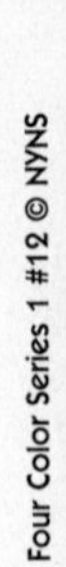
Four Color Series 1 #12 © NYNS

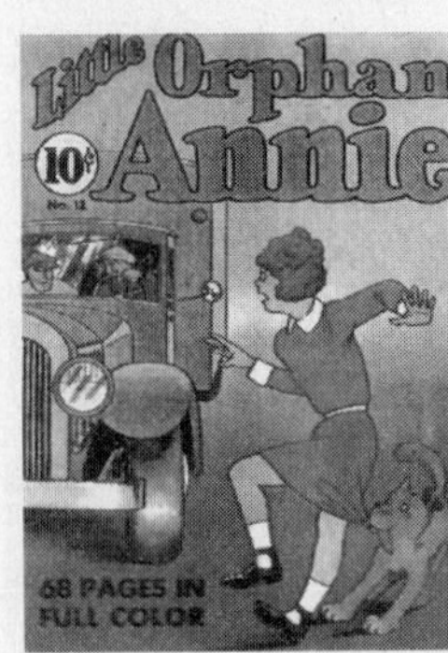

Four Color Series 2 #29 © WDC

GD VG FN VF VF/NM NM-
2.0 4.0 6.0 8.0 9.0 9.2

NOTE: *Kirby c/a(p)-1-11; #4-9 contain Sandman reprints from Adventure #85, 84, 75, 80, 77, 74 in that order.*

FOREVER PEOPLE
DC Comics: Feb, 1988 - No. 6, July, 1988 ($1.25, limited series)
1-6 3.00

FORGE
CrossGeneration Comics: Feb, 2002 - No. 13, May, 2003 ($9.95/$11.95/$7.95, TPB)
1-3: Reprints from various CrossGen titles 10.00
4-8-($11.95) 12.00
9-13-($7.95, 8-1/4" x 5-1/2") digest-sized reprints 8.00

FOR GIRLS ONLY
Bernard Baily Enterprises: 11/53 - No. 2, 6/54 (100 pgs., digest size, 25¢)
1-25% comic book, 75% articles, illos, games 14 28 42 79 107 135
2-Eddie Fisher photo & story. 10 20 30 56 73 90

FORGOTTEN FOREST OF OZ, THE (See First Comics Graphic Novel #16)

FORGOTTEN REALMS (Also see Avatar & TSR Worlds)
DC Comics: Sept, 1989 - No. 25, Sept, 1991 ($1.50/$1.75)
1, Annual 1 (1990, $2.95, 68 pgs.) 3.00
2-25: Based on TSR role-playing game. 18-Avatar story 2.25

FORLORN RIVER (See Zane Grey Four Color 395)

FOR LOVERS ONLY (Formerly Hollywood Romances)
Charlton Comics: No. 60, Aug, 1971 - No. 87, Nov, 1976
60 4 8 12 24 32 40
61-87 2 4 6 12 16 20

FORMERLY KNOWN AS THE JUSTICE LEAGUE
DC Comics: Sept, 2003 - Present ($2.50)
1-Giffen & DeMatteis-s/Maguire-a; Booster Gold, Blue Beetle, Captain Atom, Mary Marvel, Fire, and Elongated Man app. 3.00
2-6: 3,4-Roulette app. 6-JLA app. 2.50

FORT: PROPHET OF THE UNEXPLAINED
Dark Horse Comics: June, 2002 - No. 4, Sept, 2002 ($2.99, B&W, limited series)
1-4-Peter Lenkov-s/Frazer Irving-c/a 3.00
TPB (2003, $9.95) r/#1-4 10.00

FORTUNE AND GLORY
Oni Press: Dec, 1999 - No. 3, Apr, 2000 ($4.95, B&W, limited series)
1-3-Brian Michael Bendis in Hollywood 5.00
TPB ($14.95) 15.00

40 BIG PAGES OF MICKEY MOUSE
Whitman Publ. Co.: No. 945, Jan, 1936 (10-1/4x12-1/2", 44 pgs., cardboard-c)
945-Reprints Mickey Mouse Magazine #1, but with a different cover; ads were eliminated and some illustrated stories had expanded text. The book is 3/4" shorter than Mickey Mouse Mag. #1, but the reprints are same size (Rare) 160 320 480 1000 1500 2000

40 oz. COLLECTED
Image Comics: Nov, 2003 ($9.95, digest-size, B&W)
Vol. 1-Reprints Jim Mahfood's mini-comics plus 20 pgs. new material; Grrl Scouts app. 10.00

FOR YOUR EYES ONLY (See James Bond...)

FOUR COLOR
Dell Publishing Co.: Sept?, 1939 - No. 1354, Apr-June, 1962
(Series I are all 68 pgs.)

NOTE: *Four Color only appears on issues #19-25, 1-99,101. Dell Publishing Co. filed these as Series I, #1-25, and Series II, #1-1354. Issues beginning with #710? were printed with and without ads on back cover. Issues without ads are worth more.*

SERIES I:
1(nn)-Dick Tracy 628 1256 1884 4396 6748 9100
2(nn)-Don Winslow of the Navy (#1) (Rare) (11/39?) 138 276 414 1035 1518 2000
3(nn)-Myra North (1/40) 75 150 225 536 818 1100
4-Donald Duck by Al Taliaferro (1940)(Disney)(3/40?) 875 1750 2625 6563 11,032 15,500
(Prices vary widely on this book)
5-Smilin' Jack (#1) (5/40?) 58 116 174 432 646 860
6-Dick Tracy (Scarce) 146 292 438 1046 1598 2150
7-Gang Busters 36 72 108 270 405 540
8-Dick Tracy 73 146 219 519 797 1075
9-Terry and the Pirates-r/Super #9-29 50 100 150 409 622 835
10-Smilin' Jack 50 100 150 370 550 730
11-Smitty (#1) 36 72 108 261 387 510
12-Little Orphan Annie; reprints strips from 12/19/37 to 6/4/38 45 90 135 340 508 675
13-Walt Disney's Reluctant Dragon('41)-Contains 2 pgs. of photos from film; 2 pg. foreword to Fantasia by Leopold Stokowski; Donald Duck, Goofy, Baby Weems & Mickey Mouse (as the Sorcerer's Apprentice) app. (Disney) 160 320 480 1156 1766 2375
14-Moon Mullins (#1) 35 70 105 263 392 520
15-Tillie the Toiler (#1) 33 66 99 248 374 500
16-Mickey Mouse (#1) (Disney) by Gottfredson 1350 2700 4050 13,000 - -
17-Walt Disney's Dumbo, the Flying Elephant (#1)(1941)-Mickey Mouse, Donald Duck, & Pluto app. (Disney) 185 370 555 1388 2094 2800
18-Jiggs and Maggie (#1)(1936-38-r) 37 74 111 278 414 550
19-Barney Google and Snuffy Smith (#1)-(1st issue with Four Color on the cover) 38 76 115 285 418 550
20-Tiny Tim 29 58 87 210 310 410
21-Dick Tracy 61 122 183 435 667 900
22-Don Winslow 32 64 96 240 358 475
23-Gang Busters 30 60 90 218 319 420
24-Captain Easy 40 80 120 300 450 600
25-Popeye (1942) 65 130 195 485 743 1000

SERIES II:
1-Little Joe (1942) 50 100 150 400 600 800
2-Harold Teen 29 58 87 210 310 410
3-Alley Oop (#1) 46 92 138 368 554 740
4-Smilin' Jack 41 82 123 308 459 610
5-Raggedy Ann and Andy (#1) 47 94 141 376 563 750
6-Smitty 23 46 69 167 244 320
7-Smokey Stover (#1) 31 62 93 232 346 460
8-Tillie the Toiler 24 48 72 174 255 335
9-Donald Duck Finds Pirate Gold, by Carl Barks & Jack Hannah (Disney) (© 8/17/42) 750 1500 2250 5625 9313 13,000
10-Flash Gordon by Alex Raymond; reprinted from "The Ice Kingdom" 96 192 288 680 1053 1425
11-Wash Tubbs 31 62 93 228 339 450
12-Walt Disney's Bambi (#1) 59 158 177 417 639 860
13-Mr. District Attorney (#1)-See The Funnies #35 for 1st app. 30 60 90 218 319 420
14-Smilin' Jack 33 66 99 248 372 495
15-Felix the Cat (#1) 73 146 219 544 822 1100
16-Porky Pig (#1)(1942)- "Secret of the Haunted House" 80 160 240 629 965 1300
17-Popeye 47 94 141 352 531 710
18-Little Orphan Annie's Junior Commandos; Flag-c; reprints strips from 6/14/42 to 11/21/42 37 74 111 278 414 550
19-Walt Disney's Thumper Meets the Seven Dwarfs (Disney); reprinted in Silly Symphonies 50 100 150 400 600 800
20-Barney Baxter 29 58 87 209 300 390
21-Oswald the Rabbit (#1)(1943) 48 96 144 370 548 725
22-Tillie the Toiler 18 36 54 131 191 250
23-Raggedy Ann and Andy 37 74 111 278 414 550
24-Gang Busters 30 60 90 218 319 420
25-Andy Panda (#1) (Walter Lantz) 54 108 162 405 603 800
26-Popeye 47 94 141 352 531 710
27-Walt Disney's Mickey Mouse and the Seven Colored Terror 85 170 255 629 965 1300
28-Wash Tubbs 22 44 66 160 235 310
29-Donald Duck and the Mummy's Ring, by Carl Barks (Disney) (9/43) 513 1026 1539 3848 6324 8800
30-Bambi's Children (1943)-Disney 56 112 168 400 605 810
31-Moon Mullins 20 40 60 140 205 270
32-Smitty 17 34 51 121 178 235
33-Bugs Bunny "Public Nuisance #1" 115 230 345 805 1240 1675
34-Dick Tracy 41 82 123 315 470 625
35-Smokey Stover 18 36 54 127 186 245
36-Smilin' Jack 25 50 75 176 258 340
37-Bringing Up Father 20 40 60 145 213 280
38-Roy Rogers (#1, © 4/44)-1st western comic with photo-c (see Movie Comics #3) 210 420 630 1654 2577 3500
39-Oswald the Rabbit (1944) 33 66 99 248 374 500
40-Barney Google and Snuffy Smith 24 48 72 169 247 325
41-Mother Goose and Nursery Rhyme Comics (#1)-All by Walt Kelly 25 50 75 176 258 340
42-Tiny Tim (1934-r) 18 36 54 131 191 250
43-Popeye (1938-'42-r) 31 62 93 233 349 465

Four Color #55 © KING

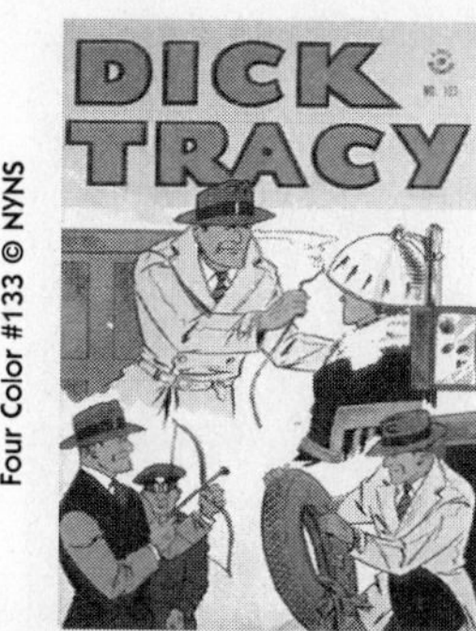

Four Color #133 © NYNS

Four Color #161 © ERB

	GD 2.0	VG 4.0	FN 6.0	VF 8.0	VF/NM 9.0	NM- 9.2
44-Terry and the Pirates (1938-r)	37	74	111	278	419	560
45-Raggedy Ann	31	62	93	231	346	460
46-Felix the Cat and the Haunted Castle	40	80	120	300	450	600
47-Gene Autry (copyright 6/16/44)	41	82	123	324	487	650
48-Porky Pig of the Mounties by Carl Barks (7/44)	92	184	276	706	1078	1450
49-Snow White and the Seven Dwarfs (Disney)	58	116	174	434	660	885
50-Fairy Tale Parade-Walt Kelly art (1944)	26	52	78	189	277	365
51-Bugs Bunny Finds the Lost Treasure	35	70	105	263	394	525
52-Little Orphan Annie; reprints strips from 6/18/38 to 11/19/38	30	60	90	218	319	420
53-Wash Tubbs	16	32	48	116	171	225
54-Andy Panda	31	62	93	228	339	450
55-Tillie the Toiler	14	28	42	102	149	195
56-Dick Tracy	35	70	105	263	394	525
57-Gene Autry	40	80	120	300	450	600
58-Smilin' Jack	25	50	75	176	258	340
59-Mother Goose and Nursery Rhyme Comics-Kelly-c/a	21	42	63	147	216	285
60-Tiny Folks Funnies	17	34	51	118	174	230
61-Santa Claus Funnies(11/44)-Kelly art	25	50	75	179	262	345
62-Donald Duck in Frozen Gold, by Carl Barks (Disney) (1/45)	162	332	498	1245	2048	2850
63-Roy Rogers; color photo-all 4 covers	47	94	141	376	563	750
64-Smokey Stover	14	28	42	99	145	190
65-Smitty	14	28	42	99	145	190
66-Gene Autry	40	80	120	300	450	600
67-Oswald the Rabbit	19	38	57	136	198	260
68-Mother Goose and Nursery Rhyme Comics, by Walt Kelly	21	42	63	147	216	285
69-Fairy Tale Parade, by Walt Kelly	26	52	78	189	277	365
70-Popeye and Wimpy	26	52	78	189	275	360
71-Walt Disney's Three Caballeros, by Walt Kelly (© 4/45)-(Disney)	75	150	225	561	856	1150
72-Raggedy Ann	27	54	81	194	285	375
73-The Gumps (#1)	13	26	39	94	137	180
74-Marge's Little Lulu (#1)	115	230	345	850	1263	1675
75-Gene Autry and the Wildcat	31	62	93	230	345	460
76-Little Orphan Annie; reprints strips from 2/28/40 to 6/24/40	26	52	78	185	270	355
77-Felix the Cat	37	74	111	278	419	560
78-Porky Pig and the Bandit Twins	27	54	81	192	281	370
79-Walt Disney's Mickey Mouse in The Riddle of the Red Hat by Carl Barks (8/45)	108	216	324	791	1208	1625
80-Smilin' Jack	16	32	48	113	167	220
81-Moon Mullins	12	24	36	82	121	160
82-Lone Ranger	40	80	120	300	450	600
83-Gene Autry in Outlaw Trail	31	62	93	230	345	460
84-Flash Gordon by Alex Raymond-Reprints from "The Fiery Desert"	41	82	123	324	487	650
85-Andy Panda and the Mad Dog Mystery	17	34	51	123	182	240
86-Roy Rogers; photo-c	35	70	105	263	394	525
87-Fairy Tale Parade by Walt Kelly; Dan Noonan-c	26	52	78	189	277	365
88-Bugs Bunny's Great Adventure (Sci/fi)	23	46	69	167	244	320
89-Tillie the Toiler	14	28	42	102	149	195
90-Christmas with Mother Goose by Walt Kelly (11/45)	19	38	57	136	198	260
91-Santa Claus Funnies by Walt Kelly (11/45)	19	38	57	136	198	260
92-Walt Disney's The Wonderful Adventures Of Pinocchio (1945); Donald Duck by Kelly, 16 pgs. (Disney)	57	114	171	432	646	860
93-Gene Autry in The Bandit of Black Rock	30	60	90	218	319	420
94-Winnie Winkle (1945)	13	26	39	90	133	175
95-Roy Rogers Comics; photo-c	35	70	105	263	394	525
96-Dick Tracy	28	56	84	203	294	385
97-Marge's Little Lulu (1946)	50	100	150	376	556	735
98-Lone Ranger, The	31	62	93	230	345	460
99-Smitty	12	24	36	82	121	160
100-Gene Autry Comics; 1st Gene Autry photo-c	31	62	93	230	345	460
101-Terry and the Pirates	26	52	78	189	275	375

NOTE: No. 101 is last issue to carry "Four Color" logo on cover; all issues beginning with No. 100 are marked "...O. S." (One Shot) which can be found in the bottom left-hand panel on the first page; the numbers following "O. S." relate to the year/month issued.

	GD 2.0	VG 4.0	FN 6.0	VF 8.0	VF/NM 9.0	NM- 9.2
102-Oswald the Rabbit-Walt Kelly art, 1 pg.	16	32	48	113	167	220
103-Easter with Mother Goose by Walt Kelly	19	38	57	136	198	260
104-Fairy Tale Parade by Walt Kelly	20	40	60	140	205	270
105-Albert the Alligator and Pogo Possum (#1) by Kelly (4/46)	66	132	198	502	764	1025
106-Tillie the Toiler (5/46)	10	20	30	73	107	140
107-Little Orphan Annie; reprints strips from 11/16/42 to 3/24/43	22	44	66	156	228	300
108-Donald Duck in The Terror of the River, by Carl Barks (Disney) (© 4/16/46)	125	250	375	938	1544	2150
109-Roy Rogers Comics; photo-c	29	58	87	210	305	400
110-Marge's Little Lulu	35	70	105	255	377	500
111-Captain Easy	15	30	45	107	156	205
112-Porky Pig's Adventure in Gopher Gulch	17	34	51	118	174	230
113-Popeye; all new Popeye stories begin	15	30	45	104	152	200
114-Fairy Tale Parade by Walt Kelly	20	40	60	140	205	270
115-Marge's Little Lulu	35	70	105	255	377	500
116-Mickey Mouse and the House of Many Mysteries (Disney)	26	52	78	189	275	360
117-Roy Rogers Comics; photo-c	23	46	69	164	240	315
118-Lone Ranger, The	31	62	93	230	345	460
119-Felix the Cat; all new Felix stories begin	35	70	105	263	392	520
120-Marge's Little Lulu	31	62	93	228	339	450
121-Fairy Tale Parade-(not Kelly)	12	24	36	87	129	170
122-Henry (#1) (10/46)	15	30	45	104	152	200
123-Bugs Bunny's Dangerous Venture	17	34	51	121	178	235
124-Roy Rogers Comics; photo-c	23	46	69	164	240	315
125-Lone Ranger, The	23	46	69	164	240	315
126-Christmas with Mother Goose by Walt Kelly (1946)	14	28	42	102	149	195
127-Popeye	15	30	45	104	152	200
128-Santa Claus Funnies- "Santa & the Angel" by Gollub; "A Mouse in the House" by Kelly	15	30	45	109	160	210
129-Walt Disney's Uncle Remus and His Tales of Brer Rabbit (#1) (1946)-Adapted from Disney movie "Song of the South"	29	58	87	210	305	400
130-Andy Panda (Walter Lantz)	12	24	36	82	121	160
131-Marge's Little Lulu	31	62	93	228	339	450
132-Tillie the Toiler (1947)	10	20	30	73	107	140
133-Dick Tracy	22	44	66	160	235	310
134-Tarzan and the Devil Ogre; Marsh-c/a	60	120	180	476	726	975
135-Felix the Cat	27	54	81	196	281	365
136-Lone Ranger, The	23	46	69	164	240	315
137-Roy Rogers Comics; photo-c	23	46	69	164	240	315
138-Smitty	10	20	30	72	104	135
139-Marge's Little Lulu (1947)	31	62	93	218	319	420
140-Easter with Mother Goose by Walt Kelly	15	30	45	109	160	210
141-Mickey Mouse and the Submarine Pirates (Disney)	22	44	66	160	235	310
142-Bugs Bunny and the Haunted Mountain	17	34	51	121	178	235
143-Oswald the Rabbit & the Prehistoric Egg	10	20	30	72	104	135
144-Roy Rogers Comics (1947)-Photo-c	23	46	69	164	240	315
145-Popeye	15	30	45	104	152	200
146-Marge's Little Lulu	31	62	93	218	319	420
147-Donald Duck in Volcano Valley, by Carl Barks (Disney) (5/47)	84	168	252	630	1040	1450
148-Albert the Alligator and Pogo Possum by Walt Kelly (5/47)	55	110	165	424	632	840
149-Smilin' Jack	11	22	33	77	114	150
150-Tillie the Toiler (6/47)	10	20	30	70	100	130
151-Lone Ranger, The	20	40	60	142	209	275
152-Little Orphan Annie; reprints strips from 1/2/44 to 5/6/44	14	28	42	102	149	195
153-Roy Rogers Comics; photo-c	21	42	63	147	216	285
154-Walter Lantz Andy Panda	12	24	36	82	121	160
155-Henry (7/47)	10	20	30	67	96	125
156-Porky Pig and the Phantom	12	24	36	84	125	165
157-Mickey Mouse & the Beanstalk (Disney)	22	44	66	160	235	310
158-Marge's Little Lulu	31	62	93	218	319	420
159-Donald Duck in the Ghost of the Grotto, by Carl Barks (Disney) (8/47)	72	144	216	540	895	1250
160-Roy Rogers Comics; photo-c	21	42	63	147	216	285
161-Tarzan and the Fires Of Tohr; Marsh-c/a	52	104	156	416	621	825
162-Felix the Cat (9/47)	21	42	63	147	216	285
163-Dick Tracy	19	38	57	138	202	265
164-Bugs Bunny Finds the Frozen Kingdom	17	34	51	121	178	235
165-Marge's Little Lulu	30	60	90	218	319	420
166-Roy Rogers Comics (52 pgs.)-Photo-c	21	42	63	147	216	285

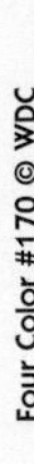
Four Color #170 © WDC

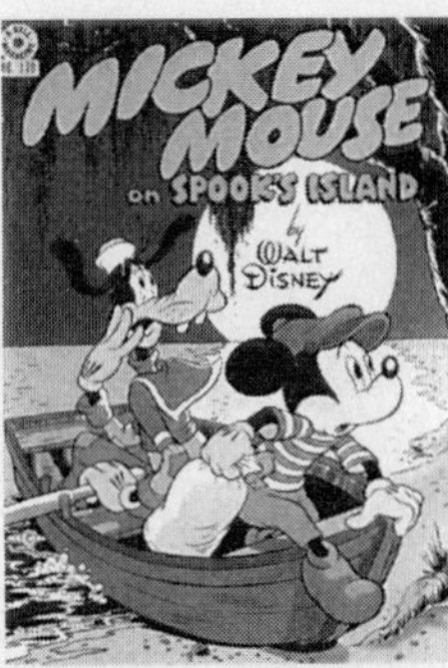

Four Color #183 © Walter Lantz

Four Color #260 © WB

	GD 2.0	VG 4.0	FN 6.0	VF 8.0	VF/NM 9.0	NM- 9.2
167-Lone Ranger, The	20	40	60	142	209	275
168-Popeye (10/47)	15	30	45	104	152	200
169-Woody Woodpecker (#1)- "Manhunter in the North"; drug use story	18	36	54	131	191	250
170-Mickey Mouse on Spook's Island (11/47)(Disney)-reprinted in Mickey Mouse #103	19	38	57	138	202	265
171-Charlie McCarthy (#1) and the Twenty Thieves	28	56	84	203	294	385
172-Christmas with Mother Goose by Walt Kelly (11/47)	14	28	42	102	149	195
173-Flash Gordon	18	36	54	131	191	250
174-Winnie Winkle	8	16	24	58	82	105
175-Santa Claus Funnies by Walt Kelly (1947)	15	30	45	109	160	210
176-Tillie the Toiler (12/47)	10	20	30	70	100	130
177-Roy Rogers Comics-(36 pgs.); Photo-c	20	40	60	145	213	280
178-Donald Duck "Christmas on Bear Mountain" by Carl Barks; 1st app. Uncle Scrooge (Disney)(12/47)	100	200	300	750	1250	1750
179-Uncle Wiggily (#1)-Walt Kelly-c	17	34	51	118	174	230
180-Ozark Ike (#1)	11	22	33	77	114	150
181-Walt Disney's Mickey Mouse in Jungle Magic	19	38	57	138	202	265
182-Porky Pig in Never-Never Land (2/48)	12	24	36	84	125	165
183-Oswald the Rabbit (Lantz)	10	20	30	72	104	135
184-Tillie the Toiler	10	20	30	70	100	130
185-Easter with Mother Goose by Walt Kelly (1948)	14	28	42	97	141	185
186-Walt Disney's Bambi (4/48)-Reprinted as Movie Classic Bambi #3 (1956)	18	36	54	127	186	245
187-Bugs Bunny and the Dreadful Dragon	12	24	36	87	129	170
188-Woody Woodpecker (Lantz, 5/48)	12	24	36	84	125	165
189-Donald Duck in The Old Castle's Secret, by Carl Barks (Disney) (6/48)	61	122	183	458	754	1050
190-Flash Gordon (6/48); bondage-c; "The Adventures of the Flying Saucers"; 5th Flying Saucer story- see The Spirit 9/28/47(1st), Shadow Comics V7#10 (2nd, 1/48),Captain Midnight #60 (3rd, 2/48) & Boy Commandos #26 (4th, 3-4/48)	21	42	63	147	216	285
191-Porky Pig to the Rescue	12	24	36	84	125	165
192-The Brownies (#1)-by Walt Kelly (7/48)	15	30	45	107	156	205
193-M.G.M. Presents Tom and Jerry (#1)(1948)	22	44	66	156	228	300
194-Mickey Mouse in The World Under the Sea (Disney)-Reprinted in Mickey Mouse #101	19	38	57	138	202	265
195-Tillie the Toiler	8	16	24	53	74	95
196-Charlie McCarthy in The Haunted Hide-Out; part photo-c	18	36	54	131	191	250
197-Spirit of the Border (#1) (Zane Grey) (1948)	13	26	39	90	133	175
198-Andy Panda	12	24	36	82	121	160
199-Donald Duck in Sheriff of Bullet Valley, by Carl Barks; Barks draws himself on wanted poster, last page; used in Love & Death (Disney) (10/48)	67	134	201	503	827	1150
200-Bugs Bunny, Super Sleuth (10/48)	12	24	36	87	129	170
201-Christmas with Mother Goose by W. Kelly	13	26	39	90	133	175
202-Woody Woodpecker	9	18	27	60	85	110
203-Donald Duck in the Golden Christmas Tree, by Carl Barks (Disney) (12/48)	46	92	138	345	573	800
204-Flash Gordon (12/48)	15	30	45	104	152	200
205-Santa Claus Funnies by Walt Kelly	14	28	42	99	145	190
206-Little Orphan Annie; reprints strips from 11/10/40 to 1/11/41	8	16	24	58	82	105
207-King of the Royal Mounted (#1) (12/48)	15	30	45	109	160	210
208-Brer Rabbit Does It Again (Disney) (1/49)	12	24	36	84	125	165
209-Harold Teen	6	12	18	38	52	65
210-Tippie and Cap Stubbs	5	10	15	36	48	60
211-Little Beaver (#1)	9	18	27	63	89	115
212-Dr. Bobbs	5	10	15	36	48	60
213-Tillie the Toiler	8	16	24	53	74	95
214-Mickey Mouse and His Sky Adventure (2/49)(Disney)-Reprinted in Mickey Mouse #105	15	30	45	104	152	200
215-Sparkle Plenty (Dick Tracy-r by Gould)	12	24	36	84	125	165
216-Andy Panda and the Police Pup (Lantz)	9	18	27	60	85	110
217-Bugs Bunny in Court Jester	12	24	36	87	129	170
218-Three Little Pigs and the Wonderful Magic Lamp (Disney) (3/49)(#1)	12	24	36	87	129	170
219-Swee'pe	10	20	30	67	96	125
220-Easter with Mother Goose by Walt Kelly	14	28	42	97	141	185
221-Uncle Wiggily-Walt Kelly cover in part	10	20	30	72	104	135
222-West of the Pecos (Zane Grey)	8	16	24	55	78	100
223-Donald Duck "Lost in the Andes" by Carl Barks (Disney-4/49) (square egg story)	64	128	192	480	790	1100
224-Little Iodine (#1), by Hatlo (4/49)	12	24	36	82	121	160
225-Oswald the Rabbit (Lantz)	7	14	21	50	68	85
226-Porky Pig and Spoofy, the Spook	10	20	30	70	100	130
227-Seven Dwarfs (Disney)	11	22	33	77	114	150
228-Mark of Zorro, The (#1) (1949)	23	46	69	167	244	320
229-Smokey Stover	7	14	21	46	63	80
230-Sunset Pass (Zane Grey)	8	16	24	55	78	100
231-Mickey Mouse and the Rajah's Treasure (Disney)	15	30	45	104	152	200
232-Woody Woodpecker (Lantz, 6/49)	9	18	27	60	85	110
233-Bugs Bunny, Sleepwalking Sleuth	12	24	36	87	129	170
234-Dumbo in Sky Voyage (Disney)	13	26	39	90	133	175
235-Tiny Tim	6	12	18	38	52	65
236-Heritage of the Desert (Zane Grey) (1949)	8	16	24	55	78	100
237-Tillie the Toiler	8	16	24	53	74	95
238-Donald Duck in Voodoo Hoodoo, by Carl Barks (Disney) (8/49)	46	92	138	345	573	800
239-Adventure Bound (8/49)	6	12	18	40	55	70
240-Andy Panda (Lantz)	9	18	27	60	85	110
241-Porky Pig, Mighty Hunter	10	20	30	70	100	130
242-Tippie and Cap Stubbs	4	8	12	28	38	48
243-Thumper Follows His Nose (Disney)	12	24	36	82	121	160
244-The Brownies by Walt Kelly	11	22	33	75	110	145
245-Dick's Adventures (9/49)	6	12	18	43	59	75
246-Thunder Mountain (Zane Grey)	6	12	18	38	52	65
247-Flash Gordon	15	30	45	104	152	200
248-Mickey Mouse and the Black Sorcerer (Disney)	15	30	45	104	152	200
249-Woody Woodpecker in the "Globetrotter" (10/49)	9	18	27	60	85	110
250-Bugs Bunny in Diamond Daze; used in **SOTI**, pg. 309	13	26	39	94	137	180
251-Hubert at Camp Moonbeam	6	12	18	38	52	65
252-Pinocchio (Disney)-not by Kelly; origin	12	24	36	82	121	160
253-Christmas with Mother Goose by W. Kelly	13	26	39	90	133	175
254-Santa Claus Funnies by Walt Kelly; Pogo & Albert story by Kelly (11/49)	14	28	42	99	145	190
255-The Ranger (Zane Grey) (1949)	6	12	18	38	52	65
256-Donald Duck in "Luck of the North" by Carl Barks (Disney) (12/49)-Shows #257 on inside	34	68	102	255	428	600
257-Little Iodine	9	18	27	60	85	110
258-Andy Panda and the Balloon Race (Lantz)	9	18	27	60	85	110
259-Santa and the Angel (Gollub art-condensed from #128) & Santa at the Zoo (12/49) -two books in one	5	10	15	36	48	60
260-Porky Pig, Hero of the Wild West (12/49)	10	20	30	70	100	130
261-Mickey Mouse and the Missing Key (Disney)	15	30	45	104	152	200
262-Raggedy Ann and Andy	10	20	30	70	100	130
263-Donald Duck in "Land of the Totem Poles" by Carl Barks (Disney) (2/50)-Has two Barks stories	33	66	100	248	412	575
264-Woody Woodpecker in the Magic Lantern (Lantz)	9	18	27	60	85	110
265-King of the Royal Mounted (Zane Grey)	9	18	27	63	89	115
266-Bugs Bunny on the "Isle of Hercules" (2/50)-Reprinted in Best of Bugs Bunny #1	10	20	30	70	100	130
267-Little Beaver; Harmon-c/a	5	10	15	36	48	60
268-Mickey Mouse's Surprise Visitor (1950)(Disney)	14	28	42	99	145	190
269-Johnny Mack Brown (#1)-Photo-c	25	50	75	176	258	340
270-Drift Fence (Zane Grey) (3/50)	6	12	18	38	52	65
271-Porky Pig in Phantom of the Plains	10	20	30	70	100	130
272-Cinderella (Disney) (4/50)	13	26	39	90	133	175
273-Oswald the Rabbit (Lantz)	7	14	21	50	68	85
274-Bugs Bunny, Hare-brained Reporter	10	20	30	70	100	130
275-Donald Duck in "Ancient Persia" by Carl Barks (Disney) (5/50)	31	62	93	233	392	550
276-Uncle Wiggily	9	18	27	60	85	110
277-Porky Pig in Desert Adventure (5/50)	10	20	30	70	100	130
278-Bill Elliott Comics (#1)-Photo-c	14	28	42	102	149	195
279-Mickey Mouse and Pluto Battle the Giant Ants (Disney); reprinted in Mickey Mouse #102 & 245	11	22	33	75	110	145
280-Andy Panda in The Isle Of Mechanical Men (Lantz)	9	18	27	60	85	110
281-Bugs Bunny in The Great Circus Mystery	10	20	30	70	100	130
282-Donald Duck and the Pixilated Parrot by Carl Barks (Disney) (© 5/23/50)	31	62	93	233	392	550
283-King of the Royal Mounted (7/50)	9	18	27	63	89	115

Four Color #292 © Cisco Kid Prod.

Four Color #355 © WB

Four Color #361 © DELL

	GD 2.0	VG 4.0	FN 6.0	VF 8.0	VF/NM 9.0	NM- 9.2
284-Porky Pig in The Kingdom of Nowhere	10	20	30	70	100	130
285-Bozo the Clown & His Minikin Circus (#1) (TV)	21	42	63	149	220	290
286-Mickey Mouse in The Uninvited Guest (Disney	11	22	33	75	110	145
287-Gene Autry's Champion in The Ghost Of Black Mountain; photo-c	12	24	36	84	125	165
288-Woody Woodpecker in Klondike Gold (Lantz)	9	18	27	60	85	110
289-Bugs Bunny in "Indian Trouble"	10	20	30	70	100	130
290-The Chief (#1) (8/50)	7	14	21	50	68	85
291-Donald Duck in "The Magic Hourglass" by Carl Barks (Disney) (9/50)	31	62	93	233	392	550
292-The Cisco Kid Comics (#1)	26	52	78	189	277	365
293-The Brownies-Kelly-c/a	11	22	33	75	110	145
294-Little Beaver	5	10	15	36	48	60
295-Porky Pig in President Porky (9/50)	10	20	30	70	100	130
296-Mickey Mouse in Private Eye for Hire (Disney)	11	22	33	75	110	145
297-Andy Panda in The Haunted Inn (Lantz, 10/50)	9	18	27	60	85	110
298-Bugs Bunny in Sheik for a Day	10	20	30	70	100	130
299-Buck Jones & the Iron Horse Trail (#1)	14	28	42	99	145	190
300-Donald Duck in "Big-Top Bedlam" by Carl Barks (Disney) (11/50)	31	62	93	233	392	550
301-The Mysterious Rider (Zane Grey)	6	12	18	38	52	65
302-Santa Claus Funnies (11/50)	6	12	18	43	59	75
303-Porky Pig in The Land of the Monstrous Flies	7	14	21	51	71	90
304-Mickey Mouse in Tom-Tom Island (Disney) (12/50)	9	18	27	65	93	120
305-Woody Woodpecker (Lantz)	6	12	18	43	59	75
306-Raggedy Ann	8	16	24	55	78	100
307-Bugs Bunny in Lumber Jack Rabbit	9	18	27	63	89	115
308-Donald Duck in "Dangerous Disguise" by Carl Barks (Disney) (1/51)	27	54	81	203	342	480
309-Betty Betz' Dollface and Her Gang (1951)	6	12	18	40	55	70
310-King of the Royal Mounted (1/51)	7	14	21	51	71	90
311-Porky Pig in Midget Horses of Hidden Valley	7	14	21	51	71	90
312-Tonto (#1)	11	22	33	77	114	150
313-Mickey Mouse in The Mystery of the Double-Cross Ranch (#1) (Disney) (2/51)	9	18	27	65	93	120
Note: Beginning with the above comic in 1951 Dell/Western began adding #1 in small print on the covers of several long running titles with the evident intention of switching these titles to their own monthly numbers, but when the conversions were made, there was no connection. It is thought that the post office may have stepped in and decreed the sequences should commence as though the first four colors printed had each begun with number one, or the first issues sold by subscription. Since the regular series' numbers don't correctly match to the numbers of earlier issues published, it's not known whether or not the numbering was in error.						
314-Ambush (Zane Grey)	6	12	18	38	52	65
315-Oswald the Rabbit (Lantz)	6	12	18	43	59	75
316-Rex Allen (#1)-Photo-c; Marsh-a	16	32	48	113	167	220
317-Bugs Bunny in Hair Today Gone Tomorrow (#1)	9	18	27	63	89	115
318-Donald Duck in "No Such Varmint" by Carl Barks (#1)-Indicia shows #317 (Disney, © 1/23/51)	27	54	81	203	342	480
319-Gene Autry's Champion; painted-c	6	12	18	43	59	75
320-Uncle Wiggily (#1)	9	18	27	60	85	110
321-Little Scouts (#1) (3/51)	4	8	12	28	38	48
322-Porky Pig in Roaring Rockets (#1 on-c)	7	14	21	51	71	90
323-Susie Q. Smith (#1) (3/51)	5	10	15	33	44	55
324-I Met a Handsome Cowboy (3/51)	10	20	30	67	96	125
325-Mickey Mouse in The Haunted Castle (#2) (Disney) (4/51)	9	18	27	65	93	120
326-Andy Panda (#1) (Lantz)	6	12	18	43	59	75
327-Bugs Bunny and the Rajah's Treasure (#2)	9	18	27	63	89	115
328-Donald Duck in Old California (#2) by Carl Barks-Peyote drug use issue (Disney) (5/51)	28	56	84	210	350	490
329-Roy Roger's Trigger (#1)(5/51)-Painted-c	16	32	48	111	163	215
330-Porky Pig Meets the Bristled Bruiser (#2)	7	14	21	51	71	90
331-Alice in Wonderland (Disney) (1951)	16	32	48	111	163	215
332-Little Beaver	5	10	15	36	48	60
333-Wilderness Trek (Zane Grey) (5/51)	6	12	18	38	52	65
334-Mickey Mouse and Yukon Gold (Disney) (6/51)	9	18	27	65	93	120
335-Francis the Famous Talking Mule (#1, 6/51)-1st Dell non animated movie comic (all issues based on movie)	11	22	33	77	114	150
336-Woody Woodpecker (Lantz)	6	12	18	43	59	75
337-The Brownies-not by Walt Kelly	5	10	15	33	44	55
338-Bugs Bunny and the Rocking Horse Thieves	9	18	27	63	89	115
339-Donald Duck and the Magic Fountain-not by Carl Barks (Disney) (7-8/51)	9	18	27	65	93	120
340-King of the Royal Mounted (7/51)	7	14	21	51	71	90
341-Unbirthday Party with Alice in Wonderland (Disney) (7/51)	16	32	48	111	163	215
342-Porky Pig the Lucky Peppermint Mine; r/in Porky Pig #3	6	12	18	38	52	65
343-Mickey Mouse in The Ruby Eye of Homar-Guy-Am (Disney)-Reprinted in Mickey Mouse #104	8	16	24	55	78	100
344-Sergeant Preston from Challenge of The Yukon (#1) (TV)	13	26	39	90	133	175
345-Andy Panda in Scotland Yard (8-10/51) (Lantz)	6	12	18	43	59	75
346-Hideout (Zane Grey)	6	12	18	38	52	65
347-Bugs Bunny the Frigid Hare (8-9/51)	9	18	27	63	89	115
348-Donald Duck "The Crocodile Collector"; Barks-c only (Disney) (9-10/51)	17	34	51	123	182	240
349-Uncle Wiggily	7	14	21	51	71	90
350-Woody Woodpecker (Lantz)	6	12	18	43	59	75
351-Porky Pig & the Grand Canyon Giant (9-10/51)	6	12	18	38	52	65
352-Mickey Mouse in The Mystery of Painted Valley (Disney)	8	16	24	55	78	100
353-Duck Album (#1)-Barks-c (Disney)	10	20	30	67	96	125
354-Raggedy Ann & Andy	8	16	24	55	78	100
355-Bugs Bunny Hot-Rod Hare	9	18	27	63	89	115
356-Donald Duck in "Rags to Riches"; Barks-c only	17	34	51	123	182	240
357-Comeback (Zane Grey)	5	10	15	33	44	55
358-Andy Panda (Lantz) (11-1/52)	6	12	18	43	59	75
359-Frosty the Snowman (#1)	10	20	30	70	100	130
360-Porky Pig in Tree of Fortune (11-12/51)	6	12	18	38	52	65
361-Santa Claus Funnies	6	12	18	43	59	75
362-Mickey Mouse and the Smuggled Diamonds (Disney)	8	16	24	55	78	100
363-King of the Royal Mounted	6	12	18	43	59	75
364-Woody Woodpecker (Lantz)	5	10	15	36	48	60
365-The Brownies-not by Kelly	5	10	15	33	44	55
366-Bugs Bunny Uncle Buckskin Comes to Town (12-1/52)	9	18	27	63	89	115
367-Donald Duck in "A Christmas for Shacktown" by Carl Barks (Disney) (1-2/52)	25	50	75	188	314	440
368-Bob Clampett's Beany and Cecil (#1)	29	58	87	210	305	400
369-The Lone Ranger's Famous Horse Hi-Yo Silver (#1); Silver's origin	10	20	30	73	107	140
370-Porky Pig in Trouble in the Big Trees	6	12	18	38	52	65
371-Mickey Mouse in The Inca Idol Case (1952) (Disney)	8	16	24	55	78	100
372-Riders of the Purple Sage (Zane Grey)	5	10	15	33	44	55
373-Sergeant Preston (TV)	8	16	24	58	82	105
374-Woody Woodpecker (Lantz)	5	10	15	36	48	60
375-John Carter of Mars (E. R. Burroughs)-Jesse Marsh-a; origin	27	54	81	192	281	370
376-Bugs Bunny, "The Magic Sneeze"	9	18	27	63	89	115
377-Susie Q. Smith	4	8	12	25	33	42
378-Tom Corbett, Space Cadet (#1) (TV)-McWilliams-a	19	38	57	136	198	260
379-Donald Duck in "Southern Hospitality"; Not by Barks (Disney)	9	18	27	65	93	120
380-Raggedy Ann & Andy	8	16	24	55	78	100
381-Marge's Tubby (#1)	22	44	66	160	235	310
382-Snow White and the Seven Dwarfs (Disney)-origin; partial reprint of Four Color #49 (Movie)	11	22	33	77	114	150
383-Andy Panda (Lantz)	5	10	15	33	44	55
384-King of the Royal Mounted (3/52)(Zane Grey)	6	12	18	43	59	75
385-Porky Pig inThe Isle of Missing Ships (3-4/52)	6	12	18	38	52	65
386-Uncle Scrooge (#1)-by Carl Barks (Disney) in "Only a Poor Old Man" (3/52)	91	182	273	774	1187	1600
387-Mickey Mouse in High Tibet (Disney) (4-5/52)	8	16	24	55	78	100
388-Oswald the Rabbit (Lantz)	6	12	18	43	59	75
389-Andy Hardy Comics (#1)	5	10	15	33	44	55
390-Woody Woodpecker (Lantz)	5	10	15	36	48	60
391-Uncle Wiggily	7	14	21	51	71	90
392-Hi-Yo Silver	6	12	18	40	55	70
393-Bugs Bunny	9	18	27	63	89	115
394-Donald Duck in Malayalaya-Barks-c only (Disney)	17	34	51	123	182	240
395-Forlorn River(Zane Grey)-First Nevada (5/52)	5	10	15	33	44	55
396-Tales of the Texas Rangers(#1)(TV)-Photo-c	12	24	36	82	121	160

Four Color #409 © Walter Lantz

Four Color #450 © WDC

Four Color #517 © WDC

	GD 2.0	VG 4.0	FN 6.0	VF 8.0	VF/NM 9.0	NM- 9.2
397-Sergeant Preston of the Yukon (TV) (5/52)	8	16	24	58	82	105
398-The Brownies-not by Kelly	5	10	15	33	44	55
399-Porky Pig in The Lost Gold Mine	6	12	18	38	52	65
400-Tom Corbett, Space Cadet (TV)-McWilliams-c/a	11	22	33	75	110	145
401-Mickey Mouse and Goofy's Mechanical Wizard (Disney) (6-7/52)	6	12	18	43	59	75
402-Mary Jane and Sniffles	9	18	27	60	85	110
403-Li'l Bad Wolf (Disney) (6/52)(#1)	8	16	24	55	78	100
404-The Range Rider (#1) (Flying A's...)(TV)-Photo-c	12	24	36	82	121	160
405-Woody Woodpecker (Lantz) (6-7/52)	5	10	15	36	48	60
406-Tweety and Sylvester (#1)	10	20	30	73	107	140
407-Bugs Bunny, Foreign-Legion Hare	8	16	24	53	74	95
408-Donald Duck and the Golden Helmet by Carl Barks (Disney) (7-8/52)	25	50	75	188	314	440
409-Andy Panda (7-9/52)	5	10	15	33	44	55
410-Porky Pig in The Water Wizard (7/52)	6	12	18	38	52	65
411-Mickey Mouse and the Old Sea Dog (Disney) (8-9/52)	6	12	18	43	59	75
412-Nevada (Zane Grey)	5	10	15	33	44	55
413-Robin Hood (Disney-Movie) (8/52)-Photo-c (1st Disney movie four color book)	11	22	33	77	114	150
414-Bob Clampett's Beany and Cecil (TV)	17	34	51	123	182	240
415-Rootie Kazootie (#1) (TV)	11	22	33	77	114	150
416-Woody Woodpecker (Lantz)	5	10	15	36	48	60
417-Double Trouble with Goober (#1) (8/52)	4	8	12	27	36	45
418-Rusty Riley, a Boy, a Horse, and a Dog (#1)-Frank Godwin-a (strip reprints) (8/52)	5	10	15	36	48	60
419-Sergeant Preston (TV)	8	16	24	58	82	105
420-Bugs Bunny in The Mysterious Buckaroo (8-9/52)	8	16	24	53	74	95
421-Tom Corbett, Space Cadet(TV)-McWilliams-a	11	22	33	75	110	145
422-Donald Duck and the Gilded Man, by Carl Barks (Disney) (9-10/52) (#423 on inside)	25	50	75	188	314	440
423-Rhubarb, Owner of the Brooklyn Ball Club (The Millionaire Cat) (#1)-Painted cover	6	12	18	40	55	70
424-Flash Gordon-Test Flight in Space (9/52)	11	22	33	77	114	150
425-Zorro, the Return of	13	26	39	90	133	175
426-Porky Pig in The Scalawag Leprechaun	6	12	18	38	52	65
427-Mickey Mouse and the Wonderful Whizzix (Disney) (10-11/52)-Reprinted in Mickey Mouse #100	6	12	18	43	59	75
428-Uncle Wiggily	6	12	18	38	52	65
429-Pluto in "Why Dogs Leave Home" (Disney) (10/52)(#1)	10	20	30	72	104	135
430-Marge's Tubby, the Shadow of a Man-Eater	12	24	36	87	129	170
431-Woody Woodpecker (10/52) (Lantz)	5	10	15	36	48	60
432-Bugs Bunny and the Rabbit Olympics	8	16	24	53	74	95
433-Wildfire (Zane Grey) (11-1/52-53)	5	10	15	33	44	55
434-Rin Tin Tin "In Dark Danger" (#1) (TV) (11/52)-Photo-c	16	32	48	113	167	220
435-Frosty the Snowman (11/52)	6	12	18	38	52	65
436-The Brownies-not by Kelly (11/52)	4	8	12	29	40	50
437-John Carter of Mars (E.R. Burroughs)-Marsh-a	17	34	51	118	174	230
438-Annie Oakley (#1) (TV)	16	32	48	113	167	220
439-Little Hiawatha (Disney) (12/52)j(#1)	6	12	18	43	59	75
440-Black Beauty (12/52)	4	8	12	27	36	45
441-Fearless Fagan	4	8	12	28	38	48
442-Peter Pan (Disney) (Movie)	11	22	33	80	118	155
443-Ben Bowie and His Mountain Men (#1)	8	16	24	55	78	100
444-Marge's Tubby	12	24	36	87	129	170
445-Charlie McCarthy	6	12	18	40	55	70
446-Captain Hook and Peter Pan (Disney)(Movie)(1/53)	10	20	30	70	100	130
447-Andy Hardy Comics	4	8	12	22	30	38
448-Bob Clampett's Beany and Cecil (TV)	17	34	51	123	182	240
449-Tappan's Burro (Zane Grey) (2-4/53)	5	10	15	33	44	55
450-Duck Album; Barks-c (Disney)	8	16	24	53	74	95
451-Rusty Riley-Frank Godwin-a (strip-r) (2/53)	4	8	12	28	38	48
452-Raggedy Ann & Andy (1953)	8	16	24	55	78	100
453-Susie Q. Smith (2/53)	4	8	12	25	33	42
454-Krazy Kat Comics; not by Herriman	5	10	15	33	44	55
455-Johnny Mack Brown Comics(3/53)-Photo-c	7	14	21	51	71	90
456-Uncle Scrooge Back to the Klondike (#2) by Barks (3/53) (Disney)	55	110	165	434	667	900
457-Daffy (#1)	10	20	30	70	100	130
458-Oswald the Rabbit (Lantz)	5	10	15	33	44	55

	GD 2.0	VG 4.0	FN 6.0	VF 8.0	VF/NM 9.0	NM- 9.2
459-Rootie Kazootie (TV)	8	16	24	55	78	100
460-Buck Jones (4/53)	6	12	18	40	55	70
461-Marge's Tubby	11	22	33	77	114	150
462-Little Scouts	3	6	9	19	25	32
463-Petunia (4/53)	4	8	12	28	38	48
464-Bozo (4/53)	10	20	30	70	100	130
465-Francis the Famous Talking Mule	6	12	18	43	59	75
466-Rhubarb, the Millionaire Cat; painted-c	5	10	15	36	48	60
467-Desert Gold (Zane Grey) (5-7/53)	5	10	15	33	44	55
468-Goofy (#1) (Disney)	13	26	39	94	137	180
469-Beetle Bailey (#1) (5/53	11	22	33	77	114	150
470-Elmer Fudd	7	14	21	46	63	80
471-Double Trouble with Goober	3	6	9	18	23	28
472-Wild Bill Elliott (6/53)-Photo-c	5	10	15	36	48	60
473-Li'l Bad Wolf (Disney) (6/53)(#2)	5	10	15	36	48	60
474-Mary Jane and Sniffles	8	16	24	55	78	100
475-M.G.M.'s The Two Mouseketeers (#1)	8	16	24	58	82	105
476-Rin Tin Tin (TV)-Photo-c	9	18	27	60	85	110
477-Bob Clampett's Beany and Cecil (TV)	17	34	51	123	182	240
478-Charlie McCarthy	6	12	18	40	55	70
479-Queen of the West Dale Evans (#1)-Photo-c	24	48	72	169	247	325
480-Andy Hardy Comics	4	8	12	22	30	38
481-Annie Oakley And Tagg (TV)	10	20	30	70	100	130
482-Brownies-not by Kelly	4	8	12	29	40	50
483-Little Beaver (7/53)	4	8	12	29	40	50
484-River Feud (Zane Grey) (8-10/53)	5	10	15	33	44	55
485-The Little People-Walt Scott (#1)	8	16	24	55	78	100
486-Rusty Riley-Frank Godwin strip-r	4	8	12	28	38	48
487-Mowgli, the Jungle Book (Rudyard Kipling's)	6	12	18	43	59	75
488-John Carter of Mars (Burroughs)-Marsh-a; painted-c	17	34	51	118	174	230
489-Tweety and Sylvester	6	12	18	40	55	70
490-Jungle Jim (#1)	8	16	24	55	78	100
491-Silvertip (#1) (Max Brand)-Kinstler-a (8/53)	9	18	27	63	89	115
492-Duck Album (Disney)	6	12	18	40	55	70
493-Johnny Mack Brown; photo-c	7	14	21	51	71	90
494-The Little King (#1)	10	20	30	72	104	135
495-Uncle Scrooge (#3) (Disney)-by Carl Barks (9/53)	41	82	123	324	487	650
496-The Green Hornet; painted-c	27	54	81	192	281	370
497-Zorro (Sword of...)-Kinstler-a	14	18	42	97	141	185
498-Bugs Bunny's Album (9/53)	6	12	18	40	55	70
499-M.G.M.'s Spike and Tyke (#1) (9/53)	6	12	18	38	52	65
500-Buck Jones	6	12	18	40	55	70
501-Francis the Famous Talking Mule	5	10	15	36	48	60
502-Rootie Kazootie (TV)	8	16	24	55	78	100
503-Uncle Wiggily (10/53)	6	12	18	38	52	65
504-Krazy Kat; not by Herriman	5	10	15	33	44	55
505-The Sword and the Rose (Disney) (10/53)(Movie)-Photo-c	10	20	30	67	96	125
506-The Little Scouts	3	6	9	19	25	32
507-Oswald the Rabbit (Lantz)	5	10	15	33	44	55
508-Bozo (10/53)	10	20	30	70	100	130
509-Pluto (Disney) (10/53)	7	14	21	46	63	80
510-Son of Black Beauty	4	8	12	25	33	42
511-Outlaw Trail (Zane Grey)-Kinstler-a	6	12	18	38	52	65
512-Flash Gordon (11/53)	8	16	24	55	78	100
513-Ben Bowie and His Mountain Men	4	8	12	29	40	50
514-Frosty the Snowman (11/53)	6	12	18	38	52	65
515-Andy Hardy	4	8	12	22	30	38
516-Double Trouble With Goober	3	6	9	18	23	28
517-Chip 'N' Dale (#1) (Disney)	11	22	33	77	114	150
518-Rivets (11/53)	4	8	12	22	30	38
519-Steve Canyon (#1)-Not by Milton Caniff	10	20	30.	67	96	125
520-Wild Bill Elliott-Photo-c	5	10	15	36	48	60
521-Beetle Bailey (12/53)	6	12	18	43	59	75
522-The Brownies	4	8	12	29	40	50
523-Rin Tin Tin (TV)-Photo-c (12/53)	9	18	27	60	85	110
524-Tweety and Sylvester	6	12	18	40	55	70
525-Santa Claus Funnies	6	12	18	43	59	75
526-Napoleon	3	6	9	19	25	32
527-Charlie McCarthy	6	12	18	40	55	70
528-Queen of the West Dale Evans; photo-c	12	24	36	82	121	160
529-Little Beaver	4	8	12	29	40	50

Four Color #538 © Johnston McCulley

Four Color #559 © Desilu

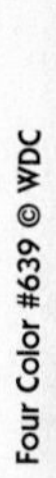
Four Color #639 © WDC

	GD 2.0	VG 4.0	FN 6.0	VF 8.0	VF/NM 9.0	NM- 9.2
530-Bob Clampett's Beany and Cecil (TV) (1/54)	17	34	51	123	182	240
531-Duck Album (Disney)	6	12	18	40	55	70
532-The Rustlers (Zane Grey) (2-4/54)	5	10	15	33	44	55
533-Raggedy Ann and Andy	8	16	24	55	78	100
534-Western Marshal(Ernest Haycox's)-Kinstler-a	7	14	21	46	63	80
535-I Love Lucy (#1) (TV) (2/54)-Photo-c	53	106	159	400	600	800
536-Daffy (3/54)	6	12	18	38	52	65
537-Stormy, the Thoroughbred... (Disney-Movie) on top 2/3 of each page; Pluto story on bottom 1/3 of each page (2/54)	5	10	15	33	44	55
538-The Mask of Zorro; Kinstler-a	14	18	42	97	141	185
539-Ben and Me (Disney) (3/54)	4	8	12	28	38	48
540-Knights of the Round Table (3/54) (Movie)-Photo-c	8	16	24	55	78	100
541-Johnny Mack Brown; photo-c	7	14	21	51	71	90
542-Super Circus Featuring Mary Hartline (TV) (3/54)	8	16	24	57	76	100
543-Uncle Wiggily (3/54)	6	12	18	38	52	65
544-Rob Roy (Disney-Movie)-Manning-a; photo-c	9	18	27	60	85	110
545-The Wonderful Adventures of Pinocchio-Partial reprint of Four Color #92 (Disney-Movie)	8	16	24	55	78	100
546-Buck Jones	6	12	18	40	55	70
547-Francis the Famous Talking Mule	5	10	15	36	48	60
548-Krazy Kat; not by Herriman (4/54)	4	8	12	29	40	50
549-Oswald the Rabbit (Lantz)	5	10	15	33	44	55
550-The Little Scouts	3	6	9	19	25	32
551-Bozo (4/54)	10	20	30	70	100	130
552-Beetle Bailey	6	12	18	43	59	75
553-Susie Q. Smith	4	8	12	25	33	42
554-Rusty Riley (Frank Godwin strip-r)	4	8	12	28	38	48
555-Range War (Zane Grey)	5	10	15	33	44	55
556-Double Trouble With Goober (5/54)	3	6	9	18	23	28
557-Ben Bowie and His Mountain Men	4	8	12	29	40	50
558-Elmer Fudd (5/54)	4	8	12	29	40	50
559-I Love Lucy (#2) (TV)-Photo-c	32	64	96	240	358	475
560-Duck Album (Disney) (5/54)	6	12	18	40	55	70
561-Mr. Magoo (5/54)	12	24	36	82	121	160
562-Goofy (Disney)(#2)	8	16	24	55	78	100
563-Rhubarb, the Millionaire Cat (6/54)	5	10	15	36	48	60
564-Li'l Bad Wolf (Disney)(#3)	5	10	15	36	48	60
565-Jungle Jim	5	10	15	33	44	55
566-Son of Black Beauty	4	8	12	25	33	42
567-Prince Valiant (#1)-By Bob Fuje (Movie)-Photo-c	12	24	36	87	129	170
568-Gypsy Colt (Movie) (6/54)	5	10	15	36	48	60
569-Priscilla's Pop	4	8	12	27	36	45
570-Bob Clampett's Beany and Cecil (TV)	17	34	51	123	182	240
571-Charlie McCarthy	6	12	18	40	55	70
572-Silvertip (Max Brand) (7/54); Kinstler-a	5	10	15	36	48	60
573-The Little People by Walt Scott	5	10	15	33	44	55
574-The Hand of Zorro; Kinstler-a	14	18	42	97	141	185
575-Annie Oakley and Tagg (TV)-Photo-c	10	20	30	70	100	130
576-Angel (#1) (8/54)	3	7	10	21	28	35
577-M.G.M.'s Spike and Tyke	4	8	12	22	30	38
578-Steve Canyon (8/54)	6	12	18	40	55	70
579-Francis the Famous Talking Mule	5	10	15	36	48	60
580-Six Gun Ranch (Luke Short-8/54)	4	8	12	28	38	48
581-Chip 'N' Dale (#2) (Disney)	6	12	18	43	59	75
582-Mowgli Jungle Book (Kipling) (8/54)	5	10	15	36	48	60
583-The Lost Wagon Train (Zane Grey)	5	10	15	33	44	55
584-Johnny Mack Brown-Photo-c	7	14	21	51	71	90
585-Bugs Bunny's Album	6	12	18	40	55	70
586-Duck Album (Disney)	6	12	18	40	55	70
587-The Little Scouts	3	6	9	19	25	32
588-King Richard and the Crusaders (Movie) (10/54) Matt Baker-a; photo-c	10	20	30	73	107	140
589-Buck Jones	6	12	18	40	55	70
590-Hansel and Gretel; partial photo-c	7	14	21	51	71	90
591-Western Marshal(Ernest Haycox's)-Kinstler-a	6	12	18	40	55	70
592-Super Circus (TV)	7	14	21	53	69	90
593-Oswald the Rabbit (Lantz)	5	10	15	33	44	55
594-Bozo (10/54)	10	20	30	70	100	130
595-Pluto (Disney)	5	10	15	33	44	55
596-Turok, Son of Stone (#1)	55	110	165	425	650	875
597-The Little King	6	12	18	40	55	70

	GD 2.0	VG 4.0	FN 6.0	VF 8.0	VF/NM 9.0	NM- 9.2
598-Captain Davy Jones	5	10	15	36	48	60
599-Ben Bowie and His Mountain Men	4	8	12	29	40	50
600-Daisy Duck's Diary (#1) (Disney) (11/54)	8	16	24	53	74	95
601-Frosty the Snowman	6	12	18	38	52	65
602-Mr. Magoo and Gerald McBoing-Boing	12	24	36	82	121	160
603-M.G.M.'s The Two Mouseketeers	6	12	18	38	52	65
604-Shadow on the Trail (Zane Grey)	5	10	15	33	44	55
605-The Brownies-not by Kelly (12/54)	4	8	12	29	40	50
606-Sir Lancelot (not TV)	8	16	24	55	78	100
607-Santa Claus Funnies	6	12	18	43	59	75
608-Silvertip- "Valley of Vanishing Men" (Max Brand)-Kinstler-a	5	10	15	36	48	60
609-The Littlest Outlaw (Disney-Movie) (1/55)-Photo-c	7	14	21	51	71	90
610-Drum Beat (Movie); Alan Ladd photo-c	10	20	30	67	96	125
611-Duck Album (Disney)	6	12	18	40	55	70
612-Little Beaver (1/55)	4	8	12	29	40	50
613-Western Marshal (Ernest Haycox's) (2/55)-Kinstler-a	6	12	18	40	55	70
614-20,000 Leagues Under the Sea (Disney) (Movie) (2/55)-Painted-c	10	20	30	70	100	130
615-Daffy	6	12	18	38	52	65
616-To the Last Man (Zane Grey)	5	10	15	33	44	55
617-The Quest of Zorro	13	26	39	90	133	175
618-Johnny Mack Brown; photo-c	7	14	21	51	71	90
619-Krazy Kat; not by Herriman	4	8	12	29	40	50
620-Mowgli Jungle Book (Kipling)	5	10	15	36	48	60
621-Francis the Famous Talking Mule (4/55)	4	8	12	29	40	50
622-Beetle Bailey	6	12	18	43	59	75
623-Oswald the Rabbit (Lantz)	4	8	12	27	36	45
624-Treasure Island(Disney-Movie)(4/55)-Photo-c	9	18	27	65	93	120
625-Beaver Valley (Disney-Movie)	7	14	21	50	68	85
626-Ben Bowie and His Mountain Men	4	8	12	29	40	50
627-Goofy (Disney) (5/55)	8	16	24	55	78	100
628-Elmer Fudd	4	8	12	29	40	50
629-Lady and the Tramp with Jock (Disney)	8	16	24	55	78	100
630-Priscilla's Pop	4	8	12	27	36	45
631-Davy Crockett, Indian Fighter (#1) (Disney) (5/55) (TV)-Fess Parker photo-c	21	42	63	147	216	285
632-Fighting Caravans (Zane Grey)	5	10	15	33	44	55
633-The Little People by Walt Scott (6/55)	5	10	15	33	44	55
634-Lady and the Tramp Album (Disney) (6/55)	6	12	18	38	52	65
635-Bob Clampett's Beany and Cecil (TV)	17	34	51	123	182	240
636-Chip 'N' Dale (Disney)	6	12	18	43	59	75
637-Silvertip (Max Brand)-Kinstler-a	5	10	15	36	48	60
638-M.G.M.'s Spike and Tyke (8/55)	4	8	12	22	30	38
639-Davy Crockett at the Alamo (Disney) (7/55) (TV)-Fess Parker photo-c	17	34	51	118	174	230
640-Western Marshal(Ernest Haycox's)-Kinstler-a	6	12	18	40	55	70
641-Steve Canyon (1955)-by Caniff	6	12	18	40	55	70
642-M.G.M.'s The Two Mouseketeers	6	12	18	38	52	65
643-Wild Bill Elliott; photo-c	4	8	12	29	40	50
644-Sir Walter Raleigh (5/55)-Based on movie "The Virgin Queen"; photo-c	8	16	24	53	74	95
645-Johnny Mack Brown; photo-c	7	14	21	51	71	90
646-Dotty Dripple and Taffy (#1)	4	8	12	29	40	50
647-Bugs Bunny's Album (9/55)	6	12	18	40	55	70
648-Jace Pearson of the Texas Rangers (TV)-Photo-c	6	12	18	40	55	70
649-Duck Album (Disney)	6	12	18	40	55	70
650-Prince Valiant; by Bob Fuje	8	16	24	55	78	100
651-King Colt (Luke Short) (9/55)-Kinstler-a	4	8	12	28	38	48
652-Buck Jones	4	8	12	29	40	50
653-Smokey the Bear (#1) (10/55)	12	24	36	84	125	165
654-Pluto (Disney)	5	10	15	33	44	55
655-Francis the Famous Talking Mule	4	8	12	29	40	50
656-Turok, Son of Stone (#2) (10/55)	33	66	99	248	369	490
657-Ben Bowie and His Mountain Men	4	8	12	29	40	50
658-Goofy (Disney)	8	16	24	55	78	100
659-Daisy Duck's Diary (Disney)(#2)	6	12	18	43	59	75
660-Little Beaver	4	8	12	29	40	50
661-Frosty the Snowman	6	12	18	38	52	65
662-Zoo Parade (TV)-Marlin Perkins (11/55)	6	12	18	38	52	65
663-Winky Dink (TV)	9	18	27	63	89	115

Four Color #668 © WDC

Four Color #691 © ME

Four Color #757 © 20th Century Fox

	GD 2.0	VG 4.0	FN 6.0	VF 8.0	VF/NM 9.0	NM- 9.2
664-Davy Crockett in the Great Keelboat Race (TV) (Disney) (11/55)-Fess Parker photo-c	16	32	48	113	167	220
665-The African Lion (Disney-Movie) (11/55)	6	12	18	43	59	75
666-Santa Claus Funnies	6	12	18	43	59	75
667-Silvertip and the Stolen Stallion (Max Brand) (12/55)-Kinstler-a	5	10	15	36	48	60
668-Dumbo (Disney) (12/55)-First of two printings. Dumbo on cover with starry sky. Reprints 4-Color #234?; same-c as #234	10	20	30	73	107	140
668-Dumbo (Disney) (1/58)-Second printing. Same cover altered, with Timothy Mouse added. Same contents as above	8	16	24	53	74	95
669-Robin Hood (Disney-Movie) (12/55)-Reprints #413 plus-c; photo-c	6	12	18	43	59	75
670-M.G.M's Mouse Musketeers (#1) (1/56)-Formerly the Two Mouseketeers	5	10	15	33	44	55
671-Davy Crockett and the River Pirates (TV) (Disney) (12/55)-Jesse Marsh-a; Fess Parker photo-c	16	32	48	113	167	220
672-Quentin Durward (1/56) (Movie)-Photo-c	8	16	24	53	74	95
673-Buffalo Bill, Jr. (#1) (TV)-James Arness photo-c	8	16	24	58	82	105
674-The Little Rascals (#1) (TV)	9	18	27	65	93	120
675-Steve Donovan, Western Marshal (#1) (TV)-Kinstler-a; photo-c	9	18	27	63	89	115
676-Will-Yum!	4	8	12	22	30	38
677-Little King	6	12	18	40	55	70
678-The Last Hunt (Movie)-Photo-c	9	18	27	60	85	110
679-Gunsmoke (#1) (TV)-Photo-c	19	38	57	136	198	260
680-Out Our Way with the Worry Wart (2/56)	4	8	12	22	30	38
681-Forever Darling (Movie) with Lucille Ball & Desi Arnaz (2/56)-; photo-c	12	24	36	84	125	165
682-The Sword & the Rose (Disney-Movie)-Reprint of #505; Renamed When Knighthood Was in Flower for the novel; photo-c	8	16	24	55	78	100
683-Hi and Lois (3/56)	4	8	12	28	38	48
684-Helen of Troy (Movie)-Buscema-a; photo-c	11	22	33	77	114	150
685-Johnny Mack Brown; photo-c	7	14	21	51	71	90
686-Duck Album (Disney)	6	12	18	40	55	70
687-The Indian Fighter (Movie)-Kirk Douglas photo-c	9	18	27	60	85	110
688-Alexander the Great (Movie) (5/56)-Buscema-a; photo-c	8	16	24	55	78	100
689-Elmer Fudd (3/56)	4	8	12	29	40	50
690-The Conqueror (Movie) - John Wayne photo-c	18	36	54	131	191	250
691-Dotty Dripple and Taffy	3	7	10	21	28	35
692-The Little People-Walt Scott	5	10	15	33	44	55
693-Song of the South (Disney) (1956)-Partial reprint of #129	10	20	30	67	96	125
694-Super Circus (TV)-Photo-c	7	14	21	53	69	90
695-Little Beaver	4	8	12	29	40	50
696-Krazy Kat; not by Herriman (4/56)	4	8	12	29	40	50
697-Oswald the Rabbit (Lantz)	4	8	12	27	36	45
698-Francis the Famous Talking Mule (4/56)	4	8	12	29	40	50
699-Prince Valiant-by Bob Fuje	8	16	24	55	78	100
700-Water Birds and the Olympic Elk (Disney-Movie) (4/56)	6	12	18	40	55	70
701-Jiminy Cricket (#1) (Disney) (5/56)	10	20	30	67	96	125
702-The Goofy Success Story (Disney)	8	16	24	55	78	100
703-Scamp (#1) (Disney)	10	20	30	67	96	125
704-Priscilla's Pop (5/56)	4	8	12	27	36	45
705-Brave Eagle (#1) (TV)-Photo-c	7	14	21	51	71	90
706-Bongo and Lumpjaw (Disney) (6/56)	6	12	18	43	59	75
707-Corky and White Shadow (Disney) (5/56)-Mickey Mouse Club (TV); photo-c	8	16	24	55	78	100
708-Smokey the Bear	7	14	21	50	68	85
709-The Searchers (Movie) - John Wayne photo-c	28	56	84	203	294	385
710-Francis the Famous Talking Mule	4	8	12	29	40	50
711-M.G.M's Mouse Musketeers	4	8	12	24	32	40
712-The Great Locomotive Chase (Disney-Movie) (9/56)-Photo-c	8	16	24	55	78	100
713-The Animal World (Movie) (8/56)	4	8	12	25	33	42
714-Spin and Marty (#1) (TV) (Disney)-Mickey Mouse Club (6/56); photo-c	14	28	42	97	141	185
715-Timmy (8/56)	5	10	15	33	44	55
716-Man in Space (Disney)(A science feature from Tomorrowland)	10	20	30	67	96	125
717-Moby Dick (Movie)-Gregory Peck photo-c	10	20	30	67	96	125
718-Dotty Dripple and Taffy	3	7	10	21	28	35
719-Prince Valiant; by Bob Fuje (8/56)	8	16	24	55	78	100
720-Gunsmoke (TV)-James Arness photo-c	10	20	30	70	100	130
721-Captain Kangaroo (TV)-Photo-c	18	36	54	131	191	250
722-Johnny Mack Brown-Photo-c	7	14	21	51	71	90
723-Santiago (Movie)-Kinstler-a (9/56); Alan Ladd photo-c	10	20	30	73	107	140
724-Bugs Bunny's Album	5	10	15	36	48	60
725-Elmer Fudd (9/56)	4	8	12	24	32	40
726-Duck Album (Disney) (9/56)	6	12	18	40	55	70
727-The Nature of Things (TV) (Disney)-Jesse Marsh-a	6	12	18	40	55	70
728-M.G.M's Mouse Musketeers	4	8	12	24	32	40
729-Bob Son of Battle (11/56)	4	8	12	27	36	45
730-Smokey Stover	5	10	15	36	48	60
731-Silvertip and The Fighting Four (Max Brand)-Kinstler-a	5	10	15	36	48	60
732-Zorro, the Challenge of (10/56)	13	26	39	90	133	175
733-Buck Jones	4	8	12	29	40	50
734-Cheyenne (#1) (TV) (10/56)-Clint Walker photo-c	18	36	54	131	191	250
735-Crusader Rabbit (#1) (TV)	31	62	93	233	352	470
736-Pluto (Disney)	5	10	15	33	44	55
737-Steve Canyon-Caniff-a	6	12	18	40	55	70
738-Westward Ho, the Wagons (Disney-Movie)-Fess Parker photo-c	10	20	30	73	107	140
739-Bounty Guns (Luke Short)-Drucker-a	4	8	12	27	36	45
740-Chilly Willy (#1) (Walter Lantz)	6	12	18	43	59	75
741-The Fastest Gun Alive (Movie)(9/56)-Photo-c	8	16	24	55	78	100
742-Buffalo Bill, Jr. (TV)-Photo-c	6	12	18	38	52	65
743-Daisy Duck's Diary (Disney) (11/56)	6	12	18	43	59	75
744-Little Beaver	4	8	12	29	40	50
745-Francis the Famous Talking Mule	4	8	12	29	40	50
746-Dotty Dripple and Taffy	3	7	10	21	28	35
747-Goofy (Disney)	8	16	24	55	78	100
748-Frosty the Snowman (11/56)	5	10	15	36	48	60
749-Secrets of Life (Disney-Movie)-Photo-c	6	12	18	38	52	65
750-The Great Cat Family (Disney-TV/Movie)-Pinocchio & Alice app.	7	14	21	51	71	90
751-Our Miss Brooks (TV)-Photo-c	9	18	27	60	85	110
752-Mandrake, the Magician	11	22	33	80	118	155
753-Walt Scott's Little People (11/56)	5	10	15	33	44	55
754-Smokey the Bear	7	14	21	50	68	85
755-The Littlest Snowman (12/56)	6	12	18	38	52	65
756-Santa Claus Funnies	6	12	18	43	59	75
757-The True Story of Jesse James (Movie)-Photo-c	10	20	30	70	100	130
758-Bear Country (Disney-Movie)	6	12	18	40	55	70
759-Circus Boy (TV)-The Monkees' Mickey Dolenz photo-c (12/56)	14	28	42	102	149	195
760-The Hardy Boys (#1) (TV) (Disney)-Mickey Mouse Club; photo-c	12	24	36	82	121	160
761-Howdy Doody (TV) (1/57)	11	22	33	80	118	155
762-The Sharkfighters (Movie) (1/57); Buscema-a; photo-c	9	18	27	60	85	110
763-Grandma Duck's Farm Friends (#1) (Disney)	8	16	24	55	78	100
764-M.G.M's Mouse Musketeers	4	8	12	24	32	40
765-Will-Yum!	4	8	12	22	30	38
766-Buffalo Bill, Jr. (TV)-Photo-c	6	12	18	38	52	65
767-Spin and Marty (TV) (Disney)-Mickey Mouse Club (2/57)	10	20	30	70	100	130
768-Steve Donovan, Western Marshal (TV)-Kinstler-a; photo-c	7	14	21	51	71	90
769-Gunsmoke (TV)-James Arness photo-c	10	20	30	70	100	130
770-Brave Eagle (TV)-Photo-c	4	8	12	28	38	48
771-Brand of Empire (Luke Short)(3/57)-Drucker-a	4	8	12	27	36	45
772-Cheyenne (TV)-Clint Walker photo-c	9	18	27	65	93	120
773-The Brave One (Movie)-Photo-c	6	12	18	40	55	70
774-Hi and Lois (3/57)	3	6	9	19	25	32
775-Sir Lancelot and Brian (TV)-Buscema-a; photo-c	10	20	30	73	107	140
776-Johnny Mack Brown; photo-c	7	14	21	51	71	90
777-Scamp (Disney) (3/57)	7	14	21	51	71	90
778-The Little Rascals (TV)	6	12	18	43	59	75
779-Lee Hunter, Indian Fighter (3/57)	5	10	15	36	48	60
780-Captain Kangaroo (TV)-Photo-c	15	30	45	104	152	200
781-Fury (#1) (TV) (3/57)-Photo-c	9	18	27	60	85	110

Four Color #785 © Norbert

Four Color #846 © Loew's Inc.

Four Color #876 © DELL

	GD 2.0	VG 4.0	FN 6.0	VF 8.0	VF/NM 9.0	NM- 9.2
782-Duck Album (Disney)	6	12	18	40	55	70
783-Elmer Fudd	4	8	12	24	32	40
784-Around the World in 80 Days (Movie) (2/57)-Photo-c	7	14	21	51	71	90
785-Circus Boy (TV) (4/57)-The Monkees' Mickey Dolenz photo-c	12	24	36	82	121	160
786-Cinderella (Disney) (3/57)-Partial-r of #272	8	16	24	53	74	95
787-Little Hiawatha (Disney) (4/57)(#2)	5	10	15	36	48	60
788-Prince Valiant; by Bob Fuje	8	16	24	53	74	95
789-Silvertip-Valley Thieves (Max Brand) (4/57)-Kinstler-a	5	10	15	36	48	60
790-The Wings of Eagles (Movie) (John Wayne)-Toth-a; John Wayne photo-c; 10¢ & 15¢ editions exist	16	32	48	113	167	220
791-The 77th Bengal Lancers (TV)-Photo-c	8	16	24	55	78	100
792-Oswald the Rabbit (Lantz)	4	8	12	27	36	45
793-Morty Meekle	3	6	9	19	25	32
794-The Count of Monte Cristo (5/57) (Movie)-Buscema-a	10	20	30	67	96	125
795-Jiminy Cricket (Disney)(#2)	7	14	21	51	71	90
796-Ludwig Bemelman's Madeleine and Genevieve	4	8	12	25	33	42
797-Gunsmoke (TV)-Photo-c	10	20	30	70	100	130
798-Buffalo Bill, Jr. (TV)-Photo-c	6	12	18	38	52	65
799-Priscilla's Pop	4	8	12	27	36	45
800-The Buccaneers (TV)-Photo-c	8	16	24	55	78	100
801-Dotty Dripple and Taffy	3	7	10	21	28	35
802-Goofy (Disney) (5/57)	8	16	24	55	78	100
803-Cheyenne (TV)-Clint Walker photo-c	9	18	27	65	93	120
804-Steve Canyon-Caniff-a (1957)	6	12	18	40	55	70
805-Crusader Rabbit (TV)	26	52	78	185	270	355
806-Scamp (Disney) (6/57)	7	14	21	51	71	90
807-Savage Range (Luke Short)-Drucker-a	4	8	12	27	36	45
808-Spin and Marty (TV)(Disney)-Mickey Mouse Club; photo-c	10	20	30	70	100	130
809-The Little People (Walt Scott)	5	10	15	33	44	55
810-Francis the Famous Talking Mule	4	8	12	27	36	45
811-Howdy Doody (TV) (7/57)	11	22	33	80	118	155
812-The Big Land (Movie); Alan Ladd photo-c	10	20	30	72	104	135
813-Circus Boy (TV)-The Monkees' Mickey Dolenz photo-c	12	24	36	82	121	160
814-Covered Wagons, Ho! (Disney)-Donald Duck (TV) (6/57); Mickey Mouse app.	6	12	18	40	55	70
815-Dragoon Wells Massacre (Movie)-photo-c	9	18	27	60	85	110
816-Brave Eagle (TV)-photo-c	4	8	12	28	38	48
817-Little Beaver	4	8	12	29	40	50
818-Smokey the Bear (6/57)	7	14	21	50	68	85
819-Mickey Mouse in Magicland (Disney) (7/57)	5	10	15	36	48	60
820-The Oklahoman (Movie)-Photo-c	10	20	30	70	100	130
821-Wringle Wrangle (Disney)-Based on movie "Westward Ho, the Wagons"; Marsh-a; Fess Parker photo-c	9	18	27	63	89	115
822-Paul Revere's Ride with Johnny Tremain (TV) (Disney)-Toth-a	10	20	30	70	100	130
823-Timmy	4	8	12	24	32	40
824-The Pride and the Passion (Movie) (8/57)-Frank Sinatra & Cary Grant photo-c	10	20	30	70	100	130
825-The Little Rascals (TV)	6	12	18	43	59	75
826-Spin and Marty and Annette (TV) (Disney)-Mickey Mouse Club; Annette Funicello photo-c	25	50	75	176	258	340
827-Smokey Stover (8/57)	5	10	15	36	48	60
828-Buffalo Bill, Jr. (TV)-Photo-c	6	12	18	38	52	65
829-Tales of the Pony Express (TV) (8/57)-Painted-c	5	10	15	36	48	60
830-The Hardy Boys (TV) (Disney)-Mickey Mouse Club (8/57); photo-c	10	20	30	70	100	130
831-No Sleep 'Til Dawn (Movie)-Karl Malden photo-c	7	14	21	51	71	90
832-Lolly and Pepper (#1)	4	8	12	28	38	48
833-Scamp (Disney) (9/57)	7	14	21	51	71	90
834-Johnny Mack Brown; photo-c	7	14	21	51	71	90
835-Silvertip-The False Rider (Max Brand)	5	10	15	36	48	60
836-Man in Flight (Disney) (TV) (9/57)	8	16	24	55	78	100
837-All-American Athlete Cotton Woods	4	8	12	25	33	42
838-Bugs Bunny's Life Story Album (9/57)	5	10	15	36	48	60
839-The Vigilantes (Movie)	8	16	24	55	78	100
840-Duck Album (Disney) (9/57)	6	12	18	40	55	70
841-Elmer Fudd	4	8	12	24	32	40
842-The Nature of Things (Disney-Movie) ('57)-Jesse Marsh-a (TV series)	6	12	18	40	55	70
843-The First Americans (Disney) (TV)-Marsh-a	10	20	30	67	96	125
844-Gunsmoke (TV)-Photo-c	10	20	30	70	100	130
845-The Land Unknown (Movie)-Alex Toth-a	13	26	39	90	133	175
846-Gun Glory (Movie)-by Alex Toth; photo-c	10	20	30	70	100	130
847-Perri (squirrels) (Disney-Movie)-Two different covers published	6	12	18	40	55	70
848-Marauder's Moon (Luke Short)	4	8	12	27	36	45
849-Prince Valiant; by Bob Fuje	8	16	24	53	74	95
850-Buck Jones	4	8	12	29	40	50
851-The Story of Mankind (Movie) (1/58)-Hedy Lamarr & Vincent Price photo-c	8	16	24	55	78	100
852-Chilly Willy (2/58) (Lantz)	4	8	12	29	40	50
853-Pluto (Disney) (10/57)	5	10	15	33	44	55
854-The Hunchback of Notre Dame (Movie)-Photo-c	14	28	42	97	141	185
855-Broken Arrow (TV)-Photo-c	6	12	18	43	59	75
856-Buffalo Bill, Jr. (TV)-Photo-c	6	12	18	38	52	65
857-The Goofy Adventure Story (Disney) (11/57)	8	16	24	55	78	100
858-Daisy Duck's Diary (Disney) (11/57)	6	12	18	38	52	65
859-Topper and Neil (TV) (11/57)	5	10	15	36	48	60
860-Wyatt Earp (#1) (TV)-Manning-a; photo-c	11	22	33	77	114	150
861-Frosty the Snowman	5	10	15	36	48	60
862-The Truth About Mother Goose (Disney-Movie) (11/57)	8	16	24	58	82	105
863-Francis the Famous Talking Mule	4	8	12	27	36	45
864-The Littlest Snowman	6	12	18	38	52	65
865-Andy Burnett (TV) (Disney) (12/57)-Photo-c	10	20	30	70	100	130
866-Mars and Beyond (Disney-TV)(A science feature from Tomorrowland)	10	20	30	67	96	125
867-Santa Claus Funnies	6	12	18	43	59	75
868-The Little People (12/57)	5	10	15	33	44	55
869-Old Yeller (Disney-Movie)-Photo-c	6	12	18	40	55	70
870-Little Beaver (1/58)	4	8	12	29	40	50
871-Curly Kayoe	4	8	12	24	32	40
872-Captain Kangaroo (TV)-Photo-c	15	30	45	104	152	200
873-Grandma Duck's Farm Friends (Disney)	6	12	18	40	55	70
874-Old Ironsides (Disney-Movie with Johnny Tremain) (1/58)	7	14	21	51	71	90
875-Trumpets West (Luke Short) (2/58)	4	8	12	27	36	45
876-Tales of Wells Fargo (#1)(TV)(2/58)-Photo-c	10	20	30	72	104	135
877-Frontier Doctor with Rex Allen (TV)-Alex Toth-a; Rex Allen photo-c	11	22	33	75	110	145
878-Peanuts (#1)-Schulz-c only (2/58)	17	34	51	123	182	240
879-Brave Eagle (TV) (2/58)-Photo-c	4	8	12	28	38	48
880-Steve Donovan, Western Marshal-Drucker-a (TV)-Photo-c	5	10	15	36	48	60
881-The Captain and the Kids (2/58)	4	8	12	27	36	45
882-Zorro (Disney)-1st Disney issue; by Alex Toth (TV) (2/58); photo-c	17	34	51	123	182	240
883-The Little Rascals (TV)	6	12	18	43	59	75
884-Hawkeye and the Last of the Mohicans (TV) (3/58); photo-c	8	16	24	55	78	100
885-Fury (TV) (3/58)-Photo-c	8	16	24	53	74	95
886-Bongo and Lumpjaw (Disney) (3/58)	5	10	15	36	48	60
887-The Hardy Boys (Disney) (TV)-Mickey Mouse Club (1/58)-Photo-c	10	20	30	70	100	130
888-Elmer Fudd (3/58)	4	8	12	24	32	40
889-Clint and Mac (Disney) (TV) (3/58)-Alex Toth-a; photo-c	14	28	42	97	141	185
890-Wyatt Earp (TV)-by Russ Manning; photo-c	8	16	24	58	82	105
891-Light in the Forest (Disney-Movie) (3/58)-Fess Parker photo-c	8	16	24	61	83	110
892-Maverick (#1) (TV) (4/58)-James Garner photo-c	26	52	78	189	275	360
893-Jim Bowie (TV)-Photo-c	6	12	18	43	59	75
894-Oswald the Rabbit (Lantz)	4	8	12	27	36	45
895-Wagon Train (#1) (TV) (3/58)-Photo-c	12	24	36	87	129	170
896-The Adventures of Tinker Bell (Disney)	10	20	30	67	96	125
897-Jiminy Cricket (Disney)	7	14	21	51	71	90
898-Silvertip (Max Brand)-Kinstler-a (5/58)	5	10	15	36	48	60
899-Goofy (Disney) (5/58)	6	12	18	38	52	65
900-Prince Valiant; by Bob Fuje	8	16	24	53	74	95
901-Little Hiawatha (Disney)	5	10	15	36	48	60
902-Will-Yum!	4	8	12	22	30	38

Four Color #970 © WB

Four Color #992 © WB

Four Color #1010 © WDC

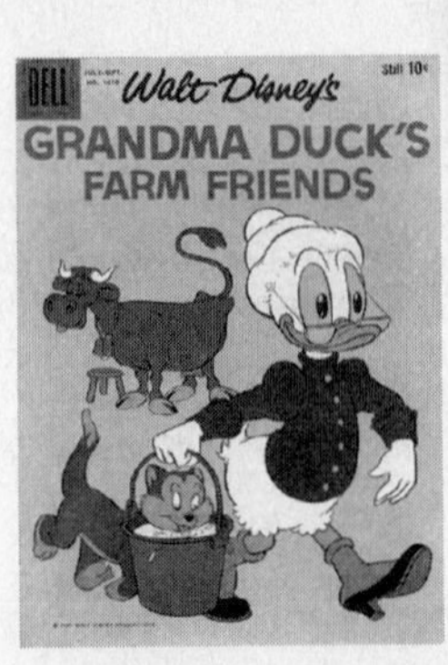

	GD 2.0	VG 4.0	FN 6.0	VF 8.0	VF/NM 9.0	NM- 9.2
903-Dotty Dripple and Taffy	3	7	10	21	28	35
904-Lee Hunter, Indian Fighter	4	8	12	25	33	42
905-Annette (Disney) (TV) (5/58)-Mickey Mouse Club; Annette Funicello photo-c	31	62	93	223	329	435
906-Francis the Famous Talking Mule	4	8	12	27	36	45
907-Sugarfoot (#1) (TV)Toth-a; photo-c	14	28	42	99	145	190
908-The Little People and the Giant-Walt Scott (5/58)	5	10	15	33	44	55
909-Smitty	4	8	12	27	36	45
910-The Vikings (Movie)-Buscema-a; Kirk Douglas photo-c	9	18	27	65	93	120
911-The Gray Ghost (TV)-Photo-c	10	20	30	70	100	125
912-Leave It to Beaver (#1) (TV)-Photo-c	18	36	54	131	191	250
913-The Left-Handed Gun (Movie) (7/58); Paul Newman photo-c	10	20	30	73	107	140
914-No Time for Sergeants (Movie)-Andy Griffith photo-c; Toth-a	11	22	33	77	114	150
915-Casey Jones (TV)-Alan Hale photo-c	6	12	18	40	55	70
916-Red Ryder Ranch Comics (7/58)	5	10	15	36	48	60
917-The Life of Riley (TV)-Photo-c	12	24	36	87	129	170
918-Beep Beep, the Roadrunner (#1) (7/58)-Published with two different back covers	11	22	33	77	114	150
919-Boots and Saddles (#1) (TV)-Photo-c	9	18	27	60	85	110
920-Zorro (Disney) (TV) (6/58)Toth-a; photo-c	13	26	39	90	133	175
921-Wyatt Earp (TV)-Manning-a; photo-c	8	16	24	58	82	105
922-Johnny Mack Brown by Russ Manning; photo-c	8	16	24	53	74	95
923-Timmy	4	8	12	24	32	40
924-Colt .45 (#1) (TV) (8/58)-W. Preston photo-c	11	22	33	77	114	150
925-Last of the Fast Guns (Movie) (8/58)-Photo-c	8	16	24	55	78	100
926-Peter Pan (Disney)-Reprint of #442	5	10	15	36	48	60
927-Top Gun (Luke Short) Buscema-a	4	8	12	27	36	45
928-Sea Hunt (#1) (9/58) (TV)-Lloyd Bridges photo-c	13	26	39	94	137	180
929-Brave Eagle (TV)-Photo-c	4	8	12	28	38	48
930-Maverick (TV) (7/58)-James Garner photo-c	12	24	36	82	121	160
931-Have Gun, Will Travel (#1) (TV)-Photo-c	15	30	45	104	152	200
932-Smokey the Bear (His Life Story)	7	14	21	50	68	85
933-Zorro (Disney, 9/58) (TV)-Alex Toth-a; photo-c	13	26	39	90	133	175
934-Restless Gun (#1) (TV)-Photo-c	12	24	36	87	129	170
935-King of the Royal Mounted	4	8	12	29	40	50
936-The Little Rascals (TV)	6	12	18	43	59	75
937-Ruff and Reddy (#1) (9/58) (TV) (1st Hanna-Barbera comic book)	14	28	42	99	145	190
938-Elmer Fudd (9/58)	4	8	12	24	32	40
939-Steve Canyon - not by Caniff	6	12	18	40	55	70
940-Lolly and Pepper (10/58)	3	6	9	19	25	32
941-Pluto (Disney) (10/58)	4	8	12	29	40	50
942-Pony Express (TV)	5	10	15	36	48	60
943-White Wilderness (Disney-Movie) (10/58)	7	14	21	51	71	90
944-The 7th Voyage of Sinbad (Movie) (9/58)-Buscema-a; photo-c	14	28	42	99	145	190
945-Maverick (TV)-James Garner/Jack Kelly photo-c	12	24	36	82	121	160
946-The Big Country (Movie)-Photo-c	8	16	24	55	78	100
947-Broken Arrow (TV)-Photo-c (11/58)	6	12	18	38	52	65
948-Daisy Duck's Diary (Disney) (11/58)	6	12	18	38	52	65
949-High Adventure(Lowell Thomas')(TV)-Photo-c	6	12	18	43	59	75
950-Frosty the Snowman	5	10	15	36	48	60
951-The Lennon Sisters Life Story (TV)-Toth-a, 32 pgs.; photo-c	15	30	45	107	156	205
952-Goofy (Disney) (11/58)	6	12	18	38	52	65
953-Francis the Famous Talking Mule	4	8	12	27	36	45
954-Man in Space-Satellites (TV)	8	16	24	55	78	100
955-Hi and Lois (11/58)	3	6	9	19	25	32
956-Ricky Nelson (#1) (TV)-Photo-c	20	40	60	145	213	280
957-Buffalo Bee (#1) (TV)	10	20	30	70	100	130
958-Santa Claus Funnies	6	12	18	40	55	70
959-Christmas Stories-(Walt Scott's Little People) (1951-56 strip reprints)	5	10	15	33	44	55
960-Zorro (Disney) (TV) (12/58)-Toth art; photo-c	13	26	39	90	133	175
961-Jace Pearson's Tales of the Texas Rangers (TV)-Spiegle-a; photo-c	6	12	18	38	52	65
962-Maverick (TV) (1/59)-James Garner/Jack Kelly photo-c	12	24	36	82	121	160
963-Johnny Mack Brown; photo-c	7	14	21	51	71	90
964-The Hardy Boys (TV) (Disney) (1/59)-Mickey Mouse Club; photo-c	10	20	30	70	100	130
965-Grandma Duck's Farm Friends (Disney)(1/59)	5	10	15	36	48	60
966-Tonka (starring Sal Mineo; Disney-Movie)-Photo-c	9	18	27	65	93	120
967-Chilly Willy (2/59) (Lantz)	4	8	12	29	40	50
968-Tales of Wells Fargo (TV)-Photo-c	10	20	30	67	96	125
969-Peanuts (2/59)	12	24	36	82	121	160
970-Lawman (#1) (TV)-Photo-c	14	28	42	97	141	185
971-Wagon Train (TV)-Photo-c	8	16	24	53	74	95
972-Tom Thumb (Movie)-George Pal (1/59)	10	20	30	70	100	130
973-Sleeping Beauty and the Prince(Disney)(5/59)	12	24	36	87	129	170
974-The Little Rascals (TV) (3/59)	6	12	18	43	59	75
975-Fury (TV)-Photo-c	8	16	24	53	74	95
976-Zorro (Disney) (TV)-Toth-a; photo-c	13	26	39	90	133	175
977-Elmer Fudd (3/59)	4	8	12	24	32	40
978-Lolly and Pepper	3	6	9	19	25	32
979-Oswald the Rabbit (Lantz)	4	8	12	27	36	45
980-Maverick (TV) (4-6/59)-James Garner/Jack Kelly photo-c	12	24	36	82	121	160
981-Ruff and Reddy (TV) (Hanna-Barbera)	9	18	27	63	89	115
982-The New Adventures of Tinker Bell (TV) (Disney)	9	18	27	63	89	115
983-Have Gun, Will Travel (TV) (4-6/59)-Photo-c	10	20	30	67	96	125
984-Sleeping Beauty's Fairy Godmothers (Disney)	10	20	30	67	96	125
985-Shaggy Dog (Disney-Movie)-Photo-all four covers; Annette on back-c(5/59)	9	18	27	60	85	110
986-Restless Gun (TV)-Photo-c	9	18	27	63	89	115
987-Goofy (Disney) (7/59)	6	12	18	38	52	65
988-Little Hiawatha (Disney)	5	10	15	36	48	60
989-Jiminy Cricket (Disney) (5-7/59)	7	14	21	51	71	90
990-Huckleberry Hound (#1)(TV)(Hanna-Barbera); 1st app. Huck, Yogi Bear, & Pixie & Dixie & Mr. Jinks	13	26	39	94	137	180
991-Francis the Famous Talking Mule	4	8	12	27	36	45
992-Sugarfoot (TV)-Toth-a; photo-c	13	26	39	90	133	175
993-Jim Bowie (TV)-Photo-c	6	12	18	40	55	70
994-Sea Hunt (TV)-Lloyd Bridges photo-c	9	18	27	63	89	115
995-Donald Duck Album (Disney) (5-7/59)(#1)	7	14	21	46	63	80
996-Nevada (Zane Grey)	5	10	15	33	44	55
997-Walt Disney Presents-Tales of Texas John Slaughter (#1) (TV) (Disney)-Photo-c; photo of W. Disney inside-c	8	16	24	58	82	105
998-Ricky Nelson (TV)-Photo-c	20	40	60	145	213	280
999-Leave It to Beaver (TV)-Photo-c	15	30	45	109	160	210
1000-The Gray Ghost (TV) (6-8/59)-Photo-c	10	20	30	70	100	125
1001-Lowell Thomas' High Adventure (TV) (8-10/59)-Photo-c	6	12	18	40	55	70
1002-Buffalo Bee (TV)	8	16	24	53	74	95
1003-Zorro (TV) (Disney)-Toth-a; photo-c	13	26	39	90	133	175
1004-Colt .45 (TV) (6-8/59)-Photo-c	11	22	33	77	114	150
1005-Maverick (TV)-James Garner/Jack Kelly photo-c	12	24	36	82	121	160
1006-Hercules (Movie)-Buscema-a; photo-c	10	20	30	72	104	135
1007-John Paul Jones (Movie)-Robert Stack photo-c	6	12	18	40	55	70
1008-Beep Beep, the Road Runner (7-9/59)	6	12	18	43	59	75
1009-The Rifleman (#1) (TV)-Photo-c	27	54	81	194	285	375
1010-Grandma Duck's Farm Friends (Disney)-by Carl Barks	14	28	42	97	141	185
1011-Buckskin (#1) (TV)-Photo-c	8	16	24	55	78	100
1012-Last Train from Gun Hill (Movie) (7/59)-Photo-c	10	20	30	67	96	125
1013-Bat Masterson (#1) (TV) (8/59)-Gene Barry photo-c	13	26	39	94	137	180
1014-The Lennon Sisters (TV)-Toth-a; photo-c	14	28	42	102	149	195
1015-Peanuts-Schulz-c	12	24	36	82	121	160
1016-Smokey the Bear Nature Stories	5	10	15	33	44	55
1017-Chilly Willy (Lantz)	4	8	12	29	40	50
1018-Rio Bravo (Movie)(6/59)-John Wayne; Toth-a; John Wayne, Dean Martin & Ricky Nelson photo-c	25	50	75	176	258	340
1019-Wagon Train (TV)-Photo-c	8	16	24	53	74	95
1020-Jungle Jim-McWilliams-a	4	8	12	27	36	45
1021-Jace Pearson's Tales of the Texas Rangers (TV)-Photo-c	6	12	18	38	52	65
1022-Timmy	4	8	12	24	32	40
1023-Tales of Wells Fargo (TV)-Photo-c	10	20	30	67	96	125
1024-Darby O'Gill and the Little People (Disney-Movie)-Toth-a; photo-c	11	22	33	77	114	150

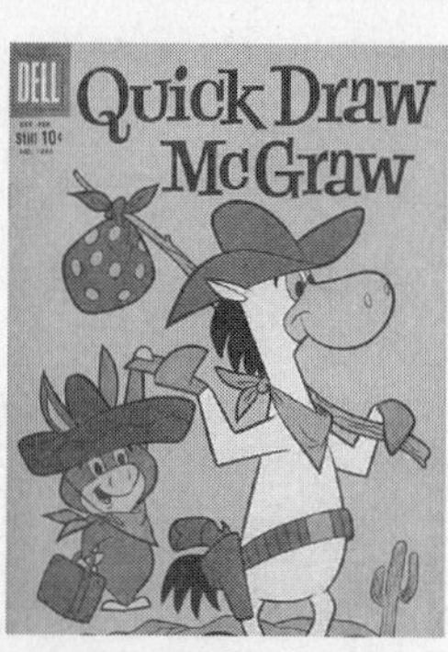

Four Color #1040 © H-B

Four Color #1085 © Loew's Inc.

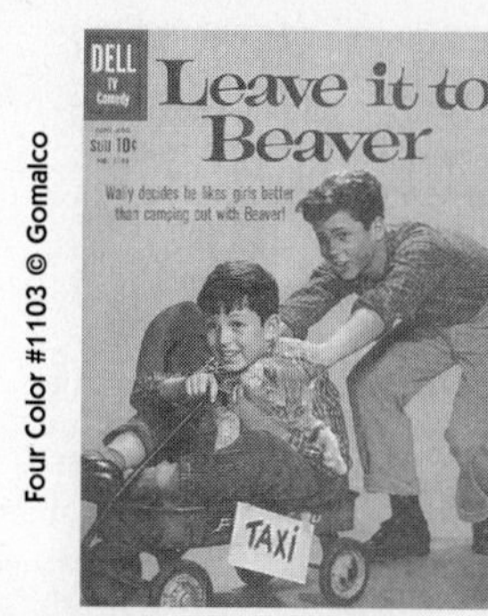

Four Color #1103 © Gomalco

	GD 2.0	VG 4.0	FN 6.0	VF 8.0	VF/NM 9.0	NM- 9.2
1025-Vacation in Disneyland (8-10/59)-Carl Barks-a(24pgs.) (Disney)	19	38	57	136	198	260
1026-Spin and Marty (TV) (Disney) (9-11/59)-Mickey Mouse Club; photo-c	9	18	27	60	85	110
1027-The Texan (#1)(TV)-Photo-c	10	20	30	67	96	125
1028-Rawhide (#1) (TV) (9-11/59)-Clint Eastwood photo-c; Tufts-a	25	50	75	181	266	350
1029-Boots and Saddles (TV) (9/59)-Photo-c	6	12	18	40	55	70
1030-Spanky and Alfalfa, the Little Rascals (TV)	6	12	18	43	59	75
1031-Fury (TV)-Photo-c	8	16	24	53	74	95
1032-Elmer Fudd	4	8	12	24	32	40
1033-Steve Canyon-not by Caniff; photo-c	6	12	18	40	55	70
1034-Nancy and Sluggo Summer Camp (9-11/59)	5	10	15	33	44	55
1035-Lawman (TV)-Photo-c	8	16	24	55	78	100
1036-The Big Circus (Movie)-Photo-c	7	14	21	51	71	90
1037-Zorro (Disney) (TV)-Tufts-a; Annette Funicello photo-c	16	32	48	113	167	220
1038-Ruff and Reddy (TV)(Hanna-Barbera)(1959)	9	18	27	63	89	115
1039-Pluto (Disney) (11-1/60)	4	8	12	29	40	50
1040-Quick Draw McGraw (#1) (TV) (Hanna-Barbera) (12-2/60)	15	30	45	104	152	200
1041-Sea Hunt (TV) (10-12/59)-Toth-a; Lloyd Bridges photo-c	9	18	27	65	93	120
1042-The Three Chipmunks (Alvin, Simon & Theodore) (#1) (TV) (10-12/59)	7	14	21	46	63	80
1043-The Three Stooges (#1)-Photo-c	26	52	78	189	275	360
1044-Have Gun, Will Travel (TV)-Photo-c	10	20	30	67	96	125
1045-Restless Gun (TV)-Photo-c	9	18	27	63	89	115
1046-Beep Beep, the Road Runner (11-1/60)	6	12	18	43	59	75
1047-Gyro Gearloose (#1) (Disney)-All Barks-c/a	19	38	57	136	198	260
1048-The Horse Soldiers (Movie) (John Wayne)-Sekowsky-a; painted cover featuring John Wayne	15	30	45	104	152	200
1049-Don't Give Up the Ship (Movie) (8/59)-Jerry Lewis photo-c	9	18	27	65	93	120
1050-Huckleberry Hound (TV) (Hanna-Barbera) (10-12/59)	9	18	27	63	89	115
1051-Donald in Mathmagic Land (Disney-Movie)	10	20	30	67	96	125
1052-Ben-Hur (Movie) (11/59)-Manning-a	10	20	30	73	107	140
1053-Goofy (Disney) (11-1/60)	6	12	18	38	52	65
1054-Huckleberry Hound Winter Fun (TV) (Hanna-Barbera) (12/59)	9	18	27	63	89	115
1055-Daisy Duck's Diary (Disney)-by Carl Barks (11-1/60)	10	20	30	70	100	130
1056-Yellowstone Kelly (Movie)-Clint Walker photo-c	6	12	18	43	59	75
1057-Mickey Mouse Album (Disney)	4	8	12	29	40	50
1058-Colt .45 (TV)-Photo-c	11	22	33	77	114	150
1059-Sugarfoot (TV)-Photo-c	10	20	30	67	96	125
1060-Journey to the Center of the Earth (Movie)-Pat Boone & James Mason photo-c	12	24	36	87	129	170
1061-Buffalo Bee (TV)	8	16	24	53	74	95
1062-Christmas Stories (Walt Scott's Little People strip-r)	5	10	15	33	44	55
1063-Santa Claus Funnies	6	12	18	40	55	70
1064-Bugs Bunny's Merry Christmas (12/59)	5	10	15	36	48	60
1065-Frosty the Snowman	5	10	15	36	48	60
1066-77 Sunset Strip (#1) (TV)-Toth-a (1-3/60)-Efrem Zimbalist, Jr. & Edd "Kookie" Byrnes photo-c	12	24	36	87	129	170
1067-Yogi Bear (#1) (TV) (Hanna-Barbera)	12	24	36	87	129	170
1068-Francis the Famous Talking Mule	4	8	12	27	36	45
1069-The FBI Story (Movie)-Toth-a; James Stewart photo on-c	10	20	30	73	107	140
1070-Solomon and Sheba (Movie)-Sekowsky-a; photo-c	10	20	30	70	100	130
1071-The Real McCoys (#1) (TV) (1-3/60)-Toth-a; Walter Brennan photo-c	10	20	30	72	104	135
1072-Blythe (Marge's)	6	12	18	40	55	70
1073-Grandma Duck's Farm Friends-Barks-c/a (Disney)	14	28	42	97	141	185
1074-Chilly Willy (Lantz)	4	8	12	29	40	50
1075-Tales of Wells Fargo (TV)-Photo-c	10	20	30	67	96	125
1076-The Rebel (#1) (TV)-Sekowsky-a; photo-c	11	22	33	77	114	150
1077-The Deputy (#1) (TV)-Buscema-a; Henry Fonda photo-c	14	28	42	99	145	190
1078-The Three Stooges (2-4/60)-Photo-c	14	28	42	97	141	185

	GD 2.0	VG 4.0	FN 6.0	VF 8.0	VF/NM 9.0	NM- 9.2
1079-The Little Rascals (TV) (Spanky & Alfalfa)	6	12	18	43	59	75
1080-Fury (TV) (2-4/60)-Photo-c	8	16	24	53	74	95
1081-Elmer Fudd	4	8	12	24	32	40
1082-Spin and Marty (Disney) (TV)-Photo-c	9	18	27	60	85	110
1083-Men into Space (TV)-Anderson-a; photo-c	6	12	18	40	55	70
1084-Speedy Gonzales	6	12	18	40	55	70
1085-The Time Machine (H.G. Wells) (Movie) (3/60)-Alex Toth-a; Rod Taylor photo-c	16	32	48	113	167	220
1086-Lolly and Pepper	3	6	9	19	25	32
1087-Peter Gunn (TV)-Photo-c	10	20	30	70	100	130
1088-A Dog of Flanders (Movie)-Photo-c	5	10	15	36	48	60
1089-Restless Gun (TV)-Photo-c	9	18	27	63	89	115
1090-Francis the Famous Talking Mule	4	8	12	27	36	45
1091-Jacky's Diary (4-6/60)	5	10	15	36	48	60
1092-Toby Tyler (Disney-Movie)-Photo-c	7	14	21	51	71	90
1093-MacKenzie's Raiders (Movie/TV)-Richard Carlson photo-c from TV show	7	14	21	51	71	90
1094-Goofy (Disney)	6	12	18	38	52	65
1095-Gyro Gearloose (Disney)-All Barks-c/a	10	20	30	73	107	140
1096-The Texan (TV)-Rory Calhoun photo-c	9	18	27	63	89	115
1097-Rawhide (TV)-Manning-a; Clint Eastwood photo-c	16	32	48	113	167	220
1098-Sugarfoot (TV)-Photo-c	10	20	30	67	96	125
1099-Donald Duck Album (Disney) (5-7/60)-Barks-c	7	14	21	51	71	90
1100-Annette's Life Story (Disney-Movie) (5/60)-Annette Funicello photo-c	25	50	75	181	266	350
1101-Robert Louis Stevenson's Kidnapped (Disney-Movie) (5/60); photo-c	7	14	21	51	71	90
1102-Wanted: Dead or Alive (#1) (TV) (5-7/60); Steve McQueen photo-c	14	28	42	99	145	190
1103-Leave It to Beaver (TV)-Photo-c	15	30	45	109	160	210
1104-Yogi Bear Goes to College (TV) (Hanna-Barbera) (6-8/60)	8	16	24	58	82	105
1105-Gale Storm (Oh! Susanna) (TV)-Toth-a; photo-c	14	28	42	97	141	185
1106-77 Sunset Strip(TV)(6-8/60)-Toth-a; photo-c	10	20	30	70	100	130
1107-Buckskin (TV)-Photo-c	7	14	21	51	71	90
1108-The Troubleshooters (TV)-Keenan Wynn photo-c	6	12	18	40	55	70
1109-This Is Your Life, Donald Duck (Disney) (TV) (8-10/60)-Gyro flashback to WDC&S #141; origin Donald Duck (1st told)	15	30	45	104	152	200
1110-Bonanza (#1) (TV) (6-8/60)-Photo-c	36	72	108	270	405	540
1111-Shotgun Slade (TV)-Photo-c	7	14	21	51	71	90
1112-Pixie and Dixie and Mr. Jinks (#1) (TV) (Hanna-Barbera) (7-9/60)	9	18	27	60	85	110
1113-Tales of Wells Fargo (TV)-Photo-c	10	20	30	67	96	125
1114-Huckleberry Finn (Movie) (7/60)-Photo-c	6	12	18	40	55	70
1115-Ricky Nelson (TV)-Manning-a; photo-c	16	32	48	111	163	215
1116-Boots and Saddles (TV) (8/60)-Photo-c	6	12	18	40	55	70
1117-Boy and the Pirates (Movie)-Photo-c	7	14	21	51	71	90
1118-The Sword and the Dragon (Movie) (6/60)-Photo-c	9	18	27	60	85	110
1119-Smokey the Bear Nature Stories	5	10	15	33	44	55
1120-Dinosaurus (Movie)-Painted-c	9	18	27	60	85	110
1121-Hercules Unchained (Movie) (8/60)-Crandall/Evans-a	10	20	30	72	104	135
1122-Chilly Willy (Lantz)	4	8	12	29	40	50
1123-Tombstone Territory (TV)-Photo-c	10	20	30	70	100	130
1124-Whirlybirds (#1) (TV)-Photo-c	10	20	30	67	96	125
1125-Laramie (#1) (TV)-Photo-c; G. Kane/Heath-a	10	20	30	70	100	130
1126-Sundance (TV) (8-10/60)-Earl Holliman photo-c	7	14	21	51	71	90
1127-The Three Stooges-Photo-c (8-10/60)	14	28	42	97	141	185
1128-Rocky and His Friends (#1) (TV) (Jay Ward) (8-10/60)	35	70	105	263	392	520
1129-Pollyanna (Disney-Movie)-Hayley Mills photo-c	9	18	27	60	85	110
1130-The Deputy (TV)-Buscema-a; Henry Fonda photo-c	10	20	30	73	107	140
1131-Elmer Fudd (9-11/60)	4	8	12	24	32	40
1132-Space Mouse (Lantz) (8-10/60)	5	10	15	36	48	60
1133-Fury (TV)-Photo-c	8	16	24	53	74	95
1134-Real McCoys (TV)-Toth-a; photo-c	10	20	30	72	104	135
1135-M.G.M.'s Mouse Musketeers (9-11/60)	3	7	10	21	28	35
1136-Jungle Cat (Disney-Movie)-Photo-c	7	14	21	51	71	90
1137-The Little Rascals (TV)	6	12	18	43	59	75

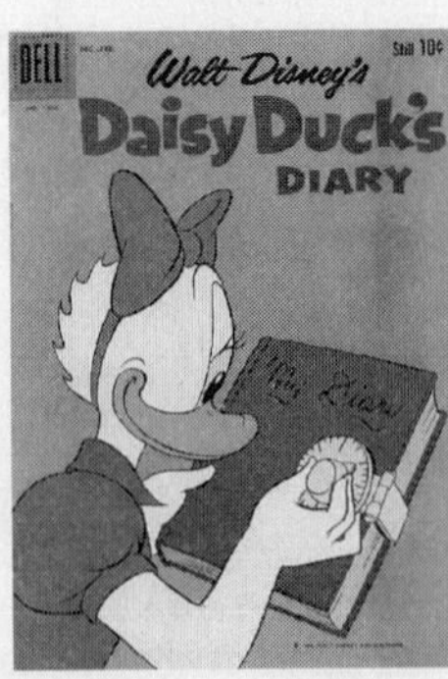

Four Color #1150 © WDC

Four Color #1192 © Ozzie Nelson

Four Color #1237 © Desilu

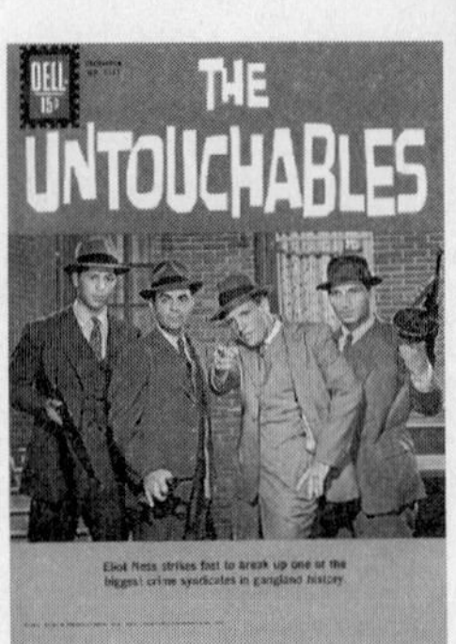

	GD 2.0	VG 4.0	FN 6.0	VF 8.0	VF/NM 9.0	NM- 9.2
1138-The Rebel (TV)-Photo-c	10	20	30	67	96	125
1139-Spartacus (Movie) (11/60)-Buscema-a; Kirk Douglas photo-c	14	28	42	97	141	185
1140-Donald Duck Album (Disney)-Barks-c	7	14	21	51	71	90
1141-Huckleberry Hound for President (TV) (Hanna-Barbera) (10/60)	9	18	27	60	85	110
1142-Johnny Ringo (TV)-Photo-c	8	16	24	55	78	100
1143-Pluto (Disney) (11-1/61)	4	8	12	29	40	50
1144-The Story of Ruth (Movie)-Photo-c	10	20	30	70	100	130
1145-The Lost World (Movie)-Gil Kane-a; photo-c; 1 pg. Conan Doyle biography by Torres	10	20	30	73	107	140
1146-Restless Gun (TV)-Photo-c; Wildey-a	9	18	27	63	89	115
1147-Sugarfoot (TV)-Photo-c	10	20	30	67	96	125
1148-I Aim at the Stars-the Wernher Von Braun Story (Movie) (11-1/61)-Photo-c	8	16	24	55	78	100
1149-Goofy (Disney) (11-1/61)	6	12	18	38	52	65
1150-Daisy Duck's Diary (Disney) (12-1/61) by Carl Barks	10	20	30	70	100	130
1151-Mickey Mouse Album (Disney) (11-1/61)	4	8	12	29	40	50
1152-Rocky and His Friends (TV) (Jay Ward) (12-2/61)	24	48	72	174	255	335
1153-Frosty the Snowman	5	10	15	36	48	60
1154-Santa Claus Funnies	6	12	18	40	55	70
1155-North to Alaska (Movie)-John Wayne photo-c	18	36	54	131	191	250
1156-Walt Disney Swiss Family Robinson (Movie) (12/60)-Photo-c	8	16	24	58	82	105
1157-Master of the World (Movie) (7/61)	6	12	18	43	59	75
1158-Three Worlds of Gulliver (2 issues exist with different covers) (Movie)-Photo-c	8	16	24	53	74	95
1159-77 Sunset Strip (TV)-Toth-a; photo-c	10	20	30	70	100	130
1160-Rawhide (TV)-Clint Eastwood photo-c	16	32	48	113	167	220
1161-Grandma Duck's Farm Friends (Disney) by Carl Barks (2-4/61)	14	28	42	97	141	185
1162-Yogi Bear Joins the Marines (TV) (Hanna-Barbera) (5-7/61)	8	16	24	58	82	105
1163-Daniel Boone (3-5/61); Marsh-a	6	12	18	40	55	70
1164-Wanted: Dead or Alive (TV)-Steve McQueen photo-c	10	20	30	73	107	140
1165-Ellery Queen (#1) (3-5/61)	12	24	36	84	125	165
1166-Rocky and His Friends (TV) (Jay Ward)	24	48	72	174	255	335
1167-Tales of Wells Fargo (TV)-Photo-c	9	18	27	63	89	115
1168-The Detectives (TV)-Robert Taylor photo-c	11	22	33	77	114	150
1169-New Adventures of Sherlock Holmes	17	34	51	121	178	235
1170-The Three Stooges (3-5/61)-Photo-c	14	28	42	97	141	185
1171-Elmer Fudd	4	8	12	24	32	40
1172-Fury (TV)-Photo-c	8	16	24	53	74	95
1173-The Twilight Zone (#1) (TV) (5/61)-Crandall/Evans-c/a; Crandall tribute to Ingles	23	46	69	167	244	320
1174-The Little Rascals (TV)	5	10	15	36	48	60
1175-M.G.M.'s Mouse Musketeers (3-5/61)	3	7	10	21	28	35
1176-Dondi (Movie)-Origin; photo-c	5	10	15	36	48	60
1177-Chilly Willy (Lantz) (4-6/61)	4	8	12	29	40	50
1178-Ten Who Dared (Disney-Movie) (12/60)-Painted-c; cast member photo on back-c	8	16	24	58	82	105
1179-The Swamp Fox (TV) (Disney)-Leslie Nielson photo-c	10	20	30	67	96	125
1180-The Danny Thomas Show (TV)-Toth-a; photo-c	18	36	54	131	191	250
1181-Texas John Slaughter (TV) (Disney) (4-6/61)-Photo-c	8	16	24	55	78	100
1182-Donald Duck Album (Disney) (5-7/61)	5	10	15	36	48	60
1183-101 Dalmatians (Disney-Movie) (3/61)	11	22	33	77	114	150
1184-Gyro Gearloose; All Barks-c/a (Disney) (5-7/61) Two variations exist	10	20	30	73	107	140
1185-Sweetie Pie	5	10	15	33	44	55
1186-Yak Yak (#1) by Jack Davis (2 versions - one minus 3-pg. Davis-c/a)	10	20	30	67	96	125
1187-The Three Stooges (6-8/61)-Photo-c	14	28	42	97	141	185
1188-Atlantis, the Lost Continent (Movie) (5/61)-Photo-c	12	24	36	82	121	150
1189-Greyfriars Bobby (Disney-Movie) (11/61)-Photo-c (scarce)	8	16	24	55	78	100
1190-Donald and the Wheel (Disney-Movie) (11/61); Barks-c	8	16	24	55	78	100

	GD 2.0	VG 4.0	FN 6.0	VF 8.0	VF/NM 9.0	NM- 9.2
1191-Leave It to Beaver (TV)-Photo-c	15	30	45	109	160	210
1192-Ricky Nelson (TV)-Manning-a; photo-c	16	32	48	111	163	215
1193-The Real McCoys (TV) (6-8/61)-Photo-c	10	20	30	67	96	125
1194-Pepe (Movie) (4/61)-Photo-c	3	6	9	18	24	30
1195-National Velvet (#1) (TV)-Photo-c	8	16	24	55	78	100
1196-Pixie and Dixie and Mr. Jinks (TV) (Hanna-Barbera) (7-9/61)	6	12	18	43	59	75
1197-The Aquanauts (TV) (5-7/61)-Photo-c	8	16	24	55	78	100
1198-Donald in Mathmagic Land (Disney-Movie)-Reprint of #1051	7	14	21	51	71	90
1199-The Absent-Minded Professor (Disney-Movie) (4/61)-Photo-c	9	18	27	60	85	110
1200-Hennessey (TV) (8-10/61)-Gil Kane-a; photo-c	8	16	24	55	78	100
1201-Goofy (Disney) (8-10/61)	6	12	18	38	52	65
1202-Rawhide (TV)-Clint Eastwood photo-c	16	32	48	113	167	220
1203-Pinocchio (Disney) (3/62)	6	12	18	40	55	70
1204-Scamp (Disney)	5	10	15	33	44	55
1205-David and Goliath (Movie) (7/61)-Photo-c	7	14	21	51	71	90
1206-Lolly and Pepper (9-11/61)	3	6	9	19	25	32
1207-The Rebel (TV)-Sekowsky-a; photo-c	10	20	30	67	96	125
1208-Rocky and His Friends (Jay Ward) (TV)	24	48	72	174	255	335
1209-Sugarfoot (TV)-Photo-c (10-12/61)	10	20	30	67	96	125
1210-The Parent Trap (Disney-Movie) (8/61)-Hayley Mills photo-c	10	20	30	72	104	135
1211-77 Sunset Strip (TV)-Manning-a; photo-c	9	18	27	65	93	120
1212-Chilly Willy (Lantz) (7-9/61)	4	8	12	29	40	50
1213-Mysterious Island (Movie)-Photo-c	10	20	30	67	96	125
1214-Smokey the Bear	5	10	15	33	44	55
1215-Tales of Wells Fargo (TV) (10-12/61)-Photo-c	9	18	27	63	89	115
1216-Whirlybirds (TV)-Photo-c	9	18	27	63	89	115
1218-Fury (TV)-Photo-c	8	16	24	53	74	95
1219-The Detectives (TV)-Robert Taylor & Adam West photo-c	10	20	30	67	96	125
1220-Gunslinger (TV)-Photo-c	10	20	30	67	96	125
1221-Bonanza (TV) (9-11/61)-Photo-c	20	40	60	140	205	270
1222-Elmer Fudd (9-11/61)	4	8	12	24	32	40
1223-Laramie (TV)-Gil Kane-a; photo-c	7	14	21	51	71	90
1224-The Little Rascals (TV) (10-12/61)	5	10	15	36	48	60
1225-The Deputy (TV)-Henry Fonda photo-c	10	20	30	73	107	140
1226-Nikki, Wild Dog of the North (Disney-Movie) (9/61)-Photo-c	6	12	18	40	55	70
1227-Morgan the Pirate (Movie)-Photo-c	9	18	27	60	85	110
1229-Thief of Baghdad (Movie)-Crandall/Evans-a; photo-c	8	16	24	53	74	95
1230-Voyage to the Bottom of the Sea (#1) (Movie)-Photo insert on-c	12	24	36	82	121	160
1231-Danger Man (TV) (9-11/61)-Patrick McGoohan photo-c	12	24	36	84	125	165
1232-On the Double (Movie)	5	10	15	36	48	60
1233-Tammy Tell Me True (Movie) (1961)	7	14	21	51	71	90
1234-The Phantom Planet (Movie) (1961)	8	16	24	55	78	100
1235-Mister Magoo (#1) (12-2/62)	10	20	30	67	96	125
1235-Mister Magoo (3-5/65) 2nd printing; reprint of 12-2/62 issue	7	14	21	50	68	85
1236-King of Kings (Movie)-Photo-c	9	18	27	60	85	110
1237-The Untouchables (#1) (TV)-Not by Toth; photo-c	24	48	72	174	255	335
1238-Deputy Dawg (TV)	12	24	36	87	129	170
1239-Donald Duck Album (Disney) (10-12/61)-Barks-c	7	14	21	51	71	90
1240-The Detectives (TV)-Tufts-a; Robert Taylor photo-c	10	20	30	67	96	125
1241-Sweetie Pie	4	8	12	25	33	42
1242-King Leonardo and His Short Subjects (#1) (TV) (11-1/62)	14	28	42	102	149	195
1243-Ellery Queen	10	20	30	67	96	125
1244-Space Mouse (Lantz) (11-1/62)	5	10	15	36	48	60
1245-New Adventures of Sherlock Holmes	15	30	45	109	160	210
1246-Mickey Mouse Album (Disney)	4	8	12	29	40	50
1247-Daisy Duck's Diary (Disney) (12-2/62)	6	12	18	38	52	65
1248-Pluto (Disney)	4	8	12	29	40	50
1249-The Danny Thomas Show (TV)-Manning-a; photo-c	17	34	51	121	178	235
1250-The Four Horsemen of the Apocalypse (Movie)-Photo-c						

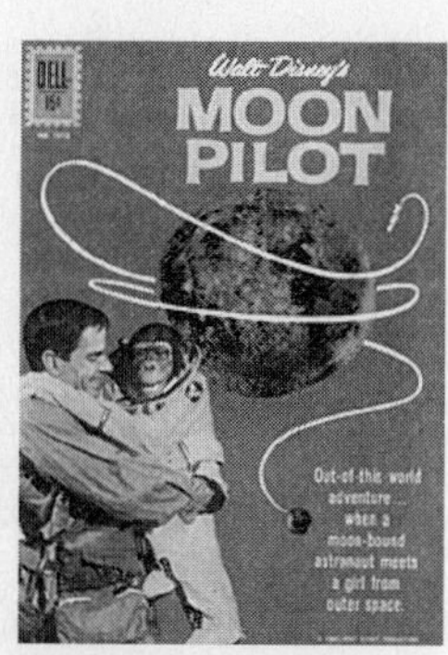

Four Color #1313 © WDC

Four Color #1328 © Columbia Pictures

Four Favorites #7 © ACE

	GD 2.0	VG 4.0	FN 6.0	VF 8.0	VF/NM 9.0	NM- 9.2
	7	14	21	51	71	90
1251-Everything's Ducky (Movie) (1961)	5	10	15	36	48	60
1252-The Andy Griffith Show (TV)-Photo-c; 1st show aired 10/3/60	38	76	114	285	430	575
1253-Space Man (#1) (1-3/62)	8	16	24	58	82	105
1254- "Diver Dan" (#1) (TV) (2-4/62)-Photo-c	6	12	18	40	55	70
1255-The Wonders of Aladdin (Movie) (1961)	7	14	21	51	71	90
1256-Kona, Monarch of Monster Isle (#1) (2-4/62)-Glanzman-a	9	18	27	60	85	110
1257-Car 54, Where Are You? (#1) (TV) (3-5/62)-Photo-c	9	18	27	65	93	120
1258-The Frogmen (#1)-Evans-a	9	18	27	60	85	110
1259-El Cid (Movie) (1961)-Photo-c	8	16	24	55	78	100
1260-The Horsemasters (TV, Movie) (Disney) (12-2/62)-Annette Funicello photo-c	14	28	42	99	145	190
1261-Rawhide (TV)-Clint Eastwood photo-c	16	32	48	113	167	220
1262-The Rebel (TV)-Photo-c	10	20	30	67	96	125
1263-77 Sunset Strip (TV) (12-2/62)-Manning-a; photo-c	9	18	27	65	93	120
1264-Pixie and Dixie and Mr. Jinks (TV) (Hanna-Barbera)	6	12	18	43	59	75
1265-The Real McCoys (TV)-Photo-c	10	20	30	67	96	125
1266-M.G.M.'s Spike and Tyke (12-2/62)	3	6	9	18	24	30
1267-Gyro Gearloose; Barks-c/a, 4 pgs. (Disney) (12-2/62)	8	16	24	58	82	105
1268-Oswald the Rabbit (Lantz)	4	8	12	27	36	45
1269-Rawhide (TV)-Clint Eastwood photo-c	16	32	48	113	167	220
1270-Bullwinkle and Rocky (#1) (TV) (Jay Ward) (3-5/62)	21	42	63	149	220	290
1271-Yogi Bear Birthday Party (TV) (Hanna-Barbera) (11/61) (Given away for 1 box top from Kellogg's Corn Flakes)	6	12	18	43	59	75
1272-Frosty the Snowman	5	10	15	36	48	60
1273-Hans Brinker (Disney-Movie)-Photo-c (2/62)	7	14	21	51	71	90
1274-Santa Claus Funnies (12/61)	6	12	18	40	55	70
1275-Rocky and His Friends (TV) (Jay Ward)	24	48	72	174	255	335
1276-Dondi	3	7	10	21	28	35
1278-King Leonardo and His Short Subjects (TV)	14	28	42	102	149	195
1279-Grandma Duck's Farm Friends (Disney)	5	10	15	36	48	60
1280-Hennesey (TV)-Photo-c	7	14	21	51	71	90
1281-Chilly Willy (Lantz) (4-6/62)	4	8	12	29	40	50
1282-Babes in Toyland (Disney-Movie) (1/62); Annette Funicello photo-c	15	30	45	104	152	200
1283-Bonanza (TV) (2-4/62)-Photo-c	20	40	60	140	205	270
1284-Laramie (TV)-Heath-a; photo-c	7	14	21	51	71	90
1285-Leave It to Beaver (TV)-Photo-c	15	30	45	109	160	210
1286-The Untouchables (TV)-Photo-c	17	34	51	118	174	230
1287-Man from Wells Fargo (TV)-Photo-c	6	12	18	43	59	75
1288-Twilight Zone (TV) (4/62)-Crandall/Evans-c/a	13	26	39	90	133	175
1289-Ellery Queen	10	20	30	67	96	125
1290-M.G.M.'s Mouse Musketeers	3	7	10	21	28	35
1291-77 Sunset Strip (TV)-Manning-a; photo-c	9	18	27	65	93	120
1293-Elmer Fudd (3-5/62)	4	8	12	24	32	40
1294-Ripcord (TV)	8	16	24	55	78	100
1295-Mister Ed, the Talking Horse (#1) (TV) (3-5/62)-Photo-c	14	28	42	102	149	195
1296-Fury (TV) (3-5/62)-Photo-c	8	16	24	53	74	95
1297-Spanky, Alfalfa and the Little Rascals (TV)	5	10	15	36	48	60
1298-The Hathaways (TV)-Photo-c	5	10	15	36	48	60
1299-Deputy Dawg (TV)	12	24	36	87	129	170
1300-The Comancheros (Movie) (1961)-John Wayne photo-c	17	34	51	123	182	240
1301-Adventures in Paradise (TV) (2-4/62)	6	12	18	43	59	75
1302-Johnny Jason, Teen Reporter (2-4/62)	4	8	12	25	33	42
1303-Lad: A Dog (Movie)-Photo-c	5	10	15	33	44	55
1304-Nellie the Nurse (3-5/62)-Stanley-a	8	16	24	55	78	100
1305-Mister Magoo (3-5/62)	10	20	30	67	96	125
1306-Target: The Corruptors (#1) (TV) (3-5/62)-Photo-c	6	12	18	43	59	75
1307-Margie (TV) (3-5/62)	6	12	18	43	59	75
1308-Tales of the Wizard of Oz (TV) (3-5/62)	13	26	39	90	133	175
1309-87th Precinct (#1) (TV) (4-6/62)-Krigstein-a; photo-c	11	22	33	77	114	150
1310-Huck and Yogi Winter Sports (TV) (Hanna-Barbera) (3/62)	10	20	30	67	96	125
1311-Rocky and His Friends (TV) (Jay Ward)	24	48	72	174	255	335
1312-National Velvet (TV)-Photo-c	4	8	12	29	40	50
1313-Moon Pilot (Disney-Movie)-Photo-c	8	16	24	55	78	100
1328-The Underwater City (Movie) (1961)-Evans-a; photo-c	8	16	24	55	78	100
1329-See Gyro Gearloose #01329-207						
1330-Brain Boy (#1)-Gil Kane-a	14	28	42	99	145	190
1332-Bachelor Father (TV)	9	18	27	60	85	110
1333-Short Ribs (4-6/62)	6	12	18	40	55	70
1335-Aggie Mack (4-6/62)	4	8	12	28	38	48
1336-On Stage; not by Leonard Starr	5	10	15	36	48	60
1337-Dr. Kildare (#1) (TV) (4-6/62)-Photo-c	10	20	30	67	96	125
1341-The Andy Griffith Show (TV) (4-6/62)-Photo-c	35	70	105	263	394	525
1348-Yak Yak (#2)-Jack Davis-c/a	9	18	27	63	89	115
1349-Yogi Bear Visits the U.N. (TV) (Hanna-Barbera) (1/62)-Photo-c	10	20	30	70	100	130
1350-Comanche (Disney-Movie)(1962)-Reprints 4-Color #966 (title change from "Tonka" to "Comanche") (4-6/62)-Sal Mineo photo-c	6	12	18	40	55	70
1354-Calvin & the Colonel (#1) (TV) (4-6/62)	10	20	30	67	96	125

NOTE: *Missing numbers probably do not exist.*

4-D MONKEY, THE (Adventures of... #? on)
Leung's Publications: 1988 - No. 11, 1990 ($1.80/$2.00, 52 pgs.)

	GD	VG	FN	VF	VF/NM	NM-
1-11: 1-Karate Pig, Ninja Flounder & 4-D Monkey (48 pgs., centerfold is a Christmas card). 2-4 (52pgs.)						2.50

FOUR FAVORITES (Crime Must Pay the Penalty No. 33 on)
Ace Magazines: Sept, 1941 - No. 32, Dec, 1947

	GD	VG	FN	VF	VF/NM	NM-
1-Vulcan, Lash Lightning (formerly Flash Lightning in Sure-Fire), Magno the Magnetic Man & The Raven begin; flag/Hitler-c	160	320	480	1000	1500	2000
2-The Black Ace only app.	57	114	171	356	538	720
3-Last Vulcan	48	96	144	288	432	575
4,5: 4-The Raven & Vulcan end; Unknown Soldier begins (see Our Flag), ends #28. 5-Captain Courageous begins (5/42), ends #28 (moves over from Captain Courageous #6); not in #6	44	88	132	264	395	525
6-8: 6-The Flag app.; Mr. Risk begins (7/42)	42	84	126	252	359	465
9-Kurtzman-a (Lash Lightning); robot-c	44	88	132	264	395	525
10-Classic Kurtzman-c/a (Magno & Davey)	50	100	150	300	450	600
11-Kurtzman-a; Hitler, Mussolini, Hirohito-c; L.B. Cole-a; Unknown Soldier by Kurtzman	57	114	171	356	538	720
12-L.B. Cole-a	37	74	111	213	299	385
13-20: 18,20-Palais-c/a	32	64	96	182	259	335
21-No Unknown Soldier; The Unknown app.	24	48	72	138	194	250
22-26: 22-Captain Courageous drops costume. 23-Unknown Soldier drops costume. 25-29-Hap Hazard app. 26-Last Magno	24	48	72	138	194	250
27-29: Hap Hazard app. in all	22	44	66	127	176	225
30-32: 30-Funny-c begin (teen humor), end #32	15	30	45	86	118	150

NOTE: ***Dave Berg** c-5. **Jim Mooney** a-6; c-1-3. **Palais** a-18-20; c-18-25. Torture chamber c-5.*

FOUR HORSEMEN, THE (See The Crusaders)

FOUR HORSEMEN
DC Comics (Vertigo): Feb, 2000 - No. 4, May, 2000 ($2.50, limited series)

	GD	VG	FN	VF	VF/NM	NM-
1-4-Essad Ribic-c/a; Robert Rodi-s						2.50

FOUR HORSEMEN OF THE APOCALYPSE, THE (Movie)
Dell Publishing Co.: No. 1250, Jan-Mar, 1962 (one-shot)

	GD	VG	FN	VF	VF/NM	NM-
Four Color 1250-Photo-c	7	14	21	51	71	90

4MOST (Foremost Boys No. 32-40; becomes Thrilling Crime Cases #41 on)
Novelty Publications/Star Publications No. 37-on:
Winter, 1941-42 - V8#5(#36), 9-10/49; #37, 11-12/49 - #40, 4-5/50

	GD	VG	FN	VF	VF/NM	NM-
V1#1-The Target by Sid Greene, The Cadet & Dick Cole begin with origins retold; produced by Funnies Inc.; quarterly issues begin, end V6#3	140	280	420	875	1313	1750
2-Last Target (Spr/42); WWII cover	60	120	180	375	563	750
3-Dan'l Flannel begins; flag-c	44	88	132	264	395	525
4-1pg. Dr. Seuss (signed) (Aut/42); fish in the face-c	44	88	132	264	395	525
V2#1-3	17	34	51	98	134	170
4-Hitler, Tojo & Mussolini app. as pumpkins on-c	31	62	93	178	252	325
V3#1-4	14	28	42	81	111	140
V4#1-4: 2-Walter Johnson-c	11	22	33	66	88	110
V5#1-4: 1-The Target & Targeteers app.	10	20	30	58	77	95
V6#1-4	9	18	27	52	66	80
5-L. B. Cole-c	21	42	63	118	164	210

411 #2 © MAR

Fox Giants - Love Problems © FOX

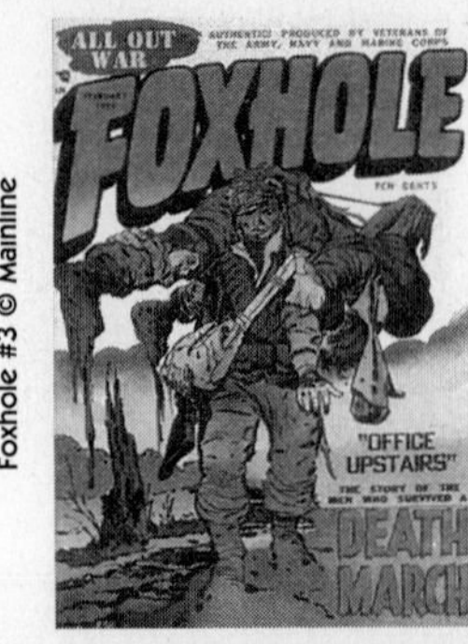

Foxhole #3 © Mainline

	GD 2.0	VG 4.0	FN 6.0	VF 8.0	VF/NM 9.0	NM- 9.2
V7#1,3,5, V8#1, 37	9	18	27	52	66	80
2,4,6-L. B. Cole-c. 6-Last Dick Cole	21	42	63	118	164	210
V8#2,3,5-L. B. Cole-c/a	24	48	72	138	194	250
4-L. B. Cole-a	14	28	42	81	111	140
38-40: 38-Johnny Weismuller (Tarzan) life story & Jim Braddock (boxer) life story. 38-40-L.B. Cole-c. 40-Last White Rider	18	36	54	104	142	180
Accepted Reprint 38-40 (nd): 40-r/Johnny Weismuller life story; all have L.B. Cole-c	10	20	30	56	73	90

411
Marvel Comics: June, 2003 - No. 3 ($3.50, limited series)

1,2-Tributes to peacemakers; s/a by various. 1-Millar, Quitely, Mack, Winslade & others-s/a. 2-Harris, Phillips, Manco, Bruce Jones. 3.50

FOUR-STAR BATTLE TALES
National Periodical Publications: Feb-Mar, 1973 - No. 5, Nov-Dec, 1973

	GD	VG	FN	VF	VF/NM	NM-
1-Reprints begin	3	6	9	18	24	30
2-5	2	4	6	10	13	16

NOTE: ***Drucker** r-1, 3-5. **Heath** r-2, 5; c-1. **Krigstein** r-5. **Kubert** r-4; c-2.*

FOUR STAR SPECTACULAR
National Periodical Publications: Mar-Apr, 1976 - No. 6, Jan-Feb, 1977

	GD	VG	FN	VF	VF/NM	NM-
1	2	4	6	11	14	18
2-6: Reprints in all. 2-Infinity cover	1	3	4	6	8	10

NOTE: *All contain DC Superhero reprints. #1 has 68 pgs.; #2-6, 52 pgs.. #1, 4-Hawkman app.; #2-Kid Flash app.; #3-Green Lantern app; #2, 4, 5-Wonder Woman, Superboy app; #5-Green Arrow, Vigilante app; #6-Blackhawk G.A.-r.*

FOUR TEENERS (Formerly Crime Must Pay The Penalty; Dotty No. 35 on)
A. A. Wyn: No. 34, April, 1948 (52 pgs.)

	GD	VG	FN	VF	VF/NM	NM-
34-Teen-age comic; Dotty app.; Curly & Jerry continue from Four Favorites	7	14	21	35	43	50

FOURTH WORLD GALLERY, THE (Jack Kirby's...)
DC Comics: 1996 (9/96) ($3.50, one-shot)

nn-Pin-ups of Jack Kirby's Fourth World characters (New Gods, Forever People & Mister Miracle) by John Byrne, Rick Burchett, Dan Jurgens, Walt Simonson & others 3.50

FOUR WOMEN
DC Comics (Homage): Dec, 2001 - No. 5, Apr, 2002 ($2.95, limited series)

1-5-Sam Kieth-s/a 3.00
TPB (2002, $17.95) r/series; foreward by Kieth 18.00

FOX AND THE CROW (Stanley & His Monster No. 109 on) (See Comic Cavalcade & Real Screen Comics)
National Periodical Publications: Dec-Jan, 1951-52 - No. 108, Feb-Mar, 1968

	GD	VG	FN	VF	VF/NM	NM-
1	110	220	330	688	1032	1375
2(Scarce)	52	104	156	312	469	625
3-5	37	74	111	213	299	385
6-10	27	54	81	153	214	275
11-20	20	40	60	112	156	200
21-30: 22-Last precode issue (2/55)	14	28	42	81	111	140
31-40	11	22	33	66	88	110
41-60	7	14	21	50	68	85
61-80	6	12	18	38	52	65
81-94: 94-(11/65)-The Brat Finks begin	4	8	12	27	36	45
95-Stanley & His Monster begins (origin & 1st app)	6	12	18	38	52	65
96-99,101-108	3	7	10	21	28	35
100 (10-11/66)	4	8	12	24	32	40

NOTE: *Many covers by **Mort Drucker.***

FOX AND THE HOUND, THE (Disney)(Movie)
Whitman Publishing Co.: Aug, 1981 - No. 3, Oct, 1981

	GD	VG	FN	VF	VF/NM	NM-
11292(#1),2,3-Based on animated movie	1	2	3	5	7	9

FOXFIRE (See The Phoenix Resurrection)
Malibu Comics (Ultraverse): Feb, 1996 - No. 4, May, 1996 ($1.50)

1-4: Sludge, Ultraforce app. 4-Punisher app. 2.25

FOX GIANTS (Also see Giant Comics Edition)
Fox Features Syndicate: 1944 - 1950 (25¢, 132 - 196 pgs.)

	GD	VG	FN	VF	VF/NM	NM-
Album of Crime nn(1949, 132p)	46	92	138	276	413	550
Album of Love nn(1949, 132p)	42	84	126	252	359	465
All Famous Crime Stories nn('49, 132p)	46	92	138	276	413	550
All Good Comics 1(1944, 132p)(R.W. Voigt)-The Bouncer, Purple Tigress,Rick Evans, Puppeteer, Green Mask; Infinity-c	40	80	120	240	350	460
All Great nn(1944, 132p)-Capt. Jack Terry, Rick Evans, Jaguar Man	40	80	120	240	350	460
All Great nn(Chicago Nite Life News)(1945, 132p)-Green Mask, Bouncer, Puppeteer, Rick Evans, Rocket Kelly	40	80	120	240	355	470
All-Great Confessions nn(1949, 132p)	40	80	120	240	340	440
All Great Crime Stories nn('49, 132p)	46	92	138	276	413	550
All Great Jungle Adventures nn('49, 132p)	55	110	165	330	495	660
All Real Confession Magazine 3 (3/49, 132p)	40	80	120	240	340	440
All Real Confession Magazine 4 (4/49, 132p)	40	80	120	240	340	440
All Your Comics 1(1944, 132p)-The Puppeteer, Red Robbins, & Merciless the Sorcerer	42	84	126	252	359	465
Almanac Of Crime nn(1948, 148p)-Phantom Lady	50	100	150	300	450	600
Almanac Of Crime 1(1950, 132p)	44	88	132	264	395	525
Book Of Love nn(1950, 132p)	39	78	117	230	325	420
Burning Romances 1(1949, 132p)	44	88	132	264	395	525
Crimes Incorporated nn(1950, 132p)	41	82	123	246	368	490
Daring Love Stories nn(1950, 132p)	39	78	117	233	329	425
Everybody's Comics 1(1944, 50¢, 196p)-The Green Mask, The Puppeteer, The Bouncer, Rocket Kelly, Rick Evans	46	92	138	276	413	550
Everybody's Comics 1(1946, 196p)-Green Lama, The Puppeteer	39	78	117	233	329	425
Everybody's Comics 1(1946, 196p)-Same as 1945 Ribtickler	32	64	96	182	259	335
Everybody's Comics nn(1947, 132p)-Jo-Jo, Purple Tigress, Cosmo Cat, Bronze Man	38	76	114	219	310	400
Exciting Romance Stories nn(1949, 132p)	39	78	117	230	325	420
Famous Love nn(1950, 132p)	39	78	117	230	325	420
Intimate Confessions nn(1950, 132p)	39	78	117	233	329	425
Journal Of Crime nn(1949, 132p)	46	92	138	276	413	550
Love Problems nn(1949, 132p)	40	80	120	240	340	440
Love Thrills nn(1950, 132p)	40	80	120	240	340	440
March of Crime nn('48, 132p)-Female w/rifle-c	41	82	123	246	368	490
March of Crime nn('49, 132p)-Cop w/pistol-c	40	80	120	240	360	480
March of Crime nn(1949, 132p)-Coffin & man w/machine-gun-c	40	80	120	240	360	480
Revealing Love Stories nn(1950, 132p)	39	78	117	233	329	425
Ribtickler nn(1945, 50¢, 196p)-Chicago Nite Life News; Marvel Mutt, Cosmo Cat, Flash Rabbit, The Nebbs app.	39	78	117	230	325	420
Romantic Thrills nn(1950, 132p)	39	78	117	230	325	420
Secret Love Stories nn(1949, 132p)	39	78	117	230	325	420
Strange Love nn(1950, 132p)-Photo-c	41	82	123	246	368	490
Sweetheart Scandals nn(1950, 132p)	39	78	117	230	325	420
Teen-Age Love nn(1950, 132p)	39	78	117	230	325	420
Throbbing Love nn(1950, 132p)-Photo-c; used in **POP**, pg. 107	41	82	123	246	368	490
Truth About Crime nn(1949, 132p)	46	92	138	276	413	550
Variety Comics 1(1946, 132p)-Blue Beetle, Jungle Jo	40	80	120	240	350	460
Variety Comics nn(1950, 132p)-Jungle Jo, My Secret Affair(w/Harrison/Wood-a), Crimes by Women & My Story	40	80	120	240	340	440
Western Roundup nn('50, 132p)-Hoot Gibson; Cody of the Pony Express app.	40	80	120	240	350	460

NOTE: *Each of the above usually contain four remaindered Fox books minus covers. Since these missing covers often had the first page of the first story, most Giants therefore are incomplete. Approximate values are listed. Books with appearances of Phantom Lady, Rulah, Jo-Jo, etc. could bring more.*

FOXHOLE (Becomes Never Again #8?)
Mainline/Charlton No. 5 on: 9-10/54 - No. 4, 3-4/55; No. 5, 7/55 - No. 7, 3/56

	GD	VG	FN	VF	VF/NM	NM-
1-Classic Kirby-c	44	88	132	264	395	525
2-Kirby-c/a(2); Kirby scripts based on his war time experiences	33	66	99	190	270	350
3-5-Kirby-c only	19	38	57	107	149	190
6-Kirby-c/a(2)	28	56	84	159	225	290
7	9	18	27	54	70	85
Super Reprints #10,15-17: 10-r/? 15,16-r/United States Marines #5,8. 17-r/Monty Hall #?	2	4	6	12	16	20
11,12,18-r/Foxhole #1,2,3; Kirby-c	3	6	9	19	25	32

NOTE: ***Kirby** a(r)-Super #11, 12. **Powell** a(r)-Super #15, 16. Stories by actual veterans.*

FOX KIDS FUNHOUSE (TV)
Acclaim Books: 1997 ($4.50, digest size)

1-The Tick 4.50

FOXY FAGAN COMICS (Funny Animal)
Dearfield Publishing Co.: Dec, 1946 - No. 7, Summer, 1948

	GD	VG	FN	VF	VF/NM	NM-
1-Foxy Fagan & Little Buck begin	13	26	39	74	100	125
2	8	16	24	40	50	60
3-7: 6-Rocket ship-c	7	14	21	35	43	50

Frankenstein Mobster #0 © Mark Wheatley

Frankie Comics #4 © MAR

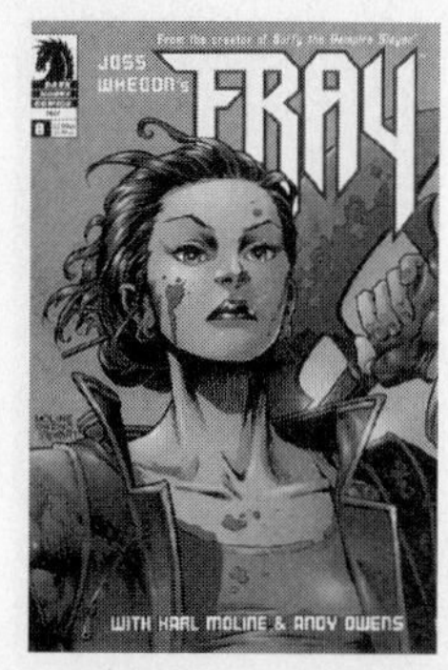

Fray #8 © Joss Whedon

	GD 2.0	VG 4.0	FN 6.0	VF 8.0	VF/NM 9.0	NM- 9.2

FRACTURED FAIRY TALES (TV)
Gold Key: Oct, 1962 (Jay Ward)

	GD	VG	FN	VF	VF/NM	NM-
1 (10022-210)-From Bullwinkle TV show	12	24	36	87	129	170

FRAGGLE ROCK (TV)
Marvel Comics (Star Comics)/Marvel V2#1 on: Apr, 1985 - No. 8, Sept, 1986; V2#1, Apr, 1988 - No. 6, Sept, 1988

	GD	VG	FN	VF	VF/NM	NM-
1-6 (75¢-c)						5.00
7,8						6.00
V2#1-6-($1.00): Reprints 1st series						2.25

FRANCIS, BROTHER OF THE UNIVERSE
Marvel Comics Group: 1980 (75¢, 52 pgs., one-shot)

	GD	VG	FN	VF	VF/NM	NM-
nn-John Buscema/Marie Severin-a; story of Francis Bernadone celebrating his 800th birthday in 1982						4.00

FRANCIS THE FAMOUS TALKING MULE (All based on movie)
Dell Publishing Co.: No. 335 (#1), June, 1951 - No. 1090, March, 1960

	GD	VG	FN	VF	VF/NM	NM-
Four Color 335 (#1)	11	22	33	77	114	150
Four Color 465	6	12	18	43	59	75
Four Color 501,547,579	5	10	15	36	48	60
Four Color 621,655,698,710,745	4	8	12	29	40	50
Four Color 810,863,906,953,991,1068,1090	4	8	12	27	36	45

FRANK
Nemesis Comics (Harvey): Apr (Mar inside), 1994 - No. 4, 1994 ($1.75/$2.50, limited series)

	GD	VG	FN	VF	VF/NM	NM-
1-4-($2.50, direct sale): 1-Foil-c Edition						3.00
1-4-($1.75)-Newsstand Editions; Cowan-a in all						2.25

FRANK
Fantagraphics Books: Sept, 1996 ($2.95, B&W)

	GD	VG	FN	VF	VF/NM	NM-
1-Woodring-c/a/scripts						3.00

FRANK BUCK (Formerly My True Love)
Fox Features Syndicate: No. 70, May, 1950 - No. 3, Sept, 1950

	GD	VG	FN	VF	VF/NM	NM-
70-Wood a(p)(3 stories)-Photo-c	34	68	102	196	278	360
71-Wood-a (9 pgs.); photo/painted-c	18	36	54	104	142	180
3: 3-Photo/painted-c	14	28	42	79	107	135

NOTE: *Based on "Bring 'Em Back Alive" TV show.*

FRANKENSTEIN (See Dracula, Movie Classics & Werewolf)
Dell Publishing Co.: Aug-Oct, 1964; No. 2, Sept, 1966 - No. 4, Mar, 1967

	GD	VG	FN	VF	VF/NM	NM-
1(12-283-410)(1964)(2nd printing; see Movie Classics for 1st printing)	6	12	18	43	59	75
2-Intro. & origin super-hero character (9/66)	4	8	12	28	38	48
3,4	3	6	9	18	24	30

FRANKENSTEIN (The Monster of...; also see Monsters Unleashed #2, Power Record Comics, Psycho & Silver Surfer #7)
Marvel Comics Group: Jan, 1973 - No. 18, Sept, 1975

	GD	VG	FN	VF	VF/NM	NM-
1-Ploog-c/a begins, ends #6	6	12	18	40	55	70
2	4	8	12	24	32	40
3-5	3	6	9	18	23	28
6,7,10: 7-Dracula cameo	2	4	6	14	18	22
8,9-Dracula c/sty. 9-Death of Dracula	4	8	12	27	36	45
11-17	2	4	6	10	13	16
18-Wrightson-c(i)	2	4	6	12	16	20

NOTE: ***Adkins** c-17i. **Buscema** a-7-10p. **Ditko** a-12r. **G. Kane** c-15p. **Orlando** a-8r. **Ploog** a-1-3, 4p, 5p, 6; c-1-6. **Wrightson** c-18i.*

FRANKENSTEIN (Mary Wollstonecraft Shelley's...; A Marvel Illustrated Novel)
Marvel Pub.: 1983 ($8.95, B&W, 196 pgs., 8x11" TPB)

	GD	VG	FN	VF	VF/NM	NM-
nn-Wrightson-a; 4 pg. intro. by Stephen King	4	8	12	27	36	45

FRANKENSTEIN COMICS (Also See Prize Comics)
Prize Publ. (Crestwood/Feature): Sum, 1945 - V5#5(#33), Oct-Nov, 1954

	GD	VG	FN	VF	VF/NM	NM-
1-Frankenstein begins by Dick Briefer (origin); Frank Sinatra parody	110	220	330	688	1032	1375
2	53	106	159	318	479	640
3-5	40	80	120	240	358	475
6-10: 7-S&K a(r)/Headline Comics. 8(7-8/47)-Superman satire	37	74	111	212	301	390
11-17(1-2/49)-11-Boris Karloff parody-c/story. 17-Last humor issue	32	64	96	182	259	335
18(3/52)-New origin, horror series begins	40	80	120	240	358	475
19,20(V3#4, 8-9/52)	28	56	84	159	225	290
21(V3#5), 22(V3#6), 23(V4#1) - #28(V4#6)	25	50	75	147	202	260
29(V5#1) - #33(V5#5)	25	50	75	147	202	260

NOTE: ***Briefer** c/a-all. **Meskin** a-21, 29.*

FRANKENSTEIN/DRACULA WAR, THE
Topps Comics: Feb, 1995 - No. 3, May, 1995 ($2.50, limited series)

	GD	VG	FN	VF	VF/NM	NM-
1-3						3.00

FRANKENSTEIN, JR. (...& the Impossibles) (TV)
Gold Key: Jan, 1966 (Hanna-Barbera)

	GD	VG	FN	VF	VF/NM	NM-
1-Super hero (scarce)	12	24	36	82	121	160

FRANKENSTEIN MOBSTER
Image Comics: No. 0, Oct, 2003 - Present ($2.95)

	GD	VG	FN	VF	VF/NM	NM-
0,1: 0-Two covers by Wheatley and Hughes; Wheatley-s/a. 1-Variant-c by Wieringo						3.00

FRANKENSTEIN: OR THE MODERN PROMETHEUS
Caliber Press: 1994 ($2.95, one-shot)

	GD	VG	FN	VF	VF/NM	NM-
1						3.00

FRANK FRAZETTA FANTASY ILLUSTRATED (Magazine)
Quantum Cat Entertainment: Spring 1998 - No. 8 ($5.95, quarterly)

	GD	VG	FN	VF	VF/NM	NM-
1-Anthology; art by Corben, Horley, Jusko						6.00
1-Linsner variant-c						10.00
2-Battle Chasers by Madureira; Harris-a						8.00
2-Madureira Battle Chasers variant-c						12.00
3-8-Frazetta-c						6.00
3-Tony Daniel variant-c						15.00
5,6-Portacio variant-c, 7,8-Alex Nino variant-c						10.00
8-Alex Ross Chicago Comicon variant-c						10.00

FRANK FRAZETTA'S THUN'DA TALES
Fantagraphics Books: 1987 ($2.00, one-shot)

	GD	VG	FN	VF	VF/NM	NM-
1-Frazetta-r						6.00

FRANK FRAZETTA'S UNTAMED LOVE (Also see Untamed Love)
Fantagraphics Books: Nov, 1987 ($2.00, one-shot)

	GD	VG	FN	VF	VF/NM	NM-
1-Frazetta-r from 1950's romance comics						6.00

FRANKIE COMICS (...& Lana No. 13-15) (Formerly Movie Tunes; becomes Frankie Fuddle No. 16 on)
Marvel Comics (MgPC): No. 4, Wint, 1946-47 - No. 15, June, 1949

	GD	VG	FN	VF	VF/NM	NM-
4-Mitzi, Margie, Daisy app.	13	26	39	76	103	130
5-9	8	16	24	46	58	70
10-15: 13-Anti-Wertham editorial	8	16	24	40	50	60

FRANKIE DOODLE (See Sparkler, both series)
United Features Syndicate: No. 7, 1939

	GD	VG	FN	VF	VF/NM	NM-
Single Series 7	33	66	99	190	270	350

FRANKIE FUDDLE (Formerly Frankie & Lana)
Marvel Comics: No. 16, Aug, 1949 - No. 17, Nov, 1949

	GD	VG	FN	VF	VF/NM	NM-
16,17	8	16	24	40	50	60

FRANK LUTHER'S SILLY PILLY COMICS (See Jingle Dingle...)
Children's Comics (Maltex Cereal): 1950 (10¢)

	GD	VG	FN	VF	VF/NM	NM-
1-Characters from radio, records, & TV	8	16	24	40	50	60

FRANK MERRIWELL AT YALE (Speed Demons No. 5 on?)
Charlton Comics: June, 1955 - No. 4, Jan, 1956 (Also see Shadow Comics)

	GD	VG	FN	VF	VF/NM	NM-
1	7	14	21	37	46	55
2-4	5	10	15	24	30	35

FRANTIC (Magazine) (See Ratfink & Zany)
Pierce Publishing Co.: Oct, 1958 - V2#2, Apr, 1959 (Satire)

	GD	VG	FN	VF	VF/NM	NM-
V1#1	10	20	30	60	80	100
2	8	16	24	46	58	70
V2#1,2: 1-Burgos-a, Severin-c/a; Powell-a?	7	14	21	35	43	50

FRAY
Dark Horse Comics: June, 2001 - No. 8, July, 2003 ($2.99, limited series)

	GD	VG	FN	VF	VF/NM	NM-
1-Joss Whedon-s/Moline & Owens-a	1	2	3	5	6	8
1-DF Gold edition	2	4	6	10	12	15
2-8: 6-(3/02). 7-(4/03)						4.00

FREAK FORCE (Also see Savage Dragon)
Image Comics (Highbrow Ent.): Dec, 1993 - No. 18, July, 1995 ($1.95/$2.50)

	GD	VG	FN	VF	VF/NM	NM-
1-18-Superpatriot & Mighty Man in all; Erik Larsen scripts in all. 4-Vanguard app. 8-Begin $2.50-c. 9-Cyberforce-c & app. 13-Variant-c						3.00

FREAK FORCE (Also see Savage Dragon)

Freckles and His Friends #8 © STD

Freemind #5 © Michelinie & Layton

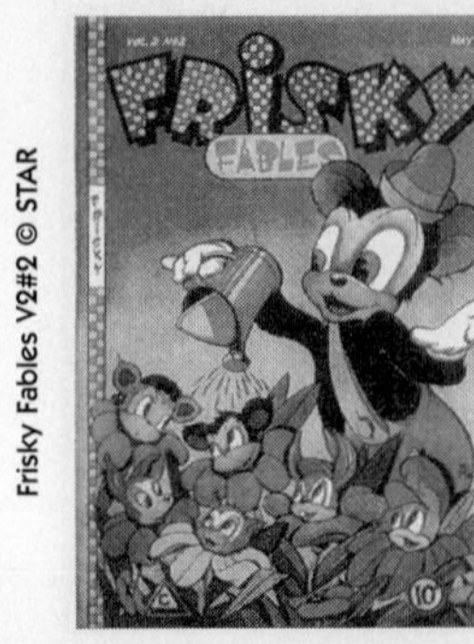

Frisky Fables V2#2 © STAR

Image Comics: Apr, 1997 - No. 3, July, 1997 ($2.95)

	GD 2.0	VG 4.0	FN 6.0	VF 8.0	VF/NM 9.0	NM- 9.2
1-3-Larsen-s						3.00

FRECKLES AND HIS FRIENDS (See Crackajack Funnies, Famous Comics Cartoon Book, Honeybee Birdwhistle... & Red Ryder)

FRECKLES AND HIS FRIENDS
Standard Comics/Argo: No. 5, 11/47 - No. 12, 8/49; 11/55 - No. 4, 6/56

	GD 2.0	VG 4.0	FN 6.0	VF 8.0	VF/NM 9.0	NM- 9.2
5-Reprints	8	16	24	46	58	70
6-12-Reprints. 7-9-Airbrush-c (by Schomburg?). 11-Lingerie panels	6	12	18	28	34	40

NOTE: *Some copies of No. 8 & 9 contain a printing oddity. The negatives were elongated in the engraving process, probably to conform to page dimensions on the filler pages. Those pages only look normal when viewed at a 45 degree angle.*

	GD 2.0	VG 4.0	FN 6.0	VF 8.0	VF/NM 9.0	NM- 9.2
1(Argo,'55)-Reprints (NEA Service)	6	12	18	28	34	40
2-4	4	8	12	18	22	25

FREDDY (Formerly My Little Margie's Boy Friends) (Also see Blue Bird)
Charlton Comics: V2#12, June, 1958 - No. 47, Feb, 1965

	GD 2.0	VG 4.0	FN 6.0	VF 8.0	VF/NM 9.0	NM- 9.2
V2#12	4	8	12	24	32	40
13-15	3	6	9	16	20	25
16-47	2	4	6	11	14	18

FREDDY
Dell Publishing Co.: May-July, 1963 - No. 3, Oct-Dec, 1964

	GD 2.0	VG 4.0	FN 6.0	VF 8.0	VF/NM 9.0	NM- 9.2
1	3	6	9	19	25	32
2,3	2	4	6	14	18	22

FREDDY KRUEGER'S A NIGHTMARE ON ELM STREET
Marvel Comics: Oct, 1989 - No. 2, Dec, 1989 ($2.25, B&W, movie adaptation)

	GD 2.0	VG 4.0	FN 6.0	VF 8.0	VF/NM 9.0	NM- 9.2
1,2: Origin Freddy Krueger; Buckler/Alcala-a						3.00

FREDDY'S DEAD: THE FINAL NIGHTMARE
Innovation Publishing: Oct, 1991 - No. 3, Dec 1991 ($2.50, color mini-series, adapts movie)

	GD 2.0	VG 4.0	FN 6.0	VF 8.0	VF/NM 9.0	NM- 9.2
1-3: Dismukes (film poster artist) painted-c						3.00

FRED HEMBECK DESTROYS THE MARVEL UNIVERSE
Marvel Comics: July, 1989 ($1.50, one-shot)

	GD 2.0	VG 4.0	FN 6.0	VF 8.0	VF/NM 9.0	NM- 9.2
1-Punisher app.; Staton-i (5 pgs.)						3.00

FRED HEMBECK SELLS THE MARVEL UNIVERSE
Marvel Comics: Oct, 1990 ($1.25, one-shot)

	GD 2.0	VG 4.0	FN 6.0	VF 8.0	VF/NM 9.0	NM- 9.2
1-Punisher, Wolverine parodies; Hembeck/Austin-c						3.00

FREEDOM AGENT (Also see John Steele)
Gold Key: Apr, 1963 (12¢)

	GD 2.0	VG 4.0	FN 6.0	VF 8.0	VF/NM 9.0	NM- 9.2
1 (10054-304)-Painted-c	4	8	12	29	40	50

FREEDOM FIGHTERS (See Justice League of America #107,108)
National Periodical Publ./DC Comics: Mar-Apr, 1976 - No. 15, July-Aug, 1978

	GD 2.0	VG 4.0	FN 6.0	VF 8.0	VF/NM 9.0	NM- 9.2
1-Uncle Sam, The Ray, Black Condor, Doll Man, Human Bomb, & Phantom Lady begin (all former Quality characters)	2	4	6	11	14	18
2-9: 4,5-Wonder Woman x-over. 7-1st app. Crusaders	1	3	4	6	8	10
10-15: 10-Origin Doll Man; Cat-Man-c/story (4th app; 1st revival since Detective #325). 11-Origin The Ray. 12-Origin Firebrand. 13-Origin Black Condor. 14-Batgirl & Batwoman app. 15-Batgirl & Batwoman app.; origin Phantom Lady	2	4	6	8	10	12

NOTE: ***Buckler** c-5-11p, 13p, 14p.*

FREEMIND
Future Comics: No. 0, Aug, 2002; Nov, 2002 - No. 7, June, 2003 ($3.50)

	GD 2.0	VG 4.0	FN 6.0	VF 8.0	VF/NM 9.0	NM- 9.2
0-($2.25) Giordano-c						2.25
0-($2.25) Variant-c by Layton						2.25
1-7 ($3.50) 1-Two covers by Giordano & Layton; Giordano-a thru #3. 4,5-Leeke-a						3.50

FREE SPEECHES
Oni Press: Aug, 1998 ($2.95, one-shot)

	GD 2.0	VG 4.0	FN 6.0	VF 8.0	VF/NM 9.0	NM- 9.2
1-Speeches against comic censorship; Frank Miller-c						3.00

FREEX
Malibu Comics (Ultraverse): July, 1993 - No. 18, Mar, 1995 ($1.95)

	GD 2.0	VG 4.0	FN 6.0	VF 8.0	VF/NM 9.0	NM- 9.2
1-3,5-14,16-18: 1-Polybagged w/trading card. 2-Some were polybagged w/card. 6-Nightman-c/story. 7-2 pg. origin Hardcase by Zeck. 17-Rune app.						2.25
1-Holographic-c edition						6.00
1-Ultra 5,000 limited silver ink-c						3.00
4-($2.50, 48 pgs.)-Rune flip-c/story by B. Smith (3 pgs.); 3 pg. Night Man preview						2.50
15 ($3.50)-w/Ultraverse Premiere #9 flip book; Alec Swan & Rafferty app.						3.50
Giant Size 1 (1994, $2.50)-Prime app.						2.50

NOTE: ***Simonson** c-1.*

FRENZY (Magazine) (Satire)
Picture Magazine: Apr, 1958 - No. 6, Mar, 1959

	GD 2.0	VG 4.0	FN 6.0	VF 8.0	VF/NM 9.0	NM- 9.2
1	10	20	30	60	80	100
2-6	7	14	21	37	46	55

FRIDAY FOSTER
Dell Publishing Co.: October, 1972

	GD 2.0	VG 4.0	FN 6.0	VF 8.0	VF/NM 9.0	NM- 9.2
1	3	7	10	23	29	38

FRIENDLY GHOST, CASPER, THE (Becomes Casper... #254 on)
Harvey Publications: Aug, 1958 - No. 224, Oct, 1982; No. 225, Oct, 1986 - No. 253, June, 1990

	GD 2.0	VG 4.0	FN 6.0	VF 8.0	VF/NM 9.0	NM- 9.2
1-Infinity-c	31	62	93	228	339	450
2	15	30	45	104	152	200
3-10: 6-X-Mas-c	8	16	24	55	78	100
11-20: 18-X-Mas-c	6	12	18	40	55	70
21-30	4	8	12	27	36	45
31-50	3	7	10	21	28	35
51-70,100: 54-X-Mas-c	3	6	9	18	24	30
71-99	3	6	9	16	20	24
101-131: 131-Last 12¢ issue	2	4	6	14	18	22
132-159	2	4	6	11	14	18
160-163: All 52 pg. Giants	3	6	9	16	20	24
164-199: 173,179,185-Cub Scout Specials	1	3	4	6	8	10
200	2	4	6	8	10	12
201-224	1	2	3	5	6	8
225-237: 230-X-mas-c. 232-Valentine's-c						5.00
238-253: 238-Begin $1.00-c. 238,244-Halloween-c. 243-Last new material						4.00

FRIENDS OF MAXX (Also see Maxx)
Image Comics (I Before E): Apr, 1996 ($2.95)

	GD 2.0	VG 4.0	FN 6.0	VF 8.0	VF/NM 9.0	NM- 9.2
1-Featuring Dude Japan; Sam Kieth-c/a/scripts						3.00

FRIGHT
Atlas/Seaboard Periodicals: June, 1975 (Aug on inside)

	GD 2.0	VG 4.0	FN 6.0	VF 8.0	VF/NM 9.0	NM- 9.2
1-Origin/1st app. The Son of Dracula; Frank Thorne-c/a	1	2	3	5	7	9

FRIGHT NIGHT
Now Comics: Oct, 1988 - No. 22, 1990 ($1.75)

	GD 2.0	VG 4.0	FN 6.0	VF 8.0	VF/NM 9.0	NM- 9.2
1-22: 1,2 Adapts movie. 8, 9-Evil Ed horror photo-c from movie						2.25

FRIGHT NIGHT II
Now Comics: 1989 ($3.95, 52 pgs.)

	GD 2.0	VG 4.0	FN 6.0	VF 8.0	VF/NM 9.0	NM- 9.2
1-Adapts movie sequel						4.00

FRISKY ANIMALS (Formerly Frisky Fables; Super Cat #56 on)
Star Publications: No. 44, Jan, 1951 - No. 55, Sept, 1953

	GD 2.0	VG 4.0	FN 6.0	VF 8.0	VF/NM 9.0	NM- 9.2
44-Super Cat; L.B. Cole	24	48	72	135	190	245
45-Classic L. B. Cole-c	34	68	102	196	278	360
46-51,53-55: Super Cat. 54-Super Cat-c begin	22	44	66	127	176	225
52-L. B. Cole-c/a, 3 1/2 pgs.; X-Mas-c	24	48	72	135	190	245

NOTE: *All have **L. B. Cole**-c. No. 47-No Super Cat. **Disbrow** a-49, 52. **Fago** a-51.*

FRISKY ANIMALS ON PARADE (Formerly Parade Comics; becomes Superspook)
Ajax-Farrell Publ. (Four Star Comic Corp.): Sept, 1957 - No. 3, Dec-Jan, 1957-1958

	GD 2.0	VG 4.0	FN 6.0	VF 8.0	VF/NM 9.0	NM- 9.2
1-L. B. Cole-c	20	40	60	112	156	200
2-No L. B. Cole-c	9	18	27	52	66	80
3-L. B. Cole-c	17	34	51	98	134	170

FRISKY FABLES (Frisky Animals No. 44 on)
Premium Group/Novelty Publ./Star Publ. V5#4 on: Spring, 1945 - No. 43, Oct, 1950

	GD 2.0	VG 4.0	FN 6.0	VF 8.0	VF/NM 9.0	NM- 9.2
V1#1-Funny animal; Al Fago-c/a #1-38	22	44	66	124	172	220
2,3(Fall & Winter, 1945)	11	22	33	63	84	105
V2#1(#4, 4/46) - 9,11,12(#15, 3/47): 4-Flag-c	9	18	27	52	66	80
10-Christmas-c	9	18	27	54	70	85
V3#1(#16, 4/47) - 12(#27, 3/48): 4-Flag-c. 7,9-Infinity-c. 10-X-Mas-c	8	16	24	43	54	65
V4#1(#28, 4/48) - 7(#34, 2-3/49)	8	16	24	40	50	60
V5#1(#35, 4-5/49) - 4(#38, 10-11/49)	8	16	24	40	50	60
39-43-L. B. Cole-c; 40-Xmas-c	24	48	72	135	190	245
Accepted Reprint No. 43 (nd); L.B. Cole-c	9	18	27	52	66	80

FRITZI RITZ (See Comics On Parade, Single Series #5, 1(reprint), Tip Top & United Comics)

FRITZI RITZ (United Comics No. 8-26) (Also see Tip Topper for early Peanuts by Schulz)
United Features Synd./St. John No. 37-55/Dell No. 56 on:
Fall, 1948; No. 3, 1949 - No. 7, 1949; No. 27, 3-4/53 - No. 36, 9-10/54; No. 37 - No. 55, 9-11/57; No. 56, 12-2/57-58 - No. 59, 9-11/58

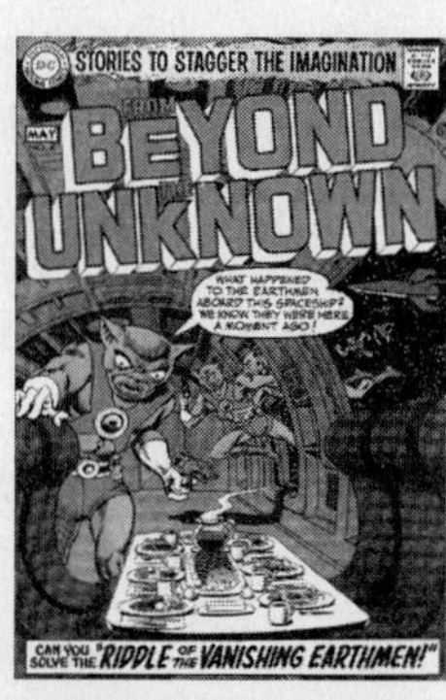

From Beyond the Unknown #4 © DC

From Hell #3
© Alan Moore & Eddie Campbell

Frontline Combat #3 © WMG

	GD 2.0	VG 4.0	FN 6.0	VF 8.0	VF/NM 9.0	NM- 9.2
nn(1948)-Special Fall issue; by Ernie Bushmiller	16	32	48	92	126	160
3(#1)	10	20	30	58	77	95
4-7(1949): 6-Abbie & Slats app.	8	16	24	46	58	70
27(1953)-33,37-50,57-59-Early Peanuts (1-4 pgs.) by Schulz. 29-Five pg. Abbie & Slats; 1 pg. Mamie by Russell Patterson. 38(9/55)-41(4/56)-Low print run	8	16	24	43	54	65
34-36,51-56: 36-1 pg. Mamie by Patterson	7	14	21	35	43	50

NOTE: *Abbie & Slats in #6,7, 27-31. Li'l Abner in #32-36.*

FROGMAN COMICS
Hillman Periodicals: Jan-Feb, 1952 - No. 11, May, 1953

	GD 2.0	VG 4.0	FN 6.0	VF 8.0	VF/NM 9.0	NM- 9.2
1	15	30	45	84	115	145
2	9	18	27	49	62	75
3,4,6-11: 4-Meskin-a	8	16	24	40	50	60
5-Krigstein-a	8	16	24	46	58	70

FROGMEN, THE
Dell Publishing Co.: No. 1258, Feb-Apr, 1962 - No. 11, Nov-Jan, 1964-65 (Painted-c)

	GD 2.0	VG 4.0	FN 6.0	VF 8.0	VF/NM 9.0	NM- 9.2
Four Color 1258(#1)-Evans-a	9	18	27	60	85	110
2,3-Evans-a; part Frazetta inks in #2,3	6	12	18	43	59	75
4,6-11	4	8	12	27	36	45
5-Toth-a	5	10	15	33	44	55

FROM BEYOND THE UNKNOWN
National Periodical Publications: 10-11/69 - No. 25, 11-12/73

	GD 2.0	VG 4.0	FN 6.0	VF 8.0	VF/NM 9.0	NM- 9.2
1	5	10	15	36	48	60
2-6	3	6	9	18	24	30
7-11: (64 pgs.) 7-Intro Col. Glenn Merrit	3	7	10	21	28	35
12-17: (52 pgs.) 13-Wood-a(i)(r). 17-Pres. Nixon-c	3	6	9	18	23	28
18-25: Star Rovers-r begin #18,19. Space Museum in #23-25	2	4	6	11	14	18

NOTE: ***N. Adams** c-3, 6, 8, 9. **Anderson** c-2, 4, 5, 10, 11i, 15-17, 22; reprints-3, 4, 6-8, 10, 11, 13-16, 24, 25. **Infantino** r-1-5, 7-19, 23-25; c-11p. **Kaluta** c-18, 19. **Gil Kane** a-9r. **Kubert** c-1, 7, 12-14. **Toth** a-2r. **Wood** a-13i. Photo c-22.*

FROM DUSK TILL DAWN (Movie)
Big Entertainment: 1996 ($4.95, one-shot)

	GD 2.0	VG 4.0	FN 6.0	VF 8.0	VF/NM 9.0	NM- 9.2
nn-Adaptation of the film; Brereton-c						5.00
nn-($9.95)Deluxe Ed. w/ new material						10.00

FROM HELL
Mad Love/Tundra Publishing/Kitchen Sink: 1991 - No. 11, Sept, 1998 (B&W)

	GD 2.0	VG 4.0	FN 6.0	VF 8.0	VF/NM 9.0	NM- 9.2
1-Alan Moore and Eddie Campbell's Jack The Ripper story collected from the Taboo anthology series	2	4	6	12	16	20
1-(2nd printing)	2	4	6	8	10	12
1-(3rd printing)	1	2	3	4	5	7
2	1	2	3	5	6	8
2-(2nd printing)						6.00
2-(3rd printing)						4.00
3-1st Kitchen Sink Press issue	1	2	3	5	6	8
3-(2nd printing)						5.00
4-10: 10-(8/96)	1	2	3	4	5	7
11-Dance of the Gull Catchers (9/98, $4.95) Epilogue	2	4	6	10	12	15
Tundra Publishing reprintings 1-5 ('92)	1	2	3	4	5	7
HC						125.00
HC Ltd. Edition of 1,000 (signed and numbered)						225.00
TPB-1st printing (11/99)						60.00
TPB-2nd printing (3/00)						50.00
TPB-3rd printing (11/00)						40.00
TPB-4th printing (7/01) Regular and movie covers						35.00
TPB-5th printing - Regular and movie covers						35.00

FROM HERE TO INSANITY (Satire) (Formerly Eh! #1-7) (See Frantic & Frenzy)
Charlton Comics: No. 8, Feb, 1955 - V3#1, 1956

	GD 2.0	VG 4.0	FN 6.0	VF 8.0	VF/NM 9.0	NM- 9.2
8	17	34	51	98	134	170
9	15	30	45	86	118	150
10-Ditko-c/a (3 pgs.)	24	48	72	135	190	245
11,12-All Kirby except 4 pgs.	33	66	99	190	270	350
V3#1(1956)-Ward-c/a(2) (signed McCartney); 5 pgs. Wolverton-a; 3 pgs. Ditko-a; magazine format (cover says "Crazy, Man, Crazy" and becomes Crazy, Man, Crazy with V2#2)	40	80	120	240	340	440

FROM THE PIT
Fantagor Press: 1994 ($4.95, one-shot, mature)

	GD 2.0	VG 4.0	FN 6.0	VF 8.0	VF/NM 9.0	NM- 9.2
1-R. Corben-a; HP Lovecraft back-up story	1	2	3	5	6	8

FRONTIER DOCTOR (TV)
Dell Publishing Co.: No. 877, Feb, 1958 (one-shot)

	GD 2.0	VG 4.0	FN 6.0	VF 8.0	VF/NM 9.0	NM- 9.2
Four Color 877-Toth-a, Rex Allen photo-c	11	22	33	75	110	145

FRONTIER FIGHTERS
National Periodical Publications: Sept-Oct, 1955 - No. 8, Nov-Dec, 1956

	GD 2.0	VG 4.0	FN 6.0	VF 8.0	VF/NM 9.0	NM- 9.2
1-Davy Crockett, Buffalo Bill (by Kubert), Kit Carson begin (Scarce)	56	112	168	350	525	700
2	40	80	120	240	345	450
3-8	39	78	117	230	325	420

NOTE: *Buffalo Bill by **Kubert** in all.*

FRONTIER ROMANCES
Avon Periodicals/I. W.: Nov-Dec, 1949 - No. 2, Feb-Mar, 1950 (Painted-c)

	GD 2.0	VG 4.0	FN 6.0	VF 8.0	VF/NM 9.0	NM- 9.2
1-Used in **SOTI**, pg. 180 (General reference) & illo. "Erotic spanking in a western comic book"	48	96	144	288	432	575
2 (Scarce)-Woodish-a by Stallman	39	78	117	230	325	420
I.W. Reprint #1-Reprints Avon's #1	4	8	12	27	36	45
I.W. Reprint #9-Reprints ?	3	6	9	18	23	28

FRONTIER SCOUT: DAN'L BOONE (Formerly Death Valley; The Masked Raider No. 14 on)
Charlton Comics: No. 10, Jan, 1956 - No. 13, Aug, 1956; V2#14, Mar, 1965

	GD 2.0	VG 4.0	FN 6.0	VF 8.0	VF/NM 9.0	NM- 9.2
10	10	20	30	56	73	90
11-13(1956)	6	12	18	31	38	45
V2#14(3/65)	5	10	14	20	24	28

FRONTIER TRAIL (The Rider No. 1-5)
Ajax/Farrell Publ.: No. 6, May, 1958

	GD 2.0	VG 4.0	FN 6.0	VF 8.0	VF/NM 9.0	NM- 9.2
6	6	12	18	28	34	40

FRONTIER WESTERN
Atlas Comics (PrPl): Feb, 1956 - No. 10, Aug, 1957

	GD 2.0	VG 4.0	FN 6.0	VF 8.0	VF/NM 9.0	NM- 9.2
1	20	40	60	112	156	200
2,3,6-Williamson-a, 4 pgs. each	14	28	42	79	107	135
4,7,9,10: 10-Check-a	9	18	27	52	66	80
5-Crandall, Baker, Davis-a; Williamson text illos	13	26	39	74	100	125
8-Crandall, Morrow, & Wildey-a	9	18	27	54	70	85

NOTE: ***Baker** a-9. **Colan** a-2, 6. **Drucker** a-3, 4. **Heath** c-5. **Maneely** c/a-2, 7, 9. **Maurera** a-2. **Romita** a-7. **Severin** c-6, 8, 10. **Tuska** a-2. **Wildey** a-5, 8. Ringo Kid in No. 4.*

FRONTLINE COMBAT
E. C. Comics: July-Aug, 1951 - No. 15, Jan, 1954

	GD 2.0	VG 4.0	FN 6.0	VF 8.0	VF/NM 9.0	NM- 9.2
1-Severin/Kurtzman-a	64	128	192	480	690	900
2	36	72	108	270	385	500
3	28	56	84	210	298	385
4-Used in **SOTI**, pg. 257; contains "Airburst" by Kurtzman which is his personal all-time favorite story	25	50	75	188	269	350
5	22	44	66	165	238	310
6-10	19	38	57	143	204	265
11-15	14	28	42	105	148	190

NOTE: ***Davis** a-in all; c-11, 12. **Evans** a-10-15. **Heath** a-1. **Kubert** a-14. **Kurtzman** a-1-5; c-1-9. **Severin** a-5-7, 9, 13, 15. **Severin/Elder** a-2-11; c-10. **Toth** a-8, 12. **Wood** a-1-4, 6-10, 12-15; c-13-15. Special issues: No. 7 (Iwo Jima), No. 9 (Civil War), No. 12 (Air Force).*

(Canadian reprints known; see Table of Contents.)

FRONTLINE COMBAT
Russ Cochran/Gemstone Publishing: Aug, 1995 - No. 14 ($2.00/$2.50)

	GD 2.0	VG 4.0	FN 6.0	VF 8.0	VF/NM 9.0	NM- 9.2
1-14-E.C. reprints in all						3.00

FRONT PAGE COMIC BOOK
Front Page Comics (Harvey): 1945

	GD 2.0	VG 4.0	FN 6.0	VF 8.0	VF/NM 9.0	NM- 9.2
1-Kubert-a; intro. & 1st app. Man in Black by Powell; Fuje-c	40	80	120	240	340	440

FROST AND FIRE (See DC Science Fiction Graphic Novel)

FROSTY THE SNOWMAN
Dell Publishing Co.: No. 359, Nov, 1951 - No. 1272, Dec-Feb?/1961-62

	GD 2.0	VG 4.0	FN 6.0	VF 8.0	VF/NM 9.0	NM- 9.2
Four Color 359 (#1)	10	20	30	70	100	130
Four Color 435,514,601,661	6	12	18	38	52	65
Four Color 748,861,950,1065,1153,1272	5	10	15	36	48	60

FRUITMAN SPECIAL
Harvey Publications: Dec, 1969 (68 pgs.)

	GD 2.0	VG 4.0	FN 6.0	VF 8.0	VF/NM 9.0	NM- 9.2
1-Funny super hero	4	8	12	22	30	38

F-TROOP (TV)
Dell Publishing Co.: Aug, 1966 - No. 7, Aug, 1967 (All have photo-c)

	GD 2.0	VG 4.0	FN 6.0	VF 8.0	VF/NM 9.0	NM- 9.2
1	10	20	30	73	107	140
2-7	6	12	18	43	59	75

FUGITIVES FROM JUSTICE

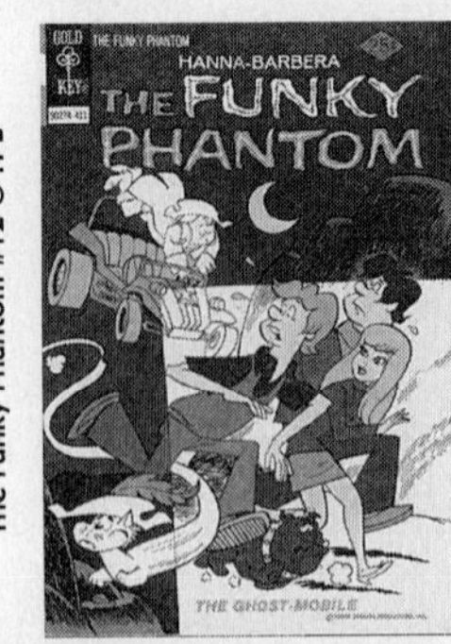

The Funky Phantom #12 © H-B

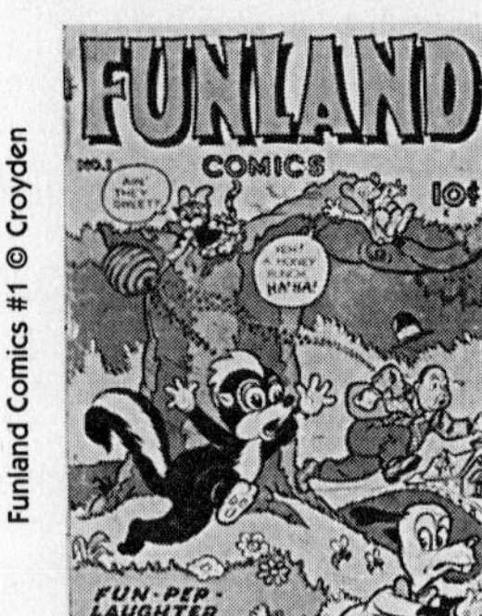

Funland Comics #1 © Croyden

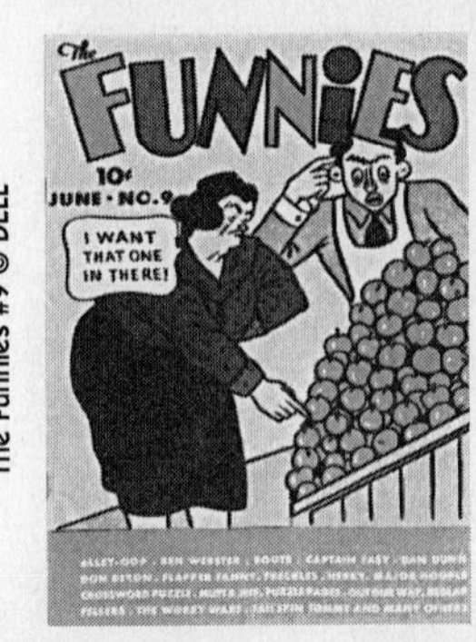

The Funnies #9 © DELL

GD VG FN VF VF/NM NM-
2.0 4.0 6.0 8.0 9.0 9.2

St. John Publishing Co.: Feb, 1952 - No. 5, Oct, 1952

1 22 44 66 124 172 220
2-Matt Baker-r/Northwest Mounties #2; Vic Flint strip reprints begin
22 44 66 124 172 220
3-Reprints panel from Authentic Police Cases that was used in **SOTI** with changes; Tuska-a
21 42 63 118 164 210
4 10 20 30 58 77 95
5-Last Vic Flint-r; bondage-c 12 24 36 69 92 115

FUGITOID
Mirage Studios: 1985 (B&W, magazine size, one-shot)

1-Ties into Teenage Mutant Ninja Turtles #5 6.00

FULL OF FUN
Red Top (Decker Publ.)(Farrell)/I. W. Enterprises: Aug, 1957 - No. 2, Nov, 1957; 1964

1(1957)-Funny animal; Dave Berg-a 7 14 21 37 46 55
2-Reprints Bingo, the Monkey Doodle Boy 5 10 15 22 26 30
8-I.W. Reprint('64) 2 4 6 10 12 15

FUN AT CHRISTMAS (See March of Comics No. 138)

FUN CLUB COMICS (See Interstate Theatres...)

FUN COMICS (Formerly Holiday Comics #1-8; Mighty Bear #13 on)
Star Publications: No. 9, Jan, 1953 - No. 12, Oct, 1953

9-(25¢ Giant)-L. B. Cole X-Mas-c; X-Mas issue 24 48 72 135 190 245
10-12-L. B. Cole-c. 12-Mighty Bear-c/story 20 40 60 112 156 200

FUNDAY FUNNIES (See Famous TV..., and Harvey Hits No. 35,40)

FUN-IN (TV)(Hanna-Barbera)
Gold Key: Feb, 1970 - No. 10, Jan, 1972; No. 11, 4/74 - No. 15, 12/74

1-Dastardly & Muttley in Their Flying Machines; Perils of Penelope Pitstop in #1-4;
It's the Wolf in all 7 14 21 50 68 85
2-4,6-Cattanooga Cats in 2-4 4 8 12 24 32 40
5,7-Motormouse & Autocat, Dastardly & Muttley in both; It's the Wolf in #7
4 8 12 27 36 45
8,10-The Harlem Globetrotters, Dastardly & Muttley in #10
4 8 12 27 36 45
9-Where's Huddles?, Dastardly & Muttley, Motormouse & Autocat app.
4 8 12 27 36 45
11-Butch Cassidy 3 6 9 21 28 35
12-15: 12,15-Speed Buggy. 13-Hair Bear Bunch. 14-Inch High Private Eye
3 6 9 21 28 35

FUNKY PHANTOM, THE (TV)
Gold Key: Mar, 1972 - No. 13, Mar, 1975 (Hanna-Barbera)

1 6 12 18 38 52 65
2-5 3 6 9 19 25 32
6-13 3 6 9 16 20 24

FUNLAND
Ziff-Davis (Approved Comics): No date (1940s) (25¢)

nn-Contains games, puzzles, cut-outs, etc. 19 38 57 106 146 185

FUNLAND COMICS
Croyden Publishers: 1945

1-Funny animal 16 32 48 92 126 160

FUNNIES, THE (New Funnies No. 65 on)
Dell Publishing Co.: Oct, 1936 - No. 64, May, 1942

1-Tailspin Tommy, Mutt & Jeff, Alley Oop (1st app?), Capt. Easy (1st app.), Don Dixon begin
360 720 1080 1980 2840 3700
2 (11/36)-Scribbly by Mayer begins (see Popular Comics #6 for 1st app.)
168 336 504 924 1300 1675
3 118 236 354 649 912 1175
4,5: 4(1/37)-Christmas-c 89 178 267 490 695 900
6-10 68 136 204 374 525 675
11-20: 16-Christmas-c 63 126 189 347 486 625
21-29: 25-Crime Busters by McWilliams(4pgs.) 50 100 150 275 388 500
30-John Carter of Mars (origin/1st app.) begins by Edgar Rice Burroughs;
Warner Bros.' Bosko-c (4/39) 132 264 396 825 1238 1650
31-44: 33-John Coleman Burroughs art begins on John Carter. 34-Last funny-c.
35-(9/39)-Mr. District Attorney begins; based on radio show; 1st cover app. John Carter
of Mars 76 152 228 475 713 950
45-Origin/1st app. Phantasmo, the Master of the World (Dell's 1st super-hero, 7/40) & his
sidekick Whizzer McGee 88 176 264 550 825 1100
46-50: 46-The Black Knight begins, ends #62 55 110 165 340 508 675
51-56-Last ERB John Carter of Mars 48 96 144 288 432 575
57-Intro. & origin Captain Midnight (7/41) 333 666 1000 2165 3333 4500
58-60: 58-Captain Midnight-c begin, end #63 96 192 288 600 900 1200
61-Andy Panda begins by Walter Lantz 84 168 252 525 788 1050
62,63: 63-Last Captain Midnight-c; bondage-c 66 132 198 413 619 825
64-Format change; Oswald the Rabbit, Felix the Cat, Li'l Eight Ball app.; origin & 1st app.
Woody Woodpecker in Oswald; last Capt. Midnight; Oswald, Andy Panda, Li'l Eight Ball-c
118 236 354 738 1107 1475

NOTE: ***Mayer** c-26, 48. **McWilliams** art in many issues on "Rex King of the Deep". Alley Oop c-17, 20. Captain Midnight c-57(i/2), 58-63. John Carter c-35-37, 40. Phantasmo c-45-56, 57(1/2), 58-61(part). Rex King c-38, 39, 42. Tailspin Tommy c-41.*

FUNNIES ANNUAL, THE
Avon Periodicals: 1959 ($1.00, approx. 7x10", B&W; tabloid-size)

1-(Rare)-Features the best newspaper comic strips of the year: Archie, Snuffy Smith, Beetle Bailey, Henry, Blondie, Steve Canyon, Buz Sawyer, The Little King, Hi & Lois, Popeye, & others. Also has a chronological history of the comics from 2000 B.C. to 1959.
44 88 132 264 395 525

FUNNIES ON PARADE (See Promotional Comics section)

FUNNY ANIMALS (See Fawcett's Funny Animals)
Charlton Comics: Sept, 1984 - No. 2, Nov, 1984

1,2-Atomic Mouse-r; low print 6.00

FUNNYBONE (... The Laugh-Book of Comical Comics)
La Salle Publishing Co.: 1944 (25¢, 132 pgs.)

nn 30 60 90 170 240 310

FUNNY BOOK (...Magazine for Young Folks) (Hocus Pocus No. 9)
Parents' Magazine Press (Funny Book Publishing Corp.):
Dec, 1942 - No. 9, Aug-Sept, 1946 (Comics, stories, puzzles, games)

1-Funny animal; Alice In Wonderland app. 15 30 45 86 118 150
2-Gulliver in Giant-Land 9 18 27 52 66 80
3-9: 4-Advs. of Robin Hood. 9-Hocus-Pocus strip 8 16 24 40 50 60

FUNNY COMICS
Modern Store Publ.: 1955 (7¢, 5x7", 36 pgs.)

1-Funny animal 4 8 12 27 36 45

FUNNY COMIC TUNES (See Funny Tunes)

FUNNY FABLES
Decker Publications (Red Top Comics): Aug, 1957 - V2#2, Nov, 1957

V1#1 6 12 18 31 38 45
V1#2,V2#1,2: V1#2 (11/57)-Reissue of V1#1 5 10 14 20 24 28

FUNNY FILMS (Features funny animal characters from films)
American Comics Group(Michel Publ./Titan Publ.): Sept-Oct, 1949 - No. 29, May-June, 1954 (No. 1-4: 52 pgs.)

1-Puss An' Boots, Blunderbunny begin 20 40 60 112 156 200
2 11 22 33 63 84 105
3-10: 3-X-Mas-c 8 16 24 46 58 70
11-20 6 12 18 31 38 45
21-29 5 10 15 24 30 35

FUNNY FOLKS (Hollywood... on cover only No. 16-26; becomes Hollywood Funny Folks No. 27 on)
National Periodical Publ.: April-May, 1946 - No. 26, June-July, 1950 (52 pgs., #16 on)

1-Nutsy Squirrel begins (1st app.) by Rube Grossman
40 80 120 240 340 440
2 20 40 60 112 156 200
3-5: 4-1st Nutsy Squirrel-c 15 30 45 84 115 145
6-10: 6,9-Nutsy Squirrel-c begin 11 22 33 63 84 105
11-26: 16-Begin 52 pg. issues (10-11/48) 10 20 30 56 73 90

NOTE: ***Sheldon Mayer** a-in some issues. **Post** a-18. Christmas c-12.*

FUNNY FROLICS
Timely/Marvel Comics (SPI): Summer, 1945 - No. 5, Dec, 1946

1-Sharpy Fox, Puffy Pig, Krazy Krow 24 48 72 135 190 245
2 13 26 39 74 100 125
3,4 10 20 30 56 73 90
5-Kurtzman-a 11 22 33 63 84 105

FUNNY FUNNIES
Nedor Publishing Co.: April, 1943 (68 pgs.)

1-Funny animals; Peter Porker app. 20 40 60 112 156 200

FUNNYMAN (Also see Cisco Kid Comics & Extra Comics)
Magazine Enterprises: Dec, 1947; No. 1, Jan, 1948 - No. 6, Aug, 1948

nn(12/47)-Prepublication B&W undistributed copy by Siegel & Shuster-(5-3/4x8"), 16 pgs.;

Funny Pages V2#8 © CEN

Fury V3#1 © MAR

Fury of Firestorrm #4 © DC

	GD 2.0	VG 4.0	FN 6.0	VF 8.0	VF/NM 9.0	NM- 9.2

Sold at auction in 1997 for $575.00
1-Siegel & Shuster-a in all; Dick Ayers 1st pro work (as assistant) on 1st few issues
46 92 138 276 413 550
2 29 58 87 164 232 300
3-6 24 48 72 135 190 245

FUNNY MOVIES (See 3-D Funny Movies)

FUNNY PAGES (Formerly The Comics Magazine)
Comics Magazine Co./Ultem Publ.(Chesler)/Centaur Publications:
No. 6, Nov, 1936 - No. 42, Oct, 1940

V1#6 (nn, nd)-The Clock begins (2 pgs., 1st app.), ends #11; The Clock is the 1st masked comic book hero 228 456 684 1425 2138 2850
7-11 88 176 264 550 825 1100
V2#1-V2#3: V2#1 (9/37)(V2#2 on-c; V2#1 in indicia). V2#2 (10/37)(V2#3 on-c; V2#2 in indicia). V2#3(11/37)-5 62 124 186 388 582 775
6(1st Centaur, 3/38) 88 176 264 550 825 1100
7-9 63 126 189 394 590 785
10(Scarce, 9/38)-1st app. of The Arrow by Gustavson (Blue costume)
300 600 900 1925 2963 4000
11,12 116 232 348 725 1088 1450
V3#1-Bruce Wayne prototype in "Case of the Missing Heir," by Bob Kane, 3 months before app. Batman (See Det. Pic. Stories #5) 120 240 360 750 1125 1500
2-6,8: 6,8-Last funny covers 107 214 321 669 1005 1340
7-1st Arrow-c (9/39) 232 464 696 1450 2175 2900
9-Tarpe Mills jungle-c 112 224 336 700 1050 1400
10-2nd Arrow-c 180 360 540 1125 1688 2250
V4#1(1/40, Arrow-c)-(Rare)-The Owl & The Phantom Rider app.; origin Mantoka, Maker of Magic by Jack Cole. Mad Ming begins, ends #42; Tarpe Mills-a
232 464 696 1450 2175 2900
35-Classic Arrow-c 232 464 696 1450 2175 2900
36-38-Mad Ming-c 109 218 327 681 1021 1360
39-41-Arrow-c 172 344 516 1075 1613 2150
42 (Scarce,10/40)-Last Arrow; Arrow-c 180 360 540 1125 1688 2250
NOTE: ***Biro*** *c-V2#9.* ***Burgos*** *c-V3#10.* ***Jack Cole*** *a-V2#3, 7, 8, 10, 11, V3#2, 6, 9, 10, V4#1, 37; c-V3#2, 4.* ***Eisner*** *a-V1#7, 8?, 10.* ***Ken Ernst*** *a-V1#7, 8.* ***Everett*** *a-V2#11 (illos).* ***Filchock*** *c-V2#10, V3#6.* ***Gill Fox*** *a-V2#11.* ***Sid Greene*** *a-39.* ***Guardineer*** *a-V2#2, 3, 5.* ***Gustavson*** *a-V2#5, 11, 12, V3#1-10, 35, 38-42; c-V3#7, 35, 39-42.* ***Bob Kane*** *a-V3#1.* ***McWilliams*** *a-V2#12, V3#1, 3-6.* ***Tarpe Mills*** *a-V3#8-10, V4#1; c-V3#9.* ***Ed Moore Jr.*** *a-V2#12.* ***Schwab*** *c-V3#1.* ***Bob Wood*** *a-V2#2, 3, 8, 11, V3#6, 9, 10; c-V2#6, 7. Arrow c-V3#7, 10, V4#1, 35, 40-42.*

FUNNY PICTURE STORIES (Comic Pages V3#4 on)
Comics Magazine Co./Centaur Publications: Nov, 1936 - V3#3, May, 1939

V1#1-The Clock begins (c-feature)(see Funny Pages for 1st app.)
319 638 957 2074 3187 4300
2 116 232 348 725 1088 1450
3-7(6/37): 4-Eisner-a; X-Mas-c. 7-Racial humor-c 78 156 234 488 732 975
V2#1 (9/37; V1#10 on-c; V2#1 in indicia)-Jack Strand begins
55 110 165 330 495 660
2 (10/37; V1#11 on-c; V2#2 in indicia) 55 110 165 330 495 660
3-5,7-11(11/38): 4-Xmas-c 46 92 138 276 413 550
6-(1st Centaur, 3/38) 78 156 234 488 732 975
V3#1(1/39)-3 44 88 132 264 395 525
NOTE: ***Biro*** *c-V2#1, 8, 9, 11.* ***Guardineer*** *a-V1#11; c-V2#6, V3#5.* ***Bob Wood*** *c/a-V1#11, V2#2; c-V2#3, 5.*

FUNNY STUFF (Becomes The Dodo & the Frog No. 80)
All-American/National Periodical Publications No. 7 on: Summer, 1944 - No. 79, July-Aug, 1954 (#1-7 are quarterly)

1-The Three Mouseketeers (ends #28) & The "Terrific Whatzit" begin; Sheldon Mayer-a 88 176 264 550 825 1100
2-Sheldon Mayer-a 42 84 126 252 376 500
3-5: 3-Flash parody. 5-All Mayer-a/scripts issue 31 62 93 175 248 320
6-10 10-(6/46) 21 42 63 118 164 210
11-17,19 16 32 48 92 126 160
18-The Dodo & the Frog (2/47, 1st app?) begin?; X-Mas-c
28 56 84 159 225 290
19-1st Dodo & the Frog-c (3/47) 19 38 57 106 146 185
20-2nd Dodo & the Frog-c (4/47) 13 26 39 76 103 130
21,23-30: 24-Infinity-c 10 20 30 60 80 100
22-Superman cameo 40 80 120 240 340 440
31-79: 70-1st Bo Bunny by Mayer & begins 9 18 27 54 70 85
NOTE: ***Mayer*** *a-1-8, 55, ,57, 58, 61, 62, 64, 65, 68, 70, 72, 74-79; c-2, 5, 6, 8.*

FUNNY STUFF STOCKING STUFFER
DC Comics: Mar, 1985 ($1.25, 52 pgs.)

1-Almost every DC funny animal featured 3.00

FUNNY 3-D
Harvey Publications: December, 1953 (25¢, came with 2 pair of glasses)

	GD 2.0	VG 4.0	FN 6.0	VF 8.0	VF/NM 9.0	NM- 9.2

1-Shows cover in 3-D on inside 12 24 36 69 92 115

FUNNY TUNES (Animated Funny Comic Tunes No. 16-22; Funny Comic Tunes No. 23, on covers only; formerly Krazy Komics #15; Oscar No. 24 on)
U.S.A. Comics Magazine Corp. (Timely): No. 16, Summer, 1944 - No. 23, Fall, 1946

16-Silly Seal, Ziggy Pig, Krazy Krow begin 15 30 45 86 118 150
17 (Fall/44)-Becomes Gay Comics #18 on? 12 24 36 69 92 115
18-22: 21-Super Rabbit app. 10 20 30 56 73 90
23-Kurtzman-a 11 22 33 63 84 105

FUNNY TUNES (Becomes Space Comics #4 on)
Avon Periodicals: July, 1953 - No. 3, Dec-Jan, 1953-54

1-Space Mouse, Peter Rabbit, Merry Mouse, Spotty the Pup, Cicero the Cat begin; all continue in Space Comics 11 22 33 63 84 105
2,3 8 16 24 46 58 70

FUNNY WORLD
Marbak Press: 1947 - No. 3, 1948

1-The Berrys, The Toodles & other strip-r begin 8 16 24 46 58 70
2,3 6 12 18 31 38 45

FUNTASTIC WORLD OF HANNA-BARBERA, THE (TV)
Marvel Comics Group: Dec, 1977 - No. 3, June, 1978 ($1.25, oversized)

1-3: 1-The Flintstones Christmas Party(12/77). 2-Yogi Bear's Easter Parade(3/78). 3-Laff-a-lympics(6/78) 4 8 12 29 40 50

FUN TIME
Ace Periodicals: Spring, 1953; No. 2, Sum, 1953; No. 3(nn), Fall, 1953; No. 4, Wint, 1953-54

1-(25¢, 100 pgs.)-Funny animal 18 36 54 104 142 180
2-4 (All 25¢, 100 pgs.) 15 30 45 84 115 145

FUN WITH SANTA CLAUS (See March of Comics No. 11, 108, 325)

FURTHER ADVENTURES OF CYCLOPS AND PHOENIX (Also see Adventures of Cyclops and Phoenix, Uncanny X-Men & X-Men)
Marvel Comics: June, 1996 - No. 4, Sept, 1996 ($1.95, limited series)

1-4: Origin of Mr. Sinister; Milligan scripts; John Paul Leon-c/a(p). 2-4-Apocalypse app. 3.00
Trade Paperback (1997, $14.99) r/1-4 15.00

FURTHER ADVENTURES OF INDIANA JONES, THE (Movie) (Also see Indiana Jones and the Last Crusade & Indiana Jones and the Temple of Doom)
Marvel Comics Group: Jan, 1983 - No. 34, Mar, 1986

1-Byrne/Austin-a; Austin-c 4.00
2-34: 2-Byrne/Austin-c/a 2.50
NOTE: ***Austin*** *a-1i, 2i, 6i, 9i; c-1, 2i, 6i, 9i.* ***Byrne*** *a-1p, 2p; c-2p.* ***Chaykin*** *a-6p; c-6p, 8p-10p.* ***Ditko*** *a-21p, 25-28, 34.* ***Golden*** *c-24, 25.* ***Simonson*** *c-9. Painted c-14.*

FURTHER ADVENTURES OF NYOKA, THE JUNGLE GIRL, THE (See Nyoka)
AC Comics: 1988 - No. 5, 1989 ($1.95, color; $2.25/$2.50, B&W)

1-5 : 1,2-Bill Black-a plus reprints. 3-Photo-c. 5-(B&W)-Reprints plus movie photos 2.50

FURY (Straight Arrow's Horse...) (See A-1 No. 119)

FURY (TV) (See March Of Comics #200)
Dell Publishing Co./Gold Key: No. 781, Mar, 1957 - Nov, 1962 (All photo-c)

Four Color 781 9 18 27 60 85 110
Four Color 885,975,1031,1080,1133,1172,1218,1296 8 16 24 53 74 95
01292-208(#1-'62), 10020-211(11/62-G.K.) 7 14 21 51 71 90

FURY
Marvel Comics: May, 1994 ($2.95, one-shot)

1-Iron Man, Red Skull, FF, Hatemonger, Logan app.; Origin Nick Fury 3.00

FURY (Volume 3)
Marvel Comics (MAX): Nov, 2001 - No. 6, Apr, 2002 ($2.99, mature content)

1-6-Ennis-s/Robertson-a 3.00

FURY/ AGENT 13
Marvel Comics: June, 1998 - No. 2, July, 1998 ($2.99, limited series)

1,2-Nick Fury returns 3.00

FURY OF FIRESTORM, THE (Becomes Firestorm The Nuclear Man on cover with #50, in indicia with #65) (Also see Firestorm)
DC Comics: June, 1982 - No. 64, Oct, 1987 (75¢ on)

1-Intro The Black Bison; brief origin 6.00
2-40,43-64: 4-JLA x-over. 17-1st app. Firehawk. 21-Death of Killer Frost. 22-Origin. 23-Intro. Byte. 24-(6/84)-1st app. Blue Devil & Bug (origin); origin Byte. 34-1st app./origin Killer Frost II. 39-Weasel's ID revealed. 48-Intro. Moonbow. 53-Origin/1st app. Silver Shade. 55,56-Legends x-over. 58-1st app./origin new Parasite 2.50
41,42-Crisis x-over 3.00

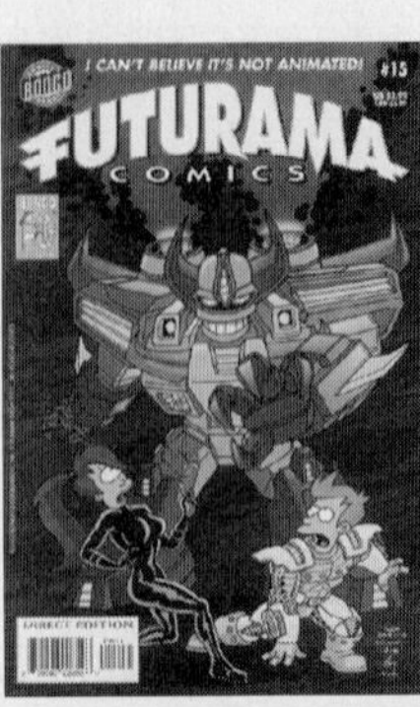

Futurama Comics #15 © Bongo

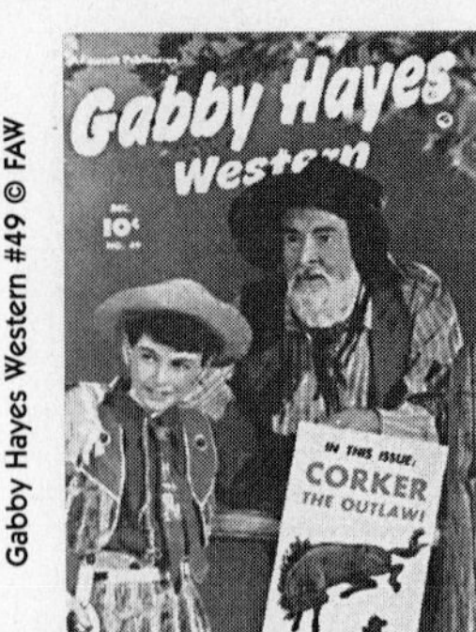

Gabby Hayes Western #49 © FAW

Gambit #2 © MAR

	GD 2.0	VG 4.0	FN 6.0	VF 8.0	VF/NM 9.0	NM- 9.2
61-Test cover variant; Superman logo	3	7	10	21	28	35
Annual 1-4: 1(1983), 2(1984), 3(1985), 4(1986)						3.00

NOTE: ***Colan** a-19p, Annual 4p. **Giffen** a-Annual 4p. **Gil Kane** c-30. **Nino** a-37. **Tuska** a-(p)-17, 18, 32, 45.*

FURY OF SHIELD
Marvel Comics: Apr, 1995 - No. 4, July, 1995 ($2.50/$1.95, limited series)

1 ($2.50)-Foil-c						3.00
2-4: 4-Bagged w/ decoder						2.50

FUSED
Image Comics: Mar, 2002 - Present ($2.95)

1-4-Steve Niles-s. 1,2-Paul Lee-a. 3-Brad Rader-a. 4-Templesmith-a — 3.00

FUSION
Eclipse Comics: Jan, 1987 - No. 17, Oct, 1989 ($2.00, B&W, Baxter paper)

1-17: 11-The Weasel Patrol begins (1st app.?) — 2.25

FUTURAMA (TV)
Bongo Comics: 2000 - Present ($2.50, bi-monthly)

1-Based on the FOX-TV animated series; Groening/Morrison-c						3.50
1-San Diego Comic-Con Premiere Edition						5.00
2-15: 8-CGC cover spoof; X-Men parody						3.00
Futurama-O-Rama TPB (2002, $12.95) r/#1-4; sketch pages of Fry's development						13.00

FUTURAMA/SIMPSONS INFINITELY SECRET CROSSOVER CRISIS (TV)
Bongo Comics: 2002 - No. 2, 2002 ($2.50, limited series)

1,2-Evil Brain Spawns put Futurama crew into the Simpsons' Springfield — 2.50

FUTURE COMICS
David McKay Publications: June, 1940 - No. 4, Sept, 1940

1-(6/40, 64 pgs.)-Origin The Phantom (1st in comics) (4 pgs.); The Lone Ranger (8 pgs.) & Saturn Against the Earth (4 pgs.) begin	264	528	792	1650	2475	3300
2	124	248	372	775	1163	1550
3,4	100	200	300	625	938	1250

FUTURE COP L.A.P.D. (Electronic Arts video game) (Also see PromotionalComics section)
DC Comics (WildStorm): Jan, 1999 ($4.95, magazine sized)

1-Stories & art by various — 5.00

FUTURETECH
Mushroom Comics: Jan, 1996 ($2.50, limited series)

1-Flipbook w/SWARM — 2.50

FUTURE WORLD COMICS
George W. Dougherty: Summer, 1946 - No. 2, Fall, 1946

1,2: H. C. Kiefer-c; preview of the World of Tomorrow	33	66	99	190	270	350

FUTURE WORLD COMIX (Warren Presents...)
Warren Publications: Sept, 1978 (B&W magazine, 84 pgs.)

1-Corben, Maroto, Morrow, Nino, Sutton-a; Todd-c/a; contains nudity panels	2	4	6	8	10	12

FUTURIANS, THE (See Marvel Graphic Novel #9)
Lodestone Publishing/Eternity Comics: Sept, 1985 - No. 3, 1985 ($1.50)

1-3: Indicia title "Dave Cockrum's..."						2.25
Graphic Novel 1 ($9.95, Eternity)-r/#1-3, plus never published #4 issue						10.00

G-8 (Listed at G-Eight)

GABBY (Formerly Ken Shannon) (Teen humor)
Quality Comics Group: No. 11, Jul, 1953; No. 2, Sep, 1953 - No. 9, Sep, 1954

11(#1)(7/53)	8	16	24	46	58	70
2	6	12	18	28	34	40
3-9	5	10	15	23	28	32

GABBY GOB (See Harvey Hits No. 85, 90, 94, 97, 100, 103, 106, 109)

GABBY HAYES ADVENTURE COMICS
Toby Press: Dec, 1953

1-Photo-c	16	32	48	89	122	155

GABBY HAYES WESTERN (Movie star)(See Monte Hale, Real Western Hero & Western Hero)
Fawcett Publications/Charlton Comics No. 51 on: Nov, 1948 - No. 50, Jan, 1953; No. 51, Dec, 1954 - No. 59, Jan, 1957

1-Gabby & his horse Corker begin; photo front/back-c begin	50	100	150	300	450	600
2	26	52	78	150	210	270
3-5	19	38	57	106	146	185
6-10: 9-Young Falcon begins	15	30	45	86	118	150
11-20: 19-Last photo back-c	12	24	36	71	96	120
21-49: 20,22,24,26,28,29-(52 pgs.)	10	20	30	56	73	90
50-(1/53)-Last Fawcett issue; last photo-c?	11	22	33	63	84	105
51-(12/54)-1st Charlton issue; photo-c	11	22	33	66	88	110
52-59(1955-57): 53,55-Photo-c. 58-Swayze-a	8	16	24	43	54	65

GAGS
United Features Synd./Triangle Publ. No. 9 on: Jul, 1937 - V3#10, Oct, 1944 (13-3/4x10-3/4")

1(7/37)-52 pgs.; 20 pgs. Grin & Bear It, Fellow Citizen	9	18	27	52	66	80
V1#9 (36 pgs.) (7/42)	6	12	18	28	34	40
V3#10	5	10	15	24	30	35

GALACTIC
Dark Horse Comics: Aug, 2003 - Present ($2.99)

1-3-Krueger-s/Greene-a/Pearson-c — 3.00

GALACTICA: THE NEW MILLENNIUM
Realm Press: Sept, 1999 ($2.99)

1-Stories by Shooter, Braden, Kuhoric — 3.00

GALACTIC GUARDIANS
Marvel Comics: July, 1994 - No. 4, Oct, 1994 ($1.50, limited series)

1-4 — 2.25

GALACTIC WARS COMIX (Warren Presents... on cover)
Warren Publications: Dec, 1978 (B&W magazine, 84 pgs.)

nn-Wood, Williamson-r; Battlestar Galactica/Flash Gordon photo/text stories	2	4	6	8	10	12

GALACTUS THE DEVOURER
Marvel Comics: Sept, 1999 - No. 6, Mar, 2000 ($3.50/$2.50, limited series)

1-($3.50) L. Simonson-s/Muth & Sienkiewicz-a						3.50
2-5-($2.50) Buscema & Sienkiewicz-a						2.50
6-($3.50) Death of Galactus; Buscema & Sienkiewicz-a						3.50

GALAXIA (Magazine)
Astral Publ.: 1981 ($2.50, B&W, 52 pgs.)

1-Buckler/Giordano-c; Texeira/Guice-a; 1st app. Astron, Sojourner, Bloodwing, Warlords; Buckler-s/a	1	3	4	6	8	10

GALLANT MEN, THE (TV)
Gold Key: Oct, 1963 (Photo-c)

1(1008-310)-Manning-a	3	7	10	21	28	35

GALLEGHER, BOY REPORTER (Disney, TV)
Gold Key: May, 1965

1(10149-505)-Photo-c	3	6	9	18	23	28

GAMBIT (See X-Men #266 & X-Men Annual #14)
Marvel Comics: Dec, 1993 - No. 4, Mar, 1994 ($2.00, limited series)

1-($2.50)-Lee Weeks-c/a in all; gold foil stamped-c.						5.00
1 (Gold)	2	4	6	10	12	15
2-4						3.00

GAMBIT
Marvel Comics: Sept, 1997 - No. 4, Dec, 1997 ($2.50, limited series)

1-4-Janson-a/ Mackie & Kavanagh-s — 3.00

GAMBIT
Marvel Comics: Feb, 1999 - No. 25, Feb, 2001 ($2.99/$1.99)

1-($2.99) Five covers; Nicieza-a/Skroce-a						4.00
2-11,13-16-($1.99): 2-Two covers (Skroce & Adam Kubert)						2.50
12-($2.99)						3.50
17-24: 17-Begin $2.25-c. 21-Mystique-c/app.						2.25
25-($2.99) Leads into "Gambit & Bishop"						3.00
...1999 Annual ($3.50) Nicieza-s/McDaniel-a						3.50
...2000 Annual ($3.50) Nicieza-s/Derenick & Smith-a						3.50

GAMBIT & BISHOP (... : Sons of the Atom on cover)
Marvel Comics: Feb, 2001 - No. 6, May, 2001 ($2.25, bi-weekly limited series)

Alpha (2/01) Prelude to series; Nord-a						2.25
1-6-Jeanty-a/Williams-c						2.25
Genesis (3/01, $3.50) reprints their first apps. and first meeting						3.50

GAMBIT AND THE X-TERNALS
Marvel Comics: Mar, 1995 - No. 4, July, 1995 ($1.95, limited series)

1-4-Age of Apocalypse — 2.50

GAMEBOY (Super Mario covers on all)

Gang Busters #12 © DC

Garrison's Gorillas #2 © DELL

Gay Comics #27 © MAR

Valiant: 1990 - No. 5 ($1.95, coated-c)

	GD 2.0	VG 4.0	FN 6.0	VF 8.0	VF/NM 9.0	NM- 9.2
1-5: 3,4-Layton-c. 4-Morrow-a. 5-Layton-c(i)						4.00

GAMERA
Dark Horse Comics: Aug, 1996 - No. 4, Nov, 1996 ($2.95, limited series)

	GD 2.0	VG 4.0	FN 6.0	VF 8.0	VF/NM 9.0	NM- 9.2
1-4						3.00

GAMMARAUDERS
DC Comics: Jan, 1989 - No. 10, Dec, 1989 ($1.25/$1.50/$2.00)

	GD 2.0	VG 4.0	FN 6.0	VF 8.0	VF/NM 9.0	NM- 9.2
1-10-Based on TSR game						2.25

GAMORRA SWIMSUIT SPECIAL
Image Comics (WildStorm Productions): June, 1996 ($2.50, one-shot)

	GD 2.0	VG 4.0	FN 6.0	VF 8.0	VF/NM 9.0	NM- 9.2
1-Campbell wraparound-c; pinups						2.50

GANDY GOOSE (Movies/TV)(See All Surprise, Giant Comics Edition #5A &10, Paul Terry's Comics & Terry-Toons)
St. John Publ. Co./Pines No. 5,6: Mar, 1953 - No. 5, Nov, 1953; No. 5, Fall, 1956 - No. 6, Sum/58

	GD 2.0	VG 4.0	FN 6.0	VF 8.0	VF/NM 9.0	NM- 9.2
1-All St. John issues are pre-code	10	20	30	56	73	90
2	6	12	18	31	38	45
3-5(1953)(St. John)	6	12	18	28	34	40
5,6(1956-58)(Pines)-CBS Television Presents...	5	10	15	22	26	30

GANG BUSTERS (See Popular Comics #38)
David McKay/Dell Publishing Co.: 1938 - 1943

	GD 2.0	VG 4.0	FN 6.0	VF 8.0	VF/NM 9.0	NM- 9.2
Feature Books 17(McKay)('38)-1st app.	52	104	156	384	580	775
Large Feature Comic 10('39)-(Scarce)	52	104	156	384	580	775
Large Feature Comic 17('41)	33	66	99	248	374	500
Four Color 7(1940)	36	72	108	270	405	540
Four Color 23,24('42-43)	30	60	90	218	319	420

GANG BUSTERS (Radio/TV)(Gangbusters #14 on)
National Periodical Publ.: Dec-Jan, 1947-48 - No. 67, Dec-Jan, 1958-59 (No. 1-23: 52 pgs.)

	GD 2.0	VG 4.0	FN 6.0	VF 8.0	VF/NM 9.0	NM- 9.2
1	88	176	264	550	825	1100
2	40	80	120	240	358	475
3-5	33	66	99	190	270	350
6-10: 9-Dan Barry-a. 9,10-Photo-c	25	50	75	147	202	260
11-13-Photo-c	21	42	63	118	164	210
14,17-Frazetta-a, 8 pgs. each. 14-Photo-c	40	80	120	240	340	440
15,16,18-20,26: 26-Kirby-a	16	32	48	92	126	160
21-25,27-30	14	28	42	79	107	135
31-44: 44-Last Pre-code (2-3/55)	12	24	36	69	92	115
45-67	10	20	30	56	73	90

NOTE: ***Barry** a-6, 8, 10. **Drucker** a-51. **Moreira** a-48, 50, 59. **Roussos** a-8.*

GANGLAND
DC Comics (Vertigo): Jun, 1998 - No. 4, Sept, 1998 ($2.95, limited series)

	GD 2.0	VG 4.0	FN 6.0	VF 8.0	VF/NM 9.0	NM- 9.2
1-4:Crime anthology by various. 2-Corben-a						3.00
TPB-(2000, $12.95) r/#1-4; Bradstreet-c						13.00

GANGSTERS AND GUN MOLLS
Avon Per./Realistic Comics: Sept, 1951 - No. 4, June, 1952 (Painted c-1-3)

	GD 2.0	VG 4.0	FN 6.0	VF 8.0	VF/NM 9.0	NM- 9.2
1-Wood-a, 1 pg; c-/Avon paperback #292	48	96	144	288	432	575
2-Check-a, 8 pgs.; Kamen-a; Bonnie Parker story	40	80	120	240	340	440
3-Marijuana mentioned; used in **POP**, pg. 84,85	37	74	111	212	301	390
4-Syd Shores-c	29	58	87	164	232	300

GANGSTERS CAN'T WIN
D. S. Publishing Co.: Feb-Mar, 1948 - No. 9, June-July, 1949 (All 52 pgs?)

	GD 2.0	VG 4.0	FN 6.0	VF 8.0	VF/NM 9.0	NM- 9.2
1-True crime stories	35	70	105	201	288	370
2	18	36	54	104	142	180
3,5,6	16	32	48	92	126	160
4-Acid in face story	20	40	60	112	156	200
7-9	12	24	36	71	96	120

NOTE: ***Ingles** a-5, 6. **McWilliams** a-5, 7. **Reinman** c-6.*

GANG WORLD
Standard Comics: No. 5, Nov, 1952 - No. 6, Jan, 1953

	GD 2.0	VG 4.0	FN 6.0	VF 8.0	VF/NM 9.0	NM- 9.2
5-Bondage-c	20	40	60	112	156	200
6	15	30	45	84	115	145

GARGOYLE (See The Defenders #94)
Marvel Comics Group: June, 1985 - No. 4, Sept, 1985 (75¢, limited series)

	GD 2.0	VG 4.0	FN 6.0	VF 8.0	VF/NM 9.0	NM- 9.2
1-Wrightson-c; character from Defenders						3.50
2-4						2.50

GARGOYLES (TV cartoon)
Marvel Comics: Feb, 1995 - No. 17, June, 1996 ($2.50)

	GD 2.0	VG 4.0	FN 6.0	VF 8.0	VF/NM 9.0	NM- 9.2
1-17: Based on animated series						3.00

GARRISON'S GORILLAS (TV)
Dell Publishing Co.: Jan, 1968 - No. 4, Oct, 1968; No. 5, Oct, 1969 (Photo-c)

	GD 2.0	VG 4.0	FN 6.0	VF 8.0	VF/NM 9.0	NM- 9.2
1	5	10	15	36	48	60
2-5: 5-Reprints #1	4	8	12	22	30	38

GARY GIANNI'S THE MONSTERMEN
Dark Horse Comics: Aug, 1999 ($2.95, one-shot)

	GD 2.0	VG 4.0	FN 6.0	VF 8.0	VF/NM 9.0	NM- 9.2
1-Gianni-s/c/a; back-up Hellboy story by Mignola						3.00

GASM
Stories, Layouts & Press, Inc.: Nov, 1977 - nn(No. 4), Jun, 1978 (B&W/color)

	GD 2.0	VG 4.0	FN 6.0	VF 8.0	VF/NM 9.0	NM- 9.2
1-Mark Wheatley-s/a; Gene Day-s/a; Workman-a	2	4	6	12	16	20
nn(#2, 2/78) Day-s/a; Wheatley-a; Workman-a	2	4	6	9	11	14
nn(#3, 4/78) Day-s/a; Wheatley-a; Corben-a	2	4	6	14	18	22
nn(#4, 6/78) Hempel-a; Howarth-a; Corben-a	3	6	9	16	20	24

GASOLINE ALLEY (Top Love Stories No. 3 on?)
Star Publications: Sept-Oct, 1950 - No. 2, Dec, 1950 (Newspaper-r)

	GD 2.0	VG 4.0	FN 6.0	VF 8.0	VF/NM 9.0	NM- 9.2
1-Contains 1 pg. intro. history of the strip (The Life of Skeezix); reprints 15 scenes of highlights from 1921-1935, plus an adventure from 1935 and 1936 strips; a 2-pg. filler is included on the life of the creator Frank King, with photo of the cartoonist.	22	44	66	127	176	225
2-(1936-37 reprints)-L. B. Cole-c	26	52	78	147	206	265

(See Super Book No. 21)

GASP!
American Comics Group: Mar, 1967 - No. 4, Aug, 1967 (12¢)

	GD 2.0	VG 4.0	FN 6.0	VF 8.0	VF/NM 9.0	NM- 9.2
1	4	8	12	29	40	50
2-4	3	6	9	18	24	30

GATECRASHER
Black Bull Entertainment: Mar, 2000 - No. 4, Jun, 2000 ($2.50, limited series)

	GD 2.0	VG 4.0	FN 6.0	VF 8.0	VF/NM 9.0	NM- 9.2
1,2-Waid-s/Conner & Palmiotti-c/a; 1,2-variant-c by J.G. Jones						2.50
3,4: 3-Jusko var-c. 4-Linsner-c						2.50
... Ring of Fire TPB (11/00, $12.95) r/#1-4; Hughes-c; Ennis intro.						13.00

GATECRASHER (Regular series)
Black Bull Entertainment: Aug, 2000 - No. 6, Jan, 2001 ($2.50, limited series)

	GD 2.0	VG 4.0	FN 6.0	VF 8.0	VF/NM 9.0	NM- 9.2
1-6-Waid-s/Conner & Palmiotti-c/a; 1-3-Variant-c by Fabry. 4-Hildebrandts variant-c. 5-Art Adams var-c. 6-Texeira var-c						2.50

GAY COMICS (Honeymoon No. 41)
Timely Comics/USA Comic Mag. Co. No. 18-24: Mar, 1944 (no month); No. 18, Fall, 1944 - No. 40, Oct, 1949

	GD 2.0	VG 4.0	FN 6.0	VF 8.0	VF/NM 9.0	NM- 9.2
1-Wolverton's Powerhouse Pepper; Tessie the Typist begins; 1st app. Willie (one shot)	48	96	144	288	432	575
18-(Formerly Funny Tunes #17?)-Wolverton-a	32	64	96	182	259	335
19-29: Wolverton-a in all. 21,24-6 pg., 7 pg. Powerhouse Pepper; additional 2 pg. story in 24). 23-7 pg Wolverton story & 2 two pg stories(total of 11pgs.). 24,29-Kurtzman-a (24-"Hey Look"(2))	26	52	78	147	206	265
30,33,36,37-Kurtzman's "Hey Look"	10	20	30	58	77	95
31-Kurtzman's "Hey Look" (1), Giggles 'N' Grins (1-1/2)	10	20	30	58	77	95
32,35,38-40: 35-Nellie The Nurse begins?	9	18	27	54	70	85
34-Three Kurtzman's "Hey Look"	11	22	33	63	84	105

GAY COMICS (Also see Smile, Tickle, & Whee Comics)
Modern Store Publ.: 1955 (7¢, 5x7-1/4", 52 pgs.)

	GD 2.0	VG 4.0	FN 6.0	VF 8.0	VF/NM 9.0	NM- 9.2
1	4	8	12	27	36	45

GAY PURR-EE (See Movie Comics)

GAZILLION
Image Comics: Nov, 1998 ($2.50, one-shot)

	GD 2.0	VG 4.0	FN 6.0	VF 8.0	VF/NM 9.0	NM- 9.2
1-Howard Shum-s/ Keron Grant-a						2.50

GEAR STATION, THE
Image Comics: Mar, 2000 - No. 5, Nov, 2000 ($2.50)

	GD 2.0	VG 4.0	FN 6.0	VF 8.0	VF/NM 9.0	NM- 9.2
1-Four covers by Ross, Turner, Pat Lee, Fraga						2.50
1-($6.95) DF Cover						7.00
2-5: 2-Two covers by Fraga and Art Adams						2.50

GEEK, THE (See Brother Power... & Vertigo Visions)

GEEKSVILLE (Also see 3 Geeks, The)
3 Finger Prints/ Image: Aug, 1999 - No. 6, Mar, 2001 ($2.75/$2.95, B&W)

	GD 2.0	VG 4.0	FN 6.0	VF 8.0	VF/NM 9.0	NM- 9.2
1,2,4-6-The 3 Geeks by Koslowski; Innocent Bystander by Sassaman						3.00
3-Includes "Babes & Blades" mini-comic						5.00

Gemini Blood #2 © DC

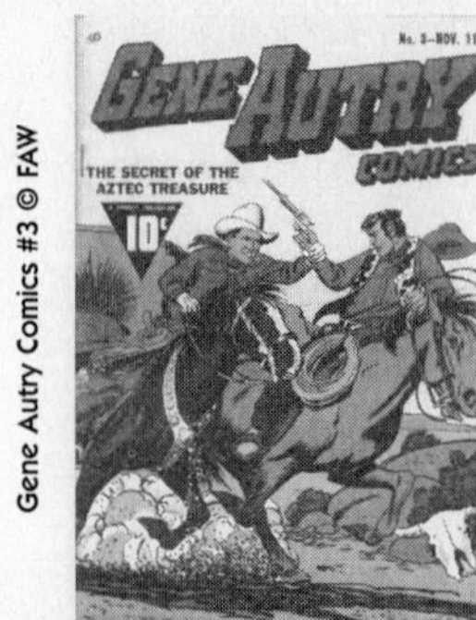

Gene Autry Comics #3 © FAW

Generation X #6 © MAR

	GD 2.0	VG 4.0	FN 6.0	VF 8.0	VF/NM 9.0	NM- 9.2

0-(3/00) First Image issue 3.00
(Vol. 2) 1-4-($2.95) 3-Mini-comic insert by the Geeks 3.00

G-8 AND HIS BATTLE ACES (Based on pulps)
Gold Key: Oct, 1966

1 (10184-610)-Painted-c 4 8 12 27 36 45

G-8 AND HIS BATTLE ACES
Blazing Comics: 1991 ($1.50, one-shot)

1-Glanzman-a; Truman-c 2.50
NOTE: *Flip book format with "The Spider's Web" #1 on other side w/**Glanzman**-a, **Truman**-c.*

GEISHA (Also see Oni Press Summer Vacation Supercolor Fun Special)
Oni Press: Sept, 1998 - No. 4, Dec, 1998 ($2.95, limited series)

1-4-Andi Watson-s/a. 2-Adam Warren-c 3.00
...One Shot (5/00, $4.50) 4.50
The Complete Geisha TPB (5/03, $15.95, digest size) r/#1-4, One Shot & story from Oni Press Summer Vacation Supercolor Fun Special 16.00

GEM COMICS
Spotlight Publishers: Apr, 1945 (52 pgs)

1-Little Mohee, Steve Strong app.; Jungle bondage-c 44 88 132 264 395 525

GEMINAR
Image Comics: July, 2000 ($4.95, B&W)

1-(72-Page Special) Terry Collins-s/Al Bigley-a 5.00

GEMINI BLOOD
DC Comics (Helix): Sept, 1996 - No. 9, May, 1997 ($2.25, limited series)

1-9: 5-Simonson-c 2.25

GEN ACTIVE
DC Comics (WildStorm): May, 2000 - No. 6, Aug, 2001 ($3.95)

1-6: 1-Covers by Campbell and Madureira; Gen 13 & DV8 app. 5-Mahfood-a; Quitely and Stelfreeze-c. 6-Portacio-a/c 4.00

GENE AUTRY (See March of Comics No. 25, 28, 39, 54, 78, 90, 104, 120, 135, 150 in the Promotional Comics section & Western Roundup under Dell Giants)

GENE AUTRY COMICS (Movie, Radio star; singing cowboy)
Fawcett Publications: 1941 (On sale 12/31/41) - No. 10, 1943 (68 pgs.)
(Dell takes over with No. 11)

	GD	VG	FN	VF	VF/NM	NM-
1 (Rare)-Gene Autry & his horse Champion begin	759	1518	2277	5313	8157	11,000
2-(1942)	152	304	456	950	1425	1900
3-5: 3-(11/1/42)	98	196	294	613	919	1225
6-10	80	160	240	500	750	1000

GENE AUTRY COMICS (...& Champion No. 102 on)
Dell Publishing Co.: No. 11, 1943 - No. 121, Jan-Mar, 1959 (TV - later issues)

	GD	VG	FN	VF	VF/NM	NM-
11 (1943, 60 pgs.)-Continuation of Fawcett series; photo back-c; first Dell issue	56	112	168	425	650	875
12 (2/44, 60 pgs.)	50	100	150	392	589	785
Four Color 47 (1944, 60 pgs.)	41	82	123	324	487	650
Four Color 57 (11/44),66('45)(52 pgs. each)	40	80	120	300	450	600
Four Color 75,83 ('45, 36 pgs. each)	31	62	93	230	345	460
Four Color 93 ('45, 36 pgs.)	30	60	90	218	319	420
Four Color 100 ('46, 36 pgs.) First Gene Autry photo-c	31	62	93	230	345	460
1 (5-6/46, 52 pgs.)	41	82	123	324	487	650
2 (7-8/46)-Photo-c begin, end #111	25	50	75	181	266	350
3-5: 4-Intro Flapjack Hobbs	20	40	60	140	205	270
6-10	17	34	51	118	174	230
11-20: 20-Panhandle Pete begins	14	28	42	99	145	190
21-29 (36pgs.)	11	22	33	80	118	155
30-40 (52pgs.)	10	20	30	70	100	130
41-56 (52pgs.)	9	18	27	60	85	110
57-66 (36pgs.): 58-X-mas-c	7	14	21	51	71	90
67-80 (52pgs.)	7	14	21	46	63	80
81-90 (52pgs.): 82-X-mas-c. 87-Blank inside-c	6	12	18	40	55	70
91-99 (36pgs. No. 91-on). 94-X-mas-c	5	10	15	36	48	60
100	6	12	18	38	52	65
101-111-Last Gene Autry photo-c	5	10	15	33	44	55
112-121-All Champion painted-c, most by Savitt	4	8	12	29	40	50

NOTE: *Photo back covers 4-18, 20-45, 48-65. **Manning** a-118. **Jesse Marsh** art: 4-Color No. 66, 75, 93, 100, No. 1-25, 27-37, 39, 40.*

GENE AUTRY'S CHAMPION (TV)
Dell Publ. Co.: No. 287, 8/50; No. 319, 2/51; No. 3, 8-10/51 - No. 19, 8-10/55

	GD	VG	FN	VF	VF/NM	NM-
Four Color 287(#1)('50, 52pgs.)-Photo-c	12	24	36	84	125	165
Four Color 319(#2, '51), 3: 2-Painted-c begin, most by Sam Savitt	6	12	18	43	59	75
4-19: 19-Last painted-c	5	10	15	33	44	55

GENE DOGS
Marvel Comics UK: Oct, 1993 - No. 4, Jan, 1994 ($1.75, limited series)

1-($2.75)-Polybagged w/4 trading cards 3.00
2-4: 2-Vs. Genetix 2.25

GENE POOL
IDW Publishing: Oct, 2003 ($6.99, squarebound)

nn-Wein & Wolfman-s/Cummings-a 7.00

GENERAL DOUGLAS MACARTHUR
Fox Features Syndicate: 1951

nn-True life story 21 42 63 118 164 210

GENERIC COMIC, THE
Marvel Comics Group: Apr, 1984 (one-shot)

1 3.00

GENERATION HEX
DC Comics (Amalgam): June, 1997 ($1.95, one-shot)

1-Milligan-s/ Pollina & Morales-a 2.50

GENERATION NEXT
Marvel Comics: Mar, 1995 - No. 4, June, 1995 ($1.95, limited series)

1-4-Age of Apocalypse; Scott Lobdell scripts & Chris Bachalo-c/a 2.50

GENERATION X (See Gen 13/ Generation X)
Marvel Comics: Oct, 1994 - No. 75, June, 2001 ($1.50/$1.95/$1.99/$2.25)

Collectors Preview ($1.75), "Ashcan" Edition 2.25
-1(7/97) Flashback story 3.00
1/2 (San Diego giveaway) 2 4 6 8 10 12
1-($3.95)-Wraparound chromium-c; Scott Lobdell scripts & Chris Bachalo-a begins 6.00
2-($1.95)-Deluxe edition, Bachalo-a 4.00
3,4-($1.95)-Deluxe Edition; Bachalo-a 3.00
2-10: 2-4-Standard Edition. 5-Returns from "Age of Apocalypse," begin $1.95-c. 6-Bachalo-a(p) ends, returns #17. 7-Roger Cruz-a(p). 10-Omega Red-c/app. 3.00
11-24, 26-28: 13,14-Bishop-app. 17-Stan Lee app. (Stan Lee scripts own dialogue); Bachalo/Buckingham-a; Onslaught update. 18-Toad cameo. 20-Franklin Richards app; Howard the Duck cameo. 21-Howard the Duck app. 22-Nightmare app. 2.50
25-($2.99)-Wraparound-c. Black Tom, Howard the Duck app. 3.50
29-37: 29-Begin $1.99-c, "Operation Zero Tolerance". 33-Hama-s 2.50
38-49: 38-Dodson-a begins. 40-Penance ID revealed. 49-Maggott app. 2.50
50,57-($2.99): 50-Crossover w/X-Man #50 3.50
51-56, 58-62: 59-Avengers & Spider-Man app. 2.25
63-74: 63-Ellis-s begin. 64-Begin $2.25-c. 69-71-Art Adams-c 2.25
75-($2.99) Final issue; Chamber joins the X-Men; Lim-a 3.00
'95 Special-($3.95) 4.00
'96 Special-($2.95)-Wraparound-c; Jeff Johnson-c/a 3.50
'97 Special-($2.99)-Wraparound-c; 3.50
'98 Annual-($3.50)-vs. Dracula 3.50
'99 Annual-($3.50)-Monet leaves 3.50
75¢ Ashcan Edition 3.00
...Holiday Special 1 (2/99, $3.50) Pollina-a 3.50
...Underground Special 1 (5/98, $2.50, B&W) Mahfood-a 2.50

GENERATION X/ GEN 13 (Also see Gen 13/ Generation X)
Marvel Comics: 1997 ($3.99, one-shot)

1-Robinson-s/Larroca-a(p) 4.00

GENE RODDENBERRY'S LOST UNIVERSE
Tekno Comix: Apr, 1995 - No. 7, Oct, 1995 ($1.95)

1-7: 1-3-w/ bound-in game piece & trading card. 4-w/bound-in trading card 2.25

GENE RODDENBERRY'S XANDER IN LOST UNIVERSE
Tekno Comix: No. 0, Nov, 1995; No. 1, Dec, 1995 - No. 8, July, 1996 ($2.25)

0,1-8: 1-5-Jae Lee-c. 4-Polybagged. 8-Pt. 5 of The Big Bang x-over 2.25

GENESIS (See DC related titles)
DC Comics: Oct, 1997 - No. 4, Oct, 1997 ($1.95, weekly limited series)

1-4: Byrne-s/Wagner-a(p) in all. 3.00

GENESIS: THE #1 COLLECTION (WildStorm Archives)
WildStorm Productions: 1998 ($9.99, TPB, B&W)

Gen13 #8 © WSP

Gen 13 #1 © WSP

Gen13 Bootleg #8 © WSP

GD VG FN VF VF/NM NM-
2.0 4.0 6.0 8.0 9.0 9.2

nn-Reprints #1 issues of WildStorm titles and pin-ups 10.00

GENETIX
Marvel Comics UK: Oct, 1993 - No. 6, Mar, 1994 ($1.75, limited series)
1-($2.75)-Polybagged w/4 cards; Dark Guard app. 3.00
2-6: 2-Intro Tektos. 4-Vs. Gene Dogs 2.25

GEN 12 (Also see Gen13 and Team 7)
Image Comics (WildStorm Productions): Feb, 1998 - No. 5, June, 1998 ($2.50, lim. series)
1-5: 1-Team 7 & Gen13 app.; wraparound-c 3.00

GEN 13 (Also see Wild C.A.T.S. #1 & Deathmate Black #2)
Image Comics (WildStorm Productions): Feb, 1994 - No. 5, July 1994 ($1.95, limited series)
0 (8/95, $2.50)-Ch. 1 w/Jim Lee-p; Ch.4 w/Charest-p 3.00
1/2 1 2 3 4 5 7
1-($2.50)-Created by Jim Lee 1 3 4 6 8 10
1-2nd printing 2.50
1-"3-D" Edition (9/97, $4.95)-w/glasses 5.00
2-($2.50) 1 2 3 4 5 7
3-Pitt-c & story 4.00
4-Pitt-c & story; wraparound-c 3.00
5 4.00
5-Alternate Portacio-c; see Deathblow #5 6.00
...Collected Edition ('94, $12.95)-r/#1-5 13.00
...Rave ($1.50, 3/95)-wraparound-c 3.00
NOTE: *Issues 1-4 contain coupons redeemable for the ashcan edition of Gen 13 #0. Price listed is for a complete book.*

GEN 13
Image Comics (WildStorm Productions): Mar, 1995 - No. 36, Dec, 1998;
DC Comics (WildStorm): No. 37, Mar, 1999 - No. 77, Jul, 2002 ($2.95/$2.50)
1-A (Charge)-Campbell/Garner-c 4.50
1-B (Thumbs Up)-Campbell/Garner-c 4.50
1-C-1-F,1-I-1-M: 1-C (Lil' GEN 13)-Art Adams-c. 1-D (Barbari-GEN)-Simon Bisley-c. 1-E (Your Friendly Neighborhood Grunge)-Cleary-c. 1-F (GEN 13 Goes Madison Ave.)-Golden-c. 1-I (That's the way we became GEN 13)-Campbell/Gibson-c. 1-J (All Dolled Up)-Campbell/McWeeney-c. 1-K (Verti-GEN)-Dunn-c. 1-L (Picto-Fiction). 1-M (Do it Yourself Cover) 1 2 3 4 5 7
1-G (Lin-GEN-re)-Michael Lopez-c 2 4 6 8 10 12
1-H (GEN-et Jackson)-Jason Pearson-c 2 4 6 8 10 12
1-Chromium-c by Campbell 60.00
1-Chromium-c by Jim Lee 80.00
1-"3-D" Edition (2/98, $4.95)-w/glasses 5.00
2 ($1.95, Newsstand)-WildStorm Rising Pt. 4; bound-in card 2.50
2-12: 2-($2.50, Direct Market)-WildStorm Rising Pt. 4, bound-in card. 6,7-Jim Lee-c/a(p). 9-Ramos-a. 10,11-Fire From Heaven Pt. 3. & Pt.9 3.00
11-($4.95)-Special European Tour Edition; chromium-c 2 4 6 11 14 18
13A,13B,13C-($1.30, 13 pgs.): 13A-Archie & Friends app. 13B-Bone-c/app.; Teenage Mutant Ninja Turtles, Madman, Spawn & Jim Lee app. 3.00
14-24: 20-Last Campbell-a 2.50
25-($3.50)-Two covers by Campbell and Charest 3.50
25-($3.50)-Voyager Pack w/Danger Girl preview 4.50
25-Foil-c 10.00
26-32,34: 26-Arcudi-s/Frank-a begins. 34-Back-up story by Art Adams 2.50
33-Flip book w/Planetary preview 4.00
35-49: 36,38,40-Two covers. 37-First DC issue. 41-Last Frank-a 2.50
50-($3.95) Two covers by Lee and Benes; art by various 4.00
51-76: 51-Moy-a; Fairchild loses her powers. 60-Warren-s/a. 66-Art by various incl. Campbell (3 pgs.). 70,75,76-Mays-a. 76-Original team dies 2.50
77-($3.50) Mays, Andrews, Warren-a 3.50
Annual 1 (1997, $2.95) Ellis-s/ Dillon-c/a. 3.50
Annual 1999 ($3.50, DC) Slipstream x-over w/ DV8 3.50
Annual 2000 ($3.50) Devil's Night x-over w/WildStorm titles; Bermejo-c 3.50
...: A Christmas Caper (1/00, $5.95, one-shot) McWeeney-s/a 6.00
... Archives (4/98, $12.99) B&W reprints of mini-series, #0,1/2,1-13ABC; includes cover gallery and sourcebook 13.00
...: Carny Folk (2/00, $3.50) Collect back-up stories 3.50
... European Vacation TPB ($6.95) r/#6,7 7.00
.../ Fantastic Four (2001, $5.95) Maguire-s/c/a(p) 6.00
...: Going West (6/99, $2.50, one-shot) Pruett-s 2.50
...: Grunge Saves the World (5/99, $5.95, one-shot) Altieri-c/a 6.00
... I Love New York TPB ($9.95) r/part #25, 26-29; Frank-c 10.00
... London, New York, Hell TPB ($6.95) r/Annual #1 & Bootleg Ann. #1 7.00
... Lost in Paradise TPB ($6.95) r/#3-5 7.00
.../ Maxx (12/95, $3.50, one-shot) Messner-Loebs-s, 1st Coker-c/a. 3.50
...: Meanwhile (2003, $17.95) r/#43,44,66-70; all Warren-s; art by various 18.00
...: Medicine Song (2001, $5.95) Brent Anderson-c/a(p)/Raab-s 6.00
... Science Friction (2001, $5.95) Haley & Lopresti-a 6.00
... Starting Over TPB ($14.95) r/#1-7 15.00
... Superhuman Like You TPB ($12.95) r/#60-65; Warren-c 13.00
... #13 A,B&C Collected Edition ($6.95, TPB) r/#13A,B&C 7.00
... 3-D Special (1997, $4.95, one-shot) Art Adams-s/a(p) 5.00
...: The Unreal World (7/96, $2.95, one-shot) Humberto Ramos-c/a 3.00
... We'll Take Manhattan TPB ($14.95) r/#45-50; new Benes-c 15.00
...: Wired (4/99, $2.50, one-shot) Richard Bennett-c/a 2.50
...: 'Zine (12/96, $1.95, B&W, digest size) Campbell/Garner-c 2.25
Variant Collection-Four editions (all 13 variants w/Chromium variant-limited, signed) 100.00

GEN 13
DC Comics (WildStorm): No. 0, Sept, 2002 - No. 16, Feb, 2004 ($2.95)
0-(13¢-c) Intro. new team; includes previews of 21 Down & The Resistance 2.50
1-Claremont-s/Garza-c/a; Fairchild app. 3.00
2-16: 8-13-Bachs-a. 16-Original team returns 3.00
...: September Song TPB (2003, $19.95) r/#0-6; Garza sketch pages 20.00

GEN 13 BOOTLEG
Image Comics (WildStorm): Nov, 1996 - No. 20, Jul, 1998 ($2.50)
1-Alan Davis-a; alternate costumes-c 2.50
1-Team falling variant-c 3.00
2-7: 2-Alan Davis-a. 5,6-Terry Moore-s. 7-Robinson-s/Scott Hampton-a 2.50
8-10-Adam Warren-s/a 4.00
11-20: 11,12-Lopresti-s/a & Simonson-s. 13-Wieringo-s/a. 14-Mariotte-s/Phillips-a. 15,16-Strnad-s/Shaw-a. 18-Altieri-s/a(p)/c, 18-Variant-c by Bruce Timm 2.50
Annual 1 (2/98, $2.95) Ellis-s/Dillon-c/a 3.00
... Grunge: The Movie (12/97, $9.95) r/#8-10, Warren-c 10.00
...Vol. 1 TPB (10/98, $11.95) r/#1-4 12.00

GEN 13/ GENERATION X (Also see Generation X / Gen 13)
Image Comics (WildStorm Publications): July, 1997 ($2.95, one-shot)
1-Choi-s/ Art Adams-p/Garner-i. Variant covers by Adams/Garner and Campbell/McWeeney 3.00
1-($4.95) 3-D Edition w/glasses; Campbell-c 5.00

GEN 13 INTERACTIVE
Image Comics (WildStorm): Oct, 1997 - No. 3, Dec, 1997 ($2.50, lim. series)
1-3-Internet voting used to determine storyline 2.50
... Plus! (7/98, $11.95) r/series & 3-D Special (in 2-D) 12.00

GEN 13 : MAGICAL DRAMA QUEEN ROXY
Image Comics (WildStorm): Oct, 1998 - No. 3, Dec, 1998 ($3.50, lim. series)
1-3-Adam Warren-s/c/a; manga style, 2-Variant-c by Hiroyuki Utatane 3.50
1-($6.95) Dynamic Forces Ed. w/Variant Warren-c 7.00

GEN 13 /MONKEYMAN & O'BRIEN
Image Comics (WildStorm): Jun, 1998 - No. 2, July, 1998 ($2.50, lim. series)
1,2-Art Adams-s/a(p); 1-Two covers 2.50
1-($4.95) Chromium-c 5.00
1-($6.95) Dynamic Forces Ed. 7.00

GEN 13: ORDINARY HEROES
Image Comics (WildStorm Publications): Feb, 1996 - No. 2, July, 1996 ($2.50, limited series)
1,2-Adam Hughes-c/a/scripts 3.00

GENTLE BEN (TV)
Dell Publishing Co.: Feb, 1968 - No. 5, Oct, 1969 (All photo-c)
1 4 8 12 29 40 50
2-5: 5-Reprints #1 3 6 9 18 23 28

GEOMANCER (Also see Eternal Warrior: Fist & Steel)
Valiant: Nov, 1994 - No. 8, June, 1995 ($3.75/$2.25)
1 ($3.75)-Chromium wraparound-c; Eternal Warrior app. 3.75
2-8 2.25

GEORGE OF THE JUNGLE (TV)(See America's Best TV Comics)
Gold Key: Feb, 1969 - No. 2, Oct, 1969 (Jay Ward)
1 14 28 42 97 141 185
2 9 18 27 65 93 120

GEORGE PAL'S PUPPETOONS (Funny animal puppets)
Fawcett Publications: Dec, 1945 - No. 18, Dec, 1947; No. 19, 1950
1-Captain Marvel-c 42 84 126 252 376 500
2 24 48 72 135 190 245
3-10 15 30 45 84 115 145

Georgie Comics #12 © MAR

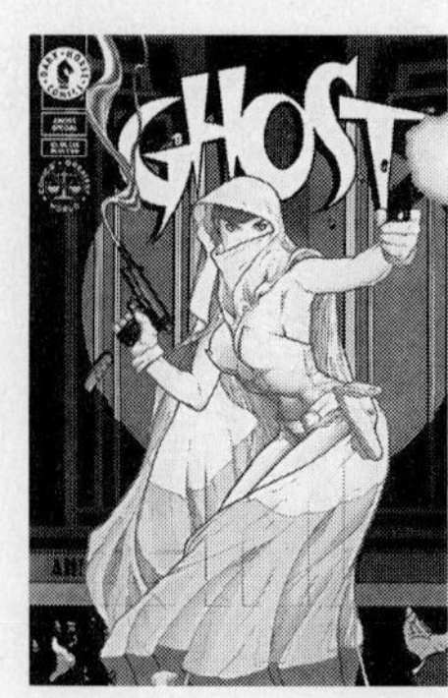

Ghost Special #1 © DH

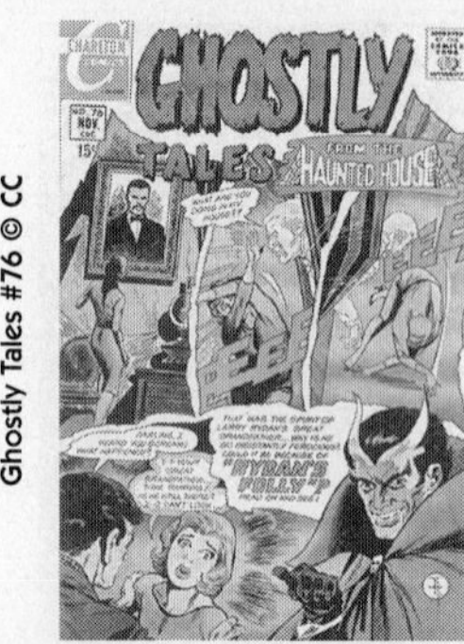

Ghostly Tales #76 © CC

	GD 2.0	VG 4.0	FN 6.0	VF 8.0	VF/NM 9.0	NM- 9.2
11-19	12	24	36	71	96	120
GEORGIE COMICS (...& Judy Comics #20-35?; see All Teen & Teen Comics)						
Timely Comics/GPI No. 1-34: Spr, 1945 - No. 39, Oct, 1952 (#1-3 are quarterly)						
1-Dave Berg-a	26	52	78	150	210	270
2	14	28	42	79	107	135
3-5,7,8	11	22	33	63	84	105
6-Georgie visits Timely Comics	14	28	42	79	107	135
9,10-Kurtzman's "Hey Look" (1 & ?); Margie app.	11	22	33	66	88	110
11,12: 11-Margie, Millie app.	9	18	27	49	62	75
13-Kurtzman's "Hey Look", 3 pgs.	9	18	27	54	70	85
14-Wolverton-a(1 pg.); Kurtzman's "Hey Look"	10	20	30	58	77	95
15,16,18-20	8	16	24	43	54	65
17,29-Kurtzman's "Hey Look", 1 pg.	9	18	27	49	62	75
21-24,27,28,30-39: 21-Anti-Wertham editorial	7	14	21	37	46	55
25-Painted-c by classic pin-up artist Peter Driben	10	20	30	58	77	95
26-Logo design swipe from Archie Comics	8	16	24	40	50	60
GERALD McBOING-BOING AND THE NEARSIGHTED MR. MAGOO (TV) (Mr. Magoo No. 6 on)						
Dell Publishing Co.: Aug-Oct, 1952 - No. 5, Aug-Oct, 1953						
1	14	28	42	102	149	195
2-5	11	22	33	80	118	155
GERONIMO (See Fighting Indians of the Wild West!)						
Avon Periodicals: 1950 - No. 4, Feb, 1952						
1-Indian Fighter; Maneely-a; Texas Rangers-r/Cowpuncher #1; Fawcette-c	19	38	57	106	146	185
2-On the Warpath; Kit West app.; Kinstler-c/a	12	24	36	69	92	115
3-And His Apache Murderers; Kinstler-c/a(2); Kit West-r/Cowpuncher #6	12	24	36	69	92	115
4-Savage Raids of; Kinstler-c & inside front-c; Kinstlerish-a by McCann(3)	11	22	33	63	84	105
GERONIMO JONES						
Charlton Comics: Sept, 1971 - No. 9, Jan, 1973						
1	2	4	6	12	16	20
2-9	1	3	4	6	8	10
Modern Comics Reprint #7('78)						4.00
GETALONG GANG, THE (TV)						
Marvel Comics (Star Comics): May, 1985 - No. 6, Mar, 1986						
1-6: Saturday morning TV stars						3.00
GET LOST						
Mikeross Publications/New Comics: Feb-Mar, 1954 - No. 3, June-July, 1954 (Satire)						
1-Andru/Esposito-a in all?	31	62	93	175	248	320
2-Andru/Esposito-c; has 4 pg. E.C. parody featuring "The Sewer Keeper"	21	42	63	118	164	210
3-John Wayne 'Hondo' parody	17	34	51	98	134	170
1,2 (10,12/87-New Comics)-B&W r-original						2.25
GET SMART (TV)						
Dell Publ. Co.: June, 1966 - No. 8, Sept, 1967 (All have Don Adams photo-c)						
1	11	22	33	77	114	150
2,3-Ditko-a	8	16	24	55	78	100
4-8: 8-Reprints #1 (cover and insides)	6	12	18	43	59	75
GHOST (...Comics #9)						
Fiction House Magazines: 1951(Winter) - No. 11, Summer, 1954						
1-Most covers by Whitman	70	140	210	438	657	875
2-Ghost Gallery & Werewolf Hunter stories	39	78	117	230	325	420
3-9: 3,6,7,9-Bondage-c. 9-Abel, Discount-a	33	66	99	190	270	350
10,11-Dr. Drew by Grandenetti in each, reprinted from Rangers; 11-Evans-r/Rangers #39; Grandenetti-r/Rangers #49	29	58	87	164	232	300
GHOST (See Comic's Greatest World)						
Dark Horse Comics: Apr, 1995 - No. 36, Apr, 1998 ($2.50/$2.95)						
1-Adam Hughes-a	1	2	3	5	6	8
2,3-Hughes-a						4.00
4-24: 4-Barb Wire app. 5,6-Hughes-c. 12-Ghost/Hellboy preview. 15,21-X app. 18,19-Barb Wire app.						3.00
25-($3.50)-48 pgs. special						3.50
26-36: 26-Begin $2.95-c. 29-Flip book w/Timecop. 33-36-Jade Cathedral; Harris painted-c						3.00
Special 1 (7/94, $3.95, 48 pgs.)	1	2	3	4	5	7
Special 2 (6/98, $3.95) Barb Wire app.						4.00
...Black October (1/99, $14.95, trade paperback)-r/#6-9,26,27						15.00

	GD 2.0	VG 4.0	FN 6.0	VF 8.0	VF/NM 9.0	NM- 9.2
...Nocturnes (1996, $9.95, trade paperback)-r/#1-3 & 5						10.00
...Stories (1995, $9.95, trade paperback)-r/Early Ghost app.						10.00
GHOST (Volume 2)						
Dark Horse Comics: Sept, 1998 - No. 22, Aug, 2000 ($2.95)						
1-22: 1-4-Ryan Benjamin-c/Zanier-a						3.00
Handbook (8/99, $2.95) guide to issues and characters						3.00
Special 3 (12/98, $3.95)						4.00
GHOST AND THE SHADOW						
Dark Horse Comics: Dec, 1995 ($2.95, one-shot)						
1-Moench scripts						3.00
GHOST/BATGIRL						
Dark Horse Comics: Aug, 2000 - No. 4, Dec, 2000 ($2.95, limited series)						
1-4-New Batgirl; Oracle & Bruce Wayne app.; Benjamin-c/a						3.00
GHOST/HELLBOY						
Dark Horse Comics: May, 1996 - No. 2, June, 1996 ($2.50, limited series)						
1,2: Mike Mignola-c/scripts & breakdowns; Scott Benefiel finished-a						3.00
GHOST BREAKERS (Also see Racket Squad in Action, Red Dragon & (CC) Sherlock Holmes Comics)						
Street & Smith Publications: Sept, 1948 - No. 2, Dec, 1948 (52 pgs.)						
1-Powell-c/a(3); Dr. Neff (magician) app.	40	80	120	240	358	475
2-Powell-c/a(2); Maneely-a	35	70	105	201	288	370
GHOSTBUSTERS (TV) (Also, see Real...and Slimer)						
First Comics: Feb, 1987 - No. 6, Aug, 1987 ($1.25)						
1-6: Based on new animated TV series						3.00
GHOSTBUSTERS II						
Now Comics: Oct, 1989 - No. 3, Dec, 1989 ($1.95, mini-series)						
1-3: Movie Adaptation						3.00
GHOST CASTLE (See Tales of...)						
GHOSTDANCING						
DC Comics (Vertigo): Mar, 1995 - No. 6, Sept, 1995 ($1.95, limited series)						
1-6: Case-c/a						2.25
GHOST IN THE SHELL (Manga)						
Dark Horse: Mar, 1995 - No. 8, Oct, 1995 ($3.95, B&W/color, lim. series)						
1,2	2	4	6	15	19	22
3	2	4	6	8	10	12
4-8	1	2	3	5	6	8
GHOST IN THE SHELL 2: MAN-MADE INTERFACE (Manga)						
Dark Horse Comics: Jan, 2003 - No. 11 ($3.50, color/B&W, lim. series)						
1-9-Masamune Shirow-s/a. 5-B&W						3.50
GHOSTLY HAUNTS (Formerly Ghost Manor)						
Charlton Comics: #20, 9/71 - #53, 12/76; #54, 9/77 - #55, 10/77; #56, 1/78 - #58, 4/78						
20	3	6	9	18	23	28
21	2	4	6	10	13	16
22-25,27,31-34,36,37-Ditko-c/a. 27-Dr. Graves x-over. 32-New logo. 33-Back to old logo	2	4	6	14	18	22
26,29,30,35-Ditko-c	2	4	6	10	13	16
28,38-40-Ditko-a. 39-Origin & 1st app. Destiny Fox	2	4	6	10	13	16
41,42: 41-Sutton-c; Ditko-a. 42-Newton-c/a	2	4	6	11	14	18
43-46,48,50,52-Ditko-a	2	4	6	10	12	15
47,54,56-Ditko-c/a. 56-Ditko-a(r).	2	4	6	11	14	18
49,51,53,55,57	1	3	4	6	8	10
58 (4/78) Last issue	2	4	6	11	14	18
40,41(Modern Comics-r, 1977, 1978)						4.00

NOTE: ***Ditko** a-22-25, 27, 28, 31-34, 36-41, 43-48, 50, 52, 54, 56r; c-22-27, 29, 30, 33-37, 47, 54, 56. **Glanzman** a-20. **Howard** a-27, 30, 35, 40-43, 48, 54, 57. **Kim** a-38, 41, 57. **Larson** a-48, 50. **Newton** c/a-42. **Staton** a-32, 35; c-28, 46. **Sutton** c-33, 37, 39, 41.*

	GD 2.0	VG 4.0	FN 6.0	VF 8.0	VF/NM 9.0	NM- 9.2
GHOSTLY TALES (Formerly Blue Beetle No. 50-54)						
Charlton Comics: No. 55, 4-5/66 - No. 124, 12/76; No. 125, 9/77 - No. 169, 10/84						
55-Intro. & origin Dr. Graves; Ditko-a	6	12	18	40	55	70
56-58,60,61,70,71-Ditko-a. 70-Dr. Graves ends. 71-Last 12¢ issue	3	7	10	21	28	35
59,62-66,68	3	6	9	16	20	25
67,69-Ditko-c/a	4	8	12	24	32	40
72,75,76,79-82,85-Ditko-a	2	4	6	14	18	22
73,77,78,83,84,86-90,92-95,97,99-Ditko-c/a	3	6	9	18	23	28
74,91,98,119,123,124,127-130: 127,130-Sutton-a	2	4	6	9	11	14

Ghost Manor #19 © CC

The Ghost Rider #5 © ME

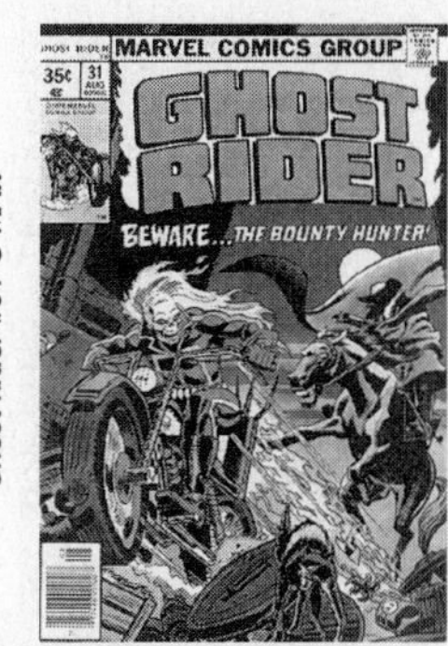

Ghost Rider #31 © MAR

	GD 2.0	VG 4.0	FN 6.0	VF 8.0	VF/NM 9.0	NM- 9.2
96-Ditko-c	2	4	6	12	16	20
100-Ditko-c; Sutton-a	2	4	6	12	16	20
101,103-105-Ditko-a	2	4	6	11	14	18
102,109-Ditko-c/a	2	4	6	14	18	22
110,113-Sutton-c; Ditko-a	2	4	6	11	14	18
106-Ditko & Sutton-a; Sutton-c	2	4	6	11	14	18
107-Ditko, Wood, Sutton-a	2	4	6	12	16	20
108,116,117,126-Ditko-a	2	4	6	11	14	18
111,118,120-122,125-Ditko-c/a	2	4	6	14	18	22
112,114,115: 112,114-Ditko, Sutton-a. 114-Newton-a. 115-Newton, Ditko-a.	2	4	6	11	14	18
131-133,163-Ditko-c/a	2	4	6	10	13	16
134,135,142,145-151,153,154,156-160	1	2	3	5	6	8
136-141,143,144,152,155-Ditko-a	1	3	4	6	8	10
161,162,164-168-Lower print run. 162-Nudity panel	2	4	6	9	11	14
169 (10/84) Last issue; lower print run	2	4	6	11	14	18

NOTE: ***Aparo** a-65, 66, 68, 72, 141r, 142r; c-71, 72, 74-76, 81, 146r. **Ditko** a-55-58, 60, 61, 67, 69-73, 75-90, 92-95, 97, 99-118, 120-122, 125r, 126r, 131-133r, 136-141r, 143r, 144r, 152, 155, 161, 163; c-67, 69, 73, 77, 78, 83, 84, 86-90, 92-97, 99, 102, 109, 111, 118, 120-122, 125, 131-133, 163. **Glanzman** a-167. **Howard** a-95, 98, 99, 108, 117, 129; c-98, 107, 120, 121, 161. **Larson** a-117, 119. **Morisi** a-83, 84, 86. **Newton** a-114; c-115(painted). **Palais** a-61. **Staton** a-161; c-117. **Sutton** a-106, 107, 111-114, 127, 130, 162; c-100, 106, 110, 113(painted). **Wood** a-107.*

GHOSTLY WEIRD STORIES (Formerly Blue Bolt Weird)
Star Publications: No. 120, Sept, 1953 - No. 124, Sept, 1954

	GD 2.0	VG 4.0	FN 6.0	VF 8.0	VF/NM 9.0	NM- 9.2
120-Jo-Jo-r	40	80	120	240	340	440
121-124: 121-Jo-Jo-r. 122-The Mask-r/Capt. Flight #5; Rulah-r; has 1pg. story 'Death and the Devil Pills'-r/Western Outlaws #17. 123-Jo-Jo; Disbrow-a(2). 124-Torpedo Man	36	72	108	204	290	375

NOTE: ***Disbrow** a-120-124. **L. B. Cole** covers-all issues (#122 is a sci-fi cover).*

GHOST MANOR (Ghostly Haunts No. 20 on)
Charlton Comics: July, 1968 - No. 19, July, 1971

	GD 2.0	VG 4.0	FN 6.0	VF 8.0	VF/NM 9.0	NM- 9.2
1	5	10	15	36	48	60
2-6: 6-Last 12¢ issue	3	6	9	18	24	30
7-12,17: 17-Morisi-a	3	6	9	16	20	24
13,14,16-Ditko-a	3	6	9	18	24	30
15,18,19-Ditko-c/a	4	8	12	22	30	38

GHOST MANOR (2nd Series)
Charlton Comics: Oct, 1971-No. 32, Dec, 1976; No. 33, Sept, 1977-No. 77, 11/84

	GD 2.0	VG 4.0	FN 6.0	VF 8.0	VF/NM 9.0	NM- 9.2
1	4	8	12	27	36	45
2,3,5-7,9-Ditko-c	2	4	6	14	18	22
4,10-Ditko-c/a	3	6	9	18	23	28
8-Wood, Ditko-a; Sutton-c	3	6	9	18	23	28
11,14-Ditko-c/a	3	6	9	16	20	24
12,17,27,30	2	4	6	9	11	14
13,15,16,23-26,29: 13-Ditko-a. 15,16-Ditko-c. 23-Sutton-a. 24-26,29-Ditko-a. 25-Sutton-a. 26-Early Zeck-a; Boyette-c	2	4	6	11	14	18
18-Newton's 1st pro art; Ditko-a; Sutton-c	3	6	9	16	20	25
19-21: 19-Newton, Sutton-a; nudity panels. 20-Ditko-a. 21-E-Man, Blue Beetle, Capt. Atom cameos; Ditko-a.	2	4	6	11	14	18
22-Newton-c/a; Ditko-a	2	4	6	12	16	20
28,31,37,38-Ditko-c/a: 28-Nudity panels	2	4	6	12	16	20
32-36,39,41,45,48-50,53	1	2	3	5	7	9
40-Ditko-a; torture & drug use	2	4	6	11	14	18
42,43,46,47,51,52,60,62-Ditko-c/a	2	4	6	10	13	16
44,54,71-Ditko-a	2	4	6	8	10	12
55,56,58,59,61,63,65-70	1	2	3	4	5	7
57-Wood, Ditko, Howard-a	2	4	6	9	11	14
64-Ditko & Newton-a	2	4	6	8	10	12
71-76	1	2	3	4	5	7
77-(11/84) Last issueAparo-r/Space Adventures V3#60 (Paul Mann)	2	4	6	10	13	16
19 (Modern Comics reprint, 1977)						4.00

NOTE: ***Ditko** a-4, 8, 10, 11(2), 13, 14, 18, 20-22, 24-26, 28, 29, 31, 37r, 38r, 40r, 42-44r, 46r, 47, 51r, 52r, 54r, 57, 60, 62(4), 64r, 71; c-2-7, 9-11, 14-16, 28, 31, 37, 38, 42, 43, 46, 47, 51, 52, 60, 62, 64. **Howard** a-4, 8, 12, 17, 19-21, 31, 41, 45, 57. **Newton** a-18-20, 22, 64; c-22. **Staton** a-13, 38, 44, 45. **Sutton** a-19, 23, 25, 45;c-8, 18.*

GHOST RIDER (See A-1 Comics, Best of the West, Black Phantom, Bobby Benson, Great Western, Red Mask & Tim Holt)
Magazine Enterprises: 1950 - No. 14, 1954

NOTE: *The character was inspired by Vaughn Monroe's "Ghost Riders in the Sky", and Disney's movie "The Headless Horseman".*

	GD 2.0	VG 4.0	FN 6.0	VF 8.0	VF/NM 9.0	NM- 9.2
1(A-1 #27)-Origin Ghost Rider	96	192	288	600	900	1200
2-5: 2(A-1 #29), 3(A-1 #31), 4(A-1 #34), 5(A-1 #37)-All Frazetta-c only	70	140	210	438	657	875
6,7: 6(A-1 #44)-Loco weed story, 7(A-1 #51)	31	62	93	178	252	325
8,9: 8(A-1 #57)-Drug use story, 9(A-1 #69)	26	52	78	150	210	270
10(A-1 #71)-Vs. Frankenstein	28	56	84	159	225	290
11-14: 11(A-1 #75). 12(A-1 #80)-Bondage-c; one-eyed Devil-c. 13(A-1 #84). 14(A-1 #112)	23	46	69	130	183	235

NOTE: ***Dick Ayers** art in all; c-1, 6-14.*

GHOST RIDER, THE (See Night Rider & Western Gunfighters)
Marvel Comics Group: Feb, 1967 - No. 7, Nov, 1967 (Western hero)(12¢)

	GD 2.0	VG 4.0	FN 6.0	VF 8.0	VF/NM 9.0	NM- 9.2
1-Origin & 1st app. Ghost Rider; Kid Colt-reprints begin	9	18	27	60	85	110
2	5	10	15	33	44	55
3-7: 6-Last Kid Colt-r; All Ayers-c/a(p)	4	8	12	27	36	45

GHOST RIDER (See The Champions, Marvel Spotlight #5, Marvel Team-Up #15, 58, Marvel Treasury Edition #18, Marvel Two-In-One #8, The Original Ghost Rider & The Original Ghost Rider Rides Again)
Marvel Comics Group: Sept, 1973 - No. 81, June, 1983 (Super-hero)

	GD 2.0	VG 4.0	FN 6.0	VF 8.0	VF/NM 9.0	NM- 9.2
1-Johnny Blaze, the Ghost Rider begins; 1st app. Daimon Hellstrom (Son of Satan) in cameo	8	16	24	53	74	95
2-1st full app. Daimon Hellstrom; gives glimpse of costume (1 panel); story continues in Marvel Spotlight #12	4	8	12	24	32	40
3-5: 3-Ghost Rider gets new cycle; Son of Satan app.	3	6	9	18	24	30
6-10: 10-Reprints origin/1st app. from Marvel Spotlight #5; Ploog-a	2	4	6	12	16	20
11-16	2	4	6	9	11	14
17,19-(Reg. 25¢ editions)(4,8/76)	2	4	6	9	11	14
17,19-(30¢-c variants, limited distribution)	2	4	6	11	14	18
18-(Reg. 25¢ edition)(6/76). Spider-Man-c & app.	2	4	6	10	13	16
18-(30¢-c variant, limited distribution)	2	4	6	14	18	22
20-Daredevil x-over; ties into D.D. #138; Byrne-a	2	4	6	12	16	20
21-30: 22-1st app. Enforcer. 29,30-Vs. Dr. Strange	1	2	3	5	7	9
24-26-(35¢-c variants, limited distribution)	2	4	6	8	10	12
31-34,36-49	1	2	3	4	5	7
35-Death Race classic; Starlin-c/a/sty	2	4	6	8	10	12
50-Double size	1	2	3	5	7	9
51-76,78-80: 80-Brief origin recap. 68,77-Origin retold						5.00
81-Death of Ghost Rider (Demon leaves Blaze)	2	4	6	10	12	15

NOTE: ***Anderson** c-64p. **Infantino** a(p)-43, 44, 51. **G. Kane** a-21p; c(p)-1, 2, 4, 5, 8, 9, 11-13, 19, 20, 24, 25. **Kirby** c-21-23. **Mooney** a-2-9p, 30i. **Nebres** c-26i. **Newton** a-23i. **Perez** c-26p. **Shores** a-2i. J. **Sparling** a-62p, 64p, 65p. **Starlin** a(p)-35. **Sutton** a-1p, 44i, 64i, 65i, 66, 67i. **Tuska** a-13p, 14p, 16p.*

GHOST RIDER (Volume 2) (Also see Doctor Strange/Ghost Rider Special, Marvel Comics Presents & Midnight Sons Unlimited)
Marvel Comics (Midnight Sons imprint #44 on): V2#1, May, 1990 - No. 93, Feb, 1998 ($1.50/$1.75/$1.95)

	GD 2.0	VG 4.0	FN 6.0	VF 8.0	VF/NM 9.0	NM- 9.2
1-($1.95, 52 pgs.)-Origin/1st app. new Ghost Rider; Kingpin app.						6.00
1-2nd printing (not gold)						2.50
2-5: 3-Kingpin app. 5-Punisher app.; Jim Lee-c						3.00
5-Gold background 2nd printing						2.50
6-14,16-24,29,30,32-39: 6-Punisher app. 6,17-Spider-Man/Hobgoblin-c/story. 9-X-Factor app. 10-Reintro Johnny Blaze on the last pg. 11-Stroman-c/a(p). 12,13-Dr. Strange x-over cont'd in D.S. #28. 13-Painted-c. 14-Johnny Blaze vs. Ghost Rider; origin recap 1st Ghost Rider (Blaze). 18-Painted-c by Nelson. 29-Wolverine-c/story. 32-Dr. Strange x-over; Johnny Blaze app. 34-Williamson-a(i). 36-Daredevil app. 37-Archangel app.						2.50
15-Glow in the dark-c						3.00
25-27: 25-($2.75)-Contains pop-up scene insert. 26,27-X-Men x-over; Lee/Williams-c on both						3.00
28,31-($2.50, 52 pgs.)-Polybagged w/poster; part 1 & part 6 of Rise of the Midnight Sons storyline (see Ghost Rider/Blaze #1)						3.00
40-Outer-c is Darkhold envelope made of black parchment w/gold ink; Midnight Massacre; Demogoblin app.						3.00
41-48: 41-Lilith & Centurious app.; begin $1.75-c. 41-43-Neon ink-c. 43-Has free extra 16 pg. insert on Siege of Darkness. 44,45-Siege of Darkness parts 2 & 10. 44-Spot varnish-c. 46-Intro new Ghost Rider. 48-Spider-Man app.						2.25
49,51-60,62-74: 49-Begin $1.95-c; bound-in trading card sheet; Hulk app. 55-Werewolf by Night app. 65-Punisher app. 67,68-Gambit app. 68-Wolverine app. 73,74-Blaze, Vengeance app.						2.25
50,61: 50-($2.50, 52 pgs.)-Regular edition						2.50
50-($2.95, 52 pgs.)-Collectors Ed. die cut foil-c						3.00
75-92: 76-Vs. Vengeance. 77,78-Dr. Strange-app. 78-New costume						2.25
93-($2.99)-Saltares & Texeira-a						3.00
#(-1) Flashback (7/97) Saltares-a						2.25
Annual 1,2 ('93, '94, $2.95, 68 pgs.) 1-Bagged w/card						3.00
...And Cable 1 (9/92, $3.95, stiff-c, 68 pgs.)-Reprints Marvel Comics Presents #90-98 w/new Kieth-c						4.00

Ghost Rider 2099 #4 © MAR

Ghosts #76 © DC

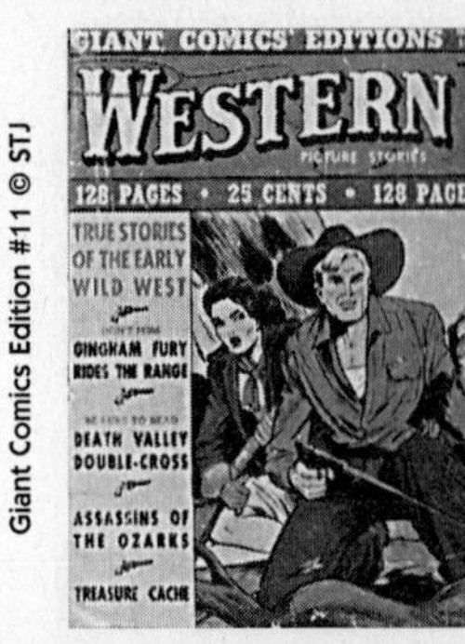

Giant Comics Edition #11 © STJ

GD 2.0 | VG 4.0 | FN 6.0 | VF 8.0 | VF/NM 9.0 | NM- 9.2

...:Crossroads (11/95, $3.95) Die cut cover; Nord-a 5.00
Highway to Hell (2001, $3.50) Reprints origin from Marvel Spotlight #5 3.50
...: Resurrected TPB (2001, $12.95) r/#1-7 13.00
NOTE: ***Andy & Joe Kubert*** *c/a-28-31.* ***Quesada*** *c-21.* ***Williamson*** *a(i)-33-35; c-33i.*

GHOST RIDER (Volume 3)
Marvel Comics: Aug, 2001 - No. 6, Jan, 2002 ($2.99, limited series)
1-6-Grayson-s/Kaniuga-a/c 3.00
...: The Hammer Lane TPB (6/02, $15.95) r/#1-6 16.00

GHOST RIDER/BALLISTIC
Marvel Comics: Feb, 1997 ($2.95, one-shot)
1-Devil's Reign pt. 3 3.00

GHOST RIDER/BLAZE: SPIRITS OF VENGEANCE (Also see Blaze)
Marvel Comics (Midnight Sons imprint #17 on): Aug, 1992 - No. 23, June, 1994 ($1.75)
1-($2.75, 52 pgs.)-Polybagged w/poster; part 2 of Rise of the Midnight Sons storyline; Adam Kubert-c/a begins 3.00
2-11,14-21: 4-Art Adams & Joe Kubert-p. 5,6-Spirits of Venom parts 2 & 4 cont'd from Web of Spider-Man #95,96 w/Demogoblin. 14-17-Neon ink-c. 15-Intro Blaze's new costume & power. 17,18-Siege of Darkness parts 8 & 13. 17-Spot varnish-c 2.25
12-($2.95)-Glow-in-the-dark-c 3.00
13-($2.25)-Outer-c is Darkhold envelope made of black parchment w/gold ink; Midnight Massacre x-over 2.50
22,23: 22-Begin $1.95-c; bound-in trading card sheet 2.25
NOTE: ***Adam & Joe Kubert*** *c-7, 8.* ***Adam Kubert/Steacy*** *c-6.* ***J. Kubert*** *a-13p(6 pgs.)*

GHOST RIDER/CAPTAIN AMERICA: FEAR
Marvel Comics: Oct, 1992 ($5.95, 52 pgs.)
nn-Wraparound gatefold-c; Williamson inks 6.00

GHOST RIDER 2099
Marvel Comics: May, 1994 - No. 25, May, 1996 ($1.50/$1.95)
1 ($2.25)-Collector's Edition w/prismatic foil-c 3.00
1 ($1.50)-Regular Edition; bound-in trading card sheet 2.25
2-24: 7-Spider-Man 2099 app. 2.25
2-(Variant; polybagged with Sega Sub-Terrania poster) 5.00
25 ($2.95) 3.00

GHOST RIDER, WOLVERINE, PUNISHER: THE DARK DESIGN
Marvel Comics: Dec, 1994 ($5.95, one-shot)
nn-Gatefold-c 6.00

GHOST RIDER; WOLVERINE; PUNISHER: HEARTS OF DARKNESS
Marvel Comics: Dec, 1991 ($4.95, one-shot, 52 pgs.)
1-Double gatefold-c; John Romita, Jr.-c/a(p) 5.00

GHOSTS (Ghost No. 1)
National Periodical Publications/DC Comics: Sept-Oct, 1971 - No. 112, May, 1982 (No. 1-5: 52 pgs.)

	GD	VG	FN	VF	VF/NM	NM-
1-Aparo-a	12	24	36	87	129	170
2-Wood-a(i)	7	14	21	46	63	80
3-5	5	10	15	36	48	60
6-10	3	6	9	18	24	30
11-20	2	4	6	12	16	20
21-39	2	4	6	8	10	12
40-(68 pgs.)	3	6	9	16	20	24
41-60	1	2	3	5	6	8
61-96						6.00
97-99-The Spectre vs. Dr. 13 by Aparo. 97,98-Spectre-c by Aparo.	2	4	6	8	10	12
100-Infinity-c	1	2	3	4	5	7
101-112						5.00

NOTE: ***B. Baily*** *a-77.* ***Buckler*** *c-99, 100.* ***J. Craig*** *a-108.* ***Ditko*** *a-77, 111.* ***Giffen*** *a-104p, 106p, 111p.* ***Glanzman*** *a-2.* ***Golden*** *a-88.* ***Infantino*** *a-8.* ***Kaluta*** *c-7, 93, 101.* ***Kubert*** *a-8; c-89, 105-108, 111.* ***Mayer*** *a-111.* ***McWilliams*** *a-99.* ***Win Mortimer*** *a-89, 91, 94.* ***Nasser/Netzer*** *a-97.* ***Newton*** *a-92p, 94p.* ***Nino*** *a-35, 37, 57.* ***Orlando*** *a-74i; c-80.* ***Redondo*** *a-8, 13, 45.* ***Sparling*** *a(p)-90, 93, 94.* ***Spiegle*** *a-103, 105.* ***Tuska*** *a-2i. Dr. 13, the Ghostbreaker back-ups in 95-99, 101.*

GHOSTS SPECIAL (See DC Special Series No. 7)

GHOST STORIES (See Amazing Ghost Stories)

GHOST STORIES
Dell Publ. Co.: Sept-Nov, 1962; No. 2, Apr-June, 1963 - No. 37, Oct, 1973

	GD	VG	FN	VF	VF/NM	NM-
12-295-211(#1)-Written by John Stanley	6	12	18	43	59	75
2	4	8	12	22	30	38
3-10: Two No. 6's exist with different c/a(12-295-406 & 12-295-503) #12-295-503 is actually #9 with indicia to #6	3	6	9	19	25	32
11-21: 21-Last 12¢ issue	3	6	9	16	20	25
22-37	2	4	6	11	14	18

NOTE: *#21-34, 36, 37 all reprint earlier issues.*

GHOUL TALES (Magazine)
Stanley Publications: Nov, 1970 - No. 5, July, 1971 (52 pgs.) (B&W)

	GD	VG	FN	VF	VF/NM	NM-
1-Aragon pre-code reprints; Mr. Mystery as host; bondage-c	7	14	21	50	68	85
2,3: 2-(1/71)Reprint/Climax #1. 3-(3/71)	4	8	12	24	32	40
4-(5/71)Reprints story "The Way to a Man's Heart" used in **SOTI**	4	8	12	29	40	50
5-ACG reprints	3	7	10	21	28	35

NOTE: *No. 1-4 contain pre-code Aragon reprints.*

GIANT BOY BOOK OF COMICS (Also see Boy Comics)
Newsbook Publications (Gleason): 1945 (240 pgs., hard-c)

	GD	VG	FN	VF	VF/NM	NM-
1-Crimebuster & Young Robin Hood; Biro-c	91	182	273	569	855	1140

GIANT COMIC ALBUM
King Features Syndicate: 1972 (59¢, 11x14", 52 pgs., B&W, cardboard-c)

	GD	VG	FN	VF	VF/NM	NM-
Newspaper reprints: Barney Google, Little Iodine, Katzenjammer Kids, Henry, Beetle Bailey, Blondie, & Snuffy Smith each...	3	6	9	18	24	30
Flash Gordon ('68-69 Dan Barry)	4	8	12	24	32	40
Mandrake the Magician ('59 Falk), Popeye	3	7	10	21	28	35

GIANT COMICS
Charlton Comics: Summer, 1957 - No. 3, Winter, 1957 (25¢, 100 pgs.)

	GD	VG	FN	VF	VF/NM	NM-
1-Atomic Mouse, Hoppy app.	22	44	66	124	172	220
2,3: 2-Romance. 3-Christmas Book; Atomic Mouse, Atomic Rabbit, Li'l Genius, Li'l Tomboy & Atom the Cat stories	16	32	48	89	122	155

NOTE: *The above may be rebound comics; contents could vary.*

GIANT COMICS (See Wham-O Giant Comics)

GIANT COMICS EDITION (See Terry-Toons) (Also see Fox Giants)
St. John Publishing Co.: 1947 - No. 17, 1950 (25¢, 100-164 pgs.)

	GD	VG	FN	VF	VF/NM	NM-
1-Mighty Mouse	46	92	138	288	444	600
2-Abbie & Slats	22	44	66	138	214	290
3-Terry-Toons Album; 100 pgs.	35	70	105	219	340	460
4-Crime comics; contains Red Seal No. 16, used & illo. in **SOTI**	52	104	156	325	500	675
5-Police Case Book (4/49, 132 pgs.)-Contents varies; contains remaindered St. John books - some volumes contain 5 copies rather than 4, with 160 pages; Matt Baker-c	50	100	150	313	482	650
5A-Terry-Toons Album (132 pgs.)-Mighty Mouse, Heckle & Jeckle, Gandy Goose & Dinky stories	32	64	96	200	305	410
6-Western Picture Stories; Baker-c/a(3); Tuska-a; The Sky Chief, Blue Monk, Ventrilo app., 132 pgs.	48	96	144	300	463	625
7-Contains a teen-age romance plus 3 Mopsy comics	29	58	87	181	276	370
8-The Adventures of Mighty Mouse (10/49)	32	64	96	200	305	410
9-Romance and Confession Stories; Kubert-a(4); Baker-a; photo-c (132 pgs.)	52	104	156	325	500	675
10-Terry-Toons Album (132 pgs.)-Mighty Mouse, Heckle & Jeckle, Gandy Goose stories	32	64	96	200	305	410
11-Western Picture Stories-Baker-c/a(4); The Sky Chief, Desperado, & Blue Monk app.; another version with Son of Sinbad by Kubert (132 pgs.)	46	92	138	288	444	600
12-Diary Secrets; Baker prostitute-c; 4 St. John romance comics; Baker-a	108	216	324	675	1038	1400
13-Romances; Baker, Kubert-a	46	92	138	288	444	600
14-Mighty Mouse Album (132 pgs.)	32	64	96	200	305	410
15-Romances (4 love comics)-Baker-c	52	104	156	325	500	675
16-Little Audrey; Abbott & Costello, Casper	34	68	102	213	327	440
17(nn)-Mighty Mouse Album (nn, no date, but did follow No. 16); 100 pgs. on cover but has 148 pgs.	32	64	96	200	305	410

NOTE: *The above books contain remaindered comics and contents could vary with each issue. No. 11, 12 have part photo magazine insides.*

GIANT COMICS EDITIONS
United Features Syndicate: 1940's (132 pgs.)

	GD	VG	FN	VF	VF/NM	NM-
1-Abbie & Slats, Abbott & Costello, Jim Hardy, Ella Cinders, Iron Vic, Gordo, & Bill Bumlin	40	80	120	240	340	440
2-Jim Hardy, Ella Cinders, Elmo & Gordo	30	60	90	170	240	310

NOTE: *Above books contain rebound copies; contents can vary.*

GIANT GRAB BAG OF COMICS (See Archie All-Star Specials under Archie Comics)

GIANTKILLER
DC Comics: Aug, 1999 - No. 6, Jan, 2000 ($2.50, limited series)

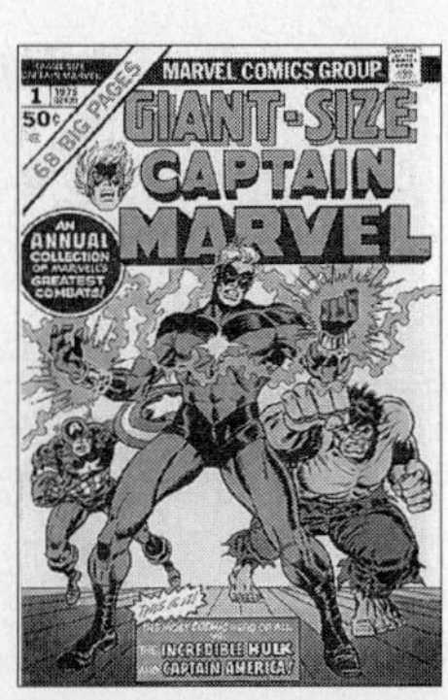

Giant-Size Captain Marvel #1 © MAR

Giant-Size Spider-Man #1 © MAR

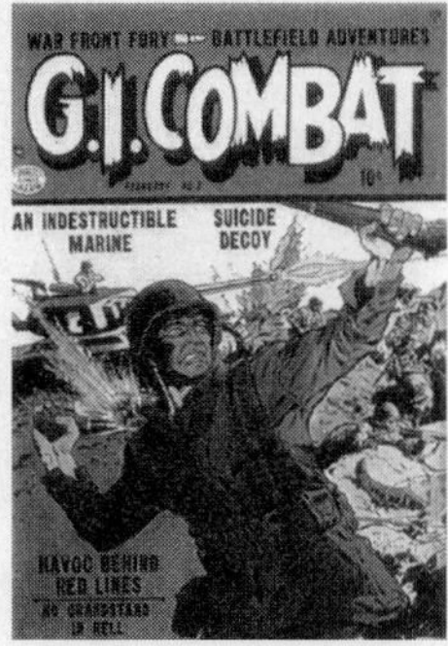

G.I. Combat #3 © QUA

	GD 2.0	VG 4.0	FN 6.0	VF 8.0	VF/NM 9.0	NM- 9.2
1-6-Story and painted art by Dan Brereton						2.50
...A to Z: A Field Guide to Big Monsters (8/99)						2.50
GIANTS (See Thrilling True Story of the Baseball...)						
GIANT-SIZE...						
Marvel Comics Group: May, 1974 - Dec, 1975 (35/50¢, 52/68 pgs.) (Some titles quarterly) (Scarce in strict NM or better due to defective cutting, gluing and binding; warping, splitting and off-center pages are common)						
Avengers 1(8/74)-New-a plus G.A. H. Torch-r; 1st modern app. The Whizzer; 1st & only modern app. Miss America; 2nd app. Invaders; Kang, Rama-Tut, Mantis app.	4	8	12	27	36	45
Avengers 2,3,5: 2(11/74)-Death of the Swordsman; origin of Rama-Tut. 3(2/75). 5(12/75)-Reprints Avengers Special #1	3	6	9	16	20	25
Avengers 4 (6/75)-Vision marries Scarlet Witch.	3	7	10	21	28	35
Captain America 1(12/75)-r/stories T.O.S. 59-63 by Kirby (#63 reprints origin)	4	8	12	22	30	38
Captain Marvel 1(12/75)-r/Capt. Marvel #17, 20, 21 by Gil Kane (p)	3	6	9	16	20	24
Chillers 1(6/74, 52 pgs)-Curse of Dracula; origin/1st app. Lilith, Dracula's daughter; Heath-r, Colan-c/a(p); becomes Giant-Size Dracula #2 on	4	8	12	29	40	50
Chillers 1(2/75, 50¢, 68 pgs.)-Alcala-a	3	6	9	18	23	28
Chillers 2(5/75)-All-r; Everett-r from Advs. into Weird Worlds	2	4	6	14	18	22
Chillers 3(8/75)-Wrightson-c(new)/a(r); Colan, Kirby, Smith-r	3	6	9	18	23	28
Conan 1(9/74)-B. Smith-r/#3; start adaptation of Howard's "Hour of the Dragon" (ends #4); 1st app. Belit; new-a begins	3	6	9	18	24	30
Conan 2(12/74)-B. Smith-r/#5; Sutton-a(i)(#1 also); Buscema-c	2	4	6	14	18	22
Conan 3-5: 3(4/75)-B. Smith-r/#6; Sutton-a(i). 4(6/75)-B. Smith-r/#7. 5(1975)-B. Smith-r/#14,15; Kirby-c	2	4	6	11	14	18
Creatures 1(5/74, 52 pgs.)-Werewolf app; 1st app. Tigra (formerly Cat); Crandall-r; becomes Giant-Size Werewolf w/#2	4	8	12	24	32	40
Daredevil 1(1975)-Reprints Daredevil Annual #1	2	4	6	14	18	22
Defenders 1(7/74)-Silver Surfer app.; Starlin-a; Ditko, Everett & Kirby reprints	3	7	10	21	28	35
Defenders 2(10/74, 68 pgs.)-New G. Kane-c/a(p); Son of Satan app.; Sub-Mariner-r by Everett; Ditko-r/Strange Tales #119 (Dr. Strange); Maneely-r	3	6	9	16	20	24
Defenders 3-5: 3(1/75)-1st app. Korvac.; Newton, Starlin-a; Ditko, Everett-r. 4(4/75)-Ditko, Everett-r; G. Kane-c. 5-(7/75)-Guardians app.	2	4	6	12	16	20
Doc Savage 1(1975, 68 pgs.)-r/#1,2; Mooney-r	2	4	6	11	14	18
Doctor Strange 1(11/75)-Reprints stories from Strange Tales #164-168; Lawrence, Tuska-r	2	4	6	14	18	22
Dracula 2(9/74, 50¢)-Formerly Giant-Size Chillers	3	6	9	16	20	24
Dracula 3(12/74)-Fox-r/Uncanny Tales #6	2	4	6	14	18	22
Dracula 4(3/75)-Ditko-r(2)	2	4	6	14	18	22
Dracula 5(6/75)-1st Byrne art at Marvel	4	8	12	27	36	45
Fantastic Four 2-4: 2(8/74)-Formerly Giant-Size Super-Stars; Ditko-r. 3(11/74). 4(2/75)-1st Madrox; 2-4-All have Buscema-a	3	6	9	16	20	25
Fantastic Four 5,6: 5(5/75)-All-r; Kirby, G. Kane-r. 6(10/75)-All-r; Kirby-r	2	4	6	12	16	20
Hulk 1(1975) r/Hulk Special #1	3	6	9	18	23	28
Invaders 1(6/75, 50¢, 68 pgs.)-Origin; G.A. Sub-Mariner-r/Sub-Mariner #1; intro Master Man	3	6	9	18	24	30
Iron Man 1(1975)-Ditko reprint	3	6	9	16	20	25
Kid Colt 1-3: 1(1/75). 2(4/75). 3(7/75)-new Ayers-a	5	10	15	36	48	60
Man-Thing 1(8/74)-New Ploog-c/a (25 pgs.); Ditko-r/Amazing Adv. #11; Kirby-r/ Strange Tales Ann. #2 & T.O.S. #15; (#1-5 all have new Man-Thing stories, pre-hero-r & are 68 pgs.)	3	6	9	18	24	30
Man-Thing 2,3: 2(11/74)-Buscema-c/a(p); Kirby, Powell-r. 3(2/75)-Alcala-a; Ditko, Kirby, Sutton-r; Gil Kane-c	2	4	6	12	16	20
Man-Thing 4,5: 4(5/75)-Howard the Duck by Brunner-c/a; Ditko-r. 5(8/75)-Howard the Duck by Brunner (p); Dracula cameo in Howard the Duck; Buscema-a(p); Sutton-a(i); G. Kane-c	3	6	9	18	23	28
Marvel Triple Action 1,2: 1(5/75). 2(7/75)	2	4	6	12	16	20
Master of Kung Fu 1(9/74)-Russell-a; Yellow Claw-r in #1-4; Gulacy-a in #1,2	3	6	9	18	23	28
Master of Kung Fu 2-4: 2-(12/74)-r/Yellow Claw #1. 3(3/75)-Gulacy-a; Kirby-a. 4(6/75)-Kirby-a	2	4	6	12	16	20
Power Man 1(1975)	2	4	6	12	16	20
Spider-Man 1(7/74)-Spider-Man /Human Torch-r by Kirby/Ditko; Byrne-r plus new-a (Dracula-c/story)	6	12	18	40	55	70
Spider-Man 2,3: 2(10/74)-Shang-Chi-c/app. 3(1/75)-Doc Savage-c/app.; Daredevil/ Spider-Man-r w/Ditko-a	4	8	12	22	30	38
Spider-Man 4(4/75)-3rd Punisher app.; Byrne, Ditko-r	9	18	27	65	93	120
Spider-Man 5,6: 5(7/75)-Man-Thing/Lizard-c. 6(9/75)	3	6	9	18	24	30
Super-Heroes Featuring Spider-Man 1(6/74, 35¢, 52 pgs.)-Spider-Man vs. Man-Wolf; Morbius, the Living Vampire app.; Ditko-r; G. Kane-a(p); Spidey villains app.	6	12	18	40	55	70
Super-Stars 1(5/74, 35¢, 52 pgs.)-Fantastic Four; Thing vs. Hulk; Kirbyish-c/a by Buckler/Sinnott; F.F. villains profiled; becomes Giant-Size Fantastic Four #2 on	4	8	12	27	36	45
Super-Villain Team-Up 1(3/75, 68 pgs.)-Craig-r(i) (Also see Fantastic Four #6 for 1st super-villain team-up)	2	4	6	14	18	22
Super-Villain Team-Up 2(6/75, 68 pgs.)-Dr. Doom, Sub-Mariner app.; Spider-Man-r from Amazing Spider-Man #8 by Ditko; Sekowsky-a(p)	2	4	6	11	14	18
Thor 1(7/75)	3	6	9	18	24	30
Werewolf 2(10/74, 68 pgs.)-Formerly Giant-Size Creatures; Ditko-r; Frankenstein app.	2	4	6	14	18	22
Werewolf 3,5: 3(1/75, 68 pgs.). 5(7/75, 68 pgs.)	2	4	6	14	18	22
Werewolf 4(4/75, 68 pgs.)-Morbius the Living Vampire app.	3	6	9	18	23	28
X-Men 1(Summer, 1975, 50¢, 68 pgs.)-1st app. new X-Men; intro. Nightcrawler, Storm, Colossus & Thunderbird; 2nd full app. Wolverine after Incredible Hulk #181	69	138	207	587	894	1200
X-Men 2 (11/75)-N. Adams-r (51 pgs)	8	16	24	53	74	95
GIANT SPECTACULAR COMICS (See Archie All-Star Special under Archie Comics)						
GIANT SUMMER FUN BOOK (See Terry-Toons...)						
G. I. COMBAT						
Quality Comics Group: Oct, 1952 - No. 43, Dec, 1956						
1-Crandall-c; Cuidera a-1-43i	66	132	198	413	619	825
2	34	68	102	196	278	360
3-5,10-Crandall-c/a	31	62	93	175	248	320
6-Crandall-a	27	54	81	155	218	280
7-9	23	46	69	130	183	235
11-20	18	36	54	104	142	180
21-31,33,35-43: 41-1st S.A. issue	16	32	48	89	122	155
32-Nuclear attack-c/story "Atomic Rocket Assault"	19	38	57	106	146	185
34-Crandall-a	17	34	51	98	134	170
G. I. COMBAT (See DC Special Series #22)						
National Periodical Publ./DC Comics: No. 44, Jan, 1957 - No. 288, Mar, 1987						
44-Grey tone-c	50	100	150	400	600	800
45	27	54	81	196	288	380
46-50	21	42	63	152	224	295
51-Grey tone-c	22	44	66	160	235	310
52-54,59,60	17	34	51	123	182	240
55-minor Sgt. Rock prototype by Finger	20	40	60	142	209	275
56-Sgt. Rock prototype by Kanigher/Kubert	23	46	69	167	244	320
57,58-Pre-Sgt. Rock Easy Co. stories	21	42	63	149	220	290
61-65,69-74: 74-American flag-c	14	28	42	97	141	185
66-Pre-Sgt. Rock Easy Co. story	20	40	60	140	205	270
67-1st Tank Killer	22	44	66	160	235	310
68-(1/59) Introduces "The Rock", Sgt. Rock prototype by Kanigher/Kubert; once considered his actual 1st app. (see Our Army at War #82,83)	53	106	159	451	688	925
75-80: 75-Greytone-c begin, end #109	16	32	48	113	167	220
81,82,84-86	13	26	39	90	133	175
83-1st Big Al, Little Al, & Charlie Cigar	15	30	45	109	160	210
87-1st Haunted Tank; series begins	50	100	150	413	632	850
88-2nd Haunted Tank	21	42	63	149	220	290
89,90: 90-Last 10¢ issue	13	26	39	90	133	175
91-1st Haunted Tank-c	16	32	48	116	171	225
92-99: 92-Grey tone-c	10	20	30	73	107	140
100,108: 108-1st Sgt. Rock x-over	11	22	33	80	118	155
101-107,109: 109-Grey tone-c	9	18	27	60	85	110
110-112,115-120	7	14	21	50	68	85
113-Grey tone-c	8	16	24	55	78	100
114-Origin Haunted Tank	14	28	42	99	145	190
121-136: 121-1st app. Sgt. Rock's father. 136-Last 12¢ issue	5	10	15	36	48	60
137,139,140	4	8	12	27	36	45
138-Intro. The Losers (Capt. Storm, Gunner/Sarge, Johnny Cloud) in Haunted Tank (10-11/69)	9	18	27	65	93	120
141-143	3	6	9	18	23	28
144-148 (68 pgs.)	4	8	12	22	30	38

G.I. Jane #5 © Stanhall

G.I. Joe #6 © Hasbro

G.I. Joe, A Real American Hero #94 © Hasbro

GD 2.0 | VG 4.0 | FN 6.0 | VF 8.0 | VF/NM 9.0 | NM- 9.2

149,151-154 (52 pgs.): 151-Capt. Storm story. 151,153-Medal of Honor series by Maurer 3 6 9 18 23 28
150- (52 pgs.) Ice Cream Soldier story (tells how he got his name); Death of Haunted Tank-c/s 4 8 12 22 30 38
155-167,169,170,200 2 4 6 9 11 14
168-Neal Adams-c 2 4 6 14 18 22
171-199 2 4 6 8 10 12
201,202 ($1.00 size) Neal Adams-c 2 4 6 11 14 18
203-210 ($1.00 size) 2 4 6 9 11 14
211-230 ($1.00 size) 1 3 4 6 8 10
231-259 ($1.00 size).232-Origin Kana the Ninja. 244-Death of Slim Stryker; 1st app. The Mercenaries. 246-(76 pgs., $1.50)-30th Anniversary issue. 257-Intro. Stuart's Raiders 1 2 3 5 7 9
260-281: 260-Begin $1.25, 52 pg. issues, end #281. 264-Intro Sgt. Bullet; origin Kana. 269-Intro. The Bravos of Vietnam. 274-Cameo of Monitor from Crisis on Infinite Earths 6.00
282-288 (75¢): 282-New advs. begin 6.00

NOTE: ***N. Adams** c-168, 201, 202. **Check** a-168, 173. **Drucker** a-48, 61, 63, 66, 71, 72, 76, 134, 140, 141, 144, 147, 148, 153. **Evans** a-135, 138, 158, 164, 166, 201, 202, 204, 205, 215, 256. Giffen a-267. **Glanzman** a-most issues. **Kubert/Heath** a-most issues; **Kubert** covers most issues. **Morrow** a-159-161(2 pgs.). **Redondo** a-189, 240i, 243i. **Sekowsky** a-162p. **Severin** a-147, 152, 154. **Simonson** c-169. **Thorne** a-152, 156. **Wildey** a-153. Johnny Cloud app.-112, 115, 120. Mlle. Marie app.-123, 132, 200. Sgt. Rock app.-111-113, 115, 120, 125, 141, 146, 147, 149, 200. USS Stevens by **Glanzman**-145, 150-153, 157. **Grandenetti** c-44-48.*

GIDGET (TV)
Dell Publishing Co.: Apr, 1966 - No. 2, Dec, 1966

1-Sally Field photo-c 10 20 30 72 104 135
2 7 14 21 51 71 90

GIFT (See The Crusaders)

GIFT COMICS
Fawcett Publications: 1942 - No. 4, 1949 (50¢/25¢, 324 pgs./152 pgs.)

1-Captain Marvel, Bulletman, Golden Arrow, Ibis the Invincible, Mr. Scarlet, & Spy Smasher begin; not rebound, remaindered comics, printed at same time as originals; 50¢-c & 324 pgs. begin, end #3. 264 528 792 1650 2475 3300
2-Commando Yank, Phantom Eagle, others app. 160 320 480 1000 1500 2000
3 108 216 324 675 1013 1350
4-(25¢, 152 pgs.)-The Marvel Family, Captain Marvel, etc.; each issue can vary in contents 68 136 204 425 638 850

GIFTS FROM SANTA (See March of Comics No. 137)

GIFTS OF THE NIGHT
DC Comics (Vertigo): Feb, 1999 - No. 4, May, 1999 ($2.95, limited series)

1-4-Bolton-c/a; Chadwick-s 3.00

GIGGLE COMICS (Spencer Spook No. 100) (Also see Ha Ha Comics)
Creston No.1-63/American Comics Group No. 64 on; Oct, 1943 - No. 99, Jan-Feb, 1955

1-Funny animal 33 66 99 190 270 350
2 16 32 48 92 126 160
3-5: Ken Hultgren-a begins? 12 24 36 69 92 115
6-10: 9-1st Superkatt (6/44) 10 20 30 56 73 90
11-20 8 16 24 46 58 70
21-40: 32-Patriotic-c. 37,61-X-Mas-c 8 16 24 40 50 60
41-54,56-59,61-99: 95-Spencer Spook begins? 7 14 21 35 43 50
55,60-Milt Gross-a 8 16 24 40 50 60

G-I IN BATTLE (G-I No. 1 only)
Ajax-Farrell Publ./Four Star: Aug, 1952 - No. 9, July, 1953; Mar, 1957 - No. 6, May, 1958

1 11 22 33 66 88 110
2 7 14 21 37 46 55
3-9 7 14 21 35 43 50
Annual 1(1952, 25¢, 100 pgs.) 26 52 78 150 210 270
1(1957-Ajax) 8 16 24 40 50 60
2-6 6 12 18 27 33 38

G. I. JANE
Stanhall/Merit No. 11: May, 1953 - No. 11, Mar, 1955 (Misdated 3/54)

1-PX Pete begins; Bill Williams-c/a 13 26 39 76 103 130
2-7(5/54) 8 16 24 43 54 65
8-10(12/54, Stanhall) 7 14 21 37 46 55
11 (3/55, Merit) 7 14 21 35 43 50

G. I. JOE (Also see Advs. of..., Showcase #53, 54 & The Yardbirds)
Ziff-Davis Publ. Co. (Korean War): No. 10, 1950; No. 11, 4-5/51 - No. 51, 6/57(52pgs.: 10-14,6-17?)

10(#1, 1950)-Saunders painted-c begin 16 32 48 92 126 160
11-14(#2-5, 10/51): 11-New logo. 12-New logo 10 20 30 58 77 95
V2#6(12/51)-17-(11/52; Last 52 pgs.?) 10 20 30 56 73 90

GD 2.0 | VG 4.0 | FN 6.0 | VF 8.0 | VF/NM 9.0 | NM- 9.2

18-(25¢, 100 pg. Giant, 12-1/52-53) 24 48 72 135 190 245
19-30: 20-22,24,28-31-The Yardbirds app. 9 18 27 49 62 75
31-47,49-51 8 16 24 46 58 70
48-Atom bomb story 9 18 27 49 62 75

NOTE: ***Powell** a-V2#7, 8, 11. **Norman Saunders** painted c-10-14, V2#6-14, 26, 30, 31, 35, 38, 39. **Tuska** a-7. Bondage c-29, 35, 38.*

G. I. JOE (America's Movable Fighting Man)
Custom Comics: 1967 (5-1/8x8-3/8", 36 pgs.)

nn-Schaffenberger-a; based on Hasbro toy 4 8 12 24 32 40

G.I. JOE
Dark Horse Comics: Dec, 1995 - No. 4, Apr, 1996 ($1.95, limited series)

1-4: Mike W. Barr scripts. 1-Three Frank Miller covers with title logos in red, white and blue. 2-Breyfogle-c. 3-Simonson-c 3.00

G.I. JOE
Dark Horse Comics: V2#1, June, 1996 - V2#4, Sept, 1996 ($2.50)

V2#1-4: Mike W. Barr scripts. 4-Painted-c 3.00

G.I. JOE
Image Comics: 2001 - Present ($2.95)

1-Campbell-c; back-c painted by Beck; Blaylock-s 2 4 6 8 10 12
1-2nd printing with front & back covers switched 6.00
2,3 5.00
4-($3.50) 4.00
5-20,22-25: 6-SuperPatriot preview. 18-Brereton-c. 3.00
21-Silent issue; Zeck-a; two covers by Campbell and Zeck 3.00
...: Malfunction (2003, $15.95) r/#11-15 16.00
...: M. I. A. (2002, $4.95) r/#1&2; Beck back-c from #1 on cover 5.00
...: Reckonings (2002, $12.95) r/#6-9; Zeck-c 13.00
...: Reinstated (2002, $14.95) r/#1-4 15.00

G. I. JOE AND THE TRANSFORMERS
Marvel Comics Group: Jan, 1987 - No. 4, Apr, 1987 (Limited series)

1-4 4.00

G. I. JOE, A REAL AMERICAN HERO (...Starring Snake-Eyes on-c #135 on)
Marvel Comics Group: June, 1982 - No. 155, Dec, 1994

1-Printed on Baxter paper; based on Hasbro toy 3 6 9 16 20 25
2-Printed on reg. paper 2 4 6 14 18 22
3-10 2 4 6 10 12 15
11-20: 11-Intro Airborne 2 4 6 8 10 12
21-1st Storm Shadow; silent issue 3 6 9 16 20 25
22 1 3 4 6 8 10
23-25,28-30,60: 60-Todd McFarlane-a 1 2 3 4 5 7
26,27-Origin Snake-Eyes parts 1 & 2 2 4 6 9 11 14
31-50: 33-New headquarters 5.00
51-59,61-90 4.00
91,92,94-99 5.00
93-Snake-Eyes' face first revealed 2 4 6 10 13 16
100,135-138: 135-138-($1.75)-Bagged w/trading card 1 2 3 5 7 9
101-134: 110-1st Ron Garney-a 6.00
139-142-New Transformers app. 1 3 4 6 8 10
143,145-149 1 2 3 5 6 8
144-Origin Snake-Eyes 2 4 6 8 10 12
150-Low print thru #155 2 4 6 14 18 22
151-154 2 4 6 12 16 20
155-Last issue 3 7 10 21 28 35
All 2nd printings 2.25
Special #1 (2/95, $1.50) r/#60 w/McFarlane-a 3 6 9 19 25 32
Special Treasury Edition (1982)-r/#1 3 6 9 17 21 26
Volume 1 TPB (4/02, $24.95) r/#1-10; new cover by Michael Golden 25.00
Volume 2 TPB (6/02, $24.95) r/#11-20; new cover by J. Scott Campbell 25.00
Volume 3 TPB (2002, $24.99) r/#21-30; new cover by J. Scott Campbell 25.00
Volume 4 TPB (2002, $25.99) r/#31-40; new cover by J. Scott Campbell 26.00
Volume 5 TPB (2002, $24.99) r/#42-50; new cover by J. Scott Campbell 25.00
Yearbook 1-4: (3/85-3/88)-r/#1; Golden-c. 2-Golden-c/a 5.00

NOTE: ***Garney** a(p)-110. **Golden** c-23, 29, 34, 36. **Heath** a-24. **Rogers** a(p)-75, 77-82, 84, 86; c-77.*

G.I. JOE: BATTLE FILES
Image Comics: 2002 - No. 3, 2002 ($5.95)

1-3-Profile pages of characters and history; Beck-c 6.00

G. I. JOE COMICS MAGAZINE
Marvel Comics Group: Dec, 1986 - No. 13, 1988 ($1.50, digest-size)

1-13: G.I. Joe-r 1 3 4 6 8 10

G.I. Joe: Frontline #1 © Hasbro

Ginger #5 © AP

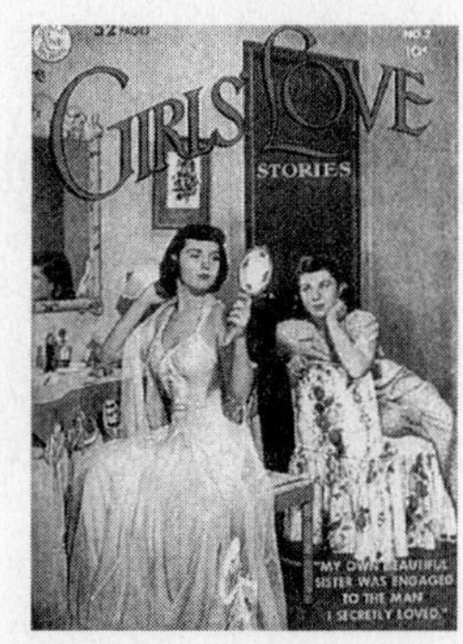

Girls' Love Stories #2 © DC

G.I. JOE EUROPEAN MISSIONS (Action Force in indicia)
Marvel Comics Ltd. (British): Jun, 1988 - No. 15, Dec, 1989 ($1.50/$1.75)
(Series reprints Action Force)

	GD 2.0	VG 4.0	FN 6.0	VF 8.0	VF/NM 9.0	NM- 9.2
1,3-Snake Eyes & Storm Shadow-c/s	1	2	3	5	7	9
2,4-15						6.00

G.I. JOE: FRONT LINE
Image Comics: 2002 - Present ($2.95)

	GD 2.0	VG 4.0	FN 6.0	VF 8.0	VF/NM 9.0	NM- 9.2
1-18: 1-Jurgens-a/Hama-s. 1-Two covers by Dorman & Sharpe. 7,8-Harris-c						3.00
...Vol. 1 - The Mission That Never Was TPB (2003, $14.95) r/ #1-4; script pages						15.00

G. I. JOE ORDER OF BATTLE, THE
Marvel Comics Group: Dec, 1986 - No. 4, Mar, 1987 (limited series)

	GD 2.0	VG 4.0	FN 6.0	VF 8.0	VF/NM 9.0	NM- 9.2
1-4						6.00

G. I. JOE SPECIAL MISSIONS (Indicia title: Special Missions)
Marvel Comics Group: Oct, 1986 - No. 28, Dec, 1989 ($1.00)

	GD 2.0	VG 4.0	FN 6.0	VF 8.0	VF/NM 9.0	NM- 9.2
1-20						4.00
21-28						5.00

G.I. JOE VS. THE TRANSFORMERS
Image Comics: Jun, 2003 - No. 6, Nov, 2003 ($2.95, limited series)

	GD 2.0	VG 4.0	FN 6.0	VF 8.0	VF/NM 9.0	NM- 9.2
1-Blaylock-s/Mike Miller-a; three covers by Miller, Campbell & Andrews						3.00
1-2nd printing; black cover with logo; back-c by Campbell						3.00
2-6: 2-Two covers by Miller & Brooks						3.00

G. I. JUNIORS (See Harvey Hits No. 86,91,95,98,101,104,107,110,112,114,116,118,120,122)

GILGAMESH II
DC Comics: 1989 - No. 4, 1989 ($3.95, limited series, prestige format, mature)

	GD 2.0	VG 4.0	FN 6.0	VF 8.0	VF/NM 9.0	NM- 9.2
1-4: Starlin-c/a/scripts						4.00

GIL THORP
Dell Publishing Co.: May-July, 1963

	GD 2.0	VG 4.0	FN 6.0	VF 8.0	VF/NM 9.0	NM- 9.2
1-Caniffish-a	4	8	12	25	33	42

GINGER
Archie Publications: 1951 - No. 10, Summer, 1954

	GD 2.0	VG 4.0	FN 6.0	VF 8.0	VF/NM 9.0	NM- 9.2
1-Teenage humor	14	28	42	81	111	140
2-(1952)	9	18	27	49	62	75
3-6: 6-(Sum/53)	8	16	24	40	50	60
7-10-Katy Keene app.	9	18	27	54	70	85

GINGER FOX (Also see The World of Ginger Fox)
Comico: Sept, 1988 - No. 4, Dec, 1988 ($1.75, limited series)

	GD 2.0	VG 4.0	FN 6.0	VF 8.0	VF/NM 9.0	NM- 9.2
1-4: Part photo-c on all						2.25

G.I. R.A.M.B.O.T.
Wonder Color Comics/Pied Piper #2: Apr, 1987 - No. 2? ($1.95)

	GD 2.0	VG 4.0	FN 6.0	VF 8.0	VF/NM 9.0	NM- 9.2
1,2: 2-Exist?						2.25

GIRL
DC Comics (Vertigo Verite): Jul, 1996 - No. 3, 1996 ($2.50, lim. series, mature)

	GD 2.0	VG 4.0	FN 6.0	VF 8.0	VF/NM 9.0	NM- 9.2
1-3: Peter Milligan scripts; Fegredo-c/a						2.50

GIRL COMICS (Becomes Girl Confessions No. 13 on)
Marvel/Atlas Comics(CnPC): Oct, 1949 - No. 12, Jan, 1952 (#1-4: 52 pgs.)

	GD 2.0	VG 4.0	FN 6.0	VF 8.0	VF/NM 9.0	NM- 9.2
1-Photo-c	23	46	69	129	180	230
2-Kubert-a; photo-c	13	26	39	74	100	125
3-Everett-a; Liz Taylor photo-c	23	46	69	129	180	230
4-11: 4-Photo-c. 10-12-Sol Brodsky-c	10	20	30	58	77	95
12-Krigstein-a; Al Hartley-c	11	22	33	63	84	105

GIRL CONFESSIONS (Formerly Girl Comics)
Atlas Comics (CnPC/ZPC): No. 13, Mar, 1952 - No. 35, Aug, 1954

	GD 2.0	VG 4.0	FN 6.0	VF 8.0	VF/NM 9.0	NM- 9.2
13-Everett-a	12	24	36	71	96	120
14,15,19,20	9	18	27	49	62	75
16-18-Everett-a	10	20	30	58	77	95
21-35: Robinson-a	7	14	21	37	46	55

GIRL CRAZY
Dark Horse Comics: May, 1996 - No. 3, July, 1996 ($2.95, B&W, limited series)

	GD 2.0	VG 4.0	FN 6.0	VF 8.0	VF/NM 9.0	NM- 9.2
1-3: Gilbert Hernandez-a/scripts.						3.00

GIRL FROM U.N.C.L.E., THE (TV) (Also see The Man From...)
Gold Key: Jan, 1967 - No. 5, Oct, 1967

	GD 2.0	VG 4.0	FN 6.0	VF 8.0	VF/NM 9.0	NM- 9.2
1-McWilliams-a; Stephanie Powers photo front/back-c & pin-ups (no ads, 12¢)	10	20	30	72	104	135
2-5-Leonard Swift-Courier No. 5	7	14	21	51	71	90

GIRLS' FUN & FASHION MAGAZINE (Formerly Polly Pigtails)
Parents' Magazine Institute: V5#44, Jan, 1950 - V5#48, Sept., 1950

	GD 2.0	VG 4.0	FN 6.0	VF 8.0	VF/NM 9.0	NM- 9.2
V5#44	6	12	18	28	34	40
45-48	5	10	14	20	24	28

GIRLS IN LOVE
Fawcett Publications: May, 1950 - No. 2, July, 1950

	GD 2.0	VG 4.0	FN 6.0	VF 8.0	VF/NM 9.0	NM- 9.2
1-Photo-c	12	24	36	71	96	120
2-Photo-c	10	20	30	56	73	90

GIRLS IN LOVE (Formerly G. I. Sweethearts No. 45)
Quality Comics Group: No. 46, Sept, 1955 - No. 57, Dec, 1956

	GD 2.0	VG 4.0	FN 6.0	VF 8.0	VF/NM 9.0	NM- 9.2
46	8	16	24	46	58	70
47-53,55,56	6	12	18	33	41	48
54- 'Commie' story	7	14	21	37	46	55
57-Matt Baker-c/a	9	18	27	52	66	80

GIRLS IN WHITE (See Harvey Comics Hits No. 58)

GIRLS' LIFE (Patsy Walker's Own Magazine For Girls!)
Atlas Comics (BFP): Jan, 1954 - No. 6, Nov, 1954

	GD 2.0	VG 4.0	FN 6.0	VF 8.0	VF/NM 9.0	NM- 9.2
1	11	22	33	66	88	110
2-Al Hartley-c	8	16	24	40	50	60
3-6	7	14	21	35	43	50

GIRLS' LOVE STORIES
National Comics(Signal Publ. No. 9-65/Arleigh No. 83-117): Aug-Sept, 1949 - No. 180, Nov-Dec, 1973 (No. 1-13: 52 pgs.)

	GD 2.0	VG 4.0	FN 6.0	VF 8.0	VF/NM 9.0	NM- 9.2
1-Toth, Kinstler-a, 8 pgs. each; photo-c	55	110	165	330	495	660
2-Kinstler-a?	32	64	96	180	255	330
3-10: 1-9-Photo-c. 7-Infantino-c(p)	22	44	66	124	172	220
11-20	17	34	51	95	130	165
21-33: 21-Kinstler-a. 33-Last pre-code (1-2/55)	11	22	33	63	84	105
34-50	9	18	27	52	66	80
51-70	6	12	18	40	55	70
71-99: 83-Last 10¢ issue	4	8	12	29	40	50
100	5	10	15	33	44	55
101-146: 113-117-April O'Day app.	3	6	9	19	25	32
147-151- "Confessions" serial. 150-Wood-a	3	6	9	19	25	32
152-160,171-179	2	4	6	14	18	22
161-170 (52 pgs.)	4	8	12	22	30	38
180 Last issue	3	6	9	19	25	32

GIRLS' ROMANCES
National Periodical Publ.(Signal Publ. No. 7-79/Arleigh No. 84): Feb-Mar, 1950 - No. 160, Oct, 1971 (No. 1-11: 52 pgs.)

	GD 2.0	VG 4.0	FN 6.0	VF 8.0	VF/NM 9.0	NM- 9.2
1-Photo-c	53	106	159	318	479	640
2-Photo-c; Toth-a	31	62	93	175	248	320
3-10: 3-6-Photo-c	22	44	66	124	172	220
11,12,14-20	15	30	45	84	115	145
13-Toth-c	16	32	48	89	122	155
21-31: 31-Last pre-code (2-3/55)	10	20	30	58	77	95
32-50	6	12	18	43	59	75
51-99: 80-Last 10¢ issue	4	8	12	29	40	50
100	5	10	15	33	44	55
101-108,110-120	3	6	9	19	25	32
109-Beatles-c/story	12	24	36	87	129	170
121-133,135-140	3	6	9	18	23	28
134-Neal Adams-c (splash pg. is same as-c)	5	10	15	33	44	55
141-158	2	4	6	14	18	22
159,160-52 pgs.	4	8	12	22	30	38

GIRL WHO WOULD BE DEATH, THE
DC Comics (Vertigo): Dec, 1998 - No. 4, March, 1999 ($2.50, lim. series)

	GD 2.0	VG 4.0	FN 6.0	VF 8.0	VF/NM 9.0	NM- 9.2
1-4-Kiernan-s/Ormston-a						2.50

G. I. SWEETHEARTS (Formerly Diary Loves; Girls In Love #46 on)
Quality Comics Group: No. 32, June, 1953 - No. 45, May, 1955

	GD 2.0	VG 4.0	FN 6.0	VF 8.0	VF/NM 9.0	NM- 9.2
32	9	18	27	49	62	75
33-45: 44-Last pre-code (3/55)	7	14	21	35	43	50

G.I. TALES (Formerly Sgt. Barney Barker No. 1-3)
Atlas Comics (MCI): No. 4, Feb, 1957 - No. 6, July, 1957

	GD 2.0	VG 4.0	FN 6.0	VF 8.0	VF/NM 9.0	NM- 9.2
4-Severin-a(4)	9	18	27	49	62	75
5	7	14	21	35	43	50
6-Orlando, Powell, & Woodbridge-a	7	14	21	37	46	55

G.I. War Brides #1 © SUPR

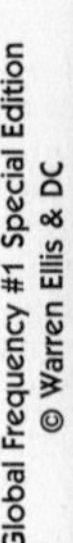
Global Frequency #1 Special Edition © Warren Ellis & DC

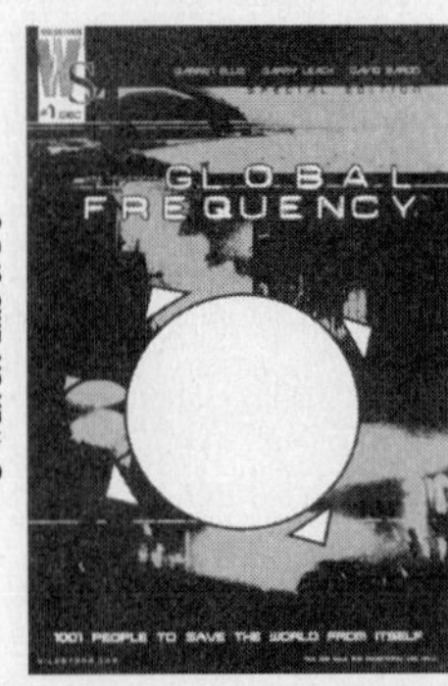

Glory #4 © Rob Liefeld

GD VG FN VF VF/NM NM-
2.0 4.0 6.0 8.0 9.0 9.2

GD VG FN VF VF/NM NM-
2.0 4.0 6.0 8.0 9.0 9.2

GIVE ME LIBERTY (Also see Dark Horse Presents Fifth Anniversary Special, Dark Horse Presents #100-4, Happy Birthday Martha Washington, Martha Washington Goes to War, Martha Washington Stranded In Space & San Diego Comicon Comics #2)
Dark Horse Comics: June, 1990 - No. 4, 1991 ($4.95, limited series, 52 pgs.)

1-4: 1st app. Martha Washington; Frank Miller scripts, Dave Gibbons-c/a in all 5.00

G. I. WAR BRIDES
Superior Publishers Ltd.: Apr, 1954 - No. 8, June, 1955

1 9 18 27 49 62 75
2 6 12 18 28 34 40
3-8: 4-Kamen*esque*-a; lingerie panels 5 10 15 24 30 35

G. I. WAR TALES
National Periodical Publications: Mar-Apr, 1973 - No. 4, Oct-Nov, 1973

1-Reprints in all; dinosaur-c/s 3 6 9 18 23 28
2-N. Adams-a(r) 2 4 6 11 14 18
3,4: 4-Krigstein-a(r) 2 4 6 10 13 16
NOTE: ***Drucker** a-3r, 4r. **Heath** a-4r. **Kubert** a-2, 3; c-4r.*

GIZMO (Also see Domino Chance)
Chance Ent.: May-June, 1985 (B&W, one-shot)

1 6.00

GIZMO
Mirage Studios: 1986 - No. 6, July, 1987 ($1.50, B&W)

1-6 2.50

GLADSTONE COMIC ALBUM
Gladstone: 1987 - No. 28, 1990 ($5.95/$9.95, 8-1/2x11")(All Mickey Mouse albums are by Gottfredson)

1-10: 1-Uncle Scrooge; Barks-r; Beck-c. 2-Donald Duck; r/F.C. #108 by Barks. 3-Mickey Mouse-r by Gottfredson. 4-Uncle Scrooge; r/F.C. #456 by Barks w/unedited story. 5-Donald Duck Advs.; r/F.C. #199. 6-Uncle Scrooge-r by Barks. 7-Donald Duck-r by Barks. 8-Mickey Mouse-r. 9-Bambi; r/F.C. #186? 10-Donald Duck Advs.; r/F.C. #275
1 3 4 6 8 10
11-20: 11-Uncle Scrooge; r/U.S. #4. 12-Donald And Daisy; r/F.C. #1055, WDC&S. 13-Donald Duck Advs.; r/F.C. #408. 14-Uncle Scrooge; Barks-r/U.S #21. 15-Donald And Gladstone; Barks-r. 16-Donald Duck Advs.; r/F.C. #238. 17-Mickey Mouse strip-r (The World of Tomorrow, The Pirate Ghost Ship). 18-Donald Duck and the Junior Woodchucks; Barks-r. 19-Uncle Scrooge; r/U.S. #12; Rosa-c. 20-Uncle Scrooge; r/F.C. #386; Barks-c/a(r)
1 3 4 6 8 10
21-25: 21-Donald Duck Family; Barks-c/a(r). 22-Mickey Mouse strip-r. 23-Donald Duck; Barks-r/D.D. #26 w/unedited story. 24-Uncle Scrooge; Barks-r; Rosa-c. 25-D. Duck; Barks-c/a-r/F.C. #367 1 3 4 6 8 10
26-28: All have $9.95-c. 26-Mickey and Donald; Gottfredson-c/a(r). 27-Donald Duck; r/WDC&S by Barks; Barks painted-c. 28-Uncle Scrooge & Donald Duck; Rosa-c/a (4 stories)
1 3 4 6 8 10
Special 1-7: 1 ('89-'90, $9.95/13.95)-1-Donald Duck Finds Pirate Gold; r/F.C. #9. 2 ('89, $8.95)-Uncle Scrooge and Donald Duck; Barks-r/Uncle Scrooge #5; Rosa-c. 3 ('89, $8.95)-Mickey Mouse strip-r. 4 ('89, $11.95)-Uncle Scrooge; Rosa-c/a-r/Son of the Sun from U.S. #219 plus Barks-r/U.S. 5 ('90, $11.95)-Donald Duck Advs.; Barks-r/F.C. #282 & 422 plus Barks painted-c. 6 ('90, $12.95)-Uncle Scrooge; Barks-c/a-r/Uncle Scrooge. 7 ('90, $13.95)-Mickey Mouse; Gottfredson strip-r 2 4 6 9 11 14

GLADSTONE COMIC ALBUM (2nd Series)(Also see The Original Dick Tracy)
Gladstone Publishing: 1990 ($5.95, 8-1/2 x 11," stiff-c, 52 pgs.)

1,2-The Original Dick Tracy. 2-Origin of the 2-way wrist radio 6.00
3-D Tracy Meets the Mole-r by Gould ($6.95). 1 2 3 5 6 8

GLAMOROUS ROMANCES (Formerly Dotty)
Ace Magazines (A. A. Wyn): No. 41, July, 1949 - No. 90, Oct, 1956 (Photo-c 68-90)

41-Dotty app. 9 18 27 49 62 75
42-72,74-80: 44-Begin 52 pg. issues. 45,50-61-Painted-c. 80-Last pre-code (2/55) 7 14 21 35 43 50
73-L.B. Cole-r/All Love #27 7 14 21 37 46 55
81-90 6 12 18 31 38 45

GLOBAL FREQUENCY
DC Comics (WildStorm): Dec, 2002 - No. 12 ($2.95, limited series)

1-10-Warren Ellis-s. 1-Leach-a. 2-Fabry-a. 3-Dillon-a. 5-Muth-a. 7-Bisley-a 3.00
1-Special Edition variant-c; promotional giveaway for retailers (200 printed) 10.00
...: Planet Ablaze TPB (2003, $14.95) r/#1-6 15.00

GLOOMCOOKIE
SLG Publishing: June, 1999 - Present ($2.95, B&W)

1-18-Serena Valentino-s. 1-6-Ted Naifeh-a. 7-12-Gebbia-a 3.00
...Presents: A Monster's Christmas (12/02, $3.95, color) 4.00

GLORY
Image Comics (Extreme Studios)/Maximum Press: Mar, 1995 - No. 22, Apr, 1997 ($2.50)

0-Deodato-c/a, 1-(3/95)-Deodato-a 2.50
1A-Variant-c 4.00
2-11,13-22: 4-Variant-c by Quesada & Palmiotti. 5-Bagged w/Youngblood gaming card. 7,8-Deodato-c/a(p). 8-Babewatch x-over. 9-Cruz-c; Extreme Destroyer Pt. 5; polybagged w/card. 10-Angela-c/app. 11-Deodato-c. 2.50
12-($3.50)-Photo-c 3.50
Trade Paperback (1995, $9.95)-r/#1-4 10.00

GLORY
Awesome Comics: Mar, 1999 ($2.50)

0-Liefeld-c; story and sketch pages 2.50

GLORY (ALAN MOORE'S...)
Avatar Press: Dec, 2001 - Present ($3.50)

Preview-(9/01, $1.99) B&W pages and cover art; Alan Moore-s 2.25
0-Four regular covers 3.50
1,2: 1-Alan Moore-s/Mychaels & Gebbie-a; nine covers by various. 2-Five covers 3.50

GLORY & FRIENDS BIKINI FEST
Image Comics (Extreme): Sept, 1995 - No. 2, Oct, 1995 ($2.50, limited series)

1,2: 1-Photo-c; centerfold photo; pin-ups 2.50

GLORY & FRIENDS CHRISTMAS SPECIAL
Image Comics (Extreme Studios): Dec, 1995 ($2.50, one-shot)

1-Deodato-c 2.50

GLORY & FRIENDS LINGERIE SPECIAL
Image Comics (Extreme Studios): Sept, 1995 ($2.95, one-shot)

1-Pin-ups w/photos; photo-c; varant-c exists 3.00

GLORY/ANGELA: ANGELS IN HELL (See Angela/Glory: Rage of Angels)
Image Comics (Extreme Studios): Apr, 1996 ($2.50, one-shot)

1-Flip book w/Darkchylde #1 2.50

GLORY/AVENGELYNE
Image Comics (Extreme Studios): Oct, 1995 ($3.95, one-shot)

1-Chromium-c, 1-Regular-c 4.00

GLORY/CELESTINE: DARK ANGEL
Image Comics/Maximum Press (Extreme Studios): Sept, 1996 - No. 3, Nov, 1996 ($2.50, limited series)

1-3 2.50

GNOME MOBILE, THE (See Movie Comics)

GOBBLEDYGOOK
Mirage Studios: 1984 - No. 2, 1984 (B&W)(1st Mirage comics, published at same time)

1-(24 pgs.)-1st Teenage Mutant Ninja Turtles 31 62 93 228 339 450
2-(24 pgs.) 25 50 75 181 266 350

GOBBLEDYGOOK
Mirage Studios: Dec, 1986 ($3.50, B&W, one-shot, 100 pgs.)

1-New 8 pg. TMNT story plus a Donatello/Michaelangelo 7 pg. story & a Gizmo story; Corben-i(r)/TMNT #7 5.00

GOBLIN, THE
Warren Publishing Co.: June, 1982 - No. 3, Dec, 1982 ($2.25, B&W magazine with 8 pg. color insert comic in all)

1-The Gremlin app. Philo Photon & the Troll Patrol, Micro-Buccaneers & Wizard Wormglow begin & app. in all. Tin Man app. Golden-a(p). Nebres-c/a in all
2 4 6 12 16 20
2,3: 2-1st Hobgoblin. 3-Tin Man app. 2 4 6 9 11 14
NOTE: ***Bermejo** a-1-3. **Elias** a-1-3. **Laxamana** a-1-3. **Nino** a-3.*

GO BOY 7
Dark Horse Comics: July, 2003 - Present ($2.99)

1-3-Peyer-s/Sommariva-a 3.00

GODDESS
DC Comics (Vertigo): June, 1995 - No. 8, Jan, 1996 ($2.95, limited series)

1-Garth Ennis scripts; Phil Winslade-c/a in all 5.00
2-8 4.00
TPB (2002, $19.95) r/#1-8; foreword and sketch pages by Winslade 20.00

GODFATHERS, THE (See The Crusaders)

GOD IS
Spire Christian Comics (Fleming H. Revell Co.): 1973, 1975 (35-49¢)

Goddess #8 © Garth Ennis & Phil Winslade

Godzilla Color Special #1 © Toho Co. Ltd.

Go Girl! #2 © Trina Robbins

	GD 2.0	VG 4.0	FN 6.0	VF 8.0	VF/NM 9.0	NM- 9.2
nn-By Al Hartley	1	3	4	6	8	10

GODS AND TULIPS
Westhampton House: Aug, 1999 ($3.00, B&W, one-shot for the CBLDF)

	GD 2.0	VG 4.0	FN 6.0	VF 8.0	VF/NM 9.0	NM- 9.2
nn-Neil Gaiman speeches; Kaluta-c						3.00

GOD'S COUNTRY (Also see Marvel Comics Presents)
Marvel Comics: 1994 ($6.95)

	GD 2.0	VG 4.0	FN 6.0	VF 8.0	VF/NM 9.0	NM- 9.2
nn-P. Craig Russell-a; Colossus story; r/Marvel Comics Presents #10-17						7.00

GODS FOR HIRE
Hot Comics: Dec, 1986 - No. 3 ($1.50)

	GD 2.0	VG 4.0	FN 6.0	VF 8.0	VF/NM 9.0	NM- 9.2
1-3: Barry Crain-c/a(p)						2.25

GOD'S HEROES IN AMERICA
Catechetical Guild Educational Society: 1956 (nn) (25¢/35¢, 68 pgs.)

	GD 2.0	VG 4.0	FN 6.0	VF 8.0	VF/NM 9.0	NM- 9.2
307	3	6	9	16	20	24

GOD'S SMUGGLER (Religious)
Spire Christian Comics/Fleming H. Revell Co.: 1972 (39¢/40¢)

	GD 2.0	VG 4.0	FN 6.0	VF 8.0	VF/NM 9.0	NM- 9.2
1-Two variations exist	1	3	4	6	8	10

GODWHEEL
Malibu Comics (Ultraverse): No. 0, Jan, 1995 - No. 3, Feb, 1995 ($2.50, limited series)

	GD 2.0	VG 4.0	FN 6.0	VF 8.0	VF/NM 9.0	NM- 9.2
0-3: 0-Flip-c. 1-1st app. of Primevil; Thor cameo (1 panel). 3-Perez-a in Chapter 3, Thor app.						2.50

GODZILLA (Movie)
Marvel Comics : August, 1977 - No. 24, July, 1979 (Based on movie series)

	GD 2.0	VG 4.0	FN 6.0	VF 8.0	VF/NM 9.0	NM- 9.2
1-(Regular 30¢ edition)-Mooney-i	2	4	6	14	18	22
1-(35¢-c variant, limited distribution)	3	7	10	21	28	35
2-(Regular 30¢ edition)-Tuska-i.	1	3	4	6	8	10
2,3-(35¢-c variant, limited distribution)	2	4	6	11	14	18
3-(30¢-c) Champions app.(w/o Ghost Rider)	2	4	6	8	10	12
4-10: 4,5-Sutton-a	1	2	3	5	7	9
11-23: 14-Shield app. 20-F.F. app. 21,22-Devil Dinosaur app.	1	2	3	5	6	8
24-Last issue	1	3	4	6	8	10

GODZILLA (Movie)
Dark Horse Comics: May, 1988 - No. 6, 1988 ($1.95, B&W, limited series) (Based on movie series)

	GD 2.0	VG 4.0	FN 6.0	VF 8.0	VF/NM 9.0	NM- 9.2
1						6.00
2-6						4.00
...Collection (1990, $10.95)-r/1-6 with new-c						11.00
...Color Special 1 (Sum, 1992, $3.50, color, 44 pgs.)-Arthur Adams wraparound-c/a & part scripts						5.00
...King Of The Monsters Special (8/87, $1.50)-Origin; Bissette-c/a						4.00
...Vs. Barkley nn (12/93, $2.95, color)-Dorman painted-c						4.00

GODZILLA (King of the Monsters) (Movie)
Dark Horse Comics: May, 1995 - No. 16, Sept, 1996 ($2.50) (Based on movies)

	GD 2.0	VG 4.0	FN 6.0	VF 8.0	VF/NM 9.0	NM- 9.2
0-16: 0-r/Dark Horse Comics #10,11. 1-3-Kevin Maguire scripts. 3-8-Art Adams-c						4.00
...Vs. Hero Zero ($2.50)						3.00

GOG (VILLAINS) (See Kingdom Come)
DC Comics: Feb, 1998 ($1.95, one-shot)

	GD 2.0	VG 4.0	FN 6.0	VF 8.0	VF/NM 9.0	NM- 9.2
1-Waid-s/Ordway-a(p)/Pearson-c						3.00

GO GIRL!
Image Comics: Aug, 2000 - Present ($3.50, B&W, quarterly)

	GD 2.0	VG 4.0	FN 6.0	VF 8.0	VF/NM 9.0	NM- 9.2
1-5-Trina Robbins-s/Anne Timmons-a; pin-up gallery						3.50

GO-GO
Charlton Comics: June, 1966 - No. 9, Oct, 1967

	GD 2.0	VG 4.0	FN 6.0	VF 8.0	VF/NM 9.0	NM- 9.2
1-Miss Bikini Luv begins w/Jim Aparo's 1st published work; Rolling Stones, Beatles, Elvis, Sonny & Cher, Bob Dylan, Sinatra, parody; Herman's Hermits pin-ups; D'Agostino-c/a in #1-8	8	16	24	55	78	100
2-Ringo Starr, David McCallum & Beatles photos on cover; Beatles story and photos	8	16	24	55	78	100
3,4: 3-Blooperman begins, ends #6; 1 pg. Batman & Robin satire; full pg. photo pin-ups Lovin' Spoonful & The Byrds	5	10	15	33	44	55
5,7,9: 5 (2/67)-Super Hero & TV satire by Jim Aparo & Grass Green begins. 6-8-Aparo-a. 7-Photo of Brian Wilson of Beach Boys on-c & Beach Boys photo inside f/b-c. 9-Aparo-c/a	5	10	15	33	44	55
6-Parody of JLA & DC heroes vs. Marvel heroes; Aparo-a; Elvis parody; Petula Clark photo-c	6	12	18	38	52	65
8-Monkees photo on-c & photo inside f/b-c	6	12	18	43	59	75

GO-GO AND ANIMAL (See Tippy's Friends...)

GOING STEADY (Formerly Teen-Age Temptations)
St. John Publ. Co.: No. 10, Dec, 1954 - No. 13, June, 1955; No. 14, Oct, 1955

	GD 2.0	VG 4.0	FN 6.0	VF 8.0	VF/NM 9.0	NM- 9.2
10(1954)-Matt Baker-c/a	21	42	63	118	164	210
11(2/55, last precode), 12(4/55)-Baker-c	12	24	36	69	92	115
13(6/55)-Baker-c/a	15	30	45	84	115	145
14(10/55)-Matt Baker-c/a, 25 pgs.	17	34	51	95	130	165

GOING STEADY (Formerly Personal Love)
Prize Publications/Headline: V3#3, Feb, 1960 - V3#6, Aug, 1960; V4#1, Sept-Oct, 1960

	GD 2.0	VG 4.0	FN 6.0	VF 8.0	VF/NM 9.0	NM- 9.2
V3#3-6, V4#1	3	6	9	17	21	26

GOING STEADY WITH BETTY (Becomes Betty & Her Steady No. 2)
Avon Periodicals: Nov-Dec, 1949

	GD 2.0	VG 4.0	FN 6.0	VF 8.0	VF/NM 9.0	NM- 9.2
1	15	30	45	84	115	145

GOLDEN AGE, THE
DC Comics (Elseworlds): 1993 - No. 4, 1994 ($4.95, limited series)

	GD 2.0	VG 4.0	FN 6.0	VF 8.0	VF/NM 9.0	NM- 9.2
1-4: James Robinson scripts; Paul Smith-c/a; gold foil embossed-c						6.00
Trade Paperback (1995, $19.95)						20.00

GOLDEN AGE SECRET FILES
DC Comics: Feb, 2001 ($4.95, one-shot)

	GD 2.0	VG 4.0	FN 6.0	VF 8.0	VF/NM 9.0	NM- 9.2
1-Origins and profiles of JSA members and other G.A. heroes; Lark-c						5.00

GOLDEN ARROW (See Fawcett Miniatures, Mighty Midget & Whiz Comics)

GOLDEN ARROW (...Western No. 6)
Fawcett Publications: Spring, 1942 - No. 6, Spring, 1947 (68 pgs.)

	GD 2.0	VG 4.0	FN 6.0	VF 8.0	VF/NM 9.0	NM- 9.2
1-Golden Arrow begins	85	170	255	531	796	1060
2-(1943)	42	84	126	252	376	500
3-5: 3-(Win/45-46). 4-(Spr/46). 5-(Fall/46)	34	68	102	193	274	355
6-Krigstein-a	36	72	108	204	290	375

GOLDEN COMICS DIGEST
Gold Key: May, 1969 - No. 48, Jan, 1976

NOTE: *Whitman editions exist of many titles and are generally valued the same.*

	GD 2.0	VG 4.0	FN 6.0	VF 8.0	VF/NM 9.0	NM- 9.2
1-Tom & Jerry, Woody Woodpecker, Bugs Bunny	5	10	15	36	48	60
2-Hanna-Barbera TV Fun Favorites; Space Ghost, Flintstones, Atom Ant, Jetsons, Yogi Bear, Banana Splits, others app.	7	14	21	50	68	85
3-Tom & Jerry, Woody Woodpecker	3	6	9	16	20	24
4-Tarzan; Manning & Marsh-a	4	8	12	29	40	50
5,8-Tom & Jerry, W. Woodpecker, Bugs Bunny	2	4	6	14	18	22
6-Bugs Bunny	2	4	6	14	18	22
7-Hanna-Barbera TV Fun Favorites	5	10	15	36	48	60
9-Tarzan	4	8	12	29	40	50
10,12-17: 10-Bugs Bunny. 12-Tom & Jerry, Bugs Bunny, W. Woodpecker Journey to the Sun. 13-Tom & Jerry. 14-Bugs Bunny Fun Packed Funnies. 15-Tom & Jerry, Woody Woodpecker, Bugs Bunny. 16-Woody Woodpecker Cartoon Special. 17-Bugs Bunny	2	4	6	14	18	22
11-Hanna-Barbera TV Fun Favorites	6	12	18	38	52	65
18-Tom & Jerry; Barney Bear-r by Barks	3	6	9	16	20	24
19-Little Lulu	4	8	12	25	33	42
20-22: 20-Woody Woodpecker Falltime Funtime. 21-Bugs Bunny Showtime. 22-Tom & Jerry Winter Wingding	2	4	6	14	18	22
23-Little Lulu & Tubby Fun Fling	4	8	12	25	33	42
24-26,28: 24-Woody Woodpecker Fun Festival. 25-Tom & Jerry. 26-Bugs Bunny Halloween Hulla-Boo-Loo; Dr. Spektor article, also #25. 28-Tom & Jerry	2	4	6	12	16	20
27-Little Lulu & Tubby in Hawaii	4	8	12	24	32	40
29-Little Lulu & Tubby	4	8	12	24	32	40
30-Bugs Bunny Vacation Funnies	2	4	6	12	16	20
31-Turok, Son of Stone; r/4-Color #596,656; c-r/#9	4	8	12	27	36	45
32-Woody Woodpecker Summer Fun	2	4	6	12	16	20
33,36: 33-Little Lulu & Tubby Halloween Fun; Dr. Spektor app. 36-Little Lulu & Her Friends	4	8	12	24	32	40
34,35,37-39: 34-Bugs Bunny Winter Funnies. 35-Tom & Jerry Snowtime Funtime. 37-Woody Woodpecker County Fair. 39-Bugs Bunny Summer Fun	2	4	6	12	16	20
38-The Pink Panther	3	6	9	16	20	24
40,43: 40-Little Lulu & Tubby Trick or Treat; all by Stanley. 43-Little Lulu in Paris	4	8	12	24	32	40
41,42,44,47: 41-Tom & Jerry Winter Carnival. 42-Bugs Bunny. 44-Woody Woodpecker Family Fun Festival. 47-Bugs Bunny	2	4	6	11	14	18
45-The Pink Panther	3	6	9	16	20	24
46-Little Lulu & Tubby	3	7	10	21	28	35

Golden Lad #1 © Spark Publ.

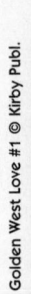

Golden West Love #1 © Kirby Publ.

Gon Again © Kodansha Ltd.

	GD 2.0	VG 4.0	FN 6.0	VF 8.0	VF/NM 9.0	NM- 9.2
48-The Lone Ranger	3	6	9	18	23	28

NOTE: *#1-30, 164 pgs.; #31 on, 132 pgs..*

GOLDEN LAD
Spark/Fact & Fiction Publ.: July, 1945 - No. 5, June, 1946 (#4, 5: 52 pgs.)

	GD 2.0	VG 4.0	FN 6.0	VF 8.0	VF/NM 9.0	NM- 9.2
1-Origin & 1st app. Golden Lad & Swift Arrow; Sandusky and the Senator begins	74	148	222	463	694	925
2-Mort Meskin-c/a	39	78	117	230	325	420
3,4-Mort Meskin-c/a	35	70	105	201	288	370
5-Origin & 1st app. Golden Girl; Shaman & Flame app.	39	78	117	230	325	420

NOTE: *All have* ***Robinson****, and* ***Roussos*** *art plus* ***Meskin*** *covers and art.*

GOLDEN LEGACY
Fitzgerald Publishing Co.: 1966 - 1972 (Black History) (25¢)

	GD 2.0	VG 4.0	FN 6.0	VF 8.0	VF/NM 9.0	NM- 9.2
1-12,14-16: 1-Toussaint L'Ouverture (1966), 2-Harriet Tubman (1967), 3-Crispus Attucks & the Minutemen (1967), 4-Benjamin Banneker (1968), 5-Matthew Henson (1969), 6-Alexander Dumas & Family (1969), 7-Frederick Douglass, Part 1 (1969), 8-Frederick Douglass, Part 2 (1970), 9-Robert Smalls (1970), 10-J. Cinque & the Amistad Mutiny (1970), 11-Men in Action: White, Marshall J. Wilkins (1970), 12-Black Cowboys (1972), 14-The Life of Alexander Pushkin (1971), 15-Ancient African Kingdoms (1972), 16-Black Inventors (1972) each....	2	4	6	12	16	20
13-The Life of Martin Luther King, Jr. (1972)	3	6	9	16	20	25
1-10,12,13,15,16(1976)-Reprints	1	2	3	5	6	8

GOLDEN LOVE STORIES (Formerly Golden West Love)
Kirby Publishing Co.: No. 4, April, 1950

	GD 2.0	VG 4.0	FN 6.0	VF 8.0	VF/NM 9.0	NM- 9.2
4-Powell-a; Glenn Ford/Janet Leigh photo-c	16	32	48	89	122	155

GOLDEN PICTURE CLASSIC, A
Western Printing Co. (Simon & Shuster): 1956-1957 (Text stories w/illustrations in color; 100 pgs. each)

	GD 2.0	VG 4.0	FN 6.0	VF 8.0	VF/NM 9.0	NM- 9.2
CL-401: Treasure Island	10	20	30	58	77	95
CL-402,403: 402: Tom Sawyer. 403: Black Beauty	9	18	27	49	62	75
CL-404, 405: CL-404: Little Women. CL-405: Heidi	9	18	27	49	62	75
CL-406: Ben Hur	7	14	21	37	46	55
CL-407: Around the World in 80 Days	7	14	21	37	46	55
CL-408: Sherlock Holmes	8	16	24	43	54	65
CL-409: The Three Musketeers	7	14	21	37	46	55
CL-410: The Merry Advs. of Robin Hood	7	14	21	37	46	55
CL-411,412: 411: Hans Brinker. 412: The Count of Monte Cristo	8	16	24	43	54	65

(Both soft & hardcover editions are valued the same)

NOTE: *Recent research has uncovered new information. Apparently #s 1-6 were issued in 1956 and #7-12 in 1957. But they can be found in five different series listings: CL-1 to CL-12 (softbound); CL-401 to CL-412 (also softbound); CL-101 to CL-112 (hardbound); plus two new series discoveries: A Golden Reading Adventure, publ. by Golden Press; edited down to 60 pages and reduced in size to 6x9"; only #s discovered so far are #381 (CL-4), #382 (CL-6) & #387 (CL-3). They have no reorder list and some have covers different from GPC. There have also been found British hardbound editions of GPC with dust jackets. Copies of all five listed series vary from scarce to very rare. Some editions of some series have not yet been found at all.*

GOLDEN PICTURE STORY BOOK
Racine Press (Western): Dec, 1961 (50¢, Treasury size, 52 pgs.) (All are scarce)

	GD 2.0	VG 4.0	FN 6.0	VF 8.0	VF/NM 9.0	NM- 9.2
ST-1-Huckleberry Hound (TV); Hokey Wolf, Pixie & Dixie, Quick Draw McGraw, Snooper and Blabber, Augie Doggie app.	20	40	60	145	213	280
ST-2-Yogi Bear (TV); Snagglepuss, Yakky Doodle, Quick Draw McGraw, Snooper and Blabber, Augie Doggie app.	20	40	60	145	213	280
ST-3-Babes in Toyland (Walt Disney's...)-Annette Funicello photo-c	25	50	75	181	266	350
ST-4-(...of Disney Ducks)-Walt Disney's Wonderful World of Ducks (Donald Duck, Uncle Scrooge, Donald's Nephews, Grandma Duck, Ludwig Von Drake, & Gyro Gearloose stories)	25	50	75	181	266	350

GOLDEN RECORD COMIC (See Amazing Spider-Man #1, Avengers #4, Fantastic Four #1, Journey Into Mystery #83)

GOLDEN STORY BOOKS
Western Printing Co. (Simon & Shuster): 1949 (Heavy covers, digest size, 128 pgs.) (Illustrated text in color)

	GD 2.0	VG 4.0	FN 6.0	VF 8.0	VF/NM 9.0	NM- 9.2
7-Walt Disney's Mystery in Disneyville, a book-length adventure starring Donald and Nephews, Mickey and Nephews, and with Minnie, Daisy and Goofy. Art by Dick Moores & Manuel Gonzales (scarce)	30	60	90	170	240	310
10-Bugs Bunny's Treasure Hunt, a book-length adventure starring Bugs & Porky Pig, with Petunia Pig & Nephew, Cicero. Art by Tom McKimson (scarce)	21	42	63	118	164	210

GOLDEN WEST LOVE (Golden Love Stories No. 4)
Kirby Publishing Co.: Sept-Oct, 1949 - No. 3, Feb, 1950 (All 52 pgs.)

	GD 2.0	VG 4.0	FN 6.0	VF 8.0	VF/NM 9.0	NM- 9.2
1-Powell-a in all; Roussos-a; painted-c	22	44	66	124	172	220
2,3: Photo-c	16	32	48	89	122	155

GOLDEN WEST RODEO TREASURY (See Dell Giants)

GOLDFISH (See A.K.A. Goldfish)

GOLDILOCKS (See March of Comics No. 1)

GOLD KEY CHAMPION
Gold Key: Mar, 1978 - No. 2, May, 1978 (50¢, 52pgs.)

	GD 2.0	VG 4.0	FN 6.0	VF 8.0	VF/NM 9.0	NM- 9.2
1,2: 1-Space Family Robinson; half-r. 2-Mighty Samson; half-r	1	3	4	6	8	10

GOLD KEY SPOTLIGHT
Gold Key: May, 1976 - No. 11, Feb, 1978

	GD 2.0	VG 4.0	FN 6.0	VF 8.0	VF/NM 9.0	NM- 9.2
1-Tom, Dick & Harriet	2	4	6	8	10	12
2-11: 2-Wacky Advs. of Cracky. 3-Wacky Witch. 4-Tom, Dick & Harriet. 5-Wacky Advs. of Cracky. 6-Dagar the Invincible; Santos-a; origin Demonomicon. 7-Wacky Witch & Greta Ghost 10-O. G. Whiz.11-Tom, Dick & Harriet. 8-The Occult Files of Dr. Spektor, Simbar, Lu-sai; Santos-a. 9-Tragg	1	2	3	5	7	9

GOLD MEDAL COMICS
Cambridge House: 1945 (25¢, one-shot, 132 pgs.)

	GD 2.0	VG 4.0	FN 6.0	VF 8.0	VF/NM 9.0	NM- 9.2
nn-Captain Truth by Fugitani, Crime Detector, The Witch of Salem, Luckyman, others app.	29	58	87	164	232	300

GOMER PYLE (TV)
Gold Key: July, 1966 - No. 3, Jan, 1967

	GD 2.0	VG 4.0	FN 6.0	VF 8.0	VF/NM 9.0	NM- 9.2
1-Photo front/back-c	9	18	27	65	93	120
2,3	7	14	21	46	63	80

GON
DC Comics (Paradox Press): July, 1996 - No. 4, Oct, 1996; No. 5, 1997 ($5.95, B&W, digest-size, limited series)

	GD 2.0	VG 4.0	FN 6.0	VF 8.0	VF/NM 9.0	NM- 9.2
1-5: Misadventures of baby dinosaur; 1-Gon. 2-Gon Again. 3-Gon: Here Today, Gone Tomorrow. 4-Gon: Going, Going...Gon. 5-Gon Swimmin'. Tanaka-c/a/scripts in all	1	2	3	5	6	8

GON COLOR SPECTACULAR
DC Comics (Paradox Press): 1998 ($5.95, square-bound)

	GD 2.0	VG 4.0	FN 6.0	VF 8.0	VF/NM 9.0	NM- 9.2
nn-Tanaka-c/a/scripts	1	2	3	5	6	8

GON ON SAFARI
DC Comics (Paradox Press): 2000 ($7.95, B&W, digest-size)

	GD 2.0	VG 4.0	FN 6.0	VF 8.0	VF/NM 9.0	NM- 9.2
nn-Tanaka-c/a/scripts	1	2	3	5	6	8

GON UNDERGROUND
DC Comics (Paradox Press): 1999 ($7.95, B&W, digest-size)

	GD 2.0	VG 4.0	FN 6.0	VF 8.0	VF/NM 9.0	NM- 9.2
nn-Tanaka-c/a/scripts	1	2	3	5	6	8

GON WILD
DC Comics (Paradox Press): 1997 ($9.95, B&W, digest-size)

	GD 2.0	VG 4.0	FN 6.0	VF 8.0	VF/NM 9.0	NM- 9.2
nn-Tanaka-c/a/scripts in all. (Rep. Gon #3,4)	1	3	4	6	8	10

GOODBYE, MR. CHIPS (See Movie Comics)

GOOD GIRL ART QUARTERLY
AC Comics: Summer, 1990 - No. 15, Spring, 1994 (B&W/color, 52 pgs.)

	GD 2.0	VG 4.0	FN 6.0	VF 8.0	VF/NM 9.0	NM- 9.2
1,3-15 ($3.50)-All have one new story (often FemForce) & rest reprints by Baker, Ward & other "good girl" artists						4.00
2 ($3.95)						4.00

GOOD GIRL COMICS (Formerly Good Girl Art Quarterly)
AC Comics: No. 16, Summer, 1994 - No. 18, 1995 (B&W)

	GD 2.0	VG 4.0	FN 6.0	VF 8.0	VF/NM 9.0	NM- 9.2
16-18						4.00

GOOD GUYS, THE
Defiant: Nov, 1993 - No. 9, July, 1994 ($2.50/$3.25/$3.50)

	GD 2.0	VG 4.0	FN 6.0	VF 8.0	VF/NM 9.0	NM- 9.2
1-($3.50, 52 pgs.)-Glory x-over from Plasm						3.50
2,3,5-9: 9-Pre-Schism issue						2.50
4-($3.25, 52 pgs.)						3.25

GOOD TRIUMPHS OVER EVIL! (Also see Narrative Illustration)
M.C. Gaines: 1943 (12 pgs., 7-1/4"x10", B&W) (not a comic book) (Rare)

	GD 2.0	VG 4.0	FN 6.0	VF 8.0	VF/NM 9.0	NM- 9.2
nn-A pamphlet, sequel to Narrative Illustration	96	192	288	600	900	1200

GOOFY (Disney)(See Dynabrite Comics, Mickey Mouse Magazine V4#7, Walt Disney Showcase #35 & Wheaties)
Dell Publishing Co.: No. 468, May, 1953 - Sept-Nov, 1962

	GD 2.0	VG 4.0	FN 6.0	VF 8.0	VF/NM 9.0	NM- 9.2
Four Color 468 (#1)	13	26	39	94	137	180
Four Color 562,627,658,702,747,802,857	8	16	24	55	78	100
Four Color 899,952,987,1053,1094,1149,1201	6	12	18	38	52	65

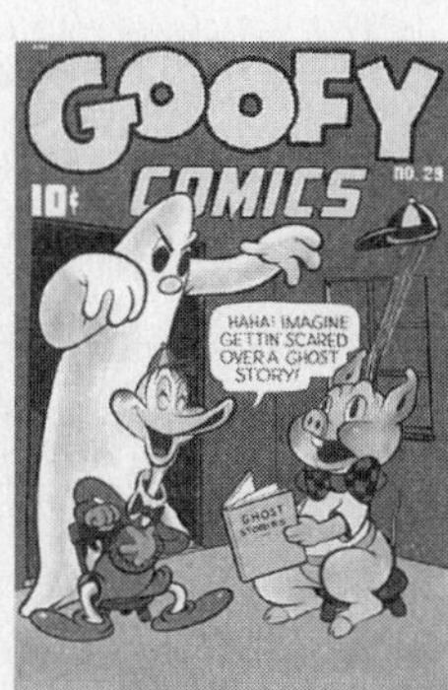

Goofy Comics #25 © STD

Gotham Central #1 © DC

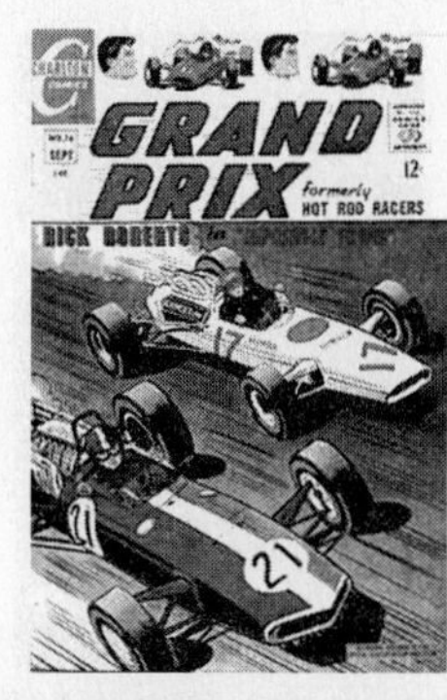

Grand Prix #16 © CC

	GD 2.0	VG 4.0	FN 6.0	VF 8.0	VF/NM 9.0	NM- 9.2
12-308-211(Dell, 9-11/62)	6	12	18	38	52	65

GOOFY ADVENTURES
Disney Comics: June, 1990 - No. 17, 1991 ($1.50)

	GD	VG	FN	VF	VF/NM	NM-
1-17: Most new stories. 2-Joshua Quagmire-a w/free poster. 7-WDC&S-r plus new-a. 9-Gottfredson-r. 14-Super Goof story. 15-All Super Goof issue. 17-Gene Colan-a(p)						3.00

GOOFY ADVENTURE STORY (See Goofy No. 857)

GOOFY COMICS (Companion to Happy Comics)(Not Disney)
Nedor Publ. Co. No. 1-14/Standard No. 14-48: June, 1943 - No. 48, 1953 (Animated Cartoons)

	GD	VG	FN	VF	VF/NM	NM-
1-Funny animal; Oriolo-c	29	58	87	164	232	300
2	15	30	45	86	118	150
3-10	12	24	36	69	92	115
11-19	10	20	30	56	73	90
20-35-Frazetta text illos in all	11	22	33	63	84	105
36-48	8	16	24	46	58	70

GOOFY SUCCESS STORY (See Goofy No. 702)

GOON, THE
Avatar Press: Mar, 1999 - No. 3, July, 1999 ($3.00, B&W)

	GD	VG	FN	VF	VF/NM	NM-
1- Eric Powell-s/a						20.00
2						12.00
3						8.00

GOON, THE
Albatross Exploding Funny Books: Oct, 2002 - No. 4, Feb, 2003 ($2.95)

	GD	VG	FN	VF	VF/NM	NM-
1- Eric Powell-s/a						10.00
2-4						6.00
...Color Special 1 (8/02)						10.00
...: Rough Stuff (1/03, $15.95) r/Avatar Press series #1-3						16.00

GOON, THE
Dark Horse Comics: June, 2003 - Present ($2.99)

	GD	VG	FN	VF	VF/NM	NM-
1-3- Eric Powell-s/a						3.00
...: Nothin' But Misery Vol. 1 (7/03, $15.95, TPB) - Reprints The Goon #1-4 (Albatross series), Color Special, and story from DHP #157						16.00

GOOSE (Humor magazine)
Cousins Publ. (Fawcett): Sept, 1976 - No. 3, 1976 (75¢, 52 pgs., B&W)

	GD	VG	FN	VF	VF/NM	NM-
1-Nudity in all	2	4	6	14	18	22
2,3: 2-(10/76) Fonz-c/s; Lone Ranger story. 3-Wonder Woman, King Kong, Six Million Dollar Man stories	2	4	6	10	12	15

GORDO (See Comics Revue No. 5 & Giant Comics Edition)

GORGO (Based on M.G.M. movie) (See Return of...)
Charlton Comics: May, 1961 - No. 23, Sept, 1965

	GD	VG	FN	VF	VF/NM	NM-
1-Ditko-a, 22 pgs.	24	48	72	171	251	330
2,3-Ditko-c/a	12	24	36	84	125	165
4-Ditko-c	8	16	24	55	78	100
5-11,13-16: 11,13-16-Ditko-a	7	14	21	51	71	90
12,17-23: 12-Reptisaurus x-over; Montes/Bache-a-No. 17-23. 20-Giordano-c	4	8	12	29	40	50
Gorgo's Revenge('62)-Becomes Return of...	6	12	18	38	52	65

GOSPEL BLIMP, THE
Spire Christian Comics (Fleming H. Revell Co.): 1973,1974 (35¢/39¢, 36 pgs.)

	GD	VG	FN	VF	VF/NM	NM-
nn	1	3	4	6	8	10

G.O.T.H.
Verotik: Dec, 1995 - No. 3, June, 1996 ($2.95, limited series, mature)

	GD	VG	FN	VF	VF/NM	NM-
1-3: Danzig scripts; Liam Sharpe-a.						3.00

GOTHAM BY GASLIGHT (A Tale of the Batman)(See Batman: Master of...)
DC Comics: 1989 ($3.95, one-shot, squarebound, 52 pgs.)

	GD	VG	FN	VF	VF/NM	NM-
nn-Mignola/Russell-a; intro by Robert Bloch						4.00

GOTHAM CENTRAL
DC Comics: Early Feb, 2003 - Present ($2.50)

	GD	VG	FN	VF	VF/NM	NM-
1-15-Stories of Gotham City Police; Brubaker & Rucka-s/Lark-c/a. 10-Two-Face app. 13,15-Joker-c						2.50

GOTHAM GIRLS
DC Comics: Oct, 2002 - No. 5, Feb, 2003 ($2.25, limited series)

	GD	VG	FN	VF	VF/NM	NM-
1-5-Catwoman, Batgirl, Poison Ivy, Harley Quinn from animated series						2.25

GOTHAM NIGHTS (See Batman: Gotham Nights II)
DC Comics: Mar, 1992 - No. 4, June, 1992 ($1.25, limited series)

	GD 2.0	VG 4.0	FN 6.0	VF 8.0	VF/NM 9.0	NM- 9.2
1-4: Featuring Batman						2.25

GOTHIC ROMANCES
Atlas/Seaboard Publ.: Dec, 1974 (75¢, B&W, magazine, 76 pgs.)

	GD	VG	FN	VF	VF/NM	NM-
1-Text w/ illos by N. Adams, Chaykin, Heath (2 pgs. ea.); painted cover (scarce)	11	22	33	77	114	150

GOTHIC TALES OF LOVE (Magazine)
Marvel Comics: Apr, 1975 - No. 2, Jun, 1975 (B&W, 76 pgs.)

	GD	VG	FN	VF	VF/NM	NM-
1,2-painted-c/a (scarce)	11	22	33	77	114	150

GOVERNOR & J. J., THE (TV)
Gold Key: Feb, 1970 - No. 3, Aug, 1970 (Photo-c)

	GD	VG	FN	VF	VF/NM	NM-
1	4	8	12	29	40	50
2,3	3	7	10	21	28	35

GRACKLE, THE
Acclaim Comics: Jan, 1997 - No. 4, Apr, 1997 ($2.95, B&W)

	GD	VG	FN	VF	VF/NM	NM-
1-4: Mike Baron scripts & Paul Gulacy-c/a. 1-4-Doublecross						3.00

GRAFIK MUSIK
Caliber Press: Nov, 1990 - No. 4, Aug, 1991 ($3.50/$2.50)

	GD	VG	FN	VF	VF/NM	NM-
1-($3.50, 48 pgs., color) Mike Allred-c/a/scripts-1st app. in color of Frank Einstein (Madman)	3	6	9	16	20	25
2-($2.50, 24 pgs., color)	2	4	6	10	12	15
3,4-($2.50, 24 pgs., B&W)	2	4	6	8	10	12

GRANDMA DUCK'S FARM FRIENDS(See Walt Disney's C&S 293 & Wheaties)
Dell Publishing Co.: No. 763, Jan, 1957 - No. 1279, Feb, 1962 (Disney)

	GD	VG	FN	VF	VF/NM	NM-
Four Color 763 (#1)	8	16	24	55	78	100
Four Color 873	6	12	18	40	55	70
Four Color 965,1279	5	10	15	36	48	60
Four Color 1010,1073,1161-Barks-a; 1073,1161-Barks c/a	14	28	42	97	141	185

GRAND PRIX (Formerly Hot Rod Racers)
Charlton Comics: No. 16, Sept, 1967 - No. 31, May, 1970

	GD	VG	FN	VF	VF/NM	NM-
16-Features Rick Roberts	4	8	12	24	32	40
17-20	3	6	9	18	24	30
21-31	3	6	9	16	20	25

GRAPHIQUE MUSIQUE
Slave Labor Graphics: Dec, 1989 - No. 3, May, 1990 ($2.95, 52 pgs.)

	GD	VG	FN	VF	VF/NM	NM-
1-Mike Allred-c/a/scripts	4	8	12	24	32	40
2,3	3	6	9	18	24	30

GRAVEDIGGERS
Acclaim Comics: Nov, 1996 - No. 4, Feb, 1997 ($2.95, B&W)

	GD	VG	FN	VF	VF/NM	NM-
1-4: Moretti scripts						3.00

GRAVESTONE
Malibu Comics: July, 1993 - No. 7, Feb, 1994 ($2.25)

	GD	VG	FN	VF	VF/NM	NM-
1-6: 3-Polybagged w/Skycap						2.25
7-($2.50)						2.50

GRAVE TALES
Hamilton Comics: Oct, 1991 - No. 3, Feb, 1992 ($3.95, B&W, mag., 52 pgs.)

	GD	VG	FN	VF	VF/NM	NM-
1-Staton-c/a	1	2	3	5	6	8
2,3: 2-Staton-a; Morrow-c						6.00

GRAY GHOST, THE
Dell Publishing Co.: No. 911, July, 1958; No. 1000, June-Aug, 1959

	GD	VG	FN	VF	VF/NM	NM-
Four Color 911 (#1), 1000-Photo-c each	10	20	30	70	100	125

GREAT ACTION COMICS
I. W. Enterprises: 1958 (Reprints with new covers)

	GD	VG	FN	VF	VF/NM	NM-
1-Captain Truth reprinted from Gold Medal #1	3	6	9	18	24	30
8,9-Reprints Phantom Lady #15 & 23	9	18	27	60	85	110

GREAT AMERICAN COMICS PRESENTS - THE SECRET VOICE
Peter George 4-Star Publ./American Features Syndicate: 1945 (10¢)

	GD	VG	FN	VF	VF/NM	NM-
1-Anti-Nazi; "What Really Happened to Hitler"	34	68	102	196	278	360

GREAT AMERICAN WESTERN, THE
AC Comics: 1987 - No. 4, 1990? ($1.75/$2.95/$3.50, B&W with some color)

	GD	VG	FN	VF	VF/NM	NM-
1-4: 1-Western-r plus Bill Black-a. 2-Tribute to ME comics; Durango Kid photo-c 3-Tribute to Tom Mix plus Roy Rogers, Durango Kid; Billy the Kid-r by Severin; photo-c. 4- ($3.50, 52 pgs., 16 pgs. color)-Tribute to Lash LaRue; photo-c & interior photos; Fawcett-r						4.00
...Presents 1 (1991, $5.00) New Sunset Carson; film history						5.00

The Great Gazoo #3 © H-B

Great Western #11 © ME

Green Arrow #15 © DC

GD VG FN VF VF/NM NM-
2.0 4.0 6.0 8.0 9.0 9.2

GREAT CAT FAMILY, THE (Disney-TV/Movie)
Dell Publishing Co.: No. 750, Nov, 1956 (one-shot)
Four Color 750-Pinocchio & Alice app. 7 14 21 51 71 90

GREAT COMICS
Great Comics Publications: Nov, 1941 - No. 3, Jan, 1942
1-Origin/1st app. The Great Zarro; Madame Strange & Guy Gorham, Wizard of Science & The Great Zarro begin 128 256 384 800 1200 1600
2-Buck Johnson, Jungle Explorer app.; X-Mas-c 64 128 192 400 570 800
3-Futuro Takes Hitler to Hell-c/s; "The Lost City" movie story (starring William Boyd); continues in Choice Comics #3 256 512 768 1600 2400 3200

GREAT COMICS
Novack Publishing Co./Jubilee Comics/Knockout/Barrel O' Fun: 1945
1-(Four publ. variations: Barrel O-Fun, Jubilee, Knockout & Novack)-The Defenders, Capt. Power app.; L. B. Cole-c 40 80 120 240 340 440
1-(Jubilee)-Same cover; Boogey Man, Satanas, & The Sorcerer & His Apprentice 30 60 90 170 240 310
1-(Barrel O' Fun)-L. B. Cole-c; Barrel O' Fun overprinted in indicia; Li'l Cactus, Cuckoo Sheriff (humorous) 20 40 60 112 156 200

GREAT DOGPATCH MYSTERY (See Mammy Yokum & the...)

GREATEST BATMAN STORIES EVER TOLD, THE
DC Comics
Hardcover ($24.95) 50.00
Softcover ($15.95) "Greatest DC Stories Vol. 2" on spine 18.00
Vol. 2 softcover (1992, $16.95)"Greatest DC Stories Vol. 7" on spine 18.00

GREATEST FLASH STORIES EVER TOLD, THE
DC Comics: 1991
nn-Hardcover ($29.95); Infantino-c 45.00
nn-Softcover ($14.95) 16.00

GREATEST GOLDEN AGE STORIES EVER TOLD, THE
DC Comics: 1990 ($24.95, hardcover)
nn-Ordway-c 60.00

GREATEST JOKER STORIES EVER TOLD, THE (See Batman)
DC Comics: 1983
Hardcover ($19.95)-Kyle Baker painted-c 45.00
Softcover ($14.95) 20.00
Stacked Deck...Expanded Edition (1992, $29.95)-Longmeadow Press Publ. 32.00

GREATEST 1950s STORIES EVER TOLD, THE
DC Comics: 1990
Hardcover ($29.95)-Kubert-c 55.00
Softcover ($14.95) "Greatest DC Stories Vol. 5" on spine 20.00

GREATEST TEAM-UP STORIES EVER TOLD, THE
DC Comics: 1989
Hardcover ($24.95)-DeVries and Infantino painted-c 55.00
Softcover ($14.95) "Greatest DC Stories Vol. 4" on spine; Adams-c 20.00

GREATEST SUPERMAN STORIES EVER TOLD, THE
DC Comics: 1987
Hardcover ($24.95) 50.00
Softcover ($15.95) 20.00

GREAT EXPLOITS
Decker Publ./Red Top: Oct, 1957
1-Krigstein-a(2) (re-issue on cover); reprints Daring Advs. #6 by Approved Comics 8 16 24 40 50 60

GREAT FOODINI, THE (See Foodini)

GREAT GAZOO, THE (The Flintstones)(TV)
Charlton Comics: Aug, 1973 - No. 20, Jan, 1977 (Hanna-Barbera)
1 4 8 12 24 32 40
2-10 2 4 6 12 16 20
11-20 2 4 6 10 12 15

GREAT GRAPE APE, THE (TV)(See TV Stars #1)
Charlton Comics: Sept, 1976 - No. 2, Nov, 1976 (Hanna-Barbera)
1 3 6 9 18 24 30
2 2 4 6 11 14 18

GREAT LOCOMOTIVE CHASE, THE (Disney)
Dell Publishing Co.: No. 712, Sept, 1956 (one-shot)
Four Color 712-Movie, photo-c 8 16 24 55 78 100

GREAT LOVER ROMANCES (Young Lover Romances #4,5)
Toby Press: 3/51; #2, 1951(nd); #3, 1952 (nd); #6, Oct?, 1952 - No. 22, May, 1955 (Photo-c #1-5, 10 ,13, 15, 17) (no #4, 5)
1-Jon Juan story-r/Jon Juan #1 by Schomburg; Dr. Anthony King app. 17 34 51 98 134 170
2-Jon Juan, Dr. Anthony King app. 10 20 30 56 73 90
3,7,9-14,16-22: 10-Rita Hayworth photo-c. 17-Rita Hayworth & Aldo Ray photo-c 7 14 21 37 46 55
6-Kurtzman-a (10/52) 10 20 30 56 73 90
8-Five pgs. of "Pin-Up Pete" by Sparling 10 20 30 56 73 90
15-Liz Taylor photo-c 18 36 54 107 138 175

GREAT RACE, THE (See Movie Classics)

GREAT SCOTT SHOE STORE (See Bulls-Eye)

GREAT SOCIETY COMIC BOOK, THE (Political parody)
Pocket Books Inc./Parallax Pub.: 1966 ($1.00, 36 pgs., 7"x10", one-shot)
nn-Super-LBJ-c/story; 60s politicians app. as super-heroes; Tallarico-a 3 6 9 18 23 28

GREAT WEST (Magazine)
M. F. Enterprises: 1969 (B&W, 52 pgs.)
V1#1 2 4 6 11 14 18

GREAT WESTERN
Magazine Enterprises: No. 8, Jan-Mar, 1954 - No. 11, Oct-Dec, 1954
8(A-1 93)-Trail Colt by Guardineer; Powell Red Hawk-r/Straight Arrow begins, ends #11; Durango Kid story 22 44 66 124 172 220
9(A-1 105), 11(A-1 127)-Ghost Rider, Durango Kid app. in each. 9-Red Mask-c, but no app. 14 28 42 79 107 135
10(A-1 113)-The Calico Kid by Guardineer-r/Tim Holt #8; Straight Arrow, Durango Kid app. 14 28 42 79 107 135
I.W. Reprint #1,2 9: 1,2-r/Straight Arrow #36,42. 9-r/Straight Arrow #? 3 6 9 18 23 28
I.W. Reprint #8-Origin Ghost Rider(r/Tim Holt #11); Tim Holt app.; Bolle-a 3 6 9 19 25 32
NOTE: *Guardineer c-8. Powell a(r)-8-11 (from Straight Arrow).*

GREEN ARROW (See Action #440, Adventure, Brave & the Bold, DC Super Stars #17, Detective #521, Flash #217, Green Lantern #76, Justice League of America #4, Leading Comics, More Fun #73 (1st app.), Showcase '95 #9 & World's Finest Comics)

GREEN ARROW
DC Comics: May, 1983 - No. 4, Aug, 1983 (limited series)
1-Origin; Speedy cameo; Mike W. Barr scripts, Trevor Von Eeden-c/a 5.00
2-4 4.00

GREEN ARROW
DC Comics: Feb, 1988 - No. 137, Oct, 1998 ($1.00-$2.50) (Painted-c #1-3)
1-Mike Grell scripts begin, ends #80 5.00
2-49,51-74,76-86: 27,28-Warlord app. 35-38-Co-stars Black Canary; Bill Wray-i. 40-Grell-a. 47-Begin $1.50-c. 63-No longer has mature readers on-c. 63-66-Shado app. 81-Aparo-a begins, ends #100; Nuklon app. 82-Intro & death of Rival. 83-Huntress-c/story. 84-Deathstroke cameo. 85-Deathstroke-c/app. 86-Catwoman-c/story w/Jim Balent layouts 2.50
50,75-($2.50, 52 pgs.): Anniversary issues. 75-Arsenal (Roy Harper) & Shado app. 3.00
0,87-96: 87-$1.95-c begins. 88-Guy Gardner, Martian Manhunter, & Wonder Woman-c/app.; Flash-c. 89-Anarky app. 90-(9/94)-Zero Hour tie-in. 0-(10/94)-1st app. Connor Hawke; Aparo-a(p). 91-(11/94). 93-1st app. Camorouge. 95-Hal Jordan cameo. 96-Intro new Force of July; Hal Jordan (Parallax) app; Oliver Queen learns that Connor Hawke is his son 2.50
97-99,102-109: 97-Begin $2.25-c; no Aparo-a. 97-99-Arsenal app. 102,103-Underworld Unleashed x-over. 104-GL(Kyle Rayner)-c/app. 105-Robin-c/app. 107-109-Thorn app. 109-Lois Lane cameo; Weeks-c. 2.50
100-($3.95)-Foil-c; Superman app. 1 3 4 6 8 10
101-Death of Oliver Queen; Superman app. 3 6 9 18 24 30
110,111-124: 110,111-GL x-over. 110-Intro Hatchet. 114-Final Night. 115-117-Black Canary & Oracle app. 2.50
125-($3.50, 48 pgs)-GL x-over cont. in GL #92 3.50
126-136: 126-Begin $2.50-c. 130-GL & Flash x-over. 132,133-JLA app. 134,135-Brotherhood of the Fist pts. 1,5. 136-Hal Jordan-c/app. 2.50
137-Last issue; Superman app.; last panel cameo of Oliver Queen 2 4 6 10 12 15
#1,000,000 (11/98) 853rd Century x-over 2.50
Annual 1-6 ('88-'94, 68 pgs.)-1-No Grell scripts. 2-No Grell scripts; recaps origin Green Arrow, Speedy, Black Canary & others. 3-Bill Wray-a. 4-50th anniversary issue. 5-Batman, Eclipso app. 6-Bloodlines; Hook app. 3.50

Green Arrow (2nd series) #21 © DC

Green Hornet Comics #1 © HOKE

Green Lantern #19 © DC

	GD 2.0	VG 4.0	FN 6.0	VF 8.0	VF/NM 9.0	NM- 9.2
Annual 7-('95, $3.95)-Year One story						4.00

NOTE: *Aparo a-0, 81-85, 86 (partial),87p, 88p, 91-95, 96i, 98-100p, 109p; c-81,98-100p.* ***Austin*** *c-96i.* ***Balent*** *lay-outs-86.* ***Burchett*** *c-91-95.* ***Campanella*** *a-100-108i, 110-113i; c-99i, 101-108i,110-113i.* ***Denys Cowan*** *a-39p, 41-43p, 47p, 48p, 60p; c-41-43.* ***Damaggio*** *a(p)-97p, 100-108p, 110-112p; c-97-99p, 101-108p, 110-113p.* ***Mike Grell*** *c-1-4, 10p, 11, 39, 40, 44, 45, 47-80, Annual 4, 5.* ***Nasser/Netzer*** *a-89, 96.* ***Sienkiewicz*** *a-109i.* ***Springer*** *a-67, 68.* ***Weeks*** *c-109.*

GREEN ARROW
DC Comics: Apr, 2001 - Present ($2.50)

	GD	VG	FN	VF	VF/NM	NM-
1-Oliver Queen returns; Kevin Smith-s/Hester-a/Wagner-painted-c	2	4	6	10	13	16
1-2nd-4th printings						3.00
2-Batman cameo	1	2	3	4	5	7
2-2nd printing						2.50
3-5: 4-JLA app.						5.00
6-15: 7-Barry Allen & Hal Jordan app. 9,10-Stanley & his Monster app. 10-Oliver regains his soul. 12-Hawkman-c/app.						3.00
16-25: 16-Brad Meltzer-s begin; The Shade app. 18-Solomon Grundy-c/app. 19-JLA app. 22-Beatty-s; Count Vertigo app. 23-25-Green Lantern app.; Raab-s/Adlard-a						2.50
26-34: 26-Winick-s begin						2.50
...: Quiver HC (2002, $24.95) r/#1-10; Smith intro.						25.00
...: Quiver SC (2003, $17.95) r/#1-10; Smith intro.						18.00
...Secret Files & Origins 1-(12/02, $4.95)1- Origin stories & profiles; Wagner-c						5.00
...: Sounds of Violence HC (2003, $19.95) r/#11-15; Hester intro. & sketch pages						20.00
...: The Archer's Quest HC (2003, $19.95) r/#16-21; pitch,script and sketch pages						20.00

GREEN ARROW: THE LONG BOW HUNTERS
DC Comics: Aug, 1987 - No. 3, Oct, 1987 ($2.95, limited series, mature)

	GD	VG	FN	VF	VF/NM	NM-
1-Grell-c/a in all						6.00
1,2-2nd printings						3.00
2,3						4.00
Trade paperback (1989, $12.95)-r/#1-3						13.00

GREEN ARROW: THE WONDER YEAR
DC Comics: Feb, 1993 - No. 4, May, 1993 ($1.75, limited series)

	GD	VG	FN	VF	VF/NM	NM-
1-4: Mike Grell-a(p)/scripts & Gray Morrow-a(i)						2.50

GREEN BERET, THE (See Tales of...)

GREEN CANDLES
DC Comics (Paradox Press): Sept, 1995 - No. 3, Dec, 1995 ($5.95, B&W, limited series, digest size)

	GD	VG	FN	VF	VF/NM	NM-
1-3						6.00
Paperback ($9.95)						10.00

GREEN GIANT COMICS (Also see Colossus Comics)
Pelican Publ. (Funnies, Inc.): 1940 (No price on cover; distributed in New York City only)

	GD	VG	FN	VF	VF/NM	NM-
1-Dr. Nerod, Green Giant, Black Arrow, Mundoo & Master Mystic app.; origin Colossus (Rare)	1000	2000	3000	7500	11,750	16,000

NOTE: *The idea for this book came from George Kapitan. Printed by Moreau Publ. of Orange, N.J. as an experiment to see if they could profitably use the idle time of their 40-page Hoe color press. The experiment failed due to the difficulty of obtaining good quality color registration and Mr. Moreau believes the book never reached the stands. The book has no price or date which lends credence to this. Contains five pages reprinted from Motion Picture Funnies Weekly.*

GREEN GOBLIN
Marvel Comics: Oct, 1995 - No. 13, Oct, 1996 ($2.95/$1.95)

	GD	VG	FN	VF	VF/NM	NM-
1-($2.95)-Scott McDaniel-c/a begins, ends #7; foil-c						3.50
2-13: 2-Begin $1.95-c. 4-Hobgoblin-c/app; Thing app. 6-Daredevil-c/app. 8-Robertson-a; McDaniel-c. 12,13-Onslaught x-over. 13-Green Goblin quits; Spider-Man app.						2.25

GREENHAVEN
Aircel Publishing: 1988 - No. 3, 1988 ($2.00, limited series, 28 pgs.)

	GD	VG	FN	VF	VF/NM	NM-
1-3						2.25

GREEN HORNET, THE (TV)
Dell Publishing Co./Gold Key: Sept, 1953; Feb, 1967 - No. 3, Aug, 1967

	GD	VG	FN	VF	VF/NM	NM-
Four Color 496-Painted-c.	27	54	81	192	281	370
1-All have Bruce Lee photo-c	23	46	69	164	240	315
2,3	15	30	45	109	160	210

GREEN HORNET, THE (Also see Kato of the... & Tales of the...)
Now Comics: Nov, 1989 - No. 14, Feb, 1991 ($1.75)
V2#1, Sept, 1991 - V2#40, Jan, 1995 ($1.95)

	GD	VG	FN	VF	VF/NM	NM-
1 ($2.95, double-size)-Steranko painted-c; G.A. Green Hornet						5.00
1,2: 1-2nd printing ('90, $3.95)-New Butler-c						4.00
3-14: 5-Death of original ('30s) Green Hornet. 6-Dave Dorman painted-c. 11-Snyder-c						3.00
V2#1-11,13-21,24-26,28-30,32-37: 1-Butler painted-c. 9-Mayerik-c						2.50
12-($2.50)-Color Green Hornet button polybagged inside						4.00
22,23-($2.95)-Bagged w/color hologravure card						4.00
27-($2.95)-Newsstand ed. polybagged w/multi-dimensional card (1993 Anniversary Special on cover), 27-($2.95)-Direct Sale ed. polybagged w/multi-dimensional card; cover variations						3.00
31,38: 31-($2.50)-Polybagged w/trading card						2.50
39,40-Low print run						6.00
1-($2.50)-Polybagged w/button (same as #12)						2.50
2,3-($1.95)-Same as #13 & 14						2.25
Annual 1 (12/92, $2.50), Annual 1994 (10/94, $2.95)						3.50

GREEN HORNET: DARK TOMORROW
Now Comics: Jun, 1993 - No. 3, Aug, 1993 ($2.50, limited series)

	GD	VG	FN	VF	VF/NM	NM-
1-3: Future Green Hornet						3.00

GREEN HORNET: SOLITARY SENTINEL, THE
Now Comics: Dec, 1992 - No. 3, 1993 ($2.50, limited series)

	GD	VG	FN	VF	VF/NM	NM-
1-3						3.00

GREEN HORNET COMICS (...Racket Buster #44) (Radio, movies)
Helnit Publ. Co.(Holyoke) No. 1-6/Family Comics(Harvey) No. 7-on:
Dec, 1940 - No. 47, Sept, 1949 (See All New #13,14)(Early issues: 68 pgs.)

	GD	VG	FN	VF	VF/NM	NM-
1-1st app. Green Hornet & Kato; origin of Green Hornet on inside front-c; intro the Black Beauty (Green Hornet's car); painted-c	483	966	1449	3381	5191	7000
2-Early issues based on radio adventures	192	384	576	1200	1800	2400
3	140	280	420	875	1313	1750
4-6: 6-(8/41)	112	224	336	700	1050	1400
7 (6/42)-Origin The Zebra & begins; Robin Hood, Spirit of '76, Blonde Bomber & Mighty Midgets begin; new logo	94	188	282	588	882	1175
8,10	78	156	234	488	732	975
9-Kirby-c	98	196	294	613	919	1225
11,12-Mr. Q in both	78	156	234	488	732	975
13-1st Nazi-c; shows Hitler poster on-c	85	170	255	531	796	1060
14-19	60	120	180	375	563	750
20-Classic-c	66	132	198	413	617	820
21-23,25-30	48	96	144	288	432	575
24-Sci-Fi-c	52	104	156	312	469	625
31-The Man in Black Called Fate begins (11-12/45, early app.)	50	100	150	300	450	600
32-36	40	80	120	240	350	460
37,38: Shock Gibson app. by Powell. 37-S&K Kid Adonis reprinted from Stuntman #3. 38-Kid Adonis app.	40	80	120	240	350	460
39-Stuntman story by S&K	50	100	150	300	450	600
40-47: 42-47-Kerry Drake in all. 45-Boy Explorers on-c only. 46- "Case of the Marijuana Racket" cover/story; Kerry Drake app.	35	70	105	201	288	370

NOTE: ***Fuje*** *a-23, 24, 26.* ***Henkle*** *c-7-9.* ***Kubert*** *a-20, 30.* ***Powell*** *a-7-10, 12, 14, 16-21, 30, 31(2), 32(3), 33, 34(3), 35, 36, 37(2), 38.* ***Robinson*** *a-27.* ***Schomburg*** *c-15, 17-23. Kirbyish c-7, 15. Bondage c-8, 14, 18, 26, 36.*

GREEN JET COMICS, THE (See Comic Books, Series 1)

GREEN LAMA (Also see Comic Books, Series 1, Daring Adventures #17 & Prize Comics #7)
Spark Publications/Prize No. 7 on: Dec, 1944 - No. 8, Mar, 1946

	GD	VG	FN	VF	VF/NM	NM-
1-Intro. Lt. Hercules & The Boy Champions; Mac Raboy-c/a #1-8	128	256	384	800	1200	1600
2-Lt. Hercules borrows the Human Torch's powers for one panel	76	152	228	475	713	950
3-6,8: 4-Dick Tracy take-off in Lt. Hercules story by H. L. Gold (science fiction writer). 5-Lt. Hercules story; Little Orphan Annie, Smilin' Jack & Snuffy Smith take-off (5/45)	61	122	183	381	571	760
7-X-mas-c; Raboy craft tint-c/a (note: a small quantity of NM copies surfaced)	39	78	117	224	317	410

NOTE: ***Robinson*** *a-3-5, 8.* ***Roussos*** *a-8. Formerly a pulp hero who began in 1940.*

GREEN LANTERN (1st Series) (See All-American, All Flash Quarterly, All Star Comics, The Big All-American & Comic Cavalcade)
National Periodical Publications/All-American: Fall, 1941 - No. 38, May-June, 1949 (#1-18 are quarterly)

	GD	VG	FN	VF	VF/NM	NM-
1-Origin retold; classic Purcell-c	2941	5882	8823	23,500	36,750	50,000
2-1st book-length story	655	1310	1965	4585	7043	9500
3-Classic German war-c by Mart Nodell	483	966	1449	3381	5191	7000
4-Green Lantern & Doiby Dickles join the Army	400	800	1200	2600	4000	5400
5	280	560	840	1750	2625	3500
6,8: 8-Hop Harrigan begins; classic-c	220	440	660	1375	2063	2750
7-Robot-c.	236	472	708	1475	2213	2950
9,10: 10-Origin/1st app. Vandal Savage	188	376	564	1175	1763	2350
11-15: 12-Origin/1st app. Gambler	140	280	420	875	1313	1750
16-Classic jungle-c (scarce in high grade)	144	288	432	900	1350	1800
17,19,20	130	260	390	813	1219	1625

Green Lantern (2nd series) #40 © DC

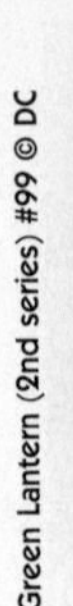

Green Lantern (2nd series) #99 © DC

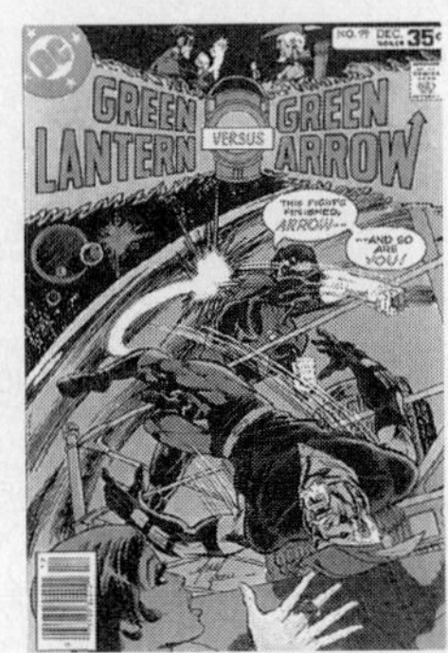

Green Lantern (3rd series) #101 © DC

	GD 2.0	VG 4.0	FN 6.0	VF 8.0	VF/NM 9.0	NM- 9.2
18-Christmas-c	160	320	480	1000	1500	2000
21-26,28	118	236	355	738	1107	1475
27-Origin/1st app. Sky Pirate	124	248	372	775	1163	1550
29-All Harlequin issue; classic Harlequin-c	128	256	384	800	1200	1600
30-Origin/1st app. Streak the Wonder Dog by Toth (2-3/48) (scarce)	148	296	444	925	1388	1850
31-35: 35-Kubert-c. 35-38-New logo	100	200	300	625	938	1250
36-38: 37-Sargon the Sorcerer app.	124	248	372	775	1163	1550

NOTE: *Book-length stories #2-7.* ***Mayer/Moldoff*** *c-9.* ***Mayer/Purcell*** *c-8.* ***Purcell*** *c-1.* ***Mart Nodell*** *c-2, 3, 7.* ***Paul Reinman*** *c-11, 12, 15-22.* ***Toth*** *a-28, 30, 31, 34-38; c-28, 30, 34p, 36-38p. Cover to #8 says Fall while the indicia says Summer Issue. Streak the Wonder Dog c-30 (w/Green Lantern), 34, 36, 38.*

GREEN LANTERN (See Action Comics Weekly, Adventure Comics, Brave & the Bold, Day of Judgment, DC Special, DC Special Series, Flash, Guy Gardner, Guy Gardner Reborn, JLA, JSA, Justice League of America, Parallax: Emerald Night, Showcase, Showcase '93 #12 & Tales of The...Corps)

GREEN LANTERN (2nd Series)(Green Lantern Corps #206 on) (See Showcase #22-24)
National Periodical Publ./DC Comics: Jul/Aug. 1960 - No. 89, Apr/May 1972; No. 90, Aug/Sept. 1976 - No. 205, Oct, 1986

	GD 2.0	VG 4.0	FN 6.0	VF 8.0	VF/NM 9.0	NM- 9.2
1-(7-8/60)-Origin retold; Gil Kane-c/a continues; 1st app. Guardians of the Universe	317	634	951	2900	4700	6500
2-1st Pieface	67	134	201	536	943	1350
3-Contains readers poll	44	88	132	319	535	750
4,5: 5-Origin/1st app. Hector Hammond	32	64	96	232	391	550
6-Intro Tomar-Re the alien G.L.	29	58	87	210	355	500
7-Origin/1st app. Sinestro (7-8/61)	26	52	78	189	315	440
8-10: 8-1st 5700 A.D. story; grey tone-c. 9-1st Jordan Brothers; last 10¢ issue	23	46	69	167	269	370
11,12	18	36	54	131	191	250
13-Flash x-over	24	48	72	174	287	400
14-20: 14-Origin/1st app. Sonar. 16-Origin & 1st app. Star Sapphire. 20-Flash x-over	16	32	48	113	167	220
21-30: 21-Origin & 1st app. Dr. Polaris. 23-1st Tattooed Man. 24-Origin & 1st app. Shark. 29-JLA cameo; 1st Blackhand	13	26	39	94	137	180
31-39: 37-1st app. Evil Star (villain)	11	22	33	77	114	150
40-1st app. Crisis (10/65); 2nd solo G.A. Green Lantern in Silver Age (see Showcase #55); origin The Guardians; Doiby Dickles app.	45	90	135	360	540	720
41-44,46-50: 42-Zatanna x-over. 43-Flash x-over	9	18	27	65	93	125
45-2nd S.A. app. G.A. Green Lantern in title (6/66)	15	30	45	104	152	200
51,53-58	8	16	24	53	74	95
52-G.A. Green Lantern x-over	10	20	30	67	96	125
59-1st app. Guy Gardner (3/68)	21	42	63	149	220	290
60,62-69: 69-Wood inks; last 12¢ issue	6	12	18	40	55	70
61-G.A. Green Lantern x-over	7	14	21	50	68	85
70-75	5	10	15	33	44	55
76-(4/70)-Begin Green Lantern/Green Arrow series (by Neal Adams #76-89) ends #122 (see Flash #217 for 2nd series)	27	54	81	196	310	425
77	8	16	24	58	82	105
78-80	7	14	21	46	63	80
81-84: 82-Wrightson-i(1 pg.). 83-G.L. reveals i.d. to Carol Ferris. 84-N. Adams/Wrightson-a (22 pgs.); last 15¢-c; partial photo-c	6	12	18	43	59	75
85,86-(52 pgs.)-Anti-drug issues. 86-G.A. Green Lantern-r; Toth-a	8	16	24	55	78	100
87-(52 pgs.): 2nd app. Guy Gardner (cameo); 1st app. John Stewart (12-1/71-72) (becomes 3rd Green Lantern in #182)	6	12	18	38	52	65
88-(2-3/72, 52 pgs.)-Unpubbed G.A. Green Lantern story; Green Lantern-r/Showcase #23. N. Adams-c/a (1 pg.)	4	8	12	25	33	42
89-(4-5/72, 52 pgs.)-G.A. Green Lantern-r; Green Lantern & Green Arrow move to Flash #217 (2nd team-up series)	6	12	18	38	52	65
90 (8-9/76)-Begin 3rd Green Lantern/Green Arrow team-up series; Mike Grell-c/a begins, ends #111	2	4	6	12	16	20
91-99	1	3	4	6	8	10
100-(1/78, Giant)-1st app. Air Wave II	2	4	6	11	14	18
101-107,111,113-115,117-119: 107-1st Tales of the G.L. Corps story	1	2	3	5	6	8
108-110-(44 pgs)-G.A. Green Lantern back-ups in each. 111-Origin retold; G.A. Green Lantern app.	1	2	3	5	7	9
112-G.A. Green Lantern origin retold	2	4	6	10	12	15
116-1st app. Guy Gardner as a G.L. (5/79)	4	8	12	24	32	40
117-119,121-(Whitman variants; low print run; none have issue # on cover)	1	3	4	6	8	10
120-122,124-150: 22-Last Green Lantern/Green Arrow team-up. 130-132-Tales of the G.L. Corps. 132-Adam Strange series begins, ends147. 136,137-1st app. Citadel; Space Ranger app. 141-1st app. Omega Men (6/81). 142,143-Omega Men app.;Perez-c. 144-Omega Men cameo. 148-Tales of the G.L. Corps begins, ends #173. 150-Anniversary issue, 52 pgs.; no G.L. Corps						6.00
123-Green Lantern back to solo action; 2nd app. Guy Gardner as Green Lantern	1	2	3	4	5	7
151-180,183,184,186,187: 159-Origin Evil Star. 160,161-Omega Men app.						4.00
181,182,185,188: 181-Hal Jordan resigns as G.L. 182-John Stewart becomes new G.L.; origin recap of Hal Jordan as G.L. 185-Origin new G.L. (John Stewart).188-I.D. revealed; Alan Moore back-up scripts.						5.00
189-193,196-199,201-205: 191-Re-intro Star Sapphire (cameo). 192-Re-intro & origin of Star Sapphire (1st full app.). 194,198-Crisis x-over. 199-Hal Jordan returns as a member of G.L. Corps (3 G.L.s now). 201-Green Lantern Corps begins (is cover title, says premiere issue); intro. Kilowog						3.50
194-Hal Jordan/Guy Gardner battle; Guardians choose Guy Gardner to become new Green Lantern						4.00
195-Guy Gardner becomes Green Lantern; Crisis on Infinite Earths x-over	1	3	4	6	8	10
200-Double-size						4.00
Annual 1 (Listed as Tales Of The Green Lantern Corps Annual 1)						
Annual 2,3 (See Green Lantern Corps Annual #2,3)						3.50
Special 1 (1988), 2 (1989)-(Both $1.50, 52 pgs.)						3.50

NOTE: ***N. Adams*** *a-76, 77-87p, 89; c-63, 76-89.* ***M. Anderson*** *a-137i.* ***Austin*** *a-93i, 94i, 171i.* ***Chaykin*** *c-196.* ***Greene*** *a-39-49i, 58-63i; c-54-58i.* ***Grell*** *a-90-106, 108-111; c-90-106, 108-112.* ***Heck*** *a-120-122p.* ***Infantino*** *a-137p, 145-147p, 151, 152p.* ***Gil Kane*** *a-1-49p, 50-57, 58-61p, 68-75p, 85p(r), 87p(r), 88p(r), 156, 177, 184p; c-1-52, 54-61p, 67-75, 123, 154, 156, 165-171, 177, 184.* ***Newton*** *a-148p, 149p, 181.* ***Perez*** *c-132p, 141-144.* ***Sekowsky*** *a-65p, 170p.* ***Simonson*** *c-200.* ***Sparling*** *a-63p.* ***Starlin*** *c-129, 133.* ***Staton*** *a-117p, 123-127p, 128, 129-131p, 132-139, 140p, 141-146, 147p, 148-150, 151-155p; c-107p, 117p, 135(i), 136p, 145p, 146, 147, 148-152p, 155p.* ***Toth*** *a-86r, 171p.* ***Tuska*** *a-166-168p, 170p.*

GREEN LANTERN (3rd Series)
DC Comics: June, 1990 - Present ($1.00/$1.25/$1.50/$1.75/$1.95/$1.99/$2.25)

	NM- 9.2
1-Hal Jordan, John Stewart & Guy Gardner return; Batman & JLA app.	5.00
2-26: 9-12-Guy Gardner solo story. 13-(52 pgs.). 18-Guy Gardner solo story. 19-($1.75, 52 pgs.)-50th anniversary issue; Mart Nodell (original G.A. artist) part-p on G.A. Gr.Lantern; G. Kane-c. 25-($1.75, 52 pgs.)-Hal Jordan/Guy Gardner battle	4.00
27-45,47: 30,31-Gorilla Grodd-c/story(see Flash #69). 38,39-Adam Strange-c/story. 42-Deathstroke-c/s. 47-Green Arrow x-over	3.00
46,48,49,50: 46-Superman app. cont'd in Superman #82. 48-Emerald Twilight part 1. 50-($2.95, 52 pgs.)-Glow-in-the-dark-c	6.00
0, 51-62: 51-1st app. New Green Lantern (Kyle Rayner) with new costume. 53-Superman-c/story. 55-(9/94)-Zero Hour. 0-(10/94). 56-(11/94)	4.00
63,64-Kyle Rayner vs. Hal Jordan.	4.00
65-80,82-92: 63-Begin $1.75-c. 65-New Titans app. 66,67-Flash app. 71-Batman & Robin app. 72-Shazam!-c/app. 73-Wonder Woman-c/app. 73-75-Adam Strange app. 76,77-Green Arrow x-over. 80-Final Night x-over. 87-JLA app. 91-Genesis x-over. 92-Green Arrow x-over	3.00
81-(Regular Ed.)-Memorial for Hal Jordan (Parallax); most DC heroes app.	5.00
81-($3.95, Deluxe Edition)-Embossed prism-c	6.00
93-99: 93-Begin $1.95-c; Deadman app. 94-Superboy app. 95-Starlin-a(p). 98,99-Legion of Super-Heroes-c/app.	2.50
100-($2.95) Two covers (Jordan & Rayner); vs. Sinestro	5.00
101-106: 101-106-Hal Jordan-c/app. 103-JLA-c/app. 104-Green Arrow app. 105,106-Parallax app.	3.00
107-126: 107-Jade becomes a Green Lantern. 119-Hal Jordan/Spectre app. 125-JLA app.	2.25
127-149: 127-Begin $2.25-c. 129-Winick-s begin. 134-136-JLA-c/app. 143-Joker: Last Laugh; Lee-c. 145-Kyle becomes The Ion. 149-Superman-c/app.	2.25
150-($3.50) Jim Lee-c; Kyle becomes Green Lantern again; new costume	3.50
151-172: 151-155-Jim Lee-c: 154-Terry attacked. 155-Spectre-c/app. 162-164-Crossover with Green Arrow #23-25. 165-Raab-s begin. 169-Kilowog returns	2.25
#1,000,000 (11/98) 853rd Century x-over; Hitch & Neary-a/c	3.00
Annual 1-3: ('92-'94, 68 pgs.)-1-Eclipso app. 2 -Intro Nightblade. 3-Elseworlds story	3.50
Annual 4 (1995, $3.50)-Year One story	4.00
Annual 5,7,8 ('96, '98, '99, $2.95): 5-Legends of the Dead Earth. 7-Ghosts; Wrightson-c. 8-JLApe; Art Adams-c	3.00
Annual 6 (1997, $3.95)-Pulp Heroes story	5.00
Annual 9 (2000, $3.50) Planet DC	3.50
...80 Page Giant (12/98, $4.95) Stories by various	5.00
...80 Page Giant 2 (6/99, $4.95) Team-ups	5.00
...80 Page Giant 3 (8/00, $5.95) Darkseid vs. the GL Corps	6.00
....: 1001 Emerald Nights (2001, $6.95) Elseworlds; Guay-a/c; LaBan-s	7.00
...3-D #1 (12/98, $3.95) Jeanty-a	4.00
....: A New Dawn TPB (1998, $9.95)-r/#50-55	10.00
....: Baptism of Fire TPB (1999, $12.95)-r/#59,66,67,70-75	13.00
....: Brother's Keeper (2003, $12.95)-r/#151-155; Green Lantern Secret Files #3	13.00
....: Emerald Allies TPB (2000, $14.95)-r/GL/GA team-ups	15.00
....: Emerald Knights TPB (1998, $12.95)-r/Hal Jordan's return	13.00
....: Emerald Twilight nn (1994, $5.95)-r/#48-50	6.00
....: Emerald Twilight/New Dawn TPB (2003, $19.95)-r/#48-55	20.00
....: Ganthet's Tale nn (1992, $5.95, 68 pgs.)-Silver foil logo; Niven scripts; Byrne-c/a	6.00
.../Green Arrow Collection, Vol. 2-r/Gl #84-87,89 & Flash #217-219 & GL/GA	

Green Lantern: Brightest Day; Blackest Night © DC

The Green Mask #6 © FOX

Grendel #3 © Matt Wagner

	GD	VG	FN	VF	VF/NM	NM-
	2.0	4.0	6.0	8.0	9.0	9.2

#5-7 by O'Neil/Adams/Wrightson 13.00
...: New Journey, Old Path TPB (2001, $12.95)-r/#129-136 13.00
... : Our Worlds at War (8/01, $2.95) Jae Lee-c; prelude to x-over 3.00
...Plus 1 (12/1996, $2.95)-The Ray & Polaris-c/app. 3.00
...Secret Files 1-3- (7/98-7/02, $4.95)1- Origin stories & profiles. 2-Grell-c 5.00
.../Superman: Legend of the Green Flame (2000, $5.95) 1988 unpub. Neil Gaiman story of Hal Jordan with new art by various; Frank Miller-c 6.00
...: The Power of Ion (2003, $14.95, TPB) r/#142-150 15.00
...The Road Back nn (1992, $8.95)-r/1-8 w/covers 9.00
...: Traitor TPB (2001, $12.95) r/Legends of the DCU #20,21,28,29,37,38 13.00
...: Willworld (2001, $24.95, HC) Seth Fisher-a/J.M. DeMatteis-s; Hal Jordan 25.00
...: Willworld (2003, $17.95, SC) Seth Fisher-a/J.M. DeMatteis-s; Hal Jordan 18.00
NOTE: *Staton a(p)-9-12; c-9-12.*

GREEN LANTERN (See Tangent Comics/ Green Lantern)

GREEN LANTERN ANNUAL NO. 1, 1963
DC Comics: 1998 ($4.95, one-shot)
1-Reprints Golden Age & Silver Age stories in 1963-style 80 pg. Giant format; new Gil Kane sketch art 5.00

GREEN LANTERN: BRIGHTEST DAY; BLACKEST NIGHT
DC Comics: 2002 ($5.95, squarebound, one-shot)
nn-Alan Scott vs. Solomon Grundy in 1944; Snyder III-c/a; Seagle-s 6.00

GREEN LANTERN: CIRCLE OF FIRE
DC Comics: Early Oct, 2000 - No. 2, Late Oct, 2000 (limited series)
1-($4.95) Intro. other Green Lanterns 5.00
2-($3.75) 4.00
Green Lantern (x-overs)- .../Adam Strange; .../Atom; .../Firestorm; ... /Green Lantern, Winick-s; .../Power Girl (all $2.50-c) 2.50
TPB (2002, $17.95) r/#1,2 & x-overs 18.00

GREEN LANTERN CORPS, THE (Formerly Green Lantern; see Tales of...)
DC Comics: No. 206, Nov, 1986 - No. 224, May, 1988
206-223: 212-John Stewart marries Katma Tui. 220,221-Millennium tie-ins 3.00
224-Double-size last issue 4.00
...Corps Annual 2,3- (12/86,8/87) 1-Formerly Tales of ...Annual #1; Alan Moore scripts. 3-Indicia says Green Lantern Annual #3; Moore scripts; Byrne-a 3.00
NOTE: ***Austin** a-Annual 3i. **Gil Kane** a-223, 224p; c-223, 224, Annual 2. **Russell** a-Annual 3i. **Staton** a-207-213p, 217p, 221p, 222p, Annual 3; c-207-213p, 217p, 221p, 222p. **Willingham** a-213p, 219p, 220p, 218p, 219p, Annual 2, 3p; c-218p, 219p.*

GREEN LANTERN CORPS QUARTERLY
DC Comics: Summer, 1992 - No. 8, Spring, 1994 ($2.50/$2.95, 68 pgs.)
1,7,8: 1-G.A. Green Lantern story; Staton-a(p). 7-Painted-c; Tim Vigil-a. 8-Lobo-c/s 3.50
2-6: 2-G.A. G.L.-c/story; Austin-c(i); Gulacy-a(p). 3-G.A. G.L. story. 4-Austin-i 3.00

GREEN LANTERN: DRAGON LORD
DC Comics: 2001 - No. 3, 2001 ($4.95, squarebound, limited series)
1-3: A G.L. in ancient China; Moench-s/Gulacy-c/a 5.00

GREEN LANTERN: EMERALD DAWN (Also see Emerald Dawn)
DC Comics: Dec, 1989 - No. 6, May, 1990 ($1.00, limited series)
1-Origin retold; Giffen plots in all 5.00
2-6: 4-Re-intro. Tomar-Re 4.00

GREEN LANTERN: EMERALD DAWN II (Emerald Dawn II #1 & 2)
DC Comics: Apr, 1991 - No. 6, Sept, 1991 ($1.00, limited series)
1-6 2.50
TPB (2003, $12.95) r/#1-6; Alan Davis-c 13.00

GREEN LANTERN: EVIL'S MIGHT (Elseworlds)
DC Comics: 2002 - No. 3 ($5.95, squarebound, limited series)
1-3-Kyle Rayner in 19th century NYC; Rogers-a; Chaykin & Tischman-s 6.00

GREEN LANTERN: FEAR ITSELF
DC Comics: 1999 (Graphic novel)
Hardcover ($24.95) Ron Marz-s/Brad Parker painted-a 25.00
Softcover ($14.95) 15.00

GREEN LANTERN/FLASH: FASTER FRIENDS (See Flash/Green Lantern...)
DC Comics: 1997 ($4.95, limited series)
1-Marz-s 5.00

GREEN LANTERN GALLERY
DC Comics: Dec, 1996 ($3.50, one-shot)
1-Wraparound-c; pin-ups by various 3.50

GREEN LANTERN/GREEN ARROW (Also see The Flash #217)
DC Comics: Oct, 1983 - No. 7, April, 1984 (52-60 pgs.)
1-7- r-Green Lantern #76-89 4.00
NOTE: ***Neal Adams** r-1-7; c-1-4. **Wrightson** r-4, 5.*

GREEN LANTERN • LEGACY: THE LAST WILL & TESTAMENT OF HAL JORDAN
DC Comics: 2002 ($24.95, hardcover graphic novel)
Hardcover-Anderson & Sienkiewicz-a/c; Kelly-s; Return of Oa 25.00

GREEN LANTERN: MOSAIC (Also see Cosmic Odyssey #2)
DC Comics: June, 1992 - No. 18, Nov, 1993 ($1.25)
1-18: Featuring John Stewart. 1-Painted-c by Cully Hamner 2.25

GREEN LANTERN/SENTINEL: HEART OF DARKNESS
DC Comics: Mar, 1998 - No. 3, May, 1998 ($1.95, limited series)
1-3-Marz-s/Pelletier-a 3.00

GREEN LANTERN/SILVER SURFER: UNHOLY ALLIANCES
DC Comics: 1995 ($4.95, one-shot)(Prelude to DC Versus Marvel)
nn-Hal Jordan app. 5.00

GREEN LANTERN: THE NEW CORPS
DC Comics:1999 - No. 2, 1999 ($4.95, limited series)
1,2-Kyle recruits new GLs; Eaton-a 5.00

GREEN LANTERN VS. ALIENS
Dark Horse Comics: Sept, 2000 - No. 4, Dec, 2000 ($2.95, limited series)
1-4: 1-Hal Jordan and GL Corps vs. Aliens; Leonardi-p. 2-4-Kyle Rayner 3.00

GREEN MASK, THE (See Mystery Men)
Summer, 1940 - No. 9, 2/42; No. 10, 8/44 - No. 11, 11/44;
Fox Features Syndicate: V2#1, Spring, 1945 - No. 6, 10-11/46

	GD 2.0	VG 4.0	FN 6.0	VF 8.0	VF/NM 9.0	NM- 9.2
V1#1-Origin The Green Mask & Domino; reprints/Mystery Men #1-3,5-7; Lou Fine-c	370	740	1110	2405	3703	5000
2-Zanzibar The Magician by Tuska	132	264	396	825	1238	1650
3-Powell-a; Marijuana story	82	164	246	513	769	1025
4-Navy Jones begins, ends #6	66	132	198	413	619	825
5	55	110	165	330	495	660
6-The Nightbird begins, ends #9; bondage/torture-c	44	88	132	264	395	525
7-9: 9(2/42)-Becomes The Bouncer #10(nn) on? & Green Mask #10 on	39	78	117	230	325	420
10,11: 10-Origin One Round Hogan & Rocket Kelly	32	64	96	184	262	340
V2#1	24	48	72	138	194	250
2-6	21	42	63	118	164	210

GREEN PLANET, THE
Charlton Comics: 1962 (one-shot) (12¢)

	GD 2.0	VG 4.0	FN 6.0	VF 8.0	VF/NM 9.0	NM- 9.2
nn-Giordano-c; sci-fi	7	14	21	51	71	90

GREEN TEAM (See Cancelled Comic Cavalcade & 1st Issue Special)

GREETINGS FROM SANTA (See March of Comics No. 48)

GRENDEL (Also see Primer #2, Mage and Comico Collection)
Comico: Mar, 1983 - No. 3, Feb, 1984 ($1.50, B&W)(#1 has indicia to Skrog #1)

	GD 2.0	VG 4.0	FN 6.0	VF 8.0	VF/NM 9.0	NM- 9.2
1-Origin Hunter Rose	10	20	30	73	107	140
2,3: 2-Origin Argent	8	16	24	55	78	100

GRENDEL
Comico: Oct, 1986 - No. 40, Feb, 1990 ($1.50/$1.95/$2.50, mature)

	GD 2.0	VG 4.0	FN 6.0	VF 8.0	VF/NM 9.0	NM- 9.2
1	1	2	3	5	6	8
1,2: 2nd printings						3.00
2,3,5-15: 13-15-Ken Steacy-c.						4.00
4,16: 4-Dave Stevens-c(i). 16-Re-intro Mage (series begins, ends #19)						6.00
17-40: 24-25,27-28,30-31-Snyder-c/a						3.00
Devil by the Deed (Graphic Novel, 10/86, $5.95, 52 pgs.)-r/Grendel back-ups/ Mage 6-14; Alan Moore intro.	1	2	3	4	5	7
Devil's Legacy ($14.95, 1988, Graphic Novel)	2	4	6	10	12	15
Devil's Vagary (10/87, B&W & red)-No price; included in Comico Collection	2	4	6	8	10	12

GRENDEL (Title series): **Dark Horse Comics**
--BLACK, WHITE, AND RED, 11/98 - No. 4, 2/99 ($3.95, anthology)
1-Wagner-s in all. Art by Sale, Leon and others 5.00
2-4: 2-Mack, Chadwick-a. 3-Allred, Kristensen-a. 4-Pearson, Sprouse-a 4.00
--CLASSICS, 7/95 - 8/95 ($3.95, mature) 1,2-reprints; new Wagner-c 4.00
--CYCLE, 10/95 ($5.95) 1-nn-history of Grendel by M. Wagner & others 6.00

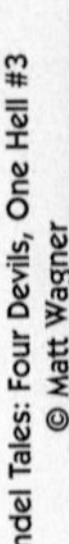
Grendel Tales: Four Devils, One Hell #3 © Matt Wagner

Grifter #1 © WSP

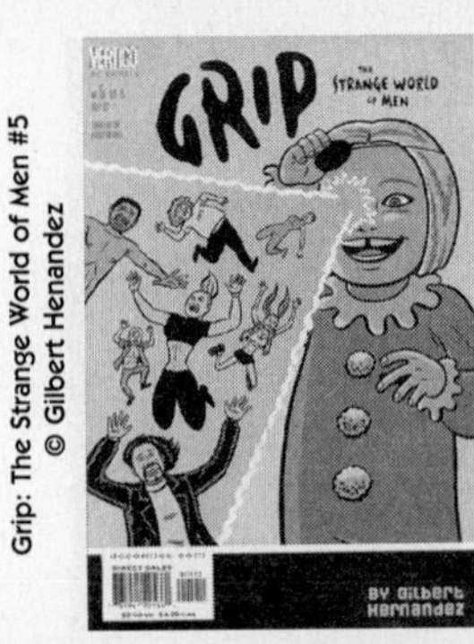

Grip: The Strange World of Men #5 © Gilbert Hernandez

GD 2.0 VG 4.0 FN 6.0 VF 8.0 VF/NM 9.0 NM- 9.2

--DEVIL BY THE DEED, 7/93 ($3.95, varnish-c) 1-nn-M. Wagner-c/a/scripts; r/Grendel back-ups from Mage #6-14 4.00
Reprint (12/97, $3.95) w/pin-ups by various 4.00

--DEVIL CHILD, 6/99 - No. 2, 7/99 ($2.95, mature) 1,2-Sale & Kristiansen-a/Schutz-s 3.00

--DEVIL QUEST, 11/95 ($4.95) 1-nn-Prequel to Batman/Grendel II; M. Wagner story & art; r/back-up story from Grendel Tales series. 5.00

--DEVILS AND DEATHS, 10/94 - 11/94 ($2.95, mature) 1,2 3.00

: DEVIL'S LEGACY, 3/00 - No. 12, 2/01 ($2.95, reprints 1986 series, recolored)
1-12-Wagner-s/c; Pander Bros.-a 3.00

: GOD AND THE DEVIL, No. 0, 1/03 - No. 10 ($3.50, reprints 1986 series, recolored)
0-8: 0-Sale-c/a; r/#23. 1-8-Snyder-c 3.50

--RED, WHITE & BLACK, 9/02 - No. 4, 12/02 ($4.99, anthology)
1-4-Wagner-s in all. 1-Art by Thompson, Sakai, Mahfood and others. 2-Kelley Jones, Watson, Brereton, Hester & Parks-a. 3-Oeming, Noto, Cannon, Ashley Wood, Huddleston-a 4-Chiang, Dalrymple, Robertson, Snyder III and Zulli-a 5.00

--TALES: DEVIL'S CHOICES, 3/95 - 6/95 ($2.95, mature) 1-4 3.00

--TALES: FOUR DEVILS, ONE HELL, 8/93 - 1/94 ($2.95, mature)
1-6-Wagner painted-c 3.00
TPB (12/94, $17.95) r/#1-6 18.00

--TALES: HOMECOMING, 12/94 - 2/95 ($2.95, mature) 1-3 3.00

--TALES: THE DEVIL IN OUR MIDST, 5/94 - 9/95 ($2.95, mature) 1-5-Wagner painted-c 3.00

--TALES: THE DEVIL MAY CARE, 12/95 - No. 6, 5/96 ($2.95, mature)
1-6-Terry LaBan scripts. 5-Batman/Grendel II preview 3.00

--TALES: THE DEVIL'S APPRENTICE, 9/97 - No. 3, 11/97 ($2.95, mature)
1-3 3.00

: THE DEVIL INSIDE, 9/01 - No. 3, 11/01 ($2.99)
1-3-r/#13-15 with new Wagner-c 3.00

GRENDEL: WAR CHILD
Dark Horse Comics: Aug, 1992 - No. 10, Jun, 1993 ($2.50, lim. series, mature)
1-9: 1-4-Bisley painted-c; Wagner-i & scripts in all 3.00
10-($3.50, 52 pgs.) Wagner-c 4.00
Limited Edition Hardcover ($99.95) 100.00

GREYFRIARS BOBBY (Disney)(Movie)
Dell Publishing Co.: No. 1189, Nov, 1961 (one-shot)
Four Color 1189-Photo-c (scarce) 8 16 24 55 78 100

GREYLORE
Sirius: 12/85 - No. 5, Sept, 1986 ($1.50/$1.75, high quality paper)
1-5: Bo Hampton-a in all 2.25

GREYSHIRT: INDIGO SUNSET (Also see Tomorrow Stories)
America's Best Comics: Dec, 2001 - No. 6, Aug, 2002 ($3.50, limited series)
1-6-Veitch-s/a. 4-Back-up w/John Severin-a. 6-Cho-a 3.50
TPB (2002, $19.95) r/#1-6; preface by Alan Moore 20.00

GRIDIRON GIANTS
Ultimate Sports Ent.: 2000 - No. 2 ($3.95, cardstock covers)
1,2-NFL players Sanders, Marino, Plummer, T. Davis battle evil 4.00

GRIFFIN, THE
DC Comics: 1991 - No. 6, 1991 ($4.95, limited series, 52 pgs.)
Book 1-6: Matt Wagner painted-c 5.00

GRIFTER (Also see Team 7 & WildC.A.T.S)
Image Comics (WildStorm Prod.): May, 1995 - No. 10, Mar, 1996 ($1.95)
1 ($1.95, Newsstand)-WildStorm Rising Pt. 5 2.50
1-10:1 ($2.50, Direct)-WildStorm Rising Pt. 5, bound-in trading card 3.00

GRIFTER
Image Comics (WildStorm Prod.): V2#1, July, 1996 - No. 14, Aug, 1997 ($2.50)
V2#1-14: Steven Grant scripts 3.00

GRIFTER AND THE MASK
Dark Horse Comics: Sept, 1996 - No. 2, Oct, 1996 ($2.50, limited series)
(1st Dark Horse Comics/Image x-over)
1,2: Steve Seagle scripts 3.00

GRIFTER/BADROCK (Also see WildC.A.T.S & Youngblood)
Image Comics (Extreme Studios): Oct, 1995 - No.2, Nov, 1995 ($2.50, unfinished lim. series)
1,2: 2-Flip book w/Badrock #2 2.50

GRIFTER: ONE SHOT
Image Comics (WildStorm Productions): Jan, 1995 ($4.95, one-shot)
1-Flip-c 5.00

GRIFTER/SHI
Image Comics (WildStorm Productions): Apr, 1996 - No. 2, May, 1996 ($2.95, limited series)
1,2: 1-Jim Lee-c/a(p); Travis Charest-a(p). 2-Billy Tucci-c/a(p); Travis Charest-a(p) 3.00

GRIM GHOST, THE
Atlas/Seaboard Publ.: Jan, 1975 - No. 3, July, 1975
1-3: Fleisher-s in all. 1-Origin. 2-Son of Satan; Colan-a. 3-Heath-c
1 2 3 4 5 7

GRIMJACK (Also see Demon Knight & Starslayer)
First Comics: Aug, 1984 - No. 81, Apr, 1991 ($1.00/$1.95/$2.25)
1-John Ostrander scripts & Tim Truman-c/a begins. 3.00
2-25: 20-Sutton-c/a begins. 22-Bolland-a. 2.25
26-2nd color Teenage Mutant Ninja Turtles 4.00
27-74,76-81 (Later issues $1.95, $2.25): 30-Dynamo Joe x-over; 31-Mandrake-c/a begins. 73,74-Kelley Jones-a 2.50
75-($5.95, 52 pgs.)-Fold-out map; coated stock 6.00
NOTE: *Truman c/a-1-17.*

GRIMJACK CASEFILES
First Comics: Nov, 1990 - No. 5, Mar, 1991 ($1.95, limited series)
1-5 Reprints 1st stories from Starslayer #10 on 2.25

GRIMM'S GHOST STORIES (See Dan Curtis)
Gold Key/Whitman No. 55 on: Jan, 1972 - No. 60, June, 1982 (Painted-c #1-42,44,46-56)

	GD	VG	FN	VF	VF/NM	NM-
1	3	7	10	21	28	35
2-5,8: 5,8-Williamson-a	2	4	6	11	14	18
6,7,9,10	2	4	6	9	11	14
11-20	1	3	4	6	8	10
21-42,45-54: 32,34-Reprints. 45-Photo-c	1	2	3	5	6	8
43,44,55-60: 43,44-(52 pgs.). 43-Photo-c. 58(2/82). 59(4/82)-Williamson-a(r/#8). 60(6/82)	1	3	4	6	8	10
Mini-Comic No. 1 (3-1/4x6-1/2", 1976)	1	2	3	5	7	9

NOTE: *Reprints-#32?, 34?, 39, 43, 44, 47?, 53; 56-60(1/3).* **Bolle** *a-8, 17, 22-25, 27, 29(2), 33, 35, 41, 43r, 45(2), 48(2), 50, 52.* **Celardo** *a-17, 26, 28p, 30, 31, 43(2), 45.* **Lopez** *a-24, 25.* **McWilliams** *a-33, 44r, 48, 54(2), 57, 58.* **Win Mortimer** *a-31, 33, 49, 51, 55, 56, 58(2), 59, 60.* **Roussos** *a-25, 30.* **Sparling** *a-23, 24, 28, 30, 31, 33, 43r, 44, 45, 51(2), 52, 56, 58, 59(2), 60.* **Spiegle** *a-44.*

GRIN (The American Funny Book) (Satire)
APAG House Pubs: Nov, 1972 - No. 3, April, 1973 (Magazine, 52 pgs.)
1-Parodies-Godfather, All in the Family 3 6 9 16 20 25
2,3 2 4 6 10 12 15

GRIN & BEAR IT (See Gags)
Dell Publishing Co.: No. 28, 1941
Large Feature Comic 28 12 24 36 84 125 165

GRIPS (Extreme violence)
Silverwolf Comics: Sept, 1986 - No. 4, Dec, 1986 ($1.50, B&W, mature)
1-Tim Vigil-c/a in all 6.00
2-4 4.00

GRIP: THE STRANGE WORLD OF MEN
DC Comics (Vertigo): Jan, 2002 - No. 5, May, 2002 ($2.50, limited series)
1-4-Gilbert Hernandez-s/a 2.50

GRIT GRADY (See Holyoke One-Shot No. 1)

GROO (Sergio Aragonés'...)
Image Comics: Dec, 1994 - No. 12, Dec, 1995 ($1.95)
1-12: 2-Indicia reads #1, Jan, 1995; Aragonés-c/a in all 3.50

GROO (Sergio Aragonés'...)
Dark Horse Comics: Jan, 1998 - No. 4, Apr, 1998 ($2.95)
1-4: Aragonés-c/a in all 4.00

GROO CHRONICLES, THE (Sergio Aragonés)
Marvel Comics (Epic Comics): June, 1989 - No. 6, Feb, 1990 ($3.50)
Book 1-6: Reprints early Pacific issues 3.50

GROO SPECIAL
Eclipse Comics: Oct, 1984 ($2.00, 52 pgs., Baxter paper)
1-Aragonés-c/a 2 4 6 14 18 22

GROO THE WANDERER (See Destroyer Duck #1 & Starslayer #5)
Pacific Comics: Dec, 1982 - No. 8, Apr, 1984
1-Aragonés-c/a(p) in all; Aragonés bio., photo 2 4 6 12 16 20

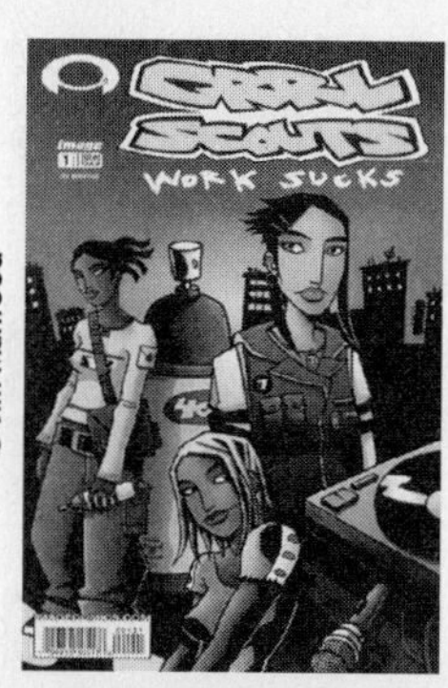

Grrl Scouts: Work Sucks #1 © Jim Mahfood

Guardian Angel #1 © Blue Dolphin Press

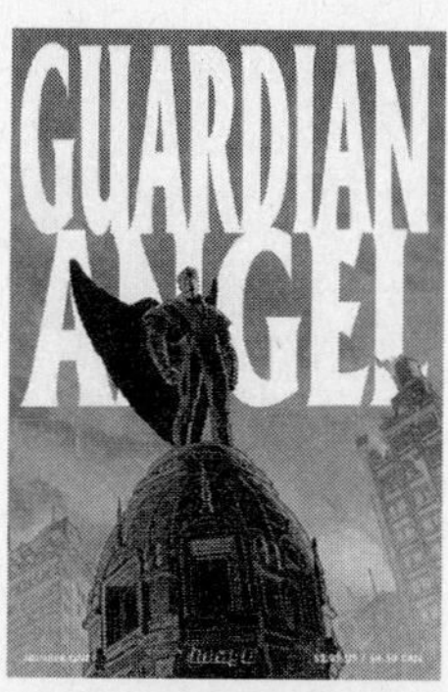

Gunhawks #1 © MAR

	GD 2.0	VG 4.0	FN 6.0	VF 8.0	VF/NM 9.0	NM- 9.2
2-5: 5-Deluxe paper (1.00-c)	2	4	6	9	11	14
6-8	2	4	6	10	13	16

GROO THE WANDERER (Sergio Aragonés'...) (See Marvel Graphic Novel #32)
Marvel Comics (Epic Comics): March, 1985 - No. 120, Jan, 1995

1-Aragonés-c/a in all	2	4	6	9	11	14
2-10	1	2	3	4	5	7
11-20,50-($1.50, double size)						5.00
21-49,51-99: 87-direct sale only, high quality paper						3.00
100-($2.95, 52 pgs.)						5.00
101-120						4.00
Groo Carnival, The (12/91, $8.95)-r/#9-12						11.00
Groo Garden, The (4/94, $10.95)-r/#25-28						11.00

GROOVY (Cartoon Comics - not CCA approved)
Marvel Comics Group: March, 1968 - No. 3, July, 1968

1-Monkees, Ringo Starr, Sonny & Cher, Mamas & Papas photos	9	18	27	60	85	110
2,3	6	12	18	40	55	70

GROSS POINT
DC Comics: Aug, 1997 - No. 14, Aug, 1998 ($2.50)

1-14: 1-Waid/Augustyn-s 2.50

GROUP LARUE, THE
Innovation Publishing: 1989 - No. 4, 1990 ($1.95, mini-series)

1-4-By Mike Baron 2.25

GRRL SCOUTS (Jim Mahfood's...) (Also see 40 oz. Collected)
Oni Press: Mar,1999 - No. 4, Dec, 1999 ($2.95, B&W, limited series)

1-4-Mahfood-s/c/a 3.00
TPB (2003, $12.95) r/#1-4; pin-ups by Warren, Winick, Allred, Fegredo and others 13.00

GRRL SCOUTS: WORK SUCKS
Image Comics: Feb, 2003 - No. 4, May, 2003 ($2.95, B&W, limited series)

1-4-Mahfood-s/c/a 3.00

GUADALCANAL DIARY (See American Library)

GUARDIAN ANGEL
Image Comics: May, 2002 - Present ($2.95)

1,2-Peterson-s/Wiesenfeld-a 3.00

GUARDIANS OF JUSTICE & THE O-FORCE
Shadow Comics: 1990 (no date) ($1.50, 7-1/2 x10-1/4)

1-Super-hero group 2.25

GUARDIANS OF METROPOLIS
DC Comics: Nov, 1995 - Feb, 1995 ($1.50, limited series)

1-4: 1-Superman & Granny Goodness app. 2.25

GUARDIANS OF THE GALAXY (Also see The Defenders #26, Marvel Presents #3, Marvel Super-Heroes #18, Marvel Two-In-One #5)
Marvel Comics: June, 1990 - No. 62, July, 1995 ($1.00/$1.25)

1-Valentino-c/a(p) begin. 3.00
2-16: 2-Zeck-c(i). 5-McFarlane-c(i). 7-Intro Malevolence (Mephisto's daughter); Perez-c(i). 8-Intro Rancor (descendant of Wolverine) in cameo. 9-1st full app. Rancor; Rob Liefeld-c(i). 10-Jim Lee-c(i). 13,14-1st app. Spirit of Vengeance (futuristic Ghost Rider). 14-Spirit of Vengeance vs. The Guardians. 15-Starlin-c(i). 16-($1.50, 52 pgs.)-Starlin-c(i) 2.50
17-24,26-38,40-47: 17-20-31st century Punishers storyline. 20-Last $1.00-c. 21-Rancor app. 22-Reintro Starhawk. 24-Silver Surfer-c/story; Ron Lim-c. 26-Origin retold. 27-28-Infinity War x-over; 27-Inhumans app. 43-Intro Wooden (son of Thor) 2.25
25-($2.50)-Prism foil-c; Silver Surfer/Galactus-c/s 3.00
25-($2.50)-Without foil-c; newsstand edition 2.50
39-($2.95, 52 pgs.)-Embossed & holo-grafx foil-c; Dr. Doom vs. Rancor 3.00
48,49,51-62: 48-bound-in trading card sheet 2.25
50-($2.00, 52 pgs.)-Newsstand edition 2.25
50-($2.95, 52 pgs.)-Collectors ed. w/foil embossed-c 3.00
Annual 1-4: ('91-'94, 68 pgs.)-1-Origin. 2-Spirit of Vengeance-c/story. 3,4-Bagged w/card 3.00

GUERRILLA WAR (Formerly Jungle War Stories)
Dell Publishing Co.: No. 12, July-Sept, 1965 - No. 14, Mar, 1966

12-14	3	6	9	16	20	24

GUFF
Dark Horse Comics: Apr, 1998 ($1.95, B&W)

1-Flip book; Aragonés-c 2.25

GUILTY (See Justice Traps the Guilty)

	GD 2.0	VG 4.0	FN 6.0	VF 8.0	VF/NM 9.0	NM- 9.2

GULLIVER'S TRAVELS (See Dell Jr. Treasury No. 3)
Dell Publishing Co.: Sept-Nov, 1965 - No. 3, May, 1966

1	6	12	18	40	55	70
2,3	4	8	12	28	38	48

GUMBY'S SUMMER FUN SPECIAL
Comico: July, 1987 ($2.50)

1-Art Adams-c/a; B. Burden scripts 3.00

GUMBY'S WINTER FUN SPECIAL
Comico: Dec, 1988 ($2.50, 44 pgs.)

1-Art Adams-c/a 3.00

GUMPS, THE (See Merry Christmas..., Popular & Super Comics)
Dell Publ. Co./Bridgeport Herald Corp.: No. 73, 1945; Mar-Apr, 1947 - No. 5, Nov-Dec, 1947

Four Color 73 (Dell)(1945)	13	26	39	94	137	180
1 (3-4/47)	16	32	48	92	126	160
2-5	10	20	30	58	77	95

GUNFIGHTER (Fat & Slat #1-4) (Becomes Haunt of Fear #15 on)
E. C. Comics (Fables Publ. Co.): No. 5, Sum, 1948 - No. 14, Mar-Apr, 1950

5,6-Moon Girl in each	55	110	165	330	495	660
7-14: 14-Bondage-c	40	80	120	240	350	460

NOTE: *Craig & H. C. Kiefer art in most issues.* **Craig** *c-5, 6, 13, 14.* **Feldstein/Craig** *a-10.* **Feldstein** *a-7-11.* **Harrison/Wood** *a-13, 14.* **Ingels** *a-5-14; c-7-12.*

GUNFIGHTERS, THE
Super Comics (Reprints): 1963 - 1964

10-12,15,16,18: 10,11-r/Billy the Kid #s? 12-r/The Rider #5(Swift Arrow). 15-r/Straight Arrow #42; Powell-r. 16-r/Billy the Kid #?(Toby). 18-r/The Rider #3; Severin-c	2	4	6	11	14	18

GUNFIGHTERS, THE (Formerly Kid Montana)
Charlton Comics: No. 51, 10/66 - No. 52, 10/67; No. 53, 6/79 - No. 85, 7/84

51,52	2	4	6	12	16	20
53,54,56:53,54-Williamson/Torres-r/Six Gun Heroes #47,49. 56-Williamson/Severin-c; Severin-r/Sheriff of Tombstone #1	1	3	4	6	8	10
55,57-80						6.00
81-84-Lower print run	1	2	3	5	6	8
85-S&K-r/1955 Bullseye	1	3	4	6	8	10

GUNFIRE (See Deathstroke Annual #2 & Showcase 94 #1,2)
DC Comics: May, 1994 - No. 13, June, 1995 ($1.75/$2.25)

1-5,0,6-13: 2-Ricochet-c/story. 5-(9/94). 0-(10/94). 6-(11/94) 2.25

GUN GLORY (Movie)
Dell Publishing Co.: No. 846, Oct, 1957 (one-shot)

Four Color 846-Toth-a, photo-c.	10	20	30	70	100	130

GUNHAWK, THE (Formerly Whip Wilson)(See Wild Western)
Marvel Comics/Atlas (MCI): No. 12, Nov, 1950 - No. 18, Dec, 1951
(Also see Two-Gun Western #5)

12	20	40	60	112	156	200
13-18: 13-Tuska-a. 16-Colan-a. 18-Maneely-c	14	28	42	79	107	135

GUNHAWKS (Gunhawk No. 7)
Marvel Comics Group: Oct, 1972 - No. 7, October, 1973

1,6: 1-Reno Jones, Kid Cassidy; Shores-c/a(p). 6-Kid Cassidy dies	3	6	9	16	20	24
2-5,7: 7-Reno Jones solo	2	4	6	11	14	18

GUNHED
Vix Comics: 1990 - No. 3, 1991? ($4.95, 7-1/8 x 9-1/8, 52 pgs., bi-monthly)

1-3: Japanese sci-fi based on 1991 movie 5.00

GUNMASTER (Becomes Judo Master #89 on)
Charlton Comics: 9/64 - No. 4, 1965; No. 84, 7/65 - No. 88, 3-4/66; No. 89, 10/67

V1#1	4	8	12	24	32	40
2,4, V5#84-86: 84-Formerly Six-Gun Heroes	3	6	9	16	20	25
V5#87-89	2	4	6	11	14	18

NOTE: *Vol. 5 was originally cancelled with #88 (3-4/66). #89 on, became Judo Master, then later in 1967, Charlton issued #89 as a Gunmaster one-shot.*

GUN RUNNER
Marvel Comics UK: Oct, 1993 - No. 6, Mar, 1994 ($1.75, limited series)

1-($2.75)-Polybagged w/4 trading cards; Spirits of Vengeance app. 3.00
2-6: 2-Ghost Rider & Blaze app. 2.25

GUNS AGAINST GANGSTERS (True-To-Life Romances #8 on)

Gunsmith Cats: Mister V #1 © Kenichi Sonoda

Gunsmoke #25 © CBS

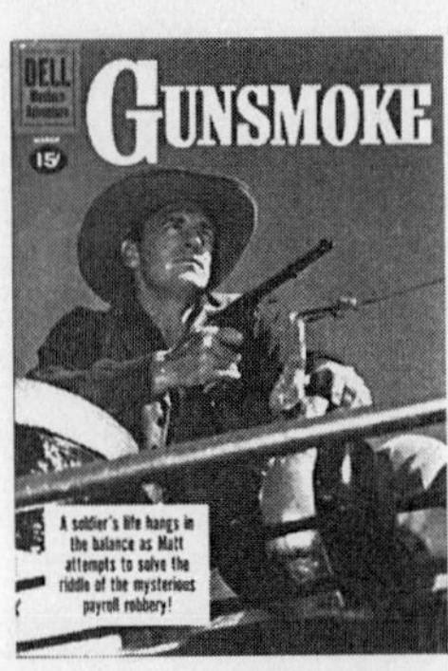

Guy Gardner #21 © DC

GD VG FN VF VF/NM NM-
2.0 4.0 6.0 8.0 9.0 9.2

Curtis Publications/Novelty Press: Sept-Oct, 1948 - No. 6, July-Aug, 1949; V2#1, Sept-Oct, 1949

1-Toni & Greg Gayle begins by Schomburg; L.B. Cole-c 39 78 117 230 325 420
2-L.B. Cole-c 30 60 90 170 240 310
3-6, V2#1: 6-Toni Gayle-c 25 50 75 147 202 260

NOTE: ***L. B. Cole*** *c-1-6, V2#1, 2; a-1, 2, 3(2), 4-6.*

GUNSLINGER
Dell Publishing Co.: No. 1220, Oct-Dec, 1961 (one-shot)

Four Color 1220-Photo-c 10 20 30 67 96 125

GUNSLINGER (Formerly Tex Dawson...)
Marvel Comics Group: No. 2, Apr, 1973 - No. 3, June, 1973

2,3 2 4 6 12 16 20

GUNSLINGERS
Marvel Comics: Feb, 2000 ($2.99)

1-Reprints stories of Two-Gun Kid, Rawhide Kid and Caleb Hammer 3.00

GUNSMITH CATS: (Title series), **Dark Horse Comics**

--BAD TRIP (Manga), 6/98 - No. 6, 11/98 ($2.95, B&W) 1-6 3.00
--BEAN BANDIT (Manga), 1/99 - No. 9 ($2.95, B&W, limited series) 1-9 3.00
--GOLDIE VS. MISTY (Manga), 11/97 - No. 7, 5/98 ($2.95, B&W) 1-7 3.00
--KIDNAPPED (Manga), 11/99 - No. 10, 8/00 ($2.95, B&W) 1-10 3.00
--MISTER V (Manga), 10/00 - No. 11, 8/01 ($3.50/$2.99), B&W) 1-7,9-11 3.50
8-($2.99) 3.00
--THE RETURN OF GRAY (Manga), 8/96 - No. 7, 2/97 ($2.95, B&W) 1-7 3.00
--SHADES OF GRAY (Manga), 5/97 - No. 5, 9/97 ($2.95, B&W) 1-5 3.00
--SPECIAL (Manga) Nov, 2001 ($2.99, B&W, one-shot) 3.00

GUNSMOKE (Blazing Stories of the West)
Western Comics (Youthful Magazines): Apr-May, 1949 - No. 16, Jan, 1952

1-Gunsmoke & Masked Marvel begin by Ingels; Ingels bondage-c 40 80 120 240 360 480
2-Ingels-c/a(2) 29 58 87 164 232 300
3-Ingels bondage-c/a 24 48 72 138 194 250
4-6: Ingels-c 19 38 57 109 152 195
7-10 11 22 33 63 84 105
11-16: 15,16-Western/horror stories 10 20 30 58 77 95

NOTE: ***Stallman*** *a-11, 14.* ***Wildey*** *a-15, 16.*

GUNSMOKE (TV)
Dell Publishing Co./Gold Key (All have James Arness photo-c): No. 679, Feb, 1956 - No. 27, Feb, 1969 - No. 6, Feb, 1970

Four Color 679(#1) 19 38 57 136 198 260
Four Color 720,769,797,844 (#2-5),6(11-1/57-58) 10 20 30 70 100 130
7,8,9,11,12-Williamson-a in all, 4 pgs. each 10 20 30 72 104 135
10-Williamson/Crandall-a, 4 pgs. 10 20 30 72 104 135
13-27 8 16 24 58 82 105
1 (Gold Key) 7 14 21 46 63 80
2-6('69-70) 4 8 12 25 33 42

GUNSMOKE TRAIL
Ajax-Farrell Publ./Four Star Comic Corp.: June, 1957 - No. 4, Dec, 1957

1 11 22 33 63 84 105
2-4 7 14 21 35 43 50

GUNSMOKE WESTERN (Formerly Western Tales of Black Rider)
Atlas Comics No. 32-35(CPS/NPI); Marvel No. 36 on: No. 32, Dec, 1955 - No. 77, July, 1963

32-Baker & Drucker-a 17 34 51 98 134 170
33,35,36-Williamson-a in each: 5,6 & 4 pgs. plus Drucker-a #33. 33-Kinstler-a? 14 28 42 79 107 135
34-Baker-a, 4 pgs.; Kirby-c 12 24 36 69 92 115
37-Davis-a(2); Williamson text illo 11 22 33 63 84 105
38,39: 39-Williamson text illo (unsigned) 9 18 27 52 66 80
40-Williamson/Mayo-a (4 pgs.) 10 20 30 56 73 90
41,42,45,46,48,49,52-54,57,58,60: 49,52-Kid from Texas story. 57-1st Two Gun Kid by Severin. 60-Sam Hawk app. in Kid Colt 8 16 24 40 50 60
43,44-Torres-a 8 16 24 40 50 60
47,51,59,61: 47,51,59-Kirby-a. 61-Crandall-a 9 18 27 49 62 75
50-Kirby, Crandall-a 10 20 30 56 73 90
55,56-Matt Baker-a 9 18 27 52 66 80
62-67,69,71-73,77-Kirby-a. 72-Origin Kid Colt 6 12 18 38 52 65

GD VG FN VF VF/NM NM-
2.0 4.0 6.0 8.0 9.0 9.2

68,70,74-76: 68-(10¢-c) 4 8 12 29 40 50
68-(10¢ cover price blacked out, 12¢ printed on) 8 16 24 58 82 105

NOTE: ***Colan*** *a-35-37, 39, 72, 76.* ***Davis*** *a-37, 52, 54, 55; c-50, 54.* ***Ditko*** *a-66; c-56p.* ***Drucker*** *a-.32-34.* ***Heath*** *c-33.* ***Jack Keller*** *a-35, 40, 60, 72; c-72.* ***Kirby*** *a-47, 50, 51, 59, 62(3), 63-67, 69, 71, 73, 77; c-56(w/****Ditko****),57, 58, 60, 61(w/****Ayers****), 62, 63, 66, 68, 69, 71-77.* ***Robinson*** *a-35.* ***Severin*** *a-35, 59-61; c-34, 35, 39, 42, 43.* ***Tuska*** *a-34.* ***Wildey*** *a-10, 37, 42, 56, 57. Kid Colt in all. Two-Gun Kid in No. 57, 59, 60-63. Wyatt Earp in No. 45, 48, 49, 52, 54, 55, 58.*

GUNS OF FACT & FICTION (Also see A-1 Comics)
Magazine Enterprises: No. 13, 1948 (one-shot)

A-1 13-Used in **SOTI**, pg. 19; Ingels & J. Craig-a 30 60 90 170 240 310

GUNS OF THE DRAGON
DC Comics: Oct, 1998 - No. 4, Jan, 1999 ($2.50, limited series)

1-4-DCU in the 1920's; Enemy Ace & Bat Lash app. 2.50

GUN THEORY
Marvel Comics (Epic): Oct, 2003 - No. 4 ($2.50, limited series)

1,2-Daniel Way-s/Jon Proctor-a 2.50

GUNWITCH, THE : OUTSKIRTS OF DOOM (See The Nocturnals)
Oni Press: June, 2001 - No. 3, Oct, 2001 ($2.95, B&W, limited series)

1-3-Brereton-s/painted-c/Naifeh-s 3.00

GUY GARDNER (Guy Gardner: Warrior #17 on)(Also see Green Lantern #59)
DC Comics: Oct, 1992 - No. 44, July, 1996 ($1.25/$1.50/$1.75)

1-24,0,26-30: 1-Staton-c/a(p) begins. 6-Guy vs. Hal Jordan. 8-Vs. Lobo-c/story. 5-JLA x-over, begin $1.50-c. 18-Begin 4-part Emerald Fallout story; splash page x-over GL #50. 18-21-Vs. Hal Jordan. 24-(9/94)-Zero Hour. 0-(10/94) 2.50
25 (11/94, $2.50, 52 pgs.) 3.00
29 ($2.95)-Gatefold-c 3.50
29-Variant-c (Edward Hopper's Nighthawks) 2.50
31-44: 31-$1.75-c begins. 40-Gorilla Grodd-c/app. 44-Parallax-app. (1 pg.) 2.50
Annual 1 (1995, $3.50)-Year One story 4.00
Annual 2 (1996, $2.95)-Legends of the Dead Earth story 3.00

GUY GARDNER REBORN
DC Comics: 1992 - Book 3, 1992 ($4.95, limited series)

1-3: Staton-c/a(p). 1-Lobo-c/cameo. 2,3-Lobo-c/s 5.00

GYPSY COLT
Dell Publishing Co.: No. 568, June, 1954 (one-shot)

Four Color 568--Movie 5 10 15 36 48 60

GYRO GEARLOOSE (See Dynabrite Comics, Walt Disney's C&S #140 &Walt Disney Showcase #18)
Dell Publishing Co.: No. 1047, Nov-Jan/1959-60 - May-July, 1962 (Disney)

Four Color 1047 (No. 1)-All Barks-c/a 19 38 57 136 198 260
Four Color 1095,1184-All by Carl Barks 10 20 30 73 107 140
Four Color 1267-Barks c/a, 4 pgs. 8 16 24 58 82 105
01329-207 (#1, 5-7/62)-Barks-c only (intended as 4-Color 1329?) 6 12 18 43 59 75

HACKER FILES, THE
DC Comics: Aug, 1992 - No. 12, July, 1993 ($1.95)

1-12: 1-Sutton-a(p) begins; computer generated-c 2.25

HAGAR THE HORRIBLE (See Comics Reading Libraries in the Promotional Comics section)

HA HA COMICS (Teepee Tim No. 100 on; also see Giggle Comics)
Scope Mag.(Creston Publ.) No. 1-80/American Comics Group: Oct, 1943 - No. 99, Jan, 1955

1-Funny animal 33 66 99 190 270 350
2 16 32 48 92 126 160
3-5: Ken Hultgren-a begins? 12 24 36 69 92 115
6-10 10 20 30 56 73 90
11-20: 14-Infinity-c 8 16 24 46 58 70
21-40 8 16 24 40 50 60
41-94,96-99: 49-X-Mas-c 7 14 21 35 43 50
95-3-D effect-c 15 30 45 84 115 145

HAIR BEAR BUNCH, THE (TV) (See Fun-In No. 13)
Gold Key: Feb, 1972 - No. 9, Feb, 1974 (Hanna-Barbera)

1 4 8 12 27 36 45
2-9 3 6 9 18 23 28

HALLELUJAH TRAIL, THE (See Movie Classics)

HALL OF FAME FEATURING THE T.H.U.N.D.E.R. AGENTS
JC Productions(Archie Comics Group): May, 1983 - No. 3, Dec, 1983

Hammer of the Gods: Hammer Hits China #1 © Oeming & Wheatley

The Hand of Fate #13 © ACE

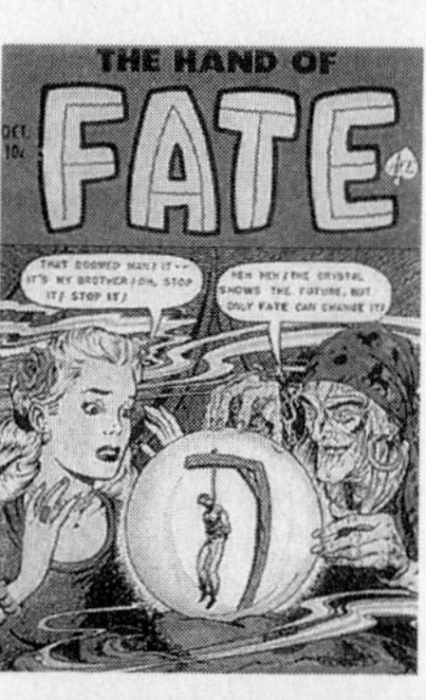

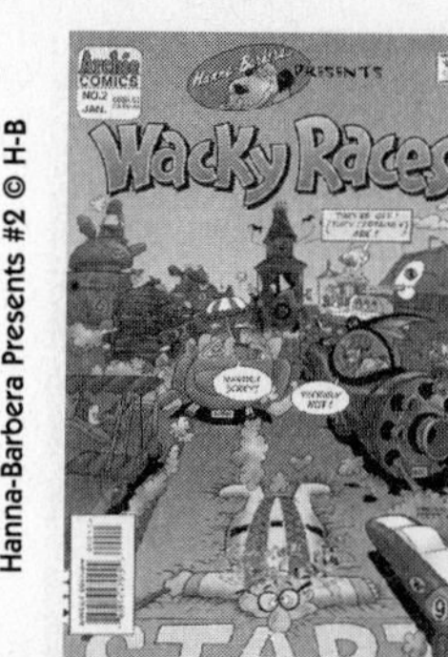

Hanna-Barbera Presents #2 © H-B

GD VG FN VF VF/NM NM-
2.0 4.0 6.0 8.0 9.0 9.2

GD VG FN VF VF/NM NM-
2.0 4.0 6.0 8.0 9.0 9.2

1-3: Thunder Agents-r(Crandall, Kane, Tuska, Wood-a). 2-New Ditko-c 3.00

HALLOWEEN (Movie)
Chaos! Comics: Nov, 2000; Apr, 2001 ($2.95/$2.99, one-shots)
1-Brewer-a; Michael Myers childhood at the Sanitarium 3.00
...II: The Blackest Eyes (4/01, $2.99) Beck-a 3.00
...III: The Devil's Eyes (11/01, $2.99) Justiniano-a 3.00

HALLOWEEN HORROR
Eclipse Comics: Oct, 1987 (Seduction of the Innocent #7)($1.75)
1-Pre-code horror-r 3.00

HALLOWEEN MEGAZINE
Marvel Comics: Dec, 1996 ($3.95, one-shot, 96 pgs.)
1-Reprints Tomb of Dracula 4.00

HALO JONES (See The Ballad of...)

HAMMER, THE
Dark Horse Comics: Oct, 1997 - No. 4, Jan, 1998 ($2.95, limited series)
1-4-Kelley Jones-s/c/a, ...: Uncle Alex (8/98, $2.95) 3.00

HAMMER, THE: THE OUTSIDER
Dark Horse Comics: Feb, 1999 - No. 3, Apr, 1999 ($2.95, limited series)
1-3-Kelley Jones-s/c/a 3.00

HAMMERLOCKE
DC Comics: Sept, 1992 - No. 9, May, 1993 ($1.75, limited series)
1-($2.50, 52 pgs.)-Chris Sprouse-c/a in all 3.00
2-9 2.25

HAMMER OF GOD (Also see Nexus)
First Comics: Feb, 1990 - No. 4, May, 1990 ($1.95, limited series)
1-4 2.50

HAMMER OF GOD: BUTCH
Dark Horse Comics: May, 1994 - No. 4, Aug, 1994 ($2.50, limited series)
1-3 2.50

HAMMER OF GOD: PENTATHLON
Dark Horse Comics: Jan, 1994 ($2.50, one shot)
1-character from Nexus 2.50

HAMMER OF GOD: SWORD OF JUSTICE
First Comics: Feb 1991 - Mar 1991 ($4.95, lim. series, squarebound, 52 pgs.)
V2#1,2 5.00

HAMMER OF THE GODS
Insight Studio Groups: 2001 - No. 5, 2001 ($2.95, limited series)
1-Michael Oeming & Mark Wheatley-s/a; Frank Cho-c 6.00
2-5: 3-Hughes-c. 5-Dave Johnson-c 3.00
The ColorSaga (2002, $4.95) r/"Enemy of the Gods" internet strip 5.00
Mortal Enemy TPB (2002, $18.95) r/#1-5; intro. by Peter David; afterword by Raven 19.00

HAMMER OF THE GODS: HAMMER HITS CHINA
Image Comics: Feb, 2003 - No. 3, Sept, 2003 ($2.95, limited series)
1-3-Oeming & Wheatley-s/a; Oeming-c. 2-Frankenstein Mobster by Wheatley 3.00

HANDBOOK OF THE CONAN UNIVERSE, THE
Marvel Comics: June, 1985 ($1.25, one-shot)
1-Kaluta-c. 4.00

HAND OF FATE (Formerly Men Against Crime)
Ace Magazines: No. 8, Dec, 1951 - No. 25, Dec, 1954 (Weird/horror stories) (Two #25's)

	GD 2.0	VG 4.0	FN 6.0	VF 8.0	VF/NM 9.0	NM- 9.2
8-Surrealistic text story	40	80	120	240	353	465
9,10,21-Necronomicon sty; drug belladonna used	24	48	72	138	194	250
11-18,20,22,23	20	40	60	115	160	205
19-Bondage, hypo needle scenes	22	44	66	127	176	225
24-Electric chair-c	32	64	96	182	259	335
25a(11/54), 25b(12/54)-Both have Cameron-a	17	34	51	98	134	170

NOTE: *Cameron a-9, 10, 19-25a, 25b; c-13.* ***Sekowsky*** *a-8, 9, 13, 14.*

HAND OF FATE
Eclipse Comics: Feb, 1988 - No. 3, Apr, 1988 ($1.75/$2.00, Baxter paper)
1-3; 3-B&W 2.25

HANDS OF THE DRAGON
Seaboard Periodicals (Atlas): June, 1975

	GD 2.0	VG 4.0	FN 6.0	VF 8.0	VF/NM 9.0	NM- 9.2
1-Origin/1st app.; Craig-a(p)/Mooney inks	1	2	3	5	7	9

HANGMAN COMICS (Special Comics No. 1; Black Hood No. 9 on)
(Also see Flyman, Mighty Comics, Mighty Crusaders & Pep Comics)
MLJ Magazines: No. 2, Spring, 1942 - No. 8, Fall, 1943

	GD 2.0	VG 4.0	FN 6.0	VF 8.0	VF/NM 9.0	NM- 9.2
2-The Hangman, Boy Buddies begin	192	384	576	1200	1800	2400
3-Beheading splash pg.; 1st Nazi war-c	124	248	372	775	1163	1550
4-8: 5-1st Jap war-c. 8-2nd app. Super Duck (ties w/Jolly Jingles #11)	109	218	327	681	1021	1360

NOTE: *Fuje a-7(3), 8(3); c-3.* ***Reinman*** *c/a-3. Bondage c-3.* ***Sahle*** *c-6.*

HANK
Pentagon Publishing Co.: 1946

	GD 2.0	VG 4.0	FN 6.0	VF 8.0	VF/NM 9.0	NM- 9.2
nn-Coulton Waugh's newspaper reprint	8	16	24	46	58	70

HANNA-BARBERA (See Golden Comics Digest No. 2, 7, 11)

HANNA-BARBERA ALL-STARS
Archie Publications: Oct, 1995 - No. 6, Sept, 1996 ($1.50, bi-monthly)
1-6 3.00

HANNA-BARBERA BANDWAGON (TV)
Gold Key: Oct, 1962 - No. 3, Apr, 1963

	GD 2.0	VG 4.0	FN 6.0	VF 8.0	VF/NM 9.0	NM- 9.2
1-Giant, 84 pgs. 1-Augie Doggie app.; 1st app. Lippy the Lion, Touché Turtle & Dum Dum, Wally Gator, Loopy de Loop,	14	28	42	99	145	190
2-Giant, 84 pgs.; Mr. & Mrs. J. Evil Scientist (1st app.) in Snagglepuss story; Yakky Doodle, Ruff and Reddy and others app.	10	20	30	72	104	135
3-Regular size; Mr. & Mrs. J. Evil Scientist app. (pre-#1), Snagglepuss, Wally Gator and others app.	8	16	24	55	78	100

HANNA-BARBERA GIANT SIZE
Harvey Comics: Oct, 1992 - No. 3 ($2.25, 68 pgs.)
V2#1-3:Flintstones, Yogi Bear, Magilla Gorilla, Huckleberry Hound, Quick Draw McGraw, Yakky Doodle & Chopper, Jetsons & others 5.00

HANNA-BARBERA HI-ADVENTURE HEROES (See Hi-Adventure...)

HANNA-BARBERA PARADE (TV)
Charlton Comics: Sept, 1971 - No. 10, Dec, 1972

	GD 2.0	VG 4.0	FN 6.0	VF 8.0	VF/NM 9.0	NM- 9.2
1	9	18	27	60	85	110
2,4-10	5	10	15	33	44	55
3-(52 pgs.)- "Summer Picnic"	7	14	21	46	63	80

NOTE: *No. 4 (1/72) went on sale late in 1972 with the January 1973 issues.*

HANNA-BARBERA PRESENTS
Archie Publications: Nov, 1995 - No. 6 ($1.50, bi-monthly)
1-8: 1-Atom Ant & Secret Squirrel. 2-Wacky Races. 3-Yogi Bear. 4-Quick Draw McGraw & Magilla Gorilla. 5-A Pup Named Scooby-Doo. 6-Superstar Olympics. 7-Wacky Races. 8-Frankenstein Jr. & the Impossibles 3.00

HANNA-BARBERA SPOTLIGHT (See Spotlight)

HANNA-BARBERA SUPER TV HEROES (TV)
Gold Key: Apr, 1968 - No. 7, Oct, 1969 (Hanna-Barbera)

	GD 2.0	VG 4.0	FN 6.0	VF 8.0	VF/NM 9.0	NM- 9.2
1-The Birdman, The Herculoids(ends #6; not in #2), Moby Dick, Young Samson & Goliath (ends #2,4), and The Mighty Mightor begin; Spiegle-a in all	19	38	57	136	198	260
2-The Galaxy Trio app.; Shazzan begins; 12¢ & 15¢ versions exist	13	26	39	90	133	175
3,6,7-The Space Ghost app.	12	24	36	84	125	165
4,5	10	20	30	73	107	140

NOTE: *Birdman in #1,2,4,5. Herculoids in #2,4-7. Mighty Mightor in #1,2,4-7. Moby Dick in all. Shazzan in #2-5. Young Samson & Goliath in #1,3.*

HANNA-BARBERA TV FUN FAVORITES (See Golden Comics Digest #2,7,11)

HANNA-BARBERA (TV STARS) (See TV Stars)

HANS BRINKER (Disney)
Dell Publishing Co.: No. 1273, Feb, 1962 (one-shot)

	GD 2.0	VG 4.0	FN 6.0	VF 8.0	VF/NM 9.0	NM- 9.2
Four Color 1273-Movie, photo-c	7	14	21	51	71	90

HANS CHRISTIAN ANDERSEN
Ziff-Davis Publ. Co.: 1953 (100 pgs., Special Issue)

	GD 2.0	VG 4.0	FN 6.0	VF 8.0	VF/NM 9.0	NM- 9.2
nn-Danny Kaye (movie)-Photo-c; fairy tales	17	34	51	95	130	165

HANSEL & GRETEL
Dell Publishing Co.: No. 590, Oct, 1954 (one-shot)

	GD 2.0	VG 4.0	FN 6.0	VF 8.0	VF/NM 9.0	NM- 9.2
Four Color 590-Partial photo-c	7	14	21	51	71	90

HANSI, THE GIRL WHO LOVED THE SWASTIKA
Spire Christian Comics (Fleming H. Revell Co.): 1973, 1976 (39¢/49¢)

	GD 2.0	VG 4.0	FN 6.0	VF 8.0	VF/NM 9.0	NM- 9.2
1973 edition with 39¢-c	4	8	12	24	32	40
1976 edition with 49¢-c	3	6	9	18	24	30

Hap Hazard Comics #1 © ACE

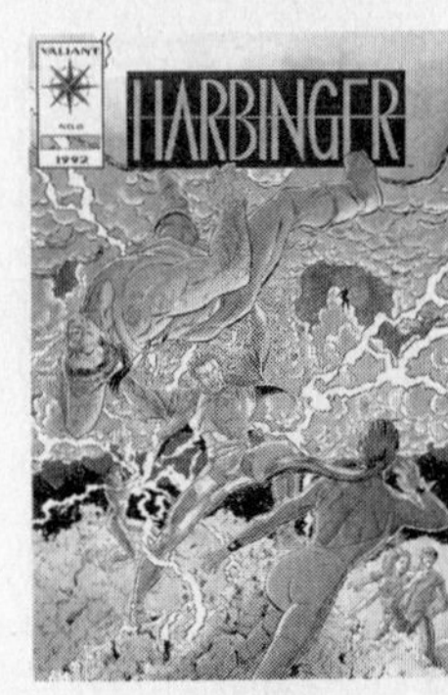

Harbinger #0 (1st printing) © Voyager Comm.

The H.A.R.D. Corps #8 © Voyager Comm.

HAP HAZARD COMICS (Real Love No. 25 on)
Ace Magazines (Readers' Research): Summer, 1944 - No. 24, Feb, 1949
(#1-6 are quarterly issues)

	GD 2.0	VG 4.0	FN 6.0	VF 8.0	VF/NM 9.0	NM- 9.2
1	15	30	45	86	118	150
2	9	18	27	49	62	75
3-10	8	16	24	40	50	60
11-13,15-24	7	14	21	35	43	50
14-Feldstein-c (4/47)	9	18	27	52	66	80

HAP HOPPER (See Comics Revue No. 2)

HAPPIEST MILLIONAIRE, THE (See Movie Comics)

HAPPI TIM (See March of Comics No. 182)

HAPPY BIRTHDAY MARTHA WASHINGTON (Also see Give Me Liberty, Martha Washington Goes To War, & Martha Washington Stranded In Space)
Dark Horse Comics: Mar, 1995 ($2.95, one-shot)

	GD 2.0	VG 4.0	FN 6.0	VF 8.0	VF/NM 9.0	NM- 9.2
1-Miller script; Gibbons-c/a						3.00

HAPPY COMICS (Happy Rabbit No. 41 on)
Nedor Publ./Standard Comics (Animated Cartoons): Aug, 1943 - No. 40, Dec, 1950
(Companion to Goofy Comics)

	GD 2.0	VG 4.0	FN 6.0	VF 8.0	VF/NM 9.0	NM- 9.2
1-Funny animal	27	54	81	153	214	275
2	14	28	42	79	107	135
3-10	10	20	30	56	73	90
11-19	8	16	24	46	58	70
20-31,34-37-Frazetta text illos in all (2 in #34&35, 3 in #27,28,30). 27-Al Fago-a	10	20	30	56	73	90
32-Frazetta-a, 7 pgs. plus 2 text illos; Roussos-a	21	42	63	118	164	210
33-Frazetta-a(2), 6 pgs. each (Scarce)	29	58	87	164	232	300
38-40	7	14	21	37	46	55

HAPPYDALE: DEVILS IN THE DESERT
DC Comics (Vertigo): 1999 - No. 2, 1999 ($6.95, limited series)

	GD 2.0	VG 4.0	FN 6.0	VF 8.0	VF/NM 9.0	NM- 9.2
1,2-Andrew Dabb-s/Seth Fisher-a						7.00

HAPPY DAYS (TV)(See Kite Fun Book)
Gold Key: Mar, 1979 - No. 6, Feb, 1980

	GD 2.0	VG 4.0	FN 6.0	VF 8.0	VF/NM 9.0	NM- 9.2
1-Photo-c of TV cast; 35¢-c	3	6	9	16	20	25
2-6-(40¢-c)	2	4	6	8	10	12

HAPPY HOLIDAY (See March of Comics No. 181)

HAPPY HOULIHANS (Saddle Justice No. 3 on; see Blackstone, The Magician Detective)
E. C. Comics: Fall, 1947 - No. 2, Winter, 1947-48

	GD 2.0	VG 4.0	FN 6.0	VF 8.0	VF/NM 9.0	NM- 9.2
1-Origin Moon Girl (same date as Moon Girl #1)	50	100	150	300	450	600
2	30	60	90	170	240	310

HAPPY JACK
Red Top (Decker): Aug, 1957 - No. 2, Nov, 1957

	GD 2.0	VG 4.0	FN 6.0	VF 8.0	VF/NM 9.0	NM- 9.2
V1#1,2	5	10	15	22	26	30

HAPPY JACK HOWARD
Red Top (Farrell)/Decker: 1957

	GD 2.0	VG 4.0	FN 6.0	VF 8.0	VF/NM 9.0	NM- 9.2
nn-Reprints Handy Andy story from E. C. Dandy Comics #5, renamed "Happy Jack"	5	10	15	22	26	30

HAPPY RABBIT (Formerly Happy Comics)
Standard Comics (Animated Cartoons): No. 41, Feb, 1951 - No. 48, Apr, 1952

	GD 2.0	VG 4.0	FN 6.0	VF 8.0	VF/NM 9.0	NM- 9.2
41-Funny animal	7	14	21	35	43	50
42-48	5	10	15	24	30	35

HARBINGER (Also see Unity)
Valiant: Jan, 1992 - No. 41, June, 1995 ($1.95/$2.50)

	GD 2.0	VG 4.0	FN 6.0	VF 8.0	VF/NM 9.0	NM- 9.2
0-Prequel to the series; available by redeeming coupons in #1-6; cover image has pink sky; title logo is blue	3	6	9	18	23	28
0-(2nd printing) cover has blue sky & red logo						3.00
1-1st app.						6.00
2-4: 4-Low print run						5.00
5,6: 5-Solar app. 6-Torque dies						4.00
7-10: 8,9-Unity x-overs. 8-Miller-c. 9-Simonson-c. 10-1st app. H.A.R.D Corps (10/92)						3.00
11-24,26-41: 14-1st app. Stronghold. 18-Intro Screen. 19-1st app. Stunner. 22-Archer & Armstrong app. 24-Cover similar to #1. 26-Intro New Harbingers. 29-Bound-in trading card. 30-H.A.R.D. Corps app. 32-Eternal Warrior app. 33-Dr. Eclipse app.						2.50
25-($3.50, 52 pgs.)-Harada vs. Sting						3.50
...Files 1,2 (8/94,2/95 $2.50)						2.50
Trade paperback nn (11/92, $9.95)-Reprints #1-4 & comes polybagged with a copy of Harbinger #0 w/new-c. Price for TPB only						10.00

NOTE: *Issues 1-6 have coupons with origin of Harada and are redeemable for Harbinger #0 .*

HARD BOILED
Dark Horse Comics: Sept, 1990 - No. 3, Mar, 1992 ($4.95/$5.95, 8 1/2x11", lim. series)

	GD 2.0	VG 4.0	FN 6.0	VF 8.0	VF/NM 9.0	NM- 9.2
1-3-Miller-s; Darrow-c/a; sexually explicit & violent	1	2	3	4	5	7
TPB (5/93, $15.95)						16.00
Big Damn Hard Boiled (12/97, $29.95, B&W) r/#1-3						30.00

HARDCASE (See Break Thru, Flood Relief & Ultraforce, 1st Series)
Malibu Comics (Ultraverse): June, 1993 - No. 26, Aug, 1995 ($1.95/$2.50)

	GD 2.0	VG 4.0	FN 6.0	VF 8.0	VF/NM 9.0	NM- 9.2
1-Intro Hardcase; Dave Gibbons-c; has coupon for Ultraverse Premiere #0; Jim Callahan-a(p) begin, ends #3						3.00
1-With coupon missing						2.25
1-Platinum Edition						4.00
1-Holographic Cover Edition; 1st full-c holograph tied w/Prime 1 & Strangers 1						7.00
1-Ultra Limited silver foil-c						4.00
2,3-Callahan-a, 2-($2.50)-Newsstand edition bagged w/trading card						2.50
4,6-15, 17-19: 4-Strangers app. 7-Break-Thru x-over. 8-Solution app. 9-Vs. Turf. 12-Silver foil logo, wraparound-c. 17-Prime app.						2.50
5-($2.50, 48 pgs.)-Rune flip-c/story by B. Smith (3 pgs.)						2.50
16 ($3.50, 68 pgs.)-Rune pin-up						3.50
20-26: 23-Loki app.						2.50

NOTE: *Perez a-8(2); c-20i.*

HARDCORE STATION
DC Comics: July, 1998 - No. 6, Dec, 1998 ($2.50, limited series)

	GD 2.0	VG 4.0	FN 6.0	VF 8.0	VF/NM 9.0	NM- 9.2
1-6-Starlin-s/a(p). 3-Green Lantern-c/app. 5,6-JLA-c/app.						3.00

H.A.R.D. CORPS, THE (See Harbinger #10)
Valiant: Dec, 1992 - No. 30, Feb, 1995 ($2.25) (Harbinger spin-off)

	GD 2.0	VG 4.0	FN 6.0	VF 8.0	VF/NM 9.0	NM- 9.2
1-($2.50)-Gatefold-c by Jim Lee & Bob Layton						3.00
1-Gold variant						5.00
2-30: 5-Bloodshot-c/story cont'd from Bloodshot #3. 5-Variant edition; came w/Comic Defense System. 10-Turok app. 17-vs. Armorines. 18-Bound-in trading card. 20-Harbinger app.						2.25

HARDWARE
DC Comics (Milestone): Apr, 1993 - No. 50, Apr, 1997 ($1.50/$1.75/$2.50)

	GD 2.0	VG 4.0	FN 6.0	VF 8.0	VF/NM 9.0	NM- 9.2
1-($2.95)-Collector's Edition polybagged w/poster & trading card (direct sale only)						4.00
1-Platinum Edition						5.00
1-15,17-19: 11-Shadow War x-over. 11,14-Simonson-c. 12-Buckler-a(p). 17-Worlds Collide Pt. 2. 18-Simonson-c; Worlds Collide Pt. 9. 15-1st Humberto Ramos DC work						2.50
16,50-($3.95, 52 pgs.)-16-Collector's Edition w/gatefold 2nd cover by Byrne; new armor; Icon app.						4.00
16,20-24,26-49: 16-($2.50, 52 pgs.)-Newsstand Ed. 49-Moebius-c						2.50
25-($2.95, 52 pgs.)						3.00

HARDY BOYS, THE (Disney
Dell Publ. Co.: No. 760, Dec, 1956 - No. 964, Jan, 1959 (Mickey Mouse Club)

	GD 2.0	VG 4.0	FN 6.0	VF 8.0	VF/NM 9.0	NM- 9.2
Four Color 760 (#1)-Photo-c	12	24	36	82	121	160
Four Color 830(8/57), 887(1/58), 964-Photo-c	10	20	30	70	100	130

HARDY BOYS, THE (TV)
Gold Key: Apr, 1970 - No. 4, Jan, 1971

	GD 2.0	VG 4.0	FN 6.0	VF 8.0	VF/NM 9.0	NM- 9.2
1	5	10	15	33	44	55
2-4	3	6	9	19	25	32

HARLAN ELLISON'S DREAM CORRIDOR
Dark Horse Comics: Mar, 1995 - No. 5, July, 1995 ($2.95, anthology)

	GD 2.0	VG 4.0	FN 6.0	VF 8.0	VF/NM 9.0	NM- 9.2
1-5: Adaptation of Ellison stories. 1-4-Byrne-a.						3.00
Special (1/95, $4.95)						5.00
Trade paperback-(1996, $18.95, 192 pgs)-r/#1-5 & Special #1						19.00

HARLAN ELLISON'S DREAM CORRIDOR QUARTERLY
Dark Horse Comics: V2#1, Aug, 1996 ($5.95, anthology, squarebound)

	GD 2.0	VG 4.0	FN 6.0	VF 8.0	VF/NM 9.0	NM- 9.2
V2#1-Adaptations of Ellison's stories w/new material; Neal Adams-a						6.00

HARLEM GLOBETROTTERS (TV) (See Fun-In No. 8, 10)
Gold Key: Apr, 1972 - No. 12, Jan, 1975 (Hanna-Barbera)

	GD 2.0	VG 4.0	FN 6.0	VF 8.0	VF/NM 9.0	NM- 9.2
1	4	8	12	27	36	45
2-5	2	4	6	14	18	22
6-12	2	4	6	11	14	18

NOTE: *#4, 8, and 12 contain 16 extra pages of advertising.*

HARLEQUIN ROMANCE
Dark Horse Comics: Nov, 2001 ($10.95, hardcover, one-shot)

	GD 2.0	VG 4.0	FN 6.0	VF 8.0	VF/NM 9.0	NM- 9.2
nn-Neil Gaiman-s; painted-a/c by John Bolton						11.00

HARLEY QUINN
DC Comics: Dec, 2000 - No. 38, Jan, 2004 ($2.95/$2.25/$2.50)

Harley Quinn #25 © DC

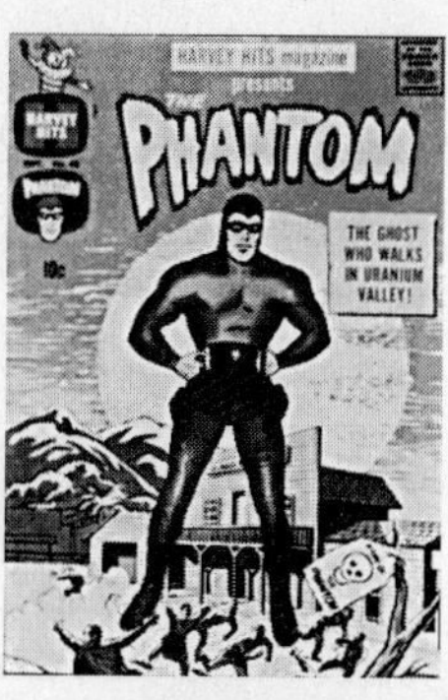

Harvey Comics Hits #48 © UFS

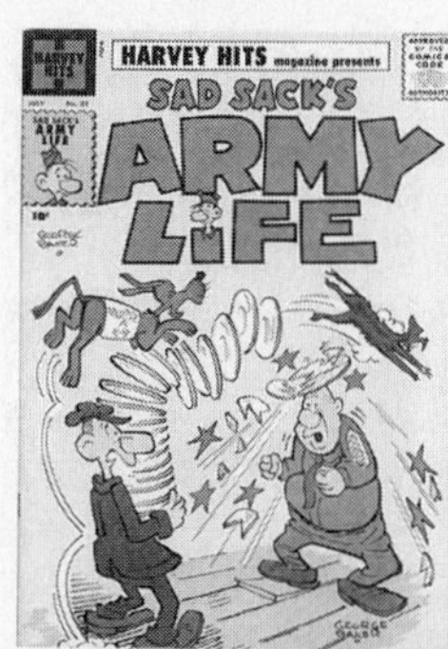

Harvey Hits #22 © HARV

	GD 2.0	VG 4.0	FN 6.0	VF 8.0	VF/NM 9.0	NM- 9.2
1-Joker and Poison Ivy app.; Terry & Rachel Dodson-a/c						4.00
2-11-($2.25). 2-Two-Face-c/app. 3-Slumber party. 6,7-Riddler app.						2.50
12-($2.95) Batman app.						3.00
13-38: 13-Joker: Last Laugh. 17,18-Bizarro-c/app. 23-Begin $2.50-c. 23,24-Martian Manhunter app. 25,32-Joker-c/app.						2.50
Harley & Ivy: Love on the Lam (2001, $5.95) Winick-s/Chiodo-c/a						6.00
...: Our Worlds at War (10/01, $2.95) Jae Lee-c; art by various						3.00

HAROLD TEEN (See Popular Comics, & Super Comics)
Dell Publishing Co.: No. 2, 1942 - No. 209, Jan, 1949

	GD 2.0	VG 4.0	FN 6.0	VF 8.0	VF/NM 9.0	NM- 9.2
Four Color 2	29	58	87	210	310	410
Four Color 209	6	12	18	38	52	65

HARRIERS
Entity Comics: June, 1995 - No. 3, 1995 ($2.50)

	GD 2.0	VG 4.0	FN 6.0	VF 8.0	VF/NM 9.0	NM- 9.2
1-Foil-c; polybagged w/PC game, 1-3 ($2.50)						3.00

HARROWERS, THE (See Clive Barker's...)

HARSH REALM (Inspired 1999 TV series)
Harris Comics: 1993- No. 6, 1994 ($2.95, limited series)

	GD 2.0	VG 4.0	FN 6.0	VF 8.0	VF/NM 9.0	NM- 9.2
1-6: Painted-c. Hudnall-s/Paquette & Ridgway-a						3.50
TPB (2000, $14.95) r/series						15.00

HARVEY
Marvel Comics: Oct, 1970; No. 2, 12/70; No. 3, 6/72 - No. 6, 12/72

	GD 2.0	VG 4.0	FN 6.0	VF 8.0	VF/NM 9.0	NM- 9.2
1	9	18	27	60	85	110
2-6	6	12	18	38	52	65

HARVEY COLLECTORS COMICS (Richie Rich Collectors Comics #10 on, cover title only)
Harvey Publ.: Sept, 1975 - No. 15, Jan, 1978; No. 16, Oct, 1979 (52 pgs.)

	GD 2.0	VG 4.0	FN 6.0	VF 8.0	VF/NM 9.0	NM- 9.2
1-Reprints Richie Rich #1,2	2	4	6	12	16	20
2-10: 7-Splash pg. shows cover to Friendly Ghost Casper #1	1	3	4	6	8	10
11-16: 16-Sad Sack-r	1	2	3	4	5	7

NOTE: *All reprints: Casper-#2, 7, Richie Rich-#1, 3, 5, 6, 8-15, Sad Sack-#16. Wendy-#4. #6 titled 'Richie Rich...'on inside.*

HARVEY COMICS HITS (Formerly Joe Palooka #50)
Harvey Publications: No. 51, Oct, 1951 - No. 62, Apr, 1953

	GD 2.0	VG 4.0	FN 6.0	VF 8.0	VF/NM 9.0	NM- 9.2
51-The Phantom	32	64	96	182	259	335
52-Steve Canyon's Air Power(Air Force sponsored)	14	28	42	79	107	135
53-Mandrake the Magician	24	48	72	138	194	250
54-Tim Tyler's Tales of Jungle Terror	14	28	42	79	107	135
55-Love Stories of Mary Worth	9	18	27	49	62	75
56-The Phantom; bondage-c	27	54	81	155	218	280
57-Rip Kirby Exposes the Kidnap Racket; entire book by Alex Raymond	17	34	51	98	134	170
58-Girls in White (nurses stories)	9	18	27	49	62	75
59-Tales of the Invisible featuring Scarlet O'Neil	13	26	39	74	100	125
60-Paramount Animated Comics #1 (9/52) (3rd app. Baby Huey); 2nd Harvey app. Baby Huey & Casper the Friendly Ghost (1st in Little Audrey #25 (8/52)); 1st app. Herman & Catnip (c/story) & Buzzy the Crow	40	80	120	240	345	450
61-Casper the Friendly Ghost #6 (3rd Harvey Casper, 10/52)-Casper-c	42	84	126	252	376	500
62-Paramount Animated Comics #2; Herman & Catnip, Baby Huey & Buzzy the Crow	16	32	48	92	126	160

HARVEY COMICS LIBRARY
Harvey Publications: Apr, 1952 - No. 2, 1952

	GD 2.0	VG 4.0	FN 6.0	VF 8.0	VF/NM 9.0	NM- 9.2
1-Teen-Age Dope Slaves as exposed by Rex Morgan, M.D.; drug propaganda story; used in **SOTI**, pg. 27	112	224	336	700	1050	1400
2-Dick Tracy Presents Sparkle Plenty in "Blackmail Terror"	24	48	72	138	194	250

HARVEY COMICS SPOTLIGHT
Harvey Comics: Sept, 1987 - No. 4, Mar, 1988 (75¢/$1.00)

	GD 2.0	VG 4.0	FN 6.0	VF 8.0	VF/NM 9.0	NM- 9.2
1-New material; begin 75¢, ends #3; Sand Sack						5.00
2-4: 2,4-All new material. 2-Baby Huey. 3-Little Dot; contains reprints w/5 pg. new story. 4-$1.00-c; Little Audrey						4.00

NOTE: No. 5 was advertised but not published.

HARVEY HITS
Harvey Publications: Sept, 1957 - No. 122, Nov, 1967

	GD 2.0	VG 4.0	FN 6.0	VF 8.0	VF/NM 9.0	NM- 9.2
1-The Phantom	28	56	84	200	293	385
2-Rags Rabbit (10/57)	5	10	15	33	44	55
3-Richie Rich (11/57)-r/Little Dot; 1st book devoted to Richie Rich; see Little Dot for 1st app.	103	206	309	876	1338	1800
4-Little Dot's Uncles (12/57)	17	34	51	123	182	240
5-Stevie Mazie's Boy Friend (1/58)	4	8	12	27	36	45
6-The Phantom (2/58); Kirby-c; 2pg. Powell-a	19	38	57	138	202	265
7-Wendy the Good Little Witch (3/58, pre-dates Wendy #1; 1st book devoted to Wendy)	25	50	75	181	266	350
8-Sad Sack's Army Life; George Baker-c	7	14	21	51	71	90
9-Richie Rich's Golden Deeds; reprints (2nd book devoted to Richie Rich)	41	82	123	324	487	650
10-Little Lotta's Lunch Box	12	24	36	82	121	160
11-Little Audrey Summer Fun (7/58)	9	18	27	65	93	120
12-The Phantom; Kirby-c; 2pg. Powell-a (8/58)	15	30	45	109	160	210
13-Little Dot's Uncles (9/58); Richie Rich 1pg.	11	22	33	77	114	150
14-Herman & Katnip (10/58, TV/movies)	4	8	12	24	32	40
15-The Phantom (12/58)-1 pg. origin	15	30	45	109	160	210
16-Wendy the Good Little Witch (1/59); Casper app.	12	24	36	82	121	160
17-Sad Sack's Army Life (2/59)	6	12	18	43	59	75
18-Buzzy & the Crow	4	8	12	27	36	45
19-Little Audrey (4/59)	6	12	18	40	55	70
20-Casper & Spooky	8	16	24	58	82	105
21-Wendy the Witch	8	16	24	58	82	105
22-Sad Sack's Army Life	5	10	15	36	48	60
23-Wendy the Witch (8/59)	8	16	24	58	82	105
24-Little Dot's Uncles (9/59); Richie Rich 1pg.	9	18	27	65	93	120
25-Herman & Katnip (10/59)	3	7	10	21	28	35
26-The Phantom (11/59)	12	24	36	84	125	165
27-Wendy the Good Little Witch (12/59)	8	16	24	58	82	105
28-Sad Sack's Army Life (1/60)	4	8	12	27	36	45
29-Harvey-Toon (No.1)('60); Casper, Buzzy	6	12	18	38	52	65
30-Wendy the Witch (3/60)	8	16	24	58	82	105
31-Herman & Katnip (4/60)	3	7	10	21	28	35
32-Sad Sack's Army Life (5/60)	4	8	12	24	32	40
33-Wendy the Witch (6/60)	8	16	24	53	74	95
34-Harvey-Toon (7/60)	4	8	12	27	36	45
35-Funday Funnies (8/60)	3	7	10	21	28	35
36-The Phantom (1960)	11	22	33	77	114	150
37-Casper & Nightmare	6	12	18	43	59	75
38-Harvey-Toon	4	8	12	27	36	45
39-Sad Sack's Army Life (12/60)	4	8	12	24	32	40
40-Funday Funnies (1/61)	3	6	9	18	24	30
41-Herman & Katnip	3	6	9	18	24	30
42-Harvey-Toon (3/61)	3	7	10	21	28	35
43-Sad Sack's Army Life (4/61)	3	7	10	21	28	35
44-The Phantom (5/61)	10	20	30	73	107	140
45-Casper & Nightmare	5	10	15	36	48	60
46-Harvey-Toon (7/61)	3	6	9	18	24	30
47-Sad Sack's Army Life (8/61)	3	6	9	18	24	30
48-The Phantom (9/61)	10	20	30	73	107	140
49-Stumbo the Giant (1st app. in Hot Stuff)	10	20	30	72	104	135
50-Harvey-Toon (11/61)	3	6	9	18	23	28
51-Sad Sack's Army Life (12/61)	3	6	9	18	23	28
52-Casper & Nightmare	5	10	15	33	44	55
53-Harvey-Toons (2/62)	3	6	9	16	20	25
54-Stumbo the Giant	6	12	18	40	55	70
55-Sad Sack's Army Life (4/62)	3	6	9	18	23	28
56-Casper & Nightmare	4	8	12	29	40	50
57-Stumbo the Giant	6	12	18	40	55	70
58-Sad Sack's Army Life	3	6	9	18	23	28
59-Casper & Nightmare (7/62)	4	8	12	29	40	50
60-Stumbo the Giant (9/62)	6	12	18	40	55	70
61-Sad Sack's Army Life	3	6	9	16	20	25
62-Casper & Nightmare	4	8	12	27	36	45
63-Stumbo the Giant	5	10	15	33	44	55
64-Sad Sack's Army Life (1/63)	3	6	9	16	20	25
65-Casper & Nightmare	4	8	12	27	36	45
66-Stumbo The Giant (3/63)	5	10	15	33	44	55
67-Sad Sack's Army Life (4/63)	3	6	9	16	20	25
68-Casper & Nightmare	4	8	12	27	36	45
69-Stumbo the Giant (6/63)	5	10	15	33	44	55
70-Sad Sack's Army Life (7/63)	3	6	9	16	20	25
71-Casper & Nightmare (8/63)	4	8	12	24	32	40
72-Stumbo the Giant	5	10	15	33	44	55
73-Little Sad Sack (10/63)	3	6	9	16	20	25
74-Sad Sack's Muttsy... (11/63)	3	6	9	16	20	25
75-Casper & Nightmare	3	7	10	21	28	35

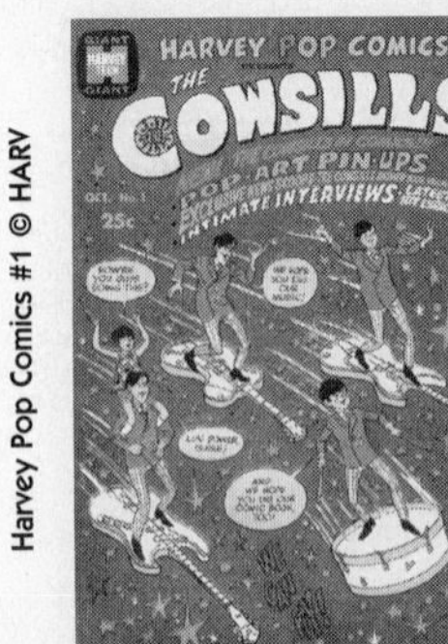

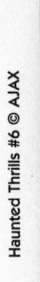

Harvey Pop Comics #1 © HARV

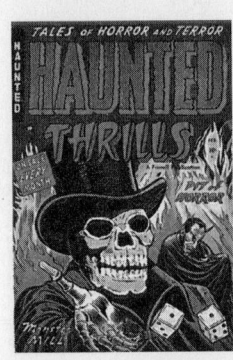

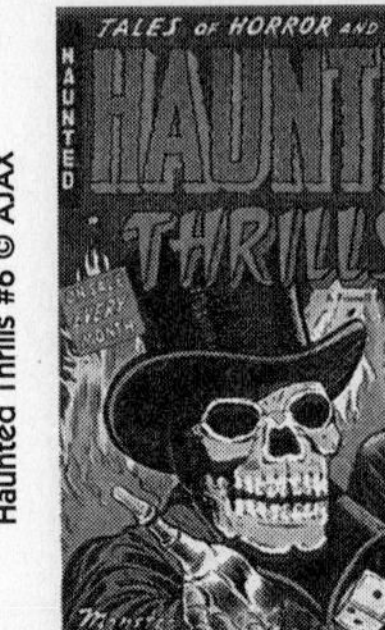

Haunted Thrills #6 © AJAX

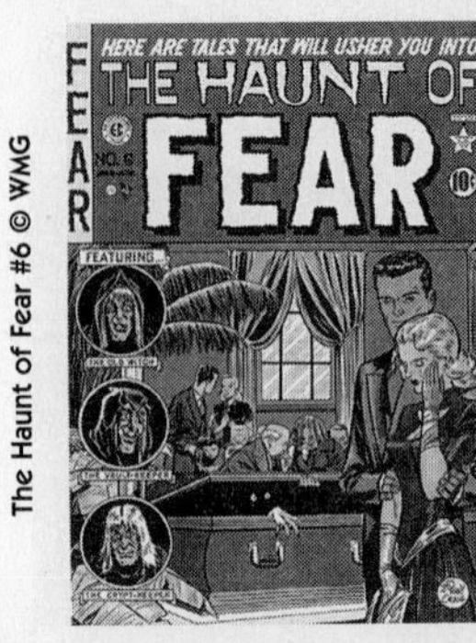

The Haunt of Fear #6 © WMG

	GD 2.0	VG 4.0	FN 6.0	VF 8.0	VF/NM 9.0	NM- 9.2
76-Little Sad Sack	3	6	9	16	20	25
77-Sad Sack's Muttsy...	3	6	9	16	20	25
78-Stumbo the Giant (3/64); JFK caricature	5	10	15	33	44	55
79-87: 79-Little Sad Sack (4/64). 80-Sad Sack's Muttsy... (5/64). 81-Little Sad Sack. 82-Sad Sack's Muttsy... 83-Little Sad Sack(8/64). 84-Sad Sack's Muttsy... 85-Gabby Gob (#1) (10/64). 86-G. I. Juniors (#1)(11/64). 87-Sad Sack's Muttsy... (12/64)	3	6	9	16	20	25
88-Stumbo the Giant (1/65)	5	10	15	33	44	55
89-122: 89-Sad Sack's Muttsy... 90-Gabby Gob. 91-G. I. Juniors. 92-Sad Sack's Muttsy... (5/65). 93-Sadie Sack (6/65). 94-Gabby Gob. 95-G. I. Juniors (8/65). 96-Sad Sack's Muttsy... (9/65). 97-Gabby Gob (10/65). 98-G. I. Juniors (11/65). 99-Sad Sack's Muttsy... (12/65). 100-Gabby Gob(1/66). 101-G. I. Juniors (2/66). 102-Sad Sack's Muttsy... (3/66). 103-Gabby Gob. 104- G. I. Juniors. 105-Sad Sack's Muttsy... 106-Gabby Gob (7/66). 107-G. I. Juniors (8/66). 108-Sad Sack's Muttsy...109-Gabby Gob. 110-G. I. Juniors (11/66). 111-Sad Sack's Muttsy... (12/66). 112-G. I. Juniors. 113-Sad Sack's Muttsy... 114-G. I. Juniors. 115-Sad Sack's Muttsy... 116-G. I. Juniors (5/67). 117-Sad Sack's Muttsy... 118-G. I. Juniors. 119-Sad Sack's Muttsy... (8/67). 120-G. I. Juniors (9/67). 121-Sad Sack's Muttsy... (10/67). 122-G. I. Juniors (11/67)	2	4	6	10	13	16

HARVEY HITS COMICS
Harvey Publications: Nov, 1986 - No. 6, Oct, 1987

	GD	VG	FN	VF	VF/NM	NM-
1-Little Lotta, Little Dot, Wendy & Baby Huey	1	2	3	4	5	7
2-6: 3-Xmas-c						4.50

HARVEY POP COMICS (Rock Happening) (Teen Humor)
Harvey Publications: Oct, 1968 - No. 2, Nov, 1969 (Both are 68 pg. Giants)

	GD	VG	FN	VF	VF/NM	NM-
1-The Cowsills	6	12	18	40	55	70
2-Bunny	5	10	15	36	48	60

HARVEY 3-D HITS (See Sad Sack)

HARVEY-TOON (...S) (See Harvey Hits No. 29, 34, 38, 42, 46, 50, 53)

HARVEY WISEGUYS (...Digest #? on)
Harvey Comics: Nov, 1987; #2, Nov, 1988; #3, Apr, 1989 - No. 4, Nov, 1989 (98 pgs., digest-size, $1.25/$1.75)

	GD	VG	FN	VF	VF/NM	NM-
1-Hot Stuff, Spooky, etc.	1	2	3	4	5	7
2-4: 2 (68 pgs.)						4.50

HATARI (See Movie Classics)

HATE
Fantagraphics Books: Spr, 1990 - No. 30, 1998 ($2.50/$2.95, B&W/color)

	GD	VG	FN	VF	VF/NM	NM-
1	2	4	6	10	12	15
2-3	1	2	3	5	6	8
4-10						5.00
11-20: 16- color begins						4.00
21-29						3.00
30-($3.95) Last issue						4.00
Annual 1 (2/01, $3.95) Peter Bagge-s/a						4.00
Annual 2-4 (12/01, 12/02, 12/03; $4.95) Peter Bagge-s/a						5.00
Buddy Bites the Bullet! (2001, $16.95) r/Buddy stories in color						17.00
Buddy Go Home! (1997, $16.95) r/Buddy stories in color						17.00
Hate-Ball Special Edition ($3.95, giveaway)-reprints						4.00
Hate Jamboree (10/98, $4.50) old & new cartoons						4.50

HATHAWAYS, THE (TV)
Dell Publishing Co.: No. 1298, Feb-Apr, 1962 (one-shot)

	GD	VG	FN	VF	VF/NM	NM-
Four Color 1298-Photo-c	5	10	15	36	48	60

HAUNTED (See This Magazine Is Haunted)

HAUNTED (Baron Weirwulf's Haunted Library on-c #21 on)
Charlton Comics: 9/71 - No. 30, 11/76; No. 31, 9/77 - No. 75, 9/84

	GD	VG	FN	VF	VF/NM	NM-
1-All Ditko issue	4	8	12	29	40	50
2-7-Ditko-c/a	3	6	9	16	20	25
8,12,28-Ditko-a	2	4	6	11	14	18
9,19	2	4	6	9	11	14
10,20,15,18: 10,20-Sutton-a. 15,18-Sutton-c	2	4	6	9	11	14
11,13,14,16-Ditko-c/a	2	4	6	12	16	20
17-Sutton-c/a; Newton-a	2	4	6	10	12	15
21-Newton-c/a; Sutton-a; 1st Baron Weirwulf	3	6	9	18	23	28
22-Newton-c; Sutton-a	2	4	6	10	13	16
23,24-Sutton-c; Ditko-a	2	4	6	10	13	16
25-27,29,32,33	1	3	4	6	8	10
30,41,47,49-52,74-Ditko-c/a: 51-Reprints #1	2	4	6	10	13	16
31,35,37,38-Sutton-a	1	3	4	6	8	10
34,36,39,40,42,57,60-Ditko-a	2	4	6	8	10	12
43-46,48,53-56,58,59,61-73: 59-Newton-a. 64-Sutton-c. 71-73-Low print	1	2	3	5	6	8
75-(9/84) Last issue; low print	2	4	6	10	12	15

NOTE: ***Aparo** c-45. **Ditko** a-1-8, 11-16, 18, 23, 24, 28, 30, 34r, 36r, 39-42r, 47r, 49-52r, 57, 60, 74. c-1-7, 11, 13, 14, 16, 30, 41, 47, 49-52, 74. **Howard** a-6, 9, 18, 22, 25, 32. **Kim** a-9, 19. **Morisi** a-13. **Newton** a-17, 21, 59r; c-21, 22(painted). **Staton** a-11, 12, 18, 21, 22, 30, 33, 35, 38; c-18, 33. **Sutton** a-10, 17, 20-22, 31, 35, 37, 38; c-15, 17, 18, 23(painted), 24(painted), 64r. #49 reprints Tales of the Mysterious Traveler #4.*

HAUNTED, THE
Chaos! Comics: Jan, 2002 - No. 4, Apr, 2002 ($2.99, limited series)

	GD	VG	FN	VF	VF/NM	NM-
1-4-Peter David-s/Nat Jones-a						3.00
...: Gray Matters (7/02, $2.99) David-s/Jones-a						3.00

HAUNTED LOVE
Charlton Comics: Apr, 1973 - No. 11, Sept, 1975

	GD	VG	FN	VF	VF/NM	NM-
1-Tom Sutton-a (16 pgs.)	5	10	15	36	48	60
2,3,6,7,10,11	3	6	9	16	20	25
4,5-Ditko-a	3	6	9	19	25	32
8,9-Newton-c	3	6	9	18	23	28
Modern Comics #1(1978)	2	4	6	9	11	14

NOTE: ***Howard** a-8i. **Kim** a-7-9. **Newton** c-8, 9. **Staton** a-1-6. **Sutton** a-1, 3-5, 10, 11.*

HAUNTED MAN, THE
Dark Horse Comics: Mar, 2000 ($2.95, unfinished limited series)

	GD	VG	FN	VF	VF/NM	NM-
1-Gerald Jones-s/Mark Badger-a						3.00

HAUNTED THRILLS (Tales of Horror and Terror)
Ajax/Farrell Publications: June, 1952 - No. 18, Nov-Dec, 1954

	GD	VG	FN	VF	VF/NM	NM-
1-r/Ellery Queen #1	46	92	138	276	413	550
2-L. B. Cole-a r-/Ellery Queen #1	34	68	102	196	278	360
3-5: 3-Drug use story	30	60	90	173	244	315
6-10,12: 7-Hitler story.	25	50	75	147	202	260
11-Nazi death camp story	27	54	81	155	218	280
13-18: 18-Lingerie panels. 14-Jesus Christ apps. in story by Webb. 15-Jo-Jo-r	20	40	60	115	160	205

NOTE: ***Kamenish** art in most issues. **Webb** a-12.*

HAUNT OF FEAR (Formerly Gunfighter)
E. C. Comics: No. 15, May-June, 1950 - No. 28, Nov-Dec, 1954

	GD	VG	FN	VF	VF/NM	NM-
15(#1, 1950)(Scarce)	271	542	813	2033	2917	3800
16-1st app. "The Witches Cauldron" & the Old Witch (by Kamen); begin series as hostess of Haunt of Fear	116	232	348	870	1248	1625
17-Origin of Crypt of Terror, Vault of Horror, & Haunt of Fear; used in **SOTI**, pg. 43; last pg. Ingels-a used by N.Y. Legis. Comm.; story "Monster Maker" based on Frankenstein. Old Witch by Feldstein	116	232	348	870	1248	1625
4-Ingles becomes regular artist for Old Witch. 1st Vault Keeper & Crypt Keeper app. in HOF; begin series	71	142	213	533	767	1000
5-Injury-to-eye panel, pg. 4 of Wood story	55	110	165	413	589	765
6,7,9,10: 6-Crypt Keeper by Feldstein begins. 9-Crypt Keeper by Davis begins. 10-Ingels biog.	41	82	123	308	439	570
8-Classic Feldstein Shrunken Head-c	44	88	132	330	470	610
11,12: Classic Ingels-c; 11-Kamen biog. 12-Feldstein biog.	33	66	99	248	354	460
13,15,16,18,20: 11-Kamen biog. 12-Feldstein biog. 16,18-Ray Bradbury adaptations. 18-Ray Bradbury biography. 20-Feldstein-r/Vault of Horror #12	31	62	93	233	332	430
14-Origin Old Witch by Ingels; classic-ingels-c	46	92	138	345	493	640
17-Classic Ingels-c	32	64	96	240	345	450
19-Used in **SOTI**, ill. "A comic book baseball game" & Senate investigation on juvenile delinq. bondage/decapitation-c	41	82	123	308	439	570
21-27: 23-Used in **SOTI**, pg. 241. 24-Used in Senate Investigative Report, pg.8. 26-Contains anti-censorship editorial, 'Are you a Red Dupe?' 27-Cannibalism story; Wertham cameo	21	42	63	158	229	300
28-Low distribution	29	58	87	218	314	410

NOTE: *(Canadian reprints known; see Table of Contents). **Craig** a-15-17, 5, 7, 10, 12, 13; c-15-17, 5-7. **Crandall** a-20, 21, 26, 27. **Davis** a-4-26, 28. **Evans** a-15-19, 22-25, 27. **Feldstein** a-15-17, 20; c-4, 8-10. **Ingels** a-16, 17, 4-28; c-11-28. **Kamen** a-16, 4, 6, 7, 9-11, 13-19, 21-28. **Krigstein** a-28. **Kurtzman** a-15(#1), 17(#3). **Orlando** a-9, 12. **Wood** a-15, 16, 4-6.*

HAUNT OF FEAR, THE
Gladstone Publishing: May, 1991 - No. 2, July, 1991 ($2.00, 68 pgs.)

	GD	VG	FN	VF	VF/NM	NM-
1,2: 1-Ghastly Ingels-c(r); 2-Craig-c(r)						3.00

HAUNT OF FEAR
Russ Cochran/Gemstone Publ.: Sept, 1991 - No. 5, 1992 ($2.00, 68 pgs.); Nov, 1992 - Present ($1.50/$2.00/$2.50)

	GD	VG	FN	VF	VF/NM	NM-
1-25: 1-Ingels-c(r). 1-3-r/HOF #15-17 with original-c. 4,5-r/HOF #4,5 with original-c						2.50
Annual 1-5: 1- r/#1-5. 2- r/#6-10. 3- r/#11-15. 4- r/#16-20. 5- r/#21-25						14.00
Annual 6-r/#26-28						9.00

Have Gun, Will Travel #9 © DELL

Hawkeye #2 © MAR

Hawkman V4#8 © DC

HAUNT OF HORROR, THE (Digest)
Marvel Comics: Jun, 1973 - No. 2, Aug, 1973 (164 pgs.; text and art)

	GD 2.0	VG 4.0	FN 6.0	VF 8.0	VF/NM 9.0	NM- 9.2
1-Morrow painted skull-c; stories by Ellison, Howard, and Leiber; Brunner-a	3	7	10	21	28	35
2-Kelly Freas painted bondage-c; stories by McCaffrey, Goulart, Leiber, Ellison; art by Simonson, Brunner, and Buscema	3	6	9	16	20	25

HAUNT OF HORROR, THE (Magazine)
Cadence Comics Publ. (Marvel): May, 1974 - No. 5, Jan, 1975 (75¢) (B&W)

	GD 2.0	VG 4.0	FN 6.0	VF 8.0	VF/NM 9.0	NM- 9.2
1,2: 2-Origin & 1st app. Gabriel the Devil Hunter; Satana begins	2	4	6	10	13	16
3-5: 4-Neal Adams-a. 5-Evans-a(2)	2	4	6	14	18	22

NOTE: ***Alcala** a-2. **Colan** a-2p. **Heath** r-1. **Krigstein** r-3. **Reese** a-1. **Simonson** a-1.*

HAVE GUN, WILL TRAVEL (TV)
Dell Publishing Co.: No. 931, 8/58 - No. 14, 7-9/62 (All Richard Boone photo-c)

	GD 2.0	VG 4.0	FN 6.0	VF 8.0	VF/NM 9.0	NM- 9.2
Four Color 931 (#1)	15	30	45	104	152	200
Four Color 983,1044 (#2,3)	10	20	30	67	96	125
4 (1-3/60) - 10	9	18	27	60	85	110
11-14	8	16	24	58	82	105

HAVEN: THE BROKEN CITY (See JLA/Haven: Arrival and JLA/Haven: Anathema)
DC Comics: Feb, 2002 - No. 9, Oct, 2002 ($2.50, limited series)

1-9-Olivetti-c/a: 1- JLA app. Series concludes in JLA/Haven: Anathema 2.50

HAVOK & WOLVERINE - MELTDOWN (See Marvel Comics Presents #24)
Marvel Comics (Epic Comics): Mar, 1989 - No. 4, Oct, 1989 ($3.50, mini-series, square-bound, mature)

1-4: Art by Kent Williams & Jon J. Muth; story by Walt & Louise Simonson 4.00

HAWAIIAN DICK
Image Comics: Dec, 2002 - No. 3, Feb, 2003 ($2.95, limited series)

1-3-B. Clay Moore-s/Steven Griffin-a 3.00
...: Byrd of Paradise TPB (8/03, $14.95) r/#1-3, script & sketch pages 15.00

HAWAIIAN EYE (TV)
Gold Key: July, 1963 (Troy Donahue, Connie Stevens photo-c)

	GD 2.0	VG 4.0	FN 6.0	VF 8.0	VF/NM 9.0	NM- 9.2
1 (10073-307)	6	12	18	38	52	65

HAWAIIAN ILLUSTRATED LEGENDS SERIES
Hogarth Press: 1975 (B&W)(Cover printed w/blue, yellow, and green)

1-Kalelealuaka, the Mysterious Warrior 5.00

HAWK, THE (Also see Approved Comics #1, 7 & Tops In Adventure)
Ziff-Davis/St. John Publ. Co. No. 4 on: Wint/51 - No. 3, 11-12/52; No. 4, 1-2/53; No. 8, 9/54 - No. 12, 5/55 (Painted c-1-4)(#5-7 don't exist)

	GD 2.0	VG 4.0	FN 6.0	VF 8.0	VF/NM 9.0	NM- 9.2
1-Anderson-a	21	42	63	118	164	210
2 (Sum, '52)-Kubert, Infantino-a	12	24	36	69	92	115
3-4,11: 11-Buckskin Belle & The Texan app.	10	20	30	56	73	90
8-10,12: 8(9/54)-Reprints #3 w/different-c by Baker. 9-Baker-c/a; Kubert-a(r)/#2. 10-Baker-c/a; r/one story from #2. 12-Baker-c/a; Buckskin Belle app.	13	26	39	74	100	125
3-D 1(11/53, 25¢)-Came w/glasses; Baker-c	34	68	102	196	278	360

NOTE: ***Baker** c-8-12. **Larsen** a-10. **Tuska** a-1, 9, 12. Painted c-1, 4, 7.*

HAWK AND THE DOVE, THE (See Showcase #75 & Teen Titans) (1st series)
National Periodical Publications: Aug-Sept, 1968 - No. 6, June-July, 1969

	GD 2.0	VG 4.0	FN 6.0	VF 8.0	VF/NM 9.0	NM- 9.2
1-Ditko-c/a	9	18	27	60	85	110
2-6: 5-Teen Titans cameo	6	12	18	38	52	65

NOTE: ***Ditko** c/a-1, 2. **Gil Kane** a-3p, 4p, 5, 6p; c-3-6.*

HAWK AND DOVE (2nd Series)
DC Comics: Oct, 1988 - No. 5, Feb, 1989 ($1.00, limited series)

1-Rob Liefeld-c/a(p) in all 4.00
2-5 3.00
Trade paperback ('93, $9.95)-Reprints #1-5 10.00

HAWK AND DOVE
DC Comics: June, 1989 - No. 28, Oct, 1991 ($1.00)

1-28 2.50
Annual 1,2 ('90, '91; $2.00) 1-Liefeld pin-up. 2-Armageddon 2001 x-over 3.00

HAWK AND DOVE
DC Comics: Nov, 1997 - No. 5, Mar, 1998 ($2.50, limited series)

1-5-Baron-s/Zachary & Giordano-a 2.50

HAWK AND WINDBLADE (See Elflord)
Warp Graphics: Aug, 1997 - No.2, Sept, 1997 ($2.95, limited series)

1,2-Blair-s/Chan-c/a 3.00

HAWKEYE (See The Avengers #16 & Tales Of Suspense #57)
Marvel Comics Group: Sept, 1983 - No. 4, Dec, 1983 (limited series)

1-4: Mark Gruenwald-a/scripts. 1-Origin Hawkeye. 3-Origin Mockingbird. 4-Hawkeye & Mockingbird elope 3.00

HAWKEYE
Marvel Comics: Jan, 1994 - No. 4, Apr, 1994 ($1.75, limited series)

1-4 2.25

HAWKEYE (Volume 2)
Marvel Comics: Dec, 2003 - Present ($2.99)

1-3-Nicieza-s/Raffaele-a 3.00

HAWKEYE & THE LAST OF THE MOHICANS (TV)
Dell Publishing Co.: No. 884, Mar, 1958 (one-shot)

	GD 2.0	VG 4.0	FN 6.0	VF 8.0	VF/NM 9.0	NM- 9.2
Four Color 884-Photo-c	8	16	24	55	78	100

HAWKEYE: EARTH'S MIGHTIEST MARKSMAN
Marvel Comics: Oct, 1998 ($2.99, one-shot)

1-Justice and Firestar app.; DeFalco-s 3.00

HAWKMAN (See Atom & Hawkman, The Brave & the Bold, DC Comics Presents, Detective Comics, Flash Comics, Hawkworld, JSA, Justice League of America #31, Legend of the Hawkman, Mystery in Space, Shadow War Of..., Showcase, & World's Finest #256)

HAWKMAN (1st Series) (Also see The Atom #7 & Brave & the Bold #34-36, 42-44, 51)
National Periodical Publications: Apr-May, 1964 - No. 27, Aug-Sept, 1968

	GD 2.0	VG 4.0	FN 6.0	VF 8.0	VF/NM 9.0	NM- 9.2
1-(4-5/64)-Anderson-c/a begins, ends #21	51	102	153	434	667	900
2	24	48	72	169	247	325
3,5: 5-2nd app. Shadow Thief	15	30	45	104	152	200
4-Origin & 1st app. Zatanna (10-11/64)	19	38	57	136	198	260
6	12	24	36	82	121	160
7	11	22	33	75	110	145
8-10: 9-Atom cameo; Hawkman & Atom learn each other's I.D.; 3rd app. Shadow Thief	10	20	30	67	96	125
11-15	7	14	21	51	71	90
16,17-27: 18-Adam Strange x-over (cameo #19). 25-G.A. Hawkman-r by Moldoff. 26-Kirby-a(r). 27-Kubert-c	6	12	18	40	55	70

HAWKMAN (2nd Series)
DC Comics: Aug, 1986 - No. 17, Dec, 1987

1-17: 10-Byrne-c, Special #1 (1986, $1.25) 2.50
Trade paperback (1989, $19.95)-r/Brave and the Bold #34-36,42-44 by Kubert; Kubert-c 20.00

HAWKMAN (4th Series)(See both Hawkworld limited & ongoing series)
DC Comics: Sept, 1993 - No. 33, July, 1996 ($1.75/$1.95/$2.25)

1-($2.50)-Gold foil embossed-c; storyline cont'd from Hawkworld ongoing series; new costume & powers. 3.00
2-13,0,14-33: 2-Green Lantern x-over. 3-Airstryke app. 4,6-Wonder Woman app. 13-(9/94)-Zero Hour. 0-(10/94). 14-(11/94). 15-Aquaman-c & app. 23-Wonder Woman app. 25-Kent Williams-c. 29,30-Chaykin-c. 32-Breyfogle-c 2.50
Annual 1 (1993, $2.50, 68 pgs.)-Bloodlines Earthplague 3.00
Annual 2 (1995, $3.95)-Year One story 4.00

HAWKMAN (See JSA #23 for return)
DC Comics: May, 2002 - Present ($2.50)

1-Johns & Robinson-s/Morales-a 5.00
1-2nd printing 2.50
2-23: 2-4-Shadow Thief app. 5,6-Green Arrow-c/app. 8-Atom-c/app. 13-Van Sciver-a. 14-Gentleman Ghost app. 15-Hawkwoman app. 16-Byth returns. 23-Black Reign x-over 2.50
...: Endless Flight TPB (2003, $12.95) r/#1-6 & Secret Files and Origins 13.00
... Secret Files and Origins (10/02, $4.95) profiles and pin-ups by various 5.00

HAWKMOON: THE JEWEL IN THE SKULL
First Comics: May, 1986 - No. 4, Nov, 1986 ($1.75, limited series, Baxter paper)

1-4: Adapts novel by Michael Moorcock 2.50

HAWKMOON: THE MAD GOD'S AMULET
First Comics: Jan, 1987 - No. 4, July, 1987 ($1.75, limited series, Baxter paper)

1-4: Adapts novel by Michael Moorcock 2.50

HAWKMOON: THE RUNESTAFF
First Comics: Jun, 1988 -No. 4, Dec, 1988 ($1.75-$1.95, lim. series, Baxter paper)

1-4: ($1.75) Adapts novel by Michael Moorcock. 3,4 ($1.95) 2.50

HAWKMOON: THE SWORD OF DAWN
First Comics: Sept, 1987 - No. 4, Mar, 1988 ($1.75, lim. series, Baxter paper)

1-4: Dorman painted-c; adapts Moorcock novel 2.50

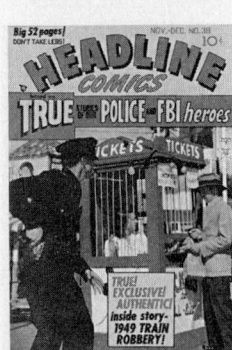

Headline Comics #38 © PRIZE

Heartbreakers #3 © Guinan & Bennett

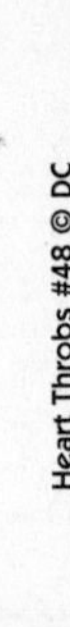

Heart Throbs #48 © DC

HAWKS OF THE SEAS (WILL EISNER'S...)
Dark Horse Comics: July, 2003 ($19.95, B&W, hardcover)

nn-Reprints 1937-1939 weekly Pirate serial by Will Eisner; Williamson intro. 20.00

HAWKWORLD
DC Comics: 1989 - No. 3, 1989 ($3.95, prestige format, limited series)

Book 1-3: 1-Tim Truman story & art in all; Hawkman dons new costume; reintro Byth 4.00
TPB (1991, $16.95) r/#1-3 17.00

HAWKWORLD (3rd Series)
DC Comics: June, 1990 - No. 32, Mar, 1993 ($1.50/$1.75)

1-Hawkman spin-off; story cont'd from limited series. 3.00
2-32: 15,16-War of the Gods x-over. 22-J'onn J'onzz app. 2.25
Annual 1-3 ('90-'92, $2.95, 68 pgs.), 2-2nd printing with silver ink-c 3.00
NOTE: ***Truman** a-30-32; c-27-32, Annual 1.*

HAYWIRE
DC Comics: Oct, 1988 - No. 13, Sept, 1989 ($1.25, mature)

1-13 2.25

HAZARD
Image Comics (WildStorm Prod.): June, 1996 - No. 7, Nov, 1996 ($1.75)

1-7: 1-Intro Hazard; Jeff Mariotte scripts begin; Jim Lee-c(p) 3.00

HEADHUNTERS
Image Comics: Apr, 1997 - No. 3, June, 1997 ($2.95, B&W)

1-3: Chris Marrinan-s/a 3.00

HEADLINE COMICS (...For the American Boy) (...Crime No. 32-39)
Prize Publ./American Boys' Comics: Feb, 1943 - No. 22, Nov-Dec, 1946; No. 23, 1947 - No. 77, Oct, 1956

	GD 2.0	VG 4.0	FN 6.0	VF 8.0	VF/NM 9.0	NM- 9.2
1-Junior Rangers-c/stories begin; Yank & Doodle x-over in Junior Rangers (Junior Rangers are Uncle Sam's nephews)	50	100	150	300	450	600
2	28	56	84	157	221	285
3-Used in **POP**, pg. 84	21	42	63	118	164	210
4-7,9,10: 4,9,10-Hitler stories in each	18	36	54	104	142	180
8-Classic Hitler-c	55	110	165	340	508	675
11,12	16	32	48	92	126	160
13-15-Blue Streak in all	18	36	54	101	138	175
16-Origin & 1st app. Atomic Man (11-12/45)	28	56	84	157	221	285
17,18,20,21: 21-Atomic Man ends (9-10/46)	14	28	42	81	111	140
19-S&K-a	31	62	93	175	248	320
22-Last Junior Rangers; Kiefer-c	11	22	33	66	88	110
23,24: (All S&K-a). 23-Valentine's Day Massacre story; content changes to true crime. 24-Dope-crazy killer story	29	58	87	164	232	300
25-35-S&K-c/a. 25-Powell-a	27	54	81	155	218	280
36-S&K-a; photo-c begin	21	42	63	118	164	210
37-1 pg. S&K, Severin-a; rare Kirby photo-c app.	21	42	63	118	164	210
38,40-Meskin-a	9	18	27	49	62	75
39,41-43,46-50,52-55: 41-J. Edgar Hoover 26th Anniversary Issue with photo on-c. 43,49-Meskin-a	8	16	24	40	50	60
44-S&K-c; Severin/Elder, Meskin-a	13	26	39	74	100	125
45-Kirby-a	11	22	33	63	84	105
51-Kirby-c	8	16	24	46	58	70
56-S&K-a	13	26	39	74	100	125
57-77: 72-Meskin-c/a(i)	6	12	18	31	38	45

NOTE: ***Hollingsworth** a-30. Photo c-36-43. **H. C. Kiefer** c-12-16, 22. Atomic Man c-17-19.*

HEADMAN
Innovation Publishing: 1990 ($2.50, mature)

1-Sci/fi 2.50

HEAP, THE
Skywald Publications: Sept, 1971 (52 pgs.)

	GD 2.0	VG 4.0	FN 6.0	VF 8.0	VF/NM 9.0	NM- 9.2
1-Kinstler-r/Strange Worlds #8	3	6	9	18	24	30

HEART AND SOUL
Mikeross Publications: April-May, 1954 - No. 2, June-July, 1954

	GD 2.0	VG 4.0	FN 6.0	VF 8.0	VF/NM 9.0	NM- 9.2
1,2	8	16	24	40	50	60

HEARTBREAKERS (Also see Dark Horse Presents)
Dark Horse Comics: Apr, 1996 - No. 4, July, 1996 ($2.95, limited series)

1-4: 1-W/paper doll & pin-up. 2-Alex Ross pin-up. 3-Evan Dorkin pin-ups. 4-Brereton-c; Matt Wagner pin-up 3.00
...Superdigest (7/98, $9.95, digest-size) new stories 10.00

HEARTLAND (See Hellblazer)
DC Comics (Vertigo): Mar, 1997 ($4.95, one-shot, mature)

1-Garth Ennis-s/Steve Dillon-c/a 5.00

HEART OF DARKNESS
Hardline Studios: 1994 ($2.95)

1-Brereton-c 3.00

HEART OF EMPIRE
Dark Horse Comics: Apr, 1999 - No. 9, Dec, 1999 ($2.95, limited series)

1-9-Bryan Talbot-s/a 3.00

HEART OF THE BEAST, THE
DC Comics (Vertigo): 1994 ($19.95, hardcover, mature)

1-Dean Motter scripts 20.00

HEARTS OF DARKNESS (See Ghost Rider; Wolverine; Punisher: Hearts of...)

HEART THROBS (Love Stories No. 147 on)
Quality Comics/National Periodical #47(4-5/57) on (Arleigh #48-101): 8/49 - No. 8, 10/50; No. 9, 3/52 - No. 146, Oct, 1972

	GD 2.0	VG 4.0	FN 6.0	VF 8.0	VF/NM 9.0	NM- 9.2
1-Classic Ward-c, Gustavson-a, 9 pgs.	40	80	120	240	350	460
2-Ward-c/a (9 pgs); Gustavson-a	26	52	78	147	206	265
3-Gustavson-a	10	20	30	56	73	90
4,6,8-Ward-a, 8-9 pgs.	14	28	42	79	107	135
5,7	8	16	24	43	54	65
9-Robert Mitchum, Jane Russell photo-c	11	22	33	63	84	105
10,15-Ward-a	11	22	33	63	84	105
11-14,16-20: 12 (7/52)	7	14	21	37	46	55
21-Ward-c	10	20	30	56	73	90
22,23-Ward-a(p)	8	16	24	43	54	65
24-33: 33-Last pre-code (3/55)	7	14	21	35	43	50
34-39,41-46 (12/56; last Quality issue)	6	12	18	31	38	45
40-Ward-a; r-7 pgs./#21	7	14	21	37	46	55
47-(4-5/57; 1st DC issue)	23	46	69	167	244	320
48-60, 100	9	18	27	65	93	120
61-70	7	14	21	46	63	80
71-99: 74-Last 10 cent issue	6	12	18	38	52	65
101-The Beatles app. on-c	14	28	42	99	145	190
102-120: 102-123-(Serial)-Three Girls, Their Lives, Their Loves	3	6	9	19	25	32
121-132,143-146	3	6	9	16	20	25
133-142-(52 pgs.)	4	8	12	22	30	38

NOTE: ***Gustavson** a-8. **Tuska** a-128. Photo c-4, 5, 8-10, 15, 17.*

HEART THROBS - THE BEST OF DC ROMANCE COMICS (See Fireside Book Series)

HEART THROBS
DC Comics (Vertigo): Jan, 1999 - No. 4, Apr, 1999 ($2.95, lim. series)

1-4-Romance anthology. 1-Timm-c. 3-Corben-a 3.00

HEATHCLIFF (See Star Comics Magazine)
Marvel Comics (Star Comics)/Marvel Comics No. 23 on: Apr, 1985 - No. 56, Feb, 1991 (#16-on, $1.00)

1-Post-a most issues 6.00
2-10,47: 47-Batman parody (Catman vs. the Soaker) 4.00
11-46,48-56: 43-X-Mas issue 3.00
Annual 1 ('87) 3.00

HEATHCLIFF'S FUNHOUSE
Marvel Comics (Star Comics)/Marvel No. 6 on: May, 1987 - No. 10, 1988

1 4.00
2-10 3.00

HEAVEN'S DEVILS
Image Comics: Sept, 2003 - No. 4 ($2.95, B&W, limited series)

1,2-Jai Nitz-s/Zach Howard-a 3.00

HEAVY HITTERS
Marvel Comics (Epic Comics): 1993 ($3.75, 68 pgs.)

1-Bound w/trading card; Lawdog, Feud, Alien Legion, Trouble With Girls, & Spyke 3.75

HEAVY LIQUID
DC Comics (Vertigo): Oct, 1999 - No. 5, Feb, 2000 ($5.95, limited series)

1-5-Paul Pope-s/a; flip covers 6.00
TPB (2001, $29.95) r/#1-5 30.00

HECKLE AND JECKLE (Paul Terry's...)(See Blue Ribbon, Giant Comics Edition #5A & 10, Paul Terry's, Terry-Toons Comics)
St. John Publ. Co. No. 1-24/Pines No. 25 on: No. 3, 2/52 - No. 24, 10/55; No. 25, Fall/56 - No. 34, 6/59

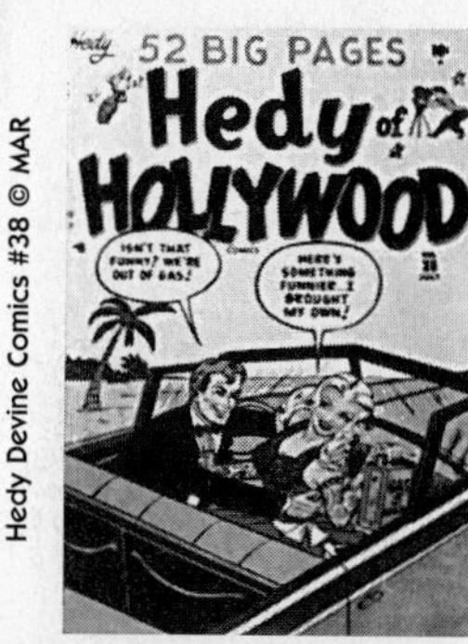

Hedy Devine Comics #38 © MAR

Hellblazer #144 © DC

Hellboy: Seed of Destruction #2 © Michael Mignola

	GD 2.0	VG 4.0	FN 6.0	VF 8.0	VF/NM 9.0	NM- 9.2
3(#1)-Funny animal	26	52	78	150	210	270
4(6/52), 5	12	24	36	71	96	120
6-10(4/53)	8	16	24	46	58	70
11-20	8	16	24	40	50	60
21-34: 25-Begin CBS Television Presents on-c	6	12	18	28	34	40

HECKLE AND JECKLE (TV) (See New Terrytoons)
Gold Key/Dell Publ. Co.: 11/62 - No. 4, 8/63; 5/66; No. 2, 10/66; No. 3, 8/67

	GD	VG	FN	VF	VF/NM	NM-
1 (11/62; Gold Key)	7	14	21	51	71	90
2-4	4	8	12	25	33	42
1 (5/66; Dell)	4	8	12	29	40	50
2,3	3	7	10	21	28	35

(See March of Comics No. 379, 472, 484)

HECKLE AND JECKLE 3-D
Spotlight Comics: 1987 - No. 2?, 1987 ($2.50)

	GD	VG	FN	VF	VF/NM	NM-
1,2						4.50

HECKLER, THE
DC Comics: Sept, 1992 - No. 6, Feb, 1993 ($1.25)

	GD	VG	FN	VF	VF/NM	NM-
1-6-T&M Bierbaum-s/Keith Giffen-c/a						2.25

HECTIC PLANET
Slave Labor Graphics 1998 ($12.95/$14.95)

	GD	VG	FN	VF	VF/NM	NM-
Book 1,2-r-Dorkin-s/a from Pirate Corp$ Vol. 1 & 2						15.00

HECTOR COMICS (The Keenest Teen in Town)
Key Publications: Nov, 1953 - No. 3, 1954

	GD	VG	FN	VF	VF/NM	NM-
1-Teen humor	6	12	18	28	34	40
2,3	4	8	12	17	21	24

HECTOR HEATHCOTE (TV)
Gold Key: Mar, 1964

	GD	VG	FN	VF	VF/NM	NM-
1 (10111-403)	8	16	24	55	78	100

HECTOR THE INSPECTOR (See Top Flight Comics)

HEDGE KNIGHT, THE
Image Comics: Aug, 2003 - Present ($2.95)

	GD	VG	FN	VF	VF/NM	NM-
1,2-George R.R. Martin-s/Mark Miller-a. 1-Two covers by Kaluta and Miller						3.00

HEDY DEVINE COMICS (Formerly All Winners #21? or Teen #22?(6/47); Hedy of Hollywood #36 on; also see Annie Oakley, Comedy & Venus)
Marvel Comics (RCM)/Atlas #50: No. 22, Aug, 1947 - No. 50, Sept, 1952

	GD	VG	FN	VF	VF/NM	NM-
22-1st app. Hedy Devine (also see Joker #32)	26	52	78	147	206	265
23,24,27-30: 23-Wolverton-a, 1 pg; Kurtzman's "Hey Look", 2 pgs. 24,27-30- "Hey Look" by Kurtzman, 1-3 pgs.	18	36	54	104	142	180
25-Classic "Hey Look" by Kurtzman, "Optical Illusion"	19	38	57	109	152	195
26- "Giggles 'n' Grins" by Kurtzman	15	30	45	84	115	145
31-34,36-50: 32-Anti-Wertham editorial	10	20	30	58	77	95
35-Four pgs. "Rusty" by Kurtzman	15	30	45	86	118	150

HEDY-MILLIE-TESSIE COMEDY (See Comedy Comics)

HEDY WOLFE (Also see Patsy & Hedy & Miss America Magazine V1#2)
Atlas Publishing Co. (Emgee): Aug, 1957

	GD	VG	FN	VF	VF/NM	NM-
1-Patsy Walker's rival; Al Hartley-c	11	22	33	63	84	105

HEE HAW (TV)
Charlton Press: July, 1970 - No. 7, Aug, 1971

	GD	VG	FN	VF	VF/NM	NM-
1	4	8	12	29	40	50
2-7	3	6	9	18	24	30

HEIDI (See Dell Jr. Treasury No. 6)

HEIRS OF ETERNITY
Image Comics: Apr, 2003 - Present ($2.95)

	GD	VG	FN	VF	VF/NM	NM-
1-5-Jae Tsai-a/José Torres-s. 4,5-B&W						3.00

HELEN OF TROY (Movie)
Dell Publishing Co.: No. 684, Mar, 1956 (one-shot)

	GD	VG	FN	VF	VF/NM	NM-
Four Color 684-Buscema-a, photo-c	11	22	33	77	114	150

HELL
Dark Horse Comics: July, 2003 - Present ($2.99)

	GD	VG	FN	VF	VF/NM	NM-
1-3-Augustyn-s/Demong-a/Meglia-c						3.00

HELLBLAZER (John Constantine) (See Saga of Swamp Thing #37)
(Also see Books of Magic limited series)
DC Comics (Vertigo #63 on): Jan, 1988 - Present ($1.25/$1.50/$1.95/$2.25/$2.50/$2.75)

	GD 2.0	VG 4.0	FN 6.0	VF 8.0	VF/NM 9.0	NM- 9.2
1-(44 pgs.)-John Constantine; McKean-c thru #21	2	4	6	8	10	12
2-5	1	2	3	4	5	7
6-8,10: 10-Swamp Thing cameo						5.00
9,19: 9-X-over w/Swamp Thing #76. 19-Sandman app.						6.00
11-18,20						5.00
21-26,28-30: 22-Williams-c. 24-Contains bound-in Shocker movie poster. 25,26-Grant Morrison scripts.						5.00
27-Gaiman scripts; Dave McKean-a; low print run	2	4	6	10	12	15
31-39: 36-Preview of World Without End.						4.00
40-($2.25, 52 pgs.)-Dave McKean-a & colors; preview of Kid Eternity						4.00
41-Ennis scripts begin; ends #83						5.00
42-120: 44,45-Sutton-a(i). 50-($3.00, 52 pgs.). 52-Glenn Fabry painted-c begin. 62-Special Death insert by McKean. 63-Silver metallic ink on-c. 77-Totleben-c. 84-Sean Phillips-c/a begins; Delano story. 85-88-Eddie Campbell story. 75-($2.95, 52 pgs.). 89-Paul Jenkins scripts begin; 108-Adlard-a. 100,120 ($3.50,48 pgs.)						3.50
121-191: 129-Ennis-s, begin $2.50-c. 141-Bradstreet-a. 146-150-Corben-a 151-Azzarello-s begin. 175-Carey-s begin; Dillon-a. 176-Begin $2.75-c. 182,183-Bermejo-a						2.75
Annual 1 (1989, $2.95, 68 pgs.)-Bryan Talbot's 1st work in American comics						5.00
Special 1 (1993, $3.95, 68 pgs.)-Ennis story; w/pin-ups.						4.00
...Damnation's Flame (1999, $16.95, TPB) r/#72-77						17.00
...Dangerous Habits (1997, $14.95, TPB) r/#41-46						15.00
...Fear and Loathing (1997, $14.95, TPB) r/#62-67						18.00
...Fear and Loathing (2nd printing, $17.95)						18.00
...: Freezes Over (2003, $14.95, TPB) r/#157-163						15.00
...Good Intentions (2002, $12.95, TPB) r/#151-156						13.00
...Hard Time (2001, $9.95, TPB) r/#146-150						10.00
...Haunting (2003, $12.95, TPB) r/#134-139						13.00
...Original Sins (1993, $19.95, TPB) r/#1-9						20.00
...Rake at the Gates of Hell (2003, $19.95, TPB) r/#78-83; Heartland #1						20.00
...Tainted Love (1998, $16.95, TPB) r/#68-71, Vertigo Jam #1 and Hellblazer Special #1						17.00

NOTE: ***Alcala** a-8i, 9i, 18-22i. **Gaiman** scripts-27. **McKean** a-27,40; c-1-21. **Sutton** a-44i, 45i. **Talbot** a-Annual 1.*

HELLBLAZER SPECIAL: BAD BLOOD
DC Comics (Vertigo): Sept, 2000 - No. 4, Dec, 2000 ($2.95, mini-series)

	GD	VG	FN	VF	VF/NM	NM-
1-4-Delano-s/Bond-a; Constantine in 2025 London						3.00

HELLBLAZER SPECIAL: LADY CONSTANTINE
DC Comics (Vertigo): Feb, 2003 - No. 4, May, 2003 ($2.95, mini-series)

	GD	VG	FN	VF	VF/NM	NM-
1-4-Story of Johanna Constantine in 1785; Diggle-s/Sudzuka-a/Noto-c						3.00

HELLBLAZER/THE BOOKS OF MAGIC
DC Comics (Vertigo): Dec, 1997 - No. 2, Jan, 1998 ($2.50, mini-series)

	GD	VG	FN	VF	VF/NM	NM-
1,2-John Constantine and Tim Hunter						2.50

HELLBOY (Also see Danger Unlimited #4, Dark Horse Presents, Gen[13] #13B, Ghost/Hellboy, John Byrne's Next Men, San Diego Comic Con #2, & Savage Dragon)

HELLBOY: ALMOST COLOSSUS
Dark Horse Comics (Legend): Jun, 1997 - No. 2, Jul, 1997 ($2.95, lim. series)

	GD	VG	FN	VF	VF/NM	NM-
1,2-Mignola-s/a						3.00

HELLBOY: BOX FULL OF EVIL
Dark Horse Comics: Aug, 1999 - No. 2, Sept, 1999 ($2.95, lim. series)

	GD	VG	FN	VF	VF/NM	NM-
1,2-Mignola-s/a; back-up story w/ Matt Smith-a						3.00

HELLBOY CHRISTMAS SPECIAL
Dark Horse Comics: Dec, 1997 ($3.95, one-shot)

	GD	VG	FN	VF	VF/NM	NM-
nn-Christmas stories by Mignola, Gianni, Darrow, Purcell						4.00

HELLBOY: CONQUEROR WORM
Dark Horse Comics: May, 2001 - No. 4, Aug, 2001 ($2.99, lim. series)

	GD	VG	FN	VF	VF/NM	NM-
1-4-Mignola-s/a/c						3.00

HELLBOY, JR.
Dark Horse Comics: Oct, 1999 - No. 2, Nov, 1999 ($2.95, limited series)

	GD	VG	FN	VF	VF/NM	NM-
1,2-Stories and art by various						3.00

HELLBOY, JR., HALLOWEEN SPECIAL
Dark Horse Comics: Oct, 1997 ($3.95, one-shot)

	GD	VG	FN	VF	VF/NM	NM-
nn-"Harvey" style renditions of Hellboy characters; Bill Wray, Mike Mignola & various-s/a; wraparound-c by Wray						4.00

HELLBOY: SEED OF DESTRUCTION
Dark Horse Comics (Legend): Mar, 1994 - No. 4, Jun, 1994 ($2.50, lim. series)

	GD	VG	FN	VF	VF/NM	NM-
1-4-Mignola-c/a w/Byrne scripts; Monkeyman & O'Brien back-up story (origin) by Art Adams.						4.00
Trade paperback (1994, $17.95)-collects all four issues plus r/Hellboy's 1st app. in San Diego Comic Con #2 & pin-ups						18.00
Limited edition hardcover (1995, $99.95)-includes everything in trade paperback						

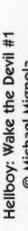

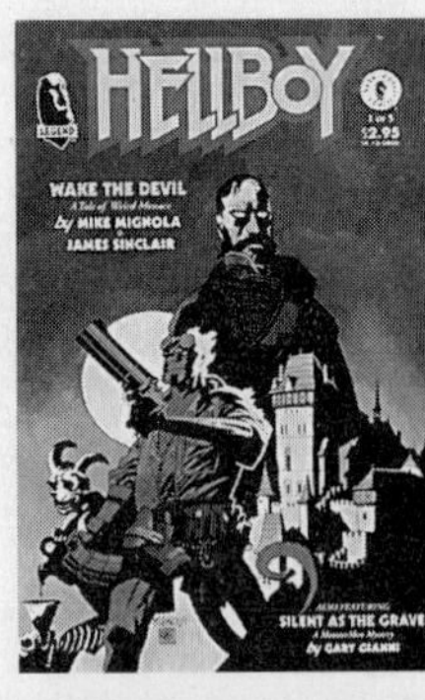
Hellboy: Wake the Devil #1 © Michael Mignola

Hellstorm: Prince of Lies #18 © MAR

Henry #1 © DELL

	GD 2.0	VG 4.0	FN 6.0	VF 8.0	VF/NM 9.0	NM- 9.2

plus additional material. 100.00

HELLBOY: THE CHAINED COFFIN AND OTHERS
Dark Horse Comics (Legend): Aug, 1998 ($17.95, TPB)
nn-Mignola-c/a/s; reprints out-of-print one shots; pin-up gallery 18.00

HELLBOY: THE CORPSE AND THE IRON SHOES
Dark Horse Comics (Legend): Jan, 1996 ($2.95, one-shot)
nn-Mignola-c/a/scripts; reprints "The Corpse" serial from Capitol City's Advance Comics catalog w/new story 3.00

HELLBOY: THE RIGHT HAND OF DOOM
Dark Horse Comics (Legend): Apr, 2000 ($17.95, TPB)
nn-Mignola-c/a/s; reprints 18.00

HELLBOY: THE THIRD WISH
Dark Horse Comics (Maverick): July, 2002 - No. 2, Aug, 2002 ($2.99, limited series)
1,2-Mignola-c/a/s 3.00

HELLBOY: THE WOLVES OF ST. AUGUST
Dark Horse Comics (Legend): 1995 ($4.95, squarebound, one-shot)
nn-Mignola--c/a/scripts; r/Dark Horse Presents #88-91 with additional story 5.00

HELLBOY: WAKE THE DEVIL (Sequel to Seed of Destruction)
Dark Horse Comics (Legend): Jun, 1996 - No. 5, Oct, 1996 ($2.95, lim. series)
1-5: Mignola-c/a & scripts; The Monstermen back-up story by Gary Gianni 3.00
TPB (1997, $17.95) r/#1-5 18.00

HELLBOY: WEIRD TALES
Dark Horse Comics: Feb, 2003 - No. 8 ($2.99, limited series, anthology)
1-5-Hellboy stories from other creators. 1-Cassaday-c/s/a; Watson-s/a 3.00

HELLCAT
Marvel Comics: Sept, 2000 - No. 3, Nov, 2000 ($2.99)
1-3-Englehart-s/Breyfogle-a; Hedy Wolfe app. 3.00

HELLCOP
Image Comics (Avalon Studios): Aug, 1998 - No. 4, Mar, 1999 ($2.50)
1-4: 1-(Oct. on-c) Casey-s 2.50

HELL ETERNAL
DC Comics (Vertigo Verité): 1998 ($6.95, squarebound, one-shot)
1-Delano-s/Phillips-a 7.00

HELLHOLE
Image Comics: July, 1999 - No. 3, Oct, 1999 ($2.50)
1-3-Lobdell-s/Polina-a 2.50

HELLHOUNDS (...: Panzer Cops #3-6)
Dark Horse Comics: 1994 - No. 6, July, 1994 ($2.50, B&W, limited series)
1-6: 1-Hamner-c. 3-(4/94). 2-Joe Phillips-c 3.00

HELLHOUNDS
Image Comics: Aug, 2003 - Present ($2.95)
1-3: 1-Five covers; Singley-s/Abraham-a 3.00

HELLHOUND, THE REDEMPTION QUEST
Marvel Comics (Epic Comics): Dec, 1993 - No. 4, Mar, 1994 ($2.25, lim. series, coated stock)
1-4 2.25

HELLO, I'M JOHNNY CASH
Spire Christian Comics (Fleming H. Revell Co.): 1976 (39¢/49¢)

	GD	VG	FN	VF	VF/NM	NM-
nn-(39¢-c)	2	4	6	10	12	15
nn-(49¢-c)	1	3	4	6	8	10

HELL ON EARTH (See DC Science Fiction Graphic Novel)

HELLO PAL COMICS (Short Story Comics)
Harvey Publications: Jan, 1943 - No. 3, May, 1943 (Photo-c)

	GD	VG	FN	VF	VF/NM	NM-
1-Rocketman & Rocketgirl begin; Yankee Doodle Jones app.; Mickey Rooney photo-c	66	132	198	413	619	825
2-Charlie McCarthy photo-c (scarce)	55	110	165	330	495	660
3-Bob Hope photo-c (scarce)	58	116	174	363	544	725

HELLRAISER/NIGHTBREED – JIHAD (Also see Clive Barker's...)
Epic Comics (Marvel Comics): 1991 - Book 2, 1991 ($4.50, 52 pgs.)
Book 1,2 4.50

HELL-RIDER (Motorcycle themed magazine)
Skywald Publications: Aug, 1971 - No. 2, Oct, 1971 (B&W, 68 pgs.)

	GD	VG	FN	VF	VF/NM	NM-
1-Origin & 1st app.; Butterfly & the Wild Bunch begin; 1st Hell-Rider by Andru, Esposito and Friedrich	5	10	15	36	48	60
2-Andru, Ayers, Buckler, Shores-a	4	8	12	24	32	40

NOTE: *#3 advertised in Psycho #5 but did not come out.* ***Buckler*** *a-1, 2.* ***Rosenbaum*** *c-1,2.*

HELL'S ANGEL (Becomes Dark Angel #6 on)
Marvel Comics UK: July, 1992 - No. 5, Nov, 1993 ($1.75)
1-5: X-Men (Wolverine, Cyclops)-c/stories. 1-Origin. 3-Jim Lee cover swipe 2.25

HELLSHOCK
Image Comics: July, 1994 - No. 4, Nov, 1994 ($1.95, limited series)
1-4-Jae Lee-c/a & scripts. 4-Variant-c. 2.50

HELLSHOCK
Image Comics: Jan, 1997 - No. 3, Jan, 1998 ($2.95/$2.50, limited series)
1-($2.95)-Jae Lee-c/s/a, Villarrubia-painted-a 4.00
2-($2.50) 2.50
Book 3: The Science of Faith (1/98, $2.50) Jae Lee-c/s/a, Villarrubia-painted-a 2.50

HELLSPAWN
Image Comics: Aug, 2000 - Present ($2.50)
1-Bendis-s/Ashley Wood-c/a; Spawn and Clown app. 2.50
2-9: 6-Last Bendis-s; Mike Moran (Miracleman app.). 7-Niles-s 2.50
10-16-Templesmith-a 2.50

HELLSTORM: PRINCE OF LIES (See Ghost Rider #1 & Marvel Spotlight #12)
Marvel Comics: Apr, 1993 - No. 21, Dec, 1994 ($2.00)
1-($2.95)-Parchment-c w/red thermographic ink 3.00
2-21: 14-Bound-in trading card sheet. 18-P. Craig Russell-c 2.50

HE-MAN (See Masters Of The Universe)

HE-MAN (Also see Tops In Adventure)
Ziff-Davis Publ. Co. (Approved Comics): Fall, 1952

	GD	VG	FN	VF	VF/NM	NM-
1-Kinstler painted-c; Powell-a	17	34	51	95	130	165

HE-MAN
Toby Press: May, 1954 - No. 2, July, 1954 (Painted-c by B. Safran)

	GD	VG	FN	VF	VF/NM	NM-
1	16	32	48	92	126	160
2-Shark-c	15	30	45	86	118	150

HENNESSEY (TV)
Dell Publishing Co.: No. 1200, Aug-Oct, 1961 - No. 1280, Mar-May, 1962

	GD	VG	FN	VF	VF/NM	NM-
Four Color 1200-Gil Kane-a, photo-c	8	16	24	55	78	100
Four Color 1280-Photo-c	7	14	21	51	71	90

HENRY (Also see Little Annie Rooney)
David McKay Publications: 1935 (52 pgs.) (Daily B&W strip reprints)(10"x10" cardboard-c)

	GD	VG	FN	VF	VF/NM	NM-
1-By Carl Anderson	40	80	120	240	340	440

HENRY (See King Comics & Magic Comics)
Dell Publishing Co.: No. 122, Oct, 1946 - No. 65, Apr-June, 1961

	GD	VG	FN	VF	VF/NM	NM-
Four Color 122-All new stories begin	15	30	45	104	152	200
Four Color 155 (7/47), 1 (1-3/48)-All new stories	10	20	30	67	96	125
2	6	12	18	38	52	65
3-10	4	8	12	29	40	50
11-20: 20-Infinity-c	3	7	10	21	28	35
21-30	3	6	9	18	24	30
31-40	2	4	6	14	18	22
41-65	2	4	6	11	14	18

HENRY (See Giant Comic Album and March of Comics No. 43, 58, 84, 101, 112, 129, 147, 162, 178, 189)

HENRY ALDRICH COMICS (TV)
Dell Publishing Co.: Aug-Sept, 1950 - No. 22, Sept-Nov, 1954

	GD	VG	FN	VF	VF/NM	NM-
1-Part series written by John Stanley; Bill Williams-a	10	20	30	70	100	130
2	6	12	18	38	52	65
3-5	5	10	15	33	44	55
6-10	4	8	12	27	36	45
11-22	3	7	10	21	28	35

HENRY BREWSTER
Country Wide (M.F. Ent.): Feb, 1966 - V2#7, Sept, 1967 (All 25¢ Giants)

	GD	VG	FN	VF	VF/NM	NM-
1	3	6	9	18	24	30
2-6(12/66), V2#7-Powell-a in most	2	4	6	10	12	15

HEPCATS
Antarctic Press: Nov, 1996 - No. 12 ($2.95, B&W)
0-12-Martin Wagner-c/s/a: 0-color 3.00
0-($9.95) CD Edition 10.00

Hercules: The Legendary Journeys #4 © MCA TV

H-E-R-O #1 © DC

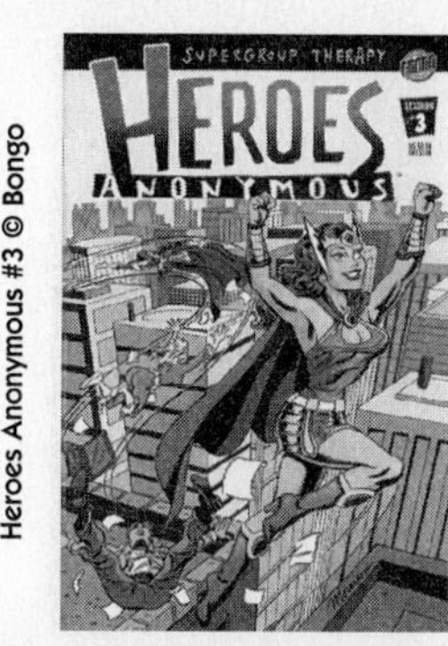

Heroes Anonymous #3 © Bongo

	GD	VG	FN	VF	VF/NM	NM-
	2.0	4.0	6.0	8.0	9.0	9.2

HERBIE (See Forbidden Worlds & Unknown Worlds)
American Comics Group: April-May, 1964 - No. 23, Feb, 1967 (All 12¢)

1-Whitney-c/a in most issues	17	34	51	123	182	240
2-4	9	18	27	65	93	120
5-Beatles, Dean Martin, F. Sinatra app.	10	20	30	73	107	140
6,7,9,10	8	16	24	53	74	95
8-Origin & 1st app. The Fat Fury	9	18	27	65	93	120
11-23: 14-Nemesis & Magicman app. 17-r/2nd Herbie from Forbidden Worlds #94. 23-r/1st Herbie from F.W. #73	6	12	18	40	55	70

HERBIE
Dark Horse Comics: Oct, 1992 - No. 12, 1993 ($2.50, limited series)

1-Whitney-r plus new-c/a in all; Byrne-c/a & scripts 3.00
2-6: 3-Bob Burden-c/a. 4-Art Adams-c 2.50

HERBIE GOES TO MONTE CARLO, HERBIE RIDES AGAIN (See Walt Disney Showcase No. 24, 41)

HERCULES (See Hit Comics #1-21, Journey Into Mystery Annual, Marvel Graphic Novel #37, Marvel Premiere #26 & The Mighty...)

HERCULES (See Charlton Classics)
Charlton Comics: Oct, 1967 - No. 13, Sept, 1969; Dec, 1968

1-Thane of Bagarth begins; Glanzman-a in all	4	8	12	25	33	42
2-13: 1-5,7-10-Aparo-a. 8-(12¢-c)	2	4	6	14	18	22
8-(Low distribution)(12/68, 35¢, B&W); magazine format; new Hercules story plus-r story/#1; Thane-r/#1-3	6	12	18	38	52	65
Modern Comics reprint 10('77), 11('78)						6.00

HERCULES (Prince of Power) (Also see The Champions)
Marvel Comics Group: V1#1, Sept, 1982 - V1#4, Dec, 1982; V2#1, Mar, 1984 - V2#4, Jun, 1984 (color, both limited series)

1-4, V2#1-4: Layton-c/a. 4-Death of Zeus. 3.00
NOTE: *Layton a-1, 2, 3p, 4p, V2#1-4; c-1-4, V2#1-4.*

HERCULES: HEART OF CHAOS
Marvel Comics: Aug, 1997 - No. 3, Oct, 1997 ($2.50, limited series)

1-3-DeFalco-s, Frenz-a 2.50

HERCULES: OFFICIAL COMICS MOVIE ADAPTION
Acclaim Books: 1997 ($4.50, digest size)

nn-Adaption of the Disney animated movie 4.50

HERCULES: THE LEGENDARY JOURNEYS (TV)
Topps Comics: June, 1996 - No. 5, Oct, 1996 ($2.95)

1-2: 1-Golden-c.						3.00
3-Xena-c/app.	1	2	3	4	5	7
3-Variant-c	2	4	6	10	12	15
4,5: Xena-c/app.						5.00

HERCULES UNBOUND
National Periodical Publications: Oct-Nov, 1975 - No. 12, Aug-Sept, 1977

1-Wood-i begins	2	4	6	8	10	12
2-12: 7-Adams ad. 10-Atomic Knights x-over	1	2	3	4	5	7

NOTE: ***Buckler** c-7p. **Layton** inks-No. 9, 10. **Simonson** a-7-10p, 11, 12; c- 8p, 9-12. **Wood** a-1-8i; c-7i, 8i.*

HERCULES (...Unchained #1121) (Movie)
Dell Publishing Co.: No. 1006, June-Aug, 1959 - No.1121, Aug, 1960

Four Color 1006-Buscema-a, photo-c	10	20	30	72	104	135
Four Color 1121-Crandall/Evans-a	10	20	30	72	104	135

HERE COMES SANTA (See March of Comics No. 30, 213, 340)

HERE'S HOWIE COMICS
National Periodical Publications: Jan-Feb, 1952 - No. 18, Nov-Dec, 1954

1	26	52	78	150	210	270
2	14	28	42	79	107	135
3-5: 5-Howie in the Army issues begin (9-10/52)	10	20	30	60	80	100
6-10	9	18	27	52	66	80
11-18	8	16	24	46	58	70

HERETIC, THE
Dark Horse (Blanc Noir): Nov, 1996 - No. 4, Mar, 1997 ($2.95, lim. series)

1-4:-w/back-up story 3.00

HERITAGE OF THE DESERT (See Zane Grey, 4-Color 236)

HERMAN & KATNIP (See Harvey Comics Hits #60 & 62, Harvey Hits #14,25,31,41 & Paramount Animated Comics #1)

HERMES VS. THE EYEBALL KID
Dark Horse Comics: Dec, 1994 - No. 3,Feb, 1995 ($2.95, B&W, limited series)

1-3: Eddie Campbell-c/a/scripts 3.00

	GD	VG	FN	VF	VF/NM	NM-
	2.0	4.0	6.0	8.0	9.0	9.2

H-E-R-O (Dial H For HERO)
DC Comics: Apr, 2003 - Present ($2.50)

1-Will Pfeiffer-s/Kano-a/Van Fleet-c 3.00
2-12: 2-6-Kano-a. 7,8-Gleason-a. 12-Kirk-a 2.50
...: Double Feature (6/03, $4.95) r/#1&2 5.00
...: Powers and Abilities (2003, $9.95) r/#1-6; intro. by Geoff Johns 10.00

HERO (Warrior of the Mystic Realms)
Marvel Comics: May, 1990 - No. 6, Oct, 1990 ($1.50, limited series)

1-6: 1-Portacio-i 2.25

HERO ALLIANCE, THE
Sirius Comics: Dec, 1985 - No. 2, Sept, 1986 (B&W)

1,2: 2-($1.50), Special Edition 1 (7/86, color) 2.25

HERO ALLIANCE
Wonder Color Comics: May, 1987 ($1.95)

1-Ron Lim-a 2.25

HERO ALLIANCE
Innovation Publishing: V2#1, Sept, 1989 - V2#17, Nov, 1991 ($1.95, 28 pgs.)

V2#1-17: 1,2-Ron Lim-a 2.25
Annual 1 (1990, $2.75, 36 pgs.)-Paul Smith-c/a 2.75
Special 1 (1992, $2.50, 32 pgs.)-Stuart Immonen-a (10 pgs.) 2.50

HERO ALLIANCE: END OF THE GOLDEN AGE
Innovation Publ.: July, 1989 - No. 3, Aug, 1989 ($1.75, bi-weekly lim. series)

1-3: Bart Sears & Ron Lim-c/a; reprints & new-a 2.25

HEROES
Marvel Comics: Dec, 2001 ($3.50, magazine-size, one-shot)

1-Pin-up tributes to the rescue workers of the Sept. 11 tragedy; art and text by various; cover by Alex Ross 3.50
1-2nd and 3rd printings 3.50

HEROES (Also see Shadow Cabinet & Static)
DC Comics (Milestone): May, 1996 - No. 6, Nov, 1996 ($2.50, limited series)

1-6: 1-Intro Heroes (Iota, Donner, Blitzen, Starlight, Payback & Static) 2.50

HEROES AGAINST HUNGER
DC Comics: 1986 ($1.50; one-shot for famine relief)

1-Superman, Batman app.; Neal Adams-c(p); includes many artists work; Jeff Jones assist (2 pg.) on B. Smith-a; Kirby-a 4.00

HEROES ALL CATHOLIC ACTION ILLUSTRATED
Heroes All Co.: 1943 - V6#5, Mar 10, 1948 (paper covers)

V1#1-(16 pgs., 8x11")	24	48	72	135	190	245
V1#2-(16 pgs., 8x11")	20	40	60	112	156	200
V2#1(1/44)-3(3/44)-(16 pgs., 8x11")	17	34	51	98	134	170
V3#1(1/45)-10(12/45)-(16 pgs., 8x11")	15	30	45	86	118	150
V4#1-35 (12/20/46)-(16 pgs.)	13	26	39	76	103	130
V5#1(1/10/47)-8(2/28/47)-(16 pgs.), V5#9(3/7/47)-20(11/25/47)-(32 pgs.), V6#1(1/10/48)-5(3/10/48)-(32 pgs.)	11	22	33	63	84	105

HEROES ANONYMOUS
Bongo Comics: 2003 - No. 6 ($2.99, limited series)

1-3-($2.99)-Bill Morrison-c. 2-Guerra-a. 3-Pepoy-a 3.00

HEROES FOR HIRE
Marvel Comics: July, 1997 - No. 19, Jan, 1999 ($2.99/$1.99)

1-($2.99)-Wraparound cover 5.00
2-19: 2-Variant cover. 7-Thunderbolts app. 9-Punisher-c/app. 10,11-Deadpool-c/app. 18,19-Wolverine-c/app. 3.00
.../Quicksilver '98 Annual ($2.99) Siege of Wundagore pt.5 3.00

HEROES FOR HOPE STARRING THE X-MEN
Marvel Comics Group: Dec, 1985 ($1.50, one-shot, 52 pgs., proceeds donated to famine relief)

1-Stephen King scripts; Byrne, Miller, Corben-a; Wrightson/J. Jones-a (3 pgs.); Art Adams-c; Starlin back-c 5.00

HEROES, INC. PRESENTS CANNON
Wally Wood/CPL/Gang Publ.: 1969 - No. 2, 1976 (Sold at Army PX's)

nn-Ditko, Wood-a; Wood-c; Reese-a(p)	2	4	6	10	12	15
2-Wood-c; Ditko, Byrne, Wood-a; 8-1/2x10-1/2"; B&W; $2.00	2	4	6	14	18	22

NOTE: *First issue not distributed by publisher; 1,800 copies were stored and 900 copies were stolen from warehouse. Many copies have surfaced in recent years.*

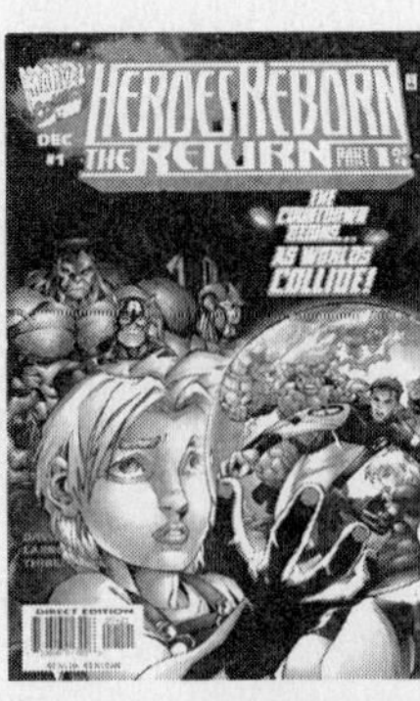

Heroes Reborn: The Return #1 © MAR

Heroic Comics #22 © EAS

High Roads #3 © Leinil Yu

HEROES OF THE WILD FRONTIER (Formerly Baffling Mysteries)
Ace Periodicals: No. 27, Jan, 1956 - No. 2, Apr, 1956

	GD 2.0	VG 4.0	FN 6.0	VF 8.0	VF/NM 9.0	NM- 9.2
27(#1),2-Davy Crockett, Daniel Boone, Buffalo Bill	6	12	18	28	34	40

HEROES REBORN (one-shots)
Marvel Comics: Jan, 2000 ($1.99)

	GD 2.0	VG 4.0	FN 6.0	VF 8.0	VF/NM 9.0	NM- 9.2
...:Ashema; ...:Doom; ...:Doomsday; ...:Masters of Evil; ...:Rebel; ...:Remnants; ...:Young Allies						2.25

HEROES REBORN: THE RETURN
Marvel Comics: Dec, 1997 - No. 4 ($2.50, weekly mini-series)

	GD 2.0	VG 4.0	FN 6.0	VF 8.0	VF/NM 9.0	NM- 9.2
1-4-Avengers, Fantastic Four, Iron Man & Captain America rejoin regular Marvel Universe; Peter David-s/Larocca-c/a						4.00
1-4-Variant-c for each						6.00
Wizard 1/2	1	2	3	5	7	9
Return of the Heroes TPB ('98, $14.95) r/#1-4						15.00

HERO FOR HIRE (Power Man No. 17 on; also see Cage)
Marvel Comics Group: June, 1972 - No. 16, Dec, 1973

	GD 2.0	VG 4.0	FN 6.0	VF 8.0	VF/NM 9.0	NM- 9.2
1-Origin & 1st app. Luke Cage; Tuska-a(p)	7	14	21	50	68	85
2-Tuska-a(p)	3	7	10	21	28	35
3-5: 3-1st app. Mace. 4-1st app. Phil Fox of the Bugle	2	4	6	15	19	25
6-10: 8,9-Dr. Doom app. 9-F.F. app.	2	4	6	10	12	15
11-16: 14-Origin retold. 15-Everett Sub-Mariner-r('53). 16-Origin Stilletto; death of Rackham	1	3	4	7	9	10

HERO HOTLINE (1st app. in Action Comics Weekly #637)
DC Comics: April, 1989 - No. 6, Sept, 1989 ($1.75, limited series)

	GD 2.0	VG 4.0	FN 6.0	VF 8.0	VF/NM 9.0	NM- 9.2
1-6: Super-hero humor; Schaffenberger-i						2.25

HEROIC ADVENTURES (See Adventures)

HEROIC COMICS (Reg'lar Fellers...#1-15; New Heroic #41 on)
Eastern Color Printing Co./Famous Funnies(Funnies, Inc. No. 1): Aug, 1940 - No. 97, June, 1955

	GD 2.0	VG 4.0	FN 6.0	VF 8.0	VF/NM 9.0	NM- 9.2
1-Hydroman (origin) by Bill Everett, The Purple Zombie (origin) & Mann of India by Tarpe Mills begins (all 1st apps.)	176	352	528	1100	1650	2200
2	76	152	228	475	713	950
3,4	51	102	153	306	458	610
5,6	42	84	126	252	376	500
7-Origin & 1st app. Man O'Metal (1 pg.)	44	88	132	264	400	535
8-10: 10-Lingerie panels	34	68	102	196	278	360
11,13: 13-Crandall/Fine-a	32	64	96	182	259	335
12-Music Master (origin/1st app.) begins by Everett, ends No. 31; last Purple Zombie & Mann of India	36	72	108	204	290	375
14,15-Hydroman x-over in Rainbow Boy. 14-Origin & 1st app. Rainbow Boy (super hero). 15-1st app. Downbeat	34	68	102	196	278	360
16-20: 16-New logo. 17-Rainbow Boy x-over in Hydroman. 19-Rainbow Boy x-over in Hydroman & vice versa	24	48	72	138	194	250
21-30:25-Rainbow Boy x-over in Hydroman. 28-Last Man O'Metal. 29-Last Hydroman	17	34	51	98	134	170
31,34,38	8	16	24	40	50	60
32,36,37-Toth-a (3-4 pgs. each)	9	18	27	49	62	75
33,35-Toth-a (8 & 9 pgs.)	9	18	27	52	66	80
39-42-Toth, Ingels-a	9	18	27	52	66	80
43,46,47,49-Toth-a (2-4 pgs.). 47-Ingels-a	8	16	24	46	58	70
44,45,50-Toth-a (6-9 pgs.)	9	18	27	49	62	75
48,53,54	7	14	21	37	46	55
51-Williamson-a	9	18	27	49	62	75
52-Williamson-a (3 pg. story)	8	16	24	40	50	60
55-Toth-a	8	16	24	46	58	70
56-60: 60-Everett-a	8	16	24	40	50	60
61-Everett-a	7	14	21	37	46	55
62,64-Everett-c/a	8	16	24	40	50	60
63-Everett-c	7	14	21	37	46	55
65-Williamson/Frazetta-a; Evans-a (2 pgs.)	10	20	30	58	77	95
66,75,94-Frazetta-a (2 pgs. each)	8	16	24	40	50	60
67,73-Frazetta-a (4 pgs. each)	9	18	27	49	62	75
68,74,76-80,84,85,88-93,95-97: 95-Last pre-code	7	14	21	35	43	50
69,72-Frazetta-a (6 & 8 pgs. each); 1st (?) app. Frazetta Red Cross ad	10	20	30	58	77	95
70,71,86,87-Frazetta, 3-4 pgs. each; 1 pg. ad by Frazetta in #70	8	16	24	43	54	65
81,82-Frazetta art (1 pg. each): 81-1st (?) app. Frazetta Boy Scout ad (tied w/ Buster Crabbe #9	7	14	21	37	46	55
83-Frazetta-a (1/2 pg.)	7	14	21	37	46	55

NOTE: ***Evans*** *a-64, 65.* ***Everett*** *a-(Hydroman-c/a-No. 1-9), 44, 60-64; c-1-9, 62-64.* ***Harvey Fuller*** *c-28-35.* ***Sid Greene*** *a-38-43, 46.* ***Guardineer*** *a-42(3), 43, 44, 45(2), 49(3), 50, 60, 61(2), 65, 67(2) 70-72.* ***Ingels*** *c-41.* ***Kiefer*** *a-46, 48; c-19-22, 24, 44, 46, 48, 51-53, 65, 67-69, 71-74, 76, 77, 79, 80, 82, 85, 86, 88, 89, 94, 95.* ***Mort Lawrence*** *a-45.* ***Tarpe Mills*** *a-2(2), 3(2), 10.* ***Ed Moore*** *a-49, 52-54, 56-63, 65-69, 72-74, 76, 77.* ***H.G. Peter*** *a-58-74, 76, 77, 87.* ***Paul Reinman*** *a-49.* ***Rico*** *a-31. Captain Tootsie by* ***Beck****-31, 32. Painted-c #16 on. Hydroman c-1-11. Music Master c-12, 13, 15. Rainbow Boy c-14.*

HERO ZERO (Also see Comics' Greatest World & Godzilla Versus Hero Zero)
Dark Horse Comics: Sept, 1994 ($2.50)

	GD 2.0	VG 4.0	FN 6.0	VF 8.0	VF/NM 9.0	NM- 9.2
0						2.50

HEX (Replaces Jonah Hex)
DC Comics: Sept, 1985 - No. 18, Feb, 1987 (Story cont'd from Jonah Hex # 92)

	GD 2.0	VG 4.0	FN 6.0	VF 8.0	VF/NM 9.0	NM- 9.2
1-Hex in post-atomic war world; origin	1	2	3	5	6	8
2-18: 6-Origin Stiletta. 11-13: All contain future Batman storyline. 13-Intro The Dogs of War (origin #15)						5.00

NOTE: ***Giffen*** *a(p)-15-18; c(p)-15,17,18.* ***Texeira*** *a-1, 2p, 3p, 5-7p, 9p, 11-14p; c(p)-1, 2, 4-7, 12.*

HEXBREAKER (See First Comics Graphic Novel #15)

HEY THERE, IT'S YOGI BEAR (See Movie Comics)

HI-ADVENTURE HEROES (TV)
Gold Key: May, 1969 - No. 2, Aug, 1969 (Hanna-Barbera)

	GD 2.0	VG 4.0	FN 6.0	VF 8.0	VF/NM 9.0	NM- 9.2
1-Three Musketeers, Gulliver, Arabian Knights	6	12	18	38	52	65
2-Three Musketeers, Micro-Venture, Arabian Knights	5	10	15	33	44	55

HI AND LOIS
Dell Publishing Co.: No. 683, Mar, 1956 - No. 955, Nov, 1958

	GD 2.0	VG 4.0	FN 6.0	VF 8.0	VF/NM 9.0	NM- 9.2
Four Color 683 (#1)	4	8	12	28	38	48
Four Color 774(3/57),955	3	6	9	19	25	32

HI AND LOIS
Charlton Comics: Nov, 1969 - No. 11, July, 1971

	GD 2.0	VG 4.0	FN 6.0	VF 8.0	VF/NM 9.0	NM- 9.2
1	3	6	9	16	20	25
2-11	2	4	6	10	12	15

HICKORY (See All Humor Comics)
Quality Comics Group: Oct, 1949 - No. 6, Aug, 1950

	GD 2.0	VG 4.0	FN 6.0	VF 8.0	VF/NM 9.0	NM- 9.2
1-Sahl-c/a in all; Feldstein?-a	17	34	51	98	134	170
2	10	20	30	56	73	90
3-6	9	18	27	52	66	80

HIDDEN CREW, THE (See The United States Air Force Presents:...)

HIDE-OUT (See Zane Grey, Four Color No. 346)

HIDING PLACE, THE
Spire Christian Comics (Fleming H. Revell Co.): 1973 (39¢/49¢)

	GD 2.0	VG 4.0	FN 6.0	VF 8.0	VF/NM 9.0	NM- 9.2
nn	1	3	4	6	8	10

HIEROGLYPH
Dark Horse Comics: Nov, 1999 - No. 4, Feb, 2000 ($2.95, limited series)

	GD 2.0	VG 4.0	FN 6.0	VF 8.0	VF/NM 9.0	NM- 9.2
1-4-Ricardo Delgado-s/a						3.00

HIGH ADVENTURE
Red Top(Decker) Comics (Farrell): Oct, 1957

	GD 2.0	VG 4.0	FN 6.0	VF 8.0	VF/NM 9.0	NM- 9.2
1-Krigstein-r from Explorer Joe (re-issue on-c)	5	10	15	23	28	32

HIGH ADVENTURE (TV)
Dell Publishing Co.: No. 949, Nov, 1958 - No. 1001, Aug-Oct, 1959 (Lowell Thomas)

	GD 2.0	VG 4.0	FN 6.0	VF 8.0	VF/NM 9.0	NM- 9.2
Four Color 949 (#1)-Photo-c	6	12	18	43	59	75
Four Color 1001-Lowell Thomas'...(#2)	6	12	18	40	55	70

HIGH CHAPPARAL (TV)
Gold Key: Aug, 1968 (Photo-c)

	GD 2.0	VG 4.0	FN 6.0	VF 8.0	VF/NM 9.0	NM- 9.2
1 (10226-808)-Tufts-a	6	12	18	38	52	65

HIGH ROADS
DC Comics (Cliffhanger): June, 2002 - No. 6, Nov, 2002 ($2.95, limited series)

	GD 2.0	VG 4.0	FN 6.0	VF 8.0	VF/NM 9.0	NM- 9.2
1-6-Leinil Yu-c/a; Lobdell-s						3.00
TPB (2003, $14.95) r/#1-6; sketch pages						15.00

HIGH SCHOOL CONFIDENTIAL DIARY (Confidential Diary #12 on)
Charlton Comics: June, 1960 - No. 11, Mar, 1962

	GD 2.0	VG 4.0	FN 6.0	VF 8.0	VF/NM 9.0	NM- 9.2
1	5	10	15	33	44	55
2-11	3	6	9	19	25	32

HI-HO COMICS
Four Star Publications: nd (2/46?) - No. 3, 1946

	GD 2.0	VG 4.0	FN 6.0	VF 8.0	VF/NM 9.0	NM- 9.2
1-Funny Animal; L. B. Cole-c	39	78	117	230	325	420
2,3: 2-L. B. Cole-c	22	44	66	127	176	225

Hi-School Romance #5 © HARV

Hit Comics #6 © QUA

Hitman #21 © DC

HI-JINX (Teen-age Animal Funnies)
La Salle Publ. Co./B&I Publ. Co. (American Comics Group)/Creston: 1945; July-Aug, 1947 - No. 7, July-Aug, 1948

	GD 2.0	VG 4.0	FN 6.0	VF 8.0	VF/NM 9.0	NM- 9.2
nn-(© 1945, 25 cents, 132 Pgs.)(La Salle)	24	48	72	138	194	250
1-Teen-age, funny animal	17	34	51	98	134	170
2,3	10	20	30	58	77	95
4-7-Milt Gross. 4-X-Mas-c	15	30	45	86	118	150

HI-LITE COMICS
E. R. Ross Publishing Co.: Fall, 1945

	GD 2.0	VG 4.0	FN 6.0	VF 8.0	VF/NM 9.0	NM- 9.2
1-Miss Shady	20	40	60	112	156	200

HILLBILLY COMICS
Charlton Comics: Aug, 1955 - No. 4, July, 1956 (Satire)

	GD 2.0	VG 4.0	FN 6.0	VF 8.0	VF/NM 9.0	NM- 9.2
1-By Art Gates	9	18	27	52	66	80
2-4	6	12	18	31	38	45

HILLY ROSE'S SPACE ADVENTURES
Astro Comics: May, 1995 - No. 9 ($2.95, B&W)

	GD 2.0	VG 4.0	FN 6.0	VF 8.0	VF/NM 9.0	NM- 9.2
1	1	2	3	5	7	9
2-5						5.00
6-9						3.00
Trade Paperback (1996, $12.95)-r/#1-5						13.00

HIP FLASK UNNATURAL SELECTION
Active Images: Sept, 2002 - Present ($2.99)

	GD 2.0	VG 4.0	FN 6.0	VF 8.0	VF/NM 9.0	NM- 9.2
1-Casey & Starkings-s/Ladronn-a; var.-c by Madureira, Campbell, Churchill						3.00

HIP-IT-TY HOP (See March of Comics No. 15)

HI-SCHOOL ROMANCE (...Romances No. 41 on)
Harvey Publ./True Love(Home Comics): Oct, 1949 - No. 5, June, 1950; No. 6, Dec, 1950 - No. 73, Mar, 1958; No. 74, Sept, 1958 - No. 75, Nov, 1958

	GD 2.0	VG 4.0	FN 6.0	VF 8.0	VF/NM 9.0	NM- 9.2
1-Photo-c	16	32	48	92	126	160
2-Photo-c	9	18	27	52	66	80
3-9: 3,5-Photo-c	8	16	24	40	50	60
10-Rape story	9	18	27	52	66	80
11-20	6	12	18	31	38	45
21-31	5	10	15	24	30	35
32- "Unholy passion" story	8	16	24	40	50	60
33-36: 36-Last pre-code (2/55)	5	10	15	23	28	32
37-53,59-72,74,75	4	8	12	18	22	25
54-58,73-Kirby-c	5	10	15	22	26	30

NOTE: ***Powell** a-1-3, 5, 8, 12-16, 18, 21-23, 25-27, 30-34, 36, 37, 39, 45-48, 50-52, 57, 58, 60, 64, 65, 67, 69.*

HI-SCHOOL ROMANCE DATE BOOK
Harvey Publications: Nov, 1962 - No. 3, Mar, 1963 (25¢ Giants)

	GD 2.0	VG 4.0	FN 6.0	VF 8.0	VF/NM 9.0	NM- 9.2
1-Powell, Baker-a	5	10	15	36	48	60
2,3	3	7	10	21	28	35

HIS NAME IS SAVAGE (Magazine format)
Adventure House Press: June, 1968 (35¢, 52 pgs.)

	GD 2.0	VG 4.0	FN 6.0	VF 8.0	VF/NM 9.0	NM- 9.2
1-Gil Kane-a	4	8	12	29	40	50

HI-SPOT COMICS (Red Ryder No. 1 & No. 3 on)
Hawley Publications: No. 2, Nov, 1940

	GD 2.0	VG 4.0	FN 6.0	VF 8.0	VF/NM 9.0	NM- 9.2
2-David Innes of Pellucidar; art by J. C. Burroughs; written by Edgar Rice Burroughs	120	240	360	750	1125	1500

HISTORY OF THE DC UNIVERSE (Also see Crisis on Infinite Earths)
DC Comics: Sept, 1986 - No. 2, Nov, 1986 ($2.95, limited series)

	GD 2.0	VG 4.0	FN 6.0	VF 8.0	VF/NM 9.0	NM- 9.2
1,2: 1-Perez-c/a						3.00
Limited Edition hardcover	5	10	15	33	44	55
Softcover (2002, $9.95) new Alex Ross wraparound-c						10.00

HISTORY OF VIOLENCE, A
DC Comics (Paradox Press) 1998?

	GD 2.0	VG 4.0	FN 6.0	VF 8.0	VF/NM 9.0	NM- 9.2
nn-Paperback ($9.95)						10.00

HITCHHIKERS GUIDE TO THE GALAXY (See Life, the Universe and Everything & Restaraunt at the End of the Universe)
DC Comics: 1993 - No. 3, 1993 ($4.95, limited series)

	GD 2.0	VG 4.0	FN 6.0	VF 8.0	VF/NM 9.0	NM- 9.2
1-3: Adaptation of Douglas Adams book						5.00
TPB (1997, $14.95) r/#1-3						15.00

HIT COMICS
Quality Comics Group: July, 1940 - No. 65, July, 1950

	GD 2.0	VG 4.0	FN 6.0	VF 8.0	VF/NM 9.0	NM- 9.2
1-Origin/1st app. Neon, the Unknown & Hercules; intro. The Red Bee; Bob & Swab, Blaze Barton, the Strange Twins, X-5 Super Agent, Casey Jones & Jack & Jill (ends #7) begin	634	1268	1902	4438	6819	9200
2-The Old Witch begins, ends #14	262	524	786	1638	2457	3275
3-Casey Jones ends; transvestism story "Jack & Jill"	244	488	732	1525	2288	3050
4-Super Agent (ends #17), & Betty Bates (ends #65) begin; X-5 ends	218	436	654	1363	2044	2725
5-Classic Lou Fine cover	531	1062	1593	3717	5709	7700
6-10: 10-Old Witch by Crandall (4 pgs.); 1st work in comics (4/41)	188	376	564	1175	1763	2350
11-Classic cover	168	336	504	1050	1575	2100
12-17: 13-Blaze Barton ends. 17-Last Neon; Crandall Hercules in all; Last Lou Fine-c	116	232	348	725	1088	1450
18-Origin & 1st app. Stormy Foster, the Great Defender (12/41); The Ghost of Flanders begins; Crandall-c	126	252	378	788	1182	1575
19,20	100	200	300	625	938	1250
21-24: 21-Last Hercules. 24-Last Red Bee & Strange Twins	96	192	288	600	900	1200
25-Origin & 1st app. Kid Eternity and begins by Moldoff (12/42); 1st app. The Keeper (Kid Eternity's aide)	182	364	546	1138	1707	2275
26-Blackhawk x-over in Kid Eternity	100	200	300	625	938	1250
27-29	50	100	150	300	450	600
30,31- "Bill the Magnificent" by Kurtzman, 11 pgs. in each	46	92	138	276	413	550
32-40: 32-Plastic Man x-over. 34-Last Stormy Foster	29	58	87	164	232	300
41-50	21	42	63	118	164	210
51-60-Last Kid Eternity	20	40	60	112	156	200
61-63-Crandall-c/a; 61-Jeb Rivers begins	21	42	63	118	164	210
64,65-Crandall-a	20	40	60	112	156	200

NOTE: ***Crandall** a-11-17(Hercules), 23, 24(Stormy Foster); c-18-20, 23, 24. **Fine** c-1-14, 16, 17(most). **Ward** c-33. Bondage c-7, 64. Hercules c-3, 10-17. Jeb Rivers c-61-65. Kid Eternity c-25-60 (w/Keeper-28-34, 36, 39-43, 45-55). Neon the Unknown c-2, 4, 8, 9. Red Bee c-1, 5-7. Stormy Foster c-18-24.*

HITLER'S ASTROLOGER (See Marvel Graphic Novel #35)

HITMAN (Also see Bloodbath #2, Batman Chronicles #4, Demon #43-45 & Demon Annual #2)
DC Comics: May, 1996 - No. 60, Apr, 2001 ($2.25/$2.50)

	GD 2.0	VG 4.0	FN 6.0	VF 8.0	VF/NM 9.0	NM- 9.2
1-Garth Ennis-s & John McCrea-c/a begin; Batman app.	1	2	3	5	7	9
2-Joker-c;Two Face, Mad Hatter, Batman app.						6.00
3-5: 3-Batman-c/app.; Joker app. 4-1st app. Nightfist						4.00
6-20: 8-Final Night x-over. 10-GL cameo. 11-20: 11,12-GL-c/app. 15-20-"Ace of Killers". 16-18-Catwoman app. 17-19-Demon-app.						3.00
21-59: 34-Superman-c/app.						2.50
60-($3.95) Final issue; includes pin-ups by various						4.00
#1,000,000 (11/98) Hitman goes to the 853rd Century						2.50
Annual 1 (1997, $3.95) Pulp Heroes						4.00
.../Lobo: That Stupid Bastich (7/00, $3.95) Ennis-s/Mahnke-a						4.00
TPB-(1997, $9.95) r/#1-3, Demon Ann. #2, Batman Chronicles #4						10.00
Ace of Killers TPB ('00, $17.95) r/#15-22						18.00
Local Heroes TPB ('99, $17.95) r/#9-14 & Annual #1						18.00
10,000 Bullets TPB ('98, $9.95) r/#4-8						10.00
Who Dares Wins TPB ('01, $12.95) r/#23-28						13.00

HI-YO SILVER (See Lone Ranger's Famous Horse... and The Lone Ranger; and March of Comics No. 215 in the Promotional Comics section)

HOBBIT, THE
Eclipse Comics: 1989 - No. 3, 1990 ($4.95, squarebound, 52 pgs.)

	GD 2.0	VG 4.0	FN 6.0	VF 8.0	VF/NM 9.0	NM- 9.2
Book 1-3: Adapts novel; Wenzel-a						7.00
Book 1-Second printing						5.00
Graphic Novel (1990, Ballantine)-r/#1-3						20.00

HOCUS POCUS (Formerly Funny Book)
Parents' Magazine Press: No. 9, Aug-Sept, 1946

	GD 2.0	VG 4.0	FN 6.0	VF 8.0	VF/NM 9.0	NM- 9.2
9	7	14	21	35	43	50

HOGAN'S HEROES (TV)
Dell Publishing Co.: June, 1966 - No. 8, Sept, 1967; No. 9, Oct, 1969

	GD 2.0	VG 4.0	FN 6.0	VF 8.0	VF/NM 9.0	NM- 9.2
1: #1-7 photo-c	9	18	27	65	93	120
2,3-Ditko-a(p)	6	12	18	40	55	70
4-9: 9-Reprints #1	5	10	15	33	44	55

HOKUM & HEX (See Razorline)
Marvel Comics (Razorline): Sept, 1993 - No. 9, May, 1994 ($1.75/$1.95)

	GD 2.0	VG 4.0	FN 6.0	VF 8.0	VF/NM 9.0	NM- 9.2
1-($2.50)-Foil embossed-c; by Clive Barker						3.00
2-9: 5-Hyperkind x-over						2.25

HOLIDAY COMICS

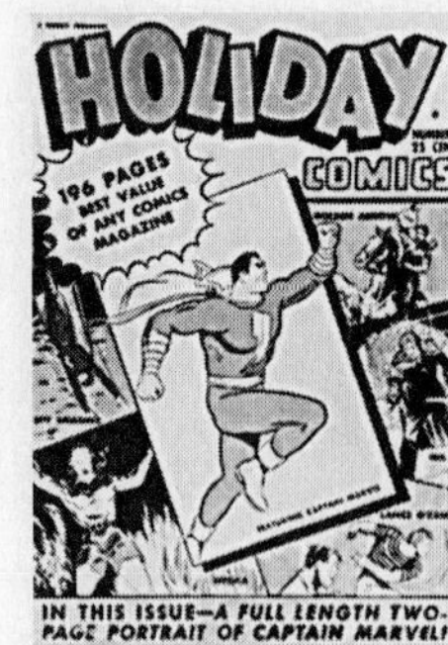

Holiday Comics #1 © FAW

Hollywood Diary #1 © QUA

Holyoke One-Shot #1 © HOKE

	GD 2.0	VG 4.0	FN 6.0	VF 8.0	VF/NM 9.0	NM- 9.2
Fawcett Publications: 1942 (25¢, 196 pgs.)						
1-Contains three Fawcett comics plus two page portrait of Captain Marvel; Capt. Marvel, Nyoka #1, & Whiz. Not rebound, remaindered comics; printed at the same time as originals	158	316	474	988	1482	1975
HOLIDAY COMICS (Becomes Fun Comics #9-12)						
Star Publications: Jan, 1951 - No. 8, Oct, 1952						
1-Funny animal contents (Frisky Fables) in all; L. B. Cole X-Mas-c	38	76	114	219	310	400
2-Classic L. B. Cole-c	39	78	117	230	325	420
3-8: 5,8-X-Mas-c; all L.B. Cole-c	25	50	75	147	202	260
Accepted Reprint 4 (nd)-L.B. Cole-c	11	22	33	63	84	105
HOLIDAY DIGEST						
Harvey Comics: 1988 ($1.25, digest-size)						
1	1	2	3	5	7	9
HOLIDAY PARADE (Walt Disney's...)						
W. D. Publications (Disney): Winter, 1990-91(no year given) - No. 2, Winter, 1990-91 ($2.95, 68 pgs.)						
1-Reprints 1947 Firestone by Barks plus new-a						4.00
2-Barks-r plus other stories						4.00
HOLI-DAY SURPRISE (Formerly Summer Fun)						
Charlton Comics: V2#55, Mar, 1967 (25¢ Giant)						
V2#55	4	8	12	24	32	40
HOLLYWOOD COMICS						
New Age Publishers: Winter, 1944 (52 pgs.)						
1-Funny animal	19	38	57	106	146	185
HOLLYWOOD CONFESSIONS						
St. John Publishing Co.: Oct, 1949 - No. 2, Dec, 1949						
1-Kubert-c/a (entire book)	31	62	93	175	248	320
2-Kubert-c/a (entire book) (Scarce)	35	70	105	201	288	370
HOLLYWOOD DIARY						
Quality Comics Group: Dec, 1949 - No. 5, July-Aug, 1950						
1-No photo-c	21	42	63	118	164	210
2-Photo-c	13	26	39	76	103	130
3-5-Photo-c. 5-June Allyson/Peter Lawford photo-c	11	22	33	66	88	110
HOLLYWOOD FILM STORIES						
Feature Publications/Prize: April, 1950 - No. 4, Oct, 1950 (All photo-c; "Fumetti" type movie comic)						
1-June Allyson photo-c	21	42	63	118	164	210
2-4: 2-Lizabeth Scott photo-c. 3-Barbara Stanwick photo-c. 4-Betty Hutton photo-c	15	30	45	84	115	145
HOLLYWOOD FUNNY FOLKS (Formerly Funny Folks; Becomes Nutsy Squirrel #61 on)						
National Periodical Publ.: No. 27, Aug-Sept, 1950 - No. 60, July-Aug, 1954						
27	14	28	42	79	107	135
28-40	10	20	30	56	73	90
41-60	9	18	27	49	62	75
NOTE: ***Sheldon Mayer** a-27-35, 37-40, 43-46, 48-51, 53, 56, 57, 60.*						
HOLLYWOOD LOVE DOCTOR (See Doctor Anthony King...)						
HOLLYWOOD PICTORIAL (...Romances on cover)						
St. John Publishing Co.: No. 3, Jan, 1950						
3-Matt Baker-a; photo-c	24	48	72	135	190	245
(Becomes a movie magazine - Hollywood Pictorial Western with No. 4.)						
HOLLYWOOD ROMANCES (Formerly Brides In Love; becomes For Lovers Only #60 on)						
Charlton Comics: V2#46, 11/66; #47, 10/67; #48, 11/68;V3#49,11/69-V3#59, 6/71						
V2#46-Rolling Stones-c/story	9	18	27	65	93	120
V2#47-V3#59: 56- "Born to Heart Break" begins	2	4	6	11	14	18
HOLLYWOOD SECRETS						
Quality Comics Group: Nov, 1949 - No. 6, Sept, 1950						
1-Ward-c/a (9 pgs.)	34	68	102	196	278	360
2-Crandall-a, Ward-c/a (9 pgs.)	23	46	69	130	183	235
3-6: All photo-c. 5-Lex Barker (Tarzan)-c	12	24	36	71	96	120
...of Romance, I.W. Reprint #9; r/#2 above w/Kinstler-c	2	4	6	11	14	18
HOLLYWOOD SUPERSTARS						
Marvel Comics (Epic Comics): Nov, 1990 - No. 5, Apr, 1991 ($2.25)						
1-($2.95, 52 pgs.)-Spiegle-c/a in all; Aragones-a, inside front-c plus 2-4 pgs.						3.00

| | GD 2.0 | VG 4.0 | FN 6.0 | VF 8.0 | VF/NM 9.0 | NM- 9.2 |

	GD 2.0	VG 4.0	FN 6.0	VF 8.0	VF/NM 9.0	NM- 9.2
2-5 ($2.25)						2.25
HOLO-MAN (See Power Record Comics)						
HOLYOKE ONE-SHOT						
Holyoke Publishing Co. (Tem Publ.): 1944 - No. 10, 1945 (All reprints)						
1,2: 1-Grit Grady (on cover only), Miss Victory, Alias X (origin)-All reprints from Captain Fearless. 2-Rusty Dugan (Corporal); Capt. Fearless (origin), Mr. Miracle (origin) app.	16	32	48	92	126	160
3-Miss Victory; r/Crash #4; Cat Man (origin), Solar Legion by Kirby app.; Miss Victory on cover only (1945)	29	58	87	164	232	300
4,6,8: 4-Mr. Miracle; The Blue Streak app. 6-Capt. Fearless, Alias X, Capt. Stone (splash used as-c to #10); Diamond Jim & Rusty Dugan (splash from cover of #2). 8-Blue Streak, Strong Man (story matches cover to #7)-Crash reprints	14	28	42	79	107	135
5,7: 5-U.S. Border Patrol Comics (Sgt. Dick Carter of the...), Miss Victory (story matches cover to #3), Citizen Smith, & Mr. Miracle app. 7-Secret Agent Z-2, Strong Man, Blue Streak (story matches cover to #8); Reprints from Crash #2	16	32	48	92	126	160
9-Citizen Smith, The Blue Streak, Solar Legion by Kirby & Strongman, the Perfect Human app.; reprints from Crash #4 & 5; Citizen Smith on cover only-from story in #5 (1944-before #3)	19	38	57	109	152	195
10-Captain Stone; r/Crash; Solar Legion by S&K	19	38	57	109	152	195
HOLY TERROR						
Image Comics: Aug, 2002 - Present ($2.95)						
1,2-Phil Hester-a/c; Jason Caskey-s						3.00
HOMER COBB (See Adventures of...)						
HOMER HOOPER						
Atlas Comics: July, 1953 - No. 4, Dec, 1953						
1-Teenage humor	10	20	30	56	73	90
2-4	8	16	24	40	50	60
HOMER, THE HAPPY GHOST (See Adventures of...)						
Atlas(ACI/PPI/WPI)/Marvel: 3/55 - No. 22, 11/58; V2#1, 11/69 - V2#4, 5/70						
V1#1-Dan DeCarlo-c/a begins, ends #22	22	44	66	124	172	220
2-1st code approved issue	11	22	33	66	88	110
3-10	10	20	30	56	73	90
11-22	9	18	27	49	62	75
V2#1 (11/69)	10	20	30	70	100	130
2-4	6	12	18	38	52	65
HOME RUN (Also see A-1 Comics)						
Magazine Enterprises: No. 89, 1953 (one-shot)						
A-1 89 (#3)-Powell-a; Stan Musial photo-c	13	26	39	74	100	125
HOMICIDE (Also see Dark Horse Presents)						
Dark Horse Comics: Apr, 1990 ($1.95, B&W, one-shot)						
1-Detective story						2.25
HONEYMOON (Formerly Gay Comics)						
A Lover's Magazine(USA) (Marvel): No. 41, Jan, 1950						
41-Photo-c; article by Betty Grable	10	20	30	56	73	90
HONEYMOONERS, THE (TV)						
Lodestone: Oct, 1986 ($1.50)						
1-Photo-c						4.00
HONEYMOONERS, THE (TV)						
Triad Publications: Sept, 1987 - No. 13? ($2.00)						
1-13						4.00
HONEYMOON ROMANCE						
Artful Publications (Canadian): Apr, 1950 - No. 2, July, 1950 (25¢, digest size)						
1,2-(Rare)	38	76	114	219	310	400
HONEY WEST (TV)						
Gold Key: Sept, 1966 (Photo-c)						
1 (10186-609)	11	22	33	77	114	150
HONG KONG PHOOEY (TV)						
Charlton Comics: June, 1975 - No. 9, Nov, 1976 (Hanna-Barbera)						
1	6	12	18	38	52	65
2	3	6	9	19	25	32
3-9	3	6	9	16	20	24
HONG ON THE RANGE						
Image/Flypaper Press: Dec, 1997 - No. 3, Feb, 1998 ($2.50, lim. series)						

Hook #1 © TriStar Pictures

Hopalong Cassidy #9 © FAW

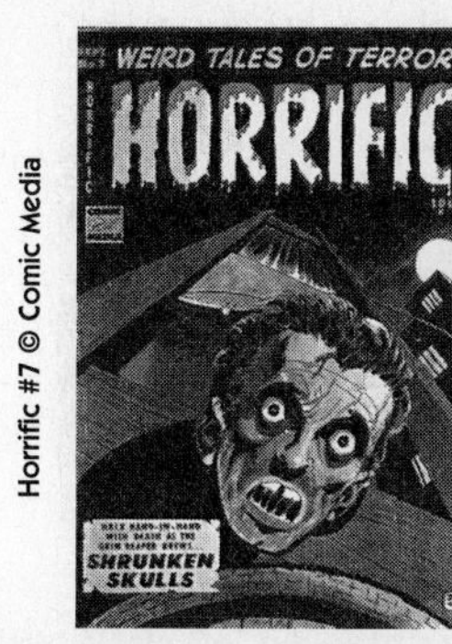

Horrific #7 © Comic Media

	GD 2.0	VG 4.0	FN 6.0	VF 8.0	VF/NM 9.0	NM- 9.2
1-3: Wu-s/Lafferty-a						2.50

HOOD, THE
Marvel Comics (MAX): Jul, 2002 - No. 6, Dec, 2002 ($2.99, limited series)

	GD 2.0	VG 4.0	FN 6.0	VF 8.0	VF/NM 9.0	NM- 9.2
1-6-Vaughan-s/Hotz-c/a						3.00
Vol. 1 Blood From Stones TPB (2003, $14.99) r/#1-6						15.00

HOODED HORSEMAN, THE (Formerly Blazing West)
American Comics Group (Michel Publ.): No. 21, 1-2/52 - No. 27, 1-2/54; No. 18, 12-1/54-55 - No. 22, 8-9/55

	GD 2.0	VG 4.0	FN 6.0	VF 8.0	VF/NM 9.0	NM- 9.2
21(1-2/52)-Hooded Horseman, Injun Jones cont.	15	30	45	86	118	150
22	10	20	30	56	73	90
23,24,27(1-2/54)	9	18	27	49	62	75
25 (9-10/53)-Cowboy Sahib on cover only; Hooded Horseman i.d. revealed	9	18	27	52	66	80
26-Origin/1st app. Cowboy Sahib by L. Starr	11	22	33	63	84	105
18(12-1/54-55)(Formerly Out of the Night)	10	20	30	56	73	90
19,21,22: 19-Last precode (1-2/55)	8	16	24	46	58	70
20-Origin Johnny Injun	9	18	27	52	66	80

NOTE: ***Whitney** c/a-21('52), 20-22.*

HOODED MENACE, THE (Also see Daring Adventures)
Realistic/Avon Periodicals: 1951 (one-shot)

	GD 2.0	VG 4.0	FN 6.0	VF 8.0	VF/NM 9.0	NM- 9.2
nn-Based on a band of hooded outlaws in the Pacific Northwest, 1900-1906; reprinted in Daring Advs. #15	48	96	144	288	432	575

HOODS UP
Fram Corp.: 1953 (15¢, distributed to service station owners, 16 pgs.)

	GD 2.0	VG 4.0	FN 6.0	VF 8.0	VF/NM 9.0	NM- 9.2
1-(Very Rare; only 2 known); Eisner-c/a in all.	48	96	144	288	432	575
2-6-(Very Rare; only 1 known of #3, 4, 2 known of #2)	48	96	144	288	432	575

NOTE: *Convertible Connie gives tips for service stations, selling Fram oil filters.*

HOOK (Movie)
Marvel Comics: Early Feb, 1992 - No. 4, Late Mar, 1992 ($1.00, limited series)

	GD 2.0	VG 4.0	FN 6.0	VF 8.0	VF/NM 9.0	NM- 9.2
1-4: Adapts movie; Vess-c; 1-Morrow-a(p)						2.25
nn (1991, $5.95, 84 pgs.)-Contains #1-4; Vess-c						6.00
1 (1991, $2.95, magazine, 84 pgs.)-Contains #1-4; Vess-c (same cover as nn issue)						3.00

HOOT GIBSON'S WESTERN ROUNDUP (See Western Roundup under Fox Giants)

HOOT GIBSON WESTERN (Formerly My Love Story)
Fox Features Syndicate: No. 5, May, 1950 - No. 3, Sept, 1950

	GD 2.0	VG 4.0	FN 6.0	VF 8.0	VF/NM 9.0	NM- 9.2
5,6(#1,2): 5-Photo-c. 6-Photo/painted-c	29	58	87	164	232	300
3-Wood-a; painted-c	31	62	93	175	248	320

HOPALONG CASSIDY (Also see Bill Boyd Western, Master Comics, Real Western Hero, Six Gun Heroes & Western Hero; Bill Boyd starred as H. Cassidy in the movies; H. Cassidy in movies, radio & TV)
Fawcett Publications: Feb, 1943; No. 2, Summer, 1946 - No. 85, Nov, 1953

	GD 2.0	VG 4.0	FN 6.0	VF 8.0	VF/NM 9.0	NM- 9.2
1 (1943, 68 pgs.)-H. Cassidy & his horse Topper begin (on sale 1/8/43)-Captain Marvel app. on-c	470	940	1410	3290	5045	6800
2-(Sum, '46)	78	156	234	488	732	975
3,4: 3-(Fall, '46, 52 pgs. begin)	40	80	120	240	345	450
5- "Mad Barber" story mentioned in **SOTI**, pgs. 308,309; photo-c	36	72	108	204	290	375
6-10: 8-Photo-c	28	56	84	159	225	290
11-19: 11,13-19-Photo-c	21	42	63	118	164	210
20-29 (52 pgs.)-Painted/photo-c	17	34	51	98	134	170
30,31,33,34,37-39,41 (52 pgs.)-Painted-c	12	24	36	69	92	115
32,40 (36pgs.)-Painted-c	10	20	30	60	80	100
35,42,43,45-47,49-51,53,54,56 (52 pgs.)-Photo-c	11	22	33	63	84	105
36,44,48 (36 pgs.)-Photo-c	10	20	30	58	77	95
52,55,57-70 (36 pgs.)-Photo-c	9	18	27	54	70	85
71-84-Photo-c	8	16	24	46	58	70
85-Last Fawcett issue; photo-c	9	18	27	54	70	85

NOTE: *Line-drawn c-1-4, 6, 7, 9, 10, 12.*

	GD 2.0	VG 4.0	FN 6.0	VF 8.0	VF/NM 9.0	NM- 9.2
... & The 5 Men of Evil (AC Comics, 1991, $12.95) r/newspaper strips and Fawcett story "Signature of Death"						13.00

HOPALONG CASSIDY
National Periodical Publications: No. 86, Feb, 1954 - No. 135, May-June, 1959 (All-36 pgs.)

	GD 2.0	VG 4.0	FN 6.0	VF 8.0	VF/NM 9.0	NM- 9.2
86-Gene Colan-a begins, ends #117; photo covers continue	40	80	120	240	340	440
87	23	46	69	129	180	230
88-91: 91-1 pg. Superboy-sty (6/54)	15	30	45	86	118	150
92-99 (98 has #93 on-c; last precode issue, 2/55). 95-Reversed photo-c to #52. 98-Reversed photo-c to #61. 99-Reversed photo-c to #60	14	28	42	79	107	135
100-Same cover as #50	15	30	45	86	118	150
101-108: 105-Same photo-c as #54. 107-Same photo-c as #51. 108-Last photo-c	8	16	24	53	74	95
109-130: 118-Gil Kane-a begins. 123-Kubert-a (2 pgs.). 124-Painted-c	7	14	21	50	68	85
131-135	7	14	21	51	71	90

HOPELESS SAVAGES (Also see Too Much Hopeless Savages; and the Promotional Comics section for Free Comic Book Day edition)
Oni Press: Aug, 2001 - No. 4, Nov, 2001 ($2.95, B&W, limited series)

	GD 2.0	VG 4.0	FN 6.0	VF 8.0	VF/NM 9.0	NM- 9.2
1-4-Van Meter-s/Norrie-a/Clugston-Major-a/Watson-c						3.00
TPB (2002, $13.95, 8" x 5.75") r/#1-4; plus color stories; Watson-c						14.00

HOPELESS SAVAGES: GROUND ZERO
Oni Press: June, 2002 - No. 4, Oct, 2002 ($2.95, B&W, limited series)

	GD 2.0	VG 4.0	FN 6.0	VF 8.0	VF/NM 9.0	NM- 9.2
1-4-Van Meter-s/O'Malley-a/Dodson-c. 1-Watson-a						3.00
TPB (2003, $11.95, 8" x 5.75") r/#1-4; Dodson-c						12.00

HOPE SHIP
Dell Publishing Co.: June-Aug, 1963

	GD 2.0	VG 4.0	FN 6.0	VF 8.0	VF/NM 9.0	NM- 9.2
1	3	6	9	17	21	26

HOPPY THE MARVEL BUNNY (See Fawcett's Funny Animals)
Fawcett Publications: Dec, 1945 - No. 15, Sept, 1947

	GD 2.0	VG 4.0	FN 6.0	VF 8.0	VF/NM 9.0	NM- 9.2
1	30	60	90	170	240	310
2	15	30	45	86	118	150
3-15: 7-Xmas-c	13	26	39	74	100	125

HORACE & DOTTY DRIPPLE (Dotty Dripple No. 1-24)
Harvey Publications: No. 25, Aug, 1952 - No. 43, Oct, 1955

	GD 2.0	VG 4.0	FN 6.0	VF 8.0	VF/NM 9.0	NM- 9.2
25-43	4	7	10	14	17	20

HORIZONTAL LIEUTENANT, THE (See Movie Classics)

HOROBI
Viz Premiere Comics: 1990 - No. 8, 1990 ($3.75, B&W, mature readers, 84 pgs.) V2#1, 1990 - No. 7, 1991 ($4.25, B&W, 68 pgs.)

	GD 2.0	VG 4.0	FN 6.0	VF 8.0	VF/NM 9.0	NM- 9.2
1-8: Japanese manga, Part Two, #1-7						4.50

HORRIFIC (Terrific No. 14 on)
Artful/Comic Media/Harwell/Mystery: Sept, 1952 - No. 13, Sept, 1954

	GD 2.0	VG 4.0	FN 6.0	VF 8.0	VF/NM 9.0	NM- 9.2
1	50	100	150	300	450	600
2	30	60	90	170	240	310
3-Bullet in head-c	52	104	156	312	469	625
4,5,7,9,10: 4-Shrunken head-c. 7-Guillotine-c	26	52	78	150	210	270
6-Jack The Ripper story	27	54	81	155	218	280
8-Origin & 1st app. The Teller (E.C. parody)	30	60	90	173	244	315
11-13: 11-Swipe/Witches Tales #6,27; Devil-c	21	42	63	121	168	215

NOTE: ***Don Heck** a-8; c-3-13. **Hollingsworth** a-4. **Morisi** a-8. **Palais** a-5, 7-12.*

HORROR FROM THE TOMB (Mysterious Stories No. 2 on)
Premier Magazine Co.: Sept, 1954

	GD 2.0	VG 4.0	FN 6.0	VF 8.0	VF/NM 9.0	NM- 9.2
1-Woodbridge/Torres, Check-a; The Keeper of the Graveyard is host	40	80	120	240	350	460

HORRORIST, THE (Also see Hellblazer)
DC Comics (Vertigo): Dec, 1995 - No. 2, Jan, 1996 ($5.95, lim. series, mature)

	GD 2.0	VG 4.0	FN 6.0	VF 8.0	VF/NM 9.0	NM- 9.2
1,2: Jamie Delano scripts, David Lloyd-c/a; John Constantine (Hellblazer) app.						6.00

HORROR OF COLLIER COUNTY
Dark Horse Comics: Oct, 1999 - No. 5, Feb, 2000 ($2.95, B&W, limited series)

	GD 2.0	VG 4.0	FN 6.0	VF 8.0	VF/NM 9.0	NM- 9.2
1-5-Rich Tommaso-s/a						3.00

HORRORS, THE (Formerly Startling Terror Tales #10)
Star Publications: No. 11, Jan, 1953 - No. 15, Apr, 1954

	GD 2.0	VG 4.0	FN 6.0	VF 8.0	VF/NM 9.0	NM- 9.2
11-Horrors of War; Disbrow-a(2)	31	62	93	175	248	320
12-Horrors of War; color illo in **POP**	29	58	87	164	232	300
13-Horrors of Mystery; crime stories	27	54	81	153	214	275
14,15-Horrors of the Underworld; crime stories	29	58	87	164	232	300

NOTE: *All have **L. B. Cole** covers; a-12. **Hollingsworth** a-13. **Palais** a-13r.*

HORROR TALES (Magazine)
Eerie Publications: V1#7, 6/69 - V6#6, 12/74; V7#1, 2/75; V7#2, 5/76 - V8#5, 1977; V9#1-3, 8/78; V10#1(2/79) (V1-V6: 52 pgs.; V7, V8#2: 112 pgs.; V8#4 on: 68 pgs.) (No V5#3, V8#1,3)

	GD 2.0	VG 4.0	FN 6.0	VF 8.0	VF/NM 9.0	NM- 9.2
V1#7	4	8	12	29	40	50
V1#8,9	3	7	10	21	28	35
V2#1-6('70), V3#1-6('71), V4#1-3,5-7('72)	3	6	9	18	24	30
V4#4-LSD story reprint/Weird V3#5	4	8	12	25	33	42

Hot Rods and Racing Cars #2 © CC

Hot Stuff, The Little Devil #3 © HARV

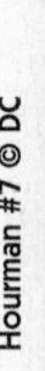
Hourman #7 © DC

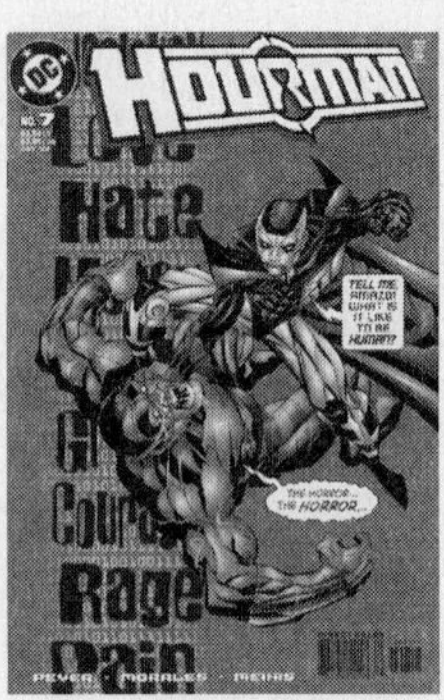

	GD 2.0	VG 4.0	FN 6.0	VF 8.0	VF/NM 9.0	NM- 9.2
V5#1,2,4,5(6/73),5(10/73),6(12/73),V6#1-6('74),V7#1,2,4('76),V7#3('76)-Giant issue, V8#2,4,5('77)	3	6	9	18	24	30
V9#1-3(11/78, $1.50), V10#1(2/79)	4	8	12	22	30	38

NOTE: *Bondage-c-V6#1, 3, V7#2.*

HORSE FEATHERS COMICS
Lev Gleason Publ.: Nov, 1945 - No. 4, July(Summer on-c), 1948 (52 pgs.)

	GD	VG	FN	VF	VF/NM	NM-
1-Wolverton's Scoop Scuttle, 2 pgs.	20	40	60	112	156	200
2	10	20	30	58	77	95
3,4: 3-(5/48)	8	16	24	46	58	70

HORSEMAN
Crusade Comics/Kevlar Studios: Mar, 1996 - No. 3, Nov, 1997 ($2.95)

	GD	VG	FN	VF	VF/NM	NM-
0-1st Kevlar Studios issue, 1-(3/96)-Crusade issue; Shi-c/app., 1-(11/96)-3-(11/97)-Kevlar Studios						3.00

HORSEMASTERS, THE (Disney)(TV, Movie)
Dell Publishing Co.: No. 1260, Dec-Feb, 1961/62

	GD	VG	FN	VF	VF/NM	NM-
Four Color 1260-Annette Funicello photo-c	14	28	42	99	145	190

HORSE SOLDIERS, THE
Dell Publishing Co.: No. 1048, Nov-Jan, 1959/60 (John Wayne movie)

	GD	VG	FN	VF	VF/NM	NM-
Four Color 1048-Painted-c, Sekowsky-a	15	30	45	104	152	200

HORSE WITHOUT A HEAD, THE (See Movie Comics)

HOT DOG
Magazine Enterprises: June-July, 1954 - No. 4, Dec-Jan, 1954-55

	GD	VG	FN	VF	VF/NM	NM-
1(A-1 #107)	8	16	24	46	58	70
2,3(A-1 #115),4(A-1 #136)	6	12	18	31	38	45

HOT DOG (See Jughead's Pal, Hotdog)

HOTEL DEPAREE - SUNDANCE (TV)
Dell Publishing Co.: No. 1126, Aug-Oct, 1960 (one-shot)

	GD	VG	FN	VF	VF/NM	NM-
Four Color 1126-Earl Holliman photo-c	7	14	21	51	71	90

HOT ROD AND SPEEDWAY COMICS
Hillman Periodicals: Feb-Mar, 1952 - No. 5, Apr-May, 1953

	GD	VG	FN	VF	VF/NM	NM-
1	29	58	87	164	232	300
2-Krigstein-a	20	40	60	112	156	200
3-5	11	22	33	66	88	110

HOT ROD COMICS (...Featuring Clint Curtis) (See XMas Comics)
Fawcett Publications: Nov, 1951 (no month given) - V2#7, Feb, 1953

	GD	VG	FN	VF	VF/NM	NM-
nn (V1#1)-Powell-c/a in all	34	68	102	196	278	360
2 (4/52)	19	38	57	106	146	185
3-6, V2#7	14	28	42	79	107	135

HOT ROD KING (Also see Speed Smith the Hot Rod King)
Ziff-Davis Publ. Co.: Fall, 1952

	GD	VG	FN	VF	VF/NM	NM-
1-Giacoia-a; Saunders painted-c	28	56	84	159	225	290

HOT ROD RACERS (Grand Prix No. 16 on)
Charlton Comics: Dec, 1964 - No. 15, July, 1967

	GD	VG	FN	VF	VF/NM	NM-
1	8	16	24	58	82	105
2-5	5	10	15	36	48	60
6-15	4	8	12	27	36	45

HOT RODS AND RACING CARS
Charlton Comics (Motor Mag. No. 1): Nov, 1951 - No. 120, June, 1973

	GD	VG	FN	VF	VF/NM	NM-
1-Speed Davis begins; Indianapolis 500 story	29	58	87	164	232	300
2	15	30	45	86	118	150
3-10	10	20	30	60	80	100
11-20	9	18	27	52	66	80
21-33,36-40	8	16	24	43	54	65
34, 35 (? & 6/58, 68 pgs.)	10	20	30	58	77	95
41-60	7	14	21	35	43	50
61-80	3	7	10	21	28	35
81-100	3	6	9	16	20	25
101-120	2	4	6	12	16	20

HOT SHOT CHARLIE
Hillman Periodicals: 1947 (Lee Elias)

	GD	VG	FN	VF	VF/NM	NM-
1	10	20	30	58	77	95

HOT SHOTS: AVENGERS
Marvel Comics: Oct, 1995 ($2.95, one-shot)

	GD	VG	FN	VF	VF/NM	NM-
nn-pin-ups						3.00

HOTSPUR
Eclipse Comics: Jun, 1987 - No. 3, Sep, 1987 ($1.75, lim. series, Baxter paper)

	GD	VG	FN	VF	VF/NM	NM-
1-3						3.00

HOT STUFF (See Stumbo Tinytown)
Harvey Comics: V2#1, Sept, 1991 - No. 12, June, 1994 ($1.00)

	GD	VG	FN	VF	VF/NM	NM-
V2#1-Stumbo back-up story						4.00
2-12 ($1.50)						3.00
...Big Book 1 (11/92), 2 (6/93) (Both $1.95, 52 pgs.)						4.00

HOT STUFF CREEPY CAVES
Harvey Publications: Nov, 1974 - No. 7, Nov, 1975

	GD	VG	FN	VF	VF/NM	NM-
1	4	8	12	25	33	42
2-7	3	6	9	16	20	24

HOT STUFF DIGEST
Harvey Comics: July, 1992 - No. 5, Nov, 1993 ($1.75, digest-size)

	GD	VG	FN	VF	VF/NM	NM-
V2#1-Hot Stuff, Stumbo, Richie Rich stories						6.00
2-5						4.00

HOT STUFF GIANT SIZE
Harvey Comics: Oct, 1992 - No. 3, Oct, 1993 ($2.25, 68 pgs.)

	GD	VG	FN	VF	VF/NM	NM-
V2#1-Hot Stuff & Stumbo stories						4.50
2,3						3.50

HOT STUFF SIZZLERS
Harvey Publications: July, 1960 - No. 59, Mar, 1974; V2#1, Aug, 1992

	GD	VG	FN	VF	VF/NM	NM-
1- 84 pgs. begin, ends #5; Hot Stuff, Stumbo begin	15	30	45	104	152	200
2-5	7	14	21	51	71	90
6-10: 6-68 pgs. begin, ends #45	5	10	15	36	48	60
11-20	4	8	12	27	36	45
21-45	3	6	9	18	24	30
46-52: 52 pgs. begin	2	4	6	14	18	22
53-59	2	4	6	10	12	15
V2#1-(8/92, $1.25)-Stumbo back-up						5.00

HOT STUFF, THE LITTLE DEVIL (Also see Devil Kids & Harvey Hits)
Harvey Publications (Illustrated Humor): 10/57 - No. 141, 7/77; No. 142, 2/78 - No. 164, 8/82; No. 165, 10/86 - No. 171, 11/87; No. 172, 11/88; No. 173, Sept, 1990 - No. 177, 1/91

	GD	VG	FN	VF	VF/NM	NM-
1	40	80	120	300	450	600
2-1st app. Stumbo the Giant (12/57)	21	42	63	147	216	285
3-5	15	30	45	104	152	200
6-10	9	18	27	65	93	120
11-20	7	14	21	50	68	85
21-40	5	10	15	33	44	55
41-60	3	7	10	21	28	35
61-80	3	6	9	18	23	28
81-105	2	4	6	12	16	20
106-112: All 52 pg. Giants	3	6	9	18	23	28
113-125	2	4	6	8	10	12
126-141	1	2	3	5	7	9
142-177: 172-177-($1.00)						6.00

HOT WHEELS (TV)
National Periodical Publications: Mar-Apr, 1970 - No. 6, Jan-Feb, 1971

	GD	VG	FN	VF	VF/NM	NM-
1	10	20	30	70	100	130
2,4,5	6	12	18	38	52	65
3-Neal Adams-c	6	12	18	43	59	75
6-Neal Adams-c/a	8	16	24	53	75	95

NOTE: ***Toth** a-1p, 2-5; c-1p, 5.*

HOURMAN (Justice Society member, see Adventure Comics #48)

HOURMAN (See JLA and DC One Million)
DC Comics: Apr, 1999 - No. 25, Apr, 2001 ($2.50)

	GD	VG	FN	VF	VF/NM	NM-
1-25: 1-JLA app.; McDaniel-c. 2-Tomorrow Woman-c/app. 6,7-Amazo app. 11-13-Justice Legion A app. 16-Silver Age flashback. 18,19-JSA-c/app. 22-Harris-c/a. 24-Hourman Vs. Rex Tyler						2.50

HOUSE OF MYSTERY (See Brave and the Bold #93, Elvira's House of Mystery, Limited Collectors' Edition & Super DC Giant)

HOUSE OF MYSTERY, THE
National Periodical Publications/DC Comics: Dec-Jan, 1951-52 - No. 321, Oct, 1983 (No. 194-203: 52 pgs.)

	GD	VG	FN	VF	VF/NM	NM-
1-DC's first horror comic	228	456	684	1425	2138	2850
2	90	180	270	563	844	1125
3	64	128	192	400	600	800
4,5	51	102	153	306	458	610

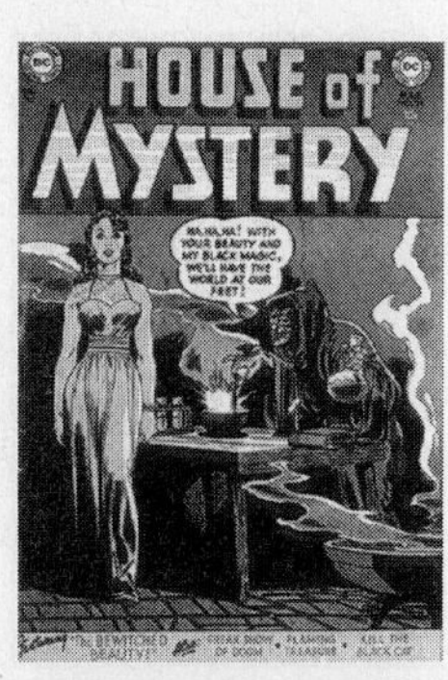

House of Mystery #24 © DC

House of Mystery #204 © DC

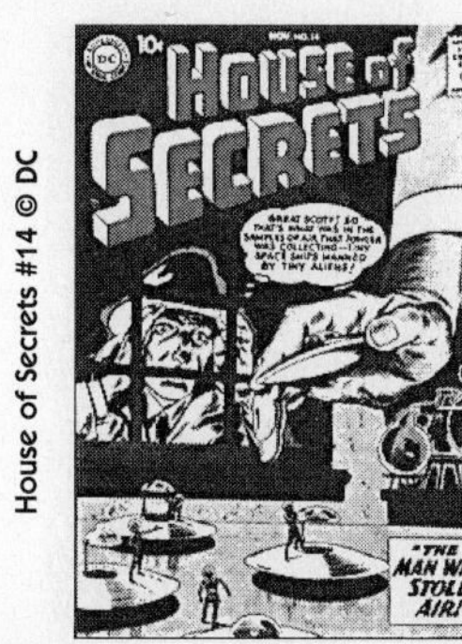

House of Secrets #14 © DC

	GD 2.0	VG 4.0	FN 6.0	VF 8.0	VF/NM 9.0	NM- 9.2
6-10	44	88	132	264	395	525
11-15	39	78	117	230	325	420
16(7/53)-25	30	60	90	170	240	310
26-35(2/55)-Last pre-code issue; 30-Woodish-a	24	48	72	135	190	245
36-50: 50-Text story of Orson Welles' War of the Worlds broadcast	14	28	42	99	145	190
51-60: 55-1st S.A. issue	11	22	33	77	114	150
61,63,65,66,70,72,76,85-Kirby-a	13	26	39	90	133	175
62,64,67-69,71,73-75,77-83,86-99	10	20	30	67	96	125
84-Prototype of Negative Man (Doom Patrol)	13	26	39	90	133	175
100 (7/60)	10	20	30	72	104	135
101-116: 109-Toth, Kubert-a. 116-Last 10¢ issue	9	18	27	63	89	115
117-130: 117-Swipes-c to HOS #20. 120-Toth-a	8	16	24	55	78	100
131-142	7	14	21	50	68	85
143-J'onn J'onzz, Manhunter begins (6/64), ends #173; story continues from Detective #326; intro. Idol-Head of Diabolu	22	44	66	156	228	300
144	10	20	30	70	100	130
145-155,157-159: 149-Toth-a. 155-The Human Hurricane app. (12/65), Red Tornado prototype. 158-Origin Diabolu Idol-Head	7	14	21	50	68	85
156-Robby Reed begins (origin/1st app.), ends #173	9	18	27	63	89	115
160-(7/66)-Robby Reed becomes Plastic Man in this issue only; 1st S.A. app. Plastic Man; intro Marco Xavier (Martian Manhunter) & Vulture Crime Organization; ends #173	11	22	33	75	110	145
161-173: 169-Origin/1st app. Gem Girl	5	10	15	36	48	60
174-Mystery format begins.	8	16	24	53	74	95
175-1st app. Cain (House of Mystery host)	6	12	18	40	55	70
176,177	5	10	15	36	48	60
178-Neal Adams-a (2/69)	6	12	18	43	59	75
179-N. Adams/Orlando, Wrightson-a (1st pro work, 3 pgs.)	8	16	24	58	82	105
180,181,183: Wrightson-a (3,10, & 3 pgs.). 180-Last 12¢ issue; Kane/Wood-a(2). 183-Wood-a	5	10	15	36	48	60
182,184: 182-Toth-a. 184-Kane/Wood, Toth-a	4	8	12	24	32	40
185-Williamson/Kaluta-a; Howard-a (3 pgs.)	4	8	12	27	36	45
186-N. Adams-c/a; Wrightson-a (10 pgs.)	5	10	15	36	48	60
187,190: Adams-c. 187-Toth-a. 190-Toth-a(r)	3	7	10	21	28	35
188-Wrightson-a (8 & 3pgs.); Adams-c	4	8	12	29	40	50
189,192,197: Adams-c on all. 189-Wood-a(i). 192-Last 15¢-c	3	7	10	21	28	35
191-Wrightson-a (8 & 3pgs.); Adams-c	4	8	12	29	40	50
193-Wrightson-c	4	8	12	22	30	38
194-Wrightson-c; 52 pgs begin, end #203; Toth,Kirby-a	4	8	12	29	40	50
195: Wrightson-c. Swamp creature story by Wrightson similar to Swamp Thing (10 pgs.)(10/71)	6	12	18	40	55	70
196,198	4	8	12	22	30	38
199-Adams-c; Wood-a(8pgs.); Kirby-a	4	8	12	27	36	45
200-(25¢, 52 pgs.)-One third-r (3/72)	4	8	12	28	38	48
201-203-(25¢, 52 pgs.)-One third-r	4	8	12	22	30	38
204-Wrightson-c/a, 9 pgs.	3	7	10	21	28	35
205,206,208,210,212,215,216,218	2	4	6	14	18	22
207-Wrightson c/a; Starlin, Redondo-a	3	6	9	19	25	32
209,211,213,214,217,219-Wrightson-c	3	6	9	16	20	25
220,222,223	2	4	6	11	14	18
221-Wrightson/Kaluta-a(8 pgs.)	3	6	9	19	25	32
224-229: 224-Wrightson-r from Spectre #9; Dillin/Adams-r from House of Secrets #82; begin 100 pg. issues; Phantom Stranger-r. 225,227-(100 pgs.): 225-Spectre app. 226-Wrightson/Redondo-a Phantom Stranger-r. 228-N. Adams inks; Wrightson-r. 229-Wrightson-a(r); Toth-r; last 100 pg. issue	5	10	15	33	44	55
230,232-235,237-250	2	4	6	9	11	14
231-Classic Wrightson-c	3	6	9	18	23	28
236-Wrightson-c; Ditko-a(p); N. Adams-i	2	4	6	11	14	18
251-254-(84 pgs.)-Adams-c. 251-Wood-a	2	4	6	14	18	22
255,256-(84 pgs.)-Wrightson-c	2	4	6	14	18	22
257-259-(84 pgs.)	2	4	6	12	16	20
260-289: 282-(68 pgs.)-Has extra story "The Computers That Saved Metropolis" Radio Shack giveaway by Jim Starlin	1	2	3	5	7	9
290-1st "I, Vampire"	2	4	6	12	16	20
291-299- "I, Vampire"	2	4	6	8	10	12
300,319,321: Death of "I, Vampire"	2	4	6	9	11	14
301-318,320: 301-318-"I, Vampire"	2	4	6	8	10	12
Welcome to the House of Mystery (7/98, $5.95) reprints stories with new framing story by Gaiman and Aragonés						6.00

NOTE: ***Neal Adams*** *a-236i; c-175-192, 197, 199, 251-254.* ***Alcala*** *a-209, 217, 219, 224, 227.* ***M. Anderson*** *a-212; c/a-37.* ***Aparo*** *a-209.* ***Aragones*** *a-185, 186, 194, 196, 200, 202, 229, 251.* ***Baily*** *a-279p.* ***Cameron*** *a-76, 79.* ***Colan*** *a-202r.* ***Craig*** *a-263, 275, 295, 300.* ***Dillin/Adams*** *r-224.* ***Ditko*** *a-236p, 247, 254, 258, 276; c-277.* ***Drucker*** *a-37.* ***Evans*** *c-218.* ***Fraden*** *a-251.* ***Giffen*** *a-284.* ***Giunta*** *a-199, 227r.* ***Golden*** *a-257, 259.* ***Heath*** *a-194r; c-203.* ***Howard*** *a-182, 185, 187, 196, 229r, 247i, 254, 279i.* ***Kaluta*** *a-195, 200, 250r; c-200-202, 210, 212, 233, 260, 261, 263, 265, 267, 268, 273, 276, 284, 287, 288, 293-295, 300, 302, 304, 305, 309-319, 321.* ***Bob Kane*** *a-84.* ***Gil Kane*** *a-196p, 253p, 300p.* ***Kirby*** *a-194r, 199r; c-65, 76, 78, 79, 85.* ***Kubert*** *c-282, 283, 285, 286, 289-292, 297-299, 301, 303, 306-308.* ***Maneely*** *a-68, 227r.* ***Mayer*** *a-317p.* ***Meskin*** *a-52-144 (most), 195r, 224r, 229r; c-63, 66, 124, 127.* ***Mooney*** *a-24, 159, 160.* ***Moreira*** *a-3, 4, 20-50, 58, 59, 62, 68, 77, 79, 90, 108, 113, 123, 201r, 228; c-4-28, 44, 47, 50, 54, 59, 62, 64, 68, 70, 73.* ***Morrow*** *a-192, 196, 255, 320i.* ***Mortimer*** *a-204(3 pgs.).* ***Nasser*** *a-276.* ***Newton*** *a-259, 272.* ***Nino*** *a-204, 212, 213, 220, 224, 225, 245, 250, 252-256, 283.* ***Orlando*** *a-175(2 pgs.), 178, 240i; c-240, 258p, 262, 264p, 270p, 271, 272, 274, 275, 278, 296i.* ***Redondo*** *a-194, 195, 197, 202, 203, 207, 211, 214, 217, 219, 226, 227, 229, 235, 241, 287(layout), 302p, 303i, 308; c-229.* ***Reese*** *a-195, 200, 205i.* ***Rogers*** *a-254, 274, 277.* ***Roussos*** *a-65, 84, 224i.* ***Sekowsky*** *a-282p.* ***Sparling*** *a-203.* ***Starlin*** *a-207(2 pgs.), 282p; c-281.* ***Leonard Starr*** *a-9.* ***Staton*** *a-300p.* ***Sutton*** *a-189, 271, 290, 291, 293, 295, 297-299, 302, 303, 306-309, 310-313i, 314.* ***Tuska*** *a-293p, 294p, 316p.* ***Wrightson*** *c-193-195, 204, 207, 209, 211, 213, 214, 217, 219, 221, 231, 236, 255, 256; r-224.*

HOUSE OF SECRETS (Combined with The Unexpected after #154)
National Periodical Publications/DC Comics: 11-12/56 - No. 80, 9-10/66; No. 81, 8-9/69 - No. 140, 2-3/76; No. 141, 8-9/76 - No. 154, 10-11/78

	GD 2.0	VG 4.0	FN 6.0	VF 8.0	VF/NM 9.0	NM- 9.2
1-Drucker-a; Moreira-c	111	222	333	944	1447	1950
2-Moreira-a	42	84	126	336	506	675
3-Kirby-c/a	37	74	111	278	414	550
4-Kirby-a	29	58	87	210	305	400
5-7	20	40	60	140	205	270
8-Kirby-a	23	46	69	167	244	320
9-11: 11-Lou Cameron-a (unsigned)	17	34	51	123	182	240
12-Kirby-c/a; Lou Cameron-a	19	38	57	138	202	265
13-15: 14-Flying saucer-c	13	26	39	94	137	180
16-20	12	24	36	82	121	160
21,22,24-30	10	20	30	72	104	135
23-1st app. Mark Merlin & begin series (8/59)	12	24	36	82	121	160
31-50: 48-Toth-a. 50-Last 10¢ issue	9	18	27	65	93	120
51-60: 58-Origin Mark Merlin	8	16	24	55	78	100
61-First Eclipso (7-8/63) and begin series	17	34	51	123	182	240
62	9	18	27	65	93	120
63-65-Toth-a on Eclipso (see Brave and the Bold #64)	8	16	24	53	74	95
66-1st Eclipso-c (also #67,70,78,79); Toth-a	9	18	27	65	93	120
67,73: 67-Toth-a on Eclipso. 73-Mark Merlin becomes Prince Ra-Man (1st app.)	8	16	24	53	74	95
68-72,74-80: 76-Prince Ra-Man vs. Eclipso. 80-Eclipso, Prince Ra-Man end	7	14	21	50	68	85
81-Mystery format begins; 1st app. Abel (House Of Secrets host); (cameo in DC Special #4)	7	14	21	51	71	90
82-84: 82-Neal Adams-c(i)	4	8	12	27	36	45
85,90: 85-N. Adams-a(i). 90-Buckler (early work)/N. Adams-a(i)	4	8	12	29	40	50
86,88,89,91	4	8	12	22	30	38
87-Wrightson & Kaluta-a	5	10	15	33	44	55
92-1st app. Swamp Thing-c/story (8 pgs.)(6-7/71) by Berni Wrightson(p) w/JeffJones/Kaluta/Weiss ink assists; classic-c.	50	100	150	400	600	800
93,95,97,98-(52 pgs.)-Wrightson-c	4	8	12	27	36	45
94,96-(52 pgs.)-Wrightson-c. 94-Wrightson-a(i); 96-Wood-a	4	8	12	27	36	45
99-Wrightson splash pg.	3	7	10	21	28	35
100-Classic Wrightson-c	4	8	12	28	38	48
101,102,104,105,108-120	2	4	6	11	14	18
103,106,107-Wrightson-c	3	6	9	16	20	25
121-133	2	4	6	8	10	12
134-136,139-Wrightson-a	2	4	6	10	13	16
137,138,141-154	1	2	3	5	7	9
140-1st solo origin of the Patchworkman (see Swamp Thing #3)	3	6	9	16	20	24

NOTE: ***Neal Adams*** *c-81, 82, 84-88, 90, 91.* ***Alcala*** *a-104-107.* ***Anderson*** *a-91. Aparo a-93, 97, 105.* ***B. Bailey*** *a-107.* ***Cameron*** *a-13, 15.* ***Colan*** *a-63.* ***Ditko*** *a-139p, 148.* ***Elias*** *a-58.* ***Evans*** *a-118.* ***Finlay*** *a-7r(Real Fact?).* ***Glanzman*** *a-91.* ***Golden*** *a-151.* ***Heath*** *a-31.* ***Heck*** *a-85.* ***Kaluta*** *a-87, 98, 99; c-98, 99, 101, 102, 105, 149, 151, 154.* ***Bob Kane*** *a-18, 21.* ***G. Kane*** *a-85p.* ***Kirby*** *c-3, 11, 12.* ***Kubert*** *a-39.* ***Meskin*** *a-2-68 (most), 94r; c-55-60.* ***Moreira*** *a-7, 8, 51, 54, 102-104, 106, 108, 113, 116, 118, 121, 123, 127; c-1, 2, 4-10, 13-20.* ***Morrow*** *a-86, 89, 90; c-89, 146-148.* ***Nino*** *a-101, 103, 106, 109, 115, 117, 126, 128, 131, 147, 153.* ***Redondo*** *a-95, 99, 102, 104p, 113, 116, 134, 136, 139, 140.* ***Reese*** *a-85.* ***Severin*** *a-91.* ***Starlin*** *c-150.* ***Sutton*** *a-154.* ***Toth*** *a-63-67, 83, 93r, 94r, 96r-98r, 123.* ***Tuska*** *a-90, 104.* ***Wrightson*** *a-134; c-92-94, 96, 100, 103, 106, 107, 135, 136, 139.*

HOUSE OF SECRETS
DC Comics (Vertigo): Oct, 1996 - No. 25, Dec, 1998 ($2.50) (Creator-owned series)

	NM- 9.2
1-Steven Seagle-s/Kristiansen-c/a.	3.50
2-25: 5,7-Kristiansen-c/a. 6-Fegrado-a	3.00
TPB-(1997, $14.95) r/1-5	15.00

HOUSE OF SECRETS: FACADE

Howard the Duck #11 © MAR

Howdy Doody #3 © Cal. Nat. Prod.

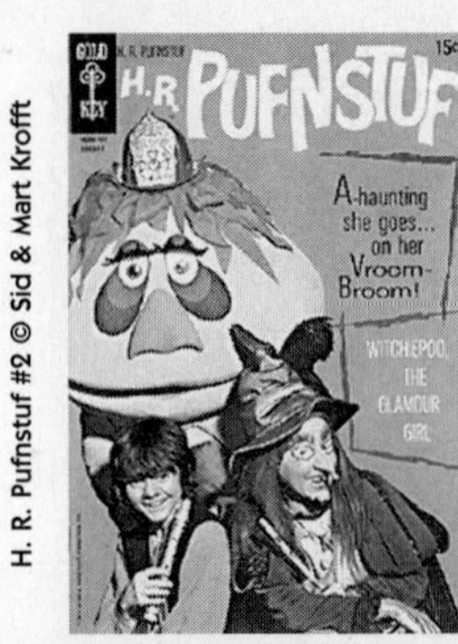

H. R. Pufnstuf #2 © Sid & Mart Krofft

	GD 2.0	VG 4.0	FN 6.0	VF 8.0	VF/NM 9.0	NM- 9.2

DC Comics (Vertigo): 2001 - No. 2, 2001 ($5.95, limited series)

1,2-Steven Seagle-s/Teddy Kristiansen-c/a. 6.00

HOUSE OF TERROR (3-D)
St. John Publishing Co.: Oct, 1953 (25¢, came w/glasses)

1-Kubert, Baker-a 33 66 99 190 270 350

HOUSE OF YANG, THE (See Yang)
Charlton Comics: July, 1975 - No. 6, June, 1976; 1978

1-Sanho Kim-a in all 2 4 6 11 14 18
2-6 1 2 3 5 7 9
Modern Comics #1,2(1978) 4.00

HOUSE ON THE BORDERLAND
DC Comics (Vertigo): 2000 ($29.95, hardcover, one-shot)

HC-Adaptation of William Hope Hodgson book; Corben-a 30.00
SC (2003, $19.95) 20.00

HOUSE II: THE SECOND STORY
Marvel Comics: Oct, 1987 (One-shot)

1-Adapts movie 2.50

HOWARD CHAYKIN'S AMERICAN FLAGG (See American Flagg!)
First Comics: V2#1, May, 1988 - V2#12, Apr, 1989 ($1.75/$1.95, Baxter paper)

V2#1-9,11,12-Chaykin-c(p) in all 2.25
10-Elvis Presley photo-c 3.00

HOWARD THE DUCK (See Bizarre Adventures #34, Crazy Magazine, Fear, Man-Thing, Marvel Treasury Edition & Sensational She-Hulk #14-17)
Marvel Comics Group: Jan, 1976 - No. 31, May, 1979; No. 32, Jan, 1986; No. 33, Sept, 1986

1-Brunner-c/a; Spider-Man x-over (low distr.) 3 6 9 18 23 28
2-Brunner-c/a 2 4 6 8 10 12
3,4-(Regular 25¢ edition). 3-Buscema-a(p), (7/76) 1 2 3 5 7 9
3,4-(30¢-c, limited distribution) 2 4 6 10 12 15
5 1 2 3 5 7 9
6-11: 8-Howard The Duck for president. 9-1st Sgt. Preston Dudley of RCMP.
10-Spider-Man-c/sty 6.00
12-1st app. Kiss (cameo, 3/77) 3 6 9 18 24 30
13-(30¢-c) Kiss app. (1st full story, 6/77); Daimon Hellstrom app. plus cameo of Howard as Son of Satan 3 7 10 21 28 35
13-(35¢-c, limited distribution) 4 8 12 29 40 50
14-32: 14-17-(Regular 30¢-c). 14-Howard as Son of Satan-c/story; Son of Satan app. 16-Album issue; 3 pgs. comics. 22,23-Man-Thing-c/stories; Star Wars parody. 30,32-P. Smith-a 4.00
14-17-(35¢-c, limited distribution) 6.00
33-Last issue; low print run 6.00
Annual 1(1977, 52 pgs.)-Mayerik-a 1 2 3 4 5 7

NOTE: ***Austin*** *c-29i.* ***Bolland*** *c-33.* ***Brunner*** *a-1p, 2p; c-1, 2.* ***Buckler*** *c-3p.* ***Buscema*** *a-3p.* ***Colan*** *a(p)-4-15, 17-20, 24-27, 30, 31; c(p)-4-31, Annual 1p.* ***Leialoha*** *a-1-13i; c(i)-3-5, 8-11.* ***Mayerik*** *a-22, 23, 33.* ***Paul Smith*** *a-30p, 32. Man-Thing app. in #22, 23.*

HOWARD THE DUCK (Magazine)
Marvel Comics Group: Oct, 1979 - No. 9, Mar, 1981 (B&W, 68 pgs.)

1-Art by Colan, Janson, Golden. Kidney Lady app. 1 3 4 6 8 10
2,3,5-9 (nudity in most): 2-Mayerick-c. 3-Xmas issue; Jack Davis-c; Duck World flashback. 5-Dracula app. 6-1st Street People back-up story. 7-Has poster by Byrne; Man-Thing-c/s (46 pgs.). 8-Batman parody w/Marshall Rogers-a; Dave Sim-a (1 pg.). 9-Marie Severin-a; John Pound painted-c 5.00
4-Beatles, John Lennon, Elvis, Kiss & Devo cameos; Hitler app. 2 4 6 8 10 12

NOTE: ***Buscema*** *a-4p.* ***Colan*** *a-1-5p, 7-9p.* ***Jack Davis*** *c-3.* ***Golden*** *a(p)-1, 5, 6(51pgs.).* ***Rogers*** *a-7, 8.* ***Simonson*** *a-7.*

HOWARD THE DUCK (Volume 2)
Marvel Comics: Mar, 2002 - No. 6, Aug, 2002 ($2.99)

1-Gerber-s/Winslade-a/Fabry-c 4.00
2-6: 2,4-6-Gerber-s/Winslade-a/Fabry-c. 3-Fabry-a/c 3.00
TPB (9/02, $14.99) r/#1-6 15.00

HOWARD THE DUCK HOLIDAY SPECIAL
Marvel Comics: Feb, 1997 ($2.50, one-shot)

1-Wraparound-c; Hama-s 2.50

HOWARD THE DUCK: THE MOVIE
Marvel Comics Group: Dec, 1986 - No. 3, Feb, 1987 (Limited series)

1-3: Movie adaptation; r/Marvel Super Special 2.50

HOW BOYS AND GIRLS CAN HELP WIN THE WAR
The Parents' Magazine Institute: 1942 (10¢, one-shot)

1-All proceeds used to buy war bonds 26 52 78 150 210 270

HOWDY DOODY (TV)(See Jackpot of Fun-- & Poll Parrot)
Dell Publishing Co.: 1/50 - No. 38, 7-9/56; No. 761, 1/57; No. 811, 7/57

1-(Scarce)-Photo-c; 1st TV comic 92 184 276 731 1116 1500
2-Photo-c 40 80 120 300 450 600
3-5: All photo-c 25 50 75 176 258 340
6-Used in **SOTI**, pg. 309; classic-c; painted covers begin 26 52 78 189 275 360
7-10 17 34 51 118 174 230
11-20: 13-X-Mas-c 14 28 42 99 145 190
21-38, Four Color 761,811 11 22 33 80 118 155

HOW IT BEGAN
United Features Syndicate: No. 15, 1939 (one-shot)

Single Series 15 34 68 102 196 278 360

HOW SANTA GOT HIS RED SUIT (See March of Comics No. 2)

HOW THE WEST WAS WON (See Movie Comics)

HOW TO DRAW FOR THE COMICS
Street and Smith: No date (1942?) (10¢, 64 pgs., B&W & color, no ads)

nn-Art by Robert Winsor McCay (recreating his father's art), George Marcoux (Supersnipe artist), Vernon Greene (The Shadow artist), Jack Binder (with biog.), Thorton Fisher, Jon Small, & Jack Farr; has biographies of each artist 29 58 87 164 232 300

H. P. LOVECRAFT'S CTHULHU
Millennium Publications: Dec, 1991 - No. 3, May, 1992 ($2.50, limited series)

1-3: 1-Contains trading cards on thin stock 3.00

H. R. PUFNSTUF (TV) (See March of Comics #360)
Gold Key: Oct, 1970 - No. 8, July, 1972

1-Photo-c 21 42 63 149 220 290
2-8-Photo-c on all. 6,7-Both Gold Key and Whitman editions exist 11 22 33 75 110 145

HUBERT AT CAMP MOONBEAM
Dell Publishing Co.: No. 251, Oct, 1949 (one shot)

Four Color 251 6 12 18 38 52 65

HUCK & YOGI JAMBOREE (TV)
Dell Publishing Co.: Mar, 1961 ($1.00, 6-1/4x9", 116 pgs., cardboard-c, high quality paper) (B&W original material)

nn (scarce) 10 20 30 73 107 140

HUCK & YOGI WINTER SPORTS (TV)
Dell Publishing Co.: No. 1310, Mar, 1962 (Hanna-Barbara) (one-shot)

Four Color 1310 10 20 30 67 96 125

HUCK FINN (See The New Adventures of... & Power Record Comics)

HUCKLEBERRY FINN (Movie)
Dell Publishing Co.: No. 1114, July, 1960

Four Color 1114-Photo-c 6 12 18 40 55 70

HUCKLEBERRY HOUND (See Dell Giant #31,44, Golden Picture Story Book, Kite Fun Book, March of Comics #199, 214, 235, Spotlight #1 & Whitman Comic Books)

HUCKLEBERRY HOUND (TV)
Dell/Gold Key No. 18 (10/62) on: No. 990, 5-7/59 - No. 43, 10/70 (Hanna-Barbera)

Four Color 990(#1)-1st app. Huckleberry Hound, Yogi Bear, & Pixie & Dixie & Mr. Jinks 13 26 39 94 137 180
Four Color 1050,1054 (12/59) 9 18 27 63 89 115
3(1-2/60) - 7 (9-10/60), Four Color 1141 (10/60) 9 18 27 60 85 110
8-10 7 14 21 50 68 85
11,13-17 (6-8/62) 5 10 15 36 48 60
12-1st Hokey Wolf & Ding-a-Ling 6 12 18 40 55 70
18,19 (84pgs.; 18-20 titled ...Chuckleberry Tales) 9 18 27 60 85 110
20-Titled Chuckleberry Tales 5 10 15 33 44 55
21-30: 28-30-Reprints 4 8 12 27 36 45
31-43: 31,32,35,37-43-Reprints 3 7 10 21 28 35

HUCKLEBERRY HOUND (TV)
Charlton Comics: Nov, 1970 - No. 8, Jan, 1972 (Hanna-Barbera)

1 6 12 18 38 52 65
2-8 3 6 9 19 25 32

HUEY, DEWEY, & LOUIE (See Donald Duck, 1938 for 1st app. Also see Mickey Mouse Magazine V4#2, V5#7 & Walt Disney's Junior Woodchucks Limited Series)

Hulk: Gray #1 © MAR

Human Target #4 © DC

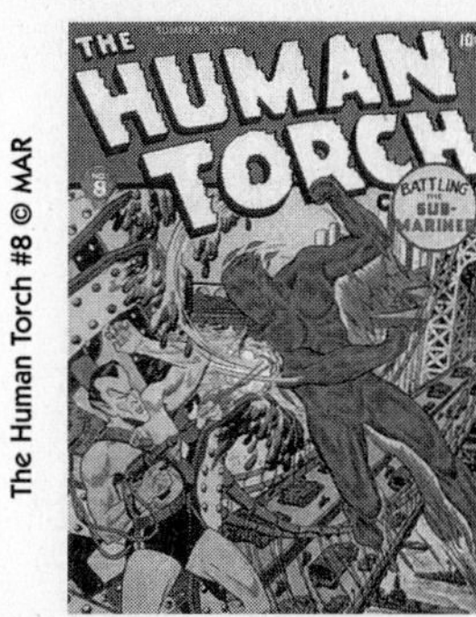

The Human Torch #8 © MAR

GD VG FN VF VF/NM NM-
2.0 4.0 6.0 8.0 9.0 9.2

HUEY, DEWEY, & LOUIE BACK TO SCHOOL (See Dell Giant #22, 35, 49 & Dell Giants)

HUEY, DEWEY, AND LOUIE JUNIOR WOODCHUCKS (Disney)
Gold Key No. 1-61/Whitman No. 62 on: Aug, 1966 - No. 81, July, 1984
(See Walt Disney's Comics & Stories #125)

1 6 12 18 43 59 75
2,3(12/68) 4 8 12 24 32 40
4,5(4/70)-r/two WDC&S D.Duck stories by Barks 4 8 12 22 30 38
6-17 3 6 9 19 25 32
18,27-30 3 6 9 16 20 24
19-23,25-New storyboarded scripts by Barks, 13-25 pgs. per issue
3 7 10 21 28 35
24,26: 26-r/Barks Donald Duck WDC&S stories 3 6 9 18 23 28
31-57,60,61: 35,41-r/Barks J.W. scripts 2 4 6 9 11 14
58,59: 58-r/Barks Donald Duck WDC&S stories 2 4 6 10 13 16
62-64 (Whitman) 2 4 6 10 13 16
65-(9/80), 66 (Pre-pack? scarce) 3 6 9 18 23 28
67 (1/81),68 2 4 6 12 16 20
69-74: 72(2/82), 73(2-3/82), 74(3/82) 2 4 6 11 14 18
75-81 (all #90183; pre-pack; nd, nd code; scarce): 75(4/83), 76(5/83), 77(7/83),
78(8/83), 79(4/84), 80(5/84), 81(7/84) 2 4 6 12 16 20

HUGGA BUNCH (TV)
Marvel Comics (Star Comics): Oct, 1986 - No. 6, Aug, 1987

1-6 4.00

HULK (Magazine)(Formerly The Rampaging Hulk)(Also see The Incredible Hulk)
Marvel Comics: No. 10, Aug., 1978 - No. 27, June, 1981 ($1.50)

10-18: 10-Bill Bixby interview. 11-Moon Knight begins. 12-15,17,18-Moon Knight stories.
12-Lou Ferrigno interview. 2 4 6 8 10 12
19-27: 20-Moon Knight story. 23-Last full color issue; Banner is attacked. 24-Part color,
Lou Ferrigno interview. 25-Part color. 26,27-are B&W
1 2 3 5 6 8

NOTE: #10-20 have fragile spines which split easily. ***Alcala*** *a(i)-15, 17-20, 22, 24-27.* ***Buscema*** *a-23; c-26.* ***Chaykin*** *a-21-25.* ***Colan*** *a(p)-11, 19, 24-27.* ***Jusko*** *painted c-12.* ***Nebres*** *a-16.* ***Severin*** *a-19i. Moon Knight by* ***Sienkiewicz*** *in 13-15, 17, 18, 20.* ***Simonson*** *a-27; c-23. Dominic Fortune appears in #21-24.*

HULK (Becomes Incredible Hulk Vol. 2 with issue #12)
Marvel Comics: Apr, 1999 - No. 11, Feb, 2000 ($2.99/$1.99)

1-($2.99) Byrne-s/Garney-a 5.00
1-Variant-c 9.00
1-DFE Remarked-c 50.00
1-Gold foil variant 10.00
2-7-($1.99): 2-Two covers. 5-Art by Jurgens, Buscema & Texeira. 7-Avengers app. 4.00
8-Hulk battles Wolverine 7.00
9-11: 11-She-Hulk app. 3.00
1999 Annual ($3.50) Chapter One story; Byrne-s/Weeks-a 3.50
Hulk Vs. The Thing (12/99, $3.99, TPB) reprints their notable battles 4.00

HULK: FUTURE IMPERFECT
Marvel Comics: Jan, 1993 - No. 2, Dec, 1992 (In error) ($5.95, 52 pgs., squarebound, limited series)

1,2: Embossed-c; Peter David story & George Perez-c/a. 1-1st app. Maestro.
1 2 3 5 6 8

HULK: GRAY
Marvel Comics: Dec, 2003 - No. 6 ($3.50, limited series)

1-4-Hulk's origin & early days; Loeb-s/Sale-a/c 3.50

HULK: NIGHTMERICA
Marvel Comics: Aug, 2003 - No. 6 ($2.99, limited series)

1-4-Brian Ashmore painted-a/c 3.00

HULK/ PITT
Marvel Comics: 1997 ($5.99, one-shot)

1-David-s/Keown-c/a 6.00

HULK SMASH
Marvel Comics: Mar, 2001 - No. 2, Apr, 2001 ($2.99, limited series)

1,2-Ennis-s/McCrea & Janson-a/Nowlan painted-c 3.00

HULK: THE MOVIE
Marvel Comics

...Adaptation (8/03, $3.50) Bruce Jones-s/Bagley-a/Keown-c 3.50
TPB (2003, $12.99) r/Adaptation, Ultimates #5, Inc. Hulk #34, Ult. Marvel Team-Up #2&3 13.00

HULK 2099
Marvel Comics: Dec, 1994 - No. 10, Sept, 1995 ($1.50/$1.95)

GD VG FN VF VF/NM NM-
2.0 4.0 6.0 8.0 9.0 9.2

1-($2.50)-Green foil-c 3.00
2-10: 2-A. Kubert-c 2.25

HULK/WOLVERINE: 6 HOURS
Marvel Comics: Mar, 2003 - No. 4, May, 2003 ($2.99, limited series)

1-4-Bruce Jones-s/Scott Kolins-a; Bisley-c 3.00
Hulk Legends Vol. 1: Hulk/Wolverine: 6 Hours (2003, $13.99, TPB) r/#1-4 & 1st Wolverine app.
from Incredible Hulk #181 14.00

HUMAN DEFENSE CORPS
DC Comics: Jul, 2003 - No. 6, Dec, 2003 ($2.50, limited series)

1-6-Ty Templeton-s/Sauve, Jr & Vlasco-a. 1-Lois Lane app. 2.50

HUMAN FLY
I.W. Enterprises/Super: 1963 - 1964 (Reprints)

I.W. Reprint #1-Reprints Blue Beetle #44('46) 2 4 6 14 18 22
Super Reprint #10-R/Blue Beetle #46('47) 2 4 6 14 18 22

HUMAN FLY, THE
Marvel Comics Group: Sept, 1977 - No. 19, Mar, 1979

1,2,9,19: 1,2-(Regular 30¢-c). 1-Origin; Spider-Man x-over. 2-Ghost Rider app.
9-Daredevil x-over; Byrne-c(p). 19-Last issue 1 2 3 5 6 8
1,2-(35¢-c, limited distribution) 2 4 6 8 10 12
3-8,10-18 4.00

NOTE: ***Austin*** *c-4i, 9i.* ***Elias*** *a-1, 3p, 4p, 7p, 10-12p, 15p, 18p, 19p.* ***Layton*** *c-19.*

HUMAN TARGET
DC Comics (Vertigo): Apr, 1999 - No. 4, July, 1999 ($2.95, limited series)

1-4-Milligan-s/Bradstreet-c/Biuković-a 3.00
TPB (2000, $12.95) new Bradstreet-c 13.00

HUMAN TARGET
DC Comics (Vertigo): Oct, 2003 - Present ($2.95)

1-5-Milligan-s/Pulido-a/c 3.00

HUMAN TARGET: FINAL CUT
DC Comics (Vertigo): 2002 ($29.95/$19.95, graphic novel)

Hardcover (2002, $29.95) Milligan-s/Pulido-a/c 30.00
Softcover (2003, $19.95) 20.00

HUMAN TARGET SPECIAL (TV)
DC Comics: Nov, 1991 ($2.00, 52 pgs., one-shot)

1 3.00

HUMAN TORCH, THE (Red Raven #1)(See All-Select, All Winners, Marvel Mystery, Men's Adventures, Mystic Comics (2nd series), Sub-Mariner, USA & Young Men)
Timely/Marvel Comics (TP 2,3/TCI 4-9/SePI 10/SnPC 11-25/CnPC 26-35/Atlas Comics (CPC 36-38)): No. 2, Fall, 1940 - No. 15, Spring, 1944; No. 16, Fall, 1944 - No. 35, Mar, 1949 (Becomes Love Tales #36 on); No. 36, April, 1954 - No. 38, Aug, 1954

2(#1)-Intro & Origin Toro; The Falcon, The Fiery Mask, Mantor the Magician, & Microman only app.; Human Torch by Burgos, Sub-Mariner by Everett begin (origin of each in text)
2750 5500 8250 20,800 32,400 44,000
3(#2)-40 pg. H.T. story; H.T. & S.M. battle over who is best artist in text-Everett or Burgos
497 994 1491 3479 5340 7200
4(#3)-Origin The Patriot in text; last Everett Sub-Mariner; Sid Greene-a
419 838 1257 2724 4187 5650
5(#4)-The Patriot app; Angel x-over in Sub-Mariner (Summer, 1941); 1st Nazi war-c this title
326 652 978 2119 3260 4400
5-Human Torch battles Sub-Mariner (Fall, '41); 60 pg. story
483 966 1449 3381 5191 7000
6,9 220 440 660 1375 2063 2750
7-1st Japanese war-c 228 456 684 1425 2138 2850
8-Human Torch battles Sub-Mariner; 52 pg. story; Wolverton-a, 1 pg.
326 652 978 2119 3260 4400
10-Human Torch battles Sub-Mariner, 45 pg. story; Wolverton-a, 1 pg.
288 576 864 1800 2700 3600
11,13-15: 14-1st Atlas Globe logo (Winter, 1943-44; see All Winners #11 also)
172 344 516 1075 1613 2150
12-Classic-c 308 616 924 1925 2888 3850
16-20: 20-Last War issue 122 244 366 763 1144 1525
21,22,24-30: 27-2nd app. (1st-c) Asbestos Lady (see Capt. America Comics #63 for 1st app.)
109 218 327 681 1021 1360
23 (Sum/46)-Becomes Junior Miss 24? Classic Schomburg Robot-c
128 256 384 800 1200 1600
31,32: 31-Namora x-over in Sub-Mariner (also #30); last Toro. 32-Sungirl,
Namora app.; Sungirl-c 94 188 282 588 882 1175
33-Capt. America x-over 98 196 294 606 916 1225

Humphrey Comics #16 © HARV

Hunter: The Age of Magic #4 © DC

Ibis, The Invincible #1 © FAW

	GD	VG	FN	VF	VF/NM	NM-
	2.0	4.0	6.0	8.0	9.0	9.2

34-Sungirl solo 85 170 255 531 796 1060
35-Captain America & Sungirl app. (1949) 94 188 282 588 882 1175
36-38(1954)-Sub-Mariner in all 85 170 255 531 796 1060
NOTE: ***Ayers*** *Human Torch in 36(3).* ***Brodsky*** *c-25, 31-33?, 37, 38.* ***Burgos*** *c-36.* ***Everett*** *a-1-3, 27, 28, 30, 37, 38.* ***Powell*** *a-36(Sub-Mariner).* ***Schomburg*** *c-1-3, 5-8, 10-23.* ***Sekowsky*** *c-28, 34?, 35?* ***Shores*** *c-24, 26, 27, 29, 30.* ***Mickey Spillane*** *text 4-6. Bondage c-2, 12, 19.*

HUMAN TORCH, THE (Also see Avengers West Coast, Fantastic Four, The Invaders, Saga of the Original... & Strange Tales #101)
Marvel Comics Group: Sept, 1974 - No. 8, Nov, 1975
1: 1-8-r/stories from Strange Tales #101-108 2 4 6 11 14 18
2-8: 1st H.T. title since G.A. 7-vs. Sub-Mariner 1 3 4 6 8 10
NOTE: *Golden Age & Silver Age Human Torch-r #1-8.* ***Ayers*** *r-6, 7.* ***Kirby/Ayers*** *r-1-5, 8.*

HUMAN TORCH (From the Fantastic Four)
Marvel Comics: June, 2003 - Present ($2.50/$2.99)
1-7-Skottie Young-c/a; Karl Kesel-s 2.50
8-($2.99) Dodd-a 3.00

HUMBUG (Satire by Harvey Kurtzman)
Humbug Publications: Aug, 1957 - No. 9, May, 1958; No. 10, June, 1958; No. 11, Oct, 1958
1-Wood-a (intro pgs. only) 29 58 87 164 232 300
2 14 28 42 81 111 140
3-9: 8-Elvis in Jailbreak Rock 12 24 36 71 96 120
10,11-Magazine format. 10-Photo-c 16 32 48 92 126 160
Bound Volume(#1-9)(extremely rare) 66 132 198 413 619 825
NOTE: ***Davis*** *a-1-11.* ***Elder*** *a-2-4, 6-9, 11.* ***Heath*** *a-2, 4-8, 10.* ***Jaffee*** *a-2, 4-9.* ***Kurtzman*** *a-11.*

HUMDINGER (Becomes White Rider and Super Horse #3 on?)
Novelty Press/Premium Group: May-June, 1946 - V2#2, July-Aug, 1947
1-Jerkwater Line, Mickey Starlight by Don Rico, Dink begin
36 72 108 204 290 375
2 16 32 48 92 126 160
3-6, V2#1,2 11 22 33 66 88 110

HUMONGOUS MAN
Alternative Press (Ikon Press): Sept, 1997 -No. 3 ($2.25, B&W)
1-3-Stepp & Harrison-c/s/a. 2.25

HUMOR (See All Humor Comics)

HUMPHREY COMICS (Joe Palooka Presents...; also see Joe Palooka)
Harvey Publications: Oct, 1948 - No. 22, Apr, 1952
1-Joe Palooka's pal (r); (52 pgs.)-Powell-a 13 26 39 76 103 130
2,3: Powell-a 8 16 24 43 54 65
4-Boy Heroes app.; Powell-a 8 16 24 46 58 70
5-8,10: 5,6-Powell-a. 7-Little Dot app. 7 14 21 35 43 50
9-Origin Humphrey 8 16 24 43 54 65
11-22 6 12 18 31 38 45

HUNCHBACK OF NOTRE DAME, THE
Dell Publishing Co.: No. 854, Oct, 1957 (one shot)
Four Color 854-Movie, photo-c 14 28 42 97 141 185

HUNGER DOGS, THE (See DC Graphic Novel #4)

HUNK
Charlton Comics: Aug, 1961 - No. 11, 1963
1 4 8 12 28 38 48
2-11 3 6 9 16 20 24

HUNTED (Formerly My Love Memoirs)
Fox Features Syndicate: No. 13, July, 1950; No. 2, Sept, 1950
13(#1)-Used in **SOTI**, pg. 42 & illo. "Treating police contemptuously" (lower left); Hollingsworth bondage-c 36 72 108 204 290 375
2 16 32 48 92 126 160

HUNTER'S HEART
DC Comics: June, 1995 - No. 3, Aug, 1995 ($5.95, B&W, limited series)
1-3 6.00

HUNTER: THE AGE OF MAGIC (See Books of Magic)
DC Comics (Vertigo): Sept, 2001 - No. 25, Sept, 2003 ($2.50/$2.75)
1-25: Horrocks-s/Case-a. 1-8-Bolton-c. 14-Begin $2.75-c. 19-Bachalo-c 2.75

HUNTRESS, THE (See All-Star Comics #69, Batman Family, Brave & the Bold #62, DC Super Stars #17, Detective #652, Infinity, Inc. #1, Sensation Comics #68 & Wonder Woman #271)
DC Comics: Apr, 1989 - No. 19, Oct, 1990 ($1.00, mature)
1-16: Staton-c/a(p) in all 2.50
17-19-Batman-c/stories 3.00

HUNTRESS, THE
DC Comics: June, 1994 - No. 4, Sept, 1994 ($1.50, limited series)
1-4-Netzer-c/a: 2-Batman app. 2.25

HURRICANE COMICS
Cambridge House: 1945 (52 pgs.)
1-(Humor, funny animal) 24 48 72 135 190 245

HYBRIDS
Continuity Comics: Jan, 1994 ($2.50, one-shot)
1-Neal Adams-c(p) & part-a(i); embossed-c. 3.50

HYBRIDS DEATHWATCH 2000
Continuity Comics: Apr, 1993 - No. 3, Aug, 1993 ($2.50)
0-(Giveaway)-Foil-c; Neal Adams-c(i) & plots (also #1,2) 3.50
1-3: 1-Polybagged w/card; die-cut-c. 2-Thermal-c. 3-Polybagged w/card; indestructible-c; Adams plot 3.00

HYBRIDS ORIGIN
Continuity Comics: 1993 - No. 5, Jan, 1994 ($2.50)
1-5: 2,3-Neal Adams-c. 4,5-Valeria the She-Bat app. Adams-c(i) 3.25

HYDE-25
Harris Publications: Apr, 1995 ($2.95, one-shot)
0-coupon for poster; r/Vampirella's 1st app. 3.00

HYDROMAN (See Heroic Comics)

HYPERKIND (See Razorline)
Marvel Comics: Sept, 1993 - No. 9, May, 1994 ($1.75/$1.95)
1-($2.50)-Foil embossed-c; by Clive Barker 3.00
2-9 2.25

HYPERKIND UNLEASED
Marvel Comics: Aug, 1994 ($2.95, 52 pgs., one-shot)
1 3.00

HYPER MYSTERY COMICS
Hyper Publications: May, 1940 - No. 2, June, 1940 (68 pgs.)
1-Hyper, the Phenomenal begins; Calkins-a 200 400 600 1250 1875 2500
2 104 208 312 650 975 1300

HYPERSONIC
Dark Horse Comics: Nov, 1997 - No. 4, Feb, 1998 ($2.95, limited series)
1-4: Abnett & White/Erskine-a 3.00

I AIM AT THE STARS (Movie)
Dell Publishing Co.: No. 1148, Nov-Jan/1960-61 (one-shot)
Four Color 1148-The Werner Von Braun Sty-photo-c 8 16 24 55 78 100

I AM COYOTE (See Eclipse Graphic Album Series & Eclipse Magazine #2)

I AM LEGEND
Eclipse Books: 1991 - No. 4, 1991 ($5.95, B&W, squarebound, 68 pgs.)
1-4: Based on 1954 novel by Richard Matheson 6.00

IBIS, THE INVINCIBLE (See Fawcett Miniatures, Mighty Midget & Whiz)
Fawcett Publications: 1942 (Fall?); #2, Mar.,1943; #3, Wint, 1945 - #5, Fall, 1946; #6, Spring, 1948
1-Origin Ibis; Raboy-c; on sale 1/2/43 200 400 600 1250 1875 2500
2-Bondage-c (on sale 2/5/43) 96 192 288 600 900 1200
3-Wolverton-a #3-6 (4 pgs. each) 74 148 222 463 694 925
4-6: 5-Bondage-c 50 100 150 300 450 600
NOTE: ***Mac Raboy*** *c(p)-3-5.* ***Schaffenberger*** *c-6.*

I-BOTS (See Isaac Asimov's I-BOTS)

iCANDY
DC Comics: Nov, 2003 - Present ($2.50, limited series)
1-4: 1-3-Abnett & Lanning-s/Andrasofszky-a. 4-Udon-a 2.50

ICE AGE ON THE WORLD OF MAGIC: THE GATHERING (See Magic The Gathering)

ICE KING OF OZ, THE (See First Comics Graphic Novel #13)

ICEMAN (Also see The Champions & X-Men #94)
Marvel Comics Group: Dec, 1984 - No. 4, June, 1985 (Limited series)
1,2,4: Zeck covers on all 3.50
3-The Defenders, Champions (Ghost Rider) & the original X-Men x-over 4.00

ICEMAN (X-Men)
Marvel Comics: Dec, 2001 - No. 4, Mar, 2002 ($2.50, limited series)

Icon #15 © Milestone Media

Ideal Comics #1 © MAR

I, Lusiphur #2 © Drew Hayes

	GD 2.0	VG 4.0	FN 6.0	VF 8.0	VF/NM 9.0	NM- 9.2
1-4-Abnett & Lanning-s/Kerschl-a						3.00

ICON
DC Comics (Milestone): May, 1993 - No. 42, Feb, 1997($1.50/$1.75/$2.50)

	GD 2.0	VG 4.0	FN 6.0	VF 8.0	VF/NM 9.0	NM- 9.2
1-($2.95)-Collector's Edition polybagged w/poster & trading card (direct sale only)						3.00
1-24,30-42: 9-Simonson-c. 15,16-Worlds Collide Pt. 4 & 11. 15-Superboy app. 16-Superman-c/story. 40-Vs. Blood Syndicate						2.50
25-($2.95, 52 pgs.)						3.00

IDAHO
Dell Publishing Co.: June-Aug, 1963 - No. 8, July-Sept, 1965

	GD 2.0	VG 4.0	FN 6.0	VF 8.0	VF/NM 9.0	NM- 9.2
1	3	6	9	18	24	30
2-8: 5-7-Painted-c	2	4	6	10	13	16

IDEAL (... a Classical Comic) (2nd Series) (Love Romances No. 6 on)
Timely Comics: July, 1948 - No. 5, March, 1949 (Feature length stories)

	GD 2.0	VG 4.0	FN 6.0	VF 8.0	VF/NM 9.0	NM- 9.2
1-Antony & Cleopatra	36	72	108	204	290	375
2-The Corpses of Dr. Sacotti	31	62	93	175	248	320
3-Joan of Arc; used in **SOTI**, pg. 308 'Boer War'	29	58	87	164	232	300
4-Richard the Lion-hearted; titled "...the World's Greatest Comics"; The Witness app.	40	80	120	240	340	440
5-Ideal Love & Romance; change to love; photo-c	19	38	57	107	149	190

IDEAL COMICS (1st Series) (Willie Comics No. 5 on)
Timely Comics (MgPC): Fall, 1944 - No. 4, Spring, 1946

	GD 2.0	VG 4.0	FN 6.0	VF 8.0	VF/NM 9.0	NM- 9.2
1-Funny animal; Super Rabbit in all	24	48	72	135	190	245
2	14	28	42	79	107	135
3,4	13	26	39	74	100	125

IDEAL LOVE & ROMANCE (See Ideal, A Classical Comic)

IDEAL ROMANCE (Formerly Tender Romance)
Key Publ.: No. 3, April, 1954 - No. 8, Feb, 1955 (Diary Confessions No. 9 on)

	GD 2.0	VG 4.0	FN 6.0	VF 8.0	VF/NM 9.0	NM- 9.2
3-Bernard Baily-c	9	18	27	52	66	80
4-8: 4-6-B. Baily-c	6	12	18	33	41	48

IDEALS (Secret Stories)
Ideals Publ., USA: 1981 (68 pgs, graphic novels, 7x10", stiff-c)

	GD 2.0	VG 4.0	FN 6.0	VF 8.0	VF/NM 9.0	NM- 9.2
Captain America - Star Spangled Super Hero	3	6	9	19	25	32
Fantastic Four - Cosmic Quartet	3	6	9	19	25	32
Incredible Hulk - Gamma Powered Goliath	3	6	9	19	25	32
Spider-Man - World Famous Wall Crawler	4	8	12	25	33	42

I DIE AT MIDNIGHT (Vertigo V2K)
DC Comics (Vertigo): 2000 ($6.95, prestige format, one-shot)

	GD 2.0	VG 4.0	FN 6.0	VF 8.0	VF/NM 9.0	NM- 9.2
1-Kyle Baker-s/a						7.00

IDOL
Marvel Comics (Epic Comics): 1992 - No. 3, 1992 ($2.95, mini-series, 52 pgs.)

	GD 2.0	VG 4.0	FN 6.0	VF 8.0	VF/NM 9.0	NM- 9.2
Book 1-3						3.00

I DREAM OF JEANNIE (TV)
Dell Publishing Co.: Apr, 1965 - No. 2, Dec, 1966 (Photo-c)

	GD 2.0	VG 4.0	FN 6.0	VF 8.0	VF/NM 9.0	NM- 9.2
1-Barbara Eden photo-c, each	17	34	51	123	182	240
2	13	26	39	90	133	175

I FEEL SICK
Slave Labor Graphics: Aug, 1999 - No. 2, May, 2000 ($3.95, limited series)

	GD 2.0	VG 4.0	FN 6.0	VF 8.0	VF/NM 9.0	NM- 9.2
1,2-Jhonen Vasquez-s/a						4.00

ILLUMINATOR
Marvel Comics/Nelson Publ.: 1993 - No. 4, 1993 ($4.99/$2.95, 52 pgs.)

	GD 2.0	VG 4.0	FN 6.0	VF 8.0	VF/NM 9.0	NM- 9.2
1,2-($4.99) Religious themed						5.00
3,4						3.00

ILLUSTRATED GAGS
United Features Syndicate: No. 16, 1940

	GD 2.0	VG 4.0	FN 6.0	VF 8.0	VF/NM 9.0	NM- 9.2
Single Series 16	17	34	51	95	130	165

ILLUSTRATED LIBRARY OF..., AN (See Classics Illustrated Giants)

ILLUSTRATED STORIES OF THE OPERAS
Baily (Bernard) Publ. Co.: 1943 (16 pgs.; B&W) (25 cents) (cover-B&W & red)

	GD 2.0	VG 4.0	FN 6.0	VF 8.0	VF/NM 9.0	NM- 9.2
nn-(Rare)(4 diff. issues)-Faust (part-r in Cisco Kid #1), nn-Aida, nn-Carmen; Baily-a, nn-Rigoleito	55	110	165	330	495	660

ILLUSTRATED STORY OF ROBIN HOOD & HIS MERRY MEN, THE (See Classics Giveaways, 12/44)

ILLUSTRATED TARZAN BOOK, THE (See Tarzan Book)

I LOVED (Formerly Rulah; Colossal Features Magazine No. 33 on)
Fox Features Syndicate: No. 28, July, 1949 - No. 32, Mar, 1950

	GD 2.0	VG 4.0	FN 6.0	VF 8.0	VF/NM 9.0	NM- 9.2
28	10	20	30	60	80	100
29-32	8	16	24	43	54	65

I LOVE LUCY
Eternity Comics : 6/90 - No. 6, 1990;V2#1, 11/90 - No. 6, 1991 ($2.95, B&W, mini-series)

	GD 2.0	VG 4.0	FN 6.0	VF 8.0	VF/NM 9.0	NM- 9.2
1-6: Reprints 1950s comic strip; photo-c						4.00
Book II #1-6: Reprints comic strip; photo-c						4.00
...In Full Color 1 (1991, $5.95, 52 pgs.)-Reprints I Love Lucy Comics #4,5,8,16; photo-c with embossed logo (2 versions exist, one with pgs. 18 & 19 reversed, the other corrected)	1	2	3	5	6	8
...In 3-D 1 (1991, $3.95, w/glasses)-Reprints I Love Lucy Comics; photo-c; bagged						6.00

I LOVE LUCY COMICS (TV) (Also see The Lucy Show)
Dell Publishing Co.: No. 535, Feb, 1954 - No. 35, Apr-June, 1962 (Lucille Ball photo-c on all)

	GD 2.0	VG 4.0	FN 6.0	VF 8.0	VF/NM 9.0	NM- 9.2
Four Color 535(#1)	53	106	159	400	600	800
Four Color 559(#2, 5/54)	32	64	96	240	358	475
3 (8-10/54) - 5	21	42	63	147	216	285
6-10	16	32	48	116	171	225
11-20	12	24	36	82	121	160
21-35	10	20	30	72	104	135

I LOVE NEW YORK
Linsner.com: 2002 ($2.95, B&W, one-shot)

	GD 2.0	VG 4.0	FN 6.0	VF 8.0	VF/NM 9.0	NM- 9.2
1-Linsner-s/a; benefit book for the Sept. 11 charities						3.00

I LOVE YOU
Fawcett Publications: June, 1950 (one-shot)

	GD 2.0	VG 4.0	FN 6.0	VF 8.0	VF/NM 9.0	NM- 9.2
1-Photo-c	15	30	45	84	115	145

I LOVE YOU (Formerly In Love)
Charlton Comics: No. 7, 9/55 - No. 121, 12/76; No. 122, 3/79 - No. 130, 5/80

	GD 2.0	VG 4.0	FN 6.0	VF 8.0	VF/NM 9.0	NM- 9.2
7-Kirby-c; Powell-a	9	18	27	65	93	120
8-10	4	8	12	29	40	50
11-16,18-20	4	8	12	27	36	45
17-(68 pg. Giant)	7	14	21	51	71	90
21-50: 26-No Torres-a	3	6	9	19	25	32
51-59	2	4	6	14	18	22
60-(1/66)-Elvis Presley line drawn c/story	16	32	48	113	167	220
61-85	2	4	6	10	13	16
86-110	1	2	3	5	7	9
111-130						6.00

I, LUSIPHUR (Becomes Poison Elves, 1st series #8 on)
Mulehide Graphics: 1991 - No. 7, 1992 (B&W, magazine size)

	GD 2.0	VG 4.0	FN 6.0	VF 8.0	VF/NM 9.0	NM- 9.2
1-Drew Hayes-c/a/scripts	4	8	12	27	36	45
2,4,5	2	4	6	12	16	20
3-Low print run	4	8	12	29	40	50
6,7	2	4	6	8	10	12
Poison Elves: Requiem For An Elf (Sirius Ent., 6/96, $14.95, trade paperback) -Reprints I, Lusiphur #1,2 as text, and 3-6						15.00

I'M A COP
Magazine Enterprises: 1954 - No. 3, 1954?

	GD 2.0	VG 4.0	FN 6.0	VF 8.0	VF/NM 9.0	NM- 9.2
1(A-1 #111)-Powell-c/a in all	16	32	48	92	126	160
2(A-1 #126), 3(A-1 #128)	10	20	30	56	73	90

IMAGE GRAPHIC NOVEL
Image Int.: 1984 ($6.95)(Advertised as Pacific Comics Graphic Novel #1)

	GD 2.0	VG 4.0	FN 6.0	VF 8.0	VF/NM 9.0	NM- 9.2
1-The Seven Samuroid; Brunner-c/a						7.00

IMAGE INTRODUCES...
Image Comics: Oct, 2001 - Present ($2.95, anthology)

	GD 2.0	VG 4.0	FN 6.0	VF 8.0	VF/NM 9.0	NM- 9.2
Believer #1-Schamberger-s/Thurman & Molder-a; Legend of Isis preview						3.00
Cryptopia #1-Raab-s/Quinn-a						3.00
Dog Soldiers #1-Hunter-s/Pachoumis-a						3.00
Legend of Isis #1-Valdez-a						3.00
Primate #1-Two covers; Beau Smith & Bernhardt-s/Byrd-a						3.00

IMAGES OF A DISTANT SOIL
Image Comics: Feb, 1997 ($2.95, B&W, one-shot)

	GD 2.0	VG 4.0	FN 6.0	VF 8.0	VF/NM 9.0	NM- 9.2
1-Sketches by various						3.00

IMAGES OF SHADOWHAWK (Also see Shadowhawk)
Image Comics: Sept, 1993 - No. 3, 1994 ($1.95, limited series)

	GD 2.0	VG 4.0	FN 6.0	VF 8.0	VF/NM 9.0	NM- 9.2
1-3: Keith Giffen-c/a; Trencher app.						2.25

IMAGE TWO-IN-ONE
Image Comics: Mar, 2001 ($2.95, 48 pgs., B&W, one-shot)

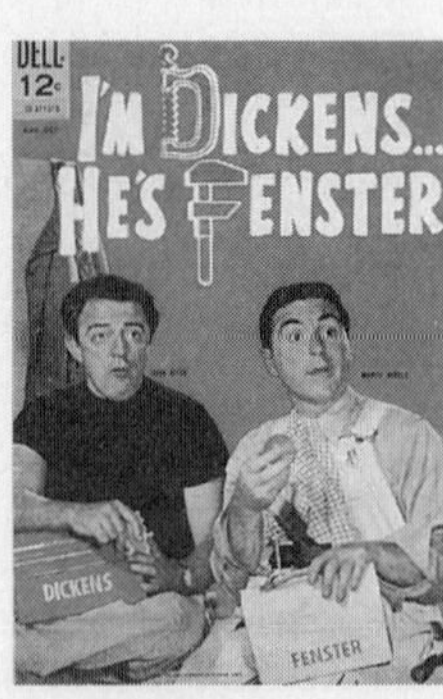

I'm Dickens - He's Fenster #2 © DELL

Impulse #9 © DC

Incredible Hulk #235 © MAR

GD VG FN VF VF/NM NM-
2.0 4.0 6.0 8.0 9.0 9.2

1-Two stories; 24 pages produced in 24 hrs. by Larsen and Eliopoulos 3.00

IMAGE ZERO
Image Comics: 1993 (Received through mail w/coupons from Image books)

0-Savage Dragon, StormWatch, Shadowhawk, Strykeforce; 1st app. Troll; 1st app. McFarlane's Freak, Blotch, Sweat and Bludd 5.00

I'M DICKENS - HE'S FENSTER (TV)
Dell Publishing Co.: May-July, 1963 - No. 2, Aug-Oct, 1963 (Photo-c)

1 6 12 18 43 59 75
2 6 12 18 38 52 65

I MET A HANDSOME COWBOY
Dell Publishing Co.: No. 324, Mar, 1951

Four Color 324 10 20 30 67 96 125

IMMORTAL DOCTOR FATE, THE
DC Comics: Jan, 1985 - No. 3, Mar, 1985 ($1.25, limited series)

1-3: 1-Simonson-c/a. 2-Giffen-c/a(p) 4.00

IMMORTALIS (See Mortigan Goth: Immortalis)

IMMORTAL II
Image Comics: Apr, 1997 - No. 5, Feb, 1998 ($2.50, B&W&Grey, limited series)

1-5: 1-B&W w/ color pull-out poster 2.50

IMPACT
E. C. Comics: Mar-Apr, 1955 - No. 5, Nov-Dec, 1955

1-Not code approved 16 32 48 120 175 230
2 10 20 30 75 110 145
3-5: 4-Crandall-a 8 16 24 60 90 120

NOTE: ***Crandall*** *a-1-4.* ***Davis*** *a-2-4; c-1-5.* ***Evans*** *a-1, 4, 5.* ***Ingels*** *a-in all.* ***Kamen*** *a-3.* ***Krigstein*** *a-1, 5.* ***Orlando*** *a-2, 5.*

IMPACT
Gemstone Publishing: Apr, 1999 - No. 5, Aug, 1999 ($2.50)

1-5-Reprints E.C. series 2.50

IMPACT CHRISTMAS SPECIAL
DC Comics (Impact Comics): 1991 ($2.50, 68 pgs.)

1-Gift of the Magi by Infantino/Rogers; The Black Hood, The Fly, The Jaguar, & The Shield stories 2.50

IMPOSSIBLE MAN SUMMER VACATION SPECTACULAR, THE
Marvel Comics: Aug, 1990; No. 2, Sept, 1991 ($2.00, 68 pgs.) (See Fantastic Four#11)

1-Spider Man, Quasar, Dr. Strange, She-Hulk, Punisher & Dr. Doom stories; Barry Crain, Guice-a; Art Adams-c(i) 2.50
2-Ka Zar & Thor app.; Cable Wolverine-c app. 2.50

IMPERIAL GUARD
Marvel Comics: Jan, 1997 - No. 3, Mar, 1997 ($1.95, limited series)

1-3: Augustyn-s in all; 1-Wraparound-c 2.25

IMPULSE (See Flash #92, 2nd Series for 1st app.) (Also see Young Justice)
DC Comics: Apr, 1995 - No. 89, Oct, 2002 ($1.50/$1.75/$1.95/$2.25/$2.50)

1-Mark Waid scripts & Humberto Ramos-c/a(p) begin; brief retelling of origin 6.00
2-12: 9-XS from Legion (Impulse's cousin) comes to the 20th Century, returns to the 30th Century in #12. 10-Dead Heat Pt. 3 (cont'd in Flash #110). 11-Dead Heat Pt. 4 (cont'd in Flash #111); Johnny Quick dies. 3.00
13-25: 14-Trickster app. 17-Zatanna-c/app. 21-Legion-c/app. 22-Jesse Quick-c/app. 24-Origin; Flash app. 25-Last Ramos-a. 2.50
26-55: 26-Rousseau-a begins. 28-1st new Arrowette (see World's Finest #113). 30-Genesis x-over.41-Arrowette-c/app. 47-Superman-c/app. 50-Batman & Joker-c/app. Van Sciver-a begins. 52,53-Simonson art pages 2.50
56-62: 56-Young Justice app. 2.50
63-89: 63-Begin $2.50-c. 66-JLA,JSA-c/app. 68,69-Adam Strange, GL app. 77-Our Worlds at War x-over; Young Justice-c/app. 79-Amancio-a. 85-World Without Young Justice x-over pt. 2. 86-JLA app. 2.50
#1,000,000 (11/98) John Fox app. 2.50
Annual 1 (1996, $2.95)-Legends of the Dead Earth; Parobeck-a 4.00
Annual 2 (1997, $3.95)-Pulp Heroes stories; Orbik painted-c 4.00
.../Atom Double-Shot 1(2/98, $1.95) Jurgens-s/Mhan-a 3.00
...: Bart Saves the Universe (4/99, $5.95) JSA app. 6.00
...Plus(9/97, $2.95) w/Gross Out (Scare Tactics)-c/app. 3.00
...Reckless Youth (1997, $14.95, TPB) r/Flash #92-94, Impulse #1-6 15.00

INCAL, THE
Marvel Comics (Epic): Nov, 1988 - No. 3, Jan, 1989 ($10.95/$12.95, mature)

1-3: Moebius-c/a in all; sexual content 14.00

INCOMPLETE DEATH'S HEAD (Also see Death's Head)
Marvel Comics UK: Jan, 1993 - No. 12, Dec, 1993 ($1.75, limited series)

1-($2.95, 56 pgs.)-Die-cut cover 3.00
2-11: 2-Re-intro original Death's Head. 3-Original Death's Head vs. Dragon's Claws 2.25
12-($2.50, 52 pgs.)-She Hulk app. 2.50

INCREDIBLE HULK, THE (See Aurora, The Avengers #1, The Defenders #1, Giant-Size..., Hulk, Marvel Collectors Item Classics, Marvel Comics Presents #26, Marvel Fanfare, Marvel Treasury Edition, Power Record Comics, Rampaging Hulk, She-Hulk & 2099 Unlimited)

INCREDIBLE HULK, THE
Marvel Comics: May, 1962 - No. 6, Mar, 1963; No. 102, Apr, 1968 - No. 474, Mar, 1999

1-Origin & 1st app. (skin is grey colored); Kirby pencils begin, end #5
667 1334 2000 7400 15,200 23,000
2-1st green skinned Hulk; Kirby/Ditko-a 220 440 660 1760 3080 4400
3-Origin retold; 1st app. Ringmaster & Hercules (9/62)
137 274 411 1096 1848 2600
4,5: 4-Brief origin retold 126 252 378 1008 1704 2400
6-(3/63) Intro. Teen Brigade; all Ditko-a 168 336 504 1344 2272 3200
102-(4/68) (Formerly Tales to Astonish)-Origin retold; story continued from Tales to Astonish #101 24 48 72 169 247 325
103 10 20 30 73 107 140
104-Rhino app. 10 20 30 73 107 140
105-108: 105-1st Missing Link. 107-Mandarin app.(9/68). 108-Mandarin & Nick Fury app. (10/68) 8 16 24 53 74 95
109,110: 109-Ka-Zar app. 6 12 18 43 59 75
111-117: 117-Last 12¢ issue 5 10 15 36 48 60
118-Hulk vs. Sub-Mariner 6 12 18 40 55 70
119-121,123-125 4 8 12 27 36 45
122-Hulk battles Thing (12/69) 7 14 21 50 68 85
126-1st Barbara Norriss (Valkyrie) 4 8 12 29 40 50
127-139: 131-Hulk vs. Iron Man; 1st Jim Wilson, Hulk's new sidekick. 136-1st Xeron, The Star-Slayer 3 6 9 18 24 30
140-Written by Harlan Ellison; 1st Jarella, Hulk's love 3 7 10 21 28 35
140-2nd printing (1994) 2 4 6 8 10 12
141-1st app. Doc Samson (7/71) 5 10 15 36 48 60
142-144: 144-Last 15¢ issue 3 6 9 16 20 25
145-(52 pgs.)-Origin retold 3 7 10 21 28 35
146-160: 149-1st app. The Inheritor. 155-1st app. Shaper. 158-Warlock cameo(12/72)
2 4 6 11 14 18
161-The Mimic dies; Beast app. 3 6 9 18 23 28
162-1st app. The Wendigo (4/73); Beast app. 3 7 10 21 28 35
163-171,173-176: 163-1st app. The Gremlin. 164-1st Capt. Omen & Colonel John D. Armbruster. 166-1st Zzzax. 168-1st The Harpy; nudity panels of Betty Brant. 169-1st app. Bi-Beast.176-Warlock cameo (2 panels only); same date as Strange Tales #178 (6/74)
2 4 6 9 11 14
172-X-Men cameo; origin Juggernaut retold 3 6 9 18 24 30
177-1st actual death of Warlock (last panel only) 2 4 6 11 14 18
178-Rebirth of Warlock 2 4 6 11 14 18
179 2 4 6 9 11 14
180-(10/74)-1st app. Wolverine (cameo last pg.) 12 24 36 82 121 160
181-(11/74)-1st full Wolverine story; Trimpe-a 71 142 213 604 927 1250
182-Wolverine cameo; see Giant-Size X-Men #1 for next app.; 1st Crackajack Jackson
10 20 30 73 107 140
183-199: 185-Death of Col. Armbruster 2 4 6 8 10 12
198,199, 201,202-(30¢-c variants, lim. distribution) 2 4 6 11 14 18
200-(25¢-c) Silver Surfer app.; anniversary issue 3 6 9 18 24 30
200-(30¢-c variant, limited distribution)(6/76) 4 8 12 27 36 45
201-220: 201-Conan swipe-c/sty. 212-1st app. The Constrictor 6.00
212-216-(35¢-c variant, limited distribution) 1 2 3 5 7 9
221-249: 227-Original Avengers app. 232-Capt. America x-over from C.A. #230. 233-Marvel Man app. 234-(4/79)-1st app. Quasar (formerly called Marvel Man. 243-Cage app. 5.00
250-Giant size; Silver Surfer app. 2 4 6 8 10 12
251-277,280-299: 271-Rocket Raccoon app. 272-Sasquatch & Wendigo app.; Wolverine & Alpha Flight cameo in flashback. 282-284-She-Hulk app. 293-F.F. app. 4.00
278,279-Most Marvel characters app. (Wolverine in both). 279-X-Men & Alpha Flight cameos 5.00
300-(11/84, 52 pgs.)-Spider-Man app in new black costume on-c & 2 pg. cameo 6.00
301-313: 312-Origin Hulk retold 3.00
314-Byrne-c/a begins, ends #319 5.00
315-319: 319-Bruce Banner & Betty Talbot wed 4.00
320-323,325,327-329 3.00
324-1st app. Grey Hulk since #1 (c-swipe of #1) 2 4 6 8 10 12
326-Grey vs. Green Hulk 5.00
330,331: 330-1st McFarlane ish (4/87); Thunderbolt Ross dies. 331-Grey Hulk series begins

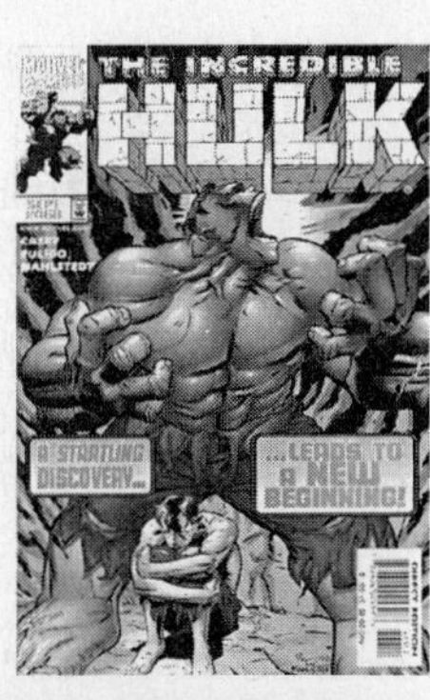

Incredible Hulk #468 © MAR

Incredible Hulk V2#56 © MAR

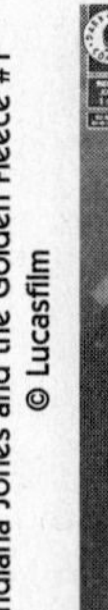
Indiana Jones and the Golden Fleece #1 © Lucasfilm

	GD 2.0	VG 4.0	FN 6.0	VF 8.0	VF/NM 9.0	NM- 9.2
	2	4	6	14	18	22
332-334,336-339: 336,337-X-Factor app.	2	4	6	8	10	12
335-No McFarlane-a						4.00
340-Hulk battles Wolverine by McFarlane	4	8	12	24	32	40
341-346: 345-($1.50, 52 pgs.). 346-Last McFarlane issue	1	2	3	4	5	7
347-349,351-358,360-366: 347-1st app. Marlo						3.00
350-Hulk/Thing battle						6.00
359-Wolverine app. (illusion only)						3.00
367,372,377: 367-1st Dale Keown-a on Hulk (3/90). 372-Green Hulk app.;Keown-c/a. 377-1st all new Hulk; fluorescent-c; Keown-c/a	1	2	3	5	6	8
368-371,373-376: 368-Sam Kieth-c/a, 1st app. Pantheon. 369,370-Dale Keown-c/a. 370,371-Original Defenders app. 371,373-376: Keown-c/a. 376-Green vs. Grey Hulk						5.00
377-Fluorescent green logo 2nd printing						3.00
378,380,389: No Keown-a. 380-Doc Samson app.						3.00
379,381-388,390-392-Keown-a. 385-Infinity Gauntlet x-over. 389-Last $1.00-c. 392-X-Factor app.						4.00
393-($2.50, 72 pgs.)-30th anniversary issue; green foil stamped-c; swipes-c to #1; has pin-ups of classic battles; Keown-c/a						5.00
393-2nd printing						2.50
394-399: 394-No Keown-c/a; intro Trauma. 395,396-Punisher-c/stories; Keown-c/a. 397-Begin "Ghost of the Past" 4-part sty; Keown c/a. 398-Last Keown-c/a						2.50
400-($2.50, 68 pgs.)-Holo-grafx foil-c & r/TTA #63						3.00
400-416: 400-2nd print-Diff. color foil-c. 402-Return of Doc Samson						2.50
417-424: 417-Begin $1.50-c; Rick Jones' bachelor party; Hulk returns from "Future Imperfect"; bound-in trading card sheet. 418-(Regular edition)-Rick Jones marries Marlo; includes cameo apps of various Marvel characters as well as DC's Death & Peter David. 420-Death of Jim Wilson						2.50
418-($2.50)-Collector's Edition w/gatefold die-cut-c						3.00
425 ($2.25, 52 pgs.)						2.50
425 ($3.50, 52 pgs.)-Holographic-c						4.00
426-434, 436-442: 426-Begin $1.95-c. 427, 428-Man-Thing app. 431,432-Abomination app. 434-Funeral for Nick Fury. 436-Ghosts of the Future begins, ends #440. 439-Hulk becomes Maestro, Avengers app. 440-Thor-c/app. 441,442-She-Hulk-c/app.						2.50
435 ($2.50)-Rhino-app; excerpt from "What Savage Beast"						3.00
443,446-448: 443-Begin $1.50-c; re-app. of Hulk. 446-w/card insert. 447-Begin Deodato-c/a(p)						2.50
444,445: 444-Cable-c/app.; "Onslaught". 445-"Onslaught"						4.00
447-Variant cover						4.00
449-1st app. Thunderbolts						6.00
450-($2.95)-Thunderbolts app.; 2 stories; Heroes Reborn-c/app.						5.00
451-470: 455-X-Men-c/app. 460-Bruce Banner returns. 464-Silver Surfer-c/app. 466,467: Betty dies. 467-Last Peter David-s/Kubert-a. 468-Casey-s/Pulido-a begin						2.50
471-473						3.00
474-($2.99) Last issue; Abomination app.						4.00
#(-1) Flashback (7/97) Kubert-a						2.50
Special 1 (10/68, 25¢, 68 pg.)-New 51 pg. story, Hulk battles The Inhumans (early app.); Steranko-c.	10	20	30	70	100	130
Special 2 (10/69, 25¢, 68 pg.)-Origin retold	6	12	18	38	52	65
Special 3,4: 3-(1/71, 25¢, 68 pg.). 4-(1/72, 52pgs.)	3	6	9	16	20	25
Annual 5 (1976)	2	4	6	10	12	15
Annual 6-8 ('77-79)-7-Byrne/Layton-c/a; Iceman & Angel app. in book-length story. 8-Book-length Sasquatch-c/sty	1	3	4	6	8	10
Annual 9,10: 9('80). 10 ('81)						6.00
Annual 11('82)-Doc Samson back-up by Miller(p)(5 pgs.); Spider-Man & Avengers app. Buckler-a(p)						5.00
Annual 12-17: 12 ('83). 13('84). 14('85). 15('86). 16('90, $2.00, 68 pgs.)-She-Hulk app. 17(1991, $2.00)-Origin retold						3.50
Annual 18-20 ('92-'94 68 pgs.)-18-Return of the Defenders, Pt. I; no Keown-c/a 19-Bagged w/card						3.00
...'97 ($2.99) Pollina-c						3.00
...And Wolverine 1 (10/86, $2.50)-r/1st app. (#180-181)	1	3	4	6	8	10
...: Beauty and the Behemoth ('98, $19.95, TPB) r/Bruce & Betty stories						20.00
...Ground Zero ('95, $12.95) r/#340-346						13.00
...Hercules Unleashed (10/96, $2.50) David-s/Deodato-c/a						2.50
.../Sub-Mariner '98 Annual ($2.99)						3.00
...Versus Quasimodo 1 (3/83, one-shot)-Based on Saturday morning cartoon						4.00
...Vs. Superman 1 (7/99, $5.95, one-shot)-painted-c by Rude						6.00
...Versus Venom 1 (4/94, $2.50, one-shot)-Embossed-c; red foil logo						3.00
Wizard #1 Ace Edition - Reprints #1 with new Andy Kubert-c						14.00
Wizard #181 Ace Edition - Reprints #181 with new Chen-c						14.00

(Also see titles listed under **Hulk**)

NOTE: ***Adkins*** *a-111-116i.* ***Austin*** *a(i)-350, 351, 353, 354; c-302i, 350i.* ***Ayers*** *a-3-5i.* ***Buckler*** *a-Annual 5; c-252.* ***John Buscema*** *c-202p.* ***Byrne*** *a-314-319p; c-314-316, 318, 319, 359, Annual 14i.* ***Colan*** *c-363.* ***Ditko*** *a-2i, 6, 249, Annual 2r(5), 3r, 9p; c-2i, 6, 235, 249.* ***Everett*** *c-133i.* ***Golden*** *c-248, 251.* ***Kane*** *c(p)-193, 194, 196, 198.* ***Dale Keown*** *a(p)-367, 369-377, 379, 381-388, 390-393, 395-398; c-369-377p, 381, 382p, 384, 385, 386, 387p, 388, 390p, 391-393, 395p, 396, 397p, 398.* ***Kirby*** *a-1-5p, Special 2, 3p, Annual 5p; c-1-5, Annual 5.* ***McFarlane*** *a-330-334p, 336-339p, 340-343, 344-346p; c-330p, 340p, 341-343, 344p, 345, 346p.* ***Mignola*** *c-302, 305, 313.* ***Miller*** *c-258p, 261, 264, 268.* ***Mooney*** *a-230p, 287i, 288i.* ***Powell*** *a-Special 3r(2).* ***Romita*** *a-Annual 17p.* ***Severin*** *a(i)-108-110, 131-133, 141-151, 153-155; c(i)-109, 110, 132, 142, 144-155.* ***Simonson*** *c-283, 364-367.* ***Starlin*** *a-222p; c-217.* ***Staton*** *a(i)-187-189, 191-209.* ***Tuska*** *a-102i, 105i, 106i, 218p.* ***Williamson*** *a-310i; c-310i, 311i.* ***Wrightson*** *c-197.*

INCREDIBLE HULK (Vol. 2) (Formerly Hulk #1-11)
Marvel Comics: No. 12, Mar, 2000 - Present ($1.99-$3.50)

	GD 2.0	VG 4.0	FN 6.0	VF 8.0	VF/NM 9.0	NM- 9.2
12-Jenkins-s/Garney & McKone-a						3.00
13,14-($1.99) Garney & Buscema-a						2.50
15-24,26-32: 15-Begin $2.25-c. 21-Maximum Security x-over. 24-($1.99-c)						2.25
25-($2.99) Hulk vs. The Abomination; Romita Jr.-a						3.00
33-($3.50, 100 pgs.) new Bogdanove-a/Priest-s; reprints						3.50
34-Bruce Jones-s begin; Romita Jr.-a						5.00
35-49,51-54: 35-39-Jones-s/Romita Jr.-a. 40-43-Weeks-a. 44-49-Immonen-a						3.00
50-($3.50) Deodato-a begins; Abomination app. thru #54						3.50
55-65: 55(25¢-c) Absorbing Man returns; Fernandez-a. 60-65-Deodato-a						2.25
Annual 2000 ($3.50) Texeira-a/Jenkins-s; Avengers app.						3.50
Annual 2001 ($2.99) Thor-c/app.; Larsen-s/Williams III-c						3.00
... : Boiling Point (Volume 2, 2002, $8.99, TPB) r/#40-43; Andrews-c						9.00
Dogs of War (6/01, $19.95, TPB) r/#12-20						20.00
... : Return of the Monster (7/02, $12.99, TPB) r/#34-39						13.00
...: The End (8/02, $5.95) David-s/Keown-a; Hulk in the far future						6.00
...Volume 1 HC (2002, $29.99, oversized) r/#34-43 & Startling Stories: Banner #1-4						30.00
...Volume 2 HC (2003, $29.99, oversized) r/#44-54; sketch pages and cover gallery						30.00
Volume 3: Transfer of Power (2003, $12.99, TPB) r/#44-49						13.00
Volume 4: Abominable (2003, $11.99, TPB) r/#50-54; Abomination app.; Deodato-a						12.00
Volume 5: Hide in Plain Sight (2003, $11.99, TPB) r/#55-59; Fernandez-a						12.00

INCREDIBLE MR. LIMPET, THE (See Movie Classics)

INCREDIBLE SCIENCE FICTION (Formerly Weird Science-Fantasy)
E. C. Comics: No. 30, July-Aug, 1955 - No. 33, Jan-Feb, 1956

	GD 2.0	VG 4.0	FN 6.0	VF 8.0	VF/NM 9.0	NM- 9.2
30,33: 33-Story-r/Weird Fantasy #18	37	74	111	278	399	520
31-Williamson/Krenkel-a, Wood-a(2)	38	76	114	285	410	535
32-Williamson/Krenkel-a	38	76	114	285	410	535

NOTE: ***Davis*** *a-30, 32, 33; c-30-32.* ***Krigstein*** *a-in all.* ***Orlando*** *a-30, 32, 33("Judgement Day" reprint).* ***Wood*** *a-30, 31, 33; c-33.*

INCREDIBLE SCIENCE FICTION (Formerly Weird Science-Fantasy)
Russ Cochran/Gemstone Publ.: No. 8, Aug, 1994 - No. 11, May, 1995 ($2.00)

	GD 2.0	VG 4.0	FN 6.0	VF 8.0	VF/NM 9.0	NM- 9.2
8-11: Reprints #30-33 of E.C. series						2.50

INDEPENDENCE DAY (Movie)
Marvel Comics: No. 0, June, 1996 - No. 2, Aug, 1996 ($1.95, limited series)

	GD 2.0	VG 4.0	FN 6.0	VF 8.0	VF/NM 9.0	NM- 9.2
0-Special Edition; photo-c						5.00
0-2						2.50

INDEPENDENT VOICES
Peregrine Entertainment: Sept, 1998; Sept, 1999 ($1.95/$2.95, B&W)

	GD 2.0	VG 4.0	FN 6.0	VF 8.0	VF/NM 9.0	NM- 9.2
1-Sampler of Indy titles for CBLDF						2.25
2-(9/99, $2.95); 2nd printing-(5/00)						3.00

INDIANA JONES (Title series), **Dark Horse Comics**

	GD 2.0	VG 4.0	FN 6.0	VF 8.0	VF/NM 9.0	NM- 9.2
--AND THE ARMS OF GOLD, 2/94 - 5/94 ($2.50) 1-4						2.50
--AND THE FATE OF ATLANTIS, 3/91 - 9/91 ($2.50) 1-4-Dorman painted-c on all; contain trading cards (#1 has a 2nd printing, 10/91)						2.50
--AND THE GOLDEN FLEECE, 6/94 - 7/94 ($2.50) 1,2						2.50
--AND THE IRON PHOENIX, 12/94 - 3/95 ($2.50) 1-4						2.50

INDIANA JONES AND THE LAST CRUSADE
Marvel Comics: 1989 - No. 4, 1989 ($1.00, limited series, movie adaptation)

	GD 2.0	VG 4.0	FN 6.0	VF 8.0	VF/NM 9.0	NM- 9.2
1-4: Williamson-i assist						3.00
1-(1989, $2.95, B&W mag., 80 pgs.)						4.00
--AND THE SHRINE OF THE SEA DEVIL: Dark Horse, 9/94 ($2.50, one shot) 1-Gary Gianni-a						2.50
--AND THE SPEAR OF DESTINY: Dark Horse, 4/95 - 8/95 ($2.50) 1-4						2.50
--THUNDER IN THE ORIENT: Dark Horse, 9/93 - '94 ($2.50) 1-6: Dan Barry story & art in all; 1-Dorman painted-c						2.50

INDIANA JONES AND THE TEMPLE OF DOOM
Marvel Comics Group: Sept, 1984 - No. 3, Nov, 1984 (Movie adaptation)

	GD 2.0	VG 4.0	FN 6.0	VF 8.0	VF/NM 9.0	NM- 9.2
1-3-r/Marvel Super Special; Guice-a						3.00

INDIAN BRAVES (Baffling Mysteries No. 5 on)
Ace Magazines: March, 1951 - No. 4, Sept, 1951

Inferior Five #2 © DC

Inferno #1 © DC

The Inhumans #5 © MAR

GD VG FN VF VF/NM NM-
2.0 4.0 6.0 8.0 9.0 9.2

1-Green Arrowhead begins, ends #3 13 26 39 76 103 130
2 8 16 24 43 54 65
3,4 7 14 21 37 46 55
I.W. Reprint #1 (nd)-r/Indian Braves #4 2 4 6 10 13 16

INDIAN CHIEF (White Eagle...) (Formerly The Chief, Four Color 290)
Dell Publ. Co.: No. 3, July-Sept, 1951 - No. 33, Jan-Mar, 1959 (All painted-c)

3 5 10 15 33 44 55
4-11: 6-White Eagle app. 4 8 12 27 36 45
12-1st White Eagle(10-12/53)-Not same as earlier character
5 10 15 33 44 55
13-29 3 7 10 21 28 35
30-33-Buscema-a 4 8 12 22 30 38

INDIAN CHIEF (See March of Comics No. 94, 110, 127, 140, 159, 170, 187)

INDIAN FIGHTER, THE (Movie)
Dell Publishing Co.: No. 687, May, 1956 (one-shot)

Four Color 687-Kirk Douglas photo-c 9 18 27 60 85 110

INDIAN FIGHTER
Youthful Magazines: May, 1950 - No. 11, Jan, 1952

1 13 26 39 76 103 130
2-Wildey-a/c(bondage) 9 18 27 52 66 80
3-11: 3,4-Wildey-a 7 14 21 37 46 55
NOTE: ***Walter Johnson*** *c-1, 3, 4, 6.* ***Palais*** *a-10.* ***Stallman*** *a-7.* ***Wildey*** *a-2-4; c-2, 5.*

INDIAN LEGENDS OF THE NIAGARA (See American Graphics)

INDIANS
Fiction House Magazines (Wings Publ. Co.): Spring, 1950 - No. 17, Spr, 1953 (1-8: 52 pgs.)

1-Manzar The White Indian, Long Bow & Orphan of the Storm begin
29 58 87 164 232 300
2-Starlight begins 15 30 45 86 118 150
3-5: 5-17-Most-c by Whitman 13 26 39 74 100 125
6-10 11 22 33 63 84 105
11-17 10 20 30 56 73 90

INDIANS OF THE WILD WEST
I. W. Enterprises: Circa 1958? (no date) (Reprints)

9-Kinstler-c; Whitman-a; r/Indians #? 2 4 6 11 14 18

INDIANS ON THE WARPATH
St. John Publishing Co.: No date (Late 40s, early 50s) (132 pgs.)

nn-Matt Baker-c; contains St. John comics rebound. Many combinations possible
34 68 102 196 278 360

INDIAN TRIBES (See Famous Indian Tribes)

INDIAN WARRIORS (Formerly White Rider and Super Horse; becomes Western Crime Cases #9)
Star Publications: No. 7, June, 1951 - No. 8, Sept, 1951

7-White Rider & Superhorse continue; "Last of the Mohicans" serial begins;
L.B. Cole-c 19 38 57 107 149 190
8-L. B. Cole-c 18 36 54 101 138 175
3-D 1(12/53, 25¢)-Came w/glasses; L. B. Cole-c 39 78 117 230 325 420
Accepted Reprint(nn)(inside cover shows White Rider & Superhorse #11)-r/cover to #7;
origin White Rider &...; L. B. Cole-c 7 14 21 35 43 50
Accepted Reprint #8 (nd); L.B. Cole-c (r-cover to #8) 7 14 21 35 43 50

INDOORS-OUTDOORS (See Wisco)

INDOOR SPORTS
National Specials Co.: nd (6x9", 64 pgs., B&W-r, hard-c)

nn-By Tad 5 10 15 24 30 35

INDUSTRIAL GOTHIC
DC Comics (Vertigo): Dec, 1995 - No. 5, Apr, 1996 ($2.50, limited series)

1-5: Ted McKeever-c/a/scripts 2.50

INFERIOR FIVE, THE (Inferior 5 #11, 12) (See Showcase #62, 63, 65)
National Periodical Publications (#1-10: 12¢): 3-4/67 - No. 10, 9-10/68; No. 11, 8-9/72 - No. 12, 10-11/72

1-(3-4/67)-Sekowsky-a(p); 4th app. 6 12 18 38 52 65
2-5: 2-Plastic Man, F.F. app. 4-Thor app. 3 6 9 19 25 32
6-9: 6-Stars DC staff 3 6 9 16 20 24
10-Superman x-over; F.F., Spider-Man & Sub-Mariner app.
3 6 9 18 24 30
11,12: Orlando-c/a; both r/Showcase #62,63 2 4 6 12 16 20

INFERNO
Caliber Comics: 1995 - No. 5 ($2.95, B&W)

1-5 3.00

INFERNO (See Legion of Super-Heroes)
DC Comics: Oct, 1997 - No. 4, Feb, 1998 ($2.50, limited series)

1-Immonen-s/c/a in all 4.00
2-4 3.00

INFERNO: HELLBOUND
Image Comics (Top Cow): Jan, 2002 - Present ($2.50/$2.99)

1,2: 1-Seven covers; Silvestri-a/Silvestri and Wohl-s 2.50
3-($2.99) Tan-a 3.00
#0 (7/02, $3.00) Tan-a 3.00
Wizard #0- Previews series; bagged with Wizard Top Cow Special mag 2.25

INFINITY ABYSS (Also see Marvel Universe: The End)
Marvel Comics: Aug, 2002 - No. 6 ($2.99, limited series)

1-5-Starlin-s/a; Thanos, Captain Marvel, Spider-Man, Dr. Strange app. 3.00
6-($3.50) 3.50
Thanos Vol. 2: Infinity Abyss TPB (2003, $17.99) r/ #1-6 18.00

INFINITY CRUSADE
Marvel Comics: June, 1993 - No. 6, Nov, 1993 ($2.50, limited series, 52 pgs.)

1-6: By Jim Starlin & Ron Lim 2.50

INFINITY GAUNTLET (The... #2 on; see Infinity Crusade, The Infinity War & Warlock & the Infinity Watch)
Marvel Comics: July, 1991 - No. 6, Dec, 1991 ($2.50, limited series)

1-6:Thanos-c/stories in all; Starlin scripts in all; 5,6-Ron Lim-c/a 3.00
TPB (4/99, $24.95) r/#1-6 25.00
NOTE: ***Lim*** *a-3p(part), 5p, 6p; c-5i, 6i.* ***Perez*** *a-1-3p, 4p(part); c-1(painted), 2-4, 5i, 6i.*

INFINITY, INC. (See All-Star Squadron #25)
DC Comics: Mar, 1984 - No. 53, Aug, 1988 ($1.25, Baxter paper, 36 pgs.)

1-Brainwave, Jr., Fury, The Huntress, Jade, Northwind, Nuklon, Obsidian, Power Girl, Silver Scarab & Star Spangled Kid begin 4.00
2-13,38-49,51-53: 2-Dr. Midnite, G.A. Flash, W. Woman, Dr. Fate, Hourman, Green Lantern, Wildcat app. 5-Nudity panels. 46,47-Millennium tie-ins 3.00
14-Todd McFarlane-a (5/85, 2nd full story) 1 2 3 6 8 9
15-37-McFarlane-a (20,23,24: 5 pgs. only; 33: 2 pgs.); 18-24-Crisis x-over. 21-Intro new Hourman & Dr. Midnight. 26-New Wildcat app. 31-Star Spangled Kid becomes Skyman. 32-Green Fury becomes Green Flame. 33-Origin Obsidian. 35-1st modern app. G.A. Fury
4.00
50 ($2.50, 52 pgs.) 3.00
Annual 1,2: 1(12/85)-Crisis x-over. 2('88, $2.00), Special 1 ('87, $1.50) 3.00
NOTE: ***Kubert*** *r-4.* ***McFarlane*** *a-14-37p, Annual 1p; c(p)-14-19, 22, 25, 26, 31-33, 37, Annual 1.* ***Newton*** *a-12p, 13p(last work 4/85).* ***Tuska*** *a-11p. JSA app. 3-10.*

INFINITY WAR, THE (Also see Infinity Gauntlet & Warlock and the Infinity...)
Marvel Comics: June, 1992 - No. 6, Nov, 1992 ($2.50, mini-series)

1-Starlin scripts, Lim-c/a(p), Thanos app. in all 2.50
2-6: All have wraparound gatefold covers 2.50

INFORMER, THE
Feature Television Productions: April, 1954 - No. 5, Dec, 1954

1-Sekowsky-a begins 12 24 36 71 96 120
2 9 18 27 49 62 75
3-5 8 16 24 43 54 65

IN HIS STEPS
Spire Christian Comics (Fleming H. Revell Co.): 1973, 1977 (39/49¢)

nn 1 3 4 6 8 10

INHUMANOIDS, THE (TV)
Marvel Comics (Star Comics): Jan, 1987 - No. 4, July 1987

1-4: Based on Hasbro toys 3.00

INHUMANS, THE (See Amazing Adventures, Fantastic Four #54 & Special #5, Incredible Hulk Special #1, Marvel Graphic Novel & Thor #146)
Marvel Comics Group: Oct, 1975 - No. 12, Aug, 1977

1: #1-4,6 are 25¢ issues 2 4 6 12 16 20
2-12: 9-Reprints Amazing Adventures #1,2('70). 12-Hulk app.
1 2 3 5 7 9
4,6-(30¢-c variants, limited distribution)(4,8/76) 2 4 6 11 14 18
11,12-(35¢-c variants, limited distribution) 2 4 6 11 14 18
Special 1(4/90, $1.50, 52 pgs.)-F.F. cameo 3.00
NOTE: ***Buckler*** *c-2-4p, 5.* ***Gil Kane*** *a-5-7p; c-1p, 7p, 8p.* ***Kirby*** *a-9r.* ***Mooney*** *a-11i.* ***Perez*** *a-1-4p, 8p.*

INHUMANS (Marvel Knights)
Marvel Comics: Nov, 1998 - No. 12, Oct, 1999 ($2.99, limited series)

Inhumans V6#2 © MAR

Instant Piano #3 © DH

Intimate Confessions #2 © REAL

	GD 2.0	VG 4.0	FN 6.0	VF 8.0	VF/NM 9.0	NM- 9.2
1-Jae Lee-c/a; Paul Jenkins-s						10.00
1-($6.95) DF Edition; Jae Lee variant-c						7.00
2-Two covers by Lee and Darrow						4.00
3-12						3.00
TPB (10/00, $24.95) r/#1-12						25.00

INHUMANS (Volume 3)
Marvel Comics: Jun, 2000 - No. 4, Oct, 2000 ($2.99, limited series)

	GD	VG	FN	VF	VF/NM	NM-
1-4-Ladronn-c/Pacheco & Marin-s. 1-3-Ladronn-a. 4-Lucas-a						3.00

INHUMANS (Volume 6)
Marvel Comics: Jun, 2003 - Present ($2.50/$2.99)

	GD	VG	FN	VF	VF/NM	NM-
1-8: 1-6-McKeever-s/Clark-a/JH Williams III-c. 7-Begin $2.99-c. 7,8-Teranishi-a						3.00

INHUMANS: THE GREAT REFUGE
Marvel Comics: May, 1995 ($2.95, one-shot)

	GD	VG	FN	VF	VF/NM	NM-
1						3.00

INKY & DINKY (See Felix's Nephews...)

IN LOVE (...Magazine on-c; I Love You No. 7 on)
Mainline/Charlton No. 5 (5/55)-on: Aug-Sept, 1954 - No. 6, July, 1955 ('Adult Reading' on-c)

	GD	VG	FN	VF	VF/NM	NM-
1-Simon & Kirby-a; book-length novel in all issues	39	78	117	230	325	420
2,3-S&K-a. 3-Last pre-code (12-1/54-55)	24	48	72	135	190	245
4-S&K-a.(Rare)	25	50	75	144	198	255
5-S&K-c only	10	20	30	60	80	100
6-No S&K-a	8	16	24	40	50	60

INNOVATION SPECTACULAR
Innovation Publishing: 1991 - No. 2, 1991 ($2.95, squarebound, 100 pgs.)

	GD	VG	FN	VF	VF/NM	NM-
1,2: Contains rebound comics w/o covers						3.00

INNOVATION SUMMER FUN SPECIAL
Innovation Publishing: 1991 ($3.50, B&W/color, squarebound)

	GD	VG	FN	VF	VF/NM	NM-
1-Contains rebound comics (Power Factory)						3.50

INSANE
Dark Horse Comics: Feb, 1988 - No. 2 ($1.75, B&W)

	GD	VG	FN	VF	VF/NM	NM-
1,2: 1-X-Men, Godzilla parodies. 2-Concrete						2.25

INSANE CLOWN POSSE
Chaos Comics: June, 1999 - No. 3, Nov, 1999 ($2.95)

	GD	VG	FN	VF	VF/NM	NM-
1-3-McCann-s						4.00
TPB ('00, $8.95) r/#1-3						9.00

INSANE CLOWN POSSE: THE PENDULUM
Chaos Comics: Jan, 2000 - No. 12, Dec, 2001 ($2.95)

	GD	VG	FN	VF	VF/NM	NM-
1-12-($5.95) polybagged w/CD						6.00
...: Hallowicked 1 (11/01, $2.99)						3.00
...: Halls of Illusion 1 (6/02, $2.99)						3.00

IN SEARCH OF THE CASTAWAYS (See Movie Comics)

INSIDE CRIME (Formerly My Intimate Affair)
Fox Features Syndicate (Hero Books): No. 3, July, 1950 - No. 2, Sept, 1950

	GD	VG	FN	VF	VF/NM	NM-
3-Wood-a (10 pgs.); L. B. Cole-c	29	58	87	164	232	300
2-Used in **SOTI**, pg. 182,183; r/Spook #24	23	46	69	129	180	230
nn(no publ. listed, nd)	10	20	30	56	73	90

INSPECTOR, THE (TV) (Also see The Pink Panther)
Gold Key: July, 1974 - No. 19, Feb, 1978

	GD	VG	FN	VF	VF/NM	NM-
1	3	7	10	21	28	35
2-5	2	4	6	14	18	22
6-9	2	4	6	11	14	18
10-19: 11-Reprints	2	4	6	8	10	12

INSPECTOR GILL OF THE FISH POLICE (See Fish Police)

INSPECTOR WADE
David McKay Publications: No. 13, May, 1938

	GD	VG	FN	VF	VF/NM	NM-
Feature Books 13	21	42	63	147	216	285

INSTANT PIANO
Dark Horse Comics: Aug, 1994 - No. 4, Feb, 1995 ($3.95, B&W, bimonthly, mature)

	GD	VG	FN	VF	VF/NM	NM-
1-4						4.00

INTERFACE
Marvel Comics (Epic Comics): Dec, 1989 - No. 8, Dec, 1990 ($1.95, mature, coated paper)

	GD	VG	FN	VF	VF/NM	NM-
1-8: Cont. from 1st ESPers series; painted-c/a						2.25
Espers: Interface TPB ('98, $16.95) r/#1-6						17.00

INTERNATIONAL COMICS (...Crime Patrol No. 6)
E. C. Comics: Spring, 1947 - No. 5, Nov-Dec, 1947

	GD 2.0	VG 4.0	FN 6.0	VF 8.0	VF/NM 9.0	NM- 9.2
1-Schaffenberger-a begins, ends #4	58	116	174	363	542	720
2	43	86	129	258	384	510
3-5	40	80	120	240	340	440

INTERNATIONAL CRIME PATROL (Formerly International Comics #1-5; becomes Crime Patrol No. 7 on)
E. C. Comics: No. 6, Spring, 1948

	GD	VG	FN	VF	VF/NM	NM-
6-Moon Girl app.	58	116	174	363	542	720

IN THE DAYS OF THE MOB (Magazine)
Hampshire Dist. Ltd. (National): Fall, 1971 (B&W)

	GD	VG	FN	VF	VF/NM	NM-
1-Kirby-a; John Dillinger wanted poster inside (1/2 value if poster is missing)	8	16	24	55	78	100

IN THE PRESENCE OF MINE ENEMIES
Spire Christian Comics/Fleming H. Revell Co.: 1973 (35/49¢)

	GD	VG	FN	VF	VF/NM	NM-
nn	1	3	4	6	8	10

IN THE SHADOW OF EDGAR ALLAN POE
DC Comics (Vertigo): 2002 (Graphic novel)

	GD	VG	FN	VF	VF/NM	NM-
Hardcover (2002, $24.95) Fuqua-s/Phillips and Parke photo-a						25.00
Softcover (2003, $17.95)						18.00

INTIMATE
Charlton Comics: Dec, 1957 - No. 3, May, 1958

	GD	VG	FN	VF	VF/NM	NM-
1	5	10	15	24	30	35
2,3	4	8	11	16	19	22

INTIMATE CONFESSIONS (See Fox Giants)

INTIMATE CONFESSIONS
Realistic Comics: July-Aug, 1951 - No. 7, Aug, 1952; No. 8, Mar, 1953 (All painted-c)

	GD	VG	FN	VF	VF/NM	NM-
1-Kinstler-c/a; c/Avon paperback #222	76	152	228	475	713	950
2	22	44	66	124	172	220
3-c/Avon paperback #250; Kinstler-c/a	25	50	75	147	202	260
4-8: 4-c/Avon paperback #304; Kinstler-c. 6-c/Avon paperback #120. 8-c/Avon paperback #375; Kinstler-a	22	44	66	124	172	220

INTIMATE CONFESSIONS
I. W. Enterprises/Super Comics: 1964

	GD	VG	FN	VF	VF/NM	NM-
I.W. Reprint #9,10, Super Reprint #10,12,18	2	4	6	11	14	18

INTIMATE LOVE
Standard Comics: No. 5, 1950 - No. 28, Aug, 1954

	GD	VG	FN	VF	VF/NM	NM-
5-8: 6-8-Severin/Elder-a	9	18	27	49	62	75
9	6	12	18	31	38	45
10-Jane Russell, Robert Mitchum photo-c	10	20	30	60	80	100
11-18,20,23,25,27,28	6	12	18	28	34	40
19,21,22,24,26-Toth-a	7	14	21	37	46	55

NOTE: *Celardo a-8, 10.* ***Colletta*** *a-23.* ***Moreira*** *a-13(2). Photo-c-6, 7, 10, 12, 14, 15, 18-20, 24, 26, 27.*

INTIMATE SECRETS OF ROMANCE
Star Publications: Sept, 1953 - No. 2, Apr, 1954

	GD	VG	FN	VF	VF/NM	NM-
1,2-L. B. Cole-c	20	40	60	112	156	200

INTRIGUE
Quality Comics Group: Jan, 1955

	GD	VG	FN	VF	VF/NM	NM-
1-Horror; Jack Cole reprint/Web of Evil	33	66	99	190	270	350

INTRIGUE
Image Comics: Aug, 1999 - No. 3, Feb, 2000 ($2.50/$2.95)

	GD	VG	FN	VF	VF/NM	NM-
1,2: 1-Two covers (Andrews, Wieringo); Shum-s/Andrews-a						2.50
3-($2.95)						3.00

INTRUDER
TSR, Inc.: 1990 - No. 10, 1991 ($2.95, 44 pgs.)

	GD	VG	FN	VF	VF/NM	NM-
1-10						3.00

INVADERS, THE (TV)
Gold Key: Oct, 1967 - No. 4, Oct, 1968 (All have photo-c)

	GD	VG	FN	VF	VF/NM	NM-
1-Spiegle-a in all	11	22	33	77	114	150
2-4	8	16	24	55	78	100

INVADERS, THE (Also see The Avengers #71 & Giant-Size Invaders)
Marvel Comics Group: August, 1975 - No. 40, May, 1979; No. 41, Sept, 1979

	GD	VG	FN	VF	VF/NM	NM-
1-Captain America & Bucky, Human Torch & Toro, & Sub-Mariner begin; cont'd. from Giant Size Invaders #1; #1-7 are 25¢ issues	4	8	12	29	40	50
2-5: 2-1st app. Brain-Drain. 3-Battle issue; Cap vs. Namor vs. Torch; intro U-Man						

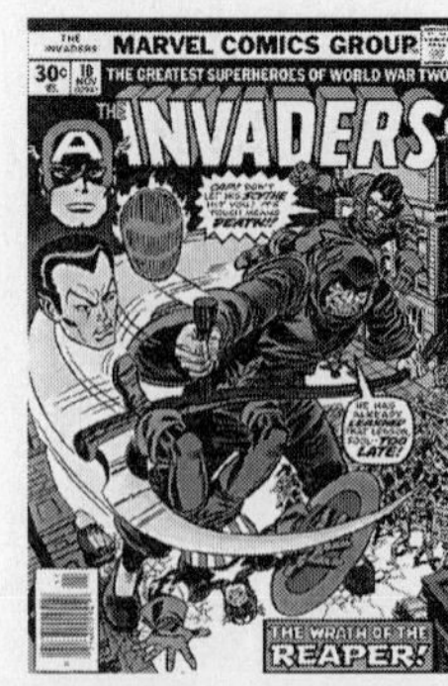

The Invaders #10 © MAR

Invincible #1 © Kirkman & Walker

Iron Fist #14 © MAR

GD VG FN VF VF/NM NM-
2.0 4.0 6.0 8.0 9.0 9.2

2 4 6 12 16 20
6-10: 6,7-(Regular 25¢ edition). 6-(7/76) Liberty Legion app. 7-Intro Baron Blood & intro/1st app. Union Jack; Human Torch origin retold. 8-Union Jack-c/story. 9-Origin Baron Blood. 10-G.A. Capt. America-r/C.A #22 2 4 6 8 10 12
6,7-(30¢-c variants, limited distribution) 2 4 6 14 18 22
11-19: 11-Origin Spitfire; intro The Blue Bullet. 14-1st app. The Crusaders. 16-Re-intro The Destroyer. 17-Intro Warrior Woman. 18-Re-intro The Destroyer w/new origin. 19-Hitler-c/story 1 2 3 5 7 9
17-19,21-(35¢-c variants, limited distribution) 2 4 6 9 11 14
20-(Regular 30¢-c) Reprints origin/1st app. Sub-Mariner from Motion Picture Funnies Weekly with color added & brief write-up about MPFW; 1st app. new Union Jack II 2 4 6 8 10 12
20-(35¢-c variant, limited distribution) 2 4 6 12 16 20
21-(Regular 30¢ edition)-r/Marvel Mystery #10 (battle issue) 1 2 3 5 7 9
22-30,34-40: 22-New origin Toro. 24-r/Marvel Mystery #17 (team-up issue; all-r). 25-All new-a begins. 28-Intro new Human Top & Golden Girl. 29-Intro Teutonic Knight. 34-Mighty Destroyer joins. 35-The Whizzer app. 6.00
31-33: 31-Frankenstein-c/sty. 32,33-Thor app. 1 2 3 5 7 9
41-Double size last issue 2 4 6 10 12 15
Annual 1 (9/77)-Schomburg, Rico stories (new); Schomburg-c/a (1st for Marvel in 30 years); Avengers app.; re-intro The Shark & The Hyena 3 7 10 21 28 35
NOTE: ***Buckler*** *a-5.* ***Everett*** *r-20('39), 21(1940), 24, Annual 1.* ***Gil Kane*** *c(p)-13, 17, 18, 20-27.* ***Kirby*** *c(p)-3-12, 14-16, 32, 33.* ***Mooney*** *a-5i, 16, 22.* ***Robbins*** *a-1-4, 6-9, 10(3 pg.), 11-15, 17-21, 23, 25-28; c-28.*

INVADERS (See Namor, the Sub-Mariner #12)
Marvel Comics Group: May, 1993 - No. 4, Aug, 1993 ($1.75, limited series)
1-4 2.50

INVADERS FROM HOME
DC Comics (Piranha Press): 1990 - No. 6, 1990 ($2.50, mature)
1-6 2.50

INVASION
DC Comics: Holiday, 1988-'89 - No. 3, Jan, 1989 ($2.95, lim. series, 84 pgs.)
1-3:1-McFarlane/Russell-a. 2-McFarlane/Russell & Giffen/Gordon-a 3.00

INVINCIBLE
Image Comics: Jan, 2003 - Present ($2.95)
1-7-Kirkman-s/Walker-a. 4-Preview of The Moth 3.00
Vol. 1: Family Matters TPB (8/03, $12.95) r/#1-4; intro. by Busiek; sketch pages 13.00

INVINCIBLE FOUR OF KUNG FU & NINJA
Leung Publications: April, 1988 - No. 6, 1989 ($2.00)
1-($2.75) 3.00
2-6: 2-Begin $2.00-c 2.25

INVISIBLE BOY (See Approved Comics)

INVISIBLE MAN, THE (See Superior Stories #1 & Supernatural Thrillers #2)

INVISIBLE PEOPLE
Kitchen Sink Press: 1992 (B&W, lim. series)
Book One: Sanctum; Book Two: "The Power": Will Eisner-s/a in all 2.25
Book Three: "Mortal Combat" 4.00
Hardcover ($34.95) 35.00
TPB (DC Comics, 9/00, $12.95) reprints series 13.00

INVISIBLES, THE (1st Series)
DC Comics (Vertigo): Sept, 1994 - No. 25, Oct, 1996 ($1.95/$2.50, mature)
1-($2.95, 52 pgs.)-Intro King Mob, Ragged Robin, Boy, Lord Fanny & Dane (Jack Frost); Grant Morrison scripts in all 6.00
2-8: 4-Includes bound-in trading cards. 5-1st app. Orlando; brown paper-c 4.00
9-25: 10-Intro Jim Crow. 13-15-Origin Lord Fanny. 19-Origin King Mob; polybagged. 20-Origin Boy. 21-Mister Six revealed. 25-Intro Division X 2.50
Apocalipstick (2001, $19.95, TPB)-r/#9-16; Bolland-c 20.00
Entropy in the U.K. (2001, $19.95, TPB)-r/#17-25; Bolland-c 20.00
Say You Want A Revolution (1996, $17.50, TPB)-r/#1-8 18.00
NOTE: ***Buckingham*** *a-25p.* ***Rian Hughes*** *c-1, 5.* ***Phil Jimenez*** *a-17p-19p.* ***Paul Johnson*** *a-16, 21.* ***Sean Phillips*** *c-2-4, 6-25.* ***Weston*** *a-10p.* ***Yeowell*** *a-1p-4p, 22p-24p.*

INVISIBLES, THE (2nd Series)
DC Comics (Vertigo): V2#1, Feb, 1997 - No. 22, Feb, 1999 ($2.50, mature)
1-Intro Jolly Roger; Grant Morrison scripts, Phil Jimenez-a, & Brian Bolland-c begins 4.00
2-22: 9,14-Weston-a 2.50
Bloody Hell in America TPB ('98, $12.95) r/#1-4 13.00
Counting to None TPB ('99, $19.95) r/#5-13 20.00
Kissing Mr. Quimper TPB ('00, $19.95) r/#14-22 20.00

INVISIBLES, THE (3rd Series) (Issue #'s go in reverse from #12 to #1)

GD VG FN VF VF/NM NM-
2.0 4.0 6.0 8.0 9.0 9.2

DC Comics (Vertigo): V3#12, Apr, 1999 - No. 1, June, 2000 ($2.95, mature)
1-12-Bolland-c; Morrison-s on all. 1-Quitely-a. 2-4-Art by various. 5-8-Phillips-a. 9-12-Phillip Bond-a. 3.00
The Invisible Kingdom TPB ('02, $19.95) r/#12-1; new Bolland-c 20.00

INVISIBLE SCARLET O'NEIL (Also see Famous Funnies #81 & Harvey Comics Hits #59)
Famous Funnies (Harvey): Dec, 1950 - No. 3, Apr, 1951 (2-3 pgs. of Powell-a in each issue.)
1 15 30 45 86 118 150
2,3 11 22 33 63 84 105

I, PAPARAZZI
DC Comics (Vertigo): 2001 ($29.95, HC, digitally manipulated photographic art)
nn-Pat McGreal-s/Steven Parke-digital-a/Stephen John Phillips-photos 30.00

IRON CORPORAL, THE (See Army War Heroes #22)
Charlton Comics: No. 23, Oct, 1985 - No. 25, Feb, 1986
23-25: Glanzman-a(r); low print 5.00

IRON FIST (See Deadly Hands of Kung Fu, Marvel Premiere & Power Man)
Marvel Comics: Nov, 1975 - No. 15, Sept, 1977
1-Iron Fist battles Iron Man (#1-6: 25¢) 5 10 15 36 48 60
2 3 6 9 18 24 30
3-10: 4-6-(Regular 25¢ edition)(4-6/76). 8-Origin retold 2 4 6 14 18 22
4-6-(30¢-c variant, limited distribution) 3 7 10 21 28 35
11,13: 13-(30¢-c) 2 4 6 10 13 16
12-Capt. America app. 2 4 6 12 16 20
13-(35¢-c variant, limited distribution) 3 6 9 16 20 24
14-1st app. Sabretooth (8/77)(see Power Man) 11 22 33 77 114 150
14-(35¢-c variant, limited distribution) 27 54 81 194 285 375
15-(Regular 30¢ ed.) X-Men app., Byrne-a 6 12 18 38 52 65
15-(35¢-c variant, limited distribution) 10 20 30 70 100 130
NOTE: ***Adkins*** *a-8p, 10i, 13i; c-8i.* ***Byrne*** *a-1-15p; c-8p, 15p.* ***G. Kane*** *c-4-6p.* ***McWilliams*** *a-1i.*

IRON FIST
Marvel Comics: Sept, 1996 - No. 2, Oct, 1996 ($1.50, limited series)
1,2 3.00

IRON FIST
Marvel Comics: Jul, 1998 - No. 3, Sept, 1998 ($2.50, limited series)
1-3: Jurgens-s/Guice-a 2.50

IRON FIST: WOLVERINE
Marvel Comics: Nov, 2000 - No. 4, Feb, 2001 ($2.99, limited series)
1-4-Igle-c/a; Kingpin app. 2-Iron Man app. 3,4-Capt. America app. 3.00

IRONHAND OF ALMURIC (Robert E. Howard's...)
Dark Horse Comics: Aug, 1991 - No. 4, 1991 ($2.00, B&W, mini-series)
1-4: 1-Conrad painted-c 2.25

IRON HORSE (TV)
Dell Publishing Co.: March, 1967 - No. 2, June, 1967
1-Dale Robertson photo covers on both 3 6 9 19 25 32
2 3 6 9 16 20 24

IRONJAW (Also see The Barbarians)
Atlas/Seaboard Publ.: Jan, 1975 - No. 4, July, 1975
1,2-Neal Adams-c. 1-1st app. Iron Jaw; Sekowsky-a(p); Fleisher-s 1 3 4 6 8 10
3,4-Marcos. 4-Origin 1 2 3 4 5 7

IRON LANTERN
Marvel Comics (Amalgam): June, 1997 ($1.95, one-shot)
1-Kurt Busiek-s/Paul Smith & Al Williamson-a 2.50

IRON MAN (Also see The Avengers #1, Giant-Size..., Marvel Collectors Item Classics, Marvel Double Feature, Marvel Fanfare & Tales of Suspense #39)
Marvel Comics: May, 1968 - No. 332, Sept, 1996
1-Origin; Colan-c/a(p); story continued from Iron Man & Sub-Mariner #1 37 74 111 278 414 550
2 12 24 36 87 129 170
3 9 18 27 60 85 110
4,5 7 14 21 51 71 90
6-10: 9-Iron Man battles green Hulk-like android 6 12 18 43 59 75
11-15: 15-Last 12¢ issue 5 10 15 36 48 60
16-20 4 8 12 24 32 40
21-24,26-30: 22-Death of Janice Cord. 27-Intro Fire Brand 3 6 9 18 24 30

Iron Man #125 © MAR

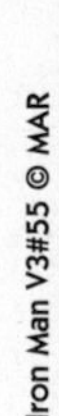

Iron Man V3#55 © MAR

Iron Man: The Iron Age #1 © MAR

GD 2.0 | VG 4.0 | FN 6.0 | VF 8.0 | VF/NM 9.0 | NM- 9.2

25-Iron Man battles Sub-Mariner 3 7 10 21 28 35
31-42: 33-1st app. Spymaster. 35-Nick Fury & Daredevil x-over. 42-Last 15¢ issue 3 6 9 16 20 24
43-Intro The Guardsman; 25¢ giant (52 pgs.) 3 7 10 21 28 35
44-46,48-50: 43-Giant-Man back-up by Ayers. 44-Ant-Man by Tuska. 46-The Guardsman dies. 50-Princess Python app. 2 4 6 12 16 20
47-Origin retold; Barry Smith-a(p) 3 6 9 18 23 28
51-53: 53-Starlin part pencils 2 4 6 11 14 18
54-Iron Man battles Sub-Mariner; 1st app. Moondragon (1/73) as Madame MacEvil; Everett part-c 3 6 10 21 28 35
55-1st app. Thanos (cameo), Drax the Destroyer, Mentor, Starfox & Kronos (2/73); Starlin-c/a 10 20 30 70 100 130
56-Starlin-a 3 6 9 18 23 28
57-65,67-70: 59-Firebrand returns. 65-Origin Dr. Spectrum. 67-Last 20¢ issue. 68-Sunfire & Unicorn app.; origin retold; Starlin-c 2 4 6 9 11 14
66-Iron Man vs. Thor. 2 4 6 14 18 22
71-84: 72-Cameo portraits of N. Adams. 73-Rename Stark Industries to Stark International; Brunner. 76-r/#9. 2 4 6 8 10 12
85-89-(Regular 25¢ editions): 86-1st app. Blizzard. 87-Origin Blizzard. 88-Thanos app. 89-Daredevil app.; last 25¢-c 2 4 6 8 10 12
85-89-(30¢-c variants, limited distribution)(4-8/76) 2 4 6 11 14 18
90-99: 96-1st app. new Guardsman 1 3 4 6 8 10
99,101-103-(35¢-c variants, limited dist.) 2 4 6 8 10 12
100-(7/77)-Starlin-c 3 6 9 16 20 25
100-(35¢-c variant, limited dist.) 4 8 12 22 30 38
101-117: 101-Intro DreadKnight. 109-1st app. new Crimson Dynamo; 1st app. Vanguard. 110-Origin Jack of Hearts retold; death of Count Nefaria. 114-Avengers app. 1 2 3 5 6 8
118-Byrne-a(p); 1st app. Jim Rhodes 1 2 3 5 7 9
119-127: 120,121-Sub-Mariner x-over. 122-Origin. 123-128-Tony Stark treated for alcohol problem. 125-Ant-Man app. 1 2 3 5 6 8
128-Classic Tony Stark alcoholism cover 2 4 6 8 10 12
129,130,133-149 5.00
131,132-Hulk x-over 1 2 3 4 5 7
150-Double size 1 2 3 5 6 8
151-168: 152-New armor. 161-Moon Knight app. 167-Tony Stark alcohol problem resurfaces 4.00
169-New Iron Man (Jim Rhodes replaces Tony Stark) 6.00
170,171 4.00
172-199: 172-Captain America x-over. 186-Intro Vibro. 190-Scarlet Witch app. 191-198-Tony Stark returns as original Iron Man. 192-Both Iron Men battle 3.00
200-(11/85, $1.25, 52 pgs.)-Tony Stark returns as new Iron Man (red & white armor) thru #230 5.00
201-213,215-224: 213-Intro new Dominic Fortune 3.00
214,225,228,231,234,247: 214-Spider-Woman app. in new black costume (1/87). 225-Double size ($1.25). 228-vs. Capt. America. 231-Intro new Iron Man. 234-Spider-Man x-over. 247-Hulk x-over 4.00
226,227,229,230,232,233,235-243,245,246,248,249: 233-Ant-Man app. 243-Tony Stark loses use of legs 2.50
244-($1.50, 52 pgs.)-New Armor makes him walk 3.00
250-($1.50, 52 pgs.)-Dr. Doom-c/story 3.00
251-274,276-281,283,285-287,289,291-299: 258-277-Byrne scripts. 271-Fin Fang Foom app. 276-Black Widow-c/story; last $1.00-c. 281-1st app.; War Machine (cameo). 283-2nd full app. War Machine 2.50
275-($1.50, 52 pgs.) 3.00
282-1st full app. War Machine (7/92) 4.00
284-Death of Iron Man (Tony Stark) 4.00
288-($2.50, 52pg.)-Silver foil stamped-c; Iron Man's 350th app. in comics 3.00
290-($2.95, 52pg.)-Gold foil stamped-c; 30th ann. 3.00
300-($3.95, 68 pgs.)-Collector's Edition w/embossed foil-c; anniversary issue; War Machine-c/story 4.00
300-($2.50, 68 pgs.)-Newsstand Edition 2.50
301-303: 302-Venom-c/story (cameo #301) 2.50
304-316,318-324,326-331: 304-Begin $1.50-c; bound-in trading card sheet; Thunderstrike-c/story. 310-Orange logo. 312-w/bound-in Power Ranger Card. 319-Prologue to "The Crossing." 326-New Tony Stark; Pratt-c. 330-War Machine & Stockpile app; return of Morgan Stark 2.50
310,325: 310 ($2.95)-Polybagged w/ 16 pg. Marvel Action Hour preview & acetate print; white logo. 325-($2.95)-Wraparound-c 3.00
317 ($2.50)-Flip book 2.50
332-Onslaught x-over 4.00
Special 1 (8/70)-Sub-Mariner x-over; Everett-c 4 8 12 24 32 40
Special 2 (11/71, 52 pgs.)-r/TOS #81,82,91 (all-r) 2 4 6 14 18 22
Annual 3 (1976)-Man-Thing app. 2 4 6 9 11 14

King Size 4 (8/77)-The Champions (w/Ghost Rider) app.; Newton-a(i) 1 3 4 6 8 10
Annual 5 ('82) New-a 6.00
Annual 6-8: ('83-'85) 6-New Iron Man (J. Rhodes) app. 8-X-Factor app. 5.00
Annual 9-15: ('86-'94) 10-Atlantis Attacks x-over; P. Smith-a; Layton/Guice-a; Sub-Mariner app. 11-(1990)-Origin of Mrs. Arbogast by Ditko (p&i). 12-1 pg. origin recap; Ant-Man back-up-s. 13-Darkhawk & Avengers West Coast app.; Colan/Williamson-a. 14-Bagged w/card 3.00
Manual 1 (1993, $1.75)-Operations handbook 2.50
Graphic Novel: Crash (1988, $12.95, Adults, 72 pgs.)-Computer generated art & color; violence & nudity 13.00
...Collector's Preview 1(11/94, $1.95)-wraparound-c; text & illos-no comics 2.50
...Vs. Dr. Doom (12/94, $12.95)-r/#149-150, 249,250. Julie Bell-c 13.00
NOTE: ***Austin*** *c-105i, 109-111i, 151i.* ***Byrne*** *a-118p; c-109p, 197, 253.* ***Colan*** *a-1p, 253, Special 1p(3); c-1p.* ***Craig*** *a-1i, 2-4, 5-13i, 14, 15-19i, 24p, 25p, 26-28i; c-2-4.* ***Ditko*** *a-160p.* ***Everett*** *c-29.* ***Guice*** *a-233-241p.* ***G. Kane*** *c(p)-52-54, 63, 67, 72-75, 77-79, 88, 98.* ***Kirby*** *a-Special 1p; c-13, 80p, 90, 92-95.* ***Mooney*** *a-40i, 43i, 47i.* ***Perez*** *c-103p.* ***Simonson*** *c-Annual 8.* ***B. Smith*** *a-232p, 243i; c-232.* ***P. Smith*** *a-159p, 245p, Annual 10p; c-159.* ***Starlin*** *a-53p(part), 55p, 56p; c-55p, 160, 163.* ***Tuska*** *a-5-13p, 15-23p, 24i, 32p, 38-46p, 48-54p, 57-61p, 63-69p, 70-72p, 78p, 86-92p, 95-106p, Annual 4p.* ***Wood*** *a-Special 1i.*

IRON MAN (The Invincible...) (Volume Two)
Marvel Comics: Nov, 1996 - No. 13, Nov, 1997 ($2.95/$1.95/$1.99)
(Produced by WildStorm Productions)

V2#1-3-Heroes Reborn begins; Scott Lobdell scripts & Whilce Portacio-c/a begin; new origin Iron Man & Hulk. 2-Hulk app. 3-Fantastic Four app. 4.00
1-Variant-c 5.00
4-11: 4-Two covers. 6-Fantastic Four app.; Industrial Revolution; Hulk app. 7-Return of Rebel. 11-($1.99) Dr. Doom-c/app. 3.00
12-($2.99) "Heroes Reunited"-pt. 3; Hulk-c/app. 3.50
13-($1.99) "World War 3"-pt. 3, x-over w/Image 3.00

IRON MAN (The Invincible...) (Volume Three)
Marvel Comics: Feb, 1998 - Present ($2.99/$1.99/$2.25)

V3#1-($2.99)-Follows Heroes Return; Busiek scripts & Chen-c/a begin; Deathsquad app. 5.00
1-Alternate Ed. 1 2 3 5 6 8
2-12: 2-Two covers. 6-Black Widow-c/app. 7-Warbird-c/app. 8-Black Widow app. 9-Mandarin returns 3.00
13-($2.99) battles the Controller 3.50
14-24: 14-Fantastic Four-c/app. 3.00
25-($2.99) Iron Man and Warbird battle Ultimo; Avengers app. 3.00
26-30-Quesada-s. 28-Whiplash killed. 29-Begin $2.25-c. 2.50
31-45,47-49,51-54: 35-Maximum Security x-over; FF-c/app. 41-Grant-a begins. 44-New armor debut. 48-Ultron-c/app. 2.25
46-($3.50, 100 pgs.) Sentient armor returns; r/V1#78,140,141 3.50
50-($3.50) Grell-s begin; Black Widow app. 3.50
55-($3.50) 400th issue; Asamiya-c; back-up story Stark reveals ID; Grell-a 3.50
56-66: 56-Reis-a. 57,58-Ryan-a. 59-61-Grell-c/a. 62,63-Ryan-a. 64-Davis-a; Thor-c/app. 2.25
67-75: 67-Begin $2.99-c; Gene Ha-c 3.00
.../Captain America '98 Annual ($3.50) vs. Modok 3.50
1999, 2000 Annual ($3.50) 3.50
2001 Annual ($2.99) Claremont-s/Ryan-a 3.00
Mask in the Iron Man (5/01, $14.95, TPB) r/#26-30, #1/2 15.00

IRON MAN & SUB-MARINER
Marvel Comics Group: Apr, 1968 (12¢, one-shot) (Pre-dates Iron Man #1 & Sub-Mariner #1)

1-Iron Man story by Colan/Craig continued from Tales of Suspense #99 & continued in Iron Man #1; Sub-Mariner story by Colan continued from Tales to Astonish #101 & continued in Sub-Mariner #1; Colan/Everett-c 15 30 45 104 152 200

IRON MAN: BAD BLOOD
Marvel Comics: Sept, 2000 - No. 4, Dec, 2000 ($2.99, limited series)

1-4-Micheline-s/Layton-a 3.00

IRON MAN: THE IRON AGE
Marvel Comics: Aug, 1998 - No. 2, Sept, 1998 ($5.99, limited series)

1,2-Busiek-s; flashback story from gold armor days 6.00

IRON MAN: THE LEGEND
Marvel Comics: Sept, 1996 ($3.95, one-shot)

1-Tribute issue 4.50

IRON MAN 2020 (Also see Machine Man limited series)
Marvel Comics: June, 1994 ($5.95, one-shot)

nn 6.00

IRON MAN/X-O MANOWAR: HEAVY METAL (See X-O Manowar/Iron Man: In Heavy Metal)
Marvel Comics: Sept, 1996 ($2.50, one-shot) (1st Marvel/Valiant x-over)

1-Pt. II of Iron Man/X-O Manowar x-over; Fabian Nicieza scripts; 1st app. Rand Banion 2.50

I Spy #5 © CBS

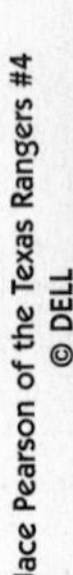
Jace Pearson of the Texas Rangers #4 © DELL

Jackie Robinson #2 © FAW

GD 2.0 | VG 4.0 | FN 6.0 | VF 8.0 | VF/NM 9.0 | NM- 9.2

IRON MARSHALL
Jademan Comics: July, 1990 - No. 32, Feb, 1993 ($1.75, plastic coated-c)
1,32: Kung Fu stories. 1-Poster centerfold 2.25
2-31-Kung Fu stories in all 2.25

IRON VIC (See Comics Revue No. 3 & Giant Comics Editions)
United Features Syndicate/St. John Publ. Co.: 1940
Single Series 22 34 68 102 193 274 355

IRON WINGS
Image Comics: Apr, 2000 - No. 2, May, 2000 ($2.50)
1,2: 1-Two covers 2.50

IRONWOLF
DC Comics: 1986 ($2.00, one shot)
1-r/Weird Worlds 8-10; Chaykin story & art 2.25

IRONWOLF: FIRES OF THE REVOLUTION (See Weird Worlds #8-10)
DC Comics: 1992 ($29.95, hardcover)
nn-Chaykin/Moore story, Mignola-a w/Russell inks. 30.00

ISAAC ASIMOV'S I-BOTS
Tekno Comix: Dec, 1995 - No. 7, May, 1996 ($1.95)
1-7: 1-6-Perez-c/a. 2-Chaykin variant-c exists. 3-Polybagged. 7-Lady Justice-c/app. 2.25

ISAAC ASIMOV'S I-BOTS
BIG Entertainment: V2#1, June, 1996 - No. 9, Feb, 1997 ($2.25)
V2#1-9: 1-Lady Justice-c/app. 6-Gil Kane-c 2.25

ISIS (TV) (Also see Shazam)
National Per.l Publ./DC Comics: Oct-Nov, 1976 - No. 8, Dec-Jan, 1977-78
1-Wood inks 2 4 6 10 13 16
2-8: 5-Isis new look. 7-Origin 1 2 3 5 7 9

ISLAND AT THE TOP OF THE WORLD (See Walt Disney Showcase #27)

ISLAND OF DR. MOREAU, THE (Movie)
Marvel Comics Group: Oct, 1977 (52 pgs.)
1-Gil Kane-c 1 2 3 4 5 7

I SPY (TV)
Gold Key: Aug, 1966 - No. 6, Sept, 1968 (All have photo-c)
1-Bill Cosby, Robert Culp photo covers 23 46 69 167 244 320
2-6: 3,4-McWilliams-a. 5-Last 12¢-c 14 28 42 97 141 185

IT! (See Astonishing Tales No. 21-24 & Supernatural Thrillers No. 1)

ITCHY & SCRATCHY COMICS (The Simpsons TV show)
Bongo Comics: 1993 - No. 3, 1993 ($1.95)
1-3: 1-Bound-in jumbo poster. 3-w/decoder screen trading card 4.00
Holiday Special ('94, $1.95) 4.00

IT GIRL (Also see Atomics, and Madman Comics)
Oni Press: May, 2002 ($2.95, one-shot)
1-Allred-s/Clugston-Major-c/a; Atomics and Madman app. 3.00

IT REALLY HAPPENED
William H. Wise No. 1,2/Standard (Visual Editions): 1944 - No. 11, Oct, 1947
1-Kit Carson & Ben Franklin stories 21 42 63 118 164 210
2 11 22 33 63 84 105
3,4,6,9,11: 6-Joan of Arc story. 9-Captain Kidd & Frank Buck stories 10 20 30 56 73 90
5-Lou Gehrig & Lewis Carroll stories 16 32 48 89 122 155
7-Teddy Roosevelt story 11 22 33 63 84 105
8-Story of Roy Rogers 17 34 51 95 130 165
10-Honus Wagner & Mark Twain stories 13 26 39 74 100 125
NOTE: *Guardineer a-7(2), 8(2), 11. Schomburg c-1-7, 9-11.*

IT RHYMES WITH LUST (Also see Bold Stories & Candid Tales)
St. John Publishing Co.: 1950 (Digest size, 128 pgs.)
nn (Rare)-Matt Baker & Ray Osrin-a 61 122 183 381 573 765

IT'S ABOUT TIME (TV)
Gold Key: Jan, 1967
1 (10195-701)-Photo-c 5 10 15 33 44 55

IT'S A DUCK'S LIFE
Marvel Comics/Atlas(MMC): Feb, 1950 - No. 11, Feb, 1952
1-Buck Duck, Super Rabbit begin 15 30 45 86 118 150
2 9 18 27 49 62 75
3-11 8 16 24 43 54 65

IT'S GAMETIME
National Periodical Publications: Sept-Oct, 1955 - No. 4, Mar-Apr, 1956
1-(Scarce)-Infinity-c; Davy Crockett app. in puzzle 76 152 228 475 713 950
2,3 (Scarce): 2-Dodo & The Frog 60 120 180 375 563 750
4 (Rare) 63 126 189 394 592 790

IT'S LOVE, LOVE, LOVE
St. John Publishing Co.: Nov, 1957 - No. 2, Jan, 1958 (10¢)
1,2 6 12 18 28 34 40

IVANHOE (See Fawcett Movie Comics No. 20)

IVANHOE
Dell Publishing Co.: July-Sept, 1963
1 (12-373-309) 4 8 12 24 32 40

IWO JIMA (See Spectacular Features Magazine)

JACE PEARSON OF THE TEXAS RANGERS (Radio/TV)(4-Color #396 is titled Tales of the Texas Rangers; ...'s Tales of ... #11-on)(See Western Roundup under Dell Giants)
Dell Publishing Co.: No. 396, 5/52 - No. 1021, 8-10/59 (No #10) (All-Photo-c)
Four Color 396 (#1) 12 24 36 82 121 160
2(5-7/53) - 9(2-4/55) 7 14 21 51 71 90
Four Color 648(#10, 9/55) 6 12 18 40 55 70
11(11-2/55-56) - 14,17-20(6-8/58) 6 12 18 38 52 65
15,16-Toth-a 6 12 18 40 55 70
Four Color 961, 1021: 961-Spiegle-a 6 12 18 38 52 65
NOTE: *Joel McCrea photo c-1-9, F.C. 648 (starred on radio show only); Willard Parker photo c-11-on (starred on TV series).*

JACK ARMSTRONG (Radio)(See True Comics)
Parents' Institute: Nov, 1947 - No. 9, Sept, 1948; No. 10, Mar, 1949 - No. 13, Sept, 1949
1-(Scarce) (odd size) Cast intro. inside front-c 44 88 132 264 395 525
2 21 42 63 118 164 210
3-5 15 30 45 86 118 150
6-13: 7-Vic Hardy's Crime Lab begins? 12 24 36 71 96 120

JACK HUNTER
Blackthorne Publishing: July, 1987 - No. 3 ($1.25)
1-3 2.25

JACKIE CHAN'S SPARTAN X
Topps Comics: May, 1997 - No. 3 ($2.95, limited series)
1-3-Michael Golden-s/a; variant photo-c 3.00

JACKIE CHAN'S SPARTAN X: HELL BENT HERO FOR HIRE
Image Comics (Little Eva Ink): Mar, 1998 - No. 3 ($2.95, B&W)
1-3-Michael Golden-s/a: 1-variant photo-c 3.00

JACKIE GLEASON (TV) (Also see The Honeymooners)
St. John Publishing Co.: Sept, 1955 - No. 4, Dec, 1955?
1(1955)(TV)-Photo-c 60 120 180 375 563 750
2-4 40 80 120 240 360 480

JACKIE GLEASON AND THE HONEYMOONERS (TV)
National Periodical Publications: June-July, 1956 - No. 12, Apr-May, 1958
1-1st app. Ralph Kramden 88 176 264 550 825 1100
2 54 108 162 324 487 650
3-11 40 80 120 240 360 480
12 (Scarce) 60 120 180 375 563 750

JACKIE JOKERS (Became Richie Rich &...)
Harvey Publications: March, 1973 - No. 4, Sept, 1973 (#5 was advertised, but not published)
1-1st app. 3 6 9 18 23 28
2-4: 2-President Nixon app. 2 4 6 9 11 14

JACKIE ROBINSON (Famous Plays of...) (Also see Negro Heroes #2 & Picture News #4)
Fawcett Publications: May, 1950 - No. 6, 1952 (Baseball hero) (All photo-c)
nn 92 184 276 575 863 1150
2 55 110 165 330 495 660
3-6 46 92 138 276 413 550

JACK IN THE BOX (Formerly Yellowjacket Comics #1-10; becomes Cowboy Western Comics #17 on)
Frank Comunale/Charlton Comics No. 11 on: Feb, 1946; No. 11, Oct, 1946 - No. 16, Nov-Dec, 1947
1-Stitches, Marty Mouse & Nutsy McKrow 15 30 45 86 118 150
11-Yellowjacket (early Charlton comic) 20 40 60 112 156 200

Jack Kirby's Fourth World #10 © DC

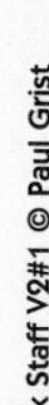
Jack Staff V2#1 © Paul Grist

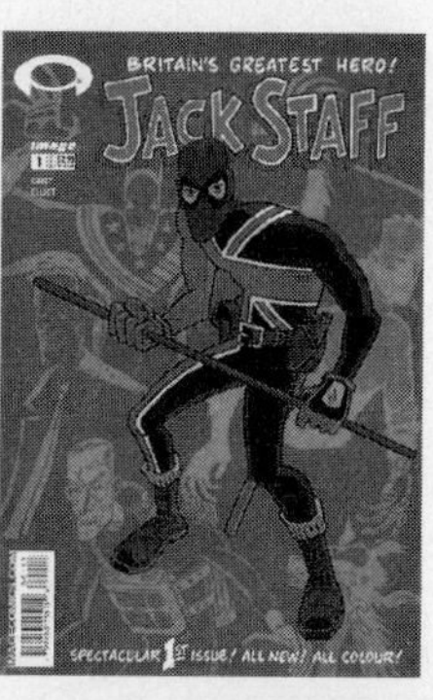

James Bond Jr. #1 © Eon Prod. Ltd.

	GD 2.0	VG 4.0	FN 6.0	VF 8.0	VF/NM 9.0	NM- 9.2
12,14,15	9	18	27	54	70	85
13-Wolverton-a	21	42	63	118	164	210
16-12 pg. adapt. of Silas Marner; Kiefer-a	11	22	33	63	84	105

JACK KIRBY'S FOURTH WORLD (See Mister Miracle & New Gods, 3rd Series)
DC Comics: Mar, 1997 - No. 20, Oct, 1998 ($1.95/$2.25)

1-20: 1-Byrne-a/scripts & Simonson-c begin; story cont'd from New Gods, 3rd Series #15; retells "The Pact" (New Gods, 1st Series #7); 1st DC app. Thor (cameo). 2-Thor vs. Big Barda; "Apokolips Then" back-up begins; Kirby-c/swipe (Thor #126) 8-Genesis x-over. 10-Simonson-s/a 13-Simonson back-up story. 20-Superman-c/app. 2.25

JACK KIRBY'S SECRET CITY SAGA
Topps Comics (Kirbyverse): No. 0, Apr, 1993; No. 1, May, 1993 - No. 4, Aug, 1993 ($2.95, limited series)

0-(No cover price, 20 pgs.)-Simonson-c/a 3.00
0-Red embossed-c (limited ed.) 5.00
1-4-Bagged w/3 trading cards; Ditko-c/a: 1-Ditko/Art Adams-c. 2-Ditko/Byrne-c; has coupon for Pres. Clinton holo-foil trading card. 3-Dorman poster; has coupon for Gore holo-foil trading card. 4-Ditko/Perez-c 3.00

NOTE: *Issues #1-4 contain coupons redeemable for Kirbychrome version of #1*

JACK KIRBY'S SILVER STAR (Also see Silver Star)
Topps Comics (Kirbyverse): Oct, 1993 ($2.95)(Intended as a 4-issue limited series)

1-Silver ink-c; Austin-c/a(i); polybagged w/3 cards 3.00

JACK KIRBY'S TEENAGENTS (See Satan's Six)
Topps Comics (Kirbyverse): Aug, 1993 - No. 3, Oct, 1993 ($2.95)(Intended as a 4-issue limited series)

1-3: Bagged with/3 trading cards; 1-3-Austin-c(i): 3-Liberty Project app. 3.00

JACK OF HEARTS (Also see The Deadly Hands of Kung Fu #22 & Marvel Premiere #44)
Marvel Comics Group: Jan, 1984 - No. 4, Apr, 1984 (60¢, limited series)

1-4 2.50

JACKPOT COMICS (Jolly Jingles #10 on)
MLJ Magazines: Spring, 1941 - No. 9, Spring, 1943

	GD	VG	FN	VF	VF/NM	NM-
1-The Black Hood, Mr. Justice, Steel Sterling & Sgt. Boyle begin; Biro-c	305	610	915	1983	3042	4100
2-S. Cooper-c	140	280	420	875	1313	1750
3-Hubbell-c	104	208	312	650	975	1300
4-Archie begins (Win/41; on sale 12/41)-(also see Pep Comics #22); 1st app. Mrs. Grundy, the principal; Novick-c	370	740	1110	2405	3703	5000
5-Hitler, Tojo, Mussolini-c by Montana; 1st definitive Mr. Weatherbee; 1st app. Reggie in 1 panel cameo	152	304	456	950	1425	1900
6-9: 6,7-Bondage-c by Novick. 8,9-Sahle-c	107	214	321	669	1005	1340

JACK Q FROST (See Unearthly Spectaculars)

JACK STAFF (Vol. 2; previously published in Britain)
Image Comics: Feb, 2003 - Present ($2.95)

1-4-Paul Grist-s/a 3.00

JACK THE GIANT KILLER (See Movie Classics)

JACK THE GIANT KILLER (New Adventures of...)
Bimfort & Co.: Aug-Sept, 1953

	GD	VG	FN	VF	VF/NM	NM-
V1#1-H. C. Kiefer-c/a	24	48	72	135	190	245

JACKY'S DIARY
Dell Publishing Co.: No. 1091, Apr-June, 1960 (one-shot)

	GD	VG	FN	VF	VF/NM	NM-
Four Color 1091	5	10	15	36	48	60

JADE (Chaos! Presents: ...)
Chaos! Comics: May, 2001 - No. 4, Aug, 2001 ($2.99, limited series)

1-4-Lashley-a/Golden & Sniegoski-a 3.00
...Redemption 1-4 (12/01 - No. 4, 3/02) Tortosa-a 3.00

JADEMAN COLLECTION
Jademan Comics: Dec, 1989 - No. 3, 1990 ($2.50, plastic coated-c, 68 pgs.)

1-3: 1-Wraparound-c w/fold-out poster 2.50

JADEMAN KUNG FU SPECIAL
Jademan Comics: 1988 ($1.50, 64 pgs.)

1 2.50

JADE WARRIORS (Mike Deodato's...)
Image Comics (Glass House Graphics): Nov, 1999 - No. 3, 2000 ($2.50)

1-3-Deodato-a 2.50
1-Variant-c 2.50

JAGUAR, THE (Also see The Adventures of...)

Impact Comics (DC): Aug, 1991 - No. 14, Oct, 1992 ($1.00)

1-14: 4-The Black Hood x-over. 7-Sienkiewicz-c. 9-Contains Crusaders trading card 2.25
Annual 1 (1992, $2.50, 68 pgs.)-With trading card 2.50

JAGUAR GOD
Verotik: Mar, 1995 - No. 7, June, 1997 ($2.95, mature)

0 (2/96, $3.50)-Embossed Frazetta-c; Bisley-a; w/pin-ups. 4.00
1-Frazetta-c. 4.00
2-7: 2-Frazetta-c. 3-Bisley-c. 4-Emond-c. 7-($2.95)-Frazetta-c 3.00

JAKE THRASH
Aircel Publishing: 1988 - No. 3, 1988 ($2.00)

1-3 2.25

JAM, THE (...Urban Adventure)
Slave Labor Nos. 1-5/Dark Horse Comics Nos. 6-8/Caliber Comics No. 9 on: Nov, 1989 - No. 14, 1997 ($1.95/$2.50/$2.95, B&W)

1-14: Bernie Mireault-c/a/scripts. 6-1st Dark Horse issue. 9-1st Caliber issue 3.00

JAMBOREE
Round Publishing Co.: Feb, 1946(no month given) - No. 3, Apr, 1946

	GD	VG	FN	VF	VF/NM	NM-
1-Funny animal	26	52	78	150	210	270
2,3	16	32	48	92	126	160

JAMES BOND 007: A SILENT ARMAGEDDON
Dark Horse Comics/Acme Press: Mar, 1993 - Apr 1993 (limited series)

1,2 3.50

JAMES BOND 007: GOLDENEYE (Movie)
Topps Comics: Jan, 1996 ($2.95, unfinished limited series of 3)

1-Movie adaptation; Stelfreeze-c 3.00

JAMES BOND 007: SERPENT'S TOOTH
Dark Horse Comics/Acme Press: July 1992 - Aug 1992 ($4.95, limited series)

1-3-Paul Gulacy-c/a 5.00

JAMES BOND 007: SHATTERED HELIX
Dark Horse Comics: Jun 1994 - July 1994 ($2.50, limited series)

1,2 3.00

JAMES BOND 007: THE QUASIMODO GAMBIT
Dark Horse Comics: Jan 1995 - May 1995 ($3.95, limited series)

1-3 4.50

JAMES BOND FOR YOUR EYES ONLY
Marvel Comics Group: Oct, 1981 - No. 2, Nov, 1981

1,2-Movie adapt.; r/Marvel Super Special #19 3.00

JAMES BOND JR. (TV)
Marvel Comics: Jan, 1992 - No. 12, Dec, 1992 (#1: $1.00, #2-on: $1.25)

1-12: Based on animated TV show 2.25

JAMES BOND: LICENCE TO KILL (See Licence To Kill)

JAMES BOND: PERMISSION TO DIE
Eclipse Comics/ACME Press: 1989 - No. 3, 1991 ($3.95, lim. series, squarebound, 52 pgs.)

1-3: Mike Grell-c/a/scripts in all. 3-($4.95) 5.00

JAM, THE: SUPER COOL COLOR INJECTED TURBO ADVENTURE #1 FROM HELL!
Comico: May, 1988 ($2.50, 44 pgs., one-shot)

1 2.50

JANE ARDEN (See Feature Funnies & Pageant of Comics)
St. John (United Features Syndicate): Mar, 1948 - No. 2, June, 1948

	GD	VG	FN	VF	VF/NM	NM-
1-Newspaper reprints	16	32	48	92	126	160
2	12	24	36	69	92	115

JANN OF THE JUNGLE (Jungle Tales No. 1-7)
Atlas Comics (CSI): No. 8, Nov, 1955 - No. 17, June, 1957

	GD	VG	FN	VF	VF/NM	NM-
8(#1)	34	68	102	193	274	355
9,11-15	20	40	60	112	156	200
10-Williamson/Colletta-c	20	40	60	115	160	205
16,17-Williamson/Mayo-a(3), 5 pgs. each	21	42	63	121	168	215

NOTE: ***Everett** c-15-17. **Heck** a-8, 15, 17. **Maneely** c-11. **Shores** a-8.*

JAR OF FOOLS
Penny Dreadful Press: 1994 ($5.95, B&W)

1-Jason Lutes-c/a/scripts 6.00

JAR OF FOOLS

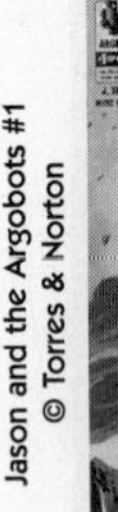
Jason and the Argobots #1 © Torres & Norton

Jesse James #4 © AVON

Jet Aces #4 © FH

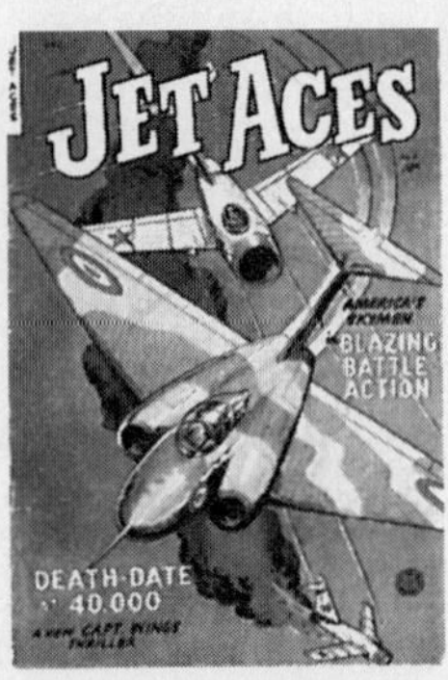

GD 2.0 | VG 4.0 | FN 6.0 | VF 8.0 | VF/NM 9.0 | NM- 9.2

Black Eye Productions: 1994 - No. 2, 1994 ($6.95, B&W)
1,2: 1-Reprints of earlier ed. Jason Lutes-c/a/scripts 7.00

JASON & THE ARGOBOTS
Oni Press: Aug, 2002 - No. 4, Dec, 2002 ($2.95, B&W, limited series)
1-4-Torres-s/Norton-c/a 3.00
Vol. 1 Birthquake TPB (6/03, $11.95, digest size) r/#1-4, Sunday comic strips 12.00
Vol. 2 Machina Ex Deus TPB (9/03, $11.95, digest size) new story 12.00

JASON & THE ARGONAUTS (See Movie Classics)

JASON GOES TO HELL: THE FINAL FRIDAY (Movie)
Topps Comics: July, 1993 - No. 3, Sept, 1993 ($2.95, limited series)
1-3: Adaptation of film. 1-Glow-in-the-dark-c 3.00

JASON'S QUEST (See Showcase #88-90)

JASON VS. LEATHERFACE
Topps Comics: Oct, 1995 - No. 3, Jan, 1996 ($2.95, limited series)
1-3: Collins scripts; Bisley-c 3.00

JAWS 2 (See Marvel Comics Super Special, A)

JAY & SILENT BOB (See Clerks & Oni Double Feature)
Oni Press: July, 1998 - No. 4, Oct, 1999 ($2.95, B&W, limited series)
1-Kevin Smith-s/Fegredo-a; photo-c & Quesada/Palmiotti-c 8.00
1-San Diego Comic Con variant covers (2 different covers, came packaged with action figures) 10.00
1-2nd & 3rd printings, 2-4: 2-Allred-c. 3-Flip-c by Jaime Hernandez 3.00
Chasing Dogma TPB (1999, $11.95) r/#1-4; Alanis Morissette intro. 12.00
Chasing Dogma TPB (2001, $12.95) r/#1-4 in color; Morissette intro. 13.00
Chasing Dogma HC (1999, $69.95, S&N) r/#1-4 in color; Morissette intro. 70.00

JCP FEATURES
J.C. Productions (Archie): Feb, 1982-c; Dec, 1981-indicia ($2.00, one-shot, B&W magazine)
1-T.H.U.N.D.E.R. Agents; Black Hood by Morrow & Neal Adams; Texeira-a; 2 pgs. S&K-a from Fly #1 1 3 4 6 8 10

JEANIE COMICS (Formerly All Surprise; Cowgirl Romances #28)
Marvel Comics/Atlas(CPC): No. 13, April, 1947 - No. 27, Oct, 1949
13-Mitzi, Willie begin 19 38 57 109 152 195
14,15 14 28 42 79 107 135
16-Used in Love and Death by Legman; Kurtzman's "Hey Look" 16 32 48 89 122 155
17-19,22-Kurtzman's "Hey Look", (1-3 pgs. each) 11 22 33 66 88 110
20,21,23-27 10 20 30 58 77 95

JEEP COMICS (Also see G.I. Comics and Overseas Comics)
R. B. Leffingwell & Co.: Winter, 1944 - No. 3, Mar-Apr, 1948
1-Capt. Power, Criss Cross & Jeep & Peep (costumed) begin 55 110 165 330 495 660
2 37 74 111 212 301 390
3-L. B. Cole dinosaur-c 46 92 138 276 413 550

JEFF JORDAN, U.S. AGENT
D. S. Publishing Co.: Dec, 1947 - Jan, 1948
1 15 30 45 86 118 150

JEMM, SON OF SATURN
DC Comics: Sept, 1984 - No. 12, Aug, 1985 (Maxi-series, mando paper)
1-12: 3-Origin 2.50
NOTE: *Colan a-1-12p; c-1-5, 7-12p.*

JENNY FINN
Oni Press: June, 1999 - No. 2, Sept, 1999 ($2.95, B&W, unfinished lim. series)
1,2-Mignola & Nixey-s/Nixey-a/Mignola-c 3.00

JENNY SPARKS: THE SECRET HISTORY OF THE AUTHORITY
DC Comics (WildStorm): Aug, 2000 - No. 5, Mar, 2001 ($2.50, limited series)
1-Millar-s/McCrea & Hodgkins-a/Hitch & Neary-c 3.50
1-Variant-c by McCrea 1 3 4 6 8 10
2-5: 2-Apollo & Midnighter. 3-Jack Hawksmoor. 4-Shen. 5-Engineer 3.00
TPB (2001, $14.95) r/#1-5; Ellis intro. 15.00

JERRY DRUMMER (Formerly Soldier & Marine V2#9)
Charlton Comics: V2#10, Apr, 1957 - V3#12, Oct, 1957
V2#10, V3#11,12: 11-Whitman-c/a 6 12 18 29 36 42

JERRY IGER'S... (All titles, Blackthorne/First)(Value: cover or less)

JERRY LEWIS (See The Adventures of...)

JESSE JAMES (The True Story Of..., also seeThe Legend of...)
Dell Publishing Co.: No. 757, Dec, 1956 (one shot)
Four Color 757-Movie, photo-c 10 20 30 70 100 130

JESSE JAMES (See Badmen of the West & Blazing Sixguns)
Avon Periodicals: 8/50 - No. 9, 11/52; No. 15, 10/53 - No. 29, 8-9/56
1-Kubert Alabam-r/Cowpuncher #1 17 34 51 98 134 170
2-Kubert-a(3) 14 28 42 79 107 135
3-Kubert Alabam-r/Cowpuncher #2 13 26 39 76 103 130
4,9-No Kubert 8 16 24 40 50 60
5,6-Kubert Jesse James-a(3); 5-Wood-a(1pg.) 13 26 39 76 103 130
7-Kubert Jesse James-a(2) 11 22 33 66 88 110
8-Kinstler-a(3) 8 16 24 46 58 70
15-Kinstler-r/#3 7 14 21 35 43 50
16-Kinstler-r/#3 & story-r/Butch Cassidy #1 7 14 21 37 46 55
17-19,21: 17-Jesse James-r/#4; Kinstler-c idea from Kubert splash in #6. 18-Kubert Jesse James-r/#5. 19-Kubert Jesse James-r/#6. 21-Two Jesse James-r/#4, Kinstler-r/#4 6 12 18 33 41 48
20-Williamson/Frazetta-a; r/Chief Vic. Apache Massacre; Kubert Jesse James-r/#6; Kit West story by Larsen 14 28 42 79 107 135
22-29: 22,23-No Kubert. 24-New McCarty strip by Kinstler; Kinstler-r. 25-New McCarty Jesse James strip by Kinstler; Jesse James-r/#7,9. 26,27-New McCarty Jesse James strip plus a Kinstler/McCann Jesse James-r. 28-Reprints most of Red Mountain, Featuring Quantrells Raiders 6 12 18 33 41 48
Annual nn (1952; 25¢, 100 pgs.)- "...Brings Six-Gun Justice to the West"- 3 earlier issues rebound; Kubert, Kinstler-a(3) 29 58 87 164 232 300
NOTE: *Mostly reprints #10 on.* **Fawcette** *c-1, 2.* **Kida** *a-5.* **Kinstler** *a-3, 4, 7-9, 15r, 16r(2), 21-27; c-3, 4, 9, 17-27. Painted c-5-8. 22 has 2 stories r/Sheriff Bob Dixon's Chuck Wagon #1 with name changed to Sheriff Bob Trent.*

JESSE JAMES
Realistic Publications: July, 1953
nn-Reprints Avon's #1; same-c, colors different 9 18 27 54 70 85

JEST (Formerly Snap; becomes Kayo #12)
Harry 'A' Chesler: No. 10, 1944; No. 11, 1944
10-Johnny Rebel & Yankee Boy app. in text 17 34 51 98 134 170
11-Little Nemo in Adventure Land 17 34 51 98 134 170

JESTER
Harry 'A' Chesler: No. 10, 1945
10 15 30 45 86 118 150

JESUS
Spire Christian Comics (Fleming H. Revell Co.): 1979 (49¢)
nn 2 4 6 8 10 12

JET (See Jet Powers)

JET (Crimson from Wildcore & Backlash)
DC Comics (WildStorm): Nov, 2000 - No. 4, Feb, 2001 ($2.50, limited series)
1-4-Nguyen-a/Abnett & Lanning-s 2.50

JET ACES
Fiction House Magazines: 1952 - No. 4, 1953
1 16 32 48 92 126 160
2-4 9 18 27 54 70 85

JETCAT CLUBHOUSE (Also see Land of Nod, The)
Oni Press: Apr, 2001 - No. 3, Aug, 2001 ($3.25)
1-3-Jay Stephens-s/a. 1-Wraparound-c 3.25
TPB (8/02, $10.95, 8 3/4" x 5 3/4") r/#1-3 & stories from Nickelodeon mag. & other 11.00

JET DREAM (...and Her Stunt-Girl Counterspies)(See The Man from Uncle #7)
Gold Key: June, 1968 (12¢)
1-Painted-c 4 8 12 25 33 42

JET FIGHTERS (Korean War)
Standard Magazines: No. 5, Nov, 1952 - No. 7, Mar, 1953
5,7-Toth-a. 5-Toth-c 12 24 36 69 92 115
6-Celardo-a 7 14 21 35 43 50

JET POWER
I.W. Enterprises: 1963
I.W. Reprint 1,2-r/Jet Powers #1,2 3 6 9 19 25 32

JET POWERS (American Air Forces No. 5 on)
Magazine Enterprises: 1950 - No. 4, 1951
1(A-1 #30)-Powell-c/a begins 36 72 108 204 290 375
2(A-1 #32) Powell dinosaur-c/a; classic-c 34 68 102 196 278 360

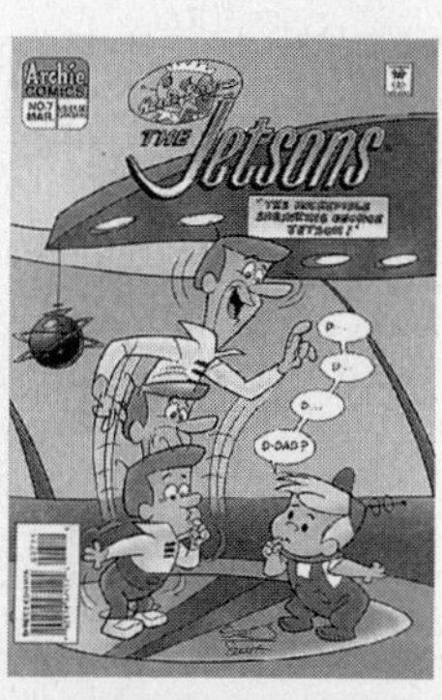

The Jetsons #7 © H-B

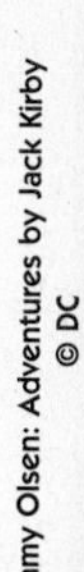

Jimmy Olsen: Adventures by Jack Kirby © DC

Jingle Belle Winter Wingding © Paul Dini

	GD 2.0	VG 4.0	FN 6.0	VF 8.0	VF/NM 9.0	NM- 9.2
3(A-1 #35)-Williamson/Evans-a	40	80	120	240	345	450
4(A-1 #38)-Williamson/Wood-a; "The Rain of Sleep" drug story	40	80	120	240	345	450
JET PUP (See 3-D Features)						
JETSONS, THE (TV) (See March of Comics #276, 330, 348 & Spotlight #3) **Gold Key:** Jan, 1963 - No. 36, Oct, 1970 (Hanna-Barbera)						
1-1st comic book app.	27	54	81	192	281	370
2	13	26	39	90	133	175
3-10	10	20	30	70	100	130
11-22	8	16	24	55	78	100
23-36-Reprints	6	12	18	43	59	75
JETSONS, THE (TV) (Also see Golden Comics Digest) **Charlton Comics:** Nov, 1970 - No. 20, Dec, 1973 (Hanna-Barbera)						
1	9	18	27	65	93	120
2	5	10	15	36	48	60
3-10	4	8	12	24	32	40
11-20	3	6	9	18	24	30
JETSONS, THE (TV) **Harvey Comics:** V2#1, Sept, 1992 - No. 5, Nov, 1993 ($1.25/$1.50) (Hanna-Barbera)						
V2#1-5						4.00
...Big Book V2#1,2,3 ($1.95, 52 pgs.): 1-(11/92). 2-(4/93). 3-(7/93)						4.00
...Giant Size 1,2,3 ($2.25, 68 pgs): 1-(10/92). 2-(4/93). 3-(10/93)						4.00
JETSONS, THE (TV) **Archie Comics:** Sept, 1995 - No. 17, Aug, 1996 ($1.50)						
1-17						3.00
JETTA OF THE 21ST CENTURY **Standard Comics:** No. 5, Dec, 1952 - No. 7, Apr, 1953 (Teen-age Archie type)						
5	24	48	72	135	190	245
6,7: 6-Robot-c	14	28	42	79	107	135
JEZEBEL JADE (Hanna-Barbara) **Comico:** Oct, 1988 - No. 3, Dec, 1988 ($2.00, mini-series)						
1-3: Johnny Quest spin-off						3.00
JEZEBELLE (See Wildstorm 2000 Annuals) **DC Comics (WildStorm):** Mar, 2001 - No. 6, Aug, 2001 ($2.50, limited series)						
1-6-Ben Raab-s/Steve Ellis-a						2.50
JIGGS & MAGGIE **Dell Publishing Co.:** No. 18, 1941 (one shot)						
Four Color 18 (#1)-(1936-38-r)	37	74	111	278	414	550
JIGGS & MAGGIE **Standard Comics/Harvey Publications No. 22 on:** No. 11, 1949(June) - No. 21, 2/53; No. 22, 4/53 - No. 27, 2-3/54						
11	12	24	36	71	96	120
12-15,17-21	8	16	24	43	54	65
16-Wood text illos.	9	18	27	49	62	75
22-24-Little Dot app.	8	16	24	46	58	70
25,27	7	14	21	35	43	50
26-Four pgs. partially in 3-D	14	28	42	79	107	135

NOTE: *Sunday page reprints by McManus loosely blended into story continuity. Based on Bringing Up Father strip. Advertised on covers as "All New."*

	GD 2.0	VG 4.0	FN 6.0	VF 8.0	VF/NM 9.0	NM- 9.2
JIGSAW (Big Hero Adventures) **Harvey Publ. (Funday Funnies):** Sept, 1966 - No. 2, Dec, 1966 (36 pgs.)						
1-Origin & 1st app.; Crandall-a (5 pgs.)	3	7	10	21	28	35
2-Man From S.R.A.M.	2	4	6	14	18	22
JIGSAW OF DOOM (See Complete Mystery No. 2)						
JIM BOWIE (Formerly Danger?; Black Jack No. 20 on) **Charlton Comics:** No. 16, 1955? - No. 19, Apr, 1957						
16	8	16	24	43	54	65
17-19	6	12	18	29	36	42
JIM BOWIE (TV, see Western Tales) **Dell Publishing Co.:** No. 893, Mar, 1958 - No. 993, May-July, 1959						
Four Color 893 (#1)	6	12	18	43	59	75
993-Photo-c	6	12	18	40	55	70
JIM DANDY **Dandy Magazine (Lev Gleason):** May, 1956 - No. 3, Sept, 1956 (Charles Biro)						
1-Biro-c	8	16	24	46	58	70
2,3	6	12	18	28	34	40
JIM HARDY (See Giant Comics Eds., Sparkler & Treasury of Comics #2 & 5) **United Features Syndicate/Spotlight Publ.:** 1939; 1942; 1947 - No. 2, 1947						
Single Series 6 ('39)	40	80	120	240	345	450
Single Series 27('42)	36	72	108	204	290	375
1('47)-Spotlight Publ.	15	30	45	86	118	150
2	9	18	27	52	66	80
JIM HARDY **Spotlight/United Features Synd.:** 1944 (25¢, 132 pgs.) (Tip Top, Sparkler-r)						
nn-Origin Mirror Man; Triple Terror app.	40	80	120	240	340	440
JIMINY CRICKET (Disney,, see Mickey Mouse Mag. V5#3 & Walt Disney Showcase #37) **Dell Publishing Co.:** No. 701, May, 1956 - No. 989, May-July, 1959						
Four Color 701	10	20	30	67	96	125
Four Color 795, 897, 989	7	14	21	51	71	90
JIM LEE SKETCHBOOK **DC Comics (WildStorm):** 2002 (no price, 16 pgs.)						
nn-Various DC and WildStorm character sketches by Lee						2.50
JIMMY CORRIGAN (See Acme Novelty Library)						
JIMMY DURANTE (Also see A-1 Comics) **Magazine Enterprises:** No. 18, 1949 - No. 20, 1949						
A-1 18,20-Photo-c	43	86	129	258	389	520
JIMMY OLSEN (See Superman's Pal...)						
JIMMY OLSEN: ADVENTURES BY JACK KIRBY **DC Comics:** 2003 ($19.95, TPB)						
nn-Reprints Jack Kirby's early issues of Superman's Pal Jimmy Olsen #133-139,141; Mark Evanier intro.; cover by Kirby and Steve Rude						20.00
JIMMY WAKELY (Cowboy movie star) **National Per. Publ.:** Sept-Oct, 1949 - No. 18, July-Aug, 1952 (1-13: 52pgs.)						
1-Photo-c, 52 pgs. begin; Alex Toth-a; Kit Colby Girl Sheriff begins	111	222	333	694	1040	1385
2-Toth-a	46	92	138	276	413	550
3,4,6,7-Frazetta-a in all, 3 pgs. each; Toth-a in all. 7-Last photo-c. 4-Kurtzman "Pot-Shot Pete", 1 pg; Toth-a	47	94	141	282	424	565
5,8-15-Toth-a; 12,14-Kubert-a (3 & 2 pgs.)	39	78	117	230	325	420
16-18	33	66	99	190	268	345

NOTE: *Gil Kane c-10-19p.*

	GD 2.0	VG 4.0	FN 6.0	VF 8.0	VF/NM 9.0	NM- 9.2
JIM RAY'S AVIATION SKETCH BOOK **Vital Publishers:** Mar-Apr, 1946 - No. 2, May-June, 1946						
1-Picture stories about planes and pilots	39	78	117	230	325	420
2	27	54	81	153	214	275
JIM SOLAR (See Wisco/Klarer in the Promotional Comics section)						
JINGLE BELLE (Paul Dini's...) **Oni Press:** Nov, 1999 - No. 2, Dec, 1999 ($2.95, B&W, limited series)						
1,2-Paul Dini-s. 2-Alex Ross flip-c						3.00
Jingle Belle: Dash Away All (12/03, $11.95, digest-size) Dini-s/Garibaldi-a						12.00
Jingle Belle's Cool Yule (11/02, $13.95,TPB) r/All-Star Holiday Hullabaloo, The Mighty Elves, and Jubilee; internet strips and a color section w/DeStefano-a						14.00
Paul Dini's Jingle Belle Jubilee (11/01, $2.95) Dini-s; art by Rolston, DeCarlo, Morrison and Bone; pin-ups by Thompson and Aragonés						3.00
Paul Dini's Jingle Belle's All-Star Holiday Hullabaloo (11/00, $4.95) stories by various including Dini, Aragonés, Jeff Smith, Bill Morrison; Frank Cho-c						5.00
Paul Dini's Jingle Belle: The Mighty Elves (7/01, $2.95) Dini-s/Bone-a						3.00
Paul Dini's Jingle Belle Winter Wingding (11/02, $2.95) Dini-s/Clugston-Major-c						3.00
TPB (10/00, $8.95) r/#1&2, and app. from Oni Double Feature #13						9.00
JINGLE BELLS (See March of Comics No. 65)						
JINGLE DINGLE CHRISTMAS STOCKING COMICS (See Foodini #2) **Stanhall Publications:** V2#1, 1951 (no date listed) (25¢, 100 pgs.; giant-size) (Publ. annually)						
V2#1-Foodini & Pinhead, Silly Pilly plus games & puzzles	19	38	57	109	152	195
JINGLE JANGLE COMICS (Also see Puzzle Fun Comics) **Eastern Color Printing Co.:** Feb, 1942 - No. 42, Dec, 1949						
1-Pie-Face Prince of Old Pretzleburg, Jingle Jangle Tales by George Carlson, Hortense, & Benny Bear begin	46	92	138	276	413	550
2-4: 2,3-No Pie-Face Prince. 4-Pie-Face Prince-c	22	44	66	124	172	220
5	20	40	60	112	156	200
6-10: 8-No Pie-Face Prince	15	30	45	86	118	150

Jinx #5 © Brian Michael Bendis

JLA #50 © DC

JLA/Avengers #1 © DC & MAR

	GD 2.0	VG 4.0	FN 6.0	VF 8.0	VF/NM 9.0	NM- 9.2
11-15	12	24	36	69	92	115
16-30: 17,18-No Pie-Face Prince. 30-XMas-c	10	20	30	56	73	90
31-42: 36,42-Xmas-c	9	18	27	52	66	80

NOTE: ***George Carlson** a-(2) in all except No. 2, 3, 8; c-1-6. **Carlson** 1 pg. puzzles in 9, 10, 12-15, 18, 20. **Carlson** illustrated a series of Uncle Wiggily books in 1930's.*

JING PALS
Victory Publishing Corp.: Feb, 1946 - No. 4, Aug?, 1946 (Funny animal)

	GD 2.0	VG 4.0	FN 6.0	VF 8.0	VF/NM 9.0	NM- 9.2
1-Wishing Willie, Puggy Panda & Johnny Rabbit begin	15	30	45	86	118	150
2-4	9	18	27	49	62	75

JINKS, PIXIE, AND DIXIE (See Kite Fun Book & Whitman Comic Books)

JINN
Image Comics (Avalon Studios): Mar, 2000 - No. 3, Oct, 2000 ($2.50)

1-3-Rearte-c/a 3.00

JINX
Caliber Press: 1996 - No. 7, 1996 ($2.95, B&W, 32 pgs.)

1-7: Brian Michael Bendis-c/a/scripts. 2-Photo-c 3.00

JINX (Volume 2)
Image Comics: 1997 - No. 5, 1998 ($2.95, B&W, bi-monthly)

1-4: Brian Michael Bendis-c/a/scripts. 3.00
5-($3.95) Brereton-c 4.00
...Buried Treasures ('98, $3.95) short stories, ...Confessions ('98, $3.95) short stories, ...Pop Culture Hoo-Hah ('98, $3.95) humor shorts 4.00
TPB (1997, $10.95) r/Vol 1,#1-4 11.00
...: The Definitive Collection ('01, $24.95) remastered #1-5, sketch pages, art gallery, script excerpts, Mack intro. 25.00

JINX: TORSO
Image Comics: 1998 - No. 6, 1999 ($3.95/$4.95, B&W)

1-6-Based on Eliot Ness' pursuit of America's first serial killer; Brian Michael Bendis & Marc Andreyko-s/Bendis-a. 3-6-($4.95) 5.00
Softcover (2000, $24.95) r/#1-6; intro. by Greg Rucka; photo essay of the actual murders and police documents 25.00
Hardcover (2000, $49.95) signed & numbered 50.00

JLA (See Justice League of America and Justice Leagues)
DC Comics: Jan, 1997 - Present ($1.95/$1.99/$2.25)

	GD 2.0	VG 4.0	FN 6.0	VF 8.0	VF/NM 9.0	NM- 9.2
1-Morrison-s/Porter & Dell-a. The Hyperclan app.	2	4	6	10	12	15
2	1	3	4	6	8	10
3,4	1	2	3	5	7	9

5-Membership drive; Tomorrow Woman app. 6.00
6-9: 8-Green Arrow joins. 6.00
10-21: 10-Rock of Ages begins. 11-Joker and Luthor-c/app. 15-($2.95) Rock of Ages concludes. 16-New members join; Prometheus app. 17,20-Jorgensen-a. 18-21-Waid-s. 20,21-Adam Strange c/app. 5.00
22-40: 22-Begin $1.99-c; Sandman (Daniel) app. 27-Amazo app. 28-31-JSA app. 35-Hal Jordan/Spectre app. 36-40-World War 3 2.50
41-($2.99) Conclusion of World War 3; last Morrison-s 3.00
42-46: 43-Waid-s; Ra's al Ghul app. 44-Begin $2.25-c. 46-Batman leaves 2.25
47-49: 47-Hitch & Neary-a begins; JLA battles Queen of Fables 2.25
50-($3.75) JLA vs. Dr. Destiny; art by Hitch & various 3.75
51-74: 52-55-Hitch-a. 59-Joker: Last Laugh. 61-68-Kelly-s/Mahnke-a. 69-73-Hunt for Aquaman; bi-monthly with alternating art by Mahnke and Guichet 2.25
75-(1/03, $3.95) leads into Aquaman (4th series) #1 4.00
76-92: 76-Firestorm app. 77-Banks-a. 79-Kanjar Ro app. 91,92-O'Neil-s/Huat-a 2.25
#1,000,000 (11/98) 853rd Century x-over 2.50
Annual 1 (1997, $3.95) Pulp Heroes; Augustyn-s/Olivetti & Ha-a 4.00
Annual 2 (1998, $2.95) Ghosts; Wrightson-c 4.00
Annual 3 (1999, $2.95) JLApe; Art Adams-c 3.00
Annual 4 (2000, $3.50) Planet DC x-over; Steve Scott-c/a 3.50
...80-Page Giant 1 (7/98, $4.95) stories & art by various 6.00
...80-Page Giant 2 (11/99, $4.95) Green Arrow & Hawkman app. Hitch-c 6.00
...80-Page Giant 3 (10/00, $5.95) Pariah & Harbinger; intro. Moon Maiden 6.00
...Foreign Bodies (1999, $5.95) Kobra app.; Semeiks-a 6.00
...Gallery (1997, $2.95) pin-ups by various; Quitely-c 3.00
...God & Monsters (2001, $6.95) Benefiel-a/c 7.00
.../ Haven: Anathema (2002, $6.95) Concludes the Haven: The Broken City series 7.00
.../ Haven: Arrival (2001, $6.95) Leads into the Haven: The Broken City series 7.00
...In Crisis Secret Files 1 (11/98, $4.95) recap of JLA in DC x-overs 5.00
...: Island of Dr. Moreau, The (2002, $6.95) Elseworlds; Pugh-c/a; Thomas-s 7.00
.../ JSA: Virtue and Vice HC (2002, $24.95) Teams battle Despero & Johnny Sorrow; Goyer & Johns-s/Pacheco-a/c 25.00
.../ JSA: Virtue and Vice SC (2003, $17.95) 18.00
...: Obsidian Age Book One, The (2003, $12.95) r/#66-71 13.00
...: Obsidian Age Book Two, The (2003, $12.95) r/#72-76 13.00
...: Our Worlds at War (9/01, $2.95) Jae Lee-c; Aquaman presumed dead 3.00
...Primeval (1999, $5.95) Abnett & Lanning-s/Olivetti-a 6.00
...: Riddle of the Beast HC (2001, $24.95) Grant-s/painted-a by various; Sweet-c 25.00
...: Riddle of the Beast SC (2003, $14.95) Grant-s/painted-a by various; Kaluta-c 15.00
...: Seven Caskets (2000, $5.95) Brereton-s/painted-c/a 6.00
...Showcase 80-Page Giant (2/00, $4.95) Hitch-c 5.00
...Superpower (1999, $5.95) Arcudi-s/Eaton-a; Mark Antaeus joins 6.00
...: Shogun of Steel (2002, $6.95) Elseworlds; Justiniano-c/a 7.00
...Vs. Predator (DC/Dark Horse, 2000, $5.95) Nolan-c/a 6.00
...: Welcome to the Working Week (2003, $6.95) Patton Oswalt-s 7.00
...: Zatanna's Search (2003, $12.95) rep. Zatanna's early app. & origin; Bolland-c 13.00
American Dreams (1998, $7.95, TPB) r/#5-9 8.00
Divided We Fall (2001, $17.95, TPB) r/#47-54 18.00
Golden Perfect (2003, $12.95, TPB) r/#61-65 13.00
Justice For All (1999, $14.95, TPB) r/#24-33 15.00
New World Order (1997, $5.95, TPB) r/#1-4 6.00
Rock of Ages (1998, $9.95, TPB) r/#10-15 10.00
Strength in Numbers (1998, $12.95, TPB) r/#16-23, Secret Files #2 and Prometheus #1 13.00
Terror Incognita (2002, $12.95, TPB) r/#55-60 13.00
Tower of Babel (2001, $12.95, TPB) r/#42-46, Secret Files #3, 80-Page Giant #1 13.00
World War III (2000, $12.95, TPB) r/#34-41 13.00

JLA: ACT OF GOD
DC Comics: 2000 - No. 3, 2001 ($4.95, limited series)

1-3-Elseworlds; metahumans lose their powers; Moench-s/Dave Ross-a 5.00

JLA: AGE OF WONDER
DC Comics: 2003 - No. 2, 2003 ($5.95, limited series)

1,2-Elseworlds; Superman and the League of Science during the Industrial Revolution 6.00

JLA: A LEAGUE OF ONE
DC Comics: 2000 (Graphic novel)

Hardcover ($24.95) Christopher Moeller-s/painted-a 25.00
Softcover (2002, $14.95) 15.00

JLA/AVENGERS (See Avengers/JLA for #2 & #4)
Marvel Comics: Sept, 2003; No. 3, Dec, 2003 ($5.95, limited series)

1-Busiek-s/Pérez-a; wraparound-c; Krona, Starro, Grandmaster, Terminus app. 6.00
3-Busiek-s/Pérez-a; wraparound-c; Phantom Stranger app. 6.00

JLA: BLACK BAPTISM
DC Comics: May, 2001 - No. 4, Aug, 2001 ($2.50, limited series)

1-4-Saiz-a(p)/Bradstreet-c; Zatanna app. 2.50

JLA: CREATED EQUAL
DC Comics: 2000 - No. 2, 2000 ($5.95, limited series, prestige format)

1,2-Nicieza-s/Maguire-a; Elseworlds-Superman as the last man on Earth 6.00

JLA: DESTINY
DC Comics: 2002 - No. 4, 2002 ($5.95, prestige format, limited series)

1-4-Elseworlds; Arcudi-s/Mandrake-a 6.00

JLA: EARTH 2
DC Comics: 2000 (Graphic novel)

Hardcover ($24.95) Morrison-s/Quitely-a; Crime Syndicate app. 25.00
Softcover ($14.95) 15.00

JLA: GATEKEEPER
DC Comics: 2001 - No. 3, 2001 ($4.95, prestige format, limited series)

1-3-Truman-s/a 5.00

JLA: HEAVEN'S LADDER
DC Comics: 2000 ($9.95, Treasury-size one-shot)

nn-Bryan Hitch & Paul Neary-c/a; Mark Waid-s 10.00

JLA: INCARNATIONS
DC Comics: Jul, 2001 - No. 7, Feb, 2002 ($3.50, limited series)

1-7-Ostrander-s/Semeiks-a; different eras of the Justice League 3.50

JLA: LIBERTY AND JUSTICE
DC Comics: Nov, 2003 ($9.95, Treasury-size one-shot)

nn-Alex Ross-c/a; Paul Dini-s; story of the classic Justice League 10.00

JLA PARADISE LOST
DC Comics: Jan, 1998 - No. 3, Mar, 1998 ($1.95, limited series)

1-3-Millar-s/Olivetti-a 2.50

JLA: Year One #12 © DC

Joe College #1 © HILL

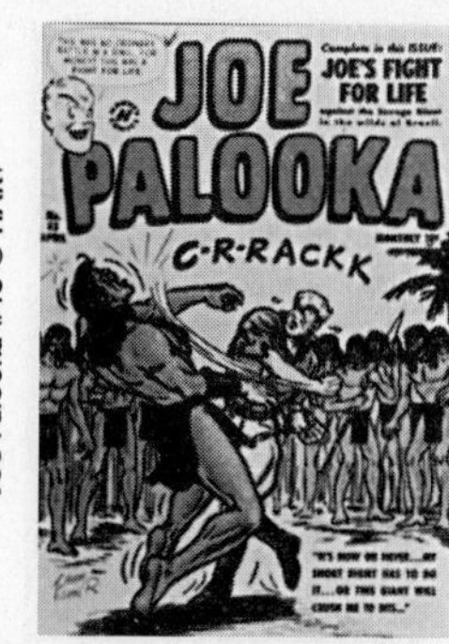

Joe Palooka #43 © HARV

GD 2.0 | VG 4.0 | FN 6.0 | VF 8.0 | VF/NM 9.0 | NM- 9.2

JLA: SCARY MONSTERS
DC Comics: May, 2003 - No. 6, Oct, 2003 ($2.50, limited series)
1-6-Claremont-s/Art Adams-c 2.50

JLA SECRET FILES
DC Comics: Sept, 1997 - Present ($4.95)
1-Standard Ed. w/origin-s & pin-ups 5.00
1-Collector's Ed. w/origin-s & pin-ups; cardstock-c 6.00
2,3: 2-(8/98) origin-s of JLA #16's newer members. 3-(12/00) 5.00

JLA: SECRET ORIGINS
DC Comics: Nov, 2002 ($7.95, Treasury-size one-shot)
nn-Alex Ross 2-page origins of Justice League members; text by Paul Dini 8.00

JLA: SECRET SOCIETY OF SUPER-HEROES
DC Comics: 2000 - No. 2, 2000 ($5.95, limited series, prestige format)
1,2-Elseworlds JLA; Chaykin and Tischman-s/McKone-a 6.00

JLA /SPECTRE: SOUL WAR
DC Comics: 2003 - No. 2, 2003 ($5.95, limited series, prestige format)
1,2-DeMatteis-s/Banks & Neary-a 6.00

JLA: THE NAIL (Elseworlds)
DC Comics: Aug, 1998 - No. 3, Oct, 1998 ($4.95, prestige format)
1-3-JLA in a world without Superman; Alan Davis-s/a(p) 5.00
TPB ('98, $12.95) r/series w/new Davis-c 13.00

JLA / TITANS
DC Comics: Dec, 1998 - No. 3, Feb, 1999 ($2.95, limited series)
1-3-Grayson-s; P. Jimenez-c/a 3.00
...:The Technis Imperative ('99, $12.95, TPB) r/#1-3; Titans Secret Files 13.00

JLA: TOMORROW WOMAN (Girlfrenzy)
DC Comics: June, 1998 ($1.95, one-shot)
1-Peyer-s; story takes place during JLA #5 2.50

JLA / WILDC.A.T.S
DC Comics: 1997 ($5.95, one-shot, prestige format)
1-Morrison-s/Semeiks & Conrad-a 6.00

JLA /WITCHBLADE
DC Comics/Top Cow: 2000 ($5.95, prestige format, one-shot)
1-Pararillo-c/a 6.00

JLA / WORLD WITHOUT GROWN-UPS (See Young Justice)
DC Comics: Aug, 1998 - No. 2, Sept, 1998 ($4.95, prestige format)
1,2-JLA, Robin, Impulse & Superboy app.; Ramos & McKone-a 6.00
TPB ('98, $9.95) r/series & Young Justice: The Secret #1 10.00

JLA: YEAR ONE
DC Comics: Jan, 1998 - No. 12, Dec, 1998 ($2.95/$1.95, limited series)
1-($2.95)-Waid & Augustyn-s/Kitson-a 5.00
1-Platinum Edition 10.00
2-8-($1.95): 5-Doom Patrol-c/app. 7-Superman app. 4.00
9-12 3.00
TPB ('99, $19.95) r/#1-12; Busiek intro. 20.00

JLA-Z
DC Comics: Nov, 2003 - No. 3, Jan, 2004 ($2.50, limited series)
1-3-Pin-ups and info on current and former JLA members and villains; art by various 2.50

JLX
DC Comics (Amalgam): Apr, 1996 ($1.95, one-shot)
1-Mark Waid scripts 2.50

JLX UNLEASHED
DC Comics (Amalgam): June, 1997 ($1.95, one-shot)
1-Priest-s/ Oscar Jimenez & Rodriquez/a 2.50

JOAN OF ARC (Also see A-1 Comics & Ideal a Classical Comic)
Magazine Enterprises: No. 21, 1949 (one shot)
A-1 21-Movie adaptation; Ingrid Bergman photo-covers & interior photos;
Whitney-a 29 58 87 164 232 300

JOE COLLEGE
Hillman Periodicals: Fall, 1949 - No. 2, Wint, 1950 (Teen-age humor, 52 pgs.)
1-Powell-a; Briefer-a 12 24 36 71 96 120
2-Powell-a 10 20 30 56 73 90

JOE JINKS
United Features Syndicate: No. 12, 1939
Single Series 12 31 62 93 175 248 320

JOE LOUIS (See Fight Comics #2, Picture News #6 & True Comics #5)
Fawcett Publications: Sept, 1950 - No. 2, Nov, 1950 (Photo-c) (Boxing champ) (See Dick Cole #10)
1-Photo-c; life story 55 110 165 344 515 685
2-Photo-c 40 80 120 240 340 440

JOE PALOOKA (1st Series)(Also see Big Shot Comics, Columbia Comics & Feature Funnies)
Columbia Comic Corp. (Publication Enterprises): 1942 - No. 4, 1944
1-1st to portray American president; gov't permission required
88 176 264 550 825 1100
2 (1943)-Hitler-c 55 110 165 330 495 660
3-Nazi Sub-c 39 78 117 230 325 420
4 34 68 102 196 278 360

JOE PALOOKA (2nd Series) (Battle Adv. #68-74; ...Advs. #75, 77-81, 83-85, 87; Champ of the Comics #76, 82, 86, 89-93) (See All-New)
Harvey Publications: Nov, 1945 - No. 118, Mar, 1961
1 48 96 144 288 432 575
2 25 50 75 147 202 260
3,4,6,7-1st Flyin' Fool, ends #25 16 32 48 92 126 160
5-Boy Explorers by S&K (7-8/46) 22 44 66 124 172 220
8-10 13 26 39 74 100 125
11-14,16,18-20: 14-Black Cat text-s(2). 18-Powell-a.; Little Max app. 19-Freedom Train-c
10 20 30 58 77 95
15-Origin & 1st app. Humphrey (12/47); Super-heroine Atoma app. by Powell
16 32 48 92 126 160
17-Humphrey vs. Palooka-c/s; 1st app. Little Max 16 32 48 92 126 160
21-26,29,30: 22-Powell-a. 30-Nude female painting 9 18 27 52 66 80
27-Little Max app.; Howie Morenz-s 9 18 27 54 70 85
28-Babe Ruth 4 pg. sty. 9 18 27 54 70 85
31,39,51: 31-Dizzy Dean 4 pg. sty. 39-(12/49) Humphrey & Little Max begin; Sonny Baugh football-s; Sherlock Max-s. 51-Babe Ruth 2 pg. sty; Jake Lamotta 1/2 pg. sty
8 16 24 46 58 70
32-38,40-50,52-61: 35-Little Max-c/story(4 pgs.); Joe Louis 1 pg. sty. 36-Humphrey story. 41-Bing Crosby photo on-c. 44-Palooka marries Ann Howe. 50-(11/51)-Becomes Harvey Comics Hits #51 8 16 24 40 50 60
62-S&K Boy Explorers-r 8 16 24 46 58 70
63-65,73-80,100: 79-Story of 1st meeting with Ann 7 14 21 35 43 50
66,67-'Commie' torture story "Drug-Diet Horror" 8 16 24 46 58 70
68,70-72: 68,70-Joe vs. "Gooks"-c. 71-Bloody bayonets-c. 72-Tank-c
8 16 24 43 54 65
69-1st "Battle Adventures" issue; torture & bondage 8 16 24 46 58 70
81-99,101-115: 104,107-Humphrey & Little Max-s 6 12 18 31 38 45
116-S&K Boy Explorers-r (Giant, '60) 8 16 24 43 54 65
117-(84 pg. Giant) r/Commie issues #66,67; Powell-a 8 16 24 46 58 70
118-(84 pg. Giant) Jack Dempsey 2 pg. sty, Powell-a 8 16 24 43 54 65
...Visits the Lost City nn (1945)(One Shot)(50¢)-164 page continuous story strip reprint. Has biography & photo of Ham Fisher; possibly the single longest comic book story published in that era (159 pgs.?) 161 322 483 1006 1428 2050
NOTE: ***Nostrand/Powell** a-73. **Powell** a-7, 8, 10, 12, 14, 17, 19, 26-45, 47-53, 70, 73 at least. Black Cat text stories #8, 12, 13, 19.*

JOE PSYCHO & MOO FROG
Goblin Studios: 1996 - No. 5, 1997 ($2.50, B&W)
1-5: 4-Two covers 2.50
...Full Color Extravagarbonzo ($2.95, color) 3.00

JOE YANK (Korean War)
Standard Comics (Visual Editions): No. 5, Mar, 1952 - No. 16, 1954
5-Toth, Celardo, Tuska-a 9 18 27 52 66 80
6-Toth, Severin/Elder-a 9 18 27 52 66 80
7 6 12 18 31 38 45
8-Toth-c 8 16 24 40 50 60
9-16: 9-Andru-c. 12-Andru-a 6 12 18 28 34 40

JOHN BOLTON'S HALLS OF HORROR
Eclipse Comics: June, 1985 - No. 2, June, 1985 ($1.75, limited series)
1,2-British-r; Bolton-c/a 3.00

JOHN BOLTON'S STRANGE WINK
Dark Horse Comics: Mar, 1998 - No. 3, May, 1998 ($2.95, B&W, limited series)
1-3-Anthology; Bolton-s/c/a 3.00

JOHN BYRNE'S NEXT MEN (See Dark Horse Presents #54)

John Byrne's Next Men #21 © John Byrne & Mike Mignola

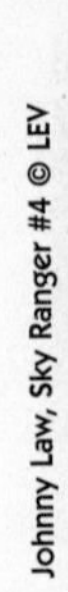
Johnny Law, Sky Ranger #4 © LEV

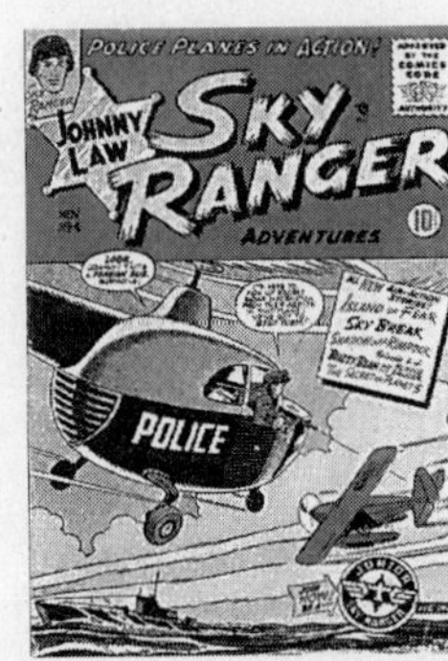

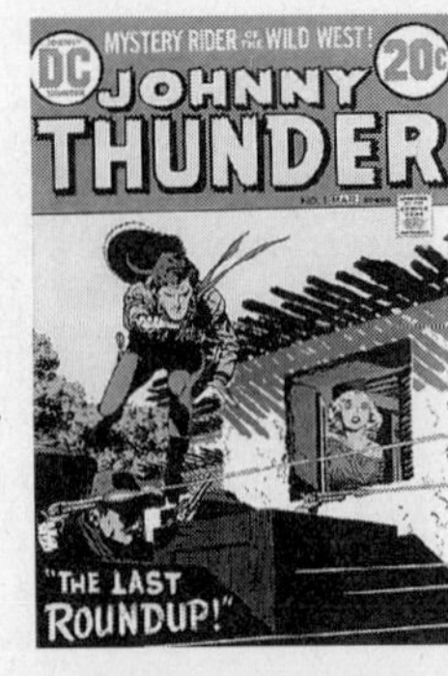

Johnny Thunder #1 © DC

GD 2.0 | VG 4.0 | FN 6.0 | VF 8.0 | VF/NM 9.0 | NM- 9.2

Dark Horse Comics (Legend imprint #19 on): Jan, 1992 - No. 30, Dec, 1994 ($2.50, mature)

1-Silver foil embossed-c; Byrne-c/a/scripts in all 4.00
1-4: 1-2nd printing with gold ink logo 2.50
0-(2/92)-r/chapters 1-4 from DHP w/new Byrne-c 2.50
5-20,22-30: 7-10-MA #1-4 mini-series on flip side. 16-Origin of Mark IV. 17-Miller-c. 19-22-Faith storyline. 23-26-Power storyline. 27-30-Lies storyline Pt. 1-4 2.50
21-(12/93) 1st Hellboy; cover and Hellboy pages by Mike Mignola; Byrne other pages 3 6 9 16 20 24
...Parallel, Book 2 ($16.95)-TPB; r/#7-12 17.00
...Fame, Book 3($16.95)-TPB r/#13-18 17.00
...Faith, Book 4($14.95)-TPB r/#19-22 15.00

NOTE: *Issues 1 through 6 contain certificates redeemable for an exclusive Next Men trading card set by Byrne. Prices are for complete books.* ***Cody*** *painted c-23-26.* ***Mignola*** *a-21(part); c-21.*

JOHN BYRNE'S 2112
Dark Horse Comics (Legend): Oct, 1994 ($9.95, TPB)

1-Byrne-c/a/s 10.00

JOHN CARTER OF MARS (See The Funnies & Tarzan #207)
Dell Publishing Co.: No. 375, Mar-May, 1952 - No. 488, Aug-Oct, 1953
(Edgar Rice Burroughs)

Four Color 375 (#1)-Origin; Jesse Marsh-a 27 54 81 192 281 370
Four Color 437, 488-Painted-c 17 34 51 118 174 230

JOHN CARTER OF MARS
Gold Key: Apr, 1964 - No. 3, Oct, 1964

1(10104-404)-r/4-Color #375; Jesse Marsh-a 7 14 21 46 63 80
2(407), 3(410)-r/4-Color #437 & 488; Marsh-a 5 10 15 33 44 55

JOHN CARTER OF MARS
House of Greystroke: 1970 (10-1/2x16-1/2", 72 pgs., B&W, paper-c)

1941-42 Sunday strip-r; John Coleman Burroughs-a 4 8 12 22 30 38

JOHN CARTER, WARLORD OF MARS (Also see Weird Worlds)
Marvel Comics: June, 1977 - No. 28, Oct, 1979

1,18: 1-Origin. 18-Frank Miller-a(p)(1st publ. Marvel work) 1 2 3 5 7 9
1-(35¢-c variant, limited dist.) 2 4 6 11 14 18
2-5-(35¢-c variants, limited dist.) 6.00
2-17,19-28: 11-Origin Dejah Thoris 4.00
Annuals 1-3: 1(1977). 2(1978). 3(1979)-All 52 pgs. with new book-length stories 4.00

NOTE: ***Austin*** *c-24i.* ***Gil Kane*** *a-1-10p; c-1p, 2p, 3, 4-9p, 10, 15p, Annual 1p.* ***Layton*** *a-17i.* ***Miller*** *c-25, 26p.* ***Nebres*** *a-2-4i, 8-16i; c(i)-6-9, 11-22, 25, Annual 1.* ***Perez*** *c-24p.* ***Simonson*** *a-15p.* ***Sutton*** *a-7i.*

JOHN F. KENNEDY, CHAMPION OF FREEDOM
Worden & Childs: 1964 (no month) (25¢)

nn-Photo-c 8 16 24 58 82 105

JOHN F. KENNEDY LIFE STORY
Dell Publishing Co.: Aug-Oct, 1964; Nov, 1965; June, 1966 (12¢)

12-378-410-Photo-c 7 14 21 50 68 85
12-378-511 (reprint, 11/65) 4 8 12 24 32 40
12-378-606 (reprint, 6/66) 3 7 10 21 28 35

JOHN FORCE (See Magic Agent)

JOHN HIX SCRAP BOOK, THE
Eastern Color Printing Co. (McNaught Synd.): Late 1930's (no date)
(10¢, 68 pgs., regular size)

1-Strange As It Seems (resembles Single Series books) 39 78 117 230 325 420
2-Strange As It Seems 27 54 81 153 214 275

JOHN JAKES' MULLKON EMPIRE
Tekno Comix: Sept, 1995 - No. 6, Feb, 1996 ($1.95)

1-6 2.25

JOHN LAW DETECTIVE (See Smash Comics #3)
Eclipse Comics: April, 1983 ($1.50, Baxter paper)

1-Three Eisner stories originally drawn in 1948 for the never published John Law #1; original cover pencilled in 1948 & inked in 1982 by Eisner 3.00

JOHNNY APPLESEED (See Story Hour Series)

JOHNNY CASH (See Hello, I'm...)

JOHNNY DANGER (See Movie Comics, 1946)
Toby Press: 1950 (Based on movie serial)

1-Photo-c; Sparling-a 18 36 54 101 138 175

JOHNNY DANGER PRIVATE DETECTIVE
Toby Press: Aug, 1954 (Reprinted in Danger #11 by Super)

1-Photo-c; Opium den story 14 28 42 79 107 135

JOHNNY DYNAMITE (Formerly Dynamite #1-9; Foreign Intrigues #14 on)
Charlton Comics: No. 10, June, 1955 - No. 12, Oct, 1955

10-12 10 20 30 56 73 90

JOHNNY DYNAMITE
Dark Horse Comics: Sept, 1994 - Dec, 1994 ($2.95, B&W & red, limited series)

1-4: Max Allan Collins scripts in all; Terry Beatty-a 3.00
...: Underworld GN (AiT/Planet Lar, 3/03, $12.95, B&W) r/#1-4 in B&W without red 13.00

JOHNNY HAZARD
Best Books (Standard Comics) (King Features): No. 5, Aug, 1948 - No. 8, May, 1949; No. 35, date?

5-Strip reprints by Frank Robbins (c/a) 20 40 60 112 156 200
6,8-Strip reprints by Frank Robbins 17 34 51 95 130 165
7,35: 7-New art, not Robbins 11 22 33 63 84 105

JOHNNY JASON (...Teen Reporter)
Dell Publishing Co.: Feb-Apr, 1962 - No. 2, June-Aug, 1962

Four Color 1302, 2(01380-208) 4 8 12 25 33 42

JOHNNY LAW, SKY RANGER
Good Comics (Lev Gleason): Apr, 1955 - No. 3, Aug, 1955; No. 4, Nov, 1955

1-Edmond Good-c/a 10 20 30 58 77 95
2-4 7 14 21 35 43 50

JOHNNY MACK BROWN (Western star; see Western Roundup under Dell Giants)
Dell Publishing Co.: No. 269, Mar, 1950 - No. 963, Feb, 1959 (All Photo-c)

Four Color 269(#1)(3/50, 52pgs.)-Johnny Mack Brown & his horse Rebel begin; photo front/back-c begin; Marsh-a in #1-9 25 50 75 176 258 340
2(10-12/50, 52pgs.) 12 24 36 87 129 170
3(1-3/51, 52pgs.) 10 20 30 67 96 125
4-10 (9-11/52)(36pgs.), Four Color 455,493,541,584,618,645,685,722,776,834,963 7 14 21 51 71 90
Four Color 922-Manning-a 8 16 24 53 74 95

JOHNNY NEMO
Eclipse Comics: Sept, 1985 - No. 3, Feb, 1986 (Mini-series)

1-3 2.50

JOHNNY PERIL (See Comic Cavalcade #15, Danger Trail #5, Sensation Comics #107 & Sensation Mystery)

JOHNNY RINGO (TV)
Dell Publishing Co.: No. 1142, Nov-Jan, 1960/61 (one shot)

Four Color 1142-Photo-c 8 16 24 55 78 100

JOHNNY STARBOARD (See Wisco)

JOHNNY THE HOMICIDAL MANIAC
Slave Labor Graphics: Aug, 1995 - No. 7, Jan, 1997 ($2.95, B&W, lim. series)

1-Jhonen Vasquez-c/s/a 1 3 4 6 8 10
1-Signed & numbered edition 2 4 6 10 12 15
2,3: 2-(11/95). 3-(2/96) 6.00
4-7: 4-(5-96). 5-(8/96) 4.00
Hardcover-($29.95) r/#1-7 30.00
TPB-($19.95) 20.00

JOHNNY THUNDER
National Periodical Publications: Feb-Mar, 1973 - No. 3, July-Aug, 1973

1-Johnny Thunder & Nighthawk-r. in all 2 4 6 12 16 20
2,3: 2-Trigger Twins app. 2 4 6 8 10 12

NOTE: *All contain 1950s DC reprints from All-American Western.* ***Drucker*** *r-2, 3.* ***G. Kane*** *r-2, 3.* ***Moriera*** *r-1.* ***Toth*** *r-1, 3; c-1r, 3r. Also see All-American, All-Star Western, Flash Comics, Western Comics, World's Best & World's Finest.*

JOHN PAUL JONES
Dell Publishing Co.: No. 1007, July-Sept, 1959 (one-shot)

Four Color 1007-Movie, Robert Stack photo-c 6 12 18 40 55 70

JOHN STEED & EMMA PEEL (See The Avengers, Gold Key series)

JOHN STEELE SECRET AGENT (Also see Freedom Agent)
Gold Key: Dec, 1964

1-Freedom Agent 9 18 27 63 89 115

JOHN WAYNE ADVENTURE COMICS (Movie star; See Big Tex, Oxydol-Dreft, Tim McCoy, & With The Marines...#1)
Toby Press: Winter, 1949-50 - No. 31, May, 1955 (Photo-c: 1-12,17,25-on)

1 (36pgs.)-Photo-c begin (1st time in comics on-c) 158 316 474 988 1482 1975

Jo-Jo Comics #17 © FOX

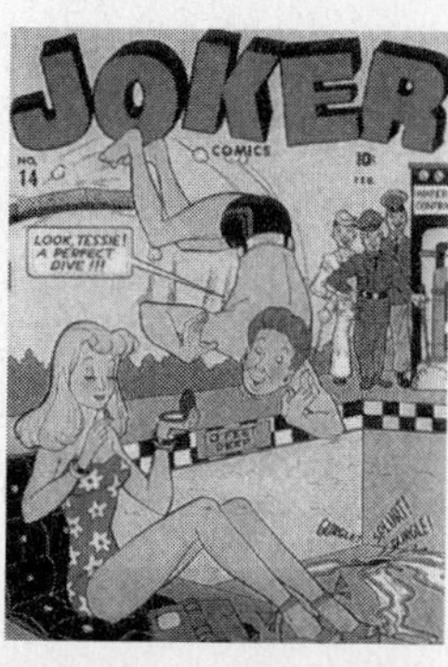

Joker Comics #14 © MAR

Jonah Hex #3 © DC

	GD 2.0	VG 4.0	FN 6.0	VF 8.0	VF/NM 9.0	NM- 9.2
2-4: 2-(4/50, 36pgs.)-Williamson/Frazetta-a(2) 6 & 2 pgs. (one story-r/Billy the Kid #1); photo back-c. 3-(36pgs.)-Williamson/Frazetta-a(2), 16 pgs. total; photo back-c. 4-(52pgs.)-Williamson/Frazetta-a(2), 16 pgs. total	69	138	207	431	646	860
5 (52pgs.)-Kurtzman-a-(Alfred "L" Newman in Potshot Pete)	50	100	150	300	450	600
6 (52pgs.)-Williamson/Frazetta-a (10 pgs.); Kurtzman-a "Pot-Shot Pete", (5 pgs.); & "Genius Jones", (1 pg.)	60	120	180	375	563	750
7 (52pgs.)-Williamson/Frazetta-a (10 pgs.)	54	108	162	324	487	650
8 (36pgs.)-Williamson/Frazetta-a(2) (12 & 9 pgs.)	66	132	198	413	619	825
9-11: Photo western-c	39	78	117	230	325	420
12,14-Photo war-c. 12-Kurtzman-a(2 pg.) "Genius"	39	78	117	230	325	420
13,15: 13,15-Line-drawn-c begin, end #24	35	70	105	201	283	365
16-Williamson/Frazetta-r/Billy the Kid #1	38	76	114	219	310	400
17-Photo-c	38	76	114	219	310	400
18-Williamson/Frazetta-a (r/#4 & 8, 19 pgs.)	40	80	120	240	340	440
19-24: 23-Evans-a?	32	64	96	182	259	335
25-Photo-c resume; end #31; Williamson/Frazetta-r/Billy the Kid #3	40	80	120	240	340	440
26-28,30-Photo-c	36	72	108	204	290	375
29,31-Williamson/Frazetta-a in each (r/#4, 2)	39	78	117	230	325	420

NOTE: *Williamsonish art in later issues by* ***Gerald McCann.***

JO-JO COMICS (...Congo King #7-29; My Desire #30 on)(Also see Fantastic Fears and Jungle Jo)
Fox Feature Syndicate: 1945 - No. 29, July, 1949 (Two No.7's; no #13)

	GD 2.0	VG 4.0	FN 6.0	VF 8.0	VF/NM 9.0	NM- 9.2
nn(1945)-Funny animal, humor	17	34	51	98	134	170
2(Sum,'46)-6(4-5/47): Funny animal. 2-Ten pg. Electro story (Fall/46)	10	20	30	56	73	90
7(7/47)-Jo-Jo, Congo King begins (1st app.); Bronze Man & Purple Tigress app.	90	180	270	563	844	1125
7(#8) (9/47)	64	128	192	400	600	800
8-10(#9-11): 8-Tanee begins	55	110	165	330	495	660
11,12(#12,13),14,16: 11,16-Kamen bondage-c	48	96	144	288	432	575
15,17: 15-Cited by Dr. Wertham in 5/47 Saturday Review of Literature. 17-Kamen bondage-c	50	100	150	300	450	600
18-20	48	96	144	288	432	575
21-29: 21-Hollingsworth-a(4 pgs.; 23-1 pg.)	42	84	126	252	359	465

NOTE: *Many bondage-c/a by* ***Baker/Kamen/Feldstein/Good.*** *No. 7's have Princesses Gwenna, Geesa, Yolda, & Safra before settling down on Tanee.*

JOKEBOOK COMICS DIGEST ANNUAL (...Magazine No. 5 on)
Archie Publications: Oct, 1977 - No. 13, Oct, 1983 (Digest Size)

	GD 2.0	VG 4.0	FN 6.0	VF 8.0	VF/NM 9.0	NM- 9.2
1(10/77)-Reprints; Neal Adams-a	2	4	6	12	16	20
2(4/78)-5	2	4	6	9	11	14
6-11	1	3	4	6	8	10

JOKER, THE (See Batman #1, Batman: The Killing Joke, Brave & the Bold, Detective, Greatest Joker Stories & Justice League Annual #2)
National Periodical Publications: May, 1975 - No. 9, Sept-Oct, 1976

	GD 2.0	VG 4.0	FN 6.0	VF 8.0	VF/NM 9.0	NM- 9.2
1-Two-Face app.	4	8	12	29	40	50
2,3: 3-The Creeper app.	3	6	9	16	20	25
4-9: 4-Green Arrow-c/sty. 6-Sherlock Holmes-c/sty. 7-Lex Luthor-c/story. 8-Scarecrow-c/story. 9-Catwoman-c/story	2	4	6	11	14	18

JOKER, THE (See Tangent Comics/ The Joker)

JOKER COMICS (Adventures Into Terror No. 43 on)
Timely/Marvel Comics No. 36 on (TCI/CDS): Apr, 1942 - No. 42, Aug, 1950

	GD 2.0	VG 4.0	FN 6.0	VF 8.0	VF/NM 9.0	NM- 9.2
1-(Rare)-Powerhouse Pepper (1st app.) begins by Wolverton; Stuporman app. from Daring Comics	264	528	792	1650	2475	3300
2-Wolverton-a; 1st app. Tessie the Typist & begin series	88	176	264	550	825	1100
3-5-Wolverton-a	55	110	165	330	495	660
6-10-Wolverton-a. 6-Tessie-c begin	40	80	120	240	353	465
11-20-Wolverton-a	36	72	108	207	294	380
21,22,24-27,29,30-Wolverton cont'd. & Kurtzman's "Hey Look" in #23-27	31	62	93	178	252	325
23-1st "Hey Look" by Kurtzman; Wolverton-a	33	66	99	190	270	350
28,32,34,37-41: 28-Millie the Model begins. 32-Hedy begins. 41-Nellie the Nurse app.	11	22	33	63	84	105
31-Last Powerhouse Pepper; not in #28	24	48	72	138	194	250
33,35,36-Kurtzman's "Hey Look"	12	24	36	69	92	115
42-Only app. 'Patty Pinup,' clone of Millie the Model	11	22	33	66	88	110

JOKER: DEVIL'S ADVOCATE
DC Comics: 1996 ($24.95/$12.95, one-shot)

	GD 2.0	VG 4.0	FN 6.0	VF 8.0	VF/NM 9.0	NM- 9.2
nn-(Hardcover)-Dixon scripts/Nolan & Hanna-a						25.00
nn-(Softcover)						13.00

JOKER: LAST LAUGH
DC Comics: Dec, 2001 - No. 6, Jan, 2002 ($2.95, weekly limited series)

	GD 2.0	VG 4.0	FN 6.0	VF 8.0	VF/NM 9.0	NM- 9.2
1-6: 1,6-Bolland-c						3.00
...Secret Files (12/01, $5.95) Short stories by various; Simonson-c						6.00

JOKER / MASK
Dark Horse Comics: May, 2000 - No. 4, Aug, 2000 ($2.95, limited series)

	GD 2.0	VG 4.0	FN 6.0	VF 8.0	VF/NM 9.0	NM- 9.2
1-4-Batman, Harley Quinn, Poison Ivy app.						3.00

JOLLY CHRISTMAS, A (See March of Comics No. 269)

JOLLY COMICS: Four Star Publishing Co.: 1947 (Advertised, not published)

JOLLY JINGLES (Formerly Jackpot Comics)
MLJ Magazines: No. 10, Sum, 1943 - No. 16, Wint, 1944/45

	GD 2.0	VG 4.0	FN 6.0	VF 8.0	VF/NM 9.0	NM- 9.2
10-Super Duck begins (origin & 1st app.); Woody The Woodpecker begins (not same as Lantz character)	39	78	117	230	325	420
11 (Fall, '43)-2nd Super Duck(see Hangman #8)	20	40	60	112	156	200
12-Hitler-c	25	50	75	144	198	225
13-16: 13-Sahle-c. 15-Vigoda-c	13	26	39	74	100	125

JONAH HEX (See All-Star Western, Hex and Weird Western Tales)
National Periodical Pub./DC Comics: Mar-Apr, 1977 - No. 92, Aug, 1985

	GD 2.0	VG 4.0	FN 6.0	VF 8.0	VF/NM 9.0	NM- 9.2
1	10	20	30	73	107	140
2	5	10	15	36	48	60
3,4,9: 9-Wrightson-c.	4	8	12	27	36	45
5,6,10: 5-Rep 1st app. from All-Star Western #10	3	7	10	21	28	35
7,8-Explains Hex's face disfigurement (origin)	4	8	12	29	40	50
11-20: 12-Starlin-c	2	4	6	14	18	22
21-32: 31,32-Origin retold	2	4	6	10	12	15
33-50	1	2	3	5	7	9
51-80						5.00
81-91: 89-Mark Texeira-a						6.00
92-Story cont'd in Hex #1	2	4	6	14	18	22

NOTE: ***Ayers*** *a(p)-35-37, 40, 41, 44-53, 56, 58-82.* ***Buckler*** *a-11; c-11, 13-16.* ***Kubert*** *c-43-46.* ***Morrow*** *a-90-92; c-10.* ***Spiegle(Tothish)*** *a-34, 38, 40, 49, 52.* ***Texeira*** *a-89p. Batlash back-ups in 49, 52. El Diablo back-ups in 48, 56-60, 73-75. Scalphunter back-ups in 40, 41, 45-47.*

JONAH HEX AND OTHER WESTERN TALES (Blue Ribbon Digest)
DC Comics: Sept-Oct, 1979 - No. 3, Jan-Feb, 1980 (100 pgs.)

	GD 2.0	VG 4.0	FN 6.0	VF 8.0	VF/NM 9.0	NM- 9.2
1-3: 1-Origin Scalphunter-r, Ayers/Evans, Neal Adams-a.; painted-c. 2-Weird Western Tales-r; Neal Adams, Toth, Aragones-a. 3-Outlaw-r, Scalphunter-r; Gil Kane, Wildey-a	2	4	6	10	12	15

JONAH HEX: RIDERS OF THE WORM AND SUCH
DC Comics (Vertigo): Mar, 1995 - No. 5, July, 1995 ($2.95, limited series)

	GD 2.0	VG 4.0	FN 6.0	VF 8.0	VF/NM 9.0	NM- 9.2
1-5-Lansdale story, Truman -a						4.00

JONAH HEX: SHADOWS WEST
DC Comics (Vertigo): Feb, 1999 - No. 3, Apr, 1999 ($2.95, limited series)

	GD 2.0	VG 4.0	FN 6.0	VF 8.0	VF/NM 9.0	NM- 9.2
1-3-Lansdale-s/Truman -a						4.00

JONAH HEX SPECTACULAR (See DC Special Series No. 16)

JONAH HEX: TWO-GUN MOJO
DC Comics (Vertigo): Aug, 1993 - No. 5, Dec, 1993 ($2.95, limited series)

	GD 2.0	VG 4.0	FN 6.0	VF 8.0	VF/NM 9.0	NM- 9.2
1-Lansdale scripts in all; Truman/Glanzman-a in all w/Truman-c						6.00
1-Platinum edition with no price on cover						20.00
2-5						4.00
TPB-(1994, $12.95) r/#1-5						13.00

JONESY (Formerly Crack Western)
Comic Favorite/Quality Comics Group: No. 85, Aug, 1953; No. 2, Oct, 1953 - No. 8, Oct, 1954

	GD 2.0	VG 4.0	FN 6.0	VF 8.0	VF/NM 9.0	NM- 9.2
85(#1)-Teen-age humor	8	16	24	43	54	65
2	5	10	15	24	30	35
3-8	5	10	15	22	26	30

JON JUAN (Also see Great Lover Romances)
Toby Press: Spring, 1950

	GD 2.0	VG 4.0	FN 6.0	VF 8.0	VF/NM 9.0	NM- 9.2
1-All Schomburg-a (signed Al Reid on-c); written by Siegel; used in **SOTI**, pg. 38 (Scarce)	62	124	186	388	582	775

JONNI THUNDER (...A.K.A. Thunderbolt)
DC Comics: Feb, 1985 - No. 4, Aug, 1985 (75¢, limited series)

	GD 2.0	VG 4.0	FN 6.0	VF 8.0	VF/NM 9.0	NM- 9.2
1-4: 1-Origin & 1st app.						2.25

JONNY DEMON
Dark Horse Comics: May, 1994 - No. 3, July, 1994 ($2.50, limited series)

Jonny Double #1 © DC

Journey Into Mystery #14 © MAR

Journey Into Mystery #86 © MAR

GD 2.0 | VG 4.0 | FN 6.0 | VF 8.0 | VF/NM 9.0 | NM- 9.2

1-3 2.50

JONNY DOUBLE
DC Comics (Vertigo): Sept, 1998 - No. 4, Dec, 1998 ($2.95, limited series)

1-4-Azzarello-s 3.00
TPB (2002, $12.95) r/#1-4; Chiarello-c 13.00

JONNY QUEST (TV)
Gold Key: Dec, 1964 (Hanna-Barbera)

1 (10139-412) 35 70 105 263 394 525

JONNY QUEST (TV)
Comico: June 1986 - No. 31, Dec, 1988 ($1.50/$1.75)(Hanna-Barbera)

1 5.00
2,3,5: 3,5-Dave Stevens-c 4.00
4,6-31: 30-Adapts TV episode 3.00
Special 1(9/88, $1.75), 2(10/88, $1.75) 4.00
NOTE: ***M. Anderson*** *a-9.* ***Mooney*** *a-Special 1.* ***Pini*** *a-2.* ***Quagmire*** *a-31p.* ***Rude*** *a-1; c-2i.* ***Sienkiewicz*** *c-11.* ***Spiegle*** *a-7, 12, 21; c-21* ***Staton*** *a-2i, 11p.* ***Steacy*** *c-8.* ***Stevens*** *a-4i; c-3,5.* ***Wildey*** *a-1, c-1, 7, 12.* ***Williamson*** *a-4i; c-4i.*

JONNY QUEST CLASSICS (TV)
Comico: May, 1987 - No. 3, July, 1987 ($2.00) (Hanna-Barbera)

1-3: Wildey-c/a; 3-Based on TV episode 3.00

JON SABLE, FREELANCE (Also see Mike Grell's Sable & Sable)
First Comics: 6/83 - No. 56, 2/88 (#1-17, $1; #18-33, $1.25, #34-on, $1.75)

1-Mike Grell-c/a/scripts 3.00
2-56: 3-5-Origin, parts 1-3. 6-Origin, part 4. 11-1st app. of Maggie the Cat. 14-Mando paper begins. 16-Maggie the Cat. app. 25-30-Shatter app. 34-Deluxe format begins ($1.75) 2.25
NOTE: ***Aragones*** *a-33; c-33(part).* ***Grell*** *a-1-43;c-1-52, 53p, 54-56.*

JOSEPH & HIS BRETHREN (See The Living Bible)

JOSIE (She's... #1-16) (...& the Pussycats #45 on) (See Archie's Pals 'n' Gals #23 for 1st app.) (Also see Archie Giant Series Magazine #528, 540, 551, 562, 571, 584, 597, 610, 622)
Archie Publ./Radio Comics: Feb, 1963; No. 2, Aug, 1963 - No. 106, Oct, 1982

1 17 34 51 123 182 240
2 9 18 27 65 93 120
3-5 7 14 21 46 63 80
6-10 5 10 15 33 44 55
11-20 4 8 12 24 32 40
21, 23-30 3 6 9 18 24 30
22 (9/66)-Mighty Man & Mighty (Josie Girl) app. 4 8 12 27 36 45
31-44 3 6 9 16 20 24
45 (12/69)-Josie and the Pussycats begins (Hanna Barbera TV cartoon); 1st app. of the Pussycats 10 20 30 73 107 140
46-2nd app./1st cover Pussycats 7 14 21 51 71 90
47-3rd app. of the Pussycats 5 10 15 33 44 55
48,49-Pussycats band-c/s 6 12 18 38 52 65
50-J&P-c; go to Hollywood, meet Hanna & Barbera 7 14 21 46 63 80
51-54 3 6 9 19 25 32
55-74 (2/74)(52 pg. issues) 3 6 9 18 24 30
75-90(8/76) 2 4 6 11 14 18
91-99 2 4 6 10 12 15
100 (10/79) 2 4 6 12 16 20
101-106 2 4 6 11 14 18

JOSIE & THE PUSSYCATS (TV)
Archie Comics: 1993 - No. 2, 1994 ($2.00, 52 pgs.)(Published annually)

1,2-Bound-in pull-out poster in each. 2-(Spr/94) 5.00

JOURNAL OF CRIME (See Fox Giants)

JOURNEY
Aardvark-Vanaheim #1-14/Fantagraphics Books #15-on: 1983 - No. 14, Sept, 1984; No. 15, Apr, 1985 - No. 27, July, 1986 (B&W)

1 3.00
2-27: 20-Sam Kieth-a 2.25

JOURNEY INTO FEAR
Superior-Dynamic Publications: May, 1951 - No. 21, Sept, 1954

1-Baker-r(2) 67 134 210 419 630 840
2 46 92 138 276 413 550
3,4 40 80 120 240 345 450
5-10,15: 15-Used in **SOTI**, pg. 389 29 58 87 164 232 300
11-14,16-21 27 54 81 153 214 275
NOTE: *Kamenish 'headlight'-a most issues.* ***Robinson*** *a-10.*

JOURNEY INTO MYSTERY (1st Series) (Thor Nos. 126-502)

GD 2.0 | VG 4.0 | FN 6.0 | VF 8.0 | VF/NM 9.0 | NM- 9.2

Atlas(CPS No. 1-48/AMI No. 49-68/Marvel No. 69 (6/61) on): 6/52 - No. 48, 8/57; No. 49, 11/58 - No. 125, 2/66; 503, 11/96 - No. 521, June, 1998

1-Weird/horror stories begin 300 600 900 1925 2963 4000
2 104 208 312 650 975 1300
3,4 78 156 234 488 732 975
5-11 55 110 165 330 495 660
12-20,22: 15-Atomic explosion panel. 22-Davis*esque*-a; last pre-code issue (2/55) 42 84 126 252 381 510
21-Kubert-a; Tothish-a by Andru 43 86 129 258 389 520
23-32,35-38,40: 24-Torres?-a. 38-Ditko-a 31 62 93 175 248 320
33-Williamson-a; Ditko-a (his 1st for Atlas?) 34 68 102 193 274 355
34,39: 34-Krigstein-a. 39-1st S.A. issue; Wood-a 32 64 96 180 255 330
41-Crandall-a; Frazetta*esque*-a by Morrow 20 40 60 142 209 275
42,46,48: 42,48-Torres-a. 46-Torres & Krigstein-a 19 38 57 138 202 265
43,44-Williamson/Mayo-a in both 21 42 63 147 216 285
45,47,50,52-54: 50-Davis-a. 54-Williamson-a 19 38 57 133 194 255
49-Matt Fox, Check-a 19 38 57 138 202 265
51-Kirby/Wood-a 21 42 63 149 220 290
55-61,63-65,67-69,71,72,74,75: 74-Contents change to Fantasy. 75-Last 10¢ issue 19 38 57 133 194 255
62-Prototype ish. (The Hulk); 1st app. Xemnu (Titan) called "The Hulk" 29 58 87 210 305 400
66-Prototype ish. (The Hulk)-Return of Xemnu "The Hulk" 26 52 78 185 270 355
70-Prototype ish. (The Sandman)(7/61); similar to Spidey villain 25 50 75 176 258 340
73-Story titled "The Spider" where a spider is exposed to radiation & gets powers of a human and shoots webbing; a reverse prototype of Spider-Man's origin 36 72 108 270 405 540
76,77,80-82: 80-Anti-communist propaganda story 15 30 45 109 160 210
76-(10¢ cover price blacked out, 12¢ printed on) 36 72 108 270 405 540
78-The Sorceror (Dr. Strange prototype) app. (3/62) 25 50 75 176 258 340
79-Prototype issue. (Mr. Hyde) 21 42 63 149 220 290
83-Origin & 1st app. The Mighty Thor by Kirby (8/62) and begin series; Thor-c also begin 400 800 1200 4000 6500 9000
83-Reprint from the Golden Record Comic Set 13 26 39 94 137 180
With the record (1966) 20 40 60 140 205 270
84-2nd app. Thor 110 220 330 880 1540 2200
85-1st app. Loki & Heimdall; Odin cameo (1 panel) 70 140 210 560 980 1400
86-1st full app. Odin 49 98 147 416 658 900
87-89: 89-Origin Thor retold 35 70 105 262 431 600
90-No Kirby-a 26 52 78 188 319 450
91,92,94,96-Sinnott-a 24 48 72 174 287 400
93,97-Kirby-a; Tales of Asgard series begins #97 (origin which concludes in #99); origin/1st app. Lava Man 26 52 78 188 319 450
95-Sinnott-a 24 48 72 174 287 400
98-100-Kirby/Heck-a. 98-Origin/1st app. The Human Cobra. 99-1st app. Surtur & Mr. Hyde 19 38 57 137 218 300
101,108: 101-(2/64)-2nd Avengers x-over (w/o Capt. America); see Tales Of Suspense #49 for 1st x-over. 108-(9/64)-Early Dr. Strange & Avengers x-over; ten extra pgs. Kirby-a 14 28 42 101 163 225
102,104-107,110: 102-Intro Sif. 105-109-Ten extra pgs. Kirby-a in each. 107-1st app. Grey Gargoyle 13 26 39 94 147 200
103-1st app. Enchantress 16 32 48 116 183 250
109-Magneto-c & app. (1st x-over, 10/64) 29 58 87 210 355 500
111,113,116-123,125: 113-Origin Loki. 118-1st app. Destroyer. 119-Intro Hogun, Fandrall, Volstagg 11 22 33 80 127 175
112-Thor Vs. Hulk (1/65); Origin Loki 32 64 96 232 391 550
114-Origin/1st app. Absorbing Man 16 32 48 116 183 250
115-Detailed origin of Loki 15 30 45 109 174 240
124-Hercules-c/story 12 24 36 87 138 190
503-521: 503-(11/96, $1.50)-The Lost Gods begin; Tom DeFalco scripts & Deodato Studios-c/a. 505-Spider-Man-c/app. 509-Loki-c/app. 514-516-Shang-Chi 2.50
#(-1) Flashback (7/97) Tales of Asgard Donald Blake app. 2.50
Annual 1(1965, 25¢, 72 pgs.)-New Thor vs. Hercules(1st app.)-c/story (see Incredible Hulk #3); Kirby-c/a; r/#85,93,95,97 21 42 63 149 220 290
NOTE: ***Ayers*** *a-14, 39, 64i, 71i, 74i, 80i.* ***Bailey*** *a-43.* ***Briefer*** *a-5, 12.* ***Cameron*** *a-35.* ***Check*** *a-17.* ***Colan*** *a-23, 81; c-14.* ***Ditko*** *a-33, 38, 50-96; c-58, 67, 71, 88i.* ***Kirby/Ditko*** *a-50-83.* ***Everett*** *a-20, 48; c-4-7, 9, 36, 37, 39-42, 44, 45, 47.* ***Forte*** *a-19, 35, 40, 53.* ***Heath*** *a-4-6, 11, 14; c-1, 8, 11, 15, 51.* ***Heck*** *a-53, 73.* ***Kirby*** *a(p)-51, 52, 56, 57, 60, 62, 64, 66, 69, 71-74, 76, 79, 80-89, 93, 97, 98, 100(w/****Heck****), 101-125; c-50-57, 59-66, 68-70, 72-82, 88(w/****Ditko****), 83 & 84(w/****Sinnott****), 85-96(w/****Ayers****), 97-125p.* ***Leiber/Fox*** *a-93, 98-102.* ***Maneely*** *c-20-22.* ***Morisi*** *a-42.* ***Morrow*** *a-41, 42.* ***Orlando*** *a-30, 45, 57.* ***Mac Pakula*** *(Tothish) a-9, 35, 41.* ***Powell*** *a-20, 27, 34.* ***Reinman*** *a-39, 87, 92, 96i.* ***Robinson*** *a-9.* ***Roussos*** *a-39.* ***Robert Sale*** *a-14.* ***Severin*** *a-27; c-30.* ***Sinnott*** *a-41; c-50.* ***Tuska*** *a-11.* ***Wildey*** *a-16.*

JOURNEY INTO MYSTERY (2nd Series)

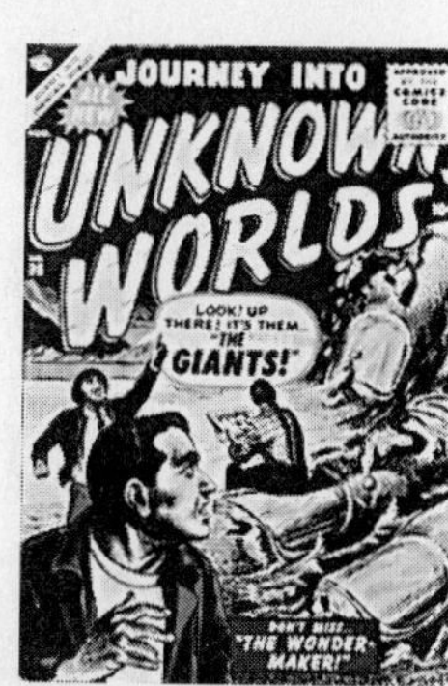

Journey Into Unknown Worlds #36 © MAR

JSA #54 © DC

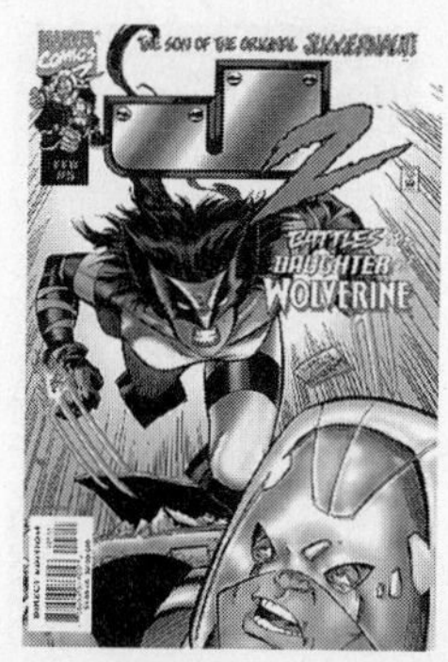

J2 #5 © MAR

GD VG FN VF VF/NM NM-
2.0 4.0 6.0 8.0 9.0 9.2

Marvel Comics: Oct, 1972 - No. 19, Oct, 1975
1-Robert Howard adaptation; Starlin/Ploog-a 3 6 9 18 24 30
2-5: 2,3,5-Bloch adapt. 4-H. P. Lovecraft adapt. 2 4 6 12 16 20
6-19: Reprints 2 4 6 10 12 15
NOTE: ***N. Adams** a-2i. **Ditko** r-7, 10, 12, 14, 15, 19; c-10. **Everett** r-9, 14. **G. Kane** a-1p, 2p; c-1-3p. **Kirby** r-7, 13, 15, 18, 19; c-7. **Mort Lawrence** r-2. **Maneely** r-3. **Orlando** r-16. **Reese** a-1, 2i. **Starlin** a-1p, 3p. **Torres** r-16. **Wildey** r-9, 14.*

JOURNEY INTO UNKNOWN WORLDS (Formerly Teen)
Atlas Comics (WFP): No. 36, Sept, 1950 - No. 38, Feb, 1951; No. 4, Apr, 1951 - No. 59, Aug, 1957
36(#1)-Science fiction/weird; "End Of The Earth" c/story
232 464 696 1450 2175 2900
37(#2)-Science fiction; "When Worlds Collide" c/story; Everett-c/a; Hitler story
100 200 300 625 938 1250
38(#3)-Science fiction 85 170 255 531 796 1060
4-6,8,10-Science fiction/weird 55 110 165 330 495 660
7-Wolverton-a "Planet of Terror", 6 pgs; electric chair c-inset/story
90 180 270 563 844 1125
9-Giant eyeball story 66 132 198 413 619 825
11,12-Krigstein-a 40 80 120 240 340 440
13,16,17,20 35 70 105 201 288 370
14-Wolverton-a "One of Our Graveyards Is Missing", 4 pgs; Tuska-a
67 134 201 419 630 840
15-Wolverton-a "They Crawl by Night", 5 pgs.; 2 pg. Maneely s/f story
67 134 201 419 630 840
18,19-Matt Fox-a 40 80 120 240 340 440
21-33: 21-Decapitation-c. 24-Sci/fic story. 26-Atom bomb panel. 27-Sid Check-a. 33-Last pre-code (2/55) 27 54 81 153 214 275
34-Kubert, Torres-a 21 42 63 118 164 210
35-Torres-a 19 38 57 106 146 185
36-45,48,50,53,55,59: 43-Krigstein-a. 44-Davis-a. 45,55,59-Williamson-a in all; with Mayo #55,59. 55-Crandall-a. 48,53-Crandall-a (4 pgs. #48). 48-Check-a. 50-Davis, Crandall-a
18 36 54 101 138 175
46,47,49,52,54,56-58: 54-Torres-a 16 32 48 92 126 160
51-Ditko, Wood-a 20 40 60 112 156 200
NOTE: ***Ayers** a-24, 43. **Berg** a-38(#3), 43. **Lou Cameron** a-33. **Colan** a-37(#2), 6, 17, 19, 20, 23, 39. **Ditko** a-45, 51. **Drucker** a-35, 58. **Everett** a-37(#2), 11, 14, 41, 55, 56; c-37(#2), 11, 13, 14, 17, 22, 47, 48, 50, 53-55, 59. **Forte** a-49. **Fox** a-21i. **Heath** a-36(#1), 4, 6-8, 17, 20, 22, 36i; c-18. **Keller** a-15. **Mort Lawrence** a-38, 39. **Maneely** a-7, 8, 15, 16, 22, 49, 58; c-19, 25, 52. **Morrow** a-48. **Orlando** a-44, 57. **Pakula** a-36. **Powell** a-42, 53, 54. **Reinman** a-8. **Rico** a-21. **Robert Sale** a-24, 49. **Sekowsky** a-4, 5, 9. **Severin** a-38, 51; c-38, 48i, 56. **Sinnott** a-9, 21, 24. **Tuska** a-38(#3), 14. **Wildey** a-25, 43, 44.*

JOURNEYMAN
Image Comics: Aug, 1999 - No. 3, Oct, 1999 ($2.95, B&W, limited series)
1-3-Brandon McKinney-s/a 3.00

JOURNEY TO THE CENTER OF THE EARTH (Movie)
Dell Publishing Co.: No. 1060, Nov-Jan, 1959/60 (one-shot)
Four Color 1060-Pat Boone & James Mason photo-c 12 24 36 87 129 170

JSA (Justice Society of America) (Also see All Star Comics)
DC Comics: Aug, 1999 - Present ($2.50)
1-Robinson and Goyer-s; funeral of Wesley Dodds 2 4 6 8 10 12
2-5: 4-Return of Dr. Fate 6.00
6-24: 6-Black Adam-c/app. 11,12-Kobra. 16-20-JSA vs. Johnny Sorrow. 19,20-Spectre app. 22-Hawkgirl origin. 23-Hawkman returns 4.00
25-($3.75) Hawkman rejoins the JSA 1 2 3 5 7 9
26-36, 38-49: 27-Capt. Marvel app. 29-Joker: Last Laugh. 31,32-Snejbjerg-a. 33-Ultra-Humanite. 34-Intro. new Crimson Avenger and Hourman. 42-G.A. Mr. Terrific and the Freedom Fighters app. 46-Eclipso returns 3.00
37-($3.50) Johnny Thunder merges with the Thunderbolt; origin new Crimson Avenger 3.50
50-($3.95) Wraparound-c by Pacheco; Sentinel becomes Green Lantern again 4.00
51-56: 51-Kobra killed. 54-JLA app. 55-Ma Hunkle (Red Tornado) app. 56-Black Reign x-over with Hawkman 2.50
Annual 1 (10/00, $3.50) Planet DC; intro. Nemesis 3.50
Darkness Falls TPB (2002, $19.95) r/#6-15 20.00
Fair Play TPB (2003, $14.95) r/#26-31 & Secret Files #2 15.00
Justice Be Done TPB (2000, $14.95) r/Secret Files & #1-5 15.00
...: Our Worlds at War 1 (9/01, $2.95) Jae Lee-c; Saltares-a 3.00
... Secret Files 1 (8/99, $4.95) Origin stories and pin-ups; death of Wesley Dodds (G.A. Sandman); intro new Hawkgirl 5.00
... Secret Files 2 (9/01, $4.95) Short stories and profile pages 5.00
...: Stealing Thunder TPB (2003, $14.95) r/#32-38; JSA vs. The Ultra-Humanite 15.00
...: The Return of Hawkman TPB (2002, $19.95) r/#16-26 & Secret Files #1 20.00

JSA: ALL STARS

GD VG FN VF VF/NM NM-
2.0 4.0 6.0 8.0 9.0 9.2

DC Comics: July, 2003 - No. 8, Feb, 2004 ($2.50/$3.50, limited series, back-up stories in Golden Age style)
1-6,8-Goyer & Johns-s/Cassaday-c. 1-Velluto-a; intro. Legacy. 2-Hawkman by Loeb/Sale 3-Dr. Fate by Cooke. 4-Starman by Robinson/Harris. 5-Hourman by Chaykin. 6-Dr. Mid-nite by Azzarello/Risso 2.50
7-($3.50) Mr. Terrific back-up story by Chabon; Lark-a 3.50

JSA: THE LIBERTY FILE (Elseworlds)
DC Comics: Feb, 2000 - No. 2, Mar, 2000 ($6.95, limited series)
1,2-Batman, Dr. Mid-Nite and Hourman vs. WW2 Joker; Tony Harris-c/a 7.00

JSA: THE UNHOLY THREE (Elseworlds)(Sequel to JSA: The Liberty File)
DC Comics: 2003 - No. 2, 2003 ($6.95, limited series)
1,2-Batman, Superman and Hourman; Tony Harris-c/a 7.00

J2 (Also see A-Next and Juggernaut)
Marvel Comics: Oct, 1998 - No. 12, Sept, 1999 ($1.99)
1-12:1-Juggernaut's son; Lim-a. 2-Two covers; X-People app. 3-J2 battles the Hulk 2.25

JUDE, THE FORGOTTEN SAINT
Catechetical Guild Education Soc.: 1954 (16 pgs.; 8x11"; full color; paper-c)
nn 4 8 12 18 22 25

J.U.D.G.E.: THE SECRET RAGE
Image Comics: Mar, 2000 - No. 3, May, 2000 ($2.95)
1-3-Greg Horn-s/c/a 3.00

JUDGE COLT
Gold Key: Oct, 1969 - No. 4, Sept, 1970
1 3 6 9 18 23 28
2-4 2 4 6 10 13 16

JUDGE DREDD (...Classics #62 on; also see Batman - Judge Dredd, The Law of Dredd & 2000 A.D. Monthly)
Eagle Comics/IPC Magazines Ltd./Quality Comics #34-35, V2#1-37/ Fleetway #38 on: Nov, 1983 - No. 35, 1986; V2#1, Oct, 1986 - No. 77, 1993
1-Bolland-c/a 6.00
2-35 3.00
V2#1-77: 1-('86)-New look begins. 20-Begin $1.50-c. 21/22, 23/24-Two issue numbers in one. 28-1st app. Megaman (super-hero). 39-Begin $1.75-c. 51-Begin $1.95-c. 53-Bolland-a. 57-Reprints 1st published Judge Dredd story 2.50
Special 1 2.50
NOTE: ***Bolland** a-1-6, 8, 10; c-1-10, 15. **Guice** c-V2#23/24, 26, 27.*

JUDGE DREDD (3rd Series)
DC Comics: Aug, 1994 - No. 18, Jan, 1996 ($1.95)
1-18: 12-Begin $2.25-c 2.50
nn ($5.95)-Movie adaptation, Sienkiewicz-c 6.00

JUDGE DREDD'S CRIME FILE
Eagle Comics: Aug, 1989 - No. 6, Feb, 1986 ($1.25, limited series)
1-6: 1-Byrne-a 2.50

JUDGE DREDD: LEGENDS OF THE LAW
DC Comics: Dec, 1994 - No. 13, Dec, 1995 ($1.95)
1-13: 1-5-Dorman-c 2.50

JUDGE DREDD: THE EARLY CASES
Eagle Comics: Feb, 1986 - No. 6, Jul, 1986 ($1.25, Mega-series, Mando paper)
1-6: 2000 A.D.-r 2.50

JUDGE DREDD: THE JUDGE CHILD QUEST (Judge Child in indicia)
Eagle Comics: Aug, 1984 - No. 5, Oct, 1984 ($1.25, Lim. series, Baxter paper)
1-5: 2000A.D.-r; Bolland-c/a 2.50

JUDGE DREDD: THE MEGAZINE
Fleetway/Quality: 1991 - Present ($4.95, stiff-c, squarebound, 52 pgs.)
1-3 5.00

JUDGE DREDD VS. ALIENS: INCUBUS
Dark Horse Comics: March, 2003 - No. 4, June, 2003 ($2.99, limited series)
1-4-Flint-a/Wagner & Diggle-s 3.00

JUDGE PARKER
Argo: Feb, 1956 - No. 2, 1956
1-Newspaper strip reprints 7 14 21 35 43 50
2 5 10 15 24 30 35

JUDGMENT DAY
Awesome Entertainment: June, 1997 - No. 3, Oct, 1997 ($2.50, limited series)

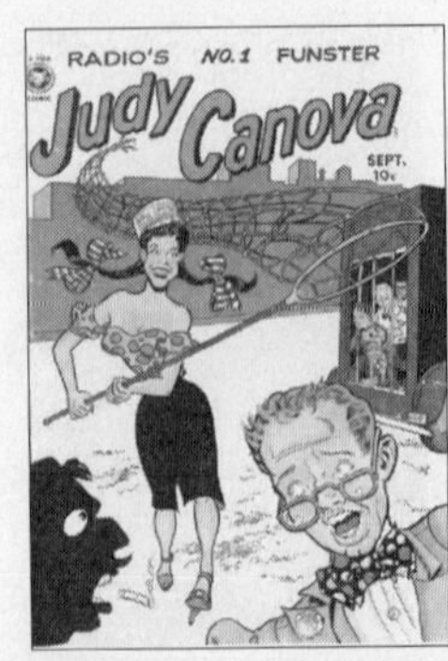

Judy Canova #3 © FOX

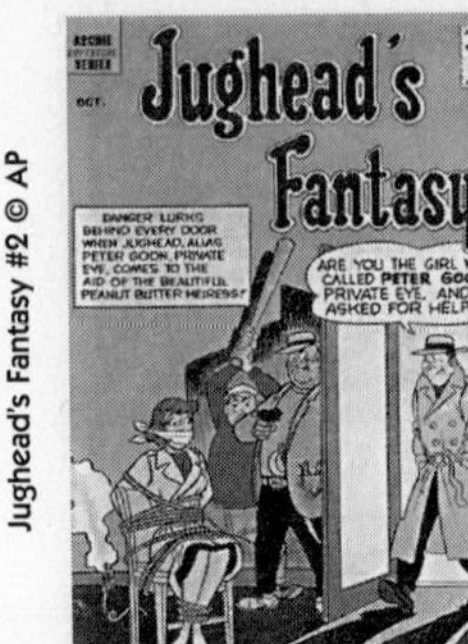

Jughead's Fantasy #2 © AP

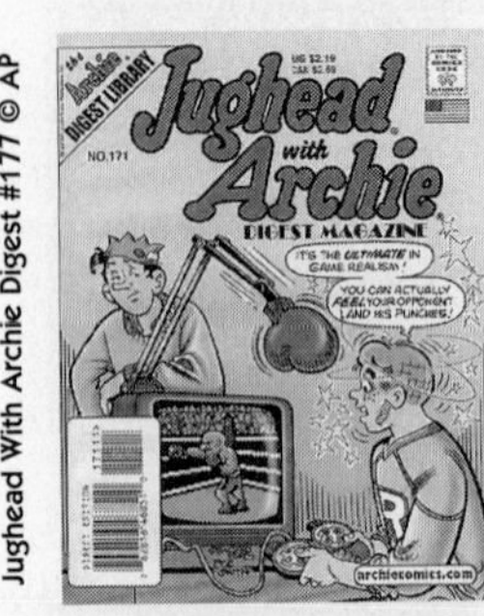

Jughead With Archie Digest #177 © AP

	GD 2.0	VG 4.0	FN 6.0	VF 8.0	VF/NM 9.0	NM- 9.2
1-3: 1 Alpha-Moore-s/Liefeld-c/a(p) flashback art by various in all. 2 Omega. 3 Final Judgment. All have a variant cover by Dave Gibbons						2.50
...Aftermath-($3.50) Moore-s/Kane-a; Youngblood, Glory, New Men, Maximage, Allies and Spacehunter short stories. Also has a variant cover by Dave Gibbons						3.50

JUDO JOE
Jay-Jay Corp.: Aug, 1953 - No. 3, Dec, 1953 (Judo lessons in each issue)

	GD	VG	FN	VF	VF/NM	NM-
1-Drug ring story	9	18	27	52	66	80
2,3: 3-Hypo needle story	7	14	21	35	43	50

JUDOMASTER (Gun Master #84-89) (Also see Crisis on Infinite Earths, Sarge Steel #6 & Special War Series)
Charlton Comics: No. 89, May-June, 1966 - No. 98, Dec, 1967 (Two No. 89's)

	GD	VG	FN	VF	VF/NM	NM-
89-3rd app. Judomaster	4	8	12	28	38	48
90,92-98: 93-Intro. Tiger	4	8	12	22	30	38
91-Sarge Steel begins	4	8	12	24	32	40
93,94,96,98 (Modern Comics reprint, 1977)						4.00

NOTE: *Morisi Thunderbolt #90. #91 has 1 pg. biography on writer/artist Frank McLaughlin.*

JUDY CANOVA (Formerly My Experience) (Stage, screen, radio)
Fox Features Syndicate: No. 23, May, 1950 - No. 3, Sept, 1950

	GD	VG	FN	VF	VF/NM	NM-
23(#1)-Wood-c,a(p)?	23	46	69	129	180	230
24-Wood-a(p)	22	44	66	124	172	220
3-Wood-c; Wood/Orlando-a	24	48	72	135	190	245

JUDY GARLAND (See Famous Stars)

JUDY JOINS THE WAVES
Toby Press: 1951 (For U.S. Navy)

	GD	VG	FN	VF	VF/NM	NM-
nn	7	14	21	35	43	50

JUGGERNAUT (See X-Men)
Marvel Comics: Apr, 1997, Nov, 1999 ($2.99, one-shots)

	GD	VG	FN	VF	VF/NM	NM-
1-(4/97) Kelly-s/ Rouleau-a						3.00
1-(11/99) Casey-s; Eighth Day x-over; Thor, Iron Man, Spidey app.						3.00

JUGHEAD (Formerly Archie's Pal...)
Archie Publications: No. 127, Dec, 1965 - No. 352, June, 1987

	GD	VG	FN	VF	VF/NM	NM-
127-130	3	6	9	18	23	28
131,133,135-160(9/68)	2	4	6	14	18	22
132,134: 132-Shield-c; The Fly & Black Hood app.; Shield cameo. 134-Shield-c	3	7	10	21	28	35
161-180	2	4	6	10	13	16
181-199	2	4	6	8	10	12
200(1/72)	2	4	6	9	11	14
201-240(5/75)	1	2	3	5	7	9
241-270(11/77)	1	2	3	4	5	7
271-299						6.00
300(5/80)-Anniversary issue; infinity-c	1	2	3	4	5	7
301-320(1/82)						4.00
321-324,326-352						3.00
325-(10/82) Cheryl Blossom app. (not on cover); same month as intro. (cover & story) in Archie's Girls, Betty & Veronica #320; Jason Blossom app.; DeCarlo-a	3	6	9	16	20	24

JUGHEAD (2nd Series)(Becomes Archie's Pal Jughead Comics #46 on)
Archie Enterprises: Aug, 1987 - No. 45, May, 1993 (.75/$1.00/$1.25)

	GD	VG	FN	VF	VF/NM	NM-
1	1	2	3	4	5	7
2-10						4.00
11-45: 4-X-Mas issue. 17-Colan-c/a						3.00

JUGHEAD AS CAPTAIN HERO (See Archie as Pureheart the Powerful, Archie Giant Series Magazine #142 & Life With Archie)
Archie Publications: Oct, 1966 - No. 7, Nov, 1967

	GD	VG	FN	VF	VF/NM	NM-
1-Super hero parody	7	14	21	46	63	80
2	4	8	12	29	40	50
3-7	4	8	12	24	32	40

JUGHEAD JONES COMICS DIGEST, THE (...Magazine No. 10-64; Jughead Jones Digest Magazine #65)
Archie Publ.: June, 1977 - No. 100, May, 1996 ($1.35/$1.50/$1.75, digest-size, 128 pgs.)

	GD	VG	FN	VF	VF/NM	NM-
1-Neal Adams-a; Capt. Hero-r	3	7	10	21	28	35
2(9/77)-Neal Adams-a	3	6	9	16	20	24
3-6,8-10	2	4	6	10	13	16
7-Origin Jaguar-r; N. Adams-a.	2	4	6	12	16	20
11-20: 13-r/1957 Jughead's Folly	1	3	4	6	8	10
21-50	1	2	3	4	5	7
51-70						5.00
71-100						3.00

JUGHEAD'S BABY TALES
Archie Comics: Spring, 1994 - No. 2, Wint. 1994 ($2.00, 52 pgs.)

	GD	VG	FN	VF	VF/NM	NM-
1,2: 1-Bound-in pull-out poster						4.00

JUGHEAD'S DINER
Archie Comics: Apr, 1990 - No. 7, Apr, 1991 ($1.00)

	GD	VG	FN	VF	VF/NM	NM-
1						4.00
2-7						2.50

JUGHEAD'S DOUBLE DIGEST (...Magazine #5)
Archie Comics: Oct, 1989 - Present ($2.25 - $3.59)

	GD	VG	FN	VF	VF/NM	NM-
1	1	3	4	6	8	10
2-10: 2,5-Capt. Hero stories	1	2	3	4	5	7
11-25						4.00
26-100: 58-Begin $2.99-c. 66-Begin $3.19-c. 75-Begin $3.29-c. 91-Begin $3.59-c						3.60

JUGHEAD'S EAT-OUT COMIC BOOK MAGAZINE (See Archie Giant Series Magazine No. 170)

JUGHEAD'S FANTASY
Archie Publications: Aug, 1960 - No. 3, Dec, 1960

	GD	VG	FN	VF	VF/NM	NM-
1	18	36	54	131	191	250
2	12	24	36	82	121	160
3	10	20	30	67	96	125

JUGHEAD'S FOLLY
Archie Publications (Close-Up): 1957 (36 pgs.)(one-shot)

	GD	VG	FN	VF	VF/NM	NM-
1-Jughead a la Elvis (Rare) (1st reference to Elvis in comics?)	50	100	150	300	450	600

JUGHEAD'S JOKES
Archie Publications: Aug, 1967 - No. 78, Sept, 1982
(No. 1-8, 38 on: reg. size; No. 9-23: 68 pgs.; No. 24-37: 52 pgs.)

	GD	VG	FN	VF	VF/NM	NM-
1	7	14	21	51	71	90
2	4	8	12	27	36	45
3-8	3	6	9	18	24	30
9,10 (68 pgs.)	3	7	10	21	28	35
11-23(4/71) (68 pgs.)	3	6	9	18	23	28
24-37(1/74) (52 pgs.)	2	4	6	11	14	18
38-50(9/76)	1	2	3	5	6	8
51-78						5.00

JUGHEAD'S PAL HOT DOG (See Laugh #14 for 1st app.)
Archie Comics: Jan, 1990 - No. 5, Oct, 1990 ($1.00)

	GD	VG	FN	VF	VF/NM	NM-
1						4.00
2-5						2.50

JUGHEAD'S SOUL FOOD
Spire Christian Comics (Fleming H. Revell Co.): 1979 (49 cents)

	GD	VG	FN	VF	VF/NM	NM-
nn-Low print run	2	4	6	10	12	15

JUGHEAD'S TIME POLICE
Archie Comics: July, 1990 - No. 6, May, 1991 ($1.00, bi-monthly)

	GD	VG	FN	VF	VF/NM	NM-
1						4.00
2-6: Colan a-3-6p; c-3-6						2.50

JUGHEAD WITH ARCHIE DIGEST (...Plus Betty & Veronica & Reggie Too No. 1,2; ...Magazine #33-?, 101-on; ...Comics Digest Mag.)
Archie Pub.: Mar, 1974 - Present ($1.00-$2.39)

	GD	VG	FN	VF	VF/NM	NM-
1	6	12	18	38	52	65
2	4	8	12	24	32	40
3-10	3	6	9	18	24	30
11-13,15-17,19,20: Capt. Hero-r in #14-16; Capt. Pureheart #17,19	2	4	6	10	12	15
14,18,21,22-Pureheart the Powerful in #18,21,22	2	4	6	11	14	18
23-30: 29-The Shield-r. 30-The Fly-r	1	3	4	6	8	10
31-50,100	1	2	3	5	6	8
51-99	1	2	3	4	5	7
101-121						4.00
122-189: 156-Begin $2.19-c. 180-Begin $2.39-c						2.50

JUKE BOX COMICS
Famous Funnies: Mar, 1948 - No. 6, Jan, 1949

	GD	VG	FN	VF	VF/NM	NM-
1-Toth-c/a; Hollingsworth-a	40	80	120	240	340	440
2-Transvestism story	27	54	81	153	214	275
3-6: 3-Peggy Lee story. 4-Jimmy Durante line drawn-c. 6-Features Desi Arnaz plus Arnaz line drawn-c	21	42	63	118	164	210

Jumbo Comics #96 © FH

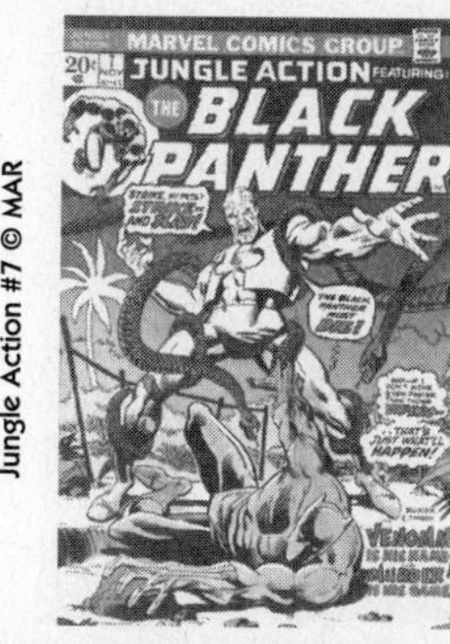

Jungle Action #7 © MAR

Jungle Comics #30 © FH

GD 2.0 | VG 4.0 | FN 6.0 | VF 8.0 | VF/NM 9.0 | NM- 9.2

JUMBO COMICS (Created by S.M. Iger)
Fiction House Magazines (Real Adv. Publ. Co.): Sept, 1938 - No. 167, Mar, 1953 (No. 1-3: 68 pgs.; No. 4-8: 52 pgs.)(No. 1-8 oversized-10-1/2x14-1/2"; black & white)

1-(Rare)-Sheena Queen of the Jungle(1st app.) by Meskin, Hawks of the Seas (The Hawk #10 on; see Feature Funnies #3) by Eisner, The Hunchback by Dick Briefer (ends #8), Wilton of the West (ends #24), Inspector Dayton (ends #67) & ZX-5 (ends #140) begin; 1st comic art by Jack Kirby (Count of Monte Cristo & Wilton of the West); Mickey Mouse appears (1 panel) with brief biography of Walt Disney; 1st app. Peter Pupp by Bob Kane. Note: Sheena was created by Iger for publication in England as a newspaper strip. The early issues of Jumbo contain Sheena strip-r; multiple panel-c 1,2,7 — 2050 4100 6150 20,500 - -
2-(Rare)-Origin Sheena. Diary of Dr. Hayward by Kirby (also #3) plus 2 other stories; contains strip from Universal Film featuring Edgar Bergen & Charlie McCarthy plus-c (preview of film) — 660 1320 1980 6600 - -
3-Last Kirby issue — 460 920 1380 4600 - -
4-(Scarce)-Origin The Hawk by Eisner; Wilton of the West by Fine (ends #14)(1st comic work); Count of Monte Cristo by Fine (ends #15); The Diary of Dr. Hayward by Fine (cont'd #8,9) — 430 860 1290 4300 - -
5-Christmas-c — 360 740 1110 3700 - -
6-8-Last B&W issue. #8 was a 1939 N. Y. World's Fair Special Edition; Frank Buck's Jungleland story — 330 660 990 3300 - -
9-Stuart Taylor begins by Fine (ends #140); Fine-c; 1st color issue (8-9/39)-1st Sheena (jungle) cover; 8-1/4x10-1/4" (oversized in width only) — 310 620 930 3100 - -
10-Regular size 68 pg. issues begin; Sheena dons new costume w/origin costume; Stuart Taylor sci/fi-c; classic Lou Fine-c. — 184 368 552 1150 1725 2300
11-13: 12-The Hawk-c by Eisner. 13-Eisner-c — 124 248 372 775 1163 1550
14-Intro. Lightning (super-hero) on-c only — 128 256 384 800 1200 1600
15,17-20: 15-1st Lightning story and begins, ends #41. 17-Lightning part-c — 78 156 234 488 732 975
16-Lightning-c — 96 192 288 600 900 1200
21-30: 22-1st Tom, Dick & Harry; origin The Hawk retold. 25-Midnight the Black Stallion begins, ends #65 — 61 122 183 381 571 760
31-40: 31-(9/41)-1st app. Mars God of War in Stuart Taylor story (see Planet Comics #15. 35-Shows V2#11 (correct number does not appear) — 50 100 150 300 450 600
41-50: 42-Ghost Gallery begins, ends #167 — 40 80 120 240 345 450
51-60: 52-Last Tom, Dick & Harry — 36 72 108 204 290 375
61-70: 68-Sky Girl begins, ends #130; not in #79 — 27 54 81 155 218 280
71-93,95-99: 89-ZX5 becomes a private eye. — 22 44 66 124 172 220
94-Used in Love and Death by Legman — 24 48 72 135 190 245
100 — 24 48 72 135 190 245
101-121 — 21 42 63 121 168 215
121-140,150-158: 155-Used in **POP**, pg. 98 — 18 36 54 104 142 180
141-149-Two Sheena stories. 141-Long Bow, Indian Boy begins, ends #160 — 17 34 51 98 134 170
159-163: Space Scouts serial in all. 160-Last jungle-c (6/52). 161-Ghost Gallery covers begin, end #167. 163-Suicide Smith app. — 16 32 48 92 126 160
164-The Star Pirate begins, ends #165 — 16 32 48 92 126 160
165-167: 165,167-Space Rangers app. — 16 32 48 92 126 160

NOTE: *Bondage covers, negligee panels, torture, etc. are common in this series. Hawks of the Seas, Inspector Dayton, Spies in Action, Sports Shorts, & Uncle Otto by Eisner, #1-7. Hawk by* ***Eisner****-#10-15.* ***Eisner*** *c-1-8, 12-14. 1pg. Patsy pin-ups in 92-97, 99-101. Sheena by* ***Meskin****-#1, 4; by* ***Powell****-#2, 3, 5-28;* ***Powell*** *c-14, 16, 17, 19.* ***Powell/Eisner*** *c-15. Sky Girl by* ***Matt Baker****-#69-78, 80-130. ZX-5 & Ghost Gallery by* ***Kamen****-#90-130.* ***Bailey*** *a-3-8.* ***Briefer*** *a-1-8, 10.* ***Fine*** *a-14; c-9-11.* ***Kamen*** *a-101, 105, 123, 132; c-105, 121-145.* ***Bob Kane*** *a-1-8.* ***Whitman*** *c-146-167(most). Jungle c-9, 13, 15, 17 on.*

JUNGLE ACTION
Atlas Comics (IPC): Oct, 1954 - No. 6, Aug, 1955

1-Leopard Girl begins by Al Hartley (#1,3); Jungle Boy by Forte; Maneely-a in all — 39 78 117 230 325 420
2-(3-D effect cover) — 39 78 117 230 325 420
3-6: 3-Last precode (2/55) — 25 50 75 144 198 255

NOTE: ***Maneely*** *c-1, 2, 5, 6.* ***Romita*** *a-3, 6.* ***Shores*** *a-3, 6; c-3, 4?.*

JUNGLE ACTION (...& Black Panther #18-21?)
Marvel Comics Group: Oct, 1972 - No. 24, Nov, 1976

1-Lorna, Jann-r (All reprints in 1-4) — 2 4 6 12 16 20
2-4 — 2 4 6 8 10 12
5-Black Panther begins (r/Avengers #62) — 3 6 9 16 20 25
6-New solo Black Panther stories begin — 2 4 6 14 18 22
7,9,10: 9-Contains pull-out centerfold ad by Mark Jewelers — 2 4 6 8 10 12
8-Origin Black Panther — 2 4 6 10 13 16
11-20,23,24: 19-23-KKK x-over. 23-r/#22. 24-1st Wind Eagle; story contd in Marvel Premiere #51-#53 — 1 2 3 5 6 8
21,22-(Regular 25¢ edition)(5,7/76) — 1 2 3 5 6 8
21,22-(30¢-c variant, limited distribution) — 2 4 6 8 10 12

NOTE: ***Buckler*** *a-6-9p, 22; c-8p, 12p.* ***Buscema*** *a-5p; c-22.* ***Byrne*** *c-23.* ***Gil Kane*** *a-8p; c-2, 4, 10p, 11p, 13-17, 19, 24.* ***Kirby*** *c-18.* ***Maneely*** *r-1.* ***Russell*** *a-13i.* ***Starlin*** *c-3p.*

JUNGLE ADVENTURES
Super Comics: 1963 - 1964 (Reprints)

10,12,15,17,18: 10-r/Terrors of the Jungle #4 & #10(Rulah). 12-r/Zoot #14(Rulah).15-r/Kaanga from Jungle #152 & Tiger Girl. 17-All Jo-Jo-r. 18-Reprints/White Princess of the Jungle #1; no Kinstler-a; origin of both White Princess & Cap'n Courage — 4 8 12 22 30 38

JUNGLE ADVENTURES
Skywald Comics: Mar, 1971 - No. 3, June, 1971 (25¢, 52 pgs.)

1-Zangar origin; reprints of Jo-Jo, Blue Gorilla(origin)/White Princess #3, Kinstler-r/White Princess #2 — 3 6 9 16 20 25
2,3: 2-Zangar, Sheena-r/Sheena #17 & Jumbo #162, Jo-Jo, origin Slave Girl-r. 3-Zangar, Jo-Jo, White Princess, Rulah-r — 2 4 6 10 13 16

JUNGLE BOOK (See King Louie and Mowgli, Movie Comics, Mowgli..., Walt Disney Showcase #45 & Walt Disney's The Jungle Book)

JUNGLE CAT (Disney)
Dell Publishing Co.: No. 1136, Sept-Nov, 1960 (one shot)

Four Color 1136-Movie, photo-c — 7 14 21 51 71 90

JUNGLE COMICS
Fiction House Magazines: 1/40 - No. 157, 3/53; No. 158, Spr, 1953 - No. 163, Summer, 1954

1-Origin The White Panther, Kaanga, Lord of the Jungle, Tabu, Wizard of the Jungle; Wambi, the Jungle Boy, Camilla & Capt. Terry Thunder begin (all 1st app.). Lou Fine-c — 448 896 1344 3136 4818 6500
2-Fantomah, Mystery Woman of the Jungle begins, ends #51; The Red Panther begins, ends #26 — 164 328 492 1025 1538 2050
3,4 — 134 268 402 838 1257 1675
5-Classic Eisner-c — 144 288 432 900 1350 1800
6-10: 7,8-Powell-c — 76 152 228 475 713 950
11-20: 13-Tuska-c — 55 110 165 330 495 660
21-30: 25-Shows V2#1 (correct number does not appear). #27-New origin Fantomah, Daughter of the Pharoahs; Camilla dons new costume — 44 88 132 264 395 525
31-40 — 36 72 108 204 290 375
41,43-50 — 31 62 93 178 252 325
42-Kaanga by Crandall, 12 pgs. — 34 68 102 193 274 355
51-60 — 27 54 81 155 218 280
61-70: 67-Cover swipes Crandall splash pg. in #42 — 24 48 72 135 190 245
71-80: 79-New origin Tabu — 21 42 63 118 164 210
81-97,99,101-110: 104-In Camilla story, villain is Dr. Wertham — 19 38 57 107 149 190
98-Used in **SOTI**, pg. 185 & illo "In ordinary comic books, there are pictures within pictures for children who know how to look;" used by N.Y. Legis. Comm. — 33 66 99 190 270 350
100 — 24 48 72 135 190 245
111-120: 118-Clyde Beatty app. — 20 40 60 112 156 200
121-130 — 18 36 54 101 138 175
131-163: 135-Desert Panther begins in Terry Thunder (origin), not in #137; ends (dies) #138. 139-Last 52 pg. issue. 141-Last Tabu. 143,145-Used in **POP**, pg. 99. 151-Last Camilla & Terry Thunder. 152-Tiger Girl begins. 158-Last Wambi; Sheena app. — 17 34 51 95 130 165
I.W. Reprint #1,9: 1-r/? 9-r/#151 — 3 6 9 16 25 32

NOTE: *Bondage covers, negligee panels, torture, etc. are common to this series. Camilla by* ***Fran Hopper****-#70-92; by* ***Baker****-#69, 100-113, 115, 116; by* ***Lubbers****-#97-99 by* ***Tuska****-#63, 65. Kaanga by* ***John Celardo****-#80-113; by* ***Larsen****-#71, 75-79; by* ***Moreira****-#58, 60, 61, 63-70, 72-74; by* ***Tuska****-#37, 62; by* ***Whitman****-#114-163. Tabu by* ***Larsen****-#59-75, 82-92; by* ***Whitman****-#93-115. Terry Thunder by* ***Hopper****-#71, 72; by* ***Celardo****-#78, 79; by* ***Lubbers****-#80-85. Tiger Girl-r by* ***Baker****-#152, 153, 155-157, 159. Wambi by* ***Baker****-#62-67, 74.* ***Astarita*** *c-45, 46.* ***Celardo*** *a-78; c-98-113.* ***Crandall*** *c-67 from splash pg.* ***Eisner*** *c-2, 5, 6.* ***Fine*** *c-1.* ***Larsen*** *a-65, 66, 71, 72, 74, 75, 79, 83, 84, 87-90.* ***Moriera*** *c-43, 44.* ***Morisi*** *a-51.* ***Powell*** *c-7, 8.* ***Sultan*** *c-3, 4.* ***Tuska*** *c-13.* ***Whitman*** *c-132-163(most).* ***Zolnerowich*** *c-11, 12, 18-41.*

JUNGLE COMICS
Blackthorne Publishing: May, 1988 - No. 4 ($2.00, B&W/color)

1-Dave Stevens-c; B. Jones scripts in all. — 3.00
2-4: 2-B&W-a begins — 2.25

JUNGLE GIRL (See Lorna, the...)

JUNGLE GIRL (Nyoka, Jungle Girl No. 2 on)
Fawcett Publications: Fall, 1942 (one-shot)(No month listed)

1-Bondage-c; photo of Kay Aldridge who played Nyoka in movie serial app. on-c. Adaptation of the classic Republic movie serial Perils of Nyoka. 1st comic to devote entire contents to

Jungle Jo #2 © FOX

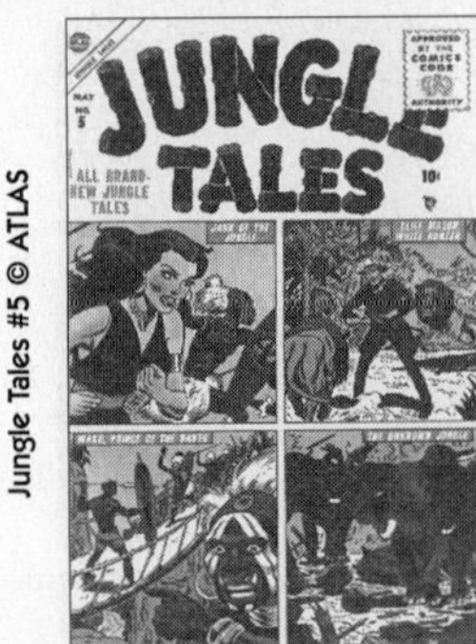

Jungle Tales #5 © ATLAS

Jurassic Park #1 © Universal Studios & Amblin Entertainment

	GD 2.0	VG 4.0	FN 6.0	VF 8.0	VF/NM 9.0	NM- 9.2
a movie serial adaptation	130	260	390	813	1219	1625

JUNGLE GIRLS
AC Comics: 1989 - No. 16, 1993 (B&W)

	GD 2.0	VG 4.0	FN 6.0	VF 8.0	VF/NM 9.0	NM- 9.2
1-16: 1-4,10,13-16-New story & "good girl" reprints. 5-9,11,12-All g.g. reprints (Baker, Powell, Lubbers, others)						3.00

JUNGLE JIM (Also see Ace Comics)
Standard Comics (Best Books): No. 11, Jan, 1949 - No. 20, Apr, 1951

	GD 2.0	VG 4.0	FN 6.0	VF 8.0	VF/NM 9.0	NM- 9.2
11	10	20	30	58	77	95
12-20	7	14	21	35	43	50

JUNGLE JIM
Dell Publishing Co.: No. 490, 8/53 - No. 1020, 8-10/59 (Painted-c)

	GD 2.0	VG 4.0	FN 6.0	VF 8.0	VF/NM 9.0	NM- 9.2
Four Color 490(#1)	8	16	24	55	78	100
Four Color 565(#2, 6/54)	5	10	15	33	44	55
3(10-12/54)-5	4	8	12	29	40	50
6-19(1-3/59), Four Color 1020(#20)	4	8	12	27	36	45

JUNGLE JIM
King Features Syndicate: No. 5, Dec, 1967

	GD 2.0	VG 4.0	FN 6.0	VF 8.0	VF/NM 9.0	NM- 9.2
5-Reprints Dell #5; Wood-c	2	4	6	11	14	18

JUNGLE JIM (Continued from Dell series)
Charlton Comics: No. 22, Feb, 1969 - No. 28, Feb, 1970 (#21 was an overseas edition only)

	GD 2.0	VG 4.0	FN 6.0	VF 8.0	VF/NM 9.0	NM- 9.2
22-Dan Flagg begins; Ditko/Wood-a	4	8	12	24	32	40
23-26: 23-Last Dan Flagg; Howard-c. 24-Jungle People begin	3	6	9	16	20	24
27,28: 27-Ditko/Howard-a. 28-Ditko-a	3	6	9	18	24	30

NOTE: *Ditko cover of #22 reprints story panels*

JUNGLE JO
Fox Feature Syndicate (Hero Books): Mar, 1950 - No. 3, Sept, 1950

	GD 2.0	VG 4.0	FN 6.0	VF 8.0	VF/NM 9.0	NM- 9.2
nn-Jo-Jo blanked out, leaving Congo King; came out after Jo-Jo #29 (intended as Jo-Jo #30?)	43	86	129	258	389	520
1-Tangi begins; part Wood-a	46	92	138	276	413	550
2,3	38	76	114	219	310	400

JUNGLE LIL (Dorothy Lamour #2 on; also see Feature Stories Magazine)
Fox Feature Syndicate (Hero Books): April, 1950

	GD 2.0	VG 4.0	FN 6.0	VF 8.0	VF/NM 9.0	NM- 9.2
1	40	80	120	240	340	440

JUNGLE TALES (Jann of the Jungle No. 8 on)
Atlas Comics (CSI): Sept, 1954 - No. 7, Sept, 1955

	GD 2.0	VG 4.0	FN 6.0	VF 8.0	VF/NM 9.0	NM- 9.2
1-Jann of the Jungle	39	78	117	230	325	420
2-7: 3-Last precode (1/55)	27	54	81	153	214	275

NOTE: *Heath c-5.* ***Heck*** *a-6, 7.* ***Maneely*** *a-2; c-1, 3.* ***Shores*** *a-5-7; c-4, 6.* ***Tuska*** *a-2.*

JUNGLE TALES OF CAVEWOMAN
Basement Comics: 1998 ($2.95, B&W)

	GD 2.0	VG 4.0	FN 6.0	VF 8.0	VF/NM 9.0	NM- 9.2
1-Budd Root-s/a						3.00

JUNGLE TALES OF TARZAN
Charlton Comics: Dec, 1964 - No. 4, July, 1965

	GD 2.0	VG 4.0	FN 6.0	VF 8.0	VF/NM 9.0	NM- 9.2
1	6	12	18	40	55	70
2-4	4	8	12	27	36	45

NOTE: ***Giordano*** *c-3p.* ***Glanzman*** *a-1-3.* ***Montes/Bache*** *a-4.*

JUNGLE TERROR (See Harvey Comics Hits No. 54)

JUNGLE THRILLS (Formerly Sports Thrills; Terrors of the Jungle #17 on)
Star Publications: No. 16, Feb, 1952; Dec, 1953; No. 7, 1954

	GD 2.0	VG 4.0	FN 6.0	VF 8.0	VF/NM 9.0	NM- 9.2
16-Phantom Lady & Rulah story-reprint/All Top No. 15; used in **POP**, pg. 98,99; L. B. Cole-c	50	100	150	300	450	600
3-D 1(12/53, 25¢)-Came w/glasses; Jungle Lil & Jungle Jo appear; L. B. Cole-c	50	100	150	300	450	600
7-Titled 'Picture Scope Jungle Adventures;' (1954, 36 pgs, 15¢)-3-D effect c/stories; story & coloring book; Disbrow-a/script; L.B. Cole-c	49	98	147	294	442	590

JUNGLE TWINS, THE (Tono & Kono)
Gold Key/Whitman No. 18: Apr, 1972 - No. 17, Nov, 1975; No. 18, May, 1982

	GD 2.0	VG 4.0	FN 6.0	VF 8.0	VF/NM 9.0	NM- 9.2
1	2	4	6	14	18	22
2-5	1	3	4	6	8	10
6-18: 18(Whitman, 5/82)-Reprints	1	2	3	4	5	7

NOTE: *UFO c/story No. 13. Painted-c No. 1-17.* ***Spiegle*** *c-18.*

JUNGLE WAR STORIES (Guerrilla War No. 12 on)
Dell Publishing Co.: July-Sept, 1962 - No. 11, Apr-June, 1965 (Painted-c)

	GD 2.0	VG 4.0	FN 6.0	VF 8.0	VF/NM 9.0	NM- 9.2
01-384-209 (#1)	4	8	12	25	33	42
2-11	3	6	9	18	23	28

JUNIE PROM (Also see Dexter Comics)
Dearfield Publishing Co.: Winter, 1947-48 - No. 7, Aug, 1949

	GD 2.0	VG 4.0	FN 6.0	VF 8.0	VF/NM 9.0	NM- 9.2
1-Teen-age	13	26	39	76	103	130
2	8	16	24	46	58	70
3-7	7	14	21	37	46	55

JUNIOR
Fantagraphics Books: June, 2000 - No. 5, Jan, 2001 ($2.95, B&W)

	GD 2.0	VG 4.0	FN 6.0	VF 8.0	VF/NM 9.0	NM- 9.2
1-5-Peter Bagge-s/a						3.00

JUNIOR CARROT PATROL (Jr. Carrot Patrol #2)
Dark Horse Comics: May, 1989; No. 2, Nov, 1990 ($2.00, B&W)

	GD 2.0	VG 4.0	FN 6.0	VF 8.0	VF/NM 9.0	NM- 9.2
1,2-Flaming Carrot spin-off. 1-Bob Burden-c(i)						2.50

JUNIOR COMICS (Formerly Li'l Pan; becomes Western Outlaws with #17)
Fox Feature Syndicate: No. 9, Sept, 1947 - No. 16, July, 1948

	GD 2.0	VG 4.0	FN 6.0	VF 8.0	VF/NM 9.0	NM- 9.2
9-Feldstein-c/a; headlights-c	84	168	252	525	788	1050
10-16-Feldstein-c/a; headlights-c on all	75	105	225	469	705	940

JUNIOR FUNNIES (Formerly Tiny Tot Funnies No. 9)
Harvey Publ. (King Features Synd.): No. 10, Aug, 1951 - No. 13, Feb, 1952

	GD 2.0	VG 4.0	FN 6.0	VF 8.0	VF/NM 9.0	NM- 9.2
10-Partial reprints in all; Blondie, Dagwood, Daisy, Henry, Popeye, Felix, Katzenjammer Kids	6	12	18	27	33	38
11-13	5	10	15	23	28	32

JUNIOR HOPP COMICS
Stanmor Publ.: Feb, 1952 - No. 3, July, 1952

	GD 2.0	VG 4.0	FN 6.0	VF 8.0	VF/NM 9.0	NM- 9.2
1-Teenage humor	10	20	30	56	73	90
2,3: 3-Dave Berg-a	6	12	18	31	38	45

JUNIOR MEDICS OF AMERICA, THE
E. R. Squire & Sons: No. 1359, 1957 (15¢)

	GD 2.0	VG 4.0	FN 6.0	VF 8.0	VF/NM 9.0	NM- 9.2
1359	4	8	12	17	21	24

JUNIOR MISS
Timely/Marvel (CnPC): Wint, 1944; No. 24, Apr, 1947 - No. 39, Aug, 1950

	GD 2.0	VG 4.0	FN 6.0	VF 8.0	VF/NM 9.0	NM- 9.2
1-Frank Sinatra & June Allyson life story	29	58	87	164	232	300
24-Formerly The Human Torch #23?	14	28	42	79	107	135
25-38: 29,31,34-Cindy-c/stories (others?)	8	16	24	46	58	70
39-Kurtzman-a	10	20	30	56	73	90

NOTE: *Painted-c 35-37. 35, 37-all romance. 36, 38-mostly teen humor.*

JUNIOR PARTNERS (Formerly Oral Roberts' True Stories)
Oral Roberts Evangelistic Assn.: No. 120, Aug, 1959 - V3#12, Dec, 1961

	GD 2.0	VG 4.0	FN 6.0	VF 8.0	VF/NM 9.0	NM- 9.2
120(#1)	4	8	12	29	40	50
2(9/59)	3	6	9	19	25	32
3-12(7/60)	2	4	6	14	18	22
V2#1(8/60)-5(12/60)	2	4	6	10	13	16
V3#1(1/61)-12	2	4	6	8	10	12

JUNIOR TREASURY (See Dell Junior...)

JUNIOR WOODCHUCKS GUIDE (Walt Disney's...)
Danbury Press: 1973 (8-3/4"x5-3/4", 214 pgs., hardcover)

	GD 2.0	VG 4.0	FN 6.0	VF 8.0	VF/NM 9.0	NM- 9.2
nn-Illustrated text based on the long-standing J.W. Guide used by Donald Duck's nephews Huey, Dewey & Louie by Carl Barks. The guidebook was a popular plot device to enable the nephews to solve problems facing their uncle or Scrooge McDuck (scarce)	6	12	18	38	52	65

JUNIOR WOODCHUCKS LIMITED SERIES (Walt Disney's...)
W. D. Publications (Disney): July, 1991 - No. 4, Oct, 1991 ($1.50, limited series; new & reprint-a)

	GD 2.0	VG 4.0	FN 6.0	VF 8.0	VF/NM 9.0	NM- 9.2
1-4: 1-The Beagle Boys app.; Barks-r						2.50

JUNIOR WOODCHUCKS (See Huey, Dewey & Louie...)

JUNK CULTURE
DC Comics (Vertigo): July, 1997 - No. 2, Aug, 1997 ($2.50, limited series)

	GD 2.0	VG 4.0	FN 6.0	VF 8.0	VF/NM 9.0	NM- 9.2
1,2: Ted McKeever-s/a in all						3.00

JURASSIC PARK
Topps Comics: June, 1993 - No. 4, Aug, 1993; No. 5, Oct, 1994 - No. 10, Feb, 1995

	GD 2.0	VG 4.0	FN 6.0	VF 8.0	VF/NM 9.0	NM- 9.2
1-($2.50)-Newsstand Edition; Kane/Perez-a in all; 1-4: movie adaptation						2.50
1-($2.95)-Collector's Ed.; polybagged w/3 cards						4.00
1-Amberchrome Edition w/no price or ads	1	2	3	4	5	7
2-4-($2.50)-Newsstand Edition						2.50
2,3-($2.95)-Collector's Ed.; polybagged w/3 cards						3.00
4-10: 4-($2.95)-Collector's Ed.; polybagged w/1 of 4 different action hologram trading card;						

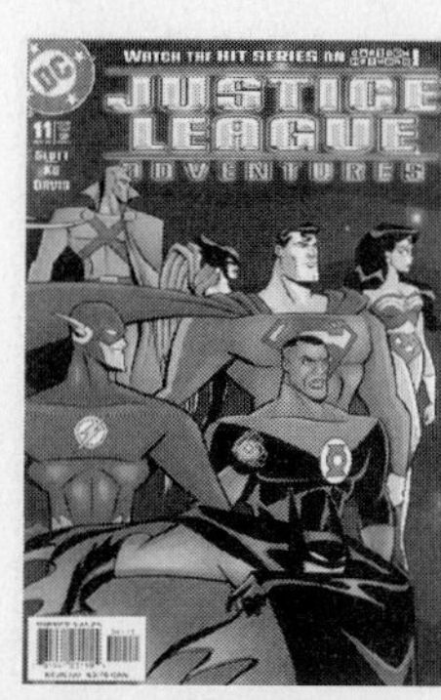

Justice League Adventures #11 © DC

Justice League Europe #32 © DC

Justice League of America #4 © DC

Gil Kane/Perez-a. 5-becomes Advs. of 3.00
Annual 1 ($3.95, 5/95) 4.00
Trade paperback (1993, $9.95)-r/#1-4; bagged w/#0 10.00

JURASSIC PARK: RAPTOR
Topps Comics: Nov, 1993 - No. 2, Dec, 1993 ($2.95, limited series)
1,2: 1-Bagged w/3 trading cards & Zorro #0; Golden c-1,2 3.00

JURASSIC PARK: RAPTORS ATTACK
Topps Comics: Mar, 1994 - No. 4, June, 1994 ($2.50, limited series)
1-4-Michael Golden-c/frontispiece 2.50

JURASSIC PARK: RAPTORS HIJACK
Topps Comics: July, 1994 - No. 4, Oct, 1994 ($2.50, limited series)
1-4: Michael Golden-c/front piece 2.50

JUST A PILGRIM
Black Bull Entertainment: May, 2001 - No. 5, Sept, 2001 ($2.99)
Limited Preview Edition (12/00, $7.00) Ennis & Ezquerra interviews 7.00
1-Ennis-s/Ezquerra-a; two covers by Texeira & JG Jones 3.00
2-5: 2-Fabry-c. 3-Nowlan-c. 4-Sienkiewicz-c 3.00
TPB (11/01, $12.99) r/#1-5; Waid intro. 13.00

JUST A PILGRIM: GARDEN OF EDEN
Black Bull Entertainment: May, 2002 - No. 4, Aug, 2002 ($2.99, limited series)
Limited Preview Ed. (1/02, $7.00) Ennis & Ezquerra interviews; Jones-c 7.00
1-4-Ennis-s/Ezquerra-a 3.00
TPB (11/02, $12.99) r/#1-4; Gareb Shamus intro. 13.00

JUSTICE
Marvel Comics Group (New Universe): Nov, 1986 - No. 32, June, 1989
1-32: 26-32-$1.50-c (low print run) 2.25

JUSTICE COMICS (Formerly Wacky Duck; Tales of Justice #53 on)
Marvel/Atlas Comics (NPP 7-9,4-19/CnPC 20-23/MjMC 24-38/Male 39-52:
No. 7, Fall/47 - No. 9, 6/48; No. 4, 8/48 - No. 52, 3/55
7(#1, 1947) 29 58 87 164 232 300
8(#2)-Kurtzman-a "Giggles 'n' Grins" (3) 20 40 60 112 156 200
9(#3, 6/48) 18 36 54 101 138 175
4 16 32 48 92 126 160
5(9/48)-9: 8-Anti-Wertham editorial 14 28 42 79 107 135
10-15-Photo-c 11 22 33 63 84 105
16-30 10 20 30 56 73 90
31-40,42-52: 35-Gene Colan-a. 48-Last precode; Pakula & Tuska-a.
9 18 27 52 66 80
41-Electrocution-c 17 34 51 98 134 170
NOTE: ***Heath** a-24. **Maneely** c-44, 52. **Pakula** a-43, 45, 48. **Louis Ravielli** a-39. **Robinson** a-22, 25, 41. **Shores** c-7(#1), 8(#2)? **Tuska** a-48. **Wildey** a-52.*

JUSTICE: FOUR BALANCE
Marvel Comics: Sept, 1994 - No. 4, Dec, 1994 ($1.75, limited series)
1-4: 1-Thing & Firestar app. 2.25

JUSTICE, INC. (The Avenger) (Pulp)
National Periodical Publications: May-June, 1975 - No. 4, Nov-Dec, 1975
1-McWilliams-a, Kubert-c; origin 2 4 6 8 10 12
2-4: 2-4-Kirby-a(p), c-2,3p. 4-Kubert-c 1 3 4 6 8 10
NOTE: *Adapted from Kenneth Robeson novel, creator of Doc Savage.*

JUSTICE, INC. (Pulp)
DC Comics: 1989 - No. 2, 1989 ($3.95, 52 pgs., squarebound, mature)
1,2: Re-intro The Avenger; Andrew Helfer scripts & Kyle Baker-c/a 4.00

JUSTICE LEAGUE (...International #7-25; ...America #26 on)
DC Comics: May, 1987 - No. 113, Aug, 1996 (Also see Legends #6)
1-Batman, Green Lantern (Guy Gardner), Blue Beetle, Mr. Miracle, Capt. Marvel & Martian Manhunter begin 1 2 3 4 5 7
2,3: 3-Regular-c (white background) 5.00
3-Limited-c (yellow background, Superman logo) 4 8 12 29 40 50
4-10: 4-Booster Gold joins. 5-Origin Gray Man; Batman vs. Guy Gardner; Creeper app. 7-($1.25, 52 pgs.)-Capt. Marvel & Dr. Fate resign; Capt. Atom & Rocket Red join. 9,10-Millennium x-over 3.00
11-17,22,23,25-49,51-68,72-82: 16-Bruce Wayne-c/story. 31,32-J. L. Europe x-over. 58-Lobo app. 61-New team begins; swipes-c to J.L. of A. #1('60). 70-Newsstand version w/o outer-c. 71-Direct sales version w/black outer-c. 71-Newsstand version w/o outer-c. 80-Intro new Booster Gold. 82,83-Guy Gardner-c/stories 2.50
18-21,24,50: 18-21-Lobo app. 24-($1.50)-1st app. Justice League Europe. 50-($1.75, 52 pgs.) 3.00
69-Doomsday tie-in; takes place between Superman: The Man of Steel #18 & Superman #74 5.00
69,70-2nd printings 2.25
70-Funeral for a Friend part 1; red 3/4 outer-c 4.00
83-99,101-113: 92-(9/94)-Zero Hour x-over; Triumph app. 113-Green Lantern, Flash & Hawkman app. 2.50
100 ($3.95)-Foil-c; 52 pgs. 4.00
100 ($2.95)-Newstand 3.00
#0-(10/94) Zero Hour (publ between #92 & #93); new team begins (Hawkman, Flash, Wonder Woman, Metamorpho, Nuklon, Crimson Fox, Obsidian & Fire) 2.50
Annual 1-8,10 ('87-'94, '96, 68 pgs.): 2-Joker-c/story; Batman cameo. 5-Armageddon 2001 x-over; Silver ink 2nd print. 7-Bloodlines x-over. 8-Elseworlds story. 10-Legends of the Dead Earth 3.00
Annual 9 (1995, $3.50)-Year One story 3.50
Special 1,2 ('90,'91, 52 pgs.): 1-Giffen plots. 2-Staton-a(p) 3.00
Spectacular 1 (1992, $1.50, 52 pgs.)-Intro new JLI & JLE teams; ties into JLI #61 & JLE #37; two interlocking covers by Jurgens 3.00
A New Beginning Trade Paperback (1989, $12.95)-r/#1-7 13.00
NOTE: ***Anderson** c-61i. **Austin** a-1i, 60i; c-1i. **Giffen** a-13; c-21p. **Guice** a-62i. **Maguire** a-1-12, 16-19, 22, 23. **Russell** a-Annual 1i; c-54i. **Willingham** a-30p, Annual 2.*

JUSTICE LEAGUE ADVENTURES (Based on Cartoon Network series)
DC Comics: Jan, 2002 - Present ($1.99/$2.25)
1-Timm & Ross-c 3.00
2-27: 3-Nicieza-s. 5-Starro app. 10-Begin $2.25-c. 14-Includes 16 pg. insert for VERB with Haberlin CG-art. 15-Amancio-a. 16-McCloud-s. 20-Psycho Pirate app. 25,26-Adam Strange-c/app. 2.25
Free Comic Book Day giveaway - (See Promotional Comics section)
TPB (2003, $9.95) r/#1,3,6,10-13; Timm/Ross-c from #1 10.00

JUSTICE LEAGUE: A MIDSUMMER'S NIGHTMARE
DC Comics: Sept, 1996 - No. 3, Nov, 1996 ($2.95, limited series, 38 pgs.)
1-3: Re-establishes Superman, Batman, Green Lantern, The Martian Manhunter, Flash, Aquaman & Wonder Woman as the Justice League; Mark Waid & Fabian Nicieza co-scripts; Jeff Johnson & Darick Robertson-a(p); Kevin Maguire-c 5.00
TPB-(1997, $8.95) r/1-3 9.00

JUSTICE LEAGUE EUROPE (Justice League International #51 on)
DC Comics: Apr, 1989 - No. 68, Sept., 1994 (75¢/ $1.00/$1.25/$1.50)
1-Giffen plots in all, breakdowns in #1-8,13-30; Justice League #1-c/swipe 3.00
2-10: 7-9-Batman app. 7,8-JLA x-over. 8,9-Superman app. 2.50
11-49: 12-Metal Men app. 20-22-Rogers-c/a(p). 33,34-Lobo vs. Despero. 37-New team begins; swipes-c to JLA #9; see JLA Spectacular 2.50
50-($2.50, 68 pgs.)-Battles Sonar 3.00
51-68: 68-Zero Hour x-over; Triumph joins Justice League Task Force (See JLTF #17) 2.25
Annual 1-5 ('90-'94, 68 pgs.)-1-Return of the Global Guardians; Giffen plots/breakdowns. 2-Armageddon 2001; Giffen-a(p); Rogers-a(p); Golden-a(i). 3-Eclipso app. 4-Intro Lionheart. 5-Elseworlds story 3.00
NOTE: ***Phil Jimenez** a-68p. **Rogers** c/a-20-22. **Sears** a-1-12, 14-19, 23-29; c-1-10, 12, 14-19, 23-29.*

JUSTICE LEAGUE INTERNATIONAL (See Justice League Europe)

JUSTICE LEAGUE OF AMERICA (See Brave & the Bold #28-30, Mystery In Space #75 & Official... Index)
National Periodical Publ./DC Comics: Oct-Nov, 1960 - No. 261, Apr, 1987 (#91-99,139-157: 52 pgs.)
1-(10-11/60)-Origin & 1st app. Despero; Aquaman, Batman, Flash, Green Lantern, J'onn J'onzz, Superman & Wonder Woman continue from Brave and the Bold
300 600 900 2685 4843 7000
2 71 142 213 568 1034 1500
3-Origin/1st app. Kanjar Ro (see Mystery in Space #75)(scarce in high grade due to black-c)
60 120 180 480 865 1250
4-Green Arrow joins JLA 44 88 132 319 535 750
5-Origin & 1st app. Dr. Destiny 38 76 114 275 463 650
6-8,10: 6-Origin & 1st app. Prof. Amos Fortune. 7-(10-11/61)-Last 10¢ issue. 10-(3/62)-Origin & 1st app. Felix Faust; 1st app. Lord of Time 31 62 93 225 357 490
9-(2/62)-Origin JLA (1st origin) 38 76 114 275 463 650
11-15: 12-(6/62)-Origin & 1st app. Dr. Light. 13-(8/62)-Speedy app. 14-(9/62)-Atom joins JLA. 22 44 66 156 228 300
16-20: 17-Adam Strange flashback 19 38 57 136 198 260
21-(8/63)-"Crisis on Earth-One"; re-intro. of JSA in this title (see Flash #129) (1st S.A. app. Hourman & Dr. Fate) 31 62 93 225 362 500
22- "Crisis on Earth-Two"; JSA x-over (story continued from #21)
30 60 90 218 322 425
23-28: 24-Adam Strange app. 27-Robin app. 14 28 42 99 145 190
29-JSA x-over; 1st S.A. app. Starman; "Crisis on Earth-Three"
17 34 51 123 182 240

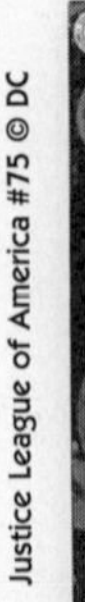
Justice League of America #75 © DC

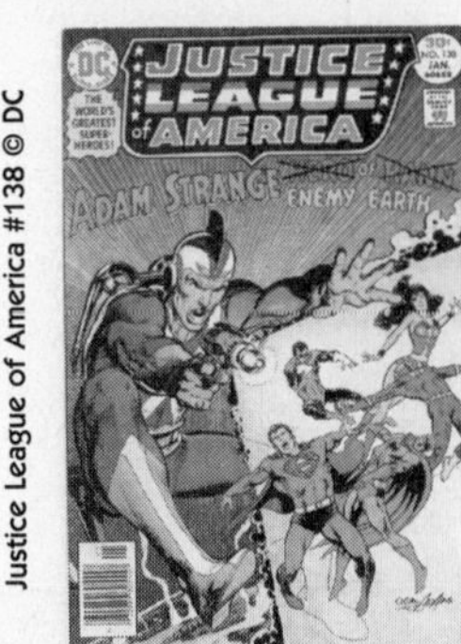

Justice League of America #138 © DC

Justice Society of America #3 © DC

	GD 2.0	VG 4.0	FN 6.0	VF 8.0	VF/NM 9.0	NM- 9.2

30-JSA x-over 16 32 48 111 163 215

31-Hawkman joins JLA, Hawkgirl cameo (11/64) 12 24 36 82 121 160

32,34: 32-Intro & Origin Brain Storm. 34-Joker-c/sty 10 20 30 67 96 125

33,35,36,40,41: 40-3rd S.A. Penguin app. 41-Intro & origin The Key 9 18 27 60 85 110

37-39: 37,38-JSA x-over. 37-1st S.A. app. Mr. Terrific; Batman cameo. 38-"Crisis on Earth-A". 39-Giant G-16; r/B&B #28,30 & JLA #5 12 24 36 82 121 160

42-45: 42-Metamorpho app. 43-Intro. Royal Flush Gang 7 14 21 51 71 90

46-JSA x-over; 1st S.A. app. Sandman; 3rd S.A. app. of G.A. Spectre (8/66) 12 24 36 87 129 170

47-JSA x-over; 4th S.A. app of G.A. Spectre. 9 18 27 63 89 115

48-Giant G-29; r/JLA #2,3 & B&B #29 9 18 27 60 85 110

49-54,57,59,60 7 14 21 46 63 80

55-Intro. Earth 2 Robin (1st G.A. Robin in S.A.) 9 18 27 60 85 110

56-JLA vs. JSA (1st G.A. Wonder Woman in S.A.) 8 16 24 53 74 95

58-Giant G-41; r/JLA #6,8,1 8 16 24 53 74 95

61-63,66,68-72: 69-Wonder Woman quits. 71-Manhunter leaves. 72-Last 12¢ issue 5 10 15 36 48 60

64,65-JSA story. 64-(8/68)-Origin/1st app. S.A. Red Tornado 6 12 18 40 55 70

67-Giant G-53; r/JLA #4,14,31 7 14 21 51 71 90

73-1st S.A. app. of G.A. Superman 6 12 18 40 55 70

74-Black Canary joins; 1st meeting of G.A. & S.A. Superman. 6 12 18 40 55 70

75-2nd app. Green Arrow in new costume (see Brave & the Bold #85) 6 12 18 38 52 65

76-Giant G-65 6 12 18 40 55 70

77-80: 78-Re-intro Vigilante (1st S.A. app?) 4 8 12 24 32 40

81-84,86-90: 82-1st S.A. app. of G.A. Batman (cameo). 83-Death of Spectre. 90-Last 15¢ issue 3 7 10 21 28 35

85,93-(Giant G-77,G-89; 68 pgs.) 5 10 15 33 44 55

91,92: 91-1st meeting of the G.A. & S.A. Robin; begin 25¢, 52 pgs. issues, ends #99. 92-S.A. Robin tries on costume that is similar to that of G.A. Robin in All Star Comics #58 4 8 12 27 36 45

94-Reprints 1st Sandman story (Adv. #40) & origin/1st app. Starman (Adventure #61); Deadman x-over; N. Adams-a (4 pgs.) 9 18 27 60 85 110

95,96: 95-Origin Dr. Fate & Dr. Midnight -r/ More Fun #67, All-American #25). 96-Origin Hourman (Adv. #48); Wildcat-r 4 8 12 28 38 48

97-99: 97-Origin JLA retold; Sargon, Starman-r. 98-G.A. Sargon, Starman-r. 99-G.A. Sandman, Atom-r; last 52 pg. issue 4 8 12 24 32 40

100-(8/72)-1st meeting of G.A. & S.A. W. Woman 4 8 12 29 40 50

101,102: JSA x-overs. 102-Red Tornado dies 3 7 10 21 28 35

103-106,109: 103-Rutland Vermont Halloween x-over; Phantom Stranger joins. 105-Elongated Man joins. 106-New Red Tornado joins. 109-Hawkman resigns 2 4 6 14 18 22

107,108-JSA x-over; 1st revival app. of G.A. Uncle Sam, Black Condor, The Ray, Dollman, Phantom Lady & The Human Bomb 3 6 9 16 20 24

110-116: All 100 pgs. 111-JLA vs. Injustice Gang; Shining Knight, Green Arrow-r. 112-Amazo app; Crimson Avenger, Vigilante-r; origin Starman-r/Adv. #81. 115-Martian Manhunter app. 4 8 12 28 38 48

117-122,125-134: 117-Hawkman rejoins. 120,121-Adam Strange app. 125,126-Two-Face-app. 128-Wonder Woman rejoins. 129-Destruction of Red Tornado 2 4 6 10 12 15

123-(10/75),124: JLA/JSA x-over. DC editor Julie Schwartz & JLA writers Cary Bates & Elliot S! Maggin appear in story as themselves. 1st named app. Earth-Prime (3rd app. after Flash; 1st Series #179 & 228) 2 4 6 11 14 18

135-136: 135-137-G.A. Bulletman, Bulletgirl, Spy Smasher, Mr. Scarlet, Pinky & Ibis x-over, 1st appearances since G.A. 2 4 6 11 14 18

137-Superman battles G.A. Capt. Marvel 2 4 6 14 18 22

138,139-157: 138-Adam Strange app. w/c by Neal Adams; 1st app. Green Lantern of the 73rd Century. 139-157-(52 pgs.): 139-Adam Strange app. 144-Origin retold; origin J'onn J'onzz. 145-Red Tornado resurrected. 147,148-Legion of Super-Heroes x-over 2 4 6 10 12 15

158-160-(44 pgs.) 1 3 4 6 8 10

158,160-162,168,169,171,172,176,179,181-(Whitman variants; low print run, none show issue # on cover) 2 4 6 8 10 12

161-182: 161-Zatanna joins & new costume. 171-Mr. Terrific murdered. 178-Cover similar to #1; J'onn J'onzz app. 179-Firestorm joins. 181-Green Arrow leaves JLA 6.00

183-185-JSA/New Gods/Darkseid/Mr.Miracle x-over 1 2 3 4 5 7

186-199: 192,193-Real origin Red Tornado. 193-1st app. All-Star Squadron as free 16 pg. insert 5.00

200 ($1.50, Anniversary issue, 76pgs.)-JLA origin retold; Green Arrow rejoins; Bolland, Aparo, Giordano, Gil Kane, Infantino, Kubert-a; Perez-c/a 6.00

	GD 2.0	VG 4.0	FN 6.0	VF 8.0	VF/NM 9.0	NM- 9.2

201-206,209-243,246-259: 203-Intro/origin new Royal Flush Gang. 219,220-True origin Black Canary. 228-Re-intro Martian Manhunter. 228-230-War of the Worlds storyline; JLA Satellite destroyed by Martians. 233-Story cont'd from Annual #2. 243-Aquaman leaves. 250-Batman rejoins. 253-Origin Despero. 258-Death of Vibe. 258-261-Legends x-over 3.00

207,208-JSA, JLA, & All-Star Squadron team-up 4.00

244,245-Crisis x-over 4.00

260-Death of Steel 5.00

261-Last issue 1 2 3 4 5 7

Annual 1-3 ('83-'85), 2-Intro new J.L.A. (Aquaman, Martian Manhunter, Steel, Gypsy, Vixen, Vibe, Elongated Man, & Zatanna). 3-Crisis x-over 3.00

NOTE: ***Neal Adams*** *c-63, 66, 67, 70, 74, 79, 81, 82, 86-89, 91, 92, 94, 96-98, 138, 139.* ***M. Anderson*** *c-1-4, 6, 7, 10, 12-14.* ***Aparo*** *a-200.* ***Austin*** *a-200i.* ***Baily*** *a-96r.* ***Bolland*** *a-200.* ***Buckler*** *c-158, 163, 164.* ***Burnley*** *r-94, 98, 99.* ***Greene*** *a-46-61i, 64-73i, 110i(r).* ***Grell*** *c-117, 122.* ***Kaluta*** *c-154p.* ***Gil Kane*** *a-200.* ***Krigstein*** *a-96(r/Sensation #84).* ***Kubert*** *a-200; c-72, 73.* ***Nino*** *a-228i, 230i.* ***Orlando*** *c-151i.* ***Perez*** *a-184-186p, 192-197p, 200p; c-184p, 186, 192-195, 196p, 197p, 199, 200, 201p, 202, 203-205p, 207-209, 212-215, 217, 219, 220.* ***Reinman*** *r-97.* ***Roussos*** *a-62i.* ***Sekowsky*** *a-37, 38, 44-63p, 110-112p(r); c-46-48p, 51p.* ***Sekowsky/Anderson*** *c-5, 8, 9, 11, 15.* ***B. Smith*** *c-185i.* ***Starlin*** *c-178-180, 183, 185p.* ***Staton*** *a-244p; c-157p, 244p.* ***Toth*** *r-110.* ***Tuska*** *a-153, 228p, 241-243p. JSA x-overs-21, 22, 29, 30, 37, 38, 46, 47, 55, 56, 64, 65, 73, 74, 82, 83, 91, 92, 100, 101, 102, 107, 108, 110, 113, 115, 123, 124, 135-137, 147, 148, 159, 160, 171, 172, 183-185, 195-197, 207-209, 219, 220, 231, 232, 244.*

JUSTICE LEAGUE OF AMERICA SUPER SPECTACULAR
DC Comics: 1999 ($5.95, mimics format of DC 100 Page Super Spectaculars)

1-Reprints Silver Age JLA and Golden Age JSA 6.00

JUSTICE LEAGUE QUARTERLY (...International Quarterly #6 on)
DC Comics: Winter, 1990-91 - No. 17, Winter, 1994 ($2.95/$3.50, 84 pgs.)

1-12,14-17: 1-Intro The Conglomerate (Booster Gold, Praxis, Gypsy, Vapor, Echo, Maxi-Man, & Reverb); Justice League #1-c/swipe. 1,2-Giffen plots/breakdowns. 3-Giffen plot; 72 pg. story. 4-Rogers/Russell-a in back-up. 5,6-Waid scripts. 8,17-Global Guardians app. 12-Waid script 3.50

13-Linsner-c 6.00

NOTE: ***Phil Jimenez*** *a-17p.* ***Sprouse*** *a-1p.*

JUSTICE LEAGUES...
DC Comics: Mar, 2001 ($2.50, limited series)

JL?, Justice League of Amazons, Justice League of Atlantis, Justice League of Arkham, Justice League of Aliens, JLA: JLA split by the Advance Man; Perez-c in all; s&a by various 2.50

JUSTICE LEAGUE TASK FORCE
DC Comics: June, 1993 - No. 37, Aug, 1996 ($1.25/$1.50/$1.75)

1-16,0,17-37: Aquaman, Nightwing, Flash, J'onn J'onzz, & Gypsy form team. 5,6-Knight-quest tie-ins (new Batman cameo #5, 1 pg.). 15-Triumph cameo. 16-(9/94)-Zero Hour x-over; Triumph app. 0-(10/94). 17-(11/94)-Triumph becomes part of Justice League Task Force (See JLE #68). 26-Impulse app. 35-Warlord app. 37-Triumph quits team 2.25

JUSTICE MACHINE, THE
Noble Comics: June, 1981 - No. 5, Nov, 1983 ($2.00, nos. 1-3 are mag. size)

1-Byrne-c(p) 3 6 9 16 20 24

2-Austin-c(i) 2 4 6 9 11 14

3 1 2 3 5 7 9

4,5, Annual 1 (1/84, 68 pgs.)(published by Texas Comics); 1st app. The Elementals; Golden-c(p) 5.00

JUSTICE MACHINE (Also see The New Justice Machine)
Comico/Innovation Publishing: Jan, 1987 - No. 29, May 1989 ($1.50/$1.75)

1-29 2.25

Annual 1(6/89, $2.50, 36 pgs.)-Last Comico ish. 3.00

Summer Spectacular 1 ('89, $2.75)-Innovation Publ.; Byrne/Gustovich-c 3.00

JUSTICE MACHINE, THE
Innovation Publishing: 1990 - No. 4, 1990 ($1.95/$2.25, deluxe format, mature)

1-4: Gustovich-c/a in all 2.25

JUSTICE MACHINE FEATURING THE ELEMENTALS
Comico: May, 1986 - No. 4, Aug, 1986 ($1.50, limited series)

1-4 2.25

JUSTICE RIDERS
DC Comics: 1997 ($5.95, one-shot, prestige format)

1-Elseworlds; Dixon-s/Williams & Gray-a 6.00

JUSTICE SOCIETY OF AMERICA (See Adventure #461 & All-Star #3)
DC Comics: April, 1991 - No. 8, Nov, 1991 ($1.00, limited series)

1-8: 1-Flash. 2-Black Canary. 3-Green Lantern. 4-Hawkman. 5-Flash/Hawkman. 6-Green Lantern/Black Canary. 7-JSA 2.50

JUSTICE SOCIETY OF AMERICA (Also see Last Days of the... Special)
DC Comics: Aug, 1992 - No. 10, May, 1993 ($1.25)

1-10 2.50

Justice Traps the Guilty #3 © PRIZE

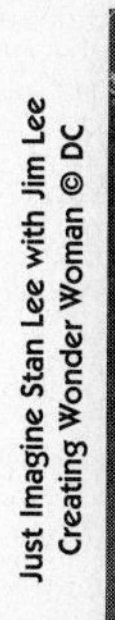

Just Imagine Stan Lee with Jim Lee Creating Wonder Woman © DC

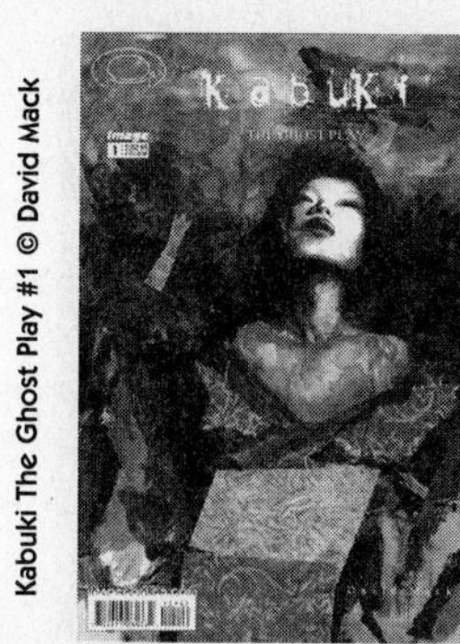

Kabuki The Ghost Play #1 © David Mack

JUSTICE SOCIETY OF AMERICA 100-PAGE SUPER SPECTACULAR
DC Comics: 2000 ($6.95, mimics format of DC 100 Page Super Spectaculars)

	GD 2.0	VG 4.0	FN 6.0	VF 8.0	VF/NM 9.0	NM- 9.2
1-"1975 Issue" reprints Flash team-up and Golden Age JSA						7.00

JUSTICE SOCIETY RETURNS, THE (See All Star Comics (1999) for related titles)
DC Comics: 2003 ($19.95, TPB)

	GD 2.0	VG 4.0	FN 6.0	VF 8.0	VF/NM 9.0	NM- 9.2
TPB-Reprints 1999 JSA x-over from All-Star Comics #1,2 and related one-shots						20.00

JUSTICE TRAPS THE GUILTY (Fargo Kid V11#3 on)
Prize/Headline Publications: Oct-Nov, 1947 - V11#2(#92), Apr-May, 1958 (True FBI Cases)

	GD 2.0	VG 4.0	FN 6.0	VF 8.0	VF/NM 9.0	NM- 9.2
V2#1-S&K-c/a; electrocution-c	58	116	174	363	544	725
2-S&K-c/a	37	74	111	213	299	385
3-5-S&K-c/a	34	68	102	196	278	360
6-S&K-c/a; Feldstein-a	36	72	108	204	290	375
7,9-S&K-c/a. 7-9-V2#1-3 in indicia; #7-9 on-c	30	60	90	173	244	315
8-Krigstein-a; S&K-c	29	58	87	164	232	300
10-Krigstein-a; S&K-c/a	30	60	90	173	244	315
11,18,19-S&K-c	15	30	45	86	118	150
12,14-17,20-No S&K. 14-Severin/Elder-a (8pg.)	9	18	27	52	66	80
13-Used in **SOTI**, pg. 110-111	10	20	30	58	77	95
21,30-S&K-c/a	15	30	45	86	118	150
22,23,27-S&K-c	10	20	30	58	77	95
24-26,29,31-50: 32-Meskin story	8	16	24	43	54	65
28-Kirby-c	9	18	27	52	66	80
51-55,57,59-70	7	14	21	37	46	55
56-Ben Oda, Joe Simon, Joe Genola, Mort Meskin & Jack Kirby app. in police line-up on classic-c	10	20	30	58	77	95
58-Illo. in **SOTI**, "Treating police contemptuously" (top left); text on heroin	27	54	81	155	218	280
71-92: 76-Orlando-a	6	12	18	31	38	45

NOTE: ***Bailey** a-12, 13. **Elder** a-8. **Kirby** a-19p. **Meskin** a-22, 27, 63, 64; c-45, 46. **Robinson/Meskin** a-5, 19. **Severin** a-8, 11p. Photo c-12, 15-17.*

JUST IMAGINE STAN LEE WITH... (Stan Lee re-invents DC icons)
DC Comics: 2001 - 2002 ($5.95, prestige format, one-shots)
(Adam Hughes back-c on all)(Michael Uslan back-up stories in all, diff. artists)

	GD 2.0	VG 4.0	FN 6.0	VF 8.0	VF/NM 9.0	NM- 9.2
Scott McDaniel Creating **Aquaman**- Back-up w/Fradon-a						6.00
Joe Kubert Creating **Batman**- Back-up w/Kaluta-a						6.00
Chris Bachalo Creating **Catwoman**- Back-up w/Cooke & Allred-a						6.00
John Cassaday Creating **Crisis**- no back-up story						6.00
Kevin Maguire Creating **The Flash**- Back-up w/Aragonés-a						6.00
Dave Gibbons Creating **Green Lantern**- Back-up w/Giordano-a						6.00
Jerry Ordway Creating **JLA**						6.00
John Byrne Creating **Robin**- Back-up w/John Severin-a						6.00
Walter Simonson Creating **Sandman**- Back-up w/Corben-a						6.00
Gary Frank Creating **Shazam!**- Back-up w/Kano-a						6.00
John Buscema Creating **Superman**- Back-up w/Kyle Baker-a						6.00
Jim Lee Creating **Wonder Woman**- Back-up w/Gene Colan-a						6.00
Secret Files and Origins #1 (3/02, $4.95) Crisis prologue; Jurgens-a						5.00
TPB -Just Imagine Stan Lee Creating the DC Universe: Book One (2002, $19.95) r/Batman, Wonder Woman, Superman, Green Lantern						20.00
TPB -Just Imagine Stan Lee Creating the DC Universe: Book Two (2003, $19.95) r/Flash, JLA, Secret Files and Origins, Robin, Shazam; sketch pages						20.00

JUST MARRIED
Charlton Comics: January, 1958 - No. 114, Dec, 1976

	GD 2.0	VG 4.0	FN 6.0	VF 8.0	VF/NM 9.0	NM- 9.2
1	7	14	21	50	68	85
2	4	8	12	25	33	42
3-10	3	6	9	19	25	32
11-30	3	6	9	16	20	24
31-50	2	4	6	11	14	18
51-70	2	4	6	10	12	15
71-90	2	4	6	8	10	12
91-114	1	3	4	6	8	10

JUSTY
Viz Comics: Dec 6, 1988 - No. 9, 1989 ($1.75, B&W, bi-weekly mini-series)

	GD 2.0	VG 4.0	FN 6.0	VF 8.0	VF/NM 9.0	NM- 9.2
1-9: Japanese manga						2.50

KA'A'NGA COMICS (...Jungle King)(See Jungle Comics)
Fiction House Magazines (Glen-Kel Publ. Co.): Spring, 1949 - No. 20, Summer, 1954

	GD 2.0	VG 4.0	FN 6.0	VF 8.0	VF/NM 9.0	NM- 9.2
1-Ka'a'nga, Lord of the Jungle begins	52	104	157	312	469	625
2 (Winter, '49-'50)	30	60	90	170	240	310
3,4	22	44	66	127	176	225
5-Camilla app.	17	34	51	98	134	170
6-10: 7-Tuska-a. 9-Tabu, Wizard of the Jungle app. 10-Used in **POP**, pg. 99	15	30	45	84	115	145
11-15: 15-Camilla-r by Baker/Jungle #106	12	24	36	69	92	115
16-Sheena app.	13	26	39	74	100	125
17-20	11	22	33	63	84	105
I.W. Reprint #1,8: 1-r/#18; Kinstler-c. 8-r/#10	3	6	9	16	20	25

NOTE: ***Celardo** c-1. **Whitman** c-8-20(most).*

KABOOM
Awesome Entertainment: Sept, 1997 - No. 3, Nov, 1997 ($2.50)

	GD 2.0	VG 4.0	FN 6.0	VF 8.0	VF/NM 9.0	NM- 9.2
1-3: 1-Matsuda-a/Loeb-s; 4 covers exist (Matsuda, Sale, Pollina and McGuinness), 1-Dynamic Forces Edition, 2-Regular, 2-Alicia Watcher variant-c, 2-Gold logo variant-c, 3-Two covers by Liefeld & Matsuda, 3-Dynamic Forces Ed., Prelude Ed.						2.50
Prelude Gold Edition						4.00

KABOOM (2nd series)
Awesome Entertainment: July, 1999 - No. 3, Dec, 1999 ($2.50)

	GD 2.0	VG 4.0	FN 6.0	VF 8.0	VF/NM 9.0	NM- 9.2
1-3: 1-Grant-a(p); at least 4 variant covers						2.50

KABUKI
Caliber: Nov, 1994 ($3.50, B&W, one-shot)

	GD 2.0	VG 4.0	FN 6.0	VF 8.0	VF/NM 9.0	NM- 9.2
nn-(Fear The Reaper) 1st app.; David Mack-c/a/s	1	2	3	5	6	8
Color Special (1/96, $2.95)-Mack-c/a/scripts; pin-ups by Tucci, Harris & Quesada						4.00
Gallery (8/95, $2.95)- pinups from Mack, Bradstreet, Paul Pope & others						3.00

KABUKI
Image Comics: Oct, 1997 - Present ($2.95, color)

	GD 2.0	VG 4.0	FN 6.0	VF 8.0	VF/NM 9.0	NM- 9.2
1-David Mack-c/s/a						5.00
1-($10.00)-Dynamic Forces Edition	1	3	4	6	8	10
2-5						4.00
6-9						3.00
#1/2 (9/01, $2.95) r/Wizard 1/2; Eklipse Mag. article; bio						3.00
...Classics (2/99, $3.95) Reprints Fear the Reaper						4.00
...Classics 2 (3/99, $3.95) Reprints Dance of Dance						4.00
...Classics 3-5 (3-6/99, $4.95) Reprints Circle of Blood-Acts 1-3						5.00
...Classics 6-12 (7/99-3/00, $3.25) Various reprints						3.25
...Images (6/98, $4.95) r/#1 with new pin-ups						5.00
...Images 2 (1/99, $4.95) r/#1 with new pin-ups						5.00
...Metamorphosis TPB (10/00, $24.95) r/#1-9; Sienkiewicz intro.						25.00
...Reflections 1-4 (7/98-5/02; $4.95) new story plus art techniques						5.00
... The Ghost Play (11/02, $2.95) new story plus interview						3.00

KABUKI AGENTS (SCARAB)
Image Comics: Aug, 1999 - No. 8, Aug, 2001 ($2.95, B&W)

	GD 2.0	VG 4.0	FN 6.0	VF 8.0	VF/NM 9.0	NM- 9.2
1-8-David Mack-s/Rick Mays-a						3.00
Lost in Translation HC (3/02, $29.95) r/#1-8; intro. by Paul Pope						30.00
Lost in Translation SC (3/02, $19.95) r/#1-8; intro. by Paul Pope						20.00

KABUKI: CIRCLE OF BLOOD
Caliber Press: Jan, 1995 - No. 6, Nov, 1995 ($2.95, B&W)

	GD 2.0	VG 4.0	FN 6.0	VF 8.0	VF/NM 9.0	NM- 9.2
1-David Mack story/a in all						5.00
2-6: 3-#1 on inside indicia.						3.00
6-Variant-c						3.00
TPB ($16.95) r/#1-6, intro. by Steranko						17.00
TPB (1997, $17.95) Image Edition-r/#1-6, intro. by Steranko						18.00
TPB ($24.95) Deluxe Edition						25.00

KABUKI: DANCE OF DEATH
London Night Studios: Jan, 1995 ($3.00, B&W, one-shot)

	GD 2.0	VG 4.0	FN 6.0	VF 8.0	VF/NM 9.0	NM- 9.2
1-David Mack-c/a/scripts	1	2	3	5	6	8

KABUKI: DREAMS
Image Comics: Jan, 1998 ($4.95, TPB)

	GD 2.0	VG 4.0	FN 6.0	VF 8.0	VF/NM 9.0	NM- 9.2
nn-Reprints Color Special & Dreams of the Dead						5.00

KABUKI: DREAMS OF THE DEAD
Caliber: July, 1996 ($2.95, one-shot)

	GD 2.0	VG 4.0	FN 6.0	VF 8.0	VF/NM 9.0	NM- 9.2
nn-David Mack-c/a/scripts						3.00

KABUKI FAN EDITION
Gemstone Publ./Caliber: Feb, 1997 (mail-in offer, one-shot)

	GD 2.0	VG 4.0	FN 6.0	VF 8.0	VF/NM 9.0	NM- 9.2
nn-David Mack-c/a/scripts						4.00

KABUKI: MASKS OF THE NOH
Caliber: May, 1996 - No. 4, Feb, 1997 ($2.95, limited series)

	GD 2.0	VG 4.0	FN 6.0	VF 8.0	VF/NM 9.0	NM- 9.2
1-4: 1-Three-c (1A-Quesada, 1B-Buzz, &1C-Mack). 3-Terry Moore pin-up						3.00
TPB-(4/98, $10.95) r/#1-4; intro by Terry Moore						11.00

KABUKI: SKIN DEEP
Caliber Comics: Oct, 1996 - No. 3, May, 1997 ($2.95)

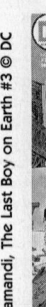

Kamandi, The Last Boy on Earth #3 © DC

Karate Kid #8 © DC

Katy Keene #38 © AP

	GD 2.0	VG 4.0	FN 6.0	VF 8.0	VF/NM 9.0	NM- 9.2
1-3:David Mack-c/a/scripts. 2-Two-c (1-Mack, 1-Ross)						3.00
TPB-(5/98, $9.95) r/#1-3; intro by Alex Ross						10.00

KAMANDI: AT EARTH'S END
DC Comics: June, 1993 - No. 6, Nov, 1993 ($1.75, limited series)

	GD	VG	FN	VF	VF/NM	NM-
1-6: Elseworlds storyline						2.50

KAMANDI, THE LAST BOY ON EARTH (Also see Alarming Tales #1, Brave and the Bold #120 & 157 & Cancelled Comic Cavalcade)
National Periodical Publ./DC Comics: Oct-Nov, 1972 - 59, Sept-Oct, 1978

	GD	VG	FN	VF	VF/NM	NM-
1-Origin & 1st app. Kamandi	6	12	18	43	59	75
2,3	4	8	12	24	32	40
4,5: 4-Intro. Prince Tuftan of the Tigers	3	6	9	18	24	30
6-10	2	4	6	14	18	22
11-20	2	4	6	10	13	16
21-28,30,31,33-40: 24-Last 20¢ issue. 31-Intro Pyra.	2	4	6	9	11	14
29,32: 29-Superman x-over. 32-(68 pgs.)-r/origin from #1 plus one new story; 4 pg. biog. of Jack Kirby with B&W photos	2	4	6	11	14	18
41-57	1	3	4	6	8	10
58-(44 pgs.)-Karate Kid x-over from LSH	2	4	6	10	13	16
59-(44 pgs.)-Cont'd in B&B #157; The Return of Omac back-up by Starlin-c/a(p)	2	4	6	10	13	16

NOTE: ***Ayers** a(p)-48-59 (most). **Giffen** a-44p, 45p. **Kirby** a-1-40p; c-1-33. **Kubert** c-34-41. **Nasser** a-45p, 46p. **Starlin** a-59p; c-57, 59p.*

KAMIKAZI
DC Comics (Cliffhanger): Dec, 2003 - Present ($2.95)

	GD	VG	FN	VF	VF/NM	NM-
1-3-Herrera-a						3.00

KAMUI (Legend Of...#2 on)
Eclipse Comics/Viz Comics: May 12, 1987 - No. 37, Nov. 15, 1988 ($1.50, B&W, bi-weekly)

	GD	VG	FN	VF	VF/NM	NM-
1-37: 1-3 have 2nd printings						2.50

KAOS MOON (Also see Negative Burn #34)
Caliber Comics: 1996 - No. 4, 1997 ($2.95, B&W)

	GD	VG	FN	VF	VF/NM	NM-
1-4-David Boller-s/a						3.00
3,4-Limited Alternate-c						4.00
3,4-Gold Alternate-c, Full Circle TPB ($5.95) r/#1,2						6.00

KARATE KID (See Action, Adventure, Legion of Super-Heroes, & Superboy)
National Periodical Publications/DC Comics: Mar-Apr, 1976 - No. 15, July-Aug, 1978 (Legion of Super-Heroes spin-off)

	GD	VG	FN	VF	VF/NM	NM-
1,15: 1-Meets Iris Jacobs; Estrada/Staton-a. 15-Continued into Kamandi #58	2	4	6	8	10	12
2-14: 2-Major Disaster app. 14-Robin x-over	1	2	3	4	5	7

NOTE: ***Grell** c-1-4, 5p, 6p, 7, 8. **Staton** a-1-9i. Legion x-over-No. 1, 2, 4, 6, 10, 12, 13. Princess Projectra x-over-#8, 9.*

KATHY
Standard Comics: Sept, 1949 - No. 17, Sept, 1955

	GD	VG	FN	VF	VF/NM	NM-
1-Teen-age	11	22	33	66	88	110
2-Schomburg-c	8	16	24	46	58	70
3-5	6	12	18	31	38	45
6-17: 17-Code approved	5	10	15	24	30	35

KATHY (The Teenage Tornado)
Atlas Comics/Marvel (ZPC): Oct, 1959 - No. 27, Feb, 1964

	GD	VG	FN	VF	VF/NM	NM-
1-Teen-age	7	14	21	50	68	85
2	4	8	12	25	33	42
3-15	3	6	9	18	24	30
16-27	2	4	6	12	16	20

KAT KARSON
I. W. Enterprises: No date (Reprint)

	GD	VG	FN	VF	VF/NM	NM-
1-Funny animals	2	4	6	10	12	15

KATO OF THE GREEN HORNET (Also see The Green Hornet)
Now Comics: Nov, 1991 - No. 4, Feb, 1992 ($2.50, mini-series)

	GD	VG	FN	VF	VF/NM	NM-
1-4: Brent Anderson-c/a						2.50

KATO OF THE GREEN HORNET II (Also see The Green Hornet)
Now Comics: Nov, 1992 - No. 2, Dec, 1993 ($2.50, mini-series)

	GD	VG	FN	VF	VF/NM	NM-
1,2-Baron-s/Mayerik & Sherman-a						2.50

KATY KEENE (Also see Kasco Komics, Laugh, Pep, Suzie, & Wilbur)
Archie Publ./Close-Up/Radio Comics: 1949 - No. 4, 1951; No. 5, 3/52 - No. 62, Oct, 1961 (50-53-Adventures of...on-c) (Cut and missing pages are common)

	GD	VG	FN	VF	VF/NM	NM-
1-Bill Woggon-c/a begins; swipes-c to Mopsy #1	100	200	300	625	938	1250
2-(1950)	48	96	144	288	432	575
3-5: 3-(1951). 4-(1951)	40	80	120	240	340	440
6-10	34	68	102	196	278	360
11,13-21: 21-Last pre-code issue (3/55)	29	58	87	164	232	300
12-(Scarce)	34	68	102	196	278	360
22-40	21	42	63	118	164	210
41-60: 54-Wedding Album plus wedding pin-up	17	34	51	95	130	165
61,62: 62-Robot-c	19	38	57	106	146	185
Annual 1('54, 25¢)-All new stories; last pre-code	46	92	138	276	413	550
Annual 2-6('55-59, 25¢)-All new stories	29	58	87	164	232	300
3-D 1(1953, 25¢, large size)-Came w/glasses	40	80	120	240	340	440
Charm 1(9/58)-Woggon-c/a; new stories, and cut-outs	29	58	87	164	232	300
Glamour 1(1957)-Puzzles, games, cut-outs	29	58	87	164	232	300
Spectacular 1('56)	29	58	87	164	232	300

NOTE: *Debby's Diary in #45, 47-49, 52, 57.*

KATY KEENE COMICS DIGEST MAGAZINE
Close-Up, Inc. (Archie Ent.): 1987 - No. 10, July, 1990 ($1.25/$1.35/$1.50, digest size)

	GD	VG	FN	VF	VF/NM	NM-
1	2	4	6	9	11	14
2-10	1	2	3	5	6	8

KATY KEENE FASHION BOOK MAGAZINE
Radio Comics/Archie Publications: 1955 - No. 13, Sum, '56 - N. 23, Wint, '58-59 (nn 3-10)

	GD	VG	FN	VF	VF/NM	NM-
1-Bill Woggon-c/a	46	92	138	276	413	550
2	29	58	87	164	232	300
11-18: 18-Photo Bill Woggon	21	42	63	118	164	210
19-23	17	34	51	95	130	165

KATY KEENE HOLIDAY FUN (See Archie Giant Series Magazine No. 7, 12)

KATY KEENE PINUP PARADE
Radio Comics/Archie Publications: 1955 - No. 15, Summer, 1961 (25¢) (Cut-out & missing pages are common)

	GD	VG	FN	VF	VF/NM	NM-
1-Cut-outs in all?; last pre-code issue	46	92	138	276	413	550
2-(1956)	28	56	84	159	225	290
3-5: 3-(1957)	25	50	75	144	198	255
6-10,12-14: 8-Mad parody. 10-Bill Woggon photo	21	42	63	118	164	210
11-Story of how comics get CCA approved, narrated by Katy	26	52	78	147	206	265
15(Rare)-Photo artist & family	40	80	120	240	345	450

KATY KEENE SPECIAL (Katy Keene #7 on; see Laugh Comics Digest)
Archie Ent.: Sept, 1983 - No. 33, 1990 (Later issues published quarterly)

	GD	VG	FN	VF	VF/NM	NM-
1-10: 1-Woggon-r; new Woggon-c. 3-Woggon-r						5.00
11-25						6.00
26-32-(Low print run)	1	2	3	5	6	8
33	1	3	4	6	8	10

KATZENJAMMER KIDS, THE (See Captain & the Kids & Giant Comic Album)
David McKay Publ./Standard No. 12-21(Spring/'50 - 53)/Harvey No. 22, 4/53 on: 1945-1946; Summer, 1947 - No. 27, Feb-Mar, 1954

	GD	VG	FN	VF	VF/NM	NM-
Feature Books 30	20	40	60	112	156	200
Feature Books 32,35('45),41,44('46)	18	36	54	101	138	175
Feature Book 37-Has photos & biography of Harold Knerr	19	38	57	107	149	190
1(1947)-All new stories begin	19	38	57	107	149	190
2	10	20	30	58	77	95
3-11	8	16	24	42	54	65
12-14(Standard)	6	12	18	33	41	48
15-21(Standard)	6	12	18	29	36	42
22-25,27(Harvey): 22-24-Henry app.	6	12	18	29	36	42
26-Half in 3-D	17	34	51	95	130	165

KAYO (Formerly Bullseye & Jest; becomes Carnival Comics)
Harry 'A' Chesler: No. 12, Mar, 1945

	GD	VG	FN	VF	VF/NM	NM-
12-Green Knight, Capt. Glory, Little Nemo (not by McCay)	17	34	51	95	130	165

KA-ZAR (Also see Marvel Comics #1, Savage Tales #6 & X-Men #10)
Marvel Comics Group: Aug, 1970 - No. 3, Mar, 1971 (Giant-Size, 68 pgs.)

	GD	VG	FN	VF	VF/NM	NM-
1-Reprints earlier Ka-Zar stories; Avengers x-over in Hercules; Daredevil, X-Men app.; hidden profanity-c	3	7	10	21	28	35
2,3-Daredevil-r. 2-r/Daredevil #13 w/Kirby layouts; Ka-Zar origin, Angel-r from X-Men by Tuska. 3-Romita & Heck-a (no Kirby)	3	6	9	16	20	24

NOTE: ***Buscema** r-2. **Colan** a-1p(r). **Kirby** c/a-1, 2. #1-Reprints X-Men #10 & Daredevil #24*

KA-ZAR
Marvel Comics Group: Jan, 1974 - No. 20, Feb, 1977 (Regular Size)

Ka-Zar V2#6 © MAR

Keen Detective Funnies #9 © CEN

The Kents #1 © DC

	GD 2.0	VG 4.0	FN 6.0	VF 8.0	VF/NM 9.0	NM- 9.2
1	2	4	6	10	13	16
2-10	1	2	3	5	6	8
11-14,16,18-20						5.00
15,17-(Regular 25¢ edition)(8/76)						5.00
15,17-(30¢-c variants, limited distribution)	1	2	3	4	5	7

NOTE: ***Alcala** a-6i, 8i. **Brunner** c-4. **J. Buscema** a-6-10p; c-1, 5, 7. **Heath** a-12. **G. Kane** c(p)-3, 5, 8-11, 15, 20. **Kirby** c-12p. **Reinman** a-1p.*

KA-ZAR (Volume 2)
Marvel Comics: May, 1997 - No. 20, Dec, 1998 ($1.95/$1.99)

1-Waid-s/Andy Kubert-c/a. thru #4 3.00
1-2nd printing; new cover 2.25
2,4: 2-Two-c 2.50
3-Alpha Flight #1 preview 3.00
5-13,15-20: 8-Includes Spider-Man Cybercomic CD-ROM. 9-11-Thanos app. 15-Priest-s/Martinez & Rodriguez-a begin; Punisher app. 2.25
14-($2.99) Last Waid/Kubert issue; flip book with 2nd story previewing new creative team of Priest-s/Martinez & Rodriguez-a 3.00
'97 Annual ($2.99)-Wraparound-c 3.00

KA-ZAR OF THE SAVAGE LAND
Marvel Comics: Feb, 1997 ($2.50, one-shot)

1-Wraparound-c 2.50

KA-ZAR: SIBLING RIVALRY
Marvel Comics: July, 1997 ($1.95, one-shot)

(# -1) Flashback story w/Alpha Flight #1 preview 2.25

KA-ZAR THE SAVAGE (See Marvel Fanfare)
Marvel Comics Group: Apr, 1981 - No. 34, Oct, 1984 (Regular size)(Mando paper #10 on)

1 4.00
2-20,24,27,28,30-34: 11-Origin Zabu. 12-One of two versions with panel missing on pg. 10. 20-Kraven the Hunter-c/story (also apps. in #21) 2.50
12-Version with panel on pg. 10 (1600 printed) 6.00
21-23, 25,26-Spider-Man app. 26-Photo-c. 3.00
29-Double size; Ka-Zar & Shanna wed 3.00

NOTE: ***B. Anderson** a-1-15p, 18, 19; c-1-17, 18p, 20(back). **G. Kane** a(back-up)-11, 12, 14.*

KEEN DETECTIVE FUNNIES (Formerly Detective Picture Stories?)
Centaur Publications: No. 8, July, 1938 - No. 24, Sept, 1940

	GD 2.0	VG 4.0	FN 6.0	VF 8.0	VF/NM 9.0	NM- 9.2
V1#8-The Clock continues-r/Funny Picture Stories #1; Roy Crane-a (1st?)	228	456	684	1425	2138	2850
9-Tex Martin by Eisner; The Gang Buster app.	85	170	255	531	796	1060
10,11: 11-Dean Denton story (begins?)	76	152	228	475	713	950
V2#1,2-The Eye Sees by Frank Thomas begins; ends #23(Not in V2#3&5). 2-Jack Cole-a	70	140	210	438	654	870
3-6: 3-TNT Todd begins. 4-Gabby Flynn begins. 5,6-Dean Denton story	65	130	195	406	613	820
7-The Masked Marvel by Ben Thompson begins (7/39, 1st app.)(scarce)	240	480	720	1500	2250	3000
8-Nudist ranch panel w/four girls	85	170	255	531	796	1060
9-11	74	148	222	463	694	925
12(12/39)-Origin The Eye Sees by Frank Thomas; death of Masked Marvel's sidekick ZL	92	184	276	575	863	1150
V3#1,2	68	136	204	425	638	850
18,19,21,22: 18-Bondage/torture-c	68	136	204	425	638	850
20-Classic Eye Sees-c by Thomas	96	192	288	600	900	1200
23-Air Man begins (intro); Air Man-c	91	182	273	569	855	1140
24-(scarce) Air Man-c	96	192	288	600	900	1200

NOTE: ***Burgos** a-V2#2. **Jack Cole** a-V2#2. **Eisner** a-10, V2#6r. **Ken Ernst** a-V2#4-7, 9, 10, 19, 21; c-V2#4. **Everett** a-V2#6, 7, 9, 11, 12, 20. **Guardineer** a-V2#5, 66. **Gustavson** a-V2#4-6. **Simon** c-V3#1. **Thompson** c-V2#7, 9, 10, 22.*

KEEN KOMICS
Centaur Publications: V2#1, May, 1939 - V2#3, Nov, 1939

	GD 2.0	VG 4.0	FN 6.0	VF 8.0	VF/NM 9.0	NM- 9.2
V2#1(Large size)-Dan Hastings (s/f), The Big Top, Bob Phantom the Magician, The Mad Goddess app.	96	192	288	600	900	1200
V2#2(Reg. size)-The Forbidden Idol of Machu Picchu; Cut Carson by Burgos begins	61	122	183	381	571	760
V2#3-Saddle Sniffl by Jack Cole, Circus Pays, Kings Revenge app.	61	122	183	381	571	760

NOTE: ***Binder** a-V2#2. **Burgos** a-V2#2, 3. **Ken Ernst** a-V2#3. **Gustavson** a-V2#2. **Jack Cole** a-V2#3.*

KEEN TEENS (Girls magazine)
Life's Romances Publ./Leader/Magazine Ent.: 1945 - No. 6, Aug-Sept, 1947

	GD 2.0	VG 4.0	FN 6.0	VF 8.0	VF/NM 9.0	NM- 9.2
nn (#1)-14 pgs. Claire Voyant (cont'd. in other nn issue) movie photos, Dotty Dripple, Gertie O'Grady & Sissy; Van Johnson, Frank Sinatra photo-c	38	76	114	219	310	400
nn (#2, 1946)-16 pgs. Claire Voyant & 16 pgs. movie photos	28	56	84	159	225	290
3-6: 4-Glenn Ford photo-c. 5-Perry Como-c	12	24	36	69	92	115

KEIF LLAMA
Oni Press: Mar, 1999 ($2.95, B&W, one-shot)

1-Matt Howarth-s/a 3.00

KELLYS, THE (Formerly Rusty Comics; Spy Cases No. 26 on)
Marvel Comics (HPC): No. 23, Jan, 1950 - No. 25, June, 1950 (52 pgs.)

	GD 2.0	VG 4.0	FN 6.0	VF 8.0	VF/NM 9.0	NM- 9.2
23-Teenage	12	24	36	71	96	120
24,25: 24-Margie app.	8	16	24	46	58	70

KELVIN MACE
Vortex Publications: 1986 - No. 2, 1986 ($2.00, B&W)

1,2: 1-(B&W). 1-2nd print (1/87, $1.75). 2-(Color) 2.25

KEN MAYNARD WESTERN (Movie star)(See Wow Comics, 1936)
Fawcett Publ.: Sept, 1950 - No. 8, Feb, 1952 (All 36 pgs; photo front/back-c)

	GD 2.0	VG 4.0	FN 6.0	VF 8.0	VF/NM 9.0	NM- 9.2
1-Ken Maynard & his horse Tarzan begin	60	120	180	375	563	750
2	39	78	117	230	325	420
3-8: 6-Atomic bomb explosion panel	30	60	90	170	240	310

KEN SHANNON (Becomes Gabby #11 on) (Also see Police Comics #103)
Quality Comics Group: Oct, 1951 - No. 10, Apr, 1953 (A private eye)

	GD 2.0	VG 4.0	FN 6.0	VF 8.0	VF/NM 9.0	NM- 9.2
1-Crandall-a	39	78	117	230	325	420
2-Crandall c/a(2)	31	62	93	175	248	320
3-5-Crandall-a. 3-Horror-c	22	44	66	124	172	220
6-Crandall-c/a; "The Weird Vampire Mob"-c/s	25	50	75	144	198	255
7,10: 7-Crandall-a. 10-Crandall-c	18	36	54	101	138	175
8,9: 8-Opium den drug use story	17	34	51	98	134	170

NOTE: ***Crandall/Cuidera** c-1-10. **Jack Cole** a-1-9. #1-15 published after title change to Gabby.*

KEN STUART
Publication Enterprises: Jan, 1949 (Sea Adventures)

	GD 2.0	VG 4.0	FN 6.0	VF 8.0	VF/NM 9.0	NM- 9.2
1-Frank Borth-c/a	10	20	30	56	73	90

KENT BLAKE OF THE SECRET SERVICE (Spy)
Marvel/Atlas Comics(20CC): May, 1951 - No. 14, July, 1953

	GD 2.0	VG 4.0	FN 6.0	VF 8.0	VF/NM 9.0	NM- 9.2
1-Injury to eye, bondage, torture; Brodsky-c	21	42	63	118	164	210
2-Drug use w/hypo scenes; Brodsky-c	15	30	45	84	115	145
3-14: 8-R.Q. Sale-a (2 pgs.)	9	18	27	52	66	80

NOTE: ***Heath** c-5, 7, 8. **Infantino** c-12. **Maneely** c-3. **Sinnott** a-2(3). **Tuska** a-8(3pg.).*

KENTS, THE
DC Comics: Aug, 1997 - No. 12, July, 1998 ($2.50, limited series)

1-12-Ostrander-s/art by Truman and Bair (#1-8), Mandrake (#9-12) 3.00
TPB ($19.95) r/#1-12 20.00

KERRY DRAKE (Also see A-1 Comics)
Argo: Jan, 1956 - No. 2, March, 1956

	GD 2.0	VG 4.0	FN 6.0	VF 8.0	VF/NM 9.0	NM- 9.2
1,2-Newspaper-r	8	16	24	46	58	70

KERRY DRAKE DETECTIVE CASES (…Racket Buster No. 32,33)
(Also see Chamber of Clues & Green Hornet Comics #42-47)
Life's Romances/Com/Magazine Ent. No.1-5/Harvey No.6 on: 1944 - No. 5, 1944; No. 6, Jan, 1948 - No. 33, Aug, 1952

	GD 2.0	VG 4.0	FN 6.0	VF 8.0	VF/NM 9.0	NM- 9.2
nn(1944)(A-1 Comics)(slightly over-size)	31	62	93	175	248	320
2	19	38	57	106	146	185
3-5(1944)	16	32	48	92	126	160
6,8(1948): Lady Crime by Powell. 8-Bondage-c	11	22	33	63	84	105
7-Kubert-a; biog of Andriola (artist)	12	24	36	71	96	120
9,10-Two-part marijuana story; Kerry smokes marijuana in #10	16	32	48	92	126	160
11-15	10	20	30	56	73	90
16-33	8	16	24	46	58	70

NOTE: ***Andiola** c-6-9. **Berg** a-5. **Powell** a-10-23, 28, 29.*

KEWPIES
Will Eisner Publications: Spring, 1949

	GD 2.0	VG 4.0	FN 6.0	VF 8.0	VF/NM 9.0	NM- 9.2
1-Feiffer-a; Kewpie Doll ad on back cover	46	92	138	276	413	550

KEY COMICS
Consolidated Magazines: Jan, 1944 - No. 5, Aug, 1946

	GD 2.0	VG 4.0	FN 6.0	VF 8.0	VF/NM 9.0	NM- 9.2
1-The Key, Will-O-The-Wisp begin	40	80	120	240	355	470
2 (3/44)	23	46	69	130	183	235
3,4: 4-(5/46)-Origin John Quincy The Atom (begins); Walter Johnson c-3-5	20	40	60	112	156	200

5-4pg. Faust Opera adaptation; Kiefer-a; back-c advertises "Masterpieces Illustrated" by

Kid Colt Outlaw #5 © MAR

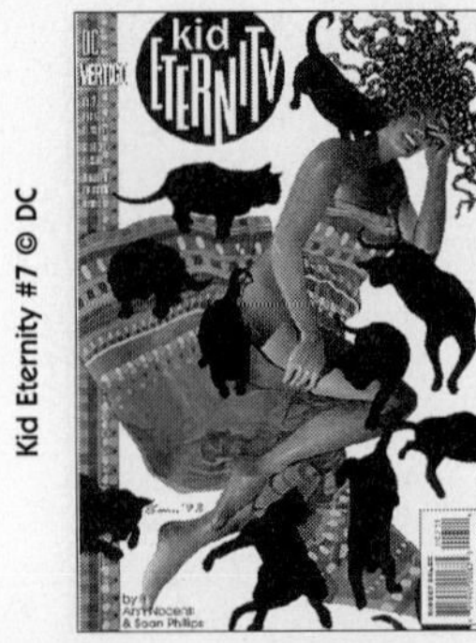

Kid Eternity #7 © DC

Kid Komics #4 © MAR

GD VG FN VF VF/NM NM-
2.0 4.0 6.0 8.0 9.0 9.2

Lloyd Jacquet after he left Classic Comics (no copies of Masterpieces Illustrated known)
25 50 75 144 198 255

KEY RING COMICS
Dell Publishing Co.: 1941 (16 pgs.; two colors) (sold 5 for 10¢)

1-Sky Hawk, 1-Viking Carter, 1-Features Sleepy Samson, 1-Origin Greg Gilday-
r/War Comics #2 8 16 24 43 54 65
1-Radior (Super hero) 9 18 27 52 66 80
NOTE: *Each book has two holes in spine to put in binder.*

KICKERS, INC.
Marvel Comics Group: Nov, 1986 - No. 12, Oct, 1987

1-12 2.25

KID CARROTS
St. John Publishing Co.: September, 1953

1-Funny animal 8 16 24 40 50 60

KID COLT OUTLAW (Kid Colt #1-4; ...Outlaw #5-on)(Also see All Western Winners, Best Western, Black Rider, Giant-Size..., Two-Gun Kid, Two-Gun Western, Western Winners, Wild Western, Wisco)
Marvel Comics(LCC) 1-16; Atlas(LMC) 17-102; Marvel 103-on: 8/48 - No. 139, 3/68; No. 140, 11/69 - No. 229, 4/79

1-Kid Colt & his horse Steel begin. 100 200 300 625 938 1250
2 50 100 150 300 450 600
3-5: 4-Anti-Wertham editorial; Tex Taylor app. 5-Blaze Carson app.
40 80 120 240 358 475
6-8: 6-Tex Taylor app; 7-Nimo the Lion begins, ends #10
29 58 87 164 232 300
9,10 (52 pgs.) 29 58 87 164 232 300
11-Origin 33 66 99 190 270 350
12-20 21 42 63 118 164 200
21-32 17 34 51 95 130 165
33-45: Black Rider in all 13 26 39 74 100 125
46,47,49,50 11 22 33 63 84 105
48-Kubert-a 11 22 33 66 88 110
51-53,55,56 9 18 27 52 66 80
54-Williamson/Maneely-c 10 20 30 56 73 90
57-60,66: 4-pg. Williamson-a in all 8 16 24 53 74 95
61-63,67-78,80-86: 70-Severin-c. 73-Maneely-c. 86-Kirby-a(r).
6 12 18 38 52 65
64,65-Crandall-a 6 12 18 40 55 70
79,87: 79-Origin retold. 87-Davis-a(r) 6 12 18 40 55 70
88,89-Williamson-a in both (4 pgs.). 89-Redrawn Matt Slade #2
6 12 18 43 59 75
90-99,101-106,108,109: 91-Kirby/Ayers-c. 95-Kirby/Ayers-c/story. 102-Last 10¢ issue
5 10 15 33 44 55
100 5 10 15 36 48 60
107-Only Kirby sci-fi cover of title; Kirby -a. 6 12 18 38 52 65
110-(5/63)-1st app. Iron Mask (Iron Man type villain) 6 12 18 38 52 65
111-120: 114-(1/64)-2nd app. Iron Mask 4 8 12 25 33 42
121-129,133-139: 121-Rawhide Kid x-over. 125-Two-Gun Kid x-over. 139-Last 12¢ issue
3 6 9 19 25 32
130-132 (68 pgs.)-one new story each. 130-Origin 4 8 12 25 33 42
140-155: 140-Reprints begin (later issues mostly-r). 155-Last 15¢ issue
2 4 6 11 14 18
156-Giant; reprints (52 pgs.) 3 6 9 18 23 28
157-180,200: 170-Origin retold. 2 4 6 10 13 16
181-199 2 4 6 8 10 12
201-229: 201-New material w/Rawhide Kid app; Kane-c. 229-Rawhide Kid-r
1 3 4 6 8 10
205-209-(30¢-c variants, limited dist.) 2 4 6 11 14 18
218-220-(35¢-c variants, limited dist.) 2 4 6 11 14 18
...Album (no date; 1950's; Atlas Comics)-132 pgs.; random binding, cardboard cover,
B&W stories; contents can vary (Rare) 78 156 234 488 732 975
NOTE: ***Ayers*** *a-many.* ***Colan*** *a-52, 53; c(p)-223, 228, 229.* ***Crandall*** *a-140r, 167r.* ***Everett*** *a-90, 137i, 225i(r).* ***Heath*** *a-8(2); c-34, 35, 39, 44, 46, 48, 49, 57, 64.* ***Heck*** *a-135, 139.* ***Jack Keller*** *a-25(2), 26-68(3-4), 78, 94p, 98, 99, 108, 110, 130, 132, 140-150r.* ***Kirby*** *a-86r, 93, 96, 107, 119, 176(part); c-87, 92-95, 97, 99-112, 114-117, 121-123, 197r; w/****Ditko*** *c-89.* ***Maneely*** *a-12, 68, 81; c-17, 19, 40-43, 47, 52, 53, 62, 65, 68, 78, 81, 142r, 150r.* ***Morrow*** *a-173r, 216r.* ***Rico*** *a-13, 18.* ***Severin*** *c-58, 59, 143, 148, 149i.* ***Shores*** *a-39, 41-43, 143r; c-1-10(most), 24.* ***Sutton*** *a-136, 137p, 225p(r).* ***Wildey*** *a-47, 54, 82, 144r.* ***Williamson*** *r-147, 170, 172, 216.* ***Woodbridge*** *a-64, 81. Black Rider in #33-45, 74, 86. Iron Mask in #110, 114, 121, 127. Sam Hawk in #84, 101, 111, 121, 146, 174, 181, 188.*

KID COWBOY (Also see Approved Comics #4 & Boy Cowboy)
Ziff-Davis Publ./St. John (Approved Comics) #11,14: 1950 - No. 11, Wint, '52-'53; No. 14, June, 1954 (No #12,13) (Painted covers #1-10, 14)

1-Lucy Belle & Red Feather begin 16 32 48 92 126 160

GD VG FN VF VF/NM NM-
2.0 4.0 6.0 8.0 9.0 9.2

2-Maneely-c 10 20 30 58 77 95
3-11,14: (#3, spr. '51). 5-Berg-a. 14-Code approved 9 18 27 52 66 80

KID DEATH & FLUFFY HALLOWEEN SPECIAL
Event Comics: Oct, 1997 ($2.95, B&W, one-shot)

1-Variant-c by Cebollero & Quesada/Palmiotti 3.00

KID DEATH & FLUFFY SPRING BREAK SPECIAL
Event Comics: July, 1996 ($2.50, B&W, one-shot)

1-Quesada & Palmiotti-c/scripts 2.50

KIDDIE KAPERS
Kiddie Kapers Co., 1945/Decker Publ. (Red Top-Farrell): 1945?(nd); Oct, 1957; 1963 - 1964

1(nd, 1945-46?, 36 pgs.)-Infinity-c; funny animal 9 18 27 52 66 80
1(10/57)(Decker)-Little Bit-r from Kiddie Karnival 5 10 15 22 26 30
Super Reprint #7, 10('63), 12, 14('63), 15,17('64), 18('64): 10, 14-r/Animal Adventures #1. 15-Animal Adventures #? 17-Cowboys 'N' Injuns #?
2 4 6 9 11 14

KIDDIE KARNIVAL
Ziff-Davis Publ. Co. (Approved Comics): 1952 (25¢, 100 pgs.) (One Shot)

nn-Rebound Little Bit #1,2; painted-c 38 76 114 219 310 400

KID ETERNITY (Becomes Buccaneers) (See Hit Comics)
Quality Comics Group: Spring, 1946 - No. 18, Nov, 1949

1 96 192 288 600 900 1200
2 40 80 120 240 345 450
3-Mac Raboy-a 40 80 120 240 353 465
4-10 25 50 75 144 198 255
11-18 20 40 60 112 156 200

KID ETERNITY
DC Comics: 1991 - No. 3, Nov, 1991 ($4.95, limited series)

1-3: Grant Morrison scripts 6.00

KID ETERNITY
DC Comics (Vertigo): May, 1993 - No. 16, Sept, 1994 ($1.95, mature)

1-16: 1-Gold ink-c. 6-Photo-c. All Sean Phillips-c/a except #15 (Phillips-c/i only) 2.25

KID FROM DODGE CITY, THE
Atlas Comics (MMC): July, 1957 - No. 2, Sept, 1957

1-Don Heck-c 10 20 30 56 73 90
2-Everett-c 7 14 21 35 43 50

KID FROM TEXAS, THE (A Texas Ranger)
Atlas Comics (CSI): June, 1957 - No. 2, Aug, 1957

1-Powell-a; Severin-c 10 20 30 56 73 90
2 7 14 21 35 43 50

KID KOKO
I. W. Enterprises: 1958

Reprint #1,2-(r/M.E.'s Koko & Kola #4, 1947) 2 4 6 9 11 14

KID KOMICS (Kid Movie Komics No. 11)
Timely Comics (USA 1,2/FCI 3-10): Feb, 1943 - No. 10, Spring, 1946

1-Origin Captain Wonder & sidekick Tim Mullrooney, & Subbie; intro the Sea-Going Lad, Pinto Pete, & Trixie Trouble; Knuckles & Whitewash Jones (from Young Allies) app.;
Wolverton-a (7 pgs.) 423 846 1269 2751 4226 5700
2-The Young Allies, Red Hawk, & Tommy Tyme begin; last Captain Wonder & Subbie
184 368 552 1150 1725 2300
3-The Vision, Daredevils & Red Hawk app. 140 280 420 875 1313 1750
4-The Destroyer begins; Sub-Mariner app.; Red Hawk & Tommy Tyme end
118 236 354 738 1107 1475
5,6: 5-Tommy Tyme begins, ends #10 90 180 270 563 844 1125
7-10: 7,10-The Whizzer app. Destroyer not in #7,8. 10-Last Destroyer, Young Allies &
Whizzer 80 160 240 500 750 1000
NOTE: ***Brodsky*** *c-5.* ***Schomburg*** *c-2-4, 6-10.* ***Shores*** *c-1. Captain Wonder c-1, 2. The Young Allies c-3-10.*

KID MONTANA (Formerly Davy Crockett Frontier Fighter; The Gunfighters No. 51 on)
Charlton Comics: V2#9, Nov, 1957 - No. 50, Mar, 1965

V2#9 (#1) 5 10 15 36 48 60
10 4 8 12 24 32 40
11,12,14-20 3 6 9 18 23 28
13-Williamson-a 4 8 12 24 32 40
21-35: 25,31-Giordano-c. 32-Origin Kid Montana. 34-Geronimo-c/s. 35-Snow Monster-c/s
2 4 6 12 16 20
36-50: 36-Dinosaur-c/s. 37,48-Giordano-c 2 4 6 10 12 15
NOTE: *Title change to Montana Kid on cover only #44 & 45; remained Kid Montana on inside.* ***Chasal*** *a-29,30.* ***Giordano*** *c-25,31,37,48.* ***Giordano/Alascia*** *c-12.* ***Mastroserio*** *a-9,11,13,14,22; c-11,14.* ***Masulli/Mastroserio*** *c-*

Kid Supreme #1 © Rob Liefeld

Kin #6 © Gary Frank

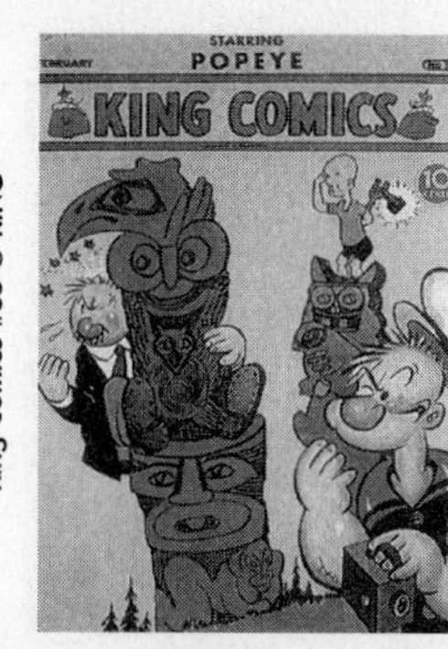

King Comics #35 © KING

GD VG FN VF VF/NM NM-
2.0 4.0 6.0 8.0 9.0 9.2

*13. **Montes/Bache** c-42. **Morisi** c-16,32-34,36?,40,41,44,46; a-13,15;16,31-50. **Nicholas/Alascia** a-44,48.*

KID MOVIE KOMICS (Formerly Kid Komics; Rusty Comics #12 on)
Timely Comics: No. 11, Summer, 1946

	GD	VG	FN	VF	VF/NM	NM-
11-Silly Seal & Ziggy Pig; 2 pgs. Kurtzman "Hey Look" plus 6 pg. "Pigtales" story	27	54	81	153	214	275

KIDNAPPED (Robert Louis Stevenson's...also see Movie Comics)(Disney)
Dell Publishing Co.: No. 1101, May, 1960

	GD	VG	FN	VF	VF/NM	NM-
Four Color 1101-Movie, photo-c	7	14	21	51	71	90

KIDNAP RACKET (See Harvey Comics Hits No. 57)

KID SLADE GUNFIGHTER (Formerly Matt Slade...)
Atlas Comics (SPI): No. 5, Jan, 1957 - No. 8, July, 1957

	GD	VG	FN	VF	VF/NM	NM-
5-Maneely, Roth, Severin-a in all; Maneely-c	13	26	39	74	100	125
6,8-Severin-c	8	16	24	43	54	65
7-Williamson/Mayo-a, 4 pgs.	10	20	30	56	73	90

KID SUPREME (See Supreme)
Image Comics (Extreme Studios): Mar, 1996 - No. 3, July, 1996 ($2.50)

	GD	VG	FN	VF	VF/NM	NM-
1-3: Fraga-a/scripts. 3-Glory-c/app.						2.50

KID TERRIFIC
Image Comics: Nov, 1998 ($2.95, B&W)

	GD	VG	FN	VF	VF/NM	NM-
1-Snyder & Diliberto-s/a						3.00

KID ZOO COMICS
Street & Smith Publications: July, 1948 (52 pgs.)

	GD	VG	FN	VF	VF/NM	NM-
1-Funny Animal	28	56	84	157	225	290

KILLER (...Tales By Timothy Truman)
Eclipse Comics: March, 1985 ($1.75, one-shot, Baxter paper)

	GD	VG	FN	VF	VF/NM	NM-
1-Timothy Truman-c/a						2.50

KILLER INSTINCT (Video game)
Acclaim Comics: June, 1996 - No. 6 ($2.50, limited series)

	GD	VG	FN	VF	VF/NM	NM-
1-6: 1-Bart Sears-a(p). 4-Special #1. 5-Special #2. 6-Special #3						3.00

KILLER PRINCESSES
Oni Press: Dec, 2001 - No. 3, Apr, 2003 ($2.95, limited series)

	GD	VG	FN	VF	VF/NM	NM-
1-3-Gail Simone-s/Lea Hernandez-a						3.00

KILLERS, THE
Magazine Enterprises: 1947 - No. 2, 1948 (No month)

	GD	VG	FN	VF	VF/NM	NM-
1-Mr. Zin, the Hatchet Killer; mentioned in **SOTI**, pgs. 179,180; used by N.Y. Legis. Comm.; L. B. Cole-c	107	214	321	669	1005	1340
2-(Scarce)-Hashish smoking story; "Dying, Dying, Dead" drug story; Whitney, Ingels-a; Whitney hanging-c	88	176	264	550	825	1100

KILLING JOKE, THE (See Batman: The Killing Joke under Batman one-shots)

KILLPOWER: THE EARLY YEARS
Marvel Comics UK: Sept, 1993 - No. 4, Dec, 1993 ($1.75, mini-series)

	GD	VG	FN	VF	VF/NM	NM-
1-($2.95)-Foil embossed-c						3.00
2-4: 2-Genetix app. 3-Punisher app.						2.25

KILLRAVEN (See Amazing Adventures #18 (5/73))
Marvel Comics: Feb, 2001 ($2.99, one-shot)

	GD	VG	FN	VF	VF/NM	NM-
1-Linsner-s/a/c						3.00

KILLRAVEN
Marvel Comics: Dec, 2002 - No. 6, May, 2003 ($2.99, limited series)

	GD	VG	FN	VF	VF/NM	NM-
1-6-Alan Davis-s/a(p)/Mark Farmer-i						3.00

KILLRAZOR
Image Comics (Top Cow Productions): Aug, 1995 ($2.50, one-shot)

	GD	VG	FN	VF	VF/NM	NM-
1						2.50

KILL YOUR BOYFRIEND
DC Comics (Vertigo): June, 1995 ($4.95, one-shot)

	GD	VG	FN	VF	VF/NM	NM-
1-Grant Morrison story						6.00
1($5.95, 1998) 2nd printing						6.00

KILROY (Volume 2)
Caliber Press: 1998 ($2.95, B&W)

	GD	VG	FN	VF	VF/NM	NM-
1-Pruett-s						3.00

KILROY IS HERE
Caliber Press: 1995 ($2.95, B&W)

	GD	VG	FN	VF	VF/NM	NM-
1-10						3.00

KILROYS, THE
B&I Publ. Co. No. 1-19/American Comics Group: June-July, 1947 - No. 54, June-July, 1955

	GD	VG	FN	VF	VF/NM	NM-
1	23	46	69	129	180	230
2	12	24	36	69	92	115
3-5: 5-Gross-a	10	20	30	56	73	90
6-10: 8-Milt Gross's Moronica	8	16	24	46	58	70
11-20: 14-Gross-a	8	16	24	40	50	60
21-30	7	14	21	35	43	50
31-47,50-54	6	12	18	31	38	45
48,49-(3-D effect-c/stories)	18	36	54	101	138	175

KILROY: THE SHORT STORIES
Caliber Press: 1995 ($2.95, B&W)

	GD	VG	FN	VF	VF/NM	NM-
1						3.00

KIN
Image Comics (Top Cow): Mar, 2000 - Sept, 2000 ($2.95)

	GD	VG	FN	VF	VF/NM	NM-
1-5-Gary Frank-s/c/a						3.00
1-($6.95) DF Alternate footprint cover						7.00
6-($3.95)						4.00
... Descent of Man TPB (2002, $19.95) r/ #1-6						20.00

KINDRED, THE
Image Comics (WildStorm Productions): Mar, 1994 - No. 4, July, 1995 ($1.95, limited series)

	GD	VG	FN	VF	VF/NM	NM-
1-($2.50)-Grifter & Backlash app. in all; bound-in trading card						2.50
2-4						2.50
2,3: 2-Variant-c. 3-Alternate-c by Portacio, see Deathblow #5						4.00
Trade paperback (2/95, $9.95)						10.00

NOTE: *Booth c/a-1-4. The first four issues contain coupons redeemable for a Jim Lee Grifter/Backlash print.*

KINDRED II, THE
DC Comics (WildStorm): Mar, 2002 - No. 4, June, 2002 ($2.50, limited series)

	GD	VG	FN	VF	VF/NM	NM-
1-4-Booth-s/Booth & Regla-a						2.50

KING ARTHUR AND THE KNIGHTS OF JUSTICE
Marvel Comics UK: Dec, 1993 - No. 3, Feb, 1994 ($1.25, limited series)

	GD	VG	FN	VF	VF/NM	NM-
1-3: TV adaptation						2.25

KING CLASSICS
King Features : 1977 (36 pgs., cardboard-c)
(Printed in Spain for U.S. distr.)

1-Connecticut Yankee, 2-Last of the Mohicans, 3-Moby Dick, 4-Robin Hood, 5-Swiss Family Robinson, 6-Robinson Crusoe, 7-Treasure Island, 8-20,000 Leagues, 9-Christmas Carol, 10-Huck Finn, 11-Around the World in 80 Days, 12-Davy Crockett, 13-Don Quixote, 14-Gold Bug, 15-Ivanhoe, 16-Three Musketeers, 17-Baron Munchausen, 18-Alice in Wonderland, 19-Black Arrow, 20-Five Weeks in a Balloon, 21-Great Expectations, 22-Gulliver's Travels, 23-Prince & Pauper, 24-Lawrence of Arabia (Originals, 1977-78)

	GD	VG	FN	VF	VF/NM	NM-
each....	2	4	6	10	12	15
Reprints (1979; HRN-24)	1	2	3	5	7	9

NOTE: *The first eight issues were not numbered. Issues No. 25-32 were advertised but not published. The 1977 originals have HRN 32a; the 1978 originals have HRN 32b.*

KING COLT (See Luke Short's Western Stories)

KING COMICS (Strip reprints)
David McKay Publications/Standard #156-on: 4/36 - No. 155, 11-12/49; No. 156, Spr/50 - No. 159, 2/52 (Winter on-c)

	GD	VG	FN	VF	VF/NM	NM-
1-1st app. Flash Gordon by Alex Raymond; Brick Bradford (1st app.), Popeye, Henry (1st app.) & Mandrake the Magician (1st app.) begin; Popeye-c begin	1225	2450	3675	9500	-	-
2	344	688	1032	1892	2596	3300
3	233	466	699	1282	1766	2250
4	178	356	534	979	1340	1700
5	128	256	384	704	977	1250
6-10: 9-X-Mas-c	89	178	267	490	683	875
11-20	69	138	207	380	528	675
21-30: 21-X-Mas-c	50	100	150	275	388	500
31-40: 33-Last Segar Popeye	40	80	120	220	310	400
41-50: 46-Text illos by Marge Buell contain characters similar to Lulu, Alvin & Tubby. 50-The Lone Ranger begins	34	68	102	193	274	355
51-60: 52-Barney Baxter begins?	24	48	72	135	190	245
61-The Phantom begins	25	50	75	147	202	260
62-80: 76-Flag-c. 79-Blondie begins	18	36	54	101	138	175
81-99	14	28	42	79	107	135
100	17	34	51	95	130	165
101-114: 114-Last Raymond issue (1 pg.); Flash Gordon by Austin Briggs begins, ends #155	13	26	39	74	100	125
115-145: 117-Phantom origin retold	10	20	30	56	73	90
146,147-Prince Valiant in both	9	18	27	49	62	75

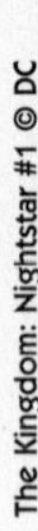

The Kingdom: Nightstar #1 © DC

Kingpin #1 © MAR

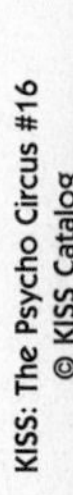
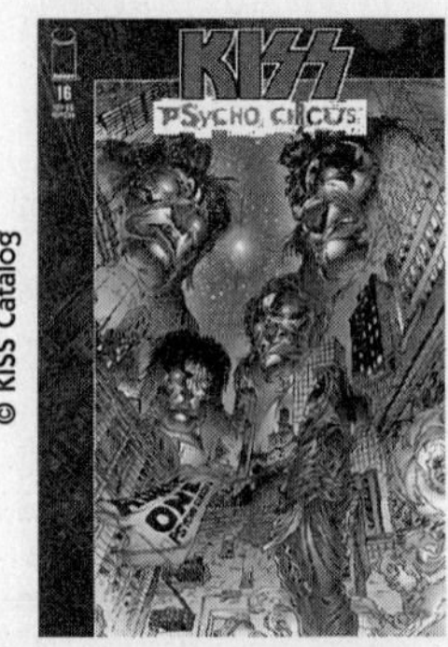

KISS: The Psycho Circus #16 © KISS Catalog

	GD 2.0	VG 4.0	FN 6.0	VF 8.0	VF/NM 9.0	NM- 9.2
148-155: 155-Flash Gordon ends (11-12/49)	9	18	27	49	62	75
156-159: 156-New logo begins (Standard)	8	16	24	46	58	70

NOTE: *Marge Buell text illos in No. 24-46 at least.*

KING CONAN (Conan The King No. 20 on)
Marvel Comics Group: Mar, 1980 - No. 19, Nov, 1983 (52 pgs.)

1 — 6.00
2-19: 4-Death of Thoth Amon. 7-1st Paul Smith-a, 1 pg. pin-up (9/81) — 4.00

NOTE: ***J. Buscema*** *a-1-9p, 17p; c(p)-1-5, 7-9, 14, 17.* ***Kaluta*** *c-19.* ***Nebres*** *a-17i, 18, 19i.* ***Severin*** *c-18.* ***Simonson*** *c-6.*

KING DAVID
DC Comics (Vertigo): 2002 ($19.95, 8 1/2" x 11")

nn-Story of King David; Kyle Baker-s/a — 20.00

KINGDOM, THE
DC Comics: Feb, 1999 - No. 2, Feb, 1999 ($2.95/$1.99, limited series)

1,2-Waid-s; sequel to Kingdom Come; introduces Hypertime — 4.00
...: Kid Flash 1 (2/99, $1.99) Waid-s/Pararillo-a, ...: Nightstar 1 (2/99, $1.99) Waid-s/Haley-a, ...: Offspring 1 (2/99, $1.99) Waid-s/Quitely-a, ...: Planet Krypton 1 (2/99, $1.99) Waid-s/Kitson-a, ...: Son of the Bat 1 (2/99, $1.99) Waid-s/Apthorp-a — 2.25

KINGDOM COME
DC Comics: 1996 - No. 4, 1996 ($4.95, painted limited series)

	GD	VG	FN	VF	VF/NM	NM-
1-Mark Waid scripts & Alex Ross-painted c/a in all; tells the last days of the DC Universe; 1st app. Magog	1	2	3	5	6	8
2-Superman forms new Justice League	1	2	3	4	5	7
3-Return of Captain Marvel						5.00
4-Final battle of Superman and Captain Marvel	1	2	3	4	5	7
Deluxe Slipcase Edition-($89.95) w/Revelations companion book, 12 new story pages, foil stamped covers, signed and numbered						120.00
Hardcover Edition-($29.95)-Includes 12 new story pages and artwork from Revelations, new cover artwork with gold foil inlay						35.00
Hardcover 2nd printing						30.00
Softcover Ed.-($14.95)-Includes 12 new story pgs. & artwork from Revelations, new c-artwork						15.00

KING KONG (See Movie Comics)

KING LEONARDO & HIS SHORT SUBJECTS (TV)
Dell Publishing Co./Gold Key: Nov-Jan, 1961-62 - No. 4, Sept, 1963

	GD	VG	FN	VF	VF/NM	NM-
Four Color 1242,1278	14	28	42	102	149	195
01390-207(5-7/62)(Dell)	10	20	30	73	107	140
1 (10/62)	12	24	36	87	129	170
2-4	10	20	30	67	96	125

KING LOUIE & MOWGLI (See Jungle Book under Movie Comics)
Gold Key: May, 1968 (Disney)

	GD	VG	FN	VF	VF/NM	NM-
1 (#10223-805)-Characters from Jungle Book	3	6	9	19	25	32

KING OF DIAMONDS (TV)
Dell Publishing Co.: July-Sept, 1962

	GD	VG	FN	VF	VF/NM	NM-
01-391-209-Photo-c	4	8	12	28	38	48

KING OF KINGS (Movie)
Dell Publishing Co.: No. 1236, Oct-Nov, 1961

	GD	VG	FN	VF	VF/NM	NM-
Four Color 1236-Photo-c	9	18	27	60	85	110

KING OF THE BAD MEN OF DEADWOOD
Avon Periodicals: 1950 (See Wild Bill Hickok #16)

	GD	VG	FN	VF	VF/NM	NM-
nn-Kinstler-c; Kamen/Feldstein-r/Cowpuncher #2	16	32	48	89	122	155

KING OF THE ROYAL MOUNTED (See Famous Feature Stories, King Comics, Red Ryder #3 & Super Book #2, 6)

KING OF THE ROYAL MOUNTED (Zane Grey's...)
David McKay/Dell Publishing Co.: No. 1, May, 1937; No. 9, 1940; No. 207, Dec, 1948 - No. 935, Sept-Nov, 1958

	GD	VG	FN	VF	VF/NM	NM-
Feature Books 1 (5/37)(McKay)	73	146	219	519	785	1050
Large Feature Comic 9 (1940)	38	76	114	285	430	575
Four Color 207(#1, 12/48)	15	30	45	109	160	210
Four Color 265,283	9	18	27	63	89	115
Four Color 310,340	7	14	21	51	71	90
Four Color 363,384, 8(6-8/52)-10	6	12	18	43	59	75
11-20	6	12	18	38	52	65
21-28(3-5/58), Four Color 935(9-11/58)	4	8	12	29	40	50

NOTE: *4-Color No. 207, 265, 283, 310, 340, 363, 384 are all newspaper reprints with* ***Jim Gary*** *art. No. 8 on are all Dell originals. Painted c-No. 9-on.*

KINGPIN
Marvel Comics: Nov, 1997 ($5.99, squarebound, one-shot)

nn-Spider-Man & Daredevil vs. Kingpin; Stan Lee-s/ John Romita Sr.-a — 6.00

KINGPIN
Marvel Comics: Aug, 2003 - No. 7, Jan, 2004 ($2.50/$2.99, limited series)

1-6-Bruce Jones-s/Sean Phillips & Klaus Janson-a — 2.50
7-($2.99) — 3.00

KING RICHARD & THE CRUSADERS
Dell Publishing Co.: No. 588, Oct, 1954

	GD	VG	FN	VF	VF/NM	NM-
Four Color 588-Movie, Matt Baker-a, photo-c	10	20	30	73	107	140

KINGS OF THE NIGHT
Dark Horse Comics: 1990 - No. 2, 1990 ($2.25, limited series)

1,2-Robert E. Howard adaptation; Bolton-c — 2.25

KING SOLOMON'S MINES (Movie)
Avon Periodicals: 1951

	GD	VG	FN	VF	VF/NM	NM-
nn (#1 on 1st page)	40	80	120	240	340	440

KING TIGER & MOTORHEAD
Dark Horse Comics: Aug, 1996 - No. 2, Sept, 1996 ($2.95, limited series)

1,2: Chichester scripts — 3.00

KIPLING, RUDYARD (See Mowgli, The Jungle Book)

KISS (See Crazy Magazine, Howard the Duck #12, 13, Marvel Comics Super Special #1, 5, Rock Fantasy Comics #10 & Rock N' Roll Comics #9)

KISS
Dark Horse Comics: June, 2002 - No. 13, Sept, 2003 ($2.99, limited series)

1-Photo-c and J. Scott Campbell-c; Casey-s — 4.00
2-13: 2-Photo-c and J. Scott Campbell-c. 3-Photo-c and Leinil Yu-c — 3.00
...: Men and Monsters TPB (9/03, $12.95) r/#7-10 — 13.00
...: Rediscovery TPB (2003, $9.95) r/#1-3 — 10.00
...: Return of the Phantom TPB (2003, $9.95) r/#4-6 — 10.00

KISS: THE PSYCHO CIRCUS
Image Comics: Aug, 1997 - No. 31, June, 2000 ($1.95/$2.25/$2.50)

	GD	VG	FN	VF	VF/NM	NM-
1-Holguin-s/Medina-a(p)	1	2	3	5	6	8
1-2nd & 3rd printings						2.50
2						5.00
3,4: 4-Photo-c						4.00
5-8: 5-Begin $2.25-c						3.00
9-29						2.50
30,31: 30-Begin $2.50-c						2.50
Book 1 TPB ('98, $12.95) r/#1-6						13.00
Book 2 Destroyer TPB (8/99, $9.95) r/#10-13						10.00
Book 3 Whispered Scream TPB ('00, $9.95) r/#7-9,18						10.00
...Magazine 1 ($6.95) r/#1-3 plus interviews						7.00
...Magazine 2-5 ($4.95) 2-r/#4,5 plus interviews. 3-r/#6,7. 4-r/#8,9						5.00
Wizard Edition ('98, supplement) Bios, tour preview and interviews						2.25

KISSING CHAOS
Oni Press: Sept, 2001 - No. 8, Mar, 2002 ($2.25, B&W, 6" x 9", limited series)

1-8-Arthur Dela Cruz-s/a — 2.25
...: 1000 Words (7/03, $2.99, regular comic-sized) — 3.00
TPB (9/02, $17.95) r/#1-8 — 18.00

KISSING CHAOS: NONSTOP BEAUTY
Oni Press: Oct, 2002 - No. 4, March, 2003 ($2.95, B&W, 6" x 9", limited series)

1-4-Arthur Dela Cruz-s/a — 3.00
TPB (9/03, $11.95) r/#1-4 — 12.00

KISS KISS BANG BANG
CrossGen Comics: Feb, 2004 - Present ($2.95)

1-Bedard-s/Perkins-a — 3.00

KISSYFUR (TV)
DC Comics: 1989 (Sept.) ($2.00, 52 pgs., one-shot)

1-Based on Saturday morning cartoon — 4.00

KIT CARSON (Formerly All True Detective Cases No. 4; Fighting Davy Crockett No. 9; see Blazing Sixguns & Frontier Fighters)
Avon Periodicals: 1950; No. 2, 8/51 - No. 3, 12/51; No. 5, 11-12/54 - No. 8, 9/55 (No #4)

	GD	VG	FN	VF	VF/NM	NM-
nn(#1) (1950)- "...Indian Scout" ; r-Cowboys 'N' Injuns #?	14	28	42	79	107	135
2(8/51)	10	20	30	56	73	90
3(12/51)- "...Fights the Comanche Raiders"	9	18	27	49	62	75
5-6,8(11-12/54-9/55): 5-Formerly All True Detective Cases (last pre-code); titled "...and the Trail of Doom"	8	16	24	46	58	70

Kitty Pryde, Agent of S.H.I.E.L.D. #3 © MAR

Kobalt #6 © Milestone Media

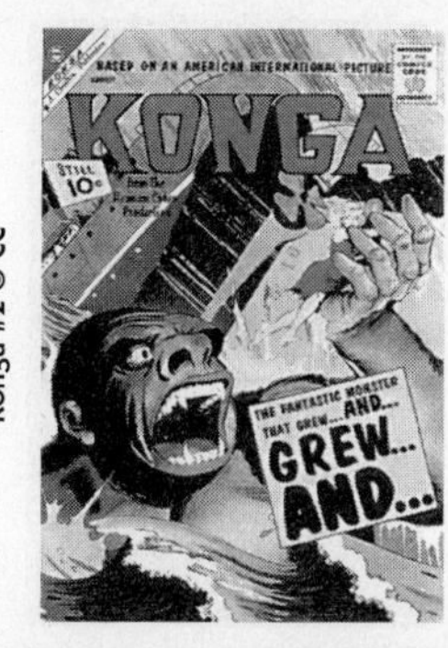

Konga #2 © CC

GD 2.0 VG 4.0 FN 6.0 VF 8.0 VF/NM 9.0 NM- 9.2

7-McCann-a? 8 16 24 46 58 70
I.W. Reprint #10('63)-r/Kit Carson #1; Severin-c 2 4 6 12 16 20
NOTE: *Kinstler c-1-3, 5-8.*

KIT CARSON & THE BLACKFEET WARRIORS
Realistic: 1953
nn-Reprint; Kinstler-c 9 18 27 54 70 85

KIT KARTER
Dell Publishing Co.: May-July, 1962
1 3 7 10 21 28 35

KITTY
St. John Publishing Co.: Oct, 1948
1-Teenage; Lily Renee-c/a 8 16 24 40 50 60

KITTY PRYDE, AGENT OF S.H.I.E.L.D. (Also see Excalibur and Mekanix)
Marvel Comics: Dec, 1997 - No. 3, Feb, 1998 ($2.50, limited series)
1-3-Hama-s 2.50

KITTY PRYDE AND WOLVERINE (Also see Uncanny X-Men & X-Men)
Marvel Comics Group: Nov, 1984 - No. 6, Apr, 1985 (Limited series)
1-6: Characters from X-Men 4.50

KLARER GIVEAWAYS (See Wisco in the Promotional Comics section)

KNIGHTHAWK
Acclaim Comics (Windjammer): Sept, 1995 - No. 6, Nov, 1995 ($2.50, lim. series)
1-6: 6-origin 2.50

KNIGHTMARE
Antarctic Press: July, 1994 - May, 1995 ($2.75, B&W, mature readers)
1-6 2.75

KNIGHTMARE
Image Comics (Extreme Studios): Feb, 1995 - No. 5, June, 1995 ($2.50)
0 ($3.50) 3.50
1-5: 4-Quesada & Palmiotti variant-c, 5-Flip book w/Warcry 2.50

KNIGHTS OF PENDRAGON, THE (Also see Pendragon)
Marvel Comics Ltd.: July, 1990 - No. 18, Dec, 1991 ($1.95)
1-18: 1-Capt. Britain app. 2,8-Free poster inside. 9,10-Bolton-c. 11,18-Iron Man app. 2.25

KNIGHTS OF THE ROUND TABLE
Dell Publishing Co.: No. 540, Mar, 1954
Four Color 540-Movie, photo-c 8 16 24 55 78 100

KNIGHTS OF THE ROUND TABLE
Pines Comics: No. 10, April, 1957
10 5 10 15 24 30 35

KNIGHTS OF THE ROUND TABLE
Dell Publishing Co.: Nov-Jan, 1963-64
1 (12-397-401)-Painted-c 4 8 12 24 32 40

KNIGHTSTRIKE (Also see Operation: Knightstrike)
Image Comics (Extreme Studios): Jan, 1996 ($2.50)
1-Rob Liefeld & Eric Stephenson story; Extreme Destroyer Part 6. 2.50

KNIGHT WATCHMAN (See Big Bang Comics & Dr. Weird)
Image Comics: June, 1998 - No. 4, Oct, 1998 ($2.95/$3.50, B&W, lim. series)
1-3-Ben Torres-c/a in all 3.00
4-($3.50) 3.50

KNIGHT WATCHMAN: GRAVEYARD SHIFT
Caliber Press: 1994 ($2.95, B&W)
1,2-Ben Torres-a 3.00

KNOCK KNOCK (...Who's There?)
Whitman Publ./Gerona Publications: No. 801, 1936 (52 pgs.) (8x9", B&W)
801-Joke book; Bob Dunn-a 8 16 24 46 58 70

KNOCKOUT ADVENTURES
Fiction House Magazines: Winter, 1953-54
1-Reprints Fight Comics #53 w/Rip Carson-c/s 14 28 42 79 107 135

KNUCKLES (Spin-off of Sonic the Hedgehog)
Archie Publications: Apr, 1997 - Present ($1.50/$1.75/$1.79)
1-29 2.25

KNUCKLES' CHAOTIX
Archie Publications: Jan, 1996 ($2.00, annual)

GD 2.0 VG 4.0 FN 6.0 VF 8.0 VF/NM 9.0 NM- 9.2

1 3.00

KOBALT
DC Comics (Milestone): June, 1994 - No. 16, Sept, 1995 ($1.75/$2.50)
1-16: 1-Byrne-c. 4-Intro Page. 16-Kent Williams-c 2.50

KOBRA (Unpublished #8 appears in DC Special Series No. 1)
National Periodical Publications: Feb-Mar, 1976 - No. 7, Mar-Apr, 1977
1-1st app.; Kirby-a redrawn by Marcos; only 25¢-c 1 3 4 6 8 10
2-7: (All 30¢ issues) 3-Giffen-a 6.00
NOTE: *Austin a-3i. Buckler a-5p; c-5p. Kubert c-4. Nasser a-6p, 7; c-7.*

KOKEY KOALA (...and the Magic Button)
Toby Press: May, 1952
1 11 22 33 63 84 105

KOKO AND KOLA (Also see A-1 Comics #16 & Tick Tock Tales)
Com/Magazine Enterprises: Fall, 1946 - No. 5, May, 1947; No. 6, 1950
1-Funny animal 11 22 33 63 84 105
2-X-Mas-c 8 16 24 40 50 60
3-6: 6(A-1 28) 7 14 21 35 43 50

KO KOMICS
Gerona Publications: Oct, 1945 (scarce)
1-The Duke of Darkness & The Menace (hero) 70 140 210 438 657 875

KOLCHAK: THE NIGHT STALKER (TV)
Moonstone: 2002 - Present ($6.50/$6.95)
1-($6.50) Jeff Rice-s/Gordon Purcell-a 6.50
... Devil in the Details (2003, $6.95) Trevor Von Eeden-a 7.00
... Fever Pitch (2002, $6.95) Christopher Jones-a 7.00
... Get of Belial (2002, $6.95) Art Nichols-a 7.00
... Lambs to the Slaughter (2003, $6.95) Trevor Von Eeden-a 7.00
... Tales of the Night Stalker (2003, $3.50) two covers by Moore & Ulanski; Marrinan-a 3.50

KOMIC KARTOONS
Timely Comics (EPC): Fall, 1945 - No. 2, Winter, 1945
1,2-Andy Wolf, Bertie Mouse 20 40 60 112 156 200

KOMIK PAGES (Formerly Snap; becomes Bullseye #11)
Harry 'A' Chesler, Jr. (Our Army, Inc.): Apr, 1945 (All reprints)
10(#1 on inside)-Land O' Nod by Rick Yager (2 pgs.), Animal Crackers, Foxy GrandPa, Tom, Dick & Mary, Cheerio Minstrels, Red Starr plus other 1-2 pg. strips; Cole-a 24 48 72 135 190 245

KONA (...Monarch of Monster Isle)
Dell Publishing Co.: Feb-Apr, 1962 - No. 21, Jan-Mar, 1967 (Painted-c)
Four Color 1256 (#1) 9 18 27 60 85 110
2-10: 4-Anak begins. 6-Gil Kane-c 5 10 15 33 44 55
11-21 4 8 12 24 32 40
NOTE: *Glanzman a-all issues.*

KONGA (Fantastic Giants No. 24) (See Return of...)
Charlton Comics: 1960; No. 2, Aug, 1961 - No. 23, Nov, 1965
1(1960)-Based on movie; Giordano-c 25 50 75 176 258 340
2-5: 2-Giordano-c; no Ditko-a 11 22 33 77 114 150
6-15 9 18 27 65 93 120
16-23 6 12 18 38 52 65
NOTE: *Ditko a-1, 3-15; c-4, 6-9. Glanzman a-12. Montes & Bache a-16-23.*

KONGA'S REVENGE (Formerly Return of...)
Charlton Comics: No. 2, Summer, 1963 - No. 3, Fall, 1964; Dec, 1968
2,3: 2-Ditko-c/a 7 14 21 46 63 80
1(12/68)-Reprints Konga's Revenge #3 3 6 9 19 25 32

KONG THE UNTAMED
National Periodical Publications: June-July, 1975 - V2#5, Feb-Mar, 1976
1-1st app. Kong; Wrightson-c; Alcala-a 2 4 6 8 10 12
2-Wrightson-c; Alcala-a 1 2 3 5 7 9
3-5: 3-Alcala-a 5.00

KOOKIE
Dell Publishing Co.: Feb-Apr, 1962 - No. 2, May-July, 1962 (15 cents)
1-Written by John Stanley; Bill Williams-a 9 18 27 65 93 120
2 8 16 24 58 82 105

KOOSH KINS
Archie Comics: Oct, 1991 - No. 3, Feb, 1992 ($1.00, bi-monthly, limited series)
1-3 2.25

Kore #2 © Devil's Due Publ. Inc.

Krofft Supershow #1 © Sid & Marty Krofft TV Prod.

Kull and the Barbarians #1 © MAR

GD 2.0 | VG 4.0 | FN 6.0 | VF 8.0 | VF/NM 9.0 | NM- 9.2

NOTE: *No. 4 was planned, but cancelled.*

KORAK, SON OF TARZAN (Edgar Rice Burroughs)(See Tarzan #139)
Gold Key: Jan, 1964 - No. 45, Jan, 1972 (Painted-c No. 1-?)

1-Russ Manning-a 8 16 24 55 78 100
2-11-Russ Manning-a 4 8 12 29 40 50
12-23: 12,13-Warren Tufts-a. 14-Jon of the Kalahari ends. 15-Mabu, Jungle Boy begins. 21-Manning-a. 23-Last 12¢ issue 4 8 12 24 32 40
24-30 3 6 9 18 24 30
31-45 2 4 6 14 18 22

KORAK, SON OF TARZAN (Tarzan Family #60 on; see Tarzan #230)
National Periodical Publications: V9#46, May-June, 1972 - V12#56, Feb-Mar, 1974; No. 57, May-June, 1975 - No. 59, Sept-Oct, 1975 (Edgar Rice Burroughs)

46-(52 pgs.)-Carson of Venus begins (origin), ends #56; Pellucidar feature; Weiss-a 2 4 6 12 16 20
47-59: 49-Origin Korak retold 1 2 3 5 7 9

NOTE: *All have covers by **Joe Kubert**. **Manning** strip reprints-No. 57-59. **Murphy Anderson** a-52. **Michael Kaluta** a-46-56. **Frank Thorne** a-46-51.*

KORE
Image Comics: Apr, 2003 - No. 5, Sept, 2003 ($2.95)

1-5: 1-Two covers by Capullo and Seeley; Seeley-a (p) 3.00

KORG: 70,000 B. C. (TV)
Charlton Publications: May, 1975 - No. 9, Nov, 1976 (Hanna-Barbera)

1,2: 1-Boyette-c/a. 2-Painted-c; Byrne text illos 2 4 6 11 14 18
3-9 2 4 6 8 10 12

KORNER KID COMICS: Four Star Publications: 1947 (Advertised, not pub.)

KOSMIC KAT ACTIVITY BOOK (See Deity)
Image Comics: Aug, 1999 ($2.95, one-shot)

1-Stories and games by various 3.00

KRAZY KAT
Holt: 1946 (Hardcover)

Reprints daily & Sunday strips by Herriman 60 120 180 375 563 750
dust jacket only 46 92 138 276 413 550

KRAZY KAT (See Ace Comics & March of Comics No. 72, 87)

KRAZY KAT COMICS (...& Ignatz the Mouse early issues)
Dell Publ. Co./Gold Key: May-June, 1951 - F.C. #696, Apr, 1956; Jan, 1964 (None by Herriman)

1(1951) 9 18 27 60 85 110
2-5 (#5, 8-10/52) 5 10 15 36 48 60
Four Color 454,504 5 10 15 33 44 55
Four Color 548,619,696 (4/56) 4 8 12 29 40 50
1(10098-401)(1/64-Gold Key)(TV) 4 8 12 29 40 50

KRAZY KOMICS (1st Series) (Cindy Comics No. 27 on) (Also see Ziggy Pig)
Timely Comics (USA No. 1-21/JPC No. 22-26): July, 1942 - No. 26, Spr, 1947

1-Toughy Tomcat, Ziggy Pig (by Jaffee) & Silly Seal begin 58 116 174 363 544 725
2 28 56 84 159 225 290
3-8,10 20 40 60 112 156 200
9-Hitler parody 21 42 63 118 164 210
11,13,14 14 28 42 81 111 140
12-Timely's entire art staff drew themselves into a Creeper story 26 52 78 147 206 265
15-(8-9/44)-Becomes Funny Tunes #16; has "Super Soldier" by Pfc. Stan Lee 14 28 42 81 111 140
16-24,26: 16-(10-11/44). 26-Super Rabbit-c/story 12 24 36 69 92 115
25-Wacky Duck-c/story & begin; Kurtzman-a (6pgs.) 14 28 42 81 111 140

KRAZY KOMICS (2nd Series)
Timely/Marvel Comics: Aug, 1948 - No. 2, Nov, 1948

1-Wolverton (10 pgs.) & Kurtzman (8 pgs.)-a; Eustice Hayseed begins (Li'l Abner swipe) 42 84 126 252 376 500
2-Wolverton-a (10 pgs.); Powerhouse Pepper cameo 33 66 99 190 270 350

KRAZY KROW (Also see Dopey Duck, Film Funnies, Funny Frolics & Movie Tunes)
Marvel Comics (ZPC): Summer, 1945 - No. 3, Wint, 1945/46

1 21 42 63 118 164 210
2,3 13 26 39 74 100 125
I.W. Reprint #1('57), 2('58), 7 2 4 6 12 16 20

KRAZYLIFE (Becomes Nutty Life #2)
Fox Feature Syndicate: 1945 (no month)

1-Funny animal 18 36 54 104 142 180

GD 2.0 | VG 4.0 | FN 6.0 | VF 8.0 | VF/NM 9.0 | NM- 9.2

KREE/SKRULL WAR STARRING THE AVENGERS, THE
Marvel Comics: Sept, 1983 - No. 2, Oct, 1983 ($2.50, 68 pgs., Baxter paper)

1,2 4.00

NOTE: ***Neal Adams** p-1r, 2. **Buscema** a-1r, 2r. **Simonson** a-1p; c-1p.*

KROFFT SUPERSHOW (TV)
Gold Key: Apr, 1978 - No. 6, Jan, 1979

1-Photo-c 3 6 9 18 23 28
2-6: 6-Photo-c 2 4 6 11 14 18

KRULL
Marvel Comics Group: Nov, 1983 - No. 2, Dec, 1983

1,2-Adaptation of film; r/Marvel Super Special. 1-Photo-c from movie 2.50

KRUSTY COMICS (TV)(See Simpsons Comics)
Bongo Comics: 1995 - No. 3, 1995 ($2.25, limited series)

1-3 2.50

KRYPTON CHRONICLES
DC Comics: Sept, 1981 - No. 3, Nov, 1981

1-3: 1-Buckler-c(p) 4.00

KULL AND THE BARBARIANS
Marvel Comics: May, 1975 - No. 3, Sept, 1975 ($1.00, B&W, magazine)

1-(84 pgs.) Andru/Wood-r/Kull #1; 2 pgs. Neal Adams; Gil Kane(p), Marie & John Severin-a(r); Krenkel text illo. 2 4 6 11 14 18
2,3: 2-(84 pgs.) Red Sonja by Chaykin begins; Solomon Kane by Weiss/Adams; Gil Kane-a; Solomon Kane pin-up by Wrightson. 3-(76 pgs.) Origin Red Sonja by Chaykin; Adams-a; Solomon Kane app. 2 4 6 9 11 14

KULL THE CONQUEROR (...the Destroyer #11 on; see Conan #1, Creatures on the Loose #10, Marvel Preview, Monsters on the Prowl)
Marvel Comics Group: June, 1971 - No. 2, Sept, 1971; No. 3, July, 1972 - No. 15, Aug, 1974; No. 16, Aug, 1976 - No. 29, Oct, 1978

1-Andru/Wood-a; 2nd app. & origin Kull; 15¢ issue 4 8 12 27 36 45
2-5: 2-3rd Kull app. Last 15¢ iss. 3-13: 20¢ issues 2 4 6 11 14 18
6-10 2 4 6 8 10 12
11-15: 11-15-Ploog-a. 14,15: 25¢ issues 1 2 3 5 7 9
16-(Regular 25¢ edition)(8/76) 1 2 3 4 5 7
16-(30¢-c variant, limited distribution) 1 3 4 6 8 10
17-29: 21-23-(Reg. 30¢ editions) 1 2 3 4 5 7
21-23-(35¢-c variants, limited distribution) 1 3 4 6 8 10

NOTE: *No. 1, 2, 7-9, 11 are based on Robert E. Howard stories. **Alcala** a-17p, 18-20i; c-24. **Ditko** a-12r, 15r. **Gil Kane** c-15p, 21. **Nebres** a-22i-27i; c-25i, 27i. **Ploog** c-11, 12p, 13. **Severin** a-2-9i; c-2-10i, 19. **Starlin** c-14.*

KULL THE CONQUEROR
Marvel Comics Group: Dec, 1982 - No. 2, Mar, 1983 (52 pgs., Baxter paper)

1,2: 1-Buscema-a(p) 4.00

KULL THE CONQUEROR (No. 9,10 titled "Kull")
Marvel Comics Group: 5/83 - No. 10, 6/85 (52 pgs., Baxter paper)

V3#1-10: Buscema-a in #1-3,5-10 3.00

NOTE: *Bolton a-4. Golden painted c-3-8. Guice a-4p. Sienkiwicz a-4; c-2.*

KUNG FU (See Deadly Hands of..., & Master of...)

KUNG FU FIGHTER (See Richard Dragon...)

KURT BUSIEK'S ASTRO CITY (Limited series) (Also see Astro City: Local Heroes)
Image Comics (Juke Box Productions): Aug, 1995 - No. 6, Jan, 1996 ($2.25)

1-Kurt Busiek scripts, Brent Anderson-a & Alex Ross front & back-c begins; 1st app. Samaritan & Honor Guard (Cleopatra, MHP, Beautie, The Black Rapier, Quarrel & N-Forcer) 2 4 6 8 10 12
2-6: 2-1st app. The Silver Agent, The Old Soldier, & the "original" Honor Guard (Max O'Millions, Starwoman, the "original" Cleopatra, the "original" N-Forcer, the Bouncing Beatnik, Leopardman & Kitkat). 3-1st app. Jack-in-the-Box & The Deacon. 4-1st app. Winged Victory (cameo), The Hanged Man & The First Family. 5-1st app. Crackerjack, The Astro City Irregulars, Nightingale & Sunbird. 6-Origin Samaritan; 1st full app. Winged Victory 1 3 4 6 8 10
Life In The Big City-(8/96, $19.95, trade paperback)-r/Image Comics limited series w/sketchbook & cover gallery; Ross-c 20.00
Life In The Big City-(8/96, $49.95, hardcover, 1000 print run)-r/Image Comics limited series w/sketchbook & cover gallery; Ross-c 50.00

KURT BUSIEK'S ASTRO CITY (1st Homage Comics series)
Image Comics (Homage Comics): V2#1, Sept, 1996 - No. 15, Dec, 1998;
DC Comics (Homage Comics): No. 16, Mar, 1999 - No. 22, Aug, 2000 ($2.50)

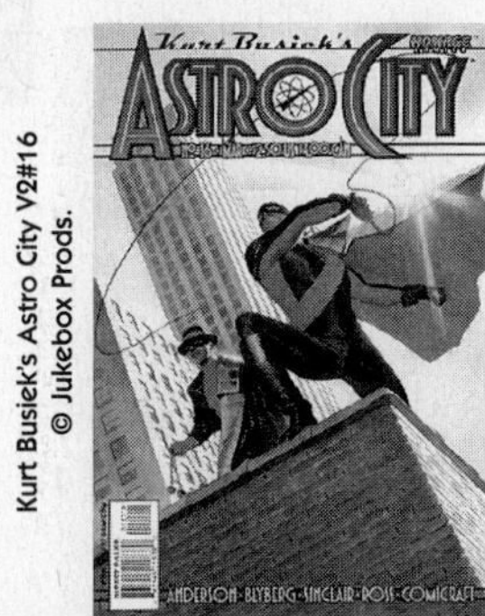

Kurt Busiek's Astro City V2#16 © Jukebox Prods.

Lab Rats #3 © John Byrne

Lady Death: The Gauntlet #1 © Chaos!

	GD 2.0	VG 4.0	FN 6.0	VF 8.0	VF/NM 9.0	NM- 9.2
1/2-(10/96)-The Hanged Man story; 1st app. The All-American & Slugger, The Lamplighter, The Time-Keeper & Eterneon	1	3	4	6	8	10
1/2-(1/98) 2nd printing w/new cover						2.50
1- Kurt Busiek scripts, Alex Ross-c, Brent Anderson-p & Will Blyberg-i begin; intro The Gentleman, Thunderhead & Helia.	1	2	3	5	6	8
1-(12/97, $4.95) "3-D Edition" w/glasses						5.00
2-Origin The First Family; Astra story	1	2	3	4	5	7
3-5: 4-1st app. The Crossbreed, Ironhorse, Glue Gun & The Confessor (cameo)						6.00
6-10						5.00
11-22: 14-20-Steeljack story arc. 16-(3/99) First DC issue						2.50
TPB-($19.95) Ross-c, r/#4-9, #1/2 w/sketchbook						20.00
Family Album TPB ($19.95) r/#1-3,10-13						20.00
The Tarnished Angel HC ($29.95) r/#14-20; new Ross dust jacket; sketch pages by Anderson & Ross; cover gallery with reference photos						30.00
The Tarnished Angel SC ($19.95) r/#14-20; new Ross-c						20.00

LABMAN
Image Comics: Nov, 1996 ($3.50, one-shot)

	GD	VG	FN	VF	VF/NM	NM-
1-Allred-c						4.00

LAB RATS
DC Comics: June, 2002 - No. 8, Jan, 2003 ($2.50)

	GD	VG	FN	VF	VF/NM	NM-
1-8-John Byrne-s/a. 5,6-Superman app.						2.50

LABYRINTH
Marvel Comics Group: Nov, 1986 - No. 3, Jan, 1987 (Limited series)

	GD	VG	FN	VF	VF/NM	NM-
1-3: David Bowie movie adaptation; r/Marvel Super Special #40						4.00

LA COSA NOSTROID (See Scud: The Disposible Assassin)
Fireman Press: Mar, 1996 - No. 9, 1998 ($2.95, B&W)

	GD	VG	FN	VF	VF/NM	NM-
1-9-Dan Harmon-s/Rob Schrab-c/a						3.00

LAD: A DOG (Movie)
Dell Publishing Co.: 1961 - No. 2, July-Sept, 1962

	GD	VG	FN	VF	VF/NM	NM-
Four Color 1303	5	10	15	33	44	55
2	4	8	12	28	38	48

LADY AND THE TRAMP (Disney, See Dell Giants & Movie Comics)
Dell Publishing Co.: No. 629, May, 1955 - No. 634, June, 1955

	GD	VG	FN	VF	VF/NM	NM-
Four Color 629 (#1)-..with Jock	8	16	24	55	78	100
Four Color 634-...Album	6	12	18	38	52	65

LADY COP (See 1st Issue Special)

LADY DEATH (See Evil Ernie)
Chaos! Comics: Jan, 1994 - No. 3, Mar, 1994 ($2.75, limited series)

	GD	VG	FN	VF	VF/NM	NM-
1/2-S. Hughes-c/a in all, 1/2 Velvet	1	2	3	4	5	7
1/2 Gold	1	3	4	6	8	10
1/2 Signed Limited Edition	2	4	6	8	10	12
1-($3.50)-Chromium-c	2	4	6	11	14	18
1-Commemorative	2	4	6	10	13	16
1-(9/96, $2.95) "Encore Presentation"; r/#1						3.00
2	1	2	3	5	6	8
3						5.00
... And Jade (4/02, $2.99) Augustyn-s/Reis-a						3.00
...And The Women of Chaos! Gallery #1 (11/96, $2.25) pin-ups by various						3.00
.../Bad Kitty (9/01, $2.99) Mota-c/a						3.00
.../Bedlam (6/02, $2.99) Augustyn-s/Reis-c						3.00
...By Steven Hughes (6/00, $2.95) Tribute issue to Steven Hughes						3.00
...By Steven Hughes Deluxe Edition(6/00, $15.95)						16.00
.../Chastity (1/02, $2.99) Mota-c/a; Augustyn-s						3.00
...Death Becomes Her #0 (11/97, $2.95) Hughes-c/a						3.00
...FAN Edition: All Hallow's Eve #1 (1/97, mail-in)						5.00
...In Lingerie #1 (8/95, $2.95) pin-ups, wraparound-c						3.00
...In Lingerie #1-Leather Edition (10,000)						12.00
...In Lingerie #1-Micro Premium Edition; Lady Demon-c (2,000)						35.00
...: Love Bites (3/01, $2.99) Kaminski-s/Luke Ross-a						3.00
.../Medieval Witchblade (8/01, $3.50) covers by Molenaar and Silvestri						3.50
.../Medieval Witchblade Preview Ed. (8/01, $1.99) Molenaar-c						2.25
...: Mischief Night (11/01, $2.99) Ostrander-s/Reis-a						3.00
...: Re-Imagined (7/02, $2.99) Gossett-c						3.00
...: River of Fear (4/01, $2.99) Bennett-a(p)/Cleavenger-c						3.00
...Swimsuit Special #1-($2.50)-Wraparound-c						3.00
...Swimsuit Special #1-Red velvet-c						14.00
...Swimsuit 2001 #1-(2/01, $2.99)-Reis-c; art by various						3.00
...: The Reckoning (7/94, $6.95)-r/#1-3						7.00
...: The Reckoning (8/95, $12.95)- new printing including Lady Death 1/2 & Swimsuit Special #1						13.00
.../Vampirella (3/99, $3.50) Hughes-c/a						3.50
.../Vampirella 2 (3/00, $3.50) Deodato-c/a						3.50
... Vs. Purgatori (12/99, $3.50) Deodato-a						3.50
... Vs. Vampirella Preview (2/00, $1.00) Deodato-a/c						2.25

LADY DEATH (Ongoing series)
Chaos! Comics: Feb, 1998 - No. 16, May, 1999 ($2.95)

	GD	VG	FN	VF	VF/NM	NM-
1-16: 1-4: Pulido-s/Hughes-c/a. 5-8,13-16-Deodato-a. 9-11-Hughes-a						3.00
...Retribution (8/98, $2.95) Jadsen-a						3.00
...Retribution Premium Ed.						6.00

LADY DEATH: ALIVE
Chaos! Comics: May, 2001 - No. 4, Aug, 2001 ($2.99, limited series)

	GD	VG	FN	VF	VF/NM	NM-
1-4-Ivan Reis-a; Lady Death becomes mortal						3.00

LADY DEATH: A MEDIEVAL TALE (Brian Pulido's...)
CG Entertainment: Mar, 2003 - Present ($2.95)

	GD	VG	FN	VF	VF/NM	NM-
1-12: 1-Brian Pulido-s/Ivan Reis-a; Lady Death in the CrossGen Universe						3.00
Vol.1 TPB (2003, $9.95) digest-sized reprint of #1-6						10.00

LADY DEATH: DARK ALLIANCE
Chaos! Comics: July, 2002 - No. 5, ($2.99, limited series)

	GD	VG	FN	VF	VF/NM	NM-
1-3-Reis-a/Ostrander-s						3.00

LADY DEATH: DARK MILLENNIUM
Chaos! Comics: Feb, 2000 - No. 3, Apr, 2000 ($2.95, limited series)

	GD	VG	FN	VF	VF/NM	NM-
Preview (6/00, $5.00)						5.00
1-3-Ivan Reis-a						3.00

LADY DEATH: GODDESS RETURNS
Chaos! Comics: Jun, 2002 - No. 2, Aug, 2002 ($2.99, limited series)

	GD	VG	FN	VF	VF/NM	NM-
1,2-Mota-a/Ostrander-s						3.00

LADY DEATH: HEARTBREAKER
Chaos! Comics: Mar, 2002 - No. 4, ($2.99, limited series)

	GD	VG	FN	VF	VF/NM	NM-
1-Molenaar-a/Ostrander-s						3.00

LADY DEATH: JUDGEMENT WAR
Chaos! Comics: Nov, 1999 - No. 3, Jan, 2000 ($2.95, limited series)

	GD	VG	FN	VF	VF/NM	NM-
Prelude (10/99) two covers						3.00
1-3-Ivan Reis-a						3.00

LADY DEATH: LAST RITES
Chaos! Comics: Oct, 2001 - No. 4, Feb, 2001 ($2.99, limited series)

	GD	VG	FN	VF	VF/NM	NM-
1-4-Ivan Reis-a/Ostrander-s						3.00

LADY DEATH: THE CRUCIBLE
Chaos! Comics: Nov, 1996 - No. 6, Oct, 1997 ($3.50/$2.95, limited series)

	GD	VG	FN	VF	VF/NM	NM-
1/2						4.00
1/2 Cloth Edition						8.00
1-Wraparound silver foil embossed-c						4.00
2-6-($2.95)						3.00

LADY DEATH: THE GAUNTLET
Chaos! Comics: Apr, 2002 - No. 2, May, 2002 ($2.99, limited series)

	GD	VG	FN	VF	VF/NM	NM-
1,2: 1-J. Scott Campbell-c/redesign of Lady Death's outfit; Mota-a						3.00

LADY DEATH: THE ODYSSEY
Chaos! Comics: Apr, 1996 - No. 4, Aug, 1996 ($3.50/$2.95)

	GD	VG	FN	VF	VF/NM	NM-
1-($1.50)-Sneak Peek Preview						2.25
1-($1.50)-Sneak Peek Preview Micro Premium Edition (2500 print run)	2	4	6	8	10	12
1-($3.50)-Embossed, wraparound goil foil-c						5.00
1-Black Onyx Edition (200 print run)	7	14	21	46	63	80
1-($19.95)-Premium Edition (10,000 print run)						20.00
2-4-($2.95)						3.00

LADY DEATH: THE RAPTURE
Chaos! Comics: Jun, 1999 - No. 4, Sept, 1999 ($2.95, limited series)

	GD	VG	FN	VF	VF/NM	NM-
1-4-Ivan Reis-c/a; Pulido-s						3.00

LADY DEATH: TRIBULATION
Chaos! Comics: Dec, 2000 - No. 4, Mar, 2001 ($2.95, limited series)

	GD	VG	FN	VF	VF/NM	NM-
1-4-Ivan Reis-a; Kaminski-s						3.00

LADY DEATH II: BETWEEN HEAVEN & HELL
Chaos! Comics: Mar, 1995 - No. 4, July, 1995 ($3.50, limited series)

	GD	VG	FN	VF	VF/NM	NM-
1-Chromium wraparound-c; Evil Ernie cameo						5.00

Lady Luck #88 © QUA

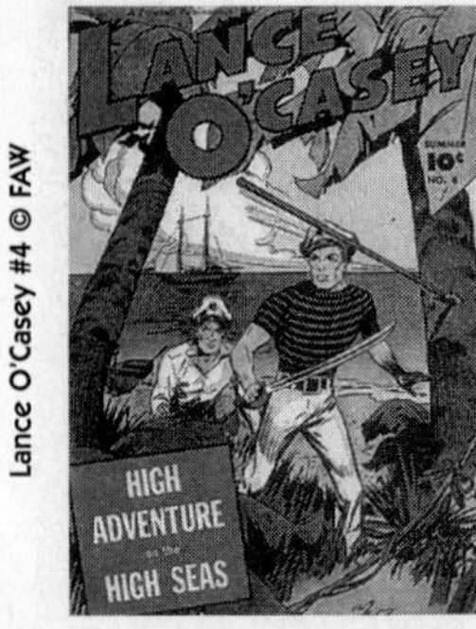

Lance O'Casey #4 © FAW

Large Feature Comic #8 © Chicago Tribune

	GD 2.0	VG 4.0	FN 6.0	VF 8.0	VF/NM 9.0	NM- 9.2
1-Commemorative (4,000), 1-Black Velvet-c	2	4	6	11	14	18
1-Gold	1	3	4	6	8	10
1-"Refractor" edition (5,000)	2	4	6	12	16	20
2-4						3.50
4-Lady Demon variant-c	1	2	3	5	7	9
Trade paperback-($12.95)-r/#1-4						13.00

LADY DEMON
Chaos! Comics: Mar, 2000 - No. 3, May, 2000 ($2.95, limited series)

	GD	VG	FN	VF	VF/NM	NM-
1-3-Kaminski-s/Brewer-a						3.00
1-Premium Edition						10.00

LADY FOR A NIGHT (See Cinema Comics Herald)

LADY JUSTICE (See Neil Gaiman's...)

LADY LUCK (Formerly Smash #1-85) (Also see Spirit Sections #1)
Quality Comics Group: No. 86, Dec, 1949 - No. 90, Aug, 1950

	GD	VG	FN	VF	VF/NM	NM-
86(#1)	88	176	264	550	825	1100
87-90	64	128	192	400	600	800

LADY PENDRAGON
Maximum Press: Mar, 1996 ($2.50)

	GD	VG	FN	VF	VF/NM	NM-
1-Matt Hawkins script						2.50

LADY PENDRAGON
Image Comics: Nov, 1998 - No. 3, Jan, 1999 ($2.50, mini-series)

	GD	VG	FN	VF	VF/NM	NM-
Preview (6/98) Flip book w/ Deity preview						3.00
1-3: 1-Matt Hawkins-s/Stinsman-a						3.00
1-($6.95) DF Ed. with variant-c by Jusko						7.00
2-($4.95)Variant edition						5.00
0-(3/99) Origin; flip book						2.50

LADY PENDRAGON (Volume 3)
Image Comics: Apr, 1999 - No. 9, Mar, 2000 ($2.50, mini-series)

	GD	VG	FN	VF	VF/NM	NM-
1,2,4-6,8-10: 1-Matt Hawkins-s/Stinsman-a. 2-Peterson-c						2.50
3-Flip book w/Alley Cat preview (1st app.)						3.00
7-($3.95) Flip book; Stinsman-a/Cleavenger painted-a						4.00
Gallery Edition (10/99, $2.95) pin-ups						3.00
...Merlin (1/00, $2.95) Stinsman-a						3.00

LADY PENDRAGON/ MORE THAN MORTAL
Image Comics: May, 1999 ($2.50, one-shot)

	GD	VG	FN	VF	VF/NM	NM-
Preview (2/99) Diamond Dateline suppl.						2.25
1-Scott-s/Norton-a; 2 covers by Norton & Finch						2.50

LADY RAWHIDE
Topps Comics: July, 1995 - No. 5, Mar, 1996 ($2.95, bi-monthly, limited series)

	GD	VG	FN	VF	VF/NM	NM-
1-5: Don McGregor scripts & Mayhew-a. in all. 2-Stelfreeze-c. 3-Hughes-c. 4-Golden-c. 5-Julie Bell-c.						3.00
It Can't Happen Here TPB (8/99, $16.95) r/#1-5						17.00
Mini Comic 1 (7/95) Maroto-a; Zorro app.						2.25
Special Edition 1 (6/95, $3.95)-Reprints						4.00

LADY RAWHIDE (Volume 2)
Topps Comics: Oct, 1996 -No. 5, June, 1997 ($2.95, limited series)

	GD	VG	FN	VF	VF/NM	NM-
1-5: 1-Julie Bell-c.						3.00

LADY RAWHIDE OTHER PEOPLE'S BLOOD (ZORRO'S ...)
Image Comics: Mar, 1999 - No. 5, July, 1999 ($2.95, B&W)

	GD	VG	FN	VF	VF/NM	NM-
1-5-Reprints Lady Rawhide series in B&W						3.00

LADY SUPREME (See Asylum)(Also see Supreme & Kid Supreme)
Image Comics (Extreme): May, 1996 - No. 2, June, 1996 ($2.50, limited series)

	GD	VG	FN	VF	VF/NM	NM-
1,2-Terry Moore -s: 1-Terry Moore-c. 2-Flip book w/Newmen preview						2.50

LAFF-A-LYMPICS (TV)(See The Funtastic World of Hanna-Barbera)
Marvel Comics: Mar, 1978 - No. 13, Mar, 1979 (Newsstand sales only)

	GD	VG	FN	VF	VF/NM	NM-
1-Yogi Bear, Scooby Doo, Pixie & Dixie, etc.	3	6	9	18	24	30
2-8	2	4	6	12	16	20
9-13: 11-Jetsons x-over; 1 pg. illustrated bio of Mighty Mightor, Herculoids, Shazzan, Galaxy Trio & Space Ghost	3	6	9	16	20	25

LAFFY-DAFFY COMICS
Rural Home Publ. Co.: Feb, 1945 - No. 2, Mar, 1945

	GD	VG	FN	VF	VF/NM	NM-
1,2-Funny animal	9	18	27	54	70	85

LANA (Little Lana No. 8 on)
Marvel Comics (MjMC): Aug, 1948 - No. 7, Aug, 1949 (Also see Annie Oakley)

	GD	VG	FN	VF	VF/NM	NM-
1-Rusty, Millie begin	21	42	63	118	164	210
2-Kurtzman's "Hey Look" (1); last Rusty	12	24	36	69	92	115
3-7: 3-Nellie begins	9	18	27	52	66	80

LANCELOT & GUINEVERE (See Movie Classics)

LANCELOT LINK, SECRET CHIMP (TV)
Gold Key: Apr, 1971 - No. 8, Feb, 1973

	GD	VG	FN	VF	VF/NM	NM-
1-Photo-c	7	14	21	50	68	85
2-8: 2-Photo-c	4	8	12	27	36	45

LANCELOT STRONG (See The Shield)

LANCE O'CASEY (See Mighty Midget & Whiz Comics)
Fawcett Publications: Spring, 1946 - No. 3, Fall, 1946; No. 4, Summer, 1948

	GD	VG	FN	VF	VF/NM	NM-
1-Captain Marvel app. on-c	36	72	108	204	290	375
2	24	48	72	135	190	245
3,4	18	36	54	101	138	175

NOTE: *The cover for the 1st issue was done in 1942 but was not published until 1946. The cover shows 68 pages but actually has only 36 pages.*

LANCER (TV)(Western)
Gold Key: Feb, 1969 - No. 3, Sept, 1969 (All photo-c)

	GD	VG	FN	VF	VF/NM	NM-
1	4	8	12	28	38	48
2,3	3	6	9	19	25	32

LAND OF NOD, THE
Dark Horse Comics: July, 1997 - No. 3, Feb, 1998 ($2.95, B&W)

	GD	VG	FN	VF	VF/NM	NM-
1-3-Jetcat; Jay Stephens-s/a						3.00

LAND OF OZ
Arrow Comics: 1998 - No. 9 ($2.95, B&W)

	GD	VG	FN	VF	VF/NM	NM-
1-9-Bishop-s/Bryan-s/a						3.00

LAND OF THE GIANTS (TV)
Gold Key: Nov, 1968 - No. 5, Sept, 1969 (All have photo-c)

	GD	VG	FN	VF	VF/NM	NM-
1	7	14	21	50	68	85
2-5	4	8	12	29	40	50

LAND OF THE LOST COMICS (Radio)
E. C. Comics: July-Aug, 1946 - No. 9, Spring, 1948

	GD	VG	FN	VF	VF/NM	NM-
1	37	74	111	213	299	385
2	24	48	72	138	194	250
3-9	20	40	60	112	156	200

LAND UNKNOWN, THE (Movie)
Dell Publishing Co.: No. 845, Sept, 1957

	GD	VG	FN	VF	VF/NM	NM-
Four Color 845-Alex Toth-a	13	26	39	90	133	175

LA PACIFICA
DC Comics (Paradox Press): 1994/1995 ($4.95, B&W, limited series, digest size, mature readers)

	GD	VG	FN	VF	VF/NM	NM-
1-3						5.00

LARAMIE (TV)
Dell Publishing Co.: Aug, 1960 - July, 1962 (All photo-c)

	GD	VG	FN	VF	VF/NM	NM-
Four Color 1125-Gil Kane/Heath-a	10	20	30	70	100	130
Four Color 1223,1284, 01-418-207 (7/62)	7	14	21	51	71	90

LAREDO (TV)
Gold Key: June, 1966

	GD	VG	FN	VF	VF/NM	NM-
1 (10179-606)-Photo-c	4	8	12	25	33	42

LARGE FEATURE COMIC (Formerly called Black & White in previous guides)
Dell Publishing Co.: 1939 - No. 13, 1943

Note: See individual alphabetical listings for prices

1 (Series I)-Dick Tracy Meets the Blank
3-Heigh-Yo Silver! The Lone Ranger (text & ill.)(76 pgs.); also exists as a Whitman #710; based on radio
6-Terry & the Pirates & The Dragon Lady; reprints dailies from 1936
8-Dick Tracy the Racket Buster
9-King of the Royal Mounted (Zane Grey's...)
10-(Scarce)-Gang Busters (No. appears on inside front cover); first slick cover (based on radio program)
13-Dick Tracy and Scottie of Scotland Yard
15-Dick Tracy and the Kidnapped Princes
17-Gang Busters (1941)
2-Terry and the Pirates (#1)
4-Dick Tracy Gets His Man
5-Tarzan of the Apes (#1) by Harold Foster (origin); reprints 1st Tarzan dailies from 1929
7-(Scarce, 52 pgs.)-Hi-Yo Silver the Lone Ranger to the Rescue; also exists as a Whitman #715, based on radio program
11-Dick Tracy Foils the Mad Doc Hump
12-Smilin' Jack; no number on-c
14-Smilin' Jack Helps G-Men Solve a Case!
16-Donald Duck; 1st app. Daisy Duck on back cover (6/41-Disney)

Large Feature Comic #29 © NYNS

Lassie #37 © MGM

The Last American #4 © MAR

GD 2.0 | VG 4.0 | FN 6.0 | VF 8.0 | VF/NM 9.0 | NM- 9.2

GD 2.0 | VG 4.0 | FN 6.0 | VF 8.0 | VF/NM 9.0 | NM- 9.2

18-Phantasmo (see The Funnies #45)
20-Donald Duck Comic Paint Book (rarer than #16) (Disney)
21,22: 21-Private Buck. 22-Nuts & Jolts
24-Popeye in "Thimble Theatre" by Segar
26-Smitty
28-Grin and Bear It
30-Tillie the Toiler
2-Winnie Winkle (#1)
3-Dick Tracy
4-Tiny Tim (#1)
6-Terry and the Pirates; Caniff-a
8-Bugs Bunny (#1)('42)
9-Bringing Up Father
10-Popeye (Thimble Theatre)
11-Barney Google and Snuffy Smith
13-(nn)-1001 Hours Of Fun; puzzles & games; by A. W. Nugent. This book was bound as #13 with Large Feature Comics in publisher's files
19-Dumbo Comic Paint Book (Disney); partial-r from 4-Color #17
23-The Nebbs
25-Smilin' Jack-1st issue to show title on-c
27-Terry and the Pirates; Caniff-c/a
29-Moon Mullins
1 (Series II)-Peter Rabbit by Harrison Cady; arrival date-3/27/42
5-Toots and Casper
7-Pluto Saves the Ship (#1) (Disney)-Written by Carl Barks, Jack Hannah, & Nick George (Barks' 1st comic book work)
12-Private Buck

NOTE: *The Black & White Feature Books are oversized 8-1/2x11-3/8" comics with color covers and black and white interiors. The first nine issues all have rough, heavy stock covers and, except for #7, all have 76 pages, including covers. #7 and #10-on all have 52 pages. Beginning with #10 the covers are slick and thin and, because of their size, are difficult to handle without damaging. For this reason, they are seldom found in fine to mint condition. The paper stock, unlike Wow #1 and Capt. Marvel #1, is itself not unstable ...just thin.*

LARRY DOBY, BASEBALL HERO
Fawcett Publications: 1950 (Cleveland Indians)

nn-Bill Ward-a; photo-c 76 152 228 475 713 950

LARRY HARMON'S LAUREL AND HARDY (...Comics)
National Periodical Publ.: July-Aug, 1972 (Digest advertised, not published)

1-Low print run 9 18 27 60 85 110

LARS OF MARS
Ziff-Davis Publishing Co.: No. 10, Apr-May, 1951 - No. 11, July-Aug, 1951 (Painted-c) (Created by Jerry Siegel, editor)

10-Origin; Anderson-a(3) in each; classic robot-c 80 160 240 500 750 1000
11-Gene Colan-a; classic-c 64 128 192 400 600 800

LARS OF MARS 3-D
Eclipse Comics: Apr, 1987 ($2.50)

1-r/Lars of Mars #10,11 in 3-D plus new story 3.00
2-D limited edition (B&W, 100 copies) 5.00

LASER ERASER & PRESSBUTTON (See Axel Pressbutton & Miracle Man 9)
Eclipse Comics: Nov, 1985 - No. 6, 1987 (95¢/$2.50, limited series)

1-6: 5,6-(95¢) 2.25
...In 3-D 1 (8/86, $2.50) 3.00
2-D 1 (B&W, limited to 100 copies signed & numbered) 7.00

LASH LARUE WESTERN (Movie star; King of the bullwhip)(See Fawcett Movie Comic, Motion Picture Comics & Six-Gun Heroes)
Fawcett Publications: Sum, 1949 - No. 46, Jan, 1954 (36pgs., 1-7,9,13,16-on)

1-Lash & his horse Black Diamond begin; photo front/back-c begin
109 218 327 681 1021 1360
2(11/49) 46 92 138 276 413 550
3-5 40 80 120 240 340 440
6,7,9: 6-Last photo back-c; intro. Frontier Phantom (Lash's twin brother)
34 68 102 196 278 360
8,10 (52pgs.) 36 72 108 204 290 375
11,12,14,15 (52pgs.) 24 48 72 135 190 245
13,16-20 (36pgs.) 21 42 63 118 164 210
21-30: 21-The Frontier Phantom app. 18 36 54 101 138 175
31-45 15 30 45 86 118 150
46-Last Fawcett issue & photo-c 16 32 48 92 126 160

LASH LARUE WESTERN (Continues from Fawcett series)
Charlton Comics: No. 47, Mar-Apr, 1954 - No. 84, June, 1961

47-Photo-c 20 40 60 112 156 200
48 15 30 45 86 118 150
49-60, 67,68-(68 pgs.). 68-Check-a 11 22 33 66 88 110
61-66,69,70: 52-r/#8; 53-r/#22 10 20 30 58 77 95
71-83 8 16 24 46 58 70
84-Last issue 10 20 30 56 73 90

LASH LARUE WESTERN
AC Comics: 1990 ($3.50, 44 pgs) (24 pgs. of color, 16 pgs. of B&W)

1-Photo covers; r/Lash #6; r/old movie posters 3.50
Annual 1 (1990, $2.95, B&W, 44 pgs.)-Photo covers 3.00

LASSIE (TV)(M-G-M's... #1-36; see Kite Fun Book)
Dell Publ. Co./Gold Key No. 59 (10/62) on: June, 1950 - No. 70, July, 1969

1 (52 pgs.)-Photo-c; inside lists One Shot #282 in error
16 32 48 113 167 220
2-Painted-c begin 8 16 24 55 78 100
3-10 6 12 18 40 55 70
11-19: 12-Rocky Langford (Lassie's master) marries Gerry Lawrence. 15-1st app. Timbu
5 10 15 33 44 55
20-22-Matt Baker-a 5 10 15 36 48 60
23-38,40: 33-Robinson-a. 4 8 12 29 40 50
39-1st app. Timmy as Lassie picks up her TV family 6 12 18 43 59 75
41-50 4 8 12 29 40 50
51-58 4 8 12 27 36 45
59 (10/62)-1st Gold Key 5 10 15 33 44 55
60-70: 63-Last Timmy (10/63). 64-r/#19. 65-Forest Ranger Corey Stuart begins, ends #69. 70-Forest Rangers Bob Ericson & Scott Turner app. (Lassie's new masters)
4 8 12 24 32 40
11193(1978, $1.95, 224 pgs., Golden Press)-Baker-r (92 pgs.)
4 8 12 29 40 50

NOTE: *Photo c-57, 63. (See March of Comics #210, 217, 230, 254, 266, 278, 296, 308, 324, 334, 346, 358, 370, 381, 394, 411, 432)*

LAST AMERICAN, THE
Marvel Comics (Epic): Dec, 1990 - No. 4, March, 1991 ($2.25, mini-series)

1-4: Alan Grant scripts 2.25

LAST AVENGERS STORY, THE (Last Avengers #1)
Marvel Comics: Nov, 1995 - No. 2, Dec, 1995 ($5.95, painted, limited series) (Alterniverse)

1,2: Peter David story; acetate-c in all. 1-New team (Hank Pym, Wasp, Human Torch, Cannonball, She-Hulk, Hotshot, Bombshell, Tommy Maximoff, Hawkeye & Mockingbird) forms to battle Ultron 59, Kang the Conqueror, The Grim Reaper & Oddball 6.00

LAST DAYS OF THE JUSTICE SOCIETY SPECIAL
DC Comics: 1986 ($2.50, one-shot, 68 pgs.)

1-62 pg. JSA story plus unpubbed G.A. pg. 1 2 3 5 7 9

LAST GENERATION, THE
Black Tie Studios: 1986 - No. 5, 1989 ($1.95, B&W, high quality paper)

1-5 2.25
Book 1 (1989, $6.95)-By Caliber Press 7.00

LAST HUNT, THE
Dell Publishing Co.: No. 678, Feb, 1956

Four Color 678-Movie, photo-c 9 18 27 60 85 110

LAST KISS
ACME Press (Eclipse): 1988 ($3.95, B&W, squarebound, 52 pgs.)

1-One story adapts E.A. Poe's The Black Cat 4.00

LAST OF THE COMANCHES (Movie) (See Wild Bill Hickok #28)
Avon Periodicals: 1953

nn-Kinstler-c/a, 21pgs.; Ravielli-a 16 32 48 89 122 155

LAST OF THE ERIES, THE (See American Graphics)

LAST OF THE FAST GUNS, THE
Dell Publishing Co.: No. 925, Aug, 1958

Four Color 925-Movie, photo-c 8 16 24 55 78 100

LAST OF THE MOHICANS (See King Classics & White Rider and...)

LAST OF THE VIKING HEROES, THE (Also see Silver Star #1)
Genesis West Comics: Mar, 1987 - No. 12 ($1.50/$1.95)

1-4,5A,5B,6-12: 4-Intro The Phantom Force, 1-Signed edition ($1.50), 5A-Kirby/Stevens-c. 5B,6 ($1.95). 7-Art Adams-c. 8-Kirby back-c. 4.00
Summer Special 1-3: 1-(1988)-Frazetta-c & illos. 2 (1990, $2.50)-A TMNT app. 3 (1991, $2.50)-Teenage Mutant Ninja Turtles 4.00
Summer Special 1-Signed edition (sold for $1.95) 4.00

NOTE: ***Art Adams** c-7. **Byrne** c-3. **Kirby** c-1p, 5p. **Perez** c-2i. **Stevens** c-5Ai.*

LAST ONE, THE
DC Comics (Vertigo): July, 1993 - No. 6, Dec, 1993 ($2.50, lim. series, mature)

1-6 2.50

LAST SHOT

The Last Temptation #2 © MAR

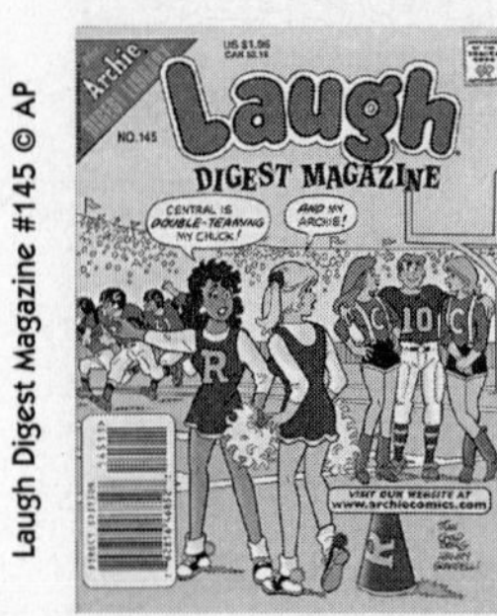

Laugh Digest Magazine #145 © AP

Lawbreakers Suspense Stories #15 © CC

Image Comics: Aug, 2001 - No. 4, Mar, 2002 ($2.95, limited series)

	GD 2.0	VG 4.0	FN 6.0	VF 8.0	VF/NM 9.0	NM- 9.2
1-4: 1-Wraparound-c; by Studio XD						3.00
...: First Draw (5/01, $2.95) Introductory one-shot						3.00

LAST STARFIGHTER, THE
Marvel Comics Group: Oct, 1984 - No. 3, Dec, 1984 (75¢, movie adaptation)

	GD 2.0	VG 4.0	FN 6.0	VF 8.0	VF/NM 9.0	NM- 9.2
1-3: r/Marvel Super Special; Guice-c						2.25

LAST TEMPTATION, THE
Marvel Comics: 1994 - No. 3, 1994 ($4.95, limited series)

	GD 2.0	VG 4.0	FN 6.0	VF 8.0	VF/NM 9.0	NM- 9.2
1-3-Alice Cooper story; Neil Gaiman scripts; McKean-c; Zulli-a: 1-Two covers						5.00

LAST TRAIN FROM GUN HILL
Dell Publishing Co.: No. 1012, July, 1959

	GD 2.0	VG 4.0	FN 6.0	VF 8.0	VF/NM 9.0	NM- 9.2
Four Color 1012-Movie, photo-c	10	20	30	67	96	125

LATEST ADVENTURES OF FOXY GRANDPA (See Foxy Grandpa)

LATEST COMICS (Super Duper No. 3?)
Spotlight Publ./Palace Promotions (Jubilee): Mar, 1945 - No. 2, 1945?

	GD 2.0	VG 4.0	FN 6.0	VF 8.0	VF/NM 9.0	NM- 9.2
1-Super Duper	17	34	51	95	130	165
2-Bee-29 (nd); Jubilee in indicia blacked out	13	26	39	74	100	125

LAUGH
Archie Enterprises: June, 1987 - No. 29, Aug, 1991 (75¢/$1.00)

	GD 2.0	VG 4.0	FN 6.0	VF 8.0	VF/NM 9.0	NM- 9.2
V2#1						5.00
2-10,14,24: 5-X-Mas issue. 14-1st app. Hot Dog. 24-Re-intro Super Duck						4.00
11-13,15-23,25-29: 19-X-Mas issue						3.00

LAUGH COMICS (Teenage) (Formerly Black Hood #9-19) (Laugh #226 on)
Archie Publications (Close-Up): No. 20, Fall, 1946 - No. 400, Apr, 1987

	GD 2.0	VG 4.0	FN 6.0	VF 8.0	VF/NM 9.0	NM- 9.2
20-Archie begins; Katy Keene & Taffy begin by Woggon; Suzie & Wilbur also begin; Archie covers begin	62	124	186	388	582	775
21-23,25	35	70	105	201	288	370
24- "Pipsy" by Kirby (6 pgs.)	36	72	108	207	294	380
26-30	19	38	57	107	149	190
31-40	15	30	45	84	115	145
41-60: 41,54-Debbi by Woggon	11	22	33	63	84	105
61-80: 67-Debbi by Woggon	9	18	27	49	62	75
81-99	5	10	15	36	48	60
100	6	12	18	38	52	65
101-126: 125-Debbi app.	4	8	12	29	40	50
127-144: Super-hero app. in all (see note)	5	10	15	33	44	55
145-156,158-160	3	7	10	21	28	35
157-Josie app.(4/64)	4	8	12	25	33	42
161-165,167-180, 200 (12/67)	3	6	9	18	23	28
166-Beatles-c (1/65)	5	10	15	36	48	60
181-199	2	4	6	14	18	22
201-240(3/71)	2	4	6	10	12	15
241-280(7/74)	2	4	6	8	10	12
281-299	1	2	3	5	7	9
300(3/76)	1	3	4	6	8	10
301-340 (7/79)	1	2	3	4	5	7
341-370 (1/82)						5.00
371-380,385-399						4.00
381-384,400: 381-384-Katy Keene app.; by Woggon-381,382						5.00

NOTE: *The Fly app. in 128, 129, 132, 134, 138, 139. Flygirl app. in 136, 137, 143. Flyman app. in 137. The Jaguar app. in 127, 130, 131, 133, 135, 140-142, 144. Josie app. in 145, 160, 164. Katy Keene app. in 20-125, 129, 130, 133. Many issues contain paper dolls.* ***Al Fagaly*** *c-20-29.* ***Montana*** *c-33, 36, 37, 42.* ***Bill Vigoda*** *c-30, 50.*

LAUGH COMICS DIGEST (...Magazine #23-89; Laugh Digest Mag. #90 on)
Archie Publ. (Close-Up No. 1, 3 on): 8/74; No. 2, 9/75; No. 3, 3/76 - Present (Digest-size) (Josie and Sabrina app. in most issues)

	GD 2.0	VG 4.0	FN 6.0	VF 8.0	VF/NM 9.0	NM- 9.2
1-Neal Adams-a	5	10	15	33	44	55
2,7,8,19-Neal Adams-a	3	6	9	18	24	30
3-6,9,10	2	4	6	12	16	20
11-18,20	2	4	6	10	12	15
21-40	2	4	6	8	10	12
41-80	1	2	3	5	6	8
81-99						5.00
100						6.00
101-138						3.00
139-190: 139-Begin $1.95-c. 148-Begin $1.99-c. 156-Begin $2.19-c. 180-Begin $2.39-c						2.50

NOTE: *Katy Keene in 23, 25, 27, 32-38, 40, 45-48, 50. The Fly-r in 19, 20. The Jaguar-r in 25, 27. Mr. Justice-r in 21. The Web-r in 23.*

LAUGH COMIX (Formerly Top Notch Laugh; Suzie Comics No. 49 on)
MLJ Magazines: No. 46, Summer, 1944 - No. 48, Winter, 1944-45

	GD 2.0	VG 4.0	FN 6.0	VF 8.0	VF/NM 9.0	NM- 9.2
46-Wilbur & Suzie in all; Harry Sahle-c	24	48	72	135	190	245
47,48: 47-Sahle-c. 48-Bill Vigoda-c	16	32	48	92	126	160

LAUGH-IN MAGAZINE (TV)(Magazine)
Laufer Publ. Co.: Oct, 1968 - No. 12, Oct, 1969 (50¢) (Satire)

	GD 2.0	VG 4.0	FN 6.0	VF 8.0	VF/NM 9.0	NM- 9.2
V1#1	5	10	15	36	48	60
2-12	4	8	12	24	32	40

LAUREL & HARDY (See Larry Harmon's... & March of Comics No. 302, 314)

LAUREL AND HARDY (...Comics)
St. John Publ. Co.: 3/49 - No. 3, 9/49; No. 26, 11/55 - No. 28, 3/56 (No #4-25)

	GD 2.0	VG 4.0	FN 6.0	VF 8.0	VF/NM 9.0	NM- 9.2
1	70	140	210	438	657	875
2	40	80	120	240	345	450
3	31	62	93	175	248	320
26-28 (Reprints)	17	34	51	95	130	165

LAUREL AND HARDY (TV)
Dell Publishing Co.: Oct, 1962 - No. 4, Sept-Nov, 1963

	GD 2.0	VG 4.0	FN 6.0	VF 8.0	VF/NM 9.0	NM- 9.2
12-423-210 (8-10/62)	7	14	21	46	63	80
2-4 (Dell)	5	10	15	33	44	55

LAUREL AND HARDY (Larry Harmon's...)
Gold Key: Jan, 1967 - No. 2, Oct, 1967

	GD 2.0	VG 4.0	FN 6.0	VF 8.0	VF/NM 9.0	NM- 9.2
1-Photo back-c	6	12	18	38	52	65
2	5	10	15	33	44	55

LAUREL AND HARDY DIGEST: DC Comics. 1972 (Advertised, not published)

L.A.W., THE (LIVING ASSAULT WEAPONS)
DC Comics: Sept, 1999 - No. 6, Feb, 2000 ($2.50, limited series)

	GD 2.0	VG 4.0	FN 6.0	VF 8.0	VF/NM 9.0	NM- 9.2
1-6-Blue Beetle, Question, Judomaster, Capt. Atom app.; Giordano-a 5-JLA app.						2.50

LAW AGAINST CRIME (Law-Crime on cover)
Essenkay Publishing Co.: April, 1948 - No. 3, Aug, 1948 (Real Stories from Police Files)

	GD 2.0	VG 4.0	FN 6.0	VF 8.0	VF/NM 9.0	NM- 9.2
1-(#1-3 are half funny animal, half crime stories)-L. B. Cole-c/a in all; electrocution-c	72	144	216	450	675	900
2-L. B. Cole-c/a	55	110	165	330	495	660
3-Used in **SOTI**, pg. 180,181 & illo "The wish to hurt or kill couples in lovers' lanes;" reprinted in All-Famous Crime #9	68	136	204	425	638	850

LAW AND ORDER
Maximum Press: Sept, 1995 - No. 2, 1995 ($2.50, unfinished limited series)

	GD 2.0	VG 4.0	FN 6.0	VF 8.0	VF/NM 9.0	NM- 9.2
1,2						2.50

LAWBREAKERS (...Suspense Stories No. 10 on)
Law and Order Magazines (Charlton): Mar, 1951 - No. 9, Oct-Nov, 1952

	GD 2.0	VG 4.0	FN 6.0	VF 8.0	VF/NM 9.0	NM- 9.2
1	39	78	117	230	325	420
2	23	46	69	130	183	235
3,5,6,8,9	18	36	54	104	142	180
4- "White Death" junkie story	22	44	66	127	176	225
7- "The Deadly Dopesters" drug story	22	44	66	127	176	225

LAWBREAKERS ALWAYS LOSE!
Marvel Comics (CBS): Spring, 1948 - No. 10, Oct, 1949

	GD 2.0	VG 4.0	FN 6.0	VF 8.0	VF/NM 9.0	NM- 9.2
1-2pg. Kurtzman-a, "Giggles 'n' Grins"	35	70	105	201	288	370
2	19	38	57	106	146	185
3-5: 4-Vampire story	14	28	42	81	111	140
6(2/49)-Has editorial defense against charges of Dr. Wertham	16	32	48	92	126	160
7-Used in **SOTI**, illo "Comic-book philosophy"	31	62	93	175	248	320
8-10: 9,10-Photo-c	13	26	39	74	100	125

NOTE: ***Brodsky*** *c-4, 5.* ***Shores*** *c-1-3, 6-8.*

LAWBREAKERS SUSPENSE STORIES (Formerly Lawbreakers; Strange Suspense Stories No. 16 on)
Capitol Stories/Charlton Comics: No. 10, Jan, 1953 - No. 15, Nov, 1953

	GD 2.0	VG 4.0	FN 6.0	VF 8.0	VF/NM 9.0	NM- 9.2
10	39	78	117	233	329	425
11 (3/53)-Severed tongues-c/story & woman negligee scene	96	192	288	600	900	1200
12-14: 13-Giordano-c begin, end #15	24	48	72	138	194	250
15-Acid-in-face-c/story; hands dissolved in acid sty	50	100	150	300	450	600

LAW-CRIME (See Law Against Crime)

LAWDOG
Marvel Comics (Epic Comics): May, 1993 - No. 10, Feb, 1993

	GD 2.0	VG 4.0	FN 6.0	VF 8.0	VF/NM 9.0	NM- 9.2
1-10						2.25

LAWDOG/GRIMROD: TERROR AT THE CROSSROADS
Marvel Comics (Epic Comics): Sept, 1993 ($3.50)

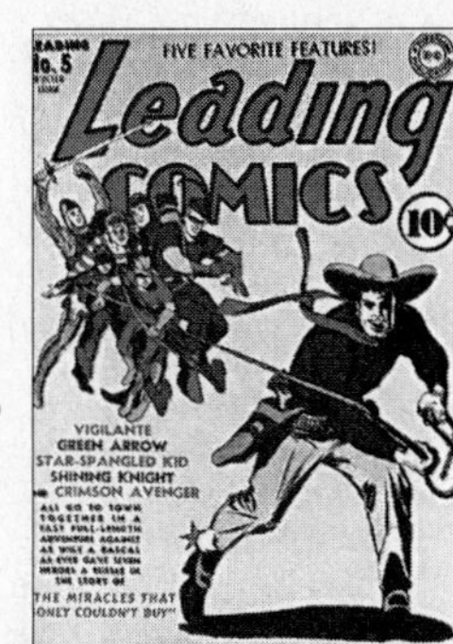

Leading Comics #5 © DC

The League of Extraordinary Gentlemen V2#2 © Alan Moore & Kevin O'Neil

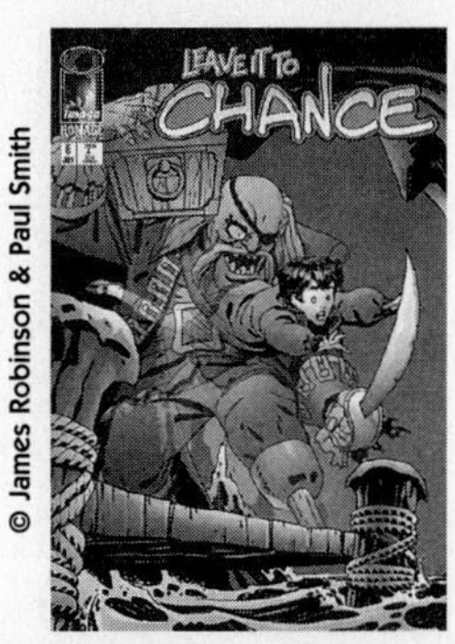

Leave It to Chance #6 © James Robinson & Paul Smith

GD VG FN VF VF/NM NM-
2.0 4.0 6.0 8.0 9.0 9.2

1 3.50

LAWMAN (TV)
Dell Publishing Co.: No. 970, Feb, 1959 - No. 11, Apr-June, 1962 (All photo-c)

Four Color 970(#1) 14 28 42 97 141 185
Four Color 1035('60), 3(2-4/60)-Toth-a 8 16 24 55 78 100
4-11 6 12 18 40 55 70

LAW OF DREDD, THE (Also see Judge Dredd)
Quality Comics/Fleetway #8 on: 1989 - No. 33, 1992 ($1.50/$1.75)

1-33: Bolland a-1-6,8,10-12,14(2 pg),15,19 2.50

LAWRENCE (See Movie Classics)

LAZARUS CHURCHYARD
Tundra Publishing: June, 1992 - No. 3, 1992 ($3.95, 44 pgs., coated stock)

1-3 4.00
The Final Cut (Image, 1/01, $14.95, TPB) Reprints Ellis/D'Israeli strips 15.00

LAZARUS FIVE
DC Comics: July, 2000 - No. 5, Nov, 2000 ($2.50, limited series)

1-5-Harris-c/Abell-a(p) 2.50

LEADING COMICS (...Screen Comics No. 42 on)
National Periodical Publications: Winter, 1941-42 - No. 41, Feb-Mar, 1950

1-Origin The Seven Soldiers of Victory; Crimson Avenger, Green Arrow & Speedy, Shining Knight, The Vigilante, Star Spangled Kid & Stripesy begin; The Dummy (Vigilante villain) 1st app. 448 896 1344 3136 4818 6500
2-Meskin-a; Fred Ray-c 160 320 480 1000 1500 2000
3 124 248 372 775 1163 1550
4,5 88 176 264 550 825 1100
6-10 77 154 231 481 723 965
11,12,14(Spring, 1945) 55 110 165 330 495 660
13-Classic robot-c 94 188 282 588 882 1175
15-(Sum,'45)-Contents change to funny animal 29 58 87 164 232 300
16-22,24-30: 16-Nero Fox-c begin, end #22 13 26 39 74 100 125
23-1st app. Peter Porkchops by Otto Feur & begins 29 58 87 164 232 300
31,32,34-41: 34-41-Leading Screen... on-c only 10 20 30 58 77 95
33-(Scarce) 21 42 63 118 164 210

NOTE: ***Rube Grossman**-a(Peter Porkchops)-most #15-on; c-15-41. **Post** a-23-37, 39, 41.*

LEADING SCREEN COMICS (Formerly Leading Comics)
National Periodical Publ.: No. 42, Apr-May, 1950 - No. 77, Aug-Sept, 1955

42-Peter Porkchops-c/stories continue 11 22 33 63 84 105
43-77 10 20 30 56 73 90

NOTE: ***Grossman** a-most. **Mayer** a-45-48, 50, 54-57, 60, 62-74, 75(3), 76, 77.*

LEAGUE OF CHAMPIONS, THE (Also see The Champions)
Hero Graphics: Dec, 1990 - No. 12, 1992 ($2.95, 52 pgs.)

1-12: 1-Flare app. 2-Origin Malice 3.00

LEAGUE OF EXTRAORDINARY GENTLEMEN, THE
America's Best Comics: Mar, 1999 - No. 6, Sept, 2000 ($2.95, limited series)

1-Alan Moore-s/Kevin O'Neill-a 1 2 3 5 7 9
1-DF Edition ($10.00) O'Neill-c 2 4 6 8 10 12
2,3 5.00
4-6: 5-Revised printing with "Wonder Co. Syringe" parody ad 3.50
5-Initial printing recalled because of "Marvel Co. Syringe" parody ad 30.00
... Compendium 1,2: 1-r/#1,2. 2-r/#3,4 6.00
Hardcover (2000, $24.95) r/#1-6 plus cover gallery 25.00

LEAGUE OF EXTRAORDINARY GENTLEMEN, THE (Volume 2)
America's Best Comics: Sept, 2002 - No. 6, Nov, 2003 ($3.50, limited series)

1-6-Alan Moore-s/Kevin O'Neill-a 3.50
... Bumper Compendium 1,2: 1-r/#1,2. 2-r/#3,4 6.00

LEAGUE OF JUSTICE
DC Comics (Elseworlds): 1996 - No. 2, 1996 ($5.95, 48 pgs., squarebound)

1,2: Magic-based alternate DC Universe story; Giordano-i 6.00

LEATHERFACE
Arpad Publishing: May (April on-c), 1991 - No. 4, May, 1992 ($2.75, painted-c)

1-4-Based on Texas Chainsaw movie; Dorman-c 3.00

LEATHERNECK THE MARINE (See Mighty Midget Comics)

LEAVE IT TO BEAVER (TV)
Dell Publishing Co.: No. 912, June, 1958; May-July, 1962 (All photo-c)

Four Color 912 18 36 54 131 191 250
Four Color 999,1103,1191,1285, 01-428-207 15 30 45 109 160 210

GD VG FN VF VF/NM NM-
2.0 4.0 6.0 8.0 9.0 9.2

LEAVE IT TO BINKY (Binky No. 72 on) (Super DC Giant) (No. 1-22: 52 pgs.)
National Periodical Publications: 2-3/48 - #60, 10/58; #61, 6-7/68 - #71, 2-3/70 (Teen-age humor)

1-Lucy wears Superman costume 36 72 108 204 290 375
2 19 38 57 106 146 185
3,4 11 22 33 66 88 110
5-Superman cameo 18 36 54 101 138 175
6-10 10 20 30 56 73 90
11-14,16-22: Last 52 pg. issue 9 18 27 49 62 75
15-Scribbly story by Mayer 10 20 30 58 77 95
23-28,30-45: 45-Last pre-code (2/55) 7 14 21 37 46 55
29-Used in **POP**, pg. 78 8 16 24 40 50 60
46-60: 60-(10/58) 4 8 12 29 40 50
61 (6-7/68) 1950's reprints with art changes 5 10 15 36 48 60
62-69: 67-Last 12¢ issue 4 8 12 22 30 38
70-7pg. app. Bus Driver who looks like Ralph from Honeymooners 4 8 12 27 36 45
71-Last issue 4 8 12 25 33 42

NOTE: ***Aragones**-a-61, 62, 67. **Drucker** a-28. **Mayer** a-1, 2, 15. Created by **Mayer**.*

LEAVE IT TO CHANCE (Also see Promotional Comics section for FCBD Ed.)
Image Comics (Homage Comics): Sept, 1996 - No. 11, Sept, 1998; No. 13, July, 2002
DC Comics (Homage Comics): No. 12, Jun, 1999 ($2.50/$2.95/$4.95)

1-3: 1-Intro Chance Falconer & St. George; James Robinson scripts & Paul Smith-c/a 5.00
4-12: 12-(6/99) 3.00
13-(7/02, $4.95) includes sketch pages and pin-ups 5.00
Shaman's Rain TPB (1997, $9.95) r/#1-4 10.00
Shaman's Rain HC (2002, $14.95, over-sized 8 1/4" x 12") r/#1-4 15.00
Trick or Threat TPB (1997, $12.95) r/#5-8 13.00
Trick or Threat TPB (2002, $14.95, over-sized 8 1/4" x 12") r/#5-8 15.00

LEE HUNTER, INDIAN FIGHTER
Dell Publishing Co.: No. 779, Mar, 1957; No. 904, May, 1958

Four Color 779 (#1) 5 10 15 36 48 60
Four Color 904 4 8 12 25 33 42

LEFT-HANDED GUN, THE (Movie)
Dell Publishing Co.: No. 913, July, 1958

Four Color 913-Paul Newman photo-c 10 20 30 73 107 140

LEGACY
Majestic Entertainment: Oct, 1993 - No. 2, Nov, 1993; No. 0, 1994 ($2.25)

1-2,0: 1-Glow-in-the-dark-c. 0-Platinum 2.25

LEGACY
Image Comics: May, 2003 - Present ($2.95)

1-3-Francisco-a/Treffiletti-s 3.00

LEGACY OF KAIN (Based on the Eidos video game)
Top Cow Productions: Oct, 1999; Jan, 2004 ($2.99)

...Defiance 1 (1/04, $2.99) Cha-c; Kirkham-a 3.00
...Soul Reaver 1 (10/99, Diamond Dateline supplement) Benitez-c 2.25

LEGEND OF CUSTER, THE (TV)
Dell Publishing Co.: Jan, 1968

1-Wayne Maunder photo-c 3 6 9 19 25 32

LEGEND OF JESSE JAMES, THE (TV)
Gold Key: Feb, 1966

10172-602-Photo-c 3 6 9 19 25 32

LEGEND OF KAMUI, THE (See Kamui)

LEGEND OF LOBO, THE (See Movie Comics)

LEGEND OF MOTHER SARAH (Manga)
Dark Horse Comics: Apr, 1995 - No. 8, Nov, 1995 ($2.50, limited series)

1-8: Katsuhiro Otomo scripts 4.00

LEGEND OF MOTHER SARAH: CITY OF THE ANGELS (Manga)
Dark Horse Comics: Oct, 1996 - No. 9 ($3.95, B&W, limited series)

1(10/96), 2(12/97),3-9: Otomo scripts 4.00

LEGEND OF MOTHER SARAH: CITY OF THE CHILDREN (Manga)
Dark Horse Comics: Jan, 1996 - No. 7, July, 1996 ($3.95, B&W, limited series)

1-7:Otomo scripts 4.00

LEGEND OF SUPREME
Image Comics (Extreme): Dec, 1994 - No. 3, Feb, 1995 ($2.50, limited series)

Legend of the Sage #4 © Chaos!

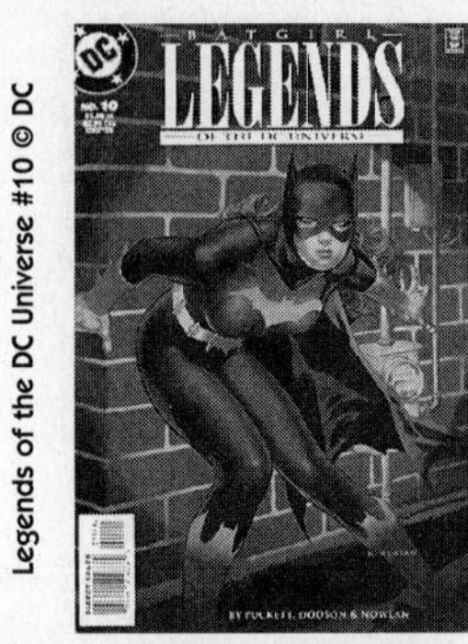

Legends of the DC Universe #10 © DC

The Legion #8 © DC

GD VG FN VF VF/NM NM-
2.0 4.0 6.0 8.0 9.0 9.2

1-3 2.50

LEGEND OF THE ELFLORD
DavDez Arts: July, 1998 - No. 2, Sept, 1998 ($2.95)
1,2-Barry Blair & Colin Chin-s/a 3.00

LEGEND OF THE HAWKMAN
DC Comics: 2000 - No. 3, 2000 ($4.95, limited series)
1-3-Raab-s/Lark-c/a 5.00

LEGEND OF THE SAGE
Chaos Comics: Aug, 2001 - No. 4, Dec, 2001 ($2.99, limited series)
Preview Book (6/01, $1.99) 2.50
1-4-($2.99) Augustyn-s/Molenaar-a/c 3.00

LEGEND OF THE SHIELD, THE
DC Comics (Impact Comics): July, 1991 - No. 16, Oct, 1992 ($1.00)
1-16: 6,7-The Fly x-over. 12-Contains trading card 2.50
Annual 1 (1992, $2.50, 68 pgs.)-Snyder-a; w/trading card 2.50

LEGEND OF WONDER WOMAN, THE
DC Comics: May, 1986 - No. 4, Aug, 1986 (75¢, limited series)
1-4 4.00

LEGEND OF YOUNG DICK TURPIN, THE (Disney)(TV)
Gold Key: May, 1966
1 (10176-605)-Photo/painted-c 3 6 9 19 25 32

LEGEND OF ZELDA, THE (Link: The Legend... in indicia)
Valiant Comics: 1990 - No. 4, 1990 ($1.95, coated stiff-c) V2#1, 1990 - No. 5, 1990 ($1.50)
1-4: 4-Layton-c(i) 3.00
V2#1-5 3.00

LEGENDS
DC Comics: Nov, 1986 - No. 6, Apr, 1987 (75¢, limited series)
1-5: 1-Byrne-c/a(p) in all; 1st app. new Capt. Marvel. 3-1st app. new Suicide Squad; death of Blockbuster 4.00
6-1st app. new Justice League 6.00

LEGENDS OF DANIEL BOONE, THE (...Frontier Scout)
National Periodical Publications: Oct-Nov, 1955 - No. 8, Dec-Jan, 1956-57
1 (Scarce)-Nick Cardy c-1-8 59 118 177 369 552 735
2 (Scarce) 43 86 129 258 384 510
3-8 (Scarce) 39 78 117 230 325 420

LEGENDS OF KID DEATH AND FLUFFY
Event Comics: Feb, 1997 ($2.95, B&W, one-shot)
1-Five covers 3.00

LEGENDS OF NASCAR, THE
Vortex Comics: Nov, 1990 - No. 14, 1992? (#1 3rd printing (1/91) says 2nd printing inside)
1-Bill Elliott biog.; Trimpe-a ($1.50) 5.00
1-2nd printing (11/90, $2.00) 2.25
1-3rd print; contains Maxx racecards ($3.00) 3.00
2-14: 2-Richard Petty. 3-Ken Schrader (7/91). 4-Bobby Allison; Spiegle-a(p); Adkins part-i. 5-Sterling Marlin. 6-Bill Elliott. 7-Junior Johnson; Spiegle-c/a. 8-Benny Parsons; Heck-a 3.00
1-13-Hologram cover versions. 2-Hologram shows Bill Elliott's car by mistake (all are numbered & limited) 5.00
2-Hologram corrected version 5.00
Christmas Special ($5.95) 6.00

LEGENDS OF THE DARK CLAW
DC Comics (Amalgam): Apr, 1996 ($1.95)
1-Jim Balent-c/a 3.00

LEGENDS OF THE DARK KNIGHT (See Batman: ...)

LEGENDS OF THE DC UNIVERSE
DC Comics: Feb, 1998 - No. 41, June, 2001 ($1.95/$1.99/$2.50)
1-13,15-21: 1-3-Superman; Robinson-s/Semeiks-a/Orbik-painted-c. 4,5-Wonder Woman; Deodato-a/Rude painted-c. 8-GL/GA, O'Neil-s. 10,11-Batgirl; Dodson-a. 12,13-Justice League. 15-17-Flash. 18-Kid Flash; Guice-a. 19-Impulse; prelude to JLApe Annuals. 20,21-Abin Sur 3.00
14-($3.95) Jimmy Olsen; Kirby-esque-c by Rude 4.00
22-27,30: 22,23-Superman; Rude-c/Ladronn-a. 26,27-Aquaman/Joker 2.50
28,29: Green Lantern & the Atom; Gil Kane-a; covers by Kane and Ross 2.50
31,32: 32-Begin $2.50-c; Wonder Woman; Texeira-c 2.50
33-36-Hal Jordan as The Spectre; DeMatteis-s/Zulli-a; Hale painted-c 2.50
37-41: 37,38-Kyle Rayner. 39-Superman. 40,41-Atom; Harris-c 2.50

GD VG FN VF VF/NM NM-
2.0 4.0 6.0 8.0 9.0 9.2

... Crisis on Infinite Earths 1 (2/99, $4.95) Untold story during and after Crisis on Infinite Earths #4; Wolfman-s/Ryan-a/Orbik-c 5.00
... 80 Page Giant 1 (9/98, $4.95) Stories and art by various incl. Ditko, Perez, Gibbons, Mumy; Joe Kubert-c 5.00
... 80 Page Giant 2 (1/00, $4.95) Stories and art by various incl. Challengers by Art Adams; Sean Phillips-c 5.00
... 3-D Gallery (12/98, $2.95) Pin-ups w/glasses 3.00

LEGENDS OF THE LEGION (See Legion of Super-Heroes)
DC Comics: Feb, 1998 - No. 4, May, 1998 ($2.25, limited series)
1-4:1-Origin-s of Ultra Boy. 2-Spark. 3-Umbra. 4-Star Boy 3.00

LEGENDS OF THE STARGRAZERS (See Vanguard Illustrated #2)
Innovation Publishing: Aug, 1989 - No. 6, 1990 ($1.95, limited series, mature)
1-6: 1-Redondo part inks 2.25

LEGENDS OF THE WORLD'S FINEST (See World's Finest)
DC Comics: 1994 - No. 3, 1994 ($4.95, squarebound, limited series)
1-3: Simonson scripts; Brereton-c/a; embossed foil logos 6.00
TPB-(1995, $14.95) r/#1-3 15.00

L.E.G.I.O.N. (The # to right of title represents year of print)(Also see Lobo & R.E.B.E.L.S.)
DC Comics: Feb, 1989 - No. 70, Sept, 1994 ($1.50/$1.75)
1-Giffen plots/breakdowns in #1-12,28 5.00
2-22,24-47: 3-Lobo app. #3 on. 4-1st Lobo-c this title. 5-Lobo joins L.E.G.I.O.N. 13-Lar Gand app. 16-Lar Gand joins L.E.G.I.O.N., leaves #19. 31-Capt. Marvel app. 35-L.E.G.I.O.N. '92 begins 3.00
23,70-($2.50, 52 pgs.)-L.E.G.I.O.N. '91 begins. 70-Zero Hour 4.00
48,49,51-69: 48-Begin $1.75-c. 63-L.E.G.I.O.N. '94 begins; Superman x-over 3.00
50-($3.50, 68 pgs.) 4.00
Annual 1-5 ('90-94, 68 pgs.): 1-Lobo, Superman app. 2-Alan Grant scripts. 5-Elseworlds story; Lobo app. 4.00
NOTE: *Alan Grant scripts in #1-39, 51, Annual 1, 2.*

LEGION, THE (Continued from Legion Lost & Legion Worlds)
DC Comics: Dec, 2001 - Present ($2.50)
1-Abnett & Lanning-s; Coipel & Lanning-c/a 4.00
2-24: 3-8-Ra's al Ghul app. 5-Snejbjerg-a. 9-DeStefano-a. 12-Legion vs. JLA. 16-Fatal Five app.; Walker-a 17,18-Ra's al Ghul app. 20-23-Universo app. 2.50
25-($3.95) Art by Harris, Cockrum, Rivoche; teenage Clark Kent app.; Harris-c 4.00
26-28-Superboy app. in classic costume 2.50
...Secret Files 3003 (1/04, $4.95) Kirk-a, Harris-c/a; Superboy app. 5.00

LEGION LOST (Continued from Legion of Super-Heroes [4th series] #125)
DC Comics: May, 2000 - No. 12, Apr, 2001 ($2.50, limited series)
1-Abnett & Lanning-s. Coipel & Lanning-c/a 6.00
2-12-Abnett & Lanning-s. Coipel & Lanning-c/a in most. 4,9-Alixe-a 2.50

LEGIONNAIRES (See Legion of Super-Heroes #40, 41 & Showcase 95 #6)
DC Comics: Apr, 1992 - No. 81, Mar, 2000 ($1.25/$1.50/$2.25)
0-(10/94)-Zero Hour restart of Legion; released between #18 & #19 2.50
1-49,51-77: 1-(4/92)-Chris Sprouse-c/a; polybagged w/SkyBox trading card. 11-Kid Quantum joins. 18-(9/94)-Zero Hour. 19(11/94). 37-Valor (Lar Gand) becomes M'onel (5/96). 43-Legion tryouts; reintro Princess Projectra, Shadow Lass & others. 47-Forms one cover image with LSH #91. 60-Karate Kid & Kid Quantum join. 61-Silver Age & 70's Legion app. 76-Return of Wildfire. 79,80-Coipel-c/a; Legion vs. the Blight 2.50
50-($3.95) Pullout poster by Davis/Farmer 4.00
#1,000,000 (11/98) Sean Phillips-a 2.50
Annual 1,3 ('94,'96 $2.95)-1-Elseworlds-s. 3-Legends of the Dead Earth-s 3.00
Annual 2 (1995, $3.95)-Year One-s 4.50

LEGIONNAIRES THREE
DC Comics: Jan, 1986 - No. 4, May, 1986 (75¢, limited series)
1-4 3.00

LEGION OF MONSTERS (Also see Marvel Premiere #28 & Marvel Preview #8)
Marvel Comics Group: Sept, 1975 ($1.00, B&W, magazine, 76 pgs.)
1-Origin & 1st app. Legion of Monsters; Neal Adams-c; Morrow-a; origin & only app. The Manphibian; Frankenstein by Mayerik; Bram Stoker's Dracula adaptation; Reese-a; painted-c (#2 was advertised with Morbius & Satana, but was never published) 3 7 10 21 28 35

LEGION OF NIGHT, THE
Marvel Comics: Oct, 1991 - No. 2, Oct, 1991 ($4.95, 52 pgs.)
1,2-Whilce Portacio-c/a(p) 5.00

LEGION OF SUBSTITUTE HEROES SPECIAL (See Adventure Comics #306)
DC Comics: July, 1985 ($1.25, one-shot, 52 pgs.)

Legion of Super-Heroes (3rd series) #26 © DC

Legion of Super-Heroes (4th series) #101 © DC

Lenore #10 © Roman Dirge

GD 2.0 | VG 4.0 | FN 6.0 | VF 8.0 | VF/NM 9.0 | NM- 9.2

1-Giffen-c/a(p) 3.00

LEGION OF SUPER-HEROES (See Action Comics, Adventure, All New Collectors Edition, Legionnaires, Legends of the Legion, Limited Collectors Edition, Secrets of the..., Superboy & Superman)
National Periodical Publications: Feb, 1973 - No. 4, July-Aug, 1973

1-Legion & Tommy Tomorrow reprints begin 3 6 9 18 24 30
2-4: 2-Forte-r. 3-r/Adv. #340. Action #240. 4-r/Adv. #341, Action #233; Mooney-r 2 4 6 10 12 15

LEGION OF SUPER-HEROES, THE (Formerly Superboy and...; Tales of The Legion No. 314 on)
DC Comics: No. 259, Jan, 1980 - No. 313, July, 1984

259(#1)-Superboy leaves Legion 2 4 6 8 10 12
260-270,285-290,294: 265-Contains 28 pg. insert "Superman & the TRS-80 computer"; origin Tyroc; Tyroc leaves Legion. 290-294-Great Darkness saga. 294-Double size (52 pgs.) 1 2 3 4 5 7
261,263,264,266-(Whitman variants; low print run; no cover #'s) 1 3 4 6 8 10
271-284,291-293: 272-Blok joins; origin; 20 pg. insert-Dial 'H' For Hero. 277-Intro. Reflecto. 280-Superboy re-joins Legion. 282-Origin Reflecto. 283-Origin Wildfire 5.00
295-299,301-313: 297-Origin retold. 298-Free 16pg. Amethyst preview. 306-Brief origin Star Boy (Swan art). 311-Colan-a 3.00
300-(68 pgs., Mando paper)-Anniversary issue; has c/a by almost everyone at DC 5.00
Annual 1-3(82-84, 52 pgs.)-1-Giffen-c/a; 1st app./origin new Invisible Kid who joins Legion. 2-Karate Kid & Princess Projectra wed & resign 3.00
...The Great Darkness Saga (1989, $17.95, 196 pgs.)-r/LSH #287,290-294 & Annual #3; Giffen-c/a 2 4 6 11 14 18
NOTE: ***Aparo*** *c-282, 283, 300(part).* ***Austin*** *c-268i.* ***Buckler*** *c-273p, 274p, 276p.* ***Colan*** *a-311p.* ***Ditko*** *a(p)-267, 268, 272, 274, 276, 281.* ***Giffen*** *a-285-313p, Annual 1p; c-287p, 288p, 289, 290p, 291p, 292, 293, 294-299p, 300, 301-313p, Annual 1p, 2p.* ***Perez*** *c-268p, 277-280, 281p.* ***Starlin*** *a-265.* ***Staton*** *a-259p, 260p, 280.* ***Tuska*** *a-308p.*

LEGION OF SUPER-HEROES (3rd Series) (Reprinted in Tales of the Legion)
DC Comics: Aug, 1984 - No. 63, Aug, 1989 ($1.25/$1.75, deluxe format)

1-Silver ink logo 5.00
2-36,39-44,46-49,51-62: 4-Death of Karate Kid. 5-Death of Nemesis Kid. 12-Cosmic Boy, Lightning Lad, & Saturn Girl resign. 14-Intro new members: Tellus, Sensor Girl, Quislet. 15-17-Crisis tie-ins. 18-Crisis x-over. 25-Sensor Girl i.d. revealed as Princess Projectra. 35-Saturn Girl rejoins. 42,43-Millennium tie-ins. 44-Origin Quislet 3.00
37,38-Death of Superboy 2 4 6 9 11 14
45,50: 45 ($2.95, 68 pgs.)-Anniversary ish. 50-Double size ($2.50-c) 4.00
63-Final issue 4.00
Annual 1-4 (10/85-'88, 52 pgs.)-1-Crisis tie-in 3.00
NOTE: ***Byrne*** *c-36p.* ***Giffen*** *a(p)-1, 2, 50-55, 57-63, Annual 1p, 2; c-1-5p, 54p, Annual 1.* ***Orlando*** *a-6p.* ***Steacy*** *c-45-50, Annual 3.*

LEGION OF SUPER-HEROES (4th Series)
DC Comics: Nov, 1989 - No. 125, Mar, 2000 ($1.75/$1.95/$2.25)

0-(10/94)-Zero Hour restart of Legion; released between #61 & #62 2.50
1-Giffen-c/a(p)/scripts begin (4 pg.-a only #18) 4.00
2-20,26-49,51-53,55-58: 4-Mon-El (Lar Gand) destroys Time Trapper, changes reality. 5-Alt. reality story where Mordru rules all; Ferro Lad app. 6-1st app. of Laurel Gand (Lar Gand's cousin). 8-Origin. 13-Free poster by Giffen showing new costumes. 15-(2/91)-1st reference of Lar Gand as Valor. 26-New map of headquarters. 34-Six pg. preview of Timber Wolf mini-series. 40-Minor Legionnaires app. 41-(3/93)-SW6 Legion renamed Legionnaires w/new costumes and some new code-names 3.00
21-25: 21-24-Lobo & Darkseid storyline. 24-Cameo SW6 younger Legion duplicates. 25-SW6 Legion full intro. 3.50
50-($3.50, 68 pgs.) 4.00
54-($2.95)-Die-cut & foil stamped-c 4.00
59-99: 61-(9/94)-Zero Hour. 62-(11/94). 75-XS travels back to the 20th Century (cont'd in Impulse #9). 77-Origin of Brainiac 5. 81-Reintro Sun Boy. 85-Half of the Legion sent to the 20th century, Superman-c/app. 86-Final Night. 87-Deadman-c/app. 88-Impulse-c/app. Adventure Comics #247 cover swipe. 91-Forms one cover image with Legionnaires #47. 96-Wedding of Ultra Boy and Apparition. 99-Robin, Impulse, Superboy app. 2.50
100-($5.95, 96 pgs.)-Legionnaires return to the 30th Century; gatefold-c; 5 stories-art by Simonson, Davis and others 1 2 3 4 5 7
101-121: 101-Armstrong-a(p) begins. 105-Legion past & present vs. Time Trapper. 109-Moder-a. 110-Thunder joins. 114,115-Bizarro Legion. 120,121-Fatal Five. 2.50
122-124: 122,123-Coipel-c/a. 124-Coipel-c 3.00
125-Leads into "Legion Lost" maxi-series; Coipel-c 5.00
#1,000,000 (11/98) Giffen-a 2.50
Annual 1-5 (1990-1994, $3.50, 68 pgs.): 4-Bloodlines. 5-Elseworlds story 3.50
Annual 6 (1995,$3.95)-Year One story 4.00
Annual 7 (1996, $3.50, 48 pgs.)-Legends of the Dead Earth story; intro 75th Century Legion of Super-Heroes; Wildfire app. 3.50
Legion: Secret Files 1 (1/98, $4.95) Retold origin & pin-ups 5.00
Legion: Secret Files 2 (6/99, $4.95) Story and profile pages 5.00
The Beginning of Tomorrow TPB ('99, $17.95) r/post-Zero Hour reboot 18.00
NOTE: ***Giffen*** *a-1-24; breakdowns-26-32, 34-36; c-1-7, 8(part), 9-24.* ***Brandon Peterson*** *a(p)-15(1st for DC), 16, 18, Annual 2(54 pgs.); c-Annual 2p.* ***Swan/Anderson*** *c-8(part).*

LEGION: SCIENCE POLICE (See Legion of Super-Heroes)
DC Comics: Aug, 1998 - No. 4, Nov, 1998 ($2.25, limited series)

1-4-Ryan-a 2.50

LEGION WORLDS (Follows Legion Lost series)
DC Comics: Jun, 2001 - No. 6, Nov, 2001 ($3.95, limited series)

1-6-Abnett & Lanning-s; art by various. 5-Dillon-a. 6-Timber Wolf app. 4.00

LEMONADE KID, THE (See Bobby Benson's B-Bar-B Riders)
AC Comics: 1990 ($2.50, 28 pgs.)

1-Powell-c(r); Red Hawk-r by Powell; Lemonade Kid-r/Bobby Benson by Powell (2 stories) 2.50

LENNON SISTERS LIFE STORY, THE
Dell Publishing Co.: No. 951, Nov, 1958 - No. 1014, Aug, 1959

Four Color 951 (#1)-Toth-a, 32pgs, photo-c 15 30 45 107 156 205
Four Color 1014-Toth-a, photo-c 14 28 42 102 149 195

LENORE
Slave Labor Graphics: Feb, 1998 - Present ($2.95, B&W)

1-10: 1-Roman Dirge-s/a, 1,2-2nd printing 3.00
...: Noogies TPB ($11.95) r/#1-4 12.00
...: Wedgies TPB (2000, $13.95) r/#5-8 14.00

LEONARD NIMOY'S PRIMORTALS
Tekno Comix: Mar, 1995 - No. 15, May, 1996 ($1.95)

1-15: Concept by Leonard Nimoy & Isaac Asimov 1-3-w/bound-in game piece & trading card. 4-w/Teknophage Steel Edition coupon. 13,14-Art Adams-c. 15-Simonson-c 2.25

LEONARD NIMOY'S PRIMORTALS
BIG Entertainment: V2#0, June, 1996 - No. 8, Feb, 1997 ($2.25)

V2#0-8: 0-Includes Pt. 9 of "The Big Bang" x-over. 0,1-Simonson-c. 3-Kelley Jones-c 2.25

LEONARD NIMOY'S PRIMORTALS ORIGINS
Tekno Comix: Nov, 1995 - No. 2, Dec, 1995 ($2.95, limited series)

1,2: Nimoy scripts; Art Adams-c; polybagged 3.00

LEONARDO (Also see Teenage Mutant Ninja Turtles)
Mirage Studios: Dec, 1986 ($1.50, B&W, one-shot)

1 5.00

LEO THE LION
I. W. Enterprises: No date(1960s) (10¢)

1-Reprint 2 4 6 10 13 16

LEROY (Teen-age)
Standard Comics: Nov, 1949 - No. 6, Nov, 1950

1 10 20 30 56 73 90
2-Frazetta text illo. 8 16 24 40 50 60
3-6: 3-Lubbers-a 6 12 18 31 38 45

LETHAL (Also see Brigade)
Image Comics (Extreme Studios): Feb, 1996 ($2.50, unfinished limited series)

1-Marat Mychaels-c/a. 2.50

LETHAL FOES OF SPIDER-MAN (Sequel to Deadly Foes of Spider-Man)
Marvel Comics: Sept, 1993 - No. 4, Dec, 1993 ($1.75, limited series)

1-4 2.50

LETHARGIC LAD
Crusade Ent.: June, 1996 - No. 3, Sept, 1996 ($2.95, B&W, limited series)

1,2 3.00
3-Alex Ross-c/swipe (Kingdom Come) 4.00
...Jumbo Sized Annual #1 (Summer 2002, $3.99) prints comic stories from internet 4.00

LETHARGIC LAD ADVENTURES
Crusade Ent./Destination Ent.#3 on: Oct, 1997 - No. 12, Sept./Oct. 1999 ($2.95, B&W)

1-12-Hyland-s/a. 9-Alex Ross sketch page & back-c 3.00

LET'S PRETEND (CBS radio)
D. S. Publishing Co.: May-June, 1950 - No. 3, Sept-Oct, 1950

1 17 34 51 98 134 170
2,3 13 26 39 74 100 125

LET'S READ THE NEWSPAPER

Liberty Meadows #22 © Creators Syndicate

Lidsville #2 © Sid & Marty Krofft

The Life Eaters HC © David Brin

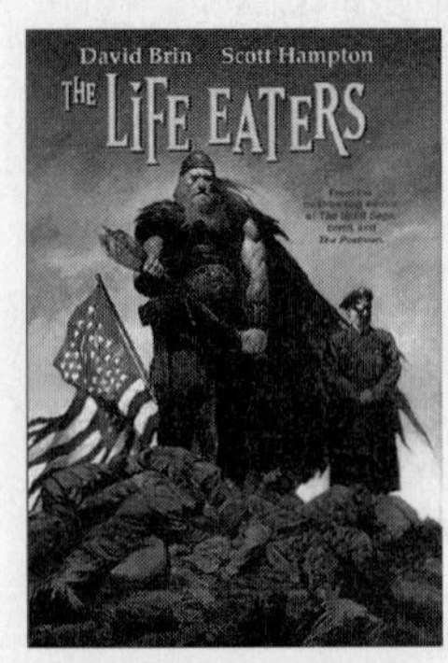

	GD 2.0	VG 4.0	FN 6.0	VF 8.0	VF/NM 9.0	NM- 9.2
Charlton Press: 1974						
nn-Features Quincy by Ted Sheares	1	3	4	6	8	10
LET'S TAKE A TRIP (TV) (CBS Television Presents) **Pines Comics:** Spring, 1958						
1-Marv Levy-c/a	5	10	15	23	28	32
LETTERS TO SANTA (See March of Comics No. 228)						
LEX LUTHOR: THE UNAUTHORIZED BIOGRAPHY **DC Comics:** 1989 ($3.95, 52 pgs., one-shot, squarebound)						
1-Painted-c; Clark Kent app.						4.00
LIBERTY COMICS (Miss Liberty No. 1) **Green Publishing Co.:** No. 5, May, '46 - No. 15, July, 1946 (MLJ & other-r)						
5 (5/46)-The Prankster app; Starr-a	21	42	63	118	164	210
10-Hangman & Boy Buddies app.; reprints 3 Hangman stories, incl. Hangman #8	22	44	66	124	172	220
11(V2#2, 1/46)-Wilbur in women's clothes	18	36	54	101	138	175
12-Black Hood & Suzie app.; classic Skull-c	40	80	120	240	358	475
14,15-Patty of Airliner; Starr-a in both	13	26	39	76	103	130
LIBERTY GUARDS **Chicago Mail Order:** No date (1946?)						
nn-Reprints Man of War #1 with cover of Liberty Scouts #1; Gustavson-c	37	74	111	212	301	390
LIBERTY MEADOWS **Insight Studios Group/Image Comics #27 on:** 1999 - Present ($2.95, B&W)						
1-Frank Cho-s/a; reprints newspaper strips	3	6	9	16	20	25
2,3	2	4	6	9	11	14
4-10	1	2	3	4	5	7
11-25,27-34: 20-Adam Hughes-c. 22-Evil Brandy vs. Brandy. 27-1st Image issue, printed sideways						3.00
...: Eden Book 1 SC (Image, 2002, $14.95) r/#1-9; sketch gallery						15.00
...: Eden Book 1 HC (Image, 2003, $24.95, with dustjacket) r/#1-9; sketch gallery						25.00
... Wedding Album(#26) (2002, $2.95)						3.00
LIBERTY PROJECT, THE **Eclipse Comics:** June, 1987 - No. 8, May, 1988 ($1.75, color, Baxter paper)						
1-8: 6-Valkyrie app.						2.25
LIBERTY SCOUTS (See Liberty Guards & Man of War) **Centaur Publications:** No. 2, June, 1941 - No. 3, Aug, 1941						
2(#1)-Origin The Fire-Man, Man of War; Vapo-Man & Liberty Scouts begin; intro Liberty Scouts; Gustavson-c/a in both	128	256	384	800	1200	1600
3(#2)-Origin & 1st app. The Sentinel	94	188	282	588	882	1175
LICENCE TO KILL (James Bond 007) (Movie) **Eclipse Comics:** 1989 ($7.95, slick paper, 52 pgs.)						
nn-Movie adaptation; Timothy Dalton photo-c	1	2	3	5	6	8
Limited Hardcover ($24.95)						25.00
LIDSVILLE (TV) **Gold Key:** Oct, 1972 - No. 5, Oct, 1973						
1-Photo-c	6	12	18	38	52	65
2-5	4	8	12	22	30	38
LIEUTENANT, THE (TV) **Dell Publishing Co.:** April-June, 1964						
1-Photo-c	3	6	9	19	25	32
LIEUTENANT BLUEBERRY (Also see Blueberry) **Marvel Comics (Epic Comics):** 1991 - No. 3, 1991 (Graphic novel)						
1,2 ($8.95)-Moebius-a in all						9.00
3 ($14.95)						15.00
LT. ROBIN CRUSOE, U.S.N. (See Movie Comics & Walt Disney Showcase #26)						
LIFE EATERS, THE **DC Comics (WildStorm):** 2003 ($29.95, hardcover with dust jacket)						
nn-David Brin-s; Scott Hampton-painted-a/c; Norse Gods team with the Nazis						30.00
LIFE OF CAPTAIN MARVEL, THE **Marvel Comics Group:** Aug, 1985 - No. 5, Dec, 1985 ($2.00, Baxter paper)						
1-5: 1-All reprint Starlin issues of Iron Man #55, Capt. Marvel #25-34 plus Marvel Feature #12 (all with Thanos). 4-New Thanos back-c by Starlin						3.00
LIFE OF CHRIST, THE **Catechetical Guild Educational Society:** No. 301, 1949 (35¢, 100 pgs.)						
301-Reprints from Topix(1949)-V5#11,12	9	18	27	49	62	75
LIFE OF CHRIST: THE CHRISTMAS STORY, THE **Marvel Comics/Nelson:** Feb, 1993 ($2.99, slick stock)						
nn						5.00
LIFE OF CHRIST: THE EASTER STORY, THE **Marvel Comics/Nelson:** 1993 ($2.99, slick stock)						
nn						5.00
LIFE OF CHRIST VISUALIZED **Standard Publishers:** 1942 - No. 3, 1943						
1-3: All came in cardboard case, each...	8	16	24	40	50	60
Case only.....	10	20	30	56	73	90
LIFE OF CHRIST VISUALIZED **The Standard Publ. Co.:** 1946? (48 pgs. in color)						
nn	5	10	15	24	30	35
LIFE OF ESTHER VISUALIZED **The Standard Publ. Co.:** No. 2062, 1947 (48 pgs. in color)						
2062	5	10	15	24	30	35
LIFE OF JOSEPH VISUALIZED **The Standard Publ. Co.:** No. 1054, 1946 (48 pgs. in color)						
1054	5	10	15	24	30	35
LIFE OF PAUL (See The Living Bible)						
LIFE OF POPE JOHN PAUL II, THE **Marvel Comics Group:** Jan, 1983 ($1.50/$1.75)						
1						6.00
LIFE OF RILEY, THE (TV) **Dell Publishing Co.:** No. 917, July, 1958						
Four Color 917-Photo-c	12	24	36	87	129	170
LIFE ON ANOTHER PLANET **Kitchen Sink Press:** 1978 (B&W, graphic novel, magazine size)						
nn-Will Eisner-s/a						13.00
Reprint (DC Comics, 5/00, $12.95)						13.00
LIFE'S LIKE THAT **Croyden Publ. Co.:** 1945 (25¢, B&W, 68 pgs.)						
nn-Newspaper Sunday strip-r by Neher	7	14	21	35	43	50
LIFE STORIES OF AMERICAN PRESIDENTS (See Dell Giants)						
LIFE STORY **Fawcett Publications:** Apr, 1949 - V8#46, Jan, 1953; V8#47, Apr, 1953 (All have photo-c?)						
V1#1	14	28	42	79	107	135
2	8	16	24	43	54	65
3-6, V2#7-12	7	14	21	37	46	55
V3#13-Wood-a	14	28	42	79	107	135
V3#14-18, V4#19-24, V5#25-30, V6#31-35	6	12	18	33	41	48
V6#36- "I sold drugs" on-c	8	16	24	43	54	65
V7#37,40-42, V8#44,45	6	12	18	29	36	42
V7#38, V8#43-Evans-a	6	12	18	33	41	48
V7#39-Drug Smuggling & Junkie story	7	14	21	37	46	55
V8#46,47 (Scarce)	7	14	21	37	46	55

NOTE: ***Powell*** *a-13, 23, 24, 26, 28, 30, 32, 39.* ***Marcus Swayze*** *a-1-3, 10-12, 15, 16, 20, 21, 23-25, 31, 35, 37, 40, 44, 46.*

	GD 2.0	VG 4.0	FN 6.0	VF 8.0	VF/NM 9.0	NM- 9.2
LIFE, THE UNIVERSE AND EVERYTHING (See Hitchhikers Guide to the Galaxy & Restaurant at the End of the Universe) **DC Comics:** 1996 - No. 3, 1996 ($6.95, squarebound, limited series)						
1-3: Adaptation of novel by Douglas Adams.	1	2	3	4	5	7
LIFE WITH ARCHIE **Archie Publications:** Sept, 1958 - No. 285, July, 1991						
1	28	56	84	203	297	390
2-(9/59)	14	28	42	99	145	190
3-5: 3-(7/60)	10	20	30	67	96	125
6-10	8	16	24	53	74	95
11-20	6	12	18	40	55	70
21(7/63)-30	4	8	12	29	40	50
31-41	4	8	12	24	32	40
42-Pureheart begins (1st app.-c/s, 10/65)	7	14	21	51	71	90
43,44	5	10	15	33	44	55
45(1/66) 1st Man From R.I.V.E.R.D.A.L.E.	6	12	18	43	59	75

Life With Archie #50 © AP

Limited Collectors' Edition C-32 © DC

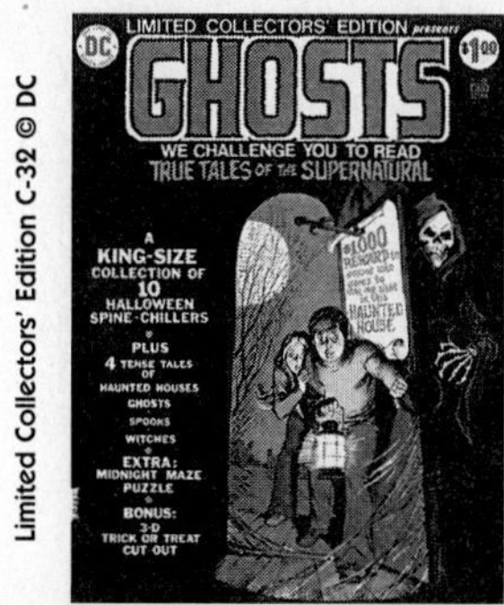

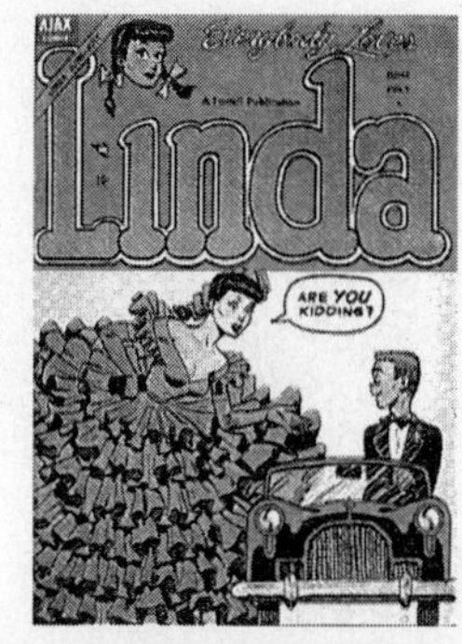

Linda #2 © AJAX

	GD 2.0	VG 4.0	FN 6.0	VF 8.0	VF/NM 9.0	NM- 9.2

46-Origin Pureheart 5 10 15 33 44 55
47-49 4 8 12 25 33 42
50-United Three begin: Pureheart (Archie), Superteen (Betty), Captain Hero (Jughead)
5 10 15 33 44 55
51-59: 59-Pureheart ends 4 8 12 25 33 42
60-Archie band begins, ends #66 5 10 15 33 44 55
61-66: 61-Man From R.I.V.E.R.D.A.L.E.-c/s 4 8 12 22 30 38
67-80 2 4 6 14 18 22
81-99 2 4 6 12 16 20
100 (8/70), 113-Sabrina & Salem app. 3 6 9 18 24 30
101-112, 114-130(2/73), 139(11/73)-Archie Band c/s 2 4 6 10 12 15
131,134-138,140-146,148-161,164-170(6/76) 1 3 4 6 8 10
132,133,147,163-all horror-c/s 2 4 6 10 12 15
162-UFO c/s 2 4 6 10 12 15
171,173-175,177-184,186,189,191-194,196 1 2 3 4 5 7
172,185,197 : 172-(9/77)-Bi-Cent. spec. ish, 185-2nd 24th cent.-c/s, 197-Time machine/ SF-c/s 1 2 3 5 6 8
176(12/76)-1st app. Capt. Archie of Starship Rivda, in 24th century c/s; 1st app. Stella the Robot 2 4 6 10 12 15
187,188,195,198,199-all horror-c/s 1 2 3 5 6 8
190-1st Dr. Doom-c/s 1 2 3 5 6 8
200 (12/78) Maltese Pigeon-s 1 2 3 5 7 9
201-203,205-237,239,240(1/84): 208-Reintro Veronica. 5.00
204-Flying saucer-c/s 1 2 3 4 5 7
238-(9/83)-25th anniversary issue; Ol' Betsy (jalopy) replaced 6.00
241-278,280-284: 250-Comic book convention-s 4.00
279,285: 279-Intro Mustang Sally ($1.00, 7/90) 5.00

NOTE: ***Gene Colan** a-272-279, 285, 286.*

LIFE WITH MILLIE (Formerly A Date With Millie) (Modeling With Millie #21 on)
Atlas/Marvel Comics Group: No. 8, Dec, 1960 - No. 20, Dec, 1962

8-Teenage 8 16 24 55 78 100
9-11 6 12 18 38 52 65
12-20 5 10 15 33 44 55

LIFE WITH SNARKY PARKER (TV)
Fox Feature Syndicate: Aug, 1950

1-Early TV comic; photo-c from TV puppet show 27 54 81 153 214 275

LIGHT AND DARKNESS WAR, THE
Marvel Comics (Epic Comics): Oct, 1988 - No. 6, Dec, 1989 ($1.95, lim. series)

1-6 2.25

LIGHT FANTASTIC, THE (Terry Pratchett's)
Innovation Publishing: June, 1992 - No. 4, Sept, 1992 ($2.50, mini-series)

1-4: Adapts 2nd novel in Discworld series 2.50

LIGHT IN THE FOREST (Disney)
Dell Publishing Co.: No. 891, Mar, 1958

Four Color 891-Movie, Fess Parker photo-c 8 16 24 61 83 110

LIGHTNING COMICS (Formerly Sure-Fire No. 1-3)
Ace Magazines: No. 4, Dec, 1940 - No. 13(V3#1), June, 1942

4-Characters continue from Sure-Fire 100 200 300 625 938 1250
5,6: 6-Dr. Nemesis begins 68 136 204 425 638 850
V2#1-6: 2- "Flash Lightning" becomes "Lash..." 55 110 165 330 495 660
V3#1-Intro. Lightning Girl & The Sword 55 110 165 330 495 660

NOTE: ***Anderson** a-V2#6. **Mooney** c-V1#5, 6, V2#1-6, V3#1. Bondage c-V2#6. Lightning-c on all.*

LIGHTNING COMICS PRESENTS
Lightning Comics: May, 1994 ($3.50)

1-Red foil-c distr. by Diamond Distr., 1-Black/yellow/blue-c distrib. by Capital Distr., 1-Red/yellow-c distributed by H. World, 1-Platinum 3.50

LI'L ... (See Little ...)

LILI
Image Comics: No. 0, 1999 ($4.95, B&W)

0-Bendis & Yanover-s 5.00

LILLITH (See Warrior Nun...)
Antarctic Press: Sept, 1996 - No. 3, Feb, 1997 ($2.95, limited series)

1-3: 1-Variant-c 3.00

LIMITED COLLECTORS' EDITION (See Famous First Edition, Marvel Treasury #28, Rudolph The Red-Nosed Reindeer, & Superman Vs. The Amazing Spider-Man; becomes All-New Collectors' Edition)
National Periodical Publications/DC Comics:
(#21-34,51-59: 84 pgs.; #35-41: 68 pgs.; #42-50: 60 pgs.)
C-21, Summer, 1973 - No. C-59, 1978 ($1.00) (10x13-1/2")
(Rudolph...C-20 (implied), 12/72)-See Rudolph The Red-Nosed Reindeer

C-21: Shazam (TV); r/Captain Marvel Jr. #11 by Raboy; C.C. Beck-c, biog. & photo 4 8 12 22 30 38
C-22: Tarzan; complete origin reprinted from #207-210; all Kubert-c/a; Joe Kubert biography & photo inside 3 6 9 18 24 30
C-23: House of Mystery; Wrightson, N. Adams/Orlando, G. Kane/Wood, Toth, Aragones, Sparling reprints 4 8 12 27 36 45
C-24: Rudolph The Red-Nosed Reindeer 8 16 24 53 74 95
C-25: Batman; Neal Adams-c/a(r); G.A. Joker-r; Batman/Enemy Ace-r; Novick-a(r); has photos from TV show 4 8 12 29 40 50
C-26: See Famous First Edition C-26 (same contents)
C-27,C-29,C-31: C-27: Shazam (TV); G.A. Capt. Marvel & Mary Marvel-r; Beck-r. C-29: Tarzan; reprints "Return of Tarzan" from #219-223 by Kubert; Kubert-c. C-31: Superman; origin-r; Giordano-a; photos of George Reeves from 1950s TV show on inside b/c; Burnley, Boring-r 3 6 9 18 23 28
C-32: Ghosts (new-a) 4 8 12 25 33 42
C-33: Rudolph The Red-Nosed Reindeer(new-a) 7 14 21 50 68 85
C-34: Christmas with the Super-Heroes; unpublished Angel & Ape story by Oksner & Wood; Batman & Teen Titans-r 3 6 9 18 23 28
C-35: Shazam (TV); photo cover features TV's Captain Marvel, Jackson Bostwick; Beck-r; TV photos inside b/c 3 6 9 16 20 25
C-36: The Bible; all new adaptation beginning with Genesis by Kubert, Redondo & Mayer; Kubert-c 3 6 9 16 20 25
C-37: Batman; r-1946 Sundays; inside b/c photos of Batman TV show villains (all villain issue; r/G.A. Joker, Catwoman, Penguin, Two-Face, & Scarecrow stories plus 1946 Sundays-r) 3 6 9 19 25 32
C-38: Superman; 1 pg. N. Adams; part photo-c; photos from TV show on inside back-c 3 6 9 16 20 25
C-39: Secret Origins of Super-Villains; N. Adams-i(r); collection reprints 1950's Joker origin, Luthor origin from Adv. Comics #271, Captain Cold origin from Showcase #8 among others; G.A. Batman-r; Beck-r 3 6 9 16 20 25
C-40: Dick Tracy by Gould featuring Flattop; newspaper-r from 12/21/43 - 5/17/44; biog. of Chester Gould 3 6 9 16 20 25
C-41: Super Friends (TV); JLA-r(1965); Toth-c/a 3 6 9 18 23 28
C-42: Rudolph 5 10 15 33 44 55
C-43-C-47: C-43: Christmas with the Super-Heroes; Wrightson, S&K, Neal Adams-a. C-44: Batman; N. Adams-p(r) & G.A.-r; painted-c. C-45: More Secret Origins of Super-Villains; Flash-r/#105; G.A. Wonder Woman & Batman/Catwoman-r. C-46: Justice League of America(1963-r); 3 pgs. Toth-a C-47: Superman Salutes the Bicentennial (Tomahawk interior); 2 pgs. new-a 3 6 9 16 20 24
C-48,C-49: C-48: Superman Vs. The Flash (Superman/Flash race); swipes-c to Superman #199; r/Superman #199 & Flash #175; 6 pgs. Neal Adams-a. C-49: Superboy & the Legion of Super-Heroes 3 6 9 18 23 28
C-50: Rudolph The Red-Nosed Reindeer 5 10 15 33 44 55
C-51: Batman; Neal Adams-c/a 3 6 9 18 24 30
C-52,C-57: C-52: The Best of DC; Neal Adams-c/a; Toth, Kubert-a. C-57: Welcome Back, Kotter-r(TV)(5/78) includes unpublished #11 3 6 9 16 20 25
C-59: Batman's Strangest Cases; N. Adams-r; Wrightson-r/Swamp Thing #7; N. Adams/Wrightson-c 3 6 9 16 20 25

NOTE: *All-r with exception of some special features and covers. **Aparo** a-52r; c-37. **Grell** c-49. **Infantino** a-25, 39, 44, 45, 52. **Bob Kane** r-25. **Robinson** r-25, 44. **Sprang** r-44. Issues #21-31, 35-39, 45, 48 have back cover cut-outs.*

LINDA (Everybody Loves...) (Phantom Lady No. 5 on)
Ajax-Farrell Publ. Co.: Apr-May, 1954 - No. 4, Oct-Nov, 1954

1-Kamenish-a 16 32 48 92 126 160
2-Lingerie panel 13 26 39 74 100 125
3,4 10 20 30 58 77 95

LINDA CARTER, STUDENT NURSE
Atlas Comics (AMI): Sept, 1961 - No. 9, Jan, 1963

1-Al Hartley-c 5 10 15 36 48 60
2-9 4 8 12 24 32 40

LINDA LARK
Dell Publishing Co.: Oct-Dec, 1961 - No. 8, Aug-Oct, 1963

1 3 7 10 21 28 35
2-8 2 4 6 14 18 22

LINUS, THE LIONHEARTED (TV)
Gold Key: Sept, 1965

1 (10155-509) 9 18 27 65 93 120

LION, THE (See Movie Comics)

LIONHEART

Lippy the Lion and Hardy Har Har #1 © GK

Little Archie #5 © AP

Little Audrey #27 © HARV

Awesome Comics: Sept, 1999 - No. 2 ($2.99/$2.50)

	GD 2.0	VG 4.0	FN 6.0	VF 8.0	VF/NM 9.0	NM- 9.2
1-Ian Churchill-story/a, Jeph Loeb-s; Coven app.						3.00
2-Flip book w/Coven #4						2.50

LION OF SPARTA (See Movie Classics)

LIPPY THE LION AND HARDY HAR HAR (TV)
Gold Key: Mar, 1963 (12¢) (See Hanna-Barbera Band Wagon #1)

	GD 2.0	VG 4.0	FN 6.0	VF 8.0	VF/NM 9.0	NM- 9.2
1 (10049-303)	10	20	30	73	107	140

LISA COMICS (TV)(See Simpsons Comics)
Bongo Comics: 1995 ($2.25)

	GD 2.0	VG 4.0	FN 6.0	VF 8.0	VF/NM 9.0	NM- 9.2
1-Lisa in Wonderland						3.00

LI'L ABNER (See Comics on Parade, Sparkle, Sparkler Comics, Tip Top Comics & Tip Topper)
United Features Syndicate: 1939 - 1940

	GD 2.0	VG 4.0	FN 6.0	VF 8.0	VF/NM 9.0	NM- 9.2
Single Series 4 ('39)	74	148	222	463	694	925
Single Series 18 ('40) (#18 on inside, #2 on-c)	60	120	180	375	563	750

LI'L ABNER (Al Capp's; continued from Comics on Parade #58)
Harvey Publ. No. 61-69 (2/49)/Toby Press No. 70 on: No. 61, Dec, 1947 - No. 97, Jan, 1955
(See Oxydol-Dreft in Promotional Comics section)

	GD 2.0	VG 4.0	FN 6.0	VF 8.0	VF/NM 9.0	NM- 9.2
61(#1)-Wolverton & Powell-a	35	70	105	201	288	370
62-65: 63-The Wolf Girl app. 65-Powell-a	21	42	63	118	164	210
66,67,69,70	19	38	57	106	146	185
68-Full length Fearless Fosdick-c/story	20	40	60	112	156	200
71-74,76,80	15	30	45	86	118	150
75,77-79,86,91-All with Kurtzman art; 86-Sadie Hawkins Day. 91-r/#77	19	38	57	106	146	185
81-85,87-90,92-94,96,97: 83-Evil-Eye Fleegle & Double Whammy app. 88-Cousin Weakeyes goes hunting. 94-Six lessons from Adam Lazonga. 96-Football issue	14	28	42	81	111	140
95-Full length Fearless Fosdick story	16	32	48	92	126	160

LI'L ABNER
Toby Press: 1951

	GD 2.0	VG 4.0	FN 6.0	VF 8.0	VF/NM 9.0	NM- 9.2
1	19	38	57	106	146	185

LI'L ABNER'S DOGPATCH (See Al Capp's...)

LITTLE AL OF THE F.B.I.
Ziff-Davis Publications: No. 10, 1950 (no month) - No. 11, Apr-May, 1951 (Saunders painted-c)

	GD 2.0	VG 4.0	FN 6.0	VF 8.0	VF/NM 9.0	NM- 9.2
10(1950)	17	34	51	98	134	170
11(1951)	14	28	42	79	107	135

LITTLE AL OF THE SECRET SERVICE
Ziff-Davis Publications: No. 10, 7-8/51; No, 2, 9-10/51; No. 3, Winter, 1951 (Saunders painted-c)

	GD 2.0	VG 4.0	FN 6.0	VF 8.0	VF/NM 9.0	NM- 9.2
10(#1)	17	34	51	98	134	170
2,3	14	28	42	79	107	135

LITTLE AMBROSE
Archie Publications: September, 1958

	GD 2.0	VG 4.0	FN 6.0	VF 8.0	VF/NM 9.0	NM- 9.2
1-Bob Bolling-c	15	30	45	84	115	145

LITTLE ANGEL
Standard (Visual Editions)/Pines: No. 5, Sept, 1954; No. 6, Sept, 1955 - No. 16, Sept, 1959

	GD 2.0	VG 4.0	FN 6.0	VF 8.0	VF/NM 9.0	NM- 9.2
5-Last pre-code issue	8	16	24	40	50	60
6-16	5	10	15	24	30	35

LITTLE ANNIE ROONEY (Also see Henry)
David McKay Publ.: 1935 (25¢, B&W dailies, 48 pgs.)(10"x10", cardboard-c)

	GD 2.0	VG 4.0	FN 6.0	VF 8.0	VF/NM 9.0	NM- 9.2
Book 1-Daily strip-r by Darrell McClure	39	78	117	230	325	420

LITTLE ANNIE ROONEY (See King Comics & Treasury of Comics)
David McKay/St. John/Standard: 1938; Aug, 1948 - No. 3, Oct, 1948

	GD 2.0	VG 4.0	FN 6.0	VF 8.0	VF/NM 9.0	NM- 9.2
Feature Books 11 (McKay, 1938)	39	78	117	230	325	420
1 (St. John)	16	32	48	92	126	160
2,3	9	18	27	52	66	80

LITTLE ARCHIE (The Adventures of... #13-on) (See Archie Giant Series Mag. #527, 534, 538, 545, 549, 556, 560, 566, 570, 583, 594, 596, 607, 609, 619)
Archie Publications: 1956 - No. 180, Feb, 1983 (Giants No. 3-84)

	GD 2.0	VG 4.0	FN 6.0	VF 8.0	VF/NM 9.0	NM- 9.2
1-(Scarce)	55	110	165	468	714	960
2 (1957)	26	52	78	189	275	360
3-5: 3-(1958)-Bob Bolling-c & giant issues begin	15	30	45	104	152	200
6-10	11	22	33	77	114	150
11-22 (84 pgs.)	8	16	24	55	78	100
23-39 (68 pgs.)	6	12	18	43	59	75
40 (Fall/66)-Intro. Little Pureheart-c/s (68 pgs.)	7	14	21	50	68	85
41,44-Little Pureheart (68 pgs.)	6	12	18	40	55	70
42-Intro The Little Archies Band, ends #66 (68 pgs.)	7	14	21	46	63	80
43-1st Boy From R.I.V.E.R.D.A.L.E. (68 pgs.)	6	12	18	43	59	75
45-58 (68pgs.)	4	8	12	29	40	50
59 (68pgs.)-Little Sabrina begins	8	16	24	58	82	105
60-66 (68 pgs.)	4	8	12	27	36	45
67(9/71)-84: 84-Last 52pg. Giant-Size (2/74)	3	6	9	18	23	28
85-99	2	4	6	9	11	14
100	2	4	6	10	13	16
101-112,114-116,118-129	1	2	3	5	7	9
113,117,130: 113-Halloween Special issue(12/76). 117-Donny Osmond-c cameo 130-UFO cover (5/78)	2	4	6	8	10	12
131-150(1/80), 180(Last issue, 2/83)						6.00
151-179						4.00
...In Animal Land 1 (1957)	13	26	39	90	133	175
...In Animal Land 17 (Winter, 1957-58)-19 (Summer,1958)-Formerly Li'l Jinx	8	16	24	53	74	95

NOTE: *Little Archie Band app. 42-66. Little Sabrina in 59-78,80-180*

LITTLE ARCHIE CHRISTMAS SPECIAL (See Archie Giant Series #581)

LITTLE ARCHIE COMICS DIGEST ANNUAL (...Magazine #5 on)
Archie Publications: 10/77 - No. 48, 5/91 (Digest-size, 128 pgs., later issues $1.35-$1.50)

	GD 2.0	VG 4.0	FN 6.0	VF 8.0	VF/NM 9.0	NM- 9.2
1(10/77)-Reprints	3	6	9	16	20	25
2(4/78,3(11/78)-Neal Adams-a. 3-The Fly-r by S&K	2	4	6	14	18	22
4(4/79) - 10	2	4	6	10	12	15
11-20	1	3	4	6	8	10
21-30: 28-Christmas-c	1	2	3	4	5	7
31-48: 40,46-Christmas-c						5.00

NOTE: *Little Archie, Little Jinx, Little Jughead & Little Sabrina in most issues.*

LITTLE ARCHIE DIGEST MAGAZINE
Archie Comics: July, 1991 - No. 25 ($1.50/$1.79/$1.89, digest size, bi-annual)

	GD 2.0	VG 4.0	FN 6.0	VF 8.0	VF/NM 9.0	NM- 9.2
V2#1						6.00
2-10						3.50
11-25						2.50

LITTLE ARCHIE MYSTERY
Archie Publications: Aug, 1963 - No. 2, Oct, 1963 (12¢ issues)

	GD 2.0	VG 4.0	FN 6.0	VF 8.0	VF/NM 9.0	NM- 9.2
1	12	24	36	82	121	160
2	7	14	21	46	63	80

LITTLE ASPIRIN (See Little Lenny & Wisco)
Marvel Comics (CnPC): July, 1949 - No. 3, Dec, 1949 (52 pgs.)

	GD 2.0	VG 4.0	FN 6.0	VF 8.0	VF/NM 9.0	NM- 9.2
1-Oscar app.; Kurtzman-a (4 pgs.)	17	34	51	98	134	170
2-Kurtzman-a (4 pgs.)	10	20	30	56	73	90
3-No Kurtzman-a	8	16	24	40	50	60

LITTLE AUDREY (Also see Playful...)
St. John Publ.: Apr, 1948 - No. 24, May, 1952

	GD 2.0	VG 4.0	FN 6.0	VF 8.0	VF/NM 9.0	NM- 9.2
1-1st app. Little Audrey	42	84	126	252	376	500
2	24	48	72	138	194	250
3-5	16	32	48	92	126	160
6-10	12	24	36	69	92	115
11-20: 16-X-Mas-c	9	18	27	52	66	80
21-24	8	16	24	43	54	65

LITTLE AUDREY (See Harvey Hits #11, 19)
Harvey Publications: No. 25, Aug, 1952 - No. 53, April, 1957

	GD 2.0	VG 4.0	FN 6.0	VF 8.0	VF/NM 9.0	NM- 9.2
25-(Paramount Pictures Famous Star... on-c); 1st Harvey Casper and Baby Huey (1 month earlier than Harvey Comic Hits #60(9/52))	14	28	42	97	141	185
26-30: 26-28-Casper app.	7	14	21	51	71	90
31-40: 32-35-Casper app.	6	12	18	43	59	75
41-53	4	8	12	29	40	50
...Clubhouse 1 (9/61, 68 pg. Giant)-New stories & reprints	9	18	27	63	89	115

LITTLE AUDREY
Harvey Comics: Aug, 1992 - No. 8, July, 1994 ($1.25/$1.50)

	GD 2.0	VG 4.0	FN 6.0	VF 8.0	VF/NM 9.0	NM- 9.2
V2#1						3.00
2-8						2.25

LITTLE AUDREY (...Yearbook)
St. John Publishing Co.: 1950 (50¢, 260 pgs.)

	GD 2.0	VG 4.0	FN 6.0	VF 8.0	VF/NM 9.0	NM- 9.2
Contains 8 complete 1949 comics rebound; Casper, Alice in Wonderland, Little Audrey, Abbott & Costello, Pinocchio, Moon Mullins, Three Stooges (from Jubilee), Little Annie Rooney app. (Rare)	66	132	198	413	619	825

Little Dot #13 © HARV

Little Eva #2 © STJ

Li'l Genius #55 © CC

	GD 2.0	VG 4.0	FN 6.0	VF 8.0	VF/NM 9.0	NM- 9.2

(Also see All Good & Treasury of Comics)
NOTE: *This book contains remaindered St. John comics; many variations possible.*

LITTLE AUDREY & MELVIN (Audrey & Melvin No. 62)
Harvey Publications: May, 1962 - No. 61, Dec, 1973

	GD 2.0	VG 4.0	FN 6.0	VF 8.0	VF/NM 9.0	NM- 9.2
1	10	20	30	70	100	130
2-5	6	12	18	38	52	65
6-10	4	8	12	29	40	50
11-20	3	6	9	18	24	30
21-40: 22-Richie Rich app.	2	4	6	14	18	22
41-50,55-61	2	4	6	10	13	16
51-54: All 52 pg. Giants	2	4	6	14	18	22

LITTLE AUDREY TV FUNTIME
Harvey Publ.: Sept, 1962 - No. 33, Oct, 1971 (#1-31: 68 pgs.; #32,33: 52 pgs.)

	GD 2.0	VG 4.0	FN 6.0	VF 8.0	VF/NM 9.0	NM- 9.2
1-Richie Rich app.	10	20	30	70	100	130
2,3: Richie Rich app.	6	12	18	40	55	70
4,5: 5-25¢ & 35¢ issues exist	5	10	15	36	48	60
6-10	4	8	12	22	30	38
11-20	3	6	9	16	20	24
21-33	2	4	6	12	16	20

LITTLE BAD WOLF (Disney; seeWalt Disney's C&S #52, Walt Disney Showcase #21 & Wheaties)
Dell Publishing Co.: No. 403, June, 1952 - No. 564, June, 1954

	GD 2.0	VG 4.0	FN 6.0	VF 8.0	VF/NM 9.0	NM- 9.2
Four Color 403 (#1)	8	16	24	55	78	100
Four Color 473 (6/53), 564	5	10	15	36	48	60

LITTLE BEAVER
Dell Publishing Co.: No. 211, Jan, 1949 - No. 870, Jan, 1958 (All painted-c)

	GD 2.0	VG 4.0	FN 6.0	VF 8.0	VF/NM 9.0	NM- 9.2
Four Color 211('49)-All Harman-a	9	18	27	63	89	115
Four Color 267,294,332(5/51)	5	10	15	36	48	60
3(10-12/51)-8(1-3/53)	5	10	15	33	44	55
Four Color 483(8-10/53),529	4	8	12	29	40	50
Four Color 612,660,695,744,817,870	4	8	12	29	40	50

LITTLE BIT
Jubilee/St. John Publishing Co.: Mar, 1949 - No. 2, June, 1949

	GD 2.0	VG 4.0	FN 6.0	VF 8.0	VF/NM 9.0	NM- 9.2
1	9	18	27	54	70	85
2	7	14	21	37	46	55

LITTLE DOT (See Humphrey, Li'l Max, Sad Sack, and Tastee-Freez Comics)
Harvey Publications: Sept, 1953 - No. 164, Apr, 1976

	GD 2.0	VG 4.0	FN 6.0	VF 8.0	VF/NM 9.0	NM- 9.2
1-Intro./1st app. Richie Rich & Little Lotta	160	320	480	1000	1500	2000
2-1st app. Freckles & Pee Wee (Richie Rich's poor friends)	60	120	180	375	563	750
3	42	84	126	252	376	500
4	37	74	111	213	299	385
5-Origin dots on Little Dot's dress	42	84	126	252	376	500
6-Richie Rich, Little Lotta, & Little Dot all on cover; 1st Richie Rich cover featured	42	84	126	252	376	500
7-10: 9-Last pre-code issue (1/55)	24	48	72	138	194	250
11-20	17	34	51	95	130	165
21-30	11	22	33	66	88	110
31-40	9	18	27	54	70	85
41-50	8	16	24	40	50	60
51-60	7	14	21	35	43	50
61-80	4	8	12	24	32	40
81-100	3	6	9	18	24	30
101-141	2	4	6	14	18	22
142-145: All 52 pg. Giants	3	6	9	16	20	25
146-164	2	4	6	9	11	14

NOTE: *Richie Rich & Little Lotta in all.*

LITTLE DOT
Harvey Comics: Sept, 1992 - No. 7, June, 1994 ($1.25/$1.50)

	GD 2.0	VG 4.0	FN 6.0	VF 8.0	VF/NM 9.0	NM- 9.2
V2#1-Little Dot, Little Lotta, Richie Rich in all						3.00
2-7 ($1.50)						2.50

LITTLE DOT DOTLAND (Dot Dotland No. 62, 63)
Harvey Publications: July, 1962 - No. 61, Dec, 1973

	GD 2.0	VG 4.0	FN 6.0	VF 8.0	VF/NM 9.0	NM- 9.2
1-Richie Rich begins	12	24	36	82	121	160
2,3	7	14	21	46	63	80
4,5	6	12	18	40	55	70
6-10	4	8	12	29	40	50
11-20	3	7	10	21	28	35
21-30	3	6	9	16	20	25
31-50	2	4	6	14	18	22
51-54: All 52 pg. Giants	3	6	9	16	20	25
55-61	2	4	6	10	12	15

LITTLE DOT'S UNCLES & AUNTS (See Harvey Hits No. 4, 13, 24)
Harvey Enterprises: Oct, 1961; No. 2, Aug, 1962 - No. 52, Apr, 1974

	GD 2.0	VG 4.0	FN 6.0	VF 8.0	VF/NM 9.0	NM- 9.2
1-Richie Rich begins; 68 pgs. begin	14	28	42	99	145	190
2,3	8	16	24	53	74	95
4,5	6	12	18	40	55	70
6-10	5	10	15	33	44	55
11-20	4	8	12	24	32	40
21-37: Last 68 pg. issue	3	6	9	18	23	28
38-52: All 52 pg. Giants	2	4	6	14	18	22

LITTLE DRACULA
Harvey Comics: Jan, 1992 - No. 3, May, 1992 ($1.25, quarterly, mini-series)

	GD 2.0	VG 4.0	FN 6.0	VF 8.0	VF/NM 9.0	NM- 9.2
1-3						3.00

LITTLE ENDLESS STORYBOOK, THE (See The Sandman titles)
DC Comics: 2001 ($5.95, Prestige format, one-shot)

	GD 2.0	VG 4.0	FN 6.0	VF 8.0	VF/NM 9.0	NM- 9.2
nn-Jill Thompson-s/painted-a/c; puppy Barnabas searches for Delirium						20.00

LITTLE EVA
St. John Publishing Co.: May, 1952 - No. 31, Nov, 1956

	GD 2.0	VG 4.0	FN 6.0	VF 8.0	VF/NM 9.0	NM- 9.2
1	16	32	48	92	126	160
2	9	18	27	52	66	80
3-5	8	16	24	40	50	60
6-10	7	14	21	35	43	50
11-31	6	12	18	31	38	45
3-D 1,2(10/53, 11/53, 25¢)-Both came w/glasses. 1-Infinity-c	23	46	69	129	180	230
I.W. Reprint #1-3,6-8: 1-r/Little Eva #28. 2-r/Little Eva #29. 3-r/Little Eva #24	2	4	6	9	11	14
Super Reprint #10,12('63),14,16,18('64): 18-r/Little Eva #25.	2	4	6	9	11	14

LI'L GENIUS (Formerly Super Brat; Summer Fun No. 54) (See Blue Bird & Giant Comics #3)
Charlton Comics: 1954 - No. 52, 1/65; No. 53, 10/65; No. 54, 10/85 - No. 55, 1/86

	GD 2.0	VG 4.0	FN 6.0	VF 8.0	VF/NM 9.0	NM- 9.2
5(#1?)	11	22	33	66	88	110
6-10	7	14	21	37	46	55
11-15,19,20	6	12	18	29	36	42
16,17-(68 pgs.)	8	16	24	40	50	60
18-(100 pgs., 10/58)	11	22	33	63	84	105
21-35	3	6	9	18	23	28
36-53	2	4	6	11	14	18
54,55 (Low print)						5.00

LI'L GHOST
St. John Publ. Co./Fago No. 1 on: 2/58; No. 2,1/59 - No. 3, Mar, 1959

	GD 2.0	VG 4.0	FN 6.0	VF 8.0	VF/NM 9.0	NM- 9.2
1(St. John)	9	18	27	52	66	80
2,3	6	12	18	28	34	40

LITTLE GIANT COMICS
Centaur Publications: 7/38 - No. 3, 10/38; No. 4, 2/39 (132 pgs.) (6-3/4x4-1/2")

	GD 2.0	VG 4.0	FN 6.0	VF 8.0	VF/NM 9.0	NM- 9.2
1-B&W with color-c; stories, puzzles, magic	66	132	198	413	617	820
2,3-B&W with color-c	55	110	165	344	515	685
4 (6-5/8x9-3/8")(68 pgs., B&W inside)	55	110	165	344	515	685

NOTE: ***Filchock** c-2, 4. **Gustavson** a-1. **Pinajian** a-4. **Bob Wood** a-1.*

LITTLE GIANT DETECTIVE FUNNIES
Centaur Publ.: Oct, 1938; No. 4, Jan, 1939 (6-3/4x4-1/2", 132 pgs., B&W)

	GD 2.0	VG 4.0	FN 6.0	VF 8.0	VF/NM 9.0	NM- 9.2
1-B&W with color-c	76	152	228	475	713	950
4(1/39, B&W; color-c; 68 pgs., 6-1/2x9-1/2")-Eisner-r	55	110	165	344	515	685

LITTLE GIANT MOVIE FUNNIES
Centaur Publ.: Aug, 1938 - No. 2, Oct, 1938 (6-3/4x4-1/2", 132 pgs., B&W)

	GD 2.0	VG 4.0	FN 6.0	VF 8.0	VF/NM 9.0	NM- 9.2
1-Ed Wheelan's "Minute Movies" reprints	76	152	228	475	713	950
2-Ed Wheelan's "Minute Movies" reprints	55	110	165	344	515	685

LITTLE GROUCHO (...the Red-Headed Tornado; ...Grouchy No. 2)
Reston Publ. Co.: No. 16; Feb-Mar, 1955 - No. 2, June-July, 1955 (See Tippy Terry)

	GD 2.0	VG 4.0	FN 6.0	VF 8.0	VF/NM 9.0	NM- 9.2
16, 1 (2-3/55)	8	16	24	43	54	65
2(6-7/55)	6	12	18	27	33	38

LITTLE HIAWATHA (Disney; see Walt Disney's C&S #143)
Dell Publishing Co.: No. 439, Dec, 1952 - No. 988, May-July, 1959

	GD 2.0	VG 4.0	FN 6.0	VF 8.0	VF/NM 9.0	NM- 9.2
Four Color 439 (#1)	6	12	18	43	59	75

Little Lotta #6 © HARV

Little Lulu #215 © Marjorie Buell

Little Max Comics #3 © HARV

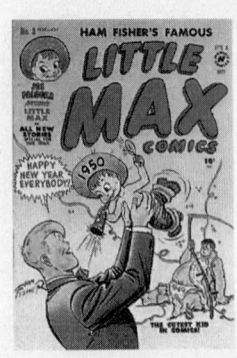

	GD 2.0	VG 4.0	FN 6.0	VF 8.0	VF/NM 9.0	NM- 9.2
Four Color 787 (4/57), 901 (5/58), 988	5	10	15	36	48	60

LITTLE IKE
St. John Publishing Co.: April, 1953 - No. 4, Oct, 1953

	GD 2.0	VG 4.0	FN 6.0	VF 8.0	VF/NM 9.0	NM- 9.2
1	10	20	30	56	73	90
2	6	12	18	31	38	45
3,4	5	10	15	24	30	35

LITTLE IODINE (See Giant Comic Album)
Dell Publ. Co.: No. 224, 4/49 - No. 257, 1949: 3-5/50 - No. 56, 4-6/62 (1-4-52pgs.)

	GD 2.0	VG 4.0	FN 6.0	VF 8.0	VF/NM 9.0	NM- 9.2
Four Color 224-By Jimmy Hatlo	12	24	36	82	121	160
Four Color 257	9	18	27	60	85	110
1(3-5/50)	10	20	30	72	104	135
2-5	5	10	15	36	48	60
6-10	4	8	12	27	36	45
11-20	3	7	10	21	28	35
21-30: 27-Xmas-c	3	6	9	19	25	32
31-40	3	6	9	18	23	28
41-56	2	4	6	14	18	22

LITTLE JACK FROST
Avon Periodicals: 1951

	GD 2.0	VG 4.0	FN 6.0	VF 8.0	VF/NM 9.0	NM- 9.2
1	10	20	30	58	77	95

LI'L JINX (Little Archie in Animal Land #17) (Also see Pep Comics #62)
Archie Publications: No. 11, Nov, 1956 - No. 16, Sept, 1957

	GD 2.0	VG 4.0	FN 6.0	VF 8.0	VF/NM 9.0	NM- 9.2
11-By Joe Edwards	13	26	39	74	100	125
12(1/57)-16	10	20	30	56	73	90

LI'L JINX (See Archie Giant Series Magazine No. 223)

LI'L JINX CHRISTMAS BAG (See Archie Giant Series Mag. No. 195, 206, 219)

LI'L JINX GIANT LAUGH-OUT (See Archie Giant Series Mag. No. 176, 185)
Archie Publications: No. 33, Sept, 1971 - No. 43, Nov, 1973 (52 pgs.)

	GD 2.0	VG 4.0	FN 6.0	VF 8.0	VF/NM 9.0	NM- 9.2
33-43 (52 pgs.)	2	4	6	11	14	18

LITTLE JOE (See Popular Comics & Super Comics)
Dell Publishing Co.: No. 1, 1942

	GD 2.0	VG 4.0	FN 6.0	VF 8.0	VF/NM 9.0	NM- 9.2
Four Color 1	50	100	150	400	600	800

LITTLE JOE
St. John Publishing Co.: Apr, 1953

	GD 2.0	VG 4.0	FN 6.0	VF 8.0	VF/NM 9.0	NM- 9.2
1	5	10	15	23	28	32

LI'L KIDS (Also see Li'l Pals)
Marvel Comics Group: 8/70 - No. 2, 10/70; No. 3, 11/71 - No. 12, 6/73

	GD 2.0	VG 4.0	FN 6.0	VF 8.0	VF/NM 9.0	NM- 9.2
1	6	12	18	43	59	75
2-9	4	8	12	24	32	40
10-12-Calvin app.	4	8	12	27	36	45

LITTLE KING
Dell Publishing Co.: No. 494, Aug, 1953 - No. 677, Feb, 1956

	GD 2.0	VG 4.0	FN 6.0	VF 8.0	VF/NM 9.0	NM- 9.2
Four Color 494 (#1)	10	20	30	72	104	135
Four Color 597, 677	6	12	18	40	55	70

LITTLE LANA (Formerly Lana)
Marvel Comics (MjMC): No. 8, Nov, 1949; No. 9, Mar, 1950

	GD 2.0	VG 4.0	FN 6.0	VF 8.0	VF/NM 9.0	NM- 9.2
8,9	9	18	27	52	66	80

LITTLE LENNY
Marvel Comics (CDS): June, 1949 - No. 3, Nov, 1949

	GD 2.0	VG 4.0	FN 6.0	VF 8.0	VF/NM 9.0	NM- 9.2
1-Little Aspirin app.	12	24	36	69	92	115
2,3	8	16	24	40	50	60

LITTLE LIZZIE
Marvel Comics (PrPI)/Atlas (OMC): 6/49 - No. 5, 4/50; 9/53 - No. 3, Jan, 1954

	GD 2.0	VG 4.0	FN 6.0	VF 8.0	VF/NM 9.0	NM- 9.2
1	13	26	39	74	100	125
2-5	8	16	24	43	54	65
1 (9/53, 2nd series by Atlas)-Howie Post-c	9	18	27	49	62	75
2,3	7	14	21	35	43	50

LITTLE LOTTA (See Harvey Hits No. 10)
Harvey Publications: 11/55 - No. 110, 11/73; No. 111, 9/74 - No. 120, 5/76
V2#1, Oct, 1992 - No. 4, July, 1993 ($1.25)

	GD 2.0	VG 4.0	FN 6.0	VF 8.0	VF/NM 9.0	NM- 9.2
1-Richie Rich (r) & Little Dot begin	33	66	99	248	374	500
2,3	16	32	48	116	171	225
4,5	10	20	30	72	104	135
6-10	8	16	24	55	78	100
11-20	6	12	18	40	55	70
21-40	4	8	12	24	32	40
41-60	3	7	10	21	28	35
61-80: 62-1st app. Nurse Jenny	3	6	9	16	20	25
81-99	2	4	6	11	14	18
100-103: All 52 pg. Giants	2	4	6	14	18	22
104-120	1	3	4	6	8	10
V2#1-4 (1992-93)						3.00

NOTE: *No. 121 was advertised, but never released.*

LITTLE LOTTA FOODLAND
Harvey Publications: 9/63 - No. 14, 10/67; No. 15, 10/68 - No. 29, Oct, 1972

	GD 2.0	VG 4.0	FN 6.0	VF 8.0	VF/NM 9.0	NM- 9.2
1-Little Lotta, Little Dot, Richie Rich, 68 pgs. begin	13	26	39	94	137	180
2,3	9	18	27	60	85	110
4,5	6	12	18	43	59	75
6-10	5	10	15	33	44	55
11-20	3	6	9	19	25	32
21-26: 26-Last 68 pg. issue	3	6	9	16	20	24
27,28: Both 52 pgs.	2	4	6	14	18	22
29-(36 pgs.)	2	4	6	9	11	14

LITTLE LULU (Formerly Marge's Little Lulu)
Gold Key 207-257/Whitman 258 on: No. 207, Sept, 1972 - No. 268, Mar, 1984

	GD 2.0	VG 4.0	FN 6.0	VF 8.0	VF/NM 9.0	NM- 9.2
207,209,220-Stanley-r. 207-1st app. Henrietta	2	4	6	11	14	18
208,210-219: 208-1st app. Snobbly, Wilbur's butler	2	4	6	9	11	14
221-240,242-249, 250(r/#166), 251-254(r/#206)	1	2	3	5	7	9
241,263-Stanley-r	1	3	4	6	8	10
255-257(Gold Key): 256-r/#212	1	2	3	5	6	8
258,259,262,264(2/82),265(3/82) (Whitman)	2	4	6	8	10	12
260-(9/80)(Whitman pre-pack only - low distribution)	13	26	39	94	137	180
261-(11/80)(Whitman pre-pack only)	3	7	10	21	28	35
266-268 (All #90028 on-c; no date, no date code; 3-pack): 266(7/83). 267(8/83). 268(3/84)-Stanley-r	2	4	6	12	16	20

LITTLE MARY MIXUP (See Comics On Parade)
United Features Syndicate: No. 10, 1939, - No. 26, 1940

	GD 2.0	VG 4.0	FN 6.0	VF 8.0	VF/NM 9.0	NM- 9.2
Single Series 10, 26	36	72	108	204	290	375

LITTLE MAX COMICS (Joe Palooka's Pal; see Joe Palooka)
Harvey Publications: Oct, 1949 - No. 73, Nov, 1961

	GD 2.0	VG 4.0	FN 6.0	VF 8.0	VF/NM 9.0	NM- 9.2
1-Infinity-c; Little Dot begins; Joe Palooka on-c	22	44	66	124	172	220
2-Little Dot app.; Joe Palooka on-c	11	22	33	66	88	110
3-Little Dot app.; Joe Palooka on-c	9	18	27	52	66	80
4-10: 5-Little Dot app., 1pg.	8	16	24	40	50	60
11-20	7	14	21	35	43	50
21-40: 23-Little Dot app. 38-r/#20	6	12	18	28	34	40
41-73: 63-65,67-73-Include new five pg. Richie Rich stories. 70-73-Little Lotta app.	3	6	9	18	24	30

LI'L MENACE
Fago Magazine Co.: Dec, 1958 - No. 3, May, 1959

	GD 2.0	VG 4.0	FN 6.0	VF 8.0	VF/NM 9.0	NM- 9.2
1-Peter Rabbit app.	8	16	24	46	58	70
2-Peter Rabbit (Vincent Fago's)	7	14	21	35	43	50
3	6	12	18	28	34	40

LITTLE MERMAID, THE (Walt Disney's...; also see Disney's...)
W. D. Publications (Disney): 1990 (no date given)($5.95, no ads, 52 pgs.)

	GD 2.0	VG 4.0	FN 6.0	VF 8.0	VF/NM 9.0	NM- 9.2
nn-Adapts animated movie	1	2	3	4	5	7
nn-Comic version ($2.50)						3.00

LITTLE MERMAID, THE
Disney Comics: 1992 - No. 4, 1992 ($1.50, mini-series)

	GD 2.0	VG 4.0	FN 6.0	VF 8.0	VF/NM 9.0	NM- 9.2
1-4: Based on movie						3.00
1-4: 2nd printings sold at Wal-Mart w/different-c						2.25

LITTLE MISS MUFFET
Best Books (Standard Comics)/King Features Synd.: No. 11, Dec, 1948 - No. 13, March, 1949

	GD 2.0	VG 4.0	FN 6.0	VF 8.0	VF/NM 9.0	NM- 9.2
11-Strip reprints; Fanny Cory-c/a	8	16	24	43	54	65
12,13-Strip reprints; Fanny Cory-c/a	6	12	18	28	34	40

LITTLE MISS SUNBEAM COMICS
Magazine Enterprises/Quality Bakers of America: June-July, 1950 - No. 4, Dec-Jan, 1950-51

	GD 2.0	VG 4.0	FN 6.0	VF 8.0	VF/NM 9.0	NM- 9.2
1	17	34	51	98	134	170
2-4	10	20	30	56	73	90
...Advs. In Space ('55)	7	14	21	35	43	50

LITTLE MONSTERS, THE (See March of Comics #423, Three Stooges #17)
Gold Key: Nov, 1964 - No. 44, Feb, 1978

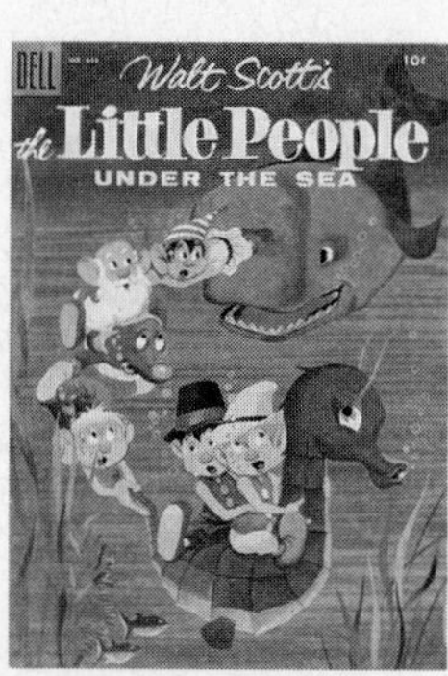

Little People Four Color #633 © DELL

Little Red Hot: Bound #3 © Dawn Brown

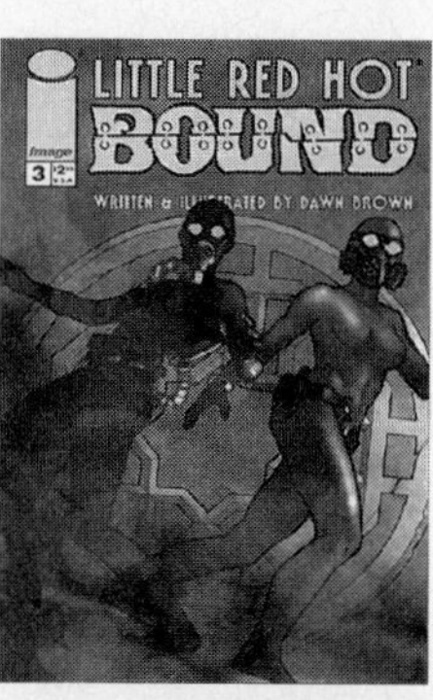

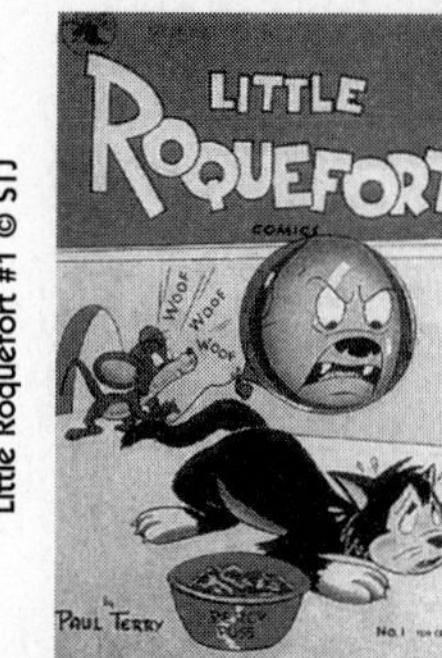

Little Roquefort #1 © STJ

	GD 2.0	VG 4.0	FN 6.0	VF 8.0	VF/NM 9.0	NM- 9.2
1	6	12	18	43	59	75
2	4	8	12	22	30	38
3-10	3	6	9	18	24	30
11-20	3	6	9	16	20	24
21-30	2	4	6	11	14	18
31-44: 20,34-39,43-Reprints	2	4	6	8	10	12

LITTLE MONSTERS (Movie)
Now Comics: 1989 - No. 6, June, 1990 ($1.75)

	GD 2.0	VG 4.0	FN 6.0	VF 8.0	VF/NM 9.0	NM- 9.2
1-6: Photo-c from movie						2.25

LITTLE NEMO (See Cocomalt, Future Comics, Help, Jest, Kayo, Punch, Red Seal, & Superworld; most by Winsor McCay Jr., son of famous artist) (Other McCay books: see Little Sammy Sneeze & Dreams of the Rarebit Fiend)

LITTLE NEMO (...in Slumberland)
McCay Features/Nostalgia Press('69): 1945 (11x7-1/4", 28 pgs., B&W)

	GD 2.0	VG 4.0	FN 6.0	VF 8.0	VF/NM 9.0	NM- 9.2
1905 & 1911 reprints by Winsor McCay	10	20	30	56	73	90
1969-70 (Exact reprint)	2	4	6	10	12	15

LITTLE ORPHAN ANNIE (See Annie, Famous Feature Stories, Marvel Super Special, Merry Christmas..., Popular Comics, Super Book #7, 11, 23 & Super Comics)

LITTLE ORPHAN ANNIE
David McKay Publ./Dell Publishing Co.: No. 7, 1937 - No. 3, Sept-Nov, 1948; No. 206, Dec, 1948

	GD 2.0	VG 4.0	FN 6.0	VF 8.0	VF/NM 9.0	NM- 9.2
Feature Books(McKay) 7-(1937) (Rare)	80	160	240	580	878	1175
Four Color 12(1941)	45	90	135	340	508	675
Four Color 18(1943)-Flag-c	37	74	111	278	414	550
Four Color 52(1944)	30	60	90	218	319	420
Four Color 76(1945)	26	52	78	185	270	355
Four Color 107(1946)	22	44	66	156	228	300
Four Color 152(1947)	14	28	42	102	149	195
1(3-5/48)-r/strips from 5/7/44 to 7/30/44	14	28	42	102	149	195
2-r/strips from 7/21/40 to 9/9/40	10	20	30	70	100	130
3-r/strips from 9/10/40 to 11/9/40	10	20	30	70	100	130
Four Color 206(12/48)	8	16	24	58	82	105

LI'L PALS (Also see Li'l Kids)
Marvel Comics Group: Sept, 1972 - No. 5, May, 1973

	GD 2.0	VG 4.0	FN 6.0	VF 8.0	VF/NM 9.0	NM- 9.2
1	6	12	18	40	55	70
2-5	4	8	12	24	32	40

LI'L PAN (Formerly Rocket Kelly; becomes Junior Comics with #9)
Fox Features Syndicate: No. 6, Dec-Jan, 1946-47 - No. 8, Apr-May, 1947
(Also see Wotalife Comics)

	GD 2.0	VG 4.0	FN 6.0	VF 8.0	VF/NM 9.0	NM- 9.2
6	10	20	30	56	73	90
7,8: 7-Atomic bomb story; robot-c	8	16	24	40	50	60

LITTLE PEOPLE (Also see Darby O'Gill & the...)
Dell Publishing Co.: No. 485, Aug-Oct, 1953 - No. 1062, Dec, 1959
(Walt Scott's)

	GD 2.0	VG 4.0	FN 6.0	VF 8.0	VF/NM 9.0	NM- 9.2
Four Color 485 (#1)	8	16	24	55	78	100
Four Color 573(7/54), 633(6/55)	5	10	15	33	44	55
Four Color 692(3/56),753(11/56),809(7/57),868(12/57),908(5/58), 959(12/58), 1062	5	10	15	33	44	55

LITTLE RASCALS
Dell Publishing Co.: No. 674, Jan, 1956 - No. 1297, Mar-May, 1962

	GD 2.0	VG 4.0	FN 6.0	VF 8.0	VF/NM 9.0	NM- 9.2
Four Color 674 (#1)	9	18	27	65	93	120
Four Color 778(3/57),825(8/57)	6	12	18	43	59	75
Four Color 883(3/58),936(9/58),974(3/59),1030(9/59),1079(2-4/60),1137(9-11/60)	6	12	18	43	59	75
Four Color 1174(3-5/61),1224(10-12/61),1297	5	10	15	36	48	60

LI'L RASCAL TWINS (Formerly Nature Boy)
Charlton Comics: No. 6, 1957 - No. 18, Jan, 1960

	GD 2.0	VG 4.0	FN 6.0	VF 8.0	VF/NM 9.0	NM- 9.2
6-Li'l Genius & Tomboy in all	6	12	18	29	36	42
7-18: 7-Timmy the Timid Ghost app.	4	8	12	18	22	25

LITTLE RED HOT: (CHANE OF FOOLS)
Image Comics: Feb, 1999 - No. 3, Apr, 1999 ($2.95/$3.50, B&W, limited series)

	GD 2.0	VG 4.0	FN 6.0	VF 8.0	VF/NM 9.0	NM- 9.2
1-3-Dawn Brown-s/a. 2,3-($3.50-c)						3.50
The Foolish Collection TPB ($12.95) r/#1-3						13.00

LITTLE RED HOT: BOUND
Image Comics: July, 2001 - No. 3, Nov, 2001 ($2.95, color, limited series)

	GD 2.0	VG 4.0	FN 6.0	VF 8.0	VF/NM 9.0	NM- 9.2
1-3-Dawn Brown-s/a.						3.00

LITTLE ROQUEFORT COMICS (See Paul Terry's Comics #105)
St. John Publishing Co.(all pre-code)/Pines No. 10: June, 1952 - No. 9, Oct, 1953; No. 10, Summer, 1958

	GD 2.0	VG 4.0	FN 6.0	VF 8.0	VF/NM 9.0	NM- 9.2
1-By Paul Terry	10	20	30	56	73	90
2	6	12	18	31	38	45
3-10: 10-CBS Television Presents on-c	5	10	15	24	30	35

LITTLE SAD SACK (See Harvey Hits No. 73, 76, 79, 81, 83)
Harvey Publications: Oct, 1964 - No. 19, Nov, 1967

	GD 2.0	VG 4.0	FN 6.0	VF 8.0	VF/NM 9.0	NM- 9.2
1-Richie Rich app. on cover only	6	12	18	38	52	65
2-10	3	6	9	19	25	32
11-19	3	6	9	16	20	25

LITTLE SCOUTS
Dell Publishing Co.: No. 321, Mar, 1951 - No. 587, Oct, 1954

	GD 2.0	VG 4.0	FN 6.0	VF 8.0	VF/NM 9.0	NM- 9.2
Four Color #321 (#1, 3/51)	4	8	12	28	38	48
2(10-12/51) - 6(10-12/52)	3	6	9	19	25	32
Four Color #462,506,550,587	3	6	9	19	25	32

LITTLE SHOP OF HORRORS SPECIAL (Movie)
DC Comics: Feb, 1987 ($2.00, 68 pgs.)

	GD 2.0	VG 4.0	FN 6.0	VF 8.0	VF/NM 9.0	NM- 9.2
1-Colan-c/a						4.00

LITTLE SPUNKY
I. W. Enterprises: No date (1963?) (10¢)

	GD 2.0	VG 4.0	FN 6.0	VF 8.0	VF/NM 9.0	NM- 9.2
1-r/Frisky Fables #1	2	4	6	9	11	14

LITTLE STOOGES, THE (The Three Stooges' Sons)
Gold Key: Sept, 1972 - No. 7, Mar, 1974

	GD 2.0	VG 4.0	FN 6.0	VF 8.0	VF/NM 9.0	NM- 9.2
1-Norman Maurer cover/stories in all	4	8	12	22	30	38
2-7	2	4	6	14	18	22

LITTLEST OUTLAW (Disney)
Dell Publishing Co.: No. 609, Jan, 1955

	GD 2.0	VG 4.0	FN 6.0	VF 8.0	VF/NM 9.0	NM- 9.2
Four Color 609-Movie, photo-c	7	14	21	51	71	90

LITTLEST SNOWMAN, THE
Dell Publishing Co.: No. 755, 12/56; No. 864, 12/57; 12-2/1963-64

	GD 2.0	VG 4.0	FN 6.0	VF 8.0	VF/NM 9.0	NM- 9.2
Four Color #755,864, 1(1964)	6	12	18	38	52	65

LI'L TOMBOY (Formerly Fawcett's Funny Animals; see Giant Comics #3)
Charlton Comics: V14#92, Oct, 1956; No. 93, Mar, 1957 - No. 107, Feb, 1960

	GD 2.0	VG 4.0	FN 6.0	VF 8.0	VF/NM 9.0	NM- 9.2
V14#92	5	10	15	24	30	35
93-107: 97-Atomic Bunny app.	5	10	14	20	24	28

LI'L WILLIE COMICS (Formerly & becomes Willie Comics #22 on)
Marvel Comics (MgPC): No. 20, July, 1949 - No. 21, Sept, 1949

	GD 2.0	VG 4.0	FN 6.0	VF 8.0	VF/NM 9.0	NM- 9.2
20,21: 20-Little Aspirin app.	10	20	30	58	77	95

LITTLE WOMEN (See Power Record Comics)

LIVE IT UP
Spire Christian Comics (Fleming H. Revell Co.): 1973, 1976 (39-49 cents)

	GD 2.0	VG 4.0	FN 6.0	VF 8.0	VF/NM 9.0	NM- 9.2
nn	1	3	4	6	8	10

LIVING BIBLE, THE
Living Bible Corp.: Fall, 1945 - No. 3, Spring, 1946

	GD 2.0	VG 4.0	FN 6.0	VF 8.0	VF/NM 9.0	NM- 9.2
1-The Life of Paul; all have L. B. Cole-c	40	80	120	240	340	440
2-Joseph & His Brethren; Jonah & the Whale	30	60	90	170	240	310
3-Chaplains At War (classic-c)	40	80	120	240	350	460

LOBO
Dell Publishing Co.: Dec, 1965; No. 2, Oct, 1966

	GD 2.0	VG 4.0	FN 6.0	VF 8.0	VF/NM 9.0	NM- 9.2
1-1st black character to have his own title	4	8	12	22	30	38
2	3	6	9	18	23	28

LOBO (Also see Action #650, Adventures of Superman, Demon (2nd series), Justice League, L.E.G.I.O.N., Mister Miracle, Omega Men #3 & Superman #41)
DC Comics: Nov, 1990 - No. 4, Feb, 1991 ($1.50, color, limited series)

	GD 2.0	VG 4.0	FN 6.0	VF 8.0	VF/NM 9.0	NM- 9.2
1-(99¢)-Giffen plots/Breakdowns in all						4.00
1-2nd printing						2.50
2-4: 2-Legion '89 spin-off. 1-4 have Bisley painted covers & art						2.50
...: Blazing Chain of Love 1 (9/92, $1.50)-Denys Cowan-c/a; Alan Grant scripts, ...Convention Special 1 (1993, $1.75), ...Paramilitary Christmas Special 1 (1991, $2.39, 52 pgs.) -Bisley-c/a, ...: Portrait of a Victim 1 (1993, $1.75)						2.50

LOBO (Also see Showcase '95 #9)
DC Comics: Dec, 1993 - No. 64, Jul, 1999 ($1.75/$1.95/$2.25/$2.50, mature)

	GD 2.0	VG 4.0	FN 6.0	VF 8.0	VF/NM 9.0	NM- 9.2
1 ($2.95)-Foil enhanced-c; Alan Grant scripts begin						3.00

2-9,0,10-64: 2-7-Alan Grant scripts. 9-(9/94). 0-(10/94)-Origin retold. 50-Lobo

Lobo #26 © DC

Lone #1 © DH

Lone Ranger #39 © Lone Ranger Inc.

	GD 2.0	VG 4.0	FN 6.0	VF 8.0	VF/NM 9.0	NM- 9.2
vs. the DCU. 58-Giffen-a						2.50
#1,000,000 (11/98) 853rd Century x-over						2.50
Annual 1 (1993, $3.50, 68 pgs.)-Bloodlines x-over						3.50
Annual 2 (1994, $3.50)-21 artists (20 listed on-c); Alan Grant script; Elseworlds story						3.50
Annual 3 (1995, $3.95)-Year One story						4.00
...Big Babe Spring Break Special (Spr, '95, $1.95)-Balent-a						2.50
...Bounty Hunting for Fun and Profit ('95)-Bisley-c						5.00
... Chained (5/97, $2.50)-Alan Grant story						2.50
.../Deadman: The Brave And The Bald (2/95, $3.50)						3.50
.../Demon: Helloween (12/96, $2.25)-Giarrano-a						2.50
...Fragtastic Voyage 1 ('97, $5.95)-Mejia painted-c/a						6.00
...Gallery (9/95, $3.50)-pin-ups.						3.50
...In the Chair 1 (8/94, $1.95, 36 pgs.), ...I Quit-(12/95, $2.25)						2.50
.../Judge Dredd ('95, $4.95).						5.00
...Lobocop 1 (2/94, $1.95)-Alan Grant scripts; painted-c						2.50

LOBO: (Title Series), DC Comics

	GD 2.0	VG 4.0	FN 6.0	VF 8.0	VF/NM 9.0	NM- 9.2
--A CONTRACT ON GAWD, 4/94 - 7/94 (mature) 1-4: Alan Grant scripts. 3-Groo cameo						2.50
--DEATH AND TAXES, 10/96 - No. 4, 1/97, 1-4-Giffen/Grant scripts						2.50
--GOES TO HOLLYWOOD, 8/96 ($2.25), 1-Grant scripts						2.50
--INFANTICIDE, 10/92 - 1/93 ($1.50, mature), 1-4-Giffen-c/a; Grant scripts						2.50
--/ MASK, 2/97 - No. 2, 3/97 ($5.95), 1,2						6.00
--'S BACK, 5/92 - No. 4, 11/92 ($1.50, mature), 1-4: 1-Has 3 outer covers. Bisley painted-c 1,2; a-1-3. 3-Sam Kieth-c; all have Giffen plots/breakdown & Grant scripts						2.50
Trade paperback (1993, $9.95)-r/1-4						10.00
--THE DUCK, 6/97 ($1.95), 1-A. Grant-s/V. Semeiks & R. Kryssing-a						2.50
--UNAMERICAN GLADIATORS, 6/93 - No. 4, 9/93 ($1.75, mature), 1-4-Mignola-c; Grant/Wagner scripts						2.50
--UNBOUND, 8/03 - No. 6 ($2.95, mature), 1-4-Giffen-s/Horley-c/a. 4-Ambush Bug app.						3.00

LOCKE!
Blackthorne Publishing: 1987 - No. 3, ($1.25, limited series)

	GD 2.0	VG 4.0	FN 6.0	VF 8.0	VF/NM 9.0	NM- 9.2
1-3						2.25

LOCO (Magazine) (Satire)
Satire Publications: Aug, 1958 - V1#3, Jan, 1959

	GD 2.0	VG 4.0	FN 6.0	VF 8.0	VF/NM 9.0	NM- 9.2
V1#1-Chic Stone-a	8	16	24	46	58	70
V1#2,3-Severin-a, 2 pgs. Davis; 3-Heath-a	7	14	21	35	43	50

LOGAN: PATH OF THE WARLORD
Marvel Comics: Feb, 1996 ($5.95, one-shot)

	GD 2.0	VG 4.0	FN 6.0	VF 8.0	VF/NM 9.0	NM- 9.2
1-John Paul Leon-a						6.00

LOGAN: SHADOW SOCIETY
Marvel Comics: 1996 ($5.95, one-shot)

	GD 2.0	VG 4.0	FN 6.0	VF 8.0	VF/NM 9.0	NM- 9.2
1						6.00

LOGAN'S RUN
Marvel Comics Group: Jan, 1977 - No. 7, July, 1977

	GD 2.0	VG 4.0	FN 6.0	VF 8.0	VF/NM 9.0	NM- 9.2
1: 1-5-Based on novel & movie	1	3	4	6	8	10
2-5,7: 6,7-New stories adapted from novel						6.00
6-1st Thanos (also see Iron Man #55) solo story (back-up) by Zeck (6/77)	2	4	6	12	16	20
6-(35¢-c variant, limited distribution)	3	6	9	18	24	30
7-(35¢-c variant, limited distribution)	1	2	3	5	7	9

NOTE: ***Austin*** *a-6i.* ***Gulacy*** *c-6.* ***Kane*** *c-7p.* ***Perez*** *a-1-5p; c-1-5p.* ***Sutton*** *a-6p, 7p.*

LOIS & CLARK, THE NEW ADVENTURES OF SUPERMAN
DC Comics: 1994 ($9.95, one-shot)

	GD 2.0	VG 4.0	FN 6.0	VF 8.0	VF/NM 9.0	NM- 9.2
1-r/Man of Steel #2, Superman Ann. 1, Superman #9 & 11, Action #600 & 655, Adventures of Superman #445, 462 & 466	1	3	4	6	8	10

LOIS LANE (Also see Daring New Adventures of Supergirl, Showcase #9,10 & Superman's Girlfriend...)
DC Comics: Aug, 1986 - No. 2, Sept, 1986 ($1.50, 52 pgs.)

	GD 2.0	VG 4.0	FN 6.0	VF 8.0	VF/NM 9.0	NM- 9.2
1,2-Morrow-c/a in each						4.00

LOLLY AND PEPPER
Dell Publishing Co.: No. 832, Sept, 1957 - July, 1962

	GD 2.0	VG 4.0	FN 6.0	VF 8.0	VF/NM 9.0	NM- 9.2
Four Color 832(#1)	4	8	12	28	38	48
Four Color 940,978,1086,1206	3	6	9	19	25	32
01-459-207 (7/62)	3	6	9	18	24	30

LOMAX (See Police Action)

LONDON'S DARK
Escape/Titan: 1989 ($8.95, B&W, graphic novel)

	GD 2.0	VG 4.0	FN 6.0	VF 8.0	VF/NM 9.0	NM- 9.2
nn-James Robinson script; Paul Johnson-c/a	1	2	3	5	7	9

LONE
Dark Horse Comics: Sept, 2003 - Present ($2.99)

	GD 2.0	VG 4.0	FN 6.0	VF 8.0	VF/NM 9.0	NM- 9.2
1,2-Stuart Moore-s/Jerome Opeña-a						3.00

LONE EAGLE (The Flame No. 5 on)
Ajax/Farrell Publications: Apr-May, 1954 - No. 4, Oct-Nov, 1954

	GD 2.0	VG 4.0	FN 6.0	VF 8.0	VF/NM 9.0	NM- 9.2
1	13	26	39	74	100	125
2-4: 3-Bondage-c	9	18	27	52	66	80

LONE GUNMEN, THE (From the X-Files)
Dark Horse Comics: June, 2001 ($2.99, one-shot)

	GD 2.0	VG 4.0	FN 6.0	VF 8.0	VF/NM 9.0	NM- 9.2
1-Paul Lee-a; photo-c						3.00

LONELY HEART (Formerly Dear Lonely Hearts; Dear Heart #15 on)
Ajax/Farrell Publ. (Excellent Publ.): No. 9, Mar, 1955 - No. 14, Feb, 1956

	GD 2.0	VG 4.0	FN 6.0	VF 8.0	VF/NM 9.0	NM- 9.2
9-Kamenesque-a; (Last precode)	10	20	30	56	73	90
10-14	7	14	21	35	43	50

LONE RANGER, THE (See Ace Comics, Aurora, Dell Giants,Future Comics, Golden Comics Digest #48, King Comics, Magic Comics & March of Comics #165, 174, 193, 208, 225, 238, 310, 322, 338, 350)

LONE RANGER, THE
Dell Publishing Co.: No. 3, 1939 - No. 167, Feb, 1947

	GD 2.0	VG 4.0	FN 6.0	VF 8.0	VF/NM 9.0	NM- 9.2
Large Feature Comic 3(1939)-Heigh-Yo Silver; text with illus. by Robert Weisman; also exists as a Whitman #710	126	252	378	788	1182	1575
Large Feature Comic 7(1939)-Illustr. by Henry Vallely; Hi-Yo Silver the Lone Ranger to the Rescue; also exists as a Whitman #715	122	244	366	763	1144	1525
Feature Book 21(1940), 24(1941)	78	156	234	488	732	975
Four Color 82(1945)	40	80	120	300	450	600
Four Color 98(1945),118(1946)	31	62	93	230	345	460
Four Color 125(1946),136(1947)	23	46	69	164	240	315
Four Color 151,167(1947)	20	40	60	142	209	275

LONE RANGER, THE (Movie, radio & TV; Clayton Moore starred as Lone Ranger in the movies; No. 1-37: strip reprints)(See Dell Giants)
Dell Publishing Co.: Jan-Feb, 1948 - No. 145, May-July, 1962

	GD 2.0	VG 4.0	FN 6.0	VF 8.0	VF/NM 9.0	NM- 9.2
1 (36 pgs.)-The Lone Ranger, his horse Silver, companion Tonto & his horse Scout begin	60	120	180	459	705	950
2 (52 pgs. begin, end #41)	31	62	93	223	324	425
3-5	23	46	69	167	244	320
6,7,9,10	19	38	57	138	202	265
8-Origin retold; Indian back-c begin, end #35	23	46	69	167	244	320
11-20: 11- "Young Hawk" Indian boy serial begins, ends #145	14	28	42	97	141	185
21,22,24-31: 51-Reprint. 31-1st Mask logo	11	22	33	77	114	150
23-Origin retold	14	28	42	99	145	190
32-37: 32-Painted-c begin. 36-Animal photo back-c begin, end #49. 37-Last newspaper-r issue; new outfit; red shirt becomes blue; most known copies show the blue shirt on-c & inside	9	18	27	65	93	120
37-Variant issue; Long Ranger wears a red shirt on-c and inside. A few copies of the red shirt outfit were printed before catching the mistake and changing the color to blue (rare)	17	34	51	123	182	240
38-41 (All 52 pgs.) 38-Paul S. Newman-s (wrote most of the stories #38-on)	9	18	27	65	93	120
42-50 (36 pgs.)	8	16	24	53	74	95
51-74 (52 pgs.): 56-One pg. origin story of Lone Ranger & Tonto. 71-Blank inside-c	8	16	24	53	74	95
75,77-99: 79-X-mas-c	7	14	21	50	68	85
76-Classic flag-c	8	16	24	53	74	95
100	8	16	24	58	82	105
101-111: Last painted-c	7	14	21	46	63	80
112-Clayton Moore photo-c begin, end #145	20	40	60	140	205	270
113-117: 117-10¢ &15¢-c exist	11	22	33	77	114	150
118-Origin Lone Ranger, Tonto, & Silver retold; Special anniversary issue	25	50	75	176	258	340
119-140: 139-Fran Striker-s	10	20	30	70	100	130
141-145	10	20	30	73	107	140

NOTE: ***Hank Hartman*** *painted c(signed)-65, 66, 70, 75, 82; unsigned-64?, 67-69?, 71, 72, 73?, 74?, 76-78, 80, 81, 83-91, 92?, 93-111.* ***Ernest Nordli*** *painted c(signed)-42, 50, 52, 53, 56, 59, 60; unsigned-39-41, 44-49, 51, 54, 55, 57, 58, 61-63?*

LONE RANGER, THE
Gold Key (Reprints in #13-20): 9/64 - No. 16, 12/69; No. 17, 11/72; No. 18, 9/74 - No. 28, 3/77

	GD 2.0	VG 4.0	FN 6.0	VF 8.0	VF/NM 9.0	NM- 9.2
1-Retells origin	7	14	21	46	63	80

Lone Rider #4 © Farrell Pub.

Lone Wolf and Cub #15 © FC

Looney Tunes and Merrie Melodies #21 © WB

	GD 2.0	VG 4.0	FN 6.0	VF 8.0	VF/NM 9.0	NM- 9.2
2	4	8	12	24	32	40
3-10: Small Bear-r in #6-12. 10-Last 12¢ issue	3	7	10	21	28	35
11-17	3	6	9	16	20	24
18-28	2	4	6	11	14	18
Golden West 1(30029-610, 10/66)-Giant; r/most Golden West #3 including Clayton Moore photo front/back-c	8	16	24	53	74	95

LONE RANGER AND TONTO, THE
Topps Comics: Aug, 1994 - No. 4, Nov, 1994 ($2.50, limited series)

	GD	VG	FN	VF	VF/NM	NM-
1-4: 3-Origin of Lone Ranger; Tonto leaves; Lansdale story, Truman-c/a in all.						2.50
1-4: Silver logo. 1-Signed by Lansdale and Truman						6.00
Trade paperback (1/95, $9.95)						10.00

LONE RANGER'S COMPANION TONTO, THE (TV)
Dell Publishing Co.: No. 312, Jan, 1951 - No. 33, Nov-Jan/58-59 (All painted-c)

	GD	VG	FN	VF	VF/NM	NM-
Four Color 312(#1, 1/51)	11	22	33	77	114	150
2(8-10/51),3: (#2 titled "Tonto")	6	12	18	43	59	75
4-10	6	12	18	38	52	65
11-20	5	10	15	33	44	55
21-33	4	8	12	27	36	45

NOTE: *Ernest Nordli painted c(signed)-2, 7; unsigned-3-6, 8-11, 12?, 13, 14, 18?, 22-24? See Aurora Comic Booklets.*

LONE RANGER'S FAMOUS HORSE HI-YO SILVER, THE (TV)
Dell Publishing Co.: No. 369, Jan, 1952 - No. 36, Oct-Dec, 1960 (All painted-c, most by Sam Savitt) (Lone Ranger appears in most issues)

	GD	VG	FN	VF	VF/NM	NM-
Four Color 369(#1)-Silver's origin as told by The Lone Ranger	10	20	30	73	107	140
Four Color 392(#2, 4/52)	6	12	18	40	55	70
3(7-9/52)-10(4-6/52)	5	10	15	36	48	60
11-36	4	8	12	29	40	50

LONE RIDER (Also see The Rider)
Superior Comics(Farrell Publ.): Apr, 1951 - No. 26, Jul, 1955 (#3-on: 36 pgs.)

	GD	VG	FN	VF	VF/NM	NM-
1 (52 pgs.)-The Lone Rider & his horse Lightnin' begin; Kamenish-a begins	31	62	93	175	248	320
2 (52 pgs.)-The Golden Arrow begins (origin)	16	32	48	92	126	160
3-6: 6-Last Golden Arrow	15	30	45	86	118	150
7-Golden Arrow becomes Swift Arrow; origin of his shield	16	32	48	92	126	160
8-Origin Swift Arrow	17	34	51	98	134	170
9,10	10	20	30	58	77	95
11-14	8	16	24	46	58	70
15-Golden Arrow origin-r from #2, changing name to Swift Arrow	9	18	27	54	70	85
16-20,22-26: 23-Apache Kid app.	8	16	24	40	50	60
21-3-D effect-c	16	32	48	92	126	160

LONE WOLF AND CUB
First Comics: May, 1987 - No. 45, Apr, 1991 ($1.95-$3.25, B&W, deluxe size)

	GD	VG	FN	VF	VF/NM	NM-
1-Frank Miller-c & intro.; reprints manga series by Koike & Kojima	1	2	3	6	8	10
1-2nd print, 3rd print, 2-2nd print						3.25
2-12: 6-72 pgs. origin issue						5.50
13-38,40: 40-Ploog-c						4.00
39-($5.95, 120 pgs.)-Ploog-c						6.50
41-44: 41-($3.95, 84 pgs.)-Ploog-c. 42-Ploog-c						6.00
45-Last issue; low print						7.00
Deluxe Edition ($19.95, B&W)						20.00

NOTE: *Sienkiewicz c-13-24. Matt Wagner c-25-30.*

LONE WOLF AND CUB (Trade paperbacks)
Dark Horse Comics: Aug, 2000 - No. 28 ($9.95, B&W, 4" x 6", approx. 300 pgs.)

	GD	VG	FN	VF	VF/NM	NM-
1-Collects First Comics reprint series; Frank Miller-c						18.00
1-(2nd printing)						12.00
1-(3rd-5th printings)						10.00
2,3-(1st printings)						12.00
2,3-(2nd printings)						10.00
4-28						10.00

LONE WOLF 2100 (Also see Reveal)
Dark Horse Comics: May, 2002 - Present ($2.99, color)

	GD	VG	FN	VF	VF/NM	NM-
1-New homage to Lone Wolf and Cub; Kennedy-s/Velasco-a						4.00
2-10						3.00
...: The Red File (1/03, $2.99) character and story background files						3.00
... Vol. 1 - Shadows on Saplings TPB (2003, $12.95, 6" x 9") r/#1-4						13.00
... Vol. 2 - The Language of Chaos TPB (2003, $12.95, 6" x 9") r/#5-8, Dirty Tricks short story from Reveal						13.00

LONG BOW (...Indian Boy)(See Indians & Jumbo Comics #141)
Fiction House Mag. (Real Adventures Publ.): 1951 - No. 9, Wint, 1952/53

	GD	VG	FN	VF	VF/NM	NM-
1-Most covers by Maurice Whitman	17	34	51	98	134	170
2	10	20	30	58	77	95
3-9	9	18	27	52	66	80

LONG HOT SUMMER, THE
DC Comics (Milestone): Jul, 1995 - No. 3, Sept, 1995 ($2.95/$2.50, lim. series)

	GD	VG	FN	VF	VF/NM	NM-
1-3: 1-($2.95-c). 2,3-($2.50-c)						3.00

LONG JOHN SILVER & THE PIRATES (Formerly Terry & the Pirates)
Charlton Comics: No. 30, Aug, 1956 - No. 32, March, 1957 (TV)

	GD	VG	FN	VF	VF/NM	NM-
30-32: Whitman-c	10	20	30	56	73	90

LONGSHOT (Also see X-Men, 2nd Series #10)
Marvel Comics: Sept, 1985 - No. 6, Feb, 1986 (60¢, limited series)

	GD	VG	FN	VF	VF/NM	NM-
1-6: 1-Art Adams/Whilce Portacio-c/a in all. 4-Spider-Man app. 6-Double size	1	2	3	4	5	7
Trade Paperback (1989, $16.95)-r/#1-6						17.00

LONGSHOT
Marvel Comics: Feb, 1998 ($3.99, one-shot)

	GD	VG	FN	VF	VF/NM	NM-
1-DeMatteis-s/Zulli-a						4.00

LOONEY TUNES (2nd Series) (TV)
Gold Key/Whitman: April, 1975 - No. 47, June, 1984

	GD	VG	FN	VF	VF/NM	NM-
1-Reprints	4	8	12	22	30	38
2-10: 2,4-reprints	2	4	6	12	16	20
11-20: 16-reprints	2	4	6	9	11	14
21-30	1	2	3	5	7	9
31,32,36-42(2/82)	1	2	3	4	5	7
33-(8/80)-35 (Whitman pre-pack only , scarce)	2	4	6	14	18	22
43(4/82),44(6/83) (low distribution)	2	4	6	9	11	14
45-47 (All #90296 on-c; nd, nd code, pre-pack) 45(8/83), 46(3/84), 47(6/84)	2	4	6	12	16	20

LOONEY TUNES (3rd Series) (TV)
DC Comics: Apr, 1994 - Present ($1.50/$1.75/$1.95/$1.99/$2.25)

	GD	VG	FN	VF	VF/NM	NM-
1-10: 1-Marvin Martian-c/sty; Bugs Bunny, Roadrunner, Daffy begin						3.00
11-110: 23-34-($1.75-c). 35-43-($1.95-c). 44-Begin $1.99-c. 83-Giffen-s. 93-Begin $2.25-c. 100-Art by various incl. Kyle Baker, Marie Severin, Darwyn Cooke, Jill Thompson						2.25
...Back In Action Movie Adaptation (12/03, $3.95) photo-c						4.00

LOONEY TUNES AND MERRIE MELODIES COMICS ("Looney Tunes" #166(8/55) on) (Also see Porky's Duck Hunt)
Dell Publishing Co.: 1941 - No. 246, July-Sept, 1962

	GD	VG	FN	VF	VF/NM	NM-
1-Porky Pig, Bugs Bunny, Daffy Duck, Elmer Fudd, Mary Jane & Sniffles, Pat Patsy and Pete begin (1st comic book app. of each). Bugs Bunny story by Win Smith (early Mickey Mouse artist)	1025	2050	3075	7175	11,588	16,000
2 (11/41)	150	300	450	1216	1858	2500
3-Kandi the Cave Kid begins by Walt Kelly; also in #4-6,8,11,15	115	230	345	901	1376	1850
4-Kelly-a	115	230	345	901	1376	1850
5-Bugs Bunny The Super-Duper Rabbit story (1st funny animal super hero, 3/42; also see Coo Coo); Kelly-a	90	180	270	706	1078	1450
6,8-Kelly-a	65	130	195	510	780	1050
7,9,10: 9-Painted-c. 10-Flag-c	52	104	156	416	621	825
11,15-Kelly-a; 15-X-Mas-c	52	104	156	416	621	825
12-14,16-19	40	80	120	300	450	600
20-25: Pat, Patsy & Pete by Walt Kelly in all	33	66	99	248	374	500
26-30	26	52	78	189	275	360
31-40: 33-War bond-c. 39-X-Mas-c	22	44	66	156	228	300
41-50	16	32	48	113	167	220
51-60	12	24	36	87	129	170
61-80	9	18	27	60	85	110
81-99: 87-X-Mas-c	7	14	21	51	71	90
100	8	16	24	55	78	100
101-120	6	12	18	43	59	75
121-150	5	10	15	36	48	60
151-200: 159-X-Mas-c	4	8	12	29	40	50
201-240	4	8	12	27	36	45
241-246	4	8	12	29	40	50

LOONY SPORTS (Magazine)
3-Strikes Publishing Co.: Spring, 1975 (68 pgs.)

The Losers #1 © DC

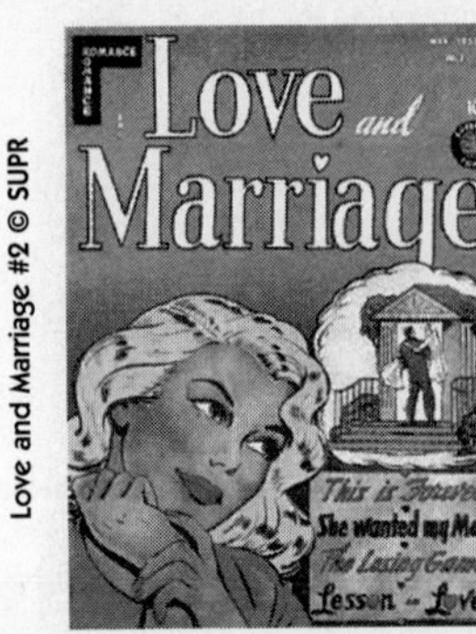

Love and Marriage #2 © SUPR

Love and Rockets V2#5 © Fantagraphics Books

	GD 2.0	VG 4.0	FN 6.0	VF 8.0	VF/NM 9.0	NM- 9.2
1-Sports satire	2	4	6	9	11	14

LOOSE CANNON (Also see Action Comics Annual #5 & Showcase '94 #5)
DC Comics: June, 1995 - No. 4, Sept, 1995 ($1.75, limited series)

	GD 2.0	VG 4.0	FN 6.0	VF 8.0	VF/NM 9.0	NM- 9.2
1-4: Adam Pollina-a. 1-Superman app.						2.50

LOOY DOT DOPE
United Features Syndicate: No. 13, 1939

	GD 2.0	VG 4.0	FN 6.0	VF 8.0	VF/NM 9.0	NM- 9.2
Single Series 13	31	62	93	175	248	320

LORD JIM (See Movie Comics)

LORD PUMPKIN
Malibu Comics (Ultraverse): Oct, 1994 ($2.50, one-shot)

	GD 2.0	VG 4.0	FN 6.0	VF 8.0	VF/NM 9.0	NM- 9.2
0-Two covers						2.50

LORD PUMPKIN/NECROMANTRA
Malibu Comics (Ultraverse): Apr, 1995 - No. 4, July, 1995 ($2.95, limited series, flip book)

	GD 2.0	VG 4.0	FN 6.0	VF 8.0	VF/NM 9.0	NM- 9.2
1-4						3.00

LORDS OF MISRULE
Dark Horse Comics: Jan, 1997 - No. 6, Jun, 1997 ($2.95, B&W, limited series)

	GD 2.0	VG 4.0	FN 6.0	VF 8.0	VF/NM 9.0	NM- 9.2
1-6: 1-Wraparound-c						3.00

LORDS OF THE ULTRA-REALM
DC Comics: June, 1986 - No. 6, Nov, 1986 (Mini-series)

	GD 2.0	VG 4.0	FN 6.0	VF 8.0	VF/NM 9.0	NM- 9.2
1-6, Special 1(12/87, $2.25)						2.25

LORE
IDW Publishing: Dec, 2003 - Present ($5.99)

	GD 2.0	VG 4.0	FN 6.0	VF 8.0	VF/NM 9.0	NM- 9.2
1-Ashley Wood-a/c; T P Louise & Wood-s						6.00

LORNA THE JUNGLE GIRL (...Jungle Queen #1-5)
Atlas Comics (NPI 1/OMC 2-11/NPI 12-26): July, 1953 - No. 26, Aug, 1957

	GD 2.0	VG 4.0	FN 6.0	VF 8.0	VF/NM 9.0	NM- 9.2
1-Origin & 1st app.	39	78	117	230	325	420
2-Intro. & 1st app. Greg Knight	20	40	60	112	156	200
3-5	17	34	51	98	134	170
6-11: 11-Last pre-code (1/55)	14	28	42	79	107	135
12-17,19-26: 14-Colletta & Maneely-c	11	22	33	63	84	105
18-Williamson/Colletta-c	12	24	36	69	92	115

NOTE: ***Brodsky*** *c-1-3, 5, 9.* ***Everett*** *c-21, 23-26.* ***Heath*** *c-6, 7.* ***Maneely*** *c-12, 15.* ***Romita*** *a-20, 22, 24, 26.* ***Shores*** *a-14-16, 24, 26; c-11, 13, 16.* ***Tuska*** *a-6.*

LOSERS
DC Comics (Vertigo): Aug, 2003 - Present ($2.95)

	GD 2.0	VG 4.0	FN 6.0	VF 8.0	VF/NM 9.0	NM- 9.2
1-Andy Diggle-s/Jock-a						5.00
2-7						3.00

LOSERS SPECIAL (See Our Fighting Forces #123)(Also see G.I. Combat & Our Fighting Forces)
DC Comics: Sept, 1985 ($1.25, one-shot)

	GD 2.0	VG 4.0	FN 6.0	VF 8.0	VF/NM 9.0	NM- 9.2
1-Capt. Storm, Gunner & Sarge; Crisis x-over						5.00

LOST, THE
Chaos! Comics: Dec, 1997 - No. 3 ($2.95, B&W, unfinished limited series)

	GD 2.0	VG 4.0	FN 6.0	VF 8.0	VF/NM 9.0	NM- 9.2
1-3-Andreyko-script: 1-Russell back-c						3.00

LOST CONTINENT
Eclipse Int'l: Sept, 1990 - No. 6, 1991 ($3.50, B&W, squarebound, 60 pgs.)

	GD 2.0	VG 4.0	FN 6.0	VF 8.0	VF/NM 9.0	NM- 9.2
1-6: Japanese story translated to English						3.50

LOST HEROES
Davdez Arts: Mar, 1998 - No. 4 ($2.95)

	GD 2.0	VG 4.0	FN 6.0	VF 8.0	VF/NM 9.0	NM- 9.2
0-4-Rob Prior-s/painted-a						3.00

LOST IN SPACE (Movie)
Dark Horse Comics: Apr, 1998 - No. 3, July, 1998 ($2.95, limited series)

	GD 2.0	VG 4.0	FN 6.0	VF 8.0	VF/NM 9.0	NM- 9.2
1-3-Continuation of 1998 movie; Erskine-c						3.00

LOST IN SPACE (TV)(Also see Space Family Robinson)
Innovation Publishing: Aug, 1991 - No. 12, Jan, 1993 ($2.50, limited series)

	GD 2.0	VG 4.0	FN 6.0	VF 8.0	VF/NM 9.0	NM- 9.2
1-12: Bill Mumy (Will Robinson) scripts in #1-9. 9-Perez-c						3.00
1,2-Special Ed.; r/#1,2 plus new art & new-c						3.00
Annual 1,2 (1991, 1992, $2.95, 52 pgs.)						3.00
...: Project Robinson (11/93, $2.50) 1st & only part of intended series						3.00

LOST IN SPACE: VOYAGE TO THE BOTTOM OF THE SOUL
Innovation Publishing: No. 13, Aug, 1993 - No. 18, 1994 ($2.50, limited series)

	GD 2.0	VG 4.0	FN 6.0	VF 8.0	VF/NM 9.0	NM- 9.2
13(V1#1, $2.95)-Embossed silver logo edition; Bill Mumy scripts begin; painted-c						3.00
13(V1#1, $4.95)-Embossed gold logo edition bagged w/poster						5.00
14-18: Painted-c						3.00

NOTE: *Originally intended to be a 12 issue limited series.*

LOST ONES, THE
Image Comics: Mar, 2000 ($2.95)

	GD 2.0	VG 4.0	FN 6.0	VF 8.0	VF/NM 9.0	NM- 9.2
1-Ken Penders-s/a						3.00

LOST PLANET
Eclipse Comics: 5/87 - No. 5, 2/88; No. 6, 3/89 (Mini-series, Baxter paper)

	GD 2.0	VG 4.0	FN 6.0	VF 8.0	VF/NM 9.0	NM- 9.2
1-6-Bo Hampton-c/a in all						2.25

LOST WAGON TRAIN, THE (See Zane Grey Four Color 583)

LOST WORLD, THE
Dell Publishing Co.: No. 1145, Nov-Jan, 1960-61

	GD 2.0	VG 4.0	FN 6.0	VF 8.0	VF/NM 9.0	NM- 9.2
Four Color 1145-Movie, Gil Kane-a, photo-c; 1pg. Conan Doyle biography by Torres	10	20	30	73	107	140

LOST WORLD, THE (See Jurassic Park)
Topps Comics: May, 1997 - No. 4, Aug, 1997 ($2.95, limited series)

	GD 2.0	VG 4.0	FN 6.0	VF 8.0	VF/NM 9.0	NM- 9.2
1-4-Movie adaption						3.00

LOST WORLDS (Weird Tales of the Past and Future)
Standard Comics: No. 5, Oct, 1952 - No. 6, Dec, 1952

	GD 2.0	VG 4.0	FN 6.0	VF 8.0	VF/NM 9.0	NM- 9.2
5- "Alice in Terrorland" by Alex Toth; J. Katz-a	43	86	129	258	389	520
6-Toth-a	38	76	114	219	310	400

LOTS 'O' FUN COMICS
Robert Allen Co.: 1940's? (5¢, heavy stock, blue covers)

nn-Contents can vary; Felix, Planet Comics known; contents would determine value. Similar to Up-To-Date Comics. Remainders - re-packaged.

LOU GEHRIG (See The Pride of the Yankees)

LOVE ADVENTURES (Actual Confessions #13)
Marvel (IPS)/Atlas Comics (MPI): Oct, 1949; No. 2, Jan, 1950; No. 3, Feb, 1951 - No. 12, Aug, 1952

	GD 2.0	VG 4.0	FN 6.0	VF 8.0	VF/NM 9.0	NM- 9.2
1-Photo-c	17	34	51	98	134	170
2-Powell-a; Tyrone Power, Gene Tierney photo-c	15	30	45	86	118	150
3-8,10-12: 8-Robinson-a	9	18	27	49	62	75
9-Everett-a	9	18	27	52	66	80

LOVE AND MARRIAGE
Superior Comics Ltd. (Canada): Mar, 1952 - No. 16, Sept, 1954

	GD 2.0	VG 4.0	FN 6.0	VF 8.0	VF/NM 9.0	NM- 9.2
1	14	28	42	79	107	135
2	8	16	24	43	54	65
3-10	7	14	21	37	46	55
11-16	6	12	18	31	38	45
I.W. Reprint #1,2,8,11,14: 8-r/Love and Marriage #3. 11-r/Love and Marriage #11	2	4	6	10	13	16
Super Reprint #10('63),15,17('64):15-Love and Marriage #?	2	4	6	10	13	16

NOTE: *All issues have* ***Kamenish*** *art.*

LOVE AND ROCKETS
Fantagraphics Books: July, 1982 - No. 50, May, 1996 ($2.95/$2.50/$4.95, B&W, mature)

	GD 2.0	VG 4.0	FN 6.0	VF 8.0	VF/NM 9.0	NM- 9.2
1-B&W-c (6/82, $2.95; small size, publ. by Hernandez Bros.)(800 printed)	4	8	12	27	36	45
1 (Fall, '82; color-c)	3	6	9	18	23	28
1-2nd & 3rd printing, 2-11,29-31: 2nd printings						3.00
2	1	2	3	5	7	9
3-10	1	2	3	4	5	7
11-49: 30 ($2.95, 52 pgs.)						4.00
50-($4.95)						5.00

LOVE AND ROCKETS (Volume 2)
Fantagraphics Books: Spring, 2001 - Present ($3.95, B&W, mature)

	GD 2.0	VG 4.0	FN 6.0	VF 8.0	VF/NM 9.0	NM- 9.2
1-9-Gilbert, Jaime and Mario Hernandez-s/a						4.00

LOVE AND ROMANCE
Charlton Comics: Sept, 1971 - No. 24, Sept, 1975

	GD 2.0	VG 4.0	FN 6.0	VF 8.0	VF/NM 9.0	NM- 9.2
1	3	6	9	19	25	32
2-10	2	4	6	10	13	16
11-24	1	3	4	6	8	10

LOVE AT FIRST SIGHT
Ace Magazines (RAR Publ. Co./Periodical House): Oct, 1949 - No. 43, Nov, 1956 (Photo-c: 21-42)

	GD 2.0	VG 4.0	FN 6.0	VF 8.0	VF/NM 9.0	NM- 9.2
1-Painted-c	14	28	42	81	111	140
2-Painted-c	8	16	24	46	58	70
3-10: 4-Painted-c	7	14	21	37	46	55

Lovebunny and Mr. Hell: A Day in the Lovelife #1 © IM

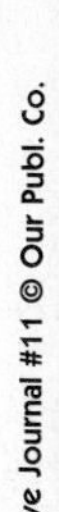
Love Journal #11 © Our Publ. Co.

Love Lessons #3 © HARV

	GD 2.0	VG 4.0	FN 6.0	VF 8.0	VF/NM 9.0	NM- 9.2
11-20	7	14	21	35	43	50
21-33: 33-Last pre-code	6	12	18	31	38	45
34-43	6	12	18	28	34	40

LOVE BUG, THE (See Movie Comics)

LOVEBUNNY AND MR. HELL
Devil's Due Publ./Image Comics: 2002 - Present ($2.95, B&W, one-shots)

	GD 2.0	VG 4.0	FN 6.0	VF 8.0	VF/NM 9.0	NM- 9.2
1-Tim Seeley-s						3.00
...: A Day in the Lovelife (Image, 2003) Blaylock-a						3.00
...: Savage Love (Image, 2003) Seeley-s/a; Savage Dragon app.; Seeley & Larsen-c						3.00

LOVE CLASSICS
A Lover's Magazine/Marvel: Nov, 1949 - No. 2, Feb, 1950 (Photo-c, 52 pgs.)

	GD 2.0	VG 4.0	FN 6.0	VF 8.0	VF/NM 9.0	NM- 9.2
1,2: 2-Virginia Mayo photo-c; 30 pg. story "I Was a Small Town Flirt"	14	28	42	81	111	140

LOVE CONFESSIONS
Quality Comics: Oct, 1949 - No. 54, Dec, 1956 (Photo-c: 3,4,6,7,9,11-18,21)

	GD 2.0	VG 4.0	FN 6.0	VF 8.0	VF/NM 9.0	NM- 9.2
1-Ward-c/a, 9 pgs; Gustavson-a	31	62	93	178	252	325
2-Gustavson-a; Ward-c	15	30	45	84	115	145
3	9	18	27	52	66	80
4-Crandall-a	10	20	30	58	77	95
5-Ward-a, 7 pgs.	12	24	36	69	92	115
6,7,9,11-13,15,16,18: 7-Van Johnson photo-c. 8-Robert Mitchum & Jane Russell photo-c	8	16	24	40	50	60
8,10-Ward-a (2 stories in #10)	12	24	36	69	92	115
14,17,19,22-Ward-a; 17-Faith Domerque photo-c	11	22	33	63	84	105
20-Ward-a(2)	12	24	36	69	92	115
21,23-28,30-38,40-42: Last precode, 4/55	6	12	18	31	38	45
29-Ward-a	10	20	30	58	77	95
39-Matt Baker-a	8	16	24	43	54	65
43,44,46-48,50-54: 47-Ward-c?	6	12	18	28	34	40
45-Ward-a	8	16	24	40	50	60
49-Baker-c/a	9	18	27	49	62	75

LOVE DIARY
Our Publishing Co./Toytown/Patches: July, 1949 - No. 48, Oct, 1955 (Photo-c: 1-24,27-29) (52 pgs. #1-11?)

	GD 2.0	VG 4.0	FN 6.0	VF 8.0	VF/NM 9.0	NM- 9.2
1-Krigstein-a	20	40	60	112	156	200
2,3-Krigstein & Mort Leav-a in each	12	24	36	71	96	120
4-8	8	16	24	43	54	65
9,10-Everett-a	8	16	24	46	58	70
11-20: 16- Mort Leav-a, 3 pg. Baker-sty. Leav-a	8	16	24	40	50	60
21-30,32-48: 45-Leav-a. 47-Last precode(12/54)	7	14	21	37	46	55
31-John Buscema headlights-c	8	16	24	43	54	65

LOVE DIARY (Diary Loves #2 on; title change due to previously published title)
Quality Comics Group: Sept, 1949

	GD 2.0	VG 4.0	FN 6.0	VF 8.0	VF/NM 9.0	NM- 9.2
1-Ward-c/a, 9 pgs.	32	64	96	182	259	335

LOVE DIARY
Charlton Comics: July, 1958 - No. 102, Dec, 1976

	GD 2.0	VG 4.0	FN 6.0	VF 8.0	VF/NM 9.0	NM- 9.2
1	9	18	27	52	66	80
2	6	12	18	33	41	48
3-5,7-10: 10-Photo-c	6	12	18	27	33	38
6-Torres-a	6	12	18	31	38	45
11-20: 20-Photo-c	3	6	9	18	24	30
21-40	3	6	9	16	20	24
41-60	2	4	6	11	14	18
61-80,100-102	2	4	6	9	11	14
81-99	1	3	4	6	8	10

LOVE DOCTOR (See Dr. Anthony King...)

LOVE DRAMAS (True Secrets No. 3 on?)
Marvel Comics (IPS): Oct, 1949 - No. 2, Jan, 1950

	GD 2.0	VG 4.0	FN 6.0	VF 8.0	VF/NM 9.0	NM- 9.2
1-Jack Kamen-a; photo-c	19	38	57	106	146	185
2	13	26	39	74	100	125

LOVE EXPERIENCES (Challenge of the Unknown No. 6)
Ace Periodicals (A.A. Wyn/Periodical House): Oct, 1949 - No. 5, June, 1950; No. 6, Apr, 1951 - No. 38, June, 1956

	GD 2.0	VG 4.0	FN 6.0	VF 8.0	VF/NM 9.0	NM- 9.2
1-Painted-c	13	26	39	76	103	130
2	8	16	24	43	54	65
3-5: 5-Painted-c	7	14	21	37	46	55
6-10	7	14	21	35	43	50
11-30: 30-Last pre-code (2/55)	6	12	18	28	34	40

	GD 2.0	VG 4.0	FN 6.0	VF 8.0	VF/NM 9.0	NM- 9.2
31-38: 38-Indicia date-6/56; c-date-8/56	5	10	15	24	30	35

NOTE: ***Anne Brewster** a-15. Photo c-4, 15-35, 38.*

LOVE FIGHTS
Oni Press: June, 2003 - Present ($2.99, B&W)

1-6-Andi Watson-s/a

LOVE JOURNAL
Our Publishing Co.: No. 10, Oct, 1951 - No. 25, July, 1954

	GD 2.0	VG 4.0	FN 6.0	VF 8.0	VF/NM 9.0	NM- 9.2
10	10	20	30	58	77	95
11-25: 19-Mort Leav-a	7	14	21	37	46	55

LOVELAND
Mutual Mag./Eye Publ. (Marvel): Nov, 1949 - No. 2, Feb, 1950 (52 pgs.)

	GD 2.0	VG 4.0	FN 6.0	VF 8.0	VF/NM 9.0	NM- 9.2
1,2-Photo-c	11	22	33	63	84	105

LOVE LESSONS
Harvey Comics/Key Publ. No. 5: Oct, 1949 - No. 5, June, 1950

	GD 2.0	VG 4.0	FN 6.0	VF 8.0	VF/NM 9.0	NM- 9.2
1-Metallic silver-c printed over the cancelled covers of Love Letters #1; indicia title is "Love Letters"	14	28	42	81	111	140
2-Powell-a; photo-c	8	16	24	46	58	70
3-5: 3-Photo-c	7	14	21	37	46	55

LOVE LETTERS (10/49, Harvey; advertised but never published; covers were printed before cancellation and were used as the cover to Love Lessons #1)

LOVE LETTERS (Love Secrets No. 32 on)
Quality Comics: 11/49 - #6, 9/50; #7, 3/51 - #31, 6/53; #32, 2/54 - #51, 12/56

	GD 2.0	VG 4.0	FN 6.0	VF 8.0	VF/NM 9.0	NM- 9.2
1-Ward-c, Gustavson-a	25	50	75	147	202	260
2-Ward-c, Gustavson-a	20	40	60	112	156	200
3-Gustavson-a	14	28	42	81	111	140
4-Ward-a, 9 pgs.	19	38	57	107	149	190
5-8,10	8	16	24	43	54	65
9-One pg. Ward "Be Popular with the Opposite Sex"; Robert Mitchum photo-c	9	18	27	52	66	80
11-Ward-r/Broadway Romances #2 & retitled	9	18	27	52	66	80
12-15,18-20	7	14	21	37	46	55
16,17-Ward-a; 16-Anthony Quinn photo-c. 17-Jane Russell photo-c	12	24	36	69	92	115
21-29	7	14	21	35	43	50
30,31(6/53)-Ward-a	8	16	24	46	58	70
32(2/54)-39: 38-Crandall-a. 39-Last precode (4/55)	6	12	18	31	38	45
40-48	6	12	18	28	34	40
49,50-Baker-a	9	18	27	52	66	80
51-Baker-c	8	16	24	43	54	65

NOTE: *Photo-c on most 3-28.*

LOVE LIFE
P. L. Publishing Co.: Nov, 1951

	GD 2.0	VG 4.0	FN 6.0	VF 8.0	VF/NM 9.0	NM- 9.2
1	10	20	30	58	77	95

LOVELORN (Confessions of the Lovelorn #52 on)
American Comics Group (Michel Publ./Regis Publ.): Aug-Sept, 1949 - No. 51, July, 1954 (No. 1-26: 52 pgs.)

	GD 2.0	VG 4.0	FN 6.0	VF 8.0	VF/NM 9.0	NM- 9.2
1	16	32	48	92	126	160
2	9	18	27	54	70	85
3-10	8	16	24	43	54	65
11-20,22-48: 18-Drucker-a(2 pgs.). 46-Lazarus-a	7	14	21	37	46	55
21-Prostitution story	9	18	27	49	62	75
49-51-Has 3-D effect-c/stories	16	32	48	92	126	160

LOVE MEMORIES
Fawcett Publications: 1949 (no month) - No. 4, July, 1950 (All photo-c)

	GD 2.0	VG 4.0	FN 6.0	VF 8.0	VF/NM 9.0	NM- 9.2
1	16	32	48	92	126	160
2-4: 2-(Win/49-50)	9	18	27	54	70	85

LOVE MYSTERY
Fawcett Publications: June, 1950 - No. 3, Oct, 1950 (All photo-c)

	GD 2.0	VG 4.0	FN 6.0	VF 8.0	VF/NM 9.0	NM- 9.2
1-George Evans-a	23	46	69	129	180	230
2,3-Evans-a. 3-Powell-a	17	34	51	98	134	170

LOVE PROBLEMS (See Fox Giants)

LOVE PROBLEMS AND ADVICE ILLUSTRATED (see True Love...)

LOVE ROMANCES (Formerly Ideal #5)
Timely/Marvel/Atlas(TCI No. 7-71/Male No. 72-106): No. 6, May, 1949 - No. 106, July, 1963

	GD 2.0	VG 4.0	FN 6.0	VF 8.0	VF/NM 9.0	NM- 9.2
6-Photo-c	16	32	48	92	126	160
7-Photo-c; Kamen-a	10	20	30	56	73	90
8-Kubert-a; photo-c	10	20	30	56	73	90

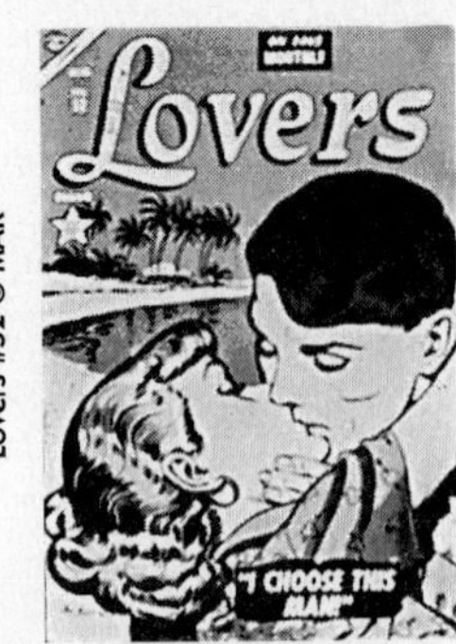

Lovers #52 © MAR

Lucifer #9 © DC

Lucky "7" Comics #1 © Howard Pub.

	GD 2.0	VG 4.0	FN 6.0	VF 8.0	VF/NM 9.0	NM- 9.2
9-20: 9-12-Photo-c	9	18	27	49	62	75
21,24-Krigstein-a	9	18	27	54	70	85
22,23,25-35,37,39,40	8	16	24	46	58	70
36,38-Krigstein-a	9	18	27	49	62	75
41-44,46,47: Last precode (2/55)	8	16	24	43	54	65
45,57-Matt Baker-a	9	18	27	54	70	85
48,50-52,54-56,58-74	5	10	15	33	44	55
49,53-Toth-a, 6 & ? pgs.	6	12	18	38	52	65
75,77,82-Matt Baker-a	6	12	18	43	59	75
76,78-81,86,88-90,92-95: 80-Heath-c. 95-Last 10¢-c?	4	8	12	29	40	50
83,84,87,91-Kirby-c. 83-Severin-a	6	12	18	43	59	75
85,96,97,99-106-Kirby-c/a	8	16	24	53	74	95
98-Kirby-c/a	8	16	24	55	78	100

NOTE: ***Anne Brewster** a-67, 72. **Colletta** a-37, 40, 42, 44, 67(2); c-42, 44, 49, 54, 80. **Everett** c-70. **Heath** a-87. **Kirby** c-80, 85, 88. **Robinson** a-29.*

LOVERS (Formerly Blonde Phantom)
Marvel Comics No. 23,24/Atlas No. 25 on (ANC): No. 23, May, 1949 - No. 86, Aug?, 1957

	GD 2.0	VG 4.0	FN 6.0	VF 8.0	VF/NM 9.0	NM- 9.2
23-Photo-c begin, end #28	16	32	48	92	126	160
24-Toth-*ish* plus Robinson-a	9	18	27	52	66	80
25,30-Kubert-a; 7, 10 pgs.	9	18	27	54	70	85
26-29,31-36,39,40	8	16	24	43	54	65
37,38-Krigstein-a	9	18	27	52	66	80
41-Everett-a(2)	9	18	27	52	66	80
42,44-65: 65-Last pre-code (1/55)	7	14	21	37	46	55
43-Frazetta 1 pg. ad	8	16	24	40	50	60
66,68-86	7	14	21	35	43	50
67-Toth-a	8	16	24	40	50	60

NOTE: ***Anne Brewster** a-86. **Colletta** a-54, 59, 62, 64, 65, 69, 85; c-61, 64, 65, 75. **Heath** a-61. **Maneely** a-57. **Powell** a-27, 30. **Robinson** a-54, 56.*

LOVERS' LANE
Lev Gleason Publications: Oct, 1949 - No. 41, June, 1954 (No. 1-18: 52 pgs.)

	GD 2.0	VG 4.0	FN 6.0	VF 8.0	VF/NM 9.0	NM- 9.2
1-Biro-c	11	22	33	66	88	110
2-Biro-c	8	16	24	40	50	60
3-20: 3,4-Painted-c. 20-Frazetta 1 pg. ad	7	14	21	35	43	50
21-38,40,41	6	12	18	28	34	40
39-Story narrated by Frank Sinatra	8	16	24	40	50	60

NOTE: ***Briefer** a-6, 21. **Fuje** a-4, 16; c-many. **Guardineer** a-1. **Kinstler** c-41. **Tuska** a-6. Painted c-3-18. Photo c-19-22, 26-28.*

LOVE SCANDALS
Quality Comics: Feb, 1950 - No. 5, Oct, 1950 (Photo-c #2-5) (All 52 pgs.)

	GD 2.0	VG 4.0	FN 6.0	VF 8.0	VF/NM 9.0	NM- 9.2
1-Ward-c/a, 9 pgs.	27	54	81	155	218	280
2,3: 2-Gustavson-a	11	22	33	66	88	110
4-Ward-a, 18 pgs; Gil Fox-a	21	42	63	118	164	210
5-C. Cuidera-a; tomboy story "I Hated Being a Woman"	11	22	33	66	88	110

LOVE SECRETS
Marvel Comics(IPC): Oct, 1949 - No. 2, Jan, 1950 (52 pgs., photo-c)

	GD 2.0	VG 4.0	FN 6.0	VF 8.0	VF/NM 9.0	NM- 9.2
1	16	32	48	92	126	160
2	10	20	30	56	73	90

LOVE SECRETS (Formerly Love Letters #31)
Quality Comics Group: No. 32, Aug, 1953 - No. 56, Dec, 1956

	GD 2.0	VG 4.0	FN 6.0	VF 8.0	VF/NM 9.0	NM- 9.2
32	10	20	30	60	80	100
33,35-39	7	14	21	35	43	50
34-Ward-a	10	20	30	60	80	100
40-Matt Baker-c	8	16	24	43	54	65
41-43: 43-Last precode (3/55)	7	14	21	35	43	50
44,47-50,53,54	6	12	18	28	34	40
45,46-Ward-a. 46-Baker-a	9	18	27	49	62	75
51,52-Ward(r). 52-r/Love Confessions #17	7	14	21	35	43	50
55,56: 55-Baker-a. 56-Baker-c	8	16	24	40	50	60

LOVE STORIES (See Top Love Stories)

LOVE STORIES (Formerly Heart Throbs)
National Periodical Publ.: No. 147, Nov, 1972 - No. 152, Oct-Nov, 1973

	GD 2.0	VG 4.0	FN 6.0	VF 8.0	VF/NM 9.0	NM- 9.2
147-152	2	4	6	12	16	20

LOVE STORIES OF MARY WORTH (See Harvey Comics Hits #55 & Mary Worth)
Harvey Publications: Sept, 1949 - No. 5, May, 1950

	GD 2.0	VG 4.0	FN 6.0	VF 8.0	VF/NM 9.0	NM- 9.2
1-1940's newspaper reprints-#1-4	8	16	24	46	58	70
2-5: 3-Kamen/Baker-a?	6	12	18	31	38	45

LOVE TALES (Formerly The Human Torch #35)
Marvel/Atlas Comics (ZPC No. 36-50/MMC No. 67-75): No. 36, 5/49 - No. 58, 8/52; No. 59, date? - No. 75, Sept, 1957

	GD 2.0	VG 4.0	FN 6.0	VF 8.0	VF/NM 9.0	NM- 9.2
36-Photo-c	16	32	48	92	126	160
37	9	18	27	52	66	80
38-44,46-50: 39-41-Photo-c	8	16	24	46	58	70
45,51,52,69: 45-Powell-a. 51,69-Everett-a. 52-Krigstein-a	9	18	27	49	62	75
53-60: 60-Last pre-code (2/55)	7	14	21	35	43	50
61-68,70-75: 75-Brewster, Cameron, Colletta-a	6	12	18	31	38	45

LOVE THRILLS (See Fox Giants)

LOVE TRAILS (Western romance)
A Lover's Magazine (CDS)(Marvel): Dec, 1949 - No. 2, Mar, 1950 (52 pgs.)

	GD 2.0	VG 4.0	FN 6.0	VF 8.0	VF/NM 9.0	NM- 9.2
1,2: 1-Photo-c	15	30	45	86	118	150

LOWELL THOMAS' HIGH ADVENTURE (See High Adventure)

LT. (See Lieutenant)

LUBA
Fantographics Books: Feb, 1998 - Present ($2.95/$3.50, B&W, mature)

	NM- 9.2
1-4-Gilbert Hernandez-s/a	3.00
5-7-($3.50)	3.50

LUBA'S COMICS AND STORIES
Fantographics Books: Mar, 2000 - Present ($2.95/$3.50, B&W, mature)

	NM- 9.2
1-Gilbert Hernandez-s/a	3.00
2-3-($3.50)	3.50

LUCIFER (See The Sandman #4)
DC Comics (Vertigo): Jun, 2000 - Present ($2.50)

	NM- 9.2
1-Carey-s/Weston-a/Fegredo-c	8.00
2,3-Carey-s/Weston-a/Fegredo-c	5.00
4-10: 4-Pleece-a. 5-Gross-a	4.00
11-45: 16-Moeller-c begin. 25,26-Death app. 45-Naifeh-a	2.50
Preview-16 pg. flip book w/Swamp Thing Preview	3.00
A Dalliance With the Damned TPB ('02, $14.95) r/#14-20	15.00
Children and Monsters TPB ('01, $17.95) r/#5-13	18.00
Devil in the Gateway TPB ('01, $14.95) r/#1-4 & Sandman Presents:..#1-3	15.00
...: Inferno TPB (2003, $14.95) r/#29-35	15.00
...: Nirvana (2002, $5.95) Carey-s/Muth-painted-c/a; Daniel app.	6.00
...: The Divine Comedy TPB (2003, $17.95) r/#21-28	18.00

LUCIFER'S HAMMER (Larry Niven & Jerry Pournelle's...)
Innovation Publishing: Nov, 1993 - No. 6, 1994 ($2.50, painted, limited series)

	NM- 9.2
1-6: Adaptatin of novel, painted-c & art	2.50

LUCKY COMICS
Consolidated Magazines: Jan, 1944; No. 2, Sum, 1945 - No. 5, Sum, 1946

	GD 2.0	VG 4.0	FN 6.0	VF 8.0	VF/NM 9.0	NM- 9.2
1-Lucky Starr & Bobbie begin	22	44	66	127	176	225
2-5: 5-Devil-c by Walter Johnson	12	24	36	71	96	120

LUCKY DUCK
Standard Comics (Literary Ent.): No. 5, Jan, 1953 - No. 8, Sept, 1953

	GD 2.0	VG 4.0	FN 6.0	VF 8.0	VF/NM 9.0	NM- 9.2
5-Funny animal; Irving Spector-a	11	22	33	63	84	105
6-8-Irving Spector-a	10	20	30	56	73	90

NOTE: *Harvey Kurtzman tried to hire Spector for Mad #1.*

LUCKY "7" COMICS
Howard Publishers Ltd.: 1944 (No date listed)

	GD 2.0	VG 4.0	FN 6.0	VF 8.0	VF/NM 9.0	NM- 9.2
1-Pioneer, Sir Gallagher, Dick Royce, Congo Raider, Punch Powers; bondage-c	39	78	117	230	325	420

LUCKY STAR (Western)
Nation Wide Publ. Co.: 1950 - No. 7, 1951; No. 8, 1953 - No. 14, 1955 (5x7-1/4"; full color, 5¢)

	GD 2.0	VG 4.0	FN 6.0	VF 8.0	VF/NM 9.0	NM- 9.2
nn (#1)-(5¢, 52 pgs.)-Davis-a	18	36	54	101	138	175
2,3-(5¢, 52 pgs.)-Davis-a	11	22	33	63	84	105
4-7-(5¢, 52 pgs.)-Davis-a	10	20	30	56	73	90
8-14-(36 pgs.)(Exist?)	8	16	24	42	54	65
Given away with Lucky Star Western Wear by the Juvenile Mfg. Co.	6	12	18	31	38	45

LUCY SHOW, THE (TV) (Also see I Love Lucy)
Gold Key: June, 1963 - No. 5, June, 1964 (Photo-c: 1,2)

	GD 2.0	VG 4.0	FN 6.0	VF 8.0	VF/NM 9.0	NM- 9.2
1	14	28	42	99	145	190
2	8	16	24	55	78	100
3-5: Photo back c-1,2,4,5	7	14	21	51	71	90

LUCY, THE REAL GONE GAL (Meet Miss Pepper #5 on)

Luftwaffe 1946 V2#5 © Ted Nomura

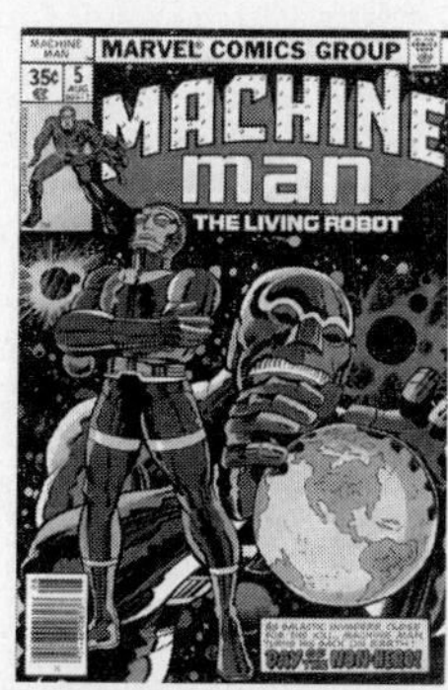

Machine Man #5 © MAR

Mad #28 © EC Publ.

GD VG FN VF VF/NM NM-
2.0 4.0 6.0 8.0 9.0 9.2

GD VG FN VF VF/NM NM-
2.0 4.0 6.0 8.0 9.0 9.2

St. John Publishing Co.: June, 1953 - No. 4, Dec, 1953
1-Negligee panels 13 26 39 76 103 130
2 8 16 24 46 58 70
3,4: 3-Drucker-a 8 16 24 40 50 60

LUDWIG BEMELMAN'S MADELEINE & GENEVIEVE
Dell Publishing Co.: No. 796, May, 1957
Four Color 796 4 8 12 25 33 42

LUDWIG VON DRAKE (TV)(Disney)(See Walt Disney's C&S #256)
Dell Publishing Co.: Nov-Dec, 1961 - No. 4, June-Aug, 1962
1 8 16 24 53 74 95
2-4 6 12 18 38 52 65

LUFTWAFFE: 1946 (Volume 1)
Antarctic Press: July, 1996 - No. 4, Jan, 1997 ($2.95, B&W, limited series)
1-4-Ben Dunn & Ted Nomura-s/a, ...Special Ed. 3.00

LUFTWAFFE: 1946 (Volume 2)
Antarctic Press: Mar, 1997 - No. 18 ($2.95/$2.99, B&W, limited series)
1-18: 8-Reviews Tigers of Terra series 3.00
Annual 1 (4/98, $2.95)-Reprints early Nomura pages 3.00
...Color Special (4/98) 3.00
...Technical Manual 1,2 (2/98, 4/99) 4.00

LUGER
Eclipse Comics: Oct, 1986 - No. 3, Feb, 1987 ($1.75, miniseries, Baxter paper)
1-3: Bruce Jones scripts; Yeates-c/a 2.25

LUKE CAGE (See Cage & Hero for Hire)

LUKE SHORT'S WESTERN STORIES
Dell Publishing Co.: No. 580, Aug, 1954 - No. 927, Aug, 1958
Four Color 580(8/54), 651(9/55)-Kinstler-a 4 8 12 28 38 48
Four Color 739,771,807,848,875,927 4 8 12 27 36 45

LUNATIC FRINGE, THE
Innovation Publishing: July, 1989 - No. 2, 1989 ($1.75, deluxe format)
1,2 2.25

LUNATICKLE (Magazine) (Satire)
Whitstone Publ.: Feb, 1956 - No. 2, Apr, 1956
1,2-Kubert-a (scarce) 6 12 18 28 34 40

LUNATIK
Marvel Comics: Dec, 1995 - No. 3, Feb, 1996 ($1.95, limited series)
1-3 2.25

LUST FOR LIFE
Slave Labor Graphics: Feb, 1997 - No. 4, Jan, 1998 ($2.95, B&W)
1-4: 1-Jeff Levin-s/a 3.00

LYCANTHROPE LEO
Viz Communications: 1994 - No. 7($2.95, B&W, limited series, 44 pgs.)
1-7 3.00

LYNCH (See Gen 13)
Image Comics (WildStorm Productions): May, 1997 ($2.50, one-shot)
1-Helmut-c/app. 2.50

LYNCH MOB
Chaos! Comics: June, 1994 - No. 4, Sept, 1994 ($2.50, limited series)
1-4 2.50
1-Special edition full foil-c 5.00

LYNDON B. JOHNSON
Dell Publishing Co.: Mar, 1965
12-445-503-Photo-c 3 7 10 21 28 35

M
Eclipse Books: 1990 - No. 4, 1991 ($4.95, painted, 52 pgs.)
1-Adapts movie; contains flexi-disc ($5.95) 6.00
2-4 5.00

MACE GRIFFIN BOUNTY HUNTER (Based on video game)
Image Comics (Top Cow): May, 2003 ($2.99, one-shot)
1-Nocon-a 3.00

MACHINE, THE
Dark Horse Comics: Nov, 1994 - No. 4, Feb, 1995 ($2.50, limited series)
1-4 2.50

MACHINE MAN (Also see 2001, A Space Odyssey)
Marvel Comics Group: Apr, 1978 - No. 9, Dec, 1978; No. 10, Aug, 1979 - No. 19, Feb, 1981
1-Jack Kirby-c/a/scripts begin; end #9 2 4 6 10 13 16
2-9-Kirby-c/a/s. 9-(12/78) 1 2 3 5 6 8
10-17: 10-(8/79) Marv Wolfman scripts & Ditko-a begins 5.00
18-Wendigo, Alpha Flight-ties into X-Men #140 2 4 6 11 14 18
19-Intro/1st app. Jack O'Lantern (Macendale), later becomes 2nd Hobgoblin
2 4 6 9 11 14
NOTE: *Austin c-7i, 19i.* ***Buckler*** *c-17p, 18p.* ***Byrne*** *c-14p.* ***Ditko*** *a-10-19; c-10-13, 14i, 15, 16.* ***Kirby*** *a-1-9p; c-1-5, 7-9p.* ***Layton*** *c-7i.* ***Miller*** *c-19p.* ***Simonson*** *c-6.*

MACHINE MAN (Also see X-51)
Marvel Comics Group: Oct, 1984 - No. 4, Jan, 1985 (Limited-series)
1-4-Barry Smith-c/a(i) & colors in all 4.00
TPB (1988, $6.95) r/ #1-4; Barry Smith-c 7.00
.../Bastion '98 Annual ($2.99) wraparound-c 3.00

MACHINE MAN 2020
Marvel Comics: Aug, 1994 - Nov, 1994 ($2.00, 52 pgs., limited series)
1-4: Reprints Machine Man limited series; Barry Windsor-Smith-c/i(r) 2.25

MACK BOLAN: THE EXECUTIONER (Don Pendleton's...)
Innovation Publishing: July, 1993 ($2.50)
1-3-($2.50) 2.50
1-($3.95)-Indestructible Cover Edition 4.00
1-($2.95)-Collector's Gold Edition; foil stamped 3.00
1-($3.50)-Double Cover Edition; red foil outer-c 3.50

MACKENZIE'S RAIDERS (Movie, TV)
Dell Publishing Co.: No. 1093, Apr-June, 1960
Four Color 1093-Richard Carlson photo-c from TV show
7 14 21 51 71 90

MACROSS (Becomes Robotech: The Macross Saga #2 on)
Comico: Dec, 1984 ($1.50)(Low print run)
1-Early manga app. 3 6 9 16 20 25

MACROSS II
Viz Select Comics: 1992 - No. 10, 1993 ($2.75, B&W, limited series)
1-10: Based on video series 2.75

MAD (Tales Calculated to Drive You...)
E. C. Comics (Educational Comics): Oct-Nov, 1952 - Present (No. 24-on are magazine format) (Kurtzman editor No. 1-28, Feldstein No. 29 - No. ?)
1-Wood, Davis, Elder start as regulars 500 1000 1500 3500 5250 7000
2-Dick Tracy cameo 141 282 423 1058 1517 1975
3,4: 3-Stan Lee mentioned. 4-Reefer mention story "Flob Was a Slob" by Davis; Superman parody 86 172 258 645 923 1200
5-Low distr.; W.M. Gaines biog. 150 300 450 1125 1613 2100
6-11: 6-Popeye cameo. 7,8- "Hey Look" reprints by Kurtzman. 11-Wolverton-a; Davis story was-r/Crime Suspenstories #12 w/new Kurtzman dialogue
61 122 183 458 659 860
12-15: 15,18-Pot Shot Pete-r by Kurtzman 48 96 144 360 518 675
16-23(5/55): 18-Alice in Wonderland by Jack Davis. 21-1st app. Alfred E. Neuman on-c in fake ad. 22-All by Elder plus photo-montages by Kurtzman.
23-Special cancel announcement 39 78 117 293 422 550
24(7/55)-1st magazine issue (25¢); Kurtzman logo & border on-c; 1st "What? Me Worry?" on-c; 2nd printing exists 91 182 273 683 979 1275
25-Jaffee starts as regular writer 41 82 123 308 442 575
26,27: 27-Jaffee starts as story artist; new logo 39 78 117 244 360 475
28-Last issue edited by Kurtzman; (three cover variations exist with different wording on contents banner on lower right of cover; value of each the same)
32 64 96 200 293 385
29-Kamen-a; Don Martin starts as regular; Feldstein editing begins
32 64 96 200 293 385
30-1st A. E. Neuman cover by Mingo; last Elder-a; Bob Clarke starts as regular; Disneyland & Elvis Presley spoof 50 100 150 313 457 600
31-Freas starts as regular; last Davis-a until #99 29 58 87 181 266 350
32,33: 32-Orlando, Drucker, Woodbridge start as regulars; Wood back-c. 33-Orlando back-c
25 50 75 156 228 300
34-Berg starts as regular 21 42 63 131 191 250
35-Mingo wraparound-c; Crandall-a 21 42 63 131 191 250
36-40 (7/58) 15 30 45 94 140 185
41-50: 42-Danny Kaye-s. 44-Xmas-c. 47-49-Sid Caesar-s. 48-Uncle Sam-c.
50 (10/59)-Peter Gunn-s 13 26 39 81 116 150

Mad #64 © EC Publ.

Mad #192 © EC Publ.

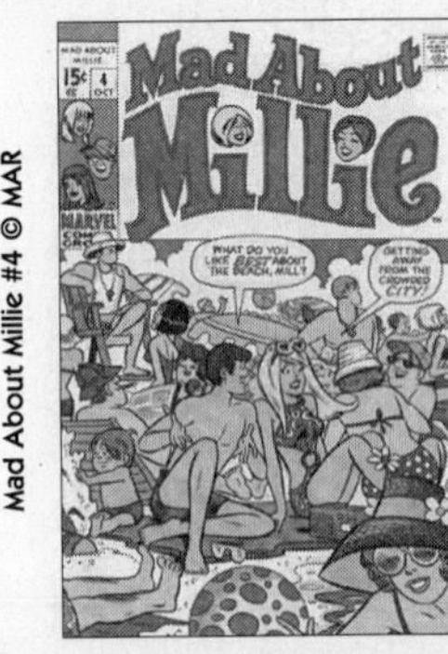

Mad About Millie #4 © MAR

51-59: 52-Xmas-c; 77 Sunset Strip. 53-Rifleman-s. 55-Sid Caesar-s. 59-Strips of Superman, Flash Gordon, Donald Duck & others. 59-Halloween/Headless Horseman-c 11 22 33 69 100 130
60 (1/61)-JFK/Nixon flip-c; 1st Spy vs. Spy by Prohias, who starts as regular 13 26 39 81 116 150
61-70: 64-Rickard starts as regular. 65-JFK-s. 66-JFK-c. 68-Xmas-c by Martin. 70-Route 66-s 8 16 24 50 73 95
71-75,77-80 (7/63): 72-10th Anniv. special; 1/3 pg. strips of Superman, Tarzan & others. 73-Bonanza-s. 74-Dr. Kildare-s 6 12 18 38 52 65
76-Aragonés starts as regular 6 12 18 43 59 75
81-85: 81-Superman strip. 82-Castro-c. 85-Lincoln-c 5 10 15 33 44 55
86-1st Fold-in; commonly creased back covers makes these and later issues scarcer in NM 6 12 18 38 52 65
87,88 5 10 15 36 48 60
89,90: 89-One strip by Walt Kelly; Frankenstein-c; Fugitive-s. 90-Ringo back-c by Frazetta; Beatles app. 6 12 18 38 52 65
91,94,96,100: 91-Jaffee starts as story artist. 94-King Kong-c. 96-Man From U.N.C.L.E. 100-(1/66)-Anniversary issue 5 10 15 33 44 55
92,93,95,97-99: 99-Davis-a resumes 4 8 12 29 40 50
101,104,106,108,114,115,119,121: 101-Infinity-c; Voyage to the Bottom of the Sea-s. 104-Lost in Space-s. 106-Tarzan back-c by Frazetta; 2 pg. Batman by Aragonés. 108-Hogan's Heroes by Davis. 114-Rat Patrol-s. 115-Star Trek. 119-Invaders (TV). 121-Beatles-c; Ringo pin-up; flip-c of Sik-Teen; Flying Nun-s 4 8 12 24 32 40
102,103,107,109-113,116-118,120(7/68): 118-Beatles cameo 3 7 10 21 28 35
105-Batman-c/s, TV show parody (9/66) 4 8 12 28 38 48
122,124,126,128,129,131-134,136,137,139,140: 122-Ronald Reagan photo inside; Drucker & Mingo-c. 126-Family Affair-s. 128-Last Orlando. 131-Reagan photo back-c. 132-Xmas-c. 133-John Wayne/True Grit. 136-Room 222 3 6 9 16 20 25
123-Three different covers 3 6 9 18 23 28
125,127,130,135,138: 125-2001 Space Odyssey; Hitler back-c. 127-Mod Squad-c/s. 130-Land of the Giants-s; Torres begins as reg. 135-Easy Rider-c by Davis. 138-Snoopy-c; MASH-s 3 6 9 18 24 30
141-149,151-156,158-170: 141-Hawaii Five-0. 147-All in the Family-s. 153-Dirty Harry-s. 155-Godfather-c/s. 156-Columbo-s. 159-Clockwork Orange-c/s. 161-Tarzan-s. 164-Kung Fu (TV)-s. 165-James Bond-s; Dean Martin-c. 169-Drucker-c; McCloud-s. 170-Exorcist-s 2 4 6 14 18 22
150-(4/72) Partridge Family-s 3 6 9 16 20 24
157-(4/72) Planet of the Apes-c/s 3 6 9 18 23 28
171-185,187,189-192,194,195,198,199: 172-Six Million Dollar Man-s; Hitler back-c. 178-Godfather II-c/s. 180-Jaws-c/s (1/76). 182-Bob Jones starts as regular.185-Starsky & Hutch-s. 187-Fonz/Happy Days-c/s; Harry North starts as regular. 189-Travolta/Kotter-c/s. 190-John Wayne-c/s. 192-King Kong-c/s. 194-Rocky-c/s; Laverne & Shirley-s. 199-James Bond-s 2 4 6 10 13 16
186,188,197,200: 186-Star Trek-c/s. 188-Six Million Dollar Man/ Bionic Woman. 197-Spock-s; Star Wars-s. 200-Close Encounters 2 4 6 12 16 20
193,196: 193-Farrah/Charlie's Angels-c/s. 196-Star Wars-c/s 2 4 6 14 18 22
201,203,205,220: 201-Sat. Night Fever-c/s. 203-Star Wars. 205-Travolta/Grease. 220-Yoda-c, Empire Strikes Back-s 2 4 6 10 12 15
202,204,206,207,209,211-219,221-227,229,230: 204-Hulk TV show. 206-Tarzan. 208-Superman movie. 209-Mork & Mindy. 212-Spider-Man-s; Alien (movie)-s. 213-James Bond, Dracula, Rocky II-s 216-Star Trek. 219-Martin-c. 221-Shining-s. 223-Dallas-c/s. 225-Popeye. 226-Superman II. 229-James Bond. 230-Star Wars 1 3 4 6 8 10
208,228: 208-Superman movie-c/s; Battlestar Galactica-s. 228-Raiders of the Lost Ark-c/s 2 4 6 9 11 14
210-Lord of the Rings 2 4 6 10 12 15
231-235,237-241,243-249,251-260: 233-Pac-Man-c. 234-MASH-c/s. 235-Flip-c with Rocky III & Conan; Boris-a. 239-Mickey Mouse-c. 241-Knight Rider-s. 243-Superman III. 245- Last Rickard-a. 247-Seven Dwarfs-c. 253-Supergirl movie-s; Prince/Purple Rain-s. 254-Rock stars-s. 255-Reagan-c; Cosby-s. 256-Last issue edited by Feldstein; Dynasty, Bev. Hills Cop. 259-Rambo. 260-Back to the Future-c/s; Honeymooners-s 1 2 3 5 6 8
236,242,250: 236-E.T.-c/s;Star Trek II-s. 242-Star Wars/A-Team-c/s. 250-Temple of Doom-c/s; Tarzan-s 1 2 3 5 7 9
261-267,269-276,278-288,290-297: 261-Miami Vice. 262-Rocky IV-c/s, Leave It To Beaver-s. 263-Young Sherlock Holmes-s. 264-Hulk Hogan-c; Rambo-s. 267-Top Gun. 271-Star Trek IV-c/s. 272-ALF-c; Get Smart-s. 273-Pee Wee Herman-c/s. 274-Last Martin-a. 281-California Raisins-c. 282-Star Trek:TNG-s; ALF-s. 283-Rambo III-c/s. 284-Roger Rabbit-c/s. 285-Hulk Hogan-c. 287-3 pgs. Eisner-a. 291-TMNT-c; Indiana Jones-s. 292-Super Mario Bros.-c; Married with Children-s. 295-Back to the Future II. 297-Mike Tyson-c 1 2 3 4 5 7
268,277,289,298-300: 268-Aliens-c/s. 277-Michael Jackson-c/s; Robocop-s. 289-Batman movie parody. 298-Gremlins II-c/s; Robocop II. Batman-s. 299-Simpsons-c/story; Total Recall-s. 300(1/91) Casablanca-s, Dick Tracy-s, Wizard of Oz-s, Gone With The Wind-s 1 2 3 5 6 8
300-303 (1/91-6/91)-Special Hussein Asylum Editions; only distributed to the troops in the Middle East (see Mad Super Spec.) 2 4 6 12 16 20
301-310,312,313,315-320,322,324,326-334,337-349: 303-Home Alone-c/s. 305-Simpsons-s. 306-TMNT II movie. 308-Terminator II. 315-Tribute to William Gaines. 316-Photo-c. 319-Dracula-c/s. 320-Disney's Aladdin-s. 322-Batman Animated series. 327-Seinfeld-s; X-Men-s. 331-Flintstones-c/s. 332-O.J. Simpson-c/s; Simpsons app. in Lion King. 334-Frankenstein-c/s. 338-Judge Dredd-c by Frazetta. 341-Pocahontas-s. 345-Beatles app. (1 pg.) 347-Broken Arrow & Mission Impossible 5.00
311,314,321,323,325,335,336,350,354,358: 311-Addams Family-c/story, Home Improvement-s. 314-Batman Returns-c/story. 321-Star Trek DS9-c/s. 323-Jurassic Park-c/s. 325,336-Beavis & Butthead-c/s. 335-X-Files-s; Pulp Fiction-s; Interview with the Vampire-s. 336-Lois & Clark-s. 350-Polybagged w/CD Rom. 354-Star Wars; Beavis & Butthead-s. 358-X-Files 6.00
351-353,355-357,359-400 4.00
401-439 3.50
Mad About Super Heroes (2002, $9.95) r/super hero app.; Alex Ross-c 10.00

NOTE: ***Aragones*** *c-210, 293.* ***Davis*** *c-2, 27, 135, 139, 173, 178, 212, 213, 219, 246, 260, 296, 308.* ***Drucker*** *c-122, 169, 176, 225, 234, 264, 266, 274, 280, 285, 297, 299, 303, 314, 315, 321.* ***Elder*** *c-5, 259, 261, 268.* ***Elder/Kurtzman*** *a-258-274.* ***Jules Feiffer*** *a(r)-42.* ***Freas*** *c-39-59, 62-67, 69-70, 72, 74.* ***Heath*** *a-14, 27.* ***Jaffee*** *c-199, 217, 224, 258.* ***Kamen*** *a-29.* ***Krigstein*** *a-12, 17, 24, 26.* ***Kurtzman*** *c-1, 3, 4, 6-10, 13, 16, 18.* ***Martin*** *c-68, 165, 229.* ***Mingo*** *c-30-37, 61, 71, 75-80, 82-114, 117-124, 126, 129, 131, 133, 134, 136, 140, 143-148, 150-162, 164, 166-168, 171, 172, 174, 175, 177, 179, 181, 183, 185, 198, 206, 209, 211, 214, 218, 221, 222, 300.* ***John Severin*** *a-1-6, 9, 10.* ***Wolverton*** *c-11; a-11, 17, 29, 31, 36, 40, 82, 137.* ***Wood*** *a-24-45, 59; c-26, 28, 29.* ***Woodbridge*** *a-43. Issues 1-23 are 36 pgs.; 24-28 are 58 pgs.; 29 on are 52 pgs.*

MAD (See Mad Follies, ...Special, More Trash from..., and The Worst from...)

MAD ABOUT MILLIE (Also see Millie the Model)
Marvel Comics Group: April, 1969 - No. 16, Nov, 1970

1-Giant issue 8 16 24 53 74 95
2,3 (Giants) 5 10 15 36 48 60
4-10 3 7 10 21 28 35
11-16: 16-r 3 6 9 18 24 30
Annual 1(11/71, 52 pgs.) 3 7 10 21 28 35

MADAME XANADU
DC Comics: July, 1981 ($1.00, no ads, 36 pgs.)

1-Marshall Rogers-a(25 pgs.); Kaluta-c/a(2pgs.); pin-up 5.00

MADBALLS
Star Comics/Marvel Comics #9 on: Sept, 1986 - No. 3, Nov, 1986; No. 4, June, 1987 - No. 10, June, 1988

1-10: Based on toys. 9-Post-a 4.00

MAD DISCO
E.C. Comics: 1980 (one-shot, 36 pgs.)

1-Includes 30 minute flexi-disc of Mad disco music 2 4 6 12 16 20

MAD-DOG
Marvel Comics: May, 1993 - No. 6, Oct, 1993 ($1.25)

1-6-Flip book w/2nd story "created" by Bob Newhart's character from his TV show "Bob" set at a comic book company; actual s/a-Ty Templeton 2.50

MAD DOGS
Eclipse Comics: Feb, 1992 - No. 3, July, 1992 ($2.50, B&W, limited series)

1-3 2.50

MAD 84 (Mad Extra)
E.C. Comics: 1984 (84 pgs.)

1 1 2 3 5 7 9

MAD FOLLIES (Special)
E. C. Comics: 1963 - No. 7, 1969

nn(1963)-Paperback book covers 25 50 75 181 266 350
2(1964)-Calendar 19 38 57 138 202 265
3(1965)-Mischief Stickers 15 30 45 104 152 200
4(1966)-Mobile; Frazetta-r/back-c Mad #90 11 22 33 77 114 150
5,6: 5(1967)-Stencils. 6(1968)-Mischief Stickers 9 18 27 60 85 110
7(1969)-Nasty Cards 9 18 27 60 85 110
(If bonus is missing, issue is half price)

NOTE: ***Clarke*** *c-4.* ***Frazetta*** *r-4, 6 (1 pg. ea.).* ***Mingo*** *c-1-3.* ***Orlando*** *a-5.*

MAD HATTER, THE (Costumed Hero)
O. W. Comics Corp.: Jan-Feb, 1946; No. 2, Sept-Oct, 1946

1-Freddy the Firefly begins; Giunta-c/a 88 176 264 550 825 1100
2-Has ad for E.C.'s Animal Fables #1 42 84 126 252 376 500

MADHOUSE

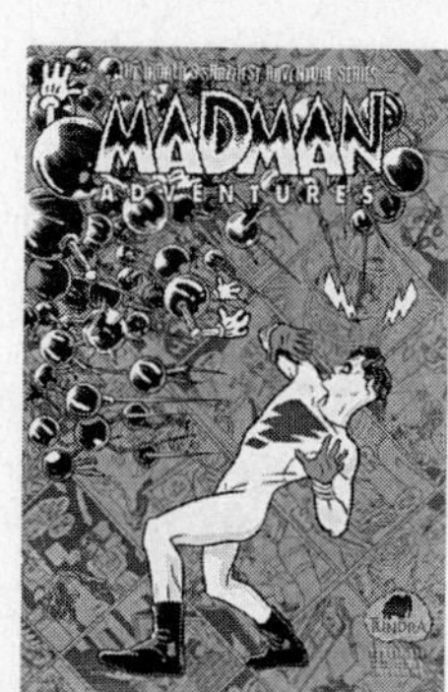

Madman Adventures #1 © Mike Allred

Mad Super Special #109 © EC Publ.

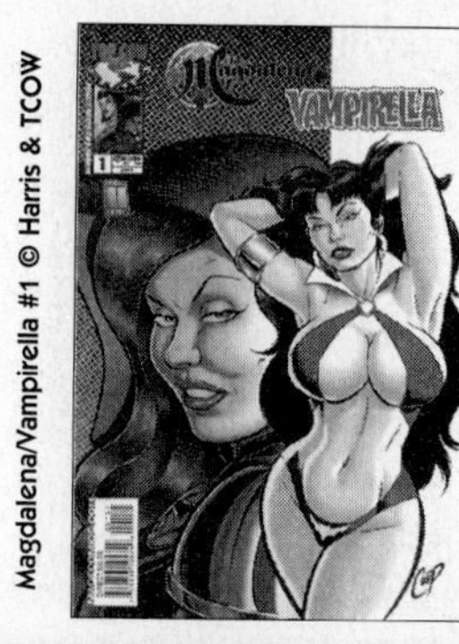

Magdalena/Vampirella #1 © Harris & TCOW

GD 2.0 | VG 4.0 | FN 6.0 | VF 8.0 | VF/NM 9.0 | NM- 9.2

Ajax/Farrell Publ. (Excellent Publ./4-Star): 3-4/54 - No. 4, 9-10/54; 6/57 - No. 4, Dec?, 1957
1(1954) 32 64 96 184 262 340
2,3 17 34 51 98 134 170
4-Surrealistic-c 26 52 78 150 210 270
1(1957, 2nd series) 14 28 42 81 111 140
2-4 (#4 exist?) 10 20 30 56 73 90

MAD HOUSE (Formerly Madhouse Glads; ...Comics #104? on)
Red Circle Productions/Archie Publications: No. 95, 9/74 - No. 97, 1/75; No. 98, 8/75 - No. 130, 10/82
95,96-Horror stories through #97; Morrow-c 2 4 6 10 13 16
97-Intro. Henry Hobson; Morrow-a/c, Thorne-a 2 4 6 8 10 12
98,99,101-120-Satire/humor stories. 110-Sabrina app.,1pg. 1 2 3 5 7 9
100 1 3 4 6 8 10
121-129 1 3 4 6 8 10
130 2 4 6 10 12 15
Annual 8(1970-71)-Formerly Madhouse Ma-ad Annual; Sabrina app. (6 pgs.) 4 8 12 27 36 45
Annual 9- 12(1974-75): 11-Wood-a(r) 2 4 6 12 16 20
...Comics Digest 1('75-76) 2 4 6 11 14 18
2-8(8/82)(...Mag. #5 on)-Sabrina in many 2 4 6 9 11 14
NOTE: *B. Jones a-96. McWilliams a-97. Wildey a-95, 96. See Archie Comics Digest #1, 13.*

MADHOUSE GLADS (Formerly ...Ma-ad; Madhouse #95 on)
Archie Publ.: No. 73, May, 1970 - No. 94, Aug, 1974 (No. 78-92: 52 pgs.)
73-77,93,94: 74-1 pg. Sabrina 2 4 6 10 13 16
78-92 (52 pgs.) 2 4 6 12 16 20

MADHOUSE MA-AD (...Jokes #67-70; ...Freak-Out #71-74)
(Formerly Archie's Madhouse) (Becomes Madhouse Glads #73 on)
Archie Publications: No. 67, April, 1969 - No. 72, Jan, 1970
67-71: 70-1 pg. Sabrina 2 4 6 14 18 22
72-6 pgs. Sabrina 3 7 10 21 28 35
...Annual 7(1969-70)-Formerly Archie's Madhouse Annual; becomes Madhouse Annual; 6 pgs. Sabrina 4 8 12 27 36 45

MADMAN (See Creatures of the Id #1)
Tundra Publishing: Mar, 1992 - No. 3, 1992 ($3.95, duotone, high quality, lim. series, 52 pgs.)
1-Mike Allred-c/a in all 2 4 6 8 10 12
1-2nd printing 4.00
2,3 6.00

MADMAN ADVENTURES
Tundra Publishing: 1992 - No. 3, 1993 ($2.95, limited series)
1-Mike Allred-c/a in all 1 2 3 5 7 9
2,3 5.00
TPB (Oni Press, 2002, $14.95) r/#1-3 & first app. of Frank Einstein from Creatures of the Id in color; gallery pages 15.00

MADMAN COMICS (Also see The Atomics)
Dark Horse Comics (Legend No. 2 on): Apr, 1994 - No. 20, Dec, 2000 ($2.95/$2.99)
1-Allred-c/a; F. Miller back-c. 1 2 3 5 6 8
2-3: 3-Alex Toth back-c. 5.00
4-11: 4-Dave Stevens back-c. 6,7-Miller/Darrow's Big Guy app. 6-Bruce Timm back-c. 7-Darrow back-c. 8-Origin?; Bagge back-c. 10-Allred/Ross-c; Ross back-c. 11-Frazetta back-c 4.00
12-16: 12-(4/99) 3.00
17-20: 17-The G-Men From Hell #1 on cover; Brereton back-c. 18-(#2). 19,20-($2.99-c). 20-Clowes back-c 3.00
... Boogaloo TPB (6/99, $8.95) r/Nexus Meets Madman & Madman/The Jam 9.00
Ltd. Ed. Slipcover (1997, $99.95, signed and numbered) w/Vol.1 & Vol. 2. Vol.1- reprints #1-5; Vol. 2- reprints #6-10 100.00
The Complete Madman Comics: Vol. 2 (11/96, $17.95, TPB) r/#6-10 plus new material 18.00
Madman King-Size Super Groovy Special (Oni Press, 7/03, $6.95) new short stories by Allred, Derington, Krall and Weissman 7.00
Madman Picture Exhibition No. 1-4 (4-7/02, $3.95) pin-ups by various 4.00
Madman Picture Exhibition Limited Edition (10/02, $29.95) Hardcover collects MPE #1-4 30.00
Yearbook '95 (1996, $17.95, TPB)-r/#1-5, intro by Teller 18.00

MADMAN / THE JAM
Dark Horse Comics: Jul, 1998 - No. 2, Aug, 1998 ($2.95, mini-series)
1,2-Allred & Mireault-s/a 3.00

MAD MONSTER PARTY (See Movie Classics)

MADNESS IN MURDERWORLD
Marvel Comics: 1989 (Came with computer game from Paragon Software)
V1#1-Starring The X-Men 2.25

MADRAVEN HALLOWEEN SPECIAL
Hamilton Comics: Oct, 1995 ($2.95, one-shot)
nn-Morrow-a 3.00

MAD SPECIAL (...Super Special)
E. C. Publications, Inc.: Fall, 1970 - Present (84 - 116 pgs.)
(If bonus is missing, issue is one half price)
Fall 1970(#1)-Bonus-Voodoo Doll; contains 17 pgs. new material 9 18 27 65 93 120
Spring 1971(#2)-Wall Nuts; 17 pgs. new material 6 12 18 38 52 65
3-Protest Stickers 6 12 18 38 52 65
4-8: 4-Mini Posters. 5-Mad Flag. 6-Mad Mischief Stickers. 7-Presidential candidate posters, Wild Shocking Message posters. 8-TV Guise 5 10 15 33 44 55
9(1972)-Contains Nostalgic Mad #1 (28 pgs.) 4 8 12 25 33 42
10-13: 10-Nonsense Stickers (Don Martin). 13-Sickie Stickers; 3 pgs. Wolverton-r/Mad #137. 11-Contains 33-1/3 RPM record. 12-Contains Nostalgic Mad #2 (36 pgs.); Davis, Wolverton-a 3 7 10 21 28 35
14,16-21,24: 4-Vital Message posters & Art Depreciation paintings. 16-Mad-hesive Stickers. 17-Don Martin posters. 20-Martin Stickers. 18-Contains Nostalgic Mad #4 (36 pgs.). 21,24-Contains Nostalgic Mad #5 (28 pgs.) & #6 (28 pgs.) 3 6 9 16 20 25
15-Contains Nostalgic Mad #3 (28 pgs.) 3 6 9 18 23 28
22,23,25,27-29,30: 22-Diplomas. 23-Martin Stickers. 25-Martin Posters.27-Mad Shock-Sticks. 28-Contains Nostalgic Mad #7 (36 pgs.). 29-Mad Collectable-Correctables Posters. 30-The Movies 2 4 6 10 13 16
26-Has 33-1/3 RPM record 2 4 6 14 18 22
31,33-35,37-50 2 4 6 9 11 14
32-Contains Nostalgic Mad #8. 36-Has 96 pgs. of comic book & comic strip spoofs: titles "The Comics" on-c 2 4 6 10 13 16
51-70 1 3 4 6 8 10
71-88,90-100: 71-Batman parodies-r by Wood, Drucker. 72-Wolverton-c r-from 1st panel in Mad #11; Wolverton-s r/new dialogue. 83-All Star Trek spoof issue 1 2 3 5 6 8
76-(Fall, 1991)-Special Hussein Asylum Edition; distributed only to the troops in the Middle East (see Mad #300-303) 2 4 6 12 16 20
89-($3.95)-Polybagged w/1st of 3 Spy vs. Spy hologram trading cards (direct sale only issue) (other cards came w/card set) 1 3 4 6 8 10
101-135: 117-Sci-Fi parodies-r. 4.00
NOTE: *#28-30 have no number on cover. Freas c-76. Mingo c-9, 11, 15, 19, 23.*

MAGDALENA, THE (See The Darkness)
Image Comics (Top Cow): Apr, 2000 - No. 3, Jan, 2001 ($2.50)
Preview Special ('00, $4.95) Flip book w/Blood Legacy preview 5.00
1-Benitez-c/a; variant covers by Silvestri & Turner 2.50
2,3: 2-Two covers 2.50
.../Angelus #1/2 (11/01, $2.95) Benitez-c/Ching-a 3.00
...Blood Divine (2002, $9.95) r/#1-3 & #1/2; cover gallery 10.00
.../Vampirella (7/03, $2.99) Wohl-s/Benitez-a; two covers 3.00

MAGDALENA, THE (Volume 2)
Image Comics (Top Cow): Aug, 2003 - Present ($2.99)
Preview (6/03) B&W preview; Wizard World East logo on cover 2.25
1-4-Holguin-s/Basaldua-a 3.00
1-Variant-c by Jim Silke benefitting ACTOR charity 5.00

MAGE (The Hero Discovered...; also see Grendel #16)
Comico: Feb, 1984 (no month) - No. 15, Dec, 1986 ($1.50, Mando paper)
1-Comico's 1st color comic 2 4 6 9 11 14
2-5: 3-Intro Edsel 6.00
6-Grendel begins (1st in color) 3 6 9 16 20 25
7-1st new Grendel story 2 4 6 8 10 12
8-14: 13-Grendel dies. 14-Grendel story ends 6.00
15-($2.95) Double size w/pullout poster 1 2 3 5 6 8
TPB Volume 1-4 (Image, $5.95) 1- r/#1,2. 2- r/#3,4. 3- r/#5,6. 4- r/#7,8 7.00
TPB Volume 5-7 (Image, $6.95) 5- r/#9,10. 6- r/#11,12. 7- r/#13,14 7.00
TPB Volume 8 (Image, 9/99, $7.50) r/#15 7.50

MAGE (The Hero Defined)
Image Comics: July, 1997 - No. 15, Oct, 1999 ($2.50)
0-(7/97, $5.00) American Ent. Ed. 5.00
1-14:Matt Wagner-c/s/a in all. 13-Three covers 2.50
1-"3-D Edition" (2/98, $4.95) w/glasses 5.00
15-($5.95) Acetate cover 6.00
Volume 1,2 TPB ('98,'99, $9.95) 1- r/#1-4. 2-r/#5-8 10.00

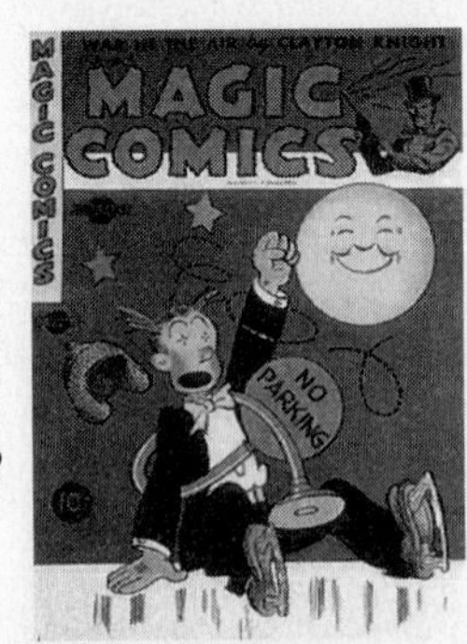

Magic Comics #43 © DMP

Magilla Gorilla #1 © H-B

Magnus Robot Fighter #50 © VAL

GD 2.0 | VG 4.0 | FN 6.0 | VF 8.0 | VF/NM 9.0 | NM- 9.2

Volume 3 TPB ('00, $12.95) r/#9-12 13.00
Volume 4 TPB ('01, $14.95) r/#13-15 15.00

MAGE KNIGHT: STOLEN DESTINY (Based on the fantasy game Mage Knight)
Idea + Design Works: Oct, 2002 - No. 5, Feb, 2003 ($3.50, limited series)
1-5: 1-J. Scott Campbell-c; Cabrera-a/Dezago-s, 2-Dave Johnson-c 3.50

MAGGIE AND HOPEY COLOR SPECIAL (See Love and Rockets)
Fantagraphics Books: May, 1997 ($3.50, one-shot)
1 3.50

MAGGIE THE CAT (Also see Jon Sable, Freelance #11 & Shaman's Tears #12)
Image Comics (Creative Fire Studio): Jan, 1996 - No. 2, Feb, 1996 ($2.50, unfinished limited series)
1,2: Mike Grell-c/a/scripts 2.50

MAGICA DE SPELL (See Walt Disney Showcase #30)

MAGIC AGENT (See Forbidden Worlds & Unknown Worlds)
American Comics Group: Jan-Feb, 1962 - No. 3, May-June, 1962

	GD	VG	FN	VF	VF/NM	NM-
1-Origin & 1st app. John Force	4	8	12	28	38	48
2,3	3	6	9	19	25	32

MAGICAL POKÉMON JOURNEY
Viz Comics: 2000 - Present ($4.95, B&W, magazine-size)
1-4 5.00
Part 2: 1-3; Part 3: 1-4: 1-Includes color poster; Part 4: 1-4; Part 5: 1-4; Part 6: 1-4 5.00

MAGIC COMICS
David McKay Publications: Aug, 1939 - No. 123, Nov-Dec, 1949

	GD	VG	FN	VF	VF/NM	NM-
1-Mandrake the Magician, Henry, Popeye , Blondie, Barney Baxter, Secret Agent X-9 (not by Raymond), Bunky by Billy DeBeck & Thornton Burgess text stories illustrated by Harrison Cady begin; Henry covers begin	340	680	1020	1870	2635	3400
2	120	240	360	660	930	1200
3	90	180	270	495	698	900
4	70	140	210	385	543	700
5	55	110	165	303	427	550
6-10: 8-11,21-Mandrake/Henry-c	45	90	135	248	349	450
11-16,18,20: 12-Mandrake-c begin.	38	76	114	209	295	380
17-The Lone Ranger begins	42	84	126	231	326	420
19-Robot-c	45	90	135	248	349	450
21-30: 25-Only Blondie-c. 26-Dagwood-c begin	25	50	75	138	194	250
31-40: 36-Flag-c	18	36	54	99	140	180
41-50	14	28	42	77	109	140
51-60	12	24	36	66	93	120
61-70	10	20	30	55	75	100
71-99, 107,108-Flash Gordon app; not by Raymond	8	16	24	44	62	80
100	9	18	26	50	70	90
101-106,109-123: 123-Last Dagwood-c	7	14	21	39	55	70

MAGIC FLUTE, THE (See Night Music #9-11)

MAGIC PICKLE
Oni Press: Sept, 2001 - No. 4, Dec, 2001 ($2.95, limited series)
1-4-Scott Morse-s/a; Mahfood-a (2 pgs.) 3.00

MAGIC SWORD, THE (See Movie Classics)

MAGIC THE GATHERING (Title Series), **Acclaim Comics (Armada)**
...ANTIQUITIES WAR,11/95 - 2/96 ($2.50), 1-4-Paul Smith-a(p) 2.50
...ARABIAN NIGHTS, 12/95 - 1/96 ($2.50), 1,2 2.50
...COLLECTION ,'95 ($4.95), 1,2-polybagged 5.00
...CONVOCATIONS, '95 ($2.50), 1-nn-pin-ups 2.50
...ELDER DRAGONS ,'95 ($2.50), 1,2-Doug Wheatley-a 2.50
...FALLEN ANGEL ,'95 ($5.95), nn 6.00
...FALLEN EMPIRES ,9/95 - 10/95 ($2.75), 1,2 3.00
...Collection ($4.95)-polybagged 5.00
...HOMELANDS ,'95 ($5.95), nn-polybagged w/card; Hildebrandts-c 6.00
... ICE AGE (On The World of...) ,7/5 -11/95 ($2.50), 1-4: 1,2-bound-in Magic Card. 3,4-bound-in insert 2.50
...LEGEND OF JEDIT OJANEN, '96 ($2.50), 1,2 2.50
...NIGHTMARE, '95 ($2.50, one shot), 1 2.50
...THE SHADOW MAGE, 7/95 - 10/95 ($2.50), 1-4-bagged w/Magic The Gathering card 2.50
...Collection 1,2 (1995, $4.95)-Trade paperback; polybagged 5.00
...SHANDALAR ,'96 ($2.50), 1,2 2.50
...WAYFARER ,11/95 - 2/96 ($2.50), 1-5 2.50

MAGIC: THE GATHERING: GERRARD'S QUEST
Dark Horse Comics: Mar, 1998 - No. 4, June, 1998 ($2.95, limited series)
1-4: Grell-s/Mhan-a 3.00

MAGIK (Illyana and Storm Limited Series)
Marvel Comics Group: Dec, 1983 - No. 4, Mar, 1984 (60¢, limited series)
1-4: 1-Characters from X-Men; Inferno begins; X-Men cameo (Buscema pencils in #1,2; c-1p. 2-4: 2-Nightcrawler app. & X-Men cameo 3.00

MAGIK (See Black Sun mini-series)
Marvel Comics: Dec, 2000 - No. 4, Mar, 2001 ($2.99, limited series)
1-4-Liam Sharp-a/Abnett & Lanning-s; Nightcrawler app. 3.00

MAGILLA GORILLA (TV) (See Kite Fun Book)
Gold Key: May, 1964 - No. 10, Dec, 1968 (Hanna-Barbera)

	GD	VG	FN	VF	VF/NM	NM-
1-1st comic app.	11	22	33	77	114	150
2-4: 3-Vs. Yogi Bear for President. 4-1st Punkin Puss & Mushmouse, Ricochet Rabbit & Droop-a-Long	7	14	21	51	71	90
5-10: 10-Reprints	6	12	18	43	59	75

MAGILLA GORILLA (TV)(See Spotlight #4)
Charlton Comics: Nov, 1970 - No. 5, July, 1971 (Hanna-Barbera)

	GD	VG	FN	VF	VF/NM	NM-
1	6	12	18	38	52	65
2-5	4	8	12	22	30	38

MAGNETIC MEN FEATURING MAGNETO
Marvel Comics (Amalgam): June, 1997 ($1.95, one-shot)
1-Tom Peyer-s/Barry Kitson & Dan Panosian-a 2.50

MAGNETO (See X-Men #1)
Marvel Comics: nd (Sept, 1993) (Giveaway) (one-shot)
0-Embossed foil-c by Sienkiewicz; r/Classic X-Men #19 & 12 by Bolton 5.00

MAGNETO
Marvel Comics: Nov, 1996 - No. 4, Feb, 1997 ($1.95, limited series)
1-4: Peter Milligan scripts & Kelley Jones-a(p) 2.50

MAGNETO AND THE MAGNETIC MEN
Marvel Comics (Amalgam): Apr, 1996 ($1.95, one-shot)
1-Jeff Matsuda-a(p) 2.50

MAGNETO ASCENDANT
Marvel Comics: May, 1999 ($3.99, squarebound one-shot)
1-Reprints early Magneto appearances 4.00

MAGNETO: DARK SEDUCTION
Marvel Comics: Jun, 2000 - No. 4, Sept, 2000 ($2.99, limited series)
1-4: Nicieza-s/Cruz-a. 3,4-Avengers-c/app. 3.00

MAGNETO REX
Marvel Comics: Apr, 1999 - No. 3, July, 1999 ($2.50, limited series)
1-3-Rogue, Quicksilver app.; Peterson-a(p) 2.50

MAGNUS, ROBOT FIGHTER (...4000 A.D.)(See Doctor Solar)
Gold Key: Feb, 1963 - No. 46, Jan, 1977 (All painted covers except #5,31)

	GD	VG	FN	VF	VF/NM	NM-
1-Origin & 1st app. Magnus; Aliens (1st app.) series begins	25	50	75	176	258	340
2,3	11	22	33	77	114	150
4-10: 10-Simonson fan club illo (5/65, 1st-a?)	7	14	21	53	74	90
11-20	5	10	15	36	48	60
21,24-28: 28-Aliens ends	4	8	12	24	32	40
22,23: 22-Origin-r/#1; last 12¢ issue	4	8	12	25	33	42
29-46-Mostly reprints	2	4	6	11	14	18

NOTE: *Manning a-1-22, 28-43(r). Spiegle a-23, 44r.*

MAGNUS ROBOT FIGHTER (Also see Vintage Magnus)
Valiant/Acclaim Comics: May, 1991 - No. 64, Feb, 1996 ($1.75/$1.95/$2.25/$2.50)
1-Nichols/Layton-c/a; 1-8 have trading cards 6.00
2-8: 4-Rai cameo. 5-Origin & 1st full app. Rai (10/91); 5-8 are in flip book format and back-c & half of book are Rai #1-4 mini-series. 6-1st Solar x-over. 7-Magnus vs. Rai-c/story; 1st X-O Armor 4.00
0-Origin issue; Layton-a; ordered through mail w/coupons from 1st 8 issues plus 50¢; B. Smith trading card 6.00
0-Sold thru comic shops without trading card 3.00
9-11 3.00

	GD	VG	FN	VF	VF/NM	NM-
12-(3.25, 44 pgs.)-Turok-c/story (1st app. in Valiant universe, 5/92); has 8 pg. Magnus story insert	1	2	3	5	6	8

Major Bummer #15 © Arcudi & Mahnke

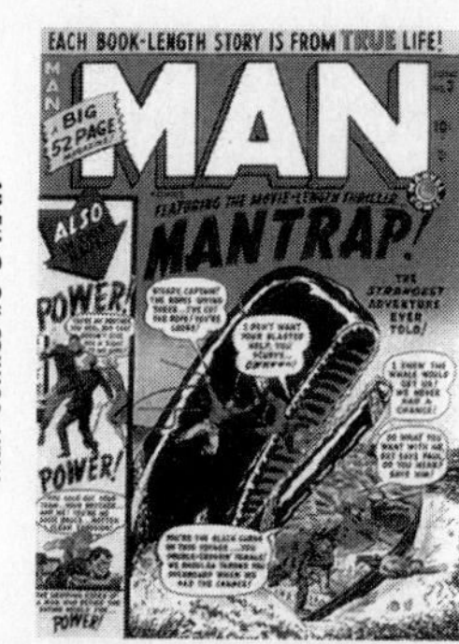

Man Comics #3 © MAR

Man From Atlantis #4 © SOLOW Prod.

	GD 2.0	VG 4.0	FN 6.0	VF 8.0	VF/NM 9.0	NM- 9.2
13-24,26-48: 14-1st app. Isak. 15,16-Unity x-overs. 15-Miller-c. 16-Birth of Magnus. 21-New direction & new logo. 21-Gold ink variant. 24-Story cont'd in Rai & the Future Force #9. 33-Timewalker app.36-Bound-in trading cards. 37-Rai & Starwatchers app. 44-Bound-in sneak peek card.						2.50
25-($2.95)-Embossed silver foil-c; new costume						3.00
49-63						3.00
64-($2.50): 64-Magnus dies?						3.00
...Invasion (1994, $9.95)-r/Rai #1-4 & Magnus #5-8						10.00
Magnus Steel Nation (1994, $9.95) r/#1-4						10.00
Yearbook (1994, $3.95, 52 pgs.)						4.00

NOTE: ***Ditko/Reese** a-18. **Layton** a(i)-5; c-6-9i, 25; back(i)-5-8. **Reese** a(i)-22, 25, 28; c(i)-22, 24, 28. **Simonson** c-16. Prices for issues 1-8 are for trading cards and coupons intact.*

MAGNUS ROBOT FIGHTER
Acclaim Comics (Valiant Heroes): V2#1, May, 1997 - No. 18, Jun, 1998 ($2.50)

	GD	VG	FN	VF	VF/NM	NM-
1-18: 1-Reintro Magnus; Donavon Wylie (X-O Manowar) cameo; Tom Peyer scripts & Mike McKone-c/a begin; painted variant-c exists						2.50

MAGNUS ROBOT FIGHTER/NEXUS
Valiant/Dark Horse Comics: Dec, 1993 - No. 2, Apr, 1994 ($2.95, lim. series)

	GD	VG	FN	VF	VF/NM	NM-
1,2: Steve Rude painted-c & pencils in all						3.00

MAID OF THE MIST (See American Graphics)

MAI, THE PSYCHIC GIRL
Eclipse Comics: May, 1987 - No. 28, July, 1989 ($1.50, B&W, bi-weekly, 44pgs.)

	GD	VG	FN	VF	VF/NM	NM-
1-28, 1,2-2nd print						2.50

MAJOR BUMMER
DC Comics: Aug, 1997 - No. 15, Oct, 1998 ($2.50)

	GD	VG	FN	VF	VF/NM	NM-
1-15: 1-Origin and 1st app. Major Bummer						2.50

MAJOR HOOPLE COMICS (See Crackajack Funnies)
Nedor Publications: nd (Jan, 1943)

	GD	VG	FN	VF	VF/NM	NM-
1-Mary Worth, Phantom Soldier app. by Moldoff	40	80	120	240	345	450

MAJOR VICTORY COMICS (Also see Dynamic Comics)
H. Clay Glover/Service Publ./Harry 'A' Chesler: 1944 - No. 3, Summer, 1945

	GD	VG	FN	VF	VF/NM	NM-
1-Origin Major Victory (patriotic hero) by C. Sultan (reprint from Dynamic #1); 1st app. Spider Woman	64	128	192	400	600	800
2-Dynamic Boy app.	40	80	120	240	345	450
3-Rocket Boy app.	39	78	117	230	325	420

MALIBU ASHCAN: RAFFERTY (See Firearm #12)
Malibu Comics (Ultraverse): Nov, 1994 (99¢, B&W w/color-c; one-shot)

	GD	VG	FN	VF	VF/NM	NM-
1-Previews "The Rafferty Saga" storyline in Firearm; Chaykin-c						2.25

MALTESE FALCON
David McKay Publications: No. 48, 1946

	GD	VG	FN	VF	VF/NM	NM-
Feature Books 48-by Dashiell Hammett	76	152	228	475	713	950

MALU IN THE LAND OF ADVENTURE
I. W. Enterprises: 1964 (See White Princess of Jungle #2)

	GD	VG	FN	VF	VF/NM	NM-
1-r/Avon's Slave Girl Comics #1; Severin-c	6	12	18	38	52	65

MAMMOTH COMICS
Whitman Publishing Co.(K. K. Publ.): 1938 (84 pgs.) (B&W, 8-1/2x11-1/2")

	GD	VG	FN	VF	VF/NM	NM-
1-Alley Oop, Terry & the Pirates, Dick Tracy, Little Orphan Annie, Wash Tubbs, Moon Mullins, Smilin' Jack, Tailspin Tommy, Don Winslow, Dan Dunn, Smokey Stover & other reprints (scarce)	200	400	600	1250	1875	2500

MAN AGAINST TIME
Image Comics (Motown Machineworks): May, 1996 - No. 4, Aug, 1996 ($2.25, limited series)

	GD	VG	FN	VF	VF/NM	NM-
1-4: 1-Simonson-c. 2,3-Leon-c. 4-Barreto & Leon-c						2.25

MAN-BAT (See Batman Family, Brave & the Bold, & Detective #400)
National Periodical Publ./DC Comics: Dec-Jan, 1975-76 - No. 2, Feb-Mar, 1976; Dec, 1984

	GD	VG	FN	VF	VF/NM	NM-
1-Ditko-a(p); Aparo-c; Batman app.; 1st app. She-Bat?	2	4	6	12	16	20
2-Aparo-c	2	4	6	8	10	12
1 (12/84)-N. Adams-r(3)/Det.(Vs. Batman on-c)						4.00

MAN-BAT
DC Comics: Feb, 1996 - No. 3, Apr, 1996 ($2.25, limited series)

	GD	VG	FN	VF	VF/NM	NM-
1-3: Dixon scripts in all. 2-Killer Croc-c/app.						2.25

MAN CALLED A-X, THE
Malibu Comics (Bravura): Nov, 1994 - No. 4, Jun, 1995 ($2.95, limited series)

	GD	VG	FN	VF	VF/NM	NM-
0-4: Marv Wolfman scripts & Shawn McManus-c/a. 0-(2/95). 1-"1A" on cover						3.00

MAN CALLED A-X, THE
DC Comics: Oct, 1997 - No. 8, May, 1998 ($2.50)

	GD	VG	FN	VF	VF/NM	NM-
1-8: Marv Wolfman scripts & Shawn McManus-c/a.						2.50

MAN COMICS
Marvel/Atlas Comics (NPI): Dec, 1949 - No. 28, Sept, 1953 (#1-6: 52 pgs.)

	GD	VG	FN	VF	VF/NM	NM-
1-Tuska-a	24	48	72	135	190	245
2-Tuska-a	14	28	42	79	107	135
3-6	10	20	30	58	77	95
7,8	10	20	30	56	73	90
9-13,15: 9-Format changes to war	8	16	24	43	54	65
14-Henkel (3 pgs.); Pakula-a	9	18	27	49	62	75
16-21,23-28: 28-Crime issue (Bob Brant)	7	14	21	37	46	55
22-Krigstein-a, 5 pgs.	9	18	27	49	62	75

NOTE: ***Berg** a-14, 15, 19. **Colan** a-9, 21. **Everett** a-8, 22; c-22, 25. **Heath** a-11, 17, 21. Kubertish a-by **Bob Brown**-3. **Maneely** a-11; c-10, 11. **Reinman** a-11. **Robinson** a-7, 10, 14. **Robert Sale** a-9, 11. **Sinnott** a-22, 23. **Tuska** a-14, 23.*

MANDRAKE THE MAGICIAN (See Defenders Of The Earth, 123, 46, 52, 55, Giant Comic Album, King Comics, Magic Comics, The Phantom #21, Tiny Tot Funnies & Wow Comics, '36)

MANDRAKE THE MAGICIAN (See Harvey Comics Hits #53)
David McKay Publ./Dell/King Comics (All 12¢): 1938 - 1948; Sept, 1966 - No. 10, Nov, 1967 (Also see Four Color #752)

	GD	VG	FN	VF	VF/NM	NM-
Feature Books 18,19,23 (1938)	59	118	177	369	555	740
Feature Books 46	44	88	132	264	395	525
Feature Books 52,55	37	74	111	212	301	390
Four Color 752 (11/56)	11	22	33	80	118	155
1-Begin S.O.S. Phantom, ends #3	6	12	18	38	52	65
2-7,9: 4-Girl Phantom app. 5-Flying Saucer-c/story. 5,6-Brick Bradford app. 7-Origin Lothar. 9-Brick Bradford app.	3	7	10	21	28	35
8-Jeff Jones-a (4 pgs.)	4	8	12	24	32	40
10-Rip Kirby app.; Raymond-a (14 pgs.)	4	8	12	28	38	48

MANDRAKE THE MAGICIAN
Marvel Comics: Apr, 1995 - No. 2, May, 1995 ($2.95, unfinished limited series)

	GD	VG	FN	VF	VF/NM	NM-
1,2: Mike Barr scripts						3.00

MAN-EATING COW (See Tick #7,8)
New England Comics: July, 1992 - No. 10, 1994? ($2.75, B&W, limited series)

	GD	VG	FN	VF	VF/NM	NM-
1-10						3.00
Man-Eating Cow Bonanza (6/96, $4.95, 128 pgs.)-r/#1-4.						5.00

MAN FROM ATLANTIS (TV)
Marvel Comics: Feb, 1978 - No. 7, Aug, 1978

	GD	VG	FN	VF	VF/NM	NM-
1-(84 pgs.)-Sutton-a(p), Buscema-c; origin & cast photos	1	3	4	6	8	10
2-7						4.00

MAN FROM PLANET X, THE
Planet X Productions: 1987 (no price; probably unlicensed)

	GD	VG	FN	VF	VF/NM	NM-
1-Reprints Fawcett Movie Comic						2.25

MAN FROM U.N.C.L.E., THE (TV) (Also see The Girl From Uncle)
Gold Key: Feb, 1965 - No. 22, Apr, 1969 (All photo-c)

	GD	VG	FN	VF	VF/NM	NM-
1	16	32	48	113	167	220
2-Photo back c-2-8	9	18	27	63	89	115
3-10: 7-Jet Dream begins (1st app., also see Jet Dream) (all new stories)	7	14	21	50	68	85
11-22: 19-Last 12¢ issue. 21,22-Reprint #10 & 7	6	12	18	43	59	75

MAN FROM U.N.C.L.E., THE (TV)
Entertainment Publishing: 1987 - No. 11 ($1.50/$1.75, B&W)

	GD	VG	FN	VF	VF/NM	NM-
1-7 ($1.50), 8-11 ($1.75)						3.00

MAN FROM WELLS FARGO (TV)
Dell Publishing Co.: No. 1287, Feb-Apr, 1962 - May-July, 1962 (Photo-c)

	GD	VG	FN	VF	VF/NM	NM-
Four Color 1287, #01-495-207	6	12	18	43	59	75

MANGA SHI (See Tomoe)
Crusade Entertainment: Aug, 1996 ($2.95)

	GD	VG	FN	VF	VF/NM	NM-
1-Printed backwards (manga-style)						3.00

MANGA SHI 2000
Crusade Entertainment: Feb, 1997 - No. 3, June, 1997 ($2.95, mini-series)

	GD	VG	FN	VF	VF/NM	NM-
1-3: 1-Two covers						3.00

MANGA ZEN (Also see Zen Intergalactic Ninja)
Zen Comics (Fusion Studios): 1996 - No. 3, 1996 ($2.50, B&W)

	GD	VG	FN	VF	VF/NM	NM-
1-3						2.50

MANGAZINE

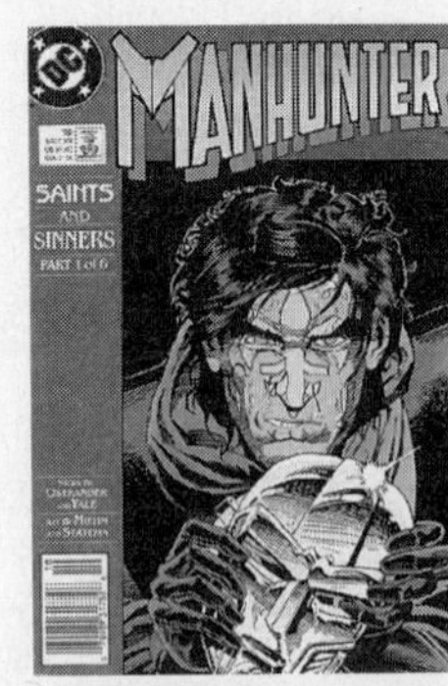

Manhunter #18 © DC

The Man of Steel #5 © DC

Man-Thing #14 © MAR

Antarctic Press: Aug, 1985 - No. 4, Sept, 1986 (B&W)

	GD 2.0	VG 4.0	FN 6.0	VF 8.0	VF/NM 9.0	NM- 9.2
1-Soft paper-c	2	4	6	11	14	18
2-4	2	4	6	8	10	12

MANGLE TANGLE TALES
Innovation Publishing: 1990 ($2.95, deluxe format)

	GD 2.0	VG 4.0	FN 6.0	VF 8.0	VF/NM 9.0	NM- 9.2
1-Intro by Harlan Ellison						3.00

MANHUNT! (Becomes Red Fox #15 on)
Magazine Enterprises: 10/47 - No. 11, 8/48; #13,14, 1953 (no #12)

	GD 2.0	VG 4.0	FN 6.0	VF 8.0	VF/NM 9.0	NM- 9.2
1-Red Fox by L. B. Cole, Undercover Girl by Whitney, Space Ace begin (1st app.); negligee panels	50	100	150	300	450	600
2-Electrocution-c	40	80	120	240	340	440
3-6	34	68	102	193	274	355
7-10: 7-Space Ace ends. 8-Trail Colt begins (intro/1st app., 5/48) by Guardineer; Trail Colt-c. 10-G. Ingels-a	30	60	90	170	240	310
11(8/48)-Frazetta-a, 7 pgs.; The Duke, Scotland Yard begin	40	80	120	240	350	460
13(A-1 #63)-Frazetta, r-/Trail Colt #1, 7 pgs.	40	80	120	237	334	430
14(A-1 #77)-Bondage/hypo-c; last L. B. Cole Red Fox; Ingels-a	33	66	99	190	270	350

NOTE: *Guardineer a-1-5; c-8. Whitney a-2-14; c-1-6, 10. Red Fox by L. B. Cole-#1-14. #15 was advertised but came out as Red Fox #15. Bondage c-6.*

MANHUNTER (See Adventure #58, 73, Brave & the Bold, Detective Comics, 1st Issue Special, House of Mystery #143 and Justice League of America)
DC Comics: 1984 ($2.50, 76 pgs; high quality paper)

	GD 2.0	VG 4.0	FN 6.0	VF 8.0	VF/NM 9.0	NM- 9.2
1-Simonson-c/a(r)/Detective; Batman app.						3.50

MANHUNTER
DC Comics: July, 1988 - No. 24, Apr, 1990 ($1.00)

	GD 2.0	VG 4.0	FN 6.0	VF 8.0	VF/NM 9.0	NM- 9.2
1-24: 8,9-Flash app. 9-Invasion. 17-Batman-c/sty						2.25

MANHUNTER
DC Comics: No. 0, Nov, 1994 - No. 12, Nov, 1995 ($1.95/$2.25)

	GD 2.0	VG 4.0	FN 6.0	VF 8.0	VF/NM 9.0	NM- 9.2
0-12						2.25

MANHUNTER: THE SPECIAL EDITION
DC Comics: 1999 ($9.95)

	GD 2.0	VG 4.0	FN 6.0	VF 8.0	VF/NM 9.0	NM- 9.2
TPB-Reprints Detective Comics stories by Goodwin and Simonson						10.00

MAN IN BLACK (See Thrill-O-Rama) (Also see All New Comics, Front Page, Green Hornet #31, Strange Story & Tally-Ho Comics)
Harvey Publications: Sept, 1957 - No. 4, Mar, 1958

	GD 2.0	VG 4.0	FN 6.0	VF 8.0	VF/NM 9.0	NM- 9.2
1-Bob Powell-c/a	18	36	54	104	142	180
2-4: Powell-c/a	14	28	42	79	107	135

MAN IN BLACK
Lorne-Harvey Publications (Recollections): 1990 - No. 2, July, 1991 (B&W)

	GD 2.0	VG 4.0	FN 6.0	VF 8.0	VF/NM 9.0	NM- 9.2
1,2						2.25

MAN IN FLIGHT (Disney, TV)
Dell Publishing Co.: No. 836, Sept, 1957

	GD 2.0	VG 4.0	FN 6.0	VF 8.0	VF/NM 9.0	NM- 9.2
Four Color 836	8	16	24	55	78	100

MAN IN SPACE (Disney, TV, see Dell Giant #27)
Dell Publishing Co.: No. 716, Aug, 1956 - No. 954, Nov, 1958

	GD 2.0	VG 4.0	FN 6.0	VF 8.0	VF/NM 9.0	NM- 9.2
Four Color 716-A science feat. from Tomorrowland	10	20	30	67	96	125
Four Color 954-Satellites	8	16	24	55	78	100

MANKIND (WWF Wrestling)
Chaos Comics: Sept, 1999 ($2.95, one-shot)

	GD 2.0	VG 4.0	FN 6.0	VF 8.0	VF/NM 9.0	NM- 9.2
1-Regular and photo-c						3.00
1-Premium Edition ($10.00) Dwayne Turner & Danny Miki-c						10.00

MANN AND SUPERMAN
DC Comics: 2000 ($5.95, prestige format, one-shot)

	GD 2.0	VG 4.0	FN 6.0	VF 8.0	VF/NM 9.0	NM- 9.2
nn-Michael T. Gilbert-s/a						6.00

MAN OF STEEL, THE (Also see Superman: The Man of Steel)
DC Comics: 1986 (June release) - No. 6, 1986 (75¢, limited series)

	GD 2.0	VG 4.0	FN 6.0	VF 8.0	VF/NM 9.0	NM- 9.2
1-6: 1-Silver logo; Byrne-c/a/scripts in all; origin, 1-Alternate-c for newsstand sales,1-Distr. to toy stores by So Much Fun, 2-6: 2-Intro. Lois Lane, Jimmy Olsen. 3-Intro/origin Magpie; Batman-c/story. 4-Intro. new Lex Luthor						4.00
1-6-Silver Editions (1993, $1.95)-r/1-6						3.00
...The Complete Saga nn-Contains #1-6, given away in contest						26.00
Limited Edition, softcover	5	10	15	36	48	60

NOTE: *Issues 1-6 were released between Action #583 (9/86) & Action #584 (1/87) plus Superman #423 (9/86) & Advs. of Superman #424 (1/87).*

MAN OF THE ATOM (See Solar, Man of the Atom Vol. 2)

MAN OF WAR (See Liberty Guards & Liberty Scouts)
Centaur Publications: Nov, 1941 - No. 2, Jan, 1942

	GD 2.0	VG 4.0	FN 6.0	VF 8.0	VF/NM 9.0	NM- 9.2
1-The Fire-Man, Man of War, The Sentinel, Liberty Guards, & Vapo-Man begin; Gustavson-c/a; Flag-c	168	336	504	1050	1575	2100
2-Intro The Ferret; Gustavson-c/a	124	248	372	775	1163	1550

MAN OF WAR
Eclipse Comics: Aug, 1987 - No. 3, Feb, 1988 ($1.75, Baxter paper)

	GD 2.0	VG 4.0	FN 6.0	VF 8.0	VF/NM 9.0	NM- 9.2
1-3: Bruce Jones scripts						2.25

MAN OF WAR (See The Protectors)
Malibu Comics: 1993 - No, 8, Feb, 1994 ($1.95/$2.50/$2.25)

	GD 2.0	VG 4.0	FN 6.0	VF 8.0	VF/NM 9.0	NM- 9.2
1-5 ($1.95)-Newsstand Editions w/different-c						2.25
1-8-1-5-Collector's Edi. w/poster. 6-8 ($2.25): 6-Polybagged w/Skycap. 8-Vs. Rocket Rangers						2.50

MAN O' MARS
Fiction House Magazines: 1953; 1964

	GD 2.0	VG 4.0	FN 6.0	VF 8.0	VF/NM 9.0	NM- 9.2
1-Space Rangers; Whitman-c	42	84	126	252	376	500
I.W. Reprint #1-r/Man O'Mars #1 & Star Pirate; Murphy Anderson-a	6	12	18	38	52	65

MANTECH ROBOT WARRIORS
Archie Enterprises, Inc.: Sept, 1984 - No. 4, Apr, 1985 (75¢)

	GD 2.0	VG 4.0	FN 6.0	VF 8.0	VF/NM 9.0	NM- 9.2
1-4: Ayers-c/a(p). 1-Buckler-c(i)						3.00

MAN-THING (See Fear, Giant-Size..., Marvel Comics Presents, Marvel Fanfare, Monsters Unleashed, Power Record Comics & Savage Tales)
Marvel Comics Group: Jan, 1974 - No. 22, Oct, 1975; V2#1, Nov, 1979 - V2#11, July, 1981

	GD 2.0	VG 4.0	FN 6.0	VF 8.0	VF/NM 9.0	NM- 9.2
1-Howard the Duck(2nd app.) cont'd/Fear #19	4	8	12	29	40	50
2	2	4	6	14	18	22
3-1st app. original Foolkiller	2	4	6	11	14	18
4-Origin Foolkiller; last app. 1st Foolkiller	2	4	6	10	13	16
5-11-Ploog-a. 11-Foolkiller cameo (flashback)	2	4	6	10	13	16
12-22: 19-1st app. Scavenger. 20-Spidey cameo. 21-Origin Scavenger, Man-Thing. 22-Howard the Duck cameo	1	2	3	5	7	9
V2#1(1979)	1	2	3	5	6	8
V2#2-11: 4-Dr. Strange-c/app. 11-Mayerik-a						4.00

NOTE: *Alcala a-14. Brunner c-1. J. Buscema a-12p, 13p, 16p. Gil Kane c-4p, 10p, 12-20p, 21. Mooney a-17, 18, 19p, 20-22, V2#1-3p. Ploog Man-Thing-5p, 6p, 7, 8, 9-11p; c-5, 6, 8, 9, 11. Sutton a-13i. No. 19 says #10 in indicia.*

MAN-THING (Volume Three, continues in Strange Tales #1 (9/98))
Marvel Comics: Dec, 1997 - No. 8, July, 1998 ($2.99)

	GD 2.0	VG 4.0	FN 6.0	VF 8.0	VF/NM 9.0	NM- 9.2
1-8-DeMatteis-s/Sharp-a. 2-Two covers. 6-Howard the Duck-c/app.						3.00

MANTRA
Malibu Comics (Ultraverse): July, 1993 - No. 24, Aug, 1995 ($1.95/$2.50)

	GD 2.0	VG 4.0	FN 6.0	VF 8.0	VF/NM 9.0	NM- 9.2
1-Polybagged w/trading card & coupon						3.00
1-Newsstand edition w/o trading card or coupon						2.25
1-Full cover holographic edition	1	3	4	6	8	10
1-Ultra-limited silver foil-c						5.00
2-9,11-24: 3-Intro Warstrike & Kismet. 6-Break-Thru x-over. 2-($2.50-Newsstand edition bagged w/card. 4-($2.50, 48 pgs.)-Rune flip-c/story by B. Smith (3 pgs.). 7-Prime app.; origin Prototype by Jurgens/Austin (2 pgs.). 11-New costume. 17-Intro NecroMantra & Pinnacle; prelude to Godwheel						2.50
10-($3.50, 68 pgs.)-Flip-c w/Ultraverse Premiere #2						3.50
Giant Size 1 (7/94, $2.50, 44 pgs.)						2.50
...Spear of Destiny 1,2 (4/95, $2.50, 36pgs.)						2.50

MANTRA (2nd Series) (Also See Black September)
Malibu Comics (Ultraverse): Infinity, Sept, 1995 - No. 7, Apr, 1996 ($1.50)

	GD 2.0	VG 4.0	FN 6.0	VF 8.0	VF/NM 9.0	NM- 9.2
Infinity (9/95, $1.50)-Black September x-over, Intro new Mantra						2.25
1-7: 1-(10/95). 5-Return of Eden (original Mantra). 6,7-Rush app.						2.25

MAN WITH THE X-RAY EYES, THE (See X,... under Movie Comics)

MANY GHOSTS OF DR. GRAVES, THE (Doctor Graves #73 on)
Charlton Comics: 5/67 - No. 60, 12/76; No. 61, 9/77 - No. 62, 10/77; No. 63, 2/78 - No. 65, 4/78; No. 66, 6/81 - No. 72, 5/82

	GD 2.0	VG 4.0	FN 6.0	VF 8.0	VF/NM 9.0	NM- 9.2
1-Ditko-a; Palais-a; early issues 12¢-c	5	10	15	36	48	60
2-6,8,10	3	6	9	16	20	25
7,9-Ditko-a	3	6	9	18	24	30
11-13,16-18-Ditko-c/a	2	4	6	12	16	20
14,19,23,25	2	4	6	9	11	14
15,20,21-Ditko-a	2	4	6	10	13	16
22,24,26,27,29-35,38,40-Ditko-c/a	2	4	6	10	13	16

Many Ghosts of Dr. Graves #42 © CC

Marc Spector: Moon Knight #15 © MAR

Marge's Little Lulu #25 © Marjorie Buell

	GD 2.0	VG 4.0	FN 6.0	VF 8.0	VF/NM 9.0	NM- 9.2
28-Ditko-c	2	4	6	9	11	14
36,46,56,57,59,66-69,71	1	2	3	5	7	9
37,41,43,51,54,60,61-Ditko-a	2	4	6	8	10	12
39,58-Ditko-c. 39-Sutton-a. 58-Ditko-a	2	4	6	8	10	12
42,44,53-Sutton-c; Ditko-a. 42-Sutton-a	2	4	6	8	10	12
45-1st Newton comic work (8 pgs.); new logo; Sutton-c	2	4	6	10	13	16
47-Newton, Sutton, Ditko-a	2	4	6	9	11	14
48-Ditko, Sutton-a	2	4	6	8	10	12
49-Newton-c/a; Sutton-a.	1	3	4	6	8	10
50-Sutton-a	1	2	3	5	7	9
52-Newton-c; Ditko-a	2	4	6	8	10	12
55-Ditko-c; Sutton-a	2	4	6	8	10	12
62-65-Ditko-c/a. 65-Sutton-a	2	4	6	9	11	14
70,72-Ditko-a	2	4	6	9	11	14
Modern Comics Reprint 12,25 (1978)						4.00

NOTE: ***Aparo** a-4, 5, 7, 8, 66r, 69r; c-8, 14, 19, 66r, 67r. **Byrne** c-54. **Ditko** a-1, 7, 9, 11-13, 15-18, 20-22, 24, 26, 27, 29, 30-35, 37, 38, 40-44, 47, 48, 51-54, 58, 60r-65r, 70, 72; c-11-13, 16-18, 22, 24, 26-35, 38, 40, 55, 58, 62-65. **Howard** a-38, 39, 45i, 65; c-48. **Kim** a-36, 46, 52. **Larson** a-58. **Morisi** a-13, 14, 23, 26. **Newton** a-45, 47p, 49p; c-49, 52. **Staton** a-36, 37, 41, 43. **Sutton** a-39, 42, 47-50, 55, 65; c-42, 44, 45; painted c-53. **Zeck** a-56, 59.*

MANY LOVES OF DOBIE GILLIS (TV)
National Periodical Publications: May-June, 1960 - No. 26, Oct, 1964

	GD 2.0	VG 4.0	FN 6.0	VF 8.0	VF/NM 9.0	NM- 9.2
1-Most covers by Bob Oskner	25	50	75	181	266	350
2-5	14	28	42	97	141	185
6-10: 10-Last 10¢-c	9	18	27	65	93	120
11-26: 20-Drucker-a. 24-(3-4/64). 25-(9/64)	9	18	27	60	85	110

MANY WORLDS OF TESLA STRONG, THE (Also see Tom Strong)
America's Best Comics: July, 2003 ($5.95, one-shot)

	GD 2.0	VG 4.0	FN 6.0	VF 8.0	VF/NM 9.0	NM- 9.2
1-Two covers by Timm & Art Adams; art by various incl. Campbell, Cho, Noto, Hughes						6.00

MARAUDER'S MOON (See Luke Short, Four Color #848)

MARCH OF COMICS (See Promotional Comics section)

MARCH OF CRIME (Formerly My Love Affair #1-6) (See Fox Giants)
Fox Features Synd.: No. 7, July, 1950 - No. 2, Sept, 1950; No. 3, Sept, 1951

	GD 2.0	VG 4.0	FN 6.0	VF 8.0	VF/NM 9.0	NM- 9.2
7(#1)(7/50)-True crime stories; Wood-a	40	80	120	240	340	440
2(9/50)-Wood-a (exceptional)	39	78	117	230	325	420
3(9/51)	19	38	57	106	146	185

MARCO POLO
Charlton Comics Group: 1962 (Movie classic)

	GD 2.0	VG 4.0	FN 6.0	VF 8.0	VF/NM 9.0	NM- 9.2
nn (Scarce)-Glanzman-c/a (25 pgs.)	11	22	33	77	114	150

MARC SPECTOR: MOON KNIGHT (Also see Moon Knight)
Marvel Comics: June, 1989 - No. 60, Mar, 1994 ($1.50/$1.75, direct sales)

	GD 2.0	VG 4.0	FN 6.0	VF 8.0	VF/NM 9.0	NM- 9.2
1-24,26-49,51-54,58,59: 4-Intro new Midnight. 8,9-Punisher app. 15-Silver Sable app. 19-21-Spider-Man & Punisher app. 25-(52 pgs.)-Ghost Rider app. 32,33-Hobgoblin II (Macendale) & Spider-Man (in black costume) app. 35-38-Punisher story. 42-44-Infinity War x-over. 46-Demogoblin app. 51,53-Gambit app. 55-New look. 57-Spider-Man-c/story. 60-Moon Knight dies						2.50
50-(56 pgs.)-Special die-cut-c						3.00
55-57,60-Platt a						3.50
...: Divided We Fall ($4.95, 52 pgs.)						5.00
Special 1 (1992, $2.50)						2.50

NOTE: *Cowan c(p) 20-23. Guice c-20. Heath c/a-4. Platt -a 55-57,60; c-55-60.*

MARGARET O'BRIEN (See The Adventures of...)

MARGE'S LITTLE LULU (Continues as Little Lulu from #207 on)
Dell Publishing Co./Gold Key #165-206: No. 74, 6/45 - No. 164, 7-9/62; No. 165, 10/62 - No. 206, 8/72

Marjorie Henderson Buell, born in Philadelphia, Pa., in 1904, created Little Lulu, a cartoon character that appeared weekly in the Saturday Evening Post from Feb. 23, 1935 through Dec. 30, 1944. She was not responsible for any of the comic books. **John Stanley** did pencils only on all Little Lulu comics through at least #135 (1959). He did pencils and inks on Four Color #74 & 97. **Irving Tripp** began inking stories from #1 on, and remained the comic's illustrator throughout its entire run. **Stanley** did storyboards (layouts), pencils, and scripts in all cases and inking only on covers. His word balloons were written in cursive. **Tripp** and occasionally other artists at Western Publ. in Poughkeepsie, N.Y. blew up the pencilled pages, inked the blowups, and lettered them. **Arnold Drake** did storyboards, pencils and scripts starting with #197 (1970) on, amidst reprinted issues. **Buell** sold her rights exclusively to Western Publ. in Dec., 1971. The earlier issues had to be approved by **Buell** prior to publication.

	GD 2.0	VG 4.0	FN 6.0	VF 8.0	VF/NM 9.0	NM- 9.2
Four Color 74('45)-Intro Lulu, Tubby & Alvin	115	230	345	850	1263	1675
Four Color 97(2/46)	50	100	150	376	556	735
(Above two books are all John Stanley - cover, pencils, and inks.)						
Four Color 110('46)-1st Alvin Story Telling Time; 1st app. Willy; variant cover may exist	35	70	105	255	377	500
Four Color 115-1st app. Boys' Clubhouse	35	70	105	255	377	500
Four Color 120, 131: 120-1st app. Eddie	31	62	93	228	339	450
Four Color 139('47),146,158	31	62	93	218	319	420
Four Color 165 (10/47)-Smokes doll hair & has wild hallucinations. 1st Tubby detective story	30	60	90	218	319	420
1(1-2/48)-Lulu's Diary feature begins	60	120	180	420	660	900
2-1st app. Gloria; 1st Tubby story in a L.L. comic; 1st app. Miss Feeny	31	62	93	218	319	420
3-5	28	56	84	203	297	390
6-10: 7-1st app. Annie; Xmas-c	22	44	66	156	228	300
11-20: 18-X-Mas-c. 19-1st app. Wilbur. 20-1st app. Mr. McNabbem	19	38	57	136	198	260
21-30: 26-r/F.C. 110. 30-Xmas-c	15	30	45	109	160	210
31-38,40: 35-1st Mumday story	13	26	39	90	133	175
39-Intro. Witch Hazel in "That Awful Witch Hazel"	14	28	42	99	145	190
41-60: 42-Xmas-c. 45-2nd Witch Hazel app. 49-Gives Stanley & others credit	12	24	36	82	121	160
61-80: 63-1st app. Chubby (Tubby's cousin). 68-1st app. Prof. Cleff. 78-Xmas-c. 80-Intro. Little Itch (2/55)	9	18	27	65	93	120
81-99: 90-Xmas-c	8	16	24	53	74	95
100	8	16	24	55	78	100
101-130: 123-1st app. Fifi	6	12	18	43	59	75
131-164: 135-Last Stanley-p	6	12	18	38	52	65
165-Giant; ...in Paris ('62)	12	24	36	87	129	170
166-Giant; ...Christmas Diary (1962 - '63)	12	24	36	87	129	170
167-169	5	10	15	33	44	55
170,172,175,176,178-196,198-200-Stanley-r. 182-1st app. Little Scarecrow Boy	3	6	9	18	23	28
171,173,174,177,197	2	4	6	14	18	22
201,203,206-Last issue to carry Marge's name	2	4	6	12	16	20
202,204,205-Stanley-r	2	4	6	14	18	22
...& Tubby in Japan (12¢)(5-7/62) 01476-207	8	16	24	53	74	95
...Summer Camp 1(8/67-G.K.-Giant) '57-58-r	6	12	18	40	55	70
...Trick 'N' Treat 1(12¢)(12/62-Gold Key)	7	14	21	46	63	80

NOTE: *See Dell Giant Comics #23, 29, 36, 42, 50, & Dell Giants for annuals. All Giants not by Stanley from L.L. on Vacation (7/54) on. Irving Tripp a-#1-on. Christmas c-7, 18, 30, 42, 78, 90, 126, 166, 250. Summer Camp issues #173, 177, 181, 189, 197, 201, 206.*

MARGE'S LITTLE LULU (See Golden Comics Digest #19, 23, 27, 29, 33, 36, 40, 43, 46, & March of Comics #251, 267, 275, 293, 307, 323, 335, 349, 355, 369, 385, 406, 417, 427, 439, 456, 468, 475, 488)

MARGE'S TUBBY (Little Lulu)(See Dell Giants)
Dell Publishing Co./Gold Key: No. 381, Aug, 1952 - No. 49, Dec-Feb, 1961-62

	GD 2.0	VG 4.0	FN 6.0	VF 8.0	VF/NM 9.0	NM- 9.2
Four Color 381(#1)-Stanley script; Irving Tripp-a	22	44	66	160	235	310
Four Color 430,444-Stanley-a	12	24	36	87	129	170
Four Color 461 (4/53)-1st Tubby & Men From Mars story; Stanley-a	11	22	33	77	114	150
5 (7-9/53)-Stanley-a	9	18	27	65	93	120
6-10	8	16	24	53	74	95
11-20	6	12	18	38	52	65
21-30	4	8	12	29	40	50
31-49	4	8	12	27	36	45
...& the Little Men From Mars No. 30020-410(10/64-G.K.)-25¢, 68 pgs.	9	18	27	60	85	110

NOTE: ***John Stanley** did all storyboards & scripts through at least #35 (1959). **Lloyd White** did all art except F.C. 381, 430, 444, 461 & #5.*

MARGIE (See My Little...)

MARGIE (TV)
Dell Publ. Co.: No. 1307, Mar-May, 1962 - No. 2, July-Sept, 1962 (Photo-c)

	GD 2.0	VG 4.0	FN 6.0	VF 8.0	VF/NM 9.0	NM- 9.2
Four Color 1307(#1)	6	12	18	43	59	75
2	5	10	15	36	48	60

MARGIE COMICS (Formerly Comedy Comics; Reno Browne #50 on)
(Also see Cindy Comics & Teen Comics)
Marvel Comics (ACI): No. 35, Winter, 1946-47 - No. 49, Dec, 1949

	GD 2.0	VG 4.0	FN 6.0	VF 8.0	VF/NM 9.0	NM- 9.2
35	16	32	48	92	126	160
36-38,42,45,47-49	9	18	27	52	66	80
39,41,43(2),44,46-Kurtzman's "Hey Look"	10	20	30	58	77	95
40-Three "Hey Looks", three "Giggles 'n' Grins" by Kurtzman	12	24	36	69	92	115

MARINES (See Tell It to the...)

MARINES ATTACK
Charlton Comics: Aug, 1964 - No. 9, Feb-Mar, 1966

	GD 2.0	VG 4.0	FN 6.0	VF 8.0	VF/NM 9.0	NM- 9.2
1-Glanzman-a begins	4	8	12	25	33	42
2-9	2	4	6	14	18	22

MARINES AT WAR (Formerly Tales of the Marines #4)
Atlas Comics (OPI): No. 5, Apr, 1957 - No. 7, Aug, 1957

Marines in Battle #2 © MAR

The Mark #3 © DH

M.A.R.S. Patrol Total War #2 © GK

	GD 2.0	VG 4.0	FN 6.0	VF 8.0	VF/NM 9.0	NM- 9.2
5-7	8	16	24	46	58	70

NOTE: ***Colan*** *a-5.* ***Drucker*** *a-5.* ***Everett*** *a-5.* ***Maneely*** *a-5.* ***Orlando*** *a-7.* ***Severin*** *c-5.*

MARINES IN ACTION
Atlas News Co.: June, 1955 - No. 14, Sept, 1957

	GD 2.0	VG 4.0	FN 6.0	VF 8.0	VF/NM 9.0	NM- 9.2
1-Rock Murdock, Boot Camp Brady begin	11	22	33	63	84	105
2-14	8	16	24	46	58	70

NOTE: ***Berg*** *a-2, 8, 9, 11, 14.* ***Heath*** *c-2, 9.* ***Maneely*** *c-1.* ***Severin*** *a-4; c-7-11, 14.*

MARINES IN BATTLE
Atlas Comics (ACI No. 1-12/WPI No. 13-25): Aug, 1954 - No. 25, Sept, 1958

	GD 2.0	VG 4.0	FN 6.0	VF 8.0	VF/NM 9.0	NM- 9.2
1-Heath-c; Iron Mike McGraw by Heath; history of U.S. Marine Corps. begins	21	42	63	118	164	210
2-Heath-c	11	22	33	63	84	105
3-6,8-10: 4-Last precode (2/55)	9	18	27	52	66	80
7-Kubert/Moskowitz-a (6 pgs.)	9	18	27	54	70	85
11-16,18-21,24	8	16	24	46	58	70
17-Williamson-a (3 pgs.)	10	20	30	56	73	90
22,25-Torres-a	9	18	27	49	62	75
23-Crandall-a; Mark Murdock app.	9	18	27	52	66	80

NOTE: ***Berg*** *a-22.* ***G. Colan*** *a-22, 23.* ***Drucker*** *a-6.* ***Everett*** *a-4, 15; c-21.* ***Heath*** *c-1, 2, 4.* ***Maneely*** *c-23, 24.* ***Orlando*** *a-14.* ***Pakula*** *a-6, 23.* ***Powell*** *a-16.* ***Severin*** *a-22; c-12.* ***Sinnott*** *a-23.* ***Tuska*** *a-15.*

MARINE WAR HEROES (Charlton Premiere #19 on)
Charlton Comics: Jan, 1964 - No. 18, Mar, 1967

	GD 2.0	VG 4.0	FN 6.0	VF 8.0	VF/NM 9.0	NM- 9.2
1-Montes/Bache-c/a	4	8	12	25	33	42
2-18: 14,18-Montes/Bache-a	2	4	6	14	18	22

MARK, THE (Also see Mayhem)
Dark Horse Comics: Dec, 1993 - No. 4, Mar, 1994 ($2.50, limited series)

	GD 2.0	VG 4.0	FN 6.0	VF 8.0	VF/NM 9.0	NM- 9.2
1-4						2.50

MARK HAZZARD: MERC
Marvel Comics Group: Nov, 1986 - No. 12, Oct, 1987 (75¢)

	GD 2.0	VG 4.0	FN 6.0	VF 8.0	VF/NM 9.0	NM- 9.2
1-12: Morrow-a, Annual 1 (11/87, $1.25)						2.25

MARK OF CHARON (See Negation)
CG Entertainment: Apr, 2003 - No. 5, Aug, 2003 ($2.95, limited series)

	GD 2.0	VG 4.0	FN 6.0	VF 8.0	VF/NM 9.0	NM- 9.2
1-5-Bedard-s/Bennett-a						3.00

MARK OF ZORRO (See Zorro, Four Color #228)

MARK 1 COMICS (Also see Shaloman)
Mark 1 Comics: Apr, 1988 - No. 3, Mar, 1989 ($1.50)

	GD 2.0	VG 4.0	FN 6.0	VF 8.0	VF/NM 9.0	NM- 9.2
1-3: Early Shaloman app. 2-Origin						2.25

MARKSMAN, THE (Also see Champions)
Hero Comics: Jan, 1988 - No. 5, 1988 ($1.95)

	GD 2.0	VG 4.0	FN 6.0	VF 8.0	VF/NM 9.0	NM- 9.2
1-5: 1-Rose begins. 1-3-Origin The Marksman						2.25
Annual 1 ('88, $2.75, 52pgs)-Champions app.						2.75

MARK TRAIL
Standard Magazines (Hall Syndicate)/Fawcett Publ. No. 5: Oct, 1955; No. 5, Summer, 1959

	GD 2.0	VG 4.0	FN 6.0	VF 8.0	VF/NM 9.0	NM- 9.2
1(1955)-Sunday strip-r	7	14	21	37	46	55
5(1959)	5	10	15	22	26	30
...Adventure Book of Nature 1 (Summer, 1958, 25¢, Pines)-100 pg. Giant; Special Camp Issue; contains 78 Sunday strip-r	9	18	27	54	70	85

MARMADUKE MONK
I. W. Enterprises/Super Comics: No date; 1963 (10¢)

	GD 2.0	VG 4.0	FN 6.0	VF 8.0	VF/NM 9.0	NM- 9.2
I.W. Reprint 1 (nd)	2	4	6	9	11	14
Super Reprint 14 (1963)-r/Monkeyshines Comics #?	2	4	6	8	10	12

MARMADUKE MOUSE
Quality Comics Group (Arnold Publ.): Spring, 1946 - No. 65, Dec, 1956 (Early issues: 52 pgs.)

	GD 2.0	VG 4.0	FN 6.0	VF 8.0	VF/NM 9.0	NM- 9.2
1-Funny animal	18	36	54	104	142	180
2	10	20	30	56	73	90
3-10	8	16	24	40	50	60
11-30	6	12	18	31	38	45
31-65: Later issues are 36 pgs.	5	10	15	24	30	35
Super Reprint #14(1963)	2	4	6	10	12	15

MARQUIS, THE
Oni Press

	GD 2.0	VG 4.0	FN 6.0	VF 8.0	VF/NM 9.0	NM- 9.2
...: A Sin of One ($2.99, 5/03) Guy Davis-s/a; Michael Gaydos-c						3.00
...: Intermezzo TPB ($11.95, 12/03) r/A Sin of One and Hell's Courtesan #1,2						12.00

MARQUIS, THE: DANSE MACABRE
Oni Press: May, 2000 - No. 5, Feb, 2001 ($2.95, B&W, limited series)

	GD 2.0	VG 4.0	FN 6.0	VF 8.0	VF/NM 9.0	NM- 9.2
1-5-Guy Davis-s/a. 1-Wagner-c. 2-Mignola-c. 3-Vess-c. 5-K. Jones-c						3.00
TPB (8/2001, $18.95) r/1-5 & Les Preludes; Seagle intro.						19.00

MARQUIS, THE: DEVIL'S REIGN: HELL'S COURTESAN
Oni Press: Feb, 2002 - No. 2, Apr, 2002 ($2.95, B&W, limited series)

	GD 2.0	VG 4.0	FN 6.0	VF 8.0	VF/NM 9.0	NM- 9.2
1,2-Guy Davis-s/a						3.00

MARRIAGE OF HERCULES AND XENA, THE
Topps Comics: July, 1998 ($2.95, one-shot)

	GD 2.0	VG 4.0	FN 6.0	VF 8.0	VF/NM 9.0	NM- 9.2
1-Photo-c; Lopresti-a; Alex Ross pin-up, 1-Alex Ross painted-c						3.00
1-Gold foil logo-c						5.00

MARRIED ... WITH CHILDREN (TV)(Based on Fox TV show)
Now Comics: June, 1990 - No. 7, Feb, 1991(12/90 inside) ($1.75)
V2#1, Sept, 1991 - No. 12, 1992 ($1.95)

	GD 2.0	VG 4.0	FN 6.0	VF 8.0	VF/NM 9.0	NM- 9.2
1-7: 2-Photo-c, 1,2-2nd printing, V2#1-12: 1,4,5,9-Photo-c						2.25
...Buck's Tale (6/94, $1.95)						2.25
...1994 Annual nn (2/94, $2.50, 52 pgs.)-Flip book format						2.50
Special 1 (7/92, $1.95)-Kelly Bundy photo-c/poster						2.25

MARRIED ... WITH CHILDREN: KELLY BUNDY
Now Comics: Aug, 1992 - No. 3, Oct, 1992 ($1.95, limited series)

	GD 2.0	VG 4.0	FN 6.0	VF 8.0	VF/NM 9.0	NM- 9.2
1-3: Kelly Bundy photo-c & poster in each						2.25

MARRIED ... WITH CHILDREN: QUANTUM QUARTET
Now Comics: Oct, 1993 - No. 4, 1994, ($1.95, limited series)

	GD 2.0	VG 4.0	FN 6.0	VF 8.0	VF/NM 9.0	NM- 9.2
1-4: Fantastic Four parody						2.25

MARRIED ... WITH CHILDREN: 2099
Now Comics: June, 1993 - No. 3, Aug, 1993 ($1.95, limited series)

	GD 2.0	VG 4.0	FN 6.0	VF 8.0	VF/NM 9.0	NM- 9.2
1-3						2.25

MARS
First Comics: Jan, 1984 - No. 12, Jan, 1985 ($1.00, Mando paper)

	GD 2.0	VG 4.0	FN 6.0	VF 8.0	VF/NM 9.0	NM- 9.2
nn: 1-12: Marc Hempel & Mark Wheatley story & art. 2-The Black Flame begins. 10-Dynamo Joe begins						2.25

MARS & BEYOND (Disney, TV)
Dell Publishing Co.: No. 866, Dec, 1957

	GD 2.0	VG 4.0	FN 6.0	VF 8.0	VF/NM 9.0	NM- 9.2
Four Color 866-A Science feat. from Tomorrowland	10	20	30	67	96	125

MARS ATTACKS
Topps Comics: May, 1994 - No. 5, Sept, 1994 ($2.95, limited series)

	GD 2.0	VG 4.0	FN 6.0	VF 8.0	VF/NM 9.0	NM- 9.2
1-5-Giffen story; flip books						4.50
Special Edition	2	4	6	8	10	12
Trade paperback (12/94, $12.95)-r/limited series plus new 8 pg. story						13.00

MARS ATTACKS
Topps Comics: V2#1, 8/95 - V2#3, 10/95; V2#4, 1/96 - No. 7, 5/96($2.95, bi-monthly #6 on)

	GD 2.0	VG 4.0	FN 6.0	VF 8.0	VF/NM 9.0	NM- 9.2
V2#1-7: 1-Counterstrike storyline begins. 4-(1/96). 5-(1/96). 5,7-Brereton-c. 6-(3/96)-Simonson-c. 7-Story leads into Baseball Special #1						3.00
Baseball Special 1 (6/96, $2.95)-Bisley-c.						3.00

MARS ATTACKS HIGH SCHOOL
Topps Comics: May, 1997 - No. 2, Sept, 1997 ($2.95, B&W, limited series)

	GD 2.0	VG 4.0	FN 6.0	VF 8.0	VF/NM 9.0	NM- 9.2
1,2-Stelfreeze-c						3.00

MARS ATTACKS IMAGE
Topps Comics: Dec, 1996 - No. 4, Mar, 1997 ($2.50, limited series)

	GD 2.0	VG 4.0	FN 6.0	VF 8.0	VF/NM 9.0	NM- 9.2
1-4-Giffen-s/Smith/Sienkiewicz-a						3.00

MARS ATTACKS THE SAVAGE DRAGON
Topps Comics: Dec, 1996 - No. 4, Mar, 1997 ($2.95, limited series)

	GD 2.0	VG 4.0	FN 6.0	VF 8.0	VF/NM 9.0	NM- 9.2
1-4: 1-w/bound-in card						3.00

MARSHAL BLUEBERRY (See Blueberry)
Marvel Comics (Epic Comics): 1991 ($14.95, graphic novel)

	GD 2.0	VG 4.0	FN 6.0	VF 8.0	VF/NM 9.0	NM- 9.2
1-Moebius-a						15.00

MARSHAL LAW (Also see Crime And Punishment: Marshall Law...)
Marvel Comics (Epic Comics): Oct, 1987 - No. 6, May, 1989 ($1.95, mature)

	GD 2.0	VG 4.0	FN 6.0	VF 8.0	VF/NM 9.0	NM- 9.2
1-6						2.25

M.A.R.S. PATROL TOTAL WAR (Formerly Total War #1,2)
Gold Key: No. 3, Sept, 1966 - No. 10, Aug, 1969 (All-Painted-c except #7)

	GD 2.0	VG 4.0	FN 6.0	VF 8.0	VF/NM 9.0	NM- 9.2
3-Wood-a; aliens invade USA	7	14	21	46	63	80
4-10	4	8	12	27	36	45

MARTHA WASHINGTON (Also see Dark Horse Presents Fifth Anniversary Special, Dark Horse Presents #100-4, Give Me Liberty, Happy Birthday Martha Washington & San Diego Comicon Comics #2)

Martian Manhunter #0 © DC

Marvel Boy #1 © MAR

Marvel Classics Comics #28 © MAR

	GD	VG	FN	VF	VF/NM	NM-
	2.0	4.0	6.0	8.0	9.0	9.2

MARTHA WASHINGTON GOES TO WAR
Dark Horse Comics (Legend): May, 1994 - No. 5, Sep, 1994 ($2.95, lim. series)

1-5-Miller scripts; Gibbons-c/a 3.00
TPB ($17.95) r/#1-5 18.00

MARTHA WASHINGTON SAVES THE WORLD
Dark Horse Comics: Dec, 1997 - No. 3, Feb, 1998 ($2.95/$3.95, lim. series)

1,2-Miller scripts; Gibbons-c/a in all 3.00
3-($3.95) 4.00

MARTHA WASHINGTON STRANDED IN SPACE
Dark Horse Comics (Legend): Nov, 1995 ($2.95, one-shot)

nn-Miller-s/Gibbons-a; Big Guy app. 3.00

MARTHA WAYNE (See The Story of...)

MARTIAN MANHUNTER (See Detective Comics & Showcase '95 #9)
DC Comics: May, 1988 - No. 4, Aug,. 1988 ($1.25, limited series)

1-4: 1,4-Batman app. 2-Batman cameo 2.50
Special 1-(1996, $3.50) 3.50

MARTIAN MANHUNTER (See JLA)
DC Comics: No. 0, Oct, 1998 - No. 36, Nov, 2001 ($1.99)

0-(10/98) Origin retold; Ostrander-s/Mandrake-c/a 3.00
1-36: 1-(12/98). 6-9-JLA app. 18,19-JSA app. 24-Mahnke-a 2.50
#1,000,000 (11/98) 853rd Century x-over 2.50
Annual 1,2 (1998,1999; $2.95) 1-Ghosts; Wrightson-c. 2-JLApe 3.00

MARTIAN MANHUNTER: AMERICAN SECRETS
DC Comics: 1992 - Book Three, 1992 ($4.95, limited series, prestige format)

1-3: Barreto-a 5.00

MARTIN KANE (William Gargan as... Private Eye)(Stage/Screen/Radio/TV)
Fox Features Syndicate (Hero Books): No. 4, June, 1950 - No. 2, Aug, 1950 (Formerly My Secret Affair)

4(#1)-True crime stories; Wood-c/a(2); used in **SOTI**, pg. 160; photo back-c 31 62 93 175 248 320
2-Wood/Orlando story, 5 pgs; Wood-a(2) 24 48 72 135 190 245

MARTIN MYSTERY
Dark Horse (Bonelli Comics): Mar, 1999 - No. 6, Aug, 1999 ($4.95, B&W, digest size)

1-6-Reprints Italian series in English; Gibbons-c on #1-3 5.00

MARTY MOUSE
I. W. Enterprises: No date (1958?) (10¢)

1-Reprint 2 4 6 10 12 15

MARVEL ACTION HOUR FEATURING IRON MAN (TV cartoon)
Marvel Comics: Nov, 1994 - No. 8, June, 1995 ($1.50/$2.95)

1-8: Based on cartoon series 2.25
1 ($2.95)-Polybagged w/16 pg Marvel Action Hour Preview & acetate print 3.00

MARVEL ACTION HOUR FEATURING THE FANTASTIC FOUR (TV cartoon)
Marvel Comics: Nov, 1994 - No. 8, June, 1995 ($1.50/$2.95)

1-8: Based on cartoon series 2.25
1-($2.95)-Polybagged w/ 16 pg. Marvel Action Hour Preview & acetate print 3.00

MARVEL ACTION UNIVERSE (TV cartoon)
Marvel Comics: Jan, 1989 ($1.00, one-shot)

1-r/Spider-Man And His Amazing Friends 4.00

MARVEL ADVENTURES
Marvel Comics: Apr, 1997 - No. 18, Sept, 1998 ($1.50)

1-18-"Animated style": 1,4,7-Hulk-c/app. 2,11-Spider-Man. 3,8,15-X-Men. 5-Spider-Man & X-Men. 6-Spider-Man & Human Torch. 9,12-Fantastic Four. 10,16-Silver Surfer. 13-Spider-Man & Silver Surfer. 14-Hulk & Dr. Strange. 18-Capt. America 2.25

MARVEL ADVENTURES STARRING DAREDEVIL (...Adventure #3 on)
Marvel Comics Group: Dec, 1975 - No. 6, Oct, 1976

1 1 3 4 6 8 10
2-6-r/Daredevil #22-27 by Colan. 3-5-(25¢-c) 6.00
3-5-(30¢-c variants, limited distribution)(4,6,8/76) 2 4 6 10 13 16

MARVEL AND DC PRESENT FEATURING THE UNCANNY X-MEN AND THE NEW TEEN TITANS
Marvel Comics/DC Comics: 1982 ($2.00, 68 pgs., one-shot, Baxter paper)

1-3rd app. Deathstroke the Terminator; Darkseid app.; Simonson/Austin-c/a 2 4 6 12 16 20

MARVEL BOY (Astonishing #3 on; see Marvel Super Action #4)
Marvel Comics (MPC): Dec, 1950 - No. 2, Feb, 1951

1-Origin Marvel Boy by Russ Heath 107 214 321 669 1005 1340
2-Everett-a 76 152 228 475 713 950

MARVEL BOY (Marvel Knights)
Marvel Comics: Aug, 2000 - No. 6, Mar, 2001 ($2.99, limited series)

1-Intro. Marvel Boy; Morrison-s/J.G. Jones-c/a 3.50
1-DF Variant-c 5.00
2-6 3.00
TPB (6/01, $15.95) 16.00

MARVEL CHILLERS (Also see Giant-Size Chillers)
Marvel Comics Group: Oct, 1975 - No. 7, Oct, 1976 (All 25¢ issues)

1-Intro. Modred the Mystic, ends #2; Kane-c(p) 2 4 6 9 11 14
2,4,5,7: 4-Kraven app. 5,6-Red Wolf app. 7-Kirby-c; Tuska-p 1 2 3 5 6 8
3-Tigra, the Were-Woman begins (origin), ends #7 (see Giant-Size Creatures #1). Chaykin/Wrightson-c. 2 4 6 12 16 20
4-6-(30¢-c variants, limited distribution)(4-8/76) 2 4 6 11 14 18
6-Byrne-a(p); Buckler-c(p) 1 3 4 6 8 10
NOTE: ***Bolle** a-1. **Buckler** c-2. **Kirby** c-7.*

MARVEL CLASSICS COMICS SERIES FEATURING...
(Also see Pendulum Illustrated Classics)
Marvel Comics Group: 1976 - No. 36, Dec, 1978 (52 pgs., no ads)

1-Dr. Jekyll and Mr. Hyde 2 4 6 11 14 18
2-10,28: 28-1st Golden-c/a; Pit and the Pendulum 2 4 6 8 10 12
11-27,29-36 1 2 3 5 7 9
NOTE: ***Adkins** c-1i, 4i, 12i. **Alcala** a-34i; c-34. **Bolle** a-35. **Buscema** c-17p, 19p, 26p. **Golden** c/a-28. **Gil Kane** c-1-16p, 21p, 22p, 24p, 32p. **Nebres** a-5; c-24i. **Nino** a-2, 8, 12. **Redondo** a-1, 9. No. 1-12 were reprinted from Pendulum Illustrated Classics.*

MARVEL COLLECTIBLE CLASSICS: AVENGERS
Marvel Comics: 1998 ($10.00, reprints with chromium wraparound-c)

1-Reprints Avengers Vol.3, #1; Perez-c 10.00

MARVEL COLLECTIBLE CLASSICS: SPIDER-MAN
Marvel Comics: 1998 ($10.00, reprints with chromium wraparound-c)

1-Reprints Amazing Spider-Man #300; McFarlane-c 10.00
2-Reprints Spider-Man #1; McFarlane-c 10.00

MARVEL COLLECTIBLE CLASSICS: X-MEN
Marvel Comics: 1998 ($10.00, reprints with chromium wraparound-c)

1-6: 1-Reprints (Uncanny) X-Men #1 & 2; Adam Kubert-c. 2-Reprints Uncanny X-Men #141 & 142; Byrne-c. 3-Reprints (Uncanny) X-Men #137; Larroca-c. 4-Reprints X-Men #25; Andy Kubert-c. 5-Reprints Giant Size X-Men #1; Gary Frank-c. 6-Reprints X-Men V2#1; Ramos-c 10.00

MARVEL COLLECTOR'S EDITION
Marvel Comics: 1992 (Ordered thru mail with Charleston Chew candy wrapper)

1-Flip-book format; Spider-Man, Silver Surfer, Wolverine (by Sam Kieth), & Ghost Rider stories; Wolverine back-c by Kieth 3.00

MARVEL COLLECTORS' ITEM CLASSICS (Marvel's Greatest #23 on)
Marvel Comics Group(ATF): Feb, 1965 - No. 22, Aug, 1969 (25¢, 68 pgs.)

1-Fantastic Four, Spider-Man, Thor, Hulk, Iron Man-r begin 10 20 30 70 100 130
2 (4/66) 6 12 18 38 52 65
3,4 4 8 12 28 38 48
5-10 4 8 12 22 30 38
11-22: 22-r/The Man in the Ant Hill/TTA #27 3 6 9 18 23 28
NOTE: *All reprints; **Ditko, Kirby** art in all.*

MARVEL COMICS (Marvel Mystery Comics #2 on)
Timely Comics (Funnies, Inc.): Oct, Nov, 1939

NOTE: The first issue was originally dated October 1939. Most copies have a black circle stamped over the date (on cover and inside) with "November" printed over it. However, some copies do not have the November overprint and could have a higher value. Most No. 1's have printing defects, i.e., tilted pages which caused trimming into the panels usually on right side and bottom. Covers exist with and without gloss finish.

1-Origin Sub-Mariner by Bill Everett(1st newsstand app.); 1st 8 pgs. were produced for Motion Picture Funnies Weekly #1 which was probably not distributed outside of advance copies; intro Human Torch by Carl Burgos, Kazar the Great (1st Tarzan clone), & Jungle Terror(only app.); intro. The Angel by Gustavson, The Masked Raider & his horse Lightning (ends #12); cover by sci/fi pulp illustrator Frank R. Paul 19,250 38,500 57,750 138,000 234,500 330,000

MARVEL COMICS PRESENTS
Marvel Comics (Midnight Sons imprint #143 on): Early Sept, 1988 - No. 175, Feb, 1995

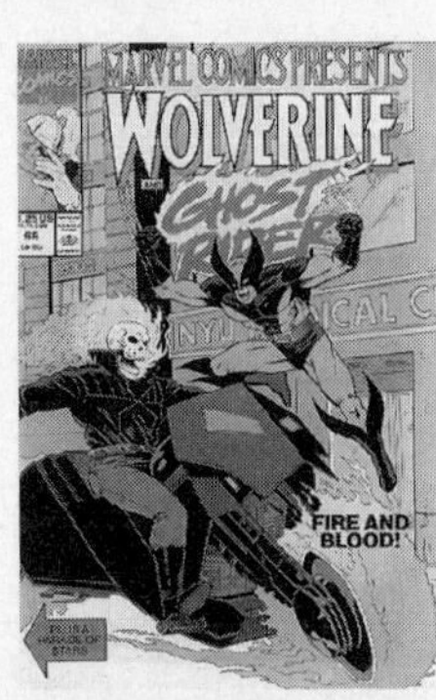

Marvel Comics Presents #66 © MAR

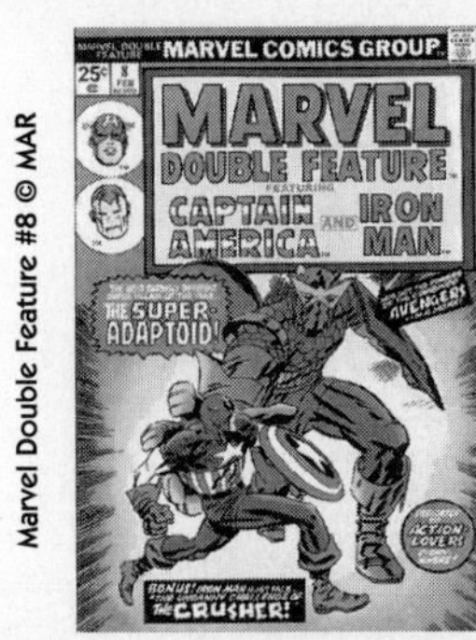

Marvel Double Feature #8 © MAR

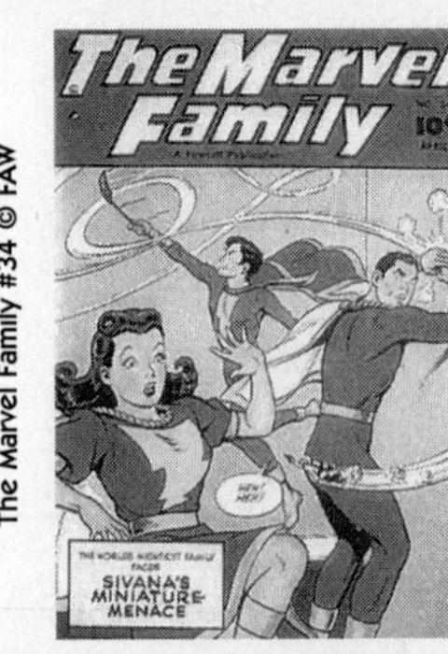

The Marvel Family #34 © FAW

GD 2.0 | VG 4.0 | FN 6.0 | VF 8.0 | VF/NM 9.0 | NM- 9.2

($1.25/$1.50/$1.75, bi-weekly)
1-Wolverine by Buscema in #1-10 6.00
2-5 4.00
6-10: 6-Sub-Mariner app. 10-Colossus begins 3.00
11-47,51-71: 17-Cyclops begins. 19-1st app. Damage Control. 24-Havok begins. 25-Origin/1st app. Nth Man. 26-Hulk begins by Rogers. 29-Quasar app. 31-Excalibur begins by Austin (i). 32-McFarlane-a(p). 37-Devil-Slayer app. 33-Capt. America; Jim Lee-a. 38-Wolverine begins by Buscema; Hulk app. 39-Spider-Man app. 46-Liefeld Wolverine-c. 51-53-Wolverine by Rob Liefeld. 54-61-Wolverine/Hulk story: 54-Werewolf by Night begins; The Shroud by Ditko. 58-Iron Man by Ditko. 59-Punisher. 62-Deathlok & Wolverine stories 63-Wolverine. 64-71-Wolverine/Ghost Rider 8-part story. 70-Liefeld Ghost Rider/ Wolverine-c 2.50
48-50-Wolverine & Spider-Man team-up by Erik Larsen-c/a. 48-Wasp app. 49,50-Savage Dragon prototype app. by Larsen. 50-Silver Surfer. 50-53-Comet Man; Mumy scripts 4.00
72-Begin 13-part Weapon-X story (Wolverine origin) by B. Windsor-Smith (prologue) 5.00
73-Weapon-X part 1; Black Knight, Sub-Mariner 4.00
74-84: 74-Weapon-X part 2; Black Knight, Sub-Mariner. 76-Death's Head story. 77-Mr. Fantastic story. 78-Iron Man by Steacy. 80,81-Capt. America by Ditko/Austin. 81-Daredevil by Rogers/Williamson. 82-Power Man. 83-Human Torch by Ditko(a&scripts); $1.00-c direct, $1.25 newsstand. 84-Last Weapon-X (24 pg. conclusion) 3.00
85-Begin 8-part Wolverine story by Sam Kieth (c/a); 1st Kieth-a on Wolverine; begin 8-part Beast story by Jae Lee(p) with Liefeld part pencils #85,86; 1st Jae Lee-a (assisted w/Liefeld, 1991) 4.00
86-90: 86-89-Wolverine, Beast stories continue. 90-Begin 8-part Ghost Rider & Cable story, ends #97; begin flip book format w/two-c 3.00
91-175: 93-Begin 6-part Wolverine story, ends #98. 98-Begin 2-part Ghost Rider story. 99-Spider-Man story. 101-Begin 6-part Ghost Rider/Dr. Strange story & begin 8-part Wolverine/Nightcrawler story by Colan/Williamson; Punisher story. 107-Begin 6-part Ghost Rider/Werewolf by Night story. 112-Demogoblin story by Colan/Williamson; Pip the Troll story w/Starlin scripts & Gamora cameo. 113-Begin 6-part Giant-Man & begin 6-part Ghost Rider/Iron Fist stories. 100-Full-length Ghost Rider/Wolverine story by Sam Kieth w/Tim Vigil assists; anniversary issue, non flip-book. 108-Begin 4 part Thanos story; Starlin scripts. 109-Begin 8 part Wolverine/Typhoid Mary story. 111-Iron Fist. 117-Preview of Ravage 2099 (1st app.); begin 6 part Wolverine/Venom story w/Kieth-a. 118-Preview of Doom 2099 (1st app.). 119-Begin Ghost Rider/Cloak & Dagger by Colan. 120,136,138-Spider-Man. 123-Begin 8-part Ghost Rider/Typhoid Mary story; begin 4-part She Hulk story; begin 8-part Wolverine/Lynx story. 125-Begin 6-part Iron Fist story. 129-Jae Lee back-c. 130-Begin 6-part Ghost Rider/ Cage story. 131-Begin 6-part Ghost Rider/Cage story. 132-Begin 5-part Wolverine story. 133-136-Iron Fist vs. Sabretooth. 136-Daredevil. 137-Begin 6-part Wolverine story & 6-part Ghost Rider story. 147-Begin 2-part Vengeance-c/story w/new Ghost Rider. 149-Vengeance-c/story w/new Ghost Rider. 150-Silver ink-c; begin 2-part Bloody Mary story w/Typhoid Mary,Wolverine, Daredevil, new Ghost Rider; intro Steel Raven. 152-Begin 4-part Wolverine, 4-part War Machine, 4-part Vengeance, 3-part Moon Knight stories; same date as War Machine #1. 143-146: Siege of Darkness parts 3,6,11,14; all have spot-varnished-c. 143-Ghost Rider/Scarlet Witch; intro new Werewolf. 144-Begin 2-part Morbius story. 145-Begin 2-part Nightstalkers story. 153-155-Bound-in Spider-Man trading card sheet 2.50
...Colossus: God's Country (1994, $6.95) r/#10-17 1 2 3 4 5 7

NOTE: ***Austin** a-31-37i; c(i)-48, 50, 99, 122. **Buscema** a-1-10, 38-47; c-6. **Byrne** a-79; c-71. **Colan** a(p)-36, 37. **Colan/Williamson** a-101-108. **Ditko** a-7p, 10, 56p, 58, 80, 81, 83. **Guice** a-62. **Sam Kieth** a-85-92, 117-122; c-85-98, 99p, 100-108, 117, 118, 120-122; back c-109-113, 117. **Jae Lee** c-129(back). **Liefeld** a-51, 52, 53p(2), 85p; c-46, 70. **McFarlane** c-32. **Mooney** a-73. **Rogers** a-26, 38, 46i, 81p. **Russell** a-10-14,16,17i; c-4,19, 30,31i. **Saltares** a-8p(early), 38-45p. **Simonson** c-1. **B. Smith** a-72-84; c-72-84. **P. Smith** c-34. **Sparling** a-33. **Starlin** a-89i. **Staton** a-74. **Steacy** a-78. **Sutton** a-101-105. **Williamson** c-62i. Two Gun Kid by **Gil Kane** in #116, 122.*

MARVEL COMICS SUPER SPECIAL, A (Marvel Super Special #5 on)
Marvel Comics: Sept, 1977 - No. 41(?), Nov, 1986 (nn 7) ($1.50, magazine)

1-Kiss, 40 pgs. comics plus photos & features; Simonson-a(p); also see Howard the Duck #12; ink contains real KISS blood; Dr. Doom, Spider-Man, Avengers, Fantastic Four, Mephisto app. 12 24 36 82 121 160
2-Conan (1978) 2 4 6 11 14 18
3-Close Encounters of the Third Kind (1978); Simonson-a 2 4 6 8 10 12
4-The Beatles Story (1978)-Perez/Janson-a; has photos & articles 4 8 12 27 36 45
5-Kiss (1978)-Includes poster 12 24 36 82 121 160
6-Jaws II (1978) 2 4 6 8 10 12
7-Sgt. Pepper; Beatles movie adaptation; withdrawn from U.S. distribution (French ed. exists)
8-Battlestar Galactica; tabloid size ($1.50, 1978); adapts TV show 2 4 6 11 14 18
8-Modern-r of tabloid size 2 4 6 11 14 18
8-Battlestar Galactica; publ. in regular magazine format; low distribution ($1.50, 8-1/2x11") 2 4 6 11 14 18
9-Conan 2 4 6 9 11 14
10-Star-Lord 1 3 4 6 8 10
11-13-Weirdworld begins #11; 25 copy special press run of each with gold seal and signed by artists (Proof quality), Spring-June, 1979 9 18 27 60 85 110
11-15: 11-13-Weirdworld (regular issues): 11-Fold-out centerfold. 14-Miller-c(p); adapts movie "Meteor." 15-Star Trek with photos & pin-ups ($1.50-c) 1 2 3 5 6 8
15-With $2.00 price; the price was changed at tail end of a 200,000 press run 1 3 4 6 8 10
16-Empire Strikes Back adaption; Williamson-a 1 3 4 6 8 10
17-20 (Movie adaptations):17-Xanadu. 18-Raiders of the Lost Ark. 19-For Your Eyes Only (James Bond). 20-Dragonslayer 6.00
21-26,28-30 (Movie adaptations): 21-Conan. 22-Blade Runner; Williamson-a; Steranko-c. 23-Annie. 24-The Dark Crystal. 25-Rock and Rule-w/photos; artwork is from movie. 26-Octopussy (James Bond). 28-Krull; photo-c. 29-Tarzan of the Apes (Greystoke movie). 30-Indiana Jones and the Temple of Doom 1 2 3 4 5 7
27,31-41: 27-Return of the Jedi. 31-The Last Star Fighter. 32-The Muppets Take Manhattan. 33-Buckaroo Banzai. 34-Sheena. 35-Conan The Destroyer. 36-Dune. 37-2010. 38-Red Sonja. 39-Santa Claus:The Movie. 40-Labyrinth. 41-Howard The Duck 1 2 3 5 7 9

NOTE: ***J. Buscema** a-1, 2, 9, 11-13, 18p, 21, 35, 40; c-11(part), 12. **Chaykin** a-9, 19p; c-18, 19. **Colan** a(p)-6, 10, 14. **Morrow** a-34; c-1i, 34. **Nebres** a-11. **Spiegle** a-29. **Stevens** a-27. **Williamson** a-27. #22-28 contain photos from movies.*

MARVEL COMICS: 2001
Marvel Comics: 2001 (no cover price, one-shot)

1-Previews new titles for Fall 2001; Wolverine-c 2.25

MARVEL DOUBLE FEATURE
Marvel Comics Group: Dec, 1973 - No. 21, Mar, 1977

1-Capt. America, Iron Man-r/T.O.S. begin 2 4 6 10 13 16
2-10: 3-Last 20¢ issue 1 3 4 6 8 10
11-17,20,21:17-Story-r/Iron Man & Sub-Mariner #1; last 25¢ issue 6.00
15-17-(30¢-c variants, limited distribution)(4,6,8/76) 1 3 4 6 8 10
18,19-Colan/Craig-r from Iron Man #1 in both 1 2 3 5 6 8

NOTE: ***Colan** r-1-19p. **Craig** r-17-19i. **G. Kane** r-15p; c-15p. **Kirby** r-1-16p, 20, 21; c-17-20.*

MARVEL DOUBLE SHOT
Marvel Comics: Jan, 2003 - No. 4, April, 2003 ($2.99, limited series)

1-4: 1-Hulk by Haynes; Thor w/Asamiya-a; Jusko-c. 2-Dr. Doom by Rivera; Simpsons-style Avengers by Bill Morrison 3.00

MARVEL FAMILY (Also see Captain Marvel Adventures No. 18)
Fawcett Publications: Dec, 1945 - No. 89, Jan, 1954

	GD 2.0	VG 4.0	FN 6.0	VF 8.0	VF/NM 9.0	NM- 9.2
1-Origin Captain Marvel, Captain Marvel Jr., Mary Marvel, & Uncle Marvel retold; origin/1st app. Black Adam	168	336	504	1050	1575	2100
2-The 3 Lt. Marvels & Uncle Marvel app.	76	152	228	475	713	950
3	55	110	165	330	495	660
4,5	44	88	132	264	395	525
6-10: 7-Shazam app.	39	78	117	230	325	420
11-20	30	60	90	170	240	310
21-30	25	50	75	147	202	260
31-40	21	42	63	118	164	210
41-46,48-50	17	34	51	98	134	170
47-Flying Saucer-c/story (5/50)	23	46	69	132	186	240
51-76	15	30	45	86	118	150
77-Communist Threat-c	24	48	72	138	194	250
78,81-Used in **POP**, pg. 92,93.	18	36	54	101	138	175
79,80,82-89: 79-Horror satire-c	17	34	51	98	134	170

MARVEL FANFARE (1st Series)
Marvel Comics Group: Mar, 1982 - No. 60, Jan, 1992 ($1.25/$2.25, slick paper, direct sales)

1-Spider-Man/Angel team-up; 1st Paul Smith-a (1st full story; see King Conan #7); Daredevil app. (many copies were printed missing the centerfold) 6.00
2-Spider-Man, Ka-Zar, The Angel. F.F. origin retold 5.00
3,4-X-Men & Ka-Zar. 4-Deathlok, Spidey app. 4.00
5-14: 5-Dr. Strange, Capt. America. 6-Spider-Man, Scarlet Witch. 7-Incredible Hulk; D.D. back-up(also 15). 8-Dr. Strange; Wolf Boy begins. 9-Man-Thing. 10-13-Black Widow. 14-The Vision 3.00
15,24,33: 15-The Thing by Barry Smith, c/a. 24-Weirdworld; Wolverine back-up. 33-X-Men, Wolverine app.; Punisher pin-up 4.00
16-23,25-32,34-44,46-50: 16,17-Skywolf. 16-Sub-Mariner back-up. 17-Hulk back-up. 18-Capt. America by Miller. 19-Cloak and Dagger. 20-Thing/Dr. Strange. 21-Thing/Dr. Strange /Hulk. 22,23-Iron Man vs. Dr. Octopus. 25,26-Weirdworld. 27-Daredevil/Spider-Man. 28-Alpha Flight. 29-Hulk. 30-Moon Knight. 31,32-Captain America. 34-37-Warriors Three. 38-Moon Knight/Dazzler. 39-Moon Knight/Hawkeye. 40-Angel/Rogue & Storm. 41-Dr. Strange. 42-Spider-Man. 43-Sub-Mariner/Human Torch. 44-Iron Man vs. Dr. Doom by Ken Steacy. 46-Fantastic Four. 47-Hulk. 48-She-Hulk/Vision. 49-Dr. Strange/Nick Fury. 50-X-Factor 2.50

Marvel Feature #7 © MAR

Marvel Holiday Special 1993 © MAR

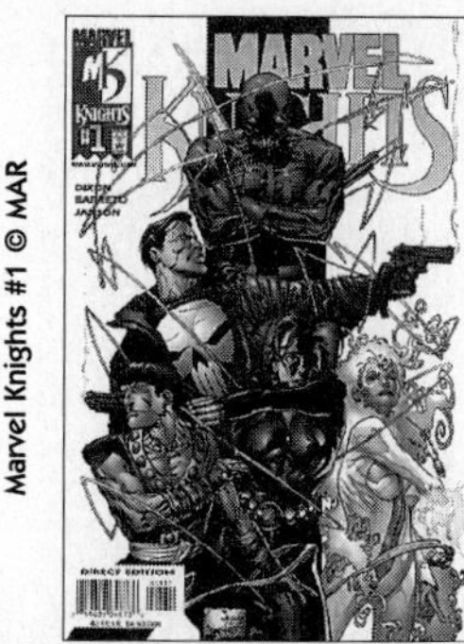
Marvel Knights #1 © MAR

GD VG FN VF VF/NM NM-
2.0 4.0 6.0 8.0 9.0 9.2

45-All pin-up issue by Steacy, Art Adams & others 4.00
51-($2.95, 52 pgs.)-Silver Surfer; Fantastic Four & Capt. Marvel app.; 51,52-Colan/Williamson back-up (Dr. Strange) 3.00
52,53,56-60: 52,53-Black Knight; 53-Iron Man back up. 56-59-Shanna the She-Devil. 58-Vision & Scarlet Witch back-up. 60-Black Panther/Rogue/Daredevil stories 2.50
54,55-Wolverine back-ups. 54-Black Knight. 55-Power Pack 4.00
NOTE: ***Art Adams*** *c-13.* ***Austin*** *a-1i, 4i, 33i, 38i; c-8i, 33i.* ***Buscema*** *a-51p.* ***Byrne*** *a-1p, 29, 48; c-29.* ***Chiodo*** *painted c-56-59.* ***Colan*** *a-51p.* ***Cowan/Simonson*** *c/a-60.* ***Golden*** *a-1, 2, 4p, 47; c-1, 2, 47.* ***Infantino*** *c/a(p)-8.* ***Gil Kane*** *a-8-11p.* ***Miller*** *a-18; c-1(Back-c), 18.* ***Perez*** *a-10, 11p, 12, 13p; c-10-13p.* ***Rogers*** *a-5p; c-5p.* ***Russell*** *a-5i, 6i, 8-11i, 43i; c-5i, 6.* ***Paul Smith*** *a-1p, 4p, 32, 60; c-4p. Staton c/a-50(p).* ***Williamson*** *a-30i, 51i.*

MARVEL FANFARE (2nd Series)
Marvel Comics: Sept, 1996 - No. 6, Feb, 1997 (99¢)

1-6: 1-Capt. America & The Falcon-c/story; Deathlok app. 2-Wolverine & Hulk-c/app. 3-Ghost Rider & Spider-Man-c/app. 5-Longshot-c/app. 6-Sabretooth, Power Man, & Iron Fist-c/app 2.25

MARVEL FEATURE (See Marvel Two-In-One)
Marvel Comics Group: Dec, 1971 - No. 12, Nov, 1973 (1,2: 25¢, 52 pg. giants) (#1-3: quarterly)

1-Origin/1st app. The Defenders (Sub-Mariner, Hulk & Dr. Strange); see Sub-Mariner #34,35 for prequel; Dr. Strange solo story (predates Dr.Strange #1) plus 1950s Sub-Mariner-r; Neal Adams-c 15 30 45 109 160 210
2-2nd app. Defenders; 1950s Sub-Mariner-r. Rutland, Vermont Halloween x-over 8 16 24 53 74 95
3-Defenders ends 6 12 18 38 52 65
4-Re-intro Antman (1st app. since 1960s), begin series; brief origin; Spider-Man app. 3 6 9 18 24 30
5-7,9,10: 6-Wasp app. & begins team-ups. 9-Iron Man app. 10-Last Antman 2 4 6 9 11 14
8-Origin Antman & Wasp-r/TTA #44; Kirby-a 2 4 6 11 14 18
11-Thing vs. Hulk; 1st Thing solo book (9/73); origin Fantastic Four retold 5 10 15 36 48 60
12-Thing/Iron Man; early Thanos app.; occurs after Capt. Marvel #33; Starlin-a(p) 3 6 9 18 24 30
NOTE: ***Bolle*** *a-9i.* ***Everett*** *a-1i, 3i.* ***Hartley*** *r-10.* ***Kane*** *c-3p, 7p.* ***Russell*** *a-7-10p.* ***Starlin*** *a-8, 11, 12; c-8.*

MARVEL FEATURE (Also see Red Sonja)
Marvel Comics: Nov, 1975 - No. 7, Nov, 1976 (Story cont'd in Conan #68)

1,7: 1-Red Sonja begins (pre-dates Red Sonja #1); adapts Howard short story; Adams-r/Savage Sword of Conan #1. 7-Battles Conan 1 3 4 6 8 10
2-6: Thorne-c/a in #2-7. 4,5-(Regular 25¢ edition)(5,7/76) 6.00
4,5-(30¢-c variants, limited distribution) 2 4 6 11 14 18

MARVEL FRONTIER COMICS UNLIMITED
Marvel Frontier Comics: Jan, 1994 ($2.95, 68 pgs.)

1-Dances with Demons, Immortalis, Children of the Voyager, Evil Eye, The Fallen stories 3.00

MARVEL FUMETTI BOOK
Marvel Comics Group: Apr, 1984 ($1.00, one-shot)

1-All photos; Stan Lee photo-c; Art Adams touch-ups 4.00

MARVEL FUN & GAMES
Marvel Comics Group: 1979/80 (color comic for kids)

1,11: 1-Games, puzzles, etc. 11-X-Men-c 1 2 3 5 7 9
2-10,12,13: (beware marked pages) 6.00

MARVEL GRAPHIC NOVEL
Marvel Comics Group (Epic Comics): 1982 - No. 38, 1990? ($5.95/$6.95)

1-Death of Captain Marvel (2nd Marvel graphic novel); Capt. Marvel battles Thanos by Jim Starlin (c/a/scripts) 2 4 6 12 16 20
1 (2nd & 3rd printings) 1 2 3 5 6 8
2-Elric: The Dreaming City 2 4 6 8 10 12
3-Dreadstar; Starlin-c/a, 52 pgs. 2 4 6 9 11 14
4-Origin/1st app. The New Mutants (1982) 2 4 6 9 11 14
4,5-2nd printings 1 2 3 4 5 7
5-X-Men; book-length story (1982) 2 4 6 11 14 18
6-15,20,23,25,30,31: 6-The Star Slammers. 7-Killraven. 8-Super Boxers; Byrne scripts. 9-The Futurians. 10-Heartburst. 11-Void Indigo. 12-Dazzler. 13-Starstruck. 14-The Swords Of The Swashbucklers. 15-The Raven Banner (a Tale of Asgard). 20-Greenberg the Vampire. 23-Dr. Strange. 25-Alien Legion. 30-A Sailor's Story. 31-Wolfpack 1 2 3 5 7 9
16,17,21,29: 16-The Aladdin Effect (Storm, Tigra, Wasp, She-Hulk). 17-Revenge Of The Living Monolith (Spider-Man, Avengers, FF app.). 21-Marada the She-Wolf. 29-The Big Chance (Thing vs. Hulk) 1 2 3 5 7 9
18,19,26-28: 18-She Hulk. 19-Witch Queen of Acheron (Conan). 26-Dracula. 27-Avengers (Emperor Doom). 28-Conan the Reaver 2 4 6 9 11 13

GD VG FN VF VF/NM NM-
2.0 4.0 6.0 8.0 9.0 9.2

22-Amaz. Spider-Man in Hooky by Wrightson 2 4 6 10 12 15
24-Love and War (Daredevil); Miller scripts 2 4 6 9 11 14
32-Death of Groo 2 4 6 10 12 15
32-2nd printing ($5.95) 1 2 3 5 6 8
33,34,36,37: 33-Thor. 34-Predator & Prey (Cloak & Dagger). 36-Willow (movie adapt.). 37-Hercules 1 3 4 6 8 10
35-Hitler's Astrologer (The Shadow, $12.95, HC) 2 4 6 10 13 16
35-Soft-c reprint (1990, $10.95) 2 4 6 8 10 12
38-Silver Surfer (Judgement Day)($14.95, HC) 2 4 6 11 14 18
38-Soft-c reprint (1990, $10.95) 2 4 6 9 11 14
nn-Abslom Daak: Dalak Killer (1990, $8.95) Dr. Who 1 3 4 6 8 10
nn-Arena by Bruce Jones (1989, $5.95) Dinosaurs 1 2 3 5 6 8
nn- A-Team Storybook Comics Illustrated (1983) r/ A-Team mini-series #1-3 1 3 4 6 8 10
nn-Ax (1988, $5.95) Ernie Colan-s/a 1 3 4 6 8 10
nn-Black Widow Coldest War (4/90, $9.95) 2 4 6 8 10 12
nn-Chronicles of Genghis Grimtoad (1990, $8.95)-Alan Grant-s 1 3 4 6 8 10
nn-Conan the Barbarian in the Horn of Azoth (1990, $8.95) 2 4 6 8 10 12
nn-Conan of Isles ($8.95) 2 4 6 8 10 12
nn-Conan Ravagers of Time (1992, $9.95) Kull & Red Sonja app. 2 4 6 8 10 12
nn-Conan -The Skull of Set 2 4 6 8 10 12
nn-Doctor Strange and Doctor Doom Triumph and Torment (1989, $17.95, HC) 2 4 6 14 18 22
nn-Dreamwalker (1989, $6.95)-Morrow-a 1 2 3 5 7 9
nn-Excalibur Weird War III (1990, $9.95) 2 4 6 8 10 12
nn-G.I. Joe - The Trojan Gambit (1983, 68 pgs.) 2 4 6 8 10 12
nn-Harvey Kurtzman Strange Adventures (Epic, $19.95, HC) Aragonés, Crumb 3 6 9 16 20 25
nn-Hearts and Minds (1990, $8.95) Heath-a 1 3 4 6 8 10
nn-Inhumans (1988, $7.95)-Williamson-i 1 2 3 5 7 9
nn-Jhereg (Epic, 1990, $8.95) 1 3 4 6 8 10
nn-Kazar-Guns of the Savage Land (7/90, $8.95) 1 3 4 6 8 10
nn-Kull-The Vale of Shadow ('89, $6.95) 1 3 4 6 8 10
nn-Last of the Dragons (1988, $6.95) Austin-a(i) 1 2 3 4 5 7
nn-Nightraven: House of Cards (1991, $14.95) 2 4 6 10 12 15
nn-Nightraven: The Collected Stories (1990, $9.95) Bolton-r/British Hulk mag.; David Lloyd-c/a 2 4 6 8 10 12
nn-Original Adventures of Cholly and Flytrap (Epic, 1991, $9.95) Suydam-s/c/a 2 4 6 10 12 15
nn-Rick Mason Agent (1989, $9.95) 1 3 4 6 8 10
nn-Roger Rabbit In The Resurrection Of Doom (1989, $8.95) 1 3 4 6 8 10
nn-A Sailor's Story Book II: Winds, Dreams and Dragons ('86, $6.95, softcover) Glansman-s/c/a 1 3 4 6 8 10
nn-Squadron Supreme: Death of a Universe (1989, $9.95) Gruenwald-s; Ryan & Williamson-a 1 3 4 6 8 10
nn-Who Framed Roger Rabbit (1989, $6.95) 1 3 4 6 8 10
NOTE: ***Aragones*** *a-27, 32.* ***Buscema*** *a-38.* ***Byrne*** *c/a-18.* ***Heath*** *a-35i.* ***Kaluta*** *a-13, 35p; c-13.* ***Miller*** *a-24p.* ***Simonson*** *a-6; c-6.* ***Starlin*** *c/a-1,3.* ***Williamson*** *a-34.* ***Wrightson*** *c-29i.*

MARVEL-HEROES & LEGENDS
Marvel Comics: Oct, 1996; 1997 ($2.95)

nn-Wraparound-c, ...1997 ($2.99) -Original Avengers story 3.00

MARVEL HOLIDAY SPECIAL
Marvel Comics: No. 1, 1991 ($2.25, 84 pgs.) - 1996

1-X-Men, Fantastic Four, Punisher, Thor, Capt. America, Ghost Rider, Capt. Ultra, Spidey stories; Art Adams-c/a 3.00
nn (1/93)-Wolverine, Thanos (by Starlin/Lim/Austin) 3.00
nn (1994)-Capt. America, X-Men, Silver Surfer 3.00
...1996-Spider-Man by Waid & Olliffe; X-Men, Silver Surfer 3.00
NOTE: ***Art Adams*** *c-'93.* ***Golden*** *a-'93.* ***Perez*** *c-'94.*

MARVEL ILLUSTRATED: SWIMSUIT ISSUE (Also see Marvel Swimsuit Special)
Marvel Comics: 1991 ($3.95, magazine, 52 pgs.)

V1#1-Parody of Sports Illustrated swimsuit issue; Mary Jane Parker centerfold pin-up by Jusko; 2nd print exists 1 3 4 6 8 10

MARVEL KNIGHTS (See Black Panther, Daredevil, Inhumans, & Punisher)
Marvel Comics: 1998 (Previews for upcoming series)

Sketchbook-Wizard suppl.; Quesada & Palmiotti-c 3.00
Tourbook-($2.99) Interviews and art previews 3.00

MARVEL KNIGHTS

Marvel Mangaverse: Spider-Man #1 © MAR

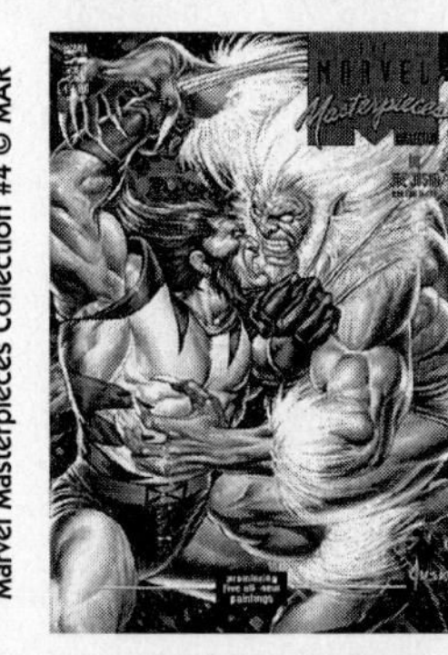
Marvel Masterpieces Collection #4 © MAR

Marvel Mystery Comics #70 © MAR

GD VG FN VF VF/NM NM-
2.0 4.0 6.0 8.0 9.0 9.2

Marvel Comics: July, 2000 - No. 15, Sept, 2001 ($2.99)

1-Daredevil, Punisher, Black Widow, Shang-Chi, Dagger app. 4.00
2-15: 2-Two covers by Barreto & Quesada 3.00
.../Marvel Boy Genesis Edition (6/00) Sketchbook preview 2.25
...: Millennial Visions (2/02, $3.99) Pin-ups by various; Harris-c 4.00

MARVEL KNIGHTS (Volume 2)
Marvel Comics: May, 2002 - No. 6, Oct, 2002 ($2.99)

1-6-Daredevil, Punisher, Black Widow app.; Ponticelli-a 3.00

MARVEL KNIGHTS: DOUBLE SHOT
Marvel Comics: June, 2002 - No. 4 ($2.99, limited series)

1-5: 1-Punisher by Ennis & Quesada; Daredevil by Haynes; Fabry-c 3.00

MARVEL KNIGHTS MAGAZINE
Marvel Comics: May, 2001 - No. 6, Oct, 2001 ($3.99, magazine size)

1-6-Reprints of recent Daredevil, Punisher, Black Widow, Inhumans 4.00

MARVEL MANGAVERSE:... (one-shots)
Marvel Comics: March 2002 ($2.25, manga-inspired one-shots)

Avengers Assemble! - Udon Studio-s/a 2.25
Eternity Twilight ($3.50) - Ben Dunn-s/a/wrap-around-c 3.50
Fantastic Four - Adam Warren-s/Keron Grant-a 2.25
Ghost Riders - Chuck Austen-s/a 2.25
Punisher - Peter David-s/Lea Hernandez-a 2.25
Spider-Man - Kaare Andrews-s/a 2.25
X-Men - C.B. Cebulski-s/Jeff Matsuda-a 2.25

MARVEL MANGAVERSE (Manga series)
Marvel Comics: June, 2002 - No. 6, Nov., 2002 ($2.25)

1-6: 1-Ben Dunn-s/a; intro. manga Captain Marvel 2.25
Vol. 1 TPB (2002, $24.95) r/one-shots 25.00
Vol. 2 TPB (2002, $12.99) r/#1-6 13.00
Vol. 3: Spider-Man-Legend of the Spider-Clan (2003, $11.99, TPB) r/series 12.00

MARVEL MASTERPIECES COLLECTION, THE
Marvel Comics: May, 1993 - No. 4, Aug, 1993 ($2.95, coated paper, lim. series)

1-4-Reprints Marvel Masterpieces trading cards w/ new Jusko paintings in each; Jusko painted-c/a 3.00

MARVEL MASTERPIECES 2 COLLECTION, THE
Marvel Comics: July, 1994 - No. 3, Sept, 1994 ($2.95, limited series)

1-3: 1-Kaluta-c; r/trading cards; new Steranko centerfold 3.00

MARVEL MILESTONE EDITION
Marvel Comics: 1991 - 1999 ($2.95, coated stock)(r/originals with original ads w/silver ink-c)

...: X-Men #1-Reprints X-Men #1 (1991) 3.00
...: Giant Size X-Men #1-(1991, $3.95, 68 pgs.) 4.00
...: Fantastic Four #1 (11/91), ...: Incredible Hulk #1 (3/92, says 3/91 by error), ...: Amazing Fantasy #15 (3/92), ...: Fantastic Four #5 (11/92), ...: Amazing Spider-Man #129 (11/92), ...: Iron Man #55 (11/92), ...: Iron Fist #14 (11/92), ...: Amazing Spider-Man #1 (1/93), ...: Amazing Spider-Man #1 (1/93) variation- no price on-c, ...: Tales of Suspense #39 (3/93), ...: Avengers #1 (9/93), ...: X-Men #9 (10/93), ...: Avengers #16 (10/93), ...:Amazing Spider-Man #149 (11/94, $2.95), ...:X-Men #28 (11/94, $2.95) 3.00
...:Captain America #1 (3/95, $3.95) 4.00
...:Amazing Spider-Man #3 (3/95, $2.95), ...:Avengers #4 (3/95, $2.95), ...:Strange Tales-r/Dr. Strange stories from #110, 111, 114, & 115 3.00
....:Hulk #181 (8/99, $2.99) 3.00

MARVEL MINI-BOOKS (See Promotional Comics section)

MARVEL MOVIE PREMIERE (Magazine)
Marvel Comics Group: Sept, 1975 (B&W, one-shot)

1-Burroughs' "The Land That Time Forgot" adapt. 1 3 4 6 8 10

MARVEL MOVIE SHOWCASE FEATURING STAR WARS
Marvel Comics Group: Nov, 1982 - No. 2, Dec, 1982 ($1.25, 68 pgs.)

1,2-Star Wars movie adaptation; reprints Star Wars #1-6 by Chaykin; 1-Reprints-c to Star Wars #1. 2-Stevens-r 4.00

MARVEL MOVIE SPOTLIGHT FEATURING RAIDERS OF THE LOST ARK
Marvel Comics Group: Nov, 1982 ($1.25, 68 pgs.)

1-Edited-r/Raiders of the Lost Ark #1-3; Buscema-c/a(p); movie adapt. 3.00

MARVEL MUST HAVES (Reprints of recent sold-out issues)
Marvel Comics: Dec, 2001 - Present ($3.99/$2.99)

1,2,4-6: 1-r/Wolverine: Origin #1, Startling Stories: Banner #1, Tangled Web #4 and Cable #97. 2-Amazing Spider-Man #36 and others. 4-Truth #1, Capt. America V4 #1, and The Ultimates #1. 5-r/Ultimate War #1, Ult. X-Men #26, Ult Spider-Man #33. 6-Ult. Spider-Man #33-36 4.00
3-r/Call of Duty: The Brotherhood #1 & Daredevil #32,33 3.00
Amazing Spider-Man #30-32; Incredible Hulk #34-36; The Ultimates #1-3; Ultimate Spider-Man #1-3; Ultimate X-Men #1-3; (New) X-Men #114-116 each.... 4.00

MARVEL MYSTERY COMICS (Formerly Marvel Comics) (Becomes Marvel Tales No. 93 on)
Timely /Marvel Comics (TP #2-17/TCI #18-54/MCI #55-92): No. 2, Dec, 1939 - No. 92, June, 1949

2-(Rare)-American Ace begins, ends #3; Human Torch (blue costume) by Burgos, Sub-Mariner by Everett continue; 2 pg. origin recap of Human Torch
2375 4750 7125 17,800 27,900 38,000
3-New logo from Marvel pulp begins; 1st app. of television in comics? in Human Torch story (1/40) 1188 2376 3563 8910 13,955 19,000
4-Intro. Electro, the Marvel of the Age (ends #19), The Ferret, Mystery Detective (ends #9); 1st Sub-Mariner-c by Schomburg; 2nd German swastika on-c of a comic (2/40); one month after Top-Notch Comics #2 1031 2062 3093 7733 12,117 16,500
5 Classic Schomburg-c (Scarce) 1875 3750 5625 14,000 22,000 30,000
6,7: 6-Gustavson Angel story 690 1380 2070 4830 7415 10,000
8-1st Human Torch & Sub-Mariner battle(6/40) 1000 2000 3000 7000 10,750 14,500
9-(Scarce)-Human Torch & Sub-Mariner battle (cover/story); classic-c
2250 4500 6750 17,000 26,500 36,000
10-Human Torch & Sub-Mariner battle, conclusion; Terry Vance, the Schoolboy Sleuth begins, ends #57 724 1448 2172 5068 7784 10,500
11 341 682 1023 2217 3409 4600
12-Classic Kirby-c 385 770 1155 2503 3852 5200
13-Intro. & 1st app. The Vision by S&K (11/40); Sub-Mariner dons new costume, ends #15
483 966 1449 3381 5191 7000
14-16: 14-Shows-c to Human Torch #1 on-c (12/40). 15-S&K Vision, Gustavson Angel story
248 496 744 1550 2325 3100
17-Human Torch/Sub-Mariner team-up by Burgos/Everett; pin-up on back-c; shows-c to Human Torch #2 on-c 284 568 852 1775 2663 3550
18 232 464 696 1450 2175 2900
19,20: 19-Origin Toro in text; shows-c to Sub-Mariner #1 on-c. 20-Origin The Angel in text
240 480 720 1500 2250 3000
21-The Patriot begins, (intro. in Human Torch #4 (#3)); not in #46-48; pin-up on back-c (7/41)
232 464 696 1450 2175 2900
22-25: 23-Last Gustavson Angel; origin The Vision in text. 24-Injury-to-eye story
208 416 624 1300 1950 2600
26-30: 27-Ka-Zar ends; last S&K Vision who battles Satan. 28-Jimmy Jupiter in the Land of Nowhere begins, ends #48; Sub-Mariner vs. The Flying Dutchman. 30-1st Japanese war-c
184 368 552 1150 1725 2300
31-33,35,36,38,39: 31-Sub-Mariner by Everett ends, resumes #84. 32-1st app. The Boboes
164 328 492 1025 1538 2050
34-Everett, Burgos, Martin Goodman, Funnies, Inc. office appear in story & battles Hitler; last Burgos Human Torch 188 376 564 1175 1763 2350
37-Classic Hitler-c 188 376 564 1175 1763 2350
40-Classic Zeppelin-c 180 360 540 1125 1688 2250
41-43,45,47,48: 48-Last Vision; flag-c 136 272 408 850 1275 1700
44-Classic Super Plane-c 152 304 456 950 1425 1900
46-Classic Hitler-c 152 304 456 950 1425 1900
49-Origin Miss America 176 352 528 1100 1650 2200
50-Mary becomes Miss Patriot (origin) 144 288 432 900 1350 1800
51-60: 54-Bondage-c 122 244 366 763 1144 1525
61,62,64-Last German war-c 118 236 354 738 1107 1475
63-Classic Hitler War-c; The Villainess Cat-Woman only app.
136 272 408 850 1275 1700
65,66-Last Japanese War-c 118 236 354 738 1107 1475
67-78: 74-Last Patriot. 75-Young Allies begin. 76-Ten Chapter Miss America serial begins, ends #85 109 218 327 681 1021 1360
79-New cover format; Super Villains begin on cover; last Angel
112 224 336 700 1050 1400
80-1st app. Capt. America in Marvel Comics 132 264 396 825 1238 1650
81-Captain America app. 104 208 312 650 975 1300
82-Origin & 1st app. Namora (5/47); 1st Sub-Mariner/Namora team-up; Captain America app.
264 528 792 1650 2475 3300
83,85: 83-Last Young Allies. 85-Last Miss America; Blonde Phantom app.
92 184 276 575 863 1150
84-Blonde Phantom begins (on-c of #84,88,89); Sub-Mariner by Everett begins; Captain America app. 130 260 390 813 1219 1625
86-Blonde Phantom i.d. revealed; Captain America app.; last Bucky app.
100 200 300 625 938 1250
87-1st Capt. America/Golden Girl team-up; last Toro app. (8/48)
109 218 327 681 1021 1360
88-Golden Girl, Namora, & Sun Girl (1st in Marvel Comics) x-over; Captain America, Blonde Phantom app. 100 200 300 625 938 1250

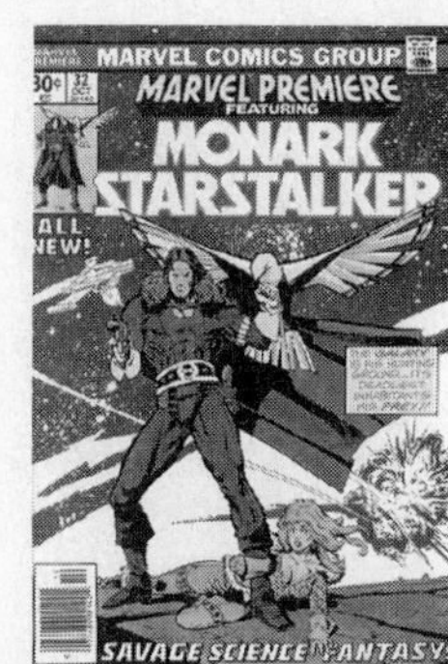

Marvel Prremiere #32 © MAR

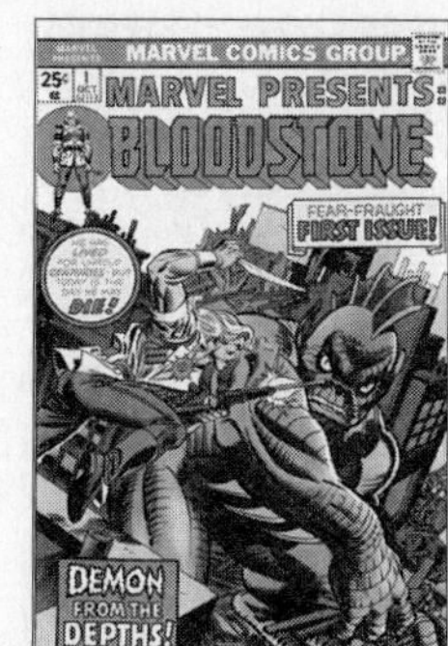

Marvel Presents #1 © MAR

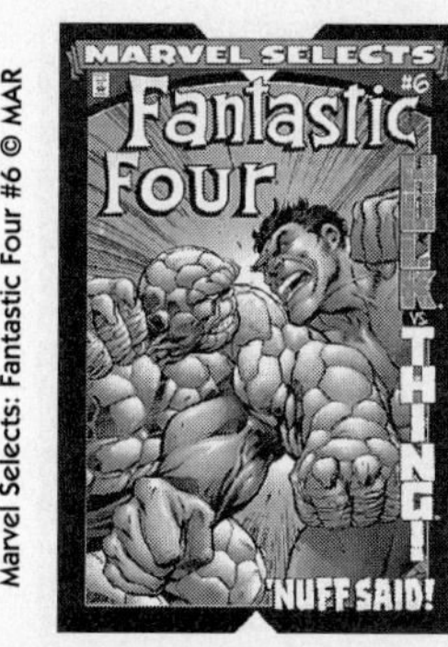

Marvel Selects: Fantastic Four #6 © MAR

GD VG FN VF VF/NM NM-
2.0 4.0 6.0 8.0 9.0 9.2

89-1st Human Torch/Sun Girl team-up; 1st Captain America solo; Blonde Phantom app.
100 200 300 625 938 1250

90,91: 90-Blonde Phantom un-masked; Captain America app. 91-Capt. America app.; Blonde Phantom & Sub-Mariner end; early Venus app. (4/49) (scarce)
122 244 366 763 1144 1525

92-Feature story on the birth of the Human Torch and the death of Professor Horton (his creator); 1st app. The Witness in Marvel Comics; Captain America app. (scarce)
296 592 888 1850 2775 3700

132 Pg. issue, B&W, 25¢ (1943-44)-printed in N. Y.; square binding, blank inside covers); has Marvel No. 33-c in color; contains Capt. America #18 & Marvel Mystery Comics #33; same contents as Captain America Annual (Less than 5 copies known to exist)
3250 6500 9750 23,000 - -

132 Pg. issue (with variant contents), B&W, 25¢ (1942-'43)- square binding, blank inside covers; has same Marvel No. 33-c in color but contains Capt. America #22 & Marvel Mystery Comics #41 instead (possibly scarcer than other version)
(a G+ copy sold in 2002 for $7,500)

NOTE: ***Brodsky*** *c-49, 72, 86, 88-92.* ***Crandall*** *a-26i.* ***Everett*** *c-7-9, 27, 84.* ***Gabrielle*** *c-30-32.* ***Schomburg*** *c-3-11, 13-29, 33-36, 39-48, 50-59, 63-69, 74, 76, 132 pg. issue.* ***Shores*** *c-37, 38, 75p, 77, 78p, 79p, 80, 81p, 82-84, 85p, 87p.* ***Sekowsky*** *c-73. Bondage covers-3, 4, 7, 12, 28, 29, 49, 50, 52, 56, 57, 58, 59, 65. Angel c-2, 3, 8, 12. Remember Pearl Harbor issues-#30-32.*

MARVEL MYSTERY COMICS
Marvel Comics: Dec, 1999 ($3.95, reprints)

1-Reprints original 1940s stories; Schomburg-c from #74 4.00

MARVEL NO-PRIZE BOOK, THE (The Official… on-c)
Marvel Comics Group: Jan, 1983 (one-shot, direct sales only)

1-Golden-c; Kirby-a 4.00

MARVELOUS ADVENTURES OF GUS BEEZER
Marvel Comics: May, 2003; Feb, 2004 ($2.99, one-shots)

...: Gus Beezer & Spider-Man 1 - (5/03) Gurihiru-a 3.00
...: Hulk 1 - (5/03) Simone-s/Lethcoe-a; She-Hulk app. 3.00
...: Spider-Man 1 - (5/03) Simone-s/Lethcoe-a; The Lizard & Dr. Doom app. 3.00
...: X-Men 1 - (5/03) Simone-s/Lethcoe-a 3.00

MARVEL PREMIERE
Marvel Comics Group: April, 1972 - No. 61, Aug, 1981 (A tryout book for new characters)

1-Origin Warlock (pre-#1) by Gil Kane/Adkins; origin Counter-Earth; Hulk & Thor cameo (#1-14 are 20¢-c) 6 12 18 43 59 75
2-Warlock ends; Kirby Yellow Claw-r 3 6 9 19 25 32
3-Dr. Strange series begins (pre #1, 7/72), B. Smith-c/a(p)
6 12 18 38 52 65
4-Smith/Brunner-a 3 6 9 16 20 25
5-9: 8-Starlin-c/a(p) 2 4 6 10 13 16
10-Death of the Ancient One 2 4 6 14 18 22
11-14: 11-Dr. Strange origin-r by Ditko. 14-Last Dr. Strange (3/74), gets own title 3 months later 1 3 4 6 8 10
15-Origin/1st app. Iron Fist (5/74), ends #25 7 14 21 51 71 90
16,25: 16-2nd app. Iron Fist; origin cont'd from #15; Hama's 1st Marvel-a. 25-1st Byrne Iron Fist (moves to own title next) 3 6 9 19 25 32
17-24: Iron Fist in all 2 4 6 12 16 20
26-Hercules. 1 2 3 4 5 7
27-Satana 1 2 3 5 7 9
28-Legion of Monsters (Ghost Rider, Man-Thing, Morbius, Werewolf)
2 4 6 11 14 18
29-46,49: 29,30-The Liberty Legion. 29-1st modern app. Patriot. 31-1st app. Woodgod; last 25¢ issue. 32-1st app. Monark Starstalker. 33,34-1st color app. Solomon Kane (Robert E. Howard adaptation "Red Shadows".) 35-Origin/1st app. 3-D Man. 36,37-3-D Man. 38-1st Weirdworld. 39,40-Torpedo. 41-1st Seeker 3000! 42-Tigra. 43-Paladin. 44-Jack of Hearts (1st solo book, 10/78). 45,46-Man-Wolf. 49-The Falcon (1st solo book, 8/79) 4.00
29-31-(30¢-c variants, limited distribution)(4,6,8/76) 2 4 6 10 12 15
36-38-(35¢-c variants, limited distribution)(6,8,10/77) 2 4 6 10 12 15
47,48-Byrne-a: 47-Origin/1st app. new Ant-Man. 48-Ant-Man
1 2 3 5 6 8
50-1st app. Alice Cooper; co-plotted by Alice 2 4 6 10 12 15
51-56,58-61: 51-53-Black Panther. 54-1st Caleb Hammer. 55-Wonder Man. 56-1st color app. Dominic Fortune. 58-60-Dr. Who. 61-Star Lord 3.00
57-Dr. Who (2nd U.S. app.-see Movie Classics) 5.00

NOTE: ***N. Adams*** *(Crusty Bunkers) part inks-10, 12, 13.* ***Austin*** *a-50i, 56i; c-46i, 50i, 56i, 58.* ***Brunner*** *a-4i, 6p, 9-14p; c-9-14.* ***Byrne*** *a-47p, 48p.* ***Chaykin*** *a-32-34; c-32, 33, 56.* ***Giffen*** *a-31p, 44p; c-44.* ***Gil Kane*** *a(p)-1, 2, 15; c(p)-1, 2, 15, 16, 22-24, 27, 36, 37.* ***Kirby*** *c-26, 29-31, 35.* ***Layton*** *a-47i, 48i; c-47.* ***McWilliams*** *a-25i.* ***Miller*** *c-49p, 53p, 58p.* ***Nebres*** *a-44i; c-38i.* ***Nino*** *a-38i.* ***Perez*** *c/a-38p, 45p, 46p.* ***Ploog*** *a-38; c-5-7.* ***Russell*** *a-7p.* ***Simonson*** *a-60(2pgs.); c-57.* ***Starlin*** *a-8p; c-8.* ***Sutton*** *a-41, 43, 50p, 61; c-50p, 61. #57-60 publ'd w/two different prices on-c.*

MARVEL PRESENTS
Marvel Comics: October, 1975 - No. 12, Aug, 1977 (#1-6 are 25¢ issues)

GD VG FN VF VF/NM NM-
2.0 4.0 6.0 8.0 9.0 9.2

1-Origin & 1st app. Bloodstone 2 4 6 8 10 12
2-Origin Bloodstone continued; Kirby-c 1 2 3 4 5 7
3-Guardians of the Galaxy (1st solo book, 2/76) begins, ends #12
2 4 6 10 12 15
4-7,9-12: 9,10-Origin Starhawk 1 2 3 5 6 8
4-6-(30¢-c variants, limited distribution)(4-8/76) 2 4 6 8 10 12
8-r/story from Silver Surfer #2 plus 4 pgs. new-a 1 2 3 5 6 8
11,12-(35¢-c variants, limited distribution)(6,8/77) 2 4 6 8 10 12

NOTE: ***Austin*** *a-6i.* ***Buscema*** *r-8p.* ***Chaykin*** *a-5p.* ***Kane*** *c-1p.* ***Starlin*** *layouts-10.*

MARVEL PREVIEW (Magazine) (Bizarre Adventures #25 on)
Marvel Comics: Feb (no month), 1975 - No. 24, Winter, 1980 (B&W) ($1.00)

1-Man-Gods From Beyond the Stars; Crusty Bunkers (Neal Adams)-a(i) & cover; Nino-a
2 4 6 10 13 16
2-1st origin The Punisher (see Amaz. Spider-Man #129 & Classic Punisher); 1st app. Dominic Fortune; Morrow-c 8 16 24 58 82 105
3,8,10: 3-Blade the Vampire Slayer. 8-Legion of Monsters; Morbius app. 10-Thor the Mighty; Starlin frontispiece 2 4 6 12 16 20
4,5: 4-Star-Lord & Sword in the Star (origins & 1st app.). 5,6-Sherlock Holmes.
2 4 6 9 11 14
6,9: 6-Sherlock Holmes; N. Adams frontispiece. 9-Man-God; origin Star Hawk, ends #20
1 3 4 6 8 10
7-Satana, Sword in the Star app. 2 4 6 8 10 12
11,12,16,19: 11-Star-Lord; Byrne-a; Starlin frontispiece. 12-Haunt of Horror. 16-Masters of Terror. 19-Kull 1 2 3 5 6 8
13-15,17,18,20-24: 14,15-Star-Lord. 14-Starlin painted-c. 17-Blackmark by G. Kane (see SSOC #1-3). 18-Star-Lord. 20-Bizarre Advs. 21-Moon Knight (Spr/80)-Predates Moon Knight #1; The Shroud by Ditko. 22-King Arthur. 23-Bizarre Advs.; Miller-a. 24-Debut Paradox 5.00

NOTE: ***N. Adams*** *(C. Bunkers) r-20i.* ***Buscema*** *a-22, 23.* ***Byrne*** *a-11.* ***Chaykin*** *a-20r; c-20 (new).* ***Colan*** *a-8, 16p(3), 18p, 23p; c-16p.* ***Elias*** *a-18.* ***Giffen*** *a-7.* ***Infantino*** *a-14p.* ***Kaluta*** *a-12; c-15.* ***Miller*** *a-23.* ***Morrow*** *a-8i; c-2-4.* ***Perez*** *a-20p.* ***Ploog*** *a-8.* ***Starlin*** *c-13, 14. Nudity in some issues*

MARVEL RIOT
Marvel Comics: Dec, 1995 ($1.95, one-shot)

1-"Age of Apocalypse" spoof; Lobdell script 2.25

MARVELS
Marvel Comics: Jan, 1994 - No. 4, Apr, 1994 ($5.95, painted lim. series)
No. 1 (2nd Printing), Apr, 1996 - No. 4 (2nd Printing), July, 1996 ($2.95)

1-4: Kurt Busiek scripts & Alex Ross painted-c/a in all; double-c w/acetate overlay
1 2 3 5 6 8
Marvel Classic Collectors Pack ($11.90)-Issues #1 & 2 boxed (1st printings).
2 4 6 10 13 16
0-(8/94, $2.95)-no acetate overlay. 4.00
1-4-(2nd printing): r/original limited series w/o acetate overlay 3.00
Hardcover (1994, $59.95)-r/#0-4; w/intros by Stan Lee, John Romita, Sr., Kurt Busiek & Scott McCloud. 60.00
Trade paperback ($19.95) 20.00

MARVEL SAGA, THE
Marvel Comics Group: Dec, 1985 - No. 25, Dec, 1987

1,21-25 2.25
2-20 2.25

NOTE: ***Williamson*** *a(i)-9, 10; c(i)-7, 10-12, 14, 16.*

MARVELS COMICS: ... (Marvel-type comics read in the Marvel Universe)
Marvel Comics: Jul, 2000 ($2.25, one-shots)

...Captain America #1 -Frenz & Sinnott-a; ...Daredevil #1 -Isabella-s/Newell-a; ...Fantastic Four #1 -Kesel-s/Paul Smith-a; Spider-Man #1 -Oliff-a; ...Thor #1 -Templeton-s/Aucoin-a 2.25
...X-Men #1 -Millar-s/ Sean Phillips & Duncan Fegredo-a 2.25
The History of Marvels Comics (no cover price)-Faux history; previews titles 2.25

MARVEL SELECTS:
Marvel Comics: Jan, 2000 - No. 6, June, 2000 ($2.75/$2.99, reprints)

...Fantastic Four 1-6: Reprints F.F. #107-112; new Davis-c 2.75
...Spider-Man 1,2,4-6: Reprints AS-M #100,101,103,104,93; Wieringo-c 2.75
...Spider-Man 3 ($2.99): Reprints AS-M #102; new Wieringo-c 3.00

MARVEL'S GREATEST COMICS (Marvel Collectors' Item Classics #1-22)
Marvel Comics Group: No. 23, Oct, 1969 - No. 96, Jan, 1981

23-34 (Giants). Begin Fantastic Four-r/#30s?-116 2 4 6 14 18 22
35-37-Silver Surfer-r/Fantastic Four #48-50 2 4 6 8 10 12
38-50: 42-Silver Surfer-r/F.F.(others?) 1 2 3 5 6 8
51-70: 63,64-(25¢ editions) 5.00
63,64-(30¢-c variants, limited distribution)(5,7/76) 1 2 3 4 5 7
71-96: 71-73-(30¢ editions) 4.00

Marvel 1602 #1 © MAR

Marvel Spotlight #32 © MAR

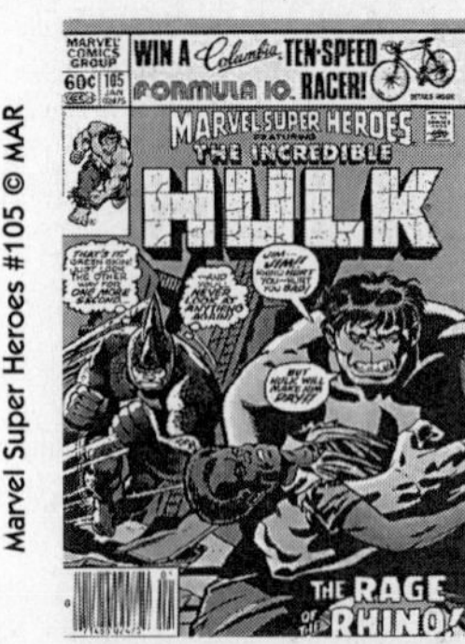

Marvel Super Heroes #105 © MAR

GD 2.0 | VG 4.0 | FN 6.0 | VF 8.0 | VF/NM 9.0 | NM- 9.2

71-73-(35¢-c variants, limited distribution)(7,9-10/77) 6.00

NOTE: *Dr. Strange, Fantastic Four, Iron Man, Watcher-#23, 24. Capt. America, Dr. Strange, Iron Man, Fantastic Four-#25-28. Fantastic Four-#38-96.* **Buscema** *r-85-92; c-87-92r.* **Ditko** *r-23-28.* **Kirby** *r-23-82; c-75, 77p, 80p. #81 reprints Fantastic Four #100.*

MARVEL'S GREATEST SUPERHERO BATTLES (See Fireside Book Series)

MARVEL: SHADOWS AND LIGHT
Marvel Comics: Feb, 1997 ($2.95, B&W, one-shot)

1-Tony Daniel-c 3.00

MARVEL 1602
Marvel Comics: Nov, 2003 - No. 8 ($3.50, limited series)

1-6-Neil Gaiman-s; Andy Kubert & Richard Isanove-a 3.50

MARVELS OF SCIENCE
Charlton Comics: March, 1946 - No. 4, June, 1946

1-A-Bomb story 24 48 72 138 194 250
2-4 14 28 42 79 107 135

MARVEL SPECIAL EDITION FEATURING... (Also see Special Collectors' Ed.)
Marvel Comics Group: 1975 - 1978 (84 pgs.) (Oversized)

1-The Spectacular Spider-Man ($1.50); r/Amazing Spider-Man #6,35, Annual 1; Ditko-a(r) 3 6 9 18 24 30
1,2-Star Wars ('77,'78; r/Star Wars #1-3 & #4-6; regular edition and Whitman variant exist 2 4 6 10 13 16
3-Star Wars ('78, $2.50, 116 pgs.); r/S. Wars #1-6; regular edition and Whitman variant exist 2 4 6 14 18 22
3-Close Encounters of the Third Kind (1978, $1.50, 56 pgs.)-Movie adaptation; Simonson-a(p) 2 4 6 10 12 15
V2#2(Spring, 1980, $2.00, oversized)- "Star Wars: The Empire Strikes Back"; r/Marvel Comics Super Special #16 3 6 9 18 23 28

NOTE: **Chaykin** *c/a(r)-1(1977), 2, 3.* **Stevens** *a(r)-2i, 3i.* **Williamson** *a(r)-V2#2.*

MARVEL SPECTACULAR
Marvel Comics Group: Aug, 1973 - No. 19, Nov, 1975

1-Thor-r from mid-sixties begin by Kirby 2 4 6 8 10 12
2-19 6.00

MARVELS: PORTRAITS
Marvel Comics: Mar, 1995 - No. 4, June, 1995 ($2.95, limited series)

1-4:Different artists renditions of Marvel characters 3.00

MARVEL SPOTLIGHT (...& Son of Satan #19, 20, 23, 24)
Marvel Comics Group: Nov, 1971 - No. 33, Apr, 1977; V2#1, July, 1979 - V2#11, Mar, 1981 (A try-out book for new characters)

1-Origin Red Wolf (western hero)(1st solo book, pre-#1); Wood inks, Neal Adams-c; only 15¢ issue 4 8 12 27 36 45
2-(25¢, 52 pgs.)-Venus-r by Everett; origin/1st app. Werewolf By Night (begins) by Ploog; N. Adams-c 16 32 48 113 167 220
3,4: 4-Werewolf By Night ends (6/72); gets own title 9/72 6 12 18 38 52 65
5-Origin/1st app. Ghost Rider (8/72) & begins 15 30 45 104 152 200
6-8: 6-Origin G.R. retold. 8-Last Ploog issue 4 8 12 29 40 50
9-11-Last Ghost Rider (gets own title next mo.) 4 8 12 22 30 38
12-Origin & 2nd full app. The Son of Satan (10/73); story cont'd from Ghost Rider #2 & into #3; series begins, ends #24 4 8 12 22 30 38
13-24: 13-Partial origin Son of Satan. 14-Last 20¢ issue. 22-Ghost Rider-c & cameo (5 panels). 24-Last Son of Satan (10/75); gets own title 12/75 2 4 6 8 10 12
25,27,30,31: 27-(Regular 25¢-c), Sub-Mariner app. 30-The Warriors Three. 31-Nick Fury 6.00
26-Scarecrow 1 3 4 6 8 10
27-(30¢-c variant, limited distribution) 2 4 6 11 14 18
28-(Regular 25¢-c) 1st solo Moon Knight app. 3 6 9 18 24 30
28-(30¢-c variant, limited distribution) 5 10 15 36 48 60
29,32: 29-(Regular 25¢-c) (8/76) Moon Knight app.; last 25¢ issue. 32-1st app./partial origin Spider-Woman (2/77); Nick Fury app. 2 4 6 14 18 22
29-(30¢-c variant, limited distribution) 4 8 12 29 40 50
33-Deathlok; 1st app. Devil-Slayer 1 2 3 5 6 8
V2#1-7,9-11: 1-4-Capt. Marvel. 5-Dragon Lord. 6,7-StarLord; origin #6. 9-11-Capt. Universe (see Micronauts #8) 3.00
1-Variant copy missing issue #1 on cover 2 4 6 8 10 12
8-Capt. Marvel; Miller-c/a(p) 6.00

NOTE: **Austin** *c-V2#2i, 8.* **J. Buscema** *c/a-30p.* **Chaykin** *a-31; c-26, 31.* **Colan** *a-18p, 19p.* **Ditko** *a-V2#4, 5, 9-11; c-V2#4, 9-11.* **Kane** *c-21p, 32p.* **Kirby** *c-29p.* **McWilliams** *a-20i.* **Miller** *a-V2#8p; c(p)-V2#2, 5, 7, 8.* **Mooney** *a-8i, 10i, 14p, 15, 16p, 17p, 24p, 27, 32i.* **Nasser** *a-33p.* **Ploog** *a-2-5, 6-8p; c-3-9.* **Romita** *c-13.* **Sutton** *a-9-11p, V2#6, 7. #29-25¢ & 30¢ issues exist.*

MARVEL SUPER ACTION (Magazine)
Marvel Comics Group: Jan, 1976 (B&W, 76 pgs.)

1-Origin/2nd app. Dominic Fortune(see Marvel Preview); early Punisher app.; Weird World & The Huntress; Evans, Ploog-a 6 12 18 40 55 70

MARVEL SUPER ACTION
Marvel Comics Group: May, 1977 - No. 37, Nov, 1981

1-Reprints Capt. America #100 by Kirby 2 4 6 8 10 12
2-13: 2,3,5-13 reprint Capt. America #101,102,103-111. 4-Marvel Boy-r(origin)/M. Boy #1. 11-Origin-r. 12,13-Classic Steranko-c/a(r). 1 2 3 4 5 7
2,3-(35¢-c variants, limited distribution)(6,8/77) 1 2 3 6 8 10
14-20: r/Avengers #55,56, Annual 2, others 4.00
21-37: 30-r/Hulk #6 from U.K. 3.50

NOTE: **Buscema** *a(r)-14p, 15p; c-18-20, 22, 35r-37.* **Everett** *a-4.* **Heath** *a-4r.* **Kirby** *r-1-3, 5-11.* **B. Smith** *a-27r, 28r.* **Steranko** *a(r)-12p, 13p; c-12r, 13r.*

MARVEL SUPER HERO CONTEST OF CHAMPIONS
Marvel Comics Group: June, 1982 - No. 3, Aug, 1982 (Limited series)

1-3: Features nearly all Marvel characters currently appearing in their comics; 1st Marvel limited series 1 2 3 5 6 8

MARVEL SUPER HEROES
Marvel Comics Group: October, 1966 (25¢, 68 pgs.) (1st Marvel one-shot)

1-r/origin Daredevil from D.D. #1; r/Avengers #2; G.A. Sub-Mariner-r/Marvel Mystery #8 (Human Torch app.). Kirby-a 11 22 33 77 114 150

MARVEL SUPER-HEROES (Formerly Fantasy Masterpieces #1-11)
(Also see Giant-Size Super Heroes) (#12-20: 25¢, 68 pgs.)
Marvel Comics: No. 12, 12/67 - No. 31, 11/71; No. 32, 9/72 - No. 105, 1/82

12-Origin & 1st app. Capt. Marvel of the Kree; G.A. Human Torch, Destroyer, Capt. America, Black Knight, Sub-Mariner-r (#12-20 all contain new stories and reprints) 13 26 39 90 133 175
13-2nd app. Capt. Marvel; G.A. Black Knight, Torch, Vision, Capt. America, Sub-Mariner-r 7 14 21 46 63 80
14-Amazing Spider-Man (5/68, new-a by Andru/Everett); G.A. Sub-Mariner, Torch, Mercury (1st Kirby-a at Marvel), Black Knight, Capt. America reprints 9 18 27 60 85 110
15-17: 15-Black Bolt cameo in Medusa (new-a); Black Knight, Sub-Mariner, Black Marvel, Capt. America-r. 16-Origin & 1st app. S. A. Phantom Eagle; G.A. Torch, Capt. America, Black Knight, Patriot, Sub-Mariner-r. 17-Origin Black Knight (new-a); G.A. Torch, Sub-Mariner-r; reprint from All-Winners Squad #21 (cover & story) 4 8 12 24 32 40
18-Origin/1st app. Guardians of the Galaxy (1/69); G.A. Sub-Mariner, All-Winners Squad-r 5 10 15 36 48 60
19-Ka-Zar (new-a); G.A. Torch, Marvel Boy, Black Knight, Sub-Mariner reprints; Smith-c(p); Tuska-a(r) 3 6 9 16 20 25
20-Doctor Doom (5/69); r/Young Men #24 w/-c 3 7 10 21 28 35
21-31: All-r issues. 21-X-Men, Daredevil, Iron Man-r begin, end #31. 31-Last Giant issue 2 4 6 10 12 15
32-50: 32-Hulk/Sub-Mariner-r begin from TTA. 6.00
51-70,100: 56-r/origin Hulk/Inc. Hulk #102; Hulk-r begin 4.00
57,58-(30¢-c variants, limited distribution)(5,7/76) 5.00
65,66-(35¢-c variants, limited distribution)(7,9/77) 5.00
71-99,101-105 3.00

NOTE: **Austin** *a-104.* **Colan** *a(p)-12, 13, 15, 18; c-12, 13, 15, 18.* **Everett** *a-14i(new); r-14, 15i, 18, 19, 33; c-85(r). New* **Kirby** *c-22, 27, 54.* **Maneely** *r-14, 15, 19.* **Severin** *r-83-85i, 100-102; c-100-102r.* **Starlin** *c-47.* **Tuska** *a-19p. Black Knight-r by* **Maneely** *in 12-16, 19. Sub-Mariner-r by* **Everett** *in 12-20.*

MARVEL SUPER-HEROES
Marvel Comics: May, 1990 - V2#15, Oct, 1993 ($2.95/$2.50, quart., 68-84 pgs.)

1-Moon Knight, Hercules, Black Panther, Magik, Brother Voodoo, Speedball (by Ditko) & Hellcat; Hembeck-a 3.00
2,4,5,V2#3,6-15: 2-Summer Special(7/90); Rogue, Speedball (by Ditko), Iron Man, Falcon, Tigra & Daredevil. 4-Spider-Man/Nick Fury, Daredevil,Speedball, Wonder Man, Spitfire & Black Knight; Byrne-c. 5-Thor, Dr. Strange, Thing & She-Hulk; Speedball by Ditko(p). V2#3-Retells origin Capt. America w/new facts; Blue Shield, Capt. Marvel,Speedball, Wasp; Hulk by Ditko/Rogers V2#6-9: 6-8-$2.25-c. 6,7-X-Men, Cloak & Dagger, The Shroud (by Ditko) & Marvel Boy in each. 8-X-Men, Namor & Iron Man (by Ditko); Larsen-c. 9-West Coast Avengers, Iron Man app.; Kieth-c(p). V2#10-Ms. Marvel/Sabretooth-c/story (intended for Ms. Marvel #24; shows-c to #24); Namor, Vision, Scarlet Witch stories. V2#11,12 :11-Original Ghost Rider-c/story; Giant-Man, Ms. Marvel stories. 12-Dr. Strange, Falcon, Iron Man. V2#13-15 ($2.75, 84 pgs.): 13-All Iron Man 30th anniversary. 15-Iron Man/Thor/Volstagg/Dr. Druid 2.75

MARVEL SUPER-HEROES MEGAZINE
Marvel Comics: Oct, 1994 - No. 6, Mar, 1995 ($2.95, 100 pgs.)

1-6: 1-r/FF #232, DD #159, Iron Man #115, Incred. Hulk #314 3.00

Marvel Super-Heroes Secret Wars #8 © MAR

Marvel Tales #120 © MAR

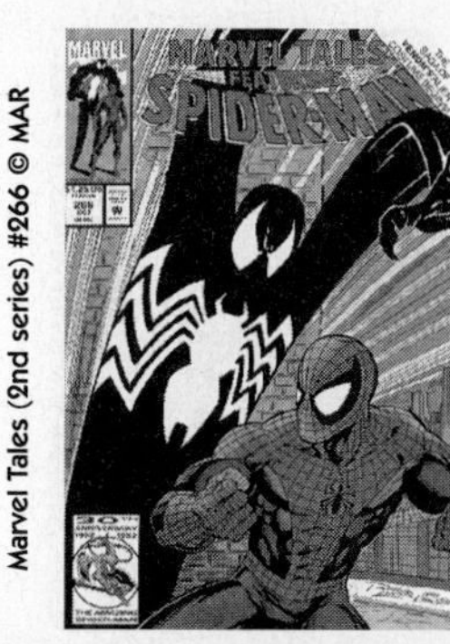

Marvel Tales (2nd series) #266 © MAR

GD VG FN VF VF/NM NM-
2.0 4.0 6.0 8.0 9.0 9.2

MARVEL SUPER-HEROES SECRET WARS (See Secret Wars II)
Marvel Comics Group: May, 1984 - No. 12, Apr, 1985 (limited series)

1 1 2 3 5 6 8
1-3-(2nd printings, sold in multi-packs) 2.50
2-6,9-11: 6-The Wasp dies 6.00
7,12: 7-Intro. new Spider-Woman. 12-($1.00, 52 pgs.) 1 2 3 4 5 7
8-Spider-Man's new black costume explained as alien costume (1st app. Venom as alien costume) 3 6 9 18 23 28

NOTE: ***Zeck*** *a-1-12; c-1,3,8-12. Additional artists (John Romita Sr., Art Adams and others) had uncreditted art in #12.*

MARVEL SUPER SPECIAL, A (See Marvel Comics Super...)

MARVEL SWIMSUIT SPECIAL (Also see Marvel Illustrated...)
Marvel Comics: 1992 - No. 4, 1995 ($3.95/$4.50, magazine, 52 pgs.)

1-4-Silvestri-c; pin-ups by diff. artists. 2-Jusko-c. 3-Hughes-c 1 2 3 5 6 8

MARVEL TAILS STARRING PETER PORKER THE SPECTACULAR SPIDER-HAM (Also see Peter Porker...)
Marvel Comics Group: Nov, 1983 (one-shot)

1-Peter Porker, the Spectacular Spider-Ham, Captain Americat, Goose Rider, Hulk Bunny app. 4.00

MARVEL TALES (Formerly Marvel Mystery Comics #1-92)
Marvel/Atlas Comics (MCI): No. 93, Aug, 1949 - No. 159, Aug, 1957

93-Horror/weird stories begin 144 288 432 900 1350 1800
94-Everett-a 94 188 282 588 882 1175
95,96,99,101,103,105: 95-New logo 64 128 192 400 600 800
97-Sun Girl, 2 pgs; Kirbyish-a; one story used in N.Y. State Legislative document 76 152 228 475 713 950
98,100: 98-Krigstein-a 66 132 198 413 619 825
102-Wolverton-a "The End of the World", (6 pgs.) 92 184 276 575 863 1150
104-Wolverton-a "Gateway to Horror", (6 pgs.) 90 180 270 563 844 1125
106,107-Krigstein-a. 106-Decapitation story 54 108 162 324 487 650
108-120: 118-Hypo-c/panels in End of World story. 120-Jack Katz-a 40 80 120 240 345 450
121,123-131: 128-Flying Saucer-c. 131-Last precode (2/55) 34 68 102 193 274 355
122-Kubert-a 34 68 102 196 278 360
132,133,135-141,143,145 22 44 66 127 176 225
134-Krigstein, Kubert-a; flying saucer-c 24 48 72 135 190 245
142-Krigstein-a 23 46 69 130 183 235
144-Williamson/Krenkel-a, 3 pgs. 23 46 69 130 183 235
146,148-151,154-156,158: 150-1st S.A. issue. 156-Torres-a 17 34 51 98 134 170
147,152: 147-Ditko-a. 152-Wood, Morrow-a 20 40 60 112 156 200
153-Everett End of World c/story 22 44 66 124 172 220
157,159-Krigstein-a 18 36 54 101 138 175

NOTE: ***Andru*** *a-103.* ***Briefer*** *a-118.* ***Check*** *a-147.* ***Colan*** *a-105, 107, 118, 120, 121, 127, 131.* ***Drucker*** *a-127, 135, 141, 146, 150.* ***Everett*** *a-98, 104, 106(2), 108(2), 131, 148, 151, 153, 155; c-107, 109, 111, 112, 114, 117, 127, 143, 147-151, 153, 155, 156.* ***Forte*** *a-119, 125, 130.* ***Heath*** *a-110, 113, 118, 119; c-104-106, 110, 130.* ***Gil Kane*** *a-117.* ***Lawrence*** *a-130.* ***Maneely*** *a-111, 126, 129; c-108, 116, 120, 129, 152.* ***Mooney*** *a-114.* ***Morisi*** *a-153.* ***Morrow*** *a-150, 152, 156.* ***Orlando*** *a-149, 151, 157.* ***Pakula*** *a-119, 121, 135, 144, 150, 152, 156.* ***Powell*** *a-136, 137, 150, 154.* ***Ravielli*** *a-117.* ***Rico*** *a-97, 99.* ***Romita*** *a-108.* ***Sekowsky*** *a-96-98.* ***Shores*** *a-110; c-96.* ***Sinnott*** *a-105, 116.* ***Tuska*** *a-114.* ***Whitney*** *a-107.* ***Wildey*** *a-126, 138.*

MARVEL TALES (...Annual #1,2; ...Starring Spider-Man #123 on)
Marvel Comics Group (NPP earlier issues): 1964 - No. 291, Nov, 1994 (No. 1-32: 72 pgs.)
(#1-3 have Canadian variants; back & inside-c are blank, same value)

1-Reprints origins of Spider-Man/Amazing Fantasy #15, Hulk/Inc. Hulk#1, Ant-Man/T.T.A. #35, Giant Man/T.T.A. #49, Iron Man/T.O.S. #39,48, Thor/J.I.M. #83 & r/Sgt. Fury #1 30 60 90 219 322 425
2 ('65)-r/X-Men #1(origin), Avengers #1(origin), origin Dr. Strange-r/Strange Tales #115 & origin Hulk(Hulk #3) 11 22 33 77 114 150
3 (7/66)-Spider-Man, Strange Tales (H. Torch), Journey into Mystery (Thor), Tales to Astonish (Ant-Man)-r begin (r/Strange Tales #101) 6 12 18 40 55 70
4,5 4 8 12 27 36 45
6-8,10: 10-Reprints 1st Kraven/Amaz. S-M #15 3 6 9 18 23 28
9-r/Amazing Spider-Man #14 w/cover 3 6 9 19 25 32
11-33: 11-Spider-Man battles Daredevil-r/Amaz. Spider-Man #16. 13-Origin Marvel Boy-r from M. Boy #1. 22-Green Goblin-c/story-r/Amaz. Spider-Man #27. 30-New Angel story (x-over w/Ka-Zar #2,3). 32-Last 72 pg. iss. 33-(52 pgs.) Kraven-r 2 4 6 12 16 20
34-50: 34-Begin regular size issues 1 2 3 4 5 7
51-65 5.00
66-70-(Regular 25¢ editions)(4-8/76) 4.00

GD VG FN VF VF/NM NM-
2.0 4.0 6.0 8.0 9.0 9.2

66-70-(30¢-c variants, limited distribution) 6.00
71-105: 75-Origin Spider-Man-r. 77-79-Drug issues-r/Amaz. Spider-Man #96-98. 98-Death of Gwen Stacy-r/Amaz. Spider-Man #121 (Green Goblin). 99-Death Green Goblin-r/Amaz. Spider-Man #122. 100-(52 pgs.)-New Hawkeye/Two Gun Kid story.
101-105-All Spider-Man-r 3.00
80-84-(35¢-c variants, limited distribution)(6-10/77) 5.00
106-r/1st Punisher-Amazing Spider-Man #129 6.00
107-136: 107-133-All Spider-Man-r. 111,112-r/Spider-Man #134,135 (Punisher). 113,114-r/Spider-Man #136,137(Green Goblin). 126-128-r/clone story from Amazing Spider-Man #149-151. 134-136-Dr. Strange-r begin; SpM stories continue. 134-Dr. Strange-r/Strange Tales #110 3.00
137-Origin-r Dr. Strange; shows original unprinted-c & origin Spider-Man/Amazing Fantasy #15 6.00
137-Nabisco giveaway 1 2 3 4 5 7
138-Reprints all Amazing Spider-Man #1; begin reprints of Spider-Man with covers similar to originals 5.00
139-144: r/Amazing Spider-Man #2-7 3.00
145-149,151-190,193-199: Spider-Man-r continue w/#8 on. 149-Contains skin "Tattooz" decals. 153-r/1st Kraven/Spider-Man #15. 155-r/2nd Green Goblin/Spider-Man #17. 161,164,165-Gr. Goblin-c/stories-r/Spider-Man #23,26,27. 178,179-Green Goblin-c/story-r/Spider-Man #39,40. 187,189-Kraven-r. 193-Byrne-r/Marvel Team-Up begin w/scripts 2.50
150,191,192,200: 150-($1.00, 52pgs.)-r/Spider-Man Annual #1(Kraven app.). 191-($1.50, 68 pgs.)-r/Spider-Man #96-98. 192-($1.25, 52 pgs.)-r/Spider-Man #121,122. 200-Double size ($1.25)-Miller-c & r/Annual #14 4.00
201-257: 208-Last Byrne-r. 210,211-r/Spidey #134,135. 212,213-r/Giant-Size Spidey #4. 213-r/1st solo Silver Surfer story/F.F. Annual #5. 214,215-r/Spidey #161,162. 222-Reprints origin Punisher/Spectacular Spider-Man #83; last Punisher reprint. 209-Reprints 1st app. The Punisher/Amazing Spider-Man #129; Punisher reprints begin, end #222. 223-McFarlane-c begins, end #239. 233-Spider-Man/X-Men team-ups begin; r/X-Men #35. 234-r/Marvel Team-Up #4. 235,236-r/M. Team-Up Annual #1. 237,238-r/M. Team-Up #150. 239,240-r/M. Team-Up #38,90(Beast). 242-r/M.Team-Up #89. 243-r/M. Team-Up #117 (Wolverine). 250-($1.50, 52pgs.)-r/1st Karma/M. Team-Up #100. 251-r/Spider-Man #100 (Green Goblin-c/story). 252-r/1st app. Morbius/Amaz. Spider-Man #101. 253-($1.50, 52 pgs.) -r/Amaz. S-M #102254-r/M. Team-Up #15(Ghost Rider); new painted-c. 255,256-Spider-Man & Ghost Rider-r/Marvel Team-Up #58,91. 257-Hobgoblin-r begin (r/Amazing Spider-Man #238) 2.25
258-291: 258-261-r/A. Spider-Man #239,249-251(Hobgoblin). 262,263-r/Marv. Team-Up #53,54. 262-New X-Men vs. Sunstroke story. 263-New Woodgod origin story. 264,265-r/Amazing Spider-Man Annual 5. 266-273-Reprints alien costume stories/A. S-M 252-259. 277-r/1st Silver Sable/A. S-M 265. 283-r/A. S-M 275 (Hobgoblin). 284-r/A. S-M 276 (Hobgoblin) 2.25
285-variant w/Wonder-Con logo on c-no price-giveaway 2.25
286-($2.95)-p/bagged w/16 page insert & animation print 3.00

NOTE: *All contain reprints; some have new art. #89-97-r/Amazing Spider-Man #110-118; #98-136-r/#121-159; #137-150-r/Amazing Fantasy #15, #1-12 & Annual 1; #151-167-r/#13-28 & Annual 2; #168-186-r/#29-46.* ***Austin*** *a-100i; c-272i, 273i.* ***Byrne*** *a(r)-193-198p, 201-208p.* ***Ditko*** *a-1-30, 83, 100, 137-155.* ***G. Kane*** *a-71, 81, 98-101p, 249r; c-125-127p, 130p, 137-155.* ***Sam Kieth*** *c-255, 262, 263.* ***Ron Lim*** *c-266p-281p, 283p-285p.* ***McFarlane*** *c-223-239.* ***Mooney*** *a-63, 95-97i, 103(i).* ***Nasser*** *a-100p.* ***Nebres*** *a-242i.* ***Perez*** *c-259-261.* ***Rogers*** *c-240, 241, 243-252.*

MARVEL TEAM-UP (See Marvel Treasury Edition #18 & Official Marvel Index To...)
(Replaced by Web of Spider-Man)
Marvel Comics Group: March, 1972 - No. 150, Feb, 1985
NOTE: *Spider-Man team-ups in all but Nos. 18, 23, 26, 29, 32, 35, 97, 104, 105, 137.*

1-Human Torch 13 26 39 94 137 180
2-Human Torch 5 10 15 33 44 55
3-Spider-Man/Human Torch vs. Morbius (part 1); 3rd app. of Morbius (7/72) 6 12 18 38 52 65
4-Spider-Man/X-Men vs. Morbius (part 2 of story); 4th app. of Morbius 6 12 18 38 52 65
5-10: 5-Vision. 6-Thing. 7-Thor. 8-The Cat (4/73, came out between The Cat #3 & 4). 9-Iron Man. 10-H-T 3 6 9 16 20 24
11,13,14,16-20: 11-Inhumans. 13-Capt. America. 14-Sub-Mariner. 16-Capt. Marvel. 17-Mr. Fantastic. 18-H-T/Hulk. 19-Ka-Zar. 20-Black Panther; last 20¢ issue 2 4 6 10 12 15
12-Werewolf (8/73, 1 month before Werewolf #1). 3 6 9 18 23 28
15-1st Spider-Man/Ghost Rider team-up (11/73) 2 4 6 14 18 22
21-30: 21-Dr. Strange. 22-Hawkeye. 23-H-T/Iceman (X-Men cameo). 24-Brother Voodoo. 25-Daredevil. 26-H-T/Thor. 27-Hulk. 28-Hercules. 29-H-T/Iron Man. 30-Falcon 1 2 3 5 7 9
31-45,47-50: 31-Iron Fist. 32-H-T/Son of Satan. 33-Nighthawk. 34-Valkyrie. 35-H-T/Dr. Strange. 36-Frankenstein. 37-Man-Wolf. 38-Beast. 39-H-T. 40-Sons of the Tiger/H-T. 41-Scarlet Witch. 42-The Vision. 43-Dr. Doom; retells origin. 44-Moondragon. 45-Killraven. 47-Thing. 48-Iron Man; last 25¢ issue. 49-Dr. Strange; Iron Man app. 50-Iron Man; Dr. Strange app. 6.00
44-48-(30¢-c variants, limited distribution)(4-8/76) 2 4 6 11 14 18
46-Spider-Man/Deathlok team-up 1 2 3 4 5 7

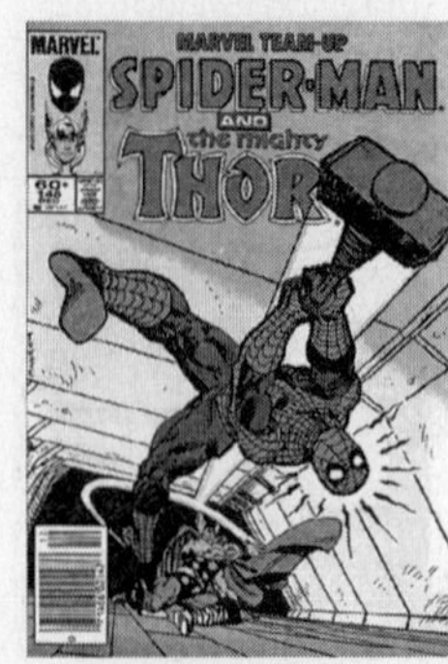

Marvel Team-Up #148 © MAR

Marvel Triple Action #45 © MAR

Marvel Two-In-One #42 © MAR

GD VG FN VF VF/NM NM-
2.0 4.0 6.0 8.0 9.0 9.2

51,52,56,57: 51-Iron Man; Dr. Strange app. 52-Capt. America. 56-Daredevil. 57-Black Widow 5.00

53-Hulk; Woodgod & X-Men app., 1st Byrne-a on X-Men (1/77) 3 6 9 18 24 30

54,55,58-60: 54,59,60: 54-Hulk; Woodgod app. 59-Yellowjacket/The Wasp. 60-The Wasp (Byrne-a in all). 55-Warlock-c/story; Byrne-a. 58-Ghost Rider 1 2 3 4 5 7

58-62-(35¢-c variants, limited distribution)(6-10/77) 2 4 6 11 14 18

61-70: All Byrne-a; 61-H-T. 62-Ms. Marvel; last 30¢ issue. 63-Iron Fist. 64-Daughters of the Dragon. 65-Capt. Britain (1st U.S. app.). 66-Capt. Britain; 1st app. Arcade. 67-Tigra; Kraven the Hunter app. 68-Man-Thing. 69-Havok (from X-Men). 70-Thor 6.00

71-74,76-78,80: 71-Falcon. 72-Iron Man. 73-Daredevil. 74-Not Ready for Prime Time Players (Belushi). 76-Dr. Strange. 77-Ms. Marvel. 78-Wonder Man. 80-Dr. Strange/Clea; last 35¢ issue 4.00

75,79,81: Byrne-a(p). 75-Power Man; Cage app. 79-Mary Jane Watson as Red Sonja; Clark Kent cameo (1 panel, 3/79). 81-Death of Satana 5.00

82-99: 82-Black Widow. 83-Nick Fury. 84-Shang-Chi. 86-Guardians of the Galaxy. 89-Nightcrawler (from X-Men). 91-Ghost Rider. 92-Hawkeye. 93-Werewolf by Night. 94-Spider-Man vs. The Shroud. 95-Mockingbird (intro.); Nick Fury app. 96-Howard the Duck; last 40¢ issue. 97-Spider-Woman/ Hulk. 98-Black Widow. 99-Machine Man. 85-Shang-Chi/ Black Widow/Nick Fury. 87-Black Panther. 88-Invisible Girl. 90-Beast 3.00

100-(Double-size)-Fantastic Four/Storm/Black Panther; origin/1st app. Karma, one of the New Mutants; origin Storm; X-Men x-over; Miller-c/a(p); Byrne-a (on X-Men app. only) 6.00

101-116: 101-Nighthawk(Ditko-a). 102-Doc Samson. 103-Ant-Man. 104-Hulk/Ka-Zar. 105-Hulk/Powerman/Iron Fist. 106-Capt. America. 107-She-Hulk. 108-Paladin; Dazzler cameo. 109-Dazzler; Paladin app. 110-Iron Man. 111-Devil-Slayer. 112-King Kull; last 50¢ issue. 113-Quasar. 114-Falcon. 115-Thor. 116-Valkyrie 3.00

117-Wolverine-c/story 1 3 4 6 8 10

118-140,142-149: 118-Professor X; Wolverine app. (4 pgs.); X-Men cameo. 119-Gargoyle. 120-Dominic Fortune. 121-Human Torch. 122-Man-Thing. 123-Daredevil. 124-The Beast. 125-Tigra. 126-Hulk & Powerman/Son of Satan. 127-The Watcher. 128-Capt. America; Spider-Man/Capt. America photo-c. 129-The Vision. 130-Scarlet Witch. 131-Frogman. 132-Mr. Fantastic. 133-Fantastic Four. 134-Jack of Hearts. 135-Kitty Pryde; X-Men cameo. 136-Wonder Man. 137-Aunt May/Franklin Richards. 138-Sandman. 139-Nick Fury. 140-Black Widow. 142-Capt. Marvel. 143-Starfox. 144-Moon Knight. 145-Iron Man. 146-Nomad. 147-Human Torch; Spider-Man back to old costume. 148-Thor. 149-Cannonball 2.50

141-Daredevil; SpM/Black Widow app. (Spidey in new black costume; ties w/ Amazing Spider-Man #252 for 1st black costume) 1 3 4 6 8 10

150-X-Men ($1.00, double-size); B. Smith-c 5.00

Annual 1 (1976)-Spider-Man/X-Men (early app.) 3 6 9 18 23 28

Annual 2 (1979)-Spider-Man/Hulk 1 2 3 5 6 8

Annuals 3,4: 3 (1980)-Hulk/Power Man/Machine Man/Iron Fist; Miller-c(p). 4 (1981)-Spider-Man /Daredevil/Moon Knight/Power Man/Iron Fist; brief origins of each; Miller-c; Miller scripts on Daredevil 5.00

Annuals 5-7: 5 (1982)-SpM/The Thing/Scarlet Witch/Dr. Strange/Quasar. 6 (1983)-Spider-Man/ New Mutants (early app.), Cloak & Dagger. 7(1984)-Alpha Flight; Byrne-c(i) 4.00

NOTE: ***Art Adams*** *c-141p.* ***Austin*** *a-79i; c-76i, 79i, 96i, 101i, 112i, 130i.* ***Bolle*** *a-9i.* ***Byrne*** *a(p)-53-55, 59-70, 75, 79, 100; c-68p, 70p, 72p, 75, 76p, 79p, 129i, 133i.* ***Colan*** *a-87p.* ***Ditko*** *a-101.* ***Kane*** *a(p)-4-6, 13, 14, 16-19, 23; c(p)-4, 13, 14, 17-19, 23, 25, 26, 32-35, 37, 41, 44, 45, 47, 53, 54.* ***Miller*** *a-100p; c-95p, 99p, 100p, 102p, 106.* ***Mooney*** *a-2i, 7i, 8, 10p, 11p, 16i, 24-31p, 72, 93i, Annual 5i.* ***Nasser*** *a-89p; c-101p.* ***Simonson*** *c-99i, 148.* ***Paul Smith*** *c-131, 132.* ***Starlin*** *c-27.* ***Sutton*** *a-93p. "H-T" means Human Torch; "SpM" means Spider-Man; "S-M" means Sub-Mariner.*

MARVEL TEAM-UP (2nd Series)
Marvel Comics: Sept, 1997 - No. 11, July, 1998 ($1.99)

1-11: 1-Spider-Man team-ups begin, Generation x-app. 2-Hercules-c/app.; two covers. 3-Sandman. 4-Man-Thing. 7-Blade. 8-Namor team-ups begin, Dr. Strange app. 9-Capt. America. 10-Thing. 11-Iron Man 2.25

MARVEL: THE LOST GENERATION
Marvel Comics: No. 12, Mar, 2000 - No. 1, Feb, 2001 ($2.99, issue #s go in reverse)

1-12-Stern-s/Byrne-s/a; untold story of The First Line. 5-Thor app. 3.00

MARVEL TREASURY EDITION
Marvel Comics Group/Whitman #17,18: 1974; #2, Dec, 1974 - #28, 1981 ($1.50/$2.50, 100 pgs., oversized, new-a &-r)(Also see Amazing Spider-Man, The, Marvel Spec. Ed. Feat.--, Savage Fists of Kung Fu, Superman Vs. , & 2001, A Space Odyssey)

1-Spectacular Spider-Man; story-r/Marvel Super-Heroes #14; Romita-c/a(r); G. Kane, Ditko-r; Green Goblin/Hulk-r 5 10 15 36 48 60

1-1,000 numbered copies signed by Stan Lee & John Romita on front-c & sold thru mail for $5.00; these were the1st 1,000 copies off the press 11 22 33 75 110 145

2-10: 2-Fantastic Four-r/F.F. 6,11,48-50(Silver Surfer). 3-The Mighty Thor-r/Thor #125-130. 4-Conan the Barbarian; Barry Smith-c/a(r)/Conan #11. 5-The Hulk (origin-r/Hulk #3). 6-Dr. Strange. 7-Mighty Avengers. 8-Giant Superhero Holiday Grab-Bag; Spider-Man, Hulk, Nick Fury. 9-Giant; Super-hero Team-up. 10-Thor; r/Thor #154-157 3 6 9 16 20 24

11-20: 11-Fantastic Four. 12-Howard the Duck (r/#H. the Duck #1 & G.S. Man-Thing #4,5) plus new Defenders story. 13-Giant Super-Hero Holiday Grab-Bag. 14-The Sensational Spider-Man; r/1st Morbius from Amazing S-M #101,102 plus #100 & r/Not Brand Echh #6. 15-Conan; B. Smith, Neal Adams-i; r/Conan #24. 16-The Defenders (origin) & Valkyrie; r/Defenders #1,4,13,14. 17-The Hulk. 18-The Astonishing Spider-Man; r/Spider-Man's 1st team-ups with Iron Fist, The X-Men, Ghost Rider & Werewolf by Night; inside back-c has photos from 1978 Spider-Man TV show. 19-Conan the Barbarian. 20-Hulk 2 4 6 10 13 16

21-25,27: 21-Fantastic Four. 22-Spider-Man. 23-Conan. 24-Rampaging Hulk. 25-Spider-Man vs. The Hulk. 27-Spider-Man 2 4 6 10 13 16

26-The Hulk; 6 pg. new Wolverine/Hercules-s 2 4 6 12 16 20

28-Spider-Man/Superman; (origin of each) 4 8 12 27 36 45

NOTE: *Reprints-2, 3, 5, 7-9, 13, 14, 16, 17.* ***Neal Adams*** *a(i)-6, 15.* ***Brunner*** *a-6, 12; c-6.* ***Buscema*** *a-15, 19, 28; c-28.* ***Colan*** *a-6r; c-12p.* ***Ditko*** *a-1, 6.* ***Gil Kane*** *c-16p.* ***Kirby*** *a-1-3, 5, 7, 9-11; c-7.* ***Perez*** *a-26.* ***Romita*** *c-1, 5.* ***B. Smith*** *a-4, 15, 19; c-4, 19.*

MARVEL TREASURY OF OZ FEATURING THE MARVELOUS LAND OF OZ
Marvel Comics Group: 1975 ($1.50, oversized) (See MGM's Marvelous...)

1-Buscema-a; Romita-c 2 4 6 14 18 22

MARVEL TREASURY SPECIAL (Also see 2001: A Space Odyssey)
Marvel Comics Group: 1974; 1976 ($1.50, oversized, 84 pgs.)

Vol. 1-Spider-Man, Torch, Sub-Mariner, Avengers "Giant Superhero Holiday Grab-Bag"; Wood, Colan/Everett, plus 2 Kirby-r; reprints Hulk vs. Thing from Fantastic Four #25,26 2 4 6 14 18 22

Vol. 1-... Featuring Captain America's Bicentennial Battles (6/76)-Kirby-a; B. Smith inks, 11 pgs. 3 6 9 16 20 24

MARVEL TRIPLE ACTION (See Giant-Size...)
Marvel Comics Group: Feb, 1972 - No. 24, Mar, 1975; No. 25, Aug, 1975 - No. 47, Apr, 1979

1-(25¢ giant, 52 pgs.)-Dr. Doom, Silver Surfer, The Thing begin, end #4 ('66 reprints from Fantastic Four) 2 4 6 14 18 22

2-5 2 4 6 8 10 12

6-10 1 2 3 4 5 7

11-47: 45-r/X-Men #45. 46-r/Avengers #53(X-Men) 4.00

29,30-(30¢-c variants, limited distribution)(5,7/76) 6.00

36,37-(35¢-c variants, limited distribution)(7,9/77) 6.00

NOTE: *#5-44, 46, 47 reprint Avengers #11 thru ?. #40-r/Avengers #48(1st Black Knight).* ***Buscema*** *a(r)-35p, 36p, 38p, 39p, 41, 42, 43p, 44p, 46p, 47p.* ***Ditko*** *a-2r; c-47.* ***Kirby*** *a(r)-1-4p; c-1-4, 9-19, 22, 24, 29.* ***Starlin*** *c-7.* ***Tuska*** *a(r)-40p, 43i, 46i, 47i. #2 through #17 are 20¢-c.*

MARVEL TWO-IN-ONE (...Featuring ... #82 on; also see The Thing)
Marvel Comics Group: January, 1974 - No. 100, June, 1983

1-Thing team-ups begin; Man-Thing 6 12 18 40 55 70

2,3: 2-Sub-Mariner; last 20¢ issue. 3-Daredevil 3 6 9 16 20 25

4-6: 4-Capt. America. 5-Guardians of the Galaxy (9/74, 2nd app.?). 6-Dr. Strange (11/74) 2 4 6 11 14 18

7,9,10 2 4 6 8 10 12

8-Early Ghost Rider app. (3/75) 2 4 6 9 11 14

11-14,19,20: 13-Power Man. 14-Son of Satan (early app.) 1 2 3 5 6 8

15-18-(Regular 25¢ editions)(5-7/76) 17-Spider-Man. 1 2 3 5 6 8

15-18-(30¢-c variants, limited distribution) 2 4 6 11 14 18

21-29: 27-Deathlok. 29-Master of Kung Fu; Spider-Woman cameo 5.00

28,29,31-(35¢-c variants, limited distribution) 2 4 6 11 14 18

30-2nd full app. Spider-Woman (see Marvel Spotlight #32 for 1st app.) 1 2 3 5 7 9

30-(35¢-c variant, limited distribution)(8/77) 2 4 6 12 16 20

31-40: 31-33-Spider-Woman. 39-Vision 5.00

41,42,44,45,47-49: 42-Capt. America. 45-Capt. Marvel 3.00

43,50,53,55-Byrne-a(p). 53-Quasar(7/79, 2nd app.) 5.00

46-Thing battles Hulk-c/story 1 2 3 5 7 9

51-The Beast, Nick Fury, Ms. Marvel; Miller-p 6.00

52-Moon Knight app. 3.00

54-Death of Deathlok: Byrne-a 1 2 3 5 7 9

56-60,64-74,76-79,81,82: 60-Intro. Impossible Woman. 68-Angel. 69-Guardians of the Galaxy. 71-1st app. Maelstrom. 76-Iceman 3.00

61-63: 61-Starhawk (from Guardians); "The Coming of Her" storyline begins, ends #63; cover similar to F.F. #67 (Him-c). 62-Moondragon; Thanos & Warlock cameo in flashback; Starhawk app. 63-Warlock revived shortly; Starhawk & Moondragon app. 4.00

75-Avengers (52 pgs.) 4.00

80,90,100: 80-Ghost Rider. 90-Spider-Man. 100-Double size, Byrne-s 4.00

83-89,91-99: 83-Sasquatch. 84-Alpha Flight app. 93-Jocasta dies. 96-X-Men-c & cameo 3.00

Annual 1(1976, 52 pgs.)-Thing/Liberty Legion; Kirby-c 1 3 4 6 8 10

Annual 2(1977, 52 pgs.)-Thing/Spider-Man; 2nd death of Thanos; end of Thanos saga;

Marvel Universe #1 © MAR

Mary Marvel Comics #13 © FAW

The Masked Man #11 © ECL

	GD 2.0	VG 4.0	FN 6.0	VF 8.0	VF/NM 9.0	NM- 9.2

Warlock app.; Starlin-c/a 3 7 10 21 28 35
Annual 3,4 (1978-79, 52 pgs.): 3-Nova. 4-Black Bolt 5.00
Annual 5-7 (1980-82, 52 pgs.): 5-Hulk. 6-1st app. American Eagle. 7-The Thing/Champion; Sasquatch, Colossus app.; X-Men cameo (1 pg.) 4.00
NOTE: ***Austin*** *c(i)-42, 54, 56, 58, 61, 63, 66.* ***John Buscema*** *a-30p, 45; c-30p.* ***Byrne*** *(p)-43, 50, 53-55; c-43, 53p, 56p, 98i, 99i.* ***Gil Kane*** *a-1p, 2p; c(p)-1-3, 9, 11, 14, 28.* ***Kirby*** *c-10, 12, 19p, 20, 25, 27.* ***Mooney*** *a-18i, 38i, 90i.* ***Nasser*** *a-70p.* ***Perez*** *a(p)-56-58, 60, 64, 65; c(p)-32, 33, 42, 50-52, 54, 55, 57, 58, 61-66, 70.* ***Roussos*** *a-Annual 1i.* ***Simonson*** *c-43i, 97p, Annual 6i.* ***Starlin*** *c-6, Annual 1.* ***Tuska*** *a-6p.*

MARVEL UNIVERSE (See Official Handbook Of The...)

MARVEL UNIVERSE (Title on variant covers for newsstand editions of some 2001 Marvel titles. See indicia for actual titles and issue numbers)

MARVEL UNIVERSE
Marvel Comics: June, 1998 - No. 7, Dec, 1998 ($2.99/$1.99)
1-($2.99)-Invaders stories from WW2; Stern-s 3.00
2-7-($1.99): 2-Two covers. 4-7-Monster Hunters; Manley-a/Stern-s 2.25

MARVEL UNIVERSE: MILLENNIAL VISIONS
Marvel Comics: Feb, 2002 ($3.99, one-shot)
1-Pin-ups by various; wraparound-c by JH Williams & Gray 4.00

MARVEL UNIVERSE: THE END (Also see Infinity Abyss)
Marvel Comics: May, 2003 - No. 6, Aug, 2003 ($3.50/$2.99, limited series)
1-($3.50)-Thanos, X-Men, FF, Avengers, Spider-Man, Daredevil app.; Starlin-s/a(p) 3.50
2-6-($2.99) Akhenaten, Eternity, Living Tribunal app. 3.00
Thanos Vol. 3: Marvel Universe - The End (2003, $16.99) r/#1-6 17.00

MARVEL UNLIMITED (Title on variant covers for newsstand editions of some 2001 Daredevil issues. See indicia for actual titles and issue numbers)

MARVEL VALENTINE SPECIAL
Marvel Comics: Mar, 1997 ($2.99, one-shot)
1-Valentine stories w/Spider-Man, Daredevil, Cyclops, Phoenix 3.00

MARVEL VERSUS DC (See DC Versus Marvel) (Also see Amazon, Assassins, Bruce Wayne: Agent of S.H.I.E.L.D., Bullets & Bracelets, Doctor Strangefate, JLX, Legend of the Dark Claw, Magneto & The Magnetic Men, Speed Demon, Spider-Boy, Super Soldier, & X-Patrol)
Marvel Comics: No. 2, 1996 - No. 3, 1996 ($3.95, limited series)
2,3: 2-Peter David script. 3-Ron Marz script; Dan Jurgens-a(p). 1st app. of Super Soldier, Spider-Boy, Dr. Doomsday, Doctor Strangefate, The Dark Claw, Nightcreeper, Amazon, Wraith & others. Storyline continues in Amalgam books. 4.00

MARVEL VISIONARIES
Marvel Comics: 2002 - Present (various prices, TPB)
...: Gil Kane (8/02, $24.95) r/Amazing Spider-Man #99, Marvel Premiere #1,#15, TOA #76 & others; plus sketch pages and a cover gallery 25.00
...: Jim Steranko (9/02, $14.95) r/Captain America #110,111,113; X-Men #50,51 and stories from Tower of Shadows #1 and Our Love Story #5; plus a cover gallery 15.00

MARVEL X-MEN COLLECTION, THE
Marvel Comics: Jan, 1994 - No. 3, Mar, 1994 ($2.95, limited series)
1-3-r/X-Men trading cards by Jim Lee 3.00

MARVEL - YEAR IN REVIEW (Magazine)
Marvel Comics: 1989 - No. 3, 1991 (52 pgs.)
1-3: 1-Spider-Man-c by McFarlane. 2-Capt. America-c. 3-X-Men/Wolverine-c 5.00

MARVILLE
Marvel Comics: Nov, 2002 - No. 7, Jul, 2003 ($2.25, limited series)
1-6-Satire on DC/AOL-Time-Warner; Jemas-a/Bright-a/Horn-c 2.25
1-($3.95) Variant foil cover by Udon Studios; bonus sketch pages and Jemas afterword 4.00
7-($2.99) Intro. to Epic Comics line with submission guidelines 3.00

MARVIN MOUSE
Atlas Comics (BPC): September, 1957
1-Everett-c/a; Maneely-a 13 26 39 74 100 125

MARY JANE & SNIFFLES (See Looney Tunes)
Dell Publishing Co.: No. 402, June, 1952 - No. 474, June, 1953
Four Color 402 (#1) 9 18 27 60 85 110
Four Color 474 8 16 24 55 78 100

MARY MARVEL COMICS (Monte Hale #29 on) (Also see Captain Marvel #18, Marvel Family, Shazam, & Wow Comics)
Fawcett Publications: Dec, 1945 - No. 28, Sept, 1948
1-Captain Marvel introduces Mary on-c; intro/origin Georgia Sivana
200 400 600 1250 1875 2500
2 76 152 228 475 713 950
3,4: 3-New logo 53 106 159 318 479 640
5-8: 8-Bulletgirl x-over in Mary Marvel; X-Mas-c 40 80 120 240 345 450
9,10 38 76 114 219 310 400
11-20 25 50 75 144 198 255
21-28: 28-Western-c 21 42 63 118 164 210

MARY POPPINS (See Movie Comics & Walt Disney Showcase No. 17)

MARY SHELLEY'S FRANKENSTEIN
Topps Comics: Oct, 1994 - Jan, 1995 ($2.95, limited series)
1-4-polybagged w/3 trading cards 3.00
1-4 ($2.50)-Newstand ed. 2.50

MARY WORTH (See Harvey Comics Hits #55 & Love Stories of...)
Argo: March, 1956 (Also see Romantic Picture Novelettes)
1 8 16 24 43 54 65

MASK (TV)
DC Comics: Dec, 1985 - No. 4, Mar, 1986; Feb, 1987 - No. 9, Oct, 1987
1-4; 1-9 (2nd series)-Sat. morning TV show. 2.50

MASK, THE (Also see Mayhem)
Dark Horse Comics: Aug, 1991 - No. 4, Oct, 1991; No. 0, Dec, 1991 ($2.50, 36 pgs., limited series)
1-4: 1-1st app. Lt. Kellaway as The Mask (see Dark Horse Presents #10 for 1st app.) 5.00
0-(12/91, B&W, 56 pgs.)-r/Mayhem #1-4 4.00
...: HUNT FOR GREEN OCTOBER July, 1995 - Oct, 1995 ($2.50, lim. series)
1-4-Evan Dorkin scripts 2.50
.../ MARSHALL LAW Feb, 1998 - No. 2, Mar, 1998 ($2.95, lim. series)
1,2-Mills-s/O'Neill-a 3.00
...: OFFICIAL MOVIE ADAPTATION July, 1994 - Aug, 1994 ($2.50, lim. series)
1,2 2.50
... RETURNS Oct, 1992 - No. 4, Mar, 1993 ($2.50, limited series)
1-4 4.00
... SOUTHERN DISCOMFORT Mar, 1996 - No. 4, July, 1996 ($2.50, lim. series)
1-4 2.50
... STRIKES BACK Feb, 1995 - No. 5, Jun, 1995 ($2.50, limited series)
1-5 2.50
... SUMMER VACATION July, 1995 ($10.95, one shot, hard-c)
1-nn-Rick Geary-c/a 11.00
... TOYS IN THE ATTIC Aug, 1998 - No. 4, Nov, 1998 ($2.95, limited series)
1-4-Fingerman-s 3.00
... VIRTUAL SURREALITY July, 1997 ($2.95, one shot)
nn-Mignola, Aragonés, and others-s/a 3.00
... WORLD TOUR Dec, 1995 - No. 4, Mar, 1996 ($2.50, limited series)
1-4: 3-X & Ghost-c/app. 2.50

MASK COMICS
Rural Home Publ.: Feb-Mar, 1945 - No. 2, Apr-May, 1945; No. 2, Fall, 1945
1-Classic L. B. Cole Satan-c/a; Palais-a 280 560 840 1750 2625 3500
2-(Scarce)-Classic L. B. Cole Satan-c; Black Rider, The Boy Magician, & The Collector app.
176 352 528 1100 1650 2200
2-(Fall, 1945)-No publ.-same as regular #2; L. B. Cole-c
140 280 420 875 1313 1750

MASKED BANDIT, THE
Avon Periodicals: 1952
nn-Kinstler-a 17 34 51 95 130 165

MASKED MAN, THE
Eclipse Comics: 12/84 - #10, 4/86; #11, 10/87; #12, 4/88 ($1.75/$2.00, color/B&W #9 on, Baxter paper)
1-12: 1-Origin retold. 3-Origin Aphid-Man; begin $2.00-c 2.25

MASKED MARVEL (See Keen Detective Funnies)
Centaur Publications: Sept, 1940 - No. 3, Dec, 1940
1-The Masked Marvel begins 168 336 504 1050 1575 2100
2,3: 2-Gustavson, Tarpe Mills-a 112 224 336 700 1050 1400

MASKED RAIDER, THE (Billy The Kid #9 on; Frontier Scout, Daniel Boone #10-13) (Also see Blue Bird)
Charlton Comics: June, 1955 - No. 8, July, 1957; No. 14, Aug, 1958 - No. 30, June, 1961
1-Masked Raider & Talon the Golden Eagle begin; painted-c
13 26 39 74 100 125
2 8 16 24 43 54 65
3-8,15: 8-Billy The Kid app. 15-Williamson-a, 7 pgs. 6 12 18 31 38 45

Masks: Too Hot For TV! #1 © WSP

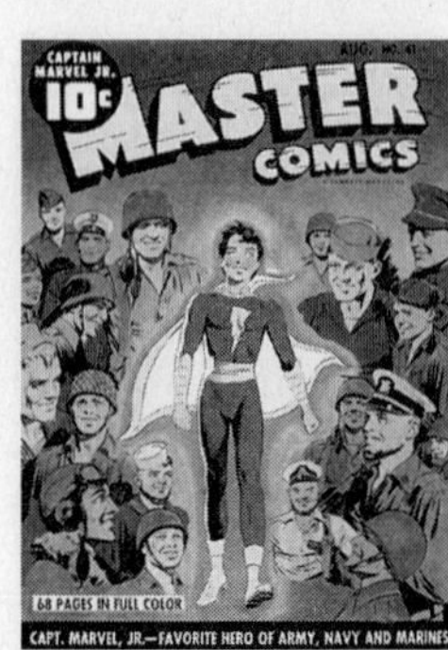

Master Comics #41 © FAW

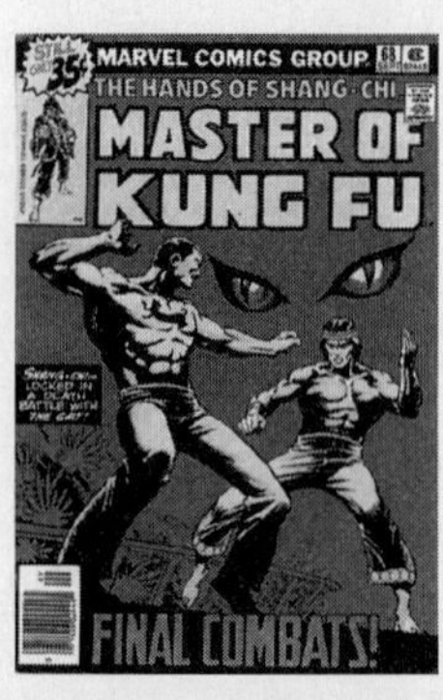

Master of Kung Fu #68 © MAR

GD VG FN VF VF/NM NM-
2.0 4.0 6.0 8.0 9.0 9.2

14,16-30: 22-Rocky Lane app. 5 10 15 24 30 35

MASKED RANGER
Premier Magazines: Apr, 1954 - No. 9, Aug, 1955
1-The Masked Ranger, his horse Streak, & The Crimson Avenger (origin) begin, end #9; Woodbridge/Frazetta-a 40 80 120 240 345 450
2,3 14 28 42 79 107 135
4-8-All Woodbridge-a. 5-Jesse James by Woodbridge. 6-Billy The Kid by Woodbridge. 7-Wild Bill Hickok by Woodbridge. 8-Jim Bowie's Life Story 15 30 45 84 115 145
9-Torres-a; Wyatt Earp by Woodbridge; Says Death of Masked Ranger on-c 16 32 48 89 122 155
NOTE: *Check a-1. **Woodbridge** c/a-1, 4-9.*

MASK OF DR. FU MANCHU, THE (See Dr. Fu Manchu)
Avon Periodicals: 1951
1-Sax Rohmer adapt.; Wood-c/a (26 pgs.); Hollingsworth-a 92 184 276 575 863 1150

MASK OF ZORRO, THE
Image Comics: Aug, 1998 - No. 4, Dec, 1998 ($2.95, limited series)
1-4-Movie adapt. Photo variant-c 3.00

MASKS: TOO HOT FOR TV!
DC Comics (WildStorm): Feb, 2004 ($4.95)
1-Short stories by various incl. Thompson, Brubaker, Mahnke, Conner; Fabry-c 5.00

MASQUE OF THE RED DEATH (See Movie Classics)

MASTER COMICS (Combined with Slam Bang Comics #7 on)
Fawcett Publications: Mar, 1940 - No. 133, Apr, 1953 (No. 1-6: oversized issues) (#1-3: 15¢, 52 pgs.; #4-6: 10¢, 36 pgs.; #7-Begin 68 pg. issues)
1-Origin & 1st app. Master Man; The Devil's Dagger, El Carim, Master of Magic, Rick O'Say, Morton Murch, White Rajah, Shipwreck Roberts, Frontier Marshal, Streak Sloan, Mr. Clue begin (all features end #6) 759 1518 2277 5313 8157 11,000
2 228 456 684 1425 2138 2850
3-6: 6-Last Master Man 168 336 504 1050 1575 2100
NOTE: *#1-6 rarely found in near mint or very fine condition due to large-size format.*
7-(10/40)-Bulletman, Zoro, the Mystery Man (ends #22), Lee Granger, Jungle King, & Buck Jones begin; only app. The War Bird & Mark Swift & the Time Retarder; Zoro, Lee Granger, Jungle King & Mark Swift all continue from Slam Bang; Bulletman moves from Nickel 296 592 888 1850 2775 3700
8-The Red Gaucho (ends #13), Captain Venture (ends #22) & The Planet Princess begin 152 304 456 950 1425 1900
9,10: 10-Lee Granger ends 120 240 360 750 1125 1500
11-Origin & 1st app. Minute-Man (2/41) 264 528 792 1650 2475 3300
12 128 256 384 800 1200 1600
13-Origin & 1st app. Bulletgirl; Hitler-c 200 400 600 1250 1875 2500
14-16: 14-Companions Three begins, ends #31 108 216 324 675 1013 1350
17-20: 17-Raboy-a on Bulletman begins. 20-Captain Marvel cameo app. in Bulletman 100 200 300 625 938 1250
21-(12/41; Scarce)-Captain Marvel & Bulletman team up against Capt. Nazi; origin & 1st app. Capt. Marvel Jr's most famous nemesis Captain Nazi who will cause creation of Capt. Marvel Jr. in Whiz #25. Part I of trilogy origin of Capt. Marvel Jr.; 1st Mac Raboy-c for Fawcett; Capt. Nazi-c 504 1008 1512 3528 5414 7300
22-(1/42)-Captain Marvel Jr. moves over from Whiz #25 & teams up with Bulletman against Captain Nazi; part III of trilogy origin of Capt. Marvel Jr. & his 1st cover and adventure 448 896 1344 3136 4818 6500
23-Capt. Marvel Jr. c/stories begin (1st solo story); fights Capt. Nazi by himself. 288 576 864 1800 2700 3600
24,25 96 192 288 600 900 1200
26-28,30-Captain Marvel Jr. vs. Capt. Nazi. 30-Flag-c 85 170 255 531 796 1060
29-Hitler & Hirohito-c 108 216 324 675 1013 1350
31-33,35: 32-Last El Carim & Buck Jones; intro Balbo, the Boy Magician in El Carim story; classic Eagle-c by Raboy. 33-Balbo, the Boy Magician (ends #47), Hopalong Cassidy (ends #49) begins 64 128 192 400 600 800
34-Capt. Marvel Jr. vs. Capt. Nazi-c/story 73 146 219 456 688 920
36-40: 40-Flag-c 60 120 180 375 563 750
41-(8/43)-Bulletman, Capt. Marvel Jr. & Bulletgirl x-over in Minute-Man; only app. Crime Crusaders Club (Capt. Marvel Jr., Minute-Man, Bulletman & Bulletgirl) 64 128 192 400 600 800
42-47,49: 47-Hitler becomes Corpl. Hitler Jr. 49-Last Minute-Man 40 80 120 240 345 450
48-Intro. Bulletboy; Capt. Marvel cameo in Minute-Man 46 92 138 276 413 550
50-Intro Radar & Nyoka the Jungle Girl & begin series (5/44); Radar also intro in Captain Marvel #35 (same date); Capt. Marvel x-over in Radar; origin Radar; Capt. Marvel & Capt. Marvel, Jr. introduce Radar on-c 43 86 129 258 364 470
51-58 24 48 72 138 194 250
59-62: Nyoka serial "Terrible Tiara" in all; 61-Capt. Marvel Jr. 1st meets Uncle Marvel 27 54 81 153 214 275
63-80 19 38 57 106 146 185
81,83-87,89-91,95-99: 88-Hopalong Cassidy begins (ends #94). 95-Tom Mix begins (cover only in #123, ends #133) 16 32 48 92 126 160
82,88,92-94-Krigstein-a 17 34 51 98 134 170
100 17 34 51 98 134 170
101-106-Last Bulletman (not in #104) 15 30 45 86 118 150
107-120: 118-Mary Marvel 14 28 42 81 111 140
121-131-(lower print run): 123-Tom Mix-c only 15 30 45 86 118 150
132-B&W and color illos in **POP**; last Nyoka 16 32 48 89 122 155
133-Bill Battle app. 20 40 60 112 156 200
NOTE: ***Mac Raboy** a-15-39, 40(part), 42, 58. c-21-49, 51, 52, 54, 56, 58, 68(part), 69(part). Bulletman c-7-11, 13(half), 15, 18(part), 19, 20, 21(w/Capt. Marvel & Capt. Nazi), 22(w/Capt. Marvel, Jr.). Capt. Marvel, Jr. c-23-133. Master Man c-1-6. Minute Man c-12, 13(half), 14, 16, 17, 18(part).*

MASTER DARQUE
Acclaim Comics (Valiant): Feb, 1998 ($3.95)
1-Manco-a/Christina Z.-s 4.00

MASTER DETECTIVE
Super Comics: 1964 (Reprints)
17-r/Criminals on the Loose V4 #2; r/Young King Cole #?; McWilliams-r 2 4 6 9 11 14

MASTER OF KUNG FU (Formerly Special Marvel Edition; see Deadly Hands of Kung Fu & Giant-Size...)
Marvel Comics Group: No. 17, April, 1974 - No. 125, June, 1983
17-Starlin-a; intro Black Jack Tarr; 3rd Shang-Chi (ties w/Deadly Hands #1) 3 6 9 16 20 25
18,20 2 4 6 8 10 12
19-Man-Thing-c/story 2 4 6 10 12 15
21-23,25-30 1 2 3 5 7 9
24-Starlin, Simonson-a 1 2 3 6 8 10
31-50: 33-1st Leiko Wu. 43-Last 25¢ issue 5.00
39-43-(30¢-c variants, limited distribution)(5-7/76) 2 4 6 10 12 15
51-99 4.00
53-57-(35¢-c variants, limited distribution)(6-10/77) 2 4 6 10 12 15
100,118,125-Double size 5.00
101-117,119-124 3.00
Annual 1(4/76)-Iron Fist app. 2 4 6 12 16 20
NOTE: ***Austin** c-63i, 74i. **Buscema** c-44p. **Gulacy** a(p)-18-20, 22, 25, 29-31, 33-35, 38, 39, 40(p&i), 42-50, 53r(#20); c-51, 55, 64, 67. **Gil Kane** c(p)-20, 38, 39, 42, 45, 59, 63. **Nebres** c-73i. **Starlin** a-17p, 24; c-54. **Sutton** a-42i. #53 reprints #20.*

MASTER OF KUNG-FU, SHANG-CHI:... (2002 series, see Shang Chi:...)

MASTER OF KUNG-FU: BLEEDING BLACK
Marvel Comics: Feb, 1991 ($2.95, 84 pgs., one-shot)
1-The Return of Shang-Chi 3.00

MASTER OF THE WORLD
Dell Publishing Co.: No. 1157, July, 1961
Four Color 1157-Movie 6 12 18 43 59 75

MASTERS OF TERROR (Magazine)
Marvel Comics Group: July, 1975 - No. 2, Sept, 1975 (B&W) (All reprints)
1-Brunner, Barry Smith-a; Morrow/Steranko-c; Starlin-a(p); Gil Kane-a 2 4 6 11 14 18
2-Reese, Kane, Mayerik-a; Adkins/Steranko-c 2 4 6 9 11 14

MASTERS OF THE UNIVERSE (See DC Comics Presents #47 for 1st app.)
DC Comics: Dec, 1982 - No. 3, Feb, 1983 (Mini-series)
1 6.00
2,3: 2-Origin He-Man & Ceril 4.00
NOTE: ***Alcala** a-1i, 2i. **Tuska** a-1-3p; c-1-3p. #2 has 75 & 95 cent cover price.*

MASTERS OF THE UNIVERSE (Comic Album)
Western Publishing Co.: 1984 (8-1/2x11", $2.95, 64 pgs.)
11362-Based on Mattel toy & cartoon 2 4 6 9 11 14

MASTERS OF THE UNIVERSE
Star Comics/Marvel #7 on: May 1986 - No. 13, May, 1988 (75¢/$1.00)
1 5.00
2-11: 8-Begin $1.00-c 3.00
12-Death of He-Man (1st Marvel app.) 1 2 3 4 5 7

Masters of the Universe V2#1 © Mattel

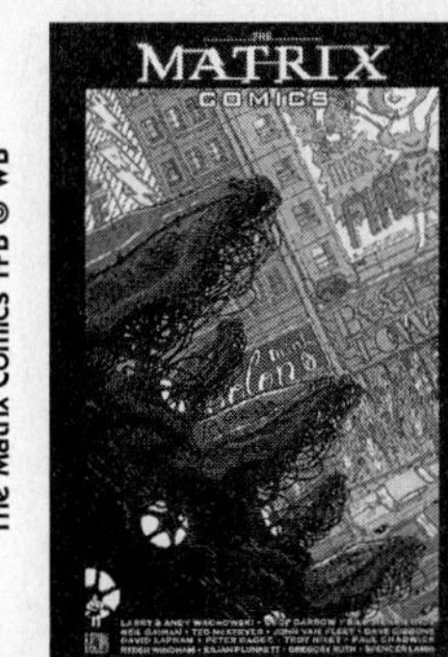

The Matrix Comics TPB © WB

Mazie #8 © Magazine Publ.

	GD 2.0	VG 4.0	FN 6.0	VF 8.0	VF/NM 9.0	NM- 9.2
13-Return of He-Man & death of Skeletor	1	2	3	4	5	7
The Motion Picture (11/87, $2.00)-Tuska-p						4.00

MASTERS OF THE UNIVERSE
Image Comics: Nov, 2002 - No. 4, March, 2003 ($2.95, limited series)

	GD 2.0	VG 4.0	FN 6.0	VF 8.0	VF/NM 9.0	NM- 9.2
1-($2.95) Two covers by Santalucia and Campbell; Santalucia-a						3.00
1-($5.95) Variant-c by Norem w/gold foil logo						6.00
2-4($2.95) 2-Two covers by Santalucia and Manapul. 3,4-Two covers						3.00
TPB (CrossGen, 2003, $9.95, 8-1/4" x 5-1/2") digest-sized reprints #1-4						10.00

MASTERS OF THE UNIVERSE (Volume 2)
Image Comics: March, 2003 - Present ($2.95)

	GD 2.0	VG 4.0	FN 6.0	VF 8.0	VF/NM 9.0	NM- 9.2
1-6-($2.95) 1-Santalucia-c. 2-Two covers by Santalucia & JJ Kirby						3.00
1-($5.95) Wraparound variant-c by Struzan w/silver foil logo						6.00
3,4-($5.95) Wraparound variant holofoil-c. 3-By Edwards 4-By Boris Vallejo & Julie Bell						6.00

MASTERS OF THE UNIVERSE...
CrossGen Comics

	GD 2.0	VG 4.0	FN 6.0	VF 8.0	VF/NM 9.0	NM- 9.2
...Rise of the Snake-Men (Nov, 2003 - No. 3, $2.95) Meyers-a						3.00
...The Power of Fear (12/03, $2.95, one-shot) Santalucia-a						3.00

MASTERS OF THE UNIVERSE, ICONS OF EVIL
Image Comics/CrossGen Comics: Jun, 2003 - Present ($4.95, one-shots)

	GD 2.0	VG 4.0	FN 6.0	VF 8.0	VF/NM 9.0	NM- 9.2
...Beastman -(Image) Origin of Beast Man; Tony Moore-a						5.00
...Mer-Man -(CrossGen)						5.00
...Trapjaw -(CrossGen)						5.00
...Tri-Klops -(CrossGen) Walker-c						5.00

MASTERWORKS SERIES OF GREAT COMIC BOOK ARTISTS, THE
Sea Gate Dist./DC Comics: May, 1983 - No. 3, Dec, 1983 (Baxter paper)

	GD 2.0	VG 4.0	FN 6.0	VF 8.0	VF/NM 9.0	NM- 9.2
1-3: 1,2-Shining Knight by Frazetta r-/Adventure. 2-Tomahawk by Frazetta-r. 3-Wrightson-c/a(r)						5.00

MATRIX COMICS, THE (Movie)
Burlyman Entertainment: 2003 ($21.95, trade paperback)

	GD 2.0	VG 4.0	FN 6.0	VF 8.0	VF/NM 9.0	NM- 9.2
nn-Short stories by various incl. Wachowskis, Darrow, Gaiman, Sienkiewicz, Bagge						22.00

MATT SLADE GUNFIGHTER (Kid Slade Gunfighter #5 on; See Western Gunfighters)
Atlas Comics (SPI): May, 1956 - No. 4, Nov, 1956

	GD 2.0	VG 4.0	FN 6.0	VF 8.0	VF/NM 9.0	NM- 9.2
1-Intro Matt & horse Eagle; Williamson/Torres-a	21	42	63	118	164	210
2-Williamson-a	13	26	39	74	100	125
3,4	10	20	30	58	77	95

*NOTE: **Maneely** a-1, 3, 4; c-1, 2, 4. **Roth** a-2-4. **Severin** a-1, 3, 4. **Maneely** c/a-1. Issue #s stamped on cover after printing.*

MAUS: A SURVIVOR'S TALE (First graphic novel to win a Pulitzer Prize)
Pantheon Books: 1986, 1991 (B&W)

	GD 2.0	VG 4.0	FN 6.0	VF 8.0	VF/NM 9.0	NM- 9.2
Vol. 1-(...: My Father Bleeds History)(1986) Art Spiegelman-s/a; recounts stories of Spiegelman's father in 1930s-40s Nazi-occupied Poland; collects first six stories serialized in Raw Magazine from 1980-1985						20.00
Vol. 2-(...: And Here My Troubles Began)(1991)						20.00
Complete Maus Survivor's Tale -HC Vols. 1& 2 w/slipcase						35.00
Hardcover Vol. 1 (1991)						24.00
Hardcover Vol. 2 (1991)						24.00
TPB (1992, $14.00) Vols. 1& 2						14.00

MAVERICK (TV)
Dell Publishing Co.: No. 892, 4/58 - No. 19, 4-6/62 (All have photo-c)

	GD 2.0	VG 4.0	FN 6.0	VF 8.0	VF/NM 9.0	NM- 9.2
Four Color 892 (#1)-James Garner photo-c begin	26	52	78	189	275	360
Four Color 930,945,962,980,1005 (6-8/59): 945-James Garner/Jack Kelly photo-c begin	12	24	36	82	121	160
7 (10-12/59) - 14: Last Garner/Kelly-c	10	20	30	67	96	125
15-18: Jack Kelly/Roger Moore photo-c	8	16	24	55	78	100
19-Jack Kelly photo-c (last issue)	8	16	24	58	82	105

MAVERICK (See X-Men)
Marvel Comics: Jan, 1997 ($2.95, one-shot)

	GD 2.0	VG 4.0	FN 6.0	VF 8.0	VF/NM 9.0	NM- 9.2
1-Hama-s						3.00

MAVERICK (See X-Men)
Marvel Comics: Sept, 1997 - No. 12, Aug, 1998 ($2.99/$1.99)

	GD 2.0	VG 4.0	FN 6.0	VF 8.0	VF/NM 9.0	NM- 9.2
1,12: 1-($2.99)-Wraparound-c. 12-($2.99) Battles Omega Red						4.00
2-11: 2-Two covers. 4-Wolverine app. 6,7-Sabretooth app.						3.00

MAVERICK MARSHAL
Charlton Comics: Nov, 1958 - No. 7, May, 1960

	GD 2.0	VG 4.0	FN 6.0	VF 8.0	VF/NM 9.0	NM- 9.2
1	6	12	18	31	38	45
2-7	5	10	15	22	26	30

MAVERICKS
Daggar Comics Group: Jan, 1994 - No. 5, 1994 (#1-$2.75, #2-5-$2.50)

	GD 2.0	VG 4.0	FN 6.0	VF 8.0	VF/NM 9.0	NM- 9.2
1-5: 1-Bronze. 1-Gold. 1-Silver						2.75

MAX BRAND (See Silvertip)

MAX HAMM FAIRY TALE DETECTIVE
Nite Owl Comix: 2002; 2003 ($4.95, B&W, 6 1/2" x 8")

	GD 2.0	VG 4.0	FN 6.0	VF 8.0	VF/NM 9.0	NM- 9.2
1-Frank Cammuso-s/a						5.00
Vol. 2 (2003) Frank Cammuso-s/a						5.00

MAXIMAGE
Image Comics (Extreme Studios): Dec, 1995 - No. 7, June 1996 ($2.50)

	GD 2.0	VG 4.0	FN 6.0	VF 8.0	VF/NM 9.0	NM- 9.2
1-7: 1-Liefeld-c. 2-Extreme Destroyer Pt. 2; polybagged w/card. 4-Angela & Glory-c/app.						2.50

MAXIMUM SECURITY (Crossover)
Marvel Comics: Oct, 2000 - No. 3, Jan, 2001 ($2.99)

	GD 2.0	VG 4.0	FN 6.0	VF 8.0	VF/NM 9.0	NM- 9.2
1-3-Busiek-s/Ordway-a; Ronan the Accuser, Avengers app.						3.00
...Dangerous Planet 1: Busiek-s/Ordway-a; Ego, the Living Planet						3.00
Thor vs. Ego (11/00, $2.99) Reprints Thor #133,160,161; Kirby-a						3.00

MAXX (Also see Darker Image, Primer #5, & Friends of Maxx)
Image Comics (I Before E): Mar, 1993 - No. 35, Feb, 1998 ($1.95)

	GD 2.0	VG 4.0	FN 6.0	VF 8.0	VF/NM 9.0	NM- 9.2
1/2	1	3	4	6	8	10
1/2 (Gold)						20.00
1-Sam Kieth-c/a/scripts						4.00
1-Glow-in-the-dark variant	2	4	6	8	10	12
1-"3-D Edition" (1/98, $4.95) plus new back-up story						5.00
2-12: 6-Savage Dragon cameo(1 pg.). 7,8-Pitt-c & story						2.50
13-16						2.50
17-35: 21-Alan Moore-s						2.50
Volume 1 TPB (DC/WildStorm, 2003, $17.95) r/#1-6						18.00

MAYA (See Movie Classics)
Gold Key: Mar, 1968

	GD 2.0	VG 4.0	FN 6.0	VF 8.0	VF/NM 9.0	NM- 9.2
1 (10218-803)(TV)	3	6	9	18	24	30

MAYHEM
Dark Horse Comics: May, 1989 - No. 4, Sept, 1989 ($2.50, B&W, 52 pgs.)

	GD 2.0	VG 4.0	FN 6.0	VF 8.0	VF/NM 9.0	NM- 9.2
1- Four part Stanley Ipkiss/Mask story begins; Mask-c	1	3	4	6	8	10
2-4: 2-Mask 1/2 back-c. 4-Mask-c	1	2	3	5	7	9

MAZE AGENCY, THE
Comico/Innovation Publ. #8 on: Dec, 1988 - No. 20, 1991 ($1.95-$2.50, color)

	GD 2.0	VG 4.0	FN 6.0	VF 8.0	VF/NM 9.0	NM- 9.2
1-20: 9-Ellery Queen app. 7 ($2.50)-Last Comico issue						2.50
Annual 1 (1990, $2.75)-Ploog-c; Spirit tribute ish						2.75
Special 1 (1989, $2.75)-Staton-p (Innovation)						2.75

MAZE AGENCY, THE (Vol. 2)
Caliber Comics: July, 1997 - Present ($2.95, B&W)

	GD 2.0	VG 4.0	FN 6.0	VF 8.0	VF/NM 9.0	NM- 9.2
1-3: 1-Barr-s/Gonzales-a(p). 3-Hughes-c						3.00

MAZIE (...& Her Friends) (See Flat-Top, Mortie, Stevie & Tastee-Freez)
Mazie Comics(Magazine Publ.)/Harvey Publ. No. 13-on: 1953 - #12, 1954; #13, 12/54 - #22, 9/56; #23, 9/57 - #28, 8/58

	GD 2.0	VG 4.0	FN 6.0	VF 8.0	VF/NM 9.0	NM- 9.2
1-(Teen-age)-Stevie's girlfriend	9	18	27	52	66	80
2	6	12	18	28	34	40
3-10	5	10	15	24	30	35
11-28	4	8	12	18	22	25

MAZIE
Nation Wide Publishers: 1950 - No. 7, 1951 (5¢) (5x7-1/4"-miniature)(52 pgs.)

	GD 2.0	VG 4.0	FN 6.0	VF 8.0	VF/NM 9.0	NM- 9.2
1-Teen-age	16	32	48	92	126	160
2-7	9	18	27	51	66	80

MAZINGER (See First Comics Graphic Novel #17)

'MAZING MAN
DC Comics: Jan, 1986 - No. 12, Dec, 1986

	GD 2.0	VG 4.0	FN 6.0	VF 8.0	VF/NM 9.0	NM- 9.2
1-11: 7,8-Hembeck-a						2.50
12-Dark Knight part-c by Miller						3.00
Special 1 ('87), 2 (4/88), 3 ('90)-All $2.00, 52pgs.						2.50

McCANDLESS & COMPANY
Mandalay Books: 2001 ($7.95)

	GD 2.0	VG 4.0	FN 6.0	VF 8.0	VF/NM 9.0	NM- 9.2
...: Dead Razor - J.C. Vaughn-s/Busch & Sheehan-a; 3 covers						8.00

McHALE'S NAVY (TV) (See Movie Classics)
Dell Publ. Co.: May-July, 1963 - No. 3, Nov-Jan, 1963-64 (All have photo-c)

Medal of Honor #4 © DH

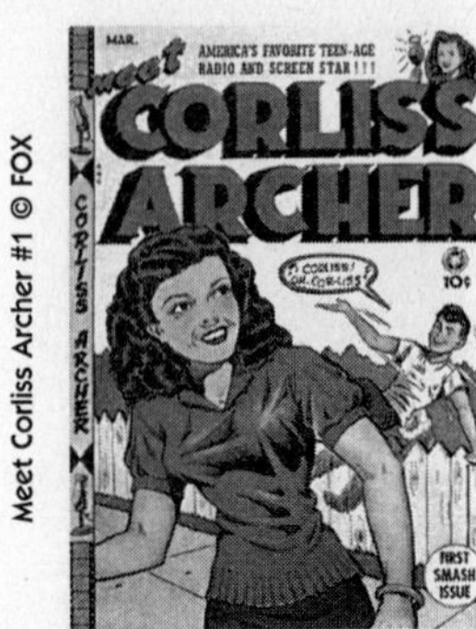

Meet Corliss Archer #1 © FOX

Mega Man #1 © Capcom Co. Ltd.

	GD 2.0	VG 4.0	FN 6.0	VF 8.0	VF/NM 9.0	NM- 9.2
1	7	14	21	51	71	90
2,3	6	12	18	38	52	65

McKEEVER & THE COLONEL (TV)
Dell Publishing Co.: Feb-Apr, 1963 - No. 3, Aug-Oct, 1963

	GD	VG	FN	VF	VF/NM	NM-
1-Photo-c	7	14	21	46	63	80
2,3	5	10	15	36	48	60

McLINTOCK (See Movie Comics)

MD
E. C. Comics: Apr-May, 1955 - No. 5, Dec-Jan, 1955-56

	GD	VG	FN	VF	VF/NM	NM-
1-Not approved by code; Craig-c	13	26	39	98	139	180
2-5	9	18	27	68	94	120

NOTE: *Crandall, Evans, Ingels, Orlando art in all issues; Craig c-1-5.*

MD
Russ Cochran/Gemstone Publishing: Sept, 1999 - No. 5, Jan, 2000 ($2.50)

	NM-
1-5-Reprints original EC series	2.50
Annual 1 (1999, $13.50) r/#1-5	14.00

M.D. GEIST
CPM Comics: 1995 - No. 3, 1995 (Limited series)

	NM-
1-3	3.00

M.D. GEIST DATA ALBUM
CPM Comics: June, 1996 ($9.95, trade paperback)

	NM-
1	10.00

M.D. GEIST: GROUND ZERO
CPM Comics: Mar, 1996 - No. 3, May, 1996 ($2.95, limited series)

	NM-
1-3	3.00

MEASLES
Fantagraphics Books: Christmas 1998 - Present ($2.95, B&W, quarterly)

	NM-
1-8-Anthology: 1-Venus-s by Hernandez	3.00

MEAT CAKE
Iconographix: 1992 (B&W)

	NM-
1	2.50

MEAT CAKE
Fantagraphics Books: No. 1, Oct, 1993 - Present (B&W)

	NM-
0-8: 3-Sal Buscema-a. 0-(1996)-r/Meat Cake #1 from Iconographix	2.50
9-($3.95) Alan Moore-s	4.00

MECHA (Also see Mayhem)
Dark Horse Comics: June, 1987 - No. 6, 1988 ($1.50/$1.95, color/B&W)

	NM-
1-6: 1,2 ($1.95, color), 3,4-($1.75, B&W), 5,6-($1.50, B&W)	2.50

MECHANIC, THE
Image Comics: 1998 ($5.95, one-shot, squarebound)

	NM-
1-Chiodo-painted art; Peterson-s	6.00
1-($10.00) DF Alternate Cover Ed.	10.00

MECHA SPECIAL
Dark Horse Comics: May, 1995 ($2.95, one-shot)

	NM-
1	3.00

MECH DESTROYER
Image Comics: Apr, 2001 - No. 4, Sept, 2001 ($2.95, limited series)

	NM-
1-4-Jae Kim-c/a; Robert Chong-s	3.00

MEDAL FOR BOWZER, A
American Visuals: 1966 (8 pgs.)

	GD	VG	FN	VF	VF/NM	NM-
nn-Eisner-c/script	27	54	81	153	214	275

MEDAL OF HONOR COMICS
A. S. Curtis: Spring, 1946

	GD	VG	FN	VF	VF/NM	NM-
1-War stories	12	24	36	71	96	120

MEDAL OF HONOR SPECIAL
Dark Horse Comics: 1994 ($2.50, one-shot)

	NM-
1-Kubert-c/a (first story)	2.50

MEDIA STARR
Innovation Publ.: July, 1989 - No. 3, Sept, 1989 ($1.95, mini-series, 28pgs.)

	NM-
1-3: Deluxe format	2.25

MEDIEVAL SPAWN/WITCHBLADE
Image Comics (Top Cow Productions): May, 1996 - No. 3, June, 1996 ($2.95, limited series)

	NM-
1-3-Garth Ennis scripts in all	6.00
1-Platinum foil-c (500 copies from Pittsburgh Con)	35.00
1-Gold	10.00
1-ETM Exclusive Edition; gold foil logo	7.00
TPB ($9.95) r/#1-3	10.00

MEET ANGEL (Formerly Angel & the Ape)
National Periodical Publications: No. 7, Nov-Dec, 1969

	GD	VG	FN	VF	VF/NM	NM-
7-Wood-a(i)	3	6	9	19	25	32

MEET CORLISS ARCHER (Radio/Movie)(My Life #4 on)
Fox Features Syndicate: Mar, 1948 - No. 3, July, 1948

	GD	VG	FN	VF	VF/NM	NM-
1-(Teen-age)-Feldstein-c/a; headlight-c	100	200	300	625	938	1250
2	55	110	165	341	511	680
3-Part Feldstein-c only	50	100	150	300	450	600

NOTE: *No. 1-3 used in Seduction of the Innocent, pg. 39.*

MEET HERCULES (See Three Stooges)

MEET MERTON
Toby Press: Dec, 1953 - No. 4, June, 1954

	GD	VG	FN	VF	VF/NM	NM-
1-(Teen-age)-Dave Berg-c/a	9	18	27	52	66	80
2-Dave Berg-c/a	6	12	18	28	34	40
3,4-Dave Berg-c/a	6	12	18	27	33	38
I.W. Reprint #9, Super Reprint #11('63), 18	2	4	6	9	11	14

MEET MISS BLISS (Becomes Stories Of Romance #5 on)
Atlas Comics (LMC): May, 1955 - No. 4, Nov, 1955

	GD	VG	FN	VF	VF/NM	NM-
1-Al Hartley-c/a	14	28	42	79	107	135
2-4	9	18	27	52	66	80

MEET MISS PEPPER (Formerly Lucy, The Real Gone Gal)
St. John Publishing Co.: No. 5, April, 1954 - No. 6, June, 1954

	GD	VG	FN	VF	VF/NM	NM-
5-Kubert/Maurer-a	21	42	63	118	164	210
6-Kubert/Maurer-a; Kubert-c	17	34	51	95	130	165

MEGA DRAGON & TIGER
Image Comics: Mar, 1999 - No. 5 ($2.95)

	NM-
1-5-Tony Wong-s/a	3.00

MEGAHURTZ
Image Comics: Aug, 1997 - No. 3, Oct, 1997 ($2.95, B&W)

	NM-
1-3-St. Pierre-s	3.00

MEGALITH (Megalith Deathwatch 2000 #1,2 of second series)
Continuity: 1989 - No. 9, Mar, 1992; No, 0, Apr, 1993 - No. 7, Jan, 1994

	NM-
1-9-($2.00-c) 1-Neal Adams & Mark Texiera-c/Texiera & Nebres-a	3.00
2nd series: 0-(4/93)-Foil-c; no c-price, giveaway; Adams plot	3.00
1-7: 1-3-Bagged w/card: 1-Gatefold-c by Nebres; Adams plot. 2-Fold-out-c; Adams plot. 3-Indestructible-c. 4-7-Embossed-c: 4-Adams/Nebres-c; Adams part-i. 5-Sienkiewicz-i. 6-Adams part-i. 7-Adams-c(p); Adams plot	3.00

MEGAMAN
Dreamwave Productions: Sept, 2003 - Present ($2.95)

	NM-
1-4-Brian Augustyn-s/Mic Fong-a	3.00
1-($5.95) Chromium wraparound variant-c	6.00

MEGATON (A super hero)
Megaton Publ.: Nov, 1983; No. 2, Oct, 1985 - No. 8, Aug, 1987 (B&W)

	GD	VG	FN	VF	VF/NM	NM-
1-($2.00, 68 pgs.)-Erik Larsen's 1st pro work; Vanguard by Larsen begins (1st app.), ends #4; 1st app. Megaton, Berzerker, & Ethrian; Guice-c/a(p); Gustovich-a(p) in #1,2	2	4	6	8	10	12
2-($2.00, 68 pgs.)-The Dragon cameo (1 pg.) by Larsen (later The Savage Dragon in Image Comics); Guice-c/a(p)	1	3	4	6	8	10
3-(44 pgs.)-1st full app. Savage Dragon-c/story by Larsen; 1st comic book work by Angel Medina (pin-up)	2	4	6	10	13	16
4-(52 pgs.)-2nd full app. Savage Dragon by Larsen; 4,5-Wildman by Grass Green	1	2	3	5	7	9
5-1st Liefeld published-a (inside f/c, 6/86)						6.00
6,7: 6-Larsen-c						5.00
8-1st Liefeld story-a (7 pg. super hero story) plus 1 pg. Youngblood ad	1	2	3	4	6	8
...Explosion (6/87, 16 pg. color giveaway)-1st app. Youngblood by Rob Liefeld (2 pg. spread); shows Megaton heroes	2	4	6	12	16	20
...Holiday Special 1 (1994, $2.95, color, 40 pgs., publ. by Entity Comics)-Gold foil logo; bagged w/Kelley Jones card; Vanguard, Megaton plus shows unpublished-c to 1987 Youngblood #1 by Liefeld/Ordway						4.00

NOTE: *Copies of Megaton Explosion were also released in early 1992 all signed by Rob Liefeld and were made available to retailers.*

Mekanix #1 © MAR

The Men in Black #1 © Lowell Cunningham

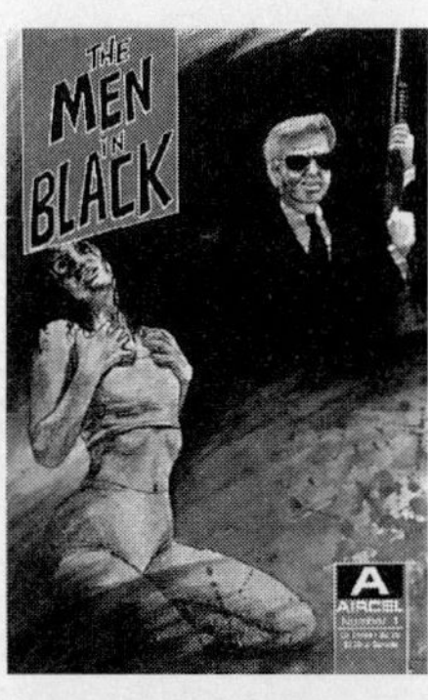

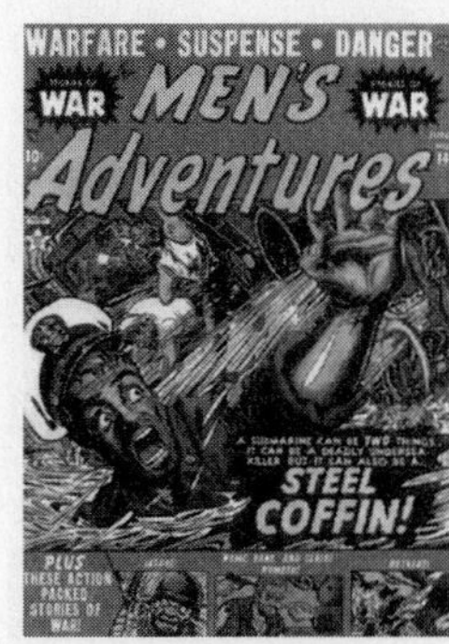

Men's Adventures #14 © MAR

MEGATON MAN (See Don Simpson's Bizarre Heroes)
Kitchen Sink Enterprises: Nov, 1984 - No. 10, 1986

	GD 2.0	VG 4.0	FN 6.0	VF 8.0	VF/NM 9.0	NM- 9.2
1-10, 1-2nd printing (1989)						3.00
...Meets The Uncategorizable X-Thems 1 (4/89, $2.00)						3.00

MEGATON MAN: BOMB SHELL
Image Comics: Jul, 1999 - No. 2 ($2.95, B&W, mini-series)

	GD 2.0	VG 4.0	FN 6.0	VF 8.0	VF/NM 9.0	NM- 9.2
1-Reprints stories from Megaton Man internet site						3.00

MEGATON MAN: HARD COPY
Image Comics: Feb, 1999 - No. 2, Apr, 1999 ($2.95, B&W, mini-series)

	GD 2.0	VG 4.0	FN 6.0	VF 8.0	VF/NM 9.0	NM- 9.2
1,2-Reprints stories from Megaton Man internet site						3.00

MEGATON MAN VS. FORBIDDEN FRANKENSTEIN
Fiasco Comics: Apr, 1996 ($2.95, B&W, one-shot)

	GD 2.0	VG 4.0	FN 6.0	VF 8.0	VF/NM 9.0	NM- 9.2
1-Intro The Tomb Team (Forbidden Frankenstein, Drekula, Bride of the Monster, & Moon Wolf).						3.00

MEK
DC Comics (Homage): Jan, 2003 - No. 3, Mar, 2003 ($2.95, limited series)

	GD 2.0	VG 4.0	FN 6.0	VF 8.0	VF/NM 9.0	NM- 9.2
1-3-Warren Ellis-s/Steve Rolston-a						3.00

MEKANIX (See X-Men titles) (See X-Treme X-Men Vol. 4 for TPB)
Marvel Comics: Dec, 2002 - No. 6, May, 2003 ($2.99, limited series)

	GD 2.0	VG 4.0	FN 6.0	VF 8.0	VF/NM 9.0	NM- 9.2
1-6-Kitty Pryde in college; Claremont-s/Bobillo & Sosa-a						3.00

MEL ALLEN SPORTS COMICS (The Voice of the Yankees)
Standard Comics: No. 5, Nov, 1949; No. 6, June, 1950

	GD 2.0	VG 4.0	FN 6.0	VF 8.0	VF/NM 9.0	NM- 9.2
5(#1 on inside)-Tuska-a	24	48	72	135	190	245
6(#2)-Lou Gehrig story	16	32	48	92	126	160

MELTING POT
Kitchen Sink Press: Dec, 1993 - No. 4, Sept, 1994 ($2.95)

	GD 2.0	VG 4.0	FN 6.0	VF 8.0	VF/NM 9.0	NM- 9.2
1-4: Bisley-painted-c						3.00

MELVIN MONSTER
Dell Publishing Co.: Apr-June, 1965 - No. 10, Oct, 1969

	GD 2.0	VG 4.0	FN 6.0	VF 8.0	VF/NM 9.0	NM- 9.2
1-By John Stanley	11	22	33	77	114	150
2-10-All by Stanley. #10-r/#1	8	16	24	58	82	105

MELVIN THE MONSTER (See Peter, the Little Pest & Dexter The Demon #7)
Atlas Comics (HPC): July, 1956 - No. 6, July, 1957

	GD 2.0	VG 4.0	FN 6.0	VF 8.0	VF/NM 9.0	NM- 9.2
1-Maneely-c/a	14	28	42	79	107	135
2-6: 4-Maneely-c/a	10	20	30	56	73	90

MENACE
Atlas Comics (HPC): Mar, 1953 - No. 11, May, 1954

	GD 2.0	VG 4.0	FN 6.0	VF 8.0	VF/NM 9.0	NM- 9.2
1-Horror & sci/fi stories begin; Everett-c/a	66	132	198	413	619	825
2-Post-atom bomb disaster by Everett; anti-Communist propaganda/torture scenes; Sinnott sci/fi story "Rocket to the Moon"	46	92	138	276	413	550
3,4,6-Everett-a. 4-Sci/fi story "Escape to the Moon". 6-Romita sci/fi story "Science Fiction"	39	78	117	233	329	425
5-Origin & 1st app. The Zombie by Everett (reprinted in Tales of the Zombie #1)(7/53); 5-Sci/fi story "Rocket Ship"	55	110	165	330	495	660
7,8,10,11: 7-Frankenstein story. 8-End of world story; Heath 3-D art(3 pgs.). 10-H-Bomb panels	31	62	93	175	248	320
9-Everett-a r-in Vampire Tales #1	35	70	105	201	288	370

NOTE: ***Brodsky** c-7, 8, 11. **Colan** a-6; c-9. **Everett** a-1-6, 9; c-1-6. **Heath** a-1-8; c-10. **Katz** a-11. **Maneely** a-3, 5, 7-9. **Powell** a-11. **Romita** a-3, 6, 8, 11. **Shelly** a-10. **Shores** a-7. **Sinnott** a-2, 7. **Tuska** a-1, 2, 5.*

MENACE
Awesome-Hyperwerks: Nov, 1998 ($2.50)

	GD 2.0	VG 4.0	FN 6.0	VF 8.0	VF/NM 9.0	NM- 9.2
1-Jada Pinkett Smith-s/Fraga-a						2.50

MEN AGAINST CRIME (Formerly Mr. Risk; Hand of Fate #8 on)
Ace Magazines: No. 3, Feb, 1951 - No. 7, Oct, 1951

	GD 2.0	VG 4.0	FN 6.0	VF 8.0	VF/NM 9.0	NM- 9.2
3-Mr. Risk app.	11	22	33	63	84	105
4-7: 4-Colan-a; entire book-r as Trapped! #4. 5-Meskin-a	8	16	24	46	58	70

MEN, GUNS, & CATTLE (See Classics Illustrated Special Issue)

MEN IN ACTION (Battle Brady #10 on)
Atlas Comics (IPS): April, 1952 - No. 9, Dec, 1952 (War stories)

	GD 2.0	VG 4.0	FN 6.0	VF 8.0	VF/NM 9.0	NM- 9.2
1-Berg, Reinman-a	17	34	51	98	134	170
2,3: 3-Heath-c/a	10	20	30	56	73	90
4-6,8,9	9	18	27	49	62	75
7-Krigstein-a; Heath-c	10	20	30	56	73	90

NOTE: ***Brodsky** c-1, 4-6. **Maneely** c-5. **Pakula** a-1, 6. **Robinson** c-8. **Shores** c-9.*

MEN IN ACTION
Ajax/Farrell Publications: April, 1957 - No. 6, 1958

	GD 2.0	VG 4.0	FN 6.0	VF 8.0	VF/NM 9.0	NM- 9.2
1	9	18	27	52	66	80
2	6	12	18	31	38	45
3-6	6	12	18	27	33	38

MEN IN BLACK, THE (1st series)
Aircel Comics (Malibu): Jan, 1990 - No. 3 Mar, 1990 ($2.25, B&W, lim. series)

	GD 2.0	VG 4.0	FN 6.0	VF 8.0	VF/NM 9.0	NM- 9.2
1-Cunningham-s/a in all	4	8	12	27	36	45
2,3	3	6	9	17	21	25
Graphic Novel (Jan, 1991) r/#1-3	3	6	9	16	20	25

MEN IN BLACK (2nd series)
Aircel Comics (Malibu): May, 1991 - No. 3, Jul, 1991 ($2.50, B&W, lim. series)

	GD 2.0	VG 4.0	FN 6.0	VF 8.0	VF/NM 9.0	NM- 9.2
1-Cunningham-s/a in all	3	6	9	16	20	25
2,3	2	4	6	8	10	12

MEN IN BLACK: FAR CRY
Marvel Comics: Aug, 1997 ($3.99, color, one-shot)

	GD 2.0	VG 4.0	FN 6.0	VF 8.0	VF/NM 9.0	NM- 9.2
1-Cunningham-s						4.00

MEN IN BLACK: RETRIBUTION
Marvel Comics: Dec, 1997 ($3.99, color, one-shot)

	GD 2.0	VG 4.0	FN 6.0	VF 8.0	VF/NM 9.0	NM- 9.2
1-Cunningham-s; continuation of the movie						4.00

MEN IN BLACK: THE MOVIE
Marvel Comics: Oct, 1997 ($3.99, one-shot, movie adaption)

	GD 2.0	VG 4.0	FN 6.0	VF 8.0	VF/NM 9.0	NM- 9.2
1-Cunningham-s						4.00

MEN INTO SPACE
Dell Publishing Co.: No. 1083, Feb-Apr, 1960

	GD 2.0	VG 4.0	FN 6.0	VF 8.0	VF/NM 9.0	NM- 9.2
Four Color 1083-Anderson-a, photo-c	6	12	18	40	55	70

MEN OF BATTLE (Also see New Men of Battle)
Catechetical Guild: V1#5, March, 1943 (Hardcover)

	GD 2.0	VG 4.0	FN 6.0	VF 8.0	VF/NM 9.0	NM- 9.2
V1#5-Topix reprints	6	12	18	27	33	38

MEN OF WAR
DC Comics, Inc.: August, 1977 - No. 26, March, 1980 (#9,10: 44 pgs.)

	GD 2.0	VG 4.0	FN 6.0	VF 8.0	VF/NM 9.0	NM- 9.2
1-Enemy Ace, Gravedigger (origin #1,2) begin	2	4	6	11	14	18
2-4,8-10,12-14,19,20: All Enemy Ace stories. 4-1st Dateline Frontline. 9-Unknown Soldier app.	1	2	3	5	7	9
5-7,11,15-18,21-25: 17-1st app. Rosa	1	2	3	4	5	7
26-Sgt. Rock & Easy Co.-c/s	2	4	6	9	11	14

NOTE: ***Chaykin** a-9, 10, 12-14, 19, 20. **Evans** c-25. **Kubert** c-2-23, 24p, 26.*

MEN'S ADVENTURES (Formerly True Adventures)
Marvel/Atlas Comics (CCC): No. 4, Aug, 1950 - No. 28, July, 1954

	GD 2.0	VG 4.0	FN 6.0	VF 8.0	VF/NM 9.0	NM- 9.2
4(#1)(52 pgs.)	33	66	99	190	270	350
5-Flying Saucer story	21	42	63	118	164	210
6-8: 7-Buried alive story. 8-Sci/fic story	19	38	57	106	146	185
9-20: All war format	12	24	36	69	92	115
21,22,24,26: All horror format	21	42	63	118	164	210
23-Crandall-a; Fox-a(i); horror format	22	44	66	124	172	220
25-Shrunken head-c	34	68	102	193	274	355
27,28-Human Torch & Toro-c/stories; Captain America & Sub-Mariner stories in each (also see Young Men #24-28)	100	200	300	625	938	1250

NOTE: ***Ayers** a-27(H. Torch). **Berg** a-15, 16. **Brodsky** c-4-9, 11, 12, 16-18, 24. **Burgos** c-27, 28(Human Torch). **Colan** a-14, 19. **Everett** a-10, 14, 22, 25, 28; c-14, 21-23. **Heath** a-8, 11, 24; c-13, 20, 26. **Lawrence** a-23; 27(Captain America). **Maneely** a-24; c-10, 15. **Mac Pakula** a-15, 25. **Post** a-23. **Powell** a-27(Sub-Mariner). **Reinman** a-11, 12. **Robinson** c-19. **Romita** a-22. **Shores** c-25. **Sinnott** a-21. **Tuska** a-24. Adventure-#4-8; War-#9-20; Weird/Horror-#21-26.*

MENZ INSANA
DC Comics (Vertigo): 1997 ($7.95, one-shot)

	GD 2.0	VG 4.0	FN 6.0	VF 8.0	VF/NM 9.0	NM- 9.2
nn-Fowler-s/Bolton painted art	1	2	3	5	6	8

MEPHISTO VS... (See Silver Surfer #3)
Marvel Comics Group: Apr, 1987 - No. 4, July, 1987 ($1.50, mini-series)

	GD 2.0	VG 4.0	FN 6.0	VF 8.0	VF/NM 9.0	NM- 9.2
1-4: 1-Fantastic Four; Austin-i. 2-X-Factor. 3-X-Men. 4-Avengers						3.00

MERC (See Mark Hazzard: Merc)

MERCHANTS OF DEATH
Acme Press (Eclipse): Jul, 1988 - No. 4, Nov, 1988 ($3.50, B&W/16 pgs. color, 44 pg. mag.)

	GD 2.0	VG 4.0	FN 6.0	VF 8.0	VF/NM 9.0	NM- 9.2
1-4: 4-Toth-c						3.50

MERCY
DC Comics (Vertigo): 1993 ($5.95, 68 pgs., mature)

	GD 2.0	VG 4.0	FN 6.0	VF 8.0	VF/NM 9.0	NM- 9.2
nn						6.00

Meridian #23 © CRO

Metal Men #29 © DC

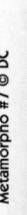

Metamorpho #7 © DC

MERIDIAN
CrossGeneration Comics: Jul, 2000 - No. 44, Apr, 2004 ($2.95)

	GD 2.0	VG 4.0	FN 6.0	VF 8.0	VF/NM 9.0	NM- 9.2
1-44: Barbara Kesel-s						3.00
Flying Solo Vol. 1 TPB (2001, $19.95) r/#1-7; cover by Steve Rude						20.00
Going to Ground Vol. 2 TPB (2002, $19.95) r/#8-14						20.00
Taking the Skies Vol. 3 TPB (2002, $15.95) r/#15-20						16.00
Vol. 4: Coming Home (12/02, $15.95) r/#21-26						16.00
Vol. 5: Minister of Cadador (7/03, $15.95) r/#27-32						16.00
Vol. 6: Changing Course (1/04, $15.95) r/#33-38						16.00
Traveler Vol. 1-4 ($9.95): Digest-size reprints of TPBs						10.00

MERLIN JONES AS THE MONKEY'S UNCLE (See Movie Comics and The Misadventures of... under Movie Comics)

MERRILL'S MARAUDERS (See Movie Classics)

MERRY CHRISTMAS (See A Christmas Adventure, Donald Duck..., Dell Giant #39, & March of Comics #153 in the PromotionalComics section)

MERRY COMICS
Carlton Publishing Co.: Dec, 1945 (No cover price)

	GD 2.0	VG 4.0	FN 6.0	VF 8.0	VF/NM 9.0	NM- 9.2
nn-Boogeyman app.	21	42	63	118	164	210

MERRY COMICS: Four Star Publications: 1947 (Advertised, not published)

MERRY-GO-ROUND COMICS
LaSalle Publ. Co./Croyden Publ./Rotary Litho.: 1944 (25¢, 132 pgs.); 1946; 9-10/47 - No. 2, 1948

	GD 2.0	VG 4.0	FN 6.0	VF 8.0	VF/NM 9.0	NM- 9.2
nn(1944)(LaSalle)-Funny animal; 29 new features	19	38	57	106	146	185
21 (Publisher?)	8	16	24	46	58	70
1(1946)(Croyden)-Al Fago-c; funny animal	10	20	30	58	77	95
V1#1,2(1947-48; 52 pgs.)(Rotary Litho. Co. Ltd., Canada); Ken Hultgren-a	8	16	24	46	58	70

MERRY MAILMAN (See Fawcett's Funny Animals #87-89)

MERRY MOUSE (Also see Funny Tunes & Space Comics)
Avon Periodicals: June, 1953 - No. 4, Jan-Feb, 1954

	GD 2.0	VG 4.0	FN 6.0	VF 8.0	VF/NM 9.0	NM- 9.2
1-1st app.; funny animal; Frank Carin-c/a	10	20	30	56	73	90
2-4	7	14	21	35	43	50

MERV PUMPKINHEAD, AGENT OF D.R.E.A.M. (See The Sandman)
DC Comics (Vertigo): 2000 ($5.95, one-shot)

	GD 2.0	VG 4.0	FN 6.0	VF 8.0	VF/NM 9.0	NM- 9.2
1-Buckingham-a(p); Nowlan painted-c						6.00

MESSENGER, THE
Image Comics: July, 2000 ($5.95, one-shot)

	GD 2.0	VG 4.0	FN 6.0	VF 8.0	VF/NM 9.0	NM- 9.2
1-Ordway-s/c/a						6.00

META-4
First Comics: Feb, 1991 - No. 4, 1991 ($2.25)

	GD 2.0	VG 4.0	FN 6.0	VF 8.0	VF/NM 9.0	NM- 9.2
1-($3.95, 52pgs.)						4.00
2-4						2.25

METALLIX (Also see Promotional Comics section for FCBD Ed.)
Future Comics: Dec, 2002 - No. 6, June, 2003 ($3.50)

	GD 2.0	VG 4.0	FN 6.0	VF 8.0	VF/NM 9.0	NM- 9.2
0-6-Ron Lim-a. 0-(6/03) Origin. 1-Layton-c						3.50
1-Collector's Edition with variant cover by Lim						3.50

METAL MEN (See Brave & the Bold, DC Comics Presents, and Showcase #37-40)
National Periodical Publications/DC Comics: 4-5/63 - No. 41, 12-1/69-70; No. 42, 2-3/73 - No. 44, 7-8/73; No. 45, 4-5/76 - No. 56, 2-3/78

	GD 2.0	VG 4.0	FN 6.0	VF 8.0	VF/NM 9.0	NM- 9.2
1-(4-5/63)-5th app. Metal Men	50	100	150	425	650	875
2	20	40	60	142	209	275
3-5	13	26	39	90	133	175
6-10	9	18	27	60	85	110
11-20: 12-Beatles cameo (12/65)	7	14	21	46	63	80
21-Batman, Robin & Flash x-over	5	10	15	36	48	60
22-26,28-30	5	10	15	33	44	55
27-Origin Metal Men retold	7	14	21	50	68	85
31-41(1968-70): 38-Last 12¢ issue. 41-Last 15¢	4	8	12	27	36	45
42-44(1973)-Reprints	2	4	6	10	12	15
45('76)-49-Simonson-a in all: 48,49-Re-intro Eclipso	1	2	3	6	8	10
50-56: 50-Part-r. 54,55-Green Lantern x-over	1	2	3	6	8	10

NOTE: ***Andru/Esposito** c-1-30. **Aparo** c-53-56. **Giordano** c-45, 46. **Kane/Esposito** a-30, 31; c-31. **Simonson** a-45-49; c-47-52. **Staton** a-50-56.*

METAL MEN
DC Comics: Oct, 1993 - No. 4, Jan, 1994 ($1.25, mini-series)

	GD 2.0	VG 4.0	FN 6.0	VF 8.0	VF/NM 9.0	NM- 9.2
1-($2.50)-Multi-colored foil-c						4.00
2-4: 2-Origin						2.50

METAL MEN (See Tangent Comics/ Metal Men)

METAMORPHO (See Action Comics #413, Brave & the Bold #57,58, 1st Issue Special, & World's Finest #217)
National Periodical Publications: July-Aug, 1965 - No. 17, Mar-Apr, 1968 (All 12¢ issues)

	GD 2.0	VG 4.0	FN 6.0	VF 8.0	VF/NM 9.0	NM- 9.2
1-(7-8/65)-3rd app. Metamorpho	12	24	36	87	129	170
2,3	7	14	21	46	63	80
4-6,10:10-Origin & 1st app. Element Girl (1-2/67)	5	10	15	36	48	60
7-9	4	8	12	29	40	50
11-17: 17-Sparling-c/a	4	8	12	24	32	40

NOTE: ***Ramona Fradon** a-B&B 57, 58, 1-4. **Orlando** a-5, 6; c-5-9, 11. **Trapani** a(p)-7-16; i-16.*

METAMORPHO
DC Comics: Aug, 1993 - No. 4, Nov, 1993 ($1.50, mini-series)

	GD 2.0	VG 4.0	FN 6.0	VF 8.0	VF/NM 9.0	NM- 9.2
1-4						2.50

METAPHYSIQUE
Malibu Comics (Bravura): Apr, 1995 - No. 6, Oct, 1995 ($2.95, limited series)

	GD 2.0	VG 4.0	FN 6.0	VF 8.0	VF/NM 9.0	NM- 9.2
1-6: Norm Breyfogle-c/a/scripts						3.00

METEOR COMICS
L. L. Baird (Croyden): Nov, 1945

	GD 2.0	VG 4.0	FN 6.0	VF 8.0	VF/NM 9.0	NM- 9.2
1-Captain Wizard, Impossible Man, Race Wilkins app.; origin Baldy Bean, Capt. Wizard's sidekick; bare-breasted mermaids story	40	80	120	240	340	440

METEOR MAN
Marvel Comics: Aug, 1993 - No. 6, Jan, 1994 ($1.25, limited series)

	GD 2.0	VG 4.0	FN 6.0	VF 8.0	VF/NM 9.0	NM- 9.2
1-6: 1-Regular unbagged. 4-Night Thrasher-c/story. 6-Terry Austin-c(i)						2.25
1-Polybagged w/button & rap newspaper						4.00
...: The Movie (4/93 [7/93 on cover], $2.25) movie adaptation						2.25

METROPOL (See Ted McKeever's...)

METROPOL A.D. (See Ted McKeever's...)

METROPOLIS S.C.U. (Also see Showcase '96 #1)
DC Comics: Nov, 1995 - No. 4, Feb, 1996 ($1.50, limited series)

	GD 2.0	VG 4.0	FN 6.0	VF 8.0	VF/NM 9.0	NM- 9.2
1-4:1-Superman-c & app.						2.25

MEZZ: GALACTIC TOUR 2494 (Also See Nexus)
Dark Horse Comics: May, 1994 ($2.50, one-shot)

	GD 2.0	VG 4.0	FN 6.0	VF 8.0	VF/NM 9.0	NM- 9.2
1						2.50

MGM'S MARVELOUS WIZARD OF OZ (See Marvel Treasury of Oz)
Marvel Comics Group/National Periodical Publications: 1975 ($1.50, 84 pgs.; oversize)

	GD 2.0	VG 4.0	FN 6.0	VF 8.0	VF/NM 9.0	NM- 9.2
1-Adaptation of MGM's movie; J. Buscema-a	2	4	6	14	18	22

M.G.M'S MOUSE MUSKETEERS (Formerly M.G.M.'s The Two Mouseketeers)
Dell Publishing Co.: No. 670, Jan, 1956 - No. 1290, Mar-May, 1962

	GD 2.0	VG 4.0	FN 6.0	VF 8.0	VF/NM 9.0	NM- 9.2
Four Color 670 (#4)	5	10	15	33	44	55
Four Color 711,728,764	4	8	12	24	32	40
8 (4-6/57) - 21 (3-5/60)	3	7	10	21	28	35
Four Color 1135,1175,1290	3	7	10	21	28	35

M.G.M.'S SPIKE AND TYKE (also see Tom & Jerry #79)
Dell Publishing Co.: No. 499, Sept, 1953 - No. 1266, Dec-Feb, 1961-62

	GD 2.0	VG 4.0	FN 6.0	VF 8.0	VF/NM 9.0	NM- 9.2
Four Color 499 (#1)	6	12	18	38	52	65
Four Color 577,638	4	8	12	22	30	38
4(12-2/55-56)-10	3	6	9	19	25	32
11-24(12-2/60-61)	3	6	9	18	23	28
Four Color 1266	3	6	9	18	24	30

M.G.M.'S THE TWO MOUSKETEERS
Dell Publishing Co.: No. 475, June, 1953 - No. 642, July, 1955

	GD 2.0	VG 4.0	FN 6.0	VF 8.0	VF/NM 9.0	NM- 9.2
Four Color 475 (#1)	8	16	24	58	82	105
Four Color 603 (11/54), 642	6	12	18	38	52	65

MICHAELANGELO CHRISTMAS SPECIAL (See Teenage Mutant Ninja Turtles Christmas Special)

MICHAELANGELO, TEENAGE MUTANT NINJA TURTLE
Mirage Studios: 1986 (One shot) ($1.50, B&W)

	GD 2.0	VG 4.0	FN 6.0	VF 8.0	VF/NM 9.0	NM- 9.2
1						4.00
1-2nd printing ('89, $1.75)-Reprint plus new-a						2.25

MICHAEL MOORCOCK'S MULTIVERSE
DC Comics (Helix): Nov, 1997 - No. 12, Oct, 1998 ($2.50, limited series)

	GD 2.0	VG 4.0	FN 6.0	VF 8.0	VF/NM 9.0	NM- 9.2
1-12: Simonson, Reeve & Ridgway-a						2.50
TPB (1999, $19.95) r/#1-12						20.00

MICHAEL TURNER PRESENTS: ASPEN (See Aspen)

MICKEY AND DONALD (See Walt Disney's...)

Mickey Mouse #30 © WDC

GOLD KEY
WALT DISNEY
MICKEY MOUSE
12¢
Mickey and Goofy are attacked by a mechanical shark while searching for THE UNDERWATER PIRATES!

Mickey Mouse #112 © WDC

Mickey Mouse Magazine #1 © WDC

	GD 2.0	VG 4.0	FN 6.0	VF 8.0	VF/NM 9.0	NM- 9.2

MICKEY AND DONALD IN VACATIONLAND (See Dell Giant No. 47)

MICKEY & THE BEANSTALK (See Story Hour Series)

MICKEY & THE SLEUTH (See Walt Disney Showcase #38, 39, 42)

MICKEY FINN (Also see Big Shot Comics #74 & Feature Funnies)
Eastern Color 1-4/McNaught Synd. #5 on (Columbia)/Headline V3#2:
Nov?, 1942 - V3#2, May, 1952

	GD	VG	FN	VF	VF/NM	NM-
1	31	62	93	175	248	320
2	16	32	48	92	126	160
3-Charlie Chan story	11	22	33	66	88	110
4	9	18	27	52	66	80
5-10	8	16	24	43	54	65
11-15(1949): 12-Sparky Watts app.	7	14	21	35	43	50
V3#1,2(1952)	6	12	18	28	34	40

MICKEY MALONE
Hale Nass Corp.: 1936 (Color, punchout-c) (B&W-a on back)

	GD	VG	FN	VF	VF/NM	NM-
nn-1pg. of comics	175	350	700	-	-	-

MICKEY MANTLE (See Baseball's Greatest Heroes #1)

MICKEY MOUSE (See Adventures of Mickey Mouse, The Best of Walt Disney Comics, Cheerios giveaways, Donald and ..., Dynabrite Comics, 40 Big Pages..., Gladstone Comic Album, Merry Christmas From..., Walt Disney's Mickey and Donald, Walt Disney's Comics & Stories, Walt Disney's..., & Wheaties)

MICKEY MOUSE (...Secret Agent #107-109; Walt Disney's... #148-205?)
(See Dell Giants for annuals) (#204 exists from both G.K. & Whitman)
Dell Publ. Co./Gold Key #85-204/Whitman #204-218/Gladstone #219 on:
#16, 1941 - #84, 7-9/62; #85, 11/62 - #218, 6/84; #219, 10/86 - #256, 4/90

	GD	VG	FN	VF	VF/NM	NM-
Four Color 16(1941)-1st Mickey Mouse comic book; "...vs. the Phantom Blot" by Gottfredson	1350	2700	4050	13,000	-	-
Four Color 27(1943)- "7 Colored Terror"	85	170	255	629	965	1300
Four Color 79(1945)-By Carl Barks (1 story)	108	216	324	791	1208	1625
Four Color 116(1946)	26	52	78	189	275	360
Four Color 141,157(1947)	22	44	66	160	235	310
Four Color 170,181,194('48)	19	38	57	138	202	265
Four Color 214('49),231,248,261	15	30	45	104	152	200
Four Color 268-Reprints/WDC&S #22-24 by Gottfredson ("Surprise Visitor")	14	28	42	99	145	190
Four Color 279,286,296	11	22	33	75	110	145
Four Color 304,313(#1),325(#2),334	9	18	27	65	93	120
Four Color 343,352,362,371,387	8	16	24	55	78	100
Four Color 401,411,427(10-11/52)	6	12	18	43	59	75
Four Color 819-Mickey Mouse in Magicland	5	10	15	36	48	60
Four Color 1057,1151,1246(1959-61)-Album; #1057 has 10¢ & 12¢ editions; back covers are different	4	8	12	29	40	50
28(12-1/52-53)-32,34	5	10	15	36	48	60
33-(Exists with 2 dates, 10-11/53 & 12-1/54)	5	10	15	36	48	60
35-50	4	8	12	29	40	50
51-73,75-80	4	8	12	24	32	40
74-Story swipe "The Rare Stamp Search" from 4-Color #422- "The Gilded Man"	4	8	12	27	36	45
81-105: 93,95-titled "Mickey Mouse Club Album". 100-105: Reprint 4-Color #427,194,279, 170,343,214 in that order	3	7	10	21	28	35
106-120	3	6	9	16	20	25
121-130	2	4	6	12	16	20
131-146	2	4	6	11	14	18
147,148: 147-Reprints "The Phantom Fires" from WDC&S #200-202.148-Reprints "The Mystery of Lonely Valley" from WDC&S #208-210	2	4	6	11	14	18
149-158	2	4	6	8	10	12
159-Reprints "The Sunken City" from WDC&S #205-207	2	4	6	8	10	12
160-178: 162-165,167-170-r	2	4	6	9	11	14
179-(52 pgs.)	1	3	4	6	8	10
180-203: 200-r/Four Color #371	1	2	3	5	7	9
204-(Whitman or G.K.), 205,206	2	4	6	9	11	14
207(8/80), 209(pre-pack?)	3	6	9	18	24	30
208-(8-12/80)-Only distr. in Whitman 3-pack	7	14	21	50	68	85
210(2/81),211-214	2	4	6	8	10	12
215-218: 215(2/82), 216(4/82), 217(3/84), 218(misdated 8/82; actual date 7/84)	2	4	6	10	13	16
219-1st Gladstone issue; The Seven Ghosts serial-r begins by Gottfredson	2	4	6	11	14	18
220,221	1	2	3	5	7	9
222-225: 222-Editor-in Grief strip-r						4.00
226-230						4.00
231-243,246-254: 240-r/March of Comics #27. 245-r/F.C. #279. 250-r/F.C. #248						3.00
244 (1/89, $2.95, 100 pgs.)-Squarebound 60th anniversary issue; gives history of Mickey						4.00
245, 256: 245-r/F.C. #279. 256-$1.95, 68 pgs.						4.00
255 ($1.95, 68 pgs.)						3.00

NOTE: *Reprints #195-197, 198(2/3), 199(1/3), 200-208, 211(1/2), 212, 213, 215(1/3), 216-on.* ***Gottfredson*** *Mickey Mouse serials in #219-239, 241-244, 246-249, 251-253, 255.*

	GD	VG	FN	VF	VF/NM	NM-
Album 01-518-210(Dell), 1(10082-309)(9/63-Gold Key)	3	7	10	21	28	35
...Club 1(1/64-Gold Key)(TV)	4	8	12	24	32	40
Mini Comic 1(1976)(3-1/4x6-1/2")-Reprints 158	1	2	3	5	6	8
Surprise Party 1(30037-901, G.K.)(1/69)-40th Anniversary (see Walt Disney Showcase #47)	4	8	12	24	32	40
Surprise Party 1(1979)-r/1969 issue	1	2	3	5	6	8

MICKEY MOUSE ADVENTURES
Disney Comics: June, 1990 - No. 18, Nov, 1991 ($1.50)

	GD	VG	FN	VF	VF/NM	NM-
1,8,9: 1-Bradbury, Murry-r/M.M. #45,73 plus new-a. 8-Byrne-c. 9-Fantasia 50th ann. issue w/new adapt. of movie						3.00
2-7,10-18: 2-Begin all new stories. 10-r/F.C. #214						2.50

MICKEY MOUSE CLUB FUN BOOK
Golden Press: 1977 (1.95, 228 pgs.)(square bound)

	GD	VG	FN	VF	VF/NM	NM-
11190-1950s-r; 20,000 Leagues, M. Mouse Silly Symphonys, The Reluctant Dragon, etc.	4	8	12	24	32	40

MICKEY MOUSE CLUB MAGAZINE (See Walt Disney...)

MICKEY MOUSE COMICS DIGEST
Gladstone: 1986 - No. 5, 1987 (96 pgs.)

	GD	VG	FN	VF	VF/NM	NM-
1 ($1.25-c)	1	2	3	5	6	8
2-5: 3-5 ($1.50-c)						5.00

MICKEY MOUSE IN COLOR
Another Rainbow/Pantheon: 1988 (Deluxe, 13"x17", hard-c, $250.00)
(Trade, 9-7/8"x11-1/2", hard-c, $39.95)

	GD	VG	FN	VF	VF/NM	NM-
Deluxe limited edition of 3,000 copies signed by Floyd Gottfredson and Carl Barks, designated as the "Official Mickey Mouse 60th Anniversary" book. Mickey Sunday and daily reprints, plus Barks "Riddle of the Red Hat" from Four Color #79. Comes with 45 r.p.m. record interview with Gottfredson and Barks. 240 pgs.	20	40	60	142	209	275
Deluxe, limited to 100 copies, as above, but with a unique colored pencil original drawing of Mickey Mouse by Carl Barks. Add value of art to book price.						800.00
Pantheon trade edition, edited down & without Barks, 192 pgs.	4	8	12	24	32	40

MICKEY MOUSE MAGAZINE (Becomes Walt Disney's Comics & Stories)
K. K. Publ./Western Publishing Co.: Summer, 1935 (June-Aug, indicia) - V5#12, Sept, 1940; V1#1-5, V3#11,12, V4#1-3 are 44 pgs; V2#3-100 pgs; V5#12-68 pgs; rest are 36 pgs.(No V3#1, V4#6)

	GD	VG	FN	VF	VF/NM	NM-
V1#1 (Large size, 13-1/4x10-1/4"; 25¢)-Contains puzzles, games, cels, stories & comics of Disney characters. Promotional magazine for Disney cartoon movies and paraphernalia	1200	2400	3600	7800	16,000	-

Note: *Some copies were autographed by the editors & given away with all early one year subscriptions.*

	GD	VG	FN	VF	VF/NM	NM-
2 (Size change, 11-1/2x8-1/2"; 10/35; 10¢)-High quality paper begins; Messmer-a	200	400	600	1700	-	-
3,4: 3-Messmer-a	100	200	300	875	-	-
5-1st Donald Duck solo-c; 2nd cover app. ever; last 44 pg. & high quality paper issue	160	320	480	1400	-	-
6-9: 6-36 pg. issues begin; Donald becomes editor. 8-2nd Donald solo-c. 9-1st Mickey/Minnie-c	95	190	285	825	-	-
10-12, V2#1,2: 11-1st Pluto/Mickey-c; Donald fires himself and appoints Mickey as editor	90	180	270	775	-	-
V2#3-Special 100 pg. Christmas issue (25¢); Messmer-a; Donald becomes editor of Wise Quacks	330	660	990	3000	-	-
4-Mickey Mouse Comics & Roy Ranger (adventure strip) begin; both end V2#9; Messmer-a	75	150	225	650	-	-
5-9: 5-Ted True (adventure strip, ends V2#9) & Silly Symphony Comics (ends V3#3) begin. 6-1st solo Minnie-c. 6-9-Mickey Mouse Movies cut-out in each	48	96	144	288	432	575
10-1st full color issue; Mickey Mouse (by Gottfredson; ends V3#12) & Silly Symphony (ends V3#3) full color Sunday-r, Peter The Farm Detective (ends V5#8) & Ole Of The North (ends V3#3) begins	72	144	216	450	675	900
11-13: 12-Hiawatha-c & feature story	46	92	138	276	418	560
V3#2-Big Bad Wolf Halloween-c	55	110	165	344	515	685
3 (12/37)-1st app. Snow White & The Seven Dwarfs (before release of movie) (possibly 1st in print); Mickey X-Mas-c	100	200	300	625	938	1250

4 (1/38)-Snow White & The Seven Dwarfs serial begins (on stands before release of

Mickey Mouse Magazine V5#6 © WDC

Micronauts #1 © Takara, Ltd.

Midnight Nation #12 © J. Michael Straczynski & TCOW

movie); Ducky Symphony (ends V3#11) begins
82 164 246 513 769 1025
5-1st Snow White & Seven Dwarfs-c (St. Valentine's Day)
102 204 306 638 957 1275
6-Snow White serial ends; Lonesome Ghosts app. (2 pp.)
55 110 165 337 506 675
7-Seven Dwarfs Easter-c 53 106 159 318 479 640
8-10: 9-Dopey-c. 10-1st solo Goofy-c 43 86 129 258 389 520
11,12 (44 pgs; 8 more pgs. color added). 11-Mickey the Sheriff serial (ends V4#3) & Donald Duck strip-r (ends V3#12) begin. Color feature on Snow White's Forest Friends 48 96 144 288 429 570
V4#1 (10/38; 44 pgs.)-Brave Little Tailor-c/feature story, nominated for Academy Award; Bobby & Chip by Otto Messmer (ends V4#2) & The Practical Pig (ends V4#2) begin
48 96 144 288 429 570
2 (44 pgs.)-1st Huey, Dewey & Louie-c 49 98 147 294 440 585
3 (12/38, 44 pgs.)-Ferdinand The Bull-c/feature story, Academy Award winner; Mickey Mouse & The Whalers serial begins, ends V4#12
48 96 144 288 429 570
4-Spotty, Mother Pluto strip-r begin, end V4#8 43 86 129 258 389 520
5-St. Valentine's day-c. 1st Pluto solo-c 51 102 153 306 458 610
7 (3/39)-The Ugly Duckling-c/feature story, Academy Award winner
48 96 144 288 429 570
7 (4/39)-Goofy & Wilbur The Grasshopper classic-c/feature story from 1st Goofy solo cartoon movie; Timid Elmer begins, ends V5#5
48 96 144 288 429 570
8-Big Bad Wolf-c from Practical Pig movie poster; Practical Pig feature story
48 96 144 288 429 570
9-Donald Duck & Mickey Mouse Sunday-r begin; The Pointer feature story, nominated for Academy Award 48 96 144 288 429 570
10-Classic July 4th drum & fife-c; last Donald Sunday-r
58 116 174 363 544 725
11-1st slick-c; last over-sized issue 43 86 129 258 389 520
12 (9/39; format change, 10-1/4x8-1/4")-1st full color, cover to cover issue; Donald's Penguin-c/feature story 53 106 159 318 479 640
V5#1-Black Pete-c; Officer Duck-c/feature story; Autograph Hound feature story; Robinson Crusoe serial begins 52 104 156 312 469 625
2-Goofy-c; 1st app. Pinocchio (cameo) 68 136 204 425 638 850
3 (12/39)-Pinocchio Christmas-c (Before movie release). 1st app. Jiminy Cricket; Pinocchio serial begins 77 154 231 481 721 960
4,5: 5-Jiminy Cricket-c; Pinocchio serial ends; Donald's Dog Laundry feature story
52 104 156 312 469 625
6,7: 6-Tugboat Mickey feature story; Rip Van Winkle feature begins, ends V5#8. 7-2nd Huey, Dewey & Louie-c 51 102 153 306 458 610
8-Last magazine size issue; 2nd solo Pluto-c; Figaro & Cleo feature story
52 104 156 312 469 625
9-11: 9 (6/40; change to comic book size)-Jiminy Cricket feature story; Donald-c & Sunday-r begin. 10-Special Independence Day issue. 11-Hawaiian Holiday & Mickey's Trailer feature stories; last 36 pg. issue 55 110 165 344 515 685
12 (Format change)-The transition issue (68 pgs.) becoming a comic book. With only a title change to follow, becomes Walt Disney's Comics & Stories #1 with the next issue 434 868 1302 3038 4669 6300

NOTE: *Otto Messmer-a is in many issues of the first two-three years. The following story titles and issues have gags created by* ***Carl Barks:*** *V4#3(12/38)-'Donald's Better Self' & 'Donald's Golf Game;' V4#4(1/39)-'Donald's Lucky Day;' V4#7(3/39)-'Hockey Champ;' V4#7(4/39)-'Donald's Cousin Gus;' V4#9(6/39)-'Sea Scouts;' V4#12(9/39)-'Donald's Penguin;' V5#9 (6/40)-'Donald's Vacation;' V5#10(7/40)-'Bone Trouble;' V5#12(9/40)-'Window Cleaners.'*

MICKEY MOUSE MAGAZINE (Russian Version)
May 16, 1991 (1st Russian printing of a modern comic book)
1-Bagged w/gold label commemoration in English 10.00

MICKEY MOUSE MARCH OF COMICS (See March of Comics #8,27,45,60,74)

MICKEY MOUSE'S SUMMER VACATION (See Story Hour Series)

MICKEY MOUSE SUMMER FUN (See Dell Giants)

MICKEY SPILLANE'S MIKE DANGER
Tekno Comix: Sept, 1995 - No. 11, May, 1996 ($1.95)
1-11: 1-Frank Miller-c. 7-polybagged; Simonson-c. 8,9-Simonson-c 2.25

MICKEY SPILLANE'S MIKE DANGER
Big Entertainment: V2#1, June, 1996 - No. 10, Apr, 1997 ($2.25)
V2#1-10: Max Allan Collins scripts 2.25

MICROBOTS, THE
Gold Key: Dec, 1971 (one-shot)
1 (10271-112) 3 6 9 16 20 24

GD VG FN VF VF/NM NM-
2.0 4.0 6.0 8.0 9.0 9.2

MICRONAUTS (Toys)
Marvel Comics Group: Jan, 1979 - No. 59, Aug, 1984 (Mando paper #53 on)
1-Intro/1st app. Baron Karza 5.00
2-10,35,37,57: 7-Man-Thing app. 8-1st app. Capt. Universe (8/79). 9-1st app. Cilicia. 35-Double size; origin Microverse; intro Death Squad; Dr. Strange app. 37-Nightcrawler app.; X-Men cameo (2 pgs.). 57-(52 pgs.) 3.00
11-34,36,38-56,58,59: 13-1st app. Jasmine. 15-Death of Microtron. 15-17-Fantastic Four app. 17-Death of Jasmine. 20-Ant-Man app. 21-Microverse series begins. 25-Origin Baron Karza. 25-29-Nick Fury app. 27-Death of Biotron. 34-Dr. Strange app. 38-First direct sale. 40-Fantastic Four app. 48-Early Guice-a begins. 59-Golden painted-c 2.50
nn-Reprints #1-3; blank UPC; diamond on top 2.25
Annual 1,2 (12/79,10/80)-Ditko-c/a 3.00

NOTE: *#38-on distributed only through comic shops.* ***N. Adams*** *c-7i.* ***Chaykin*** *a-13-18p.* ***Ditko*** *a-39p.* ***Giffen*** *a-36p, 37p(part).* ***Golden*** *a-1-12p; c-2-7p, 8-23, 24p, 38, 39, 59.* ***Guice*** *a-48-58p; c-49-58.* ***Gil Kane*** *a-38, 40-45p; c-40-45.* ***Layton*** *c-33-37.* ***Miller*** *c-31.*

MICRONAUTS (Toys)
Marvel Comics Group: Oct, 1984 - No. 20, May, 1986
V2#1-20 2.50

NOTE: ***Kelley Jones*** *a-1; c-1, 6.* ***Guice*** *a-4p; c-2p.*

MICRONAUTS
Image Comics: 2002 - Present ($2.95)
2002 Convention Special (no cover price, B&W) previews series 2.25
1-11: 1-3-Hanson-a; Dave Johnson-c. 4-Su-a; 2 covers by Linsner & Hanson 3.00
...Vol. 1: Revolution (2003, $12.95, digest size) r/#1-5 13.00

MICRONAUTS: KARZA
Image Comics: Feb, 2003 - No. 4, May, 2003 ($2.95)
1-4-Krueger-s/Kurth-a 3.00

MICRONAUTS SPECIAL EDITION
Marvel Comics Group: Dec, 1983 - No. 5, Apr, 1984 ($2.00, limited series, Baxter paper)
1-5: r-/original series 1-12; Guice-c(p)-all 3.00

MIDGET COMICS (Fighting Indian Stories)
St. John Publishng Co.: Feb, 1950 - No. 2, Apr, 1950 (5-3/8x7-3/8", 68 pgs.)
1-Fighting Indian Stories; Matt Baker-c 20 40 60 112 156 200
2-Tex West, Cowboy Marshal (also in #1) 10 20 30 56 73 90

MIDNIGHT (See Smash Comics #18)

MIDNIGHT
Ajax/Farrell Publ. (Four Star Comic Corp.): Apr, 1957 - No. 6, June, 1958
1-Reprints from Voodoo & Strange Fantasy with some changes
15 30 45 86 118 150
2-6 9 18 27 52 66 80

MIDNIGHT EYE
Viz Premiere Comics: 1991 - No. 6, 1992 ($4.95, 44 pgs., mature)
1-6: Japanese stories translated into English 5.00

MIDNIGHT MASS
DC Comics (Vertigo): Jun, 2002 - No. 8, Jan, 2003 ($2.50)
1-8-Rozum-s/Saiz & Palmiotti-a 2.50

MIDNIGHT MEN
Marvel Comics (Epic Comics/Heavy Hitters): June, 1993 - No. 4, Sept, 1993 ($2.50/$1.95, limited series)
1-($2.50)-Embossed-c; Chaykin-c/a & scripts in all 3.00
2-4 2.25

MIDNIGHT MYSTERY
American Comics Group: Jan-Feb, 1961 - No. 7, Oct, 1961
1-Sci/Fi story 9 18 27 65 93 120
2-7: 7-Gustavson-a 5 10 15 36 48 60

NOTE: ***Reinman*** *a-1, 3.* ***Whitney*** *a-1, 4-6; c-1-3, 5, 7.*

MIDNIGHT NATION
Image Comics (Top Cow): Oct, 2000 - No. 12, July, 2002 ($2.50/$2.95)
1-Straczynski-s/Frank-a; 2 covers 3.00
2-11: 9-Twin Towers cover 2.50
12-($2.95)Last issue 3.00
Wizard #1/2 (2001) Michael Zulli-a; two covers by Frank 3.00
Vol. 1 ('03, $29.99, TPB) r/#1-12 & Wizard #1/2; cover gallery; afterword by Straczynski 30.00

MIDNIGHT SONS UNLIMITED
Marvel Comics (Midnight Sons imprint #4 on): Apr, 1993 - No. 9, May, 1995 ($3.95, 68 pgs.)
1-9: Blaze, Darkhold (by Quesada #1), Ghost Rider, Morbius & Nightstalkers in all.

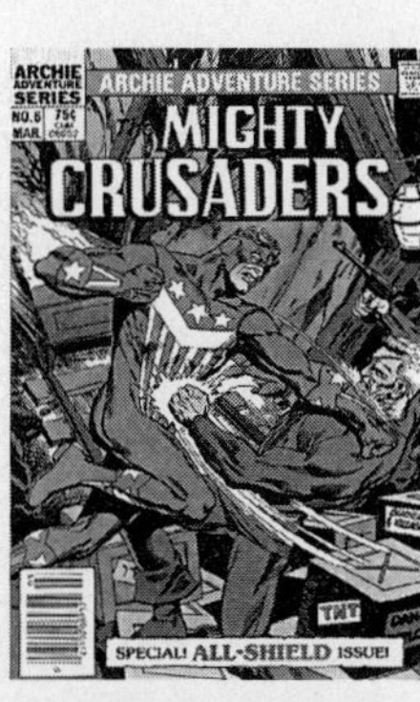

Mightly Crusaders #6 © Red Circle

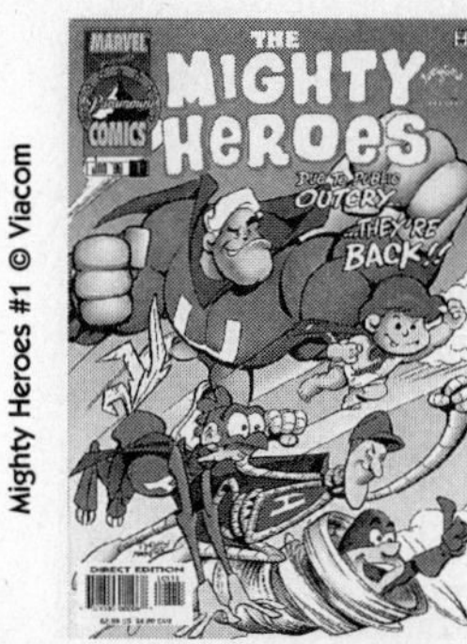

Mighty Heroes #1 © Viacom

Mighty Marvel Western #1 © MAR

	GD 2.0	VG 4.0	FN 6.0	VF 8.0	VF/NM 9.0	NM- 9.2

1-Painted-c. 3-Spider-Man app. 4-Siege of Darkness part 17; new Dr. Strange & new Ghost Rider app.; spot varnish-c 4.00
NOTE: *Sears a-2.*

MIDNIGHT TALES
Charlton Press: Dec, 1972 - No. 18, May, 1976

V1#1 2 4 6 14 18 22
2-10 2 4 6 9 11 14
11-18: 11-14-Newton-a(p) 1 3 4 6 8 10
12,17(Modern Comics reprint, 1977) 5.00
NOTE: ***Adkins** a-12i, 13i. **Ditko** a-12. **Howard** (Wood imitator) a-1-15, 17, 18; c-1-18. **Don Newton** a-11-14p. **Staton** a-1, 3-11, 13. **Sutton** a-3-10.*

MIGHTY ATOM, THE (...& the Pixies #6) (Formerly The Pixies #1-5)
Magazine Enterprises: No. 6, 1949; Nov, 1957 - No. 6, Aug-Sept, 1958

6(1949-M.E.)-no month (1st Series) 7 14 21 35 43 50
1-6(2nd Series)-Pixies-r 4 8 12 18 22 25
I.W. Reprint #1(nd) 2 4 6 9 11 14

MIGHTY BEAR (Formerly Fun Comics; becomes Unsane #15)
Star Publ. No. 13,14/Ajax-Farrell (Four Star): No. 13, Jan, 1954 - No. 14, Mar, 1954; 9/57 - No. 3, 2/58

13,14-L. B. Cole-c 19 38 57 106 146 185
1-3('57-58)Four Star; becomes Mighty Ghost #4 7 14 21 35 43 50

MIGHTY COMICS (...Presents) (Formerly Flyman)
Radio Comics (Archie): No. 40, Nov, 1966 - No. 50, Oct, 1967 (All 12¢ issues)

40-Web 4 8 12 22 30 38
41-50: 41-Shield, Black Hood. 42-Black Hood. 43-Shield, Web & Black Hood. 44-Black Hood, Steel Sterling & The Shield. 45-Shield & Hangman; origin Web retold. 46-Steel Sterling, Web & Black Hood. 47-Black Hood & Mr. Justice. 48-Shield & Hangman; Wizard x-over in Shield. 49-Steel Sterling & Fox; Black Hood x-over in Steel Sterling. 50-Black Hood & Web; Inferno x-over in Web 3 6 9 19 25 32
NOTE: ***Paul Reinman** a-40-50.*

MIGHTY CRUSADERS, THE (Also see Adventures of the Fly, The Crusaders & Fly Man)
Mighty Comics Group (Radio Comics): Nov, 1965 - No. 7, Oct, 1966 (All 12¢)

1-Origin The Shield 6 12 18 43 59 75
2-Origin Comet 4 8 12 24 32 40
3,5-7: 3-Origin Fly-Man. 5-Intro. Ultra-Men (Fox, Web, Capt. Flag) & Terrific Three (Jaguar, Mr. Justice, Steel Sterling). 7-Steel Sterling feature; origin Fly-Girl 4 8 12 22 30 38
4-1st S.A. app. Fireball, Inferno & Fox; Firefly, Web, Bob Phantom, Blackjack, Hangman, Zambini, Kardak, Steel Sterling, Mr. Justice, Wizard, Capt. Flag, Jaguar x-over 4 8 12 25 33 42
Volume 1: Origin of a Super Team TPB (2003, $12.95) r/#1 & Fly Man #31-33 13.00
NOTE: ***Reinman** a-6.*

MIGHTY CRUSADERS, THE (All New Advs. of...#2)
Red Circle Prod./Archie Ent. No. 6 on: Mar, 1983 - No. 13, Sept, 1985 ($1.00, 36 pgs, Mando paper)

1-Origin Black Hood, The Fly, Fly Girl, The Shield, The Wizard, The Jaguar, Pvt. Strong & The Web. 6.00
2-10: 2-Mister Midnight begins. 4-Darkling replaces Shield. 5-Origin Jaguar, Shield begins. 7-Untold origin Jaguar. 10-Veitch-a 4.00
11-13-Lower print run 5.00
NOTE: ***Buckler** a-1-3, 4i, 5p, 7p, 8i, 9i; c-1-10p.*

MIGHTY GHOST (Formerly Mighty Bear #1-3)
Ajax/Farrell Publ.: No. 4, June, 1958

4 6 12 18 28 34 40

MIGHTY HERCULES, THE (TV)
Gold Key: July, 1963 - No. 2, Nov, 1963

1 (10072-307) 16 32 48 113 167 220
2 (10072-311) 15 30 45 104 152 200

MIGHTY HEROES, THE (TV) (Funny)
Dell Publishing Co.: Mar, 1967 - No. 4, July, 1967

1-Also has a 1957 Heckle & Jeckle-r 15 30 45 104 152 200
2-4: 4-Has two 1958 Mighty Mouse-r 10 20 30 72 104 135

MIGHTY HEROES
Spotlight Comics: 1987 (B&W, one-shot)

1-Heckle & Jeckle backup 4.00

MIGHTY HEROES
Marvel Comics: Jan, 1998 ($2.99, one-shot)

1-Origin of the Mighty Heroes 3.00

MIGHTY MARVEL TEAM-UP THRILLERS
Marvel Comics: 1983 ($5.95, trade paperback)

1-Reprints team-up stories 35.00

MIGHTY MARVEL WESTERN, THE
Marvel Comics Group (LMC earlier issues): Oct, 1968 - No. 46, Sept, 1976 (#1-14: 68 pgs.; #15,16: 52 pgs.)

1-Begin Kid Colt, Rawhide Kid, Two-Gun Kid-r 6 12 18 38 52 65
2-5: (2-14 are 68 pgs.) 4 8 12 25 33 42
6-16: (15,16 are 52 pgs.) 4 8 12 22 30 38
17-20 2 4 6 12 16 20
21-30,32,37: 24-Kid Colt-r end. 25-Matt Slade-r begin. 32-Origin-r/Rawhide Kid #23; Williamson-r/Kid Slade #7. 37-Williamson, Kirby-r/Two-Gun Kid 51 2 4 6 10 12 15
31,33-36,38-46: 31-Baker-r. 2 4 6 8 10 12
45-(30¢-c variant, limited distribution)(6/76) 2 4 6 11 14 18
NOTE: ***Jack Davis** a(r)-21-24. **Keller** r-1-13, 22. **Kirby** a(r)-1-3, 6, 9, 12-14, 16, 25-29, 32-38, 40, 41, 43-46; c-29. **Maneely** a(r)-22. **Severin** c-3i, 9. No Matt Slade-#43.*

MIGHTY MIDGET COMICS, THE (Miniature)
Samuel E. Lowe & Co.: No date; circa 1942-1943 (Sold 2 for 5¢, B&W and red, 36 pgs, approx. 5x4")

Bulletman #11(1943)-r/cover/Bulletman #3 23 46 69 129 180 230
Captain Marvel Adventures #11 23 46 69 129 180 230
Captain Marvel #11 (Same as above except for full color ad on back cover; this issue was glued to cover of Captain Marvel #20 and is not found in fine-mint condition) 330 660 990 - - -
Captain Marvel Jr. #11 (Same-c as Master #27 23 46 69 129 180 230
Captain Marvel Jr. #11 (Same as above except for full color ad on back-c; this issue was glued to cover of Captain Marvel #21 and is not found in fine-mint condition) 330 660 990 - - -
Golden Arrow #11 21 42 63 118 164 210
Golden Arrow #11 (Same as above except for full color ad on back-c; this issue was glued to cover of Captain Marvel #21 and is not found in fine-mint condition) 270 540 810 - - -
Ibis the Invincible #11(1942)-Origin; reprints cover to Ibis #1 (Predates Fawcett's Ibis the Invincible #1). 23 46 69 129 180 230
Spy Smasher #11(1942) 23 46 69 129 180 230
NOTE: *The above books came in a box called "box full of books" and was distributed with other Samuel Lowe puzzles, paper dolls, coloring books, etc. They are not titled Mighty Midget Comics. All have a war bond seal on back cover which is otherwise blank. These books came in a "Mighty Midget" flat cardboard counter display rack.*
Balbo, the Boy Magician #12 (1943)-1st book devoted entirely to character. 12 24 36 71 96 120
Bulletman #12 17 34 51 98 134 170
Commando Yank #12 (1943)-Only comic devoted entirely to character. 14 28 42 79 107 135
Dr. Voltz the Human Generator (1943)-Only comic devoted entirely to character. 12 24 36 71 96 120
Lance O'Casey #12 (1943)-1st comic devoted entirely to character (Predates Fawcett's Lance O'Casey #1). 12 24 36 71 96 120
Leatherneck the Marine (1943)-Only comic devoted entirely to character. 12 24 36 71 96 120
Minute Man #12 17 34 51 98 134 170
Mister "Q" (1943)-Only comic devoted entirely to character. 12 24 36 71 96 120
Mr. Scarlet and Pinky #12 (1943)-Only comic devoted entirely to character. 14 28 42 81 111 140
Pat Wilton and His Flying Fortress (1943)-1st comic devoted entirely to character. 12 24 36 71 96 120
The Phantom Eagle #12 (1943)-Only comic devoted entirely to character. 12 24 36 71 96 120
State Trooper Stops Crime (1943)-Only comic devoted entirely to character. 12 24 36 71 96 120
Tornado Tom (1943)-Origin, r/from Cyclone #1-3; only comic devoted entirely to character. 12 24 36 71 96 120

MIGHTY MORPHIN' POWER RANGERS: THE MOVIE (Also see Saban's Mighty Morphin' Power Rangers)
Marvel Comics: Sept, 1995 ($3.95, one-shot)

nn-adaptation of movie 4.00

MIGHTY MOUSE (See Adventures of..., Dell Giant #43, Giant Comics Edition, March of Comics #205, 237, 247, 257, 447, 459, 471, 483, Oxydol-Dreft, Paul Terry's, & Terry-Toons Comics)

MIGHTY MOUSE (1st Series)
Timely/Marvel Comics (20th Century Fox): Fall, 1946 - No. 4, Summer, 1947

1 124 248 372 775 1163 1550

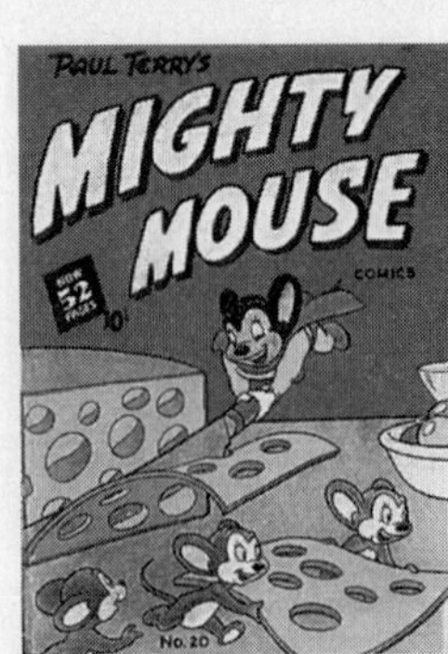

Mighty Mouse #20 © Terry Toons

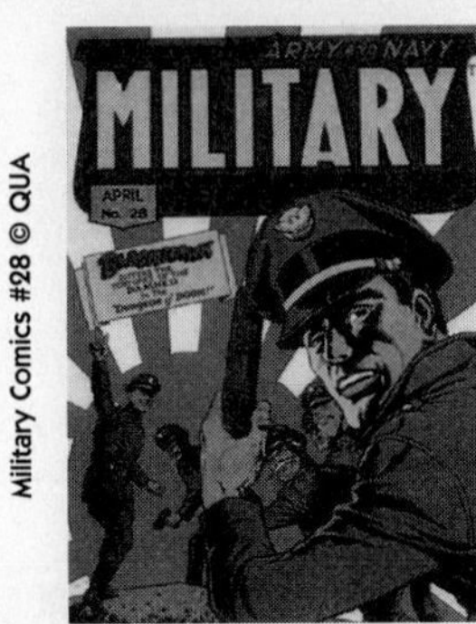

Military Comics #28 © QUA

Milk and Cheese #7 © Evan Dorkin

	GD 2.0	VG 4.0	FN 6.0	VF 8.0	VF/NM 9.0	NM- 9.2
2	55	110	165	344	515	685
3,4	40	80	120	240	345	450

MIGHTY MOUSE (2nd Series) (Paul Terry's... #62-71)
St. John Publishing Co./Pines No. 68 (3/56) on (TV issues #72 on):
Aug, 1947 - No. 67, 11/55; No. 68, 3/56 - No. 83, 6/59

	GD	VG	FN	VF	VF/NM	NM-
5(#1)	39	78	117	233	329	425
6-10	20	40	60	112	156	200
11-19	13	26	39	76	103	130
20 (11/50) - 25-(52 pg. editions)	10	20	30	58	77	95
20-25-(36 pg. editions)	9	18	27	52	66	80
26-37: 35-Flying saucer-c	8	16	24	43	54	65
38-45-(100 pgs.)	19	38	57	106	146	185
46-83: 62-64,67-Painted-c. 82-Infinity-c	8	16	24	40	50	60
Album nn (nd, 1952/53?, St. John)(100 pgs.)(Rebound issues w/new cover)	23	46	69	132	186	240
Album 1(10/52, 25¢, 100 pgs., St. John)-Gandy Goose app.	29	58	87	164	232	300
Album 2,3(11/52 & 12/52, St. John) (100 pgs.)	23	46	69	132	186	240
Fun Club Magazine 1(Fall, 1957-Pines, 25¢, 100 pgs.) (CBS TV)-Tom Terrific, Heckle & Jeckle, Dinky Duck, Gandy Goose	16	32	48	92	126	160
Fun Club Magazine 2-6(Winter, 1958-Pines)	10	20	30	58	77	95
3-D 1-(1st printing-9/53, 25¢)(St. John)-Came w/glasses; stiff covers; says World's First! on-c; 1st 3-D comic	31	62	93	175	248	320
3-D 1-(2nd printing-10/53, 25¢)-Came w/glasses; slick, glossy covers, slightly smaller	27	54	81	153	214	275
3-D 2,3(11/53, 12/53, 25¢)-(St. John)-With glasses	26	52	78	147	206	265

MIGHTY MOUSE (TV)(3rd Series)(Formerly Adventures of Mighty Mouse)
Gold Key/Dell Publ. Co. No. 166-on: No. 161, Oct, 1964 - No. 172, Oct, 1968

	GD	VG	FN	VF	VF/NM	NM-
161(10/64)-165(9/65)-(Becomes Adventures of... No. 166 on)	5	10	15	36	48	60
166(3/66), 167(6/66)-172	4	8	12	24	32	40

MIGHTY MOUSE (TV)
Spotlight Comics: 1987 - No. 2, 1987 ($1.50, color)

	NM-
1,2-New stories	3.00
...And Friends Holiday Special (11/87, $1.75)	3.00

MIGHTY MOUSE (TV)
Marvel Comics: Oct, 1990 - No. 10, July, 1991 ($1.00)(Based on Sat. cartoon)

	NM-
1-10: 1-Dark Knight-c parody. 2-10: 3-Intro Bat-Bat; Byrne-c. 4,5-Crisis-c/story parodies w/Perez-c. 6-Spider-Man-c parody. 7-Origin Bat-Bat	2.25

MIGHTY MOUSE ADVENTURE MAGAZINE
Spotlight Comics: 1987 ($2.00, B&W, 52 pgs., magazine size, one-shot)

	NM-
1-Deputy Dawg, Heckle & Jeckle backup stories	5.00

MIGHTY MOUSE ADVENTURES (Adventures of... #2 on)
St. John Publishing Co.: November, 1951

	GD	VG	FN	VF	VF/NM	NM-
1	34	68	102	193	274	355

MIGHTY MOUSE ADVENTURE STORIES (Paul Terry's... on-c only)
St. John Publishing Co.: 1953 (50¢, 384 pgs.)

	GD	VG	FN	VF	VF/NM	NM-
nn-Rebound issues	43	86	129	258	389	520

MIGHTY MUTANIMALS (See Teenage Mutant Ninja Turtles Adventures #19)
May, 1991 - No. 3, July, 1991 ($1.00, limited series)
Archie Comics: Apr, 1992 - No. 8, June, 1993 ($1.25)

	NM-
1-3: 1-Story cont'd from TMNT Advs. #19.	2.25
1-9 (1992): 7-1st app. Merdude	2.25

MIGHTY SAMSON (Also see Gold Key Champion)
Gold Key/Whitman #32: July, 1964 - No. 20, Nov, 1969; No. 21, Aug, 1972; No. 22, Dec, 1973 - No. 31, Mar, 1976; No. 32, Aug, 1982 (Painted-c #1-31)

	GD	VG	FN	VF	VF/NM	NM-
1-Origin/1st app.; Thorne-a begins	9	18	27	65	93	120
2-5	5	10	15	36	48	60
6-10: 7-Tom Morrow begins, ends #20	4	8	12	24	32	40
11-20	3	6	9	18	24	30
21-31: 21,22-r	2	4	6	14	18	22
32(Whitman, 8/82)-r	2	4	6	8	10	12

MIGHTY THOR (See Thor)

MIKE BARNETT, MAN AGAINST CRIME (TV)
Fawcett Publications: Dec, 1951 - No. 6, Oct, 1952

	GD	VG	FN	VF	VF/NM	NM-
1	20	40	60	112	156	200
2	12	24	36	69	92	115
3,4,6	10	20	30	58	77	95
5- "Market for Morphine" cover/story	13	26	39	76	103	130

MIKE DANGER (See Mickey Spillane's...)

MIKE DEODATO'S...
Caliber Comics: 1996, ($2.95, B&W)

	NM-
...FALLOUT 3000 #1, ...JONAS (mag. size) #1,...PRIME CUTS (mag. size) #1, ...PROTHEUS #1,2, ...RAMTHAR #1,...RAZOR NIGHTS #1	3.00

MIKE GRELL'S SABLE (Also see Jon Sable & Sable)
First Comics: Mar, 1990 - No. 10, Dec, 1990 ($1.75)

	NM-
1-10: r/Jon Sable Freelance #1-10 by Grell	2.25

MIKE MIST MINUTE MIST-ERIES (See Ms. Tree/Mike Mist in 3-D)
Eclipse Comics: April, 1981 ($1.25, B&W, one-shot)

	NM-
1	2.25

MIKE SHAYNE PRIVATE EYE
Dell Publishing Co.: Nov-Jan, 1962 - No. 3, Sept-Nov, 1962

	GD	VG	FN	VF	VF/NM	NM-
1	4	8	12	25	33	42
2,3	3	6	9	18	23	28

MILITARY COMICS (Becomes Modern Comics #44 on)
Quality Comics Group: Aug, 1941 - No. 43, Oct, 1945

	GD	VG	FN	VF	VF/NM	NM-
1-Origin/1st app. Blackhawk by C. Cuidera (Eisner scripts); Miss America, The Death Patrol by Jack Cole (also #2-7,27-30), & The Blue Tracer by Guardineer; X of the Underground, The Yankee Eagle, Q-Boat & Shot & Shell, Archie Atkins, Loops & Banks by Bud Ernest (Bob Powell)(ends #13) begin	931	1862	2793	6517	10,009	13,500
2-Secret War News begins (by McWilliams #2-16); Cole-a; new uniform with yellow circle & hawk's head for Blackhawk	264	528	792	1650	2475	3300
3-Origin/1st app. Chop Chop (9/41)	228	456	684	1425	2138	2850
4	184	368	552	1150	1725	2300
5-The Sniper begins; Miss America in costume #4-7	152	304	456	950	1425	1900
6-9: 8-X of the Underground begins (ends #13). 9-The Phantom Clipper begins (ends #16)	110	220	330	688	1032	1375
10-Classic Eisner-c	120	240	360	750	1125	1500
11-Flag-c	90	180	270	563	844	1125
12-Blackhawk by Crandall begins, ends #22	112	224	336	700	1050	1400
13-15: 14-Private Dogtag begins (ends #83)	85	170	255	531	796	1060
16-20: 16-Blue Tracer ends. 17-P.T. Boat begins	74	148	222	463	692	920
21-31: 22-Last Crandall Blackhawk. 23-Shrunken head-c. 27-Death Patrol revived	63	126	189	394	592	790
32-43	55	110	165	330	495	660

NOTE: ***Berg** a-6. **Al Bryant** c-31-34, 38, 40-43. **J. Cole** a-1-3, 27-32. **Crandall** a-12-22; c-13-20. **Cuidera** c-2-9. **Eisner** c-1, 2(part), 9, 10. **Kotsky** c-21-29, 35, 37, 39. **McWilliams** a-2-16. **Powell** a-1-13. **Ward** Blackhawk-30, 31(15 pgs. each); c-30.*

MILK AND CHEESE (Also see Cerebus Bi-Weekly #20)
Slave Labor: 1991 - Present ($2.50, B&W)

	GD	VG	FN	VF	VF/NM	NM-
1-Evan Dorkin story & art in all.	4	8	12	29	40	50
1-2nd-6th printings						4.00
2-"Other #1"	3	6	9	18	24	30
2-reprint						3.00
3-"Third #1"	2	4	6	12	16	20
4-"Fourth #1", 5-"First Second Issue"	1	3	4	6	8	10
6,7: 6-"#666"						5.00

NOTE: *Multiple printings of all issues exist and are worth cover price unless listed here.*

MILLENNIUM
DC Comics: Jan, 1988 - No. 8, Feb, 1988 (Weekly limited series)

	NM-
1-Staton c/a(p) begins	3.00
2-8	2.50

MILLENNIUM EDITION:... (Reprints of classic DC issues)
DC Comics: Feb, 2000 - Feb, 2001 (gold foil cover stamps)

	NM-
Action Comics #1, Adventure Comics #61, All Star Comics #3, All Star Comics #8, Batman #1, Detective Comics #1, Detective Comics #27, Detective Comics #38, Flash Comics #1, Military Comics #1, More Fun Comics #73, Police Comics #1, Sensation Comics #1, Superman #1, Whiz Comics #2, Wonder Woman #1 -($3.95-c)	4.00

Action Comics #252, Adventure Comics #247, Brave and the Bold #28, Brave and the Bold #85, Crisis on Infinte Earths #1, Detective #225, Detective #327, Detective #359, Detective #395, Flash #123, Gen13 #1, Green Lantern #76, House of Mystery #1, House of Secrets #92, JLA #1, Justice League #1, Mad #1, Man of Steel #1, Mysterious Suspense #1, New Gods, #1, New Teen Titans #1, Our Army at War #81, Plop! #1, Saga of the Swamp Thing #21, Shadow #1, Showcase #4, Showcase #9, Showcase #22, Superman #233, Superman (2nd) #75, Superman's Pal Jimmy Olsen #1, Watchmen #1, WildC.A.T.s #1,

Millie the Model #7 © MAR

Minute Man #1 © FAW

Miracleman #1 © ECL

	GD 2.0	VG 4.0	FN 6.0	VF 8.0	VF/NM 9.0	NM- 9.2
Wonder Woman (2nd) #1, World's Finest #71 -($2.50-c)						2.50
All-Star Western #10, Hellblazer #1, More Fun Comics #101, Preacher #1, Sandman #1, Spirit #1, Superboy #1, Superman #76, Young Romance #1-($2.95-c)						3.00
Batman: The Dark Knight Returns #1, Kingdom Come #1 -($5.95-c)						6.00
All Star Comics #3, Batman #1, Justice League #1: Chromium cover						10.00
Crisis on Infinite Earths #1 Chromium cover						20.00

MILLENNIUM FEVER
DC Comics (Vertigo): Oct, 1995 - No.4, Jan, 1996 ($2.50, limited series)

	GD	VG	FN	VF	VF/NM	NM-
1-4: Duncan Fegredo-c/a						2.50

MILLENNIUM INDEX
Independent Comics Group: Mar, 1988 - No. 2, Mar, 1988 ($2.00)

	GD	VG	FN	VF	VF/NM	NM-
1,2						2.25

MILLENNIUM 2.5 A.D.
ACG Comics: No. 1, 2000 ($2.95)

	GD	VG	FN	VF	VF/NM	NM-
1-Reprints 1934 Buck Rogers daily strips #1-48						3.00

MILLIE, THE LOVABLE MONSTER
Dell Publishing Co.: Sept-Nov, 1962 - No. 6, Jan, 1973

	GD	VG	FN	VF	VF/NM	NM-
12-523-211	6	12	18	38	52	65
2(8-10/63)-Bill Woggon c/a	5	10	15	33	44	55
3(8-10/64)	4	8	12	27	36	45
4(7/72), 5(10/72), 6(1/73)	2	4	6	12	16	20

NOTE: ***Woggon** a-3-6; c-3-6. 4 reprints 1; 5 reprints 2; 6 reprints 3.*

MILLIE THE MODEL (See Comedy Comics, A Date With..., Joker Comics #28, Life With..., Mad About..., Marvel Mini-Books, Misty & Modeling With...)
Marvel/Atlas/Marvel Comics(CnPC #1)(SPI/Male/VPI):1945 - No. 207, Dec, 1973

	GD	VG	FN	VF	VF/NM	NM-
1-Origin	82	164	246	513	769	1025
2 (10/46)-Millie becomes The Blonde Phantom to sell Blonde Phantom perfume; a pre-Blonde Phantom app. (see All-Select #11, Fall, 1946)	43	86	129	258	364	470
3-8,10: 4-7-Willie app. 7-Willie smokes extra strong tobacco. 8,10-Kurtzman's "Hey Look". 8-Willie & Rusty app.	30	60	90	170	240	310
9-Powerhouse Pepper by Wolverton, 4 pgs.	34	68	102	193	274	355
11-Kurtzman-a, "Giggles 'n' Grins"	20	40	60	115	160	205
12,15,17-20: 12-Rusty & Hedy Devine app.	15	30	45	84	115	145
13,14,16-Kurtzman's "Hey Look". 13-Hedy Devine app.	16	32	48	89	122	155
21-30	10	20	30	60	80	100
31-40	7	14	21	50	68	85
41-60	6	12	18	40	55	70
61-99	4	8	12	29	40	50
100	5	10	15	36	48	60
101-130: 107-Jack Kirby app. in story	4	8	12	27	36	45
131-134,136,138-153: 141-Groovy Gears-c/s	3	7	10	21	28	35
135-(2/66) 1st app. Groovy Gears	4	8	12	27	36	45
137-2nd app. Groovy Gears	4	8	12	24	32	40
154-New Millie begins (10/67)	4	8	12	29	40	50
155-190	3	6	9	19	25	32
191,193-199,201-206	3	6	9	16	20	25
192-(52 pgs.)	4	8	12	22	30	38
200,207(Last issue)	4	8	12	22	30	38
(Beware: cut-up pages are common in all Annuals)						
Annual 1(1962)-Early Marvel annual (2nd?)	21	42	63	147	216	285
Annual 2(1963)	14	28	42	99	145	190
Annual 3-5 (1964-1966)	9	18	27	60	85	110
Annual 6-10(1967-11/71)	7	14	21	51	71	90
Queen-Size 11(9/74), 12(1975)	6	12	18	43	59	75

NOTE: ***Dan DeCarlo** a-18-93.*

MILLION DOLLAR DIGEST (Richie Rich... #23 on; also see Richie Rich...)
Harvey Publications: 11/86 - No. 7, 11/87; No. 8, 4/88 - No. 34, Nov, 1994 ($1.25/$1.75, digest size)

	GD	VG	FN	VF	VF/NM	NM-
1						6.00
2-8: 8-(68 pgs.)						4.00
9-34: 9-Begin $1.75-c. 14-May not exist						3.00

MILT GROSS FUNNIES (Also see Picture News #1)
Milt Gross, Inc. (ACG?): Aug, 1947 - No. 2, Sept, 1947

	GD	VG	FN	VF	VF/NM	NM-
1	20	40	60	112	156	200
2	14	28	42	79	107	135

MILTON THE MONSTER & FEARLESS FLY (TV)
Gold Key: May, 1966

	GD	VG	FN	VF	VF/NM	NM-
1 (10175-605)	10	20	30	73	107	140

MINIMUM WAGE
Fantagraphics Books: V1#1, July, 1995 ($9.95, B&W, graphic novel, mature)
V2#1, 1995 - Present ($2.95, B&W, mature)

	GD	VG	FN	VF	VF/NM	NM-
V1#1-Bob Fingerman story & art	1	3	4	6	8	10
V2#1-9($2.95): Bob Fingerman story & art. 2-Kevin Nowlan back-c. 4-w/pin-ups. 5-Mignola back-c						3.00
Book Two TPB ('97, $12.95) r/V2#1-5						13.00

MINISTRY OF SPACE
Image Comics: Apr, 2001 - No. 3 ($2.95, limited series)

	GD	VG	FN	VF	VF/NM	NM-
1,2-Warren Ellis-s/Chris Weston-a						3.00

MINOR MIRACLES
DC Comics: 2000 ($12.95, B&W, squarebound)

	GD	VG	FN	VF	VF/NM	NM-
nn-Will Eisner-s/a						13.00

MINUTE MAN (See Master Comics & Mighty Midget Comics)
Fawcett Publications: Summer, 1941 - No. 3, Spring, 1942 (68 pgs.)

	GD	VG	FN	VF	VF/NM	NM-
1	200	400	600	1250	1875	2500
2,3	124	248	372	775	1163	1550

MINX, THE
DC Comics (Vertigo): Oct, 1998 - No. 8, May, 1999 ($2.50, limited series)

	GD	VG	FN	VF	VF/NM	NM-
1-8-Milligan-s/Phillips-c/a						3.00

MIRACLE COMICS
Hillman Periodicals: Feb, 1940 - No. 4, Mar, 1941

	GD	VG	FN	VF	VF/NM	NM-
1-Sky Wizard Master of Space, Dash Dixon, Man of Might, Pinkie Parker, Dusty Doyle, The Kid Cop, K-7, Secret Agent, The Scorpion, & Blandu, Jungle Queen begin; Masked Angel only app. (all 1st app.)	184	368	552	1150	1725	2300
2	92	184	276	575	863	1150
3,4: 3-Bill Colt, the Ghost Rider begins. 4-The Veiled Prophet & Bullet Bob (by Burnley) app.	78	156	234	488	732	975

MIRACLEMAN
Eclipse Comics: Aug, 1985 - No. 15, Nov, 1988; No. 16, Dec, 1989 - No. 24, 1994

	GD	VG	FN	VF	VF/NM	NM-
1-r/British Marvelman series; Alan Moore scripts in #1-16	1	2	3	5	7	9
1-Gold variant (edition of 400, signed by Alan Moore, came with signed & #'d certificate of authenticity)						1500.00
1-Blue variant (edition of 600, came with signed & #'d certificate of authenticity)						800.00
2-12: 8-Airboy preview. 9,10-Origin Miracleman. 9-Shows graphic scenes of childbirth. 10-Snyder-c	1	2	3	5	6	8
13,14	2	4	6	10	12	15
15-($1.75-c, scarce) end of Kid Miracleman	6	12	18	38	52	65
16-Last Alan Moore-s; 1st $1.95-c (low print)	2	4	6	12	16	20
17,18-($1.95): 17-"The Golden Age" begins, ends #22. Dave McKean-c begins, end #22; Neil Gaiman scripts in #17-24	2	4	6	8	10	12
19-23-($2.50); 23-"The Silver Age" begins; BWS-c	1	2	3	5	6	8
24-Last issue; B. Smith-c	2	4	6	9	11	14
3-D 1 (12/85)	1	2	3	5	6	8
Book One: A Dream of Flying (1988, $9.95, TPB) r/#1-5; Leach-c						22.00
Book One: A Dream of Flying-Hardcover (1988, $29.95) r/#1-5						70.00
Book Two: The Red King Syndrome (1990, $12.95, TPB) r/#6-10; Bolton-c						22.00
Book Two: The Red King Syndrome-Hardcover (1990, $30.95) r/#6-10						85.00
Book Three: Olympus (1990, $12.95, TPB) r/#11-16						100.00
Book Three: Olympus-Hardcover (1990, $30.95) r/#11-16						200.00
Book Four: The Golden Age (1992, $15.95, TPB) r/#17-22						30.00
Book Four: The Golden Age Hardcover (1992, $33.95) r/#17-22						50.00
Book Four: The Golden Age (1993, $12.99, TPB) new McKean-c						15.00

NOTE: ***Chaykin** c-3. **Gulacy** c-7. **McKean** c-17-22. **B. Smith** c-23, 24. **Starlin** c-4. **Totleben** a-11-13; c-9, 11-13. **Truman** c-6.*

MIRACLEMAN: APOCRYPHA
Eclipse Comics: Nov, 1991 - No. 3, Feb, 1992 ($2.50, limited series)

	GD	VG	FN	VF	VF/NM	NM-
1-3: 1-Stories by Neil Gaiman, Mark Buckingham, Alex Ross & others. 3-Stories by James Robinson, Kelley Jones, Matt Wagner, Neil Gaiman, Mark Buckingham & others	1	2	3	4	5	7
TPB (12/92, $15.95) r/#1-3; Buckingham-c						20.00

MIRACLEMAN FAMILY
Eclipse Comics: May, 1988 - No. 2, Sept, 1988 ($1.95, lim. series, Baxter paper)

	GD	VG	FN	VF	VF/NM	NM-
1,2: 2-Gulacy-c						5.00

MIRACLE OF THE WHITE STALLIONS, THE (See Movie Comics)

MIRACLE SQUAD, THE

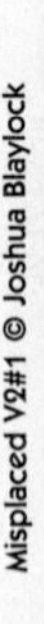

Misplaced V2#1 © Joshua Blaylock

Miss America Comics #1 © MAR

Mission Impossible #1 © DELL

	GD 2.0	VG 4.0	FN 6.0	VF 8.0	VF/NM 9.0	NM- 9.2

Upshot Graphics (Fantagraphics Books): Aug, 1986 - No. 4, 1987 ($2.00)

1-4						2.25

MIRACLE SQUAD: BLOOD AND DUST, THE
Apple Comics: Jan, 1989 - No. 4, July, 1989 ($1.95, B&W, limited series)

1-4						2.25

MISADVENTURES OF MERLIN JONES, THE (See Movie Comics & Merlin Jones as the Monkey's Uncle under Movie Comics)

MISPLACED
Image Comics: May, 2003 - Present ($2.95)

1,2: 1-Three covers by Blaylock, Green and Clugston-Major; Blaylock-s/a						3.00

MISS AMERICA COMICS (Miss America Magazine #2 on; also see Blonde Phantom & Marvel Mystery Comics)
Marvel Comics (20CC): 1944 (one-shot)

1-2 pgs. pin-ups	158	316	474	988	1482	1975

MISS AMERICA MAGAZINE (Formerly Miss America; Miss America #51 on)
Miss America Publ. Corp./Marvel/Atlas (MAP): V1#2, Nov, 1944 - No. 93, Nov, 1958

	GD	VG	FN	VF	VF/NM	NM-
V1#2-Photo-c of teenage girl in Miss America costume; Miss America, Patsy Walker (intro.) comic stories plus movie reviews & stories; intro. Buzz Baxter & Hedy Wolfe; 1 pg. origin Miss America	128	256	384	800	1200	1600
3-5-Miss America & Patsy Walker stories	48	96	144	288	432	575
6-Patsy Walker only	15	30	45	86	118	150
V2#1(4/45)-6(9/45)-Patsy Walker continues	10	20	30	56	73	90
V3#1(10/45)-6(4/46)	9	18	27	52	66	80
V4#1(5/46),2,5(9/46)	9	18	27	49	62	75
V4#3(7/46)-Liz Taylor photo-c	20	40	60	112	156	200
V4#4 (8/46; 68 pgs.), V4#6 (10/46; 92 pgs.)	8	16	24	43	54	65
V5#1(11/46)-6(4/47), V6#1(5/47)-3(7/47)	8	16	24	43	54	65
V7#1(8/47)-14,16-23(#56, 6/49)	8	16	24	40	50	60
V7#15-All comics	8	16	24	46	58	70
V7#24(#57, 7/49)-Kamen-a (becomes Best Western #58 on?)	8	16	24	43	54	65
V7#25(8/49), 27-44(3/52), VII,nn(5/52)	7	14	21	37	46	55
V7#26(9/49)-All comics	8	16	24	43	54	65
V1,nn(7/52)-V1,nn(1/53)(#46-49), V7#50(Spring '53), V1#51-V7?#54(7/53), 55-93	7	14	21	35	43	50

NOTE: *Photo-c #1, 4, V2#1, 4, 5, V3#5, V4#3, 4, 6, V7#15, 16, 24, 26, 34, 37, 38. Painted c-3.* ***Powell*** *a-V7#31.*

MISS BEVERLY HILLS OF HOLLYWOOD (See Adventures of Bob Hope)
National Periodical Publ.: Mar-Apr, 1949 - No. 9, July-Aug, 1950 (52 pgs.)

	GD	VG	FN	VF	VF/NM	NM-
1 (Meets Alan Ladd)	60	120	180	375	563	750
2-William Holden photo on-c	44	88	132	264	395	525
3-5: 2-9-Part photo-c. 5-Bob Hope photo on-c	40	80	120	240	340	440
6,7,9: 6-Lucille Ball photo on-c	36	72	108	204	290	375
8-Reagan photo on-c	40	80	120	240	345	450

NOTE: *Beverly meets Alan Ladd in #1, Eve Arden #2, Betty Hutton #4, Bob Hope #5.*

MISS CAIRO JONES
Croyden Publishers: 1945

1-Bob Oksner daily newspaper-r (1st strip story); lingerie panels	21	42	63	118	164	210

MISS FURY COMICS (Newspaper strip reprints)
Timely Comics (NPI 1/CmPI 2/MPC 3-8): Winter, 1942-43 - No. 8, Winter, 1946 (Published quarterly)

	GD	VG	FN	VF	VF/NM	NM-
1-Origin Miss Fury by Tarpe' Mills (68 pgs.) in costume w/pin-ups	370	740	1110	2405	3703	5000
2-(60 pgs.)-In costume w/pin-ups	184	368	552	1150	1725	2300
3-(60 pgs.)-In costume w/pin-ups; Hitler-c	148	296	444	925	1388	1850
4-(52 pgs.)-In costume, 2 pgs. w/pin-ups	112	224	336	700	1050	1400
5-(52 pgs.)-In costume w/pin-ups	94	188	282	588	882	1175
6-(52 pgs.)-Not in costume in inside stories, w/pin-ups	90	180	270	563	844	1125
7,8-(36 pgs.)-In costume 1 pg. each; no pin-ups	78	156	234	488	732	975

NOTE: ***Schomburg*** *c-1, 5, 6.*

MISS FURY
Adventure Comics: 1991 - No. 4, 1991 ($2.50, limited series)

	GD	VG	FN	VF	VF/NM	NM-
1-4: 1-Origin; granddaughter of original Miss Fury						3.00
1-Limited ed. ($4.95)						5.00

MISSION IMPOSSIBLE (TV)
Dell Publ. Co.: May, 1967 - No. 4, Oct, 1968; No. 5, Oct, 1969 (All have photo-c)

	GD	VG	FN	VF	VF/NM	NM-
1	10	20	30	67	96	125
2-5: 5-Reprints #1	7	14	21	50	68	85

MISSION IMPOSSIBLE (Movie)
Marvel Comics (Paramount Comics): May, 1996 ($2.95, one-shot)
(1st Paramount Comics book)

1-Liefeld-c & back-up story						3.00

MISS LIBERTY (Becomes Liberty Comics)
Burten Publishing Co.: 1945 (MLJ reprints)

1-The Shield & Dusty, The Wizard, & Roy, the Super Boy app.; r/Shield-Wizard #13	30	60	90	170	240	310

MISS MELODY LANE OF BROADWAY (See The Adventures of Bob Hope)
National Periodical Publ.: Feb-Mar, 1950 - No. 3, June-July, 1950 (52 pgs.)

	GD	VG	FN	VF	VF/NM	NM-
1-Movie stars photos app. on all-c.	60	120	180	375	563	750
2,3: 3-Ed Sullivan photo on-c.	40	80	120	240	340	440

MISS PEACH
Dell Publishing Co.: Oct-Dec, 1963; 1969

	GD	VG	FN	VF	VF/NM	NM-
1-Jack Mendelsohn-a/script	9	18	27	63	89	115
...Tells You How to Grow (1969; 25¢)-Mel Lazarus-a; also given away (36 pgs.)	5	10	15	36	48	60

MISS PEPPER (See Meet Miss Pepper)

MISS SUNBEAM (See Little Miss...)

MISS VICTORY (See Captain Fearless #1,2, Holyoke One-Shot #3, Veri Best Sure Fire & Veri Best Sure Shot Comics)

MISTER AMERICA
Endeavor Comics: Apr, 1994 - No. 2, May, 1994 ($2.95, limited series)

1,2						3.00

MR. & MRS. BEANS
United Features Syndicate: No. 11, 1939

Single Series 11	36	72	108	204	290	375

MR. & MRS. J. EVIL SCIENTIST (TV)(See The Flintstones & Hanna-Barbera Band Wagon #3)
Gold Key: Nov, 1963 - No. 4, Sept, 1966 (Hanna-Barbera, all 12¢)

	GD	VG	FN	VF	VF/NM	NM-
1	9	18	27	63	89	115
2-4	6	12	18	40	55	70

MR. ANTHONY'S LOVE CLINIC (Based on radio show)
Hillman Periodicals: Nov, 1949 - No. 5, Apr-May, 1950 (52 pgs.)

	GD	VG	FN	VF	VF/NM	NM-
1-Photo-c	14	28	42	81	111	140
2	9	18	27	52	66	80
3-5: 5-Photo-c	8	16	24	46	58	70

MISTER BLANK
Amaze Ink: No. 0, Jan, 1996 - No. 14, May, 2000 ($1.75/$2.95, B&W)

	GD	VG	FN	VF	VF/NM	NM-
0-($1.75, 16 pgs.) Origin of Mr. Blank						2.25
1-14-($2.95) Chris Hicks-s/a						3.00

MR. DISTRICT ATTORNEY (Radio/TV)
National Per. Publ.: Jan-Feb, 1948 - No. 67, Jan-Feb, 1959 (1-23: 52 pgs.)

	GD	VG	FN	VF	VF/NM	NM-
1-Howard Purcell c-5-23 (most)	100	200	300	625	938	1250
2	46	92	138	276	413	550
3-5	36	72	108	204	290	375
6-10	29	58	87	164	232	300
11-20	22	44	66	124	172	220
21-43: 43-Last pre-code (1-2/55)	15	30	45	86	118	150
44-67	12	24	36	71	96	120

MR. DISTRICT ATTORNEY (SeeThe Funnies #35)
Dell Publishing Co.: No. 13, 1942

Four Color 13-See The Funnies #35 for 1st app.	30	60	90	218	319	420

MISTER E (Also see Books of Magic limited series)
DC Comics: Jun, 1991- No. 4, Sept, 1991($1.75, limited series)

1-4-Snyder III-c/a; follow-up to Books of Magic limited series						3.00

MISTER ED, THE TALKING HORSE (TV)
Dell Publishing Co./Gold Key: Mar-May, 1962 - No. 6, Feb, 1964 (All photo-c; photo back-c: 1-6)

	GD	VG	FN	VF	VF/NM	NM-
Four Color 1295	14	28	42	102	149	195
1(11/62) (Gold Key)-Photo-c	10	20	30	70	100	130
2-6: Photo-c	6	12	18	43	59	75

(See March of Comics #244, 260, 282, 290)

MR. GUM (From The Atomics)

Mister Miracle #18 © DC

Mister Mystery #6 © Media Pub.

Mr. T and the T-Force #1 © NOW

	GD 2.0	VG 4.0	FN 6.0	VF 8.0	VF/NM 9.0	NM- 9.2

Oni Press: April, 2003 ($2.99, one-shot)
1-Mike Allred-s/J. Bone-a; Madman & The Atomics app. 3.00

MR. HERO, THE NEWMATIC MAN (See Neil Gaiman's...)

MR. MAGOO (TV) (The Nearsighted..., ...& Gerald McBoing Boing 1954 issues; formerly Gerald McBoing-Boing And ...)
Dell Publishing Co.: No. 6, Nov-Jan, 1953-54; 5/54 - 3-5/62; 9-11/63 - 3-5/65

	GD	VG	FN	VF	VF/NM	NM-
6	12	24	36	82	121	160
Four Color 561(5/54),602(11/54)	12	24	36	82	121	160
Four Color 1235(#1, 12-2/62),1305(#2, 3-5/62)	10	20	30	67	96	125
3(9-11/63) - 5	9	18	27	60	85	110
Four Color 1235(12-536-505)(3-5/65)-2nd Printing	7	14	21	50	68	85

MR. MAJESTIC (See WildC.A.T.S.)
DC Comics (WildStorm): Sept, 1999 - No. 9, May, 2000 ($2.50)
1-9: 1-McGuinness-a/Casey & Holguin-s. 2-Two covers 2.50
TPB (2002, $14.95) r/#1-6 & Wildstorm Spotlight #1

MISTER MIRACLE (1st series) (See Cancelled Comic Cavalcade)
National Periodical Publications/DC Comics: 3-4/71 - V4#18, 2-3/74; V5#19, 9/77 - V6#25, 8-9/78; 1987 (Fourth World)

	GD	VG	FN	VF	VF/NM	NM-
1-1st app. Mr. Miracle (#1-3 are 15¢)	7	14	21	50	68	85
2,3: 3-Last 15¢ issue	4	8	12	27	36	45
4-8: 4-Intro. Barda; Boy Commandos-r begin; all 52 pgs.	4	8	12	27	36	45
9-18: 9-Origin Mr. Miracle; Darkseid cameo. 15-Intro/1st app. Shilo Norman. 18-Barda & Scott Free wed; New Gods app. & Darkseid cameo; Last Kirby issue.	2	4	6	14	18	22
19-25 (1977-78)	1	2	3	5	7	9

Special 1(1987, $1.25, 52 pgs.) 3.00
Jack Kirby's Fourth World TPB ('01, $12.95) B&W&Grey-toned reprint of #11-18; Mark Evanier intro. 13.00
Jack Kirby's Mister Miracle TPB ('98, $12.95) B&W&Grey-toned reprint of #1-10; David Copperfield intro. 13.00
NOTE: **Austin** *a-19i.* **Ditko** *a-6r.* **Golden** *a-23-25p; c-25p.* **Heath** *a-24i, 25i; c-25i.* **Kirby** *a(p)/c-1-18.* **Nasser** *a-19i.* **Rogers** *a-19-22p; c-19, 20p, 21p, 22-24. 4-8 contain* **Simon & Kirby** *Boy Commandos reprints from Detective 82,76, Boy Commandos 1, 3 & Detective 64 in that order.*

MISTER MIRACLE (2nd Series) (See Justice League)
DC Comics: Jan, 1989 - No. 28, June, 1991 ($1.00/$1.25)
1-28: 13,14-Lobo app. 22-1st new Mr. Miracle w/new costume 2.50

MISTER MIRACLE (3rd Series)
DC Comics: Apr, 1996 - No. 7, Oct, 1996 ($1.95)
1-7: 2-Vs. JLA. 6-Simonson-c 2.25

MR. MIRACLE (See Capt. Fearless #1 & Holyoke One-Shot #4)

MR. MONSTER (1st Series)(Doc Stearn... #7 on; See Airboy-Mr. Monster Special, Dark Horse Presents, Super Duper Comics & Vanguard Illustrated #7)
Eclipse Comics: Jan, 1985 - No. 10, June, 1987 ($1.75, Baxter paper)
1-3: 1-1st story-r from Vanguard Ill. #7(1st app.). 2-Dave Stevens-c. 3-Alan Moore scripts; Wolverton-r/Weird Mysteries #5. 5.00
4-10: 6-Ditko-r/Fantastic Fears #5 plus new Giffen-a. 10- "6-D" issue 4.00

MR. MONSTER
Dark Horse Comics: Feb, 1988 - No. 8, July, 1991 ($1.75, B&W)
1-7 3.00
8-($4.95, 60 pgs.)-Origins conclusion 5.00

MR. MONSTER ATTACKS! (Doc Stearn...)
Tundra Publ.: Aug, 1992 - No. 3, Oct, 1992 ($3.95, limited series, 32 pgs.)
1-3: Michael T. Gilbert-a/scripts; Gilbert/Dorman painted-c 4.00

MR. MONSTER PRESENTS (CRACK-A-BOOM!)
Caliber Comics: 1997 - No. 3, 1997 ($2.95, B&W&Red, limited series)
1-3: Michael T. Gilbert-a/scripts: 1-Wraparound-c 3.00

MR. MONSTER'S GAL FRIDAY...KELLY!
Image Comics: Jan, 2000 - Present ($3.50, B&W)
1-3- Michael T. Gilbert-c; story & art by various. 3-Alan Moore-s 3.50

MR. MONSTER'S SUPER-DUPER SPECIAL
Eclipse Comics: May, 1986 - No. 8, July, 1987
1-(5/86)...3-D High Octane Horror #1 5.00
1-(5/86)...2-D version, 100 copies 2 4 6 10 13 16
2-(8/86)...High Octane Horror #1, 3-(9/86)...True Crime #1, 4-(11/86)...True Crime #2, 5-(1/87)...Hi-Voltage Super Science #1, 6-(3/87)...High Shock Schlock #1, 7-(5/87)...High Shock Schlock #2, 8-(7/87)...Weird Tales Of The Future #1 4.00
NOTE: **Jack Cole** *r-3, 4.* **Evans** *a-2r.* **Kubert** *a-1r.* **Powell** *a-5r.* **Wolverton** *a-2r, 7r, 8r.*

MR. MONSTER VS. GORZILLA
Image Comics: July, 1998 ($2.95, one-shot)
1-Michael T. Gilbert-a 3.00

MR. MUSCLES (Formerly Blue Beetle #18-21)
Charlton Comics: No. 22, Mar, 1956; No. 23, Aug, 1956
22,23 8 16 24 46 58 70

MR. MXYZPTLK (VILLAINS)
DC Comics: Feb, 1998 ($1.95, one-shot)
1-Grant-s/Morgan-a/Pearson-c 2.25

MISTER MYSTERY (Tales of Horror and Suspense)
Mr. Publ. (Media Publ.) No. 1-3/SPM Publ./Stanmore (Aragon): Sept, 1951 - No. 19, Oct, 1954

	GD	VG	FN	VF	VF/NM	NM-
1-Kurtzmanesque horror story	88	176	264	550	825	1100
2,3-Kurtzmanesque story. 3-Anti-Wertham edit.	58	116	174	363	544	725
4,6: Bondage-c; 6-Torture	58	116	174	363	544	725
5,8,10	55	110	165	330	495	660
7- "The Brain Bats of Venus" by Wolverton; partially re-used in Weird Tales of the Future #7	120	240	360	750	1125	1500
9-Nostrand-a	55	110	165	330	495	660
11-Wolverton "Robot Woman" story/Weird Mysteries #2, cut up, rewritten & partially redrawn	80	160	240	500	750	1000
12-Classic injury to eye-c	122	244	366	763	1144	1525
13-17,19: 15- "Living Dead" junkie story. 17-Severed heads-c. 19-Reprints	40	80	120	240	353	465
18- "Robot Woman" by Wolverton reprinted from Weird Mysteries #2; decapitation, bondage-c	60	120	180	375	563	750

NOTE: **Andru** *a-1, 2p, 3p.* **Andru/Esposito** *c-1-3.* **Baily** *c-10-18(most).* **Mortellaro** *c-5-7. Bondage c-7. Some issues have graphic dismemberment scenes.*

MR. PUNCH
DC Comics (Vertigo): 1994 ($24.95, one-shot)
nn (Hard-c)-Gaiman scripts; McKean-c/a 40.00
nn (Soft-c) 15.00

MISTER Q (See Mighty Midget Comics & Our Flag Comics #5)

MR. RISK (Formerly All Romances; Men Against Crime #3 on)(Also see Our Flag Comics & Super-Mystery Comics)
Ace Magazines: No. 7, Oct, 1950; No. 2, Dec, 1950
7,2 9 18 27 52 66 80

MR. SCARLET & PINKY (See Mighty Midget Comics)

MR. T AND THE T-FORCE
Now Comics: June, 1993 - No. 10, May, 1994 ($1.95, color)
1-10-Newsstand editions: 1-7-polybagged with photo trading card in each. 1,2-Neal Adams-c/a(p). 3-Dave Dorman painted-c 2.25
1-10-Direct Sale editions polybagged w/line drawn trading cards. 1-Contains gold foil trading card by Neal Adams 2.25

MISTER UNIVERSE (Professional wrestler)
Mr. Publications Media Publ. (Stanmor, Aragon): July, 1951; No. 2, Oct, 1951 - No. 5, April, 1952

	GD	VG	FN	VF	VF/NM	NM-
1	22	44	66	127	176	225
2- "Jungle That Time Forgot", (24 pg. story); Andru/Esposito-c	14	28	42	79	107	135
3-Marijuana story	14	28	42	79	107	135
4,5- "Goes to War" cover/stories	10	20	30	58	77	95

MISTER X (See Vortex)
Mr. Publications/Vortex Comics/Caliber V3#1 on: 6/84 - No. 14, 8/88 ($1.50/$2.25, direct sales, coated paper);V2#1, Apr, 1989 - V2#12, Mar, 1990 ($2.00/$2.50, B&W, newsprint) V3#1, 1996 - Present ($2.95, B&W)
1-14: 11-Dave McKean story & art (6 pgs.) 4.00
V2 #1-12: 1-11 (Second Coming, B&W): 1-Four diff.-c. 10-Photo-c 3.00
V3 #1-4 3.00
Return of... ($11.95, graphic novel)-r/V1#1-4 12.00
Return of... ($34.95, hardcover limited edition)-r/1-4 35.00
Special (no date, 1990?) 3.00

MISTY
Marvel Comics (Star Comics): Dec, 1985 - No. 6, May, 1986 (Limited series)
1-6: Millie The Model's niece 3.00

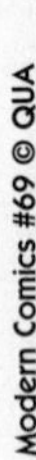
Modern Comics #69 © QUA

Mod Wheels #12 © GK

Monkees #4 © Raybert Prod.

	GD 2.0	VG 4.0	FN 6.0	VF 8.0	VF/NM 9.0	NM- 9.2

MITZI COMICS (Becomes Mitzi's Boy Friend #2-7)(See All Teen)
Timely Comics: Spring, 1948 (one-shot)

	GD	VG	FN	VF	VF/NM	NM-
1-Kurtzman's "Hey Look" plus 3 pgs. "Giggles 'n' Grins"	26	52	78	150	210	270

MITZI'S BOY FRIEND (Formerly Mitzi Comics; becomes Mitzi's Romances)
Marvel Comics (TCI): No. 2, June, 1948 - No. 7, April, 1949

	GD	VG	FN	VF	VF/NM	NM-
2	14	28	42	79	107	135
3-7	10	20	30	60	80	100

MITZI'S ROMANCES (Formerly Mitzi's Boy Friend)
Timely/Marvel Comics (TCI): No. 8, June, 1949 - No. 10, Dec, 1949

	GD	VG	FN	VF	VF/NM	NM-
8-Becomes True Life Tales #8 (10/49) on?	11	22	33	66	88	110
9,10: 10-Painted-c	9	18	27	54	70	85

MOBFIRE
DC Comics (Vertigo): Dec, 1994 - No. 6, May, 1995 ($2.50, limited series)

	GD	VG	FN	VF	VF/NM	NM-
1-6						2.50

MOBY DICK (See Feature Presentations #6, and King Classics)
Dell Publishing Co.: No. 717, Aug, 1956

	GD	VG	FN	VF	VF/NM	NM-
Four Color 717-Movie, Gregory Peck photo-c	10	20	30	67	96	125

MOBY DUCK (See Donald Duck #112 & Walt Disney Showcase #2,11)
Gold Key (Disney): Oct, 1967 - No. 11, Oct, 1970; No. 12, Jan, 1974 - No. 30, Feb, 1978

	GD	VG	FN	VF	VF/NM	NM-
1	4	8	12	24	32	40
2-5	2	4	6	12	16	20
6-11	2	4	6	10	13	16
12-30: 21,30-r	1	3	4	6	8	10

MODEL FUN (With Bobby Benson)
Harle Publications: No. 3, Winter, 1954-55 - No. 5, July, 1955

	GD	VG	FN	VF	VF/NM	NM-
3-Bobby Benson	7	14	21	35	43	50
4,5-Bobby Benson	5	10	15	23	28	32

MODELING WITH MILLIE (Formerly Life With Millie)
Atlas/Marvel Comics (Male Publ.): No. 21, Feb, 1963 - No. 54, June, 1967

	GD	VG	FN	VF	VF/NM	NM-
21	8	16	24	58	82	105
22-30	5	10	15	36	48	60
31-54	4	8	12	27	36	45

MODERN COMICS (Formerly Military Comics #1-43)
Quality Comics Group: No. 44, Nov, 1945 - No. 102, Oct, 1950

	GD	VG	FN	VF	VF/NM	NM-
44-Blackhawk continues	55	110	165	330	495	660
45-52: 49-1st app. Fear, Lady Adventuress	40	80	120	240	340	440
53-Torchy by Ward begins (9/46)	42	84	126	252	376	500
54-60: 55-J. Cole-a	35	70	105	201	288	370
61-77,79,80: 73-J. Cole-a	33	66	99	190	268	345
78-1st app. Madame Butterfly	35	70	105	201	288	370
81-99,101: 82,83-One pg. J. Cole-a. 83-Last 52 pg. issue 99-Blackhawks on the moon-c/story	31	62	93	175	248	320
100	33	66	99	190	268	345
102-(Scarce)-J. Cole-a; Spirit by Eisner app.	38	76	114	219	310	400

NOTE: ***Al Bryant*** *c-44-51, 54, 55, 66, 69.* ***Jack Cole*** *a-55, 73.* ***Crandall*** *Blackhawk-#46, 47, 50, 51, 54, 56, 58-60, 64, 67-70, 73, 74, 76-78, 80-83; c-60-65, 67, 68, 70-95.* ***Crandall/Cuidera*** *c-56-59, 96-102.* ***Gustavson*** *a-47, 49.* ***Ward*** *Blackhawk-#52, 53, 55 (15 pgs. each). Torchy in #53-102; by* ***Ward*** *only in #53-89(9/49); by* ***Gil Fox*** *#92, 93, 102.*

MODERN LOVE
E. C. Comics: June-July, 1949 - No. 8, Aug-Sept, 1950

	GD	VG	FN	VF	VF/NM	NM-
1-Feldstein, Ingels-a	66	132	198	495	660	825
2-Craig/Feldstein-c/s	43	86	129	258	384	510
3	40	80	120	240	345	450
4-6 (Scarce): 4-Bra/panties panels	51	102	153	306	458	610
7,8	40	80	120	240	345	450

NOTE: ***Craig*** *a-3.* ***Feldstein*** *a-in most issues; c-1, 2i, 3-8.* ***Harrison*** *a-4.* ***Iger*** *a-6-8.* ***Ingels*** *a-1, 2, 4-7.* ***Palais*** *a-5.* ***Wood*** *a-7.* ***Wood/Harrison*** *a-5-7. (Canadian reprints known; see Table of Contents.)*

MOD LOVE
Western Publishing Co.: 1967 (50¢, 36 pgs.)

	GD	VG	FN	VF	VF/NM	NM-
1-(Low print)	5	10	15	36	48	60

MODNIKS, THE
Gold Key: Aug, 1967 - No. 2, Aug, 1970

	GD	VG	FN	VF	VF/NM	NM-
10206-708(#1)	4	8	12	22	30	38
2	3	6	9	16	20	24

MOD SQUAD (TV)
Dell Publishing Co.: Jan, 1969 - No. 3, Oct, 1969 - No. 8, April, 1971

	GD	VG	FN	VF	VF/NM	NM-
1-Photo-c	7	14	21	51	71	90
2-4: 2-4-Photo-c	4	8	12	29	40	50
5-8: 8-Photo-c; Reprints #2	4	8	12	25	33	42

MOD WHEELS
Gold Key: Mar, 1971 - No. 19, Jan, 1976

	GD	VG	FN	VF	VF/NM	NM-
1	4	8	12	27	36	45
2-9	3	6	9	16	20	25
10-19: 11,15-Extra 16 pgs. ads	2	4	6	12	16	20

MOE & SHMOE COMICS
O. S. Publ. Co.: Spring, 1948 - No. 2, Summer, 1948

	GD	VG	FN	VF	VF/NM	NM-
1	9	18	27	49	62	75
2	6	12	18	31	38	45

MOEBIUS (Graphic novel)
Marvel Comics (Epic Comics): Oct, 1987 - No. 6, 1988; No. 7, 1990; No. 8, 1991 ($9.95, 8x11", mature)

	GD	VG	FN	VF	VF/NM	NM-
1,2,4-6,8: (#2, 2nd printing, $9.95)						10.00
3,7,0: 3-(1st & 2nd printings, $12.95). 0 (1990, $12.95)						13.00
Moebius I-Signed & #'d hard-c ($45.95, Graphitti Designs, 1,500 copies printed)-r/#1-3						46.00

MOEBIUS COMICS
Caliber: May, 1996 - No. 6 ($2.95, B&W)

	GD	VG	FN	VF	VF/NM	NM-
1-6: Moebius-c/a. 1-William Stout-a						3.00

MOEBIUS: THE MAN FROM CIGURI
Dark Horse Comics: 1996 ($7.95, digest-size)

	GD	VG	FN	VF	VF/NM	NM-
nn-Moebius-c/a						8.00

MOLLY MANTON'S ROMANCES (Romantic Affairs #3)
Marvel Comics (SePI): Sept, 1949 - No. 2, Dec, 1949 (52 pgs.)

	GD	VG	FN	VF	VF/NM	NM-
1-Photo-c (becomes Blaze the Wonder Collie #2 (10/49) on? & Molly Manton's Romances #2	16	32	48	92	126	160
2-Titled "Romances of..."; photo-c	10	20	30	60	80	100

MOLLY O'DAY (Super Sleuth)
Avon Periodicals: February, 1945 (1st Avon comic)

	GD	VG	FN	VF	VF/NM	NM-
1-Molly O'Day, The Enchanted Dagger by Tuska (r/Yankee #1), Capt'n Courage, Corporal Grant app.	54	108	162	324	487	650

MOMENT OF SILENCE
Marvel Comics: Feb, 2002 ($3.50, one-shot)

	GD	VG	FN	VF	VF/NM	NM-
1-Tributes to the heroes and victims of Sept. 11; s/a by various						3.50

MONA
Kitchen Sink Press: 1999 ($4.95, B&W, one-shot)

	GD	VG	FN	VF	VF/NM	NM-
1-Cartoons by Kurtzman and various; Hernandez-c						5.00

MONARCHY, THE (Also see The Authority and StormWatch)
DC Comics (WildStorm): Apr, 2001 - No. 12, May, 2002 ($2.50)

	GD	VG	FN	VF	VF/NM	NM-
1-McCrea & Leach-a/Young-s						2.50
2-12						2.50
Bullets Over Babylon TPB (2001, $12.95) r/#1-4, Authority #21						13.00

MONKEES, THE (TV)(Also see Circus Boy, Groovy, Not Brand Echh #3, Teen-Age Talk, Teen Beam & Teen Beat)
Dell Publishing Co.: March, 1967 - No. 17, Oct, 1969

	GD	VG	FN	VF	VF/NM	NM-
1-Photo-c	11	22	33	77	114	150
2-17: All photo-c. 17-Reprints #1	7	14	21	50	68	85

MONKEY AND THE BEAR, THE
Atlas Comics (ZPC): Sept, 1953 - No. 3, Jan, 1954

	GD	VG	FN	VF	VF/NM	NM-
1-Howie Post-c/a in all; funny animal	9	18	27	49	62	75
2,3	6	12	18	31	38	45

MONKEYMAN AND O'BRIEN (Also see Dark Horse Presents #80, 100-5, Gen[13]/..., Hellboy: Seed of Destruction, & San Diego Comic Con #2)
Dark Horse Comics (Legend): Jul, 1996 - No. 3, Sept, 1996 ($2.95, lim. series)

	GD	VG	FN	VF	VF/NM	NM-
1-3: New stories; Art Adams-c/a/scripts						3.50
nn-(2/96, $2.95)-r/back-up stories from Hellboy: Seed of Destruction; Adams-c/a/scripts						3.50

MONKEYSHINES COMICS
Ace Periodicals/Publishers Specialists/Current Books/Unity Publ.: Summer, 1944 - No. 27, July, 1949

	GD	VG	FN	VF	VF/NM	NM-
1-Funny animal	13	26	39	76	103	130
2-(Aut/44)	8	16	24	43	54	65
3-10: 3-(Win/44)	7	14	21	37	46	55
11-18,20-27: 23,24-Fago-c/a	7	14	21	35	43	50

The Monroes #1 © DELL

Monsters on the Prowl #16 © MAR

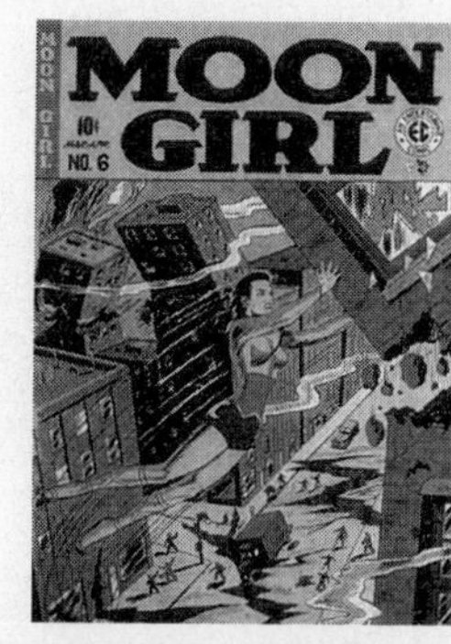

Moon Girl #6 © WMG

	GD 2.0	VG 4.0	FN 6.0	VF 8.0	VF/NM 9.0	NM- 9.2
19-Frazetta-a	8	16	24	43	54	65

MONKEY'S UNCLE, THE (See Merlin Jones As... under Movie Comics)

MONROES, THE (TV)
Dell Publishing Co.: Apr, 1967

1-Photo-c	3	6	9	19	25	32

MONSTER
Fiction House Magazines: 1953 - No. 2, 1953

1-Dr. Drew by Grandenetti; reprint from Rangers Comics #48; Whitman-c	50	100	150	300	450	600
2-Whitman-c	40	80	120	240	340	440

MONSTER CRIME COMICS (Also see Crime Must Stop)
Hillman Periodicals: Oct, 1952 (15¢, 52 pgs.)

1 (Scarce)	100	200	300	625	938	1250

MONSTER FIGHTERS INC.
Image Comics (Bright Anvil Studios): Apr, 1999; Dec, 1999 ($3.50/$3.95)

1-Torres-s/Lubera & Yeung-a						3.50
...: The Black Book 1 (9/00, $3.50) Manapul-a						3.50
...The Ghosts of Christmas 1 (12/99, $3.95)						4.00

MONSTER HOWLS (Magazine)
Humor-Vision: December, 1966 (Satire) (35¢, 68 pgs.)

1	5	10	15	36	48	60

MONSTER HUNTERS
Charlton Comics: Aug, 1975 - No. 9, Jan, 1977; No. 10, Oct, 1977 - No. 18, Feb, 1979

1-Howard-a; Newton-c	3	6	9	18	24	30
2-Sutton-c/a; Ditko-a	2	4	6	12	16	20
3,4,5,7: 4-Sutton-c/a	2	4	6	8	10	12
6,8,10: 6,8,10-Ditko-a	2	4	6	10	12	15
9,11,12	1	2	3	5	7	9
13,15,18-Ditko-c/a. 18-Sutton-a	2	4	6	10	12	15
14-Special all-Ditko issue	3	6	9	18	23	28
16,17-Sutton-a	1	2	3	5	7	9
1,2 (Modern Comics reprints, 1977)						4.00

NOTE: ***Ditko** a-2, 6, 8, 10, 13-15r, 18r; c-13-15, 18. **Howard** a-1, 3, 17; r-13. **Morisi** a-1. **Staton** a-1, 13. **Sutton** a-2, 4; c-2, 4; r-16-18. **Zeck** a-4-9. Reprints in #12-18.*

MONSTER MADNESS (Magazine)
Marvel Comics: 1972 - No. 3, 1973 (60¢, B&W)

1-3: Stories by "Sinister" Stan Lee	3	6	9	19	25	32

MONSTER MAN
Image Comics (Action Planet): Sept, 1997 ($2.95, B&W)

1-Mike Manley-c/s/a						3.00

MONSTER MASTERWORKS
Marvel Comics: 1989 ($12.95, TPB)

nn-Reprints 1960's monster stories; art by Kirby, Ditko, Ayers, Everett						13.00

MONSTER MATINEE
Chaos! Comics: Oct, 1997 - No. 3, Oct, 1997 ($2.50, limited series)

1-3: pin-ups						2.50

MONSTER MENACE
Marvel Comics: Dec, 1993 - No. 4, Mar, 1994 ($1.25, limited series)

1-4: Pre-code Atlas horror reprints.						3.00

NOTE: ***Ditko**-r & **Kirby**-r in all.*

MONSTER OF FRANKENSTEIN (See Frankenstein)

MONSTERS ATTACKS (Magazine)
Globe Communications Corpse: Sept, 1989 - No. 3, July, 1990 (B&W)

1-3-Ditko, Morrow, J. Severin-a						4.00

MONSTERS ON THE PROWL (Chamber of Darkness #1-8)
Marvel Comics Group (No. 13,14: 52 pgs.): No. 9, 2/71 - No. 27, 11/73; No. 28, 6/74 - No. 30, 10/74

9-Barry Smith inks	3	7	10	21	28	35
10-12,15: 12-Last 15¢ issue	2	4	6	12	16	20
13,14-(52 pgs.)	3	6	9	16	20	25
16-(4/72)-King Kull 4th app.; Severin-c	2	4	6	14	18	22
17-30	2	4	6	10	13	16

NOTE: ***Ditko** r-9, 14, 16. **Kirby** r-10-17, 21, 23, 25, 27, 28, 30; c-9, 25. **Kirby/Ditko** r-14, 17-20, 22, 24, 26, 29. **Marie/John Severin** a-16(Kull). 9-13, 15 contain one new story. Woodish art by **Reese**-11. King Kull created by Robert E. Howard.*

MONSTERS TO LAUGH WITH (Magazine) (Becomes Monsters Unlimited #4)
Marvel Comics Group: 1964 - No. 3, 1965 (B&W)

1-Humor by Stan Lee	7	14	21	46	63	80
2,3	4	8	12	25	33	42

MONSTERS UNLEASHED (Magazine)
Marvel Comics Group: July, 1973 - No. 11, Apr, 1975; Summer, 1975 (B&W)

1-Soloman Kane sty; Werewolf app.	4	8	12	22	30	38
2-4: 2-The Frankenstein Monster begins, ends #10. 3-Neal Adams-c/a; The Man-Thing begins (origin-r); Son of Satan preview. 4-Werewolf app.	3	6	9	19	25	32
5-7: Werewolf in all. 5-Man-Thing. 7-Williamson-a(r)	2	4	6	14	18	22
8-11: 8-Man-Thing; N. Adams-r. 9-Man-Thing; Wendigo app. 10-Origin Tigra	3	6	9	16	20	25
Annual 1 (Summer,1975, 92 pgs.)-Kane-a	2	4	6	14	18	22

NOTE: ***Boris** c-2, 6. **Brunner** a-2; c-11. **J. Buscema** a-2p, 4p, 5p. **Colan** a-1, 4r. **Davis** a-3r. **Everett** a-2r. **G. Kane** a-3. **Krigstein** r-4. **Morrow** a-3; c-1. **Perez** a-8. **Ploog** a-6. **Reese** a-1, 2. **Tuska** a-3p. **Wildey** a-1r.*

MONSTERS UNLIMITED (Magazine) (Formerly Monsters To Laugh With)
Marvel Comics Group: No. 4, 1965 - No. 7, 1966 (B&W)

4-7	4	8	12	24	32	40

MONSTER WORLD
DC Comics (WildStorm): Jul, 2001 - No. 4, Oct, 2001 ($2.50, limited series)

1-4-Lobdell-s/Meglia-c/a						2.50

MONTANA KID, THE (See Kid Montana)

MONTE HALE WESTERN (Movie star; Formerly Mary Marvel #1-28; also see Fawcett Movie Comic, Motion Picture Comics, Picture News #8, Real Western Hero, Six-Gun Heroes, Western Hero & XMas Comics)
Fawcett Publ./Charlton No. 83 on: No. 29, Oct, 1948 - No. 88, Jan, 1956

29-(#1, 52 pgs.)-Photo-c begin, end #82; Monte Hale & his horse Pardner begin	50	100	150	300	450	600
30-(52 pgs.)-Big Bow and Little Arrow begin, end #34; Captain Tootsie by Beck	27	54	81	153	214	275
31-36,38-40-(52 pgs.): 34-Gabby Hayes begins, ends #80. 39-Captain Tootsie by Beck	20	40	60	112	156	200
37,41,45,49-(36 pgs.)	15	30	45	84	115	145
42-44,46-48,50-(52 pgs.): 47-Big Bow & Little Arrow app.	16	32	48	92	126	160
51,52,54-56,58,59-(52 pgs.)	12	24	36	71	96	120
53,57-(36 pgs.): 53-Slim Pickens app.	10	20	30	58	77	95
60-81: 36 pgs. #60-on. 80-Gabby Hayes ends	10	20	30	56	73	90
82-Last Fawcett issue (6/53)	12	24	36	69	92	115
83-1st Charlton issue (2/55); B&W photo back-c begin. Gabby Hayes returns, ends #86	14	28	42	79	107	135
84 (4/55)	10	20	30	58	77	95
85-86	10	20	30	56	73	90
87,88: 87-Wolverton-r, 1/2 pg. 88-Last issue	10	20	30	58	77	95

NOTE: ***Gil Kane** a-33?, 34? Rocky Lane -1 pg. (Carnation ad)-38, 40, 41, 43, 44, 46, 55.*

MONTY HALL OF THE U.S. MARINES (See With the Marines...)
Toby Press: Aug, 1951 - No. 11, Apr, 1953

1	11	22	33	63	84	105
2	7	14	21	37	46	55
3-5	7	14	21	35	43	50
6-11	6	12	18	31	38	45

NOTE: *Full page pin-ups (Pin-Up Pete) by **Jack Sparling** in #1-9.*

MOON, A GIRL...ROMANCE, A (Becomes Weird Fantasy #13 on; formerly Moon Girl #1-8)
E. C. Comics: No. 9, Sept-Oct, 1949 - No. 12, Mar-Apr, 1950

9-Moon Girl cameo	70	140	210	438	657	875
10,11	57	114	171	356	533	710
12-(Scarce)	70	140	210	438	657	875

NOTE: ***Feldstein, Ingels** art in all. **Feldstein** c-9-12. **Wood/Harrison** a-10-12. Canadian reprints known; see Table of Contents.*

MOON GIRL AND THE PRINCE (#1) (Moon Girl #2-6; Moon Girl Fights Crime #7, 8; becomes A Moon, A Girl, Romance #9 on)(Also see Animal Fables #7 and Happy Houlihans)
E. C. Comics: Fall, 1947 - No. 8, Summer, 1949

1-Origin Moon Girl (see Happy Houlihans #1)	92	184	276	575	863	1150
2	53	106	159	318	479	640
3,4: 4-Moon Girl vs. a vampire	47	94	141	282	421	560
5-E.C.'s 1st horror story, "Zombie Terror"	102	204	306	638	957	1275
6-8 (Scarce): 7-Origin Star (Moongirl's sidekick)	53	106	159	318	479	640

NOTE: ***Craig** a-2, 5.; c-1,2. **Moldoff** a-1-8; c-2-6. **Wheelan's** Fat and Slat app. in #3, 4, 6. #2 & #3 are 52 pgs., #4 on, 36 pgs. Canadian reprints known; (see Table of Contents.)*

MOON KNIGHT (Also see The Hulk, Marc Spector..., Marvel Preview #21, Marvel Spotlight & Werewolf by Night #32)

Moon Knight #1 © MAR

Moonshadow #12 © DeMatteis & Muth

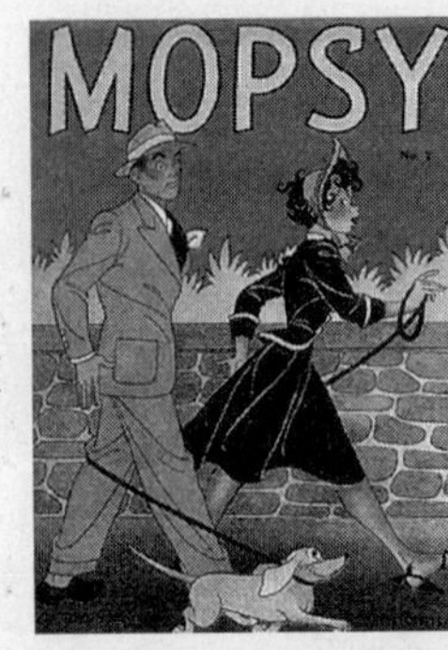

Mopsy #2 © STJ

GD 2.0 | VG 4.0 | FN 6.0 | VF 8.0 | VF/NM 9.0 | NM- 9.2

Marvel Comics Group: Nov, 1980 - No. 38, Jul, 1984 (Mando paper #33 on)
1-Origin resumed in #4 5.00
2-15,25,35: 4-Intro Midnight Man. 25-Double size. 35-($1.00, 52 pgs.)-X-Men app.; F.F. cameo 3.00
16-24,26-34,36-38: 16-The Thing app. 2.50
NOTE: ***Austin** c-27i, 31i. **Cowan** a-16; c-16, 17. **Kaluta** c-36-38; back c-35. **Miller** c-9, 12p, 13p, 15p, 27p. **Ploog** back c-35. **Sienkiewicz** a-1-15, 17-20, 22-26, 28-30, 33i, 36(4), 37; c-1-5, 7, 8, 10, 11, 14-16, 18-26, 28-30, 31p, 33, 34.*

MOON KNIGHT
Marvel Comics Group: June, 1985 - V2#6, Dec, 1985
V2#1-6: 1-Double size; new costume. 6-Sienkiewicz painted-c. 2.50

MOON KNIGHT
Marvel Comics: Jan, 1998 - No. 4, Apr, 1998 ($2.50, limited series)
1-4-Moench-s/Edwards-c/a 2.50

MOON KNIGHT (Volume 3)
Marvel Comics: Jan, 1999 - No. 4, Feb, 1999 ($2.99, limited series)
1-4-Moench-s/Texeira-a(p) 3.00

MOON KNIGHT: DIVIDED WE FALL
Marvel Comics: 1992 ($4.95, 52 pgs.)
nn-Denys Cowan-c/a(p) 5.00

MOON KNIGHT SPECIAL
Marvel Comics: Oct, 1992 ($2.50, 52 pgs.)
1-Shang Chi, Master of Kung Fu-c/story 2.50

MOON KNIGHT SPECIAL EDITION
Marvel Comics Group: Nov, 1983 - No. 3, Jan, 1984 ($2.00, limited series, Baxter paper)
1-3: Reprints from Hulk mag. by Sienkiewicz 3.00

MOON MULLINS (See Popular Comics, Super Book #3 & Super Comics)
Dell Publishing Co.: 1941 - 1945
Four Color 14(1941) 35 70 105 263 392 520
Large Feature Comic 29(1941) 26 52 78 189 277 365
Four Color 31(1943) 20 40 60 140 205 270
Four Color 81(1945) 12 24 36 82 121 160

MOON MULLINS
Michel Publ. (American Comics Group)#1-6/St. John #7,8: Dec-Jan, 1947-48 - No. 8, 1949 (52 pgs)
1-Alternating Sunday & daily strip-r 22 44 66 124 172 220
2 11 22 33 66 88 110
3-8: 7,8-St. John Publ. 8-...Featuring Kayo on-c 10 20 30 60 80 100
NOTE: ***Milt Gross** a-2-6, 8. **Frank Willard** r-all.*

MOON PILOT
Dell Publishing Co.: No. 1313, Mar-May, 1962
Four Color 1313-Movie, photo-c 8 16 24 55 78 100

MOONSHADOW (Also see Farewell, Moonshadow)
Marvel Comics (Epic Comics): 5/85 - #12, 2/87 ($1.50/$1.75, mature) (1st fully painted comic book)
1-Origin; J. M. DeMatteis scripts & Jon J. Muth painted-c/a. 6.00
2-12: 11-Origin 4.00
Trade paperback (1987?)-r/#1-12 14.00
Signed & numbered hard-c ($39.95, 1,200 copies)-r/#1-12 5 10 15 36 48 60

MOONSHADOW
DC Comics (Vertigo): Oct, 1994 - No. 12, Aug, 1995 ($2.25/$2.95)
1-11: Reprints Epic series. 2.50
12 ($2.95)-w/expanded ending 3.00
The Complete Moonshadow TPB ('98, $39.95) r/#1-12 and Farewell Moonshadow; new Muth painted-c 40.00

MOON-SPINNERS, THE (See Movie Comics)

MOONSTONE MONSTERS
Moonstone: 2003 ($2.95, B&W)
...: Ghosts ($2.95) - Short stories by various; Frenz-c 3.00
...: Sea Creatures ($2.95) - Short stories by various; Frenz-c 3.00

MOONSTONE NOIR
Moonstone: 2003 ($2.95/$4.95/$5.50, B&W)
...: Johnny Dollar ($4.95) - Gallaher-s/Theriault-a 5.00
...: Mr. Keen, Tracer of Lost Persons 1,2 ($2.95, limited series) - Ferguson-a 3.00
...: Mysterious Traveler ($5.50) - Trevor Von Eeden-a/Joe Gentile-s 5.50
...: The Lone Wolf ($4.95) - Jolley-s/Croall-a 5.00

MOPSY (See Pageant of Comics & TV Teens)
St. John Publ. Co.: Feb, 1948 - No. 19, Sept, 1953
1-Part-r; reprints "Some Punkins" by Neher 19 38 57 107 149 190
2 10 20 30 58 77 95
3-10(1953): 8-Lingerie panels 9 18 27 52 66 80
11-19: 19-Lingerie-c 8 16 24 46 58 70
NOTE: *#1, 3-6, 13, 18, 19 have paper dolls.*

MORBIUS REVISITED
Marvel Comic: Aug, 1993 - No. 5, Dec, 1993 ($1.95, mini-series)
1-5-Reprints Fear #27-31 2.25

MORBIUS: THE LIVING VAMPIRE (Also see Amazing Spider-Man #101,102, Fear #20, Marvel Team-Up #3, 4, Midnight Sons Unl. & Vampire Tales)
Marvel Comics (Midnight Sons imprint #16 on): Sep, 1992 - No. 32, Apr, 1995 ($1.75/$1.95)
1-($2.75, 52 pgs.)-Polybagged w/poster; Ghost Rider & Johnny Blaze x-over (part 3 of Rise of the Midnight Sons) 3.00
2-11,13-24,26-32: 3,4-Vs. Spider-Man-c/s.15-Ghost Rider app. 16-Spot varnish-c. 16,17-Siege of Darkness,parts 5 &13. 18-Deathlok app. 21-Bound-in Spider-Man trading card sheet; Spider-Man app. 2.25
12-($2.25)-Outer-c is a Darkhold envelope made of black parchment w/gold ink; Midnight Massacre x-over 2.50
25-($2.50, 52 pgs.)-Gold foil logo 2.50

MORE FUN COMICS (Formerly New Fun Comics #1-6)
National Periodical Publications: No. 7, Jan, 1936 - No. 127, Nov-Dec, 1947 (No. 7,9-11: paper-c)
7(1/36)-Oversized, paper-c; 1 pg. Kelly-a 769 1538 2310 5400 - -
8(2/36)-Oversized (10x12"), paper-c; 1 pg. Kelly-a; Sullivan-c 769 1538 2310 5400 - -
9(3-4/36)(Very rare, 1st standard-sized comic book with original material)-Last multiple panel-c 923 1849 2770 6500 - -
10,11(7/36): 10-Last Henri Duval by Siegel & Shuster. 11-1st "Calling All Cars" by Siegel & Shuster; new classic logo begins 538 1076 1615 3750 - -
12(8/36)-Slick-c begin 415 830 1245 2950 - -
V2#1(9/36, #13) 385 770 1154 2700 - -
2(10/36, #14)-Dr. Occult in costume (1st in color)(Superman proto-type; 1st DC appearance) continues from The Comics Magazine, ends #17 1846 3692 5539 12,900 - -
V2#3(11/36, #15), 16(V2#4), 17(V2#5): 16-Cover numbering begins; Xmas-c; last Superman tryout issue 738 1476 2215 5100 - -
18-20(V2#8, 5/37) 292 584 877 2050 - -
21(V2#9)-24(V2#12, 9/37) 276 552 828 1518 1972 2425
25(V3#1, 10/37)-27(V3#3, 12/37): 27-Xmas-c 276 552 828 1518 1972 2425
28-30: 30-1st non-funny cover 250 500 750 1375 1775 2175
31-Has ad for Action #1 265 530 795 1458 1892 2325
32-35: 32-Last Dr. Occult 250 500 750 1375 1775 2175
36-40: 36-(10/38)-The Masked Ranger & sidekick Pedro begins; Ginger Snap by Bob Kane (2 pgs.; 1st-a?). 39-Xmas-c 250 500 750 1375 1775 2175
41-50: 41-Last Masked Ranger 212 424 636 1166 1558 1950
51-The Spectre app. (in costume) in one panel ad at end of Buccaneer story 741 1482 2223 4076 5438 6800
52-(2/40)-Origin/1st app. The Spectre (in costume splash panel only), part 1 by Bernard Baily (parts 1 & 2 written by Jerry Siegel; Spectre's costume changes color from purple & blue to green & grey; last Wing Brady; Spectre-c 5250 10,500 15,750 39,500 61,750 84,000
53-Origin The Spectre (in costume at end of story), part 2; Capt. Desmo begins; Spectre-c 2530 5060 7590 17,800 30,400 43,000
54-The Spectre in costume; last King Carter; classic-Spectre-c 1063 2126 3189 7973 12,487 17,000
55-(Scarce, 5/40)-Dr. Fate begins (1st app.); last Bulldog Martin; Spectre-c 1188 2376 3563 8910 13,955 19,000
56-1st Dr. Fate-c (classic), origin continues. Congo Bill begins (6/40), 1st app.; 586 1172 1758 4102 6301 8500
57-60-All Spectre-c 356 712 1068 2314 3557 4800
61,65: 61-Classic Dr. Fate-c. 65-Classic Spectre-c 326 652 978 2119 3260 4400
62-64,66: 63-Last St. Bob Neal. 64-Lance Larkin begins; all Spectre-c 296 592 888 1850 2775 3700
67-(5/41)-Origin (1st) Dr. Fate; last Congo Bill & Biff Bronson (Congo Bill continues in Action Comics #37, 6/41)-Spectre-c 634 1268 1902 4438 6819 9200
68-70: 68-Clip Carson begins. 70-Last Lance Larkin; all Dr. Fate-c 232 464 696 1450 2175 2900
71-Origin & 1st app. Johnny Quick by Mort Weisinger (9/41); classic sci/fi Dr. Fate-c 504 1008 1512 3528 5414 7300
72-Dr. Fate's new helmet; last Sgt. Carey, Sgt. O'Malley & Captain Desmo;

More Fun Comics #80 © DC

More Than Mortal: Otherworlds #4 © IM

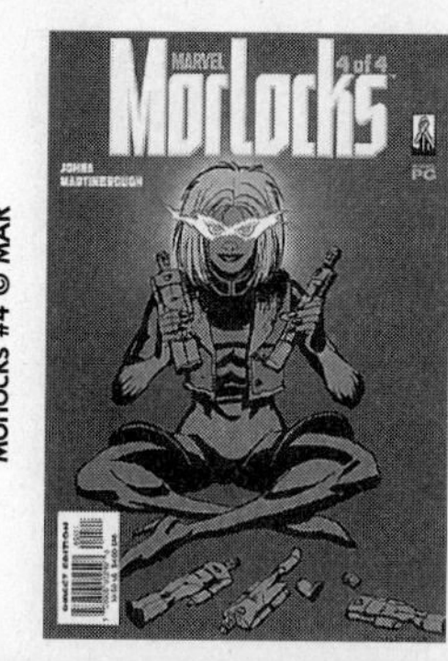

Morlocks #4 © MAR

GD VG FN VF VF/NM NM-
2.0 4.0 6.0 8.0 9.0 9.2

German submarine-c (only German war-c) 228 456 684 1425 2138 2850
73-Origin & 1st app. Aquaman (11/41) by Paul Norris; intro. Green Arrow & Speedy;
Dr. Fate-c 1125 2250 3375 8438 13,219 18,000
74-2nd Aquaman; 1st Percival Popp, Supercop; Dr. Fate-c
280 560 840 1750 2625 3500
75,76: 75-New origin Spectre; Nazi spy ring cover w/Hitler's photo. 76-Last Dr. Fate-c;
Johnny Quick (by Meskin #76-97) begins, ends #107; last Clip Carson
232 464 696 1450 2175 2900
77-80: 77-Green Arrow-c begin 200 400 600 1250 1875 2500
81-83,85,88,90: 81-Last large logo. 82-1st small logo.
128 256 384 800 1200 1600
84-Green Arrow Japanese war-c 132 264 395 825 1238 1650
86,87-Johnny Quick-c. 87-Last Radio Squad 128 256 384 800 1200 1600
89-Origin Green Arrow & Speedy Team-up 139 278 417 869 1305 1740
91-97,99: 91-1st bi-monthly issue. 93-Dover & Clover begin (1st app., 9-10/43).
97-Kubert-a 78 156 234 488 732 975
98-Last Dr. Fate (scarce) 100 200 300 625 938 1250
100 (11-12/44)-Johnny Quick-c 118 236 354 738 1107 1475
101-Origin & 1st app. Superboy (1-2/45)(not by Siegel & Shuster); last Spectre issue;
Green Arrow-c 827 1654 2481 5789 8895 12,000
102-2nd Superboy app; 1st Dover & Clover-c 128 256 384 800 1200 1600
103-3rd Superboy app; last Green Arrow-c 96 192 288 600 900 1200
104-1st Superboy-c w/Dover & Clover 84 168 252 525 788 1050
105,106-Superboy-c 78 156 234 488 732 975
107-Last Johnny Quick & Superboy 78 156 234 488 732 975
108-120: 108-Genius Jones begins; 1st c-app. (3-4/46; cont'd from Adventure Comics #102)
24 48 72 138 194 250
121-124,126: 121-123,126-Post funny animal (Jimminy & the Magic Book)-c
22 44 66 127 176 225
125-Superman c-app.w/Jimminy 76 152 228 475 713 950
127-(Scarce)-Post-c/a 36 72 108 204 290 375

NOTE: *All issues are scarce to rare. Cover features: The Spectre-#52-55, 57-60, 62-67. Dr. Fate-#56, 61, 68-76. The Green Arrow & Speedy-#77-85, 88-97, 99, 101 (w/Dover & Clover-#98, 103). Johnny Quick-#86, 87, 100. Dover & Clover-#102, (104, 106 w/Superboy), 107, 108(w/Genius Jones), 110, 112, 114, 117, 119. Genius Jones-#109, 111, 113, 115, 118, 120.* **Baily** *a-45, 52-on; c-52-55, 57-60, 62-67.* **Al Capp** *a-45(signed Koppy).* **Ellsworth** *c-7.* **Creig Flessel** *c-30, 31, 35-48(most).* **Guardineer** *c-47, 49, 50.* **Kiefer** *a-20.* **Meskin** *c-86, 87, 100?* **Moldoff** *c-51.* **George Papp** *c-77-85.* **Post** *c-121-127.* **Vincent Sullivan** *c-8-28, 32-34.*

MORE FUND COMICS (Benefit book for the Comic Book Legal Defense Fund)
Sky Dog Press: Sept, 2003 ($10.00, B&W, trade paperback)
nn-Anthology of short stories and pin-ups by various; Hulk-c by Pérez 10.00

MORE SEYMOUR (See Seymour My Son)
Archie Publications: Oct, 1963
1-DeCarlo-a? 3 6 9 25 24 32

MORE THAN MORTAL (Also see Lady Pendragon/...)
Liar Comics: June, 1997 - No. 4, Apr, 1998 ($2.95, limited series)
Image Comics: No. 5, Dec, 1999 - Present ($2.95)
1-Blue forest background-c, 1-Variant-c 4.00
1-White-c 6.00
1-2nd printing; purple sky cover 3.00
2-4: 3-Silvestri-c, 4-Two-c, one by Randy Queen 3.00
5,6: 5-1st Image Comics issue 3.00

MORE THAN MORTAL: OTHERWORLDS
Image Comics: July, 1999 - No. 4, Dec, 1999 ($2.95, limited series)
1-4-Firchow-a. 1-Two covers 3.00

MORE THAN MORTAL SAGAS
Liar Comics: Jun, 1998 - No. 3, Dec, 1998 ($2.95, limited series)
1,2-Painted art by Romano. 2-Two-c, one by Firchow 3.00
1-Variant-c by Linsner 5.00

MORE THAN MORTAL TRUTHS AND LEGENDS
Liar Comics: Aug, 1998 - No. 6, Apr, 1999 ($2.95)
1-6-Firchow-a(p) 3.00
1-Variant-c by Dan Norton 4.50

MORE TRASH FROM MAD (Annual)
E. C. Comics: 1958 - No. 12, 1969
(Note: Bonus missing = half price)
nn(1958)-8 pgs. color Mad reprint from #20 21 42 63 149 220 290
2(1959)-Market Product Labels 15 30 45 109 160 210
3(1960)-Text book covers 14 28 42 102 149 195
4(1961)-Sing Along with Mad booklet 14 28 42 102 149 195
5(1962)-Window Stickers; r/from Mad #39 10 20 30 72 104 135
6(1963)-TV Guise booklet 10 20 30 72 104 135
7(1964)-Alfred E. Neuman commemorative stamps 8 16 24 58 82 105
8(1965)-Life size poster-Alfred E. Neuman 6 12 18 43 59 75
9-12: 9,10(1966-67)-Mischief Sticker. 11(1968)-Campaign poster & bumper sticker.
12(1969)-Pocket medals 6 12 18 43 59 75
NOTE: **Kelly Freas** *c-1, 2, 4.* **Mingo** *c-3, 5-9, 12.*

MORGAN THE PIRATE (Movie)
Dell Publishing Co.: No. 1227, Sept-Nov, 1961
Four Color 1227-Photo-c 9 18 27 60 85 110

MORLOCKS
Marvel Comics: June, 2002 - No. 4, Sept, 2002 ($2.50, limited series)
1-4-Johns-s/Martinbrough-c/a 2.50

MORLOCK 2001
Atlas/Seaboard Publ.: Feb, 1975 - No. 3, July, 1975
1,2: 1-(Super-hero)-Origin & 1st app.; Milgrom-c 1 2 3 5 6 8
3-Ditko/Wrightson-a; origin The Midnight Man & The Mystery Men
1 3 4 6 8 10

MORNINGSTAR SPECIAL
Comico: Apr, 1990 ($2.50)
1-From the Elementals; Willingham-c/a/scripts 3.00

MORRIGAN
Dimension X: Aug, 1993 ($2.75, B&W)
1-Foil stamped-c 3.00

MORRIGAN
Sirius Entertainment: 1997 ($2.95, limited series)
1-Tenuta-c/a 3.00

MORTAL KOMBAT
Malibu Comics: July, 1994 - No. 6, Dec, 1994 ($2.95)
1-6: 1-Two diff. covers exist 3.00
1-Limited edition gold foil embossed-c 4.00
0 (12/94), Special Edition 1 (11/94) 3.00
Tournament Edition I12/94, $3.95), II('95)($3.95) 4.00
...: **BARAKA** ,June, 1995 ($2.95, one-shot) #1; ...**BATTLEWAVE** ,2/95 - No. 6, 7/95 , #1-6; ...**GORO, PRINCE OF PAIN** ,9/94 - No. 3, 11/94, #1-3; ...**KITANA AND MILEENA** ,8/95 , ...**KUNG LAO** ,7/95 , #1; ... **RAYDON & KANO** ,3/95 - No. 3, 5/95, #1-3: ...(all $2.95-c)
3.00
...: **U.S. SPECIAL FORCES** ,1/95 - No. 2, ($3.50), #1,2 3.50

MORTIE (Mazie's Friend; also see Flat-Top)
Magazine Publishers: Dec, 1952 - No. 4, June, 1953?
1 8 16 24 46 58 70
2-4 5 10 15 24 30 35

MORTIGAN GOTH: IMMORTALIS (See Marvel Frontier Comics Unlimited)
Marvel Comics: Sept, 1993 - No. 4, Mar, 1994 ($1.95, mini-series)
1-($2.95)-Foil-c 3.00
2-4 2.25

MORT THE DEAD TEENAGER
Marvel Comics: Nov, 1993 - No. 4, Mar, 1994 ($1.75, mini-series)
1-4 2.25

MORTY MEEKLE
Dell Publishing Co.: No. 793, May, 1957
Four Color 793 3 6 9 19 25 32

MOSES & THE TEN COMMANDMENTS (See Dell Giants)

MOSTLY WANTED
DC Comics (WildStorm): Jul, 2000 - No. 4, Nov, 2000 ($2.50, limited series)
1-4-Lobdell-s/Flores-a 2.50

MOTHER GOOSE AND NURSERY RHYME COMICS (See Christmas With Mother Goose)
Dell Publishing Co.: No. 41, 1944 - No. 862, Nov, 1957
Four Color 41-Walt Kelly-c/a 25 50 75 176 258 340
Four Color 59, 68-Kelly c/a 21 42 63 147 216 285
Four Color 862-The Truth About..., Movie (Disney) 8 16 24 58 82 105

MOTHER TERESA OF CALCUTTA
Marvel Comics Group: 1984
1-(52 pgs.) No ads 4.00

MOTION PICTURE COMICS (See Fawcett Movie Comics)
Fawcett Publications: No. 101, 1950 - No. 114, Jan, 1953 (All-photo-c)

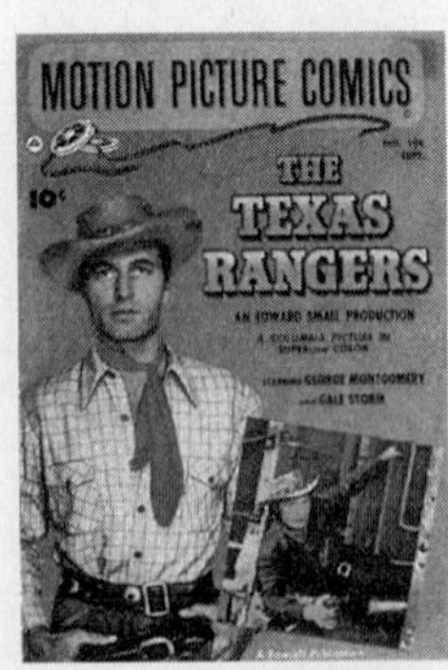

Motion Picture Comics #106 © FAW

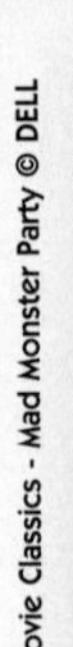
Movie Classics - Mad Monster Party © DELL

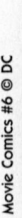

Movie Comics #6 © DC

	GD 2.0	VG 4.0	FN 6.0	VF 8.0	VF/NM 9.0	NM- 9.2
101- "Vanishing Westerner"; Monte Hale (1950)	31	62	93	175	248	320
102- "Code of the Silver Sage"; Rocky Lane (1/51)	28	56	84	159	225	290
103- "Covered Wagon Raid"; Rocky Lane (3/51)	28	56	84	159	225	290
104- "Vigilante Hideout"; Rocky Lane (5/51)-Book length Powell-a	28	56	84	159	225	290
105- "Red Badge of Courage"; Audie Murphy; Bob Powell-a (7/51)	34	68	102	196	278	360
106- "The Texas Rangers"; George Montgomery (9/51)	29	58	87	164	232	300
107- "Frisco Tornado"; Rocky Lane (11/51)	26	52	78	147	206	265
108- "Mask of the Avenger"; John Derek	19	38	57	109	152	195
109- "Rough Rider of Durango"; Rocky Lane	27	54	81	153	214	275
110- "When Worlds Collide"; George Evans-a (5/52); Williamson & Evans drew themselves in story; (also see Famous Funnies No. 72-88)	96	192	288	600	900	1200
111- "The Vanishing Outpost"; Lash LaRue	32	64	96	184	262	340
112- "Brave Warrior"; Jon Hall & Jay Silverheels	19	38	57	106	146	185
113- "Walk East on Beacon"; George Murphy; Schaffenberger-a	14	28	42	79	107	135
114- "Cripple Creek"; George Montgomery (1/53)	15	30	45	84	115	145

MOTION PICTURE FUNNIES WEEKLY (See Promotional Comics section)

MOTORHEAD (See Comic's Greatest World)
Dark Horse Comics: Aug, 1995 - No. 6, Jan, 1996 ($2.50)

1-6: Bisley-c on all. 1-Predator app. 2.50
Special 1 (3/94, $3.95, 52pgs.)-Jae Lee-c; Barb Wire, The Machine & Wolf Gang app. 4.00

MOTORMOUTH (... & Killpower #7? on)
Marvel Comics UK: June, 1992 - No. 12, May, 1993 ($1.75)

1-13: 1,2-Nick Fury app. 3-Punisher-c/story. 5,6-Nick Fury & Punisher app. 6-Cable cameo. 7-9-Cable app. 2.25

MOUNTAIN MEN (See Ben Bowie)

MOUSE MUSKETEERS (See M.G.M.'s...)

MOUSE ON THE MOON, THE (See Movie Classics)

MOVIE CLASSICS
Dell Publishing Co.: Apr, 1956; May-Jul, 1962 - Dec, 1969

(Before 1963, most movie adaptations were part of the 4-Color series)
(Disney movie adaptations after 1970 are in Walt Disney Showcase)

	GD 2.0	VG 4.0	FN 6.0	VF 8.0	VF/NM 9.0	NM- 9.2
Around the World Under the Sea 12-030-612 (12/66)	4	8	12	22	30	38
Bambi 3(4/56)-Disney; r/4-Color #186	4	8	12	27	36	45
Battle of the Bulge 12-056-606 (6/66)	4	8	12	24	32	40
Beach Blanket Bingo 12-058-509	8	16	24	53	74	95
Bon Voyage 01-068-212 (12/62)-Disney; photo-c	4	8	12	25	33	42
Castilian, The 12-110-401	4	8	12	22	30	38
Cat, The 12-109-612 (12/66)	3	7	10	21	28	35
Cheyenne Autumn 12-112-506 (4-6/65)	6	12	18	40	55	70
Circus World, Samuel Bronston's 12-115-411; John Wayne app.; John Wayne photo-c	10	20	30	73	107	140
Countdown 12-150-710 (10/67)-James Caan photo-c	4	8	12	24	32	40
Creature, The 1 (12-142-302) (12-2/62-63)	8	16	24	53	74	95
Creature, The 12-142-410 (10/64)	5	10	15	36	48	60
David Ladd's Life Story 12-173-212 (10-12/62)-Photo-c	8	16	24	55	78	100
Die, Monster, Die 12-175-603 (3/66)-Photo-c	6	12	18	38	52	65
Dirty Dozen 12-180-710 (10/67)	5	10	15	33	44	55
Dr. Who & the Daleks 12-190-612 (12/66)-Peter Cushing photo-c; 1st U.S. app. of Dr. Who	10	20	30	73	107	140
Dracula 12-231-212 (10-12/62)	7	14	21	46	63	80
El Dorado 12-240-710 (10/67)-John Wayne; photo-c	13	26	39	94	137	180
Ensign Pulver 12-257-410 (8-10/64)	3	7	10	21	28	35
Frankenstein 12-283-305 (3-5/63)(see Frankenstein 8-10/64 for 2nd printing)	7	14	21	50	68	85
Great Race, The 12-299-603 (3/66)-Natallie Wood, Tony Curtis photo-c	5	10	15	33	44	55
Hallelujah Trail, The 12-307-602 (2/66) (Shows 1/66 inside); Burt Lancaster, Lee Remick photo-c	5	10	15	36	48	60
Hatari 12-340-301 (1/63)-John Wayne	9	18	27	60	85	110
Horizontal Lieutenant, The 01-348-210 (10/62)	3	7	10	21	28	35
Incredible Mr. Limpet, The 12-370-408; Don Knotts photo-c	4	8	12	28	38	48
Jack the Giant Killer 12-374-301 (1/63)	9	18	27	60	85	110
Jason & the Argonauts 12-376-310 (8-10/63)-Photo-c	10	20	30	67	96	125
Lancelot & Guinevere 12-416-310 (10/63)	6	12	18	38	52	65
Lawrence 12-426-308 (8/63)-Story of Lawrence of Arabia; movie ad on back-c; not exactly like movie	6	12	18	38	52	65
Lion of Sparta 12-439-301 (1/63)	4	8	12	25	33	42
Mad Monster Party 12-460-801 (9/67)-Based on Kurtzman's screenplay	8	16	24	55	78	100
Magic Sword, The 01-496-209 (9/62)	6	12	18	40	55	70
Masque of the Red Death 12-490-410 (8-10/64)-Vincent Price photo-c	7	14	21	46	63	80
Maya 12-495-612 (12/66)-Clint Walker & Jay North part photo-c	4	8	12	28	38	48
McHale's Navy 12-500-412 (10-12/64)	5	10	15	33	44	55
Merrill's Marauders 12-510-301 (1/63)-Photo-c	3	7	10	21	28	35
Mouse on the Moon, The 12-530-312 (10/12/63)-Photo-c	4	8	12	25	33	42
Mummy, The 12-537-211 (9-11/62) 2 versions with different back-c	7	14	21	51	71	90
Music Man, The 12-538-301 (1/63)	4	8	12	22	30	38
Naked Prey, The 12-545-612 (12/66)-Photo-c	6	12	18	40	55	70
Night of the Grizzly, The 12-558-612 (12/66)-Photo-c	4	8	12	25	33	42
None But the Brave 12-565-506 (4-6/65)	6	12	18	40	55	70
Operation Bikini 12-597-310 (10/63)-Photo-c	4	8	12	22	30	38
Operation Crossbow 12-590-512 (10-12/65)	4	8	12	22	30	38
Prince & the Pauper, The 01-654-207 (5-7/62)-Disney	4	8	12	25	33	42
Raven, The 12-680-309 (9/63)-Vincent Price photo-c	6	12	18	43	59	75
Ring of Bright Water 01-701-910 (10/69) (inside shows #12-701-909)	4	8	12	25	33	42
Runaway, The 12-707-412 (10-12/64)	3	7	10	21	28	35
Santa Claus Conquers the Martians #? (1964)-Photo-c	10	20	30	67	96	125
Santa Claus Conquers the Martians 12-725-603 (3/66, 12¢)-Reprints 1964 issue; photo-c	8	16	24	55	78	100
Another version given away with a Golden Record, SLP 170, nn, no price (3/66)-Complete with record	15	30	45	104	152	200
Six Black Horses 12-750-301 (1/63)-Photo-c	4	8	12	22	30	38
Ski Party 12-743-511 (9-11/65)-Frankie Avalon photo-c; photo inside-c; Adkins-a	5	10	15	36	48	60
Smoky 12-746-702 (2/67)	3	7	10	21	28	35
Sons of Katie Elder 12-748-511 (9-11/65); John Wayne app.; photo-c	14	28	42	97	141	185
Tales of Terror 12-793-302 (2/63)-Evans-a	6	12	18	40	55	70
Three Stooges Meet Hercules 01-828-208 (8/62)-Photo-c	10	20	30	67	96	125
Tomb of Ligeia 12-830-506 (4-6/65)	6	12	18	40	55	70
Treasure Island 01-845-211 (7-9/62)-Disney; r/4-Color #624	4	8	12	22	30	38
Twice Told Tales (Nathaniel Hawthorne) 12-840-401 (11-1/63-64); Vincent Price photo-c	6	12	18	43	59	75
Two on a Guillotine 12-850-506 (4-6/65)	4	8	12	25	33	42
Valley of Gwangi 01-880-912 (12/69)	10	20	30	70	100	130
War Gods of the Deep 12-900-509 (7-9/65)	4	8	12	22	30	38
War Wagon, The 12-533-709 (9/67); John Wayne app.	9	18	27	63	89	115
Who's Minding the Mint? 12-924-708 (8/67)	3	7	10	21	28	35
Wolfman, The 12-922-308 (6-8/63)	7	14	21	50	68	85
Wolfman, The 1(12-922-410)(8-10/64)-2nd printing; r/#12-922-308	4	8	12	27	36	45
Zulu 12-950-410 (8-10/64)-Photo-c	8	16	24	58	82	105

MOVIE COMICS (See Cinema Comics Herald & Fawcett Movie Comics)

MOVIE COMICS
National Periodical Publications/Picture Comics: April, 1939 - No. 6, Sept-Oct, 1939 (Most all photo-c)

	GD 2.0	VG 4.0	FN 6.0	VF 8.0	VF/NM 9.0	NM- 9.2
1- "Gunga Din", "Son of Frankenstein", "The Great Man Votes", "Fisherman's Wharf", & "Scouts to the Rescue" part 1; Wheelan "Minute Movies" begin	326	652	978	2119	3260	4400
2- "Stagecoach", "The Saint Strikes Back", "King of the Turf","Scouts to the Rescue" part 2, "Arizona Legion", Andy Devine photo-c	228	456	684	1425	2138	2850
3- "East Side of Heaven", "Mystery in the White Room", "Four Feathers", "Mexican Rose" with Gene Autry, "Spirit of Culver", "Many Secrets", "The Mikado" (1st Gene Autry photo cover)	164	328	492	1025	1538	2050
4- "Captain Fury", Gene Autry in "Blue Montana Skies", "Streets of N.Y." with Jackie Cooper, "Oregon Trail" part 1 with Johnny Mack Brown, "Big Town Czar" with Barton MacLane, & "Star Reporter" with Warren Hull	130	260	390	813	1219	1625

Movie Comics #2 © FH

Movie Comics - Bambi #1 © WDC

Movie Comics - Merlin Jones as the Monkey's Uncle © WDC

GD VG FN VF VF/NM NM-
2.0 4.0 6.0 8.0 9.0 9.2

5- "The Man in the Iron Mask", "Five Came Back", "Wolf Call", "The Girl & the Gambler", "The House of Fear", "The Family Next Door", "Oregon Trail" part 2
152 304 456 950 1425 1900
6- "The Phantom Creeps", "Chumps at Oxford", & "The Oregon Trail" part 3; 2nd Robot-c
192 384 576 1200 1800 2400

NOTE: *Above books contain many original movie stills with dialogue from movie scripts. All issues are scarce.*

MOVIE COMICS
Fiction House Magazines: Dec, 1946 - No. 4, 1947

1-Big Town (by Lubbers), Johnny Danger begin; Celardo-a; Mitzi of the Movies by Fran Hopper 55 110 165 330 495 660
2-(2/47)- "White Tie & Tails" with William Bendix; Mitzi of the Movies begins by Matt Baker, ends #4 40 80 120 240 350 460
3-(6/47)-Andy Hardy starring Mickey Rooney 40 80 120 240 350 460
4-Mitzi In Hollywood by Matt Baker; Merton of the Movies with Red Skelton; Yvonne DeCarlo & George Brent in "Slave Girl" 48 96 144 288 432 575

MOVIE COMICS
Gold Key/Whitman: Oct, 1962 - 1984

Alice in Wonderland 10144-503 (3/65)-Disney; partial reprint of 4-Color #331
4 8 12 27 36 45
Alice In Wonderland #1 (Whitman, 3/84) 1 2 3 5 7 9
Aristocats, The 1 (30045-103)(3/71)-Disney; with pull-out poster (25¢)
(No poster = half price) 8 16 24 55 78 100
Bambi 1 (10087-309)(9/63)-Disney; r/4-C #186 4 8 12 28 38 48
Bambi 2 (10087-607)(7/66)-Disney; r/4-C #186 4 8 12 22 30 38
Beneath the Planet of the Apes 30044-012 (12/70)-with pull-out poster; photo-c
(No poster = half price) 10 20 30 70 100 130
Big Red 10026-211 (11/62)-Disney; photo-c 4 8 12 22 30 38
Big Red 10026-503 (3/65)-Disney; reprints 10026-211; photo-c
3 6 9 18 24 30
Blackbeard's Ghost 10222-806 (6/68)-Disney 3 7 10 21 28 35
Bullwhip Griffin 10181-706 (6/67)-Disney; Spiegle-a; photo-c
4 8 12 25 33 42
Captain Sindbad 10077-309 (9/63)-Manning-a; photo-c
7 14 21 46 63 80
Chitty Chitty Bang Bang 1 (30038-902)(2/69)-with pull-out poster; Disney; photo-c
(No poster = half price) 7 14 21 51 71 90
Cinderella 10152-508 (8/65)-Disney; r/4-C #786 4 8 12 25 33 42
Darby O'Gill & the Little People 10251-001(1/70)-Disney; reprints 4-Color #1024 (Toth-a); photo-c 6 12 18 38 52 65
Dumbo 1 (10090-310)(10/63)-Disney; r/4-C #668 4 8 12 25 33 42
Emil & the Detectives 10120-502 (11/64)-Disney; photo-c
4 8 12 22 30 38
Escapade in Florence 1 (10043-301)(1/63)-Disney; starring Annette Funicello
9 18 27 60 85 110
Fall of the Roman Empire 10118-407 (7/64); Sophia Loren photo-c
4 8 12 25 33 42
Fantastic Voyage 10178-702 (2/67)-Wood/Adkins-a; photo-c
6 12 18 40 55 70
55 Days at Peking 10081-309 (9/63)-Photo-c 4 8 12 22 30 38
Fighting Prince of Donegal, The 10193-701 (1/67)-Disney
3 7 10 21 28 35
First Men in the Moon 10132-503 (3/65)-Fred Fredericks-a; photo-c
4 8 12 24 32 40
Gay Purr-ee 30017-301(1/63, 84 pgs.) 6 12 18 38 52 65
Gnome Mobile, The 10207-710 (10/67)-Disney 4 8 12 25 33 42
Goodbye, Mr. Chips 10246-006 (6/70)-Peter O'Toole photo-c
4 8 12 22 30 38
Happiest Millionaire, The 10221-804 (4/68)-Disney 4 8 12 25 33 42
Hey There, It's Yogi Bear 10122-409 (9/64)-Hanna-Barbera
7 14 21 51 71 90
Horse Without a Head, The 10109-401 (1/64)-Disney 3 7 10 21 28 35
How the West Was Won 10074-307 (7/63)-Based on the L'Amour novel; Tufts-a
5 10 15 33 44 55
In Search of the Castaways 10048-303 (3/63)-Disney; Hayley Mills photo-c
7 14 21 51 71 90
Jungle Book, The 1 (6022-801)(1/68-Whitman)-Disney; large size (10x13-1/2"); 59¢
7 14 21 51 71 90
Jungle Book, The 1 (30033-803)(3/68, 68 pgs.)-Disney; same contents as Whitman #1
4 8 12 28 38 48
Jungle Book, The 1 (6/78, $1.00 tabloid) 3 6 9 18 24 30
Jungle Book (7/84)-r/Giant 1 2 3 5 7 9
Kidnapped 10080-306 (6/63)-Disney; reprints 4-Color #1101; photo-c
4 8 12 22 30 38

GD VG FN VF VF/NM NM-
2.0 4.0 6.0 8.0 9.0 9.2

King Kong 30036-809(9/68-68 pgs.)-painted-c 4 8 12 28 38 48
King Kong nn-Whitman Treasury($1.00, 68 pgs.,1968), same cover as Gold Key issue
6 12 18 38 52 65
King Kong 11299(#1-786, 10x13-1/4", 68 pgs., $1.00, 1978)
3 6 9 18 24 30
Lady and the Tramp 10042-301 (1/63)-Disney; r/4-Color #629
4 8 12 25 33 42
Lady and the Tramp 1 (1967-Giant; 25¢)-Disney; reprints part of Dell #1
6 12 18 43 59 75
Lady and the Tramp 2 (10042-203)(3/72)-Disney; r/4-Color #629
3 6 9 18 24 30
Legend of Lobo, The 1 (10059-303)(3/63)-Disney; photo-c
3 6 9 18 24 30
Lt. Robin Crusoe, U.S.N. 10191-610 (10/66)-Disney; Dick Van Dyke photo-c
3 6 9 19 25 32
Lion, The 10035-301 (1/63)-Photo-c 3 6 9 18 24 30
Lord Jim 10156-509 (9/65)-Photo-c 3 6 9 18 24 30
Love Bug, The 10237-906 (6/69)-Disney; Buddy Hackett photo-c
4 8 12 22 30 38
Mary Poppins 10136-501 (1/65)-Disney; photo-c 5 10 15 33 44 55
Mary Poppins 30023-501 (1/65-68 pgs.)-Disney; photo-c
7 14 21 51 71 90
McLintock 10110-403 (3/64); John Wayne app.; John Wayne & Maureen O'Hara photo-c
13 26 39 90 133 175
Merlin Jones as the Monkey's Uncle 10115-510 (10/65)-Disney; Annette Funicello front/back photo-c 6 12 18 43 59 75
Miracle of the White Stallions, The 10065-306 (6/63)-Disney
3 7 10 21 28 35
Misadventures of Merlin Jones, The 10115-405 (5/64)-Disney; Annette Funicello photo front/back-c 6 12 18 43 59 75
Moon-Spinners, The 10124-410 (10/64)-Disney; Haley Mills photo-c
7 14 21 51 69 90
Mutiny on the Bounty 1 (10040-302)(2/63)-Marlon Brando photo-c
4 8 12 22 30 38
Nikki, Wild Dog of the North 10141-412 (12/64)-Disney; reprints 4-Color #1226
3 6 9 18 24 30
Old Yeller 10168-601 (1/66)-Disney; reprints 4-Color #869; photo-c
3 6 9 18 24 30
One Hundred & One Dalmations 1 (10247-002) (2/70)-Disney; reprints Four Color #1183
3 7 10 21 28 35
Peter Pan 1 (10086-309)(9/63)-Disney; reprints Four Color #442
4 8 12 25 33 42
Peter Pan 2 (10086-909)(9/69)-Disney; reprints Four Color #442
3 6 9 18 24 30
Peter Pan 1 (3/84)-r/4-Color #442 1 2 3 4 5 7
P.T. 109 10123-409 (9/64)-John F. Kennedy 5 10 15 36 48 60
Rio Conchos 10143-503(3/65) 4 8 12 25 33 42
Robin Hood 10163-506 (6/65)-Disney; reprints Four Color #413
3 6 9 19 25 32
Shaggy Dog & the Absent-Minded Professor 30032-708 (8/67-Giant, 68 pgs.) Disney; reprints 4-Color #985,1199 6 12 18 40 55 70
Sleeping Beauty 1 (30042-009)(9/70)-Disney; reprints Four Color #973; with pull-out poster
(No poster = half price) 7 14 21 51 71 90
Snow White & the Seven Dwarfs 1 (10091-310)(10/63)-Disney; reprints Four Color #382
4 8 12 22 30 38
Snow White & the Seven Dwarfs 10091-709 (9/67)-Disney; reprints Four Color #382
3 6 9 18 24 30
Snow White & the Seven Dwarfs 90091-204 (2/84)-Reprints Four Color #382
1 2 3 4 5 7
Son of Flubber 1 (10057-304)(4/63)-Disney; sequel to "The Absent-Minded Professor"
4 8 12 25 33 42
Summer Magic 10076-309 (9/63)-Disney; Hayley Mills photo-c; Manning-a
7 14 21 51 71 90
Swiss Family Robinson 10236-904 (4/69)-Disney; reprints Four Color #1156; photo-c
3 7 10 21 28 35
Sword in the Stone, The 30019-402 (2/64-Giant, 68 pgs.)-Disney (see March of Comics #258 & Wart and the Wizard 7 14 21 51 71 90
That Darn Cat 10171-602 (2/66)-Disney; Hayley Mills photo-c
7 14 21 51 71 90
Those Magnificent Men in Their Flying Machines 10162-510 (10/65); photo-c
4 8 12 22 30 38
Three Stooges in Orbit 30016-211 (11/62-Giant, 32 pgs.)-All photos from movie; stiff-photo-c
11 22 33 77 114 150
Tiger Walks, A 10117-406 (6/64)-Disney; Torres?, Tufts-a; photo-c

Movie Love #11 © FF

Ms. Tree #33 © Max Collins & Terry Beatty

Mucha Lucha #1 © WB

GD VG FN VF VF/NM NM-
2.0 4.0 6.0 8.0 9.0 9.2

4 8 12 28 38 48
Toby Tyler 10142-502 (2/65)-Disney; reprints Four Color #1092; photo-c
3 7 10 21 28 35
Treasure Island 1 (10200-703)(3/67)-Disney; reprints Four Color #624; photo-c
3 6 9 18 24 30
20,000 Leagues Under the Sea 1 (10095-312)(12/63)-Disney; reprints Four Color #614
3 7 10 21 28 35
Wonderful Adventures of Pinocchio, The 1 (10089-310)(10/63)-Disney; reprints Four Color #545 (see Wonderful Advs. of...) 4 8 12 25 33 42
Wonderful Adventures of Pinocchio, The 10089-109 (9/71)-Disney; reprints Four Color #545
3 6 9 18 24 30
Wonderful World of the Brothers Grimm 1 (10008-210)(10/62)
5 10 15 33 44 55
X, the Man with the X-Ray Eyes 10083-309 (9/63)-Ray Milland photo on-c
8 16 24 55 78 100
Yellow Submarine 35000-902 (2/69-Giant, 68 pgs.)-With pull-out poster;
The Beatles cartoon movie; Paul S. Newman-s 25 50 75 176 258 340
Without poster 9 18 27 63 89 115

MOVIE LOVE (Also see Personal Love)
Famous Funnies: Feb, 1950 - No. 22, Aug, 1953 (All photo-c)
1-Dick Powell, Evelyn Keyes, & Mickey Rooney photo-c
16 32 48 92 126 160
2-Myrna Loy photo-c 9 18 27 52 66 80
3-7,9: 6-Ricardo Montalban photo-c. 9-Gene Tierney, John Lund, Glenn Ford, & Rhonda Fleming photo-c. 8 16 24 46 58 70
8-Williamson/Frazetta-a, 6 pgs. 40 80 120 240 360 480
10-Frazetta-a, 6 pgs. 41 82 123 246 368 490
11,14-16: 14-Janet Leigh photo-c 8 16 24 43 54 65
12-Dean Martin & Jerry Lewis photo-c (12/51, pre-dates Advs. of Dean Martin & Jerry Lewis comic) 16 32 48 92 126 160
13-Ronald Reagan photo-c with 1 pg. biog. 24 48 72 135 190 245
17-Leslie Caron & Ralph Meeker photo-c; 1 pg. Frazetta ad
8 16 24 46 58 70
18-22: 19-John Derek photo-c. 20-Donald O'Connor & Debbie Reynolds photo-c. 21-Paul Henreid & Patricia Medina photo-c. 22-John Payne & Coleen Gray photo-c
8 16 24 40 50 60
NOTE: *Each issue has a full-length movie adaptation with photo covers.*

MOVIE THRILLERS (Movie)
Magazine Enterprises: 1949
1-Adaptation of "Rope of Sand" w/Burt Lancaster; Burt Lancaster photo-c
31 62 93 175 248 320

MOVIE TOWN ANIMAL ANTICS (Formerly Animal Antics; becomes Raccoon Kids #52 on)
National Periodical Publ.: No. 24, Jan-Feb, 1950 - No. 51, July-Aug, 1954
24-Raccoon Kids continue 12 24 36 69 92 115
25-51 10 20 30 56 73 90
NOTE: ***Sheldon Mayer** a-28-33, 35, 37-41, 43, 44, 47, 49-51.*

MOVIE TUNES COMICS (Formerly Animated...; Frankie No. 4 on)
Marvel Comics (MgPC): No. 3, Fall, 1946
3-Super Rabbit, Krazy Krow, Silly Seal & Ziggy Pig 13 26 39 74 100 125

MOWGLI JUNGLE BOOK (Rudyard Kipling's...)
Dell Publ. Co.: No. 487, Aug-Oct, 1953 - No. 620, Apr, 1955
Four Color 487 (#1) 6 12 18 43 59 75
Four Color 582 (8/54), 620 5 10 15 36 48 60

MR. (See Mister)

M. REX
Image Comics: July, 1999 - No. 2, Dec, 1999 ($2.95)
Preview ($5.00) B&W pages and sketchbook; Rouleau-a 5.00
1,2-($2.95) 1-Joe Kelly-s/Rouleau-a/Anacleto-c. 2-Rouleau-c 3.00

MS. CYANIDE & ICE
Blackout Comics: June, 1995 - No. 1, 1995 ($2.95, B&W)
0,1 3.00

MS. FORTUNE
Image Comics: Jan, 1998 ($2.95, B&W, one-shot)
1-Chris Marrinan-s/a 3.00

MS. MARVEL (Also see The Avengers #183)
Marvel Comics Group: Jan, 1977 - No. 23, Apr, 1979
1-1st app. Ms. Marvel; Scorpion app. in #1,2 2 4 6 8 10 12
2-10: 2-Origin. 5-Vision app. 6-10-(Reg. 30¢-c). 10-Last 30¢ issue 6.00
6-10-(35¢-c variants, limited dist.)(6/77) 1 2 3 5 7 9
11-15,19-23: 19-Capt. Marvel app. 20-New costume. 23-Vance Astro (leader of the Guardians) app. 5.00
16,17-Mystique cameo 2 4 6 8 10 12
18-1st full Mystique; Avengers x-over 2 4 6 12 16 20
NOTE: ***Austin** c-14i, 16i, 17i, 22i. **Buscema** a-1-3p; c(p)-2, 4, 6, 7, 15. **Infantino** a-14p, 19p. **Gil Kane** c-8. **Mooney** a-4-8p, 13p, 15-18p. **Starlin** c-12.*

MS. MYSTIC
Pacific Comics: Oct, 1982 - No. 2, Feb, 1984 ($1.00/$1.50)
1,2: Neal Adams-c/a/script. 1-Origin; intro Erth, Ayre, Fyre & Watr 4.00

MS. MYSTIC
Continuity Comics: 1988 - No. 9, May, 1992 ($2.00)
1-9: 1,2-Reprint Pacific Comics issues 3.00

MS. MYSTIC
Continunity Comics: V2#1, Oct, 1993 - V2#4, Jan, 1994 ($2.50)
V2#1-4: 1-Adams-c(i)/part-i. 2-4-Embossed-c. 2-Nebres part-i. 3-Adams-c(i)/plot. 4-Adams-c(p)/plot 2.50

MS. MYSTIC DEATHWATCH 2000 (Ms. Mystic #3)
Continuity: May, 1993 - No. 3, Aug, 1993 ($2.50)
1-3-Bagged w/card; Adams plots 2.50

MS. TREE QUARTERLY / SPECIAL
DC Comics: Summer, 1990 -No. 10, 1992 ($3.95/$3.50, 84 pgs, mature)
1-10: 1-Midnight story; Batman text story, Grell-a. 2,3-Midnight stories; The Butcher text stories 4.00
NOTE: ***Cowan** c-2. **Grell** c-1, 6. **Infantino** a-8.*

MS. TREE'S THRILLING DETECTIVE ADVS (Ms. Tree #4 on; also see The Best of Ms. Tree) (Baxter paper #4-9)
Eclipse Comics/Aardvark-Vanaheim 10-18/Renegade Press 19 on:
2/83 - #9, 7/84; #10, 8/84 - #18, 5/85; #19, 6/85 - #50, 6/89
1 3.00
2-49: 2-Schythe begins. 9-Last Eclipse & last color issue. 10,11-two-tone 2.50
50-Contains flexi-disc ($3.95, 52pgs.) 4.00
Summer Special 1 (8/86) 3.00
1950s 3-D Crime (7/87, no glasses)-Johnny Dynamite in 3-D 3.00
Mike Mist in 3-D (8/85)-With glasses 3.00
NOTE; ***Miller** pin-up 1-4. Johnny Dynamite-r begin #36 by **Morisi**.*

MS. VICTORY SPECIAL(Also see Capt. Paragon & Femforce)
Americomics: Jan, 1985 (nd)
1 2.50

MUCHA LUCHA (Based on Kids WB animated TV show)
DC Comics: Jun, 2003 - No. 3, Aug, 2003 ($2.25, limited series)
1-3-Rikochet, Buena Girl and The Flea app. 2.25

MUGGSY MOUSE (Also see Tick Tock Tales)
Magazine Enterprises: 1951 - No. 3, 1951; No. 4, 1954 - No. 5, 1954; 1963
1(A-1 #33) 8 16 24 43 54 65
2(A-1 #36)-Racist-c 10 20 30 56 73 90
3(A-1 #39), 4(A-1 #95), 5(A-1 #99) 6 12 18 28 34 40
Super Reprint #14(1963), I.W. Reprint #1,2 (nd) 2 4 6 9 11 14

MUGGY-DOO, BOY CAT
Stanhall Publ.: July, 1953 - No. 4, Jan, 1954
1-Funny animal; Irving Spector-a 8 16 24 46 58 70
2-4 5 10 15 24 30 35
Super Reprint #12('63), 16('64) 2 4 6 9 11 14

MUKTUK WOLFSBREATH: HARD-BOILED SHAMAN
DC Comics (Vertigo): Aug, 1998 - No. 3, Oct, 1998 ($2.50)
1-3-Terry LaBan-s/Steve Parkhouse-a 2.50

MULLKON EMPIRE (See John Jake's...)

MUMMY, THE (See Universal Presents... under Dell Giants & Movie Classics)

MUMMY, THE: VALLEY OF THE GODS (Movie adaption)
Chaos! Comics: May, 2001 - No. 3 ($2.99, limited series)
1-Based on "The Mummy Returns" movie; Broome-a; Broome & photo-c 3.00

MUNDEN'S BAR ANNUAL
First Comics: Apr, 1988; 1989 ($2.95/$5.95)
1-($2.95)-r/from Grimjack; Fish Police story; Ordway-c 3.00
2-($5.95)-Teenage Mutant Ninja Turtles app. 6.00

Murder Incorporated #14 © FOX

Muties #1 © MAR

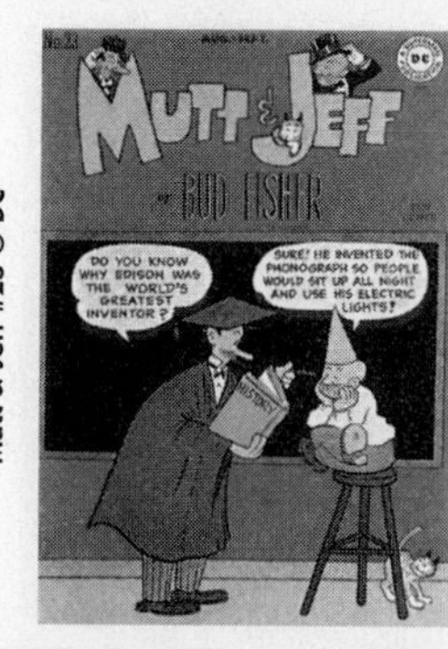

Mutt & Jeff #23 © DC

	GD 2.0	VG 4.0	FN 6.0	VF 8.0	VF/NM 9.0	NM- 9.2

MUNSTERS, THE (TV)
Gold Key: Jan, 1965 - No. 16, Jan, 1968 (All photo-c)

	GD	VG	FN	VF	VF/NM	NM-
1 (10134-501)	20	40	60	145	213	280
2	10	20	30	73	107	140
3-5	9	18	27	63	89	115
6-16	8	16	24	53	74	95

MUNSTERS, THE (TV)
TV Comics!: Aug, 1997 - No. 4 ($2.95, B&W)

	GD	VG	FN	VF	VF/NM	NM-
1-4-All have photo-c						3.00
1,4-($7.95)-Variant-c						8.00
2-Variant-c w/Beverly Owens as Marilyn						3.00
Special Comic Con Ed. (7/97, $9.95)						10.00

MUPPET BABIES, THE (TV)(See Star Comics Magazine)
Marvel Comics (Star Comics)/Marvel #18 on: Aug, 1985 - No. 26, July, 1989 (Children's book)

	GD	VG	FN	VF	VF/NM	NM-
1-26						3.00

MUPPETS TAKE MANHATTAN, THE
Marvel Comics (Star Comics): Nov, 1984 - No. 3, Jan, 1985

	GD	VG	FN	VF	VF/NM	NM-
1-3-Movie adapt. r-/Marvel Super Special						3.00

MURCIELAGA, SHE-BAT
Heroic Publishing: Jan, 1993 - No. 2, 1993 (B&W)

	GD	VG	FN	VF	VF/NM	NM-
1-($1.50, 28 pgs.)						2.50
2-($2.95, 36 pgs.)-Coated-c						3.00

MURDER CAN BE FUN
Slave Labor Graphics: Feb, 1996 - No. 12 ($2.95, B&W)

	GD	VG	FN	VF	VF/NM	NM-
1-12: 1-Dorkin-c. 2-Vasquez-c.						3.00

MURDER INCORPORATED (My Private Life #16 on)
Fox Feature Syndicate: 1/48 - No. 15, 12/49; (2 No.9's); 6/50 - No. 3, 8/51

	GD	VG	FN	VF	VF/NM	NM-
1 (1st Series); 1,2 have 'For Adults Only' on-c	50	100	150	300	450	600
2-Electrocution story	40	80	120	240	345	450
3-7,9(4/49),10(5/49),11-15	24	48	72	135	190	245
8-Used in **SOTI**, pg. 160	26	52	78	150	210	270
9(3/49)-Possible use in **SOTI**, pg. 145; r/Blue Beetle #56('48)	24	48	72	135	190	245
5(#1, 6/50)(2nd Series)-Formerly My Desire #4; bondage-c.	19	38	57	106	146	185
2(8/50)-Morisi-a	16	32	48	92	126	160
3(8/51)-Used in **POP**, pg. 81; Rico-a; lingerie-c/panels	18	36	54	101	138	175

MURDER ME DEAD
El Capitán Books: July, 2000 - No. 9, Oct, 2001 ($2.95/$4.95, B&W)

	GD	VG	FN	VF	VF/NM	NM-
1-8-David Lapham-s/a						3.00
9-($4.95)						5.00

MURDEROUS GANGSTERS
Avon Per./Realistic No. 3 on: Jul, 1951; No. 2, Dec, 1951 - No. 4, Jun, 1952

	GD	VG	FN	VF	VF/NM	NM-
1-Pretty Boy Floyd, Leggs Diamond; 1 pg. Wood-a	44	88	132	264	395	525
2-Baby-Face Nelson; 1 pg. Wood-a; painted-c	30	60	90	170	240	310
3-Painted-c	24	48	72	135	190	245
4- "Murder by Needle" drug story; Mort Lawrence-a; Kinstler-c	30	60	90	170	240	310

MURDER MYSTERIES (Neil Gaiman's...)
Dark Horse Comics: 2002 ($13.95, HC, one-shot)

	GD	VG	FN	VF	VF/NM	NM-
HC-Adapts Gaiman story; P. Craig Russell-script/art						14.00

MURDER TALES (Magazine)
World Famous Publications: V1#10, Nov, 1970 - V1#11, Jan, 1971 (52 pgs.)

	GD	VG	FN	VF	VF/NM	NM-
V1#10-One pg. Frazetta ad	4	8	12	24	32	40
11-Guardineer-r; bondage-c	3	6	9	18	24	30

MUSHMOUSE AND PUNKIN PUSS (TV)
Gold Key: September, 1965 (Hanna-Barbera)

	GD	VG	FN	VF	VF/NM	NM-
1 (10153-509)	10	20	30	70	100	130

MUSIC MAN, THE (See Movie Classics)

MUTANT CHRONICLES (Video game)
Acclaim Comics (Armada): May, 1996 - No. 4, Aug, 1996 ($2.95, lim. series)

	GD	VG	FN	VF	VF/NM	NM-
1-4: Simon Bisley-c on all, Sourcebook (#5)						3.00

MUTANT EARTH (Stan Winston's...)
Image Comics: April, 2002 - No. 4, Jan, 2003 ($2.95)

	GD	VG	FN	VF	VF/NM	NM-
1-4-Flip book w/Realm of the Claw						3.00
Trakk...His Adventures in Mutant Earth TPB (2003, $16.95) r/#1-4; Winston interview						17.00

MUTANT MISADVENTURES OF CLOAK AND DAGGER, THE
(Becomes Cloak and Dagger #14 on)
Marvel Comics: Oct, 1988 - No. 19, Aug, 1991 ($1.25/$1.50)

	GD	VG	FN	VF	VF/NM	NM-
1-8,10-15: 1-X-Factor app. 10-Painted-c. 12-Dr. Doom app. 14-Begin new direction						2.25
9,16-19: 9-(52 pgs.) The Avengers x-over; painted-c. 16-18-Spider-Man x-over. 18-Infinity Gauntlet x-over; Thanos cameo; Ghost Rider app. 19-(52 pgs.) Origin Cloak & Dagger						2.50

NOTE: ***Austin*** *a-12i; c(i)-4, 12, 13; scripts-all.* ***Russell*** *a-2i.* ***Williamson*** *a-14i-16i; c-15i.*

MUTANTS & MISFITS
Silverline Comics (Solson): 1987 - No. 3, 1987 ($1.95)

	GD	VG	FN	VF	VF/NM	NM-
1-3						2.25

MUTANTS VS. ULTRAS
Malibu Comics (Ultraverse): Nov, 1995 ($6.95, one-shot)

	GD	VG	FN	VF	VF/NM	NM-
1-r/Exiles vs. X-Men, Night Man vs. Wolverine, Prime vs. Hulk						7.00

MUTANT, TEXAS: TALES OF SHERIFF IDA RED (Also see Jingle Belle)
Oni Press: May, 2002 - No. 4, Nov, 2002 ($2.95, B&W, limited series)

	GD	VG	FN	VF	VF/NM	NM-
1-4-Paul Dini-s/J. Bone-c/a						3.00
TPB (2003, $11.95) r/#1-4; intro. by Joe Lansdale						12.00

MUTANT X (See X-Factor)
Marvel Comics: Nov, 1998 - No. 32, June, 2001 ($2.99/$1.99/$2.25)

	GD	VG	FN	VF	VF/NM	NM-
1-($2.99) Alex Summers with alternate world's X-Men						3.00
2-11,13-19-($1.99): 2-Two covers. 5-Man-Spider-c/app.						2.25
12,25-($2.99): 12-Pin-up gallery by Kaluta, Romita, Byrne						3.00
20-24,26-32: 20-Begin $2.25-c. 28-31-Logan-c/app. 32-Last issue						2.25
Annual '99, '00 (5/99,'00, $3.50) '00-Doran-a(p)						3.50
Annual 2001 ($2.99) Story oocurs between #31 & #32; Dracula app.						3.00

MUTANT X (Based on TV show)
Marvel Comics: May, 2002 - Present ($3.50)

	GD	VG	FN	VF	VF/NM	NM-
...: Dangerous Decisions (6/02) -Kuder-s/Immonen-a						3.50
...: Origin (5/02) -Tischman & Chaykin-s/Ferguson-a						3.50

MUTATIS
Marvel Comics (Epic Comics): 1992 - No. 3, 1992 ($2.25, mini-series)

	GD	VG	FN	VF	VF/NM	NM-
1-3: Painted-c						2.25

MUTIES
Marvel Comics: Apr, 2002 - No. 6, Sept, 2002 ($2.50)

	GD	VG	FN	VF	VF/NM	NM-
1-6: 1-Bollars-s/Ferguson-a. 2-Spaziante-a. 3-Haspiel-a. 4-Kanuiga-a						2.50

MUTINY (Stormy Tales of the Seven Seas)
Aragon Magazines: Oct, 1954 - No. 3, Feb, 1955

	GD	VG	FN	VF	VF/NM	NM-
1	17	34	51	98	134	170
2,3: 2-Capt. Mutiny. 3-Bondage-c	14	28	42	79	107	135

MUTINY ON THE BOUNTY (See Classics Illustrated #100 & Movie Comics)

MUTT AND JEFF (See All-American, All-Flash #18, Cicero's Cat, Comic Cavalcade, Famous Feature Stories, The Funnies, Popular & Xmas Comics)
All American/National 1-103(6/58)/Dell 104(10/58)-115 (10-12/59)/ Harvey 116(2/60)-148: Summer, 1939 (nd) - No. 148, Nov, 1965

	GD	VG	FN	VF	VF/NM	NM-
1(nn)-Lost Wheels	128	256	384	800	1200	1600
2(nn)-Charging Bull (Summer, 1940, nd; on sale 6/20/40)	66	132	200	413	619	825
3(nn)-Bucking Broncos (Summer, 1941, nd)	48	96	144	288	432	575
4(Winter, '41), 5(Summer, '42)	43	86	129	258	389	520
6-10	24	48	72	138	194	250
11-20: 20-X-Mas-c	17	34	51	98	134	170
21-30	12	24	36	71	96	120
31-50: 32-X-Mas-c	10	20	30	56	73	90
51-75-Last Fisher issue. 53-Last 52 pgs.	8	16	24	46	58	70
76-99,101-103: 76-Last pre-code issue(1/55)	5	10	15	33	44	55
100	5	10	15	36	48	60
104-115,132-148	4	8	12	27	36	45
116-131-Richie Rich app.	4	8	12	29	40	50
...Jokes 1-3(8/60-61, Harvey)-84 pgs.; Richie Rich in all; Little Dot in #2,3; Lotta in #2	4	8	12	28	38	48
...New Jokes 1-4(10/63-11/65, Harvey)-68 pgs.; Richie Rich in #1-3; Stumbo in #1	3	7	10	21	28	35

NOTE: *Most all issues by* ***Al Smith****. Issues from 1963 on have* ***Fisher*** *reprints. Clarification: early issues signed by Fisher are mostly drawn by Smith.*

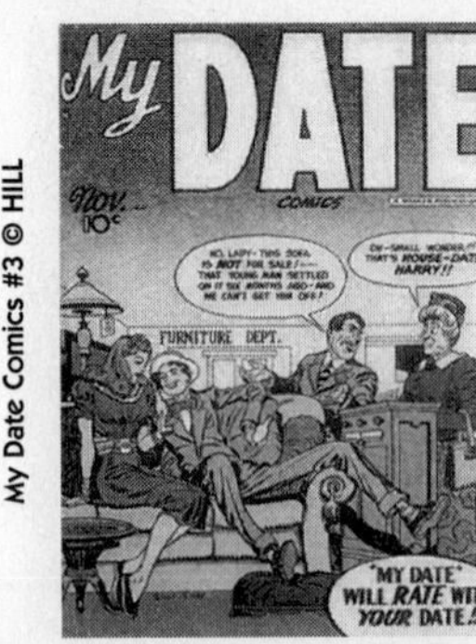

My Date Comics #3 © HILL

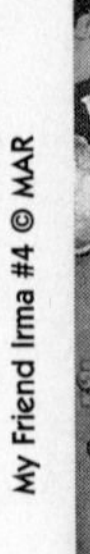
My Friend Irma #4 © MAR

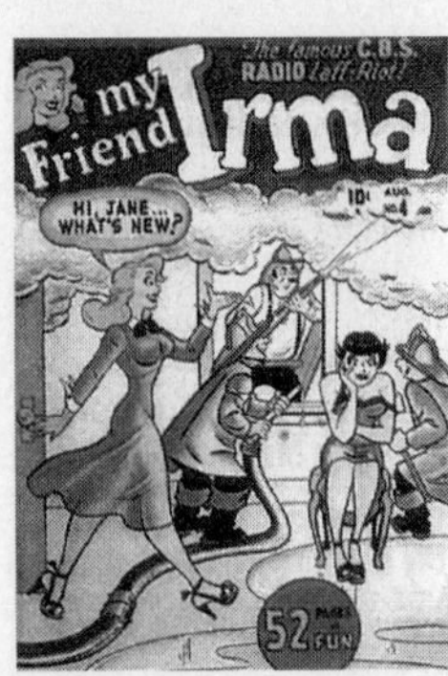

My Intimate Affair #1 © FOX

MY BROTHERS' KEEPER
Spire Christian Comics (Fleming H. Revell Co.): 1973 (35/49¢, 36 pgs.)

	GD 2.0	VG 4.0	FN 6.0	VF 8.0	VF/NM 9.0	NM- 9.2
nn	1	3	4	6	8	10

MY CONFESSIONS (My Confession #7&8; formerly Western True Crime; A Spectacular Feature Magazine #11)
Fox Feature Syndicate: No. 7, Aug, 1949 - No. 10, Jan-Feb, 1950

	GD 2.0	VG 4.0	FN 6.0	VF 8.0	VF/NM 9.0	NM- 9.2
7-Wood-a (10 pgs.)	24	48	72	135	190	245
8,9: 8-Harrison/Wood-a (19 pgs.). 9-Wood-a	22	44	66	124	172	220
10	10	20	30	58	77	95

MY DATE COMICS (Teen-age)
Hillman Periodicals: July, 1947 - V1#4, Jan, 1948 (2nd Romance comic; see Young Romance)

	GD 2.0	VG 4.0	FN 6.0	VF 8.0	VF/NM 9.0	NM- 9.2
1-S&K-c/a	38	76	114	219	310	400
2-4-S&K-c/a; Dan Barry-a	26	52	78	150	210	270

MY DESIRE (Formerly Jo-Jo Comics; becomes Murder, Inc. #5 on)
Fox Feature Syndicate: No. 30, Aug, 1949 - No. 4, April, 1950

	GD 2.0	VG 4.0	FN 6.0	VF 8.0	VF/NM 9.0	NM- 9.2
30(#1)	17	34	51	98	134	170
31 (#2, 10/49),3(2/50),4	11	22	33	66	88	110
31 (Canadian edition)	8	16	24	40	50	60
32(12/49)-Wood-a	21	42	63	118	164	210

MY DIARY (Becomes My Friend Irma #3 on?)
Marvel Comics (A Lovers Mag.): Dec, 1949 - No. 2, Mar, 1950

	GD 2.0	VG 4.0	FN 6.0	VF 8.0	VF/NM 9.0	NM- 9.2
1,2-Photo-c	15	30	45	86	118	150

MY EXPERIENCE (Formerly All Top; becomes Judy Canova #23 on)
Fox Feature Syndicate: No. 19, Sept, 1949 - No. 22, Mar, 1950

	GD 2.0	VG 4.0	FN 6.0	VF 8.0	VF/NM 9.0	NM- 9.2
19,21: 19-Wood-a. 21-Wood-a(2)	26	52	78	150	210	270
20	11	22	33	66	88	110
22-Wood-a (9 pgs.)	21	42	63	118	164	210

MY FAITH IN FRANKIE
DC Comics (Vertigo): March, 2004 - No. 4 ($2.95, limited series)

	GD 2.0	VG 4.0	FN 6.0	VF 8.0	VF/NM 9.0	NM- 9.2
1-Mike Carey-s/Sonny Liew & Marc Hempel-a						3.00

MY FAVORITE MARTIAN (TV)
Gold Key: 1/64; No.2, 7/64 - No. 9, 10/66 (No. 1,3-9 have photo-c)

	GD 2.0	VG 4.0	FN 6.0	VF 8.0	VF/NM 9.0	NM- 9.2
1-Russ Manning-a	14	28	42	99	145	190
2	8	16	24	53	74	95
3-9	7	14	21	50	68	85

MY FRIEND IRMA (Radio/TV) (Formerly My Diary? and/or Western Life Romances?)
Marvel/Atlas Comics (BFP): No. 3, June, 1950 - No. 47, Dec, 1954; No. 48, Feb, 1955

	GD 2.0	VG 4.0	FN 6.0	VF 8.0	VF/NM 9.0	NM- 9.2
3-Dan DeCarlo-a in all; 52 pgs. begin, end ?	17	34	51	98	134	170
4-Kurtzman-a (10 pgs.)	19	38	57	106	146	185
5- "Egghead Doodle" by Kurtzman (4 pgs.)	15	30	45	84	115	145
6,8-10: 9-Paper dolls, 1 pg; Millie app. (5 pgs.)	10	20	30	60	80	100
7-One pg. Kurtzman-a	11	22	33	63	84	105
11-23: 23-One pg. Frazetta-a	8	16	24	43	54	65
24-48: 41,48-Stan Lee & Dan DeCarlo app.	7	14	21	35	43	50

MY GIRL PEARL
Atlas Comics: 4/55 - #4, 10/55; #5, 7/57 - #6, 9/57; #7, 8/60 - #11, ?/61

	GD 2.0	VG 4.0	FN 6.0	VF 8.0	VF/NM 9.0	NM- 9.2
1-Dan DeCarlo-c/a in #1-6	15	30	45	84	115	145
2	8	16	24	46	58	70
3-6	7	14	21	35	43	50
7-11	4	8	12	24	32	40

MY GREATEST ADVENTURE (Doom Patrol #86 on)
National Periodical Publications: Jan-Feb, 1955 - No. 85, Feb, 1964

	GD 2.0	VG 4.0	FN 6.0	VF 8.0	VF/NM 9.0	NM- 9.2
1-Before CCA	130	260	390	875	1438	2000
2	50	100	150	400	600	800
3-5	36	72	108	270	405	540
6-10: 6-Science fiction format begins	31	62	93	228	339	450
11-14: 12-1st S.A. issue	23	46	69	167	244	320
15-17: Kirby-a in all	25	50	75	181	266	350
18-Kirby-c/a	29	58	87	210	305	400
19,22-25	19	38	57	138	202	265
20,21,28-Kirby-a	23	46	69	167	244	320
26,27,29,30	14	28	42	99	145	190
31-40	12	24	36	82	121	160
41,42,44-57,59	10	20	30	70	100	130
43-Kirby-a	11	22	33	75	110	145
58,60,61-Toth-a; Last 10¢ issue	10	20	30	72	104	135
62-76,78,79: 79-Promotes "Legion of the Strange" for next issue; renamed Doom Patrol for #80	7	14	21	51	71	90
77-Toth-a; Robotman prototype	8	16	24	53	74	95
80-(6/63)-Intro/origin Doom Patrol and begin series; origin & 1st app. Negative Man, Elasti-Girl & S.A. Robotman	44	88	132	352	526	700
81,85-Toth-a	18	36	54	127	186	245
82-84	16	32	48	113	167	220

NOTE: ***Anderson** a-42. **Cameron** a-24. **Colan** a-77. **Meskin** a-25, 26, 32, 39, 45, 50, 56, 57, 61, 64, 70, 73, 74, 76, 79; c-76. **Moreira** a-11, 12, 15, 17, 20, 23, 25, 27, 37, 40-43, 46, 48, 55-57, 59, 60, 62-65, 67, 69, 70; c-1-4, 7-10. **Roussos** c/a-71-73. **Wildey** a-32.*

MY GREAT LOVE (Becomes Will Rogers Western #5)
Fox Feature Syndicate: Oct, 1949 - No. 4, Apr, 1950

	GD 2.0	VG 4.0	FN 6.0	VF 8.0	VF/NM 9.0	NM- 9.2
1	15	30	45	86	118	150
2-4	9	18	27	52	66	80

MY INTIMATE AFFAIR (Inside Crime #3)
Fox Feature Syndicate: Mar, 1950 - No. 2, May, 1950

	GD 2.0	VG 4.0	FN 6.0	VF 8.0	VF/NM 9.0	NM- 9.2
1	15	30	45	86	118	150
2	9	18	27	52	66	80

MY LIFE (Formerly Meet Corliss Archer)
Fox Feature Syndicate: No. 4, Sept, 1948 - No. 15, July, 1950

	GD 2.0	VG 4.0	FN 6.0	VF 8.0	VF/NM 9.0	NM- 9.2
4-Used in **SOTI**, pg. 39; Kamen/Feldstein-a	40	80	120	240	340	440
5-Kamen-a	24	48	72	135	190	245
6-Kamen/Feldstein-a	25	50	75	147	202	260
7-Wood-a; wash cover	21	42	63	118	164	210
8,9,11-15	10	20	30	58	77	95
10-Wood-a	19	38	57	107	149	190

MY LITTLE MARGIE (TV)
Charlton Comics: July, 1954 - No. 54, Nov, 1964

	GD 2.0	VG 4.0	FN 6.0	VF 8.0	VF/NM 9.0	NM- 9.2
1-Photo front/back-c	36	72	108	204	290	375
2-Photo front/back-c	18	36	54	104	142	180
3-7,10	10	20	30	60	80	100
8,9-Infinity-c	11	22	33	63	84	105
11-14: Part-photo-c (#13, 8/56)	9	18	27	54	70	85
15-19	9	18	27	49	62	75
20-(25¢, 100 pg. issue)	15	30	45	86	118	150
21-40: 40-Last 10¢ issue	5	10	15	36	48	60
41-53	4	8	12	29	40	50
54-(11/64) Beatles on cover; lead story spoofs the Beatle haircut craze of the 1960's; Beatles app. (scarce)	18	36	54	131	191	250

NOTE: *Doll cut-outs in 32, 33, 40, 45, 50.*

MY LITTLE MARGIE'S BOY FRIENDS (TV) (Freddy V2#12 on)
Charlton Comics: Aug, 1955 - No. 11, Apr?, 1958

	GD 2.0	VG 4.0	FN 6.0	VF 8.0	VF/NM 9.0	NM- 9.2
1-Has several Archie swipes	15	30	45	86	118	150
2	9	18	27	52	66	80
3-11	8	16	24	43	54	65

MY LITTLE MARGIE'S FASHIONS (TV)
Charlton Comics: Feb, 1959 - No. 5, Nov, 1959

	GD 2.0	VG 4.0	FN 6.0	VF 8.0	VF/NM 9.0	NM- 9.2
1	14	28	42	79	107	135
2-5	8	16	24	43	54	65

MY LOVE (Becomes Two Gun Western #5 (11/50) on?)
Marvel Comics (CLDS): July, 1949 - No. 4, Apr, 1950 (All photo-c)

	GD 2.0	VG 4.0	FN 6.0	VF 8.0	VF/NM 9.0	NM- 9.2
1	14	28	42	81	111	140
2,3	9	18	27	52	66	80
4-Bettie Page photo-c (see Cupid #2)	33	66	99	190	270	350

MY LOVE
Marvel Comics Group: Sept, 1969 - No. 39, Mar, 1976

	GD 2.0	VG 4.0	FN 6.0	VF 8.0	VF/NM 9.0	NM- 9.2
1	6	12	18	40	55	70
2-9: 4-6-Colan-a	3	7	10	21	28	35
10-Williamson-r/My Own Romance #71; Kirby-a	4	8	12	22	30	38
11-13,15-19	3	6	9	18	23	28
14-(52 pgs.)-Woodstock-c/sty; Morrow-c/a; Kirby/Colletta-r	4	8	12	29	40	50
20-Starlin-a	3	6	9	19	25	32
21,22,24-27,29-38: 38-Reprints	3	6	9	16	20	24
23-Steranko-r/Our Love Story #5	3	6	9	19	25	32
28-Kirby-a	3	6	9	18	23	28
39-Last issue; reprints	3	6	9	18	23	28
Special 1 (12/71)(52 pgs.)	4	8	12	29	40	50

NOTE: ***John Buscema** a-1-7, 10, 18-21, 22r(2), 24r, 25r, 29r, 34r, 36r, 37r, Spec. (r)(4); c-13, 15, 25, 27, Spec. **Colan** a-4, 5, 6, 8, 9, 16, 17, 20, 21, 22, 24r, 27r, 30r, 35r, 39r. **Colan/Everett** a-13, 15, 16, 27(r/#13). **Kirby** a-(r)-10, 14, 26, 28. **Romita** a-1-3, 19, 20, 25, 34, 38; c-1-3, 15.*

My Love Story #2 © FOX

My Only Love #9 © CC

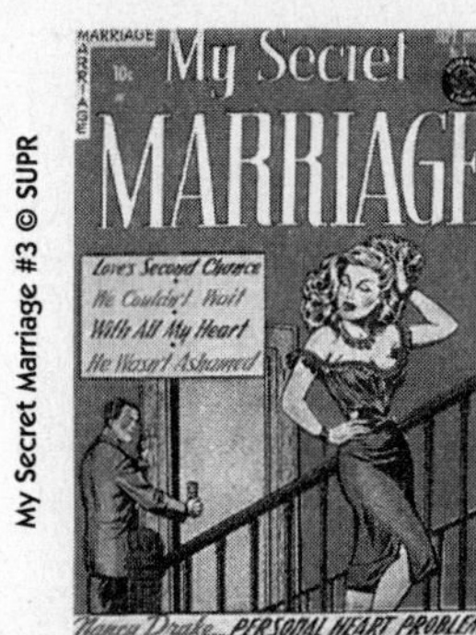

My Secret Marriage #3 © SUPR

MY LOVE AFFAIR (March of Crime #7 on)
Fox Feature Syndicate: July, 1949 - No. 6, May, 1950

	GD 2.0	VG 4.0	FN 6.0	VF 8.0	VF/NM 9.0	NM- 9.2
1	15	30	45	86	118	150
2	9	18	27	52	66	80
3-6-Wood-a. 5-(3/50)-Becomes Love Stories #6	19	38	57	107	149	190

MY LOVE LIFE (Formerly Zegra)
Fox Feature Synd.: No. 6, June, 1949 - No. 13, Aug, 1950; No. 13, Sept, 1951

	GD 2.0	VG 4.0	FN 6.0	VF 8.0	VF/NM 9.0	NM- 9.2
6-Kamenish-a	16	32	48	92	126	160
7-13	9	18	27	52	66	80
13 (9/51)(Formerly My Story #12)	9	18	27	49	62	75

MY LOVE MEMOIRS (Formerly Women Outlaws; Hunted #13 on)
Fox Feature Syndicate: No. 9, Nov, 1949 - No. 12, May, 1950

	GD 2.0	VG 4.0	FN 6.0	VF 8.0	VF/NM 9.0	NM- 9.2
9,11,12-Wood-a	19	38	57	106	146	185
10	9	18	27	52	66	80

MY LOVE SECRET (Formerly Phantom Lady; Animal Crackers #31)
Fox Feature Syndicate/M. S. Distr.: No. 24, June, 1949 - No. 30, June, 1950; No. 53, 1954

	GD 2.0	VG 4.0	FN 6.0	VF 8.0	VF/NM 9.0	NM- 9.2
24-Kamen/Feldstein-a	19	38	57	106	146	185
25-Possible caricature of Wood on-c?	11	22	33	66	88	110
26,28-Wood-a	19	38	57	106	146	185
27,29,30: 30-Photo-c	10	20	30	56	73	90
53-(Reprint, M.S. Distr.) 1954? nd given; formerly Western Thrillers; becomes Crimes by Women #54; photo-c	7	14	21	35	43	50

MY LOVE STORY (Hoot Gibson Western #5 on)
Fox Feature Syndicate: Sept, 1949 - No. 4, Mar, 1950

	GD 2.0	VG 4.0	FN 6.0	VF 8.0	VF/NM 9.0	NM- 9.2
1	15	30	45	86	118	150
2	9	18	27	52	66	80
3,4-Wood-a	19	38	57	107	149	190

MY LOVE STORY
Atlas Comics (GPS): April, 1956 - No. 9, Aug, 1957

	GD 2.0	VG 4.0	FN 6.0	VF 8.0	VF/NM 9.0	NM- 9.2
1	11	22	33	66	88	110
2	7	14	21	37	46	55
3,7: Matt Baker-a. 7-Toth-a	9	18	27	52	66	80
4-6,8,9	7	14	21	35	43	50

NOTE: ***Brewster** a-3. **Colletta** a-1(2), 3, 4(2), 5; c-3.*

MY NAME IS CHAOS
DC Comics: 1992 - No. 4, 1992 ($4.95, limited series, 52 pgs.)

	GD 2.0	VG 4.0	FN 6.0	VF 8.0	VF/NM 9.0	NM- 9.2
Book 1-4: Tom Veitch scripts; painted-c						5.00

MY NAME IS HOLOCAUST
DC Comics: May, 1995 - No. 5, Sept, 1995 ($2.50, limited series)

	GD 2.0	VG 4.0	FN 6.0	VF 8.0	VF/NM 9.0	NM- 9.2
1-5						2.50

MY ONLY LOVE
Charlton Comics: July, 1975 - No. 9, Nov, 1976

	GD 2.0	VG 4.0	FN 6.0	VF 8.0	VF/NM 9.0	NM- 9.2
1	2	4	6	14	18	22
2,4-9	2	4	6	10	12	15
3-Toth-a	2	4	6	11	14	18

MY OWN ROMANCE (Formerly My Romance; Teen-Age Romance #77 on)
Marvel/Atlas (MjPC/RCM No. 4-59/ZPC No. 60-76): No. 4, Mar, 1949 - No. 76, July, 1960

	GD 2.0	VG 4.0	FN 6.0	VF 8.0	VF/NM 9.0	NM- 9.2
4-Photo-c	16	32	48	92	126	160
5-10: 5,6,8-10-Photo-c	9	18	27	52	66	80
11-20: 14-Powell-a	8	16	24	46	58	70
21-42,55: 42-Last precode (2/55). 55-Toth-a	8	16	24	43	54	65
43-54,56-60	4	8	12	29	40	50
61-70,72,73,75,76	4	8	12	27	36	45
71-Williamson-a	5	10	15	33	44	55
74-Kirby-a	5	10	15	33	44	55

NOTE: ***Brewster** a-59. **Colletta** a-45(2), 48, 50, 55, 57(2), 59; c-58i, 59, 61. **Everett** a-25; c-58p. **Kirby** c-71, 75, 76. **Morisi** a-18. **Orlando** a-61. **Romita** a-36. **Tuska** a-10.*

MY PAL DIZZY (See Comic Books, Series I)

MY PAST (...Confessions) (Formerly Western Thrillers)
Fox Feature Syndicate: No. 7, Aug, 1949 - No. 11, Apr, 1950 (Crimes Inc. #12)

	GD 2.0	VG 4.0	FN 6.0	VF 8.0	VF/NM 9.0	NM- 9.2
7	15	30	45	86	118	150
8-10	9	18	27	52	66	80
11-Wood-a	19	38	57	106	146	185

MY PERSONAL PROBLEM
Ajax/Farrell/Steinway Comic: 11/55; No. 2, 2/56; No. 3, 9/56 - No. 4, 11/56; 10/57 - No. 3, 5/58

	GD 2.0	VG 4.0	FN 6.0	VF 8.0	VF/NM 9.0	NM- 9.2
1	9	18	27	52	66	80
2-4	6	12	18	33	41	48
1-3('57-'58)-Steinway	6	12	18	27	33	38

MY PRIVATE LIFE (Formerly Murder, Inc.; becomes Pedro #18)
Fox Feature Syndicate: No. 16, Feb, 1950 - No. 17, April, 1950

	GD 2.0	VG 4.0	FN 6.0	VF 8.0	VF/NM 9.0	NM- 9.2
16,17	13	26	39	74	100	125

MYRA NORTH (See The Comics, Crackajack Funnies & Red Ryder)
Dell Publishing Co.: No. 3, Jan, 1940

	GD 2.0	VG 4.0	FN 6.0	VF 8.0	VF/NM 9.0	NM- 9.2
Four Color 3	75	150	225	536	818	1100

MY REAL LOVE
Standard Comics: No. 5, June, 1952 (Photo-c)

	GD 2.0	VG 4.0	FN 6.0	VF 8.0	VF/NM 9.0	NM- 9.2
5-Toth-a, 3 pgs.; Tuska, Cardy, Vern Greene-a	14	28	42	79	107	135

MY ROMANCE (Becomes My Own Romance #4 on)
Marvel Comics (RCM): Sept, 1948 - No. 3, Jan, 1949

	GD 2.0	VG 4.0	FN 6.0	VF 8.0	VF/NM 9.0	NM- 9.2
1	15	30	45	86	118	150
2,3: 2-Anti-Wertham editorial (11/48)	9	18	27	52	66	80

MY ROMANTIC ADVENTURES (Formerly Romantic Adventures)
American Comics Group: No. 68, 8/56 - No. 115, 12/60; No. 116, 7/61 - No. 138, 3/64

	GD 2.0	VG 4.0	FN 6.0	VF 8.0	VF/NM 9.0	NM- 9.2
68	9	18	27	52	66	80
69-85	6	12	18	28	34	40
86-Three pg. Williamson-a (2/58)	8	16	24	43	54	65
87-100	3	6	9	18	24	30
101-138	2	4	6	14	18	22

NOTE: ***Whitney** art in most issues.*

MY SECRET (Becomes Our Secret #4 on)
Superior Comics, Ltd.: Aug, 1949 - No. 3, Oct, 1949

	GD 2.0	VG 4.0	FN 6.0	VF 8.0	VF/NM 9.0	NM- 9.2
1	14	28	42	79	107	135
2,3	9	18	27	52	66	80

MY SECRET AFFAIR (Becomes Martin Kane #4)
Hero Book (Fox Feature Syndicate): Dec, 1949 - No. 3, April, 1950

	GD 2.0	VG 4.0	FN 6.0	VF 8.0	VF/NM 9.0	NM- 9.2
1-Harrison/Wood-a (10 pgs.)	22	44	66	127	176	225
2-Wood-a	18	36	54	104	142	180
3-Wood-a	19	38	57	106	146	185

MY SECRET CONFESSION
Sterling Comics: September, 1955

	GD 2.0	VG 4.0	FN 6.0	VF 8.0	VF/NM 9.0	NM- 9.2
1-Sekowsky-a	9	18	27	52	66	80

MY SECRET LIFE (Formerly Western Outlaws; Romeo Tubbs #26 on)
Fox Feature Syndicate: No. 22, July, 1949 - No. 27, July, 1950; No. 27, 9/51

	GD 2.0	VG 4.0	FN 6.0	VF 8.0	VF/NM 9.0	NM- 9.2
22	11	22	33	63	84	105
23,26-Wood-a, 6 pgs.	18	36	54	101	138	175
24,25,27	9	18	27	54	70	85
27 (9/51)	9	18	27	49	62	75

NOTE: *The title was changed to Romeo Tubbs after #25 even though #26 & 27 did come out.*

MY SECRET LIFE (Formerly Young Lovers; Sue & Sally Smith #48)
Charlton Comics: No. 19, Aug, 1957 - No. 47, Sept, 1962

	GD 2.0	VG 4.0	FN 6.0	VF 8.0	VF/NM 9.0	NM- 9.2
19	4	8	12	24	32	40
20-35	2	4	6	14	18	22
36-47: 44-Last 10¢ issue	2	4	6	11	14	18

MY SECRET MARRIAGE
Superior Comics, Ltd.: May, 1953 - No. 24, July, 1956 (Canadian)

	GD 2.0	VG 4.0	FN 6.0	VF 8.0	VF/NM 9.0	NM- 9.2
1	13	26	39	76	103	130
2	8	16	24	43	54	65
3-24	7	14	21	35	43	50
I.W. Reprint #9	2	4	6	9	11	14

NOTE: *Many issues contain **Kamen-ish** art.*

MY SECRET ROMANCE (Becomes A Star Presentation #3)
Hero Book (Fox Feature Syndicate): Jan, 1950 - No. 2, March, 1950

	GD 2.0	VG 4.0	FN 6.0	VF 8.0	VF/NM 9.0	NM- 9.2
1	14	28	42	81	111	140
2-Wood-a	19	38	57	106	146	185

MY SECRET STORY (Formerly Captain Kidd #25; Sabu #30 on)
Fox Feature Syndicate: No. 26, Oct, 1949 - No. 29, April, 1950

	GD 2.0	VG 4.0	FN 6.0	VF 8.0	VF/NM 9.0	NM- 9.2
26	15	30	45	86	118	150
27-29	9	18	27	51	66	80

MYS-TECH WARS
Marvel Comics UK: Mar, 1993 - No. 4, June, 1993 ($1.75, mini-series)

	GD 2.0	VG 4.0	FN 6.0	VF 8.0	VF/NM 9.0	NM- 9.2
1-4: 1-Gatefold-c						2.25

Mysteries #3 © SUPR

Mysterious Adventures #2 © Story

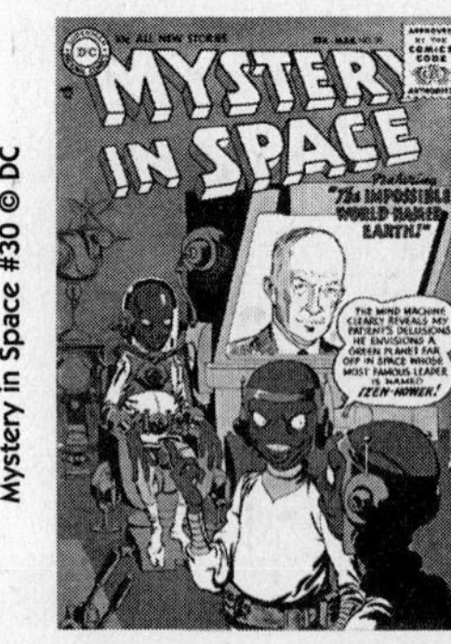

Mystery in Space #30 © DC

GD 2.0 | VG 4.0 | FN 6.0 | VF 8.0 | VF/NM 9.0 | NM- 9.2

MYSTERIES (...Weird & Strange)
Superior/Dynamic Publ. (Randall Publ. Ltd.): May, 1953 - No. 11, Jan, 1955
1-All horror stories 41 82 123 246 348 450
2-A-Bomb blast story 26 52 78 150 210 270
3-11: 10-Kamenish-c/a reprinted from Strange Mysteries #2; cover is from a panel in Strange Mysteries #2 23 46 69 132 186 240

MYSTERIES IN SPACE (See Fireside Book Series)

MYSTERIES OF SCOTLAND YARD (Also see A-1 Comics)
Magazine Enterprises: No. 121, 1954 (one shot)
A-1 121-Reprinted from Manhunt (5 stories) 17 34 51 95 130 165

MYSTERIES OF UNEXPLORED WORLDS (See Blue Bird)(Becomes Son of Vulcan V2#49 on)
Charlton Comics: Aug, 1956; No. 2, Jan, 1957 - No. 48, Sept, 1965
1 37 74 111 212 301 390
2-No Ditko 15 30 45 86 118 150
3,4,8,9 Ditko-a. 3-Diko c/a (4). 4-Ditko c/a (2). 29 58 87 164 232 300
5,6,10,11: 5,6-Ditko-c/a (all). 10-Ditko-c/a(4). 11-Ditko-c/a(3); signed J. Kotdi 31 62 93 175 248 320
7-(2/58, 68 pgs.) 4 stories w/Ditko-a 34 68 102 193 274 355
12,19,21-24,26-Ditko-a. 12-Ditko sty (3); Baker story "The Charm Bracelet." 22 44 66 127 176 225
13-18,20 9 18 27 49 62 75
25,27-30 4 8 12 29 40 50
31-45 4 8 12 24 32 40
46(5/65)-Son of Vulcan begins (origin/1st app.) 5 10 15 33 44 55
47,48 4 8 12 24 32 40
NOTE: ***Ditko** c-3-6, 10, 11, 19, 21-24. Covers to #19, 21-24 reprint story panels.*

MYSTERIOUS ADVENTURES
Story Comics: Mar, 1951 - No. 24, Mar, 1955; No. 25, Aug, 1955
1-All horror stories 60 120 180 375 563 750
2 36 72 108 204 290 375
3,4,6,10 32 64 96 184 262 340
5-Bondage-c 36 72 108 204 290 375
7-Daggar in eye panel 40 80 120 240 350 460
8-Eyeball story 47 94 141 282 421 560
9-Extreme violence (8/52) 38 76 114 219 310 400
11(12/52)-Used in **SOTI**, pg. 84 38 76 114 219 310 400
12,14: 14-E.C. Old Witch swipe 32 64 96 184 262 340
13-Classic skull-c 37 74 111 212 301 390
15-21: 18-Used in Senate Investigative report, pgs. 5,6; E.C. swipe/TFTC #35; The Coffin-Keeper & Corpse (hosts). 20-Used by Wertham in the Senate hearings. 21-Bondage/beheading-c 40 80 120 240 340 440
22- "Cinderella" parody 33 66 99 190 270 350
23-Disbrow-a (6 pgs.); E.C. swipe "The Mystery Keeper's Tale" (host) and "Mother Ghoul's Nursery Tale" 33 66 99 190 270 350
24,25 25 50 75 147 202 260
NOTE: ***Tothish** art by **Ross Andru**-#22, 23. **Bache** a-8. **Cameron** a-5-7. **Harrison** a-12. **Hollingsworth** a-3-8, 12. **Schaffenberger** a-24, 25. **Wildey** a-15, 17.*

MYSTERIOUS ISLAND
Dell Publishing Co.: No. 1213, July-Sept, 1961
Four Color 1213-Movie, photo-c 10 20 30 67 96 125

MYSTERIOUS ISLE
Dell Publishing Co.: Nov-Jan, 1963/64 (Jules Verne)
1 4 8 12 22 30 38

MYSTERIOUS RIDER, THE (See Zane Grey, 4-Color 301)

MYSTERIOUS STORIES (Formerly Horror From the Tomb #1)
Premier Magazines: No. 2, Dec-Jan, 1954-1955 - No. 7, Dec, 1955
2-Woodbridge-c; last pre-code issue 46 92 138 276 413 550
3-Woodbridge-c/a 32 64 96 182 259 335
4-7: 5-Cinderella parody. 6-Woodbridge-c 30 60 90 170 240 310
NOTE: ***Hollingsworth** a-2, 4.*

MYSTERIOUS SUSPENSE (Also see Blue Beetle #1 (1967))
Charlton Comics: Oct, 1968 (12¢)
1-Return of the Question by Ditko (c/a) 7 14 21 51 71 90

MYSTERIOUS TRAVELER (See Tales of the...)

MYSTERIOUS TRAVELER COMICS (Radio)
Trans-World Publications: Nov, 1948
1-Powell-c/a(2); Poe adaptation, "Tell Tale Heart" 55 110 165 330 495 660

MYSTERY COMICS
William H. Wise & Co.: 1944 - No. 4, 1944 (No months given)
1-The Magnet, The Silver Knight, Brad Spencer, Wonderman, Dick Devins, King of Futuria, & Zudo the Jungle Boy begin (all 1st app.); Schomburg-c on all 112 224 336 700 1050 1400
2-Bondage-c 69 138 207 431 646 860
3,4: 3-Lance Lewis, Space Detective begins (1st app.); Robot-c. 4(V2#1 inside) 61 122 183 381 573 765

MYSTERY COMICS DIGEST
Gold Key/Whitman?: Mar, 1972 - No. 26, Oct, 1975
1-Ripley's Believe It or Not; reprint of Ripley's #1 origin Ra-Ka-Tep the Mummy; Wood-a 4 8 12 27 36 45
2-9: 2-Boris Karloff Tales of Mystery; Wood-a; 1st app. Werewolf Count Wulfstein. 3-Twilight Zone (TV); Crandall, Toth & George Evans-a; 1st app. Tragg & Simbar the Lion Lord; (2) Crandall/Frazetta-r/Twilight Zone #1 4-Ripley's Believe It or Not; 1st app. Baron Tibor, the Vampire. 5-Boris Karloff Tales of Mystery; 1st app. Dr. Spektor. 6-Twilight Zone (TV); 1st app. U.S. Marshal Reid & Sir Duane; Evans-r. 7-Ripley's Believe It or Not; origin The Lurker in the Swamp; 1st app. Duroc. 8-Boris Karloff Tales of Mystery; McWilliams-r; Orlando-r. 9-Twilight Zone (TV); Williamson, Crandall, McWilliams-a; 2nd Tragg app.;Torres, Evans, Heck/Tuska-r 3 6 9 19 25 32
10-26: 10,13-Ripley's Believe It or Not: 13-Orlando-r. 11,14-Boris Karloff Tales of Mystery. 14-1st app. Xorkon. 12,15-Twilight Zone (TV). 16,19,22,25-Ripley's Believe It or Not. 17-Boris Karloff Tales of Mystery; Williamson-r; Orlando-r. 18,21,24-Twilight Zone (TV). 20,23,26-Boris Karloff Tales of Mystery 3 6 9 16 20 24
NOTE: *Dr. Spektor app.-#5, 10-12, 21. Durak app.-#15. Duroc app.-#14 (later called Durak). King George 1st app.-#8.*

MYSTERY IN SPACE (Also see Fireside Book Series and Pulp Fiction Library: ...)
National Periodical Pub.: 4-5/51 - No. 110, 9/66; No. 111, 9/80 - No. 117, 3/81 (#1-3: 52 pgs.)
1-Frazetta-a, 8 pgs.; Knights of the Galaxy begins, ends #8 226 452 678 1978 3189 4400
2 89 178 267 757 1154 1550
3 71 142 213 604 927 1250
4,5 59 118 177 502 764 1025
6-10: 7-Toth-a 48 96 144 384 580 775
11-15 37 74 111 278 414 550
16-18,20-25: Interplanetary Insurance feature by Infantino in all. 21-1st app. Space Cabbie. 24-Last pre-code issue 32 64 96 240 360 480
19-Virgil Finlay-a 36 72 108 270 405 540
26-40: 26-Space Cabbie feature begins. 34-1st S.A. issue 29 58 87 210 305 400
41-52: 47-Space Cabbie feature ends 22 44 65 156 228 300
53-Adam Strange begins (8/59, 10pg. sty); robot-c 149 298 447 1267 1934 2600
54 44 88 132 352 526 700
55-Grey tone-c 37 74 111 278 414 550
56-60: 59-Kane/Anderson-a 22 44 66 160 235 310
61-71: 61-1st app. Adam Strange foe Ulthoon. 62-1st app. A.S. foe Mortan. 63-Origin Vandor. 66-Star Rovers begin (1st app.). 68-1st app. Dust Devils (6/61). 69-1st Mailbag. 70-2nd app. Dust Devils. 71-Last 10¢ issue 17 34 51 123 182 240
72-74,76-80 12 24 36 84 125 165
75-JLA x-over in Adam Strange (5/62)(sequel to J.L.A. #3) 25 50 75 181 266 350
81-86 10 20 30 72 104 135
87-(11/63)-Adam Strange/Hawkman double feat begins; 3rd Hawkman tryout series 19 38 57 138 202 265
88-Adam Strange & Hawkman stories 17 34 51 121 178 235
89-Adam Strange & Hawkman stories 16 32 48 116 171 225
90-Adam Strange & Hawkman team-up for 1st time (3/64); Hawkman moves to own title next month 19 38 57 133 194 255
91-102: 91-End Infantino art on Adam Strange; double-length Adam Strange story. 92-Space Ranger begins (6/64), ends #103. 92-94,96,98-Space Ranger-c. 94,98-Adam Strange/Space Ranger team-up. 102-Adam Strange ends (no Space Ranger) 6 12 18 40 55 70
103-Origin Ultra, the Multi-Alien; last Space Ranger 6 12 18 40 55 70
104-110: 110-(9/66)-Last 12¢ issue 4 8 12 29 40 50
V17#111(9/80)-117: 117-Newton-a(3 pgs.) 1 2 3 5 7 9
NOTE: ***Anderson** a-2, 4, 8-10, 12-17, 19, 45-48, 51, 57, 59i, 61-64, 70, 76, 87-91; c-9, 10, 15-25, 87, 89, 105-108, 110. **Aparo** a-111. **Austin** a-112i. **Bolland** a-115. **Craig** a-114, 116. **Ditko** a-111, 114-116. **Drucker** a-13, 14. **Elias** a-98, 102, 103. **Golden** a-113p. **Sid Greene** a-78, 91. **Infantino** a-1-8, 11, 14-25, 27-46, 48, 49, 51, 53-91, 103, 117; c-60-86, 88, 90, 91, 105, 107. **Gil Kane** a-14p, 15p, 18p, 19p, 26p, 29-59p(most), 100-102; c-52, 101. **Kubert** a-113; c-111-115. **Moriera** c-27, 28. **Rogers** a-111. **Sekowsky** a-52. **Simon** & **Kirby** a-4(2 pgs.). **Spiegle** a-111, 114. **Starlin** c-116. **Sutton** a-112. **Tuska** a-115p, 117p.*

MYSTERY MEN COMICS
Fox Features Syndicate: Aug, 1939 - No. 31, Feb, 1942
1-Intro. & 1st app. The Blue Beetle, The Green Mask, Rex Dexter of Mars by Briefer, Zanzibar

Mystery Men Comics #15 © FOX

Mystic #23 © CRO

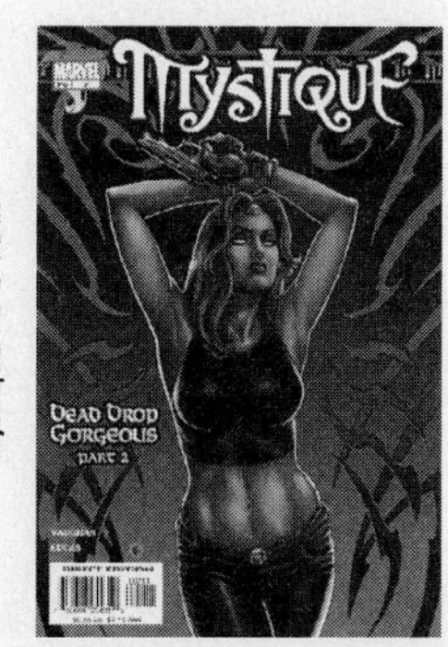

Mystique #2 © MAR

	GD 2.0	VG 4.0	FN 6.0	VF 8.0	VF/NM 9.0	NM- 9.2
by Tuska, Lt. Drake, D-13-Secret Agent by Powell, Chen Chang, Wing Turner, & Captain Denny Scott	1000	2000	3000	7000	10,750	14,500
2-Robot & sci/fi-c (2nd Robot-c w/Movie #6)	326	652	978	2119	3260	4400
3 (10/39)-Classic Lou Fine-c	407	814	1221	2646	4073	5500
4,5: 4-Capt. Savage begins (11/39)	248	496	744	1550	2325	3100
6-Tuska-c	200	400	600	1250	1875	2500
7-1st Blue Beetle-c app.	248	496	744	1550	2325	3100
8-Lou Fine-c	224	448	672	1400	2100	2800
9-The Moth begins; Lou Fine-c	114	228	342	713	1069	1425
10-12: All Joe Simon-c. 10-Wing Turner by Kirby; Simon-c. 11-Intro. Domino	96	192	288	600	900	1200
13-Intro. Lynx & sidekick Blackie (8/40)	64	128	192	400	600	800
14-18	61	122	183	381	571	760
19-Intro. & 1st app. Miss X (ends #21)	64	128	192	400	600	800
20-31: 26-The Wraith begins	58	116	174	363	549	735

NOTE: ***Briefer** a-1-15, 20, 24; c-9. **Cuidera** a-22. **Lou Fine** c-1-5,8,9. **Powell** a-1-15, 24. **Simon** c-10-12. **Tuska** a-1-16, 22, 24, 27; c-6. Bondage-c 1, 3, 7, 8, 25, 27-29, 31. Blue Beetle c-7, 8, 10-31. D-13 Secret Agent c-6. Green Mask c-1, 3-5. Rex Dexter of Mars c-2, 9.*

MYSTERY MEN MOVIE ADAPTION
Dark Horse Comics: July, 1999 - No. 2, Aug, 1999 ($2.95, mini-series)

	GD	VG	FN	VF	VF/NM	NM-
1,2-Fingerman-s; photo-c						3.00

MYSTERY PLAY, THE
DC Comics (Vertigo): 1994 ($19.95, one-shot)

	GD	VG	FN	VF	VF/NM	NM-
nn-Hardcover-Morrison-s/Muth-painted art						25.00
Softcover ($9.95)-New Muth cover						10.00

MYSTERY TALES
Atlas Comics (20CC): Mar, 1952 - No. 54, Aug, 1957

	GD	VG	FN	VF	VF/NM	NM-
1-Horror/weird stories in all	85	170	255	531	796	1060
2-Krigstein-a	46	92	138	276	413	550
3-10: 6-A-Bomb panel. 10-Story similar to "The Assassin" from Shock SuspenStories	40	80	120	240	340	440
11,13-21: 14-Maneely s/f story. 20-Electric chair issue. 21-Matt Fox-a; decapitation story	30	60	90	170	240	310
12,22: 12-Matt Fox-a. 22-Forte/Matt Fox-c; a(i)	33	66	99	190	270	350
23-26 (2/55)-Last precode issue	24	48	72	135	190	245
27,29-35,37,38,41-43,48,49: 43-Morisi story contains Frazetta art swipes from Untamed Love	19	38	57	107	149	190
28,36,39,40,45: 28-Jack Katz-a. 36,39-Krigstein-a. 40,45-Ditko-a (#45 is 3 pgs. only)	20	40	60	112	156	200
44,51-Williamson/Krenkel-a	21	42	63	121	168	215
46-Williamson/Krenkel-a; Crandall text illos	21	42	63	121	168	215
47-Crandall, Ditko, Powell-a	21	42	63	121	168	215
50,52,53: 50-Torres, Morrow-a	19	38	57	107	149	190
54-Crandall, Check-a	20	40	60	112	156	200

NOTE: ***Ayers** a-18, 49, 52. **Berg** a-17, 51. **Colan** a-1, 3, 18, 35, 43. **Colletta** a-18. **Drucker** a-41. **Everett** a-2, 29, 33, 35, 41; c-8-11, 14, 38, 39, 41, 43, 44, 46, 48-51, 53. **Fass** a-16. **Forte** a-21, 22, 45, 46. **Matt Fox** a-12?, 21, 22; c-22. **Heath** a-3; c-3, 15, 17, 26. **Heck** a-25. **Kinstler** a-15. **Mort Lawrence** a-26, 32, 34. **Maneely** a-1, 9, 14, 22; c-12, 23, 24, 27. **Mooney** a-3, 40. **Morisi** a-43, 49, 52. **Morrow** a-50. **Orlando** a-51. **Pakula** a-16. **Powell** a-21, 29, 37, 38, 47. **Reinman** a-1, 14, 17. **Robinson** a-7p, 42. **Romita** a-37. **Roussos** a-4, 44. **R.Q. Sale** a-45, 46, 49. **Severin** c-52. **Shores** a-17, 45. **Tuska** a-10, 12, 14. **Whitney** a-2. **Wildey** a-37.*

MYSTERY TALES
Super Comics: 1964

	GD	VG	FN	VF	VF/NM	NM-
Super Reprint #16,17('64): 16-r/Tales of Horror #2. 17-r/Eerie #14(Avon), 18-Kubert-r/Strange Terrors #4	3	6	9	16	20	25

MYSTIC (3rd Series)
Marvel/Atlas Comics (CLDS 1/CSI 2-21/OMC 22-35/CSI 35-61): March, 1951 - No. 61, Aug, 1957

	GD	VG	FN	VF	VF/NM	NM-
1-Atom bomb panels; horror/weird stories in all	90	180	270	563	844	1125
2	50	100	150	300	450	600
3-Eyes torn out	44	88	132	264	395	525
4- "The Devil Birds" by Wolverton (6 pgs.)	78	156	234	488	732	975
5,7-10	34	68	102	196	278	360
6- "The Eye of Doom" by Wolverton (7 pgs.)	78	156	234	488	732	975
11-20: 16-Bondage/torture c/story	29	58	87	164	232	300
21-25,27-36-Last precode (3/55). 25-E.C. swipe	24	48	72	135	190	245
26-Atomic War, severed head stories	26	52	78	150	210	270
37-51,53-56,61	20	40	60	112	156	200
52-Wood-a; Crandall-a?	22	44	66	127	176	225
57-Story "Trapped in the Ant-Hill" (1957) is very similar to "The Man in the Ant Hill" in TTA #27	23	46	69	130	183	235
58,59-Krigstein-a	20	40	60	115	160	205
60-Williamson/Mayo-a (4 pgs.)	20	40	60	115	160	205

NOTE: ***Andru** a-23, 25. **Ayers** a-35, 53; c-8. **Berg** a-49. **Cameron** a-49, 51. **Check** a-31, 60. **Colan** a-3, 7, 12, 21, 37, 60. **Colletta** a-29. **Drucker** a-46, 52, 56. **Everett** a-8, 9, 17, 40, 44, 57; c-13, 18, 21, 42, 47, 49, 51-55, 57-59, 61. **Forte** a-35, 52, 58. **Fox** a-24i. **Al Hartley** a-35. **Heath** a-10; c-10, 20, 22, 23, 25, 30. **Infantino** a-12. **Kane** a-8, 24p. **Jack Katz** a-31, 33. **Mort Law.rence** a-19, 37. **Maneely** a-22, 24, 58; c-7, 15, 28, 29, 31. **Moldoff** a-29. **Morisi** a-48, 49, 52. **Morrow** a-51. **Orlando** a-57, 61. **Pakula** a-52, 57, 59. **Powell** a-52, 54-56. **Robinson** a-5. **Romita** a-11, 15. **R.Q. Sale** a-35, 53, 58. **Sekowsky** a-1, 2, 4, 5. **Severin** c-56, 60. **Tuska** a-15. **Whitney** a-33. **Wildey** a-28, 30. **Ed Win** a-17, 20. Canadian reprints known-title 'Startling.'*

MYSTIC (Also see CrossGen Chronicles)
CrossGeneration Comics: Jul, 2000 - No. 43, Jan, 2004 ($2.95)

	GD	VG	FN	VF	VF/NM	NM-
1-43: 1-Marz-s/Peterson & Dell-a. 15-Cameos by DC & Marvel characters						3.00
...: Rite of Passage Vol. 1 TPB (5/01, $19.95) r/#1-7; Linsner-c						20.00
...: The Demon Queen Vol. 2 TPB (2002, $19.95) r/#8-14						20.00
...: Siege of Scales Vol. 3 TPB (2002, $15.95) r/#15-20						16.00
...: Out All Night Vol.4 TPB (2003, $15.95) r/#21-26						16.00
Vol. 5: Master Class (2003, $15.95) r/#27-32						16.00

MYSTICAL TALES
Atlas Comics (CCC 1/EPI 2-8): June, 1956 - No. 8, Aug, 1957

	GD	VG	FN	VF	VF/NM	NM-
1-Everett-c/a	48	96	144	288	432	575
2-4: 2-Berg-a. 3,4-Crandall-a.	27	54	81	155	218	280
5-Williamson-a (4 pgs.)	29	58	87	164	232	300
6-Torres, Krigstein-a	25	50	75	147	202	260
7-Bolle, Forte, Torres, Orlando-a	25	50	75	144	198	255
8-Krigstein, Check-a	25	50	75	147	202	260

NOTE: ***Everett** a-1; c-1-4, 6, 7. **Orlando** a-1, 2, 7. **Pakula** a-3. **Powell** a-1, 4.*

MYSTIC COMICS (1st Series)
Timely Comics (TPI 1-5/TCI 8-10): March, 1940 - No. 10, Aug, 1942

	GD	VG	FN	VF	VF/NM	NM-
1-Origin The Blue Blaze, The Dynamic Man, & Flexo the Rubber Robot; Zephyr Jones, 3X's & Deep Sea Demon app.; The Magician begins (all 1st app.); c-from Spider pulp V18#1, 6/39	1281	2562	3843	9608	15,054	20,500
2-The Invisible Man & Master Mind Excello begin; Space Rangers, Zara of the Jungle, Taxi Taylor app. (scarce)	423	846	1269	2856	4428	6000
3-Origin Hercules, who last appears in #4	311	622	933	2022	3111	4200
4-Origin The Thin Man & The Black Widow; Merzak the Mystic app.; last Flexo, Dynamic Man, Invisible Man & Blue Blaze (some issues have date sticker on cover; others have July w/August overprint in silver color); Roosevelt assassination-c	333	666	1000	2165	3333	4500
5-(3/41)-Origin The Black Marvel, The Blazing Skull, The Sub-Earth Man, Super Slave & The Terror; The Moon Man & Black Widow app.; 5-German war-c begin, end #10	311	622	933	2022	3111	4200
6-(10/41)-Origin The Challenger & The Destroyer (1st app.?; also see All-Winners #2, Fall, 1941)	370	740	1110	2405	3703	5000
7-The Witness begins (12/41, origin & 1st app.); origin Davey & the Demon; last Black Widow; Hitler opens his trunk of terror-c by Simon & Kirby (classic-c)	393	786	1179	2555	3928	5300
8,10: 10-Father Time, World of Wonder, & Red Skeleton app.; last Challenger & Terror	212	424	636	1325	1988	2650
9-Gary Gaunt app.; last Black Marvel, Mystic & Blazing Skull; Hitler-c	228	456	684	1425	2138	2850

NOTE: ***Gabrielle** c-8-10. **Kirby/Schomburg** c-6. **Rico** a-9(2). **Schomburg** a-1-4; c-1-5. **Sekowsky** a-9. **Sekowsky/Klein** a-8(Challenger). Bondage c-1, 2, 9.*

MYSTIC COMICS (2nd Series)
Timely Comics (ANC): Oct, 1944 - No. 3, Win, 1944-45; No. 4, Mar, 1945

	GD	VG	FN	VF	VF/NM	NM-
1-The Angel, The Destroyer, The Human Torch, Terry Vance the Schoolboy Sleuth, & Tommy Tyme begin	236	472	708	1475	2213	2950
2-(Fall/44)-Last Human Torch & Terry Vance; bondage/hypo-c	122	244	366	763	1144	1525
3-Last Angel (two stories) & Tommy Tyme	115	230	345	719	1080	1440
4-The Young Allies-c & app.; Schomburg-c	108	216	324	675	1018	1360

MYSTIC EDGE (Manga)
Antarctic Press: Oct, 1998 ($2.95, one-shot)

	GD	VG	FN	VF	VF/NM	NM-
1-Ryan Kinnaird-s/a/c						3.00

MYSTIQUE (See X-Men titles)
Marvel Comics: June, 2003 - Present ($2.99)

	GD	VG	FN	VF	VF/NM	NM-
1-9: 1-6-Linsner-c/Vaughan-s/Lucas-a. 7-Ryan-a begins. 8-Horn-c. 9-Mayhew-c						3.00

MYSTIQUE & SABRETOOTH (Sabretooth and Mystique on-c)
Marvel Comics: Dec, 1996 - No. 4, Mar, 1997 ($1.95, limited series)

	GD	VG	FN	VF	VF/NM	NM-
1-4: Characters from X-Men						3.00

MY STORY (...True Romances in Pictures #5,6; becomes My Love Life #13) (Formerly Zago)
Hero Books (Fox Features Syndicate): No. 5, May, 1949 - No. 12, Aug, 1950

	GD	VG	FN	VF	VF/NM	NM-
5-Kamen/Feldstein-a	21	42	63	118	164	210
6-8,11,12: 12-Photo-c	10	20	30	58	77	95

Naked Brain #1 © Marc Hempel

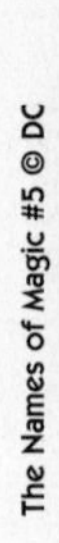

The Names of Magic #5 © DC

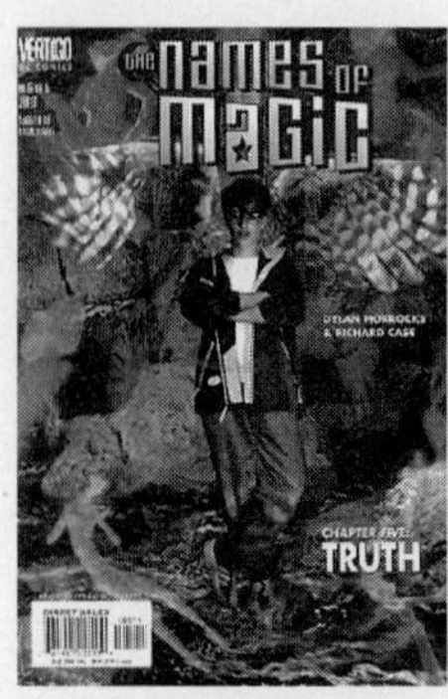

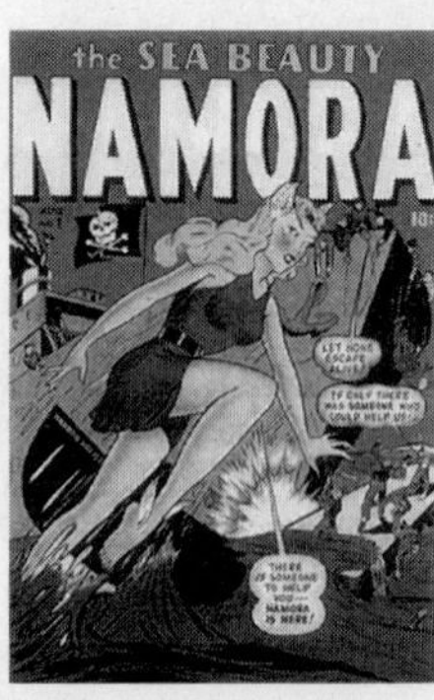

Namora #1 © MAR

	GD 2.0	VG 4.0	FN 6.0	VF 8.0	VF/NM 9.0	NM- 9.2

9,10-Wood-a 19 38 57 107 149 190

MYTHOGRAPHY
Bardic Press: Sept, 1996 - No. 8, May, 1998 ($3.95/$4.25, B&W, anthology)

1-3: 1-Drew Hayes-s/a 5.00
4-8 4.25

MYTHOS: THE FINAL TOUR
DC Comics/Vertigo: Dec, 1996 - No. 3, Feb, 1997 ($5.95, limited series)

1-3: 1-Ney Rieber-s/Amaro-a. 2-Snejbjerg-a; Constantine-app. 3-Kristiansen-a; Black Orchid-app. 6.00

MYTHSTALKERS
Image Comics: Mar, 2003 - Present ($2.95)

1-6-Jiro-a 3.00

MY TRUE LOVE (Formerly Western Killers #64; Frank Buck #70 on)
Fox Features Syndicate: No. 65, July, 1949 - No. 69, March, 1950

65 16 32 48 92 126 160
66,68,69: 69-Morisi-a 10 20 30 58 77 95
67-Wood-a 19 38 57 107 149 190

NAKED BRAIN (Marc Hempel's...)
Insight Studios Group: 2002 - No. 3, 2002 ($2.95, B&W, limited series)

1-3-Marc Hempel cartoons and sketches; Tug & Buster app. 3.00

NAKED PREY, THE (See Movie Classics)

'NAM, THE (See Savage Tales #1, 2nd series & Punisher Invades...)
Marvel Comics Group: Dec, 1986 - No. 84, Sept, 1993

1-Golden a(p)/c begins, ends #13 3.00
1 (2nd printing) 2.25
2-8,10-66,70-74: 7-Golden-a (2 pgs.). 32-Death R. Kennedy. 52,53-Frank Castle (The Punisher) app. 52,53-Gold 2nd printings. 58-Silver logo. 65-Heath-c/a. 70-Lomax scripts begin 2.25
9-1st app. Fudd Verzyl, Tunnel Rat 3.00
67-69,76-84: 67-69-Punisher 3 part story 3.00
75-($2.25, 52 pgs.) 2.50
Trade Paperback 1,2: 1-r/#1-4. 2-r/#5-8 5.00
TPB ('99, $14.95) r/#1-4; recolored 15.00

'NAM MAGAZINE, THE
Marvel Comics: Aug, 1988 - No. 10, May, 1989 ($2.00, B&W, 52pgs.)

1-10: Each issue reprints 2 issues of the comic 2.25

NAMELESS, THE
Image Comics: May, 1997 - No. 5, Sept, 1997 ($2.95, B&W)

1-5: Pruett/Hester-s/a 3.00

NAMES OF MAGIC, THE (Also see Books of Magic)
DC Comics (Vertigo): Feb, 2001 - No. 5, June, 2001 ($2.50, limited series)

1-5: Bolton painted-c on all; Case-a; leads into Hunter: The Age of Magic 2.50
TPB (2002, $14.95) r/#1-5 15.00

NAME OF THE GAME, THE
DC Comics: 2001 ($29.95, graphic novel)

Hardcover ($29.95) Will Eisner-s/a 30.00

NAMOR (Volume 2)
Marvel Comics: June, 2003 - No. 12 (25¢/$2.25)

1-(25¢-c)Young Namor in the 1920s; Larroca-c/a 2.25
2-6-($2.25) Larroca-a 2.25
7-10-($2.99): 7-Olliffe-a begins 3.00

NAMORA (See Marvel Mystery Comics #82 & Sub-Mariner Comics)
Marvel Comics (PrPl): Fall, 1948 - No. 3, Dec, 1948

1-Sub-Mariner x-over in Namora; Namora by Everett(2), Sub-Mariner by Rico (10 pgs.) 248 496 744 1550 2325 3100
2-The Blonde Phantom & Sub-Mariner story; Everett-a 126 252 378 788 1182 1575
3-(Scarce)-Sub-Mariner app.; Everett-a 135 270 405 844 1265 1685

NAMOR, THE SUB-MARINER (See Prince Namor & Sub-Mariner)
Marvel Comics: Apr, 1990 - No. 62, May, 1995 ($1.00/$1.25/$1.50)

1-Byrne-c/a/scripts in 1-25 (scripts only #26-32) 4.00
2-5: 5-Iron Man app. 3.00
6-11,13-23,25,27-49,51-62: 16-Re-intro Iron Fist (8-cameo only). 18-Punisher cameo (1 panel); 21-23,25-Wolverine cameos. 22,23-Iron Fist app. 28-Iron Fist-c/story. 31-Dr. Doom-c/story. 33,34-Iron Fist cameo. 35-New Tiger Shark-c/story. 37-Aqua holografx foil-c. 48-The Thing app. 2.25
12,24: 12-(52pgs.)-Re-intro. The Invaders. 24-Namor vs. Wolverine 2.50
26-Namor w/new costume; 1st Jae Lee-c/a this title (5/92) & begins 3.00
50-($1.75, 52 pgs.)-Newsstand ed.; w/bound-in S-M trading card sheet (both versions) 2.25
50-($2.95, 52 pgs.)-Collector edition w/foil-c 3.00
Annual 1-4 ('91-94, 68 pgs.): 1-3 pg. origin recap. 2-Return/Defenders. 3-Bagged w/card. 4-Painted-c 3.00

NOTE: *Jae Lee a-26-30p, 31-37, 38p, 39, 40; c-26-40.*

NANCY AND SLUGGO (See Comics On Parade & Sparkle Comics)
United Features Syndicate: No. 16, 1949 - No. 23, 1954

16(#1) 9 18 27 52 66 80
17-23 6 12 18 33 41 48

NANCY & SLUGGO (Nancy #146-173; formerly Sparkler Comics)
St. John/Dell #146-187/Gold Key #188 on: No. 121, Apr, 1955-No. 192, Oct, 1963

121(4/55)(St. John) 8 16 24 43 54 65
122-145(7/57)(St. John) 7 14 21 35 43 50
146(9/57)-Peanuts begins, ends #192 (Dell) 6 12 18 40 55 70
147-161 (Dell) Peanuts in all 5 10 15 36 48 60
162-165,177-180-John Stanley-a 8 16 24 55 78 100
166-176-Oona & Her Haunted House series; Stanley-a 9 18 27 63 89 115
181-187(3-5/62)(Dell) 5 10 15 33 44 55
188(10/62)-192 (Gold Key) 5 10 15 33 44 55
Four Color 1034(9-11/59)-Summer Camp 5 10 15 33 44 55
(See Dell Giant #34, 45 & Dell Giants)

NANNY AND THE PROFESSOR (TV)
Dell Publishing Co.: Aug, 1970 - No. 2, Oct, 1970 (Photo-c)

1-(01-546-008) 6 12 18 38 52 65
2 4 8 12 29 40 50

NAPOLEON
Dell Publishing Co.: No. 526, Dec, 1953

Four Color 526 3 6 9 19 25 32

NAPOLEON & SAMANTHA (See Walt Disney Showcase No. 10)

NAPOLEON & UNCLE ELBY (See Clifford McBride's...)
Eastern Color Printing Co.: July, 1942 (68 pgs.) (One Shot)

1 44 88 132 264 395 525
1945-American Book-Strafford Press (128 pgs.) (8x10-1/2"; B&W reprints; hardcover) 15 30 45 86 118 150

NARRATIVE ILLUSTRATION, THE STORY OF THE COMICS (Also see Good Triumphs Over Evil!)
M.C. Gaines: Summer, 1942 (32 pgs., 7-1/4"x10", B&W w/color inserts)

nn-16 pgs. text with illustrations of ancient art, strips and comic covers; 4 pg. WWII War Bond promo, "The Minute Man Answers the Call" color comic drawn by Shelly and a special 8-page color comic insert of "The Story of Saul" from Picture Stories from the Bible #1 or soon to appear in PS #1. Insert has special title page indicating it was No. 10 of a Sunday newspaper supplement insert series that had already run in a New England "Sunday Herald." (very rare; only two known copies.) Estimated value... 1400.00

NASH (WCW Wrestling)
Image Comics: July, 1999 - No. 2, July, 1999 ($2.95)

1,2-Regular and photo-c 3.00
1-($6.95) Photo-split-cover Edition 7.00

NATHANIEL DUSK
DC Comics: Feb, 1984 - No. 4, May, 1984 ($1.25, mini-series, direct sales, Baxter paper)

1-4: 1-Intro/origin; Gene Colan-c/a in all 2.25

NATHANIEL DUSK II
DC Comics: Oct, 1985 - No. 4, Jan, 1986 ($2.00, mini-series, Baxter paper)

1-4: Gene Colan-c/a in all 2.25

NATHAN NEVER
Dark Horse (Bonelli Comics): Mar, 1999 - No. 6, Aug, 1999 ($4.95, B&W, digest size)

1-6-Reprints Italian series in English. 1-4-Art Adams-c 5.00

NATIONAL COMICS
Quality Comics Group: July, 1940 - No. 75, Nov, 1949

1-Uncle Sam begins (1st app.); origin sidekick Buddy by Eisner; origin Wonder Boy & Kid Dixon; Merlin the Magician (ends #45); Cyclone, Kid Patrol, Sally O'Neil Policewoman, Pen Miller (by Klaus Nordling; ends #22), Prop Powers (ends #26), & Paul Bunyan (ends #22) begin 517 1034 1551 3619 5560 7500
2 240 480 720 1500 2250 3000

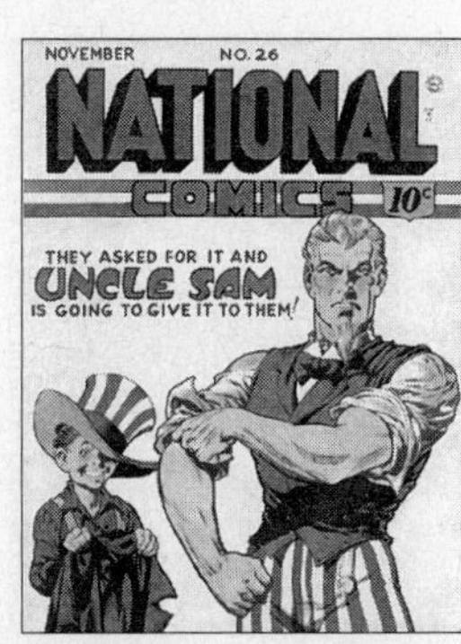

National Comics #26 © QUA

Necrowar #1 © Dreamwave Prod.

Negative Burn #47 © Caliber

	GD 2.0	VG 4.0	FN 6.0	VF 8.0	VF/NM 9.0	NM- 9.2
3-Last Eisner Uncle Sam	168	336	504	1050	1575	2100
4-Last Cyclone	132	264	396	825	1238	1650
5-(11/40)-Quicksilver begins (1st app.; 3rd w/lightning speed?; re-intro'd by DC in 1993 as Max Mercury in Flash #76, 2nd series); origin Uncle Sam; bondage-c	152	304	456	950	1425	1900
6,8-11: 8-Jack & Jill begins (ends #22). 9-Flag-c	128	256	384	800	1200	1600
7-Classic Lou Fine-c	224	448	672	1400	2100	2800
12	96	192	288	600	900	1200
13-16-Lou Fine-a	86	172	258	538	807	1075
17,19-22: 22-Last Pen Miller (moves to Crack #23)	66	132	198	413	619	825
18-(12/41)-Shows orientals attacking Pearl Harbor; on stands one month before actual event	120	240	360	750	1125	1500
23-The Unknown & Destroyer 171 begin	68	136	204	425	638	850
24-Japanese War-c	68	136	204	425	638	850
25-30: 26-Wonder Boy ends. 27- G-2 the Unknown begins (ends #46). 29-Origin The Unknown	48	96	144	288	432	575
31-33: 33-Chic Carter begins (ends #47)	44	88	132	264	395	525
34-37,40: 35-Last Kid Patrol	39	78	117	233	329	425
38-Hitler, Tojo, Mussolini-c	43	86	129	258	384	510
39-Hitler-c	44	88	132	264	397	530
41-50: 42-The Barker begins (1st app?, 5/44); The Barker covers begin. 48-Origin The Whistler	24	48	72	138	194	250
51-Sally O'Neil by Ward, 8 pgs. (12/45)	29	58	87	164	232	300
52-60	20	40	60	112	156	200
61-67: 67-Format change; Quicksilver app.	15	30	45	86	118	150
68-75: The Barker ends	12	24	36	71	96	120

NOTE: ***Cole*** *Quicksilver-13; Barker-43; c-43, 46, 47, 49-51.* ***Crandall*** *Uncle Sam-11-13 (with* ***Fine****), 25, 26; c-24-26, 30-33, 43.* ***Crandall*** *Paul Bunyan-10-13.* ***Fine*** *Uncle Sam-13 (w/****Crandall****), 17, 18; c-1-14, 16, 18, 21.* ***Gill Fox*** *c-69-74.* ***Guardineer*** *Quicksilver-27, 35.* ***Gustavson*** *Quicksilver-14-26.* ***McWilliams*** *a-23-28, 55, 57. Uncle Sam c-1-41. Barker c-42-75.*

NATIONAL COMICS (Also see All Star Comics 1999 crossover titles)
DC Comics: May, 1999 ($1.99, one-shot)

	GD	VG	FN	VF	VF/NM	NM-
1-Golden Age Flash and Mr. Terrific; Waid-s/Lopresti-a						2.25

NATIONAL CRUMB, THE (Magazine-Size)
Mayfair Publications: August, 1975 (52 pgs., B&W) (Satire)

	GD	VG	FN	VF	VF/NM	NM-
1-Grandenetti-c/a, Ayers-a	2	4	6	11	14	18

NATIONAL VELVET (TV)
Dell Publishing Co./Gold Key: May-July, 1961 - No. 2, Mar, 1963 (All photo-c)

	GD	VG	FN	VF	VF/NM	NM-
Four Color 1195 (#1)	8	16	24	55	78	100
Four Color 1312, 01-556-207, 12-556-210 (Dell)	4	8	12	29	40	50
1,2: 1(12/62) (Gold Key). 2(3/63)	4	8	12	29	40	50

NATION OF SNITCHES
Piranha Press (DC): 1990 ($4.95, color, 52 pgs.)

	GD	VG	FN	VF	VF/NM	NM-
nn						5.00

NATURE BOY (Formerly Danny Blaze; Li'l Rascal Twins #6 on)
Charlton Comics: No. 3, March, 1956 - No. 5, Feb, 1957

	GD	VG	FN	VF	VF/NM	NM-
3-Origin; Blue Beetle story; Buscema-c/a	24	48	72	135	190	245
4,5	17	34	51	98	134	170

NOTE: ***John Buscema*** *a-3, 4p, 5; c-3.* ***Powell*** *a-4.*

NATURE OF THINGS (Disney, TV/Movie)
Dell Publishing Co.: No. 727, Sept, 1956 - No. 842, Sept, 1957

	GD	VG	FN	VF	VF/NM	NM-
Four Color 727 (#1), 842-Jesse Marsh-a	6	12	18	40	55	70

NAUSICAA OF THE VALLEY OF WIND
Viz Comics: 1988 - No. 7, 1989; 1989 - No. 4, 1990 ($2.50, B&W, 68pgs.)

	GD	VG	FN	VF	VF/NM	NM-
Book 1-7: 1-Contains Moebius poster						3.25
Part II, Book 1-4 ($2.95)						3.25

NAVY ACTION (Sailor Sweeney #12-14)
Atlas Comics (CDS): Aug, 1954 - No. 11, Apr, 1956; No. 15, 1/57 - No. 18, 8/57

	GD	VG	FN	VF	VF/NM	NM-
1-Powell-a	19	38	57	107	149	190
2-Lawrence-a	10	20	30	58	77	95
3-11: 4-Last precode (2/55)	8	16	24	46	58	70
15-18	8	16	24	43	54	65

NOTE: ***Berg*** *a-7, 9.* ***Colan*** *a-8.* ***Drucker*** *a-7, 17.* ***Everett*** *a-3, 7, 16; c-16, 17.* ***Heath*** *c-1, 2, 6.* ***Maneely*** *a-7, 8, 18; c-9, 11.* ***Pakula*** *a-2, 3, 9.* ***Reinman*** *a-17.*

NAVY COMBAT
Atlas Comics (MPI): June, 1955 - No. 20, Oct, 1958

	GD	VG	FN	VF	VF/NM	NM-
1-Torpedo Taylor begins by Don Heck	19	38	57	107	149	190
2	10	20	30	58	77	95
3-10	8	16	24	46	58	70
11,13,15,16,18-20	8	16	24	43	54	65
12-Crandall-a	10	20	30	56	73	90
14-Torres-a	8	16	24	46	58	70
17-Williamson-a, 4 pgs.; Torres-a	9	18	27	49	62	75

NOTE: ***Berg*** *a-10, 11.* ***Colan*** *a-11.* ***Drucker*** *a-7.* ***Everett*** *a-3, 20; c-8 & 9 w/****Tuska****, 10, 13-16.* ***Heck*** *a-11(2).* ***Maneely*** *c-1, 6, 11, 17.* ***Morisi*** *a-8.* ***Pakula*** *a-7.* ***Powell*** *a-20.*

NAVY HEROES
Almanac Publishing Co.: 1945

	GD	VG	FN	VF	VF/NM	NM-
1-Heavy in propaganda	12	24	36	71	96	120

NAVY PATROL
Key Publications: May, 1955 - No. 4, Nov, 1955

	GD	VG	FN	VF	VF/NM	NM-
1	8	16	24	40	50	60
2-4	5	10	15	24	30	35

NAVY TALES
Atlas Comics (CDS): Jan, 1957 - No. 4, July, 1957

	GD	VG	FN	VF	VF/NM	NM-
1-Everett-c; Berg, Powell-a	16	32	48	92	126	160
2-Williamson/Mayo-a(5 pgs); Crandall-a	14	28	42	79	107	135
3,4-Reinman-a; Severin-c. 4-Crandall-a	12	24	36	69	92	115

NOTE: ***Colan*** *a-4.* ***Maneely*** *c-2.* ***Sinnott*** *a-4.*

NAVY TASK FORCE
Stanmor Publications/Aragon Mag. No. 4-8: Feb, 1954 - No. 8, April, 1956

	GD	VG	FN	VF	VF/NM	NM-
1	8	16	24	46	58	70
2	5	10	15	24	30	35
3-8: #8-r/Navy Patrol #1	5	10	15	22	26	30

NAVY WAR HEROES
Charlton Comics: Jan, 1964 - No. 7, Mar-Apr, 1965

	GD	VG	FN	VF	VF/NM	NM-
1	3	7	10	21	28	35
2-7	2	4	6	12	16	20

NAZA (Stone Age Warrior)
Dell Publishing Co.: Nov-Jan, 1963-64 - No. 9, March, 1966

	GD	VG	FN	VF	VF/NM	NM-
12-555-401 (#1)-Painted-c	5	10	15	33	44	55
2-9: 2-4-Painted-c	3	7	10	21	28	35

NAZZ, THE
DC Comics: 1990 - No. 4, 1991 ($4.95, 52 pgs., mature)

	GD	VG	FN	VF	VF/NM	NM-
1-4						5.00

NEBBS, THE (Also see Crackajack Funnies)
Dell Publishing Co./Croydon Publishing Co.: 1941; 1945

	GD	VG	FN	VF	VF/NM	NM-
Large Feature Comic 23(1941)	15	30	45	109	160	210
1(1945, 36 pgs.)-Reprints	13	26	39	74	100	125

NECROMANCER: THE GRAPHIC NOVEL
Marvel Comics (Epic Comics): 1989 ($8.95)

	GD	VG	FN	VF	VF/NM	NM-
nn						9.00

NECROWAR
Dreamwave Productions: July, 2003 - No. 3, Sept, 2003 ($2.95)

	GD	VG	FN	VF	VF/NM	NM-
1-3-Furman-s/Granov-digital art						3.00

NEGATION
CrossGeneration Comics: Dec, 2001 - Present ($2.95)

	GD	VG	FN	VF	VF/NM	NM-
Prequel (12/01)						3.00
1-26: 1-(1/02) Pelletier-a/Bedard & Waid-s						3.00
... Lawbringer (11/02, $2.95) Nebres-a						3.00
Vol. 1: Bohica! (10/02, $19.95, TPB) r/ Prequel & #1-6						20.00
Vol. 2: Baptism of Fire (5/03, $15.95, TPB) r/#7-12						16.00
Vol. 3: Hounded (12/03, $15.95, TPB) r/#13-18						16.00

NEGATIVE BURN
Caliber: 1993 - No. 50, 1997 ($2.95, B&W, anthology)

	GD	VG	FN	VF	VF/NM	NM-
1,2,4-12,14-47: Anthology by various including Bolland, Burden, Doran, Gaiman, Moebius, Moore, & Pope						4.00
3,13: 3-Bone story. 13-Strangers in Paradise story	2	4	6	8	10	12
48,49-($4.95)						5.00
50-($6.95, 96 pgs.)-Gaiman, Robinson, Bolland						7.00

NEGRO (See All-Negro)

NEGRO HEROES (Calling All Girls, Real Heroes, & True Comics reprints)
Parents' Magazine Institute: Spring, 1947 - No. 2, Summer, 1948

	GD	VG	FN	VF	VF/NM	NM-
1	85	170	255	531	796	1060
2-Jackie Robinson-c/story	92	184	276	575	863	1150

Neil Gaiman's Lady Justice #3 © BIG

New Adventure Comics #17 © DC

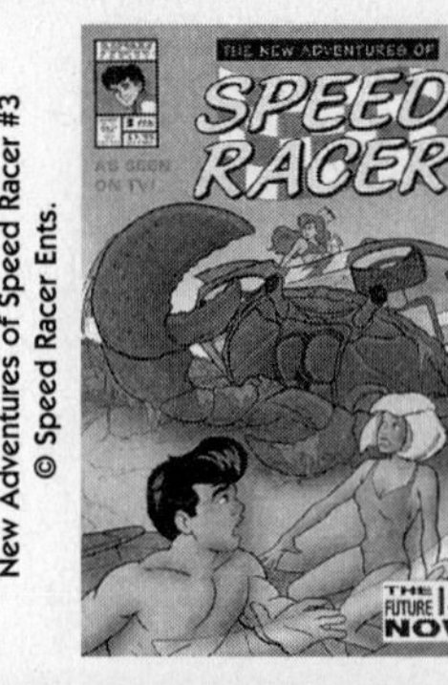

New Adventures of Speed Racer #3 © Speed Racer Ents.

NEGRO ROMANCE (Negro Romances #4)
Fawcett Publications: June, 1950 - No. 3, Oct, 1950 (All photo-c)

	GD 2.0	VG 4.0	FN 6.0	VF 8.0	VF/NM 9.0	NM- 9.2
1-Evans-a	114	228	342	713	1069	1425
2,3	85	170	255	531	796	1060

NEGRO ROMANCES (Formerly Negro Romance; Romantic Secrets #5 on)
Charlton Comics: No. 4, May, 1955

	GD 2.0	VG 4.0	FN 6.0	VF 8.0	VF/NM 9.0	NM- 9.2
4-Reprints Fawcett #2	69	138	207	431	646	860

NEIL GAIMAN AND CHARLES VESS' STARDUST
DC Comics (Vertigo): 1997 - No. 4, 1998 ($5.95/$6.95, square-bound, lim. series)

	NM- 9.2
1-4: Gaiman text with Vess paintings in all	7.00
Hardcover (1998, $29.95) r/series with new sketches	35.00
Softcover (1999, $19.95) oversized; new Vess-c	20.00

NEIL GAIMAN'S LADY JUSTICE
Tekno Comix: Sept, 1995 - No. 11, May, 1996 ($1.95/$2.25)

	NM- 9.2
1-11: 1-Sienkiewicz-c; pin-ups. 1-5-Brereton-c. 7-Polybagged. 11-The Big Bang Pt. 7	2.25

NEIL GAIMAN'S LADY JUSTICE
BIG Entertainment: V2#1, June, 1996 - No. 9, Feb, 1997 ($2.25)

	NM- 9.2
V2#1-9: Dan Brereton-c on all. 6-8-Dan Brereton script	2.25

NEIL GAIMAN'S MIDNIGHT DAYS
DC Comics (Vertigo): 1999 ($17.95, trade paperback)

	NM- 9.2
nn-Reprints Gaiman's short stories; new Swamp Thing w/ Bissette-a	18.00

NEIL GAIMAN'S MR. HERO-THE NEWMATIC MAN
Tekno Comix: Mar, 1995 - No. 17, May, 1996 ($1.95/$2.25)

	NM- 9.2
1-17: 1-Intro Mr. Hero & Teknophage; bound-in game piece and trading card. 4-w/Steel edition Neil Gaiman's Teknophage #1 coupon. 13-Polybagged	2.25

NEIL GAIMAN'S MR. HERO-THE NEWMATIC MAN
BIG Entertainment: V2#1, June, 1996 ($2.25)

	NM- 9.2
V2#1-Teknophage destroys Mr. Hero; includes The Big Bang Pt. 10	2.25

NEIL GAIMAN'S PHAGE-SHADOWDEATH
BIG Entertainment: June, 1996 - No. 6, Nov, 1996 ($2.25, limited series)

	NM- 9.2
1-6: Bryan Talbot-c & scripts in all. 1-1st app. Orlando Holmes	2.25

NEIL GAIMAN'S TEKNOPHAGE
Tekno Comix: Aug, 1995 - No. 10, Mar, 1996 ($1.95/$2.25)

	NM- 9.2
1-6-Rick Veitch scripts & Bryan Talbot-c/a.	2.25
1-Steel Edition	4.00
7-10: Paul Jenkins scripts in all. 8-polybagged	2.25

NEIL GAIMAN'S WHEEL OF WORLDS
Tekno Comix: Apr, 1995 - No. 1, May, 1996 ($2.95/$3.25)

	NM- 9.2
0-1st app. Lady Justice; 48 pgs.; bound-in poster	3.25
0-Regular edition	2.25
1 ($3.25, 5/96)-Bruce Jones scripts; Lady Justice & Teknophage app.; CGI photo-c	3.25

NEIL THE HORSE (See Charlton Bullseye #2)
Aardvark-Vanaheim #1-10/Renegade Press #11 on: 2/83 - No. 10, 12/84; No. 11, 4/85 - #15, 1985 (B&W)

	NM- 9.2
1($1.40)	4.00
1-2nd print	2.25
2-13: 13-Double size; 11,13-w/paperdolls	2.25
14,15: Double size ($3.00). 15 is a flip book(2-c)	3.00

NELLIE THE NURSE (Also see Gay Comics & Joker Comics)
Marvel/Atlas Comics (SPI/LMC): 1945 - No. 36, Oct, 1952; 1957

	GD 2.0	VG 4.0	FN 6.0	VF 8.0	VF/NM 9.0	NM- 9.2
1-(1945)	40	80	120	240	340	440
2-(Spring/46)	20	40	60	112	156	200
3,4: 3-New logo (9/46)	15	30	45	86	118	150
5-Kurtzman's "Hey Look" (3); Georgie app.	17	34	51	98	134	170
6-8,10: 7,8-Georgie app. 10-Millie app.	14	28	42	81	111	140
9-Wolverton-a (1 pg.); Mille the Model app.	15	30	45	84	115	145
11,14-16,18-Kurtzman's "Hey Look"	15	30	45	86	118	150
12- "Giggles 'n' Grins" by Kurtzman	14	28	42	81	111	140
13,17,19,20: 17-Annie Oakley app.	10	20	30	60	80	100
21-27,29,30	10	20	30	56	73	90
28-Mr. Nexdoor-r (3 pgs.) by Kurtzman/Rusty #22	10	20	30	56	73	90
31-36: 36-Post-c	9	18	27	49	62	75
1('57)-Leading Mag. (Atlas)-Everett-a, 20 pgs	9	18	27	54	70	85

NELLIE THE NURSE
Dell Publishing Co.: No. 1304, Mar-May, 1962

	GD 2.0	VG 4.0	FN 6.0	VF 8.0	VF/NM 9.0	NM- 9.2
Four Color 1304-Stanley-a	8	16	24	55	78	100

NEMESIS THE WARLOCK (Also see Spellbinders)
Eagle Comics: Sept, 1984 - No. 7, Mar, 1985 (limited series, Baxter paper)

	NM- 9.2
1-7: 2000 A.D. reprints	2.25

NEMESIS THE WARLOCK
Quality Comics/Fleetway Quality #2 on: 1989 - No. 19, 1991 ($1.95, B&W)

	NM- 9.2
1-19	2.25

NEON CYBER
Image Comics (Dreamwave Prod.): Jul, 1999 - No. 8, Jun, 2000 ($2.50)

	NM- 9.2
1-8-Adrian Tsang-s	2.50

NEUTRO
Dell Publishing Co.: Jan, 1967

	GD 2.0	VG 4.0	FN 6.0	VF 8.0	VF/NM 9.0	NM- 9.2
1-Jack Sparling-c/a (super hero); UFO-s	4	8	12	29	40	50

NEVADA (See Zane Grey's Four Color 412, 996 & Zane Grey's Stories of the West #1)

NEVADA (Also see Vertigo Winter's Edge #1)
DC Comics (Vertigo): May, 1998 - No. 6, Oct, 1998 ($2.50, limited series)

	NM- 9.2
1-6-Gerber-s/Winslade-c/a	2.50
TPB-(1999, $14.95) r/#1-6 & Vertigo Winter's Edge preview	15.00

NEVER AGAIN (War stories; becomes Soldier & Marine V2#9)
Charlton Comics: Aug, 1955; No. 8, July, 1956 (No #2-7)

	GD 2.0	VG 4.0	FN 6.0	VF 8.0	VF/NM 9.0	NM- 9.2
1	9	18	27	52	66	80
8-(Formerly Foxhole?)	6	12	18	28	34	40

NEVERMEN, THE (See Dark Horse Presents #148-150)
Dark Horse Comics: May, 2000 - No. 4, Aug, 2000 ($2.95, limited series)

	NM- 9.2
1-4-Phil Amara-s/Guy Davis-a	3.00

NEVERMEN, THE: STREETS OF BLOOD
Dark Horse Comics: Jan, 2003 - No. 3, Apr, 2003 ($2.99, limited series)

	NM- 9.2
1-3-Phil Amara-s/Guy Davis-a	3.00
TPB (7/03, $9.95) r/#1-3; Paul Jenkins intro.; Davis sketch pages	10.00

NEW ADVENTURE COMICS (Formerly New Comics; becomes Adventure Comics #32 on; V1#12 indicia says NEW COMICS #12)
National Periodical Publications: V1#12, Jan, 1937 - No. 31, Oct, 1938

	GD 2.0	VG 4.0	FN 6.0	VF 8.0	VF/NM 9.0	NM- 9.2
V1#12-Federal Men by Siegel & Shuster continues; Jor-L mentioned; Whitney Ellsworth-c begin, end #14	508	1016	1523	3500	-	-
V2#1(2/37, #13)-(Rare)	477	954	1431	3300	-	-
V2#2 (#14)	415	830	1246	2900	-	-
15(V2#3)-20(V2#8): 15-1st Adventure logo; Creig Flessel-c begin, end #31. 16-1st non-funny cover. 17-Nadir, Master of Magic begins, ends #30	356	712	1068	1958	2679	3400
21(V2#9),22(V2#10, 2/37): 22-X-Mas-c	317	634	951	1744	2322	2900
23-31	267	534	800	1469	1960	2450

NEW ADVENTURES OF ABRAHAM LINCOLN, THE
Image Comics (Homage): 1998 ($19.95, one-shot)

	NM- 9.2
1-Scott McCloud-s/computer art	20.00

NEW ADVENTURES OF CHARLIE CHAN, THE (TV)
National Periodical Publications: May-June, 1958 - No. 6, Mar-Apr, 1959

	GD 2.0	VG 4.0	FN 6.0	VF 8.0	VF/NM 9.0	NM- 9.2
1 (Scarce)-Gil Kane/Sid Greene-a in all	70	140	210	438	657	875
2 (Scarce)	46	92	138	276	413	550
3-6 (Scarce)-Greene/Giella-a	40	80	120	240	345	450

NEW ADVENTURES OF HUCK FINN, THE (TV)
Gold Key: December, 1968 (Hanna-Barbera)

	GD 2.0	VG 4.0	FN 6.0	VF 8.0	VF/NM 9.0	NM- 9.2
1- "The Curse of Thut"; part photo-c	4	8	12	27	36	45

NEW ADVENTURES OF PINOCCHIO (TV)
Dell Publishing Co.: Oct-Dec, 1962 - No. 3, Sept-Nov, 1963

	GD 2.0	VG 4.0	FN 6.0	VF 8.0	VF/NM 9.0	NM- 9.2
12-562-212(#1)	10	20	30	67	96	125
2,3	8	16	24	53	74	95

NEW ADVENTURES OF ROBIN HOOD (See Robin Hood)

NEW ADVENTURES OF SHERLOCK HOLMES (Also see Sherlock Holmes)
Dell Publishing Co.: No. 1169, Mar-May, 1961 - No. 1245, Nov-Jan, 1961/62

	GD 2.0	VG 4.0	FN 6.0	VF 8.0	VF/NM 9.0	NM- 9.2
Four Color 1169(#1)	17	34	51	121	178	235
Four Color 1245	15	30	45	109	160	210

NEW ADVENTURES OF SPEED RACER
Now Comics: Dec, 1993 - No. 7, 1994? ($1.95)

	NM- 9.2
1-7	2.25

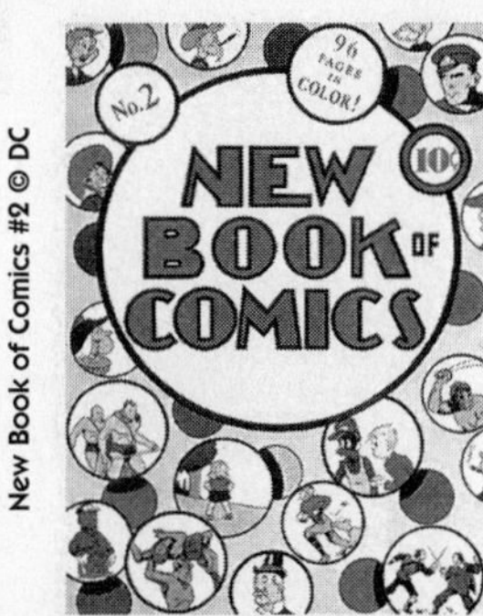

New Book of Comics #2 © DC

New Fun Comics #1 © DC

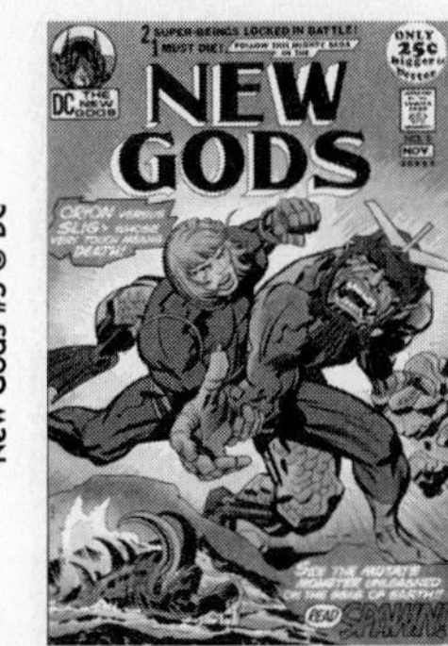

New Gods #5 © DC

GD VG FN VF VF/NM NM-
2.0 4.0 6.0 8.0 9.0 9.2

0-(Premiere)-3-D cover 3.00

NEW ADVENTURES OF SUPERBOY, THE (Also see Superboy)
DC Comics: Jan, 1980 - No. 54, June, 1984
1 5.00
2-6,8-10 4.00
11-49,51-54: 11-Superboy gets new power. 14-Lex Luthor app. 15-Superboy gets new parents. 28-Dial "H" For Hero begins, ends #49. 45-47-1st app. Sunburst. 48-Begin 75¢-c. 3.00
2,5,6,8 (Whitman variants; low print run; no issue # shown on cover)
1 2 3 4 5 7
7,50: 7-Has extra story "The Computers That Saved Metropolis" by Starlin (Radio Shack giveaway w/indicia). 50-Legion app. 5.00
NOTE: *Buckler a-9p; c-36p.* ***Giffen*** *a-50; c-50. 40i.* ***Gil Kane*** *c-32p, 33p, 35, 39, 41-49.* ***Miller*** *c-51.* ***Starlin*** *a-7. Krypto back-ups in 17, 22. Superbaby in 11, 14, 19, 24.*

NEW ADVENTURES OF THE PHANTOM BLOT, THE (See The Phantom Blot)

NEW AMERICA
Eclipse Comics: Nov, 1987 - No. 4, Feb, 1988 ($1.75, Baxter paper)
1-4: Scout limited series 2.25

NEW ARCHIES, THE (TV)
Archie Comic Publications: Oct, 1987 - No. 22, May, 1990 (75¢)
1 5.00
2-10: 3-Xmas issue 4.00
11-22: 17-22 (95¢-$1.00): 21-Xmas issue 3.00

NEW ARCHIES DIGEST (TV)(...Comics Digest Magazine #4?-10; ...Digest Magazine #11 on)
Archie Comics: May, 1988 - No. 14, July, 1991 ($1.35/$1.50, quarterly)
1 6.00
2-14: 6-Begin $1.50-c 3.50

NEW BOOK OF COMICS (Also see Big Book Of Fun)
National Periodical Publ.: 1937; No. 2, Spring, 1938 (100 pgs. each) (Reprints)
1(Rare)-1st regular size comic annual; 2nd DC annual; contains r/New Comics #1-4 & More Fun #9; r/Federal Men (8 pgs.), Henri Duval (1 pg.), & Dr. Occult in costume (1 pg.) by Siegel & Shuster; Moldoff, Sheldon Mayer (15 pgs.)-a
2000 4000 6000 13,000 - -
2-Contains-r/More Fun #15 & 16; r/Dr. Occult in costume (a Superman prototype), & Calling All Cars (4 pgs.) by Siegel & Shuster 1000 2000 3000 6500 - -

NEW COMICS (New Adventure #12 on)
National Periodical Publ.: 12/35 - No. 11, 12/36 (No. 1-6: paper cover) (No. 1-5: 84 pgs.)
V1#1-Billy the Kid, Sagebrush 'n' Cactus, Jibby Jones, Needles, The Vikings, Sir Loin of Beef, Now-When I Was a Boy, & other 1-2 pg. strips; 2 pgs. Kelly art(1st)-(Gulliver's Travels); Sheldon Mayer-a(1st)(2 2pg. strips); Vincent Sullivan-c(1st)
2850 5700 8550 19,500 - -
2-1st app. Federal Men by Siegel & Shuster & begins (also see The Comics Magazine #2); Mayer, Kelly-a (Rare)(1/36) 1000 2000 3000 7000 - -
3-6: 3,4-Sheldon Mayer-a which continues in The Comics Magazine #1. 3-Vincent Sullivan-c. 4-Dickens' "A Tale of Two Cities" adaptation begins. 5-Junior Federal Men Club; Kiefer-a. 6- "She" adaptation begins 575 1150 1725 4900 - -
7-11: 11-Christmas-c 475 950 1425 3300 - -
NOTE: *#1-6 rarely occur in mint condition.* ***Whitney Ellsworth*** *c-4-11.*

NEW DEFENDERS (See Defenders)

NEW DNAGENTS, THE (Formerly DNAgents)
Eclipse Comics: V2#1, Oct, 1985 - V2#17, Mar, 1987 (Whole #s 25-40; Mando paper)
V2#1-17: 1-Origin recap. 7-Begin 95 cent-c. 9,10-Airboy preview 2.25
3-D 1 (1/86, $2.25) 2.25
2-D 1 (1/86)-Limited ed. (100 copies) 10.00

NEW ETERNALS: APOCALYPSE NOW (Also see Eternals, The)
Marvel Comics: Feb, 2000 ($3.99, one-shot)
1-Bennett & Hanna-a; Ladronn-c 4.00

NEWFORCE (Also see Newmen)
Image Comics (Extreme Studios): Jan, 1996-No. 4, Apr, 1996 ($2.50, lim. series)
1-4: 1-"Extreme Destroyer" Pt. 8; polybagged w/gaming card. 4-Newforce disbands 2.50

NEW FUN COMICS (More Fun #7 on; see Big Book of Fun Comics)
National Periodical Publications: Feb, 1935 - No. 6, Oct, 1935 (10x15", No. 1-4,: slick-c) (No. 1-5: 36 pgs; 40 pgs. No. 6)
V1#1 (1st DC comic); 1st app. Oswald The Rabbit; Jack Woods (cowboy) begins
6500 13,000 19,500 45,000 - -
2(3/35)-(Very Rare) 2750 5500 8250 18,700 - -
3-5(8/35): 3-Don Drake on the Planet Soro-c/story (sci/fi, 4/35). 5-Soft-c
1400 2800 4200 9,400 - -
6(10/35)-1st Dr. Occult by Siegel & Shuster (Leger & Reuths); last "New Fun" title. "New Comics" #1 begins in Dec. which is reason for title change to More Fun; Henri Duval (ends #10) by Siegel & Shuster begins; paper-c
3100 6200 9300 20,700 - -

GD VG FN VF VF/NM NM-
2.0 4.0 6.0 8.0 9.0 9.2

NEW FUNNIES (The Funnies #1-64; Walter Lantz...#109 on; New TV... #259, 260, 272, 273; TV Funnies #261-271)
Dell Publishing Co.: No. 65, July, 1942 - No. 288, Mar-Apr, 1962
65(#1)-Andy Panda in a world of real people, Raggedy Ann & Andy, Oswald the Rabbit (with Woody Woodpecker x-overs), Li'l Eight Ball & Peter Rabbit begin; Bugs Bunny and Elmer app. 66 132 198 561 856 1150
66-70: 66-Felix the Cat begins. 67-Billy & Bonny Bee by Frank Thomas begins. 69-Kelly-a (2 pgs.); The Brownies begin (not by Kelly) 31 62 93 233 352 470
71-75: 72-Kelly illos. 75-Brownies by Kelly? 22 44 66 156 228 300
76-Andy Panda (Carl Barks & Pabian-a); Woody Woodpecker x-over in Oswald ends
85 170 255 655 1003 1350
77,78: 77-Kelly-c. 78-Andy Panda in a world with real people ends
22 44 66 156 228 300
79-81 15 30 45 109 160 210
82-Brownies by Kelly begins; Homer Pigeon begins 16 32 48 113 167 220
83-85-Brownies by Kelly in ea. 83-X-mas-c; Homer Pigeon begins. 85-Woody Woodpecker, 1 pg. strip begins 16 32 48 113 167 220
86-90: 87-Woody Woodpecker stories begin 11 22 33 80 118 155
91-99 9 18 27 60 85 110
100 (6/45) 9 18 27 63 89 115
101-120: 119-X-Mas-c 7 14 21 50 68 85
121-150: 131,143-X-Mas-c 6 12 18 40 55 70
151-200: 155-X-Mas-c. 167-X-Mas-c. 182-Origin & 1st app. Knothead & Splinter. 191-X-Mas-c 5 10 15 33 44 55
201-240 4 8 12 27 36 45
241-288: 270,271-Walter Lantz c-app. 281-1st story swipes/WDC&S #100
4 8 12 24 32 40
NOTE: *Early issues written by* ***John Stanley.***

NEW GODS, THE (1st Series)(New Gods #12 on)(See Adventure #459, DC Graphic Novel #4, 1st Issue Special #13 & Super-Team Family)
National Periodical Publications/DC Comics: 2-3/71 - V2#11, 10-11/72; V3#12, 7/77 - V3#19, 7-8/78 (Fourth World)
1-Intro/1st app. Orion; 4th app. Darkseid (cameo; 3 weeks after Forever People #1) (#1-3 are 15¢ issues) 9 18 27 65 93 120
2-Darkseid-c/story (2nd full app., 4-5/71) 5 10 15 36 48 60
3-1st app. Black Racer; last 15¢ issue 4 8 12 24 32 40
4-9: (25¢, 52 pg. giants): 4-Darkseid cameo; origin Manhunter-r. 5,7,8-Young Gods feature. 7-Darkseid app. (2-3/72); origin Orion; 1st origin of all New Gods as a group. 9-1st app. Forager 4 8 12 24 32 40
10,11: 11-Last Kirby issue. 3 6 9 16 20 25
12-19: Darkseid storyline w/minor apps. 12-New costume Orion (see 1st Issue Special #13 for 1st new costume). 19-Story continued in Adventure Comics #459,460
1 2 3 5 6 8
Jack Kirby's New Gods TPB ('98, $11.95, B&W&Grey) r/#1-11 plus cover gallery of original series and "84 reprints 12.00
NOTE: *#4-9(25¢, 52 pgs.) contain Manhunter-r by* ***Simon*** *&* ***Kirby*** *from Adventure #73, 74, 75, 76, 77, 78 with covers in that order.* ***Adkins*** *i-12-14, 17-19.* ***Buckler*** *a(p)-15.* ***Kirby*** *c/a-1-11p.* ***Newton*** *a(p)-12-14, 16-19.* ***Starlin*** *c-17.* ***Staton*** *c-19p.*

NEW GODS (Also see DC Graphic Novel #4)
DC Comics: June, 1984 - No. 6, Nov, 1984 ($2.00, Baxter paper)
1-5: New Kirby-c; r/New Gods #1-10. 4.00
6-Reprints New Gods #11 w/48 pgs of new Kirby story & art; leads into DC Graphic Novel #4
2 4 6 8 10 12

NEW GODS (2nd Series)
DC Comics: Feb, 1989 - No. 28, Aug, 1991 ($1.50)
1-28 2.50

NEW GODS (3rd Series) (Becomes Jack Kirby's Fourth World) (Also see Showcase '94 #1 & Showcase '95 #7)
DC Comics: Oct, 1995 - No. 15, Feb, 1997 ($1.95)
1-11,13-15: 9-Giffen-a(p). 10,11-Superman app. 13-Takion, Mr. Miracle & Big Barda app. 13-15-Byrne-a(p)/scripts & Simonson-c. 15-Apokolips merged w/ New Genesis; story cont'd in Jack Kirby's Fourth World 2.50
12-(11/96, 99¢)-Byrne-a(p)/scripts & Simonson-c begin; Takion cameo; indicia reads October 1996 2.50
...Secret Files 1 (9/98, $4.95) Origin-s 5.00

NEW GUARDIANS, THE

The New Guardians #7 © DC

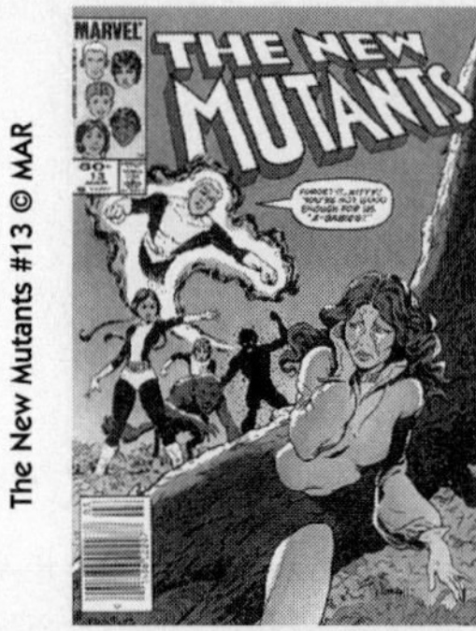

The New Mutants #13 © MAR

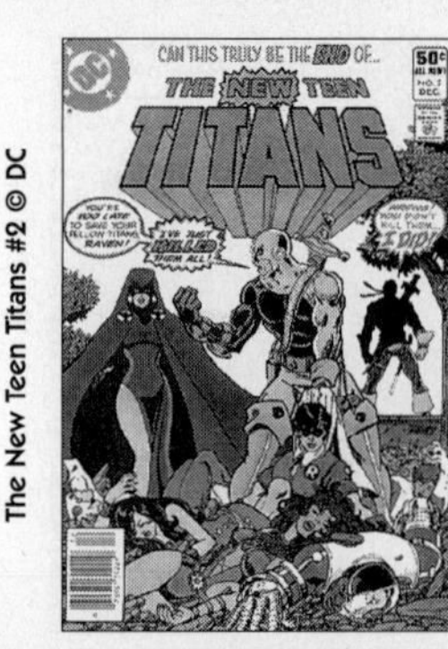

The New Teen Titans #2 © DC

GD VG FN VF VF/NM NM-
2.0 4.0 6.0 8.0 9.0 9.2

GD VG FN VF VF/NM NM-
2.0 4.0 6.0 8.0 9.0 9.2

DC Comics: Sept, 1988 - No. 12, Sept, 1989 ($1.25)

1-($2.00, 52pgs)-Staton-c/a in #1-9 3.00
2-12 2.25

NEW HEROIC (See Heroic)

NEW JUSTICE MACHINE, THE (Also see The Justice Machine)
Innovation Publishing: 1989 - No. 3, 1989 ($1.95, limited series)

1-3 2.25

NEW KIDS ON THE BLOCK, THE (Also see Richie Rich and...)
Harvey Comics: Dec, 1990 - No. 8, Dec, 1991 ($1.25)

1-8 2.25
...**Back Stage Pass** 1(12/90) - 7(11/91) **Chillin'** 1(12/90) - 7(12/91): 1-Photo-c ...**Comic Tour** '90/91 1 (12/90) - 7(12/91) **Digest** 1(1/91) - 5(1/92) **Hanging Tough** 1 (2/91) **Magic Summer Tour** 1 (Fall/90) **Magic Summer Tour** nn (Fall/90, sold at concerts) **Step By Step** 1 (Fall/90, one-shot) **Valentine Girl** 1 (Fall/90, one-shot)-Photo-c 2.25

NEW LOVE (See Love & Rockets)
Fantagraphics Books: Aug, 1996 - No. 6, Dec, 1997 ($2.95, B&W, lim. series)

1-6: Gilbert Hernandez-s/a 3.00

NEWMAN
Image Comics (Extreme Studios): Jan, 1996 - No. 4, Apr, 1996 ($2.50, lim. series)

1-4: 1-Extreme Destroyer Pt. 3; polybagged w/card. 4-Shadowhunt tie-in; Eddie Collins becomes new Shadowhawk 2.50

NEWMEN (becomes The Adventures Of The...#22)
Image Comics (Extreme Studios): Apr, 1994 - No. 20, Nov, 1995; No. 21, Nov, 1996 ($1.95/$2.50)

1-21: 1-5: Matsuda-c/a. 1-Liefeld/Matsuda plot. 10-Polybagged w/trading card. 11-Polybagged. 20-Has a variant-c; Babewatch! x-over. 21-(11/96)-Series relaunch; Chris Sprouse-a begins; pin-up. 16-Has a variant-c by Quesada & Palmiotti 2.50
TPB-(1996, $12.95) r/#1-4 w/pin-ups 13.00

NEW MEN OF BATTLE, THE
Catechetical Guild: 1949 (nn) (Carboard-c)

nn(V8#1-3,5,6)-192 pgs.; contains 5 issues of Topix rebound 8 16 24 46 58 70
nn(V8#7-V8#11)-160 pgs.; contains 5 iss. of Topix 8 16 24 46 58 70

NEW MUTANTS, THE (See Marvel Graphic Novel #4 for 1st app.)(Also see X-Force & Uncanny X-Men #167)
Marvel Comics Group: Mar, 1983 - No. 100, Apr, 1991

1 5.00
2-10: 3,4-Ties into X-Men #167. 10-1st app. Magma 3.00
11-17,19,20: 13-Kitty Pryde app. 16-1st app. Warpath (w/out costume); see X-Men #193 2.50
18,21: 18-Intro. new Warlock. 21-Double size; origin new Warlock; newsstand version has cover price written in by Sienkiewicz 3.00
22-24,27-30: 23-25-Cloak & Dagger app. 2.50
25,26: 25-Legion app. (cameo). 26-1st full Legion app. 4.00
31-58: 35-Magneto intro'd as new headmaster. 43-Portacio-i. 50-Double size. 58-Contains pull-out mutant registration form 2.50
59-61: Fall of The Mutants series. 60(52 pgs.) 3.00
62-85: 68-Intro Spyder. 63-X-Men & Wolverine clones app. 73-(52 pgs.). 76-X-Factor & X-Terminator app. 85-Liefeld-c begin 2.50
86-Rob Liefeld-a begins; McFarlane-c(i) swiped from Ditko splash pg.; Cable cameo (last page teaser) 6.00
87-1st full app. Cable (3/90) 2 4 6 12 16 20
87-2nd printing; gold metallic ink-c ($1.00) 2.50
88-2nd app. Cable 1 2 3 4 5 7
92-No Liefeld-a; Liefeld-c 4.00
89,90,91,93-100: 89-3rd app. Cable. 90-New costumes. 90,91-Sabretooth app. 93,94-Cable vs. Wolverine. 95-97-X-Tinction Agenda x-over. 95-Death of new Warlock. 97-Wolverine & Cable-c, but no app. 98-1st app. Deadpool, Gideon & Domino (2/91); 2nd Shatterstar (cameo). 99-1st app. of Feral (of X-Force); Byrne-c/swipe (X-Men, 1st Series #138). 100-(52 pgs.)-1st app. X-Force (cameo) 5.00
95,100-Gold 2nd printing. 100-Silver ink 3rd printing 2.50
Annual 1 (1984) 4.00
Annual 2 (1986, $1.25)-1st Psylocke 1 2 3 5 6 8
Annual 3,4,6,7 ('87, '88,'90,'91, 68 pgs.): 4-Evolutionary War x-over. 6-1st new costumes by Liefeld (3 pgs.); 1st app. (cameo) Shatterstar (of X-Force). 7-Liefeld pin-up only; X-Terminators back-up story; 2nd app. X-Force (cont'd in New Warriors Annual #1) 3.00
Annual 5 (1989, $2.00, 68 pgs.)-Atlantis Attacks; 1st Liefeld-a on New Mutants 4.00
Special 1-Special Edition ('85, 68 pgs.)-Ties in w/X-Men Alpha Flight limited series; cont'd in X-Men Annual #9; Art Adams/Austin-a 5.00
Summer Special 1(Sum/90, $2.95, 84 pgs.) 3.00
NOTE: ***Art Adams*** *c-38, 39.* ***Austin*** *c-57i.* ***Byrne*** *c/a-75p.* ***Liefeld*** *a-86-91p, 93-96p, 98-100, Annual 5p, 6(3 pgs.); c-85-91p, 92, 93p, 94, 95, 96p, 97-100, Annual 5, 6p.* ***McFarlane*** *c-85-89i, 93i.* ***Portacio*** *a(i)-43.* ***Russell*** *a-48i.* ***Sienkiewicz*** *a-18-31, 35-38i; c-17-31, 35i, 37i, Annual 1.* ***Simonson*** *c-11p.* ***B. Smith*** *c-36, 40-48.* ***Williamson*** *a(i)-69, 71-73, 78-80, 82, 83; c(i)-69, 72, 73, 78i.*

NEW MUTANTS
Marvel Comics: July, 2003 - Present ($2.50)

1-7: 1-6-Josh Middleton-c. 7-Bachalo-c 2.50

NEW MUTANTS, THE: TRUTH OR DEATH
Marvel Comics: Nov, 1997 - No. 3, Jan, 1998 ($2.50, limited series)

1-3-Raab-s/Chang-a(p) 2.50

NEW ORDER, THE
CFD Publishing: Nov, 1994 ($2.95)

1 3.00

NEW PEOPLE, THE (TV)
Dell Publishing Co.: Jan, 1970 - No. 2, May, 1970

1 3 6 9 18 24 30
2 3 6 9 16 20 24

NEW ROMANCES
Standard Comics: No. 5, May, 1951 - No. 21, May, 1954

5-Photo-c 13 26 39 76 103 130
6-9: 6-Barbara Bel Geddes, Richard Basehart "Fourteen Hours" photo-c. 7-Ray Milland & Joan Fontaine photo-c. 9-Photo-c from '50s movie 8 16 24 46 58 70
10,14,16,17-Toth-a 9 18 27 52 66 80
11-Toth-a; Liz Taylor, Montgomery Cliff photo-c 22 44 66 127 176 225
12,13,15,18-21 8 16 24 40 50 60
NOTE: ***Celardo*** *a-9.* ***Moreira*** *a-6.* ***Tuska*** *a-7, 20. Photo c-5-16.*

NEW SHADOWHAWK, THE (Also see Shadowhawk & Shadowhunt)
Image Comics (Shadowline Ink): June, 1995 - No. 7, Mar, 1996 ($2.50)

1-7: Kurt Busiek scripts in all 3.00

NEW STATESMEN, THE
Fleetway Publications (Quality Comics): 1989 - No. 5, 1990 ($3.95, limited series, mature readers, 52pgs.)

1-5: Futuristic; squarebound; 3-Photo-c 4.00

NEWSTRALIA
Innovation Publ.: July, 1989 - No. 5, 1989 ($1.75, color)(#2 on, $2.25, B&W)

1-5: 1,2: Timothy Truman-c/a; Gustovich-i 2.25

NEW TALENT SHOWCASE (Talent Showcase #16 on)
DC Comics: Jan, 1984 - No. 19, Oct, 1985 (Direct sales only)

1-19: Features new strips & artists. 18-Williamson-c(i) 2.25

NEW TEEN TITANS, THE (See DC Comics Presents #26, Marvel and DC Present & Teen Titans; Tales of the Teen Titans #41 on)
DC Comics: Nov, 1980 - No. 40, Mar, 1984

1-Robin, Kid Flash, Wonder Girl, The Changeling (1st app.), Starfire, The Raven, Cyborg begin; partial origin 1 3 4 6 8 10
2-1st app. Deathstroke the Terminator 6.00
3-10: 3-Origin Starfire; Intro The Fearsome Five. 4-Origin continues; J.L.A. app. 6-Origin Raven. 7-Cyborg origin. 8-Origin Kid Flash retold. 9-Minor cameo Deathstroke on last pg. 10-2nd app. Deathstroke the Terminator (see Marvel & DC Present for 3rd app.); origin Changeling retold 5.00
11-40: 13-Return of Madame Rouge & Capt. Zahl; Robotman revived. 14-Return of Mento; origin Doom Patrol. 15-Death of Madame Rouge & Capt. Zahl; intro. new Brotherhood of Evil. 16-1st app. Captain Carrot (free 16 pg. preview). 18-Return of Starfire. 19-Hawkman teams-up. 21-Intro Night Force in free 16 pg. insert; intro Brother Blood. 23-1st app. Vigilante (not in costume), & Blackfire. 24-Omega Men app. 25-Omega Men cameo; free 16 pg. preview Masters of the Universe. 26-1st app. Terra. 27-Free 16 pg. preview Atari Force. 29-The New Brotherhood of Evil & Speedy app. 30-Terra joins the Titans. 34-4th app. Deathstroke the Terminator. 37-Batman & The Outsiders x-over. 38-Origin Wonder Girl. 39-Last Dick Grayson as Robin; Kid Flash quits 3.00
Annual 1(11/82)-Omega Men app. 4.00
Annual V2#2(9/83)-1st app. Vigilante in costume 3.50
Annual 3 (See Tales of the Teen Titans Annual #3)
...: The Judas Contract TPB (2003, $19.95) r/#39,40 plus Tales of the Teen Titans #41-44 & Annual #3 20.00
NOTE: ***Perez*** *a-1-4p, 6-34p, 37-40p, Annual 1p, 2p; c-1-12, 13-17p, 18-21, 22p, 23p, 24-37, 38, 39(painted), 40, Annual 1, 2.*

NEW TEEN TITANS, THE (Becomes The New Titans #50 on)

The New Titans #120 © DC

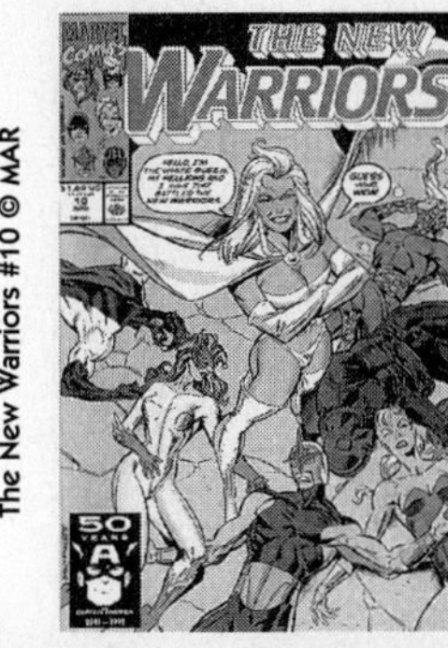

The New Warriors #10 © MAR

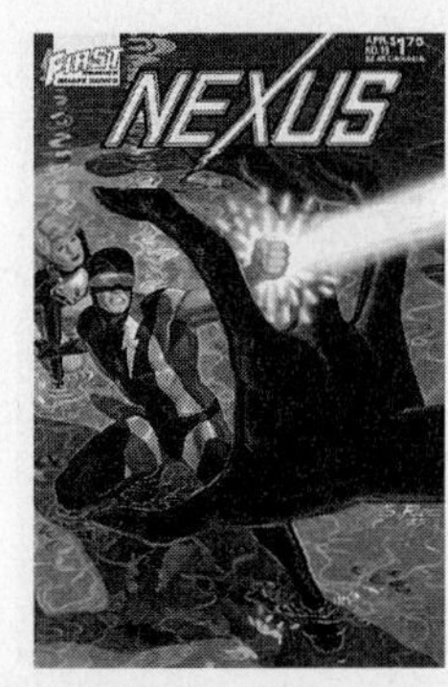

Nexus #19 © FC

DC Comics: Aug, 1984 - No. 49, Nov, 1988 ($1.25/$1.75; deluxe format)

1-New storyline; Perez-c/a begins 5.00
2,3: 2-Re-intro Lilith 4.00
4-10: 5-Death of Trigon. 7-9-Origin Lilith. 8-Intro Kole. 10-Kole joins 3.00
11-49: 13,14-Crisis x-over. 20-Robin (Jason Todd) joins; original Teen Titans return. 38-Infinity, Inc. x-over. 47-Origin of all Titans; Titans (East & West) pin-up by Perez 2.50
Annual 1-4 (9/85-'88): 1-Intro. Vanguard. 2-Byrne c/a(p); origin Brother Blood; intro new Dr. Light. 3-Intro. Danny Chase. 4-Perez-c 3.00
...: The Terror of Trigon TPB (2003, $17.95) r/#1-5; new cover by Phil Jimenez 18.00

NOTE: ***Buckler*** *c-10.* ***Kelley Jones*** *a-47, Annual 4.* ***Erik Larsen*** *a-33.* ***Orlando*** *c-33p.* ***Perez*** *a-1-5; c-1-7, 19-23, 43.* ***Steacy*** *c-47.*

NEW TERRYTOONS (TV)
Dell Publishing Co./Gold Key: 6-8/60 - No. 8, 3-5/62; 10/62 - No. 54, 1/79

1(1960-Dell)-Deputy Dawg, Dinky Duck & Hashimoto-San begin (1st app. of each)
7 14 21 50 68 85
2-8(1962) 4 8 12 27 36 45
1(30010-210)(10/62-Gold Key, 84 pgs.)-Heckle & Jeckle begins
9 18 27 60 85 110
2(30010-301)-84 pgs. 8 16 24 53 74 95
3-5 4 8 12 24 32 40
6-10 3 6 9 19 25 32
11-20 2 4 6 14 18 22
21-30 2 4 6 9 11 14
31-43 1 2 3 5 7 9
44-54: Mighty Mouse-c/s in all 2 4 6 8 10 12

NOTE: *Reprints: #4-12, 38, 40, 47. (See March of Comics #379, 393, 412, 435)*

NEW TESTAMENT STORIES VISUALIZED
Standard Publishing Co.: 1946 - 1947

"New Testament Heroes–Acts of Apostles Visualized, Book I"
"New Testament Heroes–Acts of Apostles Visualized, Book II"
"Parables Jesus Told" Set.... 16 32 48 92 126 160

NOTE: *All three are contained in a cardboard case, illustrated on front and info about the set.*

NEW TITANS, THE (Formerly The New Teen Titans)
DC Comics: No. 50, Dec, 1988 - No. 130, Feb, 1996 ($1.75/$2.25)

50-Perez-c/a begins; new origin Wonder Girl 6.00
51-59: 50-55-Painted-c. 55-Nightwing (Dick Grayson) forces Danny Chase to resign; Batman app. in flashback, Wonder Girl becomes Troia 3.00
60,61: 60-A Lonely Place of Dying Part 2 continues from Batman #440; new Robin tie-in; Timothy Drake app. 61-A Lonely Place of Dying Part 4 3.00
62-99,101-124,126-130: 62-65: Deathstroke the Terminator app. 65-Tim Drake (Robin) app. 70-1st Deathstroke solo cover/sty. 71-(44 pgs.)-10th anniversary issue; Deathstroke cameo. 72-79-Deathstroke in all: 74-Intro. Pantha. 79-Terra brought back to life; 1 panel cameo Team Titans (1st app.). Deathstroke in #80-84,86. 80-2nd full app. Team Titans. 83,84-Deathstroke kills his son, Jericho. 85-Team Titans app. 86-Deathstroke vs. Nightwing-c/story; last Deathstroke app. 87-New costume Nightwing. 90-92-Parts 2,5,8 Total Chaos (Team Titans). 115-(11/94) 2.50
100-($3.50, 52 pgs.)-Holo-grafx foil-c 3.50
125 (3.50)-wraparound-c 3.50
#0-(10/94) Zero Hour, released between #114 & 115 2.50
Annual 5-10 ('89-'94, 68 pgs.. 7-Armaggedon 2001 x-over; 1st full app. Teen (Team) Titans (new group). 8-Deathstroke app.; Eclipso app. (minor). 10-Elseworlds story 3.50
Annual 11 (1995, $3.95)-Year One story 4.00

NOTE: ***Perez*** *a-50-55p, 57,60p, 58,59,61(layouts); c-50-61, 62-67i, Annual 5i; co-plots-66.*

NEW TV FUNNIES (See New Funnies)

NEW TWO-FISTED TALES, THE
Dark Horse Comics/Byron Preiss: 1993 ($4.95, limited series, 52 pgs.)

1-Kurtzman-r & new-a 5.00

NOTE: ***Elsner*** *c-1i.* ***Kurtzman*** *c-1p, 2.*

NEW WARRIORS, THE (See Thor #411,412)
Marvel Comics: July, 1990 - No. 75, 1996 ($1.00/$1.25/$1.50)

1-Williamson-i; Bagley-c/a(p) in 1-13, Annual 1 5.00
1-Gold 2nd printing (7/91) 2.25
2-5: 1,3-Guice-c(i). 2-Williamson-c/a(i). 3.00
6-24,26-49,51-75: 7-Punisher cameo (last pg.). 8,9-Punisher app. 14-Darkhawk & Namor x-over. 17-Fantastic Four & Silver Surfer x-over. 19-Gideon (of X-Force) app. 28-Intro Turbo & Cardinal. 31-Cannonball & Warpath app. 42-Nova vs. Firelord. 46-Photo-c. 47-Bound-in S-M trading card sheet. 52-12 pg. ad insert. 62-Scarlet Spider-c/app. 70-Spider-Man-c/app. 72-Avengers-c/app. 2.25
25-($2.50, 52 pgs.)-Die-cut cover 2.50
40,60: 40-($2.25)-Gold foil collector's edition 2.50
50-($2.95, 52 pgs.)-Glow in the dark-c 3.00
Annual 1-4('91-'94,68 pgs.)-1-Origins all members; 3rd app. X-Force (cont'd from New Mutants Ann. #7 & cont'd in X-Men Ann. #15); x-over before X-Force #1. 3-Bagged w/card 3.00

NEW WARRIORS, THE
Marvel Comics: Oct, 1999 - No. 10, July, 2000 ($2.99/$2.50)

0-Wizard supplement; short story and preview sketchbook 2.25
1-($2.99) 3.00
2-10: 2-Two covers. 5-Generation X app. 9-Iron Man-c 2.50

NEW WAVE, THE
Eclipse Comics: 6/10/86 - No. 13, 3/87 (#1-8: bi-weekly, 20pgs; #9-13: monthly)

1-13:1-Origin, concludes #5. 6-Origin Megabyte. 8,9-The Heap returns. 13-Snyder-c 2.25
...Versus the Volunteers 3-D #1,2(4/87): 1-Snyder-c 2.50

NEW WORLD (See Comic Books, series I)

NEW WORLDS
Caliber: 1996 - No. 6 ($2.95/$3.95, 80 pgs., B&W, anthology)

1-6: 1-Mister X & other stories 4.00

NEW X-MEN (See X-Men *2nd series* #114-on)

NEW YORK GIANTS (See Thrilling True Story of the Baseball Giants)

NEW YORK STATE JOINT LEGISLATIVE COMMITTEE TO STUDY THE PUBLICATION OF COMICS, THE
N.Y. State Legislative Document: 1951, 1955

This document was referenced by Wertham for **Seduction of the Innocent.** Contains numerous repros from comics showing violence, sadism, torture, and sex. 1955 version (196p, No. 37, 2/23/55) - Sold for $180 in 1986.

NEW YORK, THE BIG CITY
Kitchen Sink Press: 1986 ($10.95, B&W); **DC Comics:** July, 2000 ($12.95, B&W)

nn-Will Eisner-s/a 13.00

NEW YORK WORLD'S FAIR (Also see Big Book of Fun & New Book of Fun)
National Periodical Publ.: 1939, 1940 (100 pgs.; cardboard covers)
(DC's 4th & 5th annuals)

1939-Scoop Scanlon, Superman (blond haired Superman on-c), Sandman, Zatara, Slam Bradley, Ginger Snap by Bob Kane begin; 1st published app. The Sandman (see Adventure #40 for his 1st drawn story); Vincent Sullivan-c; cover background by Guardineer
2100 4200 6300 14,700 30,000 –
1940-Batman, Hourman, Johnny Thunderbolt, Red, White & Blue & Hanko (by Creig Flessel) app.; Superman, Batman & Robin-c (1st time they all appear together); early Robin app.; 1st Burnley-c/a (per Burnley) 1128 2256 3384 7895 16,800 –

NOTE: *The 1939 edition was published 4/29/39 and released 4/30/39, the day the fair opened, at 25¢, and was first sold only at the fair. Since all other comics were 10¢, it didn't sell. Remaining copies were advertised beginning in the August issues of most DC comics for 25¢, but soon the price was dropped to 15¢. Everyone that sent a quarter through the mail for it received a free Superman #1 or a #2 to make up the dime difference. 15¢ stickers were placed over the 25¢ price. Four variations on the 15¢ stickers are known. The 1940 edition was published 5/11/40 and was priced at 15¢. It was a precursor to World's Best #1.*

NEW YORK: YEAR ZERO
Eclipse Comics: July, 1988 - No. 4, Oct, 1988 ($2.00, B&W, limited series)

1-4 2.25

NEXT MAN
Comico: Mar, 1985 - No. 5, Oct, 1985 ($1.50, color, Baxter paper)

1-5 2.25

NEXT MEN (See John Byrne's...)

NEXT NEXUS, THE
First Comics: Jan, 1989 - No. 4, April, 1989 ($1.95, limited series, Baxter paper)

1-4: Mike Baron scripts & Steve Rude-c/a. 2.25
TPB (10/89, $9.95) r/series 10.00

NEXUS (See First Comics Graphic Novel #4, 19 & The Next Nexus)
Capital Comics/First Comics No. 7 on: June, 1981 - No. 6, Mar, 1984; No. 7, Apr, 1985 - No. 80?, May, 1991 (Direct sales only, 36 pgs.; V2#1('83)-printed on Baxter paper)

1-B&W version; mag. size; w/double size poster 3 6 9 16 20 24
1-B&W 1981 limited edition; 500 copies printed and signed; same as above except this version has a 2-pg. poster & a pencil sketch on paperboard by Steve Rude
4 8 12 24 32 40
2-B&W, magazine size 2 4 6 11 14 18
3-B&W, magazine size; Brunner back-c; contains 33-1/3 rpm record ($2.95 price)
2 4 6 9 11 14
V2#1-Color version 4.00
2-49,51-80: 2-Nexus' origin begins. 67-Snyder-c/a 2.25
50-($3.50, 52 pgs.) 3.50

NOTE: ***Bissette*** *c-V2#29.* ***Giffen*** *c/a-V2#23.* ***Gulacy*** *c-1 (B&W), 2(B&W).* ***Mignola*** *c/a-V2#28.* ***Rude*** *c-3(B&W), V2#1-22, 24-27, 33-36, 39-42, 45-48, 50, 58-60, 75; a-1-3, V2#1-7, 8-16p, 18-22p, 24-27p, 33-36p, 39-42p, 45-48p, 50, 58, 59p, 60.* ***Paul Smith*** *a-V2#37, 38, 43, 44, 51-55p; c-V2#37, 38, 43, 44, 51-55.*

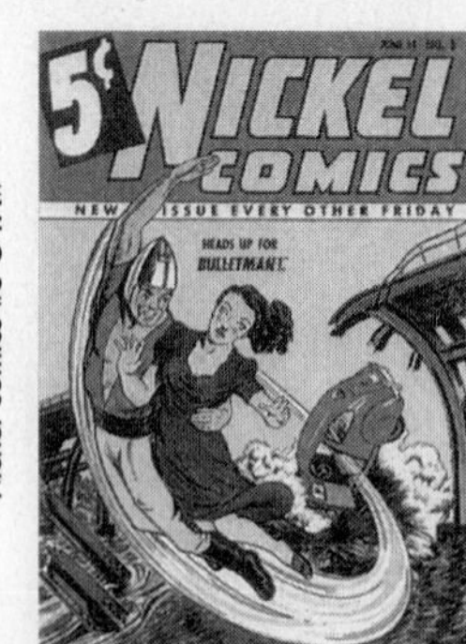

Nickel Comics #3 © FAW

Nick Fury, Agent of S.H.I.E.L.D. #16 © MAR

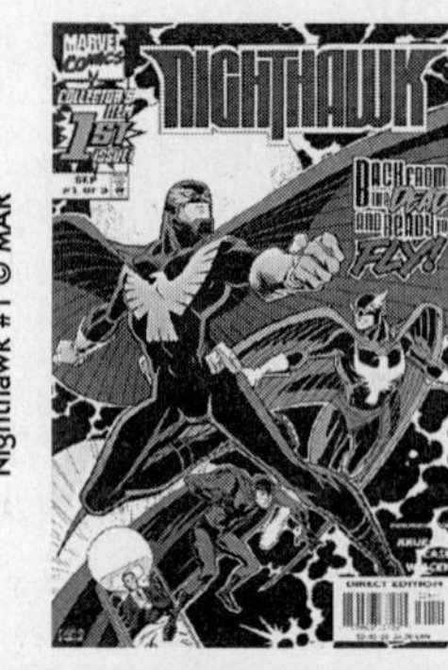

Nighthawk #1 © MAR

	GD 2.0	VG 4.0	FN 6.0	VF 8.0	VF/NM 9.0	NM- 9.2

NEXUS: ALIEN JUSTICE
Dark Horse Comics: Dec, 1992 - No. 3, Feb, 1993 ($3.95, limited series)
1-3: Mike Baron scripts & Steve Rude-c/a 4.00

NEXUS: EXECUTIONER'S SONG
Dark Horse Comics: June, 1996 - No. 4, Sept, 1996 ($2.95, limited series)
1-4: Mike Baron scripts & Steve Rude-c/a 3.00

NEXUS FILES
First Comics: 1989 ($4.50, color/16pgs. B&W, one-shot, squarebound, 52pgs.)
1-New Rude-a; info on Nexus 4.50

NEXUS: GOD CON
Dark Horse Comics: Apr, 1997 - No. 2, May, 1997 ($2.95, limited series)
1,2-Baron-s/Rude-c/a 3.00

NEXUS LEGENDS
First Comics: May, 1989 - No. 23, Mar, 1991 ($1.50, Baxter paper)\
1-23: R/1-3(Capital) & early First Comics issues w/new Rude covers #1-6,9,10 2.25

NEXUS MEETS MADMAN (...Special)
Dark Horse Comics: May, 1996 ($2.95, one-shot)
nn-Mike Baron & Mike Allred scripts, Steve Rude-c/a. 3.00

NEXUS: NIGHTMARE IN BLUE
Dark Horse Comics: July, 1997 - No. 4, Oct, 1997 ($2.95, limited series)
1-4: 1,2,4-Adam Hughes-c 3.00

NEXUS: THE LIBERATOR
Dark Horse Comics: Aug, 1992 - No. 4, Nov, 1992 ($2.95, limited series)
1-4 3.00

NEXUS: THE ORIGIN
Dark Horse Comics: July, 1996 ($3.95, one-shot)
nn-Mike Baron- scripts, Steve Rude-c/a. 4.00

NEXUS: THE WAGES OF SIN
Dark Horse Comics: Mar, 1995 - No. 4, June, 1995 ($2.95, limited series)
1-4 3.00

NFL SUPERPRO
Marvel Comics: Oct, 1991 - No. 12, Sept, 1992 ($1.00)
1-12: 1-Spider-Man-c/app. 2.25
Special Edition (9/91, $2.00) Jusko painted-c 3.00
Super Bowl Edition (3/91, squarebound) Jusko painted-c 4.00

NICKEL COMICS
Dell Publishing Co.: 1938 (Pocket size - 7-1/2x5-1/2")(68 pgs.)
1- "Bobby & Chip" by Otto Messmer, Felix the Cat artist. Contains some English reprints
78 156 234 488 732 975

NICKEL COMICS
Fawcett Publications: May, 1940 - No. 8, Aug, 1940 (36 pgs.; Bi-Weekly; 5¢)
1-Origin/1st app. Bulletman 400 800 1200 2600 4000 5400
2 128 256 384 800 1200 1600
3 96 192 288 600 900 1200
4-The Red Gaucho begins 80 160 240 500 750 1000
5-7 76 152 228 475 713 950
8-World's Fair-c; Bulletman moved to Master Comics #7 in October (scarce)
88 176 264 550 825 1100
NOTE: *Beck c-5-8. Jack Binder c-1-4. Bondage c-5. Bulletman c-1-8.*

NICK FURY, AGENT OF SHIELD (See Fury, Marvel Spotlight #31 & Shield)
Marvel Comics Group: 6/68 - No. 15, 11/69; No. 16, 11/70 - No. 18, 3/71
1 11 22 33 77 114 150
2-4: 4-Origin retold 7 14 21 46 63 80
5-Classic-c 7 14 21 50 68 85
6,7: 7-Salvador Dali painting swipe 5 10 15 33 44 55
8-11,13: 9-Hate Monger begins, ends #11. 10-Smith layouts/pencil. 11-Smith-c.
13-1st app. Super-Patriot; last 12¢ issue 3 6 9 19 25 32
12-Smith-c/a 3 7 10 21 28 35
14-Begin 15¢ issues 3 6 9 18 23 28
15-1st app. & death of Bullseye-c/story(11/69); Nick Fury shot & killed; last 15¢ issue
6 12 18 43 59 75
16-18-(25¢, 52 pgs.)-r/Str. Tales #135-143 3 6 9 16 20 24
TPB (May 2000, $19.95) r/ Strange Tales #150-168 20.00
...: Who is Scorpio? TPB (11/00, $12.95) r/#1-3,5; Steranko-c 13.00
NOTE: *Adkins a-3i. Craig a-10i. Sid Greene a-12i. Kirby a-16-18r. Springer a-4, 6, 7, 8p, 9, 10p, 11; c-8, 9. Steranko a(p)-1-3, 5; c-1-7.*

NICK FURY AGENT OF SHIELD (Also see Strange Tales #135)
Marvel Comics: Dec, 1983 - No. 2, Jan, 1984 (2.00, 52 pgs., Baxter paper)
1,2-r/Nick Fury #1-4; new Steranko-c 3.50

NICK FURY, AGENT OF S.H.I.E.L.D.
Marvel Comics: Sept, 1989 - No. 47, May, 1993 ($1.50/$1.75)
V2#1-26,30-47: 10-Capt. America app. 13-Return of The Yellow Claw. 15-Fantastic Four app. 30,31-Deathlok app. 36-Cage app. 37-Woodgod c/story. 38-41-Flashes back to pre-Shield days after WWII. 44-Capt. America-c/s. 45-Viper-c/s. 46-Gideon x-over 2.25
27-29-Wolverine-c/stories 2.50
NOTE: *Alan Grant scripts-11. Guice a(p)-20-23, 25, 26; c-20-28.*

NICK FURY VS. S.H.I.E.L.D.
Marvel Comics: June, 1988 - No. 6, Nov, 1988 ($3.50, 52 pgs, deluxe format)
1,2: 1-Steranko-c. 2-(Low print run) Sienkiewicz-c 5.00
3-6 4.00

NICK HALIDAY (Thrill of the Sea)
Argo: May, 1956
1-Daily & Sunday strip-r by Petree 8 16 24 46 58 70

NIGHT AND THE ENEMY (Graphic Novel)
Comico: 1988 (8-1/2x11") ($11.95, color, 80 pgs.)
1-Harlan Ellison scripts/Ken Steacy-c/a; r/Epic Illustrated & new-a (1st & 2nd printings) 12.00
1-Limited edition ($39.95) 40.00

NIGHT BEFORE CHRISTMAS, THE (See March of Comics No. 152 in the Promotional Comics section)

NIGHT BEFORE CHRISTMASK, THE
Dark Horse Comics: Nov, 1994 ($9.95, one-shot)
nn-Hardcover book; The Mask; Rick Geary-c/a 10.00

NIGHTBREED (See Clive Barker's Nightbreed)

NIGHTCRAWLER
Marvel Comics Group: Nov, 1985 - No. 4, Feb, 1986 (Mini-series from X-Men)
1-4: 1-Cockrum-c/a 3.50

NIGHTCRAWLER (Volume 2)
Marvel Comics: Feb, 2002 - No. 4, May, 2002 ($2.50, limited series)
1-4-Matt Smith-a 2.50

NIGHTFALL: THE BLACK CHRONICLES
DC Comics (Homage): Dec, 1999 - No. 3, Feb, 2000 ($2.95, limited series)
1-3-Coker-a/Gilmore-s 3.00

NIGHT FORCE, THE (See New Teen Titans #21)
DC Comics: Aug, 1982 - No. 14, Sept, 1983 (60¢)
1 4.00
2-14: 13-Origin Baron Winter. 14-Nudity panels 3.00
NOTE: *Colan c/a-1-14p. Giordano c-1i, 2i, 4i, 5i, 7i, 12i.*

NIGHT FORCE
DC Comics: Dec, 1996 - No. 12, Nov, 1997 ($2.25)
1-12: 1-3-Wolfman-s/Anderson-a(p). 8-"Convergence" part 2 2.25

NIGHT GLIDER
Topps Comics (Kirbyverse): April, 1993 ($2.95, one-shot)
1-Kirby c-1, Heck-a; polybagged w/Kirbychrome trading card 3.00

NIGHTHAWK
Marvel Comics: Sept, 1998 - No. 3, Nov, 1998 ($2.99, mini-series)
1-3-Krueger-s; Daredevil app. 3.00

NIGHTINGALE, THE
Henry H. Stansbury Once-Upon-A-Time Press, Inc.: 1948 (10¢, 7-1/4x10-1/4", 14 pgs., 1/2 B&W)
(Very Rare)-Low distribution; distributed to Westchester County & Bronx, N.Y. only; used in **Seduction of the Innocent**, pg. 312,313 as the 1st and only "good" comic book ever published. Ill. by Dong Kingman; 1,500 words of text, printed on high quality paper & no word balloons. Copyright registered 10/22/48, distributed week of 12/5/48. (By Hans Christian Andersen)
Estimated value........ $250

NIGHT MAN, THE (See Sludge #1)
Malibu Comics (Ultraverse): Oct, 1993 - No. 23, Aug, 1995 ($1.95/$2.50)
1-($2.50, 48 pgs.)-Rune flip-c/story by B. Smith (3 pgs.) 2.50
1-Ultra-Limited silver foil-c 6.00
2-15, 17: 3-Break-Thru x-over; Freex app. 4-Origin Firearm (2 pgs.) by Chaykin. 6-TNTNT app. 8-1st app. Teknight 2.50
16 ($3.50)-flip book (Ultraverse Premiere #11) 3.50
...:The Pilgrim Conundrum Saga (1/95, $3.95, 68 pgs.)-Strangers app. 4.00

Nightmare #1 © Skywald

Nightside #2 © MAR

Night Terrors #1 © Berni Wrightson & Chanting Monks Studios

GD VG FN VF VF/NM NM-
2.0 4.0 6.0 8.0 9.0 9.2

GD VG FN VF VF/NM NM-
2.0 4.0 6.0 8.0 9.0 9.2

18-23: 22-Loki-c/a 2.50
Infinity ($1.50) 2.50
...Vs. Wolverine #0-Kelley Jones-c; mail in offer 1 3 4 6 8 10
*NOTE: **Zeck** a-16.*

NIGHT MAN, THE
Malibu Comics (Ultraverse): Sept, 1995 - No.4, Dec, 1995 ($1.50, lim. series)
1-4: Post Black September storyline 2.50

NIGHT MAN, THE /GAMBIT
Malibu Comics (Ultraverse): Mar, 1996 - No. 3, May, 1996 ($1.95, lim. series)
0-Limited Premium Edition 4.00
1-3: David Quinn scripts in all. 3-Rhiannon discovered to be The Night Man's mother 2.50

NIGHTMARE
Ziff-Davis (Approved Comics)/St. John No. 3: Summer, 1952 - No. 3, Winter, 1952, 53 (Painted-c)
1-1 pg. Kinstler-a; Tuska-a(2) 55 110 165 330 495 660
2-Kinstler-a-Poe's "Pit & the Pendulum" 40 80 120 240 340 440
3-Kinstler-a 35 70 105 201 288 370

NIGHTMARE (Weird Horrors #1-9) (Amazing Ghost Stories #14 on)
St. John Publishing Co.: No. 10, Dec, 1953 - No. 13, Aug, 1954
10-Reprints Ziff-Davis Weird Thrillers #2 w/new Kubert-c plus 2 pgs. Kinstler-a; Anderson, Colan & Toth-a 55 110 165 330 495 660
11-Krigstein-a; painted-c; Poe adapt., "Hop Frog" 40 80 120 240 340 440
12-Kubert bondage-c; adaptation of Poe's "The Black Cat"; Cannibalism story 39 78 117 230 325 420
13-Reprints Z-D Weird Thrillers #3 with new cover; Powell-a(2), Tuska-a; Baker-c 29 58 87 164 232 300

NIGHTMARE (Magazine) (Also see Psycho)
Skywald Publishing Corp.: Dec, 1970 - No. 23, Feb, 1975 (B&W, 68 pgs.)
1-Everett-a; Heck-a; Shores-a 7 14 21 51 71 90
2-5,8,9: 2,4-Decapitation story. 5-Nazi-s; Boris Karloff 4 pg. photo/text-s. 8-Features E.C. movie "Tales From the Crypt"; reprints some E.C. comics panels. 9-Wrightson-a; bondage-c; 1st Lovecraft Saggoth Chronicles/Cthulhu 4 8 12 27 36 45
6-Kaluta-a; Jeff Jones-c, photo & interview; 1st Living Gargoyle; Love Witch-s w/nudity; Boris Karloff-s 4 8 12 29 40 50
7 3 7 10 21 28 35
10-Wrightson-a (1 pg.); Princess of Earth-c/s; Edward & Mina Sartyros, the Human Gargoyles series continues from Psycho #8 4 8 12 29 40 50
11-19: 12-Excessive gore, severed heads. 13-Lovecraft-s. 15-Dracula-c/s. 17-Vampires issue; Autobiography of a Vampire series begins 3 6 9 18 24 30
20-John Byrne's 1st artwork (2 pgs.)(8/74); severed head-c; Hitler app. 6 12 18 40 55 70
21-23: 21-(1974 Summer Special)-Kaluta-a. 22-Tomb of Horror issue. 23-(1975 Winter Special) 4 8 12 22 30 38
Annual 1(1972)-Squarebound; B. Jones-a 4 8 12 22 30 38
Winter Special 1(1973)-All new material 3 6 9 18 24 30
Yearbook nn(1974)-B. Jones, Reese, Wildey-a 3 6 9 18 24 30
*NOTE: **Adkins** a-5. **Boris** c-2, 3, 5 (#4 is not by Boris). **Buckler** a-3, 15. **Byrne** a-20p. **Everett** a-1, 2, 4, 5, 12. **Jeff Jones** a-6, 21r(Psycho #6); c-6. **Katz** a-3, 5, 21. **Reese** a-4, 5. **Wildey** a-4, 5, 6, 21, '74 Yearbook. **Wrightson** a-9, 10.*

NIGHTMARE (Alex Nino's)
Innovation Publishing: 1989 ($1.95)
1-Alex Nino-a 2.25

NIGHTMARE
Marvel Comics: Dec, 1994 - No. 4, Mar, 1995 ($1.95, limited series)
1-4 2.25

NIGHTMARE & CASPER (See Harvey Hits #71) (Casper & Nightmare #6 on) (See Casper The Friendly Ghost #19)
Harvey Publications: Aug, 1963 - No. 5, Aug, 1964 (25¢)
1-All reprints? 9 18 27 60 85 110
2-5: All reprints? 5 10 15 36 48 60

NIGHTMARE ON ELM STREET, A (See Freddy Krueger's...)

NIGHTMARES (See Do You Believe in Nightmares)

NIGHTMARES
Eclipse Comics: May, 1985 - No. 2, May, 1985 ($1.75, Baxter paper)
1,2 3.00

NIGHTMARE THEATER
Chaos! Comics: Nov, 1997 - No. 4, Nov, 1997 ($2.50, mini-series)
1-4-Horror stories by various; Wrightson-a 2.50

NIGHTMARK: BLOOD & HONOR
Alpha Productions: 1994 - No. 3, 1994 ($2.50, B&W, mini-series)
1,2 2.50

NIGHTMARK MYSTERY SPECIAL
Alpha Productions: Jan, 1994 ($2.50, B&W)
1 2.50

NIGHTMASK
Marvel Comics Group: Nov, 1986 - No. 12, Oct, 1987
1-12 2.25

NIGHT MASTER
Silverwolf: Feb, 1987 ($1.50, B&W)
1-Tim Vigil-c/a 3.00

NIGHT MUSIC (See Eclipse Graphic Album Series, The Magic Flute)
Eclipse Comics: Dec, 1984 - No. 11, 1990 ($1.75/$3.95/$4.95, Baxter paper)
1-7: 3-Russell's Jungle Book adapt. 4,5-Pelleas And Melisande (double titled) 6-Salomé (double titled). 7-Red Dog #1 2.25
8-($3.95) Ariane and Bluebeard 4.00
9-11-($4.95) The Magic Flute; Russell adapt. 5.00

NIGHT NURSE
Marvel Comics Group: Nov, 1972 - No. 4, May, 1973
1 11 22 33 77 114 150
2-4 8 16 24 55 78 100

NIGHT OF MYSTERY
Avon Periodicals: 1953 (no month) (one-shot)
nn-1 pg. Kinstler-a, Hollingsworth-c 44 88 132 264 395 525

NIGHT OF THE GRIZZLY, THE (See Movie Classics)

NIGHTRAVEN (See Marvel Graphic Novel)

NIGHT RIDER (Western)
Marvel Comics Group: Oct, 1974 - No. 6, Aug, 1975
1: 1-6 reprint Ghost Rider #1-6 (#1-origin) 2 4 6 10 13 16
2-6 1 3 4 6 8 10

NIGHT'S CHILDREN: THE VAMPIRE
Millenium: July, 1995 - No. 2, Aug, 1995 ($2.95, B&W)
1,2: Wendy Snow-Lang story & art 3.00

NIGHTSIDE
Marvel Comics: Dec, 2001 - No. 4, Mar, 2002 ($2.99)
1-4: 1-Weinberg-s/Derenick-a; intro Sydney Taine 3.00

NIGHTS INTO DREAMS (Based on video game)
Archie Comics: Feb, 1998 -No. 6, Oct, 1998 ($1.75, limited series)
1-6 2.25

NIGHTSTALKERS (Also see Midnight Sons Unlimited)
Marvel Comics (Midnight Sons #14 on): Nov, 1992 - No. 18, Apr, 1994 ($1.75)
1-($2.75, 52 pgs.)-Polybagged w/poster; part 5 of Rise of the Midnight Sons storyline; Garney/Palmer-c/a begins; Hannibal King, Blade & Frank Drake begin (see Tomb of Dracula for & Dr. Strange) 3.00
2-9,11-18: 5-Punisher app. 7-Ghost Rider app. 8,9-Morbius app. 14-Spot varnish-c. 14,15-Siege of Darkness Pts 1 & 9 2.25
10-($2.25)-Outer-c is a Darkhold envelope made of black parchment w/gold ink; Midnight Massacre part 1 2.50

NIGHT TERRORS, THE
Chanting Monks Studios: 2000 ($2.75, B&W)
1-Bernie Wrightson-c; short stories, one by Wrightson-s/a 2.75

NIGHT THRASHER (Also see The New Warriors)
Marvel Comics: Aug, 1993 - No. 21, Apr, 1995 ($1.75/$1.95)
1-($2.95, 52 pgs.)-Red holo-grafx foil-c; origin 3.00
2-21: 2-Intro Tantrum. 3-Gideon (of X-Force) app. 10-Bound-in trading card sheet; Iron Man app. 15-Hulk app. 2.25

NIGHT THRASHER: FOUR CONTROL
Marvel Comics: Oct, 1992 - No. 4, Jan, 1993 ($2.00, limited series)
1-4: 2-Intro Tantrum. 3-Gideon (of X-Force) app. 2.25

NIGHT TRIBES
DC Comics (WildStorm): July, 1999 ($4.95, one-shot)
1-Golden & Sniegoski-s/Chin-a 5.00

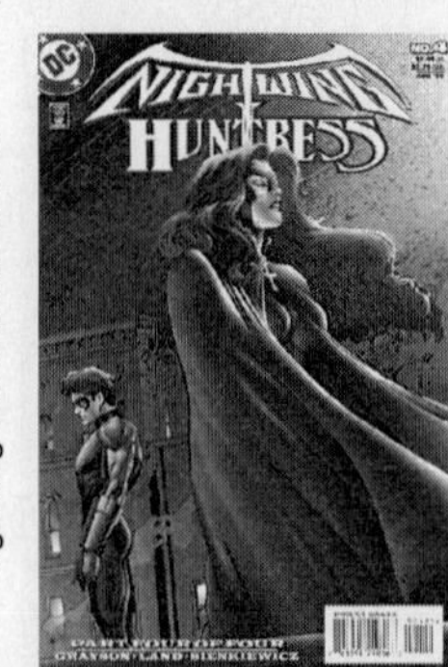

Nightwing and Huntress #4 © DC

9-11: Emergency Relief © Alternative Comics

Ninja Boy #3 © Ale Garza

GD 2.0 | VG 4.0 | FN 6.0 | VF 8.0 | VF/NM 9.0 | NM- 9.2

NIGHTVEIL (Also see Femforce)
Americomics/AC Comics: Nov, 1984 - No. 7, 1987 ($1.75)

1-7 2.25
...'s Cauldron Of Horror 1 (1989, B&W)-Kubert, Powell, Wood-r plus new Nightveil story 3.00
...'s Cauldron Of Horror 2 (1990, $2.95, B&W)-Pre-code horror-r by Kubert & Powell 3.00
...'s Cauldron Of Horror 3 (1991) 3.00
Special 1 ('88, $1.95)-Kaluta-c 2.25
One Shot ('96, $5.95)-Flip book w/ Colt 6.00

NIGHTWATCH
Marvel Comics: Apr, 1994 - No. 12, Mar, 1995 ($1.50)

1-($2.95)-Collectors edition; foil-c; Ron Lim-c/a begins; Spider-Man app. 3.00
1-12-Regular edition. 2-Bound-in S-M trading card sheet; 5,6-Venom-c & app. 7,11-Cardiac app. 2.25

NIGHTWING (Also see New Teen Titans, New Titans, Showcase '93 #11,12, Tales of the New Teen Titans & Teen Titans Spotlight)
DC Comics: Sept, 1995 - No. 4, Dec, 1995 ($2.25, limited series)

1-Dennis O'Neil story/Greg Land-a in all 5.00
2-4 4.00
...: Alfred's Return (7/95, $3.50) Giordano-a 4.00
...Ties That Bind (1997, $12.95, TPB) r/mini-series & Alfred's Return 13.00

NIGHTWING
DC Comics: Oct, 1996 - Present ($1.95/$1.99/$2.25)

1-Chuck Dixon scripts & Scott McDaniel-c/a 2 4 6 9 11 12
2,3 6.00
4-10: 6-Robin-c/app. 4.00
11-20: 13-15-Batman app. 19,20-Cataclysm pts. 2,11 3.00
21-49,51-64: 23-Green Arrow app. 26-29-Huntress-c/app. 30-Superman-c/app. 35-39-No Man's Land. 41-Land/Geraci-a begins. 46-Begin $2.25-c. 47-Texiera-c. 52-Catwoman-c/app. 54-Shrike app. 2.50
50-($3.50) Nightwing battles Torque 3.50
65-74,76-89: 65,66-Bruce Wayne: Murderer x-over pt. 3,9. 68,69: B.W.: Fugitive pt. 6,9. 70-Last Dixon-s. 71-Devin Grayson-s begin. 81-Batgirl vs. Deathstroke 2.50
75-(1/03, $2.95) Intro. Tarantula 3.00
#1,000,000 (11/98) teams with future Batman 2.25
Annual 1(1997, $3.95) Pulp Heroes 4.00
...Eighty Page Giant 1 (12/00, $5.95) Intro. of Hella; Dixon-s/Haley-c 6.00
...: A Darker Shade of Justice (2001, $19.95, TPB) r/#30-39,Secret Files #1 20.00
...: A Knight in Blüdhaven (1998, $14.95, TPB) r/#1-8 15.00
...: Love and Bullets (2000, $17.95, TPB) r/#1/2, 19,21,22,24-29 18.00
...: Our Worlds at War (9/01, $2.95) Jae Lee-c 3.00
...: Rough Justice (1999, $17.95, TPB) r/#9-18 18.00
Secret Files 1 (10/99, $4.95) Origin-s and pin-ups 5.00
...: The Hunt for Oracle (2003, $14.95, TPB) r/#41-46 & Birds of Prey #20,21 15.00
...: The Target (2001, $5.95) McDaniel-c/a 6.00
Wizard 1/2 (Mail offer) 5.00

NIGHTWING (See Tangent Comics/ Nightwing)

NIGHTWING AND HUNTRESS
DC Comics: May, 1998 - No. 4, Aug, 1998 ($1.95, limited series)

1-4-Grayson-s/Land & Sienkiewicz-a 2.50
TPB (2003, $9.95) r/#1/4; cover gallery 10.00

NIGHTWINGS (See DC Science Fiction Graphic Novel)

NIKKI, WILD DOG OF THE NORTH (Disney, see Movie Comics)
Dell Publishing Co.: No. 1226, Sept, 1961

Four Color 1226-Movie, photo-c 6 12 18 40 55 70

9-11 - ARTISTS RESPOND
Dark Horse Comics: 2002 ($9.95, TPB, proceeds donated to charities)

Volume 1-Short stories about the September 11 tragedies by various Dark Horse, Chaos! and Image writers and artists; Eric Drooker-c 10.00

9-11: EMERGENCY RELIEF
Alternative Comics: 2002 ($14.95, TPB, proceeds donated to the Red Cross)

nn-Short stories by various inc. Pekar, Eisner, Hester, Oeming, Noto; Cho-c 15.00

9-11 - THE WORLD'S FINEST COMIC BOOK WRITERS AND ARTISTS TELL STORIES TO REMEMBER
DC Comics: 2002 ($9.95, TPB, proceeds donated to charities)

Volume 2-Short stories about the September 11 tragedies by various DC, MAD, and WildStorm writers and artists ; Alex Ross-c 10.00

NINE RINGS OF WU-TANG
Image Comics: July, 1999 - No. 5, July, 2000 ($2.95)

Preview (7/99, $5.00, B&W) 5.00
1-5: 1-(11/99, $2.95) Clayton Henry-a 3.00
Tower Records Variant-c 5.00
Wizard #0 Prelude 2.25
TPB (1/01, $19.95) r/#1-5, Preview & Prelude; sketchbook & cover gallery 20.00

1963
Image Comics (Shadowline Ink): Apr, 1993 - No. 6, Oct, 1993 ($1.95, lim. series)

1-6: Alan Moore scripts; Veitch, Bissette & Gibbons-a(p) 2.25
1-Gold 3.00

*NOTE: **Bissette** a-2-4; **Gibbons** a-1i, 2i, 6i; c-2.*

1984 (Magazine) (1994 #11 on)
Warren Publishing Co.: June, 1978 - No. 10, Jan, 1980 ($1.50, B&W with color inserts, mature content with nudity; 84 pgs. except #4 has 92 pgs.)

1-Nino-a in all; Mutant World begins by Corben 2 4 6 12 16 20
2-10: 4-Rex Havoc begins. 7-1st Ghita of Alizarr by Thorne. 9-1st Starfire 2 4 6 8 10 12

NOTE: ***Alcala** a-1-3,5,7i. **Corben** a-1-8; c-1,2. **Nebres** a-1-8,10. **Thorne** a-7,8,10. **Wood** a-1,2,5i.*

1994 (Formerly 1984) (Magazine)
Warren Publishing Co.: No. 11, Feb, 1980 - No. 29, Feb, 1983 (B&W with color; mature; #11-(84 pgs.); #12-16,18-21,24-(76 pgs.); #17,22,23,25-29-(68 pgs.)

11,17,18,20,22,23,29: 11,17-8 pgs. color insert. 18-Giger-c. 20-1st Diana Jacklighter Manhuntress by Maroto. 22-1st Sigmund Pavlov by Nino; 1st Ariel Hart by Hsu. 23-All Nino issue 2 4 6 8 10 12
12-16,19,21,24-28: 21-1st app. Angel by Nebres. 27-The Warhawks return 1 2 3 5 6 8

*NOTE: **Corben** c-26. **Maroto** a-20, 21, 24-28. **Nebres** a-11-13, 15, 16, 18, 21, 22, 25, 28. **Nino** a-11-19, 20(2), 21, 25, 26, 28; c-21. **Redondo** c-20. **Thorne** a-11-14, 17-21, 24-26, 28, 29.*

NINE VOLT
Image Comics (Top Cow Productions): July, 1997 - No. 4, Oct, 1997 ($2.50)

1-4 2.50

NINJA BOY
DC Comics (WildStorm): Oct, 2001 - No. 6, Mar, 2002 ($3.50/$2.95)

1-($3.50) Ale Garza-a/c 3.50
2-6-($2.95) 3.00
...: Faded Dreams TPB (2003, $14.95) r/#1-6; sketch pages 15.00

NINJA HIGH SCHOOL (1st series)
Antarctic Press: 1986 - No. 3, Aug, 1987 (B&W)

1-Ben Dunn-s/c/a; early Manga series 2 4 6 10 12 15
2,3 1 3 4 6 8 10

NINJAK (See Bloodshot #6, 7 & Deathmate)
Valiant/Acclaim Comics (Valiant) No. 16 on: Feb, 1994 - No. 26, Nov. 1995 ($2.25/$2.50)

1 ($3.50)-Chromium-c; Quesada-c/a(p) in #1-3 3.50
1-Gold 5.00
2-13: 3-Batman, Spawn & Random (from X-Factor) app. as costumes at party (cameo). 4-w/bound-in trading card. 5,6-X-O app. 2.50
0,00,14-26: 14-(4/95)-Begin $2.50-c. 0-(6/95, $2.50). 00-(6/95, $2.50) 2.50
Yearbook 1 (1994, $3.95) 4.00

NINJAK
Acclaim Comics (Valiant Heroes): V2#1, Mar, 1997 -No. 12, Feb, 1998 ($2.50)

V2#1-12: 1-Intro new Ninjak; 1st app. Brutakon; Kurt Busiek scripts begin; painted variant-c exists. 2-1st app. Karnivor & Zeer. 3-1st app. Gigantik, Shurikai, & Nixie. 4-Origin; 1st app. Yasuiti Motomiya; intro The Dark Dozen; Colin King cameo. 9-Copycat-c 2.50

NINTENDO COMICS SYSTEM (Also see Adv. of Super Mario Brothers)
Valiant Comics: Feb, 1990 - No. 9, Oct, 1991 ($4.95, card stock-c, 68pgs.)

1-9: 1-Featuring Game Boy, Super Mario, Clappwall. 3-Layton-c. 5-8-Super Mario Bros. 9-Dr. Mario 1st app. 5.00

N.I.O.
Acclaim Comics: Nov, 1998 - No. 4, Feb, 1999 ($2.50, limited series)

1-4-Bury-s 2.50

NOAH'S ARK
Spire Christian Comics/Fleming H. Revell Co.: 1973 (35/49¢)

nn-By Al Hartley 1 3 4 6 8 10

NOBLE CAUSES
Image Comics: July, 2001; Jan, 2002 - No. 4, May, 2002 ($2.95)

...First Impressions (7/01) Intro. the Noble family; Faerber-s 3.00
1-4: 1-(1/02) Back-up-s with Conner-a. 2-Igle back-up-a. 2-4-Two covers 3.00
...: Extended Family (5/03, $6.95) short stories by various 7.00

No Honor #2 © TCOW

Northwest Mounties #2 © STJ

Nova #20 © MAR

GD VG FN VF VF/NM NM-
2.0 4.0 6.0 8.0 9.0 9.2

Vol. 1: In Sickness and in Health (2003, $12.95) r/#1-4 & ...First Impresssions 13.00

NOBLE CAUSES: DISTANT RELATIVES
Image Comics: Jul, 2003 - No. 4, Oct, 2003 ($2.95, B&W, limited series)
1-4-Faerber-s/Richardson & Ponce-a 3.00

NOBLE CAUSES: FAMILY SECRETS
Image Comics: Oct, 2002 - No. 4, Jan, 2003 ($2.95, limited series)
1-4-Faerber-s/Oeming-c. 1-Variant cover by Walker. 2,3-Valentino var-c. 4-Hester var-c 3.00

NOBODY (Amado, Cho & Adlard's...)
Oni Press: Nov, 1998 - No. 4, Feb, 1999 ($2.95, B&W, mini-series)
1-4 3.00

NOCTURNALS, THE
Malibu Comics (Bravura): Jan, 1995 - No. 6, Aug, 1995 ($2.95, limited series)
1-6: Dan Brereton painted-c/a & scripts 3.00
1-Glow-in-the-Dark premium edition 5.00

NOCTURNALS, THE
Dark Horse Comics/Oni Press: one-shots and trade paperbacks
Black Planet TPB (Oni Press, 1998, $19.95) r/#1-6 (Malibu Comics series) 20.00
Troll Bridge (Oni Press, 2000, $4.95, B&W & orange) Brereton-s/painted-c; art by Brereton, Chin, Art Adams, Sakai, Timm, Warren, Thompson, Purcell, Stephens and others 5.00
Unhallowed Eve TPB (Oni Press, 10/02, $9.95) r/Witching Hour & Troll Bridge one-shots 10.00
Witching Hour (Dark Horse, 5/98, $4.95) Brereton-s/a; reprints DHP stories + 8 new pgs. 5.00

NOCTURNALS: THE DARK FOREVER
Oni Press: Jul, 2001 -No. 3, Feb, 2002 ($2.95, limited series)
1-3-Brereton-s/painted-a/c 3.00
TPB (5/02, $9.95) r/#1-3; afterword & pin-ups by Alex Ross 10.00

NOCTURNE
Marvel Comics: June, 1995 - No. 4, Sept. 1995 ($1.50, limited series)
1-4 2.25

NO ESCAPE (Movie)
Marvel Comics: June, 1994 - No. 3, Aug, 1994 ($1.50)
1-3: Based on movie 2.25

NO HONOR
Image Comics (Top Cow): Feb, 2001 - No. 4, July, 2001 ($2.50)
Preview (12/00, B&W) Silvestri-c 2.25
1-4-Avery-s/Crain-a 2.50
TPB (8/03, $12.99) r/#1-4; intro. by Straczynski 13.00

NOMAD (See Captain America #180)
Marvel Comics: Nov, 1990 - No. 4, Feb, 1991 ($1.50, limited series)
1-4: 1,4-Captain America app. 2.25

NOMAD
Marvel Comics: V2#1, May, 1992 - No. 25, May, 1994 ($1.75)
V2#1-25: 1-Has gatefold-c w/map/wanted poster. 4-Deadpool x-over. 5-Punisher vs. Nomad-c/story. 6-Punisher & Daredevil-c/story cont'd in Punisher War Journal #48. 7-Gambit-c/story. 10-Red Wolf app. 21-Man-Thing-c/story. 25-Bound-in trading card sheet 2.25

NOMAN (See Thunder Agents)
Tower Comics: Nov, 1966 - No. 2, March, 1967 (25¢, 68 pgs.)
1-Wood/Williamson-c; Lightning begins; Dynamo cameo; Kane-a(p) & Whitney-a
9 18 27 60 85 110
2-Wood-c only; Dynamo x-over; Whitney-a 6 12 18 38 52 65

NONE BUT THE BRAVE (See Movie Classics)

NOODNIK COMICS (See Pinky the Egghead)
Comic Media/Mystery/Biltmore: Dec, 1953; No. 2, Feb, 1954 - No. 5, Aug, 1954
3-D(1953, 25¢; Comic Media)(#1)-Came w/glasses 33 66 99 190 270 350
2-5 9 18 27 49 62 75

NORMALMAN (See Cerebus the Aardvark #55, 56)
Aardvark-Vanaheim/Renegade Press #6 on: Jan, 1984 - No. 12, Dec, 1985 ($1.70/$2.00)
1-12: 1-Jim Valentino-c/a in all. 6-12 ($2.00, B&W): 10-Cerebus cameo; Sim-a (2 pgs.) 2.25
...3-D 1 (Annual, 1986, $2.25) 2.25

NORMALMAN-MEGATON MAN SPECIAL
Image Comics: Aug, 1994 ($2.50, color)
1 2.50

NORTH AVENUE IRREGULARS (See Walt Disney Showcase #49)

NORTHSTAR
Marvel Comics: Apr, 1994 - No. 4, July, 1994 ($1.75, mini-series)
1-4: Character from Alpha Flight 2.25

NORTH TO ALASKA
Dell Publishing Co.: No. 1155, Dec, 1960
Four Color 1155-Movie, John Wayne photo-c 18 36 54 131 191 250

NORTHWEST MOUNTIES (Also see Approved Comics #12)
Jubilee Publications/St. John: Oct, 1948 - No. 4, July, 1949
1-Rose of the Yukon by Matt Baker; Walter Johnson-a; Lubbers-c
46 92 138 276 413 550
2-Baker-a; Lubbers-c. Ventrilo app. 39 78 117 230 325 420
3-Bondage-c, Baker-a; Sky Chief, K-9 app. 40 80 120 240 340 440
4-Baker-c/a(2 pgs.); Blue Monk & The Desperado app.
40 80 120 240 340 440

NO SLEEP 'TIL DAWN
Dell Publishing Co.: No. 831, Aug, 1957
Four Color 831-Movie, Karl Malden photo-c 7 14 21 51 71 90

NOSTALGIA ILLUSTRATED
Marvel Comics: Nov, 1974 - V2#8, Aug, 1975 (B&W, 76 pgs.)
V1#1 3 6 9 18 24 30
V1#2, V2#1-8 2 4 6 12 15 18

NOT BRAND ECHH (Brand Echh #1-4; See Crazy, 1973)
Marvel Comics Group (LMC): Aug, 1967 - No. 13, May, 1969
(1st Marvel parody book)
1: 1-8 are 12¢ issues 6 12 18 42 56 75
2-8: 3-Origin Thor, Hulk & Capt. America; Monkees, Alfred E. Neuman cameo. 4-X-Men app. 5-Origin/intro. Forbush Man. 7-Origin Fantastical-4 & Stuporman. Beatles cameo; X-Men satire; last 12¢-c 3 7 10 23 29 38
9-13 (25¢, 68 pgs., all Giants) 9-Beatles cameo. 10-All-r; The Old Witch, Crypt Keeper & Vault Keeper cameos. 12,13-Beatles cameo 4 8 12 29 37 50
NOTE: ***Colan** a(p)-4, 5, 8, 9, 13. **Everett** a-1i. **Kirby** a(p)-1, 3, 5-7, 10r; c-1p. **J. Severin** a-1; c-3, 6-8, 11. **M. Severin** a-1-13; c-2, 9, 10, 12, 13. **Sutton** a-3, 4, 5i, 6i, 8, 9, 10r, 11-13; c-5. Archie satire in #9. Avengers satire in #8, 12.*

NOTHING CAN STOP THE JUGGERNAUT
Marvel Comics: 1989 ($3.95)
1-r/Amazing Spider-Man #229 & 230 4.00

NO TIME FOR SERGEANTS (TV)
Dell Publ. Co.: No. 914, July, 1958; Feb-Apr, 1965 - No. 3, Aug-Oct, 1965
Four Color 914 (Movie)-Toth-a; Andy Griffith photo-c 11 22 33 77 114 150
1(2-4/65) (TV): Photo-c 7 14 21 46 63 80
2,3 (TV): Photo-c 5 10 15 36 48 60

NOVA (The Man Called... No. 22-25)(See New Warriors)
Marvel Comics Group: Sept, 1976 - No. 25, May, 1979
1-Origin/1st app. Nova 2 4 6 10 13 16
2-4,12: 4-Thor x-over. 12-Spider-Man x-over 1 2 3 5 6 8
5-11 6.00
10,11-(35¢-c variants, limited distribution)(6,7/77) 2 4 6 10 12 15
12-(35¢-c variant, limited distribution)(8/77) 2 4 6 12 16 20
13,14-(Regular 30¢ editions)(9/77) 13-Intro Crime-Buster. 5.00
13,14-(35¢-c variants, limited distribution) 2 4 6 10 12 15
15-24: 18-Yellow Claw app. 19-Wally West (Kid Flash) cameo 5.00
25-Last issue 6.00
NOTE: ***Austin** c-21i, 23i. **John Buscema** a(p)-1-3, 8, 21; c-1p, 2, 15. **Infantino** a(p)-15-20, 22-25; c-17-20, 21p, 23p, 24p. **Kirby** c-4p, 5, 7. **Nebres** c-25i. **Simonson** a-23i.*

NOVA
Marvel Comics: Jan, 1994 - June, 1995 ($1.75/$1.95)
(Started as 4-part mini-series)
1-($2.95, 52 pgs.)-Collector's Edition w/gold foil-c; new Nova costume 3.00
1-($2.25, 52 pgs.)-Newsstand Edition w/o foil-c 2.25
2-18: 3-Spider-Man-c/story. 5-Stan Lee app. 5-Bound-in card sheet. 13-Firestar & Night Thrasher app.14-Darkhawk 2.25

NOVA
Marvel Comics: May, 1999 - No. 7, Nov, 1999 ($2.99/$1.99)
1-($2.99) Larsen-s/Bennett-a; wraparound-c by Larsen 3.00
2-7-($1.99): 2-Two covers; Capt. America app. 5-Spider-Man. 7-Venom 2.25

NOW AGE ILLUSTRATED (See Pendulum Illustrated Classics)

NOW AGE BOOKS ILLUSTRATED (See Pendulum Illustrated Classics)

NTH MAN THE ULTIMATE NINJA (See Marvel Comics Presents #25)

Nyoka, the Jungle Girl #17 © FAW

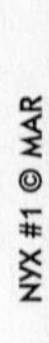
NYX #1 © MAR

Objective Five #1 © MBP Magic Beans

	GD	VG	FN	VF	VF/NM	NM-
	2.0	4.0	6.0	8.0	9.0	9.2

Marvel Comics: Aug, 1989 - No. 16, Sept, 1990 ($1.00)
1-16-Ninja mercenary. 8-Dale Keown's 1st Marvel work (1/90, pencils) 2.25

NUCLEUS (Also see Cerebus)
Heiro-Graphic Publications: May, 1979 ($1.50, B&W, adult fanzine)
1-Contains "Demonhorn" by Dave Sim; early app. of Cerebus The Aardvark (4 pg. story) 4 8 12 27 36 45

NUKLA
Dell Publishing Co.: Oct-Dec, 1965 - No. 4, Sept, 1966
1-Origin & 1st app. Nukla (super hero) 5 10 15 33 44 55
2,3 3 7 10 21 28 35
4-Ditko-a, c(p) 4 8 12 27 36 45

NURSE BETSY CRANE (Formerly Teen Secret Diary) (Also see Registered Nurse for reprints)
Charlton Comics: V2#12, Aug, 1961 - V2#27, Mar, 1964 (See Soap Opera Romances)
V2#12-27 3 6 9 16 20 24

NURSE HELEN GRANT (See The Romances of...)

NURSE LINDA LARK (See Linda Lark)

NURSERY RHYMES
Ziff-Davis Publ. Co. (Approved Comics): No. 10, July-Aug, 1951 - No. 2, Winter, 1951 (Painted-c)
10 (#1), 2: 10-Howie Post-a 16 32 48 92 126 160

NURSES, THE (TV)
Gold Key: April, 1963 - No. 3, Oct, 1963 (Photo-c: #1,2)
1 4 8 12 27 36 45
2,3 3 6 9 18 24 30

NUTS! (Satire)
Premiere Comics Group: March, 1954 - No. 5, Nov, 1954
1-Hollingsworth-a 31 62 93 175 248 320
2,4,5: 5-Capt. Marvel parody 21 42 63 118 164 210
3-Drug "reefers" mentioned 21 42 63 118 164 210

NUTS (Magazine) (Satire)
Health Knowledge: Feb, 1958 - No. 2, April, 1958
1 9 18 27 52 66 80
2 6 12 18 33 41 48

NUTS & JOLTS
Dell Publishing Co.: No. 22, 1941
Large Feature Comic 22 12 24 36 82 121 160

NUTSY SQUIRREL (Formerly Hollywood Funny Folks)(See Comic Cavalcade)
National Periodical Publications: #61, 9-10/54 - #69, 1-2/56; #70, 8-9/56 - #71, 10-11/56; #72, 11/57
61-Mayer-a; Grossman-a in all 14 28 42 79 107 135
62-72: Mayer a-62,65,67-72 10 20 30 56 73 90

NUTTY COMICS
Fawcett Publications: Winter, 1946 (Funny animal)
1-Capt. Kidd story; 1 pg. Wolverton-a 14 28 42 79 107 135

NUTTY COMICS
Home Comics (Harvey Publications): 1945; No. 4, May-June, 1946 - No. 8, June-July, 1947 (No #2,3)
nn-Helpful Hank, Bozo Bear & others (funny animal) 9 18 27 52 66 80
4 7 14 21 37 46 55
5-Rags Rabbit begins(1st app.); infinity-c 8 16 24 40 50 60
6-8 6 12 18 31 38 45

NUTTY LIFE (Formerly Krazy Life #1; becomes Wotalife Comics #3 on)
Fox Features Syndicate: No. 2, Summer, 1946
2 12 24 36 71 96 120

NYOKA, THE JUNGLE GIRL (Formerly Jungle Girl; see The Further Adventures of..., Master Comics #50 & XMas Comics)
Fawcett Publications: No. 2, Winter, 1945 - No. 77, June, 1953 (Movie serial)
2 55 110 165 344 512 680
3 34 68 102 196 278 360
4,5 29 58 87 164 232 300
6-11,13,14,16-18-Krigstein-a: 17-Sam Spade ad by Lou Fine 21 42 63 118 164 210
12,15,19,20 19 38 57 106 146 185
21-30: 25-Clayton Moore photo-c? 13 26 39 74 100 125
31-40 10 20 30 58 77 95
41-50 9 18 27 52 66 80
51-60 8 16 24 43 54 65
61-77 8 16 24 40 50 60
NOTE: *Photo-c from movies 25, 30-70, 72, 75-77. Bondage c-4, 5, 7, 8, 14, 24.*

NYOKA, THE JUNGLE GIRL (Formerly Zoo Funnies; Space Adventures #23 on)
Charlton Comics: No. 14, Nov, 1955 - No. 22, Nov, 1957
14 11 22 33 63 84 105
15-22 9 18 27 52 66 80

NYX
Marvel Comics: Nov, 2003 - Present ($2.99)
1-3-Quesada-s/Middleton-a/c 3.00

OAKLAND PRESS FUNNYBOOK, THE
The Oakland Press: 9/17/78 - 4/13/80 (16 pgs.) (Weekly)
Full color in comic book form; changes to tabloid size 4/20/80-on
Contains Tarzan by Manning, Marmaduke, Bugs Bunny, etc. (low distribution); 9/23/79 - 4/13/80 contain Buck Rogers by Gray Morrow & Jim Lawrence 2.50

OAKY DOAKS (See Famous Funnies #190)
Eastern Color Printing Co.: July, 1942 (One Shot)
1 36 72 108 204 290 375

OBERGEIST: RAGNAROK HIGHWAY
Image Comics (Top Cow/Minotaur): May, 2001 - No. 6, Nov, 2001 ($2.95, limited series)
Preview ('01, B&W, 16 pgs.) Harris painted-c 2.25
1-6-Harris-c/a/Jolley-s. 1-Three covers 3.00
... :The Directors' Cut (2002, $19.95, TPB) r/#1-6; Bruce Campbell intro. 20.00
... :The Empty Locket (3/02, $2.95, B&W) Harris & Snyder-a 3.00

OBIE
Store Comics: 1953 (6¢)
1 6 12 18 27 33 38

OBJECTIVE FIVE
Image Comics: July, 2000 - No. 6, Jan, 2001($2.95)
1-6-Lizalde-a 3.00

OBLIVION
Comico: Aug, 1995 - No. 3, May, 1996 ($2.50)
1-3: 1-Art Adams-c. 2-(1/96)-Bagged w/gaming card. 3-(5/96)-Darrow-c 2.50

OBNOXIO THE CLOWN (Character from Crazy Magazine)
Marvel Comics Group: April, 1983 (one-shot)
1-Vs. the X-Men 3.00

OCCULT FILES OF DR. SPEKTOR, THE
Gold Key/Whitman No. 25: Apr, 1973 - No. 24, Feb, 1977; No. 25, May, 1982 (Painted-c #1-24)
1-1st app. Lakota; Baron Tibor begins 4 8 12 27 36 45
2-5: 3-Mummy-c/s. 5-Jekyll & Hyde-c/s 2 4 6 12 16 20
6-10: 6,9-Frankenstein. 8,9-Dracula c/s. 9.-Jekyll & Hyde c/s. 9,10-Mummy-c/s 2 4 6 10 12 15
11-13,15-17,19-22,24: 11-1st app. Spektor as Werewolf. 11-13-Werewolf-c/s. 12,16-Frankenstein c/s. 17-Zombie/Voodoo-c. 19-Sea monster-c/s. 20-Mummy-s. 21-Swamp monster-c/s. 24-Dragon-c/s 1 3 4 6 8 10
14-Dr. Solar app. 2 4 6 14 18 22
18,23-Dr. Solar cameo 2 4 6 9 11 14
22-Return of the Owl c/s 2 4 6 9 11 14
25(Whitman, 5/82)-r/#1 with line drawn-c 1 2 3 5 7 9
NOTE: *Also see Dan Curtis, Golden Comics Digest 33, Gold Key Spotlight, Mystery Comics Digest 5, & Spine Tingling Tales.*

ODELL'S ADVENTURES IN 3-D (See Adventures in 3-D)

OFFCASTES
Marvel Comics (Epic Comics/Heavy Hitters): July, 1993 - No. 3, Sept, 1993 ($1.95, limited series)
1-3: Mike Vosburg-c/a/scripts in all 2.25

OFFICIAL CRISIS ON INFINITE EARTHS INDEX, THE
Independent Comics Group (Eclipse): Mar, 1986 ($1.75)
1 5.00

OFFICIAL CRISIS ON INFINITE EARTHS CROSSOVER INDEX, THE
Independent Comics Group (Eclipse): July, 1986 ($1.75)
1-Perez-c. 5.00

OFFICIAL DOOM PATROL INDEX, THE
Independent Comics Group (Eclipse): Feb, 1986 - No. 2, Mar, 1986 ($1.50, limited series)

The Official Legion of Super-Heroes Index #1 © DC

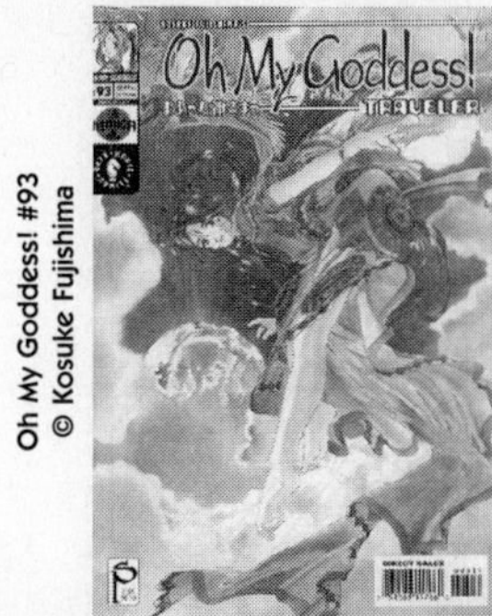

Oh My Goddess! #93 © Kosuke Fujishima

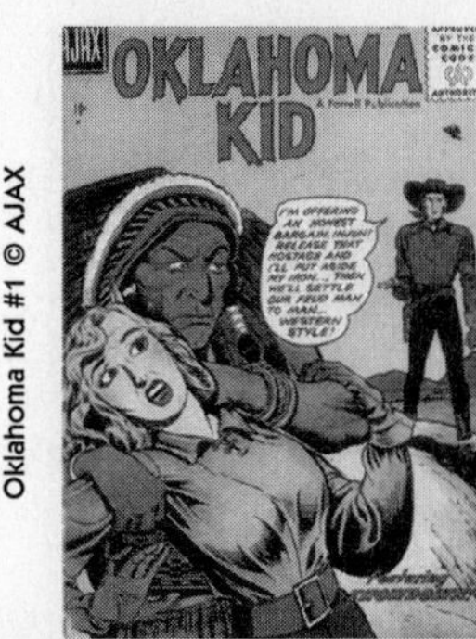

Oklahoma Kid #1 © AJAX

GD 2.0 | VG 4.0 | FN 6.0 | VF 8.0 | VF/NM 9.0 | NM- 9.2

1,2: Byrne-c. 4.00

OFFICIAL HANDBOOK OF THE CONAN UNIVERSE (See Handbook of...)

OFFICIAL HANDBOOK OF THE MARVEL UNIVERSE, THE
Marvel Comics Group: Jan, 1983 - No. 15, May, 1984 (Limited series)

1-Lists Marvel heroes & villains (letter A) 5.00
2-15: 2 (B-C, 3-(C-D). 4-(D-G). 5-(H-J), 6-(K-L). 7-(M). 8-(N-P); Punisher-c. 9-(Q-S), 10-(S). 11-(S-U). 12-(V-Z); Wolverine-c. 13,14-Book of the Dead. 15-Weaponry catalogue 4.00

NOTE: ***Bolland*** *a-8.* ***Byrne*** *c/a(p)-1-14; c-15p.* ***Grell*** *a-6, 9.* ***Kirby*** *a-1, 3.* ***Layton*** *a-2, 5, 7.* ***Mignola*** *a-3, 4, 5, 6, 8, 12.* ***Miller*** *a-4-6, 8, 10.* ***Nebres*** *a-3, 4, 8.* ***Redondo*** *a-3, 4, 8, 13, 14.* ***Simonson*** *a-1, 4, 6-13.* ***Paul Smith*** *a-1-12.* ***Starlin*** *a-5, 7, 8, 10, 13, 14.* ***Steranko*** *a-8p.* ***Zeck****-2-14.*

OFFICIAL HANDBOOK OF THE MARVEL UNIVERSE, THE
Marvel Comics Group: Dec, 1985 - No. 20, Feb, 1988 ($1.50, maxi-series)

V2#1-Byrne-c 4.00
2-20: 2,3-Byrne-c 3.00
Trade paperback Vol. 1-10 ($6.95) 1 3 4 6 8 10

NOTE: ***Art Adams*** *a-7, 8, 11, 12, 14.* ***Bolland*** *a-8, 10, 13.* ***Buckler*** *a-1, 3, 5, 10.* ***Buscema*** *a-1, 5, 8, 9, 10, 13, 14.* ***Byrne*** *a-1-14; c-1-11.* ***Ditko*** *a-1, 2, 4, 6, 7, 11, 13. a-7, 11.* ***Mignola*** *a-2, 4, 9, 11, 13.* ***Miller*** *a-2, 4, 12.* ***Simonson*** *a-1, 2, 4-13, 15.* ***Paul Smith*** *a-1-5, 7-12, 14.* ***Starlin*** *a-6, 8, 9, 12, 16.* ***Zeck*** *a-1-4, 6, 7, 9-14, 16.*

OFFICIAL HANDBOOK OF THE MARVEL UNIVERSE, THE
Marvel Comics: July, 1989 - No. 8, Mid-Dec, 1990 ($1.50, lim. series, 52 pgs.)

V3#1-8: 1-McFarlane-a (2 pgs.) 3.00

OFFICIAL HAWKMAN INDEX, THE
Independent Comics Group: Nov, 1986 - No. 2, Dec, 1986 ($2.00)

1,2 4.00

OFFICIAL JUSTICE LEAGUE OF AMERICA INDEX, THE
Independent Comics Group (Eclipse): April, 1986 - No. 8, Mar, 1987 ($2.00, Baxter paper)

1-8: 1,2-Perez-c. 6.00

OFFICIAL LEGION OF SUPER-HEROES INDEX, THE
Independent Comics Group (Eclipse): Dec, 1986 - No. 5, 1987 ($2.00, limited series)
(No Official in Title #2 on)

1-5: 4-Mooney-c 6.00

OFFICIAL MARVEL INDEX TO MARVEL TEAM-UP
Marvel Comics Group: Jan, 1986 - No. 6, 1987 ($1.25, limited series)

1-6 4.00

OFFICIAL MARVEL INDEX TO THE AMAZING SPIDER-MAN
Marvel Comics Group: Apr, 1985 - No. 9, Dec, 1985 ($1.25, limited series)

1 ($1.00)-Byrne-c. 4.00
2-9: 5,6,8,9-Punisher-c. 3.00

OFFICIAL MARVEL INDEX TO THE AVENGERS, THE
Marvel Comics: Jun, 1987 - No. 7, Aug, 1988 ($2.95, limited series)

1-7 5.00

OFFICIAL MARVEL INDEX TO THE AVENGERS, THE
Marvel Comics: V2#1, Oct, 1994 - V2#6, 1995 ($1.95, limited series)

V2#1-#6 3.00

OFFICIAL MARVEL INDEX TO THE FANTASTIC FOUR
Marvel Comics Group: Dec, 1985 - No. 12, Jan, 1987 ($1.25, limited series)

1-12: 1-Byrne-c. 1,2-Kirby back-c (unpub. art) 3.00

OFFICIAL MARVEL INDEX TO THE X-MEN, THE
Marvel Comics: May, 1987 - No. 7, July, 1988 ($2.95, limited series)

1-7 5.00

OFFICIAL MARVEL INDEX TO THE X-MEN, THE
Marvel Comics: V2#1, Apr, 1994 - V2#5, 1994 ($1.95, limited series)

V2#1-5: 1-Covers X-Men #1-51. 2-Covers #52-122,Special #1,2,Giant-Size #1,2. 3-Byrne-c; covers #123-177, Annuals 3-7, Spec. Ed. #1. 4-Covers Uncanny X-Men #178-234, Annuals 8-12. 5-Covers #235-287, Annuals 13-15 3.00

OFFICIAL SOUPY SALES COMIC (See Soupy Sales)

OFFICIAL TEEN TITANS INDEX, THE
Indep. Comics Group (Eclipse): Aug, 1985 - No. 5, 1986 ($1.50, lim. series)

1-5 4.00

OFFICIAL TRUE CRIME CASES (Formerly Sub-Mariner #23; All-True Crime Cases #26 on)
Marvel Comics (OCI): No. 24, Fall, 1947 - No. 25, Winter, 1947-48

24(#1)-Burgos-a; Syd Shores-c 24 48 72 135 190 245
25-Syd Shores-c; Kurtzman's "Hey Look" 19 38 57 106 146 185

OF SUCH IS THE KINGDOM
George A. Pflaum: 1955 (15¢, 36 pgs.)

nn-Reprints from 1951 Treasure Chest 4 7 10 14 17 20

O.G. WHIZ (See Gold Key Spotlight #10)
Gold Key: 2/71 - No. 6, 5/72; No. 7, 5/78 - No. 11, 1/79 (No. 7: 52 pgs.)

1,2-John Stanley scripts 6 12 18 43 59 75
3-6(1972) 4 8 12 22 30 38
7-11(1978-79)-Part-r: 9-Tubby issue 2 4 6 11 14 18

OH, BROTHER! (Teen Comedy)
Stanhall Publ.: Jan, 1953 - No. 5, Oct, 1953

1-By Bill Williams 8 16 24 40 50 60
2-5 5 10 15 24 30 35

OH MY GODDESS! (Manga)
Dark Horse Comics: Aug, 1994 - Present ($2.50-$3.50, B&W)

1-6-Kosuke Fujishima-s/a in all 3.00
... **PART II** 2/95 - No. 9, 9/95 ($2.50, B&W, lim.series) #1-9 3.00
... **PART III** 11/95 - No. 11, 9/96 ($2.95, B&W, lim. series) #1-11 3.00
... **PART IV** 12/96 - No. 8, 7/97 ($2.95, B&W, lim. series) #1-8 3.00
... **PART V** 9/97 - Np. 12, 8/98 ($2.95, B&W, lim. series)
1,2,5,8: 5-Ninja Master pt. 1 3.00
3,4,6,7,10-12-($3.95, 48 pgs.) 10-Fallen Angel. 11-Play The Game 4.00
9-($3.50) "It's Lonely At The Top" 3.50
... **PART VI** 10/98 - No. 5, 3/99 ($3.50/$2.95, B&W, lim. series)
1-($3.50) 3.50
2-6-($2.95)-6-Super Urd one-shot 3.00
... **PART VII** 5/99 - No. 8, 12/99 ($2.95, B&W, lim. series) #1-3 3.00
4-8-($3.50) 3.50
... **PART VIII** 1/00 - No. 6, 6/00 ($3.50, B&W, lim. series) #1-3,5,7 3.50
4-($2.95) "Hail To The Chief" begins 3.00
... **PART IX** 7/00 - No. 7, 1/01 ($3.50/$2.99) #1-4: 3-Queen Sayoko 3.50
5-7-($2.99) 3.00
... **PART X** 2/01 - No. 5, 6/01 ($3.50) #1-5 3.50
... **PART XI** 10/01 - No. 10, 3/02 ($3.50) #1,2,7,8 3.50
3-6,9-($2.99) Mystery Child 3.00
10-($3.99) 4.00
(Series adapts new numbering) 88-90-($3.50) Learning tto Love 3.50
91-94,96-103: 91-94 ($2.99) Traveler. 96-98-The Phantom Racer 3.00
95-($3.50) Traveler pt. 5 3.50

OH MY GOTH
Sirius Entertainment (Dog Star Press): 1998 - No. 4, 1999 ($2.95, B&W)

1-4-Voltaire-s/a 3.00
... Humans Suck! (2000 - No. 3) 1,2-Voltaire-s/a 3.00

OH SUSANNA (TV)
Dell Publishing Co.: No. 1105, June-Aug, 1960 (Gale Storm)

Four Color 1105-Toth-a, photo-c 14 28 42 97 141 185

OINK: BLOOD AND CIRCUS
Kitchen Sink: 1998 - No. 4, July, 1998 ($4.95, limited series)

1-4-John Mueller-s/a 5.00

OKAY COMICS
United Features Syndicate: July, 1940

1-Captain & the Kids & Hawkshaw the Detective reprints 44 88 132 264 395 525

O.K. COMICS
United Features Syndicate/Hit Publications: July, 1940 - No. 2, Oct, 1940

1-Little Giant (w/super powers), Phantom Knight, Sunset Smith, & The Teller Twins begin 75 150 225 469 705 940
2 (Rare)-Origin Mister Mist by Chas. Quinlan 77 154 231 481 723 965

OKLAHOMA KID
Ajax/Farrell Publ.: June, 1957 - No. 4, 1958

1 11 22 33 63 84 105
2-4 7 14 21 37 46 55

OKLAHOMAN, THE
Dell Publishing Co.: No. 820, July, 1957

Four Color 820-Movie, photo-c 10 20 30 70 100 130

OKTANE
Dark Horse Comics: Aug, 1995 - Nov, 1995 ($2.50, color, limited series)

1-4-Gene Ha-a 2.50

The Omega Men #30 © DC

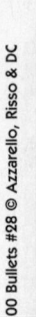

100 Bullets #28 © Azzarello, Risso & DC

100% #1 © Paul Pope

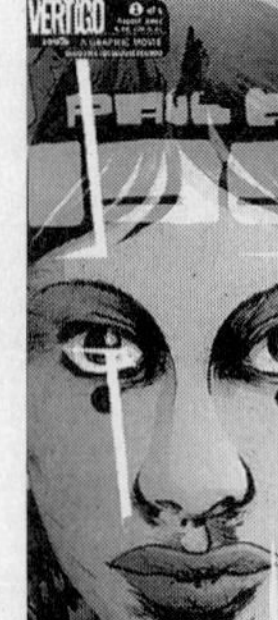

	GD 2.0	VG 4.0	FN 6.0	VF 8.0	VF/NM 9.0	NM- 9.2
OKTOBERFEST COMICS						
Now & Then Publ.: Fall 1976 (75¢, Canadian, B&W, one-shot)						
1-Dave Sim-s/a; Gene Day-a; 1st app. Uncle Hans & Natter P. Bombast; The Beavers sty; 1st Cap'n Riverrat, Sim-s/Day-a	2	4	6	12	16	20
OLD IRONSIDES (Disney)						
Dell Publishing Co.: No. 874, Jan, 1958						
Four Color 874-Movie w/Johnny Tremain	7	14	21	51	71	90
OLD YELLER (Disney, see Movie Comics, and Walt Disney Showcase #25)						
Dell Publishing Co.: No. 869, Jan, 1958						
Four Color 869-Movie, photo-c	6	12	18	40	55	70
OMAC (One Man Army; ...Corps. #4 on; also see Kamandi #59 & Warlord) (See Cancelled Comic Cavalcade)						
National Periodical Publications: Sept-Oct, 1974 - No. 8, Nov-Dec, 1975						
1-Origin	4	8	12	24	32	40
2-8: 8-2 pg. Neal Adams ad	2	4	6	11	14	18
NOTE: ***Kirby*** a-1-8p; c-1-7p. ***Kubert*** c-8.						
OMAC: ONE MAN ARMY CORPS						
DC Comics: 1991 - No. 4, 1991 ($3.95, B&W, mini-series, mature, 52 pgs.)						
Book One - Four: John Byrne-c/a & scripts						4.00
O'MALLEY AND THE ALLEY CATS						
Gold Key: April, 1971 - No. 9, Jan, 1974 (Disney)						
1	3	6	9	18	23	28
2-9	2	4	6	10	13	16
OMEGA ELITE						
Blackthorne Publishing: 1987 ($1.25)						
1-Starlin-c						3.00
OMEGA MEN, THE (See Green Lantern #141)						
DC Comics: Dec, 1982 - No. 38, May, 1986 ($1.00/$1.25/$1.50; Baxter paper)						
1,20: 20-2nd full Lobo story						3.00
2,4-9,11-19,21-25,28-30,32,33,36,38: 2-Origin Broot. 5,9-2nd & 3rd app. Lobo (cameo, 2 pgs. each). 7-Origin The Citadel. 19-Lobo cameo. 30-Intro new Primus						2.50
3-1st app. Lobo (5 pgs.)(6/83); Lobo-c	1	2	3	4	5	7
10-1st full Lobo story						5.00
26,27,31,34,35: 26,27-Alan Moore scripts. 31-Crisis x-over. 34,35-Teen Titans x-over						3.00
37-1st solo Lobo story (8 pg. back-up by Giffen)						4.00
Annual 1(11/84, 52 pgs.), 2(11/85)						3.00
NOTE: ***Giffen*** c/a-1-6p. ***Morrow*** a-24r. ***Nino*** c/a-16, 21; a-Annual 1i.						
OMEGA THE UNKNOWN						
Marvel Comics Group: March, 1976 - No. 10, Oct, 1977						
1-1st app. Omega	1	3	4	6	8	10
2,3-(Regular 25¢ editions). 2-Hulk-c/story. 3-Electro-c/story.						6.00
2,3-(30¢-c variants, limited distribution)	2	4	6	10	12	15
4-10: 8-1st app. 2nd Foolkiller (Greg Salinger), 1 panel only (cameo). 9,10-(Reg. 30¢ editions). 9-1st full app. 2nd Foolkiller						6.00
9,10-(35¢-c variants, limited distribution)	2	4	6	10	12	15
NOTE: ***Kane*** c(p)-3, 5, 8, 9. ***Mooney*** a-1-3, 4p, 5, 6p, 7, 8i, 9, 10.						
OMEN						
Northstar Publishing: 1989 - No. 3, 1989 ($2.00, B&W, mature)						
1-Tim Vigil-c/a in all	1	2	3	5	7	9
1, (2nd printing)						3.00
2,3						6.00
OMEN, THE						
Chaos! Comics: May, 1998 - No. 5, Sept, 1998 ($2.95, limited series)						
1-5: 1-Six covers, ...: Vexed (10/98, $2.95) Chaos! characters appear						3.00
OMNI MEN						
Blackthorne Publishing: 1987 - No. 3, 1987 ($1.25)						
1-3						2.25
Graphic Novel (1989, $3.50)						3.50
ONE, THE						
Marvel Comics (Epic Comics): July, 1985 - No. 6, Feb, 1986 (Limited series, mature)						
1-6: Post nuclear holocaust super-hero. 2-Intro The Other						2.25
ONE-ARM SWORDSMAN, THE						
Victory Prod./Lueng's Publ. #4 on: 1987 - No. 12, 1990 ($2.75/$1.80, 52 pgs.)						
1-3 ($2.75)						2.75
4-12: 4-6-$1.80-c. 7-12-$2.00-c						2.25

	GD 2.0	VG 4.0	FN 6.0	VF 8.0	VF/NM 9.0	NM- 9.2
ONE HUNDRED AND ONE DALMATIANS (Disney, see Cartoon Tales, Movie Comics, and Walt Disney Showcase #9, 51)						
Dell Publishing Co.: No. 1183, Mar, 1961						
Four Color 1183-Movie	11	22	33	77	114	150
101 DALMATIONS (Movie)						
Disney Comics: 1991 (52 pgs., graphic novel)						
nn-($4.95, direct sales)-r/movie adaptation & more						5.00
1-($2.95, newsstand edition)						3.00
101 WAYS TO END THE CLONE SAGA (See Spider-Man)						
Marvel Comics: Jan, 1997 ($2.50, one-shot)						
1						2.50
100 BULLETS						
DC Comics (Vertigo): Aug, 1999 - Present ($2.50)						
1-Azzarello-s/Risso-a/Dave Johnson-c						4.00
2-5						3.00
6-48: 26-Series summary; art by various. 45-Preview of Losers						2.50
A Foregone Tomorrow TPB (2002, $17.95) r/#20-30						18.00
First Shot, Last Call TPB (2000, $9.95) r/#1-5, Vertigo Winter's Edge #3						10.00
Hang Up on the Hang Low TPB (2001, $9.95) r/#15-19; Jim Lee intro.						10.00
Six Feet Under the Gun TPB (2003, $12.95) r/#37-42						13.00
Split Second Chance TPB (2001, $14.95) r/#6-14						15.00
The Counterfifth Detective TPB (2003, $12.95) r/#31-36						13.00
100 GREATEST MARVELS OF ALL TIME						
Marvel Comics: Dec, 2001 ($7.50/$3.50, limited series)						
1-5-Reprints top #6-#25 stories voted by poll for Marvel's 40th ann.						7.50
6-($3.50) (#5 on-c) Reprints X-Men (2nd series) #1						3.50
7-($3.50) (#4 on-c) Reprints Giant-Size X-Men #1						3.50
8-($3.50) (#3 on-c) Reprints (Uncanny) X-Men #137 (Death of Jean Grey)						3.50
9-($3.50) (#2 on-c) Reprints Fantastic Four #1						3.50
10-($3.50) (#1 on-c) Reprints Amazing Fantasy #15 (1st app. Spider-Man)						3.50
100 PAGES OF COMICS						
Dell Publishing Co.: 1937 (Stiff covers, square binding)						
101(Found on back cover)-Alley Oop, Wash Tubbs, Capt. Easy, Og Son of Fire, Apple Mary, Tom Mix, Dan Dunn, Tailspin Tommy, Doctor Doom	164	328	492	1066	1471	1875
100 PAGE SUPER SPECTACULAR (See DC 100 Page Super Spectacular)						
100%						
DC Comics (Vertigo): Aug, 2002 - No. 5, July, 2003 ($5.95, B&W, limited series)						
1-5-Paul Pope-s/a						6.00
100% TRUE?						
DC Comics (Paradox Press): Summer 1996 - No. 2 ($4.95, B&W)						
1,2-Reprints stories from various Paradox Press books.						5.00
$1,000,000 DUCK (See Walt Disney Showcase #5)						
ONE MILLION YEARS AGO (Tor #2 on)						
St. John Publishing Co.: Sept, 1953						
1-Origin & 1st app. Tor; Kubert-c/a; Kubert photo inside front cover	21	42	63	118	164	210
ONE PLUS ONE						
Oni Press: Sept, 2002 - No. 5, March, 2003 ($2.95, B&W, limited series)						
1-5-Shaffer-s/Krall-a						3.00
TPB (9/03, $14.95, digest-size) r/#1-5 & story from Oni Press Color Special 2002						15.00
ONE SHOT (See Four Color...)						
1001 HOURS OF FUN						
Dell Publishing Co.: No. 13, 1943						
Large Feature Comic 13 (nn)-Puzzles & games; by A.W. Nugent. This book was bound as #13 w/Large Feature Comics in publisher's files	28	56	84	159	225	290
ONE TRICK RIP OFF, THE (See Dark Horse Presents)						
ONI (Adaption of video game)						
Dark Horse Comics: Feb, 2001 - No. 3, Apr, 2001 ($2.99, limited series)						
1-3-Sunny Lee-a(p)						3.00
ONI DOUBLE FEATURE (See Clerks: The Comic Book and Jay & Silent Bob)						
Oni Press: Jan, 1998 - No. 13, Sept, 1999 ($2.95, B&W)						
1-Jay & Silent Bob; Kevin Smith-s/Matt Wagner-a	1	3	4	6	8	10
1-2nd printing						3.00
2-11,13: 2,3-Paul Pope-s/a. 3,4-Nixey-s/a. 4,5-Sienkewicz-s/a. 6,7-Gaiman-s. 9-Bagge-c.						

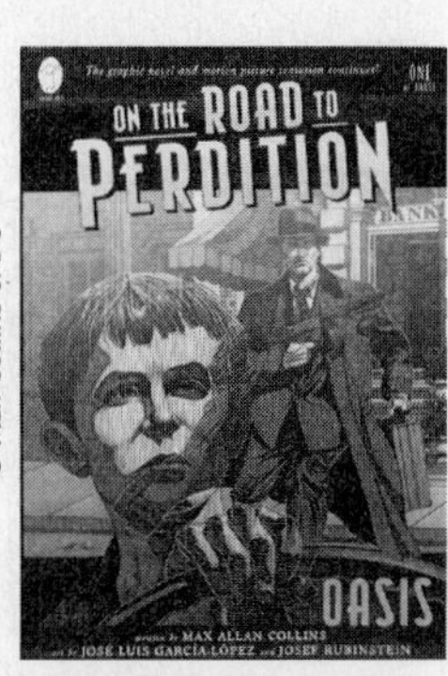

On the Road to Perdition: Oasis Book 1 © Max Collins & DC

Operation Peril #5 © ACG

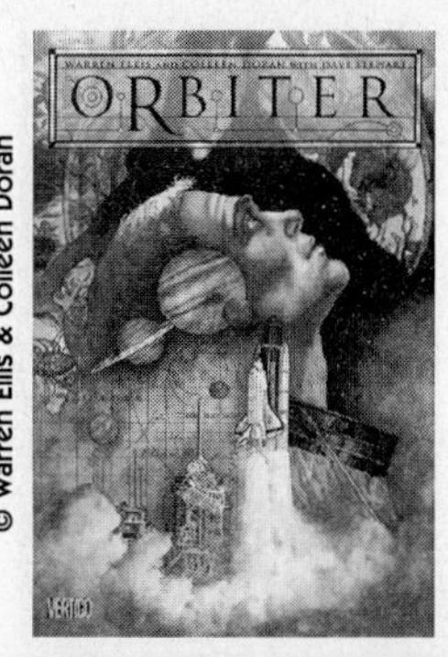

Orbiter HC © Warren Ellis & Colleen Doran

GD 2.0 | VG 4.0 | FN 6.0 | VF 8.0 | VF/NM 9.0 | NM- 9.2

13-All Paul Dini-s; Jingle Belle 3.00
12-Jay & Silent Bob as Bluntman & Chronic; Smith-s/Allred-a 5.00

ONIGAMI (See Warrior Nun Areala: Black & White)
Antarctic Press: Apr, 1998 - No. 3, July, 1998 ($2.95, B&W, limited series)
1-3-Michel Lacombe-s/a 3.00

ONI PRESS COLOR SPECIAL
Oni Press: Jun, 2001; Jul, 2002 ($5.95, annual)
...2001-Oeming "Who Killed Madman?" cover; stories & art by various 6.00
...2002-Allred wraparound-c; stories & art by various 6.00

ONSLAUGHT: EPILOGUE
Marvel Comics: Feb, 1997 ($2.95, one-shot)
1-Hama-s/Green-a; Xavier-c; Bastion-app. 3.00

ONSLAUGHT: MARVEL
Marvel Comics: Oct, 1996 ($3.95, one-shot)
1-Conclusion to Onslaught x-over; wraparound-c 1 2 3 4 5 7

ONSLAUGHT: X-MEN
Marvel Comics: Aug, 1996 ($3.95, one-shot)
1-Waid & Lobdell script; Fantastic Four & Avengers app.; Xavier as Onslaught 5.00
1-Variant-c 2 4 6 8 10 12

ON STAGE
Dell Publishing Co.: No. 1336, Apr-June, 1962
Four Color 1336-Not by Leonard Starr 5 10 15 36 48 60

ON THE DOUBLE (Movie)
Dell Publishing Co.: No. 1232, Sept-Nov, 1961
Four Color 1232 5 10 15 36 48 60

ON THE ROAD TO PERDITION (Movie)
DC Comics (Paradox Press): 2003 - Book 3 ($7.95, 8"x5 1/2", B&W, limited series)
...: Oasis, Book 1-Max Allan Collins-s/José Luis García-López-a/David Beck-c 8.00
...: Sanctuary, Book 2-Max Allan Collins-s/Steve Lieber-a/José Luis García-López-c 8.00

ON THE ROAD WITH ANDRAE CROUCH
Spire Christian Comics (Fleming H. Revell): 1973, 1977 (39¢)
nn 1 3 4 6 8 10

ON THE SCENE PRESENTS:...
Warren Publishing Co.: Oct, 1966 - No. 2, 1967 (B&W magazine, two #1 issues)
#1 "Super Heroes" (68 pgs.) Batman 1966 movie photo-c/s; has articles/photos/comic art from serials on Superman, Flash Gordon, Capt. America, Capt. Marvel and The Phantom
4 8 12 24 32 40
#1 "Freak Out, USA" (Fall/1966, 60 pgs.) (lower print run) articles on musicians like Zappa, Jefferson Airplane, Supremes 4 8 12 29 40 50
#2 "Freak Out, USA" (2/67, 52 pgs.) Beatles, Country Joe, Doors/Jim Morrison, Bee Gees
4 8 12 24 32 40

ON THE SPOT (Pretty Boy Floyd...)
Fawcett Publications: Fall, 1948
nn-Pretty Boy Floyd photo on-c; bondage-c 35 70 105 201 288 370

ONYX OVERLORD
Marvel Comics (Epic): Oct, 1992 - No. 4, Jan, 1993 ($2.75, mini-series)
1-4: Moebius scripts 2.75

OPEN SPACE
Marvel Comics: Mid-Dec, 1989 - No. 4, Aug, 1990 ($4.95, bi-monthly, 68 pgs.)
1-4: 1-Bill Wray-a; Freas-c 5.00
0-(1999) Wizard supplement; unpubl. early Alex Ross-a; new Ross-c 2.25

OPERATION BIKINI (See Movie Classics)

OPERATION BUCHAREST (See The Crusaders)

OPERATION CROSSBOW (See Movie Classics)

OPERATION: KNIGHTSTRIKE (See Knightstrike)
Image Comics (Extreme Studios): May, 1995 - No.3, July, 1995 ($2.50)
1-3 2.50

OPERATION PERIL
American Comics Group (Michel Publ.): Oct-Nov, 1950 - No. 16, Apr-May, 1953 (#1-5: 52 pgs.)
1-Time Travelers, Danny Danger (by Leonard Starr) & Typhoon Tyler (by Ogden Whitney) begin 39 78 117 230 325 420
2-War-c 24 48 72 135 190 245
3-War-c; horror story 21 42 63 118 164 210
4,5-Sci/fi-c/story 24 48 72 135 190 245
6-10: 6,8,9,10-Sci/fi-c. 6-Dinosaur-c. 7-Sabretooth-c 20 40 60 112 156 200
11,12-War-c; last Time Travelers 14 28 42 79 107 135
13-16: All war format 10 20 30 56 73 90
NOTE: *Starr a-2, 5. Whitney a-1, 2, 5-10, 12; c-1, 3, 5, 8, 9.*

OPERATION: STORMBREAKER
Acclaim Comics (Valiant Heroes): Aug, 1997 ($3.95, one-shot)
1-Waid/Augustyn-s, Braithwaite-a 4.00

OPTIC NERVE
Drawn and Quarterly: Apr, 1995 - Present ($2.95, bi-annual)
1-7: Adrian Tomine-c/a/scripts in all 3.00
8-($3.50) 3.50
32 Stories-($9.95, trade paperback)-r/Optic Nerve mini-comics 10.00
32 Stories-($29.95, hardcover)-r/Optic Nerve mini-comics; signed & numbered 30.00

ORAL ROBERTS' TRUE STORIES (Junior Partners #120 on)
TelePix Publ. (Oral Roberts' Evangelistic Assoc./Healing Waters): 1956 (no month) - No. 119, 7/59 (15¢)(No. 102: 25¢)
V1#1(1956)-(Not code approved)- "The Miracle Touch"
21 42 63 118 164 210
102-(Only issue approved by code, 10/56) "Now I See"
13 26 39 74 100 125
103-119: 115-(114 on inside) 9 18 27 52 66 80
NOTE: *Also see Happiness & Healing For You.*

ORANGE BIRD, THE
Walt Disney Educational Media Co.: No date (1980) (36 pgs.; in color; slick cover)
nn-Included with educational kit on foods, ...in Nutrition Adventures nn (1980) ...and the Nutrition Know-How Revue nn (1983) 3.00

ORB (Magazine)
Orb Publishing: 1974 - No. 6, Mar/Apr 1976 (B&W/color)
1-1st app. Northern Light & Kadaver, both series begin
3 6 9 18 24 30
2,3 (72 pgs.) 2 4 6 12 16 20
4-6 (60 pgs.): 4,5-origin Northern Light 2 4 6 10 12 15
NOTE: ***Allison** a-1-3. **Gene Day** a-1-6. **P. Hsu** a-4-6. **Steacy** s/a-3,4.*

ORBIT
Eclipse Books: 1990 - No. 3, 1990 ($4.95, 52 pgs., squarebound)
1-3: Reprints from Isaac Asimov's Science Fiction Magazine; 1-Dave Stevens-c, Bolton-a. 3-Bolton-c/a, Yeates-a 5.00

ORBITER
DC Comics (Vertigo): 2003 ($24.95, hardcover with dust jacket)
HC-Warren Ellis-s/Colleen Doran-a 25.00

ORDER, THE (cont'd from Defenders V2#12)
Marvel Comics: Apr, 2002 - No. 6, Sept, 2002 ($2.25, limited series)
1-6: 1-Haley-a/Duffy & Busiek-s. 3-Avengers-c/app. 4-Jurgens-a 2.25

ORIENTAL HEROES
Jademan Comics: Aug, 1988 - No. 55, Feb, 1993 ($1.50/$1.95, 68 pgs.)
1,55 2.25
2-54 2.25

ORIGINAL ASTRO BOY, THE
Now Comics: Sept, 1987 - No. 20, Jun, 1989 ($1.50/$1.75)
1-20-All have Ken Steacy painted-c/a 3.00

ORIGINAL BLACK CAT, THE
Recollections: Oct. 6, 1988 - No. 9, 1992 ($2.00, limited series)
1-9: Elias-r; 1-Bondage-c. 2-Murphy Anderson-c 3.00

ORIGINAL DICK TRACY, THE
Gladstone Publishing: Sept, 1990 - No. 5, 1991 ($1.95, bi-monthly, 68pgs.)
1-5: 1-Vs. Pruneface. 2-& the Evil influence; begin $2.00-c 2.25
NOTE: *#1 reprints strips 7/16/43 - 9/30/43. #2 reprints strips 12/1/46 - 2/2/47. #3 reprints 8/31/46 - 11/14/46. #4 reprints 9/17/45 - 12/23/45. #5 reprints 6/10/46 - 8/28/46.*

ORIGINAL DOCTOR SOLAR, MAN OF THE ATOM, THE
Valiant: Apr, 1995 ($2.95, one-shot)
1-Reprints Doctor Solar, Man of the Atom #1,5; Bob Fugitani-r; Paul Smith-c; afterword by Seaborn Adamson 3.00

ORIGINAL E-MAN AND MICHAEL MAUSER, THE
First Comics: Oct, 1985 - No. 7, April, 1986 ($1.75, Baxter paper)
1-7: 1-Has r-/Charlton's E-Man, Vengeance Squad. 2-Shows #4 in indicia by mistake.

Orion #25 © DC

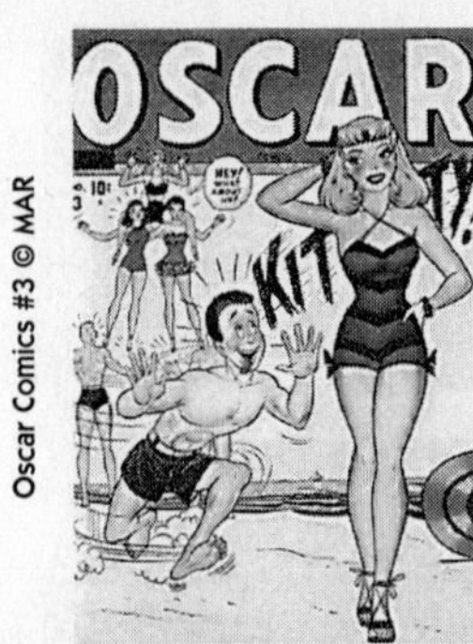

Oscar Comics #3 © MAR

Our Army at War #15 © DC

	GD 2.0	VG 4.0	FN 6.0	VF 8.0	VF/NM 9.0	NM- 9.2

7-($2.00, 44pgs.)-Staton-a 2.25

ORIGINAL GHOST RIDER, THE
Marvel Comics: July, 1992 - No. 20, Feb, 1994 ($1.75)

1-20: 1-7-r/Marvel Spotlight #5-11 by Ploog w/new-c. 3-New Phantom Rider (former Night Rider) back-ups begin by Ayers. 4-Quesada-c(p). 8-Ploog-c. 8,9-r/Ghost Rider #1,2. 10-r/Marvel Spotlight #12. 11-18,20-r/Ghost Rider #3-12. 19-r/Marvel Two-in-One #8 2.25

ORIGINAL GHOST RIDER RIDES AGAIN, THE
Marvel Comics: July, 1991 - No. 7, Jan, 1992, ($1.50, limited series, 52 pgs.)

1-7: 1-r/Ghost Rider #68(origin),69 w/covers. 2-7: R/ G.R. #70-81 w/covers 2.25

ORIGINAL MAGNUS ROBOT FIGHTER, THE
Valiant: Apr, 1995 ($2.95, one-shot)

1-Reprints Magnus, Robot Fighter 4000 #2; Russ Manning-r; Rick Leonardi-c; afterword by Seaborn Adamson 3.00

ORIGINAL NEXUS GRAPHIC NOVEL (See First Comics Graphic Novel #19)

ORIGINAL SHIELD, THE
Archie Enterprises, Inc.: Apr, 1984 - No. 4, Oct, 1984

1-4: 1,2-Origin Shield; Ayers p-1-4, Nebres c-1,2 4.00

ORIGINAL SWAMP THING SAGA, THE (See DC Special Series #2, 14, 17, 20)

ORIGINAL TUROK, SON OF STONE, THE
Valiant: Apr, 1995 - No. 2, May, 1995 ($2.95, limited series)

1,2: 1-Reprints Turok, Son of Stone #24,25,42; Alberto Gioletti-r; Rags Morales-c; afterword by Seaborn Adamson. 2-Reprints Turok, Son of Stone #24,33; Gioletti-r; McKone-c 3.00

ORIGIN OF GALACTUS (See Fantastic Four #48-50)
Marvel Comics: Feb, 1996 ($2.50, one-shot)

1-Lee & Kirby reprints w/pin-ups 2.50

ORIGIN OF THE DEFIANT UNIVERSE, THE
Defiant Comics: Feb, 1994 ($1.50, 20 pgs., one-shot)

1-David Lapham, Adam Pollina & Alan Weiss-a; Weiss-c 5.00

NOTE: *The comic was originally published as Defiant Genesis and was distributed at the 1994 Philadelphia ComicCon.*

ORIGINS OF MARVEL COMICS (See Fireside Book Series)

ORION (Manga)
Dark Horse Comics: Sept, 1992 - No. 6, July, 1993 ($2.95/$3.95, B&W, bimonthly, lim. series)

1-6:1,2,6-Squarebound): 1-Masamune Shirow-c/a/s in all 4.00

ORION (See New Gods)
DC Comics: June, 2000 - No. 25, June, 2002 ($2.50)

1-14-Simonson-s/a. 3-Back-up story w/Miller-a. 4-Gibbons-a back-up. 7-Chaykin back-up. 8-Loeb/Liefeld back-up. 10-A. Adams back-up-a 12-Jim Lee back-up-a. 13-JLA-c/app.; Byrne-a 2.50
15-($3.95) Black Racer app.; back-up story w/J.P. Leon-a 4.00
16-24-Simonson-s/a. 19-Joker: Last Laugh x-over 2.50
25-($3.95) Last issue; Mister Miracle-c/app. 4.00
The Gates of Apocalypse (2001, $12.95, TPB) r/#1-5 & various short-s 13.00

OSBORNE JOURNALS (See Spider-Man titles)
Marvel Comics: Feb, 1997 ($2.95, one-shot)

1-Hotz-c/a 3.00

OSCAR COMICS (Formerly Funny Tunes; Awful...#11 & 12) (Also see Cindy Comics)
Marvel Comics: No. 24, Spring, 1947 - No. 10, Apr, 1949; No. 13, Oct, 1949

	GD 2.0	VG 4.0	FN 6.0	VF 8.0	VF/NM 9.0	NM- 9.2
24(#1, Spring, 1947)	18	36	54	104	142	180
25(#2, Sum, 1947)-Wolverton-a plus Kurtzman's "Hey Look"	20	40	60	112	156	200
26(#3)-Same as regular #3 except #26 was printed over in black ink with #3 appearing on-c below the over print	11	22	33	66	88	110
3-9,13: 8-Margie app.	11	22	33	66	88	110
10-Kurtzman's "Hey Look"	13	26	39	76	103	130

OSWALD THE RABBIT (Also see New Fun Comics #1)
Dell Publishing Co.: No. 21, 1943 - No. 1268, 12-2/61-62 (Walter Lantz)

	GD 2.0	VG 4.0	FN 6.0	VF 8.0	VF/NM 9.0	NM- 9.2
Four Color 21(1943)	48	96	144	370	548	725
Four Color 39(1943)	33	66	99	248	374	500
Four Color 67(1944)	19	38	57	136	198	260
Four Color 102(1946)-Kelly-a, 1 pg.	16	32	48	113	167	220
Four Color 143,183	10	20	30	72	104	135
Four Color 225,273	7	14	21	50	68	85
Four Color 315,388	6	12	18	43	59	75
Four Color 458,507,549,593	5	10	15	33	44	55
Four Color 623,697,792,894,979,1268	4	8	12	27	36	45

OSWALD THE RABBIT (See The Funnies, March of Comics #7, 38, 53, 67, 81, 95, 111, 126, 141, 156, 171, 186, New Funnies & Super Book #8, 20)

OTHERS, THE
Image Comics (Shadowline Ink): 1995 - No. 3, 1995 ($2.50)

0 ($1.00)-16 pg. preview 2.25
1-3 2.50

OTIS GOES TO HOLLYWOOD
Dark Horse Comics: Apr, 1997 - No.2, May, 1997 ($2.95, B&W, mini-series)

1,2-Fingerman-c/s/a 3.00

OUR ARMY AT WAR (Becomes Sgt. Rock #302 on; also see Army At War)
National Periodical Publications: Aug, 1952 - No. 301, Feb, 1977

	GD 2.0	VG 4.0	FN 6.0	VF 8.0	VF/NM 9.0	NM- 9.2
1	143	286	429	1216	1858	2500
2	63	126	189	536	818	1100
3,4: 4-Krigstein-a	52	104	156	416	621	825
5-7	41	82	123	324	487	650
8-11,14-Krigstein-a	40	80	120	300	450	600
12,15-20	32	64	96	240	358	475
13-Krigstein-c/a; flag-c	42	84	126	315	470	625
21-31: Last precode (2/55)	24	48	72	169	247	325
32-40	20	40	60	140	205	270
41-60: 51-1st S.A. issue	16	32	48	113	167	220
61-70: 67-Minor Sgt. Rock prototype	14	28	42	99	145	190
71-80	12	24	36	82	121	160
81- (4/59)-Sgt. Rocky of Easy Co. app. by Andru & Esposito-a/ Haney-s; (the last Sgt. Rock prototype)	200	400	600	1750	2725	3700
82-1st Sgt. Rock app., in name only, in Easy Co. story (6 panels) by Kanigher & Drucker	50	100	150	413	632	850
83-(6/59)-1st true Sgt. Rock app. in "The Rock and the Wall" by Kubert & Kanigher; (most similar to prototype in G.I. Combat #68)	160	320	480	1360	2080	2800
84-Kubert-c	29	58	87	210	305	400
85-Origin & 1st app. Ice Cream Soldier	37	74	111	278	414	550
86,87-Early Sgt. Rock; Kubert-a	27	54	81	194	285	375
88-1st Sgt. Rock-c; Kubert-c/a	30	60	90	218	322	425
89	25	50	75	176	258	340
90-Kubert-c/a; How Rock got his stripes	31	62	93	228	339	450
91-All-Sgt. Rock issue; Grandenetti-c/Kubert-a	57	114	171	485	743	1000
92,94,96-99: 97-Regular Kubert-c begin	17	34	51	123	182	240
93-1st Zack Nolan	18	36	54	131	191	250
95,100: 95-1st app. Bulldozer	19	38	57	138	202	265
101,105,108,113,115: 101-1st app. Buster. 105-1st app. Junior. 113-1st app. Wildman & Jackie Johnson. 115-Rock revealed as orphan; 1st x-over Mlle. Marie. 1st Sgt. Rock's battle family	14	28	42	97	141	185
102-104,106,107,109,110,114,116-120: 104-Nurse Jane-c/s. 109-Pre Easy Co. Sgt. Rock-s. 118-Sunny injured	12	24	36	82	121	160
111-1st app. Wee Willie & Sunny	15	30	45	109	160	210
112-Classic Easy Co. roster-c	16	32	48	116	171	225
121-125,130-133,135-139,141-150: 138-1st Sparrow. 141-1st Shaker. 147,148-Rock becomes a General	9	18	27	60	85	110
126,129,134: 126-1st app. Canary; grey tone-c	9	18	27	65	93	120
127-2nd all-Sgt. Rock issue; 1st app. Little Sure	10	20	30	73	107	140
128-Training & origin Sgt. Rock; 1st Sgt. Krupp	25	50	75	176	258	340
140-3rd all-Sgt. Rock issue	9	18	27	65	93	120
151-Intro. Enemy Ace by Kubert (2/65)	37	74	111	278	414	550
152-4th all-Sgt. Rock issue	9	18	27	65	93	120
153-2nd app. Enemy Ace (4/65)	18	36	54	131	191	250
154,156,157,159-161,165-167: 157-2 pg. pin-up: 159-1st Nurse Wendy Winston-c/s. 165-2nd Iron Major	7	14	21	51	71	90
155-3rd app. Enemy Ace (6/65)(see Showcase)	12	24	36	87	129	170
158-Origin & 1st app. Iron Major(9/65), formerly Iron Captain	9	18	27	60	85	110
162,163-Viking Prince x-over in Sgt. Rock	8	16	24	58	82	105
164-Giant G-19	14	28	42	97	141	185
168-1st Unknown Soldier app.; referenced in Star-Spangled War Stories #157; (Sgt. Rock x-over) (6/66)	12	24	36	87	129	170
169,170	7	14	21	50	68	85
171-176,178-181: 171-1st Mad Emperor	6	12	18	43	59	75
177-(80 pg. Giant G-32)	9	18	27	65	93	120
182,183,186-Neal Adams-a. 186-Origin retold	7	14	21	50	68	85
184-Wee Willie dies	7	14	21	51	71	90
185,187,188,193-195,197-199	5	10	15	36	48	60
189,191,192,196: 189-Intro. The Teen-age Underground Fighters of Unit 3. 196-Hitler cameo	6	12	18	38	52	65

Our Fighting Forces #3 © DC

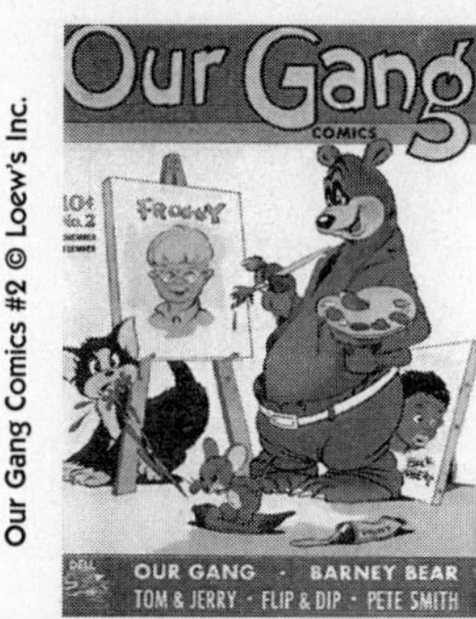

Our Gang Comics #2 © Loew's Inc.

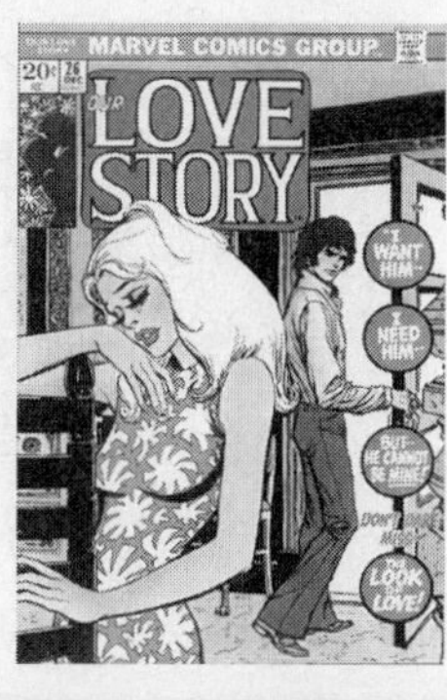

Our Love Story #26 © MAR

	GD 2.0	VG 4.0	FN 6.0	VF 8.0	VF/NM 9.0	NM- 9.2
190-(80 pg. Giant G-44)	7	14	21	51	71	90
200-12 pg. Rock story told in verse; Evans-a	6	12	18	40	55	70
201,202,204-207: 201-Krigstein-r/#14. 204,205-All reprints; no Sgt. Rock. 207-Last 12¢ cover	4	8	12	24	32	40
203-(80 pg. Giant G-56)-All-r, Sgt. Rock story	7	14	21	46	63	80
208-215	3	6	9	19	25	32
216,229-(80 pg. Giants G-68, G-80): 216-Has G-58 on-c by mistake	6	12	18	40	55	70
217-219: 218-1st U.S.S. Stevens	3	6	9	18	23	28
220-Classic dinosaur/Sgt. Rock-c/s	3	6	9	19	25	32
221-228,230-234: 231-Intro/death Rock's brother. 234-Last 15¢ issue	2	4	6	14	18	22
235-239,241: 52 pg. Giants	3	6	9	19	25	32
240-Neal Adams-a; 52 pg. Giant	4	8	12	25	33	42
242-Also listed as **DC 100 Page Super Spectacular #9**; see for price						
243-246: (All 52 pgs.) 244-No Adams-a	3	6	9	18	24	30
247-250,254-268,270: 247-Joan of Arc	2	4	6	10	13	16
251-253-Return of Iron Major	2	4	6	12	16	20
269,275-(100 pgs.)	4	8	12	27	36	45
271-274,276-279: 273-Crucifixion-c	2	4	6	10	12	15
280-(68 pgs.)-200th app. Sgt. Rock; reprints Our Army at War #81,83	3	6	9	18	24	30
281-299,301: 295-Bicentennial cover	2	4	6	9	11	14
300-Sgt. Rock-s by Kubert (2/77)	2	4	6	10	13	16

NOTE ***Alcala*** *a-251.* ***Drucker*** *a-27, 67, 68, 79, 82, 83, 96, 164, 177, 203, 212, 243r, 244, 269r, 275r, 280r.* ***Evans*** *a-165-175, 200, 266, 269, 270, 274, 276, 278, 280.* ***Glanzman*** *a-218, 220, 222, 223, 225, 227, 230-232, 238-241, 244, 247, 248, 256-259, 261, 265-267, 271, 282, 283, 298.* ***Grandenetti*** *c-91,120.* ***Grell*** *a-287.* ***Heath*** *a-50, 164, & most 176-281.* ***Kubert*** *a-38, 59, 67, 68 & most issues from 83-165, 171, 233, 236, 267, 275, 300; c-84, 280.* ***Maurer*** *a-233, 237, 239, 240, 45, 280, 284, 288, 290, 291, 295.* ***Severin*** *a-236, 252, 265, 267, 269r, 272.* ***Toth*** *a-235, 241, 254.* ***Wildey*** *a-283-285, 287p.* ***Wood*** *a-249.*

OUR FIGHTING FORCES
National Per. Publ./DC Comics: Oct-Nov, 1954 - No. 181, Sept-Oct, 1978

	GD 2.0	VG 4.0	FN 6.0	VF 8.0	VF/NM 9.0	NM- 9.2
1-Grandenetti-c/a	91	182	273	774	1187	1600
2	41	82	123	324	487	650
3-Kubert-c; last precode issue (3/55)	35	70	105	263	394	525
4,5	29	58	87	210	310	410
6-9: 7-1st S.A. issue	25	50	75	176	258	340
10-Wood-a	25	50	75	181	266	350
11-19	20	40	60	140	205	270
20-Grey tone-c (4/57)	22	44	66	160	235	310
21-30	14	28	42	99	145	190
31-40	12	24	36	87	129	170
41-Unknown Soldier tryout	16	32	48	116	171	225
42-44	11	22	33	77	114	150
45-Gunner & Sarge begins, end #94	37	74	111	278	419	560
46	16	32	48	116	171	225
47	11	22	33	80	118	155
48,50	10	20	30	73	107	140
49-1st Pooch	14	28	42	99	145	190
51-Grey tone-c	10	20	30	67	96	125
52-64: 64-Last 10¢ issue	9	18	27	60	85	110
65-70	7	14	21	46	63	80
71-Grey tone-c	6	12	18	43	59	75
72-80	5	10	15	36	48	60
81-90	5	10	15	33	44	55
91-98: 95-Devil-Dog begins, ends #98.	4	8	12	25	33	42
99-Capt. Hunter begins, ends #106	4	8	12	28	38	48
100	4	8	12	27	36	45
101-105,107-120: 116-Mlle. Marie app. 120-Last 12¢ issue	3	6	9	19	25	32
106-Hunters Hellcats begin	3	7	10	21	28	35
121,122: 121-Intro. Heller	3	6	9	18	23	28
123-The Losers (Capt. Storm, Gunner & Sarge, Johnny Cloud) begin	6	12	18	40	55	70
124-132: 132-Last 15¢ issue	2	4	6	14	18	22
133-137 (Giants). 134-Toth-a	3	6	9	18	24	30
138-150: 146-Toth-a	2	4	6	9	11	14
151-162-Kirby a(p)	2	4	6	12	16	20
163-180	2	4	6	8	10	12
181-Last issue	2	4	6	9	11	14

NOTE: ***N. Adams*** *c-147.* ***Drucker*** *a-28, 37, 39, 42-44, 49, 53, 133r.* ***Evans*** *a-149, 164-174, 177-181.* ***Glanzman*** *a-125-128, 132, 134, 138-141, 143, 144.* ***Heath*** *a-2, 16, 18, 28, 41, 44, 49, 114, 135-138r; c-51.* ***Kirby*** *a-151-162p; c-152-159.* ***Kubert*** *c/a in many issues.* ***Maurer*** *a-135.* ***Redondo*** *a-166.* ***Severin*** *a-123-130, 131i, 132-150.*

OUR FIGHTING MEN IN ACTION (See Men In Action)

OUR FLAG COMICS
Ace Magazines: Aug, 1941 - No. 5, April, 1942

	GD 2.0	VG 4.0	FN 6.0	VF 8.0	VF/NM 9.0	NM- 9.2
1-Captain Victory, The Unknown Soldier (intro.) & The Three Cheers begin	272	544	816	1700	2550	3400
2-Origin The Flag (patriotic hero); 1st app?	118	236	354	738	1107	1475
3-5: 5-Intro & 1st app. Mr. Risk	90	180	270	563	844	1125

NOTE: ***Anderson*** *a-1, 4.* ***Mooney*** *a-1, 2; c-2.*

OUR GANG COMICS (With Tom & Jerry #39-59; becomes Tom & Jerry #60 on; based on film characters)
Dell Publishing Co.: Sept-Oct, 1942 - No. 59, June, 1949

	GD 2.0	VG 4.0	FN 6.0	VF 8.0	VF/NM 9.0	NM- 9.2
1-Our Gang & Barney Bear by Kelly, Tom & Jerry, Pete Smith, Flip & Dip, The Milky Way begin (all 1st app.)	90	180	270	655	1003	1350
2-Benny Burro begins (#2 by Kelly)	44	88	132	340	508	675
3-5	30	60	90	218	322	425
6-Bumbazine & Albert only app. by Kelly	40	80	120	300	450	600
7-No Kelly story	23	46	69	164	240	315
8-Benny Burro begins by Barks	52	104	156	400	595	790
9-Barks-a(2): Benny Burro & Happy Hound; no Kelly story	47	94	141	360	535	710
10-Benny Burro by Barks	33	66	99	248	374	500
11-1st Barney Bear & Benny Burro by Barks (5-6/44); Happy Hound by Barks	47	94	141	360	535	710
12-20	24	48	72	169	247	325
21-30: 30-X-Mas-c	16	32	48	113	167	220
31-36-Last Barks issue	12	24	36	87	129	170
37-40	8	16	24	58	82	105
41-50	7	14	21	50	68	85
51-57	6	12	18	43	59	75
58,59-No Kelly art or Our Gang stories	6	12	18	38	52	65

NOTE: ***Barks*** *art in part only.* ***Barks*** *did not write Barney Bear stories #30-34. (See March of Comics #3, 26). Early issues have photo back-c.*

OUR LADY OF FATIMA
Catechetical Guild Educational Society: 3/11/55 (15¢) (36 pgs.)

	GD 2.0	VG 4.0	FN 6.0	VF 8.0	VF/NM 9.0	NM- 9.2
395	5	10	15	24	30	35

OUR LOVE (True Secrets #3 on? or Romantic Affairs #3 on?)
Marvel Comics (SPC): Sept, 1949 - No. 2, Jan, 1950

	GD 2.0	VG 4.0	FN 6.0	VF 8.0	VF/NM 9.0	NM- 9.2
1-Photo-c	15	30	45	86	118	150
2-Photo-c	10	20	30	56	73	90

OUR LOVE STORY
Marvel Comics Group: Oct, 1969 - No. 38, Feb, 1976

	GD 2.0	VG 4.0	FN 6.0	VF 8.0	VF/NM 9.0	NM- 9.2
1	6	12	18	43	59	75
2-4,6-8,10,11	3	6	9	19	25	32
5-Steranko-a	9	18	27	60	85	110
9,12-Kirby-a	3	7	10	21	28	35
13-(10/71, 52 pgs.)	4	8	12	27	36	45
14-New story by Gary Fredrich & Tarpe' Mills	3	7	10	21	28	35
15-20,27:27-Colan/Everett-a(r?); Kirby/Colletta-r	3	6	9	16	20	24
21-26,28-37	2	4	6	11	14	18
38-Last issue	3	6	9	16	20	25

NOTE: ***J. Buscema*** *a-1-3, 5-7, 9, 13r, 16r, 19r(2), 21r, 22r(2), 23r, 34r, 35r; c-11, 13, 16, 22, 23, 24, 27, 35.* ***Colan*** *a-3-6, 21r(#6), 22r, 23r(#3), 24r(#4), 27; c-19.* ***Katz*** *a-17.* ***Maneely*** *a-13r.* ***Romita*** *a-13r; c-1, 2, 4-6.* ***Weiss*** *a-16, 17, 29r(#17).*

OUR MISS BROOKS
Dell Publishing Co.: No. 751, Nov, 1956

	GD 2.0	VG 4.0	FN 6.0	VF 8.0	VF/NM 9.0	NM- 9.2
Four Color 751-Photo-c	9	18	27	60	85	110

OUR SECRET (Exciting Love Stories)(Formerly My Secret)
Superior Comics Ltd.: No. 4, Nov, 1949 - No. 8, Jun, 1950

	GD 2.0	VG 4.0	FN 6.0	VF 8.0	VF/NM 9.0	NM- 9.2
4-Kamen-a; spanking scene	19	38	57	107	149	190
5,6,8	10	20	30	58	77	95
7-Contains 9 pg. story intended for unpublished Ellery Queen #5; lingerie panels	11	22	33	63	84	105

OUTBREED 999
Blackout Comics: May, 1994 - No. 6, 1994 ($2.95)

	GD 2.0	VG 4.0	FN 6.0	VF 8.0	VF/NM 9.0	NM- 9.2
1-6: 4-1st app. of Extreme Violet in 7 pg. backup story						3.00

OUTCAST, THE
Valiant: Dec, 1995 ($2.50, one-shot)

	GD 2.0	VG 4.0	FN 6.0	VF 8.0	VF/NM 9.0	NM- 9.2
1-Breyfogle-a.						2.50

OUTCASTS
DC Comics: Oct, 1987 - No. 12, Sept, 1988 ($1.75, limited series)

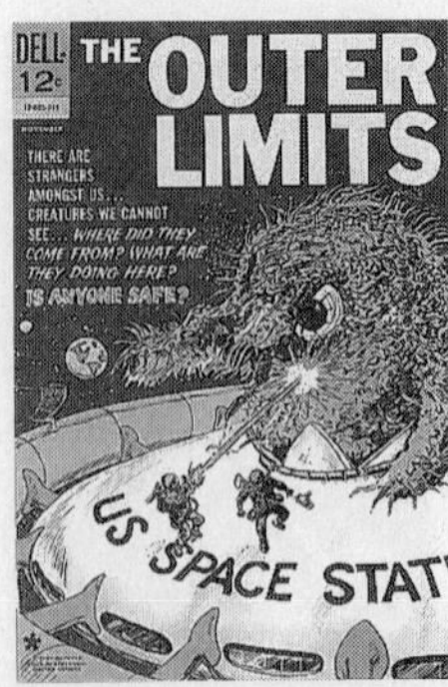

The Outer Limits #16 © DELL

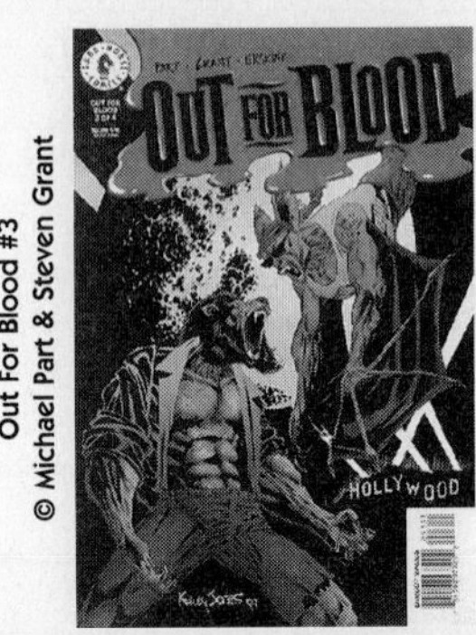

Out For Blood #3 © Michael Part & Steven Grant

Out of the Shadows #5 © STD

	GD 2.0	VG 4.0	FN 6.0	VF 8.0	VF/NM 9.0	NM- 9.2
1-12: John Wagner & Alan Grant scripts in all						2.25

OUTER LIMITS, THE (TV)
Dell Publishing Co.: Jan-Mar, 1964 - No. 18, Oct, 1969 (Most painted-c)

	GD 2.0	VG 4.0	FN 6.0	VF 8.0	VF/NM 9.0	NM- 9.2
1	13	26	39	94	137	180
2-5	8	16	24	53	74	95
6-10	6	12	18	43	59	75
11-18: 17-Reprints #1. 18-r/#2	5	10	15	36	48	60

OUTER SPACE (Formerly This Magazine Is Haunted, 2nd Series)
Charlton Comics: No. 17, May, 1958 - No. 25, Dec, 1959; Nov, 1968

	GD 2.0	VG 4.0	FN 6.0	VF 8.0	VF/NM 9.0	NM- 9.2
17-Williamson/Wood style art; not by them (Sid Check?)	15	30	45	86	118	150
18-20-Ditko-a	24	48	72	135	190	245
21-25: 21-Ditko-c	14	28	42	81	111	140
V2#1(11/68)-Ditko-a, Boyette-c	6	12	18	40	55	70

OUTER SPACE BABES, THE
Silhouette Studios: Feb, 1994 ($2.95)

	GD 2.0	VG 4.0	FN 6.0	VF 8.0	VF/NM 9.0	NM- 9.2
V3#1						3.00

OUT FOR BLOOD
Dark Horse: Sept, 1999 - No. 4, Dec, 1999 ($2.95, B&W, limited series)

	GD 2.0	VG 4.0	FN 6.0	VF 8.0	VF/NM 9.0	NM- 9.2
1-4-Kelley Jones-c; Erskine-a						3.00

OUTLANDERS (Manga)
Dark Horse Comics: Dec, 1988 - No. 33, Sept,1991 ($2.00-$2.50, B&W, 44 pgs.)

	GD 2.0	VG 4.0	FN 6.0	VF 8.0	VF/NM 9.0	NM- 9.2
1-33: Japanese Sci-fi manga						2.50

OUTLAW (See Return of the...)

OUTLAW FIGHTERS
Atlas Comics (IPC): Aug, 1954 - No. 5, Apr, 1955

	GD 2.0	VG 4.0	FN 6.0	VF 8.0	VF/NM 9.0	NM- 9.2
1-Tuska-a	14	28	42	79	107	135
2-5: 5-Heath-c/a, 7 pgs.	9	18	27	52	66	80

NOTE: ***Heath** c/a-5. **Maneely** c-2. **Pakula** a-2. **Reinman** a-2. **Tuska** a-1, 2.*

OUTLAW KID, THE (1st Series; see Wild Western)
Atlas Comics (CCC No. 1-11/EPI No. 12-29): Sept, 1954 - No. 19, Sept, 1957

	GD 2.0	VG 4.0	FN 6.0	VF 8.0	VF/NM 9.0	NM- 9.2
1-Origin; The Outlaw Kid & his horse Thunder begin; Black Rider app.	29	58	87	164	232	300
2-Black Rider app.	14	28	42	81	111	140
3-7,9: 3-Wildey-a(3)	12	24	36	71	96	120
8-Williamson/Woodbridge-a, 4 pgs.	13	26	39	76	103	130
10-Williamson-a	13	26	39	74	100	125
11-17,19: 13-Baker text illo. 15-Williamson text illo (unsigned)	9	18	27	52	66	80
18-Williamson/Mayo-a	10	20	30	56	73	90

NOTE: ***Berg** a-4, 7, 13. **Maneely** c-1-3, 5-8, 11-13, 15, 16, 18. **Pakula** a-3. **Severin** c-10, 17, 19. **Shores** a-1. **Wildey** a-1(3), 2-8, 10, 11, 12(4), 13(4), 15-19(4 each); c-4.*

OUTLAW KID, THE (2nd Series)
Marvel Comics Group: Aug, 1970 - No. 30, Oct, 1975

	GD 2.0	VG 4.0	FN 6.0	VF 8.0	VF/NM 9.0	NM- 9.2
1-Reprints; 1-Orlando-r, Wildey-r(3)	3	6	9	19	25	32
2,3,9: 2-Reprints. 3,9-Williamson-a(r)	2	4	6	11	14	18
4-7: 7-Last 15¢ issue	2	4	6	10	13	16
8-Double size (52 pgs.); Crandall-r	3	6	9	18	23	28
10-Origin	3	7	10	21	28	35
11-20: new-a in #10-16	2	4	6	11	14	18
21-30: 27-Origin-r/#10	2	4	6	8	10	12

NOTE: ***Ayers** a-10, 27r. **Berg** a-7, 25r. **Everett** a-2(2 pgs.). **Gil Kane** c-10, 11, 15, 27r, 28. **Roussos** a-10i, 27i(r). **Severin** c-1, 9, 20, 25. **Wildey** r-1-4, 6-9, 19-22, 25, 26. **Williamson** a-28r. **Woodbridge/Williamson** a-9r.*

OUTLAW NATION
DC Comics (Vertigo): Nov, 2000 - No. 19, May, 2002 ($2.50)

	GD 2.0	VG 4.0	FN 6.0	VF 8.0	VF/NM 9.0	NM- 9.2
1-19-Fabry painted-c/Delano-s/Sudzuka-a						2.50

OUTLAWS
D. S. Publishing Co.: Feb-Mar, 1948 - No. 9, June-July, 1949

	GD 2.0	VG 4.0	FN 6.0	VF 8.0	VF/NM 9.0	NM- 9.2
1-Violent & suggestive stories	35	70	105	201	288	370
2-Ingels-a; Baker-a	35	70	105	201	288	370
3,5,6: 3-Not Frazetta. 5-Sky Sheriff by Good app. 6-McWilliams-a	16	32	48	92	126	160
4-Orlando-a	18	36	54	101	138	175
7,8-Ingels-a in each	26	52	78	147	206	265
9-(Scarce)-Frazetta-a (7 pgs.)	48	96	144	288	432	575

NOTE: *Another #3 was printed in Canada with **Frazetta** art "Prairie Jinx," 7 pgs.*

OUTLAWS, THE (Formerly Western Crime Cases)
Star Publishing Co.: No. 10, May, 1952 - No. 13, Sep, 1953; No. 14, Apr, 1954

	GD 2.0	VG 4.0	FN 6.0	VF 8.0	VF/NM 9.0	NM- 9.2
10-L. B. Cole-c	22	44	66	124	172	220
11-14-L. B. Cole-c. 14-Reprints Western Thrillers #4 (Fox) w/new L.B. Cole-c; Kamen, Feldstein-r	17	34	51	95	130	165

OUTLAWS
DC Comics: Sept, 1991 - No. 8, Apr, 1992 ($1.95, limited series)

	GD 2.0	VG 4.0	FN 6.0	VF 8.0	VF/NM 9.0	NM- 9.2
1-8: Post-apocalyptic Robin Hood.						2.25

OUTLAW 7
Dark Horse Comics: Aug, 2001 - No. 4 ($2.99, limited series)

	GD 2.0	VG 4.0	FN 6.0	VF 8.0	VF/NM 9.0	NM- 9.2
1-3-Lubera & Feric-s/Lubera & Yeung-a						3.00

OUTLAWS OF THE WEST (Formerly Cody of the Pony Express #10)
Charlton Comics: No. 11, 7/57 - No. 81, 5/70; No. 82, 7/79 - No. 88, 4/80

	GD 2.0	VG 4.0	FN 6.0	VF 8.0	VF/NM 9.0	NM- 9.2
11	8	16	24	43	54	65
12,13,15-17,19,20	5	10	15	24	30	35
14-(68 pgs., 2/58)	9	18	27	49	62	75
18-Ditko-a	10	20	30	56	73	90
21-30	3	6	9	18	23	28
31-50: 34-Gunmaster app.	2	4	6	12	16	20
51-63,65,67-70: 54-Kid Montana app.	2	4	6	10	13	16
64,66: 64-Captain Doom begins (1st app.). 68-Kid Montana series begins	2	4	6	12	16	20
71-79: 73-Origin & 1st app. The Sharp Shooter, last app. #74. 75-Last Capt. Doom	2	4	6	9	11	14
80,81-Ditko-a	2	4	6	12	16	20
82-88						5.00
64,79(Modern Comics-r, 1977, '78)						4.00

OUTLAWS OF THE WILD WEST
Avon Periodicals: 1952 (25¢, 132 pgs.) (4 rebound comics)

	GD 2.0	VG 4.0	FN 6.0	VF 8.0	VF/NM 9.0	NM- 9.2
1-Wood back-c; Kubert-a (3 Jesse James-r)	34	68	102	193	274	355

OUTLAW TRAIL (See Zane Grey 4-Color 511)

OUT OF SANTA'S BAG (See March of Comics #10 in the Promotional Comics section)

OUT OF THE NIGHT (The Hooded Horseman #18 on)
Amer. Comics Group (Creston/Scope): Feb-Mar, 1952 - No. 17, Oct-Nov, 1954

	GD 2.0	VG 4.0	FN 6.0	VF 8.0	VF/NM 9.0	NM- 9.2
1-Williamson/LeDoux-a (9 pgs.)	64	128	192	400	600	800
2-Williamson-a (5 pgs.)	48	96	144	288	432	575
3,5-10: 9-Sci/Fic story	29	58	87	164	232	300
4-Williamson-a (7 pgs.)	40	80	120	240	350	460
11-17: 13-Nostrand-a? 17-E.C. Wood swipe	23	46	69	130	183	235

NOTE: ***Landau** a-14, 16, 17. **Shelly** a-12.*

OUT OF THE SHADOWS
Standard Comics/Visual Editions: No. 5, July, 1952 - No. 14, Aug, 1954

	GD 2.0	VG 4.0	FN 6.0	VF 8.0	VF/NM 9.0	NM- 9.2
5-Toth-p; Moreira, Tuska-a; Roussos-c	55	110	165	330	495	660
6-Toth/Celardo-a; Katz-a(2)	40	80	120	240	340	440
7,9: 7-Jack Katz-c/a(2). 9-Crandall-a(2)	31	62	93	175	248	320
8-Katz shrunken head-c	50	100	150	300	450	600
10-Spider-c; Sekowsky-a	31	62	93	175	248	320
11-Toth-a, 2 pgs.; Katz-a; Andru-c	31	62	93	175	248	320
12-Toth/Peppe-a(2); Katz-a	41	82	123	236	333	430
13-Cannabalism story; Sekowsky-a; Roussos-c	37	74	111	212	301	390
14-Toth-a	31	62	93	175	248	320

OUT OF THE VORTEX (Comics' Greatest World:... #1-4)
Dark Horse Comics: Oct., 1993 - No. 12, Oct, 1994 ($2.00, limited series)

	GD 2.0	VG 4.0	FN 6.0	VF 8.0	VF/NM 9.0	NM- 9.2
1-11: 1-Foil logo. 4-Dorman-c(p). 6-Hero Zero x-over						2.25
12 ($2.50)						2.50

NOTE: ***Art Adams** c-7. **Golden** c-8. **Mignola** c-2. **Simonson** c-3. **Zeck** c-10.*

OUT OF THIS WORLD
Charlton Comics: Aug, 1956 - No. 16, Dec, 1959

	GD 2.0	VG 4.0	FN 6.0	VF 8.0	VF/NM 9.0	NM- 9.2
1	26	52	78	150	210	270
2	13	26	39	76	103	130
3-6-Ditko-c/a (3) each	32	64	96	180	255	330
7-(2/58, 15¢, 68 pgs.)-Ditko-c/a(4)	33	66	99	190	270	350
8-(5/58, 15¢, 68 pgs.)-Ditko-a(2)	29	58	87	164	232	300
9,10,12,16-Ditko-a	22	44	66	127	176	225
11-Ditko c/a (3)	27	54	81	153	214	275
13-15	10	20	30	58	77	95

NOTE: ***Ditko** c-3-12, 16. **Reinman** a-10.*

OUT OF THIS WORLD
Avon Periodicals: June, 1950; Aug, 1950

1-Kubert-a(2) (one reprinted/Eerie #1, 1947) plus Crom the Barbarian by Gardner Fox &

Outsiders (3rd series) #1 © DC

Over the Edge #7 © MAR

Painkiller Jane #5 © Event

	GD 2.0	VG 4.0	FN 6.0	VF 8.0	VF/NM 9.0	NM- 9.2

John Giunta (origin); Fawcette-c 68 138 204 425 638 850
1-(8/50) Reprint; no month on cover 46 92 138 276 413 550

OUT OF THIS WORLD ADVENTURES
Avon Periodicals: July, 1950 - No. 2, Dec, 1950 (25¢ pulp)

1-Kubert-a 66 132 198 413 617 820
2-Kubert-a plus The Spider God of Akka by Gardner Fox & John Giunta pulp magazine w/comic insert 46 92 138 276 413 550

NOTE: *Out of This World Adventures is a sci-fi pulp magazine w/32 pgs. of color comics.*

OUT OUR WAY WITH WORRY WART
Dell Publishing Co.: No. 680, Feb, 1956

Four Color 680 4 8 12 22 30 38

OUTPOSTS
Blackthorne Publishing: June, 1987 - No. 4, 1987 ($1.25)

1-4: 1-Kaluta-c(p) 2.25

OUTSIDERS, THE
DC Comics: Nov, 1985 - No. 28, Feb, 1988

1 3.00
2-17 2.25
18-28: 18-26-Batman returns. 21-Intro. Strike Force Kobra; 1st app. Clayface IV 22-E.C. parody; Orlando-a. 21- 25-Atomic Knight app. 27,28-Millennium tie-ins 2.25
Annual 1 (12/86, $2.50), Special 1 (7/87, $1.50) 2.50

NOTE: ***Aparo** a-1-7, 9-14, 17-22, 25, 26; c-1-7, 9-14, 17, 19-26. **Byrne** a-11. **Bolland** a-6, 18; c-16. **Ditko** a-13p. **Erik Larsen** a-24, 27 28; c-27, 28. **Morrow** a-12.*

OUTSIDERS
DC Comics: Nov, 1993 - No. 24, Nov, 1995 ($1.75/$1.95/$2.25)

1-11,0,12-24: 1-Alpha; Travis Charest-c. 1-Omega; Travis Charest-c. 5-Atomic Knight app. 8-New Batman-c/story. 11-(9/94)-Zero Hour. 0-(10/94).12-(11/94). 21-Darkseid cameo. 22-New Gods app. 2.25

OUTSIDERS (See Titans/Young Justice: Graduation Day)
DC Comics: Aug, 2003 - Present ($2.50)

1-Nightwing, Arsenal, Metamorpho app.; Winick-s/Raney-a 5.00
2-Joker and Grodd app. 3.00
3-7: 3-Joker-c. 5,6-ChrisCross-a 2.50
... Double Feature (10/03, $4.95) r/#1,2 5.00
...: Looking For Trouble TPB (2004, $12.95) r/#1-7 & Teen Titans/Outsiders Secret Files & Origins 2003; intro. by Winick 13.00

OUT THERE
DC Comics(Cliffhanger): July, 2001 - No. 18, Aug, 2003 ($2.50/$2.95)

1-Humberto Ramos-c/a; Brian Augustyn-s 3.00
1-Variant-c by Carlos Meglia 4.00
2-8: 3-Variant-c by Bruce Timm 2.50
9-18: 9-Begin $2.95-c 3.00
...: The Evil Within TPB (2002, $12.95) r/#1-6; Ramos sketch pages 13.00

OVERKILL: WITCHBLADE/ ALIENS/ DARKNESS/ PREDATOR
Image Comics/Dark Horse Comics: Dec, 2000 - No. 2, 2001 ($5.95)

1,2-Jenkins-s/Lansing, Ching & Benitez-a 6.00

OVER THE EDGE
Marvel Comics: Nov, 1995 - No. 10, Aug, 1996 (99¢)

1-10: 1,6,10-Daredevil-c/story. 2,7-Dr. Strange-c/story. 3-Hulk-c/story. 4,9-Ghost Rider-c/story. 5-Punisher-c/story. 8-Elektra-c/story 2.25

OWL, THE (See Crackajack Funnies #25, Popular Comics #72 and Occult Files of Dr. Spektor #22)
Gold Key: April, 1967; No. 2, April, 1968

1-Written by Jerry Siegel; '40s super hero 7 14 21 46 63 80
2 5 10 15 36 48 60

OZ (See First Comics Graphic Novel, Marvel Treaury Of Oz & MGM's Marvelous...)

OZ
Caliber Press: 1994 - 1997 ($2.95, B&W)

0-20: 0-Released between #10 & #11 3.00
1 ($5.95)-Limited Edition; double-c 6.00
...Specials: Freedom Fighters. Lion. Scarecrow. Tin Man 3.00

OZARK IKE
Dell Publishing Co./Standard Comics B11 on: Feb, 1948; Nov, 1948 - No. 24, Dec, 1951; No. 25, Sept, 1952

Four Color 180(1948-Dell) 11 22 33 77 114 150
B11, B12, 13-15 9 18 27 52 66 80
16-25 8 16 24 43 54 65

OZ: DAEMONSTORM
Caliber Press: 1997 ($3.95, B&W, one-shot)

1 4.00

OZ: ROMANCE IN RAGS
Caliber Press: 1996 ($2.95, B&W, limited series)

1-3, ..Special 3.00

OZ SQUAD
Brave New Worlds/Patchwork Press: 1992 - No. 4, 1994 ($2.50/$2.75, B&W)

1-4-Patchwork Press 3.00

OZ SQUAD
Patchwork Press: Dec, 1995 - No. 10, 1996 ($3.95/$2.95, B&W)

1-($3.95) 4.00
2-10 3.00

OZ: STRAW AND SORCERY
Caliber Press: 1997 ($2.95, B&W, limited series)

1-3 3.00

OZ-WONDERLAND WARS, THE
DC Comics: Jan, 1986 - No. 3, March, 1986 (Mini-series)(Giants)

1-3-Capt Carrot app.; funny animals 4.00

OZZIE & BABS (TV Teens #14 on)
Fawcett Publications: Dec, 1947 - No. 13, Fall, 1949

1-Teen-age 9 18 27 52 66 80
2 6 12 18 28 34 40
3-13 5 10 15 23 28 32

OZZIE AND HARRIET (The Adventures of... on cover) (Radio)
National Periodical Publications: Oct-Nov, 1949 - No. 5, June-July, 1950

1-Photo-c 96 192 288 600 900 1200
2 48 96 144 288 432 575
3-5 40 80 120 240 350 460

OZZY OSBOURNE (Todd McFarland Presents)
Image Comics (Todd McFarlane Prod.): June, 1999 ($4.95, magazine-sized)

1-Bio, interview and comic story; Ormston painted-a; Ashley Wood-c 5.00

PACIFIC COMICS GRAPHIC NOVEL (See Image Graphic Novel)

PACIFIC PRESENTS (Also see Starslayer #2, 3)
Pacific Comics: Oct, 1982 - No. 2, Apr, 1983; No. 3, Mar, 1984 - No. 4, Jun, 1984

1-Chapter 3 of The Rocketeer; Stevens-c/a; Bettie Page model 1 2 3 4 5 7
2-Chapter 4 of The Rocketeer (4th app.); nudity; Stevens-c/a 1 2 3 4 5 7
3,4: 3-1st app. Vanity 3.00

NOTE: ***Conrad** a-3, 4; c-3. **Ditko** a-1-3; c-1(1/2). **Dave Stevens** a-1, 2; c-1(1/2), 2.*

PACT, THE
Image Comics: Feb, 1994 - No. 3, June, 1994 ($1.95, limited series)

1-3: Valentino co-scripts & layouts 2.25

PAGEANT OF COMICS (See Jane Arden & Mopsy)
Archer St. John: Sept, 1947 - No. 2, Oct, 1947

1,2: 1-Mopsy strip-r. 2-Jane Arden strip-r 10 20 30 56 73 90

PAINKILLER JANE
Event Comics: June, 1997 - No. 5, Nov, 1997 ($3.95/$2.95)

1-Augustyn/Waid-s/Leonardi/Palmiotti-a, variant-c 4.00
2-5: Two covers (Quesada, Leonardi) 3.00
0-(1/99, $3.95) Retells origin; two covers 4.00

PAINKILLER JANE / DARKCHYLDE
Event Comics: Oct, 1998 ($2.95, one-shot)

Preview-($6.95) DF Edition, 1-($6.95) DF Edition 7.00
1-Three covers; J.G. Jones-a 3.00

PAINKILLER JANE / HELLBOY
Event Comics: Aug, 1998 ($2.95, one-shot)

1-Leonardi & Palmiotti-a 3.00

PAINKILLER JANE VS. THE DARKNESS
Event Comics: Apr, 1997 ($2.95, one-shot)

1-Ennis-s; four variant-c (Conner, Hildebrandts, Quesada, Silvestri) 3.50

Panic #10 © WMG

Paradise X: Heralds #1 © MAR

Parliament of Justice #1 © Oeming & Vokes

GD 2.0 | VG 4.0 | FN 6.0 | VF 8.0 | VF/NM 9.0 | NM- 9.2

PAKKINS' LAND
Caliber Comics (Tapestry): Oct, 1996 - No. 6, July, 1997 ($2.95, B&W)

1-Gary and Rhoda Shipman-s/a 6.00
2,3 4.00
1-3-2nd printing 3.00
4-6 3.00
0-(6/97, $1.95) 3.00

PAKKINS' LAND: FORGOTTEN DREAMS
Caliber Comics/Image Comics #4: Apr, 1998 - No. 4, Mar, 2000 ($2.95, B&W)

1-4-Gary and Rhoda Shipman-s/a 3.00

PAKKINS' LAND: QUEST FOR KINGS
Caliber Comics: Aug, 1997 - No. 6, Mar, 1998 ($2.95, B&W)

1-6: 1-Gary and Rhoda Shipman-s/a; Jeff Smith var-c 3.00

PANCHO VILLA
Avon Periodicals: 1950

nn-Kinstler-c 25 50 75 144 198 255

PANDEMONIUM
Chaos! Comics: Sept, 1998 ($2.95, one-shot)

1-Al Rio-c 3.00

PANHANDLE PETE AND JENNIFER (TV) (See Gene Autry #20)
J. Charles Laue Publishing Co.: July, 1951 - No. 3, Nov, 1951

1 10 20 30 56 73 90
2,3 7 14 21 37 46 55

PANIC (Companion to Mad)
E. C. Comics (Tiny Tot Comics): Feb-Mar, 1954 - No. 12, Dec-Jan, 1955-56

1-Used in Senate Investigation hearings; Elder draws entire E. C. staff; Santa Claus & Mickey Spillane parody 29 58 87 218 309 400
2 14 28 42 105 148 190
3,4: 3-Senate Subcommittee parody; Davis draws Gaines, Feldstein & Kelly, 1 pg.; Old King Cole smokes marijuana. 4-Infinity-c; John Wayne parody 11 22 33 83 117 150
5-11: 8-Last pre-code issue (5/55). 9-Superman, Smilin' Jack & Dick Tracy app. on-c; has photo of Walter Winchell on-c. 11-Wheedies cereal box-c 10 20 30 75 105 135
12 (Low distribution; thousands were destroyed) 13 26 39 98 137 175

NOTE: ***Davis** a-1-12; c-12. **Elder** a-1-12. **Feldstein** c-1-3, 5. **Kamen** a-1. **Orlando** a-1-9. **Wolverton** c-4, panel-3. **Wood** a-2-9, 11, 12.*

PANIC (Magazine) (Satire)
Panic Publ.: July, 1958 - No. 6, July, 1959; V2#10, Dec, 1965 - V2#12, 1966

1 11 22 33 66 88 110
2-6 8 16 24 40 50 60
V2#10-12: Reprints earlier issues 3 6 9 18 24 30

NOTE: ***Davis** a-3(2 pgs.), 4, 5, 10; c-10. **Elder** a-5. **Powell** a-V2#10, 11. **Torres** a-1-5. **Tuska** a-V2#11.*

PANIC
Gemstone Publishing: March, 1997 - No. 11 ($2.50, quarterly)

1-11: E.C. reprints 2.50

PANTHA (See Vampirella-The New Monthly #16,17)

PANTHA: HAUNTED PASSION (Also see Vampirella Monthly #0)
Harris Comics: May, 1997 ($2.95, B&W, one-shot)

1-r/Vampirella #30,31 3.00

PARADE (See Hanna-Barbera...)

PARADE COMICS (Frisky Animals on Parade #2 on)
Ajax/Farrell Publ. (World Famous Publ.): Sept, 1957

1 9 18 27 49 62 75

NOTE: *Cover title: Frisky Animals on Parade.*

PARADE OF PLEASURE
Derric Verschoyle Ltd., London, England: 1954 (192 pgs.) (Hardback book)

By Geoffrey Wagner. Contains section devoted to the censorship of American comic books with illustrations in color and black and white. (Also see **Seduction of the Innocent**).
Distributed in USA by Library Publishers, N. Y. 50 100 150 275 363 450
with dust jacket.... 105 210 315 578 764 950

PARADIGM
Image Comics: Sept, 2002 - Present ($3.50/$2.95, B&W)

1-4,9-11-($3.50) Matthew Cashel & Jeremy Haun-s/a. 10-Savage Dragon cameo 3.50
5-8-($2.95) 3.00
12-($3.95) 4.00

Vol. 1: Segue To An Interlude TPB (8/03, $13.95) r/#1-4; sketch pages 14.00

PARADISE TOO!
Abstract Studios: 2000 - No. 14, 2003 ($2.95, B&W)

1-14-Terry Moore's unpublished newspaper strips and sketches 3.00
...: Checking For Weirdos TPB (4/03, $14.95) r/#8-12 15.00
...: Drunk Ducks! TPB (7/02, $15.95) r/#1-7 16.00

PARADISE X (Also see Earth X and Universe X)
Marvel Comics: Apr, 2002 - No. 11, July, 2003 ($4.50/$2.99)

0-Ross-c; Braithwaite-a 4.50
1-11-($2.99) Ross-c; Braithwaite-a. 7-Punisher on-c. 10-Kingpin on-c 3.00
...:A (10/03, $2.99) Braithwaite-a; Ross-c 3.00
...:Devils (11/02, $4.50) Sadowski-a; Ross-c 4.50
...:Ragnarok 1,2 (3/02, 4/03; $2.99) Yeates-a; Ross-c 3.00
...:X (11/03, $2.99) Braithwaite-a; Ross-c; conclusion of story 3.00
...:Xen (7/02, $4.50) Yeowell & Sienkiewicz-a; Ross-c 4.50
Earth X Vol. 4: Paradise X Book 1 (2003, $29.99, TPB) r/#0,1-5, ...: Xen; Heralds #1-3 30.00

PARADISE X: HERALDS (Also see Earth X and Universe X)
Marvel Comics: Dec, 2001 - No. 3, Feb, 2002 ($3.50)

1-3-Prelude to Paradise X series; Ross-c; Pugh-a 3.50
Special Edition (Wizard preview) Ross-c 2.25

PARADOX
Dark Visions Publ: June, 1994 - No. 2, Aug, 1994 ($2.95, B&W, mature)

1,2: 1-Linsner-c. 2-Boris-c. 3.00

PARALLAX: EMERALD NIGHT (See Final Night)
DC Comics: Nov, 1996 ($2.95, one-shot, 48 pgs.)

1-Final Night tie-in; Green Lantern (Kyle Rayner) app. 4.00

PARAMOUNT ANIMATED COMICS (See Harvey Comics Hits #60, 62)
Harvey Publications: No. 3, Feb, 1953 - No. 22, July, 1956

3-Baby Huey, Herman & Katnip, Buzzy the Crow begin 23 46 69 132 186 240
4-6 11 22 33 66 88 110
7-Baby Huey becomes permanent cover feature; cover title becomes Baby Huey with #9 23 46 69 129 180 230
8-10: 9-Infinity-c 11 22 33 63 84 105
11-22 9 18 27 49 62 75

PARENT TRAP, THE (Disney)
Dell Publishing Co.: No. 1210, Oct-Dec, 1961

Four Color 1210-Movie, Haley Mills photo-c 10 20 30 72 104 135

PARLIAMENT OF JUSTICE
Image Comics: Mar, 2003 ($5.95, B&W, one-shot, square-bound)

1-Michael Avon Oeming-c/s; Neil Vokes-a 6.00

PARODY
Armour Publishing: Mar, 1977 - No. 3, Aug, 1977 (B&W humor magazine)

1 2 4 6 11 14 18
2,3: 2-King Kong, Happy Days. 3-Charlie's Angels, Rocky 2 4 6 9 11 14

PAROLE BREAKERS
Avon Periodicals/Realistic #2 on: Dec, 1951 - No. 3, July, 1952

1(#2 on inside)-r-c/Avon paperback #283 (painted-c) 44 88 132 264 395 525
2-Kubert-a; r-c/Avon paperback #114 (photo-c) 33 66 99 190 270 350
3-Kinstler-c 30 60 90 170 240 310

PARTRIDGE FAMILY, THE (TV)(Also see David Cassidy)
Charlton Comics: Mar, 1971 - No. 21, Dec, 1973

1 7 14 21 46 63 80
2-4,6-10 4 8 12 24 32 40
5-Partridge Family Summer Special (52 pgs.); The Shadow, Lone Ranger, Charlie McCarthy, Flash Gordon, Hopalong Cassidy, Gene Autry & others app. 8 16 24 53 74 95
11-21 3 6 9 19 25 32

PARTS OF A HOLE
Caliber Press: 1991 ($2.50, B&W)

1-Short stories & cartoons by Brian Michael Bendis 3.00

PARTS UNKNOWN
Eclipse Comics/FX: July, 1992 - No. 4, Oct, 1992 ($2.50, B&W, mature)

1-4: All contain FX gaming cards 2.50

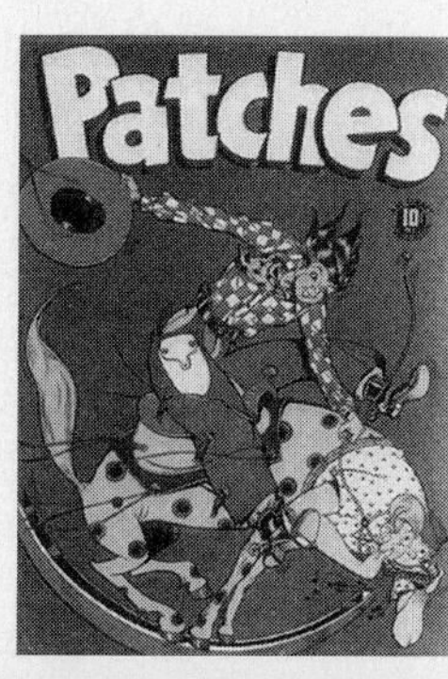

Patches #3 © Patches Publ.

The Path #2 © CRO

Patsy Walker #46 © MAR

	GD 2.0	VG 4.0	FN 6.0	VF 8.0	VF/NM 9.0	NM- 9.2

PARTS UNKNOWN
Image Comics: May, 2000 - Present ($2.95, B&W)

	GD	VG	FN	VF	VF/NM	NM-
...: Killing Attractions 1 (5/00) Beau Smith-s/Brad Gorby-a						3.00
...: Hostile Takeover 1-4 (6-9/00)						3.00

PASSION, THE
Catechetical Guild: No. 394, 1955

	GD	VG	FN	VF	VF/NM	NM-
394	5	10	15	23	28	32

PASSOVER (See Avengelyne)
Maximum Press: Dec, 1996 ($2.99, one-shot)

	GD	VG	FN	VF	VF/NM	NM-
1						3.00

PAT BOONE (TV)(Also see Superman's Girlfriend Lois Lane #9)
National Per. Publ.: Sept-Oct, 1959 - No. 5, May-Jun, 1960 (All have photo-c)

	GD	VG	FN	VF	VF/NM	NM-
1	46	92	138	276	413	550
2-5: 3-Fabian, Connie Francis & Paul Anka photos on-c. 4-Previews "Journey To The Center Of The Earth". 4-Johnny Mathis & Bobby Darin photos on-c. 5-Dick Clark & Frankie Avalon photos on-c	39	78	117	230	325	420

PATCHES
Rural Home/Patches Publ. (Orbit): Mar-Apr, 1945 - No. 11, Nov, 1947

	GD	VG	FN	VF	VF/NM	NM-
1-L. B. Cole-c	40	80	120	240	340	440
2	15	30	45	86	118	150
3,4,6,8-11: 6-Henry Aldrich story. 8-Smiley Burnette-c/s (6/47); pre-dates Smiley Burnette #1. 9-Mr. District Attorney story (radio). Leav/Keigstein-a (16 pgs.). 9-11-Leav-c. 10-Jack Carson (radio) c/story; Leav-c. 11-Red Skelton story	14	28	42	81	111	140
5-Danny Kaye-c/story; L.B. Cole-c.	21	42	63	118	164	210
7-Hopalong Cassidy-c/story	18	36	54	101	138	175

PATH, THE
CrossGeneration Comics: Apr, 2002 - No. 23, Mar, 2004 ($2.95)

	GD	VG	FN	VF	VF/NM	NM-
1-23: 1-Ron Marz-s/Bart Sears-a. 13-Matthew Smith-a begins						3.00
Vol. 1: Crisis of Faith (2002, $15.95, TPB) r/#1-6						16.00
Vol. 2: Blood on Snow (5/03, $15.95, TPB) r/#7-12						16.00
Vol. 3: Death and Dishonor ('03, $15.95, TPB) r/#13-18						16.00

PATHWAYS TO FANTASY
Pacific Comics: July, 1984

	GD	VG	FN	VF	VF/NM	NM-
1-Barry Smith-c/a; Jeff Jones-a (4 pgs.)						4.00

PATORUZU (See Adventures of...)

PATRIOTS, THE
DC Comics (WildStorm): Jan, 2000 - No. 10, Oct, 2000 ($2.50)

	GD	VG	FN	VF	VF/NM	NM-
1-10-Choi and Peterson-s/Ryan-a						2.50

PATSY & HEDY (Teenage)(Also see Hedy Wolfe)
Atlas Comics/Marvel (GPI/Male): Feb, 1952 - No. 110, Feb, 1967

	GD	VG	FN	VF	VF/NM	NM-
1-Patsy Walker & Hedy Wolfe; Al Jaffee-c	23	46	69	129	180	230
2	13	26	39	74	100	125
3-10: 3,8-Al Jaffee-c	10	20	30	58	77	95
11-20: 17-Al Jaffee-c	9	18	27	49	62	75
21-40	7	14	21	37	46	55
41-60	4	8	12	27	36	45
61-80,100: 88-Lingerie panel	3	7	10	21	28	35
81-87,89-99,101-110	3	6	9	18	24	30
Annual 1(1963)-Early Marvel annual	10	20	30	67	96	125

PATSY & HER PALS (Teenage)
Atlas Comics (PPI): May, 1953 - No. 29, Aug, 1957

	GD	VG	FN	VF	VF/NM	NM-
1-Patsy Walker	19	38	57	107	149	190
2	10	20	30	58	77	95
3-10	9	18	27	52	66	80
11-29: 24-Everett-c	8	16	24	40	50	60

PATSY WALKER (See All Teen, A Date With Patsy, Girls' Life, Miss America Magazine, Patsy & Hedy, Patsy & Her Pals & Teen Comics)
Marvel/Atlas Comics (BPC): 1945 (no month) - No. 124, Dec, 1965

	GD	VG	FN	VF	VF/NM	NM-
1-Teenage	50	100	150	300	450	600
2	27	54	81	155	218	280
3,4,6-10	21	42	63	121	168	215
5-Injury-to-eye-c	24	48	72	138	194	250
11,12,15,16,18	14	28	42	79	107	135
13,14,17,19-22-Kurtzman's "Hey Look"	15	30	45	84	115	145
23,24	10	20	30	60	80	100
25-Rusty by Kurtzman; painted-c	15	30	45	84	115	145
26-29,31: 26-31: 52 pgs.	10	20	30	56	73	90
30(52 pgs.)-Egghead Doodle by Kurtzman (1 pg.)	10	20	30	60	80	100
32-57: Last precode (3/55)	8	16	24	43	54	65
58-80,100	4	8	12	27	36	45
81-99: 92,98-Millie x-over. 99-Linda Carter x-over	3	7	10	21	28	35
101-124	3	6	9	18	24	30
Fashion Parade 1(1966, 68 pgs.) (Beware cut-out & marked pages)	9	18	27	60	85	110

NOTE: *Painted c-25-28. Anti-Wertham editorial in #21. Georgie app. in #8, 11. Millie app. in #10, 92, 98. Mitzi app. in #11. Rusty app. in #12, 25. Willie app. in #12.* ***Al Jaffee*** *c-57, 58.*

PAT THE BRAT (Adventures of Pipsqueak #34 on)
Archie Publications (Radio): June, 1953; Summer, 1955 - No. 4, 5/56; No. 15, 7/56 - No. 33, 7/59

	GD	VG	FN	VF	VF/NM	NM-
nn(6/53)	14	28	42	79	107	135
1(Summer, 1955)	10	20	30	56	73	90
2-4-(5/56) (#5-14 not published)	7	14	21	37	46	55
15-(7/56)-33	4	8	12	27	36	45

PAT THE BRAT COMICS DIGEST MAGAZINE
Archie Publications: October, 1980

	GD	VG	FN	VF	VF/NM	NM-
1-Li'l Jinx & Super Duck app.	2	4	6	9	11	14

PATTY CAKE
Permanent Press: Mar, 1995 - No. 9, Jul, 1996 ($2.95, B&W)

	GD	VG	FN	VF	VF/NM	NM-
1-9: Scott Roberts-s/a						3.00

PATTY CAKE
Caliber Press (Tapestry): Oct, 1996 - No. 3, Apr, 1997 ($2.95, B&W)

	GD	VG	FN	VF	VF/NM	NM-
1-3: Scott Roberts-s/a, ...Christmas (12/96)						3.00

PATTY CAKE & FRIENDS
Slave Labor Graphics: Nov, 1997 - Present ($2.95, B&W)

	GD	VG	FN	VF	VF/NM	NM-
Here There Be Monsters (10/97), 1-14: Scott Roberts-s/a						3.00
Volume 2 #1 (11/00, $4.95)						5.00

PATTY POWERS (Formerly Della Vision #3)
Atlas Comics: No. 4, Oct, 1955 - No. 7, Oct, 1956

	GD	VG	FN	VF	VF/NM	NM-
4	10	20	30	56	73	90
5-7	6	12	18	31	38	45

PAT WILTON (See Mighty Midget Comics)

PAUL
Spire Christian Comics (Fleming H. Revell Co.): 1978 (49¢)

	GD	VG	FN	VF	VF/NM	NM-
nn	1	3	4	6	8	10

PAULINE PERIL (See The Close Shaves of...)

PAUL REVERE'S RIDE (TV, Disney, see Walt Disney Showcase #34)
Dell Publishing Co.: No. 822, July, 1957

	GD	VG	FN	VF	VF/NM	NM-
Four Color 822-w/Johnny Tremain, Toth-a	10	20	30	70	100	130

PAUL TERRY (See Heckle and Jeckle)

PAUL TERRY'S ADVENTURES OF MIGHTY MOUSE (See Adventures of...)

PAUL TERRY'S COMICS (Formerly Terry-Toons Comics; becomes Adventures of Mighty Mouse No. 126 on)
St. John Publishing Co.: No. 85, Mar, 1951 - No. 125, May, 1955

	GD	VG	FN	VF	VF/NM	NM-
85,86-Same as Terry-Toons #85, & 86 with only a title change; published at same time?; Mighty Mouse, Heckle & Jeckle & Gandy Goose continue from Terry-Toons	11	22	33	63	84	105
87-99	8	16	24	46	58	70
100	9	18	27	52	66	80
101 104,107 125: 101,122,125 Painted c	0	10	24	40	54	05
105,106-Giant Comics Edition (25¢, 100 pgs.) (9/53 & ?). 105-Little Roquefort-c/story	19	38	57	106	146	185

PAUL TERRY'S MIGHTY MOUSE (See Mighty Mouse)

PAUL TERRY'S MIGHTY MOUSE ADVENTURE STORIES (See Mighty Mouse Adventure Stories)

PAUL THE SAMURAI (See The Tick #4)
New England Comics: July, 1992 - No. 6, July, 1993 ($2.75, B&W)

	GD	VG	FN	VF	VF/NM	NM-
1-6						2.75

PAWNEE BILL
Story Comics (Youthful Magazines?): Feb, 1951 - No. 3, July, 1951

	GD	VG	FN	VF	VF/NM	NM-
1-Bat Masterson, Wyatt Earp app.	13	26	39	74	100	125
2,3: 3-Origin Golden Warrior; Cameron-a	8	16	24	43	54	65

PAY-OFF (This Is the..., ...Crime, ...Detective Stories)
D. S. Publishing Co.: July-Aug, 1948 - No. 5, Mar-Apr, 1949 (52 pgs.)

Pebbles and Bamm Bamm #33 © H-B

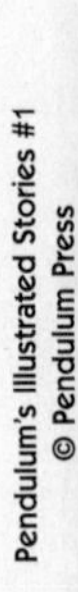
Pendulum's Illustrated Stories #1 © Pendulum Press

Pep Comics #16 © AP

GD 2.0 | VG 4.0 | FN 6.0 | VF 8.0 | VF/NM 9.0 | NM- 9.2

1-True Crime Cases #1,2 26 52 78 150 210 270
2 16 32 48 92 126 160
3-5-Thrilling Detective Stories 14 28 42 79 107 135

PEACEMAKER, THE (Also see Fightin' Five)
Charlton Comics: V3#1, Mar, 1967 - No. 5, Nov, 1967 (All 12¢ cover price)

1-Fightin' Five begins 6 12 18 38 52 65
2,3,5 3 7 10 21 28 35
4-Origin The Peacemaker 4 8 12 27 36 45
1,2(Modern Comics reprint, 1978) 5.00

PEACEMAKER (Also see Crisis On Infinite Earths & Showcase '93 #7,9,10)
DC Comics: Jan, 1988 - No. 4, Apr, 1988 ($1.25, limited series)

1-4 2.50

PEANUTS (Charlie Brown) (See Fritzi Ritz, Nancy & Sluggo, Sparkle & Sparkler, Tip Top, Tip Topper & United Comics)
Dell Publishing Co./Gold Key: 1953-54; No. 878, 2/58 - No. 13, 5-7/62; 5/63 - No. 4, 2/64

1(1953-54)-Reprints United Features' Strange As It Seems, Willie, Ferdnand
13 26 39 90 133 175
Four Color 878(#1) Schulz-s/a, with assistance from Dale Hale and Jim Sasseville thru #4
17 34 51 123 182 240
Four Color 969,1015('59) 12 24 36 82 121 160
4(2-4/60) Schulz-s/a; one story by Anthony Pocrnich, Schulz's assistant cartoonist
10 20 30 67 96 125
5-13-Schulz-c only; s/a by Pocrnich 8 16 24 58 82 105
1(Gold Key, 5/63) 12 24 36 82 121 160
2-4 8 16 24 55 78 100

PEBBLES & BAMM BAMM (TV) (See Cave Kids #7, 12)
Charlton Comics: Jan, 1972 - No. 36, Dec, 1976 (Hanna-Barbera)

1-From the Flintstones; "Teen Age..." on cover 6 12 18 38 52 65
2-10 3 6 9 19 25 32
11-20 2 4 6 14 18 22
21-36 2 4 6 10 13 16

PEBBLES & BAMM BAMM (TV)
Harvey Comics: Nov, 1993 - No. 3, Mar, 1994 ($1.50) (Hanna-Barbera)

V2#1-3 3.00
...Giant Size 1 (10/93, $2.25, 68 pgs.)("Summer Special" on-c) 4.00

PEBBLES FLINTSTONE (TV) (See The Flintstones #11)
Gold Key: Sept, 1963 (Hanna-Barbera)

1 (10088-309)-Early Pebbles app. 10 20 30 72 104 135

PEDRO (Formerly My Private Life #17; also see Romeo Tubbs)
Fox Features Syndicate: No. 18, June, 1950 - No. 2, Aug, 1950?

18(#1)-Wood-c/a(p) 24 48 72 135 190 245
2-Wood-a? 17 34 51 98 134 170

PEE-WEE PIXIES (See The Pixies)

PELLEAS AND MELISANDE (See Night Music #4, 5)

PENALTY (See Crime Must Pay the...)

PENDRAGON (Knights of... #5 on; also see Knights of...)
Marvel Comics UK, Ltd.: July, 1992 - No. 15, Sept, 1993 ($1.75)

1-15: 1-4-Iron Man app. 6-8-Spider-Man app. 2.25

PENDULUM ILLUSTRATED BIOGRAPHIES
Pendulum Press: 1979 (B&W)

19-355x-George Washington/Thomas Jefferson, 19-3495-Charles Lindbergh/Amelia Earhart, 19-3509-Harry Houdini/Walt Disney, 19-3517-Davy Crockett/Daniel Boone-Redondo-a, 19-3525-Elvis Presley/Beatles, 19-3533-Benjamin Franklin/Martin Luther King Jr, 19-3541-Abraham Lincoln/Franklin D. Roosevelt, 19-3568-Marie Curie/Albert Einstein-Redondo-a, 19-3576-Thomas Edison/Alexander Graham Bell-Redondo-a, 19-3584-Vince Lombardi/Pele, 19-3592-Babe Ruth/Jackie Robinson, 19-3606-Jim Thorpe/Althea Gibson
Softback 3.00
Hardback 5.00
NOTE: *Above books still available from publisher.*

PENDULUM ILLUSTRATED CLASSICS (Now Age Illustrated)
Pendulum Press: 1973 - 1978 (75¢, 62pp, B&W, 5-3/8x8")
(Also see Marvel Classics)

64-100x(1973)-Dracula-Redondo art, 64-131x-The Invisible Man-Nino art, 64-0968-Dr. Jekyll and Mr. Hyde-Redondo art, 64-1005-Black Beauty, 64-1010-Call of the Wild, 64-1020-Frankenstein, 64-1025-Hucklebury Finn, 64-1030-Moby Dick-Nino-a, 64-1040-Red Badge of Courage, 64-1045-The Time Machine-Nino-a, 64-1050-Tom Sawyer, 64-1055-Twenty Thousand Leagues Under the Sea, 64-1069-Treasure Island, 64-1328(1974)-Kidnapped, 64-1336-Three Musketeers-Nino art, 64-1344-A Tale of Two Cities, 64-1352-Journey to the Center of the Earth, 64-1360-The War of the Worlds-Nino-a, 64-1379-The Greatest Advs. of Sherlock Holmes-Redondo art, 64-1387-Mysterious Island, 64-1395-Hunchback of Notre Dame, 64-1409-Helen Keller-story of my life, 64-1417-Scarlet Letter, 64-1425-Gulliver's Travels, 64-2618(1977)-Around the World in Eighty Days, 64-2626-Captains Courageous, 64-2634-Connecticut Yankee, 64-2642-The Hound of the Baskervilles, 64-2650-The House of Seven Gables, 64-2669-Jane Eyre, 64-2677-The Last of the Mohicans, 64-2685-The Best of O'Henry, 64-2693-The Best of Poe-Redondo-a, 64-2707-Two Years Before the Mast, 64-2715-White Fang, 64-2723-Wuthering Heights, 64-3126(1978)-Ben Hur-Redondo art, 64-3134-A Christmas Carol, 64-3142-The Food of the Gods, 64-3150-Ivanhoe, 64-3169-The Man in the Iron Mask, 64-3177-The Prince and the Pauper, 64-3185-The Prisoner of Zenda, 64-3193-The Return of the Native, 64-3207-Robinson Crusoe, 64-3215-The Scarlet Pimpernel, 64-3223-The Sea Wolf, 64-3231-The Swiss Family Robinson, 64-3851-Billy Budd, 64-386x-Crime and Punishment, 64-3878-Don Quixote, 64-3886-Great Expectations, 64-3894-Heidi, 64-3908-The Iliad, 64-3916-Lord Jim, 64-3924-The Mutiny on Board H.M.S. Bounty, 64-3932-The Odyssey, 64-3940-Oliver Twist, 64-3959-Pride and Prejudice, 64-3967-The Turn of the Screw
Softback 3.00
Hardback 5.00

NOTE: *All of the above books can be ordered from the publisher; some were reprinted as Marvel Classic Comics #1-12. In 1972 there was another brief series of 12 titles which contained Classics Ill. artwork. They were entitled* ***Now Age Books*** *Illustrated, but can be easily distinguished from later series by the small Classics Illustrated logo at the top of the front cover. The format is the same as the later series. The 48 pg. C.I. art was stretched out to make 62 pgs. After Twin Circle Publ. terminated the Classics Ill. series in 1971, they made a one year contract with Pendulum Press to print these twelve titles of C.I. art. Pendulum was unhappy with the contract, and at the end of 1972 began their own art series, utilizing the talents of the Filipino artist group. One detail which makes this rather confusing is that when they redid the art in 1973, they gave it the same identifying no. as the 1972 series. All 12 of the 1972 C.I. editions have new covers, taken from internal art panels. In spite of their recent age, all of the 1972 C.I. series are very rare. Mint copies would fetch at least $50. Here is a list of the 1972 series, with C.I. title no. counterpart:*

64-1005 (CI#60-A2) 64-1010 (CI#91) 64-1015 (CI-Jr #503) 64-1020 (CI#26)
64-1025 (CI#19-A2) 64-1030 (CI#5-A2) 64-1035 (CI#169) 64-1040 (CI#98)
64-1045 (CI#133) 64-1050 (CI#50-A2) 64-1055 (CI#47) 64-1060 (CI-Jr#535)

PENDULUM ILLUSTRATED ORIGINALS
Pendulum Press: 1979 (In color)

94-4254-Solarman: The Beginning (See Solarman) 6.00

PENDULUM'S ILLUSTRATED STORIES
Pendulum Press: 1990 - No. 72, 1990? (No cover price ($4.95), squarebound, 68 pgs.)

1-72: Reprints Pendulum Ill. Classics series 5.00

PENNY
Avon Comics: 1947 - No. 6, Sept-Oct, 1949 (Newspaper reprints)

1-Photo & biography of creator 12 24 36 69 92 115
2-5 8 16 24 43 54 65
6-Perry Como photo on-c 9 18 27 52 66 80

PENNY CENTURY (See Love and Rockets)
Fantagraphics Books: Dec, 1997 - Present ($2.95, B&W, mini-series)

1-7-Jaime Hernandez-s/a 3.00

PENTHOUSE COMIX
General Media Int.: 1994 - No. 33, July, 1998 ($4.95, bimonthly, magazine & comic sized, mature)

1 2 4 6 8 10 12
2-5 1 2 3 5 7 9
6-33: 15-Corben-c. 16-Dorman-c. 17-Manara-c. 20-Chiodo-c. 21,23-Boris-c. 24-Scott Hampton-c. 26-33-Comic-sized 1 2 3 4 5 7

PENTHOUSE MAX
General Media International: July, 1996 - No. 3 ($4.95, magazine, mature)

1-3: 1-Giffen, Sears, Maguire-a. 2-Political satire. 3-Mr. Monster-c/app.; Dorman-c
1 2 3 4 5 7

PENTHOUSE MEN'S ADVENTURE COMIX
General Media International: 1995 - No. 7, 1996 ($4.95, magazine, mature)

1-7 (Magazine Size): 1-Boris-c, 1-5 (Comic Size): 1-Boris-c
1 2 3 4 5 7

PEP COMICS (See Archie Giant Series #576, 589, 601, 614, 624)
MLJ Magazines/Archie Publications No. 56 (3/46) on: Jan, 1940 - No. 411, Mar, 1987

1-Intro. The Shield (1st patriotic hero) by Irving Novick; origin & 1st app. The Comet by Jack Cole, The Queen of Diamonds & Kayo Ward; The Rocket, The Press Guardian (The Falcon #1 only), Sergeant Boyle, Fu Chang, & Bentley of of Scotland Yard; Robot-c; Shield-c begin
966 1932 2898 6762 10,381 14,000
2-Origin The Rocket 240 480 720 1500 2250 3000
3 176 352 528 1100 1650 2200
4-Wizard cameo; early robot-s 144 288 432 900 1350 1800
5-Wizard cameo in Shield story 144 288 432 900 1350 1800
6-10: 8-Last Cole Comet; no Cole-a in #6,7 110 220 330 688 1032 1375
11-Dusty, Shield's sidekick begins (1st app.); last Press Guardian, Fu Chang
114 228 342 713 1069 1425
12-Origin & 1st app. Fireball (2/41); last Rocket & Queen of Diamonds; Danny in Wonderland begins 136 272 408 850 1275 1700
13-15 92 184 276 575 863 1150
16-Origin Madam Satan; blood drainage-c 144 288 432 900 1350 1800

Pep Comics #85 © AP

Perfect Love #3 © Z-D

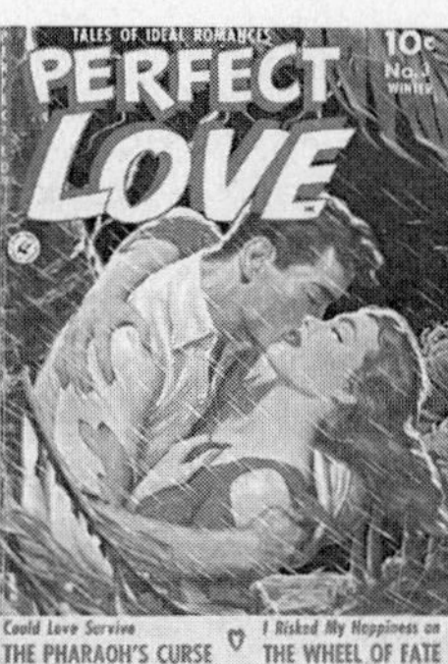

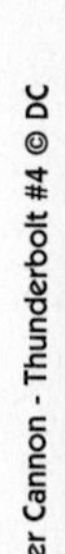
Peter Cannon - Thunderbolt #4 © DC

	GD 2.0	VG 4.0	FN 6.0	VF 8.0	VF/NM 9.0	NM- 9.2
17-Origin/1st app. The Hangman (7/41); death of The Comet; Comet is revealed as Hangman's brother	333	666	1000	2165	3333	4500
18-21: 20-Last Fireball. 21-Last Madam Satan	85	170	255	531	796	1060
22-Intro. & 1st app. Archie, Betty, & Jughead(12/41); (also see Jackpot)	1250	2500	3750	9375	14,688	20,000
23	164	328	492	1025	1538	2050
24,25: 24-Coach Kleets app. (unnamed until Archie #94); bondage/torture-c. 25-1st app. Archie's jalopy; 1st skinny Mr. Weatherbee prototype	118	236	354	738	1107	1475
26-1st app. Veronica Lodge (4/42); "Remember Pearl Harbor!" cover caption	168	336	504	1050	1575	2100
27-30: 29-Origin Shield retold; 30-Capt. Commando begins; bondage/torture-c; 1st Miss Grundy (definitive version); see Jackpot #4	92	184	276	575	863	1150
31-35: 31-MLJ offices & artists are visited in Sgt. Boyle story; 1st app. Mr. Lodge. 32-Shield dons new costume. 34-Bondage/Hypo-c. 33-Pre-Moose tryout (see Jughead #1)	74	148	222	463	694	925
36-1st Archie-c (2/43) w/Shield & Hangman	184	368	552	1150	1725	2300
37-40	55	110	165	330	495	660
41-50: 41-Archie-c begin. 47-Last Hangman issue; infinity-c. 48-Black Hood begins (5/44); ends #51,59,60	40	80	120	240	340	440
51-60: 52-Suzie begins; 1st Mr Weatherbee-c. 56-Last Capt. Commando. 59-Black Hood not in costume; lingerie panels; Archie dresses as his aunt; Suzie ends. 60-Katy Keene begins(3/47), ends #154	28	56	84	159	225	290
61-65-Last Shield. 62-1st app. Li'l Jinx (7/47)	24	48	72	138	194	250
66-80: 66-G-Man Club becomes Archie Club (2/48); Nevada Jones by Bill Woggon. 78-1st app. Dilton	15	30	45	86	118	150
81-99	11	22	33	66	88	110
100	15	30	45	84	115	145
101-130	8	16	24	43	54	65
131(2/59)-149(9/61)	4	8	12	25	33	42
150-160-Super-heroes app. in each (see note). 150 (10/61?)-2nd or 3rd app. The Jaguar? 152-157-Sci/Fi-c. 157-Li'l Jinx story	5	10	15	33	44	55
161(3/63)-167,169-180	3	6	9	18	24	30
168,200: 168-(1/64)-Jaguar app. 200-(12/66)	3	7	10	21	28	35
181(5/65)-199: 192-UFO-c. 198-Giantman-c(only)	3	6	9	16	20	24
201-217,219-226,228-240(4/70)	2	4	6	11	14	18
218,227-Archies Band-c only	2	4	6	12	16	20
241-270(10/72)	2	4	6	9	11	14
271-297,299	1	3	4	6	8	10
298-Josie and the Pussycats-c	2	4	6	9	11	14
300(4/75)	2	4	6	9	11	14
301-340(8/78)	1	2	3	5	6	8
341-382						5.00
383(4/82),393(3/84): 383-Marvelous Maureen begins (Sci/fi). 393-Thunderbunny begins						6.00
384-392,394-399,401-410						4.00
400(5/85),411: 400-Story featuring Archie staff (DeCarlo-a)						6.00

NOTE: *Biro a-2, 4, 5.* **Jack Cole** *a-1-5, 8.* **Al Fagaly** *c-55-72.* **Fuje** *a-39, 45, 47; c-34.* **Meskin** *a-2, 4, 5, 11(2).* **Montana** *c-30, 32, 33, 36, 73-87(most).* **Novick** *c-1-28, 29(w/Schomburg), 31i.* **Harry Sahle** *c-35, 39-50.* **Schomburg** *c-38.* **Bob Wood** *a-2, 4-6, 11. The Fly app. in 151, 154, 160. Flygirl app. in 153, 155, 156, 158. Jaguar app. in 150, 152, 157, 159, 168. Katy Keene by* **Bill Woggon** *in many later issues. Bondage c-7, 12, 13, 15, 18, 21, 31, 32. Cover features: Shield #1-16; Shield/Hangman #17-27, 29-41; Hangman #28. Archie #36, 41-on.*

PEPE
Dell Publishing Co.: No. 1194, Apr, 1961

	GD	VG	FN	VF	VF/NM	NM-
Four Color 1194-Movie, photo-c	3	6	9	18	24	30

PERFECT CRIME, THE
Cross Publications: Oct, 1949 - No. 33, May, 1953 (#2-12, 52 pgs.)

	GD	VG	FN	VF	VF/NM	NM-
1-Powell-a(2)	33	66	99	190	270	350
2 (4/50)	19	38	57	108	140	185
3-10: 7-Steve Duncan begins, ends #30. 10-Flag-c	16	32	48	92	126	160
11-Used in **SOTI**, pg. 159	18	36	54	101	138	175
12-14	15	30	45	86	118	150
15- "The Most Terrible Menace" 2 pg. drug editorial	16	32	48	92	126	160
16,17,19-25,27-29,31-33	11	22	33	63	84	105
18-Drug cover, heroin drug propaganda story, plus 2 pg. anti-drug editorial	24	48	72	135	190	245
26-Drug-c with hypodermic; drug propaganda story	25	50	75	147	202	260
30-Strangulation cover	25	50	75	147	202	260

NOTE: **Powell** *a-No. 1, 2, 4.* **Wildey** *a-1, 5. Bondage c-11.*

PERFECT LOVE
Ziff-Davis(Approved Comics)/St. John No. 9 on: #10, 8-9/51 (cover date; 5-6/51 indicia date); #2, 10-11/51 - #10, 12/53

	GD	VG	FN	VF	VF/NM	NM-
10(#1)(8-9/51)-Painted-c	21	42	63	118	164	210
2(10-11/51)	14	28	42	81	111	140
3,5-7: 3-Painted-c. 5-Photo-c	11	22	33	63	84	105
4,8 (Fall, 1952)-Kinstler-a; last Z-D issue	11	22	33	66	88	110
9,10 (10/53, 12/53, St. John): 9-Painted-c. 10-Photo-c	10	20	30	60	80	100

PERRI (Disney)
Dell Publishing Co.: No. 847, Jan, 1958

	GD	VG	FN	VF	VF/NM	NM-
Four Color 847-Movie, w/2 diff-c publ.	6	12	18	40	55	70

PERRY MASON
David McKay Publications: No. 49, 1946 - No. 50, 1946

	GD	VG	FN	VF	VF/NM	NM-
Feature Books 49, 59-Based on Gardner novels	31	62	93	175	248	320

PERRY MASON MYSTERY MAGAZINE (TV)
Dell Publishing Co.: June-Aug, 1964 - No. 2, Oct-Dec, 1964

	GD	VG	FN	VF	VF/NM	NM-
1	6	12	18	38	52	65
2-Raymond Burr photo-c	4	8	12	29	40	50

PERSONAL LOVE (Also see Movie Love)
Famous Funnies: Jan, 1950 - No. 33, June, 1955

	GD	VG	FN	VF	VF/NM	NM-
1-Photo-c	20	40	60	112	156	200
2-Kathryn Grayson & Mario Lanza photo-c	10	20	30	60	80	100
3-7,10: 7-Robert Walker & Joanne Dru photo-c. 10-Loretta Young & Joseph Cotton photo-c	9	18	27	54	70	85
8,9: 8-Esther Williams & Howard Keel photo-c. 9-Debra Paget & Louis Jourdan photo-c	10	20	30	56	73	90
11-Toth-a; Glenn Ford & Gene Tierney photo-c	12	24	36	69	92	115
12,16,17-One pg. Frazetta each. 17-Rock Hudson & Yvonne DeCarlo photo-c	9	18	27	54	70	85
13-15,18-23: 12-Jane Greer & William Lundigan photo-c. 14-Kirk Douglas photo-c. 15-Dale Robertson & Joanne Dru photo-c. 18-Gregory Peck & Susan Hayworth photo-c. 19-Anthony Quinn & Suzan Ball photo-c. 20-Robert Wagner & Kathleen Crowley photo-c. 21-Roberta Peters & Byron Palmer photo-c. 22-Dale Robertson photo-c. 23-Rhonda Fleming-c	9	18	27	49	62	75
24,27,28-Frazetta-a in each (8,8&6 pgs.). 27-Rhonda Fleming & Fernando Lamas photo-c. 28-Mitzi Gaynor photo-c	40	80	120	240	358	475
25-Frazetta-a (tribute to Betty Page, 7 pg. story); Tyrone Power/Terry Moore photo-c from "King of the Khyber Rifles"	49	98	147	294	440	585
26,29,30,33: 26-Constance Smith & Byron Palmer photo-c. 29-Charlton Heston & Nicol Morey photo-c. 30-Johnny Ray & Mitzi Gaynor photo-c. 33-Dana Andrews & Piper Laurie photo-c	9	18	27	49	62	75
31-Marlon Brando & Jean Simmons photo-c; last pre-code (2/55)	10	20	30	60	80	100
32-Classic Frazetta-a (8 pgs.); Kirk Douglas & Bella Darvi photo-c	54	108	162	324	487	650

NOTE: *All have photo-c. Many feature movie stars.* **Everett** *a-5, 9, 10, 24.*

PERSONAL LOVE (Going Steady V3#3 on)
Prize Publ. (Headline): V1#1, Sept, 1957 - V3#2, Nov-Dec, 1959

	GD	VG	FN	VF	VF/NM	NM-
V1#1	9	18	27	52	66	80
2	6	12	18	28	34	40
3-6(7-8/58)	6	12	18	27	33	38
V2#1(9-10/58)-V2#6(7-8/59)	5	10	15	23	28	32
V3#1-Wood?/Orlando-a	6	12	18	28	34	40
2	5	10	15	22	26	30

PETER CANNON - THUNDERBOLT (See Crisis on Infinite Earths)(Also see Thunderbolt)
DC Comics: Sept, 1992 - No. 12, Aug, 1993 ($1.25)

	GD	VG	FN	VF	VF/NM	NM-
1-12						2.25

PETER COTTONTAIL
Key Publications: Jan, 1954; Feb, 1954 - No. 2, Mar, 1954 (Says 3/53 in error)

	GD	VG	FN	VF	VF/NM	NM-
1(1/54)-Not 3-D	9	18	27	52	66	80
1(2/54)-(3-D, 25¢)-Came w/glasses; written by Bruce Hamilton	23	46	69	129	180	230
2-Reprints 3-D #1 but not in 3-D	6	12	18	31	38	45

PETER GUNN (TV)
Dell Publishing Co.: No. 1087, Apr-June, 1960

	GD	VG	FN	VF	VF/NM	NM-
Four Color 1087-Photo-c	10	20	30	70	100	130

PETE ROSE: HIS INCREDIBLE BASEBALL CAREER
Masstar Creations Inc.: 1995

	GD	VG	FN	VF	VF/NM	NM-
1-John Tartaglione-a						2.25

PETER PAN (Disney) (See Hook, Movie Classics & Comics, New Adventures of... & Walt Disney Showcase #36)

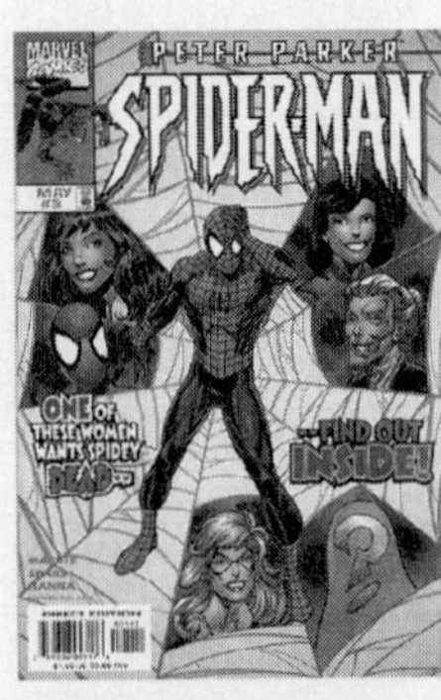

Peter Parker: Spider-Man #5 © MAR

Peter Rabbit #4 © AVON

The Phantom #73 © KING

	GD 2.0	VG 4.0	FN 6.0	VF 8.0	VF/NM 9.0	NM- 9.2
Dell Publishing Co.: No. 442, Dec, 1952 - No. 926, Aug, 1958						
Four Color 442 (#1)-Movie	11	22	33	80	118	155
Four Color 926-Reprint of 442	5	10	15	36	48	60
PETER PAN						
Disney Comics: 1991 ($5.95, graphic novel, 68 pgs.)(Celebrates video release)						
nn-r/Peter Pan Treasure Chest from 1953						7.00
PETER PANDA						
National Periodical Publications: Aug-Sept, 1953 - No. 31, Aug-Sept, 1958						
1-Grossman-c/a in all	42	84	126	252	376	500
2	24	48	72	138	194	250
3,4,6-8,10	20	40	60	112	156	200
5-Classic-c (scarce)	38	76	114	219	310	400
9-Robot-c	24	48	72	138	194	250
11-31	13	26	39	74	100	125
PETER PAN TREASURE CHEST (See Dell Giants)						
PETER PARKER (See The Spectacular Spider-Man)						
PETER PARKER: SPIDER-MAN						
Marvel Comics: Jan, 1999 - No. 57, Aug, 2003 ($2.99/$1.99/$2.25)						
1-Mackie-s/Romita Jr.-a; wraparound-c						3.00
1-($6.95) DF Edition w/variant cover by the Romitas						7.00
2-11,13-17-($1.99): 2-Two covers; Thor app. 3-Iceman-c/app. 4-Marrow-c/app. 5-Spider-Woman app. 7,8-Blade app. 9,10-Venom app. 11-Iron Man & Thor-c/app.						2.25
12-($2.99) Sinister Six and Venom app.						3.00
18-24,26-43: 18-Begin $2.25-c. 20-Jenkins-s/Buckingham-a start. 23-Intro Typeface. 24-Maximum Security x-over. 29-Rescue of MJ. 30-Ramos-c. 42,43-Mahfood-a						2.25
25-($2.99) Two covers; Spider-Man & Green Goblin						3.00
44-47-Humberto Ramos-c/a; Green Goblin-c/app.						3.00
48,49,51-57: 48,49-Buckingham-c/a. 51,52-Herrera-a. 56,57-Kieth-a; Sandman returns						2.25
50-($3.50) Buckingham-c/a						3.50
...'99 Annual (8/99, $3.50) Man-Thing app.						3.50
...'00 Annual ($3.50) Bounty app.; Joe Bennett-a; Black Cat back-up story						3.50
...'01 Annual ($2.99) Avery-s						3.00
...: A Day in the Life TPB (5/01, $14.95) r/#20-22,26; Webspinners #10-12						15.00
...: One Small Break TPB (2002, $16.95) r/#27,28,30-34; Andrews-c						17.00
Spider-Man: Return of the Goblin TPB (2002, $8.99) r/#44-47; Ramos-c						9.00
...Vol. 4: Trials & Tribulations TPB (2003, $11.99) r/#35,37,48-50; Cho-c						12.00
PETER PAT						
United Features Syndicate: No. 8, 1939						
Single Series 8	36	72	108	204	290	375
PETER PAUL'S 4 IN 1 JUMBO COMIC BOOK						
Capitol Stories (Charlton): No date (1953)						
1-Contains 4 comics bound; Space Adventures, Space Western, Crime & Justice, Racket Squad in Action	40	80	120	240	340	440
PETER PIG						
Standard Comics: No. 5, May, 1953 - No. 6, Aug, 1953						
5,6	7	14	21	35	43	50
PETER PORKCHOPS (See Leading Comics #23)						
National Periodical Publications: 11-12/49 - No. 61, 9-11/59; No. 62, 10-12/60 (1-11: 52 pgs.)						
1	35	70	105	201	288	370
2	17	34	51	98	134	170
3-10: 6- "Peter Rockets to Mars!" c/story	13	26	39	74	100	125
11-30	10	20	30	58	77	95
31-62	9	18	27	49	62	75
NOTE: *Otto Feur a-all. **Sheldon Mayer** a-30-38, 40-44, 46-52, 61.*						
PETER PORKER, THE SPECTACULAR SPIDER-HAM						
Star Comics (Marvel): May, 1985 - No. 17, Sept, 1987 (Also see Marvel Tails)						
1-Michael Golden-c						5.00
2-17: 12-Origin/1st app. Bizarro Phil. 13-Halloween issue						4.00
NOTE: *Back-up features: 2-X-Bugs. 3-Iron Mouse. 4-Croctor Strange. 5-Thrr, Dog of Thunder.*						
PETER POTAMUS (TV)						
Gold Key: Jan, 1965 (Hanna-Barbera)						
1-1st app. Peter Potamus & So-So, Breezly & Sneezly	11	22	33	75	110	145
PETER RABBIT (See New Funnies #65 & Space Comics)						
Dell Publishing Co.: No. 1, 1942						
Large Feature Comic 1	41	82	123	324	487	650
PETER RABBIT (Adventures of...; New Advs. of... #9 on)(Also see Funny Tunes & Space Comics)						
Avon Periodicals: 1947 - No. 34, Aug-Sept, 1956						
1(1947)-Reprints 1943-44 Sunday strips; contains a biography & drawing of Cady	36	72	108	204	290	375
2 (4/48)	26	52	78	147	206	265
3 ('48) - 6(7/49)-Last Cady issue	23	46	69	129	180	230
7-10(1950-8/51): 9-New logo	9	18	27	54	70	85
11(11/51)-34('56)-Avon's character	8	16	24	43	54	65
...Easter Parade (1952, 25¢, 132 pgs.)	20	40	60	112	156	200
...Jumbo Book (1954-Giant Size, 25¢)-Jesse James by Kinstler (6 pgs.); space ship-c	25	50	75	144	198	255
PETER RABBIT 3-D						
Eternity Comics: April, 1990 ($2.95, with glasses; sealed in plastic bag)						
1-By Harrison Cady (reprints)						3.00
PETER, THE LITTLE PEST (#4 titled Petey)						
Marvel Comics Group: Nov, 1969 - No. 4, May, 1970						
1	6	12	18	40	55	70
2-4-r-Dexter the Demon & Melvin the Monster	4	8	12	27	36	45
PETE'S DRAGON (See Walt Disney Showcase #43)						
PETE THE PANIC						
Stanmor Publications: November, 1955						
nn-Code approved	5	10	15	23	28	32
PETEY (See Peter, the Little Pest)						
PETTICOAT JUNCTION (TV, inspired Green Acres)						
Dell Publ. Co.: Oct-Dec, 1964 - No. 5, Oct-Dec, 1965 (#1-3, 5 have photo-c)						
1	8	16	24	55	78	100
2-5	6	12	18	38	52	65
PETUNIA (Also see Looney Tunes and Porky Pig)						
Dell Publishing Co.: No. 463, Apr, 1953						
Four Color 463	4	8	12	28	38	48
PHAGE (See Neil Gaiman's Teknophage & Neil Gaiman's Phage-Shadowdeath)						
PHANTACEA						
McPherson Publishing Co.: Sept, 1977 - No. 6, Summer, 1980 (B&W)						
1-Early Dave Sim-a (32 pgs.)	3	6	9	21	28	34
2-Dave Sim-a(10 pgs.)	2	4	6	12	16	20
3,5: 3-Flip-c w/Damnation Bridge	2	4	6	9	11	14
4,6: 4-Gene Day-a	2	4	6	9	11	14
PHANTASMO (See The Funnies #45)						
Dell Publishing Co.: No. 18, 1941						
Large Feature Comic 18	28	56	84	203	297	390
PHANTOM, THE						
David McKay Publishing Co.: 1939 - 1949						
Feature Books 20	71	142	213	510	780	1050
Feature Books 22	55	110	165	408	609	810
Feature Books 39	50	100	150	300	450	600
Feature Books 53,56,57	40	80	120	228	339	450
PHANTOM, THE (See Ace Comics, Defenders Of The Earth, Eat Right to Work and Win, Future Comics, Harvey Comics Hits #51,56, Harvey Hits #1, 6, 12, 15, 26, 36, 44, 48, & King Comics)						
PHANTOM, THE (nn (#29)-Published overseas only) (Also see Comics Reading Libraries in the Promotional Comics section)						
Gold Key(#1-17)/King(#18-28)/Charlton(#30 on): Nov, 1962 - No. 17, Jul, 1966; No. 18, Sept, 1966 - No. 28, Dec, 1967; No. 30, Feb, 1969 - No. 74, Jan, 1977						
1-Origin revealed on inside-c & back-c	17	34	51	118	174	230
2-King, Queen & Jack begins, ends #11	9	18	27	63	89	115
3-5	8	16	24	55	78	100
6-10	8	16	24	53	74	95
11-17: 12-Track Hunter begins	6	12	18	43	59	75
18-Flash Gordon begins; Wood-a	5	10	15	36	48	60
19-24: 20-Flash Gordon ends (both by Gil Kane). 21-Mandrake begins. 20,24-Girl Phantom app.	5	10	15	33	44	55
25-28: 25-Jeff Jones-a(4 pgs.); 1 pg. Williamson ad. 26-Brick Bradford app. 28(nn)-Brick Bradford app.	4	8	12	28	38	48
30-33: 33-Last 12¢ issue	3	7	10	21	28	35
34-40: 36,39-Ditko-a	3	6	9	19	25	32
41-66: 46-Intro. The Piranha. 62-Bolle-c	2	4	6	14	18	22
67-Origin retold; Newton-c/a	3	6	9	18	24	30
68-73-Newton-c/a	2	4	6	12	16	20

Phantom Lady #20 © FOX

The Phantom Stranger #3 © DC

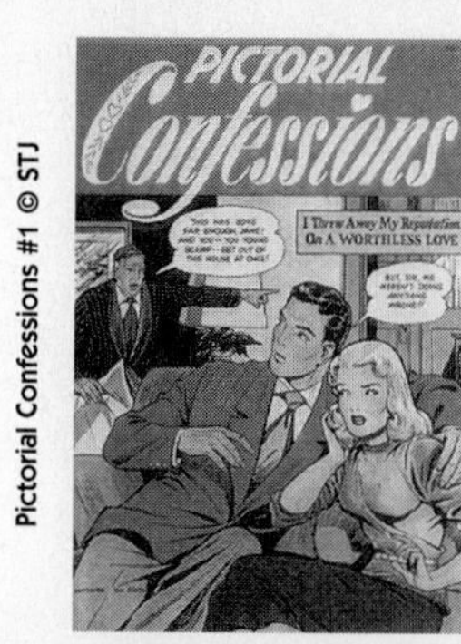

Pictorial Confessions #1 © STJ

	GD 2.0	VG 4.0	FN 6.0	VF 8.0	VF/NM 9.0	NM- 9.2

74-Classic flag-c by Newton; Newton-a; 3 6 9 18 23 28
NOTE: *Aparo a-31-34, 36-38; c-31-38, 60, 61. Painted c-1-17.*

PHANTOM, THE
DC Comics: May, 1988 - No. 4, Aug, 1988 ($1.25, mini-series)

1-4: Orlando-c/a in all 3.00

PHANTOM, THE
DC Comics: Mar, 1989 - No. 13, Mar, 1990 ($1.50)

1-13: 1-Brief origin 3.00

PHANTOM, THE
Wolf Publishing: 1992 - No. 8, 1993 ($2.25)

1-8 2.25

PHANTOM, THE
Moonstone: 2003 - Present ($3.50)

1-Cassaday-c/Raab-s/Quinn-a 3.50

PHANTOM BLOT, THE (#1 titled New Adventures of...)
Gold Key: Oct, 1964 - No. 7, Nov, 1966 (Disney)

1 (Meets The Mysterious Mr. X) 6 12 18 42 59 75
2-1st Super Goof 6 12 18 38 52 65
3-7 4 8 12 22 30 38

PHANTOM EAGLE (See Mighty Midget, Marvel Super Heroes #16 & Wow #6)

PHANTOM FORCE
Image Comics/Genesis West #0, 3-7: 12/93 - #2, 1994; #0, 3/94; #3, 5/94 - #8, 10/94 ($2.50/$3.50, limited series)

0 (3/94, $2.50)-Kirby/Jim Lee-c; Kirby-p pgs. 1,5,24-29. 3.00
1 (12/93, $2.50)-Polybagged w/trading card; Kirby Liefeld-c; Kirby plots/pencils w/inks by Liefeld, McFarlane, Jim Lee, Silvestri, Larsen, Williams, Ordway & Miki 3.00
2 ($3.50)-Kirby-a(p); Kirby/Larson-c 3.50
3-8: 3-(5/94, $2.50)-Kirby/McFarlane-c 4-(5/94)-Kirby-c(p). 5-(6/94) 3.00

PHANTOM GUARD
Image Comics (WildStorm Productions): Oct, 1997 - No. 6, Mar, 1998 ($2.50)

1-6: 1-Two covers 3.00
1-($3.50)-Voyager Pack w/Wildcore preview 3.50

PHANTOM LADY (1st Series) (My Love Secret #24 on) (Also see All Top, Daring Adventures, Freedom Fighters, Jungle Thrills, & Wonder Boy)
Fox Features Syndicate: No. 13, Aug, 1947 - No. 23, Apr, 1949

13(#1)-Phantom Lady by Matt Baker begins (1st app.); Blue Beetle story 400 800 1200 2600 4000 5400
14-16: 14(#2)-Not Baker-c. 15-P.L. injected with experimental drug. 16-Negligee-c, panels; true crime stories begin 244 488 732 1525 2288 3050
17-Classic bondage cover; used in **SOTI**, illo "Sexual stimulation by combining 'headlights' with the sadist's dream of tying up a woman" 538 1076 1614 3766 5783 7800
18,19 172 344 516 1075 1613 2150
20-22 136 272 408 850 1275 1700
23-Bondage-c 150 300 450 938 1407 1875
NOTE: ***Matt Baker** a-in all; c-13, 15-21. **Kamen** a-22, 23.*

PHANTOM LADY (2nd Series) (See Terrific Comics) (Formerly Linda)
Ajax/Farrell Publ.: V1#5, Dec-Jan, 1954/1955 - No. 4, June, 1955

V1#5(#1)-By Matt Baker 114 228 342 713 1069 1425
V1#2-Last pre-code 85 170 255 531 796 1060
3,4-Red Rocket. 3-Heroin story 69 138 207 431 646 860

PHANTOM LADY
Verotik Publications: 1994 ($9.95)

1-Reprints G. A. stories from Phantom Lady and All Top Comics; Adam Hughes-c 10.00

PHANTOM PLANET, THE
Dell Publishing Co.: No. 1234, 1961

Four Color 1234-Movie 8 16 24 55 78 100

PHANTOM STRANGER, THE (1st Series)(See Saga of Swamp Thing)
National Periodical Publications: Aug-Sept, 1952 - No. 6, June-July, 1953

1(Scarce)-1st app. 192 384 576 1200 1800 2400
2 (Scarce) 109 218 327 681 1021 1360
3-6 (Scarce) 94 188 282 588 882 1175

PHANTOM STRANGER, THE (2nd Series) (See Showcase #80)
National Periodical Publications: May-June, 1969 - No. 41, Feb-Mar, 1976

1-2nd S.A. app. P. Stranger; only 12¢ issue 10 20 30 73 107 140
2,3 5 10 15 36 48 60
4-1st new look Phantom Stranger; N. Adams-a 6 12 18 38 52 65

	GD 2.0	VG 4.0	FN 6.0	VF 8.0	VF/NM 9.0	NM- 9.2

5-7 4 8 12 27 36 45
8-14: 14-Last 15¢ issue 3 6 9 18 24 30
15-19: All 25¢ giants (52 pgs.) 3 7 10 21 28 35
20-Dark Circle begins, ends #24. 2 4 6 14 18 22
21,22 2 4 6 10 13 16
23-Spawn of Frankenstein begins by Kaluta 4 8 12 22 30 38
24,25,27-30-Last Spawn of Frankenstein 3 6 9 18 23 28
26- Book-length story featuring Phantom Stranger, Dr. 13 & Spawn of Frankenstein 3 6 9 18 24 30
31-The Black Orchid begins (6-7/74). 3 6 9 18 24 30
32,34-38: 34-Last 20¢ issue (#35 on are 25¢) 2 4 6 10 13 16
33,39-41: 33-Deadman-c/story. 39-41-Deadman app. 2 4 6 12 16 20
NOTE: ***N. Adams** a-4; c-3-19. **Anderson** a-4, 5i. **Aparo** a-7-17, 19-26; c-20-24, 33-41. **B. Bailey** a-27-30. **DeZuniga** a-12-16, 18, 19, 21, 22, 31, 34. **Grell** a-33. **Kaluta** a-23-25; c-26. **Meskin** r-15, 16, 18, 19. **Redondo** a-32, 35, 36. **Sparling** a-20. **Starr** a-17r. **Toth** a-15r. Black Orchid by **Carrilo**-38-41. Dr. 13 solo in-13, 18, 19, 20, 21, 34. Frankenstein by **Kaluta**-23-25; by **Baily**-27-30. No Black Orchid-33, 34, 37.*

PHANTOM STRANGER (See Justice League of America #103)
DC Comics: Oct, 1987 - No. 4, Jan, 1988 (75¢, limited series)

1-4-Mignola/Russell-c/a & Eclipso app. in all. 3,4-Eclipso-c 3.00

PHANTOM STRANGER (See Vertigo Visions-The Phantom Stranger)

PHANTOM: THE GHOST WHO WALKS
Marvel Comics: Feb, 1995 - No. 3, Apr, 1995 ($2.95, limited series)

1-3 4.00

PHANTOM: THE GHOST WHO WALKS
Moonstone: 2003 ($16.95, TPB)

nn-Three new stories by Raab, Goulart, Collins, Blanco and others; Klauba painted-c 17.00

PHANTOM 2040 (TV cartoon)
Marvel Comics: May, 1995 - No. 4, Aug, 1995 ($1.50)

1-4-Based on animated series; Ditko-a(p) in all 3.00

PHANTOM WITCH DOCTOR (Also see Durango Kid #8 & Eerie #8)
Avon Periodicals: 1952

1-Kinstler-c/a (7 pgs.) 46 92 138 276 413 550

PHANTOM ZONE, THE (See Adventure #283 & Superboy #100, 104)
DC Comics: January, 1982 - No. 4, April, 1982

1-4-Superman app. in all. 2-4: Batman, Green Lantern app. 3.00
NOTE: ***Colan** a-1-4p; c-1-4p. **Giordano** c-1-4i.*

PHAZE
Eclipse Comics: Apr, 1988 - No. 2, Oct, 1988 ($2.25)

1,2: 1-Sienkiewicz-c. 2-Gulacy painted-c 2.25

PHIL RIZZUTO (Baseball Hero)(See Sport Thrills, Accepted reprint)
Fawcett Publications: 1951 (New York Yankees)

nn-Photo-c 70 140 210 438 657 875

PHOENIX
Atlas/Seaboard Publ.: Jan, 1975 - No. 4, Oct, 1975

1-Origin; Rovin-s/Amendola-a 1 3 4 6 8 10
2-4: 3-Origin & only app. The Dark Avenger. 4-New origin/costume The Protector (formerly Phoenix) 1 2 3 5 7 9
NOTE: ***Infantino** appears in #1, 2. **Austin** a-3i. **Thorne** c-3.*

PHOENIX (...The Untold Story)
Marvel Comics Group: April, 1984 ($2.00, one-shot)

1-Byrne/Austin-r/X-Men #137 with original unpublished ending 2 4 6 8 10 12

PHOENIX RESURRECTION, THE
Malibu Comics (Ultraverse): 1995 - 1996 ($3.95)

Genesis #1 (12/95)-X-Men app; wraparound-c, Revelations #1 (12/95)-X-Men app; wraparound-c, Aftermath #1 (1/96)-X-Men app. 4.00
0-($1.95)-r/series 2.25
0-American Entertainment Ed. 4.00

PICNIC PARTY (See Dell Giants)

PICTORIAL CONFESSIONS (Pictorial Romances #4 on)
St. John Publishing Co.: Sept, 1949 - No. 3, Dec, 1949

1-Baker-c/a(3) 31 62 93 175 248 320
2-Baker-a; photo-c 20 40 60 112 156 200
3-Kubert, Baker-a; part Kubert-c 22 44 66 127 176 225

PICTORIAL LOVE STORIES (Formerly Tim McCoy)
Charlton Comics: No. 22, Oct, 1949 - No. 26, July, 1950 (all photo-c)

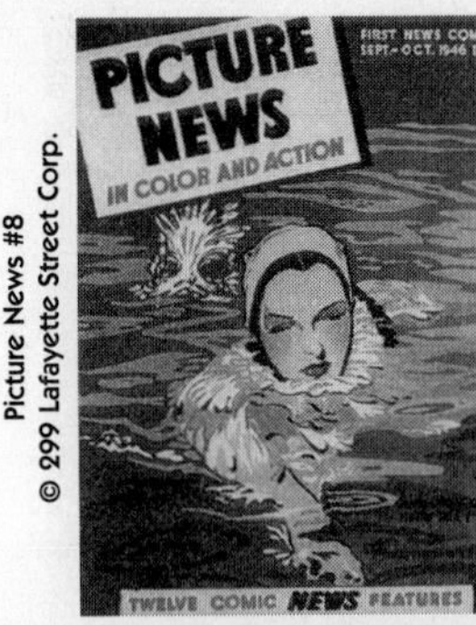

Picture News #8
© 299 Lafayette Street Corp.

Picture Parade #1 © GIL

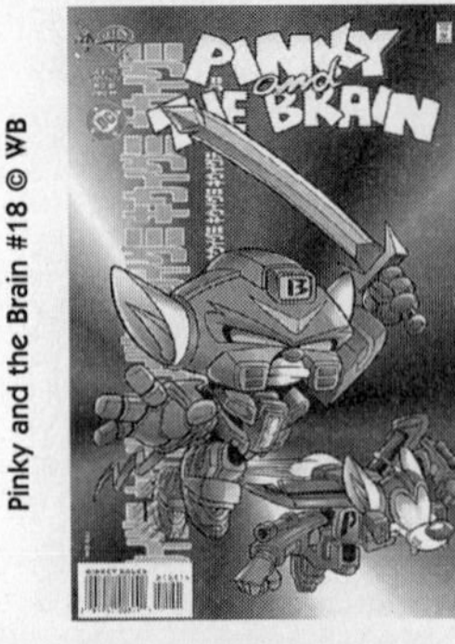

Pinky and the Brain #18 © WB

GD 2.0 VG 4.0 FN 6.0 VF 8.0 VF/NM 9.0 NM- 9.2

22-26: All have "Me-Dan Cupid". 25-Fred Astaire-c 21 42 63 118 164 210

PICTORIAL LOVE STORIES
St. John Publishing Co.: October, 1952

1-Baker-c 29 58 87 164 232 300

PICTORIAL ROMANCES (Formerly Pictorial Confessions)
St. John Publ. Co.: No. 4, Jan, 1950; No. 5, Jan, 1951 - No. 24, Mar, 1954

4-Baker-a; photo-c 30 60 90 170 240 310
5,10-All Matt Baker issues. 5-Reprints all stories from #4 w/new Baker-c
23 46 69 129 180 230
6-9,12,13,15,16-Baker-c, 2-3 stories 17 34 51 98 134 170
11-Baker-c/a(3); Kubert-r/Hollywood Confessions #1
19 38 57 106 146 185
14,21-24: Baker-c/a each. 21,24-Each has signed story by Estrada
15 30 45 86 118 150
17-20(7/53, 25¢, 100 pgs.): Baker-c/a; each has two signed stories by Estrada
31 62 93 175 248 320

NOTE: ***Matt Baker** art in most issues. **Estrada** a-17-20(2), 21, 24.*

PICTURE NEWS
Lafayette Street Corp.: Jan, 1946 - No. 10, Jan-Feb, 1947

1-Milt Gross begins, ends No. 6; 4 pg. Kirby-a; A-Bomb-c/story
40 80 120 240 345 450
2-Atomic explosion panels; Frank Sinatra/Perry Como story
22 44 66 127 176 225
3-Atomic explosion panels; Frank Sinatra, June Allyson, Benny Goodman
stories 19 38 57 106 146 185
4-Atomic explosion panels; "Caesar and Cleopatra" movie adapt. w/Claude Raines &
Vivian Leigh; Jackie Robinson story 21 42 63 118 164 210
5-7: 5-Hank Greenberg story. 6-Joe Louis-c/story 15 30 45 86 118 150
8,10: 8-Monte Hale story (9-10/46; 1st?). 10-Dick Quick; A-Bomb story; Krigstein, Gross-a
16 32 48 92 126 160
9-A-Bomb story; "Crooked Mile" movie adaptation; Joe DiMaggio story.
19 38 57 106 146 185

PICTURE PARADE (Picture Progress #5 on)
Gilberton Company (Also see A Christmas Adventure): Sept, 1953 - V1#4, Dec, 1953 (28 pgs.)

V1#1-Andy's Atomic Adventures; A-bomb blast-c; (Teachers version distributed to schools
exists) 21 42 63 118 164 210
2-Around the World with the United Nations 12 24 36 69 92 115
3-Adventures of the Lost One(The American Indian), 4-A Christmas Adventure
(r-under same title in 1969) 12 24 36 69 92 115

PICTURE PROGRESS (Formerly Picture Parade)
Gilberton Corp.: V1#5, Jan, 1954 - V3#2, Oct, 1955 (28-36 pgs.)

V1#5-9,V2#1-9: 5-News in Review 1953. 6-The Birth of America. 7-The Four Seasons.
8-Paul Revere's Ride. 9-The Hawaiian Islands(5/54). V2#1-The Story of Flight(9/54).
2-Vote for Crazy River (The Meaning of Elections). 3-Louis Pasteur. 4-The Star Spangled
Banner. 5-News in Review 1954. 6-Alaska: The Great Land. 7-Life in the Circus. 8-The
Time of the Cave Man. 9-Summer Fun(5/55) 8 16 24 43 54 65
V3#1,2: 1-The Man Who Discovered America. 2-The Lewis & Clark Expedition
8 16 24 43 54 65

PICTURE SCOPE JUNGLE ADVENTURES (See Jungle Thrills)

PICTURE STORIES FROM AMERICAN HISTORY
National/All-American/E. C. Comics: 1945 - No. 4, Sum, 1947 (#1,2: 10¢, 56 pgs.; #3,4: 15¢, 52 pgs.)

1 31 62 93 178 252 325
2-4 25 50 75 144 198 255

PICTURE STORIES FROM SCIENCE
E.C. Comics: Spring, 1947 - No. 2, Fall, 1947

1-(15¢) 31 62 93 178 252 325
2-(10¢) 27 54 81 153 214 275

PICTURE STORIES FROM THE BIBLE (See Narrative Illustration, the Story of the Comics by M.C. Gaines)
National/All-American/E.C. Comics: 1942 - No. 4, Fall, 1943; 1944-46

1-4('42-Fall, '43)-Old Testament (DC) 25 50 75 147 202 260
Complete Old Testament Edition, (12/43-DC, 50¢, 232 pgs.);-1st printing; contains #1-4;
2nd - 8th (1/47) printings exist; later printings by E.C. some with 65¢-c
29 58 87 164 232 300
Complete Old Testament Edition (1945-publ. by Bible Pictures Ltd.)-232 pgs., hardbound,
in color with dust jacket 29 58 87 164 232 300

NOTE: *Both Old and New Testaments published in England by Bible Pictures Ltd. in hardback, 1943, in color, 376 pgs. (2 vols.: O.T. 232 pgs. & N.T. 144 pgs.), and were also published by Scarf Press in 1979 (Old Test., $9.95) and in 1980 (New Test., $7.95)*

1-3(New Test.; 1944-46, DC)-52 pgs. ea. 19 38 57 107 149 190
The Complete Life of Christ Edition (1945, 25¢, 96 pgs.)-Contains #1&2 of the
New Testament Edition 29 58 87 164 232 300
1,2(Old Testament-r in comic book form)(E.C., 1946; 52 pgs.)
19 38 57 107 149 190
1(DC),2(AA),3(EC)(New Testament-r in comic book form)(E.C., 1946; 52 pgs.)
19 38 57 107 149 190
Complete New Testament Edition (1945-E.C., 40¢, 144 pgs.)-Contains #1-3
1946 printing has 50¢-c 29 58 87 164 232 300

NOTE: *Another British series entitled **The Bible Illustrated** from 1947 has recently been discovered, with the same internal artwork. This eight edition series (5-OT, 3-NT) is of particular interest to Classics Ill. collectors because it exactly copied the C.I. logo format. The British publisher was Thorpe & Porter, who in 1951 began publishing the British Classics Ill. series. All editions of The Bible Ill. have new British painted covers. While this market is still new, and not all editions have as yet been found, current market value is about the same as the first U.S. editions of Picture Stories From The Bible.*

PICTURE STORIES FROM WORLD HISTORY
E.C. Comics: Spring, 1947 - No. 2, Summer, 1947 (52, 48 pgs.)

1-(15¢) 31 62 93 178 252 325
2-(10¢) 27 54 81 153 214 275

PINHEAD
Marvel Comics (Epic Comics): Dec, 1993 - No. 6, May, 1994 ($2.50)

1-($2.95)-Embossed foil-c by Kelley Jones; Intro Pinhead & Disciples
(Snakeoil, Hangman, Fan Dancer & Dixie) 3.00
2-6 2.50

PINHEAD & FOODINI (TV)(Also see Foodini & Jingle Dingle Christmas...)
Fawcett Publications: July, 1951 - No. 4, Jan, 1952 (Early TV comic)

1-(52 pgs.)-Photo-c; based on TV puppet show 34 68 102 193 274 355
2,3-Photo-c 17 34 51 98 134 170
4 14 28 42 81 111 140

PINHEAD VS. MARSHALL LAW (Law in Hell)
Marvel Comics (Epic): Nov, 1993 - No. 2, Dec, 1993 ($2.95, lim. series)

1,2: 1-Embossed red foil-c. 2-Embossed silver foil-c 3.00

PINK DUST
Kitchen Sink Press: 1998 ($3.50, B&W, mature)

1-J. O'Barr-s/a 3.50

PINK PANTHER, THE (TV)(See The Inspector & Kite Fun Book)
Gold Key #1-70/Whitman #71-87: April, 1971 - No. 87, Mar, 1984

1-The Inspector begins 6 12 18 38 52 65
2-5 3 6 9 18 24 30
6-10 2 4 6 14 18 22
11-30: Warren Tufts-a #16-on 2 4 6 10 12 15
31-60 2 4 6 8 10 12
61-70 1 2 3 5 6 8
71-74,81-83: 81(2/82), 82(3/82), 83(4/82) 1 3 4 6 8 10
75(8/80),76-80(pre-pack?) (scarce) 2 4 6 14 18 22
84-87(All #90266 on-c, no date or date code): 84(6/83), 85(8/83), 87(3/84)
2 4 6 10 13 16
Mini-comic No. 1(1976)(3-1/4x6-1/2") 1 3 4 6 8 10

NOTE: *Pink Panther began as a movie cartoon. (See Golden Comics Digest #38, 45 and March of Comics #376, 384, 390, 409, 418, 429, 441, 449, 461, 473, 486); #37, 72, 80-85 contain reprints.*

PINK PANTHER SUPER SPECIAL (TV)
Harvey Comics: Oct, 1993 ($2.25, 68 pgs.)

V2#1-The Inspector & Wendy Witch stories also 4.00

PINK PANTHER, THE
Harvey Comics: Nov, 1993 - No. 9, July, 1994 ($1.50)

V2#1-9 3.00

PINKY & THE BRAIN (See Animaniacs)
DC Comics: July, 1996 - No. 27, Nov, 1998 ($1.75/$1.95/$1.99)

1-27, ...Christmas Special (1/96, $1.50) 3.00

PINKY LEE (See Adventures of...)

PINKY THE EGGHEAD
I.W./Super Comics: 1963 (Reprints from Noodnik)

I.W. Reprint #1,2(nd) 2 4 6 9 11 14
Super Reprint #14-r/Noodnik Comics #4 2 4 6 9 11 14

PINOCCHIO (See 4-Color #92, 252, 545, 1203, Mickey Mouse Mag. V5#3, Movie Comics under Wonderful Advs. of..., New Advs. of..., Thrilling Comics #2, Walt Disney Showcase,

Piracy #4 © WMG

Planetary/Batman: Night on Earth #1 © DC

Planet Comics #1 © FH

GD VG FN VF VF/NM NM-
2.0 4.0 6.0 8.0 9.0 9.2

Walt Disney's..., Wonderful Advs. of..., & World's Greatest Stories #2)
Dell Publishing Co.: No. 92, 1945 - No. 1203, Mar, 1962 (Disney)

Four Color 92-The Wonderful Adventures of...; 16 pg. Donald Duck story ;
entire book by Kelly 57 114 171 432 646 860
Four Color 252 (10/49)-Origin, not by Kelly 12 24 36 82 121 160
Four Color 545 (3/54)-The Wonderful Advs. of...; part-r of 4-Color #92; Disney-movie
8 16 24 55 78 100
Four Color 1203 (3/62) 6 12 18 40 55 70

PINOCCHIO AND THE EMPEROR OF THE NIGHT
Marvel Comics: Mar, 1988 ($1.25, 52 pgs.)

1-Adapts film 3.00

PINOCCHIO LEARNS ABOUT KITES (See Kite Fun Book)

PIN-UP PETE (Also see Great Lover Romances & Monty Hall...)
Toby Press: 1952

1-Jack Sparling pin-ups 19 38 57 106 146 185

PIONEER MARSHAL (See Fawcett Movie Comics)

PIONEER PICTURE STORIES
Street & Smith Publications: Dec, 1941 - No. 9, Dec, 1943

1-The Legless Air Ace begins 31 62 93 175 248 320
2 -True life story of Errol Flynn 16 32 48 92 126 160
3-9 14 28 42 81 111 140

PIONEER WEST ROMANCES (Firehair #1,2,7-11)
Fiction House Magazines: No. 3, Spring, 1950 - No. 6, Winter, 1950-51

3-(52 pgs.)-Firehair continues 21 42 63 118 164 210
4-6 21 42 63 118 164 210

PIPSQUEAK (See The Adventures of...)

PIRACY
E. C. Comics: Oct-Nov, 1954 - No. 7, Oct-Nov, 1955

1-Williamson/Torres-a 25 50 75 188 269 350
2-Williamson/Torres-a 16 32 48 120 173 225
3-7: 5-7-Comics Code symbol on cover 13 26 39 98 137 175

NOTE: ***Crandall** a-in all; c-2-4. **Davis** a-1, 2, 6. **Evans** a-3-7; c-7. **Ingels** a-3-7. **Krigstein** a-3-5, 7; c-5, 6. **Wood** a-1, 2; c-1.*

PIRACY
Gemstone Publishing: March, 1998 - No. 7, Sept, 1998 ($2.50)

1-7: E.C. reprints 2.50
Annual 1 ($10.95) Collects #1-4 11.00
Annual 2 ($7.95) Collects #5-7 8.00

PIRANA (See The Phantom #46 & Thrill-O-Rama #2, 3)

PIRATE CORP$, THE (See Hectic Planet)
Eternity Comics/Slave Labor Graphics: 1987 - No. 4, 1988 ($1.95)

1-4: 1,2-Color. 3,4-B&W 2.25
Special 1 ('89, B&W)-Slave Labor Publ. 2.25

PIRATE CORP$, THE (Volume 2)
Slave Labor Graphics: 1989 - No. 6, 1992 ($1.95)

1-6-Dorkin-s/a 2.25

PIRATE OF THE GULF, THE (See Superior Stories #2)

PIRATES COMICS
Hillman Periodicals: Feb-Mar, 1950 - No. 4, Aug-Sept, 1950 (All 52 pgs.)

1 26 52 78 150 210 270
2-Dave Berg-a 19 38 57 106 146 185
3,4-Berg-a 17 34 51 98 134 170

PIRATES OF DARK WATER, THE (Hanna Barbera)
Marvel Comics: Nov, 1991 - No. 9, Aug, 1992 ($1.95)

1-9: 9-Vess-c 3.00

P.I.'S: MICHAEL MAUSER AND MS. TREE, THE
First Comics: Jan, 1985 - No. 3, May, 1985 ($1.25, limited series)

1-3: Staton-c/a(p) 2.25

PITT, THE (Also see The Draft & The War)
Marvel Comics: Mar, 1988 ($3.25, 52 pgs., one-shot)

1-Ties into Starbrand, D.P.7 3.50

PITT (See Youngblood #4 & Gen 13 #3,#4)
Image Comics #1-9/Full Bleed #1/2,10-on: Jan, 1993 - Present ($1.95, intended as a four part limited series)

1/2-(12/95)-1st Full Bleed issue 4.00
1-Dale Keown-c/a. 1-1st app. The Pitt 4.00
2-13: All Dale Keown-c/a. 3 (Low distribution). 10 (1/96)-Indicia reads "January 1995" 3.00
14-20: 14-Begin $2.50-c, pullout poster 2.50
TPB-(1997, $9.95) r/#1/2, 1-4 10.00
TPB 2-(1999, $11.95) r/#5-9 12.00

PITT CREW
Full Bleed Studios: Aug, 1998 - Present ($2.50)

1-5: 1-Richard Pace-s/Ken Lashley-a. 2-4-Scott Lee-a 2.50

PITT IN THE BLOOD
Full Bleed Studios: Aug, 1996 ($2.50, one-shot)

nn-Richard Pace-a/script 2.50

PIXIE & DIXIE & MR. JINKS (TV)(See Jinks, Pixie, and Dixie & Whitman Comic Books)
Dell Publishing Co./Gold Key: July-Sept, 1960 - Feb, 1963 (Hanna-Barbera)

Four Color 1112 9 18 27 60 85 110
Four Color 1196,1264, 01-631-207 (Dell, 7/62) 6 12 18 43 59 75
1(2/63-Gold Key) 7 14 21 51 71 90

PIXIE PUZZLE ROCKET TO ADVENTURELAND
Avon Periodicals: Nov, 1952

1 14 28 42 79 107 135

PIXIES, THE (Advs. of...)(The Mighty Atom and ...#6 on)(See A-1 Comics #16)
Magazine Enterprises: Winter, 1946 - No. 4, Fall?, 1947; No. 5, 1948

1-Mighty Atom 9 18 27 49 62 75
2-5-Mighty Atom 6 12 18 27 33 38
I.W. Reprint #1(1958), 8-(Pee-Wee Pixies), 10-I.W. on cover, Super on inside
2 4 6 8 10 12

PIZZAZZ
Marvel Comics: Oct, 1977 - No. 16, Jan, 1979 (slick-color kids mag. w/puzzles, games, comics)

1-Star Wars photo-c/article; origin Tarzan; KISS photos/article; Iron-On bonus; 2 pg. pin-up
calendars thru #8 3 6 9 18 23 28
2-Spider-Man-c; Beatles pin-up calendar 2 4 6 10 13 16
3-8: 3-Close Encounters-s; Bradbury-s. 4-Alice Cooper, Travolta; Charlie's Angels/Fonz/Hulk/
Spider-Man-c. 5-Star Trek quiz. 6-Asimov-s. 7-James Bond; Spock/Darth Vader-c.
8-TV Spider-Man photo-c/article 2 4 6 10 13 16
9-14: 9-Shaun Cassidy-c. 10-Sgt. Pepper-c/s. 12-Battlestar Galactica-s; Spider-Man app.
13-TV Hulk-c/s. 14-Meatloaf-c/s 2 4 6 9 11 14
15,16: 15-Battlestar Galactica-s. 16-Movie Superman photo-c/s, Hulk.
2 4 6 10 13 16

NOTE: ***Star Wars** comics in all (1-6:Chaykin-a, 7-9: DeZuniga-a, 10-13:Simonson/Janson-a. 14-16:Cockrum-a). **Tarzan** comics, 1pg.-#1-8. 1pg. "Hey Look" by Kurtzman #12-16.*

PLANETARY (See Preview in flip book Gen13 #33)
DC Comics (WildStorm Prod.): Apr, 1999 - Present ($2.50/$2.95)

1-Ellis-s/Cassaday-a/c 1 3 4 6 8 10
2-5 6.00
6-10 5.00
11-15: 12-Fourth Man revealed 4.00
16-18-($2.95) 3.00
...: All Over the World and Other Stories (2000, $14.95) r/#1-6 & Preview 15.00
...: All Over the World and Other Stories-Hardcover (2000, $24.95) r/#1-6 & Preview;
with dustjacket 25.00
.../Batman: Night on Earth 1 (8/03, $5.95) Ellis-s/Cassaday-a 6.00
.../JLA: Terra Occulta (11/02, $5.95) Elseworlds; Ellis-s/Ordway-a 6.00
.../The Authority: Ruling the World (8/00, $5.95) Ellis-s/Phil Jimenez-a 6.00
...: The Fourth Man -Hardcover (2001, $24.95) r/#7-12 25.00
...: The Planetary Reader (8/03, $5.95) r/#13-15 6.00

PLANET COMICS
Fiction House Magazines: 1/40 - No. 62, 9/49; No. 63, Wint, 1949-50; No. 64, Spring, 1950; No. 65, 1951(nd); No. 66-68, 1952(nd); No. 69, Wint, 1952-53;
No. 70-72, 1953(nd); No. 73, Winter, 1953-54

1-Origin Auro, Lord of Jupiter by Briefer (ends #61); Flint Baker & The Red Comet begin;
Eisner/Fine-c 1071 2142 3213 7732 12,116 16,500
2-Lou Fine-c (Scarce) 423 846 1269 2750 4375 6000
3-Eisner-c 300 600 900 1900 2850 3800
4-Gale Allen and the Girl Squadron begins 264 528 792 1650 2475 3300
5,6-(Scarce): 5-Eisner/Fine-c 248 496 744 1550 2325 3100
7-12: 8-Robot-c. 12-The Star Pirate begins 200 400 600 1250 1875 2500
13,14: 13-Reff Ryan begins 150 300 450 938 1407 1875
15-(Scarce)-Mars, God of War begins (11/41); see Jumbo Comics #31 for 1st app.

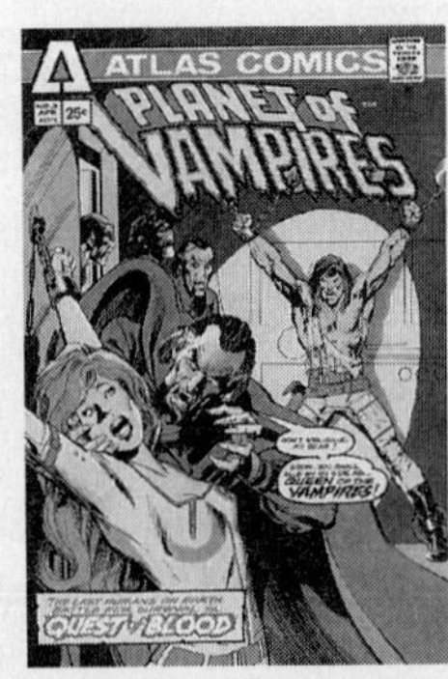

Planet of Vampires #2 © Seaboard

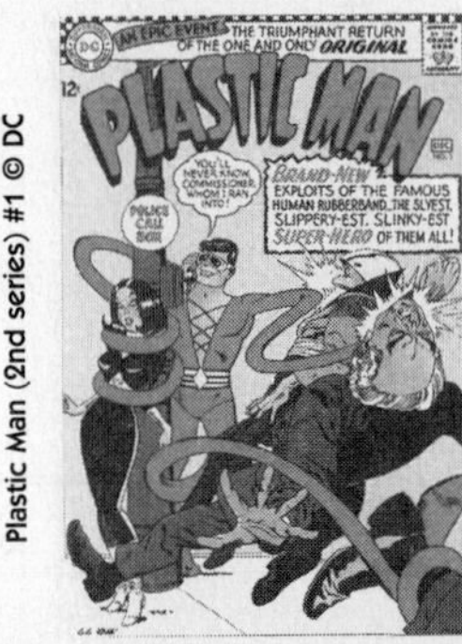

Plastic Man (2nd series) #1 © DC

Plop! #19 © DC

	GD 2.0	VG 4.0	FN 6.0	VF 8.0	VF/NM 9.0	NM- 9.2
	296	592	888	1850	2775	3700
16-20,22	132	264	395	825	1243	1660
21-The Lost World & Hunt Bowman begin	140	280	420	875	1313	1750
23-26: 26-Space Rangers begin (9/43), end #71	128	256	384	800	1200	1600
27-30	102	204	306	638	957	1275
31-35: 33-Origin Star Pirates Wonder Boots, reprinted in #52. 35-Mysta of the Moon begins, ends #62	85	170	255	531	796	1060
36-45: 38-1st Mysta of the Moon-c. 41-New origin of "Auro, Lord of Jupiter". 42-Last Gale Allen. 43-Futura begins	78	156	234	488	732	975
46-60: 48-Robot-c. 53-Used in **SOTI**, pg. 32	61	122	183	381	571	760
61-68,70: 64,70-Robot-c. 65-70-All partial-r of earlier issues. 70-r/stories from #41	48	96	144	288	432	575
69-Used in **POP**, pgs. 101,102	48	96	144	288	432	575
71-73-No series stories. 71-Space Rangers strip	39	78	117	230	325	420
I.W. Reprint 1,8,9: 1(nd)-r/#70; cover-r from Attack on Planet Mars. 8 (r/#72), 9-r/#73	9	18	27	60	85	110

NOTE: ***Anderson** a-33-38, 40-51 (Star Pirate). **Matt Baker** a-53-59 (Mysta of the Moon). **Celardo** c-12. **Bill Discount** a-71 (Space Rangers). **Elias** c-70. **Evans** a-46-49 (Auro, Lord of Jupiter), 50-64 (Lost World). **Fine** c-2, 5. **Hopper** a-31, 35 (Gale Allen), 41, 42, 48, 49 (Mysta of the Moon). **Ingels** a-24-31 (Lost World), 56-61 (Auro, Lord of Jupiter). **Lubbers** a-44-47 (Space Rangers); c-40, 41. **Moriera** a-43, 44 (Mysta of the Moon). **Renee** a-40-49 (Lost World); c-33, 35, 39. **Tuska** a-30 (Star Pirate). **M. Whitman** a-50-52 (Mysta of the Moon), 53-58 (Star Pirate); c-71-73. **Starr** a-59. **Zolnerwich** c-10. 13-25. Bondage c-53.*

PLANET COMICS
Pacific Comics: 1984 ($5.95)

1-Reprints Planet Comics #1(1940) 1 2 3 5 6 8

PLANET COMICS
Blackthorne Publishing: Apr, 1988 - No. 3 ($2.00, color/B&W #3)

1-3: New stories. 1-Dave Stevens-c 3.00

PLANET OF THE APES (Magazine) (Also see Adventures on the... & Power Record Comics)
Marvel Comics Group: Aug, 1974 - No. 29, Feb, 1977 (B&W) (Based on movies)

	GD	VG	FN	VF	VF/NM	NM-
1-Ploog-a	4	8	12	22	30	38
2-Ploog-a	3	6	9	16	20	24
3-10	2	4	6	11	14	18
11-20	2	4	6	12	16	20
21-28 (low distribution)	3	6	9	16	20	24
29 (low distribution)	5	10	15	33	44	55

NOTE: ***Alcala** a-7-11, 17-22, 24. **Ploog** a-1-4, 6, 8, 11, 13, 14, 19. **Sutton** a-11, 12, 15, 17, 19, 20, 23, 24, 29. **Tuska** a-1-6.*

PLANET OF THE APES
Adventure Comics: Apr, 1990 - No. 24, 1992 ($2.50, B&W)

1-New movie tie-in; comes w/outer-c (3 colors) 4.00
1-Limited serial numbered edition ($5.00) 5.00
1-2nd printing (no outer-c, $2.50) 2.50
2-24 3.00
Annual 1 ($3.50) 4.00
...Urchak's Folly 1-4 ($2.50, mini-series) 3.00

PLANET OF THE APES (The Human War)
Dark Horse Comics: Jun, 2001 - No. 3, Aug, 2001 ($2.99, limited series)

1-3-Follows the 2001 movie; Edginton-s 3.00

PLANET OF THE APES
Dark Horse Comics: Sept, 2001 - No. 6, Feb, 2002 ($2.99, ongoing series)

1-6: 1-3-Edginton-s. 1-Photo & Wagner covers. 2-Plunkett & photo-c 3.00

PLANET OF VAMPIRES
Seaboard Publications (Atlas): Feb, 1975 - No. 3, July, 1975

1-Neal Adams-c(i); 1st Broderick c/a(p); Hama-s 2 4 6 8 10 12
2,3: 2-Neal Adams-c. 3-Heath-c/a 1 2 3 5 7 9

PLANET TERRY
Marvel Comics (Star Comics)/Marvel: April, 1985 - No. 12, March, 1986 (Children's comic)

1-12 3.00
1-Variant with "Star Chase" game on last page & inside back-c 10.00

PLASM (See Warriors of Plasm)
Defiant Comics: June, 1993

0-Came bound into Diamond Previews V3#6 (6/93); price is for complete Previews with comic still attached 3.00
0-Comic only removed from Previews 2.25

PLASMER
Marvel Comics UK: Nov, 1993 - No. 4, Feb, 1994 ($1.95, limited series)

1-($2.50)-Polybagged w/4 trading cards 2.50
2-4: Capt. America & Silver Surfer app. 2.25

PLASTIC FORKS
Marvel Comis (Epic Comics): 1990 - No. 5, 1990 ($4.95, 68 pgs., limited series, mature)

Book 1-5: Squarebound 5.00

PLASTIC MAN (Also see Police Comics & Smash Comics #17)
Vital Publ. No. 1,2/Quality Comics No. 3 on: Sum, 1943 - No. 64, Nov, 1956

	GD	VG	FN	VF	VF/NM	NM-
nn(#1)- "In The Game of Death"; Skull-c; Jack Cole-c/a begins; ends-#64?	407	814	1221	2646	4073	5500
nn(#2, 2/44)- "The Gay Nineties Nightmare"	176	352	528	1100	1650	2200
3 (Spr, '46)	120	240	360	750	1125	1500
4 (Sum, '46)	90	180	270	563	844	1124
5 (Aut, '46)	74	148	222	463	694	925
6-10	60	120	180	375	563	750
11-20	55	110	165	330	495	660
21-30: 26-Last non-r issue?	45	90	135	270	405	540
31-40: 40-Used in POP, pg. 91	38	76	114	219	310	400
41-64: 53-Last precode issue. 54-Robot-c	31	62	93	178	252	325
Super Reprint 11,16,18: 11('63)-r/#16. 16-r/#18 & #21; Cole-a. 18('64)-Spirit-r by Eisner from Police #95	5	10	15	36	48	60

NOTE: ***Cole** r-44, 49, 56, 58, 59 at least. **Cuidera** c-32-64i.*

PLASTIC MAN (See DC Special #15 & House of Mystery #160)
National Periodical Publications/DC Comics: 11-12/66 - No. 10, 5-6/68; V4#11, 2-3/76 - No. 20, 10-11/77

	GD	VG	FN	VF	VF/NM	NM-
1-Real 1st app. Silver Age Plastic Man (House of Mystery #160 is actually tryout); Gil Kane-c/a; 12¢ issues begin	9	18	27	65	93	120
2-5: 4-Infantino-c; Mortimer-a	4	8	12	29	40	50
6-10('68): 7-G.A. Plastic Man & Woozy Winks (1st S.A. app.) app.; origin retold. 10-Sparling-a; last 12¢ issue	4	8	12	24	32	40
V4#11('76)-20: 11-20-Fradon-p. 17-Origin retold	1	2	3	5	6	8

...80-Page Giant (2003, $6.95) reprints origin and other stories in 80-Pg. Giant format 7.00
...Special 1 (8/99, $3.95) 4.00

PLASTIC MAN
DC Comics: Nov, 1988 - No. 4, Feb, 1989 ($1.00, mini-series)

1-4: 1-Origin; Woozy Winks app. 2.25

PLASTIC MAN
DC Comics: Feb, 2004 - Present ($2.95)

1,2-Kyle Baker-s/a. 1-Retells origin 3.00

PLASTRON CAFE
Mirage Studios: Dec, 1992 - No. 4, July, 1993 ($2.25, B&W)

1-4: 1-Teenage Mutant Ninja Turtles app.; Kelly Freas-c. 2-Hildebrandt painted-c. 4-Spaced & Alien Fire stories 2.25

PLAYFUL LITTLE AUDREY (TV)(Also see Little Audrey #25)
Harvey Publications: 6/57 - No. 110, 11/73; No. 111, 8/74 - No. 121, 4/76

	GD	VG	FN	VF	VF/NM	NM-
1	24	48	72	171	251	330
2	12	24	36	84	125	165
3-5	9	18	27	63	89	115
6-10	7	14	21	50	68	85
11-20	5	10	15	36	48	60
21-40	4	8	12	24	32	40
41-60	3	6	9	19	25	32
61-84: 84-Last 12¢ issue	3	6	9	16	20	24
85-99	2	4	6	11	14	18
100-52 pg. Giant	3	6	9	18	23	28
101-103: 52 pg. Giants	3	6	9	16	20	25
104-121	1	3	4	6	8	10

...In 3-D (Spring, 1988, $2.25, Blackthorne #66) 4.00

PLOP! (Also see The Best of DC #60)
National Periodical Publications: Sept-Oct, 1973 - No. 24, Nov-Dec, 1976

	GD	VG	FN	VF	VF/NM	NM-
1-Sergio Aragonés-a begins; Wrightson-a	3	7	10	21	28	35
2-4,6-20	2	4	6	11	14	18
5-Wrightson-a	2	4	6	12	16	20
21-24 (52 pgs.). 23-No Aragonés-a	2	4	6	14	18	22

NOTE: ***Alcala** a-1-3. **Anderson** a-5. **Aragonés** a-1-22, 24. **Ditko** a-16p. **Evans** a-1. **Mayer** a-1. **Orlando** a-21, 22; c-21. **Sekowsky** a-5, 6p. **Toth** a-11. **Wolverton** r-4, 22-24(1 pg.ea.); c-1-12, 14, 17, 18. **Wood** a-14, 16i, 18-24; c-13, 15, 16, 19.*

PLUTO (See Cheerios Premiums, Four Color #537, Mickey Mouse Magazine, Walt Disney Showcase #4, 7, 13, 20, 23, 33 & Wheaties)
Dell Publ. Co.: No. 7, 1942; No. 429, 10/52 - No. 1248, 11-1/61-62 (Disney)

Large Feature Comic 7(1942)-Written by Carl Barks, Jack Hannah, & Nick George (Barks' 1st comic book work) 115 230 345 876 1338 1800

Pogo Possum #1 © Walt Kelly

Poison Elves #33 © Drew Hayes

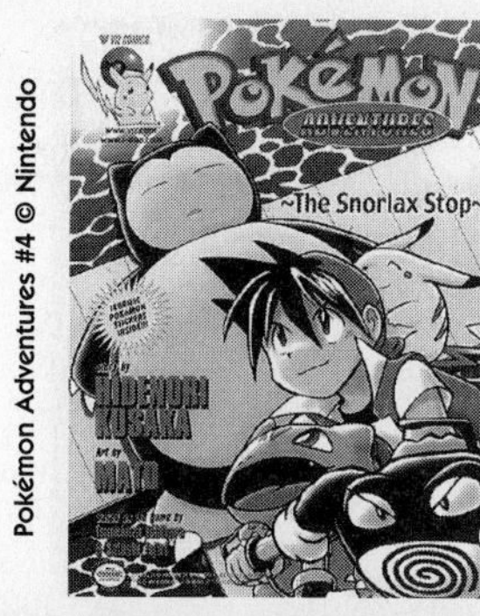

Pokémon Adventures #4 © Nintendo

	GD 2.0	VG 4.0	FN 6.0	VF 8.0	VF/NM 9.0	NM- 9.2
Four Color 429 (#1)	10	20	30	72	104	135
Four Color 509	7	14	21	46	63	80
Four Color 595,654,736,853	5	10	15	33	44	55
Four Color 941,1039,1143,1248	4	8	12	29	40	50

POCKET CLASSICS
Academic Inc. Publications: 1984 (B&W, 4 1/4" x 6 3/4", 68 pages)

C1(Black Beauty. C2(The Call of the Wild). C3(Dr. Jekyll and Mr. Hyde). C4(Dracula). C5(Frankenstein). C6(Huckleberry Finn). C7(Moby Dick). C8(The Red Badge of Courage). C9(The Time Machine). C10(Tom Sawyer). C11(Treasure Island). C12(20,000 Leagues Under the Sea). C13(The Great Adventures of Sherlock Holmes). C14(Gulliver's Travels). C15(The Hunchback of Notre Dame). C16(The Invisible Man). C17(Journey to the Center of the Earth). C18(Kidnapped). C19(The Mysterious Island). C20(The Scarlet Letter). C21(The Story of My Life). C22(A Tale of Two Cities). C23(The Three Musketeers). C24(The War of the Worlds). C25(Around the World in Eighty Days). C26(Captains Courageous). C27(A Connecticut Yankee in King Arthur's Court). C28(Sherlock Holmes - The Hound of the Baskervilles). C29(The House of the Seven Gables). C30(Jane Eyre). C31(The Last of the Mohicans). C32(The Best of O. Henry). C33(The Best of Poe). C34(Two Years Before the Mast). C35(White Fang). C36(Wuthering Heights). C37(Ben Hur). C38(A Christmas Carol). C39(The Food of the Gods). C40(Ivanhoe). C41(The Man in the Iron Mask). C42(The Prince and the Pauper). C43(The Prisoner of Zenda). C44(The Return of the Native). C45(Robinson Crusoe). C46(The Scarlet Pimpernel). C47(The Sea Wolf). C48(The Swiss Family Robinson). C49(Billy Budd). C50(Crime and Punishment). C51(Don Quixote). C52(Great Expectations). C53(Heidi). C54(The Illiad). C55(Lord Jim). C56(The Mutiny on Board H.M.S. Bounty). C57(The Odyssey). C58(Oliver Twist). C59(Pride and Prejudice). C60(The Turn of the Screw) each... 9.00

Shakespeare Series:
S1(As You Like It). S2(Hamlet). S3(Julius Caesar). S4(King Lear). S5(Macbeth). S6(The Merchant of Venice). S7(A Midsummer Night's Dream). S8(Othello). S9(Romeo and Juliet). S10(The Taming of the Shrew). S11(The Tempest). S12(Twelfth Night) each... 9.00

POCKET COMICS (Also see Double Up)
Harvey Publications: Aug, 1941 - No. 4, Jan, 1942 (Pocket size; 100 pgs.)
(1st Harvey comic)

	GD	VG	FN	VF	VF/NM	NM-
1-Origin & 1st app. The Black Cat, Cadet Blakey the Spirit of '76, The Red Blazer, The Phantom, Sphinx, & The Zebra; Phantom Ranger, British Agent #99, Spin Hawkins, Satan, Lord of Evil begin (1st app. of each); Simon-c/a in #1-3	96	192	288	600	900	1200
2 (9/41)-Black Cat on-c #2-4	64	128	192	400	600	800
3,4	50	100	150	300	450	600

POE
Cheese Comics: Sept, 1996 - No. 6, Apr, 1997 ($2.00, B&W)

1-6-Jason Asala-s/a 3.00

POE
Sirius Entertainment (Dogstar Press): Oct, 1997 - Present ($2.50/$2.95, B&W)

1-24-Jason Asala-s/a. 20-24 ($2.95) 3.00
... Color Special (12/98, $2.95) Linsner-c 3.00

POGO PARADE (See Dell Giants)

POGO POSSUM (Also see Animal Comics & Special Delivery)
Dell Publishing Co.: No. 105, 4/46 - No. 148, 5/47; 10-12/49 - No. 16, 4-6/54

	GD	VG	FN	VF	VF/NM	NM-
Four Color 105(1946)-Kelly-c/a	66	132	198	502	764	1025
Four Color 148-Kelly-c/a	55	110	165	424	632	840
1-(10-12/49)-Kelly-c/a in all	45	90	135	336	506	675
2	37	74	111	278	414	550
3-5	27	54	81	196	291	385
6-10: 10-Infinity-c	24	48	72	169	247	325
11-16: 11-X-Mas-c	18	36	54	131	191	250

NOTE: *#1-4, 9-13: 52 pgs.; #5-8, 14-16: 36 pgs.*

POINT BLANK
Acme Press (Eclipse): May, 1989 - No. 2, 1989 ($2.95, B&W, magazine)

1,2-European-r 3.00

POINT BLANK (See Wildcats)
DC Comics (WildStorm): Oct, 2002 - No. 5, Feb, 2003 ($2.95, limited series)

1-5-Brubaker-s/Wilson-a/Bisley-c. 1-Variant-c by Wilson; Grifter and John Lynch app. 3.00
TPB (2003, $14.95) r/#1-5 15.00

POISON ELVES (Formerly I, Lusiphur)
Mulehide Graphics: No. 8, 1993- No. 20, 1995 (B&W, magazine/comic size, mature readers)

	GD	VG	FN	VF	VF/NM	NM-
8-Drew Hayes-c/a/scripts.	1	3	4	6	8	10
9-11: 11-1st comic size issue	1	3	4	6	8	10
12,14,16	1	2	3	4	5	7
13,15-(low print)	2	4	6	8	10	12
15-2nd print						4.00
17-20	1	2	3	4	5	7
...Desert of the Third Sin-(1997, $14.95, TPB)-r/#13-18						15.00
...Patrons-($4.95, TPB)-r/#19,20						5.00
...Traumatic Dogs-(1996, $14.95,TPB)-Reprints I, Lusiphur #7, Poison Elves #8-12						15.00

POISON ELVES (See I, Lusiphur)
Sirius Entertainment: June, 1995 - Present ($2.50, B&W, mature readers)

	GD	VG	FN	VF	VF/NM	NM-
1-Linsner-c; Drew Hayes-a/scripts in all.						5.00
1-2nd print						2.50
2-25: 12-Purple Marauder-c/app.						3.00
26-45, 47-49						2.50
46,50-75: 61-Fillbäch Brothers-s/a. 74-Art by Crilley (3 pgs.)						3.00
... Baptism By Fire-(2003, $19.95, TPB)-r/#48-59						20.00
... Color Special #1 (12/98, $2.95)						5.00
... Companion (12/02, $3.50) Back-story and character bios						3.50
... FAN Edition #1 mail-in offer; Drew Hayes-c/s/a	1	2	3	5	6	8
... Rogues-(2002, $15.95, TPB)-r/#40-47						16.00
...Salvation-(2001, $19.95, TPB)-r/#26-39						20.00
...Sanctuary-(1999, $14.95, TPB)-r/#1-12						15.00

POISON ELVES: LUSIPHUR & LIRILITH
Sirius Entertainment: 2001 - No. 4, 2001 ($2.95, B&W, mature readers)

1-4-Drew Hayes-s/Jason Alexander-a 3.00
TPB (2002, $11.95) r/#1-4 12.00

POISON ELVES: PARINTACHIN
Sirius Entertainment: 2001 - No. 3, 2002 ($2.95, B&W, mature readers)

1-3-Drew Hayes-c/Fillbäch Brothers-s/a 3.00
TPB (2003, $8.95) r/#1-3 9.00

POKÉMON (TV) (Also see Magical Pokémon Journey)
Viz Comics: Nov, 1998 - Present ($3.25/$3.50, B&W)

...Part 1: The Electric Tale of Pikachu

	GD	VG	FN	VF	VF/NM	NM-
1-Toshiro Ono-s/a	1	3	4	6	8	10
1-4 (2nd through current printings)						3.50
2						6.00
3,4						4.00
TPB ($12.95)						13.00

...Part 2: Pikachu Strikes Back

1 5.00
2-4 4.00
TPB 13.00

...Part 3: Electric Pikachu Boogaloo

1 4.00
2-4 ($2.95-c) 3.50
TPB 13.00

...Part 4: Surf's Up Pikachu

1,3,4 4.00
2 ($2.95-c) 3.50
TPB 13.00

NOTE: Multiple printings exist for most issues

POKÉMON ADVENTURES
Viz Comics: Sept, 1999 - No. 4 ($5.95, B&W, magazine-size)

1-4-Includes stickers bound in 6.00

POKÉMON ADVENTURES
Viz Comics: 2000 - Present ($2.95/$4.95, B&W)

Part 2 (2/00-7/00) 1-6-Includes stickers bound in 3.50
Part 3 (8/00-2/01) 1-7 3.50
Part 4 (3/00-6/01) 1-4 5.00
Part 5 (7/01-10/01) 1-4 5.00
Part 6 - 1-4, Part 7 1,2 5.00

POKÉMON: THE FIRST MOVIE
Viz Comics: 1999 ($3.95)

Mewtwo Strikes Back 1-4 4.00
Pikachu's Vacation 4.00

POKÉMON: THE MOVIE 2000
Viz Comics: 2000 ($3.95)

1-Official movie adaption 4.00
Pikachu's Rescue Adventure 4.00
...:The Power of One (mini-series) 1-3 4.00

POLICE ACADEMY (TV)
Marvel Comics: Nov, 1989 - No. 6, Feb, 1990 ($1.00)

Police Comics #100 © QUA

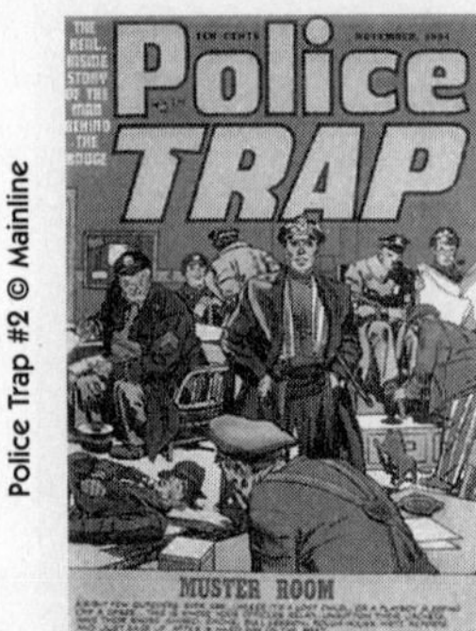

Police Trap #2 © Mainline

Popeye #2 © KING

	GD 2.0	VG 4.0	FN 6.0	VF 8.0	VF/NM 9.0	NM- 9.2

1-6: Based on TV cartoon; Post-c/a(p) in all 2.25

POLICE ACTION
Atlas News Co.: Jan, 1954 - No. 7, Nov, 1954

1-Violent-a by Robert Q. Sale 21 42 63 118 164 210
2 11 22 33 63 84 105
3-7: 7-Powell-a 10 20 30 58 77 95

NOTE: ***Ayers** a-4, 5. **Colan** a-1. **Forte** a-1, 2. **Mort Lawrence** a-5. **Maneely** a-3; c-1, 5. **Reinman** a-6, 7.*

POLICE ACTION
Atlas/Seaboard Publ.: Feb, 1975 - No. 3, June, 1975

1-3: 1-Lomax, N.Y.P.D., Luke Malone begin; McWilliams-a. 2-Origin Luke Malone, Manhunter; Ploog-a 1 2 3 5 6 8

NOTE: ***Ploog** art in all. **Sekowsky/McWilliams** a-1-3. **Thorne** c-3.*

POLICE AGAINST CRIME
Premiere Magazines: April, 1954 - No. 9, Aug, 1955

1-Disbrow-a; extreme violence (man's face slashed with knife); Hollingsworth-a
25 50 75 147 202 260
2-Hollingsworth-a 14 28 42 81 111 140
3-9 11 22 33 63 84 105

POLICE BADGE #479 (Formerly Spy Thrillers #1-4)
Atlas Comics (PrPl): No. 5, Sept, 1955

5-Maneely-c/a (6 pgs.) 11 22 33 63 84 105

POLICE CASE BOOK (See Giant Comics Editions)

POLICE CASES (See Authentic... & Record Book of...)

POLICE COMICS
Quality Comics Group (Comic Magazines): Aug, 1941 - No. 127, Oct, 1953

1-Origin/1st app. Plastic Man by Jack Cole (r-in DC Special #15), The Human Bomb by Gustavson, & No. 711; intro. Chic Carter by Eisner, The Firebrand by Reed Crandall, The Mouthpiece by Guardineer, Phantom Lady, & The Sword; Firebrand-c 1-4
724 1448 2172 5068 7784 10,500
2-Plastic Man smuggles opium 311 622 933 2022 3111 4200
3 224 448 672 1400 2100 2800
4 194 384 576 1200 1800 2400
5-Plastic Man-c begin; Plastic Man forced to smoke marijuana; Plastic Man covers begin, end #102 184 368 552 1150 1725 2300
6,7 160 320 480 1000 1500 2000
8-Manhunter begins (origin/1st app.) (3/42) 188 376 564 1175 1763 2350
9,10 128 256 384 800 1200 1600
11-The Spirit strip reprints begin by Eisner (origin-strip #1); 1st comic book app. The Spirit & 1st cover app. (9/42) 224 448 672 1400 2100 2800
12-Intro. Ebony 134 268 402 838 1257 1675
13-Intro. Woozy Winks; last Firebrand 128 256 384 800 1200 1600
14-19: 15-Last No. 711; Destiny begins 94 188 282 588 882 1175
20-The Raven x-over in Phantom Lady; features Jack Cole himself
94 188 282 588 882 1175
21,22: 21-Raven & Spider Widow x-over in Phantom Lady (cameo in #22)
80 160 240 500 750 1000
23-30: 23-Last Phantom Lady. 24-26-Flatfoot Burns by Kurtzman in all
76 152 228 475 713 950
31-41: 37-1st app. Candy by Sahle & begins (12/44). 41-Last Spirit-r by Eisner
53 106 159 318 479 640
42,43-Spirit-r by Eisner/Fine 53 106 159 318 474 630
44-Fine Spirit-r begin, end #88,90,92 50 100 150 300 463 625
45-50: 50-(#50 on-c, #49 on inside, 1/46) 40 80 120 240 358 475
51-60: 58-Last Human Bomb 36 72 108 204 290 375
61-88,90,92: 63-(Some issues have #65 printed on cover, but #63 on inside) Kurtzman-a, 6 pgs. 90,92-Spirit by Fine 27 54 81 155 218 280
89,91,93-No Spirit stories 24 48 72 138 194 250
94-99,101,102: Spirit by Eisner in all; 101-Last Manhunter. 102-Last Spirit & Plastic Man by Jack Cole 34 68 102 196 278 360
100 40 80 120 240 340 440
103-Content change to crime; Ken Shannon & T-Man begin (1st app. of each, 12/50) 28 56 84 159 225 290
104-112,114-127: Crandall-a most issues (not in 104,105,122,125-127). 109-Atomic bomb story. 112-Crandall-a 20 40 60 115 160 205
113-Crandall-c/a(2), 9 pgs. each 22 44 66 124 172 220

NOTE: *Most Spirit stories signed by Eisner are not by him; all are reprints. **Cole** c-17, 19-21, 24-26, 28-31, 36-38, 40-42, 45-48, 65-68, 69, 73, 75. **Crandall** Firebrand-1-8. Spirit by **Eisner** 1-41, 94-102; by **Eisner/Fine**-42, 43; by **Fine**-44-88, 90, 92. 103, 109. **Al Bryant** c-33, 34. **Cole** c-17-32, 35-102(most). **Crandall** c-13, 14. **Crandall/Cuidera** c-105-127. **Eisner** c-4i. **Gill Fox** c-1-3, 4p, 5-12, 15. Bondage c-103, 109, 125.*

POLICE LINE-UP
Avon Periodicals/Realistic Comics #3,4: Aug, 1951 - No. 4, July, 1952 (Painted-c #1-3)

1-Wood-a, 1 pg. plus part-c; spanking panel-r/Saint #5
40 80 120 240 340 440
2-Classic story "The Religious Murder Cult", drugs, perversion; r/Saint #5; c-r/Avon paperback #329 29 58 87 164 232 300
3,4: 3-Kubert-a(r?)/part-c; Kinstler-a (inside-c only) 22 44 66 127 176 225

POLICE TRAP (Public Defender In Action #7 on)
Mainline #1-4/Charlton #5,6: 8-9/54 - No. 4, 2-3/55; No. 5, 7/55 - No. 6, 9/55

1-S&K covers-all issues; Meskin-a; Kirby scripts 31 62 93 175 248 320
2-4 19 38 57 106 146 185
5,6-S&K-c/a 25 50 75 144 198 255

POLICE TRAP
Super Comics: No. 11, 1963; No. 16-18, 1964

Reprint #11,16-18: 11-r/Police Trap #3. 16-r/Justice Traps the Guilty #? 17-r/Inside Crime #3 & r/Justice Traps The Guilty #83; 18-r/Inside Crime #3
2 4 6 10 13 16

POLLY & HER PALS (See Comic Monthly #1)

POLLYANNA (Disney)
Dell Publishing Co.: No. 1129, Aug-Oct, 1960

Four Color 1129-Movie, Haley Mills photo-c 9 18 27 60 85 110

POLLY PIGTAILS (Girls' Fun & Fashion Magazine #44 on)
Parents' Magazine Institute/Polly Pigtails: Jan, 1946 - V4#43, Oct-Nov, 1949

1-Infinity-c; photo-c 12 24 36 69 92 115
2-Photo-c 7 14 21 37 46 55
3-5: 3,4-Photo-c 6 12 18 31 38 45
6-10: 7-Photo-c 6 12 18 28 34 40
11-30: 22-Photo-c 5 10 15 24 30 35
31-43 5 10 15 22 26 30

PONY EXPRESS (See Tales of the...)

PONYTAIL (Teen-age)
Dell Publishing Co./Charlton No. 13 on: 7-9/62 - No. 12, 10-12/65; No. 13, 11/69 - No. 20, 1/71

12-641-209(#1) 4 8 12 24 32 42
2-12 3 6 9 18 23 28
13-20 2 4 6 11 14 18

POP COMICS
Modern Store Publ.: 1955 (36 pgs.; 5x7"; in color) (7¢)

1-Funny animal 6 12 18 28 34 40

POPEYE (See Comic Album #7, 11, 15, Comics Reading Libraries *in the Promotional Comics section*, Eat Right to Work and Win, Giant Comic Album, King Comics, Kite Fun Book, Magic Comics, March of Comics #37,52, 66, 80, 96, 117, 134, 148, 157, 169, 194, 246, 264, 274, 294, 453, 465, 477 & Wow Comics, 1st series)

POPEYE
David McKay Publications: 1937 - 1939 (All by Segar)

Feature Books nn (100 pgs.) (Very Rare) 600 1200 1800 4200 5858 8100
Feature Books 2 (52 pgs.) 65 130 195 485 743 1000
Feature Books 3 (100 pgs.)-r/nn issue with a new-c 60 120 180 459 705 950
Feature Books 5,10 (76 pgs.) 53 106 159 410 625 840
Feature Books 14 (76 pgs.) (Scarce) 60 128 180 459 705 950

POPEYE (Strip reprints through 4-Color #70)
Dell #1-65/Gold Key #66-80/King #81-92/Charlton #94-138/Gold Key #139-155/Whitman #156 on: 1941 - 1947; #1, 2-4/48 - #65, 7-9/62; #66, 10/62 - #80, 5/66; #81, 8/66 - #92, 12/67; #94, 2/69 - #138, 1/77; #139, 5/78 - #171, 6/84 (no #93,160,161)

Large Feature Comic 24('41)-Half by Segar 54 108 162 400 600 800
Four Color 25('41)-by Segar 65 130 195 485 743 1000
Large Feature Comic 10('43) 41 82 123 317 476 635
Four Color 17('43),26('43)-by Segar 47 94 141 352 531 710
Four Color 43('44) 31 62 93 233 349 465
Four Color 70('45)-Title: ...& Wimpy 26 52 78 189 275 360
Four Color 113('46-original strips begin),127,145('47),168
15 30 45 104 152 200
1(2-4/48)(Dell)-All new stories continue 29 58 87 210 305 400
2 15 30 45 104 152 200
3-10: 5-Popeye on moon w/rocket-c 12 24 36 87 129 170
11-20 10 20 30 73 107 140
21-40,46: 46-Origin Swee' Pee 9 18 27 60 85 110
41-45,47-50 7 14 21 51 71 90
51-60 6 12 18 43 59 75
61-65 (Last Dell issue) 6 12 18 38 52 65

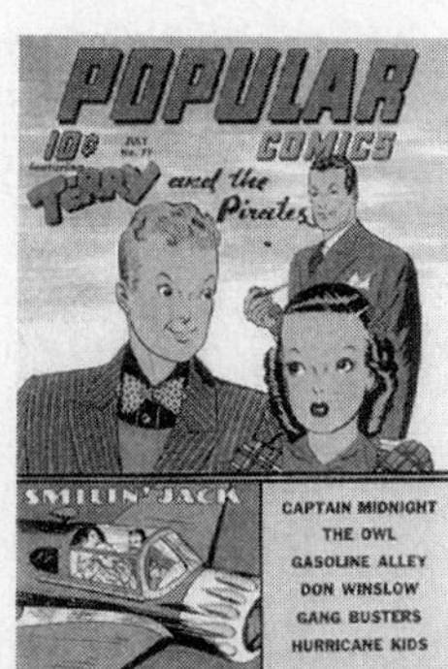

Popular Comics #77 © DELL

Popular Romance #7 © STD

The Possessed #1 © Johns & Grimminger

	GD 2.0	VG 4.0	FN 6.0	VF 8.0	VF/NM 9.0	NM- 9.2

66,67-Both 84 pgs. (Gold Key) 7 14 21 51 71 90
68-80 4 8 12 27 36 45
81-92,94-97 (no #93): 97-Last 12¢ issue 3 7 10 21 28 35
98,99,101-138 2 4 6 12 16 20
100 3 6 9 18 24 30
139-155: 144-50th Anniversary issue 1 3 4 6 8 10
156,157,162-167(Whitman)(no #160,161).167(3/82) 2 4 6 10 13 16
158(9/80),159(11/80)-pre-pack only 3 6 9 18 23 28
168-171:(All #90069 on-c; pre-pack) 168(6/83). 169(#168 on-c)(8/83). 170(3/84).
171(6/84) 2 4 6 12 16 20
NOTE: *Reprints-#145, 147, 149, 151, 153, 155, 157, 163-168(1/3), 170.*

POPEYE
Harvey Comics: Nov, 1993 - No. 7, Aug, 1994 ($1.50)
V2#1-7 3.00
...Summer Special V2#1-(10/93, $2.25, 68 pgs.)-Sagendorf-r & others 4.00

POPEYE SPECIAL
Ocean Comics: Summer, 1987 - No. 2, Sept, 1988 ($1.75/$2.00)
1,2: 1-Origin 4.00

POPPLES (TV, movie)
Star Comics (Marvel): Dec, 1986 - No. 5, Aug, 1987
1-5-Based on toys 4.00

POPPO OF THE POPCORN THEATRE
Fuller Publishing Co. (Publishers Weekly): 10/29/55 - No. 13, 1956 (weekly)
1 9 18 27 52 66 80
2-5 7 14 21 35 43 50
6-13 6 12 18 28 34 40
NOTE: *By* ***Charles Biro.*** *10¢ cover, given away by supermarkets such as IGA.*

POP-POP COMICS
R. B. Leffingwell Co.: No date (Circa 1945) (52 pgs.)
1-Funny animal 13 26 39 74 100 125

POPULAR COMICS
Dell Publishing Co.: Feb, 1936 - No. 145, July-Sept, 1948
1-Dick Tracy (1st comic book app.), Little Orphan Annie, Terry & the Pirates, Gasoline Alley, Don Winslow (1st app.), Harold Teen, Little Joe, Skippy, Moon Mullins, Mutt & Jeff, Tailspin Tommy, Smitty, Smokey Stover, Winnie Winkle & The Gumps begin (all strip-r)
615 1230 1846 4400 - -
2 215 430 646 1550 - -
3 162 324 485 1150 - -
4-6(7/36): 5-Tom Mix begins. 6-1st app. Scribbly 131 262 392 925 - -
7-10: 8,9-Scribbly & Reglar Fellers app. 100 200 300 725 - -
11-20: 12-X-Mas-c 80 160 240 460 655 850
21-27: 27-Last Terry & the Pirates, Little Orphan Annie, & Dick Tracy
60 120 180 345 493 640
28-37: 28-Gene Autry app. 31,32-Tim McCoy app. 35-Christmas-c; Tex Ritter app.
47 94 141 270 385 500
38-43: Tarzan in text only. 38-(4/39)-Gang Busters (Radio, 2nd app.) & Zane Grey's Tex Thorne begins? 43-The Masked Pilot app.; 1st non-funny-c?
46 92 138 265 375 485
44,45: 45-Hurricane Kid-c 33 66 99 190 270 350
46-Origin/1st app. Martan, the Marvel Man(12/39) 43 86 129 247 349 450
47-50 32 64 96 184 260 335
51-Origin The Voice (The Invisible Detective) strip begins (5/40)
33 66 99 190 270 350
52-Robot-c 32 64 96 184 262 340
53-59: 55-End of World story 28 56 84 161 231 300
60-Origin/1st app. Professor Supermind and Son (2/41)
31 62 93 178 252 325
61-71: 63-Smilin' Jack begins 25 50 75 144 202 260
72-The Owl & Terry & the Pirates begin (2/42); Smokey Stover reprints begin
40 80 120 230 328 425
73-75 27 54 81 155 223 290
76-78-Capt. Midnight in all (see The Funnies #57) 40 80 120 230 325 420
79-85-Last Owl 26 52 78 150 213 275
86-99: 98-Felix the Cat, Smokey Stover-r begin 18 36 54 103 147 190
100 20 40 60 115 168 220
101-130 11 22 33 63 92 120
131-145: 142-Last Terry & the Pirates 10 20 30 57 81 105
NOTE: *Martan, the Marvel Man c-47-49, 52, 57-59. Professor Supermind c-60-63, 64(1/2), 65, 66. The Voice c-53.*

POPULAR FAIRY TALES (See March of Comics #6, 18)

	GD 2.0	VG 4.0	FN 6.0	VF 8.0	VF/NM 9.0	NM- 9.2

POPULAR ROMANCE
Better-Standard Publications: No. 5, Dec, 1949 - No. 29, July, 1954
5 11 22 33 63 84 105
6-9: 7-Palais-a; lingerie panels 8 16 24 46 58 70
10-Wood-a (2 pgs.) 9 18 27 54 70 85
11,12,14-16,18-21,28,29 7 14 21 37 46 55
13,17-Severin/Elder-a (3&8 pgs.) 8 16 24 43 54 65
22-27-Toth-a 9 18 27 52 66 80
NOTE: *All have photo-c.* ***Tuska*** *art in most issues.*

POPULAR TEEN-AGERS (Secrets of Love) (School Day Romances #1-4)
Star Publications: No. 5, Sept, 1950 - No. 23, Nov, 1954
5-Toni Gay, Midge Martin & Eve Adams continue from School Day Romances; Ginger Bunn (formerly Ginger Snapp & becomes Honey Bunn #6 on) begins; all features end #8 35 70 105 201 288 370
6-8 (7/51)-Honey Bunn begins; all have L. B. Cole-c; 6-Negligee panels
32 64 96 182 259 335
9-(...Romances; 1st romance issue, 10/51) 21 42 63 121 168 215
10-(...Secrets of Love thru #23) 20 40 60 112 156 200
11,16,18,19,22,23 16 32 48 92 126 160
12,13,17,20,21-Disbrow-a 18 36 54 101 138 175
14-Harrison/Wood-a 24 48 72 135 190 245
15-Wood?, Disbrow-a 19 38 57 106 146 185
Accepted Reprint 5,6 (nd); L.B. Cole-c 9 18 27 52 66 80
NOTE: *All have* ***L. B. Cole*** *covers.*

PORKY PIG (See Bugs Bunny &..., Kite Fun Book, Looney Tunes, March of Comics #42, 57, 71, 89, 99, 113, 130, 143, 164, 175, 192, 209, 218, 367, and Super Book #6, 18, 30)

PORKY PIG (...& Bugs Bunny #40-69)
Dell Publishing Co./Gold Key No. 1-93/Whitman No. 94 on: No. 16, 1942 - No. 81, Mar-Apr, 1962; Jan, 1965 - No. 109, June, 1984
Four Color 16(#1, 1942) 80 160 240 629 965 1300
Four Color 48(1944)-Carl Barks-a 92 184 276 706 1078 1450
Four Color 78(1945) 27 54 81 192 281 370
Four Color 112(7/46) 17 34 51 118 174 230
Four Color 156,182,191('49) 12 24 36 84 125 165
Four Color 226,241('49),260,271,277,284,295 10 20 30 70 100 130
Four Color 303,311,322,330: 322-Sci/fi-c/story 7 14 21 51 71 90
Four Color 342,351,360,370,385,399,410,426 6 12 18 38 52 65
25 (11-12/52)-30 4 8 12 29 40 50
31-40 4 8 12 24 32 40
41-60 3 6 9 19 25 32
61-81(3-4/62) 3 6 9 16 20 25
1(1/65-Gold Key)(2nd Series) 5 10 15 36 48 60
2,4,5-r/4-Color 226,284 & 271 in that order 3 6 9 19 25 32
3,6-10: 3-r/Four Color #342 3 6 9 16 20 25
11-30 2 4 6 11 14 18
31-54 2 4 6 9 11 14
55-70 1 3 4 6 8 10
71-93(Gold Key) 1 2 3 5 6 8
94-96 1 2 3 5 7 9
97(9/80),98-pre-pack only 3 6 9 16 20 24
99-pre-pack only (exist?) 3 6 9 18 24 30
100 2 4 6 9 11 14
101-105: 104(2/82). 105(4/82) 1 3 4 6 8 10
106-109 (All #90140 on-c, no date or date code): 106(7/83), 107(8/83), 108(2/84), 109(6/84) low print run 2 4 6 10 13 16
NOTE: *Reprints-#1-8, 9-35(2/3); 36-46(1/4-1/2), 58, 67, 69-74, 76, 78, 102-109(1/3-1/2).*

PORKY PIG'S DUCK HUNT
Saalfield Publishing Co.: 1938 (12pgs.)(large size)(heavy linen-like paper)
2178-1st app. Porky Pig & Daffy Duck by Leon Schlesinger. Illustrated text story book written in verse.1st book ever devoted to these characters. (see Looney Tunes #1 for their 1st comic book app.) 70 140 210 438 657 875

PORTIA PRINZ OF THE GLAMAZONS
Eclipse Comics: Dec, 1986 - No. 6, Oct, 1987 ($2.00, B&W, Baxter paper)
1-6 2.25

POSSESSED, THE
DC Comics (Cliffhanger): Sept, 2003 - No. 6 ($2.95, limited series)
1-5-Johns & Grimminger-s/Sharp-a 3.00

POST GAZETTE (See Meet the New... in the Promotional Comics section)

POUNDED
Oni Press: Mar, 2002 - No. 3, June, 2002 ($2.95, B&W, limited series)

The Power Company #1 © DC

Power Man #100 © MAR

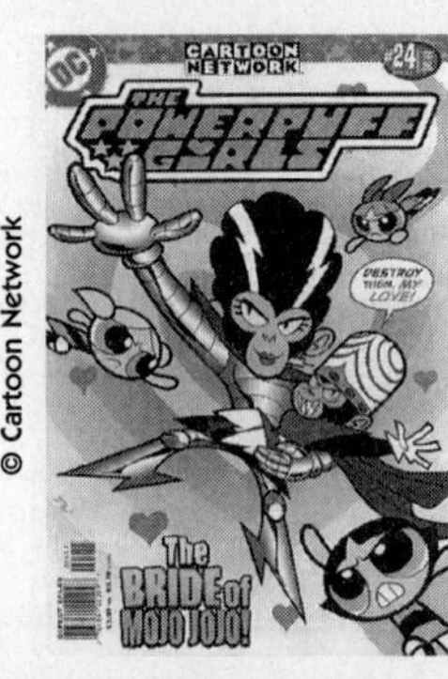

The Powerpuff Girls #24 © Cartoon Network

GD 2.0 | VG 4.0 | FN 6.0 | VF 8.0 | VF/NM 9.0 | NM- 9.2

1-3-Brian Wood-s/Steve Rolston-a 3.00
TPB (10/02, $8.95, 8 1/4" x 6") r/#1-3; intro by Kieron Dwyer; sketch pages and pin-ups 9.00

POWDER RIVER RUSTLERS (See Fawcett Movie Comics)

POWER & GLORY (See American Flagg! & Howard Chaykin's American Flagg!
Malibu Comics (Bravura): Feb, 1994 - No. 4, May, 1994 ($2.50, limited series, mature)

1A, 1B-By Howard Chaykin; w/Bravura stamp 2.50
1-Newsstand ed. (polybagged w/children's warning on bag), Gold ed., Silver-foil ed., Blue-foil ed.(print run of 10,000), Serigraph ed. (print run of 3,000)($2.95)-Howard Chaykin-c/a begin 3.00
2-4-Contains Bravura stamp 2.50
Holiday Special (Win '94, $2.95) 3.00

POWER COMICS
Holyoke Publ. Co./Narrative Publ.: 1944 - No. 4, 1945

	GD	VG	FN	VF	VF/NM	NM-
1-L. B. Cole-c	148	296	444	925	1388	1850
2-Hitler, Hirohito-c (scarce)	148	296	444	925	1388	1850
3-Classic L.B. Cole-c; Dr. Mephisto begins?	170	340	510	1063	1594	2125
4-L.B. Cole-c; Miss Espionage app. #3,4; Leav-a	148	296	444	925	1388	1850

POWER COMICS
Power Comics Co.: 1977 - No. 5, Dec, 1977 (B&W)

	GD	VG	FN	VF	VF/NM	NM-
1- "A Boy And His Aardvark" by Dave Sim; first Dave Sim aardvark (not Cerebus)	2	4	6	12	16	20
1-Reprint (3/77, black-c)	1	2	3	5	6	8
2-Cobalt Blue by Gustovich	1	3	4	6	8	10
3-5: 3-Nightwitch. 4-Northern Light. 5-Bluebird	1	3	4	6	8	10

POWER COMICS
Eclipse Comics (Acme Press): Mar, 1988 - No. 4, Sept, 1988 ($2.00, B&W, mini-series)

1-4: Bolland, Gibbons-r in all 2.25

POWER COMPANY, THE
DC Comics: Apr, 2002 - No. 18, Sep, 2003 ($2.50/$2.75)

1-6-Busiek-s/Grummett-a. 6-Green Arrow & Black Canary-c/app. 2.50
7-18: 7:Begin $2.75-c. 8,9-Green Arrow app. 11-Firestorm joins. 15-Batman app. 2.75
...Bork (3/02) Busiek-s/Dwyer-a; Batman & Flash (Barry Allen) app. 2.50
...Josiah Power (3/02) Busiek-s/Giffen-a; Superman app. 2.50
...Manhunter (3/02) Busiek-s/Jurgens-a; Nightwing app. 2.50
...Sapphire (3/02) Busiek-s/Bagley-a; JLA & Kobra app. 2.50
...Skyrocket (3/02) Busiek-s/Staton-a; Green Lantern (Hal Jordan) app. 2.50
...Striker Z (3/02) Busiek-s/Bachs-a; Superboy app. 2.50
...Witchfire (3/02) Busiek-s/Haley-a; Wonder Woman app. 2.50

POWER FACTOR
Wonder Color Comics #1/Pied Piper #2: May, 1987 - No. 2, 1987 ($1.95)

1,2: Super team. 2-Infantino-c 2.25

POWER FACTOR
Innovation Publishing: Oct, 1990 - No. 3, 1991 ($1.95/$2.25)

1-3: 1-R-/1st story + new-a, 2-r/2nd story + new-a. 3-Infantino-a 2.25

POWER GIRL (See All-Star #58, Infinity, Inc., Showcase #97-99)
DC Comics: June, 1988 - No. 4, Sept, 1988 ($1.00, color, limited series)

1-4 3.00

POWERHOUSE PEPPER COMICS (See Gay Comics, Joker Comics & Tessie the Typist)
Marvel Comics (20CC): No. 1, 1943; No. 2, May, 1948 - No. 5, Nov, 1948

	GD	VG	FN	VF	VF/NM	NM-
1-(60 pgs.)-Wolverton-a in all; c-2,3	176	352	528	1100	1650	2200
2	85	170	255	531	796	1060
3,4	78	156	234	488	732	975
5-(Scarce)	92	184	276	575	863	1150

POWER LINE
Marvel Comics (Epic Comics): May, 1988 - No. 8, Sept, 1989 ($1.25/$1.50)

1-8: 2-Williamson-i. 3-Dr. Zero app. 4-7-Morrow-a. 8-Williamson-i 2.25

POWER LORDS
DC Comics: Dec, 1983 - No. 3, Feb, 1984 (Limited series, Mando paper)

1-3: Based on Revell toys 2.25

POWER MAN (Formerly Hero for Hire; ...& Iron Fist #50 on; see Cage & Giant-Size...)
Marvel Comics Group: No. 17, Feb, 1974 - No. 125, Sept, 1986

	GD	VG	FN	VF	VF/NM	NM-
17-Luke Cage continues; Iron Man app.	2	4	6	10	12	15
18-20: 18-Last 20¢ issue	1	3	4	6	8	10
21-30	1	2	3	5	6	8
30-(30¢-c variant, limited distribution)(4/76)	2	4	6	8	10	12
31-46: 31-Part Neal Adams-i. 34-Last 25¢ issue. 36-r/Hero For Hire #12. 41-1st app. Thunderbolt. 45-Starlin-c.	1	2	3	4	5	7
31-34-(30¢-c variants, limited distribution)(5-8/76)	1	3	4	6	8	10
44-46-(35¢-c variants, limited distribution)(6-8/77)	1	3	4	6	8	10
47-Barry Smith-a	1	2	3	5	7	9
47-(35¢-c variant, limited distribution)(10/77)	2	4	6	9	11	14
48-50-Byrne-a(p); 48-Power Man/Iron Fist 1st meet. 50-Iron Fist joins Cage	2	4	6	8	10	12
51-56,58-65,67-77: 58-Intro El Aguila. 75-Double size. 77-Daredevil app.						4.00
57-New X-Men app. (6/79)	2	4	6	14	18	22
66-2nd app. Sabretooth (see Iron Fist #14)	3	7	10	21	28	35
78,84: 78-3rd app. Sabretooth (cameo under cloak). 84-4th app. Sabretooth	2	4	6	11	14	18
79-83,85-99,101-124: 87-Moon Knight app. 109-The Reaper app.						3.00
100,125-Double size: 100-Origin K'un L'un. 125-Death of Iron Fist						4.00
Annual 1(1976)-Punisher cameo in flashback	2	4	6	9	11	14

NOTE: ***Austin** c-102i. **Byrne** a-48-50; c-102, 104, 106, 107, 112-116. **Kane** c(p)-24, 25, 28, 48. **Miller** a-68, 76(2 pgs.); c-66-68, 70-74, 80i. **Mooney** a-38i, 53i, 55i. **Nebres** a-76p. **Nino** a-42i, 43i. **Perez** a-27. **B. Smith** a-47i. **Tuska** a(p)-17, 20, 24, 26, 28, 29, 36, 47. Painted c-75, 100.*

POWER OF PRIME
Malibu Comics (Ultraverse): July, 1995 - No. 4, Nov, 1995 ($2.50, lim. series)

1-4 2.50

POWER OF SHAZAM!, THE (See SHAZAM!)
DC Comics: 1994 (Painted graphic novel) (Prequel to new series)

	GD	VG	FN	VF	VF/NM	NM-
Hardcover-($19.95)-New origin of Shazam!; Ordway painted-c/a & script	3	6	9	16	20	25
Softcover-($7.50), Softcover-($9.95)-New-c.	2	4	6	8	10	12

POWER OF SHAZAM!, THE
DC Comics: Mar, 1995 - No. 47, Mar, 1999 ($1.50/$1.75/$1.95/$2.50)

1-Jerry Ordway scripts begin 4.00
2-20: 4-Begin $1.75-c. 6:Re-intro of Capt. Nazi. 8-Re-intro of Spy Smasher, Bulletman & Minuteman; Swan-a (7 pgs.). 11-Re-intro of Ibis, Swan-a(2 pgs.). 14-Gil Kane-a(p). 20-Superman-c/app.; "Final Night" 3.00
21-47: 21-Plastic Man-c/app. 22-Batman-c/app. 35,36-X-over w/Starman #39,40. 38-41-Mr. Mind. 43-Bulletman app. 45-JLA-c/app. 2.50
#1,000,000 (11/98) 853rd Century x-over; Ordway-c/s/a 3.00
Annual 1 (1996, $2.95)-Legends of the Dead Earth story; Jerry Ordway-c; Mike Manley-a 4.00

POWER OF STRONGMAN, THE (Also see Strongman)
AC Comics: 1989 ($2.95)

1-Powell G.A.-r 3.00

POWER OF THE ATOM (See Secret Origins #29)
DC Comics: Aug, 1988 - No. 18, Nov, 1989 ($1.00)

1-18: 6-Chronos returns; Byrne-p. 9-JLI app. 2.25

POWER PACHYDERMS
Marvel Comics: Sept, 1989 ($1.25, one-shot)

1-Elephant super-heroes; parody of X-Men, Elektra, & 3 Stooges 2.25

POWER PACK
Marvel Comics Group: Aug, 1984 - No. 62, Feb, 1991

1-($1.00, 52 pgs.)-Origin & 1st app. Power Pack 3.00
2-18,20-26,28,30-45,47-62 2.25
19-(52 pgs.)-Cloak & Dagger, Wolverine app. 3.00
27-Mutant massacre; Wolverine & Sabretooth app. 5.00
29,46: 29-Spider-Man & Hobgoblin app. 46-Punisher app. 2.50
Graphic Novel: Power Pack & Cloak & Dagger: Shelter From the Storm ('89, SC, $7.95) Velluto/Farmer-a 10.00
...Holiday Special 1 (2/92, $2.25, 68 pgs.) 2.25

NOTE: ***Austin** scripts-53. **Mignola** c-20. **Morrow** a-51. **Spiegle** a-55i. **Williamson** a(i)-43, 50, 52.*

POWER PACK (Volume 2)
Marvel Comics: Aug, 2000 - No. 4, Nov, 2000 ($2.99, limited series)

1-4-Doran & Austin-c/a 3.00

POWERPUFF GIRLS, THE (Also see Cartoon Network Starring... #1)
DC Comics: May, 2000 - Present ($1.99/$2.25)

1 4.00
2-45: 25-Pin-ups by Allred, Byrne, Baker, Mignola, Hernandez, Warren 2.25
...Double Whammy (12/00, $3.95) r/#1,2 & a Dexter's Lab story 4.00
...Movie: The Comic (9/02, $2.95) Movie adaptation; Phil Moy & Chris Cook-a 3.00

POWER RANGERS ZEO (TV)(Saban's...)(Also see Saban's Mighty Morphin Power Rangers)
Image Comics (Extreme Studios): Aug, 1996 ($2.50)

1-Based on TV show 2.50

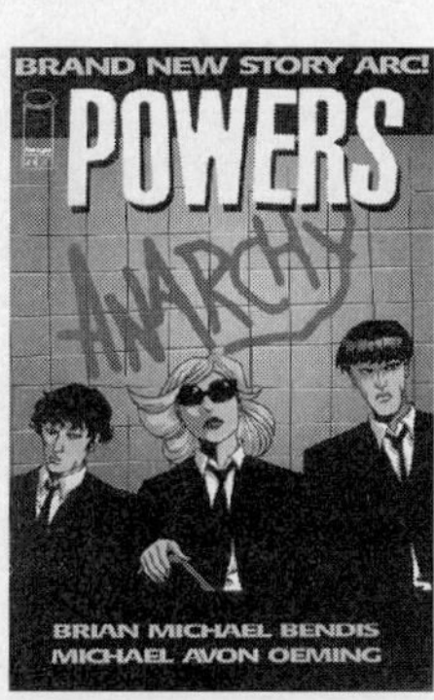

Powers #21 © Jinxworld Inc.

Preacher #34 © Ennis & Dillon

Predator: Big Game #2 © 20th Century Fox

GD 2.0 | VG 4.0 | FN 6.0 | VF 8.0 | VF/NM 9.0 | NM- 9.2

POWER RECORD COMICS (See the Promotional Comics section)

POWERS
Image Comics: 2000 - Present ($2.95)

1-Bendis-s/Oeming-a; murder of Retro Girl 1 3 4 6 8 10
2-6: 6-End of Retro Girl arc. 5.00
7-14: 7-Warren Ellis app. 12-14-Death of Olympia 3.50
15-35: 31-35-Origin of the Powers 3.00
Annual 1 (2001, $3.95) 4.00
...Coloring/Activity Book (2001, $1.50, B&W, 8 x 10.5") Oeming-a 2.25
....: Little Deaths TPB (2002, $19.95) r/#7,12-14, Ann. #1, Coloring/Activity Book; sketch pages, cover gallery 20.00
....: Roleplay TPB (2001, $13.95) r/#8-11; sketchbook, cover gallery 14.00
... Scriptbook (2001, $19.95) scripts for #1-11; Oeming sketches 20.00
....: Supergroup TPB (2003, $19.95) r/#15-20; sketchbook, cover gallery 20.00
..: Who Killed Retro Girl TPB (2000, $21.95) r/#1-6; sketchbook, cover gallery, and promotional strips from Comic Shop News 22.00

POWERS THAT BE (Becomes Star Seed No.7 on)
Broadway Comics: Nov, 1995 - No. 6, June, 1996 ($2.50)

1-6: 1-Intro of Fatale & Star Seed. 6-Begin $2.95-c. 3.00
Preview Editions 1-3 (9/95 - 11/95, B&W) 2.50

POW MAGAZINE (Bob Sproul's) (Satire Magazine)
Humor-Vision: Aug, 1966 - No. 3, Feb, 1967 (30¢)

1,2: 2-Jones-a 4 8 12 27 36 45
3-Wrightson-a 5 10 15 36 48 60

PREACHER
DC Comics (Vertigo): Apr, 1995 - No. 66, Oct, 2000 ($2.50, mature)

nn-Preview 2 4 6 12 16 20
1 ($2.95)-Ennis scripts, Dillon-a & Fabry-c in all; 1st app. Jesse, Tulip, & Cassidy 2 4 6 9 11 14
2,3: 2-1st app. Saint of Killers. 1 2 3 5 7 9
4,5 1 2 3 4 5 7
6-10 5.00
11-20: 12-Polybagged w/videogame w/Ennis text. 13-Hunters storyline begins; ends #17. 19-Saint of Killers app.; begin "Crusaders", ends #24 4.00
21-25: 21-24-Saint of Killers app. 25-Origin of Cassidy. 3.00
26-49,52-64: 52-Tulip origin 2.50
50-($3.75) Pin-ups by Jim Lee, Bradstreet, Quesada and Palmiotti 3.75
51-Includes preview of 100 Bullets; Tulip origin 4.00
65,66-($3.75) 65-Almost everyone dies. 66-Final issue 5.00
Alamo (2001, $17.95, TPB) r/#59-66; Fabry-c 18.00
All Hell's a-Coming (2000, $17.95, TPB)-r/#51-58, ...:Tall in the Saddle 18.00
...: Dead or Alive HC (2000, $29.95) Gallery of Glenn Fabry's cover paintings for every Preacher issue; commentary by Fabry & Ennis 30.00
...: Dead or Alive SC (2003, $19.95) 20.00
Dixie Fried (1998, $14.95, TPB)-r/#27-33, Special: Cassidy 15.00
Gone To Texas (1996, $14.95, TPB)-r/#1-7; Fabry-c 15.00
Proud Americans (1997, $14.95, TPB)-r/#18-26; Fabry-c 15.00
Salvation (1999, $14.95, TPB)-r/#41-50; Fabry-c 15.00
Until the End of the World (1996, $14.95, TPB)-r/#8-17; Fabry-c 15.00
War in the Sun (1999, $14.95, TPB)-r/#34-40 15.00

PREACHER SPECIAL: CASSIDY: BLOOD & WHISKEY
DC Comics (Vertigo): 1998 ($5.95, one-shot)

1-Ennis-scripts/Fabry-c /Dillon-a 6.00

PREACHER SPECIAL: ONE MAN'S WAR
DC Comics (Vertigo): Mar, 1998 ($4.95, one-shot)

1-Ennis-scripts/Fabry-c /Snejbjerg-a 5.00

PREACHER SPECIAL: SAINT OF KILLERS
DC Comics (Vertigo): Aug, 1996 - No. 4, Nov, 1996 ($2.50, lim. series, mature)

1-4: Ennis-scripts/Fabry-c. 1,2-Pugh-a. 3,4-Ezquerra-a 3.00
1-Signed & numbered 20.00

PREACHER SPECIAL: THE GOOD OLD BOYS
DC Comics (Vertigo): Aug, 1997 ($4.95, one-shot, mature)

1-Ennis-scripts/Fabry-c /Esquerra-a 5.00

PREACHER SPECIAL: THE STORY OF YOU-KNOW-WHO
DC Comics (Vertigo): Dec, 1996 ($4.95, one-shot, mature)

1-Ennis-scripts/Fabry-c/Case-a 5.00

PREACHER: TALL IN THE SADDLE
DC Comics (Vertigo): 2000 ($5.95, one-shot)

GD 2.0 | VG 4.0 | FN 6.0 | VF 8.0 | VF/NM 9.0 | NM- 9.2

1-Ennis-scripts/Fabry-c/Dillon-a; early romance of Tulip and Jesse 6.00

PREDATOR (Also see Aliens Vs. ..., Batman vs. ..., Dark Horse Comics, & Dark Horse Presents)
Dark Horse Comics: June, 1989 - No. 4, Mar, 1990 ($2.25, limited series)

1-Based on movie; 1st app. Predator 1 2 3 4 5 7
1-2nd printing 3.00
2 5.00
3,4 4.00
Trade paperback (1990, $12.95)-r/#1-4 13.00

PREDATOR: (title series) **Dark Horse Comics**

--BAD BLOOD, 12/93 - No. 4, 1994 ($2.50) 1-4 3.00
--BIG GAME, 3/91 - No. 4, 6/91 ($2.50) 1-4: 1-3-Contain 2 Dark Horse trading cards 3.00
--BLOODY SANDS OF TIME, 2/92 - No. 2, 2/92 ($2.50) 1,2-Dan Barry-c/a(p)/scripts 3.00
--CAPTIVE, 4/98 ($2.95, one-shot) 1 3.00
--COLD WAR, 9/91 - No. 4, 12/91 ($2.50) 1-4: All have painted-c 3.00
--DARK RIVER, 7/96 - No.4, 10/96 ($2.95)1-4: Miran Kim-c 3.00
--HELL & HOT WATER, 4/97 - No. 3, 6/97 ($2.95) 1-3 3.00
--HELL COME A WALKIN', 2/98 - No. 2, 3/98 ($2.95) 1,2-In the Civil War 3.00
--HOMEWORLD, 3/99 - No. 4, 6/99 ($2.95) 1-4 3.00
--INVADERS FROM THE FOURTH DIMENSION, 7/94 ($3.95, one-shot, 52 pgs.) 1 4.00
--JUNGLE TALES. 3/95 ($2.95t) 1-r/Dark Horse Comics 3.00
--KINDRED, 12/96 - No. 4, 3/97 ($2.50) 1-4 3.00
--NEMESIS, 12/97 - No. 2, 1/98 ($2.95) 1,2-Predator in Victorian England; Taggart-c 3.00
--PRIMAL, 7/97 - No. 2, 8/97 ($2.95) 1,2 3.00
--RACE WAR (See Dark Horse Presents #67), 2/93 - No. 4,10/93 ($2.50, color) 1-4,0: 1-4-Dorman painted-c #1-4, 0(4/930 3.00
--STRANGE ROUX, 11/96 ($2.95, one-shot) 1 3.00
--XENOGENESIS (Also see Aliens Xenogenesis), 8/99 - No. 4, 11/99 ($2.95) 1,2-Edginton-s 3.00

PREDATOR 2
Dark Horse Comics: Feb, 1991 - No. 2, June, 1991 ($2.50, limited series)

1,2: 1-Adapts movie; both w/trading cards & photo-c 3.00

PREDATOR VS. JUDGE DREDD
Dark Horse Comics: Oct, 1997 - No. 3 ($2.50, limited series)

1-3-Wagner-s/Alcatena-a/Bolland-c 3.00

PREDATOR VS. MAGNUS ROBOT FIGHTER
Dark Horse/Valiant: Oct, 1992 - No. 2, 1993 ($2.95, limited series)
(1st Dark Horse/Valiant x-over)

1,2: (Reg.)-Barry Smith-c; Lee Weeks-a. 2-w/trading cards 3.00
1 (Platinum edition, 11/92)-Barry Smith-c 10.00

PREHISTORIC WORLD (See Classics Illustrated Special Issue)

PREMIERE (See Charlton Premiere)

PRESTO KID, THE (See Red Mask)

PRETTY BOY FLOYD (See On the Spot)

PREZ (See Cancelled Comic Cavalcade, Sandman #54 & Supergirl #10)
National Periodical Publications: Aug-Sept, 1973 - No. 4, Feb-Mar, 1974

1-Origin; Joe Simon scripts 3 6 9 18 24 30
2-4 2 4 6 11 14 18

PRICE, THE (See Eclipse Graphic Album Series)

PRIDE & JOY
DC Comics (Vertigo): July, 1997 - No. 4, Oct, 1997 (2.50, limited series)

1-4-Ennis-s 2.50

PRIDE AND THE PASSION, THE
Dell Publishing Co.: No. 824, Aug, 1957

Four Color 824-Movie, Frank Sinatra & Cary Grant photo-c 10 20 30 70 100 130

PRIDE OF THE YANKEES, THE (See Real Heroes & Sport Comics)
Magazine Enterprises: 1949 (The Life of Lou Gehrig)

nn-Photo-c; Ogden Whitney-a 80 160 240 500 750 1000

PRIEST (Also see Asylum)
Maximum Press: Aug, 1996 - No. 2, Oct, 1996 ($2.99)

1,2 3.00

Prime #8 © MAL

Prison Break! #3 © AVON

Prize Comics #2 © PRIZE

	GD 2.0	VG 4.0	FN 6.0	VF 8.0	VF/NM 9.0	NM- 9.2

PRIMAL FORCE
DC Comics: No. 0, Oct, 1994 - No. 14, Dec, 1995 ($1.95/$2.25)
0-14: 0- Teams Red Tornado, Golem, Jack O'Lantern, Meridian & Silver Dragon. 9-begin $2.25-c — 2.25

PRIMAL MAN (See The Crusaders)

PRIMAL RAGE
Sirius Entertainment: 1996 ($2.95)
1-Dark One-c; based of video game — 3.00

PRIME (See Break-Thru, Flood Relief & Ultraforce)
Malibu Comics (Ultraverse): June, 1993 - No. 26, Aug, 1995 ($1.95/$2.50)
1-1st app. Prime; has coupon for Ultraverse Premiere #0 — 3.00
1-With coupon missing — 2.25
1-Full cover holographic edition; 1st of kind w/Hardcase #1 & Strangers #1 — 6.00
1-Ultra 5,000 edition w/silver ink-c — 4.00
2-11,14-26: 2-Polybagged w/card & coupon for U. Premiere #0. 3,4-Prototype app. 4-Direct sale w/o card.4-($2.50)-Newsstand ed. polybagged w/card. 5-($2.50, 48 pgs.)-Rune flip-c/story part B by Barry Smith; see Sludge #1 for 1st app. Rune; 3-pg. Night Man preview. 6-Bill & Chelsea Clinton app. 7-Break-Thru x-over. 8-Mantra app.; 2-pg. origin Freex by Simonson. 10-Firearm app.15-Intro Papa Verite; Perez-c/a. 16-Intro Turbo Charge — 2.50
12-($3.50, 68 pgs.)-Flip book w/Ultraverse Premiere #3; silver foil logo — 3.50
13-($2.95, 52 pgs.)-Variant covers — 3.00
...: Gross and Disgusting 1 (10/94, $3.95)-Boris-c; "Annual" on cover, published monthly in indicia — 4.00
...Month "Ashcan" (8/94, 75¢)-Boris-c — 2.25
... Time: A Prime Collection (1994, $9.95)-r/1-4 — 10.00
...Vs. The Incredible Hulk (1995)-mail away limited edition — 10.00
...Vs. The Incredible Hulk Premium edition — 10.00
...Vs. The Incredible Hulk Super Premium edition — 15.00
NOTE: *Perez a-15; c-15, 16.*

PRIME (Also see Black September)
Malibu Comics (Ultraverse): Infinity, Sept, 1995 - V2#15, Dec, 1996 ($1.50)
Infinity, V2#1-8: Post Black September storyline. 6-8-Solitaire app. 9-Breyfogle-c/a. 10-12-Ramos-c. 15-Lord Pumpkin app. — 2.25
Infinity Signed Edition (2,000 printed) — 5.00

PRIME/CAPTAIN AMERICA
Malibu Comics: Mar, 1996 ($3.95, one-shot)
1-Norm Breyfogle-a — 4.00

PRIME8: CREATION
Two Morrows Publishing: July, 2001 ($3.95, B&W)
1-Neal Adams-c — 4.00

PRIMER (Comico...)
Comico: Oct (no month), 1982 - No. 6, Feb, 1984 (B&W)

	GD	VG	FN	VF	VF/NM	NM-
1 (52 pgs.)	2	4	6	8	10	12
2-1st app. Grendel & Argent by Wagner	10	20	30	67	96	125
3,4	1	2	3	5	7	9
5-1st Sam Kieth art in comics ('83) & 1st The Maxx	3	7	10	21	28	35
6-Intro & 1st app. Evangeline	2	4	6	9	11	14

PRIMORTALS (Leonard Nimoy's...)

PRIMUS (TV)
Charlton Comics: Feb, 1972 - No. 7, Oct, 1972

	GD	VG	FN	VF	VF/NM	NM-
1-Staton-a in all	2	4	6	12	16	20
2-7: 6-Drug propaganda story	2	4	6	9	11	14

PRINCE NAMOR, THE SUB-MARINER (Also see Namor ...)
Marvel Comics Group: Sept, 1984 - No. 4, Dec, 1984 (Limited-series)
1-4 — 2.50

PRINCESS SALLY (Video game)
Archie Publications: Apr, 1995 - No. 3, June, 1995 ($1.50, limited series)
1-3: Spin-off from Sonic the Hedgehog — 4.00

PRINCE VALIANT (See Ace Comics, Comics Reading Libraries *in the Promotional Comics section*, & King Comics #146, 147)
David McKay Publ./Dell: No. 26, 1941; No. 67, June, 1954 - No. 900, May, 1958

	GD	VG	FN	VF	VF/NM	NM-
Feature Books 26 ('41)-Harold Foster-c/a; newspaper strips reprinted, pgs. 1-28,30-63; color & 68 pgs; Foster cover is only original comic book artwork by him	74	148	222	561	856	1150
Four Color 567 ((6/54)(#1)-By Bob Fuje-Movie, photo-c	12	24	36	87	129	170
Four Color 650 (9/55), 699 (4/56), 719 (8/56),-Fuje-a	8	16	24	55	78	100
Four Color 788 (4/57), 849 (1/58), 900-Fuje-a	8	16	24	53	74	95

PRINCE VALIANT
Marvel Comics: Dec, 1994 - No. 4, Mar, 1995 ($3.95, limited series)
1-4; Kaluta-c in all. — 4.00

PRINCE VANDAL
Triumphant Comics: Nov, 1993 - Apr?, 1994 ($2.50)
1-6: 1,2-Triumphant Unleashed x-over — 2.50

PRIORITY: WHITE HEAT
AC Comics: 1986 - No. 2, 1986 ($1.75, mini-series)
1,2-Bill Black-a — 3.00

PRISCILLA'S POP
Dell Publishing Co.: No. 569, June, 1954 - No. 799, May, 1957

	GD	VG	FN	VF	VF/NM	NM-
Four Color 569 (#1), 630 (5/55), 704 (5/56),799	4	8	12	27	36	45

PRISON BARS (See Behind...)

PRISON BREAK!
Avon Per./Realistic No. 3 on: Sept, 1951 - No. 5, Sept, 1952 (Painted c-3)

	GD	VG	FN	VF	VF/NM	NM-
1-Wood-c & 1 pg.; has-r/Saint #7 retitled Michael Strong Private Eye	43	86	129	258	384	510
2-Wood-c; Kubert-a; Kinstler inside front-c	33	66	99	190	270	350
3-Orlando, Check-a; c-/Avon paperback #179	27	54	81	155	218	280
4,5: 4-Kinstler-c & inside f/c; Lawrence, Lazarus-a. 5-Kinstler-c; Infantino-a	24	48	72	135	190	245

PRISONER, THE (TV)
DC Comics: 1988 - No. 4, 1989 ($3.50, squarebound, mini-series)
1-4 (Books a-d) — 3.50

PRISON RIOT
Avon Periodicals: 1952

	GD	VG	FN	VF	VF/NM	NM-
1-Marijuana Murders-1 pg. text; Kinstler-c; 2 Kubert illos on text pages	30	60	90	170	240	310

PRISON TO PRAISE
Logos International: 1974 (35¢) (Religious, Christian)

	GD	VG	FN	VF	VF/NM	NM-
nn-True Story of Merlin R. Carothers	2	4	6	9	11	14

PRIVATE BUCK
Dell Publishing Co.: No. 21, 1941 - No. 12, 1942

	GD	VG	FN	VF	VF/NM	NM-
Large Feature Comic 21 (#1)(1941)(Series I), 22 (1941)(Series I), 12 (1942)(Series II)	12	24	36	84	125	165

PRIVATEERS
Vanguard Graphics: Aug, 1987 - No. 2, 1987 ($1.50)
1,2 — 2.25

PRIVATE EYE (Cover title: Rocky Jorden...#6-8)
Atlas Comics (MCI): Jan, 1951 - No. 8, March, 1952

	GD	VG	FN	VF	VF/NM	NM-
1-Cover title: Crime Cases... #1-5	22	44	66	127	176	225
2,3-Tuska c/a(3)	14	28	42	79	107	135
4-8	11	22	33	63	84	105

NOTE: *Henkel a-6(3), 7; c-7. Sinnott a-6.*

PRIVATE EYE (See Mike Shayne...)

PRIVATE SECRETARY
Dell Publishing Co.: Dec-Feb, 1962-63 - No. 2, Mar-May, 1963

	GD	VG	FN	VF	VF/NM	NM-
1	4	8	12	24	32	40
2	3	6	9	18	24	30

PRIVATE STRONG (See The Double Life of...)

PRIZE COMICS (...Western #69 on) (Also see Treasure Comics)
Prize Publications: March, 1940 - No. 68, Feb-Mar, 1948

	GD	VG	FN	VF	VF/NM	NM-
1-Origin Power Nelson, The Futureman & Jupiter, Master Magician; Ted O'Neil, Secret Agent M-11, Jaxon of the Jungle, Bucky Brady & Storm Curtis begin (1st app. of each)	248	496	744	1550	2325	3100
2-The Black Owl begins (1st app.)	110	220	330	688	1032	1375
3,4: 4-Robot-c	92	184	276	575	863	1150
5,6: Dr. Dekkar, Master of Monsters app. in each	85	170	255	531	796	1060
7-(Scarce)-1st app. The Green Lama (12/40); Black Owl by S&K; origin/1st app. Dr. Frost & Frankenstein; Capt. Gallant, The Great Voodini & Twist Turner begin;	184	368	552	1150	1725	2300
8,9-Black Owl & Ted O'Neil by S&K	94	188	282	588	882	1175
10-12,14,15: 11-Origin Bulldog Denny. 14-War-c	70	140	210	438	657	875

Prize Comics Western #79 © PRIZE

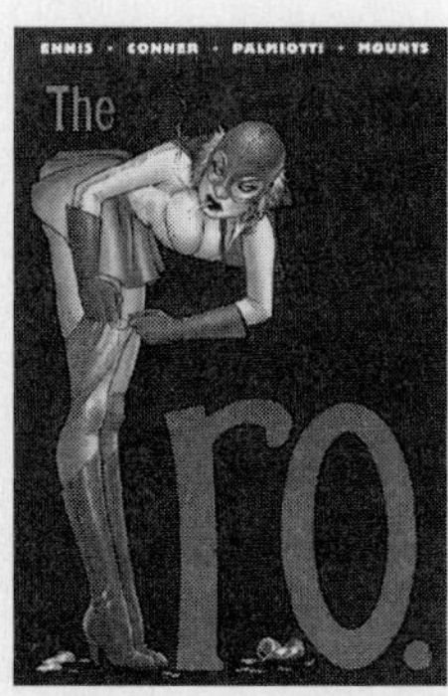

The Pro #1 © Palmiotti, Ennis & Conner

Promethea #27 © ABC

	GD 2.0	VG 4.0	FN 6.0	VF 8.0	VF/NM 9.0	NM- 9.2
13-Yank & Doodle begin (8/41, origin/1st app.)	74	148	222	463	694	925
16-20: 16-Spike Mason begins	65	130	195	406	613	820
21-24: 21-War-c. 22-Statue of Liberty jap attack war-c. 23-Uncle Sam patriotic war-c. 24-Lincoln statue patriotic-c	48	96	144	288	432	575
25-30: 25-28 War-c	32	64	96	182	259	335
31-33: 31-Jap war-c	27	54	81	155	218	280
34-Origin Airmale, Yank & Doodle; The Black Owl joins army, Yank & Doodle's father assumes Black Owl's role	32	64	96	182	259	335
35-36,38-40: 35-Flying Fist & Bingo begin	23	46	69	130	183	235
37-Intro. Stampy, Airmale's sidekick; Hitler-c	39	78	117	230	325	420
41-50: 45-Yank & Doodle learn Black Owl's I.D. (their father). 48-Prince Ra begins	18	36	54	104	142	180
51-62,64,67,68: 53-Transvestism story. 55-No Frankenstein. 57-X-Mas-c. 64-Black Owl retires	15	30	45	86	118	150
63-Simon & Kirby c/a	19	38	57	106	146	185
65,66-Frankenstein-c by Briefer	16	32	48	92	126	160

NOTE: ***Briefer** a 7-on; c-65, 66. **J. Binder** a-16; c-21-29. **Guardineer** a-62. **Kiefer** c-62. **Palais** c-68. **Simon & Kirby** c-63, 75, 83.*

PRIZE COMICS WESTERN (Formerly Prize Comics #1-68)
Prize Publications (Feature): No. 69(V7#2), Apr-May, 1948 - No. 119, Nov-Dec, 1956 (No. 69-84: 52 pgs.)

	GD	VG	FN	VF	VF/NM	NM-
69(V7#2)	15	30	45	86	118	150
70-75: 74-Kurtzman-a (8 pgs.)	13	26	39	74	100	125
76-Randolph Scott photo-c; "Canadian Pacific" movie adaptation	14	28	42	79	107	135
77-Photo-c; Severin/Elder, Mart Bailey-a; "Streets of Laredo" movie adaptation	13	26	39	74	100	125
78-Photo-c; S&K-a, 10 pgs.; Severin, Mart Bailey-a; "Bullet Code", & "Roughshod" movie adaptations	19	38	57	106	146	185
79-Photo-c; Kurtzman-a, 8 pgs.; Severin/Elder, Severin, Mart Bailey-a; "Stage To Chino" movie adaptation w/George O'Brien	19	38	57	106	146	185
80-82-Photo-c; 80,81-Severin/Elder-a(2). 82-1st app. The Preacher by Mart Bailey; Severin/Elder-a(3)	14	28	42	79	107	135
83,84	11	22	33	63	84	105
85-1st app. American Eagle by John Severin & begins (V9#6, 1-2/51)	25	50	75	144	198	255
86,101-105, 109-Severin/Williamson-a	13	26	39	74	100	125
87-99,110,111-Severin/Elder-a(2-3) each	14	28	42	79	107	135
100	15	30	45	84	115	145
106-108,112	10	20	30	56	73	90
113-Williamson/Severin-a(2)/Frazetta?	14	28	42	79	107	135
114-119: Drifter series in all; by Mort Meskin #114-118	9	18	27	52	66	80

NOTE: ***Fass** a-81. **Severin & Elder** c-84-99. **Severin** a-72, 75, 77-79, 83-86, 96, 97, 100-105; c-92,100-109(most), 110-119. **Simon & Kirby** c-75, 83.*

PRIZE MYSTERY
Key Publications: May, 1955 - No. 3, Sept, 1955

	GD	VG	FN	VF	VF/NM	NM-
1	11	22	33	63	84	105
2,3	8	16	24	46	58	70

PRO, THE
Image Comics: July, 2002 ($5.95, squarebound, one-shot)

1-Ennis-s/Conner & Palmiotti-a; prostitute gets super-powers 8.00
1-Second printing with different cover 6.00

PROFESSIONAL FOOTBALL (See Charlton Sport Library)

PROFESSOR COFFIN
Charlton Comics: No. 19, Oct, 1985 - No. 21, Feb, 1986

19-21: Wayne Howard-a(r); low print run 1 2 3 5 6 8

PROFESSOR OM
Innovation Publishing: May, 1990 - No. 2, 1990 ($2.50, limited series)

1,2-East Meets West spin-off 2.50

PROFESSOR XAVIER AND THE X-MEN (Also see X-Men, 1st series)
Marvel Comics: Nov, 1995 - No. 18 (99¢)

1-18: Stories featuring the Original X-Men. 2-vs. The Blob. 5-Vs. the Original Brotherhood of Evil Mutants. 10-Vs. The Avengers 2.25

PROJECT, THE
DC Comics (Paradox Press): No. 1,2, 1998? ($5.59)

1,2 6.00

PROJECT A-KO (Manga)
Malibu Comics: Mar, 1994 - No. 4, June, 1994 ($2.95)

1-4-Based on anime film 3.00

PROJECT A-KO 2 (Manga)
CPM Comics: May, 1995 - No. 3, Aug, 1995 ($2.95, limited series)

1-3 3.00

PROJECT A-KO VERSUS THE UNIVERSE (Manga)
CPM Comics: Oct, 1995 - No. 5, June, 1996 ($2.95, limited series, bi-monthly)

1-5 3.00

PROJECT: HERO
Vanguard Graphics (Canadian): Aug, 1987 ($1.50)

1 2.25

PROMETHEA
America's Best Comics: Aug, 1999 - Present ($3.50/$2.95)

1-Alan Moore-s/Williams III & Gray-a; Alex Ross painted-c 3.50
1-Variant-c by Williams III & Gray 3.50
2-28-($2.95): 7-Villarrubia photo-a. 10-"Sex, Stars & Serpents". 26-28-Tom Strong app. 27-Cover swipe of Superman vs. Spider-Man treasury ed. 3.00
Book 1 Hardcover ($24.95, dust jacket) r/#1-6 25.00
Book 1 TPB ($14.95) r/#1-6 15.00
Book 2 Hardcover ($24.95, dust jacket) r/#7-12 25.00
Book 2 TPB ($14.95) r/#7-12 15.00
Book 3 Hardcover ($24.95, dust jacket) r/#13-18 25.00
Book 3 TPB ($14.95) r/#13-18 15.00

PROMETHEUS (VILLAINS) (Leads into JLA #16,17)
DC Comics: Feb, 1998 ($1.95, one-shot)

1-Origin & 1st app.; Morrison-s/Pearson-c 3.00

PROPELLERMAN
Dark Horse Comics: Jan, 1993 - No. 8, Mar, 1994 ($2.95, limited series)

1-8: 2,4,8-Contain 2 trading cards 3.00

PROPHET (See Youngblood #2)
Image Comics (Extreme Studios): Oct, 1993 - No. 10, 1995 ($1.95)

1-($2.50)-Liefeld/Panosian-c/a; 1st app. Mary McCormick; Liefeld scripts in 1-4; #1-3 contain coupons for Prophet #0 2.50
1-Gold foil embossed-c edition rationed to dealers 4.00
2-10: 2-Liefeld-c(p). 3-1st app. Judas. 4-1st app. Omen; Black and White Pt. 3 by Thibert. 4-Alternate-c by Stephen Platt. 5,6-Platt-c/a. 7-(9/94, $2.50)-Platt-c/a. 8-Bloodstrike app. 10-Polybagged w/trading card; Platt-c. 2.50
0-(7/94, $2.50)-San Diego Comic Con ed. (2200 copies) 3.00

PROPHET
Image Comics (Extreme Studios): V2#1, Aug, 1995 - No. 8 ($3.50)

V2#1-8: Dixon scripts in all. 1-4-Platt-a. 1-Boris-c; F. Miller variant-c. 4-Newmen app. 5,6-Wraparound-c 3.50
Annual 1 (9/95, $2.50)-Bagged w/Youngblood gaming card; Quesada-c 2.50
Babewatch Special 1 (12/95, $2.50)-Babewatch tie-in 2.50
1995 San Diego Edition-B&W preview of V2#1. 3.00
TPB-(1996, $12.95) r/#1-7 13.00

PROPHET (Volume 3)
Awesome Comics: Mar, 2000 ($2.99)

1-Flip-c by Jim Lee and Liefeld 3.00

PROPHET/CABLE
Image Comics (Extreme): Jan, 1997 - No. 2, Mar, 1997 ($3.50, limited series)

1,2-Liefeld-c/a: 2-#1 listed on cover 3.50

PROPHET/CHAPEL: SUPER SOLDIERS
Image Comics (Extreme): May, 1996 - No. 2, June, 1996 ($2.50, limited series)

1,2: 1-Two covers exist 2.50
1-San Diego Edition; B&W-c 2.50

PROPOSITION PLAYER
DC Comics (Vertigo): Dec, 1999 - No. 6, May, 2000 ($2.50, limited series)

1-6-Willingham-s/Guinan-a/Bolton-c 2.50
TPB (2003, $14.95) r/#1-6; intro. by James McManus 15.00

PROTECTORS (Also see The Ferret)
Malibu Comics: Sept, 1992 - No. 20, May, 1994 ($1.95-$2.95)

1-20 ($2.50, direct sale)-With poster & diff-c: 1-Origin; has 3/4 outer-c. 3-Polybagged w/Skycap 2.50
1-12 ($1.95, newsstand)-Without poster 2.25

PROTOTYPE (Also see Flood Relief & Ultraforce)

Psycho #3 © Skywald

Pudgy Pig #1 © CC

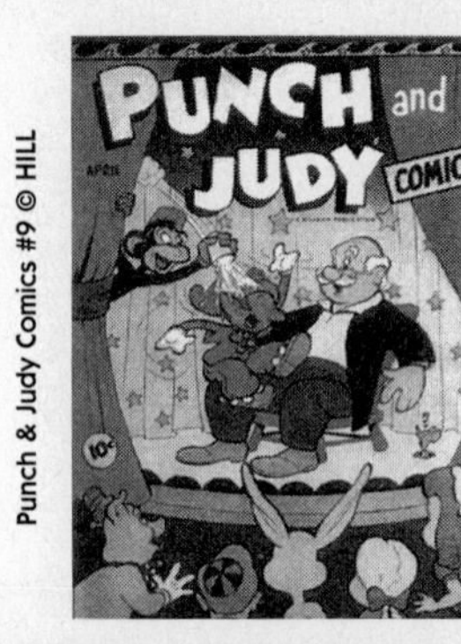

Punch & Judy Comics #9 © HILL

GD 2.0 | VG 4.0 | FN 6.0 | VF 8.0 | VF/NM 9.0 | NM- 9.2

Malibu Comics (Ultraverse): Aug, 1993 - No. 18, Feb, 1995 ($1.95/$2.50)

1-Holo-c 6.00
1-Ultra Limited silver foil-c 4.00
1-12,0,14-18: 3-($2.50, 48 pgs.)-Rune flip-c/story by B. Smith (3 pgs.). 4-Intro Wrath. 5-Break-Thru & Strangers x-over. 6-Arena cameo. 7,8-Arena-c/story. 12-(7/94). 0-(8/94, $2.50, 44 pgs.), 14(10/94) 2.50
13 (8/94, $3.50)-Flip book(Ultraverse Premiere #6) 3.50
Giant Size 1 (10/94, $2.50, 44 pgs.) 2.50

PROWLER (Also see Revenge of the...)
Eclipse Comics: July, 1987 - No. 4, Oct, 1987 ($1.75)

1-4: Snyder-c/a. 3,4-Origin 2.25

PROWLER, THE
Marvel Comics: Nov, 1994 ($1.75)

1-4: 1-Spider-Man app. 2.25

PROWLER IN "WHITE ZOMBIE", THE
Eclipse Comics: Oct, 1988 ($2.00, B&W, Baxter paper)

1-Adapts Bela Lugosi movie White Zombie 2.25

PRUDENCE & CAUTION (Also see Dogs of War & Warriors of Plasm)
Defiant: May, 1994 - No. 2, June, 1994 ($3.50/$2.50)(Spanish versions exist)

1-($3.50, 52 pgs.)-Chris Claremont scripts in all 3.50
2-($2.50) 2.50

PRYDE AND WISDOM (Also see Excalibur)
Marvel Comics: Sept, 1996 - No. 3, Nov, 1996 ($1.95, limited series)

1-3: Warren Ellis scripts; Terry Dodson & Karl Story-c/a 2.25

PSI-FORCE
Marvel Comics Group: Nov, 1986 - No. 32, June, 1989 (75¢/$1.50)

1-25: 11-13-Williamson-i 2.25
26-32 2.50
Annual 1 (10/87) 3.00

PSI-JUDGE ANDERSON
Fleetway Publications (Quality): 1989 - No. 15, 1990 ($1.95, B&W)

1-15 2.50

PSI-LORDS
Valiant: Sept, 1994 - No. 10, June, 1995 ($2.25)

1-($3.50)-Chromium wraparound-c 3.50
1-Gold 5.00
2-10: 3-Chaos Effect Epsilon Pt. 2 2.25

PSYBA-RATS (Also see Showcase '94 #3,4)
DC Comics: Apr, 1995-No. 3, June, 1995 ($2.50, limited series)

1-3 2.50

PSYCHO (Magazine) (Also see Nightmare)
Skywald Publ. Corp.: Jan, 1971 - No. 24, Mar, 1975 (68 pgs.; B&W)

	GD	VG	FN	VF	VF/NM	NM-
1-All reprints	7	14	21	50	68	85
2-Origin & 1st app. The Heap, series begins	5	10	15	36	48	60
3-Frankenstein series by Adkins begins	4	8	12	29	40	50
4,7,9,10: 4-7-Squarebound. 4-1st Out of Chaos/Satan-c/s	4	8	12	27	36	45
8-(Squarebound)1st app. Edward & Mina Sartyros, the Human Gargoyles	5	10	15	33	44	55
11-18: 13-Cannabalism; 3 pgs of Christopher Lee as Dracula photos. 18-Injury to eye-c.	3	6	9	19	25	32
19-Origin Dracula.	3	7	10	21	28	35
20-24: 20-Severed Head-c. 22-1974 Fall Special; Reese, Wildey-a(r). 24-1975 Winter Special; Dave Sim scripts	4	8	12	22	30	38
Annual 1 (1972)(68 pgs.) Dracula & the Heap app.	4	8	12	22	30	38
Yearbook (1974-nn)-Everett, Reese-a	3	6	9	18	24	30

NOTE: ***Boris** c-3, 5. **Buckler** a-2, 4, 5. **Gene Day** a-21, 23, 24. **Everett** a-3-6. **B. Jones** a-4. **Jeff Jones** a-6, 7, 9; c-12. **Kaluta** a-13. **Katz/Buckler** a-3. **Kim** a-24. **Morrow** a-1. **Reese** a-5. **Dave Sim** s-24. **Sutton** a-3. **Wildey** a-5.*

PSYCHOANALYSIS
E. C. Comics: Mar-Apr, 1955 - No. 4, Sept-Oct, 1955

	GD	VG	FN	VF	VF/NM	NM-
1-All Kamen-c/a; not approved by code	18	36	54	135	193	250
2-4-Kamen-c/a in all	13	26	39	98	137	175

PSYCHOANALYSIS
Gemstone Publishing: Oct, 1999 - No. 4, Jan, 2000 ($2.50)

1-4-Reprints E.C. series 2.50
Annual 1 (2000, $10.95) r/#1-4 11.00

PSYCHOBLAST
First Comics: Nov, 1987 - No. 9, July, 1988 ($1.75)

1-9 2.25

PSYCHONAUTS
Marvel Comics (Epic Comics): Oct, 1993 - No. 4, Jan, 1994 ($4.95, lim. series)

1-4: American/Japanese co-produced comic 5.00

PSYLOCKE & ARCHANGEL CRIMSON DAWN
Marvel Comics: Aug, 1997 - No. 4, Nov, 1997 ($2.50, limited series)

1-4-Raab-s/Larroca-a(p) 2.50

P.T. 109 (See Movie Comics)

PUBLIC DEFENDER IN ACTION (Formerly Police Trap)
Charlton Comics: No. 7, Mar, 1956 - No. 12, Oct, 1957

	GD	VG	FN	VF	VF/NM	NM-
7	10	20	30	60	80	100
8-12	8	16	24	40	50	60

PUBLIC ENEMIES
D. S. Publishing Co.: 1948 - No. 9, June-July, 1949

	GD	VG	FN	VF	VF/NM	NM-
1-True Crime Stories	26	52	78	147	206	265
2-Used in **SOTI**, pg. 95	23	46	69	129	180	230
3-5: 5-Arrival date of 10/1/48	15	30	45	84	115	145
6,8,9	14	28	42	79	107	135
7-McWilliams-a; injury to eye panel	15	30	45	84	115	145

PUBO
Dark Horse Comics: Dec, 2002 - No. 3, Mar, 2003 ($3.50, B&W, limited series)

1-3-Leland Purvis-s/a 3.50

PUDGY PIG
Charlton Comics: Sept, 1958 - No. 2, Nov, 1958

	GD	VG	FN	VF	VF/NM	NM-
1,2	3	6	9	19	25	32

PUFFED
Image Comics: Jul, 2003 - No. 3, Sept, 2003 ($2.95, B&W)

1-3-Layman-s/Crosland-a. 1-Two covers by Crosland & Quitely 3.00

PULP FANTASTIC (Vertigo V2K)
DC Comics (Vertigo): Feb, 2000 - No. 3, Apr, 2000 ($2.50, limited series)

1-3-Chaykin & Tischman-s/Burchett-a 2.50

PULP FICTION LIBRARY: MYSTERY IN SPACE
DC Comics: 1999 ($19.95, TPB)

nn-Reprints classic sci-fi stories from Mystery in Space, Strange Adventures, Real Fact Comics and My Greatest Adventure 20.00

PUMA BLUES
Aardvark One International/Mirage Studios #21 on: 1986 - No. 26, 1990 ($1.70-$1.75, B&W)

1-19, 21-26: 1-1st & 2nd printings. 25,26-$1.75-c 2.25
20 ($2.25)-By Alan Moore, Miller, Grell, others 3.00
Trade Paperback (12/88, $14.95) 15.00

PUMPKINHEAD: THE RITES OF EXORCISM (Movie)
Dark Horse Comics: 1993 - No. 2, 1993 ($2.50, limited series)

1,2: Based on movie; painted-c by McManus 2.50

PUNCH & JUDY COMICS
Hillman Per.: 1944; No. 2, Fall, 1944 - V3#2, 12/47; V3#3, 6/51 - V3#9, 12/51

	GD	VG	FN	VF	VF/NM	NM-
V1#1-(60 pgs.)	23	46	69	132	186	240
2	13	26	39	74	100	125
3-12(7/46)	10	20	30	58	77	95
V2#1(8/49),3-9	8	16	24	43	54	65
V2#2,10-12, V3#1-Kirby-a(2) each	24	48	72	135	190	245
V3#2-Kirby-a	22	44	66	124	172	220
3-9	8	16	24	43	54	65

PUNCH COMICS
Harry 'A' Chesler: 12/41; #2, 2/42; #9, 7/44 - #19, 10/46; #20, 7/47 - #23, 1/48

	GD	VG	FN	VF	VF/NM	NM-
1-Mr. E, The Sky Chief, Hale the Magician, Kitty Kelly begin	128	256	384	800	1200	1600
2-Captain Glory app.	85	170	255	531	796	1060
9-Rocketman & Rocket Girl & The Master Key begin	80	160	240	500	750	1000
10-Sky Chief app.; J. Cole-a; Master Key-r/Scoop #3	61	122	183	381	571	760
11-Origin Master Key-r/Scoop #1; Sky Chief, Little Nemo app.; Jack Cole-a; Fine-*ish* art by Sultan	55	110	165	344	512	680

Punch Comics #19 © CHES

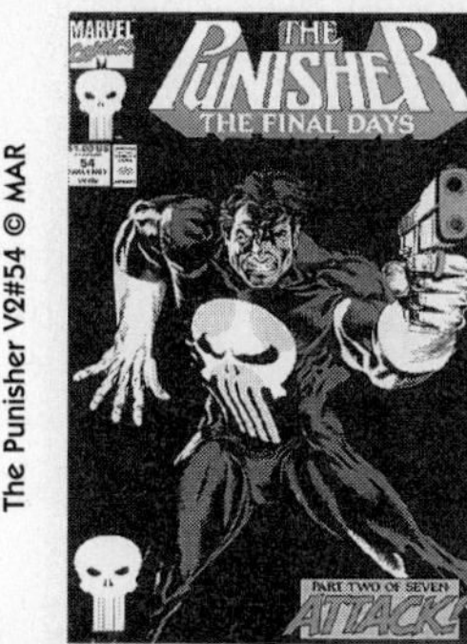

The Punisher V2#54 © MAR

The Punisher V3#6 © MAR

GD VG FN VF VF/NM NM-
2.0 4.0 6.0 8.0 9.0 9.2

GD VG FN VF VF/NM NM-
2.0 4.0 6.0 8.0 9.0 9.2

12-Rocket Boy & Capt. Glory app; classic Skull-c 224 448 672 1400 2100 2800
13-Cover has list of 4 Chesler artists' names on tombstone
61 122 183 381 571 760
14,15,19,21: 21-Hypo needle story 55 110 165 330 495 660
16,17-Gag-c 51 102 153 306 463 620
18-Bondage-c; hypodermic panels 67 134 201 419 627 835
20-Unique cover with bare-breasted women. Rocket Girl-c
96 192 288 600 900 1200
22,23-Little Nemo-not by McCay. 22-Intro Baxter (teenage)(68 pgs.)
30 60 90 170 240 310

PUNCHY AND THE BLACK CROW
Charlton Comics: No. 10, Oct, 1985 - No. 12, Feb, 1986

10-12: Al Fago funny animal-r; low print run 6.00

PUNISHER (See Amazing Spider-Man #129, Blood and Glory, Captain America #241, Classic Punisher, Daredevil #182-184, 257, Daredevil and the..., Ghost Rider V2#5, 6, Marc Spector #8 & 9, Marvel Preview #2, Marvel Super Action, Marvel Tales, Power Pack #46, Spectacular Spider-Man #81-83, 140, 141, 143 & new Strange Tales #13 & 14)

PUNISHER (The...)
Marvel Comics Group: Jan, 1986 - No. 5, May, 1986 (Limited series)

1-Double size 2 4 6 11 14 18
2-5 1 3 4 6 8 10
Trade Paperback (1988)-r/#1-5 11.00
Circle of Blood TPB (8/01, $15.95) Zeck-c 16.00
NOTE: ***Zeck** a-1-4; c-1-5.*

PUNISHER (The...) (Volume 2)
Marvel Comics: July, 1987 - No. 104, July, 1995

1 1 3 4 6 8 10
2-9: 8-Portacio/Williams-c/a begins, ends #18. 9-Scarcer, low dist. 6.00
10-Daredevil app; ties in w/Daredevil #257 1 3 4 6 8 10
11-74,76-85,87-89: 13-18-Kingpin app. 19-Stroman-c/a. 20-Portacio-c(p). 24-1st app. Shadowmasters. 25,50:($1.50,52 pgs.). 25-Shadowmasters app. 57-Photo-c; came w/outer-c (newsstand ed. w/o outer-c). 59-Punisher is severely cut & has skin grafts (has black skin). 60-62-Luke Cage app. 62-Punisher back to white skin. 68-Tarantula-c/story. 85-Prequel to Suicide Run Pt. 0. 87,88-Suicide Run Pt. 6 & 9 2.50
75-($2.75, 52 pgs.)-Embossed silver foil-c 3.00
86-($2.95, 52 pgs.)-Embossed & foil stamped-c; Suicide Run part 3 3.00
90-99: 90-bound-in cards. 99-Cringe app. 2.50
100,104: 100-($2.95, 68 pgs.). 104-Last issue 4.00
100-($3.95, 68 pgs.)-Foil cover 5.00
101-103: 102-Bullseye 3.50
"Ashcan" edition (75¢)-Joe Kubert-c 3.00
Annual 1-7 ('88-'94, 68 pgs.) 1-Evolutionary War x-over. 2-Atlantis Attacks x-over; Jim Lee-a(p) (back-up story, 6 pgs.); Moon Knight app. 4-Golden-c(p). 6-Bagged w/card. 7-Rapido app. 3.00
...: A Man Named Frank (1994, $6.95, TPB) 7.00
...and Wolverine in African Saga nn (1989, $5.95, 52 pgs.)-Reprints Punisher War Journal #6 & 7; Jim Lee-c/a(r) 6.00
... Assassin Guild ('88, $6.95, graphic novel) 10.00
Back to School Special 1-3 (11/92-10/94, $2.95, 68 pgs.) 3.00
.../Batman: Deadly Knights (10/94, $4.95) 5.00
.../Black Widow: Spinning Doomsday's Web (1992, $9.95, graphic novel) 12.00
...Bloodlines nn (1991, $5.95, 68 pgs.) 6.00
...: Die Hard in the Big Easy nn ('92, $4.95, 52 pgs.) 5.00
...: Empty Quarter nn ('94, $6.95) 7.00
...G-Force nn (1992, $4.95, 52 pgs.)-Painted-c 5.00
...Holiday Special 1-3 (1/93-1/95,, 52 pgs.,68pgs.)-1-Foil-c 3.00
...Intruder Graphic Novel (1989, $14.95, hardcover) 20.00
...Intruder Graphic Novel (1991, $9.95, softcover) 12.00
...Invades the 'Nam: Final Invasion nn (2/94, $6.95)-J. Kubert-c & chapter break art; reprints The 'Nam #84 & unpublished #85,86 7.00
...Kingdom Gone Graphic Novel (1990, $16.95, hardcover) 20.00
...Meets Archie (8/94, $3.95, 52 pgs.)-Die cut-c; no ads; same contents as Archie Meets The Punisher 5.00
...Movie Special 1 (6/90, $5.95, 68 pgs.) 6.00
...: No Escape nn (1990, $4.95, 52 pgs.)-New-a 5.00
...Return to Big Nothing Graphic Novel (Epic, 1989, $16.95, hardcover) 25.00
...Return to Big Nothing Graphic Novel (Marvel, 1989, $12.95, softcover) 15.00
...The Prize nn (1990, $4.95, 68 pgs.)-New-a 5.00
Summer Special 1-4(8/91-7/94, 52 pgs.):1-No ads. 2-Bisley-c; Austin-a(i). 3-No ads 3.00
NOTE: ***Austin** c(i)-47, 48. **Cowan** c-39. **Golden** c-50, 85, 86, 100. **Heath** a-26, 27, 89, 90; c-26, 27. **Quesada** c-56p, 62p. **Sienkiewicz** c-Back to School 1.**Stroman** a-76p(9 pgs.). **Williamson** a(i)-25, 60-62i, 64-70, 74, Annual 5; c(i)-62, 65-68.*

PUNISHER (Also see Double Edge)
Marvel Comics: Nov, 1995 - No. 18, Apr, 1997 ($2.95/$1.95/$1.50)

1 ($2.95)-Ostrander scripts begin; foil-c. 3.00
2-18: 7-Vs. S.H.I.E.L.D. 11-"Onslaught." 12-17-X-Cutioner-c/app. 17-Daredevil, Spider-Man-c/app. 2.50

PUNISHER (Marvel Knights)
Marvel Comics: Nov, 1998 - No. 4, Feb, 1999 ($2.99, limited series)

1-4: 1-Wrightson-a; Wrightson & Jusko-c 3.00
1-($6.95) DF Edition; Jae Lee variant-c 7.00

PUNISHER (Marvel Knights) (Volume 3)
Marvel Comics: Apr, 2000 - No. 12, Mar, 2001 ($2.99, limited series)

1-Ennis-s/Dillon & Palmiotti-a/Bradstreet-c 5.00
1-Bradstreet white variant-c 10.00
1-($6.95) DF Edition; Jurgens & Ordway variant-c 7.00
2-Two covers by Bradstreet & Dillon 3.00
3-($3.99) Bagged with Marvel Knights Genesis Edition; Daredevil app. 4.00
4-12: 9-11-The Russian app. 3.00
HC (6/02, $34.95) r/#1-12, Punisher Kills the Marvel Universe, and Marvel Knights Double Shot #1 35.00
.../Painkiller Jane (1/01, $3.50) Jusko-c; Ennis-s/Jusko and Dave Ross-a(p) 3.50
...: Welcome Back Frank TPB (4/01, $19.95) r/#1-12 20.00

PUNISHER (Marvel Knights) (Volume 4)
Marvel Comics: Aug, 2001 - No. 37, Feb, 2004 ($2.99)

1-Ennis-s/Dillon & Palmiotti-a/Bradstreet-c; The Russian app. 4.00
2-Two covers (Dillon & Bradstreet) Spider-Man-c/app. 3.00
3-37: 3-7-Ennis-s/Dillon-a. 9-12-Peyer-s/Gutierrez-a. 13,14-Ennis-s/Dilllon-a. 16,17-Wolverine app.; Robertson-a. 18-23,32-Dillon-a. 24-27-Mandrake-a. 27-Elektra app. 33-37-Spider-Man, Daredevil, & Wolverine app. 36,37-Hulk app. 3.00
...Army of One TPB (2/02, $15.95) r/#1-7; Bradstreet-c 16.00
Vol. 2 HC (2003, $29.95) r/#1-7,13-18; intro. by Mike Millar 30.00
Vol. 3: Business as Usual TPB (2003, $14.99) r/#13-18; Bradstreet-c 15.00
Vol. 4: Full Auto TPB (2003, $17.99) r/#20-26; Bradstreet-c 18.00
Vol. 5: Streets of Laredo TPB (2003, $17.99) r/#19,27-32 18.00

PUNISHER (Marvel MAX)
Marvel Comics: Mar, 2004 - Present ($2.99)

1-Ennis-s/Larosa-a/Bradstreet-c; flashback to his family's murder; Micro app. 3.00

PUNISHER AND WOLVERINE: DAMAGING EVIDENCE (See Wolverine and...)

PUNISHER ARMORY, THE
Marvel Comics: 7/90 ($1.50); No. 2, 6/91; No. 3, 4/92 - 10/94($1.75/$2.00)

1-10: 1-r/weapons pgs. from War Journal. 1,2-Jim Lee-c. 3-10- All new material. 3-Jusko painted-c 2.50

PUNISHER KILLS THE MARVEL UNIVERSE
Marvel Comics: Nov, 1995 ($5.95, one-shot)

1-Garth Ennis script/Doug Braithwaite-a 7.00
1-2nd printing (3/00) Steve Dillon-c 6.00

PUNISHER MAGAZINE, THE
Marvel Comics: Oct, 1989 - No. 16, Nov, 1990 ($2.25, B&W, Magazine, 52 pgs.)

1-16: 1-r/Punisher #1('86). 2,3-r/Punisher 2-5. 4-16: 4-7-r/Punisher V2#1-8. 4-Chiodo-c. 8-r/Punisher #10 & Daredevil #257; Portacio & Lee-r. 14-r/Punisher War Journal #1,2 w/new Lee-c. 16-r/Punisher W. J. #3,8 3.00
NOTE: ***Chiodo** painted c-4, 7, 16. **Jusko** painted c-6, 8. **Jim Lee** r-8, 14-16; c-14. **Portacio/Williams** r-7-12.*

PUNISHER MOVIE COMIC
Marvel Comics: Nov, 1989 - No. 3, Dec, 1989 ($1.00, limited series)

1-3: Movie adaptation 2.25
1 (1989, $4.95, squarebound)-contains #1-3 5.00

PUNISHER: ORIGIN OF MICRO CHIP, THE
Marvel Comics: July, 1993 - No. 2, Aug, 1993 ($1.75, limited series)

1,2 2.25

PUNISHER: P.O.V.
Marvel Comics: 1991 - No. 4, 1991 ($4.95, painted, limited series, 52 pgs.)

1-4: Starlin scripts & Wrightson painted-c/a in all. 2-Nick Fury app. 5.00

PUNISHER: THE GHOSTS OF INNOCENTS
Marvel Comics: Jan, 1993 - No. 2, Jan, 1993 ($5.95, 52 pgs.)

1,2-Starlin scripts 6.00

PUNISHER 2099 (See Punisher War Journal #50)
Marvel Comics: Feb, 1993 - No. 34, Nov, 1995 ($1.25/$1.50/$1.95)

1-24,26-34: 1-Foil stamped-c. 1-Second printing. 13-Spider-Man 2099 x-over; Ron Lim-c(p).

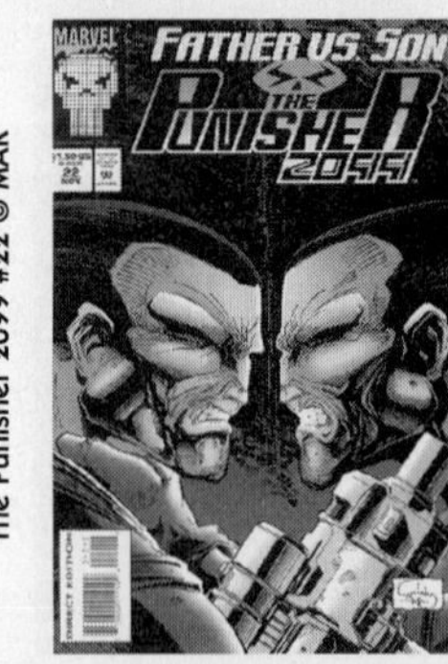

The Punisher 2099 #22 © MAR

Purgatori #3 © Chaos!

Quantum & Woody #5 © Acclaim

	GD 2.0	VG 4.0	FN 6.0	VF 8.0	VF/NM 9.0	NM- 9.2

16-bound-in card sheet 2.25
25 ($2.95, 52 pgs.)-Deluxe edition; embossed foil-cover 3.00
25 ($2.25, 52 pgs.) 2.25

PUNISHER VS. DAREDEVIL
Marvel Comics: Jun, 2000 ($3.50, one-shot)

1-Reprints Daredevil #183,#184 & #257 3.50

PUNISHER WAR JOURNAL, THE
Marvel Comics: Nov, 1988 - No. 80, July, 1995 ($1.50/$1.75/$1.95)

1-Origin The Punisher; Matt Murdock cameo; Jim Lee inks begin 5.00
2-7: 2,3-Daredevil x-over; Jim Lee-c(i). 4-Jim Lee c/a begins. 6-Two part Wolverine story begins. 7-Wolverine-c, story ends 4.00
8-49,51-60,62,63,65: 13-16,20-22: No Jim Lee-a. 13-Lee-c only. 13-15-Heath-i. 14,15-Spider-Man x-over. 19-Last Jim Lee-c/a.29,30-Ghost Rider app. 31-Andy & Joe Kubert art. 36-Photo-c. 47,48-Nomad/Daredevil-c/stories; see Nomad. 57,58-Daredevil & Ghost Rider-c/stories. 62,63-Suicide Run Pt. 4 & 7. 3.00
50,61,64($2.95, 52 pgs.): 50-Preview of Punisher 2099 (1st app.); embossed-c. 61-Embossed foil cover; Suicide Run Pt. 1. 64-Die-cut-c; Suicide Run Pt. 10 3.00
64-($2.25, 52 pgs.)-Regular cover edition 2.25
66-74,76-80: 66-Bound-in card sheet 2.25
75 ($2.50, 52 pgs.) 2.50
NOTE: *Golden c-25-30, 40, 61, 62. Jusko painted c-31, 32. Jim Lee a-1i-3i, 4p-13p, 17p-19p; c-2i, 3i, 4p-15p, 17p, 18p, 19p. Painted c-40.*

PUNISHER: WAR ZONE, THE
Marvel Comics: Mar, 1992 - No. 41, July, 1995 ($1.75/$1.95)

1-($2.25, 40 pgs.)-Die cut-c; Romita, Jr.-c/a begins 3.00
2-22,24,26,27-41: 8-Last Romita, Jr.-c/a. 19-Wolverine app. 24-Suicide Run Pt. 5. 27-Bound-in card sheet 2.25
23-($2.95, 52 pgs.)-Enbossed foil-c; Suicide Run part 2; Buscema-a(part) 3.00
25-($2.25, 52 pgs.)-Suicide Run part 8; painted-c 2.50
Annual 1,2 ('93, 94, $2.95, 68 pgs.)-1-Bagged w/card; John Buscema-a 3.00
NOTE: *Golden c-23. Romita, Jr. c/a-1-8.*

PUNISHER: YEAR ONE
Marvel Comics: Dec, 1994 - No. 4, Apr, 1995 ($2.50, limited series)

1-4 2.50

PUNX
Acclaim (Valiant): Nov, 1995 - No. 3, Jan, 1996 ($2.50, unfinished lim. series)

1-3: Giffen story & art in all. 2-Satirizes Scott McCloud's Understanding Comics 2.50
(Manga) Special 1 (3/96, $2.50)-Giffen scripts 2.50

PUPPET COMICS
George W. Dougherty Co.: Spring, 1946 - No. 2, Summer, 1946

	GD	VG	FN	VF	VF/NM	NM-
1-Funny animal in both	13	26	39	74	100	125
2	11	22	33	63	84	105

PUPPETOONS (See George Pal's...)

PUREHEART (See Archie as...)

PURGATORI
Chaos! Comics: Prelude #-1, 5/96 ($1.50, 16 pgs.); 1996 - No. 3 Dec, 1996 ($3.50/$2.95, limited series)

Prelude #-1-Pulido story; Balent-c/a; contains sketches & interviews 2.25
0-(2/01, $2.99) Prelude to "Love Bites"; Rio-c/a 3.00
1/2 (12/00, $2.95) Al Rio-c/a 3.00
1-($3.50)-Wraparound cover; red foil embossed-c; Jim Balent-a 5.00
1-($19.95)-Premium Edition (1000 print run) 20.00
2-($3.00)-Wraparound-c 3.00
2-Variant-c 5.00
...: Heartbreaker 1 (3/02, $2.99) Jolley-s 3.00
...: Love Bites 1 (3/01, $2.99) Turnbull-a/Kaminski-s 3.00
...: Mischief Night 1 (11/01, $2.99) 3.00
...: Re-Imagined 1 (7/02, $2.99) Jolley-s/Neves-a 3.00
...The Dracula Gambit-($2.95) 3.00
...The Dracula Gambit Sketchbook-($2.95) 3.00
...The Vampire's Myth 1-($19.95) Premium Ed. (10,000) 20.00
...Vs. Chastity (7/00, $2.95) Two versions (Alpha and Omega) with different endings; Rio-a 3.00
...Vs. Lady Death (1/01, $2.95) Kaminski-s 3.00
...Vs. Vampirella (4/00, $2.95) Zanier-a; Chastity app. 3.00

PURGATORI
Chaos! Comics: Oct, 1998 - No. 7, Apr, 1999 ($2.95)

1-7-Quinn-s/Rio-c/a. 2-Lady Death-c 3.00

PURGATORI: DARKEST HOUR
Chaos! Comics: Sept, 2001 - No. 2, Oct, 2001 ($2.99, limited series)

1,2 3.00

PURGATORI: EMPIRE
Chaos! Comics: May, 2000 - No. 3, July, 2000 ($2.95, limited series)

1-3-Cleavenger-c 3.00

PURGATORI: GODDESS RISING
Chaos! Comics: July, 1999 - No. 4, Oct, 1999 ($2.95, limited series)

1-4-Deodato-c/a 3.00

PURGATORI: GOD HUNTER
Chaos! Comics: Apr, 2002 - No. 2, May, 2002 ($2.99, limited series)

1,2-Molenaar-a/Jolley-s 3.00

PURGATORI: GOD KILLER
Chaos! Comics: Jun, 2002 - No. 2, July, 2002 ($2.99, limited series)

1,2-Molenaar-a/Jolley-s 3.00

PURGATORI: THE HUNTED
Chaos! Comics: Jun, 2001 - No. 2, Aug, 2001 ($2.99, limited series)

1,2 3.00

PURPLE CLAW, THE (Also see Tales of Horror)
Minoan Publishing Co./Toby Press: Jan, 1953 - No. 3, May, 1953

	GD	VG	FN	VF	VF/NM	NM-
1-Origin; horror/weird stories in all	33	66	99	190	270	350
2,3: 1-3 r-in Tales of Horror #9-11	24	48	72	135	190	245
I.W. Reprint #8-Reprints #1	3	6	9	18	24	30

PUSSYCAT (Magazine)
Marvel Comics Group: Oct, 1968 (B&W reprints from Men's magazines)

	GD	VG	FN	VF	VF/NM	NM-
1-(Scarce)-Ward, Everett, Wood-a; Everett-c	18	36	54	127	186	245

PUZZLE FUN COMICS (Also see Jingle Jangle)
George W. Dougherty Co.: Spring, 1946 - No. 2, Summer, 1946 (52 pgs.)

	GD	VG	FN	VF	VF/NM	NM-
1-Gustavson-a	24	48	72	135	190	245
2	16	32	48	92	126	160

NOTE: *#1 & 2('46) each contain a **George Carlson** cover plus a 6 pg. story "Alec in Fumbleland"; also many puzzles in each.*

PvP (Player vs. Player)
Image Comics: Mar, 2003 - Present ($2.95, B&W, reads sideways)

1-5-Scott Kurtz-s/a. 1-Frank Cho-c 3.00

QUACK!
Star Reach Productions: July, 1976 - No. 6, 1977? ($1.25, B&W)

	GD	VG	FN	VF	VF/NM	NM-
1-Brunner-c/a on Duckaneer (Howard the Duck clone); Dave Stevens, Gilbert, Shaw-a	2	4	6	8	10	12
1-2nd printing (10/76)						4.00
2-6: 2-Newton the Rabbit Wonder by Aragonés/Leialoha; Gilbert, Shaw-a; Leialoha-c. 3-The Beavers by Dave Sim begin, end #5; Gilbert, Shaw-a; Sim/Leialoha-c. 6-Brunner-a (Duckeneer); Gilbert-a	1	2	3	5	6	8

QUADRANT
Quadrant Publications: 1983 - No. 8, 1986 (B&W, nudity, adults)

	GD	VG	FN	VF	VF/NM	NM-
1-Peter Hsu-c/a in all	2	4	6	8	10	12
2-8	1	2	3	4	5	7

QUANTUM & WOODY
Acclaim Comics: June, 1997 - No. 17, No. 32 (9/99), No. 18 - No. 21, Feb, 2000 ($2.50)

1-17: 1-1st app.; two covers. 6-Copycat-c. 9-Troublemakers app. 2.50
32-(9/99); 18-(10/99),19-21 2.50
The Director's Cut TPB ('97, $7.95) r/#1-4 plus extra pages 8.00

QUANTUM LEAP (TV) (See A Nightmare on Elm Street)
Innovation Publishing: Sept, 1991 - No. 12, Jun, 1993 ($2.50, painted-c)

1-12: Based on TV show; all have painted-c. 8-Has photo gallery 3.00
Special Edition 1 (10/92)-r/#1 w/8 extra pgs. of photos & articles 3.00
Time and Space Special 1 (#13) ($2.95)-Foil logo 3.00

QUANTUM TUNNELER, THE
Revolution Studio: Oct, 2001 (no cover price, one-shot)

1-Prequel to "The One" movie; Clayton Henry-a 2.25

QUASAR (See Avengers #302, Captain America #217, Incredible Hulk #234, Marvel Team-Up #113 & Marvel Two-in-One #53)
Marvel Comics: Oct, 1989 - No. 60, Jul, 1994 ($1.00/$1.25, Direct sales #17 on)

1-Origin; formerly Marvel Boy/Marvel Man 3.00
2-49,51-60: 3-Human Torch app. 6-Venom cameo (2 pgs.). 7-Cosmic Spidey. 11-Excalibur

Queen & Country #14 © Greg Rucka

Quicksilver #10 © MAR

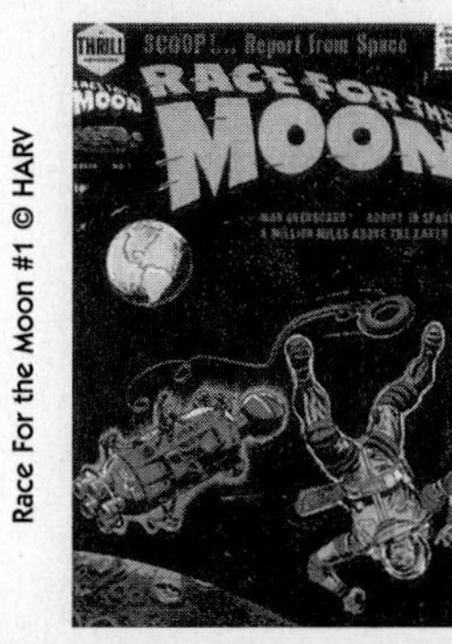

Race For the Moon #1 © HARV

	GD 2.0	VG 4.0	FN 6.0	VF 8.0	VF/NM 9.0	NM- 9.2

x-over. 14-McFarlane-c. 16-($1.50, 52 pgs.). 17-Flash parody (Buried Alien). 20-Fantastic Four app. 23-Ghost Rider x-over. 25-($1.50, 52 pgs.)-New costume Quasar. 26-Infinity Gauntlet x-over; Thanos-c/story. 27-Infinity Gauntlet x-over. 30-Thanos cameo in flashback; last $1.00-c. 31-Begin $1.25-c; D.P. 7 guest stars. 38-40-Infinity War x-overs. 38-Battles Warlock. 39-Thanos-c & cameo. 40-Thanos app. 42-Punisher-c/story. 53-Warlock & Moondragon app. 58-w/bound-in card sheet 2.50

50-($2.95, 52 pgs.)-Holo-grafx foil-c; Silver Surfer, Man-Thing, Ren & Stimpy app. 3.00

Special #1-3 ($1.25, newsstand)-Same as #32-34 2.25

QUEEN & COUNTRY (See Whiteout) (Also see Promotional Comics section for Free Comic Book Day edition)
Oni Press: Mar, 2001 - Present ($2.95/$2.99, B&W)

1-Rucka-s in all. Rolston-a/Sale-c 1 2 3 4 5 7

2-5: 2-4-Rolston-a/Sale-c. 5-Snyder-c/Hurtt-a 4.00

6-22: 6,7-Snyder-c/Hurtt-a. 13-15-Alexander-a. 16-20-McNeil-a. 21,22-Hawthorne-a 3.00

Operation: Blackwall (10/03, $8.95, TPB) r/#13-15; John Rogers intro. 9.00

Operation: Broken Ground (2002, $11.95, TPB) r/#1-4; Ellis intro. 12.00

Operation: Crystal Ball (1/03, $14.95, TPB) r/#8-12; Judd Winick intro. 15.00

Operation: Morningstar (9/02, $8.95, TPB) r/#5-7; Stuart Moore intro. 9.00

QUEEN & COUNTRY: DECLASSIFIED
Oni Press: Nov, 2002 - No. 3, Jan, 2003 ($2.95, B&W, limited series)

1-3-Rucka-s/Hurtt-a/Morse-c 3.00

TPB (7/03, $8.95) r/#1-3; intro. by Micah Wright 9.00

QUEEN OF THE WEST, DALE EVANS (TV)(See Dale Evans Comics, Roy Rogers & Western Roundup under Dell Giants)
Dell Publ. Co.: No. 479, 7/53 - No. 22, 1-3/59 (All photo-c; photo back c-4-8,15)

Four Color 479(#1, '53) 24 48 72 169 247 325

Four Color 528(#2, '54) 12 24 36 82 121 160

3,4: 3(4-6/54)-Toth-a. 4-Toth, Manning-a 9 18 27 63 89 115

5-10-Manning-a. 5-Marsh-a 8 16 24 55 78 100

11,19,21-No Manning 21-Tufts-a 6 12 18 40 55 70

12-18,20,22-Manning-a 7 14 21 46 63 80

QUENTIN DURWARD
Dell Publishing Co.: No. 672, Jan, 1956

Four Color 672-Movie, photo-c 8 16 24 53 74 95

QUESTAR ILLUSTRATED SCIENCE FICTION CLASSICS
Golden Press: 1977 (224 pgs.) ($1.95)

11197-Stories by Asimov, Sturgeon, Silverberg & Niven; Starstream-r 3 7 10 21 28 35

QUEST FOR CAMELOT
DC Comics: July, 1998 ($4.95)

1-Movie adaption 5.00

QUEST FOR DREAMS LOST (Also see Word Warriors)
Literacy Volunteers of Chicago: July 4, 1987 ($2.00, B&W, 52 pgs.)(Proceeds donated to help fight illiteracy)

1-Teenage Mutant Ninja Turtles by Eastman/Laird, Trollords, Silent Invasion, The Realm, Wordsmith, Reacto Man, Eb'nn, Aniverse 2.25

QUESTION, THE (See Americomics, Blue Beetle (1967), Charlton Bullseye & Mysterious Suspense)

QUESTION, THE (Also see Showcase '95 #3)
DC Comics: Feb, 1987 - No. 36, Mar, 1990 ($1.50)

1-36: Denny O'Neil scripts in all 2.50

Annual 1 (1988, $2.50) 2.50

Annual 2 (1989, $3.50) 3.50

QUESTION QUARTERLY, THE
DC Comics: Summer, 1990 - No. 5, Spring, 1992 ($2.50, 52pgs.)

1-5 2.50

NOTE: ***Cowan*** *a-1, 2, 4, 5; c-1-3, 5.* ***Mignola*** *a-5i.* ***Quesada*** *a-3-5.*

QUESTION RETURNS, THE
DC Comics: Feb, 1997 ($3.50, one-shot)

1-Brereton-c 3.50

QUESTPROBE
Marvel Comics: 8/84; No. 2, 1/85; No. 3, 11/85 (lim. series)

1-3: 1-The Hulk app. by Romita. 2-Spider-Man; Mooney-a(i). 3-Human Torch & Thing 3.00

QUICK DRAW McGRAW (TV) (Hanna-Barbera)(See Whitman Comic Books)
Dell Publishing Co./Gold Key No. 12 on: No. 1040, 12-2/59-60 - No. 11, 7-9/62; No. 12, 11/62; No. 13, 2/63; No. 14, 4/63; No. 15, 6/69 (1st show aired 9/29/59)

Four Color 1040(#1) 1st app. Quick Draw & Baba Looey, Augie Doggie & Doggie Daddy and Snooper & Blabber 15 30 45 104 152 200

2(4-6/60)-4,6: 2-Augie Doggie & Snooper & Blabber stories (8 pgs. each); pre-dates both of their #1 issues. 4-Augie Doggie & Snooper & Blabber stories. 8 16 24 58 82 105

5-1st Snagglepuss app.; last 10¢ issue 9 18 27 63 89 115

7-11 6 12 18 43 59 75

12,13-Title change to ...Fun-Type Roundup (84pgs.) 9 18 27 63 89 115

14,15: 15-Reprints 6 12 18 38 52 65

QUICK DRAW McGRAW (TV)(See Spotlight #2)
Charlton Comics: Nov, 1970 - No. 8, Jan, 1972 (Hanna-Barbera)

1 6 12 18 38 52 65

2-8 3 7 10 21 28 35

QUICKSILVER (See Avengers)
Marvel Comics: Nov, 1997 - No. 13, Nov, 1998 ($2.99/$1.99)

1-($2.99)-Peyer-s/Casey Jones-a; wraparound-c 3.00

2-11: 2-Two covers-variant by Golden. 4-6-Inhumans app. 2.25

12-($2.99) Siege of Wundagore pt. 4 3.00

13-Magneto-c/app.; last issue 2.25

QUICK-TRIGGER WESTERN (...Action #12; Cowboy Action #5-11)
Atlas Comics (ACI #12/WPI #13-19): No. 12, May, 1956 - No. 19, Sept, 1957

12-Baker-a 17 34 51 95 130 165

13-Williamson-a, 5 pgs. 16 32 48 89 122 155

14-Everett, Crandall, Torres-a; Heath-c 15 30 45 84 115 145

15,16: 15-Torres, Crandall-a. 16-Orlando, Kirby-a 12 24 36 69 92 115

17,18: 18-Baker-a 11 22 33 63 84 105

19 9 18 27 52 66 80

NOTE: ***Ayers*** *a-17.* ***Colan*** *a-16.* ***Maneely*** *a-15, 17; c-15, 18.* ***Morrow*** *a-18.* ***Powell*** *a-14.* ***Severin*** *a-19; c-12, 13, 16, 17, 19.* ***Shores*** *a-16.* ***Tuska*** *a-17.*

QUINCY (See Comics Reading Libraries in the Promotional Comics section)

Q-UNIT
Harris Comics: Dec, 1993 ($2.95)

1-($2.95)-Polybagged w/trading card version 1.2 3.00

RACCOON KIDS, THE (Formerly Movietown Animal Antics)
National Periodical Publications (Arleigh No. 63,64): No. 52, Sept-Oct, 1954 - No. 62, Oct-Nov, 1956; No. 63, Sept, 1957; No. 64, Nov, 1957

52-Doodles Duck by Mayer 15 30 45 86 118 150

53-64: 53-62-Doodles Duck by Mayer 11 22 33 63 84 105

RACE FOR THE MOON
Harvey Publications: Mar, 1958 - No. 3, Nov, 1958

1-Powell-a(5); 1/2-pg. S&K-a; cover redrawn from Galaxy Science Fiction pulp (5/53) 15 30 45 86 118 150

2-Kirby/Williamson-c(r)/a(3); Kirby-p 7 more stys 27 54 81 153 214 275

3-Kirby/Williamson-c/a(4); Kirby-p 6 more stys 29 58 87 164 232 300

RACE OF SCORPIONS
Dark Horse Comics: 1990 - No. 2, 1990 ($4.50/$4.95, 52pgs.)

1,2: 1-r/stories from Dark Horse Presents #23-27. 2-($4.95-c) 5.00

RACER-X
Now Comics: 8/88 - No. 11, 8/89; V2#1, 9/89 - V2#10, 1990 ($1.75)

0-Deluxe ($3.50) 3.50

1 (9/88) - 11, V2#1-10 2.25

RACER X (See Speed Racer)
DC Comics (WildStorm): Oct, 2000 - No. 3, Dec, 2000 ($2.95, limited series)

1-3: 1-Tommy Yune-s/Jo Chen-a; 2 covers by Yune. 2,3-Kabala app. 3.50

RACING PETTYS
STP Corp.: 1980 ($2.50, 68 pgs., 10 1/8" x 13 1/4")

1-Bob Kane-a. Kane bio on inside back-c. 10.00

RACK & PAIN
Dark Horse Comics: Mar, 1994 - No. 4, June, 1994 ($2.50, limited series)

1-4: Brian Pulido scripts in all. 1-Greg Capullo-c 3.00

RACK & PAIN: KILLERS
Chaos! Comics: Sept, 1996 - No. 4, Jan, 1997 ($2.95, limited series)

1-4: Reprints Dark Horse series; Jae Lee-c 3.00

RACKET SQUAD IN ACTION
Capitol Stories/Charlton Comics: May-June, 1952 - No. 29, Mar, 1958

1 29 58 87 164 232 300

2-4,6: 3,4,6-Dr. Neff, Ghost Breaker app. 15 30 45 86 118 150

Radioactive Man V2#6 © Bongo

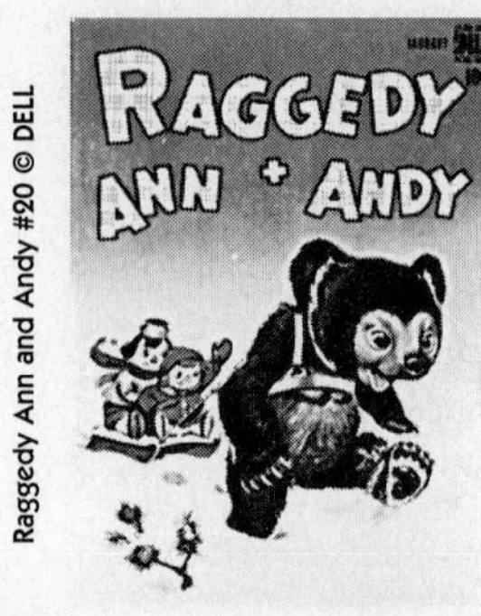

Raggedy Ann and Andy #20 © DELL

Ramar of the Jungle #1 © CC

	GD 2.0	VG 4.0	FN 6.0	VF 8.0	VF/NM 9.0	NM- 9.2
5-Dr. Neff, Ghost Breaker app; headlights-c	23	46	69	130	183	235
7-10: 10-Explosion-c	14	28	42	81	111	140
11-Ditko-c/a	31	62	93	175	248	320
12-Ditko explosion-c (classic); Shuster-a(2)	50	100	150	300	450	600
13-Shuster-c(p)/a.	11	22	33	66	88	110
14-Marijuana story "Shakedown"	14	28	42	81	111	140
15-28	10	20	30	60	80	100
29-(15¢, 68 pgs.)	12	24	36	71	96	120

RADIANT LOVE (Formerly Daring Love #1)
Gilmor Magazines: No. 2, Dec, 1953 - No. 6, Aug, 1954

	GD 2.0	VG 4.0	FN 6.0	VF 8.0	VF/NM 9.0	NM- 9.2
2	9	18	27	54	70	85
3-6	7	14	21	35	43	50

RADICAL DREAMER
Blackball Comics: No. 0, May, 1994 - No. 4, Nov, 1994 ($1.99, bi-monthly) (1st poster format comic)

	GD 2.0	VG 4.0	FN 6.0	VF 8.0	VF/NM 9.0	NM- 9.2
0-4: 0-2-($1.99, poster format): 0-1st app. Max Wrighter. 3,4-($2.50-c)						3.00

RADICAL DREAMER
Mark's Giant Economy Size Comics: V2#1, June, 1995 - V2#6, Feb, 1996 ($2.95, B&W, limited series)

	GD 2.0	VG 4.0	FN 6.0	VF 8.0	VF/NM 9.0	NM- 9.2
V2#1-6						3.00
Prime (5/96, $2.95)						3.00
Dreams Cannot Die!-(1996, $20.00, softcover)-Collects V1#0-4 & V2#1-6; intro by Kurt Busiek; afterward by Mark Waid						20.00
Dreams Cannot Die!-(1996, $60.00, hardcover)-Signed & limited edition; collects V1#0-4 & V2#1-6; intro by Kurt Busiek; afterward by Mark Waid						60.00

RADIOACTIVE MAN (Simpsons TV show)
Bongo Comics: 1993 - No. 6, 1994 ($1.95/$2.25, limited series)

	GD 2.0	VG 4.0	FN 6.0	VF 8.0	VF/NM 9.0	NM- 9.2
1-($2.95)-Glow-in-the-dark-c; bound-in jumbo poster; origin Radioactive Man; (cover dated Nov. 1952)						5.00
2-6: 2-Says #88 on-c & inside & dated May 1962; cover parody of Atlas Kirby monster-c; Superior Squad app.; origin Fallout Boy. 3-($1.95)-Cover "dated" Aug 1972 #216. 4-($2.25)-Cover "dated" Oct 1980 #412; w/trading card. 5-Cover "dated" Jan 1986 #679; w/trading card. 6-(Jan 1995 #1000)						4.00
Colossal #1-($4.95)						7.00
#4 (2001, $2.50) Faux 1953 issue; Murphy Anderson-i (6 pgs.)						2.50
#100 (2000, $2.50) Comic Book Guy-c/app.; faux 1963 issue inside						2.50
#136 (2001, $2.50) Dan DeCarlo-c/a						2.50
#222 (2001, $2.50) Batton Lash-s; Radioactive Man in 1972-style						2.50
#575 (2002, $2.50) Chaykin-c; Radioactive Man in 1984-style						2.50
1963-106 (2002, $2.50) Radioactive Man in 1960s Gold Key-style; Groening-c						2.50
#7 Bongo Super Heroes Starring... (2003, $2.50) Marvel Silver Age-style Superior Squad						2.50

RADISKULL & DEVIL DOLL
Image Comics: Nov, 2002 - Present ($2.50/$2.95, B&W, one-shots)

	GD 2.0	VG 4.0	FN 6.0	VF 8.0	VF/NM 9.0	NM- 9.2
...: Radiskull Hate Christmas (11/02, $2.50) Josh Blaylock & Tim Seeley-s/Mike Norton-a						2.50
...: Radiskull Hate Love (3/03, $2.95) Josh Blaylock & Tim Seeley-s/Jamar Nicholas-a						3.00

RADIX
Image Comics: Dec, 2001 - No. 3, Apr, 2002 ($2.95)

	GD 2.0	VG 4.0	FN 6.0	VF 8.0	VF/NM 9.0	NM- 9.2
1-3-Ray & Ben Lai-s/a						3.00

RAGAMUFFINS
Eclipse Comics: Jan, 1985 ($1.75, one shot)

	GD 2.0	VG 4.0	FN 6.0	VF 8.0	VF/NM 9.0	NM- 9.2
1-Eclipse Magazine-r, w/color; Colan-a						2.25

RAGGEDY ANN AND ANDY (See Dell Giants, March of Comics #23 & New Funnies)
Dell Publishing Co.: No. 5, 1942 - No. 533, 2/54; 10-12/64 - No. 4, 3/66

	GD 2.0	VG 4.0	FN 6.0	VF 8.0	VF/NM 9.0	NM- 9.2
Four Color 5(1942)	47	94	141	376	563	750
Four Color 23(1943)	37	74	111	278	414	550
Four Color 45(1943)	31	62	93	231	346	460
Four Color 72(1945)	27	54	81	194	285	375
1(6/46)-Billy & Bonnie Bee by Frank Thomas	32	64	96	240	358	475
2,3: 3-Egbert Elephant by Dan Noonan begins	19	38	57	136	198	260
4-Kelly-a, 16 pgs.	20	40	60	140	205	270
5,6,8-10	15	30	45	104	152	200
7-Little Black Sambo, Black Mumbo & Black Jumbo only app; Christmas-c	17	34	51	123	182	240
11-20	12	24	36	82	121	160
21-Alice In Wonderland cover/story	15	30	45	104	152	200
22-27,29-39(8/49), Four Color 262(1/50): 34-"...In Candyland"	10	20	30	70	100	130
28-Kelly-c	10	20	30	73	107	140
Four Color 306,354,380,452,533	8	16	24	55	78	100
1(10-12/64-Dell)	4	8	12	29	40	50
2,3(10-12/65), 4(3/66)	3	7	10	21	28	35

NOTE: ***Kelly** art ("Animal Mother Goose")-#1-34, 36, 37; c-28. Peterkin Pottle by **John Stanley** in 32-38.*

RAGGEDY ANN AND ANDY
Gold Key: Dec, 1971 - No. 6, Sept, 1973

	GD 2.0	VG 4.0	FN 6.0	VF 8.0	VF/NM 9.0	NM- 9.2
1	3	7	10	21	28	35
2-6	3	6	9	16	20	24

RAGGEDY ANN & THE CAMEL WITH THE WRINKLED KNEES (See Dell Jr. Treasury #8)

RAGMAN (See Batman Family #20, The Brave & The Bold #196 & Cancelled Comic Cavalcade)
National Per. Publ./DC Comics No. 5: Aug-Sept, 1976 - No. 5, Jun-Jul, 1977

	GD 2.0	VG 4.0	FN 6.0	VF 8.0	VF/NM 9.0	NM- 9.2
1-Origin & 1st app.	2	4	6	9	11	14
2-5: 2-Origin ends; Kubert-c. 4-Drug use story	1	2	3	5	6	8

NOTE: ***Kubert** a-4, 5; c-1-5. **Redondo** studios a-1-4.*

RAGMAN (2nd Series)
DC Comics: Oct, 1991 - No. 8, May, 1992 ($1.50, limited series)

	GD 2.0	VG 4.0	FN 6.0	VF 8.0	VF/NM 9.0	NM- 9.2
1-8: 1-Giffen plots/breakdowns. 3-Origin. 8-Batman-c/story						3.00

RAGMAN: CRY OF THE DEAD
DC Comics: Aug, 1993 - No. 6, Jan, 1994 ($1.75, limited series)

	GD 2.0	VG 4.0	FN 6.0	VF 8.0	VF/NM 9.0	NM- 9.2
1-6: Joe Kubert-c						3.00

RAGMOP
Image Comics: Sept, 1997 - No. 2 ($2.95, B&W)

	GD 2.0	VG 4.0	FN 6.0	VF 8.0	VF/NM 9.0	NM- 9.2
1,2-Rob Walton-c/s/a						3.00

RAGS RABBIT (Formerly Babe Ruth Sports #10 or Little Max #10?; also see Harvey Hits #2, Harvey Wiseguys & Tastee Freez)
Harvey Publications: No. 11, June, 1951 - No. 18, March, 1954 (Written & drawn for little folks)

	GD 2.0	VG 4.0	FN 6.0	VF 8.0	VF/NM 9.0	NM- 9.2
11-(See Nutty Comics #5 for 1st app.)	6	12	18	31	38	45
12-18	5	10	15	24	30	35

RAI (Rai and the Future Force #9-23) (See Magnus #5-8)
Valiant: Mar, 1992 - No. 0, Oct, 1992; No. 9, May, 1993 - No. 33, Jun, 1995 ($1.95/$2.25)

	GD 2.0	VG 4.0	FN 6.0	VF 8.0	VF/NM 9.0	NM- 9.2
1-Valiant's 1st original character	2	4	6	8	10	12
2-4,0: 4-Low print run. 0-(11/92)-Origin/1st app. new Rai (Rising Spirit) & 1st full app. & partial origin Bloodshot; also see Eternal Warrior #4; tells future of all characters	1	2	3	5	6	8
5-10: 6,7-Unity x-overs. 7-Death of Rai. 9-($2.50)-Gatefold-c; story cont'd from Magnus #24; Magnus, Eternal Warrior & X-O app.						4.00
11-33: 15-Manowar Armor app. 17-19-Magnus x-over. 21-1st app. The Starwatchers (cameo); trading card. 22-Death of Rai. 26-Chaos Effect Epsilon Pt. 3						2.50

NOTE: ***Layton** c-2i, 9i. **Miller** c-6. **Simonson** c-7.*

RAIDERS OF THE LOST ARK (Movie)
Marvel Comics Group: Sept, 1981 - No. 3, Nov, 1981 (Movie adaptation)

	GD 2.0	VG 4.0	FN 6.0	VF 8.0	VF/NM 9.0	NM- 9.2
1-3: 1-r/Marvel Comics Super Special #18						3.00

NOTE: ***Buscema** a(p)-1-3; c(p)-1. **Simonson** a-3i; scripts-1-3.*

RAIL: BROKEN THINGS
Image Comics: Nov, 2001 ($5.95, one-shot)

	GD 2.0	VG 4.0	FN 6.0	VF 8.0	VF/NM 9.0	NM- 9.2
nn-Dave Dorman-s/a						6.00

RAINBOW BRITE AND THE STAR STEALER
DC Comics: 1985

	GD 2.0	VG 4.0	FN 6.0	VF 8.0	VF/NM 9.0	NM- 9.2
nn-Movie adaptation	2	4	6	8	10	12

RALPH KINER, HOME RUN KING
Fawcett Publications: 1950 (Pittsburgh Pirates)

	GD 2.0	VG 4.0	FN 6.0	VF 8.0	VF/NM 9.0	NM- 9.2
nn-Photo-c; life story	60	120	180	375	563	750

RALPH SNART ADVENTURES
Now Comics: June, 1986 - V2#9, 1987; V3#1 - #26, Feb, 1991; V4#1, 1992 - #4, 1992

	GD 2.0	VG 4.0	FN 6.0	VF 8.0	VF/NM 9.0	NM- 9.2
1-3, V2#1-7,V3#1-23,25,26:1-($1.00, B&W)-1(B&W),V2#1(11/86), B&W), 8,9-color. V3#1(9/88)-Color begins						2.50
V3#24-($2.50)-3-D issue, V4#1-3-Direct sale versions w/cards						2.50
V4#1-3-Newsstand versions w/random cards						2.50
Book 1	1	2	3	5	6	8
3-D Special (11/92, $3.50)-Complete 12-card set w/3-D glasses						3.50

RAMAR OF THE JUNGLE (TV)
Toby Press No. 1/Charlton No. 2 on: 1954 (no month); No. 2, Sept, 1955 - No. 5, Sept, 1956

	GD 2.0	VG 4.0	FN 6.0	VF 8.0	VF/NM 9.0	NM- 9.2
1-Jon Hall photo-c; last pre-code issue	22	44	66	124	172	220
2-5: 2-Jon Hall photo-c	15	30	45	84	115	145

RAMM

The Rampaging Hulk #5 © MAR

Rangers Comics #27 © FH

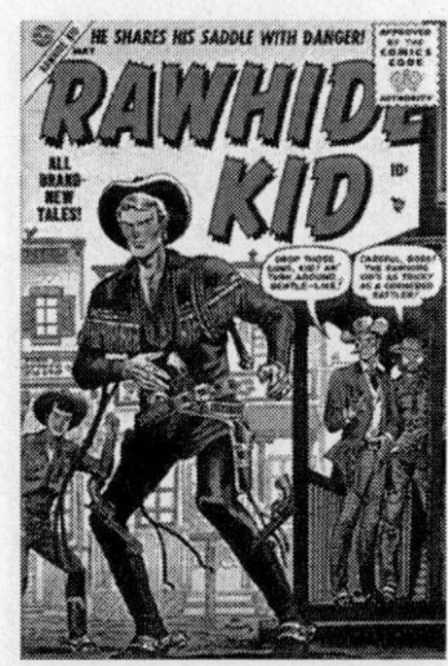
The Rawhide Kid #2 © MAR

	GD 2.0	VG 4.0	FN 6.0	VF 8.0	VF/NM 9.0	NM- 9.2

Megaton Comics: May, 1987 - No. 2, Sept, 1987 ($1.50, B&W)
1,2-Both have 1 pg. Youngblood ad by Liefeld 2.25

RAMPAGING HULK (The Hulk #10 on; also see Marvel Treasury Edition)
Marvel Comics Group: Jan, 1977 - No. 9, June, 1978 ($1.00, B&W magazine)
1-Bloodstone story w/Buscema & Nebres-a. Origin re-cap w/Simonson-a; Gargoyle, UFO story; Ken Barr-c 2 4 6 14 18 22
2-Old X-Men app; origin old w/Simonson-a & new X-Men in text w/Cockrum illos; Bloodstone story w/Brown & Nebres-a 2 4 6 10 13 16
3-9: 3-Iron Man app. 4-Gallery of villains w/Giffen-a. 5,6-Hulk vs. Sub-Mariner. 7-Man-Thing story. 8-Original Avengers app. 9-Thor vs. Hulk battle; Shanna the She-Devil story w/DeZuniga-a 2 4 6 8 10 12
NOTE: ***Alcala** a-1-3i, 5i, 8i. **Buscema** a-1. **Giffen** a-4. **Nino** a-4i. **Simonson** a-1-3p. **Starlin** a-4(w/Nino), 7; c-4, 5, 7.*

RAMPAGING HULK
Marvel Comics: Aug, 1998 - No. 6, Jan, 1999 ($2.99/$1.99)
1-($2.99) Flashback stories of Savage Hulk; Leonardi-a 3.00
2-6-($1.99): 2-Two covers 2.25

RANDOLPH SCOTT (Movie star)(See Crack Western #67, Prize Comics Western #76, Western Hearts #8, Western Love #1 & Western Winners #7)

RANDY O'DONNELL IS THE M@N
Image Comics: May, 2001 - No. 3, Sept, 2001 ($2.95)
1-3-DeFalco & Lim/s&a 3.00

RANGE BUSTERS
Fox Features Syndicate: Sept, 1950 (One shot)
1 (Exist?) 20 40 60 112 156 200

RANGE BUSTERS (Formerly Cowboy Love?; Wyatt Earp, Frontier Marshall #11 on)
Charlton Comics: No. 8, May, 1955 - No. 10, Sept, 1955
8 8 16 24 43 54 65
9,10 6 12 18 28 34 40

RANGELAND LOVE
Atlas Comics (CDS): Dec, 1949 - No. 2, Mar, 1950 (52 pgs.)
1-Robert Taylor & Arlene Dahl photo-c 17 34 51 98 134 170
2-Photo-c 14 28 42 79 107 135

RANGER, THE (See Zane Grey, Four Color #255)

RANGE RIDER, THE (TV)(See Flying A's...)

RANGE ROMANCES
Comic Magazines (Quality Comics): Dec, 1949 - No. 5, Aug, 1950 (#5: 52 pg)
1-Gustavson-c/a 27 54 81 153 214 275
2-Crandall-c/a 27 54 81 153 214 275
3-Crandall, Gustavson-a; photo-c 23 46 69 130 183 235
4-Crandall-a; photo-c 20 40 60 112 156 200
5-Gustavson-a; Crandall-a(p); photo-c 20 40 60 112 156 200

RANGERS COMICS (...of Freedom #1-7)
Fiction House Magazines: 10/41 - No. 67, 10/52; No. 68, Fall, 1952; No. 69, Winter, 1952-53 (Flying stories)
1-Intro. Ranger Girl & The Rangers of Freedom; ends #7, cover app. only #5 300 600 900 1900 2850 3800
2 88 176 264 550 825 1100
3 66 132 198 413 619 825
4,5 60 120 180 375 563 750
6-10: 8-U.S. Rangers begin 48 96 144 288 432 575
11,12-Commando Rangers app. 44 88 132 264 395 525
13-Commando Ranger begins-not same as Commando Rangers 43 86 129 258 384 510
14-20 39 78 117 230 325 420
21-Intro/origin Firehair (begins, 2/45) 40 80 120 240 345 450
22-30: 23-Kazanda begins, ends #28. 28-Tiger Man begins (origin/1st app., 4/46), ends #46. 30-Crusoe Island begins, ends #40 29 58 87 164 232 300
31-40: 33-Hypodermic panels 25 50 75 144 198 255
41-46: 41-Last Werewolf Hunter 21 42 63 118 164 210
47-56- "Eisnerish" Dr. Drew by Grandenetti. 48-Last Glory Forbes. 53-Last 52 pg. issue. 55-Last Sky Rangers 20 40 60 112 156 200
57-60-Straight Dr. Drew by Grandenetti 15 30 45 86 118 150
61-69: 64-Suicide Smith begins. 63-Used in **POP**, pgs. 85, 99. 67-Space Rangers begin, end #69 13 26 39 74 100 125
NOTE: *Bondage, discipline covers, lingerie panels are common. Crusoe Island by **Larsen**-#30-36. Firehair by **Lubbers**-#30-49. Glory Forbes by **Baker**-#36-45, 47; by **Whitman**-#34, 35. I Confess in #41-53. Jan of the Jungle in #42-58. King of the Congo in #49-53. Tiger Man by **Celardo**-#30-39. **M. Anderson** a-30? **Baker** a-36-38, 42, 44. **John Celardo** a-34, 36-39. **Lee Elias** a-21-28. **Evans** a-19, 38-46, 48-52. **Hopper** a-25, 26. **Ingels** a-13-16. **Larsen** a-34. **Bob Lubbers** a-30-38, 40-44; c-40-45. **Moreira** a-41-47. **Tuska** a-16, 17, 19, 22. **M. Whitman** c-61-66. **Zolnerwich** c-1-17.*

RANGO (TV)
Dell Publishing Co.: Aug, 1967
1-Photo-c of comedian Tim Conway 3 7 10 21 28 35

RAPHAEL (See Teenage Mutant Ninja Turtles)
Mirage Studios: 1985 ($1.50, 7-1/2x11", B&W w/2 color cover, one-shot)
1-1st Turtles one-shot spin-off; contains 1st drawing of the Turtles as a group from 1983 4.00
1-2nd printing (11/87); new-c & 8 pgs. art 2.25

RASCALS IN PARADISE
Dark Horse Comics: Aug, 1994 - No. 3, Dec, 1994 ($3.95, magazine size)
1-3-Jim Silke-a/story 4.00
Trade paperback-($16.95)-r/#1-3 17.00

RATFINK (See Frantic, Zany, & Ed "Big Daddy" Roth's Ratfink Comix)
Canrom, Inc.: Oct, 1964
1-Woodbridge-a 6 12 18 43 59 75

RAT PATROL, THE (TV)
Dell Publishing Co.: Mar, 1967 - No. 5, Nov, 1967; No. 6, Oct, 1969
1-Christopher George photo-c 8 16 24 55 78 100
2-6: 3-6-Photo-c 5 10 15 33 44 55

RAVAGE 2099 (See Marvel Comics Presents #117)
Marvel Comics: Dec, 1992 - No. 33, Aug, 1995($1.25/$1.50)
1-($1.75)-Gold foil stamped-c; Stan Lee scripts 3.00
1-($1.75)-2nd printing 2.25
2-24,26-33: 5-Last Ryan-c. 6-Last Ryan-a. 14-Punisher 2099 x-over. 15-Ron Lim-c(p). 18-Bound-in card sheet 2.25
25 ($2.25, 52 pgs.) 2.25
25 ($2.95, 52 pgs.)-Silver foil embossed-c 3.00

RAVEN, THE (See Movie Classics)

RAVEN CHRONICLES
Caliber (New Worlds): 1995 - No. 16 ($2.95, B&W)
1-16: 10-Flip book w/Wordsmith #6. 15-Flip book w/High Caliber #4 3.00

RAVENS AND RAINBOWS
Pacific Comics: Dec, 1983 (Baxter paper)(Reprints fanzine work in color)
1-Jeff Jones-c/a(r); nudity scenes 3.00

RAWHIDE (TV)
Dell Publishing Co./Gold Key: Sept-Nov, 1959 - June-Aug, 1962; July, 1963 - No. 2, Jan, 1964
Four Color 1028 (#1) 25 50 75 181 266 350
Four Color 1097,1160,1202,1261,1269 16 32 48 113 167 220
01-684-208 (8/62, Dell) 14 28 42 97 141 185
1(10071-307) (7/63, Gold Key) 14 28 42 97 141 185
2-(12¢) 13 26 39 90 133 175
NOTE: *All have Clint Eastwood photo-c. **Tufts** a-1028.*

RAWHIDE KID
Atlas/Marvel Comics (CnPC No. 1-16/AMI No. 17-30): Mar, 1955 - No. 16, Sept, 1957; No. 17, Aug, 1960 - No. 151, May, 1979
1-Rawhide Kid, his horse Apache & sidekick Randy begin; Wyatt Earp app.; #1 was not code approved; Maneely splash pg. 88 176 264 550 825 1100
2 40 80 120 240 345 450
3-5 31 62 93 175 248 320
6-10: 7-Williamson-a (4 pgs.) 24 48 72 135 190 245
11-16: 16-Torres-a 20 40 60 112 156 200
17-Origin by Jack Kirby; Kirby-a begins 32 64 96 240 360 480
18-21,24-30 13 26 39 90 133 175
22-Monster-c/story by Kirby/Ayers 16 32 48 113 167 220
23-Origin retold by Jack Kirby 20 40 60 140 205 270
31-35,40: 31,32-Kirby-a. 33-35-Davis-a. 34-Kirby-a. 35-Intro & death of The Raven. 40-Two-Gun Kid x-over. 10 20 30 72 104 135
36,37,39,41,42-No Kirby. 42-1st Larry Lieber issue 9 18 27 65 93 120
38-Red Raven-c/story; Kirby-c (2/64). 12 24 36 82 121 160
43-Kirby-a (beware: pin-up often missing) 12 24 36 82 121 160
44,46: 46-Toth-a. 46-Doc Holliday-c/s 9 18 27 60 85 110
45-Origin retold, 17 pgs. 10 20 30 73 107 140
47-49,51-60 6 12 18 38 52 65
50-Kid Colt x-over; vs. Rawhide Kid 6 12 18 40 55 70
61-70: 64-Kid Colt story. 66-Two-Gun Kid story. 67-Kid Colt story. 70-Last 12¢ issue 4 8 12 29 40 50

Rawhide Kid (3rd series) #5 © MAR

Razor #33 © Everette Hartsoe

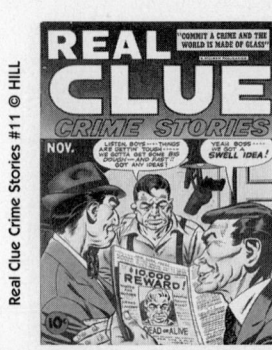

Real Clue Crime Stories #11 © HILL

	GD 2.0	VG 4.0	FN 6.0	VF 8.0	VF/NM 9.0	NM- 9.2
71-78,80-83,85	3	6	9	18	24	30
79,84,86,95: 79-Williamson-a(r). 84,86: Kirby-a. 86-Origin-r; Williamson-r/Ringo Kid #13 (4 pgs.)	3	6	9	19	25	32
87-91: 90-Kid Colt app. 91-Last 15¢ issue	3	6	9	16	20	25
92,93 (52 pg.Giants). 92-Kirby-a	4	8	12	24	32	40
94,96-99	2	4	6	14	18	22
100 (6/72)-Origin retold & expanded	3	6	9	19	25	32
101-120: 115-Last new story	2	4	6	11	14	18
121-151	2	4	6	8	10	12
133,134-(30¢-c variants, limited distribution)(5,7/76)	2	4	6	12	16	20
140,141-(35¢-c variants, limited distribution)(7,9/77)	2	4	6	12	16	20
Special 1(9/71, 25¢, 68 pgs.)-All Kirby/Ayers-r	4	8	12	27	36	45

NOTE: ***Ayers*** *a-13, 14, 16.* ***Colan*** *a-5, 35, 37; c-145p, 148p, 149p.* ***Davis*** *a-125r.* ***Everett*** *a-54i, 65, 66, 88, 96i, 148i(r).* ***Gulacy*** *c-147.* ***Heath*** *c-4.* ***G. Kane*** *c-101, 144.* ***Keller*** *a-5, 144r.* ***Kirby*** *a-17-32, 34, 42, 43, 84, 86, 92, 109r, 112r, 137r, Spec. 1; c-17-35, 37, 38, 40, 41, 43-47, 137r.* ***Maneely*** *c-1, 2, 5, 6, 14.* ***Morisi*** *a-13.* ***Morrow/Williamson*** *r-111.* ***Roussos*** *r-146i, 147i, 149-151i.* ***Severin*** *a-16; c-8, 13.* ***Sutton*** *a-93.* ***Torres*** *a-99r.* ***Tuska*** *a-14.* ***Wildey*** *r-146-151(Outlaw Kid).* ***Williamson*** *r-79, 86, 95.*

RAWHIDE KID
Marvel Comics Group: Aug, 1985 - No. 4, Nov, 1985 (Mini-series)

1-4						5.00

RAWHIDE KID
Marvel Comics (MAX): Apr, 2003 - No. 5, June, 2003 ($2.99, limited series)

1-John Severin-a/Ron Zimmerman-s; Dave Johnson-c						3.00
2-5: 3-Dodson-c. 4-Darwyn Cooke-c. 5-J. Scott Campbell-c						3.00
Vol. 1: Slap Leather TPB (2003, $12.99) r/#1-5						13.00

RAY, THE (See Freedom Fighters & Smash Comics #14)
DC Comics: Feb, 1992 - No. 6, July, 1992 ($1.00, mini-series)

1-Sienkiewicz-c; Joe Quesada-a(p) in 1-5						5.00
2-6: 3-6-Quesada-c(p). 6-Quesada layouts only						3.00
...In a Blaze of Power (1994, $12.95)-r/#1-6 w/new Quesada-c						13.00

RAY, THE
DC Comics: May, 1994 - No. 28, Oct, 1996 ($1.75/$1.95/$2.25)

1-Quesada-c(p); Superboy app.						3.00
1-($2.95)-Collectors Edition w/diff. Quesada-c; embossed foil-c						4.00
2-5,0,6-24,26-28: 2-Quesada-c(p); Superboy app. 5-(9/94). 0-(10/94)						2.25
25-($3.50)-Future Flash (Bart Allen)-c/app; double size						3.50
Annual 1 ($3.95, 68 pgs.)-Superman app.						4.00

RAY BRADBURY COMICS
Topps Comics: Feb, 1993 - V4#1, June, 1994 ($2.95)

1-5-Polybagged w/3 trading cards each. 1-All dinosaur issue; Corben-a; Williamson/Torres/Krenkel-r/Weird Science-Fantasy #25. 3-All dinosaur issue; Steacy painted-c; Stout-a						3.00
Special Edition 1 (1994, $2.95)-The Illustrated Man						3.00
...Special: Tales of Horror #1 ($2.50), ...Trilogy of Terror V3#1 (5/94, $2.50), ...Martian Chronicles V4#1 (6/94, $2.50)-Steranko-c						2.50

NOTE: ***Kelley Jones*** *a-Trilogy of Terror V3#1.* ***Kaluta*** *a-Martian Chronicles V4#1.* ***Kurtzman/Matt Wagner*** *c-2.* ***McKean*** *c-4.* ***Mignola*** *a-4.* ***Wood*** *a-Trilogy of Terror V3#1r.*

RAZOR
London Night Studios: May, 1992 - No. 51, Apr, 1999 ($3.95/$3.00, B&W)

0 (5/92, $3.95)-Direct market	1	3	4	6	8	10
0 (4/95, $3.00)-London Night edition						3.00
1/2 (4/95, mail-in offer)-1st Poizon; Linsner-c						4.00
1 (8/92, $2.50)-Fathom Press	1	3	4	6	8	10
1-2nd printing						3.00
2 ($2.95)-J. O'Barr-c	1	2	3	5	6	8
2-Limited edi. in red & blue, 2-Platinum; no c-price	1	3	4	6	8	10
3-($3.95)-Jim Balent-c						4.00
3-w/poster insert						5.00
4-Vigil-c						3.00
4-w/poster insert						4.00
5-Linsner-c						5.00
5-Platinum	1	2	3	5	6	8
6-31,33,34:10-1st app. Stryke. 1,12 -Rituals Pt. 1 & 2. 21-Rose & Gunn app. 25-Photo-c						2.50
25-Uncut ($10.00)-Nude Edition; double-c						10.00
32-($3.50)						3.50
32-($5.00)-Nude Edition; Nude-c						5.00
35-49,51						3.00
40-Uncut ($6.00)-Nude Edition						6.00
50-Uncut-Four covers incl. Tony Daniel						3.00
Annual 1 (1993, $2.95)-1st app. Shi	2	4	6	11	14	18
Annual 1-Gold (1200 printed)	2	4	6	12	16	20
Annual 2 (Late 1994, $3.00)						3.00
.../Cry No More 1-($3.95)-Origin Razor; variant-c exists						4.00
.../Embrace nn-($3.00)-Variant photo-c(Carmen Electra)						3.00
...Pictorial 1-(10/97, $5.00)						5.00
.../Shi Special 1 (7/94, $3.00)						4.00
.../Switchblade Symphony 1-($3.95)-Hartsoe-s						4.00
...: Swimsuit Special-painted-c						3.00
...: The Darkest Night 1,2 ($4.95)-painted-c						5.00
.../Warrior Nun Areala-Faith-(5/96, $3.95)						4.00
.../Warrior Nun Areala-Faith-(5/96, $3.95)-Virgin-c						5.00

RAZOR: BURN
London Night Studios: 1994 - No. 5, 1994 ($3.00, limited series, mature)

1-5						3.00
TPB-($14.95) r/ #1-5						15.00

RAZOR/DARK ANGEL: THE FINAL NAIL
Boneyard Press #1/London Night Studios #2: June, 1994 -No. 2, June, 1994 ($2.95, B&W, limited series, mature)

1,2						3.00

RAZOR• DEEP CUTS
London Night Studios: Sept, 1997 ($5.00, one-shot, mature)

1-Photo-c & insides						5.00

RAZOR/MORBID ANGEL: SOUL SEARCH
London Night Studios: Sept, 1996 - No. 3, 1997 ($3.00, limited series, mature)

1-3						3.00

RAZOR: THE SUFFERING
London Night Studios: 1994 - No. 3, 1995 ($2.95, limited series, mature)

1-3 ($2.95): 2-(9/94), 1-($3.00)-Director's Cut						3.00
1-Platinum						5.00
Trade paperback-($12.95)						13.00

RAZOR: TORTURE
London Night Studios: 1995 - No. 6, 1995 ($3.00, limited series, mature)

0-($3.95)-Wraparound, chromium-c; polybagged w/card; alternate-c exists?						4.00
1-6 ($3.00): 3-Error & corrected issues exist						3.00

RAZOR: VOLUME TWO
London Night Studios: Oct, 1996 - No. 7, June, 1997 ($3.95/$3.00, mature)

1-Wraparound foil-c; Quinn-s						4.00
2-7-($3.00): 3-Error & corrected issues exist						3.00

RAZORLINE
Marvel Comics: Sept, 1993 (75¢, one-shot)

1-Clive Barker super-heroes: Ectokid, Hokum & Hex, Hyperkind & Saint Sinner (all 1st app.)						2.25

REAL ADVENTURE COMICS (Action Adventure #2 on)
Gillmor Magazines: Apr, 1955

1	8	16	24	40	50	60

REAL ADVENTURES OF JONNY QUEST, THE
Dark Horse Comics: Sept, 1996 - No. 12, Sept, 1997 ($2.95)

1-12						3.00

REAL CLUE CRIME STORIES (Formerly Clue Comics)
Hillman Periodicals: V2#4, June, 1947 - V8#3, May, 1953

	GD 2.0	VG 4.0	FN 6.0	VF 8.0	VF/NM 9.0	NM- 9.2
V2#4(#1)-S&K c/a(3); Dan Barry-a	48	96	144	288	432	575
5-7-S&K c/a(3-4). 7-Iron Lady app.	39	78	117	233	329	425
8-12	11	22	33	66	88	110
V3#1-8,10-12, V4#1-3,5-8,11,12	10	20	30	58	77	95
V3#9-Used in **SOTI**, pg. 102	13	26	39	74	100	125
V4#4-S&K-a	14	28	42	79	107	135
V4#9,10-Krigstein-a	11	22	33	63	84	105
V5#1-5,7,8,10,12	9	18	27	49	62	75
6,9,11(1/54)-Krigstein-a	10	20	30	58	77	95
V6#1-5,8,9,11	8	16	24	43	54	65
6,7,10,12-Krigstein-a. 10-Bondage-c	10	20	30	58	77	95
V7#1-3,5-11, V8#1-3: V7#6-1 pg. Frazetta ad "Prayer" - 1st app.?	8	16	24	43	54	65
4,12-Krigstein-a	10	20	30	58	77	95

NOTE: ***Barry*** *a-9, 10; c-V2#8.* ***Briefer*** *a-V6#6.* ***Fuje*** *a- V2#7(2), 8, 11.* ***Infantino*** *a-V2#8; c-V2#11.* ***Lawrence*** *a-V3#8, V5#7.* ***Powell*** *a-V4#11, 12. V5#4, 5, 7 are 68 pgs.*

REAL EXPERIENCES (Formerly Tiny Tessie)
Atlas Comics (20CC): No. 25, Jan, 1950

Real Heroes Comics #4 © PMI

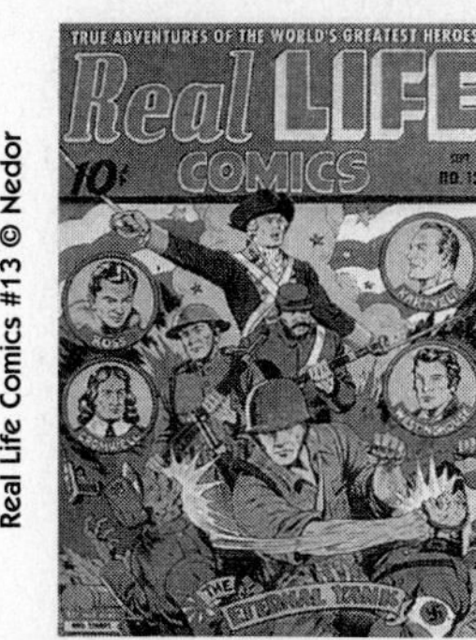

Real Life Comics #13 © Nedor

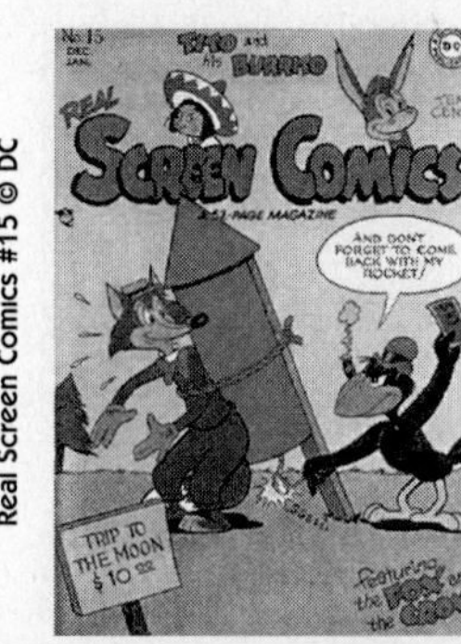

Real Screen Comics #15 © DC

	GD 2.0	VG 4.0	FN 6.0	VF 8.0	VF/NM 9.0	NM- 9.2
25-Virginia Mayo photo-c from movie "Red Light"	8	16	24	46	58	70

REAL FACT COMICS
National Periodical Publications: Mar-Apr, 1946 - No. 21, July-Aug, 1949

	GD 2.0	VG 4.0	FN 6.0	VF 8.0	VF/NM 9.0	NM- 9.2
1-S&K-c/a; Harry Houdini story; Just Imagine begins (not by Finlay); Fred Ray-a	60	120	180	375	563	750
2-S&K-a; Rin-Tin-Tin & P. T. Barnum stories	40	80	120	240	340	440
3-H.G. Wells, Lon Chaney stories; 1st DC letter column	37	74	111	212	301	390
4-Virgil Finlay-a on 'Just Imagine' begins, ends #12 (2 pgs. each); Jimmy Stewart & Jack London stories; Joe DiMaggio 1 pg. biography	40	80	120	240	340	440
5-Batman/Robin-c taken from cover of Batman #9; 5 pg. story about creation of Batman & Robin; Tom Mix story	184	368	552	1150	1725	2300
6-Origin & 1st app. Tommy Tomorrow by Weisinger and Sherman (1-2/47); Flag-c; 1st writing by Harlan Ellison (letter column, non-professional); "First Man to Reach Mars" epic-c/story	112	224	336	700	1050	1400
7-(No. 6 on inside)-Roussos-a; D. Fairbanks sty.	20	40	60	112	156	200
8-2nd app. Tommy Tomorrow by Finlay (5-6/47)	61	122	183	381	573	765
9-S&K-a; Glenn Miller, Indianapolis 500 stories	30	60	90	170	240	310
10-Vigilante by Meskin (based on movie serial); 4 pg. Finlay s/f story	29	58	87	164	232	300
11,12: 11-Annie Oakley, G-Men stories; Kinstler-a	16	32	48	92	126	160
13-Dale Evans and Tommy Tomorrow-c/stories	50	100	150	300	450	600
14,17,18: 14-Will Rogers story	15	30	45	86	118	150
15-Nuclear explosion part-c ("Last War on Earth" story); Clyde Beatty story	20	40	60	112	156	200
16-Tommy Tomorrow app.; 1st Planeteers?	46	92	138	276	413	550
19-Sir Arthur Conan Doyle story	17	34	51	98	134	170
20-Kubert-a, 4 pgs; Daniel Boone story	19	38	57	106	146	185
21-Kubert-a, 2 pgs; Kit Carson story	15	30	45	86	118	150

NOTE: ***Barry** c-16. **Virgil Finlay** c-6, 8. **Meskin** c-10. **Roussos** a-1-4, 6.*

REAL FUNNIES
Nedor Publishing Co.: Jan, 1943 - No. 3, June, 1943

	GD 2.0	VG 4.0	FN 6.0	VF 8.0	VF/NM 9.0	NM- 9.2
1-Funny animal, humor; Black Terrier app. (clone of The Black Terror)	34	68	102	193	274	355
2,3	17	34	51	98	134	170

REAL GHOSTBUSTERS, THE (Also see Slimer)
Now Comics: Aug, 1988 - No. 32, 1991 ($1.75/$1.95)

	GD 2.0	VG 4.0	FN 6.0	VF 8.0	VF/NM 9.0	NM- 9.2
1-32: 1-Based on Ghostbusters movie. #29-32 exist?						3.00

REAL HEROES COMICS
Parents' Magazine Institute: Sept, 1941 - No. 16, Oct, 1946

	GD 2.0	VG 4.0	FN 6.0	VF 8.0	VF/NM 9.0	NM- 9.2
1-Roosevelt-c/story	34	68	102	193	274	355
2-J. Edgar Hoover-c/story	15	30	45	86	118	150
3-5,7-10: 4-Churchill, Roosevelt stories	13	26	39	76	103	130
6-Lou Gehrig-c/story	21	42	63	118	164	210
11-16: 13-Kiefer-a	9	18	27	52	66	80

REALISTIC ROMANCES
Realistic Comics/Avon Periodicals: July-Aug, 1951 - No. 17, Aug-Sept, 1954 (No #9-14)

	GD 2.0	VG 4.0	FN 6.0	VF 8.0	VF/NM 9.0	NM- 9.2
1-Kinstler-a; c-/Avon paperback #211	23	46	69	130	183	235
2	11	22	33	66	88	110
3,4	10	20	30	60	80	100
5,8-Kinstler-a	11	22	33	63	84	105
6-c-/Diversey Prize Novels #6; Kinstler-a	11	22	33	66	88	110
7-Evans-a?; c-/Avon paperback #360	11	22	33	66	88	110
15,17: 17-Kinstler-c	10	20	30	56	73	90
16-Kinstler marijuana story-r/Romantic Love #6	11	22	33	63	84	105
I.W. Reprint #1,8,9: #1-r/Realistic Romances #4; Astarita-a. 9-r/Women To Love #1	2	4	6	10	13	16

NOTE: ***Astarita** a-2-4, 7, 8, 17. Photo c-1, 2. Painted c-3, 4.*

REAL LIFE COMICS
Nedor/Better/Standard Publ./Pictorial Magazine No. 13: Sept, 1941 - No. 59, Sept, 1952

	GD 2.0	VG 4.0	FN 6.0	VF 8.0	VF/NM 9.0	NM- 9.2
1-Uncle Sam-c/story; Daniel Boone story	55	110	165	330	495	660
2	27	54	81	153	214	275
3-Hitler cover	80	160	240	500	750	1000
4,5: 4-Story of American flag "Old Glory"	17	34	51	95	130	165
6-10: 6-Wild Bill Hickok story	16	32	48	89	122	155
11-20: 17-Albert Einstein story	15	30	45	84	115	145
21-23,25,26,28-30: 29-A-Bomb story	11	22	33	66	88	110
24-Story of Baseball (Babe Ruth)	20	40	60	112	156	200
27-Schomburg A-Bomb-c; story of A-Bomb	19	38	57	107	149	190
31-33,35,36,42-44,48,49: 49-Baseball issue	10	20	30	56	73	90
34,37-41,45-47: 34-Jimmy Stewart story. 37-Story of motion pictures; Bing Crosby story. 38-Jane Froman story. 39- "1,000,000 A.D." story. 40-Bob Feller. 41-Jimmie Foxx story ("Jimmy" on-c); "Home Run" Baker story. 45-Story of Olympic games; Burl Ives & Kit Carson story. 46-Douglas Fairbanks Jr. & Sr. story. 47-George Gershwin story	11	22	33	66	88	110
50-Frazetta-a (5 pgs.)	29	58	87	164	232	300
51-Jules Verne "Journey to the Moon" by Evans	20	40	60	115	160	205
52-Frazetta-a (4 pgs.); Severin/Elder-a(2); Evans-a	32	64	96	180	255	330
53-57-Severin/Elder-a. 54-Bat Masterson-c/story	15	30	45	84	115	145
58-Severin/Elder-a(2)	15	30	45	86	118	150
59-1 pg. Frazetta; Severin/Elder-a	15	30	45	84	115	145

NOTE: *Some issues had two titles. **Guardineer** a-40(2), 44. **Meskin** a-52. **Roussos** a-50. **Schomburg** c-1, 2, 4, 5, 7, 11, 13-21, 23, 24, 26, 28, 30-32, 34-40, 42, 44-47, 55. **Tuska** a-53. Photo-c 5, 6.*

REAL LIFE SECRETS (Real Secrets #2 on)
Ace Periodicals: Sept, 1949 (one-shot)

	GD 2.0	VG 4.0	FN 6.0	VF 8.0	VF/NM 9.0	NM- 9.2
1-Painted-c	12	24	36	71	96	120

REAL LIFE STORY OF FESS PARKER (Magazine)
Dell Publishing Co.: 1955

	GD 2.0	VG 4.0	FN 6.0	VF 8.0	VF/NM 9.0	NM- 9.2
1	10	20	30	70	100	130

REAL LIFE TALES OF SUSPENSE (See Suspense)

REAL LOVE (Formerly Hap Hazard)
Ace Periodicals (A. A. Wyn): No. 25, April, 1949 - No. 76, Nov, 1956

	GD 2.0	VG 4.0	FN 6.0	VF 8.0	VF/NM 9.0	NM- 9.2
25	13	26	39	74	100	125
26	9	18	27	49	62	75
27-L. B. Cole-a	11	22	33	63	84	105
28-35	8	16	24	40	50	60
36-66: 66-Last pre-code (2/55)	7	14	21	35	43	50
67-76	6	12	18	28	34	40

NOTE: *Photo c-50-76. Painted c-46.*

REALM, THE
Arrow Comics/WeeBee Comics #13/Caliber Press #14 on: Feb, 1986 - No. 21, 1991 ($1.50/$1.95/$2.50, B&W)

	GD 2.0	VG 4.0	FN 6.0	VF 8.0	VF/NM 9.0	NM- 9.2
1-21: 4-1st app. Deadworld (9/86)						2.50
Book 1 ($4.95, B&W)						5.00

REAL McCOYS, THE (TV)
Dell Publ. Co.: No. 1071, 1-3/60 - 5-7/1962 (All have Walter Brennan photo-c)

	GD 2.0	VG 4.0	FN 6.0	VF 8.0	VF/NM 9.0	NM- 9.2
Four Color 1071,1134-Toth-a in both	10	20	30	72	104	135
Four Color 1193,1265	10	20	30	67	96	125
01-689-207 (5-7/62)	9	18	27	60	85	110

REALM OF THE CLAW (Also see Mutant Earth as part of a flipbook)
Image Comics: Oct, 2003 - Present ($2.95)

	GD 2.0	VG 4.0	FN 6.0	VF 8.0	VF/NM 9.0	NM- 9.2
0-(7/03, $5.95) Convention Special; cover has gold-foil title logo						6.00
1,2-Two covers by Yardin						3.00

REAL SCREEN COMICS (#1 titled Real Screen Funnies; TV Screen Cartoons #129-138)
National Periodical Publications: Spring, 1945 - No. 128, May-June, 1959 (#1-40: 52 pgs.)

	GD 2.0	VG 4.0	FN 6.0	VF 8.0	VF/NM 9.0	NM- 9.2
1-The Fox & the Crow, Flippity & Flop, Tito & His Burrito begin	100	200	300	625	938	1250
2	48	96	144	288	432	575
3-5	34	68	102	196	278	360
6-10 (2-3/47)	22	44	66	127	176	225
11-20 (10-11/48): 13-The Crow x-over in Flippity & Flop	17	34	51	98	134	170
21-30 (6-7/50)	13	26	39	74	100	125
31-50	11	22	33	63	84	105
51-99	10	20	30	56	73	90
100	10	20	30	58	77	95
101-128	8	16	24	46	58	70

REAL SECRETS (Formerly Real Life Secrets)
Ace Periodicals: No. 2, Nov, 1950 - No. 5, May, 1950

	GD 2.0	VG 4.0	FN 6.0	VF 8.0	VF/NM 9.0	NM- 9.2
2-Painted-c	10	20	30	56	73	90
3-5: 3-Photo-c	8	16	24	40	50	60

REAL SPORTS COMICS (All Sports Comics #2 on)
Hillman Periodicals: Oct-Nov, 1948 (52 pgs.)

	GD 2.0	VG 4.0	FN 6.0	VF 8.0	VF/NM 9.0	NM- 9.2
1-Powell-a (12 pgs.)	40	80	120	240	340	440

REAL WAR STORIES
Eclipse Comics: July, 1987; No. 2, Jan, 1991 ($2.00, 52 pgs.)

	GD 2.0	VG 4.0	FN 6.0	VF 8.0	VF/NM 9.0	NM- 9.2
1-Bolland-a(p), Bissette-a, Totleben-a(i); Alan Moore scripts (2nd printing exists, 2/88)						3.00
2-($4.95)						5.00

R.E.B.E.L.S. '95 #12 © DC

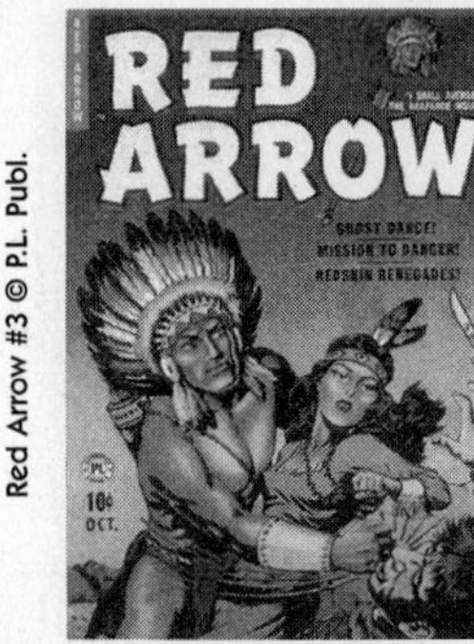

Red Arrow #3 © P.L. Publ.

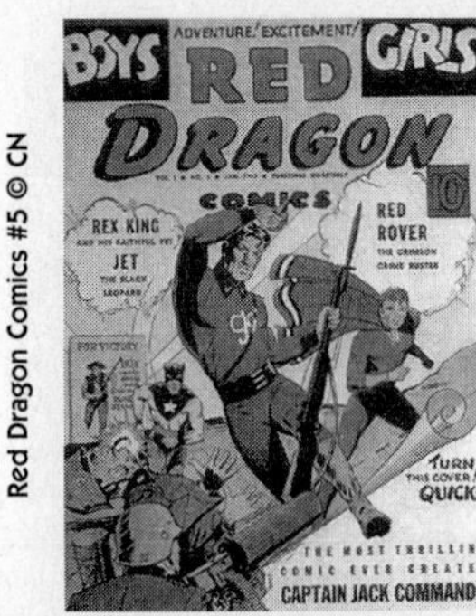

Red Dragon Comics #5 © CN

	GD	VG	FN	VF	VF/NM	NM-
	2.0	4.0	6.0	8.0	9.0	9.2

REAL WESTERN HERO (Formerly Wow #1-69; Western Hero #76 on)
Fawcett Publications: No. 70, Sept, 1948 - No. 75, Feb, 1949 (All 52 pgs.)

70(#1)-Tom Mix, Monte Hale, Hopalong Cassidy, Young Falcon begin
36 72 108 204 290 375
71-75: 71-Gabby Hayes begins. 71,72-Captain Tootsie by Beck. 75-Big Bow and Little Arrow app. 23 46 69 129 180 230
NOTE: *Painted/photo c-70-73; painted c-74, 75.*

REAL WEST ROMANCES
Crestwood Publishing Co./Prize Publ.: 4-5/49 - V1#6, 3/50; V2#1, Apr-May, 1950 (All 52 pgs. & photo-c)

V1#1-S&K-a(p) 26 52 78 147 206 265
2 13 26 39 74 100 125
3-Kirby-a(p) only 14 28 42 79 107 135
4-S&K-a; Whip Wilson, Reno Browne photo-c 20 40 60 112 156 200
5-Audie Murphy, Gale Storm photo-c; S&K-a 18 36 54 101 138 175
6-Produced by S&K, no S&K-a; Robert Preston & Cathy Downs photo-c
14 28 42 81 107 135
V2#1-Kirby-a(p) 11 22 33 63 84 105
NOTE: ***Meskin** a-V1#5, 6. **Severin/Elder** a-V1#3-6, V2#1. **Meskin** a-V1#6. **Leonard Starr** a-1-3. Photo-c V1#1-6, V2#1.*

REALWORLDS :...
DC Comics: 2000 ($5.95, one-shots, prestige format)

Batman - Marshall Rogers-a/Golden & Sniegoski-s; Justice League of America -Dematteis-s/ Barr-painted art; Superman - Vance-s/García-López & Rubenstein-a; Wonder Woman - Hanson & Neuwirth-s/Sam-a 6.00

RE-ANIMATOR IN FULL COLOR
Adventure Comics: Oct, 1991 - No. 3, 1992 ($2.95, mini-series)

1-3: Adapts horror movie. 1-Dorman painted-c 3.00

REAP THE WILD WIND (See Cinema Comics Herald)

REBEL, THE (TV)
Dell Publishing Co.: No. 1076, Feb-Apr, 1960 - No. 1262, Dec-Feb, 1961-62

Four Color 1076 (#1)-Sekowsky-a, photo-c 11 22 33 77 114 150
Four Color 1138 (9-11/60), 1207 (9-11/61), 1262-Photo-c
10 20 30 67 96 125

R.E.B.E.L.S. '94 (Becomes R.E.B.E.L.S. '95 & R.E.B.E.L.S. '96)
DC Comics: No. 0, Oct, 1994 - No. 17, Mar, 1996 ($1.95/$2.25)

0-17: 8-$2.25-c begins. 15-R.E.B.E.L.S '96 begins. 2.25

REBEL SWORD (Manga)
Dark Horse Comics: Oct, 1994 - No. 6, Feb, 1995 ($2.50, B&W)

1-6 2.50

RECORD BOOK OF FAMOUS POLICE CASES
St. John Publishing Co.: 1949 (25¢, 132 pgs.)

nn-Kubert-a(3); r/Son of Sinbad; Baker-c 39 78 117 230 325 420

RED
DC Comics (Homage): Sept, 2003 - No. 3, Feb, 2004 ($2.95, limited series)

1-3-Warren Ellis-s/Cully Hamner-a/c 3.00

RED ARROW
P. L. Publishing Co.: May-June, 1951 - No. 3, Oct, 1951

1 11 22 33 63 84 105
2,3 9 18 27 49 62 75

RED BAND COMICS
Enwil Associates: Feb, 1945 - No. 4, May, 1945

1 39 78 117 230 325 420
2-Origin Bogeyman & Santanas; c-reprint/#1 29 58 87 164 232 300
3,4-Captain Wizard app. in both (1st app.); each has identical contents/cover
27 54 81 155 218 280

REDBLADE
Dark Horse Comics: Apr, 1993 - No. 3, July, 1993 ($2.50, mini-series)

1-3: 1-Double gatefold-c 3.00

RED CIRCLE COMICS (Also see Blazing Comics & Blue Circle Comics)
Rural Home Publications (Enwil): Jan, 1945 - No. 4, April, 1945

1-The Prankster & Red Riot begin 39 78 117 230 325 420
2-Starr-a; The Judge (costumed hero) app. 30 60 90 170 240 310
3,4-Starr-c/a. 3-The Prankster not in costume 23 46 69 132 186 240
4-(Dated 4/45)-Leftover covers to #4 were later restapled over early 1950s coverless comics; variations in the coverless comics used are endless; Woman Outlaws, Dorothy Lamour, Crime Does Not Pay, Sabu, Diary Loves, Love Confessions & Young Love V3#3 known
17 34 51 95 130 165

RED CIRCLE SORCERY (Chilling Adventures in Sorcery #1-5)
Red Circle Prod. (Archie): No. 6, Apr, 1974 - No. 11, Feb, 1975 (All 25¢ iss.)

6,8,9,11: 6-Early Chaykin-a. 7-Pino-a. 8-Only app. The Cobra
1 3 4 6 8 10
7-Bruce Jones-a with Wrightson, Kaluta, Jeff Jones 2 4 6 10 12 15
10-Wood-a(i) 2 4 6 8 10 12
NOTE: ***Chaykin** a-6, 10. **McWilliams** a-10(2 & 3 pgs.). **Mooney** a-11p. **Morrow** a-6-8, 9(text illos), 10, 11i; c-6-11. **Thorne** a-8, 10. **Toth** a-8, 9.*

RED DOG (See Night Music #7)

RED DRAGON
Comico: June, 1996 ($2.95)

1-Bisley-c 3.00

RED DRAGON COMICS (1st Series) (Formerly Trail Blazers; see Super Magician V5#7, 8)
Street & Smith Publications: No. 5, Jan, 1943 - No. 9, Jan, 1944

5-Origin Red Rover, the Crimson Crimebuster; Rex King, Man of Adventure, Captain Jack Commando, & The Minute Man begin; text origin Red Dragon; Binder-c
100 200 300 625 938 1250
6-Origin The Black Crusader & Red Dragon (3/43); 1st story app. Red Dragon & 1st cover (classic-c) 224 448 672 1400 2100 2800
7-Classic-c 172 344 516 1075 1613 2150
8-The Red Knight app. 74 148 222 463 694 925
9-Origin Chuck Magnon, Immortal Man 74 148 222 463 694 925

RED DRAGON COMICS (2nd Series)(See Super Magician V2#8)
Street & Smith Publications: Nov, 1947 - No. 6, Jan, 1949; No. 7, July, 1949

1-Red Dragon begins; Elliman, Nigel app.; Edd Cartier-c/a
92 184 276 575 863 1150
2-Cartier-c 64 128 192 400 600 800
3-1st app. Dr. Neff Ghost Breaker by Powell; Elliman, Nigel app.
55 110 165 330 495 660
4-Cartier c/a 74 148 222 463 692 920
5-7 40 80 120 240 345 450
NOTE: ***Maneely** a-5, 7. **Powell** a-2-7; c-3, 5, 7.*

RED EAGLE
David McKay Publications: No. 16, Aug, 1938

Feature Books 16 18 36 54 131 191 250

REDEYE (See Comics Reading Libraries in the Promotional Comics section)

RED FOX (Formerly Manhunt! #1-14; also see Extra Comics)
Magazine Enterprises: No. 15, 1954

15(A-1 #108)-Undercover Girl story; L.B. Cole-c/a (Red Fox); r-from Manhunt; Powell-a
20 40 60 112 156 200

RED FURY
High Impact Entertainment: 1997 ($2.95, B&W)

1 3.00

RED GOOSE COMIC SELECTIONS (See Comic Selections)

RED HAWK (See A-1 Comics, Bobby Benson's ..#14-16 & Straight Arrow #2)
Magazine Enterprises: No. 90, 1953

A-1 90-Powell-c/a 13 26 39 74 120 125

RED MASK (Formerly Tim Holt; see Best Comics, Blazing Six-Guns)
Magazine Enterprises No. 42-53/Sussex No. 54 (M.E. on-c): No. 42, June-July, 1954 - No. 53, May, 1956; No. 54, Sept, 1957

42-Ghost Rider by Ayers continues, ends #50; Black Phantom continues; 3-D effect c/stories begin 22 44 66 127 176 225
43- 3-D effect-c/stories 20 40 60 112 156 200
44-52: 3-D effect stories only. 47-Last pre-code issue. 50-Last Ghost Rider. 51-The Presto Kid begins by Ayers (1st app.); Presto Kid-c begins; last 3-D effect story.
52-Origin The Presto Kid 18 36 54 101 138 175
53,54-Last Black Phantom; last Presto Kid-c 14 28 42 81 111 140
I.W. Reprint #1 (r-/#52). 2 (nd, r/#51 w/diff.-c). 3, 8 (nd; Kinstler-c); 8-r/Red Mask #52
3 6 9 18 23 28
NOTE: ***Ayers** art on Ghost Rider & Presto Kid. **Bolle** art in all (Red Mask); c-43, 44, 49. **Guardineer** a-52. Black Phantom in #42-44, 47-50, 53, 54.*

REDMASK OF THE RIO GRANDE
AC Comics: 1990 ($2.50, 28pgs.)(Has photos of movie posters)

1-Bolle-c/a(r); photo inside-c 2.50

RED MOUNTAIN FEATURING QUANTRELL'S RAIDERS (Movie)(Also see Jesse James #28)

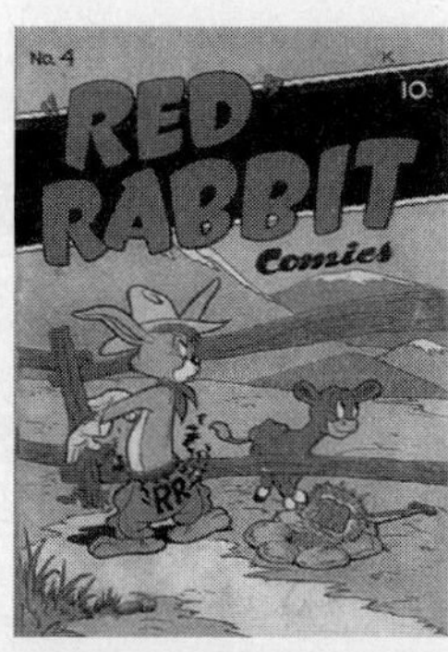

"Red" Rabbit Comics #4 © Dearfield

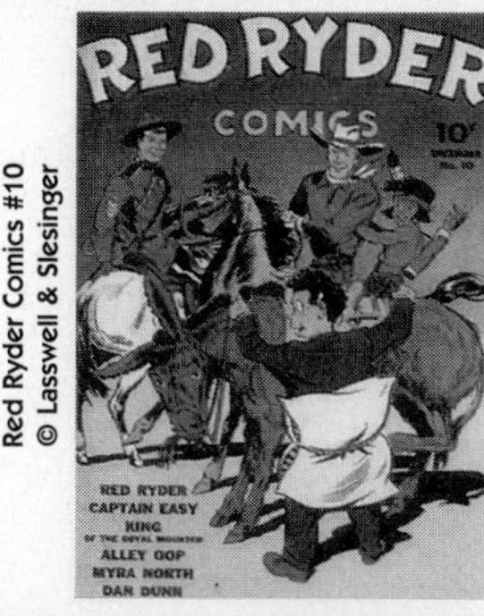

Red Ryder Comics #10 © Lasswell & Slesinger

Red Star #9 © Christian Gossett

	GD 2.0	VG 4.0	FN 6.0	VF 8.0	VF/NM 9.0	NM- 9.2
Avon Periodicals: 1952						
nn-Alan Ladd; Kinstler-c	29	58	87	164	232	300

"RED" RABBIT COMICS
Dearfield Comic/J. Charles Laue Publ. Co.: Jan, 1947 - No. 22, Aug-Sep, 1951

	GD 2.0	VG 4.0	FN 6.0	VF 8.0	VF/NM 9.0	NM- 9.2
1	14	28	42	81	111	140
2	8	16	24	46	58	70
3-10	7	14	21	37	46	55
11-17,19-22	7	14	21	35	43	50
18-Flying Saucer-c (1/51)	8	16	24	46	58	70

RED RAVEN COMICS (Human Torch #2 on)(Also see X-Men #44 & Sub-Mariner #26, 2nd series)
Timely Comics: August, 1940

	GD 2.0	VG 4.0	FN 6.0	VF 8.0	VF/NM 9.0	NM- 9.2
1-Origin & 1st app. Red Raven; Comet Pierce & Mercury by Kirby, The Human Top & The Eternal Brain; intro. Magar, the Mystic & only app.; Kirby-c (his 1st signed work)	1071	2142	3213	7973	12,487	17,000

RED ROCKET 7
Dark Horse Comics: Aug, 1997 - No. 7, June, 1998 ($3.95, square format, limited series)

	GD 2.0	VG 4.0	FN 6.0	VF 8.0	VF/NM 9.0	NM- 9.2
1-7-Mike Allred-c/s/a						4.00

RED RYDER COMICS (Hi Spot #2)(Movies, radio)(See Crackajack Funnies & Super Book of Comics)
Hawley Publ. No. 1/Dell Publishing Co.(K.K.) No. 3 on: 9/40; No. 3, 8/41 - No. 5, 12/41; No. 6, 4/42 - No. 151, 4-6/57

	GD 2.0	VG 4.0	FN 6.0	VF 8.0	VF/NM 9.0	NM- 9.2
1-Red Ryder, his horse Thunder, Little Beaver & his horse Papoose strip reprints begin by Fred Harman; 1st meeting of Red & Little Beaver; Harman line-drawn-c #1-85	300	600	900	1900	2850	3800
3-(Scarce)-Alley Oop, Capt. Easy, Dan Dunn, Freckles & His Friends, King of the Royal Mtd., Myra North strip-r begin	90	180	270	655	1003	1350
4-6: 6-1st Dell issue (4/42)	41	82	123	316	471	625
7-10	33	66	99	248	374	500
11-20	25	50	75	181	266	350
21-32-Last Alley Oop, Dan Dunn, Capt. Easy, Freckles	17	34	51	121	178	235
33-40 (52 pgs.)	12	24	36	87	129	170
41 (52 pgs.)-Rocky Lane photo back-c; photo back-c begin, end #57	13	26	39	94	137	180
42-46 (52 pgs.): 46-Last Red Ryder strip-r	10	20	30	72	104	135
47-53 (52 pgs.): 47-New stories on Red Ryder begin. 49,52-Harmon photo back-c	9	18	27	60	85	110
54-92: 54-73 (36 pgs.). 59-Harmon photo back-c. 73-Last King of the Royal Mtd; strip-r by Jim Gary. 74-85 (52 pgs.)-Harman line-drawn-c. 86-92 (52 pgs.)-Harman painted-c	7	14	21	51	71	90
93-99,101-106: 94-96 (36 pgs.)-Harman painted-c. 97,98,(36 pgs.)-Harman line-drawn-c. 99,101-106 (36 pgs.)-Jim Bannon Photo-c	6	12	18	43	59	75
100 (36 pgs.)-Bannon photo-c	7	14	21	46	63	80
107-118 (52 pgs.)-Harman line-drawn-c	6	12	18	40	55	70
119-129 (52 pgs.): 119-Painted-c begin, not by Harman, end #151	6	12	18	38	52	65
130-151 (36 pgs.): 145-Title change to Red Ryder Ranch Magazine 149-Title change to Red Ryder Ranch Comics	5	10	15	36	48	60
Four Color 916 (7/58)	5	10	15	36	48	60

NOTE: ***Fred Harman** a-1-99; c-1-98, 107-118. Don Red Barry, Allan Rocky Lane, Wild Bill Elliott & Jim Bannon starred as Red Ryder in the movies. Robert Blake starred as Little Beaver.*

RED RYDER PAINT BOOK
Whitman Publishing Co.: 1941 (8-1/2x11-1/2", 148 pgs.)

	GD 2.0	VG 4.0	FN 6.0	VF 8.0	VF/NM 9.0	NM- 9.2
nn-Reprints 1940 daily strips	78	156	234	488	732	975

RED SEAL COMICS (Formerly Carnival Comics, and/or Spotlight Comics?)
Harry 'A' Chesler/Superior Publ. No. 19 on: No. 14, 10/45 - No. 18, 10/46; No. 19, 6/47 - No. 22, 12/47

	GD 2.0	VG 4.0	FN 6.0	VF 8.0	VF/NM 9.0	NM- 9.2
14-The Black Dwarf begins (continued from Spotlight?); Little Nemo app; bondage/hypo-c; Tuska-a	74	148	222	463	694	925
15-Torture story; funny-c	48	96	144	288	432	575
16-Used in **SOTI**, pg. 181, illo "Outside the forbidden pages of de Sade, you find draining a girl's blood only in children's comics;" drug club story r-later in Crime Reporter #1; Veiled Avenger & Barry Kuda app; Tuska-a; funny-c	63	126	189	394	592	790
17,18,20: Lady Satan, Yankee Girl & Sky Chief app; 17-Tuska-a	48	96	144	288	432	575
19-No Black Dwarf (on-c only); Zor, El Tigre app.	43	86	129	258	389	520
21-Lady Satan & Black Dwarf app.	38	76	114	219	310	400
22-Zor, Rocketman app. (68 pgs.)	38	76	114	219	310	400

REDSKIN (Thrilling Indian Stories)(Famous Western Badmen #13 on)

	GD 2.0	VG 4.0	FN 6.0	VF 8.0	VF/NM 9.0	NM- 9.2
Youthful Magazines: Sept, 1950 - No. 12, Oct, 1952						
1-Walter Johnson-a (7 pgs.)	18	36	54	101	138	175
2	11	22	33	63	84	105
3-12: 3-Daniel Boone story. 6-Geronimo story	10	20	30	56	73	90

NOTE: ***Walter Johnson** c-3, 4. **Palais** a-11. **Wildey** a-5, 11. Bondage c-6, 12.*

RED SONJA (Also see Conan #23, Kull & The Barbarians, Marvel Feature & Savage Sword Of Conan #1)
Marvel Comics Group: 1/77 - No. 15, 5/79; V1#1, 2/83 - V2#2, 3/83; V3#1, 8/83 - V3#4, 2/84; V3#5, 1/85 - V3#13, 5/86

	GD 2.0	VG 4.0	FN 6.0	VF 8.0	VF/NM 9.0	NM- 9.2
1-Created by Robert E. Howard	2	4	6	9	11	14
2-10: 5-Last 30¢ issue	1	2	3	4	5	7
4,5-(35¢-c variants, limited distribution)(7,9/77)	1	2	3	6	8	10
11-15, V1#1,V2#2: 14-Last 35¢ issue						6.00
V3#1-13: #1-4 ($1.00, 52 pgs.)						3.50

NOTE: ***Brunner** c-12-14. **J. Buscema** a(p)-12, 13, 15; c-V#1. **Nebres** a-V3#3i(part). **N. Redondo** a-8i, V3#2i, 3i. **Simonson** a-V3#1. **Thorne** c/a-1-11.*

RED SONJA: SCAVENGER HUNT
Marvel Comics: Dec, 1995 ($2.95, one-shot)

	GD 2.0	VG 4.0	FN 6.0	VF 8.0	VF/NM 9.0	NM- 9.2
1						3.00

RED SONJA: THE MOVIE
Marvel Comics Group: Nov, 1985 - No. 2, Dec, 1985 (Limited series)

	GD 2.0	VG 4.0	FN 6.0	VF 8.0	VF/NM 9.0	NM- 9.2
1,2-Movie adapt-r/Marvel Super Spec. #38						3.00

RED STAR, THE
Image Comics/Archangel Studios: June, 2000 - No. 9, June, 2002 ($2.95)

	GD 2.0	VG 4.0	FN 6.0	VF 8.0	VF/NM 9.0	NM- 9.2
1-Christian Gossett-s/a(p)						4.00
2-9: 9-Beck-c						3.00
#(7.5) Reprints Wizard #1/2 story with new pages						3.00
Annual 1 (Archangel Studios, 11/02, $3.50) "Run Makita Run"						3.50
TPB (4/01, $24.95, 9x12") Oversized r/#1-4; intro. by Bendis						25.00
Nokgorka TPB (8/02, $24.95, 9x12") Oversized r/#6-9; w/sketch pages						25.00
Wizard 1/2 (mail order)						10.00

RED STAR, THE (Volume 2)
CrossGen Comics #1,2/Archangel Studios #3 on: Feb, 2003 - Present ($2.95/$2.99)

	GD 2.0	VG 4.0	FN 6.0	VF 8.0	VF/NM 9.0	NM- 9.2
1-3-Christian Gossett-s/a(p)						3.00

RED TORNADO (See All-American #20 & Justice League of America #64)
DC Comics: July, 1985 - No. 4, Oct, 1985 (Limited series)

	GD 2.0	VG 4.0	FN 6.0	VF 8.0	VF/NM 9.0	NM- 9.2
1-4: Kurt Busiek scripts in all. 1-3-Superman & Batman cameos						3.00

RED WARRIOR
Marvel/Atlas Comics (TCI): Jan, 1951 - No. 6, Dec, 1951

	GD 2.0	VG 4.0	FN 6.0	VF 8.0	VF/NM 9.0	NM- 9.2
1-Red Warrior & his horse White Wing; Tuska-a	17	34	51	98	134	170
2-Tuska-c	10	20	30	56	73	90
3-6: 4-Origin White Wing. 6-Maneely-c	9	18	27	49	62	75

RED WOLF (See Avengers #80 & Marvel Spotlight #1)
Marvel Comics Group: May, 1972 - No. 9, Sept, 1973

	GD 2.0	VG 4.0	FN 6.0	VF 8.0	VF/NM 9.0	NM- 9.2
1-(Western hero); Gil Kane/Severin-c; Shores-a	3	6	9	16	20	25
2-9: 2-Kane-c; Shores-a. 6-Tuska-r in back-up. 7-Red Wolf as super hero begins. 9-Origin sidekick, Lobo (wolf)	2	4	6	10	12	15

REESE'S PIECES
Eclipse Comics: Oct, 1985 - No.2, Oct, 1985 ($1.75, Baxter paper)

	GD 2.0	VG 4.0	FN 6.0	VF 8.0	VF/NM 9.0	NM- 9.2
1,2-B&W-r in color						2.25

REFORM SCHOOL GIRL!
Realistic Comics: 1951

	GD 2.0	VG 4.0	FN 6.0	VF 8.0	VF/NM 9.0	NM- 9.2
nn-Used in **SOTI**, pg. 358, & cover ill. with caption "Comic books are supposed to be like fairy tales"	152	304	456	950	1425	1900

(Prices vary widely on this book)

NOTE: *The cover and title originated from a digest-sized book published by Diversey Publishing Co. of Chicago in 1948. The original book "House of Fury", Doubleday, came out in 1941. The girl's real name which appears on the cover of the digest and comic is Marty Collins, Canadian model and ice skating star who posed for this special color photograph for the Diversey novel.*

REGENTS ILLUSTRATED CLASSICS
Prentice Hall Regents, Englewood Cliffs, NJ 07632: 1981 (Plus more recent reprintings) (48 pgs., B&W-a with 14 pgs. of teaching helps)

NOTE: *This series contains Classics Ill. art, and was produced from the same illegal source as **Cassette Books**. But when Twin Circle sued to stop the sale of the Cassette Books, they decided to permit this series to continue. This series was produced as a teaching aid. The 20 title series is divided into four levels based upon number of basic words used therein. There is also a teacher's manual for each level. All of the titles are still available from the publisher for about $5 each retail. The number to call for mail order purchases is (201)767-5937. Almost all of the issues have new covers taken from some interior art panel. Here is a list of the series by Regents ident. no. and the Classics Ill. counterpart.*

Reign of the Zodiac #1 © Keith Giffen & DC

The Ren & Stimpy Show #35 © Nickelodeon

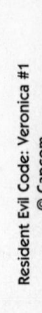

Resident Evil Code: Veronica #1 © Capcom

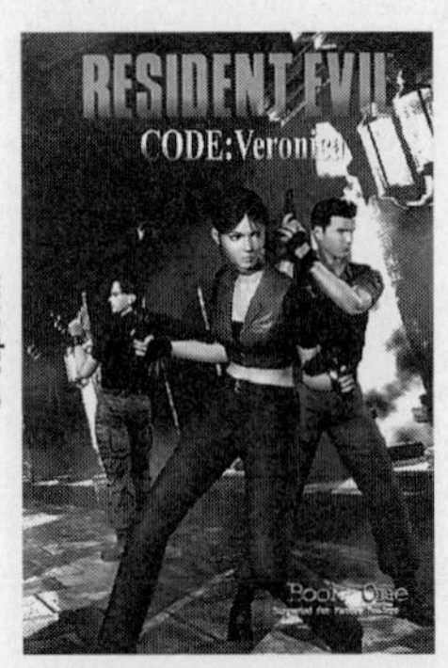

GD VG FN VF VF/NM NM-
2.0 4.0 6.0 8.0 9.0 9.2

GD VG FN VF VF/NM NM-
2.0 4.0 6.0 8.0 9.0 9.2

16770(CI#24-A2)18333(CI#3-A2)21668(CI#13-A2)32224(CI#21)33051(CI#26)35788(CI#84)37153(CI#16)44460(CI#19-A2)44808(CI#18-A2)52395(CI#4-A2)58627(CI#5-A2)60067(CI#30)68405(CI#23A1)70302(CI#29)78192(CI#7-A2)78193(CI#10-A2)79679(CI#85)92046(CI#1-A2)93062(CI#64)93512(CI#25)

RE: GEX
Awesome-Hyperwerks: Jul, 1998 - No. 0, Dec, 1998; ($2.50)

Preview (7/98) Wizard Con Edition 3.00
0-(12/98) Loeb-s/Liefeld-a/Pat Lee-c, 1-(9/98) Loeb-s/Liefeld-a/c 2.50

REGGIE (Formerly Archie's Rival...; Reggie & Me #19 on)
Archie Publications: No. 15, Sept, 1963 - No. 18, Nov, 1965

15(9/63), 16(10/64), 17(8/65), 18(11/65) 5 10 15 33 44 55
NOTE: *Cover title No. 15 & 16 is Archie's Rival Reggie.*

REGGIE AND ME (Formerly Reggie)
Archie Publ.: No. 19, Aug, 1966 - No. 126, Sept, 1980 (No. 50-68: 52 pgs.)

19-Evilheart app. 4 8 12 24 32 40
20-23-Evilheart app.; with Pureheart #22 3 6 9 18 24 30
24-40(3/70) 2 4 6 12 16 20
41-49(7/71) 2 4 6 10 12 15
50(9/71)-68 (1/74, 52 pgs.) 2 4 6 12 16 20
69-99 1 2 3 5 7 9
100(10/77) 2 4 6 8 10 12
101-126 1 2 3 4 5 7

REGGIE'S JOKES (See Reggie's Wise Guy Jokes)

REGGIE'S REVENGE!
Archie Comic Publications, Inc.: Spring, 1994 - No. 3 ($2.00, 52 pgs.) (Published semi-annually)

1-Bound-in pull-out poster 3.00
2,3 2.25

REGGIE'S WISE GUY JOKES
Archie Publications: Aug, 1968 - No. 60, Jan, 1982 (#5-28 are Giants)

1 5 10 15 33 44 55
2-4 3 6 9 18 20 24
5-16 (1/71)(68 pg. Giants) 3 6 9 18 24 30
17-28 (52 pg. Giants) 2 4 6 12 16 20
29-40(1/77) 1 2 3 5 7 9
41-60 5.00

REGISTERED NURSE
Charlton Comics: Summer, 1963

1-r/Nurse Betsy Crane & Cynthia Doyle 3 6 9 18 23 28

REG'LAR FELLERS
Visual Editions (Standard): No. 5, Nov, 1947 - No. 6, Mar, 1948

5,6 9 18 27 49 62 75

REG'LAR FELLERS HEROIC (See Heroic Comics)

REGULATORS
Image Comics: June, 1995 - No. 3, Aug, 1995 ($2.50)

1-3: Kurt Busiek scripts 2.50

REID FLEMING, WORLD'S TOUGHEST MILKMAN
Eclipse Comics/ Deep Sea Comics: 8/86; V2#1, 12/86 - V2#3, 12/88; V2#4, 11/89; V2#5, 11/90 (B&W)

1 (3rd print, large size, 8/86, $2.50), 1-4th & 5th printings ($2.50) 3.00
V2#1 (10/86, regular size, $2.00), 1-2nd print, 3rd print ($2.00, 2/89) 2.25
2-8 , V2#2-2nd & 3rd printings, V2#4-2nd printing, V2#5 ($2.00) 2.25

REIGN OF THE ZODIAC
DC Comics: Oct, 2003 - Present ($2.75)

1-5-Giffen-s/Doran-a/Harris-c 2.75

RELATIVE HEROES
DC Comics: Mar, 2000 - No. 6, Aug, 2000 ($2.50, limited series)

1-6-Grayson-s/Guichet & Sowd-a. 6-Superman-c/app. 2.50

RELOAD
DC Comics (Homage): May, 2003 - No. 3, Sept, 2003 ($2.95, limited series)

1-3-Warren Ellis-s/Paul Gulacy & Jimmy Palmiotti-a 3.00

RELUCTANT DRAGON, THE (Walt Disney's...)
Dell Publishing Co.: No. 13, 1940

Four Color 13-Contains 2 pgs. of photos from film; 2 pg. foreword to Fantasia by Leopold Stokowski; Donald Duck, Goofy, Baby Weems & Mickey Mouse (as the Sorcerer's Apprentice) app. 160 320 480 1156 1766 2375

REMARKABLE WORLDS OF PROFESSOR PHINEAS B. FUDDLE, THE
DC Comics (Paradox Press): 2000 - No. 4, 2000 ($5.95, limited series)

1-4-Boaz Yakin-s/Erez Yakin-a 6.00
TPB (2001, $19.95) r/series 20.00

REMEMBER PEARL HARBOR
Street & Smith Publications: 1942 (68 pgs.) (Illustrated story of the battle)

nn-Uncle Sam-c; Jack Binder-a 46 92 138 276 413 550

REN & STIMPY SHOW, THE (TV) (Nicklodeon cartoon characters)
Marvel Comics: Dec, 1992 - No. 44, July, 1996 ($1.75/$1.95)

1-($2.25)-Polybagged w/scratch & sniff Ren or Stimpy air fowler (equal numbers of each were made) 6.00
1-2nd & 3rd printing; different dialogue on-c 2.25
2-6: 4-Muddy Mudskipper back-up. 5-Bill Wray painted-c. 6-Spider-Man vs. Powdered Toast Man 4.00
7-17: 12-1st solo back-up story w/Tank & Brenner 2.50
18-44: 18-Powered Toast Man app. 2.50
25 ($2.95) Deluxe edition w/die cut cover 3.00
...Don't Try This at Home (3/94, $12.95, TPB)-r/#9-12 13.00
...Eenteractive Special ('95, $2.95) 3.00
...Holiday Special 1994 (2/95, $2.95, 52 pgs.) 3.00
...Mini Comic (1995) 5.00
...Pick of the Litter nn (1993, $12.95, TPB)-r/#1-4 13.00
...Radio Daze (11/95, $1.95) 2.50
...Running Joke nn (1993, $12.95, TPB)-r/#1-4 plus new-a 13.00
...Seeck Little Monkeys (1/95, $12.95)-r/#17-20 13.00
...Special 2 (7/94, $2.95, 52 pgs.), ...Special 3 (10/94, $2.95, 52 pgs.)-Choose adventure, ...Special: Around the World in a Daze ($2.95), ...Special: Four Swerks (1/95, $2.95, 52 pgs.)-FF #1 cover swipe; cover reads "Four Swerks w/5 pg. coloring book.", ...Special: Powdered Toast Man 1 (4/94, $2.95, 52 pgs.), ...Special: Powdered Toast Man's Cereal Serial (4/95, $2.95), ...Special: Sports (10/95, $2.95) 3.00
...Tastes Like Chicken nn (11/93,$12.95,TPB)-r/#5-8 13.00
...Your Pals (1994, $12.95, TPB)-r/#13-16 13.00

RENFIELD
Caliber Press:1994 - No. 3, 1995 ($2.95, B&W, limited series)

1-3 3.00

RENO BROWNE, HOLLYWOOD'S GREATEST COWGIRL (Formerly Margie Comics; Apache Kid #53 on; also see Western Hearts, Western Life Romances & Western Love)
Marvel Comics (MPC): No. 50, April, 1950 - No. 52, Sept, 1950 (52 pgs.)

50-Reno Browne photo-c on all 34 68 102 193 274 355
51,52 29 58 87 164 232 300

REPLACEMENT GOD
Amaze Ink: June, 1995 - No. 8 ($2.95, B&W)

1-8-Zander Cannon-s/a 3.00

REPLACEMENT GOD
Image Comics: May, 1997 - No. 5 ($2.95, B&W)

1-5: 1-Flip book w/"Knute's Escapes", r/original series. 2-Flip book w/"Harris Thermidor". 3-5: 3-Flip book w/"Myth and Legend" 3.00

REPTILICUS (Becomes Reptisaurus #3 on)
Charlton Comics: Aug, 1961 - No. 2, Oct, 1961

1 (Movie) 20 40 60 145 213 280
2 10 20 30 73 107 140

REPTISAURUS (Reptilicus #1,2)
Charlton Comics: V2#3, Jan, 1962 - No. 8, Dec, 1962; Summer, 1963

V2#3-8: 8-Montes/Bache-c/a 7 14 21 51 71 90
Special Edition 1 (Summer, 1963) 7 14 21 50 68 85

REQUIEM FOR DRACULA
Marvel Comics: Feb, 1993 ($2.00, 52 pgs.)

nn-r/Tomb of Dracula #69,70 by Gene Colan 2.25

RESCUERS, THE (See Walt Disney Showcase #40)

RESIDENT EVIL (Based on video game)
Image Comics (WildStorm): Mar, 1998 - No. 5 ($4.95, quarterly magazine)

1 7.00
2-5 5.00
...Code: Veronica 1-4 (2002, $14.95) English reprint of Japanese comics 15.00
...Collection One ('99, $14.95, TPB) r/#1-4 15.00

RESIDENT EVIL: FIRE AND ICE
DC Comics (WildStorm): Dec, 2000 - No. 4, May, 2001 ($2.50, limited series)

The Resistance #1 © WSP

Resurrection Man #16 © DC

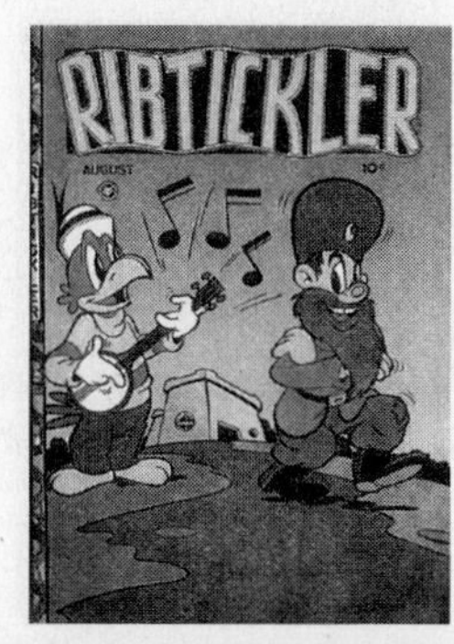

Ribtickler #9 © FOX

	GD 2.0	VG 4.0	FN 6.0	VF 8.0	VF/NM 9.0	NM- 9.2

1-4-Bermejo-c 2.50

RESISTANCE, THE
DC Comics (WildStorm): Nov, 2002 - No. 8, June, 2003 ($2.95)
1-8-Palmiotti & Gray-s/Santacruz-a 3.00

RESTAURANT AT THE END OF THE UNIVERSE, THE (See Hitchhiker's Guide to the Galaxy & Life, the Universe & Everything)
DC Comics: 1994 - No. 3, 1994 ($6.95, limited series)
1-3 7.00

RESTLESS GUN (TV)
Dell Publishing Co.: No. 934, Sept, 1958 - No. 1146, Nov-Jan, 1960-61
Four Color 934 (#1)-Photo-c 12 24 36 87 129 170
Four Color 986 (5/59), 1045 (11-1/60), 1089 (3/60), 1146-Wildey-a; all photo-c 9 18 27 63 89 115

RESURRECTION MAN
DC Comics: May, 1997 - No. 27, Aug, 1999 ($2.50)
1-Lenticular disc on cover 5.00
2-5: 2-JLA app. 4.00
6-10: 6-Genesis-x-over. 7-Batman app. 10-Hitman-c/app. 3.00
11-27: 16,17-Supergirl x-over. 18-Deadman & Phantom Stranger-c/app. 21-JLA-c/app. 2.50
#1,000,000 (11/98) 853rd Century x-over 2.50

RETIEF (Keith Laumer's)
Adventure Comics (Malibu): Dec, 1989 - Vol. 2, No.6, ($2.25, B&W)
1-6,Vol. 2, #1-6,Vol. 3 (...of The CDT) #1-6 2.50
...and The Warlords #1-6, ...: Diplomatic Immunity #1 (4/91), ...: Giant Killer #1 (9/91), ...: Crime & Punishment #1 (11/91) 2.50

RETURN FROM WITCH MOUNTAIN (See Walt Disney Showcase #44)

RETURN OF ALISON DARE: LITTLE MISS ADVENTURES, THE (Also see Alison Dare: Little Miss Adventures)
Oni Press: Apr, 2001 - No. 3, Sept, 2001 ($2.95, B&W, limited series)
1-3-J. Torres-s/J.Bone-c/a 3.00

RETURN OF GORGO, THE (Formerly Gorgo's Revenge)
Charlton Comics: No. 2, Aug, 1963; No. 3, Fall, 1964 (12¢)
2,3-Ditko-c/a; based on M.G.M. movie 8 16 24 58 82 105

RETURN OF KONGA, THE (Konga's Revenge #2 on)
Charlton Comics: 1962
nn 8 16 24 53 74 95

RETURN OF MEGATON MAN
Kitchen Sink Press: July, 1988 - No. 3, 1988 ($2.00, limited series)
1-3: Simpson-c/a 2.25

RETURN OF THE OUTLAW
Toby Press (Minoan): Feb, 1953 - No. 11, 1955
1-Billy the Kid 10 20 30 56 73 90
2 7 14 21 35 43 50
3-11 6 12 18 31 38 45

RETURN TO JURASSIC PARK
Topps Comics: Apr, 1995 - No. 9, Feb, 1996 ($2.50/$2.95)
1-9: 3-Begin $2.95-c. 9-Artist's Jam issue 3.00

RETURN TO THE AMALGAM AGE OF COMICS: THE MARVEL COMICS COLLECTION
Marvel Comics: 1997 ($12.95, TPB)
nn-Reprints Amalgam one-shots: Challengers of the Fantastic #1, The Exciting X-Patrol #1, Iron Lantern #1, The Magnetic Men Featuring Magneto #1, Spider-Boy Team-Up #1 & Thorion of the New Asgods #1 13.00

REVEAL
Dark Horse Comics: Nov, 2002 ($6.95, squarebound)
1-Short stories of Dark Horse characters by various; Lone Wolf 2100, Buffy, Spyboy app. 7.00

REVEALING LOVE STORIES (See Fox Giants)

REVEALING ROMANCES
Ace Magazines: Sept, 1949 - No. 6, Aug, 1950
1 12 24 36 71 96 120
2 8 16 24 40 50 60
3-6 7 14 21 35 43 50

REVENGE OF THE PROWLER (Also see The Prowler)
Eclipse Comics: Feb, 1988 - No. 4, June, 1988 ($1.75/$1.95)
1,3,4: 1-$1.75. 3,4-$1.95-c; Snyder III-a(p) 2.25

2 ($2.50)-Contains flexi-disc 2.50

REVENGERS FEATURING MEGALITH
Continuity Comics: Apr, 1985; 1987 - No. 6, 1989 ($2.00, Baxter paper)
1 (1985)-Origin; Neal Adams-c/a, scripts, 1-6 ('87-'89, newsstand) 2.25

REX ALLEN COMICS (Movie star)(Also see Four Color #877 & Western Roundup under Dell Giants)
Dell Publ. Co.: No. 316, Feb, 1951 - No. 31, Dec-Feb, 1958-59 (All-photo-c)
Four Color 316(#1)(52 pgs.)-Rex Allen & his horse Koko begin; Marsh-a 16 32 48 113 167 220
2 (9-11/51, 36 pgs.) 10 20 30 67 96 125
3-10 8 16 24 53 74 95
11-20 6 12 18 43 59 75
21-23,25-31 6 12 18 40 55 70
24-Toth-a 7 14 21 46 63 80
NOTE: *Manning a-20, 27-30. Photo back-c F.C. #316, 2-12, 20, 21.*

REX DEXTER OF MARS (See Mystery Men Comics)
Fox Features Syndicate: Fall, 1940 (68 pgs.)
1-Rex Dexter, Patty O'Day, & Zanzibar (Tuska-a) app.; Briefer-c/a 192 384 576 1200 1800 2400

REX HART (Formerly Blaze Carson; Whip Wilson #9 on)
Timely/Marvel Comics (USA): No. 6, Aug, 1949 - No. 8, Feb, 1950 (All photo-c)
6-Rex Hart & his horse Warrior begin; Black Rider app; Captain Tootsie by Beck 28 56 84 159 225 290
7,8: 18 pg. Thriller in each. 8-Blaze the Wonder Collie app. in text 19 38 57 106 146 185

REX MORGAN, M.D. (Also see Harvey Comics Library)
Argo Publ.: Dec, 1955 - No. 3, Apr?, 1956
1-r/Rex Morgan daily newspaper strips & daily panel-r of "These Women" by D'Alessio & "Timeout" by Jeff Keate 14 28 42 79 107 135
2,3 10 20 30 56 73 90

REX MUNDI (Latin for "King of the World")
Image Comics: No. 0, Aug, 2002 - Present ($2.95)
0-7-Arvid Nelson-s/Eric Johnson-a 3.00

REX THE WONDER DOG (See The Adventures of...)

RHUBARB, THE MILLIONAIRE CAT
Dell Publishing Co.: No. 423, Sept-Oct, 1952 - No. 563, June, 1954
Four Color 423 (#1) 6 12 18 40 55 70
Four Color 466(5/53),563 5 10 15 36 48 60

RIB
Dilemma Productions: Oct, 1995 - April, 1996 ($1.95, B&W)
Ashcan, 1 3.00

RIB
Bookmark Productions: 1996 ($2.95, B&W)
1-Sakai-c; Andrew Ford-s/a 3.00

RIB
Caliber Comics: May, 1997 - No. 5, 1998 ($2.95, B&W)
1-5: 1-"Beginnings" pts. 1 & 2 3.00

RIBIT! (Red Sonja imitation)
Comico: Jan, 1989 - No. 4, April?, 1989 ($1.95, limited series)
1-4: Frank Thorne-c/a/scripts 3.00

RIBTICKLER (Also see Fox Giants)
Fox Feature Synd./Green Publ. (1957)/Norlen (1959): 1945 - No. 9, Aug, 1947; 1957; 1959
1-Funny animal 16 32 48 92 126 160
2-(1946) 9 18 27 52 66 80
3-9: 3,7-Cosmo Cat app. 8 16 24 43 54 65
3,7,8 (Green Publ.-1957), 3,7,8 (Norlen Mag.-1959) 3 6 9 18 24 30

RICHARD DRAGON, KUNG-FU FIGHTER (See The Batman Chronicles #5, Brave & the Bold, & The Question)
National Periodical Publ./DC Comics: Apr-May, 1975 - No. 18, Nov-Dec, 1977
1-Intro Richard Dragon, Ben Stanley & O-Sensei; 1st app. Barney Ling; adaptation of Jim Dennis novel "Dragon's Fists" begins, ends #4 2 4 6 10 13 16
2,3: 2-Intro Carolyn Woosan; Starlin/Weiss-c/a; bondage-c. 3-Kirby-a(p); Giordano bondage-c 1 3 4 6 8 10
4-8-Wood inks. 4-Carolyn Woosan dies. 5-1st app. Lady Shiva 1 2 3 4 5 7

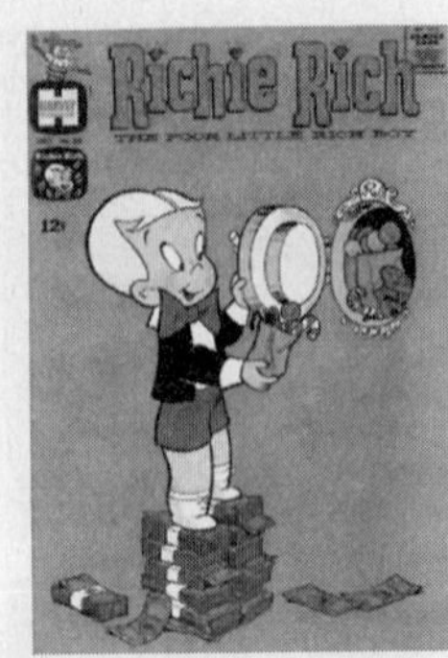

Richie Rich #35 © HARV

Richie Rich and Cadbury #16 © HARV

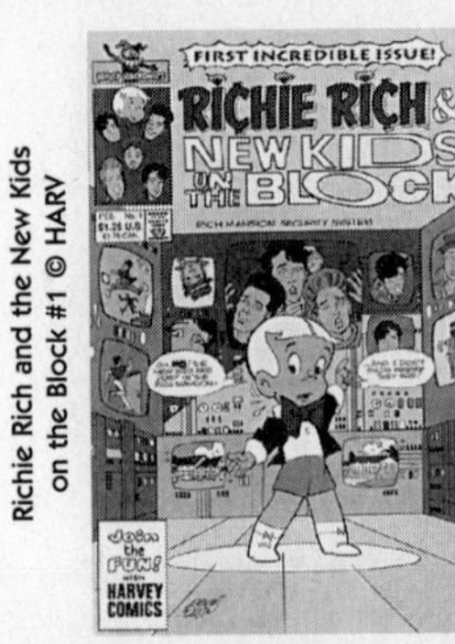

Richie Rich and the New Kids on the Block #1 © HARV

GD 2.0 VG 4.0 FN 6.0 VF 8.0 VF/NM 9.0 NM- 9.2

9-13,15-18: 9-Ben Stanley becomes Ben Turner; intro Preying Mantis. 16-1st app. Prof Ojo.
18-1st app. Ben Turner as The Bronze Tiger 1 2 3 4 5 7
14-"Spirit of Bruce Lee" 2 4 6 10 12 15
NOTE: ***Buckler** a-14. c-15, 18. **Chua** c-13. **Estrada** a-9, 13-18. **Estrada/Abel** a-10-12. **Estrada/Wood** a-4-8. **Giordano** c-1, 3-11. **Weiss** a-2(partial) c-2i.*

RICHARD THE LION-HEARTED (See Ideal a Classical Comic)

RICHIE RICH (See Harvey Collectors Comics, Harvey Hits, Little Dot, Little Lotta, Little Sad Sack, Million Dollar Digest, Mutt & Jeff, Super Richie, and 3-D Dolly)

RICHIE RICH (...the Poor Little Rich Boy) (See Harvey Hits #3, 9)
Harvey Publ.: Nov, 1960 - #218, Oct, 1982; #219, Oct, 1986 - #254, Jan, 1991

1-(See Little Dot #1 for 1st app.) 150 300 450 1216 1858 2500
2 51 102 153 434 667 900
3-5 33 66 99 248 374 500
6-10: 8-Christmas-c 22 44 66 156 228 300
11-20 14 28 42 99 145 190
21-30 10 20 30 70 100 130
31-40 9 18 27 60 85 110
41-50: 42(10/67)-Flying saucer-c 7 14 21 50 68 85
51-55,57-60: 59-Buck, prototype of Dollar the Dog 6 12 18 38 52 65
56-1st app. Super Richie 7 14 21 46 63 80
61-64,66-80: 71-Nixon & Robert Kennedy caricatures 4 8 12 27 36 45
65-1st app. Dollar the Dog 6 12 18 43 59 75
81-99 3 6 9 18 24 30
100(12/70)-1st app. Irona the robot maid 4 8 12 22 30 38
101-111,117-120 2 4 6 14 18 22
112-116: All 52 pg. Giants 3 6 9 16 20 25
121-140: 137-1st app. Mr. Cheepers 2 4 6 10 12 15
141-160: 145-Infinity-c. 155-3rd app. The Money Monster
2 4 6 8 10 12
161-180 1 3 4 6 8 10
181-199 1 2 3 5 6 8
200 1 3 4 6 8 10
201-218: 210-Stone-Age Riches app 1 2 3 4 5 7
219-254: 237-Last original material 6.00

RICHIE RICH
Harvey Comics: Mar, 1991 - No. 28, Nov, 1994 ($1.00, bi-monthly)

1-28: Reprints best of Richie Rich 2.50
Giant Size 1-4 (10/91-10/93, $2.25, 68 pgs.) 3.00

RICHIE RICH ADVENTURE DIGEST MAGAZINE
Harvey Comics: 1992 - No. 7, Sept, 1994 ($1.25, quarterly, digest-size)

1-7 4.00

RICHIE RICH AND...
Harvey Comics: Oct, 1987 - No. 11, May, 1990 ($1.00)

1-Professor Keenbean 4.00
2-11: 2-Casper. 3-Dollar the Dog. 4-Cadbury. 5 Mayda Munny. 6-Irona. 7-Little Dot. 8-Professor Keenbean. 9-Little Audrey. 10-Mayda Munny. 11-Cadbury 3.00

RICHIE RICH AND BILLY BELLHOPS
Harvey Publications: Oct, 1977 (52 pgs., one-shot)

1 2 4 6 10 12 15

RICHIE RICH AND CADBURY
Harvey Publ.: 10/77; #2, 9/78 - #23, 7/82; #24, 7/90 - #29, 1/91 (1-10: 52pgs.)

1-(52 pg. Giant) 2 4 6 12 16 20
2-10-(52 pg. Giant) 2 4 6 8 10 12
11-23 6.00
24-29: 24-Begin $1.00-c 4.00

RICHIE RICH AND CASPER
Harvey Publications: Aug, 1974 - No. 45, Sept, 1982

1 4 8 12 24 32 40
2-5 2 4 6 14 18 22
6-10: 10-Xmas-c 2 4 6 10 13 16
11-20 1 3 4 6 8 10
21-45: 22-Xmas-c 6.00

RICHIE RICH AND DOLLAR THE DOG (See Richie Rich #65)
Harvey Publications: Sept, 1977 - No. 24, Aug, 1982 (#1-10: 52 pgs.)

1-(52 pg. Giant) 2 4 6 12 16 20
2-10-(52 pg. Giant) 2 4 6 8 10 12
11-24 6.00

RICHIE RICH AND DOT
Harvey Publications: Oct, 1974 (one-shot)

GD 2.0 VG 4.0 FN 6.0 VF 8.0 VF/NM 9.0 NM- 9.2

1 3 6 9 18 23 28

RICHIE RICH AND GLORIA
Harvey Publications: Sept, 1977 - No. 25, Sept, 1982 (#1-11: 52 pgs.)

1-(52 pg. Giant) 2 4 6 12 16 20
2-11-(52 pg. Giant) 2 4 6 8 10 12
12-25 6.00

RICHIE RICH AND HIS GIRLFRIENDS
Harvey Publications: April, 1979 - No. 16, Dec, 1982

1-(52 pg. Giant) 2 4 6 10 13 16
2-(52 pg. Giant) 1 3 4 6 8 10
3-10 1 2 3 5 6 8
11-16 6.00

RICHIE RICH AND HIS MEAN COUSIN REGGIE
Harvey Publications: April, 1979 - No. 3, 1980 (50¢) (#1,2: 52 pgs.)

1 2 4 6 10 13 16
2-3: 1 3 4 6 8 10
NOTE: *No. 4 was advertised, but never released.*

RICHIE RICH AND JACKIE JOKERS (Also see Jackie Jokers)
Harvey Publications: Nov, 1973 - No. 48, Dec, 1982

1: 52 pg. Giant; contains material from unpublished Jackie Jokers #5
4 8 12 29 40 50
2,3-(52 pg. Giants). 2-R.R. & Jackie 1st meet 3 6 9 18 23 28
4,5 2 4 6 14 18 22
6-10 2 4 6 10 13 16
11-20,26: 11-1st app. Kool Katz. 26-Star Wars parody 1 3 4 6 8 10
21-25,27-40 1 2 3 4 5 7
41-48 6.00

RICHIE RICH AND PROFESSOR KEENBEAN
Harvey Comics: Sept, 1990 - No. 2, Nov, 1990 ($1.00)

1,2 3.00

RICHIE RICH AND THE NEW KIDS ON THE BLOCK
Harvey Publications: Feb, 1991 - No. 3, June, 1991 ($1.25, bi-monthly)

1-3: 1,2-New Richie Rich stories 3.00

RICHIE RICH AND TIMMY TIME
Harvey Publications: Sept, 1977 (50¢, 52 pgs, one-shot)

1 2 4 6 10 12 15

RICHIE RICH BANK BOOKS
Harvey Publications: Oct, 1972 - No. 59, Sept, 1982

1 5 10 15 36 48 60
2-5: 2-2nd app. The Money Monster 3 6 9 18 24 30
6-10 2 4 6 12 16 20
11-20: 18-Super Richie app. 2 4 6 8 10 12
21-30 1 2 3 5 7 9
31-40 1 2 3 4 5 7
41-59 6.00

RICHIE RICH BEST OF THE YEARS
Harvey Publications: Oct, 1977 - No. 6, June, 1980 (128 pgs., digest-size)

1(10/77)-Reprints 2 4 6 10 12 15
2-6(11/79-6/80, 95¢). #2(10/78)-Rep.. #3(6/79, 75¢) 1 2 3 5 7 9

RICHIE RICH BIG BOOK
Harvey Publications: Nov, 1992 - No. 2, May, 1993 ($1.50, 52 pgs.)

1,2 3.00

RICHIE RICH BIG BUCKS
Harvey Publications: Apr, 1991 - No. 8, July, 1992 ($1.00, bi-monthly)

1-8 3.00

RICHIE RICH BILLIONS
Harvey Publications: Oct, 1974 - No. 48, Oct, 1982 (#1-33: 52 pgs.)

1 4 8 12 27 36 45
2-5 3 6 9 16 20 25
6-10 2 4 6 11 14 18
11-20 2 4 6 8 10 12
21-33 1 2 3 5 6 8
34-48: 35-Onion app. 6.00

RICHIE RICH CASH
Harvey Publications: Sept, 1974 - No. 47, Aug, 1982

1-1st app. Dr. N-R-Gee 4 8 12 24 32 40

Richie Rich Cash Money #1 © HARV

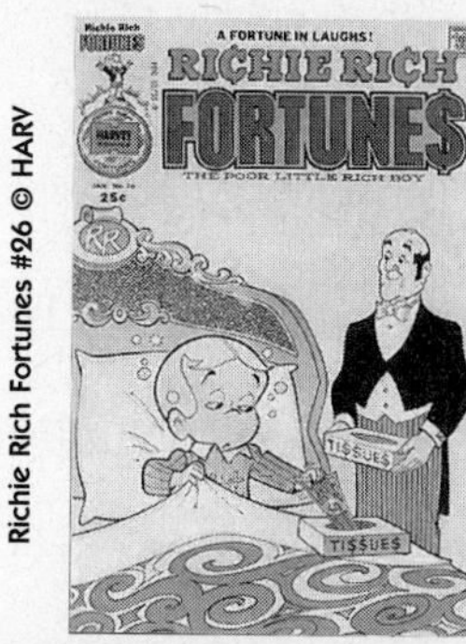

Richie Rich Fortunes #26 © HARV

Richie Rich Millions #22 © HARV

	GD 2.0	VG 4.0	FN 6.0	VF 8.0	VF/NM 9.0	NM- 9.2
2-5	2	4	6	14	18	22
6-10	2	4	6	10	13	16
11-20	1	3	4	6	8	10
21-30	1	2	3	4	5	7
31-47: 33-Dr. Blemish app.						6.00

RICHIE RICH CASH MONEY
Harvey Comics: May, 1992 - No. 2, Aug, 1992 ($1.25)

	GD	VG	FN	VF	VF/NM	NM-
1,2						3.00

RICHIE RICH COLLECTORS COMICS (See Harvey Collectors Comics)

RICHIE RICH DIAMONDS
Harvey Publications: Aug, 1972 - No. 59, Aug, 1982 (#1, 23-45: 52 pgs.)

	GD	VG	FN	VF	VF/NM	NM-
1-(52 pg. Giant)	6	12	18	38	52	65
2-5	3	6	9	18	24	30
6-10	2	4	6	12	16	20
11-22	2	4	6	8	10	12
23-30-(52 pg. Giants)	2	4	6	9	11	14
31-45: 39-r/Origin Little Dot	1	2	3	5	7	9
46-50	1	2	3	4	5	7
51-59						6.00

RICHIE RICH DIGEST
Harvey Publications: Oct, 1986 - No. 42, Oct, 1994 ($1.25/$1.75, digest-size)

	GD	VG	FN	VF	VF/NM	NM-
1	1	3	4	6	8	10
2-10						6.00
11-20						5.00
21-42						4.00

RICHIE RICH DIGEST STORIES (...Magazine #?-on)
Harvey Publications: Oct, 1977 - No., 17, Oct, 1982 (75¢/95¢, digest-size)

	GD	VG	FN	VF	VF/NM	NM-
1-Reprints	2	4	6	10	12	15
2-10: Reprints	1	2	3	5	7	9
11-17: Reprints						6.00

RICHIE RICH DIGEST WINNERS
Harvey Publications: Dec, 1977 - No. 16, Sept, 1982 (75¢/95¢, 132 pgs., digest-size)

	GD	VG	FN	VF	VF/NM	NM-
1	2	4	6	10	12	15
2-5	1	2	3	5	7	9
6-16						6.00

RICHIE RICH DOLLARS & CENTS
Harvey Publications: Aug, 1963 - No. 109, Aug, 1982 (#1-43: 68 pgs.; 44-60, 71-94: 52 pgs.)

	GD	VG	FN	VF	VF/NM	NM-
1: (#1-64 are all reprint issues)	17	34	51	123	182	240
2	9	18	27	65	93	120
3-5: 5-r/1st app. of R.R. from Little Dot #1	7	14	21	51	71	90
6-10	5	10	15	36	48	60
11-20	4	8	12	29	40	50
21-30: 25-r/1st app. Nurse Jenny (Little Lotta #62)	3	7	10	21	28	35
31-43: 43-Last 68 pg. issue	3	6	9	18	23	28
44-60: All 52 pgs.	2	4	6	11	14	18
61-71	1	3	4	6	8	10
72-94: All 52 pgs.	2	4	6	9	11	14
95-99,101-109						6.00
100-Anniversary issue	1	2	3	5	7	9

RICHIE RICH FORTUNES
Harvey Publications: Sept, 1971 - No. 63, July, 1982 (#1-15: 52 pgs.)

	GD	VG	FN	VF	VF/NM	NM-
1	6	12	18	43	59	75
2-5	3	7	10	21	28	35
6-10	2	4	6	14	18	22
11-15: 11-r/1st app. The Onion	2	4	6	10	12	15
16-30	1	2	3	5	7	9
31-40	1	2	3	4	5	7
41-63: 62-Onion app.						6.00

RICHIE RICH GEMS
Harvey Publications: Sept, 1974 - No. 43, Sept, 1982

	GD	VG	FN	VF	VF/NM	NM-
1	4	8	12	24	32	40
2-5	2	4	6	14	18	22
6-10	2	4	6	10	13	16
11-20	1	3	4	6	8	10
21-30	1	2	3	4	5	7
31-43: 36-Dr. Blemish, Onion app. 38-1st app. Stone-Age Riches						6.00

RICHIE RICH GOLD AND SILVER
Harvey Publications: Sept, 1975 - No. 42, Oct, 1982 (#1-27: 52 pgs.)

	GD 2.0	VG 4.0	FN 6.0	VF 8.0	VF/NM 9.0	NM- 9.2
1	3	7	10	21	28	35
2-5	2	4	6	12	16	20
6-10	2	4	6	9	11	14
11-27	1	2	3	5	7	9
28-42: 34-Stone-Age Riches app.						6.00

RICHIE RICH GOLD NUGGETS DIGEST
Harvey Publications: Feb., 1991 - No. 4, June, 1991 ($1.75, digest-size)

	GD	VG	FN	VF	VF/NM	NM-
1-4						3.00

RICHIE RICH HOLIDAY DIGEST MAGAZINE (...Digest #4)
Harvey Publications: Jan, 1980 - #3, Jan, 1982; #4, 3/88; #5, 2/89 (annual)

	GD	VG	FN	VF	VF/NM	NM-
1-X-Mas-c	1	3	4	6	8	10
2-5: 2,3: All X-Mas-c. 4-(3/88, $1.25), 5-(2/89, $1.75)	1	2	3	4	5	7

RICHIE RICH INVENTIONS
Harvey Publications: Oct, 1977 - No. 26, Oct, 1982 (#1-11: 52 pgs.)

	GD	VG	FN	VF	VF/NM	NM-
1	2	4	6	12	16	20
2-5	2	4	6	8	10	12
6-11	1	2	3	5	6	8
12-26						6.00

RICHIE RICH JACKPOTS
Harvey Publications: Oct, 1972 - No. 58, Aug, 1982 (#41-43: 52 pgs.)

	GD	VG	FN	VF	VF/NM	NM-
1	5	10	15	36	48	60
2-5	3	6	9	18	24	30
6-10	2	4	6	12	16	20
11-15,17-20	2	4	6	8	10	12
16-Super Richie app.	2	4	6	10	12	15
21-30	1	2	3	5	7	9
31-40,44-50: 37-Caricatures of Frank Sinatra, Dean Martin, Sammy Davis, Jr. 45-Dr. Blemish app.	1	2	3	4	5	7
41-43 (52 pgs.)	1	3	4	6	8	10
51-58						6.00

RICHIE RICH MILLION DOLLAR DIGEST (...Magazine #?-on)(See Million Dollar Digest)
Harvey Publications: Oct, 1980 - No. 10, Oct, 1982 ($1.50)

	GD	VG	FN	VF	VF/NM	NM-
1	1	3	4	6	8	10
2-10						6.00

RICHIE RICH MILLIONS
Harvey Publ.: 9/61; #2, 9/62 - #113, 10/82 (#1-48: 68 pgs.; 49-64, 85-97: 52 pgs.)

	GD	VG	FN	VF	VF/NM	NM-
1: (#1-3 are all reprint issues)	20	40	60	145	213	280
2	10	20	30	73	107	140
3-10: All other giants are new & reprints. 5-1st 15 pg. Richie Rich story	10	20	30	67	96	125
11-20	6	12	18	40	55	70
21-30	5	10	15	33	44	55
31-48: 31-1st app. The Onion. 48-Last 68 pg. Giant	4	8	12	24	32	40
49-64: 52 pg. Giants	3	6	9	16	20	25
65-67,69-73,75-84	2	4	6	8	10	12
68-1st Super Richie-c (11/74)	2	4	6	12	16	20
74-1st app. Mr. Woody; Super Richie app.	2	4	6	9	11	14
85-97: 52 pg. Giants	2	4	6	9	11	14
98,99	1	2	3	4	5	7
100	1	2	3	5	7	9
101-113						6.00

RICHIE RICH MONEY WORLD
Harvey Publications: Sept, 1972 - No. 59, Sept, 1982

	GD	VG	FN	VF	VF/NM	NM-
1-(52 pg. Giant)-1st app. Mayda Munny	6	12	18	43	59	75
2-Super Richie app.	3	7	10	21	28	35
3-5	3	6	9	18	24	30
6-10: 9,10-Richie Rich mistakenly named Little Lotta on covers	2	4	6	12	16	20
11-20: 16,20-Dr. N-R-Gee	2	4	6	8	10	12
21-30	1	2	3	5	7	9
31-50	1	2	3	4	5	7
51-59						6.00
Digest 1 (2/91, $1.75)						5.00
2-8 (12/93, $1.75)						3.00

RICHIE RICH PROFITS
Harvey Publications: Oct, 1974 - No. 47, Sept, 1982

	GD	VG	FN	VF	VF/NM	NM-
1	4	8	12	24	32	40
2-5	2	4	6	14	18	22
6-10: 10-Origin of Dr. N-R-Gee	2	4	6	10	13	16

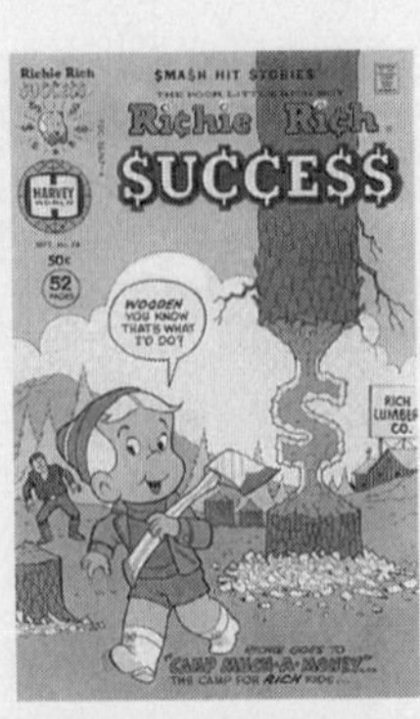

Richie Rich Success Stories #76 © HARV

The Rifleman #9 © DELL

The Ringo Kid #3 © MAR

	GD 2.0	VG 4.0	FN 6.0	VF 8.0	VF/NM 9.0	NM- 9.2
11-20: 15-Christmas-c	1	3	4	6	8	10
21-30	1	2	3	4	5	7
31-47						6.00

RICHIE RICH RELICS
Harvey Comics: Jan, 1988 - No.4, Feb, 1989 (75¢/$1.00, reprints)

	GD	VG	FN	VF	VF/NM	NM-
1-4						3.00

RICHIE RICH RICHES
Harvey Publications: July, 1972 - No. 59, Aug, 1982 (#1, 2, 41-45: 52 pgs.)

	GD	VG	FN	VF	VF/NM	NM-
1-(52 pg. Giant)-1st app. The Money Monster	6	12	18	43	59	75
2-(52 pg. Giant)	3	7	10	21	28	35
3-5	3	6	9	18	24	30
6-10	2	4	6	12	16	20
11-20: 17-Super Richie app. (3/75)	2	4	6	8	10	12
21-40	1	2	3	5	6	8
41-45: 52 pg. Giants	1	3	4	6	8	10
46-59: 56-Dr. Blemish app.						6.00

RICHIE RICH SUCCESS STORIES
Harvey Publications: Nov, 1964 - No. 105, Sept, 1982 (#1-38: 68 pgs., 39-55, 67-90: 52 pgs.)

	GD	VG	FN	VF	VF/NM	NM-
1	19	38	57	136	198	260
2-5	10	20	30	70	100	130
6-10	6	12	18	43	59	75
11-20	5	10	15	36	48	60
21-30: 27-1st Penny Van Dough (8/69)	4	8	12	27	36	45
31-38: 38-Last 68 pg. Giant	3	7	10	21	28	35
39-55-(52 pgs.): 44-Super Richie app.	2	4	6	14	18	22
56-66	2	4	6	8	10	12
67-90: 52 pgs.	2	4	6	9	11	14
91-105: 91-Onion app. 101-Dr. Blemish app.						6.00

RICHIE RICH SUMMER BONANZA
Harvey Comics: Oct, 1991 ($1.95, one-shot, 68 pgs.)

	GD	VG	FN	VF	VF/NM	NM-
1-Richie Rich, Little Dot, Little Lotta						3.00

RICHIE RICH TREASURE CHEST DIGEST (...Magazine #3)
Harvey Publications: Apr, 1982 - No. 3, Aug, 1982 (95¢, Digest Mag.)
(#4 advertised but not publ.)

	GD	VG	FN	VF	VF/NM	NM-
1	1	2	3	5	7	9
2,3	1	2	3	4	5	7

RICHIE RICH VACATION DIGEST
Harvey Comics: Oct, 1991; Oct, 1992; Oct, 1993 ($1.75, digest-size)

	GD	VG	FN	VF	VF/NM	NM-
1-(10/91), 1-(10/92), 1-(10/93)						4.00

RICHIE RICH VACATIONS DIGEST
Harvey Publ.: 11/77; No. 2, 10/78 - No. 7, 10/81; No. 8, 8/82; (Digest, 132 pgs.)

	GD	VG	FN	VF	VF/NM	NM-
1-Reprints	2	4	6	10	12	15
2-6	1	2	3	5	7	9
7,8						6.00

RICHIE RICH VAULT OF MYSTERY
Harvey Publications: Nov, 1974 - No. 47, Sept, 1982

	GD	VG	FN	VF	VF/NM	NM-
1	4	8	12	24	32	40
2-5	2	4	6	14	18	22
7-10	2	4	6	10	13	16
11-20	1	3	4	6	8	10
21-30	1	2	3	4	5	7
31-47						6.00

RICHIE RICH ZILLIONZ
Harvey Publ.: Oct, 1976 - No. 33, Sept, 1982 (#1-4: 68 pgs.; #5-18: 52 pgs.)

	GD	VG	FN	VF	VF/NM	NM-
1	3	7	10	21	28	35
2-4: 4-Last 68 pg. Giant	2	4	6	12	16	20
5-10	2	4	6	8	10	12
11-18: 18-Last 52 pg. Giant	1	2	3	5	6	8
19-33						6.00

RICK GEARY'S WONDERS AND ODDITIES
Dark Horse Comics: Dec, 1988 ($2.00, B&W, one-shot)

	GD	VG	FN	VF	VF/NM	NM-
1						2.25

RICKY
Standard Comics (Visual Editions): No. 5, Sept, 1953

	GD	VG	FN	VF	VF/NM	NM-
5-Teenage humor	6	12	18	27	33	38

RICKY NELSON (TV)(See Sweethearts V2#42)
Dell Publishing Co.: No. 956, Dec, 1958 - No. 1192, June, 1961 (All photo-c)

	GD	VG	FN	VF	VF/NM	NM-
Four Color 956,998	20	40	60	145	213	280
Four Color 1115	16	32	48	111	163	215
Four Color 1192-Manning-a	16	32	48	111	163	215

RIDER, THE (Frontier Trail #6; also see Blazing Sixguns I.W. Reprint #10, 11)
Ajax/Farrell Publ. (Four Star Comic Corp.): Mar, 1957 - No. 5, 1958

	GD	VG	FN	VF	VF/NM	NM-
1-Swift Arrow, Lone Rider begin	13	26	39	76	103	130
2-5	8	16	24	43	54	65

RIDERS OF THE PURPLE SAGE (See Zane Grey & Four Color #372)

RIFLEMAN, THE (TV)
Dell Publ. Co./Gold Key No. 13 on: No. 1009, 7-9/59 - No. 12, 7-9/62; No. 13, 11/62 - No. 20, 10/64

	GD	VG	FN	VF	VF/NM	NM-
Four Color 1009 (#1)	27	54	81	194	285	375
2 (1-3/60)	14	28	42	99	145	190
3-Toth-a (4 pgs.)	14	28	42	99	145	190
4-10: 6-Toth-a (4 pgs.)	12	24	36	84	125	165
11-20	9	18	27	65	93	120

NOTE: *Warren Tufts a-2-9. All have Chuck Connors photo-c. Photo back c-13-15.*

RIMA, THE JUNGLE GIRL
National Periodical Publications: Apr-May, 1974 - No. 7, Apr-May, 1975

	GD	VG	FN	VF	VF/NM	NM-
1-Origin, part 1 (#1-5: 20¢; 6,7: 25¢)	2	4	6	10	13	16
2-7: 2-4-Origin, parts 2-4. 7-Origin & only app. Space Marshal	1	2	3	5	6	8

NOTE: *Kubert c-1-7. Nino a-1-7. Redondo a-1-7.*

RING OF BRIGHT WATER (See Movie Classics)

RING OF THE NIBELUNG, THE
DC Comics: 1989 - No. 4, 1990 ($4.95, squarebound, 52 pgs., mature readers)

	GD	VG	FN	VF	VF/NM	NM-
1-4: Adapts novel, Gil Kane-c/a						5.00

RING OF THE NIBELUNG, THE
Dark Horse Comics: Feb, 2000 - Sept, 2001 ($2.95/$2.99/$5.99, limited series)

	GD	VG	FN	VF	VF/NM	NM-
Vol. 1 (The Rhinegold) 1-4: Adapts Wagner; P. Craig Russell-s/a						3.00
Vol. 2,3: Vol. 2 (The Valkyrie) 1-3: 1-(8/00). Vol. 3 (Siegfried) 1-3: 1-(12/00)						3.00
Vol. 4 (The Twilight of the Gods) 1-3: 1-(6/01)						3.00
4-(9/01, $5.99, 64 pgs.) Conclusion with sketch pages						6.00

RINGO KID, THE (2nd Series)
Marvel Comics Group: Jan, 1970 - No. 23, Nov, 1973; No. 24, Nov, 1975 - No. 30, Nov, 1976

	GD	VG	FN	VF	VF/NM	NM-
1-Williamson-a r-from #10, 1956.	3	6	9	18	24	30
2-11: 2-Severin-c. 11-Last 15¢ issue	2	4	6	10	13	16
12 (52 pg. Giant)	3	6	9	16	20	24
13-20: 13-Wildey-r. 20-Williamson-r/#1	2	4	6	8	10	12
21-30	1	2	3	5	7	9
27,28-(30¢-c variant, limited distribution)(5,7/76)	2	4	6	12	16	20

RINGO KID WESTERN, THE (1st Series) (See Wild Western & Western Trails)
Atlas Comics (HPC)/Marvel Comics: Aug, 1954 - No. 21, Sept, 1957

	GD	VG	FN	VF	VF/NM	NM-
1-Origin; The Ringo Kid begins	31	62	93	175	248	320
2-Black Rider app.; origin/1st app. Ringo's Horse Arab	16	32	48	92	126	160
3-5	11	22	33	63	84	105
6-8-Severin-a(3) each	12	24	36	69	92	115
9,11,12,14-21: 12-Orlando-a (4 pgs.)	9	18	27	52	66	80
10,13-Williamson-a (4 pgs.)	10	20	30	56	73	90

NOTE: *Berg a-8. Maneely a-1-5, 15, 16(text illos only), 17(4), 18, 20, 21; c-1-6, 8, 13, 15-18, 20. J. Severin c-10, 11. Sinnott a-1. Wildey a-16-18.*

RIN TIN TIN (See March of Comics #163,180,195)

RIN TIN TIN (TV) (...& Rusty #21 on; see Western Roundup under Dell Giants)
Dell Publishing Co./Gold Key: Nov, 1952 - No. 38, May-July, 1961; Nov, 1963 (All Photo-c)

	GD	VG	FN	VF	VF/NM	NM-
Four Color 434 (#1)	16	32	48	113	167	220
Four Color 476,523	9	18	27	60	85	110
4(3-5/54)-10	7	14	21	51	71	90
11-20	6	12	18	43	59	75
21-38: 36-Toth-a (4 pgs.)	5	10	15	36	48	60
... & Rusty 1 (11/63-Gold Key)	6	12	18	43	59	75

RIO (Also see Eclipse Monthly)
Comico: June, 1987 ($8.95, 64 pgs.)

	GD	VG	FN	VF	VF/NM	NM-
1-Wildey-c/a						9.00

RIO AT BAY
Dark Horse Comics: July, 1992 - No. 2, Aug, 1992 ($2.95, limited series)

	GD	VG	FN	VF	VF/NM	NM-
1,2-Wildey-c/a						3.00

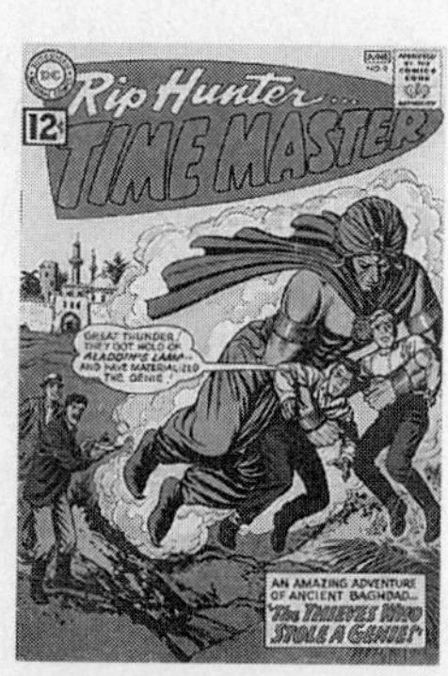

Rip Hunter Time Master #8 © DC

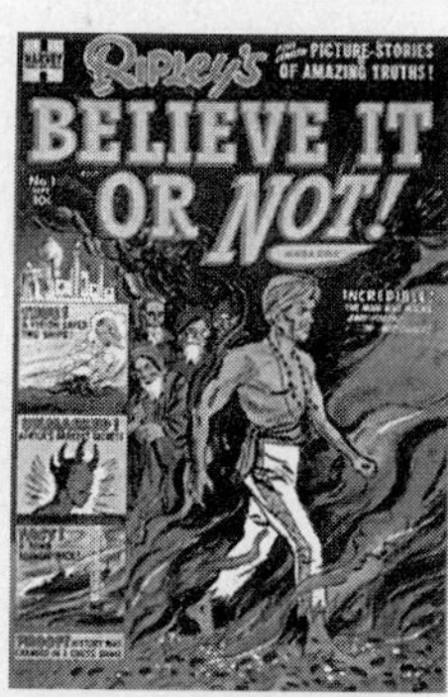

Rising Stars #14 © J. Michael Straczynski & TCOW

GD 2.0 | VG 4.0 | FN 6.0 | VF 8.0 | VF/NM 9.0 | NM- 9.2

RIO BRAVO (Movie) (See 4-Color #1018)
Dell Publishing Co.: June, 1959
Four Color #1018-Toth-a; John Wayne, Dean Martin, & Ricky Nelson photo-c. 25 50 75 176 258 340

RIO CONCHOS (See Movie Comics)

RIOT (Satire)
Atlas Comics (ACI No. 1-5/WPI No. 6): Apr, 1954 - No. 3, Aug, 1954; No. 4, Feb, 1956 - No. 6, June, 1956
1-Russ Heath-a 31 62 93 175 248 320
2-Li'l Abner satire by Post 23 46 69 130 183 235
3-Last precode (8/54) 20 40 60 112 156 200
4-Infinity-c; Marilyn Monroe "7 Year Itch" movie satire; Mad Rip-off ads 26 52 78 147 206 265
5-Marilyn Monroe, John Wayne parody; part photo-c 27 54 81 153 214 275
6-Lorna of the Jungle satire by Everett; Dennis the Menace satire-c/story; part photo-c 20 40 60 112 156 200
NOTE: *Berg a-3. Burgos c-1, 2. Colan a-1. Everett a-1, 4, 6. Heath a-1. Maneely a-1, 2, 4-6; c-3, 4, 6. Post a-1-4. Reinman a-2. Severin a-4-6.*

RIOT GEAR
Triumphant Comics: Sept, 1993 - No. 11, July, 1994 ($2.50, serially numbered)
1-11: 1-2nd app. Riot Gear. 2-1st app. Rabin. 3,4-Triumphant Unleashed x-over. 3-1st app. Surzar. 4-Death of Captain Tich 2.50
Violent Past 1,2: 1-(2/94, $2.50) 2.50

R.I.P.
TSR, Inc.: 1990 - No. 8, 1991 ($2.95, 44 pgs.)
1-8-Based on TSR game 3.00

RIPCLAW (See Cyberforce)
Image Comics (Top Cow Prod.): Apr, 1995 - No. 3, June, 1995 (Limited series)
1/2-Gold, 1/2-San Diego ed., 1/2-Chicago ed. 1 3 4 6 8 10
1-3: Brandon Peterson-a(p) 3.00
Special 1 (10/95, $2.50) 2.50

RIPCLAW
Image Comics (Top Cow Prod.): V2#1, Dec, 1995 - No. 6, June, 1996 ($2.50)
V2#1-6: 5-Medieval Spawn/Witchblade Preview 2.50

RIPCORD (TV)
Dell Publishing Co.: Mar-May, 1962
Four Color 1294 8 16 24 55 78 100

R.I.P.D.
Dark Horse Comics: Oct, 1999 - No. 4, Jan, 2000 ($2.95, limited series)
1-4 3.00
TPB (2003, $12.95) r/#1-4 13.00

RIPFIRE
Malibu Comics (Ultraverse): No. 0, Apr, 1995 ($2.50, one-shot)
0 2.50

RIP HUNTER TIME MASTER (See Showcase #20, 21, 25, 26 & Time Masters)
National Periodical Publications: Mar-Apr, 1961 - No. 29, Nov-Dec, 1965
1-(3-4/61) 50 100 150 400 600 800
2 27 54 81 192 281 370
3-5: 5-Last 10¢ issue 16 32 48 111 163 215
6,7-Toth-a in each 11 22 33 75 110 145
8-15 9 18 27 60 85 110
16-20: 20-Hitler c/s 7 14 21 50 68 85
21-29: 29-Gil Kane-c 6 12 18 40 55 70

RIP IN TIME (Also see Teenage Mutant Ninja Turtles #5-7)
Fantagor Press: Aug, 1986 - No.5, 1987 ($1.50, B&W)
1-5: Corben-c/a in all 3.00

RIP KIRBY (Also see Harvey Comics Hits #57, & Street Comix)
David McKay Publications: 1948
Feature Books 51,54: Raymond-c; 51-Origin 35 70 105 201 288 370

RIPLEY'S BELIEVE IT OR NOT! (See Ace Comics, All-American Comics, Mystery Comics Digest #1, 4, 7, 10, 13, 16, 19, 22, 25)

RIPLEY'S BELIEVE IT OR NOT!
Harvey Publications: Sept, 1953 - No. 4, March, 1954
1-Powell-a 14 28 42 79 107 135
2-4 10 20 30 56 73 90

RIPLEY'S BELIEVE IT OR NOT! (Continuation of Ripleys'...True Ghost Stories & Ripley's...True War Stories)
Gold Key: No. 4, April, 1967 - No. 94, Feb, 1980
4-Photo-c; McWilliams-a 4 8 12 27 36 45
5-Subtitled "True War Stories"; Evans-a; 1st Jeff Jones-a in comics? (2 pgs.) 4 8 12 27 36 45
6-10: 6-McWilliams-a. 10-Evans-a(2) 4 8 12 22 30 38
11-20: 15-Evans-a 3 6 9 18 23 28
21-30 2 4 6 14 18 22
31-38,40-60 2 4 6 10 13 16
39-Crandall-a 2 4 6 11 14 18
61-73 1 3 4 6 8 10
74,77-83-(52 pgs.) 2 4 6 10 13 16
75,76,84-94 1 2 3 5 6 8
Story Digest Mag. 1(6/70)-4-3/4x6-1/2", 148pp. 6 12 18 40 55 70
NOTE: *Evanish art by Luiz Dominguez #22-25, 27, 30, 31, 40. Jeff Jones a-5(2 pgs.). McWilliams a-65, 66, 70, 89. Orlando a-8. Sparling c-68. Reprints-74, 77-84, 87 (part); 91, 93 (all). Williamson, Wood a-80r/#1.*

RIPLEY'S BELIEVE IT OR NOT!
Dark Horse Comics: May, 2002 - No. 4 ($2.99, B&W, limited series)
1-3-Nord-c/a. 1-Stories of Amelia Earhart & D.B. Cooper 3.00

RIPLEY'S BELIEVE IT OR NOT! TRUE GHOST STORIES (Along with Ripley's...True War Stories, the three issues together precede the 1967 series that starts its numbering with #4) (Also see Dan Curtis)
Gold Key: June, 1965 - No. 2, Oct, 1966
1-Williamson, Wood & Evans-a; photo-c 7 14 21 51 71 90
2-Orlando, McWilliams-a; photo-c 4 8 12 29 40 50
Mini-Comic 1(1976-3-1/4x6-1/2") 2 4 6 9 11 14
11186(1977)-Golden Press; ($1.95, 224 pgs.)-All-r 4 8 12 27 36 45
11401(3/79)-Golden Press; ($1.00, 96 pgs.)-All-r 3 6 9 16 20 24

RIPLEY'S BELIEVE IT OR NOT! TRUE WAR STORIES (Along with Ripley's...True Ghost Stories, the three issues together precede the 1967 series that starts its numbering with #4)
Gold Key: Nov, 1965 (Aug, 1965 in indicia)
1-No Williamson-a 4 8 12 27 36 45

RIPLEY'S BELIEVE IT OR NOT! TRUE WEIRD
Ripley Enterprises: June, 1966 - No. 2, Aug, 1966 (B&W Magazine)
1,2-Comic stories & text 3 6 9 18 23 28

RIPTIDE
Image Comics: Sep, 1995 - No. 2, Oct, 1995 ($2.50, limited series)
1,2: Rob Liefeld-c 2.50

RISE OF APOCALYPSE
Marvel Comics: Oct, 1996 - No. 4, Jan, 1997 ($1.95, limited series)
1-4: Adam Pollina-c/a 2.25

RISING STARS
Image Comics(Top Cow): Mar, 1999 - Present ($2.50/$2.99)
Preview-(3/99, $5.00) Straczynski-s 6.00
0-(6/00, $2.50) Gary Frank-a/c 2.50
1/2-(8/01, $2.95) Anderson-c; art & sketch pages by Zanier 3.00
1-Four covers; Keu Cha-c/a 1 2 3 5 7 9
1-($10.00) Gold Editions-four covers 10.00
1-($50.00) Holofoil-c 50.00
2-7: 5-7-Zanier & Lashley-a(p) 1 2 3 5 7 9
8-21: 8-13-Zanier & Lashley-a(p). 14-Immonen-a. 15-Flip book B&W preview of Universe. 15-21-Brent Anderson-a 3.00
Born In Fire TPB (11/00, $19.95) r/#1-8; foreword by Neil Gaiman 20.00
Power TPB (2002, $19.95) r/#9-16 20.00
Prelude-(10/00, $2.95) Cha-a/Lashley-c 3.00
...: Visitations (2002, $8.99) r/#0, 1/2, Preview; new Anderson-c; cover gallery 9.00
Wizard #0-(3/99) Wizard supplement; Straczynski-s 2.00
Wizard #1/2 10.00

RISING STARS BRIGHT
Image Comics(Top Cow): Mar, 2003 - No. 3, May, 2003 ($2.99, limited series)
1-3-Avery-s/Jurgens & Gorder-a/Beck-c 3.00

RIVERDALE HIGH (Archie's... #7,8)
Archie Comics: Aug, 1990 - No. 8, Oct, 1991 ($1.00, bi-monthly)
1 4.00
2-8 3.00

RIVER FEUD (See Zane Grey & Four Color #484)

RIVETS

Roarin' Rick's Rare Bit Fiends #10 © King Hell

Robin #21 © DC

Robin Hood Tales #12 © DC

	GD 2.0	VG 4.0	FN 6.0	VF 8.0	VF/NM 9.0	NM- 9.2

Dell Publishing Co.: No. 518, Nov, 1953

Four Color 518	4	8	12	22	30	38

RIVETS (A dog)
Argo Publ.: Jan, 1956 - No. 3, May, 1956

1-Reprints Sunday & daily newspaper strips	6	12	18	31	38	45
2,3	5	10	15	22	26	30

ROACHMILL
Blackthorne Publ.: Dec, 1986 - No. 6, Oct, 1987 ($1.75, B&W)

1-6 2.25

ROACHMILL
Dark Horse Comics: May, 1988 - No. 10, Dec, 1990 ($1.75, B&W)

1-10: 10-Contains trading cards 2.25

ROAD RUNNER (See Beep Beep, the...)

ROAD TO PERDITION (Inspired the 2002 Tom Hanks/Paul Newman movie)
(Also see On the Road to Perdition: Oasis)
DC Comics/Paradox Press: 1998, 2002 ($13.95, B&W paperback graphic novel)

nn-(1st printing) Max Allan Collins-s/Richard Piers Rayner-a 30.00
2nd & 3rd printings (2002, $13.95) 14.00
Movie photo cover edition (2002) 14.00

ROADTRIP
Oni Press: Aug, 2000 ($2.95, B&W, one-shot)

1-Reprints Judd Winick's back-up stories from Oni Double Feature #9,10 3.00

ROADWAYS
Cult Press: May, 1994 ($2.75, B&W, limited series)

1 2.75

ROARIN' RICK'S RARE BIT FIENDS
King Hell Press: July, 1994 - No. 21, Aug, 1996 ($2.95, B&W, mature)

1-21: Rick Veitch-c/a/scripts in all. 20-(5/96). 21-(8/96)-Reads Subtleman #1 on cover 3.00
Rabid Eye: The Dream Art of Rick Veitch ($14.95, B&W, TPB)-r/#1-8 & the appendix from #12 15.00
Pocket Universe (6/96, $14.95, B&W, TPB)-Reprints 15.00

ROBERT E. HOWARD'S CONAN THE BARBARIAN
Marvel Comics: 1983 ($2.50, 68 pgs., Baxter paper)

1-r/Savage Tales #2,3 by Smith, c-r/Conan #21 by Smith. 4.00

ROBERT LOUIS STEVENSON'S KIDNAPPED (See Kidnapped)

ROBIN (See Aurora, Birds of Prey, Detective Comics #38, New Teen Titans, Robin II, Robin III, Robin 3000, Star Spangled Comics #65, Teen Titans & Young Justice)

ROBIN (See Batman #457)
DC Comics: Jan, 1991 - No. 5, May, 1991 ($1.00, limited series)

1-Free poster by N. Adams; Bolland-c on all 4.00
1-2nd & 3rd printings (without poster) 2.25
2-5 3.00
2-2nd printing 2.25
Annual 1,2 (1992-93, $2.50, 68 pgs.): 1-Grant/Wagner scripts; Sam Kieth-c. 2-Intro Razorsharp; Jim Balent-c(p) 3.00

ROBIN (See Detective #668)
DC Comics: Nov, 1993 - Present ($1.50/$1.95/$1.99/$2.25)

1-($2.95)-Collector's edition w/foil embossed-c; 1st app. Robin's car, The Redbird; Azrael as Batman app. 4.00
1-Newsstand ed. 2.25
0,2-49,51-66-Regular editions: 3-5-The Spoiler app. 6-The Huntress-c/story cont'd from Showcase '94 #5. 7-Knightquest: The Conclusion w/new Batman (Azrael) vs. Bruce Wayne. 8-KnightsEnd Pt. 5. 9-KnightsEnd Aftermath; Batman-c & app. 10-(9/94)-Zero Hour. 0-(10/94). 11-(11/94). 25-Green Arrow-c/app. 26-Batman app. 27-Contagion Pt. 3; Catwoman-c/app; Penguin & Azrael app. 28-Contagion Pt. 11. 29-Penguin app. 31-Wildcat-c/app. 32-Legacy Pt. 3. 33-Legacy Pt. 7. 35-Final Night. 46-Genesis. 52,53-Cataclysm pt. 7, conclusion. 55-Green Arrow app. 62-64-Flash-c/app. 2.50
14 ($2.50)-Embossed-c; Troika Pt. 4 3.00
50-($2.95)-Lady Shiva & King Snake app. 3.00
67-74,76-78: 67-72-No Man's Land 2.50
75-($2.95) 3.00
79-97: 79-Begin $2.25-c; Green Arrow app. 86-Pander Bros.-a 2.25
98,99-Bruce Wayne: Murderer x-over pt. 6, 11 2.50
100-($3.50) Last Dixon-s 3.50
101-121: 101-Young Justice x-over. 106-Kevin Lau-c. 121-Willingham-s/Mays-a 2.25
#1,000,000 (11/98) 853rd Century x-over 2.50
Annual 3-5: 3-(1994, $2.95)-Elseworlds story. 4-(1995, $2.95)-Year One story. 5-(1996, $2.95)-Legends of the Dead Earth story 3.00
Annual 6 (1997, $3.95)-Pulp Heroes story. 4.00
.../Argent 1 (2/98, $1.95) Argent (Teen Titans) app. 2.25
...Eighty-Page Giant 1 (9/00, $5.95) Chuck Dixon-s/Diego Barreto-a 6.00
...: Flying Solo (2000, $12.95, TPB) r/#1-6, Showcase '94 #5,6 13.00
...Plus 1 (12/96, $2.95) Impulse-c/app.; Waid-s 3.00
...Plus 2 (12/97, $2.95) Fang (Scare Tactics) app. 3.00

ROBIN: A HERO REBORN
DC Comics: 1991 ($4.95, squarebound, trade paperback)

nn-r/Batman #455-457 & Robin #1-5; Bolland-c 5.00

ROBIN HOOD (See The Advs. of..., Brave and the Bold, Four Color #413, 669, King Classics, Movie Comics & Power Record Comics)

ROBIN HOOD (...& His Merry Men, The Illustrated Story of...) (See Classic Comics #7 & Classics Giveaways, 12/44)

ROBIN HOOD (Adventures of... #7, 8)
Magazine Enterprises (Sussex Pub. Co.): No. 52, Nov, 1955 - No. 6, Jun, 1957

52 (#1)-Origin Robin Hood & Sir Gallant of the Round Table	17	34	51	95	130	165
53 (#2), 3-6: 6-Richard Greene photo-c (TV)	13	26	39	74	100	125
I.W. Reprint #1,2,9: 1-r/#3. 2-r/#4. 9-r/#52 (1963)	2	4	6	12	16	20
Super Reprint #10,15: 10-r/#53. 15-r/#5	2	4	6	12	16	20

NOTE: ***Bolle** a-in all; c-52. **Powell** a-6.*

ROBIN HOOD (Not Disney)
Dell Publishing Co.: May-July, 1963 (one-shot)

1	3	6	9	18	24	30

ROBIN HOOD (Disney) (Also see Best of Walt Disney)
Western Publishing Co.: 1973 ($1.50, 8-1/2x11", 52 pgs., cardboard-c)

96151- "Robin Hood", based on movie, 96152- "The Mystery of Sherwood Forest", 96153- "In King Richard's Service", 96154- "The Wizard's Ring" each....	3	6	9	18	23	28

ROBIN HOOD
Eclipse Comics: July, 1991 - No. 3, Dec, 1991 ($2.50, limited series)

1-3: Timothy Truman layouts 2.50

ROBIN HOOD AND HIS MERRY MEN (Formerly Danger & Adventure)
Charlton Comics: No. 28, Apr, 1956 - No. 38, Aug, 1958

28	10	20	30	56	73	90
29-37	8	16	24	43	54	65
38-Ditko-a (5 pgs.); Rocke-c	14	28	42	79	107	135

ROBIN HOOD TALES (Published by National Periodical #7 on)
Quality Comics Group (Comic Magazines): Feb, 1956 - No. 6, Nov-Dec, 1956

1-All have Baker/Cuidera-c	35	70	105	201	288	370
2-6-Matt Baker-a	34	68	102	196	278	360

ROBIN HOOD TALES (Cont'd from Quality series)(See Brave & the Bold #5)
National Periodical Publ.: No. 7, Jan-Feb, 1957 - No. 14, Mar-Apr, 1958

7-All have Andru/Esposito-c	39	78	117	230	325	420
8-14	34	68	102	196	278	360

ROBINSON CRUSOE (See King Classics & Power Record Comics)
Dell Publishing Co.: Nov-Jan, 1963-64

1	3	6	9	16	20	24

ROBIN II (The Joker's Wild)
DC Comics: Oct, 1991 - No. 4, Dec, 1991 ($1.50, mini-series)

1-(Direct sales, $1.50)-With 4 diff.-c; same hologram on each 3.00
1-(Newsstand, $1.00)-No hologram; 1 version 2.25
1-Collector's set ($10.00)-Contains all 5 versions bagged with hologram trading card inside 12.00
2-(Direct sales, $1.50)-With 3 different-c 2.50
2-4-(Newsstand, $1.00)-1 version of each 2.25
2-Collector's set ($8.00)-Contains all 4 versions bagged with hologram trading card inside 9.00
3-(Direct sale, $1.50)-With 2 different-c 2.50
3-Collector's set ($6.00)-Contains all 3 versions bagged with hologram trading card inside 7.00
4-(Direct sales, $1.50)-Only one version 2.50
4-Collector's set ($4.00)-Contains both versions bagged with Bat-Signal hologram trading card 5.00
Multi-pack (All four issues w/hologram sticker) 8.00

Robocop #14 © Orion Pictures

Robo Dojo #6 © WSP

Robotech #0 © Harmony Gold USA

GD	VG	FN	VF	VF/NM	NM-
2.0	4.0	6.0	8.0	9.0	9.2

Deluxe Complete Set ($30.00)-Contains all 14 versions of #1-4 plus a new hologram trading card; numbered & limited to 25,000; comes with slipcase & 2 acid free backing boards 35.00

ROBIN III: CRY OF THE HUNTRESS
DC Comics: Dec, 1992 - No. 6, Mar, 1993 (Limited series)

1-6 ($2.50, collector's ed.)-Polybagged w/movement enhanced-c plus mini-poster of newsstand-c by Zeck 3.00
1-6 ($1.25, newsstand ed.): All have Zeck-c 2.25

ROBIN 3000
DC Comics (Elseworlds): 1992 - No. 2, 1992 ($4.95, mini-series, 52 pgs.)

1,2-Foil logo; Russell-c/a 5.00

ROBIN: YEAR ONE
DC Comics: 2000 - No. 4, 2001 ($4.95, square-bound, limited series)

1-4: Earliest days of Robin's career; Javier Pulido-c/a. 2,4-Two-Face app. 5.00
TPB (2002, $14.95) r/#1-4 15.00

ROBOCOP
Marvel Comics: Oct, 1987 ($2.00, B&W, magazine, one-shot)

1-Movie adaptation 4.00

ROBOCOP (Also see Dark Horse Comics)
Marvel Comics: Mar, 1990 - No. 23, Jan, 1992 ($1.50)

1-Based on movie 3.00
2-23 2.50
nn (7/90, $4.95, 52 pgs.)-r/B&W magazine in color; adapts 1st movie 5.00

ROBOCOP (FRANK MILLER'S...) (Also see Promotional Comics section for FCBD Ed.)
Avatar Press: July, 2003 - No. 3 ($3.50, limited series)

1,2-Frank Miller-s/Juan Ryp-a. 1-Three covers by Miller, Ryp, and Barrows. 2-Two covers 3.50

ROBOCOP: MORTAL COILS
Dark Horse Comics: Sept, 1993 - No. 4, Dec, 1993 ($2.50, limited series)

1-4: 1,2-Cago painted-c 2.50

ROBOCOP: PRIME SUSPECT
Dark Horse Comics: Oct, 1992 - No. 4, Jan, 1993 ($2.50, limited series)

1-4: 1,3-Nelson painted-c. 2,4-Bolton painted-c 2.50

ROBOCOP: ROULETTE
Dark Horse Comics: Dec, 1993 - No. 4, 1994 ($2.50, limited series)

1-4: 1,3-Nelson painted-c. 2,4-Bolton painted-c 2.50

ROBOCOP 2
Marvel Comics: Aug, 1990 ($2.25, B&W, magazine, 68 pgs.)

1-Adapts movie sequel 2.50

ROBOCOP 2
Marvel Comics: Aug, 1990; Late Aug, 1990 - #3, Late Sept, 1990 ($1.00, limited series)

nn-(8/90, $4.95, 68 pgs., color)-Same contents as B&W magazine 5.00
1: #1-3 reprint no number issue 3.00
2,3: 2-Guice-c(i) 2.50

ROBOCOP 3
Dark Horse Comics: July, 1993 - No. 3, Nov, 1993 ($2.50, limited series)

1-3: Nelson painted-c; Nguyen-a(p) 2.50

ROBOCOP VERSUS THE TERMINATOR
Dark Horse Comics: Sept, 1992 - No. 4, 1992 (Dec.) ($2.50, limited series)

1-4: Miller scripts & Simonson-c/a in all 3.00
1-Platinum Edition 6.00
NOTE: *All contain a different Robocop cardboard cut-out stand-up.*

ROBO DOJO
DC Comics (WildStorm): Apr, 2002 - No. 6, Sept, 2002 ($2.95, limited series)

1-6-Wolfman-s 3.00

ROBO-HUNTER (Also see Sam Slade...)
Eagle Comics: Apr, 1984 - No. 5, 1984 ($1.00)

1-5-2000 A.D. 2.25

R.O.B.O.T. BATTALION 2050
Eclipse Comics: Mar, 1988 ($2.00, B&W, one-shot)

1 2.25

ROBOT COMICS
Renegade Press: No. 0, June, 1987 ($2.00, B&W, one-shot)

0-Bob Burden story & art 2.25

GD	VG	FN	VF	VF/NM	NM-
2.0	4.0	6.0	8.0	9.0	9.2

ROBOTECH
Antarctic Press: Mar, 1997 - No. 11, Nov, 1998 ($2.95)

1-11, Annual 1 (4/98, $2.95) 3.00
...Class Reunion (12/98, $3.95, B&W) 4.00
...Escape (5/98, $2.95, B&W), ...Final Fire (12/98, $2.95, B&W) 3.00

ROBOTECH
DC Comics (WildStorm): No. 0, Feb, 2003 - No. 6, Jul, 2003 ($2.50/$2.95, limited series)

0-Tommy Yune-s; art by Jim Lee, Garza, Bermejo and others; pin-up pages by various 2.50
1-6 ($2.95)-Long Vo-a 3.00
...: From the Stars (2003, $9.95, digest-size) r/#0-6 & Sourcebook 10.00
... Sourcebook (3/03, $2.95) pin-ups and info on characters and mecha; art by various 3.00

ROBOTECH: COVERT-OPS
Antarctic Press: Aug, 1998 - No. 2, Sept, 1998 ($2.95, B&W, limited series)

1,2-Gregory Lane-s/a 3.00

ROBOTECH DEFENDERS
DC Comics: Mar, 1985 - No. 2, Apr, 1985 (Mini-series)

1,2 3.00

ROBOTECH IN 3-D (TV)
Comico: Aug, 1987 ($2.50)

1-Steacy painted-c 4.00

ROBOTECH: INVASION
DC Comics (WildStorm): Feb, 2004 - No. 5 ($2.95, limited series)

1-Faerber & Yune-s/Miyazawa & Dogan-a 3.00

ROBOTECH: LOVE AND WAR
DC Comics (WildStorm): Aug, 2003 - No. 6, Jan, 2004 ($2.95, limited series)

1-6-Long Vo & Charles Park-a/Faerber & Yune-s. 2-Variant-c by Warren 3.00

ROBOTECH MASTERS (TV)
Comico: July, 1985 - No. 23, Apr, 1988 ($1.50)

1-23 3.00

ROBOTECH: SENTINELS - RUBICON
Antarctic Press: July, 1998 ($2.95, B&W)

1 3.00

ROBOTECH SPECIAL
Comico: May, 1988 ($2.50, one-shot, 44 pgs.)

1-Steacy wraparound-c; partial photo-c 4.00

ROBOTECH THE GRAPHIC NOVEL
Comico: Aug, 1986 ($5.95, 8-1/2x11", 52 pgs.)

1-Origin SDF-1; intro T.R. Edwards, Steacy-c/a; 2nd printing also exists (12/86) 7.00

ROBOTECH: THE MACROSS SAGA (TV)(Formerly Macross)
Comico: No. 2, Feb, 1985 - No. 36, Feb, 1989 ($1.50)

2-10 4.00
11-36: 12,17-Ken Steacy painted-c. 26-Begin $1.75-c. 35,36-($1.95) 3.00
Volume 1-4 TPB (WildStorm, 2003, $14.95, 5-3/4" x 8-1/4")1-Reprints #2-6 & Macross #1. 2- r/#7-12. 3-r/#13-18. 4-r/#19-24 15.00

ROBOTECH: THE NEW GENERATION
Comico: July, 1985 - No. 25, July, 1988

1-25 3.00

ROBOTECH: VERMILION
Antarctic Press: Mar, 1997 - No. 4, ($2.95, B&W, limited series)

1-4 3.00

ROBOTECH: WINGS OF GIBRALTAR
Antarctic Press: Aug, 1998 - No. 2, Sept, 1998 ($2.95, B&W, limited series)

1,2-Lee Duhig-s/a 3.00

ROBOTIX
Marvel Comics: Feb, 1986 (75¢, one-shot)

1-Based on toy 3.00

ROBOTMEN OF THE LOST PLANET (Also see Space Thrillers)
Avon Periodicals: 1952 (Also see Strange Worlds #19)

1-McCann-a (3 pgs.); Fawcette-a 107 214 321 669 1005 1340

ROB ROY
Dell Publishing Co.: 1954 (Disney-Movie)

Four Color 544-Manning-a, photo-c 9 18 27 60 85 110

Rocket Comics #2 © HILL

Rock Fantasy Comics #11 © Rock Fantasy Comics

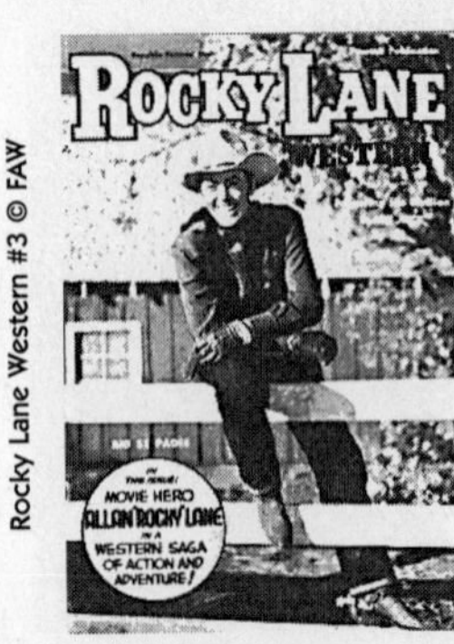

Rocky Lane Western #3 © FAW

GD VG FN VF VF/NM NM-
2.0 4.0 6.0 8.0 9.0 9.2

ROB ZOMBIE'S SPOOKSHOW INTERNATIONAL
CrossGen Comics: Nov, 2003 - No. 5 ($3.50/$2.95, limited series)
1-($3.50) Campbell-c; Rob Zombie-s/Colan, Dwyer & others-a 3.50
2,3-($2.95): 2-Edwards-c 3.00

ROCK, THE (WWF Wrestling)
Chaos! Comics: June, 2001 ($2.99, one-shot)
1-Photo-c; Grant-s/Neves-a 3.00

ROCK & ROLL HIGH SCHOOL
Roger Corman's Cosmic Comics: Oct, 1995 ($2.50)
1-Bob Fingerman scripts 2.50

ROCK AND ROLLO (Formerly TV Teens)
Charlton Comics: V2#14, Oct, 1957 - No. 19, Sept, 1958
V2#14-19 6 12 18 28 34 40

ROCK COMICS
Landgraphic Publ.: Jul/Aug, 1979 ($1.25, tabloid size, 28 pgs.)
1-N. Adams-c; Thor(not Marvel's) story by Adams 2 4 6 12 16 20

ROCKET COMICS
Hillman Periodicals: Mar, 1940 - No. 3, May, 1940
1-Rocket Riley, Red Roberts the Electro Man (origin), The Phantom Ranger, The Steel Shark, The Defender, Buzzard Barnes and his Sky Devils, Lefty Larson, & The Defender, the Man with a Thousand Faces begin (1st app. of each); all have Rocket Riley-c
248 496 744 1550 2325 3100
2,3 124 248 372 775 1163 1550

ROCKETEER, THE (See Eclipse Graphic Album Series, Pacific Presents & Starslayer)

ROCKETEER ADVENTURE MAGAZINE, THE
Comico/Dark Horse Comics No. 3: July, 1988 ($2.00); No. 2, July, 1989 ($2.75); No. 3, Jan, 1995 ($2.95)
1-(7/88, $2.00)-Dave Stevens-c/a in all; Kaluta back-up-a; 1st app. Jonas (character based on The Shadow) 1 2 3 5 7 9
2-(7/89, $2.75)-Stevens/Dorman painted-c 6.00
3-(1/95, $2.95)-Includes pinups by Stevens, Gulacy, Plunkett, & Mignola 3.50
Volume 2-(9/96, $9.95, magazine size TPB)-Reprints #1-3 10.00

ROCKETEER SPECIAL EDITION, THE
Eclipse Comics: Nov, 1984 ($1.50, Baxter paper)(Chapter 5 of Rocketeer serial)
1-Stevens-c/a; Kaluta back-c; pin-ups inside 2 4 6 8 10 12
NOTE: *Originally intended to be published in Pacific Presents.*

ROCKETEER: THE OFFICIAL MOVIE ADAPTATION, THE
W. D. Publications (Disney): 1991
nn-($5.95, 68 pgs.)-Squarebound deluxe edition 6.00
nn-($2.95, 68 pgs.)-Stapled regular edition 3.00
3-D Comic Book (1991, $7.98, 52 pgs.) 8.00

ROCKET KELLY (See The Bouncer, Green Mask #10); becomes Li'l Pan #6)
Fox Feature Syndicate: 1944; Fall, 1945 - No. 5, Oct-Nov, 1946
nn (1944), 1 35 70 105 201 288 370
2-The Puppeteer app. (costumed hero) 26 52 78 147 206 265
3-5: 5-(#5 on cover, #4 inside) 23 46 69 130 183 235

ROCKETMAN (Strange Fantasy #2 on) (See Hello Pal & Scoop Comics)
Ajax/Farrell Publications: June, 1952 (Strange Stories of the Future)
1-Rocketman & Cosmo 40 80 120 240 345 450

ROCKET RACCOON
Marvel Comics: May, 1985 - No. 4, Aug, 1985 (color, limited series)
1-4: Mignola-a 2.25

ROCKET SHIP X
Fox Features Syndicate: September, 1951; 1952
1 61 122 183 381 573 765
1952 (nn, nd, no publ.)-Edited 1951-c (exist?) 40 80 120 240 340 440

ROCKET TO ADVENTURE LAND (See Pixie Puzzle...)

ROCKET TO THE MOON
Avon Periodicals: 1951
nn-Orlando-c/a; adapts Otis Aldebert Kline's "Maza of the Moon"
107 214 321 669 1005 1340

ROCK FANTASY COMICS
Rock Fantasy Comics: Dec, 1989 - No. 16?, 1991 ($2.25/$3.00, B&W)(No cover price)
1-Pink Floyd part 1 5.00
1-2nd printing ($3.00-c) 3.00
2,3: 2-Rolling Stones #1. 3-Led Zeppelin #1 4.00
2,3: 2nd printings ($3.00-c, 1/90 & 2/90) 3.00
4-Stevie Nicks Not published
5-Monstrosities of Rock #1; photo back-c 4.00
5-2nd printing ($3.00, 3/90 indicia, 2/90-c) 3.00
6-9,11-15,17,18: 6-Guns n' Roses #1 (1st & 2nd printings, 3/90)-Begin $3.00-c. 7-Sex Pistols #1. 8-Alice Cooper; not published. 9-Van Halen #1; photo back-c. 11-Jimi Hendrix #1; wraparound-c 3.00
10-Kiss #1; photo back-c 2 4 6 8 10 12
16-($5.00, 68 pgs.)-The Great Gig in the Sky(Floyd) 5.00

ROCK HAPPENING (See Bunny and Harvey Pop Comics:...)

ROCK N' ROLL COMICS
Revolutionary Comics: Jun, 1989 - No. 65 ($1.50/$1.95/$2.50, B&W/col. #15 on)
1-Guns N' Roses 1 2 3 5 6 8
1-2nd thru 7th printings. 7th printing (full color w/new-c/a) 2.25
2-Metallica 1 3 4 6 8 10
2-2nd thru 6th printings (6th in color) 2.25
3-Bon Jovi (no reprints) 1 2 3 5 6 8
4-8,10-65: 4-Motley Crue(2nd printing only, 1st destroyed). 5-Def Leppard (2 printings). 6-Rolling Stones(4 printings). 7-The Who (3 printings). 8-Skid Row; not published. 10-Warrant/Whitesnake(2 printings; 1st has 2 diff.-c). 11-Aerosmith (2 printings?). 12-New Kids on the Block(2 printings). 12-3rd printing; rewritten & titled NKOTB Hate Book. 13-Led Zeppelin. 14-Sex Pistols. 15-Poison; 1st color issue. 16-Van Halen. 17-Madonna. 18-Alice Cooper. 19-Public Enemy/2 Live Crew. 20-Queensryche/Tesla. 21-Prince? 22-AC/DC; begin $2.50-c. 23-Living Colour. 24-Anthrax. 29-Ozzy. 45,46-Grateful Dead. 49-Rush. 50,51-Bob Dylan. 56-David Bowie 5.00
9-Kiss 2 4 6 8 10 12
9-2nd & 3rd printings 2.25
NOTE: *Most issues were reprinted except #3. Later reprints are in color. #8 was not released.*

ROCKO'S MODERN LIFE (TV)
Marvel Comics: June, 1994 - No. 7, Dec, 1994 ($1.95) (Nickelodeon cartoon)
1-7 2.25

ROCKY AND HIS FIENDISH FRIENDS (TV)(Bullwinkle)
Gold Key: Oct, 1962 - No. 5, Sept, 1963 (Jay Ward)
1 (25¢, 80 pgs.) 22 44 66 160 235 310
2,3 (25¢, 80 pgs.) 15 30 45 107 156 205
4,5 (Regular size, 12¢) 10 20 30 72 104 135

ROCKY AND HIS FRIENDS (See Kite Fun Book & March of Comics #216 in the Promotional Comics section)

ROCKY AND HIS FRIENDS (TV)
Dell Publishing Co.: No. 1128, 8-10/60 - No.1311,1962 (Jay Ward)
Four Color #1128 (#1) (8-10/60) 35 70 105 263 392 520
Four Color #1152 (12-2/61), 1166, 1208, 1275, 1311('62)
24 48 72 174 255 335

ROCKY HORROR PICTURE SHOW THE COMIC BOOK, THE
Caliber Press: Jul, 1990 - No. 3, Jan, 1991 ($2.95, mini-series, 52 pgs.)
1-3: 1-Adapts cult film plus photos, etc., 1-2nd printing 3.00
...Collection ($4.95) 5.00

ROCKY JONES SPACE RANGER (See Space Adventures #15-18)

ROCKY JORDEN PRIVATE EYE (See Private Eye)

ROCKY LANE WESTERN (Allan Rocky Lane starred in Republic movies & TV for a short time as Allan Lane, Red Ryder & Rocky Lane) (See Black Jack Fawcett Movie Comics, Motion Picture Comics & Six-Gun Heroes)
Fawcett Publications/Charlton No. 56 on: May, 1949 - No. 87, Nov, 1959
1 (36 pgs.)-Rocky, his stallion Black Jack, & Slim Pickens begin; photo-c begin, end #57; photo back-c 100 200 300 625 938 1250
2 (36 pgs.)-Last photo back-c 40 80 120 240 350 460
3-5 (52 pgs.): 4-Captain Tootsie by Beck 31 62 93 175 248 320
6,10 (36 pgs.): 10-Complete western novelette "Badman's Reward"
22 44 66 127 176 225
7-9 (52 pgs.) 24 48 72 135 190 245
11-13,15-17,19,20 (52 pgs.): 15-Black Jack's Hitching Post begins, ends #25. 20-Last Slim Pickens 18 36 54 101 138 175
14,18 (36 pgs.) 15 30 45 86 118 150
21,23,24 (52 pgs.): 21-Dee Dickens begins, ends #55,57,65-68
15 30 45 86 118 150
22,25-28,30 (36 pgs. begin) 14 28 42 81 111 140
29-Classic complete novel "The Land of Missing Men" with hidden land of ancient temple ruins (r-in #65) 20 40 60 112 156 200

Rod Cameron Western #10 © FAW

The Rogues #1 © DC

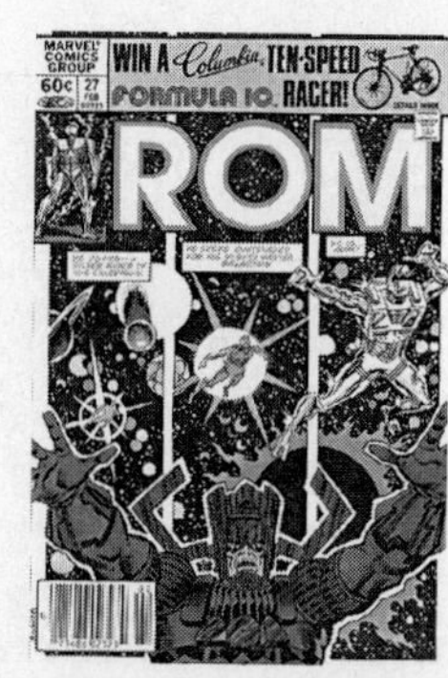

ROM #27 © Parker Bros.

	GD 2.0	VG 4.0	FN 6.0	VF 8.0	VF/NM 9.0	NM- 9.2

31-40 13 26 39 74 100 125
41-54 11 22 33 63 84 105
55-Last Fawcett issue (1/54) 12 24 36 69 92 115
56-1st Charlton issue (2/54)-Photo-c 20 40 60 112 156 200
57,60-Photo-c 12 24 36 69 92 115
58,59,61-64,66-78,80-86: 59-61-Young Falcon app. 64-Slim Pickens app.
66-68: Reprints #30,31,32 10 20 30 56 73 90
65-r/#29, "The Land of Missing Men" 11 22 33 63 84 105
79-Giant Edition (68 pgs.) 12 24 36 69 92 115
87-Last issue 11 22 33 63 84 105
NOTE: *Complete novels in #10, 14, 18, 22, 25, 30-32, 36, 38, 39, 49. Captain Tootsie in #4, 12, 20. Big Bow and Little Arrow in #11, 28, 63. Black Jack's Hitching Post in #15-25, 64, 73.*

ROCKY LANE WESTERN
AC Comics: 1989 ($2.50, B&W, one-shot?)
1-Photo-c; Giordano reprints 4.00
Annual 1 (1991, $2.95, B&W, 44 pgs.)-photo front/back & inside-c; reprints 4.00

ROD CAMERON WESTERN (Movie star)
Fawcett Publications: Feb, 1950 - No. 20, Apr, 1953
1-Rod Cameron, his horse War Paint, & Sam The Sheriff begin; photo front/back-c begin
54 108 162 324 487 650
2 29 58 87 164 232 300
3-Novel length story "The Mystery of the Seven Cities of Cibola"
24 48 72 138 194 250
4-10: 9-Last photo back-c 20 40 60 112 156 200
11-19 16 32 48 92 126 160
20-Last issue & photo-c 17 34 51 98 134 170
NOTE: *Novel length stories in No. 1-8, 12-14.*

RODEO RYAN (See A-1 Comics #8)

ROEL
Sirius: Feb, 1997 ($2.95, B&W, one-shot)
1 3.00

ROGAN GOSH
DC Comics (Vertigo): 1994 ($6.95, one-shot)
nn-Peter Milligan scripts 7.00

ROGER DODGER (Also in Exciting Comics #57 on)
Standard Comics: No. 5, Aug, 1952
5-Teen-age 6 12 18 28 34 40

ROGER RABBIT (Also see Marvel Graphic Novel)
Disney Comics: June, 1990 - No. 18, Nov, 1991 ($1.50)
1-18-All new stories 3.00
In 3-D 1 (1992, $2.50)-Sold at Wal-Mart?; w/glasses 4.00

ROGER RABBIT'S TOONTOWN
Disney Comics: Aug, 1991 - No. 5, Dec, 1991 ($1.50)
1-5 2.50

ROGER ZELAZNY'S AMBER: THE GUNS OF AVALON
DC Comics: 1996 - No. 3, 1996 ($6.95, limited series)
1-3: Based on novel 7.00

ROG 2000
Pacific Comics: June, 1982 ($2.95, 44 pgs., B&W, one-shot, magazine)
nn-Byrne-c/a (r) 2 4 6 8 10 12
2nd printing (7/82) 1 2 3 4 5 7

ROG 2000
Fantagraphics Books: 1987 - No. 2, 1987 ($2.00, limited series)
1,2-Byrne-r 3.00

ROGUE
Marvel Comics: Jan, 1995 - No. 4, Apr, 1995 ($2.95, limited series)
1-4: 1-Gold foil logo 4.00
TPB-($12.95) r/#1-4 13.00

ROGUE (Volume 2)
Marvel Comics: Sept, 2001 - No. 4, Dec, 2001 ($2.50, limited series)
1-4-Julie Bell painted-c/Lopresti-a; Rogue's early days with X-Men 2.50

ROGUES GALLERY
DC Comics: 1996 ($3.50, one-shot)
1-Pinups of DC villains by various artists 3.50

ROGUES, THE (VILLAINS) (See The Flash)

	GD 2.0	VG 4.0	FN 6.0	VF 8.0	VF/NM 9.0	NM- 9.2

DC Comics: Feb, 1998 ($1.95, one-shot)
1-Augustyn-s/Pearson-c 2.25

ROGUE TROOPER
Quality Comics/Fleetway Quality #38-on : Oct, 1986 - No. 49, 1991 ($1.25/$1.50/$1.75)
1-49: 6-Double size. 21,22,25-27-Guice-c. 47,48-Alan Moore scripts 2.25

ROLLING STONES: VOODOO LOUNGE
Marvel Comics: 1995 ($6.95, Prestige format, one-shot)
nn-Dave McKean-script/design/art 7.00

ROLY POLY COMIC BOOK
Green Publishing Co.: 1945 - No. 15, 1946 (MLJ reprints)
1-Red Rube & Steel Sterling begin; Sahle-c 31 62 93 175 248 320
6-The Blue Circle & The Steel Fist app. 19 38 57 106 146 185
10-Origin Red Rube retold; Steel Sterling story (Zip #41)
27 54 81 155 218 280
11,12: The Black Hood app. in both 19 38 57 106 146 185
14-Classic decapitation-c; the Black Hood app. 39 78 117 230 325 420
15-The Blue Circle & The Steel Fist app.; cover exact swipe from Fox Blue Beetle #1
33 66 99 190 270 350

ROM (Based on the Parker Brothers toy)
Marvel Comics Group: Dec, 1979 - No. 75, Feb, 1986
1-Origin/1st app. 1 3 4 6 8 10
2-16,19-23,28-30: 5-Dr. Strange. 13-Saga of the Space Knights begins. 19-X-Men cameo. 23-Powerman & Iron Fist app. 4.00
17,18-X-Men app. 1 2 3 5 6 8
24-27: 24-F.F. cameo; Skrulls, Nova & The New Champions app. 25-Double size. 26,27-Galactus app. 5.00
31-49,51-60: 31,32-Brotherhood of Evil Mutants app. 32-X-Men cameo. 34,35-Sub-Mariner app. 41,42-Dr. Strange app. 56,57-Alpha Flight app. 58,59-Ant-Man app. 2.25
50-Skrulls app. (52 pgs.) Pin-ups by Konkle, Austin 3.00
61-74: 65-West Coast Avengers & Beta Ray Bill app. 65,66-X-Men app. 2.25
75-Last issue 6.00
Annual 1-4: (1982-85, 52 pgs.) 3.00
NOTE: ***Austin** c-3i, 18i, 61i. **Byrne** a-74i; c-56, 57, 74. **Ditko** a-59-75p, Annual 4. **Golden** c-7-12, 19. **Guice** a-61i; c-55, 58, 60p, 70p. **Layton** a-59i, 72i; c-15, 59i, 69. **Miller** c-2p?, 3p, 17p, 18p. **Russell** a(i)-64, 65, 67, 69, 71, 75; c-64, 65i, 66, 71i, 75. **Severin** c-41p. **Sienkiewicz** a-53i; c-46, 47, 52-54, 68, 71p, Annual 2. **Simonson** c-18. **P. Smith** c-59p. **Starlin** c-67. **Zeck** c-50.*

ROMANCE (See True Stories of...)

ROMANCE AND CONFESSION STORIES (See Giant Comics Edition)
St. John Publishing Co.: No date (1949) (25¢, 100 pgs.)
1-Baker-c/a; remaindered St. John love comics 40 80 120 240 340 440

ROMANCE DIARY
Marvel Comics (CDS)(CLDS): Dec, 1949 - No. 2, Mar, 1950
1,2 14 28 42 81 111 140

ROMANCE OF FLYING, THE
David McKay Publications: 1942
Feature Books 33 (nn)-WW II photos 15 30 45 86 118 150

ROMANCES OF MOLLY MANTON (See Molly Manton)

ROMANCES OF NURSE HELEN GRANT, THE
Atlas Comics (VPI): Aug, 1957
1 8 16 24 43 54 65

ROMANCES OF THE WEST (Becomes Romantic Affairs #3?)
Marvel Comics (SPC): Nov, 1949 - No. 2, Mar, 1950 (52 pgs.)
1-Movie photo-c of Yvonne DeCarlo & Howard Duff (Calamity Jane & Sam Bass)
24 48 72 138 194 250
2-Photo-c 15 30 45 86 118 150

ROMANCE STORIES OF TRUE LOVE (Formerly True Love Problems & Advice Illustrated)
Harvey Publications: No. 45, 5/57 - No. 50, 3/58; No. 51, 9/58 - No. 52, 11/58
45-51: 45,46,48-50-Powell-a 6 12 18 31 38 45
52-Matt Baker-a 8 16 24 46 58 70

ROMANCE TALES (Formerly Western Winners #6?)
Marvel Comics (CDS): No. 7, Oct, 1949 - No. 9, Mar, 1950 (7,8: photo-c)
7 14 28 42 79 107 135
8,9: 8-Everett-a 10 20 30 56 73 90

ROMANCE TRAIL
National Periodical Publications: July-Aug, 1949 - No. 6, May-June, 1950
(All photo-c & 52 pgs.)

Romantic Adventures #32 © ACG

Romantic Picture Novelettes #1 © ME

Ronin #4 © Frank Miller

	GD 2.0	VG 4.0	FN 6.0	VF 8.0	VF/NM 9.0	NM- 9.2
1-Kinstler, Toth-a; Jimmy Wakely photo-c	60	120	180	375	563	750
2-Kinstler-a; Jim Bannon photo-c	33	66	99	190	270	350
3-Photo-c; Kinstler, Toth-a	36	72	108	204	290	375
4-Photo-c; Toth-a	26	52	78	147	206	265
5,6: Photo-c on both. 5-Kinstler-a	23	46	69	129	180	250

ROMAN HOLIDAYS, THE (TV)
Gold Key: Feb, 1973 - No. 4, Nov, 1973 (Hanna-Barbera)

	GD	VG	FN	VF	VF/NM	NM-
1	5	10	15	33	44	55
2-4	3	6	9	19	25	32

ROMANTIC ADVENTURES (My... #49-67, covers only)
American Comics Group (B&I Publ. Co.): Mar-Apr, 1949 - No. 67, July, 1956 (Becomes My... #68 on)

	GD	VG	FN	VF	VF/NM	NM-
1	18	36	54	104	142	180
2	10	20	30	58	77	95
3-10	8	16	24	43	54	65
11-20 (4/52)	7	14	21	37	46	55
21-45,51,52: 52-Last Pre-code (2/55)	6	12	18	31	38	45
46-49-3-D effect-c/stories (TrueVision)	11	22	33	63	84	105
50-Classic cover/story "Love of A Lunatic"	10	20	30	58	77	95
53-67	6	12	18	28	34	40

NOTE: *#1-23, 52 pgs.* ***Shelly*** *a-40. Whitney c/art in many issues.*

ROMANTIC AFFAIRS (Formerly Molly Manton's Romances #2 and/or Romances of the West #2 and/or Our Love #2?)
Marvel Comics (SPC): No. 3, Mar, 1950

	GD	VG	FN	VF	VF/NM	NM-
3-Photo-c from Molly Manton's Romances #2	9	18	27	52	66	80

ROMANTIC CONFESSIONS
Hillman Periodicals: Oct, 1949 - V3#1, Apr-May, 1953

	GD	VG	FN	VF	VF/NM	NM-
V1#1-McWilliams-a	16	32	48	92	126	160
2-Briefer-a; negligee panels	10	20	30	56	73	90
3-12	8	16	24	43	54	65
V2#1,2,4-8,10-12: 2-McWilliams-a	7	14	21	37	46	55
3-Krigstein-a	9	18	27	49	62	75
9-One pg. Frazetta ad	7	14	21	37	46	55
V3#1	7	14	21	35	43	50

ROMANTIC HEARTS
Story Comics/Master/Merit Pubs.: Mar, 1951 - No. 10, Oct, 1952; July, 1953 - No. 12, July, 1955

	GD	VG	FN	VF	VF/NM	NM-
1(3/51) (1st Series)	14	28	42	81	111	140
2	8	16	24	46	58	70
3-10: Cameron-a	8	16	24	40	50	60
1(7/53) (2nd Series)-Some say #11 on-c	9	18	27	52	66	80
2	7	14	21	37	46	55
3-12	6	12	18	31	38	45

ROMANTIC LOVE
Avon Periodicals/Realistic (No #14-19): 9-10/49 - #3, 1-2/50; #4, 2-3/51 - #13, 10/52; #20, 3-4/54 - #23, 9-10/54

	GD	VG	FN	VF	VF/NM	NM-
1-c-/Avon paperback #252	25	50	75	147	202	260
2-5: 3-c-/paperback Novel Library #12. 4-c-/paperback Diversey Prize Novel #5. 5-c-/paperback Novel Library #34	15	30	45	86	118	150
6- "Thrill Crazy" marijuana story; c-/Avon paperback #207; Kinstler-a	21	42	63	118	164	210
7,8: 8-Astarita-a(2)	14	28	42	81	111	140
9-12: 9-c-/paperback Novel Library #41; Kinstler-a. 10-c-/Avon paperback #212. 11-c-/paperback Novel Library #17; Kinstler-a. 12-c-/paperback Novel Library #13	15	30	45	86	118	150
13,21-23: 22,23-Kinstler-c	14	28	42	79	107	135
20-Kinstler-c/a	14	28	42	81	111	140
nn(1-3/53)(Realistic-r)	10	20	30	56	73	90

NOTE: ***Astarita*** *a-7, 10, 11, 21. Painted c-1-3, 5, 7-11, 13. Photo c-4, 6.*

ROMANTIC LOVE
Quality Comics Group: 1963-1964

	GD	VG	FN	VF	VF/NM	NM-
I.W. Reprint #2,3,8: 2-r/Romantic Love #2	2	4	6	10	12	15

ROMANTIC MARRIAGE (Cinderella Love #25 on)
Ziff-Davis/St. John No. 18 on (#1-8: 52 pgs.): #1-3 (1950, no months); #4, 5-6/51 - #17, 9/52; #18, 9/53 - #24, 9/54

	GD	VG	FN	VF	VF/NM	NM-
1-Photo-c; Cary Grant/Betsy Drake photo back-c.	21	42	63	118	164	210
2-Painted-c; Anderson-a (also #15)	14	28	42	79	107	135
3-9: 3,4,8,9-Painted-c; 5-7-Photo-c	12	24	36	69	92	115
10-Unusual format; front-c is a painted-c; back-c is a photo-c complete with logo, price, etc.	19	38	57	107	149	190
11-17 13-Photo-c. 15-Signed story by Anderson. 17-(9/52)-Last Z-D issue	10	20	30	60	80	100
18-22,24: 20-Photo-c	10	20	30	60	80	100
23-Baker-c; all stories are reprinted from #15	11	22	33	63	84	105

ROMANTIC PICTURE NOVELETTES
Magazine Enterprises: 1946

	GD	VG	FN	VF	VF/NM	NM-
1-Mary Worth-r; Creig Flessel-c	17	34	51	95	130	165

ROMANTIC SECRETS (Becomes Time For Love)
Fawcett/Charlton Comics No. 5 (10/55) on: Sept, 1949 - No. 39, 4/53; No. 5, 10/55 - No. 52, 11/64 (#1-5: photo-c)

	GD	VG	FN	VF	VF/NM	NM-
1-(52 pg. issues begin, end #?)	16	32	48	92	126	160
2,3	10	20	30	58	77	95
4,9-Evans-a	11	22	33	63	84	105
5-8,10	8	16	24	43	54	65
11-23	8	16	24	40	50	60
24-Evans-a	8	16	24	46	58	70
25-39('53)	7	14	21	37	46	55
5 (Charlton, 2nd Series)(10/55, formerly Negro Romances #4)	10	20	30	56	73	90
6-10	8	16	24	43	54	65
11-20	4	8	12	25	33	42
21-35: Last 10¢ issue?	3	7	10	21	28	35
36-52('64)	3	6	9	18	23	28

NOTE: ***Bailey*** *a-20.* ***Powell*** *a(1st series)-5, 7, 10, 12, 16, 17, 20, 26, 29, 33, 34, 36, 37.* ***Sekowsky*** *a-26. Photo c(1st series)-1-5, 16, 25, 27, 33.* ***Swayze*** *a(1st series)-16, 18, 19, 23, 26-28, 31, 32, 39.*

ROMANTIC STORY (Cowboy Love #28 on)
Fawcett/Charlton Comics No. 23 on: 11/49 - #22, Sum, 1953; #23, 5/54 - #27, 12/54; #28, 8/55 - #130, 11/73

	GD	VG	FN	VF	VF/NM	NM-
1-Photo-c begin, end #24; 52 pgs. begins	18	36	54	104	142	180
2	10	20	30	58	77	95
3-5	9	18	27	52	66	80
6-14	8	16	24	46	58	70
15-Evans-a	9	18	27	52	66	80
16-22(Sum, '53; last Fawcett issue). 21-Toth-a?	7	14	21	37	46	55
23-39: 26,29-Wood swipes	7	14	21	35	43	50
40-(100 pgs.)	11	22	33	63	84	105
41-50	4	8	12	24	32	40
51-80: 57-Hypo needle story	3	6	9	18	23	28
81-99	2	4	6	10	13	16
100	2	4	6	12	16	20
101-130	2	4	6	9	11	14

NOTE: ***Jim Aparo*** *a-94.* ***Powell*** *a-7, 8, 16, 20, 30.* ***Marcus Swayze*** *a-2, 12, 20, 32.*

ROMANTIC THRILLS (See Fox Giants)

ROMANTIC WESTERN
Fawcett Publications: Winter, 1949 - No. 3, June, 1950 (All Photo-c)

	GD	VG	FN	VF	VF/NM	NM-
1	23	46	69	129	180	230
2-(Spr/50)-Williamson, McWilliams-a	21	42	63	118	164	210
3	15	30	45	86	118	150

ROMEO TUBBS (...That Lovable Teenager; formerly My Secret Life)
Fox Feature Syndicate/Green Publ. Co. No. 27: No. 26, 5/50 - No. 28, 7/50; No. 1, 1950; No. 27, 12/52

	GD	VG	FN	VF	VF/NM	NM-
26-Teen-age	11	22	33	63	84	105
28 (7/50)	10	20	30	56	73	90
27 (12/52)-Contains Pedro on inside; Wood-a (exist?)	16	32	48	89	122	155

RONALD McDONALD (TV)
Charlton Press (King Features Synd.): Sept, 1970 - No. 4, March, 1971

	GD	VG	FN	VF	VF/NM	NM-
1	9	18	27	60	85	110
2-4	5	10	15	33	44	55
V2#1,3-Special reprint for McDonald systems; "Not for resale" on cover	6	12	18	40	55	70

RONIN
DC Comics: July, 1983 - No. 6, Aug, 1984 ($2.50, limited series, 52 pgs.)

	GD	VG	FN	VF	VF/NM	NM-
1-5-Frank Miller-c/a/scripts in all						5.00
6-Scarcer; has fold-out poster.	1	2	3	5	6	8
Trade paperback (1987, $12.95)-Reprints #1-6						13.00

RONNA
Knight Press: Apr, 1997 ($2.95, B&W, one-shot)

Route 666 #1 © CRO

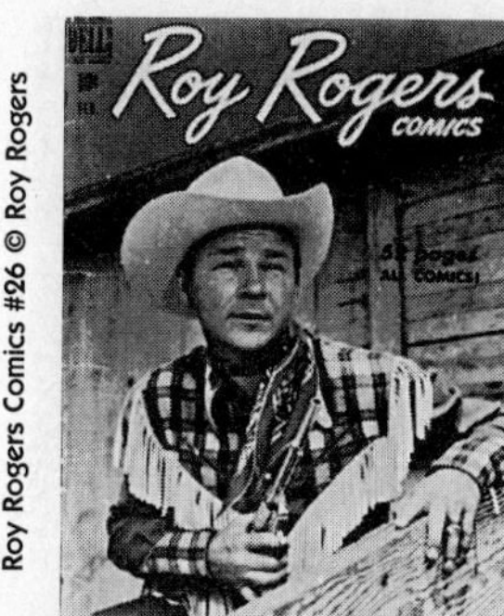

Roy Rogers Comics #26 © Roy Rogers

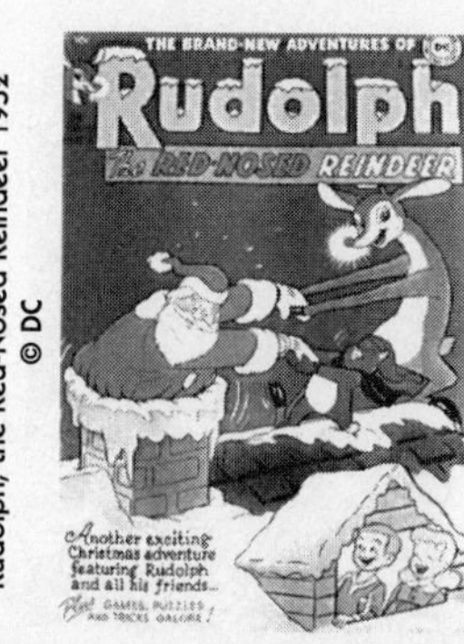

Rudolph, the Red-Nosed Reindeer 1952 © DC

	GD 2.0	VG 4.0	FN 6.0	VF 8.0	VF/NM 9.0	NM- 9.2
1-Beau Smith-s						3.00

ROOK (See Eerie Magazine & Warren Presents: The Rook)
Warren Publications: Oct, 1979 - No. 14, April, 1982 (B&W magazine)

	GD 2.0	VG 4.0	FN 6.0	VF 8.0	VF/NM 9.0	NM- 9.2
1-Nino-a/Corben-c; with 8 pg. color insert	2	4	6	11	14	18
2-4,6,7: 2-Voltar by Alcala begins. 3,4-Toth-a	1	3	4	6	8	10
5,8-14: 11-Zorro-s. 12-14-Eagle by Severin	1	3	4	6	8	10

ROOK
Harris Comics: No. 0, Jun, 1995 - No. 4, 1995 ($2.95)

	GD 2.0	VG 4.0	FN 6.0	VF 8.0	VF/NM 9.0	NM- 9.2
0-4: 0-short stories (3) w/preview. 4-Brereton-c.						3.00

ROOKIE COP (Formerly Crime and Justice?)
Charlton Comics: No. 27, Nov, 1955 - No. 33, Aug, 1957

	GD 2.0	VG 4.0	FN 6.0	VF 8.0	VF/NM 9.0	NM- 9.2
27	9	18	27	49	62	75
28-33	6	12	18	31	38	45

ROOM 222 (TV)
Dell Publishing Co.: Jan, 1970; No. 2, May, 1970 - No. 4, Jan, 1971

	GD 2.0	VG 4.0	FN 6.0	VF 8.0	VF/NM 9.0	NM- 9.2
1	6	12	18	40	55	70
2-4: 2,4-Photo-c. 3-Marijuana story. 4 r/#1	4	8	12	24	32	40

ROOTIE KAZOOTIE (TV)(See 3-D-ell)
Dell Publishing Co.: No. 415, Aug, 1952 - No. 6, Oct-Dec, 1954

	GD 2.0	VG 4.0	FN 6.0	VF 8.0	VF/NM 9.0	NM- 9.2
Four Color 415 (#1)	11	22	33	77	114	150
Four Color 459,502(#2,3), 4(4-6/54)-6	8	16	24	55	78	100

ROOTS OF THE SWAMP THING
DC Comics: July, 1986 - No.5, Nov, 1986 ($2.00, Baxter paper, 52 pgs.)

	GD 2.0	VG 4.0	FN 6.0	VF 8.0	VF/NM 9.0	NM- 9.2
1-5: r/Swamp Thing #1-10 by Wrightson & House of Mystery-r. 1-new Wrightson-c (2-5 reprinted covers).						4.00

ROSE (See Bone)
Cartoon Books: Nov, 2000 - No. 3, Feb, 2002 ($5.95, lim. series, square-bound)

	GD 2.0	VG 4.0	FN 6.0	VF 8.0	VF/NM 9.0	NM- 9.2
1-3-Prequel to Bone; Jeff Smith-s/Charles Vess painted-a/c						6.00
HC (2001, $29.95) r/#1-3; new Vess cover painting						30.00
SC (2002, $19.95) r/#1-3; new Vess cover painting						20.00
1-($6.00)-Blood & Glory Edition						6.00

ROSE AND THORN
DC Comics: Feb, 2004 - No. 6 ($2.95, limited series)

	GD 2.0	VG 4.0	FN 6.0	VF 8.0	VF/NM 9.0	NM- 9.2
1-Simone-sMelo-a/Hughes-c						3.00

ROSWELL: LITTLE GREEN MAN (See Simpsons Comics #19-22)
Bongo Comics: 1996 - No. 6 ($2.95, quarterly)

	GD 2.0	VG 4.0	FN 6.0	VF 8.0	VF/NM 9.0	NM- 9.2
1-6						3.50
...Walks Among Us ('97, $12.95, TPB) r/ #1-3 & Simpsons flip books						13.00

ROTOGIN: JUNKBOTZ
Image Comics: No. 0, Feb, 2003 - Present ($2.50)

	GD 2.0	VG 4.0	FN 6.0	VF 8.0	VF/NM 9.0	NM- 9.2
0-3-J. Korim-a/c						2.50

ROUNDUP (...Western Crime Stories)
D. S. Publishing Co.: July-Aug, 1948 - No. 5, Mar-Apr, 1949 (All 52 pgs.)

	GD 2.0	VG 4.0	FN 6.0	VF 8.0	VF/NM 9.0	NM- 9.2
1-Kiefer-a	21	42	63	118	164	210
2-5: 2-Marijuana drug mention story	15	30	45	84	115	145

ROUTE 666
CrossGeneration Comics: July, 2002 - Present ($2.95)

	GD 2.0	VG 4.0	FN 6.0	VF 8.0	VF/NM 9.0	NM- 9.2
1-20-Bedard-s/Moline-a in most. 5-Richards-a. 15-McCrea-a						3.00
...: Highway to Horror (4/03, $15.95, TPB) r/#1-6						16.00
Vol. 2: Three-Ring Circus (2003, $15.95) r/#7-12						16.00

ROYAL ROY
Marvel Comics (Star Comics): May, 1985 - No.6, Mar, 1986 (Children's book)

	GD 2.0	VG 4.0	FN 6.0	VF 8.0	VF/NM 9.0	NM- 9.2
1-6						4.00

ROY CAMPANELLA, BASEBALL HERO
Fawcett Publications: 1950 (Brooklyn Dodgers)

	GD 2.0	VG 4.0	FN 6.0	VF 8.0	VF/NM 9.0	NM- 9.2
nn-Photo-c; life story	60	120	180	375	563	750

ROY ROGERS (See March of Comics #17, 35, 47, 62, 68, 73, 77, 86, 91, 100, 105, 116, 121, 131, 136, 146, 151, 161, 167, 176, 191, 206, 221, 236, 250)

ROY ROGERS AND TRIGGER
Gold Key: Apr, 1967

	GD 2.0	VG 4.0	FN 6.0	VF 8.0	VF/NM 9.0	NM- 9.2
1-Photo-c; reprints	6	12	18	38	52	65

ROY ROGERS ANNUAL
Wilson Publ. Co., Toronto/Dell: 1947 ("Giant Edition" on-c)(132 pgs., 50¢)

nn-Less than 5 known copies. Front and back cover art are from Roy Rogers #2. Stories reprinted from Roy Rogers #2, Four Color #137 and Four Color #153. (A copy in VG/FN was sold in 1986 for $400, & in 1996 for $1200 & in 2000 for $1500)

ROY ROGERS COMICS (See Western Roundup under Dell Giants)
Dell Publishing Co.: No. 38, 4/44 - No. 177, 12/47 (#38-166: 52 pgs.)

	GD 2.0	VG 4.0	FN 6.0	VF 8.0	VF/NM 9.0	NM- 9.2
Four Color 38 (1944)-49 pg. story; photo front/back-c on all 4-Color issues (1st western comic with photo-c)	210	420	630	1654	2577	3500
Four Color 63 (1945)-Color photos on all four-c	47	94	141	376	563	750
Four Color 86,95 (1945)	35	70	105	263	394	525
Four Color 109 (1946)	29	58	87	210	305	400
Four Color 117,124,137,144	23	46	69	164	240	315
Four Color 153,160,166: 166-48 pg. story	21	42	63	147	216	285
Four Color 177 (36 pgs.)-32 pg. story	20	40	60	145	213	280

ROY ROGERS COMICS (...& Trigger #92(8/55)-on)(Roy starred in Republic movies, radio & TV) (Singing cowboy) (Also see Dale Evans, It Really Happened #8, Queen of the West Dale Evans, & Roy Rogers' Trigger)
Dell Publishing Co.: Jan, 1948 - No. 145, Sept-Oct, 1961 (#1-19: 36 pgs.)

	GD 2.0	VG 4.0	FN 6.0	VF 8.0	VF/NM 9.0	NM- 9.2
1-Roy, his horse Trigger, & Chuck Wagon Charley's Tales begin; photo-c begin, end #145	78	156	234	629	965	1300
2	30	60	90	218	319	420
3-5	22	44	66	156	228	300
6-10	17	34	51	123	182	240
11-19: 19-Chuck Wagon Charley's Tales ends	14	28	42	99	145	190
20 (52 pgs.)-Trigger feature begins, ends #46	14	28	42	102	149	195
21-30 (52 pgs.)	12	24	36	84	125	165
31-46 (52 pgs.): 37-X-Mas-c	10	20	30	70	100	130
47-56 (36 pgs.): 47-Chuck Wagon Charley's Tales returns, ends #133. 49-X-mas-c. 55-Last photo back-c	8	16	24	53	74	95
57 (52 pgs.)-Heroin drug propaganda story	8	16	24	55	78	100
58-70 (52 pgs.): 58-Heroin drug use/dealing story. 61-X-Mas-c	8	16	24	53	74	95
71-80 (52 pgs.): 73-X-Mas-c	7	14	21	50	68	85
81-91 (36 pgs. #81-on): 85-X-Mas-c	7	14	21	46	63	80
92-99,101-110,112-118: 92-Title changed to Roy Rogers and Trigger (8/55)	6	12	18	43	59	75
100-Trigger feature returns, ends #131	8	16	24	53	74	95
111,119-124-Toth-a	8	16	24	55	78	100
125-131: 125-Toth-a (1 pg.)	6	12	18	40	55	70
132-144-Manning-a. 132-1st Dale Evans-sty by Russ Manning. 138,144-Dale Evans featured	7	14	21	50	68	85
145-Last issue	8	16	24	55	78	100

NOTE: ***Buscema*** *a-74-108(2 stories each).* ***Manning*** *a-123, 124, 132-144.* ***Marsh*** *a-110. Photo back-c No. 1-9, 11-35, 38-55.*

ROY ROGERS' TRIGGER
Dell Publishing Co.: No. 329, May, 1951 - No. 17, June-Aug, 1955

	GD 2.0	VG 4.0	FN 6.0	VF 8.0	VF/NM 9.0	NM- 9.2
Four Color 329 (#1)-Painted-c	16	32	48	111	163	215
2 (9-11/51)-Photo-c	13	26	39	94	137	180
3-5: 3-Painted-c begin, end #17, most by S. Savitt	7	14	21	50	68	85
6-17: Title merges with Roy Rogers after #17	6	12	18	38	52	65

ROY ROGERS WESTERN CLASSICS
AC Comics: 1989 -No. 4 ($2.95/$3.95, 44pgs.) (24 pgs. color, 16 pgs. B&W)

	GD 2.0	VG 4.0	FN 6.0	VF 8.0	VF/NM 9.0	NM- 9.2
1-4: 1-Dale Evans-r by Manning, Trigger-r by Buscema; photo covers & interior photos by Roy & Dale. 2-Buscema-r (3); photo-c & B&W photos inside. 3-Dale Evans-r by Manning; Trigger-r by Buscema plus other Buscema-r; photo-c						4.00

RUDOLPH, THE RED-NOSED REINDEER
National Per. Publ.: 1950 - No. 13, Winter, 1962-63 (Issues are not numbered)

	GD 2.0	VG 4.0	FN 6.0	VF 8.0	VF/NM 9.0	NM- 9.2
1950 issue (#1); Grossman-c/a begins	23	46	69	129	180	230
1951-53 issues (3 total)	13	26	39	74	100	125
1954/55, 55/56, 56/57	11	22	33	63	84	105
1957/58, 58/59, 59/60, 60/61, 61/62	7	14	21	51	71	90
1962/63 (rare)(84 pgs.)(shows "Annual" in indicia)	12	24	36	82	121	160

NOTE: *13 total issues published. Has games & puzzles also.*

RUDOLPH, THE RED-NOSED REINDEER (Also see Limited Collectors' Edition C-20, C-24, C-33, C-42, C-50; and All-New Collectors' Edition C-53 & C-60)
National Per. Publ.: Christmas 1972 (Treasury-size)

	GD 2.0	VG 4.0	FN 6.0	VF 8.0	VF/NM 9.0	NM- 9.2
nn-Precursor to Limited Collectors' Edition title (scarce) (implied to be Lim. Coll .Ed. C-20)	25	50	75	176	258	340

RUFF AND REDDY (TV)
Dell Publ. Co.: No. 937, 9/58 - No. 12, 1-3/62 (Hanna-Barbera)(#9 on: 15¢)

	GD 2.0	VG 4.0	FN 6.0	VF 8.0	VF/NM 9.0	NM- 9.2
Four Color 937(#1)(1st Hanna-Barbera comic book)	14	28	42	99	145	190
Four Color 981,1038	9	18	27	63	89	115

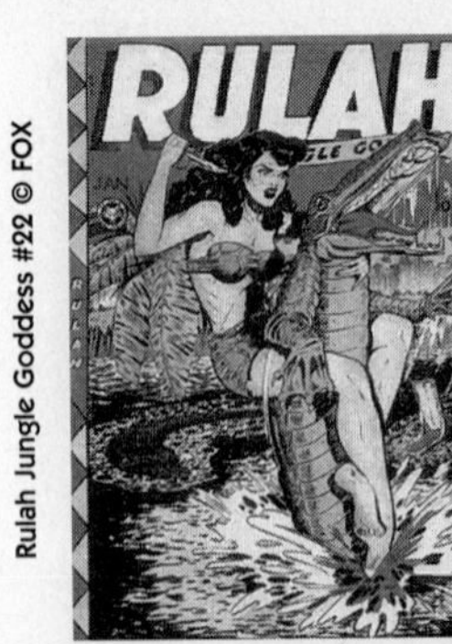

Rulah Jungle Goddess #22 © FOX

Ruse #18 © CRO

Rusty Comics #17 © MAR

	GD 2.0	VG 4.0	FN 6.0	VF 8.0	VF/NM 9.0	NM- 9.2

4(1-3/60)-12: 8-Last 10¢ issue 8 16 24 53 74 95

RUGGED ACTION (Strange Stories of Suspense #5 on)
Atlas Comics (CSI): Dec, 1954 - No. 4, June, 1955

1-Brodsky-c 14 28 42 79 107 135
2-4: 2-Last precode (2/55) 10 20 30 56 73 90
NOTE: *Ayers a-2, 3. **Maneely** c-2, 3. **Severin** a-2.*

RUGRATS COMIC ADVENTURES (TV)
Nickelodeon Magazines: 1999 - Present ($2.95, magazine size)

1-5, Volume 2: 1-6 3.00

RUINS
Marvel Comics (Alterniverse): July, 1995 - No. 2, Sept, 1995 ($5.00, painted, limited series)

1,2: Phil Sheldon from Marvels; Warren Ellis scripts; acetate-c 5.00

RULAH JUNGLE GODDESS (Formerly Zoot; I Loved #28 on) (Also see All Top Comics & Terrors of the Jungle)
Fox Features Syndicate: No. 17, Aug, 1948 - No. 27, June, 1949

17 96 192 288 600 900 1200
18-Classic girl-fight interior splash 66 132 198 413 619 825
19,20 64 128 192 400 600 800
21-Used in **SOTI**, pg. 388,389 66 132 198 413 619 825
22-Used in **SOTI**, pg. 22,23 64 128 192 400 600 800
23-27 50 100 150 300 450 600
NOTE: *Kamen c-17-19, 21, 22.*

RUMBLE GIRLS: SILKY WARRIOR TANSIE
Image Comics: Apr, 2000 - Present ($3.50, B&W)

1-6-Lea Hernandez-s/a. 2-Warren flip-c. 5,6-Warren Ellis short story 3.50

RUNAWAY, THE (See Movie Classics)

RUNAWAYS
Marvel Comics: July, 2003 - Present ($2.95/$2.25)

1-($2.95) Vaughan-s/Alphona-a/JoChen-c 3.00
2-9-($2.50) 2.50

RUN BABY RUN
Logos International: 1974 (39¢, Christian religious)

nn-By Tony Tallarico from Nicky Cruz's book 2 4 6 8 10 12

RUN, BUDDY, RUN (TV)
Gold Key: June, 1967 (Photo-c)

1 (10204-706) 3 6 9 19 25 32

RUNE (See Curse of Rune, Sludge & all other Ultraverse titles for previews)
Malibu Comics (Ultraverse): 1994 - No. 9, Apr, 1995 ($1.95)

0-Obtained by sending coupons from 11 comics; came w/Solution #0, poster, temporary tattoo, card 1 2 3 5 6 8
1,2,4-9: 1-Barry Windsor-Smith-c/a/stories begin, ends #6. 5-1st app. of Gemini. 6-Prime & Mantra app. 2.25
1-(1/94)-"Ashcan" edition flip book w/Wrath #1 2.25
1-Ultra 5000 Limited silver foil edition 4.00
3-(3/94, $3.50, 68 pgs.)-Flip book w/Ultraverse Premiere #1 3.50
Giant Size 1 ($2.50, 44 pgs.)-B.Smith story & art. 2.50

RUNE (2nd Series)(Formerly Curse of Rune)(See Ultraverse Unlimited #1)
Malibu Comics (Ultraverse): Infinity, Sept, 1995 - V2#7, Apr, 1996 ($1.50)

Infinity, V2#1-7: Infinity-Black September tie-in; black-c & painted-c exist. 1,3-7-Marvel's Adam Warlock app; regular & painted-c exist. 2-Flip book w/ "Phoenix Resurrection" Pt. 6 2.25
...Vs. Venom 1 (12/95, $3.95) 4.00

RUNE: HEARTS OF DARKNESS
Malibu Comics (Ultraverse): Sept, 1996 - No. 3, Nov, 1996 ($1.50, lim. series)

1-3: Moench scripts & Kyle Hotz-c/a; flip books w/6 pg. Rune story by the Pander Bros. 2.25

RUNE/SILVER SURFER
Marvel Comics/Malibu Comics (Ultraverse): Apr, 1995 ($5.95/$2.95, one-shot)

1 ($5.95, direct market)-BWS-c 6.00
1 ($2.95, newstand)-BWS-c 3.00
1-Collector's limited edition 6.00

RUSE (Also see Archard's Agents)
CrossGeneration Comics: Nov, 2001 - No. 26, Jan, 2004 ($2.95)

1-Waid-s/Guice & Perkins-a 5.00
2-26: 6-Jeff Johnson-a. 11,15-Paul Ryan-a. 12-Last Waid-s 3.00
Enter the Detective Vol. 1 TPB (2002, $15.95) r/#1-6; Guice-c 16.00
...: The Silent Partner Vol. 2 (3/03, $15.95, TPB) r/#7-12 16.00
...: Criminal Intent Vol. 3 ('03, $15.95, TPB) r/#13-18 16.00
Traveler 1,2 ($9.95): Digest-size editions of the TPBs 10.00

RUST
Now Comics: 7/87 - No. 15, 11/88; V2#1, 2/89 - No. 7, 1989 ($1.50/$1.75)

1-15,V2#1-7: 12-(8/88)-5 pg. preview of The Terminator (1st app.) 3.00

RUST
Caliber Comics: 1996/1997 ($2.95, B&W)

1,2 3.00

RUSTLERS, THE (See Zane Grey Four Color 532)

RUSTY, BOY DETECTIVE
Good Comics/Lev Gleason: Mar-April, 1955 - No. 5, Nov, 1955

1-Bob Wood, Carl Hubbell-a begins 9 18 27 49 62 75
2-5 6 12 18 31 38 45

RUSTY COMICS (Formerly Kid Movie Comics; Rusty and Her Family #21, 22; The Kelleys #23 on; see Millie The Model)
Marvel Comics (HPC): No. 12, Apr, 1947 - No. 22, Sept, 1949

12-Mitzi app. 20 40 60 112 156 200
13 11 22 33 63 84 105
14-Wolverton's Powerhouse Pepper (4 pgs.) plus Kurtzman's "Hey Look" 23 46 69 129 180 230
15-17-Kurtzman's "Hey Look" 16 32 48 92 126 160
18,19 10 20 30 58 77 95
20-Kurtzman-a (5 pgs.) 17 34 51 98 134 170
21,22-Kurtzman-a (17 & 22 pgs.) 22 44 66 124 172 220

RUSTY DUGAN (See Holyoke One-Shot #2)

RUSTY RILEY
Dell Publishing Co.: No. 418, Aug, 1952 - No. 554, April, 1954 (Frank Godwin strip reprints)

Four Color 418 (...a Boy, a Horse, and a Dog #1) 5 10 15 36 48 60
Four Color #451(2/53), 486 ('53), 554 4 8 12 28 38 48

RUULE
Beckett Comics: Dec, 2003 - No. 5 ($2.99)

1-David Mack-c/Mike Hawthorne-a 3.00

SAARI ("The Jungle Goddess")
P. L. Publishing Co.: November, 1951

1 44 88 132 264 395 525

SABAN POWERHOUSE (TV)
Acclaim Books: 1997 ($4.50, digest size)

1,2-Power Rangers, BeetleBorgs, and others 4.50

SABAN PRESENTS POWER RANGERS TURBO VS. BEETLEBORGS METALLIX (TV)
Acclaim Books: 1997 ($4.50, digest size, one-shot)

nn 4.50

SABAN'S MIGHTY MORPHIN POWER RANGERS
Hamilton Comics: Dec, 1994 - No. 6, May, 1995 ($1.95, limited series)

1-6: 1-w/bound-in Power Ranger Barcode Card 2.25

SABAN'S MIGHTY MORPHIN POWER RANGERS (TV)
Marvel Comics: 1995 - No. 8, 1996 ($1.75)

1-8 2.25

SABAN'S NINJA RANGERS
Hamilton Comics: Dec, 1995 - No. 4, Mar, 1995 ($1.95, limited series)

1-4: Flip book w/Saban's V.R. Troopers 2.25

SABAN'S V.R. TROOPERS (See Saban's Ninja Rangers)

SABLE (Formerly Jon Sable, Freelance; also see Mike Grell's...)
First Comics: Mar, 1988 - No. 27, May, 1990 ($1.75/$1.95)

1-27: 10-Begin $1.95-c 2.25

SABRE (See Eclipse Graphic Album Series)
Eclipse Comics: Aug, 1982 - No. 14, Aug, 1985 (Baxter paper #4 on)

1-14: 1-Sabre & Morrigan Tales begin. 4-6-Incredible Seven origin 2.25

SABRETOOTH (See Iron Fist, Power Man, X-Factor #10 & X-Men)
Marvel Comics: Aug, 1993 - No. 4, Nov, 1993 ($2.95, lim. series, coated paper)

1-4: 1-Die-cut-c. 3-Wolverine app. 4.00
...Special 1 "In the Red Zone" (1995, $4.95) Chromium wraparound-c 6.00
V2 #1 (1/98, $5.95, one-shot) Wildchild app. 6.00
Trade paperback (12/94, $12.95) r/#1-4 13.00

SABRETOOTH AND MYSTIQUE (See Mystique and Sabretooth)

Sabrina #32 © AP

Sabu, "Elephant Boy" #1 © FOX

Sad Sack Comics #4 © HARV

SABRETOOTH CLASSIC
Marvel Comics: May, 1994 - No. 15, July, 1995 ($1.50)

	GD 2.0	VG 4.0	FN 6.0	VF 8.0	VF/NM 9.0	NM- 9.2
1-15: 1-3-r/Power Man & Iron Fist #66,78,84. 4-r/Spec. S-M #116. 9-Uncanny X-Men #212, 10-r/Uncanny X-Men #213. 11-r/ Daredevil #238. 12-r/Classic X-Men #10						3.00

SABRETOOTH: MARY SHELLEY OVERDRIVE
Marvel Comics: Aug, 2002 - No. 4, Nov, 2002 ($2.99, limited series)

	GD 2.0	VG 4.0	FN 6.0	VF 8.0	VF/NM 9.0	NM- 9.2
1-4-Jolley-s; Harris-c						3.00

SABRINA (Volume 2) (Based on animated series)
Archie Publications: Jan, 2000 - Present ($1.79/$1.99/$2.19)

	GD 2.0	VG 4.0	FN 6.0	VF 8.0	VF/NM 9.0	NM- 9.2
1-Teen-age Witch magically reverted to 12 years old						3.00
2-54: 4-Begin $1.99-c. 38-Sabrina aged back to 16 years old. 39-Begin $2.19-c						2.50

SABRINA'S CHRISTMAS MAGIC (See Archie Giant Series Magazine #196, 207, 220, 231, 243, 455, 467, 479, 491, 503, 515)

SABRINA'S HALLOWEEN SPOOOKTACULAR
Archie Publications: 1993 - 1995 ($2.00, 52 pgs.)

	GD 2.0	VG 4.0	FN 6.0	VF 8.0	VF/NM 9.0	NM- 9.2
1-Neon orange ink-c; bound-in poster	1	2	3	5	6	8
2,3						5.00

SABRINA'S HOLIDAY SPECTACULAR
Archie Publications: 1993 - 1995 ($2.00, 52 pgs.)

	GD 2.0	VG 4.0	FN 6.0	VF 8.0	VF/NM 9.0	NM- 9.2
1	1	2	3	5	6	8
2,3						5.00

SABRINA, THE TEEN-AGE WITCH (TV)(See Archie Giant Series, Archie's Madhouse 22, Archie's TV..., Chilling Advs. In Sorcery, Little Archie #59)
Archie Publications: April, 1971 - No. 77, Jan, 1983 (52 pg.Giants No. 1-17)

	GD 2.0	VG 4.0	FN 6.0	VF 8.0	VF/NM 9.0	NM- 9.2
1-52 pgs. begin, end #17	15	30	45	104	152	200
2-Archie's group x-over	8	16	24	53	74	95
3-5: 3,4-Archie's Group x-over	6	12	18	38	52	65
6-10	5	10	15	33	44	55
11-17(2/74)	4	8	12	27	36	45
18-30	3	6	9	18	24	30
31-40(8/77)	2	4	6	12	16	20
41-60(6/80)	2	4	6	9	11	14
61-70	1	3	4	6	8	10
71-76-low print run	2	4	6	9	11	14
77-Last issue; low print run	2	4	6	12	16	20

SABRINA, THE TEEN-AGE WITCH
Archie Publications: 1996 ($1.50, 32 pgs., one-shot)

	GD 2.0	VG 4.0	FN 6.0	VF 8.0	VF/NM 9.0	NM- 9.2
1-Updated origin						5.00

SABRINA, THE TEEN-AGE WITCH (Continues in Sabrina, Vol. 2)
Archie Publications: May, 1997 - No. 32, Dec, 1999 ($1.50/$1.75/$1.79)

	GD 2.0	VG 4.0	FN 6.0	VF 8.0	VF/NM 9.0	NM- 9.2
1-Photo-c with Melissa Joan Hart	1	2	3	5	6	8
2-10: 9-Begin $1.75-c						5.00
11-20						4.00
21-32: 24-Begin $1.79-c. 28-Sonic the Hedgehog-c/app.						3.00

SABU, "ELEPHANT BOY" (Movie; formerly My Secret Story)
Fox Features Syndicate: No. 30, June, 1950 - No. 2, Aug, 1950

	GD 2.0	VG 4.0	FN 6.0	VF 8.0	VF/NM 9.0	NM- 9.2
30(#1)-Wood-a; photo-c from movie	27	54	81	153	214	275
2-Photo-c from movie; Kamen-a	20	40	60	112	156	200

SACHS & VIOLENS
Marvel Comics (Epic Comics): Nov, 1993 - No. 4, July, 1994 ($2.25, limited series, mature)

	GD 2.0	VG 4.0	FN 6.0	VF 8.0	VF/NM 9.0	NM- 9.2
1-($2.75)-Embossed-c w/bound-in trading card						2.75
1-($3.50)-Platinum edition (1 for each 10 ordered)						4.00
2-4: Perez-c/a; bound-in trading card: 2-(5/94)						2.25

SACRAMENTS, THE
Catechetical Guild Educational Society: Oct, 1955 (25¢)

	GD 2.0	VG 4.0	FN 6.0	VF 8.0	VF/NM 9.0	NM- 9.2
304	5	10	14	20	24	28

SACRED AND THE PROFANE, THE (See Eclipse Graphic Album Series #9 & Epic Illustrated #20)

SADDLE JUSTICE (Happy Houlihans #1,2) (Saddle Romances #9 on)
E. C. Comics: No. 3, Spring, 1948 - No. 8, Sept-Oct, 1949

	GD 2.0	VG 4.0	FN 6.0	VF 8.0	VF/NM 9.0	NM- 9.2
3-The 1st E.C. by Bill Gaines to break away from M. C. Gaines' old Educational Comics format. Craig, Feldstein, H. C. Kiefer, & Stan Asch-a; mentioned in Love and Death	48	96	144	288	432	575
4-1st Graham Ingels-a for E.C.	43	86	129	258	389	520
5-8-Ingels-a in all	40	80	120	240	350	460

NOTE: ***Craig** and **Feldstein** art in most issues. Canadian reprints known; see Table of Contents. **Craig** c-3, 4. **Ingels** c-5-8. #4 contains a biography of **Craig**.*

SADDLE ROMANCES (Saddle Justice #3-8; Weird Science #12 on)
E. C. Comics: No. 9, Nov-Dec, 1949 - No. 11, Mar-Apr, 1950

	GD 2.0	VG 4.0	FN 6.0	VF 8.0	VF/NM 9.0	NM- 9.2
9,11: 9-Ingels-c/a. 11-Ingels-a; Feldstein-c	43	86	129	258	389	520
10-Wally Wood's 1st work at E. C.; Ingels-a; Feldstein-c	44	88	132	264	397	530

NOTE: *Canadian reprints known; see Table of Contents. **Wood/Harrison** a-10, 11.*

SADIE SACK (See Harvey Hits #93)

SAD SACK AND THE SARGE
Harvey Publications: Sept, 1957 - No. 155, June, 1982

	GD 2.0	VG 4.0	FN 6.0	VF 8.0	VF/NM 9.0	NM- 9.2
1	13	26	39	94	137	180
2	7	14	21	50	68	85
3-10	6	12	18	38	52	65
11-20	5	10	15	33	44	55
21-30	3	7	10	21	28	35
31-50	2	4	6	14	18	22
51-70	2	4	6	10	13	16
71-90,97-99	1	3	4	6	8	10
91-96: All 52 pg. Giants	2	4	6	10	13	16
100	2	4	6	8	10	12
101-120	1	2	3	4	5	7
121-155						5.00

SAD SACK COMICS (See Harvey Collector's Comics #16, Little Sad Sack, Tastee Freez Comics #4 & True Comics #55)
Harvey Publications/Lorne-Harvey Publications (Recollections) #288 On: Sept, 1949 - No. 287, Oct, 1982; No. 288, 1992 - No. 293?, 1993

	GD 2.0	VG 4.0	FN 6.0	VF 8.0	VF/NM 9.0	NM- 9.2
1-Infinity-c; Little Dot begins (1st app.); civilian issues begin, end #21; based on comic strip	45	90	135	360	543	725
2-Flying Fool by Powell	24	48	72	174	255	335
3	14	28	42	97	141	185
4-10	10	20	30	72	104	135
11-21	7	14	21	51	71	90
22-("Back In The Army Again" on covers #22-36); "The Specialist" story about Sad Sack's return to Army	8	16	24	55	78	100
23-30	6	12	18	38	52	65
31-50	4	8	12	29	40	50
51-80,100: 62-"The Specialist" reprinted	3	7	10	21	28	35
81-99	3	6	9	18	23	28
101-140	2	4	6	14	18	22
141-170,200	2	4	6	11	14	18
171-199	2	4	6	9	11	14
201-207: 207-Last 12¢ issue	2	4	6	8	10	12
208-222	1	2	3	5	6	8
223-228 (25¢ Giants, 52 pgs.)	2	4	6	9	11	14
229-250	1	3	4	6	8	10
251-285						6.00
286,287-Limited distribution	1	2	3	5	7	9
288,289 ($2.75, 1992): 289-50th anniversary issue						6.00
290-293 ($1.00, 1993, B&W)						3.00
3-D 1 (1/54, 25¢)-Came with 2 pairs of glasses; titled "Harvey 3-D Hits"	18	36	54	127	186	245
...At Home for the Holidays 1 (1993, no-c price)-Publ. by Lorne-Harvey' X-Mas issue						4.00

NOTE: *The Sad Sack Comics comic book was a spin-off from a Sunday Newspaper strip launched through John Wheeler's Bell Syndicate. The previous Sunday page and the first 21 comics depicted the Sad Sack in civvies. Unpopularity caused the Sunday page to be discontinued in the early '50s. Meanwhile Sad Sack returned to the Army, by popular demand, in issue No. 22, remaining there ever since. Incidentally, relatively few of the first 21 issues were ever collected and remain scarce due to this.*

SAD SACK FUN AROUND THE WORLD
Harvey Publications: 1974 (no month)

	GD 2.0	VG 4.0	FN 6.0	VF 8.0	VF/NM 9.0	NM- 9.2
1-About Great Britain	2	4	6	12	16	20

SAD SACK GOES HOME
Harvey Publications: 1951 (16 pgs. in color, no cover price)

	GD 2.0	VG 4.0	FN 6.0	VF 8.0	VF/NM 9.0	NM- 9.2
nn-By George Baker	6	12	18	38	52	65

SAD SACK LAUGH SPECIAL
Harvey Publications: Winter, 1958-59 - No. 93, Feb, 1977 (#1-9: 84 pgs.; #10-60: 68 pgs.; #61-76: 52 pgs.)

	GD 2.0	VG 4.0	FN 6.0	VF 8.0	VF/NM 9.0	NM- 9.2
1-Giant 25¢ issues begin	10	20	30	73	107	140
2	6	12	18	40	55	70
3-10	5	10	15	33	44	55
11-30	4	8	12	27	36	45
31-60: 31-1st app. Hi-Fi Tweeter. 60-Last 68 pg. Giant	3	6	9	16	20	25

Sad Sack's Funny Friends #1 © HARV

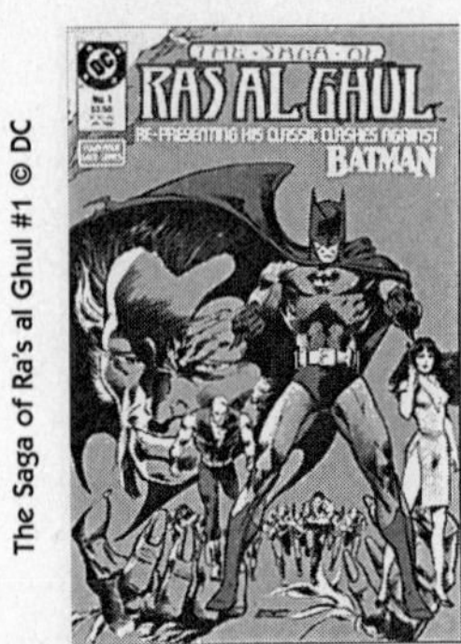

The Saga of Ra's al Ghul #1 © DC

Saint Sinner #4 © Clive Barker

	GD 2.0	VG 4.0	FN 6.0	VF 8.0	VF/NM 9.0	NM- 9.2
61-76-(All 52 pg. issues)	2	4	6	11	14	18
77-93	1	2	3	5	6	8

SAD SACK NAVY, GOBS 'N' GALS
Harvey Publications: Aug, 1972 - No. 8, Oct, 1973

	GD	VG	FN	VF	VF/NM	NM-
1: 52 pg. Giant	3	6	9	18	24	30
2-8	2	4	6	10	12	15

SAD SACK'S ARMY LIFE (See Harvey Hits #8, 17, 22, 28, 32, 39, 43, 47, 51, 55, 58, 61, 64, 67, 70)

SAD SACK'S ARMY LIFE (...Parade #1-57, ...Today #58 on)
Harvey Publications: Oct, 1963 - No. 60, Nov, 1975; No. 61, May, 1976

	GD	VG	FN	VF	VF/NM	NM-
1-(68 pg. issues begin)	7	14	21	51	71	90
2-10	4	8	12	27	36	45
11-20	3	6	9	18	24	30
21-34: Last 68 pg. issue	2	4	6	12	16	20
35-51: All 52 pgs.	2	4	6	10	13	16
52-61	1	2	3	5	7	9

SAD SACK'S FUNNY FRIENDS (See Harvey Hits #75)
Harvey Publications: Dec, 1955 - No. 75, Oct, 1969

	GD	VG	FN	VF	VF/NM	NM-
1	10	20	30	73	107	140
2-10	6	12	18	40	55	70
11-20	4	8	12	22	30	38
21-30	3	6	9	18	23	28
31-50	2	4	6	12	16	20
51-75	2	4	6	10	12	15

SAD SACK'S MUTTSY (See Harvey Hits #74, 77, 80, 82, 84, 87, 89, 92, 96, 99, 102, 105, 108, 111, 113, 115, 117, 119, 121)

SAD SACK USA (...Vacation #8)
Harvey Publications: Nov, 1972 - No. 7, Nov, 1973; No. 8, Oct, 1974

	GD	VG	FN	VF	VF/NM	NM-
1	3	6	9	16	20	25
2-8	2	4	6	8	10	12

SAD SACK WITH SARGE & SADIE
Harvey Publications: Sept, 1972 - No. 8, Nov, 1973

	GD	VG	FN	VF	VF/NM	NM-
1-(52 pg. Giant)	3	6	9	16	20	25
2-8	2	4	6	8	10	12

SAD SAD SACK WORLD
Harvey Publ.: Oct, 1964 - No. 46, Dec, 1973 (#1-31: 68 pgs.; #32-38: 52 pgs.)

	GD	VG	FN	VF	VF/NM	NM-
1	7	14	21	46	63	80
2-10	4	8	12	24	32	40
11-20	3	6	9	18	24	30
21-31: 31-Last 68 pg. issue	3	6	9	16	20	25
32-39-(All 52 pgs)	2	4	6	11	14	18
40-46	1	3	4	6	8	10

SAFEST PLACE IN THE WORLD, THE
Dark Horse Comics: 1993 ($2.50, one-shot)

1-Steve Ditko-c/a/scripts 2.50

SAFETY-BELT MAN
Sirius Entertainment: June, 1994 - No. 6, 1995 ($2.50, B&W)

1-6: 1-Horan-s/Dark One-a/Sprouse-c. 2,3-Warren-c. 4-Linsner back-up story. 5,6-Crilley-a 3.00

SAFETY-BELT MAN ALL HELL
Sirius Entertainment: June, 1996 - No. 6, Mar, 1997 ($2.95, color)

1-6-Horan-s/Fillbach Bros.-a 3.00

SAFFIRE
Image Comics: Apr, 2000 - No. 3, Feb, 2001 ($2.95)

1-3-Broome-a(p)/c 3.00
Preview-Color & B&W pages 2.25

SAGA OF BIG RED, THE
Omaha World-Herald: Sept, 1976 ($1.25) (In color)

nn-by Win Mumma; story of the Nebraska Cornhuskers (sports) 6.00

SAGA OF CRYSTAR, CRYSTAL WARRIOR, THE
Marvel Comics: May, 1983 - No. 11, Feb, 1985 (Remco toy tie-in)

1 (Baxter paper) 4.00
2-11: 3-Dr. Strange app. 3-11-Golden-c (painted-4,5). 6-Nightcrawler app; Golden-c. 11-Alpha Flight app. 3.00

SAGA OF RA'S AL GHUL, THE
DC Comics: Jan, 1988 - No. 4, Apr, 1988 ($2.50, limited series)

1-4-r/N. Adams Batman 6.00

SAGA OF SABAN'S MIGHTY MORPHIN POWER RANGERS (Also see Saban's Mighty Morphin Power Rangers)
Hamilton Comics: 1995 - No. 4, 1995 ($1.95, limited series)

1-4 2.25

SAGA OF SEVEN SUNS, THE : VEILED ALLIANCES
DC Comics (WildStorm): 2004 ($24.95, hardcover graphic novel with dustjacket)

nn-Kevin J. Anderson-s/Robert Teranishi-a 25.00

SAGA OF THE SWAMP THING, THE (See Swamp Thing)

SAGA OF THE ORIGINAL HUMAN TORCH
Marvel Comics: Apr, 1990 - No. 4, July, 1990 ($1.50, limited series)

1-4: 1-Origin; Buckler-c/a(p). 3-Hitler-c 2.25

SAGA OF THE SUB-MARINER, THE
Marvel Comics: Nov, 1988 - No. 12, Oct, 1989 ($1.25/$1.50 #5 on, maxi-series)

1-12: 9-Original X-Men app. 3.00

SAILOR MOON (Manga)
Mixx Entertainment Inc.: 1998 - Present ($2.95)

	GD	VG	FN	VF	VF/NM	NM-
1	2	4	6	11	14	18
1-(San Diego edition)	2	4	6	12	16	20
2-5	2	4	6	8	10	12
6-25						5.00
26-35						3.00
... Rini's Moon Stick 1						15.00

SAILOR ON THE SEA OF FATE (See First Comics Graphic Novel #11)

SAILOR SWEENEY (Navy Action #1-11, 15 on)
Atlas Comics (CDS): No. 12, July, 1956 - No. 14, Nov, 1956

	GD	VG	FN	VF	VF/NM	NM-
12-14: 12-Shores-a. 13,14-Severin-c	9	18	27	52	66	80

SAINT, THE (Also see Movie Comics(DC) #2 & Silver Streak #18)
Avon Periodicals: Aug, 1947 - No. 12, Mar, 1952

	GD	VG	FN	VF	VF/NM	NM-
1-Kamen bondage-c/a	76	152	228	475	713	950
2	40	80	120	240	345	450
3-5: 4-Lingerie panels	36	72	108	204	290	375
6-Miss Fury app. by Tarpe Mills (14 pgs.)	44	88	132	264	395	525
7-c-/Avon paperback #118	28	56	84	157	221	285
8,9(12/50): Saint strip-r in #8-12; 9-Kinstler-c	25	50	75	144	198	255
10-Wood-a, 1 pg; c-/Avon paperback #289	25	50	75	144	198	255
11	18	36	54	101	138	175
12-c-/Avon paperback #123	21	42	63	118	164	210

NOTE: *Lucky Dale, Girl Detective in #1,2,4,6.* ***Hollingsworth*** *a-4, 6. Painted-c 7, 8, 10-12.*

SAINT ANGEL
Image Comics: Mar, 2000 - No. 4, Mar, 2001 ($2.95/$3.95)

0-Altstaetter & Napton-s/Altstaetter-a 3.00
1-4-($3.95) Flip book w/Deity. 1-(6/00). 2-(10/00) 4.00

ST. GEORGE
Marvel Comics (Epic Comics): June, 1988 - No.8, Oct, 1989 ($1.25,/$1.50)

1-8: Sienkiewicz-c. 3-begin $1.50-c 2.25

SAINT GERMAINE
Caliber Comics: 1997 - No. 8, 1998 ($2.95)

1-8: 1,5-Alternate covers 3.00

SAINT SINNER (See Razorline)
Marvel Comics (Razorline): Oct, 1993 - No. 7, Apr, 1994 ($1.75)

1-($2.50)-Foil embossed-c; created by Clive Barker 2.50
2-7: 5-Ectokid x-over 2.25

ST. SWITHIN'S DAY
Trident Comics: Apr, 1990 ($2.50, one-shot)

1-Grant Morrison scripts 3.00

ST. SWITHIN'S DAY
Oni Press: Mar, 1998 ($2.95, B&W, one-shot)

1-Grant Morrison-s/Paul Grist-a 3.00

SALOMÉ (See Night Music #6)

SAM AND MAX, FREELANCE POLICE SPECIAL
Fishwrap Prod./Comico: 1987 ($1.75, B&W); Jan, 1989 ($2.75, 44 pgs.)

1 ($1.75, B&W, Fishwrap) 3.00
2 ($2.75, color, Comico) 2.75

Sammy: Tourist Trap #1 © Guerrilla Comics

Sandman #59 © DC

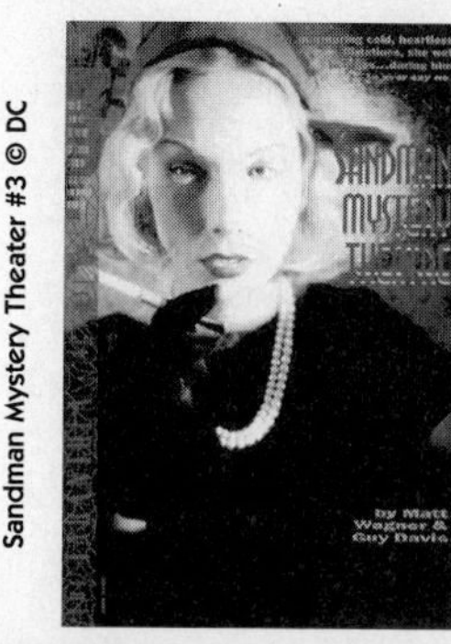

Sandman Mystery Theater #3 © DC

GD VG FN VF VF/NM NM-
2.0 4.0 6.0 8.0 9.0 9.2

SAM AND TWITCH (See Spawn and Case Files:...)
Image Comics (Todd McFarlane Prod.): Aug, 1999 - Present ($2.50)

1-25: 1-19-Bendis-s. 1-14-Medina-a. 15-19-Maleev-a. 20-24-McFarlane-s/Maleev-a 2.50
Book One: Udaku (2000, $21.95, TPB) B&W reprint of #1-8 22.00

SAM HILL PRIVATE EYE
Close-Up (Archie): 1950 - No. 7, 1951

1 17 34 51 98 134 170
2 10 20 30 58 77 95
3-7 10 20 30 56 73 90

SAMMY: TOURIST TRAP
Image Comics: Feb, 2003 - No. 4, May, 2003 ($2.95, B&W, limited series)

1-4-Azad-s/a 3.00

SAM SLADE ROBOHUNTER
Quality Comics: Oct, 1986 - No. 31, 1989 ($1.25/$1.50)

1-31 2.25

SAMSON (1st Series) (Captain Aero #7 on; see Big 3 Comics)
Fox Features Syndicate: Fall, 1940 - No. 6, Sept, 1941 (See Fantastic Comics)

1-Samson begins, ends #6; Powell-a, signed 'Rensie;' Wing Turner by Tuska app; Fine-c?
264 528 792 1650 2475 3300
2-Dr. Fung by Powell; Fine-c? 90 180 270 563 844 1125
3-Navy Jones app.; Joe Simon-c 69 138 207 431 646 860
4-Yarko the Great, Master Magician begins 59 118 177 369 555 740
5,6: 6-Origin The Topper 48 96 144 288 432 575

SAMSON (2nd Series) (Formerly Fantastic Comics #10, 11)
Ajax/Farrell Publications (Four Star): No. 12, April, 1955 - No. 14, Aug, 1955

12-Wonder Boy 31 62 93 175 248 320
13,14: 13-Wonder Boy, Rocket Man 27 54 81 153 214 275

SAMSON (See Mighty Samson)

SAMSON & DELILAH (See A Spectacular Feature Magazine)

SAM STORIES: LEGS
Image Comics: Dec, 1999 ($2.50, one-shot)

1-Sam Kieth-s/a 2.50

SAMUEL BRONSTON'S CIRCUS WORLD (See Circus World under Movie Classics)

SAMURAI (Also see Eclipse Graphic Album Series #14)
Aircel Publications: 1985 - No. 23, 1987 ($1.70, B&W)

1, 14-16-Dale Keown-a 3.00
1-(reprinted),2-12,17-23: 2 (reprinted issue exists) 2.25
13-Dale Keown's 1st published artwork (1987) 5.00

SAMURAI
Warp Graphics: May, 1997 ($2.95, B&W)

1 3.00

SAMURAI CAT
Marvel Comics (Epic Comics): June, 1991 - No. 3, Sept, 1991 ($2.25, limited series)

1-3: 3-Darth Vader-c/story parody 2.25

SAMURAI JACK SPECIAL (TV)
DC Comics: Sept, 2002 ($3.95, one-shot)

1-Adaptation of pilot episode with origin story; Tartakovsky-s 4.00

SAMUREE
Continuity Comics: May, 1987 - No. 9, Jan, 1991

1-9 3.00

SAMUREE
Continuity Comics: V2#1, May, 1993 - V2#4, Jan,1994 ($2.50)

V2#1-4-Embossed-c: 2,4-Adams plot, Nebres-i. 3-Nino-c(i) 2.50

SAMUREE
Acclaim Comics (Windjammer): Oct, 1995 - No. 2, Nov,1995 ($2.50, lim. series)

1,2 2.50

SAN DIEGO COMIC CON COMICS
Dark Horse Comics: 1992 - No.4, 1995 (B&W, promo comic for the San Diego Comic Con)

1-(1992)-Includes various characters published from Dark Horse including Concrete, The Mask, RoboCop and others; 1st app. of Sprint from John Byrne's Next Men; art by Quesada, Byrne, Rude, Burden, Moebius & others; pin-ups by Rude, Dorkin, Allred & others; Chadwick-c 1 2 3 4 5 7
2-(1993)-Intro of Legend imprint; 1st app. of John Byrne's Danger Unlimited, Mike Mignola's Hellboy, Art Adams' Monkeyman & O'Brien; contains stories featuring Concrete, Sin City, Martha Washington & others; Grendel, Madman, & Big Guy pin-ups; Don Martin-c.
2 4 6 10 12 15
3-(1994)-Contains stories featuring Barb Wire, The Mask, The Dirty Pair, & Grendel by Matt Wagner; contains pin-ups of Ghost, Predator & Rascals In Paradise; The Mask-c. 6.00
4-(1995)-Contains Sin City story by Miller (3pg.), Star Wars, The Mask, Tarzan, Foot Soldiers; Sin City & Star Wars flip-c 6.00

GD VG FN VF VF/NM NM-
2.0 4.0 6.0 8.0 9.0 9.2

SANDMAN, THE (1st Series) (Also see Adventure Comics #40, New York World's Fair & World's Finest #3)
National Periodical Publ.: Winter, 1974; No. 2, Apr-May, 1975 - No. 6, Dec-Jan, 1975-76

1-1st app. Bronze Age Sandman by Simon & Kirby (last S&K collaboration)
5 10 15 36 48 60
2-6: 6-Kirby/Wood-c/a 3 6 9 16 20 25

NOTE: *Kirby a-1p, 4-6p; c-1-5, 6p.*

SANDMAN (2nd Series) (See Books of Magic, Vertigo Jam & Vertigo Preview)
DC Comics (Vertigo imprint #47 on): Jan, 1989 - No. 75, Mar, 1996 ($1.50-$2.50, mature)

1 ($2.00, 52 pgs.)-1st app. Modern Age Sandman (Morpheus); Neil Gaiman scripts begin; Sam Kieth-a(p) in #1-5; Wesley Dodds (G.A. Sandman) cameo.
4 8 12 22 30 38
2-Cain & Abel app. (from HOM & HOS) 2 4 6 10 13 16
3-5: 3-John Constantine app. 2 4 6 9 11 14
6,7 1 3 4 6 8 10
8-Death-c/story (1st app.)-Regular ed. has Jeanette Kahn publishorial & American Cancer Society ad w/no indicia on inside front-c
2 4 6 14 18 22
8-Limited ed. (600+ copies?); has Karen Berger editorial and next issue teaser on inside covers (has indicia) 5 10 15 36 48 60
9-14: 10-Has explaination about #8 mixup; has bound-in Shocker movie poster.
14-(52 pgs.)-Bound-in Nightbreed fold-out 1 2 3 5 7 9
15-20: 16-Photo-c. 17,18-Kelley Jones-a. 19-Vess-a. 6.00
18-Error version w/1st 3 panels on pg. 1 in blue ink 3 6 9 16 20 25
19-Error version w/pages 18 & 20 facing each other 2 4 6 12 16 20
21,23-27: Seasons of Mist storyline. 22-World Without End preview. 24-Kelley Jones/Russell-a 6.00
22-1st Daniel (Later becomes new Sandman) 2 4 6 8 10 12
28-30 5.00
31-49,51-74: 41,44-48-Metallic ink on-c. 48-Cerebus appears as a doll. 36-(52 pgs.). 54-Re-intro Prez; Death app.; Belushi, Nixon & Wildcat cameos. 57-Metallic ink on c. 65-w/bound-in trading card. 69-Death of Sandman. 70-73-Zulli-a. 74-Jon J. Muth-a. 4.00
50-($2.95, 52 pgs.)-Black-c w/metallic ink by McKean; Russell-a; McFarlane pin-up 5.00
50-($2.95)-Signed & limited (5,000) Treasury Edition with sketch of Neil Gaiman
1 2 3 5 6 8
50-Platinum 20.00
75-($3.95)-Vess-a. 5.00
Special 1 (1991, $3.50, 68 pgs.)-Glow-in-the-dark-c 5.00
...: A Gallery of Dreams ($2.95)-Intro by N. Gaiman 3.00
...: Preludes & Nocturnes ($29.95, HC)-r/#1-8. 30.00
...: The Doll's House (1990, $29.95, HC)-r/#8-16. 30.00
...: Dream Country ($29.95, HC)-r/#17-20. 30.00
...: Season of Mists ($29.95, Leatherbound HC)-r/#21-28. 50.00
...: A Game of You ($29.95, HC)-r/32-37, ...: Fables and Reflections ($29.95, HC)-r/Vertigo Preview #1, Sandman Special #1, #29-31, #38-40 & #50. ...: Brief Lives ($29.95, HC)-r/#41-49. ...: World's End ($29.95, HC)-r/#51-56 30.00
...: The Kindly Ones (1996, $34.95, HC)-r/#57-69 & Vertigo Jam #1 35.00
...: The Wake ($29.95, HC)-r/#70-75. 30.00

NOTE: *A new set of hardcover printings with new covers was introduced in 1998-99. Multiple printings exist of softcover collections.* ***Bachalo*** *a-12;* ***Kelley Jones*** *a-17, 18, 22, 23, 26, 27.* ***Vess*** *a-19, 75.*

SANDMAN: ENDLESS NIGHTS
DC Comics (Vertigo): 2003 ($24.95, hardcover, with dust jacket)

HC-Neil Gaiman stories of Morpheus and the Endless illustrated by Fabry, Manara, Prado, Quitely, Russell, Sienkiewicz, and Storey; McKean-c 25.00
...Special (11/03, $2.95) Previews hardcover; Dream story w/Prado-a; McKean-c 3.00

SANDMAN MIDNIGHT THEATRE
DC Comics (Vertigo): Sept, 1995 ($6.95, squarebound, one-shot)

nn-Modern Age Sandman (Morpheus) meets G.A. Sandman; Gaiman & Wagner story; McKean-c; Kristiansen-a 7.00

SANDMAN MYSTERY THEATRE (Also see Sandman (2nd Series) #1)
DC Comics (Vertigo): Apr, 1993 - No. 70, Feb, 1999 ($1.95/$2.25/$2.50)

1-G.A. Sandman advs. begin; Matt Wagner scripts begin 4.50
2-49: 5-Neon ink logo. 29-32-Hourman app. 38-Ted Knight (G.A. Starman) app. 42-Jim Corrigan (Spectre) app. 45-48-Blackhawk app. 2.50
50-($3.50, 48 pgs.) w/bonus story of S.A. Sandman, Torres-a 3.50

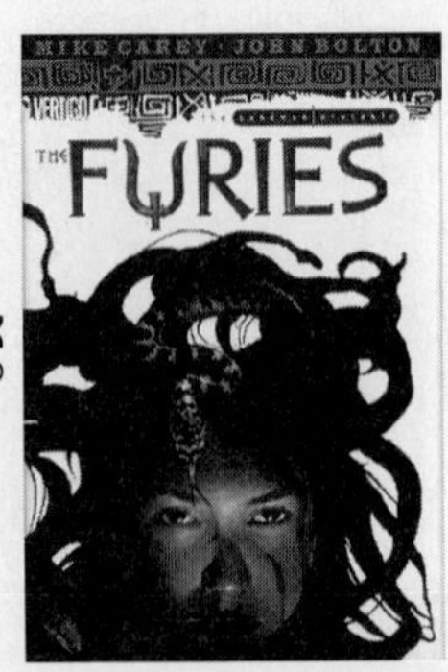
The Sandman Presents: The Furies SC © DC

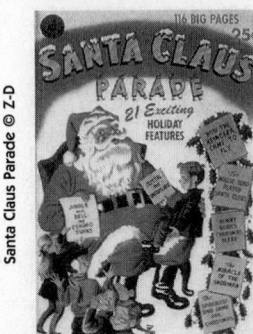

Santa Claus Parade © Z-D

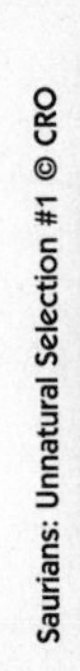
Saurians: Unnatural Selection #1 © CRO

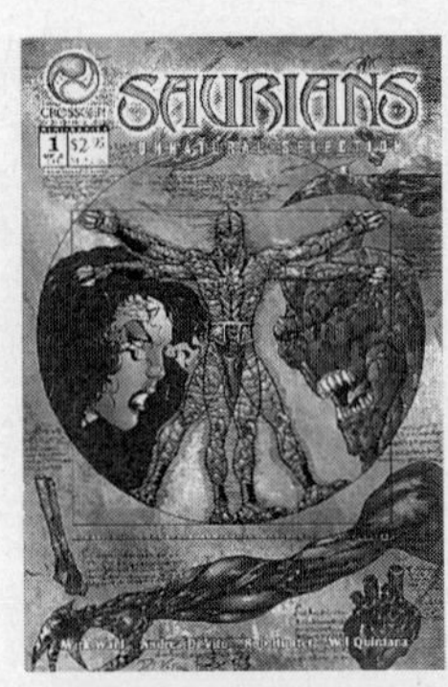

	GD 2.0	VG 4.0	FN 6.0	VF 8.0	VF/NM 9.0	NM- 9.2
51-70						2.50
Annual 1 (10/94, $3.95, 68 pgs.)-Alex Ross, Bolton & others-a						5.00

SANDMAN PRESENTS...
DC Comics (Vertigo)

Taller Tales TPB (2003, $19.95) r/S.P: The Thessaliad #1-4; Merv Pumpkinhead, Agent...; The Dreaming #55; S.P. Everything You Always...; new McKean-c; intro by Willingham 20.00

SANDMAN PRESENTS: BAST
DC Comics (Vertigo): Mar, 2003 - No. 3, May, 2003 ($2.95, limited series)

1-3-Kiernan-s/Bennett-a/McKean-c 3.00

SANDMAN PRESENTS: DEADBOY DETECTIVES (See Sandman #21-28)
DC Comics (Vertigo): Aug, 2001 - No. 4, Nov, 2001 ($2.50, limited series)

1-4:Talbot-a/McKean-c/Brubaker-s 2.50

SANDMAN PRESENTS: EVERYTHING YOU ALWAYS WANTED TO KNOW ABOUT DREAMS...BUT WERE AFRAID TO ASK
DC Comics (Vertigo): Jul, 2001 ($3.95, one-shot)

1-Short stories by Willingham; art by various; McKean-c 4.00

SANDMAN PRESENTS: LOVE STREET
DC Comics (Vertigo): Jul, 1999 - No. 3, Sept, 1999 ($2.95, limited series)

1-3: Teenage Hellblazer in 1968 London; Zulli-a 3.00

SANDMAN PRESENTS: LUCIFER
DC Comics (Vertigo): Mar, 1999 - No. 3, May, 1999 ($2.95, limited series)

1-3: Scott Hampton painted-c/a 3.00

SANDMAN PRESENTS: PETREFAX
DC Comics (Vertigo): Mar, 2000 - No. 4, Jun, 2000 ($2.95, limited series)

1-4-Carey-s/Leialoha-a 3.00

SANDMAN PRESENTS: THE CORINTHIAN
DC Comics (Vertigo): Dec, 2001 - No. 3, Feb, 2002 ($2.95, limited series)

1-3-Macan-s/Zezelj-a/McKean-c 3.00

SANDMAN PRESENTS, THE: THE FURIES
DC Comics (Vertigo): 2002 ($24.95, one-shot)

Hardcover-Mike Carey-s/John Bolton-painted art; Lyta Hall's reunion with Daniel 30.00
Softcover-(2003, $17.95) 18.00

SANDMAN PRESENTS: THE THESSALIAD
DC Comics (Vertigo): Mar, 2002 - No. 4, Jun, 2002 ($2.95, limited series)

1-4-Willingham-s/McManus-a/McKean-c 3.00

SANDMAN, THE: THE DREAM HUNTERS
DC Comics (Vertigo): Oct, 1999 ($29.95/$19.95, one-shot)

Hardcover-Neil Gaiman-s/Yoshitaka Amano-painted art 30.00
Softcover-(2000, $19.95) new Amano-c 20.00

SANDSCAPE
Dreamwave Productions: Jan, 2003 - No. 4, May, 2003 ($2.95)

1-4: 1-Gatefold wraparound-c 3.00

SANDS OF THE SOUTH PACIFIC
Toby Press: Jan, 1953

	GD	VG	FN	VF	VF/NM	NM-
1	22	44	66	124	172	220

SANTA AND HIS REINDEER (See March of Comics #166)

SANTA AND THE ANGEL (See Dell Junior Treasury #7)
Dell Publishing Co.: Dec, 1949 (Combined w/Santa at the Zoo) (Gollub-a condensed from FC#128)

	GD	VG	FN	VF	VF/NM	NM-
Four Color 259	5	10	15	36	48	60

SANTA AT THE ZOO (See Santa And The Angel)

SANTA CLAUS AROUND THE WORLD (See March of Comics #241 in Promotional Comics section)

SANTA CLAUS CONQUERS THE MARTIANS (See Movie Classics)

SANTA CLAUS FUNNIES (Also see Dell Giants)
Dell Publishing Co.: Dec?, 1942 - No. 1274, Dec, 1961

	GD	VG	FN	VF	VF/NM	NM-
nn(#1)(1942)-Kelly-a	36	72	108	270	405	540
2(12/43)-Kelly-a	26	52	78	185	270	355
Four Color 61(1944)-Kelly-a	25	50	75	179	262	345
Four Color 91(1945)-Kelly-a	19	38	57	136	198	260
Four Color 128('46),175('47)-Kelly-a	15	30	45	109	160	210
Four Color 205,254-Kelly-a	14	28	42	99	145	190
Four Color 302,361,525,607,666,756,867	6	12	18	43	59	75
Four Color 958,1063,1154,1274	6	12	18	40	55	70

NOTE: *Most issues contain only one Kelly story.*

SANTA CLAUS PARADE
Ziff-Davis (Approved Comics)/St. John Publishing Co.: 1951; No. 2, Dec, 1952; No. 3, Jan, 1955 (25¢)

	GD	VG	FN	VF	VF/NM	NM-
nn(1951-Ziff-Davis)-116 pgs. (Xmas Special 1,2)	29	58	87	164	232	300
2(12/52-Ziff-Davis)-100 pgs.; Dave Berg-a	23	46	69	129	180	230
V1#3(1/55-St. John)-100 pgs.; reprints-c/#1	20	40	60	112	156	200

SANTA CLAUS' WORKSHOP (See March of Comics #50,168 in Promotional Comics section)

SANTA IS COMING (See March of Comics #197 in Promotional Comics section)

SANTA IS HERE (See March of Comics #49 in Promotional Comics section)

SANTA'S BUSY CORNER (See March of Comics #31 in Promotional Comics section)

SANTA'S CANDY KITCHEN (See March of Comics #14 in Promotional Comics section)

SANTA'S CHRISTMAS BOOK (See March of Comics #123 in Promotional Comics section)

SANTA'S CHRISTMAS COMICS
Standard Comics (Best Books): Dec, 1952 (100 pgs.)

	GD	VG	FN	VF	VF/NM	NM-
nn-Supermouse, Dizzy Duck, Happy Rabbit, etc.	19	38	57	107	149	190

SANTA'S CHRISTMAS LIST (See March of Comics #255 in Promotional Comics section)

SANTA'S HELPERS (See March of Comics #64, 106, 198 in Promotional Comics section)

SANTA'S LITTLE HELPERS (See March of Comics #270 in Promotional Comics section)

SANTA'S SHOW (See March of Comics #311 in Promotional Comics section)

SANTA'S SLEIGH (See March of Comics #298 in Promotional Comics section)

SANTA'S SURPRISE (See March of Comics #13 in Promotional Comics section)

SANTA'S TINKER TOTS
Charlton Comics: 1958

	GD	VG	FN	VF	VF/NM	NM-
1-Based on "The Tinker Tots Keep Christmas"	4	8	12	22	30	38

SANTA'S TOYLAND (See March of Comics #242 in Promotional Comics section)

SANTA'S TOYS (See March of Comics #12 in Promotional Comics section)

SANTA'S VISIT (See March of Comics #283 in Promotional Comics section)

SANTA THE BARBARIAN
Maximum Press: Dec, 1996 ($2.99, one-shot)

1-Fraga/Mhan-s/a 3.00

SANTIAGO (Movie)
Dell Publishing Co.: Sept, 1956 (Alan Ladd photo-c)

	GD	VG	FN	VF	VF/NM	NM-
Four Color 723-Kinstler-a	10	20	30	73	107	140

SARGE SNORKEL (Beetle Bailey)
Charlton Comics: Oct, 1973 - No. 17, Dec, 1976

	GD	VG	FN	VF	VF/NM	NM-
1	2	4	6	12	16	20
2-10	2	4	6	8	10	12
11-17	1	2	3	5	7	9

SARGE STEEL (Becomes Secret Agent #9 on; also see Judomaster)
Charlton Comics: Dec, 1964 - No. 8, Mar-Apr, 1966 (All 12¢ issues)

	GD	VG	FN	VF	VF/NM	NM-
1-Origin & 1st app.	4	8	12	27	36	45
2-5,7,8	3	6	9	18	23	28
6-2nd app. Judomaster	4	8	12	22	30	38

SATAN'S SIX
Topps Comics (Kirbyverse): Apr, 1993 - No. 4, July, 1993 ($2.95, lim. series)

1-4: 1-Polybagged w/Kirbychrome trading card; Kirby/McFarlane-c plus 8 pgs. Kirby-a(p); has coupon for Kirbychrome ed. of Secret City Saga #0. 2-4-Polybagged w/3 cards. 4-Teenagents preview 3.00

NOTE: ***Ditko** a-1. **Miller** a-1.*

SATAN'S SIX: HELLSPAWN
Topps Comics (Kirbyverse): June, 1994 - No. 3, July, 1994 ($2.50, limited series)

1-3: 1-(6/94)-Indicia incorrectly shows "Vol 1 #2". 2-(6/94) 2.50

SAURIANS: UNNATURAL SELECTION (See Sigil)
CrossGeneration Comics: Feb, 2002 - No. 2, Mar, 2002 ($2.95, limited series)

1,2-Waid-s/DiVito-a 3.00

SAVAGE COMBAT TALES
Atlas/Seaboard Publ.: Feb, 1975 - No. 3, July, 1975

	GD	VG	FN	VF	VF/NM	NM-
1,3: 1-Sgt. Stryker's Death Squad begins (origin); Goodwin-s	1	2	3	5	7	9
2-Toth-a; only app. War Hawk; Goodwin-s	2	4	6	8	10	12

NOTE: ***Buckler** c-3. **McWilliams** a-1-3; c-1. **Sparling** a-1, 3.*

Savage Dragon #97 © Erik Larsen

Savage She-Hulk #23 © MAR

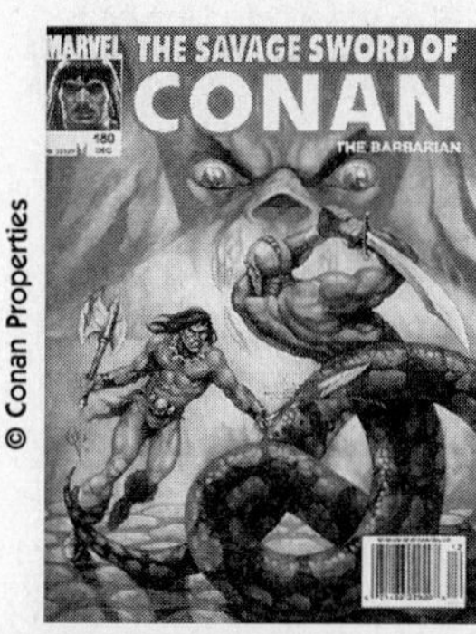

Savage Sword of Conan #180 © Conan Properties

GD VG FN VF VF/NM NM-
2.0 4.0 6.0 8.0 9.0 9.2

SAVAGE DRAGON, THE (See Megaton #3 & 4)
Image Comics (Highbrow Entertainment): July, 1992 - No. 3, Dec, 1992 ($1.95, lim. series)

1-Erik Larsen-c/a/scripts & bound-in poster in all; 4 cover color variations w/4 different posters; 1st Highbrow Entertainment title 4.00
2-Intro SuperPatriot-c/story (10/92) 3.00
3-Contains coupon for Image Comics #0 3.00
3-With coupon missing 2.25
...Vs. Savage Megaton Man 1 (3/93, $1.95)-Larsen & Simpson-c/a. 3.00
TPB-('93, $9.95) r/#1-3 10.00

SAVAGE DRAGON, THE
Image Comics (Highbrow Entertainment): June, 1993 - Present ($1.95/$2.50)

1-Erik Larsen-c/a/scripts 4.00
2-30: 2-(Wondercon Exclusive): 2-($2.95, 52 pgs.)-Teenage Mutant Ninja Turtles-c/story; flip book features Vanguard #0 (See Megaton for 1st app.). 3-7: Erik Larsen-c/a/scripts. 3-Mighty Man back-up story w/Austin-a(i). 4-Flip book w/Ricochet. 5-Mighty Man flip-c & back-up plus poster. 6-Jae Lee poster. 7-Vanguard poster. 8-Deadly Duo poster by Larsen. 13A (10/94)-Jim Lee-c/a; 1st app. Max Cash (Condition Red). 13B (6/95)-Larsen story. 15-Dragon poster by Larsen. 22-TMNT-c/a; Bisley pin-up. 27-"Wondercon Exclusive" new-c. 28-Maxx-c/app. 29-Wildstar-c/app. 30-Spawn app. 3.00
25 ($3.95)-variant-c exists. 4.00
31-49,51-71: 31-God vs. The Devil; alternate version exists w/o expletives (has "God Is Good" inside Image logo) 33-Birth of Dragon/Rapture's baby. 34,35-Hellboy-c/app. 51-Origin of She-Dragon. 70-Ann Stevens killed 2.50
50-($5.95, 100 pgs.) Kaboom and Mighty Man app.; Matsuda back-c; pin-ups by McFarlane, Simonson, Capullo and others 6.00
72-74: 72-Begin $2.95-c 3.00
75-($5.95) 6.00
76-99,101-106,108-112: 76-New direction starts. 83,84-Madman-c/app. 84-Atomics app. 97-Dragon returns home; Mighty Man app. 3.00
100-($8.95) Larsen-s/a; inked by various incl. Sienkiewicz, Timm, Austin, Simonson, Royer; plus pin-ups by Timm, Silvestri, Miller, Cho, Art Adams, Pacheco 9.00
107-($3.95) Firebreather, Invincible, Major Damage-c/app.; flip book w/Major Damage 4.00
...Companion (7/02, $2.95) guide to issues #1-100, character backgrounds 3.00
The Fallen (11/97, $12.95, TPB) r/#7-11, ...Possessed (9/98, $12.95, TPB) r/#12-16, ...Revenge (1998, $12.95, TPB) r/#17-21 13.00
...Gang War (4/00, $16.95, TPB) r/#22-26 17.00
.../Hellboy (10/02, $5.95) r/#34 & #35; Mignola-c 6.00
...Team-Ups (10/98, $19.95, TPB) r/team-ups 20.00
...: Terminated HC (2/03, $28.95) r/#34-40 & #1/2 29.00
...: This Savage World HC (2002, $24.95) r/#76-81; intro. by Larsen 25.00
...: This Savage World SC (2003, $15.95) r/#76-81; intro. by Larsen 16.00

SAVAGE DRAGON ARCHIVES (See Dragon Archives, The)

SAVAGE DRAGONBERT: FULL FRONTAL NERDITY
Image Comics: Oct, 2002 ($5.95, B&W, one-shot)

1-Reprints of the Savage Dragon/Dilbert spoof strips 6.00

SAVAGE DRAGON/DESTROYER DUCK, THE
Image Comics/ Highbrow Entertainment: Nov, 1996 ($3.95, one-shot)

1 4.00

SAVAGE DRAGON/MARSHALL LAW
Image Comics: July, 1997 - No. 2, Aug, 1997 ($2.95, B&W, limited series)

1,2-Pat Mills-s, Kevin O'Neill-a 3.00

SAVAGE DRAGON: SEX & VIOLENCE
Image Comics: Aug, 1997 - No. 2, Sept, 1997 ($2.50, limited series)

1,2-T&M Bierbaum-s, Mays, Lupka, Adam Hughes-a 3.00

SAVAGE DRAGON/TEENAGE MUTANT NINJA TURTLES CROSSOVER
Mirage Studios: Sept, 1993 ($2.75, one-shot)

1-Erik Larsen-c(i) only 3.00

SAVAGE DRAGON: THE RED HORIZON
Image Comics/ Highbrow Entertainment: Feb, 1997 - No. 3 ($2.50, lim. series)

1-3 3.00

SAVAGE FISTS OF KUNG FU
Marvel Comics Group: 1975 (Marvel Treasury)

1-Iron Fist, Shang Chi, Sons of Tiger; Adams, Starlin-a 3 6 9 18 23 28

SAVAGE HENRY
Vortex Comics: Jan, 1987 - No. 16?, 1990 ($1.75/$2.00, B&W, mature)

1-16 2.50

GD VG FN VF VF/NM NM-
2.0 4.0 6.0 8.0 9.0 9.2

SAVAGE HULK, THE (Also see Incredible Hulk)
Marvel Comics: Jan, 1996 ($6.95, one-shot)

1-Bisley-c; David, Lobdell, Wagner, Loeb, Gibbons, Messner-Loebs scripts; McKone, Kieth, Ramos & Sale-a. 7.00

SAVAGE RAIDS OF GERONIMO (See Geronimo #4)

SAVAGE RANGE (See Luke Short, Four Color 807)

SAVAGE RETURN OF DRACULA
Marvel Comics: 1992 ($2.00, 52 pgs.)

1-r/Tomb of Dracula #1,2 by Gene Colan 3.00

SAVAGE SHE-HULK, THE (See The Avengers, Marvel Graphic Novel #18 & The Sensational She-Hulk)
Marvel Comics Group: Feb, 1980 - No. 25, Feb, 1982

1-Origin & 1st app. She-Hulk 2 4 6 8 10 12
2-5,25: 25-(52 pgs.) 6.00
6-24: 6-She-Hulk vs. Iron Man. 8-Vs. Man-Thing 5.00
NOTE: ***Austin*** *a-25i; c-23i-25i.* ***J. Buscema*** *a-1p; c-1, 2p.* ***Golden*** *c-8-11.*

SAVAGE SWORD OF CONAN (The... #41 on; ...The Barbarian #175 on)
Marvel Comics Group: Aug, 1974 - No. 235, July, 1995 ($1.00/$1.25/$2.25, B&W magazine, mature)

1-Smith-r; J. Buscema/N. Adams/Krenkel-a; origin Blackmark by Gil Kane (part 1, ends #3); Blackmark's 1st app. in magazine form-r/from paperback) & Red Sonja (3rd app.) 8 16 24 58 82 105
2-Neal Adams-c; Chaykin/N. Adams-a 4 8 12 25 33 42
3-Severin/B. Smith-a; N. Adams-a 3 6 9 18 23 28
4-Neal Adams/Kane-a(r) 2 4 6 14 18 22
5-10: 5-Jeff Jones frontispiece (r) 2 4 6 11 14 18
11-20 2 4 6 9 11 14
21-30 2 4 6 8 10 12
31-50: 34-3 pg. preview of Conan newspaper strip. 35-Cover similar to Savage Tales #1. 45-Red Sonja returns; begin $1.25-c 1 3 4 6 8 10
51-100: 63-Toth frontispiece. 65-Kane-a w/Chaykin/Miller/Simonson/Sherman finishes. 70-Article on movie. 83-Red Sonja-r by Neal Adams from #1 1 2 3 4 5 7
101-176: 163-Begin $2.25-c. 169-King Kull story. 171-Soloman Kane by Williamson (i). 172-Red Sonja story 6.00
177-220: 179,187,192-Red Sonja app. 190-193-4 part King Kull story. 196, 202-King Kull story. 200-New Buscema-a; Robert E. Howard app. with Conan in story. 204-60th anniversary (1932-92). 211-Rafael Kayanan's 1st Conan-a. 214-Sequel to Red Nails by Howard 5.00
221-234 6.00
235-Last issue 2 4 6 9 11 14
Special 1(1975, B&W)-B. Smith-r/Conan #10,13 2 4 6 14 18 22
NOTE: ***N. Adams*** *a-14p, 60, 83p(r).* ***Alcala*** *a-2 ,4, 7, 12, 15-20, 23, 24, 28, 59, 67, 69, 75, 76i, 80i, 82i, 83i, 89, 180i, 184i, 187i, 189i, 216p.* ***Austin*** *a-78i.* ***Boris*** *painted c-1, 4, 5, 7, 9, 10, 12, 15.* ***Brunner*** *a-30; c-8, 30.* ***Buscema*** *a-1-5, 7, 10-12, 15-24, 26-28, 31, 32, 36-43, 45, 47-58p, 60-67p, 70, 71-74p, 76-81p, 87-96p, 98, 99-101p, 190-204p; painted c-40.* ***Chaykin*** *c-31.* ***Chiodo*** *painted c-71, 76, 79, 81, 84, 85, 178.* ***Conrad*** *c-215, 217.* ***Corben*** *a-4, 16, 29.* ***Finlay*** *a-16.* ***Golden*** *a-98, 101; c-98, 101, 105, 106, 117, 124, 150.* ***Kaluta*** *a-11, 18; c-3, 91, 93.* ***Gil Kane*** *a-2, 3, 8, 13r, 29, 47, 64, 65, 67, 85p, 86p.* ***Rafael Kayanan*** *a-211-213, 215, 217.* ***Krenkel*** *a-9, 11, 14, 16, 24.* ***Morrow*** *a-7.* ***Nebres*** *a-93i, 101i, 107, 114.* ***Newton*** *a-6.* ***Nino*** *c/a-6.* ***Redondo*** *painted c-48-50, 52, 56, 57, 85i, 90, 96i.* ***Marie & John Severin*** *a-Special 1.* ***Simonson*** *a-7, 8, 12, 15-17.* ***Barry Smith*** *a-7, 16, 24, 82r, Special 1r.* ***Starlin*** *c-26.* ***Toth*** *a-64.* ***Williamson*** *a(i)-162, 171, 186. No. 8 , 10 & 16 contain a Robert E. Howard Conan adaptation.*

SAVAGE TALES (...Featuring Conan #4 on)(Magazine)
Marvel Comics Group: May, 1971; No. 2, 10/73; No. 3, 2/74 - No. 12, Summer, 1975 (B&W)

1-Origin/1st app. The Man-Thing by Morrow; Conan the Barbarian by Barry Smith (1st Conan x-over outside his own title); Femizons by Romita-r/in #3; Ka-Zar story by Buscema 15 30 45 104 152 200
2-B. Smith, Brunner, Morrow, Williamson-a; Wrightson King Kull reprint/ Creatures on the Loose #10 4 8 12 29 40 50
3-B. Smith, Brunner, Steranko, Williamson-a 3 7 10 21 28 35
4,5-N. Adams-c; last Conan (Smith-r/#4) plus Kane/N. Adams-a. 5-Brak the Barbarian begins, ends #8 3 6 9 18 24 30
6-Ka-Zar begins; Williamson-r; N. Adams-c 2 4 6 12 16 20
7-N. Adams-i 2 4 6 9 11 14
8,9,11: 8-Shanna, the She-Devil app. thru #10; Williamson-r 2 4 6 8 10 12
10-Neal Adams-a(i), Williamson-r 2 4 6 9 11 14
...Featuring Ka-Zar Annual 1 (Summer, '75, B&W)(#12 on inside)-Ka-Zar origin by Gil Kane; B. Smith-r/Astonishing Tales 2 4 6 12 16 20
NOTE: ***Boris*** *c-7, 10.* ***Buscema*** *a-5r, 6p, 8p; c-2.* ***Colan*** *a-1p.* ***Fabian*** *c-8.* ***Golden*** *a-1, 4; c-1.* ***Heath*** *a-10p, 11p.* ***Kaluta*** *c-9.* ***Maneely*** *r-2, 4(The Crusader in both).* ***Morrow*** *a-1, 2, Annual 1.* ***Reese*** *a-2.* ***Severin*** *a-1-7.* ***Starlin*** *a-5. Robert E. Howard adaptations-1-4.*

SAVAGE TALES
Marvel Comics Group: Nov, 1985 - No. 8, Dec, 1986 ($1.50, B&W, magazine, mature)

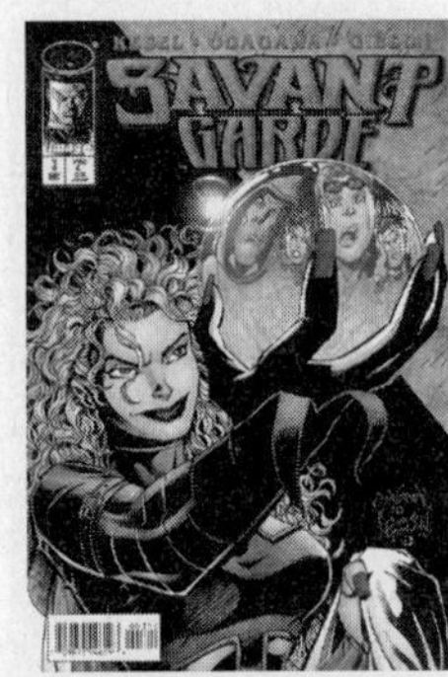

Savant Garde #3 © WSP

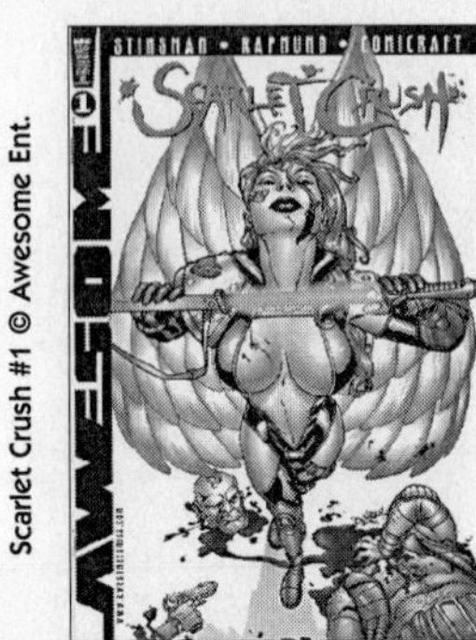

Scarlet Crush #1 © Awesome Ent.

Science Comics #2 © FOX

	GD 2.0	VG 4.0	FN 6.0	VF 8.0	VF/NM 9.0	NM- 9.2
1-1st app. The Nam; Golden, Morrow-a						5.00
2-8: 2,7-Morrow-a. 4-2nd Nam story; Golden-a						3.00

SAVANT GARDE (Also see WildC.A.T.S...)
Image Comics/WildStorm Productions: Mar, 1997 - No. 7, Sept, 1997 ($2.50)

1-7 — 2.50

SAVED BY THE BELL (TV)
Harvey Comics: Mar, 1992 - No. 5, May, 1993 ($1.25, limited series)

1-5, Holiday Special (3/92), Special 1 (9/92, $1.50)-photo-c, Summer Break 1 (10/92) — 2.25

SCAMP (Walt Disney)(See Walt Disney's Comics & Stories #204)
Dell Publ. Co./Gold Key: No. 703, 5/56 - No. 1204, 8-10/61; 11/67 - No. 45, 1/79

	GD 2.0	VG 4.0	FN 6.0	VF 8.0	VF/NM 9.0	NM- 9.2
Four Color 703(#1)	10	20	30	67	96	125
Four Color 777,806('57),833	7	14	21	51	71	90
5(3-5/58)-10(6-8/59)	6	12	18	40	55	70
11-16(12-2/60-61), Four Color 1204(1961)	5	10	15	33	44	55
1(12/67-Gold Key)-Reprints begin	4	8	12	29	40	50
2(3/69)-10	2	4	6	12	16	20
11-20	2	4	6	8	10	12
21-45						6.00

NOTE: *New stories-#20(in part), 22-25, 27, 29-31, 34, 36-40, 42-45. New covers-#11, 12, 14, 15, 17-25, 27, 29-31, 34, 36-38.*

SCARAB
DC Comics (Vertigo): Nov, 1993 - No. 8, June, 1994 ($1.95, limited series)

1-8-Glenn Fabry painted-c: 1-Silver ink-c. 2-Phantom Stranger app. — 2.25

SCAR FACE (See The Crusaders)

SCARECROW OF ROMNEY MARSH, THE (See W. Disney Showcase #53)
Gold Key: April, 1964 - No. 3, Oct, 1965 (Disney TV Show)

	GD 2.0	VG 4.0	FN 6.0	VF 8.0	VF/NM 9.0	NM- 9.2
10112-404 (#1)	4	8	12	28	38	48
2,3	3	6	9	19	25	32

SCARECROW (VILLAINS) (See Batman)
DC Comics: Feb, 1998 ($1.95, one-shot)

1-Fegredo-a/Milligan-s/Pearson-c — 2.50

SCARE TACTICS
DC Comics: Dec, 1996 - No. 12, Mar, 1998 ($2.25)

1-12: 1-1st app. — 2.25

SCARLET O'NEIL (See Harvey Comics Hits #59 & Invisible...)

SCARLET CRUSH
Awesome Entertainment: Jan, 1998 - No. 2, Feb, 1998 ($2.50)

1-Five covers by Liefeld, Stinsman(wraparound), Churchill, Skroce, and Sprouse; Stinsman-s/a(p) — 2.50
1-American Entertainment Ed.; Stinsman-c — 5.00
2-Three covers by Stinsman, McGuinness & Peterson — 2.50

SCARLET SPIDER
Marvel Comics: Nov, 1995 - No. 2, Jan, 1996 ($1.95, limited series)

1,2: Replaces Spider-Man — 2.25

SCARLET SPIDER UNLIMITED
Marvel Comics: Nov, 1995 ($3.95, one-shot)

1-Replaces Spider-Man Unlimited — 4.00

SCARLETT
DC Comics: Jan, 1993 - No. 14, Feb, 1994 (1.75)

1-($2.95) — 3.00
2-14 — 2.25

SCARLET TRACES
Dark Horse Comics: Aug, 2003 ($14.95, hardcover, one-shot)

nn-Edginton-s/D'Israeli-a — 15.00

SCARLET WITCH (See Avengers #16, Vision &... & X-Men #4)
Marvel Comics: Jan, 1994 - No. 4, Apr, 1994 ($1.75, limited series)

1-4 — 2.25

SCARY GODMOTHER (Hardcover story books)
Sirius: 1997 - Present ($19.95, HC with dust jackets, one-shots)

Volume 1 (9/97) Jill Thompson-s/a; first app. of Scary Godmother — 20.00
Vol. 2 - The Revenge of Jimmy (9/98, $19.95) — 20.00
Vol. 3 - The Mystery Date (10/99, $19.95) — 20.00
Vol. 4 - The Boo Flu (9/02, $19.95) — 20.00

SCARY GODMOTHER
Sirius: 2001 - No. 6, 2002 ($2.95, B&W, limited series)

1-6-Jill Thompson-s/a — 3.00
...: Activity Book (12/00, $2.95, B&W) Jill Thompson-s/a — 3.00
...: Bloody Valentine Special (2/98, $3.95, B&W) Jill Thompson-s/a; pin-ups by Ross, Mignola, Russell — 4.00
...: Ghoul's Out For Summer (2002,$14.95, B&W) r/#1-6 — 15.00
...: Holiday Spooktakular (11/98, $2.95, B&W) Jill Thompson-s/a; pin-ups by Brereton, LaBan, Dorkin, Fingerman — 3.00

SCARY GODMOTHER: WILD ABOUT HARRY
Sirius: 2000 - No. 3 ($2.95, B&W, limited series)

1-3-Jill Thompson-s/a — 3.00
TPB (2001, $9.95) r/series — 10.00

SCARY TALES
Charlton Comics: 8/75 - #9, 1/77; #10, 9/77 - #20, 6/79; #21, 8/80 - #46, 10/84

	GD 2.0	VG 4.0	FN 6.0	VF 8.0	VF/NM 9.0	NM- 9.2
1-Origin/1st app. Countess Von Bludd, not in #2	3	6	9	18	23	28
2,4,6,9,10: 4-Sutton-c. 9-Sutton-c/a	2	4	6	8	10	12
3-Sutton painted-c; Ditko-a	2	4	6	10	13	16
5,11-Ditko-c/a.	2	4	6	10	12	15
7,8-Ditko-a	2	4	6	9	11	14
12,15,16,19,21,39-Ditko-a	2	4	6	8	10	12
13,17,20	1	2	3	5	7	9
14,18,30,32-Ditko-c/a	2	4	6	9	11	14
22-29,31,33-40: 31-Newton-c/a. 37,38,40-New-a. 38-Mr. Jigsaw app. 39-Reprints	1	2	3	5	6	8
41-45-New-a. 41-Ditko-a(3). 42-45-(Low print)	1	2	3	5	7	9
46-Reprints (Low print)	2	4	6	9	11	14
1(Modern Comics reprint, 1977)						4.00

NOTE: ***Adkins** a-31i; c-31i. **Ditko** a-3, 5, 7, 8(2), 11, 12, 14-16r, 18(3)r, 19r, 21r, 30r, 32, 39r, 41(3); c-5, 11, 14, 18, 30, 32. **Newton** a-31p; c-31p. **Powell** a-18r. **Staton** a-1(2 pgs.), 4, 20r; c-1, 20. **Sutton** a-9; c-4, 9.*

SCATTERBRAIN
Dark Horse Comics: Jun, 1998 - No. 4, Sept, 1998 ($2.95, limited series)

1-4-Humor anthology by Aragonés, Dorkin, Stevens and others — 3.00

SCAVENGERS
Quality Comics: Feb, 1988 - No. 14, 1989 ($1.25/$1.50)

1-14: 9-13-Guice-c — 2.25

SCAVENGERS
Triumphant Comics: 1993(nd, July) - No. 11, May, 1994 ($2.50, serially numbered)

1-9,0,10,11: 5,6-Triumphant Unleashed x-over. 9-(3/94). 0-Retail edition (3/94, $2.50, 36 pgs.). 0-Giveaway edition (3/94, 20 pgs.). 0-Coupon redemption edition. 10-(4/94) — 2.50

SCENE OF THE CRIME (Also see Vertigo: Winter's Edge #2)
DC Comics (Vertigo): May, 1999 - No. 4, Aug, 1999 ($2.50, limited series)

1-4-Brubaker-s/Lark-a — 2.50
...: A Little Piece of Goodnight TPB ('00, $12.95) r/#1-4; Winter's Edge #2 — 13.00

SCHOOL DAY ROMANCES (...of Teen-Agers #4; Popular Teen-Agers #5 on)
Star Publications: Nov-Dec, 1949 - No. 4, May-June, 1950 (Teenage)

	GD 2.0	VG 4.0	FN 6.0	VF 8.0	VF/NM 9.0	NM- 9.2
1-Toni Gayle (later Toni Gay), Ginger Snapp, Midge Martin & Eve Adams begin	29	58	87	164	232	300
2,3: 3-Jane Powell photo on-c & true life story	21	42	63	118	164	210
4-Ronald Reagan photo on-c; L.B. Cole-c	32	64	96	180	255	330

NOTE: *All have **L. B. Cole** covers.*

SCHWINN BICYCLE BOOK (...Bike Thrills, 1959)
Schwinn Bicycle Co.: 1949; 1952; 1959 (10¢)

	GD 2.0	VG 4.0	FN 6.0	VF 8.0	VF/NM 9.0	NM- 9.2
1949	6	12	18	28	34	40
1952-Believe It or Not facts; comic format; 36 pgs.	5	10	14	20	24	28
1959	3	6	8	11	13	15

SCIENCE COMICS (1st Series)
Fox Features Syndicate: Feb, 1940 - No. 8, Sept, 1940

	GD 2.0	VG 4.0	FN 6.0	VF 8.0	VF/NM 9.0	NM- 9.2
1-Origin Dynamo (1st app., called Electro in #1), The Eagle (1st app.), & Navy Jones; Marga, The Panther Woman (1st app.), Cosmic Carson & Perisphere Payne, Dr. Doom begin; bondage/hypo-c; Electro-c	430	860	1290	2795	4298	5800
2-Classic Lou Fine Dynamo-c	220	440	660	1375	2063	2750
3-Classic Lou Fine Dynamo-c	180	360	540	1125	1688	2250
4-Kirby-a; Cosmic Carson-c by Joe Simon	158	316	474	988	1482	1975
5-8: 5,8-Eagle-c. 6,7-Dynamo-c	92	184	276	575	863	1150

NOTE: *Cosmic Carson by **Tuska**-#1-3; by **Kirby**-#4. **Lou Fine** c-1-3 only.*

SCIENCE COMICS (2nd Series)
Humor Publications (Ace Magazines?): Jan, 1946 - No. 5, 1946

	GD 2.0	VG 4.0	FN 6.0	VF 8.0	VF/NM 9.0	NM- 9.2
1-Palais-c/a in #1-3; A-Bomb-c	20	40	60	112	156	200

Scion #22 © CRO

Scooby-Doo #31 © H-B

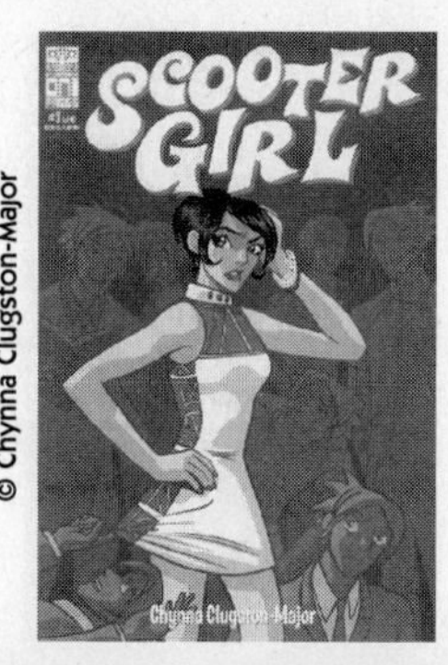

Scooter Girl #3 © Chynna Clugston-Major

	GD 2.0	VG 4.0	FN 6.0	VF 8.0	VF/NM 9.0	NM- 9.2
2	10	20	30	58	77	95
3-Feldstein-a (6 pgs.)	16	32	48	92	126	160
4,5: 4-Palais-c	8	16	24	46	58	70

SCIENCE COMICS
Ziff-Davis Publ. Co.: May, 1947 (8 pgs. in color)

	GD 2.0	VG 4.0	FN 6.0	VF 8.0	VF/NM 9.0	NM- 9.2
nn-Could be ordered by mail for 10¢; like the nn Amazing Adventures (1950) & Boy Cowboy (1950); used to test the market	39	78	117	233	329	425

SCIENCE COMICS (True Science Illustrated)
Export Publication Ent., Toronto, Canada: Mar, 1951 (Distr. in U.S. by Kable News Co.)

	GD 2.0	VG 4.0	FN 6.0	VF 8.0	VF/NM 9.0	NM- 9.2
1-Science Adventure stories plus some true science features; man on moon story	10	20	30	56	73	90

SCIENCE FICTION SPACE ADVENTURES (See Space Adventures)

SCION (Also see CrossGen Chronicles)
CrossGeneration Comics: July, 2000 - No. 44 ($2.95)

	NM- 9.2
1-44: 1-Marz-s/Cheung-a	3.00
...: Conflict of Conscience Vol. 1 TPB (5/01, $19.95) r/#1-7; Adam Hughes-c	20.00
...: Blood For Blood Vol. 2 TPB (2002, $19.95) r/#8-14 & CrossGen Chronicles #2	20.00
...: Divided Loyalties Vol. 3 TPB (2002, $15.95) r/#15-21	16.00
...: Sanctuary Vol. 4 TPB (2003, $15.95) r/#22-27	16.00
Vol. 5: The Far Kingdom (2003, $15.95) r/#28-33	16.00
Vol. 6: The Royal Wedding (2004, $15.95) r/#34-39	16.00
Traveler Vol. 1-3 ($9.95) Digest-sized reprints of TPBs	10.00

SCI-SPY
DC Comics (Vertigo): Apr, 2002 - No. 6, Sept, 2002 ($2.50, limited series)

	NM- 9.2
1-6-Moench-s/Gulacy-c/a	2.50

SCI-TECH
DC Comics (WildStorm): Sept, 1999 - No. 4, Dec, 1999 ($2.50, limited series)

	NM- 9.2
1-4-Benes-a/Choi & Peterson-s	2.50

SCOOBY DOO (TV)(...Where are you? #1-16,26; ...Mystery Comics #17-25, 27 on)
(See March Of Comics #356, 368, 382, 391 in the Promtional Comics section)
Gold Key: Mar, 1970 - No. 30, Feb, 1975 (Hanna-Barbera)

	GD 2.0	VG 4.0	FN 6.0	VF 8.0	VF/NM 9.0	NM- 9.2
1	14	28	42	99	145	190
2-5	8	16	24	55	78	100
6-10	7	14	21	46	63	80
11-20: 11-Tufts-a	5	10	15	36	48	60
21-30	4	8	12	27	36	45

SCOOBY DOO (TV)
Charlton Comics: Apr, 1975 - No. 11, Dec, 1976 (Hanna-Barbera)

	GD 2.0	VG 4.0	FN 6.0	VF 8.0	VF/NM 9.0	NM- 9.2
1	6	12	18	43	59	75
2-5	4	8	12	27	36	45
6-11	3	7	10	21	28	35

SCOOBY-DOO (TV)(Newsstand sales only) (See Dynamutt & Laff-A-Lympics)
Marvel Comics Group: Oct, 1977 - No. 9, Feb, 1979 (Hanna-Barbera)

	GD 2.0	VG 4.0	FN 6.0	VF 8.0	VF/NM 9.0	NM- 9.2
1,6-9: 1-Dyno-Mutt begins	3	6	9	18	24	30
1-(35¢-c variant, limited distribution)(10/77)	4	8	12	27	36	45
2-5	2	4	6	14	18	22

SCOOBY-DOO (TV)
Harvey Comics: Sept, 1992 - No. 3, May, 1993 ($1.25)

	GD 2.0	VG 4.0	FN 6.0	VF 8.0	VF/NM 9.0	NM- 9.2
V2#1,2						6.00
Big Book 1,2 (11/92, 4/93, $1.95, 52 pgs.)	1	2	3	4	5	7
Giant Size 1,2 (10/92, 3/93, $2.25, 68 pgs.)	1	2	3	4	5	7

SCOOBY DOO (TV)
Archie Comics: Oct, 1995 -No. 21, June, 1997 ($1.50)

	NM- 9.2
1	6.00
2-21: 12-Cover by Scooby Doo creative designer Iwao Takamoto	4.00

SCOOBY DOO (TV)
DC Comics: Aug, 1997 - Present ($1.75/$1.95/$1.99/$2.25)

	NM- 9.2
1	6.00
2-10: 5-Begin-$1.95-c	4.00
11-45: 14-Begin $1.99-c	2.50
46-80: 63-Begin $2.25-c. 75-With 2 Garbage Pail Kids stickers	2.25
...Spooky Spectacular 1 (10/99, $3.95) Comic Convention story	4.00
...Spooky Spectacular 2000 (10/00, $3.95)	4.00
...Spooky Summer Special 2001 (8/01, $3.95) Staton-a	4.00
...Super Scarefest (8/02, $3.95) r/#20,25,30-32	4.00
Vol. 1: You Meddling Kids (2003, $6.95, digest-size) r/#1-5	7.00
Vol. 2: Ruh-Roh! (2003, $6.95, digest-size) r/#6-10	7.00

SCOOP COMICS (Becomes Yankee Comics #4-7, a digest sized cartoon book not listed in this guide; becomes Snap #9)
Harry 'A' Chesler (Holyoke): November, 1941 - No. 3, Mar, 1943; No. 8, 1944

	GD 2.0	VG 4.0	FN 6.0	VF 8.0	VF/NM 9.0	NM- 9.2
1-Intro. Rocketman & Rocketgirl & begins; origin The Master Key & begins; Dan Hastings begins; Charles Sultan-c/a	128	256	384	800	1200	1600
2-Rocket Boy begins; injury to eye story (reprinted in Spotlight #3); classic-c	140	280	420	875	1313	1750
3-Injury to eye story-r from #2; Rocket Boy	66	132	198	413	617	820
8-Formerly Yankee Comics; becomes Snap	44	88	132	264	395	525

SCOOTER (See Swing With...)

SCOOTER COMICS
Rucker Publ. Ltd. (Canadian): Apr, 1946

	GD 2.0	VG 4.0	FN 6.0	VF 8.0	VF/NM 9.0	NM- 9.2
1-Teen-age/funny animal	11	22	33	63	84	105

SCOOTER GIRL
Oni Press: May, 2003 - No. 6 ($2.99, B&W, limited series)

	NM- 9.2
1-4-Chynna Clugston-Major-s/a	3.00

SCORCHED EARTH
Tundra Publishing: Apr, 1991 - No. 6, 1991 ($2.95, stiff-c)

	NM- 9.2
1-6	3.00

SCORE, THE
DC Comics (Piranha Press): 1989 - No. 4, 1990 ($4.95, 52 pgs, squarebound, mature)

	NM- 9.2
Books One - Four	5.00

SCORPION
Atlas/Seaboard Publ.: Feb, 1975 - No. 3, July, 1975

	GD 2.0	VG 4.0	FN 6.0	VF 8.0	VF/NM 9.0	NM- 9.2
1-Intro.; bondage-c by Chaykin	2	4	6	8	10	12
2-Chaykin-a w/Wrightson, Kaluta, Simonson assists(p)	2	4	6	8	10	12
3-Jim Craig-c/a	1	2	3	5	7	9

NOTE: ***Chaykin** a-1, 2; c-1. **Colon** c-2. **Craig** c/a-3.*

SCORPION KING, THE (Movie)
Dark Horse Comics: March, 2002 - No. 2, Apr, 2002 ($2.99, limited series)

	NM- 9.2
1,2-Photo-c of the Rock; Richards-a	3.00

SCORPIO ROSE
Eclipse Comics: Jan, 1983 - No. 2, Oct, 1983 ($1.25, Baxter paper)

	NM- 9.2
1,2: Dr. Orient back-up story begins. 2-origin.	4.00

SCOTLAND YARD (Inspector Farnsworth of)(Texas Rangers in Action #5 on?)
Charlton Comics Group: June, 1955 - No. 4, Mar, 1956

	GD 2.0	VG 4.0	FN 6.0	VF 8.0	VF/NM 9.0	NM- 9.2
1-Tothish-a	15	30	45	84	115	145
2-4: 2-Tothish-a	10	20	30	56	73	90

SCOUT (See Eclipse Graphic Album #16, New America & Swords of Texas)
(Becomes Scout: War Shaman)
Eclipse Comics: Dec, 1985 - No. 24, Oct, 1987($1.75/$1.25, Baxter paper)

	NM- 9.2
1-15,17,18,20-24: 19-Airboy preview. 10-Bissette-a. 11-Monday, the Eliminator begins. 15-Swords of Texas	2.50
16,19: 16-Scout 3-D Special ($2.50), 16-Scout 2-D Limited Edition, 19-contains flexidisk ($2.50)	3.00
...Handbook 1 (8/87, $1.75, B&W)	2.25
Mount Fire (1989, $14.95, TPB) r/#8-14	15.00

SCOUT: WAR SHAMAN (Formerly Scout)
Eclipse Comics: Mar, 1988 - No. 16, Dec, 1989 ($1.95)

	NM- 9.2
1-16	2.25

SCREAM (...Comics) (Andy Comics #20 on)
Humor Publications/Current Books(Ace Magazines): Autumn, 1944 - No. 19, Apr, 1948

	GD 2.0	VG 4.0	FN 6.0	VF 8.0	VF/NM 9.0	NM- 9.2
1-Teenage humor	17	34	51	98	134	170
2	10	20	30	56	73	90
3-16: 11-Racist humor (Indians). 16-Intro. Lily-Belle	8	16	24	46	58	70
17,19	8	16	24	40	50	60
18-Hypo needle story	8	16	24	46	58	70

SCREAM (Magazine)
Skywald Publ. Corp.: Aug, 1973 - No. 11, Feb, 1975 (68 pgs., B&W) (Painted-c on all)

	GD 2.0	VG 4.0	FN 6.0	VF 8.0	VF/NM 9.0	NM- 9.2
1-Nosferatu-c/1st app. (series thru #11); Morrow-a. Cthulhu/Necronomicon-s	4	8	12	29	40	50
2,3: 2-(10/73) Lady Satan 1st app. & series begins; Edgar Allan Poe adaptations begin (thru #11); Phantom of the Opera-s. 3-(12/73) Origin Lady Satan	4	8	12	22	30	38
4-1st Cannibal Werewolf and 1st Lunatic Mummy	3	6	9	19	25	32
5,7,8: 5,7-Frankenstein app. 8-Buckler-a; Werewolf-s; Slither-Slime Man-s						

Scream #1 © Skywald

Sea Devils #5 © DC

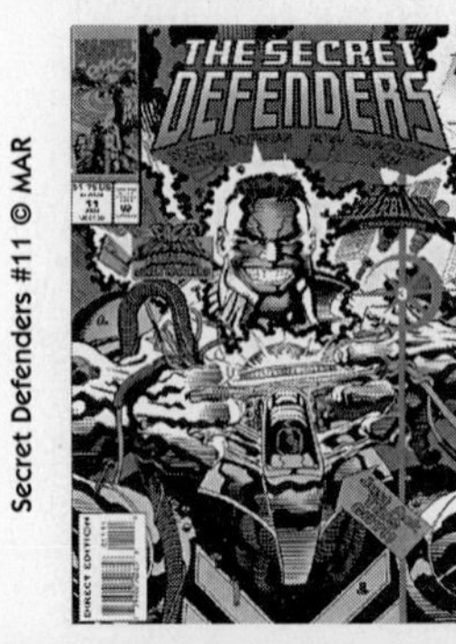

Secret Defenders #11 © MAR

	GD 2.0	VG 4.0	FN 6.0	VF 8.0	VF/NM 9.0	NM- 9.2
	3	6	9	19	25	32
6, 9,10: 6-(6/74) Saga of The Victims/ I Am Horror, classic GGA Hewetson series begins (thru #11); Frankenstein 2073-s. 9-Severed head-c; Marcos-a. 9,10-Werewolf-s. 10-Dracula-c/s	4	8	12	22	30	38
11- (1975 Winter Special) "Mr. Poe and the Raven" story	4	8	12	25	33	42

NOTE: ***Buckler** a-8. **Hewetson** s-1-11. **Marcos** a-9. **Miralles** c-2. **Morrow** a-1. **Poe** s-2-11. **Segrelles** a-7; c-1.*

SCREWBALL SQUIRREL
Dark Horse Comics: July, 1995 - No. 3, Sept, 1995 ($2.50, limited series)

	GD	VG	FN	VF	VF/NM	NM-
1-3: Characters created by Tex Avery						2.50

SCRIBBLY (See All-American Comics, Buzzy, The Funnies, Leave It To Binky & Popular Comics)
National Periodical Publ.: 8-9/48 - No. 13, 8-9/50; No. 14, 10-11/51 - No. 15, 12-1/51-52

	GD	VG	FN	VF	VF/NM	NM-
1-Sheldon Mayer-c/a in all; 52 pgs. begin	96	192	288	600	900	1200
2	61	122	184	381	571	760
3-5	50	100	150	300	450	600
6-10	39	78	117	233	329	425
11-15: 13-Last 52 pgs.	34	68	102	196	278	360

SCUD: TALES FROM THE VENDING MACHINE
Fireman Press: 1998 - No. 5 ($2.50, B&W)

	GD	VG	FN	VF	VF/NM	NM-
1-5: 1-Kaniuga-a. 2-Ruben Martinez-a						2.50

SCUD: THE DISPOSABLE ASSASSIN
Fireman Press: Feb, 1994 - No. 19, 1997 ($2.95, B&W)

	GD	VG	FN	VF	VF/NM	NM-
1						6.00
1-2nd printing in color						2.25
2,3						4.00
4-9						3.00
10-19						2.25
Heavy 3PO ($12.95, TPB) r/#1-4						13.00
Programmed For Damage ($14.95, TPB) r/#5-9						15.00
Solid Gold Bomb ($17.95, TPB) r/#10-15						18.00

SEA DEVILS (See Limited Collectors' Edition #39,45, & Showcase #27-29)
National Periodical Publications: Sept-Oct, 1961 - No. 35, May-June, 1967

	GD	VG	FN	VF	VF/NM	NM-
1-(9-10/61)	50	100	150	413	632	850
2-Last 10¢ issue	29	58	87	210	310	410
3-Begin 12¢ issues thru #35	19	38	57	136	198	260
4,5	17	34	51	118	174	230
6-10	11	22	33	75	110	145
11,12,14-20	8	16	24	55	78	100
13-Kubert, Colan-a; Joe Kubert app. in story	8	16	24	58	82	105
21-35: 22-Intro. International Sea Devils; origin & 1st app. Capt. X & Man Fish	6	12	18	38	52	65

NOTE: ***Heath** a-Showcase 27-29, 1-10; c-Showcase 27-29, 1-10, 14-16. **Moldoff** a-16i.*

SEA DEVILS (See Tangent Comics/ Sea Devils)

SEADRAGON (Also see the Epsilion Wave)
Elite Comics: May, 1986 - No. 8, 1987 ($1.75)

	GD	VG	FN	VF	VF/NM	NM-
1-8: 1-1st & 2nd printings exist						2.25

SEA HOUND, THE (Captain Silver's Log Of The...)
Avon Periodicals: 1945 (no month) - No. 2, Sept-Oct, 1945

	GD	VG	FN	VF	VF/NM	NM-
nn (#1)-29 pg. novel length sty-"The Esmeralda's Treasure"	19	38	57	107	149	190
2	13	26	39	74	100	125

SEA HOUND, THE (Radio)
Capt. Silver Syndicate: No. 3, July, 1949 - No. 4, Sept, 1949

	GD	VG	FN	VF	VF/NM	NM-
3,4	10	20	30	58	74	90

SEA HUNT (TV)
Dell Publishing Co.: No. 928, 8/58 - No. 1041, 10-12/59; No. 4, 1-3/60 - No. 13, 4-6/62 (All have Lloyd Bridges photo-c)

	GD	VG	FN	VF	VF/NM	NM-
Four Color 928(#1)	13	26	39	94	137	180
Four Color 994(#2), 4-13: Manning-a #4-6,8-11,13	9	18	27	63	89	115
Four Color 1041(#3)-Toth-a	9	18	27	65	93	120

SEAQUEST (TV)
Nemesis Comics: Mar, 1994 ($2.25)

	GD	VG	FN	VF	VF/NM	NM-
1-Has 2 diff-c stocks (slick & cardboard); Alcala-i						2.25

SEARCH FOR LOVE
American Comics Group: Feb-Mar, 1950 - No. 2, Apr-May, 1950 (52 pgs.)

	GD	VG	FN	VF	VF/NM	NM-
1	12	24	36	69	92	115
2	9	18	27	51	63	75

SEARCHERS, THE (Movie)
Dell Publishing Co.: No. 709, 1956

	GD	VG	FN	VF	VF/NM	NM-
Four Color 709-John Wayne photo-c	28	56	84	203	294	385

SEARCHERS, THE
Caliber Comics: 1996 - No. 4, 1996 ($2.95, B&W)

	GD	VG	FN	VF	VF/NM	NM-
1-4						3.00

SEARCHERS, THE : APOSTLE OF MERCY
Caliber Comics: 1997 - No. 2, 1997 ($2.95/$3.95, B&W)

	GD	VG	FN	VF	VF/NM	NM-
1-($2.95)						3.00
2-($3.95)						4.00

SEARS (See Merry Christmas From...)

SEASON'S GREETINGS
Hallmark (King Features): 1935 (6-1/4x5-1/4", 32 pgs. in color)

nn-Cover features Mickey Mouse, Popeye, Jiggs & Skippy. "The Night Before Christmas" told one panel per page, each panel by a famous artist featuring their character. Art by Alex Raymond, Gottfredson, Swinnerton, Segar, Chic Young, Milt Gross, Sullivan (Messmer), Herriman, McManus, Percy Crosby & others (22 artists in all)
Estimated value... 900.00

SEBASTIAN O
DC Comics (Vertigo): May, 1993 - No. 3, July, 1993 ($1.95, limited series)

	GD	VG	FN	VF	VF/NM	NM-
1-3-Grant Morrison scripts						2.25

SECOND LIFE OF DOCTOR MIRAGE, THE (See Shadowman #16)
Valiant: Nov, 1993 - No. 18, May, 1995 ($2.50)

	GD	VG	FN	VF	VF/NM	NM-
1-18: 1-With bound-in poster. 5-Shadowman x-over. 7-Bound-in trading card						2.50
1-Gold ink logo edition; no price on-c						3.00

SECRET AGENT (Formerly Sarge Steel)
Charlton Comics: V2#9, Oct, 1966; V2#10, Oct, 1967

	GD	VG	FN	VF	VF/NM	NM-
V2#9-Sarge Steel part-r begins	3	6	9	19	25	32
10-Tiffany Sinn, CIA app. (from Career Girl Romances #39); Aparo-a	3	6	9	16	20	24

SECRET AGENT (TV) (See Four Color #1231)
Gold Key: Nov, 1966; No. 2, Jan, 1968

	GD	VG	FN	VF	VF/NM	NM-
1-Photo-c	12	24	36	87	129	170
2-Photo-c	8	16	24	58	82	105

SECRET AGENT X-9 (See Flash Gordon #4 by King)
David McKay Publ.: 1934 (Book 1: 84 pgs.; Book 2: 124 pgs.) (8x7-1/2")

	GD	VG	FN	VF	VF/NM	NM-
Book 1-Contains reprints of the first 13 weeks of the strip by Alex Raymond; complete except for 2 dailies	44	88	132	264	395	525
Book 2-Contains reprints immediately following contents of Book 1, for 20 weeks by Alex Raymond; complete except for two dailies. Note: Raymond mis-dated the last five strips from 6/34, and while the dating sequence is confusing, the continuity is correct	40	80	120	240	340	440

SECRET AGENT X-9 (See Magic Comics)
Dell Publishing Co.: Dec, 1937 (Not by Raymond)

	GD	VG	FN	VF	VF/NM	NM-
Feature Books 8	38	76	114	285	425	565

SECRET AGENT Z-2 (See Holyoke One-Shot No. 7)

SECRET CITY SAGA (See Jack Kirby's Secret City Saga)

SECRET DEFENDERS (Also see The Defenders & Fantastic Four #374)
Marvel Comics: Mar, 1993 - No. 25, Mar, 1995 ($1.75/$1.95)

	GD	VG	FN	VF	VF/NM	NM-
1-($2.50)-Red foil stamped-c; Dr. Strange, Nomad, Wolverine, Spider Woman & Darkhawk begin						3.00
2-11,13-24: 9-New team w/Silver Surfer, Thunderstrike, Dr. Strange & War Machine. 13-Thanos replaces Dr. Strange as leader; leads into Cosmic Powers limited series; 14-Dr. Druid. 15-Bound in card sheet. 18-Giant Man & Iron Fist app.						2.25
12,25: 12-($2.50)-Prismatic foil-c. 25 ($2.50, 52 pgs.)						2.50

SECRET DIARY OF EERIE ADVENTURES
Avon Periodicals: 1953 (25¢ giant, 100 pgs., one-shot)

	GD	VG	FN	VF	VF/NM	NM-
nn-(Rare)-Kubert-a; Hollingsworth-c; Sid Check back-c	176	352	528	1100	1650	2200

SECRET FILES & ORIGINS GUIDE TO THE DC UNIVERSE
DC Comics: Mar, 2000; Feb, 2002 ($6.95/$4.95)

	GD	VG	FN	VF	VF/NM	NM-
2000 (3/00, $6.95)-Overview of DC characters; profile pages by various						7.00
2001-2002 (2/02, $4.95) Olivetti-c						5.00

SECRET FILES PRESIDENT LUTHOR
DC Comics: Mar, 2001 ($4.95, one-shot)

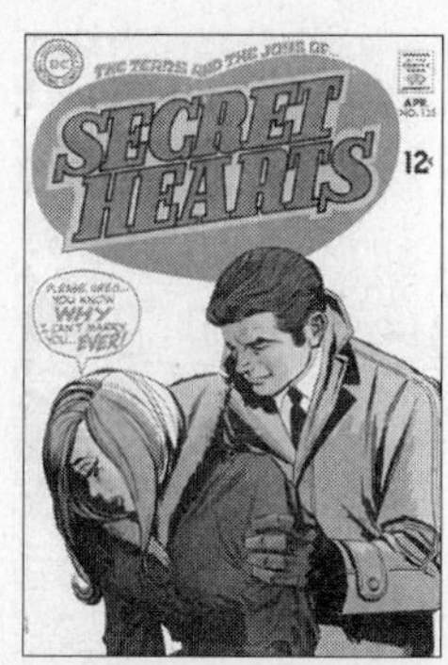

Secret Hearts #135 © DC

Secret Loves #1 © QUA

Secret Origins (3rd series) #4 © DC

	GD 2.0	VG 4.0	FN 6.0	VF 8.0	VF/NM 9.0	NM- 9.2
1-Short stories & profile pages by various; Harris-c						5.00

SECRET HEARTS
National Periodical Publications (Beverly)(Arleigh No. 50-113):
9-10/49 - No. 6, 7-8/50; No. 7, 12-1/51-52 - No. 153, 7/71

	GD 2.0	VG 4.0	FN 6.0	VF 8.0	VF/NM 9.0	NM- 9.2
1-Kinstler-a; photo-c begin, end #6	55	110	165	330	495	660
2-Toth-a (1 pg.); Kinstler-a	29	58	87	164	232	300
3,6 (1950)	25	50	75	147	202	260
4,5-Toth-a	26	52	78	150	210	270
7(12-1/51-52) (Rare)	40	80	120	240	340	440
8-10 (1952)	19	38	57	106	146	185
11-20	15	30	45	86	118	150
21-26: 26-Last precode (2-3/55)	13	26	39	74	100	125
27-40	8	16	24	53	74	95
41-50	6	12	18	38	52	65
51-60	5	10	15	33	44	55
61-75,100: 75-Last 10¢ issue	4	8	12	29	40	50
76-99,101-109	4	8	12	24	32	40
110- "Reach for Happiness" serial begins, ends #138	4	8	12	25	33	42
111-119,121-126	3	6	9	18	23	28
120,134-Neal Adams-c	4	8	12	27	36	45
127 (4/68)-Beatles cameo	4	8	12	27	36	45
128-133,135-142: 141,142- "20 Miles to Heartbreak", Chapter 2 & 3 (see Young Love for Chapters 1 & 4); Toth, Colletta-a	3	6	9	16	20	25
143-148,150-152: 144-Morrow-a	2	4	6	12	16	20
149,153: 149-Toth-a. 153-Kirby-i	2	4	6	14	18	22

SECRET ISLAND OF OZ, THE (See First Comics Graphic Novel)

SECRET LOVE (See Fox Giants & Sinister House of...)

SECRET LOVE
Ajax-Farrell/Four Star Comic Corp. No. 2 on: 12/55 - No. 3, 8/56; 4/57 - No. 5, 2/58; No. 6, 6/58

	GD 2.0	VG 4.0	FN 6.0	VF 8.0	VF/NM 9.0	NM- 9.2
1(12/55-Ajax, 1st series)	10	20	30	56	73	90
2,3	7	14	21	35	43	50
1(4/57-Ajax, 2nd series)	8	16	24	46	58	70
2-6: 5-Bakerish-a	6	12	18	31	38	45

SECRET LOVES
Comic Magazines/Quality Comics Group: Nov, 1949 - No. 6, Sept, 1950

	GD 2.0	VG 4.0	FN 6.0	VF 8.0	VF/NM 9.0	NM- 9.2
1-Ward-c	25	50	75	144	198	255
2-Ward-c	21	42	63	121	168	215
3-Crandall-a	14	28	42	81	111	140
4,6	10	20	30	60	80	100
5-Suggestive art "Boom Town Babe"; photo-c	14	28	42	81	111	140

SECRET LOVE STORIES (See Fox Giants)

SECRET MISSIONS (Admiral Zacharia's...)
St. John Publishing Co.: February, 1950

	GD 2.0	VG 4.0	FN 6.0	VF 8.0	VF/NM 9.0	NM- 9.2
1-Joe Kubert-c; stories of U.S. foreign agents	21	42	63	118	164	210

SECRET MYSTERIES (Formerly Crime Mysteries & Crime Smashers)
Ribage/Merit Publications No. 17 on: No. 16, Nov, 1954 - No. 19, July, 1955

	GD 2.0	VG 4.0	FN 6.0	VF 8.0	VF/NM 9.0	NM- 9.2
16-Horror, Palais-a; Myron Fass-c	28	56	84	159	225	290
17-19-Horror. 17-Fass-c; mis-dated 3/54?	19	38	57	107	149	190

SECRET ORIGINS (1st Series) (See 80 Page Giant #8)
National Periodical Publications: Aug-Oct, 1961 (Annual) (Reprints)

	GD 2.0	VG 4.0	FN 6.0	VF 8.0	VF/NM 9.0	NM- 9.2
1-Origin Adam Strange (Showcase #17), Green Lantern (Green Lantern #1), Challengers (partial-r/Showcase #6, 6 pgs. Kirby-a), J'onn J'onzz (Det. #225), The Flash (Showcase #4), Green Arrow (1 pg. text), Superman-Batman team (World's Finest #94), Wonder Woman (Wonder Woman #105)	48	96	144	384	580	775
Replica Edition (1998, $4.95) r/entire book and house ads						5.00
Even More Secret Origins (2003, $6.95) reprints origins of Hawkman, Eclipso, Kid Flash, Blackhawks, Green Lantern's oath, and Jimmy Olsen-Robin team in 80 pg. Giant style						7.00

SECRET ORIGINS (2nd Series)
National Periodical Publications: Feb-Mar, 1973 - No. 6, Jan-Feb, 1974; No. 7, Oct-Nov, 1974 (All 20¢ issues) (All origin reprints)

	GD 2.0	VG 4.0	FN 6.0	VF 8.0	VF/NM 9.0	NM- 9.2
1-Superman(r/1 pg. origin/Action #1, 1st time since G.A.), Batman(Detective #33), Ghost(Flash #88), The Flash(Showcase #4)	4	8	12	29	40	50
2-7: 2-Green Lantern & The Atom(Showcase #22 & 34), Supergirl(Action #252). 3-Wonder Woman(W.W. #1), Wildcat(Sensation #1). 4-Vigilante (Action #42) by Meskin, Kid Eternity(Hit #25). 5-The Spectre by Baily (More Fun #52,53). 6-Blackhawk(Military #1) & Legion of Super-Heroes(Superboy #147). 7-Robin (Detective #38), Aquaman (More Fun #73)	3	6	9	18	23	28

NOTE: ***Infantino*** *a-1.* ***Kane*** *a-2.* ***Kubert*** *a-1.*

SECRET ORIGINS (3rd Series)
DC Comics: 4/86 - No. 50, 8/90 (All origins)(52 pgs. #6 on)(#27 on: $1.50)

	GD 2.0	VG 4.0	FN 6.0	VF 8.0	VF/NM 9.0	NM- 9.2
1-Origin Superman						6.00
2-6: 2-Blue Beetle. 3-Shazam. 4-Firestorm. 5-Crimson Avenger. 6-Halo/G.A. Batman						3.00
7-9,11,12,14-20,22-26: 7-Green Lantern(Guy Gardner)/G.A. Sandman. 8-Shadow Lass/Doll Man. 9-G.A. Flash/Skyman.11-G.A. Hawkman/Power Girl. 12-Challengers of Unknown/G.A. Fury (2nd modern app.). 14-Suicide Squad; Legends spin-off. 15-Spectre/Deadman. 16-G.A. Hourman/Warlord. 17-Adam Strange story by Carmine infantino; Dr. Occult. 18-G.A. Gr. Lantern/The Creeper. 19-Uncle Sam/The Guardian. 20-Batgirl/G.A. Dr. Mid-Nite. 22-Manhunters. 23-Floronic Man/Guardians of the Universe. 24-Blue Devil/Dr. Fate. 25-LSH/Atom. 26-Black Lightning/Miss America						2.50
10-Phantom Stranger w/Alan Moore scripts; Legends spin-off						2.50
13-Origin Nightwing; Johnny Thunder app.						2.50
21-Jonah Hex/Black Condor						2.50
27-30,36-38,40-49: 27-Zatara/Zatanna. 28-Midnight/Nightshade. 29-Power of the Atom/Mr. America; new 3 pg. Red Tornado story by Mayer (last app. of Scribbly, 8/88). 30-Plastic Man/Elongated Man. 36-Poison Ivy by Neil Gaiman & Mark Buckingham/Green Lantern. 37-Legion Of Substitute Heroes/Doctor Light. 38-Green Arrow/Speedy; Grell scripts. 40-All Ape issue. 41-Rogues Gallery of Flash. 42-Phantom Girl/GrimGhost. 43-Original Hawk & Dove/Cave Carson/Chris KL-99. 44-Batman app.; story based on Det. #40. 45-Blackhawk/El Diablo. 46-JLA/LSH/New Titans. 47-LSH. 48-Ambush Bug/Stanley & His Monster/Rex the Wonder Dog/Trigger Twins. 49-Newsboy Legion/Silent Knight/Bouncing Boy						2.50
31-35,39: 31-JSA. 32-JLA. 33-35-JLI. 39-Animal Man-c/story continued in Animal Man #10; Grant Morrison scripts; Batman app.						3.00
50-($3.95, 100 pgs.)-Batman & Robin in text, Flash of Two Worlds, Johnny Thunder, Dolphin, Black Canary & Space Museum						5.00
Annual 1 (8/87)-Capt. Comet/Doom Patrol						3.00
Annual 2 ('88, $2.00)-Origin Flash II & Flash III						3.00
Annual 3 ('89, $2.95, 84 pgs.)-Teen Titans; 1st app. new Flamebird who replaces original Bat-Girl						3.00
Special 1 (10/89, $2.00)-Batman villains: Penguin, Riddler, & Two-Face; Bolland-c; Sam Kieth-a; Neil Gaiman scripts(2)						3.00

NOTE: ***Art Adams*** *a-33i(part).* ***M. Anderson*** *8, 19, 21, 25i; c-19(part).* ***Aparo*** *c/a-10.* ***Bissette*** *c-23.* ***Bolland*** *c-7.* ***Byrne*** *c/a-Annual 1.* ***Colan*** *c/a-5p.* ***Forte*** *a-37.* ***Giffen*** *a-18p, 44p, 48.* ***Infantino*** *a-17, 50p.* ***Kaluta*** *c-39.* ***Gil Kane*** *a-2, 28; c-2p.* ***Kirby*** *c-19(part).* ***Erik Larsen*** *a-13.* ***Mayer*** *a-29.* ***Morrow*** *a-21.* ***Orlando*** *a-10.* ***Perez*** *a-50i, Annual 3i; c- Annual 3.* ***Rogers*** *a-6p.* ***Russell*** *a-27i.* ***Simonson*** *c-22.* ***Staton*** *a-36, 50p.* ***Steacy*** *a-35.* ***Tuska*** *a-4p, 9p.*

SECRET ORIGINS 80 PAGE GIANT (Young Justice)
DC Comics: Dec, 1998 ($4.95, one-shot)

	GD 2.0	VG 4.0	FN 6.0	VF 8.0	VF/NM 9.0	NM- 9.2
1-Origin-s of Young Justice members; Ramos-a (Impulse)						5.00

SECRET ORIGINS FEATURING THE JLA
DC Comics: 1999 ($14.95, TPB)

	GD 2.0	VG 4.0	FN 6.0	VF 8.0	VF/NM 9.0	NM- 9.2
1-Reprints recent origin-s of JLA members; Cassaday-c						15.00

SECRET ORIGINS OF SUPER-HEROES (See DC Special Series #10, 19)

SECRET ORIGINS OF SUPER-VILLAINS 80 PAGE GIANT
DC Comics: Dec, 1999 ($4.95, one-shot)

	GD 2.0	VG 4.0	FN 6.0	VF 8.0	VF/NM 9.0	NM- 9.2
1-Origin-s of Sinestro, Amazo and others; Gibbons-c						5.00

SECRET ORIGINS OF THE WORLD'S GREATEST SUPER-HEROES
DC Comics: 1989 ($4.95, 148 pgs.)

	GD 2.0	VG 4.0	FN 6.0	VF 8.0	VF/NM 9.0	NM- 9.2
nn-Reprints Superman, JLA origins; new Batman origin-s; Bolland-c	1	2	3	4	5	7

SECRET ROMANCE
Charlton Comics: Oct, 1968 - No. 41, Nov, 1976; No. 42, Mar, 1979 - No. 48, Feb, 1980

	GD 2.0	VG 4.0	FN 6.0	VF 8.0	VF/NM 9.0	NM- 9.2
1-Begin 12¢ issues, ends #?	3	6	9	18	23	28
2-10: 9-Reese-a	2	4	6	10	13	16
11-30	2	4	6	8	10	12
31-48	1	2	3	5	7	9

NOTE: *Beyond the Stars app.-No. 9, 11, 12, 14.*

SECRET ROMANCES (Exciting Love Stories)
Superior Publications Ltd.: Apr, 1951 - No. 27, July, 1955

	GD 2.0	VG 4.0	FN 6.0	VF 8.0	VF/NM 9.0	NM- 9.2
1	15	30	45	86	118	150
2	10	20	30	60	80	100
3-10	8	16	24	46	58	70
11-13,15-18,20-27	7	14	21	37	46	55
14,19-Lingerie panels	8	16	24	40	50	60

SECRET SERVICE (See Kent Blake of the...)

SECRET SIX (See Action Comics Weekly)
National Periodical Publications: Apr-May, 1968 - No. 7, Apr-May, 1969 (12¢)

	GD 2.0	VG 4.0	FN 6.0	VF 8.0	VF/NM 9.0	NM- 9.2
1-Origin/1st app.	7	14	21	51	71	90
2-7	4	8	12	27	36	45

Secret Society of Super-Villains #7 © DC

Secrets of Haunted House #18 © DC

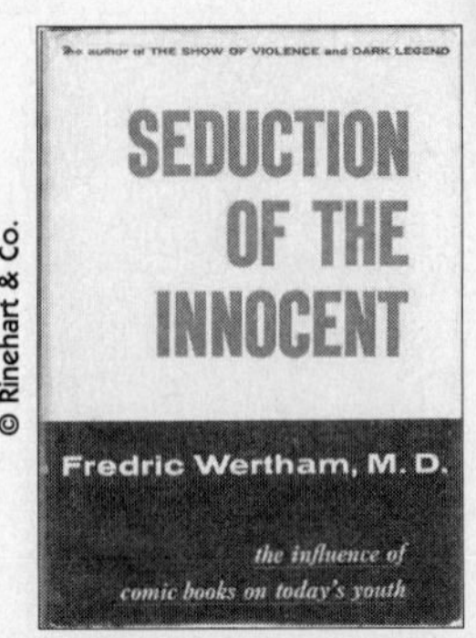

Seduction of the Innocent HC © Rinehart & Co.

	GD 2.0	VG 4.0	FN 6.0	VF 8.0	VF/NM 9.0	NM- 9.2

SECRET SIX (See Tangent Comics/ Secret Six)

SECRET SOCIETY OF SUPER-VILLAINS
National Per. Publ./DC Comics: May-June, 1976 - No. 15, June-July, 1978

	GD	VG	FN	VF	VF/NM	NM-
1-Origin; JLA cameo & Capt. Cold app.	2	4	6	11	14	18
2-5,15: 2-Re-intro/origin Capt. Comet; Green Lantern x-over. 5-Green Lantern, Hawkman x-over; Darkseid app. 15-G.A. Atom, Dr. Midnite, & JSA app.	1	3	4	6	8	10
6-14: 9,10-Creeper x-over. 11-Capt. Comet; Orlando-i	1	2	3	5	6	8

SECRET SOCIETY OF SUPER-VILLAINS SPECIAL (See DC Special Series #6)

SECRETS OF HAUNTED HOUSE
National Periodical Publications/DC Comics: 4-5/75 - #5, 12-1/75-76; #6, 6-7/77 - #14, 10-11/78; #15, 8/79 - #46, 3/82

	GD	VG	FN	VF	VF/NM	NM-
1	4	8	12	29	40	50
2-4	2	4	6	14	18	22
5-Wrightson-c	3	6	9	18	23	28
6-14	2	4	6	10	12	15
15-30	1	3	4	6	8	10
31,44: 31-Mr. E series begins, ends #41. 44-Wrightson-c	2	4	6	8	10	12
32-43,45,46	1	2	3	4	5	7

NOTE: *Aparo c-7.* ***Aragones*** *a-1.* ***B. Bailey*** *a-8.* ***Bissette*** *a-46.* ***Buckler*** *c-32-40p.* ***Ditko*** *a-9, 12, 41, 45.* ***Golden*** *a-10.* ***Howard*** *a-13i.* ***Kaluta*** *c-8, 10, 11, 14, 16, 29.* ***Kubert*** *c-41, 42.* ***Sheldon Mayer*** *a-43p.* ***McWilliams*** *a-35.* ***Nasser*** *a-24.* ***Newton*** *a-30p.* ***Nino*** *a-1, 13, 19.* ***Orlando*** *c-13, 30, 43, 45i.* ***N. Redondo*** *a-4, 5, 29.* ***Rogers*** *c-26.* ***Spiegle*** *a-31-41.* ***Wrightson*** *c-5, 44.*

SECRETS OF HAUNTED HOUSE SPECIAL (See DC Special Series #12)

SECRETS OF LIFE (Movie)
Dell Publishing Co.: 1956 (Disney)

	GD	VG	FN	VF	VF/NM	NM-
Four Color 749-Photo-c	6	12	18	38	52	65

SECRETS OF LOVE (See Popular Teen-Agers...)

SECRETS OF LOVE AND MARRIAGE
Charlton Comics: V2#1, Aug, 1956 - V2#25, June, 1961

	GD	VG	FN	VF	VF/NM	NM-
V2#1	5	10	15	33	44	55
V2#2-6	3	7	10	21	28	35
V2#7-9-(All 68 pgs.)	5	10	15	36	48	60
10-25	3	6	9	18	23	28

SECRETS OF MAGIC (See Wisco)

SECRETS OF SINISTER HOUSE (Sinister House of Secret Love #1-4)
National Periodical Publ.: No. 5, June-July, 1972 - No. 18, June-July, 1974

	GD	VG	FN	VF	VF/NM	NM-
5-(52 pgs.).	4	8	12	29	40	50
6-9: 7-Redondo-a	3	6	9	18	23	28
10-Neal Adams-a(i)	3	6	9	19	25	32
11-18: 15-Redondo-a. 17-Barry-a; early Chaykin 1 pg. strip	2	4	6	10	13	16

NOTE: ***Alcala*** *a-6, 13, 14.* ***Glanzman*** *a-7.* ***Kaluta*** *c-6, 7.* ***Nino*** *a-8, 11-13. Ambrose Bierce adapt.-#14.*

SECRETS OF THE LEGION OF SUPER-HEROES
DC Comics: Jan, 1981 - No. 3, Mar, 1981 (Limited series)

	GD	VG	FN	VF	VF/NM	NM-
1-3: 1-Origin of the Legion. 2-Retells origins of Brainiac 5, Shrinking Violet, Sun-Boy, Bouncing Boy, Ultra-Boy, Matter-Eater Lad, Mon-El, Karate Kid & Dream Girl						4.00

SECRETS OF TRUE LOVE
St. John Publishing Co.: Feb, 1958

	GD	VG	FN	VF	VF/NM	NM-
1	7	14	21	35	43	50

SECRETS OF YOUNG BRIDES
Charlton Comics: No. 5, Sept, 1957 - No. 44, Oct, 1964; July, 1975 - No. 9, Nov, 1976

	GD	VG	FN	VF	VF/NM	NM-
5	5	10	15	36	48	60
6-10: 8-Negligee panel	4	8	12	24	32	40
11-20	3	7	10	21	28	35
21-30: Last 10¢ issue?	3	6	9	18	24	30
31-44(10/64)	2	4	6	12	16	20
1-(2nd series) (7/75)	2	4	6	14	18	22
2-9	2	4	6	8	10	12

SECRET SQUIRREL (TV)(See Kite Fun Book)
Gold Key: Oct, 1966 (12¢) (Hanna-Barbera)

	GD	VG	FN	VF	VF/NM	NM-
1-1st Secret Squirrel and Morocco Mole, Squiddly Diddly, Winsome Witch	14	28	42	102	149	195

SECRET STORY ROMANCES (Becomes True Tales of Love)
Atlas Comics (TCI): Nov, 1953 - No. 21, Mar, 1956

	GD	VG	FN	VF	VF/NM	NM-
1-Everett-a; Jay Scott Pike-c	15	30	45	86	118	150
2	9	18	27	52	66	80
3-11: 11-Last pre-code (2/55)	8	16	24	43	54	65
12-21	7	14	21	37	46	55

NOTE: ***Colletta*** *a-10, 14, 15, 17, 21; c-10, 14, 17.*

SECRET VOICE, THE (See Great American Comics Presents...)

SECRET WARS II (Also see Marvel Super Heroes...)
Marvel Comics Group: July, 1985 - No. 9, Mar, 1986 (Maxi-series)

	GD	VG	FN	VF	VF/NM	NM-
1,9: 9-(52 pgs.) X-Men app., Spider-Man app.						4.00
2-8: 2,8-X-Men app. 5-1st app. Boom Boom. 5,8-Spider-Man app.						3.00

SECRET WEAPONS
Valiant: Sept, 1993 - No. 21, May, 1995 ($2.25)

	GD	VG	FN	VF	VF/NM	NM-
1-10,12-21: 3-Reese-a(i). 5-Ninjak app. 9-Bound-in trading card. 12-Bloodshot app.						2.50
11-(Sept. on envelope, Aug on-c, $2.50)-Enclosed in manilla envelope; Bloodshot app; intro new team.						2.50

SECTAURS
Marvel Comics: June, 1985 - No. 8, Sept, 1986 (75¢) (Based on Coleco Toys)

	GD	VG	FN	VF	VF/NM	NM-
1-8, 1-Giveaway; same-c with "Coleco 1985 Toy Fair Collectors' Edition"						3.00

SECTION ZERO
Image Comics (Gorilla): June, 2000 - No. 3, Sept, 2000 ($2.50)

	GD	VG	FN	VF	VF/NM	NM-
1-3-Kesel-s/Grummett-a						2.50

SEDUCTION OF THE INNOCENT (Also see New York State Joint Legislative Committee to Study...)
Rinehart & Co., Inc., N. Y.: 1953, 1954 (400 pgs.) (Hardback, $4.00)(Written by Fredric Wertham, M.D.)(Also printed in Canada by Clarke, Irwin & Co. Ltd.)

	GD	VG	FN	VF	VF/NM	NM-
(1st Version)-with bibliographical note intact (pages 399 & 400)(several copies got out before the comic publishers forced the removal of this page)	55	110	165	344	512	680
Dust jacket only	34	68	102	193	274	355
(1st Version)-without bibliographical note	34	68	102	193	274	355
Dust jacket only	16	32	48	92	126	160
(2nd Version)-Published in England by Kennikat Press, 1954, 399 pgs. has bibliographical page	11	22	33	66	88	110
1972 r-/of 2nd version; 400 pgs. w/bibliography page; Kennikat Press	4	8	12	24	32	40

NOTE: *Material from this book appeared in the November, 1953(Vol.70, pp50-53,214) issue of the* ***Ladies' Home Journal*** *under the title "What Parents Don't Know About Comic Books". With the release of this book, Dr. Wertham reveals seven years of research attempting to link juvenile delinquency to comic books. Many illustrations showing excessive violence, sex, sadism, and torture are shown. This book was used at the Kefauver Senate hearings which led to the Comics Code Authority. Because of the influence this book had on the comic industry and the collector's interest in it, we feel this listing is justified. Also see* ***Parade of Pleasure.***

SEDUCTION OF THE INNOCENT! (Also see Halloween Horror)
Eclipse Comics: Nov, 1985 - 3-D#2, Apr, 1986 ($1.75)

	GD	VG	FN	VF	VF/NM	NM-
1-6: Double listed under cover title from #7 on						3.00
3-D 1 (10/85, $2.25, 36 pgs.)-contains unpublished Advs. Into Darkness #15 (pre-code); Dave Stevens-c						4.00
2-D 1 (100 copy limited signed & #ed edition)(B&W)	1	2	3	5	6	8
3-D 2 (4/86)-Baker, Toth, Wrightson-c						5.00
2-D 2 (100 copy limited signed & #ed edition)(B&W)	1	2	3	5	7	9

NOTE: ***Anderson*** *r-2, 3.* ***Crandall*** *c/a(r)-1.* ***Meskin*** *c/a(r)-3, 3-D 1.* ***Moreira*** *r-2.* ***Toth*** *a-1-6r; c-4r.* ***Tuska*** *r-6.*

SEEKER
Sky Comics: Apr, 1994 ($2.50, one-shot)

	GD	VG	FN	VF	VF/NM	NM-
1						2.50

SEEKERS INTO THE MYSTERY
DC Comics (Vertigo): Jan, 1996 - No. 15, Apr, 1997 ($2.50)

	GD	VG	FN	VF	VF/NM	NM-
1-14: J.M. DeMatteis scripts in all. 1-4-Glenn Barr-a. 5,10-Muth-c/a. 6-9-Zulli-c/a. 11-14-Bolton-c; Jill Thompson-a						2.50
15-($2.95)-Muth-c/a						3.00

SEEKER 3000 (See Marvel Premiere #41)
Marvel Comics: Jun, 1998 - No. 4, Sept, 1998 ($2.99/$2.50, limited series)

	GD	VG	FN	VF	VF/NM	NM-
1-($2.99)-Set 25 years after 1st app.; wraparound-c						3.00
2-4-($2.50)						2.50
...Premiere 1 (6/98, $1.50) Reprints 1st app. from Marvel Premiere #41; wraparound-c						2.25

SELECT DETECTIVE (Exciting New Mystery Cases)
D. S. Publishing Co.: Aug-Sept, 1948 - No. 3, Dec-Jan, 1948-49

	GD	VG	FN	VF	VF/NM	NM-
1-Matt Baker-a	29	58	87	164	232	300
2-Baker, McWilliams-a	19	38	57	106	146	185
3	16	32	48	92	126	160

SELF-LOATHING COMICS

Sensational She-Hulk #20 © MAR

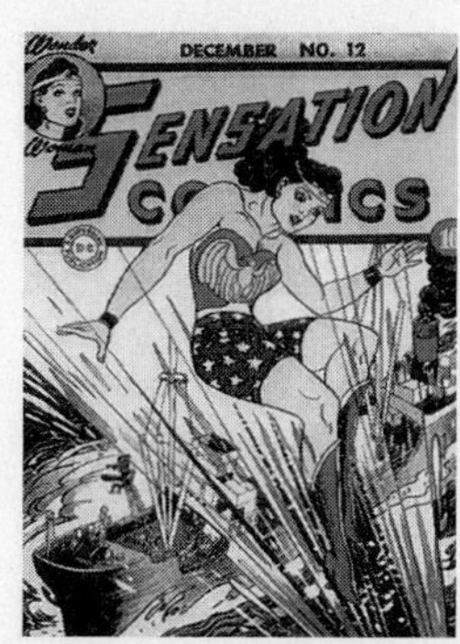

Sensation Comics #12 © DC

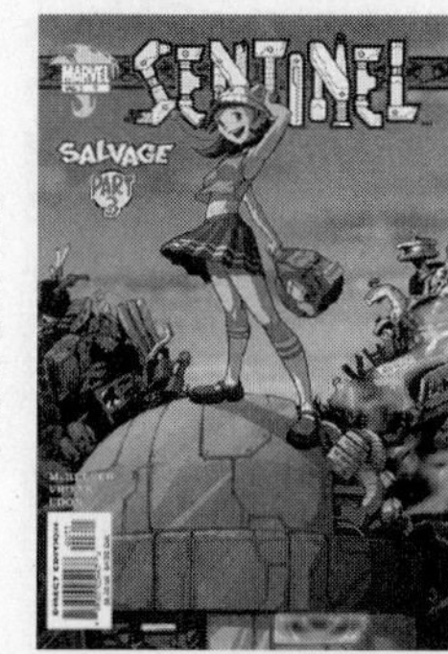

Sentinel #3 © MAR

	GD 2.0	VG 4.0	FN 6.0	VF 8.0	VF/NM 9.0	NM- 9.2

Fantagraphics Books: Feb, 1995 ($2.95, B&W)
1,2-Crumb 3.00

SEMPER FI (Tales of the Marine Corp)
Marvel Comics: Dec, 1988- No.9, Aug, 1989 (75¢)
1-9: Severin-c/a 2.25

SENSATIONAL POLICE CASES (Becomes Captain Steve Savage, 2nd Series)
Avon Periodicals: 1952; No. 2, 1954 - No. 4, July-Aug, 1954
nn-(1952, 25¢, 100 pgs.)-Kubert-a?; Check, Larsen, Lawrence & McCann-a; Kinstler-c 40 80 120 240 340 440
2-4: 2-Kirbyish-a (3-4/54). 4-Reprint/Saint #5 15 30 45 84 115 145
I.W. Reprint #5-(1963?, nd)-Reprints Prison Break #5(1952-Realistic); Infantino-a 3 6 9 18 24 30

SENSATIONAL SHE-HULK, THE (She-Hulk #21-23) (See Savage She-Hulk)
Marvel Comics: V2#1, 5/89 - No. 60, Feb, 1994 ($1.50/$1.75, deluxe format)
V2#1-Byrne-c/a(p)/scripts begin, end #8 3.00
2,3,5-8: 3-Spider-Man app. 2.25
4,14-17,21-23: 4-Reintro G.A. Blonde Phantom. 14-17-Howard the Duck app. 21-23-Return of the Blonde Phantom. 22-All Winners Squad app. 2.50
9-13,18-20,24-49,51-60: 25-Thor app. 26-Excalibur app.;Guice-c. 29-Wolverine app. (3 pgs.). 30-Hobgoblin-c & cameo. 31-Byrne-c/a/scripts begin again. 35-Last $1.50-c. 37-Wolverine/Punisher/Spidey-c, but no app. 39-Thing app. 56-War Zone app.; Hulk cameo. 57-Vs. Hulk-c/story. 58-Electro-c/story. 59-Jack O'Lantern app. 2.25
50-($2.95, 52 pgs.)-Embossed green foil-c; Byrne app.; last Byrne-c/a; Austin, Chaykin, Simonson-a; Miller-a(2 pgs.) 3.00
NOTE: ***Dale Keown** a(p)-13, 15-22.*

SENSATIONAL SHE-HULK IN CEREMONY, THE
Marvel Comics: 1989 - No. 2, 1989 ($3.95, squarebound, 52 pgs.)
nn-Part 1, nn-Part 2 4.00

SENSATIONAL SPIDER-MAN
Marvel Comics: Apr, 1989 ($5.95, squarebound, 80 pgs.)
1-r/Amazing Spider-Man Annual #14,15 by Miller & Annual #8 by Kirby & Ditko 6.00

SENSATIONAL SPIDER-MAN, THE
Marvel Comics: Jan, 1996 - No. 33, Nov, 1998 ($1.95/$1.99)
0 ($4.95)-Lenticular-c; Jurgens-a/scripts 5.00
1 5.00
1-($2.95) variant-c; polybagged w/cassette 1 2 3 5 6 8
2-5: 2-Kaine & Rhino app. 3-Giant-Man app. 4.00
6-18: 9-Onslaught tie-in; revealed that Peter & Mary Jane's unborn baby is a girl. 11-Revelations. 13-15-Ka-Zar app. 14,15-Hulk app. 3.00
19-24: Living Pharoah app. 22,23-Dr. Strange app. 2.50
25-($2.99) Spiderhunt pt. 1; Normie Osborne kidnapped 4.00
25-Variant-c 1 2 3 5 6 8
26-33: 26-Nauck-a. 27-Double-c with "The Sensational Hornet #1"; Vulture app. 28-Hornet vs. Vulture. 29,30-Black Cat-c/app. 33-Last issue; Gathering of Five concludes 2.50
#(-1) Flashback(7/97) Dezago-s/Wieringo-a 3.00
'96 Annual ($2.95) 3.00

SENSATION COMICS (Sensation Mystery #110 on)
National Per. Publ./All-American: Jan, 1942 - No. 109, May-June, 1952
1-Origin Mr. Terrific(1st app.), Wildcat(1st app.), The Gay Ghost, & Little Boy Blue; Wonder Woman (cont'd from All Star #8), The Black Pirate begin; intro. Justice & Fair Play Club 2500 5000 7500 18,750 29,375 40,000
1-Reprint, Oversize 13-1/2x10". WARNING: This comic is an exact duplicate reprint of the original except for its size. DC published it in 1974 with a second cover titling it as a Famous First Edition. There have been many reported cases of the outer cover being removed and the interior sold as the original edition. The reprint with the new outer cover removed is practically worthless. See Famous First Edition for value.
2-Etta Candy begins 434 868 1302 3038 4669 6300
3-W. Woman gets secretary's job 264 528 792 1650 2475 3300
4-1st app. Stretch Skinner in Wildcat 184 368 552 1150 1725 2300
5-Intro. Justin, Black Pirate's son 148 296 444 925 1388 1850
6-Origin/1st app. Wonder Woman's magic lasso 152 304 456 950 1425 1900
7-10 107 214 321 669 1005 1340
11,12,14-20 96 192 288 600 900 1200
13-Hitler, Tojo, Mussolini-c (as bowling pins) 134 268 402 838 1257 1675
21-30 76 152 228 475 713 950
31-33 55 110 165 344 515 685
34-Sargon, the Sorcerer begins (10/44), ends #36; begins again #52 60 120 180 375 563 750
35-40: 38-X-Mas-c 50 100 150 300 450 600
41-50: 43-The Whip app. 45 90 135 270 405 540
51-60: 51-Last Black Pirate. 56,57-Sargon by Kubert 42 84 126 252 376 500
61-67,69-80: 63-Last Mr. Terrific. 66-Wildcat by Kubert 40 80 120 240 350 460
68-Origin & 1st app. Huntress (8/47) 44 88 132 264 395 525
81-Used in **SOTI**, pg. 33,34; Krigstein-a 40 80 120 240 360 480
82-93: 83-Last Sargon. 86-The Atom app. 90-Last Wildcat. 91-Streak begins by Alex Toth. 92-Toth-a (2 pgs.) 36 72 108 204 290 375
94-1st all girl issue 48 96 144 288 432 575
95-99,101-106: 95-Unmasking of Wonder Woman-c/story. 99-1st app. Astra, Girl of the Future, ends #106. 103-Robot-c. 105-Last 52 pgs. 106-Wonder Woman ends 44 88 132 264 395 525
100-(11-12/50) 55 110 165 344 515 685
107-(Scarce, 1-2/52)-1st mystery issue; Johnny Peril by Toth(p), 8 pgs. & begins; continues from Danger Trail #5 (3-4/51)(see Comic Cavalcade #15 for 1st app.) 68 136 204 425 638 850
108-(Scarce)-Johnny Peril by Toth(p) 55 110 165 344 515 685
109-(Scarce)-Johnny Peril by Toth(p) 68 136 204 425 638 850
NOTE: ***Krigstein** a-(Wildcat)-81, 83, 84. **Moldoff** Black Pirate-1-25; Black Pirate not in 34-36, 43-48. **Oskner** c(i)-89-91, 94-106. Wonder Woman by **H. G. Peter**, all issues except #8, 17-19, 21; c-4-7, 9-18, 20-88, 92, 93. **Toth** a-91, 98; c-107. Wonder Woman c-1-106.*

SENSATION COMICS (Also see All Star Comics 1999 crossover titles)
DC Comics: May, 1999 ($1.99, one-shot)
1-Golden Age Wonder Woman and Hawkgirl; Robinson-s 2.25

SENSATION MYSTERY (Formerly Sensation Comics #1-109)
National Periodical Publ.: No. 110, July-Aug, 1952 - No. 116, July-Aug, 1953
110-Johnny Peril continues 44 88 132 264 395 525
111-116-Johnny Peril in all. 116-M. Anderson-a 44 88 132 264 395 525
NOTE: ***M. Anderson** c-110. **Colan** a-114p. **Giunta** a-112. **G. Kane** c(p)-108, 109, 111-115.*

SENSUOUS STREAKER
Marvel Publ.: 1974 (B&W magazine, 68pgs.)
1 3 6 9 17 21 26

SENTINEL
Marvel Comics: June, 2003 - No. 12, April, 2004 ($2.99/$2.50)
1-Sean McKeever-s/Udon Studios-a 3.00
2-11 3.00

SENTINELS OF JUSTICE, THE (See Americomics & Captain Paragon &...)

SENTRY
Marvel Comics: Sept, 2000 - No. 5, Jan, 2001 ($2.99, limited series)
1-5-Paul Jenkins-s/Jae Lee-a. 3-Spider-Man-c/app. 4-X-Men, FF app. 3.00
.../Fantastic Four (2/01, $2.99) Continues story from #5; Winslade-a 3.00
.../Hulk (2/01, $2.99) Sienkiewicz-c/a 3.00
.../Spider-Man (2/01, $2.99) back story of the Sentry; Leonardi-a 3.00
.../The Void (2/01, $2.99) Conclusion of story; Jae Lee-a 3.00
.../X-Men (2/01, $2.99) Sentry and Archangel; Texeira-a 3.00
TPB (10/01, $24.95) r/#1-5 & all one-shots; Stan Lee interview 25.00

SENTRY SPECIAL
Innovation Publishing: 1991 ($2.75, one-shot)(Hero Alliance spin-off)
1-Lost in Space preview (3 pgs.) 2.75

SERAPHIM
Innovation Publishing: May, 1990 ($2.50, mature readers)
1 2.50

SERGEANT BARNEY BARKER (Becomes G. I. Tales #4 on)
Atlas Comics (MCI): Aug, 1956 - No. 3, Dec, 1956
1-Severin-c/a(4) 20 40 60 112 156 200
2,3: 2-Severin-c/a(4). 3-Severin-c/a(5) 14 28 42 79 107 135

SERGEANT BILKO (Phil Silvers Starring as...) (TV)
National Periodical Publications: May-June, 1957 - No. 18, Mar-Apr, 1960
1-All have Bob Oskner-c 74 148 222 463 694 925
2 40 80 120 240 340 440
3-5 35 70 105 201 288 370
6-18: 11,12,15,17-Photo-c 29 58 87 164 232 300

SGT. BILKO'S PVT. DOBERMAN (TV)
National Periodical Publications: June-July, 1958 - No. 11, Feb-Mar, 1960
1-Bob Oskner c-1-4,7,11 34 68 102 255 383 510
2 20 40 60 140 205 270
3-5: 5-Photo-c 14 28 42 99 145 190
6-11: 6,9-Photo-c 10 20 30 67 96 125

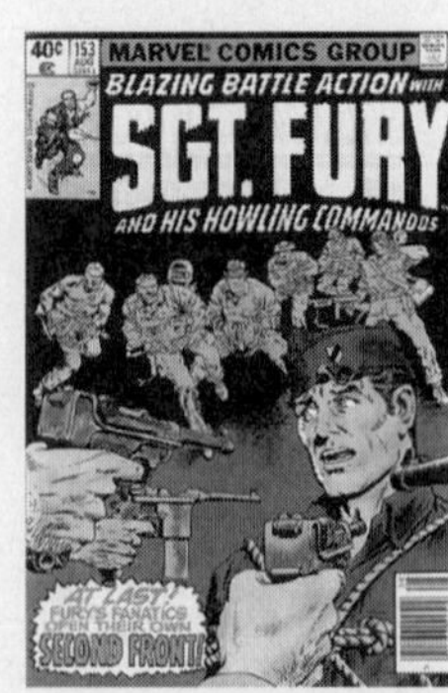

Sgt. Fury #153 © MAR

Sgt. Rock #347 © DC

Sergio Aragones' Groo & Rufferto #3 © Sergio Aragones

GD VG FN VF VF/NM NM-
2.0 4.0 6.0 8.0 9.0 9.2

SGT. DICK CARTER OF THE U.S. BORDER PATROL (See Holyoke One-Shot)

SGT. FURY (& His Howling Commandos)(See Fury & Special Marvel Edition)
Marvel Comics Group (BPC earlier issues): May, 1963 - No. 167, Dec, 1981

1-1st app. Sgt. Nick Fury (becomes agent of Shield in Strange Tales #135); Kirby/Ayers-c/a; 1st Dum-Dum Dugan & the Howlers 128 256 384 1088 1644 2200
2-Kirby-a 37 74 111 278 414 550
3-5: 3-Reed Richards x-over. 4-Death of Junior Juniper. 5-1st Baron Strucker app.; Kirby-a 22 44 66 156 228 300
6-10: 8-Baron Zemo, 1st Percival Pinkerton app. 9-Hitler-c & app. 10-1st app. Capt. Savage (the Skipper)(9/64) 13 26 39 94 137 180
11,12,14-20: 14-1st Blitz Squad. 18-Death of Pamela Hawley 8 16 24 53 74 95
13-Captain America & Bucky app.(12/64); 2nd solo Capt. America x-over outside The Avengers; Kirby-a 33 66 99 248 374 500
13-2nd printing (1994) 2 4 6 8 10 12
21-24,26,28-30 6 12 18 38 52 65
25,27: 25-Red Skull app. 27-1st app. Eric Koenig; origin Fury's eye patch 6 12 18 40 55 70
31-33,35-50: 35-Eric Koenig joins Howlers. 43-Bob Hope, Glen Miller app. 44-Flashback on Howlers' 1st mission 4 8 12 22 30 38
34-Origin Howling Commandos 4 8 12 24 32 40
51-60 3 6 9 18 24 30
61-67: 64-Capt. Savage & Raiders x-over; peace symbol-c. 67-Last 12¢ issue; flag-c 3 6 9 16 20 24
68-80: 76-Fury's Father app. in WWI story 2 4 6 14 18 22
81-91: 91-Last 15¢ issue 2 4 6 12 16 20
92-(52 pgs.) 3 6 9 16 20 24
93-99: 98-Deadly Dozen x-over 2 4 6 11 14 18
100-Capt. America, Fantastic 4 cameos; Stan Lee, Martin Goodman & others app. 3 6 9 16 20 24
101-120: 101-Origin retold 2 4 6 10 12 15
121-130: 121-123-r/#19-21 1 3 4 6 8 10
131-167: 167-Reprints (from 1963) 1 2 3 5 6 8
133,134-(30¢-c variants, limited dist.)(5,7/76) 2 4 6 8 10 12
141,142-(35¢-c variants, limited dist.)(7,9/77) 2 4 6 8 10 12
Annual 1(1965, 25¢, 72 pgs.)-r/#4,5 & new-a 15 30 45 104 152 200
Special 2(1966) 6 12 18 38 52 65
Special 3(1967) All new material 4 8 12 25 33 42
Special 4(1968) 3 6 9 18 24 30
Special 5-7(1969-11/71) 2 4 6 14 18 22

NOTE: ***Ayers** a-8, Annual 1. **Ditko** a-15i. **Gil Kane** c-37, 96. **Kirby** a-1-7, 13p, 167p(r). Special 5; c-1-20, 25, 167p. **Severin** a-44-46, 48, 162, 164; inks-49-79, Special 4, 6; c-4i, 5, 6, 44, 46, 110, 149i, 155i, 162-166. **Sutton** a-57p. Reprints in #80, 82, 85, 87, 89, 91, 93, 95, 99, 101, 103, 105, 107, 109, 111, 121-123, 145-155, 167.*

SGT. FURY AND HIS HOWLING DEFENDERS (See The Defenders #147)

SERGEANT PRESTON OF THE YUKON (TV)
Dell Publishing Co.: No. 344, Aug, 1951 - No. 29, Nov-Jan, 1958-59

Four Color 344(#1)-Sergeant Preston & his dog Yukon King begin; painted-c begin, end #18 13 26 39 90 133 175
Four Color 373,397,419('52) 8 16 24 58 82 105
5(11-1/52-53)-10(2-4/54): 6-Bondage-c. 6 12 18 43 59 75
11,12,14-17 6 12 18 38 52 65
13-Origin Sgt. Preston 6 12 18 43 59 75
18-Origin Yukon King; last painted-c 6 12 18 43 59 75
19-29: All photo-c 8 16 24 55 78 100

SGT. ROCK (Formerly Our Army at War; see Brave & the Bold #52 & Showcase #45)
National Periodical Publications/DC Comics: No. 302, Mar, 1977 - No. 422, July, 1988

302 3 7 10 21 28 35
303-310 2 4 6 11 14 18
311-320: 318-Reprints 2 4 6 8 10 12
321-350 1 2 3 5 7 9
351-399,401-421 6.00
400,422: 422-1st Joe, Adam, Andy Kubert-a team 1 2 3 5 7 9
Annual 2-4: 2(1982)-Formerly Sgt. Rock's Prize Battle Tales #1. 3(1983). 4(1984) 1 2 3 5 7 9

NOTE: ***Estrada** a-322, 327, 331, 336, 337, 341, 342i. **Glanzman** a-384, 421. **Kubert** a-302, 303, 305r, 306, 328, 351, 356, 368, 373, 422; c-317, 318r, 319-323, 325-333-on, Annual 2, 3. **Severin** a-347. **Spiegle** a-382, Annual 2, 3. **Thorne** a-384. **Toth** a-385r. **Wildey** a-307, 311, 313, 314.*

SGT. ROCK: BETWEEN HELL AND A HARD PLACE
DC Comics (Vertigo): 2003 ($24.95, hardcover one-shot)

HC-Joe Kubert-a/c; Brian Azzarello-s 25.00

SGT. ROCK SPECIAL (Sgt. Rock #14 on; see DC Special Series #3)
DC Comics: Oct, 1988 - No. 21, Feb, 1992; No. 1, 1992; No. 2, 1994
($2.00, quarterly/monthly, 52 pgs)

1-Reprint begin 1 3 4 6 8 10
2-21: All-r; 5-r/early Sgt. Rock/Our Army at War #81. 7-Tomahawk-r by Thorne. 9-Enemy Ace-r by Kubert. 10-All Rock issue. 11-r/1st Haunted Tank story. 12-All Kubert issue; begins monthly. 13-Dinosaur story by Heath(r). 14-Enemy Ace-r (22 pgs.) by Adams/Kubert. 15-Enemy Ace (22 pgs.) by Kubert. 16-Iron Major-c/story. 16,17-Enemy Ace-r. 19-r/Batman/Sgt. Rock team-up/B&B #108 by Aparo 6.00
1 (1992, $2.95, 68 pgs.)-Simonson-c; unpubbed Kubert-a; Glanzman, Russell, Pratt, & Wagner-a 5.00
2 (1994, $2.95) Brereton painted-c 4.00

NOTE: ***Neal Adams** r-1, 8, 14p. **Chaykin** a-2; r-3, 9(2pgs.); c-3. **Drucker** r-6. **Glanzman** r-20. **Golden** a-1. **Heath** a-2; r-5, 9-13, 16, 19, 21. **Krigstein** r-4, 8. **Kubert** r-1-17, 20, 21; c-1p, 2, 8, 14-21. **Miller** r-6p. **Severin** r-3, 6, 10. **Simonson** r-2, 4; c-4. **Thorne** r-7. **Toth** r-2, 8, 11. **Wood** r-4.*

SGT. ROCK SPECTACULAR (See DC Special Series #13)

SGT. ROCK'S PRIZE BATTLE TALES (Becomes Sgt. Rock Annual #2 on; see DC Special Series #18 & 80 Page Giant #7)
National Periodical Publications: Winter, 1964 (Giant - 80 pgs., one-shot)

1-Kubert, Heath-r; new Kubert-c 32 64 96 240 358 475
... Replica Edition (2000, $5.95) Reprints entire issue 6.00

SGT. STRYKER'S DEATH SQUAD (See Savage Combat Tales)

SERGIO ARAGONÉS' ACTIONS SPEAK
Dark Horse Comics: Jan, 2001 - No. 6, Jun, 2001 ($2.99, B&W, limited series)

1-6-Aragonés-c/a; wordless one-page cartoons 3.00

SERGIO ARAGONÉS' BLAIR WHICH?
Dark Horse Comics: Dec, 1999 ($2.95, B&W, one-shot)

nn-Aragonés-c/a; Evanier-s. Parody of "Blair Witch Project" movie 3.00

SERGIO ARAGONÉS' BOOGEYMAN
Dark Horse Comics: June, 1998 - No. 4, Sept, 1998 ($2.95, B&W, lim. series)

1-4-Aragonés-c/a 3.00

SERGIO ARAGONÉS DESTROYS DC
DC Comics: June, 1996 ($3.50, one-shot)

1-DC Superhero parody book; Aragonés-c/a; Evanier scripts 3.50

SERGIO ARAGONÉS' DIA DE LOS MUERTOS
Dark Horse Comics: Oct, 1998 ($2.95, one-shot)

1-Aragonés-c/a; Evanier scripts 3.00

SERGIO ARAGONÉS' GROO & RUFFERTO
Dark Horse Comics: Dec, 1998 - No. 4, Mar, 1999 ($2.95, lim. series)

1-3-Aragonés-c/a 3.00

SERGIO ARAGONÉS' GROO: DEATH AND TAXES
Dark Horse Comics: Dec, 2001 - No. 4, Apr, 2002 ($2.99, lim. series)

1-4-Aragonés-c/a; Evanier-s 3.00

SERGIO ARAGONÉS' GROO: MIGHTIER THAN THE SWORD
Dark Horse Comics: Jan, 2000 - No. 4, Apr, 2000 ($2.95, lim. series)

1-4-Aragonés-c/a; Evanier-s 3.00

SERGIO ARAGONÉS' GROO THE WANDERER (See Groo...)

SERGIO ARAGONÉS' LOUDER THAN WORDS
Dark Horse Comics: July, 1997 - No. 6, Dec, 1997 ($2.95, B&W, limited series)

1-6-Aragonés-c/a 3.00

SERGIO ARAGONÉS MASSACRES MARVEL
Marvel Comics: June, 1996 ($3.50, one-shot)

1-Marvel Superhero parody book; Aragonés-c/a; Evanier scripts 3.50

SERGIO ARAGONÉS STOMPS STAR WARS
Marvel Comics: Jan, 2000 ($2.95, one-shot)

1-Star Wars parody; Aragonés-c/a; Evanier scripts 3.00

SERRA ANGEL ON THE WORLDS OF MAGIC THE GATHERING
Acclaim Comics (Armada): Aug, 1996 ($5.95, one-shot)

1 6.00

SEVEN BLOCK
Marvel Comics (Epic Comics): 1990 ($4.50, one-shot, 52 pgs.)

1 4.50

SEVEN DEAD MEN (See Complete Mystery #1)

SEVEN DWARFS (Also see Snow White)
Dell Publishing Co.: No. 227, 1949 (Disney-Movie)

Seven Seas Comics #3
© Universal Phoenix Features

Shade, the Changing Man #57 © DC

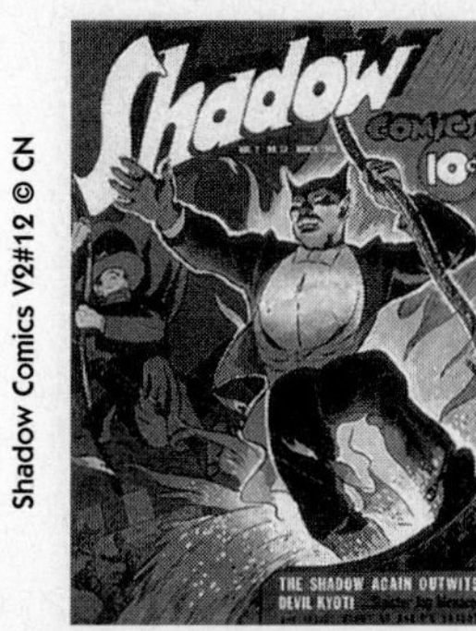

Shadow Comics V2#12 © CN

GD 2.0 | VG 4.0 | FN 6.0 | VF 8.0 | VF/NM 9.0 | NM- 9.2

Four Color #227 11 22 33 77 114 150

SEVEN MILES A SECOND
DC Comics (Vertigo Verité): 1996 ($7.95, one-shot)
nn-Wojnarowicz-s/Romberg-a 8.00

SEVEN SAMUROID, THE (See Image Graphic Novel)

SEVEN SEAS COMICS
Universal Phoenix Features/Leader No. 6: Apr, 1946 - No. 6, 1947(no month)
1-South Sea Girl by Matt Baker, Capt. Cutlass begin; Tugboat Tessie by Baker app. 85 170 255 531 796 1060
2-Swashbuckler-c 70 140 210 438 654 870
3,5,6: 3-Six pg. Feldstein-a 64 128 192 400 600 800
4-Classic Baker-c 74 148 222 463 694 925
NOTE: *Baker a-1-6; c-3-6.*

1776 (See Charlton Classic Library)

7TH VOYAGE OF SINBAD, THE (Movie)
Dell Publishing Co.: Sept, 1958 (photo-c)
Four Color 944-Buscema-a 14 28 42 99 145 190

77 SUNSET STRIP (TV)
Dell Publ. Co./Gold Key: No. 1066, Jan-Mar, 1960 - No. 2, Feb, 1963 (All photo-c)
Four Color 1066-Toth-a 12 24 36 87 129 170
Four Color 1106,1159-Toth-a 10 20 30 70 100 130
Four Color 1211,1263,1291, 01-742-209(7-9/62)-Manning-a in all 9 18 27 65 93 120
1,2: Manning-a. 1(11/62-G.K.) 10 20 30 70 100 130

77TH BENGAL LANCERS, THE (TV)
Dell Publishing Co.: May, 1957
Four Color 791-Photo-c 8 16 24 55 78 100

SEYMOUR, MY SON (See More Seymour)
Archie Publications (Radio Comics): Sept, 1963
1-DeCarlo-a? 3 7 10 21 28 35

SHADE, THE (See Starman)
DC Comics: Apr, 1997 - No. 4, July, 1997 ($2.25, limited series)
1-4-Robinson-s/Harris-c: 1-Gene Ha-a. 2-Williams/Gray-a 3-Blevins-a. 4-Zulli-a 3.00

SHADE, THE CHANGING MAN (See Cancelled Comic Cavalcade)
National Per. Publ./DC Comics: June-July, 1977 - No. 8, Aug-Sept, 1978
1-1st app. Shade; Ditko-c/a in all 2 4 6 8 10 12
2-8 1 2 3 4 5 7

SHADE, THE CHANGING MAN (2nd series) (Also see Suicide Squad #16)
DC Comics (Vertigo imprint #33 on): July, 1990 - No. 70, Apr, 1996 ($1.50-$2.25, mature)
1-($2.50, 52 pgs.)-Peter Milligan scripts in all 4.00
2-41,45-49,51-59: 6-Preview of World Without End. 17-Begin $1.75-c. 33-Metallic ink on-c. 41-Begin $1.95-c 2.25
42-44-John Constantine app. 3.00
50-($2.95, 52 pgs.) 3.50
60-70: 60-begin $2.25-c 2.25
...: The American Scream (2003, $17.95) r/#1-6 18.00
NOTE: *Bachalo a-1-9, 11-13, 15-21, 23-26, 33-39, 42-45, 47, 49, 50; c-30, 33-41.*

SHADO: SONG OF THE DRAGON (See Green Arrow #63-66)
DC Comics: 1992 - No. 4, 1992 ($4.95, limited series, 52 pgs.)
Book One - Four: Grell scripts; Morrow-a(i) 5.00

SHADOW, THE (See Batman #253, 259 & Marvel Graphic Novel #35)

SHADOW, THE (Pulp, radio)
Archie Comics (Radio Comics): Aug, 1964 - No. 8, Sept, 1965 (All 12¢)
1-Jerrry Siegel scripts in all; Shadow-c. 8 16 24 53 74 95
2-8: 2-App. in super-hero costume on-c only; Reinman-a(backup). 3-Superhero begins; Reinman-a (book-length novel). 3,4,6,7-The Fly 1 pg. strips. 4-8-Reinman-a. 5-8-Siegel scripts. 7-Shield app. 5 10 15 33 44 55

SHADOW, THE
National Periodical Publications: Oct-Nov, 1973 - No. 12, Aug-Sept, 1975
1-Kaluta-a begins 4 8 12 27 36 45
2 2 4 6 14 18 22
3-Kaluta/Wrightson-a 3 6 9 16 20 25
4,6-Kaluta-a ends. 4-Chaykin, Wrightson part-i 2 4 6 11 14 18
5,7-12: 11-The Avenger (pulp character) x-over 1 2 3 5 7 9
NOTE: *Craig a-10. Cruz a-10-12. Kaluta a-1, 2, 3p, 4, 6; c-1-4, 6, 10-12. Kubert c-9. Robbins a-5, 7-9; c-5, 7, 8.*

SHADOW, THE
DC Comics: May, 1986 - No. 4, Aug, 1986 (limited series)
1-4: Howard Chaykin art in all 3.00
Blood & Judgement ($12.95)-r/1-4 13.00

SHADOW, THE
DC Comics: Aug, 1987 - No. 19, Jan, 1989 ($1.50)
1-19: Andrew Helfer scripts in all. 3.00
Annual 1,2 (12/87, '88,)-2-The Shadow dies; origin retold (story inspired by the movie "Citizen Kane"). 4.00
NOTE: *Kyle Baker a-7i, 8-19, Annual 2. Chaykin c-Annual 1. Helfer scripts in all. Orlando a-Annual 1. Rogers c/a-7. Sienkiewicz c/a-1-6.*

SHADOW, THE (Movie)
Dark Horse Comics: June, 1994 - No. 2, July, 1994 ($2.50, limited series)
1,2-Adaptation from Universal Pictures film 3.00
NOTE: *Kaluta c/a-1, 2.*

SHADOW AND DOC SAVAGE, THE
Dark Horse Comics: July, 1995 - No. 2, Aug, 1995 ($2.95, limited series)
1,2 3.50

SHADOW AND THE MYSTERIOUS 3, THE
Dark Horse Comics: Sept, 1994 ($2.95, one-shot)
1-Kaluta co-scripts. 3.00
NOTE: *Stevens c-1.*

SHADOW CABINET (See Heroes)
DC Comics (Milestone): Jan, 1994 - No. 17, Oct, 1995 ($1.75/$2.50)
0,1-17: 0-($2.50, 52 pgs.)-Silver ink-c; Simonson-c. 1-Byrne-c 2.50

SHADOW COMICS (Pulp, radio)
Street & Smith Publications: Mar, 1940 - V9#5, Aug-Sept, 1949
NOTE: *The Shadow first appeared on radio in 1929 and was featured in pulps beginning in April, 1931, written by Walter Gibson. The early covers of this series were reprinted from the pulp covers.*
V1#1-Shadow, Doc Savage, Bill Barnes, Nick Carter (radio), Frank Merriwell, Iron Munro, the Astonishing Man begin 448 896 1344 3136 4818 6500
2-The Avenger begins, ends #6; Capt. Fury only app. 192 384 576 1200 1800 2400
3(nn-5/40)-Norgil the Magician app.; cover is exact swipe of Shadow pulp from 1/33 132 264 396 825 1238 1650
4,5: 4-The Three Musketeers begins, ends #8. 5-Doc Savage ends 102 204 306 638 957 1275
6,8,9: 9-Norgil the Magician app. 90 180 270 563 844 1125
7-Origin/1st app. The Hooded Wasp & Wasplet (11/40); series ends V3#8; Hooded Wasp/Wasplet app. on-c thru #9 96 192 288 600 900 1200
10-Origin The Iron Ghost, ends #11; The Dead End Kids begins, ends #14 90 180 270 563 844 1125
11-Origin Hooded Wasp & Wasplet retold 90 180 270 563 844 1125
12-Dead End Kids app. 78 156 234 488 732 975
V2#1(11/41) 72 144 216 450 675 900
2-(Rare) Giant ant-c; Dead End Kids story 128 256 384 800 1200 1600
3-Origin & 1st app. Supersnipe (3/42); series begins; Little Nemo story 112 224 336 700 1050 1400
4,5: 4,8-Little Nemo story 62 124 186 388 582 775
6-9: 6-Blackstone the Magician story 58 116 174 363 544 725
10,12: 10-Supersnipe app. 56 112 168 350 525 700
11-Classic Devil Kyoti World War 2 sunburst-c 60 120 180 375 563 750
V3#1-5,7-12: 10-Doc Savage begins, not in V5#5, V6#10-12, V8#4 56 112 168 336 506 675
6-Classic underwater-c 58 116 174 363 544 725
V4#1-12 45 90 135 270 405 540
V5#1-12 42 84 126 252 359 465
V6#1-11: 9-Intro. Shadow, Jr. (12/46) 39 78 117 230 325 420
12-Powell-c/a; atom bomb panels 42 84 126 252 359 465
V7#1,2,5,7-9,12: 2,5-Shadow, Jr. app.; Powell-a 40 80 120 240 360 480
3,6,11-Powell-c/a 46 92 138 276 413 550
4-Powell-c/a; Atom bomb panels 48 96 144 288 432 575
10(1/48)-Flying Saucer-c/story (2nd of this theme; see The Spirit 9/28/47); Powell-c/a 55 110 165 341 511 680
V8#1-12-Powell-a. 8-Powell Spider-c/a 46 92 138 276 413 550
V9#1,5-Powell-a 44 88 132 264 395 525
2-4-Powell-c/a 46 92 138 276 413 550
NOTE: *Binder c-V3#1. Powell art in most issues beginning V6#12. Painted c-1-6.*

SHADOWDRAGON
DC Comics: 1995 ($3.50, annual)

Shadowhawk #13 © Jim Valentino

Shadowman #23 © Voyager Comm.

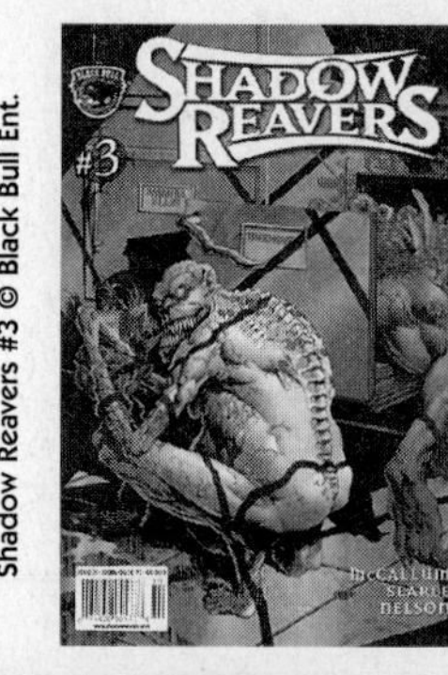

Shadow Reavers #3 © Black Bull Ent.

	GD 2.0	VG 4.0	FN 6.0	VF 8.0	VF/NM 9.0	NM- 9.2

Annual 1-Year One story 3.50

SHADOW EMPIRES: FAITH CONQUERS
Dark Horse Comics: Aug, 1994 - No. 4, Nov, 1994 ($2.95, limited series)

1-4 3.00

SHADOWHAWK (See Images of Shadowhawk, New Shadowhawk, Shadowhawk II, Shadowhawk III & Youngblood #2)
Image Comics (Shadowline Ink): Aug, 1992 - No. 4, Mar, 1993; No. 12, Aug, 1994 - No. 18, May, 1995 ($1.95/$2.50)

1-($2.50)-Embossed silver foil stamped-c; Valentino/Liefeld-c; Valentino-c/a/ scripts in all; has coupon for Image #0; 1st Shadowline Ink title 4.00
1-With coupon missing 2.25
1-($1.95)-Newsstand version w/o foil stamp 2.25
2-13,0,1418: 2-Shadowhawk poster w/McFarlane-i; brief Spawn app.; wraparound-c w/silver ink highlights. 3-($2.50)-Glow-in-the-dark-c. 4-Savage Dragon-c/story; Valentino/Larsen-c. 5-11-(See Shadowhawk II and III). 12-Cont'd from Shadowhawk III; pull-out poster by Texeira.13-w/ShadowBone poster; WildC.A.T.s app. 0 (10/94)-Liefeld c/a/story; ShadowBart poster. 14-(10/94, $2.50)-The Others app. 16-Supreme app. 17-Spawn app.; story cont'd from Badrock & Co. #6. 18-Shadowhawk dies; Savage Dragon & Brigade app. 2.50
Special 1(12/94, $3.50, 52 pgs.)-Silver Age Shadowhawk flip book 3.50
Gallery (4/94, $1.95) 2.25
Out of the Shadows ($19.95)-r/Youngblood #2, Shadowhawk #1-4, Image Zero #0, Operation: Urban Storm (Never published) 20.00
.../Vampirella (2/95, $4.95)-Pt.2 of x-over (See Vampirella/Shadowhawk for Pt. 1) 5.00
NOTE: *Shadowhawk was originally a four issue limited series. The story continued in Shadowhawk II, Shadowhawk III & then became Shadowhawk again with issue #12.*

SHADOWHAWK II (Follows Shadowhawk #4)
Image Comics (Shadowline Ink): V2#1, May, 1993 - V2#3, Aug, 1993 ($3.50/$1.95/$2.95, limited series)

V2#1 ($3.50)-Cont'd from Shadowhawk #4; die-cut mirricard-c 3.50
2 ($1.95)-Foil embossed logo; reveals identity; gold-c variant exists 2.50
3 ($2.95)-Pop-up-c w/Pact ashcan insert 3.00

SHADOWHAWK III (Follows Shadowhawk II #3)
Image Comics (Shadowline Ink): V3#1, Nov, 1993 - V3#4, Mar, 1994 ($1.95, limited series);

V3#1-4: 1-Cont'd from Shadowhawk II; intro Valentine; gold foil & red foil stamped-c variations. 2-(52 pgs.)-Shadowhawk contracts HIV virus; U.S. Male by M. Anderson (p) in free 16 pg.insert. 4-Continues in Shadowhawk #12 2.50

SHADOWHAWKS OF LEGEND
Image Comics (Shadowline Ink): Nov, 1995 ($4.95, one-shot)

nn-Stories of past Shadowhawks by Kurt Busiek, Beau Smith & Alan Moore 5.00

SHADOW, THE: HELL'S HEAT WAVE (Movie, pulp, radio)
Dark Horse Comics: Apr, 1995 - No. 3, June, 1995 ($2.95, limited series)

1-3: Kaluta story 3.00

SHADOWHUNT SPECIAL
Image Comics (Extreme Studios): Apr, 1996 ($2.50)

1-Retells origin of past Shadowhawks; Valentino script; Chapel app. 2.50

SHADOW, THE: IN THE COILS OF THE LEVIATHAN (Movie, pulp, radio)
Dark Horse Comics: Oct, 1993 - No. 4, Apr, 1994 ($2.95, limited series)

1-4-Kaluta-c & co-scripter 3.00
Trade paperback (10/94, $13.95)-r/1-4 14.00

SHADOW LADY:... (Masakazu Katsura's...)
Dark Horse Comics ($2.50, B&W, limited series, Manga)

Dangerous Love: (Oct, 1998 - No. 7, Apr, 1999) 1-7-Katsura-s/a 2.50
TPB ($17.95) r/#1-7 18.00
The Eyes of a Stranger: (No. 8, May, 1999 - No. 12, Sept, 1999) 8-12 2.50
The Awakening: (No. 13, Oct, 1999 - No. 19, Apr, 2000) 13-19 2.50
Sudden Death: (No. 20, May, 2000 - No. 24) 20-23 2.50

SHADOWLINE SAGA: CRITICAL MASS, A
Marvel Comics (Epic): Jan, 1990 - No. 7, July, 1990 ($4.95, lim. series, 68 pgs)

1-6: Dr. Zero, Powerline, St. George 5.00
7 ($5.95, 84 pgs.)-Morrow-a, Williamson-c(i) 6.00

SHADOWMAN (See X-O Manowar #4)
Valiant/Acclaim Comics (Valiant): May, 1992 - No. 43, Dec, 1995 ($2.50)

1-Partial origin 5.00
2-5: 3-1st app. Sousa the Soul Eater 4.00
6-43: 8-1st app. Master Darque. 16-1st app. Dr. Mirage (8/93). 15-Minor Turok app. 17,18-Archer & Armstrong x-over. 19-Aerosmith-c/story. 23-Dr. Mirage x-over. 24-(4/94). 25-Bound-in trading card. 29-Chaos Effect. 43-Shadowman jumps to his death 2.50
0-($2.50, 4/94)-Regular edition 2.50
0-($3.50)-Wraparound chromium-c edition 3.50
0-Gold 6.00
Yearbook 1 (12/94, $3.95) 4.00

SHADOWMAN (Volume 2)
Acclaim Comics (Valiant Heroes): Mar, 1997 - No. 20 ($2.50, mature)

1-20: 1-1st app. Zero; Garth Ennis scripts begin, end #4. 2-Zero becomes new Shadowman. 4-Origin; Jack Boniface (original Shadowman) rises from the grave. 5-Jamie Delano scripts begin. 9-Copycat-c 2.50
1-Variant painted cover 2.50
#0 Gold 5.00

SHADOWMAN (Volume 3)
Acclaim Comics: July, 1999 - No. 5, Nov, 1999 ($3.95/$2.50)

1-($3.95)-Abnett & Lanning-s/Broome & Benjamin-a 4.00
2-5-($2.50): 3,4-Flip book with Unity 2000 2.50

SHADOWMASTERS
Marvel Comics: Oct, 1989 - No.4, Jan, 1990 ($3.95, squarebound, 52 pgs.)

1-4: Heath-a(i). 1-Jim Lee-c; story cont'd from Punisher 4.00

SHADOW OF THE BATMAN
DC Comics: Dec, 1985 - No. 5, Apr, 1986 ($1.75, limited series)

1-Detective-r (all have wraparound-c) 1 2 3 4 5 7
2,3,5: 3-Penguin-c & cameo. 5-Clayface app. 5.00
4-Joker-c/story 6.00
NOTE: ***Austin** a(new)-2i, 3i; r-2-4i. **Rogers** a(new)-1, 2p, 3p, 4, 5; r-1-5p; c-1-5. **Simonson** a-1r.*

SHADOW OF THE TORTURER, THE
Innovation: July, 1991 - No. 3, 1992 ($2.50, limited series)

1-3: Based on Pocket Books novel 2.50

SHADOW ON THE TRAIL (See Zane Grey & Four Color #604)

SHADOW PLAY (Tales of the Supernatural)
Whitman Publications: June, 1982

1-Painted-c 6.00

SHADOW REAVERS
Black Bull Ent.: Oct, 2001 - Present ($2.99)

1-5-Nelson-a; two covers for each issue 3.00
Limited Preview Edition (5/01, no cover price) 2.25

SHADOW RIDERS
Marvel Comics UK, Ltd.: June, 1993 - No. 4, Sept, 1993 ($1.75, limited series)

1-($2.50)-Embossed-c; Cable-c/story 2.50
2-4-Cable app. 2-Ghost Rider app. 2.25

SHADOWS
Image Comics: Feb, 2003 - No. 4, Nov, 2003 ($2.95)

1-4-Jade Dodge-s/Matt Camp-a/c 3.00

SHADOWS & LIGHT
Marvel Comics: Feb, 1998 - No. 3, July, 1998 ($2.99, B&W, quarterly)

1-3: 1-B&W anthology of Marvel characters; Black Widow art by Gene Ha, Hulk by Wrightson, Iron Man by Ditko & Daredevil by Stelfreeze; Stelfreeze painted-c. 2-Weeks, Sharp, Starlin, Thompson-a. 3-Buscema, Grindberg, Giffen, Layton-a 3.00

SHADOW'S FALL
DC Comics (Vertigo): Nov, 1994 - No. 6, Apr, 1995 ($2.95, limited series)

1-6: Van Fleet-c/a in all. 3.00

SHADOWS FROM BEYOND (Formerly Unusual Tales)
Charlton Comics: V2#50, October, 1966

V2#50-Ditko-c 3 7 10 21 28 35

SHADOW SLASHER
Pocket Change Comics: No. 0, 1994 - No. 6, 1995? ($2.50, B&W)

0-6 2.50

SHADOW STATE
Broadway Comics: Dec, 1995 - No. 5, Apr, 1996 ($2.50)

1-5: 1,2-Fatale back-up story; Cockrum-a(p) 2.50
Preview Edition 1,2 (10-11/95, $2.50, B&W) 2.50

SHADOW STRIKES!, THE (Pulp, radio)
DC Comics: Sept, 1989 - No.31, May, 1992 ($1.75)

1-4,7-31: 31-Mignola-c 2.50
5,6-Doc Savage x-over 4.00

Shang-Chi: Master of Kung Fu #1 © MAR

Shazam! #33 © DC

Sheena, Queen of the Jungle #18 © FH

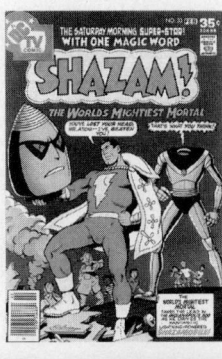

GD 2.0 | VG 4.0 | FN 6.0 | VF 8.0 | VF/NM 9.0 | NM- 9.2

Annual 1 (1989, $3.50, 68 pgs.)-Spiegle a; Kaluta-c 3.50

SHADOW WAR OF HAWKMAN
DC Comics: May, 1985 - No. 4, Aug, 1985 (limited series)
1-4 2.25

SHAGGY DOG & THE ABSENT-MINDED PROFESSOR (See Four Color #1199, Movie Comics & Walt Disney Showcase #46)(Disney-Movie)
Dell Publ. Co.: No. 985, May, 1959
Four Color #985 9 18 27 60 85 110

SHALOMAN
Al Wiesner/ Mark 1 Comics: 1989 - Present (B&W)
V1#1-Al Wiesner-s/a in all 4.50
2-9 2.50
V2 #1(The New Adventures)-4,6-10, V3 (The Legend) #1-11 2.75
V2 #5 (Color)-Shows Vol 2, No. 4 in indicia 3.00

SHAMAN'S TEARS (Also see Maggie the Cat)
Image Comics (Creative Fire Studio): 5/93 - No. 2, 8/93; No. 3, 11/94 - No. 0, 1/96 ($2.50/$1.95)
0-2: 0-(DEC-c, 1/96)-Last Issue. 1-(5/93)-Embossed red foil-c; Grell-c/a & scripts in all. 2-Cover unfolds into poster (8/93-c, 7/93 inside) 2.50
3-12: 3-Begin $1.95-c. 5-Re-intro Jon Sable. 12-Re-intro Maggie the Cat (1 pg.) 2.25

SHANG-CHI: MASTER OF KUNG-FU ("Master of Kung Fu" on cover for #1&2)
Marvel Comics: Nov, 2002 - No. 6, Apr, 2003 ($2.99, limited series)
1-6-Moench-s/Gulacy-c/a 3.00
... Vol. 1: The Hellfire Apocalypse TPB (2003, $14.99) r/#1-6 15.00

SHANGRI-LA
Image Comics: Jan, 2004 ($7.95, B&W, square-bound graphic novel)
1-Marc Bryant-s/Shepherd Hendrix-a 8.00

SHANNA, THE SHE-DEVIL (See Savage Tales #8)
Marvel Comics Group: Dec, 1972 - No. 5, Aug, 1973 (All are 20¢ issues)
1-1st app. Shanna; Steranko-c; Tuska-a(p) 3 6 9 18 24 30
2-Steranko-c; heroin drug story 2 4 6 14 18 22
3-5 2 4 6 10 12 15

SHARK FIGHTERS, THE (Movie)
Dell Publishing Co.: Jan, 1957
Four Color 762-Buscema-a; photo-c 9 18 27 60 85 110

SHARKY
Image Comics: Feb, 1998 - No. 4, 1998 ($2.50, bi-monthly)
1-4: 1-Mask app.; Elliot-s/a. Horley painted-c. 3-Three covers by Horley, Bisley, & Horley/Elliot. 4-Two covers (swipe of Avengers #4 and wraparound) 2.50
1-($2.95) "$1,000,000" variant 3.00
2-($2.50) Savage Dragon variant-c 2.50

SHARP COMICS (Slightly large size)
H. C. Blackerby: Winter, 1945-46 - V1#2, Spring, 1946 (52 pgs.)
V1#1-Origin Dick Royce Planetarian 40 80 120 240 350 460
2-Origin The Pioneer; Michael Morgan, Dick Royce, Sir Gallagher, Planetarian, Steve Hagen, Weeny and Pop app. 39 78 117 230 325 420

SHARPY FOX (See Comic Capers & Funny Frolics)
I. W. Enterprises/Super Comics: 1958; 1963
1,2-I.W. Reprint (1958): 2-r/Kiddie Kapers #1 2 4 6 8 10 12
14-Super Reprint (1963) 2 4 6 8 10 12

SHATTER (See Jon Sable #25-30)
First Comics: June, 1985; Dec, 1985 - No. 14, Apr, 1988. ($1.75, Baxter paper/deluxe paper)
1 (6/85)-1st computer generated-a in a comic book (1st printing) 3.00
1-(2nd print.); 1(12/85)-14: computer generated-a & lettering in all 2.25
Special 1 (1988) 2.25

SHATTERED IMAGE
Image Comics (WildStorm Productions): Aug, 1996 - No. 4, Dec, 1996 ($2.50, limited series)
1-4: 1st Image company-wide x-over; Kurt Busiek scripts in all. 1-Tony Daniel-c/a(p). 2-Alex Ross-c/swipe (Kingdom Come) by Ryan Benjamin & Travis Charest 2.50

SHAZAM (See Giant Comics to Color, Limited Collectors' Edition & The Power Of Shazam!)

SHAZAM! (TV)(See World's Finest #253 for story from unpublished #36)
National Periodical Publ./DC Comics: Feb, 1973 - No. 35, May-June, 1978
1-1st revival of original Captain Marvel since G.A. (origin retold), by C.C. Beck; Mary Marvel & Captain Marvel Jr. app.; Superman-c 4 8 12 24 32 40
2-5: 2-Infinity photo-c.; re-intro Mr. Mind & Tawny. 3-Capt. Marvel-r. (10/46). 4-Origin retold; Capt. Marvel-r. (1949). 5-Capt. Marvel Jr. origin retold; Capt. Marvel-r. (1948, 7 pgs.) 2 4 6 10 12 15
6,7,9-11: 6-photo-c; Capt. Marvel-r (1950, 6 pgs.). 9-Mr. Mind app. 10-Last C.C. Beck issue. 11-Schaffenberger-a begins. 2 4 6 8 10 12
8 (100 pgs.) 8-r/Capt. Marvel Jr. by Raboy; origin/C.M. #80; origin Mary Marvel/C.M.A. #18; origin Mr. Tawny/C.M.A. #79 5 10 15 36 48 60
12-17-(All 100 pgs.). 15-vs. Lex Luthor & Mr. Mind 4 8 12 29 40 50
18-24,26-30: 21-24-All reprints. 26-Sivana app. (10/76). 27-Kid Eternity teams up w/Capt. Marvel. 28-1st S.A. app. of Black Adam. 30-1st DC app. 3 Lt. Marvels 1 3 4 6 8 10
25-1st app. Isis 2 4 6 9 11 14
31-35: 31-1st DC app. Minuteman. 34-Origin Capt. Nazi & Capt. Marvel Jr. retold 2 4 6 9 11 14

NOTE: *Reprints in #1-8, 10, 12-17r, 21-24.* ***Beck*** *a-1-10, 12-17r, 21-24r; c-1, 3-9.* ***Nasser*** *c-35p.* ***Newton*** *a-35p.* ***Raboy*** *a-5r, 8r, 17r.* ***Schaffenberger*** *a-11, 14-20, 25, 26, 27p, 28, 29-31p, 33i, 35i; c-20, 22, 23, 25, 26i, 27i, 28-33.*

SHAZAM! AND THE SHAZAM FAMILY! ANNUAL
DC Comics: 2002 ($5.95, squarebound, one-shot)
1-Reprints Golden Age stories including 1st Mary Marvel and 1st Black Adam 6.00

SHAZAM!: POWER OF HOPE
DC Comics: Nov, 2000 ($9.95, treasury size, one-shot)
nn-Painted art by Alex Ross; story by Alex Ross and Paul Dini 10.00

SHAZAM: THE NEW BEGINNING
DC Comics: Apr, 1987 - No. 4, July, 1987 (Legends spin-off) (Limited series)
1-4: 1-New origin & 1st modern app. Captain Marvel; Marvel Family cameo. 2-4-Sivana & Black Adam app. 3.00

SHEA THEATRE COMICS
Shea Theatre: No date (1940's) (32 pgs.)
nn-Contains Rocket Comics; MLJ cover in one color 10 20 30 56 73 90

SHE-BAT (See Murcielaga, She-Bat & Valeria the She-Bat)

SHEENA (Movie)
Marvel Comics: Dec, 1984 - No. 2, Feb, 1985 (limited series)
1,2-r/Marvel Comics Super Special #34; Tanya Roberts movie 3.00

SHEENA, QUEEN OF THE JUNGLE (See Jerry Iger's Classic..., Jumbo Comics, & 3-D Sheena)
Fiction House Magazines: Spr, 1942; No. 2, Wint, 1942-43; No. 3, Spr, 1943; No. 4, Fall, 1948; No. 5, Sum, 1949; No. 6, Spr, 1950; No. 7-10, 1950(nd); No. 11, Spr, 1951 - No. 18, Wint, 1952-53 (#1-3: 68 pgs.; #4-7: 52 pgs.)
1-Sheena begins 248 496 744 1550 2325 3100
2 (Winter, 1942-43) 109 218 327 681 1021 1360
3 (Spring, 1943) 80 160 240 500 750 1000
4,5 (Fall, 1948, Sum, 1949): 4-New logo; cover swipe from Jumbo #20 50 100 150 300 450 600
6,7 (Spring, 1950, 1950) 43 86 129 258 389 520
8-10(1950 - Win/50, 36 pgs.) 40 80 120 240 350 460
11-18: 15-Cover swipe from Jumbo #43. 18-Used in **POP**, pg. 98 36 72 108 204 290 375
I.W. Reprint #9-r/#18; c-r/White Princess #3 5 10 15 33 44 55

NOTE: ***Baker*** *c-5-10?* ***Whitman*** *c-11-18(most).*

SHEENA-QUEEN OF THE JUNGLE
London Night: Feb, 1998 - No. 3 ($3.00)
0-($3.00)-Hartsoe-s/Sandoval-c 3.00
0-($5.00) Crocodile, Zebra, & Leopard editions 5.00
1-3-($3.00) 3.00
1-3-($5.00) Ministry Edition 5.00

SHEENA 3-D SPECIAL (Also see Blackthorne 3-D Series #1)
Eclipse Comics: Jan, 1985 ($2.00)
1-Dave Stevens-c 5.00

SHE-HULK (See The Savage She-Hulk & The Sensational She-Hulk)

SHERIFF BOB DIXON'S CHUCK WAGON (TV) (See Wild Bill Hickok #22)
Avon Periodicals: Nov, 1950
1-Kinstler-c/a(3) 14 28 42 79 107 135

SHERIFF OF TOMBSTONE
Charlton Comics: Nov, 1958 - No. 17, Sept, 1961
V1#1-Giordano-c; Severin-a 7 14 21 51 71 90
2 4 8 12 27 36 45

Sheva's War #1 © Christopher Moeller

Shidima #1 © Dreamwave Prod.

Shi: Masquerade #1 © William Tucci

	GD 2.0	VG 4.0	FN 6.0	VF 8.0	VF/NM 9.0	NM- 9.2
3-10	3	6	9	19	25	32
11-17	3	6	9	16	20	25

SHERLOCK HOLMES (See Marvel Preview, New Adventures of..., & Spectacular Stories)

SHERLOCK HOLMES (All New Baffling Adventures of...)(Young Eagle #3 on?)
Charlton Comics: Oct, 1955 - No. 2, Mar, 1956

	GD	VG	FN	VF	VF/NM	NM-
1-Dr. Neff, Ghost Breaker app.	40	80	120	240	360	480
2	38	76	114	219	310	400

SHERLOCK HOLMES (Also see The Joker)
National Periodical Publications: Sept-Oct, 1975

	GD	VG	FN	VF	VF/NM	NM-
1-Cruz-a; Simonson-c	3	6	9	18	23	28

SHERRY THE SHOWGIRL (Showgirls #4)
Atlas Comics: July, 1956 - No. 3, Dec, 1956; No. 5, Apr, 1957 - No. 7, Aug, 1957

	GD	VG	FN	VF	VF/NM	NM-
1-Dan DeCarlo-c/a in all	16	32	48	92	126	160
2	11	22	33	63	84	105
3,5-7	10	20	30	56	73	90

SHE'S JOSIE (See Josie)

SHEVA'S WAR
DC Comics (Helix): Oct, 1998 - No. 5, Feb, 1999 ($2.95, mini-series)

1-5-Christopher Moeller-s/painted-a/c 3.00

SHI (See Razor Annual #1 for 1st app.)

SHI: AKAI
Crusade Comics: 2001 ($2.99)

1-Intro. Victoria Cross; Tucci-a/c; J.C. Vaughn-s 3.00
Victoria Cross Ed. ($5.95, edition of 2000) variant Tucci-c 6.00

SHI: BLACK, WHITE AND RED
Crusade Comics: Mar, 1998 - No. 2, May, 1998 ($2.95, B&W&Red, mini-series)

1,2-J.G. Jones-painted art 3.00
...- Year of the Dragon Collected Edition (2000, $5.95) r/#1&2 6.00

SHI: C.G.I.
Crusade Comics: 2001 ($4.99)

Preview Edition 5.00

SHI/CYBLADE: THE BATTLE FOR THE INDEPENDENTS
Crusade Comics: Sept, 1995 ($2.95)

1-Tucci-c; features Cerebus, Bone, Hellboy, as well as others 3.00
1-Silvestri variant-c 4.00

SHI/DAREDEVIL: HONOR THY MOTHER (See Daredevil/Shi..)
Crusade Comics: Jan, 1997 ($2.95, one-shot)

1-Flip book 3.00

SHIDIMA
Image Comics: Jan, 2001 - No. 7, Nov, 2002 ($2.95, limited series)

1-7-Prequel to Warlands 3.00
#0-(10/01, $2.25) Short story and sketch pages 2.25

SHI: EAST WIND RAIN
Crusade Comics: Nov, 1997 - No. 2, Feb, 1998 ($3.50, limited series)

1,2-Shi at WW2 Pearl Harbor 3.50

S.H.I.E.L.D. (Nick Fury & His Agents of...) (Also see Nick Fury)
Marvel Comics Group: Feb, 1973 - No. 5, Oct, 1973 (All 20¢ issues)

	GD	VG	FN	VF	VF/NM	NM-
1-All contain reprint stories from Strange Tales #146-155; new Steranko-c	2	4	6	11	14	18
2-New Steranko flag-c	2	4	6	9	11	14
3-5: 3-Kirby/Steranko-c(r). 4-Steranko-c(r)	1	2	3	5	7	9

NOTE: ***Buscema** a-3p(r). **Kirby** layouts 1-5; c-3 (w/**Steranko**). **Steranko** a-3r, 4r(2).*

SHIELD, THE (Becomes Shield-Steel Sterling #3; #1 titled Lancelot Strong; also see Advs. of the Fly, Double Life of Private Strong, Fly Man, Mighty Comics, The Mighty Crusaders, The Original... & Pep Comics #1)
Archie Enterprises, Inc.: June, 1983 - No. 2, Aug, 1983

1,2: Steel Sterling app. 2-Kanigher-s 4.00
America's 1st Patriotic Comic Book Hero, The Shield (2002, $12.95, TPB) r/Pep Comics #1-5, Shield-Wizard Comics #1; foreward by Robert M. Overstreet 13.00

SHIELD-STEEL STERLING (Formerly The Shield)
Archie Enterprises, Inc.: No. 3, Dec, 1983 (Becomes Steel Sterling No. 4)

3-Nino-a; Steel Sterling by Kanigher & Barreto 3.00

SHIELD WIZARD COMICS (Also see Pep Comics & Top-Notch Comics)
MLJ Magazines: Summer, 1940 - No. 13, Spring, 1944

	GD	VG	FN	VF	VF/NM	NM-
1-(V1#5 on inside)-Origin The Shield by Irving Novick & The Wizard by Ed Ashe, Jr; Flag-c	470	940	1410	3290	5045	6800
2-(Winter/40)-Origin The Shield retold; Wizard's sidekick, Roy the Super Boy begins (see Top-Notch #8 for 1st app.)	232	464	696	1450	2175	2900
3,4	144	288	432	900	1350	1800
5-Dusty, the Boy Detective begins	124	248	372	775	1163	1550
6,7: 6-Roy the Super Boy app. 7-Shield dons new costume (Summer, 1942); S & K-c?	120	240	360	750	1125	1500
8-Bondage-c; Hitler photo on-c	124	248	372	775	1163	1550
9-13: 9,13-Bondage-c	86	172	258	538	807	1075

NOTE: ***Bob Montana** c-13. **Novick** c-1-6,8-11. **Harry Sahle** c-12.*

SHI: FAN EDITIONS
Crusade Comics: 1997

1-3-Two covers polybagged in FAN #19-21 3.00
1-3-Gold editions 4.00

SHI: HEAVEN AND EARTH
Crusade Comics: June, 1997 - No. 4, Apr, 1998 ($2.95)

1-4 3.00
4-($4.95) Pencil-c variant 5.00
Rising Sun Edition-signed by Tucci in FanClub Starter Pack 4.00
"Tora No Shi" variant-c 3.00

SHI: JUDGMENT NIGHT
Crusade Comics: 2000 ($3.99, one-shot)

1-Wolverine app.; Battlebook card and pages included; Tucci-a 4.00

SHI: KAIDAN
Crusade Comics: Oct, 1996 ($2.95)

1-Two covers; Tucci-c; Jae Lee wraparound-c 3.00

SHI: MASQUERADE
Crusade Comics: Mar, 1998 ($3.50, one-shot)

1-Painted art by Lago, Texeira, and others 3.50

SHI: NIGHTSTALKERS
Crusade Comics: Sept, 1997 ($3.50, one-shot)

1-Painted art by Val Mayerik 3.50

SHINING KNIGHT (See Adventure Comics #66)

SHINOBI (Based on Sega video game)
Dark Horse Comics: Aug, 2002 ($2.99, one-shot)

1-Medina-a/c 3.00

SHIP AHOY
Spotlight Publishers: Nov, 1944 (52 pgs.)

	GD	VG	FN	VF	VF/NM	NM-
1-L. B. Cole-c	20	40	60	112	156	200

SHI: PANDORA'S BOX
Avatar Press: Mar, 2003 ($3.50,B&W)

1-Four covers; Juan Jose Ryp-a 3.50

SHIP OF FOOLS
Image Comics: Aug, 1997 - No. 3 ($2.95, B&W)

0-3-Glass-s/Oeming-a 3.00

SHI: POISONED PARADISE
Avatar Press: July, 2002 - No. 2, Aug, 2002 ($3.50, limited series)

1,2-Vaughn and Tucci-s/Waller-a; 1-Four covers 3.50

SHIPWRECKED! (Disney-Movie)
Disney Comics: 1990 ($5.95, graphic novel, 68 pgs.)

nn-adaptation; Spiegle-a 6.00

SHI: REKISHI
Crusade Comics: Jan, 1997 ($2.95)

1-Character bios and story summaries of Shi: The Way of the Warrior told in Detective Joe Labianca's point of view; Christopher Golden script; Tucci-c; J.G. Jones-a; flip book w/Shi: East Wind Rain preview 3.00

SHI: SEMPO
Avatar Press: Aug, 2003 - No. 2, ($3.50, B&W, limited series)

1,2-Vaughn and Tucci-s/Alves-a; 1-Four covers 3.50

SHI: SENRYAKU
Crusade Comics: Aug, 1995 - No. 3, Nov, 1995 ($2.95, limited series)

1-3: 1-Tucci-c; Quesada, Darrow, Sim, Lee, Smith-a. 2-Tucci-c; Silvestri, Balent, Perez, Mack-a. 3-Jusko-c; Hughes, Ramos, Bell, Moore-a 3.00

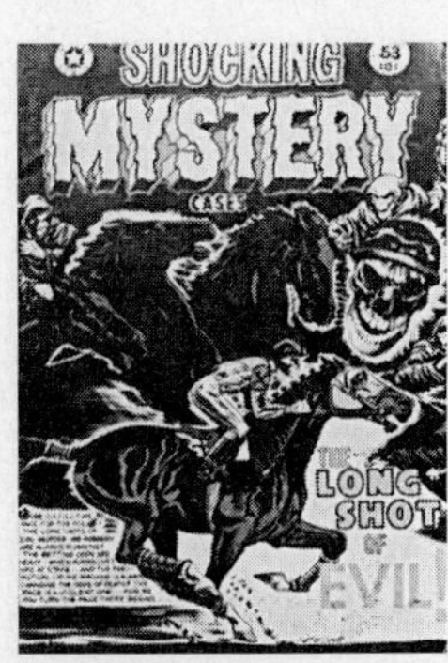

Shocking Mystery Cases #53 © STAR

Shock SuspenStories #6 © WMG

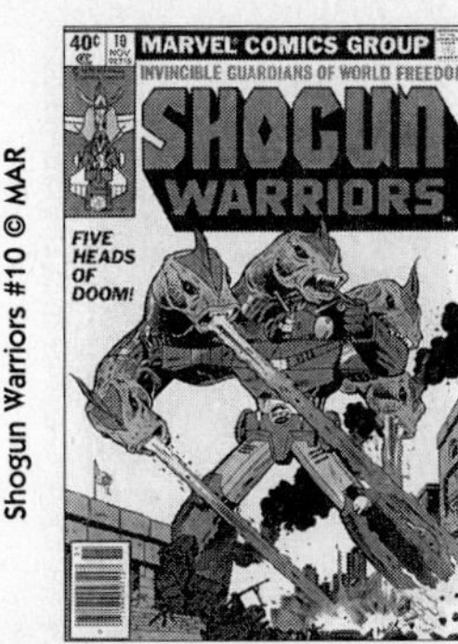

Shogun Warriors #10 © MAR

	GD 2.0	VG 4.0	FN 6.0	VF 8.0	VF/NM 9.0	NM- 9.2
1-variant-c (no logo)						4.00
Hardcover ($24.95)-r/#1-3; Frazetta-c.						25.00
Trade Paperback ($13.95)-r/#1-3; Frazetta-c.						14.00

SHI: THE ART OF WAR TOURBOOK
Crusade Comics: 1998 ($4.95, one-shot)

	GD	VG	FN	VF	VF/NM	NM-
1-Blank cover for Convention sketches; early Tucci-a inside						5.00
1-Mexico Edition ($10.00) Mexican flag-c						10.00
1-U.K. Edition ($10.00) British flag-c						10.00

SHI: THE ILLUSTRATED WARRIOR
Crusade Comics: 2002 - No. 7, 2003 ($2.99, B&W)

	GD	VG	FN	VF	VF/NM	NM-
1-7-Story text with Tucci full page art						3.00

SHI: THE SERIES
Crusade Comics: Aug, 1997 - No. 13 ($2.95, color #1-10, B&W #11)

	GD	VG	FN	VF	VF/NM	NM-
1-10						3.00
11-13: 11-B&W. 12-Color; Lau-a						3.00
#0 Convention Edition						5.00

SHI: THE WAY OF THE WARRIOR
Crusade Comics: Mar, 1994 - No. 12, Apr, 1997 ($2.50/$2.95)

	GD	VG	FN	VF	VF/NM	NM-
1/2						4.00
1	2	4	6	8	10	12
1-Commemorative ed., B&W, new-c; given out at 1994 San Diego Comic Con	2	4	6	11	14	18
1-Fan appreciation edition -r/#1						2.25
1-Fan appreciation edition (variant)						6.00
2						5.00
2-Commemorative edition (3,000)	2	4	6	10	13	16
2-Fan appreciation edition -r/#2						2.25
3						4.00
4-7: 4-Silvestri poster. 7-Tomoe app.						2.25
5,6: 5-Silvestri variant-c. 6-Tomoe #1 variant-c						3.00
5-Gold edition						12.00
6,8-12: 6-Fan appreciation edition						2.25
8-Combo Gold edition						6.00
8-Signed Edition-(5000)						3.00
Trade paperback (1995, $12.95)-r/#1-4						13.00
Trade paperback (1995, $14.95)-r/#1-4 revised; Julie Bell-c						15.00

SHI/ VAMPIRELLA
Crusade Comics: Oct, 1997 ($2.95, one-shot)

	GD	VG	FN	VF	VF/NM	NM-
1-Ellis-s/Lau-a						3.00

SHI VS. TOMOE
Crusade Comics: Aug, 1996 ($3.95, one-shot)

	GD	VG	FN	VF	VF/NM	NM-
1-Tucci-a/scripts; wraparound foil-c						4.00
1-(6/96, $5.00. B&W)-Preview Ed.; sold at San Diego Comic Con						5.00

SHI: YEAR OF THE DRAGON
Crusade Comics: 2000 - No. 3, 2000 ($2.99, limited series)

	GD	VG	FN	VF	VF/NM	NM-
1-3: 1-Two covers; Tucci-a/c; flashback to teen-aged Ana						3.00

SHMOO (See Al Capp's... & Washable Jones &...)

SHOCK (Magazine)
Stanley Publ.: May, 1969 - V3#4, Sept, 1971 (B&W reprints from horror comics, including some pre-code) (No V2#1,3)

	GD	VG	FN	VF	VF/NM	NM-
V1#1-Cover-r/Weird Tales of the Future #7 by Bernard Baily; r/Weird Chills #1	6	12	18	38	52	65
2-Wolverton-r/Weird Mysteries 5; r-Weird Mysteries #7 used in **SOTI**; cover reprints cover to Weird Chills #1	4	8	12	29	40	50
3,5,6	3	6	9	19	25	32
4-Harrison/Williamson-r/Forbid. Worlds #6	4	8	12	22	30	38
V2#2(5/70), V1#8(7/70), V2#4(9/70)-6(1/71), V3#1-4: V2#4-Cover swipe from Weird Mysteries #6	3	6	9	18	23	28

NOTE: ***Disbrow** r-V2#4; Bondage c-V1#4, V2#6, V3#1.*

SHOCK DETECTIVE CASES (Formerly Crime Fighting Detective)
(Becomes Spook Detective Cases No. 22)
Star Publications: No. 20, Sept, 1952 - No. 21, Nov, 1952

	GD	VG	FN	VF	VF/NM	NM-
20,21-L.B. Cole-c; based on true crime cases	24	48	72	138	194	250

NOTE: ***Palais** a-20. No. 21-Fox-r.*

SHOCK ILLUSTRATED (...Adult Crime Stories; Magazine format)
E. C. Comics: Sept-Oct, 1955 - No. 3, Spring, 1956 (Adult Entertainment on-c #1,2)(All 25¢)

	GD	VG	FN	VF	VF/NM	NM-
1-All by Kamen; drugs, prostitution, wife swapping	11	22	33	66	88	110
2-Williamson-a redrawn from Crime SuspenStories #13 plus Ingels, Crandall, Evans & part Torres-i; painted-c	12	24	36	69	96	120
3-Only 100 known copies bound & given away at E.C. office; Crandall, Evans-a; painted-c; shows May, 1956 on-c	92	184	276	575	863	1150

SHOCKING MYSTERY CASES (Formerly Thrilling Crime Cases)
Star Publications: No. 50, Sept, 1952 - No. 60, Oct, 1954 (All crime reprints?)

	GD	VG	FN	VF	VF/NM	NM-
50-Disbrow "Frankenstein" story	42	84	126	252	376	500
51-Disbrow-a	28	56	84	157	221	285
52-60: 56-Drug use story	26	52	78	147	206	265

NOTE: ***L. B. Cole** covers on all; a-60(2 pgs.). **Hollingsworth** a-52. **Morisi** a-55.*

SHOCKING TALES DIGEST MAGAZINE
Harvey Publications: Oct, 1981 (95¢)

	GD	VG	FN	VF	VF/NM	NM-
1-1957-58-r; Powell, Kirby, Nostrand-a	2	4	6	8	10	12

SHOCK ROCKETS
Image Comics (Gorilla): Apr, 2000 - Present ($2.50)

	GD	VG	FN	VF	VF/NM	NM-
1-6-Busiek-s/Immonen & Grawbadger-a. 6-Flip book w/Superstar preview						2.50

SHOCK SUSPENSTORIES
E. C. Comics: Feb-Mar, 1952 - No. 18, Dec-Jan, 1954-55

	GD	VG	FN	VF	VF/NM	NM-
1-Classic Feldstein electrocution-c	77	154	231	578	827	1075
2	43	86	129	323	462	600
3,4: 4-Used in **SOTI**, pg. 387,388	31	62	93	233	332	430
5-Hanging-c	36	72	108	270	385	500
6-Classic hooded vigilante bondage-c	39	78	117	293	422	550
7-Classic face melting-c	46	92	138	345	493	640
8-Williamson-a	31	62	93	233	332	430
9-11: 9-Injury to eye panel. 10-Junkie story	26	52	78	195	278	360
12- "The Monkey" classic junkie cover/story; anti-drug propaganda issue	33	66	99	248	354	460
13-Frazetta's only solo story for E.C., 7 pgs.	36	72	108	270	385	500
14-Used in Senate Investigation hearings	21	42	63	158	224	290
15-Used in 1954 Reader's Digest article, "For the Kiddies to Read"; Bill Gaines stars in prose story "The EC Caper"	19	38	57	143	204	265
16-18: 16- "Red Dupe" editorial; rape story	18	36	54	135	195	255

NOTE: ***Ray Bradbury** adaptations-1, 7, 9. **Craig** a-11; c-11. **Crandall** a-9-13, 15-18. **Davis** a-1-5. **Evans** a-7, 8, 14-18; c-16-18. **Feldstein** c-1, 7-9, 12. **Ingels** a-1, 2, 6. **Kamen** a-in all; c-10, 13, 15. **Krigstein** a-14, 18. **Orlando** a-1, 3-7, 9, 10, 12, 16, 17. **Wood** a-2-15; c-2-6, 14.*

SHOCK SUSPENSTORIES
Russ Cochran/Gemstone Publishing: Sept, 1992 - No. 18, Dec, 1996 ($1.50/$2.00/$2.50, quarterly)

	GD	VG	FN	VF	VF/NM	NM-
1-18: 1-3: Reprints with original-c. 17-r/HOF #17						2.50

SHOGUN WARRIORS
Marvel Comics Group: Feb, 1979 - No. 20, Sept, 1980 (Based on Mattel toys of the classic Japanese animation characters) (1-3: 35¢; 4-19: 40¢; 20: 50¢)

	GD	VG	FN	VF	VF/NM	NM-
1-Raydeen, Combatra, & Dangard Ace begin; Trimpe-a	2	4	6	8	10	12
2-20: 2-Lord Maurkon & Elementals of Evil app.; Rok-Korr app. 6-Shogun vs. Shogun. 7,8-Cerberus. 9-Starchild. 11-Austin-c. 12-Simonson-c. 14-16-Doctor Demonicus. 17-Juggernaut. 19,20-FF x-over	1	2	3	5	6	8
1-3: Reprints						3.00

SHOOK UP (Magazine) (Satire)
Dodsworth Publ. Co.: Nov, 1958

	GD	VG	FN	VF	VF/NM	NM-
V1#1	4	8	12	27	36	45

SHORT RIBS
Dell Publishing Co.: No. 1333, Apr - June, 1962

	GD	VG	FN	VF	VF/NM	NM-
Four Color 1333	6	12	18	40	55	70

SHORTSTOP SQUAD (Baseball)
Ultimate Sports Ent. Inc.: 1999 ($3.95, one-shot)

	GD	VG	FN	VF	VF/NM	NM-
1-Ripken Jr., Larkin, Jeter, Rodriguez app.; Edwards-c/a						4.00

SHORT STORY COMICS (See Hello Pal,...)

SHORTY SHINER (The Five-Foot Fighter in the Ten Gallon Hat)
Dandy Magazine (Charles Biro): June, 1956 - No. 3, Oct, 1956

	GD	VG	FN	VF	VF/NM	NM-
1	7	14	21	37	46	55
2,3	5	10	15	24	30	35

SHOT CALLERZ
Oni Press: May, 2002 - No. 4, Sept, 2002 ($2.95, B&W, limited series)

	GD	VG	FN	VF	VF/NM	NM-
1-4-Gary Phillips-s/Brett Weldele-a						3.00

SHOTGUN MARY
Antarctic Press: Sept, 1995 - No. 2; Mar, 1998 - No. 2, May, 1998 ($2.95)

Showcase #31 © DC

Showcase #65 © DC

Showcase #92 © DC

	GD 2.0	VG 4.0	FN 6.0	VF 8.0	VF/NM 9.0	NM- 9.2
1,2-w/pin-ups						3.00
1-($8.95)-Bagged w/CD						9.00
...Deviltown-(7/96, $2.95), ...Shooting Gallery-(6/96, $2.95), ...Son Of The Beast-(10/97, $2.95) Painted-a by Esad Ribic						3.00

SHOTGUN MARY: BLOOD LORE
Antarctic Press: Feb, 1997 - No.4, Aug, 1997 ($2.95, mini-series)

	GD 2.0	VG 4.0	FN 6.0	VF 8.0	VF/NM 9.0	NM- 9.2
1-4						3.00

SHOTGUN SLADE (TV)
Dell Publishing Co.: No. 1111, July-Sept, 1960

	GD 2.0	VG 4.0	FN 6.0	VF 8.0	VF/NM 9.0	NM- 9.2
Four Color 1111-Photo-c	7	14	21	51	71	90

SHOWCASE (See Cancelled Comic Cavalcade & New Talent...)
National Per. Publ./DC Comics: 3-4/56 - No. 93, 9/70; No. 94, 8-9/77 - No. 104, 9/78

	GD 2.0	VG 4.0	FN 6.0	VF 8.0	VF/NM 9.0	NM- 9.2
1-Fire Fighters; w/Fireman Farrell	256	512	768	2240	3620	5000
2-Kings of the Wild; Kubert-a (animal stories)	80	160	240	680	1040	1400
3-The Frogmen by Russ Heath; Heath greytone-c (early DC example, 7-8/56)	77	154	231	655	1003	1350
4-Origin/1st app. The Flash (1st DC Silver Age hero, Sept-Oct, 1956); Kanigher-s; Infantino & Kubert-c/a; 1st app. Iris West and The Turtle; r/in Secret Origins #1 ('61 & '73); Flash shown reading G.A. Flash Comics #13; back-up story w/Broome-s/Infantino & Kubert-a	1200	2400	3600	13,200	27,100	41,000
5-Manhunters	79	158	237	672	1024	1375
6-Origin/1st app. Challengers of the Unknown by Kirby, partly r/in Secret Origins #1 & Challengers #64,65 (1st S.A. hero team & 1st original concept S.A. series)(1-2/57)	282	564	846	2468	3984	5500
7-Challengers of the Unknown by Kirby (2nd app.) reprinted in Challengers of the Unknown #75	143	286	429	1216	1858	2500
8-The Flash (5-6/57, 2nd app.); origin & 1st app. Captain Cold	820	1640	2460	7503	12,152	16,800
9-Lois Lane (Pre-#1, 7-8/57) (1st Showcase character to win own series) Superman app. on-c	625	1250	1875	4700	7600	10,500
10-Lois Lane; Jor-el cameo; Superman app. on-c	226	452	678	1978	3189	4400
11-Challengers of the Unknown by Kirby (3rd)	137	274	411	1165	1783	2400
12-Challengers of the Unknown by Kirby (4th)	137	274	411	1165	1783	2400
13-The Flash (3rd app.); origin Mr. Element	312	624	936	2855	4628	6400
14-The Flash (4th app.); origin Dr. Alchemy, former Mr. Element (rare in NM)	329	658	987	3010	4880	6750
15-Space Ranger (7-8/58, 1st app.)	157	314	471	1335	2043	2750
16-Space Ranger (9-10/58, 2nd app.)	79	158	237	672	1024	1375
17-(11-12/58)-Adventures on Other Worlds; origin/1st app. Adam Strange by Gardner Fox & Mike Sekowsky	189	378	567	1654	2577	3500
18-Adventures on Other Worlds (2nd A. Strange)	100	200	300	850	1300	1750
19-Adam Strange; 1st Adam Strange logo	110	220	330	935	1430	1925
20-Rip Hunter; origin & 1st app. (5-6/59); Moriera-a	83	166	249	706	1078	1450
21-Rip Hunter (7-8/59, 2nd app.); Sekowsky-c/a	45	90	135	360	543	725
22-Origin & 1st app. Silver Age Green Lantern by Gil Kane and John Broome (9-10/59); reprinted in Secret Origins #2	341	682	1023	3120	5060	7000
23-Green Lantern (11-12/59, 2nd app.); nuclear explosion-c	128	256	384	1088	1644	2200
24-Green Lantern (1-2/60, 3rd app.)	128	256	384	1088	1644	2200
25,26-Rip Hunter by Kubert. 25-Grey tone-c	32	64	96	240	358	475
27-Sea Devils (7-8/60, 1st app.); Heath-c/a	70	140	210	595	910	1225
28-Sea Devils (9-10/60, 2nd app.); Heath-c/a	39	78	117	293	439	585
29-Sea Devils; Heath-c/a; grey tone c-27-29	39	78	117	293	439	585
30-Origin Silver Age Aquaman (1-2/61) (see Adventure #260 for 1st S.A. origin)	67	134	201	570	873	1175
31,32-Aquaman	39	78	117	293	439	585
33-Aquaman	42	84	126	315	470	625
34-Origin & 1st app. Silver Age Atom by Gil Kane & Murphy Anderson (9-10/61); reprinted in Secret Origins #2	114	288	342	969	1485	2000
35-The Atom by Gil Kane (2nd); last 10¢ issue	63	126	189	536	818	1100
36-The Atom by Gil Kane (1-2/62, 3rd app.)	52	104	156	416	621	825
37-Metal Men (3-4/62, 1st app.)	56	112	168	476	731	985
38-Metal Men (5-6/62, 2nd app.)	40	80	120	300	450	600
39-Metal Men (7-8/62, 3rd app.)	31	62	93	230	345	460
40-Metal Men (9-10/62, 4th app.)	29	58	88	210	310	410
41,42-Tommy Tomorrow (parts 1 & 2). 42-Origin	19	38	57	136	198	260
43-Dr. No (James Bond); Nodel-a; originally published as British Classics Illustrated #158A & as #6 in a European Detective series, all with diff. painted-c. This Showcase #43 version is actually censored, deleting all racial skin color and dialogue thought to be racially demeaning (1st DC S.A. movie adaptation)(based on Ian Fleming novel & movie)	42	84	126	315	475	635
44-Tommy Tomorrow	12	24	36	84	125	165
45-Sgt. Rock (7-8/63); pre-dates B&B #52; origin retold; Heath-c	30	60	90	218	322	425
46,47-Tommy Tomorrow	10	20	30	73	107	140
48,49-Cave Carson (3rd tryout series; see B&B)	9	18	27	60	85	110
50,51-I Spy (Danger Trail-r by Infantino), King Farady story (#50 has new 4 pg. story)	8	16	24	58	82	105
52-Cave Carson	8	16	24	53	74	95
53,54-G.I. Joe (11-12/64, 1-2/65); Heath-a	12	24	36	84	125	165
55-Dr. Fate & Hourman (3-4/65); origin of each in text; 1st solo app. G.A. Green Lantern in Silver Age (pre-dates Gr. Lantern #40); 1st S.A. app. Solomon Grundy	26	52	78	189	275	360
56-Dr. Fate & Hourman	15	30	45	104	152	200
57-Enemy Ace by Kubert (7-8/65, 4th app. after Our Army at War #155)	22	44	66	160	235	310
58-Enemy Ace by Kubert (5th app.)	19	38	57	136	198	260
59-Teen Titans (11-12/65, 3rd app.)	12	24	36	84	125	165
60-1st S. A. app. The Spectre; Anderson-a (1-2/66); origin in text	30	60	90	218	319	420
61-The Spectre by Anderson (2nd app.)	15	30	45	109	160	210
62-Origin & 1st app. Inferior Five (5-6/66)	10	20	30	72	104	135
63,65-Inferior Five. 63-Hulk parody. 65-X-Men parody (11-12/66)	6	12	18	43	59	75
64-The Spectre by Anderson (5th app.)	15	30	45	104	152	200
66,67-B'wana Beast	4	8	12	29	40	50
68-Maniaks (1st app.)	4	8	12	29	40	50
69,71-Maniaks. 71-Woody Allen-c/app.	4	8	12	29	40	50
70-Binky (9-10/67)-Tryout issue; 1950's Leave It To Binky reprints with art changes	6	12	18	38	52	65
72-Top Gun (Johnny Thunder-r)-Toth-a	4	8	12	29	40	50
73-Origin/1st app. Creeper; Ditko-c/a (3-4/68)	15	30	45	104	152	200
74-Intro/1st app. Anthro; Post-c/a (5/68)	10	20	30	67	96	125
75-Origin/1st app. Hawk & the Dove; Ditko-c/a	13	26	39	94	137	180
76-1st app. Bat Lash (8/68)	7	14	21	51	71	90
77-1st app. Angel & The Ape (9/68)	7	14	21	51	71	90
78-1st app. Jonny Double (11/68)	4	8	12	29	40	50
79-1st app. Dolphin (12/68); Aqualad origin-r	6	12	18	43	59	75
80-1st S.A. app. Phantom Stranger (1/69); Neal Adams-c	9	18	27	60	85	110
81-Windy & Willy; r/Many Loves of Dobie Gillis #26 with art changes	5	10	15	33	44	55
82-1st app. Nightmaster (5/69) by Grandenetti & Giordano; Kubert-c	8	16	24	53	74	95
83,84-Nightmaster by Wrightson w/Jones/Kaluta ink assist in each; Kubert-c. 83-Last 12¢ issue 84-Origin retold; begin 15¢	7	14	21	51	71	90
85-87-Firehair; Kubert-a	3	6	9	18	24	30
88-90-Jason's Quest: 90-Manhunter 2070 app.	3	6	9	16	20	25
91-93-Manhunter 2070: 92-Origin. 93-(9/70) Last 15¢ issue	3	6	9	16	20	25
94-Intro/origin new Doom Patrol & Robotman(8-9/77)	2	4	6	10	13	16
95,96-The Doom Patrol. 95-Origin Celsius	1	2	3	5	7	9
97-99-Power Girl; origin-97,98; JSA cameos	1	2	3	5	7	9
100-(52 pgs.)-Most Showcase characters featured	2	4	6	10	12	15
101-103-Hawkman; Adam Strange x-over	1	2	3	5	7	9
104-(52 pgs.)-O.S.S. Spies at War	1	2	3	5	7	9

NOTE: ***Anderson** a-22-24i, 34-36i, 55, 56, 60, 61, 64, 101-103i; c-50i, 51i, 55, 56, 60, 61, 64. **Aparo** c-94-96. **Boring** c-10. **Estrada** a-104. **Fraden** c(p)-30, 31, 33. **Heath** c-3, 27-29. **Infantino** c/a(p)-4, 8, 13, 14; c-50p, 51p. **Gil Kane** a-22-24p, 34-36p; c-17-19, 22-24p(w/**Giella**), 31. **Kane/Anderson** c-34-36. **Kirby** c-11, 12. **Kirby/Stein** c-6, 7. **Kubert** a-2, 4i, 25, 26, 45, 53, 54, 72; c-25, 26, 53, 54, 57, 58, 82-87, 101-104; c-2, 4i. **Moriera** c-5. **Orlando** a-62p, 63p, 97i; c-62, 63, 97i. **Sekowsky** a-65p. **Sparling** a-78. **Staton** a-94, 95-99p, 100; c-97-100p.*

SHOWCASE '93
DC Comics: Jan, 1993 - No. 12, Dec, 1993 ($1.95, limited series, 52 pgs.)

	GD 2.0	VG 4.0	FN 6.0	VF 8.0	VF/NM 9.0	NM- 9.2
1-12: 1-Begin 4 part Catwoman story & 6 part Blue Devil story; begin Cyborg story; Art Adams/Austin-c. 3-Flash by Travis Charest (p). 6-Azrael in Bat-costume (2 pgs.). 7,8-Knightfall parts 13 & 14. 6-10-Deathstroke app. (6,10-cameo). 9,10-Austin-i. 10-Azrael as Batman in new costume app.; Gulacy-c. 11-Perez-c. 12-Creeper app.; Alan Grant scripts.						3.00

NOTE: ***Chaykin** c-9. **Fabry** c-8. **Giffen** a-12. **Golden** c-3. **Zeck** c-6.*

SHOWCASE '94
DC Comics: Jan, 1994 - No. 12, Dec, 1994 ($1.95, limited series, 52 pgs.)

	GD 2.0	VG 4.0	FN 6.0	VF 8.0	VF/NM 9.0	NM- 9.2
1-12: 1,2-Joker & Gunfire stories. 1-New Gods. 4-Riddler story. 5-Huntress-c/story w/app. new Batman. 6-Huntress-c/story w/app. Robin; Atom story. 7-Penguin story by Peter David, P. Craig Russell, & Michael T. Gilbert; Penguin-c by Jae Lee. 8,9-Scarface origin story by Alan Grant, John Wagner,& Teddy Kristiansen; Prelude to Zero Hour. 10-Zero Hour tie-in story. 11-Man-Bat.						3.00

Showcase '95 #1 © DC

Shrek #1 © DreamWorks

Sidekicks: the Substitute © Fanboy Ent. Inc.

GD VG FN VF VF/NM NM-
2.0 4.0 6.0 8.0 9.0 9.2

NOTE: ***Alan Grant*** *scripts-3, 4.* ***Kelley Jones*** *c-12.* ***Mignola*** *c-3.* ***Nebres*** *a(i)-2.* ***Quesada*** *c-10.* ***Russell*** *a-7p.* ***Simonson*** *c-5.*

SHOWCASE '95
DC Comics: Jan, 1995 - No. 12, Dec, 1995 ($2.50/$2.95, limited series)

1-4-Supergirl story. 3-Eradicator-c.; The Question story. 4-Thorn c/story 3.00
5-12: 5-Thorn-c/story; begin $2.95-c. 8-Spectre story. 12-The Shade story by James Robinson & Wade Von Grawbadger; Maitresse story by Chris Claremont & Alan Davis 3.00

SHOWCASE '96
DC Comics: Jan, 1996 - No. 12, Dec, 1996 ($2.95, limited series)

1-12: 1-Steve Geppi cameo. 3-Black Canary & Lois Lane-c/story; Deadman story by Jamie Delano & Wade Von Grawbadger, Gary Frank-c. 4-Firebrand & Guardian-c/story; The Shade & Dr. Fate "Times Past" story by James Robinson & Matt Smith begins, ends #5. 6-Superboy-c/app.; Atom app.; Capt. Marvel (Mary Marvel)-c/app. 8-Supergirl by David & Dodson. 11-Scare Tactics app. 11,12-Legion of Super-Heroes vs. Brainiac. 12-Jesse Quick app. 3.00

SHOWGIRLS (Formerly Sherry the Showgirl #3)
Atlas Comics (MPC No. 2): No. 4, 2/57; June, 1957 - No. 2, Aug, 1957

4-(2/57) Dan DeCarlo-c/a begins 10 20 30 56 73 90
1-(6/57) Millie, Sherry, Chili, Pearl & Hazel begin 13 26 39 74 100 125
2 10 20 30 56 73 90

SHREK (Movie)
Dark Horse Comics: Sept, 2003 - No. 3 ($2.99, limited series)

1-Takes place after 1st movie; Evanier-s/Bachs-a; CGI cover 3.00

SHROUD, THE (See Super-Villain Team-Up #5)
Marvel Comics: Mar, 1994 - No. 4, June, 1994 ($1.75, mini-series)

1-4: 1,2,4-Spider-Man & Scorpion app. 2.25

SHROUD OF MYSTERY
Whitman Publications: June, 1982

1 6.00

SHUT UP AND DIE
Image Comics/Halloween: 1998 - No. 3, 1998 ($2.95,B&W, bi-monthly)

1-3: Hudnall-s 3.00

SICK (Sick Special #131) (Magazine) (Satire)
Feature Publ./Headline Publ./Crestwood Publ. Co./Hewfred Publ./ Pyramid Comm./Charlton Publ. No. 109 (4/76) on: Aug, 1960 - No. 134, Fall, 1980

V1#1-Jack Paar photo on-c; Torres-a; Untouchables-s; Ben Hur movie photo-s 15 30 45 109 160 210
2-Torres-a; Elvis app.; Lenny Bruce app. 9 18 27 65 93 120
3-5-Torres-a in all. 3-Khruschev-c; Hitler-s. 4-Newhart-s; Castro-s; John Wayne. 5-JFK/Castro-c; Elvis pin-up; Hitler. 8 16 24 55 78 100
6-Photo-s of Ricky Nelson & Marilyn Monroe; JFK 9 18 27 60 85 110
V2#1,2,4-8 (#7,8,10-14): 1-(#7) Hitler-s; Brando photo-s. 2-(#8) Dick Clark-s. 4-(#10) Untouchables-c; Candid Camera-s. 5-(#11) Nixon-c; Lone Ranger-s; JFK-s. 6-(#12) Beatnik-c/s. 8-(#14) Liz Taylor pin-up, JFK-s; Dobie Gillis-s; Sinatra & Dean Martin photo-s 7 14 21 51 71 90
3-(#9) Marilyn Monroe/JFK-c; Kingston Trio-s 8 16 24 55 78 100
V3#1-7(#15-21): 1-(#15) JFK app.; Liz Tayor/Richard Burton-s. 2-(#16) Ben Casey/ Frankenstein-c/s; Hitler photo-s. 5-(#19) Nixon back-c/s; Sinatra photo-s. 6-(#20) 1st Huckleberry Fink-c 4 8 12 29 40 50
8-(#22) Cassius Clay vs. Liston-s; 1st Civil War Blackouts-/Pvt. Bo Reargard w/ Jack Davis-a 5 10 15 36 48 60
V4#1-5 (#23-27): Civil War Blackouts-/Pvt. Bo Reargard w/ Jack Davis-a in all. 1-(#23) Smokey Bear-c; Tarzan-s. 2-(#24) Goldwater & Paar-s, Castro-s. 3-(#25) Frankenstein-c; Cleopatra/Liz Taylor-s; Steve Reeves photo-s. 4-(#26) James Bond-s; Hitler-s. 5-(#27) Taylor/Burton pin-up; Sinatra, Martin, Andress, Ekberg photo-s 4 8 12 25 33 42
28,31,36,39: 31-Pink Panther movie photo-s; Burke's Law-s. 39-Westerns; Elizabeth Montgomery photo-s; Beat mag-s 3 6 9 19 25 32
29,34,37,38: 29-Beatles-c by Jack Davis. 34-Two pg. Beatles-s & photo pin-up. 37-Playboy parody issue. 38-Addams Family-s 4 8 12 24 32 40
30,32,35,40: 30-Beatles photo pin-up; James Bond photo-s. 32-Ian Fleming-s; LBJ-s; Tarzan-s. 35-Beatles cameo; Three Stooges parody. 40-Tarzan-s; Crosby/Hope-s; Beatles parody 4 8 12 25 33 42
33-Ringo Starr photo-c & spoof on "A Hard Day's Night"; inside-c has Beatles photos 5 10 15 36 48 60
41,50,51,53,54,60: 41-Sports Illustrated parody-c/s. 50-Mod issue; flip-c w/1967 calendar w/Bob Taylor-a. 51-Get Smart-s. 53-Beatles cameo; nudity panels. 54-Monkees-c. 60-TV Daniel Boone-s 3 6 9 19 25 32
42-Fighting American-c revised from Simon/Kirby-c; "Good girl" art by Sparling; profile on Bob Powell; superhero parodies 6 12 18 38 52 65
43-49,52,55-59: 43-Sneaker set begins by Sparling. 45-Has #44 on-c & #45 on inside; TV Westerns-s; Beatles cameo. 46-Hell's Angels-s; NY Mets-s. 47-UFO/Space-c. 49-Men's Adventure mag. parody issue; nudity. 52-LBJ-s. 55-Underground culture special. 56-Alfred E. Neuman-c; inventors issue. 58-Hippie issue-c/s. 59-Hippie-s 3 6 9 16 20 25
61-64,66-69,71,73,75-80: 63-Tiny Tim-c & poster; Monkees-s. 64-Flip-c. 66-Flip-c; Mod Squad-s. 69-Beatles cameo; Peter Sellers photo-s. 71-Flip-c; Clint Eastwood0s. 76-Nixon-s; Marcus Welby-s. 78-Ma Barker-s; Courtship of Eddie's Father-s; Abbie Hoffman-s 2 4 6 14 18 22
65,70,74: 65-Cassius Clay/Brando/J. Wayne-c; Johnny Carson-s. 70-(9/69) John & Yoko-c, 1/2 pg. story. 74-Clay, Agnew, Namath & others as superheroes-c/s; Easy Rider-s; Ghost and Mrs. Muir-s 3 6 9 16 20 25
72-(84 pgs.) Xmas issue w/2 pg. slick color poster; Tarzan-s; 2 pg. Superman & superheroes-s 3 7 10 21 28 35
81-85,87-95,98,99: 81-(2/71) Woody Allen photo-s. 85 Monster Mag. parody-s; Nixon-s w/Ringo & John cameo. 88-Klute photo-s; Nixon paper dolls page. 92-Lily Tomlin; Archie Bunker pin-up. 93-Woody Allen 2 4 6 11 14 18
86,96,97,100: 86-John & Yoko, Tiny Tim-c; Love Story movie photo-s. 96-Kung Fu-c; Mummy-s, Dracula & Frankenstein app. 97-Superman-s; 1974 Calendar; Charlie Brown & Snoopy pin-up. 100-Serpico-s; Cosell-s; Jacques Cousteau-s 2 4 6 12 16 20
101-103,105-114,116,119,120: 101-Three Musketeers-s; Dick Tracy-s. 102-Young Frankenstein-s. 103-Kojak-s; Evel Knievel-s. 105-Towering Inferno-s; Peanuts/Snoopy-s. 106-Cher-c/s. 10 7-Jaws-c/s. 108-Pink Panther-c/s; Archie-s. 109-Adam & Eve-s(nudity). 110-Welcome Back Kotter-s. 111-Sonny & Cher-s. 112-King Kong-c/s. 120-Star Trek-s 2 4 6 9 11 14
104,115,117,118: 104-Muhammad Ali-c/s. 115-Charlie's Angels-s. 117-Bionic Woman & Six Million $ Man-c/s; Cher D'Flower begins by Sparling (nudity). 118-Star Wars-s; Popeye-s 2 4 6 11 14 18
121-125,128,130: 122-Darth Vader-s. 123-Jaws II-s. 128-Superman-c/movie parody. 130-Alien movie-s 2 4 6 10 13 16
126,127: 126-(68 pgs.) Battlestar Galactica-c/s; Star Wars-s; Wonder Woman-s. 127-Mork & Mindy-s; Lord of the Rings-s 2 4 6 12 16 20
131-(1980 Special) Star Wars/Star Trek/Flash Gordon wraparound-c/s; Superman parody; Battlestar Galactica-s 2 4 6 14 18 22
132,133: 132-1980 Election-c/s; Apocalypse Now-s. 133-Star Trek-s; Chips-s; Superheroes page 2 4 6 12 16 20
134 (scarce)(68 pg. Giant)-Star Wars-c; Alien-s; WKRP-s; Mork & Mindy-s; Taxi-s; MASH-s 4 8 12 22 30 38
Annual 1- 7th Annual Yearbook (1967)-Davis-c, 2 pg. glossy poster insert 4 8 12 25 33 42
Annual 2- Birthday Annual (1967)-3 pg. Huckleberry Fink fold out 3 7 10 21 28 35
Annual 3 (1968) "Big Sick Laff-in" on-c (84 pgs.)-w/psychedelic posters; Frankenstein poster 3 6 9 19 25 32
Annual 1969, 1970, 1971 3 6 9 18 24 30
Annual 12,13-(1972,1973, 84 pgs.) 13-Monster-c 3 6 9 18 24 30
Annual 14 (1974, 84 pgs.) Hitler photo-s 3 6 9 18 24 30
Annual 2-4 (1980) 2 4 6 9 11 14
Special 1 (1980) Buck Rogers-c/s; MASH-s 2 4 6 14 18 22
Special 2 (1980) Wraparound Star Wars:Empire Strikes Back-c; Charlie's Angels/Farrah-s; Rocky-s; plus reprints 2 4 6 14 18 22
Yearbook 15(1975, 84 pgs.) Paul Revere-c 3 6 9 18 23 28

NOTE: ***Davis*** *a-42, 87; c-22, 23, 25, 29, 31, 32.* ***Powell*** *a-7, 31, 57.* ***Simon*** *a-1-3, 10, 41, 42, 87, 99; c-1, 47, 57, 59, 69, 91, 95-97, 99, 100, 102, 107, 112.* ***Torres*** *a-1-3, 29, 31, 47, 49.* ***Tuska*** *a-14, 41-43. Civil War Blackouts-23, 24. #42 has biography of Bob Powell.*

SIDEKICKS
Fanboy Ent., Inc.: Jun, 2000 - No. 3, Apr, 2001 ($2.75, B&W, lim. series)

1-3-J.Torres-s/Takesi Miyazawa-a. 3-Variant-c by Wieringo 2.75
...: Super Fun Summer Special (Oni Press, 7/03, $2.99) art by various incl. Wieringo 3.00
...: The Substitute (Oni Press, 7/02, $2.95) 3.00
...: The Transfer Student TPB (Oni Press, 6/02, $8.95, 9" x 6") r/#1-3 9.00
...: The Transfer Student TPB 2nd Ed. (10/03, $11.95, 9" x 6") r/#1-3; The Substitute 12.00

SIDESHOW
Avon Periodicals: 1949 (one-shot)

1-(Rare)-Similar to Bachelor's Diary 34 68 102 196 278 360

SIEGE
Image Comics (WildStorm Prod.): Jan, 1997 - No. 4, Apr, 1997 ($2.50)

1-4 2.50

SIEGEL AND SHUSTER: DATELINE 1930s

Sigil #23 © CRO

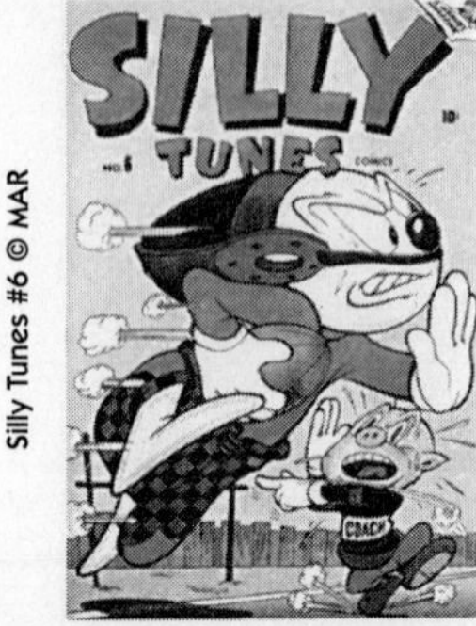

Silly Tunes #6 © MAR

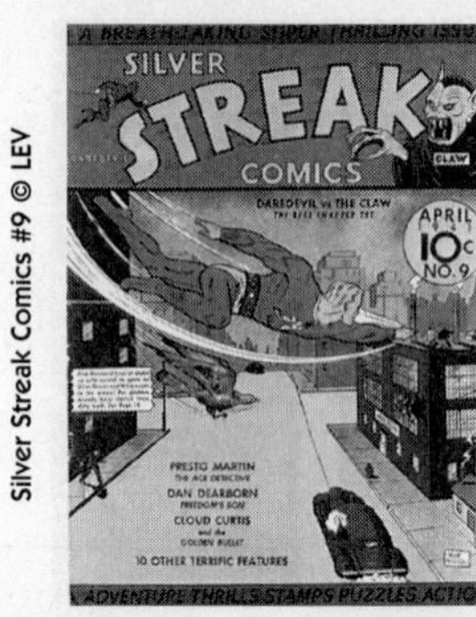

Silver Streak Comics #9 © LEV

GD 2.0 | VG 4.0 | FN 6.0 | VF 8.0 | VF/NM 9.0 | NM- 9.2

Eclipse Comics: Nov, 1984 - No. 2, Sept, 1985 ($1.50/$1.75, Baxter paper #1)
1,2: 1-Unpublished samples of strips from the '30s; includes 'Interplanetary Police'; Shuster-c. 2 ($1.75, B&W)-unpublished strips; Shuster-c 2.50

SIGIL (Also see CrossGen Chronicles)
CrossGeneration Comics: Jul, 2000 - No. 43, Jan, 2004 ($2.95)
1-43: 1-Barbara Kesel-s/Ben & Ray Lai-a. 12-Waid-s begin. 21-Chuck Dixon-s begin 3.00
...: Hostage Planet TPB (4/03, $15.95) r/#21-26 16.00
...: Mark of Power TPB (5/01, $19.95) r/#1-7; Moeller painted-c 20.00
...: The Marked Man Vol. 2 TPB (2002, $19.95) r/#8-14 20.00
...: The Lizard God Vol. 3 TPB (2002, $15.95) r/#15-20 16.00
Vol. 4: Hostage Planet (2003, $15.95) r/#21-26 16.00
Vol. 5: Death Match (2003, $15.95) r/#27-32 16.00

SIGMA
Image Comics (WildStorm Productions): March, 1996 - No. 3, June, 1996 ($2.50, limited series)
1-3: 1-"Fire From Heaven" prelude #2; Coker-a. 2-"Fire From Heaven" pt. 6. 3-"Fire From Heaven" pt. 14. 2.50

SILENT INVASION, THE
Rengade Press: Apr, 1986 - No.12, Mar, 1988 ($1.70/$2.00, B&W)
1-12-UFO sightings of the '50's 3.00
Book 1- reprints ($7.95) 8.00

SILENT MOBIUS
Viz Select Comics: 1991 - No. 5, 1992 ($4.95, color, squarebound, 44 pgs.)
1-5: Japanese stories translated to English 5.00

SILENT RAPTURE
Avatar Press: Jan, 1997 - No.2, Apr, 1997 ($3.00, B&W, limited series)
1,2 3.00

SILENT SCREAMERS (Based on the Aztech Toys figures)
Image Comics: Oct, 2000 ($4.95)
Nosferatu Issue - Alex Ross front & back-c 5.00

SILKE
Dark Horse Comics: Jan, 2001 - No. 4, Sept, 2001 ($2.95)
1-4-Tony Daniel-s/a 3.00

SILKEN GHOST
CrossGen Comics: June, 2003 - No. 5, Oct, 2003 ($2.95, limited series)
1-5-Dixon-s/Rosado-a 3.00
Traveler Vol. 1 (2003, $9.95) digest-sized reprint #1-5 10.00

SILLY PILLY (See Frank Luther's...)

SILLY SYMPHONIES (See Dell Giants)

SILLY TUNES
Timely Comics: Fall, 1945 - No. 7, June, 1947
1-Silly Seal, Ziggy Pig begin 21 42 63 118 164 210
2-(2/46) 12 24 36 69 92 115
3-7: 6-New logo 10 20 30 56 73 90

SILVER (See Lone Ranger's Famous Horse...)

SILVER AGE
DC Comics: July, 2000 ($3.95, limited series)
1-Waid-s/Dodson-a; "Silver Age" style x-over; JLA & villains switch bodies 4.00
...: Challengers of the Unknown ($2.50) Joe Kubert-c; vs. Chronos 2.50
...: Dial H For Hero ($2.50) Jim Mooney-c; vs. Martian Manhunter 2.50
...: Doom Patrol ($2.50) Ramona Fradon-c/Peyer-s 2.50
...: Flash ($2.50) Carmine Infantino-c; Kid Flash and Elongated Man app. 2.50
...: Green Lantern ($2.50) Gil Kane-c/Busiek-s/Anderson-a; vs. Sinestro 2.50
...: Justice League of America ($2.50) Ty Templeton-c 2.50
...: Showcase ($2.50) Dick Giordano-c/a; Batgirl, Adam Strange app. 2.50
... Secret Files ($4.95) Intro. Agamemno; short stories & profile pages 5.00
...: Teen Titans ($2.50) Nick Cardy-c; vs. Penguin, Mr. Element, Black Manta 2.50
...: The Brave and the Bold ($2.50) Jim Aparo-c; Batman & Metal Men 2.50
... 80-Page Giant ($5.95) Conclusion of x-over; "lost" Silver Age stories 6.00

SILVERBACK
Comico: 1989 - No. 3, 1990 ($2.50, color, limited series, mature readers)
1-3: Character from Grendel: Matt Wagner-a 3.00

SILVERBLADE
DC Comics: Sept, 1987 - No. 12, Sept, 1988
1-12: Colan-c/a in all 2.25

SILVER CROSS (See Warrior Nun series)
Antarctic Press: Nov, 1997 - No. 3, Mar, 1998 ($2.95)
1-3-Ben Dunn-s/a 3.00

SILVERHAWKS
Star Comics/Marvel Comics #6: Aug, 1987 - No. 6, June, 1988 ($1.00)
1-6 3.00

SILVERHEELS
Pacific Comics: Dec, 1983 - No. 3, May, 1984 ($1.50)
1-3 2.25

SILVER KID WESTERN
Key/Stanmor Publications: Oct, 1954 - No. 5, July, 1955
1 10 20 30 56 73 90
2 6 12 18 31 38 45
3-5 6 12 18 28 34 40
I.W. Reprint #1,2-Severin-c: 1-r/#? 2-r/#1 2 4 6 9 11 14

SILVER SABLE AND THE WILD PACK (See Amazing Spider-Man #265)
Marvel Comics: June, 1992 - No. 35, Apr, 1995 ($1.25/$1.50
1-($2.00)-Embossed & foil stamped-c; Spider-Man app. 3.00
2-35: 4,5-Dr. Doom-c/story. 6,7-Deathlok-c/story. 9-Origin Silver Sable. 10-Punisher-c/s. 15-Capt. America-c/s. 16,17-Intruders app. 18,19-Venom-c/s. 19-Siege of Darkness x-over. 23-Daredevil (in new costume) & Deadpool app. 24-Bound-in card sheet. Li'l Sylvie backup story. 25-($2.00, 52 pgs.)-Li'l Sylvie backup story 2.25

SILVER STAR (Also see Jack Kirby's...)
Pacific Comics: Feb, 1983 - No. Jan, 1984 ($1.00)
1-6: 1-1st app. Last of the Viking Heroes. 1-5-Kirby-c/a. 2-Ditko-a 5.00

SILVER STREAK COMICS (Crime Does Not Pay #22 on)
Your Guide Publs. No. 1-7/New Friday Publs. No. 8-17/Comic House Publ./Newsbook Publ.: Dec, 1939 - No. 21, May, 1942; No. 23, 1946; No # 22 (Silver logo-#1-5)
1-(Scarce)-Intro The Claw by Cole (r-/in Daredevil #21), Red Reeves, Boy Magician, & Captain Fearless; The Wasp, Mister Midnight begin; Spirit Man app. Silver metallic-c begin, end #5; Claw c-1,2,6-8 1069 2138 3207 7483 11,492 15,500
2-The Claw by Cole; Simon-c/a 385 770 1155 2503 3852 5200
3-1st app. & origin Silver Streak (2nd with lightning speed); Dickie Dean the Boy Inventor, Lance Hale, Ace Powers, Bill Wayne, & The Planet Patrol begin 330 660 990 2145 3298 4450
4-Sky Wolf begins; Silver Streak by Jack Cole (new costume); 1st app. Jackie, Lance Hale's sidekick 170 340 510 1063 1594 2125
5-Jack Cole c/a(2) 200 400 600 1250 1875 2500
6-(Scarce, 9/40)-Origin & 1st app. Daredevil (blue & yellow costume) by Jack Binder; The Claw returns; classic Cole Claw-c 1219 2438 3657 9143 14,322 19,500
7-Claw vs. Daredevil (new costume-blue & red) by Jack Cole & 3 other Cole stories (38 pgs.) 759 1518 2277 5313 8157 11,000
8-Claw vs. Daredevil by Cole; last Cole Silver Streak 322 644 966 2093 3222 4350
9-Claw vs. Daredevil by Cole 192 384 576 1200 1800 2400
10-Origin & 1st app. Captain Battle (5/41); Claw vs. Daredevil by Cole; Robot-c 170 340 510 1063 1594 2125
11-Intro. Mercury by Bob Wood, Silver Streak's sidekick; conclusion Claw vs. Daredevil by Rico; in 'Presto Martin,' 2nd pg., newspaper says 'Roussos does it again' 118 236 354 738 1107 1475
12-14: 13-Origin Thun-Dohr 85 170 255 531 796 1060
15, 17-Last Daredevil issue. 80 160 240 500 750 1000
16-Hitler-c 92 184 276 575 863 1150
18-The Saint begins (2/42, 1st app.) by Leslie Charteris (see Movie Comics #2 by DC); The Saint-c 70 140 210 438 657 875
19-21(1942): 20,21 have Wolverton's Scoop Scuttle. 21-Hitler app. in strip on cover 55 110 165 330 495 660
23(1946(An Atomic Comic)-Reprints; bondage-c 44 88 132 264 395 525
nn(11/46)(Newsbook Publ.)-R-/S.S. story from #4-7 plus 2 Captain Fearless stories, all in color; bondage/torture-c 54 108 162 324 487 650
NOTE: ***Binder*** *c-3, 4, 13-15, 17.* ***Jack Cole*** *a-(Daredevil)-#6-10, (Dickie Dean)-#3-10, (Pirate Prince)-#7, (Silver Streak)-#4-8, nn; c-5 (Silver Streak), 6 (Claw), 7, 8 (Daredevil).* ***Everett*** *Red Reed begins #20.* ***Guardineer*** *a-#8-13.* ***Don Rico*** *a-11-17 (Daredevil); c-11, 12, 16.* ***Simon*** *a-3 (Silver Streak).* ***Bob Wood*** *a-9 (Silver Streak); c-9, 10. Captain Battle c-11, 13-15, 17. Claw c-#1, 2, 6-8. Daredevil c-7, 8, 12. Dickie Dean c-19. Ned of the Navy c-20 (war). The Saint c-18. Silver Streak c-5, 9, 10, 16, 23.*

SILVER SURFER (See Fantastic Four, Fantasy Masterpieces V2#1, Fireside Book Series, Marvel Graphic Novel, Marvel Presents #8, Marvel's Greatest Comics & Tales To Astonish #92)

SILVER SURFER, THE (Also see Essential Silver Surfer)
Marvel Comics Group: Aug, 1968 - No. 18, Sept, 1970; June, 1982

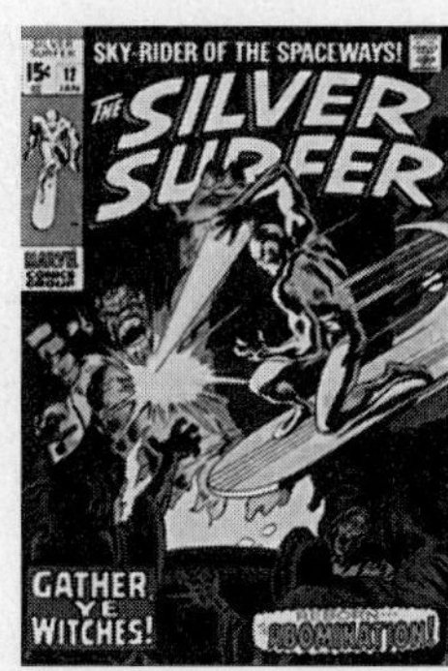

Silver Surfer #12 © MAR

Silver Surfer V4#1 © MAR

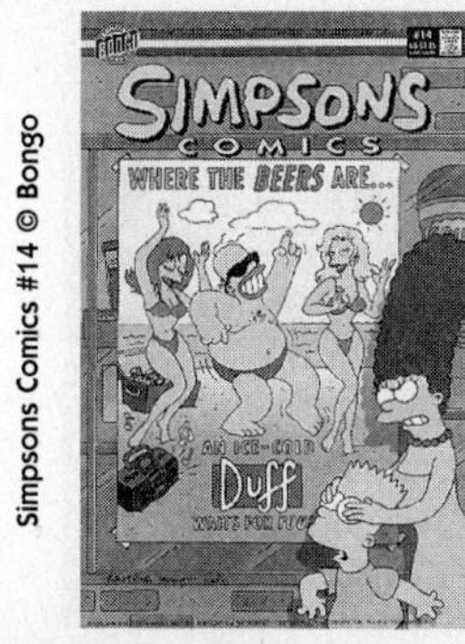

Simpsons Comics #14 © Bongo

GD VG FN VF VF/NM NM-
2.0 4.0 6.0 8.0 9.0 9.2

GD VG FN VF VF/NM NM-
2.0 4.0 6.0 8.0 9.0 9.2

1-More detailed origin by John Buscema (p); The Watcher back-up stories begin (origin), end #7; (No. 1-7: 25¢, 68 pgs.) 45 90 135 338 507 675
2 20 40 60 142 209 275
3-1st app. Mephisto 17 34 51 121 178 235
4-Lower distribution; Thor & Loki app. 40 80 120 300 450 600
5-7-Last giant size. 5-The Stranger app.; Fantastic Four app. 6-Brunner inks. 7-(8/69)-1st app. Frankenstein's monster (cameo) 11 22 33 77 114 150
8-10: 8-18-(15¢ issues) 9 18 27 60 85 110
11-13,15-18: 15-Silver Surfer vs. Human Torch; Fantastic Four app. 17-Nick Fury app. 18-Vs. The Inhumans; Kirby-c/a 8 16 24 53 74 95
14-Spider-Man x-over 11 22 33 77 114 150
V2#1 (6/82, 52 pgs.)-Byrne-c/a 1 3 4 6 8 10

NOTE: ***Adkins*** *a-8-15i.* ***Brunner*** *a-6i.* ***J. Buscema*** *a-1-17p.* ***Colan*** *a-1-3p.* ***Reinman*** *a-1-4i. #1-14 were reprinted in Fantasy Masterpieces V2#1-14.*

SILVER SURFER (Volume 3) (See Marvel Graphic Novel #38)
Marvel Comics Group: V3#1, July, 1987 - No. 146, Nov, 1998

1-Double size ($1.25) 1 2 3 5 7 9
2-17: 15-Ron Lim-c/a begins (9/88) 4.00
18-33,39-43: 25,31 ($1.50, 52 pgs.). 25-Skrulls app. 32,39-No Ron Lim-c/a. 39-Alan Grant scripts 3.00
34-Thanos returns (cameo); Starlin scripts begin 5.00
35-38: 35-1st full Thanos app. in Silver Surfer (3/90); reintro Drax the Destroyer on last pg. (cameo). 36-Recaps history of Thanos; Capt. Marvel & Warlock app. in recap. 37-1st full app. Drax the Destroyer; Drax-c. 38-Silver Surfer battles Thanos 6.00
44,45,49-Thanos stories (c-44,45) 4.00
46-48: 46-Return of Adam Warlock (2/91); re-intro Gamora & Pip the Troll. 47-Warlock battles Drax. 48-Last Starlin scripts (also #50) 4.00
50-($1.50, 52 pgs.)-Embossed & silver foil-c; Silver Surfer has brief battle w/Thanos; story cont'd in Infinity Gauntlet #1 1 2 3 4 5 7
50-2nd & 3rd printings 2.50
51-59: 51-53: Infinity Gauntlet x-over . 54-57: Infinity Gauntlet x-overs. 54-Rhino app. 55,56-Thanos-c & app. 57-Thanos-c & cameo. 58,59-Infinity Gauntlet x-overs; 58-Ron Lim-c only. 59-Thanos battles Silver Surfer-c/story; Thanos joins 3.00
60-74,76-99,101-124,126-139: 63-Capt. Marvel app. 67-69-Infinity War x-overs. 76-78-Jack of Hearts-c/s. 83-85-Infinity Crusade x-over; 83,84-Thanos cameo. 85-Storm, Wonder Man x-over. 86-Thor-c/s. 87-Dr. Strange & Warlock app. 88-Thanos-c/s. 82 (52 pgs.). 101-Bound in card sheet. 5-FF app. 96-Hulk & FF app. 97-Terrax & Nova app. 106-Doc Doom app. 121-Quasar & Beta Ray Bill app. 123-w/card insert; begin Garney-a. 126-Dr. Strange-c/app. 128-Spider-Man & Daredevil-c/app. 138-Thing-c 2.50
75-($2.50, 52 pgs.)-Embossed foil-c; Lim-c/a 3.00
100 ($2.25, 52 pgs.)-Wraparound-c 2.25
100 ($3.95, 52 pgs.)-Enhanced-c 4.00
125 ($2.95)-Wraparound-c; Vs. Hulk-c/app. 3.00
140-146: 140-142,144,145-Muth-c/a. 143,146-Cowan-a. 146-Last issue 2.50
#(-1) Flashback (7/97) 2.50
Annual 1 (1988, $1.75)-Evolutionary War app.; 1st Ron Lim-a on Silver Surfer (20 pg. back-up story & pin-ups) 5.00
Annual 2-7 ('89-'94, 68 pgs.): 2-Atlantis Attacks. 4-3 pg. origin story; Silver Surfer battles Guardians of the Galaxy. 5-Return of the Defenders, part 3; Lim-c/a (3 pgs. of pin-ups only). 6-Polybagged w/trading card; 1st app. Legacy; card is by Lim/Austin 3.00
Annual '97 ($2.99), .../Thor Annual '98 ($2.99) 3.00
...Dangerous Artifacts-(1996, $3.95)-Ron Marz scripts; Galactus-c/app. 4.00
Graphic Novel (1988, HC, $14.95) Judgment Day; Lee-s/Buscema-a 15.00
The Enslavers Graphic Novel (1990, $16.95) 17.00
Homecoming Graphic Novel (1991, $12.95, softcover) Starlin-s 15.00
Inner Demons TPB (4/98, $3.50)r/#123,125,126 3.50
...: The First Coming of Galactus nn (11/92, $5.95, 68 pgs.)-Reprints Fantastic Four #48-50 with new Lim-c 6.00
Wizard 1/2 2 4 6 10 12 15

NOTE: ***Austin*** *c(i)-7, 8, 71, 73, 74, 76, 79.* ***Cowan*** *a-143,146.* ***Cully Hamner*** *a-83p.* ***Ron Lim*** *a(p)-15-31, 33-38, 40-55, (56, 57-part-p), 60-65, 73-82, Annual 2, 4; c(p)-15-31, 32-38, 40-84, 86-92, Annual 2, 4-6.* ***Muth*** *c/a-140-142,144,145.* ***M. Rogers*** *a-1-10, 12, 19, 21; c-1-9, 11, 12, 21.*

SILVER SURFER (Volume 4)
Marvel Comics: Sept, 2003 - Present ($2.25)

1-4: 1-Milx-a; Jusko-c. 2-Jae Lee-c 2.25

SILVER SURFER, THE
Marvel Comics (Epic): Dec, 1988 - No. 2, Jan, 1989 ($1.00, lim. series)

1,2: By Stan Lee scripts & Moebius-c/a 4.00
...: Parable ('98, $5.99) r/#1&2 6.00

SILVER SURFER: LOFTIER THAN MORTALS
Marvel Comics: Oct, 1999 - No. 2, Oct, 1999 ($2.50, limited series)

1,2-Remix of Fantastic Four #57-60; Velluto-a 2.50

SILVER SURFER/SUPERMAN
Marvel Comics: 1996 ($5.95,one-shot)

1-Perez-s/Lim-c/a(p) 6.00

SILVER SURFER VS. DRACULA
Marvel Comics: Feb, 1994 ($1.75, one-shot)

1-r/Tomb of Dracula #50; Everett Vampire-r/Venus #19; Howard the Duck back-up by Brunner; Lim-c(p) 2.25

SILVER SURFER/WARLOCK: RESURRECTION
Marvel Comics: Mar, 1993 - No. 4, June, 1993 ($2.50, limited series)

1-4: Starlin-c/a & scripts 2.50

SILVER SURFER/WEAPON ZERO
Marvel Comics: Apr, 1997 ($2.95, one-shot)

1-"Devil's Reign" pt. 8 3.00

SILVERTIP (Max Brand)
Dell Publishing Co.: No. 491, Aug, 1953 - No. 898, May, 1958

Four Color 491 (#1); all painted-c 9 18 27 63 89 115
Four Color 572,608,637,667,731,789,898-Kinstler-a 5 10 15 36 48 60
Four Color 835 5 10 15 36 48 60

SIMPSONS COMICS (See Bartman, Futurama, Itchy & Scratchy & Radioactive Man)
Bongo Comics Group: 1993 - Present ($1.95/$2.50/$2.99)

1-($2.25)-FF#1-c swipe; pull-out poster; flip book 1 2 3 5 6 8
2-5: 2-Patty & Selma flip-c/sty. 3-Krusty, Agent of K.L.O.W.N. flip-c/story. 4-Infinity-c; flip-c of Busman #1; w/trading card. 5-Wraparound-c w/trading card 5.00
6-40: All Flip books. 6-w/Chief Wiggum's "Crime Comics". 7-w/"McBain Comics". 8-w/"Edna, Queen of the Congo". 9-w/"Barney Gumble". 10-w/"Apu". 11-w/"Homer". 12-w/"White Knuckled War Stories". 13-w/"Jimbo Jones' Wedgie Comics". 14-w/"Grampa". 15-w/"Itchy & Scratchy". 16-w/"Bongo Grab Bag". 17-w/"Headlight Comics". 18-w/"Milhouse". 19,20-w/"Roswell." 21,22-w/"Roswell". 23-w/"Hellfire Comics". 24-w/"Lil' Homey". 36-39-Flip book w/Radioactive Man 4.00
41-49,51-89 ($2.50): 43-Flip book w/Poochie. 52-Dini-s. 77-Dixon-s. 85-Begin $2.99-c 3.00
50-($5.95) Wraparound-c; 80 pgs.; square-bound 1 2 3 4 5 7
... A Go-Go (1999, $11.95)-r/#32-35; ...Big Bonanza (1998, $11.95)-r/#28-31, ...Extravaganza (1994, $10.00)-r/#1-4; infinity-c, ...On Parade (1998, $11.95)-r/#24-27, ...Simpsorama (1996, $10.95)-r/#11-14 12.00
Simpsons Comics Madness ('03, $14.95) r/#43-48 15.00
Simpsons Comics Royale ('01, $14.95) r/various Bongo issues 15.00

SIMPSONS COMICS AND STORIES
Welsh Publishing Group: 1993 ($2.95, one-shot)

1-(Direct Sale)-Polybagged w/Bartman poster 6.00
1-(Newsstand Edition)-Without poster 4.00

SIMPSONS COMICS PRESENTS BART SIMPSON
Bongo Comics Group: 2000 - Present ($2.50/$2.99, quarterly)

1-15: 7-9-Dan DeCarlo-layouts. 13-Begin $2.99-c 3.00
The Big Book of Bart Simpson TPB (2002, $12.95) r/#1-4 13.00
The Big Bad Book of Bart Simpson TPB (2003, $12.95) r/#5-8 13.00

SIMULATORS, THE
Neatly Chiseled Features: 1991 ($2.50, stiff-c)

1-Super hero group 2.50

SINBAD, JR (TV Cartoon)
Dell Publishing Co.: Sept-Nov, 1965 - No. 3, May, 1966

1 4 8 12 27 36 45
2,3 3 6 9 19 25 32

SIN CITY (See Dark Horse Presents, A Decade of Dark Horse, & San Diego Comic Con Comics #2,4)
Dark Horse Comics (Legend)
TPB ($15.00) Reprints early DHP stories 15.00
Booze, Broads & Bullets TPB ($15.00) 15.00

SIN CITY: A DAME TO KILL FOR
Dark Horse Comics (Legend): Nov, 1993 - No. 6, May, 1994 ($2.95, B&W, limited series)

1-6: Frank Miller-c/a & story in all. 1-1st app. Dwight. 5.00
Limited Edition Hardcover 85.00
Hardcover 25.00
TPB ($15.00) 15.00

SIN CITY: FAMILY VALUES
Dark Horse Comics (Legend): Oct, 1997 ($10.00, B&W, squarebound, one-shot)

nn-Miller-c/a & story 10.00

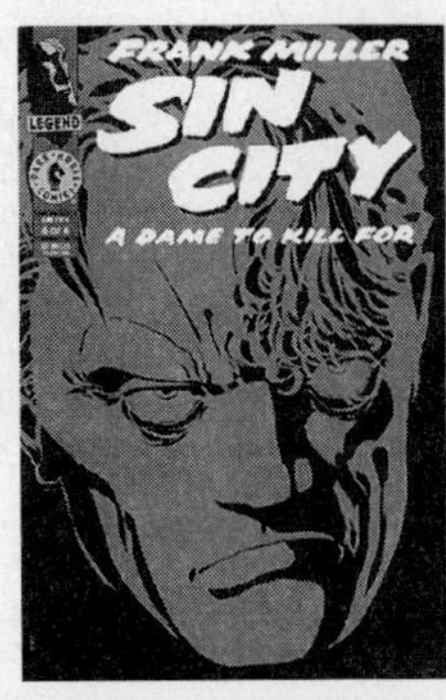

Sin City: A Dame to Kill For #6 © Frank Miller

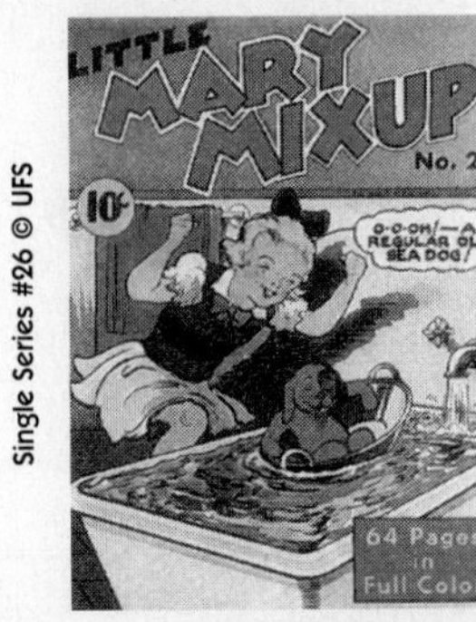

Single Series #26 © UFS

Six-Gun Heroes #1 © FAW

	GD 2.0	VG 4.0	FN 6.0	VF 8.0	VF/NM 9.0	NM- 9.2

Limited Edition Hardcover 75.00

SIN CITY: HELL AND BACK
Dark Horse (Maverick): Jul, 1999 - No. 9 ($2.95/$4.95, B&W, limited series)
1-8-Miller-c/a & story. 7-Color 3.00
9-($4.95) 5.00

SIN CITY: JUST ANOTHER SATURDAY NIGHT
Dark Horse Comics (Legend): Aug, 1997 (Wizard 1/2 offer, B&W, one-shot)
1/2-Miller-c/a & story 1 2 3 5 6 8
nn (10/98, $2.50) r/#1/2 2.50

SIN CITY: LOST, LONELY & LETHAL
Dark Horse Comics (Legend): Dec, 1996 ($2.95, B&W and blue, one-shot)
nn-Miller-c/s/a; w/pin-ups 4.00

SIN CITY: SEX AND VIOLENCE
Dark Horse Comics (Legend): Mar, 1997 ($2.95, B&W and blue, one-shot)
nn-Miller-c/a & story 4.00

SIN CITY: SILENT NIGHT
Dark Horse Comics (Legend): Dec, 1995 ($2.95, B&W, one-shot)
1-Miller-c/a & story; Marv app. 4.00

SIN CITY: THAT YELLOW BASTARD
Dark Horse Comics (Legend): Feb, 1996 - No. 6, July, 1996 ($2.95/$3.50, B&W and yellow, limited series)
1-5: Miller-c/a & story in all. 1-1st app. Hartigan. 5.00
6-($3.50) Error & corrected 5.00
Limited Edition Hardcover 25.00
TPB ($15.00) 15.00

SIN CITY: THE BABE WORE RED AND OTHER STORIES
Dark Horse Comics (Legend): Nov, 1994 ($2.95, B&W and red, one-shot)
1-r/serial run in Previews as well as other stories; Miller-c/a & scripts; Dwight app. 3.00

SIN CITY: THE BIG FAT KILL
Dark Horse Comics (Legend): Nov, 1994 - No. 5, Mar, 1995 ($2.95, B&W, limited series)
1-5-Miller story & art in all; Dwight app. 4.00
Hardcover 25.00
TPB ($15.00) 15.00

SINDBAD (See Capt. Sindbad under Movie Comics, and Fantastic Voyages of Sindbad)

SINGING GUNS (See Fawcett Movie Comics)

SINGLE SERIES (Comics on Parade #30 on)(Also see John Hix...)
United Features Syndicate: 1938 - No. 28, 1942 (All 68 pgs.)

Note: See Individual Alphabetical Listings for prices

1-Captain and the Kids (#1)	2-Broncho Bill (1939) (#1)
3-Ella Cinders (1939)	4-Li'l Abner (1939) (#1)
5-Fritzi Ritz (#1)	6-Jim Hardy by Dick Moores (#1)
7-Frankie Doodle	8-Peter Pat (On sale 7/14/39)
9-Strange As It Seems	10-Little Mary Mixup
11-Mr. and Mrs. Beans	12-Joe Jinks
13-Looy Dot Dope	14-Billy Make Believe
15-How It Began (1939)	16-Illustrated Gags (1940)-Has ad for Captain and the Kids #1 reprint listed below
17-Danny Dingle	
18-Li'l Abner (#2 on-c)	
19-Broncho Bill (#2 on-c)	20-Tarzan by Hal Foster
21-Ella Cinders (#2 on-c; on sale 3/19/40)	22-Iron Vic
23-Tailspin Tommy by Hal Forrest (#1)	24-Alice in Wonderland (#1)
25-Abbie and Slats	26-Little Mary Mixup (#2 on-c, 1940)
27-Jim Hardy by Dick Moores (1942)	28-Ella Cinders & Abbie and Slats (1942)
1-Captain and the Kids (1939 reprint)-2nd Edition	1-Fritzi Ritz (1939 reprint)-2nd ed.

NOTE: *Some issues given away at the 1939-40 New York World's Fair (#6).*

SINISTER HOUSE OF SECRET LOVE, THE (Becomes Secrets of Sinister House No. 5 on)
National Periodical Publ.: Oct-Nov, 1971 - No. 4, Apr-May, 1972

	GD	VG	FN	VF	VF/NM	NM-
1 (all 52 pgs.)	16	32	48	113	167	220
2,4: 2-Jeff Jones-c	7	14	21	51	71	90
3-Toth-a	8	16	24	53	74	95

SINS OF YOUTH... (Also see Young Justice: Sins of Youth)
DC Comics: May 2000 ($4.95/$2.50, limited crossover series)
Secret Files 1 ($4.95) Short stories and profile pages; Nauck-c 5.00
...Aquaboy/Lagoon Man; Batboy and Robin; JLA Jr.; Kid Flash/Impulse; Starwoman and the JSA, Superman, Jr./Superboy, Sr.; The Secret/ Deadboy, Wonder Girls ($2.50-c)
Old and young heroes switch ages 2.50

SIR CHARLES BARKLEY AND THE REFEREE MURDERS
Hamilton Comics: 1993 ($9.95, 8-1/2" x 11", 52 pgs.)
nn-Photo-c; Sports fantasy comic book fiction (uses real names of NBA superstars). Script by Alan Dean Foster, art by Joe Staton. Comes with bound-in sheet of 35 gummed "Moods of Charles Barkley" stamps. Photo/story on Barkley 2 4 6 8 10 12
Special Edition of 100 copies for charity signed on an affixed book plate by Barkley, Foster & Staton 150.00
Ashcan edition given away to dealers, distributors & promoters (low distribution). Four pages in color, balance of story in b&w 2 4 6 8 10 12

SIREN (Also see Eliminator & Ultraforce)
Malibu Comics (Ultraverse): Sept, 1995 - No. 3, Dec, 1995 ($1.50)
Infinity, 1-3: Infinity-Black-c & painted-c exists. 1-Regular-c & painted-c; War Machine app. 2-Flip book w/Phoenix Resurrection Pt. 3 2.25
Special 1-(2/96, $1.95, 28 pgs.)-Origin Siren; Marvel Comic's Juggernaut-c/app. 2.25

SIREN: SHAPES
Image Comics: May, 1998 - No. 3, Nov, 1998 ($2.95, B&W, limited series)
1-3-J. Torres -s 3.00

SIR LANCELOT (TV)
Dell Publishing Co.: No. 606, Dec, 1954 - No. 775, Mar, 1957

	GD	VG	FN	VF	VF/NM	NM-
Four Color 606 (not TV)	8	16	24	55	78	100
Four Color 775(...and Brian)-Buscema-a; photo-c	10	20	30	73	107	140

SIR WALTER RALEIGH (Movie)
Dell Publishing Co.: May, 1955 (Based on movie "The Virgin Queen")

	GD	VG	FN	VF	VF/NM	NM-
Four Color 644-Photo-c	8	16	24	53	74	95

SISTERHOOD OF STEEL (See Eclipse Graphic Adventure Novel #13)
Marvel Comics (Epic Comics): Dec, 1984 -No. 8, Feb, 1986 ($1.50, Baxter paper, mature)
1-8 3.00

SISTERS OF MERCY
Maximum Press/No Mercy Comics #3 on: Dec, 1995 - No. 5, Oct, 1996 ($2.50)
1-5: 1-Liefeld variant-c exists 2.50
V2#0-(3/97, $1.50) Liefeld-c 2.50

SISTERS OF MERCY: PARADISE LOST
London Night Studios/No Mercy Comics: Apr, 1997 - No. 4 ($2.50)
1-4 2.50

SISTERS OF MERCY: WHEN RAZORS CRY CRIMSON TEARS
No Mercy Comics: Oct, 1996 ($2.50, one-shot)
1 2.50

6 BLACK HORSES (See Movie Classics)

SIX FROM SIRIUS
Marvel Comics (Epic Comics): July, 1984 - No. 4, Oct, 1984 ($1.50, limited series, mature)
1-4: Moench scripts; Gulacy-c/a in all 2.25

SIX FROM SIRIUS II
Marvel Comics (Epic Comics): Feb, 1986 - No. 4, May, 1986 ($1.50, limited series, mature)
1-4: Moench scripts; Gulacy-c/a in all 2.25

SIX-GUN HEROES
Fawcett Publications: March, 1950 - No. 23, Nov, 1953 (Photo-c #1-23)

	GD	VG	FN	VF	VF/NM	NM-
1-Rocky Lane, Hopalong Cassidy, Smiley Burnette begin (same date as Smiley Burnette #1)	46	92	138	276	413	550
2	29	58	87	164	232	300
3-5: 5-Lash LaRue begins	20	40	60	112	156	200
6-15	15	30	45	84	115	145
16-22: 17-Last Smiley Burnette. 18-Monte Hale begins	13	26	39	74	100	125
23-Last Fawcett issue	14	28	42	79	107	135

NOTE: *Hopalong Cassidy photo c-1-3. Monte Hale photo c-18. Rocky Lane photo c-4, 5, 7, 9, 11, 13, 15, 17, 20, 21, 23. Lash LaRue photo c-6, 8, 10, 12, 14, 16, 19, 22.*

SIX-GUN HEROES (Cont'd from Fawcett; Gunmasters #84 on) (See Blue Bird)
Charlton Comics: No. 24, Jan, 1954 - No. 83, Mar-Apr, 1965 (All Vol. 4)

	GD	VG	FN	VF	VF/NM	NM-
24-Lash LaRue, Hopalong Cassidy, Rocky Lane & Tex Ritter begin; photo-c	21	42	63	118	164	210
25	11	22	33	63	84	105
26-30: 26-Rod Cameron story. 28-Tom Mix begins?	10	20	30	56	73	90
31-40: 38-Jingles & Wild Bill Hickok (TV)	9	18	27	49	62	75
41-46,48,50	8	16	24	46	58	70
47-Williamson-a, 2 pgs; Torres-a	9	18	27	49	62	75

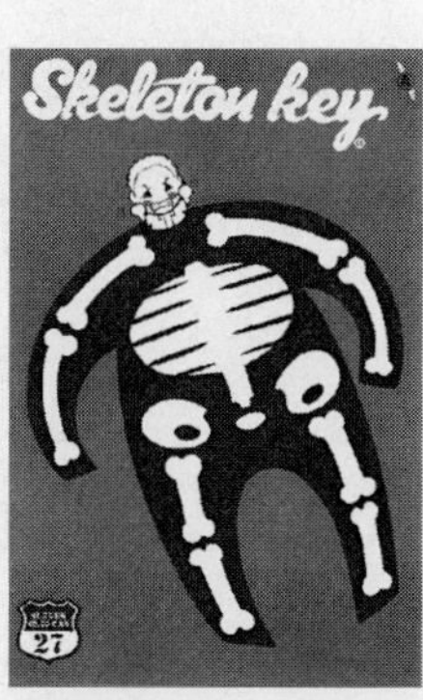

Skeleton Key #27 © Amaze Ink

Skyman #1 © CCG

Slam Bang Comics #5 © FAW

	GD 2.0	VG 4.0	FN 6.0	VF 8.0	VF/NM 9.0	NM- 9.2
49-Williamson-a (5 pgs.)	10	20	30	56	73	90
51-56,58-60: 58-Gunmaster app.	4	8	12	29	40	50
57-Origin & 1st app. Gunmaster	5	10	15	36	48	60
61,63-70	3	7	10	21	28	35
62-Origin Gunmaster	4	8	12	27	36	45
71-75,77,78,80-83	3	6	9	16	20	24
76,79: 76-Gunmaster begins. 79-1st app. & origin of Bullet, the Gun-Boy	3	6	9	18	23	28

SIXGUN RANCH (See Luke Short & Four Color #580)

SIX-GUN WESTERN
Atlas Comics (CDS): Jan, 1957 - No. 4, July, 1957

	GD 2.0	VG 4.0	FN 6.0	VF 8.0	VF/NM 9.0	NM- 9.2
1-Crandall-a; two Williamson text illos	21	42	63	118	164	210
2,3-Williamson-a in both	15	30	45	86	118	150
4-Woodbridge-a	10	20	30	60	80	100

NOTE: *Ayers a-2, 3. **Maneely** a-1; c-2, 3. **Orlando** a-2. **Pakula** a-2. **Powell** a-3. **Romita** a-1, 4. **Severin** c-1, 4. **Shores** a-2.*

SIX MILLION DOLLAR MAN, THE (TV)
Charlton Comics: 6/76 - No. 4, 12/76; No. 5, 10/77; No. 6, 2/78 - No. 9, 6/78

	GD 2.0	VG 4.0	FN 6.0	VF 8.0	VF/NM 9.0	NM- 9.2
1-Staton-c/a; Lee Majors photo on-c	2	4	6	12	16	20
2-9: 2-Neal Adams-c; Staton-a	2	4	6	10	12	15

SIX MILLION DOLLAR MAN, THE (TV)(Magazine)
Charlton Comics: July, 1976 - No. 7, Nov, 1977 (B&W)

	GD 2.0	VG 4.0	FN 6.0	VF 8.0	VF/NM 9.0	NM- 9.2
1-Neal Adams-c/a	3	6	9	16	20	25
2-Neal Adams-c	2	4	6	12	16	20
3-N. Adams part inks; Chaykin-a	2	4	6	11	14	18
4-7	2	4	6	10	12	15

SIX STRING SAMURAI
Awesome-Hyperwerks: Sept, 1998 ($2.95)

	GD 2.0	VG 4.0	FN 6.0	VF 8.0	VF/NM 9.0	NM- 9.2
1-Stinsman & Fraga-a						3.00

67 SECONDS
Marvel Comics (Epic Comics): 1992 ($15.95, 54 pgs., graphic novel)

	GD 2.0	VG 4.0	FN 6.0	VF 8.0	VF/NM 9.0	NM- 9.2
nn-James Robinson scripts; Steve Yeowell-c/a	2	4	6	11	14	18

SKATEMAN
Pacific Comics: Nov, 1983 (Baxter paper, one-shot)

	GD 2.0	VG 4.0	FN 6.0	VF 8.0	VF/NM 9.0	NM- 9.2
1-Adams-c/a						4.00

SKELETON HAND (...In Secrets of the Supernatural)
American Comics Gr. (B&M Dist. Co.): Sept-Oct, 1952 - No. 6, Jul-Aug, 1953

	GD 2.0	VG 4.0	FN 6.0	VF 8.0	VF/NM 9.0	NM- 9.2
1	44	88	132	264	375	525
2	34	68	102	196	278	360
3-6	28	56	84	159	225	290

SKELETON KEY
Amaze Ink: July, 1995 - No. 30, Jan, 1998 ($1.25/$1.50/$1.75, B&W)

	GD 2.0	VG 4.0	FN 6.0	VF 8.0	VF/NM 9.0	NM- 9.2
1-30						3.00
Special #1 (2/98, $4.95) Unpublished short stories						5.00
Sugar Kat Special (10/98, $2.95) Halloween stories						3.00
Beyond The Threshold TPB (6/96. $11.95)-r/#1-6						12.00
Cats and Dogs TPB ($12.95)-r/#25-30						13.00
The Celestial Calendar TPB ($19.95)-r/#7-18						20.00
Telling Tales TPB ($12.95)-r/#19-24						13.00

SKELETON KEY (Volume 2)
Amaze Ink: 1999 - No. 4, 1999 ($2.95, B&W)

	GD 2.0	VG 4.0	FN 6.0	VF 8.0	VF/NM 9.0	NM- 9.2
1-4-Andrew Watson-s/a						3.00

SKELETON WARRIORS
Marvel Comics: Apr, 1995 - No. 4, July, 1995 ($1.50)

	GD 2.0	VG 4.0	FN 6.0	VF 8.0	VF/NM 9.0	NM- 9.2
1-4: Based on animated series.						2.25

SKIN GRAFT: THE ADVENTURES OF A TATTOOED MAN
DC Comics (Vertigo): July, 1993 - No. 4, Oct, 1993 ($2.50, lim. series, mature)

	GD 2.0	VG 4.0	FN 6.0	VF 8.0	VF/NM 9.0	NM- 9.2
1-4						2.50

SKINWALKER (Also see Promotional Comics section for FCBD Ed.)
Oni Press: May, 2002 - No. 4, Sept, 2002 ($2.95, limited series)

	GD 2.0	VG 4.0	FN 6.0	VF 8.0	VF/NM 9.0	NM- 9.2
1-4-Hurtt & Dela Cruz-a; Talon-c						3.00

SKI PARTY (See Movie Classics)

SKREEMER
DC Comics: May, 1989 - No. 6, Oct, 1989 ($2.00, limited series, mature)

	GD 2.0	VG 4.0	FN 6.0	VF 8.0	VF/NM 9.0	NM- 9.2
1-6: Contains graphic violence; Milligan-s						2.25
TPB (2002, $19.95) r/#1-6						20.00

SKRULL KILL KREW
Marvel Comics: Sept, 1995 - No. 5, Dec, 1995 ($2.95, limited series)

	GD 2.0	VG 4.0	FN 6.0	VF 8.0	VF/NM 9.0	NM- 9.2
1-5: Grant Morrison scripts. 2,3-Cap America app.						3.00

SKUL, THE
Virtual Comics (Byron Preiss Multimedia): Oct, 1996 - No. 3, Dec, 1996 ($2.50, limited series)

	GD 2.0	VG 4.0	FN 6.0	VF 8.0	VF/NM 9.0	NM- 9.2
1-3: Ron Lim & Jimmy Palmiotti-a						2.50

SKULL & BONES
DC Comics: 1992 - No. 3, 1992 ($4.95, limited series, 52 pgs.)

	GD 2.0	VG 4.0	FN 6.0	VF 8.0	VF/NM 9.0	NM- 9.2
Book 1-3: 1-1st app.						5.00

SKULL, THE SLAYER
Marvel Comics Group: Aug, 1975 - No. 8, Nov, 1976 (20¢/25¢)

	GD 2.0	VG 4.0	FN 6.0	VF 8.0	VF/NM 9.0	NM- 9.2
1-Origin & 1st app.; Gil Kane-c	2	4	6	8	10	12
2-8: 2-Gil Kane-c. 5,6-(Regular 25¢-c). 8-Kirby-c	1	2	3	4	5	7
5,6-(30¢-c variants, limited distribution)(5,7/76)	1	3	4	6	8	10

SKY BLAZERS (CBS Radio)
Hawley Publications: Sept, 1940 - No. 2, Nov, 1940

	GD 2.0	VG 4.0	FN 6.0	VF 8.0	VF/NM 9.0	NM- 9.2
1-Sky Pirates, Ace Archer, Flying Aces begin	61	122	183	381	575	765
2-WWII aerial battle-c	40	80	120	240	340	440

SKYMAN (See Big Shot Comics & Sparky Watts)
Columbia Comics Gr.: Fall?, 1941 - No. 2, Fall?, 1942; No. 3, 1948 - No. 4, 1948

	GD 2.0	VG 4.0	FN 6.0	VF 8.0	VF/NM 9.0	NM- 9.2
1-Origin Skyman, The Face, Sparky Watts app.; Whitney-c/a; 3rd story-r from Big Shot #1; Whitney c-1-4	120	240	360	750	1125	1500
2 (1942)-Yankee Doodle	60	120	180	375	563	750
3,4 (1948)	40	80	120	240	340	440

SKYPILOT
Ziff-Davis Publ. Co.: No. 10, 1950(nd) - No. 11, Apr-May, 1951

	GD 2.0	VG 4.0	FN 6.0	VF 8.0	VF/NM 9.0	NM- 9.2
10,11-Frank Borth-a; Saunders painted-c	15	30	45	84	115	145

SKY RANGER (See Johnny Law...)

SKYROCKET
Harry 'A' Chesler: 1944

	GD 2.0	VG 4.0	FN 6.0	VF 8.0	VF/NM 9.0	NM- 9.2
nn-Alias the Dragon, Dr. Vampire, Skyrocket & The Desperado app.; WWII Jap zero-c	33	66	99	190	270	350

SKY SHERIFF (Breeze Lawson...) (Also see Exposed & Outlaws)
D. S. Publishing Co.: Summer, 1948

	GD 2.0	VG 4.0	FN 6.0	VF 8.0	VF/NM 9.0	NM- 9.2
1-Edmond Good-c/a	14	28	42	79	107	135

SKY WOLF (Also see Airboy)
Eclipse Comics: Mar, 1988 - No. 3, Oct, 1988 ($1.25/$1.50/$1.95, lim. series)

	GD 2.0	VG 4.0	FN 6.0	VF 8.0	VF/NM 9.0	NM- 9.2
1-3						2.25

SLACKER COMICS
Slave Labor Graphics: Aug, 1994 - Present ($2.95, B&W, quarterly)

	GD 2.0	VG 4.0	FN 6.0	VF 8.0	VF/NM 9.0	NM- 9.2
1-18, 1 (2nd printing)-Reads "2nd print" in indicia						3.00

SLAINE, THE BERSERKER (Slaine the King #21 on)
Quality: July, 1987 - No. 28, 1989 ($1.25/$1.50)

	GD 2.0	VG 4.0	FN 6.0	VF 8.0	VF/NM 9.0	NM- 9.2
1-28						2.25

SLAINE, THE HORNED GOD
Fleetway: 1998 - No. 3 ($6.99)

	GD 2.0	VG 4.0	FN 6.0	VF 8.0	VF/NM 9.0	NM- 9.2
1-3-Reprints series from 2000 A.D.; Bisley-a						7.00

SLAM BANG COMICS (Western Desperado #8)
Fawcett Publications: Mar, 1940 - No. 7, Sept, 1940 (Combined with Master Comics #7)

	GD 2.0	VG 4.0	FN 6.0	VF 8.0	VF/NM 9.0	NM- 9.2
1-Diamond Jack, Mark Swift & The Time Retarder, Lee Granger, Jungle King begin & continue in Master	224	448	672	1400	2100	2800
2	92	184	276	575	863	1150
3-Classic-c	140	280	420	875	1313	1750
4-7: 6-Intro Zoro, the Mystery Man (also in #7)	74	148	222	463	694	925

SLAPSTICK
Marvel Comics: Nov, 1992 - No. 4, Feb, 1993 ($1.25, limited series)

	GD 2.0	VG 4.0	FN 6.0	VF 8.0	VF/NM 9.0	NM- 9.2
1-4: Fry/Austin-c/a. 4-Ghost Rider, D.D., F.F. app.						2.25

SLAPSTICK COMICS
Comic Magazines Distributors: nd (1946?) (36 pgs.)

	GD 2.0	VG 4.0	FN 6.0	VF 8.0	VF/NM 9.0	NM- 9.2
nn-Firetop feature; Post-a(2)	25	50	75	144	198	255

SLASH-D DOUBLECROSS
St. John Publishing Co.: 1950 (Pocket-size, 132 pgs.)

Sleeper #1 © WSP

Smallville #1 © DC

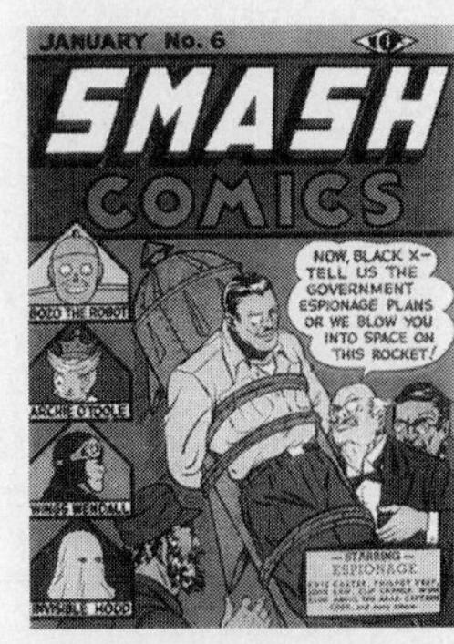

Smash Comics #6 © QUA

	GD 2.0	VG 4.0	FN 6.0	VF 8.0	VF/NM 9.0	NM- 9.2

nn-Western comics 23 46 69 129 180 230

SLASH MARAUD
DC Comics: Nov, 1987 - No. 6, Apr, 1988 ($1.75, limited series)
1-6 2.25

SLAUGHTERMAN
Comico: Feb, 1983 - No. 2, 1983 ($1.50, B&W)
1,2 3.00

SLAVE GIRL COMICS (See Malu... & White Princess of the Jungle #2)
Avon Periodicals/Eternity Comics (1989): Feb, 1949 - No. 2, Apr, 1949 (52 pgs.); Mar, 1989 (B&W, 44 pgs)
1-Larsen-c/a 92 184 276 575 863 1150
2-Larsen-a 69 138 207 431 646 860
1-(3/89, $2.25, B&W, 44 pgs.)-r/#1 3.00

SLEDGE HAMMER (TV)
Marvel Comics: Feb, 1988 - No. 2, Mar,1988 ($1.00, limited series)
1,2 3.00

SLEEPER
DC Comics (WildStorm): Mar, 2003 - Present ($2.95)
1-11-Brubaker-s/Phillips-c/a. 3-Back-up preview of The Authority: High Stakes pt. 2 3.00
...: Out in the Cold TPB (2004, $17.95) r/#1-6 18.00

SLEEPING BEAUTY (See Dell Giants & Movie Comics)
Dell Publishing Co.: No. 973, May, 1959 - No. 984, June, 1959 (Disney)
Four Color 973 (...and the Prince) 12 24 36 87 129 170
Four Color 984 (...Fairy Godmother's) 10 20 30 67 96 125

SLEEPWALKER
Marvel Comics: June, 1991 - No. 33, Feb, 1994 ($1.00/$1.25)
1-1st app. Sleepwalker 3.00
2-33: 4-Williamson-i. 5-Spider-Man-c/stor. 7-Infinity Gauntlet x-over. 8-Vs. Deathlok-c/story. 11-Ghost Rider-c/story. 12-Quesada-c/a(p) 14-Intro Spectra. 15-F.F.-c/story. 17-Darkhawk & Spider-Man x-over. 18-Infinity War x-over; Quesada/Williamson-c. 21,22-Hobgoblin app. 19-($2.00)-Die-cut Sleepwalker mask-c 2.25
25-($2.95, 52 pgs.)-Holo-grafx foil-c; origin 3.00
Holiday Special 1 (1/93, $2.00, 52 pgs.)-Quesada-c(p) 2.25

SLEEPWALKING
Hall of Heroes: Jan, 1996 ($2.50, B&W)
1-Kelley Jones-c 2.50

SLEEPY HOLLOW (Movie Adaption)
DC Comics (Vertigo): 2000 ($7.95, one-shot)
1-Kelley Jones-a/Seagle-s 8.00

SLEEZE BROTHERS, THE
Marvel Comics (Epic Comics): Aug, 1989 - No. 6, Jan, 1990 ($1.75, mature)
1-6: 4-6 (9/89 - 11/89 indicia dates) 2.25
nn-(1991, $3.95, 52 pgs.) 4.00

SLICK CHICK COMICS
Leader Enterprises: 1947(nd) - No. 3, 1947(nd)
1-Teenage humor 12 24 36 71 96 120
2,3 9 18 27 52 66 80

SLIDERS (TV)
Acclaim Comics (Armada): June, 1996 - No. 2, July, 1996 ($2.50, lim. series)
1,2: D.G. Chichester scripts; Dick Giordano-a. 2.50

SLIDERS: DARKEST HOUR (TV)
Acclaim Comics (Armada): Oct, 1996 - No. 3, Dec, 1996 ($2.50, limited series)
1-3 2.50

SLIDERS SPECIAL
Acclaim Comics (Armada): Nov, 1996 - No 3, Mar, 1997 ($3.95, limited series)
1-3: 1-Narcotica-Jerry O'Connell-s. 2-Blood and Splendor. 3-Deadly Secrets 4.00

SLIDERS: ULTIMATUM (TV)
Acclaim Comics (Armada): Sept, 1996 - No. 2, Sept, 1996 ($2.50, lim. series)
1,2 2.50

SLIMER! (TV cartoon) (Also see the Real Ghostbusters)
Now Comics: 1989 - No. 19, Feb?, 1991 ($1.75)
1-19: Based on animated cartoon 3.00

SLIM MORGAN (See Wisco)

SLINGERS (See Spider-Man: Identity Crisis issues)
Marvel Comics: Dec, 1998 - No. 12, Nov, 1999 ($2.99/$1.99)
0-(Wizard #88 supplement) Prelude story 2.25
1-($2.99) Four editions w/different covers for each hero, 16 pages common to all, the other pages from each hero's perspective 3.00
2-12: 2-Two-c. 12-Saltares-a 2.25

SLOW NEWS DAY
Slave Labor Graphics: July, 2001 - No. 6 ($3.50, B&W)
1-5-Andi Watson-s/a 3.50

SLUDGE
Malibu Comics (Ultraverse): Oct, 1993 - No. 12, Dec, 1994 ($2.50/$1.95)
1-($2.50, 48 pgs.)-Intro/1st app. Sludge; Rune flip-c/story Pt. 1 (1st app., 3 pgs.) by Barry Smith; The Night Man app. (3 pg. preview); The Mighty Magnor 1 pg strip begins by Aragonés (cont. in other titles) 3.00
1-Ultra 5000 Limited silver foil 4.00
2-11: 3-Break-Thru x-over. 4-2 pg. Mantra origin. 8-Bloodstorm app. 2.50
12 ($3.50)-Ultraverse Premiere #8 flip book; Alex Ross poster 3.50
...:Red Xmas (12/94, $2.50, 44 pgs.) 2.50

SLUGGER (Little Wise Guys Starring...)(Also see Daredevil Comics)
Lev Gleason Publications: April, 1956
1-Biro-c 7 14 21 35 43 50

SMALLVILLE (Based on TV series)
DC Comics: May, 2003 - Present ($3.50, bi-monthly)
1-6-Photo-c. 1-Plunkett-a; interviews with cast; season 1 episode guide 3.50

SMALLVILLE: THE COMIC (Based on TV series)
DC Comics: Nov, 2002 ($3.95, 64 pages, one-shot)
1-Photo-c; art by Martinez and Leon; interviews with cast; season 2 preview 4.00

SMASH COMICS (Becomes Lady Luck #86 on)
Quality Comics Group: Aug, 1939 - No. 85, Oct, 1949
1-Origin Hugh Hazard & His Iron Man, Bozo the Robot, Espionage, Starring Black X by Eisner, & Hooded Justice (Invisible Justice #2 on); Chic Carter & Wings Wendall begin; 1st Robot on the cover of a comic book (Bozo) 300 600 900 1925 2963 4000
2-The Lone Star Rider app; Invisible Hood gains power of invisibility; bondage/torture-c 112 224 336 700 1050 1400
3-Captain Cook & Eisner's John Law begin 68 136 204 425 638 850
4,5: 4-Flash Fulton begins 64 128 192 400 600 800
6-12: 12-One pg. Fine-a 55 110 165 337 506 675
13-Magno begins (8/40); last Eisner issue; The Ray app. in full page ad; The Purple Trio begins 56 112 168 350 525 700
14-Intro. The Ray (9/40) by Lou Fine & others 296 592 888 1850 2775 3700
15,16: 16-The Scarlet Seal begins 124 248 372 775 1163 1550
17-Wun Cloo becomes plastic super-hero by Jack Cole (9-months before Plastic Man) 128 256 384 800 1200 1600
18-Midnight by Jack Cole begins (origin & 1st app., 1/41) 160 320 480 1000 1500 2000
19-22: Last Ray by Fine; The Jester begins-#22 85 170 255 531 796 1060
23,24: 24-The Sword app.; last Chic Carter; Wings Wendall dons new costume #24,25 66 132 198 413 619 825
25-Origin/1st app. Wildfire; Rookie Rankin begins 76 152 228 475 713 950
26-30: 28-Midnight-c begin, end #85 66 132 198 413 617 820
31,32,34: The Ray by Rudy Palais; also #33 55 110 165 338 507 675
33-Origin The Marksman 64 128 192 400 600 800
35-37 50 100 150 300 450 600
38-The Yankee Eagle begins; last Midnight by Jack Cole; classic-c by Cole 92 184 276 575 863 1150
39,40-Last Ray issue 50 100 150 300 450 600
41,44-50 40 80 120 240 340 440
42-Lady Luck begins by Klaus Nordling 120 240 360 750 1125 1500
43-Lady Luck-c (1st & only in Smash) 45 90 135 270 405 540
51-60 30 60 90 170 240 310
61-70 24 48 72 138 194 250
71-85: 79-Midnight battles the Men from Mars-c/s 22 44 66 124 172 220

NOTE: ***Al Bryant** c-54, 63-68. **Cole** a-17-38, 68, 69, 72, 73, 78, 80, 83, 85; c-38, 60-62, 69-84. **Crandall** a-(Ray)-23-29, 35-38; c-36, 39, 40, 42-44, 46. **Fine** a(Ray)-14, 15, 16(w/**Tuska**), 17-22. **Fox** c-24-35. **Fuje** Ray-30. **Gil Fox** a-6-7, 9, 11-13. **Guardineer** a-(The Marksman)-39-?, 49, 52. **Gustavson** a-4-7, 9, 11-13 (The Jester)-22-46; (Magno)-13-21; (Midnight)-39(Cole inks), 49, 52, 63-65. **Kotzky** a-(Espionage)-33-38; c-45, 47-53. **Nordling** a-49, 52, 63-65. **Powell** a-11, 12, (Abdul the Arab)-13-24.Black X c-2, 6, 9, 11, 13, 16. Bozo the Robot c-1, 3, 5, 8, 10, 12, 14, 18, 20, 22, 24, 26. Midnight c-28-85. The Ray c-15, 17, 19, 21, 23, 25, 27. Wings Wendall c-4, 7.*

SMASH COMICS (Also see All Star Comics 1999 crossover titles)
DC Comics: May, 1999 ($1.99, one-shot)

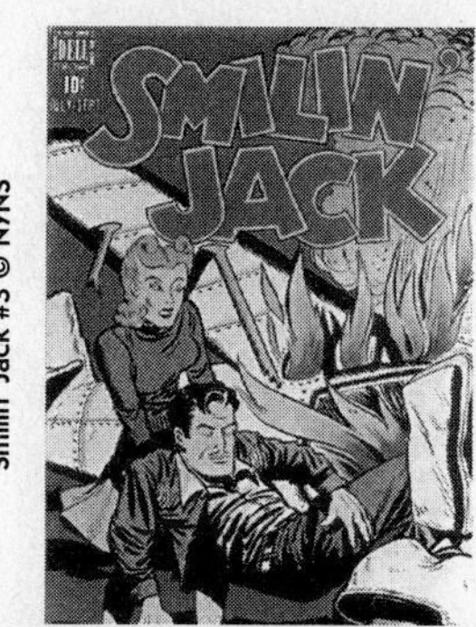

Smilin' Jack #3 © NYNS

Snagglepuss #4 © H-B

Snake Plissken Chronicles Preview © Hurricane

	GD 2.0	VG 4.0	FN 6.0	VF 8.0	VF/NM 9.0	NM- 9.2
1-Golden Age Doctor Mid-nite and Hourman						2.25

SMASH HIT SPORTS COMICS
Essankay Publications: V2#1, Jan, 1949

	GD 2.0	VG 4.0	FN 6.0	VF 8.0	VF/NM 9.0	NM- 9.2
V2#1-L.B. Cole-c/a	31	62	93	175	248	320

SMAX (Also see Top Ten)
America's Best Comics: Oct, 2003 - No. 5 ($2.95, limited series)

	GD 2.0	VG 4.0	FN 6.0	VF 8.0	VF/NM 9.0	NM- 9.2
1-4-Alan Moore-s/Zander Cannon-a						3.00

SMILE COMICS (Also see Gay Comics, Tickle, & Whee)
Modern Store Publ.: 1955 (52 pgs.; 5x7-1/4") (7¢)

	GD 2.0	VG 4.0	FN 6.0	VF 8.0	VF/NM 9.0	NM- 9.2
1	6	12	18	31	38	45

SMILEY BURNETTE WESTERN (Also see Patches #8 & Six-Gun Heroes)
Fawcett Publ.: March, 1950 - No. 4, Oct, 1950 (All photo front & back-c)

	GD 2.0	VG 4.0	FN 6.0	VF 8.0	VF/NM 9.0	NM- 9.2
1-Red Eagle begins	46	92	138	276	413	550
2-4	35	70	105	201	288	370

SMILEY (THE PSYCHOTIC BUTTON) (See Evil Ernie)
Chaos! Comics: July, 1998 - Present ($2.95, one-shots)

	GD 2.0	VG 4.0	FN 6.0	VF 8.0	VF/NM 9.0	NM- 9.2
1-Ivan Reis-a						3.00
... Holiday Special (1/99), ...'s Spring Break (4/99), ...Wrestling Special (5/99)						3.00

SMILIN' JACK (See Famous Feature Stories and Popular Comics) (Also see Super Book of Comics #1&2 and Super-Book of Comics #7&19 in the Promotional Comics section)
Dell Publishing Co.: No. 5, 1940 - No. 8, Oct-Dec, 1949

	GD 2.0	VG 4.0	FN 6.0	VF 8.0	VF/NM 9.0	NM- 9.2
Four Color 5	58	116	174	432	646	860
Four Color 10 (1940)	50	100	150	370	550	730
Large Feature Comic 12,14,25 (1941)	45	90	135	352	526	700
Four Color 4 (1942)	41	82	123	308	459	610
Four Color 14 (1943)	33	66	99	248	372	495
Four Color 36,58 (1943-44)	25	50	75	176	258	340
Four Color 80 (1945)	16	32	48	113	167	220
Four Color 149 (1947), 1 (1-3/48)	11	22	33	77	114	150
1 (1-3/48)	10	20	30	70	100	130
2	6	12	18	43	59	75
3-8 (10-12/49)	5	10	15	33	44	55

SMILING SPOOK SPUNKY (See Spunky)

SMITTY (See Popular Comics, Super Book #2, 4 & Super Comics)
Dell Publishing Co.: No. 11, 1940 - No. 7, Aug-Oct, 1949; No. 909, Apr, 1958

	GD 2.0	VG 4.0	FN 6.0	VF 8.0	VF/NM 9.0	NM- 9.2
Four Color 11 (1940)	36	72	108	261	387	510
Large Feature Comic 26 (1941)	26	52	78	189	275	360
Four Color 6 (1942)	23	46	69	167	244	320
Four Color 32 (1943)	17	34	51	121	178	235
Four Color 65 (1945)	14	28	42	99	145	190
Four Color 99 (1946)	12	24	36	82	121	160
Four Color 138 (1947)	10	20	30	72	104	135
1 (2-4/48)	10	20	30	67	96	125
2-(5-7/48)	6	12	18	38	52	65
3,4: 3-(8-10/48), 4-(11-1/48-49)	5	10	15	33	44	55
5-7, Four Color 909 (4/58)	4	8	12	27	36	45

SMOKEY BEAR (TV) (See March Of Comics #234, 362, 372, 383, 407)
Gold Key: Feb, 1970 - No. 13, Mar, 1973

	GD 2.0	VG 4.0	FN 6.0	VF 8.0	VF/NM 9.0	NM- 9.2
1	3	7	10	21	28	35
2-5	2	4	6	10	13	16
6-13	2	4	6	8	10	12

SMOKEY STOVER (See Popular Comics, Super Book #5,17,29 & Super Comics)
Dell Publishing Co.: No. 7, 1942 - No. 827, Aug, 1957

	GD 2.0	VG 4.0	FN 6.0	VF 8.0	VF/NM 9.0	NM- 9.2
Four Color 7 (1942)-Reprints	31	62	93	232	346	460
Four Color 35 (1943)	18	36	54	127	186	245
Four Color 64 (1944)	14	28	42	99	145	190
Four Color 229 (1949)	7	14	21	46	63	80
Four Color 730,827	5	10	15	36	48	60

SMOKEY THE BEAR (See Forest Fire for 1st app.)
Dell Publ. Co.: No. 653, 10/55 - No. 1214, 8/61 (See March of Comics #234)

	GD 2.0	VG 4.0	FN 6.0	VF 8.0	VF/NM 9.0	NM- 9.2
Four Color 653 (#1)	12	24	36	84	125	165
Four Color 708,754,818,932	7	14	21	50	68	85
Four Color 1016,1119,1214	5	10	15	33	44	55

SMOKY (See Movie Classics)

SMURFS (TV)
Marvel Comics: 1982 (Dec) - No. 3, 1983

	GD 2.0	VG 4.0	FN 6.0	VF 8.0	VF/NM 9.0	NM- 9.2
1-3	1	2	3	5	7	9
...Treasury Edition 1 (64 pgs.)-r/#1-3	3	6	9	18	23	28

SNAFU (Magazine)
Atlas Comics (RCM): Nov, 1955 - V2#2, Mar, 1956 (B&W)

	GD 2.0	VG 4.0	FN 6.0	VF 8.0	VF/NM 9.0	NM- 9.2
V1#1-Heath/Severin-a; Everett, Maneely-a	13	26	39	74	100	125
V2#1,2-Severin-a	10	20	30	56	73	90

SNAGGLEPUSS (TV)(See Hanna-Barbera Band Wagon, Quick Draw McGraw #5 & Spotlight #4)
Gold Key: Oct, 1962 - No. 4, Sept, 1963 (Hanna-Barbera)

	GD 2.0	VG 4.0	FN 6.0	VF 8.0	VF/NM 9.0	NM- 9.2
1	10	20	30	67	96	125
2-4	7	14	21	51	71	90

SNAKE PLISSKEN CHRONICLES, (John Carpenter's...)
Hurricane Entertainment: June, 2003 - Present ($2.99)

	GD 2.0	VG 4.0	FN 6.0	VF 8.0	VF/NM 9.0	NM- 9.2
Preview Issue (8/02, no cover price) B&W preview; John Carpenter interview						2.25
1-4: 1-Three covers; Rodriguez-a						3.00

SNAKES AND LADDERS
Eddie Campbell Comics: 2001 ($5.95, B&W, one-shot)

	GD 2.0	VG 4.0	FN 6.0	VF 8.0	VF/NM 9.0	NM- 9.2
nn-Alan Moore-s/Eddie Campbell-a						6.00

SNAP (Formerly Scoop #8; becomes Jest #10,11 & Komik Pages #10)
Harry 'A' Chesler: No. 9, 1944

	GD 2.0	VG 4.0	FN 6.0	VF 8.0	VF/NM 9.0	NM- 9.2
9-Manhunter, The Voice	20	40	60	112	156	200

SNAPPY COMICS
Cima Publ. Co. (Prize Publ.): 1945

	GD 2.0	VG 4.0	FN 6.0	VF 8.0	VF/NM 9.0	NM- 9.2
1-Airmale app.; 9 pg. Sorcerer's Apprentice adapt; Kiefer-a	34	68	102	193	274	355

SNARKY PARKER (See Life With...)

SNIFFY THE PUP
Standard Publ. (Animated Cartoons): No. 5, Nov, 1949 - No. 18, Sept, 1953

	GD 2.0	VG 4.0	FN 6.0	VF 8.0	VF/NM 9.0	NM- 9.2
5-Two Frazetta text illos	10	20	30	58	77	95
6-10	6	12	18	33	41	48
11-18	6	12	18	27	33	38

SNOOPER AND BLABBER DETECTIVES (TV) (See Whitman Comic Books)
Gold Key: Nov, 1962 - No. 3, May, 1963 (Hanna-Barbera)

	GD 2.0	VG 4.0	FN 6.0	VF 8.0	VF/NM 9.0	NM- 9.2
1	10	20	30	67	96	125
2,3	8	16	24	53	74	95

SNOW WHITE (See Christmas With... (in Promotional Comics section), Mickey Mouse Magazine, Movie Comics & Seven Dwarfs)
Dell Publishing Co.: No. 49, July, 1944 - No. 382, Mar, 1952 (Disney-Movie)

	GD 2.0	VG 4.0	FN 6.0	VF 8.0	VF/NM 9.0	NM- 9.2
Four Color 49 (...& the Seven Dwarfs)	58	116	174	434	660	885
Four Color 382 (1952)-origin; partial reprint of Four Color 49	11	22	33	77	114	150

SNOW WHITE
Marvel Comics: Jan, 1995 ($1.95, one-shot)

	GD 2.0	VG 4.0	FN 6.0	VF 8.0	VF/NM 9.0	NM- 9.2
1-r/1937 Sunday newspaper pages						2.25

SNOW WHITE AND THE SEVEN DWARFS
Whitman Publications: April, 1982 (60¢)

	GD 2.0	VG 4.0	FN 6.0	VF 8.0	VF/NM 9.0	NM- 9.2
nn-r/Four Color #49	1	2	3	4	5	7

SNOW WHITE AND THE SEVEN DWARFS GOLDEN ANNIVERSARY
Gladstone: Fall, 1987 ($2.95, magazine size, 52 pgs.)

	GD 2.0	VG 4.0	FN 6.0	VF 8.0	VF/NM 9.0	NM- 9.2
1-Contains poster	1	3	4	6	8	10

SOAP OPERA LOVE
Charlton Comics: Feb, 1983 - No. 3, June, 1983

	GD 2.0	VG 4.0	FN 6.0	VF 8.0	VF/NM 9.0	NM- 9.2
1-3-Low print run	3	6	9	18	24	30

SOAP OPERA ROMANCES
Charlton Comics: July, 1982 - No. 5, March, 1983

	GD 2.0	VG 4.0	FN 6.0	VF 8.0	VF/NM 9.0	NM- 9.2
1-5-Nurse Betsy Crane-r; low print run	3	6	9	18	24	30

SOCK MONKEY
Dark Horse Comics: Sept, 1998 - No. 2, Oct, 1998 ($2.95/$2.99, B&W)

	GD 2.0	VG 4.0	FN 6.0	VF 8.0	VF/NM 9.0	NM- 9.2
1,2-Tony Millionaire-s/a						4.00

Vol. 2 -(Tony Millionaire's Sock Monkey) July, 1999 - No. 2, Aug, 1999

	GD 2.0	VG 4.0	FN 6.0	VF 8.0	VF/NM 9.0	NM- 9.2
1,2						3.00

Vol. 3 -(Tony Millionaire's Sock Monkey) Nov, 2000 - No. 2, Dec, 2000

	GD 2.0	VG 4.0	FN 6.0	VF 8.0	VF/NM 9.0	NM- 9.2
1,2						3.00

Vol. 4 -(Tony Millionaire's Sock Monkey) May, 2003 - No. 2, Aug, 2003

Sojourn #2 © CRO

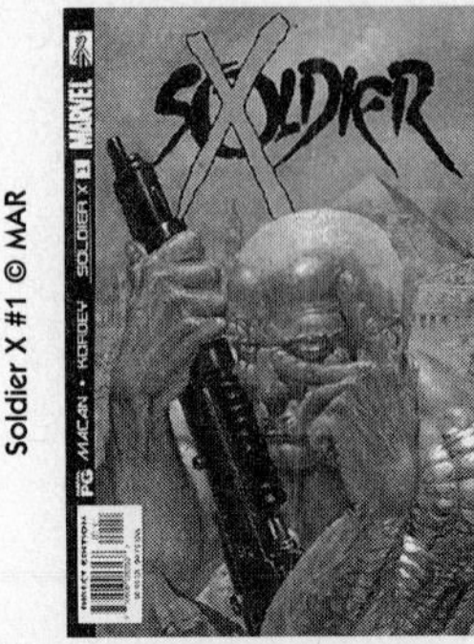

Soldier X #1 © MAR

The Solution #14 © MAL

GD 2.0 | VG 4.0 | FN 6.0 | VF 8.0 | VF/NM 9.0 | NM- 9.2

1,2 3.00

SO DARK THE ROSE
CFD Productions: Oct, 1995 ($2.95)

1-Wrightson-c 4.00

SOJOURN
White Cliffs Publ. Co.: Sept, 1977 - No. 2, 1978 ($1.50, B&W & color, tabloid size)

1,2: 1-Tor by Kubert, Eagle by Severin, E. V. Race, Private Investigator by Doug Wildey, T. C. Mars by Aragonés begin plus other strips 1 3 4 6 8 10

NOTE: Most copies came folded. Unfolded copies are worth 50% more.

SOJOURN
CrossGeneration Comics: July, 2001 - Present ($2.95)

Prequel -Ron Marz-s/Greg Land-c/a; preview pages 3.00
1-Ron Marz-s/Greg Land-c/a in most 6.00
2,3 5.00
4-24: 7-Immonen-a. 12-Brigman-a. 17-Lopresti-a. 21-Luke Ross-a 3.25
25-31: 25-$1.00-c 3.00
...: From the Ashes TPB (2001, $19.95) r/#1-6; Land painted-c 20.00
...: The Dragon's Tale TPB (2002, $15.95) r/#7-12; Jusko painted-c 16.00
...: The Warrior's Tale TPB (2003, $15.95) r/#13-18 16.00
Vol. 4:The Thief's Tale (2003, $15.95) r/#19-24 16.00
Traveler Vol.1,2 ($9.95) digest-sized reprints of TPBs 10.00

SOLAR (...Man of the Atom) (Also see Doctor Solar)
Valiant/Acclaim Comics (Valiant): Sept, 1991 - No. 60, Apr, 1996 ($1.75-$2.50, 44 pgs.)

1-Layton-a(i) on Solar; Barry Windsor-Smith-c/a 1 2 3 5 6 8
2-9: 2-Layton-a(i) on Solar, B. Smith-a. 3-1st app. Harada (11/91). 7-vs. X-O Armor 5.00
10-(6/92, $3.95)-1st app. Eternal Warrior (6 pgs.); black embossed-c; origin & 1st app. Geoff McHenry (Geomancer) 1 2 3 5 7 9
10-($3.95)-2nd printing 4.00
11-15: 11-1st full app. Eternal Warrior. 12,13-Unity x-overs. 14-1st app. Fred Bender (becomes Dr. Eclipse). 15-2nd Dr. Eclipse 3.00
16-60: 17-X-O Manowar app. 23-Solar splits. 29-1st Valiant Vision book. 33-Valiant Vision; bound-in trading card. 38-Chaos Effect Epsilion Pt.1. 46-52-Dan Jurgens-a(p)/scripts w/Giordano-i. 53,54-Jurgens scripts only. 60-Giffen scripts; Jeff Johnson-a(p) 2.50
0-($9.95, trade paperback)-r/Alpha and Omega origin story; polybagged w/poster 10.00
...:Second Death (1994, $9.95)-r/issues #1-4. 10.00

NOTE: *#1-10 all have free 8 pg. insert "Alpha and Omega" which is a 10 chapter Solar origin story. All 10 center-folds can pieced together to show climax of story.* ***Ditko*** *a-11p, 14p.* ***Giordano*** *a-46, 47, 48, 49, 50, 51, 52i.* ***Johnson*** *a-60p.* ***Jurgens*** *a-46, 47, 48, 49, 50 , 51, 52p.* ***Layton*** *a-1-3i; c-2i, 11i, 17i, 25i.* ***Miller*** *c-12.* ***Quesada*** *c-17p, 20-23p, 29p.* ***Simonson*** *c-13.* ***B. Smith*** *a-1-10; c-1, 3, 5, 7, 19i.* ***Thibert*** *c-22i, 23i.*

SOLAR LORD
Image Comics: Mar, 1999 - No. 7, Sept, 1999 ($2.50)

1-7-Khoo Fuk Lung-s/a 2.50

SOLARMAN (See Pendulum Ill. Originals)
Marvel Comics: Jan, 1989 - No. 2, May, 1990 ($1.00, limited series)

1,2 2.25

SOLAR, MAN OF THE ATOM (Man of the Atom on cover)
Acclaim Comics (Valiant Heroes): Vol. 2, May, 1997 ($3.95, one-shot, 46 pgs) (1st Valiant Heroes Special Event)

Vol. 2-Reintro Solar; Ninjak cameo; Warren Ellis scripts; Darick Robertson-a 4.00

SOLAR, MAN OF THE ATOM: HELL ON EARTH
Acclaim Comics (Valiant Heroes): Jan, 1998 - No. 4 ($2.50, limited series)

1-4-Priest-s/ Zircher-a(p) 2.50

SOLAR, MAN OF THE ATOM: REVELATIONS
Acclaim Comics (Valiant Heroes): Nov, 1997 ($3.95, one-shot, 46 pgs.)

1-Krueger-s/ Zircher-a(p) 4.00

SOLDIER & MARINE COMICS (Fightin' Army #16 on)
Charlton Comics (Toby Press of Conn. V1#11): No. 11, Dec, 1954 - No. 15, Aug, 1955; V2#9, Dec, 1956

V1#11 (12/54)-Bob Powell-a 9 18 27 49 62 75
V1#12(2/55)-15: 12-Photo-c 6 12 18 28 34 40
V2#9(Formerly Never Again; Jerry Drummer V2#10 on) 5 10 15 24 30 35

SOLDIER COMICS
Fawcett Publications: Jan, 1952 - No. 11, Sept, 1953

1 13 26 39 76 103 130
2 8 16 24 43 54 65
3-5 8 16 24 40 50 60
6-11: 8-Illo. in **POP** 7 14 21 37 46 55

SOLDIERS OF FORTUNE
American Comics Group (Creston Publ. Corp.): Mar-Apr, 1951 - No. 13, Feb-Mar, 1953

1-Capt. Crossbones by Shelly, Ace Carter, Lance Larson begin 24 48 72 135 190 245
2 14 28 42 79 107 135
3-10: 6-Bondage-c 12 24 36 69 92 115
11-13 (War format) 8 16 24 43 54 65

NOTE: ***Shelly*** *a-1-3, 5.* ***Whitney*** *a-6, 8-11, 13; c-1-3, 5, 6.*

SOLDIERS OF FREEDOM
Americomics: 1987 - No. 2, 1987 ($1.75)

1,2 3.00

SOLDIER X (Continued from Cable)
Marvel Comics: Sept, 2002 - No. 12, Aug, 2003 ($2.99/$2.25)

1,10,11,12-($2.99) 1-Kordey-a/Macan-s. 10-Bollers-s/Ranson-a 3.00
2-9-($2.25) 2.25

SOLITAIRE (Also See Prime V2#6-8)
Malibu Comics (Ultraverse): Nov, 1993 - No. 12, Dec, 1994 ($1.95)

1-($2.50)-Collector's edition bagged w/playing card 2.50
1-12: 1-Regular edition w/o playing card. 2,4-Break-Thru x-over. 3-2 pg. origin The Night Man. 4-Gatefold-c. 5-Two pg. origin the Strangers 2.25

SOLO
Marvel Comics: Sept, 1994 - No. 4, Dec, 1994 ($1.75, limited series)

1-4: Spider-Man app. 2.25

SOLO (Movie)
Dark Horse Comics: July, 1996 - No. 2, Aug, 1996 ($2.50, limited series)

1,2: Adaptation of film; photo-c 2.50

SOLO AVENGERS (Becomes Avenger Spotlight #21 on)
Marvel Comics: Dec, 1987 - No. 20, July, 1989 (75¢/$1.00)

1-Jim Lee-a on back-up story 3.00
2-20: 11-Intro Bobcat 2.50

SOLOMON AND SHEBA (Movie)
Dell Publishing Co.: No. 1070, Jan-Mar, 1960

Four Color 1070-Sekowsky-a; photo-c 10 20 30 70 100 130

SOLOMON KANE (Based on the Robert E. Howard character. Also see Blackthorne 3-D Series #60 & Marvel Premiere)
Marvel Comics: Sept, 1985 - No. 6, July, 1986 (Limited series)

1-6: 1-Double size. 3-6-Williamson-a(i) 3.00

SOLUS
CG Entertainment, Inc.: Apr, 2003 - No. 8, Jan, 2004 ($2.95)

1-8: 1-4,6,7-George Pérez-a/c; Barbara Kesel-s. 5-Ryan-a. 8-Kirk-a 3.00
Vol. 1: Genesis (1/04, $15.95) r/#1-6 16.00

SOLUTION, THE
Malibu Comics (Ultraverse): Sept, 1993 - No. 17, Feb, 1995 ($1.95)

1,3-15: 1-Intro Meathook, Deathdance, Black Tiger, Tech. 4-Break-Thru x-over; gatefold-c. 5-2 pg. origin The Strangers. 11-Brereton-c 2.50
1-($2.50)-Newsstand ed. polybagged w/trading card 2.50
1-Ultra 5000 Limited silver foil 4.00
0-Obtained w/Rune #0 by sending coupons from 11 comics 3.00
2-($2.50, 48 pgs.)-Rune flip-c/story by B. Smith; The Mighty Magnor 1 pg. strip by Aragonés 2.50
16 ($3.50)-Flip-c Ultraverse Premiere #10 3.50
17 ($2.50) 2.50

SOMERSET HOLMES (See Eclipse Graphic Novel Series)
Pacific Comics/ Eclipse Comics No. 5, 6: Sept, 1983 - No. 6, Dec, 1984 ($1.50, Baxter paper)

1-6: 1-Brent Anderson-c/a. Cliff Hanger by Williams in all 3.00

SOMETHING WICKED
Image Comics: Oct, 2003 - Present ($2.95, B&W)

1,2-Jerry Beck-a 3.00

SONG OF THE SOUTH (See Brer Rabbit)

SONIC & KNUCKLES
Archie Comics: Aug, 1995 ($2.00)

1 6.00

SONIC DISRUPTORS
DC Comics: Dec, 1987 - No. 7, July, 1988 ($1.75, unfinished limited series)

Sonic Super Special #7 © SEGA

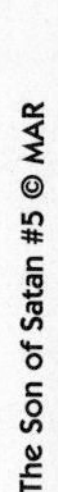

The Son of Satan #5 © MAR

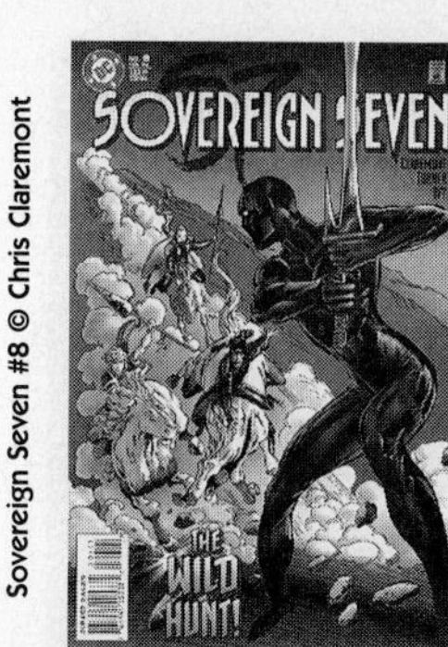

Sovereign Seven #8 © Chris Claremont

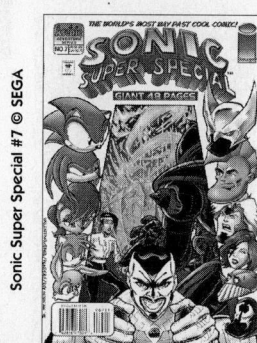

	GD 2.0	VG 4.0	FN 6.0	VF 8.0	VF/NM 9.0	NM- 9.2
1-7						3.00

SONIC'S FRIENDLY NEMESIS KNUCKLES
Archie Publications: July, 1996 - No. 3, Sept, 1996 ($1.50, limited series)

	GD 2.0	VG 4.0	FN 6.0	VF 8.0	VF/NM 9.0	NM- 9.2
1-3						4.00

SONIC SUPER SPECIAL
Archie Publications: 1997 - Present ($2.00/$2.25/$2.29, 48 pgs)

	GD 2.0	VG 4.0	FN 6.0	VF 8.0	VF/NM 9.0	NM- 9.2
1-3						4.00
4-6,8-15: 10-Sabrina-c/app. 15-Sin City spoof						3.00
7-(w/Image) Spawn, Maxx, Savage Dragon-c/app.; Valentino-a						3.00

SONIC THE HEDGEHOG (TV, video game)
Archie Comics: No. 0, Feb, 1993 - No. 3, May, 1993 ($1.25, mini-series)

	GD 2.0	VG 4.0	FN 6.0	VF 8.0	VF/NM 9.0	NM- 9.2
0(2/93),1: Shaw-a(p) & covers on all	3	6	9	18	23	28
2,3	2	4	6	11	14	18
Beginnings TPB (2003, $10.95) r/#0-3						11.00

SONIC THE HEDGEHOG (TV, video game)
Archie Comics: July, 1993 - Present ($1.25/$1.50/$1.75/$1.79/$1.99/$2.19)

	GD 2.0	VG 4.0	FN 6.0	VF 8.0	VF/NM 9.0	NM- 9.2
1	3	7	10	21	28	35
2,3	2	4	6	14	18	22
4-10: 8-Neon ink-c.	2	4	6	11	14	18
11-20	2	4	6	10	12	15
21-30 ($1.50): 25-Silver ink-c	1	3	4	6	8	10
31-50	1	2	3	4	5	7
51-93						3.50
94-131: 117-Begin $2.19-c						2.25
Triple Trouble Special (10/95, $2.00, 48 pgs.)						4.50

SONIC VS. KNUCKLES "BATTLE ROYAL" SPECIAL
Archie Publications: 1997 ($2.00, one-shot)

	GD 2.0	VG 4.0	FN 6.0	VF 8.0	VF/NM 9.0	NM- 9.2
1						4.00

SON OF AMBUSH BUG (See Ambush Bug)
DC Comics: July, 1986 - No. 6, Dec, 1986 (75¢)

	GD 2.0	VG 4.0	FN 6.0	VF 8.0	VF/NM 9.0	NM- 9.2
1-6: Giffen-c/a in all. 5-Bissette-a.						2.25

SON OF BLACK BEAUTY (Also see Black Beauty)
Dell Publishing Co.: No. 510, Oct, 1953 - No. 566, June, 1954

	GD 2.0	VG 4.0	FN 6.0	VF 8.0	VF/NM 9.0	NM- 9.2
Four Color 510, 566	4	8	12	25	33	42

SON OF FLUBBER (See Movie Comics)

SON OF MUTANT WORLD
Fantagor Press: 1990 - No. 5, 1990? ($2.00, bi-monthly)

	GD 2.0	VG 4.0	FN 6.0	VF 8.0	VF/NM 9.0	NM- 9.2
1-5: 1-3: Corben-c/a. 4,5 ($1.75, B&W)						3.00

SON OF ORIGINS OF MARVEL COMICS (See Fireside Book Series)

SON OF SATAN (Also see Ghost Rider #1 & Marvel Spotlight #12)
Marvel Comics Group: Dec, 1975 - No. 8, Feb, 1977 (25¢)

	GD 2.0	VG 4.0	FN 6.0	VF 8.0	VF/NM 9.0	NM- 9.2
1-Mooney-a; Kane-c(p), Starlin splash(p)	3	6	9	17	21	26
2,6-8: 2-Origin The Possessor. 8-Heath-a	2	4	6	10	12	15
3-5-(Regular 25¢ editions)(4-8/76): 5-Russell-p	2	4	6	10	12	15
3-5-(30¢-c variants, limited distribution)	2	4	6	14	18	22

SON OF SINBAD (Also see Abbott & Costello & Daring Adventures)
St. John Publishing Co.: Feb, 1950

	GD 2.0	VG 4.0	FN 6.0	VF 8.0	VF/NM 9.0	NM- 9.2
1-Kubert-c/a	40	80	120	240	340	440

SON OF SUPERMAN (Elseworlds)
DC Comics: 1999 ($14.95, prestige format, one-shot)

	GD 2.0	VG 4.0	FN 6.0	VF 8.0	VF/NM 9.0	NM- 9.2
nn-Chaykin & Tischman-s/Williams III & Gray-a						15.00

SON OF TOMAHAWK (See Tomahawk)

SON OF VULCAN (Formerly Mysteries of Unexplored Worlds #1-48; Thunderbolt V3#51 on)
Charlton Comics: V2#49, Nov, 1965 - V2#50, Jan, 1966

	GD 2.0	VG 4.0	FN 6.0	VF 8.0	VF/NM 9.0	NM- 9.2
V2#49,50: 50-Roy Thomas scripts (1st pro work)	3	6	9	19	25	32

SON OF YUPPIES FROM HELL (See Yuppies From Hell)
Marvel Comics: 1990 ($3.50, B&W, squarebound, 52 pgs.)

	GD 2.0	VG 4.0	FN 6.0	VF 8.0	VF/NM 9.0	NM- 9.2
nn						3.50

SONS OF KATIE ELDER (See Movie Classics)

SORCERY (See Chilling Adventures in... & Red Circle...)

SORORITY SECRETS
Toby Press: July, 1954

	GD 2.0	VG 4.0	FN 6.0	VF 8.0	VF/NM 9.0	NM- 9.2
1	9	18	27	52	66	80

SOUL OF A SAMURAI
Image Comics: May, 2003 - No. 4 ($5.95, 8 1/4" x 5 3/4", limited series)

	GD 2.0	VG 4.0	FN 6.0	VF 8.0	VF/NM 9.0	NM- 9.2
1-3-Will Dixon-s/a						6.00

SOULQUEST
Innovation: Apr, 1989 ($3.95, squarebound, 52 pgs.)

	GD 2.0	VG 4.0	FN 6.0	VF 8.0	VF/NM 9.0	NM- 9.2
1-Blackshard app.						4.00

SOUL SAGA
Image Comics (Top Cow): Feb, 2000 - No. 5, Apr, 2001 ($2.50)

	GD 2.0	VG 4.0	FN 6.0	VF 8.0	VF/NM 9.0	NM- 9.2
1-5: 1-Madureira-c; Platt & Batt-a						2.50

SOULSEARCHERS AND COMPANY
Claypool Comics: June, 1995 - Present ($2.50, B&W)

	GD 2.0	VG 4.0	FN 6.0	VF 8.0	VF/NM 9.0	NM- 9.2
1-10: Peter David scripts						5.00
11-25						3.00
26-59						2.50

SOULWIND
Image Comics: Mar, 1997 - No. 8 ($2.95, B&W, limited series)

	GD 2.0	VG 4.0	FN 6.0	VF 8.0	VF/NM 9.0	NM- 9.2
1-8: 5-"The Day I Tried To Live" pt. 1						3.00
Book Five; The August Ones (Oni Press, 3/01, $8.50)						8.50
...The Kid From Planet Earth (1997, $9.95, TPB)						10.00
...The Kid From Planet Earth (Oni Press, 1/00, $8.50, TPB)						8.50
...The Day I Tried to Live (Oni Press, 4/00, $8.50, TPB)						8.50
The Complete Soulwind TPB ($29.95, 11/03, 8" x 5 1/2") r/Oni Books #1-5						30.00

SOUPY SALES COMIC BOOK (TV)(The Official...)
Archie Publications: 1965

	GD 2.0	VG 4.0	FN 6.0	VF 8.0	VF/NM 9.0	NM- 9.2
1	10	20	30	67	96	125

SOUTHERN KNIGHTS, THE (See Crusaders #1)
Guild Publ/Fictioneer Books: No. 2, 1983 - No. 41, 1993 (B&W)

	GD 2.0	VG 4.0	FN 6.0	VF 8.0	VF/NM 9.0	NM- 9.2
2-Magazine size	1	2	3	5	6	8
3-35, 37-41						3.00
36-($3.50-c)						3.50
Dread Halloween Special 1, Primer Special 1 (Spring, 1989, $2.25)						2.25
Graphic Novels #1-4						4.00

SOVEREIGN SEVEN (Also see Showcase '95 #12)
DC Comics: July, 1995 - No. 36, July, 1998 ($1.95) (1st creator-owned mainstream DC comic)

	GD 2.0	VG 4.0	FN 6.0	VF 8.0	VF/NM 9.0	NM- 9.2
1-1st app. Sovereign Seven (Reflex, Indigo, Cascade, Finale, Cruiser, Network & Rampart); 1st app. Maitresse; Darkseid app.; Chris Claremont-s & Dwayne Turner-c/a begins						3.00
1-Gold						8.00
1-Platinum						40.00
2-25: 2-Wolverine cameo. 4-Neil Gaiman cameo. 5,8-Batman app. 7-Ramirez cameo (from the movie Highlander). 9-Humphrey Bogart cameo from Casablanca. 10-Impulse app; Manoli Wetherell & Neal Conan cameo from Uncanny X-Men #226. 11-Robin app. 16-Final Night. 24-Superman app. 25-Power Girl app.						2.25
26-36: 26-Begin $2.25-c. 28-Impulse-c/app.						2.25
Annual 1 (1995, $3.95)-Year One story; Big Barda & Lobo app.; Jeff Johnson-c/a						4.00
Annual 2 (1996, $2.95)-Legends of the Dead Earth; Leonardi-c/a						3.50
...Plus 1(2/97, $2.95)-Legion-c/app.						3.50
TPB-($12.95) r/#1-5, Annual #1 & Showcase '95 #12						13.00

SOVIET SUPER SOLDIERS
Marvel Comics: Nov, 1992 ($2.00, one-shot)

	GD 2.0	VG 4.0	FN 6.0	VF 8.0	VF/NM 9.0	NM- 9.2
1-Marvel's Russian characters; Median & Saltares-a						2.25

SPACE: ABOVE AND BEYOND (TV)
Topps Comics: Jan, 1996 - No. 3, Mar, 1996 ($2.95, limited series)

	GD 2.0	VG 4.0	FN 6.0	VF 8.0	VF/NM 9.0	NM- 9.2
1-3: Adaptation of pilot episode; Steacy-c.						3.00

SPACE: ABOVE AND BEYOND--THE GAUNTLET (TV)
Topps Comics: May, 1996 -No. 2, June, 1996 ($2.95, limited series)

	GD 2.0	VG 4.0	FN 6.0	VF 8.0	VF/NM 9.0	NM- 9.2
1,2						3.00

SPACE ACE (Also see Manhunt!)
Magazine Enterprises: No. 5, 1952

	GD 2.0	VG 4.0	FN 6.0	VF 8.0	VF/NM 9.0	NM- 9.2
5(A-1 #61)-Guardineer-a	52	104	156	312	466	620

SPACE ACE: DEFENDER OF THE UNIVERSE (Based on the Don Bluth video game)
CrossGen Comics: Oct, 2003 - No. 6 ($2.95, limited series)

	GD 2.0	VG 4.0	FN 6.0	VF 8.0	VF/NM 9.0	NM- 9.2
1,2-Kirkman-s/Borges-a						3.00

SPACE ACTION
Ace Magazines (Junior Books): June, 1952 - No. 3, Oct, 1952

	GD 2.0	VG 4.0	FN 6.0	VF 8.0	VF/NM 9.0	NM- 9.2
1-Cameron-a in all (1 story)	74	148	222	463	694	925

Space Adventures V3#29 © CC

Space Comics #4 © AVON

Spaceman #4 © MAR

GD 2.0 | VG 4.0 | FN 6.0 | VF 8.0 | VF/NM 9.0 | NM- 9.2

2,3 55 110 165 330 495 660

SPACE ADVENTURES (War At Sea #22 on)
Capitol Stories/Charlton Comics: 7/52 - No. 21, 8/56; No. 23, 5/58 - No. 59, 11/64; V3#60, 10/67; V1#2, 7/68 - V1#8, 7/69; No. 9, 5/78 - No. 13, 3/79

1 52 104 156 312 466 620
2 28 56 84 159 225 290
3-5: 4,6-Flying saucer-c/stories 22 44 66 127 176 225
6-9: 7-Sex change story "Transformation". 8-Robot-c. 9-A-Bomb panel 20 40 60 112 156 200
10,11-Ditko-c/a. 10-Robot-c. 11-Two Ditko stories 52 104 156 312 466 620
12-Ditko-c (classic) 60 120 180 375 563 750
13-(Fox-r, 10-11/54); Blue Beetle-c/story 16 32 48 92 126 160
14,15,17,18: 14-Blue Beetle-c/story; Fox-r (12-1/54-55, last pre-code). 15,17,18-Rocky Jones-c/s.(TV); 15-Part photo-c 21 42 63 118 164 210
16-Krigstein-a; Rocky Jones-c/story (TV) 23 46 69 129 180 230
19 14 28 42 81 111 140
20-Reprints Fawcett's "Destination Moon" 27 54 81 153 214 275
21-(8/56) (no #22)(Becomes War At Sea) 14 28 42 81 111 140
23-(5/58; formerly Nyoka, The Jungle Girl)-Reprints Fawcett's "Destination Moon" 24 48 72 135 190 245
24,25,31,32-Ditko-a. 24-Severin-a(signed "LePoer") 21 42 63 118 164 210
26,27-Ditko-a(4) each. 26,28-Flying saucer-c 22 44 66 124 172 220
28-30 10 20 30 56 73 90
33-Origin/1st app. Capt. Atom by Ditko (3/60) 38 76 114 285 430 575
34-40,42-All Captain Atom by Ditko 16 32 48 113 167 220
41,43,45-59: 45-Mercury Man app. 5 10 15 33 44 55
44-1st app. Mercury Man 5 10 15 36 48 60
V3#60(#1, 10/67)-Origin & 1st app. Paul Mann & The Saucers From the Future 5 10 15 36 48 60
2,5,6,8 (1968-69)-Ditko-a: 2-Aparo-c/a 3 7 10 21 28 35
3,4,7: 4-Aparo-c/a 3 6 9 16 20 25
9-13(1978-79)-Capt. Atom-r/Space Adventures by Ditko; 9-Reprints origin/1st app. Capt. Atom from #33 5.00

NOTE: *Aparo a-V3#60. c-V3#8.* ***Ditko*** *c-12, 31-42.* ***Giordano*** *c-3, 4, 7-9, 18p.* ***Krigstein*** *c-15.* ***Shuster*** *a-11. Issues 13 & 14 have Blue Beetle logos; #15-18 have Rocky Jones logos.*

SPACE ARK
Americomics (AC Comics)/ Apple Comics #3 on: June, 1985 - No. 5, Sept, 1987 ($1.75)

1-5: Funny animal (#1,2-color; #3-5-B&W) 2.25

SPACE BUSTERS
Ziff-Davis Publ. Co.: Spring, 1952 - No. 2, Fall, 1952

1-Krigstein-a(3); Painted-c by Norman Saunders 80 160 240 500 750 1000
2-Kinstler-a(2 pgs.); Saunders painted-c 63 126 189 394 590 785

NOTE: ***Anderson*** *a-2. Bondage c-2.*

SPACE CADET (See Tom Corbett,...)

SPACE CIRCUS
Dark Horse Comics: July, 2000 - No. 4, Oct, 2000 ($2.95, limited series)

1-4-Aragonés-a/Evanier-s 3.00

SPACE COMICS (Formerly Funny Tunes)
Avon Periodicals: No. 4, Mar-Apr, 1954 - No. 5, May-June, 1954

4,5-Space Mouse, Peter Rabbit, Super Pup (formerly Spotty the Pup), & Merry Mouse continue from Funny Tunes 8 16 24 40 50 60
I.W. Reprint #8 (nd)-Space Mouse-r 2 4 6 8 10 12

SPACED
Anthony Smith Publ. #1,2/Unbridled Ambition/Eclipse Comics #10 on: 1982 - No. 13, 1988 ($1.25/$1.50, B&W, quarterly)

1-($1.25-c) 3.00
2-13, Special Edition (1983, Mimeo) 2.25

SPACE DETECTIVE
Avon Periodicals: July, 1951 - No. 4, July, 1952

1-Rod Hathway, Space Detective begins, ends #4; Wood-c/a(3)-23 pgs.; "Opium Smugglers of Venus" drug story; Lucky Dale-r/Saint #4 108 216 324 675 1013 1350
2-Tales from the Shadow Squad story; Wood/Orlando-c; Wood inside layouts; "Slave Ship of Saturn" story 80 160 240 500 750 1000
3,4: 3-Kinstler-c. 4-Kinstlerish-a by McCann 40 80 120 240 358 475
I.W. Reprint #1(Reprints #2), 8(Reprints cover #1 & part Famous Funnies #191) 4 8 12 27 36 45
I.W. Reprint #9-Exist? 4 8 12 27 36 45

SPACE EXPLORER (See March of Comics #202)

SPACE FAMILY ROBINSON (TV)(...Lost in Space #15-37, ...Lost in Space On Space Station One #38 on)(See Gold Key Champion)
Gold Key: Dec, 1962 - No. 36, Oct, 1969; No. 37, 10/73 - No. 54, 11/78; No. 55, 3/81 - No. 59, 5/82 (All painted covers)

1-(Low distribution); Spiegle-a in all 25 50 75 181 266 350
2(3/63)-Family becomes lost in space 13 26 39 90 133 175
3-5 8 16 24 58 82 105
6-10: 6-Captain Venture back-up stories begin 7 14 21 51 71 90
11-20: 14-(10/65). 15-Title change (1/66) 5 10 15 36 48 60
21-36: 28-Last 12¢ issue. 36-Captain Venture ends 4 8 12 25 33 42
37-48: 37-Origin retold 2 4 6 10 13 16
49-59: Reprints #49,50,55-59 1 3 4 6 8 10

NOTE: *The TV show first aired on 9/15/65. Title changed after TV show debuted.*

SPACE FAMILY ROBINSON (See March of Comics #320, 328, 352, 404, 414)

SPACE GHOST (TV) (Also see Golden Comics Digest #2 & Hanna-Barbera Super TV Heroes #3-7)
Gold Key: March, 1967 (Hanna-Barbera) (TV debut was 9/10/66)

1 (10199-703)-Spiegle-a 33 66 99 248 374 500

SPACE GHOST (TV cartoon)
Comico: Mar, 1987 ($3.50, deluxe format, one-shot) (Hanna-Barbera)

1-Steve Rude-c/a 1 2 3 5 6 8

SPACE GIANTS, THE (TV cartoon)
FBN Publications: 1979 ($1.00, B&W, one-shots)

1-Based on Japanese TV series 2 4 6 9 11 14

SPACEHAWK
Dark Horse Comics: 1989 - No. 3, 1990 ($2.00, B&W)

1-3-Wolverton-c/a(r) plus new stories by others. 4.00

SPACE JAM
DC Comics: 1996 ($5.95, one-shot, movie adaption)

1-Wraparound photo cover of Michael Jordan 1 2 3 5 6 8

SPACE KAT-ETS (...in 3-D)
Power Publishing Co.: Dec, 1953 (25¢, came w/glasses)

1 34 68 102 193 274 355

SPACEKNIGHTS
Marvel Comics: Oct, 2000 - No. 5, Feb, 2001 ($2.99, limited series)

1-5-Starlin-s/Batista-a 3.00

SPACEMAN (Speed Carter...)
Atlas Comics (CnPC): Sept, 1953 - No. 6, July, 1954

1-Grey tone-c 66 132 198 413 619 825
2 43 86 129 258 389 520
3-6: 4-A-Bomb explosion-c 40 80 120 240 340 440

NOTE: ***Everett*** *c-1, 3.* ***Heath*** *a-1.* ***Maneely*** *a-1(3), 2(4), 3(3), 4-6; c-5, 6.* ***Romita*** *a-1.* ***Sekowsky*** *c-4.* ***Sekowsky/Abel*** *a-4(3).* ***Tuska*** *a-5(3).*

SPACE MAN
Dell Publ. Co.: No. 1253, 1-3/62 - No. 8, 3-5/64; No. 9, 7/72 - No. 10, 10/72

Four Color 1253 (#1)(1-3/62)(15¢-c) 8 16 24 58 82 105
2,3: 2-(15¢-c). 3-(12¢-c) 5 10 15 33 44 55
4-8-(12¢-c) 4 8 12 25 33 42
9,10-(15¢-c): 9-Reprints #1253. 10-Reprints #2 2 4 6 9 11 14

SPACEMAN (From the Atomics)
Oni Press: July, 2002 ($2.95, one-shot)

1-Mike Allred-s/a; Lawrence Marvit additional art 3.00

SPACE MOUSE (Also see Funny Tunes & Space Comics)
Avon Periodicals: April, 1953 - No. 5, Apr-May, 1954

1 10 20 30 56 73 90
2 7 14 21 35 43 50
3-5 6 12 18 28 34 40

SPACE MOUSE (Walter Lantz...#1; see Comic Album #17)
Dell Publishing Co./Gold Key: No. 1132, Aug-Oct, 1960 - No. 5, Nov, 1963 (Walter Lantz)

Four Color 1132,1244, 1(11/62)(G.K.) 5 10 15 36 48 60
2-5 4 8 12 28 38 48

SPACE MYSTERIES
I.W. Enterprises: 1964 (Reprints)

1-r/Journey Into Unknown Worlds #4 w/new-c 3 6 9 18 23 28
8,9: 9-r/Planet Comics #73 3 6 9 18 23 28

SPACE: 1999 (TV) (Also see Power Record Comics)

Space Patrol #2 © Z-D

Spanner's Galaxy #3 © DC

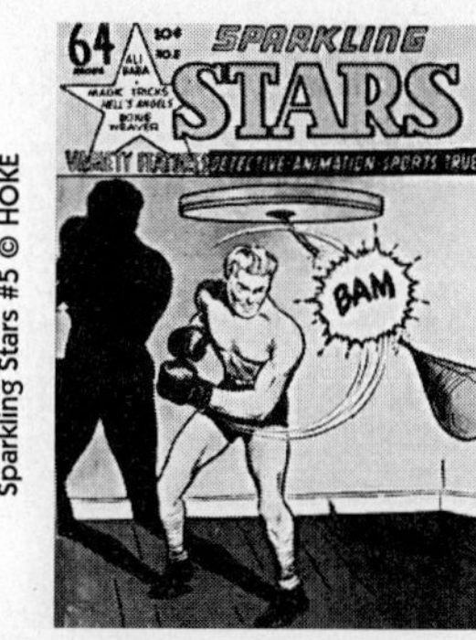

Sparkling Stars #5 © HOKE

Charlton Comics: Nov, 1975 - No. 7, Nov, 1976

	GD 2.0	VG 4.0	FN 6.0	VF 8.0	VF/NM 9.0	NM- 9.2
1-Origin Moonbase Alpha; Staton-c/a	2	4	6	11	14	18
2,7: 2-Staton-a	2	4	6	8	10	12
3-6: All Byrne-a; c-3,5,6	2	4	6	11	14	18

SPACE: 1999 (TV)(Magazine)
Charlton Comics: Nov, 1975 - No. 8, Nov, 1976 (B&W) (#7 shows #6 inside)

	GD 2.0	VG 4.0	FN 6.0	VF 8.0	VF/NM 9.0	NM- 9.2
1-Origin Moonbase Alpha; Morrow-c/a	2	4	6	12	16	20
2-8: 2,3-Morrow-c/a. 4-6-Morrow-c. 5,8-Morrow-a	2	4	6	10	12	15

SPACE PATROL (TV)
Ziff-Davis Publishing Co. (Approved Comics): Summer, 1952 - No. 2, Oct-Nov, 1952 (Painted-c by Norman Saunders)

	GD 2.0	VG 4.0	FN 6.0	VF 8.0	VF/NM 9.0	NM- 9.2
1-Krigstein-a	88	176	264	550	825	1100
2-Krigstein-a(3)	64	128	192	400	600	800

SPACE PIRATES (See Archie Giant Series #533)

SPACE RANGER (See Mystery in Space #92, Showcase #15 & Tales of the Unexpected)

SPACE SQUADRON (In the Days of the Rockets)(Becomes Space Worlds #6)
Marvel/Atlas Comics (ACI): June, 1951 - No. 5, Feb, 1952

	GD 2.0	VG 4.0	FN 6.0	VF 8.0	VF/NM 9.0	NM- 9.2
1-Space team; Brodsky c-1,5	66	132	198	413	617	820
2: Tuska c-2-4	55	110	165	344	515	685
3-5: 3-Capt. Jet Dixon by Tuska(3). 4-Weird advs. begin	46	92	138	276	413	550

SPACE THRILLERS
Avon Periodicals: 1954 (25¢ Giant)

	GD 2.0	VG 4.0	FN 6.0	VF 8.0	VF/NM 9.0	NM- 9.2
nn-(Scarce)-Robotmen of the Lost Planet; contains 3 rebound comics of The Saint & Strange Worlds. Contents could vary	115	230	345	719	1080	1440

SPACE TRIP TO THE MOON (See Space Adventures #23)

SPACE USAGI
Mirage Studios: June, 1992 - No. 3, 1992 ($2.00, B&W, mini-series)
V2#1, Nov, 1993 - V2#3, Jan, 1994 ($2.75)

	GD 2.0	VG 4.0	FN 6.0	VF 8.0	VF/NM 9.0	NM- 9.2
1-3: Stan Sakai-c/a/scripts, V2#1-3						3.00

SPACE USAGI
Dark Horse Comics: Jan, 1996 - No. 3, Mar, 1996 ($2.95, B&W, limited series)

	GD 2.0	VG 4.0	FN 6.0	VF 8.0	VF/NM 9.0	NM- 9.2
1-3: Stan Sakai-c/a/scripts						3.00

SPACE WAR (Fightin' Five #28 on)
Charlton Comics: Oct, 1959 - No. 27, Mar, 1964; No. 28, Mar, 1978 - No. 34, 3/79

	GD 2.0	VG 4.0	FN 6.0	VF 8.0	VF/NM 9.0	NM- 9.2
V1#1-Giordano-c begin, end #3	14	28	42	99	145	190
2,3	8	16	24	53	74	95
4-6,8,10-Ditko-c/a	14	28	42	99	145	190
7,9,11-15: Last 10¢ issue?	6	12	18	38	52	65
16-27 (3/64): 18,19-Robot-c	5	10	15	33	44	55
28(3/78),29-31,33,34-Ditko-c/a(r): 30-Staton, Sutton/Wood-a. 31-Ditko-c/a(3); same-c as Strange Suspense Stories #2 (1968); atom blast-c	1	3	4	6	8	10
32-r/Charlton Premiere V2#2; Sutton-a						5.00

SPACE WESTERN (Formerly Cowboy Western Comics; becomes Cowboy Western Comics #46 on)
Charlton Comics (Capitol Stories): No. 40, Oct, 1952 - No. 45, Aug, 1953

	GD 2.0	VG 4.0	FN 6.0	VF 8.0	VF/NM 9.0	NM- 9.2
40-Intro Spurs Jackson & His Space Vigilantes; flying saucer story	59	118	177	369	552	735
41,43-45: 41-Flying saucer-c. 45-Hitler app.	43	86	129	258	389	520
42-Atom bomb explosion-c	46	92	138	276	413	550

SPACE WORLDS (Formerly Space Squadron #1-5)
Atlas Comics (Male): No. 6, April, 1952

	GD 2.0	VG 4.0	FN 6.0	VF 8.0	VF/NM 9.0	NM- 9.2
6-Sol Brodsky-c	43	86	129	258	389	520

SPANKY & ALFALFA & THE LITTLE RASCALS (See The Little Rascals)

SPANNER'S GALAXY
DC Comics: Dec, 1984 - No. 6, May, 1985 (limited series)

	GD 2.0	VG 4.0	FN 6.0	VF 8.0	VF/NM 9.0	NM- 9.2
1-6: Mandrake-c/a in all.						2.25

SPARKIE, RADIO PIXIE (Radio)(Becomes Big Jon & Sparkie #4)
Ziff-Davis Publ. Co.: Winter, 1951 - No. 3, July-Aug, 1952 (Painted-c)(Sparkie #2,3; #1?)

	GD 2.0	VG 4.0	FN 6.0	VF 8.0	VF/NM 9.0	NM- 9.2
1-Based on children's radio program	29	58	87	164	232	300
2,3: 3-Big Jon and Sparkie on-c only	20	40	60	112	156	200

SPARKLE COMICS
United Features Synd.: Oct-Nov, 1948 - No. 33, Dec-Jan, 1953-54

	GD 2.0	VG 4.0	FN 6.0	VF 8.0	VF/NM 9.0	NM- 9.2
1-Li'l Abner, Nancy, Captain & the Kids, Ella Cinders (#1-3: 52 pgs.)	15	30	45	86	118	150
2	9	18	27	49	62	75
3-10	8	16	24	40	50	60
11-20	6	12	18	33	41	48
21-32	6	12	18	28	34	40
33-(2-3/54) 2 pgs. early Peanuts by Schulz	8	16	24	40	50	60

SPARKLE PLENTY (See Harvey Comics Library #2 & Dick Tracy)

SPARKLER COMICS (1st series)
United Feature Comic Group: July, 1940 - No. 2, 1940

	GD 2.0	VG 4.0	FN 6.0	VF 8.0	VF/NM 9.0	NM- 9.2
1-Jim Hardy	40	80	120	240	340	440
2-Frankie Doodle	31	62	93	175	248	320

SPARKLER COMICS (2nd series)(Nancy & Sluggo #121 on)(Cover title becomes Nancy and Sluggo #101? on)
United Features Syndicate: July, 1941 - No. 120, Jan, 1955

	GD 2.0	VG 4.0	FN 6.0	VF 8.0	VF/NM 9.0	NM- 9.2
1-Origin 1st app. Sparkman; Tarzan (by Hogarth in all issues), Captain & the Kids, Ella Cinders, Danny Dingle, Dynamite Dunn, Nancy, Abbie & Slats, Broncho Bill, Frankie Doodle, begin; Spark Man c-1-9,11,12; Hap Hopper c-10,13	240	480	720	1500	2250	3000
2	80	160	240	500	750	1000
3,4	64	128	192	400	600	800
5-9: 9-Spark Man's new costume	59	118	177	369	552	735
10-Origin Spark Man?	59	118	177	369	552	735
11,12-Spark Man war-c. 12-Spark Man's new costume (color change)	48	96	144	288	432	575
13-Hap Hopper war-c	44	88	132	264	395	525
14-Tarzan-c by Hogarth	55	110	165	330	495	660
15,17: 15-Capt & Kids-c. 17-Nancy & Sluggo-c	40	80	120	240	340	440
16,18-Spark Man war-c	45	90	135	270	403	535
19-1st Race Riley and the Commandos-c/s	44	88	132	264	395	525
20-Nancy war-c	40	80	120	240	340	440
21,25,28,31,34,37,39-Tarzan-c by Hogarth	46	92	138	276	413	550
22-24,26,27,29,30: 22-Race Riley & the Commandos strips begin, ends #44	35	70	105	201	288	370
32,33,35,36,38,40	21	42	63	118	164	210
41,43,45,46,48,49	15	30	45	84	115	145
42,44,47,50-Tarzan-c (42,47,50 by Hogarth)	29	58	87	164	232	300
51,52,54-70: 57-Li'l Abner begins (not in #58); Fearless Fosdick app. in #58	14	28	42	79	107	135
53-Tarzan-c by Hogarth	25	50	75	144	198	255
71-80	10	20	30	56	73	90
81,82,84-86: 86 Last Tarzan; lingerie panels	9	18	27	49	62	75
83-Tarzan-c; Li'l Abner ends	12	24	36	69	92	115
87-96,98-99	8	16	24	46	58	70
97-Origin Casey Ruggles by Warren Tufts	13	26	39	74	100	125
100	9	18	27	52	66	80
101-107,109-112,114-119	7	14	21	37	46	55
108,113-Toth-a	9	18	27	52	66	80
120-(10-11/54) 2 pgs. early Peanuts by Schulz	8	16	24	43	54	65

SPARKLING LOVE
Avon Periodicals/Realistic (1953): June, 1950; 1953

	GD 2.0	VG 4.0	FN 6.0	VF 8.0	VF/NM 9.0	NM- 9.2
1(Avon)-Kubert-a; photo-c	24	48	72	135	190	245
nn(1953)-Reprint; Kubert-a	9	18	27	52	66	80

SPARKLING STARS
Holyoke Publishing Co.: June, 1944 - No. 33, March, 1948

	GD 2.0	VG 4.0	FN 6.0	VF 8.0	VF/NM 9.0	NM- 9.2
1-Hell's Angels, FBI, Boxie Weaver, Petey & Pop, & Ali Baba begin	20	40	60	112	156	200
2-Speed Spaulding story	11	22	33	63	84	105
3-Actual FBI case photos & war photos	9	18	27	52	66	80
4-10: 7-X-Mas-c	8	16	24	46	58	70
11-19: 13-Origin/1st app. Jungo the Man-Beast-c/s	8	16	24	40	50	60
20-Intro Fangs the Wolf Boy	8	16	24	46	58	70
21-29,32,33: 29-Bondage-c	8	16	24	40	50	60
31-Sid Greene-a	8	16	24	40	50	60

SPARK MAN (See Sparkler Comics)
Frances M. McQueeny: 1945 (36 pgs., one-shot)

	GD 2.0	VG 4.0	FN 6.0	VF 8.0	VF/NM 9.0	NM- 9.2
1-Origin Spark Man r/Sparkler #1-3; female torture story; cover redrawn from Sparkler #1	34	68	102	193	274	355

SPARKY WATTS (Also see Big Shot Comics & Columbia Comics)
Columbia Comic Corp.: Nov?, 1942 - No. 10, 1949

	GD 2.0	VG 4.0	FN 6.0	VF 8.0	VF/NM 9.0	NM- 9.2
1(1942)-Skyman & The Face app; Hitler-c	66	132	198	413	619	825

Spawn #48 © TMP

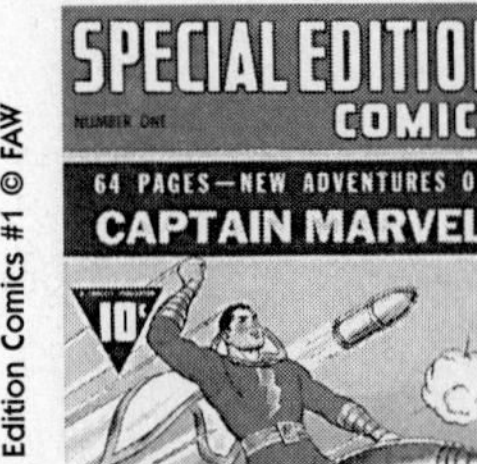

Special Edition Comics #1 © FAW

Special Marvel Edition #1 © MAR

	GD 2.0	VG 4.0	FN 6.0	VF 8.0	VF/NM 9.0	NM- 9.2
2(1943)	29	58	87	164	232	300
3(1944)	21	42	63	118	164	210
4(1944)-Origin	19	38	57	106	146	185
5(1947)-Skyman app.; Boody Rogers-c/a	16	32	48	92	126	160
6,7,9,10: 6(1947),10(1949)	10	20	30	56	73	90
8(1948)-Surrealistic-c	14	28	42	79	107	135

NOTE: ***Boody Rogers** c-1-8.*

SPARTACUS (Movie)
Dell Publishing Co.: No. 1139, Nov, 1960 (Kirk Douglas photo-c)

Four Color 1139-Buscema-a 14 28 42 97 141 185

SPARTAN: WARRIOR SPIRIT (Also see WildC.A.T.S: Covert Action Teams)
Image Comics (WildStorm Productions): July, 1995 - No. 4, Nov, 1995 ($2.50, limited series)

1-4: Kurt Busiek scripts; Mike McKone-c/a 2.50

SPAWN (Also see Curse of the Spawn and Sam & Twitch)
Image Comics (Todd McFarlane Prods.): May, 1992 - Present ($1.95/$2.50)

1-1st app. Spawn; McFarlane-c/a begins; McFarlane/Steacy-c; 1st Todd McFarlane Productions title. 1 3 4 6 8 10
1-Black & white edition 2 4 6 12 16 20
2,3: 2-1st app. Violator; McFarlane/Steacy-c 1 2 3 5 7 9
4-Contains coupon for Image Comics #0 1 2 3 5 7 9
4-With coupon missing 3.00
4-Newsstand edition w/o poster or coupon 3.00
5-Cerebus cameo (1 pg.) as stuffed animal; Spawn mobile poster #1 6.00
6-8,10: 7-Spawn Mobile poster #2. 8-Alan Moore scripts; Miller poster. 10-Cerebus app.; Dave Sim scripts; 1 pg. cameo app. by Superman 4.00
9-Neil Gaiman scripts; Jim Lee poster; 1st Angela. 6.00
11-17,19,20,22-30: 11-Miller script; Darrow poster. 12-Bloodwulf poster by Liefeld. 14,15-Violator app. 16,17-Grant Morrison scripts; Capullo-c/a(p). 23,24-McFarlane-a/stories. 25-(10/94). 19-(10/94). 20-(11/94) 3.00
18-Grant Morrison script, Capullo-c/a(p); low distr. 1 2 3 5 7 9
21-low distribution 1 2 3 5 7 9
31-49: 31-1st app. The Redeemer; new costume cameo. 32-1st full app. new costume. 38-40,42,44,46,48-Tony Daniel-c/a(p). 38-1st app. Cy-Gor. 40,41-Cy-Gor & Curse app. 4.00
50-($3.95, 48 pgs.) 3.00
51-66: 52-Savage Dragon app. 56-w/ Darkchylde preview. 57-Cy-Gor-c/app. 64-Polybagged w/McFarlane Toys catalog. 65-Photo-c of movie Spawn and McFarlane 3.00
67-97: 81-Billy Kincaid returns. 97-Angela-c/app. 2.50
98,99,101-131-($2.50): 98,99-Angela app. 2.50
100-($4.95) Angela dies; 6 covers by McFarlane, Ross, Miller, Capullo, Wood, Mignola 5.00
Annual 1-Blood & Shadows ('99, $4.95) Ashley Wood-c/a; Jenkins-s 5.00
...Bible-(8/96, $1.95)-Character bios 4.00
Book 1 TPB($9.95) r/#1-5; Book 2-r/#6-9,11; Book 3 -r/#12-15, Book 4- r/#16-20; Book 5-r/#21-25; Book 6- r/#26-30; Book 7-r/#31-34; Book 8-r/#35-38; Book 9-r/#39-42; Book 10-r/#43-47 11.00
Book 11 TPB ($10.95) r/#48-50; Book 12-r/#51-54 11.00

NOTE: ***Capullo** a-16p-18p; c-16p-18p. **Daniel** a-38-40, 42, 44, 46. **McFarlane** a-1-15; c-1-15p. **Thibert** a-16i(part). Posters come with issues 1, 4, 7-9, 11, 12. #25 was released before #19 & 20.*

SPAWN-BATMAN (Also see Batman/Spawn: War Devil under Batman: One-Shots)
Image Comics (Todd McFarlane Productions): 1994 ($3.95, one-shot)

1-Miller scripts; McFarlane-c/a 6.00

SPAWN: BLOOD FEUD
Image Comics (Todd McFarlane Productions): June, 1995 - No. 4, Sept, 1995 ($2.25, limited series)

1-4-Alan Moore scripts, Tony Daniel-a 3.50

SPAWN FAN EDITION
Image Comics (Todd McFarlane Productions): Aug, 1996 - No. 3, Oct, 1996 (Giveaway, 12 pgs.) (Polybagged w/Overstreet's FAN)

1-3: Beau Smith scripts; Brad Gorby-a(p). 1-1st app. Nordik, the Norse Hellspawn. 2-1st app. McFallon, the Dragon Master. 3-1st app. Mercy 1 2 3 5 6 8
1-3-(Gold): All retailer incentives 16.00
1-3-Variant-c 1 2 3 5 6 8
2-(Platinum)-Retailer incentive 25.00

SPAWN: THE DARK AGES
Image Comics (Todd McFarlane Productions): Mar, 1999 - No. 28, Oct, 2001 ($2.50)

1-Fabry-c; Holguin-s/Sharp-a; variant-c by McFarlane 2.50
2-28 2.50

SPAWN THE IMPALER
Image Comics (Todd McFarlane Productions): Oct, 1996 - No. 3, Dec, 1996 ($2.95, limited series)

1-3-Mike Grell scripts, painted-a 3.00

SPAWN: THE UNDEAD
Image Comics (Todd McFarlane Prod.): Jun, 1999 - No. 9, Feb, 2000 ($1.95/$2.25)

1-9-Dwayne Turner-c/a; Jenkins-s. 7-9-($2.25-c) 2.50

SPAWN/WILDC.A.T.S
Image Comics (WildStorm): Jan, 1996 - No. 4, Apr, 1996 ($2.50, lim. series)

1-4: Alan Moore scripts in all. 3.00

SPECIAL AGENT (Steve Saunders...)(Also see True Comics #68)
Parents' Magazine Institute (Commended Comics No. 2): Dec, 1947 - No. 8, Sept, 1949 (Based on true FBI cases)

1-J. Edgar Hoover photo on-c 12 24 36 69 92 115
2 8 16 24 40 50 60
3-8 7 14 21 35 43 50

SPECIAL COLLECTORS' EDITION (See Savage Fists of Kung-Fu)

SPECIAL COMICS (Becomes Hangman #2 on)
MLJ Magazines: Winter, 1941-42

1-Origin The Boy Buddies (Shield & Wizard x-over); death of The Comet; origin The Hangman retold; Hangman-c 288 576 864 1800 2700 3600

SPECIAL EDITION (See Gorgo and Reptisaurus)

SPECIAL EDITION COMICS
Fawcett Publications: 1940 (August) (68 pgs., one-shot)

1-1st book devoted entirely to Captain Marvel; C.C. Beck-c/a; only app. of Captain Marvel with belt buckle; Capt. Marvel appears with button-down flap; 1st story (came out before Captain Marvel #1) 828 1656 2484 5796 8898 12,000

NOTE: *Prices vary widely on this book. Since this book is all Captain Marvel stories, it is actually a pre-Captain Marvel #1. There is speculation that this book almost became **Captain Marvel** #1. After **Special Edition** was published, there was an editor change at Fawcett. The new editor commissioned Kirby to do a nn **Captain Marvel** book early in 1941. This book was followed by a 2nd book several months later. This 2nd book was advertised as a #3 (making Special Edition the #1, & the nn issue the #2). However, the 2nd book did come out as a #2.*

SPECIAL EDITION: SPIDER-MAN VS. THE HULK (See listing under The Amazing Spider-Man)

SPECIAL EDITION X-MEN
Marvel Comics Group: Feb, 1983 ($2.00, one-shot, Baxter paper)

1-r/Giant-Size X-Men #1 plus one new story 2 4 6 8 10 12

SPECIAL MARVEL EDITION (Master of Kung Fu #17 on)
Marvel Comics Group: Jan, 1971 - No. 16, Feb, 1974 (#1-3: 25¢, 68 pgs.; #4: 52 pgs.; #5-16: 20¢, regular ed.)

1-Thor-r by Kirby; 68 pgs. 3 6 9 18 24 30
2-4: Thor-r by Kirby; 2,3-68 pg. Giant. 4-(52 pgs.) 2 4 6 11 14 18
5-14: Sgt. Fury-r; 11-r/Sgt. Fury #13 (Capt. America) 1 3 4 6 8 10
15-Master of Kung Fu (Shang-Chi) begins (1st app., 12/73); Starlin-a; origin/1st app. Nayland Smith & Dr. Petric 8 16 24 55 78 100
16-1st app. Midnight; Starlin-a (2nd Shang-Chi) 4 8 12 24 32 40

NOTE: ***Kirby** c-10-14.*

SPECIAL MISSIONS (See G.I. Joe...)

SPECIAL WAR SERIES (Attack V4#3 on?)
Charlton Comics: Aug, 1965 - No. 4, Nov, 1965

V4#1-D-Day (also see D-Day listing) 4 8 12 27 36 45
2-Attack! 3 6 9 16 20 25
3-War & Attack (also see War & Attack) 3 6 9 16 20 25
4-Judomaster (intro/1st app.; see Sarge Steel) 8 16 24 53 74 95

SPECIES (Movie)
Dark Horse Comics: June, 1995 - No. 4, Sept, 1995 ($2.50, limited series)

1-4: Adaptation of film 3.00

SPECIES: HUMAN RACE (Movie)
Dark Horse Comics: Nov, 1996 - No. 4, Feb, 1997 ($2.95, limited series)

1-4 3.00

SPECTACULAR ADVENTURES (See Adventures)

SPECTACULAR FEATURE MAGAZINE, A (Formerly My Confessions) (Spectacular Features Magazine #12)
Fox Feature Syndicate: No. 11, April, 1950

11 (#1)-Samson and Delilah 31 62 93 175 248 320

SPECTACULAR FEATURES MAGAZINE (Formerly A Spectacular Feature Magazine)
Fox Feature Syndicate: No. 12, June, 1950 - No. 3, Aug, 1950

12 (#2)-Iwo Jima; photo flag-c 31 62 93 175 248 320
3-True Crime Cases From Police Files 25 50 75 144 198 255

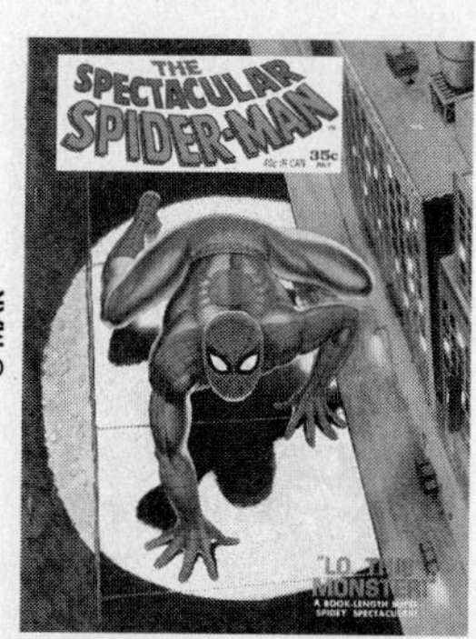

The Spectacular Spider-Man (magazine) #1 © MAR

The Spectacular Spider-Man #183 © MAR

The Spectre (4th series) #27 © DC

	GD 2.0	VG 4.0	FN 6.0	VF 8.0	VF/NM 9.0	NM- 9.2

SPECTACULAR SCARLET SPIDER
Marvel Comics: Nov, 1995 - No. 2, Dec, 1995 ($1.95, limited series)
1,2: Replaces Spectacular Spider-Man 2.25

SPECTACULAR SPIDER-MAN, THE (See Marvel Special Edition and Marvel Treasury Edition)

SPECTACULAR SPIDER-MAN, THE (Magazine)
Marvel Comics Group: July, 1968 - No. 2, Nov, 1968 (35¢)
1-(B&W)-Romita/Mooney 52 pg. story plus updated origin story with Everett-a(i)
10 20 30 70 100 130
1-Variation w/single c-price of 40¢ 10 20 30 70 100 130
2-(Color)-Green Goblin-c & 58 pg. story; Romita painted-c (story reprinted in King Size Spider-Man #9); Romita/Mooney-a 12 24 36 84 125 165

SPECTACULAR SPIDER-MAN, THE (Peter Parker...#54-132, 134)
Marvel Comics Group: Dec, 1976 - No. 263, Nov, 1998
1-Origin recap in text; return of Tarantula 5 10 15 33 44 55
2-Kraven the Hunter app. 2 4 6 12 16 20
3-5: 3-Intro Lightmaster. 4-Vulture app. 2 4 6 9 11 14
6-8-Morbius app.; 6-r/Marvel Team-Up #3 w/Morbius
2 4 6 10 13 16
7,8-(35¢-c variants, limited distribution)(6,7/77) 3 6 9 16 20 24
9-20: 9,10-White Tiger app. 11-Last 30¢-c. 17,18-Angel & Iceman app. (from Champions); Ghost Rider cameo in flashback 1 3 4 6 8 10
9-11-(35¢-c variants, limited distribution)(8-10/77) 2 4 6 10 12 15
21,24-26: 21-Scorpion app. 26-Daredevil app. 1 2 3 5 6 8
22,23-Moon Knight app. 1 2 3 5 7 9
27-Miller's 1st art on Daredevil (2/79); also see Captain America #235
3 6 9 18 23 28
28-Miller Daredevil (p) 2 4 6 12 16 20
29-55,57,59: 33-Origin Iguana. 38-Morbius app. 5.00
56-2nd app. Jack O'Lantern (Macendale) & 1st Spidey/Jack O'Lantern battle (7/81) 6.00
58-Byrne-a(p) 6.00
60-Double size; origin retold with new facts revealed 6.00
61-63,65-68,71-74: 65-Kraven the Hunter app. 4.00
64-1st app. Cloak & Dagger (3/82) 1 3 4 6 8 10
69,70-Cloak & Dagger app. 6.00
75-Double size 5.00
76-82: 78,79-Punisher cameo. 81,82-Punisher, Cloak & Dagger app. 4.00
83-Origin Punisher retold (10/83) 1 2 3 4 5 7
84,86-99: 90-Spider-man's new black costume, last panel(ties w/Amazing Spider-Man #252 & Marvel Team-Up #141 for 1st app.). 94-96-Cloak & Dagger app. 98-Intro The Spot 4.00
85-Hobgoblin (Ned Leeds) app. (12/83); gains powers of original Green Goblin (see Amazing Spider-Man #238) 1 2 3 4 5 7
100-(3/85)-Double size 5.00
101-115,117,118,120-129: 107-110-Death of Jean DeWolff. 111-Secret Wars II tie-in. 128-Black Cat new costume 3.00
116,119-Sabretooth-c/story 6.00
130-132: 30-Hobgoblin app. 131-Six part Kraven tie-in. 132-Kraven tie-in 5.00
133-140: 138-1st full app. Tombstone (origin #139). 140-Punisher cameo app. 3.00
141-143-Punisher app. 3.50
144-146,148-157: 151-Tombstone returns 3.00
147-1st app. new Hobgoblin (Macendale) in 1 pg. cameo; continued in Web of Spider-Man #48
1 3 4 6 8 10
158-Spider-Man gets new powers (1st Cosmic Spidey, cont'd in Web of Spider-Man #59) 5.00
159-Cosmic Spider-Man app. 5.00
160-170: 161-163-Hobgoblin app. 168-170-Avengers x-over. 169-1st app. The Outlaws 2.50
171-188,190-199: 180,181,183,184-Green Goblin app. 197-199-Original X-Men-c/story 2.50
189-($2.95, 52 pgs.)-Silver hologram on-c; battles Green Goblin; origin Spidey retold; Vess poster w/Spidey & Hobgoblin 4.00
189-(2nd printing)-Gold hologram on-c 3.00
195-(Deluxe ed.)-Polybagged w/"Dirt" magazine #2 & Beastie Boys/Smithereens music cassette 4.00
200-($2.95)-Holo-grafx foil-c; Green Goblin-c/story 3.00
201-219,221,222,224,226-228,230-247: 212-w/card sheet. 203-Maximum Carnage x-over. 204-Begin 4 part death of Tombstone story. 207,208-The Shroud-c/story. 208-Siege of Darkness x-over (#207 is a tie-in). 209-Black Cat back-up. 215,216-Scorpion app. 217-Power & Responsibility Pt. 4. 231-Return of Kaine; Spider-Man corpse discovered. 232-New Doc Octopus app. 233-Carnage-c/app. 235-Dragon Man cameo. 236-Dragon Man-c/app; Lizard app.; Peter Parker regains powers. 238,239-Lizard app. 239-w/card insert. 240-Revelations storyline begins. 241-Flashback 2.50
213-Collectors ed. polybagged w/16 pg. preview & animation cel; foil-c; 1st meeting Spidey & Typhoid Mary 3.00
213-Version polybagged w/Gamepro #7; no-c date, price 2.50
217,219 ($2.95)-Deluxe edition foil-c: flip book 3.00
220 ($2.25, 52 pgs.)-Flip book, Mary Jane reveals pregnancy 3.00
223,229: ($2.50) 229-Spidey quits 3.00
223,225: ($2.95)-223-Die Cut-c. 225-Newsstand ed. 3.00
225,229: ($3.95) 225-Direct Market Holodisk-c (Green Goblin). 229-Acetate-c, Spidey quits 4.00
240-Variant-c 3.00
248,249,251-254,256: 249-Return of Norman Osborn 256-1st app. Prodigy 2.50
250-($3.25) Double gatefold-c 3.25
255-($2.99) Spiderhunt pt. 4 3.00
257-262: 257-Double cover with "Spectacular Prodigy #1"; battles Jack O'Lantern. 258-Spidey is cleared. 259,260-Green Goblin & Hobgoblin app. 262-Byrne-s 2.50
263-Final issue; Byrne-c; Aunt May returns 4.00
#(-1) Flashback (7/97) 2.50
Annual 1 (1979)-Doc Octopus-c & 46 pg. story 1 3 4 6 8 10
Annual 2 (1980)-Origin/1st app. Rapier 1 2 3 4 5 7
Annual 3-5: ('81-'83) 3-Last Man-Wolf 4.00
Annual 6-14: 8 ('88,$ 1.75)-Evolutionary War x-over; Daydreamer returns Gwen Stacy "clone" back to real self (not Gwen Stacy). 9 ('89, $2.00, 68 pgs.)-Atlantis Attacks. 10 ('90, $2.00, 68 pgs.)-McFarlane-a 11 ('91, $2.00, 68 pgs.)-Iron Man app. 12 ('92, $2.25, 68 pgs.)-Venom solo story cont'd from Amazing Spider-Man Annual #26. 13 ('93, $2.95, 68 pgs.)-Polybagged w/trading card; John Romita, Sr. back-up-a 3.00
Special 1 (1995, $3.95)-Flip book 4.00
NOTE: ***Austin*** *c-21i, Annual 11i.* ***Buckler*** *a-103, 107-111, 116, 117, 119, 122, Annual 1, Annual 10; c-103, 107-111, 113, 116-119, 122, Annual 1.* ***Buscema*** *a-121.* ***Byrne*** *c(p)-17, 43, 58, 101, 102.* ***Giffen*** *a-120p.* ***Hembeck*** *c/a-86p.* ***Larsen*** *c-Annual 11p.* ***Miller*** *c-46p, 48p, 50, 51p, 52p, 54p, 55, 56p, 57, 60.* ***Mooney*** *a-7i, 11i, 21p, 23p, 25p, 26p, 29-34p, 36p, 37p, 39i, 41, 42i, 49p, 50i, 51i, 53p, 54-57i, 59-66i, 68i, 71i, 73-79i, 81-83i, 85i, 87-99i, 102i, 125p, Annual 1i, 2p.* ***Nasser*** *c-37p.* ***Perez*** *c-10.* ***Simonson*** *c-54i.* ***Zeck*** *a-118, 131, 132; c-131, 132.*

SPECTACULAR SPIDER-MAN
Marvel Comics: Sept, 2003 - Present ($2.25)
1-Jenkins-s/Ramos-a/c; Venom-c/app. 3.00
2-9: 2-5-Venom app. 6-9-Dr. Octopus app. 2.25

SPECTACULAR STORIES MAGAZINE (Formerly A Star Presentation)
Fox Feature Syndicate (Hero Books): No. 4, July, 1950; No. 3, Sept, 1950
4-Sherlock Holmes (true crime stories) 40 80 120 240 340 440
3-The St. Valentine's Day Massacre (true crime) 28 56 84 157 221 285

SPECTRE, THE (1st Series) (See Adventure Comics #431-440, More Fun & Showcase)
National Periodical Publ.: Nov-Dec, 1967 - No. 10, May-June, 1969 (All 12¢)
1-(11-12/67)-Anderson-c/a 14 28 42 102 149 195
2-5-Neal Adams-c/a; 3-Wildcat x-over 9 18 27 65 93 120
6-8,10: 6-8-Anderson inks. 7-Hourman app. 6 12 18 43 59 75
9-Wrightson-a 7 14 21 50 68 85

SPECTRE, THE (2nd Series) (See Saga of the Swamp Thing #58, Showcase '95 #8 & Wrath of the...)
DC Comics: Apr, 1987 - No. 31, Oct, 1989 ($1.00, new format)
1-Colan-a begins 4.00
2-32: 9-Nudity panels. 10-Batman cameo. 10,11-Millennium tie-ins 3.00
Annual 1 (1988, $2.00)-Deadman app. 3.00
NOTE: ***Art Adams*** *c-Annual 1.* ***Colan*** *a-1-6.* ***Kaluta*** *c-1-3.* ***Mignola*** *c-7-9.* ***Morrow*** *a-9-15.* ***Sears*** *c/a-22.* ***Vess*** *c-13-15.*

SPECTRE, THE (3rd Series) (Also see Brave and the Bold #72, 75, 116, 180, 199 & Showcase '95 #8)
DC Comics: Dec, 1992 - No. 62, Feb, 1998 ($1.75/$1.95/$2.25/$2.50)
1-($1.95)-Glow-in-the-dark-c; Mandrake-a begins 5.00
2,3 3.00
4-7,9-12,14-20: 10-Kaluta-c. 11-Hildebrandt painted-c. 16-Aparo/K. Jones-a. 19-Snyder III-c. 20-Sienkiewicz-c 2.50
8,13-($2.50)-Glow-in-the-dark-c 3.00
21-62: 22-(9/94)-Superman-c & app. 23-(11/94). 43-Kent Williams-c. 44-Kaluta-c. 47-Final Night x-over. 49-Begin Bolton-c. 51-Batman-c/app. 52-Gianni-c. 54-Corben-c. 60-Harris-c 2.50
#0 (10/94) Released between #22 & #23 2.50
Annual 1 (1995, $3.95)-Year One story 4.00
NOTE: ***Bisley*** *c-27.* ***Fabry*** *c-2.* ***Kelley Jones*** *c-31.* ***Vess*** *c-5.*

SPECTRE, THE (4th Series) (Hal Jordan; also see Day of Judgment #5 and Legends of the DC Universe #33-36)
DC Comics: Mar, 2001 - No. 27, May, 2003 ($2.50/$2.75)
1-DeMatteis-s/Ryan Sook-c/a 3.00
2-27: 3,4-Superman & Batman-c/app. 5-Two-Face-c/app. 20-Begin $2.75-c. 21-Sinestro returns. 24-JLA app. 2.75

SPEEDBALL (See Amazing Spider-Man Annual #12, Marvel Super-Heroes & The New Warriors)

Speed Comics #3 © HARV

Spellbound #3 © MAR

Spider-Girl #43 © MAR

	GD 2.0	VG 4.0	FN 6.0	VF 8.0	VF/NM 9.0	NM- 9.2

Marvel Comics: Sept, 1988(10/88-inside) - No. 11, July, 1989 (75¢)

	GD	VG	FN	VF	VF/NM	NM-
1-11: Ditko/Guice a-1-4, c-1; Ditko a-1-10; c-1-11p						2.25

SPEED BUGGY (TV)(Also see Fun-In #12, 15)
Charlton Comics: July, 1975 - No. 9, Nov, 1976 (Hanna-Barbera)

	GD	VG	FN	VF	VF/NM	NM-
1	3	6	9	16	20	25
2-9	2	4	6	10	13	16

SPEED CARTER SPACEMAN (See Spaceman)

SPEED COMICS (New Speed)(Also see Double Up)
Brookwood Publ./Speed Publ./Harvey Publications No. 14 on:
10/39 - #11, 8/40; #12, 3/41 - #44, 1-2/47 (#14-16: pocket size, 100 pgs.)

	GD	VG	FN	VF	VF/NM	NM-
1-Origin & 1st app. Shock Gibson; Ted Parrish, the Man with 1000 Faces begins; Powell-a; becomes Champion #2 on?; has earliest? full page panel in comics	326	652	978	2119	3260	4400
2-Powell-a	112	224	336	700	1050	1400
3	66	132	198	413	617	820
4,5: 4-Powell-a? 5-Dinosaur-c	54	108	162	324	487	650
6-11: 7-Mars Mason begins, ends #11	48	96	144	288	432	575
12 (3/41; shows #11 in indicia)-The Wasp begins; Major Colt app. (Capt. Colt #12)	53	106	160	318	479	640
13-Intro. Captain Freedom & Young Defenders; Girl Commandos, Pat Parker (costumed heroine), War Nurse begins; Major Colt app.	59	118	177	369	555	740
14-16 (100 pg. pocket size, 1941): 14-2nd Harvey comic (See Pocket); Shock Gibson dons new costume. 15-Pat Parker dons costume, last in costume #23; no Girl Commandos	70	140	210	438	657	875
17-Black Cat begins (4/42, early app.; see Pocket #1); origin Black Cat-r/Pocket #1; not in #40,41; S&K-c	74	148	222	463	692	920
18-20-S&K-c	58	116	174	363	542	720
21-Hitler, Tojo-c; Kirby-c	68	136	204	425	638	850
22-Kirby-c	58	116	174	363	542	720
23-Origin Girl Commandos; Kirby-c	58	116	174	363	542	720
24-Pat Parker team-up with Girl Commandos; Hitler, Tojo, & Mussolini-c	55	110	165	330	495	660
25-30: 26-Flag-c	46	92	138	276	413	550
31-Schomburg Hitler & Hirohito-c	66	132	198	413	617	820
32-36-Schomburg-c	53	106	159	318	477	635
37,39-42, 44	44	88	132	264	395	525
38-Iwo-Jima Flag-c	46	92	138	276	413	550
43-Robot-c	48	96	144	288	432	575

NOTE: ***Al Avison** c-14-16, 30, 43. **Briefer** a-6, 7. **Jon Henri** (Kirbyesque) c-17-20. **Kubert** a-37, 38, 42-44. **Kirby/Caseneuve** c-21-23. **Cecelia Munson** a-7-11(Mars Mason). **Palais** c-37, 39-42. **Powell** a-1, 2, 4-7, 28, 31, 44. **Schomburg** c-31-36. **Tuska** a-3, 6, 7. Bondage c-18, 35. Captain Freedom c-16-24, 25(part), 26-44(w/Black Cat #27, 29, 31, 32-40). Shock Gibson c-1-15.*

SPEED DEMON (Also see Marvel Versus DC #3 & DC Versus Marvel #4)
Marvel Comics (Amalgam): Apr, 1996 ($1.95, one-shot)

	GD	VG	FN	VF	VF/NM	NM-
1						2.25

SPEED DEMONS (Formerly Frank Merriwell at Yale #1-4?; Submarine Attack #11 on)
Charlton Comics: No. 5, Feb, 1957 - No. 10, 1958

	GD	VG	FN	VF	VF/NM	NM-
5-10	7	14	21	35	43	50

SPEED FORCE (See The Flash 2nd Series #143-Cobalt Blue)
DC Comics: Nov, 1997 ($3.95, one-shot)

	GD	VG	FN	VF	VF/NM	NM-
1-Flash & Kid Flash vs. Cobalt Blue; Waid-s/Aparo & Sienkiewicz-a; Flash family stories and pin-ups by various						4.00

SPEED RACER (Also see The New Adventures of...)
Now Comics: July, 1987 - No. 38, Nov, 1990 ($1.75)

	GD	VG	FN	VF	VF/NM	NM-
1-38, 1-2nd printing						2.50
Special 1 (1988, $2.00)						2.50
Special 2 (1988, $3.50)						3.50

SPEED RACER (Also see Racer X)
DC Comics (WildStorm): Oct, 1999 - No. 3, Dec, 1999 ($2.50, limited series)

	GD	VG	FN	VF	VF/NM	NM-
1-3-Tommy Yune-s/a; origin of Racer X; debut of the Mach 5						2.50
...: Born To Race (2000, $9.95, TPB) r/series & conceptual art						10.00
...: The Original Manga Vol. 1 ('00, $9.95, TPB) r/1950s B&W manga						10.00

SPEED RACER FEATURING NINJA HIGH SCHOOL
Now Comics: Aug, 1993 - No. 2, 1993 ($2.50, mini-series)

	GD	VG	FN	VF	VF/NM	NM-
1,2: 1-Polybagged w/card. 2-Exists?						2.50

SPEED RACER: RETURN OF THE GRX
Now Comics: Mar, 1994 - No. 2, Apr, 1994 ($1.95, limited series)

	GD	VG	FN	VF	VF/NM	NM-
1,2						2.50

SPEED SMITH-THE HOT ROD KING (Also see Hot Rod King)
Ziff-Davis Publishing Co.: Spring, 1952

	GD	VG	FN	VF	VF/NM	NM-
1-Saunders painted-c	24	48	72	135	190	245

SPEEDY GONZALES
Dell Publishing Co.: No. 1084, Mar, 1960

	GD	VG	FN	VF	VF/NM	NM-
Four Color 1084	6	12	18	40	55	70

SPEEDY RABBIT (See Television Puppet Show)
Realistic/I. W. Enterprises/Super Comics: nd (1953); 1963

	GD	VG	FN	VF	VF/NM	NM-
nn (1953)-Realistic Reprint?	2	4	6	10	13	16
I.W. Reprint #1 (2 versions w/diff. c/stories exist)-Peter Cottontail #? Super Reprint #14(1963)	2	4	6	8	10	12

SPELLBINDERS
Quality: Dec, 1986 - No. 12, Jan, 1988 ($1.25)

	GD	VG	FN	VF	VF/NM	NM-
1-12: Nemesis the Warlock, Amadeus Wolf						2.25

SPELLBOUND (See The Crusaders)

SPELLBOUND (Tales to Hold You... #1, Stories to Hold You...)
Atlas Comics (ACI 1-15/Male 16-23/BPC 24-34): Mar, 1952 - #23, June, 1954; #24, Oct, 1955 - #34, June, 1957

	GD	VG	FN	VF	VF/NM	NM-
1-Horror/weird stories in all	66	132	198	413	619	825
2-Edgar A. Poe app.	39	78	117	230	325	420
3-5: 3-Whitney-a; cannibalism story	34	68	102	193	274	355
6-Krigstein-a	34	68	102	193	274	355
7-10: 8-Ayers-a	29	58	87	164	232	300
11-16,18-20: 14-Ed Win-a	24	48	72	135	190	245
17-Krigstein-a	24	48	72	138	194	250
21-23: 23-Last precode (6/54)	20	40	60	112	156	200
24-28,30,31,34: 25-Orlando-a	18	36	54	101	138	175
29-Ditko-a (4 pgs.)	20	40	60	112	156	200
32,33-Torres-a	18	36	54	101	138	175

NOTE: ***Brodsky** a-5; c-1, 5-7, 10, 11, 13, 15, 25-27, 32. **Colan** a-17. **Everett** a-2, 5, 7, 10, 16, 28, 31; c-2, 8, 9, 14, 17-19, 28, 30. **Forgione/Abel** a-29. **Forte/Fox** a-16. **Al Hartley** a-2. **Heath** a-2, 4, 8, 9, 12, 14, 16; c-3, 4, 12, 16, 20, 21. **Infantino** a-15. **Keller** a-5. **Kida** a-2, 14. **Maneely** a-7, 14, 27; c-24, 29, 31. **Mooney** a-5, 13, 18. **Mac Pakula** a-22, 32. **Post** a-8. **Powell** a-19, 20, 32. **Robinson** a-1. **Romita** a-24, 26, 27. **R.Q. Sale** a-29. **Sekowsky** a-5. **Severin** c-29. **Sinnott** a-8, 16, 17.*

SPELLBOUND
Marvel Comics: Jan, 1988 - Apr, 1988 ($1.50, bi-weekly, Baxter paper)

	GD	VG	FN	VF	VF/NM	NM-
1-5						2.25
6 ($2.25, 52 pgs.)						2.50

SPELLJAMMER (Also see TSR Worlds Comics Annual)
DC Comics: Sept, 1990 - No. 15, Nov, 1991 ($1.75)

	GD	VG	FN	VF	VF/NM	NM-
1-15: Based on TSR game. 11-Heck-a.						2.25

SPENCER SPOOK (Formerly Giggle Comics; see Adventures of...)
American Comics Group: No. 100, Mar-Apr, 1955 - No. 101, May-June, 1955

	GD	VG	FN	VF	VF/NM	NM-
100,101	7	14	21	37	46	55

SPIDER, THE
Eclipse Books: 1991 - Book 3, 1991 ($4.95, 52 pgs., limited series)

	GD	VG	FN	VF	VF/NM	NM-
Book 1-3-Truman-c/a						5.00

SPIDER-BOY (Also see Marvel Versus DC #3)
Marvel Comics (Amalgam): Apr, 1996 ($1.95)

	GD	VG	FN	VF	VF/NM	NM-
1-Mike Wieringo-c/a; Karl Kesel story; 1st app. of Bizarnage, Insect Queen, Challengers of the Fantastic, Sue Storm: Agent of S.H.I.E.L. D., & King Lizard						2.25

SPIDER-BOY TEAM-UP
Marvel Comics (Amalgam): June, 1997 ($1.95, one-shot)

	GD	VG	FN	VF	VF/NM	NM-
1-Karl Kesel & Roger Stern-s/Jo Ladronn-a(p)						2.25

SPIDER-GIRL (See What If #105)
Marvel Comics: Oct, 1998 - Present ($1.99/$2.25)

	GD	VG	FN	VF	VF/NM	NM-
0-($2.99)-r/1st app. Peter Parker's daughter from What If #105; previews regular series, Avengers-Next and J2	1	2	3	4	5	7
1-DeFalco-s/Olliffe & Williamson-s	1	2	3	4	5	7
2-Two covers						4.00
3-16,18-20: 3-Fantastic Five-c/app. 10,11-Spider-Girl time-travels to meet teenaged Spider-Man						2.50
17-($2.99) Peter Parker suits up						3.00
21-24,26-49,51-59: 21-Begin $2.25-c. 31-Avengers app.						2.25
25-($2.99) Spider-Girl vs. the Savage Six						3.00
50-($3.50)						3.50
59-68-($2.99) 59-Avengers app.; Ben Parker born						3.00

Spider-Man #2 © MAR

Spider-Man Adventures #6 © MAR

Spider-Man/Black Cat: The Evil That Men Do #1 © MAR

	GD	VG	FN	VF	VF/NM	NM-
	2.0	4.0	6.0	8.0	9.0	9.2

1999 Annual ($3.99) 4.00
... A Fresh Start (1/99,$5.99, TPB) r/#1&2 6.00
TPB (10/01, $19.95) r/#0-8; new Olliffe-c 20.00

SPIDER-MAN (See Amazing..., Giant-Size..., Marvel Tales, Marvel Team-Up, Spectacular..., Spidey Super Stories, Ultimate..., Venom, & Web Of...)

SPIDER-MAN
Marvel Comics: Aug, 1990 - No. 98, Nov, 1998 ($1.75/$1.95/ $1.99)

1-Silver edition, direct sale only (unbagged) 1 2 3 5 6 8
1-Silver bagged edition; direct sale, no price on comic, but $2.00 on plastic bag (125,000 print run) 20.00
1-Regular edition w/Spidey face in UPC area (unbagged); green-c 6.00
1-Regular bagged edition w/Spidey face in UPC area; green cover (125,000) 12.00
1-Newsstand bagged w/UPC code 8.00
1-Gold edition, 2nd printing (unbagged) with Spider-Man in box (400,000-450,000) 5.00
1-Gold 2nd printing w/UPC code; (less than 10,000 print run) intended for Wal-Mart; much scarcer than originally believed 120.00
1-Platinum ed. mailed to retailers only (10,000 print run); has new McFarlane-a & editorial material instead of ads; stiff-c, no cover price 100.00
2-26: 2-McFarlane-c/a/scripts continue. 6,7-Ghost Rider & Hobgoblin app. 8-Wolverine cameo; Wolverine storyline begins. 12-Wolverine storyline ends. 13-Spidey's black costume returns; Morbius app. 14-Morbius app. 15-Erik Larsen-c/a; Beast c/s. 16-X-Force-c/story w/Liefeld assists; continues in X-Force #4; reads sideways; last McFarlane issue. 17-Thanos-c/story; Leonardi/Williamson-c/a. 13,14-Spidey in black costume. 18-Ghost Rider-c/story. 18-23-Sinister Six storyline w/Erik Larsen-c/a/scripts. 19-Hulk & Hobgoblin-c & app. 20-22-Deathlok app. 22,23-Ghost Rider, Hulk, Hobgoblin app. 23-Wrap-around gatefold-c. 24-Infinity War x-over w/Demogoblin & Hobgoblin-c/story. 24-Demogoblin dons new costume & battles Hobgoblin-c/story. 26-($3.50, 52 pgs.)-Silver hologram on-c w/gatefold poster by Ron Lim; Spidey retells his origin. 4.00
26-2nd printing; gold hologram on-c 3.50
27-45: 32-34-Punisher-c/story. 37-Maximum Carnage x-over. 39,40-Electro-c/s (cameo #38). 41-43-Iron Fist-c/stories w/Jae Lee-c/a. 42-Intro Platoon. 44-Hobgoblin app. 3.00
46-49,51-53, 55, 56,58-74,76-81: 46-Begin $1.95-c; bound-in card sheet. 51-Power & Responsibility Pt. 3. 52,53-Venom app. 60-Kaine revealed. 61-Origin Kaine. 65-Mysterio app. 66-Kaine-c/app.; Peter Parker app. 67-Carnage-c/app. 68,69-Hobgoblin-c/app. 72-Onslaught x-over; Spidey vs. Sentinels. 74-Daredevil-c/app. 77-80-Morbius-c/app. 2.50
46-($2.95)-Polybagged; silver ink-c w/16 pg. preview of cartoon series & animation style print; bound-in trading card sheet 3.00
50-($2.50)-Newsstand edition 2.50
50-($3.95)-Collectors edition w/holographic-c 4.00
51-($2.95)-Deluxe edition foil-c; flip book 3.00
54-($2.75, 52 pgs.)-Flip book 2.75
57-($2.50) 2.50
57-($2.95)-Die cut-c 3.00
65-($2.95)-Variant-c; polybagged w/cassette 3.00
75-($2.95)-Wraparound-c; return of the Green Goblin; death of Ben Reilly (who was the clone) 4.00
82-97: 84-Juggernaut app. 91-Double cover with "Dusk #1"; battles the Shocker. 93-Ghost Rider app. 2.50
98-Double cover; final issue 3.00
#(-1) Flashback (7/97) 2.50
Annual '97 ($2.99), '98 ($2.99)-Devil Dinosaur-c/app. 3.00
...and Batman ('95, $5.95) DeMatteis-s; Joker, Carnage app. 6.00
...and Daredevil ('84, $2.00) 1-r/Spectacular Spider-Man #26-28 by Miller 3.00
...: Carnage nn (6/93, $6.95, TPB)-r/Amazing S-M #344,345,359-363; spot varnish-c 7.00
.../Daredevil (10/02, $2.99) Vatche Mavlian-c/a; Brett Matthews-s 3.00
.../Dr. Strange: "The Way to Dusty Death" nn (1992, $6.95, 68 pgs.) 7.00
.../Elektra '98-($2.99) vs. The Silencer 3.00
... Fear Itself Graphic Novel (2/92, $12.95) 18.00
Giant-Sized Spider-Man (12/98, $3.99) r/team-ups 4.00
Holiday Special 1995 ($2.95) 3.00
Identity Crisis (9/98, $19.95, TPB) 20.00
...Legends Vol. 1: Todd McFarlane ('03, $19.95, TPB)-r/Amaz. S-M #298-305 20.00
...Legends Vol. 2: Todd McFarlane ('03, $19.99, TPB)-r/Amaz. S-M #306-314, & Spec. Spider-Man Annual #10 20.00
...Legends Vol. 4: Spider-Man & Wolverine ('03, $13.95, TPB) r/Spider-Man & Wolverine #1-4 and Spider-Man/Daredevil #1 14.00
.../Marrow (2/01, $2.99) Garza-a 3.00
..., Punisher, Sabretooth: Designer Genes (1993, $8.95) 9.00
...Return of the Goblin TPB (See Peter Parker: Spider-Man)
...Revelations ('97, $14.99, TPB) r/end of Clone Saga plus 14 new pages by Romita Jr. 15.00
Special Edition 1 (12/92-c, 11/92 inside)-The Trial of Venom; ordered thru mail with $5.00 donation or more to UNICEF; embossed metallic ink; came bagged w/bound-in poster; Daredevil app. 1 3 4 6 8 10
Super Special (7/95, $3.95)-Planet of the Symbiotes 4.00
The Best of Spider-Man Vol. 2 (2003, $29.99, HC with dust jacket) r/AS-M V2 #37-45, Peter Parker: S-M #44-47, and S-M's Tangled Web #10,11; Pearson-c 30.00
The Complete Frank Miller Spider-Man (2002, $29.95, HC) r/Miller-s/a 30.00
The Death of Captain Stacy ($3.50) r/AS-M#88-90 3.50
The Death of Gwen Stacy ($14.95) r/AS-M#96-98,121,122 15.00
...: The Movie ($12.95) adaptation by Stan Lee-s/Alan Davis-a; plus r/Ultimate Spider-Man #8, Peter Parker #35, Tangled Web #10; photo-c 13.00
...: The Official Movie Adaptation ($5.95) Stan Lee-s/Alan Davis-a 6.00
Torment TPB (5/01$15.95) r/#1-5, Spec. S-M #10 16.00
... Vs. Doctor Octopus ($17.95) reprints early battles; Sean Chen-c 18.00
... Vs. Punisher (7/00, $2.99) Michael Lopez-c/a 3.00
...Vs. Venom (1990, $8.95, TPB)-r/Amaz. S-M #300,315-317 w/new McFarlane-c 9.00
...Visionaries (10/01, $19.95, TPB)-r/Amaz. S-M #298-305; McFarlane-a 20.00
...Visionaries: John Romita (8/01, $19.95, TPB)-r/Amaz. S-M #39-42, 50,68,69,108,109; new Romita-c 20.00
Wizard 1/2 ($10.00) Leonardi-a; Green Goblin app. 10.00
NOTE: *Erik Larsen c/a-15, 18-23. M. Rogers/Keith Williams c/a-27, 28.*

SPIDER-MAN ADVENTURES
Marvel Comics: Dec, 1994 - No. 15, Mar, 1996 ($1.50)

1-15 ($1.50)-Based on animated series 2.25
1-($2.95)-Foil embossed-c 3.00

SPIDER-MAN AND HIS AMAZING FRIENDS (See Marvel Action Universe)
Marvel Comics Group: Dec, 1981 (one-shot)

1-Adapted from NBC TV cartoon show; Green Goblin-c/story; 1st Spidey, Firestar, Iceman team-up; Spiegle-p 5.00

SPIDER-MAN AND THE INCREDIBLE HULK (See listing under Amazing...)

SPIDER-MAN AND THE UNCANNY X-MEN
Marvel Comics: Mar, 1996 ($16.95, trade paperback)

nn-r/Uncanny X-Men #27, Uncanny X-men #35, Amazing Spider-Man #92, Marvel Team-Up Annual #1, Marvel Team-Up #150, & Spectacular Spider-Man #197-199 17.00

SPIDER-MAN & WOLVERINE (See Spider-Man Legends Vol. 4 for TPB reprint)
Marvel Comics: Aug, 2003 - No. 4, Nov, 2003 ($2.99, limited series)

1-4-Matthews-s/Mavlian-a 3.00

SPIDER-MAN AND X-FACTOR
Marvel Comics: May, 1994 - No. 3, July, 1994 ($1.95, limited series)

1-3 2.25

SPIDER-MAN /BADROCK
Maximum Press: Mar, 1997 ($2.99, mini-series)

1A, 1B(#2)-Jurgens-s 3.00

SPIDER-MAN/BLACK CAT: THE EVIL THAT MEN DO
Marvel Comics: Aug, 2002 - No. 4 ($2.99, limited series)

1-Kevin Smith-s/Terry Dodson-c/a 3.00
2,3 3.00

SPIDER-MAN: BLUE
Marvel Comics: July, 2002 - No. 6, Apr, 2003 ($3.50, limited series)

1-6: Jeph Loeb-s/Tim Sale-a/c; flashback to early MJ and Gwen Stacy 3.50
HC (2003, $21.99, with dust jacket) over-sized r/#1-6; intro. by John Romita 22.00

SPIDER-MAN: CHAPTER ONE
Marvel Comics: Dec, 1998 - No. 12, Oct, 1999 ($2.50, limited series)

1-Retelling/updating of origin; John Byrne-s/c/a 2.50
1-($6.95) DF Edition w/variant-c by Jae Lee 7.00
2-11: 2-Two covers (one is swipe of ASM #1); Fantastic Four app. 9-Daredevil. 11-Giant-Man-c/app. 2.50
12-($3.50) Battles the Sandman 3.50
0-(5/99) Origins of Vulture, Lizard and Sandman 2.50

SPIDER-MAN CLASSICS
Marvel Comics: Apr, 1993 - No. 16, July, 1994 ($1.25)

1-14,16: 1-r/Amaz. Fantasy #15 & Strange Tales #115. 2-16-r/Amaz. Spider-Man #1-15. 6-Austin-c(i) 2.25
15-($2.95)-Polybagged w/16 pg. insert & animation style print; r/Amazing Spider-Man #14 (1st Green Goblin) 3.00

SPIDER-MAN COLLECTOR'S PREVIEW
Marvel Comics: Dec, 1994 ($1.50, 100 pgs., one-shot)

1-wraparound-c; no comics 3.00

SPIDER-MAN COMICS MAGAZINE

Spider-Man/Gen13 © MAR & WSP

Spider-Man Megazine #2 © MAR

Spider-Man's Tangled Web #1 © MAR

GD 2.0 | VG 4.0 | FN 6.0 | VF 8.0 | VF/NM 9.0 | NM- 9.2

Marvel Comics Group: Jan, 1987 - No. 13, 1988 ($1.50, digest-size)
1-13-Reprints 6.00

SPIDER-MAN: DEAD MAN'S HAND
Marvel Comics: Apr, 1997 ($2.99, one-shot)
1 3.00

SPIDER-MAN: DEATH AND DESTINY
Marvel Comics: Aug, 2000 - No. 3, Oct, 2000 ($2.99, limited series)
1-3-Aftermath of the death of Capt. Stacy 3.00

SPIDER-MAN/ DOCTOR OCTOPUS: OUT OF REACH
Marvel Comics: Jan, 2004 - No. 5 ($2.99, limited series)
1,2-Keron Grant-a/Colin Mitchell-s 3.00

SPIDER-MAN: FRIENDS AND ENEMIES
Marvel Comics: Jan, 1995 - No. 4, Apr, 1995 ($1.95, limited series)
1-4-Darkhawk, Nova & Speedball app. 2.25

SPIDER-MAN: FUNERAL FOR AN OCTOPUS
Marvel Comics: Mar, 1995 - No. 3, May, 1995 ($1.50, limited series)
1-3 2.25

SPIDER-MAN/ GEN 13
Marvel Comics: Nov, 1996 ($4.95, one-shot)
nn-Peter David-s/Stuart Immonen-a 5.00

SPIDER-MAN: GET KRAVEN
Marvel Comics: Aug, 2002 - No. 6, Jan, 2003 ($2.99/$2.25, limited series)
1-($2.99) McCrea-a/Quesada-c; back-up story w/Rio-a 3.00
2-6-($2.25) 2-Sub-Mariner app. 2.25

SPIDER-MAN: HOBGOBLIN LIVES
Marvel Comics: Jan, 1997 - No. 3, Mar, 1997 ($2.50, limited series)
1-3-Wraparound-c 2.50
TPB (1/98, $14.99) r/#1-3 plus timeline 15.00

SPIDER-MAN: HOT SHOTS
Marvel Comics: Jan, 1996 ($2.95, one-shot)
nn-fold out posters by various, inc. Vess and Ross 3.00

SPIDER-MAN: LEGACY OF EVIL
Marvel Comics: June, 1996 ($3.95, one-shot)
1-Kurt Busiek script & Mark Texeira-c/a 4.00

SPIDER-MAN: LEGEND OF THE SPIDER-CLAN (See Marvel Mangaverse for TPB)
Marvel Comics: Dec, 2002 - No. 5, Apr, 2003 ($2.25, limited series)
1-5-Marvel Mangaverse Spider-Man; Kaare Andrews-s/Skottie Young-c/a 2.25

SPIDER-MAN: LIFELINE
Marvel Comics: Apr, 2001 - No. 3, June, 2001 ($2.99, limited series)
1-3-Nicieza-s/Rude-c/a; The Lizard app. 3.00

SPIDER-MAN: MADE MEN
Marvel Comics: Aug, 1998 ($5.99, one-shot)
1-Spider-Man & Daredevil vs. Kingpin 6.00

SPIDER-MAN MAGAZINE
Marvel Comics: 1994 - No. 3, 1994 ($1.95, magazine)
1-3: 1-Contains 4 S-M promo cards & 4 X-Men Ultra Fleer cards; Spider-Man story by Romita, Sr.; X-Men story; puzzles & games. 2-Doc Octopus & X-Men stories 3.00

SPIDER-MAN: MAXIMUM CLONAGE
Marvel Comics: 1995 ($4.95)
Alpha #1-Acetate-c, Omega #1-Chromium-c. 5.00

SPIDER-MAN MEGAZINE
Marvel Comics: Oct, 1994 - No. 6, Mar, 1995 ($2.95, 100 pgs.)
1-6: 1-r/ASM #16,224,225, Marvel Team-Up #1 3.00

SPIDER-MAN: POWER OF TERROR
Marvel Comics: Jan, 1995 - No. 4, Apr, 1995 ($1.95, limited series)
1-4-Silvermane & Deathlok app. 2.25

SPIDER-MAN/PUNISHER: FAMILY PLOT
Marvel Comics: Feb, 1996 - No. 2, Mar, 1996 ($2.95, limited series)
1,2 3.00

SPIDER-MAN: QUALITY OF LIFE
Marvel Comics: Jul, 2002 - No. 4, Oct, 2002 ($2.99, limited series)
1-4-All CGI art by Scott Sava; Rucka-s; Lizard app. 3.00
TPB (2002, $12.99) r/#1-4; a "Making of..." section detailing the CGI process 13.00

SPIDER-MAN: REDEMPTION
Marvel Comics: Sept, 1996 - No. 4, Dec, 1996 ($1.50, limited series)
1-4: DeMatteis scripts; Zeck-a 2.25

SPIDER-MAN: REVENGE OF THE GREEN GOBLIN
Marvel Comics: Oct, 2000 - No. 3, Dec, 2000 ($2.99, limited series)
1-3-Frenz & Olliffe-a; continues in AS-M #25 & PP:S-M #25 3.00

SPIDER-MAN SAGA
Marvel Comics: Nov, 1991 - No. 4, Feb, 1992 ($2.95, limited series)
1-4: Gives history of Spider-Man: text & illustrations 3.00

SPIDER-MAN: SWEET CHARITY
Marvel Comics: Aug, 2002 ($4.95, one-shot)
1-The Scorpion-c/app.; Campbell-c/Zimmerman-s/Robertson-a 5.00

SPIDER-MAN'S TANGLED WEB (Titled "Tangled Web" in indicia for #1-4)
Marvel Comics: Jun, 2001 - No. 22, Mar, 2003 ($2.99)
1-3: "The Thousand" on-c; Ennis-s/McCrea-a/Fabry-c 4.00
4-"Severance Package" on-c; Rucka-s/Risso-a; Kingpin-c/app. 5.00
5,6-Flowers for Rhino; Milligan-s/Fegredo-a 3.00
7-10,12,15-20,22: 7-9-Gentlemen's Agreement; Bruce Jones-s/Lee Weeks-a. 10-Andrews-s/a. 12-Fegredo-a. 15-Paul Pope-s/a. 18-Ted McKeever-s/a. 19-Mahfood-a. 20-Haspiel-a 3.00
11,13,21-($3.50) 11-Darwyn Cooke-s/a. 13-Phillips-a. 21-Christmas-s by Cooke & Bone 3.50
14-Azzarello & Scott Levy (WWE's Raven)-s about Crusher Hogan 4.00
TPB (10/01, $15.95) r/#1-6 16.00
Volume 2 TPB (4/02, $14.95) r/#7-11 15.00
Volume 3 TPB (2002, $15.99) r/#12-17; Jason Pearson-c 16.00
Volume 4 TPB (2003, $15.99) r/#18-22; Frank Cho-c 16.00

SPIDER-MAN TEAM-UP
Marvel Comics: Dec, 1995 - No. 7, June, 1996 ($2.95)
1-7: 1-w/ X-Men. 2-w/Silver Surfer. 3-w/Fantastic Four. 4-w/Avengers. 5-Gambit & Howard the Duck-c/app. 7-Thunderbolts-c/app. 3.00

SPIDER-MAN: THE ARACHNIS PROJECT
Marvel Comics: Aug, 1994 - No. 6, Jan, 1995 ($1.75, limited series)
1-6-Venom, Styx, Stone & Jury app. 2.25

SPIDER-MAN: THE CLONE JOURNAL
Marvel Comics: Mar, 1995 ($2.95, one-shot)
1 3.00

SPIDER-MAN: THE FINAL ADVENTURE
Marvel Comics: Nov, 1995 - No. 4, Feb, 1996 ($2.95, limited series)
1-4: 1-Nicieza scripts; foil-c 3.00

SPIDER-MAN: THE JACKAL FILES
Marvel Comics: Aug, 1995 ($1.95, one-shot)
1 2.25

SPIDER-MAN: THE LOST YEARS
Marvel Comics: Aug, 1995-No. 3, Oct, 1995; No. 0, 1996 ($2.95/$3.95,lim. series)
0-(1/96, $3.95)-Reprints. 4.00
1-3-DeMatteis scripts, Romita, Jr.-c/a 3.00
NOTE: ***Romita** c-0i. **Romita, Jr.** a-0r, 1-3p. c-0-3p. **Sharp** a-0r.*

SPIDER-MAN: THE MANGA
Marvel Comics: Dec, 1997 - No. 31, June, 1999 ($3.99/$2.99, B&W, bi-weekly)
1-($3.99)-English translation of Japanese Spider-Man 4.00
2-31-($2.99) 3.00

SPIDER-MAN: THE MUTANT AGENDA
Marvel Comics: No. 0, Feb, 1994; No. 1, Mar, 1994 - No. 3, May, 1994 ($1.75, limited series)
0-(2/94, $1.25, 52 pgs.)-Crosses over w/newspaper strip; has empty pages to paste in newspaper strips; gives origin of Spidey 2.25
1-3: Beast & Hobgoblin app. 1-X-Men app. 2.25

SPIDER-MAN: THE MYSTERIO MANIFESTO (Listed as "Spider-Man and Mysterio" in indicia)
Marvel Comics: Jan, 2001 - No. 3, Mar, 2001 ($2.99, limited series)
1-3-Daredevil-c/app.; Weeks & McLeod-a 3.00

SPIDER-MAN: THE PARKER YEARS
Marvel Comics: Nov, 1995 ($2.50, one-shot)
1 2.50

Spider-Man Unlimited #1 © MAR

Spider-Woman (3rd series) #5 © MAR

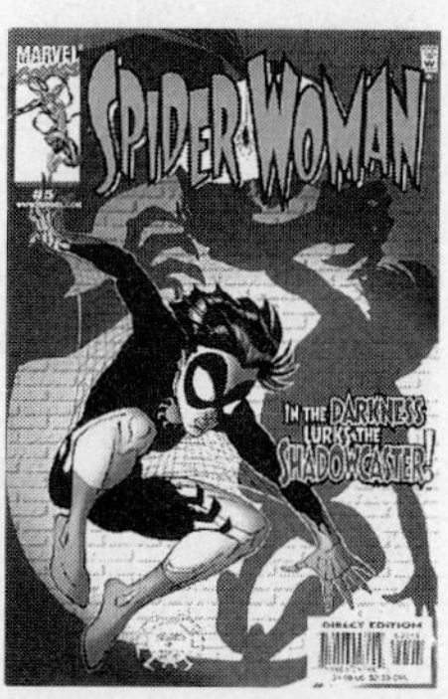

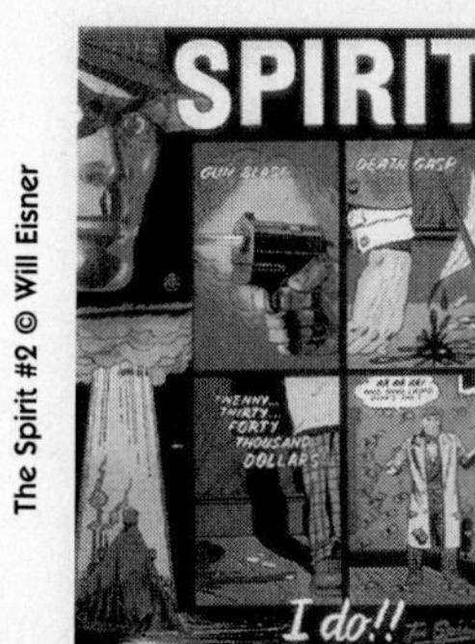

The Spirit #2 © Will Eisner

GD 2.0 | VG 4.0 | FN 6.0 | VF 8.0 | VF/NM 9.0 | NM- 9.2

SPIDER-MAN 2099 (See Amazing Spider-Man #365)
Marvel Comics: Nov, 1992 - No. 46, Aug, 1996 ($1.25/$1.50/$1.95)

1-(stiff-c)-Red foil stamped-c; begins origin of Miguel O'Hara (Spider-Man 2099); Leonardi/Williamson-c/a begins 3.00
1-2nd printing, 2-24,26-40: 2-Origin continued, ends #3. 4-Doom 2099 app. 13-Extra 16 pg. insert on Midnight Sons. 19-Bound-in trading card sheet. 35-Variant-c. 36-Two-c; Jae Lee-a. 37,38-Two-c 2.25
25-($2.25, 52 pgs.)-Newsstand edition 2.25
25-($2.95, 52 pgs.)-Deluxe edition w/embossed foil-c 3.00
41-46: 46-The Vulture app; Mike McKone-a(p)
Annual 1 (1994, $2.95, 68 pgs.) 3.00
Special 1 (1995, $3.95) 4.00
NOTE: *Chaykin c-37. Ron Lim a(p)-18; c(p)-13, 16, 18. Kelley Jones c/a-9. Leonardi/Williamson a-1-8, 10-13, 15-17, 19, 20, 22-25; c-1-13, 15, 17-19, 20, 22-25, 35.*

SPIDER-MAN 2099 MEETS SPIDER-MAN
Marvel Comics: 1995 ($5.95, one-shot)

nn-Peter David script; Leonardi/Williamson-c/a. 6.00

SPIDER-MAN UNIVERSE
Marvel Comics: Mar, 2000 - No. 7, Oct, 2000 ($4.95/$3.99, reprints)

1-5-Reprints recent issues from the various Spider-Man titles 5.00
6,7-($3.99) 4.00

SPIDER-MAN UNLIMITED
Marvel Comics: May, 1993 - No. 22, Nov, 1998 ($3.95, quarterly, 68 pgs.)

1-Begin Maximum Carnage storyline, ends; Carnage-c/story 5.00
2-12: 2-Venom & Carnage-c/story; Lim-c/a(p) in #2-6. 10-Vulture app. 4.00
13-22: 13-Begin $2.99-c; Scorpion-c/app. 15-Daniel-c; Puma-c/app. 19-Lizard-c/app. 20-Hannibal King and Lilith app. 21,22-Deodato-a 3.00

SPIDER-MAN UNLIMITED (Based on the TV animated series)
Marvel Comics: Dec, 1999 - No. 5, Apr, 2000 ($2.99/$1.99)

1-($2.99) Venom and Carnage app. 3.00
2-5: 2-($1.99) Green Goblin app. 2.25

SPIDER-MAN UNLIMITED
Marvel Comics: Mar, 2004 - Present ($2.99)

1-Short stories by various incl. Miyazawa & Chen-a 3.00

SPIDER-MAN UNMASKED
Marvel Comics: Nov, 1996 ($5.95, one-shot)

nn-Art w/text 6.00

SPIDER-MAN: VENOM AGENDA
Marvel Comics: Jan, 1998 ($2.99, one-shot)

1-Hama-s/Lyle-c/a 3.00

SPIDER-MAN VS. DRACULA
Marvel Comics: Jan, 1994 ($1.75, 52 pgs., one-shot)

1-r/Giant-Size Spider-Man #1 plus new Matt Fox-a 2.25

SPIDER-MAN VS. WOLVERINE
Marvel Comics Group: Feb, 1987; V2#1, 1990 (68 pgs.)

1-Williamson-c/a(i); intro Charlemagne; death of Ned Leeds (old Hobgoblin) 2 4 6 12 16 20
V2#1 (1990, $4.95)-Reprints #1 (2/87) 5.00

SPIDER-MAN: WEB OF DOOM
Marvel Comics: Aug, 1994 - No. 3, Oct, 1994 ($1.75, limited series)

1-3 2.25

SPIDER-MAN: YEAR IN REVIEW
Marvel Comics: Feb, 2000 ($2.99)

1-Text recaps of 1999 issues 3.00

SPIDER REIGN OF THE VAMPIRE KING, THE (Also see The Spider)
Eclipse Books: 1992 - No. 3, 1992 ($4.95, limited series, coated stock, 52 pgs.)

Book One - Three: Truman scripts & painted-c 5.00

SPIDER'S WEB, THE (See G-8 and His Battle Aces)

SPIDER-WOMAN (Also see The Avengers #240, Marvel Spotlight #32, Marvel Super Heroes Secret Wars #7 & Marvel Two-In-One #29)
Marvel Comics Group: April, 1978 - No. 50, June, 1983 (New logo #47 on)

1-New complete origin & mask added 2 4 6 10 12 15
2-5,7-18: 2-Excalibur app. 3,11,12-Brother Grimm app. 13,15-The Shroud-c/s. 16-Sienkiewicz-c 5.00
6,19,20,28,29,32: 6-Morgan LeFay app. 6,19,32-Werewolf by Night-c/s.
20,28,29-Spider-Man app. 32-Miller-c 6.00
21-27,30,31,33-36 5.00
37,38-X-Men x-over: 37-1st app. Siryn of X-Force; origin retold 1 2 3 5 6 8
39-49: 46-Kingpin app. 49-Tigra-c/story 4.00
50-(52 pgs.)-Death of Spider-Woman; photo-c 2 4 6 8 10 12
NOTE: *Austin a-37i. Byrne c-26p. Infantino a-1-19. Layton c-19. Miller c-32p.*

SPIDER-WOMAN
Marvel Comics: Nov, 1993 - No. 4, Feb, 1994 ($1.75, mini-series)

V2#1-4: 1,2-Origin; U.S. Agent app. 2.25

SPIDER-WOMAN
Marvel Comics: July, 1999 - No. 18, Dec, 2000 ($2.99/$1.99/$2.25)

1-($2.99) Byrne-s/Sears-a 3.00
2-18: 2-11-($1.99). 2-Two covers. 12-Begin $2.25-c. 15-Capt. America-c/app. 2.25

SPIDEY SUPER STORIES (Spider-Man) (Also see Fireside Books)
Marvel/Children's TV Workshop: Oct, 1974 - No. 57, Mar, 1982 (35¢, no ads)

1-Origin (stories simplified for younger readers) 4 8 12 27 36 45
2-Kraven 3 6 9 16 20 25
3-10,15: 6-Iceman. 15-Storm-c/sty 2 4 6 11 14 18
11-14,16-20: 19,20-Kirby-c 2 4 6 10 13 16
21-30: 24-Kirby-c 2 4 6 9 11 14
31-53: 31-Moondragon-c/app.; Dr. Doom app. 33-Hulk. 34-Sub-Mariner. 38-F.F. 39-Thanos-c/story. 44-Vision. 45-Silver Surfer & Dr. Doom app. 2 4 6 8 10 12
54-57: 56-Battles Jack O'Lantern-c/sty (exactly one year after 1st app. in Machine Man #19) 2 4 6 11 14 18

SPIKE AND TYKE (See M.G.M.'s...)

SPIN & MARTY (TV) (Walt Disney's)(See Walt Disney Showcase #32)
Dell Publishing Co. (Mickey Mouse Club): No. 714, June, 1956 - No. 1082, Mar-May, 1960 (All photo-c)

Four Color 714 (#1) 14 28 42 97 141 185
Four Color 767,808 (#2,3) 10 20 30 70 100 130
Four Color 826 (#4)-Annette Funicello photo-c 25 50 75 176 258 340
5(3-5/58) - 9(6-8/59) 9 18 27 60 85 110
Four Color 1026,1082 9 18 27 60 85 110

SPINE-TINGLING TALES (Doctor Spektor Presents...)
Gold Key: May, 1975 - No. 4, Jan, 1976 (All 25¢ issues)

1-1st Tragg-r/Mystery Comics Digest #3 2 4 6 9 11 14
2-4: 2-Origin Ra-Ka-Tep-r/Mystery Comics Digest #1; Dr. Spektor #12. 3-All Durak-r issue; 4-Baron Tibor's 1st app.-r/Mystery Comics Digest #4; painted-c 1 2 3 5 6 8

SPINWORLD
Amaze Ink (Slave Labor Graphics): July, 1997 - No. 4, Jan, 1998 ($2.95/$3.95, B&W, mini-series)

1-3-Brent Anderson-a(p) 3.00
4-($3.95) 4.00

SPIRAL PATH, THE
Eclipse Comics: July, 1986 - No. 2 ($1.75, Baxter paper, limited series)

1,2 2.25

SPIRAL ZONE
DC Comics: Feb, 1988 - No. 4, May, 1988 ($1.00, mini-series)

1-4-Based on Tonka toys 2.25

SPIRIT, THE (Newspaper comics - see Promotional Comics section)

SPIRIT, THE (1st Series)(Also see Police Comics #11)
Quality Comics Group (Vital): 1944 - No. 22, Aug, 1950

nn(#1)- "Wanted Dead or Alive" 76 152 228 475 713 950
nn(#2)- "Crime Doesn't Pay" 44 88 132 264 395 525
nn(#3)- "Murder Runs Wild" 39 78 117 233 329 425
4,5: 4-Flatfoot Burns begins, ends #22. 5-Wertham app. 31 62 93 178 252 325
6-10 26 52 78 150 210 270
11 24 48 72 135 190 245
12-17-Eisner-c. 19-Honeybun app. 35 70 105 201 288 370
18-21-Strip-r by Eisner; Eisner-c 40 80 120 240 345 450
22-Used by N.Y. Legis. Comm; classic Eisner-c 55 110 165 344 515 685
Super Reprint #11-r/Quality Spirit #19 by Eisner 3 7 10 21 28 35
Super Reprint #12-r/Spirit #17 by Fine; Sol Brodsky-c 3 7 10 21 28 35

SPIRIT, THE (2nd Series)

The Spirit: The New Adventures #1 © Will Eisner

Spirit of the Tao #2 © TCOW

Spook #2 © STAR

	GD 2.0	VG 4.0	FN 6.0	VF 8.0	VF/NM 9.0	NM- 9.2

GD VG FN VF VF/NM NM- 2.0 4.0 6.0 8.0 9.0 9.2

Fiction House Magazines: Spring, 1952 - No. 5, 1954

1-Not Eisner	40	80	120	240	350	460
2-Eisner-c/a(2)	40	80	120	240	340	440
3-Eisner/Grandenetti-c	33	66	99	190	270	350
4-Eisner/Grandenetti-c; Eisner-a	34	68	102	196	278	360
5-Eisner-c/a(4)	39	78	117	230	325	420

SPIRIT, THE
Harvey Publications: Oct, 1966 - No. 2, Mar, 1967 (Giant Size, 25¢, 68 pgs.)

1-Eisner-r plus 9 new pgs.(origin Denny Colt, Take 3, plus 2 filler pgs.) (#3 was advertised, but never published)	8	16	24	55	78	100
2-Eisner-r plus 9 new pgs.(origin of the Octopus)	6	12	18	43	59	75

SPIRIT, THE (Underground)
Kitchen Sink Enterprises (Krupp Comics): Jan, 1973 - No. 2, Sept, 1973 (Black & White)

1-New Eisner-c & 4 pgs. new Eisner-a plus-r (titled Crime Convention)	2	4	6	10	12	15
2-New Eisner-c & 4 pgs. new Eisner-a plus-r (titled Meets P'Gell)	2	4	6	12	16	20

SPIRIT, THE (Magazine)
Warren Publ. Co./Krupp Comic Works No. 17 on: 4/74 - No. 16, 10/76; No. 17, Winter, 1977 - No. 41, 6/83 (B&W w/color) (#6-14,16 are squarebound)

1-Eisner-r begin; 8 pg. color insert	3	7	10	21	28	35
2-5: 2-Powder Pouf-s; UFO-s. 4-Silk Satin-s	2	4	6	12	16	20
6-9,11-15: 7-All Ebony issue. 8-Female Foes issue. 8,12-Sand Seref-s. 9-P'Gell & Octupus-s. 12-X-Mas issue	2	4	6	10	12	15
10-Giant Summer Special ($1.50)-Origin	2	4	6	14	18	22
16-Giant Summer Special ($1.50)-Olga Bustle-c/s	2	4	6	11	14	18
17,18(8/78): 17-Lady Luck-r	1	2	3	5	7	9
19-21-New Eisner-a. 20,21-Wood-r (#21-r/A DP on the Moon by Wood). 20-Outer Space-r	1	2	3	5	7	9
22-41: 22,23-Wood-r (#22-r/Mission the Moon by Wood). 28-r/last story (10/5/52). 30-(7/81)-Special Spirit Jam issue w/Caniff, Corben, Bolland, Byrne, Miller, Kurtzman, Rogers, Sienkiewicz-a & 40 others. 36-Begin Spirit Section-r; r/1st story (6/2/40) in color; new Eisner-c/a(18 pgs.)($2.95). 37-r/2nd story in color plus 18 pgs. new Eisner-a. 38-41: r/3rd - 6th stories in color. 41-Lady Luck Mr. Mystic in color	1	2	3	5	6	8
Special 1(1975)-All Eisner-a (mail only, full color)	5	10	15	33	44	55

NOTE: *Covers pencilled/inked by* ***Eisner*** *only #1-9,12-16; painted by Eisner & Ken Kelly #10 & 11; painted by Eisner #17-up; one color story reprinted in #1-10.* ***Austin*** *a-30i.* ***Byrne*** *a-30p.* ***Miller*** *a-30p.*

SPIRIT, THE
Kitchen Sink Enterprises: Oct, 1983 - No. 87, Jan, 1992 ($2.00, Baxter paper)

1-60: 1-Origin-r/12/23/45 Spirit Section. 2-r/ 1/20/46-2/10/46. 3-r/2/17/46-3/10/46. 4-r/3/17/46-4/7/46. 11-Last color issue. 54-r/section 2/19/50	4.00
61-87: 85-87-Reprint the Outer Space Spirit stories by Wood. 86-r/A DP on the Moon by Wood from 1952	4.00

SPIRIT JAM
Kitchen Sink Press: Aug, 1998 ($5.95, B&W, oversized, square-bound)

nn-Reprints Spirit (Magazine) #30 by Eisner & 50 others; and "Cerebus Vs. The Spirit" from Cerebus Jam #1	6.00

SPIRIT, THE: THE NEW ADVENTURES
Kitchen Sink Press: 1997 - No. 8, Nov, 1998 ($3.50, anthology)

1-Moore-s/Gibbons-c/a	4.00
2-8: 2-Gaiman-s/Eisner-c. 3-Moore-s/Bolland-c/Moebius back-c. 4-Allred-s/a; Busiek-s/Anderson-a. 5-Chadwick-s/c/a(p); Nyberg-i. 6-S.Hampton & Mandrake-a	3.50

SPIRIT: THE ORIGIN YEARS
Kitchen Sink Press: May, 1992 - No. 10, Dec, 1993 ($2.95, B&W)

1-10: 1-r/sections 6/2/40(origin)-6/23/40 (all 1940s)	3.00

SPIRITMAN (Also see Three Comics)
No publisher listed: No date (1944) (10¢)
(Triangle Sales Co. ad on back cover)

1-Three 16pg. Spirit sections bound together, (1944, 10¢, 52 pgs.)	21	42	63	118	164	210
2-Two Spirit sections (3/26/44, 4/2/44) bound together; by Lou Fine	19	38	57	106	146	185

SPIRIT OF THE BORDER (See Zane Grey & Four Color #197)

SPIRIT OF THE TAO
Image Comics (Top Cow): Jun, 1998 - No. 15, May, 2000 ($2.50)

Preview	5.00
1-14: 1-D-Tron-s/Tan & D-Tron-a	2.50
15-($4.95)	5.00

SPIRIT OF WONDER (Manga)
Dark Horse Comics: Apr, 1996 - No. 5, Aug, 1996 ($2.95, B&W, limited series)

1-5	3.00

SPIRIT WORLD (Magazine)
National Periodical Publications: Fall, 1971 (B&W)

1-New Kirby-a; Neal Adams-c; poster inside (1/2 price without poster)	7	14	21	46	63	80

SPITFIRE
Malverne Herald (Elliot)(J. R. Mahon): No. 132, 1944 (Aug) - No. 133, 1945
(Female undercover agent)

132,133: Both have Classics Gift Box ads on b/c with checklist to #20	26	52	78	147	206	265

SPITFIRE AND THE TROUBLESHOOTERS
Marvel Comics: Oct, 1986 - No. 9, June, 1987 (Codename: Spitfire #10 on)

1-3,5-9	2.25
4-McFarlane-a	3.00

SPITFIRE COMICS (Also see Double Up)
Harvey Publications: Aug, 1941 - No. 2, Oct, 1941 (Pocket size; 100 pgs.)

1-Origin The Clown, The Fly-Man, The Spitfire & The Magician From Bagdad	78	156	234	488	732	975
2-(Scarce)	72	144	216	450	675	900

SPLITTING IMAGE
Image Comics: Mar, 1993 - No. 2, 1993 ($1.95)

1,2-Simpson-c/a; parody comic	2.25

SPOOF
Marvel Comics Group: Oct, 1970; No. 2, Nov, 1972 - No. 5, May, 1973

1-Infinity-c; Dark Shadows-c & parody	2	4	6	14	18	20
2-5: 2-All in the Family. 3-Beatles, Osmond's, Jackson 5, David Cassidy, Nixon & Agnew-c. 5-Rod Serling, Woody Allen, Ted Kennedy-c	2	4	6	9	11	14

SPOOK (Formerly Shock Detective Cases)
Star Publications: No. 22, Jan, 1953 - No. 30, Oct, 1954

22-Sgt. Spook-r; acid in face story; hanging-c	40	80	120	240	340	440
23,25,27: 25-Jungle Lil-r. 27-Two Sgt. Spook-r	30	60	90	170	240	310
24-Used in **SOTI**, pgs. 182,183-r/Inside Crime #2; Transvestism story	31	62	93	175	248	320
26,28-30: 26-Disbrow-a. 28,29-Rulah app. 29-Jo-Jo app. 30-Disbrow-c/a(2); only Star-c	30	60	90	170	240	310

NOTE: ***L. B. Cole*** *covers-all issues except #30; a-28(1 pg.).* ***Disbrow*** *a-26(2), 28, 29(2), 30(2); No. 30 r/Blue Bolt Weird Tales #114.*

SPOOK COMICS
Baily Publications/Star: 1946

1-Mr. Lucifer story	31	62	93	175	248	320

SPOOKY (The Tuff Little Ghost; see Casper The Friendly Ghost)
Harvey Publications: 11/55 - 139, 11/73; No. 140, 7/74 - No. 155, 3/77; No. 156, 12/77 - No. 158, 4/78; No. 159, 9/78; No. 160, 10/79; No. 161, 9/80

1-Nightmare begins (see Casper #19)	41	82	123	324	487	650
2	22	44	66	156	228	300
3-10(1956-57)	13	26	39	94	137	180
11-20(1957-58)	8	16	24	53	74	95
21-40(1958-59)	6	12	18	38	52	65
41-60	4	8	12	29	40	50
61-80,100	3	7	10	21	28	35
81-99	3	6	9	18	23	28
101-120	2	4	6	11	14	18
121-126,133-140	2	4	6	8	10	12
127-132: All 52 pg. Giants	2	4	6	11	14	18
141-161	1	2	3	5	6	8

SPOOKY
Harvey Comics: Nov, 1991 - No. 4, Sept, 1992 ($1.00/$1.25)

1	4.00
2-4: 3-Begin $1.25-c	3.00
...Digest 1-3 (10/92, 6/93, 10/93, $1.75, 100 pgs.)-Casper, Wendy, etc.	4.00

SPOOKY HAUNTED HOUSE
Harvey Publications: Oct, 1972 - No. 15, Feb, 1975

1	3	7	10	21	28	35
2-5	2	4	6	11	14	18

Sport Stars #1 © MAR

Spunky the Smiling Spook #1 © AJAX

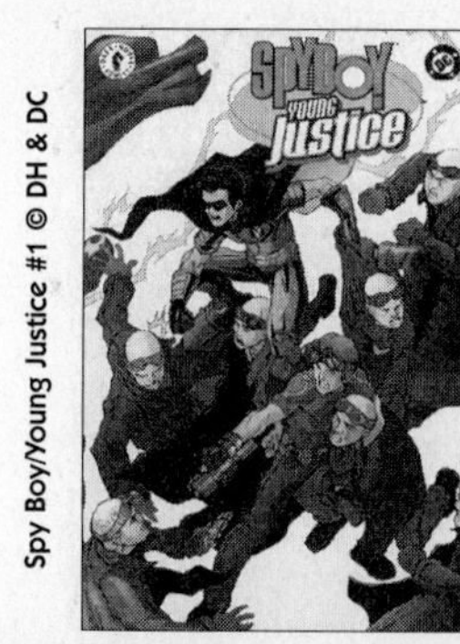

Spy Boy/Young Justice #1 © DH & DC

	GD 2.0	VG 4.0	FN 6.0	VF 8.0	VF/NM 9.0	NM- 9.2
6-10	2	4	6	8	10	12
11-15	1	2	3	5	7	9

SPOOKY MYSTERIES
Your Guide Publ. Co.: No date (1946) (10¢)

	GD	VG	FN	VF	VF/NM	NM-
1-Mr. Spooky, Super Snooper, Pinky, Girl Detective app.	20	40	60	112	156	200

SPOOKY SPOOKTOWN
Harvey Publ.: 9/61; No. 2, 9/62 - No. 52, 12/73; No. 53, 10/74 - No. 66, 12/76

	GD	VG	FN	VF	VF/NM	NM-
1-Casper, Spooky; 68 pgs. begin	17	34	51	123	182	240
2	9	18	27	65	93	120
3-5	7	14	21	46	63	80
6-10	5	10	15	36	48	60
11-20	4	8	12	24	32	40
21-39: 39-Last 68 pg. issue	3	6	9	19	25	32
40-45: All 52 pgs.	2	4	6	11	14	18
46-66: 61-Hot Stuff/Spooky team-up story	1	2	3	5	7	9

SPORT COMICS (Becomes True Sport Picture Stories #5 on)
Street & Smith Publications: Oct, 1940 (No mo.) - No. 4, Nov, 1941

	GD	VG	FN	VF	VF/NM	NM-
1-Life story of Lou Gehrig	55	110	165	330	495	660
2	31	62	93	175	248	320
3,4	27	54	81	153	214	275

SPORT LIBRARY (See Charlton Sport Library)

SPORTS ACTION (Formerly Sport Stars)
Marvel/Atlas Comics (ACI No. 2,3/SAI No. 4-14): No. 2, Feb, 1950 - No. 14, Sept, 1952

	GD	VG	FN	VF	VF/NM	NM-
2-Powell painted-c; George Gipp life story	42	84	126	252	376	500
1-(nd,no price, no publ., 52pgs, #1 on-c; has same-c as #2; blank inside-c (giveaway?)	23	46	69	129	180	230
3-Everett-a	25	50	75	144	198	255
4-11,14: Weiss-a	22	44	66	127	176	225
12,13: 12-Everett-c. 13-Krigstein-a	24	48	72	135	190	245

NOTE: *Title may have changed after No. 3, to Crime Must Lose No. 4 on, due to publisher change.* ***Sol Brodsky*** *c-4-7, 13, 14.* ***Maneely*** *c-3, 8-11.*

SPORT STARS
Parents' Magazine Institute (Sport Stars): Feb-Mar, 1946 - No. 4, Aug-Sept, 1946 (Half comic, half photo magazine)

	GD	VG	FN	VF	VF/NM	NM-
1- "How Tarzan Got That Way" story of Johnny Weissmuller	40	80	120	240	340	440
2-Baseball greats	27	54	81	155	218	280
3,4	24	48	72	135	190	245

SPORT STARS (Becomes Sports Action #2 on)
Marvel Comics (ACI): Nov, 1949 (52 pgs.)

	GD	VG	FN	VF	VF/NM	NM-
1-Knute Rockne; painted-c	44	88	132	264	395	525

SPORT THRILLS (Formerly Dick Cole; becomes Jungle Thrills #16)
Star Publications: No. 11, Nov, 1950 - No. 15, Nov, 1951

	GD	VG	FN	VF	VF/NM	NM-
11-Dick Cole begins; Ted Williams & Ty Cobb life stories	31	62	93	175	248	320
12-Joe DiMaggio, Phil Rizzuto stories & photos on-c; L.B. Cole-c/a	25	50	75	144	198	255
13-15-All L. B. Cole-c. 13-Jackie Robinson, Pee Wee Reese stories & photo on-c. 14-Johnny Weissmuler life story	25	50	75	144	198	255
Accepted Reprint #11 (#15 on-c, nd); L.B. Cole-c	9	18	27	52	66	80
Accepted Reprint #12 (nd); L.B. Cole-c; Joe DiMaggio & Phil Rizzuto life stories-r/#12	9	18	27	52	66	80

SPOTLIGHT (TV) (newsstand sales only)
Marvel Comics Group: Sept, 1978 - No. 4, Mar, 1979 (Hanna-Barbera)

	GD	VG	FN	VF	VF/NM	NM-
1-Huckleberry Hound, Yogi Bear; Shaw-a	3	7	10	21	28	35
2,4: 2-Quick Draw McGraw, Augie Doggie, Snooper & Blabber. 4-Magilla Gorilla, Snagglepuss	3	6	9	16	20	25
3-The Jetsons; Yakky Doodle	3	7	10	21	28	35

SPOTLIGHT COMICS (Becomes Red Seal Comics #14 on?)
Harry 'A' Chesler (Our Army, Inc.): Nov, 1944 - No. 3, 1945

	GD	VG	FN	VF	VF/NM	NM-
1-The Black Dwarf (cont'd in Red Seal?), The Veiled Avenger, & Barry Kuda begin; Tuska-c	66	132	198	413	619	825
2	55	110	165	330	495	660
3-Injury to eye story (reprinted from Scoop #3)	55	110	165	344	515	685

SPOTTY THE PUP (Becomes Super Pup #4, see Television Puppet Show)
Avon Periodicals/Realistic Comics: No. 2, Oct-Nov, 1953 - No. 3, Dec-Jan, 1953-54 (Also see Funny Tunes)

	GD	VG	FN	VF	VF/NM	NM-
2,3	6	12	18	31	38	45
nn (1953, Realistic-r)	4	7	9	14	16	18

SPUNKY (...Junior Cowboy)(...Comics #2 on)
Standard Comics: April, 1949 - No. 7, Nov, 1951

	GD	VG	FN	VF	VF/NM	NM-
1-Text illos by Frazetta	11	22	33	63	84	105
2-Text illos by Frazetta	9	18	27	49	62	75
3-7	6	12	18	31	38	45

SPUNKY THE SMILING SPOOK
Ajax/Farrell (World Famous Comics/Four Star Comic Corp.): Aug, 1957 - No. 4, May, 1958

	GD	VG	FN	VF	VF/NM	NM-
1-Reprints from Frisky Fables	10	20	30	56	73	90
2-4	6	12	18	31	38	45

SPY AND COUNTERSPY (Becomes Spy Hunters #3 on)
American Comics Group: Aug-Sept, 1949 - No. 2, Oct-Nov, 1949 (52 pgs.)

	GD	VG	FN	VF	VF/NM	NM-
1-Origin, 1st app. Jonathan Kent, Counterspy	27	54	81	153	214	275
2	17	34	51	95	130	165

SPYBOY
Dark Horse Comics: Oct, 1999 - Present ($2.50/$2.95/$2.99)

	NM-
1-17: 1-6-Peter David-s/Pop Mhan-a. 7,8-Meglia-a. 9-17-Mhan-a	3.00
13.1-13.3 (4/03-8/03, $2.99), 13.2,13.3-Mhan-a	3.00
... Special (5/02, $4.99) David-s/Mhan-a	5.00

SPYBOY/ YOUNG JUSTICE
Dark Horse Comics: Feb, 2002 - No. 3, Apr, 2002 ($2.99, limited series)

	NM-
1-3: 1-Peter David-s/Todd Nauck-a/Pop Mhan-c. 2-Mhan-a	3.00

SPY CASES (Formerly The Kellys)
Marvel/Atlas Comics (Hercules Publ.): No. 26, Sept, 1950 - No. 19, Oct, 1953

	GD	VG	FN	VF	VF/NM	NM-
26 (#1)	24	48	72	135	190	245
27(#2),28(#3, 2/51): 27-Everett-a; bondage-c	14	28	42	79	107	135
4(4/51) - 7,9,10	12	24	36	69	92	115
8-A-Bomb-c/story	14	28	42	79	107	135
11-19: 10-14-War format	10	20	30	56	73	90

NOTE: ***Sol Brodsky*** *c-1-5, 8, 9, 11-14, 17, 18.* ***Maneely*** *a-8; c-7, 10.* ***Tuska*** *a-7.*

SPY FIGHTERS
Marvel/Atlas Comics (CSI): March, 1951 - No. 15, July, 1953
(Cases from official records)

	GD	VG	FN	VF	VF/NM	NM-
1-Clark Mason begins; Tuska-a; Brodsky-c	25	50	75	147	202	260
2-Tuska-a	14	28	42	79	107	135
3-13: 3-5-Brodsky-c. 7-Heath-c	12	24	36	71	96	120
14,15-Pakula-a(3), Ed Win-a. 15-Brodsky-c	13	26	39	74	100	125

SPY-HUNTERS (Formerly Spy & Counterspy)
American Comics Group: No. 3, Dec-Jan, 1949-50 - No. 24, June-July, 1953 (#3-14: 52 pgs.)

	GD	VG	FN	VF	VF/NM	NM-
3-Jonathan Kent continues, ends #10	24	48	72	135	190	245
4-10: 4,8,10-Starr-a	14	28	42	79	107	135
11-15,17-22,24: 18-War-c begin. 21-War-c/stories begin	10	20	30	58	77	95
16-Williamson-a (9 pgs.)	16	32	48	92	126	160
23-Graphic torture, injury to eye panel	21	42	63	118	164	210

NOTE: ***Drucker*** *a-12.* ***Whitney*** *a-many issues; c-7, 8, 10-12, 15, 16.*

SPYMAN (Top Secret Adventures on cover)
Harvey Publications (Illustrated Humor): Sept, 1966 - No. 3, Feb, 1967 (12¢)

	GD	VG	FN	VF	VF/NM	NM-
1-Origin and 1st app. of Spyman. Steranko-a(p)-1st pro work; 1 pg. Neal Adams ad; Tuska-c/a, Crandall-a(i)	7	14	21	51	71	90
2-Simon-c; Steranko-a(p)	5	10	15	33	44	55
3-Simon-c	4	8	12	29	40	50

SPY SMASHER (See Mighty Midget, Whiz & Xmas Comics) (Also see Crime Smasher)
Fawcett Publications: Fall, 1941 - No. 11, Feb, 1943

	GD	VG	FN	VF	VF/NM	NM-
1-Spy Smasher begins; silver metallic-c	363	726	1089	2360	3630	4900
2-Raboy-c	166	332	498	1038	1557	2075
3,4: 3-Bondage-c. 4-Irvin Steinberg-c	112	224	336	700	1050	1400
5-7: Raboy-a; 6-Raboy-c/a. 7-Part photo-c (movie).	100	200	300	625	938	1250
8,11: War-c	80	160	240	500	750	1000
9-Hitler, Tojo, Mussolini-c.	94	188	282	588	882	1175
10-Hitler-c	90	180	270	563	844	1125

SPY THRILLERS (Police Badge No. 479 #5)
Atlas Comics (PrPI): Nov, 1954 - No. 4, May, 1955

	GD	VG	FN	VF	VF/NM	NM-
1-Brodsky c-1,2	22	44	66	124	172	220
2-Last precode (1/55)	13	26	39	74	100	125

Squee #3 © Jhonen Vasquez

Stanley and His Monster #3 © DC

Star Comics V2#1 © CHES

	GD 2.0	VG 4.0	FN 6.0	VF 8.0	VF/NM 9.0	NM- 9.2
3,4	10	20	30	56	73	90

SQUADRON SUPREME (Also see Marvel Graphic Novel)
Marvel Comics Group: Aug, 1985 - No. 12, Aug, 1986 (Maxi-series)

1-Double size 3.00
2-12 2.50
TPB ($24.99) r/#1-12; Alex Ross painted-c; printing inks contain some of the cremated remains of late writer Mark Gruenwald 25.00
TPB-2nd printing ($24.99): Inks contain no ashes 25.00

SQUADRON SUPREME: NEW WORLD ORDER
Marvel Comics: Sept, 1998 ($5.99, one-shot)

1-Wraparound-c; Kaminski-s 6.00

SQUALOR
First Comics: Dec, 1989 - Aug, 1990 ($2.75, limited series)

1-4: Sutton-a 2.75

SQUEE
Slave Labor Graphics: Apr, 1997 - No. 4, May, 1998 ($2.95, B&W)

1-4: Jhonen Vasquez-s/a in all 3.00

SQUEEKS (Also see Boy Comics)
Lev Gleason Publications: Oct, 1953 - No. 5, June, 1954

	GD	VG	FN	VF	VF/NM	NM-
1-Funny animal; Biro-c; Crimebuster's pet monkey "Squeeks" begins	9	18	27	49	62	75
2-Biro-c	6	12	18	27	33	38
3-5: 3-Biro-c	5	10	15	23	28	32

S.R. BISSETTE'S SPIDERBABY COMIX
SpiderBaby Grafix: Aug, 1996 - No. 2 ($3.95, B&W, magazine size)

Preview-(8/96, $3.95)-Graphic violence & nudity; Laurel & Hardy app. 4.00
1,2 4.00

S.R. BISSETTE'S TYRANT
SpiderBaby Grafix: Sept, 1994 - No. 4 ($2.95, B&W)

1-4 4.00

STAINLESS STEEL RAT
Eagle Comics: Oct, 1985 - No. 6, Mar, 1986 (Limited series)

1 (52 pgs.; $2.25-c) 3.00
2-6 ($1.50) 2.25

STALKER (Also see All Star Comics 1999 and crossover issues)
National Periodical Publications: June-July, 1975 - No. 4, Dec-Jan, 1975-76

	GD	VG	FN	VF	VF/NM	NM-
1-Origin & 1st app; Ditko/Wood-c/a	2	4	6	9	10	12
2-4-Ditko/Wood-c/a	1	2	3	4	5	7

STALKERS
Marvel Comics (Epic Comics): Apr, 1990 - No. 12, Mar, 1991 ($1.50)

1-12: 1-Chadwick-c 2.25

STAMP COMICS (Stamps... on-c; Thrilling Adventures In...#8)
Youthful Magazines/Stamp Comics, Inc.: Oct, 1951 - No. 7, Oct, 1952

	GD	VG	FN	VF	VF/NM	NM-
1-(15¢) ('Stamps' on indicia No. 1-3,5,7)	30	60	90	170	240	310
2	17	34	51	98	134	170
3-6: 3,4-Kiefer, Wildey-a	15	30	45	84	115	145
7-Roy Krenkel (4 pgs.)	19	38	57	106	146	185

NOTE: *Promotes stamp collecting; gives stories behind various commemorative stamps. No. 2, 10¢ printed over 15¢ c-price.* ***Kiefer** a-1-7.* ***Kirkel** a-1-6.* ***Napoli** a-2-7.* ***Palais** a-2-4, 7.*

STANLEY & HIS MONSTER (Formerly The Fox & the Crow)
National Periodical Publ.: No. 109, Apr-May, 1968 - No. 112, Oct-Nov, 1968

	GD	VG	FN	VF	VF/NM	NM-
109-112	3	6	9	19	25	32

STANLEY & HIS MONSTER
DC Comics: Feb, 1993 - No. 4, May, 1993 ($1.50, limited series)

1-4 2.25

STAN SHAW'S BEAUTY & THE BEAST
Dark Horse Comics: Nov, 1993 ($4.95, one-shot)

1 5.00

STAR
Image Comics (Highbrow Entertainment): June, 1995 - No. 4, Oct, 1995 ($2.50, lim. series)

1-4 2.50

STARBLAST
Marvel Comics: Jan, 1994 - No. 4, Apr, 1994 ($1.75, limited series)

1-4: 1-($2.00, 52 pgs.)-Nova, Quasar, Black Bolt; painted-c 2.25

GD VG FN VF VF/NM NM-
2.0 4.0 6.0 8.0 9.0 9.2

STAR BLAZERS
Comico: Apr, 1987 - No. 4, July, 1987 ($1.75, limited series)

1-4 3.00

STAR BLAZERS
Comico: 1989 ($1.95/$2.50, limited series)

1-5- Steacy wraparound painted-c on all 3.00

STAR BLAZERS (The Magazine of Space Battleship Yamato)
Argo Press: No. 0, Aug, 1995 - No. 3, Dec, 1995 ($2.95)

0-3 3.00

STAR BRAND
Marvel Comics (New Universe): Oct, 1986 - No. 19, May, 1989 (75¢/$1.25)

1-15: 14-begin $1.25-c 2.25
16-19-Byrne story & art; low print run 3.00
Annual 1 (10/87) 2.25

STARCHILD
Tailspin Press: 1992 - No. 12($2.25/$2.50, B&W)

1,2-('92),0(4/93),3-12: 0-Illos by Chadwick, Eisner, Sim, M. Wagner. 3-(7/93). 4-(11/93). 6-(2/94) 3.00

STARCHILD: MYTHOPOLIS
Image Comics: No. 0, July, 1997 - No. 4, Apr, 1998 ($2.95, B&W, limited series)

0-4-James Owen-s/a 3.00

STAR COMICS
Ultem Publ. (Harry 'A' Chesler)/Centaur Publications: Feb, 1937 - V2#7 (No. 23), Aug, 1939 (#1-6: large size)

	GD	VG	FN	VF	VF/NM	NM-
V1#1-Dan Hastings (s/f) begins	176	352	528	1100	1650	2200
2	80	160	240	500	750	1000
3-6 (#6, 9/37): 4,5-Little Nemo-c/stories	70	140	210	438	657	875
7-9: 8-Severed head centerspread; Impy & Little Nemo by Winsor McCay Jr, Popeye app. by Bob Wood; Mickey Mouse & Popeye app. as toys in Santa's bag on-c; X-Mas-c	64	128	192	400	600	800
10 (1st Centaur; 3/38)-Impy by Winsor McCay Jr; Don Marlow by Guardineer begins	85	170	255	531	796	1060
11-1st Jack Cole comic-a, 1 pg. (4/38)	64	128	192	400	600	800
12-15: 12-Riders of the Golden West begins; Little Nemo app. 15-Speed Silvers by Gustavson & The Last Pirate by Burgos begins	55	110	165	330	495	660
16 (12/38)-The Phantom Rider & his horse Thunder begins, ends V2#6	55	110	165	344	515	685
V2#1(#17, 2/39)-Phantom Rider-c (only non-funny-c)	59	118	177	369	555	740
2-7(#18-23): 2-Diana Deane by Tarpe Mills app. 3-Drama of Hollywood by Mills begins. 7-Jungle Queen app.	50	100	150	300	450	600

NOTE: ***Biro** c-6, 9, 10.* ***Burgos** a-15, 16, V2#1-7.* ***Ken Ernst** a-10, 12, 14.* ***Filchock** c-15, 18, 22.* ***Gill Fox** c-14, 19.* ***Guardineer** a-6, 8-14.* ***Gustavson** a-13-16, V2#1-7.* ***Winsor McCay** c-4, 5.* ***Tarpe Mills** a-15, V2#1-7.* ***Schwab** c-20, 23.* ***Bob Wood** a-10, 12, 13; c-7, 8.*

STAR COMICS MAGAZINE
Marvel Comics (Star Comics): Dec, 1986 - No. 13, 1988 ($1.50, digest-size)

	GD	VG	FN	VF	VF/NM	NM-
1,9-Spider-Man-c/s	2	4	6	8	10	12
2-8-Heathcliff, Ewoks, Top Dog, Madballs-r in #1-13	1	2	3	5	6	8
10-13	1	3	4	6	8	10

S.T.A.R. CORPS
DC Comics: Nov, 1993 - No. 6, Apr, 1994 ($1.50, limited series)

1-6: 1,2-Austin-c(i). 1-Superman app. 2.25

STAR CROSSED
DC Comics (Helix): June, 1997 - No. 3, Aug, 1997 ($2.50, limited series)

1-3-Matt Howarth-s/a 2.50

STARDUST (See Neil Gaiman and Charles Vess' Stardust)

STAR FEATURE COMICS
I. W. Enterprises: 1963

	GD	VG	FN	VF	VF/NM	NM-
Reprint #9-Stunt-Man Stetson-r/Feat. Comics #141	2	4	6	10	13	16

STARFIRE (Not the Teen Titans character)
National Periodical Publ./DC Comics: Aug-Sept, 1976 - No. 8, Oct-Nov, 1977

	GD	VG	FN	VF	VF/NM	NM-
1-Origin (CCA stamp fell off cover art; so it was approved by code)	2	4	6	8	10	12
2-8	1	2	3	4	5	7

STARGATE (Movie)

Stargate: Doomsday World #2 © MGM

Starman (2nd series) #58 © DC

Star Ranger V2#10 © CEN

GD VG FN VF VF/NM NM-
2.0 4.0 6.0 8.0 9.0 9.2

Entity Comics: July, 1996 - No. 4, Oct, 1996 ($2.95, limited series)
1-4: Based on film 3.00
1-4-($3.50): Special Edition foil-c 3.50

STARGATE: DOOMSDAY WORLD (Movie)
Entity Comics: Nov, 1996 - No. 3, Jan, 1997 ($2.95, limited series)
1-3 3.00
1-3-($3.50)-Foil-c 3.50

STARGATE: ONE NATION UNDER RA (Movie)
Entity Comics: Apr, 1997 ($2.75, B&W, one-shot)
1-($2.75) 3.00
1-($3.50)-Foil-c 3.50

STARGATE: REBELLION (Movie)
Entity Comics: May/June, 1997 - No. 3, Nov, 1997 ($2.75, B&W, limited series)
1-3 3.00
1-3-($3.50)-Gold foil-c 3.50

STARGATE: THE NEW ADVENTURES COLLECTION (Movie)
Entity Comics: Dec, 1997 ($5.95, B&W)
1-Regular and photo-c 6.00

STARGATE: UNDERWORLD (Movie)
Entity Comics: May, 1997 ($2.75, B&W, one-shot)
1 3.00

STAR HUNTERS (See DC Super Stars #16)
National Periodical Publ./DC Comics: Oct-Nov, 1977 - No. 7, Oct-Nov, 1978
1,7: 1-Newton-a(p). 7-44 pgs. 1 3 4 6 8 10
2-6 6.00
NOTE: ***Buckler** a-4-7p; c-1-7p. **Layton** a-1-5i; c-1-6i. **Nasser** a-3p. **Sutton** a-6i.*

STARJAMMERS (See X-Men Spotlight on Starjammers)

STARJAMMERS (Also see Uncanny X-Men)
Marvel Comics: Oct, 1995 - No. 4, Jan, 1996 ($2.95, limited series)
1-4: Foil-c; Ellis scripts 3.00

STARK TERROR
Stanley Publications: Dec, 1970 - No. 5, Aug, 1971 (B&W, magazine, 52 pgs.)
(1950s Horror reprints, including pre-code)
1-Bondage, torture-c 5 10 15 36 48 60
2-4 (Gillmor/Aragon-r) 3 7 10 21 28 35
5 (ACG-r) 3 6 9 18 23 28

STARLET O'HARA IN HOLLYWOOD (Teen-age) (Also see Cookie)
Standard Comics: Dec, 1948 - No. 4, Sept, 1949
1-Owen Fitzgerald-a in all 25 50 75 147 202 260
2 15 30 45 84 115 145
3,4 12 24 36 71 96 120

STAR-LORD THE SPECIAL EDITION (Also see Marvel Comics Super Special #10, Marvel Premiere & Preview & Marvel Spotlight V2#6,7)
Marvel Comics Group: Feb, 1982 (one-shot, direct sales) (1st Baxter paper comic)
1-Byrne/Austin-a; Austin-c; 8 pgs. of new-a by Golden (p); Dr. Who story by Dave Gibbons; 1st deluxe format comic 6.00

STARLORD
Marvel Comics: Dec, 1996 - No. 3, Feb, 1997 ($2.50, limited series)
1-3-Timothy Zahn-s 2.50

STARLORD MEGAZINE
Marvel Comics: Nov, 1996 ($2.95, one-shot)
1-Reprints w/preview of new series 3.00

STARMAN (1st Series) (Also see Justice League & War of the Gods)
DC Comics: Oct, 1988 - No. 45, Apr, 1992 ($1.00)
1-25,29-45: 1-Origin. 4-Intro The Power Elite. 9,10,34-Batman app. 14-Superman app. 17-Power Girl app. 38-War of the Gods x-over. 42-Lobo cameo. 42-45-Eclipso-c/stories (#43,44 with Lobo) 2.50
26-1st app. David Knight (G.A.Starman's son). 5.00
27,28: 27-Starman (David Knight) app. 28-Starman disguised as Superman; leads into Superman #50 4.00

STARMAN (2nd Series) (Also see The Golden Age, Showcase 95 #12, Showcase 96 #4,5)
DC Comics : No. 0, Oct, 1994 - No. 80, Aug, 2001 ($1.95/$2.25/$2.50)
0,1: 0-James Robinson scripts, Tony Harris-c/a(p) & Wade Von Grawbadger-a(i) begins; Sins of the Father storyline begins, ends #3; 1st app. new Starman (Jack Knight); reintro of the G.A. Mist & G.A. Shade; 1st app. Nash; David Knight dies 1 2 3 4 5 7
2-7: 2-Reintro Charity from Forbidden Tales of Dark Mansion. 3-Reintro/2nd app. "Blue" Starman (1st app. in 1st Issue Special #12); Will Payton app. (both cameos). 5-David Knight app. 6-The Shade "Times Past" story; Teddy Kristiansen-a. 7-The Black Pirate cameo 5.00
8-17: 8-Begin $2.25-c. 10-1st app. new Mist (Nash). 11-JSA "Times Past" story; Matt Smith-a. 12-16-Sins of the Child. 17-The BlackPirate app. 4.00
18-37: 18-G.A. Starman "Times Past" story; Watkiss-a. 19-David Knight app. 20-23-G.A. Sandman app. 24-26-Demon Quest; all 3 covers make-up triptych. 33-36-Batman-c/app. 37-David Knight and deceased JSA members app. 3.00
38-49,51-56: 38-Nash vs. Justice League Europe. 39,40-Crossover w/ Power of Shazam! #35,36; Bulletman app. 42-Demon-c/app. 43-JLA-c/app. 44-Phantom Lady-c/app. 46-Gene Ha-a. 51-Jor-el app. 52,53-Adam Strange-c/app. 2.50
50-($3.95) Gold foil logo on-c; Star Boy (LSH) app. 4.00
57-79: 57-62-Painted covers by Harris and Alex Ross. 72-Death of Ted Knight. 73-Eulogy. 74-Scalphunter flashback; Heath-a. 75-Superman-c/app. 2.50
80-($3.95) Final issue; cover by Harris & Robinson 4.00
#1,000,000 (11/98) 853rd Century x-over; Snejbjerg-a 2.50
Annual 1 (1996, $3.50)-Legends of the Dead Earth story; Prince Gavyn & G.A. Starman stories; J.H. Williams III, Bret Blevins, Craig Hamilton-c/a(p) 4.00
Annual 2 (1997, $3.95)-Pulp Heroes story; 4.00
...80 Page Giant (1/99, $4.95) Harris-c 5.00
...Secret Files 1 (4/98, $4.95)-Origin stories and profile pages 5.00
...The Mist (6/98, $1.95) Girlfrenzy; Mary Marvel app. 2.50
A Starry Knight-($17.95, TPB) r/#47-53 18.00
Infernal Devices-($17.95, TPB) r/#29-35,37,38 18.00
Night and Day-($14.95, TPB)-r/#7-10,12-16 15.00
Sins of the Father-($12.95, TPB)-r/#0-5 13.00
Stars My Destination-(2003, $14.95, TPB)-r/55-60 15.00
Times Past-($17.95, TPB)-r/stories of other Starmen 18.00

STARMASTERS
Americomics: Mar, 1984 ($1.50, one-shot)
1-Origin The Women of W.O.S.P. & Breed 3.00

STAR PRESENTATION, A (Formerly My Secret Romance #1,2; Spectacular Stories #4 on) (Also see This Is Suspense)
Fox Features Syndicate (Hero Books): No. 3, May, 1950
3-Dr. Jekyll & Mr. Hyde by Wood & Harrison (reprinted in Startling Terror Tales #10); "The Repulsing Dwarf" by Wood; Wood-c 55 110 165 330 495 660

STAR QUEST COMIX (Warren Presents... on cover)
Warren Publications: Oct, 1978 ($1.50, B&W magazine, 84 pgs., square-bound)
1-Corben, Maroto, Neary-a; Ken Kelly-c; Star Wars 2 4 6 8 10 12

STAR RAIDERS (See DC Graphic Novel #1)

STAR RANGER (Cowboy Comics #13 on)
Ultem Publ./Centaur Publ.: Feb, 1937 - No. 12, May, 1938 (Large size: No. 1-6)
1-(1st Western comic)-Ace & Deuce, Air Plunder; Creig Flessel-a 184 368 552 1150 1725 2300
2 84 168 252 525 788 1050
3-6 74 148 222 463 694 925
7-9: 8(12/37)-Christmas-c; Air Patrol, Gold coast app.; Guardineer centerfold 55 110 165 344 515 685
V2#10 (1st Centaur; 3/38) 85 170 255 531 796 1060
11,12 64 128 192 400 600 800
NOTE: ***J. Cole** a-10, 12; c-12. **Ken Ernst** a-11. **Gill Fox** a-8(illo), 9, 10. **Guardineer** a-1, 3, 6, 7, 8(illos), 9, 10, 12. **Gustavson** a-8-10, 12. **Fred Schwab** c-2-11. **Bob Wood** a-8-10.*

STAR RANGER FUNNIES (Formerly Cowboy Comics)
Centaur Publications: V1#15, Oct, 1938 - V2#5, Oct, 1939
V1#15-Lyin Lou, Ermine, Wild West Junior, The Law of Caribou County by Eisner, Cowboy Jake, The Plugged Dummy, Spurs by Gustavson, Red Coat, Two Buckaroos & Trouble Hunters begin 98 196 294 613 919 1225
V2#1 (1/39) 73 146 219 456 688 920
2-5: 2-Night Hawk by Gustavson. 4-Kit Carson app. 61 122 183 381 573 765
NOTE: ***Jack Cole** a-V2#1, 3; c-V2#1. **Filchock** c-V2#2, 3. **Guardineer** a-V2#3. **Gustavson** a-V2#2. **Pinajian** c/a-V2#5.*

STAR REACH
Star Reach Publ.: Apr, 1974 - No. 18 (B&W, #12-15 w/color)
1-(75¢, 52 pgs.) Art by Starlin, Simonson. Chaykin-c/a; origin Death. Cody Starbuck-sty 2 4 6 10 12 15
1-2nd, 3th, and 4th printings ($1.00-$1.50-c) 6.00
2-11: 2-Adams, Giordano-a; 1st Stephanie Starr-c/s. 3-1st Linda Lovecraft. 4-1st Sherlock

Stars and Stripes Comics #3 © CEN

Star Slammers #1 © Walt Simonson

Star Spangled Comics #83 © DC

Duck. 5-1st Gideon Faust by Chaykin. 6-Elric-c. 7-BWS-c. 9-14-Sacred & Profane-c/s by Steacy. 11-Samurai 1 2 3 4 5 7
2-2nd printing 4.00
12-15 (44 pgs.): 12-Zelazny-s. Nasser-a, Brunner-c 1 3 4 6 8 10
16-18-Magazine size: 17-Poe's Raven-c/s 1 3 4 6 8 10

NOTE: ***Adams** c-2. **Bonivert** a-17. **Brunner** a-3,5; c-3,10,12. **Chaykin** a-1,4,5; c-1(1st ed),4,5; back-c-1(2nd,3rd,4th ed). **Gene Day** a-6,8,9,11,15. **Friedrich** s-2,3,8,10. **Gasbarri** a-7. **Gilbert** a-9,12. **Giordano** a-2. **Gould** a-6. **Hirota/Mukaide** s/a-7. **Jones** c-6. **Konz** a-17. **Leialoha** a-3,4,6-i, 13,15; c-13,15. **Lyda** a-6,12-15. **Marrs** a-2-5,7,10,14,15,16,18; c-18; back-c-2. **Mukaide** a-18. **Nasser** a-12. **Nino** a-6; **Russell** a-8,10; c-8. **Dave Sim** s-7; lettering-9. **Simonson** a-1. **Skeates** a-1,2. **Starlin** a-1(x2), 2(x2); back-c-1(1st ed); c-1(2nd,3rd,4th ed). **Barry Smith** c-7. **Staton** a-5,6,7. **Steacy** a-8-14; c-9,11,14,16. **Vosburg** a-2-5,7,10. **Workman** a-2-5,8. Nudity panels in most. Wraparound-c: 3-5,7-11,13-16,18.*

STAR REACH CLASSICS
Eclipse Comics: Mar, 1984 - No. 6, Aug, 1984 ($1.50, Baxter paper)

1-6: 1-Neal Adams-r/Star Reach #1 3.00

NOTE: ***Dave Sim** a-1. **Starlin** a-1.*

STARR FLAGG, UNDERCOVER GIRL (See Undercover...)

STARRIORS
Marvel Comics: Aug, 1984 - Feb, 1985 (Limited series) (Based on Tomy toys)

1-4 3.00

STARS AND S.T.R.I.P.E. (Also see JSA)
DC Comics: July, 1999 - No. 14, Sept, 2000 ($2.95/$2.50)

0-($2.95) Moder and Weston-a; Starman app. 3.00
1-Johns and Robinson-s/Moder-a; origin new Star Spangled Kid 2.50
2-14: 4-Marvel Family app. 9-Seven Soldiers of Victory-c/app. 2.50

STARS AND STRIPES COMICS
Centaur Publications: No. 2, May, 1941 - No. 6, Dec, 1941

2(#1)-The Shark, The Iron Skull, A-Man, The Amazing Man, Mighty Man, Minimidget begin; The Voice & Dash Dartwell, the Human Meteor, Reef Kinkaid app.; Gustavson Flag-c 224 448 672 1400 2100 2800
3-Origin Dr. Synthe; The Black Panther app. 124 248 372 775 1163 1550
4-Origin/1st app. The Stars and Stripes; injury to eye-c 108 216 324 675 1013 1350
5(#5 on cover & inside) 74 148 222 463 694 925
5(#6)-(#5 on cover, #6 on inside) 74 148 222 463 694 925

NOTE: ***Gustavson** c/a-3. **Myron Strauss** c-4, 5(#5), 5(#6).*

STAR SEED (Formerly Powers That Be)
Broadway Comics: No. 7, 1996 - No. 9 ($2.95)

7-9 3.00

STARSHIP TROOPERS
Dark Horse Comics: 1997 - No. 2, 1997 ($2.95, limited series)

1,2-Movie adaption 3.00

STARSHIP TROOPERS: BRUTE CREATIONS
Dark Horse Comics: 1997 ($2.95, one-shot)

1 3.00

STARSHIP TROOPERS: DOMINANT SPECIES
Dark Horse Comics: Aug, 1998 - No. 4, Nov, 1998 ($2.95, limited series)

1-4-Strnad-s/Bolton-c 3.00

STARSHIP TROOPERS: INSECT TOUCH
Dark Horse Comics: 1997 - No. 3, 1997 ($2.95, limited series)

1-3 3.00

STAR SLAMMERS (See Marvel Graphic Novel #6)
Malibu Comics (Bravura): May, 1994 - No. 4, Aug, 1994 ($2.50, unfinished limited series)

1-4: W. Simonson-a/stories; contain Bravura stamps 2.50

STAR SLAMMERS SPECIAL
Dark Horse Comics (Legend): June, 1996 ($2.95, one-shot)

nn-Simonson-c/a/scripts; concludes Bravura limited series. 3.00

STARSLAYER
Pacific Comics/First Comics No. 7 on: Feb, 1982 - No. 6, Apr, 1983; No. 7, Aug, 1983 - No. 34, Nov, 1985

1-Origin & 1st app.; excessive blood & gore; 1 pg. Rocketeer cameo which continues in #2 5.00
2-Origin/1st full app. the Rocketeer (4/82) by Dave Stevens (Chapter 1 of Rocketeer saga; see Pacific Presents #1,2) 1 2 3 5 6 8
3-Chapter 2 of Rocketeer saga by Stevens 6.00
4,6,7: 7-Grell-a ends 3.00
5-2nd app. Groo the Wanderer by Aragones 1 2 3 4 5 7
8-34: 10-1st app. Grimjack (11/83, ends #17). 18-Starslayer meets Grimjack. 20-The Black Flame begins (9/84, 1st app.), ends #33. 27-Book length Black Flame story 2.50

NOTE: ***Grell** a-1-7; c-1-8. **Stevens** back c-2, 3. **Sutton** a-17p, 20-22p, 24-27p, 29-33p.*

STARSLAYER (The Director's Cut)
Acclaim Comics (Windjammer): June, 1994 - No. 8, Dec, 1995 ($2.50)

1-8: Mike Grell-c/a/scripts 2.50

STAR SPANGLED COMICS (Star Spangled War Stories #131 on)
National Periodical Publications: Oct, 1941 - No. 130, July, 1952

1-Origin/1st app. Tarantula; Captain X of the R.A.F., Star Spangled Kid (see Action #40), Armstrong of the Army begin; Robot-c 503 1006 1509 3521 5411 7300
2 164 328 492 1025 1538 2050
3-5 106 212 318 663 994 1325
6-Last Armstrong/Army; Penniless Palmer begins 62 124 186 388 582 775
7-(4/42)-Origin/1st app. The Guardian by S&K, & Robotman (by Paul Cassidy & created by Siegel);The Newsboy Legion (1st app.), Robotman & TNT begin; last Captain X 621 1242 1863 4347 6674 9000
8-Origin TNT & Dan the Dyna-Mite 230 460 690 1438 2157 2875
9,10 164 328 492 1025 1538 2050
11-17 122 244 366 763 1144 1525
18-Origin Star Spangled Kid 154 308 462 963 1444 1925
19-Last Tarantula 122 244 366 763 1144 1525
20-Liberty Belle begins (5/43) 132 264 396 825 1238 1650
21-29-Last S&K issue; 23-Last TNT. 25-Robotman by Jimmy Thompson begins. 29-Intro Robbie the Robotdog 102 204 306 638 959 1280
30-40: 31-S&K-c 57 114 171 356 533 710
41-51: 41,49-Kirby-c. 51-Robot-c by Kirby 53 106 159 318 474 630
52-64: 53 by S&K. 64-Last Newsboy Legion & The Guardian 48 96 144 288 432 575
65-Robin begins with c/app. (2/47); Batman cameo in 1 panel; Robin-c begins, end #95 144 288 432 900 1350 1800
66-Batman cameo in Robin story 82 164 246 513 769 1025
67,68,70-80: 68-Last Liberty Belle? 72-Burnley Robin-c 67 134 201 419 627 835
69-Origin/1st app. Tomahawk by F. Ray; atom bomb story & splash (6/47) 102 204 306 638 959 1280
81-Origin Merry, Girl of 1000 Gimmicks in Star Spangled Kid story 56 112 168 350 525 700
82,85: 82-Last Robotman? 85-Last Star Spangled Kid? 52 104 156 312 466 620
83-Tomahawk enters the lost valley, a land of dinosaurs; Capt. Compass begins, ends #130 52 104 156 312 466 620
84,87 (Rare): 87-Batman cameo in Robin 77 154 231 481 723 965
86-Batman cameo in Robin story 57 114 171 356 533 710
88(1/49)-94: Batman-c/stories in all. 91-Federal Men begin, end #93. 94-Manhunters Around the World begin, end #121 59 118 177 369 552 735
95-Batman story; last Robin-c 53 106 159 318 474 630
96,98-Batman cameo in Robin stories. 96-1st Tomahawk-c (also #97-121) 40 80 120 240 340 440
97,99 36 72 108 204 290 375
100 (1/50)-Pre-Bat-Hound tryout in Robin story (pre-dates Batman #92). 40 80 120 240 350 460
101-109,118,119,121: 121-Last Tomahawk-c 34 68 102 193 274 355
110,111,120-Batman cameo in Robin stories. 120-Last 52 pg. issue 35 70 105 201 288 370
112-Batman & Robin story 37 74 111 212 301 390
113-Frazetta-a (10 pgs.) 42 84 126 252 376 500
114-Retells Robin's origin (3/51); Batman & Robin story 44 88 132 264 395 525
115,117-Batman app. in Robin stories 37 74 111 212 301 390
116-Flag-c 37 74 111 212 301 390
122-(11/51)-Ghost Breaker-c/stories begin (origin/1st app.), ends #130 (Ghost Breaker covers #122-130) 40 80 120 240 360 480
123-126,128,129 31 62 93 178 252 325
127-Batman cameo 33 66 99 190 270 350
130-Batman cameo in Robin story 35 70 105 201 288 370

NOTE: *Most all issues after #29 signed by Simon & Kirby are not by them. **Bill Ely** c-122-130. **Mortimer** c-65-74(most), 76-95(most). **Fred Ray** c-96-106, 109, 110, 112, 113, 115-120. **S&K** c-7-31, 33, 34, 36, 37, 39, 40, 48, 49, 50-54, 56-58. **Hal Sherman** c-1-6. **Dick Sprang** c-75.*

STAR SPANGLED COMICS (Also see All Star Comics 1999 crossover titles)
DC Comics: May, 1999 ($1.99, one-shot)

1-Golden Age Sandman and the Star Spangled Kid 2.25

STAR SPANGLED KID (See Action #40, Leading Comics & Star Spangled Comics)

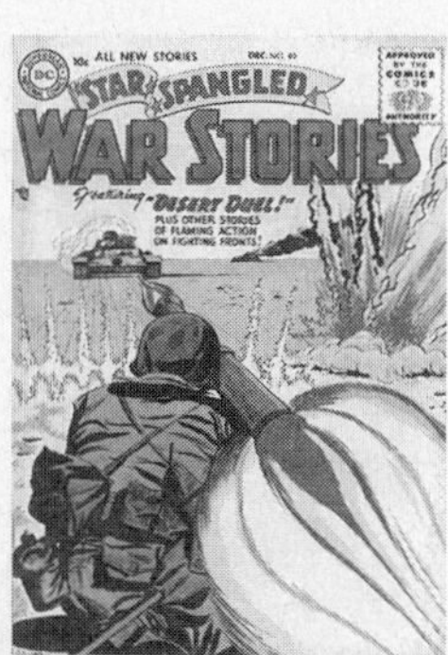

Star Spangled War Stories #40 © DC

Startling Comics #2 © Nedor

Startling Terror Tales #9 © STAR

STAR SPANGLED WAR STORIES (Formerly Star Spangled Comics #1-130; Becomes The Unknown Soldier #205 on) (See Showcase)
National Periodical Publications: No. 131, 8/52 - No. 133, 10/52; No. 3, 11/52 - No. 204, 2-3/77

	GD 2.0	VG 4.0	FN 6.0	VF 8.0	VF/NM 9.0	NM- 9.2
131(#1)	98	196	294	613	919	1225
132	66	132	198	413	619	825
133-Used in **POP**, pg. 94	55	110	165	338	507	675
3-6: 4-Devil Dog Dugan app. 6-Evans-a	31	62	93	224	332	440
7-10	25	50	75	181	266	350
11-20	21	42	63	149	220	290
21-30: 30-Last precode (2/55)	18	36	54	131	191	250
31-33,35-40	12	24	36	87	129	170
34-Krigstein-a	13	26	39	90	133	175
41-44,46-50: 50-1st S.A. issue	12	24	36	82	121	160
45-1st DC grey tone-c (5/56)	15	30	45	109	160	210
51,52,54-63,65,66, 68-83	9	18	27	63	89	115
53-"Rock Sergeant," 3rd Sgt. Rock prototype; inspired "P.I. & The Sand Fleas" in G.I. Combat #56 (1/57)	14	28	42	99	145	190
64-Pre-Sgt. Rock Easy Co. story (12/57)	12	24	36	82	121	160
67-2 Easy Co. stories without Sgt. Rock	12	24	36	87	129	170
84-Origin Mlle. Marie	17	34	51	121	178	235
85-89-Mlle. Marie in all	10	20	30	73	107	140
90-1st app. "War That Time Forgot" series; dinosaur issue-c/story (4-5/60)	35	70	105	263	394	525
91,93-No dinosaur stories	9	18	27	65	93	120
92-2nd dinosaur-c/s	14	28	42	99	145	190
94 (12/60)- "Ghost Ace" story; Baron Von Richter as The Enemy Ace (predates Our Army at War #151)	18	36	54	131	191	250
95-99: Dinosaur-c/s	12	24	36	87	129	170
100-Dinosaur-c/story.	15	30	45	104	152	200
101-115: All dinosaur issues	10	20	30	73	107	140
116-125,127-133,135-137-Last dinosaur story; Heath Birdman-#129,131	10	20	30	67	96	125
126-No dinosaur story	8	16	24	55	78	100
134-Dinosaur story; Neal Adams-a	11	22	33	77	114	150
138-New Enemy Ace-c/stories begin by Joe Kubert (4-5/68), end #150 (also see Our Army at War #151 and Showcase #57)	12	24	36	84	125	165
139-Origin Enemy Ace (7/68)	9	18	27	65	93	120
140-143,145: 145-Last 12¢ issue (6-7/69)	7	14	21	46	63	80
144-Neal Adams/Kubert-a	8	16	24	53	74	95
146-Enemy Ace-c and cameo app.	4	8	12	29	40	50
147,148-New Enemy Ace stories	6	12	18	38	52	65
149,150-Last new Enemy Ace by Kubert. Viking Prince by Kubert	5	10	15	36	48	60
151-1st solo app. Unknown Soldier (6-7/70); Enemy Ace-r begin (from Our Army at War, Showcase & SSWS); end #161	15	30	45	104	152	200
152-Reprints 2nd Enemy Ace app.	4	8	12	29	40	50
153,155-Enemy Ace reprints; early Unknown Soldier stories	4	8	12	24	32	40
154-Origin Unknown Soldier	11	22	33	77	114	150
156-1st Battle Album; Unknown Soldier story; Kubert-c/a	4	8	12	24	32	40
157-Sgt. Rock x-over in Unknown Soldier story.	3	7	10	21	28	35
158-163-(52 pgs.): New Unknown Soldier stories; Kubert-c/a. 161-Last Enemy Ace-r	3	6	9	16	20	25
164-183,200: 181-183-Enemy Ace vs. Balloon Buster serial app; Frank Thorne-a. 200-Enemy Ace back-up	2	4	6	9	11	14
184-199,201-204	1	3	4	6	8	10

NOTE: ***Anderson** a-28. **Chaykin** a-167. **Drucker** a-59, 61, 64, 66, 67, 73-84. **Estrada** a-149. **John Giunta** a-72. **Glanzman** a-167, 171, 172, 174. **Heath** a-122, 132, 133; c-67, 122, 132-134. **Kaluta** a-197i; c-167. **G. Kane** a-169. **Kubert** a-6-163(most later issues), 200. **Maurer** a-160, 165. **Severin** a-65, 162. **S&K** c-7-31, 33, 34, 37, 40. **Simonson** a-170, 172, 174, 180. **Sutton** a-168. **Thorne** a-183. **Toth** a-164. **Wildey** a-161. Suicide Squad in 110, 116-118, 120, 121, 127.*

STARSTREAM (Adventures in Science Fiction)(See Questar illustrated)
Whitman/Western Publishing Co.: 1976 (79¢, 68 pgs, cardboard-c)

	GD 2.0	VG 4.0	FN 6.0	VF 8.0	VF/NM 9.0	NM- 9.2
1-4: 1-Bolle-a. 2-4-McWilliams & Bolle-a	2	4	6	10	13	16

STARSTRUCK
Marvel Comics (Epic Comics): Feb, 1985 - No. 6, Feb, 1986 ($1.50, mature)

	GD 2.0	VG 4.0	FN 6.0	VF 8.0	VF/NM 9.0	NM- 9.2
1-6: Kaluta-a						3.00

STARSTRUCK
Dark Horse Comics: Aug, 1990 - No. 4, Nov?, 1990 ($2.95, B&W, 52pgs.)

	GD 2.0	VG 4.0	FN 6.0	VF 8.0	VF/NM 9.0	NM- 9.2
1-3:Kaluta-r/Epic series plus new-c/a in all						3.00
4 (68, pgs.)-contains 2 trading cards						3.00

STAR STUDDED
Cambridge House/Superior Publishers: 1945 (25¢, 132 pgs.); 1945 (196 pgs.)

	GD 2.0	VG 4.0	FN 6.0	VF 8.0	VF/NM 9.0	NM- 9.2
nn-Captain Combat by Giunta, Ghost Woman, Commandette, & Red Rogue app.; Infantino-a	33	66	99	190	270	350
nn-The Cadet, Edison Bell, Hoot Gibson, Jungle Lil (196 pgs.); copies vary; Blue Beetle in some	27	54	81	153	214	275

STARTLING COMICS
Better Publications (Nedor): June, 1940 - No. 53, Sept, 1948

	GD 2.0	VG 4.0	FN 6.0	VF 8.0	VF/NM 9.0	NM- 9.2
1-Origin Captain Future-Man Of Tomorrow, Mystico (By Eisner/Fine), The Wonder Man; The Masked Rider & his horse Pinto begins; Masked Rider formerly in pulps; drug use story	248	496	744	1550	2325	3100
2 -Don Davis, Espionage Ace begins	96	192	288	600	900	1200
3	80	160	240	500	750	1000
4	60	120	180	375	563	750
5-9	50	100	150	300	450	600
10-The Fighting Yank begins (9/41, origin/1st app.)	363	726	1089	2360	3630	4900
11-2nd app. Fighting Yank	112	224	336	700	1050	1400
12-Hitler, Hirohito, Mussolini-c	94	188	282	588	882	1175
13-15	60	120	180	375	563	750
16-Origin The Four Comrades; not in #32,35	64	128	192	400	600	800
17-Last Masked Rider & Mystico	48	96	144	288	432	575
18-Pyroman begins (12/42, origin)(also see America's Best Comics #3 for 1st app., 11/42)	96	192	288	600	900	1200
19	48	96	144	288	432	575
20,21: 20-The Oracle begins (3/43); not in issues 26,28,33,34. 21-Origin The Ape, Oracle's enemy	50	100	150	300	450	600
22-34: 34-Origin The Scarab & only app.	48	96	144	288	432	575
35-Hypodermic syringe attacks Fighting Yank in drug story	50	100	150	300	450	600
36-43: 36-Last Four Comrades. 38-Bondage/torture-c. 40-Last Capt. Future & Oracle. 41-Front Page Peggy begins; A-Bomb-c. 43-Last Pyroman	42	84	126	252	376	500
44,45: 44-Lance Lewis, Space Detective begins; Ingels-c; sci/fi-c begin. 45-Tygra begins (intro/origin, 5/47); Ingels-c/a (splash pg. & inside f/c B&W ad)	66	132	198	413	617	820
46-Classic Ingels-c; Ingels-a	96	192	288	600	900	1200
47,48,50-53: 50,51-Sea-Eagle app.	60	120	180	375	563	750
49-Classic Schomburg Robot-c; last Fighting Yank	356	712	1068	2314	3557	4800

NOTE: ***Ingels** a-44, 45; c-44, 45, 46(wash). **Schomburg (Xela)** c-21-43; 47-53 (airbrush). **Tuska** c-45? Bondage c-16, 21, 37, 46-49. Captain Future c-1-9, 13, 14. Fighting Yank c-10-12, 15-17, 21, 22, 24, 26, 28, 30, 32, 34, 36, 38, 40, 42. Pyroman c-18-20, 23, 25, 27, 29, 31, 33, 35, 37, 39, 41, 43.*

STARTLING STORIES: BANNER
Marvel Comics: July, 2001 - No. 4, Oct, 2001 ($2.99, limited series)

	GD 2.0	VG 4.0	FN 6.0	VF 8.0	VF/NM 9.0	NM- 9.2
1-4-Hulk story by Azzarello; Corben-c/a						3.00
TPB (11/01, $12.95) r/1-4						13.00

STARTLING STORIES: FANTASTIC FOUR - UNSTABLE MOLECULES (See Fantastic Four - ...)

STARTLING STORIES: THE MEGALOMANIACAL SPIDER-MAN
Marvel Comics: Jun, 2002 ($2.99, one-shot)

	GD 2.0	VG 4.0	FN 6.0	VF 8.0	VF/NM 9.0	NM- 9.2
1-Spider-Man spoof; Peter Bagge-s/a						3.00

STARTLING STORIES: THE THING
Marvel Comics: 2003 ($3.50, one-shot)

	GD 2.0	VG 4.0	FN 6.0	VF 8.0	VF/NM 9.0	NM- 9.2
1-Zimmerman-s/Kramer-a; Inhumans and the Hulk app.						3.50

STARTLING STORIES: THE THING - NIGHT FALLS ON YANCY STREET
Marvel Comics: Jun, 2003 - No. 4, Sept, 2003 ($3.50, limited series)

	GD 2.0	VG 4.0	FN 6.0	VF 8.0	VF/NM 9.0	NM- 9.2
1-4-Dorkin-s/Haspiel-a. 2,3-Frightful Four app.						3.50

STARTLING TERROR TALES
Star Publications: No. 10, May, 1952 - No. 14, Feb, 1953; No. 4, Apr, 1953 - No. 11, 1954

	GD 2.0	VG 4.0	FN 6.0	VF 8.0	VF/NM 9.0	NM- 9.2
10-(1st Series)-Wood/Harrison-a (r/A Star Presentation #3) Disbrow/Cole-c; becomes 4 different titles after #10; becomes Confessions of Love #11 on, The Horrors #11 on, Terrifying Tales #11 on, Terrors of the Jungle #11 on & continues w/Startling Terror #11	72	144	216	450	675	900
11-(8/52)-L. B. Cole Spider-c; r-Fox's "A Feature Presentation" #5 (blue-c)	124	248	372	775	1163	1550
11-Black-c (variant; believed to be a pressrun change) (Unique)	132	264	396	825	1238	1650
12,14	31	62	93	175	248	320
13-Jo-Jo-r; Disbrow-a	32	64	96	184	262	340
4-9,11(1953-54) (2nd Series): 11-New logo	27	54	81	155	218	280
10-Disbrow-a	34	68	102	196	278	360

Star Trek #26 © Paramount

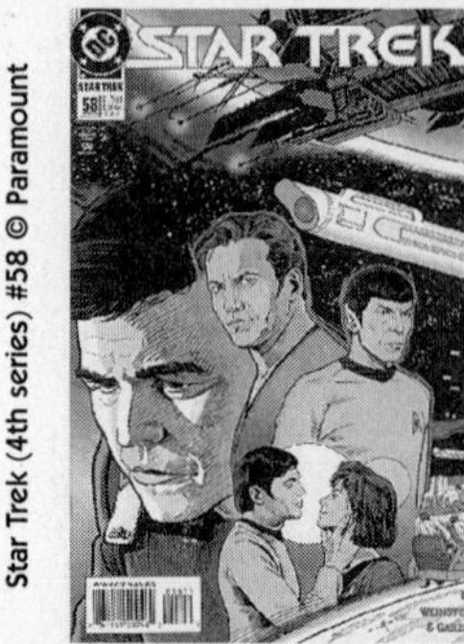

Star Trek (4th series) #58 © Paramount

Star Trek: Deep Space Nine #4 © Paramount

	GD 2.0	VG 4.0	FN 6.0	VF 8.0	VF/NM 9.0	NM- 9.2

NOTE: ***L. B. Cole** covers-all issues. **Palais** a-V2#8r, V2#11r.*

STAR TREK (TV) (See Dan Curtis Giveaways, Dynabrite Comics & Power Record Comics)
Gold Key: 7/67; No. 2, 6/68; No. 3, 12/68; No. 4, 6/69 - No. 61, 3/79

	GD	VG	FN	VF	VF/NM	NM-
1-Photo-c begin, end #9	40	80	120	300	450	600
1 (rare variation w/photo back-c)	44	88	132	352	526	700
2	24	48	72	171	251	330
2 (rare variation w/photo back-c)	35	70	105	263	392	520
3-5	16	32	48	116	171	225
3 (rare variation w/photo back-c)	26	52	78	189	275	360
6-9	13	26	39	90	133	175
10-20	8	16	24	55	78	100
21-30	6	12	18	43	59	75
31-40	5	10	15	33	44	55
41-61: 52-Drug propaganda story	4	8	12	24	32	40
...the Enterprise Logs nn (8/76)-Golden Press, ($1.95, 224 pgs.)-r/#1-8 plus 7 pgs. by McWilliams (#11185)-Photo-c	5	10	15	33	44	55
...the Enterprise Logs Vol. 2 ('76)-r/#9-17 (#11187)-Photo-c	4	8	12	29	40	50
...the Enterprise Logs Vol. 3 ('77)-r/#18-26 (#11188); McWilliams-a (4 pgs.)-Photo-c	4	8	12	29	40	50
Star Trek Vol. 4 (Winter '77)-Reprints #27,28,30-34,36,38 (#11189) plus 3 pgs. new art	4	8	12	29	40	50

NOTE: ***McWilliams** a-38, 40-44, 46-61. #29 reprints #1; #35 reprints #4; #37 reprints #5; #45 reprints #7. The tabloids all have photo covers and blank inside covers. Painted covers #10-44, 46-59.*

STAR TREK
Marvel Comics Group: April, 1980 - No. 18, Feb, 1982

	GD	VG	FN	VF	VF/NM	NM-
1: 1-3-r/Marvel Super Special; movie adapt.	2	4	6	8	10	12
2-16: 5-Miller-c	1	2	3	4	5	7
17-Low print run	2	4	6	8	10	12
18-Last issue; low print run	2	4	6	11	14	18

NOTE: ***Austin** c-18i. **Buscema** a-13. **Gil Kane** a-15. **Nasser** c/a-7. **Simonson** c-17.*

STAR TREK (Also see Who's Who In Star Trek)
DC Comics: Feb, 1984 - No. 56, Nov, 1988 (75¢, Mando paper)

	GD	VG	FN	VF	VF/NM	NM-
1-Sutton-a(p) begins	1	3	4	6	8	10
2-5						6.00
6-10: 7-Origin Saavik						5.00
11-20: 19-Walter Koenig story						4.00
21-32						3.50
33-($1.25, 52 pgs.)-20th anniversary issue						4.00
34-49: 37-Painted-c						3.00
50-($1.50, 52 pgs.)						4.00
51-56, Annual 1-3: 1(1985). 2(1986). 3(1988, $1.50)						3.00

NOTE: ***Morrow** a-28, 35, 36, 56. **Orlando** c-8i. **Perez** c-1-3. **Spiegle** a-19. **Starlin** c-24, 25. **Sutton** a-1-6p, 8-18p, 20-27p, 29p, 31-34p, 39-52p, 55p; c-4-6p, 8-22p, 46p.*

STAR TREK
DC Comics: Oct, 1989 - No. 80, Jan, 1996 ($1.50/$1.75/$1.95/$2.50)

	NM-
1-Capt. Kirk and crew	6.00
2,3	4.00
4-23,25-30: 10-12-The Trial of James T. Kirk. 21-Begin $1.75-c	3.00
24-($2.95, 68 pgs.)-40 pg. epic w/pin-ups	3.50
31-49,51-60	2.50
50-($3.50, 68 pgs.)-Painted-c	3.50
61-74,76-80	2.50
75 ($3.95)	4.00
Annual 1-6('90-'95, 68 pgs.): 1-Morrow-a. 3-Painted-c	4.00
Special 1-3 ('9-'95, 68 pgs.)-1-Sutton-a.	4.00
...: The Ashes of Eden (1995, $14.95, 100 pgs.)-Shatner story	15.00
...Generations (1994, $3.95, 68 pgs.)-Movie adaptation	4.00
...Generations (1994, $5.95, 68 pgs.)-Squarebound	6.00

STAR TREK...(TV)
DC Comics (WildStorm): one-shots

	NM-
All of Me (4/00, $5.95, prestige format) Lopresti-a	6.00
Enemy Unseen TPB (2001, $17.95) r/Perchance to Dream, Embrace the Wolf, The Killing Shadows; Struzan-c	18.00
Enter the Wolves (2001, $5.95) Crispin & Weinstein-s; Mota-a/c	6.00
New Frontier - Double Time (11/00, $5.95)-Captain Calhoun's USS Excalibur; Peter David-s; Stelfreeze-c	6.00
Other Realities TPB (2001, $14.95) r/All of Me, New Frontier - Double Time, and DS9-N-Vector; Van Fleet-c	15.00
Special (2001, $6.95) Stories from all 4 series by various; Van Fleet-c	7.00

STAR TREK: DEBT OF HONOR
DC Comics: 1992 ($24.95/$14.95, graphic novel)

	NM-
Hardcover ($24.95) Claremont-s/Hughes-a(p)	25.00
Softcover ($14.95)	15.00

STAR TREK: DEEP SPACE NINE (TV)
Malibu Comics: Aug, 1993 - No. 32, Jan, 1996 ($2.50)

	NM-
1-Direct Sale Edition w/line drawn-c	4.00
1-Newsstand Edition with photo-c	3.00
0-(1/95, $2.95)-Terok Nor	3.00
2-30: 2-Polybagged w/trading card. 9-4 pg. prelude to Hearts & Minds	2.50
31-($3.95)	4.00
32-($3.50)	3.50
Annual 1 (1/95, $3.95, 68 pgs.)	4.00
Special 1 (1995, $3.50)	3.50
Ultimate Annual 1 (12/95, $5.95)	6.00
...:Lightstorm (12/94, $3.50)	3.50

STAR TREK: DEEP SPACE NINE (TV)
Marvel Comics (Paramount Comics): Nov, 1996 - No. 15, Mar, 1998 ($1.95/$1.99)

1-15: 12,13-"Telepathy War" pt. 2,3 — 2.50

STAR TREK: DEEP SPACE NINE -- N-VECTOR (TV)
DC Comics (WildStorm): Aug, 2000 - No. 4, Nov, 2000 ($2.50, limited series)

1-4-Cypress-a — 2.50

STAR TREK DEEP SPACE NINE-THE CELEBRITY SERIES
Malibu Comics: May, 1995 ($2.95)

	NM-
1-Blood and Honor; Mark Lenard script	3.00
1-Rules of Diplomacy; Aron Eisenberg script	3.00

STAR TREK: DEEP SPACE NINE HEARTS AND MINDS
Malibu Comics: June, 1994 - No. 4, Sept, 1994 ($2.50, limited series)

	NM-
1-4	2.50
1-Holographic-c	4.00

STAR TREK: DEEP SPACE NINE, THE MAQUIS
Malibu Comics: Feb, 1995 - No. 3, Apr, 1995 ($2.50, limited series)

1-3-Newsstand-c, 1-Photo-c — 2.50

STAR TREK: DEEP SPACE NINE/THE NEXT GENERATION
Malibu Comics: Oct, 1994 - No. 2, Nov, 1994 ($2.50, limited series)

1,2: Parts 2 & 4 of x-over with Star Trek: TNG/DS9 from DC Comics — 2.50

STAR TREK: DEEP SPACE NINE WORF SPECIAL
Malibu Comics: Dec, 1995 ($3.95, one-shot)

1-Includes pinups — 4.00

STAR TREK: DIVIDED WE FALL
DC Comics (WildStorm): July, 2001 - No. 4, Oct, 2001 ($2.95, limited series)

1-4: Ordover & Mack-s; Lenara Kahn, Verad and Odan app. — 3.00

STAR TREK EARLY VOYAGES(TV)
Marvel Comics (Paramount Comics): Feb, 1997 - No. 17, Jun, 1998 ($2.95/$1.95/$1.99)

	NM-
1-($2.95)	3.00
2-17	2.50

STAR TREK: FIRST CONTACT (Movie)
Marvel Comics (Paramount Comics): Nov, 1996 ($5.95, one-shot)

nn-Movie adaption — 6.00

STAR TREK: MIRROR MIRROR
Marvel Comics (Paramount Comics): Feb, 1997 ($3.95, one-shot)

1-DeFalco-s — 4.00

STAR TREK MOVIE SPECIAL
DC Comics: 1984 (June) - No. 2, 1987 ($1.50); No. 1, 1989 ($2.00, 52 pgs)

	NM-
nn-(#1)-Adapts Star Trek III; Sutton-p (68 pgs.)	3.00
2-Adapts Star Trek IV; Sutton-a; Chaykin-c. (68 pgs.)	3.00
1 (1989)-Adapts Star Trek V; painted-c	3.00

STAR TREK: OPERATION ASSIMILATION
Marvel Comics (Paramount Comics): Dec, 1996 ($2.95, one-shot)

1 — 3.00

STAR TREK VI: THE UNDISCOVERED COUNTRY (Movie)
DC Comics: 1992

	NM-
1-($2.95, regular edition, 68 pgs.)-Adaptation of film	3.00
nn-($5.95, prestige edition)-Has photos of movie not included in regular edition; painted-c by Palmer; photo back-c	6.00

STAR TREK: STARFLEET ACADEMY

Star Trek: The Next Generation Annual #2 © Paramount

Star Trek Unlimited #8 © Paramount

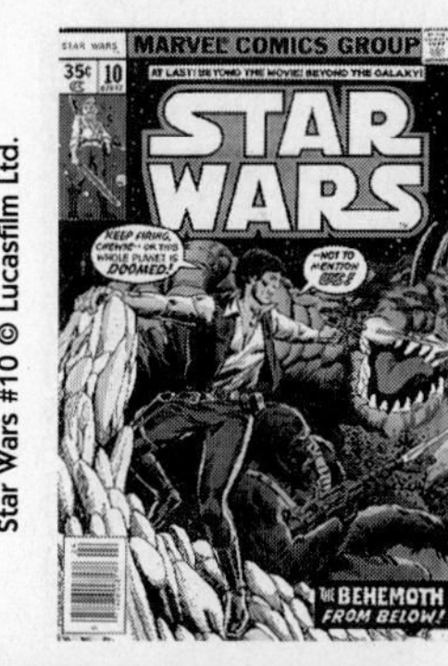

Star Wars #10 © Lucasfilm Ltd.

GD VG FN VF VF/NM NM-
2.0 4.0 6.0 8.0 9.0 9.2

Marvel Comics (Paramount Comics): Dec, 1996 - No. 19, Jun, 1998 ($1.95/$1.99)

1-19: Begin new series. 12-"Telepathy War" pt. 1. 18-English and Klingon language editions 2.50

STAR TREK: TELEPATHY WAR
Marvel Comics (Paramount Comics): Nov, 1997 ($2.99, 48 pgs., one-shot)

1-"Telepathy War" x-over pt. 6 3.00

STAR TREK - THE MODALA IMPERATIVE
DC Comics: Late July, 1991 - No. 4, Late Sept, 1991 ($1.75, limited series)

1-4 2.50
TPB ($19.95) r/series and ST:TNG - The Modala Imperative 20.00

STAR TREK: THE NEXT GENERATION (TV)
DC Comics: Feb, 1988 - No. 6, July, 1988 (limited series)

1 ($1.50, 52 pgs.)-Sienkiewicz painted-c 6.00
2-6 ($1.00) 4.00

STAR TREK: THE NEXT GENERATION (TV)
DC Comics: Oct, 1989 -No. 80, 1995 ($1.50/$1.75/$1.95)

1-Capt. Picard and crew from TV show 1 2 3 5 7 9
2,3 5.00
4-10 4.00
11-23,25-49,51-60 3.00
24,50: 24-($2.50, 52 pgs.). 50-($3.50, 68 pgs.)-Painted-c 5.00
61-74,76-80 2.50
75-($3.95, 50 pgs.) 4.00
Annual 1-6 ('90-'95, 68 pgs.) 4.00
Special 1 -3('93-'95, 68 pgs.)-1-Contains 3 stories 4.00
...-The Series Finale (1994, $3.95, 68 pgs.) 4.00

STAR TREK: THE NEXT GENERATION (TV)
DC Comics (WildStorm): one-shots

Embrace the Wolf (6/00, $5.95, prestige format) Golden & Sniegoski-s 6.00
Forgiveness (2001, $24.95, HC) David Brin-s/Scott Hampton painted-a; dust jacket-c 30.00
Forgiveness (2002, $17.95, SC) 18.00
The Gorn Crisis (1/01, $29.95, HC) Kordey painted-a/dust jacket-c 30.00
The Gorn Crisis (1/01, $17.95, SC) Kordey painted-a 18.00

STAR TREK: THE NEXT GENERATION/DEEP SPACE NINE (TV)
DC Comics: Dec, 1994 - No. 2, Jan, 1995 ($2.50, limited series)

1,2-Parts 1 & 3 of x-over with Star Trek: DS9/TNG from Malibu Comics 2.50

STAR TREK: THE NEXT GENERATION - ILL WIND
DC Comics: Nov, 1995 - No. 4, Feb, 1996 ($2.50, limited series)

1-4: Hugh Fleming painted-c on all 2.50

STAR TREK: THE NEXT GENERATION - PERCHANCE TO DREAM
DC Comics/WildStorm: Feb, 2000 - No. 4, May, 2000 ($2.50, limited series)

1-4-Bradstreet-c 2.50

STAR TREK: THE NEXT GENERATION - RIKER
Marvel Comics (Paramount Comics): July, 1998 ($3.50, one-shot)

1-Riker joins the Maquis 3.50

STAR TREK: THE NEXT GENERATION - SHADOWHEART
DC Comics: Dec, 1994 - No. 4, Mar, 1995 ($1.95, limited series)

1-4 2.50

STAR TREK: THE NEXT GENERATION - THE KILLING SHADOWS
DC Comics/WildStorm: Nov, 2000 - No. 4, Feb, 2001 ($2.50, limited series)

1-4-Scott Ciencin-s; Sela app. 2.50

STAR TREK: THE NEXT GENERATION - THE MODALA IMPERATIVE
DC Comics: Early Sept, 1991 - No. 4, Late Oct, 1991 ($1.75, limited series)

1-4 2.50

STAR TREK UNLIMITED
Marvel Comics (Paramount Comics): Nov, 1996 - No. 10, July, 1998 ($2.95/$2.99)

1,2-Stories from original series and Next Generation 4.00
3-10: 3-Begin $2.99-c. 6-"Telepathy War" pt. 4. 7-Q & Trelane swap Kirk & Picard 3.50

STAR TREK UNTOLD VOYAGES
Marvel Comics (Paramount Comics): May, 1998 - No. 5, July, 1998 ($2.50)

1-5-Kirk's crew after the 1st movie 2.50

STAR TREK: VOYAGER
Marvel Comics (Paramount Comics): Nov, 1996 - No. 15, Mar, 1998 ($1.95/$1.99)

1-15: 13-"Telepathy War" pt. 5. 14-Seven of Nine joins crew 3.00

STAR TREK: VOYAGER
DC Comics/WildStorm: one-shots and trade paperbacks

- Elite Force (7/00, $5.95) The Borg app.; Abnett & Lanning-s 6.00
... Encounters With the Unknown TPB (2001, $19.95) reprints 20.00
- False Colors (1/00, $5.95) Photo-c and Jim Lee-c; Jeff Moy-a 6.00

STAR TREK: VOYAGER-- THE PLANET KILLER
DC Comics/WildStorm: Mar, 2001 - No. 3, May, 2001 ($2.95, limited series)

1-3-Voyager vs. the Planet Killer from the ST:TOS episode; Teranishi-a 3.00

STAR TREK: VOYAGER SPLASHDOWN
Marvel Comics (Paramount Comics): Apr, 1998 - No. 4, July, 1998 ($2.50, limited series)

1-4-Voyager crashes on a water planet 3.00

STAR TREK/ X-MEN
Marvel Comics (Paramount Comics): Dec, 1996 ($4.99, one-shot)

1-Kirk's crew & X-Men; art by Silvestri, Tan, Winn & Finch; Lobdell-s 5.00

STAR TREK/ X-MEN: 2ND CONTACT
Marvel Comics (Paramount Comics): May, 1998 ($4.99, 64 pgs., one-shot)

1-Next Gen. crew & X-Men battle Kang, Sentinels & Borg following First Contact movie 5.00
1-Painted wraparound variant cover 5.00

STAR WARS (Movie) (See Classic..., Contemporary Motivators, Dark Horse Comics, The Droids, The Ewoks, Marvel Movie Showcase, Marvel Special Ed.)
Marvel Comics Group: July, 1977 - No. 107, Sept, 1986

1-(Regular 30¢ edition)-Price in square w/UPC code; #1-6 adapt first movie;
first issue on sale before movie debuted 5 10 15 36 48 60
1-(35¢-c; limited distribution - 1500 copies?)- Price in square w/UPC code
50 100 150 400 600 800

NOTE: *The rare 35¢ edition has the cover price in a square box, and the UPC box in the lower left hand corner has the UPC code lines running through it.*

2-4-(30¢ issues). 4-Battle with Darth Vader 3 6 9 18 24 30
2-4-(35¢ with UPC code; not reprints) 6 12 18 43 59 75
5,6: 5-Begin 35¢-c on all editions. 6-Dave Stevens-a(i).
2 4 6 12 16 20
7-20 2 4 6 8 10 12
21-70: 39-44-The Empire Strikes Back-r by Al Williamson in all. 50-Giant.
68-Reintro Boba Fett. 1 2 3 5 7 9
71-80 1 3 4 6 8 10
81-90: 81-Boba Fett app. 2 4 6 8 10 12
91,93-99: 98-Williamson-a. 2 4 6 10 12 15
92,100-106: 92,100-($1.00, 52 pgs.). 2 4 6 11 14 18
107(low dist.); Portacio-a(i) 6 12 18 38 52 65
1-9: Reprints; has "reprint" in upper lefthand corner of cover or on inside or price and number inside a diamond with no date or UPC on cover; 30¢ and 35¢ issues published 4.00
Annual 1 (12/79, 52 pgs.)-Simonson-c 2 4 6 8 10 12
Annual 2 (11/82, 52 pgs.), 3(12/83, 52 pgs.) 1 3 4 6 8 10
... A Long Time Ago...Vol. 1 TPB (Dark Horse Comics, 6/02, $29.95) r/#1-14 30.00
... A Long Time Ago...Vol. 2 TPB (Dark Horse Comics, 7/02, $29.95) r/#15-28 30.00
... A Long Time Ago...Vol. 3 TPB (Dark Horse Comics, 11/02, $29.95) r/#39-53 30.00
... A Long Time Ago...Vol. 4 TPB (Dark Horse Comics, 1/03, $29.95) r/#54-67 & Ann. 2 30.00
... A Long Time Ago...Vol. 5 TPB (Dark Horse Comics, 3/03, $29.95) r/#68-81 & Ann. 3 30.00
... A Long Time Ago...Vol. 6 TPB (Dark Horse Comics, 5/03, $29.95) r/#82-93 30.00
... A Long Time Ago...Vol. 7 TPB (Dark Horse Comics, 6/03, $29.95) r/#96-107 30.00

***Austin** a-11-15i, 21i, 38; c-12-15i, 21i. **Byrne** c-13p. **Chaykin** a-1-10p; c-1. **Golden** c/a-38. **Miller** c-47p; pin-up-43. **Nebres** c/a-Annual 2i. **Portacio** a-107i. **Sienkiewicz** c-92i, 98. **Simonson** a-16p, 49p, 51-63p, 65p, 66p; c-16, 49-51, 52p, 53-62, Annual 1. **Steacy** painted a-105i, 106i; c-105. **Williamson** a-39-44p, 50p, 98; c-39, 40, 41-44p. Painted c-81, 87, 92, 95, 98, 100, 105.*

STAR WARS (Monthly series)
Dark Horse Comics: Dec, 1998 - Present ($2.50/$2.95/$2.99)

1-12: 1-6-Prelude To Rebellion; Strnad-s. 4-Brereton-c. 7-12-Outlander 3.00
5,6 (Holochrome-c variants) 6.00
13, 17-18-($2.95): 13-18-Emissaries to Malastare; Truman-s 3.00
14-16-($2.50) Schultz-c 3.00
19-57: 19-22-Twilight; Duursema-a. 23-26-Infinity's End. 51-57-Republic 3.00
#0 Another Universe.com Ed.($10.00) r/serialized pages from Pizzazz Magazine; new Dorman painted-c 10.00
... A Valentine Story (2/03, $3.50) Leia & Han Solo on Hoth; Winick-s/Chadwick-a/c 3.50
...: Clone Wars Vol. 1 (2003, $14.95) 15.00
...: Clone Wars Vol. 2 (2003, $14.95) r/#51-53 & Star Wars: Jedi - Shaak Ti 15.00
...: The Stark Hyperspace War (903, $12.95) r/#36-39 13.00

STAR WARS: A NEW HOPE- THE SPECIAL EDITION
Dark Horse Comics: Jan, 1997 - No. 4, Apr, 1997 ($2.95, limited series)

1-4-Dorman-c 4.00

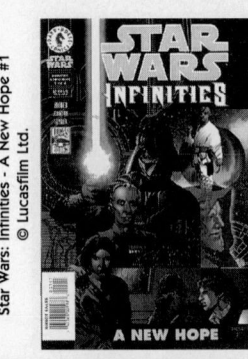

Star Wars: Empire #7 © Lucasfilm Ltd.

Star Wars: Episode 1 Queen Amidala #1 © Lucasfilm Ltd.

Star Wars: Infinities - A New Hope #1 © Lucasfilm Ltd.

	GD 2.0	VG 4.0	FN 6.0	VF 8.0	VF/NM 9.0	NM- 9.2

STAR WARS: BOBA FETT
Dark Horse Comics: Dec, 1995 - No. 3 ($3.95) (Originally intended as a one-shot)

	GD	VG	FN	VF	VF/NM	NM-
1-Kennedy-c/a						6.00
2,3						5.00
Death, Lies, & Treachery TPB (1/98, $12.95) r/#1-3						13.00
... - Agent of Doom (11/00, $2.99) Ostrander-s/Cam Kennedy-a						3.00
Twin Engines of Destruction (1/97, $2.95)						3.00

STAR WARS: BOBA FETT: ENEMY OF THE EMPIRE
Dark Horse Comics: Jan, 1999 - No. 4, Apr, 1999 ($2.95, limited series)

1-4-Recalls 1st meeting of Fett and Vader 3.00

STAR WARS: CHEWBACCA
Dark Horse Comics: Jan, 2000 - No. 4, Apr, 2000 ($2.95, limited series)

1-4-Macan-s/art by various incl. Anderson, Kordey, Gibbons; Phillips-c 3.00

STAR WARS: CRIMSON EMPIRE
Dark Horse Comics: Dec, 1997 - No. 6, May, 1998 ($2.95, limited series)

	GD	VG	FN	VF	VF/NM	NM-
1-Richardson-s/Gulacy-a	1	2	3	4	5	7
2-6						5.00

STAR WARS: CRIMSON EMPIRE II: COUNCIL OF BLOOD
Dark Horse Comics: Nov, 1998 - No. 6, Apr, 1999 ($2.95, limited series)

1-6-Richardson & Stradley-s/Gulacy-a 3.00

STAR WARS: DARK EMPIRE
Dark Horse Comics: Dec, 1991 - No. 6, Oct, 1992 ($2.95, limited series)

	GD	VG	FN	VF	VF/NM	NM-
Preview-(99¢)						3.00
1-All have Dorman painted-c	1	2	3	5	7	9
1-3-2nd printing						4.00
2-Low print run	2	4	6	8	10	12
3						6.00
4-6						4.00
Gold Embossed Set (#1-6)-With gold embossed foil logo (price is for set)						90.00
Platinum Embossed Set (#1-6)						120.00
Trade paperback (4/93, 16.95)						17.00
Dark Empire 1 - TPB 3rd printing (2003, $16.95)						17.00
Ltd. Ed. Hardcover ($99.95) Signed & numbered						100.00

STAR WARS: DARK EMPIRE II
Dark Horse Comics: Dec, 1994 - No. 6, May, 1995 ($2.95, limited series)

	GD	VG	FN	VF	VF/NM	NM-
1-Dave Dorman painted-c						5.00
2-6: Dorman-c in all.						4.00
Platinum Embossed Set (#1-6)						35.00
Trade paperback ($17.95)						18.00

STAR WARS: DARK FORCE RISING
Dark Horse Comics: May, 1997 - No. 6, Oct, 1997 ($2.95, limited series)

	GD	VG	FN	VF	VF/NM	NM-
1-6						4.00
TPB (2/98, $17.95) r/#1-6						18.00

STAR WARS: DARTH MAUL
Dark Horse Comics: Sept, 2000 - No. 4, Dec, 2000 ($2.95, limited series)

1-4-Photo-c and Struzan painted-c; takes place 6 months before Ep. 1 3.00

STAR WARS: DROIDS (See Dark Horse Comics #17-19)
Dark Horse Comics: Apr, 1994 - #6, Sept, 1994; V2#1, Apr, 1995 - V2#8, Dec, 1995 ($2.50, limited series)

	GD	VG	FN	VF	VF/NM	NM-
1-($2.95)-Embossed-c						4.00
2-6 , Special 1 (1/95, $2.50), V2#1-8						3.00

STAR WARS: EMPIRE
Dark Horse Comics: Sept, 2002 - Present ($2.99)

	GD	VG	FN	VF	VF/NM	NM-
1-12-Benjamin-a; takes place weeks before SW: A New Hope. 7-Boba Fett-c						3.00
... Volume 1 (2003, $12.95, TPB) r/#1-4						13.00

STAR WARS: EMPIRE'S END
Dark Horse Comics: Oct, 1995 - No. 2, Nov, 1995 ($2.95, limited series)

1,2-Dorman-c 3.00

STAR WARS: EPISODE 1 THE PHANTOM MENACE
Dark Horse Comics: May, 1999 - No. 4 ($2.95, movie adaptation)

	GD	VG	FN	VF	VF/NM	NM-
1-4-Regular and photo-c; Damaggio & Williamson-a						3.00
TPB ($12.95) r/#1-4						13.00
...Anakin Skywalker-Photo-c & Bradstreet-c, ...Obi-Wan Kenobi-Photo-c & Egeland-c, ...Queen Amidala-Photo-c & Bradstreet-c, ...Qui-Gon Jinn-Photo-c & Bradstreet-c						3.00
Gold foil covers; Wizard 1/2						10.00

STAR WARS: EPISODE II - ATTACK OF THE CLONES
Dark Horse Comics: Apr, 2002 - No. 4, May, 2002 ($3.99, movie adaptation)

	GD	VG	FN	VF	VF/NM	NM-
1-4-Regular and photo-c; Duursema-a						4.00
TPB ($17.95) r/#1-4; Struzan-c						18.00

STAR WARS HANDBOOK
Dark Horse Comics: July, 1998 - Present ($2.95, one-shots)

	GD	VG	FN	VF	VF/NM	NM-
...X-Wing Rogue Squadron (7/98)-Guidebook to characters and spacecraft						3.00
...Crimson Empire (7/99) Dorman-c						3.00
...Dark Empire (3/00) Dorman-c						3.00

STAR WARS: HEIR TO THE EMPIRE
Dark Horse Comics: Oct, 1995 - No.6, Apr, 1996 ($2.95, limited series)

1-6: Adaptation of Zahn novel 3.00

STAR WARS: INFINITIES - A NEW HOPE
Dark Horse Comics: May, 2001 - No. 4, Oct, 2001 ($2.99, limited series)

	GD	VG	FN	VF	VF/NM	NM-
1-4: "What If..." the Death Star wasn't destroyed in Episode 4						3.00
TPB (2002, $12.95) r/ #1-4						13.00

STAR WARS: INFINITIES - THE EMPIRE STRIKES BACK
Dark Horse Comics: July, 2002 - No. 4, Oct, 2002 ($2.99, limited series)

	GD	VG	FN	VF	VF/NM	NM-
1-4: "What If..." Luke died on the ice planet Hoth; Bachalo-c						3.00
TPB (2/03, $12.95) r/ #1-4						13.00

STAR WARS: JABBA THE HUTT
Dark Horse Comics: Apr, 1995 ($2.50, one-shots)

nn, ...The Betrayal, ...The Dynasty Trap, ...The Hunger of Princess Nampi 3.00

STAR WARS: JANGO FETT - OPEN SEASONS
Dark Horse Comics: Apr, 2002 - No. 4, July, 2002 ($2.99, limited series)

1-Bachs & Fernandez-a 3.00

STAR WARS: JEDI
Dark Horse Comics: Feb, 2003; May, 2003; Aug, 2003 ($4.99, one-shots)

	GD	VG	FN	VF	VF/NM	NM-
... - Aayla Secura (8/03) Ostrander-s/Duursema-a						5.00
... - Mace Windu (2/03) Duursema-a						5.00
... - Shaak Ti (5/03) Ostrander-s/Duursema-a						5.00

STAR WARS: JEDI ACADEMY - LEVIATHAN
Dark Horse Comics: Oct, 1998 - No. 4, Jan, 1999 ($2.95, limited series)

1-4: 1-Lago-c. 2-4-Chadwick-c 3.00

STAR WARS: JEDI COUNCIL: ACTS OF WAR
Dark Horse Comics: Jun, 2000 - No. 4, Sept, 2000 ($2.95, limited series)

1-4-Stradley-s; set one year before Episode 1 3.00

STAR WARS: JEDI QUEST
Dark Horse Comics: Sept, 2001 - No. 4, Dec, 2001 ($2.99, limited series)

1-4-Anakin's Jedi training; Windham-s/Mhan-a 3.00

STAR WARS: JEDI VS. SITH
Dark Horse Comics: Apr, 2001 - No. 6, Sept, 2001 ($2.99, limited series)

1-6: Macan-s/Bachs-a/Robinson-c 3.00

STAR WARS: MARA JADE
Dark Horse Comics: Aug, 1998 - No. 6, Jan, 1999 ($2.95, limited series)

1-6-Ezquerra-a 3.00

STAR WARS: QUI-GON & OBI-WAN - LAST STAND ON ORD MANTELL
Dark Horse Comics: Dec, 2000 - No. 3, Mar, 2001 ($2.99, limited series)

1-3: 1-Three covers (photo, Tony Daniel, Bachs) Windham-s 3.00

STAR WARS: QUI-GON & OBI-WAN - THE AURORIENT EXPRESS
Dark Horse Comics: Feb, 2002 - No. 2, Mar, 2002 ($2.99, limited series)

1,2-Six years prior to Phantom Menace; Marangon-a 3.00

STAR WARS: RETURN OF THE JEDI (Movie)
Marvel Comics Group: Oct, 1983 - No. 4, Jan, 1984 (limited series)

	GD	VG	FN	VF	VF/NM	NM-
1-4-Williamson-p in all; r/Marvel Super Special #27	1	3	4	6	8	10
Oversized issue (1983, $2.95, 10-3/4x8-1/4", 68 pgs., cardboard-c)-r/#1-4	2	4	6	10	13	16

STAR WARS: RIVER OF CHAOS
Dark Horse Comics: June, 1995 - No. 4, Sept, 1995 ($2.95, limited series)

1-4: Louise Simonson scripts 3.00

STAR WARS: SHADOWS OF THE EMPIRE
Dark Horse Comics: May, 1996 - No. 6, Oct, 1996 ($2.95, limited series)

1-6: Story details events between The Empire Strikes Back & Return of the Jedi; Russell-a(i). 3.00

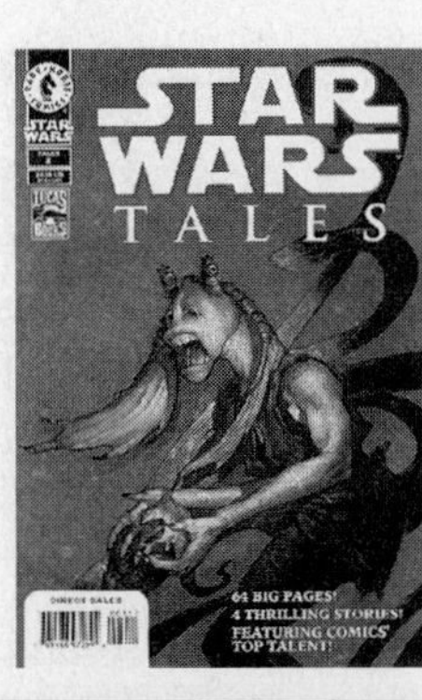

Star Wars Tales #3 © Lucasfilm Ltd.

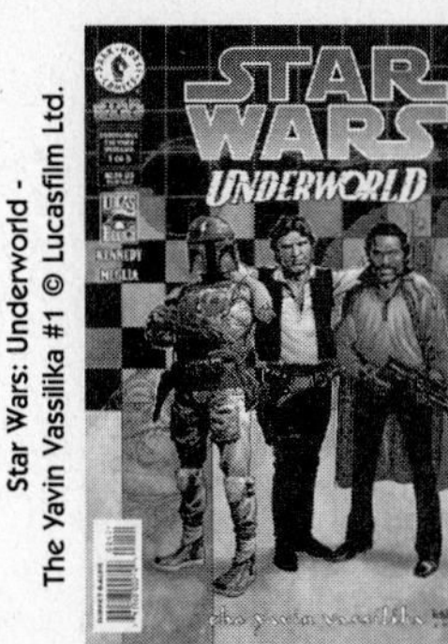

Star Wars: Underworld - The Yavin Vassilika #1 © Lucasfilm Ltd.

Steampunk #8 © Kelly & Bachalo

GD 2.0 VG 4.0 FN 6.0 VF 8.0 VF/NM 9.0 NM- 9.2

STAR WARS: SHADOWS OF THE EMPIRE - EVOLUTION
Dark Horse Comics: Feb, 1998 - No. 5, June, 1998 ($2.95, limited series)
1-5: Perry-s/Fegredo-c. 3.00

STAR WARS: SHADOW STALKER
Dark Horse Comics: Sept, 1997 ($2.95, one-shot)
nn-Windham-a. 3.00

STAR WARS: SPLINTER OF THE MIND'S EYE
Dark Horse Comics: Dec, 1995 - No. 4, June, 1996 ($2.50, limited series)
1-4: Adaption of Alan Dean Foster novel 3.00

STAR WARS: STARFIGHTER
Dark Horse Comics: Jan, 2002 - No. 3, March, 2002 ($2.99, limited series)
1-3-Williams & Gray-c 3.00

STAR WARS: TAG & BINK ARE DEAD
Dark Horse Comics: Oct, 2001 - No. 2, Nov, 2001($2.99, limited series)
1,2-Rubio-s 3.00

STAR WARS TALES
Dark Horse Comics: Sept, 1999 - Present ($4.95/$5.95/$5.99, anthology)
1-4-Short stories by various 5.00
5-17 ($5.95/$5.99-c) Art and photo-c on each 6.00
Volume 1 (1/02, $19.95) r/#1-4 20.00
Volume 2 ('02, $19.95) r/#5-8 20.00
Volume 3 (1/03, $19.95) r/#9-12 20.00

STAR WARS: TALES - A JEDI'S WEAPON (See Promotional Comics section)

STAR WARS: TALES FROM MOS EISLEY
Dark Horse Comics: Mar, 1996 ($2.95, one-shot)
nn-Bret Blevins-a. 3.00

STAR WARS: TALES OF THE JEDI (See Dark Horse Comics #7)
Dark Horse Comics: Oct, 1993 - No. 5, Feb, 1994 ($2.50, limited series)
1-5: All have Dave Dorman painted-c. 3-r/Dark Horse Comics #7-9 w/new coloring & some panels redrawn 3.00
1-5-Gold foil embossed logo; limited # printed-7500 (set) 50.00

STAR WARS: TALES OF THE JEDI-DARK LORDS OF THE SITH
Dark Horse Comics: Oct, 1994 - No. 6, Mar, 1995 ($2.50, limited series)
1-6: 1-Polybagged w/trading card 3.00

STAR WARS: TALES OF THE JEDI-REDEMPTION
Dark Horse Comics: July, 1998 - No. 5, Nov, 1998 ($2.95, limited series)
1-5: 1-Kevin J. Anderson-s/Kordey-c 3.00

STAR WARS: TALES OF THE JEDI-THE FALL OF THE SITH
Dark Horse Comics: June, 1997 - No. 5, Oct, 1997 ($2.95, limited series)
1-5 3.00

STAR WARS: TALES OF THE JEDI-THE FREEDON NADD UPRISING
Dark Horse Comics: Aug, 1994 - No. 2, Nov, 1994 ($2.50, limited series)
1,2 3.00

STAR WARS: TALES OF THE JEDI-THE GOLDEN AGE OF THE SITH
Dark Horse Comics: July, 1996 - No. 5, Feb, 1997 (99¢/$2.95, limited series)
0-(99¢)-Anderson-s 3.00
1-5-Anderson-s 3.00

STAR WARS: TALES OF THE JEDI-THE SITH WAR
Dark Horse Comics: Aug, 1995 - No. 6, Jan, 1996 ($2.50, limited series)
1-6: Anderson scripts 3.00

STAR WARS: THE BOUNTY HUNTERS
Dark Horse Comics: July, 1999 - Oct, 1999 ($2.95, one-shots)
...Aurra Sing (7/99), ...Kenix Kil (10/99), ...Scoundrel's Wages (8/99) Lando Calrissian app. 3.00

STAR WARS: THE JABBA TAPE
Dark Horse Comics: Dec, 1998 ($2.95, one-shot)
nn-Wagner-s/Plunkett-a 3.00

STAR WARS: THE LAST COMMAND
Dark Horse Comics: Nov, 1997 - No. 6, July, 1998 ($2.95, limited series)
1-6:Based on the Timothy Zaun novel 4.00

STAR WARS: THE PROTOCOL OFFENSIVE
Dark Horse Comics: Sept, 1997 ($4.95, one-shot)
nn-Anthony Daniels & Ryder Windham-s 5.00

GD 2.0 VG 4.0 FN 6.0 VF 8.0 VF/NM 9.0 NM- 9.2

STAR WARS: UNDERWORLD - THE YAVIN VASSILIKA
Dark Horse Comics: Dec, 2000 - No. 5, June, 2001 ($2.99, limited series)
1-5-(Photo and Robinson covers) 3.00

STAR WARS: UNION
Dark Horse Comics: Nov, 1999 - No. 4, Feb, 2000 ($2.95, limited series)
1-4-Wedding of Luke and Mara Jade; Teranishi-a/Stackpole-s 3.00

STAR WARS: VADER'S QUEST
Dark Horse Comics: Feb, 1999 - No. 4, May, 1999 ($2.95, limited series)
1-4-Follows destruction of 1st Death Star; Gibbons-a 3.00

STAR WARS: X-WING ROGUE SQUADRON (Star Wars: X-Wing Rogue Squadron-The Phantom Affair #5-8 appears on cover only)
Dark Horse Comics: July, 1995 - No. 35, Nov, 1998 ($2.95)
1/2 8.00
1-24,26-35: 1-4-Baron scripts. 5-20-Stackpole scripts 3.00
25-($3.95) 4.00
The Phantom Affair TPB ($12.95) r/#5-8 13.00

S.T.A.T.
Majestic Entertainment: Dec, 1993 ($2.25)
1 2.25

STATIC (Also see Eclipse Monthly)
Charlton Comics: No, 11, Oct, 1985 - No. 12, Dec, 1985
11,12-Ditko-c/a; low print run 6.00

STATIC (See Heroes)
DC Comics (Milestone): June, 1993 - No. 45, Mar, 1997 ($1.50/$1.75/$2.50)
1-($2.95)-Collector's Edition; polybagged w/poster & trading card & backing board (direct sales only) 4.00
1-24,26-45: 2-Origin. 8-Shadow War; Simonson silver ink-c. 14-($2.50, 52 pgs.)-Worlds Collide Pt. 14. 27-Kent Williams-c 2.50
25 ($3.95) 4.00
...: Trial by Fire (2000, $9.95) r/#1-4; Leon-c 10.00

STATIC SHOCK!: REBIRTH OF THE COOL (TV)
DC Comics: Jan, 2001 - No. 4, Sept, 2001 ($2.50, limited series)
1-4: McDuffie-s/Leon-c/a 2.50

STATIC-X
Chaos! Comics: Aug, 2002 ($5.99)
1-Polybagged with music CD; metal band as super-heroes; Pulido-s 6.00

STEAMPUNK
DC/WildStorm (Cliffhanger): Apr, 2000 - No. 12, Aug, 2002 ($2.50/$3.50)
Catechism (1/00) Prologue -Kelly-s/Bachalo-a 2.50
1-4,6-11: 4-Four covers by Bachalo, Madureira, Ramos, Campbell 2.50
5,12-($3.50) 3.50
...: Drama Obscura ('03, $14.95) r/#6-12 15.00
...: Manimatron ('01, $14.95) r/#1-5, Catechism, Idiosincratica 15.00

STEED AND MRS. PEEL (TV)(Also see The Avengers)
Eclipse Books/ ACME Press: 1990 - No. 3, 1991 ($4.95, limited series)
Books One - Three: Grant Morrison scripts 5.00

STEEL (Also see JLA)
DC Comics: Feb, 1994 - No. 52, July, 1998 ($1.50/$1.95/$2.50)
1-8,0,9-52: 1-From Reign of the Supermen storyline. 6,7-Worlds Collide Pt. 5 &12. 8-(9/94). 0-(10/94). 9-(11/94). 46-Superboy-c/app. 50-Millennium Giants x-over 2.50
Annual 1 (1994, $2.95)-Elseworlds story 3.00
Annual 2 (1995, $3.95)-Year One story 4.00
...Forging of a Hero TPB (1997, $19.95) r/ early app. 20.00

STEEL: THE OFFICIAL COMIC ADAPTION OF THE WARNER BROS. MOTION PICTURE
DC Comics: 1997 ($4.95, Prestige format, one-shot)
nn-Movie adaption; Bogdanove & Giordano-a 5.00

STEELGRIP STARKEY
Marvel Comics (Epic Comics): June, 1986 - No. 6, July, 1987 ($1.50, limited series, Baxter paper)
1-6 2.25

STEEL STERLING (Formerly Shield-Steel Sterling; see Blue Ribbon, Jackpot, Mighty Comics, Mighty Crusaders, Roly Poly & Zip Comics)
Archie Enterprises, Inc.: No. 4, Jan, 1984 - No. 7, July, 1984
4-7: 4-6-Kanigher-s; Barreto-a. 5,6-Infantino-a. 6-McWilliams-a 4.00

Stone #4 © Haberlin & Portacio

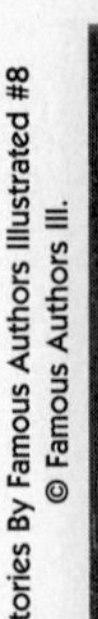

Stories By Famous Authors Illustrated #8 © Famous Authors Ill.

Stormwatch #44 © WSP

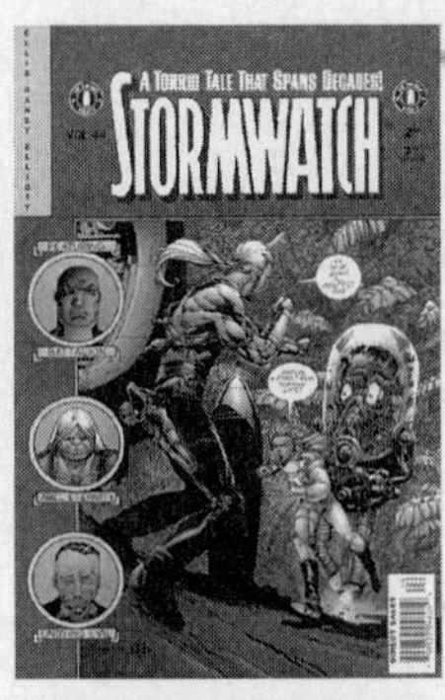

GD 2.0 | VG 4.0 | FN 6.0 | VF 8.0 | VF/NM 9.0 | NM- 9.2

STEEL, THE INDESTRUCTIBLE MAN (See All-Star Squadron #8)
DC Comics: Mar, 1978 - No. 5, Oct-Nov, 1978

1 1 3 4 6 8 10
2-5: 5-44 pgs. 6.00

STEELTOWN ROCKERS
Marvel Comics: Apr, 1987 - No. 6, Sept, 1990 ($1.00, limited series)

1-6: Small town teens form rock band 2.25

STEVE AUSTIN (See Stone Cold Steve Austin)

STEVE CANYON (See Harvey Comics Hits #52)
Dell Publishing Co.: No. 519, 11/53 - No. No. 1033, 9/59 (All Milton Caniff-a except #519, 939, 1033)

Four Color 519 (1, '53) 10 20 30. 67 96 125
Four Color 578 (8/54), 641 (7/55), 737 (10/56), 804 (5/57), 939 (10/58), 1033 (9/59) (photo-c) 6 12 18 40 55 70

STEVE CANYON
Grosset & Dunlap: 1959 (6-3/4x9", 96 pgs., B&W, no text, hardcover)

100100-Reprints 2 stories from strip (1953, 1957) 6 12 18 29 36 42
100100 (softcover edition) 5 10 15 23 28 32

STEVE CANYON COMICS
Harvey Publ.: Feb, 1948 - No. 6, Dec, 1948 (Strip reprints, No. 4,5: 52pgs.)

1-Origin; has biography of Milton Caniff; Powell-a, 2 pgs.; Caniff-a 24 48 72 135 190 245
2-Caniff, Powell-a in #2-6 15 30 45 84 115 145
3-6: 6-Intro Madame Lynx-c/story 14 28 42 79 107 135

STEVE CANYON IN 3-D
Kitchen Sink Press: June, 1986 ($2.25, one-shot)

1-Contains unpublished story from 1954 5.00

STEVE DITKO'S STRANGE AVENGING TALES
Fantagraphics Books: Feb, 1997 ($2.95, B&W)

1-Ditko-c/s/a 3.00

STEVE DONOVAN, WESTERN MARSHAL (TV)
Dell Publishing Co.: No. 675, Feb, 1956 - No. 880, Feb, 1958 (All photo-c)

Four Color 675-Kinstler-a 9 18 27 63 89 115
Four Color 768-Kinstler-a 7 14 21 51 71 90
Four Color 880 5 10 15 36 48 60

STEVE ROPER
Famous Funnies: Apr, 1948 - No. 5, Dec, 1948

1-Contains 1944 daily newspaper-r 12 24 36 71 96 120
2 8 16 24 46 58 70
3-5 8 16 24 40 50 60

STEVE SAUNDERS SPECIAL AGENT (See Special Agent)

STEVE SAVAGE (See Captain...)

STEVE ZODIAC & THE FIRE BALL XL-5 (TV)
Gold Key: Jan, 1964

10108-401 (#1) 9 18 27 63 89 115

STEVIE (Mazie's boy friend)(Also see Flat-Top, Mazie & Mortie)
Mazie (Magazine Publ.): Nov, 1952 - No. 6, Apr, 1954

1-Teenage humor; Stevie, Mortie & Mazie begin 8 16 24 46 58 70
2-6 6 12 18 28 34 40

STEVIE MAZIE'S BOY FRIEND (See Harvey Hits #5)

STEWART THE RAT (See Eclipse Graphic Album Series)

ST. GEORGE (See listing under Saint...)

STIG'S INFERNO
Vortex/Eclipse: 1985 - No. 7, Mar, 1987 ($1.95, B&W)

1-7 ($1.95) 2.25
Graphic Album (1988, $6.95, B&W, 100 pgs.) 7.00

STING OF THE GREEN HORNET (See The Green Hornet)
Now Comics: June, 1992 - No. 4, 1992 ($2.50, limited series)

1-4: Butler-c/a 2.50
1-4 ($2.75)-Collectors Ed.; polybagged w/poster 3.00

STONE
Avalon Studios: Aug, 1998 - No. 4, Apr, 1999 ($2.50, limited series)

1-4-Portacio-a/Haberlin-s 2.50
1-Alternate-c 5.00
2-($14.95) DF Stonechrome Edition 15.00

STONE (Volume 2)
Avalon Studios: Aug, 1999 - No. 4, May, 2000 ($2.50)

1-4-Portacio-a/Haberlin-s 2.50
1-Chrome-c 5.00

STONE COLD STEVE AUSTIN (WWF Wrestling)
Chaos! Comics: Oct, 1999 - No. 4, Feb, 2000 ($2.95)

1-4-Reg. & photo-c; Steven Grant-s 3.00
1-Premium Ed. ($10.00) 10.00
Preview ($5.00) 5.00

STONEY BURKE (TV)
Dell Publishing Co.: June-Aug, 1963 - No. 2, Sept-Nov, 1963

1,2-Jack Lord photo-c on both 3 6 9 18 24 30

STONY CRAIG
Pentagon Publishing Co.: 1946 (No #)

nn-Reprints Bell Syndicate's "Sgt. Stony Craig" newspaper strips 8 16 24 40 50 60

STORIES BY FAMOUS AUTHORS ILLUSTRATED (Fast Fiction #1-5)
Seaboard Publ./Famous Authors Ill.: No. 6, Aug, 1950 - No. 13, Mar, 1951

1-Scarlet Pimpernel-Baroness Orczy 36 72 108 204 290 375
2-Capt. Blood-Raphael Sabatini 35 70 105 201 288 370
3-She, by Haggard 40 80 120 240 340 440
4-The 39 Steps-John Buchan 24 48 72 135 190 245
5-Beau Geste-P. C. Wren 24 48 72 135 190 245

NOTE: *The above five issues are exact reprints of Fast Fiction #1-5 except for the title change and new Kiefer covers on #1 and 2. Kiefer c(r)-3-5. The above 5 issues were released before Famous Authors #6.*

6-Macbeth, by Shakespeare; Kiefer art (8/50); used in **SOTI**, pg. 22,143; Kiefer-c; 36 pgs. 33 66 99 190 270 350
7-The Window; Kiefer-c/a; 52 pgs. 24 48 72 135 190 245
8-Hamlet, by Shakespeare; Kiefer-c/a; 36 pgs. 29 58 87 164 232 300
9,10: 9-Nicholas Nickleby, by Dickens; G. Schrotter-a; 52 pgs. 10-Romeo & Juliet, by Shakespeare; Kiefer-c/a; 36 pgs. 24 48 72 135 190 245
11-13: 11-Ben-Hur; Schrotter-a; 52 pgs. 12-La Svengali; Schrotter-a; 36 pgs. 13-Scaramouche; Kiefer-c/a; 36 pgs. 23 46 69 130 183 235

NOTE: *Artwork was prepared/advertised for #14, The Red Badge Of Courage. Gilberton bought out Famous Authors, Ltd. and used that story as C.I. #98. Famous Authors, Ltd. then published the Classics Junior series. The Famous Authors titles were published as part of the regular Classics Ill. Series in Brazil starting in 1952.*

STORIES FROM THE TWILIGHT ZONE
Skylark Pub: Mar, 1979, 68pgs. (B&W comic digest, 5-1/4x7-5/8")

15405-2: Pfevfer-a, 56pgs, new comics 3 6 9 18 24 30

STORIES OF ROMANCE (Formerly Meet Miss Bliss)
Atlas Comics (LMC): No. 5, Mar, 1956 - No. 13, Aug, 1957

5-Baker-a? 10 20 30 56 73 90
6-10,12,13 7 14 21 35 43 50
11-Baker, Romita-a; Colletta-c/a 8 16 24 46 58 70

NOTE: ***Ann Brewster** a-13. **Colletta** a-9(2), 11; c-5, 11.*

STORM
Marvel Comics: Feb, 1996 - No. 4, May, 1996 ($2.95, limited series)

1-4-Foil-c; Dodson-a(p); Ellis-s: 2-4-Callisto; 3.50

STORMQUEST
Caliber Press (Sky Universe): Nov, 1994 - No. 6, Apr, 1995 ($1.95)

1-6 2.25

STORMWATCH (Also see The Authority)
Image Comics (WildStorm Prod.): May, 1993 - No. 50, Jul, 1997 ($1.95/$2.50)

1-8,0,9-36: 1-Intro StormWatch (Battalion, Diva, Winter, Fuji, & Hellstrike); 1st app. Weatherman; Jim Lee-c & part scripts; Lee plots in all. 1-Gold edition.1-3-Includes coupon for limited edition StormWatch trading card #00 by Lee. 3-1st app. Backlash (cameo). 0-($2.50)-Polybagged w/card; 1st full app. Backlash. 9-(4/94, $2.50)-Intro Defile. 10-(6/94),11,12-Both (8/94). 13,14-(9/94). 15-(10/94). 21-Reads #1 on-c. 22-Direct Market; Wildstorm Rising Pt. 9, bound-in card. 23-Spartan joins team. 25-(6/94, June 1995 on-c, $2.50). 35-Fire From Heaven Pt. 5. 36-Fire From Heaven Pt. 12 2.50
10-Alternate Portacio-c, see Deathblow #5 2.50
22-($1.95)-Newsstand, Wildstorm Rising Pt. 9 2.50
37-(7/96, $3.50, 38 pgs.)-Weatherman forms new team; 1st app. Jenny Sparks, Jack Hawksmoor & Rose Tattoo; Warren Ellis scripts begin; Justice League #1-c/swipe 3.50
38-49: 44-Three covers. 2.50
50-($4.50) 4.50
Special 1 ,2(1/94, 5/95, $3.50, 52 pgs.) 3.50

Stormwatch: Team Achilles #1 © WSP

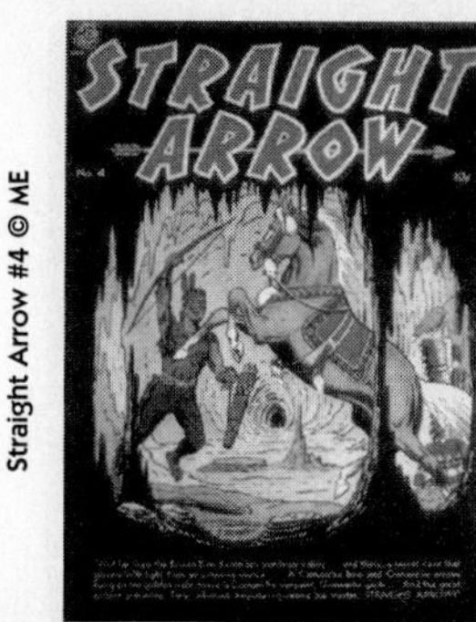

Straight Arrow #4 © ME

Strange Adventures #16 © DC

GD VG FN VF VF/NM NM-
2.0 4.0 6.0 8.0 9.0 9.2

GD VG FN VF VF/NM NM-
2.0 4.0 6.0 8.0 9.0 9.2

Sourcebook 1 (1/94, $2.50) 2.50
Forces of Nature ('99, $14.95, TPB) r/V1 #37-42 15.00
Lightning Strikes ('00, $14.95, TPB) r/V1 #43-47 15.00

STORMWATCH (Also see The Authority)
Image Comics (WildStorm): Oct, 1997 - No. 11, Sept, 1998 ($2.50)

1-Ellis-s/Jimenez-a(p); two covers by Bennett 2.50
1-($3.50)-Voyager Pack bagged w/Gen 13 preview 3.50
2-4: 4-1st app. Midnighter and Apollo 2.50
5-11: 7,8-Freefall app. 9-Gen13 & DV8 app. 2.50
A Finer World ('99, $14.95, TPB) r/V2 #4-9 15.00
Change or Die ('99, $14.95, TPB) r/V1 #48-50 & V2 #1-3 15.00
Final Orbit ('01, $9.95, TPB) r/V2 #10,11 & WildC.A.T.S./Aliens; Hitch-c 10.00

STORMWATCHER
Eclipse Comics (Acme Press): Apr, 1989 - No. 4, Dec, 1989 ($2.00, B&W)

1-4 2.25

STORMWATCH: TEAM ACHILLES
DC Comics (WildStorm): Sept, 2002 - Present ($2.95)

1-8: 1-Two covers by Portacio; Portacio-a/Wright-s. 5,6-The Authority app. 3.00
9-19: 9-Back-up preview of The Authority: High Stakes pt. 1 3.00
TPB (2003, $14.95) r/Wizard Preview and #1-6; Portacio art pages 15.00
Book 2 (2004, $14.95) r/#7-11 & short story from Eye of the Storm Annual 15.00

STORMY (Disney) (Movie)
Dell Publishing Co.: No. 537, Feb, 1954

Four Color 537 (...the Thoroughbred)-on top 2/3 of each page; Pluto story on bottom 1/3
5 10 15 33 44 55

STORY OF JESUS (See Classics Illustrated Special Issue)

STORY OF MANKIND, THE (Movie)
Dell Publishing Co.: No. 851, Jan, 1958

Four Color 851-Vincent Price/Hedy Lamarr photo-c 8 16 24 55 78 100

STORY OF MARTHA WAYNE, THE
Argo Publ.: April, 1956

1-Newspaper strip-r 6 12 18 29 36 42

STORY OF RUTH, THE
Dell Publishing Co.: No. 1144, Nov-Jan, 1961 (Movie)

Four Color #1144-Photo-c 10 20 30 70 100 130

STORY OF THE COMMANDOS, THE (Combined Operations)
Long Island Independent: 1943 (15¢, B&W, 68 pgs.) (Distr. by Gilberton)

nn-All text (no comics); photos & illustrations; ad for Classic Comics on back cover (Rare)
34 68 102 193 274 355

STORY OF THE GLOOMY BUNNY, THE (See March of Comics #9)

STRAIGHT ARROW (Radio)(See Best of the West & Great Western)
Magazine Enterprises: Feb-Mar, 1950 - No. 55, Mar, 1956 (All 36 pgs.)

1-Straight Arrow (alias Steve Adams) & his palomino Fury begin; 1st mention of Sundown Valley & the Secret Cave 46 92 138 276 413 550
2-Red Hawk begins (1st app?) by Powell (origin), ends #55
24 48 72 135 190 245
3-Frazetta-c 31 62 93 175 248 320
4,5: 4-Secret Cave-c 22 44 66 124 172 220
6-10 20 40 60 112 156 200
11-Classic story "The Valley of Time", with an ancient civilization made of gold
22 44 66 124 172 220
12-19 15 30 45 86 118 150
20-Origin Straight Arrow's Shield 17 34 51 98 134 170
21-Origin Fury 22 44 66 124 172 220
22-Frazetta-c 24 48 72 138 194 250
23,25-30: 25-Secret Cave-c. 28-Red Hawk meets The Vikings
10 20 30 60 80 100
24-Classic story "The Dragons of Doom!" with prehistoric pteradactyls
14 28 42 79 107 135
31-38: 36-Red Hawk drug story by Powell 8 16 24 46 58 70
39-Classic story "The Canyon Beast", with a dinosaur egg hatching a Tyranosaurus Rex
12 24 36 71 96 120
40-Classic story "Secret of The Spanish Specters", with Conquistadors' lost treasure
10 20 30 60 80 100
41,42,44-54: 45-Secret Cave-c 8 16 24 40 50 60
43-Intro & 1st app. Blaze, S. Arrow's Warrior dog 9 18 27 52 66 80
55-Last issue 10 20 30 56 73 90

NOTE: ***Fred Meagher** a 1-55; c-1, 2, 4-21, 23-55. **Powell** a 2-55. **Whitney** a-1. Many issues advertise the radio premiums associated with Straight Arrow.*

STRAIGHT ARROW'S FURY (Also see A-1 Comics)
Magazine Enterprises: No. 119, 1954 (one-shot)

A-1 119-Origin; Fred Meagher-c/a 16 32 48 89 122 155

STRANGE (Tales You'll Never Forget)
Ajax-Farrell Publ. (Four Star Comic Corp.): March, 1957 - No. 6, May, 1958

1 22 44 66 127 176 225
2-Censored r/Haunted Thrills 11 22 33 66 88 110
3-6 10 20 30 58 77 95

STRANGE ADVENTURES
National Periodical Publications: Aug-Sept, 1950 - No. 244, Oct-Nov, 1973 (No. 1-12: 52 pgs.)

1-Adaptation of "Destination Moon"; preview of movie w/photo-c from movie (also see Fawcett Movie Comic #2); adapt. of Edmond Hamilton's "Chris KL-99" in #1-3; Darwin Jones begins
240 480 720 2021 3261 4500
2 113 226 339 961 1468 1975
3,4 76 152 228 646 986 1325
5-8,10: 7-Origin Kris KL-99 65 130 195 553 847 1140
9-(6/51)-Origin/1st app. Captain Comet (c/story) 153 306 459 1308 2004 2700
11-20: 12,13,17,18-Toth-a. 14-Robot-c 47 94 141 376 563 750
21-30: 28-Atomic explosion panel. 30-Robot-c 37 74 111 278 414 550
31,34-38 34 68 102 255 383 510
32,33-Krigstein-a 35 70 105 263 394 525
39-Ill. in **SOTI** "Treating police contemptuously" (top right)
40 80 120 300 450 600
40-49-Last Capt. Comet; not in 45,47,48 33 66 99 248 374 500
50-53-Last precode issue (2/55) 25 50 75 176 258 340
54-70 18 36 54 131 191 250
71-99 14 28 42 99 145 190
100 16 32 48 113 167 220
101-110: 104-Space Museum begins by Sekowsky 10 20 30 73 107 140
111-116,118,119: 114-Star Hawkins begins, ends #185; Heath-a in Wood E.C. style
10 20 30 70 100 130
117-(6/60)-Origin/1st app. Atomic Knights. 50 100 150 400 600 800
120-2nd app. Atomic Knights 25 50 75 176 258 340
121,122,125,127,128,130,131,133,134: 134-Last 10¢ issue
9 18 27 60 85 110
123,126-3rd & 4th app. Atomic Knights 14 28 42 99 145 190
124-Intro/origin Faceless Creature 10 20 30 70 100 130
129,132,135,138,141,147-Atomic Knights app. 10 20 30 72 104 135
136,137,139,140,143,145,146,148,149,151,152,154,155,157-159: 159-Star Rovers app.; Gil Kane/Anderson-a. 6 12 18 43 59 75
142-2nd app. Faceless Creature 8 16 24 53 74 95
144-Only Atomic Knights-c (by M. Anderson) 11 22 33 77 114 150
150,153,156,160: Atomic Knights in each. 153-(6/63)-3rd app. Faceless Creature; atomic explosion-c. 160-Last Atomic Knights 8 16 24 53 74 95
161-179: 161-Last Space Museum. 163-Star Rovers app. 170-Infinity-c. 177-Intro/origin Immortal Man 5 10 15 33 44 55
180-Origin/1st app. Animal Man 19 38 57 133 194 255
181-183,185-189: 187-Intro/origin The Enchantress 4 8 12 27 36 45
184-2nd app. Animal Man by Gil Kane 12 24 36 82 121 160
190-1st app. Animal Man in costume 15 30 45 104 152 200
191-194,196-200,202-204 4 8 12 24 32 40
195-1st full app. Animal Man 8 16 24 55 78 100
201-Last Animal Man; 2nd full app. 6 12 18 38 52 65
205-(10/67)-Intro/origin Deadman by Infantino & begin series, ends #216
12 24 36 87 129 170
206-Neal Adams-a begins 9 18 27 60 85 110
207-210 8 16 24 55 78 100
211-216: 211-Space Museum-r. 216-(1-2/69)-Deadman story finally concludes in Brave & the Bold #86 (10-11/69); secret message panel by Neal Adams (pg. 13); tribute to Steranko
7 14 21 50 68 85
217-r/origin & 1st app. Adam Strange from Showcase #17, begin-r; Atomic Knights-r begin
2 4 6 14 18 22
218-221,223-225: 218-Last 12¢ issue. 225-Last 15¢ issue
2 4 6 12 16 20
222-New Adam Strange story; Kane/Anderson-a 3 7 10 21 28 34
226,227,230-236-(68-52 pgs.): 226, 227-New Adam Strange text story w/illos by Anderson (8,6 pgs.) 231-Last Atomic Knights-r. 235-JLA-c/s 2 4 6 12 16 20
228,229 (68 pgs.) 3 6 9 17 21 26
237-243 2 4 6 9 11 14
244-Last issue 2 4 6 9 11 14

NOTE: ***Neal Adams** a-206-216; c-207-216, 228, 235. **Anderson** a-8-52, 94, 96, 99, 115, 117, 119-163, 217r,*

Strange Fantasy #3 © AJAX

Strange Mysteries #12 © SUPR

The Strangers #2 © MAL

218r, 222, 223-225r, 226, 229r, 242i(r); c-18, 19, 21, 23, 24, 27, 30, 32-44(most); c/r-157i, 190i, 217-224, 228-231, 233, 235-239, 241-243. ***Ditko*** *a-188, 189.* ***Drucker*** *a-42, 43, 45.* ***Elias*** *a-212.* ***Finlay*** *a-2, 3, 6, 7, 210r, 229r.* ***Giunta*** *a-237r.* ***Heath*** *a-116.* ***Infantino*** *a-10-101, 106-151, 154, 157-163, 180, 190, 218-221r, 223-244p(r); c-50; c(r)-190p, 197, 199-211, 218-221, 223-244.* ***Kaluta*** *c-238, 240.* ***Gil Kane*** *a-8-116, 124, 125, 130, 138, 146-157, 173-186, 204r, 222r, 227-231r; c(p)-11-17, 25, 154, 157.* ***Kubert*** *a-55(2 pgs.), 226; c-219, 220, 225-227, 232, 234.* ***Moriera*** *c-26, 28, 29, 71.* ***Morrow*** *c-230.* ***Mortimer*** *c-8.* ***Powell*** *a-4.* ***Sekowsky*** *a-71p, 97-162p, 217p(r), 218p(r); c-206, 217-219r.* ***Simon & Kirby*** *a-2r (2 pgs)* ***Sparling*** *a-201.* ***Toth*** *a-8, 12, 13, 17-19.* ***Wood*** *a-154i. Atomic Knights in #117, 120, 123, 126, 129, 132, 135, 138, 141, 144, 147, 150, 153, 156, 160. Atomic Knights reprints by* ***Anderson*** *in 217-221, 223-231. Chris KL99 in 1-3, 5, 7, 9, 11, 15. Capt. Comet covers-9-14, 17-19, 24, 26, 27, 32-44.*

STRANGE ADVENTURES
DC Comics (Vertigo): Nov, 1999 - No. 4 ($2.50, limited series)

	GD 2.0	VG 4.0	FN 6.0	VF 8.0	VF/NM 9.0	NM- 9.2
1-3: 1-Bolland-c; art by Bolland, Gibbons, Quitely						2.50

STRANGE AS IT SEEMS (See Famous Funnies-A Carnival of Comics, Feature Funnies #1, The John Hix Scrap Book & Peanuts)

STRANGE AS IT SEEMS
United Features Syndicate: 1939

	GD 2.0	VG 4.0	FN 6.0	VF 8.0	VF/NM 9.0	NM- 9.2
Single Series 9, 1, 2	36	72	108	204	290	375

STRANGE ATTRACTORS
RetroGraphix: 1993 - No. 15, Feb, 1997 ($2.50, B&W)

	GD 2.0	VG 4.0	FN 6.0	VF 8.0	VF/NM 9.0	NM- 9.2
1-15: 1-(5/93), 2-(8/93), 3-(11/93), 4-(2/94)						2.50
Volume One-($14.95, trade paperback)-r/#1-7						15.00

STRANGE ATTRACTORS: MOON FEVER
Caliber Comics: Feb, 1997 - No. 3, June, 1997 ($2.95, B&W, mini-series)

	GD 2.0	VG 4.0	FN 6.0	VF 8.0	VF/NM 9.0	NM- 9.2
1-3						3.00

STRANGE COMBAT TALES
Marvel Comics (Epic Comics): Oct, 1993 - No. 4, Jan, 1994 ($2.50, limited series)

	GD 2.0	VG 4.0	FN 6.0	VF 8.0	VF/NM 9.0	NM- 9.2
1-4						2.50

STRANGE CONFESSIONS
Ziff-Davis Publ. Co.: Jan-Mar (Spring on-c), 1952 - No. 4, Fall, 1952 (All have photo-c)

	GD 2.0	VG 4.0	FN 6.0	VF 8.0	VF/NM 9.0	NM- 9.2
1(Scarce)-Kinstler-a	48	96	144	288	432	575
2(Scarce, 7-8/52)	37	74	111	212	301	390
3(Scarce, 9-10/52)-#3 on-c, #2 on inside; Reformatory girl story; photo-c	37	74	111	212	301	390
4(Scarce)	37	74	111	212	301	390

STRANGE DAYS
Eclipse Comics: Oct, 1984 - No. 3, Apr, 1985 ($1.75, Baxter paper)

	GD 2.0	VG 4.0	FN 6.0	VF 8.0	VF/NM 9.0	NM- 9.2
1-3: Freakwave, Johnny Nemo, & Paradax from Vanguard Illustrated; nudity, violence & strong language						2.25

STRANGE DAYS (Movie)
Marvel Comics: Dec, 1995 ($5.95, squarebound, one-shot)

	GD 2.0	VG 4.0	FN 6.0	VF 8.0	VF/NM 9.0	NM- 9.2
1-Adaptation of film						6.00

STRANGE FANTASY (Eerie Tales of Suspense!)(Formerly Rocketman #1)
Ajax-Farrell: Aug, 1952 - No. 14, Oct-Nov, 1954

	GD 2.0	VG 4.0	FN 6.0	VF 8.0	VF/NM 9.0	NM- 9.2
2(#1, 8/52)-Jungle Princess story; Kamenish-a; reprinted from Ellery Queen #1	46	92	138	276	413	550
2(10/52)-No Black Cat or Rulah; Bakerish, Kamenish-a; hypo/meathook-c	40	80	120	240	340	440
3-Rulah story, called Pulah	40	80	120	235	333	430
4-Rocket Man app. (2/53)	38	76	114	219	310	400
5,6,8,10,12,14	27	54	81	153	214	275
7-Madam Satan/Slave story	38	76	114	219	310	400
9(w/Black Cat), 9(w/Boy's Ranch; S&K-a), 9(w/War)(A rebinding of Harvey interiors; not publ. by Ajax)	34	68	102	193	274	355
9-Regular issue; Steve Ditko's 3rd published work (tied with Captain 3D)	44	88	132	264	395	525
11-Jungle story	35	70	105	201	283	365
13-Bondage-c; Rulah (Kolah) story	35	70	105	201	283	365

STRANGE GALAXY
Eerie Publications: V1#8, Feb, 1971 - No. 11, Aug, 1971 (B&W, magazine)

	GD 2.0	VG 4.0	FN 6.0	VF 8.0	VF/NM 9.0	NM- 9.2
V1#8-Reprints-c/Fantastic V19#3 (2/70) (a pulp)	3	7	10	21	28	35
9-11	3	6	9	16	20	25

STRANGEHAVEN
Abiogenesis Press: June, 1995 - Present ($2.95, B&W)

	GD 2.0	VG 4.0	FN 6.0	VF 8.0	VF/NM 9.0	NM- 9.2
1-15						3.00

STRANGE JOURNEY
America's Best (Steinway Publ.) (Ajax/Farrell): Sept, 1957 - No. 4, Jun, 1958 (Farrell reprints)

	GD 2.0	VG 4.0	FN 6.0	VF 8.0	VF/NM 9.0	NM- 9.2
1	20	40	60	112	156	200
2-4: 2-Flying saucer-c	14	28	42	79	107	135

STRANGE LOVE (See Fox Giants)

STRANGELOVE
Entity Comics: 1995 ($2.50)

	GD 2.0	VG 4.0	FN 6.0	VF 8.0	VF/NM 9.0	NM- 9.2
1						2.50

STRANGE MYSTERIES
Superior/Dynamic Publications: Sept, 1951 - No. 21, Jan, 1955

	GD 2.0	VG 4.0	FN 6.0	VF 8.0	VF/NM 9.0	NM- 9.2
1-Kamenish-a & horror stories begin	61	122	183	381	571	760
2	37	74	111	212	301	390
3-5	34	68	102	196	278	360
6-8	29	58	87	164	232	300
9-Bondage 3-D effect-c	35	70	105	201	283	365
10-Used in **SOTI**, pg. 181	26	52	78	150	210	270
11-18	23	46	69	130	183	235
19-r/Journey Into Fear #1; cover is a splash from one story; Baker-r(2)	24	48	72	138	194	250
20,21-Reprints; 20-r/#1 with new-c	18	36	54	101	138	175

STRANGE MYSTERIES
I. W. Enterprises/Super Comics: 1963 - 1964

	GD 2.0	VG 4.0	FN 6.0	VF 8.0	VF/NM 9.0	NM- 9.2
I.W. Reprint #9; Rulah-r/Spook #28; Disbrow-a	4	8	12	24	32	40
Super Reprint #10-12,15-17(1963-64): 10,11-r/Strange #2,1. 12-r/Tales of Horror #5 (3/53) less-c. 15-r/Dark Mysteries #23. 16-r/The Dead Who Walk. 17-r/Dark Mysteries #22	4	8	12	24	32	40
Super Reprint #18-r/Witchcraft #1; Kubert-a	4	8	12	24	32	40

STRANGE PLANETS
I. W. Enterprises/Super Comics: 1958; 1963-64

	GD 2.0	VG 4.0	FN 6.0	VF 8.0	VF/NM 9.0	NM- 9.2
I.W. Reprint #1(nd)-Reprints E. C. Incredible S/F #30 plus-c/Strange Worlds #3	7	14	21	50	68	85
I.W. Reprint #9-Orlando/Wood-r/Strange Worlds #4; cover-r from Flying Saucers #1	9	18	27	60	85	110
Super Reprint #10-Wood-r (22 pg.) from Space Detective #1; cover-r/Attack on Planet Mars	9	18	27	60	85	110
Super Reprint #11-Wood-r (25 pg.) from An Earthman on Venus	10	20	30	67	96	125
Super Reprint #12-Orlando-r/Rocket to the Moon	9	18	27	60	85	110
Super Reprint #15-Reprints Journey Into Unknown Worlds #8; Heath, Colan-r	5	10	15	36	48	60
Super Reprint #16-Reprints Avon's Strange Worlds #6; Kinstler, Check-a	6	12	18	38	52	65
Super Reprint #18-r/Great Exploits #1 (Daring Adventures #6); Space Busters, Explorer Joe, The Son of Robin Hood; Krigstein-a	4	8	12	29	40	50

STRANGERS
Image Comics: Mar, 2003 - No. 6, Sept, 2003 ($2.95)

	GD 2.0	VG 4.0	FN 6.0	VF 8.0	VF/NM 9.0	NM- 9.2
1-6-Randy & Jean-Marc Lofficier-s; two covers. 2-Nexus back-up story						3.00

STRANGERS, THE
Malibu Comics (Ultraverse): June, 1993 - No. 24, May, 1995 ($1.95/$2.50)

	GD 2.0	VG 4.0	FN 6.0	VF 8.0	VF/NM 9.0	NM- 9.2
1-4,6-12,14-20: 1-1st app. The Strangers; has coupon for Ultraverse Premiere #0; 1st app. the Night Man (not in costume). 2-Polybagged w/trading card. 7-Break-Thru x-over. 8-2 pg. origin Solution. 12-Silver foil logo; wraparound-c. 17-Rafferty app.						2.50
1-With coupon missing						2.25
1-Full cover holographic edition, 1st of kind w/Hardcase #1 & Prime #1						6.00
1-Ultra 5000 limited silver foil						4.00
4-($2.50)-Newsstand edition bagged w/card						2.50
5-($2.50, 52 pgs.)-Rune flip-c/story by B. Smith (3 pgs.); The Mighty Magnor 1 pg. strip by Aragones; 3-pg. Night Man preview						2.50
13-($3.50, 68 pgs.)-Mantra app.; flip book w/Ultraverse Premiere #4						3.50
21-24 ($2.50)						2.50
...:The Pilgrim Conundrum Saga (1/95, $3.95, 68pgs.)						4.00

STRANGERS IN PARADISE
Antarctic Press: Nov, 1993 - No. 3, Feb, 1994 ($2.75, B&W, limited series)

	GD 2.0	VG 4.0	FN 6.0	VF 8.0	VF/NM 9.0	NM- 9.2
1	6	12	18	38	52	65
1-2nd/3rd prints	1	2	3	5	6	8
2 (2300 printed)	4	8	12	27	36	45
3	3	6	9	18	24	30
Trade paperback (Antarctic Press, $6.95)-Red -c (5000 print run)						10.00
Trade paperback (Abstract Studios, $6.95)-Red-c (2000 print run)						15.00
Trade paperback (Abstract Studios, $6.95, 1st-4th printing)-Blue-						7.00
Hardcover ('98, $29.95) includes first draft pages						30.00

Strangers in Paradise V3#46 © Terry Moore

Strange Stories of Suspense #9 © MAR

Strange Tales #107 © MAR

	GD 2.0	VG 4.0	FN 6.0	VF 8.0	VF/NM 9.0	NM- 9.2
Gold Reprint Series ($2.75) 1-3-r/#1-3						2.75
STRANGERS IN PARADISE						
Abstract Studios: Sept, 1994 - No. 14, July, 1996 ($2.75, B&W)						
1	2	4	6	10	13	16
1,3- 2nd printings						4.00
2,3: 2-Color dream sequence	1	2	3	5	6	8
4-10						4.00
4-6-2nd printings						2.75
11-14: 14-The Letters of Molly & Poo						3.00
Gold Reprint Series ($2.75) 1-13-r/#1-13						2.75
I Dream Of You ($16.95, TPB) r/#1-9						17.00
It's a Good Life ($8.95, TPB) r/#10-13						9.00
STRANGERS IN PARADISE (Volume Three)						
Homage Comics #1-8/Abstract Studios #9-on: Oct, 1996 - Present ($2.75/$2.95, color #1-5, B&W #6-on)						
1-Terry Moore-c/s/a in all; dream seq. by Jim Lee-a						4.00
1-Jim Lee variant-c	1	2	3	6	7	8
2-5						3.50
6-16: 6-Return to B&W. 13-15-High school flashback. 16-Xena Warrior Princess parody; two covers						3.00
17-62: 33-Color issue. 46-Molly Lane. 49-Molly & Poo						3.00
...Lyrics and Poems (2/99)						2.75
...Source Book (2003, $2.95) Background on characters & story arcs, checklists						3.00
Brave New World ('02, $8.95, TPB) r/#44,45,47,48						9.00
Child of Rage ($15.95, TPB) r/#31-38						16.00
Flower to Flame ('03, $15.95, TPB) r/#55-60						16.00
Heart in Hand ('03, $12.95, TPB) r/#50-54						13.00
High School ('98, $8.95, TPB) r/#13-16						9.00
Immortal Enemies ('98, $14.95, TPB) r/#6-12						15.00
Love Me Tender ($12.95, TPB) r/#1-5 in B&W w/ color Lee seq.						13.00
My Other Life ($14.95, TPB) r/#25-30						15.00
Sanctuary ($15.95, TPB) r/#17-24						16.00
Tropic of Desire ($12.95, TPB) r/#39-43						13.00
The Complete... : Volume 3 Part 3 HC ('01, $49.95) r/#26-38						50.00
STRANGE SPORTS STORIES (See Brave & the Bold #45-49, DC Special, and DC Super Stars #10)						
National Periodical Publications: Sept-Oct, 1973 - No. 6, July-Aug, 1974						
1	3	6	9	18	24	30
2-6: 2-Swan/Anderson-a	2	4	6	10	13	16
STRANGE STORIES FROM ANOTHER WORLD (Unknown World #1)						
Fawcett Publications: No. 2, Aug, 1952 - No. 5, Feb, 1953						
2-Saunders painted-c	50	100	150	300	450	600
3-5-Saunders painted-c	40	80	120	240	340	440
STRANGE STORIES OF SUSPENSE (Rugged Action #1-4)						
Atlas Comics (CSI): No. 5, Oct, 1955 - No. 16, Aug, 1957						
5(#1)	40	80	120	240	340	440
6,9	25	50	75	144	198	255
7-E. C. swipe cover/Vault of Horror #32	26	52	78	147	206	265
8-Morrow/Williamson-a; Pakula-a	27	54	81	153	214	275
10-Crandall, Torres, Meskin-a	26	52	78	147	206	265
11-13: 12-Torres, Pakula-a. 13-E.C. art swipes	21	42	63	118	164	210
14-16: 14-Williamson/Mayo-a. 15-Krigstein-a. 16-Fox, Powell-a	23	46	69	129	180	230

NOTE: ***Everett*** *a-6, 7, 13; c-8, 9, 11-14.* ***Heath*** *a-5.* ***Maneely*** *c-5.* ***Morisi*** *a-11.* ***Morrow*** *a-13.* ***Powell*** *a-8.* ***Severin*** *c-7.* ***Wildey*** *a-14.*

	GD 2.0	VG 4.0	FN 6.0	VF 8.0	VF/NM 9.0	NM- 9.2
STRANGE STORY (Also see Front Page)						
Harvey Publications: June-July, 1946 (52 pgs.)						
1-The Man in Black Called Fate by Powell	33	66	99	190	270	350
STRANGE SUSPENSE STORIES (Lawbreakers Suspense Stories #10-15; This Is Suspense #23-26; Captain Atom V1#78 on)						
Fawcett Publications/Charlton Comics No. 16 on: 6/52 - No. 5, 2/53; No. 16, 1/54 - No. 22, 11/54; No. 27, 10/55 - No. 77, 10/65; V3#1, 10/67 - V1#9, 9/69						
1-(Fawcett)-Powell, Sekowsky-a	74	148	222	463	694	925
2-George Evans horror story	47	94	141	282	421	560
3-5 (2/53)-George Evans horror stories	41	82	123	246	348	450
16(1-2/54)-Formerly Lawbreakers S.S.	30	60	90	170	240	310
17,21: 21-Shuster-a	24	48	72	135	190	245
18-E.C. swipe/HOF 7; Ditko-c/a(2)	40	80	120	240	340	440
19-Ditko electric chair-c; Ditko-a	50	100	150	300	450	600
20-Ditko-c/a(2)	40	80	120	240	340	440
22(11/54)-Ditko-c, Shuster-a; last pre-code issue; becomes This Is Suspense	35	70	105	201	288	370
27(10/55)-(Formerly This Is Suspense #26)	15	30	45	86	118	150
28-30,38	10	20	30	60	80	100
31-33,35,37,40-Ditko-c/a(2-3 each)	22	44	66	124	172	220
34-Story of ruthless business man, Wm. B. Gaines; Ditko-c/a	46	92	138	276	413	550
36-(15¢, 68 pgs.); Ditko-a(4)	26	52	78	147	206	265
39,41,52,53-Ditko-a	18	36	54	101	138	175
42-44,46,49,54-60	6	12	18	38	52	65
45,47,48,50,51-Ditko-c/a	14	28	42	102	149	195
61-74	4	8	12	27	36	45
75(6/65)-Reprints origin/1st app. Captain Atom by Ditko from Space Advs. #33; r/Severin-a/Space Advs. #24 (75-77: 12¢ issues)	13	26	39	90	133	175
76,77-Captain Atom-r by Ditko/Space Advs.	7	14	21	46	63	80
V3#1(10/67): 12¢ issues begin	3	7	10	21	28	35
V1#2-Ditko-c/a; atom bomb-c	3	7	10	21	28	35
V1#3-9: All 12¢ issues	2	4	6	11	14	18

NOTE: ***Alascia*** *a-19.* ***Aparo*** *a-60, V3#1, 2, 4; c-V1#4, 8.* ***Baily*** *a-1-3; c-2, 5.* ***Evans*** *c-3, 4.* ***Giordano*** *c-16, 17p, 24p, 25p.* ***Montes/Bache*** *c-66.* ***Powell*** *a-4.* ***Shuster*** *a-19, 21.* ***Marcus Swayze*** *a-27.*

	GD 2.0	VG 4.0	FN 6.0	VF 8.0	VF/NM 9.0	NM- 9.2
STRANGE TALES (...Featuring Warlock #178-181; Doctor Strange #169 on)						
Atlas (CCPC #1-67/ZPC #68-79/VPI #80-85)/Marvel #86(7/61) on: June, 1951 - #168, May, 1968; #169, Sept, 1973 - #188, Nov, 1976						
1-Horror/weird stories begin	312	624	936	1950	2925	3900
2	100	200	300	625	938	1250
3,5: 3-Atom bomb panels	76	152	228	475	713	950
4-Cosmic eyeball story "The Evil Eye"	80	160	240	500	750	1000
6-9: 6-Heath-c/a. 7-Colan-a	55	110	165	343	512	680
10-Krigstein-a	59	118	177	369	555	740
11-14,16-20	40	80	120	240	345	450
15-Krigstein-a	40	80	120	240	355	470
21,23-27,29-34: 27-Atom bomb panels. 33-Davis-a. 34-Last pre-code issue (2/55)	35	70	105	201	288	370
22-Krigstein, Forte/Fox-a	36	72	108	207	294	380
28-Jack Katz story used in Senate Investigation report, pgs. 7 & 169	36	72	108	207	294	380
35-41,43,44: 37-Vampire story by Colan	20	40	60	142	209	275
42,45,59,61-Krigstein-a; #61 (2/58)	21	42	63	149	220	290
46-57,60: 51-1st S.A. issue. 53,56-Crandall-a. 60-(8/57)	18	36	54	131	191	250
58,64-Williamson-a in each, with Mayo-#58	19	38	57	133	194	255
62,63,65,66: 62-Torres-a. 66-Crandall-a	17	34	51	123	182	240
67-Prototype ish. (Quicksilver)	19	38	57	138	202	265
68,71,72,74,77,80: Ditko/Kirby-a in #67-80	18	36	54	131	191	250
69,70,73,75,76,78,79: 69-Prototype ish. (Prof. X). 70-Prototype ish. (Giant Man). 73-Prototype ish. (Ant-Man). 75-Prototype ish. (Iron Man). 76-Prototype ish. (Human Torch). 78-Prototype ish. (Ant-Man). 79-Prototype ish. (Dr. Strange) (12/60)	23	46	69	164	240	315
81-83,85-88,90,91-Ditko/Kirby-a in all: 86-Robot-c. 90-(11/61)-Atom bomb blast panel	17	34	51	118	174	230
84-Prototype ish. (Magneto)(5/61); has powers like Magneto of X-Men, but two years earlier; Ditko/Kirby-a	21	42	63	149	220	290
89-1st app. Fin Fang Foom (10/61) by Kirby	42	84	126	336	506	675
92-Prototype ish. (Ancient One); last 10¢ issue	18	36	54	131	191	250
93,95,96,98-100: Kirby-a	15	30	45	107	156	205
94-Prototype ish. (The Thing); Kirby-a	18	36	54	131	191	250
97-1st app. Aunt May & Uncle Ben by Ditko (6/62), before Amazing Fantasy #15; (see Tales Of Suspense #7); Kirby-a	37	74	111	278	414	550
101-Human Torch begins by Kirby (10/62); origin recap Fantastic Four & Human Torch; Human Torch-c begin	86	172	258	731	1116	1500
102-1st app. Wizard; robot-c	35	70	105	263	394	525
103-105: 104-1st app. Trapster. 105-2nd Wizard	30	60	90	218	319	420
106,108,109: 106-Fantastic Four guests (3/63)	20	40	60	145	213	280
107-(4/63)-Human Torch/Sub-Mariner battle; 4th S.A. Sub-Mariner app. & 1st x-over outside of Fantastic Four	26	52	78	189	275	360
110-(7/63)-Intro Doctor Strange, Ancient One & Wong by Ditko	107	214	321	910	1393	1875
111-2nd Dr. Strange	33	66	99	248	374	500
112,113	14	28	42	102	149	195
114-Acrobat disguised as Captain America, 1st app. since the G.A.; intro. & 1st app. Victoria Bentley; 3rd Dr. Strange app. & begin series (11/63)	35	70	105	263	394	525
115-Origin Dr. Strange; Human Torch vs. Sandman (Spidey villain; 2nd app. & brief origin); early Spider-Man x-over, 12/63	42	84	126	315	475	635

Strange Tales #153 © MAR

Strange Terrors #3 © STJ

Strange Worlds #1 © MAR

	GD 2.0	VG 4.0	FN 6.0	VF 8.0	VF/NM 9.0	NM- 9.2
116-(1/64)-Human Torch battles The Thing; 1st Thing x-over	12	24	36	84	125	165
117,118,120: 120-1st Iceman x-over (from X-Men)	10	20	30	67	96	125
119-Spider-Man x-over (2 panel cameo)	10	20	30	73	107	140
121,122,124,126-134: Thing/Torch team-up in 121-134. 126-Intro Clea. 128-Quicksilver & Scarlet Witch app. (1/65). 130-The Beatles cameo. 134-Last Human Torch; The Watcher-c/story; Wood-a(i)	7	14	21	50	68	85
123-1st app. The Beetle (see Amazing Spider-Man #21 for next app.); 1st Thor x-over (8/64); Loki app.	8	16	24	55	78	100
125-Torch & Thing battle Sub-Mariner (10/64)	8	16	24	55	78	100
135-Col. (formerly Sgt.) Nick Fury becomes Nick Fury Agent of Shield (origin/1st app.) by Kirby (8/65); series begins	13	26	39	94	137	180
136-140: 138-Intro Eternity	6	12	18	40	55	70
141-147,149: 145-Begins alternating-c features w/Nick Fury (odd #'s) & Dr. Strange (even #'s). 146-Last Ditko Dr. Strange who is in consecutive stories since #113; only full Ditko Dr. Strange-c this title. 147-Dr. Strange (by Everett #147-152) continues thru #168, then Dr. Strange #169	5	10	15	33	44	55
148-Origin Ancient One	7	14	21	51	71	90
150(11/66)-John Buscema's 1st work at Marvel	6	12	18	38	52	65
151-Kirby/Steranko-c/a; 1st Marvel work by Steranko	8	16	24	53	74	95
152,153-Kirby/Steranko-a	6	12	18	38	52	65
154-158-Steranko-a/script	6	12	18	38	52	65
159-Origin Nick Fury retold; Intro Val; Captain America-c/story; Steranko-a	7	14	21	46	63	80
160-162-Steranko-a/scripts; Capt. America app.	6	12	18	38	52	65
163-166,168-Steranko-a(p). 168-Last Nick Fury (gets own book next month) & last Dr. Strange who also gets own book	5	10	15	36	48	60
167-Steranko pen/script; classic flag-c	7	14	21	46	63	80
169-1st app. Brother Voodoo(origin in #169,170) & begin series, ends #173.	2	4	6	11	14	18
170-174: 174-Origin Golem	2	4	6	8	10	12
175-177: 177-Brunner-c	1	2	3	5	6	8
178-(2/75)-Warlock by Starlin begins; origin Warlock & Him retold; 1st app. Magus; Starlin-c/a/scripts in #178-181 (all before Warlock #9)	2	4	6	14	18	22
179-181-All Warlock. 179-Intro/1st app. Pip the Troll. 180-Intro Gamora. 181-(8/75)-Warlock story continued in Warlock #9	2	4	6	9	11	14
182-188: 185,186-(Regular 25¢ editions)						5.00
185,186-(30¢-c variants, limited distribution)(5,7/76)	2	4	6	11	14	18
Annual 1(1962)-Reprints from Strange Tales #73,76,78, Tales of Suspense #7,9, Tales to Astonish #1,6,7, & Journey Into Mystery #53,55,59; (1st Marvel annual?)	48	96	144	384	572	760
Annual 2(7/63)-Reprints from Strange Tales #67, Strange Worlds (Atlas) #1-3, World of Fantasy #16; new Human Torch vs. Spider-Man story by Kirby/Ditko (1st Spidey x-over; 4th app.); Kirby-c	63	126	189	536	818	1100

NOTE: ***Briefer** a-17. **Burgos** a-123p. **J. Buscema** a-174p. **Colan** a-7, 11, 20, 37, 53, 169-173p, 188p. **Davis** c-71. **Ditko** a-46, 50, 67-122, 123-125p, 126-146, 175r, 182-188r; c-51, 93, 115, 121, 146. **Everett** a-4, 21, 40-42, 73, 147-152, 164i; c-8, 10, 11, 13, 15, 24, 45, 49-54, 56, 58, 60, 61, 63, 148, 150, 152, 158i. **Forte** a-27, 43, 50, 53, 54, 60. **Heath** a-2, 6; c-6, 18-20. **Kamen** a-45. **G. Kane** c-170-173, 182p. **Kirby** Human Torch-101-105, 108, 109, 114, 120; Nick Fury-135p, 141-143p; (Layouts)-135-153; other **Kirby** a-67-100p; c-68-70, 72-74, 76-92, 94, 95, 101-114, 116-123, 125-130, 132-135, 136p, 138-145, 147, 149, 151p. **Kirby/Ayers** c-101-106, 108-110. **Kirby/Ditko** a-80, 88, 121; c-75, 93, 97, 100, 139. **Lawrence** a-29. **Leiber/ Fox** a-110-113. **Maneely** a-3, 7, 37, 42; c-33, 40. **Moldoff** a-20. **Mooney** a-174i. **Morisi** a-53, 56. **Morrow** a-54. **Orlando** a-41, 44, 46, 49, 52. **Powell** a-42, 44, 49, 54, 130-134p; c-131p. **Reinman** a-11, 50, 74, 88, 91, 95, 104, 106, 112i, 124-127i. **Robinson** a-17. **Romita** c-169. **Roussos** c-201i. **R.Q. Sale** a-56; c-16. **Sekowski** a-3, 11. **Severin** a(i)-136-138; c-137. **Starlin** a-178, 179, 180p, 181p; c-178-180, 181p. **Steranko** a-151-161, 162-168p; c-151i, 153, 155, 157, 159, 161, 163, 165, 167. **Torres** a-53, 62. **Tuska** a-14, 166p. **Whitney** a-149. **Wildey** a-42, 56. **Woodbridge** a-59. Fantastic Four cameos #101-134. Jack Katz app.-26.*

STRANGE TALES
Marvel Comics Group: Apr, 1987 - No. 19, Oct, 1988

	GD	VG	FN	VF	VF/NM	NM-
V2#1-19						2.25

STRANGE TALES
Marvel Comics: Nov, 1994 ($6.95, one-shot)

	GD	VG	FN	VF	VF/NM	NM-
V3#1-acetate-c						7.00

STRANGE TALES (Anthology; continues stories from Man-Thing #8 and Werewolf By Night #6)
Marvel Comics: Sept, 1998 - No. 2, Oct, 1998 ($4.99)

	GD	VG	FN	VF	VF/NM	NM-
1,2: 1-Silver Surfer app. 2-Two covers						5.00

STRANGE TALES: DARK CORNERS
Marvel Comics: May, 1998 ($3.99, one-shot)

	GD	VG	FN	VF	VF/NM	NM-
1-Anthology; stories by Baron & Maleev, McGregor & Dringenberg, DeMatteis & Badger; Estes painted-c						4.00

STRANGE TALES OF THE UNUSUAL
Atlas Comics (ACI No. 1-4/WPI No. 5-11): Dec, 1955 - No. 11, Aug, 1957

	GD 2.0	VG 4.0	FN 6.0	VF 8.0	VF/NM 9.0	NM- 9.2
1-Powell-a	44	88	132	264	395	525
2	29	58	87	164	232	300
3-Williamson-a (4 pgs.)	30	60	90	170	240	310
4,6,8,11	21	42	63	118	164	210
5-Crandall, Ditko-a	26	52	78	147	206	265
7,9: 7-Kirby, Orlando-a. 9-Krigstein-a	23	46	69	129	180	230
10-Torres, Morrow-a	21	42	63	118	164	210

NOTE: ***Baily** a-6. **Brodsky** c-2-4. **Everett** a-2, 6; c-6, 9, 11. **Heck** a-1. **Maneely** c-1. **Orlando** a-7. **Pakula** a-10. **Romita** a-1. **R.Q. Sale** a-3. **Wildey** a-3.*

STRANGE TERRORS
St. John Publishing Co.: June, 1952 - No. 7, Mar, 1953

	GD	VG	FN	VF	VF/NM	NM-
1-Bondage-c; Zombies spelled Zoombies on-c; Fine-*esque* -a	54	108	162	324	487	650
2	32	64	96	184	262	340
3-Kubert-a; painted-c	40	80	120	240	345	450
4-Kubert-a (reprinted in Mystery Tales #18); Ekgren painted-c; Fine-*esque* -a; Jerry Iger caricature	51	102	153	306	458	610
5-Kubert-a; painted-c	40	80	120	240	345	450
6-Giant (25¢, 100 pgs.)(1/53); bondage-c	51	102	153	306	458	610
7-Giant (25¢, 100 pgs.); Kubert-c/a	55	110	165	330	495	660

NOTE: ***Cameron** a-6, 7. **Morisi** a-6.*

STRANGE WORLD OF YOUR DREAMS
Prize Publications: Aug, 1952 - No. 4, Jan-Feb, 1953

	GD	VG	FN	VF	VF/NM	NM-
1-Simon & Kirby-a	61	122	183	381	573	765
2,3-Simon & Kirby-c/a. 2-Meskin-a	50	100	150	300	450	600
4-S&K-c; Meskin-a	40	80	120	240	350	460

STRANGE WORLDS (#18 continued from Avon's Eerie #1-17)
Avon Periodicals: 11/50 - No. 9, 11/52; No. 18, 10-11/54 - No. 22, 9-10/55
(No #11-17)

	GD	VG	FN	VF	VF/NM	NM-
1-Kenton of the Star Patrol by Kubert (r/Eerie #1 from 1947); Crom the Barbarian by John Giunta	114	228	342	713	1069	1425
2-Wood-a; Crom the Barbarian by Giunta; Dara of the Vikings app.; used in **SOTI**, pg. 112; injury to eye panel	104	208	312	650	975	1300
3-Wood/Orlando-a (Kenton), Wood/Williamson/Frazetta/Krenkel/Orlando-a (7 pgs.); Malu Slave Girl Princess app.; Kinstler-c	200	400	600	1250	1875	2500
4-Wood-c/a (Kenton); Orlando-a; origin The Enchanted Daggar; Sultan-a; classic cover	114	228	342	713	1069	1425
5-Orlando/Wood-a (Kenton); Wood-c	60	120	180	375	563	750
6-Kinstler-a(2); Orlando/Wood-c; Check-a	44	88	132	264	395	525
7-Fawcette & Becker/Alascia-a	40	80	120	240	340	440
8-Kubert, Kinstler, Hollingsworth & Lazarus-a; Lazarus Robot-c	40	80	120	240	340	440
9-Kinstler, Fawcette, Alascia-a	39	78	117	230	325	420
18-(Formerly Eerie #17)-Reprints "Attack on Planet Mars" by Kubert	33	66	99	190	270	350
19-r/Avon's "Robotmen of the Lost Planet"; last pre-code issue; Robot-c	33	66	99	190	270	350
20-War-c/story; Wood-c(r)/U.S. Paratroops #1	10	20	30	56	73	90
21,22-War-c/stories. 22-New logo	8	16	24	46	58	70
I.W. Reprint #5-Kinstler-a(r)/Avon's #9	4	8	12	27	36	45

STRANGE WORLDS
Marvel Comics (MPI No. 1,2/Male No. 3,5): Dec, 1958 - No. 5, Aug, 1959

	GD	VG	FN	VF	VF/NM	NM-
1-Kirby & Ditko-a; flying saucer issue	85	170	255	531	796	1060
2-Ditko-c/a	50	100	150	300	450	600
3-Kirby-a(2)	40	80	120	240	345	450
4-Williamson-a	39	78	117	230	325	420
5-Ditko-a	34	68	102	193	274	355

NOTE: ***Buscema** a-3, 4. **Ditko** a-1-5; c-2.. **Heck** a-2. **Kirby** a-1, 3. **Kirby/Brodsky** c-1, 3-5.*

STRAWBERRY SHORTCAKE
Marvel Comics (Star Comics): Jun, 1985 - No. 6, Feb, 1986 (Children's comic)

	GD	VG	FN	VF	VF/NM	NM-
1-6: Howie Post-a						6.00

STRAY
DC Comics (Homage Comics): 2001 ($5.95, prestige format, one-shot)

	GD	VG	FN	VF	VF/NM	NM-
1-Pollina-c/a; Lobdell & Palmiotti-s						6.00

STRAY BULLETS (Also see Promotional Comics section for Free Comic Book Day edition)
El Capitan Books: 1995 - Present ($2.95/$3.50, B&W, mature readers)

	GD	VG	FN	VF	VF/NM	NM-
1-David Lapham-c/a/scripts	2	4	6	8	10	12
2,3						6.00
4-8						3.50
9-21,31,32-($2.95)						3.00

Street Fighter #1 © Capcom

Street Sharks #1 © Streetwise

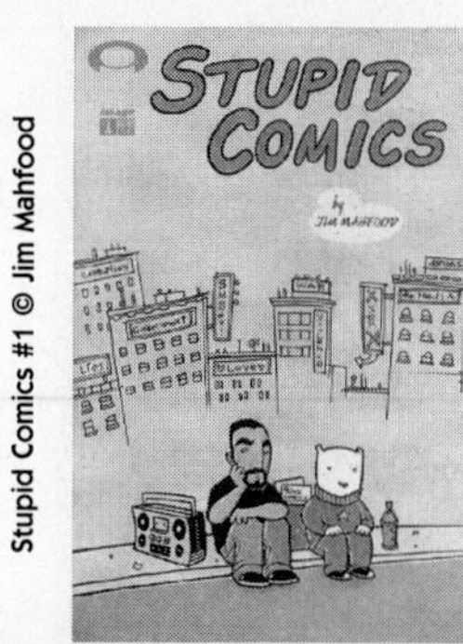

Stupid Comics #1 © Jim Mahfood

	GD 2.0	VG 4.0	FN 6.0	VF 8.0	VF/NM 9.0	NM- 9.2

22-30-($3.50) 22-Includes preview to Murder Me Dead 3.50
Innocence of Nihilism Volume 1 HC ($29.95, hardcover) r/#1-7 30.00
Somewhere Out West Volume 2 HC ($34.95, hardcover) r/#8-14 35.00
Other People Volume 3 HC ($34.95, hardcover) r/#15-22 35.00
Volume 1-3 TPB ($11.95, softcover) 1-r/#1-4. 2-r/#5-8. 3-r/ #9-12 12.00
Volume 4-7 TPB ($14.95) 4- r/#13-16. 5- r/#17-20. 6- r/#21-24. 7-r/#25-28 15.00
NOTE: *Multiple printings of most issues exist & are worth cover price.*

STRAY TOASTERS
Marvel Comics (Epic Comics): Jan, 1988 - No. 4, April, 1989 ($3.50, squarebound, limited series)
1-4: Sienkiewicz-c/a/scripts 3.50

STREET COMIX
Street Enterprises/King Features: 1973 (50¢, B&W, 36 pgs.)(20,000 print run)

	GD	VG	FN	VF	VF/NM	NM-
1-Rip Kirby	2	4	6	9	11	14
2-Flash Gordon	2	4	6	11	14	18

STREETFIGHTER
Ocean Comics: Aug, 1986 - No. 4, Spr, 1987 ($1.75, limited series)
1-4: 2-Origin begins 3.00

STREET FIGHTER
Malibu Comics: Sept, 1993 - No. 3, Nov, 1993 ($2.95)
1-3: 3-Includes poster; Ferret x-over 3.00

STREET FIGHTER
Image Comics: Sept, 2003 - Present ($2.95)
1-Back-up story w/Madureira-a; covers by Madureira and Tsang 3.00
2-4: 2-Two covers by Campbell and Warren; back-up story w/Warren-a 3.00

STREET FIGHTER: THE BATTLE FOR SHADALOO
DC Comics/CAP Co. Ltd.: 1995 ($3.95, one-shot)
1-Polybagged w/trading card & Tattoo 4.00

STREET FIGHTER II
Tokuma Comics (Viz): Apr, 1994 - No. 8, Nov, 1994 ($2.95, limited series)
1-8 3.00

STREET POET RAY
Blackthorne Publ./Marvel Comics: Spring, 1989; 1990 - No. 4, 1990 ($2.95, B&W, squarebound)
1 (Blackthorne, $2.00) 3.00
1-4 (Marvel, $2.95, thick-c & paper) 3.00

STREETS
DC Comics: 1993 - No. 3, 1993 ($4.95, limited series, 52 pgs.)
Book 1-3-Estes painted-c 5.00

STREET SHARKS
Archie Publications: Jan, 1996 - No. 3, Mar, 1996 ($1.50, limited series)
1-3 2.25

STREET SHARKS
Archie Publications: May, 1996 - No. 6 ($1.50, published 8 times a year)
1-6 2.25

STRICTLY PRIVATE (You're in the Army Now)
Eastern Color Printing Co.: July, 1942 (#1 on sale 6/15/42)

	GD	VG	FN	VF	VF/NM	NM-
1,2: Private Peter Plink. 2-Says 128 pgs. on-c	24	48	72	135	190	245

STRIKE!
Eclipse Comics: Aug, 1987 - No. 6, Jan, 1988 ($1.75)
1-6, ...Vs. Sgt. Strike Special 1 (5/88, $1.95) 2.25

STRIKEBACK! (The Hunt For Nikita)
Malibu Comics (Bravura): Oct, 1994 - No. 3, Jan, 1995 ($2.95, unfinished limited series)
1-3: Jonathon Peterson script, Kevin Maguire-c/a 3.00
1-Gold foil embossed-c 5.00

STRIKEBACK!
Image Comics (WildStorm Productions): Jan, 1996 - No. 5, May, 1996 ($2.50, limited series)
1-5: Reprints original Bravura series w/additional story & art by Kevin Maguire & Jonathon Peterson; new Maguire-c in all. 4,5-New story & art 2.50

STRIKEFORCE: AMERICA
Comico: Dec, 1995 ($2.95)
V2#1-Polybagged w/gaming card; S. Clark-a(p) 3.00

STRIKEFORCE: MORITURI
Marvel Comics Group: Dec, 1986 - No. 31, July, 1989
1-31: 14-Williamson-i. 13-Double size. 25-Heath-c 2.25

STRIKEFORCE MORITURI: ELECTRIC UNDERTOW
Marvel Comics: Dec, 1989 - No. 5, Mar, 1990 ($3.95, 52 pgs., limited series)
1-5 Squarebound 4.00

STRONG GUY REBORN (See X-Factor)
Marvel Comics: Sept, 1997 ($2.99, one-shot)
1-Dezago-s/Andy Smith, Art Thibert-a 3.00

STRONG MAN (Also see Complimentary Comics & Power of...)
Magazine Enterprises: Mar-Apr, 1955 - No. 4, Sept-Oct, 1955

	GD	VG	FN	VF	VF/NM	NM-
1(A-1 #130)-Powell-c/a	24	48	72	135	190	245
2-4: (A-1 #132,134,139)-Powell-a. 2-Powell-c	19	38	57	106	146	185

STRONTIUM DOG
Eagle Comics: Dec, 1985 - No. 4, Mar, 1986 ($1.25, limited series)
1-4, Special 1: 4-Moore script. Special 1 (1986)-Moore script 2.25

STRYFE'S STRIKE FILE
Marvel Comics: Jan, 1993 ($1.75, one-shot, no ads)
1-Stroman, Capullo, Andy Kubert, Brandon Peterson-a; silver metallic ink-c; X-Men tie-in to X-Cutioner's Song 3.00
1-Gold metallic ink 2nd printing 2.25

STUCK RUBBER BABY
DC Comics (Paradox Press): 1998 (Graphic novel)
Hardcover ($24.95) 25.00
Softcover ($13.95) 14.00

STUMBO THE GIANT (See Harvey Hits #49,54,57,60,63,66,69,72,78,88 & Hot Stuff #2)

STUMBO TINYTOWN
Harvey Publications: Oct, 1963 - No. 13, Nov, 1966 (All 25¢ giants)

	GD	VG	FN	VF	VF/NM	NM-
1-Stumbo, Hot Stuff & others begin	15	30	45	104	152	200
2	10	20	30	67	96	125
3-5	7	14	21	51	71	90
6-13	6	12	18	43	59	75

STUNT DAWGS
Harvey Comics: Mar, 1993 ($1.25, one-shot)
1 2.25

STUNTMAN COMICS (Also see Thrills Of Tomorrow)
Harvey Publ.: Apr-May, 1946 - No. 2, June-July, 1946; No. 3, Oct-Nov, 1946

	GD	VG	FN	VF	VF/NM	NM-
1-Origin Stuntman by S&K reprinted in Black Cat #9; S&K-c	112	224	336	700	1050	1400
2-S&K-c/a; The Duke of Broadway story	69	138	207	431	646	860
3-Small size (5-1/2x8-1/2"; B&W; 32 pgs.); distributed to mail subscribers only; S&K-a; Kid Adonis by S&K reprinted in Green Hornet #37	70	140	210	438	657	875

(Also see All-New #15, Boy Explorers #2, Flash Gordon #5 & Thrills of Tomorrow)

STUPID COMICS (Also see 40 oz. Collected)
Oni Press/Image Comics: July, 2000; Sept, 2002; Oct, 2003 ($2.95, B&W)
1-(Oni Press, 7/00) Jim Mahfood 1 page satire strips reprinted from JAVA magazine 3.00
1,2-(Image Comics, 9/02; 10/03) Jim Mahfood 1 page and 2 page satire strips 3.00

STUPID HEROES
Mirage Studios: Sept, 1993 - No. 3, Dec, 1994 ($2.75, unfinished limited series)
1-3-Laird-c/a & scripts; 2 trading cards bound in 2.75

STUPID, STUPID RAT TAILS (See Bone)
Cartoon Books: Dec, 1999 - No. 3, Feb, 2000 ($2.95, limited series)
1-3-Jeff Smith-a/Tom Sniegoski-s 3.00

STYGMATA
Entity Comics: No. 0, July, 1994 - No. 3, Oct, 1994 ($2.95, B&W, limited series)
0, 1-3: 0,1-Foil-c. 3-Silver foil logo 3.00
Yearbook 1 (1995, $2.95) 3.00

SUBHUMAN
Dark Horse Comics: Nov, 1998 - No. 4, Feb, 1999 ($2.95, limited series)
1-4-Mark Schultz-c 3.00

SUBMARINE ATTACK (Formerly Speed Demons)
Charlton Comics: No. 11, May, 1958 - No. 54, Feb-Mar, 1966

	GD	VG	FN	VF	VF/NM	NM-
11	4	8	12	27	36	45
12-20	3	6	9	19	25	32

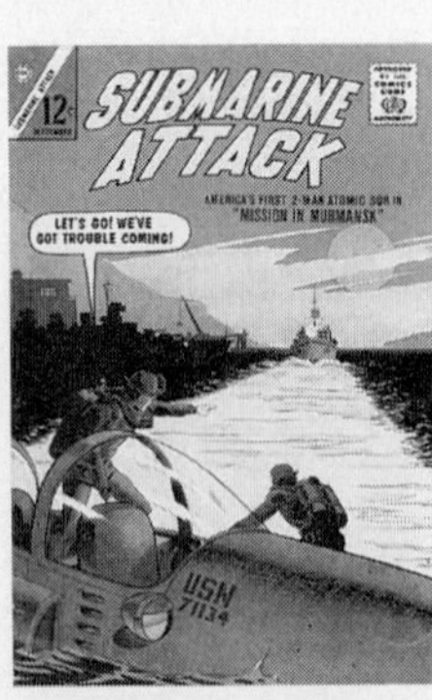

Submarine Attack #41 © CC

Sub-Mariner Comics #7 © MAR

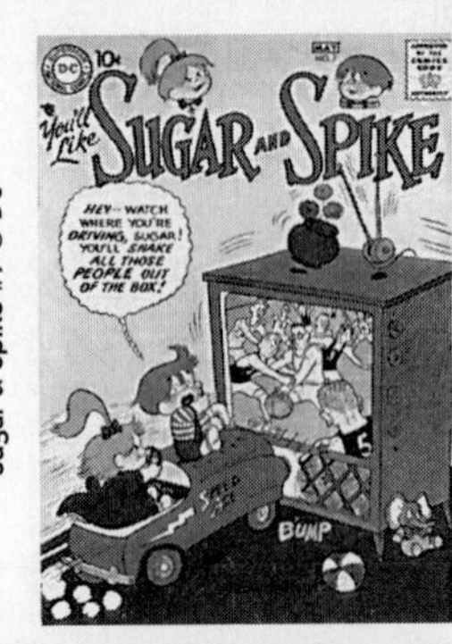

Sugar & Spike #7 © DC

	GD 2.0	VG 4.0	FN 6.0	VF 8.0	VF/NM 9.0	NM- 9.2
21-30	3	6	9	18	23	28
31-54	2	4	6	14	18	22

NOTE: ***Glanzman*** *c/a-25.* ***Montes/Bache*** *a-38, 40, 41.*

SUB-MARINER (See All-Select, All-Winners, Blonde Phantom, Daring, The Defenders, Fantastic Four #4, Human Torch, The Invaders, Iron Man &..., Marvel Mystery, Marvel Spotlight #27, Men's Adventures, Motion Picture Funnies Weekly, Namora, Namor, The..., Prince Namor, The Sub-Mariner, Saga Of The..., Tales to Astonish #70 & 2nd series, USA & Young Men)

SUB-MARINER, THE (2nd Series)(Sub-Mariner #31 on)
Marvel Comics Group: May, 1968 - No. 72, Sept, 1974 (No. 43: 52 pgs.)

	GD 2.0	VG 4.0	FN 6.0	VF 8.0	VF/NM 9.0	NM- 9.2
1-Origin Sub-Mariner; story continued from Iron Man & Sub-Mariner #1	18	36	54	131	191	250
2-Triton app.	8	16	24	55	78	100
3-5: 5-1st Tiger Shark (9/68)	6	12	18	43	59	75
6,7,9,10: 6-Tiger Shark-c & 2nd app., cont'd from #5. 7-Photo-c. (1968). 9-1st app. Serpent Crown (origin in #10 & 12)	5	10	15	33	44	55
8-Sub-Mariner vs. Thing	6	12	18	43	59	75
8-2nd printing (1994)	2	4	6	8	10	12
11-13,15: 15-Last 12¢ issue	4	8	12	22	30	38
14-Sub-Mariner vs. G.A. Human Torch; death of Toro (1st modern app. & only app. Toro, 6/69)	5	10	15	33	44	55
16-20: 19-1st Sting Ray (11/69); Stan Lee, Romita, Heck, Thomas, Everett & Kirby cameos. 20-Dr. Doom app.	3	6	9	16	20	25
21,23-33,37-39,41,42: 25-Origin Atlantis. 30-Capt. Marvel x-over. 37-Death of Lady Dorma. 38-Origin retold. 42-Last 15¢ issue.	2	4	6	12	16	20
22,40: 22-Dr. Strange x-over. 40-Spider-Man x-over	2	4	6	14	18	22
34-Prelude (w/#35) to 1st Defenders story; Hulk & Silver Surfer x-over	7	14	21	46	63	80
35-Namor/Hulk/Silver Surfer team-up to battle The Avengers-c/story (3/71); hints at teaming up again	5	10	15	36	48	60
36-Wrightson-a(i)	3	6	9	16	20	25
43-King Size Special (52 pgs.)	3	6	9	16	20	25
44,45-Sub-Mariner vs. Human Torch	2	4	6	14	18	22
46-49,56,62,64-72: 47,48-Dr. Doom app. 49-Cosmic Cube story. 62-1st Tales of Atlantis, ends #66. 64-Hitler cameo. 67-New costume; F.F. x-over. 69-Spider-Man x-over (6 panels)	1	3	4	6	8	10
50-1st app. Nita, Namor's niece (later Namorita in New Warriors)	2	4	6	10	12	15
51-55,57,58,60,61,63-Everett issues: 61-Last artwork by Everett; 1st 4 pgs. completed by Mortimer; pgs. 5-20 by Mooney	2	4	6	9	11	14
59-1st battle with Thor; Everett-a	2	4	6	14	18	22
Special 1 (1/71)-r/Tales to Astonish #70-73	3	6	9	18	23	28
Special 2 (1/72)-(52 pgs.)-r/T.T.A. #74-76; Everett-a	2	4	6	12	16	20

NOTE: ***Bolle*** *a-67i.* ***Buscema*** *a(p)-1-8, 20, 24.* ***Colan*** *a(p)-10, 11, 40, 43, 46-49, Special 1, 2; c(p)-10, 11, 40.* ***Craig*** *a-17i, 19-23i.* ***Everett*** *a-45r, 50-55, 57, 58, 59-61(plot), 63(plot); c-47, 48i, 55, 57-59i, 61, Spec. 2.* ***G. Kane*** *c(p)-42-52, 58, 66, 70, 71.* ***Mooney*** *a-24i, 25i, 32-35i, 39i, 42i, 44i, 45i, 60i, 61i, 65p, 66p, 68i.* ***Severin*** *c/a-38i.* ***Starlin*** *c-59p.* ***Tuska*** *a-41p, 42p, 69-71p.* ***Wrightson*** *a-36i. #53, 54-r/stories Sub-Mariner Comics #41 & 39.*

SUB-MARINER COMICS (1st Series) (The Sub-Mariner #1, 2, 33-42)(Official True Crime Cases #24 on; Amazing Mysteries #32 on; Best Love #33 on)
Timely/Marvel Comics (TCI 1-7/SePI 8/MPI 9-32/Atlas Comics (CCC 33-42)):
Spring, 1941 - No. 23, Sum, 1947; No. 24, Wint, 1947 - No. 31, 4/49; No. 32, 7/49; No. 33, 4/54 - No. 42, 10/55

	GD 2.0	VG 4.0	FN 6.0	VF 8.0	VF/NM 9.0	NM- 9.2
1-The Sub-Mariner by Everett & The Angel begin	2575	5150	7725	20,600	32,800	45,000
2-Everett-a	510	1020	1530	3570	5485	7400
3-Churchill assassination-c; 40 pg. S-M story	415	830	1245	2698	4149	5600
4-Everett-a, 40 pgs.; 1 pg. Wolverton-a	326	652	978	2119	3260	4400
5-Gabrielle/Klein-c	264	528	792	1650	2475	3300
6-10: 9-Wolverton-a, 3 pgs.; flag-c	228	456	684	1425	2138	2850
11-Classic Schomburg-c	224	448	672	1400	2100	2800
12-15	164	328	492	1025	1538	2050
16-20	132	264	396	825	1238	1650
21-Last Angel; Everett-a	100	200	300	625	938	1250
22-Young Allies app.	100	200	300	625	938	1250
23-The Human Torch, Namora x-over (Sum/47); 2nd app. Namora after Marvel Mystery #82	116	232	348	725	1088	1450
24-Namora x-over (3rd app.)	100	200	300	625	938	1250
25-The Blonde Phantom begins (Spr/48), ends No. 31; Kurtzman-a; Namora x-over; last quarterly issue	124	248	372	775	1163	1550
26-28: 28-Namora cover; Everett-a	100	200	300	625	938	1250
29-31 (4/49): 29-The Human Torch app. 31-Capt. America app.	100	200	300	625	938	1250
32 (7/49, Scarce)-Origin Sub-Mariner	157	314	471	981	1471	1960
33 (4/54)-Origin Sub-Mariner; The Human Torch app.; Namora x-over in Sub-Mariner #33-42	96	192	288	600	900	1200
34,35-Human Torch in each	76	152	228	475	713	950
36,37,39-41: 36,39-41-Namora app.	73	146	219	456	688	920
38-Origin Sub-Mariner's wings; Namora app.; last pre-code (2/55)	83	166	249	519	780	1040
42-Last issue	85	170	255	531	796	1060

NOTE: *Angel by* ***Gustavson****-#1, 8.* ***Brodsky*** *c-34-36, 42.* ***Everett*** *a-1-4, 22-24, 26-42; c-32, 33, 40.* ***Maneely*** *a-38; c-37, 39-41.* ***Rico*** *c-27-31.* ***Schomburg*** *c-1-4, 6, 8-18, 20.* ***Sekowsky*** *c-24. 25, 26(w/****Rico****).* ***Shores*** *c-21-23, 38. Bondage c-13, 22, 24, 25, 34.*

SUBSPECIES
Eternity Comics: May, 1991 - No. 4, Aug, 1991 ($2.50, limited series)

	GD 2.0	VG 4.0	FN 6.0	VF 8.0	VF/NM 9.0	NM- 9.2
1-4: New stories based on horror movie						2.50

SUBTLE VIOLENTS
CFD Productions: 1991 ($2.50, B&W, mature)

	GD 2.0	VG 4.0	FN 6.0	VF 8.0	VF/NM 9.0	NM- 9.2
1-Linsner-c & story	1	3	4	8	10	12
San Diego Limited Edition	4	8	12	29	40	50

SUE & SALLY SMITH (Formerly My Secret Life)
Charlton Comics: V2#48, Nov, 1962 - No. 54, Nov, 1963 (Flying Nurses)

	GD 2.0	VG 4.0	FN 6.0	VF 8.0	VF/NM 9.0	NM- 9.2
V2#48	3	6	9	18	24	30
49-54	2	4	6	12	16	20

SUGAR & SPIKE (Also see The Best of DC & DC Silver Age Classics)
National Periodical Publications: Apr-May, 1956 - No. 98, Oct-Nov, 1971

	GD 2.0	VG 4.0	FN 6.0	VF 8.0	VF/NM 9.0	NM- 9.2
1 (Scarce)	256	512	768	1600	2400	3200
2	92	184	276	575	863	1150
3-5: 3-Letter column begins	64	128	192	400	600	800
6-10	40	80	120	240	358	475
11-20	37	74	111	212	301	390
21-29: 26-Christmas-c	25	50	75	147	202	260
30-Scribbly & Scribbly, Jr. x-over	26	52	78	150	210	270
31-40	15	30	45	104	152	200
41-60	9	18	27	65	93	120
61-80: 69-1st app. Tornado-Tot-c/story. 72-Origin & 1st app. Bernie the Brain	8	16	24	53	74	95
81-84,86-95: 84-Bernie the Brain apps. as Superman in 1 panel (9/69)	6	12	18	40	55	70
85 (68 pgs.)-r/#72	7	14	21	50	68	85
96 (68 pgs.)	8	16	24	53	74	95
97,98 (52 pgs.)	7	14	21	50	68	85
No. 1 Replica Edition (2002, $2.95) reprint of #1						3.00

NOTE: *All written and drawn by* ***Sheldon Mayer.***

SUGAR BOWL COMICS (Teen-age)
Famous Funnies: May, 1948 - No. 5, Jan, 1949

	GD 2.0	VG 4.0	FN 6.0	VF 8.0	VF/NM 9.0	NM- 9.2
1-Toth-c/a	15	30	45	86	118	150
2,4,5	9	18	27	49	62	75
3-Toth-a	10	20	30	58	77	95

SUGARFOOT (TV)
Dell Publishing Co.: No. 907, May, 1958 - No. 1209, Oct-Dec, 1961

	GD 2.0	VG 4.0	FN 6.0	VF 8.0	VF/NM 9.0	NM- 9.2
Four Color 907 (#1)-Toth-a, photo-c	14	28	42	99	145	190
Four Color 992 (5-7/59), Toth-a, photo-c	13	26	39	90	133	175
Four Color 1059 (11-1/60), 1098 (5-7/60), 1147 (11-1/61), 1209-all photo-c	10	20	30	67	96	125

SUICIDE SQUAD (See Brave & the Bold and Doom Patrol & Suicide Squad Spec., Legends #3 & note under Star Spangled War stories)
DC Comics: May, 1987 - No. 66, June, 1992 (Direct sales only #32 on)

	GD 2.0	VG 4.0	FN 6.0	VF 8.0	VF/NM 9.0	NM- 9.2
1-66: 9-Millennium x-over. 10-Batman-c/story. 13-JLI app. (Batman). 16-Re-intro Shade The Changing Man. 23-1st Oracle. 27-34,36,37-Snyder-a. 40-43-"The Phoenix Gambit" Batman storyline. 40-Free Batman/Suicide Squad poster						2.25
Annual 1 (1988, $1.50)-Manhunter x-over						2.25

NOTE: ***Chaykin*** *c-1.*

SUICIDE SQUAD (2nd series)
DC Comics: Nov, 2001 - No. 12, Oct, 2002 ($2.50)

	GD 2.0	VG 4.0	FN 6.0	VF 8.0	VF/NM 9.0	NM- 9.2
1-12-Giffen-s/Medina-a; Sgt. Rock app. 4-Heath-a. 10-J. Severin-a. 12-JSA app.						2.50

SUMMER FUN (See Dell Giants)

SUMMER FUN (Formerly Li'l Genius; Holiday Surprise #55)
Charlton Comics: No. 54, Oct, 1966 (Giant)

	GD 2.0	VG 4.0	FN 6.0	VF 8.0	VF/NM 9.0	NM- 9.2
54	4	8	12	27	36	45

SUMMER FUN (Walt Disney's...)
Disney Comics: Summer, 1991 ($2.95, annual, 68 pgs.)

1-D. Duck, M. Mouse, Brer Rabbit, Chip 'n' Dale & Pluto, Li'l Bad Wolf, Super Goof,

Sun Girl #2 © MAR

Superboy #107 © DC

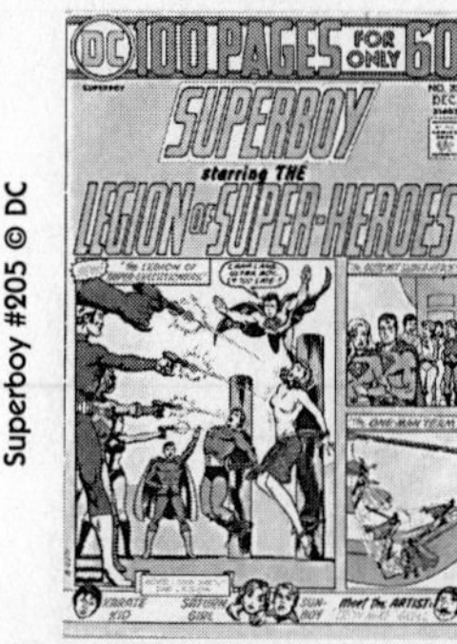

Superboy #205 © DC

	GD 2.0	VG 4.0	FN 6.0	VF 8.0	VF/NM 9.0	NM- 9.2

Scamp stories 4.00

SUMMER LOVE (Formerly Brides in Love?)
Charlton Comics: V2#46, Oct, 1965; V2#47, Oct, 1966; V2#48, Nov, 1968

	GD	VG	FN	VF	VF/NM	NM-
V2#46-Beatles-c & 8 pg. story	14	28	42	99	145	190
47-(68 pgs.) Beatles-c & 12 pg. story	10	20	30	73	107	140
48	2	4	6	14	18	22

SUMMER MAGIC (See Movie Comics)

SUNDANCE (See Hotel Deparee...)

SUNDANCE KID (Also see Blazing Six-Guns)
Skywald Publications: June, 1971 - No. 3, Sept, 1971 (52 pgs.)

	GD	VG	FN	VF	VF/NM	NM-
1-Durango Kid; Two Kirby Bullseye-r	2	4	6	14	18	22
2,3: 2-Swift Arrow, Durango Kid, Bullseye by S&K; Meskin plus 1 pg. origin.						
3-Durango Kid, Billy the Kid, Red Hawk-r	2	4	6	10	12	15

SUNDAY PIX (Christian religious)
David C. Cook Pub/USA Weekly Newsprint Color Comics: V1#1, Mar,1949 - V16#26, July 19, 1964 (7x10", 12 pgs., mail subscription only)

	GD	VG	FN	VF	VF/NM	NM-
V1#1	7	14	21	35	43	50
V1#2-up	5	10	15	23	28	32
V2#1-52 (1950)	5	10	14	20	24	28
V3-V6 (1951-1953)	4	8	11	16	19	22
V7-V11#1-7,23-52 (1954-1959)	2	4	6	11	14	18
V11#8-22 (2/22-5/31/59) H.G. Wells First Men in the Moon serial	2	4	6	12	16	20
V12#1-19,21-52; V13-V15#1,2,9-52; V16#1-26(7/19/64)	2	4	6	9	11	14
V12#20 (5/15/60) 2 page interview with Peanuts' Charles Schulz	4	8	12	25	33	42
V15#3-8 (2/24/63) John Glenn, Christian astronaut	2	4	6	12	16	20

SUN DEVILS
DC Comics: July, 1984 - No. 12, June, 1985 ($1.25, maxi series)

1-12: 6-Death of Sun Devil 2.25

SUNDIATA: A LEGEND OF AFRICA
NBM Publishing Inc.: 2002 ($15.95, hardcover with dustjacket)

nn-Will Eisner-s/a; adaptation of an African folk tale 16.00

SUN FUN KOMIKS
Sun Publications: 1939 (15¢, B&W & red)

	GD	VG	FN	VF	VF/NM	NM-
1-Satire on comics	33	66	99	190	270	350

SUNFIRE & BIG HERO SIX (See Alpha Flight)
Marvel Comics: Sept, 1998 - No. 3, Nov, 1998 ($2.50, limited series)

1-3-Lobdell-s 2.50

SUN GIRL (See The Human Torch & Marvel Mystery Comics #88)
Marvel Comics (CCC): Aug, 1948 - No. 3, Dec, 1948

	GD	VG	FN	VF	VF/NM	NM-
1-Sun Girl begins; Miss America app.	152	304	456	950	1425	1900
2,3: 2-The Blonde Phantom begins	110	220	330	688	1032	1375

SUNGLASSES
Verotik: Nov, 1995 - No. 6, Nov, 1996 ($2.95, limited series, mature)

1-5: Nancy Collins scripts; adapt. of "Sunglasses after Dark" 3.00
6-($3.95) 4.00

SUNNY, AMERICA'S SWEETHEART (Formerly Cosmo Cat #1-10)
Fox Features Syndicate: No. 11, Dec, 1947 - No. 14, June, 1948

	GD	VG	FN	VF	VF/NM	NM-
11-Feldstein-c/a	80	160	240	500	750	1000
12-14-Feldstein-c/a; 14-Lingerie panels	62	124	186	388	582	775
I.W. Reprint #8-Feldstein-a; r/Fox issue	12	24	36	84	125	165

SUN-RUNNERS (Also see Tales of the...)
Pacific Comics/Eclipse Comics/Amazing Comics: 2/84 - No. 3, 5/84; No. 4, 11/84 - No. 7, 1986 (Baxter paper)

1-7: P. Smith-a in #2-4 2.25
Christmas Special 1 (1987, $1.95)-By Amazing 2.25

SUNSET CARSON (Also see Cowboy Western)
Charlton Comics: Feb, 1951 - No. 4, 1951 (No month) (Photo-c on each)

	GD	VG	FN	VF	VF/NM	NM-
1-Photo/retouched-c (Scarce, all issues)	85	170	255	531	796	1060
2-Kit Carson story; adapts "Kansas Raiders" w/Brian Donlevy, Audie Murphy & Margaret Chapman	61	122	183	381	573	765
3,4	48	96	144	288	432	575

SUNSET PASS (See Zane Grey & 4-Color #230)

SUPER ANIMALS PRESENTS PIDGY & THE MAGIC GLASSES
Star Publications: Dec, 1953 (25¢, came w/glasses)

	GD	VG	FN	VF	VF/NM	NM-
1-(3-D Comics)-L. B. Cole-c	41	82	123	246	368	490

SUPERBOY (See Adventure, Aurora, DC Comics Presents, DC 100 Page Super Spectacular #15, DC Super Stars, 80 Page Giant #10, More Fun Comics, The New Advs. of... & Superman Family #191, Young Justice)

SUPERBOY (1st Series)(...& the Legion of Super-Heroes with #231)
(Becomes The Legion of Super-Heroes No. 259 on)
National Periodical Publications/DC Comics: Mar-Apr, 1949 - No. 258, Dec, 1979 (#1-16: 52 pgs.)

	GD	VG	FN	VF	VF/NM	NM-
1-Superman cover; intro in More Fun #101 (1-2/45)	759	1518	2277	5313	8157	11,000
2-Used in **SOTI**, pg. 35-36,226	200	400	600	1250	1875	2500
3	152	304	456	950	1425	1900
4,5: 5-1st pre-Supergirl tryout (c/story, 11-12/49)	102	204	306	638	957	1275
6-10: 8-1st Superbaby. 10-1st app. Lana Lang	90	180	270	563	844	1125
11-15	69	138	207	431	646	860
16-20: 20-2nd Jor-El cover	48	96	144	288	432	575
21-26,28-30: 21-Lana Lang app.	40	80	120	240	340	440
27-Low distribution	40	80	120	240	353	465
31-38: 38-Last pre-code issue (1/55)	34	68	102	196	278	360
39-48,50 (7/56)	30	60	90	170	240	310
49 (6/56)-1st app. Metallo (Jor-El's robot)	32	64	96	182	259	335
51-60: 52-1st S.A. issue. 56-Krypto-c	21	42	63	118	164	210
61-67	17	34	51	98	134	170
68-Origin/1st app. original Bizarro (10-11/58)	55	110	165	343	512	680
69-77,79: 76-1st Supermonkey	14	28	42	79	107	135
78-Origin Mr. Mxyzptlk & Superboy's costume	22	44	66	127	176	225
80-1st meeting Superboy/Supergirl (4/60)	19	38	57	109	152	195
81,83-85,87,88: 83-Origin/1st app. Kryptonite Kid	10	20	30	67	96	125
82-1st Bizarro Krypto	10	20	30	72	104	135
86-(1/61)-4th Legion app; Intro Pete Ross	18	36	54	131	191	250
89-(6/61)-1st app. Mon-el; 2nd Phantom Zone	28	56	84	203	294	385
90-92: 90-Pete Ross learns Superboy's I.D. 92-Last 10¢ issue	10	20	30	67	96	125
93-10th Legion app.(12/61); Chameleon Boy app.	10	20	30	72	104	135
94-97,99	8	16	24	53	74	95
98-(7/62)-18th Legion app; origin & 1st app. Ultra Boy; Pete Ross joins Legion	11	22	33	75	110	145
100-(10/62)-Ultra Boy app; 1st app. Phantom Zone villains, Dr. Xadu & Erndine. 2 pg. map of Krypton; origin Superboy retold; r-cover of Superman #1	19	38	57	133	194	255
101-120: 104-Origin Phantom Zone. 115-Atomic bomb-c. 117-Legion app.	7	14	21	46	63	80
121-128: 124-(10/65)-1st app. Insect Queen (Lana Lang). 125-Legion cameo. 126-Origin Krypto the Super Dog retold with new facts	6	12	18	43	59	75
129-(80-pg. Giant G-22)-Reprints origin Mon-el	8	16	24	55	78	100
130-137,139,140: 131-Legion statues cameo in Dog Legionnaires story. 132-1st app. Supremo. 133-Superboy meets Robin	5	10	15	36	48	60
138 (80-pg. Giant G-35)	7	14	21	46	63	80
141-146,148-155,157: 145-Superboy's parents regain their youth. 148-Legion app. 157-Last 12¢ issue	4	8	12	24	32	40
147(6/68)-Giant G-47; 1st origin of L.S.H. (Saturn Girl, Lightning Lad, Cosmic Boy); origin Legion of Super-Pets-r/Adv. #293	6	12	18	38	52	65
147 Replica Edition (2003, $6.95) reprints entire issue; cover recreation by Ordway						7.00
156,165,174 (Giants G-59,71,83): 165-r/1st app. Krypto the Superdog from Adventure Comics #210	4	8	12	27	36	45
158-164,166-171,175: 171-1st app. Aquaboy?	3	6	9	16	20	25
172,173,176-Legion app.: 172-Origin Yango (Super Ape). 176-Partial photo-c; last 15¢ issue	3	6	9	18	23	28
177-184,186,187 (All 52 pgs.): 182-All new origin of the classic World's Finest team (Superman & Batman) as teenagers (2/72, 22pgs). 184-Origin Dial H for Hero-r	3	6	9	18	24	30
185-Also listed as DC 100 Pg. Super Spectacular #12; Legion-c/story; Teen Titans, Kid Eternity(r/Hit #46), Star Spangled Kid-r(S.S. #55) (see DC 100 Pg. Super Spectacular #12 for price)						
188-190,192,194,196: 188-Origin Karkan. 196-Last Superboy solo story	2	4	6	9	11	14
191,193,195: 191-Origin Sunboy retold; Legion app. 193-Chameleon Boy & Shrinking Violet get new costumes. 195-1st app. Erg-1/Wildfire; Phantom Girl gets new costume	2	4	6	10	13	16
197-Legion series begins; Lightning Lad's new costume	3	6	9	19	25	32
198,199: 198-Element Lad & Princess Projectra get new costumes						

Superboy (3rd series) #18 © DC

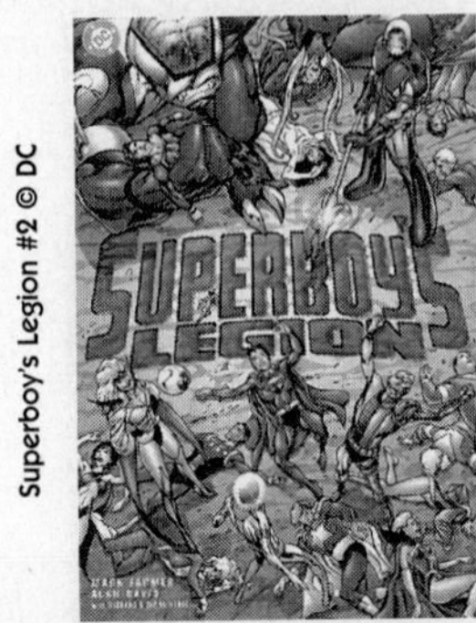

Superboy's Legion #2 © DC

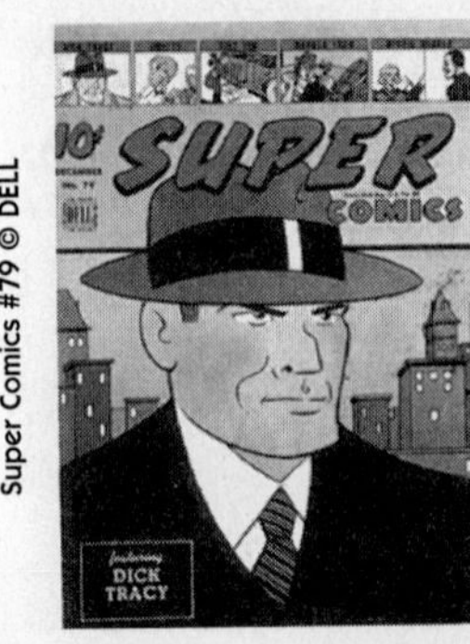

Super Comics #79 © DELL

GD VG FN VF VF/NM NM-
2.0 4.0 6.0 8.0 9.0 9.2

2 4 6 12 16 20
200-Bouncing Boy & Duo Damsel marry; J'onn J'onzz cameo
3 6 9 16 20 24
201,204,206,207,209: 201-Re-intro Erg-1 as Wildfire. 204-Supergirl resigns fromLegion. 206-Ferro Lad & Invisible Kid app. 209-Karate Kid gets new costume
2 4 6 10 13 16
202,205-(100 pgs.): 202-Light Lass gets new costume; Mike Grell's 1st comic work-i (5-6/74)
5 10 15 33 44 55
203-Invisible Kid killed by Validus 3 6 9 16 20 24
208,210: 208-(68 pgs.). 208-Legion of Super-Villains app. 210-Origin Karate Kid
2 4 6 14 18 22
211-220: 212-Matter-Eater Lad resigns. 216-1st app. Tyroc, who joins the Legion in #218
2 4 6 9 11 14
221-230,246-249: 226-Intro. Dawnstar. 228-Death of Chemical King
1 3 4 6 8 10
231-245: (Giants). 240-Origin Dawnstar. 242-(52 pgs.). 243-Legion of Substitute Heroes app. 243-245-(44 pgs.). 2 4 6 10 13 16
244,245-(Whitman variants; low print run, no issue# shown on cover)
2 4 6 12 16 20
246-248-(Whitman variants; low ...) 2 4 6 10 12 15
251-257-(Whitman variants; low ...) 2 4 6 8 10 12
250-258: 253-Intro Blok. 257-Return of Bouncing Boy & Duo Damsel by Ditko
1 2 3 5 6 8
Annual 1 (Sum/64, 84 pgs.)-Origin Krypto-r 19 38 57 136 198 260
Spectacular 1 (1980, Giant)-1st comic distributed only through comic stores; mostly-r
1 2 3 5 6 8

NOTE: ***Neal Adams** c-143, 145, 146, 148-155, 157-161, 163, 164, 166-168, 172, 173, 175, 176, 178. **M. Anderson** a-178,179, 245i. **Ditko** a-257p. **Grell** a-202i, 203-219, 220-224p, 235p; c-207-232, 235, 236p, 237, 239p, 240p, 243p, 246, 258. **Nasser** a(p)-222, 225, 226, 230, 231, 233, 236. **Simonson** a-237p. **Starlin** a(p)-239, 250, 251; c-238. **Staton** a-227p, 243-249p, 252-258p; c-247-251p. **Swan/Moldoff** c-109. **Tuska** a-172, 173, 176, 183, 235p. **Wood** inks-153-155, 157-161. Legion app.-172, 173, 176, 177, 183, 184, 188, 190, 191, 193, 195, 197-258.*

SUPERBOY (TV)(2nd Series)(The Adventures of...#19 on)
DC Comics: Feb, 1990 - No. 22, Dec, 1991 ($1.00/$1.25)

1-22: Mooney-a(p) in 1-8,18-20; 1-Photo-c from TV show. 8-Bizarro-c/story; Arthur Adams-a(i). 9-12,14-17-Swan-p 3.00
...Special 1 (1992, $1.75) Swan-a 3.00

SUPERBOY (3rd Series)
DC Comics: Feb, 1994 - No. 100, Jul, 2002 ($1.50/$1.95/$1.99/$2.25)

1-Metropolis Kid from Reign of the Supermen 4.00
2-8,0,9-24,26-76: 6,7-Worlds Collide Pts. 3 & 8. 8-(9/94)-Zero Hour x-over. 0-(10/94). 9-(11/94)-King Shark app. 21-Legion app. 28-Supergirl-c/app. 33-Final Night. 38-41-"Meltdown". 45-Legion-c/app. 47-Green Lantern-c/app. 50-Last Boy on Earth begins. 60-Crosses Hypertime. 68-Demon-c/app. 2.50
25-($2.95)-New Gods & Female Furies app.; w/pin-ups 3.50
77-99: 77-Begin $2.25-c. 79-Superboy's powers return. 80,81-Titans app. 83-New costume. 85-Batgirl app. 90,91-Our Worlds at War x-over 2.25
100-($3.50) Sienkiewicz-c; Grummett & McCrea-a; Superman cameo 3.50
#1,000,000 (11/98) 853rd Century x-over 2.50
Annual 1 (1994, $2.95, 68 pgs.)-Elseworlds story, Pt. 2 of The Super Seven (see Adventures Of Superman Annual #6) 3.00
Annual 2 (1995, $3.95)-Year One story 4.00
Annual 3 (1996, $2.95)-Legends of the Dead Earth 3.00
Annual 4 (1997, $3.95)-Pulp Heroes story 4.00
...Plus 1 (Jan, 1997, $2.95) w/Capt. Marvel Jr. 3.00
...Plus 2 (Fall, 1997, $2.95) w/Slither (Scare Tactics) 3.00
.../Risk Double-Shot 1 (Feb, 1998, $1.95) w/Risk (Teen Titans) 2.50

SUPERBOY & THE RAVERS
DC Comics: Sept, 1996 - No. 19, March, 1998 ($1.95)

1-19: 4-Adam Strange app. 7-Impulse-c/app. 9-Superman-c/app. 2.50

SUPERBOY/ROBIN: WORLD'S FINEST THREE
DC Comics: 1996 - No. 2, 1996 ($4.95, squarebound, limited series)

1,2: Superboy & Robin vs. Metallo & Poison Ivy; Karl Kesel & Chuck Dixon scripts; Tom Grummett-c(p)/a(p) 5.00

SUPERBOY'S LEGION (Elseworlds)
DC Comics: 2001 - No. 2, 2001 ($5.95, squarebound, limited series)

1,2-31st century Superboy forms Legion; Farmer-s/i; Davis-a(p)/c 6.00

SUPER BRAT (Li'l Genius #5 on)
Toby Press: Jan, 1954 - No. 4, July, 1954

1 8 16 24 43 54 65
2-4: 4-Li'l Teevy by Mel Lazarus 5 10 15 24 30 35

GD VG FN VF VF/NM NM-
2.0 4.0 6.0 8.0 9.0 9.2

I.W. Reprint #1,2,3,7,8('58): 1-r/#1 2 4 6 8 10 12
I.W. (Super) Reprint #10('63) 2 4 6 8 10 12

SUPERCAR (TV)
Gold Key: Nov, 1962 - No. 4, Aug, 1963 (All painted-c)

1 23 46 69 167 244 320
2,3 12 24 36 82 121 160
4-Last issue 15 30 45 109 160 210

SUPER CAT (Formerly Frisky Animals; also see Animal Crackers)
Star Publications #56-58/Ajax/Farrell Publ. (Four Star Comic Corp.): No. 56, Nov, 1953 - No. 58, May, 1954; Aug, 1957 - No. 4, May, 1958

56-58-L.B. Cole-c on all 21 42 63 118 164 210
1(1957-Ajax)- "The Adventures of..." c-only 10 20 30 56 73 90
2-4 7 14 21 35 43 50

SUPER CIRCUS (TV)
Cross Publishing Co.: Jan, 1951 - No. 5, Sept, 1951 (Mary Hartline)

1-(52 pgs.)-Cast photos on-c 15 30 45 86 118 150
2-Cast photos on-c 10 20 30 56 73 90
3-5 8 16 24 46 58 70

SUPER CIRCUS (TV)
Dell Publ. Co.: No. 542, Mar, 1954 - No. 694, Mar, 1956 (Mary Hartline)

Four Color 542: Mary Hartline photo-c 8 16 24 57 76 100
Four Color 592,694: Mary Hartline photo-c 7 14 21 53 69 90

SUPER COMICS
Dell Publishing Co.: May, 1938 - No. 121, Feb-Mar, 1949

1-Terry & The Pirates, The Gumps, Dick Tracy, Little Orphan Annie, Little Joe, Gasoline Alley, Smilin' Jack, Smokey Stover, Smitty, Tiny Tim, Moon Mullins, Harold Teen, Winnie Winkle begin 290 580 870 1624 2262 2900
2 107 214 321 599 837 1075
3 94 188 282 526 733 940
4,5: 4-Dick Tracy-c; also #8-10,17,26(part),31 75 150 225 420 585 750
6-10 60 120 180 336 468 600
11-20: 20-Smilin' Jack-c (also #29,32) 47 94 141 263 367 470
21-29: 21-Magic Morro begins (origin & 1st app., 2/40). 22,27-Ken Ernst-c (also #25?); Magic Morro c-22,25,27,34 38 76 113 213 297 380
30- "Sea Hawk" movie adaptation-c/story with Errol Flynn
39 78 116 218 304 390
31-40: 34-Ken Ernst-c 32 64 96 179 250 320
41-50: 41-Intro Lightning Jim. 43-Terry & The Pirates ends
27 54 81 151 211 270
51-60 20 40 60 112 156 200
61-70: 62-Flag-c. 65-Brenda Starr-r begin? 67-X-Mas-c
18 36 54 101 141 180
71-80 14 28 42 78 109 140
81-99 13 26 39 73 99 125
100 14 28 42 78 107 135
101-115-Last Dick Tracy (moves to own title) 9 18 27 50 70 90
116-121: 116,118-All Smokey Stover. 117-All Gasoline Alley. 119-121-Terry & The Pirates app. in all 8 16 24 45 60 75

SUPER COPS, THE
Red Circle Productions (Archie): July, 1974 (one-shot)

1-Morrow-c/a; art by Pino, Hack, Thorne 1 3 4 6 8 10

SUPER COPS
Now Comics: Sept, 1990 - No. 4, Dec?, 1990 ($1.75)

1-($2.75, 52 pgs.)-Dave Dorman painted-c (both printings) 2.75
2-4 2.25

SUPER CRACKED (See Cracked)

SUPER DC GIANT (25-50¢, all 68-52 pg. Giants)
National Per. Publ.: No. 13, 9-10/70 - No. 26, 7-8/71; V3#27, Summer, 1976 (No #1-12)

S-13-Binky 11 22 33 75 110 145
S-14-Top Guns of the West; Kubert-c; Trigger Twins, Johnny Thunder, Wyoming Kid-r; Moreira-r (9-10/70) 5 10 15 33 44 55
S-15-Western Comics; Kubert-c; Pow Wow Smith, Vigilante, Buffalo Bill-r; new Gil Kane-a (9-10/70) 5 10 15 33 44 55
S-16-Best of the Brave & the Bold; Batman-r & Metamorpho origin-r from Brave & the Bold; Spectre pin-up. 4 8 12 25 33 42
S-17-Love 1970 (scarce) 25 50 75 181 266 350
S-18-Three Mouseketeers; Dizzy Dog, Doodles Duck, Bo Bunny-r; Sheldon Mayer-a
10 20 30 70 100 130
S-19-Jerry Lewis; Neal Adams pin-up 10 20 30 72 104 135

Super Duck Comics #20 © MLJ

Super Friends #31 © DC

Supergirl (4th series) #68 © DC

GD VG FN VF VF/NM NM-
2.0 4.0 6.0 8.0 9.0 9.2

S-20-House of Mystery; N. Adams-c; Kirby-r(3) 7 14 21 46 63 80
S-21-Love 1971 (scarce) 29 58 87 210 310 410
S-22-Top Guns of the West; Kubert-c 3 7 10 21 28 35
S-23-The Unexpected 4 8 12 27 36 45
S-24-Supergirl 4 8 12 27 36 45
S-25-Challengers of the Unknown; all Kirby/Wood-r 3 7 10 21 28 35
S-26-Aquaman (1971)-r/S.A. Aquaman origin story from Showcase #30
3 7 10 21 28 35
27-Strange Flying Saucers Adventures (Sum, 1976) 3 6 9 19 25 32
NOTE: *Sid Greene r-27p(2), Heath r-27. G. Kane a-14r(2), 15, 27r(p). Kubert r-16.*

SUPER-DOOPER COMICS
Able Mfg. Co./Harvey: 1946 - No. 8, 1946 (10¢, 32 pgs., paper-c)
1-The Clock, Gangbuster app. 22 44 66 127 176 225
2 14 28 42 79 107 135
3,4,6 12 24 36 69 92 115
5-Capt. Freedom 14 28 42 79 107 135
7,8-Shock Gibson. 7-Where's Theres A Will by Ed Wheelan, Steve Case Crime Rover, Penny & Ullysses Jr. 8-Sam Hill app. 14 28 42 79 107 135

SUPER DUCK COMICS (The Cockeyed Wonder) (See Jolly Jingles)
MLJ Mag. No. 1-4(9/45)/Close-Up No. 5 on (Archie): Fall, 1944 - No. 94, Dec, 1960 (Also see Laugh #24)(#1-5 are quarterly)
1-Origin; Hitler & Hirohito-c 54 108 162 324 487 650
2-Bill Vigoda-c 25 50 75 144 198 255
3-5: 4-20-Al Fagaly-c (most) 17 34 51 98 134 170
6-10 14 28 42 79 107 135
11-20(6/48) 10 20 30 58 77 95
21,23-40 (10/51) 9 18 27 52 66 80
22-Used in **SOTI**, pg. 35,307,308 10 20 30 56 73 90
41-60 (2/55) 8 16 24 43 54 65
61-94 7 14 21 35 43 50

SUPER DUPER (Formerly Pocket Comics #1-4?)
Harvey Publications: No. 5, 1941 - No. 11, 1941
5-Captain Freedom & Shock Gibson app. 33 66 99 190 270 350
8,11 21 42 63 118 164 210

SUPER DUPER COMICS (Formerly Latest Comics?)
F. E. Howard Publ.: No. 3, May-June, 1947
3-1st app. Mr. Monster 15 30 45 84 115 145

SUPER FRIENDS (TV) (Also see Best of DC & Limited Collectors' Edition)
National Periodical Publications/DC Comics: Nov, 1976 - No. 47, Aug, 1981 (#14 is 44 pgs.)
1-Superman, Batman, Robin, Wonder Woman, Aquaman, Atom, Wendy, Marvin & Wonder Dog begin (1st Super Friends) 3 7 10 21 28 35
2-Penquin-c/sty 2 4 6 11 14 18
3-5 2 4 6 10 12 15
6-10,14: 7-1st app. Wonder Twins & The Seraph. 8-1st app. Jack O'Lantern. 9-1st app. Icemaiden. 14-Origin Wonder Twins 2 4 6 8 10 12
11-13,15-30: 13-1st app. Dr. Mist. 25-1st app. Fire as Green Fury. 28-Bizarro app.
1 2 3 5 7 9
14,16,21-23,32-(Whitman variants; low print run, no issue# on cover)
2 4 6 8 10 12
31,47: 31-Black Orchid app. 47-Origin Fire & Green Fury
1 3 4 6 8 10
32-46: 36,43-Plastic Man app. 1 2 3 5 6 8
TBP (2001, $14.95) r/#1,6-9,14,21,27 & L.C.E. C-41; Alex Ross-c 15.00
...: Truth, Justice and Peace TPB (2003, $14.95) r/#10,12,13,25,28,29,31,36,37 15.00
NOTE: *Estrada a-1p, 2p. Orlando a-1p. Staton a-43, 45.*

SUPER FUN
Gillmor Magazines: Jan, 1956 (By A.W. Nugent)
1-Comics, puzzles, cut-outs by A.W. Nugent 6 12 18 28 34 40

SUPER FUNNIES (...Western Funnies #3,4)
Superior Comics Publishers Ltd. (Canada): Dec, 1953 - No. 4, Sept, 1954
1-(3-D, 10¢)-...Presents Dopey Duck; make your own 3-D glasses cut-out inside front-c; did not come w/glasses 39 78 117 224 322 420
2-Horror & crime satire 14 28 42 79 107 135
3-Phantom Ranger-c/s; Geronimo, Billy the Kid app. 9 18 27 49 62 75
4-Phantom Ranger-c/story 9 18 27 49 62 75

SUPERGIRL (See Action, Adventure #281, Brave & the Bold, Crisis on Infinite Earths #7, Daring New Advs. of..., Super DC Giant, Superman Family, & Super-Team Family)

SUPERGIRL
National Periodical Publ.: Nov, 1972 - No. 9, Dec-Jan, 1973-74; No. 10, Sept-Oct, 1974 (1st solo title)(20¢)
1-Zatanna back-up stories begin, end #5 5 10 15 36 48 60
2-4,6,7,9 3 6 9 16 20 25
5,8,10: 5-Zatanna origin-r. 8-JLA x-over; Batman cameo. 10-Prez
3 6 9 18 23 28
NOTE: *Zatanna in #1-5, 7(Guest); Prez app. in #10. #1-10 are 20¢ issues.*

SUPERGIRL (Formerly Daring New Adventures of...)
DC Comics: No. 14, Dec, 1983 - No. 23, Sept, 1984
14-23: 16-Ambush Bug app. 20-JLA & New Teen Titans app. 3.00
...Movie Special (1985)-Adapts movie; Morrow-a; photo back-c 4.00

SUPERGIRL
DC Comics: Feb, 1994 - No. 4, May, 1994 ($1.50, limited series)
1-4: Guice-a(i) 3.00

SUPERGIRL (See Showcase '96 #8)
DC Comics: Sept, 1996 - No. 80, May, 2003 ($1.95/$1.99/$2.25/$2.50)
1-Peter David scripts & Gary Frank-c/a; DC cover logo in upper left is blue
1 2 3 5 6 8
1-2nd printing-DC cover logo in upper left is red 3.00
2,4-9: 4-Gorilla Grodd-c/app. 6-Superman-c/app. 9-Last Frank-a 4.00
3-Final Night, Gorilla Grodd app. 5.00
10-19: 14-Genesis x-over. 16-Power Girl app. 3.50
20-35: 20-Millennium Giants x-over; Superman app. 23-Steel-c/app. 24-Resurrection Man x-over. 25-Comet ID revealed; begin $1.99-c 3.00
36-46: 36,37-Young Justice x-over 2.50
47-49,51-74: 47-Begin $2.25-c. 51-Adopts costume from animated series. 54-Green Lantern app. 59-61-Our Worlds at War x-over. 62-Two-Face-c/app. 66,67-Demon-c/app. 68-74-Mary Marvel app. 70-Nauck-a. 73-Begin $2.50-c 2.50
50-($3.95) Supergirl's final battle with the Carnivore 4.00
75-80: 75-Re-intro. Kara Zor-El; cover swipe of Action #252 by Haynes; Benes-a. 78-Spectre app. 80-Last issue; Romita-c 2.50
#1,000,000 (11/98) 853rd Century x-over 3.00
Annual 1 (1996, $2.95)-Legends of the Dead Earth 3.00
Annual 2 (1997, $3.95)-Pulp Heroes; LSH app.; Chiodo-c 4.00
...: Many Happy Returns TPB (2003, $14.95) r/#75-80; intro. by Peter David 15.00
...Plus (2/97, $2.95) Capt.(Mary) Marvel-c/app.; David-s/Frank-a 3.00
.../Prysm Double-Shot 1 (Feb, 1998, $1.95) w/Prysm (Teen Titans) 2.50
...: Wings (2001, $5.95) Elseworlds; DeMatteis-s/Tolagson-a 6.00
TPB-('98, $14.95) r/Showcase '96 #8 & Supergirl #1-9 15.00

SUPERGIRL/LEX LUTHOR SPECIAL (Supergirl and Team Luthor on-c)
DC Comics: 1993 ($2.50, 68 pgs., one-shot)
1-Pin-ups by Byrne & Thibert 2.50

SUPER GOOF (Walt Disney) (See Dynabrite & The Phantom Blot)
Gold Key No. 1-57/Whitman No. 58 on: Oct, 1965 - No. 74, July, 1984
1 5 10 15 33 44 55
2-5 3 6 9 18 23 28
6-10 2 4 6 14 18 22
11-20 2 4 6 9 11 14
21-30 1 3 4 6 8 10
31-50 1 2 3 4 5 7
51-57 6.00
58,59 (Whitman) 1 2 3 4 5 7
60(8/80), 61(9-10/80), 62(11/80) 3-pack only (scarce) 2 4 6 14 18 22
63-66('81) 1 2 3 5 6 8
67-69: 67(2/82), 68(2-3/82), 69(3/82) 6.00
70-74 (#90180 on-c; pre-pack, nd, nd code): 70(5/83), 71(8/83), 72(5/84), 73(6/84), 74(7/84)
2 4 6 10 13 16
NOTE: *Reprints in #16, 24, 28, 29, 37, 38, 43, 45, 46, 54(1/2), 56-58, 65(1/2), 72(r-#2).*

SUPER GREEN BERET (Tod Holton...)
Lightning Comics (Milson Publ. Co.): Apr, 1967 - No. 2, Jun, 1967
1-(25¢, 68 pgs) 5 10 15 36 48 60
2-(25¢, 68 pgs) 4 8 12 24 32 40

SUPER HEROES (See Giant-Size... & Marvel...)

SUPER HEROES
Dell Publishing Co.: Jan, 1967 - No. 4, June, 1967
1-Origin & 1st app. Fab 4 4 8 12 28 38 48
2-4 3 6 9 18 24 30

SUPER-HEROES BATTLE SUPER-GORILLAS (See DC Special #16)
National Periodical Publications: Winter, 1976 (52 pgs., all reprints, one-shot)
1-Superman, Batman, Flash stories; Infantino-a(p) 2 4 6 10 12 15

Super Magician Comics V2#11 © CN

Superman #17 © DC

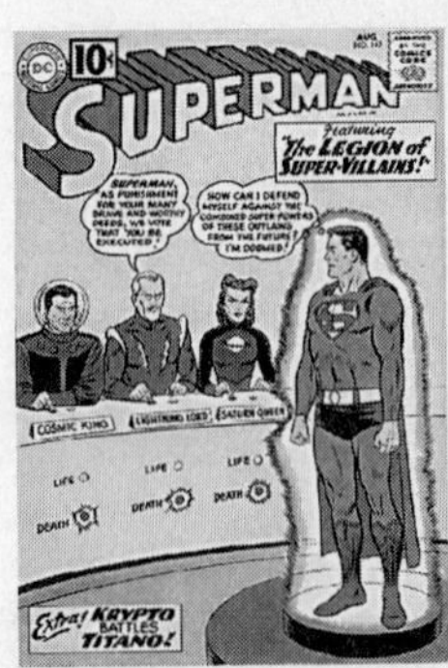

Superman #147 © DC

GD 2.0 | VG 4.0 | FN 6.0 | VF 8.0 | VF/NM 9.0 | NM- 9.2

SUPER HEROES VERSUS SUPER VILLAINS
Archie Publications (Radio Comics): July, 1966 (no month given)(68 pgs.)
1-Flyman, Black Hood, Web, Shield-r; Reinman-a 6 12 18 43 59 75

SUPERHERO WOMEN, THE - FEATURING THE FABULOUS FEMALES OF MARVEL COMICS (See Fireside Book Series)

SUPERICHIE (Formerly Super Richie)
Harvey Publications: No. 5, Oct, 1976 - No. 18, Jan, 1979 (52 pgs. giants)
5-Origin/1st app. new costumes for Rippy & Crashman 2 4 6 10 13 16
6-18 2 4 6 8 10 12

SUPERIOR STORIES
Nesbit Publishers, Inc.: May-June, 1955 - No. 4, Nov-Dec, 1955
1-The Invisible Man by H.G. Wells 24 48 72 135 190 245
2-4: 2-The Pirate of the Gulf by J.H. Ingrahams. 3-Wreck of the Grosvenor by William Clark Russell. 4-The Texas Rangers by O'Henry 11 22 33 63 84 105
NOTE: ***Morisi** c/a in all. Kiwanis stories in #3 & 4. #4 has photo of Gene Autry on-c.*

SUPER MAGIC (Super Magician Comics #2 on)
Street & Smith Publications: May, 1941
V1#1-Blackstone the Magician-c/story; origin/1st app. Rex King (Black Fury); Charles Sultan-c; Blackstone-c begin 150 300 450 938 1407 1875

SUPER MAGICIAN COMICS (Super Magic #1)
Street & Smith Publications: No. 2, Sept, 1941 - V5#8, Feb-Mar, 1947
V1#2-Blackstone the Magician continues; Rex King, Man of Adventure app. 60 120 180 375 563 750
3-Tao-Anwar, Boy Magician begins 40 80 120 240 340 440
4-7,9-12: 4-Origin Transo. 11-Supersnipe app. 39 78 117 230 325 420
8-Abbott & Costello story (1st app?, 11/42) 40 80 120 240 340 440
V2#1-The Shadow app. 40 80 120 240 350 460
2-12: 5-Origin Tigerman. 8-Red Dragon begins 21 42 63 118 164 210
V3#1-12: 5-Origin Mr. Twilight 21 42 63 118 164 210
V4#1-12: 11-Nigel Elliman Ace of Magic begins (3/46) 17 34 51 98 134 170
V5#1-6 17 34 51 98 134 170
7,8-Red Dragon by Edd Cartier-c/a 40 80 120 240 340 440
NOTE: ***Jack Binder** c-1-14(most). Red Dragon c-V5#7, 8.*

SUPERMAN (See Action Comics, Advs. of..., All-New Coll. Ed., All-Star Comics, Best of DC, Brave & the Bold, Cosmic Odyssey, DC Comics Presents, Heroes Against Hunger, JLA, The Kents, Krypton Chronicles, Limited Coll. Ed., Man of Steel, Phantom Zone, Power Record Comics, Special Edition, Steel, Super Friends, Superman: The Man of Steel, Superman: The Man of Tomorrow, Taylor's Christmas Tabloid, Three-Dimension Advs., World Of Krypton, World Of Metropolis, World Of Smallville & World's Finest)

SUPERMAN (Becomes Adventures of...#424 on)
National Periodical Publ./DC Comics: Summer, 1939 - No. 423, Sept, 1986
(#1-5 are quarterly)
1(nn)-1st four Action stories reprinted; origin Superman by Siegel & Shuster; has a new 2 pg. origin plus 4 pgs. omitted in Action story; see The Comics Magazine #1 & More Fun #14-17 for Superman prototype app.; cover r/splash page from Action #10; 1st pin-up Superman on back-c - 1st pin-up in comics 16,875 33,750 50,625 130,000 200,000 270,000
1-Reprint, Oversize 13-1/2x10". **WARNING:** This comic is an exact duplicate reprint of the original except for its size. DC published it in 1978 with a second cover titling it as a Famous First Edition. There have been many reported cases of the outer cover being removed and the interior sold as the original edition. The reprint with the new outer cover removed is practically worthless. See Famous First Edition for value.
2-All daily strip-r; full pg. ad for N.Y. World's Fair 1094 2188 3282 8205 12,853 17,500
3-2nd story-r from Action #5; 3rd story-r from Action #6 724 1448 2172 5068 7784 10,500
4-2nd mention of Daily Planet (Spr/40); also see Action #23; 2nd & 3rd app. Luthor (red-headed; also see Action #23) 552 1104 1656 3864 5932 8000
5-4th Luthor app. (red hair) 434 868 1302 3038 4669 6300
6,7: 6-1st splash pg. in a Superman comic. 7-1st Perry White? (11-12/40) 300 600 900 1925 2963 4000
8-10: 10-5th app. Luthor (1st bald Luthor, 5-6/41) 288 576 864 1800 2700 3600
11-13,15: 13-Jimmy Olsen & Luthor app. 216 432 648 1350 2025 2700
14-Patriotic Shield-c classic by Fred Ray 319 638 957 2074 3187 4300
16,18-20: 16-1st Lois Lane-c this title (5-6/42); 2nd Lois-c after Action #29 172 344 516 1075 1613 2150
17-Hitler, Hirohito-c 256 512 768 1600 2400 3200
21,22,25: 25-Clark Kent's only military service; Fred Ray's only super-hero story 128 256 384 800 1200 1600
23-Classic periscope-c 150 300 450 938 1407 1875
24-Classic Jack Burnley flag-c 196 392 588 1225 1838 2450
26-Classic war-c 188 376 564 1175 1763 2350
27-29: 27,29-Lois Lane-c. 28-Lois Lane Girl Reporter series begins, ends #40,42 120 240 360 750 1125 1500
28-Overseas edition for Armed Forces; same as reg. #28 120 240 360 750 1125 1500
30-Origin & 1st app. Mr. Mxyztplk (9-10/44)(pronounced "Mix-it-plk") in comic books; name later became Mxyzptlk ("Mix-yez-pit-l-ick"); the character was inspired by a combination of the name of Al Capp's Joe Blyfstyk (the little man with the black cloud over his head) & the devilish antics of Bugs Bunny; he 1st app. in newspapers 3/7/44 232 464 696 1450 2175 2900
31-40: 33-(3-4/45)-3rd app. Mxyztplk. 35,36-Lois Lane-c. 38-Atomic bomb story (1-2/46); delayed because of gov't censorship; Superman shown reading Batman #32 on cover. 40-Mxyztplk-c 100 200 300 625 938 1250
41-50: 42-Lois Lane-c. 45-Lois Lane as Superwoman (see Action #60 for 1st app.). 46-(5-6/47)-1st app. Superboy this title? 48-1st time Superman travels thru time 80 160 240 500 750 1000
51,52: 51-Lois Lane-c 66 132 198 413 619 825
53-Third telling of Superman origin; 10th anniversary issue ('48); classic origin-c by Boring 284 568 852 1775 2663 3550
54,56-60: 57-Lois Lane as Superwoman-c. 58-Intro Tiny Trix 66 132 198 413 619 825
55-Used in **SOTI**, pg. 33 68 136 204 425 638 850
61-Origin Superman retold; origin Green Kryptonite (1st Kryptonite story); Superman returns to Krypton for 1st time & sees his parents for 1st time since infancy, discovers he's not an Earth man 138 276 414 863 1294 1725
62-70: 62-Orson Welles-c/story. 65-1st Krypton Foes: Mala, Kizo, & U-Ban. 66-2nd Superbaby story. 67-Perry Como-c/story. 68-1st Luthor-c this title (see Action Comics) 64 128 192 400 600 800
71-75: 74-2nd Luthor-c this title. 75-Some have #74 on-c 62 124 186 388 582 775
76-Batman x-over; Superman & Batman learn each other's I.D. for the 1st time (5-6/52) (also see World's Finest #71) 172 344 516 1075 1613 2150
77-81: 78-Last 52 pg. issue. 81-Used in **POP**, pg. 88 58 116 174 363 544 725
82-87,89,90: 89-1st Curt Swan-c in title 53 106 160 318 479 640
88-Prankster, Toyman & Luthor team-up 58 116 174 363 544 725
91-95: 95-Last precode issue (2/55) 48 96 144 288 432 575
96-99: 96-Mr. Mxyztplk-c/story 40 80 120 240 350 460
100 (9-10/55)-Shows cover to #1 on-c 200 400 600 1250 1875 2500
101-105,107-110: 109-1st S.A. issue 40 80 120 240 340 440
106 (7/56)-Retells origin 40 80 120 240 350 460
111-120 36 72 108 204 290 375
121,122,124-127,129: 127-Origin/1st app. Titano. 129-Intro/origin Lori Lemaris, The Mermaid 31 62 93 175 248 320
123-Pre-Supergirl tryout-c/story (8/58). 38 76 114 219 310 400
128-(4/59)-Red Kryptonite used. Bruce Wayne x-over who protects Superman's i.d. (3rd story) 32 64 96 182 259 335
130-(7/59)-2nd app, Krypto, the Superdog with Superman (see Sup.'s Pal Jimmy Olsen #29) (all other previous app. w/Superboy) 32 64 96 182 259 335
131-139: 135-2nd Lori Lemaris app. 139-Lori Lemaris app.; 24 48 72 138 194 250
140-1st Blue Kryptonite & Bizarro Supergirl; origin Bizarro Jr. #1 25 50 75 147 202 260
141-145,148: 142-2nd Batman x-over 20 40 60 112 156 200
146-(7/61)-Superman's life story; back-up hints at Earth II. Classic-c 26 52 78 147 206 265
147(8/61)-7th Legion app; 1st app. Legion of Super-Villains; 1st app. Adult Legion; swipes-c to Adv. #247 24 48 72 138 194 250
149(11/61)-8th Legion app. (cameo); "The Death of Superman" imaginary story; last 10¢ issue 22 44 66 127 176 225
150,151,153,154,157,159,160: 157-Gold Kryptonite used (see Adv. #299); Mon-el app.; Lightning Lad cameo (11/62) 10 20 30 70 100 130
152,155,156,158,162: 152(4/62)-15th Legion app. 155-(8/62)-Legion app; Lightning Man & Cosmic Man, & Adult Legion app. 156,162-Legion app. 158-1st app. Flamebird & Nightwing & Nor-Kan of Kandor(12/62) 10 20 30 72 104 135
161-1st told death of Ma and Pa Kent 10 20 30 72 104 135
161-2nd printing (1987, $1.25)-New DC logo; sold thru So Much Fun Toy Stores (cover title: Superman Classic) 3.00
163-166,168-180: 166-XMas-c. 168-All Luthor issue; JFK tribute/memorial. 169-Bizarro Invasion of Earth-c/story; last Sally Selwyn. 170-Pres. Kennedy story is finally published after delay from #168 due to assassination. 172,173-Legion cameos. 174-Super-Mxyzptlk; Bizarro app. 8 16 24 55 78 100
167-New origin Brainiac & Brainiac 5; intro Tharla (later Luthor's wife) 10 20 30 72 104 135
181,182,184-186,188-192,194-196,198,200: 181-1st 2965 story/series. 182-1st S.A. app. of The Toyman (1/66). 189-Origin/destruction of Krypton II. 7 14 21 50 68 85

Superman Annual #2 © DC

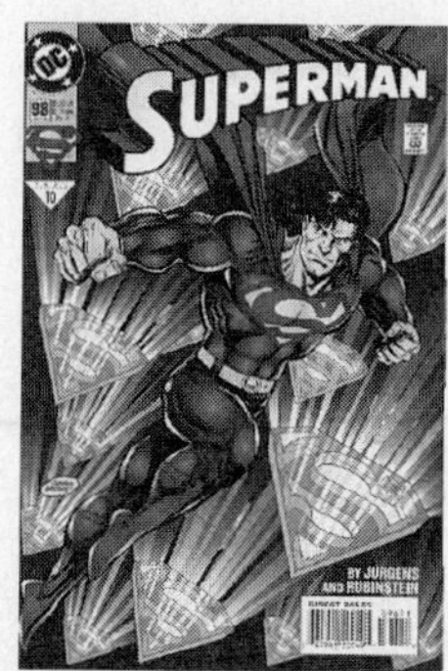

Superman (2nd series) #98 © DC

Superman (2nd series) #178 © DC

	GD 2.0	VG 4.0	FN 6.0	VF 8.0	VF/NM 9.0	NM- 9.2
183 (Giant G-18)	9	18	27	65	93	120
187,193,197 (Giants G-23,G-31,G-36)	8	16	24	55	78	100
199-1st Superman/Flash race (8/67): also see Flash #175 & World's Finest #198,199 (r-in Limited Coll. Ed. C-48)	25	50	75	181	266	350
201,203-206,208-211,213-216: 213-Brainiac-5 app. 216-Last 12¢ issue	5	10	15	33	44	55
202 (80-pg. Giant G-42)-All Bizarro issue	6	12	18	43	59	75
207,212,217 (Giants G-48,G-54,G-60): 207-30th anniversary Superman (6/68)	6	12	18	43	59	75
218-221,223-226,228-231	4	8	12	27	36	45
222,239(Giants, G-66,G-84)	6	12	18	40	55	70
227,232(Giants, G-72,G-78)-All Krypton issues	6	12	18	38	52	65
233-2nd app. Morgan Edge; Clark Kent switches from newspaper reporter to TV newscaster; all Kryptonite on earth destroyed; classic Neal Adams-c	7	14	21	46	63	80
234-238	4	8	12	24	32	40
240-Kaluta-a; last 15¢ issue	3	6	9	19	25	32
241-244 (All 52 pgs.): 241-New Wonder Woman app. 243-G.A.-r/#38	3	7	10	21	28	35
245-Also listed as DC 100 Pg. Super Spectacular #7; Air Wave, Kid Eternity, Hawkman-r; Atom-r/Atom #3 (see DC 100 Pg. Super Spectacular #7 for price)						
246-248,250,251,253 (All 52 pgs.): 246-G.A.-r/#40. 248-World of Krypton story. 251-G.A.-r/#45. 253-Finlay-a, 2 pgs., G.A.-r/#1	3	7	10	21	28	35
249,254-Neal Adams-a. 249-(52 pgs.); origin & 1st app. Terra-Man by Neal Adams (inks)	4	8	12	29	40	50
252-Also listed as DC 100 Pg. Super Spectacular #13; Ray(r/Smash #17), Black Condor, (r/Crack #18), Hawkman(r/Flash #24); Starman-r/Adv. #67; Dr. Fate & Spectre-r/More Fun #57; N. Adams-c (see DC 100 Pg. Super Spectacular #13 for price)						
255-271,273-277,279-283: 263-Photo-c. 264-1st app. Steve Lombard. 276-Intro Capt. Thunder. 279-Batman, Batgirl app.	2	4	6	10	12	15
272,278,284-All 100 pgs. G.A.-r in all. 272-r/2nd app. Mr. Mxyztplk from Action #80	4	8	12	29	40	50
285-299: 289-Partial photo-c. 292-Origin Lex Luthor retold	1	2	3	6	8	10
300-(6/76) Superman in the year 2001	3	6	9	18	24	30
301-350: 301,320-Solomon Grundy app. 323-Intro. Atomic Skull. 327-329-(44 pgs.). 330-More facts revealed about I. D. 338-The bottled city of Kandor enlarged. 344-Frankenstein & Dracula app.						6.00
321-323,325-327,329-331,336-338,340,341,343-345,348,350 (Whitman variants; low print run; no issue # on cover)	1	2	3	5	7	9
351-399: 353-Brief origin. 354,355,357-Superman 2020 stories (354-Debut of Superman III). 356-World of Krypton story (also #360,367,375). 366-Fan letter by Todd McFarlane. 372-Superman 2021 story. 376-Free 16 pg. preview Daring New Advs. of Supergirl. 377-Free 16 pg. preview Masters of the Universe						5.00
400 (10/84, $1.50, 68 pgs.)-Many top artists featured; Chaykin painted cover, Miller back-c; Steranko-s/a (10 pages)						6.00
401-422: 405-Super-Batman story. 408-Nuclear Holocaust-c/story. 411-Special Julius Schwartz tribute issue. 414,415-Crisis x-over. 422-Horror-c						4.00
423-Alan Moore scripts; Perez-a(i); last Earth I Superman story, cont'd in Action #583	1	3	4	6	8	10
Annual 1(10/60, 84 pgs.)-Reprints 1st Supergirl story/Action #252; r/Lois Lane #1; Krypto-r (1st Silver Age DC annual)	86	172	258	731	1116	1500
Annual 2(Win, 1960-61)-Super-villain issue; Brainiac, Titano, Metallo, Bizarro origin-r	42	84	126	315	470	625
Annual 3(Sum, 1961)-Strange Lives of Superman	29	58	87	210	310	410
Annual 4(Win, 1961-62)-11th Legion app; 1st Legion origins (text & pictures); advs. in time, space & on alien worlds	24	48	72	174	255	335
Annual 5(Sum, 1962)-All Krypton issue	19	38	57	133	194	255
Annual 6(Win, 1962-63)-Legion-r/Adv. #247	17	34	51	123	182	240
Annual 7(Sum, 1963)-Origin-r/Superman-Batman team/Adv. 275; r/1955 Superman dailies	13	26	39	94	137	180
Annual 8(Win, 1963-64)-All origins issue	11	22	33	80	118	155
Annual 9(8/64)-Was advertised but came out as 80 Page Giant #1 instead						
Annual 9(1983)-Toth/Austin-a						6.00
Annuals 10-12: 10(1984, $1.25)-M. Anderson inks. 11(1985)-Moore scripts. 12(1986)-Bolland-c						4.00
Special 1-3('83-'85): 1-G. Kane-c/a; contains German-r						4.00
The Amazing World of Superman "Official Metropolis Edition" (1973, $2.00, treasury-size)-Origin retold; Wood-r(i) from Superboy #153,161; poster incl. (half price if poster missing)	4	8	12	27	36	45
11195 (2/79, $1.95, 224 pgs.)-Golden Press	3	7	10	21	28	35

NOTE: ***N. Adams** a-249i, 254p; c-204-206, 210, 212-215, 219, 231i, 233-237, 240-243, 249-252, 254, 263, 307, 308, 313, 314, 317. **Adkins** a-323i. **Austin** c-368i. **Wayne Boring** art-late 1940's to early 1960's. **Buckler** a(p)-352, 363, 364, 369; c(p)-324-327, 356, 363, 368, 369, 373, 376, 378. **Burnley** a-252r; c-19-25, 30, 33, 34, 35p, 38p, 39p, 45p. **Fine** a-252r. **Kaluta** a-400. **Gil Kane** a-272r, 367, 372, 375, Special 2; c-374p, 375p, 377, 381, 382, 384-390, 392, Annual 9, Special 2. **Joe Kubert** c-216. **Morrow** a-238. **Mortimer** a-250r. **Perez** c-364p. **Fred Ray** a-25; c-6, 8-18. **Starlin** c-355. **Staton** a-354i, 355i. **Swan/Moldoff** c-149. **Williamson** a(i)-408-410, 412-416; c-408i, 409i. **Wrightson** a-400, 416.*

SUPERMAN (2nd Series)
DC Comics: Jan, 1987 - Present (75¢/$1.00/$1.25/$1.50/$1.95/$1.99)

	GD 2.0	VG 4.0	FN 6.0	VF 8.0	VF/NM 9.0	NM- 9.2
0-(10/94) Zero Hour; released between #93 & #94						2.50
1-Byrne-c/a begins; intro new Metallo						5.00
2-8,10: 3-Legends x-over; Darkseid-c & app. 7-Origin/1st app. Rampage. 8-Legion app.						3.00
9-Joker-c						4.50
11-15,17-20,22-49,51,52,54-56,58-67: 11-1st new Mr. Mxyzptlk. 12-Lori Lemaris revived. 13-1st app. new Toyman. 13,14-Millennium x-over. 20-Doom Patrol app.; Supergirl cameo. 31-Mr. Mxyzptlk app. 37-Newsboy Legion app. 41-Lobo app. 44-Batman storyline, part 1. 45-Free extra 8 pgs. 54-Newsboy Legion story. 63-Aquaman x-over. 67-Last $1.00-c						2.50
16,21: 16-1st app. new Supergirl (4/88). 21-Supergirl-c/story; 1st app. Matrix who becomes new Supergirl						4.00
50-($1.50, 52 pgs.)-Clark Kent proposes to Lois						5.00
50-2nd printing						2.25
53-Clark reveals i.d. to Lois (Cont'd from Action #662)						3.00
53-2nd printing						2.25
57-($1.75, 52 pgs.)						3.00
68-72: 65,66,68-Deathstroke-c/stories. 70-Superman & Robin team-up						2.50
73-Doomsday cameo						5.00
74-Doomsday Pt. 2 (Cont'd from Justice League #69); Superman battles Doomsday						6.00
73,74-2nd printings						2.25
75-($2.50)-Collector's Ed.; Doomsday Pt. 6; Superman dies; polybagged w/poster of funeral, obituary from Daily Planet, postage stamp & armband premiums (direct sales only)	2	4	6	11	14	18
75-Direct sales copy (no upc code, 1st print)	1	2	3	5	6	8
75-Direct sales copy (no upc code, 2nd-4th prints)						2.25
75-Newsstand copy w/upc code	1	2	3	5	6	8
75-Platinum Edition; given away to retailers						55.00
76,77-Funeral For a Friend parts 4 & 8						3.00
78-($1.95)-Collector's Edition with die-cut outer-c & mini poster; Doomsday cameo						3.00
78-($1.50)-Newsstand Edition w/poster and different-c; Doomsday-c & cameo						2.25
79-81,83-89: 83-Funeral for a Friend epilogue; new Batman (Azrael) cameo. 87,88-Bizarro-c/story						2.50
82-($3.50)-Collector's Edition w/all chromium-c; real Superman revealed; Green Lantern x-over from G.L. #46; no ads						6.00
82-($2.00, 44 pgs.)-Regular Edition w/different-c						2.50
90-99: 93-(9/94)-Zero Hour. 94-(11/94). 95-Atom app. 96-Brainiac returns						2.50
100-Death of Clark Kent foil-c						4.00
100-Newsstand						3.00
101-122: 101-Begin $1.95-c; Black Adam app. 105-Green Lantern app. 110-Plastic Man-c/app. 114-Brainiac app; Dwyer-c. 115-Lois leaves Metropolis. 116-(10/96)-1st app. Teen Titans by Jurgens & Perez in 8 pg. preview. 117-Final Night. 118-Wonder Woman app. 119-Legion app. 122-New powers						2.50
123-Collector's Edition w/glow in the dark-c, new costume						6.00
123-Standard ed., new costume						4.00
124-149: 128-Cyborg-c/app. 131-Birth of Lena Luthor. 132-Superman Red/Superman Blue. 134-Millennium Giants. 136,137-Superman 2999. 139-Starlin-a. 140-Grindberg-a						2.50
150-($2.95) Standard Ed.; Brainiac 2.0 app.; Jurgens-s						3.00
150-($3.95) Collector's Ed. w/holo-foil enhanced variant-c						4.00
151-158: 151-Loeb-s begins; Daily Planet reopens						2.25
159-174: 159-$2.25-c begin. 161-Joker-c/app. 162-Aquaman-c/app. 163-Young Justice app. 165-JLA app.; Ramos; Madureira, Liefeld, A. Adams, Wieringo, Churchill-a. 166-Collector's and reg. editions. 167-Return to Krypton. 168-Batman-c/app.(cont'd in Detective #756). 171-173-Our Worlds at War. 173-Sienkiewicz-a (2 pgs.). 174-Adopts black & red "S" logo						2.25
175-($3.50) Joker: Last Laugh x-over; Doomsday-c/app.						3.50
176-189,191-199: 176,180-Churchill-a. 180-Dracula app. 181-Bizarro-c/app. 184-Return to Krypton II. 189-Van Fleet-c. 192,193,195,197-199-New Supergirl app.						2.25
190-($2.25) Regular edition						2.25
190-($3.95) Double-Feature Issue; included reprint of Superman: The 10¢ Adventure						4.00
200-($3.50) Gene Ha-c/art by various; preview art by Yu & Bermejo						3.50
#1,000,000 (11/98) 853rd Century x-over; Gene Ha-c						2.25
Annual 1,2: 1 (1987)-No Byrne-a. 2 (1988)-Byrne-a; Newsboy Legion; Guardian returns						4.00
Annual 3-6 ('91-'94 68 pgs.): 1-Armageddon 2001 x-over; Batman app.; Austin-c(i) & part inks. 4-Eclipso app. 6-Elseworlds sty						3.00
Annual 3-2nd & 3rd printings; 3rd has silver ink						2.25
Annual 7 (1995, $3.95, 69 pgs.)-Year One story						4.00
Annual 8 (1996, $2.95)-Legends of the Dead Earth story						3.00
Annual 9 (1997, $3.95)-Pulp Heroes story						4.00
Annual 10 (1998, $2.95)-Ghosts; Wrightson-c						3.00
Annual 11 (1999, $2.95)-JLApe; Art Adams-c						3.00

Superman Adventures #58 © DC

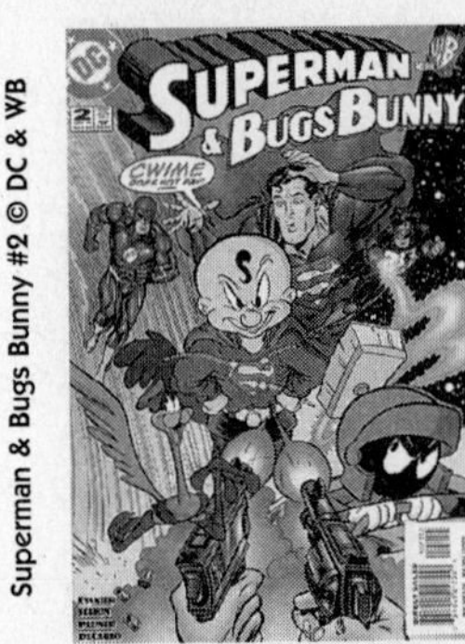

Superman & Bugs Bunny #2 © DC & WB

Superman/Batman #1 © DC

GD 2.0 VG 4.0 FN 6.0 VF 8.0 VF/NM 9.0 NM- 9.2

Annual 12 (2000, $3.50)-Planet DC 3.50
...: Critical Condition ('03, $14.95, TPB) r/2000 Kryptonite poisoning storyline 15.00
...: 80 Page Giant (2/99, $4.95) Jurgens-c 5.00
...: 80 Page Giant 2 (6/99, $4.95) Harris-c 5.00
...: 80 Page Giant 3 (11/00, $5.95) Nowlan-c; art by various 6.00
...: Endgame (2000, $14.95, TPB)-Reprints Y2K and Brainiac story line 15.00
...: Eradication! The Origin of the Eradicator (1996, $12.95, TPB) 13.00
...: Exile (1998, $14.95, TPB)-Reprints space exile following execution of Kryptonian criminals; 1st Eradicator 15.00
... In the Fifties ('02, $19.95, TPB) Intro. by Mark Waid 20.00
... In the Seventies ('00, $19.95, TPB) Intro. by Christopher Reeve 20.00
... No Limits ('00, $14.95, TPB) Reprints early 2000 stories 15.00
...: Our Worlds at War Book 1 ('02, $19.95, TPB) r/1st half of x-over 20.00
...: Our Worlds at War Book 2 ('02, $19.95, TPB) r/2nd half of x-over 20.00
...Plus 1(2/97, $2.95)-Legion of Super-Heroes-c/app. 3.00
...: President Lex TPB (2003, $17.95) r/Luthor's run for the White House; Harris-c 18.00
Special 1 (1992, $3.50, 68 pgs.)-Simonson-c/a 5.00
The Death of Clark Kent (1997, $19.95, TPB)-Reprints Man of Steel #43 (1 page), Superman #99 (1 page),#100-102, Action #709 (1 page), #710,711, Advs. of Superman #523-525, Superman:The Man of Tomorrow #1 20.00
The Death of Superman (1993, $4.95, TPB)-Reprints Man of Steel #17-19, Superman #73-75, Advs. of Superman #496,497, Action #683,684, & Justice League #69
1 2 3 5 6 8
The Death of Superman, 2nd & 3rd printings 5.00
The Death of Superman Platinum Edition 15.00
The Man of Steel Vol. 2 ('03, $19.95, TPB) r/Superman #1-3, Action #584-586, Advs. of Superman #424-426 & Who's Who Update '87 20.00
The Trial of Superman ('97, $14.95, TPB) reprints story arc 15.00
...: They Saved Luthor's Brain ('00, $14.95) r/ "death" and return of Luthor 15.00
...: 'Til Death Do Us Part ('01, $17.95) reprints; Mahnke-c 18.00
...: Time and Time Again (1994, $7.50, TPB)-Reprints 8.00
...: Transformed ('98, $12.95, TPB) r/post Final Night powerless Superman to Electric Superman 13.00
... Vs. The Revenge Squad (1999, $12.95, TPB) 13.00
NOTE: **Austin** *a(i)-1-3.* **Byrne** *a-1-16p, 17, 19-21p, 22; c-1-17, 20-22; scripts-1-22.* **Guice** *c/a-64.* **Kirby** *c-37p.* **Joe Quesada** *c-Annual 4.* **Russell** *c/a-23i.* **Simonson** *c-69i. #19-21 2nd printings sold in multi-packs.*

SUPERMAN (one-shots)
Daily News Magazine Presents DC Comics' Superman nn-(1987, 8 pgs.)-Supplement to New York Daily News; Perez-c/a 5.00
...: A Nation Divided (1999, $4.95)-Elseworlds Civil War story 5.00
... & Savage Dragon: Chicago (2002, $5.95) Larsen-a; Ross-c 6.00
... & Savage Dragon: Metropolis (11/99, $4.95) Bogdanove-a 5.00
...: At Earth's End (1995, $4.95)-Elseworlds story 5.00
...: Blood of My Ancestors (2003, $6.95)-Gil Kane & John Buscema-a 7.00
...: Distant Fires (1998, $5.95)-Elseworlds; Chaykin-s 6.00
...: Emperor Joker (10/00, $3.50)-Follows Action #769 3.50
...: End of the Century (2/00, $24.95, HC)-Immonen-s/a 25.00
...: End of the Century (2003, $17.95, SC)-Immonen-s/a 18.00
... For Earth (1991, $4.95, 52 pgs, printed on recycled paper)-Ordway wraparound-c 5.00
...IV Movie Special (1987, $2.00)-Movie adaptation; Heck-a 3.00
...Gallery, The 1 (1993, $2.95)-Poster-a 3.00
..., Inc. (1999, $6.95)-Elseworlds Clark as a sports hero; Garcia-Lopez-a 7.00
...: Kal (1995, $5.95)-Elseworlds story 6.00
...: Lex 2000 (1/01, $3.50)-Election night for the Luthor Presidency 3.50
...: Monster (1999, $5.95)-Elseworlds story; Anthony Williams-a 6.00
... Movie Special-(9/83)-Adaptation of Superman III; other versions exist with store logos on bottom 1/3 of-c 4.00
...: Our Worlds at War Secret Files 1-(8/01, $5.95)-Stories & profile pages 6.00
...'s Metropolis-(1996, $5.95, prestige format)-Elseworlds; McKeever-c/a 6.00
...: Speeding Bullets-(1993, $4.95, 52 pgs.)-Elseworlds 5.00
.../Spider-Man-(1995, $3.95)-r/DC and Marvel Presents... 4.00
... 10-Cent Adventure 1 (3/02, 10¢) McDaniel-a; intro. Cir-El Supergirl 2.25
...: The Earth Stealers 1-(1988, $2.95, 52 pgs, prestige format) Byrne script; painted-c 4.00
...: The Earth Stealers 1-2nd printing 3.00
...: The Legacy of Superman #1 (3/93, $2.50, 68 pgs.)-Art Adams-c; Simonson-a 4.00
...: The Last God of Krypton ('99,$4.95) Hildebrandt Bros.-a/Simonson-s 5.00
...: The Odyssey ('99, $4.95) Clark Kent's post-Smallville journey 5.00
...: 3-D (12/98, $3.95)-with glasses 4.00
.../Thundercats (1/04, $5.95) Winick-s/Garza-a; two covers by Garza & McGuinness 6.00
.../Toyman-(1996, $1.95) 2.50
...: Under A Yellow Sun (1994, $5.95, 68 pgs.)-A Novel by Clark Kent; embossed-c 6.00
... Vs. Darkseid: Apokolips Now! 1 (3/03, $2.95) McKone-a; Kara (Supergirl #75) app. 3.00
...: War of the Worlds (1999, $5.95)-Battles Martians 6.00
...: Where is thy Sting? (2001, $6.95)-McCormack-Sharp-c/a 7.00

GD 2.0 VG 4.0 FN 6.0 VF 8.0 VF/NM 9.0 NM- 9.2

...: Y2K (2/00, $4.95)-1st Brainiac 13 app.; Guice-c/a 5.00

SUPERMAN ADVENTURES, THE (Based on animated series)
DC Comics: Oct, 1996 - No. 66, Apr, 2002 ($1.75/$1.95/$1.99)
1-Rick Burchett-c/a begins; Paul Dini script; Lex Luthor app.; silver ink, wraparound-c 3.00
2-20,22: 2-McCloud scripts begin; Metallo-c/app. 3-Brainiac-c/app. 6-Mxyzptlk-c/app. 2.50
21-($3.95) 1st animated Supergirl 5.00
23-66: 23-Begin $1.99-c; Livewire app. 25-Batgirl-c/app. 28-Manley-a. 54-Retells Superman #233 "Kryptonite Nevermore" 58-Ross-c 2.25
Annual 1 (1997, $3.95)-Zatanna and Bruce Wayne app. 4.00
Special 1 (2/98, $2.95) Superman vs. Lobo 3.00
TPB (1998, $7.95) r/#1-6 8.00

SUPERMAN ALIENS 2: GOD WAR (Also see Superman Vs. Aliens)
DC Comics/Dark Horse Comics: May, 2002 - No. 4, Nov, 2002 ($2.99, limited series)
1-4-Bogdanove & Nowlan-a; Darkseid & New Gods app. 3.00
TPB (6/03, $12.95) r/#1-4 13.00

SUPERMAN & BATMAN: GENERATIONS (Elseworlds)
DC Comics: 1999 - No. 4, 1999 ($4.95, limited series)
1-4-Superman & Batman team-up from 1939 to the future; Byrne-c/s/a 5.00
TPB (2000, $14.95) r/series 15.00

SUPERMAN & BATMAN: GENERATIONS II (Elseworlds)
DC Comics: 2001 - No. 4, 2001 ($5.95, limited series)
1-4-Superman, Batman & others team-up from 1942-future; Byrne-c/s/a 6.00
TPB (2003, $19.95) r/series 20.00

SUPERMAN & BATMAN: GENERATIONS III (Elseworlds)
DC Comics: Mar, 2003 - No. 12, Feb, 2004 ($2.95, limited series)
1-12-Superman & Batman through the centuries; Byrne-c/s/a 3.00

SUPERMAN & BATMAN: WORLD'S FUNNEST (Elseworlds)
DC Comics: 2000 ($6.95, square-bound, one-shot)
nn-Mr. Mxyzptlk and Bat-Mite destroy each DC Universe; Dorkin-s/ art by various incl. Ross, Timm, Miller, Allred, Moldoff, Gibbons, Cho, Jimenez 7.00

SUPERMAN & BUGS BUNNY
DC Comics: Jul, 2000 - No. 4, Oct, 2000 ($2.50, limited series)
1-4-JLA & Looney Tunes characters meet 2.50

SUPERMAN/BATMAN
DC Comics: Oct, 2003 - Present ($2.95)
1-Two covers (Superman or Batman in foreground) Loeb-s/McGuinness-a; Metallo app. 5.00
1-2nd printing (Batman cover) 3.00
1-3rd printing; new McGuinness cover 3.00
1-Diamond/Alliance Retailer Summit Edition-variant cover 100.00
2-5: 2,5-Future Superman app. 3.00
...Secret Files 2003 (11/03, $4.95) Reis-a; pin-ups by various; Loeb/Sale short-s 5.00

SUPERMAN/BATMAN: ALTERNATE HISTORIES
DC Comics: 1996 ($14.95, trade paperback)
nn-Reprints Detective Comics Annual #7, Action Comics Annual #6, Steel Annual #1, Legends of the Dark Knight Annual #4 15.00

SUPERMAN: BIRTHRIGHT
DC Comics: Sept, 2003 - No. 12 ($2.95, limited series)
1-6-Waid-s/Leinil Yu-a; Clark Kent between college and early Superman years 3.00

SUPERMAN: DAY OF DOOM
DC Comics: Jan, 2003 - No. 4, Feb, 2003 ($2.95, weekly limited series)
1-4-Jurgens-s/Jurgens & Sienkiewicz-a 3.00
TPB (2003, $9.95) r/#1-4 10.00

SUPERMAN/DOOMSDAY: HUNTER/PREY
DC Comics: 1994 - No. 3, 1994 ($4.95, limited series, 52 pgs.)
1-3 5.00

SUPERMAN FAMILY, THE (Formerly Superman's Pal Jimmy Olsen)
National Per. Publ./DC Comics: No. 164, Apr-May, 1974 - No. 222, Sept, 1982
164-(100 pgs.) Jimmy Olsen, Supergirl, Lois Lane begin
4 8 12 29 40 50
165-169 (100 pgs.) 3 6 9 19 25 32
170-176 (68 pgs.) 2 4 6 12 16 20
177-190 (52 pgs.): 177-181-52 pgs. 182-Marshall Rogers-a; $1.00 issues begin; Krypto begins, ends #192. 183-Nightwing-Flamebird begins, ends #194. 189-Brainiac 5, Mon-el app. 2 4 6 9 11 14
191-193,195-199: 191-Superboy begins, ends #198 1 2 3 5 7 9
194,200: 194-Rogers-a. 200-Book length sty 1 3 4 6 8 10

Superman For All Seasons #1 © DC

Superman: Red Son #1 © DC

Superman's Girlfriend Lois Lane #135 © DC

	GD 2.0	VG 4.0	FN 6.0	VF 8.0	VF/NM 9.0	NM- 9.2
201-222: 211-Earth II Batman & Catwoman marry	1	2	3	4	5	7

NOTE: *N. Adams c-182-185. Anderson a-186i. Buckler c(p)-190, 191, 209, 210, 215, 217, 220. Jones a-191-193. Gil Kane c(p)-221, 222. Mortimer a(p)-191-193, 199, 201-222. Orlando a(i)-186, 187. Rogers a-182, 194. Staton a-191-194, 196p. Tuska a(p)-203, 207-209.*

SUPERMAN/FANTASTIC FOUR
DC Comics/Marvel Comics: 1999 ($9.95, tabloid size, one-shot)
1-Battle Galactus and the Cyborg; wraparound-c by Alex Ross and Dan Jurgens; Jurgens-s/a; Thibert-a 10.00

SUPERMAN FOR ALL SEASONS
DC Comics: 1998 - No, 4, 1998 ($4.95, limited series, prestige format)
1-Loeb-s/Sale-a/c; Superman's first year in Metropolis 6.00
2-4 5.00
Hardcover (1999, $24.95) r/#1-4 25.00

SUPERMAN FOR EARTH (See Superman one-shots)

SUPERMAN FOREVER
DC Comics: Jun, 1998 ($5.95, one-shot)
1-($5.95)-Collector's Edition with a 7-image lenticular-c by Alex Ross; Superman returns to normal; s/a by various 7.00
1-($4.95) Standard Edition with single image Ross-c 5.00

SUPERMAN/GEN13
DC Comics (WildStorm): Jun, 2000 - No. 3, Aug, 2000 ($2.50, limited series)
1-3-Hughes-s/ Bermejo-a; Campbell variant-c for each 2.50
TPB (2001, $9.95) new Bermejo-c; cover gallery 10.00

SUPERMAN: KING OF THE WORLD
DC Comics: June, 1999 ($3.95/$4.95, one-shot)
1-($3.95) Regular Ed. 4.00
1-($4.95) Collectors' Ed. with gold foil enhanced-c 5.00

SUPERMAN: LAST SON OF EARTH
DC Comics: 2000 - No. 2, 2000 ($5.95, limited series, prestige format)
1,2-Elseworlds; baby Clark rockets to Krypton; Gerber-s/Wheatley-a 6.00

SUPERMAN: LAST STAND ON KRYPTON
DC Comics: 2003 ($6.95, one-shot, prestige format)
1-Sequel to Superman: Last Son of Earth; Gerber-s/Wheatley-a 7.00

SUPERMAN: LOIS LANE (Girlfrenzy)
DC Comics: Jun, 1998 ($1.95, one shot)
1-Connor & Palmiotti-a 2.25

SUPERMAN/MADMAN HULLABALOO!
Dark Horse Comics: June, 1997 - No. 3, Aug, 1997 ($2.95, limited series)
1-3-Mike Allred-c/s/a 3.00
TPB (1997, $8.95) 9.00

SUPERMAN: METROPOLIS
DC Comics: Apr, 2003 - No. 12, Mar, 2004 ($2.95, limited series)
1-11-Focus on Jimmy Olsen; Austen-s. 1-6-Zezelj-a. 7-12-Kristiansen-a. 8,9-Creeper app. 3.00

SUPERMAN METROPOLIS SECRET FILES
DC Comics: Jun, 2000 ($4.95, one shot)
1-Short stories, pin-ups and profile pages; Hitch and Neary-c 5.00

SUPERMAN: PEACE ON EARTH
DC Comics: Jan, 1999 ($9.95, Treasury-sized, one-shot)
1-Alex Ross painted-c/a; Paul Dini-s 12.00

SUPERMAN: RED SON
DC Comics: 2003 - No. 3, 2003 ($5.95, limited series, prestige format)
1-Elseworlds; Superman's rocket lands in Russia; Mark Millar-s/Dave Johnson-c/a 10.00
2,3 6.00
TPB (2004, $17.95) r/#1-3; intro. by Tom DeSanto; sketch pages 18.00

SUPERMAN RED/ SUPERMAN BLUE
DC Comics: Feb, 1998 ($4.95, one shot)
1-Polybagged w/3-D glasses and reprint of Superman 3-D (1955); Jurgens-plot/3-D cover; script and art by various 5.00
1-($3.95)-Standard Ed.; comic only, non 3-D cover 4.00

SUPERMAN: SAVE THE PLANET
DC Comics: Oct, 1998 ($2.95, one-shot)
1-($2.95) Regular Ed.; Luthor buys the Daily Planet 3.00
1-($3.95) Collector's Ed. with acetate cover 4.00

SUPERMAN SCRAPBOOK (Has blank pages; contains no comics)

SUPERMAN: SECRET FILES
DC Comics: Jan, 1998; May 1999 ($4.95)
1,2: 1-Retold origin story, "lost" pages & pin-ups 5.00

SUPERMAN: SECRET IDENTITY
DC Comics: 2004 - No. 4, 2004 ($5.95, squarebound, mini-series)
1-Busiek-s/Immonen-a/c 6.00

SUPERMAN'S GIRLFRIEND LOIS LANE (See Action Comics #1, 80 Page Giant #3, 14, Lois Lane, Showcase #9, 10, Superman #28 & Superman Family)

SUPERMAN'S GIRLFRIEND LOIS LANE (See Showcase #9,10)
National Periodical Publ.: Mar-Apr, 1958 - No. 136, Jan-Feb, 1974; No. 137, Sept-Oct, 1974

	GD 2.0	VG 4.0	FN 6.0	VF 8.0	VF/NM 9.0	NM- 9.2
1-(3-4/58)	297	594	891	2600	4200	5800
2	77	154	231	655	1003	1350
3	51	102	153	434	667	900
4,5	44	88	132	352	526	700
6,7	35	70	105	263	394	525
8-10: 9-Pat Boone-c/story	30	60	90	220	323	425
11-13,15-19: 12-(10/59)-Aquaman app.	19	38	57	133	194	255
14-Supergirl x-over; Batman app. on-c only	19	38	57	138	202	265
20-Supergirl-c/sty	18	38	57	138	202	265
21-28: 23-1st app. Lena Thorul, Lex Luthor's sister; 1st Lois as Elastic Lass. 27-Bizarro-c/story	14	28	42	102	149	195
29-Aquaman, Batman, Green Arrow cover app. and cameo; last 10¢ issue	15	30	45	107	156	205
30-32,34-46,48,49	9	18	27	60	85	110
33(5/62)-Mon-el app.	9	18	27	65	93	120
47-Legion app.	9	18	27	65	93	120
50(7/64)-Triplicate Girl, Phantom Girl & Shrinking Violet app.	9	18	27	63	89	115
51-55,57-67,69: 59-Jor-el app.; Batman back-up sty	7	14	21	50	68	85
56-Saturn Girl app.	7	14	21	51	71	90
68-(Giant G-26)	9	18	27	60	85	110
70-Penguin & Catwoman app. (1st S.A. Catwoman, 11/66; also see Detective #369 for 3rd app.); Batman & Robin cameo	25	50	75	181	266	350
71-Batman & Robin cameos (3 panels); Catwoman story cont'd from #70 (2nd app.); see Detective #369 for 3rd app	14	28	42	102	149	195
72,73,75,76,78	6	12	18	38	52	65
74-1st Bizarro Flash (5/67); JLA cameo	6	12	18	40	55	70
77-(Giant G-39)	7	14	21	51	71	90
79-Neal Adams-c or c(i) begin, end #95,108	6	12	18	40	55	70
80-85,87,88,90-92: 92-Last 12¢ issue	4	8	12	27	36	45
86,95 (Giants G-51,G-63)-Both have Neal Adams-c	6	12	18	43	59	75
89,93: 89-Batman x-over; all N. Adams-c. 93-Wonder Woman-c/story	4	8	12	28	38	48
94,96-99,101-103,107-110	3	7	10	21	28	35
100	4	8	12	24	32	40
104-(Giant G-75)	6	12	18	38	52	65
105-Origin/1st app. The Rose & the Thorn.	6	12	18	38	52	65
106-"Black Like Me" sty; Lois changes her skin color to black	5	10	15	36	48	60
111-Justice League-c/s; Morrow-a; last 15¢ issue	4	8	12	24	32	40
112,114-123 (52 pgs.): 122-G.A. Lois Lane-r/Superman #30. 123-G.A. Batman-r/Batman #35 (w/Catwoman)	4	8	12	22	30	38
113-(Giant G-87) Kubert-a (previously unpublished G.A. story)(scarce in NM)	6	12	18	43	59	75
124-135: 130-Last Rose & the Thorn. 132-New Zatanna story	2	4	6	14	18	22
136,137: 136-Wonder Woman x-over	3	6	9	16	20	25
Annual 1(Sum, 1962)-r/L. Lane #12; Aquaman app.	22	44	66	160	235	310
Annual 2(Sum, 1963)	15	30	45	104	152	200

NOTE: *Buckler a-117-121p. Curt Swan or Kurt Schaffenberger a-1-81(most); c(p)-1-15.*

SUPERMAN: SILVER BANSHEE
DC Comics: Dec, 1998 - No. 2, Jan, 1999 ($2.25, mini-series)
1,2-Brereton-s/c; Chin-a 2.25

SUPERMAN'S NEMESIS: LEX LUTHOR
DC Comics: Mar, 1999 - No. 4, Jun, 1999 ($2.50, mini-series)
1-4-Semeiks-a 2.50

SUPERMAN'S PAL JIMMY OLSEN (Superman Family #164 on)
(See Action Comics #6 for 1st app. & 80 Page Giant)
National Periodical Publ.: Sept-Oct, 1954 - No. 163, Feb-Mar, 1974 (Fourth World #133-148)

	GD 2.0	VG 4.0	FN 6.0	VF 8.0	VF/NM 9.0	NM- 9.2
1	405	810	1215	3706	6003	8300
2	128	256	384	1088	1644	2200

Superman's Pal Jimmy Olsen #138 © DC

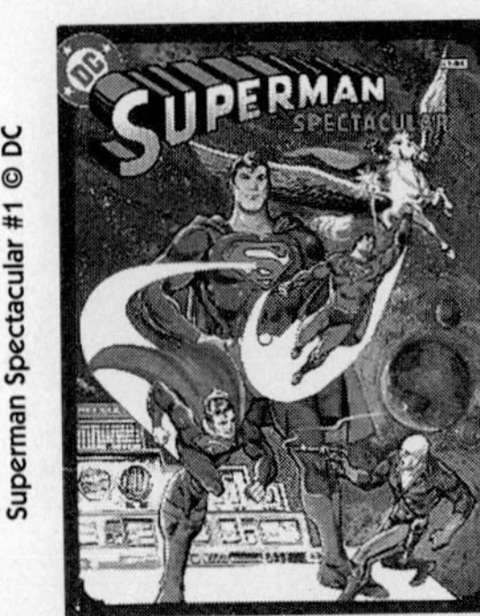

Superman Spectacular #1 © DC

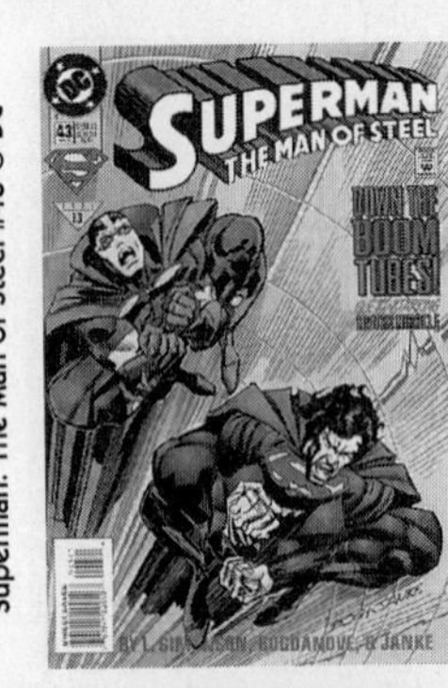

Superman: The Man of Steel #43 © DC

	GD 2.0	VG 4.0	FN 6.0	VF 8.0	VF/NM 9.0	NM- 9.2

3-Last pre-code issue 69 138 207 587 894 1200
4,5 52 104 156 416 621 825
6-10 37 74 111 278 414 550
11-20: 15-1st S.A. issue 26 52 78 189 277 365
21-30: 29-(6/58) 1st app. Krypto with Superman 17 34 51 121 178 235
31-Origin & 1st app. Elastic Lad (Jimmy Olsen) 15 30 45 109 160 210
32-40: 33-One pg. biography of Jack Larson (TV Jimmy Olsen). 36-Intro Lucy Lane. 37-2nd app. Elastic Lad & 1st cover app. 12 24 36 87 129 170
41-50: 41-1st J.O. Robot. 48-Intro/origin Superman Emergency Squad 10 20 30 72 104 135
51-56: 56-Last 10¢ issue 8 16 24 58 82 105
57-62,64-70: 57-Olsen marries Supergirl. 62-Mon-el & Elastic Lad app. but not as Legionnaires. 70-Element Boy (Lad) app. 6 12 18 43 59 75
63(9/62)-Legion of Super-Villains app. 7 14 21 46 63 80
71,74,75,78,80-84,86,89,90: 86-Jimmy Olsen Robot becomes Congorilla 5 10 15 36 48 60
72,73,76,77,79,85,87,88: 72(10/63)-Legion app; Elastic Lad (Olsen) joins. 73-Ultra Boy app. 76,85-Legion app. 76-Legion app. 77-Olsen with Colossal Boy's powers & costume; origin Titano retold. 79-(9/64)-Titled The Red-headed Beatle of 1000 B.C. 85-Legion app. 87-Legion of Super-Villains app. 88-Star Boy app. 6 12 18 38 52 65
91-94,96-98 4 8 12 29 40 50
95 (Giant G-25) 7 14 21 51 71 90
99-Olsen w/powers & costumes of Lightning Lad, Sun Boy & Element Lad 5 10 15 33 44 55
100-Legion cameo 5 10 15 36 48 60
101-103,105-112,114-120: 106-Legion app. 110-Infinity-c. 117-Batman & Legion cameo. 120-Last 12¢ issue 3 7 10 21 28 35
104 (Giant G-38) 6 12 18 40 55 70
113,122,131,140 (Giants G-50,G-62,G-74,G-86) 5 10 15 36 48 60
121,123-130,132 3 6 9 18 24 30
133-(10/70)-Jack Kirby story & art begins; re-intro Newsboy Legion; 1st app. Morgan Edge 7 14 21 46 63 80
134-1st app. Darkseid (1 panel, 12/70) 8 16 24 53 74 95
135-2nd app. Darkseid (1 pg. cameo; see New Gods & Forever People); G.A. Guardian app. 5 10 15 33 44 55
136-139: 136-Origin new Guardian. 138-Partial photo-c. 139-Last 15¢ issue 4 8 12 27 36 45
141-150: (25¢,52 pgs.). 141-Photo-c; Newsboy Legion-r by S&K begin; full pg. self-portrait of Jack Kirby; Don Rickles cameo. 149,150-G.A. Plastic Man-r in both; 150-Newsboy Legion app. 4 8 12 24 32 40
151-163 2 4 6 14 18 22

NOTE: *Issues #141-148 contain* ***Simon & Kirby*** *Newsboy Legion reprints from Star Spangled #7, 8, 9, 10, 11, 12, 13, 14 in that order.* ***N. Adams*** *c-109-112, 115, 117, 118, 120, 121, 132, 134-136, 147, 148.* ***Kirby*** *a-133-139p, 141-148p; c-133, 137, 139, 142, 145p.* ***Kirby/N. Adams*** *c-137, 138, 141-144, 146.* ***Curt Swan*** *c-1-14(most)., 140.*

SUPERMAN SPECTACULAR (Also see DC Special Series #5)
DC Comics: 1982 (Magazine size, 52 pgs., square binding)

1-Saga of Superman Red/ Superman Blue; Luthor and Terra-Man app.; Gonzales & Colletta-a 1 3 4 6 8 10

SUPERMAN / TARZAN: SONS OF THE JUNGLE
Dark Horse Comics: Oct, 2001 - No. 3, May, 2002 ($2.99, limited series)

1-3-Elseworlds; Kal-El lands in the jungle; Dixon-s/Meglia-a/Ramos-c 3.00

SUPERMAN: THE DARK SIDE
DC Comics: 1998 - No. 3, 1998 ($4.95, squarebound, mini-series)

1-3: Elseworlds; Kal-El lands on Apokolips 5.00

SUPERMAN: THE DOOMSDAY WARS
DC Comics: 1998 - No. 3, 1999 ($4.95, squarebound, mini-series)

1-3: Superman & JLA vs. Doomsday; Jurgens-s/a(p) 5.00

SUPERMAN: THE KANSAS SIGHTING
DC Comics: 2003 - No. 2, 2003 ($6.95, squarebound, mini-series)

1,2-DeMatteis-s/Tolagson-a 7.00

SUPERMAN: THE MAN OF STEEL (Also see Man of Steel, The)
DC Comics: July, 1991 - No. 134, Mar, 2003 ($1.00/$1.25/$1.50/$1.95/$2.25)

0-(10/94) Zero Hour; released between #37 & #38 2.50
1-($1.75, 52 pgs.)-Painted-c 5.00
2-16: 3-War of the Gods x-over. 5-Reads sideways. 10-Last $1.00-c. 14-Superman & Robin team-up 3.00
17-1st app. Doomsday (cameo) 1 2 3 4 5 7
17,18: 17-2nd printing. 18-2nd & 3rd printings 2.25
18-1st full app. Doomsday 1 2 3 5 7 9
19-Doomsday battle issue (c/story) 6.00
20-22: 20,21-Funeral for a Friend. 22-($1.95)-Collector's Edition w/die-cut outer-c & bound-in poster; Steel-c/story 2.50
22-($1.50)-Newsstand Ed. w/poster & different-c 2.25
23-49,51-99: 30-Regular edition. 32-Bizarro-c/story. 35,36-Worlds Collide Pt. 1 & 10. 37-(9/94)-Zero Hour x-over. 38-(11/94). 48-Aquaman app. 54-Spectre-c/app; Lex Luthor app. 56-Mxyzptlk-c/app. 57-G.A. Flash app. 58-Supergirl app. 59-Parasite-c/app.; Steel app. 60-Reintro Bottled City of Kandor. 62-Final Night. 64-New Gods app. 67-New powers. 75-"Death" of Mxyzptlk. 78,79-Millennium Giants. 80-Golden Age style. 92-JLA app. 98-Metal Men app. 2.50
30-($2.50)-Collector's Edition; polybagged with Superman & Lobo vinyl clings that stick to wraparound-c; Lobo-c/story 3.00
50 ($2.95)-The Trial of Superman 4.00
100-($2.99) New Fortress of Solitude revealed 3.00
100-($3.99) Special edition with fold out cardboard-c 4.00
101,102-101-Batman app. 2.25
103-133: 103-Begin $2.25. 105-Batman-c/app. 111-Return to Krypton. 115-117-Our Worlds at War. 117-Maxima killed. 121-Royal Flush Gang app. 128-Return to Krypton II. 2.25
134-($2.75) Last issue; Steel app.; Bogdanove-c 2.75
#1,000,000 (11/98) 853rd Century x-over; Gene Ha-c 2.50
Annual 1-5 ('92-'96,68 pgs.): 1-Eclipso app.; Joe Quesada-c(p). 2-Intro Edge. 3 -Elseworlds; Mignola-c; Batman app. 4-Year One story. 5-Legends of the Dead Earth story 3.00
Annual 6 (1997, $3.95)-Pulp Heroes story 4.00
...Gallery (1995, $3.50) Pin-ups by various 3.50

SUPERMAN: THE MAN OF TOMORROW
DC Comics: 1995 - No. 15, Fall, 1999 ($1.95, quarterly)

1-15: 1-Lex Luthor app. 3-Lex Luthor-c/app; Joker app. 4-Shazam! app. 5-Wedding of Lex Luthor. 10-Maxima-c/app. 13-JLA-c/app. 2.50
#1,000,000 (11/98) 853rd Century x-over; Gene Ha-c 2.50

SUPERMAN: THE SECRET YEARS
DC Comics: Feb, 1985 - No. 4, May, 1985 (limited series)

1-4-Miller-c on all 3.00

SUPERMAN: THE WEDDING ALBUM
DC Comics: Dec, 1996 ($4.95, 96 pgs, one-shot)

1-Standard Edition-Story & art by past and present Superman creators; gatefold back-c. Byrne-c 5.00
1-Collector's Edition-Embossed cardstock variant-c w/ metallic silver ink and matte and gloss varnishes 5.00
TPB ('97, $14.95) r/Wedding and honeymoon stories 15.00

SUPERMAN 3-D (See Three-Dimension Adventures)

SUPERMAN-TIM (See Promotional Comics section)

SUPERMAN VILLAINS SECRET FILES
DC Comics: Jun, 1998 ($4.95, one shot)

1-Origin stories, "lost" pages & pin-ups 5.00

SUPERMAN VS. ALIENS (Also see Superman Aliens 2: God War)
DC Comics/Dark Horse Comics: July, 1995 - No. 3, Sept, 1995 ($4.95, limited series)

1-3: Jurgens/Nowlan-a 5.00

SUPERMAN VS. MUHAMMAD ALI (See All-New Collectors' Edition C-56)

SUPERMAN VS. PREDATOR
DC Comics/Dark Horse Comics: 2000 - No. 3, 2000 ($4.95, limited series)

1-3-Micheline-s/Maleev-a 5.00
TPB (2001, $14.95) r/series 15.00

SUPERMAN VS. THE AMAZING SPIDER-MAN (Also see Marvel Treasury Edition No. 28)
National Periodical Publications/Marvel Comics Group: 1976 ($2.00, Treasury sized, 100 pgs.)

1-Superman and Spider-Man battle Lex Luthor and Dr. Octopus; Andru/Giordano-a; 1st Marvel/DC x-over. 7 14 21 51 71 90
1-2nd printing; 5000 numbered copies signed by Stan Lee & Carmine Infantino on front cover & sold through mail 13 26 39 90 133 175
nn-(1995, $5.95)-r/#1 6.00

SUPERMAN VS. THE TERMINATOR: DEATH TO THE FUTURE
Dark Horse/DC Comics: Dec, 1999 - No. 4, Mar, 2000 ($2.95, limited series)

1-4-Grant-s/Pugh-a/c: Steel and Supergirl app. 3.00

SUPERMAN/WONDER WOMAN: WHOM GODS DESTROY
DC Comics: 1997 ($4.95, prestige format, limited series)

1-4-Elseworlds; Claremont-s 5.00

SUPERMAN WORKBOOK
National Periodical Publ./Juvenile Group Foundation: 1945 (B&W, reprints, 68 pgs)

nn-Cover-r/Superman #14 150 300 450 938 1407 1875

Supermouse #15 © STD

Super-Mystery Comics V2#4 © ACE

Supersnipe Comics V4#6 © CN

SUPER MANGA BLAST
Dark Horse Comics: Mar, 2000 - Present ($4.95/$4.99, B&W, anthology)

	GD 2.0	VG 4.0	FN 6.0	VF 8.0	VF/NM 9.0	NM- 9.2
1-14-Reprints Oh My Goddess, 3X3 Eyes, What's Michael and others						5.00

SUPER MARIO BROS. (Also see Adventures of the..., Blip, Gameboy, and Nintendo Comics System)
Valiant Comics: 1990 - No. 5?, 1991 ($1.95, slick-c) V2#1, 1991 - No. 5, 1991

	GD 2.0	VG 4.0	FN 6.0	VF 8.0	VF/NM 9.0	NM- 9.2
1-Wildman-a						4.00
2-5, V2#1-5-($1.50)						3.00
Special Edition 1 (1990, $1.95)-Wildman-a						3.00

SUPERMEN OF AMERICA
DC Comics: Mar, 1999 ($3.95/$4.95, one-shot)

	GD 2.0	VG 4.0	FN 6.0	VF 8.0	VF/NM 9.0	NM- 9.2
1-($3.95) Regular Ed.; Immonen-s/art by various						4.00
1-($4.95) Collectors' Ed. with membership kit						5.00

SUPERMEN OF AMERICA (Mini-series)
DC Comics: Mar, 2000 - No. 6, Aug, 2000 ($2.50)

	GD 2.0	VG 4.0	FN 6.0	VF 8.0	VF/NM 9.0	NM- 9.2
1-6-Nicieza-s/Braithwaite-a						2.50

SUPERMOUSE (...the Big Cheese; see Coo Coo Comics)
Standard Comics/Pines No. 35 on (Literary Ent.): Dec, 1948 - No. 34, Sept, 1955; No. 35, Apr, 1956 - No. 45, Fall, 1958

	GD 2.0	VG 4.0	FN 6.0	VF 8.0	VF/NM 9.0	NM- 9.2
1-Frazetta text illos (3)	30	60	90	170	240	310
2-Frazetta text illos	15	30	45	84	115	145
3,5,6-Text illos by Frazetta in all	13	26	39	74	100	125
4-Two pg. text illos by Frazetta	14	28	42	79	107	135
7-10	8	16	24	43	54	65
11-20: 13-Racist humor (Indians)	7	14	21	35	43	50
21-45	6	12	18	28	34	40
1-Summer Holiday issue (Summer, 1957, 25¢, 100 pgs.)-Pines	14	28	42	79	107	135
2-Giant Summer issue (Summer, 1958, 25¢, 100 pgs.)-Pines; has games, puzzles & stories	10	20	30	56	73	90

SUPER-MYSTERY COMICS
Ace Magazines (Periodical House): July, 1940 - V8#6, July, 1949

	GD 2.0	VG 4.0	FN 6.0	VF 8.0	VF/NM 9.0	NM- 9.2
V1#1-Magno, the Magnetic Man & Vulcan begins (1st app.); Q-13, Corp. Flint, & Sky Smith begin	300	600	900	1900	2850	3800
2	96	192	288	600	900	1200
3-The Black Spider begins (1st app.)	77	154	231	481	721	960
4-Origin Davy	55	110	165	344	515	685
5-Intro. The Clown & begin series (12/40)	60	120	180	375	563	750
6(2/41)	50	100	150	300	450	600
V2#1(4/41)-Origin Buckskin	48	96	144	288	432	575
2-6(2/42): 6-Vulcan begins again	46	92	138	276	413	550
V3#1(4/42),2: 1-Black Ace begins	40	80	120	240	350	460
3-Intro. The Lancer; Dr. Nemesis & The Sword begin; Kurtzman-c/a(2) (Mr. Risk & Paul Revere Jr.); Robot-c	52	104	156	312	466	620
4-Kurtzman-c/a	45	90	135	270	403	535
5-Kurtzman-a(2); L.B. Cole-a; Mr. Risk app.	50	100	150	300	450	600
6(10/43)-Mr. Risk app.; Kurtzman's Paul Revere Jr.; L.B. Cole-a	50	100	150	300	450	600
V4#1(1/44)-L.B. Cole-a	44	88	132	264	395	525
2-6(4/45): 2,5,6-Mr. Risk app.	33	66	99	190	270	350
V5#1(7/45)-6	33	66	99	190	270	350
V6#1-6: 3-Torture c-story. 4-Last Magno. Mr. Risk app. in #2,4-6. 6-New logo	26	52	78	150	210	270
V7#1-6, V8#1-4,6	24	48	72	135	190	245
V8#5-Meskin, Tuska, Sid Greene-a	24	48	72	135	190	245

NOTE: ***Sid Greene*** *a-V7#4.* **Mooney** *c-V1#5, 6, V2#1-6.* **Palais** *a-V5#3, 4; c-V4#6-V5#4, V6#2, V8#4. Bondage c-V2#5, 6, V3#2, 5. Magno c-V1#1-V3#6, V4#2-V5#5, V6#2. The Sword c-V4#1, 6(w/Magno).*

SUPERNATURAL LAW (Formerly Wolff & Byrd, Counselors of the Macabre)
Exhibit A Press: No. 24, Oct, 1999 - Present ($2.50/$2.95, B&W)

	GD 2.0	VG 4.0	FN 6.0	VF 8.0	VF/NM 9.0	NM- 9.2
24-35-Batton Lash-s/a. 29-Marie Severin-c. 33-Cerebus spoof						2.50
36-38-($2.95). 37-Frank Cho pin-up and story panels						3.00

SUPERNATURAL LAW SECRETARY MAVIS
Exhibit A Press: 2001 - Present ($2.95/$3.50, B&W)

	GD 2.0	VG 4.0	FN 6.0	VF 8.0	VF/NM 9.0	NM- 9.2
1-3: 3-DeCarlo-c						3.00
4-($3.50) Jaime Hernandez-c						3.50

SUPERNATURALS
Marvel Comics: Dec, 1998 - No. 4, Dec, 1998 ($3.99, weekly limited series)

	GD 2.0	VG 4.0	FN 6.0	VF 8.0	VF/NM 9.0	NM- 9.2
1-4-Pulido-s/Balent-c; bound-in Halloween masks						4.00
1-4-With bound-in Ghost Rider mask (1 in 10)						4.00

SUPERNATURAL THRILLERS
Marvel Comics Group: Dec, 1972 - No. 6, Nov, 1973; No. 7, Jun, 1974 - No. 15, Oct, 1975

	GD 2.0	VG 4.0	FN 6.0	VF 8.0	VF/NM 9.0	NM- 9.2
1-It!; Sturgeon adap. (see Astonishing Tales #21)	3	6	9	18	23	28
2-4,6: 2-The Invisible Man; H.G. Wells adapt. 3-The Valley of the Worm; R.E. Howard adapt. 4-Dr. Jekyll & Mr. Hyde; R.L. Stevenson adapt.. 6-The Headless Horseman; last 20¢ issue	2	4	6	10	13	16
5-1st app. The Living Mummy	6	12	18	40	55	70
7-15: 7-The Living Mummy begins	2	4	6	14	18	22

NOTE: **Brunner** *c-11.* **Buckler** *a-5p.* **Ditko** *a-8r, 9r.* **G. Kane** *a-3p; c-3, 9p, 15p.* **Mayerik** *a-2p, 7, 8, 9p, 10p, 11.* **McWilliams** *a-14i.* **Mortimer** *a-4.* **Steranko** *c-1, 2.* **Sutton** *a-15.* **Tuska** *a-6p.*

SUPERPATRIOT (Also see Freak Force & Savage Dragon #2)
Image Comics (Highbrow Entertainment): July, 1993 - No. 4, Dec, 1993 ($1.95, lim. series)

	GD 2.0	VG 4.0	FN 6.0	VF 8.0	VF/NM 9.0	NM- 9.2
1-4: Dave Johnson-c/a; Larsen scripts; Giffen plots						2.50

SUPERPATRIOT: AMERICA'S FIGHTING FORCE
Image Comics: July, 2002 - No. 4, Oct, 2002 ($2.95, limited series)

	GD 2.0	VG 4.0	FN 6.0	VF 8.0	VF/NM 9.0	NM- 9.2
1-4-Cory Walker-a/c; Savage Dragon app.						3.00

SUPERPATRIOT: LIBERTY & JUSTICE
Image Comics (Highbrow Entertainment): July, 1995 - No. 4, Oct, 1995 ($2.50, lim. series)

	GD 2.0	VG 4.0	FN 6.0	VF 8.0	VF/NM 9.0	NM- 9.2
1-4: Dave Johnson-c/a. 1-1st app. Liberty & Justice						2.50
TPB (2002, $12.95) r/#1-4; new cover by Dave Johnson; sketch pages						13.00

SUPER POWERS (1st Series)
DC Comics: July, 1984 - No. 5, Nov, 1984

	GD 2.0	VG 4.0	FN 6.0	VF 8.0	VF/NM 9.0	NM- 9.2
1-5: 1-Joker/Penguin-c/story; Batman app.; all Kirby-c. 5-Kirby c/a						5.00

SUPER POWERS (2nd Series)
DC Comics: Sept, 1985 - No. 6, Feb, 1986

	GD 2.0	VG 4.0	FN 6.0	VF 8.0	VF/NM 9.0	NM- 9.2
1-6: Kirby-c/a; Capt. Marvel & Firestorm join; Batman cameo; Darkseid storyline in all. 4-Batman cameo. 5,6-Batman app.						5.00

SUPER POWERS (3rd Series)
DC Comics: Sept, 1986 - No. 4, Dec, 1986

	GD 2.0	VG 4.0	FN 6.0	VF 8.0	VF/NM 9.0	NM- 9.2
1-4: 1-Cyborg joins; 1st app. Samurai from Super Friends TV show. 1-4-Batman cameos; Darkseid storyline in #1-4						4.00

SUPER PUP (Formerly Spotty The Pup) (See Space Comics)
Avon Periodicals: No. 4, Mar-Apr, 1954 - No. 5, 1954

	GD 2.0	VG 4.0	FN 6.0	VF 8.0	VF/NM 9.0	NM- 9.2
4,5: 5-Robot-c	6	12	18	31	38	45

SUPER RABBIT (See All Surprise, Animated Movie Tunes, Comedy Comics, Comic Capers, Ideal Comics, It's A Duck's Life, Movie Tunes & Wisco)
Timely Comics (CmPl): Fall, 1944 - No. 14, Nov, 1948

	GD 2.0	VG 4.0	FN 6.0	VF 8.0	VF/NM 9.0	NM- 9.2
1-Hitler & Hirohito-c; war effort paper recycling PSA by S&K; Ziggy Pig & Silly begin?	70	140	210	438	657	875
2	36	72	108	204	290	375
3-5	23	46	69	130	183	235
6-Origin	25	50	75	144	198	255
7-10: 9-Infinity-c	14	28	42	81	111	140
11-Kurtzman's "Hey Look"	15	30	45	86	118	150
12-14	14	28	42	81	111	140
I.W. Reprint #1,2('58),7,10('63): 1-r/#13. 2-r/#10.	2	4	6	10	13	16

SUPER RICHIE (Superichie #5 on) (See Richie Rich Millions #68)
Harvey Publications: Sept, 1975 - No. 4, Mar, 1976 (All 52 pg. Giants)

	GD 2.0	VG 4.0	FN 6.0	VF 8.0	VF/NM 9.0	NM- 9.2
1	3	6	9	16	20	25
2-4	2	4	6	10	13	16

SUPER SLUGGERS (Baseball)
Ultimate Sports Ent. Inc.: 1999 ($3.95, one-shot)

	GD 2.0	VG 4.0	FN 6.0	VF 8.0	VF/NM 9.0	NM- 9.2
1-Bonds, Piazza, Caminiti, Griffey Jr. app.; Martinbrough-c/a						4.00

SUPERSNIPE COMICS (Formerly Army & Navy #1-5)
Street & Smith Publications: V1#6, Oct, 1942 - V5#1, Aug-Sept, 1949
(See Shadow Comics V2#3)

	GD 2.0	VG 4.0	FN 6.0	VF 8.0	VF/NM 9.0	NM- 9.2
V1#6-Rex King - Man of Adventure (costumed hero, see Super Magic/Magician) by Jack Binder begins; Supersnipe by George Marcoux continues from Army & Navy #5; Bill Ward-a	100	200	300	625	938	1250
7,10-12: 10,11-Little Nemo app.	50	100	150	300	450	600
8-Hitler, Tojo, Mussolini in Hell with Devil-c	74	148	222	463	694	925
9-Doc Savage x-over in Supersnipe; Hitler-c	78	156	234	488	732	975
V2 #1: Both V2#1(2/44) & V2#2(4/44) have V2#1 on outside-c; Huck Finn by Clare Dwiggins begins, ends V3#5 (rare)	72	144	216	450	675	900
V2#2 (4/44) has V2#1 on outside-c; classic shark-c	44	88	132	264	395	525
3-12	40	80	120	240	340	440

V3#1-12: 8-Bobby Crusoe by Dwiggins begins, ends V3#12. 9-X-Mas-c

Superworld Comics #2 © Hugo Gernsback

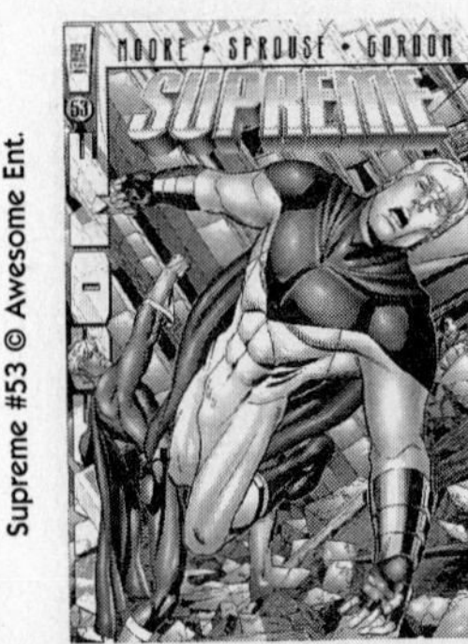

Supreme #53 © Awesome Ent.

Supreme Power #1 Special Edition © MAR

GD 2.0 | VG 4.0 | FN 6.0 | VF 8.0 | VF/NM 9.0 | NM- 9.2

35 70 105 201 288 370
V4#1-12, V5#1: V4#10-X-Mas-c 25 50 75 144 198 255
NOTE: ***George Marcoux** c-V1#6-V3#4. Doc Savage app. in some issues.*

SUPER SOLDIER (See Marvel Versus DC #3)
DC Comics (Amalgam): Apr, 1996 ($1.95, one-shot)
1-Mark Waid script & Dave Gibbons-c/a. 2.25

SUPER SOLDIER: MAN OF WAR
DC Comics (Amalgam): June, 1997 ($1.95, one-shot)
1-Waid & Gibbons-s/Gibbons & Palmiotti-c/a. 2.25

SUPER SOLDIERS
Marvel Comics UK: Apr, 1993 - No. 8, Nov, 1993 ($1.75)
1-($2.50)-Embossed silver foil logo 2.50
2-8: 5-Capt. America app. 6-Origin; Nick Fury app.; neon ink-c 2.25

SUPERSPOOK (Formerly Frisky Animals on Parade)
Ajax/Farrell Publications: No. 4, June, 1958
4 8 16 24 46 58 70

SUPER SPY (See Wham Comics)
Centaur Publications: Oct, 1940 - No. 2, Nov, 1940 (Reprints)
1-Origin The Sparkler 108 216 324 675 1013 1350
2-The Inner Circle, Dean Denton, Tim Blain, The Drew Ghost, The Night Hawk by Gustavson, & S.S. Swanson by Glanz app. 66 132 198 413 617 820

SUPERSTAR: AS SEEN ON TV
Image Comics (Gorilla): 2001 ($5.95)
1-Busiek-s/Immonen-a 6.00

SUPER STAR HOLIDAY SPECIAL (See DC Special Series #21)

SUPER-TEAM FAMILY
National Periodical Publ./DC Comics: Oct-Nov, 1975 - No. 15, Mar-Apr, 1978
1-Reprints by Neal Adams & Kane/Wood; 68 pgs. begin, ends #4. New Gods app. 2 4 6 12 16 20
2,3: New stories 2 4 6 8 10 12
4-7: Reprints. 4-G.A. JSA-r & Superman/Batman/Robin-r from World's Finest. 5-52 pgs. begin 2 4 6 8 10 12
8-14: 8-10-New Challengers of the Unknown stories. 9-Kirby-a. 11-14: New stories 2 4 6 9 11 14
15-New Gods app. New stories 2 4 6 10 13 16
NOTE: ***Neal Adams** r-1-3. **Brunner** c-3. **Buckler** c-8p. **Tuska** a-7r. **Wood** a-1i(r), 3.*

SUPER TV HEROES (See Hanna-Barbera...)

SUPER-VILLAIN CLASSICS
Marvel Comics Group: May, 1983
1-Galactus -The Origin; Kirby-a 6.00

SUPER-VILLAIN TEAM-UP (See Fantastic Four #6 & Giant-Size...)
Marvel Comics Group: 8/75 - No. 14, 10/77; No. 15, 11/78; No. 16, 5/79; No. 17, 6/80
1-Giant-Size Super-Villian Team-Up #2; Sub-Mariner & Dr. Doom begin, end #10 3 7 10 21 28 35
2-5: 5-1st app. The Shroud 2 4 6 8 10 12
5-(30¢-c variant, limited distribution)(4/76) 2 4 6 11 14 18
6,7-(25¢ editions) 6-(6/76)-F.F., Shroud app. 7-Origin Shroud 1 2 3 5 6 8
6,7-(30¢-c, limited distribution)(6,8/76) 2 4 6 8 10 12
8-17: 9-Avengers app. 11-15-Dr. Doom & Red Skull app. 1 2 3 5 6 8
12-14-(35¢-c variants, limited distribution)(6,8,10/77) 2 4 6 8 10 12
NOTE: ***Buckler** c-4p, 5p, 7p. **Buscema** c-1. **Byrne/Austin** c-14. **Evans** a-1p, 3p. **Everett** a-1p. **Giffen** a-8p, 13p; c-13p. **Kane** c-2p, 9p. **Mooney** a-4i. **Starlin** c-6. **Tuska** r-1p, 15p. **Wood** r-15p.*

SUPER WESTERN COMICS (Also see Buffalo Bill)
Youthful Magazines: Aug, 1950 (One shot)
1-Buffalo Bill begins; Wyatt Earp, Calamity Jane & Sam Slade app; Powell-c/a 14 28 42 79 107 135

SUPER WESTERN FUNNIES (See Super Funnies)

SUPERWORLD COMICS
Hugo Gernsback (Komos Publ.): Apr, 1940 - No. 3, Aug, 1940 (68 pgs.)
1-Origin & 1st app. Hip Knox, Super Hypnotist; Mitey Powers & Buzz Allen, the Invisible Avenger, Little Nemo begin; cover by Frank R. Paul (all have sci/fi-c) (Scarce) 655 1310 1965 4585 7043 9500
2-Marvo 1-2 Go+, the Super Boy of the Year 2680 (1st app.); Paul-c (Scarce) 393 786 1179 2555 3928 5300
3 (Scarce) 312 624 936 1950 2925 3900

SUPREME (Becomes ...The New Adventures #43-48)(See Youngblood #3)
(Also see Bloodwulf Special, Legend of Supreme, & Trencher #3)
Image Comics (Extreme Studios)/ Awesome Entertainment #49 on:
V2#1, Nov, 1992 - V2#42, Sept, 1996; V3#49 - No. 56, Feb, 1998
V2#1-Liefeld-a(i) & scripts; embossed foil logo 4.00
1-Gold Edition 6.00
2-(3/93)-Liefeld co-plots & inks; 1st app. Grizlock 3.00
3-42: 3-Intro Bloodstrike; 1st app. Khrome. 5-1st app. Thor. 6-The Starguard cameo. 7-1st full app. The Starguard. 10-Black and White Pt 1 (1st app.) by Art Thibert (2 pgs. ea. installment). 25-(5/94)-Platt-c. 11-Coupon #4 for Extreme Prejudice #0; Black and White Pt. 7 by Thibert. 12-(4/94)-Platt-c. 13,14-(6/94). 15 (7/94). 16 (7/94)-Stormwatch app. 18-Kid Supreme Sneak Preview; Pitt app.19,20-Polybagged w/trading card. 20-1st app. Woden & Loki (as a dog); Overtkill app. 21-1st app. Loki (in true form). 21-23-Poly-bagged trading card. 32-Lady Supreme cameo. 33-Origin & 1st full app. of Lady Supreme (Probe from the Starguard); Babewatch! tie-in. 37-Intro Loki; Fraga-c. 40-Retells Supreme's past advs. 41-Alan Moore scripts begin; Supreme revised; intro The Supremacy; Jerry Ordway-c (Joe Bennett variant-c exists). 42-New origin w/Rick Veitch-a; intro Radar, The Hound Supreme & The League of Infinity 3.00
28-Variant-c by Quesada & Palmiotti 3.00
(#43-48-**See Supreme: The New Adventures**)
V3#49,51: 49-Begin $2.99-c 3.00
50-($3.95)-Double sized, 2 covers, pin-up gallery 4.00
52a,52b-($3.50) 3.50
53-56: 53-Sprouse-a begins. 56-McGuinness-c 3.00
Annual 1-(1995, $2.95) 3.00
...: The Return TPB (Checker Book Publ., 2003, $24.95) r/#53-56 & Supreme; The Return #1-6; Ross-c; additional sketch pages by Ross 25.00
...: The Story of the Year TPB (Checker Book Publ., 2002, $26.95) r/#41-52; Ross-c 27.00
NOTE: ***Rob Liefeld** a(i)-1, 2; co-plots-2-4; scripts-1, 5, 6. **Ordway** c-41. **Platt** c-12, 25. **Thibert** c(i)-7-9.*

SUPREME: GLORY DAYS
Image Comics (Extreme Studios): Oct, 1994 - No. 2, Dec, 1994 ($2.95/$2.50, limited series)
1,2: 2-Diehard, Roman, Superpatriot, & Glory app. 3.00

SUPREME POWER
Marvel Comics (MAX): Oct, 2003 - Present ($2.99)
1-($2.99) Straczynski-s/Frank-a; Frank-c 3.00
1-($4.99) Special Edition with variant Quesada-c; includes r/early Squadron Supreme apps. 5.00
2-6 3.00

SUPREME: THE NEW ADVENTURES (Formerly Supreme)
Maximum Press: V3#43, Oct, 1996 - V3#48, May, 1997 ($2.50)
V3#43-48: 43-Alan Moore scripts begin; Joe Bennett-a; Rick Veitch-a (8 pgs.); Dan Jurgens-a (1 pg.); intro Citadel Supreme & Suprematons; 1st Allied Supermen of America 3.00

SUPREME: THE RETURN
Awesome Entertainment: May, 1999 - No. 6, June, 2000 ($2.99)
1-6: Alan Moore-s. 1,2-Sprouse & Gordon-a/c. 2,4-Liefeld-c. 6-Kirby app. 3.00

SURE-FIRE COMICS (Lightning Comics #4 on)
Ace Magazines: June, 1940 - No. 4, Oct, 1940 (Two No. 3's)
V1#1-Origin Flash Lightning & begins; X-The Phantom Fed, Ace McCoy, Buck Steele, Marvo the Magician, The Raven, Whiz Wilson (Time Traveler) begin (all 1st app.); Flash Lightning c-1-4 168 336 504 1050 1575 2100
2 78 156 234 488 732 975
3(9/40), 3(#4)(10/40)-nn on-c, #3 on inside 60 120 180 375 563 750

SURF 'N' WHEELS
Charlton Comics: Nov, 1969 - No. 6, Sept, 1970
1 4 8 12 22 30 38
2-6 2 4 6 14 18 22

SURGE
Eclipse Comics: July, 1984 - No. 4, Jan, 1985 ($1.50, lim. series, Baxter paper)
1-4 Ties into DNAgents series 2.25

SURPRISE ADVENTURES (Formerly Tormented)
Sterling Comic Group: No. 3, Mar, 1955 - No. 5, July, 1955
3-5: 3,5-Sekowsky-a 8 16 24 43 54 65

SUSIE Q. SMITH
Dell Publishing Co.: No. 323, Mar, 1951 - No. 553, Apr, 1954
Four Color 323 (#1) 5 10 15 33 44 55
Four Color 377, 453 (2/53), 553 4 8 12 25 33 42

SUSPENSE (Radio/TV issues #1-11; Real Life Tales of... #1-4) (Amazing Detective Cases #3 on?)
Marvel/Atlas Comics (CnPC No. 1-10/BFP No. 11-29): Dec, 1949 - No. 29, Apr, 1953 (#1-8, 17-23: 52 pgs.)

Suspense Comics #6 © Continental

Swamp Thing #16 © DC

Swamp Thing (3rd series) #18 © DC

	GD 2.0	VG 4.0	FN 6.0	VF 8.0	VF/NM 9.0	NM- 9.2
1-Powell-a; Peter Lorre, Sidney Greenstreet photo-c from Hammett's "The Verdict"	60	120	180	375	563	750
2-Crime stories; Dennis O'Keefe & Gale Storm photo-c from Universal movie "Abandoned"	35	70	105	201	288	370
3-Change to horror	39	78	117	230	325	420
4,7-10: 7-Dracula-sty	30	60	90	170	240	310
5-Krigstein, Tuska, Everett-a	32	64	96	182	259	335
6-Tuska, Everett, Morisi-a	31	62	93	178	252	325
11-13,15-17,19,20	24	48	72	135	190	245
14-Clasic Heath Hypo-c; A-Bomb panels	35	70	105	201	288	370
18,22-Krigstein-a	25	50	75	144	198	255
21,23,24,26-29: 24-Tuska-a	22	44	66	124	172	220
25-Electric chair-c/story	31	62	93	175	248	320

NOTE: ***Ayers** a-20. **Briefer** a-5, 7, 27. **Brodsky** c-4, 6-9, 11, 16, 17, 25. **Colan** a-8(2), 9. **Everett** a-5, 6(2), 19, 23, 28; c-21-23, 26. **Fuje** a-29. **Heath** a-5, 6, 8, 10, 12, 14; c-14, 19, 24. **Maneely** a-12, 23, 24, 28, 29; c-5, 6p, 10, 13, 15, 18. **Mooney** a-24, 28. **Morisi** a-6, 12. **Palais** a-10. **Rico** a-7-9. **Robinson** a-29. **Romita** a-20(2), 25. **Sekowsky** a-11, 13, 14. **Sinnott** a-23, 25. **Tuska** a-5, 6(2), 12; c-12. **Whitney** a-15, 16, 22. **Ed Win** a-27.*

SUSPENSE COMICS
Continental Magazines: Dec, 1943 - No. 12, Sept, 1946

	GD 2.0	VG 4.0	FN 6.0	VF 8.0	VF/NM 9.0	NM- 9.2
1-The Grey Mask begins; bondage/torture-c; L. B. Cole-a (7 pgs.)	385	770	1155	2503	3852	5200
2-Intro. The Mask; Rico, Giunta, L. B. Cole-a (7 pgs.)	284	568	852	1775	2663	3550
3-L.B. Cole-a; classic Schomburg-c (Scarce)	1700	3400	5100	10,200	14,100	18,000
4-6: 4-L. B. Cole-c begin	216	432	648	1350	2025	2700
7,9,10,12: 9-L.B. Cole eyeball-c	164	328	492	1025	1538	2050
8-Classic L. B. Cole spider-c	385	770	1155	2503	3852	5200
11-Classic Devil-c	311	622	933	2022	3111	4200

NOTE: ***L. B. Cole** c-4-12. **Fuje** a-8. **Larsen** a-11. **Palais** a-10, 11. Bondage c-1, 3, 4.*

SUSPENSE DETECTIVE
Fawcett Publications: June, 1952 - No. 5, Mar, 1953

	GD 2.0	VG 4.0	FN 6.0	VF 8.0	VF/NM 9.0	NM- 9.2
1-Evans-a (11 pgs); Baily-c/a	44	88	132	264	395	525
2-Evans-a (10 pgs.)	29	58	87	164	232	300
3-5	24	48	72	135	190	245

NOTE: ***Baily** a-4, 5; c-1-3. **Sekowsky** a-2, 4, 5; c-5.*

SUSPENSE STORIES (See Strange Suspense Stories)

SUSSEX VAMPIRE, THE (Sherlock Holmes)
Caliber Comics: 1996 ($2.95, 32 pgs., B&W, one-shot)

nn-Adapts Sir Arthur Conan Doyle's story; Warren Ellis scripts 3.00

SUZIE COMICS (Formerly Laugh Comix; see Laugh Comics, Liberty Comics #10, Pep Comics & Top-Notch Comics #28)
Close-Up No. 49,50/MLJ Mag./Archie No. 51 on: No. 49, Spring, 1945 - No. 100, Aug, 1954

	GD 2.0	VG 4.0	FN 6.0	VF 8.0	VF/NM 9.0	NM- 9.2
49-Ginger begins	24	48	72	135	190	245
50-55: 54-Transvestism story. 55-Woggon-a	15	30	45	84	115	145
56-Katy Keene begins by Woggon	14	28	42	79	107	135
57-65	11	22	33	63	84	105
66-80	10	20	30	58	77	95
81-87,89-99	10	20	30	56	73	90
88,100: 88-Used in **POP**, pgs. 76,77; Bill Woggon draws himself in story. 100-Last Katy Keene	10	20	30	58	77	95

NOTE: ***Al Fagaly** c-49-67. Katy Keene app. in 53-82, 85-100.*

SWAMP FOX, THE (TV, Disney)(See Walt Disney Presents #2)
Dell Publishing Co.: No. 1179, Dec, 1960

	GD 2.0	VG 4.0	FN 6.0	VF 8.0	VF/NM 9.0	NM- 9.2
Four Color 1179-Leslie Nielson photo-c	10	20	30	67	96	125

SWAMP THING (See Brave & the Bold, Challengers of the Unknown #82, DC Comics Presents #8 & 85, DC Special Series #2, 14, 17, 20, House of Secrets #92, Limited Collectors' Edition C-59, & Roots of the...)

SWAMP THING
National Per. Publ./DC Comics: Oct-Nov, 1972 - No. 24, Aug-Sept, 1976

	GD 2.0	VG 4.0	FN 6.0	VF 8.0	VF/NM 9.0	NM- 9.2
1-Wrightson-c/a begins; origin	13	26	39	94	137	180
2-1st app. Patchwork Man (1 panel cameo)	6	12	18	43	59	75
3-1st full app. Patchwork Man (see House of Secrets #140)	4	8	12	29	40	50
4-6,8-10: 10-Last Wrightson issue	4	8	12	27	36	45
7-Batman-c/story	4	8	12	29	40	50
11-20: 11-19-Redondo-a. 13-Origin retold (1 pg.)	2	4	6	10	13	16
21-24: 23,24-Swamp Thing reverts back to Dr. Holland. 23-New logo	2	4	6	10	13	16

NOTE: ***J. Jones** a-9i(assist). **Kaluta** a-9i. **Redondo** c-12-19, 21. **Wrightson** issues (#1-10) reprinted in DC Special Series #2, 14, 17, 20 & Roots of the Swampthing.*

SWAMP THING (Saga Of The... #1-38,42-45) (See Essential Vertigo:...)
DC Comics (Vertigo imprint #129 on): May, 1982 - No. 171, Oct, 1996

(Direct sales #65 on)

	GD 2.0	VG 4.0	FN 6.0	VF 8.0	VF/NM 9.0	NM- 9.2
1-Origin retold; Phantom Stranger series begins; ends #13; Yeates-c/a begins						6.00
2-15: 2-Photo-c from movie. 13-Last Yeates-a						4.00
16-19: Bissette-a.						5.00
20-1st Alan Moore issue	2	4	6	14	18	22
21-New origin	2	4	6	11	14	18
22,23,25: 25-John Constantine 1-panel cameo	2	4	6	8	10	12
24-JLA x-over; Last Yeates-c.	2	4	6	9	11	14
26-30	1	2	3	4	5	7
31-33,35,36: 33-r/1st app. from House of Secrets #92						5.00
34	1	2	3	5	6	8
37-1st app. John Constantine (Hellblazer) (6/85)	2	4	6	10	12	15
38-40: John Constantine app.	1	2	3	5	6	8
41-52,54-64: 44-Batman cameo. 44-51-John Constantine app. 46-Crisis x-over; Batman cameo. 49-Spectre app. 50-($1.25, 52 pgs.)-Deadman, Dr. Fate, Demon. 52-Arkham Asylum-c/story; Joker-c/cameo. 58-Spectre preview. 64-Last Moore issue						3.50
53-($1.25, 52 pgs.)-Arkham Asylum; Batman-c/story						4.50
65-83,85-99,101-124,126-149,151-153: 65-Direct sales only begins. 66-Batman & Arkham Asylum story. 70,76-John Constantine x-over; 76-X-over w/Hellblazer #9. 79-Superman-c/story. 85-Jonah Hex app. 102-Preview of World Without End. 116-Photo-c. 129-Metallic ink on-c. 140-Millar scripts begin, end #171						3.00
84-Sandman (Morpheus) cameo.						4.00
100,125,150: 100 ($2.50, 52 pgs.). 125-($2.95, 52 pgs.)-20th anniversary issue. 150 (52 pgs.)-Anniversary issue						3.00
154-171: 154-$2.25-c begins. 165-Curt Swan-a(p). 166,169,171-John Constantine & Phantom Stranger app. 168-Arcane returns						2.50
Annual 1,3-6('82-91): 1-Movie Adaptation; painted-c. 3-New format; Bolland-c. 4-Batman-c/story. 5-Batman cameo; re-intro Brother Power (Geek),1st app. since 1968						4.00
Annual 2 (1985)-Moore scripts; Bissette-a(p); Deadman, Spectre app.						7.00
Annual 7(1993, $3.95)-Children's Crusade						4.00
...A Murder of Crows (2001, $19.95)-r/#43-50; Moore-s						20.00
...: Earth To Earth (2002, $17.95)-r/#51-56; Batman app.						18.00
...Love and Death (1990, $17.95)-r/#28-34 & Annual #2; Totleben painted-c						18.00
...: Reunion (2003, $19.95, TPB) r/#57-64; Moore-s						20.00
...: Roots (1998, $7.95) Jon J Muth-s/painted-a/c						8.00
Saga of the Swamp Thing ('87, '89)-r/#21-27 (1st & 2nd print)						13.00
...: The Curse (2000, $19.95, TPB) r/#35-42; Bisley-c						20.00

NOTE: ***Bissette** a(p)-16-19, 21-27, 29, 30, 34-36, 39-42, 44, 46, 50, 64; c-17i, 24-32p, 35-37p, 40p, 44p, 46-50p, 51-58, 61, 62, 63p. **Kaluta** c/a-74. **Spiegle** a-1-3, 6. **Sutton** a-98p. **Totleben** a(i)-10, 16-27, 29, 31, 34-40, 42, 44, 46, 48, 50, 53, 55i; c-25-32i, 33, 35-40i, 42i, 44i, 46-50i, 53, 55i, 59p, 64, 65, 68, 73, 76, 80, 82, 84, 89, 91-100, Annual 4, 5. **Vess** painted c-121, 129-139, Annual 7. **Williamson** 86i. **Wrightson** a-18i(r), 33r. John Constantine appears in #37-40, 44-51, 65-67, 70-77, 80-90, 99, 114, 115, 130, 134-138.*

SWAMP THING
DC Comics (Vertigo): May, 2000 - No. 20, Dec, 2001 ($2.50)

	GD 2.0	VG 4.0	FN 6.0	VF 8.0	VF/NM 9.0	NM- 9.2
1-3-Tefé Holland's return; Vaughan-s/Petersen-a; Hale painted-c.						3.00
4-20: 7-9-Bisley-c. 10-John Constantine-c/app. 10-12-Fabry-c. 13-15-Mack-c 18-Swamp Thing app.						2.50
Preview-16 pg. flip book w/Lucifer Preview						2.25

SWARM (See Futuretech)
Mushroom Comics: Jan, 1996 ($2.50, limited series)

1-Flip book w/Futuretech #1 2.50

SWAT MALONE (America's Home Run King)
Swat Malone Enterprises: Sept, 1955

	GD 2.0	VG 4.0	FN 6.0	VF 8.0	VF/NM 9.0	NM- 9.2
V1#1-Hy Fleishman-a	11	22	33	63	84	105

SWEATSHOP
DC Comics: Jun, 2003 - No. 6, Nov, 2003 ($2.95)

1-6-Peter Bagge-s/a; Destefano-a 3.00

SWEENEY (Formerly Buz Sawyer)
Standard Comics: No. 4, June, 1949 - No. 5, Sept, 1949

	GD 2.0	VG 4.0	FN 6.0	VF 8.0	VF/NM 9.0	NM- 9.2
4,5: 5-Crane-a	9	18	27	49	62	75

SWEE'PEA (Also see Popeye #46)
Dell Publishing Co.: No. 219, Mar, 1949

	GD 2.0	VG 4.0	FN 6.0	VF 8.0	VF/NM 9.0	NM- 9.2
Four Color 219	10	20	30	67	96	125

SWEET CHILDE
Advantage Graphics Press: 1995 - No. 2, 1995 ($2.95, B&W, mature)

1,2 3.00

SWEETHEART DIARY (Cynthia Doyle #66-on)
Fawcett Publications/Charlton Comics No. 32 on: Wint, 1949; #2, Spr, 1950; #3, 6/50 - #5, 10/50; #6, 1951(nd); #7, 9/51 - #14, 1/53; #32, 10/55; #33, 4/56 - #65, 8/62 (#1-14: photo-c)

Sweethearts #119 © FAW

Sweet Sixteen #6 © PMI

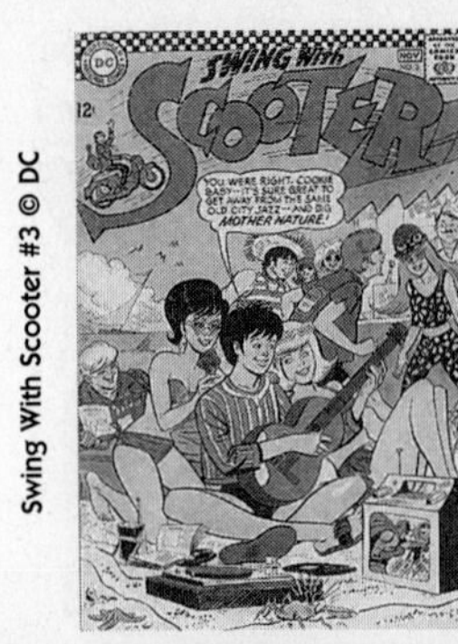

Swing With Scooter #3 © DC

	GD 2.0	VG 4.0	FN 6.0	VF 8.0	VF/NM 9.0	NM- 9.2
1	19	38	57	107	149	190
2	10	20	30	58	77	95
3,4-Wood-a	15	30	45	86	118	150
5-10: 8-Bailey-a	9	18	27	49	62	75
11-14: 13-Swayze-a. 14-Last Fawcett issue	7	14	21	37	46	55
32 (10/55; 1st Charlton issue)(Formerly Cowboy Love #31)	8	16	24	40	50	60
33-40: 34-Swayze-a	6	12	18	27	33	38
41-(68 pgs.)	6	12	18	29	36	42
42-60	3	6	9	18	24	30
61-65	3	6	9	18	23	28
SWEETHEARTS (Formerly Captain Midnight)						
Fawcett Publications/Charlton No. 122 on: #68, 10/48 - #121, 5/53; #122, 3/54; V2#23, 5/54 - #137, 12/73						
68-Photo-c begin	17	34	51	98	134	170
69,70	9	18	27	54	70	85
71-80	8	16	24	46	58	70
81-84,86-93,95-99,105	8	16	24	40	50	60
85,94,103,110,117-George Evans-a	9	18	27	49	62	75
100	8	16	24	46	58	70
101,107-Powell-a	8	16	24	43	54	65
102,104,106,108,109,112-116,118	7	14	21	37	46	55
111-1 pg. Ronald Reagan biography	9	18	27	52	66	80
119-Marilyn Monroe & Richard Widmark photo-c (1/54?); also appears in story; part Wood-a	46	92	138	276	413	550
120-Atom Bomb story	10	20	30	60	80	100
121-Liz Taylor/Fernanado Lamas photo-c	18	36	54	101	138	175
122-(1st Charlton? 3/54)-Marijuana story	10	20	30	60	80	100
V2#23 (5/54)-28: 28-Last precode issue (2/55)	7	14	21	35	43	50
29-39,41,43-45,47-50	4	8	12	24	32	40
40-Photo-c; Tommy Sands story	4	8	12	27	36	45
42-Ricky Nelson photo-c/story	9	18	27	60	85	110
46-Jimmy Rodgers photo-c/story	4	8	12	27	36	45
51-60	3	7	10	21	28	35
61-80,100	3	6	9	18	24	30
81-99	3	6	9	18	23	28
101-110	2	4	6	11	14	18
111-137	2	4	6	10	12	15
NOTE: *Photo c-68-121(Fawcett), 40, 42, 46(Charlton).* ***Swayze*** *a(Fawcett)-70-118(most).*						
SWEETHEART SCANDALS (See Fox Giants)						
SWEETIE PIE						
Dell Publishing Co.: No. 1185, May-July, 1961 - No. 1241, Nov-Jan, 1961/62						
Four Color 1185 (#1)	5	10	15	33	44	55
Four Color 1241	4	8	12	25	33	42
SWEETIE PIE						
Ajax-Farrell/Pines (Literary Ent.): Dec, 1955 - No. 15, Fall, 1957						
1-By Nadine Seltzer	9	18	27	49	62	75
2 (5/56; last Ajax?)	6	12	18	28	34	40
3-15	5	10	15	22	26	30
SWEET LOVE						
Home Comics (Harvey): Sept, 1949 - No. 5, May, 1950 (All photo-c)						
1	10	20	30	60	80	100
2	7	14	21	37	46	55
3,4: 3-Powell-a	6	12	18	31	38	45
5-Kamen, Powell-a	9	18	27	49	62	75
SWEET ROMANCE						
Charlton Comics: Oct, 1968						
1	2	4	6	12	16	20
SWEET SIXTEEN (...Comics and Stories for Girls)						
Parents' Magazine Institute: Aug-Sept, 1946 - No. 13, Jan, 1948 (All have movie stars photos on covers)						
1-Van Johnson's life story; Dorothy Dare, Queen of Hollywood Stunt Artists begins (in all issues); part photo-c	21	42	63	118	164	210
2-Jane Powell, Roddy McDowall "Holiday in Mexico" photo on-c; Alan Ladd story	14	28	42	81	111	140
3,5,6,8-11: 5-Ann Francis photo on-c; Gregory Peck story. 6-Dick Haymes story. 8-Shirley Jones photo on-c. 10-Jean Simmons photo on-c; James Stewart story	10	20	30	58	77	95
4-Elizabeth Taylor photo on-c	19	38	57	106	146	185
7-Ronald Reagan's life story	20	40	60	112	156	200

	GD 2.0	VG 4.0	FN 6.0	VF 8.0	VF/NM 9.0	NM- 9.2
12-Bob Cummings, Vic Damone story	11	22	33	63	84	105
13-Robert Mitchum's life story	11	22	33	66	88	110
SWEET XVI						
Marvel Comics: May, 1991 - No. 5, Sept, 1991($1.00, color)						
1-5: Barbara Slate story & art						3.00
SWIFT ARROW (Also see Lone Rider & The Rider)						
Ajax/Farrell Publications: Feb-Mar, 1954 - No. 5, Oct-Nov, 1954; Apr, 1957 - No. 3, Sept, 1957						
1(1954) (1st Series)	17	34	51	98	134	170
2	9	18	27	54	70	85
3-5: 5-Lone Rider story	8	16	24	46	58	70
1 (2nd Series) (Swift Arrow's Gunfighters #4)	9	18	27	49	62	75
2,3: 2-Lone Rider begins	8	16	24	40	50	60
SWIFT ARROW'S GUNFIGHTERS (Formerly Swift Arrow)						
Ajax/Farrell Publ. (Four Star Comic Corp.): No. 4, Nov, 1957						
4	8	16	24	40	50	60
SWING WITH SCOOTER						
National Periodical Publications: June-July, 1966 - No. 35, Aug-Sept, 1971; No. 36, Oct-Nov, 1972						
1	8	16	24	55	78	100
2,6-10: 9-Alfred E. Newman swipe in last panel	4	8	12	29	40	50
3-5: 3-Batman cameo on-c. 4-Batman cameo inside. 5-JLA cameo	5	10	15	33	44	55
11-13,15-19: 18-Wildcat of JSA 1pg. text. 19-Last 12¢-c	3	6	9	19	25	32
14-Alfred E. Neuman cameo	3	7	10	21	28	35
20 (68 pgs.)	4	8	12	29	40	50
21-23,25-31	3	6	9	16	20	25
24-Frankenstein-c.	3	6	9	18	24	30
32-34 (68 pgs.). 32-Batman cameo. 33-Interview with David Cassidy. 34-Interview with Rick Ely (The Rebels)	4	8	12	27	36	45
35-(52 pgs.). 1 pg. app. Clark Kent and 4 full pgs. of Superman	7	14	21	51	71	90
36-Bat-signal refererence to Batman	3	6	9	19	25	32
NOTE: ***Aragonés*** *a-13 (1pg.), 18(1pg.), 30(2pgs.)* ***Orlando*** *a-1-11; c-1-11, 13. #20, 33, 34: 68 pgs.; #35: 52 pgs.*						
SWISS FAMILY ROBINSON (Walt Disney's..; see King Classics & Movie Comics)						
Dell Publishing Co.: No. 1156, Dec, 1960						
Four Color 1156-Movie-photo-c	8	16	24	58	82	105
SWORD & THE DRAGON, THE						
Dell Publishing Co.: No. 1118, June, 1960						
Four Color 1118-Movie, photo-c	9	18	27	60	85	110
SWORD & THE ROSE, THE (Disney)						
Dell Publishing Co.: No. 505, Oct, 1953 - No. 682, Feb, 1956						
Four Color 505-Movie, photo-c	10	20	30	67	96	125
Four Color 682-When Knighthood Was in Flower-Movie, reprint of #505; Renamed the Sword & the Rose for the novel; photo-c	8	16	24	55	78	100
SWORD IN THE STONE, THE (See March of Comics #258 & Movie Comics & Wart and the Wizard)						
SWORD OF DAMOCLES						
Image Comics (WildStorm Productions): Mar, 1996 - No. 2, Apr, 1996 ($2.50, limited series)						
1,2: Warren Ellis scripts. 1-Prelude to "Fire From Heaven" x-over; 1st app. Sword						2.50
SWORD OF DRACULA						
Image Comics: Oct, 2003 - Present ($2.95, B&W, limited series)						
1,2-Tony Harris-c/Greg Scott-a						3.00
SWORD OF SORCERY						
National Periodical Publications: Feb-Mar, 1973 - No. 5, Nov-Dec, 1973 (20¢)						
1-Leiber Fafhrd & The Grey Mouser; Chaykin/Neal Adams (Crusty Bunkers) art; Kaluta-c	2	4	6	12	16	20
2,3: 2-Wrightson-c(i); Adams-a(i). 3-Wrightson-i(5 pgs.)	2	4	6	8	10	12
4,5: 5-Starlin-a(p); Conan cameo	1	2	3	5	7	9
NOTE: ***Chaykin*** *a-1-4p; c-2p, 3-5.* ***Kaluta*** *a-3i.* ***Simonson*** *a-3i, 4i, 5p; c-5.*						
SWORD OF THE ATOM						
DC Comics: Sept, 1983 - No. 4, Dec, 1983 (Limited series)						
1-4: Kane-c/a in all, Special 1-3('84, '85, '88): 1,2-Kane-c/a each						3.00
SWORDS OF TEXAS (See Scout #15)						
Eclipse Comics: Oct, 1987 - No. 4, Jan, 1988 ($1.75, color, Baxter paper)						
1-4: Scout app.						2.25

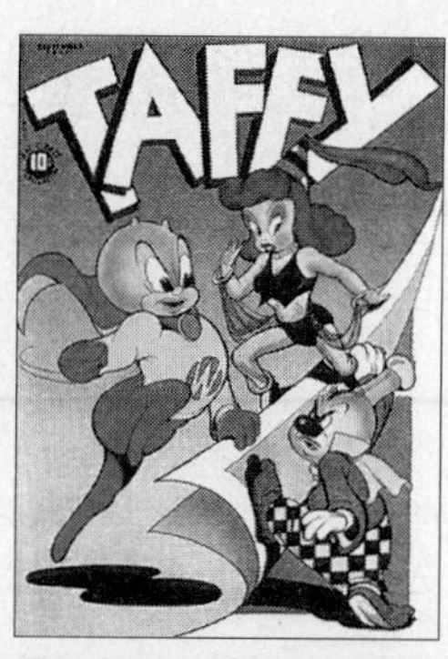

Taffy Comics #4 © Orbit Publ.

Tails #1 © SEGA

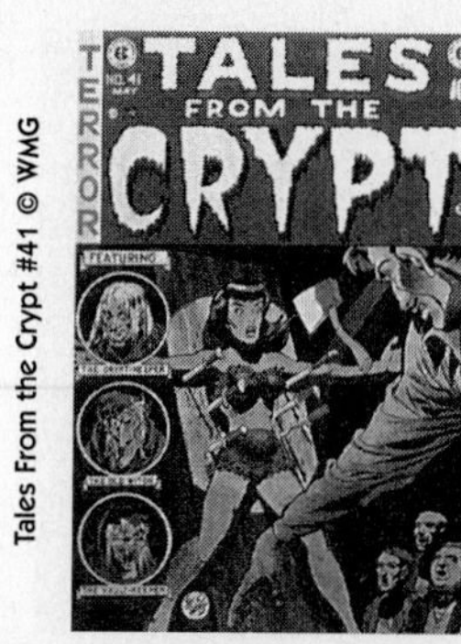

Tales From the Crypt #41 © WMG

GD VG FN VF VF/NM NM-
2.0 4.0 6.0 8.0 9.0 9.2

GD VG FN VF VF/NM NM-
2.0 4.0 6.0 8.0 9.0 9.2

SWORDS OF THE SWASHBUCKLERS (See Marvel Graphic Novel)
Marvel Comics (Epic Comics): May, 1985 - No. 12, Jun, 1987 ($1.50; mature)
1-12-Butch Guice-c/a (Cont'd from Marvel G.N.) 2.25

SWORN TO PROTECT
Marvel Comics: Sept, 1995 ($1.95) (Based on card game)
nn-Overpower Game Guide; Jubilee story 2.25

SYN
Dark Horse Comics: Aug, 2003 ($2.99)
1-3-Giffen-s/Titus-a 3.00

SYPHONS
Now Comics: V2#1, May, 1994 - V2#3, 1994 ($2.50, limited series)
V2#1-3: 1-Stardancer, Knightfire, Raze & Brigade begin 2.50

SYSTEM, THE
DC Comics (Vertigo Verite): May, 1996 - No. 3, July, 1996 ($2.95, lim. series)
1-3: Kuper-c/a 3.00
TPB (1997, $12.95) r/#1-3 13.00

TAFFY COMICS
Rural Home/Orbit Publ.: Mar-Apr, 1945 - No. 12, 1948
1-L.B. Cole-c; origin & 1st app. of Wiggles The Wonderworm plus 7 chapter WWII funny animal adventures 58 116 174 363 544 725
2-L.B. Cole-c; Wiggles-c/stories in #1-4 31 62 93 178 252 325
3,4,6-12: 6-Perry Como-c/story. 7-Duke Ellington, 2 pgs. 8-Glenn Ford-c/story. 9-Lon McCallister part photo-c & story. 10-Mort Leav-c. 11-Mickey Rooney-c/story 14 28 42 79 107 135
5-L.B. Cole-c; Van Johnson-c/story 22 44 66 127 176 225

TAILGUNNER JO
DC Comics: Sept, 1988 - No. 6, Jan, 1989 ($1.25)
1-6 2.25

TAILS
Archie Publications; Dec, 1995 - No. 3, Feb, 1996 ($1.50, limited series)
1-3: Based on Sonic, the Hedgehog video game 4.00

TAILSPIN
Spotlight Publishers: November, 1944
nn-Firebird app.; L.B. Cole-c 29 58 87 164 232 300

TAILSPIN TOMMY (Also see Popular Comics)
United Features Syndicate/Service Publ. Co.: 1940; 1946
Single Series 23(1940) 40 80 120 240 340 440
Best Seller (nd, 1946)-Service Publ. Co. 15 30 45 86 118 150

TAINTED
DC Comics (Vertigo): Jan, 1995 ($4.95, one-shot)
1-Jamie Delano scripts; Al Davison-c/a; reads February '95 on-c 5.00

TAKION
DC Comics: June, 1996 - No. 7, Dec, 1996 ($1.75)
1-7: Lopresti-c/a(p). 1-Origin; Green Lantern app. 6-Final Night x-over 2.50

TALENT SHOWCASE (See New Talent Showcase)

TALE OF ONE BAD RAT, THE
Dark Horse Comics: Oct, 1994 - No. 4, Jan, 1995 ($2.95, limited series)
1-4: Bryan Talbot-c/a/scripts 3.00
HC ($69.95, signed and numbered) R/#1-4 70.00

TALES CALCULATED TO DRIVE YOU BATS
Archie Publications: Nov, 1961 - No. 7, Nov, 1962; 1966 (Satire)
1-Only 10¢ issue; has cut-out Werewolf mask (price includes mask) 13 26 39 94 137 180
2-Begin 12¢ issues 7 14 21 51 71 90
3-6: 3-UFO cover 6 12 18 38 52 65
7-Storyline change 5 10 15 36 48 60
1(1966, 25¢, 44 pg. Giant)-r/#1; UFO cover 6 12 18 38 52 65

TALES CALCULATED TO DRIVE YOU MAD
E.C. Publications: Summer, 1997 - No. 8, Winter, 1999 ($3.99/$4.99, satire)
1-6-Full color reprints of Mad: 1-(#1-3), 2-(#4-6), 3-(#7-9), 4-(#10-12) 5-(#13-15), 6-(#16-18) 5.00
7,8-($4.99-c): 7-(#19-21), 8-(#22,23) 5.00

TALES FROM THE AGE OF APOCALYPSE
Marvel Comics: 1996 ($5.95, prestige format, one-shots)
1, ...: Sinister Bloodlines (1997, $5.95) 6.00

TALES FROM THE BOG
Aberration Press: Nov, 1995 - No. 7, Nov, 1997 ($2.95/$3.95, B&W)
1-7 4.00
Alternate #1 (Director's Cut) (1998, $2.95) 3.00

TALES FROM THE CRYPT (Formerly The Crypt Of Terror; see Three Dimensional...)
E.C. Comics: No. 20, Oct-Nov, 1950 - No. 46, Feb-Mar, 1955
20-See Crime Patrol #15 for 1st Crypt Keeper 111 222 333 833 1192 1550
21-Kurtzman-r/Haunt of Fear #15(#1) 91 182 273 683 977 1270
22-Moon Girl costume at costume party, one panel 71 142 213 533 762 990
23-25: 24-E. A. Poe adaptation 55 110 165 413 589 765
26-30: 26-Wood's 2nd EC-c 44 88 132 330 470 610
31-Williamson-a(1st at E.C.); B&W and color illos. in **POP**; Kamen draws himself, Gaines & Feldstein; Ingels, Craig & Davis draw themselves in his story 45 90 135 338 482 625
32,35-39: 38-Censored-c 39 78 117 293 417 540
33-Origin The Crypt Keeper 62 124 186 465 665 865
34-Used in **POP**, pg. 83; lingerie panels 40 80 120 300 428 555
40-Used in Senate hearings & in Hartford Cournat anti-comics editorials-1954 39 78 117 293 417 540
41-45: 45-2 pgs. showing E.C. staff 38 76 114 285 405 525
46-Low distribution; pre-advertised cover for unpublished 4th horror title "Crypt of Terror" used on this book 45 90 135 338 482 625

*NOTE: **Ray Bradbury** adaptations-34, 36. **Craig** a-20, 22-24; c-20. **Crandall** a-38, 44. **Davis** a-24-46; c-29-46. **Elder** a-37, 38. **Evans** a-32-34, 36, 40, 41, 43, 46. **Feldstein** a-20-23; c-21-25, 28. Ingels a-in all. **Kamen** a-20, 22, 25, 27-31, 33-36, 39, 41-45. **Krigstein** a-40, 42, 45. **Kurtzman** a-21. **Orlando** a-27-30, 35, 37, 39, 41-45. **Wood** a-21, 24, 25; c-26, 27. Canadian reprints known; see Table of Contents.*

TALES FROM THE CRYPT (Magazine)
Eerie Publications: No. 10, July, 1968 (35¢, B&W)
10-Contains Farrell reprints from 1950s 4 8 12 24 32 40

TALES FROM THE CRYPT
Gladstone Publishing: July, 1990 - No. 6, May, 1991 ($1.95/$2.00, 68 pgs.)
1-r/TFTC #33 & Crime S.S. #17; Davis-c(r) 3.00
2-6: 2,3,5,6-Davis-c(r). 4-Begin $2.00-c; Craig-c(r) 3.00

TALES FROM THE CRYPT
Extra-Large Comics (Russ Cochran)/Gemstone Publishing: Jul, 1991 - No. 6 ($3.95, 10 1/4 x13 1/4", 68 pgs.)
1-Davis-c(r); Craig back-c(r); E.C. reprints 4.00
2-6 ($2.00, comic sized) 3.00

TALES FROM THE CRYPT
Russ Cochran: Sept, 1991 - No. 7, July, 1992 ($2.00, 64 pgs.)
1-7 3.00

TALES FROM THE CRYPT
Russ Cochran/Gemstone: Sept, 1992 - No. 30, Dec, 1999 ($1.50, quarterly)
1-4-r/Crypt of Terror #17-19, TFTC #20 w/original-c 3.00
5-30: 5-15 ($2.00)-r/TFTC #21-23 w/original-c. 16-30 ($2.50) 3.00
Annual 1-6('93-'99) 1-r/#1-5. 2- r/#6-10. 3- r/#11-15. 4- r/#16-20. 5-r/#21-25. 6- r/#26-30 14.00

TALES FROM THE GREAT BOOK
Famous Funnies: Feb, 1955 - No. 4, Jan, 1956 (Religious themes)
1-Story of Samson; John Lehti-a in all 9 18 27 52 66 80
2-4: 2-Joshua. 3-Joash the Boy King. 4-David 7 14 21 35 43 50

TALES FROM THE HEART OF AFRICA (The Temporary Natives)
Marvel Comics (Epic Comics): Aug, 1990 ($3.95, 52 pgs.)
1 4.00

TALES FROM THE TOMB (Also see Dell Giants)
Dell Publishing Co.: Oct, 1962 (25¢ giant)
1(02-810-210)-All stories written by John Stanley 13 26 39 104 177 250

TALES FROM THE TOMB (Magazine)
Eerie Publications: V1#6, July, 1969 - V7#3, 1975 (52 pgs.)
V1#6-8 5 10 15 36 48 60
V2#1-6: 4-LSD story-r/Weird V3#5. 6-Rulah-r 4 8 12 25 33 42
V3#1-Rulah-r 4 8 12 25 33 42
2-6('71),V4#1-5('72),V5#1-6('73),V6#1-6('74),V7#1-3('75) 4 8 12 22 30 38

TALES OF ASGARD
Marvel Comics Group: Oct, 1968 (25¢, 68 pgs.); Feb, 1984 ($1.25, 52 pgs.)
1-Reprints Tales of Asgard (Thor) back-up stories from Journey into Mystery #97-106;

Tales of Ghost Castle #1 © DC

Tales of Horror #11 © Minoan Publ.

Tales of Suspense #29 © MAR

	GD 2.0	VG 4.0	FN 6.0	VF 8.0	VF/NM 9.0	NM- 9.2
new Kirby-c; Kirby-a	4	8	12	29	40	50
V2#1 (2/84)-Thor-r; Simonson-c						3.00

TALES OF EVIL
Atlas/Seaboard Publ.: Feb, 1975 - No. 3, July, 1975 (All 25¢ issues)

	GD 2.0	VG 4.0	FN 6.0	VF 8.0	VF/NM 9.0	NM- 9.2
1-3: 1-Werewolf w/Sekowsky-a. 2-Intro. The Bog Beast; Sparling-a. 3-Origin The Man-Monster; Buckler-a(p)	1	2	3	6	8	10

NOTE: *Grandenetti a-1, 2. Lieber c-1. Sekowsky a-1. Sutton a-2. Thorne c-2.*

TALES OF GHOST CASTLE
National Periodical Publications: May-June, 1975 - No. 3, Sept-Oct, 1975 (All 25¢ issues)

	GD 2.0	VG 4.0	FN 6.0	VF 8.0	VF/NM 9.0	NM- 9.2
1-Redondo-a	3	6	9	16	20	25
2,3: 2-Nino-a. 3-Redondo-a.	2	4	6	9	11	14

TALES OF G.I. JOE
Marvel Comics: Jan, 1988 - No. 15, Mar, 1989

	GD 2.0	VG 4.0	FN 6.0	VF 8.0	VF/NM 9.0	NM- 9.2
1 ($2.25, 52 pgs.)						3.00
2-15 ($1.50): 1-15-r/G.I. Joe #1-15						2.25

TALES OF HORROR
Toby Press/Minoan Publ. Corp.: June, 1952 - No. 13, Oct, 1954

	GD 2.0	VG 4.0	FN 6.0	VF 8.0	VF/NM 9.0	NM- 9.2
1	40	80	120	240	340	440
2-Torture scenes	34	68	102	193	274	355
3-13: 9-11-Reprints Purple Claw #1-3	22	44	66	127	176	225
12-Myron Fass-c/a; torture scenes	23	46	69	130	183	235

NOTE: *Andru a-5. Baily a-5. Myron Fass a-2, 3, 12; c-1-3, 12. Hollingsworth a-2. Sparling a-6, 9; c-9.*

TALES OF JUSTICE
Atlas Comics(MjMC No. 53-66/Male No. 67): No. 53, May, 1955 - No. 67, Aug, 1957

	GD 2.0	VG 4.0	FN 6.0	VF 8.0	VF/NM 9.0	NM- 9.2
53	16	32	48	92	126	160
54-57: 54-Powell-a	11	22	33	63	84	105
58,59-Krigstein-a	12	24	36	69	92	115
60-63,65: 60-Powell-a	10	20	30	56	73	90
64,66,67: 64,67-Crandall-a. 66-Torres, Orlando-a	10	20	30	58	77	95

NOTE: *Everett a-53, 60. Orlando a-65, 66. Severin a-64; c-58, 60, 65. Wildey a-64, 67.*

TALES OF SUSPENSE (Becomes Captain America #100 on)
Atlas (WPI No. 1,2/Male No. 3-12/VPI No. 13-18)/Marvel No. 19 on:
Jan, 1959 - No. 99, Mar, 1968

	GD 2.0	VG 4.0	FN 6.0	VF 8.0	VF/NM 9.0	NM- 9.2
1-Williamson-a (5 pgs.); Heck-c; #1-4 have sci/fi-c	137	274	411	1165	1783	2400
2,3: 2-Robot-c. 3-Flying saucer-c/story	52	104	156	416	621	825
4-Williamson-a (4 pgs.); Kirby/Everett-c/a	44	88	132	352	526	700
5,6,8,10: 5-Kirby monster-c begin	32	64	96	240	363	485
7-Prototype ish. (Lava Man); 1 panel app. Aunt May (see Str. Tales #97)	36	72	108	270	405	540
9-Prototype ish. (Iron Man)	38	76	114	285	425	565
11,12,15,17-19: 12-Crandall-a.	27	54	81	196	288	380
13-Elektro-c/story	28	56	84	203	297	390
14-Intro/1st app. Colossus-c/sty	32	64	96	240	363	485
16-1st Metallo-c/story (4/61, Iron Man prototype)	32	64	96	240	358	475
20-Colossus-c/story (2nd app.)	28	56	84	203	297	390
21-25: 25-Last 10¢ issue	22	44	66	156	228	300
26,27,29,30,33,34,36-38: 33-(9/62)-Hulk 1st x-over cameo (picture on wall)	18	36	54	131	191	250
28-Prototype ish. (Stone Men)	19	38	57	136	198	360
31-Prototype ish. (Dr. Doom)	22	44	66	156	228	300
32-Prototype ish. (Dr. Strange)(8/62)-Sazzik The Sorcerer app.; "The Man and the Beehive" story, 1 month before TTA #35 (2nd Antman), came out after "The Man in the Ant Hill" in TTA #27 (1/62) (1st Antman)-Characters from both stories were tested to see which got best fan response	31	62	93	232	346	460
35-Prototype issue (The Watcher)	22	44	66	156	228	300
39 (3/63)-Origin/1st app. Iron Man & begin series; 1st Iron Man story has Kirby layouts	355	710	1065	3550	5775	8000
40-2nd app. Iron Man (in new armor)	125	250	375	1000	1750	2500
41-3rd app. Iron Man; Dr. Strange (villain) app.	70	140	210	560	980	1400
42-45: 45-Intro. & 1st app. Happy & Pepper	41	82	123	297	498	700
46,47: 46-1st app. Crimson Dynamo	29	58	87	210	355	500
48-New Iron Man armor by Ditko	35	70	105	254	427	600
49-1st X-Men x-over (same date as X-Men #3, 1/64); also 1st Avengers x-over (w/o Captain America); 1st Tales of the Watcher back-up story & begins (2nd app. Watcher; see F.F. #13)	47	94	141	341	570	800
50-1st app. Mandarin	19	38	57	138	219	300
51-1st Scarecrow	17	34	51	123	199	275
52-1st app. The Black Widow (4/64)	23	46	69	167	271	375
53-Origin The Watcher; 2nd Black Widow app.	16	32	48	116	183	250
54-56: 56-1st app. Unicorn	11	22	33	79	132	185
57-Origin/1st app. Hawkeye (9/64)	23	46	69	167	283	400
58-Captain America battles Iron Man (10/64)-Classic-c; 2nd Kraven app. (Cap's 1st app. in this title)	29	58	87	210	355	500
59-Iron Man plus Captain America double feature begins (11/64); 1st S.A. Captain America solo story; intro Jarvis, Avenger's butler; classic-c	29	58	87	210	355	500
60-2nd app. Hawkeye (#64 is 3rd app.)	15	30	45	105	175	250
61,62,64: 62-Origin Mandarin (2/65)	9	18	27	65	103	140
63-1st Silver Age origin Captain America (3/65)	19	38	57	138	224	375
65-G.A. Red Skull in WWII stories(also in #66);-1st Silver-Age Red Skull (5/65).	17	34	51	107	163	275
66-Origin Red Skull	13	26	39	94	147	200
67-70: 69-1st app. Titanium Man. 70-Begin alternating-c features w/Capt. America (even #'s) & Iron Man (odd #'s)	9	18	27	63	89	115
71-75, 77,78,81-98: 75-1st app. Agent 13 later named Sharon Carter. 78-Col. Nick Fury app. 81-Intro the Adaptoid by Kirby (also in #82-84). 88-Mole Man app. in Iron Man story. 92-1st Nick Fury x-over (cameo, as Agent of S.H.I.E.L.D., 8/67). 94-Intro Modok. 95-Capt. America's i.d. revealed. 98-1st app. new Zemo (son?) in cameo (#99 is 1st full app.)	6	12	18	43	59	75
76-Intro Batroc & Sharon Carter, Agent 13 of S.H.I.E.L.D.	7	14	21	50	68	85
79-Begin 3 part Iron Man Sub-Mariner battle story; Sub-Mariner-c & cameo; 1st app. Cosmic Cube; 1st modern Red Skull	8	16	24	53	74	95
80-Iron Man battles Sub-Mariner story cont'd in Tales to Astonish #82; classic Red Skull-c	8	16	24	53	74	95
99-Captain America story cont'd in Captain America #100; Iron Man story cont'd in Iron Man & Sub-Mariner #1	8	16	24	55	78	100

NOTE: *Abel a-73-81i(as Gary Michaels), J. Buscema a-1; c-3. Colan a-39, 73-99p; c(p)-73, 75, 77, 79, 81, 83, 85-87, 89, 91, 93, 95, 97, 99. Crandall a-12. Davis a-38. Ditko a-1-15, 17-44, 46, 47-49p; c-2, 10i, 13i, 23i. Kirby/Ditko a-7; c-10, 13, 22, 28, 34. Everett a-8. Forte a-5, 9. Giacoia a-82. Heath a-2, 10. Gil Kane a-88p, 89-91; c-88, 89-91p. Kirby a(p)-2-4, 6-35, 40, 41, 43, 59-75, 77-86, 92-99; layouts-69-75, 77; c(p)4-28(most), 29-56, 58-72, 74, 76, 78, 80, 82, 84, 86, 92, 94, 96, 98. Leiber/Fox a-42, 43, 45, 51. Reinman a-26, 44i, 49i, 52i, 53i. Tuska a-58, 70-74. Wood c/a-71i.*

TALES OF SUSPENSE
Marvel Comics: V2#1, Jan, 1995 ($6.95, one-shot)

	GD 2.0	VG 4.0	FN 6.0	VF 8.0	VF/NM 9.0	NM- 9.2
V2#1-James Robinson script; acetate-c.						7.00

TALES OF SWORD & SORCERY (See Dagar)

TALES OF TERROR
Toby Press Publications: 1952 (no month)

	GD 2.0	VG 4.0	FN 6.0	VF 8.0	VF/NM 9.0	NM- 9.2
1-Fawcette-c; Ravielli-a	26	52	78	150	210	270

NOTE: *This title was cancelled due to similarity to the E.C. title.*

TALES OF TERROR (See Movie Classics)

TALES OF TERROR (Magazine)
Eerie Publications: Summer, 1964

	GD 2.0	VG 4.0	FN 6.0	VF 8.0	VF/NM 9.0	NM- 9.2
1	5	10	15	33	44	55

TALES OF TERROR
Eclipse Comics: July, 1985 - No. 13, July, 1987 ($2.00, Baxter paper, mature)

	GD 2.0	VG 4.0	FN 6.0	VF 8.0	VF/NM 9.0	NM- 9.2
1-13: 5-1st Lee Weeks-a. 7-Sam Kieth-a. 10-Snyder-a. 12-Vampire story						3.00

TALES OF TERROR ANNUAL
E.C. Comics: 1951 - No. 3, 1953 (25¢, 132 pgs., 16 stories each)

	GD 2.0	VG 4.0	FN 6.0	VF 8.0	VF/NM 9.0	NM- 9.2
nn(1951)(Scarce)-Feldstein infinity-c	550	1100	1650	4400	-	-
2(1952)-Feldstein-c	212	424	636	1590	2120	2650
3(1953)-Feldstein bondage/torture-c	164	328	492	1230	1640	2050

NOTE: *No. 1 contains three horror and one science fiction comic which came out in 1950. No. 2 contains a horror, crime, and science fiction book which generally had cover dates in 1951, and No. 3 had horror, crime, and shock books that generally appeared in 1952. All E.C. annuals contain four complete books that did not sell on the stands which were rebound in the annual format, minus the covers, and sold from the E.C. office and on the stands in key cities. The contents of each annual may vary in the same year. Crypt Keeper, Vault Keeper, Old Witch app. on all-c.*

TALES OF TERROR ILLUSTRATED (See Terror Illustrated)

TALES OF TEXAS JOHN SLAUGHTER (See Walt Disney Presents, 4-Color #997)

TALES OF THE BEANWORLD
Beanworld Press/Eclipse Comics: Feb, 1985 - No. 19, 1991; No. 20, 1993 - No. 21, 1993 ($1.50/$2.00, B&W)

	GD 2.0	VG 4.0	FN 6.0	VF 8.0	VF/NM 9.0	NM- 9.2
1-21						3.00

TALES OF THE BIZARRO WORLD
DC Comics: 2000 ($14.95, TPB)

	GD 2.0	VG 4.0	FN 6.0	VF 8.0	VF/NM 9.0	NM- 9.2
nn-Reprints early Bizarro stories; new Jaime Hernandez-c						15.00

TALES OF THE DARKNESS
Image Comics (Top Cow): Apr, 1998 - No. 4, Dec, 1998 ($2.95)

	GD 2.0	VG 4.0	FN 6.0	VF 8.0	VF/NM 9.0	NM- 9.2
1-4: 1,2-Portacio-c/a(p). 3,4-Lansing & Nocon-a(p)						3.00
1-American Entertainment Ed.						3.00
#1/2 (1/01, $2.95)						3.00

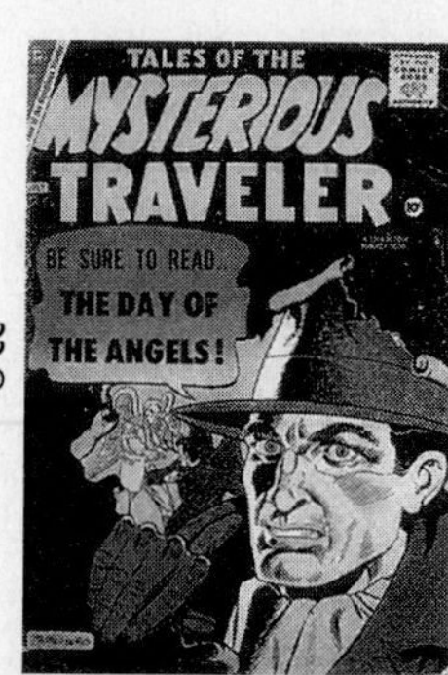

Tales of the Mysterious Traveler #8 © CC

Tales of the Teen Titans #52 © DC

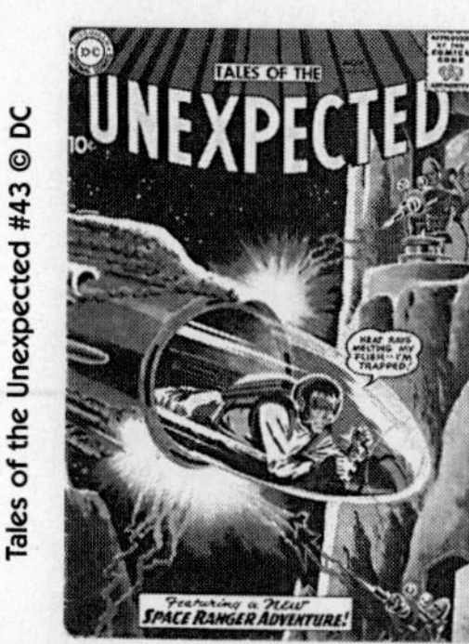

Tales of the Unexpected #43 © DC

TALES OF THE GREEN BERET
Dell Publishing Co.: Jan, 1967 - No. 5, Oct, 1969

	GD 2.0	VG 4.0	FN 6.0	VF 8.0	VF/NM 9.0	NM- 9.2
1-Glanzman-a in 1-4 & 5r	4	8	12	22	30	38
2-5: 5-Reprints #1	3	6	9	18	23	28

TALES OF THE GREEN HORNET
Now Comics: Sept, 1990 - No. 2, 1990; V2#1, Jan, 1992 - No.4, Apr, 1992; V3#1, Sept, 1992 - No. 3, Nov, 1992

	GD 2.0	VG 4.0	FN 6.0	VF 8.0	VF/NM 9.0	NM- 9.2
1,2						2.50
V2#1-4 ($1.95)						2.50
V3#1 ($2.75)-Polybagged w/hologram trading card						3.00
V3#2,3 ($2.50)						2.50

TALES OF THE GREEN LANTERN CORPS (See Green Lantern #107)
DC Comics: May, 1981 - No. 3, July, 1981 (Limited series)

	GD 2.0	VG 4.0	FN 6.0	VF 8.0	VF/NM 9.0	NM- 9.2
1-3: 1-Origin of G.L. & the Guardians, Annual 1 (1/85)-Gil Kane-c/a						3.00

TALES OF THE INVISIBLE SCARLET O'NEIL (See Harvey Comics Hits #59)

TALES OF THE KILLERS (Magazine)
World Famous Periodicals: V1#10, Dec, 1970 - V1#11, Feb, 1971 (B&W, 52 pg)

	GD 2.0	VG 4.0	FN 6.0	VF 8.0	VF/NM 9.0	NM- 9.2
V1#10-One pg. Frazetta; r/Crime Does Not Pay	4	8	12	25	33	42
11-similar-c to Crime Does Not Pay #47; contains r/Crime Does Not Pay	3	7	10	21	28	35

TALES OF THE LEGION (Formerly Legion of Super-Heroes)
DC Comics: No. 314, Aug, 1984 - No. 354, Dec, 1987

	GD 2.0	VG 4.0	FN 6.0	VF 8.0	VF/NM 9.0	NM- 9.2
314-354: 326-r-begin						2.50
Annual 4,5 (1986, 1987)-Formerly LSH Annual						3.50

TALES OF THE MARINES (Formerly Devil-Dog Dugan #1-3)
Atlas Comics (OPI): No. 4, Feb, 1957 (Marines At War #5 on)

	GD 2.0	VG 4.0	FN 6.0	VF 8.0	VF/NM 9.0	NM- 9.2
4-Powell-a; Severin-c	8	16	24	43	54	65

TALES OF THE MARVELS
Marvel Comics: 1995/1996 (all acetate, painted-c)

	GD 2.0	VG 4.0	FN 6.0	VF 8.0	VF/NM 9.0	NM- 9.2
...Blockbuster 1 (1995, $5.95, one-shot), ...Inner Demons 1 (1996, $5.95, one shot), ...Wonder Years 1,2 (1995, $4.95, limited series)						6.00

TALES OF THE MARVEL UNIVERSE
Marvel Comics: Feb, 1997 ($2.95, one-shot)

	GD 2.0	VG 4.0	FN 6.0	VF 8.0	VF/NM 9.0	NM- 9.2
1-Anthology; wraparound-c; Thunderbolts, Ka-Zar app.						3.00

TALES OF THE MYSTERIOUS TRAVELER (See Mysterious...)
Charlton Comics: Aug, 1956 - No. 13, June, 1959; V2#14, Oct, 1985 - No. 15, Dec, 1985

	GD 2.0	VG 4.0	FN 6.0	VF 8.0	VF/NM 9.0	NM- 9.2
1-No Ditko-a; Giordano/Alascia-c	46	92	138	276	413	550
2-Ditko-a(1)	40	80	120	240	345	450
3-Ditko-c/a(1)	40	80	120	240	355	470
4-6-Ditko-c/a(3-4 stories each)	48	96	144	288	432	575
7-9-Ditko-a(1-2 each). 8-Rocke-c	40	80	120	240	340	440
10,11-Ditko-c/a(3-4 each)	43	86	129	258	384	510
12	18	36	54	104	142	180
13-Baker-a (r?)	19	38	57	109	152	195
V2#14,15 (1985)-Ditko-c/a-low print run	1	2	3	5	7	9

TALES OF THE NEW TEEN TITANS
DC Comics: June, 1982 - No. 4, Sept, 1982 (Limited series)

	GD 2.0	VG 4.0	FN 6.0	VF 8.0	VF/NM 9.0	NM- 9.2
1-4						4.00

TALES OF THE PONY EXPRESS (TV)
Dell Publishing Co.: No. 829, Aug, 1957 - No. 942, Oct, 1958

	GD 2.0	VG 4.0	FN 6.0	VF 8.0	VF/NM 9.0	NM- 9.2
Four Color 829 (#1)--Painted-c	5	10	15	36	48	60
Four Color 942-Title -Pony Express	5	10	15	36	48	60

TALES OF THE REALM
CrossGen Comics: Oct, 2003 - No. 6 ($2.95, limited series)

	GD 2.0	VG 4.0	FN 6.0	VF 8.0	VF/NM 9.0	NM- 9.2
1,2-Kirkman-s						3.00

TALES OF THE SUN RUNNERS
Sirius Comics/Amazing Comics No. 3: V2#1, July, 1986 - V2#3, 1986? ($1.50)

	GD 2.0	VG 4.0	FN 6.0	VF 8.0	VF/NM 9.0	NM- 9.2
V2#1-3, Christmas Special 1(12/86)						2.25

TALES OF THE TEENAGE MUTANT NINJA TURTLES
Mirage Studios: May, 1987 - No. 7, Aug (Apr-c), 1989 (B&W, $1.50)
(See Teenage Mutant...)

	GD 2.0	VG 4.0	FN 6.0	VF 8.0	VF/NM 9.0	NM- 9.2
1-7: 2-Title merges w/Teenage Mutant Ninja...						2.25

TALES OF THE TEEN TITANS (Formerly The New Teen Titans)
DC Comics: No. 41, Apr, 1984 - No. 91, July, 1988 (75¢)

	GD 2.0	VG 4.0	FN 6.0	VF 8.0	VF/NM 9.0	NM- 9.2
41,45-49: 46-Aqualad & Aquagirl join						3.00
42-44: The Judas Contract part 1-3 with Deathstroke the Terminator in all; concludes in Annual #3. 44-Dick Grayson becomes Nightwing (3rd to be Nightwing) & joins Titans; Jericho (Deathstroke's son) joins; origin Deathstroke						3.50
50,53-55: 50-Double size; app. Betty Kane (Bat-Girl) out of costume. 53-1st full app. Azrael; Deathstroke cameo. 54,55-Deathstroke-c/stories						3.50
51,52,56-91: 52-1st app. Azrael in cameo (not same as newer character). 56-Intro Jinx. 57-Neutron app. 59-r/DC Comics Presents #26. 60-91-r/New Teen Titans Baxter series. 68-B. Smith-c. 70-Origin Kole						2.50
Annual 3(1984, $1.25)-Part 4 of The Judas Contract; Deathstroke-c/story; Death of Terra; indicia says Teen Titans Annual; previous annuals listed as New Teen Titans Annual #1,2						4.00
Annual 4-(1986, $1.25)						2.50

TALES OF THE TEXAS RANGERS (See Jace Pearson...)

TALES OF THE UNEXPECTED (Becomes The Unexpected #105 on)(See Adventure #75, Super DC Giant)
National Periodical Publications: Feb-Mar, 1956 - No. 104, Dec-Jan, 1967-68

	GD 2.0	VG 4.0	FN 6.0	VF 8.0	VF/NM 9.0	NM- 9.2
1	91	182	273	774	1187	1600
2	45	90	135	360	543	725
3-5	32	64	96	240	363	485
6-10: 6-1st Silver Age issue	27	54	81	196	291	385
11,14,19,20	17	34	51	123	182	240
12,13,15-18,21-24: All have Kirby-a. 15,17-Grey tone-c. 16-Character named 'Thor' with a magic hammer by Kirby (8/57, unlike later Thor)	23	46	69	167	244	320
25-30	15	30	45	104	152	200
31-39	13	26	39	90	133	175
40-Space Ranger begins (8/59, 3rd ap.), ends #82	90	180	270	765	1170	1575
41,42-Space Ranger stories	35	70	105	263	394	525
43-1st Space Ranger-c this title; grey tone-c	63	126	189	536	818	1100
44-46	25	50	75	181	266	350
47-50	19	38	57	136	198	260
51-60: 54-Dinosaur-c/story	15	30	45	109	160	210
61-67: 67-Last 10¢ issue	13	26	39	90	133	175
68-82: 82-Last Space Ranger	8	16	24	53	74	95
83-90,92-99	6	12	18	38	52	65
91,100: 91-1st Automan (also in #94,97)	6	12	18	40	55	70
101-104	5	10	15	33	44	55

NOTE: ***Neal Adams** c-104. **Anderson** a-50. **Brown** a-50-82(Space Ranger); c-19, 40, & many Space Ranger-c. **Cameron** a-24, 27, 29; c-24. **Heath** a-49. **Bob Kane** a-24, 48. **Kirby** a-12, 13, 15-18, 21-24; c-13, 18, 22. **Meskin** a-15, 18, 26, 27, 35, 66. **Moreira** a-16, 20, 29, 38, 44, 62, 71; c-38. **Roussos** c-10. **Wildey** a-31.*

TALES OF THE WEST (See 3-D...)

TALES OF THE WITCHBLADE
Image Comics (Top Cow Productions): Nov, 1996 - Present ($2.95)

	GD 2.0	VG 4.0	FN 6.0	VF 8.0	VF/NM 9.0	NM- 9.2
1/2	1	2	3	5	7	9
1/2 Gold						15.00
1-Daniel-c/a(p)	1	3	4	6	8	10
1-Variant-c by Turner	2	4	6	10	12	15
1-Platinum Edition						30.00
2,3						6.00
4-6: 6-Green-c						5.00
7-9: 9-Lara Croft-c						3.00
7-Variant-c by Turner	1	2	3	5	6	8
Witchblade: Distinctions (4/01, $14.95, TPB) r/#1-6; Green-c						15.00

TALES OF THE WITCHBLADE COLLECTED EDITION
Image Comics (Top Cow): May, 1998 - Present ($4.95/$5.95, square-bound)

	GD 2.0	VG 4.0	FN 6.0	VF 8.0	VF/NM 9.0	NM- 9.2
1,2: 1-r/#1,2. 2-($5.95) r/#3,4						6.00

TALES OF THE WIZARD OF OZ (See Wizard of OZ, 4-Color #1308)

TALES OF THE ZOMBIE (Magazine)
Marvel Comics Group: Aug, 1973 - No. 10, Mar, 1975 (75¢, B&W)

	GD 2.0	VG 4.0	FN 6.0	VF 8.0	VF/NM 9.0	NM- 9.2
V1#1-Reprint/Menace #5; origin	3	7	10	21	28	35
2,3: 2-Everett biog. & memorial	3	6	9	18	23	28
V2#1(#4)-Photos & text of James Bond movie "Live & Let Die"	3	6	9	16	20	24
5-10: 8-Kaluta-a	2	4	6	14	18	22
Annual 1(Summer,'75)(#11)-B&W; Everett, Buscema-a	3	6	9	16	20	25

NOTE: Brother Voodoo app. 2, 5, 6, 10. ***Alcala** a-7-9. **Boris** c-1-4. **Colan** a-2r, 6. **Heath** a-5r. **Reese** a-2. **Tuska** a-2r.*

TALES OF THUNDER
Deluxe Comics: Mar, 1985

	GD 2.0	VG 4.0	FN 6.0	VF 8.0	VF/NM 9.0	NM- 9.2
1-Dynamo, Iron Maiden, Menthor app.; Giffen-a						2.25

Tales to Astonish #8 © MAR

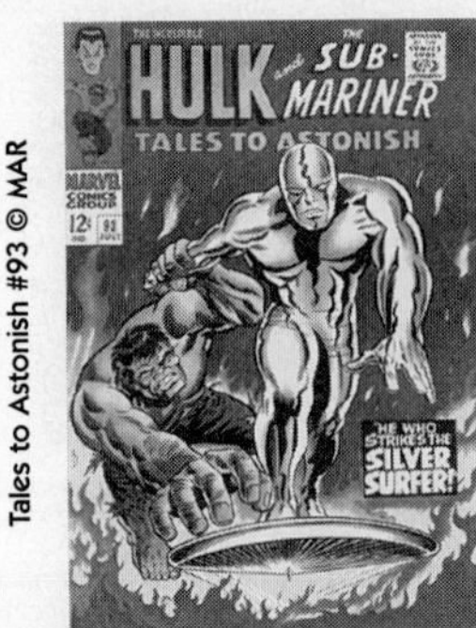

Tales to Astonish #93 © MAR

Tangent Comics/ The Joker #1 © DC

	GD 2.0	VG 4.0	FN 6.0	VF 8.0	VF/NM 9.0	NM- 9.2

TALES OF VOODOO
Eerie Publications: V1#11, Nov, 1968 - V7#6, Nov, 1974 (Magazine)

V1#11	5	10	15	33	44	55
V2#1(3/69)-V2#4(9/69)	4	8	12	24	32	40
V3#1-6('70): 4- "Claws of the Cat" redrawn from Climax #1	3	6	9	19	25	32
V4#1-6('71), V5#1-7('72), V6#1-6('73), V7#1-6('74)	3	6	9	19	25	32
Annual 1	3	7	10	21	28	35

NOTE: *Bondage-c-V1#10, V2#4, V3#4.*

TALES OF WELLS FARGO (TV)(See Western Roundup under Dell Giants)
Dell Publishing Co.: No. 876, Feb, 1958 - No. 1215, Oct-Dec, 1961

Four Color 876 (#1)-Photo-c	10	20	30	72	104	135
Four Color 968 (2/59), 1023, 1075 (3/60), 1113 (7-9/60)-All photo-c	10	20	30	67	96	125
Four Color 1167 (3-5/61), 1215-Photo-c	9	18	27	63	89	115

TALESPIN (Also see Cartoon Tales & Disney's Talespin Limited Series)
Disney Comics: June, 1991 - No. 7, Dec, 1991 ($1.50)

1-7 — 2.25

TALES TO ASTONISH (Becomes The Incredible Hulk #102 on)
Atlas (MAP No. 1/ZPC No. 2-14/VPI No. 15-21/Marvel No. 22 on: Jan, 1959 - No. 101, Mar, 1968

1-Jack Davis-a; monster-c.	137	274	411	1165	1783	2400
2-Ditko flying saucer-c (Martians); #2-4 have sci/fi-c.	56	112	168	476	731	985
3,4	44	88	132	352	526	700
5-Prototype issue (Stone Men); Williamson-a (4 pgs.); Kirby monster-c begin	45	90	135	360	543	725
6-Prototype issue (Stone Men)	36	72	108	270	405	540
7-Prototype issue (Toad Men)	36	72	108	270	405	540
8-10	32	64	96	240	363	485
11-14,17-20: 13-Swipes story from Menace #8	27	54	81	194	285	375
15-Prototype issue (Electro)	34	68	102	255	383	510
16-Prototype issue (Stone Men)	29	58	87	210	310	410
21-(7/61)-Hulk prototype	29	58	87	210	310	410
22-26,28-34	20	40	60	142	209	275
27-1st Ant-Man app. (1/62); last 10¢ issue (see Strange Tales #73,78 & Tales of Suspense #32)	289	578	867	2890	4695	6500
35-(9/62)-2nd app. Ant-Man, 1st in costume; begin series & Ant-Man-c	140	280	420	1120	1960	2800
36-3rd app. Ant-Man	64	128	192	512	894	1275
37-40: 38-1st app. Egghead	37	74	111	268	396	625
41-43	28	56	84	203	339	475
44-Origin & 1st app. The Wasp (6/63)	38	76	114	275	462	650
45-48: 48-Origin & 1st app. The Porcupine.	17	34	51	123	199	275
49-Ant-Man becomes Giant Man (11/63)	21	42	63	152	241	330
50,51,53-56,58: 50-Origin/1st app. Human Top (alias Whirlwind). 53-Origin Colossus	11	22	33	80	125	170
52-Origin/1st app. Black Knight (2/64)	13	26	39	94	152	210
57-Early Spider-Man app. (7/64)	23	46	69	167	268	370
59-Giant Man vs. Hulk feature story (9/64); Hulk's 1st app. this title	26	52	78	188	319	450
60-Giant Man & Hulk double feature begins	17	34	51	123	199	275
61-69: 61-All Ditko issue; 1st mailbag. 62-1st app./origin The Leader; new Wasp costume. 63-Origin Leader; 65-New Giant Man costume. 68-New Human Top costume. 69-Last Giant Man.	8	16	24	58	94	130
70-Sub-Mariner & Incredible Hulk begins (8/65)	9	18	27	65	107	150
71-81,83-91,94-99: 72-Begin alternating-c features w/Sub-Mariner (even #'s) & Hulk (odd #'s). 79-Hulk vs. Hercules-c/story. 81-1st app. Boomerang. 90-1st app. The Abomination. 97-X-Men cameo (brief)	6	12	18	38	52	65
82-Iron Man battles Sub-Mariner (1st Iron Man x-over outside The Avengers & TOS); story cont'd from Tales of Suspense #80	6	12	18	43	59	75
92-1st Silver Surfer x-over (outside of Fantastic Four, 6/67); 1 panel cameo only	6	12	18	40	55	70
93-Hulk battles Silver Surfer-c/story (1st full x-over)	8	16	24	53	74	95
100-Hulk battles Sub-Mariner full-length story	7	14	21	46	63	80
101-Hulk story cont'd in Incredible Hulk #102; Sub-Mariner story continued in Iron Man & Sub-Mariner #1	8	16	24	53	74	95

NOTE: ***Ayers*** *c(i)-9-12, 16, 18, 19.* ***Berg*** *a-1.* ***Burgos*** *a-62-64p.* ***Buscema*** *a-85-87p.* ***Colan*** *a(p)-70-76, 78-82, 84, 85, 101; c(p)-71-76, 78, 80, 82, 84, 86, 88, 90.* ***Ditko*** *a-1, 3-48, 50i, 60-67p; c-2, 7i, 8i, 14i, 17i.* ***Everett*** *a-78, 79i, 80-84, 85-90i, 94i, 95, 96; c(i)-79-81, 83, 86, 88.* ***Forte*** *a-6.* ***Kane*** *a-76, 88-91; c-89, 91.* ***Kirby*** *a(p)-1, 5-34-40, 44, 49-51, 68-70, 82, 83; layouts-71-84; c(p)-1, 3-48, 50-70, 72, 73, 75, 77, 78, 79, 81, 85, 90.* ***Kirby/Ditko*** *a-7, 8, 12, 13, 50; c-7, 8, 10, 13.* ***Leiber/Fox*** *a-47, 48, 50, 51.* ***Powell*** *a-65-69p, 73, 74.* ***Reinman*** *a-6, 36, 45, 46, 54i, 56-60i.*

TALES TO ASTONISH (2nd Series)
Marvel Comics Group: Dec, 1979 - No. 14, Jan, 1981

V1#1-Reprints Sub-Mariner #1 by Buscema — 6.00
2-14: Reprints Sub-Mariner #2-14 — 4.00

TALES TO ASTONISH
Marvel Comics: V3#1, Oct, 1994 ($6.95, one-shot)

V3#1-Peter David scripts; acetate, painted-c — 7.00

TALES TO HOLD YOU SPELLBOUND (See Spellbound)

TALES TO OFFEND
Dark Horse Comics: July, 1997 ($2.95, one-shot)

1-Frank Miller-s/a, EC-style cover — 3.50

TALES TOO TERRIBLE TO TELL (Becomes Terrology #10, 11)
New England Comics: Wint, 1989-90 - No. 11, Nov-Dec.1993 ($2.95/$3.50, B&W with card-stock covers)

1-($2.95) Reprints of non-EC pre-code horror; EC-style cover by Bisette — 4.00
2-8-($3.50) Story reprints, history of the pre-code titles and creators; cover galleries (B&W) inside & on back-c (color) — 4.00
9-11-($2.95) 10,11-"Terrology" on cover — 4.00

TALEWEAVER
DC Comics (WildStorm): Nov, 2001 - No. 6, Apr, 2002 ($3.50, limited series)

1-6-Philip Tan-a/Leonard Banaag-s. 2-Variant-c by Anacleto — 3.50

TALKING KOMICS
Belda Record & Publ. Co.: 1947 (20 pgs, slick-c)

	GD	VG	FN	VF	VF/NM	NM-
Each comic contained a record that followed the story - much like the Golden Record sets. Known titles: Chirpy Cricket, Lonesome Octopus, Sleepy Santa, Grumpy Shark, Flying Turtle, Happy Grasshopper with records...	3	6	9	16	20	25

TALLY-HO COMICS
Swappers Quarterly (Baily Publ. Co.): Dec, 1944

	GD	VG	FN	VF	VF/NM	NM-
nn-Frazetta's 1st work as Giunta's assistant; Man in Black horror story; violence; Giunta-c	42	84	126	252	376	500

TALOS OF THE WILDERNESS SEA
DC Comics: Aug, 1987 ($2.00, one-shot)

1 — 2.25

TALULLAH (See Comic Books Series I)

TAMMY, TELL ME TRUE
Dell Publishing Co.: No. 1233, 1961

	GD	VG	FN	VF	VF/NM	NM-
Four Color 1233-Movie	7	14	21	51	71	90

TANGENT COMICS
.../ THE ATOM, DC Comics: Dec, 1997 ($2.95, one-shot)
1-Dan Jurgens-s/Jurgens & Paul Ryan-a — 3.00
.../ THE BATMAN, DC Comics: Sept, 1998 ($1.95, one-shot)
1-Dan Jurgens-s/Klaus Janson-a — 2.25
.../ DOOM PATROL, DC Comics: Dec, 1997 ($2.95, one-shot)
1- Dan Jurgens-s/Sean Chen & Kevin Conrad-a — 3.00
.../ THE FLASH, DC Comics: Dec, 1997 ($2.95, one-shot)
1-Todd Dezago-s/Gary Frank & Cam Smith-a — 3.00
.../ GREEN LANTERN, DC Comics: Dec, '97 ($2.95, one-shot)
1-James Robinson-s/J.H. Williams III & Mick Gray-a — 3.00
.../ JLA, DC Comics: Sept, 1998 ($1.95, one-shot)
1-Dan Jurgens-s/Banks & Rapmund-a — 2.25
.../ THE JOKER, DC Comics: Dec, 1997 ($2.95, one-shot)
1-Karl Kesel-s/Matt Haley & Tom Simmons-a — 3.00
.../ THE JOKER'S WILD, DC Comics: Sept, 1998 ($1.95, one-shot)
1-Kesel & Simmons-s/Phillips & Rodriguez-a — 2.25
.../ METAL MEN, DC Comics: Dec, 1997 ($2.95, one-shot)
1-Ron Marz-s/Mike McKone & Mark McKenna-a — 3.00
.../ NIGHTWING, DC Comics: Dec, 1997 ($2.95, one-shot)
1-John Ostrander-s/Jan Duursema-a — 3.00
.../ NIGHTWING: NIGHTFORCE, DC Comics: Sept, 1998 ($1.95, one-shot)
1-John Ostrander-s/Jan Duursema-a — 2.25
.../ POWERGIRL, DC Comics: Sept, 1998 ($1.95, one-shot)
1-Marz-s/Abell & Vines-a — 2.25
.../ SEA DEVILS, DC Comics: Dec, 1997 ($2.95, one-shot)
1-Kurt Busiek-s/Vince Giarrano & Tom Palmer-a — 3.00

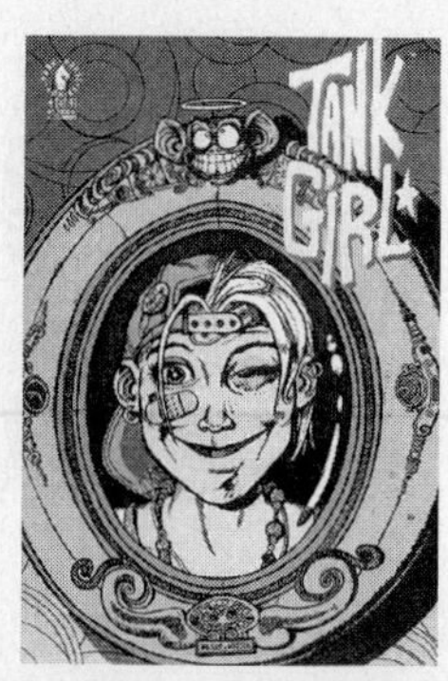

Tank Girl #4 © Deadline Magazines

Target Comics V3#2 © NOVP

Tarzan #27 © ERB

GD 2.0 VG 4.0 FN 6.0 VF 8.0 VF/NM 9.0 NM- 9.2

.../ SECRET SIX, DC Comics: Dec, 1997 ($2.95, one-shot)
1-Chuck Dixon-s/Tom Grummett & Lary Stucker-a 3.00

.../ THE SUPERMAN, DC Comics: Sept, 1998 ($1.95, one-shot)
1-Millar-s/Guice-a 2.25

.../ TALES OF THE GREEN LANTERN, DC Comics: Sept, 1998 ($1.95, one-shot)
1-Story & art by various 2.25

.../ THE TRIALS OF THE FLASH, DC Comics: Sept, 1998 ($1.95, one-shot)
1-Dezago-s/Pelletier & Lanning-a 2.25

.../ WONDER WOMAN DC Comics: Sept, 1998 ($1.95, one-shot),
1-Peter David-s/Unzueta & Mendoza-a 2.25

TANGLED WEB (See Spider-Man's Tangled Web)

TANK GIRL
Dark Horse Comics: May, 1991 - No. 4, Aug, 1991 ($2.25, B&W, mini-series)
1-Contains Dark Horse trading cards 6.00
2-4 4.00

TANK GIRL: APOCALYPSE
DC Comics: Nov, 1995 - No. 4, Feb, 1996 ($2.25, limited series)
1-4 3.00

TANK GIRL: MOVIE ADAPTATION
DC Comics: 1995 ($5.95, 68 pgs., one-shot)
nn-Peter Milligan scripts 6.00

TANK GIRL: THE ODYSSEY
DC Comics: May, 1995 - No.4, Oct, 1995 ($2.25, limited series)
1-4: Peter Milligan scripts; Hewlett-a 3.00

TANK GIRL 2
Dark Horse Comics: June, 1993 - No. 4, Sept, 1993 ($2.50, lim. series, mature)
1-4: Jamie Hewlett & Alan Martin-s/a 3.00
TPB (2/95, $17.95) r/#1-4 18.00

TAPPAN'S BURRO (See Zane Grey & 4-Color #449)

TAPPING THE VEIN (Clive Barker's...)
Eclipse Comics: 1989 - No. 5, 1992 ($6.95, squarebound, mature, 68 pgs.)
Book 1-5: 1-Russell-a, Bolton-c. 2-Bolton-a. 4-Die-cut-c 7.00
TPB (2002, $24.95, Checker Book Publ. Group) r/#1-5 25.00

TARANTULA (See Weird Suspense)

TARGET: AIRBOY
Eclipse Comics: Mar, 1988 ($1.95)
1 2.25

TARGET COMICS (...Western Romances #106 on)
Funnies, Inc./Novelty Publications/Star Publications: Feb, 1940 - V10#3 (#105), Aug-Sept, 1949

V1#1-Origin & 1st app. Manowar, The White Streak by Burgos, & Bulls-Eye Bill by Everett; City Editor (ends #5), High Grass Twins by Jack Cole (ends #4), T-Men by Joe Simon (ends #9), Rip Rory (ends #4), Fantastic Feature Films by Tarpe Mills (ends #39), & Calling 2-R (ends #14) begin; marijuana use story
497 994 1491 3479 5340 7200
2-Everett-c/a 248 496 744 1550 2325 3100
3,4-Everett, Jack Cole-a 148 296 444 925 1388 1850
5-Origin The White Streak in text; Space Hawk by Wolverton begins (6/40) (see Blue Bolt & Circus) 423 846 1269 2856 4428 6000
6-The Chameleon by Everett begins (7/40, 1st app.); White Streak origin cont'd. in text; early mention of comic collecting in letter column; 1st letter column in comics? (7/40)
192 384 576 1200 1800 2400
7-Wolverton Spacehawk-c/story (Scarce) 497 994 1491 3474 5340 7200
8-Classic sci-fi cover 144 288 432 900 1350 1800
9,12: 12-(1/41) 136 272 408 850 1275 1700
10-Intro/1st app. The Target (11/40); Simon-c 200 400 600 1250 1875 2500
11-Origin The Target & The Targeteers 172 344 516 1075 1613 2150
V2#1-Target by Bob Wood; Uncle Sam flag-c 84 168 252 525 788 1050
2-Ten part Treasure Island serial begins; Harold Delay-a; reprinted in Catholic Comics V3#1-10 (see Key Comics #5) 76 152 228 475 713 950
3-5: 4-Kit Carter, The Cadet begins 60 120 180 375 563 750
6-9: Red Seal with White Streak in #6-10 58 116 174 363 542 720
10-Classic-c 100 200 300 625 938 1250
11,12: 12-10-part Last of the Mohicans serial begins; Delay-a
56 112 168 350 525 700
V3#1-3,5-7,9,10: 10-Last Wolverton issue 55 110 165 344 517 690
4-V for Victory-c 58 116 174 363 544 725
8-Hitler, Tojo, Flag-c; 6-part Gulliver Travels serial begins; Delay-a.
70 140 210 438 657 875
11,12 19 38 57 106 146 185
V4#1-4,7-12: 8-X-Mas-c 12 24 36 71 96 120
5-Classic Statue of Liberty-c 14 28 42 81 111 140
6-Targetoons by Wolverton 14 28 42 81 111 140
V5#1-8 11 22 33 66 88 110
V6#1-4,6-10 11 22 33 63 84 105
5-Tojo-c 13 26 39 76 103 130
V7#1-12 10 20 30 58 77 95
V8#1,3-5,8,9,11,12 10 20 30 56 73 90
2,6,7-Krigstein-a 11 22 33 63 84 105
10-L.B. Cole-c 36 72 108 207 294 380
V9#1,4,6,8,10-L.B. Cole-c 35 70 105 201 288 370
2,3,5,7,9,11, V10#1 10 20 30 56 73 90
12-Classic L.B. Cole-c 39 78 117 224 317 410
V10#2,3-L.B. Cole-c 34 68 102 193 274 355

NOTE: ***Certa** c-V8#9, 11, 12, V9#5, 9, 11, V10#1. **Jack Cole** a-1-8. **Everett** a-1-9; c(signed Blake)-1, 2. **Al Fago** c-V6#8. **Sid Greene** c-V2#9, 12, V3#3. **Walter Johnson** c-V5#6, V6#4. **Tarpe Mills** a-1-4, 6, 8, 11, V3#1. **Rico** a-V7#4, 10, V8#5, 6, V9#3; c-V7#6, 8, 10, V8#2, 4, 6, 7. **Simon** a-1, 2. **Bob Wood** c-V2#2, 3, 5, 6.*

TARGET: THE CORRUPTORS (TV)
Dell Publishing Co.: No. 1306, Mar-May, 1962 - No. 3, Oct-Dec, 1962
(All have photo-c)
Four Color 1306(#1), #2,3 6 12 18 43 59 75

TARGET WESTERN ROMANCES (Formerly Target Comics; becomes Flaming Western Romances #3)
Star Publications: No. 106, Oct-Nov, 1949 - No. 107, Dec-Jan, 1949-50
106(#1)-Silhouette nudity panel; L.B. Cole-c 39 78 117 230 325 420
107(#2)-L.B. Cole-c; lingerie panels 33 66 99 190 270 350

TARGITT
Atlas/Seaboard Publ.: March, 1975 - No. 3, July, 1975
1-3: 1-Origin; Nostrand-a in all. 2-1st in costume. 3-Becomes Man-Stalker
1 2 3 5 7 9

TAROT: WITCH OF THE BLACK ROSE
Broadsword Comics: Mar, 2000 - Present ($2.95)
1-23-Jim Balent-s/c/a; two covers for each issue 3.00

TARZAN (See Aurora, Comics on Parade, Crackajack, DC 100-Page Super Spec., Edgar Rice Burroughs'..., Famous Feature Stories #1, Golden Comics Digest #4, 9, Jeep Comics #1-29, Jungle Tales of..., Limited Collectors' Edition, Popular, Sparkler, Sport Stars #1, Tip Top & Top Comics)

TARZAN
Dell Publishing Co./United Features Synd.: No. 5, 1939 - No. 161, Aug, 1947
Large Feature Comic 5('39)-(Scarce)-By Hal Foster; reprints 1st dailies from 1929
120 240 360 927 1414 1900
Single Series 20(:40)-By Hal Foster 112 224 336 700 1050 1400
Four Color 134(2/47)-Marsh-c/a 60 120 180 476 726 975
Four Color 161(8/47)-Marsh-c/a 52 104 156 416 621 825

TARZAN (...of the Apes #138 on)
Dell Publishing Co./Gold Key No. 132 on: 1-2/48 - No. 131, 7-8/62; No. 132, 11/62 - No. 206, 2/72
1-Jesse Marsh-a begins 103 206 309 799 1225 1650
2 47 94 141 376 563 750
3-5 33 66 99 248 374 500
6-10: 6-1st Tantor the Elephant. 7-1st Valley of the Monsters
29 58 87 210 305 400
11-15: 11-Two Against the Jungle begins, ends #24. 13-Lex Barker photo-c begin
24 48 72 169 247 325
16-20 19 38 57 136 198 260
21-24,26-30 15 30 45 104 152 200
25-1st "Brothers of the Spear" episode; series ends #156,160,161,196-206
17 34 51 118 174 230
31-40 11 22 33 77 114 150
41-54: Last Barker photo-c 9 18 27 60 85 110
55-60: 56-Eight pg. Boy story 7 14 21 50 68 85
61,62,64-70 6 12 18 43 59 75
63-Two Tarzan stories, 1 by Manning 7 14 21 46 63 80
71-79 6 12 18 40 55 70
80-99: 80-Gordon Scott photo-c begin 5 10 15 36 48 60
100 6 12 18 40 55 70
101-109 5 10 15 33 44 55
110 (Scarce)-Last photo-c 6 12 18 40 55 70
111-120 4 8 12 29 40 50

Tarzan #239 © ERB

Tarzan #2 © ERB

Taskmaster #4 © MAR

GD VG FN VF VF/NM NM-
2.0 4.0 6.0 8.0 9.0 9.2

121-131: Last Dell issue 4 8 12 27 36 45
132-1st Gold Key issue 5 10 15 33 44 55
133-138,140-154 4 8 12 24 32 40
139-(12/63)-1st app. Korak (Boy); leaves Tarzan & gets own book (1/64)
6 12 18 38 52 65
155-Origin Tarzan 4 8 12 29 40 50
156-161: 157-Banlu, Dog of the Arande begins, ends #159, 195. 169-Leopard Girl app.
3 6 9 21 28 35
162,165,168,171 (TV)-Ron Ely photo covers 4 8 12 22 30 38
163,164,166,167,169,170: 169-Leopard Girl app. 3 6 9 19 25 32
172-199,201-206: 178-Tarzan origin-r/#155; Leopard Girl app., also in #179, 190-193
3 6 9 18 23 28
200 3 7 10 21 28 35
Story Digest 1-(6/70, G.K., 148pp.)(scarce) 8 16 24 58 82 105

NOTE: *#162, 165, 168, 171 are TV issues. #1-153 all have* ***Marsh*** *art on Tarzan. #154-161, 163, 164, 166, 167, 172-177 all have* ***Manning*** *art on Tarzan. #178, 202 have* ***Manning*** *Tarzan reprints. No "Brothers of the Spear" in #1-24, 157-159, 162-195. #39-126, 128-156 all have* ***Russ Manning*** *art on "Brothers of the Spear". #196-201, 203-205 all have* ***Manning*** *B.O.T.S. reprints; #25-38, 127 all have Jesse* ***Marsh*** *art on B.O.T.S. #206 has a Marsh B.O.T.S. reprint.* ***Gollub*** *c-8-12.* ***Marsh*** *c-1-7.* ***Doug Wildey*** *a-162, 179-187. Many issues have front and back photo covers.*

TARZAN (Continuation of Gold Key series)
National Periodical Publications: No. 207, Apr, 1972 - No. 258, Feb, 1977

207-Origin Tarzan by Joe Kubert, part 1; John Carter begins (origin); 52 pg. issues thru #209 5 10 15 33 44 55
208,209-(52 pgs.): 208-210-Parts 2-4 of origin. 209-Last John Carter
3 6 9 18 23 28
210-220: 210-Kubert-a. 211-Hogarth, Kubert-a. 212-214: Adaptations from "Jungle Tales of Tarzan". 213-Beyond the Farthest Star begins, ends #218. 215-218,224,225-All by Kubert. 215-part Foster-r. 219-223: Adapts "The Return of Tarzan" by Kubert
2 4 6 12 16 20
221-229: 221-223-Continues adaptation of "The Return of Tarzan". 226-Manning-a
2 4 6 10 12 15
230-DC 100 Page Super Spectacular; Kubert, Kaluta-a(p); Korak begins, ends #234; Carson of Venus app. 4 8 12 24 32 40
231-235-New Kubert-a.: 231-234-(All 100 pgs.)-Adapts "Tarzan and the Lion Man"; Rex, the Wonder Dog r-#232, 233. 235-(100 pgs.)-Last Kubert issue.
4 8 12 22 30 38
236,237,239-258: 240-243 adapts "Tarzan & the Castaways". 250-256 adapts "Tarzan the Untamed." 252,253-r/#213 1 3 4 6 8 10
238-(68 pgs.) 2 4 6 12 16 20
Comic Digest 1-(Fall, 1972, 50¢, 164 pgs.)(DC)-Digest size; Kubert-c; Manning-a
5 10 15 33 44 55

NOTE: ***Anderson*** *a-207, 209, 217, 218.* ***Chaykin*** *a-216.* ***Finlay*** *a(r)-212.* ***Foster*** *strip-r #207-209, 211, 212, 221.* ***Heath*** *a-230i.* ***G. Kane*** *a(r)-232p, 233p.* ***Kubert*** *a-207-225, 227-235, 257r, 258r; c-207-249, 253.* ***Lopez*** *a-250-255p; c-250p, 251, 252, 254.* ***Manning*** *strip-r 230-235, 238.* ***Morrow*** *a-208.* ***Nino*** *a-231-234.* ***Sparling*** *a-230, 231.* ***Starr*** *a-233r.*

TARZAN (Lord of the Jungle)
Marvel Comics Group: June, 1977 - No. 29, Oct, 1979

1-New adaptions of Burrough stories; Buscema-a 1 2 3 5 6 8
1-(35¢-c variant, limited distribution)(6/77) 2 4 6 8 10 12
2-29: 2-Origin by John Buscema. 9-Young Tarzan. 12-14-Jungle Tales of Tarzan. 25-29-New stories 4.00
2-5-(35¢-c variants, limited distribution)(7-10/77) 6.00
Annual 1-3: 1-(1977). 2-(1978). 3-(1979) 4.00

NOTE: ***N. Adams*** *c-11i, 12i.* ***Alcala*** *a-9i, 10i; c-8i, 9i.* ***Buckler*** *c-25-27p, Annual 3p.* ***John Buscema*** *a-1-3, 4-18p, Annual 1; c-1-7, 8p, 9p, 10, 11p, 12p, 13, 14-19p, 21p, 22, 23p, 24p, 28p, Annual 1.* ***Mooney*** *a-22i.* ***Nebres*** *a-22i.* ***Russell*** *a-29i.*

TARZAN
Dark Horse Comics: July, 1996 - No. 20, Mar, 1998 ($2.95)

1-20: 1-6-Suydam-c 3.00

TARZAN / CARSON OF VENUS
Dark Horse Comics: May, 1998 - No. 4, Aug, 1998 ($2.95, limited series)

1-4-Darko Macan-s/Igor Korday-a 3.00

TARZAN FAMILY, THE (Formerly Korak, Son of Tarzan)
National Periodical Publications: No. 60, Nov-Dec, 1975 - No. 66, Nov-Dec, 1976

60-62-(68 pgs.): 60-Korak begins; Kaluta-r 2 4 6 10 12 15
63-66 (52 pgs.) 1 3 4 6 8 10

NOTE: *Carson of Venus-r 60-65. New John Carter-62-64, 65r, 66r. New Korak-60-66. Pellucidar feature-66. Foster strip r-60(9/4/32-10/16/32), 62(6/29/32-7/31/32), 63(10/11/31-12/13/31).* ***Kaluta*** *Carson of Venus-60-65.* ***Kubert*** *a-61, 64; c-60-64.* ***Manning*** *strip-r 60-62, 64.* ***Morrow*** *a-66r.*

TARZAN/JOHN CARTER: WARLORDS OF MARS
Dark Horse Comics: Jan, 1996 - No. 4, June, 1996 ($2.50, limited series)

1-4: Bruce Jones scripts in all. 1,2,4-Bret Blevins-c/a. 2-(4/96)-Indicia reads #3 3.00

GD VG FN VF VF/NM NM-
2.0 4.0 6.0 8.0 9.0 9.2

TARZAN KING OF THE JUNGLE (See Dell Giant #37, 51)

TARZAN, LORD OF THE JUNGLE
Gold Key: Sept, 1965 (Giant) (25¢, soft paper-c)

1-Marsh-r 9 18 27 63 89 115

TARZAN: LOVE, LIES AND THE LOST CITY (See Tarzan the Warrior)
Malibu Comics: Aug. 10, 1992 - No. 3, Sept, 1992 ($2.50, limited series)

1-($3.95, 68 pgs.)-Flip book format; Simonson & Wagner scripts 4.00
2,3-No Simonson or Wagner scripts 3.00

TARZAN MARCH OF COMICS (See March of Comics #82, 98, 114, 125, 144, 155, 172, 185, 204, 223, 240, 252, 262, 272, 286, 300, 332, 342, 354, 366)

TARZAN OF THE APES
Metropolitan Newspaper Service: 1934? (Hardcover, 4x12", 68 pgs.)

1-Strip reprints 26 52 78 147 206 265

TARZAN OF THE APES
Marvel Comics Group: July, 1984 - No. 2, Aug, 1984 (Movie adaptation)

1,2: Origin-r/Marvel Super Spec. 3.00

TARZAN'S JUNGLE ANNUAL (See Dell Giants)

TARZAN'S JUNGLE WORLD (See Dell Giant #25)

TARZAN: THE BECKONING
Malibu Comics: 1992 - No. 7, 1993 ($2.50, limited series)

1-7 3.00

TARZAN: THE LOST ADVENTURE (See Edgar Rice Burroughs' ...)

TARZAN-THE RIVERS OF BLOOD
Dark Horse Comics: Nov, 1999 - No. 8 ($2.95, limited series)

1-4: Korday-c/a 3.00

TARZAN THE SAVAGE HEART
Dark Horse Comics: Apr, 1999 - No. 4, July, 1999 ($2.95, limited series)

1-4: Grell-c/a 3.00

TARZAN THE WARRIOR (Also see Tarzan: Love, Lies and the Lost City)
Malibu Comics: Mar, 19, 1992 - No. 5, 1992 ($2.50, limited series)

1-5: 1-Bisley painted pack-c (flip book format-c) 3.00
1-2nd printing w/o flip-c by Bisley 2.50

TARZAN VS. PREDATOR AT THE EARTH'S CORE
Dark Horse Comics: Jan, 1996 - No. 4, June, 1996 ($2.50, limited series)

1-4: Lee Weeks-c/a; Walt Simonson scripts 3.00

TASKMASTER
Marvel Comics: Apr, 2002 - No. 4, July, 2002 ($2.99, limited series)

1-4-Udon Studio-s/a. 1-Iron Man app. 3.00

TASMANIAN DEVIL & HIS TASTY FRIENDS
Gold Key: Nov, 1962 (12¢)

1-Bugs Bunny & Elmer Fudd x-over 15 30 45 104 152 200

TATTERED BANNERS
DC Comics (Vertigo): Nov, 1998 - No. 4, Feb, 1999 ($2.95, limited series)

1-4-Grant & Giffen-s/McMahon-a 3.00

TEAM AMERICA (See Captain America #269)
Marvel Comics Group: June, 1982 - No. 12, May, 1983

1-12:1-Origin; Ideal Toy motorcycle characters. 9-Iron Man app. 11-Ghost Rider app. 12-Double size 2.25

TEAM ANARCHY
Dagger Comics: Oct, 1993 - No.8, 1994? ($2.50)

1-($2.75)-Red foil logo; intro Team Anarchy 2.75
1-Platinum, 2,3,3-Bronze,3-Gold,3-Silver,4-8 2.75

TEAM HELIX
Marvel Comics: Jan, 1993 - No. 4, Apr, 1993 ($1.75, limited series)

1-4: Teen Super Group. 1,2-Wolverine app. 2.25

TEAM ONE: STORMWATCH (Also see StormWatch)
Image Comics (WildStorm Productions): June, 1995 - No. 2, Aug, 1995 ($2.50, lim. series)

1,2: Steven T. Seagle scripts 2.50

TEAM ONE: WILDC.A.T.S (Also see WildC.A.T.S)
Image Comics (WildStorm Productions): July, 1995 - No. 2, Aug, 1995 ($2.50, limited series)

1,2: James Robinson scripts 2.50

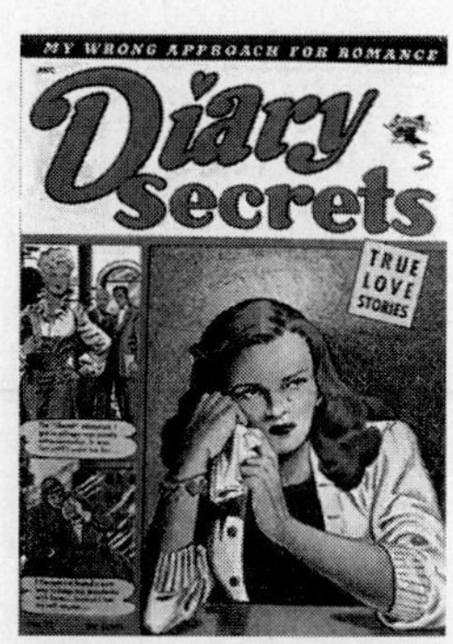

Teen-Age Diary Secrets #12 © STJ

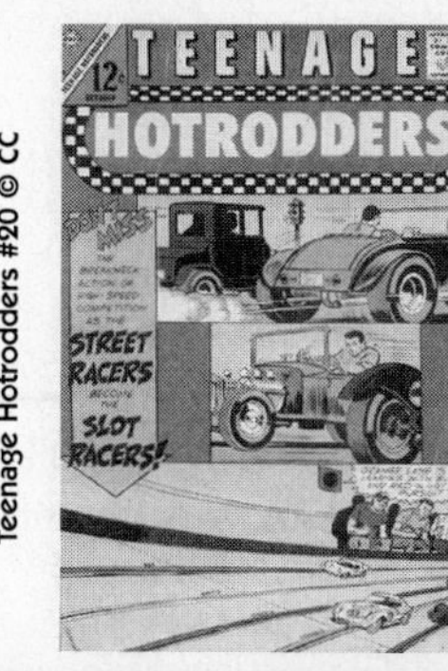

Teenage Hotrodders #20 © CC

Teenage Mutant Ninja Turtles #16 © MS

GD VG FN VF VF/NM NM-
2.0 4.0 6.0 8.0 9.0 9.2

GD VG FN VF VF/NM NM-
2.0 4.0 6.0 8.0 9.0 9.2

TEAM 7
Image Comics (WildStorm Productions): Oct, 1994 - No.4, Feb, 1995 ($2.50, limited series)
1-4: Dixon scripts in all, 1-Portacio variant-c 2.50

TEAM 7-DEAD RECKONING
Image Comics (WildStorm Productions): Jan, 1996 - No. 4, Apr, 1996 ($2.50, limited series)
1-4: Dixon scripts in all 2.50

TEAM 7-OBJECTIVE HELL
Image Comics (WildStorm Productions): May, 1995 - No. 3, July, 1995 ($1.95/$2.50, limited series)
1-($1.95)-Newstand; Dixon scripts in all; Barry Smith-c 2.25
1-3: 1-($2.50)-Direct Market; Barry Smith-c, bound-in card 2.50

TEAM SUPERMAN
DC Comics: July, 1999 ($2.95, one-shot)
1-Jeanty-a/Stelfreeze-c 3.00
...Secret Files 1 (5/98, $4.95)Origin-s and pin-ups of Superboy, Supergirl and Steel; Dave Johnson-c 5.00

TEAM TITANS (See Deathstroke & New Titans Annual #7)
DC Comics: Sept, 1992 - No. 24, Sept, 1994 ($1.75/$1.95)
1-Five different #1s exist w/origins in 1st half & the same 2nd story in each: Kilowat, Mirage, Nightrider w/Netzer/Perez-a, Redwing, & Terra w/part Perez-p; Total Chaos Pt. 3 3.00
2-24: 2-Total Chaos Pt 6. 11-Metallik app. 24-Zero Hour x-over 2.25
Annual 1,2 ('93, '94, $3.50, 68 pgs.): 2-Elseworlds tory 3.50

TEAM X/TEAM 7
Marvel Comics: Nov, 1996 ($4.95, one-shot)
1 5.00

TEAM X 2000
Marvel Comics: Feb, 1999 ($3.50, one-shot)
1-Kevin Lau-a; Bishop vs. Shi'ar Empire 3.50

TEAM YANKEE
First Comics: Jan, 1989 - No. 6, Feb, 1989 ($1.95, weekly limited series)
1-6 2.25

TEAM YOUNGBLOOD (Also see Youngblood)
Image Comics (Extreme Studios): Sept, 1993 - No. 22, Sept, 1995 ($1.95/$2.50)
1-22: 1-9-Liefeld scripts in all: 1,2,4-6,8-Thibert-c(i). 1-1st app. Dutch & Masada. 3-Spawn cameo. 5-1st app. Lynx. 7,8-Coupons 1 & 4 for Extreme Prejudice #0; Black and White Pt. 4 & 8 by Thibert. 8-Coupon #4 for E. P. #0. 9-Liefeld wraparound-c &(p)/a(p) on Pt. I. 10-Liefeld-c(p). 16,17-Polybagged w/trading card. 18-Extreme 3000 Prelude. 19-Cruz-a. 21-Angela & Glory-app. 22-Shadowhawk-c/app. 2.50

TECH JACKET
Image Comics: Nov, 2002 - Present ($2.95)
1-6-Kirkman-s/Su-a 3.00
Vol. 1: Lost and Found TPB (7/03, $12.95, 7-3/4" x 5-1/4") B&W r/#1-6; intro. by Valentino 13.00

TEDDY ROOSEVELT & HIS ROUGH RIDERS (See Real Heroes #1)
Avon Periodicals: 1950
1-Kinstler-c; Palais-a; Flag-c 19 38 57 106 146 185

TEDDY ROOSEVELT ROUGH RIDER (See Battlefield #22 & Classics Illustrated Special Issue)

TED MCKEEVER'S METROPOL (See Transit)
Marvel Comics (Epic Comics): Mar, 1991 - No. 12, Mar, 1992 ($2.95, limited series)
V1#1-12: Ted McKeever-c/a/scripts 3.50

TED MCKEEVER'S METROPOL A.D.
Marvel Comics (Epic Comics): Oct, 1992 - No. 3, Dec, 1992 ($3.50, limited series)
V2#1-3: Ted McKeever-c/a/scripts 3.50

TEENA
Magazine Enterprises/Standard Comics No. 20 on: No. 11, 1948 - No. 15, 1948; No. 20, Aug, 1949 - No. 22, Oct, 1950
A-1 #11-Teen-age; Ogden Whitney-c 9 18 27 54 70 85
A-1 #12, 15 8 16 24 46 58 70
20-22 (Standard) 6 12 18 31 38 45

TEEN-AGE BRIDES (True Bride's Experiences #8 on)
Harvey/Home Comics: Aug, 1953 - No. 7, Aug, 1954
1-Powell-a 11 22 33 63 82 110
2-Powell-a 8 16 24 45 55 70
3-7: 3,6-Powell-a 7 14 21 38 47 60

TEEN-AGE CONFESSIONS (See Teen Confessions)

TEEN-AGE CONFIDENTIAL CONFESSIONS
Charlton Comics: July, 1960 - No. 22, 1964
1 4 8 12 29 40 50
2-10 3 6 9 18 24 30
11-22 2 4 6 14 18 22

TEEN-AGE DIARY SECRETS (Formerly Blue Ribbon Comics; becomes Diary Secrets #10 on)
St. John Publishing Co.: No. 4, 9/49; nn (#5), 9/49 - No. 7, 11/49; No. 8, 2/50; No. 9, 8/50
4(9/49)-Oversized; part mag., part comic 29 58 87 164 232 300
nn(#5)(no indicia)-Oversized, all comics; contains sty "I Gave Boys the Green Light." 24 48 72 138 194 250
6,8: (Reg. size) -Photo-c; Baker-a(2-3) in each 24 48 72 135 190 245
7,9-Digest size (Pocket Comics); Baker-a(5); both have same contents; diff.-c 26 52 78 150 210 270

TEEN-AGE DOPE SLAVES (See Harvey Comics Library #1)

TEENAGE HOTRODDERS (Top Eliminator #25 on; see Blue Bird)
Charlton Comics: Apr, 1963 - No. 24, July, 1967
1 6 12 18 43 59 75
2-10 4 8 12 22 30 38
11-24 3 6 9 18 24 30

TEEN-AGE LOVE (See Fox Giants)

TEEN-AGE LOVE (Formerly Intimate)
Charlton Comics: V2#4, July, 1958 - No. 96, Dec, 1973
V2#4 5 10 15 33 44 55
5-9 4 8 12 22 30 38
10(9/59)-20 3 6 9 18 24 30
21-35 3 6 9 16 20 25
36-70 2 4 6 12 16 20
71-96: 61&62-Jonnie Love begins (origin) 2 4 6 10 12 15

TEENAGE MUTANT NINJA TURTLES (Also see Anything Goes, Donatello, First Comics Graphic Novel, Gobbledygook, Grimjack #26, Leonardo, Michaelangelo, Raphael & Tales Of The...)
Mirage Studios: 1984 - No. 62, Aug, 1993 ($1.50/$1.75, B&W; all 44-52 pgs.)
1-1st printing (3000 copies)-Only printing to have ad for Gobbledygook #1 & 2; Shredder app. (#1-4: 7-1/2x11") 31 62 93 228 339 450
1-2nd printing (6/84)(15,000 copies) 2 4 6 12 16 20
1-3rd printing (2/85)(36,000 copies) 2 4 6 8 10 12
1-4th printing, new-c (50,000 copies) 5.00
1-5th printing, new-c (8/88-c, 11/88 inside) 4.00
1-Counterfeit. **Note**: Most counterfeit copies have a half inch wide white streak or scratch marks across the center of back cover. Black part of cover is a bluish black instead of a deep black. Inside paper is very white & inside cover is bright white (no value)
2-1st printing (1984; 15,000 copies) 6 12 18 38 52 65
2-2nd printing 1 3 4 6 8 10
2-3rd printing; new Corben-c/a (2/85) 5.00
2-Counterfeit with glossy cover stock (no value).
3-1st printing (1985, 44 pgs.) 4 8 12 27 36 45
3-Variant, 500 copies, given away in NYC. Has 'Laird's Photo' in white rather than light blue 7 14 21 46 63 80
3-2nd printing; contains new back-up story 3.00
4-1st printing (1985, 44 pgs.) 3 6 9 18 24 30
4,5-2nd printing (5/87, 11/87) 2.25
5-Fugitoid begins, ends #7; 1st full color-c (1985) 2 4 6 10 12 15
6-1st printing (1986) 1 3 4 6 8 10
6-2nd printing (4/88-c, 5/88 inside) 2.25
7-4 pg. Eastman/Corben color insert; 1st color TMNT (1986, $1.75-c); Bade Biker back-up story 1 2 3 4 5 7
7-2nd printing (1/89) w/o color insert 2.25
8-Cerebus-c/story with Dave Sim-a (1986) 6.00
9,10: 9 (9/86)-Rip In Time by Corben 5.00
11-15 4.00
16-18: 18-Mark Bode'-a 3.00
18-2nd printing ($2.25, color, 44 pgs.)-New-c 2.50
19-34: 19-Begin $1.75-c. 24-26-Veitch-c/a. 2.50
32-2nd printing ($2.75, 52 pgs., full color) 3.00
35-49,51: 35-Begin $2.00-c. 2.50
50-Features pin-ups by Larsen, McFarlane, Simonson, etc. 3.00
52-62: 52-Begin $2.25-c 2.50
nn (1990, $5.95, B&W)-Movie adaptation 6.00
Book 1,2($1.50, B&W): 2-Corben-c 2.50
...Christmas Special 1 (12/90, $1.75, B&W, 52 pgs.)-Cover title: Michaelangelo Christmas Special; r/Michaelangelo one-shot plus new Raphael story 2.50

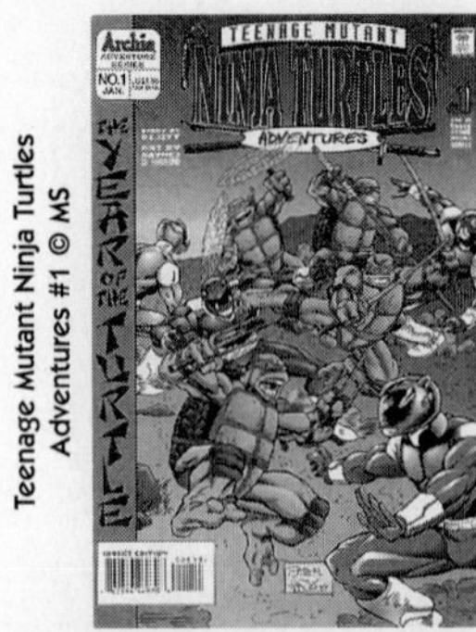

Teenage Mutant Ninja Turtles Adventures #1 © MS

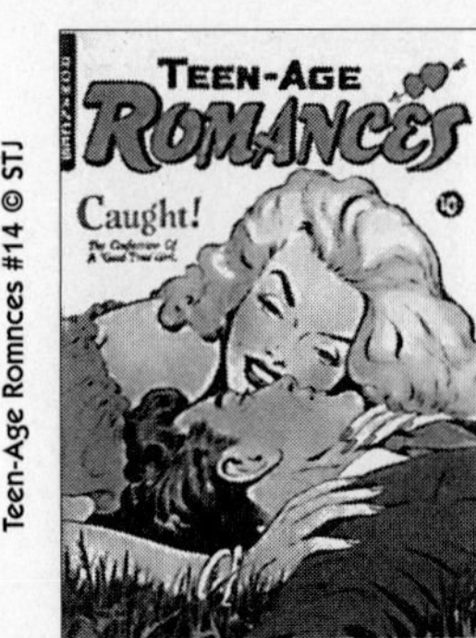

Teen-Age Romnces #14 © STJ

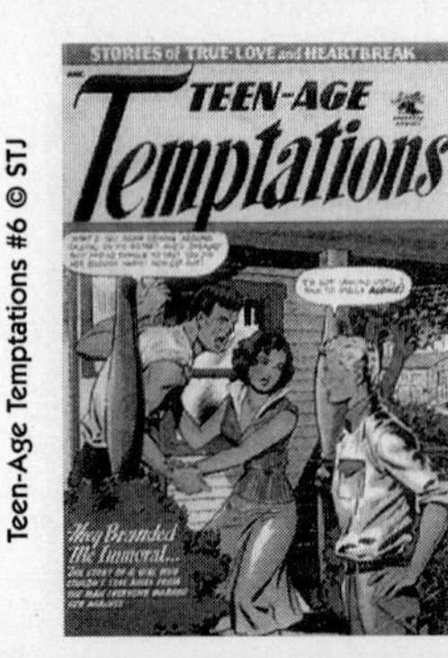

Teen-Age Temptations #6 © STJ

	GD 2.0	VG 4.0	FN 6.0	VF 8.0	VF/NM 9.0	NM- 9.2

...Special (The Maltese Turtle) nn (1/93, $2.95, color, 44 pgs.) 3.00
...Special: "Times" Pipeline nn (9/92, $2.95, color, 44 pgs.)-Mark Bode-c/a 3.00
Hardcover ($100)-r/#1-10 plus one-shots w/dust jackets - limited to 1000 w/letter of authenticity 100.00
Softcover ($40)-r/#1-10 40.00

TEENAGE MUTANT NINJA TURTLES
Mirage Studios: V2#1, Oct, 1993 - V2#13, Oct, 1995 ($2.75)
V2#1-13: 1-Wraparound-c 2.75

TEENAGE MUTANT NINJA TURTLES
Image Comics (Highbrow Ent.): June, 1996 - No. 23, Oct, 1999 ($1.95-$2.95)
1-23: 1-8: Eric Larsen-c(i) on all. 10-Savage Dragon-c/app. 3.00

TEENAGE MUTANT NINJA TURTLES
Mirage Publishing: V4#1, Dec, 2001 - Present ($2.95, B&W)
V4#1-9,11-12-Laird-s/a(i)/Lawson-a(p). 3.00
10-($3.95) Splinter dies 4.00

TEENAGE MUTANT NINJA TURTLES
Dreamwave Productions: June 2003 - Present ($2.95, color)
1-7-Animated style; Peter David-s/Lesean-a 3.00
Vol. 1 TPB (2003, $9.95) r/#1-4; cover gallery and sketch pages 10.00

TEENAGE MUTANT NINJA TURTLES (Adventures)
Archie Publications: Jan, 1996 - No. 3, Mar, 1996 ($1.50, limited series)
1-3 2.50

TEENAGE MUTANT NINJA TURTLES ADVENTURES (TV)
Archie Comics: 8/88 - No. 3, 12/88; 3/89 - No. 72, Oct, 1995 ($1.00/$1.25/$1.50/$1.75)
1-Adapts TV cartoon; not by Eastman/Laird 3.00
2,3,1-5: 2,3 (Mini-series). 1 (2nd on-going series). 5-Begins original stories not based on TV 2.50
1-11: 2nd printings 2.25
6-72: 14-Simpson-a(p). 19-1st Mighty Mutanimals (also in #20, 51-54). 22-Gene Colan-c/a. 50-Poster by Eastman/Laird. 62-w/poster 2.50
nn (1990, $2.50)-Movie adaptation 2.50
nn (Spring, 1991, $2.50, 68 pgs.)-(Meet Archie) 2.50
nn (Sum, 1991, $2.50, 68 pgs.)-(Movie II)-Adapts movie sequel 2.50
...Meet the Conservation Corps 1 (1992, $2.50, 68 pgs.) 2.50
...III The Movie: The Turtles are Back...In Time (1993, $2.50, 68 pgs.) 2.50
Special 1,4,5 (Sum/92, Spr/93, Sum/93, 68 pgs.)-1-Bill Wray-c 2.50
Giant Size Special 6 (Fall/93, $1.95, 52 pgs.) 2.50
Special 7-10 (Win/93-Fall//94, 52 pgs.): 9-Jeff Smith-c 2.50
NOTE: *There are 2nd printings of #1-11 w/B&W inside covers. Originals are color.*

TEENAGE MUTANT NINJA TURTLES CLASSICS DIGEST (TV)
Archie Comics: Aug, 1993 - No. 8, Mar, 1995? ($1.75)
1-8: Reprints TMNT Advs. 3.00

TEENAGE MUTANT NINJA TURTLES/FLAMING CARROT CROSSOVER
Mirage Publishing: Nov, 1993 - No. 4, Feb, 1994 ($2.75, limited series)
1-4: Bob Burden story 3.00

TEENAGE MUTANT NINJA TURTLES PRESENTS: APRIL O'NEIL
Archie Comics: Mar, 1993 - No. 3, June, 1993 ($1.25, limited series)
1-3 2.50

TEENAGE MUTANT NINJA TURTLES PRESENTS: DONATELLO AND LEATHERHEAD
Archie Comics: July, 1993 - No. 3, Sept, 1993 ($1.25, limited series)
1-3 2.50

TEENAGE MUTANT NINJA TURTLES PRESENTS: MERDUDE
Archie Comics: Oct, 1993 - No. 3, Dec, 1993 ($1.25, limited series)
1-3-See Mighty Mutanimals #7 for 1st app. Merdude 2.50

TEENAGE MUTANT NINJA TURTLES/SAVAGE DRAGON CROSSOVER
Mirage Studios: Aug, 1995 ($2.75, one-shot)
1 3.00

TEEN-AGE ROMANCE (Formerly My Own Romance)
Marvel Comics (ZPC): No. 77, Sept, 1960 - No. 86, Mar, 1962
77-83 4 8 12 24 32 40
84-86-Kirby-c. 84-Kirby-a(2 pgs.). 85,86-(3 pgs.) 4 8 12 29 40 50

TEEN-AGE ROMANCES
St. John Publ. Co. (Approved Comics): Jan, 1949 - No. 45, Dec, 1955
1-Baker-c/a(1) 40 80 120 240 345 450
2,3: 2-Baker-c/a. 3-Baker-c/a(3) 25 50 75 147 202 260
4,5,7,8-Photo-c; Baker-a(2-3) each 21 42 63 118 164 210
6-Slightly large size; photo-c; part magazine; Baker-a (10/49) 23 46 69 129 180 230
9-Baker-c/a; Kubert-a 27 54 81 153 214 275
10-12,20-Baker-c/a(2-3) each 20 40 60 112 156 200
13-19,21,22-Complete issues by Baker 27 54 81 153 214 275
23-25-Baker-c/a(2-3) each 19 38 57 106 146 185
26,27,33,34,36-40,42: Baker-c/a. 33,40-Signed story by Estrada. 38-Suggestive-c. 42-r/Cinderella Love #9; Last pre-code (3/55) 13 26 39 74 100 125
28-30-No Baker-a 8 16 24 43 54 65
31,32-Baker-c. 31-Estrada-s 10 20 30 60 80 100
35-Baker-c/a (16 pgs.) 14 28 42 79 107 135
41-Baker-c; Infantino-a(r); all stories are Ziff-Davis-r 11 22 33 63 84 105
43-45-Baker-c/a 14 28 42 79 107 135

TEEN-AGE TALK
I.W. Enterprises: 1964
Reprint #1 2 4 6 11 14 18
Reprint #5,8,9: 5-r/Hector #? 9-Punch Comics #?; L.B. Cole-c reprint from School Day Romances #1 2 4 6 10 13 16

TEEN-AGE TEMPTATIONS (Going Steady #10 on)(See True Love Pictorial)
St. John Publishing Co.: Oct, 1952 - No. 9, Aug, 1954
1-Baker-c/a; has story "Reform School Girl" by Estrada 45 90 135 270 403 535
2,4-Baker-c 18 36 54 104 142 180
3,5-7,9-Baker-c/a 25 50 75 144 198 255
8-Teenagers smoke reefers; Baker-c/a 25 50 75 144 198 255
NOTE: ***Estrada** a-1, 3-5.*

TEEN BEAM (Formerly Teen Beat #1)
National Periodical Publications: No. 2, Jan-Feb, 1968
2-Superman cameo; Herman's Hermits, Yardbirds, Simon & Garfunkel, Lovin Spoonful, Young Rascals app.; Orlando, Drucker-a(r); Monkees photo-c; 8 16 24 53 74 95

TEEN BEAT (Becomes Teen Beam #2)
National Periodical Publications: Nov-Dec, 1967
1-Photos & text only; Monkees photo-c; Beatles, Herman's Hermits, Animals, Supremes, Byrds app. 9 18 27 65 93 120

TEEN COMICS (Formerly All Teen; Journey Into Unknown Worlds #36 on)
Marvel Comics (WFP): No. 21, Apr, 1947 - No. 35, May, 1950
21-Kurtzman's "Hey Look"; Patsy Walker, Cindy (1st app.?), Georgie, Margie app.; Syd Shores-a begins, end #23 15 30 45 89 122 150
22,23,25,27,29,31-35: 22-(6/47)-Becomes Hedy Devine #22 (8/47) on? 11 22 33 66 88 110
24,26,28,30-Kurtzman's "Hey Look" 12 24 36 71 96 120

TEEN CONFESSIONS
Charlton Comics: Aug, 1959 - No. 97, Nov, 1976
1 8 16 24 58 82 105
2 5 10 15 33 44 55
3-10 4 8 12 25 33 42
11-30 3 6 9 19 25 32
31-Beatles-c 12 24 36 87 129 170
32-36,38-55 3 6 9 16 20 24
37 (1/66)-Beatles Fan Club story; Beatles-c 12 24 36 87 129 170
56-58,60-97: 89,90-Newton-c 2 4 6 10 13 16
59-Kaluta's 1st pro work? (12/69) 3 6 9 18 24 30

TEENIE WEENIES, THE (America's Favorite Kiddie Comic)
Ziff-Davis Publishing Co.: No. 10, 1950 - No. 11, Apr-May, 1951 (Newspaper reprints)
10,11-Painted-c 20 40 60 112 156 200

TEEN-IN (Tippy Teen)
Tower Comics: Summer, 1968 - No. 4, Fall, 1969
nn(#1, Summer, 1968) 7 14 21 50 68 85
nn(#2, Spring, 1969),3,4 5 10 15 33 44 55

TEEN LIFE (Formerly Young Life)
New Age/Quality Comics Group: No. 3, Winter, 1945 - No. 5, Fall, 1945 (Teenage magazine)
3-June Allyson photo on-c & story 13 26 39 74 100 125
4-Duke Ellington photo on-c & story 10 20 30 60 80 100
5-Van Johnson, Woody Herman & Jackie Robinson articles; Van Johnson & Woody Herman photos on-c 13 26 39 76 103 130

Teen Titans #32 © DC

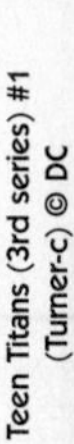
Teen Titans (3rd series) #1 (Turner-c) © DC

Tell It To The Marines #6 © TOBY

TEEN LOVE STORIES (Magazine)
Warren Publ. Co.: Sept, 1969 - No. 3, Jan, 1970 (68 pgs., photo covers, B&W)

	GD 2.0	VG 4.0	FN 6.0	VF 8.0	VF/NM 9.0	NM- 9.2
1-Photos & articles plus 36-42 pgs. new comic stories in all; Frazetta-a	5	10	15	36	48	60
2,3: 2-Anti-marijuana story	4	8	12	27	36	45

TEEN ROMANCES
Super Comics: 1964

	GD 2.0	VG 4.0	FN 6.0	VF 8.0	VF/NM 9.0	NM- 9.2
10,11,15-17-Reprints	2	4	6	8	10	12

TEEN SECRET DIARY (Nurse Betsy Crane #12 on)
Charlton Comics: Oct, 1959 - No. 11, June, 1961; No. 1, 1972

	GD 2.0	VG 4.0	FN 6.0	VF 8.0	VF/NM 9.0	NM- 9.2
1	6	12	18	38	52	65
2	4	8	12	24	32	40
3-11	3	6	9	19	25	32
1 (1972)(exist?)	3	6	9	16	20	24

TEEN TALK (See Teen)

TEEN TITANS (See Brave & the Bold #54,60, DC Super-Stars #1, Marvel & DC Present, New Teen Titans, New Titans, Official...Index and Showcase #59)
National Periodical Publications/DC Comics: 1-2/66 - No. 43, 1-2/73; No. 44, 11/76 - No. 53, 2/78

	GD 2.0	VG 4.0	FN 6.0	VF 8.0	VF/NM 9.0	NM- 9.2
1-(1-2/66)-Titans join Peace Corps; Batman, Flash, Aquaman, Wonder Woman cameos	27	54	81	194	285	375
2	12	24	36	82	121	160
3-5: 4-Speedy app.	7	14	21	51	71	90
6-10: 6-Doom Patrol app.; Beast Boy x-over; readers polled on him joining Titans	6	12	18	43	59	75
11-18: 11-Speedy app. 13-X-Mas-c	5	10	15	36	48	60
19-Wood-i; Speedy begins as regular	6	12	18	38	52	65
20-22: All Neal Adams-a. 21-Hawk & Dove app.; last 12¢ issue. 22-Origin Wonder Girl	7	14	21	50	68	85
23-31: 23-Wonder Girl dons new costume. 25-Flash, Aquaman, Batman, Green Arrow, Green Lantern, Superman, & Hawk & Dove guests; 1st app. Lilith who joins T.T. West in #50. 29-Hawk & Dove & Ocean Master app. 30-Aquagirl app. 31-Hawk & Dove app.; last 15¢ issue	4	8	12	24	32	40
32-34,40-43	3	6	9	16	20	24
35-39-(52 pgs.): 36,37-Superboy-r. 38-Green Arrow/Speedy-r; Aquaman/Aqualad story. 39-Hawk & Dove-r.	3	6	9	18	23	28
44,45,47,49,51,52: 44-Mal becomes the Guardian	2	4	6	8	10	12
46,48: 46-Joker's daughter begins (see Batman Family). 48-Intro Bumblebee; Joker's daughter becomes Harlequin	2	4	6	11	14	18
50-1st revival original Bat-Girl; intro. Teen Titans West	2	4	6	12	16	20
53-Origin retold	2	4	6	9	11	14

NOTE: ***Aparo** a-36. **Buckler** c-46-53. **Cardy** c-1-16. **Kane** a(p)-19, 22-24, 39r. **Tuska** a(p)-31, 36, 38, 39. DC Super-Stars #1 (3/76) was released before #44.*

TEEN TITANS (Also see Titans Beat in the Promotional Comics section)
DC Comics: Oct, 1996 - No. 24, Sept, 1998 ($1.95)

	NM- 9.2
1-Dan Jurgens-c/a(p)/scripts & George Pérez-c/a(i) begin; Atom forms new team (Risk, Argent, Prysm, & Joto); 1st app. Loren Jupiter & Omen; no indicia. 1-3-Origin.	4.00
2-24: 4,5-Robin, Nightwing, Supergirl, Capt. Marvel Jr. app. 12-"Then and Now" begins w/original Teen Titans-c/app. 15-Death of Joto. 17-Capt. Marvel Jr. and Fringe join. 19-Millennium Giants x-over. 23,24-Superman app.	3.00
Annual 1 (1997, $3.95)-Pulp Heroes story	4.00

TEEN TITANS (Also see Titans/Young Justice: Graduation Day)
DC Comics: Sept, 2003 - Present ($2.50)

	NM- 9.2
1-McKone-c/a;Johns-s	4.00
1-Variant-c by Michael Turner	5.00
1-2nd and 3rd printings	2.50
2-Deathstroke app.	5.00
2-2nd printing	2.50
3-7: 4-Impulse becomes Kid Flash. 5-Raven returns. 6-JLA app.	2.50
.../Outsiders Secret Files 2003 (12/03, $5.95) Reis & Jimenez-a; pin-ups by various	6.00

TEEN TITANS GO! (Based on Cartoon Network series)
DC Comics: Jan, 2004 - Present ($2.25)

	NM- 9.2
1,2-Nauck-a/Bullock-c/J. Torres-s	2.25

TEEN TITANS SPOTLIGHT
DC Comics: Aug, 1986 - No. 21, Apr, 1988

	NM- 9.2
1-21: 7-Guice's 1st work at DC. 14-Nightwing; Batman app. 15-Austin-c(i). 18,19-Millennium x-over. 21-($1.00-c)-Original Teen Titans; Spiegle-a	3.00

*Note: **Guice** a-7p, 8p; c-7,8. **Orlando** c/a-11p. **Perez** c-1, 17i, 19. **Sienkiewicz** c-10*

TEEPEE TIM (...Heap Funny Indian Boy)(Formerly Ha Ha Comics)
American Comics Group: No. 100, Feb-Mar, 1955 - No. 102, June-July, 1955

	GD 2.0	VG 4.0	FN 6.0	VF 8.0	VF/NM 9.0	NM- 9.2
100-102	6	12	18	29	36	42

TEGRA JUNGLE EMPRESS (Zegra Jungle Empress #2 on)
Fox Features Syndicate: August, 1948

	GD 2.0	VG 4.0	FN 6.0	VF 8.0	VF/NM 9.0	NM- 9.2
1-Blue Beetle, Rocket Kelly app.; used in **SOTI**, pg. 31	55	110	165	344	515	685

TEKKEN FOREVER
Image Comics: Dec, 2001 - No. 4 ($2.95, limited series)

	NM- 9.2
1-Based on the video game	3.00

TEKNO COMIX HANDBOOK
Tekno Comix: May, 1996 ($3.95, one-shot)

	NM- 9.2
1-Guide to the Tekno Universe	4.00

TEKNOPHAGE (See Neil Gaiman's...)

TEKNOPHAGE VERSUS ZEERUS
BIG Entertainment: July, 1996 ($3.25, one-shot)

	NM- 9.2
1-Paul Jenkins script	3.25

TEKWORLD (William Shatner's... on-c only)
Epic Comics (Marvel): Sept, 1992 - Aug, 1994 ($1.75)

	NM- 9.2
1-Based on Shatner's novel, TekWar, set in L.A. in the year 2120	3.00
2-24	2.25

TELEVISION (See TV)

TELEVISION COMICS (Early TV comic)
Standard Comics (Animated Cartoons): No. 5, Feb, 1950 - No. 8, Nov, 1950

	GD 2.0	VG 4.0	FN 6.0	VF 8.0	VF/NM 9.0	NM- 9.2
5-1st app. Willy Nilly	10	20	30	56	73	90
6-8: 6 has #2 on inside	8	16	24	43	54	65

TELEVISION PUPPET SHOW (Early TV comic) (See Spotty the Pup)
Avon Periodicals: 1950 - No. 2, Nov, 1950

	GD 2.0	VG 4.0	FN 6.0	VF 8.0	VF/NM 9.0	NM- 9.2
1-1st app. Speedy Rabbit, Spotty The Pup	20	40	60	112	156	200
2	14	28	42	79	107	135

TELEVISION TEENS MOPSY (See TV Teens)

TELL IT TO THE MARINES
Toby Press Publications: Mar, 1952 - No. 15, July, 1955

	GD 2.0	VG 4.0	FN 6.0	VF 8.0	VF/NM 9.0	NM- 9.2
1-Lover O'Leary and His Liberty Belles (with pin-ups), ends #6; Spike & Bat begin, end #6	20	40	60	112	156	200
2-Madame Cobra-c/story	11	22	33	63	84	105
3-5	9	18	27	49	62	75
6-12,14,15: 7-9,14,15-Photo-c	8	16	24	40	50	60
13-John Wayne photo-c	13	26	39	76	103	130
I.W. Reprint #9-r/#1 above	2	4	6	8	10	12
Super Reprint #16(1964)-r/#4 above	2	4	6	8	10	12

TELLOS
Image Comics: May, 1999 - Present ($2.50)

	NM- 9.2
1-Dezago-s/Wieringo-a	3.00
1-Variant-c ($7.95)	8.00
2-10: 4-Four covers	2.50
...: Maiden Voyage (3/01, $5.95) Didier Crispeels-a/c	6.00
...: Sons & Moons (2002, $5.95) Nick Cardy-c	6.00
...: The Last Heist (2001, $5.95) Rousseau-a/c	6.00
Prelude ($5.00, AnotherUniverse.com)	5.00
Prologue ($3.95, Dynamic Forces)	4.00
...Collected Edition 1 (12/99, $8.95) r/#1-3	9.00
...: Kindred Spirits (2/01, $17.95) r/#6-10, Section Zero #1 (Scatterjack-s)	18.00
...: Reluctant Heroes (2/01, $17.95) r/#1-5, Prelude, Prologue; sketchbook	18.00

TEMPEST (See Aquaman, 3rd Series)
DC Comics: Nov, 1996 - No. 4, Feb, 1997 ($1.75, limited series)

	NM- 9.2
1-4: Formerly Aqualad; Phil Jimenez-c/a/scripts in all	2.25

TEMPUS FUGITIVE
DC Comics: 1990 - No. 4, 1991 ($4.95, squarebound, 52 pgs.)

	NM- 9.2
Book 1,2: Ken Steacy painted-c/a & scripts	6.00
Book 3,4-($5.95-c)	6.00
TPB (Dark Horse Comics, 1/97, $17.95)	18.00

TEN COMMANDMENTS (See Moses & the... and Classics Illustrated Special)

TENDER LOVE STORIES
Skywald Publ. Corp.: Feb, 1971 - No. 4, July, 1971

The Tenth #5 © Tony Daniel

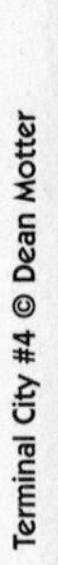

Terminal City #4 © Dean Motter

Terminator 2: Cybernetic Dawn #0 © Carolco

	GD 2.0	VG 4.0	FN 6.0	VF 8.0	VF/NM 9.0	NM- 9.2
1 (All 25¢, 52 pgs.)	3	6	9	18	24	30
2-4	2	4	6	12	16	20

TENDER ROMANCE (Ideal Romance #3 on)
Key Publications (Gilmour Magazines): Dec, 1953 - No. 2, Feb, 1954

1-Headlight & lingerie panels; B. Baily-c	18	36	54	104	142	180
2-Bernard Baily-c	10	20	30	58	77	95

TENSE SUSPENSE
Fago Publications: Dec, 1958 - No. 2, Feb, 1959

1	10	20	30	56	73	90
2	8	16	24	40	50	60

TEN STORY LOVE (Formerly a pulp magazine with same title)
Ace Periodicals: V29#3, June-July, 1951 - V36#5(#209), Sept, 1956 (#3-6: 52 pgs.)

V29#3(#177)-Part comic, part text; painted-c	11	22	33	66	88	110
4-6(1/52)	8	16	24	40	50	60
V30#1(3/52)-6(1/53)	7	14	21	37	46	55
V31#1(2/53),V32#2(4/53)-6(12/53)	7	14	21	35	43	50
V33#1(1/54)-3(5#54, #195), V34#4(7/54, #196)-6(10/54, #198)	6	12	18	31	38	45
V35#1(12/54, #199)-3(4/55, #201)-Last precode	6	12	18	28	34	40
V35#4-6(9/55, #201-204), V36#1(11/55, #205)-3, 5(9/56, #209)	5	10	15	24	30	35
V36#4-L.B. Cole-a	9	18	27	52	66	80

TENTH, THE
Image Comics: Jan, 1997 - No. 4, June, 1997 ($2.50, limited series)

1-4-Tony Daniel-c/a, Beau Smith-s 5.00
Abuse of Humanity TPB ($10.95) r/#1-4 11.00
Abuse of Humanity TPB (10/98, $11.95) r/#1-4 & 0(8/97) 12.00

TENTH, THE
Image Comics: Sept, 1997 - No. 14, Jan, 1999 ($2.50)

0-(8/97, $5.00) American Ent. Ed. 6.00
1-Tony Daniel-c/a, Beau Smith-s 6.00
2-9: 3,7-Variant-c 4.00
10-14 3.00
...Configuration (8/98) Re-cap and pin-ups 2.50
...Collected Edition 1 ('98, $4.95, square-bound) r/#1,2 5.00
...Special (4/00, $2.95) r/#0 and Wizard #1/2 3.00
Wizard #1/2-Daniel-s/Steve Scott-a 10.00

TENTH, THE (Volume 3) (The Black Embrace)
Image Comics: Mar, 1999 - No. 4, June, 1999 ($2.95)

1-4-Daniel-c/a 3.00
TPB (1/00, $12.95) r/#1-4 13.00

TENTH, THE (Volume 4) (Evil's Child)
Image Comics: Sept, 1999 - No. 4, Mar, 2000 ($2.95, limited series)

1-4-Daniel-c/a 3.00

TENTH, THE : RESURRECTED
Dark Horse Comics: July, 2001 - No. 4, Feb, 2002 ($2.99, limited series)

1-4: 1-Two covers; Daniel-s/c; Romano-a 3.00

10th MUSE
Image Comics (TidalWave Studios): Nov, 2000 - No. 9, Jan, 2002 ($2.95)

1-Character based on wrestling's Rena Mero; regular & photo covers 3.00
2-9: 2-Photo and 2 Lashley covers; flip book Dollz preview. 5-Savage Dragon app.; 2 covers by Lashley and Larsen. 6-Tellos x-over 3.00

10th MUSE (Volume 2)
Avatar Press: July, 2002 - Present ($3.50)

1-Wolfman-s; Cruz-a. 1-Five homage covers by various 3.50

TEN WHO DARED (Disney)
Dell Publishing Co.: No. 1178, Dec, 1960

Four Color 1178-Movie, painted-c; cast member photo on back-c	8	16	24	58	82	105

TERMINAL CITY
DC Comics (Vertigo): July, 1996 - No. 9, Mar, 1997 ($2.50, limited series)

1-9: Dean Motter scripts, 7,8-Matt Wagner-c 2.50
TPB ('97, $19.95) r/series 20.00

TERMINAL CITY: AERIAL GRAFFITI
DC Comics (Vertigo): Nov, 1997 - No. 5, Mar, 1998 ($2.50, limited series)

1-5: Dean Motter-s/Lark-a/Chiarello-c 2.50

	GD 2.0	VG 4.0	FN 6.0	VF 8.0	VF/NM 9.0	NM- 9.2

TERMINATOR, THE (See Robocop vs. ... & Rust #12 for 1st app.)
Now Comics: Sept, 1988 - No. 17, 1989 ($1.75, Baxter paper)

1-Based on movie	1	3	4	6	8	10

2-5 6.00
6-17: 12-($2.95, 52 pgs.)-Intro. John Connor 3.00
Trade paperback (1989, $9.95) 10.00

TERMINATOR, THE
Dark Horse Comics: Aug, 1990 - No. 4, Nov, 1990 ($2.50, limited series)

1-Set 39 years later than the movie 4.00
2-4 3.00

TERMINATOR, THE
Dark Horse Comics: 1998 - No. 4, Dec, 1998 ($2.95, limited series)

1-4-Alan Grant-s/Steve Pugh-a/c 3.00
...Special (1998, $2.95) Darrow-c/Grant-s 3.00

TERMINATOR, THE: ALL MY FUTURES PAST
Now Comics: V3#1, Aug, 1990 - V3#2, Sept, 1990 ($1.75, limited series)

V3#1,2 3.00

TERMINATOR, THE: ENDGAME
Dark Horse Comics: Sept, 1992 - No. 3, Nov, 1992 ($2.50, limited series)

1-3: Guice-a(p); painted-c 3.00

TERMINATOR, THE: HUNTERS AND KILLERS
Dark Horse Comics: Mar, 1992 - No. 3, May, 1992 ($2.50, limited series)

1-3 3.00

TERMINATOR, THE: ONE SHOT
Dark Horse Comics: July, 1991 ($5.95, 56 pgs.)

nn-Matt Wagner-a; contains stiff pop-up inside 6.00

TERMINATOR, THE: SECONDARY OBJECTIVES
Dark Horse Comics: July, 1991 - No. 4, Oct, 1991 ($2.50, limited series)

1-4: Gulacy-c/a(p) in all 3.00

TERMINATOR, THE: THE BURNING EARTH
Now Comics: V2#1, Mar, 1990 - V2#5, July, 1990 ($1.75, limited series)

V2#1: Alex Ross painted art (1st published work)	2	4	6	10	12	15
2-5: Ross-c/a in all	1	3	4	6	8	10

Trade paperback (1990, $9.95)-Reprints V2#1-5 12.00
Trade paperback (ibooks, 2003, $17.95)-Digitally remastered reprint 18.00

TERMINATOR, THE: THE DARK YEARS
Dark Horse Comics: Aug, 1999 - No. 4, Dec, 1999 ($2.95, limited series)

1-4-Alan Grant-s/Mel Rubi-a; Jae Lee-c 3.00

TERMINATOR: THE ENEMY FROM WITHIN, THE
Dark Horse Comics: Nov, 1991 - No. 4, Feb, 1992 ($2.50, limited series)

1-4: All have Simon Bisley painted-c 3.00

TERMINATOR 2: CYBERNETIC DAWN
Malibu: Nov, 1995 - No.4, Feb, 1996; No. 0. Apr, 1996 ($2.50, lim. series)

0 (4/96, $2.95)-Erskine-c/a; flip book w/Terminator 2: Nuclear Twilight 3.00
1-4: Continuation of film. 3.00

TERMINATOR 2: JUDGEMENT DAY
Marvel Comics: Early Sept, 1991 - No. 3, Early Oct, 1991 ($1.00, lim. series)

1-3: Based on movie sequel; 1-3-Same as nn issues 3.00
nn (1991, $4.95, squarebound, 68 pgs.)-Photo-c 5.00
nn (1991, $2.25, B&W, magazine, 68 pgs.) 3.00

TERMINATOR 2: NUCLEAR TWILIGHT
Malibu: Nov, 1995 - No.4, Feb, 1996; No. 0, Apr, 1996 ($2.50, lim. series)

0 (4/96, $2.95)-Erskine-c/a; flip book w/Terminator 2: Cybernetic Dawn 3.00
1-4:Continuation of film. 3.00

TERMINATOR 3: RISE OF THE MACHINES (... BEFORE THE RISE on cover)
Beckett Comics: July, 2003 - No. 6, Jan, 2004 ($5.95, limited series)

1-6: 1,2-Leads into movie; 2 covers on each. 3-6-Movie adaptation 6.00

TERRAFORMERS
Wonder Color Comics: April, 1987 - No. 2, 1987 ($1.95, limited series)

1,2-Kelley Jones-a 2.25

TERRANAUTS
Fantasy General Comics: Aug, 1986 - No. 2, 1986 ($1.75, limited series)

1,2 2.25

Terra Obscura #1 © ABC

Terry-Toons Comics #5 © Paul Terry

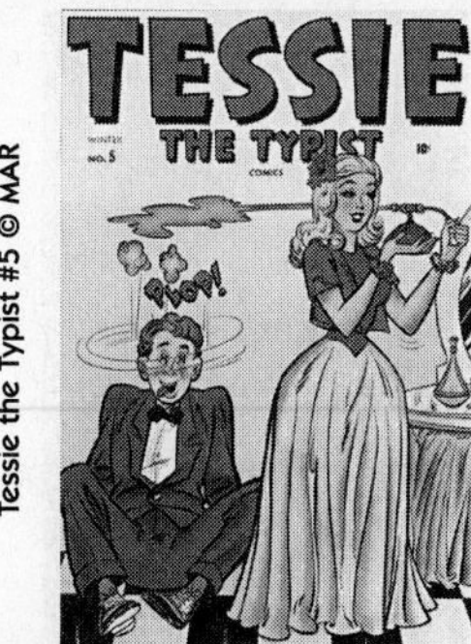

Tessie the Typist #5 © MAR

	GD 2.0	VG 4.0	FN 6.0	VF 8.0	VF/NM 9.0	NM- 9.2

TERRA OBSCURA (See Tom Strong)
America's Best Comics: Aug, 2003 - No. 6, Feb, 2004 ($2.95)

	GD	VG	FN	VF	VF/NM	NM-
1-6-Alan Moore & Peter Hogan-s/Paquette-a						3.00

TERRARISTS
Marvel Comics (Epic): Nov, 1993 - No. 4, Feb, 1994 ($2.50, limited series)

	GD	VG	FN	VF	VF/NM	NM-
1-4-Bound-in trading cards in all						2.50

TERRIFIC COMICS (Also see Suspense Comics)
Continental Magazines: Jan, 1944 - No. 6, Nov, 1944

	GD	VG	FN	VF	VF/NM	NM-
1-Kid Terrific; opium story	326	652	978	2119	3260	4400
2-1st app. The Boomerang by L.B. Cole & Ed Wheelan's "Comics" McCormick, called the world's #1 comic book fan begins	240	480	720	1500	2250	3000
3-Diana becomes Boomerang's costumed aide; L.B. Cole-c	240	480	720	1500	2250	3000
4-Classic war-c (Scarce)	385	770	1155	2503	3852	5200
5-The Reckoner begins; Boomerang & Diana by L.B. Cole; Classic Schomburg bondage & hooded vigilante-c (Scarce)	650	1300	1950	3800	5700	7600
6-L.B. Cole-c/a	220	440	660	1375	2063	2750

NOTE: ***L.B. Cole** a-1, 2(2), 3-6. **Fuje** a-5, 6. **Rico** a-2; c-1. **Schomburg** c-2, 5.*

TERRIFIC COMICS (Formerly Horrific; Wonder Boy #17 on)
Mystery Publ.(Comic Media)/(Ajax/Farrell): No. 14, Dec, 1954; No. 16, Mar, 1955 (No #15)

	GD	VG	FN	VF	VF/NM	NM-
14-Art swipe/Advs. into the Unknown #37; injury-to-eye-c; pg. 2, panel 5 swiped from Phantom Stranger #4; surrealistic Palais-a; Human Cross story; classic-c	55	110	165	330	495	660
16-Wonder Boy-c/story (last pre-code)	26	52	78	150	210	270

TERRIFYING TALES (Formerly Startling Terror Tales #10)
Star Publications: No. 11, Jan, 1953 - No. 15, Apr, 1954

	GD	VG	FN	VF	VF/NM	NM-
11-Used in **POP**, pgs. 99,100; all Jo-Jo-r	50	100	150	300	450	600
12-Reprints Jo-Jo #19 entirely; L.B. Cole splash	48	96	144	288	432	575
13-All Rulah-r; classic devil-c	55	110	165	330	495	660
14-All Rulah reprints	44	88	132	264	395	525
15-Rulah, Zago-r; used in **SOTI**-r/Rulah #22	44	88	132	264	395	525

NOTE: *All issues have **L.B. Cole** covers; bondage covers-No. 12-14.*

TERRITORY, THE
Dark Horse Comics: Jan, 1999 - No. 4, Apr, 1999 ($2.95, limited series)

	GD	VG	FN	VF	VF/NM	NM-
1-4-Delano-s/David Lloyd-c/a						3.00

TERROR ILLUSTRATED (Adult Tales of...)
E.C. Comics: Nov-Dec, 1955 - No. 2, Spring (April on-c), 1956 (Magazine, 25¢)

	GD	VG	FN	VF	VF/NM	NM-
1-Adult Entertainment on-c	18	36	54	104	142	180
2-Charles Sultan-a	12	24	36	71	96	120

NOTE: ***Craig, Evans, Ingels, Orlando** art in each. **Crandall** c-1, 2.*

TERROR INC. (See A Shadowline Saga #3)
Marvel Comics: July, 1992 - No. 13, July, 1993 ($1.75)

	GD	VG	FN	VF	VF/NM	NM-
1-8,11-13: 6,7-Punisher-c/story. 13-Ghost Rider app.						2.25
9,10-Wolverine-c/story						3.00

TERRORS OF DRACULA (Magazine)
Modern Day Periodical/Eerie Publ.: Vol. 1 #3, May, 1979 - Vol. 3 #2, Sept, 1981 (B&W)

	GD	VG	FN	VF	VF/NM	NM-
Vol. 1 #3 (5/79, 1st issue)	3	7	10	21	28	35
#4(8/79), #5(11/79)	3	6	9	16	20	25
Vol. 2 #1-4: 1-(2/80). 2-(5/80). 3-(8/80). 4-(11/80)	2	4	6	12	16	20
Vol. 3 #2 (9/81) (#1 exist?)	3	6	9	16	20	25

TERRORS OF THE JUNGLE (Formerly Jungle Thrills)
Star Publications: No. 17, 5/52 - No. 21, 2/53; No. 4, 4/53 - No. 10, 9/54

	GD	VG	FN	VF	VF/NM	NM-
17-Reprints Rulah #21, used in **SOTI**; L.B. Cole bondage-c	48	96	144	288	432	575
18-Jo-Jo-r	37	74	111	212	301	390
19,20(1952)-Jo-Jo-r; Disbrow-a	35	70	105	201	288	370
21-Jungle Jo, Tangi-r; used in **POP**, pg. 100 & color illos.; shrunken heads on-c	39	78	117	230	325	420
4-10: All Disbrow-a. 5-Jo-Jo-r. 8-Rulah, Jo-Jo-r. 9-Jo-Jo-r; Disbrow-a; Tangi by Orlando10-Rulah-r	39	78	117	230	325	420

NOTE: ***L.B. Cole** c-all; bondage c-17, 19, 21, 5, 7.*

TERROR TALES (See Beware Terror Tales)

TERROR TALES (Magazine)
Eerie Publications: V1#7, 1969 - V6#6, Dec, 1974; V7#1, Apr, 1976 - V10, 1979? (V1-V6: 52 pgs.; V7 on: 68 pgs.)

	GD	VG	FN	VF	VF/NM	NM-
V1#7	5	10	15	36	48	60
V1#8-11('69): 9-Bondage-c	4	8	12	24	32	40
V2#1-6('70), V3#1-6('71), V4#1-7('72), V5#1-6('73), V6#1-6('74), V7#1,4('76) (no V7#2), V8#1-3('77)	3	7	10	21	28	35
V7#3-(7/76) LSD story-r/Weird V3#5	3	7	10	21	28	35
V9#2-4, V10	4	8	12	22	30	38

TERRY AND THE PIRATES (See Famous Feature Stories, Merry Christmas From Sears Toyland, Popular Comics, Super Book #3,5,9,16,28, & Super Comics)

TERRY AND THE PIRATES
Dell Publishing Co.: 1939 - 1953 (By Milton Caniff)

	GD	VG	FN	VF	VF/NM	NM-
Large Feature Comic 2(1939)	60	120	180	470	715	960
Large Feature Comic 6(1938)-r/1936 dailies	56	112	168	425	650	875
Four Color 9(1940)	50	100	150	409	622	835
Large Feature Comic 27('41), 6('42)	44	88	132	352	526	700
Four Color 44('43)	37	74	111	278	419	560
Four Color 101('45)	26	52	78	189	275	375
Family Album(1942)	20	40	60	112	156	200

TERRY AND THE PIRATES (Formerly Boy Explorers; Long John Silver & the Pirates #30 on) (Daily strip-r) (Two #26's)
Harvey Publications/Charlton No. 26-28: No. 3, 4/47 - No. 26, 4/51; No. 26, 6/55 - No. 28, 10/55

	GD	VG	FN	VF	VF/NM	NM-
3(#1)-Boy Explorers by S&K; Terry & the Pirates begin by Caniff; 1st app. The Dragon Lady	40	80	120	240	345	450
4-S&K Boy Explorers	25	50	75	144	198	255
5-11: 11-Man in Black app. by Powell	12	24	36	71	96	120
12-20: 16-Girl threatened with red hot poker	10	20	30	58	77	95
21-26(4/51)-Last Caniff issue & last pre-code issue	10	20	30	56	73	90
26-28('55)(Formerly This Is Suspense)-No Caniff-a	9	18	27	49	62	75

NOTE: ***Powell** a (Tommy Tween)-5-10, 12, 14; 15-17(1/2 to 2 pgs. each).*

TERRY BEARS COMICS (TerryToons, The... #4)
St. John Publishing Co.: June, 1952 - No. 3, Mar, 1953

	GD	VG	FN	VF	VF/NM	NM-
1-By Paul Terry	9	18	27	54	70	85
2,3	7	14	21	35	43	50

TERRY-TOONS ALBUM (See Giant Comics Edition)

TERRY-TOONS COMICS (1st Series) (Becomes Paul Terry's Comics #85 on; later issues titled "Paul Terry's...")
Timely/Marvel No. 1-59 (8/47)(Becomes Best Western No. 58 on?, Marvel)/ St. John No. 60 (9/47) on: Oct, 1942 - No. 86, May, 1951

	GD	VG	FN	VF	VF/NM	NM-
1 (Scarce)-Features characters that 1st app. on movie screen; Gandy Goose & Sourpuss begin; war-c; Gandy Goose c-1-37	168	336	504	1050	1575	2100
2	61	122	183	381	573	765
3-5	44	88	132	264	395	525
6,8-10: 9,10-World War II gag-c	35	70	105	201	288	370
7-Hitler, Hirohito, Mussolini-c	46	92	138	276	413	550
11-20	22	44	66	124	172	220
21-37	15	30	45	86	118	150
38-Mighty Mouse begins (1st app., 11/45); Mighty Mouse-c begin, end #86; Gandy, Sourpuss welcome Mighty Mouse on-c	116	232	348	725	1088	1450
39-2nd app. Mighty Mouse	40	80	120	240	340	440
40-49: 43-Infinity-c	18	36	54	101	138	175
50-1st app. Heckle & Jeckle (11/46)	40	80	120	240	340	440
51-60: 55-Infinity-c. 60-(9/47)-Atomic explosion panel; 1st St. John issue	12	24	36	71	96	120
61-86: 85,86-Same book as Paul Terry's Comics #85,86 with only a title change; published at same time?	11	22	33	63	84	105

TERRY-TOONS COMICS (2nd Series)
St. John Publishing Co./Pines: June, 1952 - No. 9, Nov, 1953; 1957; 1958

	GD	VG	FN	VF	VF/NM	NM-
1-Gandy Goose & Sourpuss begin by Paul Terry	20	40	60	112	156	200
2	10	20	30	56	73	90
3-9	9	18	27	52	66	80
Giant Summer Fun Book 101,102-(Sum, 1957, Sum, 1958, 25¢, Pines)(TV) CBS Television Presents...; Tom Terrific, Mighty Mouse, Heckle & Jeckle Gandy Goose app.	14	28	42	79	107	135

TERRYTOONS, THE TERRY BEARS (Formerly Terry Bears Comics)
Pines Comics: No. 4, Summer, 1958 (CBS Television Presents...)

	GD	VG	FN	VF	VF/NM	NM-
4	6	12	18	31	38	45

TESSIE THE TYPIST (Tiny Tessie #24; see Comedy Comics, Gay Comics & Joker Comics)
Timely/Marvel Comics (20CC): Summer, 1944 - No. 23, Aug, 1949

	GD	VG	FN	VF	VF/NM	NM-
1-Doc Rockblock & others by Wolverton	64	128	192	400	600	800
2-Wolverton's Powerhouse Pepper	39	78	117	230	325	420
3-(3/45)-No Wolverton	15	30	45	86	118	150
4,5,7,8-Wolverton-a. 4-(Fall/45)	29	58	87	164	232	300

The Texan #6 © STJ

Tex Ritter Western #11 © FAW

Thanos #2 © MAR

	GD 2.0	VG 4.0	FN 6.0	VF 8.0	VF/NM 9.0	NM- 9.2
6-Kurtzman's "Hey Look", 2 pgs. Wolverton-a	29	58	87	164	232	300
9-Wolverton's Powerhouse Pepper (8 pgs.) & 1 pg. Kurtzman's "Hey Look"	32	64	96	182	259	335
10-Wolverton's Powerhouse Pepper (4 pgs.)	30	60	90	170	240	310
11-Wolverton's Powerhouse Pepper (8 pgs.)	32	64	96	182	259	335
12-Wolverton's Powerhouse Pepper (4 pgs.) & 1 pg. Kurtzman's "Hey Look"	30	60	90	170	240	310
13-Wolverton's Powerhouse Pepper (4 pgs.)	30	60	90	170	240	310
14,15: 14-Wolverton's Dr. Whackyhack (1 pg.); 1-1/2 pgs. Kurtzman's "Hey Look". 15-Kurtzman's "Hey Look" (3 pgs.) & 3 pgs. Giggles 'n' Grins	23	46	69	130	183	235
16-18-Kurtzman's "Hey Look" (?, 2 & 1 pg.)	16	32	48	89	122	155
19-Annie Oakley story (8 pgs.)	12	24	36	69	92	115
20-23: 20-Anti-Wertham editorial (2/49)	10	20	30	60	80	100

NOTE: *Lana app.-21. Millie The Model app.-13, 15, 17, 21. Rusty app.-10, 11, 13, 15, 17.*

TEXAN, THE (Fightin' Marines #15 on; Fightin' Texan #16 on)
St. John Publishing Co.: Aug, 1948 - No. 15, Oct, 1951

	GD	VG	FN	VF	VF/NM	NM-
1-Buckskin Belle	16	32	48	92	126	160
2	10	20	30	56	73	90
3,10: 10-Oversized issue	9	18	27	52	66	80
4,5,7,15-Baker-c/a	17	34	51	98	134	170
6,9-Baker-c	11	22	33	63	84	105
8,11,13,14-Baker-c/a(2-3) each	18	36	54	101	138	175
12-All Matt Baker-c/a; Peyote story	24	48	72	135	190	245

NOTE: ***Matt Baker** c-4-9, 11-15. **Larsen** a-4-6, 8-10, 15. **Tuska** a-1, 2, 7-9.*

TEXAN, THE (TV)
Dell Publishing Co.: No. 1027, Sept-Nov, 1959 - No. 1096, May-July, 1960

	GD	VG	FN	VF	VF/NM	NM-
Four Color 1027 (#1)-Photo-c	10	20	30	67	96	125
Four Color 1096-Rory Calhoun photo-c	9	18	27	63	89	115

TEXAS JOHN SLAUGHTER (See Walt Disney Presents, 4-Color #997, 1181 & #2)

TEXAS KID (See Two-Gun Western, Wild Western)
Marvel/Atlas Comics (LMC): Jan, 1951 - No. 10, July, 1952

	GD	VG	FN	VF	VF/NM	NM-
1-Origin; Texas Kid (alias Lance Temple) & his horse Thunder begin; Tuska-a	25	50	75	147	202	260
2	13	26	39	76	103	130
3-10	10	20	30	58	77	95

NOTE: ***Maneely** a-1-4; c-1, 3, 5-10.*

TEXAS RANGERS, THE (See Jace Pearson of... and Superior Stories #4)

TEXAS RANGERS IN ACTION (Formerly Captain Gallant or Scotland Yard?)
Charlton Comics: No. 5, Jul, 1956 - No. 79, Aug, 1970 (See Blue Bird Comics)

	GD	VG	FN	VF	VF/NM	NM-
5	8	16	24	46	58	70
6,7,9,10	6	12	18	28	34	40
8-Ditko-a (signed)	10	20	30	56	73	90
11-Williamson-a(5&8 pgs.); Torres/Williamson-a (5 pgs.)	10	20	30	56	73	90
12,14-20	5	10	15	23	28	32
13-Williamson-a (5 pgs); Torres, Morisi-a	8	16	24	43	54	65
21-30	3	6	9	18	23	28
31-59: 32-Both 10¢-c & 15¢-c exist	2	4	6	14	18	22
60-Riley's Rangers begin	3	6	9	16	20	24
61-65,68-70	2	4	6	9	11	14
66,67: 66-1st app. The Man Called Loco. 67-Origin	2	4	6	10	13	16
71-79	1	3	4	6	8	10
76 (Modern Comics-r, 1977)						4.00

TEXAS SLIM (See A-1 Comics)

TEX DAWSON, GUN-SLINGER (Gunslinger #2 on)
Marvel Comics Group: Jan, 1973 (20¢)(Also see Western Kid, 1st series)

	GD	VG	FN	VF	VF/NM	NM-
1-Steranko-c; Williamson-r (4 pgs.); Tex Dawson-r by Romita(3) from 1955; Tuska-r	3	6	9	16	20	25

TEX FARNUM (See Wisco)

TEX FARRELL (...Pride of the Wild West)
D. S. Publishing Co.: Mar-Apr, 1948

	GD	VG	FN	VF	VF/NM	NM-
1-Tex Farrell & his horse Lightning; Shelly-c	16	32	48	92	126	160

TEX GRANGER (Formerly Calling All Boys; see True Comics)
Parents' Magazine Inst./Commended: No. 18, Jun, 1948 - No. 24, Sept, 1949

	GD	VG	FN	VF	VF/NM	NM-
18-Tex Granger & his horse Bullet begin	12	24	36	69	92	115
19	10	20	30	56	73	90
20-24: 22-Wild Bill Hickok story. 23-Vs. Billy the Kid; Tim Holt app.	8	16	24	46	58	70

TEX MORGAN (See Blaze Carson and Wild Western)
Marvel Comics (CCC): Aug, 1948 - No. 9, Feb, 1950

	GD	VG	FN	VF	VF/NM	NM-
1-Tex Morgan, his horse Lightning & sidekick Lobo begin	29	58	87	164	232	300
2	19	38	57	106	146	185
3-6: 3,4-Arizona Annie app.	12	24	36	71	96	120
7-9: All photo-c. 7-Captain Tootsie by Beck. 8-18 pg. story "The Terror of Rimrock Valley"; Diablo app.	19	38	57	106	146	185

NOTE: *Tex Taylor app.-6, 7, 9. **Brodsky** c-6. **Syd Shores** c-2, 5.*

TEX RITTER WESTERN (Movie star; singing cowboy; see Six-Gun Heroes and Western Hero)
Fawcett No. 1-20 (1/54)/Charlton No. 21 on: Oct, 1950 - No. 46, May, 1959 (Photo-c: 1-21)

	GD	VG	FN	VF	VF/NM	NM-
1-Tex Ritter, his stallion White Flash & dog Fury begin; photo front/back-c begin	69	138	207	431	646	860
2	34	68	102	196	278	360
3-5: 5-Last photo back-c	26	52	78	150	210	270
6-10	20	40	60	112	156	200
11-19	14	28	42	81	111	140
20-Last Fawcett issue (1/54)	15	30	45	86	118	150
21-1st Charlton issue; photo-c (3/54)	19	38	57	106	146	185
22-B&W photo back-c begin, end #32	11	22	33	63	84	105
23-30: 23-25-Young Falcon app.	10	20	30	56	73	90
31-38,40-45	9	18	27	52	66	80
39-Williamson-a; Whitman-c (1/58)	10	20	30	58	77	95
46-Last issue	10	20	30	56	73	90

TEX TAYLOR (...The Fighting Cowboy on-c #1, 2)(See Blaze Carson, Kid Colt, Tex Morgan, Wild West, Wild Western, & Wisco)
Marvel Comics (HPC): Sept, 1948 - No. 9, March, 1950

	GD	VG	FN	VF	VF/NM	NM-
1-Tex Taylor & his horse Fury begin	30	60	90	170	240	310
2	16	32	48	92	126	160
3	14	28	42	81	111	140
4-6: All photo-c. 4-Anti-Wertham editorial. 5,6-Blaze Carson app.	17	34	51	98	134	170
7-9: 7-Photo-c;18 pg. Movie-Length Thriller "Trapped in Time's Lost Land!" with sabretoothed tigers, dinosaurs; Diablo app. 8-Photo-c; 18 pg. Movie-Length Thriller "The Mystery of Devil-Tree Plateau!" with dwarf horses, dwarf people & a lost miniature Inca type village; Diablo app. 9-Photo-c; 18 pg. Movie-Length Thriller "Guns Along the Border!" Captain Tootsie by Schreiber; Nimo the Mountain Lion app.	20	40	60	112	156	200

NOTE: ***Syd Shores** c-1-3.*

THANE OF BAGARTH (Also see Hercules, 1967 series)
Charlton Comics: No. 24, Oct, 1985 - No. 25, Dec, 1985

	GD	VG	FN	VF	VF/NM	NM-
24,25-Low print run						5.00

THANOS
Marvel Comics: Dec, 2003 - Present ($2.99)

	GD	VG	FN	VF	VF/NM	NM-
1-4-Starlin-s/a(p)/Milgrom-i						3.00

THANOS QUEST, THE (See Capt. Marvel #25, Infinity Gauntlet, Iron Man #55, Logan's Run, Marvel Feature #12, Marvel Universe: The End, Silver Surfer #34 & Warlock #9)
Marvel Comics: 1990 - No. 2, 1990 ($4.95, squarebound, 52 pgs.)

	GD	VG	FN	VF	VF/NM	NM-
1,2-Both have Starlin scripts & covers (both printings)	1	2	3	4	5	7
1-(3/2000, $3.99) r/material from #1&2						4.00

THAT CHEMICAL REFLEX
CFD Productions: 1994 - No. 3 ($2.50, B&W, mature)

	GD	VG	FN	VF	VF/NM	NM-
1-3: 1-Dan Brereton-c/a						2.50

THAT DARN CAT (See Movie Comics & Walt Disney Showcase #19)

THAT'S MY POP! GOES NUTS FOR FAIR
Bystander Press: 1939 (76 pgs., B&W)

	GD	VG	FN	VF	VF/NM	NM-
nn-by Milt Gross	30	60	90	170	240	310

THAT WILKIN BOY (Meet Bingo...)
Archie Publications: Jan, 1969 - No. 52, Oct, 1982

	GD	VG	FN	VF	VF/NM	NM-
1-1st app. Bingo's Band, Samantha & Tough Teddy	4	8	12	29	40	50
2-5	3	6	9	16	20	25
6-11	2	4	6	11	14	18
12-26-Giants. 12-No # on-c	2	4	6	14	18	22
27-40(1/77)	1	3	4	6	8	10
41-52						5.00

THB
Horse Press: Oct, 1994 - Present ($5.50/$2.50/$2.95, B&W)

	GD	VG	FN	VF	VF/NM	NM-
1 ($5.50) Paul Pope-s/a in all	1	2	3	5	6	8

The Thing! #14 © CC

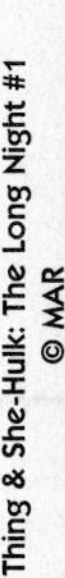

Thing & She-Hulk: The Long Night #1 © MAR

This Magazine is Haunted #10 © FAW

	GD 2.0	VG 4.0	FN 6.0	VF 8.0	VF/NM 9.0	NM- 9.2
1 (2nd Printing)-r/#1 w/new material						3.00
2 ($2.50)						5.00
3-5						4.00
69 (1995, no price, low distribution, 12 pgs.)-story reprinted in #1 (2nd Printing)						3.00
Giant THB-($4.95)						5.00
Giant THB 1 V2-(2003, $6.95)						7.00
...M3/THB: Mars' Mightiest Mek #1 (2000, $3.95)						4.00
...6A: Mek-Power #1, 6B: Mek-Power #2, 6C: Mek-Power #3 (2000, $3.95)						4.00
... 6D: Mek-Power #4 (2002, $4.95)						5.00

T.H.E. CAT (TV)
Dell Publishing Co.: Mar, 1967 - No. 4, Oct, 1967 (All have photo-c)

1	4	8	12	25	33	42
2-4	3	6	9	18	24	30

THERE'S A NEW WORLD COMING
Spire Christian Comics/Fleming H. Revell Co.: 1973 (35/49¢)

nn	1	2	3	6	8	10

THEY ALL KISSED THE BRIDE (See Cinema Comics Herald)

THIEF OF BAGHDAD
Dell Publishing Co.: No. 1229, Oct-Dec, 1961 (one-shot)

Four Color 1229-Movie, Crandall/Evans-a, photo-c	8	16	24	53	74	95

THIEVES & KINGS
I Box: 1994 - Present ($2.35, B&W, bi-monthly)

1						4.00
1-(2nd printing), 2-42						2.50

THIMK (Magazine) (Satire)
Counterpoint: May, 1958 - No. 6, May, 1959

1	9	18	27	49	62	75
2-6	6	12	18	31	38	45

THING!, THE (Blue Beetle #18 on)
Song Hits No. 1,2/Capitol Stories/Charlton: Feb, 1952 - No. 17, Nov, 1954

1-Weird/horror stories in all; shrunken head-c	84	168	252	525	788	1050
2,3	55	110	165	345	518	690
4-6,8,10: 5-Severed head-c; headlights	51	102	153	306	458	610
7-Injury to eye-c & inside panel	69	138	207	431	646	860
9-Used in **SOTI**, pg. 388 & illo "Stomping on the face is a form of brutality which modern children learn early"	79	158	237	494	740	985
11-Necronomicon story; Hansel & Gretel parody; Injury-to-eye panel; Check-a	61	122	183	381	573	765
12-1st published Ditko-c; "Cinderella" parody; lingerie panels. Ditko-a	84	168	252	525	788	1050
13,15-Ditko-c/a(3 & 5)	84	168	252	525	788	1050
14-Extreme violence/torture; Rumpelstiltskin story; Ditko-c/a(4)	86	172	258	538	807	1075
16-Injury to eye panel	31	62	93	175	248	320
17-Ditko-c; classic parody "Through the Looking Glass"; Powell-r/Beware Terror Tales #1 & recolored	74	148	222	463	694	925

NOTE: *Excessive violence, severed heads, injury to eye are common No. 5 on.* ***Al Fago*** *c-4.* ***Forgione*** *c-1i, 2, 6, 8, 9. All* ***Ditko*** *issues #14, 15.*

THING, THE (See Fantastic Four, Marvel Fanfare, Marvel Feature #11,12, Marvel Two-In-One and Startling Stories:...- Night Falls on Yancy Street)
Marvel Comics Group: July, 1983 - No. 36, June, 1986

1-Life story of Ben Grimm; Byrne scripts begin						3.00
2-36: 5-Spider-Man, She-Hulk app.						2.25

NOTE: ***Byrne*** *a-2i, 7; c-1, 7, 36i; scripts-1-13, 19-22.* ***Sienkiewicz*** *c-13i.*

THING & SHE-HULK: THE LONG NIGHT (Fantastic Four)
Marvel Comics: May, 2002 ($2.99, one-shot)

1-Hitch-c/a(pg. 1-25); Reis-a(pg. 26-39); Dezago-s						3.00

THING, THE (From Another World)
Dark Horse Comics: 1991 - No. 2, 1992 ($2.95, mini-series, stiff-c)

1,2-Based on Universal movie; painted-c/a						3.00

THING, THE: FREAKSHOW (Fantastic Four)
Marvel Comics: Aug, 2002 - No. 4, Nov, 2002 ($2.99, limited series)

1-4-Geoff Johns-s/Scott Kolins-a						3.00

THING FROM ANOTHER WORLD: CLIMATE OF FEAR, THE
Dark Horse Comics: July, 1992 - No. 4, Dec, 1992 ($2.50, mini-series)

1-4: Painted-c						3.00

THING FROM ANOTHER WORLD: ETERNAL VOWS
Dark Horse Comics: Dec, 1993 - No. 4, 1994 ($2.50, mini-series)

1-4-Gulacy-c/a						3.00

THIRD WORLD WAR
Fleetway Publ. (Quality): 1990 - No. 6, 1991 ($2.50, thick-c, mature)

1-6						2.50

THIRTEEN (...Going on 18)
Dell Publishing Co.: 11-1/61-62 - No. 25, 12/67; No. 26, 7/69 - No. 29, 1/71

1	7	14	21	46	63	80
2-10	5	10	15	36	48	60
11-25	4	8	12	28	38	48
26-29-r	4	8	12	25	33	42

NOTE: ***John Stanley*** *script-No. 3-29; art?*

13: ASSASSIN
TSR, Inc.: 1990 - No. 8, 1991 ($2.95, 44 pgs.)

1-8: Agent 13; Alcala-a(i); Springer back-up-a						3.00

30 DAYS OF NIGHT
Idea + Design Works: June, 2002 - No. 3, Oct, 2002 ($3.99, limited series)

1-Vampires in Alaska; Steve Niles-s/Ben Templesmith-a/Ashley Wood-c						30.00
1-2nd printing						10.00
2						12.00
3						6.00
TPB (2003, $17.99) r/#1-3, foreward by Clive Barker; script for #1						18.00

THIRTY SECONDS OVER TOKYO (See American Library)

THIS IS SUSPENSE! (Formerly Strange Suspense Stories; Strange Suspense Stories #27 on)
Charlton Comics: No. 23, Feb, 1955 - No. 26, Aug, 1955

23-Wood-a(r)/A Star Presentation #3 "Dr. Jekyll & Mr. Hyde"; last pre-code issue	28	56	84	159	225	290
24-Censored Fawcett-r; Evans-a (r/Suspense Detective #1)	15	30	45	86	118	150
25,26: 26-Marcus Swayze-a	10	20	30	58	77	95

THIS IS THE PAYOFF (See Pay-Off)

THIS IS WAR
Standard Comics: No. 5, July, 1952 - No. 9, May, 1953

5-Toth-a	14	28	42	81	111	140
6,9-Toth-a	11	22	33	63	84	105
7,8: 8-Ross Andru-c	8	16	24	46	58	70

THIS IS YOUR LIFE, DONALD DUCK (See Donald Duck..., Four Color #1109)

THIS MAGAZINE IS CRAZY (Crazy #? on)
Charlton Publ. (Humor Magazines): V3#2, July, 1957 - V4#8, Feb, 1959 (25¢, magazine, 68 pgs.)

V3#2-V4#7: V4#5-Russian Sputnik-c parody	8	16	24	46	58	70
V4#8-Davis-a (8 pgs.)	9	18	27	52	66	80

THIS MAGAZINE IS HAUNTED (Danger and Adventure #22 on)
Fawcett Publications/Charlton No. 15(2/54) on: Oct, 1951 - No. 14, 12/53; No. 15, 2/54 - V3#21, Nov, 1954

1-Evans-a; Dr. Death as host begins	62	124	186	388	582	775
2,5-Evans-a	44	88	132	264	395	525
3,4: 3-Vampire-c/story	36	72	108	204	290	375
6-9,11,12,14	25	50	75	147	202	260
10-Severed head-c	40	80	120	240	345	450
13-Severed head-c/story	39	78	117	230	325	420
15,20: 15-Dick Giordano-c. 20-Cover is swiped from panel in The Thing #16	21	42	63	118	164	210
16,19-Ditko-c. 19-Injury-to-eye panel; story-r/#1	40	80	120	240	340	440
17-Ditko-c/a(4); blood drainage story	46	92	138	276	413	550
18-Ditko-c/a(1 story); E.C. swipe/Haunt of Fear #5; injury-to-eye panel; reprints "Caretaker of the Dead" from Beware Terror Tales & recolored	43	86	129	258	364	470
21-Ditko-c, Evans-r/This Magazine Is Haunted #1	38	76	114	219	310	400

NOTE: ***Baily*** *a-1, 3, 4, 21r/#1.* ***Moldoff*** *c/a-1-13.* ***Powell*** *a-3-5, 11, 12, 17.* ***Shuster*** *a-18-20. Issues 19-21 have reprints which have been recolored from This Magazine is Haunted #1.*

THIS MAGAZINE IS HAUNTED (2nd Series) (Formerly Zaza the Mystic; Outer Space #17 on)
Charlton Comics: V2#12, July, 1957 - V2#16, May, 1958

V2#12-14-Ditko-c/a in all	40	80	120	240	340	440
15-No Ditko-c/a	10	20	30	56	73	90
16-Ditko-a	27	54	81	155	218	280

THIS MAGAZINE IS WILD (See Wild)

Thor #390 © MAR

Thor #492 © MAR

Thor V2#50 © MAR

GD 2.0 VG 4.0 FN 6.0 VF 8.0 VF/NM 9.0 NM- 9.2

THIS WAS YOUR LIFE (Religious)
Jack T. Chick Publ.: 1964 (3 1/2 x 5 1/2", 40 pgs., B&W and red)

nn, Another version (5x2 3/4", 26 pgs.) 2 4 6 10 12 15

THOR (See Avengers #1, Giant-Size..., Marvel Collectors Item Classics, Marvel Graphic Novel #33, Marvel Preview, Marvel Spectacular, Marvel Treasury Edition, Special Marvel Edition & Tales of Asgard)

THOR (Journey Into Mystery #1-125, 503-on)(The Mighty Thor #413-490)
Marvel Comics Group: No. 126, Mar, 1966 - No. 502, Sept, 1996

126-Thor continues (#125-130 Thor vs. Hercules) 18 36 54 131 191 250
127-130: 127-1st app. Pluto 8 16 24 55 78 100
131-133,135-140 7 14 21 50 68 85
134-Intro High Evolutionary 7 14 21 51 71 90
141-150: 146-Inhumans begin (early app.), end #151 (see Fantastic Four #45 for 1st app.). 146,147-Origin The Inhumans. 148,149-Origin Black Bolt in each. 149-Origin Medusa, Crystal, Maximus, Gorgon, Kornak 6 12 18 40 55 70
151-157,159,160 5 10 15 33 44 55
158-Origin-r/#83; 158,159-Origin Dr. Blake (Thor) 9 18 27 60 85 110
161,167,170-179: 179-Last Kirby issue 4 8 12 27 36 45
162,168,169-Origin Galactus; Kirby-a 5 10 15 36 48 60
163,164-2nd & 3th brief cameo Warlock (Him) 4 8 12 27 36 45
165-1st full app. Warlock (Him) (6/69, see Fantastic Four #67); last 12¢ issue; Kirby-a 7 14 21 50 68 85
166-2nd full app. Warlock (Him); battles Thor 6 12 18 40 55 70
180,181-Neal Adams-a 4 8 12 29 40 50
182-192: 192-Last 15¢ issue 3 6 9 18 23 28
193-(25¢, 52 pgs.); Silver Surfer x-over 6 12 18 40 55 70
194-199 2 4 6 14 18 22
200 3 6 9 18 23 28
201-206,208-224 2 4 6 8 10 12
207-Rutland, Vermont Halloween x-over 2 4 6 10 12 15
225-Intro. Firelord 2 4 6 10 12 15
226-245 1 2 3 5 7 9
246-250-(Regular 25¢ editions)(4-8/76) 1 2 3 5 7 9
246-250-(30¢-c variants, limited distribution) 2 4 6 9 11 14
251-280: 271-Iron Man x-over. 274-Death of Balder the Brave 5.00
260-264-(35¢-c variants, limited distribution)(6-10/77) 1 2 3 5 7 9
281-299: 294-Origin Asgard & Odin 4.00
300-(12/80)-End of Asgard; origin of Odin & The Destroyer 7.00
301-336,338-373,375-381,383: 316-Iron Man x-over. 340-Donald Blake returns as Thor. 341-Clark Kent & Lois Lane cameo. 373-X-Factor tie-in 3.00
337-Simonson-c/a begins, ends #382; Beta Ray Bill becomes new Thor 1 2 3 5 7 9
374-Mutant Massacre; X-Factor app. 4.00
382-($1.25)-Anniversary issue; last Simonson-a 4.00
384-Intro. new Thor 4.00
385-399,401-410,413-428: 385-Hulk x-over. 391-Spider-Man x-over; 1st Eric Masterson. 395-Intro Earth Force. 408-Eric Masterson becomes Thor. 427,428-Excalibur x-over 2.50
400,411: 400-($1.75, 68 pgs.)-Origin Loki. 411-Intro New Warriors (appears in costume in last panel); Juggernaut-c/story 4.00
412-1st full app. New Warriors (Marvel Boy, Kid Nova, Namorita, Night Thrasher, Firestar & Speedball) 6.00
429-431,434-443: 429,430-Ghost Rider x-over. 434-Capt. America x-over. 437-Thor vs. Quasar; Hercules app.;Tales of Asgard back-up stories begin. 443-Dr. Strange & Silver Surfer x-over; last $1.00-c 2.50
432,433: 432-(52 pgs.)-Thor's 300th app. (vs. Loki); reprints origin & 1st app. from Journey into Mystery #83. 433-Intro new Thor 3.00
444-449,451-473: 448-Spider-Man-c/story. 455,456-Dr. Strange back-up. 457-Old Thor returns (3 pgs.). 459-Intro Thunderstrike. 460-Starlin scripts begin. 465-Super Skrull app. 466-Drax app. 469,470-Infinity Watch x-over. 472-Intro the Godlings 2.50
450-($2.50, 68 pgs.)-Flip-book format; r/story JIM #87 (1st Loki) plus-c plus a gallery of past-c; gatefold-c 3.00
474,476-481,483-499: 474-Begin $1.50-c; bound-in trading card sheet. 459-Intro Thunderstrike, 460-Starlin scripts begin. 472-Intro the Godlings. 490-The Absorbing Man app. 491-Warren Ellis scripts begins, ends #494; Deodato-c/a begins. 492-Reintro The Enchantress; Beta Ray Bill dies. 495-Wm. Messner-Loebs scripts begin; Isherwood-c/a. 2.50
475 ($2.00, 52 pgs.)-Regular edition 2.50
475 ($2.50, 52 pgs.)-Collectors edition w/foil embossed-c 3.00
482 ($2.95, 84 pgs.)-400th issue 3.00
500 ($2.50)-Double-size; wraparound-c; Deodato-c/a; Dr. Strange app. 5.00
501-Reintro Red Norvell 3.00
502-Onslaught tie-in; Red Norvell, Jane Foster & Hela app. 4.00
Special 2(9/66)-See Journey Into Mystery for 1st annual 8 16 24 53 74 95
Special 2 (2nd printing, 1994) 2 4 6 8 10 12
King Size Special 3(1/71) 3 6 9 19 25 32
Special 4(12/71)-r/Thor #131,132 & JIM #113 3 6 9 16 20 24
Annual 5,6: 5(11/76). 6(10/77)-Guardians of the Galaxy app. 2 4 6 9 11 14
Annual 7,8: 7(1978). 8(1979)-Thor vs. Zeus-c/story 1 2 3 5 7 9
Annual 9-12: 9('81). 10('82). 11('83). 12('84) 5.00
Annual 13-19('85-'94, 68 pgs.):14-Atlantis Attacks. 16-3 pg. origin; Guardians of the Galaxy x-over.18-Polybagged w/card 3.00
...Alone Against the Celestials nn (6/92, $5.95)-r/Thor #387-389 6.00
...Legends Vol. 2: Walter Simonson Book 2 TPB (2003, $24.99) r/#349-355,357-359 25.00
...Visionaries: Walter Simonson TPB (5/01, $24.95) r/#337-348 25.00
...: Worldengine (8/96, $9.95)-r/#491-494; Deodato-c/a; story & new intermission by Warren Ellis 10.00

NOTE: ***Neal Adams*** *a-180,181; c-179-181.* ***Austin*** *a-342i, 346i; c-312i.* ***Buscema*** *a(p)-178, 182-213, 215-226, 231-238, 241-253, 254r, 256-259, 272-278, 283-285, 370, Annual 6, 8, 11i; c(p)-175, 182-196, 198-200, 202-204, 206, 211, 212, 215, 219, 221, 226, 256, 259, 261, 262, 272-278, 283, 289, 370, Annual 6.* ***Everett*** *a(i)-143, 170-175; c(i)-171, 172, 174, 176, 241.* ***Gil Kane*** *a-318p; c(p)-201, 205, 207-210, 216, 220, 222, 223, 231, 233-240, 242, 243, 318.* ***Kirby*** *a(p)-126-177, 179, 194r, 254r; c(p)-126-169, 171-174, 176-178, 249-253, 255, 257, 258, Annual 5, Special 2-4.* ***Mooney*** *a(i)-201, 204, 214-216, 218, 322i, 324i, 325i, 327i.* ***Sienkiewicz*** *c-332, 333, 335.* ***Simonson*** *a-260-271p, 337-354, 357-367, 380, Annual 7p; c-260, 263-271, 337-355, 357-369, 371, 373-382, Annual 7.* ***Starlin*** *c-213.*

THOR (Volume 2)
Marvel Comics: July, 1998 - Present ($2.99/$1.99/$2.25)

1-($2.99)-Follows Heroes Return; Jurgens-s/Romita Jr. & Janson-a; wraparound-c; battles the Destroyer 5.00
1-Variant-c 1 2 3 5 6 8
1-Rough Cut-($2.99) Features original script and pencil pages 3.00
1-Sketch cover 20.00
2-($1.99) Two covers; Avengers app. 3.00
3-11,13-23: 3-Assumes Jake Olson ID. 4-Namor-c/app. 8-Spider-Man-c/app. 14-Iron Man c/app. 17-Juggernaut-c 2.50
12-($2.99) Wraparound-c; Hercules appears 3.00
12-($10.00) Variant-c by Jusko 10.00
24,26-31,33,34: 24-Begin $2.25-c. 26-Mignola-c/Larsen-a. 29-Andy Kubert-a. 30-Maximum Security x-over; Beta Ray Bill-c/app. 33-Intro. Thor Girl 2.25
25-($2.99) Regular edition 3.00
25-($3.99) Gold foil enhanced cover 4.00
32-($3.50, 100 pgs.) new story plus reprints w/Kirby-a; Simonson-a 3.50
35-($2.99) Thor battles The Gladiator; Andy Kubert-a 3.00
36-49,51-61: 37-Starlin-a. 38,39-BWS-c. 38-42-Immonen-a. 40-Odin killed. 41-Orbik-c. 44-'Nuff Said silent issue. 51-Spider-Man app. 57-Art by various. 58-Davis-a; x-over with Iron Man #64. 60-Brereton-c 2.25
50-($4.95) Raney-c/a; back-ups w/Nuckols-a & Armenta-s/Bennett-a 5.00
62-73: 62-Begin $2.99-c. 64-Loki-c/app. 3.00
...1999 Annual ($3.50) Jurgens-s/a(p) 3.50
...2000 Annual ($3.50) Jurgens-s/Ordway-a(p); back-up stories 3.50
...2001 Annual ($3.50) Jurgens-s/Grummett-a(p); Lightle-c 3.50
...Across All Worlds (9/01, $19.95, TPB) r/#28-35 20.00
...: Gods on Earth (2003, $21.99, TPB) r/#51-58, Avengers #63, Iron Man #64, Marvel Double-Shot #1; Beck-c 22.00
...: Lord of Asgard (9/02, $15.99, TPB) r/#45-50 16.00
...Resurrection ($5.99, TPB) r/#1,2 6.00
...: The Dark Gods (7/00, $15.95, TPB) r/#9-13 16.00
...: The Death of Odin (7/02, $12.99, TPB) r/#39-44 13.00

THOR CORPS
Marvel Comics: Sept, 1993 - No. 4, Jan, 1994 ($1.75, limited series)

1-4: 1-Invaders cameo. 2-Invaders app. 3-Spider-Man 2099, Rawhide Kid, Two-Gun Kid & Kid Colt app. 4-Painted-c 2.25

THOR: GODSTORM
Marvel Comics: Nov, 2001 - No. 3, Jan, 2002 ($3.50, limited series)

1-3-Steve Rude-c/a; Busiek-s; Avengers app. 3.50

THORION OF THE NEW ASGODS
Marvel Comics (Amalgam): June, 1997 ($1.95, one-shot)

1-Keith Giffen-s/John Romita Jr.-c/a 2.25

THOR: THE LEGEND
Marvel Comics: Sept, 1996 ($3.95, one-shot)

nn-Tribute issue 4.00

THOR: VIKINGS
Marvel Comics (MAX): Sept, 2003 - No. 5, Jan, 2004 ($3.50, limited series)

1-5-Garth Ennis-s/Glenn Fabry-a/c 3.50

THOSE MAGNIFICENT MEN IN THEIR FLYING MACHINES (See Movie Comics)

3-D Batman 1953 © DC

Three-Dimension Adventures #1 © DC

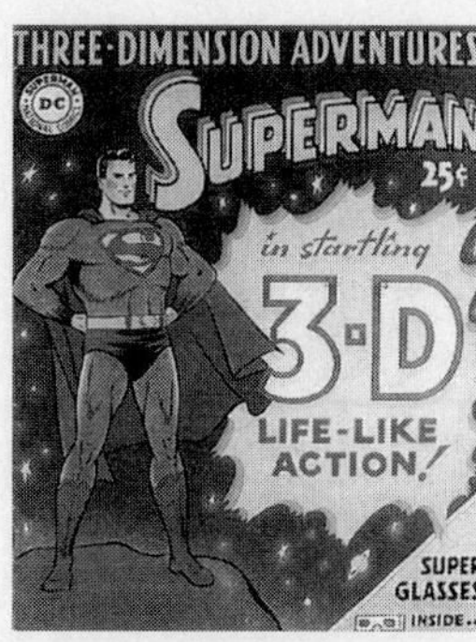

300 #2 © Frank Miller

GD 2.0 | VG 4.0 | FN 6.0 | VF 8.0 | VF/NM 9.0 | NM- 9.2

THRAX
Event Comics: Nov, 1996 ($2.95, one-shot)
1 — 3.00

THREE CABALLEROS (Walt Disney's...)
Dell Publishing Co.: No. 71, 1945
Four Color 71-by Walt Kelly, c/a — 75 150 225 561 856 1150

THREE CHIPMUNKS, THE (TV) (Also see Alvin)
Dell Publishing Co.: No. 1042, Oct-Dec, 1959
Four Color 1042 (#1)-(Alvin, Simon & Theodore) — 7 14 21 46 63 80

THREE COMICS (Also see Spiritman)
The Penny King Co.: 1944 (10¢, 52 pgs.) (2 different covers exist)
1,3,4-Lady Luck, Mr. Mystic, The Spirit app. (3 Spirit sections bound together); Lou Fine-a — 26 52 78 150 210 270
NOTE: *No. 1 contains Spirit Sections 4/9/44 - 4/23/44, and No. 4 is also from 4/44.*

3-D (NOTE: The prices of all the 3-D comics listed include glasses. Deduct 40-50 percent if glasses are missing, and reduce slightly if glasses are loose.)

3-D ACTION
Atlas Comics (ACI): Jan, 1954 (Oversized, 15¢)(2 pairs of glasses included)
1-Battle Brady; Sol Brodsky-c — 39 78 117 224 317 410

3-D ADVENTURE COMICS
Stats, Etc.: Aug, 1986 (one shot)
1-Promo material — 4.00

3-D ALIEN TERROR
Eclipse Comics: June, 1986 ($2.50)
1-Old Witch, Crypt-Keeper, Vault Keeper cameo; Morrow, John Pound-a, Yeates-c — 6.00
...in 2-D: 100 copies signed, numbered(B&W) — 1 3 4 8 10 12

3-D ANIMAL FUN (See Animal Fun)

THREE DAYS IN EUROPE
Oni Press: Nov, 2002 - No. 5, Apr, 2003 ($2.95, B&W, limited series)
1-5-Johnston-s/Hawthorne-a — 3.00
TPB (11/03, $14.95, digest-sized) r/#1-5 — 15.00

3-D BATMAN (Also see Batman 3-D)
National Periodical Publications: 1953 (Reprinted in 1966)
1953-(25¢)-Reprints Batman #42 & 48 (Penguin-c/story); Tommy Tomorrow story; came with pair of 3-D Bat glasses — 112 224 336 700 1050 1400
1966-Reprints 1953 issue; new cover by Infantino/Anderson; has inside-c photos of Batman & Robin from TV show (50¢) — 39 78 117 230 325 420

3-D CIRCUS
Fiction House Magazines (Real Adventures Publ.): 1953 (25¢, w/glasses)
1 — 39 78 117 230 325 420

3-D COMICS (See Mighty Mouse, Tor and Western Fighters)

3-D DOLLY
Harvey Publications: December, 1953 (25¢, came with 2 pairs of glasses)
1-Richie Rich story redrawn from his 1st app. in Little Dot #1; shows cover in 3-D on inside — 55 110 165 344 515 685

3-D-ELL
Dell Publishing Co.: No. 1, 1953; No. 3, 1953 (3-D comics) (25¢, came w/glasses)
1-Rootie Kazootie (#2 does not exist) — 39 78 117 224 317 410
3-Flukey Luke — 37 74 111 212 301 390

3-D EXOTIC BEAUTIES
The 3-D Zone: Nov, 1990 ($2.95, 28 pgs.)
1-L.B. Cole-c — 1 2 3 5 6 8

3-D FEATURES PRESENTS JET PUP
Dimensions Publications: Oct-Dec (Winter on-c), 1953 (25¢, came w/glasses)
1-Irving Spector-a(2) — 39 78 117 230 325 420

3-D FUNNY MOVIES
Comic Media: 1953 (25¢, came w/glasses)
1-Bugsey Bear & Paddy Pelican — 39 78 117 230 325 420

THREE-DIMENSION ADVENTURES (Superman)
National Periodical Publications: 1953 (25¢, large size, came w/glasses)
nn-Origin Superman (new art) — 112 224 336 700 1050 1400

THREE DIMENSIONAL ALIEN WORLDS (See Alien Worlds)
Pacific Comics: July, 1984 (1st Ray Zone 3-D book)(one-shot)
1-Bolton-a(p); Stevens-a(i); Art Adams 1st published-a(p) — 6.00

THREE DIMENSIONAL DNAGENTS (See New DNAgents)

THREE DIMENSIONAL E. C. CLASSICS (Three Dimensional Tales From the Crypt No. 2)
E. C. Comics: Spring, 1954 (Prices include glasses; came with 2 pair)
1-Stories by Wood (Mad #3), Krigstein (W.S. #7), Evans (F.C. #13), & Ingels (CSS #5); Kurtzman-c (rare in high grade due to unstable paper) — 88 176 264 550 825 1100
NOTE: *Stories redrawn to 3-D format. Original stories not necessarily by artists listed. CSS: Crime SuspenStories; F.C.: Frontline Combat; W.S.: Weird Science.*

THREE DIMENSIONAL TALES FROM THE CRYPT (Formerly Three Dimensional E. C. Classics)(Cover title: ...From the Crypt of Terror)
E. C. Comics: No. 2, Spring, 1954 (Prices include glasses; came with 2 pair)
2-Davis (TFTC #25), Elder (VOH #14), Craig (TFTC #24), & Orlando (TFTC #22) stories; Feldstein-c (rare in high grade) — 86 172 258 538 807 1075
NOTE: *Stories redrawn to 3-D format. Original stories not necessarily by artists listed. TFTC: Tales From the Crypt; VOH: Vault of Horror.*

3-D LOVE
Steriographic Publ. (Mikeross Publ.): Dec, 1953 (25¢, came w/glasses)
1 — 39 78 117 230 325 420

3-D NOODNICK (See Noodnick)

3-D ROMANCE
Steriographic Publ. (Mikeross Publ.): Jan, 1954 (25¢, came w/glasses)
1 — 39 78 117 230 325 420

3-D SHEENA, JUNGLE QUEEN (Also see Sheena 3-D)
Fiction House Magazines: 1953 (25¢, came w/glasses)
1-Maurice Whitman-c — 72 144 216 450 675 900

3-D SUBSTANCE
The 3-D Zone: July, 1990 ($2.95, 28 pgs.)
1-Ditko-c/a(r) — 4.00

3-D TALES OF THE WEST
Atlas Comics (CPS): Jan, 1954 (Oversized) (15¢, came with 2 pair of glasses)
1 (3-D)-Sol Brodsky-c — 39 78 117 230 325 420

3-D THREE STOOGES (Also see Three Stooges)
Eclipse Comics: Sept, 1986 - No. 2, Nov, 1986; No. 3, Oct, 1987; No. 4, 1989 ($2.50)
1-4: 3-Maurer-r. 4-r/"Three Missing Links" — 5.00
1-3 (2-D) — 5.00

3-D WHACK (See Whack)

3-D ZONE, THE
The 3-D Zone (Renegade Press)/Ray Zone: Feb, 1987 - No. 20, 1989 ($2.50)
1,3,4,7-9,11,12,14,15,17,19,20: 1-r/A Star Presentation. 3-Picture Scope Jungle Advs. 4-Electric Fear. 7-Hollywood 3-D Jayne Mansfield photo-c. 8-High Seas 3-D, 9-Redmask-r. 11-Danse Macabre; Matt Fox c/a(r). 12-3-D Presidents. 14-Tyranostar. 15-3-Dementia Comics; Kurtzman-c, Kubert, Maurer-a. 17-Thrilling Love. 19-Cracked Classics. 20-Commander Battle and His Atomic Submarine — 6.00
2,5,6,10,13,16,18: 2-Wolverton-r. 5-Krazy Kat-r. 6-Ratfink. 10-Jet 3-D; Powell & Williamson-r. 13-Flash Gordon. 16-Space Vixens; Dave Stevens-c/a. 18-Spacehawk; Wolverton-r — 6.00
NOTE: *Davis r-19.* ***Ditko*** *r-19.* ***Elder*** *r-19.* ***Everett*** *r-19.* ***Feldstein*** *r-17.* ***Frazetta*** *r-17.* ***Heath*** *r-19.* ***Kamen*** *r-17.* ***Severin*** *r-19.* ***Ward*** *r-17,19.* ***Wolverton*** *r-2,18,19.* ***Wood*** *r-1,17. Photo c-12*

3 GEEKS, THE (Also see Geeksville)
3 Finger Prints: 1996 - No. 11, Jun, 1999 (B&W)
1,2 -Rich Koslowski-s/a in all — 1 2 3 5 6 8
1-(2nd printing) — 2.50
3-7, 9-11 — 2.50
8-(48 pgs.) — 4.00
10-Variant-c — 3.50
...Full Circle (7/03, $4.95) Origin story of the 3 Geeks; "Buck Rodinski" app. — 5.00
How to Pick Up Girls If You're a Comic Book Geek (color)(7/97) — 4.00
When the Hammer Fallls TPB (2001, $14.95) r/#8-11 — 15.00

300
Dark Horse Comics: May, 1998 - No. 5, Sept, 1998 ($2.95/$3.95, limited series)
1,5: 1-Frank Miller-s/c/a; Spartans vs. Persians war. 5-($3.95-c) — 4.00
1-Second printing, 2-4 — 3.00

3 LITTLE KITTENS
BroadSword Comics: Aug, 2002 - No. 3, Dec, 2002 ($2.95, limited series)
1-3-Jim Balent-s/a; two covers — 3.00

3 LITTLE PIGS (Disney)(...and the Wonderful Magic Lamp)

The Three Mouseketeers #21 © DC

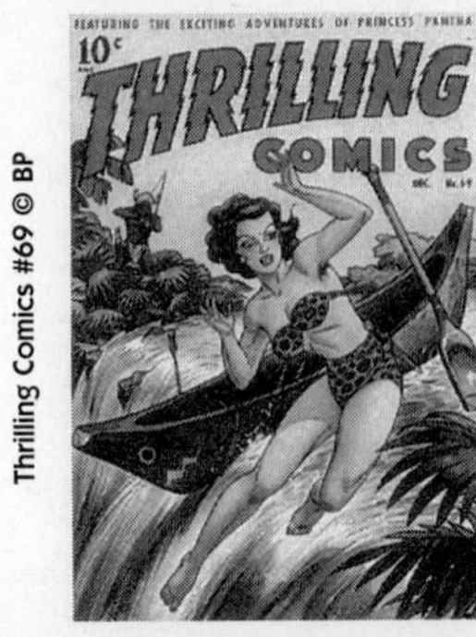

Thrilling Comics #69 © BP

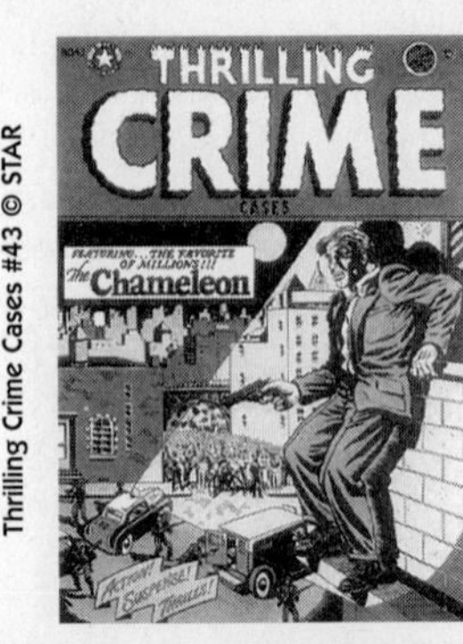

Thrilling Crime Cases #43 © STAR

	GD 2.0	VG 4.0	FN 6.0	VF 8.0	VF/NM 9.0	NM- 9.2

Dell Publishing Co.: No. 218, Mar, 1949
Four Color 218 (#1) 12 24 36 87 129 170

3 LITTLE PIGS, THE (See Walt Disney Showcase #15 & 21)
Gold Key: May, 1964; No. 2, Sept, 1968 (Walt Disney)
1-Reprints Four Color #218 4 8 12 22 30 38
2 3 6 9 16 20 24

THREE MOUSEKETEERS, THE (1st Series)(See Funny Stuff #1)
National Per. Publ.: 3-4/56 - No. 24, 9-10/59; No. 25, 8-9/60 - No. 26, 10-12/60
1 18 36 54 131 191 250
2 10 20 30 67 96 125
3-10: 6,8-Grey tone-c 8 16 24 53 74 95
11-26: 24-Cover says 11/59, inside says 9-10/59 7 14 21 46 63 80
NOTE: *Rube Grossman a-1-26. Sheldon Mayer a-1-8; c-1-7.*

THREE MOUSEKETEERS, THE (2nd Series) (See Super DC Giant)
National Periodical Publications: May-June, 1970 - No. 7, May-June, 1971 (#5-7: 68 pgs.)
1-Mayer-r in all 6 12 18 40 55 70
2-4: 4-Doodles Duck begins (1st app.) 4 8 12 24 32 40
5-7:(68 pgs.). 5-Dodo & the Frog, Bo Bunny begin 6 12 18 38 52 65

THREE MUSKETEERS, THE (See Disney's The Three Musketeers)

THREE NURSES (Confidential Diary #12-17; Career Girl Romances #24 on)
Charlton Comics: V3#18, May, 1963 - V3#23, Mar, 1964
V3#18-23 3 6 9 18 23 28

THREE RASCALS
I. W. Enterprises: 1958; 1963
I.W. Reprint #1,2,10: 1-(Says Super Comics on inside)-(M.E.'s Clubhouse Rascals). #2-(1958). 10-(1963)-r/#1 2 4 6 8 10 12

THREE RING COMICS
Spotlight Publishers: March, 1945
1-Funny animal 17 34 51 98 134 170

THREE RING COMICS (Also see Captain Wizard & Meteor Comics)
Century Publications: April, 1946
1-Prankster-c; Captain Wizard, Impossible Man, Race Wilkins, King O'Leary, & Dr. Mercy app. 35 70 105 201 288 370

THREE ROCKETEERS (See Blast-Off)

THREE STOOGES (See Comic Album #18, Top Comics, The Little Stooges, March of Comics #232, 248, 268, 280, 292, 304, 316, 336, 373, Movie Classics & Comics & 3-D Three Stooges)

THREE STOOGES
Jubilee No. 1/St. John No. 1 (9/53) on: Feb, 1949 - No. 2, May, 1949; Sept, 1953 - No. 7, Oct, 1954
1-(Scarce, 1949)-Kubert-a; infinity-c 112 224 336 700 1050 1400
2-(Scarce)-Kubert, Maurer-a 79 158 237 494 740 985
1(9/53)-Hollywood Stunt Girl by Kubert (7 pgs.) 69 138 207 431 646 860
2(3-D, 10/53, 25¢)-Came w/glasses; Stunt Girl story by Kubert 50 100 150 300 450 600
3(3-D, 10/53, 25¢)-Came w/glasses; has 3-D-c 47 94 141 282 421 560
4(3/54)-7(10/54): 4-1st app. Li'l Stooge? 40 80 120 240 338 435
NOTE: *All issues have **Kubert-Maurer** art & **Maurer** covers. 6, 7-Partial photo-c.*

THREE STOOGES
Dell Publishing Co./Gold Key No. 10 (10/62) on: No. 1043, Oct-Dec, 1959 - No. 55, June, 1972
Four Color 1043 (#1) 26 52 78 189 275 360
Four Color 1078,1127,1170,1187 14 28 42 97 141 185
6(9-11/61) - 10: 6-Professor Putter begins; ends #16 11 22 33 77 114 150
11-14,16,18-20 10 20 30 67 96 125
15-Go Around the World in a Daze (movie scenes) 10 20 30 72 104 135
17-The Little Monsters begin (5/64)(1st app.?) 10 20 30 72 104 135
21,23-30 8 16 24 58 82 105
22-Movie scenes from "The Outlaws Is Coming" 9 18 27 63 89 115
31-55 7 14 21 46 63 80
NOTE: *All Four Colors, 6-50, 52-55 have photo-c.*

THREE STOOGES IN 3-D, THE
Eternity Comics: 1991 ($3.95, high quality paper, w/glasses)
1-Reprints Three Stooges by Gold Key; photo-c 5.00

THREE STRIKES
Oni Press: Apr, 2003 - No. 5, Oct, 2003 ($2.99, B&W, limited series)
1-5-Brian Hurtt-a 3.00

3 WORLDS OF GULLIVER
Dell Publishing Co.: No. 1158, July, 1961 (2 issues exist with diff. covers)
Four Color 1158-Movie, photo-c 8 16 24 53 74 95

THRILL COMICS (See Flash Comics, Fawcett)

THRILLER
DC Comics: Nov, 1983 - No. 12, Nov, 1984 ($1.25, Baxter paper)
1-12: 1-Intro Seven Seconds; Von Eeden-c/a begins. 2-Origin. 5,6-Elvis satire 2.25

THRILLING ADVENTURES IN STAMPS COMICS (Formerly Stamp Comics)
Stamp Comics, Inc. (Very Rare): V1#8, Jan, 1953 (25¢, 100 pgs.)
V1#8-Harrison, Wildey, Kiefer, Napoli-a 74 148 222 463 692 920

THRILLING ADVENTURE STORIES (See Tigerman)
Atlas/Seaboard Publ.: Feb, 1975 - No. 2, Aug, 1975 (B&W, 68 pgs.)
1-Tigerman, Kromag the Killer begin; Heath, Thorne-a; Doc Savage movie photos of Ron Ely 2 4 6 12 16 20
2-Heath, Toth, Severin, Simonson-a; Adams-c 3 6 9 18 24 30

THRILLING COMICS
Better Publ./Nedor/Standard Comics: Feb, 1940 - No. 80, April, 1951
1-Origin & 1st app. Dr. Strange (37 pgs.), ends #?; Nickie Norton of the Secret Service begins 296 592 888 1850 2775 3700
2-The Rio Kid, The Woman in Red, Pinocchio begins 128 256 384 800 1200 1600
3-The Ghost & Lone Eagle begin 80 160 240 500 750 1000
4-6,8-10: 5-Dr. Strange changed to Doc Strange 61 122 183 381 573 765
7-Classic-c 78 156 234 488 732 975
11-18,20 55 110 165 330 495 660
19-Origin & 1st app. The American Crusader (8/41), ends #39,41 61 122 183 381 573 765
21-30: 24-Intro. Mike, Doc Strange's sidekick (1/42). 27-Robot-c. 29-Last Rio Kid 48 96 144 288 432 575
31-40: 36-Commando Cubs begin (7/43, 1st app.) 42 84 126 252 376 500
41-Classic Hitler & Mussolini-c 88 176 264 550 825 1100
42,43,45-51: 45-Hitler pict. on-c 37 74 111 212 301 390
44-Hitler-c 76 152 228 475 713 950
52-Classic Schomburg hooded bondage-c; the Ghost ends 53 106 159 318 477 635
53-The Phantom Detective begins; The Cavalier app.; no Commando Cubs 37 74 111 212 301 390
54-The Cavalier app.; no Commando Cubs 37 74 111 212 301 390
55-Lone Eagle ends 32 64 96 184 262 340
56-Princess Pantha begins (10/46, 1st app.) 48 96 144 288 432 575
57-66: 61-Ingels-a; The Lone Eagle app. 65-Last Phantom Detective & Commando Cubs. 66-Frazetta text illo 40 80 120 240 340 440
67,70-73: Frazetta-a(5-7 pgs.) in each. 72-Sea Eagle app.; Buck Ranger, Cowboy Detective begins 46 92 138 276 413 550
68,69-Frazetta-a(2), 8 & 6 pgs.; 9 & 7 pgs. 50 100 150 300 450 600
74-Last Princess Pantha; Tara app. 32 64 96 184 262 340
75-78: 75-All western format begins 15 30 45 86 118 150
79-Krigstein-a 16 32 48 92 126 160
80-Severin & Elder, Celardo, Moreira-a 16 32 48 92 126 160
NOTE: *Bondage c-5, 9, 13, 20, 22, 27-30, 38, 41, 52, 54, 70. **Kinstler** a-45. **Leo Morey** a-7. **Schomburg** (sometimes signed as **Xela**) c-7, 9-19, 36-80 (airbrush 62-71). **Tuska** a-62, 63. Woman in Red not in #19, 23, 31-33, 39-45. No. 45 exists as a Canadian reprint but numbered #48. No. 72 exists as a Canadian reprint with no **Frazetta** story.American Crusader c-20-24. Buck Ranger c-72-80. Commando Cubs c-37, 39, 41, 43, 45, 47, 49, 51. Doc Strange c-1-19, 25-36, 38, 40, 42, 44, 46, 48, 50, 52-57, 59. Princess Pantha c-58, 60-71.*

THRILLING COMICS (Also see All Star Comics 1999 crossover titles)
DC Comics: May, 1999 ($1.99, one-shot)
1-Golden Age Hawkman and Wildcat; Russ Heath-a 2.25

THRILLING CRIME CASES (Formerly 4Most; becomes Shocking Mystery Cases #50 on)
Star Publications: No. 41, June-July, 1950 - No. 49, July, 1952
41 29 58 87 164 232 300
42-45: 42-L. B. Cole-c/a (1); Chameleon story (Fox-r) 26 52 78 147 206 265
46-48: 47-Used in **POP**, pg. 84 25 50 75 144 198 255
49-(7/52)-Classic L. B. Cole-c 44 88 132 264 395 525
NOTE: ***L. B. Cole** c-all; a-43p, 45p, 46p, 49(2 pgs.). **Disbrow** a-48. **Hollingsworth** a-48.*

THRILLING ROMANCES
Standard Comics: No. 5, Dec, 1949 - No. 26, June, 1954
5 13 26 39 76 103 130
6,8 9 18 27 49 62 75

Thrills of Tomorrow #20 © HARV

Thunderbolts #29 © MAR

Thundercats #1 © WB & Ted Wolf

GD VG FN VF VF/NM NM-
2.0 4.0 6.0 8.0 9.0 9.2

7-Severin/Elder-a (7 pgs.) 10 20 30 60 80 100
9,10-Severin/Elder-a; photo-c 9 18 27 54 70 85
11,14-21,26: 12-Tyrone Power/ Susan Hayward photo-c.14-Gene Tierney & Danny Kaye photo-c from movie "On the Riviera". 15-Tony Martin/Janet Leigh photo-c
8 16 24 43 54 65
12-Wood-a (2 pgs.) 11 22 33 63 84 105
13-Severin-a 9 18 27 49 62 75
22-25-Toth-a 10 20 30 56 73 90
NOTE: *All photo-c.* ***Celardo*** *a-9, 16.* ***Colletta*** *a-23, 24(2).* ***Toth*** *text illos-19.* ***Tuska*** *a-9.*

THRILLING SCIENCE TALES
AC Comics: 1989 - No. 2 ($3.50, 2/3 color, 52 pgs.)
1,2: 1-r/Bob Colt #6(saucer); Frazetta, Guardineer (Space Ace), Wood, Krenkel, Orlando, WIlliamson-r; Kaluta-c. 2-Capt. Video-r by Evans, Capt. Science-r by Wood, Star Pirate-r by Whitman & Mysta of the Moon-r by Moreira 4.00

THRILLING TRUE STORY OF THE BASEBALL...
Fawcett Publications: 1952 (Photo-c, each)
...Giants-photo-c; has Willie Mays rookie photo-biography; Willie Mays, Eddie Stanky & others photos on-c 69 138 207 431 646 860
...Yankees-photo-c; Yogi Berra, Joe DiMaggio, Mickey Mantle & others photos on-c
66 132 198 413 619 825

THRILLING WONDER TALES
AC Comics : 1991 ($2.95, B&W)
1-Includes a Bob Powell Thun'da story 3.00

THRILLKILLER
DC Comics : Jan, 1997 - No. 3, Mar, 1997($2.50, limited series)
1-3-Elseworlds Robin & Batgirl; Chaykin-s/Brereton-c/a 3.00
...'62 ('98, $4.95, one-shot) Sequel; Chaykin-s/Brereton-c/a 5.00
TPB-(See Batman: Thrillkiller)

THRILLOGY
Pacific Comics: Jan, 1984 (One-shot, color)
1-Conrad-c/a 3.00

THRILL-O-RAMA
Harvey Publications (Fun Films): Oct, 1965 - No. 3, Dec, 1966
1-Fate (Man in Black) by Powell app.; Doug Wildey-a(2); Simon-c
6 12 18 38 52 65
2-Pirana begins (see Phantom #46); Williamson 2 pgs.; Fate (Man in Black) app.; Tuska/Simon-c 4 8 12 24 32 40
3-Fate (Man in Black) app.; Sparling-c 3 7 10 21 28 35

THRILLS OF TOMORROW (Formerly Tomb of Terror)
Harvey Publications: No. 17, Oct, 1954 - No. 20, April, 1955
17-Powell-a (horror); r/Witches Tales #7 15 30 45 84 115 145
18-Powell-a (horror); r/Tomb of Terror #1 13 26 39 74 100 125
19,20-Stuntman-c/stories by S&K (r/from Stuntman #1 & 2); 19 has origin & is last pre-code (2/55) 34 68 102 196 278 360
NOTE: ***Kirby*** *c-19, 20.* ***Palais*** *a-17.* ***Simon*** *c-18?*

THROBBING LOVE (See Fox Giants)

THROUGH GATES OF SPLENDOR
Spire Christian Comics (Flemming H. Revell Co.): 1973, 1974 (36 pages) (39-49 cents)
nn 1 3 4 6 8 10

THUMPER (Disney)
Dell Publishing Co.: No, 19, 1942 - No. 243, Sept, 1949
Four Color 19-Walt Disney's...Meets the Seven Dwarfs; reprinted in Silly Symphonies
50 100 150 400 600 800
Four Color 243-...Follows His Nose 12 24 36 82 121 160

THUN'DA (...King of the Congo)
Magazine Enterprises: 1952 - No. 6, 1953
1(A-1 #47)-Origin; Frazetta c/a; only comic done entirely by Frazetta; all Thun'da stories, no Cave Girl 140 280 420 875 1313 1750
2(A-1 #56)-Powell-c/a begins, ends #6; Intro/1st app. Cave Girl in filler strip (also app. in 3-6)
24 48 72 135 190 245
3(A-1 #73), 4(A-1 #78) 17 34 51 98 134 170
5(A-1 #83), 6(A-1 #86) 16 32 48 92 126 160

THUN'DA TALES (See Frank Frazetta's...)

THUNDER AGENTS (See Dynamo, Noman & Tales Of Thunder)
Tower Comics: 11/65 - No. 17, 12/67; No. 18, 9/68, No. 19, 11/68, No. 20, 11/69 (No. 1-16: 68 pgs.; No. 17 on: 52 pgs.)(All are 25¢)
1-Origin & 1st app. Dynamo, Noman, Menthor, & The Thunder Squad; 1st app.

GD VG FN VF VF/NM NM-
2.0 4.0 6.0 8.0 9.0 9.2

The Iron Maiden 20 40 60 140 205 270
2-Death of Egghead; A-bomb blast panel 10 20 30 73 107 140
3-5: 4-Guy Gilbert becomes Lightning who joins Thunder Squad; Iron Maiden app.
8 16 24 55 78 100
6-10: 7-Death of Menthor. 8-Origin & 1st app. The Raven
7 14 21 46 63 80
11-15: 13-Undersea Agent app.; no Raven story 6 12 18 38 52 65
16-19 6 12 18 38 52 65
20-Special Collectors Edition; all reprints 4 8 12 24 32 40
...Archives Vol. 1 (DC Comics, 2003, $49.95, HC) r/#1-4, restored and recolored 50.00
...Archives Vol. 2 (DC Comics, 2003, $49.95, HC) r/#5-7, Dynamo #1 50.00
...Archives Vol. 3 (DC Comics, 2003, $49.95, HC) r/#8-10, Dynamo #2 50.00
NOTE: ***Crandall*** *a-1, 4p, 5p, 18, 20r; c-18.* ***Ditko*** *a-6, 7p, 12p, 13?, 14p, 16, 18.* ***Giunta*** *a-6.* ***Kane*** *a-1, 5p, 6p?, 14, 16p; c-14, 15.* ***Reinman*** *a-13.* ***Sekowsky*** *a-6.* ***Tuska*** *a-1p, 7, 8, 10, 13-17, 19.* ***Whitney*** *a-9p, 10, 13, 15, 17, 18; c-17.* ***Wood*** *a-1-11, 15(w/**Ditko**-12, 18), (inks-#9, 13, 14, 16, 17), 19i, 20r; c-1-8, 9i, 10-13(#10 w/**Williamson**(p)), 16.*

T.H.U.N.D.E.R. AGENTS (See Blue Ribbon Comics, Hall of Fame Featuring the..., JCP Features & Wally Wood's...)
JC Comics (Archie Publications): May, 1983 - No. 2, Jan, 1984
1,2: 1-New Manna/Blyberg-c/a. 2-Blyberg-c 6.00

THUNDER BIRDS (See Cinema Comics Herald)

THUNDERBOLT (See The Atomic...)

THUNDERBOLT (Peter Cannon...; see Crisis on Infinite Earths & Peter...)
Charlton Comics: Jan, 1966; No. 51, Mar-Apr, 1966 - No. 60, Nov, 1967
1-Origin & 1st app. Thunderbolt 4 8 12 27 36 45
51-(Formerly Son of Vulcan #50) 3 6 9 19 25 32
52-59: 54-Sentinels begin. 59-Last Thunderbolt & Sentinels (back-up story)
2 4 6 12 16 20
60-Prankster app. 2 4 6 14 18 22
57,58 ('77)-Modern Comics-r 4.00
NOTE: ***Aparo*** *a-60.* ***Morisi*** *a-1, 51-56, 58; c-1, 51-56, 58, 59.*

THUNDERBOLTS (Also see Incredible Hulk #449)
Marvel Comics: Apr, 1997 - No. 81, Sept, 2003 ($1.95-$2.99)
1-($2.99)-Busiek-s/Bagley-c/a 1 2 3 5 7 9
1-2nd printing; new cover colors 2.50
2-4: 2-Two covers. 4-Intro. Jolt 6.00
5-11: 9-Avengers app. 3.50
12-($2.99)-Avengers and Fantastic Four-c/app. 4.00
13-24: 14-Thunderbolts return to Earth. 21-Hawkeye app. 2.50
25-($2.99) Wraparound-c 3.00
26-38: 26-Manco-a 2.25
39-($2.99) 100 Page Monster; Iron Man reprints 3.00
40-49: 40-Begin $2.25-c; Sandman-c/app. 44-Avengers app. 47-Captain Marvel app. 49-Zircher-a 2.25
50-($2.99) Last Bagley-a; Captain America becomes leader 3.00
51-74,76,77,80,81: 51,52-Zircher-a; Dr. Doom app. 80,81-Spider-Man app. 2.25
75-($3.50) Hawkeye leaves the team; Garcia-a 3.50
78,79-($2.99-c) Velasco-a begins 3.00
Annual '97 ($2.99)-Wraparound-c 3.00
Annual 2000 ($3.50) Breyfogle-a 3.50
...: Distant Rumblings (#-1) (7/97, $1.95) Busiek-s 5.00
First Strikes (1997, $4.99,TPB) r/#1,2 5.00
...: Life Sentences (7/01, $3.50) Adlard-a 3.50
...: Marvel's Most Wanted TPB ('98, $16.99) r/origin stories of original Masters of Evil 17.00
Wizard #0 (bagged with Wizard #89) 2.25

THUNDERBUNNY (See Blue Ribbon Comics #13, Charlton Bullseye & Pep Comics #393)
Red Circle Comics: Jan, 1984 (Direct sale only)
WaRP Graphics: Second series No. 1, 1985 - No. 6, 1985
Apple Comics: No. 7, 1986 - No. 12, 1987
1-Humor/parody; origin Thunderbunny; 2 page pin-up by Anderson 5.00
(2nd series) 1,2-Magazine size 3.00
3-12-Comic size 2.25

THUNDERCATS (TV)
Marvel Comics (Star Comics)/Marvel #22 on: Dec, 1985 - No. 24, June, 1988 (75¢)
1-Mooney-c/a begins 2 4 6 9 11 14
2-20: 2-(65¢ & 75¢ cover exists). 12-Begin $1.00-c. 18-20-Williamson-i
1 2 3 5 7 9
21-24: 23-Williamson-c(i) 1 3 4 6 8 10

THUNDERCATS (TV)
DC Comics (WildStorm): No. 0, Oct, 2002 - No. 5, Feb, 2003 ($2.50/$2.95, limited series)

Thundercats/Battle of the Planets #1 © WB & Ted Wolf

Thunderstrike #3 © MAR

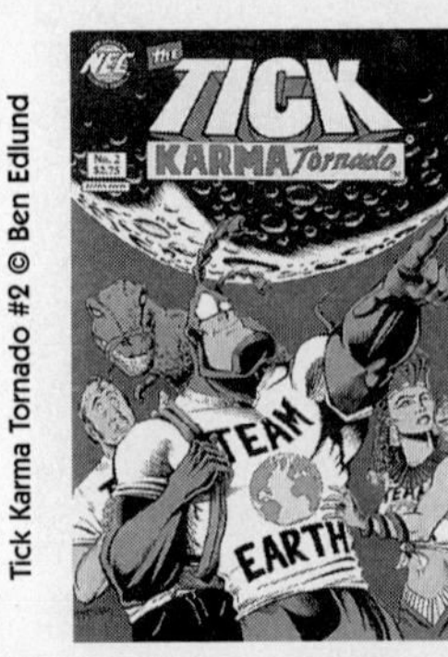

Tick Karma Tornado #2 © Ben Edlund

GD 2.0 | VG 4.0 | FN 6.0 | VF 8.0 | VF/NM 9.0 | NM- 9.2

0-($2.50) J. Scott Campbell-c/a 3.00
1-5-($2.95) 1-McGuinness-a/c; variant cover by Art Adams; rebirth of Mumm-Ra 3.00
.../ Battle of the Planets (7/03, $4.95) Kaare Andrews-s/a; 2 covers by Campbell & Ross 5.00
...: Origins-Heroes & Villains (2/04, $3.50) short stories by various 3.50
...Reclaiming Thundera TPB (2003, $12.95) r/#0-5 13.00
... Sourcebook (1/03, $2.95) pin-ups and info on characters; art by various; A. Adams-c 3.00

THUNDERCATS: DOGS OF WAR
DC Comics (WildStorm): Aug, 2003 - No. 5, Dec, 2003 ($2.95, limited series)

1-5: 1-Two covers by Booth & Pearson; Booth-a/Layman-s. 2-4-Two covers 3.00

THUNDERCATS: HAMMERHAND'S REVENGE
DC Comics (WildStorm): Dec, 2003 - No. 5 ($2.95, limited series)

1-4-Avery-s/D'Anda-a. 2-Variant-c by Warren 3.00

THUNDERCATS: THE RETURN
DC Comics (WildStorm): Apr, 2003 - No. 5, Aug, 2003 ($2.95, limited series)

1-5: 1-Two covers by Benes & Cassaday; Gilmore-s 3.00

THUNDERGOD
Crusade Entertainment: July, 1996 - No. 3 ($2.95, B&W)

1-3: Christopher Golden scripts; painted-c 3.00

THUNDERGOD
Caliber Comics: 1997 ($2.95, B&W, one-shot)

1 3.00

THUNDER MOUNTAIN (See Zane Grey, Four Color #246)

THUNDERSTRIKE (See Thor #459)
Marvel Comics: June, 1993 - No. 24, July, 1995 ($1.25)

1-($2.95, 52 pgs.)-Holo-grafx lightning patterned foil-c; Bloodaxe returns 3.00
2-24: 2-Juggernaut-c/s. 4-Capt. America app. 4-6-Spider-Man app. 8-bound-in trading card sheet. 18-Bloodaxe app. 24-Death of Thunderstrike 2.25
Marvel Double Feature...Thunderstrike/Code Blue #13 ($2.50)-Same as Thunderstrike #13 w/Code Blue flip book 2.50

TICK, THE (Also see The Chroma-Tick)
New England Comics Press: Jun, 1988 - No. 12, May, 1993
($1.75/$1.95/$2.25; B&W, over-sized)

Special Edition 1-1st comic book app. serially numbered & limited to 5,000 copies 6 12 18 38 52 65
Special Edition 1-(5/96, $5.95)-Double-c; foil-c; serially numbered (5,001 thru 14,000) & limited to 9,000 copies 6.00
Special Edition 2-Serially numbered and limited to 3000 copies 5 10 15 33 44 55
Special Edition 2-(8/96, $5.95)-Double-c; foil-c; serially numbered (5,001 thru 14,000) & limited to 9,000 copies 1 2 3 5 6 8
1-Regular Edition 1st printing; reprints Special Ed. 1 w/minor changes 4 8 12 27 36 45
1-2nd printing 6.00
1-3rd-5th printing 3.00
2-Reprints Special Ed. 2 w/minor changes 2 4 6 14 18 22
2-8-All reprints 3.00
3-5 ($1.95): 4-1st app. Paul the Samurai 1 3 4 6 8 10
6,8 ($2.25) 5.00
7-1st app. Man-Eating Cow. 6.00
8-Variant with no logo, price, issue number or company logos. 2 4 6 11 14 18
9-12 ($2.75) 4.00
12-Special Edition; card-stock, virgin foil-c; numbered edition 2 4 6 14 18 22
Pseudo-Tick #13 (11/00, $3.50) Continues story from #12 (1993) 4.00
Promo Sampler-(1990)-Tick-c/story 1 2 3 5 6 8

TICK, THE (One shots)
--BIG BACK TO SCHOOL SPECIAL
1-(10/98, $3.50, B&W) Tick and Arthur undercover in high school 3.50
--BIG CRUISE SHIP VACATION SPECIAL
1-(9/00, $3.50, B&W) 3.50
--BIG FATHER'S DAY SPECIAL
1-(6/00, $3.50, B&W) 3.50
--BIG HALLOWEEN SPECIAL
1-(10/99, $3.50, B&W) 3.50
...2000 (10/00, $3.50) 3.50
...2001 (9/01, $3.95) 4.00
--BIG MOTHER'S DAY SPECIAL
1-(4/00, $3.50, B&W) 3.50
--BIG RED-N-GREEN CHRISTMAS SPECTACLE
1-(12/01, $3.95) 4.00
--BIG SUMMER ANNUAL
1-(7/99, $3.50, B&W) Chainsaw Vigilante vs. Barry 3.50
--BIG SUMMER FUN SPECIAL
1-(8/98, $3.50, B&W) Tick and Arthur at summer camp 3.50
--BIG TAX TIME TERROR
1-(4/00, $3.50, B&W) 3.50
--BIG YEAR 2000 SPECTACLE
1-(3/00, $3.50, B&W) 3.50
--BIG YULE LOG SPECIAL
2001-(12/00, $3.50, B&W) 3.50
--INCREDIBLE INTERNET COMIC
1-(7/01, $3.95, color) reprints story from New England Comics website 4.00

INTRODUCING THE TICK
1-(4/02, $3.95, color) summary of Tick's life and adventures 3.95
--MASSIVE SUMMER DOUBLE SPECTACLE
1,2-(7,8/00, $3.50, B&W) 3.50

TICK & ARTIE
1-(6/02, $3.50, color) prints strips from Internet comic 3.50
2-(10/02, $3.95) 4.00

TICK'S BACK, THE
0-(8/97, $2.95, B&W) 3.50

TICK'S BIG ROMANTIC ADVENTURE, THE
1-(2/98, $2.95, B&W) Candy box cover with candy map on back 3.50

TICK AND ARTHUR, THE
New England Comics: Feb, 1999 - Present ($3.50, B&W)

1-6-Sean Wang-s/a 3.50

TICK BIG BLUE DESTINY, THE
New England Comics: Oct, 1997 - Present ($2.95)

1-4: 1-"Keen" Ed. 2-Two covers 3.50
1-($4.95) "Wicked Keen" Ed. w/die cut-c 5.00
5-($3.50) 3.50
6-Luny Bin Trilogy Preview #0 (7/98, $1.50) 3.50
7-9: 7-Luny Bin Trilogy begins 3.50

TICK BIG BLUE YULE LOG SPECIAL, THE
New England Comics: Dec, 1997; 1999 ($2.95, B&W)

1-"Jolly" and "Traditional" covers; flip book w/"Arthur Teaches the Tick About Hanukkah" 3.50
...1999 ($3.50) 3.50

TICK, THE : CIRCUS MAXIMUS
New England Comics: Mar, 2000 - No. 4, Jun, 2000 ($3.50, B&W)

1-4-Encyclopedia of characters from Tick comics 3.50
Giant No. 1 (8/03, $14.95) r/#1-4, Redux 15.00
Redux No. 1 (4/01, $3.50) 3.50

TICK, THE - COLOR
New England Comics: Jan, 2001 - Present ($3.95)

1-6: 1-Marc Sandroni-a 4.00

TICK, THE - HEROES OF THE CITY
New England Comics: Feb, 1999 - Present ($3.50, B&W)

1-6-Short stories by various 3.50

TICK KARMA TORNADO (The...)
New England Comics Press: Oct, 1993 - No. 9, Mar, 1995 ($2.75, B&W)

1-($3.25) 4.00
2-9: 2-$2.75-c begins 3.50

TICK'S BIG XMAS TRILOGY, THE
New England Comics: Dec, 2002 - No. 3, Dec, 2002 ($3.95, limited series)

1-3 4.00

TICK'S GOLDEN AGE COMIC, THE
New England Comics: May, 2002 - No. 3, Feb, 2003 ($4.95, Golden Age size)

1-3-Facsimile 1940s-style Tick issue; 2 covers 5.00
Giant Edition TPB (9/03, $12.95) r/#1-3 13.00

TICK'S GIANT CIRCUS OF THE MIGHTY, THE
New England Comics: Summer, 1992 - No. 3, Fall, 1993 ($2.75, B&W, magazine size)

Tick Tock Tales #3 © ME

Tigra #1 © MAR

Tim Holt #38 © ME

	GD 2.0	VG 4.0	FN 6.0	VF 8.0	VF/NM 9.0	NM- 9.2
1-(A-O). 2-(P-Z). 3-1993 Update						4.00

TICKLE COMICS (Also see Gay, Smile, & Whee Comics)
Modern Store Publ.: 1955 (7¢, 5x7-1/4", 52 pgs)

	GD	VG	FN	VF	VF/NM	NM-
1	6	12	18	28	34	40

TICK TOCK TALES
Magazine Enterprises: Jan, 1946 - V3#33, Jan-Feb, 1951

	GD	VG	FN	VF	VF/NM	NM-
1-Koko & Kola begin	14	28	42	81	111	140
2	8	16	24	46	58	70
3-10	8	16	24	40	50	60
11-33: 19-Flag-c. 23-Muggsy Mouse, The Pixies & Tom-Tom the Jungle Boy app. 25-The Pixies & Tom-Tom app.	7	14	21	35	43	50

TIGER (Also see Comics Reading Libraries in the Promotional Comics section)
Charlton Press (King Features): Mar, 1970 - No. 6, Jan, 1971 (15¢)

	GD	VG	FN	VF	VF/NM	NM-
1	3	6	9	16	20	24
2-6	2	4	6	9	11	14

TIGER BOY (See Unearthly Spectaculars)

TIGER GIRL
Gold Key: Sept, 1968 (15¢)

	GD	VG	FN	VF	VF/NM	NM-
1(10227-809)-Sparling-c/a; Jerry Siegel scripts. Some issues have a pin-up on back cover instead of advertising	4	8	12	28	38	48

TIGERMAN (Also see Thrilling Adventure Stories)
Seaboard Periodicals (Atlas): Apr, 1975 - No. 3, Sept, 1975 (All 25¢ issues)

	GD	VG	FN	VF	VF/NM	NM-
1-3: 1-Origin; Colan-c. 2,3-Ditko-p in each	1	3	4	6	8	10

TIGER WALKS, A (See Movie Comics)

TIGRA (The Avengers)
Marvel Comics: May, 2002 - No. 4, Aug, 2002 ($2.99, limited series)

	GD	VG	FN	VF	VF/NM	NM-
1-4-Christina Z-s/Deodato-c/a						3.00

TIGRESS, THE
Hero Graphics: Aug, 1992 - No. 6?, June, 1993 ($3.95/$2.95/$3.95, B&W)

	GD	VG	FN	VF	VF/NM	NM-
1,6: 1-Tigress vs. Flare. 6-44 pgs.						4.00
2-5: 2-$2.95-c begins						3.00

TILLIE THE TOILER (See Comic Monthly)
Dell Publishing Co.: No. 15, 1941 - No. 237, July, 1949

	GD	VG	FN	VF	VF/NM	NM-
Four Color 15(1941)	33	66	99	248	374	500
Large Feature Comic 30(1941)	24	48	72	174	255	335
Four Color 8(1942)	24	48	72	174	255	335
Four Color 22(1943)	18	36	54	131	191	250
Four Color 55(1944), 89(1945)	14	28	42	102	149	195
Four Color 106('45),132('46): 132-New stories begin	10	20	30	73	107	140
Four Color 150,176,184	10	20	30	70	100	130
Four Color 195,213,237	8	16	24	53	74	95

TIMBER WOLF (See Action Comics #372, & Legion of Super-Heroes)
DC Comics: Nov, 1992 - No. 5, Mar, 1993 ($1.25, limited series)

	GD	VG	FN	VF	VF/NM	NM-
1-5						2.50

TIME BANDITS
Marvel Comics Group: Feb, 1982 (one-shot, Giant)

	GD	VG	FN	VF	VF/NM	NM-
1-Movie adaptation						4.00

TIME BEAVERS (See First Comics Graphic Novel #2)

TIME BREAKERS
DC Comics (Helix): Jan, 1997 - No. 5, May, 1997 ($2.25, limited series)

	GD	VG	FN	VF	VF/NM	NM-
1-5-Pollack-s						2.50

TIMECOP (Movie)
Dark Horse Comics: Sept, 1994 - No. 2, Nov, 1994 ($2.50, limited series)

	GD	VG	FN	VF	VF/NM	NM-
1,2-Adaptation of film						2.50

TIME FOR LOVE (Formerly Romantic Secrets)
Charlton Comics: V2#53, Oct, 1966; Oct, 1967 - No. 47, May, 1976

	GD	VG	FN	VF	VF/NM	NM-
V2#53(10/66) Herman-s Hermits app.	3	7	10	21	28	35
1(10/67)	4	8	12	24	32	40
2(12/67)-10	3	6	9	16	20	24
11-20	2	4	6	11	14	18
21-29	2	4	6	9	11	14
30-(10/72)-Full-length portrait of David Cassidy	3	6	9	18	24	30
31-47	2	4	6	8	10	12

TIMELESS TOPIX (See Topix)

TIMELY PRESENTS: ALL WINNERS
Marvel Comics: Dec, 1999 ($3.99)

	GD	VG	FN	VF	VF/NM	NM-
1-Reprints All Winners Comics #19 (Fall 1946); new Lago-c						4.00

TIMELY PRESENTS: HUMAN TORCH
Marvel Comics: Feb, 1999 ($3.99)

	GD	VG	FN	VF	VF/NM	NM-
1-Reprints Human Torch Comics #5 (Fall 1941); new Lago-c						4.00

TIME MACHINE, THE
Dell Publishing Co.: No. 1085, Mar, 1960 (H.G. Wells)

	GD	VG	FN	VF	VF/NM	NM-
Four Color 1085-Movie, Alex Toth-a; Rod Taylor photo-c	16	32	48	113	167	220

TIME MASTERS
DC Comics: Feb, 1990 - No. 8, Sept, 1990 ($1.75, mini-series)

	GD	VG	FN	VF	VF/NM	NM-
1-8: New Rip Hunter series. 5-Cave Carson, Viking Prince app. 6-Dr. Fate app.						2.25

TIMESLIP COLLECTION
Marvel Comics: Nov, 1998 ($2.99, one-shot)

	GD	VG	FN	VF	VF/NM	NM-
1-Pin-ups reprinted from Marvel Vision magazine						3.00

TIMESLIP SPECIAL (The Coming of the Avengers)
Marvel Comics: Oct, 1998 ($5.99, one-shot)

	GD	VG	FN	VF	VF/NM	NM-
1-Alternate world Avengers vs. Odin						6.00

TIMESPIRITS
Marvel Comics (Epic Comics): Oct, 1984 - No. 8, Mar, 1986 ($1.50, Baxter paper, direct sales)

	GD	VG	FN	VF	VF/NM	NM-
1-8: 4-Williamson-a						2.25

TIME TUNNEL, THE (TV)
Gold Key: Feb, 1967 - No. 2, July, 1967 (12¢)

	GD	VG	FN	VF	VF/NM	NM-
1-Photo back-c on both issues	7	14	21	51	71	90
2	6	12	18	40	55	70

TIME TWISTERS
Quality Comics: Sept, 1987 - No. 21, 1989 ($1.25/$1.50)

	GD	VG	FN	VF	VF/NM	NM-
1-21: Alan Moore scripts in 1-4, 6-9, 14 (2 pg.). 14-Bolland-a (2 pg.). 15,16-Guice-c						2.25

TIME 2: THE EPIPHANY (See First Comics Graphic Novel #9)

TIMEWALKER (Also see Archer & Armstrong)
Valiant: Jan, 1994 - No. 15, Oct, 1995 ($2.50)

	GD	VG	FN	VF	VF/NM	NM-
1-15,0(3/96): 2-"JAN" on-c, February, 1995 in indicia.						2.50
Yearbook 1 (5/95, $2.95)						3.00

TIME WARP (See The Unexpected #210)
DC Comics, Inc.: Oct-Nov, 1979 - No. 5, June-July, 1980 ($1.00, 68 pgs.)

	GD	VG	FN	VF	VF/NM	NM-
1	2	4	6	8	10	12
2-5	1	2	3	5	7	9

NOTE: ***Aparo** a-1. **Buckler** a-1p. **Chaykin** a-2. **Ditko** a-1-4. **Kaluta** c-1-5. **G. Kane** a-2. **Nasser** a-4. **Newton** a-1-5p. **Orlando** a-2. **Sutton** a-1-3.*

TIME WARRIORS: THE BEGINNING
Fantasy General Comics: 1986 (Aug) - No. 2, 1986? ($1.50)

	GD	VG	FN	VF	VF/NM	NM-
1,2-Alpha Track/Skellon Empire						2.25

TIM HOLT (Movie star) (Becomes Red Mask #42 on; also see Crack Western #72, & Great Western)
Magazine Enterprises: 1948 - No. 41, April-May, 1954 (All 36 pgs.)

	GD	VG	FN	VF	VF/NM	NM-
1-(A-1 #14)-Line drawn-c w/Tim Holt photo on-c; Tim Holt, His horse Lightning & sidekick Chito begin	66	132	198	413	619	825
2-(A-1 #17)(9-10/48)-Photo-c begin, end #18	37	74	111	212	301	390
3-(A-1 #19)-Photo back-c	29	58	87	164	232	300
4(1-2/49),5: 5-Photo front/back-c	21	42	63	118	164	210
6-(5/49)-1st app. The Calico Kid (alias Rex Fury), his horse Ebony & Sidekick Sing-Song (begin series); photo back-c	35	70	105	201	288	370
7-10: 7-Calico Kid by Ayers. 8-Calico Kid by Guardineer (r-in/Great Western #10). 9-Map of Tim's Home Range	18	36	54	104	142	180
11-The Calico Kid becomes The Ghost Rider (origin & 1st app.) by Dick Ayers (r-in/Great Western I.W. #8); his horse Spectre & sidekick Sing-Song begin series	44	88	132	264	395	525
12-16,18-Last photo-c	14	28	42	81	111	140
17-Frazetta Ghost Rider-c	40	80	120	240	345	450
19,22,24: 19-Last Tim Holt-c; Bolle line-drawn-c begin; Tim Holt photo on covers #19-28,30-41. 22-interior photo-c	12	24	36	69	96	120
20-Tim Holt becomes Redmask (origin); begin series; Redmask-c #20-on	18	36	54	101	138	175
21-Frazetta Ghost Rider/Redmask-c	39	78	117	230	325	420

Tim Tyler Cowboy #15 © KFS

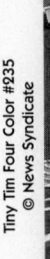

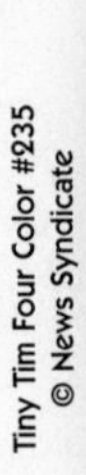
Tiny Tim Four Color #235 © News Syndicate

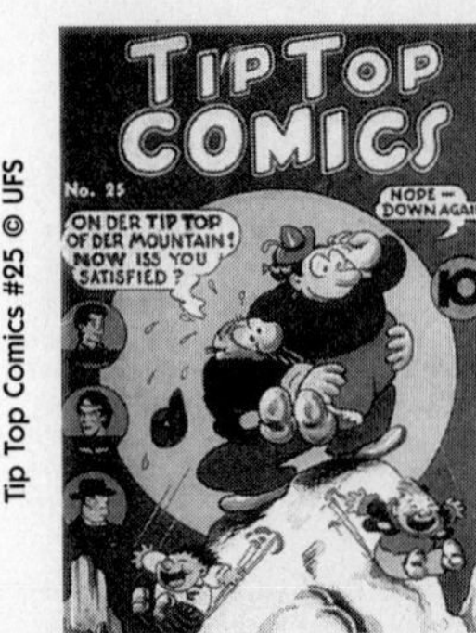

Tip Top Comics #25 © UFS

	GD 2.0	VG 4.0	FN 6.0	VF 8.0	VF/NM 9.0	NM- 9.2
23-Frazetta Redmask-c	31	62	93	175	248	320
25-1st app. Black Phantom	21	42	63	118	164	210
26-30: 28-Wild Bill Hickok, Bat Masterson team up with Redmask. 29-B&W photo-c	11	22	33	63	84	105
31-33-Ghost Rider ends	10	20	30	58	77	95
34-Tales of the Ghost Rider begins (horror)-Classic "The Flower Women" & "Hard Boiled Harry!"	14	28	42	79	107	135
35-Last Tales of the Ghost Rider	11	22	33	63	84	105
36-The Ghost Rider returns, ends #41; liquid hallucinogenic drug story	12	24	36	71	96	120
37-Ghost Rider classic "To Touch Is to Die!", about Inca treasure	12	24	36	71	96	120
38-The Black Phantom begins (not in #39); classic Ghost Rider "The Phantom Guns of Feather Gap!"	12	24	36	71	96	120
39-41: All 3-D effect c/stories	15	30	45	86	118	150

NOTE: ***Dick Ayers** a-7, 9-41. **Bolle** a-1-41; c-19, 20, 22, 24-28, 30-41.*

TIM McCOY (Formerly Zoo Funnies; Pictorial Love Stories #22 on)
Charlton Comics: No. 16, Oct, 1948 - No. 21, Aug, 1949 (Western Movie Stories)

	GD	VG	FN	VF	VF/NM	NM-
16-John Wayne, Montgomery Clift app. in "Red River"; photo back-c	44	88	132	264	395	525
17-21: 17-Allan "Rocky" Lane guest stars. 18-Rod Cameron guest stars. 19-Whip Wilson, Andy Clyde guest star; Jesse James story. 20-Jimmy Wakely guest stars. 21-Johnny Mack Brown guest stars	40	80	120	240	340	440

TIMMY
Dell Publishing Co.: No. 715, Aug, 1956 - No. 1022, Aug-Oct, 1959

	GD	VG	FN	VF	VF/NM	NM-
Four Color 715 (#1)	5	10	15	33	44	55
Four Color 823 (8/57), 923 (8/58), 1022	4	8	12	24	32	40

TIMMY THE TIMID GHOST (Formerly Win-A-Prize?; see Blue Bird)
Charlton Comics: No. 3, 2/56 - No. 44, 10/64; No. 45, 9/66; 10/67 - No. 23, 7/71; V4#24, 9/85 - No. 26, 1/86

	GD	VG	FN	VF	VF/NM	NM-
3(1956) (1st Series)	11	22	33	66	88	110
4,5	7	14	21	37	46	55
6-10	3	7	10	21	28	35
11,12(4/58,10/58)-(100 pgs.)	7	14	21	50	68	85
13-20	3	6	9	18	24	30
21-45(1966)	2	4	6	12	16	20
1(10/67, 2nd series)	3	6	9	16	20	24
2-10	2	4	6	10	12	15
11-23: 23 (7/71)	1	3	4	8	10	12
24-26 (1985-86): Fago-r (low print run)						6.00

TIM TYLER (See Harvey Comics Hits #54)

TIM TYLER (Also see Comics Reading Libraries in the Promotional Comics section)
Better Publications: 1942

	GD	VG	FN	VF	VF/NM	NM-
1	15	30	45	84	115	145

TIM TYLER COWBOY
Standard Comics (King Features Synd.): No. 11, Nov, 1948 - No. 18, 1950

	GD	VG	FN	VF	VF/NM	NM-
11-By Lyman Young	9	18	27	52	66	80
12-18: 13-15-Full length western adventures	7	14	21	35	43	50

TINCAN MAN
Image Comics: Jan, 2000 - No. 3, Mar, 2000 ($2.95, limited series)

	GD	VG	FN	VF	VF/NM	NM-
1-3-Thornton-s/Dietrich Smith & Pierre Andre-Dery-a						3.00

TINKER BELL (Disney, TV)(See Walt Disney Showcase #37)
Dell Publishing Co.: No. 896, Mar, 1958 - No. 982, Apr-June, 1959

	GD	VG	FN	VF	VF/NM	NM-
Four Color 896 (#1)-The Adventures of...	10	20	30	67	96	125
Four Color 982-The New Advs. of...	9	18	27	63	89	115

TINY FOLKS FUNNIES
Dell Publishing Co.: No. 60, 1944

	GD	VG	FN	VF	VF/NM	NM-
Four Color 60	17	34	51	118	174	230

TINY TESSIE (Tessie #1-23; Real Experiences #25)
Marvel Comics (20CC): No. 24, Oct, 1949 (52 pgs.)

	GD	VG	FN	VF	VF/NM	NM-
24	10	20	30	60	80	100

TINY TIM (Also see Super Comics)
Dell Publishing Co.: No. 4, 1941 - No. 235, July, 1949

	GD	VG	FN	VF	VF/NM	NM-
Large Feature Comic 4('41)	31	62	93	232	346	460
Four Color 20(1941)	29	58	87	210	310	410
Four Color 42(1943)	18	36	54	131	191	250
Four Color 235	6	12	18	38	52	65

TINY TOT COMICS
E. C. Comics: Mar, 1946 - No. 10, Nov-Dec, 1947 (For younger readers)

	GD 2.0	VG 4.0	FN 6.0	VF 8.0	VF/NM 9.0	NM- 9.2
1(nn)-52 pg. issues begin, end #4	39	78	117	230	325	420
2 (5/46)	22	44	66	127	176	225
3-10: 10-Christmas-c	20	40	60	112	156	200

TINY TOT FUNNIES (Formerly Family Funnies; becomes Junior Funnies)
Harvey Publ. (King Features Synd.): No. 9, June, 1951

	GD	VG	FN	VF	VF/NM	NM-
9-Flash Gordon, Mandrake, Dagwood, Daisy, etc.	8	16	24	43	54	65

TINY TOTS COMICS
Dell Publishing Co.: 1943 (Not reprints)

	GD	VG	FN	VF	VF/NM	NM-
1-Kelly-a(2); fairy tales	40	80	120	240	340	440

TIPPY & CAP STUBBS (See Popular Comics)
Dell Publishing Co.: No. 210, Jan, 1949 - No. 242, Aug, 1949

	GD	VG	FN	VF	VF/NM	NM-
Four Color 210 (#1)	5	10	15	36	48	60
Four Color 242	4	8	12	28	38	48

TIPPY'S FRIENDS GO-GO & ANIMAL
Tower Comics: July, 1966 - No. 15, Oct, 1969 (25¢)

	GD	VG	FN	VF	VF/NM	NM-
1	8	16	24	55	78	100
2-5,7,9-15: 12-15 titled "Tippy's Friend Go-Go"	4	8	12	29	40	50
6-The Monkees photo-c	7	14	21	51	71	90
8-Beatles app. on front/back-c	10	20	30	72	104	135

TIPPY TEEN (See Vicki)
Tower Comics: Nov, 1965 - No. 25, Oct, 1969 (25¢)

	GD	VG	FN	VF	VF/NM	NM-
1	9	18	27	60	85	110
2-4,6-10	5	10	15	33	44	55
5-1 pg. Beatles pin-up	5	10	15	36	48	60
11-20: 16-Twiggy photo-c	4	8	12	29	40	50
21-25	4	8	12	25	33	42
Special Collectors' Editions nn-(1969, 25¢)	5	10	15	33	44	55

TIPPY TERRY
Super/I. W. Enterprises: 1963

	GD	VG	FN	VF	VF/NM	NM-
Super Reprint #14('63)-r/Little Groucho #1	2	4	6	8	10	12
I.W. Reprint #1 (nd)-r/Little Groucho #1	2	4	6	8	10	12

TIP TOP COMICS
United Features #1-187/St. John #188-210/Dell Publishing Co. #211 on:
4/36 - No. 210, 1957; No. 211, 11-1/57-58 - No. 225, 5-7/61

	GD	VG	FN	VF	VF/NM	NM-
1-Tarzan by Hal Foster, Li'l Abner, Broncho Bill, Fritzi Ritz, Ella Cinders, Capt. & The Kids begin; strip-r (1st comic book app. of each)	950	1900	2850	5320	7410	9500
2	225	450	675	1260	1755	2250
3-Tarzan-c	200	400	600	1120	1560	2000
4	115	230	345	644	897	1150
5-8,10: 7-Photo & biography of Edgar Rice Burroughs. 8-Christmas-c	83	166	249	465	645	825
9-Tarzan-c	105	210	315	588	819	1050
11,13,16,18-Tarzan-c: 11-Has Tarzan pin-up	80	160	240	448	624	800
12,14,15,17,19,20: 20-Christmas-c	65	130	195	364	507	650
21,24,27,30-(10/38)-Tarzan-c	65	130	195	364	507	650
22,23,25,26,28,29	47	94	141	263	364	465
31,35,38,40	40	80	120	240	340	440
32,36-Tarzan-c: 32-1st published Jack Davis-a (cartoon). 36-Kurtzman panel (1st published comic work)	54	108	162	324	487	650
33,34,37,39-Tarzan-c	50	100	150	300	450	600
41-Reprints 1st Tarzan Sunday; Tarzan-c	54	108	162	324	487	650
42,44,46,48,49	35	70	105	201	288	370
43,45,47,50,52-Tarzan-c. 43-Mort Walker panel	40	80	120	240	345	450
51,53	34	68	102	193	274	355
54-Origin Mirror Man & Triple Terror, also featured on cover	40	80	120	240	340	440
55,56,58,60: Last Tarzan by Foster	27	54	81	153	214	275
57,59,61,62-Tarzan by Hogarth	34	68	102	193	274	355
63-80: 65,67-70,72-74,77,78-No Tarzan	17	34	51	95	130	165
81-90	15	30	45	84	115	145
91-99	13	26	39	74	100	125
100	14	28	42	79	107	135
101-140: 110-Gordo story. 111-Li'l Abner app. 118, 132-No Tarzan. 137-Sadie Hawkins Day story	9	18	27	52	66	80
141-170: 145,151-Gordo stories. 157-Last Li'l Abner; lingerie panels	8	16	24	40	50	60

171-188-Tarzan reprints by B. Lubbers in all. 177-Peanuts by Schulz begins?;

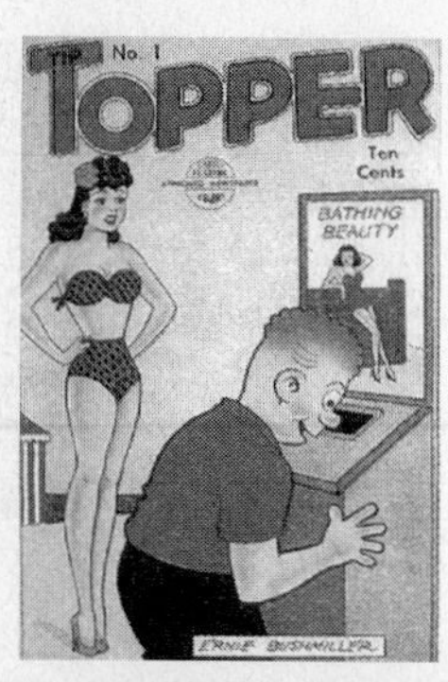

Tip Topper Comics #1 © UFS

Titans/Young Justice: Graduation Day #3 © DC

T-Man #21 © QUA

	GD 2.0	VG 4.0	FN 6.0	VF 8.0	VF/NM 9.0	NM- 9.2

no Peanuts in #178,179,181-183 8 16 24 43 54 65
189-225-Peanuts (8 pgs.) in most 7 14 21 35 43 50
Bound Volumes (Very Rare) sold at 1939 World's Fair; bound by publisher in pictorial comic boards (also see Comics on Parade)
Bound issues 1-12 264 528 792 1650 2475 3300
Bound issues 13-24 134 268 402 838 1257 1675
Bound issues 25-36 118 236 354 738 1107 1475
NOTE: *Tarzan by* **Foster***-#1-40, 44-50; by* **Rex Maxon***-#41-43; by* **Burne Hogarth***-#57, 59, 62.*

TIP TOPPER COMICS
United Features Syndicate: Oct-Nov, 1949 - No. 28, 1954
1-Li'l Abner, Abbie & Slats 10 20 30 60 80 100
2 8 16 24 40 50 60
3-5: 5-Fearless Fosdick app. 7 14 21 35 43 50
6-10: 6-Fearless Fosdick app. 6 12 18 31 38 45
11-16 5 10 15 24 30 35
17(6-7/52) (2nd app. of Peanuts by Schulz in comics?) (see United Comics #22 for 5-6/52 app.) 8 16 24 40 50 60
18-25: 18-24,26-Early Peanuts (2 pgs.). 25-Early Peanuts (3 pgs.) 26-Twin Earths 7 14 21 35 43 50
27,28-Twin Earths 7 14 21 35 43 50
NOTE: *Many lingerie panels in Fritzi Ritz stories.*

TITAN A.E.
Dark Horse Comics: May, 2000 - No. 3, July, 2000 ($2.95, limited series)
1-3-Movie prequel; Al Rio-a 3.00

TITANS (Also see Teen Titans, New Teen Titans and New Titans)
DC Comics: Mar, 1999 - No. 50, Apr, 2003 ($2.50/$2.75)
1-Titans re-form; Grayson-s; 2 covers 3.00
2-11,13-24,26-50: 2-Superman-c/app. 9,10,21,22-Deathstroke app. 24-Titans from "Kingdom Come" app. 32-36-Asamiya-c. 44-Begin $2.75-c 2.75
12-($3.50, 48 pages) 3.50
25-($3.95) Titans from "Kingdom Come" app.; Wolfman & Faerber-s; art by Pérez, Cardy, Grumment, Jimenez, Dodson, Pelletier 4.00
Annual 1 ('00, $3.50) Planet DC; intro Bushido 3.50
...Secret Files 1,2 (3/99, 10/00; $4.95) Profile pages & short stories 5.00

TITANS/ LEGION OF SUPER-HEROES: UNIVERSE ABLAZE
DC Comics: 2000 - No. 4, 2000 ($4.95, prestige format, limited series)
1-4-Jurgens-s/a; P. Jimenez-a; teams battle Universo 5.00

TITAN SPECIAL
Dark Horse Comics: June, 1994 ($3.95, one-shot)
1-($3.95, 52 pgs.) 4.00

TITANS: SCISSORS, PAPER, STONE
DC Comics: 1997 ($4.95, one-shot)
1-Manga style Elseworlds; Adam Warren-s/a(p) 5.00

TITANS SELL-OUT SPECIAL
DC Comics: Nov, 1992 ($3.50, 52 pgs., one-shot)
1-Fold-out Nightwing poster; 1st Teeny Titans 3.50

TITANS/ YOUNG JUSTICE: GRADUATION DAY
DC Comics: Early July, 2003 - No. 3, Aug, 2003 ($2.50, limited series)
1,2-Winick-s/Garza-a; leads into Teen Titans and The Outsiders series. 2-Lilith dies 2.50
3-Death of Donna Troy (Wonder Girl) 2.50
TPB (2003, $6.95) r/#1-3; plus previews of Teen Titans and The Outsiders series 7.00

T-MAN (Also see Police Comics #103)
Quality Comics Group: Sept, 1951 - No. 38, Dec, 1956
1-Pete Trask, T-Man begins; Jack Cole-a 40 80 120 240 340 440
2-Crandall-c 22 44 66 127 176 225
3,7,8: All Crandall-c 20 40 60 112 156 200
4,5-Crandall-c/a each 21 42 63 121 168 215
6-"The Man Who Could Be Hitler" c/story; Crandall-c. 22 44 66 127 176 225
9,10-Crandall-c 17 34 51 98 134 170
11-Used in **POP**, pg. 95 & color illo. 13 26 39 76 103 130
12,13,15-19,21,22-26: 21- "The Return of Mussolini" c/story. 23-H-Bomb panel. 24-Last pre-code issue (4/55). 25-Not Crandall-a 11 22 33 63 84 105
14-Hitler-c 14 28 42 81 111 140
20-H-Bomb explosion-c/story 14 28 42 81 111 140
27-38 11 22 33 63 84 105
NOTE: *Anti-communist stories common.* **Crandall** *c-2-10p.* **Cuidera** *c(i)-1-38. Bondage c-15.*

TMNT MUTANT UNIVERSE SOURCEBOOK
Archie Comics: 1992 - No. 3, 1992? ($1.95, 52 pgs.)(Lists characters from A-Z)
1-3: 3-New characters; fold-out poster 2.25

TNT COMICS
Charles Publishing Co.: Feb, 1946 (36 pgs.)
1-Yellowjacket app. 31 62 93 175 248 320

TOBY TYLER (Disney, see Movie Comics)
Dell Publishing Co.: No. 1092, Apr-June, 1960
Four Color 1092-Movie, photo-c 7 14 21 51 71 90

TODAY'S BRIDES
Ajax/Farrell Publishing Co.: Nov, 1955; No. 2, Feb, 1956; No. 3, Sept, 1956; No. 4, Nov, 1956
1 9 18 27 49 62 75
2-4 6 12 18 31 38 45

TODAY'S ROMANCE
Standard Comics: No. 5, March, 1952 - No. 8, Sept, 1952 (All photo-c?)
5-Photo-c 9 18 27 54 70 85
6-Photo-c; Toth-a 10 20 30 56 73 90
7,8 8 16 24 40 50 60

TOKA (Jungle King)
Dell Publishing Co.: Aug-Oct, 1964 - No. 10, Jan, 1967 (Painted-c #1,2)
1 4 8 12 29 40 50
2 3 6 9 18 23 28
3-10 2 4 6 14 18 22

TOKYO STORM WARNING
DC Comics (Cliffhanger): Aug, 2003 - Present ($2.95)
1-3-Warren Ellis-s/James Raiz-a 3.00

TOMAHAWK (Son of... on-c of #131-140; see Star Spangled Comics #69 & World's Finest Comics #65)
National Periodical Publications: Sept-Oct, 1950 - No. 140, May-June, 1972
1-Tomahawk & boy sidekick Dan Hunter begin by Fred Ray 160 320 480 1000 1500 2000
2-Frazetta/Williamson-a (4 pgs.) 64 128 192 400 600 800
3-5 40 80 120 240 340 440
6-10: 7-Last 52 pg. issue 33 66 99 190 270 350
11-20 24 48 72 135 190 245
21-27,30: 30-Last precode (2/55) 20 40 60 112 156 200
28-1st app. Lord Shilling (arch-foe) 21 42 63 118 164 210
29-Frazetta-r/Jimmy Wakely #3 (3 pgs.) 26 52 78 147 206 265
31-40 12 24 36 82 121 160
41-50 10 20 30 67 96 125
51-56,58-60 7 14 21 51 71 90
57-Frazetta-r/Jimmy Wakely #6 (3 pgs.) 10 20 30 70 100 130
61-77: 77-Last 10¢ issue 6 12 18 43 59 75
78-85: 81-1st app. Miss Liberty. 83-Origin Tomahawk's Rangers 5 10 15 33 44 55
86-99: 96-Origin/1st app. The Hood, alias Lady Shilling 4 8 12 22 30 38
100 4 8 12 24 32 40
101-110: 107-Origin/1st app. Thunder-Man 3 6 9 18 24 30
111-115,120,122: 122-Last 12¢ issue 3 6 9 18 23 28
116-119,121,123-130-Neal Adams-c 3 6 9 19 25 32
131-Frazetta-r/Jimmy Wakely #7 (3 pgs.); origin Firehair retold 3 6 9 18 24 30
132-135: 135-Last 15¢ issue 2 4 6 12 16 20
136-138,140 (52 pg. Giants) 3 6 9 16 20 25
139-Frazetta-r/Star Spangled #113 3 6 9 18 24 30
NOTE: **Fred Ray** *c-1, 2, 8, 11, 30, 34, 35, 40-43, 45, 46, 82. Firehair by* **Kubert***-131-134, 136.* **Maurer** *a-138.* **Severin** *a-135.* **Starr** *a-5.* **Thorne** *a-137, 140.*

TOM AND JERRY (See Comic Album #4, 8, 12, Dell Giant #21, Dell Giants, Golden Comics Digest #1, 5, 8, 13, 15, 18, 22, 25, 28, 35, Kite fun Book & March of Comics #21, 46, 61, 70, 88, 103, 119, 128, 145, 154, 173, 190, 207, 224, 281, 295, 305, 321,333, 345, 361, 365, 388, 400, 444, 451, 463, 480)

TOM AND JERRY (...Comics, early issues) (M.G.M.)
(Formerly Our Gang No. 1-59) (See Dell Giants for annuals)
Dell Publishing Co./Gold Key No. 213-327/Whitman No. 328 on: No. 193, 6/48; No. 60, 7/49 - No. 212, 7-9/62; No. 213, 11/62 - No. 291, 2/75; No. 292, 3/77 - No. 342, 5/82 - No. 344, 6/84
Four Color 193 (#1)-Titled "M.G.M. Presents..." 22 44 66 156 228 300
60-Barney Bear, Benny Burro cont. from Our Gang; Droopy begins 11 22 33 77 114 150
61 9 18 27 65 93 120
62-70: 66-X-Mas-c 8 16 24 53 74 95

Tom and Jerry #94 © DELL

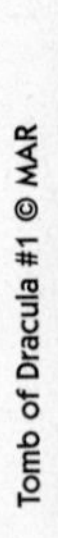
Tomb of Dracula #1 © MAR

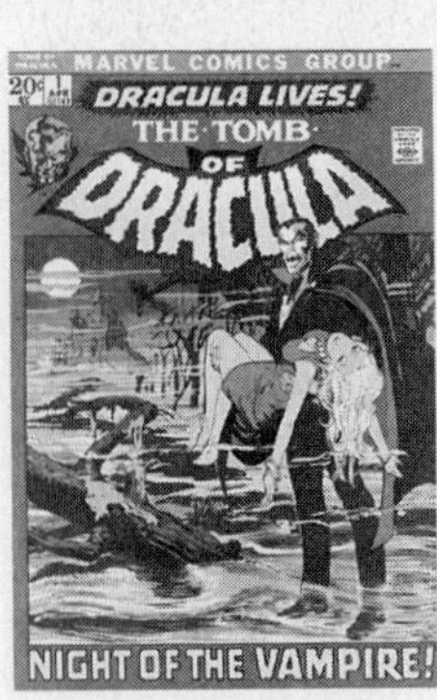

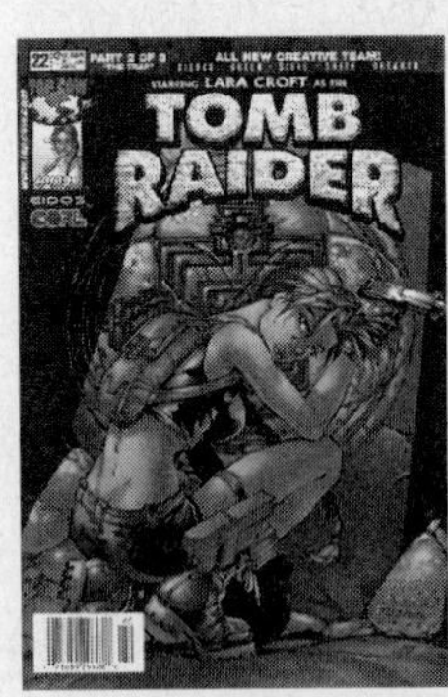

Tomb Raider: The Series #22 © Eidos

GD VG FN VF VF/NM NM-
2.0 4.0 6.0 8.0 9.0 9.2

71-80: 77,90-X-Mas-c. 79-Spike & Tyke begin 7 14 21 46 63 80
81-99 6 12 18 40 55 70
100 6 12 18 43 59 75
101-120 5 10 15 33 44 55
121-140: 126-X-Mas-c 4 8 12 29 40 50
141-160 4 8 12 27 36 45
161-200 4 8 12 24 32 40
201-212(7-9/62)(Last Dell issue) 3 7 10 21 28 35
213,214-(84 pgs.)-Titled "...Funhouse" 7 14 21 50 68 85
215-240: 215-Titled "...Funhouse" 3 6 9 18 23 28
241-270 2 4 6 11 14 18
271-300: 286- "Tom & Jerry" 2 4 6 8 10 12
301-327 (Gold Key) 1 2 3 5 7 9
328,329 (Whitman) 2 4 6 8 10 12
330(8/80),331(10/80), 332-(3-pack only) 3 6 9 16 20 24
333-341: 339(2/82), 340(2-3/82), 341(4/82) 2 4 6 8 10 12
342-344 (All #90058, no date, date code, 3-pack): 342(6/83), 343(8/83), 344(6/84)
2 4 6 11 14 18
Mouse From T.R.A.P. 1(7/66)-Giant, G. K. 5 10 15 36 48 60
Summer Fun 1(7/67, 68 pgs.)(Gold Key)-Reprints Barks' Droopy from Summer Fun #1
5 10 15 36 48 60
NOTE: *#60-87, 98-121, 268, 277, 289, 302 are 52 pgs.. Reprints-#225, 241, 245, 247, 252, 254, 266, 268, 270, 292-327, 329-342, 344.*

TOM & JERRY
Harvey Comics: Sept, 1991 - No. 18, Aug, 1994 ($1.25)
1-18: 1-Tom & Jerry, Barney Bear-r by Carl Barks 3.00
50th Anniversary Special 1 (10/91, $2.50, 68 pgs.)-Benny the Lonesome Burro-r by Barks (story/a)/Our Gang #9 4.00

TOMB OF DARKNESS (Formerly Beware)
Marvel Comics Group: No. 9, July, 1974 - No. 23, Nov, 1976
9 3 6 9 18 23 28
10-23: 11,16,18-21-Kirby-a. 15,19-Ditko-r. 17-Woodbridge-r/Astonishing #62; Powell-r. 20-Everett Venus-r/Venus #19. 22-r/Tales To Astonish #27; 1st Hank Pym. 23-Everett-r
2 4 6 10 12 15
20,21-(30¢-c variants, limited distribution)(5,7/76) 3 6 9 16 20 24

TOMB OF DRACULA (See Giant-Size Dracula, Dracula Lives, Nightstalkers, Power Record Comics & Requiem for Dracula)
Marvel Comics Group: Apr, 1972 - No. 70, Aug, 1979
1-1st app. Dracula & Frank Drake; Colan-p in all; Neal Adams-c
15 30 45 104 152 200
2 7 14 21 46 63 80
3-6: 3-Intro. Dr. Rachel Van Helsing & Inspector Chelm. 6-Neal Adams-c
5 10 15 36 48 60
7-9 4 8 12 27 36 45
10-1st app. Blade the Vampire Slayer (who app. in 1998 and 2002 movies)
11 22 33 77 114 150
11,12,14-16,20: 3 6 9 19 25 32
12-2nd app. Blade; Brunner-c(p) 4 8 12 29 40 50
13-Origin Blade 6 12 18 40 55 70
17,19: 17-Blade bitten by Dracula. 19-Blade discovers he is immune to vampire's bite. 1st mention of Blade having vampire blood in him 4 8 12 24 32 40
18-Two-part x-over cont'd in Werewolf by Night #15 3 7 10 21 28 35
21,24-Blade app. 3 6 9 16 20 24
22,23,26,27,29 2 4 6 12 16 20
25-1st app. & origin Hannibal King 3 6 9 16 20 24
25-2nd printing (1994) 2 4 6 8 10 12
28-Blade app. on-c & inside as an illusion 3 6 9 16 20 24
30,41,42-45-Blade app. 45-Intro. Deacon Frost, the vampire who bit Blade's mother
2 4 6 12 16 20
31-40 2 4 6 11 14 18
43-45-(30¢-c variants, limited distribution) 3 6 9 18 24 30
46,47-(Regular 25¢ editions)(4-8/76) 2 4 6 8 10 12
46,47-(30¢-c variants, limited distribution) 2 4 6 11 14 18
48,49,51-57,59,60: 57,59,60-(30¢-c) 2 4 6 8 10 12
50-Silver Surfer app. 2 4 6 12 16 20
57,59,60-(35¢-c variants)(6-9/77) 2 4 6 11 14 18
58-All Blade issue (Regular 30¢ edition) 3 6 9 16 20 24
58-(35¢-c variant)(7/77) 3 7 10 21 28 36
61-69 2 4 6 8 10 12
70-Double size 2 4 6 14 18 22
NOTE: ***N. Adams** c-1, 6. **Colan** a-1-70p; c(p)-8, 38-42, 44-56, 58-70. **Wrightson** c-43.*

TOMB OF DRACULA, THE (Magazine)
Marvel Comics Group: Oct, 1979 - No. 6, Aug, 1980 (B&W)
1,3: 1-Colan-a; features on movies "Dracula" and "Love at First Bite" w/photos. 3-Good girl cover-a; Miller-a (2 pg. sketch) 2 4 6 8 10 12
2,6: 2-Ditko-a (36 pgs.); Nosferatu movie feature. 6-Lilith story w/Sienkiewicz-a
1 2 3 5 7 9
4,5: Stephen King interview 2 4 6 10 13 16
NOTE: ***Buscema** a-4p, 5p. **Chaykin** c-5, 6. **Colan** a(p)-1, 3-6. **Miller** a-3. **Romita** a-2p.*

TOMB OF DRACULA
Marvel Comics (Epic Comics): 1991 - No. 4, 1992 ($4.95, 52 pgs., squarebound, mini-series)
Book 1-4: Colan/Williamson-a; Colan painted-c 5.00

TOMB OF LEGEIA (See Movie Classics)

TOMB OF TERROR (Thrills of Tomorrow #17 on)
Harvey Publications: June, 1952 - No. 16, July, 1954
1 43 86 129 258 384 510
2 26 52 78 150 210 270
3-Bondage-c; atomic disaster story 27 54 81 155 218 280
4-12: 4-Heart ripped out. 8-12-Nostrand-a 25 50 75 144 198 255
13,14-Special S/F issues. 14-Check-a 35 70 105 201 283 365
15-S/F issue; c-shows face exploding 55 110 165 330 495 660
16-Special S/F issue; Nostrand-a 32 64 96 182 259 335
NOTE: ***Edd Cartier** a-13? **Elias** c-2, 5-16. **Kremer** a-1, 7; c-1. **Nostrand** a-8-12, 15r 16. **Palais** a-2, 3, 5-7. **Powell** a-1, 3, 5, 9-16. **Sparling** a-12, 13, 15.*

TOMB RAIDER (one-shots)
Image Comics (Top Cow Prod.))
Epiphany 1 ($4.99, 8/03)-Jurgens-s/Banks-a/Haley-c; preview of Witchblade Animated 5.00
Takeover 1 ($2.99, 1/04)-Benefiel-a/Daniel-c 3.00

TOMB RAIDER: JOURNEYS
Image Comics (Top Cow Prod.): Jan, 2002 - No. 12, May, 2003 ($2.50/$2.99)
1-12: 1-Avery-s/Drew Johnson-a. 1-Two covers by Johnson & Hughes 3.00

TOMB RAIDER: THE GREATEST TREASURE OF ALL
Image Comics (Top Cow Prod.): 2002
Prelude (2002, 16 pgs., no cover price) Jusko-c/a 5.00

TOMB RAIDER: THE SERIES (Also see Witchblade/Tomb Raider)(Also see Promotional Comics section for Free Comic Book Day edition)
Image Comics (Top Cow Prod.): Dec, 1999 - Present ($2.50/$2.99)
1-Jurgens-s/Park-a; 3 covers by Park, Finch, Turner 4.00
2-24,26-29,31-36: 21-Black-c w/foil. 31-Mhan-a 3.00
25-Michael Turner-c/a; Witchblade app.; Endgame x-over with Witchblade #60 & Evo #1 3.00
30-($4.99) Tony Daniel-a 5.00
#0 (6/01, $2.50) Avery-s/Ching-a/c 2.50
#1/2 (10/01, $2.95) Early days of Lara Croft; Jurgens-s/Lopez-a 3.00
...: Chasing Shangri-La (2002, $12.95, TPB) r/#11-15 13.00
...Gallery (12/00, $2.95) Pin-ups & previous covers by various 3.00
...Magazine (6/01, $4.95) Hughes-c; r/#1,2; Jurgens interview 5.00
...: Mystic Artifacts (2001, $14.95, TPB) r/#5-10 15.00
...: Saga of the Medusa Mask (9/00, $9.95, TPB) r/#1-4; new Park-c 10.00

TOMB RAIDER/WITCHBLADE SPECIAL (Also see Witchblade/Tomb Raider)
Top Cow Prod.: Dec, 1997 (mail-in offer, one-shot)
1-Turner-s/a(p); green background cover 1 3 4 6 8 10
1-Variant-c with orange sun background 1 3 4 6 8 10
1-Variant-c with black sides 1 3 4 6 8 10
1-Revisited (12/98, $2.95) reprints #1, Turner-c 3.00
...: Trouble Seekers TPB (2002, $7.95) rep. T.R./W & W/T.R. & W/T.R. 1/2; new Turner-c 8.00

TOMBSTONE TERRITORY (See Four Color #1123)

TOM CAT (Formerly Bo; Atom The Cat #9 on)
Charlton Comics: No. 4, Apr, 1956 - No. 8, July, 1957
4-Al Fago-c/a 8 16 24 43 54 65
5-8 6 12 18 29 36 42

TOM CORBETT, SPACE CADET (TV)
Dell Publishing Co.: No. 378, Jan-Feb, 1952 - No. 11, Sept-Nov, 1954 (All painted covers)
Four Color 378 (#1)-McWilliams-a 19 38 57 136 198 260
Four Color 400,421-McWilliams-a 11 22 33 75 110 145
4(11-1/53) - 11 8 16 24 58 82 105

TOM CORBETT SPACE CADET (See March of Comics #102)

TOM CORBETT SPACE CADET (TV)
Prize Publications: V2#1, May-June, 1955 - V2#3, Sept-Oct, 1955
V2#1-Robot-c 33 66 99 190 270 350

Tom Mix Western #10 © FAW

Tomorrow Stories #1 © ABC

Tom Strong #26 © ABC

	GD 2.0	VG 4.0	FN 6.0	VF 8.0	VF/NM 9.0	NM- 9.2
2,3-Meskin-c	26	52	78	147	206	265

TOM, DICK & HARRIET (See Gold Key Spotlight)

TOM JUDGE: END OF DAYS
Image Comics: Jan, 2003 ($3.99)

	GD	VG	FN	VF	VF/NM	NM-
1-Jenkins-s/Crain-a; flip book wih Evo Preview Edition; Silvestri-c						4.00

TOM LANDRY AND THE DALLAS COWBOYS
Spire Christian Comics/Fleming H. Revell Co.: 1973 (35/49¢)

	GD	VG	FN	VF	VF/NM	NM-
nn-35¢ edition	2	4	6	12	16	20
nn-49¢ edition	2	4	6	9	11	14

TOM MIX WESTERN (Movie, radio star) (Also see The Comics, Crackajack Funnies, Master Comics, 100 Pages Of Comics, Popular Comics, Real Western Hero, Six Gun Heroes, Western Hero & XMas Comics)
Fawcett Publications: Jan, 1948 - No. 61, May, 1953 (1-17: 52 pgs.)

	GD	VG	FN	VF	VF/NM	NM-
1 (Photo-c, 52 pgs.)-Tom Mix & his horse Tony begin; Tumbleweed Jr. begins, ends #52,54,55	100	200	300	625	938	1250
2 (Photo-c)	44	88	132	264	395	525
3-5 (Painted/photo-c): 5-Billy the Kid & Oscar app.	35	70	105	201	288	370
6-8: 6,7 (Painted/photo-c). 8-Kinstler tempera-c	30	60	90	170	240	310
9,10 (Painted/photo-c)-Used in **SOTI**, pgs. 323-325	29	58	87	164	232	300
11-Kinstler oil-c	25	50	75	144	198	255
12 (Painted/photo-c)	22	44	66	127	176	225
13-17 (Painted-c, 52 pgs.)	22	44	66	127	176	225
18,22 (Painted-c, 36 pgs.)	19	38	57	107	149	190
19 (Photo-c, 52 pgs.)	20	40	60	112	156	200
20,21,23 (Painted-c, 52 pgs.)	19	38	57	107	149	190
24,25,27-29 (52 pgs.): 24-Photo-c begin, end #61. 29-Slim Pickens app.	16	32	48	92	126	160
26,30 (36 pgs.)	15	30	45	86	118	150
31-33,35-37,39,40,42 (52 pgs.): 39-Red Eagle app.	15	30	45	84	115	145
34,38 (36 pgs. begin)	13	26	39	76	103	130
41,43-60: 57-(9/52)-Dope smuggling story	10	20	30	58	77	95
61-Last issue	12	24	36	69	92	115

NOTE: *Photo-c from 1930s Tom Mix movies (he died in 1940). Many issues contain ads for Tom Mix, Rocky Lane, Space Patrol and other premiums. Captain Tootsie by* **C.C. Beck** *in #6-11, 20.*

TOM MIX WESTERN
AC Comics: 1988 - No. 2, 1989? ($2.95, B&W w/16 pgs. color, 44 pgs.)

	GD	VG	FN	VF	VF/NM	NM-
1-Tom Mix-r/Master #124,128,131,102 plus Billy the Kid-r by Severin; photo front/back/inside-c						3.50
2-($2.50, B&W)-Gabby Hayes-r; photo covers						3.00
...Holiday Album 1 (1990, $3.50, B&W, one-shot, 44 pgs.)-Contains photos & 1950s Tom Mix-r; photo inside-c						4.00

TOMMY OF THE BIG TOP (Thrilling Circus Adventures)
King Features Synd./Standard Comics: No. 10, Sep, 1948 - No. 12, Mar, 1949

	GD	VG	FN	VF	VF/NM	NM-
10-By John Lehti	8	16	24	46	58	70
11,12	6	12	18	28	34	40

TOMMY TOMORROW (See Action Comics #127, Real Fact #6, Showcase #41,42,44,46,47 & World's Finest #102)

TOMOE (Also see Shi: The Way Of the Warrior #6)
Crusade Comics: July, 1995 - No. 3, June, 1996($2.95)

	GD	VG	FN	VF	VF/NM	NM-
0-3: 2-B&W Dogs o' War preview. 3-B&W Demon Gun preview						3.00
0 (3/96, $2.95)-variant-c.						3.00
0-Commemorative edition (5,000)	2	4	6	8	10	12
1-Commemorative edition (5,000)	2	4	6	10	12	15
1-($2.95)-FAN Appreciation edition						3.00
TPB (1997, $14.95) r/#0-3						15.00

TOMOE: UNFORGETTABLE FIRE
Crusade Comics: June, 1997 ($2.95, one-shot)

	GD	VG	FN	VF	VF/NM	NM-
1-Prequel to Shi: The Series						3.00

TOMOE-WITCHBLADE/FIRE SERMON
Crusade Comics: Sept, 1996 ($3.95, one-shot)

	GD	VG	FN	VF	VF/NM	NM-
1-Tucci-c						5.00
1-($9.95)-Avalon Ed. w/gold foil-c						10.00

TOMOE-WITCHBLADE/MANGA SHI PREVIEW EDITION
Crusade Comics: July, 1996 ($5.00, B&W)

	GD	VG	FN	VF	VF/NM	NM-
nn-San Diego Preview Edition						5.00

TOMORROW KNIGHTS
Marvel Comics (Epic Comics): June, 1990 - No. 6, Mar, 1991 ($1.50)

	GD	VG	FN	VF	VF/NM	NM-
1-6: 1-($1.95, 52 pgs.)						2.25

TOMORROW STORIES
America's Best Comics: Oct, 1999 - Present ($3.50/$2.95)

	GD	VG	FN	VF	VF/NM	NM-
1-Two covers by Ross and Nowlan; Moore-s						3.50
2-12-($2.95)						3.00
Book 1 Hardcover (2002, $24.95) r/#1-6						25.00

TOM SAWYER (See Adventures of... & Famous Stories)

TOM SKINNER-UP FROM HARLEM (See Up From Harlem)

TOM STRONG (Also see Many Worlds of Tesla Strong)
America's Best Comics: June, 1999 - Present ($3.50/$2.95)

	GD	VG	FN	VF	VF/NM	NM-
1-Two covers by Ross and Sprouse; Moore-s/Sprouse-a						4.00
2-24-($2.95): 4-Art Adams-a (8 pgs.) 13-Fawcett homage w/art by Sprouse, Baker, Heath 20-Origin of Tom Stone. 22-Ordway-a						3.00
...: Book One HC ('00, $24.95) r/#1-7, cover gallery and sketchbook						25.00
...: Book One TPB ('01, $14.95) r/#1-7, cover gallery and sketchbook						15.00
...: Book Two HC ('02, $24.95) r/#8-14, sketchbook						25.00
...: Book Two TPB ('03, $14.95) r/#8-14, sketchbook						15.00

TOM STRONG'S TERRIFIC TALES
America's Best Comics: Jan, 2002 - Present ($3.50/$2.95)

	GD	VG	FN	VF	VF/NM	NM-
1-Short stories; Moore-s; art by Adams, Rivoche, Hernandez, Weiss						3.50
2-8-($2.95) 2-Adams, Ordway, Weiss-a; Adams-c. 4-Rivoche-a. 5-Pearson, Aragonés-a						3.00

TOM TERRIFIC! (TV)(See Mighty Mouse Fun Club Magazine #1)
Pines Comics (Paul Terry): Summer, 1957 - No. 6, Fall, 1958
(See Terry Toons Giant Summer Fun Book)

	GD	VG	FN	VF	VF/NM	NM-
1-1st app.?; CBS Television Presents...	24	48	72	135	190	245
2-6-(scarce)	17	34	51	95	130	165

TOM THUMB
Dell Publishing Co.: No. 972, Jan, 1959

	GD	VG	FN	VF	VF/NM	NM-
Four Color 972-Movie, George Pal	10	20	30	70	100	130

TOM-TOM, THE JUNGLE BOY (See A-1 Comics & Tick Tock Tales)
Magazine Enterprises: 1947 - No. 3, 1947; Nov, 1957 - No. 3, Mar, 1958

	GD	VG	FN	VF	VF/NM	NM-
1-Funny animal	11	22	33	63	84	105
2,3(1947): 3-Christmas issue	8	16	24	43	54	65
Tom-Tom & Itchi the Monk 1(11/57) - 3(3/58)	4	8	12	18	22	25
I.W. Reprint No. 1,2,8,10: 1,2,8-r/Koko & Kola #?	2	4	6	8	10	12

TONGUE LASH
Dark Horse Comics: Aug, 1996 - No. 2, Sept, 1996 ($2.95, lim. series, mature)

	GD	VG	FN	VF	VF/NM	NM-
1,2: Taylor-c/a						3.00

TONGUE LASH II
Dark Horse Comics: Feb, 1999 - No. 2, Mar, 1999 ($2.95, lim. series, mature)

	GD	VG	FN	VF	VF/NM	NM-
1,2: Taylor-c/a						3.00

TONKA (Disney)
Dell Publishing Co.: No. 966, Jan, 1959

	GD	VG	FN	VF	VF/NM	NM-
Four Color 966-Movie (Starring Sal Mineo)-photo-c	9	18	27	65	93	120

TONTO (See The Lone Ranger's Companion...)

TONY TRENT (The Face #1,2)
Big Shot/Columbia Comics Group: No. 3, 1948 - No. 4, 1949

	GD	VG	FN	VF	VF/NM	NM-
3,4: 3-The Face app. by Mart Bailey	19	38	57	106	146	185

TOODLES, THE (The Toodle Twins with #1)
Ziff-Davis (Approved Comics)/Argo: No. 10, July-Aug, 1951; Mar, 1956 (Newspaper-r)

	GD	VG	FN	VF	VF/NM	NM-
10-Painted-c, some newspaper-r by The Baers	11	22	33	63	84	105
...Twins 1(Argo, 3/56)-Reprints by The Baers	8	16	24	43	54	65

TOO MUCH COFFEE MAN
Adhesive Comics: July, 1993 - No. 10, Dec, 2000 ($2.50, B&W)

	GD	VG	FN	VF	VF/NM	NM-
1-Shannon Wheeler story & art	2	4	6	10	12	15
2,3	1	2	3	5	7	9
4,5						6.00
6-10						3.00
Full Color Special-nn($2.95),2-(7/97, $3.95)						4.00

TOO MUCH COFFEE MAN SPECIAL
Dark Horse Comics: July, 1997 ($2.95, B&W)

	GD	VG	FN	VF	VF/NM	NM-
nn-Reprints Dark Horse Presents #92-95						3.00

TOO MUCH HOPELESS SAVAGES
Oni Press: June, 2003 - No. 4 ($2.99, B&W, limited series)

Top Cat #9 © H-B

Topix V8#19 © CG

Top Love Stories #16 © STAR

	GD 2.0	VG 4.0	FN 6.0	VF 8.0	VF/NM 9.0	NM- 9.2

1,2-Van Meter-s/Norrie-a 3.00

TOOTH AND CLAW
Image Comics: Aug, 1999 - No. 3, Oct, 1999 ($2.95, limited series)

1-3-Mark Pacella-s/a 3.00

TOOTS & CASPER
Dell Publishing Co.: No. 5, 1942

Large Feature Comic 5	14	28	42	97	141	185

TOP ADVENTURE COMICS
I. W. Enterprises: 1964 (Reprints)

1-r/High Adv. (Explorer Joe #2); Krigstein-r	2	4	6	12	16	20
2-Black Dwarf-r/Red Seal #22; Kinstler-c	2	4	6	14	18	22

TOP CAT (TV) (Hanna-Barbera)(See Kite Fun Book)
Dell Publishing Co./Gold Key No. 4 on: 12-2/61-62 - No. 3, 6-8/62; No. 4, 10/62 - No. 31, 9/70

1 (TV show debuted 9/27/61)	16	32	48	113	167	220
2-Augie Doggie back-ups in #1-4	9	18	27	60	85	110
3-5: 3-Last 15¢ issue. 4-Begin 12¢ issues; Yakky Doodle app. in 1 pg. strip. 5-Touché Turtle app.	7	14	21	57	71	90
6-10	6	12	18	38	52	65
11-20	4	8	12	28	38	48
21-31-Reprints	3	7	10	21	28	35

TOP CAT (TV) (Hanna-Barbera)(See TV Stars #4)
Charlton Comics: Nov, 1970 - No. 20, Nov, 1973

1	6	12	18	43	59	75
2-10	4	8	12	22	30	38
11-20	3	6	9	18	24	30

NOTE: *#8 (1/72) went on sale late in 1972 between #14 and #15 with the 1/73 issues.*

TOP COMICS
K. K. Publications/Gold Key: July, 1967 (All reprints)

nn-The Gnome-Mobile (Disney-movie)	2	4	6	12	16	20
1-Beagle Boys (#7), Beep Beep the Road Runner (#5), Bugs Bunny, Chip 'n' Dale, Daffy Duck (#50), Flipper, Huey, Dewey & Louie, Junior Woodchucks, Lassie, The Little Monsters (#71), Moby Duck, Porky Pig (has Gold Key label - says Top Comics on inside), Scamp, Super Goof, Tom & Jerry, Top Cat (#21), Tweety & Sylvester (#7), Walt Disney C&S (#322), Woody Woodpecker known issues; each character given own book	2	4	6	9	11	14
1-Donald Duck (not Barks), Mickey Mouse	2	4	6	12	16	20
1-Flintstones	4	8	12	22	30	38
1-Huckleberry Hound, Yogi Bear (#30)	2	4	6	14	18	22
1-The Jetsons	5	10	15	33	44	55
1-Tarzan of the Apes (#169)	3	6	9	16	20	24
1-Three Stooges (#35)	3	6	9	19	25	32
1-Uncle Scrooge (#70)	3	6	9	18	23	28
1-Zorro (r/G.K. Zorro #7 w/Toth-a; says 2nd printing)	2	4	6	14	18	22
2-Bugs Bunny, Daffy Duck, Mickey Mouse (#114), Porky Pig, Super Goof, Tom & Jerry, Tweety & Sylvester, Walt Disney's C&S (r/#325), Woody Woodpecker	2	4	6	9	11	14
2-Donald Duck (not Barks), Three Stooges, Uncle Scrooge (#71)-Barks-c, Yogi Bear (#30), Zorro (r/#8; Toth-a)	2	4	6	11	14	18
2-Snow White & 7 Dwarfs(6/67)(1944-r)	2	4	6	10	13	16
3-Donald Duck	2	4	6	11	14	18
3-Uncle Scrooge (#72)	2	4	6	12	16	20
3,4-The Flintstones	4	8	12	22	30	38
3,4: 3-Mickey Mouse (r/#115), Tom & Jerry, Woody Woodpecker, Yogi Bear. 4-Mickey Mouse, Woody Woodpecker	2	4	6	9	11	14

NOTE: *Each book in this series is identical to its counterpart except for cover, and came out at same time. The number in parentheses is the original issue it contains.*

TOP COW BOOK OF REVELATIONS
Image Comics (Top Cow Productions): July, 2003 ($3.99, one-shot)

1-Pin-ups and background info on Top Cow characters; art by various; Gossett-c 4.00

TOP COW CLASSICS IN BLACK AND WHITE
Image Comics (Top Cow): Feb, 2000 - Present ($2.95, B&W reprints)

...: Aphrodite IX #1(9/00) B&W reprint 3.00
...: Ascension #1(4/00) B&W reprint plus time-line of series 3.00
...: Battle of the Planets #1(1/03) B&W reprint plus script and cover gallery 3.00
...: Darkness #1(3/00) B&W reprint plus time-line of series 3.00
...: Fathom #1(5/00) B&W reprint 3.00
...: Magdalena #1(10/02) B&W reprint plus time-line of series 3.00
...: Midnight Nation #1(9/00) B&W preview 3.00
...: Rising Stars #1(7/00) B&W reprint plus cover gallery 3.00
...: Tomb Raider #1(12/00) B&W reprint plus back-story 3.00
...: Witchblade #1(2/00) B&W reprint plus back-story 3.00
...: Witchblade #25(5/01) B&W reprint plus interview with Wohl & Haberlin 3.00

TOP COW PRODUCTIONS, INC./BALLISTIC STUDIOS SWIMSUIT SPECIAL
Image Comics (Top Cow Productions): May, 1995 ($2.95, one-shot)

1 4.00

TOP COW SECRETS:SPECIAL WINTER LINGERIE EDITION
Image Comics (Top Cow Productions): Jan, 1996 ($2.95, one-shot)

1-Pin-ups 3.00

TOP COW 2001 PREVIEW
Image Comics (Top Cow Productions): 2001 (no cover price, one-shot)

1-Preview pages of Tomb Raider; Jusko-a; flip cover & pages of Inferno 2.25

TOP DETECTIVE COMICS
I. W. Enterprises: 1964 (Reprints)

9-r/Young King Cole #14; Dr. Drew (not Grandenetti)	2	4	6	11	14	18

TOP DOG (See Star Comics Magazine, 75¢)
Star Comics (Marvel): Apr, 1985 - No. 14, June, 1987 (Children's book)

1-14: 10-Peter Parker & J. Jonah Jameson cameo 4.00

TOP ELIMINATOR (Teenage Hotrodders #1-24; Drag 'n' Wheels #30 on)
Charlton Comics: No. 25, Sept, 1967 - No. 29, July, 1968

25-29	3	6	9	16	20	25

TOP FLIGHT COMICS: Four Star Publ.: 1947 (Advertised, not published)

TOP FLIGHT COMICS
St. John Publishing Co.: July, 1949

1(7/49, St. John)-Hector the Inspector; funny animal	9	18	27	52	66	80

TOP GUN (See Luke Short, 4-Color #927 & Showcase #72)

TOP GUNS OF THE WEST (See Super DC Giant)

TOPIX (...Comics) (Timeless Topix-early issues) (Also see Men of Battle, Men of Courage & Treasure Chest)(V1-V5#1,V7 on-paper-c)
Catechetical Guild Educational Society: 11/42 - V10#15, 1/28/52 (Weekly - later issues)

V1#1(8 pgs.,8x11")	25	50	75	147	202	260
2,3(8 pgs.,8x11")	14	28	42	81	111	140
4-8(16 pgs.,8x11")	11	22	33	66	88	110
V2#1-10(16 pgs.,8x11"): V2#8-Pope Pius XII	10	20	30	58	77	95
V3#1-10(16 pgs.,8x11"): V3#1-(9/44)	10	20	30	56	73	90
V4#1-10: V4#1-(9/45)	9	18	27	49	62	75
V5#1(10/46,52 pgs.,2(11/46),no #3),4(1/47)-9(6/47),10(7/47), no #13,4(10/47), 14(11/47),15(12/47)	8	16	24	40	50	60
11(8/47),12(9/47)-Life of Christ editions	10	20	30	56	73	90
V6#4(1/48),5(2/48),7(3/48),8(4/48),9(5/48),11(7/48)-14 (no #1-3,6,10)	7	14	21	35	43	50
V7#1(9/1/48)-20(6/15/49), 36 pgs.	6	12	18	29	36	42
V8#1(9/19/49)-3,5-11,13-30(5/15/50)	6	12	18	28	34	40
4-Dagwood Splits the Atom(10/10/49)-Magazine format	8	16	24	40	50	60
12-Ingels-a	10	20	30	56	73	90
V9#1(9/25/50)-11,13-30(5/14/51)	6	12	18	27	33	38
12-Special 36 pg. Xmas issue, text illos format	6	12	18	28	34	40
V10#1(10/1/51)-15: 14-Hollingsworth-a	6	12	18	27	33	38

TOP JUNGLE COMICS
I. W. Enterprises: 1964 (Reprint)

1(nd)-Reprints White Princess of the Jungle #3, minus cover; Kintsler-a	3	6	9	18	24	30

TOP LOVE STORIES (Formerly Gasoline Alley #2)
Star Publications: No. 3, 5/51 - No. 19, 3/54

3(#1)	24	48	72	135	190	245
4,5,7-9: 8-Wood story	19	38	57	106	146	185
6-Wood-a	25	50	75	144	198	255
10-16,18,19-Disbrow-a	19	38	57	106	146	185
17-Wood art (Fox-r)	20	40	60	112	156	200

NOTE: *All have* **L. B. Cole** *covers.*

TOP-NOTCH COMICS (...Laugh #28-45; Laugh Comix #46 on)
MLJ Magazines: Dec, 1939 - No. 45, June, 1944

1-Origin/1st app. The Wizard; Kardak the Mystic Magician, Swift of the Secret Service

Top-Notch Comics #13 © AP

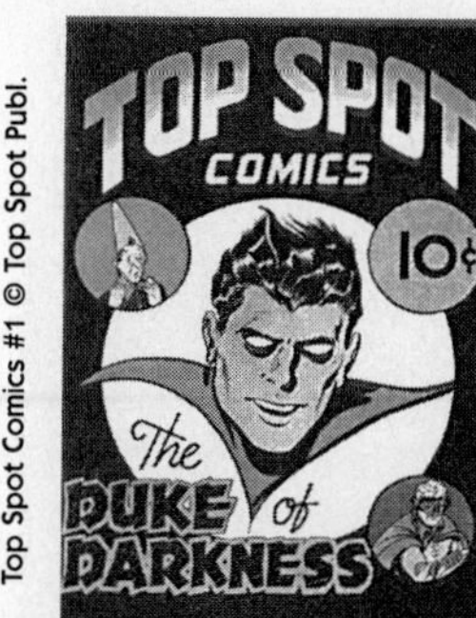

Top Spot Comics #1 © Top Spot Publ.

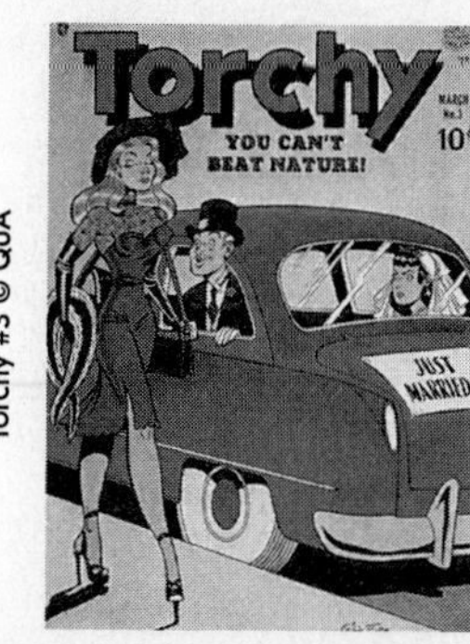

Torchy #3 © QUA

GD 2.0 | VG 4.0 | FN 6.0 | VF 8.0 | VF/NM 9.0 | NM- 9.2

(ends #3), Air Patrol, The Westpointer, Manhunters (by J. Cole), Mystic (ends #2) & Scott Rand (ends #3) begin; Wizard covers begin, end #8
579 1158 1737 4053 6227 8400
2-(1/40)-Dick Storm (ends #8), Stacy Knight M.D. (ends #4) begin; Jack Cole-a; 1st app. Nazis swastika on-c 240 480 720 1500 2250 3000
3-Bob Phantom, Scott Rand on Mars begin; J. Cole-a
164 328 492 1025 1538 2050
4-Origin/1st app. Streak Chandler on Mars; Moore of the Mounted only app.; J. Cole-a
144 288 432 900 1350 1800
5-Flag-c; origin/1st app. Galahad; Shanghai Sheridan begins (ends #8); Shield cameo; Novick-a; classic-c 156 312 468 975 1463 1950
6-Meskin-a 107 214 321 669 1005 1340
7-The Shield x-over in Wizard; The Wizard dons new costume
128 256 384 800 1200 1600
8-Origin/1st app. The Firefly & Roy, the Super Boy (9/40, 2nd costumed boy hero after Robin?; also see Toro in Human Torch #1 (Fall/40)
150 300 450 938 1407 1875
9-Origin & 1st app. The Black Hood; 1st Black Hood-c & logo (10/40); Fran Frazier begins (Scarce) 538 1076 1614 3766 5783 7800
10-2nd app. Black Hood 174 348 522 1088 1632 2175
11-15 103 206 309 644 965 1285
16-20 92 184 276 575 863 1150
21-30: 23-26-Roy app. 24-No Wizard. 25-Last Bob Phantom. 27-Last Firefly. 28-Suzie, Pokey Oakey begin. 29-Last Kardak 69 138 207 431 645 860
31-44: 33-Dotty & Ditto by Woggon begins (2/43, 1st app.). 44-Black Hood series ends
40 80 120 240 350 460
45-Last issue 46 92 138 276 413 550

NOTE: ***J. Binder** a-1-3. **Meskin** a-2, 3, 6, 15. **Bob Montana** a-30; c-28-31. **Harry Sahle** c-42-45. **Woggon** a-33-40, 42. Bondage c-17, 19. Black Hood also appeared on radio in 1944.Black Hood app. on c-9-34, 41-44. Roy the Super Boy app. on c-8, 9, 11-27. The Wizard app. on c-1-8, 11-13, 15-22, 24, 25, 27. Pokey Oakey app. on c-28-43. Suzie app. on c-44-on.*

TOPPER & NEIL (TV)
Dell Publishing Co.: No. 859, Nov, 1957

Four Color 859 5 10 15 36 48 60

TOPPS COMICS: Four Star Publications: 1947 (Advertised, not published)

TOPS
July, 1949 - No. 2, Sept, 1949 (25¢, 10-1/4x13-1/4", 68 pgs.)
Tops Magazine, Inc. (Lev Gleason): (Large size-magazine format; for the adult reader)

1 (Rare)-Story by Dashiell Hammett; Crandall/Lubbers, Tuska, Dan Barry, Fuje-a; Biro painted-c 115 288 460 805 1123 1440
2 (Rare)-Crandall/Lubbers, Biro, Kida, Fuje, Guardineer-a
107 268 428 749 1045 1340

TOPS COMICS
Consolidated Book Publishers: 1944 (10¢, 132 pgs.)

2000-(Color-c, inside in red shade & some in full color)-Ace Kelly by Rick Yager, Black Orchid, Don on the Farm, Dinky Dinkerton (Rare) 27 54 81 153 214 275

NOTE: *This book is printed in such a way that when the staple is removed, the strips on the left side of the book correspond with the same strips on the right side. Therefore, if strips are removed from the book, each strip can be folded into a complete comic section of its own.*

TOPS COMICS (See Tops in Humor)
Consolidated Book (Lev Gleason): 1944 (7-1/4x5", 32 pgs.)

2001-The Jack of Spades (costumed hero) 17 34 51 98 134 170
2002-Rip Raider 10 20 30 56 73 90
2003-Red Birch (gag cartoons) 4 8 12 18 22 25

TOP SECRET
Hillman Publ.: Jan, 1952

1 21 42 63 118 164 210

TOP SECRET ADVENTURES (See Spyman)

TOP SECRETS (...of the F.B.I.)
Street & Smith Publications: Nov, 1947 - No. 10, July-Aug, 1949

1-Powell-c/a 35 70 105 201 288 370
2-Powell-c/a 26 52 78 147 206 265
3-6,8,10-Powell-a 23 46 69 130 183 235
9-Powell-c/a 24 48 72 135 190 245
7-Used in **SOTI**, pg. 90 & illo. "How to hurt people"; used by N.Y. Legis. Comm.; Powell-c/a 35 70 105 201 288 370

NOTE: ***Powell** c-1-3, 5-10.*

TOPS IN ADVENTURE
Ziff-Davis Publishing Co.: Fall, 1952 (25¢, 132 pgs.)

1-Crusader from Mars, The Hawk, Football Thrills, He-Man; Powell-a; painted-c
46 92 138 276 413 550

TOPS IN HUMOR (See Tops Comics?)
Consolidated Book Publ. (Lev Gleason): 1944 (7-1/4x5")

2001(#1)-Origin The Jack of Spades, Ace Kelly by Rick Yager, Black Orchid (female crime fighter) app. 17 34 51 98 134 170
2 11 22 33 63 84 105

TOP SPOT COMICS
Top Spot Publ. Co.: 1945

1-The Menace, Duke of Darkness app. 36 72 108 204 290 375

TOPSY-TURVY (Teenage)
R. B. Leffingwell Publ.: Apr, 1945

1-1st app. Cookie 11 22 33 66 88 110

TOP TEN
America's Best Comics: Sept, 1999 - No. 12, Oct, 2001 ($3.50/$2.95)

1-Two covers by Ross and Ha/Cannon; Alan Moore-s/Gene Ha-a 3.50
2-11-($2.95) 3.00
12-($3.50) 3.50
Hardcover ('00, $24.95) Dust jacket with Gene Ha-a; r/#1-7 25.00
Softcover ('00, $14.95) new Gene Ha-c; r/#1-7 15.00
Book 2 HC ('02, $24.95) Dust jacket with Gene Ha-a; r/#8-12 25.00
Book 2 SC ('03, $14.95) new Gene Ha-c; r/#8-12 15.00

TOR (Prehistoric Life on Earth) (Formerly One Million Years Ago)
St. John Publ. Co.: No. 2, Oct, 1953; No. 3, May, 1954 - No. 5, Oct, 1954

3-D 2(10/53)-Kubert-c/a 14 28 42 79 107 135
3-D 2(10/53)-Oversized, otherwise same contents 12 24 36 69 92 115
3-D 2(11/53)-Kubert-c/a; has 3-D cover 12 24 36 69 92 115
3-5-Kubert-c/a: 3-Danny Dreams by Toth; Kubert 1 pg. story (w/self portrait)
14 28 42 79 107 135

NOTE: *The two October 3-D's have same contents and **Powell** art; the October & November issues are titled 3-D Comics. All 3-D issues are 25¢ and came with 3-D glasses.*

TOR (See Sojourn)
National Periodical Publications: May-June, 1975 - No. 6, Mar-Apr, 1976

1-New origin by Kubert 1 3 4 6 8 10
2-6: 2-Origin-r/St. John #1 6.00

NOTE: ***Kubert** a-1, 2-6r; c-1-6. **Toth** a(p)-3r.*

TOR (3-D)
Eclipse Comics: July, 1986 - No. 2, Aug, 1987 ($2.50)

1,2: 1-r/One Million Years Ago. 2-r/Tor 3-D #2 5.00
...2-D: 1,2-Limited signed & numbered editions 1 2 3 4 5 7

TOR
Marvel Comics (Epic Comics/Heavy Hitters): June, 1993 - No. 4, 1993 ($5.95, limited series)

1-4: Joe Kubert-c/a/scripts 6.00

TOR BY JOE KUBERT
DC Comics: 2001 - Present ($49.95, hardcover with dust jacket)

Volume 1 (2001) r/One Million Years Ago #1 & 3-D Comics #1&2 in flat color; script pages, sketch pages, proposals for TV and newspapers strips; intro. by Roy Thomas 50.00
Volume 2 (2002) r/Tor (St. John) #3-5; Danny Dreams; portfolio section 50.00
Volume 3 (2003) r/Tor (DC '75) #1; (Marvel '93) #1-4; portfolio section 50.00

TORCH OF LIBERTY SPECIAL
Dark Horse Comics (Legend): Jan, 1995 ($2.50, one-shot)

1-Byrne scripts 2.50

TORCHY (...Blonde Bombshell) (See Dollman, Military, & Modern)
Quality Comics Group: Nov, 1949 - No. 6, Sept, 1950

1-Bill Ward-c, Gil Fox-a 152 304 456 950 1425 1900
2,3-Fox-c/a 66 132 198 413 619 825
4-Fox-c/a(3), Ward-a (9 pgs.) 82 164 246 513 769 1025
5,6-Ward-c/a, 9 pgs; Fox-a(3) each 100 200 300 625 938 1250
Super Reprint #16(1964)-r/#4 with new-c 9 18 27 65 93 120

TO RIVERDALE AND BACK AGAIN (Archie Comics Presents...)
Archie Comics: 1990 ($2.50, 68 pgs.)

nn-Byrne-c, Colan-a(p); adapts NBC TV movie 5.00

TORMENTED, THE (Becomes Surprise Adventures #3 on)
Sterling Comics: July, 1954 - No. 2, Sept, 1954

1,2: Weird/horror stories 26 52 78 147 206 265

TORNADO TOM (See Mighty Midget Comics)

Total Eclipse #3 © ECL

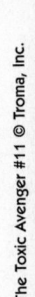

The Toxic Avenger #11 © Troma, Inc.

Transformers Comics Magazine #2 © Hasbro

GD 2.0 | VG 4.0 | FN 6.0 | VF 8.0 | VF/NM 9.0 | NM- 9.2

TORSO (See Jinx: Torso)

TOTAL ECLIPSE
Eclipse Comics: May, 1988 - No. 5, Apr, 1989 ($3.95, 52 pgs., deluxe size)
Book 1-5: 3-Intro/1st app. new Black Terror. 4-Many copies have upside down pages and are mis-cut 4.00

TOTAL ECLIPSE
Image Comics: July, 1998 (one-shot)
1-McFarlane-c; Eclipse Comics character pin-ups by Image artists 2.25

TOTAL ECLIPSE: THE SERAPHIM OBJECTIVE
Eclipse Comics: Nov, 1988 ($1.95, one-shot, Baxter paper)
1-Airboy, Valkyrie, The Heap app. 3.00

TOTAL JUSTICE
DC Comics: Oct, 1996 - No. 3, Nov, 1996 ($2.25, bi-weekly limited series) (Based on toyline)
1-3 2.25

TOTAL RECALL (Movie)
DC Comics: 1990 ($2.95, 68 pgs., movie adaptation, one-shot)
1-Arnold Schwarzenegger photo-c 3.00

TOTAL WAR (M.A.R.S. Patrol #3 on)
Gold Key: July, 1965 - No. 2, Oct, 1965 (Painted-c)
1-Wood-a in both issues 7 14 21 51 71 90
2 6 12 18 40 55 70

TOTEMS (Vertigo V2K)
DC Comics (Vertigo): Feb, 2000 ($5.95, one-shot)
1-Swamp Thing, Animal Man, Zatanna, Shade app.; Fegredo-c 6.00

TO THE HEART OF THE STORM
Kitchen Sink Press: 1991 (B&W, graphic novel)
Softcover-Will Eisner-s/a/c 15.00
Hardcover ($24.95) 25.00
TPB-(DC Comics, 9/00, $14.95) reprints 1991 edition 15.00

TO THE LAST MAN (See Zane Grey Four Color #616)

TOUCH OF SILVER, A
Image Comics: Jan, 1997 - No. 6, Nov, 1997 ($2.95, B&W, bi-monthly)
1-6-Valentino-s/a; photo-c: 5-color pgs. w/Round Table 3.00
TPB ($12.95) r/#1-6 13.00

TOUGH KID SQUAD COMICS
Timely Comics (TCI): Mar, 1942
1-(Scarce)-Origin & 1st app.The Human Top & The Tough Kid Squad; The Flying Flame app. 966 1932 2898 6762 10,381 14,000

TOWER OF SHADOWS (Creatures on the Loose #10 on)
Marvel Comics Group: Sept, 1969 - No. 9, Jan, 1971
1-Classic Steranko-c, Craig-a(p) 7 14 21 46 63 80
2,3: 2-Neal Adams-a. 3-Barry Smith, Tuska-a 4 8 12 24 32 40
4,6: 4-Marie Severin-c. 6-Wood-a 3 6 9 18 24 30
5-B. Smith-a(p), Wood-a; Wood draws himself (1st pg., 1st panel) 3 6 9 19 25 32
7-9: 7-B. Smith-a(p), Wood-a. 8-Wood-a; Wrightson-c. 9-Wrightson-c; Roy Thomas app. 4 8 12 24 32 40
Special 1(12/71, 52 pgs.)-Neal Adams-a 3 6 9 19 25 32
*NOTE: **J. Buscema** a-1p, 2p, Special 1r. **Colan** a-3p, 6p, Special 1. **J. Craig** a(r)-1p. **Ditko** a-6, 8, 9r, Special 1. **Everett** a-9(i)r; c-5i. **Kirby** a-9(p)r. **Severin** c-5p, 6. **Steranko** a-1p. **Tuska** a-3. **Wood** a-5-8. Issues 1-9 contain new stories with some pre-Marvel age reprints in 6-9. **H. P. Lovecraft** adaptation-9.*

TOWN & COUNTRY
Publisher?: May, 1940
nn-Origin The Falcon 46 92 138 276 413 550

TOXIC AVENGER (Movie)
Marvel Comics: Apr, 1991 - No. 11, Feb, 1992 ($1.50)
1-11: Based on movie character. 3,10-Photo-c 2.25

TOXIC CRUSADERS (TV)
Marvel Comics: May, 1992 - No. 8, Dec, 1992 ($1.25)
1-8: 1-3,8-Sam Kieth-c; based on USA network cartoon 2.25

TOXIC GUMBO
DC Comics (Vertigo): 1998 ($5.95, one-shot, mature)
1-McKeever-a/Lydia Lunch-s 6.00

TOYBOY
Continuity Comics: Oct, 1986 - No. 7, Mar, 1989 ($2.00, Baxter paper)
1-7 3.00
*NOTE: **N. Adams** a-1; c-1, 2,5. **Golden** a-7p; c-6,7. **Nebres** a(i)-1,2.*

TOYLAND COMICS
Fiction House Magazines: Jan, 1947 - No. 2, Mar, 1947; No. 3, July, 1947
1-Wizard of the Moon begins 31 62 93 175 248 320
2,3-Bob Lubbers-c. 3-Tuska-a 17 34 51 98 134 170
*NOTE: All above contain strips by **Al Walker.***

TOY TOWN COMICS
Toytown/Orbit Publ./B. Antin/Swapper Quarterly: 1945 - No. 7, May, 1947
1-Mertie Mouse; L. B. Cole-c/a; funny animal 40 80 120 240 340 440
2-L. B. Cole-a 24 48 72 138 194 250
3-7-L. B. Cole-a. 5-Wiggles the Wonderworm-c 21 42 63 118 164 210

TRAGG AND THE SKY GODS (See Gold Key Spotlight, Mystery Comics Digest #3,9 & Spine Tingling Tales)
Gold Key/Whitman No. 9: June, 1975 - No. 8, Feb, 1977; No. 9, May, 1982 (Painted-c #3-8)
1-Origin 2 4 6 10 13 16
2-8: 4-Sabre-Fang app. 8-Ostellon app. 1 2 3 5 7 9
9-(Whitman, 5/82) r/#1 1 2 3 5 6 8
*NOTE: **Santos** a-1, 2, 9r; c-3-7. **Spiegel** a-3-8.*

TRAIL BLAZERS (Red Dragon #5 on)
Street & Smith Publications: 1941; No. 2, Apr, 1942 - No. 4, Oct, 1942
(True stories of American heroes)
1-Life story of Jack Dempsey & Wright Brothers 35 70 105 201 288 370
2-Brooklyn Dodgers-c/story; Ben Franklin story 23 46 69 129 180 230
3,4: 3-Fred Allen, Red Barber, Yankees stories 21 42 63 118 164 210

TRAIL COLT (Also see Extra Comics & Manhunt!)
Magazine Enterprises: 1949 - No. 2, 1949
nn(A-1 #24)-7 pg. Frazetta-a r-in Manhunt #13; Undercover Girl app.; The Red Fox by L. B. Cole; Ingels-c; Whitney-a (Scarce) 40 80 120 240 340 440
2(A-1 #26)-Undercover Girl; Ingels-c; L. B. Cole-a (6 pgs.) 34 68 102 193 274 355

TRAKK: MONSTER HUNTER (Stan Winston's...)
Image Comics: Sept, 2003 - Present ($2.95)
1-Two covers by Tan & Bisley; Tan-a 3.00

TRANSFORMERS, THE (TV)(See G.I. Joe and...)
Marvel Comics Group: Sept, 1984 - No. 80, July, 1991 (75¢/$1.00)
1-Based on Hasbro Toys 2 4 6 10 12 15
2-5: 2-Golden-c. 4-Texeira-c 1 3 4 6 8 10
6-10 6.00
11-49: 21-Intro Aerialbots 4.00
50-60: 53-Jim Lee-c. 54-Intro Micromasters 6.00
61-70: 67-Jim Lee-c. 1 2 3 5 7 9
71-77: 75-($1.50, 52 pgs.) (Low print run) 2 4 6 10 13 16
78,79 (Low print run) 3 6 9 17 21 26
80-Last issue 3 7 10 21 28 35
*NOTE: Second and third printings of most early issues (1-9?) exist and are worth less than originals. Was originally planned as a four issue mini-series. **Wrightson** a-64i(4 pgs.).*

TRANSFORMERS ARMADA (Continues as Transformers Energon with #19)
(Also see Promotional Comics section for FCBD Ed.)
Dreamwave Productions: July, 2002 - No. 18, Dec, 2003 ($2.95)
1-Sarracini-s/Raiz-a; wraparound gatefold-c 3.00
2-18 3.00
Vol. 1 TPB (2003, $13.95) r/#1-5 14.00
Vol. 2 TPB (2003, $15.95) r/#6-11 16.00

TRANSFORMERS COMICS MAGAZINE
Marvel Comics: Oct, 1986 - No. 11, 1988 ($1.50, digest size)
1-11: 2-Spider-Man-c/s 4.00

TRANSFORMERS DIGEST
Marvel Comics: Jan, 1987 - No. 10, July, 1988
1,2-Spider-Man-c/s 2 4 6 10 12 15
3-10 2 4 6 8 10 12

TRANSFORMERS ENERGON (Continued from Transformers Armada #18)
Dreamwave Productions: No. 19, Jan, 2004 - Present ($2.95)
19-Furman-s 3.00

TRANSFORMERS: GENERATION 1
Dreamwave Productions: Apr, 2002 - No. 6, Oct, 2002 ($2.95)

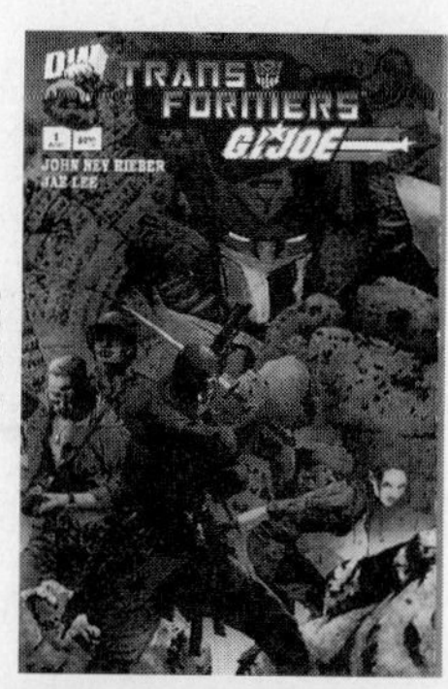

Transformers/ G.I. Joe #1 © Hasbro

Transmetropolitan #13 © Ellis & Robertson

Treasure Chest V14#18 © George A. Pflaum

GD 2.0 | VG 4.0 | FN 6.0 | VF 8.0 | VF/NM 9.0 | NM- 9.2

Preview- 6 pg. story; robot sketch pages; Pat Lee-a 2.00
1-Pat Lee-a; 2 wraparound covers by Lee 4.00
2-6: 2-Optimus Prime reactivated; 2 covers by Pat Lee 3.00
...Vol. 1 HC (2003, $49.95) r/#1-6; black hardcover with red foil lettering and art 50.00
...Vol. 1 TPB (2002, $17.95) r/#1-6 plus six page preview; 8 pg. preview of future issues 18.00

TRANSFORMERS: GENERATION 1 (Volume 2)
Dreamwave Productions: Apr, 2003 - No. 6, Sept, 2003 ($2.95)

1-6: 1-Pat Lee-a; 2 wraparound gatefold covers by Lee 3.00
1-($5.95) Chrome wraparound variant-c 6.00

TRANSFORMERS: GENERATION 1 (Volume 3)
Dreamwave Productions: No. 0, Dec, 2003 ($2.95)

0-Pat Lee-a 3.00

TRANSFORMERS: GENERATION 2
Marvel Comics: Nov, 1993 - No. 12, Oct, 1994 ($1.75)

1-($2.95, 68 pgs.)-Collector's ed. w/bi-fold metallic-c 1 2 3 5 6 8
1-11: 1-Newsstand edition (68 pgs.) 6.00
12-($2.25, 52 pgs.) 1 2 3 5 6 8

TRANSFORMERS/G.I. JOE
Dreamwave Productions: Aug, 2003 - No. 6 ($5.25)

1-Art & gatefold wraparound-c by Jae Lee; Ney Rieber-s; variant-c by Pat Lee 3.00
1-($5.95) Holofoil wraparound-c by Norton 6.00
2-4-Jae Lee-a/c 3.00

TRANSFORMERS: HEADMASTERS
Marvel Comics Group: July, 1987 - No. 4, Jan, 1988 ($1.00, limited series)

1-Springer, Akin, Garvey-a 4.00
2-4-Springer-c on all 3.00

TRANSFORMERS: MORE THAN MEETS THE EYE
Dreamwave Productions: Apr, 2003 - No. 8, Nov, 2003 ($5.25)

1-8-Pin-ups with tech info on Autobots and Decepticons; art by Pat Lee & various 5.25

TRANSFORMERS, THE MOVIE
Marvel Comics Group: Dec, 1986 - No. 3, Feb, 1987 (75¢, limited series)

1-3-Adapts animated movie 3.00

TRANSFORMERS: THE WAR WITHIN
Dreamwave Productions: Oct, 2002 - No. 6, Mar, 2003 ($2.95)

1-6-Furman-s/Figueroa-a. 1-Wraparound gatefold-c 3.00
TPB (2003, $15.95) r/#1-6; plus cover gallery 16.00

TRANSFORMERS UNIVERSE
Marvel Comics Group: Dec, 1986 - No. 4, Mar, 1987 ($1.25, limited series)

1-4-A guide to all characters 4.00

TRANSFORMERS WAR WITHIN: THE DARK AGES
Dreamwave Productions: Oct, 2003 - Present ($2.95)

1-3: 1-Furman-s/Wildman-a; two covers by Pat Lee & Figueroa 3.00

TRANSIT
Vortex Publ.: March, 1987 - No. 5, Nov, 1987 (B&W)

1-5-Ted McKeever-s/a 1 2 3 5 6 8

TRANSMETROPOLITAN
DC Comics (Vertigo): Sept, 1997 - No. 60, Nov, 2002 ($2.50)

1-Warren Ellis-s/Darick Robertson-a(p) 2 4 6 8 10 12
2,3 1 2 3 4 5 7
4-8 4.00
9-60: 15-Jae Lee-c. 25-27-Jim Lee-c. 37-39-Bradstreet-c 2.50
Back on the Street ('97, $7.95) r/#1-3 8.00
Dirge ('03, $14.95) r/#43-48 15.00
Filth of the City ('01, $5.95) Spider's columns with pin-up art by various 6.00
Gouge Away ('02, $14.95) r/#31-36 15.00
I Hate It Here ('00, $5.95) Spider's columns with pin-up art by various 6.00
Lonely City ('01, $14.95) r/#25-30; intro. by Patrick Stewart 15.00
Lust For Life ('98, $14.95) r/#4-12 15.00
Spider's Thrash ('02, $14.95) r/#37-42; intro. by Darren Aronofsky 15.00
The Cure ('03, $14.95) r/#49-54 15.00
The New Scum ('00, $12.95) r/#19-24 & Vertigo: Winter's Edge #3 13.00
Year of the Bastard ('99, $12.95) r/#13-18 13.00

TRANSMUTATION OF IKE GARUDA, THE
Marvel Comics (Epic Comics): July, 1991 - No. 2, 1991 ($3.95, 52 pgs.)

1,2 4.00

TRAPMAN
Phantom Comics: June, 1994 - No. 2, 1994? ($2.95, quarterly, unfinished limited series)

1,2 3.00

TRAPPED!
Periodical House Magazines (Ace): Oct, 1954 - No. 4, April, 1955

1 (All reprints) 10 20 30 56 73 90
2-4: 4-r/Men Against Crime #4 in its entirety 7 14 21 35 43 50
NOTE: ***Colan*** *a-1, 4.* ***Sekowsky*** *a-1.*

TRASH
Trash Publ. Co.: Mar, 1978 - No. 4, Oct, 1978 (B&W, magazine, 52 pgs.)

1,2: 1-Star Wars parody. 2-UFO-c 2 4 6 9 11 14
3-Parodies of KISS, the Beatles, and monsters 2 4 6 12 16 20
4-(84 pgs.)-Parodies of Happy Days, Rocky movies 3 6 9 16 20 24

TRAVELS OF JAIMIE McPHEETERS, THE (TV)
Gold Key: Dec, 1963

1-Kurt Russell photo on-c plus photo back-c 4 8 12 27 36 45

TREASURE CHEST (Catholic Guild; also see Topix)
George A. Pflaum: 3/12/46 - V27#8, July, 1972 (Educational comics)
(Not published during Summer)

V1#1 26 52 78 150 210 270
2-6 (5/21/46): 5-Dr. Styx app. by Baily 12 24 36 71 96 120
V2#1-20 (9/3/46-5/27/47) 10 20 30 56 73 90
V3#1-5,7-20 (1st slick cover) 9 18 27 52 66 80
V3#6-Jules Verne's "Voyage to the Moon" 11 22 33 63 84 105
V4#1-20 (9/9/48-5/31/49) 8 16 24 46 58 70
V5#1-20 (9/6/49-5/31/50) 8 16 24 43 54 65
V6#1-20 (9/14/50-5/31/51) 8 16 24 40 50 60
V7#1-20 (9/13/51-6/5/52) 7 14 21 37 46 55
V8#1-20 (9/11/52-6/4/53) 7 14 21 35 43 50
V9#1-20 ('53-'54), V10#1-20 ('54-'55) 6 12 18 31 38 45
V11('55-'56), V12('56-'57) 6 12 18 28 34 40
V13#1,3-5,7,9-V17#1 ('57-'63) 5 10 15 24 30 35
V13#2,6,8-Ingels-a 7 14 21 50 68 85
V17#2- "This Godless Communism" series begins(not in odd #'d issues); cover shows hammer & sickle over Statue of Liberty; 8 pg. Crandall-a of family life under communism 18 36 54 131 191 250
V17#3,5,7,9,11,13,15,17,19 3 6 9 18 23 28
V17#4,6,14- "This Godless Communism" stories 12 24 36 87 129 170
V17#8-Shows red octopus encompassing Earth, firing squad; 8 pgs. Crandall-a 15 30 45 109 160 210
V17#10- "This Godless Communism" - how Stalin came to power, part I; Crandall-a 14 28 42 102 149 195
V17#12-Stalin in WWII, forced labor, death by exhaustion; Crandall-a 14 28 42 102 149 195
V17#16-Kruschev takes over; de-Stalinization 14 28 42 102 149 195
V17#18-Kruschev's control; murder of revolters, brainwash, space race by Crandall 14 28 42 102 149 195
V17#20-End of series; Kruschev-people are puppets, firing squads hammer & sickle over Statue of Liberty, snake around communist manifesto by Crandall 17 34 51 121 178 235
V18#1-20, V19#11-20, V20#1-20(1964-65): V18#11-Crandall draws himself & 13 other artists on cover 3 6 9 16 20 25
V18#5- "What About Red China?" - describes how communists took over China 7 14 21 50 68 85
V19#1-10- "Red Victim" anti-communist series in all 7 14 21 50 68 85
V21-V25(1965-70)-(two V24#5's 11/7/68 & 11/21/68) (no V24#6) 2 4 6 14 18 22
V26, V27#1-8 (V26,27-68 pgs.) 3 6 9 16 20 25
Summer Edition V1#1-6('66), V2#1-6('67) 3 6 9 18 23 28
NOTE: ***Anderson*** *a-V18#13.* ***Borth*** *a-V7#10-19 (serial), V8#8-17 (serial), V9#1-10 (serial), V13#2, 6, 11, V14-V25 (except V22#1-3, 11-13), Summer Ed. V1#3-6.* ***Crandall*** *a-V16#7, 9, 12, 14, 16-18, 20; V17#1, 2, 4-6, 10, 12, 14, 16-18, 20; V18#1, 2, 3(2 pg.), 7, 9-20; V19#4, 11, 13, 16, 19, 20; V20#1, 2, 4, 6, 8-10, 12, 14-16, 18, 20; V21#1-5, 8-11, 13, 16-18; V22#3, 7, 9-11, 14; V23#3, 6, 9, 16, 18; V24#7, 8, 10, 13, 16; V25#8, 16; V27#1-7r, 8r(2 pg.), Summer Ed. V1#3-5, V2#3; c-V16#7, V18#2(part), 7, 11, V19#4, 19, 20, V20#15, V21#5, 9, V22#3, 7, 9, 11, V23#9, 16, V24#13, 16, V25#8, Summer Ed. V1#2 (back c-V1#2-5).* ***Powell*** *a-V10#11. V19#11, 15, V10#13, V13#6, 8 all have wraparound covers.*

TREASURE CHEST OF THE WORLD'S BEST COMICS
Superior, Toronto, Canada: 1945 (500 pgs., hard-c)

Contains Blue Beetle, Captain Combat, John Wayne, Dynamic Man, Nemo, Li'l Abner; contents can vary - represents random binding of extra books; Capt. America on-c 88 176 264 550 825 1100

TREASURE COMICS

Treehouse of Horror #9 © Bongo

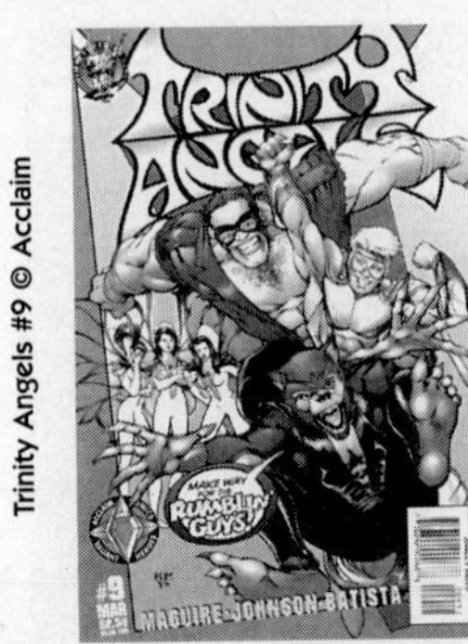

Trinity Angels #9 © Acclaim

Trouble #1 © MAR

GD 2.0 | VG 4.0 | FN 6.0 | VF 8.0 | VF/NM 9.0 | NM- 9.2

GD 2.0 | VG 4.0 | FN 6.0 | VF 8.0 | VF/NM 9.0 | NM- 9.2

Prize Publications? (no publisher listed): No date (1943) (50¢, 324 pgs., cardboard-c)
1-(Rare)-Contains rebound Prize Comics #7-11 from 1942 (blank inside-c) 220 440 660 1375 2063 2750

TREASURE COMICS
Prize Publ. (American Boys' Comics): June-July, 1945 - No. 12, Fall, 1947
1-Paul Bunyan & Marco Polo begin; Highwayman & Carrot Topp only app.; Kiefer-a 40 80 120 240 358 475
2-Arabian Knight, Gorilla King, Dr. Styx begin 23 46 69 130 183 235
3,4,9,12: 9-Kiefer-a 17 34 51 95 130 165
5-Marco Polo-c; Krigstein-a 25 50 75 147 202 260
6,11-Krigstein-a; 11-Krigstein-c 23 46 69 130 183 235
7,8-Frazetta-a (5 pgs. each). 7-Capt. Kidd Jr. app. 40 80 120 240 350 460
10-Simon & Kirby-c/a 34 68 102 196 278 360
NOTE: *Barry a-9-11; c-12.* ***Kiefer*** *a-3, 5, 7; c-2, 6, 7.* ***Roussos*** *a-11.*

TREASURE ISLAND (See Classics Illustrated #64, Doc Savage Comics #1, King Classics, Movie Classics & Movie Comics)
Dell Publishing Co.: No. 624, Apr, 1955 (Disney)
Four Color 624-Movie, photo-c 9 18 27 65 93 120

TREASURY OF COMICS
St. John Publishing Co.: 1947; No. 2, July, 1947 - No. 4, Sept, 1947; No. 5, Jan, 1948
nn(#1)-Abbie an' Slats (nn on-c, #1 on inside) 14 28 42 79 107 135
2-Jim Hardy Comics; featuring Windy & Paddles 11 22 33 63 84 105
3-Bill Bumlin 9 18 27 54 70 85
4-Abbie an' Slats 11 22 33 63 84 105
5-Jim Hardy Comics #1 11 22 33 63 84 105

TREASURY OF COMICS
St. John Publishing Co.: Mar, 1948 - No. 5, 1948 (Reg. size); 1948-1950 (Over 500 pgs., $1.00)
1 20 40 60 112 156 200
2(#2 on-c, #1 on inside) 11 22 33 63 84 105
3-5 10 20 30 56 73 90
1-(1948, 500 pgs., hard-c)-Abbie & Slats, Abbott & Costello, Casper, Little Annie Rooney, Little Audrey, Jim Hardy, Ella Cinders (16 books bound together) (Rare) 108 216 324 675 1013 1350
1(1949, 500 pgs.)-Same format as above 100 200 300 625 938 1250
1(1950, 500 pgs.)-Same format as above; different-c; (also see Little Audrey Yearbook) (Rare) 100 200 300 625 938 1250

TREASURY OF DOGS, A (See Dell Giants)

TREASURY OF HORSES, A (See Dell Giants)

TREEHOUSE OF HORROR (Bart Simpson's...)
Bongo Comics: 1995 - Present ($2.95/$2.50/$3.50/$4.50, annual)
1-(1995, $2.95)-Groening-c; Allred, Robinson & Smith stories 3.50
2-(1996, $2.50)-Stories by Dini & Bagge; infinity-c by Groening 3.00
3-(1997, $2.50)-Dorkin-s/Groening-c 3.00
4-(1998, $2.50)-Lash & Dixon-s/Groening-c 3.00
5-(1999, $3.50)-Thompson-s; Shaw & Aragonés-s/a; TenNapel-s/a 3.50
6-(2000, $4.50)-Mahfood-s/a; DeCarlo-a; Morse-s/a; Kuper-s/a 4.50
7-(2001, $4.50)-Hamill-s/Morrison-a; Ennis-s/McCrea-a; Sakai-s/a; Nixey-s/a; Brereton back-c 4.50
8-(2002, $3.50)-Templeton, Shaw, Barta, Simone, Thompson-s/a 3.50
9-(2003, $4.99)-Lord of the Rings-Brereton-a; Dini, Naifeh, Millidge, Boothby, Noto-s/a 5.00

TREKKER (See Dark Horse Presents #6)
Dark Horse Comics: May, 1987 - No. 6, Mar,1988 ($1.50, B&W)
1-6: Sci/Fi stories 2.25
Color Special 1 (1989, $2.95, 52 pgs.) 3.00
Collection ($5.95, B&W) 6.00
Special 1 (6/99, $2.95, color) 3.00

TRENCHCOAT BRIGADE, THE
DC Comics (Vertigo): Mar, 1999 - No. 4, Jun, 1999 ($2.50, limited series)
1-4: Hellblazer, Phantom Stranger, Mister E, Dr. Occult app. 2.50

TRENCHER (See Blackball Comics)
Image Comics: May, 1993 - No. 4, Oct, 1993 ($1.95, unfinished limited series)
1-4: Keith Giffen-c/a/scripts. 3-Supreme-c/story 2.25

TRIBAL FORCE
Mystic Comics: Aug, 1996 ($2.50)
1-Reads "Special Edition" on-c 2.50

TRIB COMIC BOOK, THE
Winnipeg Tribune: Sept. 24, 1977 - Vol. 4, #36, 1980 (8-1/2"x11", 24 pgs., weekly) (155 total issues)
V1# 1-Color pages (Sunday strips)-Spiderman, Asterix, Disney's Scamp, Wizard of Id, Doonesbury, Inside Woody Allen, Mary Worth, & others (similar to Spirit sections) 2 4 6 12 14 18
V1#2-15, V2#1-52, V3#1-52, V4#1-33 1 3 4 6 8 10
V4#34-36 (not distributed) 2 4 6 12 16 20
NOTE: *All issues have Spider-Man. Later issues contain Star Trek and Star Wars. 20 strips in ea. The first newspaper to put Sunday pages into a comic book format.*

TRIBE (See WildC.A.T.S #4)
Image Comics/Axis Comics No. 2 on: Apr, 1993; No. 2, Sept, 1993 - No. 3, 1994 ($2.50/$1.95)
1-By Johnson & Stroman; gold foil & embossed on black-c 2.50
1-($2.50)-Ivory Edition; gold foil & embossed on white-c; available only through the creators 2.50
2,3: 2-1st Axis Comics issue. 3-Savage Dragon app. 2.25

TRIBUTE TO STEVEN HUGHES, A
Chaos! Comics: Sept, 2000 ($6.95)
1-Lady Death & Evil Ernie pin-ups by various artists; testimonials 7.00

TRIGGER (See Roy Rogers'...)

TRIGGER TWINS
National Periodical Publications: Mar-Apr, 1973 (20¢, one-shot)
1-Trigger Twins & Pow Wow Smith-r/All-Star Western #94,103 & Western Comics #81; Infantino-r(p) 2 4 6 14 18 22

TRINITY (See DC Universe: Trinity)

TRINITY ANGELS
Acclaim Comics (Valiant Heroes): July, 1997 - No. 12, June, 1998 ($2.50)
1-12-Maguire-s/a(p):4-Copycat-c 3.00

TRIPLE GIANT COMICS (See Archie All-Star Specials under Archie Comics)

TRIPLE THREAT
Special Action/Holyoke/Gerona Publ.: Winter, 1945
1-Duke of Darkness, King O'Leary 31 62 93 175 248 320

TRIPLE-X
Dark Horse Comics: Dec, 1994 - No. 7, June, 1995 ($3.95, B&W, limited series)
1-7 4.00

TRIUMPH (Also see JLA #28-30, Justice League Task Force & Zero Hour)
DC Comics: June, 1995 - No. 4, Sept, 1995 ($1.75, limited series)
1-4: 3-Hourman, JLA app. 2.25

TRIUMPHANT UNLEASHED
Triumphant Comics: No. 0, Nov, 1993 - No. 1, Nov, 1993 ($2.50, lim. series)
0-Serially numbered, 0-Red logo, 0-White logo (no cover price; giveaway), 1-Cover is negative & reverse of #0-c 2.50

TROLL (Also see Brigade)
Image Comics (Extreme Studios): Dec, 1993 ($2.50, one-shot, 44 pgs.)
1-1st app. Troll; Liefeld scripts; Matsuda-c/a(p) 2.50
Halloween Special (1994, $2.95)-Maxx app. 3.00
...Once A Hero (8/94, $2.50) 2.50

TROLLORDS
Tru Studios/Comico V2#1 on: 2/86 - No. 15, 1988; V2#1, 11/88 - V2#4, 1989 (1-15: $1.50, B&W)
1-15: 1-Both printings. 6-Christmas issue; silver logo 2.50
V2#1-4 ($1.75, color, Comico) 2.50
Special 1 ($1.75, 2/87, color)-Jerry's Big Fun Bk. 2.50

TROLLORDS
Apple Comics: July, 1989 - No. 6, 1990 ($2.25, B&W, limited series)
1-6: 1-"The Big Batman Movie Parody" 2.50

TROLL PATROL
Harvey Comics: Jan, 1993 ($1.95, 52 pgs.)
1 2.25

TROLL II (Also see Brigade)
Image Comics (Extreme Studios): July, 1994 ($3.95, one-shot)
1 4.00

TROUBLE
Marvel Comics (Epic): Sept, 2003 - No. 5, Jan, 2004 ($2.99, limited series)

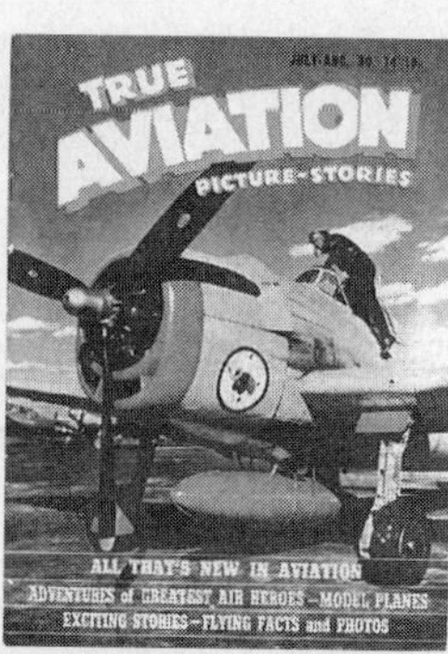

True Aviation Picture Stories #14 © PMI

True Comics #15 © PMI

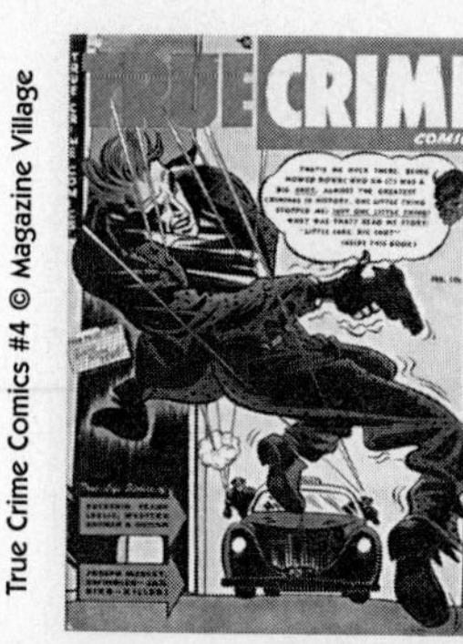

True Crime Comics #4 © Magazine Village

GD 2.0 | VG 4.0 | FN 6.0 | VF 8.0 | VF/NM 9.0 | NM- 9.2

1-Photo-c; Richard and Ben meet Mary and May; Millar-s/Dodson-a 3.00
1-2nd printing with variant Frank Cho-c 3.00
2-5 3.00

TROUBLED SOULS
Fleetway: 1990 ($9.95, trade paperback)
nn-Garth Ennis scripts & John McCrea painted-c/a. 10.00

TROUBLE MAGNET
DC Comics: Feb, 2000 - No. 4, May, 2000 ($2.50, limited series)
1-4-Windham-s/Plunkett-a 2.50

TROUBLEMAKERS
Acclaim Comics (Valiant Heroes): Apr, 1997 - No. 19, June, 1998 ($2.50)
1-19: Fabian Nicieza scripts in all. 1-1st app. XL, Rebound & Blur; 2 covers. 8-Copycat-c. 12-Shooting of Parker 2.50

TROUBLEMAN
Image Comics (Motown Machineworks): June, 1996 - No. 3, Aug, 1996 ($2.25, lim. series)
1-3 2.25

TROUBLE SHOOTERS, THE (TV)
Dell Publishing Co.: No. 1108, Jun-Aug, 1960
Four Color 1108-Keenan Wynn photo-c 6 12 18 40 55 70

TROUBLE WITH GIRLS, THE
Malibu Comics (Eternity Comics) #7-14/Comico V2#1-4/Eternity V2#5 on: 8/87 - #14, 1988; V2#1, 2/89 - V2#23, 1991? ($1.95, B&W/color)
1-14 ($1.95, B&W, Eternity)-Gerard Jones scripts & Tim Hamilton-c/a in all. 2.25
V2#1-23-Jones scripts, Hamilton-c/a. 2.25
Annual 1 (1988, $2.95) 3.00
Christmas Special 1 (12/91, $2.95, B&W, Eternity)-Jones scripts, Hamilton-c/a 3.00
Graphic Novel 1,2 (7/88, B&W)-r/#1-3 & #4-6 8.00

TROUBLE WITH GIRLS, THE: NIGHT OF THE LIZARD
Marvel Comics (Epic Comics/Heavy Hitters): 1993 - No. 4, 1993 ($2.50/$1.95, lim. series)
1-Embossed-c; Gerard Jones scripts & Bret Blevins-c/a in all 2.50
2-4: 2-Begin $1.95-c. 2.25

TROUT
Oni Press: Oct, 2001 - No. 2, Feb, 2002 ($2.95, B&W, limited series)
1,2-Troy Nixey-s/a 3.00

TRUE ADVENTURES (Formerly True Western)(Men's Adventures #4 on)
Marvel Comics (CCC): No. 3, May, 1950 (52 pgs.)
3-Powell, Sekowsky-a; Brodsky-c 17 34 51 95 130 165

TRUE ANIMAL PICTURE STORIES
True Comics Press: Winter, 1947 - No. 2, Spring-Summer, 1947
1,2 10 20 30 56 73 90

TRUE AVIATION PICTURE STORIES (Becomes Aviation Adventures & Model Building #16 on)
Parents' Mag. Institute: 1942; No. 2, Jan-Feb, 1943 - No. 15, Sept-Oct, 1946
1-(#1 & 2 titled ...Aviation Comics Digest)(not digest size) 15 30 45 86 118 150
2 10 20 30 56 73 90
3-14: 3-10-Plane photos on-c. 11,13-Photo-c 9 18 27 49 62 75
15-(Titled "True Aviation Adventures & Model Building") 8 16 24 46 58 70

TRUE BRIDE'S EXPERIENCES (Formerly Teen-Age Brides)
(True Bride-To-Be Romances No. 17 on)
True Love (Harvey Publications): No. 8, Oct, 1954 - No. 16, Feb, 1956
8 9 18 27 49 62 75
9,10: 10-Last pre-code (2/55) 7 14 21 35 43 50
11-15 6 12 18 29 36 42
16-Last issue 7 14 21 35 43 50
NOTE: *Powell a-8-10, 12, 13.*

TRUE BRIDE-TO-BE ROMANCES (Formerly True Bride's Experiences)
Home Comics/True Love (Harvey): No. 17, Apr, 1956 - No. 30, Nov, 1958
17-S&K-c, Powell-a 10 20 30 56 73 90
18-20,22,25-28,30 6 12 18 28 34 40
21,23,24,29-Powell-a. 29-Baker-a (1 pg.) 6 12 18 31 38 45

TRUE COMICS (Also see Outstanding American War Heroes)
True Comics/Parents' Magazine Press: April, 1941 - No. 84, Aug, 1950
1-Marathon run story; life story Winston Churchill 33 66 99 190 270 350
2-Red Cross story; Everett-a 16 32 48 92 126 160
3-Baseball Hall of Fame story; Chiang Kai-Shek-c/s 19 38 57 106 146 185
4,5: 4-Story of American flag "Old Glory". 5-Life story of Joe Louis 14 28 42 79 107 135
6-Baseball World Series story 17 34 51 98 134 170
7-10: 7-Buffalo Bill story. 10,11-Teddy Roosevelt 10 20 30 58 77 95
11-14,16,18-20: 11-Thomas Edison, Douglas MacArthur stories. 13-Harry Houdini story. 14-Charlie McCarthy story. 18-Story of America begins, ends #26. 19-Eisenhower-c/s 9 18 27 52 66 80
15-Flag-c; Bob Feller story 10 20 30 56 73 90
17-Brooklyn Dodgers story 11 22 33 63 84 105
21-30: 24-Marco Polo story. 28-Origin of Uncle Sam. 29-Beethoven story. 30-Cooper Brothers baseball story 8 16 24 46 58 70
31-Red Grange "Galloping Ghost" story 7 14 21 37 46 55
32-46: 33-Origin/1st app. Steve Saunders, Special Agent of the FBI, series begins. 35-Mark Twain story. 38-General Bradley-c/s. 39-FDR story. 44-Truman story. 46-George Gershwin story 7 14 21 35 43 50
47-Atomic bomb issue (c/story, 3/46) 10 20 30 56 73 90
48-54,56-65: 49-1st app. Secret Warriors. 53-Bobby Riggs story. 58-Jim Jeffries (boxer) story; Harry Houdini story. 59-Bob Hope story; pirates-c/s. 60-Speedway Speed Demon-c/story. 6 12 18 31 38 45
55-(12/46)-1st app. Sad Sack by Baker (1/2 pg.) 8 16 24 40 50 60
66-Will Rogers-c/story 7 14 21 35 43 50
67-1st oversized issue (12/47); Steve Saunders, Special Agent begins 8 16 24 40 50 60
68-70,74-77,79: 68-70,74-77-Features Steve Sanders True FBI advs. 68-Oversized; Admiral Byrd-c/s. 69-Jack Benny story. 74-Amos 'n' Andy story 6 12 18 28 34 40
71-Joe DiMaggio-c/story. 8 16 24 46 58 70
72-Jackie Robinson story; True FBI advs. 7 14 21 37 46 55
73-Walt Disney's life story 8 16 24 46 58 70
78-Stan Musial-c/story; True FBI advs. 7 14 21 37 46 55
80-84 (Scarce)-All distr. to subscribers through mail only; paper-c. 80-Rocket trip to the moon story. 81-Red Grange story 17 34 51 98 134 170
(Prices vary widely on issues 80-84)
NOTE: ***Bob Kane** a-7. **Palais** a-80. **Powell** c/a-80. #80-84 have soft covers and combined with Tex Granger, Jack Armstrong, and Calling All Kids. #68-78 featured true FBI adventures.*

TRUE COMICS AND ADVENTURE STORIES
Parents' Magazine Institute: 1965 (Giant) (25¢)
1,2: 1-Fighting Hero of Viet Nam; LBJ on-c 3 6 9 18 24 30

TRUE COMPLETE MYSTERY (Formerly Complete Mystery)
Marvel Comics (PrPI): No. 5, Apr, 1949 - No. 8, Oct, 1949
5 27 54 81 153 214 275
6-8: 6-8-Photo-c 21 42 63 118 164 210

TRUE CONFIDENCES
Fawcett Publications: 1949 (Fall) - No. 4, June, 1950 (All photo-c)
1-Has ad for Fawcett Love Adventures #1, but publ. as Love Memoirs #1 as Marvel published the title first; Swayze-a 18 36 54 101 138 175
2-4: 3-Swayze-a. 4-Powell-a 11 22 33 63 84 105

TRUE CRIME CASES (...From Official Police Files)
St. John Publishing Co.: 1944 (25¢, 100 pg. Giant)
nn-Matt Baker-c 43 86 129 258 384 510

TRUE CRIME COMICS (Also see Complete Book of...)
Magazine Village: No. 2, May, 1947; No. 3, July-Aug, 1948 - No. 6, June-July, 1949; V2#1, Aug-Sept, 1949 (52 pgs.)
2-Jack Cole-c/a; used in **SOTI**, pgs. 81,82 plus illo. "A sample of the injury-to-eye motif" & illo. "Dragging living people to death"; used in **POP**, pg. 105; "Murder, Morphine and Me" classic drug propaganda story used by N.Y. Legis. Comm. 144 288 432 900 1350 1800
3-Classic Cole-c/a; drug story with hypo, opium den & with drawing addict 107 214 321 669 1005 1340
4-Jack Cole-c/a; c-taken from a story panel in #3 (r-(2) **SOTI** & **POP** stories/#2?) 94 188 282 588 882 1175
5-Jack Cole-c, Marijuana racket story (Canadian ed. w/cover similar to #3 exists w/out drug story) 61 122 183 381 573 765
6-Not a reprint, original story (Canadian ed. reprints #4 w/different coloring on-c) 50 100 150 300 450 600
V2#1-Used in **SOTI**, pgs. 81,82 & illo. "Dragging living people to death"; Toth, Wood (3 pgs.), Roussos-a; Cole-r from #2 85 170 255 531 796 1060
NOTE: *V2#1 was reprinted in Canada as V2#9 (12/49); same-c & contents minus Wood-a.*

TRUE FAITH

True Love Pictorial #4 © STJ

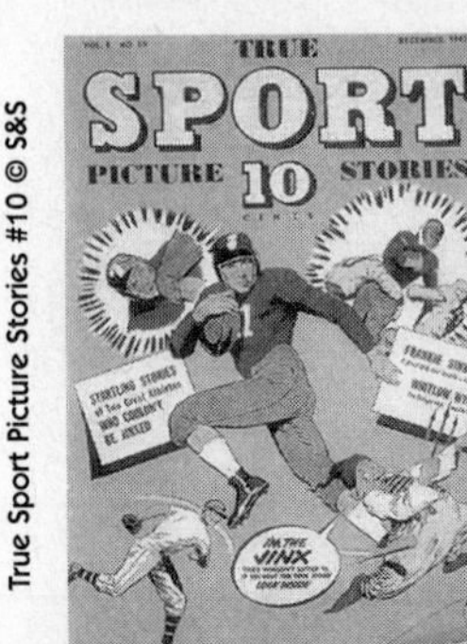

True Sport Picture Stories #10 © S&S

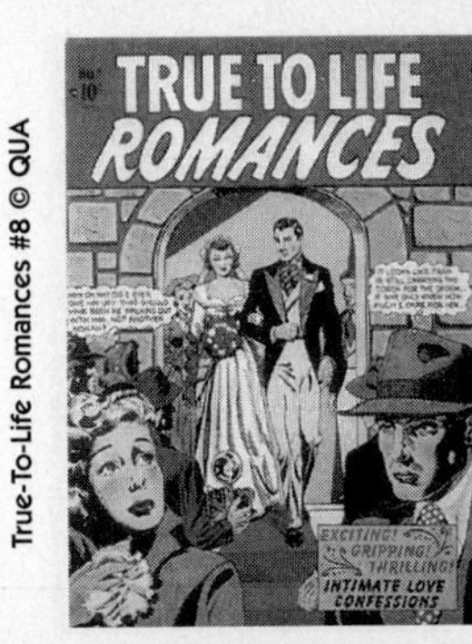

True-To-Life Romances #8 © QUA

Fleetway: 1990 ($9.95, graphic novel)

	GD 2.0	VG 4.0	FN 6.0	VF 8.0	VF/NM 9.0	NM- 9.2
nn-Garth Ennis scripts	2	4	6	12	16	20
Reprinted by DC/Vertigo ('97, $12.95)						13.00

TRUE GHOST STORIES (See Ripley's...)

TRUE LIFE ROMANCES (...Romance on cover)
Ajax/Farrell Publications: Dec, 1955 - No. 3, Aug, 1956

	GD 2.0	VG 4.0	FN 6.0	VF 8.0	VF/NM 9.0	NM- 9.2
1	10	20	30	58	77	100
2	8	16	24	40	50	60
3-Disbrow-a	8	16	24	46	58	70

TRUE LIFE SECRETS
Romantic Love Stories/Charlton: Mar-April, 1951 - No. 28, Sept, 1955; No. 29, Jan, 1956

	GD 2.0	VG 4.0	FN 6.0	VF 8.0	VF/NM 9.0	NM- 9.2
1-Photo-c begin, end #3?	14	28	42	81	111	140
2	8	16	24	46	58	70
3-19: 12-"I Was An Escort Girl" story	7	14	21	37	46	55
20-29: 25-Last precode(3/55)	6	12	18	31	38	45

TRUE LIFE TALES (Formerly Mitzi's Romances #8?)
Marvel Comics (CCC): No. 8, Oct, 1949 - No. 2, Jan, 1950 (52 pgs.)

	GD 2.0	VG 4.0	FN 6.0	VF 8.0	VF/NM 9.0	NM- 9.2
8(#1, 10/49), 2-Both have photo-c	10	20	30	58	77	95

TRUE LOVE
Eclipse Comics: Jan, 1986 - No. 2, Jan, 1986 ($2.00, Baxter paper)

	GD 2.0	VG 4.0	FN 6.0	VF 8.0	VF/NM 9.0	NM- 9.2
1,2-Love stories reprinted from pre-code Standard Comics; Toth-a(p) in both; 1-Dave Stevens-c. 2-Mayo-a						3.00

TRUE LOVE CONFESSIONS
Premier Magazines: May, 1954 - No. 11, Jan, 1956

	GD 2.0	VG 4.0	FN 6.0	VF 8.0	VF/NM 9.0	NM- 9.2
1-Marijuana story	11	22	33	66	88	110
2	7	14	21	37	46	55
3-11	6	12	18	31	38	45

TRUE LOVE PICTORIAL
St. John Publishing Co.: 1952 - No. 11, Aug, 1954

	GD 2.0	VG 4.0	FN 6.0	VF 8.0	VF/NM 9.0	NM- 9.2
1-Only photo-c	16	32	48	92	126	160
2-Baker-c/a	21	42	63	118	164	210
3-5(All 25¢, 100 pgs.): 4-Signed story by Estrada. 5-(4/53)-Formerly Teen-Age Temptations; Kubert-a in #3; Baker-a in #3-5	35	70	105	201	288	370
6,7: Baker-c/a; signed stories by Estrada	19	38	57	106	146	185
8,10,11-Baker-c/a	19	38	57	106	146	185
9-Baker-c	14	28	42	81	111	140

TRUE LOVE PROBLEMS AND ADVICE ILLUSTRATED (Becomes Romance Stories of True Love No. 45 on)
McCombs/Harvey Publ./Home Comics: June, 1949 - No. 6, Apr, 1950; No. 7, Jan, 1951 - No. 44, Mar, 1957

	GD 2.0	VG 4.0	FN 6.0	VF 8.0	VF/NM 9.0	NM- 9.2
V1#1	15	30	45	86	118	150
2	9	18	27	52	66	80
3-10: 7-9-Elias-c	7	14	21	37	46	55
11-13,15-23,25-31: 31-Last pre-code (1/55)	6	12	18	29	36	42
14,24-Rape scene	6	12	18	31	38	45
32-37,39-44	5	10	15	24	30	35
38-S&K-c	9	18	27	49	62	75

NOTE: ***Powell** a-1, 2, 7-14, 17-25, 28, 29, 33, 40, 41. #3 has True Love... on inside.*

TRUE MOVIE AND TELEVISION (Part teenage magazine)
Toby Press: Aug, 1950 - No. 3, Nov, 1950; No. 4, Mar, 1951 (52 pgs.)(1-3: 10¢)

	GD 2.0	VG 4.0	FN 6.0	VF 8.0	VF/NM 9.0	NM- 9.2
1-Elizabeth Taylor photo-c; Gene Autry, Shirley Temple, Li'l Abner app.	50	100	150	300	450	600
2-(9/50)-Janet Leigh/Liz Taylor/Ava Gardner & others photo-c; Frazetta John Wayne illo from J.Wayne Adv. Comics #2 (4/50)	39	78	117	233	329	425
3-June Allyson photo-c; Montgomery Cliff, Esther Williams, Andrews Sisters app; Li'l Abner featured; Sadie Hawkins' Day	31	62	93	175	248	320
4-Jane Powell photo-c (15¢)	19	38	57	106	146	185

NOTE: *16 pgs. in color, rest movie material in black & white.*

TRUE SECRETS (Formerly Our Love?)
Marvel (IPS)/Atlas Comics (MPI) #4 on: No. 3, Mar, 1950; No. 4, Feb, 1951 - No. 40, Sept, 1956

	GD 2.0	VG 4.0	FN 6.0	VF 8.0	VF/NM 9.0	NM- 9.2
3 (52 pgs.)(IPS one-shot)`	13	26	39	73	103	130
4,5,7-10	8	16	24	46	58	70
6,22-Everett-a	10	20	30	58	77	95
11-20	8	16	24	40	50	60
21,23-28: 24-Colletta-c. 28-Last pre-code (2/55)	7	14	21	35	43	50
29-40: 34,36-Colletta-a	6	12	18	31	38	45

TRUE SPORT PICTURE STORIES (Formerly Sport Comics)
Street & Smith Publications: V1#5, Feb, 1942 - V5#2, July-Aug, 1949

	GD 2.0	VG 4.0	FN 6.0	VF 8.0	VF/NM 9.0	NM- 9.2
V1#5-Joe DiMaggio-c/story	36	72	108	204	290	375
6-12 (1942-43): 12-Jack Dempsey story	21	42	63	118	164	210
V2#1-12 (1944-45): 7-Stan Musial-c/story; photo story of the New York Yankees	20	40	60	112	156	200
V3#1-12 (1946-47): 7-Joe DiMaggio, Stan Musial, Bob Feller & others back from the armed service story. 8-Billy Conn vs. Joe Louis-c/story	18	36	54	101	138	175
V4#1-12 (1948-49), V5#1,2	16	32	48	92	126	160

NOTE: ***Powell** a-V3#10, V4#1-4, 6-8, 10-12; V5#1, 2; c-V3#11, V4#3-7, 9-12. **Ravielli** c-V5#2.*

TRUE STORIES OF ROMANCE
Fawcett Publications: Jan, 1950 - No. 3, May, 1950 (All photo-c)

	GD 2.0	VG 4.0	FN 6.0	VF 8.0	VF/NM 9.0	NM- 9.2
1	13	26	39	76	103	130
2,3: 3-Marcus Swayze-a	9	18	27	52	66	80

TRUE STORY OF JESSE JAMES, THE (See Jesse James, Four Color 757)

TRUE SWEETHEART SECRETS
Fawcett Publications: 5/50; No. 2, 7/50; No. 3, 1951(nd); No. 4, 9/51 - No. 11, 1/53 (All photo-c)

	GD 2.0	VG 4.0	FN 6.0	VF 8.0	VF/NM 9.0	NM- 9.2
1-Photo-c; Debbie Reynolds?	15	30	45	84	115	145
2-Wood-a (11 pgs.)	18	36	54	104	142	180
3-11: 4,5-Powell-a. 8-Marcus Swayze-a. 11-Evans-a	10	20	30	60	80	100

TRUE TALES OF LOVE (Formerly Secret Story Romances)
Atlas Comics (TCI): No. 22, April, 1956 - No. 31, Sept, 1957

	GD 2.0	VG 4.0	FN 6.0	VF 8.0	VF/NM 9.0	NM- 9.2
22	9	18	27	49	62	75
23-24,26-31-Colletta-a in most:	6	12	18	31	38	45
25-Everett-a; Colletta-a	7	14	21	37	46	55

TRUE TALES OF ROMANCE
Fawcett Publications: No. 4, June, 1950

	GD 2.0	VG 4.0	FN 6.0	VF 8.0	VF/NM 9.0	NM- 9.2
4-Photo-c	9	18	27	52	66	80

TRUE 3-D
Harvey Publications: Dec, 1953 - No. 2, Feb, 1954 (25¢)(Both came with 2 pair of glasses)

	GD 2.0	VG 4.0	FN 6.0	VF 8.0	VF/NM 9.0	NM- 9.2
1-Nostrand, Powell-a	6	12	18	43	59	75
2-Powell-a	7	14	21	46	63	80

NOTE: *Many copies of #1 surfaced in 1984.*

TRUE-TO-LIFE ROMANCES (Formerly Guns Against Gangsters)
Star Publ.: #8, 11-12/49; #9, 1-2/50; #3, 4/50 - #5, 9/50; #6, 1/51 - #23, 10/54

	GD 2.0	VG 4.0	FN 6.0	VF 8.0	VF/NM 9.0	NM- 9.2
8(#1, 1949)	25	50	75	144	198	255
9(#2),4-10	18	36	54	101	138	175
3-Janet Leigh/Glenn Ford photo on-c plus true life story of each	20	40	60	112	156	200
11,22,23	15	30	45	86	118	150
12-14,17-21-Disbrow-a	17	34	51	98	134	170
15,16-Wood & Disbrow-a in each	20	40	60	112	156	200

NOTE: ***Kamen** a-13. **Kamen/Feldstein** a-14. All have **L.B. Cole** covers.*

TRUE WAR EXPERIENCES
Harvey Publications: Aug, 1952 - No. 4, Dec, 1952

	GD 2.0	VG 4.0	FN 6.0	VF 8.0	VF/NM 9.0	NM- 9.2
1	10	20	30	70	100	130
2-4	6	12	18	40	55	70

TRUE WAR ROMANCES (Becomes Exotic Romances #22 on)
Quality Comics Group: Sept, 1952 - No. 21, June, 1955

	GD 2.0	VG 4.0	FN 6.0	VF 8.0	VF/NM 9.0	NM- 9.2
1-Photo-c	14	28	42	81	111	140
2	8	16	24	46	58	70
3-10: 9-Whitney-a	8	16	24	40	50	60
11-21: 20-Last precode (4/55). 14-Whitney-a	7	14	21	35	43	50

TRUE WAR STORIES (See Ripley's...)

TRUE WESTERN (True Adventures #3)
Marvel Comics (MMC): Dec, 1949 - No. 2, March, 1950

	GD 2.0	VG 4.0	FN 6.0	VF 8.0	VF/NM 9.0	NM- 9.2
1-Photo-c; Billy The Kid story	17	34	51	98	134	170
2-Alan Ladd photo-c	21	42	63	118	164	210

TRUMP
HMH Publishing Co.: Jan, 1957 - No. 2, Mar, 1957 (50¢, magazine)

	GD 2.0	VG 4.0	FN 6.0	VF 8.0	VF/NM 9.0	NM- 9.2
1-Harvey Kurtzman satire	24	48	72	138	194	250
2-Harvey Kurtzman satire	20	40	60	112	156	200

NOTE: ***Davis, Elder, Heath, Jaffee** art-#1,2; **Wood** a-1. Article by Mel Brooks in #2.*

TRUMPETS WEST (See Luke Short, Four Color #875)

TRUTH ABOUT CRIME (See Fox Giants)

Truth Red, White & Black #1 © MAR

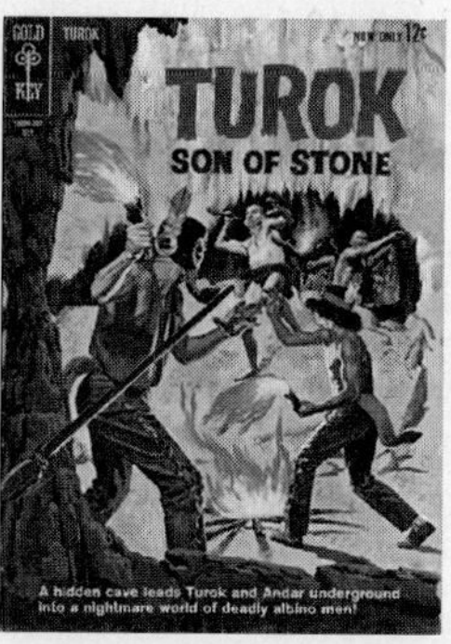

Turok, Son of Stone #34 © Acclaim

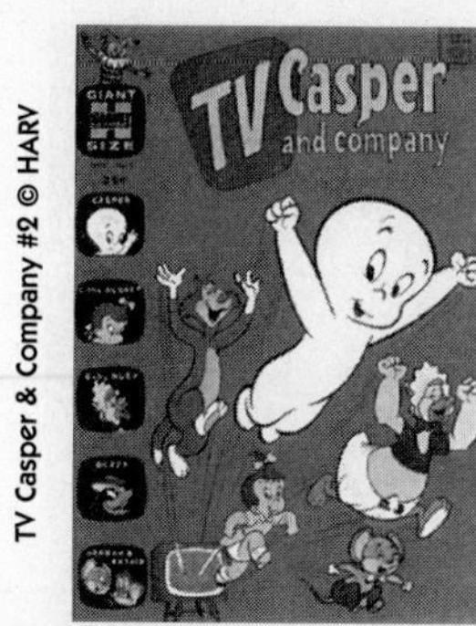

TV Casper & Company #2 © HARV

	GD	VG	FN	VF	VF/NM	NM-
	2.0	4.0	6.0	8.0	9.0	9.2

TRUTH ABOUT MOTHER GOOSE (See Mother Goose, Four Color #862)

TRUTH BEHIND THE TRIAL OF CARDINAL MINDSZENTY, THE (See Cardinal Mindszenty in the Promotional Comics section))

TRUTHFUL LOVE (Formerly Youthful Love)
Youthful Magazines: No. 2, July, 1950
2-Ingrid Bergman's true life story 10 20 30 60 80 100

TRUTH RED, WHITE & BLACK
Marvel Comics: Jan, 2003 - No. 6 ($3.50, limited series)
1-Kyle Baker-a/Robert Morales-s; the testing of Captain America's super-soldier serum 3.50
2-7: 3-Isaiah Bradley 1st dons the Captain America costume 3.50

TRY-OUT WINNER BOOK
Marvel Comics: Mar, 1988
1-Spider-Man vs. Doc Octopus 5.00

TSR WORLD (...Annual on cover only)
DC Comics: 1990 ($3.95, 84 pgs.)
1-Advanced D&D, ForgottenRealms, Dragonlance & 1st app. Spelljammer 4.00

TSUNAMI GIRL
Image Comics: 1999 - No. 3, 1999 ($2.95)
1-3-Sorayama-c/Paniccia-s/a 3.00

TUBBY (See Marge's...)

TUFF GHOSTS STARRING SPOOKY
Harvey Publications: July, 1962 - No. 39, Nov, 1970; No. 40, Sept, 1971 - No. 43, Oct, 1972
1-12¢ issues begin 13 26 39 94 137 180
2-5 7 14 21 51 71 90
6-10 5 10 15 36 48 60
11-20 4 8 12 29 40 50
21-30: 29-Hot Stuff/Spooky team-up story 3 6 9 18 24 30
31-39,43 2 4 6 14 18 22
40-42: 52 pg. Giants 3 6 9 16 20 25

TUFFY
Standard Comics: No. 5, July, 1949 - No. 9, Oct, 1950
5-All by Sid Hoff 6 12 18 31 38 45
6-9 5 10 15 22 26 30

TUFFY TURTLE
I. W. Enterprises: No date
1-Reprint 2 4 6 9 11 14

TUG & BUSTER
Art & Soul Comics: Nov, 1995 - No. 7, Feb, 1998 ($2.95, B&W, bi-monthly)
1-7: Marc Hempel-c/a/scripts 3.00
1-(Image Comics, 8/98, $2.95, B&W) 3.00

TUROK
Acclaim Comics: Mar, 1998 - No. 4, Jun, 1998 ($2.50)
1-4-Nicieza-s/Kayanan-a 2.50
..., Child of Blood 1 (1/98, $3.95) Nicieza-s/Kayanan-a 4.00
... Evolution 1 (8/02, $2.50) Nicieza-s/Kayanan-a 2.50
..., Redpath 1 (10/97, $3.95) Nicieza-s/Kayanan-a 4.00
.../ Shadowman 1 (2/99, $3.95) Priest-s/Broome & Jimenez-a 4.00
...: Spring Break in the Lost Land 1 (7/97, $3.95) Nicieza-s/Kayanan-a 4.00
...: Tales of the Lost Land 1 (4/98, $3.95) 4.00
...: The Empty Souls 1 (4/97, $3.95) Nicieza-s/Kayanan-a; variant-c 4.00

TUROK, DINOSAUR HUNTER (See Magnus Robot Fighter #12 & Archer & Armstrong #2)
Valiant/Acclaim Comics: June, 1993 - No. 47, Aug, 1996 ($2.50)
1-($3.50)-Chromium & foil-c 3.50
1-Gold foil-c variant 5.00
0, 2-47: 4-Andar app. 5-Death of Andar. 7-9-Truman/Glanzman-a. 11-Bound-in trading card. 16-Chaos Effect 2.50
Yearbook 1 (1994, $3.95, 52 pgs.) 4.00

TUROK, SON OF STONE (See Dan Curtis, Golden Comics Digest #31 & March of Comics #378, 399, 408)
Dell Publ. Co. #1-29(9/62)/Gold Key #30(12/62)-85(7/73)/Gold Key or Whitman #86(9/73)-125(1/80)/Whitman #126(3/81) on: No. 596, 12/54 - No. 29, 9/62; No. 30, 12/62 - No. 91, 7/74; No. 92, 9/74 - No. 125, 1/80; No. 126, 3/81 - No. 130, 4/82
Four Color 596 (12/54)(#1)-1st app./origin Turok & Andar; dinosaur-c. Created by Matthew H. Murphy; written by Alberto Giolitti 55 110 165 425 650 875
Four Color 656 (10/55)(#2)-1st mention of Lanok 33 66 99 248 369 490
3(3-5/56)-5: 3-Cave men 22 44 66 160 235 310
6-10: 8-Dinosaur of the deep; Turok enters Lost Valley; series begins. 9-Paul S. Newman-s (most issues thru end) 15 30 45 109 160 210
11-20: 17-Prehistoric Pygmies 11 22 33 75 110 145
21-29 8 16 24 55 78 100
30-1st Gold Key. 30-33-Painted back-c. 8 16 24 58 82 105
31-Drug use story 8 16 24 55 78 100
32-40 6 12 18 40 55 70
41-50 5 10 15 36 48 60
51-57,59,60 4 8 12 29 40 50
58-Flying Saucer c/story 5 10 15 33 44 55
61-70: 62-12¢ & 15¢ covers. 63,68-Line drawn-c 4 8 12 24 32 40
71-84: 84-Origin & 1st app. Hutec 3 6 9 18 24 30
85-99: 93-r-c/#19 w/changes. 94-r-c/#28 w/changes. 97-r-c/#31 w/changes. 98-r/#58 w/o spaceship & spacemen on-c. 99-r-c/#52 w/changes. 3 6 9 16 20 24
100 3 6 9 19 25 32
101-129: 114,115-(52 pgs.). 129(2/82) 3 6 9 18 23 28
130(4/82)-Last issue 4 8 12 24 32 40
Giant 1(30031-611) (11/66)-Slick-c; r/#10-12 & 16 plus cover to #11 10 20 30 73 107 140
Giant 1-Same as above but with paper-c 12 24 36 82 121 160
NOTE: *Most painted-c; line-drawn #63 & 130.* ***Alberto Gioletti*** *a-24-27, 30-119, 123; painted-c No. 30-129.* ***Sparling*** *a-117, 120-130. Reprints-#36, 54, 57, 75, 112, 114(1/3), 115(1/3), 118, 121, 125, 127(1/3), 128, 129(1/3), 130(1/3), Giant 1. Cover r-93, 94, 97-99, 126(all different from original covers.*

TUROK THE HUNTED
Valiant/Acclaim Comics: Mar, 1995 - No. 2, Apr, 1995 ($2.50, limited series)
1,2-Mike Deodato-a(p); price omitted on #1 2.50

TUROK THE HUNTED
Acclaim Comics (Valiant): Feb, 1996 - No. 2, Mar, 1996 ($2.50, limited series)
1,2-Mike Grell story 2.50

TUROK, TIMEWALKER
Acclaim Comics (Valiant): Aug, 1997 - No. 2, Sept, 1997 ($2.50, limited series)
1,2-Nicieza story 2.50

TUROK 2 (Magazine)
Acclaim Comics: Oct, 1998 ($4.99, magazine size)
...Seeds of Evil-Nicieza-s/Broome & Benjamin-a; origin back-up story 5.00
#2 Adon's Curse -Mack painted-c/Broome & Benjamin-a; origin pt. 2 5.00

TUROK 3: SHADOW OF OBLIVION
Acclaim Comics: Sept, 2000 ($4.95, one-shot)
1-Includes pin-up gallery 5.00

TURTLE SOUP
Mirage Studios: Sept, 1987 ($2.00, 76 pgs., B&W, one-shot)
1-Featuring Teenage Mutant Ninja Turtles 5.00

TURTLE SOUP
Mirage Studios: Nov, 1991 - No. 4, 1992 ($2.50, limited series, coated paper)
1-4: Features the Teenage Mutant Ninja Turtles 2.50

TV CASPER & COMPANY
Harvey Publications: Aug, 1963 - No. 46, April, 1974 (25¢ Giants)
1- 68 pg. Giants begin; Casper, Little Audrey, Baby Huey, Herman & Catnip, Buzzy the Crow begin 13 26 39 94 137 180
2-5 7 14 21 50 68 85
6-10 5 10 15 36 48 60
11-20 4 8 12 27 36 45
21-31: 31-Last 68 pg. issue 3 6 9 18 24 30
32-46: All 52 pgs. 3 6 9 16 20 25
NOTE: *Many issues contain reprints.*

TV FUNDAY FUNNIES (See Famous TV...)

TV FUNNIES (See New Funnies)

TV FUNTIME (See Little Audrey)

TV LAUGHOUT (See Archie's...)

TV SCREEN CARTOONS (Formerly Real Screen)
National Periodical Publ.: No. 129, July-Aug, 1959 - No. 138, Jan-Feb, 1961
129-138 (Scarce) 8 16 24 53 74 95

TV STARS (TV) (Newsstand sales only)
Marvel Comics Group: Aug, 1978 - No. 4, Feb, 1979 (Hanna-Barbera)
1-Great Grape Ape app. 3 6 9 19 25 32

Tweety and Sylvester Four Color #406 © WB

21 Down #1 © WSP

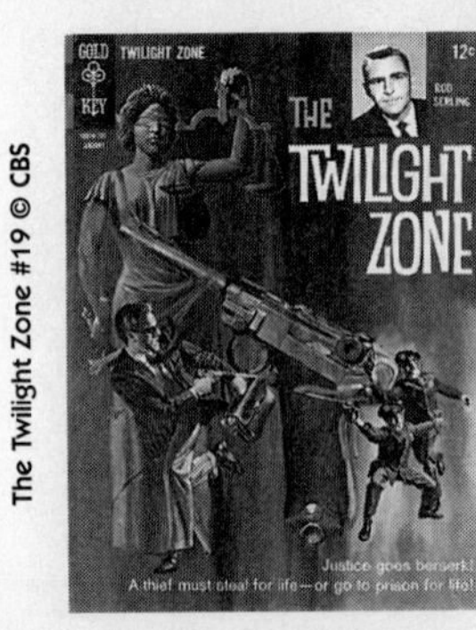

The Twilight Zone #19 © CBS

	GD 2.0	VG 4.0	FN 6.0	VF 8.0	VF/NM 9.0	NM- 9.2

2,4: 4-Top Cat app. 3 6 9 16 20 25
3-Toth-c/a; Dave Stevens inks 3 6 9 18 24 30

TV TEENS (Formerly Ozzie & Babs; Rock and Rollo #14 on)
Charlton Comics: V1#14, Feb, 1954 - V2#13, July, 1956

V1#14 (#1)-Ozzie & Babs 9 18 27 52 66 80
15 (#2) 6 12 18 28 34 40
V2#3(6/54) - 6-Don Winslow 6 12 18 29 36 42
7-13-Mopsy. 8(7/55) 6 12 18 28 34 40

TWEETY AND SYLVESTER (1st Series) (TV) (Also see Looney Tunes and Merrie Melodies)
Dell Publishing Co.: No. 406, June, 1952 - No. 37, June-Aug, 1962

Four Color 406 (#1) 10 20 30 73 107 140
Four Color 489,524 6 12 18 40 55 70
4 (3-5/54) - 20 4 8 12 29 40 50
21-37 4 8 12 24 32 40
(See March of Comics #421, 433, 445, 457, 469, 481)

TWEETY AND SYLVESTER (2nd Series)(See Kite Fun Book)
Gold Key No. 1-102/Whitman No. 103 on: Nov, 1963; No. 2, Nov, 1965 - No. 121, June, 1984

1 4 8 12 29 40 50
2-10 3 6 9 19 25 32
11-30 2 4 6 12 16 20
31-50 2 4 6 9 11 14
51-70 1 2 3 5 7 9
71-102 1 2 3 4 5 7
103,104 (Whitman) 1 2 3 5 7 9
105(9/80),106(10/80),107(12/80) 3-pack only 2 4 6 12 16 20
108-116: 113(2/82),114(2-3/82),115(3/82),116(4/82) 1 3 4 6 8 10
117-121 (All # 90094 on-c; nd, nd code): 117(6/83). 118(7/83). 119(2/84)-r(1/3). 120(5/84).
121(6/84) 2 4 6 10 13 16
Mini Comic No. 1(1976, 3-1/4x6-1/2") 1 3 4 6 8 10

12 O'CLOCK HIGH (TV)
Dell Publishing Co.: Jan-Mar, 1965 - No. 2, Apr-June, 1965 (Photo-c)

1 7 14 21 46 63 80
2 5 10 15 36 48 60

2099 A.D.
Marvel Comics: May, 1995 ($3.95, one-shot)

1-Acetate-c by Quesada & Palmiotti 4.00

2099 APOCALYPSE
Marvel Comics: Dec, 1995 ($4.95, one-shot)

1-Chromium wraparound-c; Ellis script 5.00

2099 GENESIS
Marvel Comics: Jan, 1996 ($4.95, one-shot)

1-Chromium wraparound-c; Ellis script 5.00

2099 MANIFEST DESTINY
Marvel Comics: Mar, 1998 ($5.99, one-shot)

1-Origin of Fantastic Four 2099; intro Moon Knight 2099 6.00

2099 UNLIMITED
Marvel Comics: Sept, 1993 - No. 10, 1996 ($3.95, 68 pgs.)

1-10: 1-1st app. Hulk 2099 & begins. 1-3-Spider-Man 2099 app. 9-Joe Kubert-c; Len Wein & Nancy Collins scripts 4.00

2099 WORLD OF DOOM SPECIAL
Marvel Comics: May, 1995 ($2.25, one-shot)

1-Doom's "Contract w/America" 2.25

2099 WORLD OF TOMORROW
Marvel Comics: Sept, 1996 - No. 8, Apr, 1997 ($2.50) (Replaces 2099 titles)

1-8: 1-Wraparound-c. 2-w/bound-in card. 4,5-Phalanx 2.50

21
Image Comics (Top Cow Productions): Feb, 1996 - No. 3, Apr, 1996 ($2.50)

1-3: Len Wein scripts 2.50
1-Variant-c 2.50

21 DOWN
DC Comics (WildStorm): Nov, 2002 - No. 12, Nov, 2003 ($2.95)

1-12: 1-Palmiotti & Gray-s/Saiz-a/Jusko-c 3.00
...: The Conduit (2003, $19.95, TPB) r/#1-7; intro. by Garth Ennis 20.00

2020 VISIONS
DC Comics (Vertigo): May, 1997 - No. 12, Apr, 1998 ($2.25, limited series)

1-12-Delano-s: 1-3-Quitely-a. 4-"la tormenta"-Pleece-a 2.25

20,000 LEAGUES UNDER THE SEA (Movie)(See King Classics, Movie Comics & Power Record Comics)
Dell Publishing Co.: No. 614, Feb, 1955 (Disney)

Four Color 614-Movie, painted-c 10 20 30 70 100 130

22 BRIDES (See Ash/)
Event Comics: Mar, 1996 - No. 4, Jan, 1997 ($2.95)

1-4: Fabian Nicieza scripts 3.00
2,3-Variant-c 3.00

TWICE TOLD TALES (See Movie Classics)

TWILIGHT
DC Comics: 1990 - No. 3, 1991 ($4.95, 52 pgs, lim. series, squarebound, mature)

1-3: Tommy Tomorrow app; Chaykin scripts, Garcia-Lopez-c/a 5.00

TWILIGHT AVENGER, THE
Elite Comics: July, 1986 - No. 4, 1987 ($1.75, 28 pgs, limited series)

1-4 2.25

TWILIGHT MAN
First Publishing: June, 1989 - No. 4, Sept, 1989 ($2.75, limited series)

1-4 2.75

TWILIGHT ZONE, THE (TV) (See Dan Curtis & Stories From...)
Dell Publishing Co./Gold Key/Whitman No. 92: No. 1173, 3-5/61 - No. 91, 4/79; No. 92, 5/82

Four Color 1173 (#1)-Crandall-c/a 23 46 69 167 244 320
Four Color 1288-Crandall/Evans-c/a 13 26 39 90 133 175
01-860-207 (5-7/62-Dell, 15¢) 9 18 27 65 93 120
12-860-210 on-c; 01-860-210 on inside(8-10/62-Dell)-Evans-c/a (3 stories)
9 18 27 65 93 120
1(11/62-Gold Key)-Crandall/Frazetta-a (10 & 11 pgs.); Evans-a
14 28 42 97 141 185
2 8 16 24 58 82 105
3-11: 3(11 pgs.),4(10 pgs.),9-Toth-a 6 12 18 43 59 75
12-15: 12-Williamson-a. 13,15-Crandall-a. 14-Orlando/Crandall/Torres-a
5 10 15 36 48 60
16-20 4 8 12 24 32 40
21-25: 21-Crandall-a(r). 25-Evans/Crandall-a(r); Toth-r/#4; last 12¢ issue
3 6 9 19 25 32
26,27: 26-Flying Saucer-c/story; Crandall, Evans-a(r). 27-Evans-r(2)
3 6 9 19 25 32
28-32: 32-Evans-a(r) 3 6 9 18 23 28
33-51: 43-Celardo-a. 51-Williamson-a 2 4 6 11 14 18
52-70 2 4 6 9 11 14
71-82,85-91: 71-Reprint 1 3 4 6 8 10
83-(52 pgs.) 2 4 6 10 13 16
84-(52 pgs.) Frank Miller's 1st comic book work 3 6 9 16 20 24
92-(Whitman, 5/82) Last issue; r/#1. 2 4 6 8 10 12
Mini Comic #1(1976, 3-1/4x6-1/2") 2 4 6 8 10 12

NOTE: *Bolle a-13(w/**McWilliams**), 50, 55, 57, 59, 77, 78, 80, 83, 84. **McWilliams** a-59, 78, 80, 82, 84. **Miller** a-84, 85. **Orlando** a-15, 19, 20, 22, 23. **Sekowsky** a-3. **Simonson** a-50, 54, 55, 83r. **Weiss** a-39, 79r(#39). (See Mystery Comics Digest 3, 6, 9, 12, 15, 18, 21, 24). Reprints-26(1/3), 71, 73, 79, 83, 84, 86, 92. Painted c-1-91.*

TWILIGHT ZONE, THE (TV)
Now Comics: Nov, 1990 ($2.95); Oct, 1991; V2#1, Nov, 1991 - No. 11, Oct, 1992 ($1.95); V3#1, 1993 - No. 4, 1993 ($2.50)

1-(11/90, $2.95, 52 pgs.)-Direct sale edition; Neal Adams-a, Sienkiewicz-c; Harlan Ellison scripts 3.00
1-(11/90, $1.75)-Newsstand ed. w/N. Adams-c 2.50
1-Prestige Format (10/91, $4.95)-Reprints above with extra Harlan Ellison short story 5.00
1-Collector's Edition (10/91, $2.50)-Non-code approved and polybagged; reprints 11/90 issue; gold logo, 1-Reprint ($2.50)-r/direct sale 11/90 version, 1-Reprint ($2.50)-r/newsstand 11/90 version each... 2.50
V2#1-Direct sale & newsstand ed. w/different-c 2.50
V2#2-8,10-11 2.50
V2#9-($2.95)-3-D Special; polybagged w/glasses & hologram on-c 3.00
V2#9-($4.95)-Prestige Edition; contains 2 extra stories & a different hologram on-c; polybagged w/glasses 5.00
V3#1-4, Anniversary Special 1 (1992, $2.50) 2.50
Annual 1 (4/93, $2.50)-No ads 2.50
...Science Fiction Special (3/93, $3.50) 3.50

TWINKLE COMICS
Spotlight Publishers: May, 1945

1 25 50 75 144 198 255

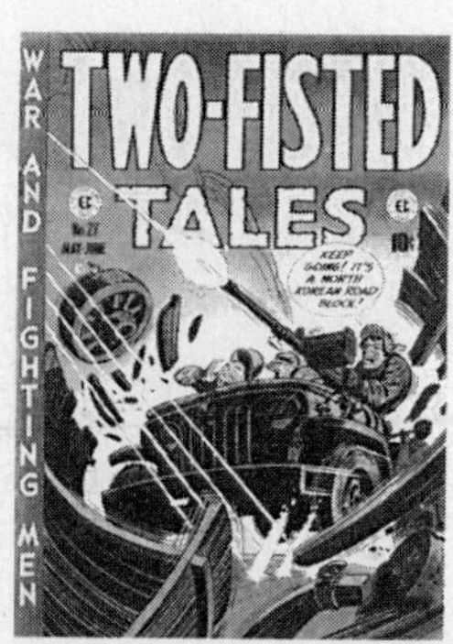

Two-Fisted Tales #27 © WMG

Two-Gun Kid #30 © MAR

2001, A Space Odyssey #9 © MAR

	GD 2.0	VG 4.0	FN 6.0	VF 8.0	VF/NM 9.0	NM- 9.2

TWIST, THE
Dell Publishing Co.: July-Sept, 1962

01-864-209-Painted-c	4	8	12	28	38	48

TWISTED TALES (See Eclipse Graphic Album Series #15)
Pacific Comics/Independent Comics Group (Eclipse) #9,10: 11/82 - No. 8, 5/84; No. 9, 11/84; No. 10, 12/84 (Baxter paper)

1-9: 1-B. Jones/Corben-c; Alcala-a; nudity/violence in al. 2-Wrightson-c; Ploog-a						4.00
10-Wrightson painted art; Morrow-a						6.00

NOTE: **Bolton** *painted c-4, 6, 7; a-7.* **Conrad** *a-1, 3, 5; c-1i, 3, 5.* **Guice** *a-8.* **Wildey** *a-3.*

TWO BIT THE WACKY WOODPECKER (See Wacky...)
Toby Press: 1951 - No. 3, May, 1953

1	10	20	30	56	73	90
2,3	6	12	18	31	38	45

TWO FACES OF TOMORROW, THE
Dark Horse: Aug, 1997 - No. 13, Aug, 1998 ($2.95/$3.95, B&W, lim. series)

1-13: 1-Manga						4.00

TWO-FISTED TALES (Formerly Haunt of Fear #15-17)
E. C. Comics: No. 18, Nov-Dec, 1950 - No. 41, Feb-Mar, 1955

18(#1)-Kurtzman-c	86	172	258	645	923	1200
19-Kurtzman-c	66	132	198	495	710	925
20-Kurtzman-c	42	84	126	315	450	585
21,22-Kurtzman-c	33	66	99	248	352	455
23-25-Kurtzman-c	26	52	78	195	278	360
26-35: 33- "Atom Bomb" by Wood	19	38	57	143	202	260
36-41	15	30	45	113	162	210
Two-Fisted Annual (1952, 25¢, 132 pgs.)	86	172	258	645	860	1075
Two-Fisted Annual (1953, 25¢, 132 pgs.)	68	136	204	510	680	850

NOTE: **Berg** *a-29.* **Colan** *a-39p.* **Craig** *a-18, 19, 32.* **Crandall** *a-35, 36.* **Davis** *a-20-36, 40; c-30, 34, 35, 41, Annual 2.* **Evans** *a-34, 40, 41; c-40.* **Feldstein** *a-18.* **Krigstein** *a-41.* **Kubert** *a-32, 33.* **Kurtzman** *a-18-25; c-18-29, 31, Annual 1.* **Severin** *a-26, 28, 29, 31, 34-41 (No. 37-39 are all-***Severin** *issues); c-36-39.* **Severin/Elder** *a-19-29, 31, 33, 36.* **Wood** *a-18-28, 30-35, 41; c-32, 33. Special issues: #26 (ChanJin Reservoir), 31 (Civil War), 35 (Civil War). Canadian reprints known; see Table of Contents. #25-Davis biog. #27-Wood biog. #28-Kurtzman biog.*

TWO-FISTED TALES
Russ Cochran/Gemstone Publishing: Oct, 1992 - No. 24, May, 1998 ($1.50/$2.00/$2.50)

1-24: 1-4r/Two-Fisted Tales #18-21 w/original-c						2.50

TWO-GUN KID (Also see All Western Winners, Best Western, Black Rider, Blaze Carson, Kid Colt, Western Winners, Wild West, & Wild Western)
Marvel/Atlas (MCI No. 1-10/HPC No. 11-59/Marvel No. 60 on): 3/48(No mo.) - No. 10, 11/49; No. 11, 12/53 - No. 59, 4/61; No. 60, 11/62 - No. 92, 3/68; No. 93, 7/70 - No. 136, 4/77

1-Two-Gun Kid & his horse Cyclone begin; The Sheriff begins	108	216	324	675	1013	1350
2	44	88	132	264	395	525
3,4: 3-Annie Oakley app.	37	74	111	212	301	390
5-Pre-Black Rider app. (Wint. 48/49); Anti-Wertham editorial (1st?)	40	80	120	240	340	440
6-10(11/49): 8-Blaze Carson app. 9-Black Rider app.	29	58	87	164	232	300
11(12/53)-Black Rider app.; 1st to have Atlas globe on-c; explains how Kid Colt became an outlaw	23	46	69	129	180	230
12-Black Rider app.	22	44	66	124	172	220
13-20: 14-Opium story	16	32	48	92	126	160
21-24,26-29	15	30	45	86	118	150
25,30: 25-Williamson-a (5 pgs.). 30-Williamson/Torres-a (4 pgs.)	16	32	48	92	126	160
31-33,35,37-40	9	18	27	60	85	110
34-Crandall-a	9	18	27	63	89	115
36,41,42,48-Origin in all	9	18	27	63	89	115
43,44,47	7	14	21	50	68	85
45,46-Davis-a	8	16	24	53	74	95
49,50,52,53-Severin-a(2/3) in each	7	14	21	46	63	80
51-Williamson-a (5 pgs.)	8	16	24	53	74	95
54,55,57,59-Severin-a(3) in each. 59-Kirby-a; last 10¢ issue (4/61)	6	12	18	43	59	75
56	6	12	18	38	52	65
58,60-New origin. 58-Kirby/Ayers-c/a "The Monster of Hidden Valley" cover/story (Kirby monster-c)	6	12	18	43	59	75
60-Edition w/handwritten issue number on cover	8	16	24	55	78	100
61,62-Kirby-a	6	12	18	40	55	70
63-74: 64-Intro. Boom-Boom	4	8	12	27	36	45
75-77-Kirby-a	5	10	15	33	44	55
78-89	3	6	9	19	25	32
90,95-Kirby-a	4	8	12	24	32	40
91,92: 92-Last new story; last 12¢ issue	3	6	9	18	24	30
93,94,96-99	2	4	6	14	18	22
100-Last 15¢-c	3	6	9	16	20	24
101-Origin retold/#58; Kirby-a	3	6	9	16	20	24
102-120-reprints	2	4	6	8	10	12
121-136-reprints. 129-131-(Regular 25¢ editions)	2	4	6	8	10	12
129-131-(30¢-c variants, limited distribution)(4-8/76)	2	4	6	11	14	18

NOTE: **Ayers** *a-26, 27.* **Davis** *c-45-47.* **Drucker** *a-23.* **Everett** *a-82, 91.* **Fuje** *a-13.* **Heath** *a-3(2), 4(3), 5(2), 7; c-13, 21, 23, 53.* **Keller** *a-16, 19, 28.* **Kirby** *a-54, 55, 57-62, 75-77, 90, 95, 101, 119, 120, 129; c-10, 52, 54-65, 67-72, 74-76, 116.* **Maneely** *a-20; c-11, 12, 16, 19, 20, 25-28, 30, 35, 49.* **Powell** *a-38, 102, 104.* **Severin** *a-9, 29, 51, 55, 57, 99r(3); c-9, 51.* **Shores** *c-1-8, 11.* **Trimpe** *c-99.* **Tuska** *a-11, 12.* **Whitney** *a-87, 89-91, 98-113, 124, 129; c-87, 89, 91, 113.* **Wildey** *a-21.* **Williamson** *a-110r. Kid Colt in #13, 14, 16-21.*

TWO GUN KID: SUNSET RIDERS
Marvel Comics: Nov, 1995 - No. 2, Dec, 1995 ($6.95, squarebound, lim. series)

1,2: Fabian Nicieza scripts in all. 1-painted-c.						7.00

TWO GUN WESTERN (1st Series) (Formerly Casey Crime Photographer #1-4? or My Love #1-4?)
Marvel/Atlas Comics (MPC): No. 5, Nov, 1950 - No. 14, June, 1952

5-The Apache Kid (Intro & origin) & his horse Nightwind begin by Buscema	27	54	81	153	214	275
6-10: 8-Kid Colt, The Texas Kid & his horse Thunder begin?	20	40	60	112	156	200
11-14: 13-Black Rider app.	14	28	42	81	111	140

NOTE: **Maneely** *a-6, 7, 9; c-6, 11-13.* **Morrow** *a-9.* **Romita** *a-8.* **Wildey** *a-8.*

2-GUN WESTERN (2nd Series) (Formerly Billy Buckskin #1-3; Two-Gun Western #5 on)
Atlas Comics (MgPC): No. 4, May, 1956

4-Colan, Ditko, Severin, Sinnott-a; Maneely-c	17	34	51	95	130	165

TWO-GUN WESTERN (Formerly 2-Gun Western)
Atlas Comics (MgPC): No. 5, July, 1956 - No. 12, Sept, 1957

5-Return of the Gun-Hawk-c/story; Black Rider app.	16	32	48	92	126	160
6,7	12	24	36	69	92	115
8,10,12-Crandall-a	13	26	39	74	100	125
9,11-Williamson-a in both (5 pgs. each)	14	28	42	79	107	135

NOTE: **Ayers** *a-9.* **Colan** *a-5.* **Everett** *c-12.* **Forgione** *a-5, 6.* **Kirby** *a-12.* **Maneely** *a-6, 8, 12; c-5, 6, 8, 11.* **Morrow** *a-9, 10.* **Powell** *a-7, 11.* **Severin** *c-10.* **Sinnott** *a-5.* **Wildey** *a-9.*

TWO MINUTE WARNING
Ultimate Sports Ent.: 2000 - No. 2 ($3.95, cardstock covers)

1,2-NFL players & Teddy Roosevelt battle evil						4.00

TWO MOUSEKETEERS, THE (See 4-Color #475, 603, 642 under M.G.M.'s...;

TWO ON A GUILLOTINE (See Movie Classics)

TWO-STEP
DC Comics (Cliffhanger): Dec, 2003 - No. 3 ($2.95, limited series)

1-Warren Ellis-s/Amanda Conner-a						3.00

2000 A.D. MONTHLY/PRESENTS (Showcase #25 on)
Eagle Comics/Quality Comics No. 5 on: 4/85 - #6, 9/85; 4/86 - #54, 1991 ($1.25-$1.50, Mando paper)

1-6,1-25:1-4 r/British series featuring Judge Dredd; Alan Moore scripts begin. 1-25 ($1.25)-Reprints from British 2000 AD						2.25
26,27/28, 29/30, 31-54: 27/28, 29/30,31-Guice-c						2.25

2001, A SPACE ODYSSEY (Movie)
Marvel Comics Group: Dec, 1976 - No. 10, Sept, 1977 (30¢)

1-Adaptation of film; Kirby-c/a in all	2	4	6	9	11	14
2-7,9,10	1	2	3	4	5	7
7,9,10-(35¢-c variants, limited distribution)(6-9/77)	1	3	4	6	8	10
8-Origin/1st app. Machine Man (called Mr. Machine)	2	4	6	10	13	16
8-(35¢-c variant, limited distribution)(6,8/77)	2	4	6	12	16	20
...Treasury 1 ('76, 84 pgs.)-All new Kirby-a	3	6	9	16	20	24

2001 NIGHTS
Viz Premiere Comics: 1990 - No. 10, 1991 ($3.75, B&W, lim. series, mature readers, 84 pgs.)

1-10: Japanese sci-fi. 1-Wraparound-c						4.25

2010 (Movie)
Marvel Comics Group: Apr, 1985 - No. 2, May, 1985

1,2-r/Marvel Super Special movie adaptation.						2.25

TYPHOID (Also see Daredevil)
Marvel Comics: Nov, 1995 - No. 4, Feb, 1996 ($3.95, squarebound, lim. series)

1-4: Van Fleet-c/a						4.00

Ultimate Marvel Team-Up #14 © MAR

Ultimate Spider-Man #25 © MAR

Ultimate X-Men #34 © MAR

GD VG FN VF VF/NM NM-
2.0 4.0 6.0 8.0 9.0 9.2

UFO & ALIEN COMIX
Warren Publishing Co.: Jan, 1978 (B&W magazine, 84 pgs., one-shot)
nn-Toth-a, J. Severin-a(r); Pie-s 2 4 6 10 12 15

UFO & OUTER SPACE (Formerly UFO Flying Saucers)
Gold Key: No. 14, June, 1978 - No. 25, Feb, 1980 (All painted covers)
14-Reprints UFO Flying Saucers #3 1 3 4 6 8 10
15,16-Reprints 1 3 4 6 8 10
17-25: 17-20-New material. 23-McWilliams-a. 24-(3 pg.-r). 25-Reprints UFO Flying Saucers #2 w/cover 1 3 4 6 8 10

UFO ENCOUNTERS
Western Publishing Co.: May, 1978 ($1.95, 228 pgs.)
11192-Reprints UFO Flying Saucers 4 8 12 22 30 38
11404-Vol.1 (128 pgs.)-See UFO Mysteries for Vol.2 3 6 9 19 25 32

UFO FLYING SAUCERS (UFO & Outer Space #14 on)
Gold Key: Oct, 1968 - No. 13, Jan, 1977 (No. 2 on, 36 pgs.)
1(30035-810) (68 pgs.) 4 8 12 29 40 50
2(11/70), 3(11/72), 4(11/74) 2 4 6 12 16 20
5(2/75)-13: Bolle-a #4 on 2 4 6 9 11 14

UFO MYSTERIES
Western Publishing Co.: 1978 ($1.00, reprints, 96 pgs.)
11400-(Vol.2)-Cont'd from UFO Encounters, pgs. 129-224 3 6 9 19 25 32

ULTIMAN GIANT ANNUAL (See Big Bang Comics)
Image Comics: Nov, 2001 ($4.95, B&W, one-shot)
1-Homage to DC 1960's annuals 5.00

ULTIMATE... (Collects 4-issue alternate titles from X-Men Age of Apocalypse crossovers)
Marvel Comics: May, 1995 ($8.95, trade paperbacks, gold foil covers)
Amazing X-Men, Astonishing X-Men, Factor-X, Gambit & the X-Ternals, Generation Next, X-Calibre, X-Man 9.00
Weapon X 10.00

ULTIMATE ADVENTURES
Marvel Comics: Nov, 2002 - No. 6, Dec, 2003 ($2.25)
1-6: 1-Intro. Hawk-Owl; Zimmerman-s/Fegredo-a. 3-Ultimates app. 2.25

ULTIMATE DAREDEVIL AND ELEKTRA
Marvel Comics: Jan, 2003 - No. 4, Mar, 2003 ($2.25, limited series)
1-4-Rucka-s/Larroca-c/a; 1st meeting of Elektra and Matt Murdock 2.25
... Vol.1 TPB (2003, $11.99) r/#1-4, Daredevil Vol. 2 #9; Larroca sketch pages 12.00

ULTIMATE FANTASTIC FOUR
Marvel Comics: Feb, 2004 - Present ($2.25)
1-Bendis & Millar-s/Adam Kubert-a/Hitch-c 2.25

ULTIMATE MARVEL MAGAZINE
Marvel Comics: Feb, 2001 - No. 11, 2002 ($3.99, magazine size)
1-11: Reprints of recent stories from the Ultimate titles plus Marvel news and features. 1-Reprints Ultimate Spider-Man #1&2. 11-Lord of the Rings-c 4.00

ULTIMATE MARVEL TEAM-UP (Spider-Man Team-up)
Marvel Comics: Apr, 2001 - No. 16, July, 2002 ($2.99/$2.25)
1-Spider-Man & Wolverine; Bendis-s in all; Matt Wagner-a/c 5.00
2,3-Hulk; Hester-a 3.50
4,5,9-16: 4,5-Iron Man; Allred-a. 9-Fantastic Four; Mahfood-a. 10-Man-Thing; Totleben-a. 11-X-Men; Clugston-Major-a. 12,13-Dr. Strange; McKeever-a.14-Black Widow; Terry Moore-a. 15,16-Shang-Chi; Mays-a 3.00
6-8-Punisher; Sienkiewicz-a. 7,8-Daredevil app. 4.00
TPB (11/01, $14.95) r/#1-5 15.00
HC (8/02, $39.99) r/#1-16 & Ult. Spider-Man Special; Bendis afterword 30.00
...: Vol. 2 TPB (2003, $11.99) r/#9-13; Mahfood-c 12.00
...: Vol. 3 TPB (2003, $12.99) r/#14-16 & Ultimate Spider-Man Super Special; Moore-c 13.00

ULTIMATES, THE (Avengers of the Ultimate line)
Marvel Comics: Mar, 2002 - Present ($2.25)
1-Intro. Capt. America; Millar-s/Hitch-a & wraparound-c 6.00
2-Intro. Giant-Man and the Wasp 4.00
3-12: 3-1st Capt. America in new costume. 4-Intro. Thor. 5-Ultimates vs. The Hulk. 8-Intro. Hawkeye 3.00
... Volume 1: Super-Human TPB (8/02, $12.99) r/#1-6 13.00

ULTIMATE SIX
Marvel Comics: Nov, 2003 - Present ($2.25)
1-The Ultimates & Spider-Man team-up; Bendis-s/Quesada & Hairsine-a; Cassaday-c 5.00
2-5-Hairsine-a; Cassaday-c 2.25

ULTIMATE SPIDER-MAN
Marvel Comics: Oct, 2000 - Present ($2.99/$2.25)
1-Bendis-s/Bagley & Thibert-a; cardstock-c; introduces revised origin and cast separate from regular Spider-continuity 7 14 21 51 71 90
1-Variant white-c (Retailer incentive) 140.00
1-DF Edition 60.00
1-Free Comic Book Day giveaway & Kay Bee Toys variant - (See Promotional Comics section)
2-Cover with Spider-Man on car 3 7 10 21 28 35
2-Cover with Spider-Man swinging past building 3 6 9 21 28 35
3,4: 4-Uncle Ben killed 3 6 9 18 24 30
5-7: 6,7-Green Goblin app. 3 7 10 21 28 35
8-13: 13-Reveals secret to MJ 1 2 3 5 7 9
14-21: 14-Intro. Gwen Stacy & Dr. Octopus 5.00
22-($3.50) Green Goblin returns 3.50
23-32 2.50
33-1st Ultimate Venom-c; intro. Eddie Brock 3.00
34-38-Ultimate Venom 2.50
39-49,51,52: 39-Nick Fury app. 43,44-X-Men app. 46-Sandman app. 51,52-Elektra app. 2.25
50-($2.99) Intro. Black Cat 3.00
Collected Edition (1/01, $3.99) r/#1-3 4.00
Hardcover (3/02, $34.95, 7x11", dust jacket) r/#1-13 & Amazing Fantasy #15; sketch pages and Bill Jemas' initial plot and character outlines 35.00
...: Double Trouble TPB (6/02, $17.95) r/#14-21 18.00
...: Learning Curve TPB (12/01, $14.95) r/#8-13 15.00
...: Legacy TPB (2002, $14.99) r/#22-27 15.00
...: Power and Responsibility TPB (4/01, $14.95) r/#1-7 15.00
...Special (7/02, $3.50) art by Bagley and various incl. Romita,Sr., Brereton, Cho, Mack, Sienkiewicz, Phillips, Pearson, Oeming, Mahfood, Russell 3.50
Vol. 6: Venom TPB (2003, $15.99) r/#33-39 16.00
Vol. 7: Irresponsible TPB (2003, $12.99) r/#40-45 13.00
Volume 2 HC (2003, $29.99, 7x11", dust jacket) r/#14-27; pin-ups &sketch pages 30.00
Volume 3 HC (2003, $29.99, 7x11", dust jacket) r/#28-39 & #1/2; script pages 30.00
Wizard #1/2 1 3 4 6 8 10

ULTIMATE WAR
Marvel Comics: Feb, 2003 - No. 4, Apr, 2003 ($2.25, limited series)
1-4-Millar-s/Bachalo-c/a; The Ultimates vs. Ultimate X-Men 2.25
Ultimate X-Men Vol. 5: Ultimate War TPB (2003, $10.99) r/#1-4 11.00

ULTIMATE X-MEN (Also see Promotional Comics section for FCBD Ed.)
Marvel Comics: Feb, 2001 - Present ($2.99/$2.25)
1-Millar-s/Adam Kubert & Thibert-a; cardstock-c; introduces revised origin and cast separate from regular X-Men continuity 3 6 9 16 20 25
1-DF Edition 30.00
1-DF Sketch Cover Edition 45.00
2 2 4 6 12 16 20
3-6 2 4 6 9 11 14
7-10 6.00
11-24,26-33: 13-Intro. Gambit. 18,19-Bachalo-a. 23,24-Andrews-a 2.25
25-($3.50) leads into the Ultimate War mini-series; Kubert-a 3.50
34-Spider-Man-c/app.; Bendis-s begin; Finch-a 2.25
35-41: 35-Spider-Man app. 36,37-Daredevil-c/app. 40-Intro. Angel 2.25
...: The Tomorrow People TPB (7/01, $14.95) r/#1-6 15.00
...: Return to Weapon X TPB (4/02, $14.95) r/#7-12 15.00
Vol. 3: World Tour TPB (2002, $17.99) r/#13-20 18.00
Vol. 4: Hellfire and Brimstone TPB (2003, $12.99) r/#21-25 13.00
Vol. 5 (See Ultimate War)
Vol. 6: Return of the King TPB (2003, $16.99) r/#26-33 17.00
Vol. 7: Blockbuster TPB (2004, $12.99) r/#34-39 13.00
Volume 1 HC (8/02, $34.99, 7x11", dust jacket) r/#1-12 & Giant-Size X-Men #1; sketch pages and Millar and Bendis' initial plot and character outlines 35.00
Volume 2 HC (2003, $29.99, 7x11", dust jacket) r/#13-25; script for #20 30.00
Volume 3 HC (2003, $29.99, 7x11", dust jacket) r/#26-33 & Utimate War #1-4 30.00
Wizard #1/2 2 4 6 10 12 15

ULTRACYBERNETIC DOLPHINDROIDS, THE
Polestar Comics: Dec, 1993 ($2.50, unfinished limited series)
1 2.50

ULTRAFORCE (1st Series) (Also see Avengers/Ultraforce #1)
Malibu Comics (Ultraverse): Aug, 1994 - No. 10, Aug, 1995 ($1.95/$2.50)
0 (9/94, $2.50)-Perez-c/a. 2.50
1-($2.50, 44 pgs.)-Bound-in trading card; team consisting of Prime, Prototype, Hardcase,

Ultraforce #7 © MAL

Ultraman Tiga #1 © Tsuburaya Prods.

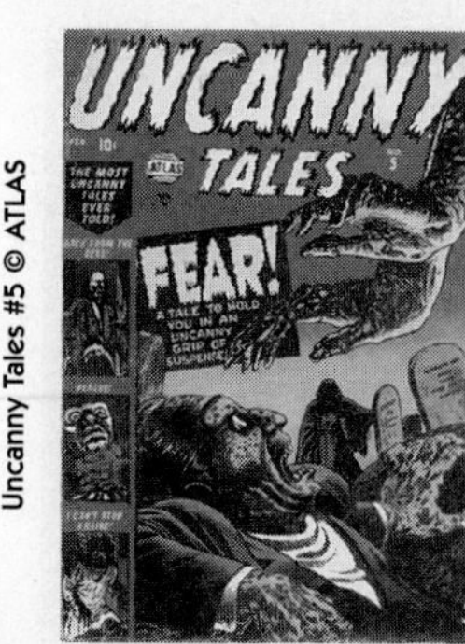

Uncanny Tales #5 © ATLAS

	GD 2.0	VG 4.0	FN 6.0	VF 8.0	VF/NM 9.0	NM- 9.2

Pixx, Ghoul, Contrary & Topaz; Gerard Jones scripts begin, ends #6; Perez-c/a begins. 2.50
1-Ultra 5000 Limited Silver Foil Edition 4.00
1-Holographic-c, no price 6.00
2-5: Perez-c/a in all. 2 (10/94, $1.95)-Prime quits, Strangers cameo. 3-Origin of Topaz; Prime rejoins. 5-Pixx dies. 2.50
2 ($2.50)-Florescent logo; limited edition stamp on-c 3.00
6-10: 6-Begin $2.50-c, Perez-c/a. 7-Ghoul story, Steve Erwin-a. 8-Marvel's Black Knight enters the Ultraverse (last seen in Avengers #375); Perez-c/a. 9,10-Black Knight app.; Perez-c. 10-Leads into Ultraforce/Avengers Prelude 2.50
Malibu "Ashcan ": Ultraforce #0A (6/94) 2.50
.../Avengers Prelude 1 (8/95, $2.50)-Perez-c. 2.50
.../Avengers 1 (8/95, $3.95)-Warren Ellis script; Perez-c/a; foil-c 4.00

ULTRAFORCE (2nd Series)(Also see Black September)
Malibu Comics (Ultraverse): Infinity, Sept, 1995 - V2#15, Dec, 1996 ($1.50)

Infinity, V2#1-15: Infinity-Team consists of Marvel's Black Knight, Ghoul, Topaz, Prime & redesigned Prototype; Warren Ellis scripts begin, ends #3; variant-c exists. 1-1st app.Cromwell, Lament & Wreckage. 2-Contains free encore presentation of Ultraforce #1; flip book "Phoenix Resurrection" Pt. 7. 7-Darick Robertson, Jeff Johnson & others-a. 8,9-Intro. Future Ultraforce (Prime, Hellblade, Angel of Destruction, Painkiller & Whipslash); Gary Erskine-c/a. 9-Foxfire app. 10-Len Wein scripts & Deodato Studios-c/a begin. 10-Lament back-up story. 11-Ghoul back-up story by Pander Bros. 12-Ultraforce vs. Maxis (cont'd in Ultraverse Unlimited #2); Exiles & Iron Clad app. 13-Prime leaves; Hardcase returns 2.25
Infinity (2000 signed) 4.00
.../Spider-Man ($3.95)-Marv Wolfman script; Green Goblin app; 2 covers exist. 4.00

ULTRAGIRL
Marvel Comics: Nov, 1996 - No. 3 Mar, 1997($1.50, limited series)

1-3: 1-1st app. 2.25

ULTRA KLUTZ
Onward Comics: 1981; 6/86 - #27, 1/89, #28, 4/90 - #31, 1990? ($1.50/$1.75/$2.00, B&W)

1 (1981)-Re-released after 2nd #1 2.25
1-30: 1-(6/86). 27-Photo back-c 2.25
31-($2.95, 52 pgs.) 3.00

ULTRAMAN
Nemesis Comics: Mar, 1994 - No. 4, Sept, 1994 ($1.75/$1.95)

1-($2.25)-Collector's edition; foil-c; special 3/4 wraparound-c 3.00
1-($1.75)-Newsstand edition 2.50
2-4: 3-$1.95-c begins 2.50
#(-1) (3/93) 2.50

ULTRAMAN TIGA
Dark Horse Comics: Aug, 2003 - No. 10 ($3.99)

1,2-Khoo Fuk Lung-a/Tony Wong-s 4.00

ULTRAVERSE DOUBLE FEATURE
Malibu Comics (Ultraverse): Jan, 1995 ($3.95, one-shot, 68 pgs.)

1-Flip-c featuring Prime & Solitaire. 4.00

ULTRAVERSE ORIGINS
Malibu Comics (Ultraverse): Jan, 1994 (99¢, one-shot)

1-Gatefold-c; 2 pg. origins all characters 2.25
1-Newsstand edition; different-c, no gatefold 2.25

ULTRAVERSE PREMIERE
Malibu Comics (Ultraverse): 1994 (one-shot)

0-Ordered thru mail w/coupons 5.00

ULTRAVERSE UNLIMITED
Malibu Comics (Ultraverse): June, 1996; No. 2, Sept, 1996 ($2.50)

1,2: 1-Adam Warlock returns to the Marvel Universe; Rune-c/app. 2-Black Knight, Reaper & Sierra Blaze return to the Marvel Universe 2.50

ULTRAVERSE YEAR ONE
Malibu Comics (Ultraverse): 1994 ($4.95, one-shot)

nn-In-depth synopsis of the first year's titles & stories. 5.00

ULTRAVERSE YEAR TWO
Malibu Comics (Ultraverse): Aug, 1995 ($4.95, one-shot)

nn-In-depth synopsis of second year's titles & stories 5.00

ULTRAVERSE YEAR ZERO: THE DEATH OF THE SQUAD
Malibu Comics (Ultraverse): Apr, 1995 - No. 4, July, 1995 ($2.95, lim. series)

1-4: 3-Codename: Firearm back-up story. 3.00

UNBIRTHDAY PARTY WITH ALICE IN WONDERLAND (See Alice In Wonderland, Four Color #341)

	GD 2.0	VG 4.0	FN 6.0	VF 8.0	VF/NM 9.0	NM- 9.2

UNBOUND
Image Comics (Desperado): Jan, 1998 ($2.95, B&W)

1-Pruett-s/Peters-a 3.00

UNCANNY ORIGINS
Marvel Comics: Sept, 1996 - No. 14, Oct, 1997 (99¢)

1-14: 1-Cyclops. 2-Quicksilver. 3-Archangel. 4-Firelord. 5-Hulk. 6-Beast. 7-Venom. 8-Nightcrawler. 9-Storm. 10-Black Cat. 11-Black Knight. 12-Dr. Strange. 13-Daredevil. 14-Iron Fist 2.25

UNCANNY TALES
Atlas Comics (PrPl/PPI): June, 1952 - No. 56, Sept, 1957

1-Heath-a; horror/weird stories begin	88	176	264	550	825	1100
2	48	96	144	288	432	575
3-5	40	80	120	240	363	485
6-Wolvertonish-a by Matt Fox	43	86	129	258	384	510
7-10: 8-Atom bomb story; Tothish-a (by Sekowsky?). 9-Crandall-a	39	78	117	230	325	420
11-20: 17-Atom bomb panels; anti-communist story; Hitler story. 19-Krenkel-a. 20-Robert Q. Sale-c	29	58	87	164	232	300
21-25,27: 25-Nostrand-a?	25	50	75	144	198	255
26-Spider-Man prototype c/story	35	70	105	201	288	370
28-Last precode issue (1/55); Kubert-a; #1-28 contain 2-3 sci/fi stories each	26	52	78	147	203	265
29-41,43-49,51	18	36	54	101	138	175
42,54,56-Krigstein-a	19	38	57	106	146	185
50,53,55-Torres-a	18	36	54	101	138	175
52-Oldest Iron Man prototype (2/57)	20	40	60	112	156	200

NOTE: ***Andru** a-15, 27. **Ayers** a-22. **Bailey** a-51. **Briefer** a-19, 20. **Brodsky** c-1, 3, 4, 6, 8, 12-16, 19. **Brodsky/Everett** c-9. **Cameron** a-47. **Colan** a-11, 16, 17, 52. **Drucker** a-37, 42, 45. **Everett** a-2, 9, 12, 32, 36, 39, 48; c-7, 11, 17, 39, 41, 50, 52, 53. **Fass** a-9, 10, 15, 24. Forte a-18, 27, 34, 52, 53. **Heath** a-13, 14; c-5, 10, 18. **Keller** a-3. **Lawrence** a-14, 17, 19, 23, 27, 28, 35. **Maneely** a-4, 8, 10, 16, 29, 35; c-2, 22, 26, 33, 38. **Moldoff** a-23. **Morisi** a-48, 52. **Morrow** a-46, 51. **Orlando** a-49, 50, 53. **Powell** a-12, 18, 34, 36, 38, 43, 50, 56. **Robinson** a-3, 13. **Reinman** a-12. **Romita** a-10. **Roussos** a-8. **Sale** a-47, 53; c-20. **Sekowsky** a-25. **Sinnott** a-15, 52. **Torres** a-53. **Tothish**-a by **Andru**-27. **Wildey** a-22, 48.*

UNCANNY TALES
Marvel Comics Group: Dec, 1973 - No. 12, Oct, 1975

1-Crandall-r/Uncanny Tales #9('50s)	3	6	9	17	23	28
2-12: 7,12-Kirby-a	2	4	6	10	12	15

NOTE: ***Ditko** reprints-#4, 6-8, 10-12.*

UNCANNY X-MEN, THE (See **X-Men, The**, 1st series, #142-on)

UNCANNY X-MEN AND THE NEW TEEN TITANS (See Marvel and DC Present...)

UNCENSORED MOUSE, THE
Eternity Comics: Apr, 1989 - No. 2, Apr, 1989 ($1.95, B&W)(Came sealed in plastic bag) (Both contain racial stereotyping & violence)

1,2-Early Gottfredson strip-r in each	2	4	6	8	10	12

NOTE: *Both issues contain unauthorized reprints. Series was cancelled. **Win Smith** r-1, 2.*

UNCLE CHARLIE'S FABLES
Lev Gleason Publ.: Jan, 1952 - No. 5, Sept, 1952 (All have Biro painted-c)

1-Norman Maurer-a; has Biro's picture	16	32	48	92	126	160
2-Fuje-a; Biro photo	10	20	30	56	73	90
3-5	9	18	27	49	62	75

UNCLE DONALD & HIS NEPHEWS DUDE RANCH (See Dell Giant #52)

UNCLE DONALD & HIS NEPHEWS FAMILY FUN (See Dell Giant #38)

UNCLE JOE'S FUNNIES
Centaur Publications: 1938 (B&W)

1-Games, puzzles & magic tricks, some interior art; Bill Everett-c	53	106	159	318	477	635

UNCLE MILTY (TV)
Victoria Publications/True Cross: Dec, 1950 - No. 4, July, 1951 (52 pgs.)(Early TV comic)

1-Milton Berle photo on-c of #1,2	53	106	159	318	477	635
2	35	70	105	201	288	370
3,4	30	60	90	170	240	310

UNCLE REMUS & HIS TALES OF BRER RABBIT (See Brer Rabbit, 4-Color #129, 208, 693)

UNCLE SAM
DC Comics (Vertigo): 1997 - No. 2, 1997 ($4.95, limited series)

1,2-Alex Ross painted c/a. Story by Ross and Steve Darnell 5.00
Hardcover (1998, $17.95) 18.00
Softcover (2000, $9.95) 10.00

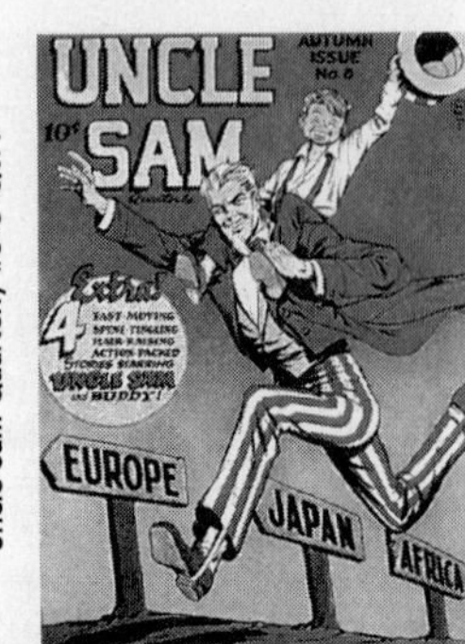

Uncle Sam Quarterly #8 © QUA

Uncle Scrooge #179 © WDC

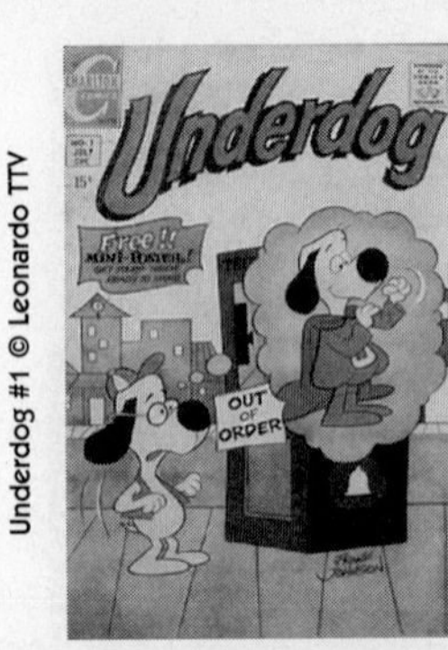

Underdog #1 © Leonardo TTV

	GD 2.0	VG 4.0	FN 6.0	VF 8.0	VF/NM 9.0	NM- 9.2

UNCLE SAM QUARTERLY (Blackhawk #9 on)(See Freedom Fighters)
Quality Comics Group: Autumn, 1941 - No. 8, Fall, 1943 (see National Comics)

1-Origin Uncle Sam; Fine/Eisner-c, chapter headings, 2 pgs. by Eisner; (2 versions: dark cover, no price; light cover with price sticker); Jack Cole-a 370 740 1110 2405 3703 5000
2-Cameos by The Ray, Black Condor, Quicksilver, The Red Bee, Alias the Spider, Hercules & Neon the Unknown; Eisner, Fine-c/a 132 264 396 825 1238 1650
3-Tuska-c/a; Eisner-a(2) 96 192 288 600 900 1200
4 85 170 255 531 796 1060
5,7-Hitler, Mussolini & Tojo-c 100 200 300 625 938 1250
6,8 69 138 207 431 646 860

NOTE: ***Kotzky** (or **Tuska**) a-3-8.*

UNCLE SCROOGE (Disney) (Becomes Walt Disney's... #210 on) (See Cartoon Tales, Dell Giants #33, 55, Disney Comic Album, Donald and Scrooge, Dynabrite, Four Color #178, Gladstone Comic Album, Walt Disney's Comics & Stories #98, Walt Disney's ...)
Dell #1-39/Gold Key #40-173/Whitman #174-209: No. 386, 3/52 - No. 39, 8-10/62; No. 40, 12/62 - No. 209, 7/84

Four Color 386(#1)-in "Only a Poor Old Man" by Carl Barks; r-in Uncle Scrooge & Donald Duck #1('65) & The Best of Walt Disney Comics (1974). The very 1st cover app. of Uncle Scrooge 91 182 273 774 1187 1600
1-(1986)-Reprints F.C. #386; given away with lithograph "Dam Disaster at Money Lake" & as a subscription offer giveaway to Gladstone subscribers 2 4 6 14 18 22
Four Color 456(#2)-in "Back to the Klondike" by Carl Barks; r-in Best of U.S. & D.D. #1('66) & Gladstone C.A. #4 55 110 165 434 667 900
Four Color 495(#3)-r-in #105 41 82 123 324 487 650
4(12-2/53-54)-r-in Gladstone Comic Album #11 33 66 99 248 369 490
5-r-in Gladstone Special #2 & Walt Disney Digest #1 29 58 87 210 305 400
6-r-in U.S. #106,165,233 & Best of U.S. & D.D. #1('66) 22 44 66 156 228 300
7-The Seven Cities of Cibola by Barks; r-in #217 & Best of D.D. & U.S. #2 ('67) 20 40 60 142 209 275
8-10: 8-r-in #111,222. 9-r-in #104,214. 10-r-in #67 17 34 51 118 174 230
11-20: 11-r-in #237. 17-r-in #215. 19-r-in Gladstone C.A. #1. 20-r-in #213 15 30 45 109 160 210
21-30: 24-X-Mas-c. 26-r-in #211 13 26 39 94 137 180
31-35,37-40: 34-r-in #228. 40-X-Mas-c 11 22 33 77 114 150
36-1st app. Magica De Spell; Number one dime 1st identified by name 13 26 39 90 133 175
41-60: 48-Magica De Spell-c/story (3/64). 49-Sci/fi-c. 51-Beagle Boys-c/story (8/64) 9 18 27 65 93 120
61-63,65,66,68-71:71-Last Barks issue w/original story (#71-he only storyboarded the script) 9 18 27 60 85 110
64-Barks Vietnam War story "Treasure of Marco Polo" banned for reprints by Disney from 1977-1989 because of its Third World revolutionary war theme. It later appeared in the hardcover Carl Barks Library set (4/89) and Walt Disney's Uncle Scrooge Adventures #42 (1/97) 11 22 33 80 118 155
67,72,73: 67,72,73-Barks-r 8 16 24 58 82 105
74-84: 74-Barks-r(1pg.). 75-81,83-Not by Barks. 82,84-Barks-r begin 6 12 18 38 52 65
85-110 5 10 15 33 44 55
111-120 3 7 10 21 28 35
121-141,143-152,154-157 3 6 9 19 25 32
142-Reprints Four Color #456 with-c 3 7 10 21 28 35
153,158,162-164,166,168-170,178,180: No Barks 2 4 6 11 14 18
159-160,165,167 2 4 6 12 16 20
161(r/#14), 171(r/#11), 177(r/#16),183(r/#6)-Barks-r 2 4 6 12 16 20
172(1/80),173(2/80)-Gold Key. Barks-a 3 6 9 16 20 24
174(3/80),175(4/80),176(5/80)-Whitman. Barks-a 3 6 9 19 25 32
177(6/80),178(7/80) 3 7 10 21 28 35
179(9/80)(r/#9)-(Very low distribution) 38 76 114 285 430 575
180(11/80),181(12/80, r/4-Color #495) pre-pack? 4 8 12 29 40 50
182-195: 184,185,187,188-Barks-a. 182,186,191-194-No Barks. 189(r/#5), 190(r/#4), 195(r/4-Color #386) 2 4 6 12 16 20
196(4/82),197(5/82): 196(r/#13) 3 6 9 16 20 24
198-209 (All #90038 on-c; pre-pack; no date or date code): 198(4/83), 199(5/83), 200(6/83), 201(6/83), 202(7/83), 203(7/83), 204(8/83), 205(8/83), 206(4/84), 207(5/83), 208(6/84), 209(7/84). 198-202,204-206: No Barks. 203(r/#12), 207(r/#93,92), 208(r/U.S. #18), 209(r/U.S. #21)-Barks-r 3 6 9 18 23 28
Uncle Scrooge & Money(G.K.)-Barks-r/from WDC&S #130 (3/67) 5 10 15 33 44 55
Mini Comic #1(1976)(3-1/4x6-1/2")-r/U.S. #115; Barks-c 2 4 6 8 10 12

NOTE: ***Barks** c-Four Color 386, 456, 495, #4-37, 39, 40, 43-71.*

UNCLE SCROOGE & DONALD DUCK
Gold Key: June, 1965 (25¢, paper cover)

1-Reprint of Four Color #386(#1) & lead story from Four Color #29 9 18 27 60 85 110

UNCLE SCROOGE COMICS DIGEST
Gladstone Publishing: Dec, 1986 - No. 5, Aug, 1987 ($1.25, Digest-size)

1,3 1 2 3 5 6 8
2,4 6.00
5 (low print run) 1 2 3 5 7 9

UNCLE SCROOGE GOES TO DISNEYLAND (See Dell Giants)
Gladstone Publishing Ltd.: Aug, 1985 ($2.50)

1-Reprints Dell Giant w/new-c by Mel Crawford, based on old cover 2 4 6 8 10 12
...Comics Digest 1 ($1.50, digest size) 2 4 6 9 11 14

UNCLE SCROOGE IN COLOR
Gladstone Publishing: 1987 ($29.95, Hardcover, 9-1/4"X12-1/4", 96 pgs.)

nn-Reprints "Christmas on Bear Mountain" from Four Color 178 by Barks; Uncle Scrooge's Christmas Carol (published as Donald Duck & the Christmas Carol, A Little Golden Book), reproduced from the original art as adapted by Norman McGary from pencils by Barks; and Uncle Scrooge the Lemonade King, reproduced from the original art, plus Barks' original pencils 4 8 12 29 40 50
nn-Slipcase edition of 750, signed by Barks, issued at $79.95 300.00

UNCLE SCROOGE THE LEMONADE KING
Whitman Publishing Co.: 1960 (A Top Top Tales Book, 6-3/8"x7-5/8", 32 pgs.)

2465-Storybook pencilled by Carl Barks, finished art adapted by Norman McGary 40 80 120 300 450 600

UNCLE WIGGILY (See March of Comics #19)
Dell Publishing Co.: No. 179, Dec, 1947 - No. 543, Mar, 1954

Four Color 179 (#1)-Walt Kelly-c 17 34 51 118 174 230
Four Color 221 (3/49)-Part Kelly-c 10 20 30 72 104 135
Four Color 276 (5/50), 320 (#1, 3/51) 9 18 27 60 85 110
Four Color 349 (9-10/51), 391 (4-5/52) 7 14 21 51 71 90
Four Color 428 (10/52), 503 (10/53), 543 6 12 18 38 52 65

UNDEAD, THE
Chaos! Comics (Black Label): Feb, 2002 ($4.99, B&W)

1-Pulido-s/Denham-a 5.00

UNDERCOVER GIRL (Starr Flagg) (See Extra Comics & Manhunt!)
Magazine Enterprises: No. 5, 1952 - No. 7, 1954

5(#1)(A-1 #62)-Fallon of the F.B.I. in all 40 80 120 240 340 440
6(A-1 #98), 7(A-1 #118)-All have Starr Flagg 39 78 117 230 325 420

NOTE: ***Powell** c-6, 7. **Whitney** a-5-7.*

UNDERDOG (TV)(See Kite Fun Book, March of Comics #426, 438, 467, 479)
Charlton Comics/Gold Key: July, 1970 - No. 10, Jan, 1972; Mar, 1975 - No. 23, Feb, 1979

1 (1st series, Charlton)-1st app. Underdog 9 18 27 65 93 120
2-10 5 10 15 36 48 60
1 (2nd series, Gold Key) 7 14 21 50 68 85
2-10 4 8 12 25 33 42
11-20: 13-1st app. Shack of Solitude 3 6 9 19 25 32
21-23 3 7 10 21 28 35

UNDERDOG
Spotlight Comics: 1987 - No. 3?, 1987 ($1.50)

1-3 4.00

UNDERDOG SUMMER SPECIAL (TV)
Harvey Comics: Oct, 1993 ($2.25, 68 pgs.)

1 4.00

UNDERSEA AGENT
Tower Comics: Jan, 1966 - No. 6, Mar, 1967 (25¢, 68 pgs.)

1-Davy Jones, Undersea Agent begins 9 18 27 65 93 120
2-6: 2-Jones gains magnetic powers. 5-Origin & 1st app. of Merman. 6-Kane/Wood-c(r) 7 14 21 46 63 80

NOTE: ***Gil Kane** a-3-6; c-4, 5. **Moldoff** a-2i.*

UNDERSEA FIGHTING COMMANDOS (See Fighting Undersea...)
I.W. Enterprises: 1964

I.W. Reprint #1,2('64): 1-r/#? 2-r/#1; Severin-c 2 4 6 10 13 16

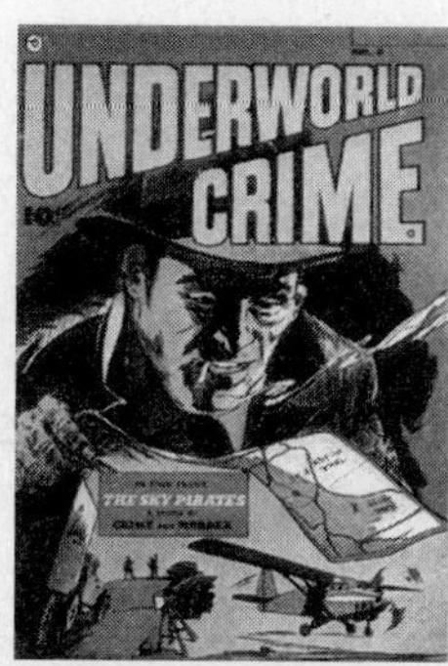

Underworld Crime #9 © FAW

The Unexpected #201 © DC

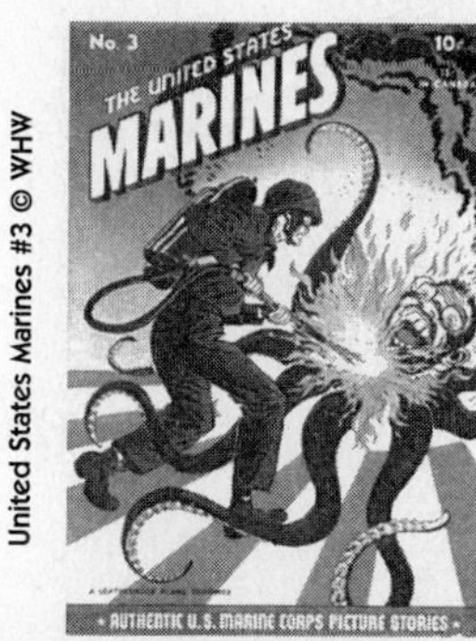

United States Marines #3 © WHW

GD VG FN VF VF/NM NM-
2.0 4.0 6.0 8.0 9.0 9.2

UNDERTAKER (World Wrestling Federation)
Chaos! Comics: Feb, 1999 - No. 10, Jan, 2000 ($2.50/$2.95)

Preview (2/99) 2.50
1-10: Reg. and photo covers for each. 1-(4/99) 3.00
1-($6.95) DF Ed.; Brereton painted-c 7.00
...Halloween Special (10/99, $2.95) Reg. & photo-c 3.00
Wizard #0 2.25

UNDERWATER CITY, THE
Dell Publishing Co.: No. 1328, 1961

Four Color 1328-Movie, Evans-a 8 16 24 55 78 100

UNDERWORLD (...True Crime Stories)
D. S. Publishing Co.: Feb-Mar, 1948 - No. 9, June-July, 1949 (52 pgs.)

1-Moldoff (Shelly)-c; excessive violence 44 88 132 264 395 525
2-Moldoff (Shelly)-c; Ma Barker story used in **SOTI**, pg. 95; female electrocution panel; lingerie art 40 80 120 240 360 480
3-McWilliams-c/a; extreme violence, mutilation 39 78 117 230 325 420
4-Used in Love and Death by Legman; Ingels-a 33 66 99 190 270 350
5-Ingels-a 24 48 72 138 194 250
6-9: 8-Ravielli-a 19 38 57 107 149 190

UNDERWORLD
DC Comics: Dec, 1987 - No. 4, Mar, 1988 ($1.00, limited series, mature)

1-4 2.25

UNDERWORLD (Movie)
IDW Publishing: Sept, 2003 ($6.99, one-shot)

1-Movie adaptation; photo-c 7.00

UNDERWORLD CRIME
Fawcett Publications: June, 1952 - No. 9, Oct, 1953

1 33 66 99 190 270 350
2 21 42 63 118 164 210
3-6,8,9 (8,9-exist?) 19 38 57 107 149 190
7-(6/53)-Bondage/torture-c 29 58 87 164 232 300

UNDERWORLD STORY, THE (Movie)
Avon Periodicals: 1950

nn-(Scarce)-Ravielli-c 30 60 90 170 240 310

UNDERWORLD UNLEASHED
DC Comics: Nov, 1995 - No. 3, Jan, 1996 ($2.95, limited series)

1-3: Mark Waid scripts & Howard Porter-c/a(p) 3.50
...: Abyss: Hell's Sentinel 1-($2.95)-Alan Scott, Phantom Stranger, Zatanna app. 3.00
...: Apokolips-Dark Uprising 1 ($1.95) 2.25
...: Batman-Devil's Asylum 1-($2.95)-Batman app. 3.00
...: Patterns of Fear-($2.95) 3.00
TPB (1998, $17.95) r/#1-3 & Abyss-Hell's Sentinel 18.00

UNEARTHLY SPECTACULARS
Harvey Publications: Oct, 1965 - No. 3, Mar, 1967

1-(12¢)-Tiger Boy; Simon-c 4 8 12 29 40 50
2-(25¢ giants)-Jack Q. Frost, Tiger Boy & Three Rocketeers app.; Williamson, Wood, Kane-a; r-1 story/Thrill-O-Rama #2 5 10 15 33 44 55
3-(25¢ giants)-Jack Q. Frost app.; Williamson/Crandall-a; r-from Alarming Advs. #1,1962 5 10 15 30 44 55

NOTE: ***Crandall*** *a-3r.* ***G. Kane*** *a-2.* ***Orlando*** *a-3.* ***Simon, Sparling, Wood*** *c-2.* ***Simon/Kirby*** *a-3r.* ***Torres*** *a-1?.* ***Wildey*** *a-1(3).* ***Williamson*** *a-2, 3r.* ***Wood*** *a-2(2).*

UNEXPECTED, THE (Formerly Tales of the...)
National Per. Publ./DC Comics: No. 105, Feb-Mar, 1968 - No. 222, May, 1982

105-Begin 12¢ cover price 6 12 18 38 52 65
106-113: 113-Last 12¢ issue (6-7/69) 4 8 12 24 32 40
114,115,117,118,120-125 3 6 9 18 24 30
116 (36 pgs.)-Wrightson-a? 3 6 9 19 25 32
119-Wrightson-a, 8pgs.(36 pgs.) 4 8 12 28 38 48
126,127,129-136-(52 pgs.) 3 6 9 19 25 32
128(52 pgs.)-Wrightson-a 4 8 12 28 38 48
137-156 2 4 6 11 14 18
157-162-(100 pgs.) 4 8 12 25 33 42
163-188: 187,188-(44 pgs.) 2 4 6 9 11 14
189,190,192-195 ($1.00, 68 pgs.): 189 on are combined with House of Secrets & The Witching Hour 2 4 6 10 13 16
191-Rogers-a(p) ($1.00, 68 pgs.) 2 4 6 11 14 18
196-222: 200-Return of Johhny Peril by Tuska. 205-213-Johnny Peril app.
210-Time Warp story 1 2 3 5 7 9

NOTE: ***Neal Adams*** *c-110, 112-115, 118, 121, 124.* ***J. Craig*** *a-195.* ***Ditko*** *a-189, 221p, 222p; c-222.* ***Drucker*** *a-107r, 132r.* ***Giffen*** *a-219, 222.* ***Kaluta*** *c-203, 212.* ***Kirby*** *a-127r, 162.* ***Kubert*** *c-204, 214-216, 219-221.* ***Mayer*** *a-217p, 220, 221p.* ***Moldoff*** *a-136r.* ***Moreira*** *a-133.* ***Mortimer*** *a-212p.* ***Newton*** *a-204p.* ***Orlando*** *a-202; c-191.* ***Perez*** *a-217p.* ***Redondo*** *a-155, 166, 195.* ***Reese*** *a-145.* ***Sparling*** *a-107, 205-209p, 212p.* ***Spiegle*** *a-217.* ***Starlin*** *c-198.* ***Toth*** *a-126r, 127r.* ***Tuska*** *a-127, 132, 134, 136, 139, 152, 180, 200p.* ***Wildey*** *a-128r, 193.* ***Wood*** *a-122i, 133i, 137i, 138i.* ***Wrightson*** *a-161r(2 pgs.). Johnny Peril in #106-114, 116, 117, 200, 205-213.*

UNEXPECTED ANNUAL, THE (See DC Special Series #4)

UNIDENTIFIED FLYING ODDBALL (See Walt Disney Showcase #52)

UNION
Image Comics (WildStorm Productions): June, 1993 - No. 0, July, 1994 ($1.95, lim. series)

0-(7/94, $2.50) 2.50
0-Alternate Portacio-c (See Deathblow #5) 5.00
1-($2.50)-Embossed foil-c; Texeira-c/a in all 2.50
1-($1.95)-Newsstand edition w/o foil-c 2.25
2-4: 4-(7/94) 2.50

UNION
Image Comics (WildStorm Prod.): Feb, 1995 - No. 9, Dec, 1995 ($2.50)

1-3,5-9: 3-Savage Dragon app. 6-Fairchild from Gen 13 app. 2.50
4-($1.95, Newsstand)-WildStorm Rising Pt. 3 2.25
4-($2.50, Direct Market)-WildStorm Rising Pt. 3, bound-in card 2.50

UNION: FINAL VENGEANCE
Image Comics (WildStorm Productions): Oct, 1997 ($2.50)

1-Golden-c/Heisler-s 2.50

UNION JACK
Marvel Comics: Dec, 1998 - No. 3, Feb, 1999 ($2.99, limited series)

1-3-Raab-s/Cassaday-s/a 3.00

UNION STATION
Oni Press: Oct, 2003 ($11.95, B&W, graphic novel)

nn-Ande Parks-s/Eduardo Barreto-a 12.00

UNITED COMICS (Formerly Fritzi Ritz #7; has Fritzi Ritz logo)
United Features Syndicate: Aug, 1940; No. 8, 1950 - No. 26, Jan-Feb, 1953

1(68 pgs.)-Fritzi Ritz & Phil Fumble 24 48 72 138 194 250
8-Fritzi Ritz, Abbie & Slats 7 14 21 37 46 55
9-21: 20-Strange As It Seems; Russell Patterson Cheesecake-a 7 14 21 35 43 50
22-(5-6/52) 2 pgs. early Peanuts by Schulz (1st in comics?) 9 18 27 49 62 75
23-26: 23-(7-8/52). 24-(9-10/52). 25-(11-12/52). 26-(1-2/53). All have 2 pgs. early Peanuts by Schulz 8 16 24 43 54 65

NOTE: *Abbie & Slats reprinted from Tip Top.*

UNITED NATIONS, THE (See Classics Illustrated Special Issue)

UNITED STATES AIR FORCE PRESENTS: THE HIDDEN CREW
U.S. Air Force: 1964 (36 pgs.)

nn-Schaffenberger-a 2 4 6 11 14 18

UNITED STATES FIGHTING AIR FORCE (Also see U.S. Fighting Air Force)
Superior Comics Ltd.: Sept, 1952 - No. 29, Oct, 1956

1 11 22 33 66 88 110
2 7 14 21 37 46 55
3-10 6 12 18 31 38 45
11-29 6 12 18 28 34 40

UNITED STATES MARINES
William H. Wise/Life's Romances Publ. Co./Magazine Ent. #5-8/Toby Press #7-11: 1943 - No. 4, 1944; No. 5, 1952 - No. 8, 1952; No. 7 - No. 11, 1953

nn-Mart Bailey-a 18 36 54 104 142 180
2-Bailey-a; Tojo classic-c 38 76 114 219 310 400
3-Tojo-c 29 58 87 164 232 300
4 10 20 30 60 80 100
5(A-1 #55)-Bailey-a, 6(A-1 #60), 7(A-1 #68), 8(A-1 #72) 9 18 27 52 66 80
7-11 (Toby) 8 16 24 40 50 60

NOTE: ***Powell*** *a-5-7.*

UNITY
Valiant: No. 0, Aug, 1992 - No. 1, 1992 (Free comics w/limited dist., 20 pgs.)

0 (Blue)-Prequel to Unity x-overs in all Valiant titles; B. Smith-c/a. (Free to everyone that bought all 8 titles that month.) 2.25
0 (Red)-Same as above, but w/red logo (5,000). 3.00
1-Epilogue to Unity x-overs; B. Smith-c/a. (1 copy available for every 8 Valiant books ordered by dealers.) 2.25

The Unknown Soldier #212 © DC

Unlimited Access #2 © MAR

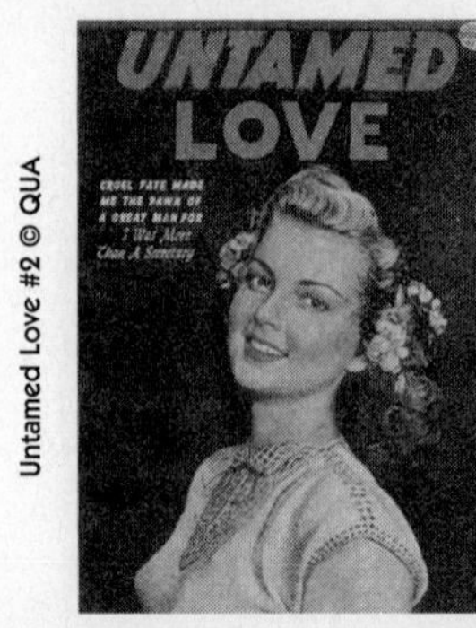

Untamed Love #2 © QUA

	GD 2.0	VG 4.0	FN 6.0	VF 8.0	VF/NM 9.0	NM- 9.2
1 (Gold), 1-(Platinum)-Promotional copy.						3.00
... : The Lost Chapter 1 (Yearbook) (2/95, $3.95)-"1994" in indicia						4.00

UNITY 2000 (See preludes in Shadowman #3,4 flipbooks)
Acclaim Comics: Nov, 1999 - No. 3, Jan, 2000 ($2.50, unfinished limited series planned for 6 issues)

	GD 2.0	VG 4.0	FN 6.0	VF 8.0	VF/NM 9.0	NM- 9.2
Preview -B&W plot preview and cover art; paper cover						2.25
1-3-Starlin-a/Shooter-s						2.50

UNIVERSAL MONSTERS
Dark Horse Comics: 1993 ($4.95/$5.95, 52 pgs.)(All adapt original movies)

	GD 2.0	VG 4.0	FN 6.0	VF 8.0	VF/NM 9.0	NM- 9.2
Creature From the Black Lagoon nn-($4.95)-Art Adams/Austin-c/a, Dracula nn-($4.95), Frankenstein nn-($3.95)-Painted-c/a, The Mummy nn-($4.95)-Painted-c	1	2	3	4	5	7

UNIVERSAL PRESENTS DRACULA-THE MUMMY& OTHER STORIES
Dell Publishing Co.: Sept-Nov, 1963 (one-shot, 84 pgs.) (Also see Dell Giants)

	GD 2.0	VG 4.0	FN 6.0	VF 8.0	VF/NM 9.0	NM- 9.2
02-530-311-r/Dracula 12-231-212, The Mummy 12-437-211 & part of Ghost Stories No. 1	14	28	42	112	206	300

UNIVERSAL SOLDIER (Movie)
Now Comics: Sept, 1992 - No. 3, Nov, 1992 (Limited series, polybagged, mature)

	GD 2.0	VG 4.0	FN 6.0	VF 8.0	VF/NM 9.0	NM- 9.2
1-3 ($2.50, Direct Sales) 1-Movie adapatation; hologram on-c (all direct sales editions have painted-c)						2.50
1-3 ($1.95, Newsstand)-Rewritten & redrawn code approved version; all newsstand editions have photo-c						2.25

UNIVERSE
Image Comics (Top Cow): Sept, 2001 - No. 8, July, 2002 ($2.50)

	GD 2.0	VG 4.0	FN 6.0	VF 8.0	VF/NM 9.0	NM- 9.2
1-7-Jenkins-s						2.50
8-($4.95) extra short-s by Jenkins; pin-up pages						5.00

UNIVERSE X (See Earth X)
Marvel Comics: Sept, 2000 - No. 12, Sept, 2001 ($3.99/$3.50, limited series)

	GD 2.0	VG 4.0	FN 6.0	VF 8.0	VF/NM 9.0	NM- 9.2
0-Ross-c/Braithwaite-a/Ross & Krueger-s						4.00
1-12: 5-Funeral of Captain America						3.50
... Beasts (6/00, $3.99) Yeates-a/Ross-c						4.00
... Cap (Capt. America) (2/01, $3.99) Yeates & Totleben-a/Ross-c; Cap dies						4.00
... 4 (Fantastic 4) (10/00, $3.99) Brent Anderson-a/Ross-c						4.00
... Iron Men (9/01, $3.99) Anderson-a/Ross-c; leads into #12						4.00
... Omnibus (6/01, $3.99) Ross B&W sketchbook and character bios						4.00
Sketchbook- Wizard supplement; B&W character sketches and bios						2.25
...Spidey (1/01, $3.99) Romita Sr. flashback-a/Guice-a/Ross-c						4.00
...X (11/01, $3.99) Series conclusion; Braithwaith-a/Ross wraparound-c						4.00
Volume 1 TPB (1/02, $24.95) r/#0-7 & Spidey, 4, & Cap; new Ross-c						25.00
Volume 2 TPB (6/02, $24.95) r/#8-12 &X, Beasts, Iron Men and Omnibus						25.00

UNKNOWN MAN, THE (Movie)
Avon Periodicals: 1951

	GD 2.0	VG 4.0	FN 6.0	VF 8.0	VF/NM 9.0	NM- 9.2
nn-Kinstler-c	29	58	87	164	232	300

UNKNOWN SOLDIER (Formerly Star-Spangled War Stories)
National Periodical Publications/DC Comics: No. 205, Apr-May, 1977 - No. 268, Oct, 1982 (See Our Army at War #168 for 1st app.)

	GD 2.0	VG 4.0	FN 6.0	VF 8.0	VF/NM 9.0	NM- 9.2
205	2	4	6	12	16	20
206-210,220,221,251: 220,221 (44pgs.). 251-Enemy Ace begins	2	4	6	9	11	14
211-218,222-247,250,252-264	1	3	4	6	8	10
219-Miller-a (44 pgs.)	2	4	6	11	14	18
248,249,265-267: 248,249-Origin. 265-267-Enemy Ace vs. Balloon Buster.	1	3	4	6	8	10
268-Death of Unknown Soldier	2	4	6	14	18	22

NOTE: ***Chaykin** a-234. **Evans** a-265-267; c-235. **Kubert** c-Most. **Miller** a-219p. **Severin** a-251-253, 260, 261, 265-267. **Simonson** a-254-256. **Spiegle** a-258, 259, 262-264.*

UNKNOWN SOLDIER, THE (Also see Brave &the Bold #146)
DC Comics: Winter, 1988-'89 - No. 12, Dec, 1989 ($1.50, maxi-series, mature)

	GD 2.0	VG 4.0	FN 6.0	VF 8.0	VF/NM 9.0	NM- 9.2
1-12: 8-Begin $1.75-c						3.00

UNKNOWN SOLDIER
DC Comics (Vertigo): Apr, 1997 - No 4, July, 1997 ($2.50, mini-series)

	GD 2.0	VG 4.0	FN 6.0	VF 8.0	VF/NM 9.0	NM- 9.2
1-Ennis-s/Plunkett-a/Bradstreet-c in all						6.00
2-4						4.00
TPB (1998, $12.95) r/#1-4						13.00

UNKNOWN WORLD (Strange Stories From Another World #2 on)
Fawcett Publications: June, 1952

	GD 2.0	VG 4.0	FN 6.0	VF 8.0	VF/NM 9.0	NM- 9.2
1-Norman Saunders painted-c	40	80	120	240	350	460

UNKNOWN WORLDS (See Journey Into...)

UNKNOWN WORLDS
American Comics Group/Best Synd. Features: Aug, 1960 - No. 57, Aug, 1967

	GD 2.0	VG 4.0	FN 6.0	VF 8.0	VF/NM 9.0	NM- 9.2
1-Schaffenberger-c	22	44	66	156	228	300
2-Dinosaur-c/story	13	26	39	90	133	175
3-5	10	20	30	73	107	140
6-11: 9-Dinosaur-c/story. 11-Last 10¢ issue	9	18	27	60	85	110
12-19: 12-Begin 12¢ issues?; ends #57	7	14	21	51	71	90
20-Herbie cameo (12-1/62-63)	8	16	24	53	74	95
21-35	6	12	18	38	52	65
36- "The People vs. Hendricks" by Craig; most popular ACG story ever	6	12	18	40	55	70
37-46	5	10	15	33	44	55
47-Williamson-a r-from Adventures Into the Unknown #96, 3 pgs.; Craig-a	5	10	15	36	48	60
48-57: 53-Frankenstein app.	4	8	12	29	40	50

NOTE: ***Ditko** a-49, 50p, 54. **Forte** a-3, 6, 11. **Landau** a-56(2). **Reinman** a-3, 9, 13, 20, 22, 23, 36, 38, 54. **Whitney** c/a-most issues. John Force, Magic Agent app.-35, 36, 48, 50, 52, 54, 56.*

UNKNOWN WORLDS OF FRANK BRUNNER
Eclipse Comics: Aug, 1985 - No. 2, Aug, 1985 ($1.75)

	GD 2.0	VG 4.0	FN 6.0	VF 8.0	VF/NM 9.0	NM- 9.2
1,2-B&W-r in color						3.50

UNKNOWN WORLDS OF SCIENCE FICTION
Marvel Comics: Jan, 1975 - No. 6, Nov, 1975; 1976 ($1.00, B&W Magazine)

	GD 2.0	VG 4.0	FN 6.0	VF 8.0	VF/NM 9.0	NM- 9.2
1-Williamson/Krenkel/Torres/Frazetta-r/Witzend #1, Neal Adams-r/Phase 1; Brunner & Kaluta-r; Freas/Romita-c	2	4	6	11	14	18
2-6: 5-Kaluta text illos	2	4	6	9	11	14
Special 1(1976,100 pgs.)-Newton painted-c	2	4	6	11	14	18

NOTE: ***Brunner** a-2; c-4, 6. **Buscema** a-Special 1p. **Chaykin** a-5. **Colan** a(p)-1, 3, 5, 6. **Corben** a-4. **Kaluta** a-2, Special 1(ext illos); c-2. **Morrow** a-3, 5. **Nino** a-3, 6, Special 1. **Perez** a-2, 3. Ray Bradbury interview in #1.*

UNLIMITED ACCESS (Also see Marvel Vs. DC))
Marvel Comics: Dec, 1997 - No. 4, Mar, 1998 ($2.99/$1.99, limited series)

	GD 2.0	VG 4.0	FN 6.0	VF 8.0	VF/NM 9.0	NM- 9.2
1-Spider-Man, Wonder Woman, Green Lantern & Hulk app.						3.50
2,3-($1.99): 2-X-Men, Legion of Super-Heroes app. 3-Original Avengers vs. original Justice League						2.50
4-($2.99) Amalgam Legion vs. Darkseid & Magneto						3.00

UNSANE (Formerly Mighty Bear #13, 14? or The Outlaws #10-14?)(Satire)
Star Publications: No. 15, June, 1954

	GD 2.0	VG 4.0	FN 6.0	VF 8.0	VF/NM 9.0	NM- 9.2
15-Disbrow-a(2); L. B. Cole-c	39	78	117	230	325	420

UNSEEN, THE
Visual Editions/Standard Comics: No. 5, 1952 - No. 15, July, 1954

	GD 2.0	VG 4.0	FN 6.0	VF 8.0	VF/NM 9.0	NM- 9.2
5-Horror stories in all; Toth-a	40	80	120	240	340	440
6,7,9,10-Jack Katz-a	31	62	93	175	248	320
8,11,13,14	23	46	69	130	183	235
12,15-Toth-a. 12-Tuska-a	31	62	93	175	248	320

NOTE: ***Nick Cardy** c-12. **Fawcette** a-13, 14. **Sekowsky** a-7, 8(2), 10, 13, 15.*

UNTAMED
Marvel Comics (Epic Comics/Heavy Hitters): June, 1993 - No. 3, Aug, 1993 ($1.95, lim. series)

	GD 2.0	VG 4.0	FN 6.0	VF 8.0	VF/NM 9.0	NM- 9.2
1-($2.50)-Embossed-c						2.50
2,3						2.25

UNTAMED LOVE (Also see Frank Frazetta's Untamed Love)
Quality Comics Group (Comic Magazines): Jan, 1950 - No. 5, Sept, 1950

	GD 2.0	VG 4.0	FN 6.0	VF 8.0	VF/NM 9.0	NM- 9.2
1-Ward-c, Gustavson-a	26	52	78	150	210	270
2,4: 2-5-Photo-c	16	32	48	92	126	160
3,5-Gustavson-a	18	36	54	101	138	175

UNTOLD LEGEND OF CAPTAIN MARVEL, THE
Marvel Comics: Apr, 1997 - No. 3, June, 1997 ($2.50, limited series)

	GD 2.0	VG 4.0	FN 6.0	VF 8.0	VF/NM 9.0	NM- 9.2
1-3						2.50

UNTOLD LEGEND OF THE BATMAN, THE (Also see Promotional section)
DC Comics: July, 1980 - No. 3, Sept, 1980 (Limited series)

	GD 2.0	VG 4.0	FN 6.0	VF 8.0	VF/NM 9.0	NM- 9.2
1-Origin; Joker-c; Byrne's 1st work at DC						6.00
2,3						4.50

NOTE: ***Aparo** a-1i, 2, 3. **Byrne** a-1p.*

UNTOLD ORIGIN OF THE FEMFORCE, THE (Also see Femforce)
AC Comics: 1989 ($4.95, 68 pgs.)

	GD 2.0	VG 4.0	FN 6.0	VF 8.0	VF/NM 9.0	NM- 9.2
1-Origin Femforce; Bill Black-a(i) & scripts						6.00

UNTOLD TALES OF CHASTITY
Chaos! Comics: Nov, 2000 ($2.95, one-shot)

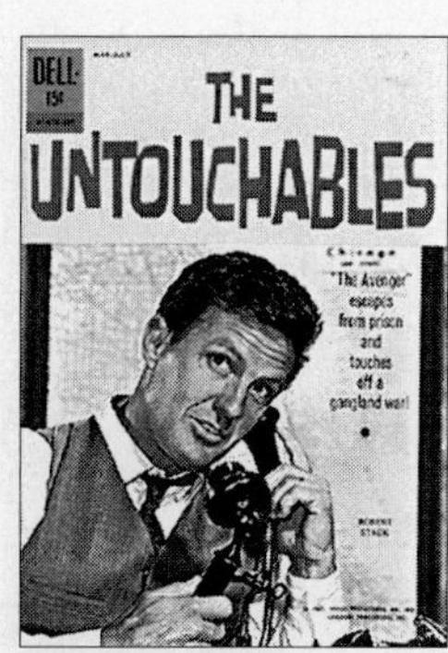

The Untouchables 01-879-207 © DELL

USA Comics #1 © TCI

Usagi Yojimbo V3#62 © Stan Sakai

	GD 2.0	VG 4.0	FN 6.0	VF 8.0	VF/NM 9.0	NM- 9.2
1-Origin; Steven Grant-s/Peter Vale-c/a						3.00
1-Premium Edition with glow in the dark cover						13.00

UNTOLD TALES OF LADY DEATH
Chaos! Comics: Nov, 2000 ($2.95, one-shot)

	GD	VG	FN	VF	VF/NM	NM-
1-Origin of Lady Death; Cremator app.; Kaminski-s						3.00
1-Premium Edition with glow in the dark cover by Steven Hughes						13.00

UNTOLD TALES OF PURGATORI
Chaos! Comics: Nov, 2000 ($2.95, one-shot)

	GD	VG	FN	VF	VF/NM	NM-
1-Purgatori in 57 B.C.; Rio-a/Grant-s						3.00
1-Premium Edition with glow in the dark cover						13.00

UNTOLD TALES OF SPIDER-MAN (Also see Amazing Fantasy #16-18)
Marvel Comics: Sept, 1995 - No. 25, Sept, 1997 (99¢)

	GD	VG	FN	VF	VF/NM	NM-
1-Kurt Busiek scripts begin; Pat Olliffe-c/a in all (except #9).						2.50
2-22, -1(7/97), 23-25: 2-1st app. Batwing. 4-1st app. The Spacemen (Gantry, Orbit, Satellite & Vacuum). 8-1st app. The Headsman; The Enforcers (The Big Man, Montana, The Ox & Fancy Dan) app. 9-Ron Frenz-a. 10-1st app. Commanda. 16-Reintro Mary Jane Watson. 21-X-Men-c/app. 25-Green Goblin						2.25
...'96-(1996, $1.95, 46 pgs.)-Kurt Busiek scripts; Mike Allred-c/a; Kurt Busiek & Pat Olliffe app. in back-up story; contains pin-ups						2.25
...'97-(1997, $1.95)-Wraparound-c						2.25
...: Strange Encounters ('98, $5.99) Dr. Strange app.						6.00

UNTOUCHABLES, THE (TV)
Dell Publishing Co.: No. 1237, 10-12/61 - No. 4, 8-10/62 (All have Robert Stack photo-c)

	GD	VG	FN	VF	VF/NM	NM-
Four Color 1237(#1)	24	48	72	174	255	335
Four Color 1286	17	34	51	118	174	230
01-879-207, 12-879-210(01879-210 on inside)	10	20	30	70	100	130

UNTOUCHABLES
Caliber Comics: Aug, 1997 - No. 4 ($2.95, B&W)

	GD	VG	FN	VF	VF/NM	NM-
1-4: 1-Pruett-s; variant covers by Kaluta & Showman						3.00

UNUSUAL TALES (Blue Beetle & Shadows From Beyond #50 on)
Charlton Comics: Nov, 1955 - No. 49, Mar-Apr, 1965

	GD	VG	FN	VF	VF/NM	NM-
1	30	60	90	170	240	310
2	15	30	45	86	118	150
3-5	11	22	33	63	84	105
6-Ditko-c only	14	28	42	81	111	140
7,8-Ditko-c/a. 8-Robot-c	27	54	81	155	218	280
9-Ditko-c/a (20 pgs.)	30	60	90	170	240	310
10-Ditko-c/a(4)	32	64	96	180	255	330
11-(3/58, 68 pgs.)-Ditko-a(4)	30	60	90	170	240	310
12,14-Ditko-a	19	38	57	107	149	190
13,16-20	7	14	21	46	63	80
15-Ditko-c/a	23	46	69	129	180	230
21,24,28	5	10	15	36	48	60
22,23,25-27,29-Ditko-a	10	20	30	72	104	135
30-49	4	8	12	27	36	45

NOTE: *Colan a-11. Ditko c-22, 23, 25-27, 31(part).*

UP FROM HARLEM (Tom Skinner...)
Spire Christian Comics (Fleming H. Revell Co.): 1973 (35/49¢)

	GD	VG	FN	VF	VF/NM	NM-
nn	1	3	4	6	8	10

UP-TO-DATE COMICS
King Features Syndicate: No date (1938) (36 pgs.; B&W cover) (10¢)

	GD	VG	FN	VF	VF/NM	NM-
nn-Popeye & Henry cover; The Phantom, Jungle Jim & Flash Gordon by Raymond, The Katzenjammer Kids, Curley Harper & others. Note: Variations in content exist.	26	52	78	150	210	270

UP YOUR NOSE AND OUT YOUR EAR (Satire)
Klevart Enterprises: Apr, 1972 - No. 2, June, 1972 (52 pgs., magazine)

	GD	VG	FN	VF	VF/NM	NM-
V1#1,2	2	4	6	11	14	18

URBAN
Moving Target Entertainment: 1994 ($1.75, B&W)

	GD	VG	FN	VF	VF/NM	NM-
1						2.25

URTH 4 (Also see Earth 4)
Continuity Comics: May, 1989 - No. 4, Dec, 1990 ($2.00, deluxe format)

	GD	VG	FN	VF	VF/NM	NM-
1-4: Ms. Mystic characters. 2-Neal Adams-c(i)						2.25

URZA-MISHRA WAR ON THE WORLD OF MAGIC THE GATHERING
Acclaim Comics (Armada): 1996 - No. 2, 1996 ($5.95, limited series)

	GD	VG	FN	VF	VF/NM	NM-
1,2						6.00

U.S. (See Uncle Sam)

USA COMICS
Timely Comics (USA): Aug, 1941 - No. 17, Fall, 1945

	GD	VG	FN	VF	VF/NM	NM-
1-Origin Major Liberty (called Mr. Liberty #1), Rockman by Wolverton, & The Whizzer by Avison; The Defender with sidekick Rusty & Jack Frost begin; The Young Avenger only app.; S&K-c plus 1 pg. art	1125	2250	3375	8438	13,219	18,000
2-Origin Captain Terror & The Vagabond; last Wolverton Rockman; Hitler-c	370	740	1110	2405	3703	5000
3-No Whizzer	296	592	888	1850	2775	3700
4-Last Rockman, Major Liberty, Defender, Jack Frost, & Capt. Terror; Corporal Dix app.	240	480	720	1500	2250	3000
5-Origin American Avenger & Roko the Amazing; The Blue Blade, The Black Widow & Victory Boys, Gypo the Gypsy Giant & Hills of Horror only app.; Sergeant Dix begins; no Whizzer; Hitler, Mussolini & Tojo-c	232	464	696	1450	2175	2900
6-Captain America (ends #17), The Destroyer, Jap Buster Johnson, Jeep Jones begin; Terror Squad only app.	300	600	900	1900	2850	3800
7-Captain Daring, Disk-Eyes the Detective by Wolverton app.; origin & only app. Marvel Boy (3/43); Secret Stamp begins; no Whizzer, Sergeant Dix; classic Schomburg-c	288	576	864	1800	2700	3600
8,10: 10-The Thunderbird only app.	192	384	576	1200	1800	2400
9-Last Secret Stamp; Hitler-c; classic-c	220	440	660	1375	2063	2750
11,12: 11-No Jeep Jones	152	304	456	950	1425	1900
13-17: 13-No Whizzer; Jeep Jones ends. 15-No Destroyer; Jap Buster Johnson ends	112	224	336	700	1050	1400

NOTE: ***Brodsky** c-14. **Gabrielle** c-4. **Schomburg** c-6, 7, 10, 12, 13, 15-17. **Shores** a-1, 4; c-9, 11. **Ed Win** a-4. Cover features: 1-The Defender; 2, 3-Captain Terror; 4-Major Liberty; 5-Victory Boys; 6-17-Captain America & Bucky.*

U.S. AGENT (See Jeff Jordan...)

U.S. AGENT (See Captain America #354)
Marvel Comics: June, 1993 - No. 4, Sept, 1993 ($1.75, limited series)

	GD	VG	FN	VF	VF/NM	NM-
1-4						2.25

U.S. AGENT
Marvel Comics: Aug, 2001 - No. 3, Oct, 2001 ($2.99, limited series)

	GD	VG	FN	VF	VF/NM	NM-
1-3: Ordway-s/a(p)/c. 2,3-Captain America app.						3.00

USAGI YOJIMBO (See Albedo, Doomsday Squad #3 & Space Usagi)
Fantagraphics Books: July, 1987 - No. 38 ($2.00/$2.25, B&W)

	GD	VG	FN	VF	VF/NM	NM-
1	1	2	3	5	6	8
1,8,10-2nd printings						2.25
2-9						4.00
10,11: 10-Leonardo app. (TMNT). 11-Aragonés-a						5.00
12-29						3.00
30-38: 30-Begin $2.25-c						3.00
Color Special 1 (11/89, $2.95, 68 pgs.)-new & r						3.50
Color Special 2 (10/91, $3.50)						3.50
Color Special #3 (10/92, $3.50)-Jeff Smith's Bone promo on inside-c						3.50
Summer Special 1 (1986, B&W, $2.75)-r/early Albedo issues						3.00

USAGI YOJIMBO
Mirage Studios: V2#1, Mar, 1993 - No. 16, 1994 ($2.75)

	GD	VG	FN	VF	VF/NM	NM-
V2#1-16: 1-Teenage Mutant Ninja Turtles app.						3.00

USAGI YOJIMBO
Dark Horse Comics: V3#1, Apr, 1996 - Present ($2.95/$2.99, B&W)

	GD	VG	FN	VF	VF/NM	NM-
V3#1-70: Stan Sakai-c/a						3.00
Color Special #4 (7/97, $2.95) "Green Persimmon"						3.00
Daisho TPB ('98, $14.95) r/Mirage series #7-14						15.00
Demon Mask TPB ('01, $15.95)						16.00
Grasscutter TPB ('99, $16.95) r/#13-22						17.00
Gray Shadows TPB ('00, $14.95) r/#23-30						15.00
Seasons TPB ('99, $14.95) r/#7-12						15.00
Shades of Death TPB ('97, $14.95) r/Mirage series #1-6						15.00
The Brink of Life and Death TPB ('98, $14.95) r/Mirage series #13,15,16 & Dark Horse series #1-6						15.00
The Shrouded Moon TPB (1/03, $15.95) r/#46-52						16.00

U.S. AIR FORCE COMICS (Army Attack #38 on)
Charlton Comics: Oct, 1958 - No. 37, Mar-Apr, 1965

	GD	VG	FN	VF	VF/NM	NM-
1	7	14	21	46	63	80
2	4	8	12	24	32	40
3-10	3	6	9	19	25	32
11-20	3	6	9	18	24	30
21-37	3	6	9	16	20	25

NOTE: *Glanzman c/a-9, 10, 12. Montes/Bache a-33.*

U.S. War Machine V2#1 © MAR

Valor #8 © DC

Vampi #18 © Harris

	GD 2.0	VG 4.0	FN 6.0	VF 8.0	VF/NM 9.0	NM- 9.2

USA IS READY
Dell Publishing Co.: 1941 (68 pgs., one-shot)

1-War propaganda	40	80	120	240	345	450

U.S. BORDER PATROL COMICS (Sgt. Dick Carter of the...) (See Holyoke One Shot)

USER
DC Comics (Vertigo): 2001 - No. 3, 2001 ($5.95, limited series)

1-3-Devin Grayson-s; Sean Phillips & John Bolton-a 6.00

U.S. FIGHTING AIR FORCE (Also see United States Fighting Air Force)
I. W. Enterprises: No date (1960s?)

1,9(nd): 1-r/United States Fighting...#?. 9-r/#1	2	4	6	9	11	14

U.S. FIGHTING MEN
Super Comics: 1963 - 1964 (Reprints)

10-r/With the U.S. Paratroops #4(Avon)	2	4	6	10	13	16
11,12,15-18: 11-r/Monty Hall #10. 12,16,17,18-r/U.S. Fighting Air Force #10,3,?&? 15-r/Man Comics #11	2	4	6	10	13	16

U.S. JONES (Also see Wonderworld Comics #28)
Fox Features Syndicate: Nov, 1941 - No. 2, Jan, 1942

1-U.S. Jones & The Topper begin; Nazi-c	124	248	372	775	1163	1550
2-Nazi-c	84	168	252	525	788	1050

U.S. MARINES
Charlton Comics: Fall, 1964 (12¢, one-shot)

1-1st app. Capt. Dude; Glanzman-a	3	7	10	21	28	35

U.S. MARINES IN ACTION
Avon Periodicals: Aug, 1952 - No. 3, Dec, 1952

1-Louis Ravielli-c/a	9	18	27	52	66	80
2,3: 3-Kinstler-c	7	14	21	35	43	50

U.S. 1
Marvel Comics Group: May, 1983 - No. 12, Oct, 1984 (7,8: painted-c)

1-12: 2-Sienkiewicz-c. 3-12-Michael Golden-c 2.25

U.S. PARATROOPS (See With the...)

U.S. PARATROOPS
I. W. Enterprises: 1964?

1,8: 1-r/With the U.S. Paratroops #1; Wood-c. 8-r/With the U.S. Paratroops #6; Kinstler-c	2	4	6	10	13	16

U.S. TANK COMMANDOS
Avon Periodicals: June, 1952 - No. 4, Mar, 1953

1-Kinstler-c	10	20	30	58	77	95
2-4: Kinstler-c	8	16	24	43	54	65
I.W. Reprint #1,8: 1-r/#1. 8-r/#3	2	4	6	10	13	16

NOTE: ***Kinstler** a-I.W. #1; c-1-4, I.W. #1, 8.*

U.S. WAR MACHINE (Also see Iron Man and War Machine)
Marvel Comics (MAX): Nov, 2001 - No. 12, Jan, 2002 ($1.50, B&W, weekly limited series)

1-12-Chuck Austen-s/a/c 2.25
TPB (12/01, $14.95) r/#1-12 15.00

U.S. WAR MACHINE 2.0
Marvel Comics (MAX): Sept, 2003 - Present ($2.99)

1-3-Austen-s/Christian Moore-CGI art 3.00

"V" (TV)
DC Comics: Feb, 1985 - No. 18, July, 1986

1-Based on TV movie & series (Sci/Fi) 3.00
2-18: 17,18-Denys Cowan-c/a 2.25

VACATION COMICS (Also see A-1 Comics)
Magazine Enterprises: No. 16, 1948 (one-shot)

A-1 16-The Pixies, Tom Tom, Flying Fredd & Koko & Kola	6	12	18	31	38	45

VACATION DIGEST
Harvey Comics: Sept, 1987 ($1.25, digest size)

1	1	2	3	5	6	8

VACATION IN DISNEYLAND (Also see Dell Giants)
Dell Publishing Co./Gold Key (1965): Aug-Oct, 1959; May, 1965 (Walt Disney)

Four Color 1025-Barks-a	19	38	57	136	198	260
1(30024-508)(G.K., 5/65, 25¢)-r/Dell Giant #30 & cover to #1 ('58); celebrates Disneyland's 10th anniversary	6	12	18	38	52	65

VACATION PARADE (See Dell Giants)

VALERIA THE SHE BAT
Continuity Comics: May, 1993 - No. 5, Nov, 1993

1-Premium; acetate-c; N. Adams-a/scripts; given as gift to retailers	1	2	3	5	6	8

5 (11/93)-Embossed-c; N. Adams-a/scripts 3.00
NOTE: *Due to lack of continuity, #2-4 do not exist.*

VALERIA THE SHE BAT
Acclaim Comics (Windjammer): Sept, 1995 - No.2, Oct, 1995 ($2.50, limited series)

1,2 2.50

VALKYRIE (See Airboy)
Eclipse Comics: May,1987 - No. 3, July, 1987 ($1.75, limited series)

1-3: 2-Holly becomes new Black Angel 2.50

VALKYRIE
Marvel Comics: Jan, 1997 ($2.95, one-shot)

1-w/pin-ups 3.00

VALKYRIE!
Eclipse Comics: July, 1988 - No. 3, Sept, 1988 ($1.95, limited series)

1-3 2.25

VALLEY OF THE DINOSAURS (TV)
Charlton Comics: Apr, 1975 - No. 11, Dec, 1976 (Hanna-Barbara)

1-W. Howard-i	2	4	6	14	18	22
2,4-11: 2-W. Howard-i	2	4	6	8	10	12
3-Byrne text illos (early work, 7/75)	2	4	6	10	13	16

VALLEY OF THE DINOSAURS (TV)
Harvey Comics: Oct, 1992 ($1.50, giant-sized)

1-Reprints 3.00

VALLEY OF GWANGI (See Movie Classics)

VALOR
E. C. Comics: Mar-Apr, 1955 - No. 5, Nov-Dec, 1955

1-Williamson/Torres-a; Wood-c/a	26	52	78	195	278	360
2-Williamson-c/a; Wood-a	21	42	63	158	229	300
3,4: 3-Williamson, Crandall-a. 4-Wood-c	16	32	48	120	170	220
5-Wood-c/a; Williamson/Evans-a	14	28	42	105	153	200

NOTE: ***Crandall** a-3, 4. **Ingels** a-1, 2, 4, 5. **Krigstein** a-1-5. **Orlando** a-3, 4; c-3. **Wood** a-1, 2, 5; c-1, 4, 5.*

VALOR
Gemstone Publishing: Oct, 1998 - No. 5, Feb, 1999 ($2.50)

1-5-Reprints 2.50

VALOR (Also see Legion of Super-Heroes & Legionnaires)
DC Comics: Nov, 1992 - No. 23, Sept, 1994 ($1.25/$1.50)

1-23: 1-Eclipso The Darkness Within aftermath. 2-Vs. Supergirl. 4-Vs. Lobo. 12-Lobo cameo. 14-Legionnaires, JLA app. 17-Austin-c(i); death of Valor. 18-22-Build-up to Zero Hour. 23-Zero Hour tie-in 2.25

VALOR THUNDERSTAR AND HIS FIREFLIES
Now Comics: Dec, 1986 ($1.50)

1-Ordway-c(p) 2.25

VAMPI (Vampirella's...)
Harris Publications (Anarchy Studios): Aug, 2000 - No. 25, Feb, 2003 ($2.95/$2.99)

Limited Edition Preview Book (5/00) Preview pages & sketchbook 3.00
1-(8/00, $2.95) Lau-a(p)/Conway-s 3.00
1-Platinum Edition 20.00
2-25: 17-Barberi-a 3.00
2-25-Deluxe Edition variants ($9.95): 4-Finch-c. 5-Wieringo-c. 6-Cha-c 10.00
...Digital 1 (11/01, $2.95) CGI art; Haberlin-s 3.00
...Digital Preview (Anarchy Studios, 7/01, $2.95) preview of CGI art 3.00
Switchblade Kiss HC (2001, $24.95) r/#1-6 25.00
Wizard #1/2 (mail order, $9.95) includes sketch pages 10.00

VAMPI VICIOUS
Anarchy Studios:

Preview Ed. (Apr, 2003, $1.99) Flip book w/ Xin: Journey of the Monkey King Preview Ed. 2.25

VAMPIRE BITES
Brainstorm Comics: May, 1995 - No. 2, Sept, 1996 ($2.95, B&W)

1,2:1-Color pin-up 3.00

VAMPIRE LESTAT, THE

Vampirella #7 © WP

Vampirella #113 © WP

Vampirella #18 © Harris

GD 2.0 VG 4.0 FN 6.0 VF 8.0 VF/NM 9.0 NM- 9.2

Innovation Publishing: Jan, 1990 - No. 12, 1991 ($2.50, painted limited series)

1-Adapts novel; Bolton painted-c on all 2 4 6 11 14 18
1-2nd printing (has UPC code, 1st prints don't) 3.00
1-3rd & 4th printings 2.50
2-1st printing 1 2 3 5 6 8
2-2nd & 3rd printings 2.50
3-5 5.00
3-6,9-2nd printings 2.50
6-12 3.00

VAMPIRELLA (Magazine)(See Warren Presents)
Warren Publishing Co./Harris Publications #113: Sept, 1969 - No. 112, Feb, 1983; No. 113, Jan, 1988? (B&W)

1-Intro. Vampirella in original costume & wings; Frazetta-c/intro. page; Adams-a; Crandall-a 40 80 120 300 450 600
2-1st app. Vampirella's cousin Evily-c/s; 1st/only app. Draculina, Vampirella's blonde twin sister 15 30 45 109 160 210
3 (Low distribution) 35 70 105 263 394 525
4,6 10 20 30 72 104 135
5,7,9: 5,7-Frazetta-c. 9-Barry Smith-a; Boris/Wood-c 10 20 30 73 107 140
8-Vampirella begins by Tom Sutton as serious strip (early issues-gag line) 11 22 33 77 114 150
10-No Vampi story; Brunner, Adams, Wood-a 6 12 18 40 55 70
11-Origin & 1st app. Pendragon; Frazetta-c 7 14 21 50 68 85
12-Vampi by Gonzales begins 7 14 21 50 68 85
13-15: 14-1st Maroto-a; Ploog-a 7 14 21 50 68 85
16,22,25: 16-1st full Dracula-c/app. 22-Color insert preview of Maroto's Dracula. 25-Vampi on cocaine-s 6 12 18 43 59 75
17,18,20,21,23,24: 17-Tomb of the Gods begins by Maroto, ends #22. 18-22-Dracula-s 6 12 18 43 59 75
19 (1973 Annual) Creation of Vampi text bio 8 16 24 53 74 95
26,28,34-36,39,40: All have 8 pg. color inserts. 28-Board game inside covers. 34,35-1st Fleur the Witch Woman. 39,40-Color Dracula-s. 40-Wrightson bio 4 8 12 27 36 45
27 (1974 Annual) New color Vampi-s; mostly-r 5 10 15 33 44 55
29,38,45: 38-2nd Vampi as Cleopatra/Blood Red Queen of Hearts; 1st Mayo-a. 4 8 12 27 36 45
30-32: 30-Intro. Pantha; Corben-a(color). 31-Origin Luana, the Beast Girl. 32-Jones-a 4 8 12 27 36 45
33-Wrightson ends; Pantha ends 4 8 12 27 36 45
36,37: 36-1st Vampi as Cleopatra/Blood Red Queen of Hearts. 37-(1975 Annual) 4 8 12 29 40 50
41-44,47,48: 41-Dracula-s 3 7 10 21 28 35
46-(10/75) Origin-r from Annual 1 4 8 12 25 33 42
49-1st Blind Priestess; The Blood Red Queen of Hearts storyline begins; Poe-s 3 7 10 21 28 35
50-Spirit cameo by Eisner; 40 pg. Vampi-s; Pantha & Fleur app.; Jones-a 3 7 10 21 28 35
51-53,56,57,59-62,65,66,68,75,79,80,82-86,88,89: 60-62,65,66-The Blood Red Queen of Hearts app. 60-1st Blind Priestess-c 3 6 9 16 20 25
54,55,63,81,87: 54-Vampi-s (42 pgs.); 8 pg. color Corben-a. 55-All Gonzales-a(r). 63-10 pgs. Wrightson-a 3 6 9 16 20 25
58,70,72: 58-(92 pgs.) 70-Rook app. 3 6 9 19 25 32
64,73: 64-(100 pg. Giant) All Mayo-a; 70 pg. Vampi-s. 73-69 pg. Vampi-s; Mayo-a 3 7 10 21 28 35
67,69,71,74,76-78-All Barbara Leigh photo-c 3 6 9 19 25 32
90-99: 90-Toth-a. 91-All-r; Gonzales-a. 93-Cassandra St. Knight begins, ends #103; new Pantha series begins, ends #108 3 6 9 16 20 25
100 (96 pg. r-special)-Origin reprinted from Ann. 1; mostly reprints; Vampirella appears topless in new 21 pg. story 7 14 21 50 68 85
101-104,106,107: All lower print run. 101,102-The Blood Red Queen of Hearts app. 107-All Maroto reprint-a issue 4 8 12 29 40 50
105,108-110: 108-Torpedo series by Toth begins; Vampi nudity splash page. 110-(100 pg. Summer Spectacular) 4 8 12 29 40 50
111,112: Low print run. 111-Giant Collector's Edition ($2.50) 112-(84 pgs.) last Warren issue 6 12 18 38 52 65
113 (1988)-1st Harris Issue; very low print run 29 58 87 210 310 410
Annual 1(1972)-New definitive origin of Vampirella by Gonzales; reprints by Neal Adams (from #1), Wood (from #9) 27 54 81 196 291 385
Special 1 (1977) Softcover (color, large-square bound)-Only available thru mail order 15 30 45 109 160 210
Special 1 (1977) Hardcover (color, large-square bound)-Only available through mail order (scarce)(500 produced, signed & #'d) 35 70 105 263 394 525
#1 1969 Commemorative Edition (2001, $4.95) reprints entire #1 5.00

GD 2.0 VG 4.0 FN 6.0 VF 8.0 VF/NM 9.0 NM- 9.2

NOTE: ***Ackerman** s-1-3. **Neal Adams** a-1, 10p, 19p(r/#10), 44(1 pg.), Annual 1. **Alcala** a-78, 90, 93i. **Bodé/Todd** c-3. **Bodé/Jones** c-4. **Boris/Wood** c-9. **Brunner** a-10, 12(1 pg.). **Corben** a-30, 31, 33, 36, 54; c-30, 31, 33, 54. **Crandall** a-1, 19(r/#1). **Frazetta** c-1, 5, 7, 11, 31. **Heath** a-58, 61, 67, 76-78, 83. **Infantino** a-57-62. **Jones** a-5, 9, 12, 27, 32 (color), 33(2 pg.), 34, 50i, 83r. **Ken Kelly** c-6, 38, 39, 40(back-c), 46, 70, 95. **Nebres** a-84, 88-90, 92-96. **Nino** a-59i, 61i, 67, 76, 85, 90. **Ploog** a-14. **Barry Smith** a-9. **Starlin** a-78. **Sutton** a-1-5, 7-11, Annual 1. **Toth** a-90i, 108, 110. **Wood** a-9, 10, 12, 19(r/#12), 27r, Annual 1; c-9(partial). **Wrightson** a-33(w/**Jones**), 40(Bio cameo) 63r. All reprint issues-19, 74, 83, 91, 105, 107, 109, 111. Annuals from 1973 on are included in regular numbering. Later annuals are same format as regular issues. Color inserts (8 pgs.) in 22, 25-28, 30-35, 39, 40, 45, 46, 49, 54, 55, 67, 72. 16 pg color insert in #36.*

VAMPIRELLA (Also see Cain/... & Vengeance of...)
Harris Publications: Nov, 1992 - No. 5, Nov, 1993 ($2.95)

0-Bagged 5.00
0-Gold 3 6 9 18 24 30
1-Jim Balent inks in #1-3; Adam Hughes c-1-3 2 4 6 12 16 20
1-2nd printing 5.00
1-(11/97) Commemorative Edition 3.00
2 2 4 6 10 12 15
3-5: 4-Snyder III-c. 5-Brereton painted-c 1 2 3 5 6 8
Trade paperback nn (10/93, $5.95)-r/#1-4; Jusko-c 1 2 3 4 5 7

NOTE: *Issues 1-5 contain certificates for free **Dave Stevens** Vampirella poster.*

VAMPIRELLA (THE NEW MONTHLY)
Harris Publications: Nov, 1997 - No. 26, Apr, 2000 ($2.95)

1-3-"Ascending Evil" -Morrison & Millar-s/Conner & Palmiotti-a. 1-Three covers by Quesada/Palmiotti, Conner, and Conner/Palmiotti 3.00
1-3-($9.95) Jae Lee variant covers 10.00
1-($24.95) Platinum Ed.w/Quesada-c 25.00
4-6-"Holy War"-Small & Stull-a, 4-Linsner variant-c 3.00
7-9-"Queen's Gambit"-Shi app. 7-Two covers. 8-Pantha-c/app. 3.00
7-($9.95) Conner variant-c 10.00
10-12-"Hell on Earth"; Small-a/Coney-s. 12-New costume 3.00
10-Jae Lee variant-c 1 3 4 6 8 10
13-15-"World's End" Zircher-p; Pantha back-up, Texeira-a 3.00
16,17: 16-Pantha-c;Texeira-a; Vampi back-up story. 17-(Pantha #2) 3.00
18-20-"Rebirth": Jae Lee-c on all. 18-Loeb-s/Sale-a. 19-Alan Davis-a. 20-Bruce Timm-a 3.00
18-20-($9.95) Variant covers: 18-Sale. 19-Davis. 20-Timm 12.00
21-26: 21,22-Dangerous Games; Small-a. 23-Lady Death-c/app.; Cleavenger-a. 24,25-Lau-a. 26-Lady Death & Pantha-c/app.; Cleavenger-a. 3.00
0-(1/99) also variant-c with Pantha #0; same contents 3.00
TPB ($7.50) r/#1-3 "Ascending Evil" 8.00
Ascending Evil Ashcan (8/97, $1.00) 2.25
Hell on Earth Ashcan (7/98, $1.00) 2.25
The End Ashcan (3/00, $6.00) 6.00
...30th Anniversary Celebration Preview (7/99) B&W preview of #18-20 10.00

VAMPIRELLA
Harris Publications: June, 2001 - No. 22, Aug, 2003 ($2.95/$2.99)

1-Four covers (Mayhew w/foil logo, Campbell, Anacleto, Jae Lee) Mayhew-a; Mark Millar-s 3.00
2-22: 2-Two covers (Mayhew & Chiodo). 3-Timm var-c. 4-Horn var-c. 7-10-Dawn Brown-a; Pantha back-up w/Texeira-a. 15-22-Conner-c 3.00
Giant-Size Ashcan (5/01, $5.95) B&W preview art and Mayhew interview 6.00
... : Nowheresville Preview Edition (3/01, $2.95)- previews Mayhew art and photo models 3.00
...Nowheresville TPB (1/02, $12.95) r/#1-3 with cover gallery 13.00

VAMPIRELLA & PANTHA SHOWCASE
Harris Publications: Jan, 1997 ($1.50, one-shot)

1-Millar-s/Texeira-c/a; flip book w/"Blood Lust"; Robinson-s/Jusko-c/a 3.00

VAMPIRELLA & THE BLOOD RED QUEEN OF HEARTS
Harris Publications: Sept, 1996 ($9.95, 96 pgs., B&W, squarebound, one-shot)

nn-r/Vampirella #49,60-62,65,66,101,102; John Bolton-c; Michael Bair back-c 1 3 4 6 8 10

VAMPIRELLA: BLOODLUST
Harris Publications: July, 1997 - No. 2, Aug, 1997 ($4.95, limited series)

1,2-Robinson-s/Jusko-painted c/a 5.00

VAMPIRELLA CLASSIC
Harris Publications: Feb, 1995 - No. 5, Nov, 1995 ($2.95, limited series)

1-5: Reprints Archie Goodwin stories. 3.00

VAMPIRELLA COMICS MAGAZINE
Harris Publications: Oct, 2003 - Present ($3.95/$9.95, magazine-sized)

1-($3.95) Texiera-c; b&w and color stories, Alan Moore interview; reviews 4.00
1,2-($9.95) 1-Three covers (Model Photo cover, Palmiotti-c, Wheatley Frankenstein-c) 10.00
2-($3.95) KISS interview 4.00

Vampirella Lives #2 © Harris

Vampirella/Witchblade #1 © Harris/TCOW

Vampire Tales #1 © MAR

GD VG FN VF VF/NM NM-
2.0 4.0 6.0 8.0 9.0 9.2

VAMPIRELLA: CROSSOVER GALLERY
Harris Publications: Sept, 1997 ($2.95, one-shot)
1-Wraparound-c by Campbell, pinups by Jae Lee, Mack, Allred, Art Adams, Quesada & Palmiotti and others 3.00

VAMPIRELLA: DEATH & DESTRUCTION
Harris Publications: July, 1996 - No. 3, Sept, 1996 ($2.95, limited series)
1-3: Amanda Conner-a(p) in all. 1-Tucci-c. 2-Hughes-c. 3-Jusko-c 3.00
1-($9.95)-Limited Edition; Beachum-c 10.00

VAMPIRELLA/DRACULA & PANTHA SHOWCASE
Harris Publications: Aug, 1997 ($1.50, one-shot)
1-Ellis, Robinson, and Moore-s; flip book w/"Pantha" 3.00

VAMPIRELLA/DRACULA: THE CENTENNIAL
Harris Publications: Oct, 1997 ($5.95, one-shot)
1-Ellis, Robinson, and Moore-s; Beachum, Frank/Smith, and Mack/Mays-a Bolton-painted-c 6.00

VAMPIRELLA: JULIE STRAIN SPECIAL
Harris Publications: Sept, 2000 ($3.95, one-shot)
1-Photo-c w/yellow background; interview and photo gallery 4.00
1-Limited Edition ($9.95); cover photo w/black background 10.00

VAMPIRELLA/LADY DEATH (Also see Lady Death/Vampirella)
Harris Publications: Feb, 1999 ($3.50, one-shot)
1-Small-a/Nelson painted-c 3.50
1-Valentine Edition ($9.95); pencil-c by Small 10.00

VAMPIRELLA: LEGENDARY TALES
Harris Publications: May, 2000 - No. 2, June, 2000 ($2.95, B&W)
1,2-Reprints from magazine; Cleavenger painted-c 3.00
1,2-($9.95) Variant painted-c by Mike Mayhew 10.00

VAMPIRELLA LIVES
Harris Publications: Dec, 1996 - No. 3, Feb, 1997 ($3.50/$2.95, limited series)
1-Die cut-c; Quesada & Palmiotti-c, Ellis-s/Conner-a 3.50
1-Deluxe Ed.-photo-c 3.50
2,3-($2.95)-Two editions (1 photo-c): 3-J. Scott Campbell-c 3.00

VAMPIRELLA: MORNING IN AMERICA
Harris Publications/Dark Horse Comics: 1991 - No. 4, 1992 ($3.95, B&W, lim. series, 52 pgs.)
1,2-All have Kaluta painted-c 1 2 3 5 6 8
3,4 1 3 4 6 8 10

VAMPIRELLA OF DRAKULON
Harris Publications: Jan, 1996 - No. 5, Sept, 1996 ($2.95)
0-5: All reprints. 0-Jim Silke-c. 3-Polybagged w/card. 4-Texeira-c 3.00

VAMPIRELLA/PAINKILLER JANE
Harris Publications: May, 1998 ($3.50, one-shot)
1-Waid & Augustyn-s/Leonardi & Palmiotti-a 3.50
1-($9.95) Variant-c 10.00

VAMPIRELLA PIN-UP SPECIAL
Harris Publications: Oct, 1995 ($2.95, one-shot)
1-Hughes-c, pin-ups by various 5.00
1-Variant-c 5.00

VAMPIRELLA: RETRO
Harris Publications: Mar, 1998 - No. 3, May, 1998 ($2.50, B&W, limited series)
1-3: Reprints; Silke painted covers 3.00

VAMPIRELLA: SAD WINGS OF DESTINY
Harris Publications: Sept, 1996 ($3.95, one-shot)
1-Jusko-c 4.00

VAMPIRELLA/SHADOWHAWK: CREATURES OF THE NIGHT (Also see Shadowhawk)
Harris Publications: 1995 ($4.95, one-shot)
1 5.00

VAMPIRELLA/SHI (See Shi/Vampirella)
Harris Publications: Oct, 1997 ($2.95, one-shot)
1-Ellis-s 3.00
1-Chromium-c 6.00

VAMPIRELLA: SILVER ANNIVERSARY COLLECTION
Harris Publications: Jan, 1997 - No. 4 Apr, 1997 ($2.50, limited series)
1-4: Two editions: Bad Girl by Beachum, Good Girl by Silke 3.00

GD VG FN VF VF/NM NM-
2.0 4.0 6.0 8.0 9.0 9.2

VAMPIRELLA'S SUMMER NIGHTS
Harris Publications: 1992 (one-shot)
1-Art Adams infinity cover; centerfold by Stelfreeze 3 7 10 21 28 35

VAMPIRELLA STRIKES
Harris Publications: Sept, 1995 - No. 8, Dec, 1996 ($2.95, limited series)
1-8: 1-Photo-c. 2-Deodato-c; polybagged w/card. 5-Eudaemon-c/app; wraparound-c; alternate-c exists. 6-(6/96)-Mark Millar script; Texeira-c; alternate-c exists. 7-Flip book 3.00
1-Newsstand Edition; diff. photo-c., 1-Limited Ed.; diff. photo-c 3.00
Annual 1-(12/96, $2.95) Delano-s; two covers 3.00

VAMPIRELLA: 25TH ANNIVERSARY SPECIAL
Harris Publications: Oct, 1996 ($5.95, squarebound, one-shot)
nn-Reintro The Blood Red Queen of Hearts; James Robinson, Grant Morrison & Warren Ellis scripts; Mark Texeira, Michael Bair & Amanda Conner-a(p); Frank Frazetta-c 6.00
nn-($6.95)-Silver Edition 7.00

VAMPIRELLA VS. HEMORRHAGE
Harris Publications: Apr, 1997($3.50)
1 3.50

VAMPIRELLA VS. PANTHA
Harris Publications: Mar, 1997 ($3.50)
1-Two covers; Millar-s/Texeira-c/a 3.50

VAMPIRELLA/WETWORKS (See Wetworks/Vampirella)
Harris Publications: June, 1997 ($2.95, one-shot)
1 3.00
1-($9.95) Alternate Edition; cardstock-c 10.00

VAMPIRELLA/WITCHBLADE
Harris Publications: 2003 ($2.99, one-shot)
1-Brian Wood-s/Steve Pugh-a; 3 covers by Texeira, Conner and Pugh 3.00

VAMPIRE'S CHRISTMAS, THE
Image Comics: Oct, 2003 ($5.95, over-sized graphic novel)
nn-Linsner-s/a; Dubisch-painted-a 6.00

VAMPIRE TALES
Marvel Comics Group: Aug, 1973 - No. 11, June, 1975 (75¢, B&W, magazine)
1-Morbius, the Living Vampire begins by Pablo Marcos (1st solo Morbius series & 5th Morbius app.) 4 8 12 29 40 50
2-Intro. Satana; Steranko-r 4 8 12 22 30 38
3,5,6: 3-Satana app. 5-Origin Morbius. 6-1st Lilith app. 3 6 9 19 25 32
4,7 3 6 9 16 20 25
8-1st solo Blade story (see Tomb of Dracula) 4 8 12 22 30 38
9-Blade app. 3 6 9 19 25 32
10,11 3 6 9 16 20 25
Annual 1(10/75)-Heath-r/#9 3 6 9 16 20 25
NOTE: ***Alcala*** *a-6, 8, 9i.* ***Boris*** *c-4, 6.* ***Chaykin*** *a-7.* ***Everett*** *a-1r.* ***Gulacy*** *a-7p.* ***Heath*** *a-9.* ***Infantino*** *a-3r.* ***Gil Kane*** *a-4, 5r.*

VAMPIRE VERSES, THE
CFD Productions: Aug, 1995 - No. 4, 1995 ($2.95, B&W, mature)
1-4 3.00

VAMPI VICIOUS
Harris Publications (Anarchy Studios): Aug, 2003 - Present ($2.99)
1-3: 1-McKeever-s/Dogan-a; 3 covers by Dogan, Lau & Noto. 3-Kau-a 3.00

VAMPS
DC Comics (Vertigo): Aug, 1994 - No. 6, Jan, 1995 ($1.95, lim. series, mature)
1-6-Bolland-c 3.00
Trade paperback ($9.95)-r/#1-6 10.00

VAMPS: HOLLYWOOD & VEIN
DC Comics (Vertigo): Feb, 1996 - No. 6, July, 1996 ($2.25, lim. series, mature)
1-6: Winslade-c 2.50

VAMPS: PUMPKIN TIME
DC Comics (Vertigo): Dec, 1998 - No. 3, Feb, 1999 ($2.50, lim. series, mature)
1-3: Quitely-c 2.50

VANDALA
Chaos! Comics: Aug, 2000 ($2.95)
1-Cleavenger-c 3.00
1-($9.95) Premium Edition 10.00
Vandala II #1 (9/01, $2.99) Benes-a 3.00

The Vault of Horror #15 © WMG

Vengeance of Vampirella #10 © Harris

Venom #2 © MAR

GD VG FN VF VF/NM NM-
2.0 4.0 6.0 8.0 9.0 9.2

VANGUARD (...Outpost: Earth) (See Megaton)
Megaton Comics: 1987 ($1.50)

1-Erik Larsen-c(p) 3.00

VANGUARD (See Savage Dragon #2)
Image Comics (Highbrow Entertainment): Oct, 1993 - No.6, 1994 ($1.95)

1-6: 1-Wraparound gatefold-c; Erik Larsen back-up-a; Supreme x-over. 3-(12/93)-Indicia says December 1994. 4-Berzerker back-up. 5-Angel Medina-a(p) 3.00

VANGUARD (See Savage Dragon #2)
Image Comics: Aug, 1996 - No.4, Feb, 1997 ($2.95, B&W, limited series)

1-4 3.00

VANGUARD: ETHEREAL WARRIORS
Image Comics: Aug, 2000 ($5.95, B&W)

1-Fosco & Larsen-a 6.00

VANGUARD ILLUSTRATED
Pacific Comics: Nov, 1983 - No. 11, Oct, 1984 (Baxter paper)(Direct sales only)

1-6,8-11: 1,7-Nudity scenes. 2-1st app. Stargrazers (see Legends of the Stargrazers; Dave Stevens-c 3.00
7-1st app. Mr. Monster (r-in Mr. Monster #1) 5.00
NOTE: ***Evans*** *a-7.* ***Kaluta*** *c-5, 7p.* ***Perez*** *a-6; c-6.* ***Rude*** *a-1-4; c-4.* ***Williamson*** *c-3.*

VANGUARD: STRANGE VISITORS
Image Comics: Oct, 1996 - No.4, Feb, 1997 ($2.95, B&W, limited series)

1-4: 3-Supreme-c/app. 3.00

VANITY (See Pacific Presents #3)
Pacific Comics: Jun, 1984 - No. 2, Aug, 1984 ($1.50, direct sales)

1,2: Origin 2.25

VARIETY COMICS (The Spice of Comics)
Rural Home Publ./Croyden Publ. Co.: 1944 - No. 2, 1945; No. 3, 1946

1-Origin Captain Valiant 22 44 66 127 176 225
2-Captain Valiant 13 26 39 76 103 130
3(1946-Croyden)-Captain Valiant 11 22 33 63 84 105

VARIETY COMICS (See Fox Giants)

VARIOGENESIS
Dagger Comics Group: June, 1994 ($3.50)

0 3.50

VARSITY
Parents' Magazine Institute: 1945

1 8 16 24 46 58 70

VAULT OF EVIL
Marvel Comics Group: Feb, 1973 - No. 23, Nov, 1975

1 (1950s reprints begin) 3 6 9 16 20 24
2-23: 3,4-Brunner-c. 11-Kirby-a 2 4 6 10 12 15
NOTE: ***Ditko*** *a-14r, 15r, 20-22r.* ***Drucker*** *a-10r(Mystic #52), 13r(Uncanny Tales #42).* ***Everett*** *a-11r(Menace #2), 13r(Menace #4); c-10.* ***Heath*** *a-5r.* ***Gil Kane*** *c-1, 6.* ***Kirby*** *a-11.* ***Krigstein*** *a-20r(Uncanny Tales #54).* ***Reinman*** *r-1.* ***Tuska*** *a-6r.*

VAULT OF HORROR (Formerly War Against Crime #1-11)
E. C. Comics: No. 12, Apr-May, 1950 - No. 40, Dec-Jan, 1954-55

12 (Scarce)-ties w/Crypt Of Terror as 1st horror comic
450 900 1350 3375 4838 6300
13-Morphine story 96 192 288 720 1035 1350
14 86 172 258 645 923 1200
15- "Terror in the Swamp" is same story w/minor changes as "The Thing in the Swamp" from Haunt of Fear #15 73 146 219 548 787 1025
16, 56 112 168 420 603 785
17-Classic werewolf-c 59 118 177 443 634 825
18,19 44 88 132 330 470 610
20-25: 22-Frankenstein-c & adaptation. 23-Used in **POP**, pg. 84; Davis-a(2). 24-Craig biography 36 72 108 270 385 500
26-B&W & color illos in **POP** 36 72 108 270 385 500
27-36: 30-Dismemberment-c. 31-Ray Bradbury biog. 32-Censored-c. 35-X-Mas-c. 36- "Pipe Dream" classic opium addict story by Krigstein; "Twin Bill" cited in articles by T.E. Murphy, Wertham 29 58 87 218 309 400
37-1st app. Drusilla, a Vampirella look alike; Williamson-a
30 60 90 225 323 420
38-39: 39-Bondage-c 28 56 84 210 300 390
40-Low distribution 36 72 108 270 385 500
NOTE: ***Craig*** *art in all but No. 13 & 33; c-12-40.* ***Crandall*** *a-33, 34, 39.* ***Davis*** *a-17-38.* ***Evans*** *a-27, 28, 30, 32, 33.* ***Feldstein*** *a-12-16.* ***Ingels*** *a-13-20, 22-40.* ***Kamen*** *a-15-22, 25, 29, 35.* ***Krigstein*** *a-36, 38-40.* ***Kurtzman*** *a-12,*

GD VG FN VF VF/NM NM-
2.0 4.0 6.0 8.0 9.0 9.2

13. ***Orlando*** *a-24, 31, 40.* ***Wood*** *a-12-14. #22, 29 & 31 have Ray Bradbury adaptations. #16 & 17 have H. P. Lovecraft adaptations.*

VAULT OF HORROR, THE
Gladstone Publ.: Aug, 1990 - No. 6, June, 1991 ($1.95, 68 pgs.)(#4 on: $2.00)

1-Craig-c(r); all contain EC reprints 4.00
2-6: 2,4-6-Craig-c(r). 3-Ingels-c(r) 3.00

VAULT OF HORROR
Russ Cochran/Gemstone Publishing: Sept, 1991 - No. 5, May, 1992 ($2.00); Oct, 1992 - No. 29, Oct, 1999 ($1.50/$2.00/$2.50)

1-29: E.C reprints. 1-4r/VOH #12-15 w/original-c 3.00

V...-COMICS (Morse code for "V" - 3 dots, 1 dash)
Fox Features Syndicate: Jan, 1942 - No. 2, Mar-Apr, 1942

1-Origin V-Man & the Boys; The Banshee & The Black Fury, The Queen of Evil, & V-Agents begin; Nazi-c 124 248 372 775 1163 1550
2-Nazi bondage/torture-c 90 180 270 563 844 1125

VECTOR
Now Comics: 1986 - No. 4, 1986? ($1.50, 1st color comic by Now Comics)

1-4: Computer-generated art 2.25

VECTOR (Formerly titled Edge #1-12)
CG Entertainment, Inc.: May, 2003 ($7.95, digest size TPB)

13-Reprints from various CrossGen titles 8.00

VEGAS KNIGHTS
Pioneer Comics: 1989 ($1.95, one-shot)

1 2.25

VEILS
DC Comics (Vertigo): 1999 ($24.95, one-shot)

Hardcover-($24.95) Painted art and photography; McGreal-s 25.00
Softcover ($14.95) 15.00

VELOCITY (Also see Cyberforce)
Image Comics (Top Cow Productions): Nov, 1995 - No. 3, Jan, 1996 ($2.50, limited series)

1-3: Kurt Busiek scripts in all. 2-Savage Dragon-c/app. 3.00

VENGEANCE OF VAMPIRELLA (Becomes Vampirella: Death & Destruction)
Harris Comics: Apr, 1994 - No. 25, Apr, 1996 ($2.95)

1-($3.50)-Quesada/Palmiotti "bloodfoil" wraparound cover 6.00
1-2nd printing; blue foil-c 3.00
1-Gold 18.00
2-8: 8-Polybagged w/trading card 4.00
9-25: 10-w/coupon for Hyde -25 poster. 11,19-Polybagged w/ trading card. 25-Quesada & Palmiotti red foil-c 3.00
...: Bloodshed (1995, $6.95) 7.00

VENGEANCE OF VAMPIRELLA: THE MYSTERY WALK
Harris Comics: Nov, 1995 ($2.95, one-shot)

0 3.00

VENGEANCE SQUAD
Charlton Comics: July, 1975 - No. 6, May, 1976 (#1-3 are 25¢ issues)

1-Mike Mauser, Private Eye begins by Staton 2 4 6 8 10 12
2-6: Morisi-a in all 1 2 3 4 5 7
5,6 (Modern Comics-r, 1977) 4.00

VENOM
Marvel Comics: June, 2003 - Present ($2.25)

1-7-Herrera-a/Way-s. 6,7-Wolverine app. 2.25
8,9-($2.99) Wolverine-c/app.; Kieth-c 3.00

VENOM: Marvel Comics (Also see Amazing Spider-Man #298-300)
... ALONG CAME A SPIDER, 1/96 - No. 4, 4/96 ($2.95)-Spider-Man & Carnage app. 3.00
... CARNAGE UNLEASHED, 4/95 - No. 4, 7/95 ($2.95) 3.00
... DEATHTRAP: THE VAULT, 3/93 ($6.95) r/Avengers: Deathtrap: The Vault 7.00
... FUNERAL PYRE, 8/93- No. 3, 10/93 ($2.95)-#1-Holo-grafx foil-c; Punisher app. in all 3.00

VENOM: LETHAL PROTECTOR
Marvel Comics: Feb, 1993 - No. 6, July, 1993 ($2.95, limited series)

1-Red holo-grafx foil-c; Bagley-c/a in all 5.00
1-Gold variant sold to retailers 15.00
1-Black-c (at least 23 copies have been authenticated by CGC since 2000)
11 22 33 77 114 150
NOTE: Counterfeit copies of the black-c exist and are valueless

Venture #1 © Faerber & Igle

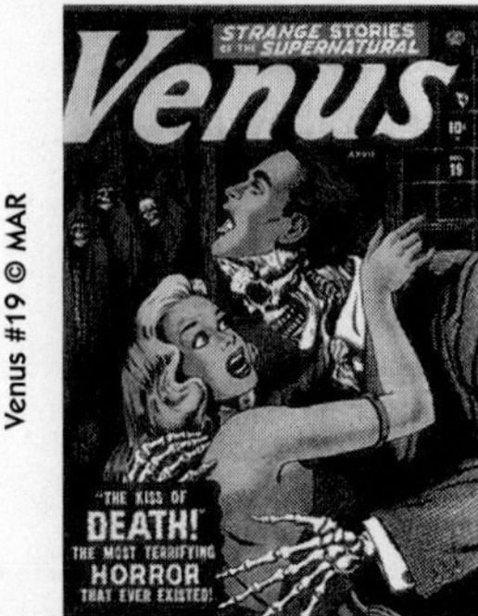

Venus #19 © MAR

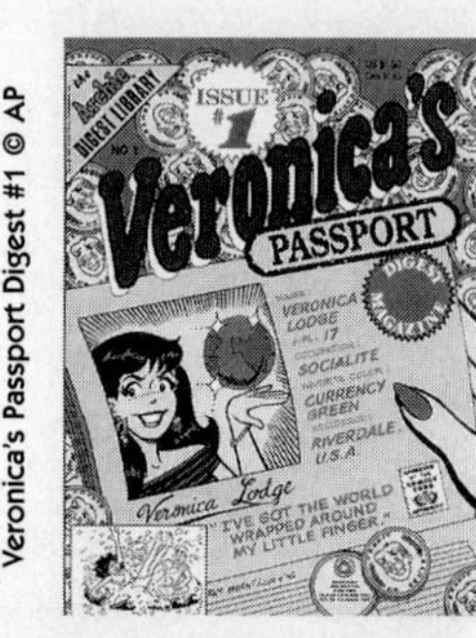

Veronica's Passport Digest #1 © AP

	GD 2.0	VG 4.0	FN 6.0	VF 8.0	VF/NM 9.0	NM- 9.2

2-6: Spider-Man app. in all 3.00
... LICENSE TO KILL,6/97 - No. 3, 8/97 ($1.95) 2.25
... NIGHTS OF VENGEANCE, 8/94 - No. 4, 11/94 ($2.95), #1-Red foil-c 3.00
... ON TRIAL, 3/97 - No. 3, 5/97 ($1.95) 2.25
... SEED OF DARKNESS, 7/97 ($1.95) #(-1) Flashback 2.25
... SEPARATION ANXIETY,12/94- No. 4, 3/95 ($2.95) #1-Embossed-c 3.00
... SIGN OF THE BOSS,3/97 - No. 2, 10/97 ($1.99) 2.25
... SINNER TAKES ALL, 8/95 - No. 5, 10/95 ($2.95) 3.00
... SUPER SPECIAL, 8/95($3.95) #1-Flip book 4.00
... THE ENEMY WITHIN, 2/94 - No. 3, 4/94 ($2.95)-Demogoblin & Morbius app.
1-Glow-in-the-dark-c 3.00
... THE FINALE, 11/97 - No. 3, 1/98 ($1.99) 2.25
... THE HUNGER, 8/96- No. 4, 11/96 ($1.95) 2.25
... THE HUNTED, 5/96-No. 3, 7/96 ($2.95) 3.00
... THE MACE, 5/94 - No. 3, 7/94 ($2.95)-#1-Embossed-c 3.00
... THE MADNESS, 11/93- No. 3, 1/94 ($2.95)-Kelley Jones-c/a(p).
1-Embossed-c; Juggernaut app. 3.00
... TOOTH AND CLAW, 12/96 - No. 3, 2/97 ($1.95)-Wolverine-c/app. 2.25

VENTURE
AC Comics (Americomics): Aug, 1986 - No. 3, 1986? ($1.75)
1-3: 1-3-Bolt. 1-Astron. 2-Femforce. 3-Fazers 2.25

VENTURE
Image Comics: Jan, 2003 - No. 4, Sept, 2003 ($2.95)
1-4-Faerber-s/Igle-a 3.00

VENUS (See Marvel Spotlight #2 & Weird Wonder Tales)
Marvel/Atlas Comics (CMC 1-9/LCC 10-19): Aug, 1948 - No. 19, Apr, 1952 (Also see Marvel Mystery #91)

	GD	VG	FN	VF	VF/NM	NM-
1-Venus & Hedy Devine begin; 1st app. Venus; Kurtzman's "Hey Look"	124	248	372	775	1163	1550
2	72	144	216	450	675	900
3,5	59	118	177	369	552	735
4-Kurtzman's "Hey Look"	60	120	180	375	563	750
6-9: 6-Loki app. 7,8-Painted-c. 9-Begin 52 pgs.; book-length feature "Whom the Gods Destroy!"	55	110	165	330	495	660
10-S/F-horror issues begin (7/50)	74	148	222	463	692	920
11-S/F end of the world (11/50)	85	170	255	531	796	1060
12-Colan-a	50	100	150	300	450	600
13-19-Venus by Everett, 2-3 stories each; covers-#13,15-19; 14-Everett part cover (Venus). 17-Bondage-c	76	152	228	475	713	950

NOTE: ***Berg** s/f story-13. **Everett** c-13, 14(part; Venus only), 15-19. **Heath** s/f story-11. **Maneely** s/f story 10(3pg.), 16. **Morisi** a-19. **Syd Shores** c-6.*

VENUS WARS, THE (Manga)
Dark Horse Comics: Apr, 1991 - No.14, May, 1992 ($2.25, B&W)
1-14: 1-3 Contain 2 Dark Horse trading cards. 1,3,7,10-(44 pgs.) 2.50

VERI BEST SURE FIRE COMICS
Holyoke Publishing Co.: No date (circa 1945) (Reprints Holyoke one-shots)

	GD	VG	FN	VF	VF/NM	NM-
1-Captain Aero, Alias X, Miss Victory, Commandos of the Devil Dogs, Red Cross, Hammerhead Hawley, Capt. Aero's Sky Scouts, Flagman app.; same-c as Veri Best Sure Shot #1	40	80	120	240	340	440

VERI BEST SURE SHOT COMICS
Holyoke Publishing Co.: No date (circa 1945) (Reprints Holyoke one-shots)

	GD	VG	FN	VF	VF/NM	NM-
1-Capt. Aero, Miss Victory by Quinlan, Alias X, The Red Cross, Flagman, Commandos of the Devil Dogs, Hammerhead Hawley, Capt. Aero's Sky Scouts; same-c as Veri Best Sure Fire #1	40	80	120	240	340	440

VERMILLION
DC Comics (Helix): Oct, 1996 - No. 12, Sept, 1997 ($2.25/$2.50)
1-12: 1-4: Lucius Shepard scripts. 4,12-Kaluta-c 2.50

VERONICA (Also see Archie's Girls, Betty &...)
Archie Comics: Apr, 1989 - Present
1-(75¢-c) 6.00
2-10: 2-(75¢-c) 4.00
11-38 3.00
39-Love Showdown pt. 4, Cheryl Blossom 5.00
40-70: 34-Neon ink-c 3.00
71-148: 134-Begin $2.19-c 2.25

VERONICA'S PASSPORT DIGEST MAGAZINE (Becomes Veronica's Digest Magazine #3 on)
Archie Comics: Nov, 1992 - No. 6 ($1.50/$1.79, digest size)
1 5.00
2-6 3.00

VERONICA'S SUMMER SPECIAL (See Archie Giant Series Magazine #615, 625)

VERTICAL
DC Comics (Vertigo): 2003 ($4.95, 3-1/4" wide pages, one-shot)
1-Seagle-s/Allred & Bond-a; odd format 1/2 width pages with some 20" long spreads 5.00

VERTIGO GALLERY, THE: DREAMS AND NIGHTMARES
DC Comics (Vertigo): 1995 ($3.50, one-shot)
1-Pin-ups of Vertigo characters by Sienkiewicz, Toth, Van Fleet & others; McKean-c 4.00

VERTIGO JAM
DC Comics (Vertigo): Aug, 1993 ($3.95, one-shot, 68 pgs.)(Painted-c by Fabry)
1-Sandman by Neil Gaiman, Hellblazer, Animal Man, Doom Patrol, Swamp Thing, Kid Eternity & Shade the Changing Man 5.00

VERTIGO POP! BANGKOK
DC Comics (Vertigo): July, 2003 - No. 4, Oct, 2003 ($2.95, limited series)
1-4-Camuncoli-c/a; Jonathan Vankin-s 3.00

VERTIGO POP! LONDON
DC Comics (Vertigo): Jan, 2003 - No. 4, Apr, 2003 ($2.95, limited series)
1-4-Philip Bond-c/a; Peter Milligan-s 3.00

VERTIGO POP! TOKYO
DC Comics (Vertigo): Sept, 2002 - No. 4, Dec, 2002 ($2.95, limited series)
1-4-Seth Fisher-c/a; Jonathan Vankin-s 3.00

VERTIGO PREVIEW
DC Comics (Vertigo): 1992 (75¢, one-shot, 36 pgs.)
1-Vertigo previews; Sandman story by Neil Gaiman 2.25

VERTIGO RAVE
DC Comics (Vertigo): Fall, 1994 (99¢, one-shot)
1-Vertigo previews 2.25

VERTIGO SECRET FILES
DC Comics (Vertigo): Aug, 2000 ($4.95)
...: Hellblazer 1 (8/00, $4.95) Background info and story summaries 5.00
...: Swamp Thing 1 (11/00, $4.95) Backstories and origins; Hale-c 5.00

VERTIGO VERITE: THE UNSEEN HAND
DC Comics (Vertigo): Sept, 1996 - No. 4, Dec, 1996 ($2.50, limited series)
1-4: Terry LaBan scripts in all 2.50

VERTIGO VISIONS
DC Comics (Vertigo): June, 1993 - Present (one-shots)
Dr. Occult 1 (7/94, $3.95) 4.00
Dr. Thirteen 1 (9/98, $5.95) Howarth-s 6.00
Prez 1 (7/95, $3.95) 4.00
The Geek 1 (6/93, $3.95) 4.00
The Eaters ($4.95, 1995)-Milligan story. 5.00
The Phantom Stranger 1 (10/93, $3.50) 3.50
Tomahawk 1 (7/98, $4.95) Pollack-s 5.00

VERTIGO WINTER'S EDGE
DC Comics (Vertigo): 1998, 1999 ($7.95/$6.95, square-bound, annual)
1-Winter stories by Vertigo creators; Desire story by Gaiman/Bolton; Bolland wraparound-c 8.00
2,3-($6.95)-Winter stories: 2-Allred-c. 3-Bond-c; Desire by Gaiman/Zulli 7.00

VERTIGO X ANNIVERSARY PREVIEW
DC Comics (Vertigo): 2003 (99¢, one-shot, 48 pgs.)
1-Previews of upcoming titles and interviews; Endless Nights, Shade, The Originals 2.25

VERY BEST OF DENNIS THE MENACE, THE
Fawcett Publ.: July, 1979 - No. 2, Apr, 1980 (95¢/$1.00, digest-size, 132 pgs.)

	GD	VG	FN	VF	VF/NM	NM-
1,2-Reprints	1	3	4	6	8	10

VERY BEST OF DENNIS THE MENACE, THE
Marvel Comics Group: Apr, 1982 - No. 3, Aug, 1982 ($1.25, digest-size)

	GD	VG	FN	VF	VF/NM	NM-
1-3: Reprints	1	2	3	5	7	9
1,2-Mistakenly printed with DC logo on cover	2	4	6	9	11	14

NOTE: ***Hank Ketcham** c-all. A few thousand of #1 & 2 were printed with DC emblem.*

V For Vendetta #5 © DC

The Vigilante #25 © DC

Violent Messiahs #4 © Hurricane Entertainment

GD 2.0 | VG 4.0 | FN 6.0 | VF 8.0 | VF/NM 9.0 | NM- 9.2

VERY VICKY
Meet Danny Ocean: 1993? - No. 8, 1995 ($2.50, B&W)
1-8, ...: Calling All Hillbillies (1995, $2.50) 2.50

VEXT
DC Comics: Mar, 1999 - No. 6, Aug, 1999 ($2.50, limited series)
1-6-Giffen-s. 1-Superman app. 2.50

V FOR VENDETTA
DC Comics: Sept, 1988 - No. 10, May, 1989 ($2.00, maxi-series)
1-10: Alan Moore scripts in all 3.00
Trade paperback (1990, $14.95) 15.00

VIC BRIDGES FAZERS SKETCHBOOK AND FACT FILE
AC Comics: Nov, 1986 ($1.75)
1 3.00

VIC FLINT(Crime Buster...)(See Authentic Police Cases #10-14 & Fugitives From Justice #2)
St. John Publ. Co.: Aug, 1948 - No. 5, Apr, 1949 (Newspaper reprints; NEA Service)
1 14 28 42 79 107 135
2 10 20 30 56 73 90
3-5 9 18 27 49 62 75

VIC FLINT (Crime Buster...)
Argo Publ.: Feb, 1956 - No. 2, May, 1956 (Newspaper reprints)
1,2 9 18 27 49 62 75

VIC JORDAN (Also see Big Shot Comics #32)
Civil Service Publ.: April, 1945
1-1944 daily newspaper-r 14 28 42 79 107 135

VICKI (Humor)
Atlas/Seaboard Publ.: Feb, 1975 - No. 4, Aug, 1975 (No. 1,2: 68 pgs.)
1,2-(68 pgs.)-Reprints Tippy Teen; Good Girl art 3 6 9 19 25 32
3,4 (Low print) 3 6 9 19 25 32

VICKI VALENTINE (...Summer Special #1)
Renegade Press: July, 1985 - No. 4, July, 1986 ($1.70, B&W)
1-4: Woggon, Rausch-a; all have paper dolls. 2-Christmas issue 3.00

VICKY
Ace Magazine: Oct, 1948 - No. 5, June, 1949
nn(10/48)-Teenage humor 7 14 21 37 46 55
4(12/48), nn(2/49), 4(4/49), 5(6/49): 5-Dotty app. 6 12 18 31 38 45

VIC TORRY & HIS FLYING SAUCER (Also see Mr. Monster's...#5)
Fawcett Publications: 1950 (one-shot)
nn-Book-length saucer story by Powell; photo/painted-c
66 132 198 413 619 825

VICTORY
Topps Comics: June, 1994 ($2.50, unfinished limited series)
1-Kurt Busiek script; Giffen-c/a; Rob Liefeld variant-c exists 2.50

VICTORY
Image Comics: May, 2003 - No. 4 ($2.95, limited series)
1-3: 1-Two covers; Francisco-a 3.00

VICTORY COMICS
Hillman Periodicals: Aug, 1941 - No. 4, Dec, 1941 (#1 by Funnies, Inc.)
1-The Conqueror by Bill Everett, The Crusader, & Bomber Burns begin; Conqueror's origin in text; Everett-c 300 600 900 1900 2850 3800
2-Everett-c/a 128 256 384 800 1200 1600
3,4 85 170 255 531 796 1060

VIC VERITY MAGAZINE
Vic Verity Publ: 1945; No. 2, Jan?, 1947 - No. 7, Sept, 1946 (A comic book)
1-C. C. Beck-c/a 22 44 66 127 176 225
2-Beck-c 13 26 39 74 100 125
3-7: 6-Beck-a. 7-Beck-c 11 22 33 66 88 110

VIDEO JACK
Marvel Comics (Epic Comics): Nov, 1987 - No. 6, Nov, 1988 ($1.25)
1-5 2.25
6-Neal Adams, Keith Giffen, Wrightson, others-a 4.00

VIETNAM JOURNAL
Apple Comics: Nov, 1987 - No. 16, Apr, 1991 ($1.75/$1.95, B&W)
1-16: Don Lomax-c/a/scripts in all, 1-2nd print 3.00
...: Indian Country Vol. 1 (1990, $12.95)-r/#1-4 plus one new story 13.00

VIETNAM JOURNAL: VALLEY OF DEATH
Apple Comics: June, 1994 - No. 2, Aug, 1994 ($2.75, B&W, limited series)
1,2: By Don Lomax 4.00

VIGILANTE, THE (Also see New Teen Titans #23 & Annual V2#2)
DC Comics: Oct, 1983 - No. 50, Feb, 1988 ($1.25, Baxter paper)
1-Origin 3.00
2-16,19-49: 3-Cyborg app. 4-1st app. The Exterminator; Newton-a(p). 6,7-Origin. 20,21-Nightwing app. 35-Origin Mad Bomber. 47-Batman-c/s 2.50
17,18-Alan Moore scripts 4.00
50-Ken Steacy painted-c 3.00
Annual nn, 2 ('85, '86) 2.50

VIGILANTE: CITY LIGHTS, PRAIRIE JUSTICE (Also see Action Comics #42, Justice League of America #78, Leading Comics & World's Finest #244)
DC Comics: Nov, 1995 - No. 4, Feb, 1996 ($2.50, limited series)
1-4: James Robinson scripts in all 2.50

VIGILANTES, THE
Dell Publishing Co.: No. 839, Sept, 1957
Four Color 839-Movie 8 16 24 55 78 100

VIGILANTE 8: SECOND OFFENSE
Chaos! Comics: Dec, 1999 ($2.95, one-shot)
1-Based on video game 3.00

VIKINGS, THE (Movie)
Dell Publishing Co.: No. 910, May, 1958
Four Color 910-Buscema-a, Kirk Douglas photo-c 9 18 27 65 93 120

VILLAINS AND VIGILANTES
Eclipse Comics: Dec, 1986 - No. 4, May, 1987 ($1.50/$1.75, limited series, Baxter paper)
1-4: Based on role-playing game. 2-4 ($1.75-c) 2.25

VILLAINY OF DOCTOR DOOM, THE
Marvel Comics: 1999 ($17.95, TPB)
nn-Reprints early battle with the Fantastic Four 18.00

VINTAGE MAGNUS (...Robot Fighter)
Valiant: Jan, 1992 - No. 4, Apr, 1992 ($2.25, limited series)
1-4: 1-Layton-c; r/origin from Magnus R.F. #22 2.25

VIOLATOR (Also see Spawn #2)
Image Comics (Todd McFarlane Productions): May, 1994 - No. 3, Aug, 1994 ($1.95, limited series)
1-Alan Moore scripts in all 5.00
2,3: Bart Sears-c(p)/a(p) 4.00

VIOLATOR VS. BADROCK
Image Comics (Extreme Studios): May, 1995 - No. 4, Aug, 1995 ($2.50, limited series)
1-4: Alan Moore scripts in all. 1-1st app Celestine; variant-c (3?) 2.50

VIOLENT MESSIAHS (...: Lamenting Pain on cover for #9-12, numbered as #1-4)
Image Comics: June, 2000 - Present ($2.95)
1-Two covers by Travis Smith and Medina 4.00
1-Tower Records variant edition 5.00
2-8: 5-Flip book sketchbook 3.00
9-12-Lamenting Pain; 2 covers on each 3.00
...: Genesis (12/01, $5.95) r/'97 B&W issue, Wizard 1/2 prologue 6.00
...: The Book of Job TPB (7/02, $24.95) r/#1-8; Foreward by Gossett 25.00

VIP (TV)
TV Comics: 2000 ($2.95, unfinished series)
1-Based on the Pamela Lee TV show; photo-c 3.00

VIPER (TV)
DC Comics: Aug, 1994 - No. 4, Nov, 1994 ($1.95, limited series)
1-4-Adaptation of television show 2.25

VIRGINIAN, THE (TV)
Gold Key: June, 1963
1(10060-306)-Part photo-c of James Drury plus photo back-c
4 8 12 29 40 50

VIRTUA FIGHTER (Video Game)
Marvel Comics: Aug, 1995 (2.95, one-shot)
1-Sega Saturn game 3.00

Vision and the Scarlet Witch #3 © MAR

Voltron: Defender of the Universe #1 © WEP

Voodoo #17 © AJAX

	GD 2.0	VG 4.0	FN 6.0	VF 8.0	VF/NM 9.0	NM- 9.2

VIRUS
Dark Horse Comics: 1993 - No. 4, 1993 ($2.50, limited series)
1-4: Ploog-c 2.50

VISION, THE
Marvel Comics: Nov, 1994 - No. 4, Feb, 1995 ($1.75, limited series)
1-4 2.25

VISION, THE (AVENGERS ICONS: ...)
Marvel Comics: Oct, 2002 - No. 4, Jan, 2003 ($2.99, limited series)
1-4-Geoff Johns-s/Ivan Reis-a 3.00

VISION AND THE SCARLET WITCH, THE (See Marvel Fanfare)
Marvel Comics Group: Nov, 1982 - No. 4, Feb, 1983 (Limited series)
1-4: 2-Nuklo & Future Man app. 3.00

VISION AND THE SCARLET WITCH, THE
Marvel Comics Group: Oct, 1985 - No. 12, Sept, 1986 (Maxi-series)
V2#1-12: 1-Origin; 1st app. in Avengers #57. 2-West Coast Avengers x-over 2.50

VISIONARIES
Marvel Comics (Star)/Marvel Comics #3 on: Nov, 1987 - No. 6, Sept, 1988
1-6 2.50

VISIONS
Vision Publications: 1979 - No. 5, 1983 (B&W, fanzine)

	GD	VG	FN	VF	VF/NM	NM-
1-Flaming Carrot begins(1st app?); N. Adams-c	4	8	12	25	33	42
2-N. Adams, Rogers-a; Gulacy back-c; signed & numbered to 2000	3	6	9	19	25	32
3-Williamson-c(p); Steranko back-c	2	4	6	12	16	20
4-Flaming Carrot-c & info.	2	4	6	12	16	20
5-1 pg. Flaming Carrot	1	3	4	6	8	10

NOTE: ***Eisner** a-4. **Miller** a-4. **Starlin** a-3. **Williamson** a-5. After #4, Visions became an annual publication of The Atlanta Fantasy Fair.*

VISITOR, THE
Valiant/Acclaim Comics (Valiant): Apr, 1995 - No. 13, Nov, 1995 ($2.50)
1-13: 8-Harbinger revealed. 13-Visitor revealed to be Sting from Harbinger 2.50

VISITOR VS. THE VALIANT UNIVERSE, THE
Valiant: Feb, 1995 - No. 2, Mar, 1995 ($2.95, limited series)
1,2 3.00

VOGUE (Also see Youngblood)
Image Comics (Extreme Studios): Oct, 1995 - No.3, Jan, 1996 ($2.50, limited series)
1-3: 1-Liefeld-c, 1-Variant-c 2.50

VOID INDIGO (Also see Marvel Graphic Novel)
Marvel Comics (Epic Comics): 11/84 - No. 2, 3/85 ($1.50, direct sales, unfinished series, mature)
1,2: Cont'd from Marvel G.N.; graphic sex & violence 2.25

VOLCANIC REVOLVER
Oni Press: Dec, 1998 - No. 3, Mar, 1999 ($2.95, B&W, limited series)
1-3: Scott Morse-s/a 3.00
TPB (12/99, $9.95, digest size) r/#1-3 and Oni Double Feature #7 prologue 10.00

VOLTRON (TV)
Modern Publishing: 1985 - No. 3, 1985 (75¢, limited series)
1-3: Ayers-a in all 4.00

VOLTRON: DEFENDER OF THE UNIVERSE (TV)
Image Comics: No. 0, May, 2003 - No. 5, Sept, 2003 ($2.50)
0-Jolley-s/Brooks-a; character pin-ups with background info 2.50
1-5-($2.95) 1-Three covers by Norton, Brooks and Andrews; Norton-a 3.00
...: Revelations TPB (2004, $11.95, digest-sized) r/#1-5; cover gallery 12.00

VOLTRON: DEFENDER OF THE UNIVERSE (TV)
Image Comics: No. 1, Jan, 2004 - Present ($2.95)
1-Jolley-s; wraparound-c 3.00

VOODA (Jungle Princess) (Formerly Voodoo)
Ajax-Farrell (Four Star Publications): No. 20, April, 1955 - No. 22, Aug, 1955

	GD	VG	FN	VF	VF/NM	NM-
20-Baker-c/a (r/Seven Seas #6)	40	80	120	240	340	440
21,22-Baker-a plus Kamen/Baker story, Kimbo Boy of Jungle, & Baker-c(p) in all. 22-Censored Jo-Jo-r (name Powaa)	36	72	108	204	290	375

NOTE: *#20-22 each contain one heavily censored-r of South Sea Girl by **Baker** from Seven Seas Comics with name changed to Vooda. #20-r/Seven Seas #6; #21-r/#4; #22-r/#3.*

VOODOO (Weird Fantastic Tales) (Vooda #20 on)
Ajax-Farrell (Four Star Publ.): May, 1952 - No. 19, Jan-Feb, 1955

	GD	VG	FN	VF	VF/NM	NM-
1-South Sea Girl-r by Baker	56	112	168	350	525	700
2-Rulah story-r plus South Sea Girl from Seven Seas #2 by Baker (name changed from Alani to El'nee)	46	92	138	276	413	550
3-Bakerish-a; man stabbed in face	39	78	117	233	329	425
4,8-Baker-r. 8-Severed head panels	39	78	117	233	329	425
5-7,9,10: 5-Nazi death camp story (flaying alive). 6-Severed head panels	32	64	96	182	259	335
11-18: 14-Zombies take over America. 15-Opium drug story-r/Ellery Queen #3. 16-Post nuclear world story.17-Electric chair panels	28	56	84	159	225	290
19-Bondage-c; Baker-r(2)/Seven Seas #5 w/minor changes & #1, heavily modified; last pre-code; contents & covers change to jungle theme	36	72	108	204	290	375
Annual 1(1952, 25¢, 100 pgs.)-Baker-a (scarce)	94	188	282	588	882	1175

VOODOO
Image Comics (WildStorm): Nov, 1997 - No. 4, Mar, 1998 ($2.50, lim. series)
1-4:Alan Moore-s in all; Hughes-c. 2-4-Rio-a 2.50
1-Platinum Ed 10.00
Dancing on the Dark TPB ('99, $9.95) r/#1-4 10.00
...-Zealot: Skin Trade (8/95, $4.95) 5.00

VOODOO (See Tales of...)

VOODOOM
Oni Press: June, 2000 ($4.95, B&W)
1-Scott Morse-s/Jim Mahfood-a 5.00

VORTEX
Vortex Publs.: Nov, 1982 - No. 15, 1988 (No month) ($1.50/$1.75, B&W)

	GD	VG	FN	VF	VF/NM	NM-
1 ($1.95)-Peter Hsu-a; Ken Steacy-c; nudity	1	2	3	5	6	8

2,12: 2-1st app. Mister X (on-c only). 12-Sam Kieth-a 5.00
3-11,13-15 2.50

VORTEX
Comico: 1991 - No. 2? ($2.50, limited series)
1,2: Heroes from The Elementals 2.50

VORTEX
Entity Comics: 1996 ($2.95)
1,1b: 1b-Kaniuga-c 3.00

VOYAGE TO THE BOTTOM OF THE SEA (Movie, TV)
Dell Publishing Co./Gold Key: No. 1230, Sept-Nov, 1961; Dec, 1964 - #16, Apr, 1970 (Painted-c)

	GD	VG	FN	VF	VF/NM	NM-
Four Color 1230 (1961)	12	24	36	82	121	160
10133-412(#1, 12/64)(Gold Key)	8	16	24	58	82	105
2(7/65) - 5: Photo back-c, 1-5	6	12	18	40	55	70
6-14	5	10	15	33	44	55
15,16-Reprints	3	7	10	21	28	35

VOYAGE TO THE DEEP
Dell Publishing Co.: Sept-Nov, 1962 - No. 4, Nov-Jan, 1964 (Painted-c)

	GD	VG	FN	VF	VF/NM	NM-
1	6	12	18	40	55	70
2-4	4	8	12	27	36	45

WACKO
Ideal Publ. Corp.: Sept, 1980 - No. 3, Oct, 1981 (84 pgs., B&W, magazine)

	GD	VG	FN	VF	VF/NM	NM-
1-3	2	4	6	8	10	12

WACKY ADVENTURES OF CRACKY (Also see Gold Key Spotlight)
Gold Key: Dec, 1972 - No. 12, Sept, 1975

	GD	VG	FN	VF	VF/NM	NM-
1	2	4	6	14	18	22
2	2	4	6	9	11	14
3-12	1	2	3	5	7	9

(See March of Comics #405, 424, 436, 448)

WACKY DUCK (...Comics #3-6; formerly Dopey Duck; Justice Comics #7 on) (See Film Funnies)
Marvel Comics (NPP): No. 3, Fall, 1946 - No. 6, Summer, 1947; Aug, 1948 - No. 2, Oct, 1948

	GD	VG	FN	VF	VF/NM	NM-
3	22	44	66	124	172	220
4-Infinity-c	20	40	60	112	156	200
5,6(1947)-Becomes Justice comics	16	32	48	92	126	160
1,2(1948)	11	22	33	66	88	110
I.W. Reprint #1,2,7('58): 1-r/Wacky Duck #6	2	4	6	10	13	16
Super Reprint #10(I.W. on-c, Super-inside)	2	4	6	10	13	16

WACKY QUACKY (See Wisco)

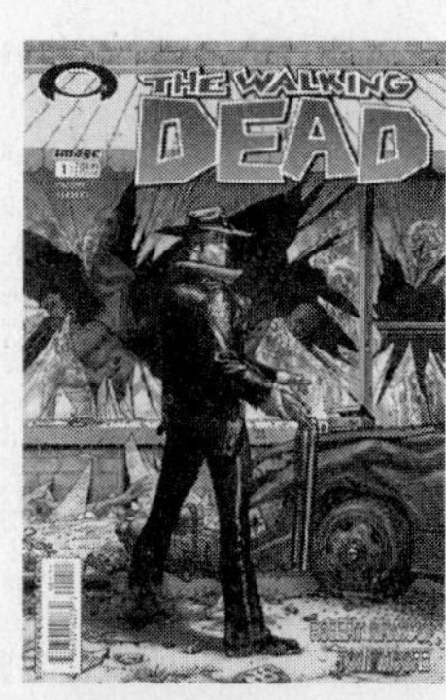

The Walking Dead #1 © Rob Kirkman

Walt Disney Comics Digest #22 © WDC

Walt Disney's Comics and Stories #5 © WDC

	GD 2.0	VG 4.0	FN 6.0	VF 8.0	VF/NM 9.0	NM- 9.2

WACKY RACES (TV)
Gold Key: Aug, 1969 - No. 7, Apr, 1972 (Hanna-Barbera)

	GD	VG	FN	VF	VF/NM	NM-
1	6	12	18	40	55	70
2-7	4	8	12	24	32	40

WACKY SQUIRREL (Also see Dark Horse Presents)
Dark Horse Comics: Oct, 1987 - No. 4, 1988 ($1.75, B&W)

	GD	VG	FN	VF	VF/NM	NM-
1-4: 4-Superman parody						2.25
Halloween Adventure Special 1 (1987, $2.00)						2.25
Summer Fun Special 1 (1988, $2.00)						2.25

WACKY WITCH (Also see Gold Key Spotlight)
Gold Key: March, 1971 - No. 21, Dec, 1975

	GD	VG	FN	VF	VF/NM	NM-
1	4	8	12	27	36	45
2	2	4	6	14	18	22
3-10	2	4	6	10	13	16
11-21	1	3	4	6	8	10

(See March of Comics #374, 398, 410, 422, 434, 446, 458, 470, 482)

WACKY WOODPECKER (See Two Bit the...)
I. W. Enterprises/Super Comics: 1958; 1963

	GD	VG	FN	VF	VF/NM	NM-
I.W. Reprint #1,2,7 (nd-reprints Two Bit...): 7-r/Two-Bit, the Wacky Woodpecker #1.	2	4	6	9	11	14
Super Reprint #10('63): 10-r/Two-Bit, The Wacky Woodpecker #?	2	4	6	9	11	14

WAGON TRAIN (1st Series) (TV) (See Western Roundup under Dell Giants)
Dell Publishing Co.: No. 895, Mar, 1958 - No. 13, Apr-June, 1962 (All photo-c)

	GD	VG	FN	VF	VF/NM	NM-
Four Color 895 (#1)	12	24	36	87	129	170
Four Color 971(#2),1019(#3)	8	16	24	53	74	95
4(1-3/60),6-13	7	14	21	46	63	80
5-Toth-a	7	14	21	51	71	90

WAGON TRAIN (2nd Series)(TV)
Gold Key: Jan, 1964 - No. 4, Oct, 1964 (All front & back photo-c)

	GD	VG	FN	VF	VF/NM	NM-
1-Tufts-a in all	6	12	18	43	59	75
2-4	5	10	15	33	44	55

WAHOO MORRIS
Image Comics: Mar, 2000 ($3.50, B&W)

	GD	VG	FN	VF	VF/NM	NM-
1-Craig Taillefer-s/a						3.50

WAITING PLACE, THE
Slave Labor Graphics: Apr, 1997 - No. 6, Sept, 1997 ($2.95)

	GD	VG	FN	VF	VF/NM	NM-
1-6-Sean McKeever-s						3.00
Vol. 2 - 1(11/99), 2-11						3.00
12-($4.95)						5.00

WAITING ROOM WILLIE (See Sad Case of...)

WALKING DEAD, THE
Image Comics: Oct, 2003 - Present ($2.95, B&W)

	GD	VG	FN	VF	VF/NM	NM-
1-3-Robert Kirkman-s/Tony Moore-a						3.00

WALLY (Teen-age)
Gold Key: Dec, 1962 - No. 4, Sept, 1963

	GD	VG	FN	VF	VF/NM	NM-
1	4	8	12	24	32	40
2-4	3	6	9	18	24	30

WALLY THE WIZARD
Marvel Comics (Star Comics): Apr, 1985 - No. 12, Mar, 1986 (Children's comic)

	GD	VG	FN	VF	VF/NM	NM-
1-12: Bob Bolling a-1,3; c-1,9,11,12						4.00
1-Variant with "Star Chase" game on last page and inside back-c						8.00

WALLY WOOD'S T.H.U.N.D.E.R. AGENTS (See Thunder Agents)
Deluxe Comics: Nov, 1984 - No. 5, Oct, 1986 ($2.00, 52 pgs.)

	GD	VG	FN	VF	VF/NM	NM-
1-5: 5-Jerry Ordway-c/a in Wood style						5.00

NOTE: ***Anderson** a-2i, 3i. **Buckler** a-4. **Ditko** a-3, 4. **Giffen** a-1p-4p. **Perez** a-1p, 2, 4; c-1-4.*

WALT DISNEY CHRISTMAS PARADE (Also see Christmas Parade)
Whitman Publ. Co. (Golden Press): Wint, 1977 ($1.95, cardboard-c, 224 pgs.)

	GD	VG	FN	VF	VF/NM	NM-
11191-Barks-r/Christmas in Disneyland #1, Dell Christmas Parade #9 & Dell Giant #53	4	8	12	25	33	42

WALT DISNEY COMICS DIGEST
Gold Key: June, 1968 - No. 57, Feb, 1976 (50¢, digest size)

	GD	VG	FN	VF	VF/NM	NM-
1-Reprints Uncle Scrooge #5; 192 pgs.	9	18	27	60	85	110
2-4-Barks-r	6	12	18	40	55	70
5-Daisy Duck by Barks (8 pgs.); last published story by Barks (art only) plus 21 pg. Scrooge-r by Barks	9	18	27	63	89	115
6-13-All Barks-r	4	8	12	27	36	45
14,15	3	6	9	18	24	30
16-Reprints Donald Duck #26 by Barks	4	8	12	25	33	42
17-20-Barks-r	3	7	10	21	28	35
21-31,33,35-37-Barks-r; 24-Toth Zorro	3	6	9	18	24	30
32,41,45,47-49	2	4	6	12	16	20
34,38,39: 34-Reprints 4-Color #318. 38-Reprints Christmas in Disneyland #1. 39-Two Barks-r/WDC&S #272, 4-Color #1073 plus Toth Zorro-r	3	6	9	18	24	30
40-Mickey Mouse-r by Gottfredson	2	4	6	14	18	22
42,43-Barks-r	2	4	6	14	18	22
44-(Has Gold Key emblem, 50¢)-Reprints 1st story of 4-Color #29,256,275,282	6	12	18	38	52	65
44-Republished in 1976 by Whitman; not identical to original; a bit smaller, blank back-c, 69¢	3	6	9	18	24	30
46,50,52-Barks-r. 52-Barks-r/WDC&S #161,132	2	4	6	12	16	20
51-Reprints 4-Color #71	3	6	9	18	24	30
53-55: 53-Reprints Dell Giant #30. 54-Reprints Donald Duck Beach Party #2. 55-Reprints Dell Giant #49	2	4	6	11	14	18
56-r/Uncle Scrooge #32 (Barks)	2	4	6	14	18	22
57-r/Mickey Mouse Almanac('57) & two Barks stories	2	4	6	12	16	20

NOTE: ***Toth** a-52r. #1-10, 196 pgs.; #11-41, 164 pgs.; #42 on, 132 pgs. Old issues were being reprinted & distributed by Whitman in 1976.*

WALT DISNEY GIANT (Disney)
Bruce Hamilton Company (Gladstone): Sept, 1995 - No. 7, Sept, 1996 ($2.25, bi-monthly, 48 pgs.)

	GD	VG	FN	VF	VF/NM	NM-
1-7: 1-Scrooge McDuck in the Yukon; Rosa-c/a/scripts plus r/F.C. #218. 2-Uncle Scrooge-r by Barks plus 17 pg. text story. 3-Donald the Mighty Duck; Rosa-c; Barks & Rosa-r. 4-Mickey and Goofy; new-a (story actually stars Goofy. Mickey Mouse by Caesar Ferioli; Donald Duck by Giorgio Cavazzano (1st in U.S.). 6-Uncle Scrooge & the Jr. Woodchucks; new-a and Barks-r. 7-Uncle Scrooge-r by Barks plus new-a						3.00

NOTE: *Series was initially solicited as Uncle Walt's Collectory. Issue #8 was advertised, but later cancelled.*

WALT DISNEY PAINT BOOK SERIES
Whitman Publ. Co.: No dates; circa 1975 (Beware! Has 1930s copyright dates) (79¢-c, 52pgs. B&W, treasury-sized) (Coloring books, text stories & comics-r)

	GD	VG	FN	VF	VF/NM	NM-
#2052 (Whitman #886-r) Mickey Mouse & Donald Duck Gag Book	4	8	12	24	32	40
#2053 (Whitman #677-r)	4	8	12	24	32	40
#2054 (Whitman #670-r) Donald-c	4	8	12	27	36	45
#2055 (Whitman #627-r) Mickey-c	4	8	12	24	32	40
#2056 (Whitman #660-r) Buckey Bug-c	3	7	10	21	28	35
#2057 (Whitman #887-r) Mickey & Donald-c	4	8	12	24	32	40

WALT DISNEY PRESENTS (TV)(Disney)
Dell Publishing Co.: No. 997, 6-8/59 - No. 6, 12-2/1960-61; No. 1181, 4-5/61 (All photo-c)

	GD	VG	FN	VF	VF/NM	NM-
Four Color 997 (#1)	8	16	24	58	82	105
2(12-2/60)-The Swamp Fox(origin), Elfego Baca, Texas John Slaughter (Disney TV show) begin	6	12	18	38	52	65
3-6: 5-Swamp Fox by Warren Tufts	5	10	15	36	48	60
Four Color 1181-Texas John Slaughter	8	16	24	55	78	100

WALT DISNEY'S CHRISTMAS PARADE (Also see Christmas Parade)
Gladstone: Winter, 1988; No. 2, Winter, 1989 ($2.95, 100 pgs.)

	GD	VG	FN	VF	VF/NM	NM-
1-Barks-r/painted-c	2	4	6	8	10	12
2-Barks-r	1	2	3	5	7	9

WALT DISNEY'S CHRISTMAS PARADE
Gemstone Publishing: Dec, 2003 ($8.95, prestige format)

	GD	VG	FN	VF	VF/NM	NM-
1-Reprints and 3 new European holiday stories						9.00

WALT DISNEY'S COMICS AND STORIES (Cont. of Mickey Mouse Magazine)
(#1-30 contain Donald Duck newspaper reprints) (Titled "Comics And Stories" #264 to #?; titled "Walt Disney's Comics And Stories" #511 on)
Dell Publishing Co./Gold Key #264-473/Whitman #474-510/Gladstone #511-547/ Disney Comics #548-585/Gladstone #586-633/Gemstone Publishing #634 on: 10/40 - #263, 8/62; #264, 10/62 - #510, 7/84; #511, 10/86 - #633, 2/99; #634, 7/03 - Present

NOTE: The whole number can always be found at the bottom of the title page in the lower left-hand or right hand panel.

	GD	VG	FN	VF	VF/NM	NM-
1(V1#1-c; V2#1-indicia)-Donald Duck strip-r by Al Taliaferro & Gottfredson's Mickey Mouse begin	1525	3050	4575	10,500	16,750	23,000
2	565	1130	1695	3673	5937	8200
3	200	400	600	1300	2000	2700

4-X-Mas-c; 1st Huey, Dewey & Louie-c this title (See Mickey Mouse Magazine

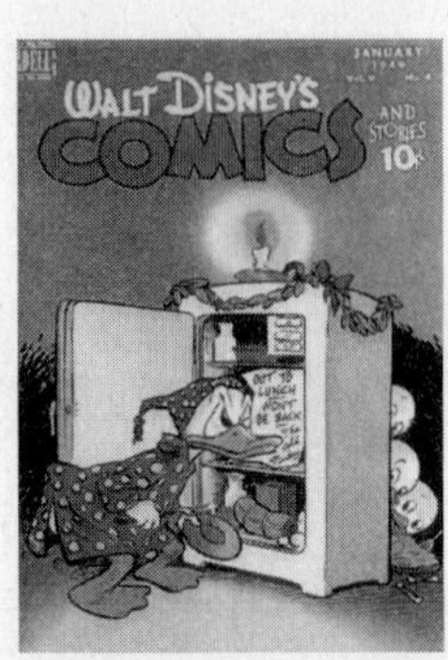

Walt Disney's Comics and Stories #100
© WDC

Walt Disney's Comics and Stories #521
© WDC

Walt Disney's Comics and Stories #634
© WDC

	GD 2.0	VG 4.0	FN 6.0	VF 8.0	VF/NM 9.0	NM- 9.2
V4#2 for 1st-c ever)	148	296	444	962	1481	2000
4-Special promotional, complimentary issue; cover same except one corner was blanked out & boxed in to identify the giveaway (not a paste-over). This special pressing was probably sent out to former subscribers to Mickey Mouse Mag. whose subscriptions had expired. (Very rare-5 known copies)	241	482	723	1567	2409	3250
5-Goofy-c	111	222	333	722	1111	1500
6-10: 8-Only Clarabelle Cow-c. 9-Taliaferro-c (1st)	89	178	267	579	890	1200
11-14: 11-Huey, Dewey & Louie-c/app.	72	142	216	468	722	975
15-17: 15-The 3 Little Kittens (17 pgs.). 16-The 3 Little Pigs (29 pgs.); X-Mas-c. 17-The Ugly Duckling (4 pgs.)	69	138	207	449	687	925
18-21	58	116	174	377	581	785
22-30: 22-Flag-c. 24-The Flying Gauchito (1st original comic book story done for WDC&S). 27-Jose Carioca by Carl Buettner (2nd original story in WDC&S)	46	92	138	299	462	625
31-New Donald Duck stories by Carl Barks begin (See F.C. #9 for 1st Barks Donald Duck)	296	592	888	1924	2962	4000
32-Barks-a	133	266	399	865	1333	1800
33-Barks-a; infinity-c	93	186	279	605	928	1250
34-Gremlins by Walt Kelly begin, end #41; Barks-a	76	152	228	494	760	1025
35,36-Barks-a	70	140	210	455	703	950
37-Donald Duck by Jack Hannah	36	72	108	234	360	485
38-40-Barks-a. 39-X-Mas-c. 40,41-Gremlins by Kelly	46	92	138	299	462	625
41-50-Barks-a. 43-Seven Dwarfs-c app. (4/44). 45-50-Nazis in Gottfredson's Mickey Mouse Stories	37	74	111	241	371	500
51-60-Barks-a. 51-X-Mas-c. 52-Li'l Bad Wolf begins, ends #203 (not in #55). 58-Kelly flag-c	25	50	75	181	266	350
61-70: Barks-a. 61-Dumbo story. 63,64-Pinocchio stories. 63-Cover swipe from New Funnies #94. 64-X-Mas-c. 65-Pluto story. 66-Infinity-c. 67,68-Mickey Mouse Sunday-r by Bill Wright	22	44	66	160	235	310
71-80: Barks-a. 75-77-Brer Rabbit stories, no Mickey Mouse. 76-X-Mas-c	17	34	51	121	178	235
81-87,89,90: Barks-a. 82-Goofy-c. 82-84-Bongo stories. 86-90-Goofy & Agnes app. 89-Chip 'n' Dale story	15	30	45	104	152	200
88-1st app. Gladstone Gander by Barks (1/48)	19	38	57	136	198	260
91-97,99: Barks-a. 95-1st WDC&S Barks-c. 96-No Mickey Mouse; Little Toot begins, ends #97. 99-X-Mas-c	13	26	39	90	133	175
98-1st Uncle Scrooge app. in WDC&S (11/48)	25	50	75	181	266	350
100-(1/49)-Barks-a	15	30	45	109	160	210
101-110-Barks-a. 107-Taliaferro-c; Donald acquires super powers	12	24	36	82	121	160
111,114,117-All Barks-a	10	20	30	70	100	130
112-Drug (ether) issue (Donald Duck)	10	20	30	70	100	130
113,115,116,118-123: No Barks. 116-Dumbo x-over. 121-Grandma Duck begins, ends #168; not in #135,142,146,155	6	12	18	43	59	75
124,126-130-All Barks-a. 124-X-Mas-c	8	16	24	58	82	105
125-1st app. Junior Woodchucks (2/51); Barks-a	12	24	36	82	121	160
131,133,135-137,139-All Barks-a	8	16	24	58	82	105
132-Barks-a(2) (D. Duck & Grandma Duck)	9	18	27	60	85	110
134-Intro. & 1st app. The Beagle Boys (11/51)	16	32	48	113	167	220
138-Classic Scrooge money story	12	24	36	87	129	170
140-(5/52)-1st app. Gyro Gearloose by Barks; 2nd Barks Uncle Scrooge-c; 3rd Uncle Scrooge cover app.	16	32	48	113	167	220
141-150-All Barks-a. 143-Little Hiawatha begins, ends #151,159	7	14	21	46	63	80
151-170-All Barks-a	6	12	18	40	55	70
171-199-All Barks-a	5	10	15	36	48	60
200	6	12	18	40	55	70
201-240: All Barks-a. 204-Chip 'n' Dale & Scamp begin	5	10	15	33	44	55
241-283: Barks-a. 241-Dumbo x-over. 247-Gyro Gearloose begins, ends #274. 256-Ludwig Von Drake begins, ends #274	4	8	12	29	40	50
284,285,287,290,295,296,309-311-Not by Barks	2	4	6	14	18	22
286,288,289,291-294,297,298,308-All Barks stories; 293-Grandma Duck's Farm Friends. 297-Gyro Gearloose. 298-Daisy Duck's Diary-r	3	6	9	18	23	28
299-307-All contain early Barks-r (#43-117). 305-Gyro Gearloose	3	6	9	19	25	32
312-Last Barks issue with original story	3	6	9	19	25	32
313-315,317-327,329-334,336-341	2	4	6	12	16	20
316-Last issue published during life of Walt Disney	2	4	6	12	16	20
328,335,342-350-Barks-r	2	4	6	12	16	20
351-360-With posters inside; Barks reprints (2 versions of each with & without posters)	4	8	12	24	32	40
351-360-Without posters...	3	6	9	18	23	28
361-400-Barks-r	2	4	6	12	16	20
401-429-Barks-r	2	4	6	11	14	18
430,433,437,438,441,444,445,466-No Barks	1	2	3	5	7	9
431,432,434-436,439,440,442,443-Barks-r	2	4	6	8	10	12
446-465,467-473-Barks-r	1	2	3	5	7	9
474(3/80),475-478 (Whitman)	2	4	6	10	13	16
479(8/80),481(10/80)-484(1/81) pre-pack only	4	8	12	27	36	45
480 (8-12/80)-(Very low distribution)	10	20	30	67	96	125
485-499: 494-r/WDC&S #98	2	4	6	10	13	16
500-510 (All #90011 on-c; pre-packs): 500(4/83), 501(5/83), 502&503(7/83), 504-506(all 8/83), 507(4/84), 508(5/84), 509(6/84), 510(7/84). 506-No Barks	2	4	6	11	14	18
511-Donald Duck by Daan Jippes (1st in U.S.; in all through #518); Gyro Gearloose Barks-r begins (in most through #547); Wuzzles by Disney Studio (1st by Gladstone)	3	6	9	18	23	28
512,513	2	4	6	10	13	16
514-516,520	1	2	3	5	7	9
517-519,521,522,525,527,529,530,532-546: 518-Infinity-c. 522-r/1st app. Huey, Dewey & Louie from D. Duck Sunday. 535-546-Barks-r. 537-1st Donald Duck by William Van Horn in WDC&S. 541-545-52 pgs. 546,547-68 pgs. 546-Kelly-r. 547-Rosa-a						5.00
523,524,526,528,531,547: Rosa-s/a in all. 523-1st Rosa 10 pager	2	4	6	9	11	14
548-($1.50, 6/90)-1st Disney issue; new-a; no M. Mouse						6.00
549,551-570,572,573,577-579,581,584 ($1.50): 549-Barks-r begin, ends #585, not in #555, 556, & 564. 551-r/1 story from F.C. #29. 556,578-r/Mickey Mouse Cheerios Premium by Dick Moores. 562,563,568-570, 572, 581-Gottfredson strip-r. 570-Valentine issue; has Mickey/Minnie centerfold. 584-Taliaferro strip-r						4.00
550 ($2.25, 52 pgs.)-Donald Duck by Barks; previously printed only in The Netherlands (1st time in U.S.); r/Chip 'n Dale & Scamp from #204						5.00
571-($2.95, 68 pgs)-r/Donald Duck's Atomic Bomb by Barks from 1947 Cheerios premium						6.00
574-576,580,582,583 ($2.95, 68 pgs.): 574-r/1st Pinocchio Sunday strip (1939-40). 575-Gottfredson-r, Pinocchio-r/WDC&S #64. 580-r/Donald Duck's 1st app. from Silly Symphony strip 12/16/34 by Taliaferro; Gottfredson strip-r begin; not in #584 & 600. 582,583-r/Mickey Mouse on Sky Island from WDC&S #1,2						5.00
585 ($2.50, 52 pgs.)-r/#140; Barks-r/WDC&S #140						5.00
586,587: 586-Gladstone issues begin again; begin $1.50-c; Gottfredson-r begins (not in #600). 587-Donald Duck by William Van Horn begins						4.00
588-597: 588,591-599-Donald Duck by William Van Horn						3.00
598,599 ($1.95, 36 pgs.): 598-r/1st drawings of Mickey Mouse by Ub Iwerks						3.00
600 ($2.95, 48 pgs.)-L.B. Cole-c(r)/WDC&S #1; Barks-r/WDC&S #32 plus Rosa, Jippes, Van Horn-r and new Rosa centerspread						4.00
601-611 ($5.95, 64 pgs., squarebound, bi-monthly): 601-Barks-c, r/Mickey Mouse V1#1, Rosa-a/scripts. 602-Rosa-c. 604-Taliaferro strip-r/1st Silly Symphony Sundays from 1932. 604,605-Jippes-a. 605-Walt Kelly-c; Gottfredson "Mickey Mouse Outwits the Phantom Blot" r/F.C. #16						6.00
612-633 ($6.95): 633-(2/99) Last Gladstone issue						7.00
634-643: 634-(7/03) First Gemstone issue; William Van Horn-c						7.00

NOTE: *(#1-38, 68 pgs.; #39-42, 60 pgs.; #43-57, 61-134, 143-168, 446, 447, 52 pgs.; #58-60, 135-142, 169-540, 36 pgs.)*

NOTE: **Barks** *art in all issues #31 on, except where noted; c-95, 96, 104, 108, 109, 130-172, 174-178, 183, 198-200, 204, 206-209, 212-216, 218, 220, 226, 228-233, 235-238, 240-243, 247, 250, 253, 256, 260, 261, 276-283, 288-292, 295-298, 301, 303, 304, 306, 307, 309, 310, 313-316, 319, 321, 322, 324, 326, 328, 329, 331, 332, 334, 341, 342, 350, 351, 527r, 530r, 540(never before published), 546r, 557-586r(most), 596p, 601p.* **Kelly** *a-24p, 34-41, 43; r-522-524, 546, 547, 582, 583; covers(most)-34-118, 531r, 537r, 541r-543r, 562r, 571r, 605r. Walt Disney's Comics & Stories featured Mickey Mouse serials which were in practically every issue from #1 through #394 and #511 to date. The titles of the serials, along with the issues they are in, are listed in previous editions of this price guide.* **Floyd Gottfredson** *Mickey Mouse serials in issues #1-14, 18-66, 69-74, 78-100, 128, 562, 563, 568-572, 582, 583, 586-599 , 601-603 , 605-present , plus "Service with a Smile" in #13; "Mickey Mouse in a Warplant" (3 pgs.), and "Pluto Catches a Nazi Spy" (4 pgs.) in #62; "Mystery Next Door", #93; "Sunken Treasure", #94; "Aunt Marissa", #95 (r in #575); "Gangland", #98 (r in #562); "Thanksgiving Dinner", #99 (r in #567); and "The Talking Dog", #100 (r in #563); "Morty's Escapade," #128. "The Brave Little Tailor", #580; "Introducing Mickey Mouse Movies ", #581; Circus Roustabout, #585; "Rumplewatt the Giant", #604. Mickey Mouse by* **Paul Murry** *#152-547 except 155-57 (***Dick Moore***), 327-29 (***Tony Strobl***), 348-50 (***Jack Manning***), 533 (***Bill Wright***).* **Don Rosa** *story/a-523, 524, 526, 528, 531, 547, 601-present.* **Al Taliaferro** *Silly Symphonies in #5-"Three Little Pigs"; #13-"Birds of a Feather"; #14-"The Boarding School Mystery"; #15-"Cookieland" and "Three Little Kittens"; #16-"The Practical Pig"; #17-"The Ugly Duckling"; "The Wise Little Hen" in #580; and "Ambrose the Robber Kitten"; #19-"Penguin Isle"; and "Bucky Bug" in #20-23, 25, 26, 28 (one continuous story from 1932-34; first 2 pgs. not Taliaferro).* **Gottfredson** *strip r-562, 563, 568-572, 581, 585, 586, 590.* **Taliaferro** *strip r-584, 580.* **Van Horn** *a-537, 545, 561, 574, 587, 588, 591-present.*

WALT DISNEY'S COMICS DIGEST
Gladstone: Dec, 1986 - No. 7, Sept, 1987

	GD 2.0	VG 4.0	FN 6.0	VF 8.0	VF/NM 9.0	NM- 9.2
1	1	2	3	5	6	8
2-7						6.00

WALT DISNEY'S COMICS PENNY PINCHER
Gladstone: May, 1997 - No. 4, Aug, 1997 (99¢, limited series)

	GD 2.0	VG 4.0	FN 6.0	VF 8.0	VF/NM 9.0	NM- 9.2
1-4						2.25

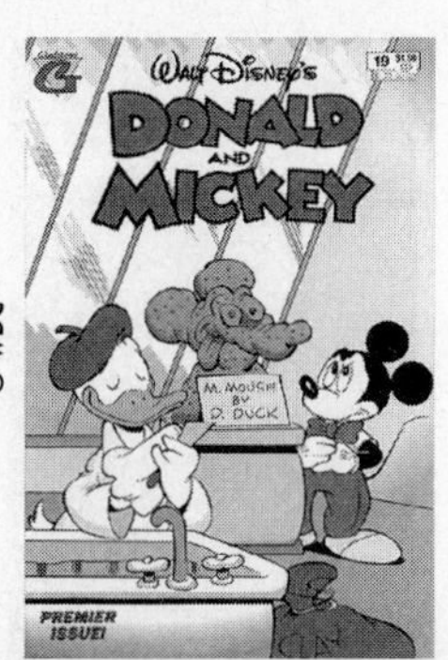

Walt Disney's Donald and Mickey #19 © WDC

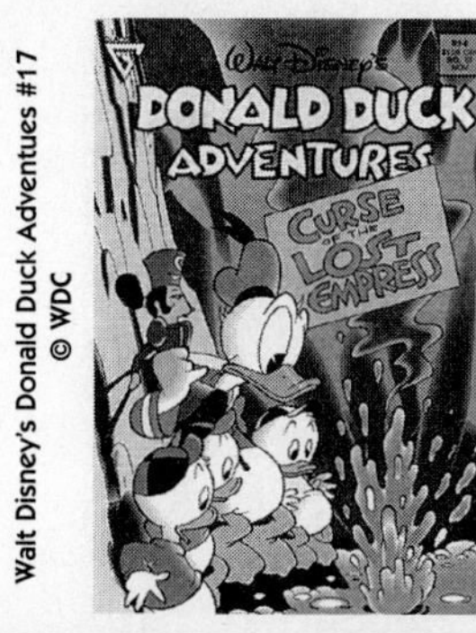

Walt Disney's Donald Duck Adventures #17 © WDC

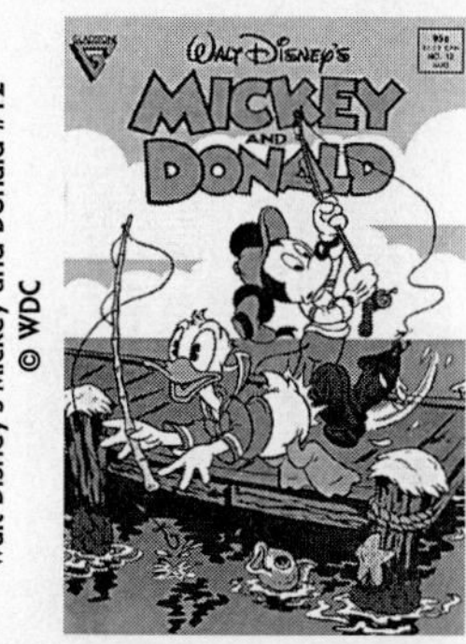

Walt Disney's Mickey and Donald #12 © WDC

GD 2.0 | VG 4.0 | FN 6.0 | VF 8.0 | VF/NM 9.0 | NM- 9.2

WALT DISNEY'S DONALD AND MICKEY (Formerly Walt Disney's Mickey and Donald)
Gladstone (Bruce Hamilton Co.): No. 19, Sept, 1993 - No. 30, 1995 ($1.50, 36 & 68 pgs.)

19,21-24,26-30: New & reprints. 19,21,23,24-Barks-r. 19,26-Murry-r. 22-Barks "Omelet" story r/WDC&S #146. 27-Mickey Mouse story by Caesar Ferioli (1st U.S work). 29-Rosa-c; Mickey Mouse story actually starring Goofy (does not include Mickey except on title page.) 4.00
20,25-($2.95, 68 pgs.): 20-Barks, Gottfredson-r 5.00
NOTE: *Donald Duck stories were all reprints.*

WALT DISNEY'S DONALD DUCK ADVENTURES (D.D. Adv. #1-3)
Gladstone: 11/87-No. 20, 4/90 (1st Series); No. 21,8/93-No. 48, 2/98(3rd Series)

1 1 2 3 4 5 7
2-r/F.C. #308 3.00
3,4,6,7,9-11,13,15-18: 3-r/F.C. #223. 4-r/F.C. #62. 9-r/F.C. #159, "Ghost of the Grotto". 11-r/F.C. #159, "Adventure Down Under." 16-r/F.C. #291; Rosa-c. 18-r/FC #318; Rosa-c 3.00
5,8-Don Rosa-c/a 5.00
12($1.50, 52pgs)-Rosa-c/a w/Barks poster 6.00
14-r/F.C. #29, "Mummy's Ring" 4.00
19($1.95, 68 pgs.)-Barks-r/F.C. #199 (1 pg.) 3.00
20($1.95, 68 pgs.)-Barks-r/F.C. #189 & cover-r; William Van Horn-a 3.00
21,22: 21-r/D.D. #46. 22-r/F.C. #282 3.00
23-25,27,29,31,32-($1.50, 36 pgs.): 21,23,29-Rosa-c. 23-Intro/1st app. Andold Wild Duck by Marco Rota. 24-Van Horn-a. 27-1st Pat Block-a, "Mystery of Widow's Gap." 31,32-Block-c 2.50
26,28($2.95, 68 pgs.): 26-Barks-r/F.C. #108, "Terror of the River". 28-Barks-r/F.C. #199, "Sheriff of Bullet Valley" 4.00
30($2.95, 68 pgs.)-r/F.C. #367, Barks' "Christmas for Shacktown" 4.00
33($1.95, 68 pgs.)-r/F.C. #408, Barks' "The Golden Helmet;"Van Horn-c 3.00
34-43: 34-Resume $1.50-c. 34,35,37-Block-a/scripts. 38-Van Horn-c/a 2.50
44-48-($1.95-c) 2.50
NOTE: ***Barks** a-1-22r, 26r, 28r, 33r, 36r; c-3r, 8r, 10r, 14r, 20r. **Block** a-27, 30, 34, 35, 37; c-27, 30-32, 34, 35, 37; c-27, 30, 31, 32, 34, 35, 37. **Rosa** a-5, 8, 12; c-13, 16, 18, 21, 23.*

WALT DISNEY'S DONALD DUCK ADVENTURES (2nd Series)
Disney Comics: June, 1990 - No. 38, July, 1993 ($1.50)

1-Rosa-a & scripts 5.00
2-21,23,25,27-33,35,36,38: 2-Barks-r/WDC&S #35; William Van Horn-a begins, ends #20. 9-Barks-r/F.C. #178. 9,11,14,17-No Van Horn-a. 11-Mad #1 cover parody. 14-Barks-r. 17-Barks-r. 21-r/FC #203 by Barks. 29-r/MOC #20 by Barks 3.00
22,24,26,34,37: 22-Rosa-a (10 pgs.) & scripts. 24-Rosa-a & scripts. 26-r/March of Comics #41 by Barks. 34-Rosa-c/a. 37-Rosa-a; Barks-r 4.00
NOTE: ***Barks** r-2, 4, 9(F.C. #178), 14(D.D. #45), 17, 21, 26, 27, 29 , 35, 36(D.D #60)-38. **Taliaferro** a-34r, 36r.*

WALT DISNEY'S DONALD DUCK ADVENTURES (Take-Along Comic)
Gemstone Publishing: July, 2003 - Present ($7.95, 5" x 7-1/2")

1-5-Mickey Mouse & Uncle Scrooge app. 8.00

WALT DISNEY'S DONALD DUCK AND FRIENDS
Gemstone Publishing: No. 308, Oct, 2003 - Present ($2.95)

308-314: 308-Numbering resumes from Gladstone Donald Duck series; Halloween-c 3.00

WALT DISNEY'S DONALD DUCK AND MICKEY MOUSE (Formerly Walt Disney's Donald and Mickey)
Gladstone (Bruce Hamilton Company): Sept, 1995 - No. 7, Sept, 1996 ($1.50, 32 pgs.)

1-7: 1-Barks-r and new Mickey Mouse stories in all. 5,6-Mickey Mouse stories by Caesar Ferioli. 7-New Donald Duck and Mickey Mouse x-over story; Barks-r/WDC&S #51 2.25
NOTE: *Issue #8 was advertised, but cancelled.*

WALT DISNEY SHOWCASE
Gold Key: Oct, 1970 - No. 54, Jan, 1980 (No. 44-48: 68pgs., 49-54: 52pgs.)

	GD	VG	FN	VF	VF/NM	NM-
1-Boatniks (Movie)-Photo-c	3	7	10	21	28	35
2-Moby Duck	3	6	9	16	20	24
3,4,7: 3-Bongo & Lumpjaw-r. 4,7-Pluto-r	2	4	6	11	14	18
5-$1,000,000 Duck (Movie)-Photo-c	3	6	9	18	23	28
6-Bedknobs & Broomsticks (Movie)	3	6	9	18	23	28
8-Daisy & Donald	2	4	6	12	16	20
9- 101 Dalmatians (cartoon feat.); r/F.C. #1183	3	6	9	19	25	32
10-Napoleon & Samantha (Movie)-Photo-c	3	6	9	18	23	28
11-Moby Duck-r	2	4	6	11	14	18
12-Dumbo-r/Four Color #668	2	4	6	12	16	20
13-Pluto-r	2	4	6	11	14	18
14-World's Greatest Athlete (Movie)-Photo-c	3	6	9	18	23	28
15- 3 Little Pigs-r	2	4	6	12	16	20
16-Aristocats (cartoon feature); r/Aristocats #1	3	6	9	18	23	28
17-Mary Poppins; r/M.P. #10136-501-Photo-c	3	6	9	18	23	28
18-Gyro Gearloose; Barks-r/F.C. #1047,1184	3	7	10	21	28	35
19-That Darn Cat; r/That Darn Cat #10171-602-Hayley Mills photo-c	3	6	9	18	23	28
20,23-Pluto-r	2	4	6	12	16	20
21-Li'l Bad Wolf & The Three Little Pigs	2	4	6	11	14	18
22-Unbirthday Party with Alice in Wonderland; r/Four Color #341	3	6	9	16	20	24
24-26: 24-Herbie Rides Again (Movie); sequel to "The Love Bug"; photo-c. 25-Old Yeller (Movie); r/F.C. #869; Photo-c. 26-Lt. Robin Crusoe USN (Movie); r/Lt. Robin Crusoe USN #10191-601; photo-c	2	4	6	12	16	20
27-Island at the Top of the World (Movie)-Photo-c	3	6	9	16	20	24
28-Brer Rabbit, Bucky Bug-r/WDC&S #58	2	4	6	12	16	20
29-Escape to Witch Mountain (Movie)-Photo-c	3	6	9	16	20	24
30-Magica De Spell; Barks-r/Uncle Scrooge #36 & WDC&S #258	4	8	12	25	33	42
31-Bambi (cartoon feature); r/Four Color #186	2	4	6	14	18	22
32-Spin & Marty-r/F.C. #1026; Mickey Mouse Club (TV)-Photo-c	3	6	9	16	20	24
33-40: 33-Pluto-r/F.C. #1143. 34-Paul Revere's Ride with Johnny Tremain (TV); r/F.C. #822. 35-Goofy-r/F.C. #952. 36-Peter Pan-r/F.C. #442. 37-Tinker Bell & Jiminy Cricket-r/F.C. #982,989. 38,39-Mickey & the Sleuth, Parts 1 & 2. 40-The Rescuers (cartoon feature)	2	4	6	10	13	16
41-Herbie Goes to Monte Carlo (Movie); sequel to "Herbie Rides Again"; photo-c	2	4	6	11	14	18
42-Mickey & the Sleuth	2	4	6	10	13	16
43-Pete's Dragon (Movie)-Photo-c	2	4	6	14	18	22
44-Return From Witch Mountain (new) & In Search of the Castaways-r (Movies)-Photo-c; 68 pg. giants begin	3	6	9	16	20	24
45-The Jungle Book (Movie); r/#30033-803	3	6	9	19	25	32
46-48: 46-The Cat From Outer Space (Movie)(new), & The Shaggy Dog (Movie)-r/F.C. #985; photo-c. 47-Mickey Mouse Surprise Party-r. 48-The Wonderful Advs. of Pinocchio-r/F.C. #1203; last 68 pg. issue	2	4	6	11	14	18
49-54: 49-North Avenue Irregulars (Movie); Zorro-r/Zorro #11; 52 pgs. begin; photo-c. 50-Bedknobs & Broomsticks-r/#6; Mooncussers-r/World of Adv. #1; photo-c. 51-101 Dalmatians-r. 52-Unidentified Flying Oddball (Movie); r/Picnic Party #8; photo-c. 53-The Scarecrow-r (TV). 54-The Black Hole (Movie)-Photo-c (predates Black Hole #1)	2	4	6	10	13	16

WALT DISNEY'S MAGAZINE (TV)(Formerly Walt Disney's Mickey Mouse Club Magazine) (50¢, bi-monthly)
Western Publishing Co.: V2#4, June, 1957 - V4#6, Oct, 1959

	GD	VG	FN	VF	VF/NM	NM-
V2#4-Stories & articles on the Mouseketeers, Zorro, & Goofy and other Disney characters & people	7	14	21	50	68	85
V2#5, V2#6(10/57)	6	12	18	43	59	75
V3#1(12/57), V3#3-5	6	12	18	38	52	65
V3#2-Annette Funicello photo-c	12	24	36	84	125	165
V3#6(10/58)-TV Zorro photo-c	8	16	24	58	82	105
V4#1(12/58) - V4#2-4,6(10/59)	6	12	18	38	52	65
V4#5-Annette Funicello photo-c, w/ 2-photo articles	12	24	36	84	125	165

NOTE: *V2#4-V3#6 were 11-1/2x8-1/2", 48 pgs.; V4#1 on were 10x8", 52 pgs. (Peak circulation of 400,000).*

WALT DISNEY'S MERRY CHRISTMAS (See Dell Giant #39)

WALT DISNEY'S MICKEY AND DONALD (M & D #1,2)(Becomes Walt Disney's Donald & Mickey #19 on)
Gladstone: Mar, 1988 - No. 18, May, 1990 (95¢)

1-Don Rosa-a; r/1949 Firestone giveaway 6.00
2-8: 3-Infinity-c. 4-8-Barks-r 3.00
9-15: 9-r/1948 Firestone giveaway; X-Mas-c 3.00
16($1.50, 52 pgs.)-r/FC #157 5.00
17-(68 pgs.) Barks M.M.-r/FC #79 plus Barks D.D.-r; Rosa-a; x-mas-c 6.00
18($1.95, 68 pgs.)-Gottfredson-r/WDC&S #13,72-74; Kelly-c(r); Barks-r 5.00
NOTE: ***Barks** reprints in 1-15, 17, 18. **Kelly** c-13r, 14 (r/Walt Disney's C&S #58), 18r.*

WALT DISNEY'S MICKEY MOUSE AND FRIENDS
Gemstone Publishing: No. 257, Oct, 2003 - Present ($2.95)

257-263: 257-Numbering resumes from Gladstone Mickey Mouse series; Halloween-c 3.00

WALT DISNEY'S MICKEY MOUSE CLUB MAGAZINE (TV)(Becomes Walt Disney's Magazine)
Western Publishing Co.: Winter, 1956 - V2#3, Apr, 1957 (11-1/2x8-1/2", quarterly, 48 pgs.)

	GD	VG	FN	VF	VF/NM	NM-
V1#1	16	32	48	113	167	220
2-4	9	18	27	60	85	110
V2#1,2	7	14	21	50	68	85
3-Annette photo-c	14	28	42	99	145	190
Annual(1956)-Two different issues; ($1.50-Whitman); 120 pgs., cardboard covers, 11-3/4x8-3/4"; reprints	16	32	48	113	167	220
Annual(1957)-Same as above	13	26	39	90	133	175

WALT DISNEY'S PINOCCHIO SPECIAL

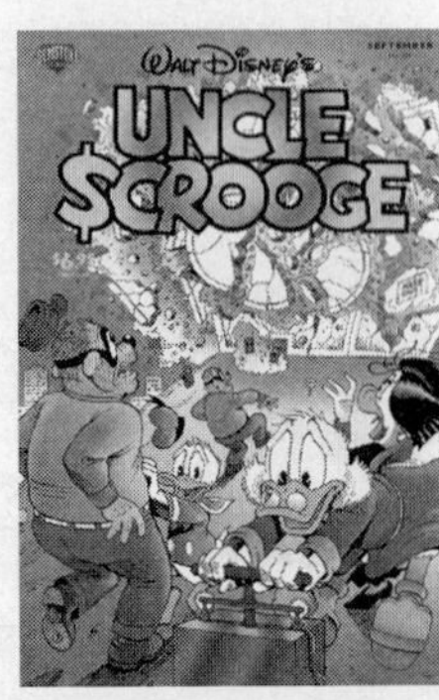

Walt Disney's Uncle Scrooge #321 © WDC

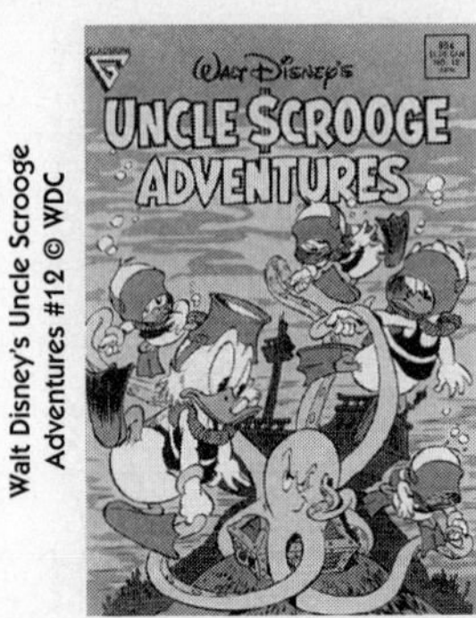

Walt Disney's Uncle Scrooge Adventures #12 © WDC

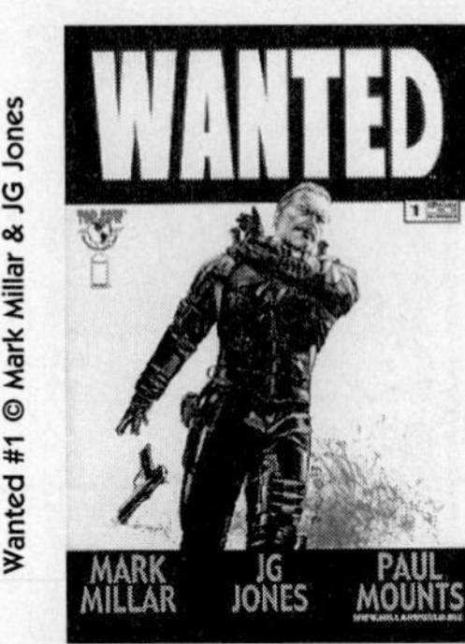

Wanted #1 © Mark Millar & JG Jones

GD VG FN VF VF/NM NM-
2.0 4.0 6.0 8.0 9.0 9.2

Gladstone: Spring, 1990 ($1.00)
1-50th anniversary edition; Kelly-r/F.C. #92 3.00

WALT DISNEY'S THE ADVENTUROUS UNCLE SCROOGE MCDUCK
Gladstone: Jan, 1998 - No. 2, Mar, 1998 ($1.95)
1,2: 1-Barks-a(r). 2-Rosa-a(r) 2.50

WALT DISNEY'S THE JUNGLE BOOK
W.D. Publications (Disney Comics): 1990 ($5.95, graphic novel, 68 pgs.)
nn-Movie adaptation; movie rereleased in 1990 6.00
nn-($2.95, 68 pgs.)-Comic edition; wraparound-c 3.00

WALT DISNEY'S UNCLE SCROOGE (Formerly Uncle Scrooge #1-209)
Gladstone #210-242/Disney Comics #243-280/Gladstone #281-318/Gemstone #319 on: No. 210, 10/86 - No. 242, 4/90; No. 243, 6/90 - No. 318, 2/99; No. 319, 7/03 - Present
210-1st Gladstone issue; r/WDC&S #134 (1st Beagle Boys) 2 4 6 10 13 16
211-218: 216-New story ("Go Slowly Sands of Time") plotted and partly scripted by Barks. 217-r/U.S. #7, "Seven Cities of Cibola" 2 4 6 10 12 15
219-"Son Of The Sun" by Rosa 3 6 9 16 20 25
220-Don Rosa-a/scripts 1 2 3 5 6 8
221-223,225,228-234,236-240 4.00
224,226,227,235: 224-Rosa-c/a. 226,227-Rosa-a. 235-Rosa-a/scripts 5.00
241-($1.95, 68 pgs.)-Rosa finishes over Barks-r 6.00
242-($1.95, 68 pgs.)-Barks-r; Rosa-a(1 pg.) 6.00
243-249,251-260,264-275,277-280,282-284-($1.50): 243-1st by Disney Comics. 274-All Barks issue. 275-Contains centerspread by Rosa. 279-All Barks issue; Rosa-c. 283-r/WDC&S #98 3.00
250-($2.25, 52 pgs.)-Barks-r; wraparound-c 4.00
261-263,276-Don Rosa-c/a 5.00
281-Gladstone issues start again; Rosa-c 6.00
285-The Life and Times of Scrooge McDuck Pt. 1; Rosa-c/a/scripts 1 3 4 6 8 10
286-293: The Life and Times of Scrooge McDuck Pt. 2-8; Rosa-c/a/scripts. 293-($1.95, 36 pgs.)-The Life and Times of Scrooge McDuck Pt. 9 6.00
294-299, 301-308-($1.50, 32 pgs.): 294-296-The Life and Times of Scrooge McDuck Pt. 10-12. 297-The Life and Times of Uncle Scrooge Pt. 0; Rosa-c/a/scripts 3.00
300-($2.25, 48 pgs.)-Rosa-c; Barks-r/WDC&S #104 and U.S. #216; r/U.S. #220; includes new centerfold. 4.00
309-318-($6.95) 318-(2/99) Last Gladstone issue 7.00
319-328: 319-(7/03) First Gemstone issue; The Dutchman's Secret by Don Rosa 7.00
NOTE: ***Barks** r-210-218, 220-223, 224(2pg.), 225-234, 236-242, 245, 246, 250-253, 255, 256, 258, 261(2 pg.), 265, 267, 268, 270(2), 272-284, 299-present; c(r)-210, 212, 221, 228, 229, 232, 233, 284. scripts-287, 293. **Rosa** a-219, 220, 224, 226, 227, 235, 261-263, 268, 275-277, 285-289; c-219, 224, 231, 261-263, 276, 278-281, 285-289; scripts-219, 220, 224, 235, 261-263, 268, 276, 285-289.*

WALT DISNEY'S UNCLE SCROOGE ADVENTURES (U. Scrooge Advs. #1-3)
Gladstone Publishing: Nov, 1987 - No. 21, May, 1990; No. 22, Sept, 1993 - No. 54, Feb, 1998
1-Barks-r begin, ends #26 1 2 3 5 6 8
2-4 4.00
5,9,14: 5-Rosa-c/a; no Barks-r. 9,14-Rosa-a 5.00
6-8,10-13,15-19: 10-r/U.S. #18(all Barks) 3.00
20,21 ($1.95, 68 pgs.) 20-Rosa-c/a. 21-Rosa-a 5.00
22 ($1.50)-Rosa-c; r/U.S. #26 5.00
23-($2.95, 68 pgs.)-Vs. The Phantom Blot-r/P.B. #3; Barks-r 4.00
24-26,29,31,32,34-36: 24,25,29,31,32-Rosa-c. 25-r/U.S. #21 2.50
27-Guardians of the Lost Library - Rosa-c/a/story; origin of Junior Woodchuck Guidebook 3.00
28-($2.95, 68 pgs.)-r/U.S. #13 w/restored missing panels 4.00
30-($2.95, 68 pgs.)-r/U.S. #12; Rosa-c 4.00
33-($2.95, 64 pgs.)-New Barks story 3.00
37-54 2.50
NOTE: ***Barks** r-1-4, 6-8, 10-13, 15-21, 23, 22, 24; c(r)-15, 16, 17, 21. **Rosa** a-5, 9, 14, 20, 21, 27; c-5, 13, 14, 17(finishes), 20, 22, 24, 25, 27, 28; scripts-5, 9, 14, 27.*

WALT DISNEY'S UNCLE SCROOGE AND DONALD DUCK
Gladstone: Jan, 1998 - No. 2, Mar, 1998 ($1.95)
1,2: 1-Rosa-a(r) 2.50

WALT DISNEY'S UNCLE SCROOGE ADVENTURES IN COLOR
Gladstone Publ.: Dec, 1995 - Present ($8.95/$9.95, squarebound, 56 issue limited series) (Polybagged w/card) (Series chronologically reprints all the stories written & drawn by Carl Barks)
1-56: 1-(12/95)-r/FC #386. 15-(12/96)-r/US #15. 16-(12/96)-r/US #16. 18-(1/97)-r/US #18 10.00

WALT DISNEY'S WHEATIES PREMIUMS (See Wheaties in the Promotional section)

GD VG FN VF VF/NM NM-
2.0 4.0 6.0 8.0 9.0 9.2

WALTER (Campaign of Terror) (Also see The Mask)
Dark Horse Comics: Feb, 1996 - No. 4, May, 1996 ($2.50, limited series)
1-4 2.50

WALTER LANTZ ANDY PANDA (Also see Andy Panda)
Gold Key: Aug, 1973 - No. 23, Jan, 1978 (Walter Lantz)
1-Reprints 2 4 6 14 18 22
2-10-All reprints 2 4 6 9 11 14
11-23: 15,17-19,22-Reprints 1 2 3 5 6 8

WALT KELLY'S...
Eclipse Comics: Dec, 1987; Apr, 1988 ($1.75/$2.50, Baxter paper)
...Christmas Classics 1 (12/87)-Kelly-r/Peter Wheat & Santa Claus Funnies, ...Springtime Tales 1 (4/88, $2.50)-Kelly-r 2.50

WALTONS, THE (See Kite Fun Book)

WALT SCOTT (See Little People)

WALT SCOTT'S CHRISTMAS STORIES (See Christmas Stories, 4-Color #959, 1062)

WAMBI, JUNGLE BOY (See Jungle Comics)
Fiction House Magazines: Spr, 1942; No. 2, Win, 1942-43; No. 3, Spr, 1943; No. 4, Fall, 1948; No. 5, Sum, 1949; No. 6, Spr, 1950; No. 7-10, 1950(nd); No. 11, Spr, 1951 - No. 18, Win, 1952-53 (#1-3: 68 pgs.)
1-Wambi, the Jungle Boy begins 92 184 276 575 863 1150
2 (1942)-Kiefer-c 50 100 150 300 450 600
3 (1943)-Kiefer-c/a 39 78 117 230 325 420
4 (1948)-Origin in text 24 48 72 135 190 245
5 (Fall, 1949, 36 pgs.)-Kiefer-c/a 20 40 60 112 156 200
6-10: 7-(52 pgs.)-New logo 19 38 57 106 146 185
11-18 13 26 39 74 100 125
I.W. Reprint #8('64)-r/#12 with new-c 3 6 9 16 20 25
NOTE: ***Alex Blum** c-8. **Kiefer** c-1-5. **Whitman** c-11-18.*

WANDERERS (See Adventure Comics #375, 376)
DC Comics: June, 1988 - No. 13, Apr, 1989 ($1.25) (Legion of Super-Heroes spin off)
1-13: 1,2-Steacy-c. 3-Legion app. 2.25

WANDERING STAR
Pen & Ink Comics/Sirius Entertainment No. 12 on: 1993 - No. 21, Mar, 1997 ($2.50/$2.75, B&W)
1-1st printing; Teri Sue Wood c/a/scripts in all 1 2 3 5 6 8
1-2nd and 3rd printings 2.75
2-1st printing. 4.00
2-21: 2-2nd printing. 12-(1/96)-1st Sirius issue 2.75
Trade paperback ($11.95)-r/1-7; 1st printing of 1000, signed and #'d 18.00
Trade paperback-2nd printing, 2000 signed 15.00
TPB Volume 2,3 (11/98, 12/98, $14.95) 2-r/#8-14, 3-r/#15-21 15.00

WANTED
Image Comics (Top Cow): Dec, 2003 - Present ($2.99)
1-Three covers; Mark Millar-s/J.G. Jones-a 3.00

WANTED COMICS
Toytown Publications/Patches/Orbit Publ.: No. 9, Sept-Oct, 1947 - No. 53, April, 1953 (#9-33: 52 pgs.)
9-True crime cases; radio's Mr. D. A. app. 23 46 69 132 186 240
10,11: 10-Giunta-a; radio's Mr. D. A. app. 14 28 42 81 111 140
12-Used in **SOTI**, pg. 277 15 30 45 84 115 145
13-Heroin drug propaganda story 13 26 39 74 100 125
14-Marijuana drug mention story (2 pgs.) 11 22 33 66 88 110
15-17,19,20 10 20 30 58 77 95
18-Marijuana story, "Satan's Cigarettes"; r-in #45 & retitled 24 48 72 135 190 245
21,22: 21-Krigstein-a. 22-Extreme violence 10 20 30 60 80 100
23,25-34,36-38,40-44,46-48,53 8 16 24 46 58 70
24-Krigstein-a; "The Dope King", marijuana mention story 11 22 33 66 88 110
35-Used in **SOTI**, pg. 160 11 22 33 63 84 105
39-Drug propaganda story "The Horror Weed" 15 30 45 86 118 150
45-Marijuana story from #18 10 20 30 58 77 95
49-Has unstable pink-c that fades easily; rare in mint condition 9 18 27 54 70 85
50-Has unstable pink-c like #49; surrealist-c by Buscema; horror stories 14 28 42 81 111 140
51- "Holiday of Horror" junkie story; drug-c 12 24 36 69 92 115
52-Classic "Cult of Killers" opium use story 12 24 36 69 92 115

Wanted, The World's Most Dangerous Villains #1 © DC

War Action #4 © ATLAS

War Comics #2 © DELL

	GD 2.0	VG 4.0	FN 6.0	VF 8.0	VF/NM 9.0	NM- 9.2

NOTE: ***Buscema*** *c-50, 51.* ***Lawrence*** *and* ***Leav*** *c/a most issues.* ***Syd Shores*** *c/a-48; c-37. Issues 9-46 have wanted criminals with their descriptions & drawn picture on cover.*

WANTED: DEAD OR ALIVE (TV)
Dell Publishing Co.: No. 1102, May-July, 1960 - No. 1164, Mar-May, 1961

	GD	VG	FN	VF	VF/NM	NM-
Four Color 1102 (#1)-Steve McQueen photo-c	14	28	42	99	145	190
Four Color 1164-Steve McQueen photo-c	10	20	30	73	107	140

WANTED, THE WORLD'S MOST DANGEROUS VILLAINS (See DC Special)
National Periodical Publ.: July-Aug, 1972 - No. 9, Aug-Sept, 1973 (All reprints & 20¢ issues)

	GD	VG	FN	VF	VF/NM	NM-
1-Batman, Green Lantern (story r-from G.L. #1), & Green Arrow	4	8	12	22	30	38
2-Batman/Joker/Penguin-c/story r-from Batman #25; plus Flash story (r-from Flash #121)	3	6	9	18	23	28
3-9: 3-Dr. Fate(r/More Fun #65), Hawkman(r/Flash #100), & Vigilante(r/Action #69). 4-Green Lantern(r/All-American #61) & Kid Eternity(r/Kid Eternity #15). 5-Dollman/Green Lantern. 6-Burnley Starman; Wildcat/Sargon. 7-Johnny Quick(r/More Fun #76), Hawkman(r/Flash #90), Hourman by Baily(r/Adv. #72). 8-Dr. Fate/Flash(r/Flash #114). 9-S&K Sandman/Superman	2	4	6	14	18	22

NOTE: ***B. Bailey*** *a-7r.* ***Infantino*** *a-2r.* ***Kane*** *r-1, 5.* ***Kubert*** *r-3i, 6, 7.* ***Meskin*** *r-3, 7.* ***Reinman*** *r-4, 6.*

WAR (See Fightin' Marines #122)
Charlton Comics: Jul, 1975 - No. 9, Nov, 1976; No. 10, Sept, 1978 - No. 49, 1984

	GD	VG	FN	VF	VF/NM	NM-
1-Boyette painted-c	2	4	6	11	14	18
2-10	1	3	4	6	8	10
11-20	1	2	3	4	5	7
21-40						6.00
41-49 (lower print run): 47-Reprints	1	2	3	4	5	7
7,9 (Modern Comics-r, 1977)						4.00

WAR, THE (See The Draft & The Pitt)
Marvel Comics: 1989 - No. 4, 1990 ($3.50, squarebound, 52 pgs.)

	GD	VG	FN	VF	VF/NM	NM-
1-4: Characters from New Universe						3.50

WAR ACTION (Korean War)
Atlas Comics (CPS): April, 1952 - No. 14, June, 1953

	GD	VG	FN	VF	VF/NM	NM-
1	21	42	63	118	164	210
2	11	22	33	63	84	105
3-10,14: 7-Pakula-a	9	18	27	54	70	85
11-13-Krigstein-a	10	20	30	58	77	95

NOTE: ***Brodsky*** *c-1-4.* ***Heath*** *a-1; c-7, 14.* ***Keller*** *a-6.* ***Maneely*** *a-1.* ***Tuska*** *a-2, 8.*

WAR ADVENTURES
Atlas Comics (HPC): Jan, 1952 - No. 13, Feb, 1953

	GD	VG	FN	VF	VF/NM	NM-
1-Tuska-a	17	34	51	98	134	170
2	10	20	30	56	73	90
3-7,9-13: 3-Pakula-a. 7-Maneely-c	8	16	24	46	58	70
8-Krigstein-a	10	20	30	56	73	90

NOTE: ***Brodsky*** *c-1-3, 6, 8, 11, 12.* ***Heath*** *a-5, 7, 10; c-4, 5, 9, 13.* ***Robinson*** *a-3; c-10.*

WAR ADVENTURES ON THE BATTLEFIELD (See Battlefield)

WAR AGAINST CRIME! (Becomes Vault of Horror #12 on)
E. C. Comics: Spring, 1948 - No. 11, Feb-Mar, 1950

	GD	VG	FN	VF	VF/NM	NM-
1-Real Stories From Police Records on-c #1-9	74	148	222	463	694	925
2,3	44	88	132	264	395	525
4-9	42	84	126	252	359	465
10-1st Vault Keeper app. & 1st Vault of Horror	193	386	579	1448	2074	2700
11-2nd Vault Keeper app.; 1st horror-c	114	228	342	855	1228	1600

NOTE: *All have* ***Johnny Craig*** *covers.* ***Feldstein*** *a-4, 7-9.* ***Harrison/Wood*** *a-11.* ***Ingels*** *a-1, 2, 8.* ***Palais*** *a-8. Changes to horror with #10.*

WAR AGAINST CRIME
Gemstone Publishing: Apr, 2000 - No. 11, Feb, 2001 ($2.50)

	GD	VG	FN	VF	VF/NM	NM-
1-11: E.C. reprints						2.50

WAR AND ATTACK (Also see Special War Series #3)
Charlton Comics: Fall, 1964; V2#54, June, 1966 - V2#63, Dec, 1967

	GD	VG	FN	VF	VF/NM	NM-
1-Wood-a (25 pgs.)	5	10	15	36	48	60
V2#54(6/66)-#63 (Formerly Fightin' Air Force)	3	6	9	16	20	25

NOTE: ***Montes/Bache*** *a-55, 56, 60, 63.*

WAR AT SEA (Formerly Space Adventures)
Charlton Comics: No. 22, Nov, 1957 - No. 42, June, 1961

	GD	VG	FN	VF	VF/NM	NM-
22	6	12	18	31	38	45
23-30	5	10	15	23	28	32
31-42	3	6	9	18	23	28

WAR BATTLES
Harvey Publications: Feb, 1952 - No. 9, Dec, 1953

	GD	VG	FN	VF	VF/NM	NM-
1-Powell-a; Elias-c	10	20	30	73	107	140
2-Powell-a	6	12	18	40	55	70
3-5,7-9: 3,7-Powell-a	6	12	18	38	52	65
6-Nostrand-a	7	14	21	46	63	80

WAR BIRDS
Fiction House Magazines: 1952(nd) - No. 3, Winter, 1952-53

	GD	VG	FN	VF	VF/NM	NM-
1	16	32	48	92	126	160
2,3	9	18	27	54	70	85

WARBLADE: ENDANGERED SPECIES (Also see WildC.A.T.S: Covert Action Teams)
Image Comics (WildStorm Productions): Jan, 1995 - No. 4, Apr, 1995 ($2.50, limited series)

	GD	VG	FN	VF	VF/NM	NM-
1-4: 1-Gatefold wraparound-c						2.50

WARCHILD
Maximum Press: Jan. 1995 - No. 4, Aug, 1995 ($2.50)

	GD	VG	FN	VF	VF/NM	NM-
1-4-Rob Liefeld-c/a/scripts						2.50
1-4: Variant-c						3.00
Trade paperback (1/96, $12.95)-r/#1-4.						13.00

WAR COMBAT (Becomes Combat Casey #6 on)
Atlas Comics (LBI No. 1/SAI No. 2-5): March, 1952 - No. 5, Nov, 1952

	GD	VG	FN	VF	VF/NM	NM-
1	15	30	45	86	118	150
2	9	18	27	52	66	80
3-5	8	16	24	43	54	65

NOTE: ***Berg*** *a-2, 4, 5.* ***Brodsky*** *c-1, 2, 4, 5.* ***Henkel*** *a-5.* ***Maneely*** *a-1, 4; c-3.*

WAR COMICS (War Stories #5 on)(See Key Ring Comics)
Dell Publishing Co.: May, 1940 (No month given) - No. 4, Sept, 1941?

	GD	VG	FN	VF	VF/NM	NM-
1-Sikandur the Robot Master, Sky Hawk, Scoop Mason, War Correspondent begin; McWilliams-c; 1st war comic	58	116	174	363	542	720
2-Origin Greg Gilday (5/41)	35	70	105	201	283	365
3-Joan becomes Greg Gilday's aide	23	46	69	132	186	240
4-Origin Night Devils	24	48	72	138	194	250

WAR COMICS
Marvel/Atlas (USA No. 1-41/JPI No. 42-49): Dec, 1950 - No. 49, Sept, 1957

	GD	VG	FN	VF	VF/NM	NM-
1	26	52	78	150	210	270
2	14	28	42	81	111	140
3-10	11	22	33	66	88	110
11-Flame thrower w/burning bodies on-c	12	24	36	71	96	120
12-20	10	20	30	56	73	90
21,23-32: 26-Valley Forge story. 32-Last precode issue (2/55)	8	16	24	46	58	70
22-Krigstein-a	10	20	30	56	73	90
33-37,39-42,44,45,47,48	8	16	24	46	58	70
38-Kubert/Moskowitz-a	9	18	27	52	66	80
43,49-Torres-a. 43-Severin/Elder E.C. swipe from Two-Fisted Tales #31	9	18	27	52	66	80
46-Crandall-a	9	18	27	52	66	80

NOTE: ***Colan*** *a-4, 36, 48, 49.* ***Drucker*** *a-37, 43, 48.* ***Everett*** *a-17.* ***Heath*** *a-7-9, 16, 19, 25, 36; c-11, 16, 19, 25, 26, 29-31, 36.* ***G. Kane*** *a-19.* ***Lawrence*** *a-36.* ***Maneely*** *a-7, 9; c-6, 27, 37.* ***Orlando*** *a-42, 48.* ***Pakula*** *a-26.* ***Ravielli*** *a-27.* ***Reinman*** *a-26.* ***Robinson*** *a-15; c-13.* ***Severin*** *a-26, 27; c-48.*

WAR DANCER (Also see Charlemagne, Doctor Chaos #2 & Warriors of Plasm)
Defiant: Feb, 1994 - No. 6, July, 1994 ($2.50)

	GD	VG	FN	VF	VF/NM	NM-
1-3,5,6: 1-Intro War Dancer; Weiss-c/a begins. 1-3-Weiss-a(p). 6-Pre-Schism issue						2.50
4-($3.25, 52 pgs.)-Charlemagne app.						3.25

WAR DOGS OF THE U.S. ARMY
Avon Periodicals: 1952

	GD	VG	FN	VF	VF/NM	NM-
1-Kinstler-c/a	15	30	45	86	118	150

WARFRONT
Harvey Publications: 9/51 - #35, 11/58; #36, 10/65; #39, 2/67

	GD	VG	FN	VF	VF/NM	NM-
1-Korean War	12	24	36	82	121	160
2	7	14	21	46	63	80
3-10	6	12	18	38	52	65
11,12,14,16-20	5	10	15	33	44	55
13,15,22-Nostrand-a	7	14	21	46	63	80
21,23-27,31-33,35	5	10	15	33	44	55
28-30,34-Kirby-c	7	14	21	50	68	85
36-(12/66)-Dynamite Joe begins, ends #39; Williamson-a	6	12	18	38	52	65
37-Wood-a (17 pgs.)	6	12	18	38	52	65
38,39-Wood-a, 2-3 pgs.; Lone Tiger app.	5	10	15	33	44	55

NOTE: ***Powell*** *a-1-6, 9-11, 14, 17, 20, 23, 25-28, 30, 31, 34, 36.* ***Powell/Nostrand*** *a-12, 13, 15.* ***Simon*** *c-36?,*

War Heroes #7 © DELL

Warlands: Dark Tide Rising #3 © Dreamwave Prod.

Warlord #53 © DC

GD 2.0 VG 4.0 FN 6.0 VF 8.0 VF/NM 9.0 NM- 9.2

38.

WAR FURY
Comic Media/Harwell (Allen Hardy Assoc.): Sept, 1952 - No. 4, Mar, 1953

1-Heck-c/a in all; Palais-a; bullet hole in forehead-c; all issues are very violent;
soldier using flame thrower on enemy 24 48 72 138 194 250
2-4: 4-Morisi-a 13 26 39 74 100 125

WAR GODS OF THE DEEP (See Movie Classics)

WARHAWKS
TSR, Inc.: 1990 - No. 10, 1991 ($2.95, 44 pgs.)

1-10-Based on TSR game, Spiegle a-1-6 3.00

WARHEADS
Marvel Comics UK: June, 1992 - No. 14, Aug, 1993 ($1.75)

1-Wolverine-c/story; indicia says #2 by mistake 3.00
2-14: 2-Nick Fury app. 3-Iron Man-c/story. 4,5-X-Force. 5-Liger vs. Cable.
6,7-Death's Head II app. (#6 is cameo) 2.25

WAR HEROES (See Marine War Heroes)

WAR HEROES
Dell Publishing Co.: 7-9/42 (no month); No. 2, 10-12/42 - No. 11, 3/45 (Published quarterly)

1-General Douglas MacArthur-c 25 50 75 147 202 260
2 14 28 42 81 111 140
3,5: 3-Pro-Russian back-c 11 22 33 63 84 105
4-Disney's Gremlins app. 19 38 57 106 146 185
6-11: 6-Tothish-a by Discount 10 20 30 56 73 90

NOTE: *No. 1 was to be released in July, but was delayed. Painted c-4, 6-9.*

WAR HEROES
Ace Magazines: May, 1952 - No. 8, Apr, 1953

1 11 22 33 66 88 110
2-Lou Cameron-a 8 16 24 43 54 65
3-8: 6,7-Cameron-a 7 14 21 37 46 55

WAR HEROES (Also see Blue Bird Comics)
Charlton Comics: Feb, 1963 - No. 27, Nov, 1967

1,2: 2-John F. Kennedy story 4 8 12 25 33 42
3-10 3 6 9 18 23 28
11-26 2 4 6 12 16 20
27-1st Devils Brigade by Glanzman 3 6 9 18 23 28

NOTE: ***Montes/Bache** a-3-7, 21, 25, 27; c-3-7.*

WAR IS HELL
Marvel Comics Group: Jan, 1973 - No. 15, Oct, 1975

1-Williamson-a(r), 5 pgs.; Ayers-a 3 6 9 18 23 28
2-8-Reprints. 6-(11/73). 7-(6/74). 7,8-Kirby-a 2 4 6 9 11 14
9-Intro Death 5 10 15 33 44 55
10-15-Death app. 3 6 9 16 20 25

NOTE: ***Bolle** a-3r. **Powell** a-1. **Woodbridge** a-1. Sgt. Fury reprints-7, 8.*

WARLANDS
Image Comics: Aug, 1999 - No. 12, Feb, 2001 ($2.50)

1-9,11,12-Pat Lee-a(p)/Adrian Tsang-s 2.50
10-($2.95) Flip book w/Shidima preview 3.00
... Chronicles 1,2 (2/00, 7/00; $7.95) 1-r/#1-3. 2-r/#4-6 8.00
...Darklyte TPB (8/01, $14.95) r/#0,1/2,1-6 w/cover gallery; new Lee-c 15.00
...Epilogue: Three Stories (3/01, $5.95) includes r/Wizard #1/2 & AE #0 6.00
Another Universe #0 3.00
Wizard #1/2 5.00

WARLANDS: THE AGE OF ICE (Volume 2)
Image Comics: July, 2001 - No. 9, Nov, 2002 ($2.95)

#0-(2/02, $2.25) 2.25
#1/2 (4/02, $2.25) 2.25
1-9: 2-Flip book preview of Banished Knights 3.00
TPB (2003, $15.95) r/#1-9 16.00

WARLANDS: DARK TIDE RISING (Volume 3)
Image Comics: Dec, 2002 - No. 6, May, 2003 ($2.95)

1-6: 1-Wraparound gatefold-c 3.00

WARLOCK (The Power of...)(Also see Avengers Annual #7, Fantastic Four #66, 67, Incredible Hulk #178, Infinity Crusade, Infinity Gauntlet, Infinity War, Marvel Premiere #1, Marvel Two-In-One Annual #2, Silver Surfer V3#46, Strange Tales #178-181 & Thor #165)
Marvel Comics Group: Aug, 1972 - No. 8, Oct, 1973; No. 9, Oct, 1975 - No. 15, Nov, 1976

1-Origin by Kane 5 10 15 33 44 55
2,3 3 6 9 18 23 28
4-8: 4-Death of Eddie Roberts 2 4 6 10 13 16
9-Starlin's 2nd Thanos saga begins, ends #15; new costume Warlock; Thanos cameo only; story cont'd from Strange Tales #178-181; Starlin-c/a in #9-15
3 6 9 16 20 25
10-Origin Thanos & Gamora; recaps events from Capt. Marvel #25-34. Thanos
vs.The Magus-c/story 3 6 9 19 25 32
11-Thanos app.; Warlock dies 2 4 6 12 16 20
12-14: (Regular 25¢ edition) 14-Origin Star Thief; last 25¢ issue
2 4 6 9 11 14
12-14-(30¢-c, limited distribution) 3 6 9 16 20 24
15-Thanos-c/story 2 4 6 10 13 16

NOTE: ***Buscema** a-2p; c-8p. **G. Kane** a-1p, 3-5p; c-1p, 2, 3, 4p, 5p, 7p. **Starlin** a-9-14p, 15; c-9, 10, 11p, 12p, 13-15. **Sutton** a-1-8i.*

WARLOCK (...Special Edition on-c)
Marvel Comics Group: Dec, 1982 - No. 6, May, 1983 ($2.00, slick paper, 52 pgs.)

1-Warlock-r/Strange Tales #178-180. 4.00
2-6: 2-r/Str. Tales #180,181 & Warlock #9. 3-r/Warlock #10-12(Thanos origin recap). 4-r/Warlock #12-15. 5-r/Warlock #15, Marvel Team-Up #55 & Avengers Ann. #7. 6-r/2nd half Avengers Annual #7 & Marvel Two-in-One Annual #2 4.00
Special Edition #1(12/83) 4.00

NOTE: ***Byrne** a-5r. **Starlin** a-1-6r; c-1-6(new). Direct sale only.*

WARLOCK
Marvel Comics: V2#1, May, 1992 - No. 6, Oct, 1992 ($2.50, limited series)

V2#1-6: 1-Reprints 1982 reprint series w/Thanos 2.50

WARLOCK
Marvel Comics: Nov, 1998 - No. 4, Feb, 1999 ($2.99, limited series)

1-4-Warlock vs. Drax 3.00

WARLOCK (M-Tech)
Marvel Comics: Oct, 1999 - No. 9, June, 2000 ($1.99/$2.50)

1-5: 1-Quesada-c. 2-Two covers 2.50
6-9: 6-Begin $2.50-c. 8-Avengers app. 2.50

WARLOCK AND THE INFINITY WATCH (Also see Infinity Gauntlet)
Marvel Comics: Feb, 1992 - No. 42, July, 1995 ($1.75) (Sequel to Infinity Gauntlet)

1-Starlin-scripts begin; brief origin recap; sequel to Infinity Gauntlet 3.00
2,3: 2-Reintro Moondragon 2.50
4-24,26: 7-Reintro The Magus; Moondragon app.; Thanos cameo on last 2 pgs. 8,9-Thanos battles Gamora-c/story. 8-Magus & Moondragon app. 10-Thanos-c/story; Magus app. 13-Hulk x-over. 21-Drax vs. Thor 2.25
25-($2.95, 52 pgs.)-Die-cut & embossed double-c; Thor & Thanos app. 3.00
28-42: 28-$1.95-c begins; bound-in card sheet 2.25

NOTE: ***Austin** c/a-1-4i, 7i. **Leonardi** a(p)-3, 4. **Medina** c/a(p)-1, 2, 5; 6, 9, 10, 14, 15, 20. **Williams** a(i)-8, 12, 13, 16-19.*

WARLOCK CHRONICLES
Marvel Comics: June, 1993 - No. 8, Feb, 1994 ($2.00, limited series)

1-($2.95)-Holo-grafx foil & embossed-c; origin retold; Starlin scripts begin;
Keith Williams-a(i) in all 3.00
2-8: 3-Thanos & Mephisto-c/story. 4-Vs. Magus-c/s. 8-Contains free 16 pg. Razorline insert 2.25

WARLOCK 5
Aircel Pub.: 11/86 - No. 22, 5/89; V2#1, June, 1989 - V2#5, 1989 ($1.70, B&W)

1-5,7-11-Gordon Derry-s/Denis Beauvais-a thru #11. 5-Green Cyborg on-c.
5-Misnumbered as #6 (no #6); Blue Girl on-c. 2.25
12-22-Barry Blair-s/a. 18-$1.95-c begins 3.00
V2#1-5 ($2.00, B&W)-All issues by Barry Blair 2.25
Compilation 1,2: 1-r/#1-5 (1988, $5.95); 2-r/#6-9 6.00

WARLORD (See 1st Issue Special #8)
National Periodical Publications/DC Comics #123 on: 1-2/76; No.2, 3-4/76; No.3, 10-11/76 - No. 133, Win, 1988-89

1-Story cont'd. from 1st Issue Special #8 3 6 9 16 20 25
2-Intro. Machiste 2 4 6 8 10 12
3-5 1 2 3 5 6 8
6-10: 6-Intro Mariah. 7-Origin Machiste. 9-Dons new costume 6.00
11-20: 11-Origin-r. 12-Intro Aton. 15-Tara returns; Warlord has son 4.00
21-36,40,41: 27-New facts about origin. 28-1st app. Wizard World. 32-Intro Shakira.
40-Warlord gets new costume 4.00
37-39: 37,38-Origin Omac by Starlin. 38-Intro Jennifer Morgan, Warlord's daughter.
39-Omac ends. 5.00
42-48: 42-47-Omac back-up series. 48-(52 pgs.)-1st app. Arak; contains free 14 pg.
Arak Son of Thunder; Claw The Unconquered app. 4.00
49-62,64-99,101-130,132: 49-Claw The Unconquered app. 50-Death of Aton. 51-Reprints #1.

War Machine #6 © MAR

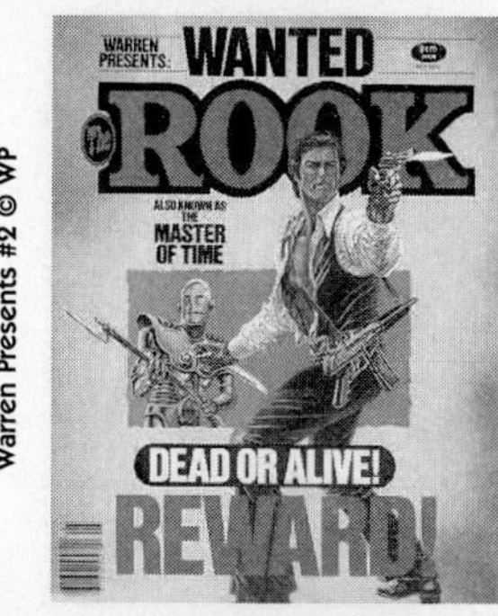

Warren Presents #2 © WP

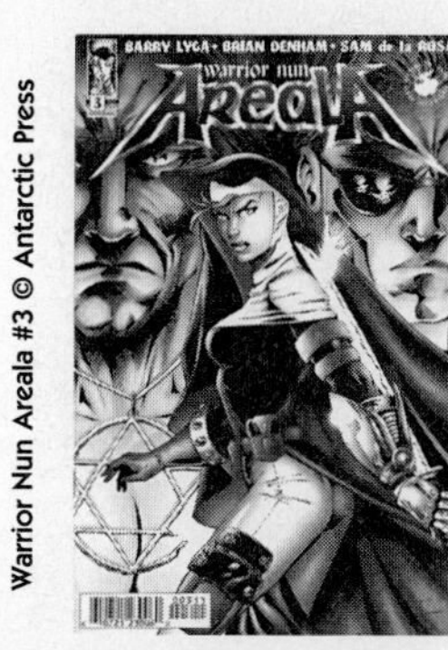

Warrior Nun Areala #3 © Antarctic Press

GD VG FN VF VF/NM NM-
2.0 4.0 6.0 8.0 9.0 9.2

55-Arion Lord of Atlantis begins, ends #62. 91-Origin w/new facts. 114,115-Legends x-over. 125-Death of Tara 3.00
63-The Barren Earth begins; free 16pg. Masters of the Universe preview 4.00
100-($1.25, 52 pgs.). 4.00
131-1st DC work by Rob Liefeld (9/88) 5.00
133-($1.50, 52 pgs.) 4.00
Remco Toy Giveaway (2-3/4x4") 5.00
Annual 1('82-'87): 1-Grell-c,/a(p). 6-New Gods app. 4.00
NOTE: *Grell a-1-15, 16-50p, 51r, 52p, 59p, Annual 1p; c-1-70, 100-104, 112, 116, 117, Annual 1, 5.* ***Wayne Howard*** *a-64i.* ***Starlin*** *a-37-39p.*

WARLORD
DC Comics: Jan, 1992 - No. 6, June, 1992 ($1.75, limited series)
1-6: Grell-c & scripts in all 2.25

WARLORDS (See DC Graphic Novel #2)

WAR MAN
Marvel Comics (Epic Comics): Nov, 1993 - No. 2, Dec, 1993 ($2.50, lim. series)
1,2 2.50

WAR MACHINE (Also see Iron Man #281,282 & Marvel Comics Presents #152)
Marvel Comics: Apr, 1994 - No. 25, Apr, 1996 ($1.50)
"Ashcan" edition (nd, 75¢, B&W, 16 pgs.) 2.25
1-($2.00, 52 pgs.)-Newsstand edition; Cable app. 2.25
1-($2.95, 52 pgs.)-Collectors ed.; embossed foil-c 3.00
2-14, 16-25: 2-Bound-in trading card sheet; Cable app. 2,3-Deathlok app. 8-red logo 2.25
8-($2.95)-Polybagged w/16 pg. Marvel Action Hour preview & acetate print; yellow logo 3.00
15 ($2.50)-Flip book 2.50

WAR OF THE GODS
DC Comics: Sept, 1991 - No. 4, Dec, 1991 ($1.75, limited series)
1-4: Perez layouts, scripts & covers. 1-Contains free mini posters (Robin, Deathstroke). 2-4-Direct sale versions include 4 pin-ups printed on cover stock plus different-c 2.25

WAR OF THE WORLDS, THE
Caliber: 1996 - No. 5 ($2.95, B&W, 32 pgs.)(Based on H. G. Wells novel)
1-5: 1-Randy Zimmerman scripts begin 3.00

WARP
First Comics: Mar, 1983 - No. 19, Feb, 1985 ($1.00/$1.25, Mando paper)
1-Sargon-Mistress of War app.; Brunner-c/a thru #9 2.25
2-19: 2-Faceless Ones begin. 10-New Warp advs., & Outrider begin 2.25
Special 1-3: 1(7/83, 36 pgs.)-Origin Chaos-Prince of Madness; origin of Warp Universe begins, ends #3. 2(1/84)-Lord Cumulus vs. Sargon Mistress of War ($1.00). 3(6/84)-Chaos-Prince of Madness 2.25

WAR PARTY
Lightning Comics: Oct, 1994 (2.95, B&W)
1-1st app. Deathmark 3.00

WARPATH (Indians on the...)
Key Publications/Stanmor: Nov, 1954 - No. 3, Apr, 1955
1 11 22 33 66 88 110
2,3 8 16 24 40 50 60

WARPED
Empire Entertainment (Solson): Jun, 1990 - No. 2, Oct-Nov, 1990 (B&W mag)
1,2 2.25

WARP GRAPHICS ANNUAL
WaRP Graphics: Dec, 1985; 1988 ($2.50)
1-Elfquest, Blood of the Innocent, Thunderbunny & Myth Adventures 5.00
1 (1988) 4.00

WARREN PRESENTS
Warren Publications: Jan, 1979 - No. 14, Nov, 1981(B&W magazine)
1-Eerie, Creepy, & Vampirella-r; Ring of the Warlords; Merlin-s; Dax-s; Sanjulian-c 2 4 6 12 16 20
2-6(10/79): 2-The Rook. 3-Alien Invasions Comix. 4-Movie Aliens. 5-Dracula '79. 6-Strange Stories of Vampires Comix 2 4 6 8 10 12
8(10/80)-r/1st app. Pantha from Vamp. #30 2 4 6 10 13 16
9(11/80) Empire Encounters Comix 2 4 6 9 11 14
13(10/81),14(11/81):13-Sword and Sorcery Comix 2 4 6 12 16 20
(#7,10,11,12 may not exist, or may be a Special below)
Special-Alien Collectors Edition (1979) 2 4 6 12 16 20
Special-Close Encounters of the Third Kind (1978) 2 4 6 8 10 12
Special-Lord of the Rings (6/79) 3 6 9 18 24 30
Special-Meteor (1/80) 2 4 6 8 10 12
Special-Moonraker/James Bond (10/79) 2 4 6 8 10 12
Special-Star Wars (1977) 3 6 9 18 24 30

WAR REPORT
Ajax/Farrell Publications (Excellent Publ.): Sept, 1952 - No. 5, May, 1953
1 11 22 33 66 88 110
2-Flame thrower w/burning bodies on-c 9 18 27 49 62 75
3-5: 4-Used in **POP**, pg. 94 7 14 21 37 46 55

WARRIOR (Wrestling star)
Ultimate Creations: May, 1996 - No. 4, 1997 ($2.95)
1-4: Warrior scripts; Callahan-c/a. 3-Wraparound-c. 4-Warrior #3 in indicia; pin-ups 3.00
1-Variant-c. 5.00

WARRIOR COMICS
H.C. Blackerby: 1945 (1930s DC reprints)
1-Wing Brady, The Iron Man, Mark Markon 23 46 69 129 180 230

WARRIOR NUN AREALA
Antarctic Press: Dec, 1994 - No. 3, Apr, 1995 ($2.95, limited series)
1 6.00
1-Special Edition (5000) 1 3 4 6 8 10
2-3, 3-Bagged w/CD 4.00

WARRIOR NUN AREALA
Antarctic Press: July, 1997 - No. 6, May, 1998 ($2.95)
1-6-Lyga-s 3.00

WARRIOR NUN AREALA (Volume 3)
Antarctic Press: July, 1999 - No. 4 ($2.50)
1-4 2.50

WARRIOR NUN AREALA AND AVENGELYNE 1996 (See Avengelyne/...)
Antarctic Press: Dec, 1996 ($2.95)
1 3.00

WARRIOR NUN AREALA AND GLORY
Antarctic Press: Sept, 1997
1-Ben Dunn-s/a ($2.95, color) 3.00
1-($5.95) Ltd. Poster Edition w/pin-ups 6.00

WARRIOR NUN AREALA: HAMMER AND THE HOLOCAUST
Antarctic Press: June, 1997- No. 2 ($2.95)
1,2 3.00

WARRIOR NUN AREALA: PORTRAITS,
Antarctic Press: Mar, 1996 ($3.95, one-shot)
1-Pin-ups 4.00

WARRIOR NUN AREALA/RAZOR
Antarctic Press: Jan, 1999 ($2.99, one-shot)
1-Dunn-c/a 3.00
1-($5.99)-Deluxe Ed. with painted-c 6.00

WARRIOR NUN AREALA: RESURRECTION
Antarctic Press: Nov, 1998 - No. 3, Mar, 1999 ($2.95)
1-3 3.00
1-($5.95)-Special Ed. with poster 6.00

WARRIOR NUN AREALA: RITUALS,
Antarctic Press: July, 1995 - No. 6, June, 1996 ($2.95/$3.50)
1-5 3.00
6-($3.50) 3.50

WARRIOR NUN AREALA: SCORPIO ROSE
Antarctic Press: Sept, 1996 - No. 4, Mar, 1997 ($2.95, color)
1-4 3.00

WARRIOR NUN AREALA VS. RAZOR (See Razor/...)
Antarctic Press: May, 1996 ($3.95, one-shot)
1-Dunn-c/a 4.00
1-($9.95)-Comic polybagged w/CD 10.00

WARRIOR NUN: BLACK AND WHITE,
Antarctic Press: Feb, 1997 - No. 21 ($2.95//$2.99/$2.50, B&W)
1-20 3.00
21-($2.50) 2.50

WARRIOR NUN DEI: AFTERTIME
Antarctic Press: Jan, 1997 - No. 2 ($2.95)

War Victory Adventures #2 © HARV

Watchmen #1 © DC

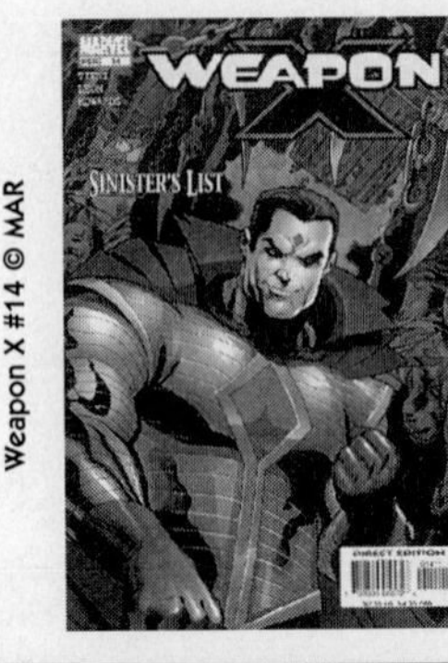

Weapon X #14 © MAR

	GD 2.0	VG 4.0	FN 6.0	VF 8.0	VF/NM 9.0	NM- 9.2
1-2-Patrick Thornton-s/a						3.00

WARRIOR NUN: FRENZY
Antarctic Press: Jan, 1998 - No. 2, Jun, 1998 ($2.95)

1,2: 1-Ribic painted-c/a. 2-Horvatic-s/a 3.00

WARRIOR NUN: RHEINTÖCHTER
Antarctic Press: Dec, 1997 - No. 2, Apr, 1998 ($2.95, B&W, limited series)

1,2-Set in medieval Europe; Paquette & Lacombe-s/a 3.00

WARRIOR OF WAVERLY STREET, THE
Dark Horse Comics: Nov, 1996 - No. 2, Dec, 1996 ($2.95, mini-series)

1,2-Darrow-c 3.00

WARRIORS
CFD Productions: 1993 (B&W, one-shot)

	GD	VG	FN	VF	VF/NM	NM-
1-Linsner, Dark One-a	2	4	6	11	14	18

WARRIORS OF PLASM (Also see Plasm)
Defiant: Aug, 1993 - No. 13, Aug, 1995 ($2.95/$2.50)

1-4: Shooter-scripts; Lapham-c/a: 1-1st app. Glory. 4-Bound-in fold-out poster 3.00
5-7,10-13: 5-Begin $2.50-c. 13-Schism issue 2.50
8,9-($2.75, 44 pgs.) 2.75
The Collected Edition (2/94, $9.95)-r/Plasm #0, WOP #1-4 & Splatterball 10.00

WAR ROMANCES (See True...)

WAR SHIPS
Dell Publishing Co.: 1942 (36 pgs.)(Similar to Large Feature Comics)

	GD	VG	FN	VF	VF/NM	NM-
nn-Cover by McWilliams; contains photos & drawings of U.S. war ships	18	36	54	104	142	180

WAR STORIES (Formerly War Comics)
Dell Publ. Co.: No. 5, 1942(nd); No. 6, Aug-Oct, 1942 - No. 8, Feb-Apr, 1943

	GD	VG	FN	VF	VF/NM	NM-
5-Origin The Whistler	27	54	81	153	214	275
6-8: 6-8-Night Devils app. 8-Painted-c	20	40	60	112	156	200

WAR STORIES (Korea)
Ajax/Farrell Publications (Excellent Publ.): Sept, 1952 - No. 5, May, 1953

	GD	VG	FN	VF	VF/NM	NM-
1	11	22	33	66	88	110
2	7	14	21	37	46	55
3-5	7	14	21	35	43	50

WAR STORIES (See Star Spangled...)

WAR STORY
DC Comics (Vertigo): Nov, 2001 - Present ($4.95, series of World War II one-shots)

...: Archangel (4/03) Ennis-s/Erskine-a 5.00
...: Condors (3/03) Ennis-s/Ezquerra-a 5.00
...: D-Day Dodgers (12/01) Ennis-s/Higgins-a 5.00
...: J For Jenny (2/03) Ennis-s/Lloyd-a 5.00
...: Johann's Tiger (11/01) Ennis-s/Weston-a 5.00
...: Nightingale (2/02) Ennis-s/Lloyd-a 5.00
...: Screaming Eagles (1/02) Ennis-s/Gibbons-a 5.00
...: The Reivers (1/03) Ennis-s/Kennedy-a 5.00

WARSTRIKE
Malibu Comics (Ultraverse): May, 1994 - No. 7, Nov, 1995 ($1.95)

1-7: 1-Simonson-c 2.25
1-Ultra 5000 Limited silver foil 4.00
Giant Size 1 (12/94, 2.50, 44pgs.)-Prelude to Godwheel 2.50

WART AND THE WIZARD (See The Sword & the Stone under Movie Comics)
Gold Key: Feb, 1964 (Walt Disney)(Characters from Sword in the Stone movie)

	GD	VG	FN	VF	VF/NM	NM-
1 (10102-402)	5	10	15	33	44	55

WARTIME ROMANCES
St. John Publishing Co.: July, 1951 - No. 18, Nov, 1953

	GD	VG	FN	VF	VF/NM	NM-
1-All Baker-c/a	34	68	102	196	278	360
2-All Baker-c/a	24	48	72	135	190	245
3,4-All Baker-c/a	22	44	66	127	176	225
5-8-Baker-c/a(2-3) each	20	40	60	112	156	200
9,11,12,16,18: Baker-c/a each. 9-Two signed stories by Estrada	15	30	45	86	118	150
10,13-15,17-Baker-c only	9	18	27	52	66	80

WAR VICTORY ADVENTURES (#1 titled War Victory Comics)
U.S. Treasury Dept./War Victory/Harvey Publ.: Summer, 1942 - No. 3, Winter, 1943-44 (5¢)

	GD	VG	FN	VF	VF/NM	NM-
1-(Promotion of Savings Bonds)-Featuring America's greatest comic art by top syndicated cartoonists; Blondie, Joe Palooka, Green Hornet, Dick Tracy, Superman, Gumps, etc.; (36 pgs.); all profits were contributed to U.S.O. & Army/Navy relief funds	40	80	120	240	345	450
2-Battle of Stalingrad story; Powell-a (8/43); flag-c	22	44	66	127	176	225
3-Capt. Red Cross-c & text only; Powell-a	20	40	60	112	156	200

WAR WAGON, THE (See Movie Classics)

WAR WINGS
Charlton Comics: Oct, 1968

	GD	VG	FN	VF	VF/NM	NM-
1	3	6	9	16	20	24

WARWORLD!
Dark Horse Comics: Feb, 1989 ($1.75, B&W, one-shot)

1-Gary Davis sci/fi art in Moebius style 2.25

WARZONE
Entity Comics: 1995 ($2.95, B&W)

1-3 3.00

WASHABLE JONES AND THE SHMOO (Also see Al Capp's Shmoo)
Toby Press: June, 1953

	GD	VG	FN	VF	VF/NM	NM-
1- "Super-Shmoo"	21	42	63	118	164	210

WASH TUBBS (See The Comics, Crackajack Funnies)
Dell Publishing Co.: No. 11, 1942 - No. 53, 1944

	GD	VG	FN	VF	VF/NM	NM-
Four Color 11 (#1)	31	62	93	228	339	450
Four Color 28 (1943)	22	44	66	160	235	310
Four Color 53	16	32	48	116	171	225

WASTELAND
DC Comics: Dec, 1987 - No. 18, May, 1989 ($1.75-$2.00 #13 on, mature)

1-5(4/88), 5(5/88), 6(5/88)-18: 13,15-Orlando-a 2.25
NOTE: ***Orlando** a-12, 13, 15. **Truman** a-10; c-13.*

WATCHMEN
DC Comics: Sept, 1986 - No. 12, Oct, 1987 (maxi-series)

	GD	VG	FN	VF	VF/NM	NM-
1-Alan Moore scripts & Dave Gibbons-c/a in all	1	2	3	4	5	7
2-12						5.00
Hardcover Collection-Slip-cased-r/#1-12 w/new material; produced by Graphitti Designs						70.00
Trade paperback (1987, $14.95)-r/#1-12						18.00

WATER BIRDS AND THE OLYMPIC ELK (Disney)
Dell Publishing Co.: No. 700, Apr, 1956

	GD	VG	FN	VF	VF/NM	NM-
Four Color 700-Movie	6	12	18	40	55	70

WATERWORLD: CHILDREN OF LEVIATHAN
Acclaim Comics: Aug, 1997 - No. 4, Nov, 1997 ($2.50, mini-series)

1-4 2.50

WAY OF THE RAT (Also see Promotional Comics section for FCBD Ed.)
CrossGeneration Comics: Jun, 2002 - Present ($2.95)

1-21: 1-Dixon-s/ Jeff Johnson-a. 5-Whigham-a. 9,14-Luke Ross-a 3.00
...: The Walls of Zhumar Vol. 1 (1/03, $15.95) r/#1-6 16.00
Vol. 2: The Dragon's Wake (2003, $15.95) r/#7-12 16.00

WEAPON X
Marvel Comics: Apr, 1994 ($12.95, one-shot)

nn-r/Marvel Comics Presents #72-84 13.00

WEAPON X
Marvel Comics: Mar, 1995 - No. 4, June, 1995 ($1.95)

1-Age of Apocalypse 4.00
2-4 2.50

WEAPON X
Marvel Comics: Nov, 2002 - Present ($2.25/$2.99)

1-7: 1-Sabretooth-c/app.; Tieri-s/Jeanty-a 2.25
8-17: 8-Begin $2.99-c. 14-Invaders app.; Leon-a. 15-Chamber joins. 16,17-Wolverine app. 3.00
Vol. 1: The Draft TPB (2003, $21.99) r/#1-5, #1/2 & The Draft one-shots 22.00
Vol. 2: The Underground TPB (2003, $19.99) r/#6-13 20.00
Wizard #1/2 (2002) 5.00

WEAPON X: THE DRAFT (Leads into 2002 Weapon X series)
Marvel Comics: Oct, 2002 ($2.25, one-shots)

...Kane 1- JH Williams-c/Raimondi-a 2.25
...Marrow 1- JH Williams-c/Badeaux-a 2.25
...Sauron 1- JH Williams-c/Kerschl-a; Emma Frost app. 2.25
...Wild Child 1- JH Williams-c/Van Sciver-a; Aurora (Alpha Flight) app. 2.25
...Zero 1- JH Williams-c/Plunkett-a; Wolverine app. 2.25

Web of Horror #1 © Major Magazines

Web of Spider-Man #116 © MAR

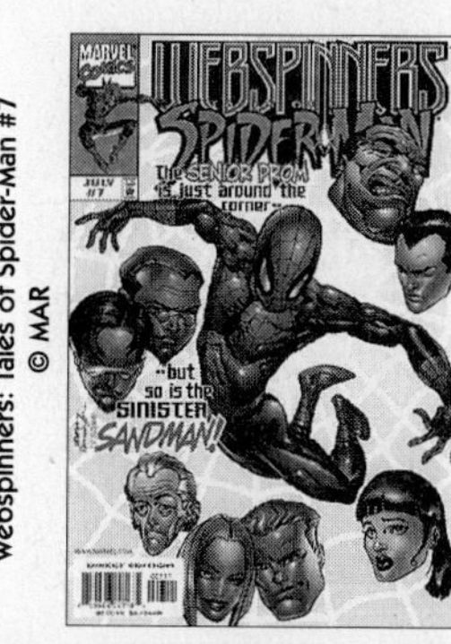

Webspinners: Tales of Spider-Man #7 © MAR

GD VG FN VF VF/NM NM-
2.0 4.0 6.0 8.0 9.0 9.2

WEAPON ZERO
Image Comics (Top Cow Productions): No. T-4(#1), June, 1995 - No. T-0(#5), Dec, 1995 ($2.50, limited series)

T-4(#1): Walt Simonson scripts in all. 5.00
T-3(#2) - T-1(#4) 4.00
T-0(#5) 3.00

WEAPON ZERO
Image Comics (Top Cow Productions): V2#1, Mar, 1996 - No. 15, Dec, 1997 ($2.50)

V2#1-Walt Simonson scripts. 3.00
2-14: 8-Begin Top Cow. 10-Devil's Reign 2.50
15-($3.50) Benitez-a 3.50

WEAPON ZERO/SILVER SURFER
Image Comics/Marvel Comics: Jan, 1997($2.95, one-shot)

1-Devil's Reign Pt. 1 3.00

WEASELGUY: ROAD TRIP
Image Comics: Sept, 1999 - No. 2 ($3.50, limited series)

1,2-Steve Buccellato-s/a 3.50
1-Variant-c by Bachalo 5.00

WEASELGUY/WITCHBLADE
Hyperwerks: July, 1998 ($2.95, one-shot)

1-Steve Buccellato-s/a; covers by Matsuda and Altstaetter 3.00

WEASEL PATROL SPECIAL, THE (Also see Fusion #17)
Eclipse Comics: Apr, 1989 ($2.00, B&W, one-shot)

1-Funny animal 2.25

WEAVEWORLD
Marvel Comics (Epic): Dec, 1991 - No. 3, 1992 ($4.95, lim. series, 68 pgs.)

1-3: Clive Barker adaptation 5.00

WEB, THE (Also see Mighty Comics & Mighty Crusaders)
DC Comics (Impact Comics): Sept, 1991 - No. 14, Oct, 1992 ($1.00)

1-14: 5-The Fly x-over 9-Trading card inside 2.25
Annual 1 (1992, $2.50, 68 pgs.)-With Trading card 2.50

NOTE: ***Gil Kane*** *c-5, 9, 10, 12-14.* ***Bill Wray*** *a(i)-1-9, 10(part).*

WEB OF EVIL
Comic Magazines/Quality Comics Group: Nov, 1952 - No. 21, Dec, 1954

1-Used in **SOTI**, pg. 388. Jack Cole-a; morphine use story
56 112 168 350 525 700
2-4,6,7: 2,3-Jack Cole-a. 4,6,7-Jack Cole-c/a 40 80 120 240 363 485
5-Electrocution-c/story; Jack Cole-c/a 46 92 138 276 413 550
8-11-Jack Cole-a 39 78 117 233 329 425
12,13,15,16,19-21 25 50 75 147 202 260
14-Part Crandall-c; Old Witch swipe 26 52 78 150 210 270
17-Opium drug propaganda story 26 52 78 147 206 265
18-Acid-in-face story 26 52 78 150 210 270

NOTE: ***Jack Cole*** *a(2 each)-2, 6, 8, 9.* ***Cuidera*** *c-1-21i.* ***Ravielli*** *a-13.*

WEB OF HORROR
Major Magazines: Dec, 1969 - No. 3, Apr, 1970 (Magazine)

1-Jeff Jones painted-c; Wrightson-a, Kaluta-a 9 18 27 65 93 120
2-Jones painted-c; Wrightson-a(2), Kaluta-a 7 14 21 51 71 90
3-Wrightson-c/a (1st published-c); Brunner, Kaluta, Bruce Jones-a
7 14 21 51 71 90

WEB OF MYSTERY
Ace Magazines (A. A. Wyn): Feb, 1951 - No. 29, Sept, 1955

1 53 106 159 318 477 635
2-Bakerish-a 31 62 93 178 252 325
3-10: 4-Colan-a 28 56 84 159 225 290
11-18,20-26: 12-John Chilly's 1st cover art. 13-Surrealistic-c. 20-r/The Beyond #1
24 48 72 138 194 250
19-Reprints Challenge of the Unknown #6 used in N.Y. Legislative Committee
24 48 72 138 194 250
27-Bakerish-a(r/The Beyond #2); last pre-code ish 23 46 69 130 183 235
28,29: 28-All-r 18 36 54 104 142 180

NOTE: *This series was to appear as "Creepy Stories", but title was changed before publication.* ***Cameron*** *a-6, 8, 11-13, 17-20, 22, 24, 25, 27; c-8, 13, 17.* ***Palais*** *a-28r.* ***Sekowsky*** *a-1-3, 7, 8, 11, 14, 21, 29.* ***Tothish*** *a-by* ***Bill Discount*** *#16. 29-all-r, 19-28-partial-r.*

WEB OF SCARLET SPIDER
Marvel Comics: Oct, 1995 - No. 4, Jan, 1996 ($1.95, limited series)

1-4: Replaces "Web of Spider-Man" 2.25

GD VG FN VF VF/NM NM-
2.0 4.0 6.0 8.0 9.0 9.2

WEB OF SPIDER-MAN (Replaces Marvel Team-Up)
Marvel Comics Group: Apr, 1985 - No. 129, Sept, 1995

1-Painted-c (5th app. black costume?) 2 4 6 10 12 15
2,3 5.00
4-8: 7-Hulk x-over; Wolverine splash 4.00
9-13: 10-Dominic Fortune guest stars; painted-c 4.00
14-17,19-28: 19-Intro Humbug & Solo 3.00
18-1st app. Venom (behind the scenes, 9/86) 3.00
29-Wolverine, new Hobgoblin (Macendale) app. 1 2 3 5 6 8
30-Origin recap The Rose & Hobgoblin I (entire book is flashback story); Punisher & Wolverine cameo 4.00
31,32-Six part Kraven storyline begins 5.00
33-37,39-47,49: 36-1st app. Tombstone (cameo) 3.00
38-Hobgoblin app.; begin $1.00-c 4.00
48-Origin Hobgoblin II(Demogoblin) cont'd from Spectacular Spider-Man #147; Kingpin app. 1 2 3 5 7 9
50-($1.50, 52 pgs.) 3.50
51-58 2.50
59-Cosmic Spidey cont'd from Spect. Spider-Man 3.50
60-89,91-99,101-106: 66,67-Green Goblin (Norman Osborn) app. as a super-hero. 69,70-Hulk x-over. 74-76-Austin-c(i). 76-Fantastic Four x-over. 78-Cloak & Dagger app. 81-Origin/1st app. Bloodshed. 84-Begin 6 part Rose & Hobgoblin II storyline; last $1.00-c. 86-Demon leaves Hobgoblin; 1st Demogoblin. 93-Gives brief history of Hobgoblin. 93,94-Hobgoblin (Macendale) Reborn-c/story, parts 1,2; MoonKnight app. 94-Venom cameo. 95-Begin 4 part x-over w/Spirits of Venom w/Ghost Rider/Blaze/Spidey vs. Venom & Demogoblin (cont'd in Ghost Rider/Blaze #5,6). 96-Spirits of Venom part 3; painted-c. 101,103-Maximum Carnage x-over. 103-Venom & Carnage app. 104-106-Nightwatch back-up stories 2.50
90-($2.95, 52 pgs.)-Polybagged w/silver hologram-c, gatefold poster showing Spider-Man & Spider-Man 2099 (Williamson-i) 3.50
90-2nd printing; gold hologram-c 3.00
100-($2.95, 52 pgs.)-Holo-grafx foil-c; intro new Spider-Armor 4.00
107-111: 107-Intro Sandstorm; Sand & Quicksand app. 2.50
112-116, 118, 119, 121-124, 126-128: 112-Begin $1.50-c; bound-in trading card sheet. 113-Regular Ed.; Gambit & Black Cat app. 118-1st solo clone story; Venom app. 2.25
113-($2.95)-Collector's ed. polybagged w/foil-c; 16 pg. preview of Spider-Man cartoon & animation cel 3.00
117-($1.50)-Flip book; Power & Responsibility Pt.1 2.25
117-($2.95)-Collector's edition; foil-c; flip book 3.00
119-($6.45)-Direct market edition; polybagged w/ Marvel Milestone Amazing Spider-Man #150 & coupon for Amazing Spider-Man #396, Spider-Man #53, & Spectacular Spider-Man #219. 7.00
120 ($2.25)-Flip book w/ preview of the Ultimate Spider-Man 2.50
125 ($3.95)-Holodisk-c; Gwen Stacy clone 4.00
125,129: 25 ($2.95)-Newsstand. 129-Last issue 3.00
Annual 1 (1985) 3.00
Annual 2 (1986)-New Mutants; Art Adams-a 1 2 3 5 6 8
Annual 3-10 ('87-'94, 68 pgs.): 4-Evolutionary War x-over. 5-Atlantis Attacks; Captain Universe by Ditko (p) & Silver Sable stories; F.F. app. 6-Punisher back-up plus Capt. Universe by Ditko; G. Kane-a. 7-Origins of Hobgoblin I, Hobgoblin II, Green Goblin I & II & Venom; Larsen/Austin-c. 8-Part 3 of Venom story; New Warriors x-over; Black Cat back-up sty. 9-Bagged w/card 3.00
Super Special 1 (1995, $3.95)-flip book 4.00

NOTE: ***Art Adams*** *a-Annual 2.* ***Byrne*** *c-3-6.* ***Chaykin*** *c-10.* ***Mignola*** *a-Annual 2.* ***Vess*** *c-1, 8, Annual 1, 2.* ***Zeck*** *a-6i, 31, 32; c-31, 32.*

WEBSPINNERS: TALES OF SPIDER-MAN
Marvel Comics: Jan, 1999 - No. 18, Jun, 2000 ($2.99/$2.50)

1-DeMatteis-s/Zulli-a; back-up story w/Romita Sr. art 3.00
1-($6.95) DF Edition 7.00
2,3: 2-Two covers 2.50
4-11,13-18: 4,5-Giffen-a; Silver Surfer-c/app. 7-9-Kelly-s/Sears and Smith-a. 10,11-Jenkins-s/Sean Phillips-a 2.50
12-($3.50) J.G. Jones-c/a; Jenkins-s 3.50

WEDDING BELLS
Quality Comics Group: Feb, 1954 - No. 19, Nov, 1956

1-Whitney-a 15 30 45 86 118 150
2 10 20 30 56 73 90
3-9: 8-Last precode (4/55) 8 16 24 40 50 60
10-Ward-a (9 pgs.) 14 28 42 79 107 135
11-14,17 7 14 21 35 43 50
15-Baker-c 8 16 24 40 50 60
16-Baker-c/a 10 20 30 56 73 90
18,19-Baker-a each 8 16 24 46 58 70

Weird Comics #4 © FOX

Weird Fantasy #17 © WMG

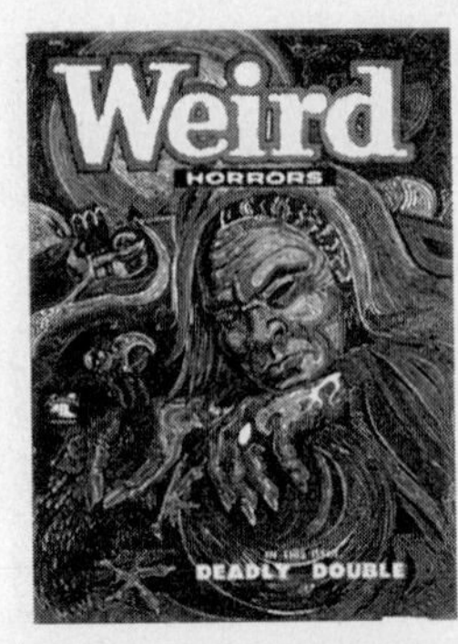

Weird Horrors #7 © STJ

GD 2.0 · VG 4.0 · FN 6.0 · VF 8.0 · VF/NM 9.0 · NM- 9.2

WEDDING OF DRACULA
Marvel Comics: Jan, 1993 ($2.00, 52 pgs.)
1-Reprints Tomb of Dracula #30,45,46 2.25

WEEKENDER, THE (Illustrated...)
Rucker Pub. Co.: V1#1, Sept, 1945? - V1#4, Nov, 1945; V2#1, Jan, 1946 - V2#3, Aug, 1946 (52 pgs.)
V1#1-4: 1-Same-c as Zip Comics #45, inside-c and back-c blank; Steel Sterling, Senor Banana, Red Rube and Ginger. 2-Capt. Victory on-c. 3-Super hero-c; Mr. E, Dan Hastings, Sky Chief and the Echo. 4-Same-c as Punch Comics #10 (9/44); r/Hale the Magician (7 pgs.) & r/Mr. E (8 pgs.-Lou Fine? or Gustavson?) plus 3 humor strips & many B&W photos & r/newspaper articles plus cheesecake photos of Hollywood stars 16 32 48 92 126 160
V2#1-Same-c as Dynamic Comics #11; 36 pgs. comics, 16 in newspaper format with photos; partial Dynamic Comics reprints; 4 pgs. of cels from the Disney film Pinocchio; Little Nemo story by Winsor McCay, Jr.; Jack Cole-a 19 38 57 106 146 185
V2#2,3: 2-Same-c as Dynamic Comics #9 by Raboy; Dan Hastings (Tuska), Rocket Boy, The Echo, Lucky Coyne. 3-Humor-c by Boddington?; Dynamic Man, Ima Slooth, Master Key, Dynamic Boy, Captain Glory 16 32 48 92 126 160

WEIRD
Eerie Publications: V1#10, 1/66 - V8#6, 12/74; V9#1, 1/75 - V14#13, Nov, 1981 (Magazine) (V1-V8: 52 pgs.; V9 on: 68 pgs.)
V1#10(#1)-Intro. Morris the Caretaker of Weird (ends V2#10); Burgos-a 7 14 21 46 63 80
11,12 4 8 12 28 38 48
V2#1-4(10/67), V3#1(1/68), V2#6(4/68)-V2#7,9,10(12/68) 4 8 12 28 38 48
V2#8-r/Ditko's 1st story/Fantastic Fears #5 5 10 15 36 48 60
V3#1(2/69)-V3#4 4 8 12 24 32 40
V3#5(12/69)-Rulah reprint; "Rulah" changed to "Pulah", LSD story reprinted in Horror Tales V4#4, Tales From the Tomb V2#4, & 20 4 8 12 24 32 40
V4#1-6('70), V5#1-6('71), V6#1-7('72), V7#1-7('73), V8#1-3, V8#4(8/74), V8#4(10/74), (V8#5 does not exist), V8#6('74), V9#1-4(1/75-'76), V10#1-3('77), V11#1-4('78), V12#1(2/79)-V14#13(11/81) 4 8 12 24 32 40
NOTE: *There are two V8#4 issues (8/74 & 10/74). V9#4 (12/76) has a cover swipe from Horror Tales V5#1 (2/73). There are two V13#3 issues (6/80 & 9/80).*

WEIRD
DC Comics (Paradox Press): Sum, 1997 - Present ($2.99, B&W, magazine)
1-4: 4-Mike Tyson-c 3.00

WEIRD, THE
DC Comics: Apr, 1988 - No. 4, July, 1988 ($1.50, limited series)
1-4: Wrightson-c/a in all 3.00

WEIRD ADVENTURES
P. L. Publishing Co. (Canada): May-June, 1951 - No. 3, Sept-Oct, 1951
1- "The She-Wolf Killer" by Matt Baker (6 pgs.) 55 110 165 330 495 660
2-Bondage/hypodermic panel 44 88 132 264 395 525
3-Male bondage/torture-c; severed head story 40 80 120 240 340 440

WEIRD ADVENTURES
Ziff-Davis Publishing Co.: No. 10, July-Aug, 1951
10-Painted-c 40 80 120 240 340 440

WEIRD CHILLS
Key Publications: July, 1954 - No. 3, Nov, 1954
1-Wolverton-r/Weird Mysteries No. 4; blood transfusion-c by Baily 80 160 240 500 750 1000
2-Extremely violent injury to eye-c by Baily; Hitler story 74 148 222 463 694 925
3-Bondage E.C. swipe-c by Baily 48 96 144 288 432 575

WEIRD COMICS
Fox Features Syndicate: Apr, 1940 - No. 20, Jan, 1942
1-The Birdman, Thor, God of Thunder (ends #5), The Sorceress of Zoom, Blast Bennett, Typhon, Voodoo Man, & Dr. Mortal begin; George Tuska bondage-c 448 896 1344 3136 4818 6500
2-Lou Fine-c 220 440 660 1375 2063 2750
3,4: 3-Simon-c. 4-Torture-c 118 236 354 738 1107 1475
5-Intro. Dart & sidekick Ace (8/40) (ends #20); bondage/hypo-c 124 248 372 775 1163 1550
6,7-Dynamite Thor app. in each. 6-Super hero covers begin 96 192 288 600 900 1200
8-Dynamo, the Eagle (11/40, early app.; see Science #1) & sidekick Buddy & Marga, the Panther Woman begin 94 188 282 588 882 1175
9,10: 10-Navy Jones app. 76 152 228 475 713 950
11-19: 16-Flag-c. 17-Origin The Black Rider. 59 118 117 369 552 735
20-Origin The Rapier; Swoop Curtis app; Churchill & Hitler-c 69 138 207 431 646 860
NOTE *Cover features: Sorceress of Zoom-4; Dr. Mortal-5; Dart & Ace-6-13, 15; Eagle-14, 16-20.*

WEIRD FANTASY (Formerly A Moon, A Girl, Romance; becomes Weird Science-Fantasy #23 on)
E. C. Comics: No. 13, May-June, 1950 - No. 22, Nov-Dec, 1953
13(#1) (1950) 186 372 558 1395 1998 2600
14-Necronomicon story; Cosmic Ray Bomb explosion-c/story by Feldstein; Feldstein & Gaines star 88 176 264 660 943 1225
15,16: 16-Used in **SOTI**, pg. 144 59 118 177 443 632 820
17 (1951) 49 98 147 367 526 685
6-10: 6-Robot-c 40 80 120 300 430 560
11-13 (1952): 12-E.C. artists cameo. 13-Anti-Wertham "Cosmic Correspondence" 33 66 99 248 354 460
14-Frazetta/Williamson(1st team-up at E.C.)/Krenkel-a (7 pgs.); Orlando draws E.C. staff 46 92 138 345 495 645
15-Williamson/Evans-a(3), 4,3,&7 pgs. 33 66 99 248 354 460
16-19-Williamson/Krenkel-a in all. 18-Williamson/Feldstein-c 31 62 93 233 332 430
20-Frazetta/Williamson-a (7 pgs.) 34 68 102 255 363 470
21-Frazetta/Williamson-c & Williamson/Krenkel-a 46 92 138 345 493 640
22-Bradbury adaptation 24 48 72 180 255 330
NOTE: ***Ray Bradbury** adaptations-13, 17-20, 22. **Crandall** a-22. **Elder** a-17. **Feldstein** a-13(#1)-8; c-13(#1)-18 (#18 w/**Williamson**), 20. **Harrison/Wood** a-13. **Kamen** a-13(#1)-16, 18-22. **Krigstein** a-22. **Kurtzman** a-13(#1)-17(#5), 6. **Orlando** a-9-22 (2 stories in #16); c-19, 22. **Severin/Elder** a-18-21. **Wood** a-13(#1)-14, 17(2 stories ea. in #10-13). Ray Bradbury adaptations in #17-19, 22. Canadian reprints exist; see Table of Contents.*

WEIRD FANTASY
Russ Cochran/Gemstone Publ.: Oct, 1992 - No. 22, Jan, 1998 ($1.50/$2.00/$2.50)
1-22: 1,2: 1,2-r/Weird Fantasy #13,14; Feldstein-c. 3-5-r/Weird Fantasy #15-17 3.00

WEIRD HORRORS (Nightmare #10 on)
St. John Publishing Co.: June, 1952 - No. 9, Oct, 1953
1-Tuska-a 55 110 165 330 495 660
2,3: 3-Hashish story 36 72 108 204 290 375
4,5 31 62 93 175 248 320
6-Ekgren-c; atomic bomb story 48 96 144 288 432 575
7-Ekgren-c; Kubert, Cameron-a 50 100 150 300 450 600
8,9-Kubert-c/a 40 80 120 240 350 460
NOTE: ***Cameron** a-7, 9. **Finesque** a-1-5. **Forgione** a-6. **Morisi** a-3. Bondage c-8.*

WEIRD MYSTERIES
Gillmore Publications: Oct, 1952 - No. 12, Sept, 1954
1-Partial Wolverton-c swiped from splash page "Flight to the Future" in Weird Tales of the Future #2; "Eternity" has an Ingels swipe 82 164 246 513 769 1025
2- "Robot Woman" by Wolverton; Bernard Baily-c reprinted in Mister Mystery #18; acid in face panel 110 220 330 688 1032 1375
3,6: Both have decapitation-c 55 110 165 344 515 685
4- "The Man Who Never Smiled" (3 pgs.) by Wolverton; Classic B. Baily skull-c 102 204 306 638 957 1275
5-Wolverton story "Swamp Monster" (6 pgs.). Classic exposed brain-c 108 216 324 675 1013 1350
7-Used in **SOTI**, illo "Indeed", illo "Sex and blood" 79 158 237 494 740 985
8-Wolverton-c panel-r/#5; used in a '54 Readers Digest anti-comics article by T. E. Murphy entitled "For the Kiddies to Read" 55 110 165 344 515 685
9-Excessive violence, gore & torture 53 106 159 318 477 635
10-Silhouetted nudity panel 47 94 141 282 421 560
11,12: 12-r/Mr. Mystery #8(2), Weird Mysteries #3 & Weird Tales of the Future #6 43 86 129 258 384 510
NOTE: ***Baily** c-2-12. Anti-Wertham column in #5. #1-12 all have 'The Ghoul Teacher' (host).*

WEIRD MYSTERIES (Magazine)
Pastime Publications: Mar-Apr, 1959 (35¢, B&W, 68 pgs.)
1-Torres-a; E. C. swipe from Tales From the Crypt #46 by Tuska "The Ragman" 8 16 24 46 58 70

WEIRD MYSTERY TALES (See DC 100 Page Super Spectacular)

WEIRD MYSTERY TALES (See Cancelled Comic Cavalcade)
National Periodical Publications: July-Aug, 1972 - No. 24, Nov, 1975
1-Kirby-a; Wrightson splash pg. 6 12 18 38 52 65
2-Titanic-c/s 3 7 10 21 28 35
3,21: 21-Wrightson-c 3 6 9 16 20 25
4-10 2 4 6 11 14 18
11-20,22-24 2 4 6 9 11 14
NOTE: ***Alcala** a-5, 10, 13, 14. **Aparo** c-4. **Bailey** a-8. **Bolle** a-8?. **Howard** a-4. **Kaluta** a-4, 24; c-1. **G. Kane** a-10.*

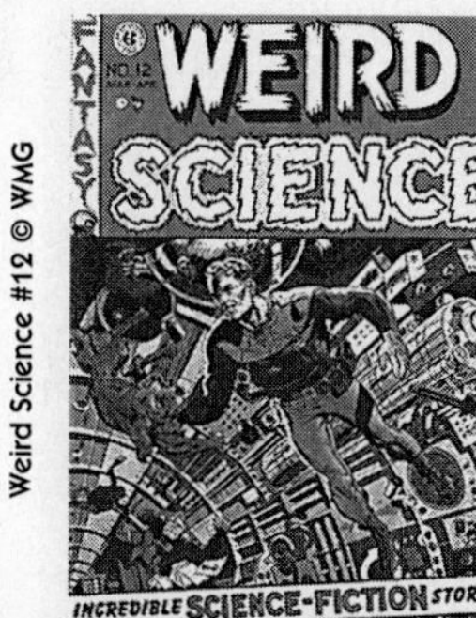

Weird Science #12 © WMG

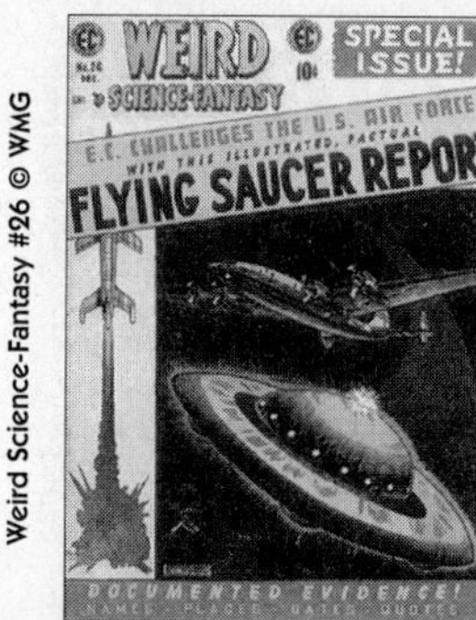

Weird Science-Fantasy #26 © WMG

Weird War Tales #14 © DC

	GD 2.0	VG 4.0	FN 6.0	VF 8.0	VF/NM 9.0	NM- 9.2

Kirby a-1, 2p, 3p. Nino a-5, 6, 9, 13, 16, 21. Redondo a-9, 17. Sparling c-6. Starlin a-3?, 4. Wood a-23.

WEIRD ROMANCE (Seduction of the Innocent #9)
Eclipse Comics: Feb, 1988 ($2.00, B&W)

1-Pre-code horror-r; Lou Cameron-r(2) 2.25

WEIRD SCIENCE (Formerly Saddle Romances) (Becomes Weird Science-Fantasy #23 on)
E. C. Comics: No. 12, May-June, 1950 - No. 22, Nov-Dec, 1953

12(#1) (1950)-"Lost in the Microcosm" classic-c/story by Kurtzman; "Dream of Doom" stars Gaines & E.C. artists 186 372 558 1395 1998 2600
13-Flying saucers over Washington-c/story, 2 years before the actual event 86 172 258 645 923 1200
14-Robot, End of the World-c/story by Feldstein 82 164 246 615 883 1150
15-War of Worlds-c/story (1950) 76 152 228 570 815 1060
5-Atomic explosion-c 58 116 174 435 623 810
6-10: 9-Wood's 1st EC-c 47 94 141 353 507 660
11-14 (1952) 33 66 99 248 354 460
15-18-Williamson/Krenkel-a in each; 15-Williamson-a. 17-Used in **POP**, pgs. 81,82. 18-Bill Gaines doll app. in story 35 70 105 263 374 485
19,20-Williamson/Frazetta-a (7 pgs. each). 19-Used in **SOTI**, illo "A young girl on her wedding night stabs her sleeping husband to death with a hatpin..." 45 90 135 338 482 625
21-Williamson/Frazetta-a (6 pgs.); Wood draws E.C. staff; Gaines & Feldstein app. in story 45 90 135 338 482 625
22-Williamson/Frazetta/Krenkel/Krigstein-a (8 pgs.); Wood draws himself in his story (last pg. & panel) 45 90 135 338 482 625

NOTE: *Elder a-14, 19. Evans a-22. Feldstein a-12(#1)-8; c-12(#1)-8, 11. Ingels a-15. Kamen a-12(#1)-13, 15-18, 20, 21. Kurtzman a-12(#1)-7. Orlando a-10-22. Wood a-12(#1), 13(#2), 5-22 (#9, 10, 12, 13 all have 2 Wood stories); c-9, 10, 12-22. Canadian reprints exist; see Table of Contents. Ray Bradbury adaptations in #17-20.*

WEIRD SCIENCE
Gladstone Publishing: Sept, 1990 - No. 4, Mar, 1991 ($1.95/$2.00, 68 pgs.)

1-4: Wood-c(r); all reprints in each 3.00

WEIRD SCIENCE
Russ Cochran/Gemstone Publishing: Sept, 1992 - No. 22, Dec, 1997 ($1.50/$2.00/$2.50)

1-22: 1,2: r/Weird Science #12,13 w/original-c. ,4-r/#14,15. 5-7-w/original-c 3.00

WEIRD SCIENCE-FANTASY (Formerly Weird Science & Weird Fantasy)
(Becomes Incredible Science Fiction #30)
E. C. Comics: No. 23 Mar, 1954 - No. 29, May-June, 1955 (#23,24: 15¢)

23-Williamson, Wood-a; Bradbury adaptation 32 64 96 240 343 445
24-Williamson & Wood-a; Harlan Ellison's 1st professional story, "Upheaval!", later adapted into a short story as "Mealtime", and then into a TV episode of Voyage to the Bottom of the Sea as "The Price of Doom" 32 64 96 240 343 445
25-Williamson-c; Williamson/Torres/Krenkel-a plus Wood-a; Bradbury adaptation; cover price back to 10¢ 35 70 105 263 374 485
26-Flying Saucer Report; Wood, Crandall-a; A-bomb panels 33 66 99 248 352 455
27-Adam Link/I Robot series begins? 32 64 96 240 343 445
28-Williamson/Krenkel/Torres-a; Wood-a 33 66 99 248 352 455
29-Frazetta-c; Williamson/Krenkel & Wood-a; last pre-code issue; new logo 63 126 189 473 674 875

NOTE: *Crandall a-26, 27, 29. Evans a-26. Feldstein c-24, 26, 28. Kamen a-27, 28. Krigstein a-23-25. Orlando a-in all. Wood a-in all; c-23, 27. The cover to #29 was originally intended for Famous Funnies #217 (Buck Rogers), but was rejected for being "too violent."*

WEIRD SCIENCE-FANTASY
Russ Cochran/Gemstone Publishing: Nov, 1992 - No. 7, May , 1994 ($1.50/$2.00/$2.50)

1-7: 1,2: r/Weird Science-Fantasy #23,24. 3-7 r/#25-29 3.00

WEIRD SCIENCE-FANTASY ANNUAL
E. C. Comics: 1952, 1953 (Sold thru the E. C. office & on the stands in some major cities) (25¢, 132 pgs.)

1952-Feldstein-c 212 424 636 1484 2067 2650
1953-Feldstein-c 136 272 408 952 1326 1700

NOTE: *The 1952 annual contains books cover-dated in 1951 & 1952, and the 1953 annual from 1952 & 1953. Contents of each annual may vary in same year.*

WEIRD SUSPENSE
Atlas/Seaboard Publ.: Feb, 1975 - No. 3, July, 1975

1-3: 1-Tarantula begins. 3-Freidrich-s 1 2 3 5 6 8

NOTE: *Boyette a-1-3. Buckler c-1, 3.*

WEIRD SUSPENSE STORIES (Canadian reprint of Crime SuspenStories #1-3; see Table of Contents)

WEIRD TALES ILLUSTRATED
Millennium Publications: 1992 - No. 2, 1992 ($2.95, high quality paper)

1,2-Bolton painted-c. 1-Adapts E.A. Poe & Harlan Ellison stories. 2-E.A. Poe & H.P. Lovecraft adaptations 3.50
1-($4.95, 52 pgs.)-Deluxe edition w/Tim Vigil-a not in regular #1; stiff-c; Bolton painted-c 5.00

WEIRD TALES OF THE FUTURE
S.P.M. Publ. No. 1-4/Aragon Publ. No. 5-8: Mar, 1952 - No. 8, July-Aug, 1953

1-Andru-a(2); Wolverton partial-c 100 200 300 625 938 1250
2,3-Wolverton-c/a(3) each. 2- "Jumpin Jupiter" satire by Wolverton begins, ends #5 135 270 405 844 1265 1685
4- "Jumpin Jupiter" satire & "The Man From the Moon" by Wolverton; partial Wolverton-c 118 236 354 738 1107 1475
5-Wolverton-c/a(2); "Jumpin Jupiter" satire 135 270 405 844 1265 1685
6-Bernard Baily-c 55 110 165 330 495 660
7- "The Mind Movers" from the art to Wolverton's "Brain Bats of Venus" from Mr. Mystery #7 which was cut apart, pasted up, partially redrawn, and rewritten by Harry Kantor, the editor; Baily-c 114 228 342 713 1069 1425
8-Reprints Weird Mysteries #1(10/52) minus cover; gory cover showing heart ripped out, by B. Baily 74 148 222 463 694 925

WEIRD TALES OF THE MACABRE (Magazine)
Atlas/Seaboard Publ.: Jan, 1975 - No. 2, Mar, 1975 (75¢, B&W)

1-Jeff Jones painted-c; Boyette-a 2 4 6 12 16 20
2-Boris Vallejo painted-c; Severin-a 3 6 9 18 23 28

WEIRD TERROR (Also see Horrific)
Allen Hardy Associates (Comic Media): Sept, 1952 - No. 13, Sept, 1954

1- "Portrait of Death", adapted from Lovecraft's "Pickman's Model"; lingerie panels, Hitler story 55 110 165 330 495 660
2,3: 2-Text on Marquis DeSade, Torture, Demonology, & St. Elmo's Fire. 3-Extreme violence, whipping, torture; article on sin eating, dowsing 46 92 138 276 413 550
4-Dismemberment, decapitation, article on human flesh for sale, Devil, whipping 46 92 138 276 413 550
5-Article on body snatching, mutilation; cannibalism story 43 86 129 258 364 470
6-Dismemberment, decapitation, man hit by lightning 42 84 126 252 376 500
7-Body burning in fireplace-c 43 86 129 258 364 470
8,11: 8-Decapitation story; Ambrose Bierce adapt. 11-End of the world story w/atomic blast panels; Tothish-a by Bill Discount 40 80 120 240 363 485
9,10,13: 13-Severed head panels 36 72 108 207 294 380
12-Discount-a 36 72 108 207 294 380

NOTE: *Don Heck a-most issues; c-1-13. Landau a-6. Morisi a-2-5, 7, 9, 12. Palais a-1, 5, 6, 8(2), 10, 12. Powell a-10. Ravielli a-11, 20.*

WEIRD THRILLERS
Ziff-Davis Publ. Co. (Approved Comics): Sept-Oct, 1951 - No. 5, Oct-Nov, 1952 (#2-5: painted-c)

1-Rondo Hatton photo-c 84 168 252 525 788 1050
2-Toth, Anderson, Colan-a 62 124 186 388 582 775
3-Two Powell, Tuska-a; classic-c 82 164 246 513 769 1025
4-Kubert, Tuska-a 58 116 174 363 544 725
5-Powell-a 54 108 162 324 487 650

NOTE: *M. Anderson a-2, 3. Roussos a-4. #2, 3 reprinted in Nightmare #10 & 13; #4, 5 reprinted in Amazing Ghost Stories #16 & #15.*

WEIRD VAMPIRE TALES (Comic magazine)
Modern Day Periodical Pub.: V3 #1, Apr, 1979 - V5 #3, Mar, 1982 (B&W)

V3 #1 (4/79) First issue, no V1 or V2 4 8 12 24 32 40
V3 #2-4 3 6 9 18 24 30
V4 #2 (4/80), V4 #3 (7/80) (no V4 #1) 3 6 9 16 20 25
V5 #1 (1/81), V5 #2 (8/81) 3 6 9 16 20 25
V5 #3 (3/82) Last issue; low print 3 7 10 21 28 35

WEIRD WAR TALES
National Periodical Publ./DC Comics: Sept-Oct, 1971 - No. 124, June, 1983 (#1-5: 52 pgs.)

1-Kubert-a in #1-4,7; c-1-7 23 46 69 167 244 320
2,3-Drucker-a: 2-Crandall-a. 3-Heath-a 9 18 27 65 93 120
4,5: 5-Toth-a; Heath-a 7 14 21 50 68 85
6,7,9,10: 6,10-Toth-a. 7-Heath-a 5 10 15 33 44 55
8-Neal Adams-c/a(i) 6 12 18 40 55 70
11-20 3 6 9 18 23 28
21-35 2 4 6 11 14 18
36-(68 pgs.)-Crandall & Kubert-r/#2; Heath-r/#3; Kubert-c 2 4 6 14 18 22
37-63: 38,39-Kubert-c 1 2 3 5 7 9
64,68-Frank Miller-a in both. 64-Miller's 1st DC work 2 4 6 12 16 20
65-67,69-92,95-99,102-124: 97-2nd Creature Commandos; series begins 6.00
93,94,100,101: 93-Intro/origin Creature Commandos. 94,99-Return of War that

Weird Western Tales #12 © DC

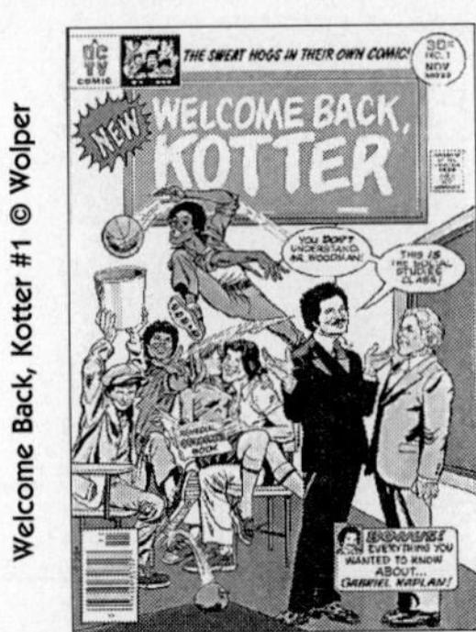

Welcome Back, Kotter #1 © Wolper

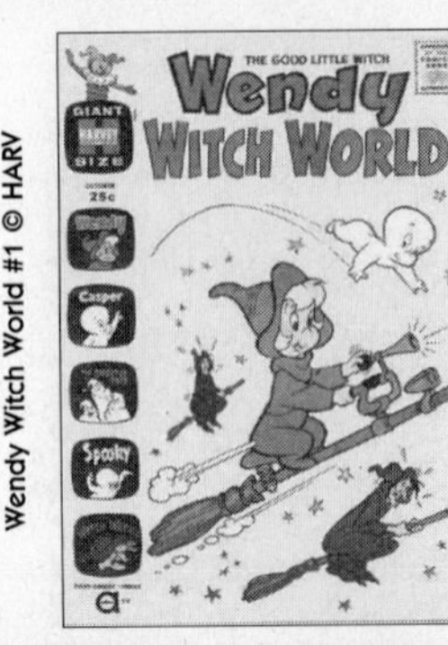

Wendy Witch World #1 © HARV

	GD 2.0	VG 4.0	FN 6.0	VF 8.0	VF/NM 9.0	NM- 9.2
time forgot-Dinosaur-c/s. 101-Intro/origin G.I. Robot						6.00

WEIRD WAR TALES
DC Comics (Vertigo): June, 1997 - No. 4, Sept, 1997 ($2.50)

	GD 2.0	VG 4.0	FN 6.0	VF 8.0	VF/NM 9.0	NM- 9.2
1-4-Anthology by various						3.00

WEIRD WAR TALES
DC Comics (Vertigo): April, 2000 ($4.95, one-shot)

	GD 2.0	VG 4.0	FN 6.0	VF 8.0	VF/NM 9.0	NM- 9.2
1-Anthology by various; last Biukovic-a						5.00

WEIRD WESTERN TALES (Formerly All-Star Western)
National Per. Publ./DC Comics: No. 12, June-July, 1972 - No. 70, Aug, 1980

	GD 2.0	VG 4.0	FN 6.0	VF 8.0	VF/NM 9.0	NM- 9.2
12-(52 pgs.)-3rd app. Jonah Hex; Bat Lash, Pow Wow Smith reprints; El Diablo by Neal Adams/Wrightson	12	24	36	82	121	160
13-Jonah Hex-c & 4th app.; Neal Adams-a	8	16	24	55	78	100
14-Toth-a	6	12	18	38	52	65
15-Adams-c/a; no Jonah Hex	4	8	12	22	30	38
16,17,19,20	3	7	10	21	28	35
18,29: 18-1st all Jonah Hex issue (7-8/73) & begins. 29-Origin Jonah Hex	4	8	12	29	40	50
21-28,30-38: Jonah Hex in all. 38-Last Jonah Hex	2	4	6	12	16	20
39-Origin/1st app. Scalphunter & begins	2	4	6	10	13	16
40-47,50-69: 64-Bat Lash-c/story	1	2	3	5	6	8
48,49: (44 pgs.)-1st & 2nd app. Cinnamon	1	2	3	5	7	9
70-Last issue	2	4	6	8	10	12

NOTE: ***Alcala** a-16, 17. **Evans** inks-39-48; c-39i, 40, 47. **G. Kane** a-15, 20. **Kubert** c-12, 33. **Starlin** c-44, 45. **Wildey** a-26. 48 & 49 are 44 pgs..*

WEIRD WESTERN TALES
DC Comics (Vertigo): Apr, 2001 - No. 4, Jul, 2001 ($2.50, limited series)

	GD 2.0	VG 4.0	FN 6.0	VF 8.0	VF/NM 9.0	NM- 9.2
1-4-Anthology by various						2.50

WEIRD WONDER TALES
Marvel Comics Group: Dec, 1973 - No. 22, May, 1977

	GD 2.0	VG 4.0	FN 6.0	VF 8.0	VF/NM 9.0	NM- 9.2
1-Wolverton-r/Mystic #6 (Eye of Doom)	3	6	9	16	20	25
2-10	2	4	6	9	11	14
11-22: 16-18-Venus-r by Everett from Venus #19,18 & 17. 19-22-Dr. Druid (Droom)-r	2	4	6	8	10	12
15-17-(30¢-c variants, limited distribution)(4-8/76)	2	4	6	11	14	18

NOTE: *All 1950s & early 1960s reprints. **Check** r-1. **Colan** r-17. **Ditko** r-4, 5, 10-13, 19-21. **Drucker** r-12, 20. **Everett** r-3(Spellbound #16), 6(Astonishing #10), 9(Adv. Into Mystery #5). **Heath** a-13r. **Heck** a-1or, 14r. **Gil Kane** c-1, 2, 10. **Kirby** r-4, 6, 10, 11, 13, 15-22; c-17, 19, 20. **Krigstein** r-19. **Kubert** r-22. **Maneely** r-8. **Mooney** r-7p. **Powell** r-3, 7. **Torres** r-7. **Wildey** r-2, 7.*

WEIRD WORLDS (See Adventures Into...)

WEIRD WORLDS (Magazine)
Eerie Publications: V1#10(12/70), V2#1(2/71) - No. 4, Aug, 1971 (52 pgs.)

	GD 2.0	VG 4.0	FN 6.0	VF 8.0	VF/NM 9.0	NM- 9.2
V1#10-Sci-fi/horror	4	8	12	24	32	40
V2#1-4	3	6	9	18	24	30

WEIRD WORLDS (Also see Ironwolf: Fires of the Revolution)
National Periodical Publications: Aug-Sept, 1972 - No. 9, Jan-Feb, 1974; No. 10, Oct-Nov, 1974 (All 20¢ issues)

	GD 2.0	VG 4.0	FN 6.0	VF 8.0	VF/NM 9.0	NM- 9.2
1-Edgar Rice Burrough's John Carter Warlord of Mars & David Innes begin (1st DC app.); Kubert-c	2	4	6	12	16	20
2-4: 2-Infantino/Orlando-c. 3-Murphy Anderson-c. 4-Kaluta-a	2	4	6	8	10	12
5-7: .5-Kaluta-c. 7-Last John Carter.	1	3	4	6	8	10
8-10: 8-Iron Wolf begins by Chaykin (1st app.)	1	2	3	5	7	9

NOTE: ***Neal Adams** a-2i, 3i. John Carter by **Andersonin** #1-3. **Chaykin** c-7, 8. **Kaluta** a-4; c-4-6, 10. **Orlando** a-4i; c-2, 3, 4i. **Wrightson** a-2i, 4i.*

WELCOME BACK, KOTTER (TV) (See Limited Collectors' Edition #57 for unpublished #11)
National Periodical Publ./DC Comics: Nov, 1976 - No. 10, Mar-Apr, 1978

	GD 2.0	VG 4.0	FN 6.0	VF 8.0	VF/NM 9.0	NM- 9.2
1-Sparling-a(p)	2	4	6	14	18	22
2-10: 3-Estrada-a	2	4	6	8	10	12

WELCOME SANTA (See March of Comics #63,183)

WELCOME TO THE LITTLE SHOP OF HORRORS
Roger Corman's Cosmic Comics: May, 1995 -No. 3, July, 1995 ($2.50, limited series)

	GD 2.0	VG 4.0	FN 6.0	VF 8.0	VF/NM 9.0	NM- 9.2
1-3						2.50

WELLS FARGO (See Tales of...)

WENDY AND THE NEW KIDS ON THE BLOCK
Harvey Comics: Mar, 1991 - No. 3, July, 1991 ($1.25)

	GD 2.0	VG 4.0	FN 6.0	VF 8.0	VF/NM 9.0	NM- 9.2
1-3						2.25

WENDY DIGEST
Harvey Comics: Oct, 1990 - No. 5, Mar, 1992 ($1.75, digest size)

	GD 2.0	VG 4.0	FN 6.0	VF 8.0	VF/NM 9.0	NM- 9.2
1-5						4.00

WENDY PARKER COMICS
Atlas Comics (OMC): July, 1953 - No. 8, July, 1954

	GD 2.0	VG 4.0	FN 6.0	VF 8.0	VF/NM 9.0	NM- 9.2
1	10	20	30	56	73	90
2	8	16	24	40	50	60
3-8	7	14	21	35	43	50

WENDY, THE GOOD LITTLE WITCH (TV)
Harvey Publ.: 8/60 - #82, 11/73; #83, 8/74 - #93, 4/76; #94, 9/90 - #97, 12/90

	GD 2.0	VG 4.0	FN 6.0	VF 8.0	VF/NM 9.0	NM- 9.2
1-Wendy & Casper the Friendly Ghost begin	25	50	75	181	266	350
2	13	26	39	90	133	175
3-5	9	18	27	65	93	120
6-10	7	14	21	50	68	85
11-20	5	10	15	36	48	60
21-30	4	8	12	27	36	45
31-50	3	6	9	19	25	32
51-64,66-69	2	4	6	12	16	20
65 (2/71)-Wendy origin.	3	6	9	18	24	30
70-74: All 52 pg. Giants	3	6	9	18	23	28
75-93	2	4	6	9	11	14
94-97 (1990, $1.00-c): 94-Has #194 on-c						4.00

(See Casper the Friendly Ghost #20 & Harvey Hits #7, 16, 21, 23, 27, 30, 33)

WENDY THE GOOD LITTLE WITCH (2nd Series)
Harvey Comics: Apr, 1991 - No. 15, Aug, 1994 ($1.00/$1.25 #7-11/$1.50 #12-15)

	GD 2.0	VG 4.0	FN 6.0	VF 8.0	VF/NM 9.0	NM- 9.2
1-15-Reprints Wendy & Casper stories. 12-Bunny app.						3.00

WENDY WITCH WORLD
Harvey Publications: 10/61; No. 2, 9/62 - No. 52, 12/73; No. 53, 9/74

	GD 2.0	VG 4.0	FN 6.0	VF 8.0	VF/NM 9.0	NM- 9.2
1-(25¢, 68 pg. Giants begin)	14	28	42	99	145	190
2-5	8	16	24	53	74	95
6-10	6	12	18	38	52	65
11-20	4	8	12	29	40	50
21-30	4	8	12	22	30	38
31-39: 39-Last 68 pg. issue	3	6	9	18	24	30
40-45: 52 pg. issues	2	4	6	12	16	20
46-53	2	4	6	9	11	14

WEREWOLF (Super Hero) (Also see Dracula & Frankenstein)
Dell Publishing Co.: Dec, 1966 - No. 3, April, 1967

	GD 2.0	VG 4.0	FN 6.0	VF 8.0	VF/NM 9.0	NM- 9.2
1-1st app.	4	8	12	24	32	40
2,3	2	4	6	14	18	22

WEREWOLF BY NIGHT (See Giant-Size..., Marvel Spotlight #2-4 & Power Record Comics)
Marvel Comics Group: Sept, 1972 - No. 43, Mar, 1977

	GD 2.0	VG 4.0	FN 6.0	VF 8.0	VF/NM 9.0	NM- 9.2
1-Ploog-a cont'd. from Marvel Spotlight #4	9	18	27	65	93	120
2	4	8	12	29	40	50
3-5	4	8	12	22	30	38
6-10	3	6	9	16	20	24
11-14,16-20	2	4	6	10	13	16
15-New origin Werewolf; Dracula-c/story cont'd from Tomb of Dracula #18; classic Ploog-c	3	6	9	16	20	25
21-31	1	3	4	6	8	10
32-Origin & 1st app. Moon Knight (8/75)	9	18	27	65	93	120
33-2nd app. Moon Knight	4	8	12	29	40	50
34-36,38-43: 35-Starlin/Wrightson-c	1	2	3	5	7	9
37-Moon Knight app; part Wrightson-c	2	4	6	8	10	12
38,39-(30¢-c variants, limited distribution)(5,7/76)	2	4	6	14	18	22

NOTE: ***Bolle** a-6i. **G. Kane** a-11p, 12p; c-21, 22, 24-30, 34p. **Mooney** a-7i. **Ploog** 1-4p, 5, 6p, 7p, 13-16p; c-5-8, 13-16. **Reinman** a-8i. **Sutton** a(i)-9, 11, 16, 35.*

WEREWOLF BY NIGHT (Vol. 2, continues in Strange Tales #1 (9/98))
Marvel Comics Group: Feb, 1998 - No. 6, July, 1998 ($2.99)

	GD 2.0	VG 4.0	FN 6.0	VF 8.0	VF/NM 9.0	NM- 9.2
1-6-Manco-a: 2-Two covers. 6-Ghost Rider-c/app.						3.00

WEREWOLVES & VAMPIRES (Magazine)
Charlton Comics: 1962 (One Shot)

	GD 2.0	VG 4.0	FN 6.0	VF 8.0	VF/NM 9.0	NM- 9.2
1	8	16	24	55	78	100

WEST COAST AVENGERS
Marvel Comics Group: Sept, 1984 - No. 4, Dec, 1984 (lim. series, Mando paper)

	GD 2.0	VG 4.0	FN 6.0	VF 8.0	VF/NM 9.0	NM- 9.2
1-Origin & 1st app. W.C. Avengers (Hawkeye, Iron Man, Mockingbird & Tigra)						4.00
2-4						3.00

WEST COAST AVENGERS (Becomes Avengers West Coast #48 on)
Marvel Comics Group: Oct, 1985 - No. 47, Aug, 1989

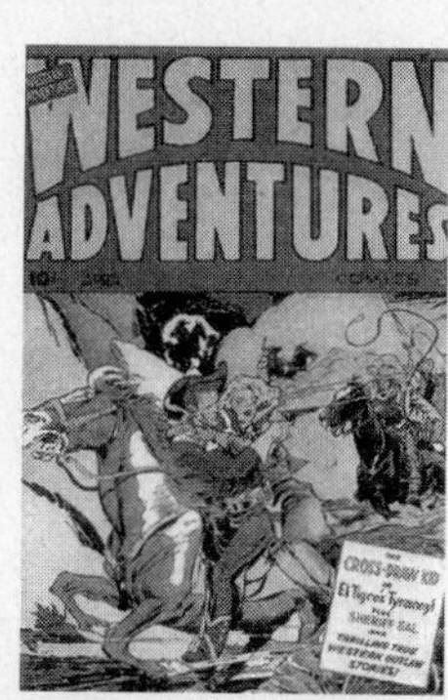

Western Adventures Comics #4 © ACE

Western Crime-Busters #4 © TM

Western Hearts #2 © STD

	GD 2.0	VG 4.0	FN 6.0	VF 8.0	VF/NM 9.0	NM- 9.2
V2#1-41						3.00
42-47: 42-Byrne-a(p)/scripts begin. 46-Byrne-c; 1st app. Great Lakes Avengers						3.00
Annual 1-3 (1986-1988): 3-Evolutionary War app.						3.00
Annual 4 (1989, $2.00)-Atlantis Attacks; Byrne/Austin-a						3.00

WESTERN ACTION
I. W. Enterprises: No. 7, 1964

	GD	VG	FN	VF	VF/NM	NM-
7-Reprints Cow Puncher #? by Avon	2	4	6	9	11	14

WESTERN ACTION
Atlas/Seaboard Publ.: Feb, 1975

	GD	VG	FN	VF	VF/NM	NM-
1-Kid Cody by Wildey & The Comanche Kid stories; intro. The Renegade	1	2	3	5	7	9

WESTERN ACTION THRILLERS
Dell Publishers: Apr, 1937 (10¢, square binding; 100 pgs.)

	GD	VG	FN	VF	VF/NM	NM-
1-Buffalo Bill, The Texas Kid, Laramie Joe, Two-Gun Thompson, & Wild West Bill app.	85	170	255	531	796	1060

WESTERN ADVENTURES COMICS (Western Love Trails #7 on)
Ace Magazines: Oct, 1948 - No. 6, Aug, 1949

	GD	VG	FN	VF	VF/NM	NM-
nn(#1)-Sheriff Sal, The Cross-Draw Kid, Sam Bass begin	24	48	72	135	190	245
nn(#2)(12/48)	13	26	39	74	100	125
nn(#3)(2/49)-Used in **SOTI**, pgs. 30,31	13	26	39	76	103	130
4-6	11	22	33	63	84	105

WESTERN BANDITS
Avon Periodicals: 1952 (Painted-c)

	GD	VG	FN	VF	VF/NM	NM-
1-Butch Cassidy, The Daltons by Larsen; Kinstler-a; c-part-r/paperback Avon Western Novel #1	17	34	51	98	134	170

WESTERN BANDIT TRAILS (See Approved Comics)
St. John Publishing Co.: Jan, 1949 - No. 3, July, 1949

	GD	VG	FN	VF	VF/NM	NM-
1-Tuska-a; Baker-c; Blue Monk, Ventrilo app.	26	52	78	150	210	270
2-Baker-c	20	40	60	112	156	200
3-Baker-c/a; Tuska-a	24	48	72	135	190	245

WESTERN COMICS (See Super DC Giant #15)
National Per. Publ: Jan-Feb, 1948 - No. 85, Jan-Feb, 1961 (1-27: 52pgs.)

	GD	VG	FN	VF	VF/NM	NM-
1-Wyoming Kid & his horse Racer, The Vigilante in "Jesse James Rides Again" (Meskin-a), Cowboy Marshal, Rodeo Rick begin	80	160	240	500	750	1000
2	40	80	120	240	340	440
3,4-Last Vigilante	37	74	111	212	301	390
5-Nighthawk & his horse Nightwind begin (not in #6); Captain Tootsie by Beck	31	62	93	175	248	320
6,7,9,10	24	48	72	135	190	245
8-Origin Wyoming Kid; 2 pg. pin-ups of rodeo queens	36	72	108	204	290	375
11-20	20	40	60	112	156	200
21-40: 24-Starr-a. 27-Last 52 pgs. 28-Flag-c	15	30	45	86	118	150
41,42,44-49: 49-Last precode issue (2/55)	14	28	42	81	111	140
43-Pow Wow Smith begins, ends #85	15	30	45	84	115	145
50-60	12	24	36	71	96	120
61-85-Last Wyoming Kid. 77-Origin Matt Savage Trail Boss. 82-1st app. Fleetfoot, Pow Wow's girlfriend	10	20	30	58	77	95

NOTE: ***G. Kane, Infantino*** *art in most.* ***Meskin*** *a-1-4.* ***Moreira*** *a-28-39.* ***Post*** *a-3-5.*

WESTERN CRIME BUSTERS
Trojan Magazines: Sept, 1950 - No. 10, Mar-Apr, 1952

	GD	VG	FN	VF	VF/NM	NM-
1-Six-Gun Smith, Wilma West, K-Bar-Kate, & Fighting Bob Dale begin; headlight-a	36	72	108	204	290	375
2	20	40	60	112	156	200
3-5: 3-Myron Fass-c	19	38	57	106	146	185
6-Wood-a	35	70	105	201	288	370
7-Six-Gun Smith by Wood	35	70	105	201	288	370
8	19	38	57	106	146	185
9-Tex Gordon & Wilma West by Wood; Lariat Lucy app.	34	68	102	193	274	355
10-Wood-a	31	62	93	175	248	320

WESTERN CRIME CASES (Formerly Indian Warriors #7,8; becomes The Outlaws #10 on)
Star Publications: No. 9, Dec, 1951

	GD	VG	FN	VF	VF/NM	NM-
9-White Rider & Super Horse; L. B. Cole-c	22	44	66	124	172	220

WESTERNER, THE (Wild Bill Pecos)
"Wanted" Comic Group/Toytown/Patches: No. 14, June, 1948 - No. 41, Dec, 1951 (#14-31: 52 pgs.)

	GD 2.0	VG 4.0	FN 6.0	VF 8.0	VF/NM 9.0	NM- 9.2
14	14	28	42	81	111	140
15-17,19-21: 19-Meskin-a	8	16	24	46	58	70
18,22-25-Krigstein-a	10	20	30	58	77	95
26(4/50)-Origin & 1st app. Calamity Kate, series ends #32; Krigstein-a	14	28	42	79	107	135
27-Krigstein-a(2)	13	26	39	74	100	125
28-41: 33-Quest app. 37-Lobo, the Wolf Boy begins	7	14	21	35	43	50

NOTE: ***Mort Lawrence*** *a-20-27, 29, 37, 39; c-19, 22-24, 26, 27.* ***Leav*** *c-14-18, 20, 31.* ***Syd Shores*** *a-39; c-34, 35, 37-41.*

WESTERNER, THE
Super Comics: 1964

	GD	VG	FN	VF	VF/NM	NM-
Super Reprint 15-17: 15-r/Oklahoma Kid #? 16-r/Crack West. #65; Severin-c; Crandall-r. 17-r/Blazing Western #2; Severin-c	2	4	6	9	11	14

WESTERN FIGHTERS
Hillman Periodicals/Star Publ.: Apr-May, 1948 - V4#7, Mar-Apr, 1953 (#1-V3#2: 52 pgs.)

	GD	VG	FN	VF	VF/NM	NM-
V1#1-Simon & Kirby-c	36	72	108	204	290	375
2-Not Kirby-a	12	24	36	71	96	120
3-Fuje-c	10	20	30	58	77	95
4-Krigstein, Ingels, Fuje-a	11	22	33	66	88	110
5,6,8,9,12	8	16	24	43	54	65
7,10-Krigstein-a	10	20	30	56	73	90
11-Williamson/Frazetta-a	31	62	93	175	248	320
V2#1-Krigstein-a	10	20	30	56	73	90
2-12: 4-Berg-a	7	14	21	35	43	50
V3#1-11,V4#1,4-7	6	12	18	31	38	45
12,V4#2,3-Krigstein-a	10	20	30	56	73	90
3-D 1(12/53, 25¢, Star Publ.)-Came w/glasses; L. B. Cole-c	39	78	117	230	325	420

NOTE: ***Kinstlerish*** *a-V2#6, 8, 9, 12; V3#2, 5-7, 11, 12; V4#1(plus cover).* ***McWilliams*** *a-11.* ***Powell*** *a-V2#2.* ***Reinman*** *a-1-12, V4#3.* ***Rowich*** *c-5, 6i.* ***Starr*** *a-5.*

WESTERN FRONTIER
P. L. Publishers: Apr-May, 1951 - No. 7, 1952

	GD	VG	FN	VF	VF/NM	NM-
1	13	26	39	74	100	125
2	8	16	24	43	54	65
3-7	7	14	21	35	43	50

WESTERN GUNFIGHTERS (1st Series) (Apache Kid #11-19)
Atlas Comics (CPS): No. 20, June, 1956 - No. 27, Aug, 1957

	GD	VG	FN	VF	VF/NM	NM-
20	13	26	39	74	100	125
21-Crandall-a	13	26	39	74	100	125
22-Wood & Powell-a	19	38	57	106	146	185
23,24: 23-Williamson-a. 24-Toth-a	13	26	39	74	100	125
25-27	10	20	30	56	73	90

NOTE: ***Berg*** *a-20.* ***Colan*** *a-20, 26, 27.* ***Crandall*** *a-21.* ***Heath*** *a-25.* ***Maneely*** *a-24, 25; c-22, 23, 25.* ***Morisi*** *a-24.* ***Morrow*** *a-26.* ***Pakula*** *a-23.* ***Severin*** *c-20, 27.* ***Torres*** *a-26.* ***Woodbridge*** *a-27.*

WESTERN GUNFIGHTERS (2nd Series)
Marvel Comics Group: Aug, 1970 - No. 33, Nov, 1975 (#1-6: 25¢, 68 pgs.)

	GD	VG	FN	VF	VF/NM	NM-
1-Ghost Rider begins; Fort Rango, Renegades & Gunhawk app.	5	10	15	36	48	60
2,3,5,6: 2-Origin Nightwind (Apache Kid's horse)	3	6	9	18	24	30
4-Barry Smith-a	4	8	12	24	32	40
7-(52 pgs) Origin Ghost Rider retold	3	6	9	18	23	28
8-14: 10-Origin Black Rider. 12-Origin Matt Slade	2	4	6	11	14	18
15-20	2	4	6	8	10	12
21-33	1	3	4	6	8	10

NOTE: ***Baker*** *r-2, 3.* ***Colan*** *r-2.* ***Drucker*** *r-3.* ***Everett*** *a-6i.* ***G. Kane*** *c-29, 31.* ***Kirby*** *a-1p(r), 5, 10-12; c-19, 21.* ***Kubert*** *r-2.* ***Maneely*** *r-2, 10.* ***Morrow*** *r-29.* ***Severin*** *c-10.* ***Shores*** *a-3, 4.* ***Barry Smith*** *a-4.* ***Steranko*** *c-14.* ***Sutton*** *a-1, 2i, 5, 4.* ***Torres*** *r-26('57).* ***Wildey*** *r-8, 9.* ***Williamson*** *r-2, 18.* ***Woodbridge*** *r-27('57). Renegades in #4, 5; Ghost Rider in #1-7.*

WESTERN HEARTS
Standard Comics: Dec, 1949 - No. 10, Mar, 1952 (All photo-c)

	GD	VG	FN	VF	VF/NM	NM-
1-Severin-a; Whip Wilson & Reno Browne photo-c	24	48	72	135	190	245
2-Beverly Tyler & Jerome Courtland photo-c from movie "Palomino"; Williamson/Frazetta-a (2 pgs.)	24	48	72	135	190	245
3-Rex Allen photo-c	14	28	42	79	107	135
4-7,10-Severin & Elder, Al Carreno-a. 5-Ray Milland & Hedy Lamarr photo-c from movie "Copper Canyon". 6-Fred MacMurray & Irene Dunn photo-c from movie "Never a Dull Moment". 7-Jock Mahoney photo-c. 10-Bill Williams & Jane Nigh photo-c	13	26	39	76	103	130
8-Randolph Scott & Janis Carter photo-c from "Santa Fe"; Severin & Elder-a	14	28	42	79	107	135
9-Whip Wilson & Reno Browne photo-c; Severin & Elder-a						

Western Hero #83 © FAW

Western Outlaws #21 © ATLAS

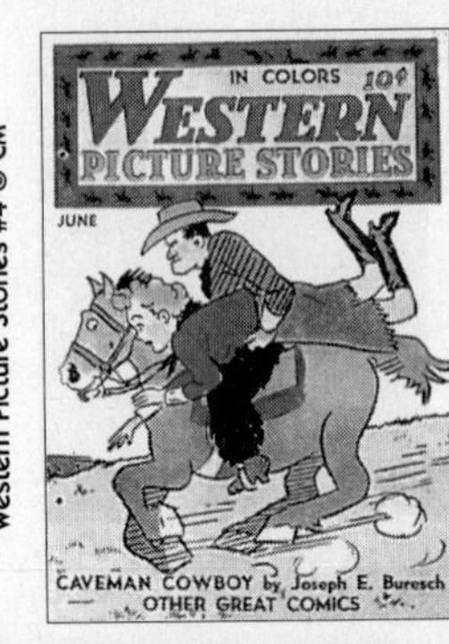

Western Picture Stories #4 © CM

	GD 2.0	VG 4.0	FN 6.0	VF 8.0	VF/NM 9.0	NM- 9.2
	15	30	45	86	118	150

WESTERN HERO (Wow Comics #1-69; Real Western Hero #70-75)
Fawcett Publications: No. 76, Mar, 1949 - No. 112, Mar, 1952

	GD 2.0	VG 4.0	FN 6.0	VF 8.0	VF/NM 9.0	NM- 9.2
76(#1, 52 pgs.)-Tom Mix, Hopalong Cassidy, Monte Hale, Gabby Hayes, Young Falcon (ends #78,80), & Big Bow and Little Arrow (ends #102,105) begin; painted-c begin	31	62	93	175	248	320
77 (52 pgs.)	18	36	54	104	142	180
78,80-82 (52 pgs.): 81-Capt. Tootsie by Beck	17	34	51	98	134	170
79,83 (36 pgs.): 83-Last painted-c	15	30	45	84	115	145
84-86,88-90 (52 pgs.): 84-Photo-c begin, end #112. 86-Last Hopalong Cassidy	15	30	45	86	118	150
87,91,95,99 (36 pgs.): 87-Bill Boyd begins, ends #95	13	26	39	76	103	130
92-94,96-98,101 (52 pgs.): 96-Tex Ritter begins. 101-Red Eagle app.	14	28	42	81	111	140
100 (52 pgs.)	15	30	45	86	118	150
102-111: 102-Begin 36 pg. issues	13	26	39	76	103	130
112-Last issue	14	28	42	81	111	140

NOTE: *1/2 to 1 pg. Rocky Lane (Carnation) in 80-83, 86, 88, 97. Photo covers feature Hopalong Cassidy #84, 86, 89; Tom Mix #85, 87, 90, 92, 94, 97; Monte Hale #88, 91, 93, 95, 98, 100, 104, 107, 110; Tex Ritter #96, 99, 101, 105, 108, 111; Gabby Hayes #103.*

WESTERN KID (1st Series)
Atlas Comics (CPC): Dec, 1954 - No. 17, Aug, 1957

	GD 2.0	VG 4.0	FN 6.0	VF 8.0	VF/NM 9.0	NM- 9.2
1-Origin; The Western Kid (Tex Dawson), his stallion Whirlwind & dog Lightning begin	21	42	63	118	164	210
2 (2/55)-Last pre-code	11	22	33	63	84	105
3-8	10	20	30	56	73	90
9,10-Williamson-a in both (4 pgs. each)	10	20	30	58	77	95
11-17	8	16	24	46	58	70

NOTE: ***Ayers** a-6, 7. **Maneely** c-2-7, 10, 14. **Romita** a-1-17; c-1, 12. **Severin** c-17.*

WESTERN KID, THE (2nd Series)
Marvel Comics Group: Dec, 1971 - No. 5, Aug, 1972 (All 20¢ issues)

	GD 2.0	VG 4.0	FN 6.0	VF 8.0	VF/NM 9.0	NM- 9.2
1-Reprints; Romita-c/a(3)	3	6	9	18	23	28
2,4,5: 2-Romita-a; Severin-c. 4-Everett-r	2	4	6	10	13	16
3-Williamson-a	2	4	6	12	16	20

WESTERN KILLERS
Fox Features Syndicate: nn, July?, 1948; No. 60, Sept, 1948 - No. 64, May, 1949; No. 6, July, 1949

	GD 2.0	VG 4.0	FN 6.0	VF 8.0	VF/NM 9.0	NM- 9.2
nn(#59?)(nd, F&J Trading Co.)-Range Busters; formerly Blue Beetle #57?	25	50	75	144	198	255
60 (#1, 9/48)-Extreme violence; lingerie panel	27	54	81	153	214	275
61-Jack Cole, Starr-a	22	44	66	127	176	225
62-64, 6 (#6-exist?)	20	40	60	112	156	200

WESTERN LIFE ROMANCES (My Friend Irma #3 on?)
Marvel Comics (IPP): Dec, 1949 - No. 2, Mar, 1950 (52 pgs.)

	GD 2.0	VG 4.0	FN 6.0	VF 8.0	VF/NM 9.0	NM- 9.2
1-Whip Wilson & Reno Browne photo-c	21	42	63	118	164	210
2-Audie Murphy & Gale Storm photo-c	17	34	51	95	130	165

WESTERN LOVE
Prize Publ.: July-Aug, 1949 - No. 5, Mar-Apr, 1950 (All photo-c & 52 pgs.)

	GD 2.0	VG 4.0	FN 6.0	VF 8.0	VF/NM 9.0	NM- 9.2
1-S&K-a; Randolph Scott photo-c from movie "Canadian Pacific" (see Prize Comics #76)	31	62	93	175	248	320
2,5-S&K-a: 2-Whip Wilson & Reno Browne photo-c. 5-Dale Robertson photo-c	24	48	72	135	190	245
3,4: 3-Reno Browne? photo-c	15	30	45	86	118	150

NOTE: ***Meskin & Severin/Elder** a-2-5.*

WESTERN LOVE TRAILS (Formerly Western Adventures)
Ace Magazines (A. A. Wyn): No. 7, Nov, 1949 - No. 9, Mar, 1950

	GD 2.0	VG 4.0	FN 6.0	VF 8.0	VF/NM 9.0	NM- 9.2
7	12	24	36	71	96	120
8,9	10	20	30	56	73	90

WESTERN MARSHAL (See Steve Donovan...)
Dell Publishing Co.: No. 534, 2-4/54 - No. 640, 7/55 (Based on Ernest Haycox's "Trailtown")

	GD 2.0	VG 4.0	FN 6.0	VF 8.0	VF/NM 9.0	NM- 9.2
Four Color 534 (#1)-Kinstler-a	7	14	21	46	63	80
Four Color 591 (10/54), 613 (2/55), 640-All Kinstler-a	6	12	18	40	55	70

WESTERN OUTLAWS (Junior Comics #9-16; My Secret Life #22 on)
Fox Features Syndicate: No. 17, Sept, 1948 - No. 21, May, 1949

	GD 2.0	VG 4.0	FN 6.0	VF 8.0	VF/NM 9.0	NM- 9.2
17-Kamen-a; Iger shop-a in all; 1 pg. "Death and the Devil Pills" r-in Ghostly Weird #122	36	72	108	204	290	375
18-21	21	42	63	118	164	210

WESTERN OUTLAWS
Atlas Comics (ACI No. 1-14/WPI No. 15-21): Feb, 1954 - No. 21, Aug, 1957

	GD 2.0	VG 4.0	FN 6.0	VF 8.0	VF/NM 9.0	NM- 9.2
1-Heath, Powell-a; Maneely hanging-c	23	46	69	129	180	230
2	12	24	36	69	92	115
3-10: 7-Violent-a by R.Q. Sale	10	20	30	56	73	90
11,14-Williamson-a in both (6 pgs. each)	11	22	33	63	84	105
12,18,20,21: Severin covers	9	18	27	52	66	80
13,15: 13-Baker-a. 15-Torres-a	10	20	30	56	73	90
16-Williamson text illo	9	18	27	52	66	80
17,19-Crandall-a. 17-Williamson text illo	10	20	30	56	73	90

NOTE: ***Ayers** a-7, 10, 18, 20. **Bolle** a-21. **Colan** a-5, 10, 11, 17. **Drucker** a-11. **Everett** a-9, 10. **Heath** a-1; c-3, 4, 8, 16. **Kubert** a-9p. **Maneely** a-13, 16, 17, 19; c-1, 5, 7, 9, 10, 12, 13. **Morisi** a-18. **Powell** a-3, 16. **Romita** a-7, 13. **Severin** a-8, 16, 19; c-17, 18, 20, 21. **Tuska** a-6, 15.*

WESTERN OUTLAWS & SHERIFFS (Formerly Best Western)
Marvel/Atlas Comics (IPC): No. 60, Dec, 1949 - No. 73, June, 1952

	GD 2.0	VG 4.0	FN 6.0	VF 8.0	VF/NM 9.0	NM- 9.2
60 (52 pgs.)	24	48	72	135	190	245
61-65: 61-Photo-c	19	38	57	106	146	185
66-Story contains 5 hangings	19	38	57	106	146	185
68-72	14	28	42	79	107	135
67-Cannibalism story	19	38	57	106	146	185
73-Black Rider story; Everett-c	15	30	45	86	118	150

NOTE: ***Maneely** a-62, 67; c-62, 69-73. **Robinson** a-68. **Sinnott** a-70. **Tuska** a-69-71.*

WESTERN PICTURE STORIES (1st Western comic)
Comics Magazine Company: Feb, 1937 - No. 4, June, 1937

	GD 2.0	VG 4.0	FN 6.0	VF 8.0	VF/NM 9.0	NM- 9.2
1-Will Eisner-a	176	352	528	1100	1650	2200
2-Will Eisner-a	100	200	300	625	938	1250
3,4: 3-Eisner-a. 4-Caveman Cowboy story	82	164	246	513	769	1025

WESTERN PICTURE STORIES (See Giant Comics Edition #6, 11)

WESTERN ROMANCES (See Target...)

WESTERN ROUGH RIDERS
Gillmor Magazines No. 1,4 (Stanmor Publ.): Nov, 1954 - No. 4, May, 1955

	GD 2.0	VG 4.0	FN 6.0	VF 8.0	VF/NM 9.0	NM- 9.2
1	9	18	27	49	62	75
2-4	7	14	21	35	43	50

WESTERN ROUNDUP (See Dell Giants & Fox Giants)

WESTERN TALES (Formerly Witches...)
Harvey Publications: No. 31, Oct, 1955 - No. 33, July-Sept, 1956

	GD 2.0	VG 4.0	FN 6.0	VF 8.0	VF/NM 9.0	NM- 9.2
31,32-All S&K-a; Davy Crockett app. in each	21	42	63	118	164	210
33-S&K-a; Jim Bowie app.	20	40	60	112	156	200

NOTE: *#32 & 33 contain Boy's Ranch reprints. **Kirby** c-31.*

WESTERN TALES OF BLACK RIDER (Formerly Black Rider; Gunsmoke Western #32 on)
Atlas Comics (CPS): No. 28, May, 1955 - No. 31, Nov, 1955

	GD 2.0	VG 4.0	FN 6.0	VF 8.0	VF/NM 9.0	NM- 9.2
28 (#1): The Spider (a villain) dies	21	42	63	118	164	210
29-31	14	28	42	79	107	135

NOTE: ***Lawrence** a-30. **Maneely** c-28-30. **Severin** a-28. **Shores** c-31.*

WESTERN TEAM-UP
Marvel Comics Group: Nov, 1973 (20¢)

	GD 2.0	VG 4.0	FN 6.0	VF 8.0	VF/NM 9.0	NM- 9.2
1-Origin & 1st app. The Dakota Kid; Rawhide Kid-r; Gunsmoke Kid-r by Jack Davis	4	8	12	22	30	38

WESTERN THRILLERS (My Past Confessions #7 on)
Fox Features Syndicate/M.S. Distr. No. 52: Aug, 1948 - No. 6, June, 1949; No. 52, 1954?

	GD 2.0	VG 4.0	FN 6.0	VF 8.0	VF/NM 9.0	NM- 9.2
1- "Velvet Rose" (Kamenish-a); "Two-Gun Sal", "Striker Sisters" (all women outlaws issue); Brodsky-c	48	96	144	288	432	575
2	22	44	66	127	176	225
3-6: 4,5-Bakerish-a; 5-Butch Cassidy app.	20	40	60	112	156	200
52-(Reprint, M.S. Dist.)-1954? No date given (becomes My Love Secret #53)	8	16	24	43	54	65

WESTERN THRILLERS (Cowboy Action #5 on)
Atlas Comics (ACI): Nov, 1954 - No. 4, Feb, 1955 (All-r/Western Outlaws & Sheriffs)

	GD 2.0	VG 4.0	FN 6.0	VF 8.0	VF/NM 9.0	NM- 9.2
1	16	32	48	89	122	155
2-4	10	20	30	56	73	90

NOTE: ***Heath** c-3. **Maneely** a-1; c-2. **Powell** a-4. **Robinson** a-4. **Romita** c-4. **Tuska** a-2.*

WESTERN TRAILS (Ringo Kid Starring in...)
Atlas Comics (SAI): May, 1957 - No. 2, July, 1957

	GD 2.0	VG 4.0	FN 6.0	VF 8.0	VF/NM 9.0	NM- 9.2
1-Ringo Kid app.; Severin-c	14	28	42	79	107	135
2-Severin-c	9	18	27	52	66	80

NOTE: ***Bolle** a-1, 2. **Maneely** a-1, 2. **Severin** c-1, 2.*

WESTERN TRUE CRIME (Becomes My Confessions)
Fox Features Syndicate: No. 15, Aug, 1948 - No. 6, June, 1949

Wetworks #42 © WSP

What If...? (2nd series) #85 © MAR

What The--?! #8 © MAR

GD 2.0 | VG 4.0 | FN 6.0 | VF 8.0 | VF/NM 9.0 | NM- 9.2

15(#1)-Kamen-a; formerly Zoot #14 (5/48)? 33 66 99 190 270 350
16(#2)-Kamenish-a; headlight panels, violence 24 48 72 135 190 245
3-Kamen-a 25 50 75 147 202 260
4-6: 4-Johnny Craig-a 16 32 48 92 126 160

WESTERN WINNERS (Formerly All-Western Winners; becomes Black Rider #8 on & Romance Tales #7 on?)
Marvel Comics (CDS): No. 5, June, 1949 - No. 7, Dec, 1949

5-Two-Gun Kid, Kid Colt, Black Rider; Shores-c 34 68 102 193 274 355
6-Two-Gun Kid, Black Rider, Heath Kid Colt story; Captain Tootsie by C.C. Beck 29 58 87 164 232 300
7-Randolph Scott Photo-c w/true stories about the West 29 58 87 164 232 300

WEST OF THE PECOS (See Zane Grey, 4-Color #222)

WESTWARD HO, THE WAGONS (Disney)
Dell Publishing Co.: No. 738, Sept, 1956 (Movie)

Four Color 738-Fess Parker photo-c 10 20 30 73 107 140

WETWORKS (See WildC.A.T.S: Covert Action Teams #2)
Image Comics (WildStorm): June, 1994 - No. 43, Aug, 1998 ($1.95/$2.50)

1-"July" on-c; gatefold wraparound-c; Portacio/Williams-c/a 3.00
1-Chicago Comicon edition 6.00
1-(2/98, $4.95) "3-D Edition" w/glasses 5.00
2-4 2.50
2-Alternate Portacio-c, see Deathblow #5 6.00
5-7,9-24: 5-($2.50). 13-Portacio-c. 16,17-Fire From Heaven Pts. 4 & 11 2.50
8 ($1.95)-Newstand, Wildstorm Rising Pt. 7 2.25
8 ($2.50)-Direct Market, Wildstorm Rising Pt. 7 2.50
25-($3.95) 4.00
26-43: 32-Variant-c by Pat Lee & Charest. 39,40-Stormwatch app. 42-Gen 13 app. 2.50
Sourcebook 1 (10/94, $2.50)-Text & illustrations (no comics) 2.50
Voyager Pack (8/97, $3.50)- #32 w/Phantom Guard preview 3.50

WETWORKS/VAMPIRELLA (See Vampirella/Wetworks)
Image Comics (WildStorm Productions): July, 1997 ($2.95, one-shot)

1-Gil Kane-c 3.00

WHACK (Satire)
St. John Publishing Co. (Jubilee Publ.): Oct, 1953 - No. 3, May, 1954

1-(3-D, 25¢)-Kubert-a; Maurer-c; came w/glasses 33 66 99 190 270 350
2,3-Kubert-a in each. 2-Bing Crosby on-c; Mighty Mouse & Steve Canyon parodies. 3-Li'l Orphan Annie parody; Maurer-c 17 34 51 98 134 170

WHACKY (See Wacky)

WHAM COMICS (See Super Spy)
Centaur Publications: Nov, 1940 - No. 2, Dec, 1940

1-The Sparkler, The Phantom Rider, Craig Carter and his Magic Ring, Detecto, Copper Slug, Speed Silvers by Gustavson, Speed Centaur & Jon Linton (s/f) begin 160 320 480 1000 1500 2000
2-Origin Blue Fire & Solarman; The Buzzard app. 108 216 324 675 1013 1350

WHAM-O GIANT COMICS
Wham-O Mfg. Co. : April, 1967 (98¢, newspaper size, one-shot)(Six issue subscription was advertised)

1-Radian & Goody Bumpkin by Wood; 1 pg. Stanley-a; Fine, Tufts-a; flying saucer reports; wraparound-c 8 16 24 53 74 95

WHAT IF? (1st Series) (What If? Featuring... #13 & #?-33)
Marvel Comics Group: Feb, 1977 - No. 47, Oct, 1984; June, 1988 (All 52 pgs.)

1-Brief origin Spider-Man, Fantastic Four 3 6 9 18 23 28
2-Origin The Hulk retold 2 4 6 8 10 12
3-5: 3-Avengers. 4-Invaders. 5-Capt. America 1 2 3 5 7 9
6-10,13,17: 8-Daredevil; Spidey parody. 9-Origins Venus, Marvel Boy, Human Robot, 3-D Man. 13-Conan app.; John Buscema-c/a(p). 17-Ghost Rider & Son of Satan app. 1 2 3 5 6 8
11,12,14-16: 11-Marvel Bullpen as F.F. 6.00
18-26,29: 18-Dr. Strange. 19-Spider-Man. 22-Origin Dr. Doom retold 5.00
27-X-Men app.; Miller-c 2 4 6 11 14 18
28-Daredevil by Miller; Ghost Rider app. 2 4 6 8 10 12
30-"What If...Spider-Man's Clone Had Lived?" 1 2 3 5 6 8
31-Begin $1.00-c; featuring Wolverine & the Hulk; X-Men app.; death of Hulk, Wolverine & Magneto 2 4 6 12 16 20
32-34,36-47: 32,36-Byrne-a. 34-Marvel crew each draw themselves. 37-Old X-Men & Silver Surfer app. 39-Thor battles Conan 4.00
35-What if Elektra had lived?; Miller/Austin-a. 5.00

Special 1 ($1.50, 6/88)-Iron Man, F.F., Thor app. 3.00

NOTE: ***Austin*** *a-27p, 32i, 34, 35i; c-35i, 36i.* ***J. Buscema*** *a-13p, 15p; c-10, 13p, 23p.* ***Byrne*** *a-32i, 36; c-36p.* ***Colan*** *a-21p; c-17p, 18p, 21p.* ***Ditko*** *a-35, Special 1.* ***Golden*** *c-29, 40-42.* ***Guice*** *a-40p.* ***Gil Kane*** *a-3p, 24p; c(p)-2-4, 7, 8.* ***Kirby*** *a-11p; c-9p, 11p.* ***Layton*** *a-32i, 33i; c-30, 32p, 33i, 34.* ***Mignola*** *c-39i.* ***Miller*** *a-28p, 32i, 34(1), 35p; c-27, 28p.* ***Mooney*** *a-8i, 30i.* ***Perez*** *a-15p.* ***Robbins*** *a-4p.* ***Sienkiewicz*** *c-43-46.* ***Simonson*** *a-15p, 32i.* ***Starlin*** *a-32i.* ***Stevens*** *a-8, 16i(part).* ***Sutton*** *a-2i, 18p, 28.* ***Tuska*** *a-5p.* ***Weiss*** *a-37p.*

WHAT IF...? (2nd Series)
Marvel Comics: V2#1, July, 1989 - No. 114, Nov, 1998 ($1.25/$1.50)

V2#1-...The Avengers Had Lost the Evol. War 4.00
2-5: 2-Daredevil, Punisher app. 3.00
6-X-Men app. 4.00
7-Wolverine app.; Liefeld-c/a(1st on Wolvie?) 5.00
8,10,11,13-15,17-30: 10-Punisher app. 11-Fantastic Four app.; McFarlane-c(i).13-Prof. X; Jim Lee-c. 14-Capt. Marvel; Lim/Austin-c.15-F.F.; Capullo-c/a(p). 17-Spider-Man/Kraven. 18-F.F. 19-Vision. 20,21-Spider-Man. 22-Silver Surfer by Lim/Austin-c/a 23-X-Men. 24-Wolverine; Punisher app. 25-(52 pgs.)-Wolverine app. 26-Punisher app. 27-Namor/F.F. 28,29-Capt. America. 29-Swipes cover to Avengers #4. 30-(52 pgs.)-F.F. 3.00
9,12-X-Men 3.50
16-Wolverine battles Conan; Red Sonja app.; X-Men cameo 4.00
31-104: 31-Cosmic Spider-Man & Venom app.; Hobgoblin cameo. 32,33-Phoenix; X-Men app. 35-Fantastic Five (w/Spidey). 36-Avengers vs. Guardians of the Galaxy. 37-Wolverine; Thibert-c(i). 38-Thor; Rogers-p(part). 40-Storm; X-Men app. 41-(52 pgs.)-Avengers vs. Galactus. 42-Spider-Man. 43-Wolverine. 44-Venom/Punisher. 45-Ghost Rider. 46-Cable. 47-Magneto. 49-Infinity Gauntlet w/Silver Surfer & Thanos. 50-(52 pgs.)-Foil embossed-c; "What If Hulk Had Killed Wolverine" 52-Dr. Doom. 54-Death's Head. 57-Punisher as Shield. 58-"What if Punisher Had Killed Spider-Man" w/cover similar to Amazing S-M #129. 59-...Wolverine led Alpha Flight. 60-X-Men Wedding Album. 61-bound-in card sheet. 61,86,88-Spider-Man. 74,77,81,84,85-X-Men. 76-Last app. Watcher in title. 78-Bisley-c. 80-Hulk. 87-Sabretooth. 89-Fantastic Four. 90-Cyclops & Havok. 91-The Hulk. 93-Wolverine. 94-Juggernaut. 95-Ghost Rider. 97-Black Knight. 100-($2.99, double-sized) Gambit and Rogue, Fantastic Four 3.00
105-Spider-Girl debut; Sienkiewicz-a 2 4 6 12 16 20
106-114: 106-Gambit. 108-Avengers. 111-Wolverine. 114-Secret Wars 2.25
#(-1) Flashback (7/97) 3.00

'WHAT'S NEW? - THE COLLECTED ADVENTURES OF PHIL & DIXIE'
Palliard Press: Oct, 1991 - No. 2, 1991 ($5.95, mostly color, sq.-bound, 52 pgs.)

1,2-By Phil Foglio 6.00

WHAT THE- -?!
Marvel Comics: Aug, 1988 - No. 26, 1993 ($1.25/$1.50/$2.50, semi-annual #5 on)

1-All contain parodies 3.00
2-24: 3-X-Men parody; Todd McFarlane-a. 5-Punisher/Wolverine parody; Jim Lee-a. 6-Punisher, Wolverine, Alpha Flight. 9-Wolverine. 16-EC back-c parody. 17-Wolverine/Punisher parody. 18-Star Trek parody w/Wolverine. 19-Punisher, Wolverine, Ghost Rider. 21-Weapon X parody. 22-Punisher/Wolverine parody 2.25
25-Summer Special 1 (1993, $2.50)-X-Men parody 2.50
26-Fall Special ($2.50, 68 pgs.)-Spider-Ham 2099-c/story; origin Silver Surfer; Hulk & Doomsday parody; indica reads "Winter Special." 2.50

NOTE: ***Austin*** *a-6i.* ***Byrne*** *a-2, 6, 10; c-2, 6-8, 10, 12, 13.* ***Golden*** *a-22.* ***Dale Keown*** *a-8p(8 pgs.).* ***McFarlane*** *a-3.* ***Rogers*** *c-15i, 16p.* ***Severin*** *a-2.* ***Staton*** *a-21p.* ***Williamson*** *a-2i.*

WHEE COMICS (Also see Gay, Smile & Tickle Comics)
Modern Store Publications: 1955 (7¢, 5x7-1/4", 52 pgs.)

1-Funny animal 6 12 18 28 34 40

WHEEDIES (See Panic #11 -EC Comics)

WHEELIE AND THE CHOPPER BUNCH (TV)
Charlton Comics: July, 1975 - No. 7, July, 1976 (Hanna-Barbera)

1-3: 1-Byrne text illo (see Nightmare for 1st art); Staton-a. 2-Byrne-a. 2,3-Mike Zeck text illos. 3-Staton-a; Byrne-c/a 3 6 9 18 23 28
4-7-Staton-a 2 4 6 11 14 18

WHEN KNIGHTHOOD WAS IN FLOWER (See The Sword & the Rose, 4-Color #505, 682)

WHEN SCHOOL IS OUT (See Wisco in Promotional Comics section)

WHERE CREATURES ROAM
Marvel Comics Group: July, 1970 - No. 8, Sept, 1971

1-Kirby/Ayers-c/a(r) 3 7 10 21 28 35
2-8-Kirby-c/a(r) 3 6 9 16 20 24

NOTE: ***Ditko*** *r-1-6, 7.* ***Heck*** *r-2, 5. All contain pre super-hero reprints.*

WHERE IN THE WORLD IS CARMEN SANDIEGO (TV)
DC Comics: June, 1996 - No. 4, Dec, 1996 ($1.75)

1-4: Adaptation of TV show 2.25

WHERE MONSTERS DWELL

Where Monsters Dwell #10 © MAR

White Princess of the Jungle #3 © AVON

Whiz Comics #22 © FAW

GD VG FN VF VF/NM NM-
2.0 4.0 6.0 8.0 9.0 9.2

Marvel Comics Group: Jan, 1970 - No. 38, Oct, 1975

1-Kirby/Ditko-r; all contain pre super-hero-r 4 8 12 22 30 38
2-10: 4-Crandall-a(r) 3 6 9 16 20 24
11,13-20: 11-Last 15¢ issue. 18,20-Starlin-c 2 4 6 11 14 18
12-Giant issue (52 pgs.) 3 6 9 18 24 30
21-37 2 4 6 10 12 15
38-Williamson-r/World of Suspense #3 2 4 6 11 14 18

NOTE: ***Colan** r-12. **Ditko** a(r)-4, 6, 8, 10, 12, 17-19, 23-25, 37. **Kirby** r-1-3, 5-16, 18-27, 30-32, 34-36, 38; c-12? **Reinman** a-3r, 4r, 12r. **Severin** c-15.*

WHERE'S HUDDLES? (TV) (See Fun-In #9)
Gold Key: Jan, 1971 - No. 3, Dec, 1971 (Hanna-Barbera)

1 3 7 10 21 28 35
2,3: 3-r/most #1 2 4 6 11 14 18

WHIP WILSON (Movie star) (Formerly Rex Hart; Gunhawk #12 on; see Western Hearts, Western Life Romances, Western Love)
Marvel Comics: No. 9, April, 1950 - No. 11, Sept, 1950 (#9,10: 52 pgs.)

9-Photo-c; Whip Wilson & his horse Bullet begin; origin Bullet; issue #23 listed on splash page; cover changed to #9 60 120 180 375 563 750
10,11: Both have photo-c. 11-36 pgs. 37 74 111 212 301 390
I.W. Reprint #1(1964)-Kinstler-c; r-Marvel #11 3 6 9 19 25 32

WHIRLWIND COMICS (Also see Cyclone Comics)
Nita Publication: June, 1940 - No. 3, Sept, 1940

1-Origin & 1st app. Cyclone; Cyclone-c 192 384 576 1200 1800 2400
2,3: Cyclone-c 102 204 306 638 957 1275

WHIRLYBIRDS (TV)
Dell Publishing Co.: No. 1124, Aug, 1960 - No. 1216, Oct-Dec, 1961

Four Color 1124 (#1)-Photo-c 10 20 30 67 96 125
Four Color 1216-Photo-c 9 18 27 63 89 115

WHISKEY DICKEL, INTERNATIONAL COWGIRL
Image Comics: Aug, 2003 ($12.95, softcover, B&W)

nn-Mark Ricketts-s/Mike Hawthorne-a; pin-up by various incl. Oeming, Thompson, Mack 13.00

WHISPER (Female Ninja)
Capital Comics: Dec, 1983 - No. 2, 1984 ($1.75, Baxter paper)

1,2: 1-Origin; Golden-c, Special (11/85, $2.50) 2.50

WHISPER (Vol. 2)
First Comics: Jun, 1986 - No. 37, June, 1990 ($1.25/$1.75/$1.95)

1-37 2.25

WHITE CHIEF OF THE PAWNEE INDIANS
Avon Periodicals: 1951

nn-Kit West app.; Kinstler-c 17 34 51 95 130 165

WHITE EAGLE INDIAN CHIEF (See Indian Chief)

WHITE FANG
Disney Comics: 1990 ($5.95, 68 pgs.)

nn-Graphic novel adapting new Disney movie 6.00

WHITE INDIAN
Magazine Enterprises: No. 11, July, 1953 - No. 15, 1954

11(A-1 94), 12(A-1 101), 13(A-1 104)-Frazetta-r(Dan Brand) in all from Durango Kid. 11-Powell-c 24 48 72 135 190 245
14(A-1 117), 15(A-1 135)-Check-a; Torres-a-#15 12 24 36 71 96 120

NOTE: *#11 contains reprints from Durango Kid #1-4; #12 from #5, 9, 10, 11; #13 from #7, 12, 13, 16. #14 & 15 contain all new stories.*

WHITEOUT (Also see Queen & Country)
Oni Press: July, 1998 - No. 4, Nov, 1998 ($2.95, B&W, limited series)

1-4: 1-Matt Wagner-c. 2-Mignola-c. 3-Gibbons-c 3.00
TPB (5/99, $10.95) r/#1-4; Miller-c 11.00

WHITEOUT: MELT
Oni Press: Sept, 1999 - No. 4, Feb, 2000 ($2.95, B&W, limited series)

1-4-Greg Rucka-s/Steve Lieber-a 3.00

WHITE PRINCESS OF THE JUNGLE (Also see Jungle Adventures & Top Jungle Comics)
Avon Periodicals: July, 1951 - No. 5, Nov, 1952

1-Origin of White Princess (Taanda) & Capt'n Courage (r); Kinstler-c 55 110 165 330 495 660
2-Reprints origin of Malu, Slave Girl Princess from Avon's Slave Girl Comics #1 w/Malu changed to Zora; Kinstler-c/a(2) 40 80 120 240 345 450
3-Origin Blue Gorilla; Kinstler-c/a 37 74 111 212 301 390

GD VG FN VF VF/NM NM-
2.0 4.0 6.0 8.0 9.0 9.2

4-Jack Barnum, White Hunter app.; r/Sheena #9 32 64 96 180 255 330
5-Blue Gorilla by McCann?; Kinstler inside-c; Fawcette/Alascia-a(3) 34 68 102 193 274 355

WHITE RIDER AND SUPER HORSE (Formerly Humdinger V2#2; Indian Warriors #7 on; also see Blue Bolt #1, 4Most & Western Crime Cases)
Novelty-Star Publications/Accepted Publ.: No. 4, 9/50 - No. 6, 3/51

4-6-Adapts "The Last of the Mohicans". 4(#1)-(9/50)-Says #11 on inside 17 34 51 98 134 170
Accepted Reprint #5(r/#5),6 (nd); L.B. Cole-c 9 18 27 52 66 80

NOTE: *All have **L. B. Cole** covers.*

WHITE WILDERNESS (Disney)
Dell Publishing Co.: No. 943, Oct, 1958

Four Color 943-Movie 7 14 21 51 71 90

WHITMAN COMIC BOOK, A
Whitman Publishing Co.: Sept., 1962 (136 pgs.; 7-3/4x5-3/4; hardcover) (B&W)

1-3,5,7: 1-Yogi Bear. 2-Huckleberry Hound. 3-Mr. Jinks and Pixie & Dixie. 5-Augie Doggie & Loopy de Loop. 7-Bugs Bunny-r from #47,51,53,54 & 55 7 14 21 51 71 90
4,6: 4-The Flintstones. 6-Snooper & Blabber Fearless Detectives/Quick Draw McGraw of the Wild West 8 16 24 55 78 100
8-Donald Duck-reprints most of WDC&S #209-213. Includes 5 Barks stories, 1 complete Mickey Mouse serial by Paul Murry & 1 Mickey Mouse serial missing the 1st episode 9 18 27 63 89 115

NOTE: *Hanna-Barbera #1-6(TV), reprints of British tabloid comics. Dell reprints-#7,8.*

WHIZ COMICS (Formerly Flash & Thrill Comics #1)(See 5 Cent Comics)
Fawcett Publications: No. 2, Feb, 1940 - No. 155, June, 1953

1-(nn on cover, #2 inside)-Origin & 1st newsstand app. Captain Marvel (formerly Captain Thunder) by C. C. Beck (created by Bill Parker), Spy Smasher, Golden Arrow, Ibis the Invincible, Dan Dare, Scoop Smith, Sivana, & Lance O'Casey begin 7000 14,000 21,000 40,000 62,000 84,000
(The only Mint copy sold in 1995 for $176,000 cash)

1-Reprint, oversize 13-1/2x10". **WARNING:** This comic is an exact duplicate reprint (except for dropping "Gangway for Captain Marvel" from-c) of the original except for its size. DC published it in 1974 with a second cover titling it as a Famous First Edition. There have been many reported cases of the outer cover being removed and the interior sold as the original edition. The reprint with the new outer cover removed is practically worthless. See Famous First Edition for value.

2-(3/40, nn on cover, #3 inside); cover to Flash #1 redrawn, pg. 12, panel 4; Spy Smasher reveals I.D. to Eve 448 896 1344 3136 4818 6500
3-(4/40, #3 on-c, #4 inside)-1st app. Beautia 315 630 945 2048 3149 4250
4-(5/40, #4 on cover, #5 inside)-Brief origin Capt. Marvel retold 288 576 864 1800 2700 3600
5-Captain Marvel wears button-down flap on splash page only 240 480 720 1500 2250 3000
6-10: 7-Dr. Voodoo begins (by Raboy-#9-22) 180 360 540 1125 1688 2250
11-14: 12-Capt. Marvel does not wear cape 124 248 372 775 1163 1550
15-Origin Sivana; Dr. Voodoo by Raboy 134 268 402 838 1257 1675
16-18-Spy Smasher battles Captain Marvel 128 256 384 800 1200 1600
19,20 85 170 255 531 796 1060
21-(9/41)-Origin & 1st cover app. Lt. Marvels, the 1st team in Fawcett comics. In this issue, Capt. Death similar to Ditko's later Dr. Strange 90 180 270 563 844 1125
22-24: 23-Only Dr. Voodoo by Tuska 69 138 207 431 646 860
25-(12/41)-Captain Nazi jumps from Master Comics #21 to take on Capt. Marvel solo after being beaten by Capt. Marvel/Bulletman team, causing the creation of Capt. Marvel Jr.; 1st app./origin of Capt. Marvel Jr. (part II of trilogy origin by CC. Beck & Mac Raboy); Captain Marvel sends Jr. back to Master #22 to aid Bulletman against Capt. Nazi; origin Old Shazam in text 538 1076 1614 3766 5783 7800
26-30 61 122 183 381 573 765
31,32: 32-1st app. The Trolls; Hitler/Mussolini satire by Beck 54 108 162 324 487 650
33-Spy Smasher, Captain Marvel x-over on cover and inside 61 122 183 381 573 765
34,36-40: 37-The Trolls app. by Swayze 40 80 120 240 345 450
35-Captain Marvel & Spy Smasher-c 50 100 150 300 450 600
41-50: 43-Spy Smasher, Ibis, Golden Arrow x-over in Capt. Marvel. 44-Flag-c. 47-Origin recap (1 pg.) 36 72 108 204 290 375
51-60: 52-Capt. Marvel x-over in Ibis. 57-Spy Smasher, Golden Arrow, Ibis cameo 30 60 90 170 240 310
61-70 28 56 84 157 221 285
71,77-80 25 50 75 147 202 260
72-76-Two Captain Marvel stories in each; 76-Spy Smasher becomes Crime Smasher 26 52 78 147 206 265
81-99: 86-Captain Marvel battles Sivana Family; robot-c. 91-Infinity-c

Who's Who: The Definitive Directory of the DC Universe #2 © DC

Wilbur Comics #8 © AP

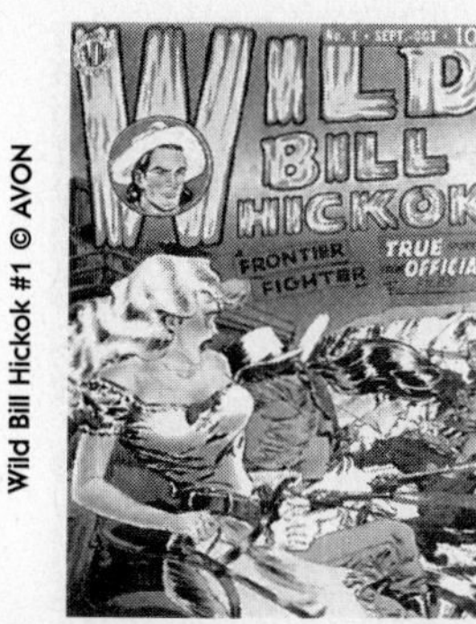

Wild Bill Hickok #1 © AVON

GD VG FN VF VF/NM NM-
2.0 4.0 6.0 8.0 9.0 9.2

100-(8/48)-Anniversary issue 25 50 75 147 202 260
101-106: 102-Commando Yank app. 106-Bulletman app. 29 58 87 164 232 300
24 48 72 138 194 250
107-149: 107-Capitol Building photo-c. 108-Brooklyn Bridge photo-c. 112-Photo-c. 139-Infinity-c. 140-Flag-c. 142-Used in **POP**, pg. 89
24 48 72 138 194 250
150-152-(Low dist.) 26 52 78 150 210 270
153-155-(Scarce):154,155-1st/2nd Dr. Death stories 34 68 102 193 274 355

NOTE: ***C.C. Beck*** *Captain Marvel-No. 25(part).* ***Krigstein*** *Golden Arrow-No. 75, 78, 91, 95, 96, 98-100.* ***Mac Raboy*** *Dr. Voodoo-No. 9-22. Captain Marvel-No. 25(part).* ***M.Swayze*** *a-37, 38, 59; c-38.* ***Schaffenberger*** *c-138-155(most).* ***Wolverton*** *1/2 pg. "Culture Corner"-No. 65-67, 68(2 1/2 pgs), 70-85, 87-96, 98-100, 102-109, 112-121, 123, 125, 126, 128-131, 133, 134, 136, 142, 143, 146.*

WHIZ KIDS (Also see Big Bang Comics)
Image Comics: Apr, 2003 ($4.95, B&W, one-shot)
1-Galahad, Cyclone, Thunder Girl and Moray app.; Jeff Austin-a 5.00

WHOA, NELLIE (Also see Love & Rockets)
Fantagraphics Books: July, 1996 - No. 3, Sept, 1996 ($2.95, B&W, lim. series)
1-3: Jamie Hernandez-c/a/scripts 3.00

WHODUNIT
D.S. Publishing Co.: Aug-Sept, 1948 - No. 3, Dec-Jan, 1948-49 (#1,2: 52 pgs.)
1-Baker-a (7 pgs.) 26 52 78 147 206 265
2,3-Detective mysteries 13 26 39 74 100 125

WHODUNNIT?
Eclipse Comics: June, 1986 - No. 3, Apr, 1987 ($2.00, limited series)
1-3: Spiegle-a. 2-Gulacy-c 2.25

WHO FRAMED ROGER RABBIT (See Marvel Graphic Novel)

WHO IS NEXT?
Standard Comics: No. 5, Jan, 1953
5-Toth, Sekowsky, Andru-a; crime stories 21 42 63 118 164 210

WHO IS THE CROOKED MAN?
Crusade: Sept, 1996 ($3.50, B&W, 40 pgs.)
1-Intro The Martyr, Scarlet 7 & Garrison 3.50

WHO'S MINDING THE MINT? (See Movie Classics)

WHO'S WHO IN STAR TREK
DC Comics: Mar, 1987 - #2, Apr, 1987 ($1.50, limited series)
1,2 6.00
NOTE: ***Byrne*** *a-1, 2.* ***Chaykin*** *c-1, 2.* ***Morrow*** *a-1, 2.* ***McFarlane*** *a-2.* ***Perez*** *a-1, 2.* ***Sutton*** *a-1, 2.*

WHO'S WHO IN THE LEGION OF SUPER-HEROES
DC Comics: Apr, 1987 - No. 7, Nov, 1988 ($1.25, limited series)
1-7 4.00

WHO'S WHO: THE DEFINITIVE DIRECTORY OF THE DC UNIVERSE
DC Comics: Mar, 1985 - No. 26, Apr, 1987 (Maxi-series, no ads)
1-DC heroes from A-Z 4.00
2-26: All have 1-2 pgs-a by most DC artists 4.00
NOTE: ***Art Adams*** *a-4, 11, 18, 20.* ***Anderson*** *a-1-5, 7-12, 14, 15, 19, 21, 23-25.* ***Aparo*** *a-2, 3, 9, 10, 12, 13, 14, 15, 17, 18, 21, 23.* ***Byrne*** *a-4, 7, 14, 16, 18i, 19, 22i, 24; c-22.* ***Cowan*** *a-3-5, 8, 10-13, 16-18, 22-25.* ***Ditko*** *a-19-22.* ***Evans*** *a-20.* ***Giffen*** *a-1, 3,-6, 8, 13, 15, 17, 18, 23.* ***Grell*** *a-6, 9, 14, 20, 23, 25, 26.* ***Infantino*** *a-1-10, 12, 15, 17-22, 24, 25.* ***Kaluta*** *a-14, 21.* ***Gil Kane*** *a-1-11, 13, 14, 16, 19, 21-23, 25.* ***Kirby*** *a-2-6, 8-18, 20, 22, 25.* ***Kubert*** *a-2, 3, 7-11, 19, 20, 25.* ***Erik Larsen*** *a-24.* ***McFarlane*** *a-10-12, 17, 19, 25, 26.* ***Morrow*** *a-4, 7, 25, 26.* ***Orlando*** *a-1, 4, 10, 11, 21i.* ***Perez*** *a-1-5, 8-19, 22-26; c-1-4, 13-18.* ***Rogers*** *a-1, 2, 5-7, 11, 12, 15, 24.* ***Starlin*** *a-13, 14, 16.* ***Stevens*** *a-4, 7, 18.*

WHO'S WHO UPDATE '87
DC Comics: Aug, 1987 - No. 5, Dec, 1987 ($1.25, limited series)
1-5: Contains art by most DC artists 3.00
NOTE: ***Giffen*** *a-1.* ***McFarlane*** *a-1-4; c-4.* ***Perez*** *a-1-4.*

WHO'S WHO UPDATE '88
DC Comics: Aug, 1988 - No. 4, Nov, 1988 ($1.25, limited series)
1-4: Contains art by most DC artists 3.00
NOTE: ***Giffen*** *a-1.* ***Erik Larsen*** *a-1.*

WICKED, THE
Avalon Studios: Dec, 1999 - No. 7, Aug, 2000 ($2.95)
Preview-(7/99, $5.00, B&W) 5.00
1-7-Anacleto-c/Martinez-a 3.00
...: Medusa's Tale (11/00, $3.95, one shot) story plus pin-up gallery 4.00
...: Vol. 1: Omnibus (2003, $19.95) r/#0-8; Drew-c 20.00

WILBUR COMICS (Teen-age) (Also see Laugh Comics, Laugh Comix, Liberty Comics #10 & Zip Comics)
MLJ Magazines/Archie Publ. No. 8, Spring, 1946 on: Sum', 1944 - No. 87, 11/59; No. 88, 9/63; No. 89, 10/64; No. 90, 10/65 (No. 1-46: 52 pgs.) (#1-11 are quarterly)
1 50 100 150 300 450 600
2(Fall, 1944) 29 58 87 164 232 300
3,4(Wint, '44-45; Spr, '45) 21 42 63 118 164 210
5-1st app. Katy Keene (Sum, '45) & begin series; Wilbur story same as Archie story in Archie #1 except Wilbur replaces Archie 84 168 252 525 788 1050
6-10: 10-(Fall, 1946) 24 48 72 135 190 245
11-20 15 30 45 84 115 145
21-30: 30-(4/50) 10 20 30 56 73 90
31-50 8 16 24 43 54 65
51-70 7 14 21 37 46 55
71-90: 88-Last 10¢ issue (9/63) 4 8 12 27 36 45
NOTE: *Katy Keene in No. 5-56, 58-69.* ***Al Fagaly*** *c-6-9, 12-24 at least.* ***Vigoda*** *c-2.*

WILD
Atlas Comics (IPC): Feb, 1954 - No. 5, Aug, 1954
1 27 54 81 155 218 280
2 16 32 48 92 126 160
3-5 14 28 42 79 107 135
NOTE: ***Berg*** *a-5; c-4.* ***Burgos*** *c-3.* ***Colan*** *a-4.* ***Everett*** *a-1-3.* ***Heath*** *a-2, 3, 5.* ***Maneely*** *a-1-3, 5; c-1, 5.* ***Post*** *a-2, 5.* ***Ed Win*** *a-1, 3.*

WILD (This Magazine Is...) (Satire)
Dell Publishing Co.: Jan, 1968 - No. 3, 1968 (Magazine, 52 pgs.)
1-3 2 4 6 14 18 22

WILD ANIMALS
Pacific Comics: Dec, 1982 ($1.00, one-shot, direct sales)
1-Funny animal; Sergio Aragones-a; Shaw-c/a 4.00

WILD BILL ELLIOTT (Also see Western Roundup under Dell Giants)
Dell Publishing Co.: No. 278, 5/50 - No. 643, 7/55 (No #11,12) (All photo-c)
Four Color 278(#1, 52pgs.)-Titled "Bill Elliott"; Bill & his horse Stormy begin; photo front/back-c begin 14 28 42 102 149 195
2 (11/50), 3 (52 pgs.) 8 16 24 58 82 105
4-10(10-12/52) 6 12 18 43 59 75
Four Color 472(6/53),520(12/53)-Last photo back-c 5 10 15 36 48 60
13(4-6/54) - 17(4-6/55) 5 10 15 33 44 55
Four Color 643 (7/55) 4 8 12 29 40 50

WILD BILL HICKOK (Also see Blazing Sixguns)
Avon Periodicals: Sept-Oct, 1949 - No. 28, May-June, 1956
1-Ingels-c 24 48 72 138 194 250
2-Painted-c; Kit West app. 12 24 36 71 96 120
3-5-Painted-c (4-Cover by Howard Winfield) 9 18 27 52 66 80
6-10,12: 8-10-Painted-c. 12-Kinsler-c? 9 18 27 52 66 80
11,13,14-Kinstler-c/a (#11-c & inside-f/c art only) 10 20 30 56 73 90
15,17,18,20: 18-Kit West story. 20-Kit West by Larsen
8 16 24 43 54 65
16-Kamen-a; r-3 stories/King of the Badmen of Deadwood
8 16 24 46 58 70
19-Meskin-a 8 16 24 43 54 65
21-Reprints 2 stories/Chief Crazy Horse 8 16 24 40 50 60
22-McCann-a?; r/Sheriff Bob Dixon's... 8 16 24 40 50 60
23-27: 23-Kinstler-c. 24-27-Kinstler-c/a(r) (24,25-r?) 8 16 24 40 50 60
28-Kinstler-c/a (new); r-/Last of the Comanches 8 16 24 43 54 65
I.W. Reprint #1-r/#2; Kinstler-c 2 4 6 10 13 16
Super Reprint #10-12: 10-r/#18. 11-r/#?. 12-r/#8 2 4 6 10 13 16
NOTE: *#23, 25 contain numerous editing deletions in both art and script due to code.* ***Kinstler*** *c-6, 7, 11-14, 17, 18, 20-22, 24-28.* ***Howard Larsen*** *a-1, 2, 4, 5, 6(3), 7-9, 11, 12, 17, 18, 20-24, 26.* ***Meskin*** *a-7.* ***Reinman*** *a-6, 17.*

WILD BILL HICKOK AND JINGLES (TV)(Formerly Cowboy Western) (Also see Blue Bird)
Charlton Comics: No. 68, Aug, 1958 - No. 75, Dec, 1959
68,69-Williamson-a (all are 10¢ issues) 11 22 33 63 84 105
70-Two pgs. Williamson-a 8 16 24 43 54 65
71-75 (#76, exist?) 6 12 18 28 34 40

WILD BILL PECOS WESTERN (Also see The Westerner)
AC Comics: 1989 ($3.50, 1/2 color/1/2 B&W, 52 pgs.)
1-Syd Shores-c/a(r)/Westerner; photo back-c 4.00

WILD BOY OF THE CONGO (Also see Approved Comics)
Ziff-Davis No. 10-12,4-8/St. John No. 9,11 on: No. 10, 2-3/51 - No. 12, 8-9/51; No. 4, 10-11/51 - No. 9, 10/53; No. 11-#15,6/55 (No #10, 1953)
10(#1)(2-3/51)-Origin; bondage-c by Saunders (painted); used in **SOTI**,

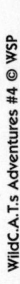

WildC.A.T.s Adventures #4 © WSP

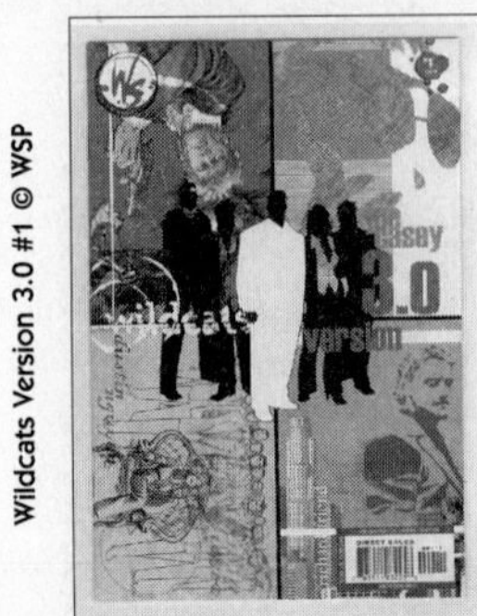
Wildcats Version 3.0 #1 © WSP

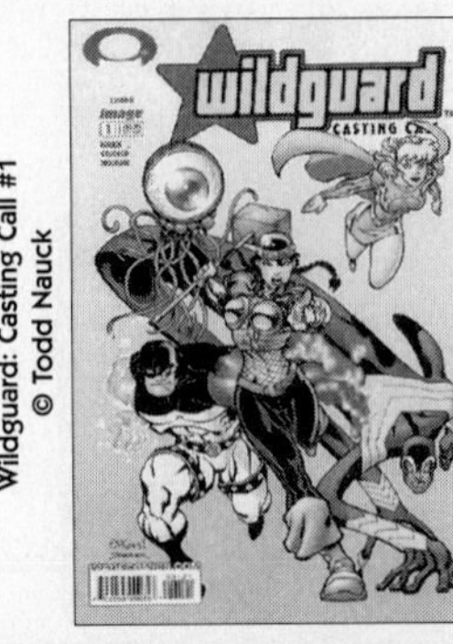
Wildguard: Casting Call #1 © Todd Nauck

	GD 2.0	VG 4.0	FN 6.0	VF 8.0	VF/NM 9.0	NM- 9.2
pg. 189; painted-c begin, end #9	24	48	72	138	194	250
11(4-5/51),12(8-9/51)-Norman Saunders painted-c	13	26	39	74	100	125
4(10-11/51)-Saunders painted bondage-c	13	26	39	74	100	125
5(Winter,'51)-Saunders painted-c	11	22	33	63	84	105
6,8,9(10/53): 6-Saunders-c. 6-9-Painted-c	11	22	33	63	84	105
7(8-9/52)-Kinstler-a	13	26	39	74	100	125
11-13-Baker-c. 11-r/#7 w/new Baker-c; Kinstler-a (2 pgs.)	14	28	42	79	107	135
14(4/55)-Baker-c; r-#12('51)	14	28	42	79	107	135
15(6/55)	10	20	30	56	73	90

WILDCAT (See Sensation Comics #1)

WILDC.A.T.S ADVENTURES (TV cartoon)
Image Comics (WildStorm): Sept, 1994 - No. 10, June, 1995 ($1.95/$2.50)

1-10 — 2.50
Sourcebook 1 (1/95, $2.95) — 3.00

WILDC.A.T.S: COVERT ACTION TEAMS
Image Comics (WildStorm Productions): Aug, 1992 - No. 4, Mar, 1993; No. 5, Nov, 1993 - No. 50, June, 1998 ($1.95/$2.50)

1-1st app; Jim Lee/Williams-c/a & Lee scripts begin; contains 2 trading cards (Two diff versions of cards inside); 1st WildStorm Productions title — 4.50
1-All gold foil signed edition — 12.00
1-All gold foil unsigned edition — 8.00
1-Newsstand edition w/o cards — 3.00
1-"3-D Special"(8/97, $4.95) w/3-D glasses; variant-c by Jim Lee. — 5.00
2-($2.50)-Prism foil stamped-c; contains coupon for Image Comics #0 & 4 pg. preview to Portacio's Wetworks (back-up) — 4.50
2-With coupon missing — 2.25
2-Direct sale misprint w/o foil-c — 3.00
2-Newsstand ed., no prism or coupon — 2.25
3-Lee/Liefeld-c (1/93-c, 12/92 inside) — 3.50
4-($2.50)-Polybagged w/Topps trading card; 1st app. Tribe by Johnson & Stroman; Youngblood cameo — 3.50
4-Variant w/red card — 6.00
5-7-Jim Lee/Williams-c/a; Lee script — 3.00
8-X-Men's Jean Grey & Scott Summers cameos — 4.00
9-12: 10-1st app. Huntsman & Soldier; Claremont scripts begin, ends #13. 11-1st app. Savant, Tapestry & Mr. Majestic. — 3.00
11-Alternate Portacio-c, see Deathblow #5 — 5.00
13-19,21-24: 15-James Robinson scripts begin, ends #20. 15,16-Black Razor story. 21-Alan Moore scripts begin, end #34; intro Tao & Ladytron; new WildC.A.T.S team forms (Mr. Majestic, Savant, Condition Red (Max Cash), Tao & Ladytron). 22-Maguire-a — 3.00
20-($2.50)-Direct Market, WildStorm Rising Pt. 2 w/bound-in card — 3.00
20-($1.95)-Newsstand, WildStorm Rising Part 2 — 2.25
25-($4.95)-Alan Moore script; wraparound foil-c. — 5.00
26-49: 29-(5/96)-Fire From Heaven Pt 7; reads Apr on-c. 30-(6/96)-Fire From Heaven Pt. 13; Spartan revealed to have transplanted personality of John Colt (from Team One: WildC.A.T.S). 31-(9/96)-Grifter rejoins team; Ladytron dies — 2.50
40-($3.50)Voyager Pack bagged w/Divine Right preview — 6.00
50-($3.50) Stories by Robinson/Lee, Choi & Peterson/Benes, and Moore/Charest; Charest sketchbook; Lee wraparound-c — 4.00
50-Chromium cover — 6.00
Annual 1 (2/98, $2.95) Robinson-s — 3.00
Compendium (1993, $9.95)-r/#1-4; bagged w/#0 — 10.00
Sourcebook 1 (9/93, $2.50)-Foil embossed-c — 2.50
Sourcebook 1-($1.95)-Newsstand ed. w/o foil embossed-c — 2.25
Sourcebook 2 (11/94, $2.50)-wraparound-c — 2.50
Special 1 (11/93, $3.50, 52 pgs.)-1st Travis Charest WildC.A.T.S-a — 3.50
...A Gathering of Eagles (5/97, $9.95, TPB) r/#10-12 — 10.00
...Gang War ('98, $16.95, TPB) r/#28-34 — 17.00
...Homecoming (8/98, $19.95, TPB) r/#21-27 — 20.00

WILDCATS
DC Comics (WildStorm): Mar, 1999 - No. 28, Dec, 2001 ($2.50)

1-Charest-a; six covers by Lee, Adams, Bisley, Campbell, Madureira and Ramos; Lobdell-s — 3.00
1-($6.95) DF Edition; variant cover by Ramos — 7.00
2-28: 2-Voodoo cover. 3-Bachalo variant-c. 5-Hitch-a/variant-c. 7-Meglia-a. 8-Phillips-a begins. 17-J.G. Jones-c. 18,19-Jim Lee-c. 20,21-Dillon-a — 2.50
Annual 2000 (12/00, $3.50) Bermejo-a; Devil's Night x-over — 3.50
...: Battery Park ('03, $17.95, TPB) r/#20-28; Phillips-c — 18.00
... Ladytron (10/00, $5.95) Origin; Casey-s/Canete-a — 6.00
... Mosaic (2/00, $3.95) Tuska-a (10 pg. back-up story) — 4.00
...: Serial Boxes ('01, $14.95, TPB) r/#14-19; Phillips-c — 15.00
...: Street Smart ('00, $24.95, HC) r/#1-6; Charest-c — 25.00
...: Street Smart ('02, $14.95, SC) r/#1-6; Charest-c — 15.00
...: Vicious Circles ('00, $14.95, TPB) r/#8-13; Phillips-c — 15.00

WILDC.A.T.S/ ALIENS
Image Comics/Dark Horse: Aug, 1998 ($4.95, one-shot)

	GD 2.0	VG 4.0	FN 6.0	VF 8.0	VF/NM 9.0	NM- 9.2
1-Ellis-s/Sprouse-a/c; Aliens invade Skywatch; Stormwatch app.; death of Winter; destruction of Skywatch	1	2	3	5	6	8
1-Variant-c by Gil Kane	1	3	4	6	8	10

WILDC.A.T.S: SAVANT GARDE FAN EDITION
Image Comics/WildStorm Productions: Feb, 1997 - No. 3, Apr, 1997 (Giveaway, 8 pgs.) (Polybagged w/Overstreet's FAN)

1-3: Barbara Kesel-s/Christian Uche-a(p) — 3.00
1-3-(Gold): All retailer incentives — 10.00

WILDC.A.T.S TRILOGY
Image Comics (WildStorm Productions): June, 1993 - No. 3, Dec, 1993 ($1.95, lim. series)

1-($2.50)-1st app. Gen 13 (Fairchild, Burnout, Grunge, Freefall) Multi-color foil-c; Jae Lee-c/a in all — 5.00
1-($1.95)-Newsstand ed. w/o foil-c — 2.25
2,3-($1.95)-Jae Lee-c/a — 2.25

WILDCATS VERSION 3.0
DC Comics (WildStorm): Oct, 2002 - Present ($2.95)

1-17: 1-Casey-s/Nguyen-a; two covers by Nguyen and Rian Hughes and Nguyen. 8-Back-up preview of The Authority: High Stakes pt. 3 — 3.00
...: Brand Building TPB (2003, $14.95) r/#1-6 — 15.00

WILDC.A.T.S/ X-MEN: THE GOLDEN AGE
Image Comics (WildStorm Productions): Feb, 1997 ($4.50, one-shot)

1-Lobdell-s/Charest-a; Two covers (Charest, Jim Lee) — 5.00
1-"3-D" Edition ($6.50) w/glasses — 7.00

WILDC.A.T.S/ X-MEN: THE MODERN AGE
Image Comics (WildStorm Productions): Aug, 1997 ($4.50, one-shot)

1-Robinson-s/Hughes-a; Two covers (Hughes, Paul Smith) — 5.00
1-"3-D" Edition ($6.50) w/glasses — 7.00

WILDC.A.T.S/ X-MEN: THE SILVER AGE
Image Comics (WildStorm Productions): June, 1997 ($4.50, one-shot)

1-Lobdell-s/Jim Lee-a; Two covers(Neal Adams, Jim Lee) — 5.00
1-"3-D" Edition ($6.50) w/glasses — 7.00

WILDCORE
Image Comics (WildStorm Prods.): Nov, 1997 - No. 10, Dec, 1998 ($2.50)

1-10: 1-Two covers (Booth/McWeeney, Charest) — 2.50
1-($3.50)-Voyager Pack w/DV8 preview — 3.50
1-Chromium-c — 5.00

WILD DOG
DC Comics: Sept, 1987 - No. 4, Dec, 1987 (75¢, limited series)

1-4 — 2.50
Special 1 (1989, $2.50, 52 pgs.) — 2.50

WILDERNESS TREK (See Zane Grey, Four Color 333)

WILDFIRE (See Zane Grey, FourColor 433)

WILD FRONTIER (Cheyenne Kid #8 on)
Charlton Comics: Oct, 1955 - No. 7, Apr, 1957

	GD 2.0	VG 4.0	FN 6.0	VF 8.0	VF/NM 9.0	NM- 9.2
1-Davy Crockett	10	20	30	56	73	90
2-6-Davy Crockett in all	7	14	21	37	46	55
7-Origin & 1st app. Cheyenne Kid	8	16	24	46	58	70

WILDGUARD: CASTING CALL
Image Comics: Sept, 2003 - Present ($2.95)

1-4: 1-Nauck-s/a; two covers by Nauck and McGuinness. 2-Wieringo var-c — 3.00

WILDSTAR (Also see The Dragon & The Savage Dragon)
Image Comics (Highbrow Entertainment): Sept, 1995 - No. 3, Jan, 1996 ($2.50, lim. series)

1-3: Al Gordon scripts; Jerry Ordway-c/a — 2.50

WILDSTAR: SKY ZERO
Image Comics (Highbrow Entertainment): Mar, 1993 - No. 4, Nov, 1993 ($1.95, lim. series)

1-4: 1-($2.50)-Embossed-c w/silver ink; Ordway-c/a in all — 2.50
1-($1.95)-Newsstand ed. w/silver ink-c, not embossed — 2.50
1-Gold variant — 6.00

WILD STARS

Wildstorm #4 © WSP

Wild Western #4 © MAR

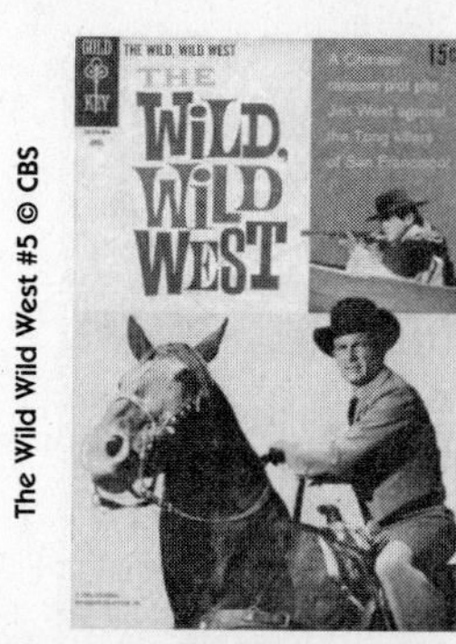

The Wild Wild West #5 © CBS

GD 2.0 | VG 4.0 | FN 6.0 | VF 8.0 | VF/NM 9.0 | NM- 9.2

Little Rocket Productions: July, 2001 - Present ($2.95, B&W)
Vol. 3: #1-6-Brunner-c; Tierney-s. 1,2-Brewer-a. 3-6-Simons-a 3.00
7-($5.95) Simons-a 6.00

WILDSTORM
Image Comics/DC Comics (WildStorm Publishing): 1994-2001 (one-shots)
...Annual 2000 (12/00, $3.50) Devil's Night x-over; Moy-a 3.50
...Chamber of Horrors (10/95, $3.50)-Bisley-c 3.50
...Fine Arts: The Gallery Collection (12/98, $19.95) Lee-c 20.00
...Halloween 1 (10/97, $2.50) Warner-c 2.50
...Rarities 1(12/94, $4.95, 52 pgs.)-r/Gen 13 1/2 & other stories 5.00
...Summer Special 1 (2001, $5.95) Short stories by various; Hughes-c 6.00
...Swimsuit Special 1 (12/94, $2.95), ...Swimsuit Special 2 (1995, $2.50) 3.00
...Swimsuit Special '97 #1 (7/97, $2.50) 2.50
...Thunderbook 1 (10/00, $6.95) Short stories by various incl. Hughes, Moy 7.00
...Ultimate Sports 1 (8/97, $2.50) 2.50
...Universe Sourcebook (5/95, $2.50) 2.50

WILDSTORM!
Image Comics (WildStorm Publishing): Aug, 1995 - No. 4, Nov, 1995 ($2.50, B&W/color, anthology)
1-4: 1-Simonson-a 2.50

WILDSTORM RISING
Image Comics (WildStorm Publishing): May, 1995 - No.2, June, 1995 ($1.95/$2.50)
1-($2.50)-Direct Market, WildStorm Rising Pt. 1 w/bound-in card 2.50
1-($1.95)-Newstand, WildStorm Rising Pt. 1 2.25
2-($2.50)-Direct Market, WildStorm Rising Pt. 10 w/bound-in card; continues in WildC.A.T.S #21. 2.50
2-($1.95)-Newstand, WildStorm Rising Pt. 10 2.25
Trade paperback (1996, $19.95)-Collects x-over; B. Smith-c 20.00

WILDSTORM SPOTLIGHT
Image Comics (WildStorm Publishing): Feb, 1997 - No. 4 ($2.50)
1-4: 1-Alan Moore-s 2.50

WILDSTORM UNIVERSE '97
Image Comics (WildStorm Publishing): Dec, 1996 - No. 3 ($2.50, limited series)
1-3: 1-Wraparound-c. 3-Gary Frank-c 2.50

WILDTHING
Marvel Comics UK: Apr, 1993 - No. 7, Oct, 1993 ($1.75)
1-($2.50)-Embossed-c; Venom & Carnage cameo 2.50
2-7: 2-Spider-Man & Venom. 6-Mysterio app. 2.25

WILD THING (Wolverine's daughter in the M2 universe)
Marvel Comics: Oct, 1999 - No. 5, Feb, 2000 ($1.99)
1-5: 1-Lim-a in all. 2-Two covers 2.25
Wizard #0 supplement; battles the Hulk 2.25

WILDTIMES
DC Comics (WildStorm Productions): Aug, 1999 ($2.50, one-shots)
...Deathblow #1 -set in 1899; Edwards-a; Jonah Hex app., ...DV8 #1 -set in 1944; Altieri-s/p; Sgt. Rock app., ...Gen13 #1 -set in 1969; Casey-s/Johnson-a; Teen Titans app., ...Grifter #1 -set in 1923; Paul Smith-a, ...Wetworks #1 -Waid-s/Lopresti-a; Superman app. 2.50
...WildC.A.T.s #0 -Wizard supplement; Charest-c 2.25

WILD WEST (Wild Western #3 on)
Marvel Comics (WFP): Spring, 1948 - No. 2, July, 1948
1-Two-Gun Kid, Arizona Annie, & Tex Taylor begin; Shores-c 36 72 108 204 290 375
2-Captain Tootsie by Beck; Shores-c 24 48 72 135 190 245

WILD WEST (Black Fury #1-57)
Charlton Comics: V2#58, Nov, 1966
V2#58 2 4 6 12 16 20

WILD WEST C.O.W.-BOYS OF MOO MESA (TV)
Archie Comics: Dec, 1992 - No. 3, Feb, 1993 (limited series)
V2#1, Mar, 1993 - No. 3, July, 1993 ($1.25)
1-3,V2#1-3 2.25

WILD WESTERN (Formerly Wild West #1,2)
Marvel/Atlas (WFP): No. 3, 9/48 - No. 57, 9/57 (3-11: 52 pgs, 12-on: 36 pgs)
3(#1)-Tex Morgan begins; Two-Gun Kid, Tex Taylor, & Arizona Annie continue from Wild West 29 58 87 164 232 300
4-Last Arizona Annie; Captain Tootsie by Beck; Kid Colt app. 21 42 63 118 164 210

GD 2.0 | VG 4.0 | FN 6.0 | VF 8.0 | VF/NM 9.0 | NM- 9.2

5-2nd app. Black Rider (1/49); Blaze Carson, Captain Tootsie (by Beck) app. 24 48 72 135 190 245
6-8: 6-Blaze Carson app; anti-Wertham editorial 15 30 45 86 118 150
9-Photo-c; Black Rider begins, ends #19 20 40 60 112 156 200
10-Charles Starrett photo-c 23 46 69 129 180 230
11-(Last 52 pg. issue) 15 30 45 86 118 150
12-14,16-19: All Black Rider-c/stories. 12-14-The Prairie Kid & his horse Fury app. 14 28 42 81 111 140
15-Red Larabee, Gunhawk (origin), his horse Blaze, & Apache Kid begin, end #22; Black Rider-c/story 15 30 45 84 115 145
20-30: 20-Kid Colt-c begin. 24-Has 2 Kid Colt stories. 26-1st app. The Ringo Kid? (2/53); 4 pg. story. 30-Katz-a 12 24 36 71 96 120
31-40 10 20 30 56 73 90
41-47,49-51,53,57 9 18 27 49 62 75
48-Williamson/Torres-a (4 pgs); Drucker-a 10 20 30 58 77 95
52-Crandall-a 10 20 30 58 77 95
54,55-Williamson-a in both (5 & 4 pgs.), #54 with Mayo plus 2 text illos 10 20 30 58 77 95
56-Baker-a? 9 18 27 49 62 75

NOTE: *Annie Oakley in #46, 47. Apache Kid in #15-22, 39. Arizona Kid in #21, 23. Arrowhead in #34-39. Black Rider in #5, 9-19, 33-44. Fighting Texan in #17. Kid Colt in #4-6, 9-11, 20-47, 52, 54-56. Outlaw Kid in #43. Red Hawkins in #13, 14. Ringo Kid in #26, 39, 41, 43, 44, 46, 47, 50, 52-56. Tex Morgan in #3, 4, 6, 9, 11. Tex Taylor in #3-6, 9, 11. Texas Kid in #23-25. Two-Gun Kid in #3-6, 9, 11, 12, 33-39, 41. Wyatt Earp in #47.* ***Ayers*** *a-41, 42.* ***Berg*** *a-26; c-24.* ***Colan*** *a-49.* ***Forte*** *a-28, 30.* ***Al Hartley*** *a-16.* ***Heath*** *a-4, 5, 8; c-34, 44.* ***Keller*** *a-24, 26(2), 29-40, 44-46, 48, 52.* ***Maneely*** *a-10, 12, 15, 16, 28, 35, 38, 40-45; c-18-22, 33, 35, 36, 38, 39, 41, 42, 45.* ***Morisi*** *a-23, 52.* ***Pakula*** *a-42, 52.* ***Powell*** *a-51.* ***Romita*** *a-24(2).* ***Severin*** *a-46, 47; c-48.* ***Shores*** *a-3, 5, 30, 31, 33, 35, 36, 38, 41; c-3-5.* ***Sinnott*** *a-34-39.* ***Wildey*** *a-43. Bondage c-19.*

WILD WESTERN ACTION (Also see The Bravados)
Skywald Publ. Corp.: Mar, 1971 - No. 3, June, 1971 (25¢, reprints, 52 pgs.)
1-Durango Kid, Straight Arrow-r; with all references to "Straight" in story relettered to "Swift"; Bravados begin; Shores-a (new) 2 4 6 14 18 22
2,3: 2-Billy Nevada, Durango Kid. 3-Red Mask, Durango Kid 2 4 6 10 12 15

WILD WESTERN ROUNDUP
Red Top/Decker Publications/I. W. Enterprises: Oct, 1957; 1960-'61
1(1957)-Kid Cowboy-r 5 10 14 20 24 28
I.W. Reprint #1('60-61)-r/#1 by Red Top 2 4 6 9 11 14

WILD WEST RODEO
Star Publications: 1953 (15¢)
1-A comic book coloring book with regular full color cover & B&W inside 8 16 24 43 54 65

WILD WILD WEST, THE (TV)
Gold Key: June, 1966 - No. 7, Oct, 1969 (All have Robert Conrad photo-c)
1-McWilliams-a 14 28 42 99 145 190
1-Variant edition with photo back-c (scarce) 15 30 45 104 152 200
2-McWilliams-a 10 20 30 72 104 135
2-Variant edition with photo back-c (scarce) 11 22 33 75 110 145
3-7 9 18 27 60 85 110

WILD, WILD WEST, THE (TV)
Millennium Publications: Oct, 1990 - No. 4, Jan?, 1991 ($2.95, limited series)
1-4-Based on TV show 3.00

WILKIN BOY (See That...)

WILL EISNER READER
Kitchen Sink Press: 1991 ($9.95, B&W, 8 1/2" x 11", TPB)
nn-Reprints stories from Will Eisner's Quarterly; Eisner-s/a/c 10.00
nn-(DC Comics, 10/00, $9.95) 10.00

WILLIE COMICS (Formerly Ideal #1-4; Crime Cases #24 on; Li'l Willie #20 & 21)
(See Gay Comics, Laugh, Millie The Model & Wisco)
Marvel Comics (MgPC): #5, Fall, 1946 - #19, 4/49; #22, 1/50 - #23, 5/50 (No #20 & 21)
5(#1)-George, Margie, Nellie the Nurse & Willie begin 21 42 63 118 164 210
6,8,9 11 22 33 66 88 110
7(1),10,11-Kurtzman's "Hey Look" 12 24 36 69 92 115
12,14-18,22,23 10 20 30 60 80 100
13,19-Kurtzman's "Hey Look" (#19-last by Kurtzman?) 11 22 33 63 84 105
NOTE: *Cindy app. in #17. Jeanie app. in #17. Little Lizzie app. in #22.*

WILLIE MAYS (See The Amazing...)

WILLIE THE PENGUIN

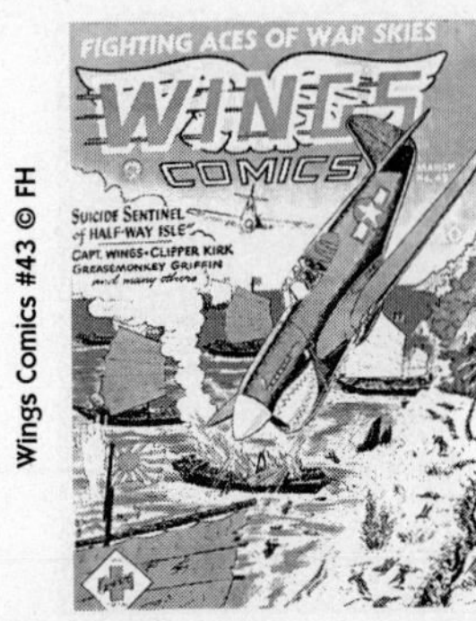

Wings Comics #43 © FH

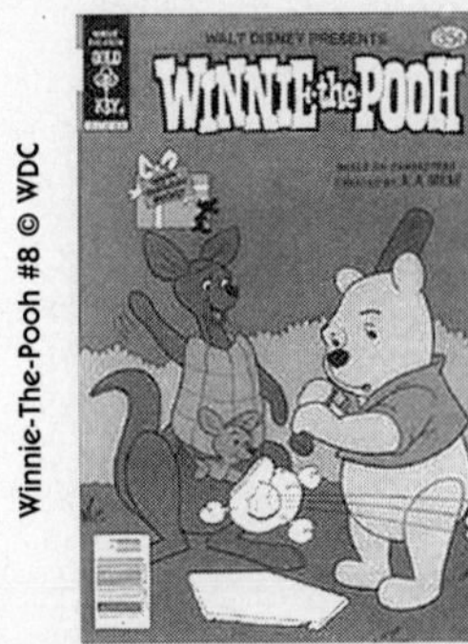

Winnie-The-Pooh #8 © WDC

Witchblade #10 © TCOW

Standard Comics: Apr, 1951 - No. 6, Apr, 1952

	GD 2.0	VG 4.0	FN 6.0	VF 8.0	VF/NM 9.0	NM- 9.2
1-Funny animal	9	18	27	49	65	75
2-6	6	12	18	28	34	40

WILLIE THE WISE-GUY (Also see Cartoon Kids)
Atlas Comics (NPP): Sept, 1957

	GD 2.0	VG 4.0	FN 6.0	VF 8.0	VF/NM 9.0	NM- 9.2
1-Kida, Maneely-a	9	18	27	49	62	75

WILLOW
Marvel Comics: Aug, 1988 - No. 3, Oct, 1988 ($1.00)

	GD 2.0	VG 4.0	FN 6.0	VF 8.0	VF/NM 9.0	NM- 9.2
1-3-R/Marvel Graphic Novel #36 (movie adaptation)						3.00

WILL ROGERS WESTERN (Formerly My Great Love #1-4; see Blazing & True Comics #66)
Fox Features Syndicate: No. 5, June, 1950 - No. 2, Aug, 1950

	GD 2.0	VG 4.0	FN 6.0	VF 8.0	VF/NM 9.0	NM- 9.2
5(#1)	36	72	108	204	290	375
2: Photo-c	31	62	93	175	248	320

WILL TO POWER (Also see Comic's Greatest World)
Dark Horse Comics: June, 1994 - No. 12, Aug, 1994 ($1.00, weekly limited series, 20 pgs.)

	GD 2.0	VG 4.0	FN 6.0	VF 8.0	VF/NM 9.0	NM- 9.2
1-12: 12-Vortex kills Titan.						2.25

NOTE: ***Mignola** c-10-12. **Sears** c-1-3.*

WILL-YUM!
Dell Publishing Co.: No. 676, Feb, 1956 - No. 902, May, 1958

	GD 2.0	VG 4.0	FN 6.0	VF 8.0	VF/NM 9.0	NM- 9.2
Four Color 676 (#1), 765 (1/57), 902	4	8	12	22	30	38

WIN A PRIZE COMICS (Timmy The Timid Ghost #3 on?)
Charlton Comics: Feb, 1955 - No. 2, Apr, 1955

	GD 2.0	VG 4.0	FN 6.0	VF 8.0	VF/NM 9.0	NM- 9.2
V1#1-S&K-a; Poe adapt; E.C. War swipe	69	138	207	431	646	860
2-S&K-a	50	100	150	300	450	600

WINDY & WILLY
National Periodical Publications: May-June, 1969 - No. 4, Nov-Dec, 1969

	GD 2.0	VG 4.0	FN 6.0	VF 8.0	VF/NM 9.0	NM- 9.2
1- r/Dobie Gillis with some art changes begin	4	8	12	27	36	45
2-4	3	6	9	16	20	25

WINGS COMICS
Fiction House Mag.: 9/40 - No. 109, 9/49; No. 110, Wint, 1949-50; No. 111, Spring, 1950; No. 112, 1950(nd); No. 113 - No. 115, 1950(nd); No. 116, 1952(nd); No. 117, Fall, 1952 - No. 122, Wint, 1953-54; No. 123 - No. 124, 1954(nd)

	GD 2.0	VG 4.0	FN 6.0	VF 8.0	VF/NM 9.0	NM- 9.2
1-Skull Squad, Clipper Kirk, Suicide Smith, Jane Martin, War Nurse, Phantom Falcons, Greasemonkey Griffin, Parachute Patrol & Powder Burns begin	240	480	720	1500	2250	3000
2	96	192	288	600	900	1200
3-5	66	132	198	413	619	825
6-10: 8-Indicia shows #7 (#8 on cover)	55	110	165	330	495	660
11-15	48	96	144	288	432	575
16-Origin & 1st app. Captain Wings & begin series	53	106	159	318	479	640
17-20	42	84	126	252	359	465
21-30	39	78	117	233	329	425
31-40	34	68	102	196	278	360
41-50	28	56	84	159	225	290
51-60: 60-Last Skull Squad	25	50	75	147	202	260
61-67: 66-Ghost Patrol begins (becomes Ghost Squadron #71 on), ends #112?	22	44	66	127	176	225
68,69: 68-Clipper Kirk becomes The Phantom Falcon-origin, Part 1; part 2 in #69	22	44	66	127	176	225
70-72: 70-1st app. The Phantom Falcon in costume, origin-Part 3; Capt. Wings battles Col. Kamikaze in all	21	42	63	121	168	215
73-99: 80-Phantom Falcon by Larsen. 99-King of the Congo begins?	21	42	63	121	168	215
100-(12/48)	23	46	69	130	183	235
101-124: 111-Last Jane Martin. 112-Flying Saucer-c/story (1950). 115-Used in **POP**, pg. 89	18	36	54	104	142	180

NOTE: *Bondage covers are common. Captain Wings battles Sky Hag-#75, 76; ...Mr. Atlantis-#85-92; ...Mr. Pupin(Red Agent)-#98-103. Capt. Wings by **Elias**-#52-64, 68, 69; by **Lubbers**-#29-32, 70-111; by **Renee**-#33-46. **Evans** a-85-106, 108-111(Jane Martin); text illos-72-84. **Larsen** a-52, 59, 64, 73-77. Jane Martin by **Fran Hopper**-#68-84; Suicide Smith by **John Celardo**-#72, 74, 76, 80-104; by **Hollingsworth**-#68-70, 105-109, 111; Ghost Squadron by **Astarita**-#67-79; by **Maurice Whitman**-#80-111. King of the Congo by **Moreira**-#99, 100. Skull Squad by **M. Baker**-#52-60; Clipper Kirk by **Baker**-#60, 61; by **Colan**-#53; by **Ingels**-(some issues?). Phantom Falcon by **Larsen**-#73-84. **Elias** c-58-72. **Fawcette** c-3-12, 16, 17, 19, 22-33. **Lubbers** c-74-109. **Tuska** a-5. **Whitman** c-110-124. **Zolnerwich** c-15, 21.*

WINGS OF THE EAGLES, THE
Dell Publishing Co.: No. 790, Apr, 1957 (10¢ & 15¢ editions exist)

	GD 2.0	VG 4.0	FN 6.0	VF 8.0	VF/NM 9.0	NM- 9.2
Four Color 790-Movie; John Wayne photo-c; Toth-a	16	32	48	113	167	220

WINKY DINK (Adventures of...)
Pines Comics: No. 75, Mar, 1957 (one-shot)

	GD 2.0	VG 4.0	FN 6.0	VF 8.0	VF/NM 9.0	NM- 9.2
75-Marv Levy-c/a	6	12	18	31	38	45

WINKY DINK (TV)
Dell Publishing Co.: No. 663, Nov, 1955

	GD 2.0	VG 4.0	FN 6.0	VF 8.0	VF/NM 9.0	NM- 9.2
Four Color 663 (#1)	9	18	27	63	89	115

WINNIE-THE-POOH (Also see Dynabrite Comics)
Gold Key No. 1-17/Whitman No. 18 on: January, 1977 - No. 33, July, 1984
(Walt Disney) (Winnie-The-Pooh began as Edward Bear in 1926 by Milne)

	GD 2.0	VG 4.0	FN 6.0	VF 8.0	VF/NM 9.0	NM- 9.2
1-New art	3	6	9	16	20	25
2-5: 5-New material	2	4	6	9	11	14
6-17: 12-up-New material	1	3	4	6	8	10
18,19(Whitman)	2	4	6	9	11	14
20,21('80) pre-pack only	3	6	9	16	20	24
22('80) (scarcer) pre-pack only	3	7	10	21	28	35
23-28: 27(2/82), 28(4/82)	2	4	6	9	11	14
29-33 (#90299 on-c, no date or date code; pre-pack): 29(4/82), 30(5/83), 31(8/83), 32(4/84), 33(7/84)	2	4	6	12	16	20

WINNIE WINKLE (See Popular Comics & Super Comics)
Dell Publishing Co.: 1941 - No. 7, Sept-Nov, 1949

	GD 2.0	VG 4.0	FN 6.0	VF 8.0	VF/NM 9.0	NM- 9.2
Large Feature Comic 2 (1941)	19	38	57	136	198	260
Four Color 94 (1945)	13	26	39	90	133	175
Four Color 174	8	16	24	58	82	105
1(3-5/48)-Contains daily & Sunday newspaper-r from 1939-1941	8	16	24	53	74	95
2 (6-8/48)	5	10	15	36	48	60
3-7	4	8	12	27	36	45

WINTERWORLD
Eclipse Comics: Sept, 1987 - No. 3, Mar, 1988 ($1.75, limited series)

	GD 2.0	VG 4.0	FN 6.0	VF 8.0	VF/NM 9.0	NM- 9.2
1-3						2.25

WISE GUYS (See Harvey...)

WISE LITTLE HEN, THE
David McKay Publ./Whitman: 1934 ,1935(48 pgs.); 1937 (Story book)

	GD 2.0	VG 4.0	FN 6.0	VF 8.0	VF/NM 9.0	NM- 9.2
nn-(1934 edition w/dust jacket)(48 pgs. with color, 8-3/4x9-3/4") -Debut of Donald Duck (see Advs. of Mickey Mouse); Donald app. on cover with Wise Little Hen & Practical Pig; painted cover; same artist as the B&W's from Silly Symphony Cartoon, The Wise Little Hen (1934) (McKay)						
Book w/dust jacket	233	466	699	1282	1941	2600
Dust jacket only	55	110	165	312	469	625
nn-(1935 edition w/dust jacket), same as 1934 ed.	139	278	417	765	1133	1500
888 (1937)(9-1/2x13", 12 pgs.)(Whitman) Donald Duck app.	34	68	102	193	274	355

WISE SON: THE WHITE WOLF
DC Comics (Milestone): Nov, 1996 - No. 4, Feb, 1997 ($2.50, limited series)

	GD 2.0	VG 4.0	FN 6.0	VF 8.0	VF/NM 9.0	NM- 9.2
1-4: Ho Che Anderson-c/a						2.50

WIT AND WISDOM OF WATERGATE (Humor magazine)
Marvel Comics: 1973, 76 pgs., squarebound

	GD 2.0	VG 4.0	FN 6.0	VF 8.0	VF/NM 9.0	NM- 9.2
1-Low print run	4	8	12	22	30	38

WITCHBLADE (Also see Cyblade/Shi, Tales Of The..., & Top Cow Classics)
Image Comics (Top Cow Productions): Nov, 1995 - Present ($2.50/$2.99)

	GD 2.0	VG 4.0	FN 6.0	VF 8.0	VF/NM 9.0	NM- 9.2
0	1	2	3	5	6	8
1/2-Mike Turner/Marc Silvestri-c.	4	8	12	24	32	40
1/2 Gold Ed., 1/2 Chromium-c	4	8	12	24	32	40
1/2-(Vol. 2, 11/02, $2.99) Wohl-s/Ching-a/c						3.00
1-Mike Turner-a(p)	4	8	12	24	32	40
1,2-American Ent. Encore Ed.	1	2	3	4	5	7
2,3	2	4	6	12	16	20
4,5	2	4	6	10	13	16
6-9: 8-Wraparound-c. 9-Tony Daniel-a(p)	1	2	3	5	7	9
9-Sunset variant-c	2	4	6	8	10	12
9-DF variant-c	2	4	6	12	16	20
10-Flip book w/Darkness #0, 1st app. the Darkness	2	4	6	8	10	12
10-Variant-c	2	4	6	10	12	15
10-Gold logo	3	6	9	18	24	30
10-($3.95) Dynamic Forces alternate-c	1	2	3	5	6	8
11-15						5.00
16-19: 18,19-"Family Ties" Darkness x-over pt. 1,4						4.00
18-Face to face variant-c, 18-American Ent. Ed., 19-AE Gold Ed.	1	2	3	5	6	8
20-25: 24-Pearson, Green-a. 25-($2.95) Turner-a(p)						3.00

Witchblade Animated #1 © TCOW

Witchcraft: La Terreur #2 © DC

The Witching Hour #31 © DC

	GD 2.0	VG 4.0	FN 6.0	VF 8.0	VF/NM 9.0	NM- 9.2
25 (Prism variant)						30.00
25 (Special)						15.00
26-39: 26-Green-a begins						2.50
27 (Variant)						10.00
40-49,51-53: 40-Begin Jenkins & Veitch-s/Keu Cha-a. 47-Zulli-c/a						2.50
40-Pittsburgh Convention Preview edition; B&W preview of #40						3.00
41-eWanted Chrome-c edition						5.00
49-Gold logo	1	2	3	5	6	8
50-($4.95) Darkness app.; Ching-a; B&W preview of Universe						5.00
54-59: 54-Black outer-c with gold foil logo; Wohl-s/Manapul-a						2.50
55-Variant Battle of the Planets Convention cover						3.00
60-72: 60-($2.99) Endgame x-over with Tomb Raider #25 & Evo #1. 64,65-Magdalena app. 71-Kirk-a						3.00
...: Animated (8/03, $2.99) Magdalena & Darkness app.; Dini-s/Bone, Bullock, Cooke-a/c						3.00
...: Blood Relations TPB (2003, $12.99) r/#54-58						13.00
.../Darkchylde (7/00, $2.50) Green-s/a(p)						2.50
.../Darkness: Family Ties Collected Edition (10/98, $9.95) r/#18,19 and Darkness #9,10						10.00
.../Darkness Special (12/99, $3.95) Green-c/a						4.00
...: Demon 1 (2003, $6.99) Mark Millar-s/Jae Lee-c/a						7.00
...: Distinctions (See Tales of the Witchblade)						
... Gallery (11/00, $2.95) Profile pages and pin-ups by various; Turner-c						3.00
Infinity (5/99, $3.50) Lobdell-s/Pollina-c/a						3.50
.../Lady Death (11/01, $4.95) Manapul-c/a						5.00
...: Prevailing TPB (2000, $14.95) r/#20-25; new Turner-c						15.00
...: Revelations TPB (2000, $24.95) r/#9-17; new Turner-c						25.00
.../Tomb Raider #1/2 (7/00, $2.95) Covers by Turner and Cha						3.00
Wizard #500						10.00
WITCHBLADE/ALIENS/THE DARKNESS/PREDATOR						
Dark Horse Comics/Top Cow Productions: Nov, 2000 ($2.99)						
1-3-Mel Rubi-a						3.00
WITCHBLADE COLLECTED EDITION						
Image Comics (Top Cow Productions): July, 1996 - Present ($4.95/$6.95, squarebound, limited series)						
1-7-($4.95): Two issues reprinted in each						5.00
8-($6.95) r/#15-17						7.00
...Slipcase (10/96, $10.95)-Packaged w/ Coll. Ed. #1-4						11.00
WITCHBLADE: DESTINY'S CHILD						
Image Comics (Top Cow): Jun, 2000 - No. 3, Sept, 2000 ($2.95, lim. series)						
1-3: 1-Boller-a/Keu Cha-c						3.00
WITCHBLADE/ ELEKTRA						
Image Comics (Top Cow Productions): Mar, 1997 ($2.95)						
1-Devil's Reign Pt. 6						3.00
WITCHBLADE: OBAKEMONO						
Image Comics (Top Cow Productions): 2002 ($9.95, one-shot graphic novel)						
1-Fiona Avery-s/Billy Tan-a; forward by Straczynski						10.00
WITCHBLADE/ TOMB RAIDER SPECIAL (Also see Tomb Raider/...)						
Image Comics (Top Cow Productions): Dec, 1998 ($2.95)						
1-Based on video game character; Turner-a(p)						3.00
1-Silvestri variant-c						5.00
1-Turner bikini variant-c						10.00
1-Prism-c						12.00
Wizard 1/2 -Turner-s						10.00
WITCHCRAFT (See Strange Mysteries, Super Reprint #18)						
Avon Periodicals: Mar-Apr, 1952 - No. 6, Mar, 1953						
1-Kubert-a; 1 pg. Check-a	68	136	204	425	638	850
2-Kubert & Check-a	52	104	156	312	466	620
3,6: 3-Lawrence-a; Kinstler inside-c	42	84	126	252	359	465
4-People cooked alive c/story	45	90	135	270	403	535
5-Kelly Freas painted-c	50	100	150	300	450	600
NOTE: ***Hollingsworth*** *a-4-6; c-4, 6.* ***McCann*** *a-3?*						
WITCHCRAFT						
DC Comics (Vertigo): June, 1994 - No. 3, Aug, 1994 ($2.95, limited series)						
1-3: James Robinson scripts & Kaluta-c in all						4.00
1-Platinum Edition						8.00
Trade paperback-(1996, $14.95)-r/#1-3; Kaluta-c						15.00
WITCHCRAFT: LA TERREUR						
DC Comics (Vertigo): Apr, 1998 - No. 3, Jun, 1998 ($2.50, limited series)						
1-3: Robinson-s/Zulli & Locke-a; interlocking cover images						2.50

	GD 2.0	VG 4.0	FN 6.0	VF 8.0	VF/NM 9.0	NM- 9.2
WITCHES TALES (Witches Western Tales #29,30)						
Witches Tales/Harvey Publications: Jan, 1951 - No. 28, Dec, 1954 (date misprinted as 4/55)						
1-Powell-a (1 pg.)	55	110	165	330	495	660
2-Eye injury panel	34	68	102	196	278	360
3-7,9,10	26	52	78	150	210	270
8-Eye injury panels	27	54	81	155	218	280
11-13,15,16: 12-Acid in face story	23	46	69	130	183	235
14,17-Powell/Nostrand-a. 17-Atomic disaster story	25	50	75	147	202	260
18-Nostrand-a; E.C. swipe/Shock S.S.	25	50	75	147	202	260
19-Nostrand-a; E.C. swipe/ "Glutton"; Devil-c	27	54	81	155	218	280
20-24-Nostrand-a. 21-E.C. swipe; rape story. 23-Wood E.C. swipes/Two-Fisted Tales #34	25	50	75	147	202	260
25-Nostrand-a; E.C. swipe/Mad Barber; decapitation-c	32	64	96	182	259	335
26-28: 27-r/#6 with diff.-c. 28-r/#8 with diff.-c	18	36	54	104	142	180
NOTE: ***Check*** *a-24.* ***Elias*** *c-8, 10, 16-27.* ***Kremer*** *a-18; c-25.* ***Nostrand*** *a-17-25; 14, 17(w/****Powell****).* ***Palais*** *a-1, 2, 4(2), 5(2), 7-9, 12, 14, 15, 17.* ***Powell*** *a-3-7, 10, 11, 19-27. Bondage-c 1, 3, 5, 6, 8, 9.*						
WITCHES TALES (Magazine)						
Eerie Publications: V1#7, July, 1969 - V7#1, Feb, 1975 (B&W, 52 pgs.)						
V1#7(7/69) - 9(11/69)	5	10	15	33	44	55
V2#1-6('70), V3#1-6('71)	4	8	12	22	30	38
V4#1-6('72), V5#1-6('73), V6#1-6('74), V7#1	3	6	9	19	25	32
NOTE: *Ajax/Farrell reprints in early issues.*						
WITCHES' WESTERN TALES (Formerly Witches Tales)(Western Tales #31 on)						
Harvey Publications: No. 29, Feb, 1955 - No. 30, Apr, 1955						
29,30-Featuring Clay Duncan & Boys' Ranch; S&K-r/from Boys' Ranch including-c. 29-Last pre-code	21	42	63	118	164	210
WITCHFINDER, THE						
Image Comics (Liar): Sept, 1999 - No. 3, Jan, 2000 ($2.95)						
1-3-Romano-a/Sharon & Matthew Scott-plot						3.00
WITCH HUNTER						
Malibu Comics (Ultraverse): Apr, 1996 ($2.50, one-shot)						
1						2.50
WITCHING HOUR ("The ..." in later issues)						
National Periodical Publ./DC Comics: Feb-Mar, 1969 - No. 85, Oct, 1978						
1-Toth-a, plus Neal Adams-a (2 pgs.)	12	24	36	82	121	160
2,6: 6-Toth-a	6	12	18	38	52	65
3,5-Wrightson-a; Toth-p. 3-Last 12¢ issue	6	12	18	40	55	70
4,7-12: Toth-a in all. 8-Toth, Neal Adams-a	4	8	12	24	32	40
13-Neal Adams-c/a, 2pgs.	4	8	12	27	36	45
14-Williamson/Garzon, Jones-a; N. Adams-c	4	8	12	29	40	50
15	3	6	9	16	20	24
16-21-(52 pg. Giants)	3	6	9	18	24	30
22-37,39,40	2	4	6	10	13	16
38-(100 pgs.)	5	10	15	33	44	55
41-60	2	4	6	8	10	12
61-83,85	1	2	3	5	7	9
84-(44 pgs.)	1	3	4	6	8	10
NOTE: *Combined with The Unexpected with #189.* ***Neal Adams*** *c-7-11, 13, 14.* ***Alcala*** *a-24, 27, 33, 41, 43.* ***Anderson*** *a-9, 38.* ***Cardy*** *c-4, 5.* ***Kaluta*** *a-7.* ***Kane*** *a-12p.* ***Morrow*** *a-10, 13, 15, 16.* ***Nino*** *a-31, 40, 45, 47.* ***Redondo*** *a-20, 23, 24, 34, 65; c-53.* ***Reese*** *a-23.* ***Sparling*** *a-1.* ***Toth*** *a-1, 3-12, 38r.* ***Tuska*** *a-11, 12.* ***Wood*** *a-15.*						
WITCHING HOUR, THE						
DC Comics (Vertigo): 1999 - No. 3, 2000 ($5.95, limited series)						
1-3-Bachalo & Thibert-c/a; Loeb & Bachalo-s						6.00
Hardcover (2000, $29.95) r/#1-3; embossed cover						30.00
Softcover (2003, $19.95) r/#1-3						20.00
WITHIN OUR REACH						
Star Reach Productions: 1991 ($7.95, 84 pgs.)						
nn-Spider-Man, Concrete by Chadwick, Gift of the Magi by Russell; X-mas stories; Chadwick-c; Spidey back-c						8.00
WITH THE MARINES ON THE BATTLEFRONTS OF THE WORLD						
Toby Press: 1953 (no month) - No. 2, Mar, 1954 (Photo covers)						
1-John Wayne story	30	60	90	170	240	310
2-Monty Hall in #1,2	9	18	27	52	66	80
WITH THE U.S. PARATROOPS BEHIND ENEMY LINES (Also see U.S. Paratroops...; #2-6 titled U.S. Paratroops...)						
Avon Periodicals: 1951 - No. 6, Dec, 1952						
1-Wood-c & inside f/c	17	34	51	98	134	170
2-Kinstler-c & inside f/c only	10	20	30	56	73	90

Wolff & Byrd, Counselors of the Macabre #10 © Batton Lash

Wolverine #25 © MAR

Wolverine #186 © MAR

GD VG FN VF VF/NM NM-
2.0 4.0 6.0 8.0 9.0 9.2

3-6: 6-Kinstler-c & inside f/c only 9 18 27 52 66 80
NOTE: *Kinstler c-2, 4-6.*

WITNESS, THE (Also see Amazing Mysteries, Captain America #71, Ideal #4, Marvel Mystery #92 & Mystic #7)
Marvel Comics (MjMe): Sept, 1948
1(Scarce)-Rico-c? 172 344 516 1075 1613 2150

WITTY COMICS
Irwin H. Rubin Publ./Chicago Nite Life News No. 2: 1945 - No. 2, 1945
1-The Pioneer, Junior Patrol; Jap war-c 29 58 87 164 232 300
2-The Pioneer, Junior Patrol 14 28 42 81 111 140

WIZARD OF FOURTH STREET, THE
Dark Horse Comics: Dec, 1987 - No. 2, 1988 ($1.75, B&W, limited series)
1,2: Adapts novel by S/F author Simon Hawke 2.25

WIZARD OF OZ (See Classics Illustrated Jr. 535, Dell Jr. Treasury No. 5, First Comics Graphic Novel, Marvelous..., & Marvel Treasury of Oz)
Dell Publishing Co.: No. 1308, Mar-May, 1962 (TV)
Four Color 1308 13 26 39 90 133 175

WIZARD'S TALE, THE
Image Comics (Homage Comics): 1997 ($19.95, squarebound, one-shot)
nn-Kurt Busiek-s/David Wenzel-painted-a/c 20.00

WOLF & RED
Dark Horse Comics: Apr, 1995 - No. 3, June, 1995 ($2.50, limited series)
1-3: Characters created by Tex Avery 2.50

WOLFF & BYRD, COUNSELORS OF THE MACABRE (Becomes Supernatural Law with issue #24)
Exhibit A Press: May, 1994 - No. 23, Aug, 1999 ($2.50, B&W)
1-23-Batton Lash-s/a 2.50

WOLF GAL (See Al Capp's...)

WOLFMAN, THE (See Movie Classics)

WOLFPACK
Marvel Comics: Feb, 1988 ($7.95); Aug, 1988 - No. 12, July, 1989 (Lim. series)
1-1st app./origin (Marvel Graphic Novel #31) 8.00
1-12 2.25

WOLVERINE (See Alpha Flight, Daredevil #196, 249, Ghost Rider; Wolverine; Punisher, Havok &..., Incredible Hulk #180, Incredible Hulk &..., Kitty Pryde And..., Marvel Comics Presents, Power Pack, Punisher and..., Spider-Man vs... & X-Men #94)

WOLVERINE (See Incredible Hulk #180 for 1st app.)
Marvel Comics Group: Sept, 1982 - No. 4, Dec, 1982 (limited series)
1-Frank Miller-c/a(p) in all 5 10 15 36 48 60
2-4 4 8 12 27 36 45
Trade paperback 1(7/87, $4.95)-Reprints #1-4 with new Miller-c.
2 4 6 11 14 18
Trade paperback nn (2nd printing, $9.95)-r/#1-4 2 4 6 8 10 12

WOLVERINE
Marvel Comics: Nov, 1988 - No. 189, June, 2003 ($1.50/$1.75/$1.95/$1.99/$2.25)
1 4 8 12 24 32 40
2 2 4 6 12 16 20
3-5: 4-BWS back-c 2 4 6 10 12 15
6-9: 6-McFarlane back-c. 7,8-Hulk app. 1 3 4 6 8 10
10-1st battle with Sabretooth (before Wolverine had his claws)
3 6 9 18 23 28
11-16: 11-New costume 1 2 3 5 6 8
17-20: 17-Byrne-c/a(p) begins, ends #23 1 2 3 4 5 7
21-30: 24,25,27-Jim Lee-c. 26-Begin $1.75-c 5.00
31-40,44,47 4.00
41-Sabretooth claims to be Wolverine's father; Cable cameo 6.00
41-Gold 2nd printing ($1.75) 2.50
42-Sabretooth, Cable & Nick Fury app.; Sabretooth proven not to be Wolverine's father
1 2 3 5 6 8
42-Gold ink 2nd printing ($1.75) 2.50
43-Sabretooth cameo (2 panels); saga ends 5.00
45,46-Sabretooth-c/stories 5.00
48-51: 48,49-Sabretooth app. 48-Begin 3 part Weapon X sequel. 50-(64 pgs.)-Die cut-c; Wolverine back to old yellow costume; Forge, Cyclops, Jubilee, Jean Grey & Nick Fury app. 51-Sabretooth-c & app. 4.00
52-74,76-80: 54-Shatterstar (from X-Force) app. 55-Gambit, Jubilee, Sunfire-c/story. 55-57,73-Gambit app. 57-Mariko Yashida dies (Late 7/92). 58,59-Terror, Inc. x-over.

GD VG FN VF VF/NM NM-
2.0 4.0 6.0 8.0 9.0 9.2

60-64-Sabretooth storyline (60,62,64-c) 4.00
75-($3.95, 68 pgs.)-Wolverine hologram on-c 5.00
81-84,86: 81-bound-in card sheet 3.00
85-($2.50)-Newsstand edition 3.00
85-($3.50)-Collectors edition 5.00
87-90 ($1.95)-Deluxe edition 3.00
87-90 ($1.50)-Regular edition 2.50
91-99,101-114: 91-Return from "Age of Apocalypse," 93-Juggernaut app. 94-Gen X app. 101-104-Elektra app. 104-Origin of Onslaught. 105-Onslaught x-over. 110-Shaman-c/app. 114-Alternate-c 3.00
100 ($3.95)-Hologram-c; Wolverine loses humanity 1 2 3 5 7 9
100 ($2.95)-Regular-c. 4.00
115-124: 115- Operation Zero Tolerance 2.50
125-($2.99) Wraparound-c; Viper secret 3.00
125-($6.95) Jae Lee variant-c 7.00
126-144: 126,127-Sabretooth-c/app. 128-Sabretooth & Shadowcat app.; Platt-a. 129-Wendigo-c/app. 131-Initial printing contained lettering error. 133-Begin Larsen-s/ Matsuda-a. 138-Galactus-c/app. 139-Cable app.; Yu-a. 142,143-Alpha Flight app. 2.50
145-($2.99) 25th Anniversary issue; Hulk and Sabretooth app. 3.00
145-($3.99) Foil enhanced cover (also see Promotional section for Nabisco mail-in ed.) 4.00
146-149: 147-Apocalypse: The Twelve; Angel-c/app. 149-Nova-c/app. 2.50
150-($2.99) Steve Skroce-s/a 3.00
151-174,176-182,184-189: 151-Begin $2.25-c. 154,155-Liefeld-s/a. 156-Churchill-a. 159-Chen-a begins. 160-Sabretooth app. 163-Texeira-a(p). 167-BWS-c. 172,173-Alpha Flight app. 176-Colossus app. 185,186-Punisher app. 2.50
175,183-($3.50) 175-Sabretooth app. 3.50
#(-1) Flashback (7/97) Logan meets Col. Fury; Nord-a 2.50
Annual nn (1990, $4.50, squarebound, 52 pgs.)-The Jungle Adventure; Simonson scripts; Mignola-c/a 5.00
Annual 2 (12/90, $4.95, squarebound, 52 pgs.)-Bloodlust 5.00
Annual nn (#3, 8/91, $5.95, 68 pgs.)-Rahne of Terror; Cable & The New Mutants app.; Andy Kubert-c/a (2nd print exists) 6.00
Annual '95 (1995, $3.95) 4.00
Annual '96 (1996, $2.95)- Wraparound-c; Silver Samurai, Yukio, and Red Ronin app. 3.00
Annual '97 ($2.99) - Wraparound-c 3.00
Annual 1999, 2000 ($3.50) : 1999-Deadpool app. 3.50
Annual 2001 ($2.99) - Tieri-s; JH Williams-c 3.00
...Battles The Incredible Hulk nn (1989, $4.95, squarebound, 52 pg.) r/Incr. Hulk #180,181 5.00
...Black Rio (11/98, $5.99)-Casey-s/Oscar Jimenez-a 6.00
...Blood Debt TPB (7/01, $12.95)-r/#150-153; Skroce-c 13.00
...Blood Hungry nn (1993, $6.95, 68 pgs.)-Kieth-r/Marvel Comics Presents #85-92 w/ new Kieth-c 7.00
...: Bloody Choices nn (1993, $7.95, 68 pgs.)-r/Graphic Novel; Nick Fury app. 8.00
... Cable Guts and Glory (10/99, $5.99) Platt-a 6.00
.../Deadpool: Weapon X TPB (7/02, $21.99)-r/#162-166 & Deadpool #57-60 22.00
... Doombringer (11/97, $5.99)-Silver Samurai-c/app. 6.00
... Evilution (9/94, $5.95) 6.00
...: Global Jeopardy 1 (12/93, $2.95, one-shot)-Embossed-c; Sub-Mariner, Zabu, Ka-Zar, Shanna & Wolverine app.; produced in cooperation with World Wildlife Fund 3.00
...:Inner Fury nn (1992, $5.95, 52 pgs.)-Sienkiewicz-c/a 6.00
...: Judgment Night (2000, $3.99) Shi app.; Battlebook 4.00
...: Killing (9/93)-Kent Williams-a 6.00
...: Knight of Terra (1995, $6.95)-Ostrander script 7.00
... Legends Vol. 2: Meltdown (2003, $19.99) r/Havok & Wolverine: Meltdown #1-4 20.00
... Legends Vol. 3 (2003, $12.99) r/#181-186 13.00
... Legends Vol. 4,5: 4-(See Wolverine: Xisle). 5-(See Wolverine: Snikt!)
.../ Nick Fury: The Scorpio Connection Hardcover (1989, $16.95) 25.00
.../ Nick Fury: The Scorpio Connection Softcover(1990, $12.95) 15.00
...: Not Dead Yet (12/98, $14.95, TPB)-r/#119-122 15.00
...: Save The Tiger 1 (7/92, $2.95, 84 pgs.)-Reprints Wolverine stories from Marvel Comics Presents #1-10 w/new Kieth-c 3.00
...Scorpio Rising ($5.95, prestige format, one-shot) 6.00
.../Shi: Dark Night of Judgment (Crusade Comics, 2000, $2.99) Tucci-a 3.00
...Triumphs And Tragedies-(1995, $16.95, trade paperback)-r/Uncanny X-Men #109,172,173, Wolverine limited series #4, & Wolverine #41,42,75 17.00
...Typhoid's Kiss (6/94, $6.95)-r/Wolverine stories from Marvel Comics Presents #109-116 7.00
...Vs. Spider-Man 1 (3/95, $2.50) -r/Marvel Comics Presents #48-50 2.50
.../Witchblade 1 (3/97, $2.95) Devil's Reign Pt. 5 4.00
Wizard #1/2 (1997) Joe Phillips-a(p) 10.00
NOTE: ***Austin*** *c-3i.* ***Bolton*** *c(back)-5.* ***Buscema*** *a-1-16,25,27p; c-1-10.* ***Byrne*** *a-17-22p, 23; c-1(back), 17-22, 23p.* ***Colan*** *a-24.* ***Andy Kubert*** *c/a-51.* ***Jim Lee*** *c-24, 25, 27.* ***Silvestri*** *a(p)-31-43, 45, 46, 48-50, 52, 53, 55-57; c-31-42p, 43, 45p, 46p, 48, 49p, 50p, 52p, 53p, 55-57p.* ***Stroman*** *a-44p; c-60p.* ***Williamson*** *a-1i, 3-8i; c(i)-1, 3-6.*

WOLVERINE (Volume 3)

Wolverine V3#2 © MAR

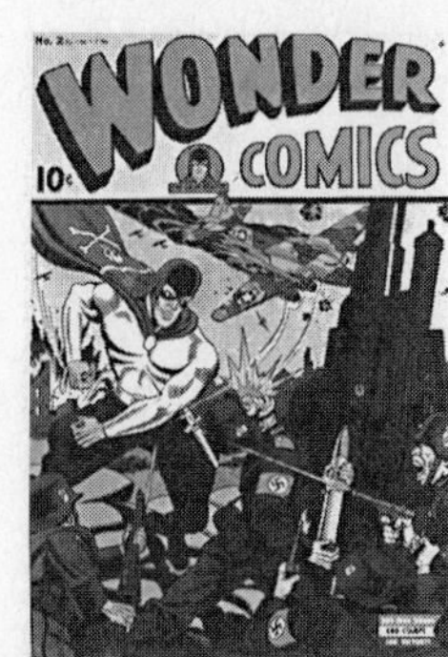

Wonder Comics #2 © GP

Wonder Man #17 © MAR

GD VG FN VF VF/NM NM-
2.0 4.0 6.0 8.0 9.0 9.2

Marvel Comics: July, 2003 - Present ($2.25)
1-Rucka-s/Robertson-a 3.00
2-9: 6-Nightcrawler app. 2.25

WOLVERINE AND THE PUNISHER: DAMAGING EVIDENCE
Marvel Comics: Oct, 1993 - No. 3, Dec, 1993 ($2.00, limited series)
1-3: 2,3-Indicia says "The Punisher and Wolverine..." 2.50

WOLVERINE: DAYS OF FUTURE PAST
Marvel Comics: Dec, 1997 - No. 3, Feb, 1998 ($2.50, limited series)
1-3: J.F. Moore-s/Bennett-a 2.50

WOLVERINE/DOOP (Also see X-Force and X-Statix)(Reprinted in X-Statix Vol. 2)
Marvel Comics: July, 2003 - No. 2, July, 2003 ($2.99, limited series)
1,2-Peter Milligan-s/Darwyn Cooke & J. Bone-a 3.00

WOLVERINE/GAMBIT: VICTIMS
Marvel Comics: Sept, 1995 - No. 4, Dec, 1995 ($2.95, limited series)
1-4: Jeph Loeb scripts & Tim Sale-a; foil-c 4.00

WOLVERINE/HULK
Marvel Comics: Apr, 2002 - No. 4, July, 2002 ($3.50, limited series)
1-4-Sam Kieth-s/a/c 3.50
Wolverine Legends Vol. 1: Wolverine/Hulk (2003, $9.99, TPB) r/#1-4 10.00

WOLVERINE: NETSUKE
Marvel Comics: Nov, 2002 - No. 4, Feb, 2003 ($3.99, limited series)
1-4-George Pratt-s/painted-a 4.00

WOLVERINE/PUNISHER REVELATIONS (Marvel Knights)
Marvel Comics: Jun, 1999 - No. 4, Sept, 1999 ($2.95, limited series)
1-4: Pat Lee-a(p) 4.00
...: Revelation (4/00, $14.95, TPB) r/#1-4 15.00

WOLVERINE SAGA
Marvel Comics: Sept, 1989 - No. 4, Mid-Dec, 1989 ($3.95, lim. series, 52 pgs.)
1-Gives history; Liefeld/Austin-c (front & back) 5.00
2-4: 2-Romita, Jr./Austin-c. 4-Kaluta-c 5.00

WOLVERINE: SNIKT!
Marvel Comics: July, 2003 - No. 5, Nov, 2003 ($2.99, limited series)
1-5-Manga-style; Tsutomu Nihei-s/a 3.00
Wolverine Legends Vol. 5: Snikt! TPB (2003, $13.99) r/#1-5 14.00

WOLVERINE: THE END
Marvel Comics: Jan, 2004 - No. 6 ($2.99, limited series)
1,2-Jenkins-s/Castellini-a 3.00
1-Wizard World Texas variant-c 20.00

WOLVERINE: THE ORIGIN
Marvel Comics: Nov, 2001 - No. 6, July, 2002 ($3.50, limited series)
1-Origin of Logan; Jenkins-s/Andy Kubert-a; Quesada-c 40.00
1-DF edition 60.00
2 15.00
3 9.00
4-6 5.00
HC (3/02, $34.95) r/#1-6; dust jacket; sketch pages and treatments 35.00
SC (2002, $14.95) r/#1-6; afterwords by Jemas and Quesada 15.00

WOLVERINE: XISLE
Marvel Comics: June, 2003 - No. 5, June, 2003 ($2.50, weekly limited series)
1-5-Bruce Jones-s/Jorge Lucas-a 2.50
Wolverine Legends Vol. 4 TPB (2003, $13.99) r/ #1-5 14.00

WOMEN IN LOVE (A Feature Presentation #5)
Fox Features Synd./Hero Books: Aug, 1949 - No. 4, Feb, 1950

	GD	VG	FN	VF	VF/NM	NM-
1	32	64	96	180	255	330
2-Kamen/Feldstein-c	26	52	78	150	210	270
3	18	36	54	101	138	175
4-Wood-a	21	42	63	118	164	210

WOMEN IN LOVE (Thrilling Romances for Adults)
Ziff-Davis Publishing Co.: Winter, 1952 (25¢, 100 pgs.)

	GD	VG	FN	VF	VF/NM	NM-
nn-(Scarce)-Kinstler-a; painted-c	53	106	159	318	477	635

WOMEN OUTLAWS (My Love Memories #9 on)(Also see Red Circle)
Fox Features Syndicate: July, 1948 - No. 8, Sept, 1949

	GD	VG	FN	VF	VF/NM	NM-
1-Used in **SOTI**, illo "Giving children an image of American womanhood"; negligee panels	74	148	222	463	694	925
2,3: 3-Kamenish-a	58	116	174	363	544	725
4-8	47	94	141	282	421	560
nn(nd)-Contains Cody of the Pony Express; same cover as #7	35	70	105	201	288	370

GD VG FN VF VF/NM NM-
2.0 4.0 6.0 8.0 9.0 9.2

WOMEN TO LOVE
Realistic: No date (1953)

	GD	VG	FN	VF	VF/NM	NM-
nn-(Scarce)-Reprints Complete Romance #1; c-/Avon paperback #165	40	80	120	240	340	440

WONDER BOY (Formerly Terrific Comics) (See Blue Bolt, Bomber Comics & Samson)
Ajax/Farrell Publ.: No. 17, May, 1955 - No. 18, July, 1955 (Code approved)

	GD	VG	FN	VF	VF/NM	NM-
17-Phantom Lady app. Bakerish-c/a	46	92	138	276	413	550
18-Phantom Lady app.	40	80	120	240	340	440

NOTE: *Phantom Lady not by Matt Baker.*

WONDER COMICS (Wonderworld #3 on)
Fox Features Syndicate: May, 1939 - No. 2, June, 1939 (68 pgs.)

	GD	VG	FN	VF	VF/NM	NM-
1-(Scarce)-Wonder Man only app. by Will Eisner; Dr. Fung (by Powell), K-51 begins; Bob Kane-a; Eisner-c	1313	2626	3939	9848	15,424	21,000
2-(Scarce)-Yarko the Great, Master Magician (see Samson) by Eisner begins; 'Spark' Stevens by Bob Kane, Patty O'Day, Tex Mason app. Lou Fine's 1st-c; Fine-a (2 pgs.); Yarko-c (Wonder Man-c #1)	448	896	1344	3136	4818	6500

WONDER COMICS
Great/Nedor/Better Publications: May, 1944 - No. 20, Oct, 1948

	GD	VG	FN	VF	VF/NM	NM-
1-The Grim Reaper & Spectro, the Mind Reader begin; Hitler/Hirohito bondage-c	140	280	420	875	1313	1750
2-Origin The Grim Reaper; Super Sleuths begin, end #8,17	68	136	204	425	638	850
3-5	61	122	183	381	573	765
6-10: 6-Flag-c. 8-Last Spectro. 9-Wonderman begins	50	100	150	300	450	600
11-14: 11-Dick Devens, King of Futuria begins, ends #14. 11,12-Ingels-c & splash pg. 14-Bondage-c	59	118	177	369	552	735
15-Tara begins (origin), ends #20	68	136	204	425	638	850
16,18: 16-Spectro app.; last Grim Reaper. 18-The Silver Knight begins	59	118	177	369	552	735
17-Wonderman with Frazetta panels; Jill Trent with all Frazetta inks	61	122	183	381	573	765
19-Frazetta panels	59	118	177	369	552	735
20-Most of Silver Knight by Frazetta	70	140	210	438	657	875

NOTE: ***Ingels** c-11, 12. **Roussos** a-19. **Schomburg (Xela)** c-1-10; (airbrush)-13-20. Bondage c-12, 13, 15. Cover features: Grim Reaper #1-8; Wonder Man #9-15; Tara #16-20.*

WONDER DUCK (See Wisco)
Marvel Comics (CDS): Sept, 1949 - No. 3, Mar, 1950

	GD	VG	FN	VF	VF/NM	NM-
1-Funny animal	16	32	48	92	126	160
2,3	10	20	30	58	77	95

WONDERFUL ADVENTURES OF PINOCCHIO, THE (See Movie Comics & Walt Disney Showcase #48)
Whitman Publishing Co.: April, 1982 (Walt Disney)
nn-(#3 Continuation of Movie Comics?); r/FC #92 6.00

WONDERFUL WORLD OF DISNEY, THE (Walt Disney)
Whitman Publishing Co.: 1978 (Digest, 116 pgs.)

	GD	VG	FN	VF	VF/NM	NM-
1-Barks-a (reprints)	3	6	9	18	24	30
2 (no date)	2	4	6	12	16	20

WONDERFUL WORLD OF THE BROTHERS GRIMM (See Movie Comics)

WONDERLAND COMICS
Feature Publications/Prize: Summer, 1945 - No. 9, Feb-Mar, 1947

	GD	VG	FN	VF	VF/NM	NM-
1-Alex in Wonderland begins; Howard Post-c	19	38	57	107	149	190
2-Howard Post-c/a(2)	10	20	30	58	77	95
3-9: 3,4-Post-c	9	18	27	52	66	80

WONDER MAN (See The Avengers #9, 151)
Marvel Comics Group: Mar, 1986 ($1.25, one-shot, 52 pgs.)
1 3.00

WONDER MAN
Marvel Comics Group: Sept, 1991 - No. 29, Jan, 1994 ($1.00)
1-29: 1-Free fold out poster by Johnson/Austin. 1-3-Johnson/Austin-c/a. 2-Avengers West Coast x-over. 4 Austin-c(i) 2.25
Annual 1 (1992, $2.25)-Immonen-a (10 pgs.) 2.50
Annual 2 (1993, $2.25)-Bagged w/trading card 2.50

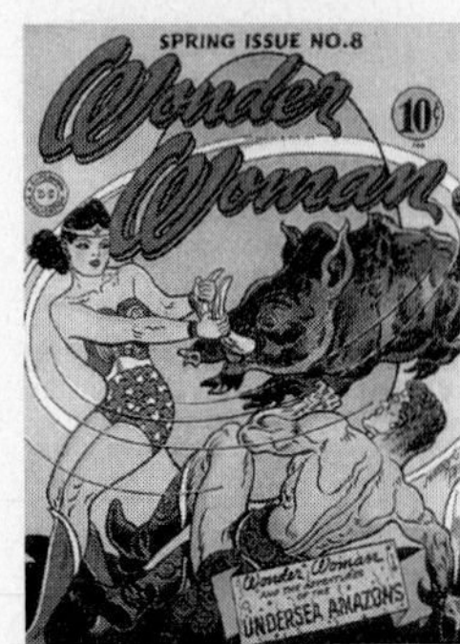

Wonder Woman #8 © DC

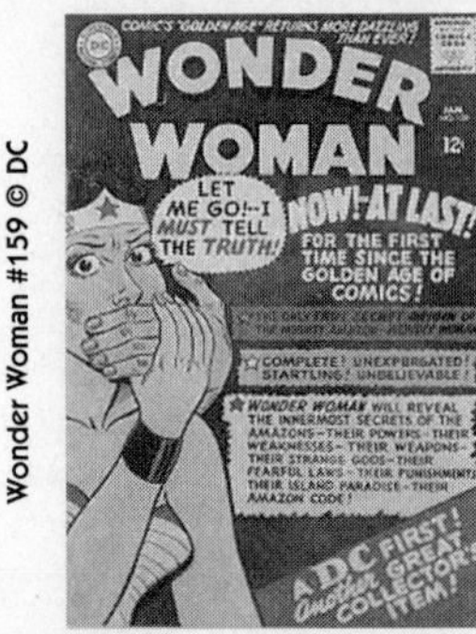

Wonder Woman #159 © DC

Wonder Woman (2nd series) #184 © DC

WONDERS OF ALADDIN, THE
Dell Publishing Co.: No. 1255, Feb-Apr, 1962

	GD 2.0	VG 4.0	FN 6.0	VF 8.0	VF/NM 9.0	NM- 9.2
Four Color 1255-Movie	7	14	21	51	71	90

WONDER WOMAN (See Adventure Comics #459, All-Star Comics, Brave & the Bold, DC Comics Presents, JLA, Justice League of America, Legend of..., Power Record Comics, Sensation Comics, Super Friends and World's Finest Comics #244)

WONDER WOMAN
National Periodical Publications/All-American Publ./DC Comics:
Summer, 1942 - No. 329, Feb, 1986

	GD 2.0	VG 4.0	FN 6.0	VF 8.0	VF/NM 9.0	NM- 9.2
1-Origin Wonder Woman retold (more detailed than All-Star #8); H. G. Peter-c/a begins	2125	4250	6375	15,950	24,975	34,000

1-Reprint, Oversize 13-1/2x10". **WARNING:** This comic is an exact reprint of the original except for its size. DC published it in 1974 with a second cover titling it as a Famous First Edition. There have been many reported cases of the outer cover being removed and the interior sold as the original edition. The reprint with the new outer cover removed is practically worthless. See Famous First Edition for value.

	GD 2.0	VG 4.0	FN 6.0	VF 8.0	VF/NM 9.0	NM- 9.2
2-Origin/1st app. Mars; Duke of Deception app.	407	814	1221	2646	4073	5500
3	220	440	660	1375	2063	2750
4,5: 5-1st Dr. Psycho app.	168	336	504	1050	1575	2100
6-9: 6-1st Cheetah app.	132	264	396	825	1238	1650
10-Invasion from Saturn classic sci-fi-c/s	144	288	432	900	1350	1800
11-20	108	216	324	675	1013	1350
21-30: 23-Story from Wonder Woman's childhood	86	172	258	538	807	1075
31-33,35-40: 38-Last H.G. Peter-c	60	120	180	375	563	750
34-Robot-c	64	128	192	400	600	800
41-44,46-49: 49-Used in **SOTI**, pgs. 234,236; last 52 pg. issue	50	100	150	300	450	600
45-Origin retold	92	184	276	575	863	1150
50-(44 pgs.)-Used in **POP**, pg. 97	50	100	150	300	450	600
51-60: 60-New logo	39	78	117	233	329	425
61-72: 62-Origin of W.W. i.d. 64-Story about 3-D movies. 70-1st Angle Man app. 72-Last pre-code (2/55)	35	70	105	201	283	365
73-90: 80-Origin The Invisible Plane. 85-1st S.A. issue. 89-Flying saucer-c/story	31	62	93	178	252	325
91-94,96,97,99: 97-Last H. G. Peter-a	25	50	75	147	202	260
95-A-Bomb-c	27	54	81	153	214	275
98-New origin & new art team (Andru & Esposito) begin (5/58); origin W.W. id w/new facts	29	58	87	164	232	300
100-(8/58)	29	58	87	164	232	300
101-104,106,108-110	22	44	66	127	176	225
105-(Scarce, 4/59)-W. W.'s secret origin; W. W. appears as girl (no costume yet) (called Wonder Girl - see DC Super-Stars #1)	92	184	276	575	863	1150
107-1st advs. of Wonder Girl; 1st Merboy; tells how Wonder Woman won her costume	31	62	93	178	252	325
111-120	18	36	54	101	138	175
121-126: 122-1st app. Wonder Tot. 124-1st app. Wonder Woman Family. 126-Last 10¢ issue	14	28	42	81	111	140
127-130: 128-Origin The Invisible Plane retold. 129-2nd app. Wonder Woman Family (#133 is 3rd app.)	9	18	27	60	85	110
131-150: 132-Flying saucer-c	7	14	21	51	71	90
151-155,157,158,160-170 (1967): 151-Wonder Girl solo issue	6	12	18	40	55	70
156-(8/65)-Early mention of a comic book shop & comic collecting; mentions DCs selling for $100 a copy	7	14	21	46	63	80
159-Origin retold (1/66); 1st S.A. origin?	9	18	27	60	85	110
171-176	5	10	15	33	44	55
177-W. Woman/Supergirl battle	7	14	21	46	63	80
178-1st new W. Woman	7	14	21	50	68	85
179-Wears no costume to issue #203.	5	10	15	36	48	60
180-195: 180-Death of Steve Trevor. 195-Wood inks	4	8	12	24	32	40
196 (52 pgs.)-Origin-r/All-Star #8 (6 out of 9 pgs.)	4	8	12	27	36	45
197,198 (52 pgs.)-Reprints	4	8	12	27	36	45
199-Jeff Jones painted-c; 52 pgs.	6	12	18	38	52	65
200 (5-6/72)-Jeff Jones-c; 52 pgs.	6	12	18	43	59	75
201,202-Catwoman app. 202-Fafhrd & The Grey Mouser debut.	3	6	9	18	24	30
203,205-210,212: 212-The Cavalier app.	2	4	6	12	16	20
204-Return to old costume; death of I Ching.	3	6	9	16	20	25
211,214-(100 pgs.)	6	12	18	40	55	70
213,215,216,218-220: 220-N. Adams assist	2	4	6	11	14	18
217: (68 pgs.)	3	6	9	18	24	30
221,222,224-227,229,230,233-236,238-240	2	4	6	8	10	12
223,228,231,232,237,241,248: 223-Steve Trevor revived as Steve Howard & learns W.W.'s I.D. 228-Both Wonder Women team up & new World War II stories begin, end #243. 231,232: JSA app. 237-Origin retold. 241-Intro Bouncer; Spectre app. 248-Steve Trevor Howard dies (44 pgs.)	2	4	6	9	11	14
242-246,252-266,269,270: 243-Both W. Women team-up again. 269-Last Wood a(i) for DC? (7/80)	1	2	3	5	6	8
247,249-251,271: 247,249 (44 pgs.). 249-Hawkgirl app. 250-Origin/1st app. Orana, the new W. Woman. 251-Orana dies. 271-Huntress & 3rd Life of Steve Trevor begin	1	2	3	5	7	9
250,251,255-262-(Whitman variants, low print run, no issue # on cover)	2	4	6	10	13	16
267,268-Re-intro Animal Man (5/80 & 6/80)	1	3	4	6	8	10
272-280,284-286,289,290,294-299,301-325						5.00
281-283: Joker-c/stories in Huntress back-ups	1	2	3	5	6	8
287,288,291-293: 287-New Teen Titans x-over. 288-New costume & logo. 291-293-Three part epic with Super-Heroines						5.00
300-($1.50, 76 pgs.)-Anniv. issue; Giffen-a; New Teen Titans, Bronze Age Sandman, JLA & G.A. Wonder Woman app.; 1st app. Lyta Trevor who becomes Fury in All-Star Squadron #25; G.A. Wonder Woman & Steve Trevor revealed as married						6.00
326-328						5.00
329 (Double size)-S.A. W.W. & Steve Trevor wed	1	3	4	6	8	10

NOTE: *Andru/Esposito c-66-160(most). **Buckler** a-300. **Colan** a-288-305p; c-288-290p. **Giffen** a-300p. **Grell** c-217. **Kaluta** c-297. **Gil Kane** c-294p, 303-305, 307, 312, 314. **Miller** c-298p. **Morrow** c-233. **Nasser** a-232p; c-231p, 232p. **Bob Oskner** c(i)-39-65(most). **Perez** c-283p, 284p. **Spiegle** a-312. **Staton** a(p)-241, 271-287, 289, 290, 294-299; c(p)-241, 245, 246. Huntress back-up stories 271-287, 289, 290, 294-299, 301-321.*

WONDER WOMAN
DC Comics: Feb, 1987 - Present (75¢/$1.00/$1.25/$1.95/$1.99/$2.25)

	GD 2.0	VG 4.0	FN 6.0	VF 8.0	VF/NM 9.0	NM- 9.2
0-(10/94) Zero Hour; released between #90 & #91	1	2	3	5	6	8
1-New origin; Perez-c/a begins	1	2	3	4	5	7
2-5						5.00
6-20: 9-Origin Cheetah. 12,13-Millennium x-over. 18,26-Free 16 pg. story						4.00
21-49: 24-Last Perez-a; scripts continue thru #62						3.00
50-($1.50, 52 pgs.)-New Titans, Justice League						4.00
51-62: Perez scripts. 60-Vs. Lobo; last Perez-c. 62-Last $1.00-c						3.00
63-New direction & Bolland-c begin; Deathstroke story continued fromW. W. Special #1						4.00
64-84						2.50
85-1st Deodato-a; ends #100	2	4	6	8	10	12
86-88: 88-Superman-c & app.						5.00
89-97: 90-(9/94)-1st Artemis. 91-(11/94). 93-Hawkman app. 96-Joker-c						4.00
98,99						3.00
100 ($2.95, Newsstand)-Death of Artemis; Bolland-c ends.						4.00
100 ($3.95, Direct Market)-Death of Artemis; foil-c.						6.00
101-119, 121-125: 101-Begin $1.95-c; Byrne-c/a/scripts begin. 101-104-Darkseid app. 105-Phantom Stranger cameo. 106-108-Phantom Stranger & Demon app. 107,108-Arion app. 111-1st app. new Wonder Girl. 111,112-Vs.Doomsday. 112-Superman app. 113-Wonder Girl-c/app; Sugar & Spike app.						2.50
120 ($2.95)-Perez-c						3.00
126-149: 128-Hippolyta becomes new W.W. 130-133-Flash (Jay Garrick) & JSA app. 136-Diana returns to W.W. role; last Byrne issue. 137-Priest-s. 139-Luke-s/Paquette-a begin; Hughes-c thru #146						2.50
150-($2.95) Hughes-c/Clark-a; Zauriel app.						3.00
151-158-Hughes-c. 153-Superboy app.						2.25
159-163: 159-Begin $2.25-c. 160,161-Clayface app. 162,163-Aquaman app.						2.25
164-171: Phil Jimenez-s/a begin; Hughes-c; Batman app. 168,169-Pérez co-plot 169-Wraparound-c.170-Lois Lane-c/app.						2.25
172-Our Worlds at War; Hippolyta killed						3.00
173,174: 173-Our Worlds at War; Darkseid app. 174-Every DC heroine app.						2.25
175-($3.50) Joker: Last Laugh; JLA app.; Jim Lee-c						3.50
176-199: 177-Paradise Island returns. 179-Jimenez-c. 184,185-Hippolyta-c/app.; Hughes-c 186-Cheetah app. 189-Simonson-s/Ordway-a begin. 190-Diana's new look. 195-Rucka-s/Drew Johnson-a begin. 197-Flash-c/app. 198,199-Noto-c						2.25
#1,000,000 (11/98) 853rd Century x-over; Deodato-c						3.00
Annual 1,2: 1 ('88, $1.50)-Art Adams-a. 2 ('89, $2.00, 68 pgs.)-All women artists issue; Perez-c(i)/a.						4.00
Annual 3 (1992, $2.50, 68 pgs.)-Quesada-c(p)						3.00
Annual 4 (1995, $3.50)-Year One						3.50
Annual 5 (1996, $2.95)-Legends of the Dead Earth story; Byrne scripts; Cockrum-a						3.00
Annual 6 (1997, $3.95)-Pulp Heroes						4.00
Annual 7,8 ('98,'99, $2.95)-7-Ghosts; Wrightson-c. 8-JLApe, A.Adams-c						3.00
...Donna Troy (6/98, $1.95) Girlfrenzy; Jimenez-a						2.50
... 80-Page Giant 1 (2002, $4.95) reprints in format of 1960s' 80-Page Giants						5.00
Gallery (1996, $3.50)-Bolland-c; pin-ups by various						4.00
...: Gods of Gotham TPB ('01, $5.95) r/#164-167; Jimenez-s/a						6.00
Lifelines TPB ('98, $9.95) r/#106-112; Byrne-c/a						10.00
...: Our Worlds at War (10/01, $2.95) History of the Amazons; Jae Lee-c						3.00
...: Paradise Found TPB ('03, $14.95) r/#171-177, Secret Files #3; Jimenez-s/a						15.00

Wonderworld Comics #14 © FOX

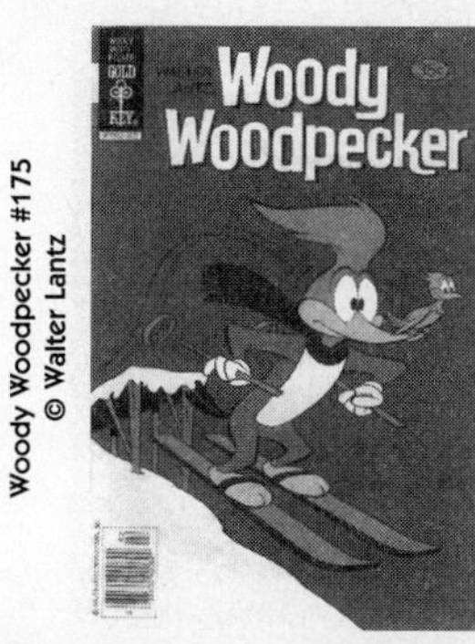

Woody Woodpecker #175 © Walter Lantz

The World Around Us #35 © GIL

GD VG FN VF VF/NM NM-
2.0 4.0 6.0 8.0 9.0 9.2

...: Paradise Lost TPB ('02, $14.95) r/#164-170; Jimenez-s/a 15.00
Plus 1 (1/97, $2.95)-Jesse Quick-c/app. 3.00
Second Genesis TPB (1997, $9.95)-r/#101-105 10.00
Secret Files 1-3 (3/98, 7/99, 5/02; $4.95) 5.00
Special 1 (1992, $1.75, 52 pgs.)-Deathstroke-c/story continued in Wonder Woman #63 4.00
...: The Blue Amazon (2003, $6.95) Elseworlds; McKeever-a 7.00
The Challenge Of Artemis TPB (1996, $9.95)-r/#94-100; Deodato-c/a 10.00
...: The Once and Future Story (1998, $4.95) Trina Robbins-s/Doran & Guice-a 5.00
NOTE: ***Art Adams*** *a-Annual 1.* ***Byrne*** *c/a 101-107.* ***Bolton*** *a-Annual 1.* ***Deodato*** *a-85-100.* ***Perez*** *a-Annual 1; c-Annual 1(i).* ***Quesada*** *c(p)-Annual 3.*

WONDER WOMAN: AMAZONIA
DC Comics: 1997 ($7.95, Graphic Album format, one shot)
1-Elseworlds; Messner-Loebs-s/Winslade-a 8.00

WONDER WOMAN SPECTACULAR (See DC Special Series #9)

WONDER WOMAN: SPIRIT OF TRUTH
DC Comics: Nov, 2001 ($9.95, treasury size, one-shot)
nn-Painted art by Alex Ross; story by Alex Ross and Paul Dini 10.00

WONDER WOMAN: THE HIKETEIA
DC Comics: 2002 ($24.95, hardcover, one-shot)
nn-Wonder Woman battles Batman; Greg Rucka-s/J.G. Jones-a 25.00
Softcover (2003, $17.95) 18.00

WONDERWORLD COMICS (Formerly Wonder Comics)
Fox Features Syndicate: No. 3, July, 1939 - No. 33, Jan, 1942
3-Intro The Flame by Fine; Dr. Fung (Powell-a), K-51 (Powell-a?), & Yarko the Great, Master Magician (Eisner-a) continues; Eisner/Fine-c
648 1296 1944 4536 6968 9400
4-Lou Fine-c 315 630 945 2048 3149 4250
5,6,9,10: Lou Fine-c 176 352 528 1100 1650 2200
7-Classic Lou Fine-c 300 600 900 1900 2850 3800
8-Classic Lou Fine-c 248 496 744 1550 2325 3100
11-Origin The Flame 134 268 402 838 1257 1675
12-15:13-Dr. Fung ends; last Fine-c 112 224 336 700 1050 1400
16-20 83 166 249 519 777 1035
21-Origin The Black Lion & Cub 76 152 228 475 713 950
22-27: 22,25-Dr. Fung app. 61 122 183 381 573 765
28-Origin & 1st app. U.S. Jones (8/41); Lu-Nar, the Moon Man begins
83 166 249 519 777 1035
29,31,33 50 100 150 300 425 600
30-Intro & Origin Flame Girl 90 180 270 563 844 1125
32-Hitler-c 70 140 210 438 657 875
NOTE: *Spies at War by* ***Eisner*** *in #13, 17. Yarko by* ***Eisner*** *in #3-11.* ***Eisner*** *text illos-3.* ***Lou Fine*** *a-3-11; c-3-13, 15; text illos-4.* ***Nordling*** *a-4-14.* ***Powell*** *a-3-12.* ***Tuska*** *a-5-9. Bondage-c 14, 15, 28, 31, 32. Cover features: The Flame-#3, 5-31; U.S. Jones-#32, 33.*

WONDERWORLDS
Innovation Publishing: 1992 ($3.50, squarebound, 100 pgs.)
1-Rebound super-hero comics, contents may vary; Hero Alliance, Terraformers, etc. 3.50

WOODSY OWL (See March of Comics #395)
Gold Key: Nov, 1973 - No. 10, Feb, 1976
1 2 4 6 14 18 22
2-10 2 4 6 8 10 12

WOODY WOODPECKER (Walter Lantz... #73 on?)(See Dell Giants for annuals)
(Also see The Funnies, Jolly Jingles, Kite Fun Book, New Funnies)
Dell Publishing Co./Gold Key No. 73-187/Whitman No. 188 on:
No. 169, 10/47 - No. 72, 5-7/62; No. 73, 10/62 - No. 201, 3/84 (nn 192)
Four Color 169(#1)-Drug turns Woody into a Mr. Hyde
18 36 54 131 191 250
Four Color 188 12 24 36 84 125 165
Four Color 202,232,249,264,288 9 18 27 60 85 110
Four Color 305,336,350 6 12 18 43 59 75
Four Color 364,374,390,405,416,431('52) 5 10 15 36 48 60
16 (12-1/52-53) - 30('55) 4 8 12 27 36 45
31-50 3 7 10 21 28 35
51-72 (Last Dell) 3 6 9 18 23 28
73-75 (Giants, 84 pgs., Gold Key) 5 10 15 36 48 60
76-80 3 6 9 16 20 24
81-103: 103-Last 12¢ issue 2 4 6 12 16 20
104-120 2 4 6 11 14 18
121-140 2 4 6 9 11 14
141-160 1 3 4 6 8 10
161-187 1 2 3 5 7 9

GD VG FN VF VF/NM NM-
2.0 4.0 6.0 8.0 9.0 9.2

188,189 (Whitman) 2 4 6 8 10 12
190(9/80),191(11/80)-pre-pack only 2 4 6 14 18 22
(No #192)
193-197: 196(2/82), 197(4/82) 2 4 6 10 13 16
198-201 (All #90062 on-c, no date or date code, pre-pack): 198(6/83), 199(7/83), 200(8/83), 201(3/84) 2 4 6 11 14 18
Christmas Parade 1(11/68-Giant)(G.K.) 4 8 12 29 40 50
Summer Fun 1(6/66-G.K.)(84 pgs.) 5 10 15 36 48 60
NOTE: *15¢ Canadian editions of the 12¢ issues exist. Reprints-No. 92, 102, 103, 105, 106, 124, 125, 152, 153, 157, 162, 165, 194(1/3)-200(1/3).*

WOODY WOODPECKER (See Comic Album #5,9,13, Dell Giant #24, 40, 54, Dell Giants, The Funnies, Golden Comics Digest #1, 3, 5, 8, 15, 16, 20, 24, 32, 37, 44, March of Comics #16, 34, 85, 93, 109, 124, 139, 158, 177, 184, 203, 222, 239, 249, 261, 420, 454, 466, 478, New Funnies & Super Book #12, 24)

WOODY WOODPECKER
Harvey Comics: Sept, 1991 - No. 15, Aug, 1994 ($1.25)
1-15: 1-r/W.W. #53 2.50
50th Anniversary Special 1 (10/91, $2.50, 68 pgs.) 3.00

WOODY WOODPECKER AND FRIENDS
Harvey Comics: Dec, 1991 - No. 4, 1992 ($1.25)
1-4 2.50

WORDSMITH (1st Series)
Renegade Press: Aug, 1985 - No. 12, Jan, 1988 ($1.70/$2.00, B&W, bi-monthly)
1-12: R. G. Taylor-c/a 3.00

WORDSMITH (2nd Series)
Caliber: 1996 - No. 9, 1997 ($2.95, B&W, limited series)
1-9: Reprints in all. 1-Contains 3 pg. sketchbook. 6-Flip book w/Raven Chronicles #10 3.00

WORD WARRIORS (Also see Quest for Dreams Lost)
Literacy Volunteers of Chicago: 1987 ($1.50, B&W)(Proceeds donated to help literacy)
1-Jon Sable by Grell, Ms. Tree, Streetwolf; Chaykin-c 3.00

WORLD AROUND US, THE (Illustrated Story of...)
Gilberton Publishers (Classics Illustrated): Sep, 1958 -No. 36, Oct, 1961 (25¢)
1-Dogs; Evans-a 8 16 24 46 58 70
2-4: 2-Indians; Check-a. 3-Horses; L. B. Cole-c. 4-Railroads; L. B. Cole-a (5 pgs.)
8 16 24 46 58 70
5-Space; Ingels-a 10 20 30 56 73 90
6-The F.B.I.; Disbrow, Evans, Ingels-a 10 20 30 56 73 90
7-Pirates; Disbrow, Ingels, Kinstler-a 9 18 27 52 66 80
8-Flight; Evans, Ingels, Crandall-a 9 18 27 52 66 80
9-Army; Disbrow, Ingels, Orlando-a 8 16 24 46 58 70
10-13: 10-Navy; Disbrow, Kinstler-a. 11-Marine Corps. 12-Coast Guard; Ingels-a (9 pgs.). 13-Air Force; L.B. Cole-c 8 16 24 46 58 70
14-French Revolution; Crandall, Evans, Kinstler-a 10 20 30 56 73 90
15-Prehistoric Animals; Al Williamson-a, 6 & 10 pgs. plus Morrow-a
10 20 30 58 77 95
16-18: 16-Crusades; Kinstler-a. 17-Festivals; Evans, Crandall-a. 18-Great Scientists; Crandall, Evans, Torres, Williamson, Morrow-a 9 18 27 52 66 80
19-Jungle; Crandall, Williamson, Morrow-a 10 20 30 58 77 95
20-Communications; Crandall, Evans, Torres-a 10 20 30 56 73 90
21-American Presidents; Crandall/Evans, Morrow-a 10 20 30 56 73 90
22-Boating; Morrow-a 8 16 24 43 54 65
23-Great Explorers; Crandall, Evans-a 9 18 27 52 66 80
24-Ghosts; Morrow, Evans-a 10 20 30 56 73 90
25-Magic; Evans, Morrow-a 10 20 30 56 73 90
26-The Civil War 11 22 33 63 84 105
27-Mountains (High Advs.); Crandall/Evans, Morrow, Torres-a
9 18 27 52 66 80
28-Whaling; Crandall, Evans, Morrow, Torres, Wildey-a; L.B. Cole-c
9 18 27 52 66 80
29-Vikings; Crandall, Evans, Torres, Morrow-a 10 20 30 58 77 95
30-Undersea Adventure; Crandall/Evans, Kirby, Morrow, Torres-a
10 20 30 56 73 90
31-Hunting; Crandall/Evans, Ingels, Kinstler, Kirby-a 9 18 27 52 66 80
32,33: 32-For Gold & Glory; Morrow, Kirby, Crandall, Evans-a. 33-Famous Teens; Torres, Crandall, Evans-a 9 18 27 52 66 80
34-36: 34-Fishing; Crandall/Evans-a. 35-Spies; Kirby, Morrow?, Evans-a. 36-Fight for Life (Medicine); Kirby-a 9 18 27 52 66 80
NOTE: See Classics Illustrated Special Edition. Another *World Around Us* issue entitled *The Sea* had been prepared in 1962 but was never published in the U.S. It was published in the British/European *World Around Us* series. Those series then continued with seven additional WAU titles not in the U.S. series.

WORLD BELOW, THE
Dark Horse Comics: Mar, 1999 - No. 4, Jun, 1999 ($2.50, limited series)

The World of Archie #5 © AP

World of Suspense #7 © MAR

World's Finest Comics #2 © DC

	GD 2.0	VG 4.0	FN 6.0	VF 8.0	VF/NM 9.0	NM- 9.2

1-4-Paul Chadwick-s/c/a 2.50

WORLD BELOW, THE: DEEPER AND STRANGER
Dark Horse Comics: Dec, 1999 - No. 4, Mar, 2000 ($2.95, B&W)

1-4-Paul Chadwick-s/c/a 3.00

WORLD CLASS COMICS
Image Comics: Aug, 2002 ($4.95, B&W)

1-Characters from Big Bang Comics 5.00

WORLD FAMOUS HEROES MAGAZINE
Comic Corp. of America (Centaur): Oct, 1941 - No. 4, Apr, 1942 (comic book)

1-Gustavson-c; Lubbers, Glanzman-a; Davy Crockett, Paul Revere, Lewis & Clark, John Paul Jones stories; Flag-c 118 236 354 738 1107 1475
2-Lou Gehrig life story; Lubbers-a 50 100 150 300 450 600
3,4-Lubbers-a. 4-Wild Bill Hickok story; 2 pg. Marlene Dietrich story 46 92 138 276 413 550

WORLD FAMOUS STORIES
Croyden Publishers: 1945

1-Ali Baba, Hansel & Gretel, Rip Van Winkle, Mid-Summer Night's Dream 14 28 42 79 107 135

WORLD IS HIS PARISH, THE
George A. Pflaum: 1953 (15¢)

nn-The story of Pope Pius XII 6 12 18 28 34 40

WORLD OF ADVENTURE (Walt Disney's...)(TV)
Gold Key: Apr, 1963 - No. 3, Oct, 1963 (12¢)

1-Disney TV characters; Savage Sam, Johnny Shiloh, Capt. Nemo, The Mooncussers 4 8 12 24 32 40
2,3 3 6 9 16 20 24

WORLD OF ARCHIE, THE (See Archie Giant Series Mag. #148, 151, 156, 160, 165, 171, 177, 182, 188, 193, 200, 208, 213, 225, 232, 237, 244, 249, 456, 461, 468, 473, 480, 485, 492, 497, 504, 509, 516, 521, 532, 543, 554, 565, 574, 587, 599, 612, 627)

WORLD OF ARCHIE
Archie Comics: Aug, 1992 - No. 22 ($1.25/$1.50)

1 4.00
2-15: 9-Neon ink-c 3.00
16-22 2.50

WORLD OF FANTASY
Atlas Comics (CPC No. 1-15/ZPC No. 16-19): May, 1956 - No. 19, Aug, 1959

1 46 92 138 276 413 550
2-Williamson-a (4 pgs.) 33 66 99 190 270 350
3-Sid Check, Roussos-a 29 58 87 164 232 300
4-7 22 44 66 127 176 225
8-Matt Fox, Orlando, Berg-a 24 48 72 135 190 245
9-Krigstein-a 23 46 69 129 180 230
10-15: 11-Torres-a 18 36 54 101 138 175
16-Williamson-a (4 pgs.); Ditko, Kirby-a 25 50 75 144 198 255
17-19-Ditko, Kirby-a 25 50 75 144 198 255

NOTE: ***Ayers*** *a-3.* ***B. Baily*** *a-4.* ***Berg*** *a-5, 6, 8.* ***Brodsky*** *c-3.* ***Check*** *a-3.* ***Ditko*** *a-17, 19.* ***Everett*** *a-2; c-4-7, 9, 12, 13.* ***Forte*** *a-4.* ***Infantino*** *a-14.* ***Kirby*** *c-15, 17-19.* ***Krigstein*** *a-9.* ***Maneely*** *c-2, 14.* ***Mooney*** *a-14.* ***Morrow*** *a-7.* ***Orlando*** *a-8, 13, 14.* ***Pakula*** *a-9.* ***Powell*** *a-4, 6.* ***R.Q. Sale*** *a-3, 9.* ***Severin*** *c-1.*

WORLD OF GIANT COMICS, THE (See Archie All-Star Specials under Archie Comics)

WORLD OF GINGER FOX, THE (Also see Ginger Fox)
Comico: Nov, 1986 ($6.95, 8 1/2 x 11", 68 pgs., mature)

Graphic Novel ($6.95) 7.00
Hardcover ($27.95) 28.00

WORLD OF JUGHEAD, THE (See Archie Giant Series Mag. #9, 14, 19, 24, 30, 136, 143, 149, 152, 157, 161, 166, 172, 178, 183, 189, 194, 202, 209, 215, 227, 233, 239, 245, 251, 457, 463, 469, 475, 481, 487, 493, 499, 505, 511, 517, 523, 531, 542, 553, 564, 577, 590, 602)

WORLD OF KRYPTON, THE (World of...#3) (See Superman #248)
DC Comics, Inc.: 7/79 - No. 3, 9/79; 12/87 - No. 4, 3/88 (Both are lim. series)

1-3 (1979, 40¢; 1st comic book mini-series): 1-Jor-El marries Lara. 3-Baby Superman sent to Earth; Krypton explodes; Mon-el app. 5.00
1-4 (75¢)-Byrne scripts; Byrne/Simonson-c 3.00

WORLD OF METROPOLIS, THE
DC Comics: Aug, 1988 - No. 4, July, 1988 ($1.00, limited series)

1-4: Byrne scripts 3.00

WORLD OF MYSTERY
Atlas Comics (GPI): June, 1956 - No. 7, July, 1957

	GD 2.0	VG 4.0	FN 6.0	VF 8.0	VF/NM 9.0	NM- 9.2

1-Torres, Orlando-a; Powell-a? 46 92 138 276 413 550
2-Woodish-a 20 40 60 112 156 200
3-Torres, Davis, Ditko-a 25 50 75 144 198 255
4-Pakula, Powell-a 25 50 75 144 198 255
5,7: 5-Orlando-a 20 40 60 112 156 200
6-Williamson/Mayo-a (4 pgs.); Ditko-a; Crandall text illo 25 50 75 144 198 255

NOTE: ***Brodsky*** *c-2.* ***Colan*** *a-7.* ***Everett*** *c-1, 3.* ***Pakula*** *a-4, 6.* ***Romita*** *a-2.* ***Severin*** *c-7.*

WORLD OF SMALLVILLE
DC Comics: Apr, 1988 - No. 4, July, 1988 (75¢, limited series)

1-4: Byrne scripts 3.00

WORLD OF SUSPENSE
Atlas News Co.: Apr, 1956 - No. 8, July, 1957

1 40 80 120 240 340 440
2-Ditko-a (4 pgs.) 24 48 72 138 194 250
3,7-Williamson-a in both (4 pgs.); #7-with Mayo 24 48 72 135 190 245
4-6,8 20 40 60 112 156 200

NOTE: ***Berg*** *a-6.* ***Cameron*** *a-2.* ***Ditko*** *a-2.* ***Drucker*** *a-1.* ***Everett*** *a-1, 5; c-6.* ***Heck*** *a-5.* ***Maneely*** *a-1; c-1-3.* ***Orlando*** *a-5.* ***Powell*** *a-6.* ***Reinman*** *a-4.* ***Roussos*** *a-6.* ***Shores*** *a-1.*

WORLD OF WHEELS (Formerly Dragstrip Hotrodders)
Charlton Comics: No. 17, Oct, 1967 - No. 32, June, 1970

17-20-Features Ken King 3 6 9 19 25 32
21-32-Features Ken King 3 6 9 16 20 25
Modern Comics Reprint 23(1978) 5.00

WORLD OF WOOD
Eclipse Comics: 1986 - No. 4, 1987; No. 5, 2/89 ($1.75, limited series)

1-4:1-Dave Stevens-c. 2-Wood/Stevens-c 4.00
5 ($2.00, B&W)-r/Avon's Flying Saucers 5.00

WORLD'S BEST COMICS (World's Finest Comics #2 on)
National Per. Publications (100 pgs.): Spring, 1941 (Cardboard-c)(DC's 6th annual format comic)

1-The Batman, Superman, Crimson Avenger, Johnny Thunder, The King, Young Dr. Davis, Zatara, Lando, Man of Magic, & Red, White & Blue begin; Superman, Batman & Robin covers begin (inside-c is blank); Fred Ray-c; 15¢ cover price 1429 2858 4287 10,080 15,790 21,500

WORLD'S BEST COMICS: GOLDEN AGE SAMPLER
DC Comics: 2003 (99¢, one-shot, samples from DC Archive editions)

1-Golden Age reprints from Superman #6, Batman #5, Sensation #11, Police #11 2.25

WORLDS BEYOND (Stories of Weird Adventure)(Worlds of Fear #2 on)
Fawcett Publications: Nov, 1951

1-Powell, Bailey-a; Moldoff-c 44 88 132 264 395 525

WORLDS COLLIDE
DC Comics: July, 1994 ($2.50, one-shot)

1-($2.50, 52 pgs.)-Milestone & Superman titles x-over 2.50
1-($3.95, 52 pgs.)-Polybagged w/vinyl clings 4.00

WORLD'S FAIR COMICS (See New York...)

WORLD'S FINEST (Also see Legends of The World's Finest)
DC Comics: 1990 - No. 3, 1990 ($3.95, squarebound, limited series, 52 pgs.)

1-3: Batman & Superman team-up against The Joker and Lex Luthor; Dave Gibbons scripts & Steve Rude-c/a. 2,3-Joker/Luthor painted-c by Steve Rude 5.00
TPB-($19.95) r/#1-3 20.00

WORLD'S FINEST COMICS (Formerly World's Best Comics #1)
National Periodical Publ./DC Comics: No. 2, Sum, 1941 - No. 323, Jan, 1986 (#1-17 have cardboard covers) (#2-9 have 100 pgs.)

2 (100 pgs.)-Superman, Batman & Robin covers continue from World's Best; (cover price 15¢ #2-70) 428 856 1284 2996 4598 6200
3-The Sandman begins; last Johnny Thunder; origin & 1st app. The Scarecrow 326 652 978 2119 3260 4400
4-Hop Harrigan app.; last Young Dr. Davis 260 520 780 1625 2438 3250
5-Intro. TNT & Dan the Dyna-Mite; last King & Crimson Avenger 260 520 780 1625 2438 3250
6-Star Spangled Kid begins (Sum/42); Aquaman app.; S&K Sandman with Sandy in new costume begins, ends #7 192 384 576 1200 1800 2400
7-Green Arrow begins (Fall/42); last Lando & Red, White & Blue; S&K art 192 384 576 1200 1800 2400
8-Boy Commandos begin (by Simon(p) #12); last The King 180 360 540 1125 1688 2250
9-Batman cameo in Star Spangled Kid; S&K-a; last 100 pg. issue; Hitler, Mussolini,

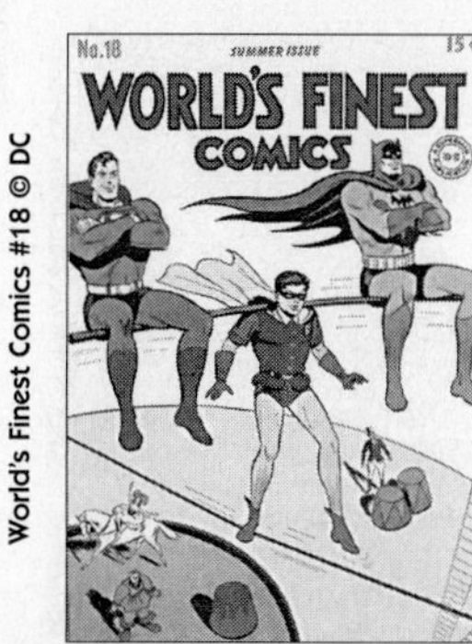

World's Finest Comics #18 © DC

World's Finest Comics #166 © DC

World's Finest Comics #322 © DC

	GD 2.0	VG 4.0	FN 6.0	VF 8.0	VF/NM 9.0	NM- 9.2
Tojo-c	200	400	600	1250	1875	2500
10-S&K-a; 76 pg. issues begin	168	336	504	1050	1575	2100
11-17: 17-Last cardboard cover issue	138	276	414	863	1294	1725
18-20: 18-Paper covers begin; last Star Spangled Kid. 20-Last quarterly issue	120	240	360	750	1125	1500
21-30: 21-Begin bi-monthly. 30-Johnny Everyman app.	85	170	255	531	796	1060
31-40: 33-35-Tomahawk app.	76	152	228	475	713	950
41-50: 41-Boy Commandos end. 42-Intro The Wyoming Kid & begins (9-10/49), ends #63. 43-Full Steam Foley begins, ends #48. 48-Last square binding. 49-Tom Sparks, Boy Inventor begins; robot-c	58	116	174	363	542	720
51-60: 51-Zatara ends. 54-Last 76 pg. issue. 59-Manhunters Around the World begins (7-8/52), ends #62	55	110	165	344	515	685
61-64: 61-Joker story. 63-Capt. Compass app.	55	110	165	330	495	660
65-Origin Superman; Tomahawk begins (7-8/53), ends #101	79	158	237	494	740	985
66-70-(15¢ issues, scarce)-Last 15¢, 68pg. issue	55	110	165	330	495	660
71-(10¢ issue, scarce)-Superman & Batman begin as team (7-8/54); were in separate stories until now; Superman & Batman exchange identities; 10¢ issues begin	90	180	270	675	1038	1400
72,73-(10¢ issue, scarce)	63	126	189	473	724	975
74-Last pre-code issue	48	96	144	360	555	750
75-(1st code approved, 3-4/55)	46	92	138	345	528	710
76-80: 77-Superman loses powers & Batman obtains them	36	72	108	270	405	540
81-90: 84-1st S.A. issue. 88-1st Joker/Luthor team-up. 89-2nd Batmen of All Nations (aka Club of Heroes). 90-Batwoman's 1st app. in World's Finest (10/57, 3rd app. anywhere) plus-c app.	29	58	87	210	310	410
91-93,95-99: 96-99-Kirby Green Arrow. 99-Robot-c	22	44	66	156	228	300
94-Origin Superman/Batman team retold	53	106	159	424	642	860
100 (3/59)	36	72	108	270	405	540
101-110: 102-Tommy Tomorrow begins, ends #124	15	30	45	109	160	210
111-121: 111-1st app. The Clock King. 113-Intro. Miss Arrowette in Green Arrow; 1st Bat-Mite/Mr. Mxyzptlk team-up (11/60). 117-Batwoman-c. 121-Last 10¢ issue	12	24	36	84	125	165
122-128: 123-2nd Bat-Mite/Mr. Mxyzptlk team-up (2/62). 125-Aquaman begins (5/62), ends #139 (Aquaman #1 is dated 1-2/62)	9	18	27	65	93	120
129-Joker/Luthor team-up-c/story	10	20	30	73	107	140
130-142: 135-Last Dick Sprang story. 140-Last Green Arrow. 142-Origin The Composite Superman (villain); Legion app.	7	14	21	51	71	90
143-150: 143-1st Mailbag. 144-Clayface/Brainiac team-up; last Clayface until Action #443	6	12	18	40	55	70
151-153,155,157-160: 156-Intro of Bizarro Batman. 157-2nd Super Sons story; last app. Kathy Kane (Bat-Woman) until Batman Family #10	5	10	15	36	48	60
154-1st Super Sons story; last Bat-Woman in costume until Batman Family #10.	6	12	18	40	55	70
156-1st Bizarro Batman; Joker-c/story	10	20	30	72	104	135
161,170 (80-Pg. Giants G-28,G-40)	6	12	18	43	59	75
162-165,167,168,171,172: 168,172-Adult Legion app.	4	8	12	27	36	45
166-Joker-c/story	5	10	15	33	44	55
169-3rd app. new Batgirl(9/67)(cover and 1 panel cameo); 3rd Bat-Mite/Mr. Mxyzptlk team-up	4	8	12	29	40	50
173-('68)-1st S.A. app. Two-Face as Batman becomes Two-Face in story	9	18	27	63	89	115
174-Adams-c	4	8	12	29	40	50
175,176-Neal Adams-c/a; both reprint J'onn J'onzz origin/Detective #225,226	5	10	15	33	44	55
177-Joker/Luthor team-up-c/story	4	8	12	29	40	50
178,180,182,183,185,186: Adams-c on all. 182-Silent Knight-r/Brave & Bold #6. 185-Last 12¢ issue. 186-Johnny Quick-r	4	8	12	24	32	40
179-(80 Page Giant G-52) -Adams-c; r/#94	6	12	18	38	52	65
181,184,187: 187-Green Arrow origin-r by Kirby (Adv. #256)	3	7	10	21	28	35
188,197:(Giants G-64,G-76; 64 pages)	5	10	15	36	48	60
189-196: 190-193-Robin-r	3	6	9	18	23	28
198,199-3rd Superman/Flash race (see Flash #175 & Superman #199). 199-Adams-c	9	18	27	60	85	110
200-Adams-c	3	6	9	19	25	32
201-203: 203-Last 15¢ issue.	3	6	9	16	20	24
204,205-(52 pgs.) Adams-c: 204-Wonder Woman app. 205-Shining Knight-r (6 pgs.) by Frazetta/Adv. #153; Teen Titans x-over	3	6	9	18	24	30
206 (Giant G-88, 64 pgs.)	5	10	15	33	44	55
207,212-(52 pgs.)	3	6	9	18	24	30
208-211(25¢-c) Adams-c: 208-(52 pgs.) Origin Robotman-r/Det. #138. 209-211-(52 pgs.)	3	6	9	19	25	32
213,214,216-222,229: 217-Metamorpho begins, ends #220; Batman/Superman team-ups resume. 229-r/origin Superman-Batman team	2	4	6	10	13	16
215-Intro. Batman Jr. & Superman Jr.	3	6	9	18	24	30
223-228-(100 pgs.). 223-N. Adams-r. 223-Deadman origin. 226-N. Adams, S&K, Toth-r; Manhunter part origin-r/Det. #225,226. 227-Deadman app.	4	8	12	29	40	50
230-(68 pgs.)	3	6	9	18	23	28
231-243,247,248: 242-Super Sons. 248-Last Vigilante	2	4	6	8	10	12
244-246-Adams-c: 244-$1.00, 84 pg. issues begin; Green Arrow, Black Canary, Wonder Woman, Vigilante begin; 246-Death of Stuff in Vigilante; origin Vigilante retold	2	4	6	12	16	20
249-252 (84 pgs.) Ditko-a: 249-The Creeper begins by Ditko, 84 pgs. 250-The Creeper origin retold by Ditko. 252-Last 84 pg. issue	2	4	6	12	16	20
253-257,259-265: 253-Capt. Marvel begins; 68 pgs. begin, end #265. 255-Last Creeper. 256-Hawkman begins. 257-Black Lightning begins. 263-Super Sons. 264-Clay Face app.	2	4	6	8	10	12
258-Adams-c	2	4	6	9	11	14
266-270,272-282-(52 pgs.). 267-Challengers of the Unknown app.; 3 Lt. Marvels return. 268-Capt. Marvel Jr. origin retold. 274-Zatanna begins. 279, 280-Capt. Marvel Jr. & Kid Eternity learn they are brothers	1	3	4	6	8	10
271-(52pgs.) Origin Superman/Batman team retold	2	4	6	8	10	12
283-299: 284-Legion app.	1	2	3	4	5	7
300-($1.25, 52pgs.)-Justice League of America, New Teen Titans & The Outsiders app.; Perez-a (3 pgs.)	1	2	3	5	6	8
301-322: 304-Origin Null and Void. 309,319-Free 16 pg. story in each (309-Flash Force 2000, 319-Mask preview)						3.00
323-Last issue						6.00

NOTE: ***Neal Adams*** *a-230ir; c-174-176, 178-180, 182, 183, 185, 186, 199-205, 208-211, 244-246, 258.* ***Austin*** *a-244-246i.* ***Burnley*** *a-8, 10; c-7-9, 11-14, 15p?, 16-18p, 20-31p.* ***Colan*** *a-274p, 297, 299.* ***Ditko*** *a-249-255.* ***Giffen*** *a-322; c-284p, 322.* ***G. Kane*** *a-38, 174r, 282, 283; c-281, 282, 289.* ***Kirby*** *a-187.* ***Kubert*** *Zatara-40-44.* ***Miller*** *c-285p.* ***Mooney*** *c-134.* ***Morrow*** *a-245-248.* ***Mortimer*** *c-16-21, 26-71.* ***Nasser*** *a(p)-244-246, 259, 260.* ***Newton*** *a-253-281p.* ***Orlando*** *a-224r.* ***Perez*** *a-300i; c-271, 276, 277p, 278p.* ***Fred Ray*** *c-1-5.* ***Fred Ray/Robinson*** *c-13-16.* ***Robinson*** *a-5, 6, 9-11, 13?, 14-16; c-6.* ***Rogers*** *a-259p.* ***Roussos*** *a-212r.* ***Simonson*** *c-291.* ***Spiegle*** *a-275-278, 284.* ***Staton*** *a-262p, 273p.* ***Swan/Moldoff*** *c-126.* ***Swan/Mortimer*** *c-79-82.* ***Toth*** *a-228r.* ***Tuska*** *a-230r, 250p, 252p, 254p, 257p, 283p, 284p, 308p. Boy Commandos by* ***Infantino*** *#39-41.*

WORLD'S FINEST COMICS DIGEST (See DC Special Series #23)

WORLD'S FINEST: OUR WORLDS AT WAR
DC Comics: Oct, 2001 ($2.95, one-shot)

	GD 2.0	VG 4.0	FN 6.0	VF 8.0	VF/NM 9.0	NM- 9.2
1-Concludes the Our Worlds at War x-over; Jae Lee-c; art by various						3.00

WORLD'S GREATEST ATHLETE (See Walt Disney Showcase #14)

WORLD'S GREATEST SONGS
Atlas Comics (Male): Sept, 1954

	GD 2.0	VG 4.0	FN 6.0	VF 8.0	VF/NM 9.0	NM- 9.2
1-(Scarce)-Heath & Harry Anderson-a; Eddie Fisher life story plus-c; gives lyrics to Frank Sinatra song "Young at Heart"	40	80	120	240	340	440

WORLD'S GREATEST STORIES
Jubilee Publications: Jan, 1949 - No. 2, May, 1949

	GD 2.0	VG 4.0	FN 6.0	VF 8.0	VF/NM 9.0	NM- 9.2
1-Alice in Wonderland; Lewis Carroll adapt.	35	70	105	201	288	370
2-Pinocchio	33	66	99	190	270	350

WORLDS OF FEAR (Stories of Weird Adventure)(Formerly Worlds Beyond #1)
Fawcett Publications: V1#2, Jan, 1952 - V2#10, June, 1953

	GD 2.0	VG 4.0	FN 6.0	VF 8.0	VF/NM 9.0	NM- 9.2
V1#2	46	92	138	276	413	550
3-Evans-a	42	84	126	252	359	465
4-6(9/52)	38	76	114	219	310	400
V2#7-9	34	68	102	196	278	360
10-Saunders painted-c; man with no eyes surrounded by eyeballs-c plus eyes ripped out story	76	152	228	475	713	950

NOTE: ***Moldoff*** *c-2-8.* ***Powell*** *a-2, 4, 5.* ***Sekowsky*** *a-4, 5.*

WORLDS UNKNOWN
Marvel Comics Group: May, 1973 - No. 8, Aug, 1974

	GD 2.0	VG 4.0	FN 6.0	VF 8.0	VF/NM 9.0	NM- 9.2
1-r/from Astonishing #54; Torres, Reese-a	2	4	6	12	16	20
2-8	2	4	6	9	11	14

NOTE: ***Adkins/Mooney*** *a-5.* ***Buscema*** *c/a-4p. W.* ***Howard*** *c/a-3i.* ***Kane*** *a(p)-1,2; c(p)-5, 6, 8.* ***Sutton*** *a-2.* ***Tuska*** *a(p)-7, 8; c-7p. No. 7, 8 has Golden Voyage of Sinbad movie adaptation.*

WORLD WAR STORIES
Dell Publishing Co.: Apr-June, 1965 - No. 3, Dec, 1965

	GD 2.0	VG 4.0	FN 6.0	VF 8.0	VF/NM 9.0	NM- 9.2
1-Glanzman-a in all	4	8	12	29	40	50
2,3	3	6	9	18	24	30

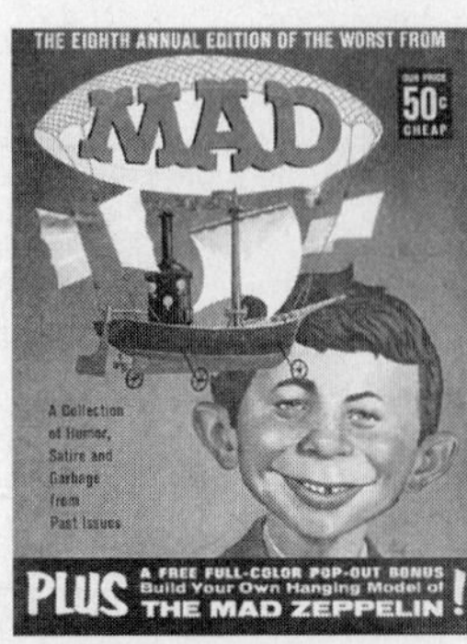

The Worst From Mad #8 © EC Publ.

Wow Comics #38 © FAW

Wyatt Earp #5 © DELL

GD 2.0 | VG 4.0 | FN 6.0 | VF 8.0 | VF/NM 9.0 | NM- 9.2

WORLD WAR II (See Classics Illustrated Special Issue)

WORLD WAR II: 1946
Antarctic Press: Oct, 1998 - No. 2 ($3.95, B&W)
1,2-Nomura-s/a 4.00

WORLD WAR III
Ace Periodicals: Mar, 1953 - No. 2, May, 1953
1-(Scarce)-Atomic bomb blast-c; Cameron-a 70 140 210 438 657 875
2-Used in **POP**, pg. 78 & B&W & color illos; Cameron-a
55 110 165 344 515 685

WORLD WITHOUT END
DC Comics: 1990 - No. 6, 1991 ($2.50, limited series, mature, stiff-c)
1-6: Horror/fantasy; all painted-c/a 2.50

WORLD WRESTLING FEDERATION BATTLEMANIA
Valiant: 1991 - No. 5?, 1991 ($2.50, magazine size, 68 pgs.)
1-5: 5-Includes 2 free pull-out posters 4.00

WORST FROM MAD, THE (Annual)
E. C. Comics: 1958 - No. 12, 1969 (Each annual cover is reprinted from the cover of the Mad issues being reprinted)(Value is 1/2 if bonus is missing)
nn(1958)-Bonus; record labels & travel stickers; 1st Mad annual; r/Mad #29-34
42 84 126 252 376 500
2(1959)-Bonus is small 33¹/3 rpm record entitled "Meet the Staff of Mad"; r/Mad #35-40
42 84 126 252 376 500
3(1960)-Has 20x30" campaign poster "Alfred E. Neuman for President"; r/Mad #41-46
20 40 60 142 209 275
4(1961)-Sunday comics section; r/Mad #47-54 19 38 57 133 194 255
5(1962)-Has 33-1/3 record; r/Mad #55-62 28 56 84 203 297 390
6(1963)-Has 33-1/3 record; r/Mad #63-70 28 56 84 203 297 390
7(1964)-Mad protest signs; r/Mad #71-76 11 22 33 75 110 145
8(1965)-Build a Mad Zeppelin 13 26 39 90 133 175
9(1966)-33-1/3 rpm record; Beatles on-c 19 38 57 138 202 265
10(1967)-Mad bumper sticker 8 16 24 53 74 95
11(1968)-Mad cover window stickers 7 14 21 51 71 90
12(1969)-Mad picture postcards; Orlando-a 7 14 21 51 71 90
NOTE: *Covers: **Bob Clarke**-#8. **Mingo**-#7, 9-12.*

WOTALIFE COMICS (Formerly Nutty Life #2; Phantom Lady #13 on)
Fox Features Syndicate/Norlen Mag.: No. 3, Aug-Sept, 1946 - No. 12, July, 1947; 1959
3-Cosmo Cat, Li'l Pan, others begin 10 20 30 56 73 90
4-12-Cosmo Cat, Li'l Pan in all 8 16 24 46 58 70
1(1959-Norlen)-Atomic Rabbit, Atomic Mouse; reprints cover to #6; reprints entire book?
8 16 24 40 50 60

WOTALIFE COMICS
Green Publications: 1957 - No. 5, 1957
1 7 14 21 35 43 50
2-5 5 10 15 22 26 30

WOW COMICS
Henle Publishing Co.: July, 1936 - No. 4, Nov, 1936 (52 pgs., magazine size)
1-Buck Jones in "The Phantom Rider" (1st app. in comics), Fu Manchu; Capt. Scott Dalton begins; Eisner-a; Briefer-c 280 560 840 1750 2625 3500
2-Ken Maynard, Fu Manchu, Popeye by Segar plus article on Popeye; Eisner-a
200 400 600 1250 1875 2500
3-Eisner-c/a(3); Popeye by Segar, Fu Manchu, Hiram Hick by Bob Kane, Space Limited app.; Jimmy Dempsey talks about Popeye's punch; Bob Ripley Believe it or Not begins; Briefer-a
184 368 552 1150 1725 2300
4-Flash Gordon by Raymond, Mandrake, Popeye by Segar, Tillie The Toiler, Fu Manchu, Hiram Hick by Bob Kane; Eisner-a(3); Briefer-c/a
228 456 684 1425 2138 2850

WOW COMICS (Real Western Hero #70 on)(See XMas Comics)
Fawcett Publ.: Winter, 1940-41; No. 2, Summer, 1941 - No. 69, Fall, 1948
nn(#1)-Origin Mr. Scarlet by S&K; Atom Blake, Boy Wizard, Jim Dolan, & Rick O'Shay begin; Diamond Jack, The White Rajah, & Shipwreck Roberts, only app.; 1st mention of Gotham City in comics; the cover was printed on unstable paper stock and is rarely found in fine or mint condition; blank inside-c; bondage-c by Beck
1250 2500 3750 9375 14,688 20,000
2 (Scarce)-The Hunchback begins 240 480 720 1500 2250 3000
3 (Fall, 1941) 116 232 348 725 1088 1450
4-Origin & 1st app. Pinky 120 240 360 750 1125 1500
5 77 154 231 481 721 960
6-Origin & 1st app. The Phantom Eagle (7/15/42); Commando Yank begins
77 154 231 481 721 960
7,8,10: 10-Swayze-c/a on Mary Marvel 60 120 180 375 563 750
9 (1/6/43)-Capt. Marvel, Capt. Marvel Jr., Shazam app.; Scarlet & Pinky x-over; Mary Marvel-c/stories begin (cameo #9) 132 264 396 825 1238 1650
11-17,19,20: 15-Flag-c 47 94 141 282 421 560
18-1st app. Uncle Marvel (10/43); infinity-c 49 98 147 294 440 585
21-30: 23-Robot-c. 28-Pinky x-over in Mary Marvel 31 62 93 175 248 320
31-40: 32-68-Phantom Eagle by Swayze 21 42 63 121 168 215
41-50 20 40 60 112 156 200
51-58: Last Mary Marvel 19 38 57 106 146 185
59-69: 59-Ozzie (teenage) begins. 62-Flying Saucer gag-c (1/48). 65-69-Tom Mix stories (cont'd in Real Western Hero) 16 32 48 92 126 160
NOTE: *Cover features: Mr. Scarlet-#1-5; Commando Yank-#6, 7, (w/Mr. Scarlet #8); Mary Marvel-#9-56, (w/Commando Yank-#46-50), (w/Mr. Scarlet & Commando Yank-#51), (w/Mr. Scarlet & Pinky #53), (w/Phantom Eagle #54, 56), (w/Commando Yank & Phantom Eagle #58); Ozzie-#59-69.*

WRATH (Also see Prototype #4)
Malibu Comics: Jan, 1994 - No. 9, Nov, 1995 ($1.95)
1-9: 2-Mantra x-over. 3-Intro/1st app. Slayer. 4,5-Freex app. 8-Mantra & Warstrike app. 9-Prime app. 2.25
1-Ultra 5000 Limited silver foil 4.00
Giant Size 1 (2.50, 44 pgs.) 2.50

WRATH OF THE SPECTRE, THE
DC Comics: May, 1988 - No. 4, Aug, 1988 ($2.50, limited series)
1-3: Aparo-r/Adventure #431-440 4.00
4-New stories 5.00

WRECK OF GROSVENOR (See Superior Stories #3)

WRETCH, THE
Caliber: 1996 ($2.95, B&W)
1-Phillip Hester-a/scripts 3.00

WRETCH, THE
Amaze Ink: 1997 - No. 4, 1998 ($2.95, B&W)
1-4-Phillip Hester-a/scripts 3.00
... Vol. 1: Everyday Doomsday (4/03, $13.95) 14.00

WRINGLE WRANGLE (Disney)
Dell Publishing Co.: No. 821, July, 1957
Four Color 821-Based on movie "Westward Ho, the Wagons"; Marsh-a; Fess Parker photo-c
9 18 27 63 89 115

WULF THE BARBARIAN
Atlas/Seaboard Publ.: Feb, 1975 - No. 4, Sept, 1975
1,2: 1-Origin; Janson-a. 2-Intro. Berithe the Swordswoman; Janson-a w/Neal Adams, Wood, Reese-a assists 2 4 6 8 10 12
3,4: 3-Skeates-s. 4-Friedrich-s 1 2 3 5 7 9

WYATT EARP
Atlas Comics/Marvel No. 23 on (IPC): Nov, 1955 - #29, June, 1960; #30, Oct, 1972 - #34, June, 1973
1 22 44 66 127 176 225
2-Williamson-a (4 pgs.) 14 28 42 79 107 135
3-6,8-11: 3-Black Bart app. 8-Wild Bill Hickok app. 11 22 33 63 84 105
7,12-Williamson-a, 4 pgs. ea.; #12 with Mayo 11 22 33 63 84 105
13-20: 17-1st app. Wyatt's deputy, Grizzly Grant 10 20 30 56 73 90
21-Davis-c 9 18 27 52 66 80
22-24,26-29: 22-Ringo Kid app. 23-Kid From Texas app. 29-Last 10¢ issue
8 16 24 43 54 65
25-Davis-a 8 16 24 46 58 70
30-Williamson-r (1972) 2 4 6 12 16 20
31-34-Reprints. 32-Torres-a(r) 2 4 6 10 13 16
NOTE: ***Ayers** a-8, 10(2), 17, 20(4). **Berg** a-9. **Everett** c-6. **Kirby** c-25, 29. **Maneely** a-1; c-1-4, 8, 12, 17, 20. **Maurer** a-2(2), 3(4), 4(4), 8(4). **Severin** a-4, 9(4), 10; c-2, 9, 10, 14. **Wildey** a-5, 17, 24, 28.*

WYATT EARP (TV) (Hugh O'Brian Famous Marshal)
Dell Publishing Co.: No. 860, Nov, 1957 - No. 13, Dec-Feb, 1960-61 (Hugh O'Brian photo-c)
Four Color 860 (#1)-Manning-a 11 22 33 77 114 150
Four Color 890,921(6/58)-All Manning-a 8 16 24 58 82 105
4 (9-11/58) - 12-Manning-a. 5-Photo back-c 6 12 18 40 55 70
13-Toth-a 6 12 18 43 59 75

WYATT EARP FRONTIER MARSHAL (Formerly Range Busters) (Also see Blue Bird)
Charlton Comics: No. 12, Jan, 1956 - No. 72, Dec, 1967
12 9 18 27 49 62 75
13-19 6 12 18 31 38 45

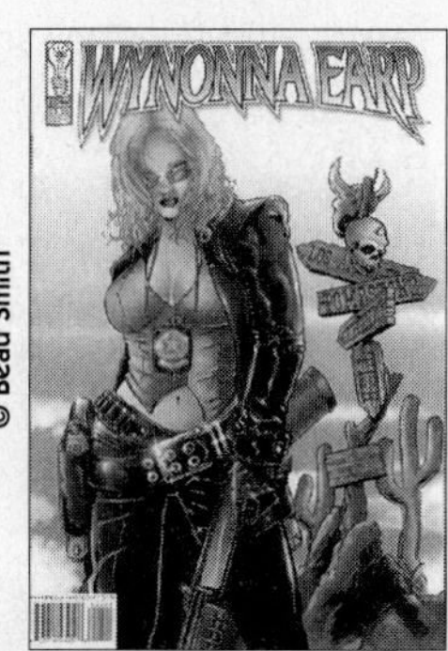

Wynonna Earp: Home on the Strange #1 © Beau Smith

Xena: Warrior Princess #2 © Universal Studios

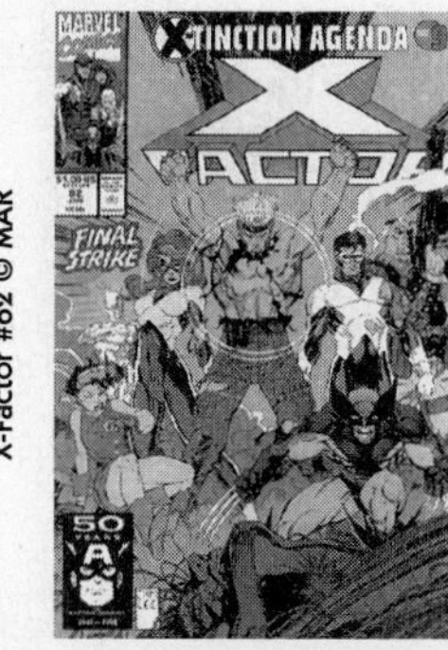

X-Factor #62 © MAR

	GD 2.0	VG 4.0	FN 6.0	VF 8.0	VF/NM 9.0	NM- 9.2
20-(68 pgs.)-Williamson-a(4), 8,5,5,& 7 pgs.	10	20	30	56	73	90
21-30	3	6	9	18	24	30
31-50	2	4	6	12	16	20
51-72 (1967)	2	4	6	9	11	14

WYNONNA EARP
Image Comics (WildStorm Productions): Dec, 1996 - No. 5, Apr, 1997 ($2.50)

1-5-Smith-s/Chin-a 2.50

WYNONNA EARP: HOME ON THE STRANGE
IDW Publishing: Dec, 2003 - Present ($3.99)

1-Smith-s/Ferreira-a 4.00

X (Comics' Greatest World: X #1 only) (Also see Comics' Greatest World & Dark Horse Comics #8)
Dark Horse Comics: Feb, 1994 - No. 25, Apr, 1996 ($2.00/$2.50)

1-25: 3-Pit Bulls x-over. 8 -Ghost-c & app. 18-Miller-c.; Predator app. 19-22-Miller-c. 2.50
Hero Illustrated Special #1,2 (1994, $1.00, 20 pgs.) 2.25
One Shot to the Head (1994, $2.50, 36 pgs.)-Miller-c. 2.50
NOTE: *Miller c-18-22.* ***Quesada*** *c-6.* ***Russell*** *a-6.*

XANADU COLOR SPECIAL
Eclipse Comics: Dec, 1988 ($2.00, one-shot)

1-Continued from Thoughts & Images 2.25

XAVIER INSTITUTE ALUMNI YEARBOOK (See X-Men titles)
Marvel Comics: Dec, 1996 ($5.95, square-bound, one-shot)

1-Text w/art by various 6.00

X-BABIES
Marvel Comics: (one-shots)

...: Murderama (8/98, $2.95) J.J. Kirby-a 3.50
...: Reborn (1/00, $3.50) J.J. Kirby-a 3.50

X-CALIBRE
Marvel Comics: Mar, 1995 - No. 4, July, 1995 ($1.95, limited series)

1-4-Age of Apocalypse 2.25

XENA: WARRIOR PRINCESS (TV)
Topps Comics: Aug, 1997 - No. 0, Oct, 1997 ($2.95)

1-Two stories by various; J. Scott Campbell-c 1 3 4 6 8 10
1,2-Photo-c 1 3 4 6 8 10
2-Stevens-c 6.00
0-(10/97)-Lopresti-c, 0-(10/97)-Photo-c 1 2 3 5 6 8
...First Appearance Collection ('97, $9.95) r/Hercules the Legendary Journeys #3-5 and 5-page story from TV Guide 10.00

XENA: WARRIOR PRINCESS (TV)
Dark Horse Comics: Sept, 1999 - No. 14, Oct, 2000 ($2.95/$2.99)

1-14: 1-Mignola-c and photo-c. 2,3-Bradstreet-c & photo-c 3.00

XENA: WARRIOR PRINCESS AND THE ORIGINAL OLYMPICS (TV)
Topps Comics: Jun, 1998 - No. 3, Aug, 1998 ($2.95, limited series)

1-3-Regular and Photo-c; Lim-a/T&M Bierbaum-s 3.00

XENA: WARRIOR PRINCESS-BLOODLINES (TV)
Topps Comics: May, 1998 - No. 2, June, 1998 ($2.95, limited series)

1,2-Lopresti-s/c/a. 2-Reg. and photo-c 3.00
1-Bath photo-c, 1-American Ent. Ed. 4.00

XENA: WARRIOR PRINCESS / JOXER: WARRIOR PRINCE (TV)
Topps Comics: Nov, 1997 - No. 3, Jan, 1998 ($2.95, limited series)

1-3-Regular and Photo-c; Lim-a/T&M Bierbaum-s 3.00

XENA: WARRIOR PRINCESS-THE DRAGON'S TEETH (TV)
Topps Comics: Dec, 1997 - No. 3, Feb, 1998 ($2.95, limited series)

1-3-Regular and Photo-c; Teranishi-a/Thomas-s 3.00

XENA: WARRIOR PRINCESS-THE ORPHEUS TRILOGY (TV)
Topps Comics: Mar, 1998 - No. 3, May, 1998 ($2.95, limited series)

1-3-Regular and Photo-c; Teranishi-a/T&M Bierbaum-s 3.00

XENA: WARRIOR PRINCESS VS. CALLISTO (TV)
Topps Comics: Feb, 1998 - No. 3, Apr, 1998 ($2.95, limited series)

1-3-Regular and Photo-c; Morgan-a/Thomas-s 3.00

XENOBROOD
DC Comics: No. 0, Oct, 1994 - No. 6, Apr, 1995 ($1.50, limited series)

0-6: 0-Indicia says "Xenobroods" 2.25

XENON
Eclipse Comics: Dec, 1987 - No. 23, Nov. 1, 1988 ($1.50, B&W, bi-weekly)

1-23 2.25

XENOTECH
Mirage Studios: Sept, 1993 - No. 3, Dec, 1994 ($2.75)

1-3: Bound with 2 trading cards. 2-(10/94) 2.75

XENOZOIC TALES (Also see Cadillacs & Dinosaurs, Death Rattle #8)
Kitchen Sink Press: Feb, 1986 - No. 14, Oct, 1996

1-Mark Schultz-s/a in all 1 3 4 6 8 10
1(2nd printing)(1/89) 3.00
2-14 5.00
Volume 1 ($14.95) r/#1-6 & Death Rattle #8 15.00
Volume 2 (5/03, $14.95, TPB) B&W r/#7-14; intro by Frank Cho 15.00

XENYA
Sanctuary Press: Apr, 1994 - No. 3 ($2.95)

1-3: 1-Hildebrandt-c; intro Xenya 3.00

XERO
DC Comics: May, 1997 - No. 12, Apr, 1998 ($1.75)

1-7 2.50
8-12 2.25

X-FACTOR (Also see The Avengers #263, Fantastic Four #286 and Mutant X)
Marvel Comics Group: Feb, 1986 - No. 149, Sept, 1998

1-($1.25, 52 pgs)-Story recaps 1st app. from Avengers #263; story cont'd from F.F. #286; return of original X-Men (now X-Factor); Guice/Layton-a; Baby Nathan app. (2nd after X-Men #201) 6.00
2-4 4.00
5-1st app. Apocalypse (2-pg. cameo) 4.00
6-1st full app. Apocalypse 1 3 4 6 8 10
7-10: 10-Sabretooth app. (11/86, 3 pgs.) cont'd in X-Men #212; 1st app. in an X-Men comic book 4.00
11-22: 13-Baby Nathan app. in flashback. 14-Cyclops vs. The Master Mold. 15-Intro wingless Angel 3.00
23-1st app. Archangel (2 pg. cameo) 1 2 3 4 5 7
24-1st full app. Archangel (now in Uncanny X-Men); Fall Of The Mutants begins; origin Apocalypse 1 2 3 5 7 9
25,26: Fall Of The Mutants; 26-New outfits 3.00
27-39,41-83,87-91,93-99,101: 35-Origin Cyclops. 38,50-(52 pgs.): 50-Liefeld/McFarlane-c. 51-53-Sabretooth app. 52-Liefeld-c(p). 54-Intro Crimson; Silvestri-c/a(p). 60-X-Tinction Agenda x-over; New Mutants (w/Cable) x-over in #60-62; Wolverine in #62. 60-Gold ink 2nd printing. 61,62-X-Tinction Agenda. 62-Jim Lee-c. 63-Portacio/Thibert-c/a(p) begins, ends #69. 65-68-Lee co-plots. 65-The Apocalypse Files begins, ends #68. 66,67-Baby Nathan app. 67-Inhumans app. 68-Baby Nathan is sent into future to save his life. 69,70-X-Men(w/Wolverine) x-over. 71-New team begins (Havok, Polaris, Strong Guy, Wolfsbane & Madrox); Stroman-c/a begins. 71-2nd printing ($1.25). 75-(52 pgs.). 77-Cannonball (of X-Force) app. 87-Quesada-c/a(p) in monthly comic begins,ends #92. 88-1st app. Random 2.50
40-Rob Liefeld-c/a (4/89, 1st at Marvel?) 3.00
84-86 -Jae Lee a(p); 85,86-Jae Lee-c. Polybagged with trading card in each; X-Cutioner's Song x-overs. 3.00
92-($3.50, 68 pgs.)-Wraparound-c by Quesada w/Havok hologram on-c; begin X-Men 30th anniversary issues; Quesada-a. 5.00
92-2nd printing 2.25
100-($2.95, 52 pgs.)-Embossed foil-c; Multiple Man dies. 5.00
100-($1.75, 52 pgs.)-Regular edition 2.25
102-105,107: 102-bound-in card sheet 2.25
106-($2.00)-Newsstand edition 2.25
106-($2.95)-Collectors edition 3.00
108-124,126-148: 112-Return from Age of Apocalypse. 115-card insert. 119-123-Sabretooth app. 123-Hound app. 124-w/Onslaught Update. 126-Onslaught x-over; Beast vs. Dark Beast 128-w/card insert; return of Multiple Man. 130-Assassination of Grayson Creed. 146,148-Moder-a 2.25
125-($2.95)-"Onslaught"; Post app.; return of Havok 4.00
149-Last issue 3.00
#(-1) Flashback (7/97) Matsuda-a 2.25
Annual 1-9: 1-(10/86-'94, 68 pgs.) 3-Evolutionary War x-over. 4-Atlantis Attacks; Byrne/Simonson-a;Byrne-c. 5-Fantastic Four, New Mutants x-over; Keown 2 pg. pin-up. 6-New Warriors app.; 5th app. X-Force cont'd from X-Men Annual #15. 7-1st Quesada-a(p) on X-Factor plus-c(p). 8-Bagged w/trading card. 9-Austin-a(i) 3.00
...Prisoner of Love (1990, $4.95, 52 pgs.)-Starlin scripts; Guice-a 5.00
NOTE: ***Art Adams*** *a-41p, 42p.* ***Buckler*** *a-50p.* ***Liefeld*** *a-40; c-40, 50i, 52p.* ***McFarlane*** *c-50i.* ***Mignola*** *c-70.* ***Brandon Peterson*** *a-78p(part).* ***Whilce Portacio*** *c/a(p)-63-69.* ***Quesada*** *a(p)-87-92, Annual 7. c(p)-78, 79, 82,*

The X-Files #6 © 20th Century Fox

X-Force #121 © MAR

X-Man #34 © MAR

	GD 2.0	VG 4.0	FN 6.0	VF 8.0	VF/NM 9.0	NM- 9.2

Annual 7. ***Simonson*** *c/a-10, 11, 13-15, 17-19, 21, 23-31, 33, 34, 36-39; c-12, 16.* ***Paul Smith*** *a-44-48; c-43.* ***Stroman*** *a(p)-71-75, 77, 78(part), 80, 81; c(p)-71-77, 80, 81, 84.* ***Zeck*** *c-2.*

X-FACTOR (Volume 2)
Marvel Comics: June, 2002 - No. 4, Oct, 2002 ($2.50)

1-4: Jensen-s/Ranson-a. 1-Phillips-c. 2,3-Edwards-c 2.50

X-51 (Machine Man)
Marvel Comics: Sept, 1999 - No. 12, Jul, 2000 ($1.99/$2.50)

1-7: 1-Joe Bennett-a. 2-Two covers 2.50
8-12: 8-Begin $2.50-c 2.50
Wizard #0 2.25

X-FILES, THE (TV)
Topps Comics: Jan, 1995 - No. 41, July, 1998 ($2.50)

	GD	VG	FN	VF	VF/NM	NM-
-2(9/96)-Black-c; r/X-Files Magazine #1&2	1	3	4	6	8	10
-1(9/96)-Silver-c; r/Hero Illustrated Giveaway	1	3	4	6	8	10
0-($3.95)-Adapts pilot episode						4.00
0-"Mulder" variant-c	1	2	3	5	6	8
0-"Scully" variant-c	1	2	3	5	6	8
1/2-W/certificate	3	6	9	16	20	25
1-New stories based on the TV show; direct market & newsstand editions; Miran Kim-c on all	3	6	9	18	24	30
2	2	4	6	11	14	18
3,4	1	2	3	5	6	8
5-10						4.00
11-41: 11-Begin $2.95-c. 21-W/bound-in card. 40,41-Reg. & photo-c						3.00
Annual 1,2 ($3.95)						4.00
Afterflight TPB ($5.95) Art by Thompson, Saviuk, Kim						6.00
Collection 1 TPB ($19.95)-r/#1-6.						20.00
Collection 2 TPB ($19.95)-r/#7-12, Annual #1.						20.00
...Fight the Future ('98, $5.95) Movie adaptation						6.00
Hero Illustrated Giveaway	2	4	6	10	12	15
Special Edition 1-5 ($4.95)-r/#1-3, 4-6, 7-9, 10-12, 13, Annual 1						5.00
Star Wars Galaxy Magazine Giveaway (B&W)	1	3	4	6	8	10
Trade paperback ($19.95)						20.00

X-FILES COMICS DIGEST, THE
Topps Comics: Dec, 1995 - No. 3 ($3.50, quarterly, digest-size)

1-3: 1,2: New X-Files stories w/Ray Bradbury Comics-r 4.00
NOTE: ***Adlard*** *a-1, 2.* ***Jack Davis*** *a-2r.* ***Russell*** *a-1r.*

X-FILES, THE: GROUND ZERO (TV)
Topps Comics: Nov, 1997 - No. 4, March, 1998 ($2.95, limited series)

1-4-Adaptation of the Kevin J. Anderson novel 3.00

X-FILES, THE: SEASON ONE (TV)
Topps Comics: July, 1997 - July, 1998 ($4.95, adaptations of TV episodes)

1,2,Squeeze, Conduit, Ice, Space, Fire, Beyond the Sea, Shadows 5.00

X-FORCE (Becomes X-Statix) (Also see The New Mutants #100)
Marvel Comics: Aug, 1991 - No. 129, Aug, 2002 ($1.00-$2.25)

1-($1.50, 52 pgs.)-Polybagged with 1 of 5 diff. Marvel Universe trading cards inside (1 each); 6th app. of X-Force; Liefeld-c/a begins 4.00
1-1st printing with Cable trading card inside 5.00
1-2nd printing; metallic ink-c (no bag or card) 2.25
2-4: 2-Deadpool-c/story. 3-New Brotherhood of Evil Mutants app. 4-Spider-Man x-over; cont'd from Spider-Man #16; reads sideways 3.00
5-10: 6-Last $1.00-c. 7,9-Weapon X back-ups. 8-Intro The Wild Pack (Cable, Kane, Domino, Hammer, G.W. Bridge, & Grizzly); Liefeld-c/a (4); Mignola-a. 10-Weapon X full-length story (part 3). 11-1st Weapon Prime (cameo); Deadpool-c/story 3.00
11-15,19-24,26-33: 15-Cable leaves X-Force 2.50
16-18-Polybagged w/trading card in each; X-Cutioner's Song x-overs 3.00
25-($3.50, 52 pgs.)-Wraparound-c w/Cable hologram on-c; Cable returns 4.00
34-37,39-45: 34-bound-in card sheet 2.50
38,40-43: 38-($2.00)-Newsstand edition. 40-43 ($1.95)-Deluxe edition 2.25
38-($2.95)-Collectors edition (prismatic) 5.00
44-49,51-67: 44-Return from Age of Apocalypse. 45-Sabretooth app. 49-Sebastian Shaw app. 52-Blob app., Onslaught cameo. 55-Vs. S.H.I.E.L.D. 56-Deadpool app. 57-Mr. Sinister & X-Man-c/app. 57,58-Onslaught x-over. 59-W/card insert; return of Longshot. 60-Dr. Strange 2.50
50 ($3.95)-Gatefold wrap-around foil-c 4.00
50 ($3.95)-Liefeld variant-c 5.00
68-74: 68-Operation Zero Tolerance 2.50
75,100-($2.99): 75-Cannonball-c/app. 3.00
76-99,101,102: 81-Pollina poster. 95-Magneto-c. 102-Ellis-s/Portacio-a 2.25
103-115: 103-Begin $2.25-c; Portacio-a thru #106. 115-Death of old team 2.25
116-New team debuts; Allred-c/a; Milligan-s; no Comics Code stamp on-c 4.00
117-129: 117-Intro. Mr. Sensitive. 120-Wolverine-c/app. 123-'Nuff Said issue. 124-Darwyn Cooke-a/c. 128-Death of U-Go Girl. 129-Fegredo-a 2.25
#(-1) Flashback (7/97) story of John Proudstar; Pollina-a 2.25
Annual 1-3 ('92-'94, 68 pgs.)-1-1st Greg Capullo-a(p) on X-Force. 2-Polybagged w/trading card; intro X-Treme & Neurtap 3.00
...And Cable '95 (12/95, $3.95)-Impossible Man app. 4.00
...And Cable '96, ...'97 ('96, 7/97) -'96-Wraparound-c 3.00
...And Spider-Man: Sabotage nn (11/92, $6.95)-Reprints X-Force #3,4 & Spider-Man #16 7.00
.../ Champions '98 ($3.50) 3.50
Annual 99 ($3.50) 3.50
...: Famous, Mutant & Mortal HC (2003, $29.99) oversized r/#116-129; foreward by Milligan; gallery of covers and pin-ups; script for #123 30.00
...New Beginnings TPB (10/01, $14.95) r/#116-120 15.00
...Rough Cut ($2.99) Pencil pages and script for #102 3.00
...Youngblood (8/96, $4.95)-Platt-c 5.00
NOTE: ***Capullo*** *a(p)-15-25, Annual 1; c(p)-14-27.* ***Rob Liefeld*** *a-1-7, 9p; c-1-9, 11p; plots-1-12.* ***Mignola*** *a-8p.*

X-FORCE MEGAZINE
Marvel Comics: Nov, 1996 ($3.95, one-shot)

1-Reprints 4.00

XIMOS: VIOLENT PAST
Triumphant Comics: Mar, 1994 - No. 2, Mar, 1994 ($2.50, limited series)

1,2 2.50

XIN: JOURNEY OF THE MONKEY KING
Anarchy Studios: May, 2003 - No. 3, July, 2003 ($2.99)

Preview Edition (Apr, 2003, $1.99) Flip book w/ Vampi Vicious Preview Edition 2.25
1-3-Kevin Lau-a. 1-Three covers by Lau, Park and Nauck. 2-Three covers 3.00

XIN: LEGEND OF THE MONKEY KING
Anarchy Studios: Nov, 2002 - No. 3, Jan, 2003 ($2.99)

Preview Edition (Summer 2002, Diamond Dateline supplement) 2.25
1-3-Kevin Lau-a. 1-Two covers by Lau & Madureira. 2-Two covers by Lau & Oeming 3.00
TPB (10/03, $12.95) r/#1-3; cover gallery and sketch pages 13.00

X-MAN (Also see X-Men Omega & X-Men Prime)
Marvel Comics: Mar, 1995 - No. 75, May, 2001 ($1.95/$1.99/$2.25)

1-Age of Apocalypse 5.00
1-2nd print 2.25
2-4,25: 25-($2.99)-Wraparound-c 3.00
5-24, 26-28: 5-Post Age of Apocalypse stories begin. 5-7-Madelyne Pryor app. 10-Professor X app. 12-vs. Excalibur. 13-Marauders, Cable app. 14-Vs. Cable; Onslaught app. 15-17-Vs. Holocaust. 17-w/Onslaught Update. 18-Onslaught x-over; X-Force-c/app; Marauders app. 19-Onslaught x-over. 20-Abomination-c/app.; w/card insert. 23-Bishop app. 24-Spider-Man, Morbius-c/app. 27-Re-appearance of Aurora(Alpha Flight) 2.50
29-49,51-62: 29-Operation Zero Tolerance. 37,38-Spider-Man-c/app. 56-Spider-Man app. 2.50
50-($2.99) Crossover with Generation X #50 3.00
63-74: 63-Ellis & Grant-s/Olivetti-a begins. 64-Begin $2.25-c 2.25
75 ($2.99) Final issue; Alcatena-a 3.00
#(-1) Flashback (7/97) 2.25
...'96, ...'97-($2.95)-Wraparound-c; '96-Age of Apocalypse 3.00
...: All Saints' Day ('97, $5.99) Dodson-a 6.00
.../Hulk '98 ($2.99) Wraparound-c; Thanos app. 3.00

XMAS COMICS
Fawcett Publications: 12?/1941 - No. 2, 12?/1942; (50¢, 324 pgs.)
No. 7, 12?/1947 (25¢, 132 pgs.)(#3-6 do not exist)

	GD	VG	FN	VF	VF/NM	NM-
1-Contains Whiz #21, Capt. Marvel #3, Bulletman #2, Wow #3, & Master #18; Raboy back-c. Not rebound, remaindered comics; printed at same time as originals	385	770	1155	2503	3852	5200
2-Capt. Marvel, Bulletman, Spy Smasher	152	304	456	950	1425	1900
7-Funny animals (Hoppy, Billy the Kid & Oscar)	60	120	180	375	563	750

XMAS COMICS
Fawcett Publications: No. 4, Dec, 1949 - No. 7, Dec, 1952 (50¢, 196 pgs.)

	GD	VG	FN	VF	VF/NM	NM-
4-Contains Whiz, Master, Tom Mix, Captain Marvel, Nyoka, Capt. Video, Bob Colt, Monte Hale, Hot Rod Comics, & Battle Stories. Not rebound, remaindered comics; printed at the same time as originals	66	132	198	413	619	825
5-7-Same as above. 7-Bill Boyd app.; stocking on cover is made of green felt (novelty cover)	53	106	159	318	477	635

X-MEN, THE (See Adventures of Cyclops and Phoenix, Amazing Adventures, Archangel, Brotherhood, Capt. America #172, Classic X-Men, Exiles, Further Adventures of Cyclops & Phoenix, Gambit, Giant-Size..., Heroes For Hope..., Kitty Pryde & Wolverine, Marvel & DC Present, Marvel Collector's Edition:..., Marvel Fanfare, Marvel Graphic Novel, Marvel Super Heroes, Marvel Team-Up, Marvel Triple Action, The Marvel X-Men Collection, New Mutants, Nightcrawler, Official Marvel Index To..., Rogue, Special Edition..., Ultimate..., Uncanny..., Wolverine, X-

X-Men #14 © MAR

X-Men #101 © MAR

The Uncanny X-Men #195 © MAR

Factor, X-Force, X-Terminators)

X-MEN, THE (1st series)(Becomes Uncanny X-Men at #142)(The X-Men #1-93; X-Men #94-141) (The Uncanny X-Men on-c only #114-141)
Marvel Comics Group: Sept, 1963 - No. 66, Mar, 1970; No. 67, Dec, 1970 - No. 141, Jan, 1981

	GD 2.0	VG 4.0	FN 6.0	VF 8.0	VF/NM 9.0	NM- 9.2
1-Origin/1st app. X-Men (Angel, Beast, Cyclops, Iceman & Marvel Girl); 1st app. Magneto & Professor X	634	1268	1902	5810	9405	13,000
2-1st app. The Vanisher	152	304	456	1292	1976	2660
3-1st app. The Blob (1/64)	68	136	204	544	947	1350
4-1st Quicksilver & Scarlet Witch & Brotherhood of the Evil Mutants (3/64); 1st app. Toad; 2nd app. Magneto	70	140	210	560	980	1400
5-Magneto & Evil Mutants-c/story	51	102	153	383	667	950
6,7: 6-Sub-Mariner app. 7-Magneto app.	44	88	132	330	565	800
8,9,11: 8-1st Unus the Untouchable. 9-Early Avengers app. (1/65); 1st Lucifer. 11-1st app. The Stranger.	35	70	105	262	431	600
10-1st S.A. app. Ka-Zar & Zabu the sabertooth (3/65)	31	62	93	225	375	525
12-Origin Prof. X; Origin/1st app. Juggernaut	38	76	114	276	463	650
13-Juggernaut and Human Torch app.	26	52	78	188	319	450
14,15: 14-1st app. Sentinels. 15-Origin Beast	28	56	84	203	339	475
16-20: 19-1st app. The Mimic (4/66)	16	32	48	116	183	250
21-27,29,30: 27-Re-enter The Mimic (r-in #75); Spider-Man cameo	13	26	39	90	133	175
28-1st app. The Banshee (1/67)(r-in #76)	17	34	51	123	199	275
28-2nd printing (1994)	2	4	6	8	10	12
31-34,36,37,39: 34-Adkins-c/a. 39-New costumes	10	20	30	73	107	140
35-Spider-Man x-over (8/67)(r-in #83); 1st app. Changeling	19	38	57	137	218	300
38,40: 38-Origins of the X-Men series begins, ends #57. 40-(1/68) 1st app. Frankenstein's monster at Marvel	11	22	33	77	114	150
41-49: 42-Death of Prof. X (Changeling disguised as). 44-1st S.A. app. G.A. Red Raven. 49-Steranko-c; 1st Polaris	9	18	27	63	89	115
50,51-Steranko-c/a	9	18	27	65	93	120
52	8	16	24	55	78	100
53-Barry Smith-c/a (his 1st comic book work)	9	18	27	65	93	120
54,55-B. Smith-c. 54-1st app. Alex Summers who later becomes Havok. 55-Summers discovers he has mutant powers	10	20	30	67	96	125
56,57,59-63,65-Neal Adams-a(p). 56-Intro Havok w/o costume. 60-1st Sauron. 65-Return of Professor X.	9	18	27	65	93	120
58-1st app. Havok in costume; N. Adams-a(p)	12	24	36	84	125	165
62,63-2nd printings (1994)	2	4	6	8	10	12
64-1st app. Sunfire	9	18	27	63	89	115
66-Last new story w/original X-Men; battles Hulk	10	20	30	70	100	130
67-93: 67-Reprints begin, end #93. 67-70,72: (52 pgs.). 71-Last 15¢ issue. 73-86-r/#25-38 w/new-c. 83-Spider-Man-c/story. 87-93-r/#39-45 with covers	6	12	18	43	59	75
94 (8/75)-New X-Men begin (see Giant-Size X-Men for 1st app.); Colossus, Nightcrawler, Thunderbird, Storm, Wolverine, & Banshee join; Angel, Marvel Girl & Iceman resign	59	118	177	502	764	1025
95-Death of Thunderbird	17	34	51	123	182	240
96,97	10	20	30	73	107	140
98,99-(Regular 25¢ edition)(4,6/76)	10	20	30	70	100	130
98,99-(30¢-c variants, limited distribution)	16	32	48	116	171	225
100-Old vs. New X-Men; part origin Phoenix; last 25¢ issue (8/76)	11	22	33	77	114	150
100-(30¢-c variant, limited distribution)	17	34	51	123	182	240
101-Phoenix origin concludes	10	20	30	72	104	135
102-104: 102-Origin Storm. 104-1st app. Starjammers (brief cameo); Magneto-c/story	6	12	18	43	59	75
105-107-(Regular 30¢ editions). 106-(8/77)Old vs. New X-Men. 107-1st full app. Starjammers; last 30¢ issue	6	12	18	43	59	75
105-107-(35¢-c variants, limited distribution)	9	18	27	63	89	115
108-Byrne-a begins (see Marvel Team-Up #53)	8	16	24	55	78	100
109-1st app. Weapon Alpha (becomes Vindicator)	7	14	21	46	63	80
110,111: 110-Phoenix joins	5	10	15	36	48	60
112-116	5	10	15	33	44	55
117-119: 117-Origin Professor X	4	8	12	27	36	45
120-1st app. Alpha Flight, story line begins (4/79); 1st app. Vindicator (formerly Weapon Alpha); last 35¢ issue	6	12	18	40	55	70
121-1st full Alpha Flight story	6	12	18	38	52	65
122-128: 123-Spider-Man x-over. 124-Colossus becomes Proletarian	3	7	10	21	28	35
129-Intro Kitty Pryde (1/80); last Banshee; Dark Phoenix saga begins; intro. Emma Frost (White Queen)	4	8	12	29	40	50
130-1st app. The Dazzler by Byrne (2/80)	3	7	10	21	28	35
131-135: 131-Dazzler app.; 1st White Queen-c. 133-Wolverine app. 134-Phoenix becomes Dark Phoenix	3	7	10	21	28	35
136,138: 138-Dazzler app.; Cyclops leaves	3	6	9	18	24	30
137-Giant; death of Phoenix	3	7	10	21	28	35
139-Alpha Flight app.; Kitty Pryde joins; new costume for Wolverine	3	7	10	21	28	35
140-Alpha Flight app.	3	7	10	21	28	35
141-Intro Future X-Men & The New Brotherhood of Evil Mutants; 1st app. Rachel (Phoenix II); Death of Franklin Richards	4	8	12	24	32	40

X-MEN: Titled THE UNCANNY X-MEN #142, Feb, 1981 - Present

	GD 2.0	VG 4.0	FN 6.0	VF 8.0	VF/NM 9.0	NM- 9.2
142-Rachel app.; deaths of alt. future Wolverine, Storm & Colossus	4	8	12	29	40	50
143-Last Byrne issue	3	6	9	19	25	32
144-150: 144-Man-Thing app. 145-Old X-Men app. 148-Spider-Woman, Dazzler app. 150-Double size	2	4	6	8	10	12
151-157,159-161,163,164: 161-Origin Magneto. 163-Origin Binary. 164-1st app. Binary as Carol Danvers	1	2	3	5	7	9
158-1st app. Rogue in X-Men (6/82, see Avengers Annual #10)	2	4	6	10	13	16
162-Wolverine solo story	2	4	6	8	10	12
165-Paul Smith-c/a begins, ends #175	1	3	4	6	8	10
166-170: 166-Double size; Paul Smith-a. 167-New Mutants app. (3/83); same date as New Mutants #1; 1st meeting w/X-Men; ties into N.M. #3,4; Starjammers app.; contains skin "Tattooz" decals. 168-1st app. Madelyne Pryor (last pg. cameo) in X-Men (see Avengers Annual #10)	1	2	3	5	7	9
171-Rogue joins X-Men; Simonson-c/a	2	4	6	10	12	15
172-174: 172,173-Two part Wolverine solo story. 173-Two cover variations, blue & black. 174-Phoenix cameo	1	2	3	5	6	8
175-(52 pgs.)-Anniversary issue; Phoenix returns	1	3	4	6	8	10
176-185,187-192,194-199: 181-Sunfire app. 182-Rogue solo story. 184-1st app. Forge (8/84). 190,191-Spider-Man & Avengers x-over. 195-Power Pack x-over	1	2	3	4	5	7
186,193: 186-Double-size; Barry Smith/Austin-a. 193-Double size; 100th app. New X-Men; 1st app. Warpath in costume (see New Mutants #16)	1	2	3	5	6	8
200-(12/85, $1.25, 52 pgs.)	1	2	3	5	6	8
201-(1/86)-1st app. Cable? (as baby Nathan; see X-Factor #1); 1st Whilce Portacio-c/a(i) on X-Men (guest artist)	3	6	9	16	20	25
202-204,206-209: 204-Nightcrawler solo story; 2nd Portacio-a(i) on X-Men. 207-Wolverine/Phoenix story	1	2	3	4	5	7
205-Wolverine solo story by Barry Smith	2	4	6	9	11	14
210,211-Mutant Massacre begins	2	4	6	14	18	22
212,213-Wolverine vs. Sabretooth (Mutant Mass.)	3	6	9	16	20	25
214-221,223,224: 219-Havok joins (7/87); brief app. Sabretooth	1	2	3	4	5	7
222-Wolverine battles Sabretooth-c/story	2	4	6	14	18	22
225-242: 225-227: Fall Of The Mutants. 226-Double size. 240-Sabretooth app. 242-Double size, X-Factor app., Inferno tie-in	1	2	3	4	5	7
243,245-247: 245-Rob Liefeld-a(p)	1	2	3	4	5	7
244-1st app. Jubilee	3	6	9	18	24	30
248-1st Jim Lee art on X-Men (1989)	2	4	6	14	18	22
248-2nd printing (1992, $1.25)						2.50
249-252: 252-Lee-c	1	2	3	4	5	7
253-255: 253-All new X-Men begin. 254-Lee-c	1	2	3	4	5	7
256,257-Jim Lee-c/a begins	1	2	3	5	7	9
258-Wolverine solo story; Lee-c/a	1	2	3	5	7	9
259-Silvestri-c/a; no Lee-a	1	2	3	4	5	7
260-265-No Lee-a. 260,261,264-Lee-c	1	2	3	4	5	7
266-1st full app. Gambit (see Ann. #14)-No Lee-a	4	8	12	27	36	45
267-Jim Lee-c/a resumes; 2nd full Gambit app.	2	4	6	10	13	16
268-Capt. America, Black Widow & Wolverine team-up; Lee-a	2	4	6	11	14	18
268,270: 268-2nd printing. 270-Gold 2nd printing						2.50
269,273-275: 269-Lee-a. 273-New Mutants (Cable) & X-Factor x-over; Golden, Byrne & Lee part pencils. 275-(52 pgs.)-Tri-fold-c by Jim Lee (p); Prof. X	1	2	3	4	5	7
270-X-Tinction Agenda begins	1	2	3	5	6	8
271,272-X-Tinction Agenda	1	2	3	5	6	8
275-Gold 2nd printing						2.50
276-280: 277-Last Lee-c/a. 280-X-Factor x-over						6.00
281-(10/91)-New team begins (Storm, Archangel, Colossus, Iceman & Marvel Girl); Whilce Portacio-c/a begins; Byrne scripts begin; wraparound-c (white logo)						

The Uncanny X-Men #308 © MAR

The Uncanny X-Men #417 © MAR

X-Men (2nd series) #33 © MAR

GD VG FN VF VF/NM NM-
2.0 4.0 6.0 8.0 9.0 9.2

1 2 3 4 5 7
281-2nd printing with red metallic ink logo w/o UPC box ($1.00-c); does not say 2nd printing inside 2.50
282-1st app. Bishop (cover & 1 pg. cameo) 2 4 6 8 10 12
282-Gold ink 2nd printing ($1.00-c) 2.50
283-1st full app. Bishop (12/91) 2 4 6 8 10 12
284-299: 284-Last $1.00-c. 286,287-Lee plots. 287-Bishop joins team. 288-Lee/Portacio plots. 290-Last Portacio-c/a. 294-Peterson-a(p) begins (#292 is 1st Peterson-c). 294-296 ($1.50)-Bagged w/trading card in each; X-Cutioner's Song x-overs; Peterson/Austin-c/a on all 4.00
300-($3.95, 68 pgs.)-Holo-grafx foil-c; Magneto app. 6.00
301-303,305-309,311 3.00
303,307-Gold Edition 1 2 3 5 6 8
304-($3.95, 68 pgs.)-Wraparound-c with Magneto hologram on-c; 30th anniversary issue; Jae Lee-a (4 pgs.) 6.00
310-($1.95)-Bound-in trading card sheet 3.00
312-$1.50-c begins; bound-in card sheet; 1st Madureira 4.00
313-321 3.00
316,317-($2.95)-Foil enhanced editions 4.00
318-321-($1.95)-Deluxe editions 3.00
322-Onslaught 5.00
323,324,326-346: 323-Return from Age of Apocalypse. 328-Sabretooth-c. 329,330-Dr. Strange app. 331-White Queen-c/app. 334-Juggernaut app.; w/Onslaught Update. 335-Onslaught, Avengers, Apocalypse, & X-Man app. 336-Onslaught. 338-Archangel's wings return to normal. 339-Havok vs. Cyclops; Spider-Man app. 341-Gladiator-c/app. 342-Deathbird cameo; two covers. 343,344-Phalanx 2.50
325-($3.95)-Anniversary issue; gatefold-c 5.00
342-Variant-c 1 3 4 6 8 10
347-349:347-Begin $1.99-c. 349-"Operation Zero Tolerance" 2.50
350-($3.99, 48 pgs.) Prismatic etched foil gatefold wraparound-c; Trial of Gambit; Seagle-s begin 1 2 3 5 6 8
351-359: 353-Bachalo-a begins. 354-Regular-c. 355-Alpha Flight-c/app. 356-Original X-Men-c 2.50
354-Dark Phoenix variant-c 4.00
360-($2.99) 35th Anniv. issue; Pacheco-c 3.00
360-($3.99) Etched Holo-foil enhanced-c 4.00
360-($6.95) DF Edition with Jae Lee variant-c 7.00
361-374: 361-Gambit returns; Skroce-a. 362-Hunt for Xavier pt. 1; Bachelo-a. 364-Yu-a. 366-Magneto-c. 369-Juggernaut-c 2.50
375-($2.99) Autopsy of Wolverine 3.00
376-379: 376,377-Apocalypse: The Twelve 2.25
380-($2.99) Polybagged with X-Men Revolution Genesis Edition preview 3.00
381,382,384-389,391-393: 381-Begin $2.25-c; Claremont-s. 387-Maximum Security 2.25
383-($2.99) 3.00
390-Colossus dies to cure the Legacy Virus 3.00
394-New look X-Men begins; Casey-s/Churchill-c/a 3.00
395-399-Poptopia. 398-Phillips & Wood-a 2.25
400-($3.50) Art by Ashley Wood, Eddie Campbell, Hamner, Phillips, Pulido and Matt Smith; wraparound-c by Wood 3.50
401-415: 401-'Nuff Said issue; Garney-a. 404,405,407-409,413-415-Phillips-a 2.25
416-421: 416-Asamiya-a begins. 421-Garney-a 2.25
422-($3.50) Alpha Flight app.; Garney-a 3.50
423-(25¢-c) Holy War pt. 1; Garney-a/Philip Tan-c 2.00
424-437: 425,426,429,430-Tan-a. 428-Birth of Nightcrawler. 434-Miyazawa-a 2.25
#(-1) Flashback (7/97) Ladronn-c/Hitch & Neary-a 2.50
Special 1(12/70)-Kirby-c/a; origin The Stranger 9 18 27 65 93 120
Special 2(11/71, 52 pgs.) 7 14 21 46 63 80
Annual 3(1979, 52 pgs.)-New story; Miller/Austin-c; Wolverine still in old yellow costume 3 7 10 21 28 35
Annual 4(1980, 52 pgs.)-Dr. Strange guest stars 2 4 6 10 12 15
Annual 5(1981, 52 pgs.) 1 2 3 5 7 9
Annual 6-8('82-'84 52 pgs.)-6-Dracula app. 6.00
Annual 9,10('85, '86)-9-New Mutants x-over cont'd from New Mutants Special Ed. #1; Art Adams-a. 10-Art Adams-a 1 2 3 5 7 9
Annual 11-13:('87-'89, 68 pgs.): 12-Evolutionary War; A.Adams-a(p). 13-Atlantis Attacks 4.00
Annual 14(1990, $2.00, 68 pgs.)-1st app. Gambit (minor app., 5 pgs.); Fantastic Four, New Mutants (Cable) & X-Factor x-over; Art Adams-c/a(p) 3 6 9 16 20 25
Annual 15 (1991, $2.00, 68 pgs.)-4 pg. origin; New Mutants x-over; 4 pg. Wolverine solo back-up story; 4th app. X-Force cont'd from New Warriors Annual #1 4.00
Annual 16-18 ('92-'94, 68 pgs.)-16-Jae Lee-c/a(p). 17-Bagged w/card 3.00
Annual '95-(11/95, $3.95)-Wraparound-c 4.00
Annual '96,'97-Wraparound-c 3.00
.../Fantastic Four Annual '98 ($2.99) Casey-s 3.00
Annual '99 ($3.50) Jubilee app. 3.50
Annual 2000 ($3.50) Cable app.; Ribic-a 3.50
Annual 2001 ($3.50, printed wide-ways) Ashley Wood-c/a; Casey-s 3.50
...At The State Fair of Texas (1983, 36 pgs., one-shot); Supplement to the Dallas Times Herald 2 4 6 10 12 15
...: The Dark Phoenix Saga TPB 1st printing (1984, $12.95) 40.00
...: The Dark Phoenix Saga TPB 2nd-5th printings 30.00
...: The Dark Phoenix Saga TPB 6th-10th printings 20.00
...From The Ashes TPB (1990, $14.95) r/#168-176 15.00
...:God Loves, Man Kills ($6.95)-r/Marvel Graphic Novel #5 7.00
...:God Loves, Man Kills - Special Edition (2003, $4.99)-reprint with new Hughes-c 5.00
...In The Days of Future Past TPB (1989, $3.95, 52 pgs.) 4.00
...Poptopia TPB (10/01, $15.95) r/#394-399 16.00
Vignettes TPB (9/01, $17.95) r/Claremont & Bolton Classic X-Men #1-13 18.00
... Vol. 1: Hope TPB (2003, $12.99) r/#410-415; Harris-c 13.00
... Vol. 2: Dominant Species TPB (2003, $11.99) r/#416-420; Asamiya-c 12.00

NOTE: ***Art Adams*** *a-Annual 9, 10p, 12p, 14p; c-218p.* ***Neal Adams*** *a-56-63p, 65p; c-56-63.* ***Adkins*** *a-34, 35p; c-31, 34, 35.* ***Austin*** *a-108i, 109i, 111-117i, 119-143i, 186i, 204i, 228i, 294-297i, Annual 3i, 7i, 9i, 13; c-109-111i, 114-122i, 123, 124-141i, 142, 143, 196i, 204i, 228i, 294-297i, Annual 3i.* ***J. Buscema*** *c-42, 43, 45.* ***Buscema/Tuska*** *a-45.* ***Byrne*** *a(p)-108, 109, 111-143, 273; c(p)-113-116, 127, 129, 131-141.* ***Capullo*** *c-14.* ***Ditko*** *r-86, 89-91, 93.* ***Everett*** *c-73.* ***Golden*** *a-273, Annual 7p.* ***Guice*** *a-216p, 217p.* ***G. Kane*** *c(p)-33, 74-76, 79, 80, 94, 95.* ***Kirby*** *a(p)-1-17 (#12-17, 67r-layouts); c(p)-1-17, 25, 30 (18, 26-parts).* ***Layton*** *a-105i; c-112i, 113i.* ***Jim Lee*** *a(p)-248, 256-258, 267-277; c(p)-252, 254, 256-261, 264, 267, 270, 275-277, 286.* ***Perez*** *a-Annual 3p; c(p)-112, 128, Annual 3.* ***Peterson*** *a(p)-294-300, 304(part); c(p)-294-299.* ***Whilce Portacio*** *a(p)-281-286, 289, 290; a(i)-267; c-281-285p, 289p, 290; c(i)-267.* ***Romita, Jr.*** *a-300; c-300.* ***Roussos*** *a-84i.* ***Simonson*** *a-171p; c-171, 217.* ***B. Smith*** *a-53, 186p, 198p, 205, 214; c-53-55, 186p, 198, 205, 212, 214, 216.* ***Paul Smith*** *a(p)-165-170, 172-175, 278; c-165-170, 172-175, 278.* ***Sparling*** *a-78p.* ***Steranko*** *a-50p, 51p; c-49-51.* ***Sutton*** *a-106i.* ***Art Thibert*** *a(i)-281-286; c(i)-281, 282, 284, 285.* ***Toth*** *a-12p, 67p(r).* ***Tuska*** *a-40-42i, 43-46p, 88i(r); c-39-41, 77p, 78p.* ***Williamson*** *a-202i, 203i, 211i; c-202i, 203i, 206i.* ***Wood*** *c-14i.*

UNCANNY X-MEN AND THE NEW TEEN TITANS (See Marvel and DC Present...)

X-MEN (2nd Series)
Marvel Comics: Oct, 1991 - Present ($1.00/$1.25/$1.95/$1.99)

1 a-d ($1.50, 52 pgs.)-Jim Lee-c/a begins, ends #11; new team begins (Cyclops, Beast, Wolverine, Gambit, Psylocke & Rogue); new Uncanny X-Men & Magneto app.; four different covers exist 4.00
1 e ($3.95)-Double gate-fold-c consisting of all four covers from 1a-d by Jim Lee; contains all pin-ups from #1a-d plus inside-c foldout poster; no ads; printed on coated stock 5.00
2-7: 4-Wolverine back to old yellow costume (same date as Wolverine #50); last $1.00-c. 5-Byrne scripts. 6-Sabretooth-c/story 5.00
8-10: 8-Gambit vs. Bishop-c/story; last Lee-a; Ghost Rider cameo cont'd in Ghost Rider #26. 9-Wolverine vs. Ghost Rider; cont'd/G.R. #26. 10-Return of Longshot 4.00
11-13,17-24,26-29,31: 12,13-Art Thibert-c/a. 28,29-Sabretooth app. 3.00
11-Silver ink 2nd printing; came with X-Men board game 2 4 6 10 12 15
14-16-($1.50)-Polybagged with trading card in each; X-Cutioner's Song x-overs; 14-Andy Kubert-c/a begins 3.00
25-($3.50, 52 pgs.)-Wraparound-c with Gambit hologram on-c; Professor X erases Magneto's mind 2 4 6 8 10 12
25-30th anniversary issue w/B&W-c with Magneto in color & Magneto hologram & no price on-c 2 4 6 10 12 15
25-Gold 30.00
30-($1.95)-Wedding issue w/bound-in trading card sheet 5.00
32-37: 32-Begin $1.50-c; bound-in card sheet. 33-Gambit & Sabretooth-c/story 3.00
36,37-($2.95)-Collectors editions (foil-c) 5.00
38-44,46-49,51-53, 55-65: 42,43- Paul Smith-a. 46,49,53-56-Onslaught app. 51-Waid scripts begin, end #56. 54-(Reg. edition)-Onslaught revealed as Professor X. 55,56-Onslaught x-over; Avengers, FF & Sentinels app. 56-Dr. Doom app. 57-Xavier taken into custody; Byrne-c/swipe (X-Men,1st Series #138). 59-Hercules-c/app. 61-Juggernaut-c/app. 62-Re-intro. Shang Chi; two covers. 63-Kingpin cameo. 64- Kingpin app. 2.50
45-($3.95)-Annual issue; gatefold-c 5.00
50-($2.95)-Vs. Onslaught, wraparound-c. 4.00
50-($3.95)-Vs. Onslaught, wraparound foil-c. 5.00
50-($2.95)-Variant gold-c. 4 8 12 24 32 40
50-($2.95)-Variant silver-c. 1 2 3 5 6 8
54-(Limited edition)-Embossed variant-c; Onslaught revealed as Professor X 3 6 9 18 24 30
66-69,71-74,76-79: 66-Operation Zero Tolerance. 76-Origin of Maggott 2.50
70-($2.99, 48 pgs.)-Joe Kelly-s begin, new members join 3.00
75-($2.99, 48 pgs.) vs. N'Garai; wraparound-c 3.00
80-($3.99) 35th Anniv. issue; holo-foil-c 5.00
80-($2.99) Regular-c 3.00
80-($6.95) Dynamic Forces Ed.; Quesada-c 7.00
81-93,95: 82-Hunt for Xavier pt. 2. 85-Davis-a. 86-Origin of Joseph. 87-Magneto War ends. 88-Juggernaut app. 2.50
94-($2.99) Contains preview of X-Men: Hidden Years 3.00
96-99: 96,97-Apocalypse: The Twelve 2.50

X-Men (2nd series) #134 © MAR

X-Men Forever #1 © MAR

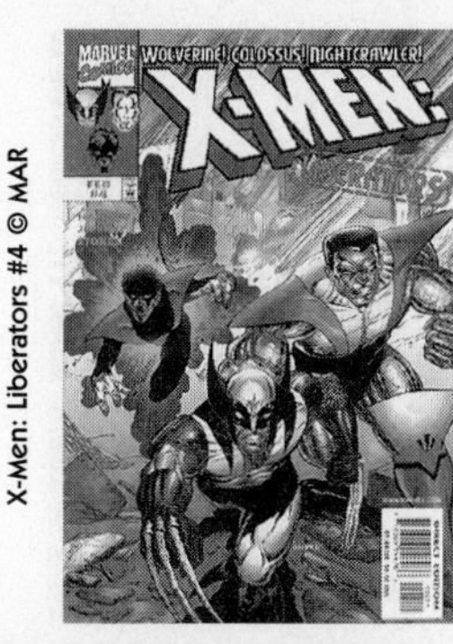

X-Men: Liberators #4 © MAR

GD 2.0 | VG 4.0 | FN 6.0 | VF 8.0 | VF/NM 9.0 | NM- 9.2

100-($2.99) Art Adams-c; begin Claremont-s/Yu-a 3.00
100-DF alternate-c 1 3 4 6 8 10
101-105,107,108,110-114: 101-Begin $2.25-c. 107-Maximum Security x-over; Bishop-c/app. 108-Moira MacTaggart dies; Senator Kelly shot. 111-Magneto-c. 112,113-Eve of Destruction 2.25
106-($2.99) X-Men battle Domina 3.00
109-($3.50, 100 pgs.) new and reprinted Christmas-themed stories 3.50
114-Title change to "New X-Men," Morrison-s/Quitely-c/a begins 4.00
115-Two covers (Quitely & BWS) 3.00
116-125,127-149: 116-Emma Frost joins. 117,118-Van Sciver-a. 121,122,135-Quitely-a. 127-Leon & Sienkiewicz-a. 128-Kordey-a. 132,139-141-Jimenez-a. 136-138-Quitely-a 142-Sabretooth app.; Bachalo-c/a thru #145. 146-Magneto returns; Jimenez-a 2.25
126-($3.25) Quitely-a; defeat of Cassanova 3.25
150-($3.50) Jean Grey dies again; last Jimenez-a 3.50
151-Silvestri-c/a 2.25
#(-1) Flashback (7/97); origin of Magneto 2.50
Annual 1-3 ('92-'94, $2.25-$2.95, 68 pgs.) 1-Lee-c & layouts; #2-Bagged w/card 4.00
Special '95 ($3.95) 4.00
... '96,...'97-Wraparound-c 3.00
.../ Dr. Doom '98 Annual ($2.99) Lopresti-a 3.00
... Annual '99 ($3.50) Adam Kubert-c 3.50
Annual 2000 ($3.50) Art Adams-c/Claremont-s/Eaton-a 3.50
...2001 Annual ($3.50) Morrison-s/Yu-a; issue printed sideways 3.50
Animation Special Graphic Novel (12/90, $10.95) adapts animated series 11.00
Ashcan #1 (1994, 75¢) Introduces new team members 2.25
Ashcan (75¢ Ashcan Edition) (1994) 2.25
... Archives Sketchbook (12/00, $2.99) Early B&W character design sketches by various incl. Lee, Davis, Yu, Pacheco, BWS, Art Adams, Liefeld 3.00
...: Declassified (10/00, $3.50) Profile pin-ups by various; Jae Lee-c 3.50
...:Fatal Attractions ('94, $17.95)-r/x-Factor #92, X-Force #25, Uncanny X-Men #304, X-Men #25, Wolverine #75, & Excalibur #71 18.00
...Millennial Visions (8/00, $3.99) Various artists interpret future X-Men 4.00
...Millennial Visions 2 (1/02, $3.50) Various artists interpret future X-Men 3.50
New X-Men: E is for Extinction TPB (11/01, $12.95) r/#114-117 13.00
New X-Men: Imperial TPB (7/02, $19.99) r/#118-126; Quitely-c 20.00
New X-Men: New Worlds TPB (2002, $14.99) r/#127-133; Quitely-c 15.00
New X-Men: Riot at Xavier's TPB (2003, $11.99) r/#134-138; Quitely-c 12.00
New X-Men: Vol. 5: Assault on Weapon Plus TPB (2003, $14.99) r/#139-145 15.00
New X-Men: Volume 1 HC (2002, $29.99) oversized r/#114-126 & 2001 Annual 30.00
New X-Men: Volume 2 HC (2003, $29.99) oversized r/#127-141; sketch & script pages 30.00
...Pizza Hut Mini-comics-(See Marvel Collector's Edition: X-Men in Promotional Comics section)
...Premium Edition #1 (1993)-Cover says "Toys 'R' Us Limited Edition X-Men" 2.25
...:Rarities (1995, $5.95)-Reprints 6.00
...:Road Trippin' ('99, $24.95, TPB) r/X-Men road trips 25.00
...:The Coming of Bishop ('95, $12.95)-r/Uncanny X-Men #282-285, 287,288 13.00
...:The Magneto War (3/99, $2.99) Davis-a 3.00
...:The Rise of Apocalypse ('98, $16.99)-r/Rise Of Apocalypse #1-4, X-Factor #5,6 17.00
... Visionaries: Chris Claremont ('98, $24.95)-r/Claremont-s; art by Byrne, BWS, Jim Lee 25.00
... Visionaries: Jim Lee ('02, $29.99)-r/Jim Lee-a from various issues between Uncanny X-Men #248 & 286; r/Classic X-Men #39 and X-Men Annual #1 30.00
... Visionaries: Joe Madureira (7/00, $17.95)-r/Uncanny X-Men #325,326,329,330,341-343; new Madureira-c 18.00
...: Zero Tolerance ('00, $24.95, TPB) r/crossover series 25.00
NOTE: ***Jim Lee*** *a-1-11p; c-1-6p, 7, 8, 9p, 10, 11p.* ***Art Thibert*** *a-6-9i, 12, 13; c-6i, 12, 13.*

X-MEN ADVENTURES (TV)
Marvel Comics: Nov, 1992 - No. 15, Jan, 1994 ($1.25)(Based on animated series)
1-Wolverine, Cyclops, Jubilee, Rogue, Gambit 3.00
2-15: 3-Magneto-c/story. 6-Sabretooth-c/story. 7-Cable-c/story. 10-Archangel guest star. 11-Cable-c/story. 15-($1.75, 52 pgs.) 2.50

X-MEN ADVENTURES II (TV)
Marvel Comics: Feb, 1994 - No. 13, Feb, 1995 ($1.25/$1.50)(Based on 2nd TV season)
1-13: 4-Bound-in trading card sheet. 5-Alpha Flight app. 2.50
...Captive Hearts/Slave Island (TPB, $4.95)-r/X-Men Adventures #5-8 5.00
...The Irresistible Force, The Muir Island Saga (5.95, 10/94, TPB) r/X-Men Advs. #9-12 6.00

X-MEN ADVENTURES III (TV)(See Adventures of the X-Men)
Marvel Comics: Mar, 1995 - No. 13, Mar, 1996 ($1.50) (Based on 3rd TV season)
1-13 2.50

X-MEN ALPHA
Marvel Comics: 1994 ($3.95, one-shot)
nn-Age of Apocalypse; wraparound chromium-c 1 2 3 5 6 8
nn ($49.95)-Gold logo 50.00

X-MEN/ALPHA FLIGHT
Marvel Comics Group: Dec, 1985 - No. 2, Dec, 1985 ($1.50, limited series)
1,2: 1-Intro The Berserkers; Paul Smith-a 5.00

X-MEN/ALPHA FLIGHT
Marvel Comics Group: May, 1998 - No. 2, June, 1998 ($2.99, limited series)
1,2-Flashback to early meeting; Raab-s/Cassaday-s/a 3.00

X-MEN AND THE MICRONAUTS, THE
Marvel Comics Group: Jan, 1984 - No. 4, Apr, 1984 (Limited series)
1-4: Guice-c/a(p) in all 4.00

X-MEN ARCHIVES
Marvel Comics: Jan, 1995 - No. 4, Apr, 1995 ($2.25, limited series)
1-4: Reprints Legion stories from New Mutants. 4-Magneto app. 2.25

X-MEN ARCHIVES FEATURING CAPTAIN BRITAIN
Marvel Comics: July, 1995 - No. 7, 1996 ($2.95, limited series)
1-7: Reprints early Capt. Britain stories 3.00

X-MEN BLACK SUN (See Black Sun:...)

X-MEN BOOKS OF ASKANI
Marvel Comics: 1995 ($2.95, one-shot)
1-Painted pin-ups w/text 3.00

X-MEN: CHILDREN OF THE ATOM
Marvel Comics: Nov, 1999 - No. 6 ($2.99, limited series)
1-6-Casey-s; X-Men before issue #1. 1-3-Rude-c/a. 4-Paul Smith-a/Rude-c. 5,6-Essad Ribic-c/a 3.00
TPB (11/01, $16.95) r/series; sketch pages; Casey intro. 17.00

X-MEN CHRONICLES
Marvel Comics: Mar, 1995 - No. 2, June, 1995 ($3.95, limited series)
1,2: Age of Apocalypse x-over. 1-wraparound-c 5.00

X-MEN: CLANDESTINE
Marvel Comics: Oct, 1996 - No. 2, Nov, 1996 ($2.95, limited series, 48 pgs.)
1,2: Alan Davis-c(p)/a(p)/scripts & Mark Farmer-c(i)/a(i) in all; wraparound-c 3.00

X-MEN CLASSIC (Formerly Classic X-Men)
Marvel Comics: No. 46, Apr, 1990 - No. 110, Aug, 1995 ($1.25/$1.50)
46-110: Reprints from X-Men. 54-(52 pgs.). 57,60-63,65-Russell-c(i); 62-r/X-Men #158(Rogue). 66-r/#162(Wolverine). 69-Begins-r of Paul Smith issues (#165 on). 70,79,90,97(52 pgs.). 70-r/X-Men #166. 90-r/#186. 100-($1.50). 104-r/X-Men #200 2.50

X-MEN CLASSICS
Marvel Comics Group: Dec, 1983 - No. 3, Feb, 1984 ($2.00, Baxter paper)
1-3: X-Men-r by Neal Adams 6.00
NOTE: ***Zeck*** *c-1-3.*

X-MEN: EARTHFALL
Marvel Comics: Sept, 1996 ($2.95, one-shot)
1-r/Uncanny X-Men #232-234; wraparound-c 3.00

X-MEN: EVOLUTION (Based on the animated series)
Marvel Comics: Feb, 2002 - No. 9, Sept, 2002 ($2.25)
1-9: 1-8-Grayson-s/Udon-a. 9-Farber-s/J.J.Kirby-a 2.25
TPB (7/02, $8.99) r/#1-4 9.00
Vol. 2 TPB (2003, $11.99) r/#5-9; Asamiya-c 12.00

X-MEN FIRSTS
Marvel Comics: Feb, 1996 ($4.95, one-shot)
1-r/Avengers Annual #10, Uncanny X-Men #266, #221; Incredible Hulk #181 5.00

X-MEN FOREVER
Marvel Comics: Jan, 2001 - No. 6, June, 2001 ($3.50, limited series)
1-6-Jean Grey, Iceman, Mystique, Toad, Juggernaut app.; Maguire-a 3.50

X-MEN: HELLFIRE CLUB
Marvel Comics: Jan, 2000 - No. 4, Apr, 2000 ($2.50, limited series)
1-4-Origin of the Hellfire Club 2.50

X-MEN: HIDDEN YEARS
Marvel Comics: Dec, 1999 - No. 22, Sept. 2001 ($3.50/$2.50)
1-New adventures from pre-#94 era; Byrne-s/a(p) 3.50
2-4,6-11,13-22-($2.50): 2-Two covers. 3-Ka-Zar app. 8,9-FF-c/app. 2.50
5-($2.75) 2.75
12-($3.50) Magneto-c/app. 3.50

X-MEN: LIBERATORS

X-Men: Ronin #1 © MAR

X-Men 2 The Movie Prequel: Nightcrawler #1 © MAR

X-Men 2099 #12 © MAR

GD VG FN VF VF/NM NM-
2.0 4.0 6.0 8.0 9.0 9.2

Marvel Comics: Nov, 1998 - No. 4, Feb, 1999 ($2.99, limited series)
1-4-Wolverine, Nightcrawler & Colossus; P. Jimenez 3.00

X-MEN LOST TALES
Marvel Comics: 1997 ($2.99)
1,2-r/Classic X-Men back-up stories 3.00

X-MEN OMEGA
Marvel Comics: June, 1995 ($3.95, one-shot)
nn-Age of Apocalypse finale 1 3 4 6 8 10
nn-($49.95)-Gold edition 50.00

X-MEN: PHOENIX
Marvel Comics: Dec, 1999 - No. 3, Mar, 2000 ($2.50, limited series)
1-3: 1-Apocalypse app. 2.50

X-MEN: PHOENIX - LEGACY OF FIRE
Marvel Comics: July, 2003 - No. 3, Sep, 2003 ($2.99, limited series)
1-3-Manga-style; Ryan Kinnard-s/a/c; intro page art by Adam Warren 3.00

X-MEN PRIME
Marvel Comics: July, 1995 ($4.95, one-shot)
nn-Post Age of Apocalyse begins 1 3 4 6 8 10

X-MEN RARITIES
Marvel Comics: 1995 ($5.95, one-shot)
nn-Reprints hard-to-find stories 6.00

X-MEN ROAD TO ONSLAUGHT
Marvel Comics: Oct, 1996 ($2.50, one-shot)
nn-Retells Onslaught Saga 2.50

X-MEN: RONIN
Marvel Comics: May, 2003 - No. 5, July, 2003 ($2.99, limited series)
1-5-Manga-style X-Men; Torres-s/Nakatsuka-a 3.00

X-MEN: SEARCH FOR CYCLOPS
Marvel Comics: Oct, 2000 - No. 4, Mar, 2001 ($2.99, limited series)
1-4-Two covers (Raney, Pollina); Raney-a 3.00

X-MEN SPOTLIGHT ON... STARJAMMERS (Also see X-Men #104)
Marvel Comics: 1990 - No. 2, 1990 ($4.50, 52 pgs.)
1,2: Features Starjammers 4.50

X-MEN SURVIVAL GUIDE TO THE MANSION
Marvel Comics: Aug, 1993 ($6.95, spiralbound)
1 7.00

X-MEN: THE EARLY YEARS
Marvel Comics: May, 1994 - No. 17, Sept, 1995 ($1.50/$2.50)
1-16: r/X-Men #1-8 w/new-c 2.25
17-$2.50-c; r/X-Men #17,18 2.50

X-MEN: THE MANGA
Marvel Comics: Mar, 1998 - No. 26, June, 1999 ($2.99, B&W)
1-26-English version of Japanese X-Men comics: 23,24-Randy Green-c 3.00

X-MEN: THE MOVIE
Marvel Comics: Aug, 2000; Sept, 2000
Adaptation (9/00, $5.95) Macchio-s/Williams & Lanning-a 6.00
Adaptation TPB (9/00, $14.95) Movie adaptation and key reprints of main characters; four photo covers (movie X, Magneto, Rogue, Wolverine) 15.00
Prequel: Magneto (8/00, $5.95) Texeira & Palmiotti-a; art & photo covers 6.00
Prequel: Rogue (8/00, $5.95) Evans & Nikolakakis-a; art & photo covers 6.00
Prequel: Wolverine (8/00, $5.95) Waller & McKenna-a; art & photo covers 6.00
TPB X-Men: Beginnings (8/00, $14.95) reprints 3 prequels w/photo-c 15.00

X-MEN 2: THE MOVIE
Marvel Comics: 2003
Adaptation (6/03, $3.50) Movie adaptation; photo-c; Austen-s/Zircher-a 3.50
Adaptation TPB (2003, $12.99) Movie adaptation & r/Prequels Nightcrawler & Wolverine 13.00
Prequel: Nightcrawler (5/03, $3.50) Kerschl-a; photo cover 3.50
Prequel: Wolverine (5/03, $3.50) Mandrake-a; photo cover; Sabretooth app. 3.50

X-MEN: THE ULTRA COLLECTION
Marvel Comics: Dec, 1994 - No. 5, Apr, 1995 ($2.95, limited series)
1-5: Pin-ups; no scripts 3.00

X-MEN: THE WEDDING ALBUM
Marvel Comics: 1994 ($2.95, magazine size, one-shot)
1-Wedding of Scott Summers & Jean Grey 3.00

X-MEN TRUE FRIENDS
Marvel Comics: Sept, 1999 - No. 3, Nov, 1999 ($2.99, limited series)
1-3-Claremont-s/Leonardi-a 3.00

X-MEN 2099 (Also see 2099: World of Tomorrow)
Marvel Comics: Oct, 1993 - No. 35, Aug, 1996 ($1.25/$1.50/$1.95)
1-($1.75)-Foil-c; Ron Lim/Adam Kubert-a begins 3.00
1-2nd printing ($1.75) 2.25
1-Gold edition (15,000 made); sold thru Diamond for $19.40 20.00
2-24,26-35: 3-Death of Tina; Lim-c/a(p) in #1-8. 8-Bound-in trading card sheet. 35-Nostromo (from X-Nation) app; storyline cont'd in 2099: World of Tomorrow 2.25
25-($2.50)-Double sized 2.50
Special 1 ($3.95) 4.00
...: Oasis ($5.95, one-shot) -Hildebrandt Bros.-c/a 6.00

X-MEN ULTRA III PREVIEW
Marvel Comics: 1995 ($2.95)
nn-Kubert-a 3.00

X-MEN UNIVERSE
Marvel Comics: Dec, 1999 - Present ($4.99/$3.99)
1-8-Reprints stories from recent X-Men titles 5.00
9-15-($3.99) 4.00

X-MEN UNIVERSE: PAST, PRESENT AND FUTURE
Marvel Comics: Feb, 1999 ($2.99, one-shot)
1-Previews 1999 X-Men events; background info 3.00

X-MEN UNLIMITED
Marvel Comics: 1993 - No. 50, Sept, 2003 ($3.95/$2.99, 68 pgs.)
1-Chris Bachalo-c/a; Quesada-a. 5.00
2-11: 2-Origin of Magneto script. 3-Sabretooth-c/story. 10-Dark Beast vs. Beast; Mark Waid script. 11-Magneto & Rogue 4.00
12-33: 12-Begin $2.99-c; Onslaught x-over; Juggernaut-c/app. 19-Caliafore-a. 20-Generation X app. 27-Origin Thunderbird. 29-Maximum Security x-over; Bishop-c/app. 30-Mahfood-a. 31-Stelfreeze-c/a. 32-Dazzler; Thompson-c/a 33-Kaluta-c 3.00
34-37,39,40-42-($3.50) 34-Von Eeden-a. 35-Finch, Conner, Maguire-a. 36-Chiodo-c/a; Larroca, Totleben-a. 39-Bachalo-c; Pearson-a. 41-Bachalo-c; X-Statix app. 3.50
38-($2.25) Kitty Pryde; Robertson-a 2.25
43-50-($2.50) 43-Sienkiewicz-c/a; Paul Smith-a. 45-Noto-c. 46-Bisley-a. 47-Warren-s/Mays-a. 48-Wolverine story w/Isanove painted-a 2.50
X-Men Legends Vol. 4: Hated and Feared TPB (2003, $19.99) r/stories by various 20.00
NOTE: *Bachalo c/a-1.* ***Quesada*** *a-1.* ***Waid*** *scripts-10*

X-MEN VS. DRACULA
Marvel Comics: Dec, 1993 ($1.75)
1-r/X-Men Annual #6; Austin-c(i) 2.25

X-MEN VS. THE AVENGERS, THE
Marvel Comics Group: Apr, 1987 - No. 4, July, 1987 ($1.50, limited series, Baxter paper)
1 4.00
2-4 3.00

X-MEN VS. THE BROOD, THE
Marvel Comics Group: Sept, 1996 - No. 2, Oct, 1996 ($2.95, limited series)
1,2-Wraparound-c; Ostrander-s/Hitch-a(p) 3.00
TPB('97, $16.99) reprints X-Men/Brood: Day of Wrath #1,2 & Uncanny X-Men #232-234 17.00

X-MEN VISIONARIES
Marvel Comics: 1995,1996,2000 (trade paperbacks)
nn-($8.95) Reprints X-Men stories; Adam & Andy Kubert-a 9.00
...2: The Neal Adams Collection (1996) r/X-Men #56-63,65 30.00
...2: The Neal Adams Col. (2nd printing, 2000, $24.95) new Adams-c 25.00

X-MEN/WILDC.A.T.S.: THE DARK AGE (See also WildC.A.T.S./X-Men...)
Marvel Comics: 1998 ($4.50, one-shot)
1-Two covers (Broome & Golden); Ellis-s 4.50

X-NATION 2099
Marvel Comics: Mar, 1996 - No. 6, Aug, 1996 ($1.95)
1-($3.95)-Humberto Ramos-a(p); wraparound, foil-c 4.00
2-6: 2,3-Ramos-a. 4-Exodus-c/app. 6-Reed Richards app 2.25

X-O MANOWAR (1st Series)
Valiant/Acclaim Comics (Valiant) No. 43 on: Feb, 1992 - No. 68, Sept, 1996 ($1.95/$2.25/$2.50, high quality)
0-(8/93, $3.50)-Wraparound embossed chromium-c by Quesada; Solar app.;

X-O Manowar #34 © Voyager Comm.

X-Statix #13 © MAR

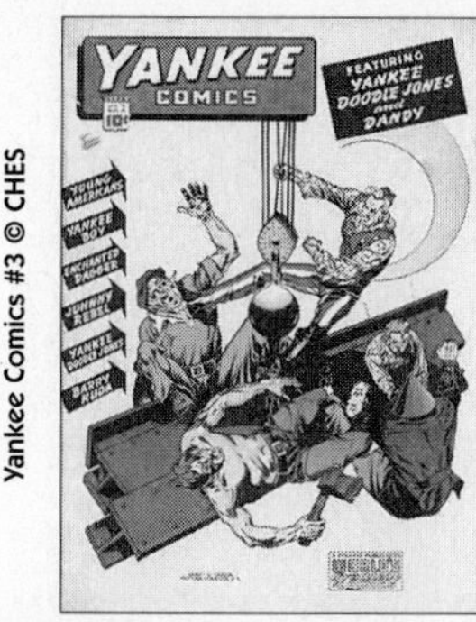

Yankee Comics #3 © CHES

GD VG FN VF VF/NM NM-
2.0 4.0 6.0 8.0 9.0 9.2

origin Aric (X-O Manowar) 3.50
0-Gold variant 5.00
1-Intro/1st app. & partial origin of Aric (X-O Manowar); Barry Smith/Layton-a 1 2 3 5 6 8
2-4: 2-B. Smith/Layton-c. 3-Layton-c(i). 4-1st app. Shadowman (cameo) 6.00
5-15: 5-B. Smith-c. 6-Begin $2.25-c; Ditko-a(p). 7,8-Unity x-overs. 7-Miller-c. 8-Simonson-c. 12-1st app. Randy Calder. 14,15-Turok-c/stories 3.00
15-Hot pink logo variant; came with Ultra Pro Rigid Comic Sleeves box; no price on cover 4.00
16-24,26-43: 20-Serial number contest insert. 27-29-Turok x-over. 28-Bound-in trading card. 30-1st app. new "good skin"; Solar app. 33-Chaos Effect Delta Pt. 3. 42-Shadowman app.; includes X-O Manowar Birthquake! Prequel 2.50
25-($3.50)-Has 16 pg. Armorines #0 bound-in w/origin 3.50
44-68: 44-Begin $2.50-c. 50-X, 50-O, 51, 52, 63-Bart Sears-c/a/scripts. 68-Revealed that Aric's past stories were premonitions of his future 2.50
Trade paperback nn (1993, $9.95)-Polybagged with copy of X-O Database #1 inside 10.00
Yearbook 1 (4/95, $2.95) 3.00
NOTE: *Layton a-1i, 2i(part); c-1, 2i, 3i, 6i, 21i.* ***Reese*** *a-4i(part); c-26i.*

X-O MANOWAR (2nd Series)(Also see Iron Man/X-O Manowar: Heavy Metal)
Acclaim Comics (Valiant Heroes): V2#1, Oct, 1996 - No. 21, Jun, 1998 ($2.50)
V2#1-21: 1-Mark Waid & Brian Augustyn scripts begin; 1st app. Donavon Wylie; Rand Banion dies; painted variant-c exists. 2-Donavon Wylie becomes new X-O Manowar. 7-9-Augustyn-s. 10-Copycat-c 2.50

X-O MANOWAR FAN EDITION
Acclaim Comics (Valiant Heroes): Feb, 1997 (Overstreet's FAN giveaway)
1-Reintro the Armorines & the Hard Corps; 1st app. Citadel; Augustyn scripts; McKone-c/a 4.00

X-O MANOWAR/IRON MAN: IN HEAVY METAL (See Iron Man/X-O Manowar: Heavy Metal)
Acclaim Comics (Valiant Heroes): Sept, 1996 ($2.50, one-shot)
(1st Marvel/Valiant x-over)
1-Pt 1 of X-O Manowar/Iron Man x-over; Arnim Zola app.; Nicieza scripts; Andy Smith-a 2.50

XOMBI
DC Comics (Milestone): Jan, 1994 - No. 21, Feb, 1996 ($1.75/$2.50)
0-($1.95)-Shadow War x-over; Simonson silver ink varnish-c 2.50
1-21: 1-John Byrne-c 2.50
1-Platinum 8.00

X-PATROL
Marvel Comics (Amalgam): Apr, 1996 ($1.95, one-shot)
1-Cruz-a(p) 2.25

XSE
Marvel Comics: Nov, 1996 - No. 4, Feb, 1997 ($1.95, limited series)
1-4: 1-Bishop & Shard app. 2.25
1-Variant-c 3.00

X-STATIX
Marvel Comics: Sept, 2002 - Present ($2.99/$2.25)
1-($2.99)Allred-a/c; intro. Venus Dee Milo; back-up w/Cooke-a 3.00
2-9-($2.25) 4-Quitely-c. 5-Pope-c/a 2.25
10-17: 10-Begin $2.99-c; Bond-a; U-Go Girl flashback. 13,14-Spider-man app. 3.00
... Vol. 1: Good Omens TPB (2003, $11.99) r/#1-5 12.00
... Vol. 2: Good Guys & Bad Guys TPB (2003, $15.99) r/#6-10 & Wolverine/Doop #1&2 16.00

X-TERMINATORS
Marvel Comics: Oct, 1988 - No. 4, Jan, 1989 ($1.00, limited series)
1-1st app.; X-Men/X-Factor tie-in; Williamson-i 3.00
2-4 2.25

X, THE MAN WITH THE X-RAY EYES (See Movie Comics)

X-TREME X-MEN (Also see Mekanix)
Marvel Comics: July, 2001 - Present ($2.99/$3.50)
1-Claremont-s/Larroca-c/a 4.00
2-24: 2-Two covers (Larroca & Pacheco); Psylocke killed 3.00
25-35: 25-30-God Loves, Man Kills II; Stryker app.; Kordey-a 3.00
36-39-($3.50) 3.50
Annual 2001 ($4.95) issue opens longways 5.00
... Vol. 1: Destiny TPB (2002, $19.95) r/#1-9 20.00
... Vol. 2: Invasion TPB (2003, $19.99) r/#10-18 20.00
... Vol. 3: Schism TPB (2003, $16.99) r/#19-23; X-Treme X-Posé #1&2 17.00
... Vol. 4: Mekanix TPB (2003, $16.99) r/Mekanix #1-6 17.00

X-TREME X-MEN: SAVAGE LAND
Marvel Comics: Nov, 2001 - No. 4, Feb, 2002 ($2.99, limited series)
1-4-Claremont-s/Sharpe-c/a; Beast app. 3.00

X-TREME X-POSE
Marvel Comics: Jan, 2003 - No. 2, Feb, 2003 ($2.99, limited series)
1,2-Claremont-s/Ranson-a/Migliari-c 3.00

X-UNIVERSE
Marvel Comics: May, 1995 - No. 2, June, 1995 ($3.50, limited series)
1,2: Age of Apocalypse 5.00

X-VENTURE (Super Heroes)
Victory Magazines Corp.: July, 1947 - No. 2, Nov, 1947
1-Atom Wizard, Mystery Shadow, Lester Trumble begin 108 216 324 675 1013 1350
2 55 110 165 344 515 685

XYR (See Eclipse Graphic Album Series #21)

YAK YAK
Dell Publishing Co.: No. 1186, May-July, 1961 - No. 1348, Apr-June, 1962
Four Color 1186 (#1)- Jack Davis-c/a; 2 versions, one minus 3pgs. 10 20 30 67 96 125
Four Color 1348 (#2)-Davis c/a 9 18 27 63 89 115

YAKKY DOODLE & CHOPPER (TV) (See Dell Giant #44)
Gold Key: Dec, 1962 (Hanna-Barbera)
1 9 18 27 60 85 110

YANG (See House of Yang)
Charlton Comics: Nov, 1973 - No. 13, May, 1976; V14#15, Sept, 1985 - No. 17, Jan, 1986 (No V14#14, series resumes with #15)
1-Origin; Sattler-a begins; slavery-s 2 4 6 11 14 18
2-13(1976) 1 2 3 6 9 10
15-17(1986): 15-Reprints #1 (Low print run) 6.00
3,10,11(Modern Comics-r, 1977) 4.00

YANKEE COMICS
Harry 'A' Chesler: Sept, 1941 - No. 7, 1942?
1-Origin The Echo, The Enchanted Dagger, Yankee Doodle Jones, The Firebrand, & The Scarlet Sentry; Black Satan app.; Yankee Doodle Jones app. on all covers 168 336 504 1050 1575 2100
2-Origin Johnny Rebel; Major Victory app.; Barry Kuda begins 78 156 234 488 732 975
3,4: 4-(3/42) 60 120 180 375 563 750
4 (nd, 1940s; 7-1/4x5", 68 pgs, distr. to the service)-Foxy Grandpa, Tom, Dick & Harry, Impy, Ace & Deuce, Dot & Dash, Ima Slooth by Jack Cole (Remington Morse publ.) 9 18 27 54 70 85
5-7 (nd; 10¢, 7-1/4x5", 68 pgs.)(Remington Morse publ.)-urges readers to send their copies to servicemen. 8 16 24 46 58 70

YANKEE DOODLE THE SPIRIT OF LIBERTY
Spire Publications: 1984 (no price, 36 pgs)
nn-Al Hartley-s/c/a 1 3 4 6 8 10

YANKS IN BATTLE
Quality Comics Group: Sept, 1956 - No. 4, Dec, 1956; 1963
1-Cuidera-c(i) 10 20 30 56 73 90
2-4: Cuidera-c(i) 7 14 21 37 46 55
I.W. Reprint #3(1963)-r/#?; exist? 2 4 6 10 12 15

YARDBIRDS, THE (G. I. Joe's Sidekicks)
Ziff-Davis Publishing Co.: Summer, 1952
1-By Bob Oskner 10 20 30 56 73 90

YARN MAN (See Megaton Man)
Kitchen Sink : Oct, 1989 ($2.00, B&W, one-shot)
1-Donald Simpson-c/a/scripts 2.25

YARNS OF YELLOWSTONE
World Color Press: 1972 (50¢, 36 pgs.)
nn-Illustrated by Bill Chapman 2 4 6 9 11 14

YEAH!
DC Comics (Homage): Oct, 1999 - No. 9, Jun, 2000 ($2.95)
1-Bagge-s/Hernandez-a 3.00
2-9: 2-Editorial page contains adult language 3.00

YELLOW CLAW (Also see Giant Size Master of Kung Fu)
Atlas Comics (MjMC): Oct, 1956 - No. 4, Apr, 1957

Yellowjacket Comics #1 © E. Levy

Young Allies Comics #12 © MAR

Youngblood V2#14 © Rob Liefeld

GD VG FN VF VF/NM NM-
2.0 4.0 6.0 8.0 9.0 9.2

1-Origin by Joe Maneely 96 192 288 600 900 1200
2-Kirby-a 77 154 231 481 721 960
3,4-Kirby-a; 4-Kirby/Severin-a 74 148 222 463 692 920
NOTE: *Everett c-3. Maneely c-1. Reinman a-2i, 3. Severin c-2, 4.*

YELLOWJACKET COMICS (Jack in the Box #11 on)(See TNT Comics)
E. Levy/Frank Comunale/Charlton: Sept, 1944 - No. 10, June, 1946

1-Intro & origin Yellowjacket; Diana, the Huntress begins; E.A. Poe's "The Black Cat" adaptation 66 132 198 413 619 825
2-Yellowjacket-c begin, end #10 42 84 126 252 359 465
3,5 40 80 120 240 340 440
4-E.A. Poe's "Fall of the House Of Usher" adaptation; Palais-a
42 84 126 252 359 465
6 48 96 144 288 432 575
7-Classic skull-c 96 192 288 600 900 1200
8-10: 1,3,4,6-10-Have stories narrated by old witch in "Tales of Terror" (1st horror series?)
46 92 138 276 413 550

YELLOWSTONE KELLY (Movie)
Dell Publishing Co.: No. 1056, Nov-Jan, 1959/60

Four Color 1056-Clint Walker photo-c 6 12 18 43 59 75

YELLOW SUBMARINE (See Movie Comics)

YIN FEI THE CHINESE NINJA
Leung's Publications: 1988 - No. 8, 1990 ($1.80/$2.00, 52 pgs.)

1-8 2.25

YOGI BEAR (See Dell Giant #41, Golden Comics Digest, Kite Fun Book, March of Comics #253, 265, 279, 291, 309, 319, 337, 344, Movie Comics under "Hey There It's..." & Whitman Comic Books)

YOGI BEAR (TV) (Hanna-Barbera) (See Four Color #990)
Dell Publishing Co./Gold Key No. 10 on: No. 1067, 12-2/59-60 - No. 9, 7-9/62; No. 10, 10/62 - No. 42, 10/70

Four Color 1067 (#1)-TV show debuted 1/30/61 12 24 36 87 129 170
Four Color 1104,1162 (5-7/61) 8 16 24 58 82 105
4(8-9/61) - 6(12-1/61-62) 6 12 18 43 59 75
Four Color 1271(11/61) 6 12 18 43 59 75
Four Color 1349(1/62)-Photo-c 10 20 30 70 100 130
7(2-3/62) - 9(7-9/62)-Last Dell 6 12 18 43 59 75
10(10/62-G.K.), 11(1/63)-titled "Yogi Bear Jellystone Jollies" (80 pgs.); 11-X-Mas-c
8 16 24 55 78 100
12(4/63), 14-20 5 10 15 36 48 60
13(7/63, 68 pgs.)-Surprise Party 8 16 24 55 78 100
21-30 4 8 12 22 30 38
31-42 3 6 9 18 24 30

YOGI BEAR (TV)
Charlton Comics: Nov, 1970 - No. 35, Jan, 1976 (Hanna-Barbera)

1 5 10 15 33 44 55
2-6,8-10 3 6 9 18 24 30
7-Summer Fun (Giant, 52 pgs.) 5 10 15 36 48 60
11-20 3 6 9 18 23 28
21-35: 28-31-partial-r 2 4 6 12 16 20
Digest (nn, 1972, 75¢-c, B&W, 100 pgs.) (scarce) 4 8 12 22 30 38

YOGI BEAR (TV)(See The Flintstones, 3rd series & Spotlight #1)
Marvel Comics Group: Nov, 1977 - No. 9, Mar, 1979 (Hanna-Barbera)

1,7-9: 1-Flintstones begin (Newsstand sales only) 3 6 9 16 23 28
2-6 2 4 6 11 14 18

YOGI BEAR (TV)
Harvey Comics: Sept, 1992 - No. 6, Mar, 1994 ($1.25/$1.50) (Hanna-Barbera)

V2#1-6 3.00
...Big Book V2#1,2 ($1.95, 52 pgs): 1-(11/92). 2-(3/93) 3.00
...Giant Size V2#1,2 ($2.25, 68 pgs.): 1-(10/92). 2-(4/93) 3.00

YOGI BEAR'S EASTER PARADE (See The Funtastic World of Hanna-Barbera #2)

YOGI BERRA (Baseball hero)
Fawcett Publications: 1951 (Yankee catcher)

nn-Photo-c (scarce) 70 140 210 438 657 875

YOSEMITE SAM (...& Bugs Bunny) (TV)
Gold Key/Whitman: Dec, 1970 - No. 81, Feb, 1984

1 5 10 15 33 44 55
2-10 3 6 9 16 20 25
11-20 2 4 6 11 14 18
21-30 2 4 6 9 11 14

GD VG FN VF VF/NM NM-
2.0 4.0 6.0 8.0 9.0 9.2

31-50 1 3 4 6 8 10
51-65 (Gold Key) 1 2 3 5 6 8
66,67 (Whitman) 2 4 6 8 10 12
68(9/80), 69(10/80), 70(12/80) 3-pack only 2 4 6 14 18 22
71-78: 76(2/82), 77(3/82), 78(4/82) 2 4 6 9 11 14
79-81 (All #90263 on-c, no date or date code; 3-pack): 79(7/83). 80(8/83). 81(2/84)-(1/3-r)
2 4 6 12 16 20
(See March of Comics #363, 380, 392)

YOUNG ALLIES COMICS (All-Winners #21; see Kid Komics #2)
Timely Comics (USA 1-7/NPI 8,9/YAI 10-20): Sum, 1941 - No. 20, Oct, 1946

1-Origin/1st app. The Young Allies (Bucky, Toro, others); 1st meeting of Captain America & Human Torch; Red Skull-c & app.; S&K-c/splash; Hitler-c; Note: the cover was altered after its preview in Human Torch #5. Stalin was shown with Hitler but was removed due to Russia becoming an ally 1313 2626 3939 9848 15,424 21,000
2-(Winter, 1941)-Captain America & Human Torch app.; Simon & Kirby-c
370 740 1110 2405 3703 5000
3-Fathertime, Captain America & Human Torch app.; Remember Pearl Harbor issue (Spring, 1942); Stan Lee scripts; Vs. Japs-c/full-length story
280 560 840 1750 2625 3500
4-The Vagabond & Red Skull, Capt. America, Human Torch app. Classic Red Skull-c
385 770 1155 2503 3852 5200
5-Captain America & Human Torch app. 184 368 552 1150 1725 2300
6,7,10: 10-Origin Tommy Tyme & Clock of Ages; ends #19
128 256 384 800 1200 1600
8-Classic Schomburg WW2 bondage-c 136 272 408 850 1275 1700
9-Hitler, Tojo, Mussolini-c. 144 288 432 900 1350 1800
11-20: 12-Classic decapitation story 96 192 288 600 900 1200
NOTE: *Brodsky c-15. Gabrielle a-3; c-3, 4. S&K c-1, 2. Schomburg c-5-14, 16-19. Shores c-20.*

YOUNG ALL-STARS
DC Comics: June, 1987 - No. 31, Nov, 1989 ($1.00, deluxe format)

1-31: 1-1st app. Iron Munro & The Flying Fox. 8,9-Millennium tie-ins 2.25
Annual 1 (1988, $2.00) 2.25

YOUNGBLOOD (See Brigade #4, Megaton Explosion & Team Youngblood)
Image Comics (Extreme Studios): Apr, 1992 - No. 4, Feb, 1993 ($2.50, lim. series); No. 6, June, 1994 (No #5) - No. 10, Dec, 1994 ($1.95/$2.50)

1-Liefeld-c/a/scripts in all; flip book format with 2 trading cards; 1st Image/Extreme Studios title. 5.00
1,2-2nd printing 2.50
2-(JUN-c, July 1992 indicia)-1st app. Shadowhawk in solo back-up story; 2 trading cards inside; flip book format; 1st app. Prophet, Kirby, Berzerkers, Darkthorn 2.50
3,0,4,5: 3-(OCT-c, August 1992 indicia)-Contains 2 trading cards inside (flip book); 1st app. Supreme in back-up story; 1st app. Showdown. 0-(12/92, $1.95)-Contains 2 trading cards; 2 cover variations exist, green or beige logo; w/Image #0 coupon. 4-(2/93)-Glow-in-the-dark cover w/2 trading cards; 2nd app. Dale Keown's The Pitt; Bloodstrike app. 5-Flip book w/Brigade #4 2.50
6-($3.50, 52 pgs.)-Wraparound-c 3.50
7-10: 7, 8-Liefeld-c(p)/a(p)/story. 8,9-(9/94) 9-Valentino story & art 2.50
Battlezone 1 (May-c, 4/93 inside, $1.95)-Arsenal book; Liefeld-c(p) 2.50
Battlezone 2 (7/94, $2.95)-Wraparound-c 3.00
Yearbook 1 (7/93, $2.50)-Fold out panel; 1st app. Tyrax & Kanan 2.50
...Super Special (Winter '97, $2.99) Sprouse -a 3.00
TPB (1996, $16.95)-r/Team Youngblood #8-10 & Youngblood #6-8,10 17.00

YOUNGBLOOD
Image Comics (Extreme Studios)/Maximum Press No. 14: V2#1, Sept, 1995 - No. 14, Dec, 1996 ($2.50)

V2#1-10,14: Roger Cruz-a in all. 4-Extreme Destroyer Pt. 4 w/gaming card. 5-Variant-c exists. 6-Angela & Glory. 7-Shadowhunt Pt. 3; Shadowhawk app. 8,10-Thor (from Supreme) app. 10-(7/96). 14-(12/96)-1st Maximum Press issue 2.50

YOUNGBLOOD (Volume 3)
Awesome/ Awesome-Hyperwerks #2 on: Feb, 1998 - No. 2, Aug, 1998 ($2.50)

1-Alan Moore-s/Skroce & Stucker-a; 12 diff. covers 2.50
1-Gold foil-c; 1+ Alter Ego Gold Foil 5.00
1-Blue foil-c Orlando Con Ed. 10.00
2-(8/98) Skroce & Liefeld covers 2.50

YOUNGBLOOD: STRIKEFILE
Image Comics (Extreme Studios): Apr, 1993 - No. 11, Feb, 1995 ($1.95/$2.50/$2.95)

1-10: 1-($1.95)-Flip book w/Jae Lee-c/a & Liefeld-c/a in #1-3; 1st app. The Allies,Giger, & Glory. 3-Thibert-i asisst. 4-Liefeld-c(p); no Lee-a. 5-Liefeld-c(p). 8-Platt-c 3.00
NOTE: *Youngblood: Strikefile began as a four issue limited series.*

YOUNGBLOOD/X-FORCE

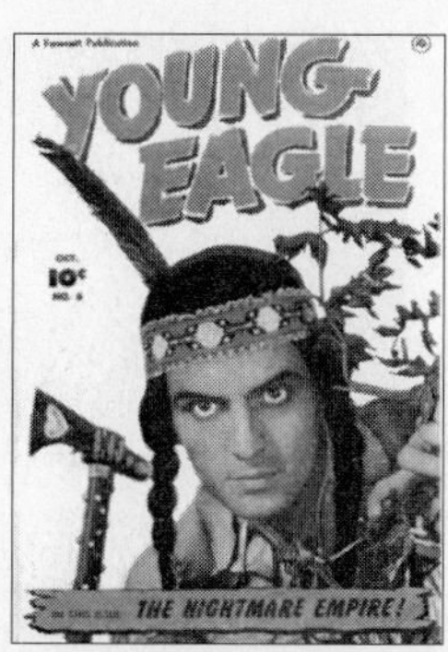

Young Eagle #6 © FAW

Young Justice #55 © DC

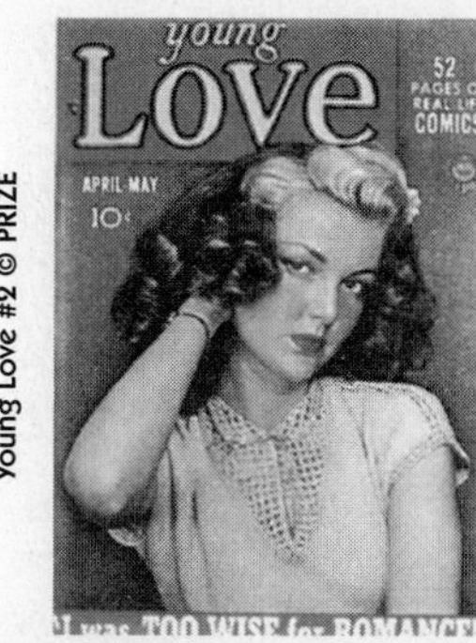

Young Love #2 © PRIZE

Image Comics (Extreme Studios): July, 1996 ($4.95, one-shot)

	GD 2.0	VG 4.0	FN 6.0	VF 8.0	VF/NM 9.0	NM- 9.2
1-Cruz-a(p); two covers exist						5.00

YOUNG BRIDES (True Love Secrets)
Feature/Prize Publ.: Sept-Oct, 1952 - No. 30, Nov-Dec, 1956 (Photo-c: 1-4)

	GD 2.0	VG 4.0	FN 6.0	VF 8.0	VF/NM 9.0	NM- 9.2
V1#1-Simon & Kirby-a	33	66	99	190	270	350
2-S&K-a	19	38	57	106	146	185
3-6-S&K-a	17	34	51	98	134	170
V2#1,3-7,10-12 (#7-18)-S&K-a	16	32	48	92	126	160
2,8,9-No S&K-a	7	14	21	37	46	55
V3#1-3(#19-21)-Last precode (3-4/55)	7	14	21	35	43	50
4,6(#22,24), V4#1,3(#25,27)	6	12	18	28	34	40
V3#5(#23)-Meskin-c	6	12	18	31	38	45
V4#2(#26)-All S&K issue	14	28	42	81	111	140
V4#4(#28)-S&K-a	11	22	33	66	88	110
V4#5,6(#29,30)	7	14	21	35	43	50

YOUNG DR. MASTERS (See The Adventures of Young Dr. Masters)

YOUNG DOCTORS, THE
Charlton Comics: Jan, 1963 - No. 6, Nov, 1963

	GD 2.0	VG 4.0	FN 6.0	VF 8.0	VF/NM 9.0	NM- 9.2
V1#1	4	8	12	24	32	40
2-6	2	4	6	14	18	22

YOUNG EAGLE
Fawcett Publications/Charlton: 12/50 - No. 10, 6/52; No. 3, 7/56 - No. 5, 4/57 (Photo-c: 1-10)

	GD 2.0	VG 4.0	FN 6.0	VF 8.0	VF/NM 9.0	NM- 9.2
1-Intro Young Eagle	19	38	57	106	146	185
2-Complete picture novelette "The Mystery of Thunder Canyon"	10	20	30	56	73	90
3-9	9	18	27	49	62	75
10-Origin Thunder, Young Eagle's Horse	8	16	24	43	54	65
3-5(Charlton)-Formerly Sherlock Holmes?	6	12	18	28	34	40

YOUNG HEARTS
Marvel Comics (SPC): Nov, 1949 - No. 2, Feb, 1950

	GD 2.0	VG 4.0	FN 6.0	VF 8.0	VF/NM 9.0	NM- 9.2
1-Photo-c	13	26	39	74	100	125
2-Colleen Townsend photo-c from movie	9	18	27	49	62	75

YOUNG HEARTS IN LOVE
Super Comics: 1964

	GD 2.0	VG 4.0	FN 6.0	VF 8.0	VF/NM 9.0	NM- 9.2
17,18: 17-r/Young Love V5#6 (4-5/62)	2	4	6	11	14	18

YOUNG HEROES (Formerly Forbidden Worlds #34)
American Comics Group (Titan): No. 35, Feb-Mar, 1955 - No. 37, Jun-Jul, 1955

	GD 2.0	VG 4.0	FN 6.0	VF 8.0	VF/NM 9.0	NM- 9.2
35-37-Frontier Scout	10	20	30	56	73	90

YOUNG HEROES IN LOVE
DC Comics: June, 1997 - No. 17; #1,000,000, Nov, 1998 ($1.75/$1.95/$2.50)

	GD 2.0	VG 4.0	FN 6.0	VF 8.0	VF/NM 9.0	NM- 9.2
1-1st app. Young Heroes; Madan-a						3.00
2-17: 3-Superman-c/app. 7-Begin $1.95-c						2.50
#1,000,000 (11/98, $2.50) 853 Century x-over						2.50

YOUNG INDIANA JONES CHRONICLES, THE
Dark Horse Comics: Feb, 1992 - No. 12, Feb, 1993 ($2.50)

	GD 2.0	VG 4.0	FN 6.0	VF 8.0	VF/NM 9.0	NM- 9.2
1-12: Dan Barry scripts in all						2.50

NOTE: ***Dan Barry** a(p)-1, 2, 5, 6, 10; c-1-10. **Morrow** a-3, 4, 5p, 6p. **Springer** a-1i, 2i.*

YOUNG INDIANA JONES CHRONICLES, THE
Hollywood Comics (Disney): 1992 ($3.95, squarebound, 68 pgs.)

	GD 2.0	VG 4.0	FN 6.0	VF 8.0	VF/NM 9.0	NM- 9.2
1-3: 1-r/YIJC #1,2 by D. Horse. 2-r/#3,4. 3-r/#5,6						4.00

YOUNG JUSTICE (Also see Teen Titans and Titans/Young Justice)
DC Comics: Sept, 1998 - No. 55, May, 2003 ($2.50/$2.75)

	GD 2.0	VG 4.0	FN 6.0	VF 8.0	VF/NM 9.0	NM- 9.2
1-Robin, Superboy & Impulse team-up; David-s/Nauck-a						4.00
2,3: 3-Mxyzptlk app.						3.00
4-20: 4-Wonder Girl, Arrowette and the Secret join. 6-JLA app. 13-Supergirl x-over. 20-Sins of Youth aftermath						3.00
21-49: 25-Empress ID revealed. 28,29-Forever People app. 32-Empress origin. 35,36-Our Worlds at War x-over. 38-Joker: Last Laugh. 41-The Ray joins. 42-Spectre-c/app. 44,45-World Without YJ x-over pt. 1,5; Ramos-c. 48-Begin $2.75-c						2.75
50-($3.95) Wonder Twins,CM3 and other various DC teen heroes app.						4.00
51-55: 53,54-Darkseid app. 55-Last issue; leads into Titans/Young Justice mini-series						2.75
#1,000,000 (11/98) 853 Century x-over						2.50
...: A League of Their Own (2000, $14.95, TPB) r/#1-7, Secret Files #1						15.00
...: 80-Page Giant (5/99, $4.95) Ramos-c; stories and art by various						5.00
...: In No Man's Land (7/99, $3.95) McDaniel-c						4.00
...: Our Worlds at War (8/01, $2.95) Jae Lee-c; Linear Men app.						3.00
...: Secret Files (1/99, $4.95) Origin-s & pin-ups						5.00
...: The Secret (6/98, $1.95) Girlfrenzy; Nauck-a						2.50

YOUNG JUSTICE: SINS OF YOUTH (Also see Sins of Youth x-over issues and Sins of Youth: Secret Files)
DC Comics: May, 2000 - No. 2, May, 2000 ($3.95, limited series)

	GD 2.0	VG 4.0	FN 6.0	VF 8.0	VF/NM 9.0	NM- 9.2
1,2-Young Justice, JLA & JSA swap ages; David-s/Nauck-a						4.00
TPB (2000, $19.95) r/#1,2 & all x-over issues)						20.00

YOUNG KING COLE (...Detective Tales)(Becomes Criminals on the Run)
Premium Group/Novelty Press: Fall, 1945 - V3#12, July, 1948

	GD 2.0	VG 4.0	FN 6.0	VF 8.0	VF/NM 9.0	NM- 9.2
V1#1-Toni Gayle begins	33	66	99	190	270	350
2	16	32	48	92	126	160
3-4	14	28	42	81	111	140
V2#1-7(8-9/46-7/47): 6,7-Certa-c	10	20	30	60	80	100
V3#1,3-6,8,9,12: 3-Certa-c. 5-McWilliams-c/a. 8,9-Harmon-c	10	20	30	58	77	95
2-L.B. Cole-a; Certa-c	17	34	51	98	134	170
7-L.B. Cole-c/a	23	46	69	132	186	240
10,11-L.B. Cole-c	20	40	60	112	156	200

YOUNG LAWYERS, THE (TV)
Dell Publishing Co.: Jan, 1971 - No. 2, Apr, 1971

	GD 2.0	VG 4.0	FN 6.0	VF 8.0	VF/NM 9.0	NM- 9.2
1	3	6	9	18	23	28
2	2	4	6	11	14	18

YOUNG LIFE (Teen Life #3 on)
New Age Publ./Quality Comics Group: Summer, 1945 - No. 2, Fall, 1945

	GD 2.0	VG 4.0	FN 6.0	VF 8.0	VF/NM 9.0	NM- 9.2
1-Skip Homeier, Louis Prima stories	15	30	45	86	118	150
2-Frank Sinatra photo on-c plus story	17	34	51	98	134	170

YOUNG LOVE (Sister title to Young Romance)
Prize(Feature)Publ.(Crestwood): 2-3/49 - No. 73, 12-1/56-57; V3#5, 2-3/60 - V7#1, 6-7/63

	GD 2.0	VG 4.0	FN 6.0	VF 8.0	VF/NM 9.0	NM- 9.2
V1#1-S&K-c/a(2)	44	88	132	264	395	525
2-Photo-c begin; S&K-a	25	50	75	147	202	260
3-S&K-a	19	38	57	107	149	190
4-5-Minor S&K-a	12	24	36	71	96	120
V2#1(#7)-S&K-a(2)	19	38	57	107	149	190
2-5(#8-11)-Minor S&K-a	10	20	30	60	80	100
6,8(#12,14)-S&K-c only. 14-S&K 1 pg. art	11	22	33	66	88	110
7,9-12(#13,15-18)-S&K-c/a	18	36	54	104	142	180
V3#1-4(#19-22)-S&K-c/a	16	32	48	92	126	160
5-7,9-12(#23-25,27-30)-Photo-c resume; S&K-a	14	28	42	81	111	140
8(#26)-No S&K-a	7	14	21	37	46	55
V4#1,6(#31,36)-S&K-a	14	28	42	79	107	135
2-5,7-12(#32-35,37-42)-Minor S&K-a	10	20	30	60	80	100
V5#1-12(#43-54), V6#1-9(#55-63)-Last precode; S&K-a in some	7	14	21	35	43	50
V6#10-12(#64-66)	4	8	12	27	36	45
V7#1-7(#67-73)	4	8	12	24	32	40
V3#5(2-3/60),6(4-5/60)(Formerly All For Love)	3	7	10	21	28	35
V4#1(6-7/60)-6(4-5/61)	3	6	9	19	25	32
V5#1(6-7/61)-6(4-5/62)	3	6	9	19	25	32
V6#1(6-7/62)-6(4-5/63), V7#1	3	6	9	18	24	30

NOTE: ***Meskin** a-14(2), 27, 42. **Powell** a-V4#6. **Severin/Elder** a-V1#3. S&K art not in #53, 57, 58, 61, 63-65. Photo-c most V3#5-V5#11.*

YOUNG LOVE
National Periodical Publ.(Arleigh Publ. Corp #49-61)/DC Comics:
#39, 9-10/63 - #120, Wint./75-76; #121, 10/76 - #126, 7/77

	GD 2.0	VG 4.0	FN 6.0	VF 8.0	VF/NM 9.0	NM- 9.2
39	5	10	15	36	48	60
40-50	4	8	12	24	32	40
51-68,70	3	7	10	21	28	35
69-(80 pg. Giant)(8-9/68)	6	12	18	40	55	70
71,72,74-77,80	3	6	9	18	24	30
73,78,79-Toth-a	3	6	9	19	25	32
81-99: 88-96-(52 pg. Giants)	3	6	9	18	23	28
100	3	6	9	18	24	30
101-106,115-120	2	4	6	14	18	22
107 (100 pgs.)	8	16	24	58	82	105
108-114 (100 pgs.)	7	14	21	51	71	90
121-126 (52 pgs.)	4	8	12	27	36	45

NOTE: ***Bolle** a-117. **Colan** a-107r. **Nasser** a-123, 124. **Orlando** a-122. **Simonson** c-125. **Toth** a-73, 78, 79, 122-125r. **Wood** a-109r(4 pgs.).*

YOUNG LOVER ROMANCES (Formerly & becomes Great Lover...)
Toby Press: No. 4, June, 1952 - No. 5, Aug, 1952

	GD 2.0	VG 4.0	FN 6.0	VF 8.0	VF/NM 9.0	NM- 9.2
4,5-Photo-c	8	16	24	40	50	60

Young Men #18 © MAR

Youthful Romances #8 © Pix-Parade

Y: The Last Man #1 © Vaughan & Guerra

GD VG FN VF VF/NM NM-
2.0 4.0 6.0 8.0 9.0 9.2

YOUNG LOVERS (My Secret Life #19 on)(Formerly Brenda Starr?)
Charlton Comics: No. 16, July, 1956 - No. 18, May, 1957

16,17('56): 16-Marcus Swayze-a 8 16 24 43 54 65
18-Elvis Presley picture-c, text story (biography)(Scarce)
60 120 180 375 563 750

YOUNG MARRIAGE
Fawcett Publications: June, 1950

1-Powell-a; photo-c 13 26 39 74 100 125

YOUNG MEN (Formerly Cowboy Romances)(...on the Battlefield #12-20(4/53); ...In Action #21)
Marvel/Atlas Comics (IPC): No. 4, 6/50 - No. 11, 10/51; No. 12, 12/51 - No. 28, 6/54

4-(52 pgs.) 20 40 60 112 156 200
5-11 13 26 39 74 100 125
12-23: 12-20-War format. 21-23-Hot Rod issues starring Flash Foster
12 24 36 71 96 120
24-(12/53)-Origin Captain America, Human Torch, & Sub-Mariner which are revived thru #28; Red Skull app. 284 568 852 1775 2663 3550
25-28: 25-Romita-c/a (see Men's Advs.) 109 218 327 681 1021 1360
25-2nd printing (1994) 2 4 6 8 10 12

NOTE: ***Berg** a-7, 14, 17, 18, 20; c-17? **Brodsky** c-4-9, 13, 14, 16, 17, 21-25. **Burgos** c-26-28. **Colan** a-14, 15. **Everett** a-18-20. **Heath** a-13, 14. **Maneely** c-10, 12, 15. **Pakula** a-14, 15. **Robinson** c-18. Captain America by **Romita**-#24?, 25, 26?, 27, 28. Human Torch by **Burgos**-#25, 27, 28. Sub-Mariner by **Everett**-#24-28.*

YOUNG REBELS, THE (TV)
Dell Publishing Co.: Jan, 1971

1-Photo-c 2 4 6 14 18 22

YOUNG ROMANCE COMICS (The 1st romance comic)
Prize/Headline (Feature Publ.) (Crestwood): Sept-Oct, 1947 - V16#4, June-July, 1963 (#1-33: 52 pgs.)

V1#1-S&K-c/a(2) 48 96 144 288 432 575
2-S&K-c/a(2-3) 32 64 96 182 259 335
3-6-S&K-c/a(2-3) each 28 56 84 159 225 290
V2#1-6(#7-12)-S&K-c/a(2-3) each 25 50 75 147 202 260
V3#1-3(#13-15): V3#1-Photo-c begin; S&K-a 17 34 51 98 134 170
4-12(#16-24)-Photo-c; S&K-a 17 34 51 98 134 170
V4#1-11(#25-35)-S&K-a 16 32 48 92 126 160
12(#36)-S&K, Toth-a 18 36 54 101 138 175
V5#1-12(#37-48), V6#4-12(#52-60)-S&K-a 16 32 48 92 126 160
V6#1-3(#49-51)-No S&K-a 8 16 24 46 58 70
V7#1-11(#61-71)-S&K-a in most 13 26 39 76 103 130
V7#12(#72), V8#1-3(#73-75)-Last precode (12-1/54-55)-No S&K-a
7 14 21 37 46 55
V8#4(#76, 4-5/55), 5(#77)-No S&K-a 6 12 18 31 38 45
V8#6-8(#78-80, 12-1/55-56)-S&K-a 10 20 30 60 80 100
V9#3,5,6(#81, 2-3/56, 83,84)-S&K-a 10 20 30 60 80 100
4, V10#1(#82,85)-All S&K-a 11 22 33 66 88 110
V10#2-6(#86-90, 10-11/57)-S&K-a 8 16 24 55 78 100
V11#1,2,5,6(#91,92,95,96)-S&K-a 8 16 24 55 78 100
3,4(#93,94), V12#2,4,5(#98,100,101)-No S&K 4 8 12 24 32 40
V12#1,3,6(#97,99,102)-S&K-a 8 16 24 55 78 100
V13#1(#103)-Powell-a; S&K's last-a for Crestwood 8 16 24 55 78 100
2,4-6(#104-108) 3 7 10 21 28 35
V13#3(#105, 4-5/60)-Elvis Presley-c app. only 5 10 15 36 48 60
V14#1-6, V15#1-6, V16#1-4(#109-124) 3 6 9 18 24 30

NOTE: ***Meskin** a-16, 24(2), 33, 47, 50. **Robinson/Meskin** a-6. **Leonard Starr** a-11. Photo c-13-32, 34-65. Issues 1-3 say "Designed for the More **Adult** Readers of **Comics**" on cover.*

YOUNG ROMANCE COMICS (Continued from Prize series)
National Periodical Publ.(Arleigh Publ. Corp. No. 127): No. 125, Aug-Sept, 1963 - No. 208, Nov-Dec, 1975

125 8 16 24 53 74 95
126-140 5 10 15 33 44 55
141-153,156-162,165-169 4 8 12 24 32 40
154-Neal Adams-c 5 10 15 36 48 60
155-1st publ. Aragonés-s (no art) 5 10 15 33 44 55
163,164-Toth-a 4 8 12 29 40 50
170-172 (68 pg. Giants): 170-Michell from Young Love ends; Lily Martin, the Swinger begins
5 10 15 33 44 55
173-183 (52 pgs.) 4 8 12 27 36 45
184-196 3 6 9 18 23 28
197-204-(100 pgs.) 7 14 21 51 71 90
205-208 3 6 9 16 20 25

YOUNG ZEN: CITY OF DEATH
Entity Comics: Late 1994 ($3.25, B&W)

1 3.25

YOUNG ZEN INTERGALACTIC NINJA (Also see Zen...)
Entity Comics: 1993 - No. 3, 1994 ($3.50/$2.95, B&W)

1-($3.50)-Polybagged w/Sam Kieth chromium trading card; gold foil logo 3.50
2,3-($2.95)-Gold foil logo 3.00

YOUR DREAMS (See Strange World of...)

YOU'RE UNDER ARREST (Manga)
Dark Horse Comics: Dec, 1995 - No. 8, July, 1996 ($2.95, limited series)

1-8 3.00

YOUR UNITED STATES
Lloyd Jacquet Studios: 1946

nn-Used in **SOTI**, pg. 309,310; Sid Greene-a 24 48 72 135 190 245

YOUTHFUL HEARTS (Daring Confessions #4 on)
Youthful Magazines: May, 1952 - No. 3, Sept, 1952

1- "Monkey on Her Back" swipes E.C. drug story/Shock SuspenStories #12; Frankie Laine photo on-c; Doug Wildey-a in al 30 60 90 170 240 310
2,3: 2-Vic Damone photo on-c. 3-Johnny Raye photo on-c
21 42 63 118 164 210

YOUTHFUL LOVE (Truthful Love #2)
Youthful Magazines: May, 1950

1 12 24 36 71 96 120

YOUTHFUL ROMANCES
Pix-Parade #1-14/Ribage #15 on: 8-9/49 - No. 5, 4/50; No. 6, 2/51; No. 7, 5/51 - #14, 10/52; #15, 1/53 - #18, 7/53; No. 5, 9/53 - No. 9, 8/54

1-(1st series)-Titled Youthful Love-Romances 27 54 81 155 218 280
2-Walter Johnson c-1-4 16 32 48 92 126 160
3-5 13 26 39 74 100 125
6,7,9-14(10/52, Pix-Parade; becomes Daring Love #15). 10(1/52)-Mel Torme photo-c/story. 12-Tony Bennett photo-c, 8pg. story & text bio.13-Richard Hayes (singer) photo-c/story; Bob & Ray photo/text story. 11 22 33 66 88 110
8-Frank Sinatra photo/text story; Wood-c/a 19 38 57 106 146 185
15-18 (Ribage)-All have photos on-c. 15-Spike Jones photo-c/story. 16-Tony Bavaar photo-c
10 20 30 60 80 100
5(9/53, Ribage)-Les Paul & Mary Ford photo-c/story; Charlton Heston photo/text story
10 20 30 56 73 90
6-9: 6-Bobby Wayne (singer) photo-c/story; Debbie Reynolds photo/text story. 7(2/54)-Tony Martin photo-c/story; Cyd Charise photo/text story. 8(5/54)-Gordon McCrae photo-c/story. (8/54)-Ralph Flanagan (band leader) photo-c/story; Audrey Hepburn photo/text story
9 18 27 49 62 75

Y: THE LAST MAN
DC Comics (Vertigo): Sept, 2002 - Present ($2.95)

1-Intro. Yorick Brown; Vaughan-s/Guerra-a/J.G. Jones-c
2 4 6 8 10 12
2 1 2 3 5 6 8
3-5 6.00
6-18: 16,17-Chadwick-a 3.00
... - Cycles TPB (2003, $12.95) r/#6-10; sketch pages by Guerra 13.00
... - Unmanned TPB (2002, $12.95) r/#1-5 13.00

Y2K: THE COMIC
New England Comics Press: Oct, 1999 ($3.95, one-shot)

1-Y2K scenarios and survival tips 4.00

YUPPIES FROM HELL (Also see Son of...)
Marvel Comics: 1989 ($2.95, B&W, one-shot, direct sales, 52 pgs.)

1-Satire 3.00

ZAGO, JUNGLE PRINCE (My Story #5 on)
Fox Features Syndicate: Sept, 1948 - No. 4, Mar, 1949

1-Blue Beetle app.; partial-r/Atomic #4 (Toni Luck) 60 120 180 375 563 750
2,3-Kamen-a 48 96 144 288 432 575
4-Baker-c 40 80 120 240 345 450

ZANE GREY'S STORIES OF THE WEST
Dell Publishing Co./Gold Key 11/64: No. 197, 9/48 - No. 996, 5-7/59; 11/64 (All painted-c)

Four Color 197(#1)(9/48) 13 26 39 90 133 175
Four Color 222,230,236('49) 8 16 24 55 78 100
Four Color 246,255,270,301,314,333,346 6 12 18 38 52 65
Four Color 357,372,395,412,433,449,467,484 5 10 15 33 44 55
Four Color 511-Kinstler-a; Kubert-a 6 12 18 38 52 65

Zatanna: Everyday Magic © DC

Zen Intergalactic Ninja #6 © S&C

Zip Comics #39 © MLJ

	GD 2.0	VG 4.0	FN 6.0	VF 8.0	VF/NM 9.0	NM- 9.2
Four Color 532,555,583,604,616,632(5/55)	5	10	15	33	44	55
27(9-11/55) - 39(9-11/58)	5	10	15	33	44	55
Four Color 996(5-7/59)	5	10	15	33	44	55
10131-411-(11/64-G.K.)-Nevada; r/4-Color #996	4	8	12	22	30	38

ZANY (Magazine)(Satire)(See Frantic & Ratfink)
Candor Publ. Co.: Sept, 1958 - No. 4, May, 1959

1-Bill Everett-c	10	20	30	56	73	90
2-4: 4-Everett-c	8	16	24	40	50	60

ZATANNA (See Adv. Comics #413, JLA #161, Supergirl #1, World's Finest Comics #274)
DC Comics: July, 1993 - No. 4, Oct, 1993 ($1.95, limited series)

1-4 2.25
...: Everyday Magic (2003, $5.95, one-shot) Dini-s/Mays-a/Bolland-c; Constantine app. 6.00
Special 1(1987, $2.00)-Gray Morrow-c/a 3.00

ZAZA, THE MYSTIC (Formerly Charlie Chan; This Magazine Is Haunted V2#12 on)
Charlton Comics: No. 10, Apr, 1956 - No. 11, Sept, 1956

10,11	12	24	36	71	96	120

ZEALOT (Also see WildC.A.T.S: Covert Action Teams)
Image Comics: Aug, 1995 - No. 3, Nov, 1995 ($2.50, limited series)

1-3 2.50

ZEGRA JUNGLE EMPRESS (Formerly Tegra)(My Love Life #6 on)
Fox Features Syndicate: No. 2, Oct, 1948 - No. 5, April, 1949

2	61	122	183	381	573	765
3-5	48	96	144	288	432	575

ZEN (Intergalactic Ninja)
Zen Comics Publishing: No. 0, Apr, 2003 - No. 4, Aug, 2003 ($2.95)

0-4-Bill Maus-a/Steve Stern-s. 0-Wraparound-c 3.00

ZEN INTERGALACTIC NINJA
No Publisher: 1987 -1993 ($1.75/$2.00, B&W)

1	2	4	6	11	14	18
2-6: Copyright-Stern & Cote	1	3	4	6	8	10

V2#1-4-($2.00) 3.00
V3#1-5-($2.95) 3.00
... :Christmas Special 1 (1992, $2.95) 3.00
... :Earth Day Special 1 (1993, $2.95) 3.00

ZEN, INTERGALACTIC NINJA (mini-series)
Zen Comics/Archie Comics: Sept, 1992 - No. 3, 1992 ($1.25)(Formerly a B&W comic by Zen Comics)

1-3: 1-Origin Zen; contains mini-poster 3.00

ZEN INTERGALACTIC NINJA
Entity Comics: No. 0, June-July, 1993 - No. 3, 1994 ($2.95, B&W, limited series)

0-Gold foil stamped-c; photo-c of Zen model 3.00
1-3: Gold foil stamped-c; Bill Maus-c/a 3.00
0-(1993, $3.50, color)-Chromium-c by Jae Lee 3.50
...Sourcebook 1-(1993, $3.50) 3.50
...Sourcebook '94-(1994, $3.50) 3.50

ZEN INTERGALACTIC NINJA: APRIL FOOL'S SPECIAL
Parody Press: 1994 ($2.50, B&W)

1-w/flip story of Renn Intergalactic Chihuahua 3.00

ZEN INTERGALACTIC NINJA COLOR
Entity Comics: 1994 - No. 7, 1995 ($2.25)

1-($3.95)-Chromium die cut-c 4.00
1, 0-($2.25)-Newsstand; Jae Lee-c; r/...All New Color Special #0 3.00
2-($2.50)-Flip book 3.00
2-($3.50)-Flip book, polybagged w/chromium trading card 3.50
3-7 3.00
Summer Special (1994, $2.95) 3.00
Yearbook: Hazardous Duty 1 (1995) 3.00
Zen-isms 1 (1995, 2.95) 3.00
Ashcan-Tour of the Universe-(no price) w/flip cover 3.00

ZEN INTERGALACTIC NINJA COMMEMORATIVE EDITION
Zen Comics Publishing: 1997 ($5.95, color)

1-Stern-s/Cote-a 6.00

ZEN INTERGALACTIC NINJA MILESTONE
Entity Comics: 1994 - No. 3, 1994 ($2.95, limited series)

1-3: Gold foil logo; r/Defend the Earth 3.00

ZEN INTERGALATIC NINJA SPRING SPECTACULAR
Entity Comics: 1994 ($2.95, B&W, one-shot)

1-Gold foil logo 3.00

ZEN INTERGALACTIC NINJA STARQUEST
Entity Comics: 1994 - No. 6, 1995 ($2.95, B&W)

1-6: Gold foil logo 3.00

ZEN, INTERGALACTIC NINJA: THE HUNTED
Entity Comics: 1993 - No. 3, 1994 ($2.95, B&W, limited series)

1-3: Newsstand Edition; foil logo 3.00
1-($3.50)-Polybagged w/chromium card by Kieth; foil logo 3.50

ZERO GIRL
DC Comics (Homage): Feb, 2001 - No. 5, Jun, 2001 ($2.95, limited series)

1-5-Sam Kieth-s/a 3.00
TPB (2001, $14.95) r/#1-5; intro. by Alan Moore 15.00

ZERO GIRL: FULL CIRCLE
DC Comics (Homage): Jan, 2003 - No. 5, May, 2003 ($2.95, limited series)

1-5-Sam Kieth-s/a 3.00
TPB (2003, $17.95) r/#1-5 18.00

ZERO HOUR: CRISIS IN TIME (Also see Showcase '94 #8-10)
DC Comics: No. 4(#1), Sept, 1994 - No. 0(#5), Oct, 1994 ($1.50, limited series)

4(#1)-0(#5) 4.00
"Ashcan"-(1994, free, B&W, 8 pgs.) several versions exist 2.25
TPB ('94, $9.95) 10.00

ZERO PATROL, THE
Continuity Comics: Nov, 1984 - No. 2 ($1.50); 1987 - No. 5, May, 1989 ($2.00)

1,2: Neal Adams-c/a; Megalith begins 4.00
1-5 (#1,2-reprints above, 1987) 3.00

ZERO TOLERANCE
First Comics: Oct, 1990 - No. 4, Jan, 1991 ($2.25, limited series)

1-4: Tim Vigil-c/a(p) (his 1st color limited series) 3.00

ZERO ZERO
Fantagraphics: Mar, 1995 -No. 27 ($3.95/$4.95, B&W, anthology, mature)

1-7,9-15,17-25 5.00
8,16 6.00
26-($4.95) Bagge-c 5.00

ZIGGY PIG-SILLY SEAL COMICS (See Animal Fun, Animated Movie-Tunes, Comic Capers, Krazy Komics, Silly Tunes & Super Rabbit)
Timely Comics (CmPL): Fall, 1944 - No. 6, Fall, 1946

1-Vs. the Japs	27	54	81	153	214	275
2	13	26	39	76	103	130
3-5	11	22	33	66	88	110
6-Infinity-c	14	28	42	81	111	140
I.W. Reprint #1(1958)-r/Krazy Komics	2	4	6	10	13	16
I.W. Reprint #2,7,8	2	4	6	10	13	16

ZIP COMICS
MLJ Magazines: Feb, 1940 - No. 47, Summer, 1944 (#1-7?: 68 pgs.)

1-Origin Kalathar the Giant Man, The Scarlet Avenger, & Steel Sterling; Mr. Satan (by Edd Ashe), Nevada Jones (masked hero) & Zambini, the Miracle Man, War Eagle, Captain Valor begins	497	994	1491	3479	5340	7200
2-Nevada Jones adds mask & horse Blaze	228	456	684	1425	2138	2850
3-Biro robot-c	176	352	528	1100	1650	2200
4,5-Biro WW2-c	148	296	444	925	1388	1850
6-8-Biro-c	128	256	384	800	1200	1600
9-Last Kalathar & Mr. Satan; classic-c	144	288	432	900	1350	1800
10-Inferno, the Flame Breather begins, ends #13	136	272	408	850	1275	1700
11,12: 11-Inferno without costume	100	200	300	625	938	1250
13-Electrocution-c	108	216	324	675	1013	1350
14,16,19	94	188	282	588	882	1175
15-Classic spider-c	116	232	348	725	1088	1450
17-Last Scarlet Avenger; women in bondage being cooked alive-c by Biro	108	216	324	675	1013	1350
18-Wilbur begins (9/41, 1st app.)	108	216	324	675	1013	1350
20-Origin & 1st app. Black Jack (11/41); Hitler-c	160	320	480	1000	1500	2000
21,23-26: 25-Last Nevada Jones. 26-Black Witch begins; last Captain Valor; "Remember Pearl Harbor!" cover caption	88	176	264	550	825	1100
22-Classic-c	124	248	372	775	1163	1550
27-Intro. Web (7/42) plus-c app.	144	288	432	900	1350	1800

Zoot #13 © FOX

Zorro #3 © Zorro Prods. Inc.

Zot! #12 © Scott McCloud

	GD 2.0	VG 4.0	FN 6.0	VF 8.0	VF/NM 9.0	NM- 9.2
28-Origin Web	124	248	372	775	1163	1550
29,30: 29-The Hyena app.	60	120	180	375	563	750
31,33-38: 34-1st Applejack app. 35-Last Zambini, Black Jack. 38-Last Web issue	48	96	144	288	432	575
32-Classic skeleton Nazi WW2-c	60	120	180	375	563	750
39-Red Rube begins (origin, 8/43)	48	96	144	288	432	575
40-46: 45-Wilbur ends	42	84	126	252	376	500
47-Last issue; scarce	45	90	135	270	403	535

NOTE: ***Biro** a-5, 9, 17; c-3-17. **Meskin** a-1-3, 5-7, 9, 10, 12, 13, 15, 16 at least. **Montana** c-29, 30, 32-35. **Novick** c-18-28, 31. **Sahle** c-37, 38, 40-46. Bondage c-8, 9, 33, 34. Cover features: Steel Sterling-1-43, 47; (w/Blackjack-20-27 & Web-27-35), 28-39; (w/Red Rube-40-43); Red Rube-44-47.*

ZIP-JET (Hero)
St. John Publishing Co.: Feb, 1953 - No. 2, Apr-May, 1953

	GD	VG	FN	VF	VF/NM	NM-
1-Rocketman-r from Punch Comics; #1-c from splash in Punch #10	74	148	222	463	694	925
2	50	100	150	300	450	600

ZIPPY THE CHIMP (CBS TV Presents...)
Pines (Literary Ent.): No. 50, March, 1957; No. 51, Aug, 1957

	GD	VG	FN	VF	VF/NM	NM-
50,51	8	16	24	40	50	60

ZODY, THE MOD ROB
Gold Key: July, 1970

	GD	VG	FN	VF	VF/NM	NM-
1	3	6	9	18	26	28

ZOMBIE WORLD (one-shots)
Dark Horse Comics

	NM-
... :Eat Your Heart Out (4/98, $2.95) Kelley Jones-c/s/a	3.00
... :Home For The Holidays (12/97, $2.95)	3.00

ZOMBIE WORLD: CHAMPION OF THE WORMS
Dark Horse Comics: Sept, 1997 - No. 3, Nov, 1997 ($2.95, limited series)

	NM-
1-3-Mignola & McEown-c/s/a	3.00

ZOMBIE WORLD: DEAD END
Dark Horse Comics: Jan, 1998 - No. 2, Feb, 1998 ($2.95, limited series)

	NM-
1,2-Stephen Blue-c/s/a	3.00

ZOMBIE WORLD: TREE OF DEATH
Dark Horse Comics: Jun, 1999 - No. 4, Oct, 1999 ($2.95, limited series)

	NM-
1-4-Mills-s/Deadstock-a	3.00

ZOMBIE WORLD: WINTER'S DREGS
Dark Horse Comics: May, 1998 - No. 4, Aug, 1998 ($2.95, limited series)

	NM-
1-4-Fingerman-s/Edwards-a	3.00

ZONE (Also see Dark Horse Presents)
Dark Horse Comics: 1990 ($1.95, B&W)

	NM-
1-Character from Dark Horse Presents	2.00

ZONE CONTINUUM, THE
Caliber Press: 1994 ($2.95, B&W)

	NM-
1	3.00

ZOO ANIMALS
Star Publications: No. 8, 1954 (15¢, 36 pgs.)

	GD	VG	FN	VF	VF/NM	NM-
8-(B&W for coloring)	6	12	18	31	38	45

ZOO FUNNIES (Tim McCoy #16 on)
Charlton Comics/Children Comics Publ.: Nov, 1945 - No. 15, 1947

	GD	VG	FN	VF	VF/NM	NM-
101(#1)(11/45, 1st Charlton comic book)-Funny animal; Al Fago-c	22	44	66	124	172	220
2(12/45, 52 pgs.) Classic-c	14	28	42	81	111	140
3-5	10	20	30	60	80	100
6-15: 8-Diana the Huntress app.	9	18	27	49	62	75

ZOO FUNNIES (Becomes Nyoka, The Jungle Girl #14 on?)
Capitol Stories/Charlton Comics: July, 1953 - No. 13, Sept, 1955; Dec, 1984

	GD	VG	FN	VF	VF/NM	NM-
1-1st app.? Timothy The Ghost; Fago-c/a	11	22	33	63	84	105
2	8	16	24	40	50	60
3-7	7	14	21	35	43	50
8-13-Nyoka app.	9	18	27	52	66	80
1(1984) (Low print run)						6.00

ZOONIVERSE
Eclipse Comics: 8/86 - No. 6, 6/87 ($1.25/$1.75, limited series, Mando paper)

	NM-
1-6	2.25

ZOO PARADE (TV)
Dell Publishing Co.: #662, 1955 (Marlin Perkins)

	GD	VG	FN	VF	VF/NM	NM-
Four Color 662	6	12	18	38	52	65

ZOOM COMICS
Carlton Publishing Co.: Dec, 1945 (one-shot)

	GD	VG	FN	VF	VF/NM	NM-
nn-Dr. Mercy, Satannas, from Red Band Comics; Capt. Milksop origin retold	40	80	120	240	345	450

ZOOT (Rulah Jungle Goddess #17 on)
Fox Features Syndicate: nd (1946) - No. 16, July, 1948 (Two #13s & 14s)

	GD	VG	FN	VF	VF/NM	NM-
nn-Funny animal only	21	42	63	118	164	210
2-The Jaguar app.	20	40	60	112	156	200
3(Fall, 1946) - 6-Funny animals & teen-age	11	22	33	63	84	105
7-(6/47)-Rulah, Jungle Goddess (origin/1st app.)	96	192	288	600	900	1200
8-10	66	132	198	413	619	825
11-Kamen bondage-c	70	140	210	438	657	875
12-Injury-to-eye panels, torture scene	48	96	144	288	432	575
13(2/48)	48	96	144	288	432	575
14(3/48)-Used in **SOTI**, pg. 104, "One picture showing a girl nailed by her wrists to trees with blood flowing from the wounds, might be taken straight from an ill. ed. of the Marquis deSade"	62	124	186	388	582	775
13(4/48),14(5/48)-Western True Crime #15 on?	48	96	144	288	432	575
15,16	48	96	144	288	432	575

ZORRO (Walt Disney with #882)(TV)(See Eclipse Graphic Album)
Dell Publishing Co.: May, 1949 - No. 15, Sept-Nov, 1961 (Photo-c 882 on)
(Zorro first appeared in a pulp story Aug 19, 1919)

	GD	VG	FN	VF	VF/NM	NM-
Four Color 228 (#1)	23	46	69	167	244	320
Four Color 425,617,732	13	26	39	90	133	175
Four Color 497,538,574-Kinstler-a	14	18	42	97	141	185
Four Color 882-Photo-c begin;1st TV Disney; Toth-a	17	34	51	123	182	240
Four Color 920,933,960,976-Toth-a in all	13	26	39	90	133	175
Four Color 1003('59)-Toth-a	13	26	39	90	133	175
Four Color 1037-Annette Funicello photo-c	16	32	48	113	167	220
8(12-2/59-60)	9	18	27	63	89	115
9-Toth-a	10	20	30	67	96	125
10,11,13-15-Last photo-c	8	16	24	58	82	105
12-Toth-a; last 10¢ issue	10	20	30	67	96	125

NOTE: ***Warren Tufts** a-4-Color 1037, 8, 9, 10, 13.*

ZORRO (Walt Disney)(TV)
Gold Key: Jan, 1966 - No. 9, Mar, 1968 (All photo-c)

	GD	VG	FN	VF	VF/NM	NM-
1-Toth-a	9	18	27	60	85	110
2,4,5,7-9-Toth-a. 5-r/F.C. #1003 by Toth	5	10	15	36	48	60
3,6-Tufts-a	5	10	15	33	44	55

NOTE: *#1-9 are reprinted from Dell issues. **Tufts** a-3, 4. #1-r/F.C. #882. #2-r/F.C. #960. #3-r/#12-c & #8 inside. #4-r/#9-c & insides. #6-r/#11(all); #7-r/#14-c. #8-r/F.C. #933 inside & back-c & #976-c. #9-r/F.C. #920.*

ZORRO (TV)
Marvel Comics: Dec, 1990 - No. 12, Nov, 1991 ($1.00)

	NM-
1-12: Based on TV show. 12-Toth-c	3.00

ZORRO (Also see Mask of Zorro)
Topps Comics: Nov, 1993 - No. 11, Nov, 1994 ($2.50/$2.95)

	GD	VG	FN	VF	VF/NM	NM-
0-(11/93, $1.00, 20 pgs.)-Painted-c; collector's ed.						2.25
1,4,6-9,11: 1-Miller-c. 4-Mike Grell-c. 6-Mignola-c. 7-Lady Rawhide-c by Gulacy. 8-Perez-c. 10-Julie Bell-c. 11-Lady Rawhide-c						3.00
2-Lady Rawhide-app. (not in costume)						5.00
3-1st app. Lady Rawhide in costume, 3-Lady Rawhide-c by Adam Hughes	1	2	3	5	6	8
5-Lady Rawhide app.						4.00
10-($2.95)-Lady Rawhide-c/app.						3.00
The Lady Wears Red (12/98, $12.95, TPB) r/#1-3						13.00
Zorro's Renegades (2/99, $14.95, TPB) r/#4-8						15.00

ZOT!
Eclipse Comics: 4/84 - No. 10, 7/85; No. 11, 1/87 - No. 36 7/91 ($1.50, Baxter-p)

	NM-
1	5.00
2,3	4.00
4-10: 4-Origin. 10-Last color issue	3.00
10 1/2 (6/86, 25¢, Not Available Comics) Ashcan; art by Feazell & Scott McCloud	4.00
11-14,15-35-($2.00-c) B&W issues	3.00
14 1/2 (Adventures of Zot! in Dimension 10 1/2)(7/87) Antisocialman app.	3.00
36-($2.95-c) B&W	4.00

Z-2 COMICS (Secret Agent...)(See Holyoke One-Shot #7)

ZULU (See Movie Classics)

The
NO. 5
NO. 6
OVERSTREET'S COMPLETELY UPDATED & REVISED EDITION
$7.50
THE COMIC BOOK
PRICE GUIDE
$9.95
COMIC BOOK
PRICE
$9.95
I'M SITTING ON TOP OF THE WORLD! EVERYBODY'S CALLING TO CONGRATULATE ME FOR BEING ON THE COVER OF THE PRICE GUIDE!
KATY KEENE
THE STARS CALLING KATY
The CONFIDENT COLLECTOR
THE OVERSTREET COMIC BOOK PRICE GUIDE
ROBERT M. OVERSTREET
22nd Edition
PRICE GUIDE
Price Guide
#33
ROBERT M. OVERSTREET
THE OVERSTREET
Comic Book
PRICE GUIDE
THE No. 1 GUIDE
Robert M. Overstreet

AMERICAN COMIC BOOK CO.

CATALOGUES AVAILABLE

(PRICE OF CATALOGUES REFUNDED WITH ANY ORDER)

1. UNDERGROUND COMIX, NEWSPAPERS, ETC. ––– $1.00
2. ORIGINAL ART, POSTERS, PORTFOLIOS, BLB'S –– $1.00
3. D.C. GOLD AND SILVER AGE, CLASSICS ILLUS. ––– $1.00
4. GOLDEN AGE: QUAL., FAW., MLJ, TIMLEY FOX, REPRINT, GLEASON, FIC. HOUSE, ETC. ––– $1.00
5. 1950'S = ART COMICS, E.C., HOR. ATLAS, WEST, WAR, CRIME, ROMANCE, ETC. –––– $1.00
6. PULPS ––– $2.00
7. DISNEY AND DELL FUNNY ––– $1.00
8. DELL T.V., MOVIE, WESTERN ––– $1.00

9. GIRLEY MAGS. (PLAYBOY, ETC., ETC., ETC.) ––– $2.00
10. MAGS. (LIFE, SPTS. ILLUS., HUMOR, MOVIE, MAD, CRIME, FAM. MON., ETC.) — 1000'S OF ITEMS ––– $2.00

11. PB'S AND DIGESTS ––– $1.00
12. MARVEL, MISC, 1960-1990 COMICS ––– $1.00
13. 50'S HUMOR COMICS, ARCHIES ––– $1.00
14. WANT LISTS: SEND $1.00 & YOUR LIST NOW!

MAKE CHECKS OUT TO = TERRY STROUD
SEND TO = P.O. BOX 23
SANTA MONICA, CA 90406
PHONE = (310) 399 4352

Let me make you the purrrrfect deal!
REEL ART
MIDWEST'S PREMIER BUYER
Some people just buy comics, others only movie memorabilia. At Reel Art, I love the whole world of Popular Culture: cult movies, classic tv shows, vintage comic books. I specialize in buying all of your comics, toys and movie memorabilia cutting you a fair price right away, without making any empty promises.
I purchase everything from one book to an entire warehouse and I am always on the prowl to buy more.
QUICK PAYMENT • PROFESSIONAL SERVICE • FAIR DEAL
CORY GLABERSON, PRESIDENT • 707 S. HARVEY
OAK PARK, IL • 60304 • TOLL-FREE 1-800-878-9378
CGLABERSON@AOL.COM • WWW.REELARTPOSTERS.COM
LOOK FOR OUR AUCTIONS ON E-BAY.
E-Bay User name: Cglaberson@aol.com
Catwoman Copyright © DC Comics, Inc. Artwork by David Voight.

BEDROCK CITY
COMIC COMPANY
TM
Sterling silver
THUNDER AGENTS
GUEST STAR APPEARANCE!
UNDERSEA AGENT
JUSTICE LEAGUE of AMERICA
12¢
THAT GLOWING METEOR—TURNING US ALL INTO TREES!
REVEALED AT LAST... "THE ORIGIN OF THE JUSTICE LEAGUE"
the AMAZING SPIDER-MAN
MARVEL COMICS GROUP
12¢
39 AUG
SPIDEY and the GREEN GOBLIN... BOTH UNMASKED!
You'll find the *best* and *brightest* Silver on-line at *www.bedrockcity.com*
Check out our Silver-*ware house* at:
6517 Westheimer (at Hillcroft)
Houston, Texas 77057
Phone (713) 780-0675 Fax (713) 780-2366
And our other *dazzling* stores:
2204-B FM 1960 W.
Houston, Texas 77090
Phone (281) 444-9763
106 W. Bay Area Blvd.
Webster, Texas 77598
Phone (281) 557-2748

COMIC SHOP LOCATOR SERVICE
COMICS
888-COMIC-BOOK
888-266-4226

WANTED

VINTAGE MOVIE POSTERS & LOBBY CARDS

FROM 1900 TO 1976

IF YOU HAVE QUALITY POSTERS FOR SALE, WE WOULD LIKE TO PURCHASE THEM FOR CASH! NO TRADE OFFERS. NO CONSIGNMENTS. JUST CASH.

STEPHEN FISHLER

873 Broadway, Suite 201, New York, NY 10003
Toll-Free (800) 229-6387 or call (212) 260-4147 • Fax (212) 260-4304
stephen@metropoliscomics.com • www.metropoliscomics.com

WANTED

COMIC BOOK

ART

COMIC STRIP ART

BEFORE YOU SELL YOUR ART, CALL ME. I CAN AND WILL PAY YOU MORE.

STEPHEN FISHLER

873 Broadway, Suite 201, New York, NY 10003
Toll-Free (800) 229-6387 or call (212) 260-4147 • Fax (212) 260-4304
stephen@metropoliscomics.com • www.metropoliscomics.com

Visit our on-line catalogue at:

www.socalcomics.com

Visit our store at:
8280 Clairemont Mesa Bl. #124
San Diego, CA 92111

858-715-8669
socalcom@aol.com

Buying and selling Golden Age to Modern comic books for plenty of years!!

COMICS - DC • MARVEL • 3-D
GOLD KEY • TOWER • ATLAS
CLASSICS ILLUS. • DELL
MAGAZINES • CREEPY • MAD
EERIE • VAMPIRELLA • PSYCHO
NIGHTMARE • PULPS • COF
MONSTER TIMES / WORLD
FAMOUS MONSTERS
FANZINES • ARKHAM HOUSE

PAUL GLAVAS
7307 WALNUT
KANSAS CITY, MO
64114-1444

E-Mail: paulglavas@yahoo.com
28 page list - $1.00
Tel. 816-523-1077

CLASSIC COMICS
AND
CLASSICS
ILLUSTRATED

Classic Comics/Illustrated and all related items
Send for FREE CATALOG

Philip Gaudino
49 Park Ave.
Port Washington, NY 11050

BUYING OR SELLING
Call (516) 883-5659
http://www.philsclassics.com

Batman and Wonder Woman Collectors

We buy pre 1975 Batman comics and memorabilia and Wonder Woman comics and memorabilia from all eras.
P.O. Box 604925
Flushing, NY 11360-4925
e-mail: batt90@aol.com
wwali@aol.com

Business Card Ads

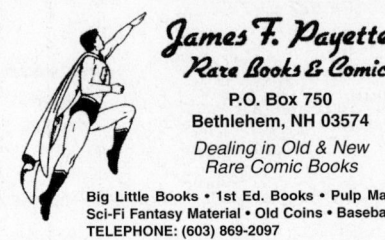

THE OVERSTREET COMIC BOOK PRICE GUIDE BUSINESS CARD ADS are a great way to advertise in the Guide! Simply send us your business card and we'll reduce it and run it as is. Have your ad seen by thousands of serious comic book collectors for an entire year! If you are a comic book or collectible dealer, retail establishment, mail-order house, etc., you can reach potential customers throughout the United States and around the world in our **BUSINESS CARDS ADS**!

For more information, contact our Advertising Dept.

Gemstone Publishing, Inc. 1966 Greenspring Drive, Suite 400, Timonium, MD 21093.

Call (888) 375-9800 Ext. 410, or fax (410) 252-4582, or e-mail **ads@gemstonepub.com**.

P.O. Box 2232
Orange, CA

James F. Payette
Rare Books & Comics
P.O. Box 750
Bethlehem, NH 03574
Dealing in Old & New
Rare Comic Books
Big Little Books • 1st Ed. Books • Pulp Magazines
Sci-Fi Fantasy Material • Old Coins • Baseball Cards
TELEPHONE: (603) 869-2097

TREASURE ISLAND COMICS
COMICS, CARDS, TOYS AND SUCH!
NEW BOOKS EVERY WEDNESDAY!
OPEN 7 DAYS A WEEK!
40819 FREMONT BLVD.
FREMONT, CA 94538
SUBSCRIPTION SERVICE AVAILABLE
WWW.TREASUREISLANDCOMICS.COM
510.770.1168

(334) 300-1106
Brent Moeshlin
Owner
QUALITY COMIX
"Specializing in High Grade Silver/Bronze"
http://www.qualitycomix.com
bmoeshlin@qualitycomix.com
7956 Vaughn Road #374
Montgomery, AL 36116

Your Virtual Comic Shop
New & Back Issues   Anime & Manga
Statues / Busts   Toys / Action Figures
Forums   AND MUCH MORE
Subscriptions & Preorders Discounted
Let Us Find What You're Looking For

GOLDEN AGE COMICS AND GAMES
PATRICK MARCHBANKS
Phone: 228.860.0256
Fax: 228.896.5472
Email: GoldenAgeCBC@aol.com
www.GoldenAgeCollectibles.com

Business Card Ads

Classified Ads

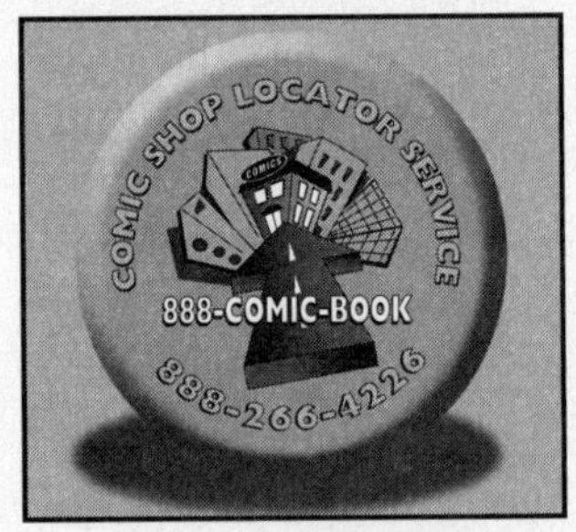

We Want Your Help!
The Overstreet Comic Book Price Guide, Overstreet's Comic Price Review, and Hake's Price Guide To Character Toys need your contributions! If you see something we've missed in The Overstreet Comic Book Price Guide, if you have comic character collectibles not included in Hake's Price Guide To Character Toys, or if you've seen something we should cover in Overstreet's Comic Price Review, we want to know about it!

Hake's Price Guide To Character Toys:
feedback@gemstonepub.com

The Overstreet Comic Book Price Guide:
feedback@gemstonepub.com

Overstreet's Comic Price Review:
gtom@gemstonepub.com

Shop Directory

(PAID ADVERTISING - STORE LISTINGS)

You can have your store listed here for very reasonable rates. Send for details for next year's Guide. The following list of stores have paid to be included in this list. We cannot assume any responsibility in your dealings with these shops. This list is provided for your information only. When planning trips, it would be advisable to make appointments in advance. Remember, to get your shop included in the next edition, contact us for rates.

Gemstone Publishing, Inc., 1966 Greenspring Dr., Suite 400, Timonium, MD 21093.
PHONE: 888-375-9800 or 410-560-5806
FAX: 410-252-4582
E-MAIL: ads@gemstonepub.com

Items stocked by these shops are noted at the end of each listing and are coded as follows:

(a) Golden Age Comics
(b) Silver Age Comics
(c) Bronze Age Comics
(d) New Comics & Magazines
(e) Back issue magazines
(f) Comic Supplies
(g) Collectible Card Games
(h) Role Playing Games
(i) Gaming Supplies
(j) Manga
(k) Anime
(l) Underground Comics
(m) Original Comic Art
(n) Pulps
(o) Big Little Books
(p) Books - Used
(q) Books - New
(r) Comic Related Posters
(s) Movie Posters
(t) Trading Cards
(u) Statues/Mini-busts, etc.
(v) Premiums (Rings, Decoders, etc.)
(w) Action Figures
(x) Other Toys
(y) Records/CDs
(z) VHS/DVD
(1) Doctor Who Items
(2) Simpsons Items
(3) Star Trek Items
(4) Star Wars Items
(5) HeroClix

ALABAMA

Sincere Comics
4667 Airport Blvd.
Mobile, AL 36608
PH: (888) 533-6008
PH: (251) 342-2603
FAX: (251) 342-2659
E-Mail: sincerecmx@aol.com
(a-l,o,r,u,w,5)

ARIZONA

Key Comics:
Discount Back-Issues
P.O. Box 5035
Mesa, AZ 85211
PH: (480) 890-0055
E-Mail: keycomics
@hotmail.com
(a,b,c,d,e,m)

All About Books & Comics
5060 N. Central
Phoenix, AZ 85012
PH: (602) 277-0757
Web: www.allaboutcomics.com
(a-l,o,q,r-u,w,x,2,3,4,5)

CALIFORNIA

www.bunkybrothers.com
Buying all comic books
Gold Silver Bronze
11590 Bari Drive
Alta Loma, CA 91701
PH: (909) 941-6402
Web: www.bunkybrothers.com
(a,b,c,e,l,m,n,p,s,t,w,x)

Terry's Comics
Buying All 10¢ & 12¢
original priced comics
P.O. Box 746
Atwood, CA 92811-0746
PH: (714) 288-8993 or
Hotline: (800) 938-0325
FAX: (714) 288-8992
E-Mail: info@terryscomics.com
Web: www.terryscomics.com
(a,b,d-h,m,n,q)

HouseOfComics.com
The Bay Area s Back Issue
Specialist --1936-present
(Website and By Appointment Only)
1678 Shattuck Avenue, #23
Berkeley, CA 94709
PH: (510) 849-2094
E-Mail:
info@houseofcomics.com
Web: www.houseofcomics.com
(a-c,m)

Crush Comics
2869 Castro Valley Blvd.
Castro Valley, CA 94546
PH: (510) 581-4779
(a-d,g,h,j-w)

Collectors Ink
2593 Highway 32
Chico, CA 95973
PH: (530) 345-0958
E-Mail: bev@collectorsink.com
Web: www.collectorsink.com
(a-g,i-l,o-r,t,u,w,z,1-5)

High Quality Comics
1106 2nd St., #110
Fallbrook, CA 92024
PH: (800) 682-3936
FAX: (760) 723-7269
E-Mail: customerservice
@highqualitycomics.com
Web:
www.highqualitycomics.com
(a-e,g,j-m,p-u,w,x,2,3,4)

Treasure Island Comics
40819 Fremont Blvd.
Fremont, CA 94538
PH: (510) 770-1168
FAX: (510) 770-1168
E-Mail:
a@treasureislandcomics.com
Web:
www.treasureislandcomics.com
(b-g,j,k,r,t,u,w,x,2,4,5)

Geoffrey's Comics
15900 Crenshaw Blvd.; Ste. B
Gardena, CA 90249
PH: (310) 538-3198
(a-g,i-n,r,t,u,w,z,5)

Back Issue Comics
695 E. Lewelling
Hayward, CA 94541
PH: (510) 276-5262
(a,b,c,e,t,x,z)

Amazing Comics & Cards
5555 Stearns St., Suite 103
Long Beach, CA 90815
PH: (562) 493-4427
Web:
www.amazingcomics.com
(b-g,i-k,q,r,t,u,w-z,1-5)

Golden Apple (Megastore)
7711 Melrose Ave.
Los Angeles, CA 90046
PH: (323) 658-6047
Web:
www.goldenapplecomics.com
(a-g,j-l,r,u,w,x,z,1-5)

Lee's Comics
1020-F N. Rengstorff Ave.
Mountain View, CA 94043
PH: (650) 965-1800
E-Mail: Lee@LCOMICS.com
Web: www.LCOMICS.com
(a-r,t-x,z,1-5)

Golden Apple
(San Fernando Valley)
8967 Reseda Blvd.
Northridge, CA 91324
PH: (818) 993-7804
(a-d,f,g,j,k,l,r,u,w,x,2,4,5)

A-1 Comics
5800 Madison Ave.
Sacramento, CA 95841
PH: (916) 331-9203
(a-z,1-5)

San Diego Comics
6937 El Cajon Blvd.
San Diego, CA 92115
PH: (619) 698-1177
Web:
www.san-diego-comics.com
(a,b,c,d,e,f,5)

Lee's Comics
2222 S. El Camino Real
San Mateo, CA 94403
PH: (650) 571-1489
(a-r,t-x,z,1-5)

Colossus Comics
Santa Clara, CA 95050
PH: (408) 802-8424
FAX: (408) 260-9108
E-Mail:
steve@colossuscomics.com
Web:
www.colossuscomics.com
ebay ID: smortensen
(a-d)

Golden Apple (Rhino)
2028 Westwood Blvd.
West Los Angeles, CA 90025
PH: (310) 474-8685 x110
(d,f,g,j,k,l,r,u,w,x,y,z,2-5)

COLORADO

Bargain Comics
21 E. Bijou St.
Colorado Springs, CO 80903
PH: (719) 578-8847
E-Mail: bargaincom@aol.com
(a-g,i,j,l,o)

RTS Unlimited Inc.
P. O. Box 150412
Lakewood, CO 80215-0412
PH: (303) 403-1840
E-Mail:
rtsunlimited@earthlink.net
(a,b,c,d,f)

CONNECTICUT

Sarge's Comics, Etc.
124 State Street
New London, CT 06320
PH: (860) 443-2004
Web: www.sargescomics.com
(a-l,p-u,w-z,1-5)

Legends of Superheros
1269 West Main St.
Waterbury, CT 06708
PH: (203) 756-2440
FAX: (203) 757-1909
E-Mail: legends@legendsofsuperheros.com
Web: www.legendsofsuperheros.com
(a-g,q,r,u,w,y,z,5)

DELAWARE

The Comic Book Shop
1711 Marsh Rd.
Wilmington, DE 19810
PH: (302) 477-1119
E-Mail: comicshop@thecomicbookshop.com
Web: www.thecomicbookshop.com
(a-g,j,l,r,u,w,x,2,4,5)

FLORIDA

The Comics Club, Inc.
723 W. Lumsden Road
Brandon, FL 33511
PH: (813) 653-4111
E-Mail: mail@comicsclub.com
Web: www.comicsclub.com
(a-j,r,s,t,u,w,3,4,5)

Emerald City Comics & Collectables, Inc.
2475-L McMullen Booth Rd.
Clearwater, FL 33759
PH: (727) 797-0664
www.EmeraldCityComics.com
(a-j,r,t-x,z,2-5)

Emerald City Comics & Collectables, Inc.
9249 Seminole Blvd.
Seminole, FL 33772
PH: (727) 398-2665
E-Mail: CowardlyLion@EmeraldCityComics.com
Web: www.EmeraldCityComics.com
(a-k,q,r,t-x,z,1-5)

Demolition Comics.com
4049 S. Dale Mabry Hwy
Tampa, FL 33611
PH: (813) 832-2692
FAX: (813) 681-9071
E-Mail: demolitioncomics @aol.com
Web: www.demolitioncomics.com
(a-m,q-u,w,x,y(records),z,2-5)

GEORGIA

Comic Company
1058 Mistletoe Rd.
Decatur, GA 30033-4312
PH: (404) 248-9846
E-Mail:mail@comiccompany.com
Web: www.comiccompany.com
(a-k,r,u,w,x,z,2,4,5)

Heroes Ink
2500 Cobb Parkway, NW,
Suite A3
Kennesaw, GA 30152
PH: (770) 428-3033
(a-g,j,p,q,r,t,w,x,z,2,3,4,5)

Odin's
360 Killian Hill Rd., Suite G-5
Lilburn, GA 30047
PH: (770) 923-0123
(a-j,r,t,u-x,2,5)

Planetary Comics
101 Crossings East, Suite 8
Peachtree City, GA 30269
PH: (770) 632-9799
(a-o,q-x,z,1-5)

ILLINOIS

Graham Crackers Comics
120 N. Bolingbrook Dr.
Bolingbrook, IL 60440
PH: (630) 739-6810
Web: www.grahamcrackers.com
(b-g,i,j,t,u,w,x,2-5)

Graham Crackers Comics
69 E. Madison St.
Chicago, IL 60603
PH: (312) 629-1810
Web: www.grahamcrackers.com
(b-g,i,j,t,u,w,x,2-5)

Graham Crackers Comics
2652 N. Clark St.
Chicago, IL 60614
PH: (773) 665-2010
Web: www.grahamcrackers.com
(a-g,i,j,t,u,w,x,2-5)

Yesterday
1143 West Addison St.
Chicago, IL 60613
PH: (773) 248-8087
(a,b,d,e,f,g,h,i,k,l,m,r,s,t)

Graham Crackers Comics
901C Lucinda Ave.
Dekalb, IL 60115
PH: (815) 748-3883
Web: www.grahamcrackers.com
(b-g,i,j,t,u,w,x,2-5)

Graham Crackers Comics
5223 S. Main St.
Downers Grove, IL 60515
PH: (630) 852-1810
Web: www.grahamcrackers.com
(b-g,i,j,t,u,w,x,2-5)

GEM Comics
125 W. First St.
Elmhurst, IL 60126
PH: (630) 833-8787
(b-j,r,t,u,w,5)

Graham Crackers Comics
1271 Rickert Dr.
Naperville, IL 60540
PH: (630) 355-4310
Web: www.grahamcrackers.com
(a-g,i,j,t,u,w,x,2-5)

Tomorrow is Yesterday, Inc.
5600 N. 2nd St.
Rockford, IL 61111
PH: (815) 633-0330
E-Mail: info@tomorrowisyesterday.com
(a-r,t,u,w-z,1-5)

Graham Crackers Comics
610 S. Randall Rd.
St. Charles, IL 60174
PH: (630) 584-0610
Web: www.grahamcrackers.com
(b-g,i,j,t,u,w,x,2-5)

Unicorn Comics & Cards
216 S. Villa Ave.
Villa Park, IL 60181
PH: (630) 279-5777
(a-g,n-z,1-5)

Graham Crackers Comics
1207 E. Butterfield Rd.
Wheaton, IL 60187
PH: (630) 668-1350
Web: www.grahamcrackers.com
(b-g,i,j,t,u,w,x,2-5)

INDIANA

Comic Quest
2260 Morgan Ave.
Evansville, IN 47711
PH: (812) 474-1133
E-Mail: sales@comicquest.com
Web: www.comicquest.com
(a-k,q,r,t,u,w,x,z,2-5)

Comic Carnival
7225 N. Keystone Avenue
Indianapolis, IN 46240
PH: (317) 253-8882
(a-h,j,l,m,n,p,r-u,w,x,z,2-5)

Comic Carnival East
9729 E. Washington St.
Indianapolis, IN 46229
PH: (317) 898-5010
(a-l,r,t-z,2-5)

Comic Carnival Southpost Center
7311 US 31 South
Indianapolis, IN 46219
PH: (317) 889-8899
(a-d,f-k,r,t-x,2,5)

Comic Carnival West
3837 N. High School Rd. #7
Indianapolis, IN 46254
PH: (317) 293-4386
(a-z,1-5)

KANSAS

Pop Culture Comix
9337 W. 87th Street
Overland Park, KS 66212
PH: (913) 341-0040
Web: www.PopCultureComix.com
(d,f,g,j,r,u,w)

Prairie Dog Comics
7130 West Maple, Suite 150
Wichita, KS 67209
PH: (316) 942-3456
FAX: (316) 942-0702
(a-z,1-5)

KENTUCKY

Comic Book World, Inc.
7130 Turfway Rd.
Florence, KY 41042
PH: (859) 371-9562
FAX: (859) 371-6925
E-Mail: cbwinfo@one.net
Web:www.comicbookworld.com
(a-l,n,r,t,u,w,z,2,5)

Comic Book World, Inc.
6905 Shepherdsville Rd.
Louisville, KY 40219
PH: (502) 964-5500
FAX: (502) 964-5500
E-Mail: cbwinfo@one.net
Web:www.comicbookworld.com
(a-l,n,r,t,u,w,z,2,5)

LOUISIANA

B.T. & S.J. Giles
P. O. Box 271
Keithville, LA 71047
PH: (318) 925-6654
(a,b,n,o,p)

MAINE

Top Shelf Comics
25 Central St.
Bangor, ME 04401
PH: (207) 947-4939
E-Mail: topshelf@tcomics.com
Web: www.tcomics.com
(a-j,q,t,u)

MARYLAND

Geppi's Comic World
1116 N. Rolling Road
Baltimore, MD 21228
PH: (410) 788-0900
FAX: (410) 455-9806
E-Mail: gdoug@diamondcomics.com
(c,d,f,g,i,j,k,t,u,w,x,z,1-5)

Alternate Worlds
72 Cranbrook Road
Cockeysville, MD 21030
PH: (410) 666-3290
(b-k,r,t,u,x,1-5)

Comics To Astonish Inc.
9400 Snowden River Pkwy.
Columbia, MD 21045
PH: (410) 381-2732
E-Mail: comics2u@aol.com
Web: www.comicstoastonish.com
(a-k,m,r,t,u,w,z,2,3,5)

Cards, Comics & Collectibles
100-A Chartley Drive
Reisterstown, MD 21136
PH: (410) 526-7410
FAX: (410) 526-4006
E-Mail: cardscomicscollectibles@yahoo.com
(a-j,r,t-x,2-5)

MASSACHUSETTS

New England Comics
131 Harvard Avenue
Allston, MA 02134
PH: (617) 783-1848
www.newenglandcomics.com
(a-d,f-k,r,t,u,w,x,z,2-5)

New England Comics
744 Crescent St.
East Crossing Plaza
Brockton, MA 02402
PH: (508) 559-5068
www.newenglandcomics.com
(a-d,f-k,r,t,u,w,x,z,2-5)

New England Comics
316 Harvard St.
Coolidge Corner
Brookline, MA 02446
PH: (617) 566-0115
www.newenglandcomics.com
(a-d,f-k,r,t,u,w,x,z,2-5)

New England Comics
14A Eliot Street
Harvard Square
Cambridge, MA 02138
PH: (617) 354-5352
www.newenglandcomics.com
(a-d,f-k,r,t,u,w,x,z,2-5)

That's Entertainment II
371 John Fitch Hwy.
Fitchburg, MA 01420
PH: (978) 342-8607
(a-z,1-5)

New England Comics
95 Pleasant St.
Malden Center
Malden, MA 02148
PH: (781) 322-2404
www.newenglandcomics.com
(a-d,f-k,r,t,u,w,x,z,2-5)

New England Comics
732 Washington Street
Norwood Center
Norwood, MA 02062
PH: (781) 769-4552
www.newenglandcomics.com
(a-d,f-k,r,t,u,w,x,z,2-5)

New England Comics
1511 Hancock St.
Quincy Center
Quincy, MA 02169
PH: (617) 770-1848
www.newenglandcomics.com
(a-d,f-k,r,t,u,w,x,z,2-5)

The Outer Limits
463 Moody St.
Waltham, MA 02453
PH: (781) 891-0444
(a-z,1-5)

That's Entertainment
244 Park Ave. (Rte. 9)
Worcester, MA 01609
PH: (508) 755-4207
Web: www.thatse.com
(a-z,1-5)

MICHIGAN

Tardy's Collector's Corner, Inc.
2009 Eastern Ave. S.E.
Grand Rapids, MI 49507
PH: (616) 247-7828
(a-f,l,n,r,u,w)

Harley Yee Rare Comics
P.O. Box 51758
Livonia, MI 48151
PH: (734) 421-7921
FAX: (734) 421-7928
E-Mail: harleycomx@aol.com
Web:www.harleyyeecomics.com
(a,b,c,i,m,n,o)

MINNESOTA

Nostalgia Zone, Inc.
3151 Hennepin Ave. South
Minneapolis, MN 55408
PH: (612) 822-2806
FAX: (612) 822-2805
Web: www.nostalgiazone.com
(a-c,e,f,j,l-o,t)

Zen Comics
742 North Snelling Ave.
St Paul, MN 55104
PH: (651) 641-0331
E-Mail: zencomics@visi.com
Web: www.zencomics.com
(a,b,c,f)

NEBRASKA

Robert Beerbohm Comic Art
P.O. Box 507
Fremont, NE 68026-0507
PH: (402) 727-4071
E-Mail:
beerbohm@teknetwork.com
(a,b,c,e,l,m,n,o,r,s,t,v,1,2,3,4)

NEVADA

Silver Cactus Comics I
480 N. Nellis Blvd. #C1A
Las Vegas, NV 89110
PH: (702) 438-4408
FAX: (702) 438-5208
(a-k,m,r-z,2-5)

Silver Cactus Comics II
4410 N. Rancho Dr.
Las Vegas, NV 89130
PH: (702) 396-8840
Web:
www.silvercactuscomics.com
(a-k,m,r-z,2-5)

NEW HAMPSHIRE

Rare Books & Comics
James F. Payette
P.O. Box 750
Bethlehem, NH 03574
PH: (603) 869-2097
FAX: (603) 869-3475
E-Mail: JimPayette@msn.com
(a-c,e,n,o)

NEW JERSEY

ZAPP! Comics
3710 Rt. 9 South
Freehold Raceway Mall
Freehold, NJ 07728
PH: (732) 866-6655
E-Mail: zappcomics@aol.com
(a-g,i,j,r,t,u,w,x,z,2,4,5)

A Time Lost... And Found
310 Evesham Road
Glendora, NJ 08029
PH: (856) 939-1909
(b,c,d,e,f,l,t,u,w)

ZAPP! Comics
(A&P Center) 574 Valley Road
Wayne, NJ 07470
PH: (973) 628-4500
E-Mail: zappcomics@aol.com
(a-g,i,j,r,t,u,w,x,z,2,4,5)

JHV Associates
(By Appointment Only)
P. O. Box 317
Woodbury Heights, NJ 08097
PH: (856) 845-4010
FAX: (856) 845-3977
E-Mail:
JHVassoc@hotmail.com
(a,b,n,s)

NEW MEXICO

Howard s Rare Comics
8019-D Menaul Blvd. N.E.
Albuquerque, NM 87111
PH: (505) 489-6258
E-Mail: hmrockman@juno.com
Web: www.howardscomics.com
(a,b,c,f,x)

NEW YORK

Excellent Adventures

Comics
110 Milton Ave. (Rt. #50)
Ballston Spa, NY 12020
PH: (518) 884-9498
(a-g,m,n,o,t,u,w,x,5)

Pinocchio Collectibles
1814 McDonald Ave.
Brooklyn, NY 11223
PH: (718) 645-2573
PH: (718) 256-7832
(b,d,e,f,g,t,w)

Ravenswood Inc.
8451 Seneca Turnpike
New Hartford, NY 13413
PH: (315) 735-3699
E-Mail:
ravens@dreamscape.com
(a-j,p-u,w,x,z)

Nuff Said Collectibles
320 E. 65th St.
New York, NY 10021
PH: (212) 861-1697
E-Mail: randy@
nuffsaidcollectibles.com
Web:
www.nuffsaidcollectibles.com
(q,u,w,x,2,3,4)

Amazing Comics
12 Gillette Ave.
Sayville, NY 11782
PH: (631) 567-8069
Web: www.amazingco.com
(a-g,t,u,w,x)

American Legends
(formerly One if By Cards, Two if By Comics)
1107 Central Park Ave.
Scarsdale, NY 10583
PH: (914) 725-2225
Web: www.amerlegends.com
(a,b,d,f,g,i,t,w,x,3,4,5)

NORTH CAROLINA

Acme Comics
2150 Lawndale Dr.
Greensboro, NC 27408
PH: (336) 574-2263
Web: www.acmecomics.com
(a-d,f,g,j,r,u,w,x,2,4,5)

OHIO

Comic Book World, Inc.
4016 Harrison Avenue
Cincinnati, OH 45211
PH: (513) 661-6300
FAX: (513) 661-6300
E-Mail: cbwinfo@one.net
Web:
www.comicbookworld.com
(a-l,n,r,t,u,w,z,2,5)

Comic Garage
349 E. Morrill Avenue
Columbus, OH 43207
PH: (614) 445-0534
E-Mail:
editor@pavementsaw.com
(a,b,c,g,k,n)(By appointment only)

Bookery Fantasy
16 West Main St.
Fairborn, OH 45324
PH: (937) 879-1408
E-Mail:bookeryfan@aol.com
Web: www.bookeryfantasy.com
(a-u,w,x,z,2-5)

Funnie Farm Bookstore
328 N. Dixie Drive
Vandalia, OH 45377
PH: (937) 898-2794
E-Mail: pdbroida@earthlink.net
(a-d,f,g,h,i,r,t,w,x,3,4)

Dark Star Books & Comics
237 Xenia Ave.
Yellow Springs, OH 45387
PH: (937) 767-9400
E-Mail: books
@darkstarbookstore.com
(a-d,f-j,p,q,r,t,w,y,1-5)

OKLAHOMA

New World Comics + Games
6219 N. Meridian
Oklahoma City, OK 73112
PH: (405) 721-7634
(a-i,r-u,w,1-5)

Want List Comics
(Appointment Only)
P.O. Box 701932
Tulsa, OK 74170-1932
PH: (918) 299-0440
E-Mail: WLC777@cox.net
(a,b,c,m,n,o,s,v)

OREGON

Nostalgia Collectibles
527 Willamette Street
Eugene, OR 97401
PH: (541) 484-9202
E-Mail: darrell7g@comcast.net
(a-g,i-u,w,x,y,1-5)

PENNSYLVANIA

Dreamscape Comics
310 West Broad Street
Bethlehem, PA 18018
PH: (610) 867-1178
Web:
www.dreamscapecomics.com
(a-l,n-u,w-z,1,3-5)

New Dimension Comics
101 Clearview Circle
Clearview Mall
Butler, PA 16001
PH: (724) 282-5283
(a-z,1-5)

New Dimension Comics
20550 Route 19,
Piazza Plaza
Cranberry Township, PA
16066-7520
PH: (724) 776-0433
Web: www.ndcomics.com
(a-z,1-5)

New Dimension Comics
508 Lawrence Ave.
Ellwood City, PA 16117
PH: (724) 758-2324
(a-z,1-5)

The Comic Store
28 McGovern Ave.
Lancaster, PA 17602
PH: (717) 397-8737
E-Mail:
comicstorepa@juno.com
Web: www.comicstorepa.com
(a-j,l,p,q,r,t,v,w,2-5)

Duncan Comics, Books, & Accessories
1047 Perry Highway
Pittsburgh, PA 15237
PH: (412) 635-0886
Web: www.duncancomics.com
(a-g,i,n,p,q,r,t,u,w,x,1-5)

Eide's Entertainment
1121 Penn Ave.
Pittsburgh, PA 15222
PH: (412) 261-0900
FAX: (412) 261-3102
E-Mail: eides@eides.com
Web: www.eides.com
(a-g, j-z,1-5)

Legends
2600 Plymouth Meeting Mall
Plymouth Meeting, PA 19462
PH: (610) 828-5848
E-Mail: fictionhs@netreach.net
(a-g,i,j,l,n,o,p,s,t,w-z,1-5)

Comic Swap, Inc.
110 South Fraser Street
State College, PA 16801
PH: (814) 234-6005
E-Mail:
comicswap.inc@verizon.net
(b-d,f-l,r,u,w,4,5)

RHODE ISLAND

The Time Capsule
537 Pontiac Ave.
Cranston, RI 02910
PH: (401) 781-5017
E-Mail: ryeremian@aol.com
(a-z,1-5)

Shadowland Comics and Collectables
2025 Smith St.
North Providence, RI 02911
PH: (401) 349-4611
Web:
www.shadowlandscomics.com
(a-i,l,p-u,w,x,z,2-5)

SOUTH CAROLINA

Planet Comics
2704 N. Main St.
Anderson, SC 29621
PH: (864) 261-3578
E-Mail:
service@planetcomics.net
(a-l,r,t,u,w,z,1-5)

Heroes and Dragons
1563-B Broad River Rd.
Columbia, SC 29210
PH: (803) 731-4376 (HERO)
(a-k,r-u,w,x,z,2-5)

TEXAS

Lone Star Comics
504 East Abram St.
Arlington, TX 76010
PH: (817) 265-0491
Web: www.mycomicshop.com/
overstreet
(a-l,n,o,q,r,t-z,1-5)

Lone Star Comics
5720 Forest Bend Dr.,
Suite #101
Arlington, TX 76017
PH: (817) 563-2550
Web: www.mycomicshop.com/
overstreet
(a-l,n,o,q,r,t-z,1-5)

Lone Star Comics
11661 Preston Rd., Suite #151
Dallas, TX 75230
PH: (214) 373-0934
Web: www.mycomicshop.com/
overstreet
(a-l,n,o,q,r,t-z,1-5)

Remember When Shop
2431 Valwood Pkwy
Dallas, TX 75234
PH: (972) 243-3439
E-Mail: rememberwh@aol.com
(a-c,e,f,m,n,r,s,t,1,2,3,4)

Titan Comics
3701 W. Northwest Hwy #125
Dallas, TX 75220
PH: (214) 350-4420
E-Mail: info@titancomics.com
(a,b,c,d,e,f,r,u)

Lone Star Comics
5429 S. Hulen St.
Ft. Worth, TX 76132
PH: (817) 346-7773
Web: www.mycomicshop.com/
overstreet
(a-l,n,o,q,r,t-z,1-5)

Bedrock City Comic Co.
6717 Westheimer
Houston, TX 77057
PH: (713) 780-0675
Web: www.bedrockcity.com
(a-g,j-o,r-x,z,1-5)

Bedrock City Comic Co.
2204-B FM1960 West
Houston, TX 77090
PH: (281) 444-9763
Web: www.bedrockcity.com
(a-g,j-o,r-x,z,1-5)

Third Planet Sci-Fi Super Store
2718 Southwest Freeway
Houston, TX 77098
PH: (713) 528-1067
E-Mail: 3planet
@third-planet.com
Web: www.third-planet.com
(a-z,1-5)

Lone Star Comics
931 Melbourne Rd.
Hurst, TX 76053
PH: (817) 595-4375
Web: www.mycomicshop.com/
overstreet
(a-l,n,o,q,r,t-z,1-5)

Lone Star Comics
2550 N. Beltline Rd.
Irving, TX 75062
PH: (972) 659-0317
Web: www.mycomicshop.com/
overstreet
(a-l,n,o,q,r,t-z,1-5)

Lone Star Comics
3600 Gus Thomasson Rd.,
Suite #107
Mesquite, TX 75150
PH: (972) 681-2040
Web: www.mycomicshop.com/
overstreet
(a-l,n,o,q,r,t-z,1-5)

Lone Star Comics
3100 Independence Pkwy
Plano, TX 75075
PH: (972) 985-1593
Web: www.mycomicshop.com/
overstreet
(a-l,n,o,q,r,t-z,1-5)

Ground Zero Comics
1700 SSE Loop 323, #302
Tyler, TX 75701
PH: (903) 566-1185
Web:
www.groundzerocomics.com
(b-k,r,t,u,w,3,4,5)

Bedrock City Comic Co.
106 W. Bay Area Blvd.
Webster, TX 77598
PH: (281) 557-2748
Web: www.bedrockcity.com
(a-g,j-o,r-x,z,1-5)

VIRGINIA

Comic & Card Collectorama
2008 Mt. Vernon Avenue
Alexandria, VA 22301
(Greater D.C. area)
PH: (703) 548-3466
E-Mail: collectram@aol.com
(a-f,j,o,p,r,s,t,v,x,1,3,4)

Trilogy Shop #2
700 E. Little Creek Rd.
Norfolk, VA 23518
PH: (757) 587-2540
FAX: (757) 587-5637
E-Mail: trilogy2
@trilogycomics.com
Web: www.trilogycomics.com
(d,f-k,5)

B & O Comic Shop
802 Elm Avenue SW
Roanoke, VA 24016
PH: (504) 342-6642
(c,d,e,f,g,h,i,r,t)

Trilogy Shop #1
5773 Princess Anne Rd.
Virginia Beach, VA 23462
PH: (757) 490-2205
FAX: (757) 671-7721
E-Mail: trilogy1
@trilogycomics.com
Web: www.trilogycomics.com
(a-k,p-x,5)

WASHINGTON

Golden Age Collectibles Ltd.
1501 Pike Place Market
410 Lower Level
Seattle, WA 98101
PH: (206) 622-9799
(a-z,1-5)

CANADA

ALBERTA

Another Dimension
130-10th Street NW
Calgary, Alberta T2N 1V3
PH: (403) 283-7078
E-Mail: comics
@another-dimension.com
Web:
www.another-dimension.com
(a-f,j,l,r,u,w,x,z,2-5)

Redd Skull Comics & CD s
720A Edmonton Trail, NE
Calgary, Alberta T2E 3J4
PH: (403) 283-2716
E-Mail: reddskullcomics
@shaw.ca
(a-d,f-m,r-z,2,4,5)

BRITISH COLUMBIA

Golden Age Collectibles Ltd.
830 Granville Street
Vancouver, B.C., V6Z 1K3
PH: (604) 683-2819
(a-o,r-x,z,1-5)

MANITOBA

The Collector's Slave
156 Imperial Ave.
WPG., MB., R2M 0K8
PH: (204) 237-4428
(a,b,c,e,f,l,m,o,p,q,t)

ONTARIO

The Comic Cave
25 Perth Street
Brockville, ONT K6V 5C3
PH: (613) 345-4349
(a-d,f-i,m,u,w,5)

The Final Stop
381 McArthur Avenue
Ottawa, ON K1L 6N5
PH: (613) 749-1247
E-Mail:
comics@thefinalstop.com
(c,d,f,g,r,t,u,w)

3RD Quadrant - CGC Dealer
226 Queen St. W.
Basement
Toronto, ON M5V 1Z6
PH: (416) 974-9211
E-Mail:
idamahn@yahoo.com
Web: www.3rdquadrant.com
(a-g,i,m,o,q,r,s,u,w,x,3,4,5)

Glossary

a - Story art; **a(i)** - Story art inks; **a(p)** - Story art pencils; **a(r)** - Story art reprint.

ADULT MATERIAL - Contains story and/or art for "mature" readers. Re: sex, violence, strong language.

ADZINE - A magazine primarily devoted to the advertising of comic books and collectibles as its first publishing priority as opposed to written articles.

ALLENTOWN COLLECTION - A collection discovered in 1987-88 just outside Allentown, Pennsylvania. The Allentown collection consisted of 135 Golden Age comics, characterized by high grade and superior paper quality.

ANNUAL - (1) A book that is published yearly; (2) Can also refer to some square bound comics.

ARRIVAL DATE - The date written (often in pencil) or stamped on the cover of comics by either the local wholesaler, newsstand owner, or distributor. The date precedes the cover date by approximately 15 to 75 days, and may vary considerably from one locale to another or from one year to another.

ASHCAN - A publisher's in-house facsimile of a proposed new title. Most ashcans have black and white covers stapled to an existing coverless comic on the inside; other ashcans are totally black and white. In modern parlance, it can also refer to promotional or sold comics, often smaller than standard comic size and usually in black and white, released by publishers to advertise the forthcoming arrival of a new title or story.

ATOM AGE - Comics published from approximately 1946-1956.

B&W - Black and white art.

BACK-UP FEATURE - A story or character that usually appears after the main feature in a comic book; often not featured on the cover.

BAD GIRL ART - A term popularized in the early '90s to describe an attitude as well as a style of art that portrays women in a sexual and often action-oriented way.

BAXTER PAPER - A high quality, heavy, white paper used in the printing of some comics.

BC - Abbreviation for Back Cover.

BI-MONTHLY - Published every two months.

BI-WEEKLY - Published every two weeks.

BONDAGE COVER - Usually denotes a female in bondage.

BOUND COPY - A comic that has been bound into a book. The process requires that the spine be trimmed and sometimes sewn into a book-like binding.

BRITISH ISSUE - A comic printed for distribution in Great Britain; these copies sometimes have the price listed in pence or pounds instead of cents or dollars.

BRITTLENESS - A severe condition of paper deterioration where paper loses its flexibility and thus chips and/or flakes easily.

BRONZE AGE - Comics published from approximately 1970 through 1985.

BROWNING - (1) The aging of paper characterized by the ever-increasing level of oxidation characterized by darkening; (2) The level of paper deterioration one step more severe than tanning and one step before brittleness.

c - Cover art; **c(i)** - Cover inks; **c(p)** - Cover pencils; **c(r)** - Cover reprint.

CAMEO - The brief appearance of one character in the strip of another.

CANADIAN ISSUE - A comic printed for distribution in Canada; these copies sometimes have no advertising.

CCA - Abbreviation for **Comics Code Authority**.

CCA SEAL - An emblem that was placed on the cover of all CCA approved comics beginning in April-May, 1955.

CENTER CREASE - See **Subscription Copy**.

CENTERFOLD or CENTER SPREAD - The two folded pages in the center of a comic book at the terminal end of the staples.

CERTIFIED GRADING - A process provided by a professional grading service that certifies a given grade for a comic and seals the book in a protective **Slab**.

CF - Abbreviation for **Centerfold**.

CFO - Abbreviation for Centerfold Out.

CGC - Abbreviation for the certified comic book grading company, Comics Guaranty, LLC.

CIRCULATION COPY - See **Subscription Copy**.

CIRCULATION FOLD - See **Subscription Fold**.

CLASSIC COVER - A cover considered by collectors to be highly desirable because of its subject matter, artwork, historical importance, etc.

CLEANING - A process in which dirt and dust is removed.

COLOR TOUCH - A restoration process by which colored ink is used to hide color flecks, color flakes, and larger areas of missing color. Short for Color Touch-Up.

COLORIST - An artist who paints the color guides for comics. Many modern colorists use computer technology.

COMIC BOOK DEALER - (1) A seller of comic books; (2) One who makes a living buying and selling comic books.

COMIC BOOK REPAIR - When a tear, loose staple or centerfold has been mended without changing or adding to the original finish of the book. Repair may involve tape, glue or nylon gossamer, and is easily detected; it is considered a defect.

COMICS CODE AUTHORITY - A voluntary organization comprised of comic book publishers formed in 1954 to review (and possibly censor) comic books before they were printed and distributed. The emblem of the CCA is a white stamp in the upper right hand corner of comics dated after February 1955. The term "post-Code" refers to the time after this practice started, or approximately 1955 to the present.

COMPLETE RUN - All issues of a given title.

CON - A convention or public gathering of fans.

CONDITION - The state of preservation of a comic book, often inaccurately used interchangeably with **Grade**.

COSMIC AEROPLANE COLLECTION - A collection from Salt Lake City, Utah discovered by Cosmic Aeroplane Books, characterized by the moderate to high grade copies of 1930s-40s comics with pencil check marks in the margins of inside pages. It is thought that these comics were kept by a commercial illustration school and the check marks were placed beside panels that instructors wanted students to draw.

COSTUMED HERO - A costumed crime fighter with "developed" human powers instead of super powers.

COUPON CUT or COUPON MISSING - A coupon has been neatly removed with scissors or razor blade from the interior or exterior of the comic as opposed to having been ripped out.

COVER GLOSS - The reflective quality of the cover inks.

COVER TRIMMED - Cover has been reduced in size by neatly cutting away rough or damaged edges.

COVERLESS - A comic with no cover attached. There is a niche demand for coverless comics, particularly in the case of hard-to-find key books otherwise impossible to locate intact. See **Remainders**.

C/P - Abbreviation for Cleaned and Pressed.

CREASE - A fold which causes ink removal, usually resulting in a white line. See **Corner Crease** and **Reading Crease**.

CROSSOVER - A story where one character appears prominently in the story of another character. See **X-Over**.

CVR - Abbreviation for Cover.

DEALER - See **Comic Book Dealer**.

DEACIDIFICATION - Several different processes that reduce acidity in paper.

DEBUT - The first time that a character appears anywhere.

DEFECT - Any fault or flaw that detracts from perfection.

DENVER COLLECTION - A collection consisting primarily of early 1940s high grade number one issues bought at auction in Pennsylvania by a Denver, Colorado dealer.

DIE-CUT COVER - A comic book cover with areas or edges precut by a printer to a special shape or to create a desired effect.

DISTRIBUTOR STRIPES - Color brushed or sprayed on the edges of comic book stacks by the distributor/wholesaler to code them for expedient exchange at the sales racks. Typical colors are red, orange, yellow, green, blue, and purple. Distributor stripes are not a defect.

DOUBLE - A duplicate copy of the same comic book.

DOUBLE COVER - When two covers are stapled to the comic interior instead of the usual one; the exterior cover often protects the interior cover from wear and damage. This is considered a desirable situation by some collectors and may increase collector value; this is not considered a defect.

DRUG PROPAGANDA STORY - A comic that makes an editorial stand about drug use.

DRUG USE STORY - A comic that shows the actual use of drugs: needle use, tripping, harmful effects, etc.

DUOTONE - Printed with black and one other color of ink. This process was common in comics printed in the 1930s.

DUST SHADOW - Darker, usually linear area at the edge of some comics stored in stacks. Some portion of the cover was not covered by the comic immediately above it and it was exposed to settling dust particles. Also see **Oxidation Shadow** and **Sun Shadow**.

EDGAR CHURCH COLLECTION - See **Mile High Collection**.

EMBOSSED COVER - A comic book cover with a pattern, shape or image pressed into the cover from the inside, creating a raised area.

ENCAPSULATION - Refers to the process of sealing certified comics in a protective plastic enclosure. Also see "slabbing."

EYE APPEAL - A term which refers to the overall look of a comic book when held at approximately arm's length. A comic may have nice eye appeal yet still possess defects which reduce grade.

FANZINE - An amateur fan publication.

FC - Abbreviation for Front Cover.

FILE COPY - A high grade comic originating from the publisher's file; contrary to what some might believe, not all file copies are in Gem Mint condition. An arrival date on the cover of a comic does not indicate that it is a file copy, though a copyright date may.

FIRST APPEARANCE - See **Debut**.

FLASHBACK - When a previous story is recalled.

FOIL COVER - A comic book cover that has had a thin metallic foil hot stamped on it. Many of these "gimmick" covers date from the early '90s, and might include chromium, prism and hologram covers as well.

FOUR COLOR - Series of comics produced by Dell, characterized by hundreds of different features; named after the four color process of printing. See **One Shot**.

FOUR COLOR PROCESS - The process of printing with the three primary colors (red, yellow, and blue) plus black.

FUMETTI - Illustration system in which individual frames of a film are colored and used for individual panels to make a comic book story. The most famous example is DC's *Movie Comics* #1-6 from 1939.

GATEFOLD COVER - A double-width fold-out cover.

GENRE - Categories of comic book subject matter; e.g. Science Fiction, Super-Hero, Romance, Funny Animal, Teenage Humor, Crime, War, Western, Mystery, Horror, etc.

GIVEAWAY - Type of comic book intended to be given away as a premium or promotional device instead of being sold.

GLASSES ATTACHED - In 3-D comics, the special blue and red cellophane and cardboard glasses are still attached to the comic.

GLASSES DETACHED - In 3-D comics, the special blue and red cellophane and cardboard glasses are not still attached to the comic; obviously less desirable than **Glasses Attached**.

GOLDEN AGE - Comics published from approximately 1938 (*Action Comics* #1) to 1945.

GOOD GIRL ART - Refers to a style of art, usually from the 1930s-50s, that portrays women in a sexually implicit way.

GREY-TONE COVER - A cover art style in which pencil or charcoal underlies the normal line drawing, used to enhance the effects of light and shadow, thus producing a richer quality. These covers, prized by most collectors, are sometimes referred to as **Painted Covers** but are not actually painted.

HB - Abbreviation for Hardback.

HEADLIGHTS - Forward illumation devices installed on all automobiles and many other vehicles...OK, OK, it's a euphemism for a comic book cover prominently featuring a woman's breasts in a provocative way. Also see **Bondage Cover** for another collecting euphemism that has long since outlived its appropriateness in these politically correct times.

HOT STAMPING - The process of pressing foil, prism paper and/or inks on cover stock.

HRN - Abbreviation for Highest Reorder Number. This refers to a method used by collectors of Gilberton's *Classic Comics* and *Classics Illustrated* series to distinguish first editions from later printings.

ILLO - Abbreviation for Illustration.

IMPAINT - Another term for **Color Touch**.

INDICIA - Publishing and title information usually located at the bottom of the first page or the bottom of the inside front cover. In rare cases and in some pre-1938 comics, it was sometimes located on internal pages.

INFINITY COVER - Shows a scene that repeats itself to infinity.

INKER - Artist that does the inking.

INTRO - Same as **Debut**.

INVESTMENT GRADE COPY - (1) Comic of sufficiently high grade and demand to be viewed by collectors as instantly liquid should the need arise to sell; (2) A comic in VF or better condition; (3) A comic purchased primarily to realize a profit.

ISSUE NUMBER - The actual edition number of a given title.

ISH - Short for Issue.

JLA - Abbreviation for Justice League of America.

JSA - Abbreviations for Justice Society of America.

KEY, KEY BOOK or KEY ISSUE - An issue that contains a first appearance, origin, or other historically or artistically important feature considered especially desirable by collectors.

LAMONT LARSON - Pedigreed collection of high grade 1940s comics with the initials or name of its original owner, Lamont Larson.

LENTICULAR COVERS or "FLICKER" COVERS - A comic book cover overlayed with a ridged plastic sheet such that the special artwork underneath appears to move when the cover is tilted at different angles perpendicular to the ridges.

LETTER COL or LETTER COLUMN - A feature in a comic book that prints and sometimes responds to letters written by its readers.

LINE DRAWN COVER - A cover published in the traditional way where pencil sketches are overdrawn with india ink and then colored. See also Grey-Tone Cover, Photo Cover, and Painted Cover.

LOGO - The title of a strip or comic book as it appears on the cover or title page.

LSH - Abbreviation for Legion of Super-Heroes.

MAGIC LIGHTNING COLLECTION - A collection of high grade 1950s comics from the San Francisco area.

MARVEL CHIPPING - A bindery (trimming/cutting) defect that results in a series of chips and tears at the top, bottom, and right edges of the cover, caused when the cutting blade of an industrial paper trimmer becomes dull. It was dubbed Marvel Chipping because it can be found quite often on Marvel comics from the late '50s and early '60s but can also occur with any company's comic books from the late 1940s through the middle 1960s.

MILE HIGH COLLECTION - High grade collection of over 22,000 comics discovered in Denver, Colorado in 1977, originally owned by Mr. Edgar Church. Comics from this collection are now famous for extremely white pages, fresh smell, and beautiful cover ink reflectivity.

MODERN AGE - A catch-all term usually applied to comics published from the 1980s to the present.

MYLAR™ - An inert, very hard, space-age plastic used to make high quality protective bags and sleeves for comic book storage. "Mylar" is a trademark of the DuPont Co.

ND - Abbreviation for No Date.

NN - Abbreviation for No Number.

NO DATE - When there is no date given on the cover or indicia page.

NO NUMBER - No issue number is given on the cover or indicia page; these are usually first issues or one-shots.

N.Y. LEGIS. COMM. - New York Legislative Committee to Study the Publication of Comics (1951).

ONE-SHOT - When only one issue is published of a title, or when a series is published where each issue is a different title (e.g. Dell's *Four Color Comics*).

ORIGIN - When the story of a character's creation is given.

OVER GUIDE - When a comic book is priced at a value over Guide list.

OXIDATION SHADOW - Darker, usually linear area at the edge of some comics stored in stacks. Some portion of the cover was not covered by the comic immediately above it, and it was exposed to the air. Also see Dust Shadow and Sun Shadow.

p - Art pencils.

PAINTED COVER - (1) Cover taken from an actual painting instead of a line drawing; (2) Inaccurate name for a grey-toned cover.

PANELOLOGIST - One who researches comic books and/or comic strips.

PANNAPICTAGRAPHIST - One possible term for someone who collects comic books; can you figure out why it hasn't exactly taken off in common parlance?

PAPER COVER - Comic book cover made from the same newsprint as the interior pages. These books are extremely rare in high grade.

PARADE OF PLEASURE - A book about the censorship of comics.

PB - Abbreviation for Paperback.

PEDIGREE - A book from a famous and usually high grade collection - e.g. Allentown, Lamont Larson, Edgar Church/Mile High, Denver, San Francisco, Cosmic Aeroplane, etc. Beware of non-pedigree collections being promoted as pedigree books; only outstanding high grade collections similar to those listed qualify.

PENCILER - Artist that does the pencils...you're figuring out some of these definitions without us by now, aren't you?

PERFECT BINDING - Pages are glued to the cover as opposed to being stapled to the cover, resulting in a flat binded side. Also known as Square Back or Square Bound.

PG - Abbreviation for Page.

PHOTO COVER - Comic book cover featuring a photographic image instead of a line drawing or painting.

PLATINUM AGE - Comics published from approximately 1900-1938.

POLYPROPALENE - A type of plastic used in the manufacture of comic book bags; now considered harmful to paper and not recommended for long term storage of comics.

POP - Abbreviation for the anti-comic book volume, *Parade of Pleasure*.

POST-CODE - Describes comics published after February 1955 and usually displaying the CCA stamp in the upper right-hand corner.

POUGHKEEPSIE - Refers to a large collection of Dell Comics file copies believed to have originated from the warehouse of Western Publishing in Poughkeepsie, NY.

PP - Abbreviation for Pages.

PRE-CODE - Describes comics published before the Comics Code Authority seal began appearing on covers in 1955.

PRE-HERO DC - A term used to describe *More Fun* #1-51 (pre-Spectre), *Adventure* #1-39 (pre-Sandman), and *Detective* #1-26 (pre-Batman). The term is actually inaccurate because technically there were "heroes" in the above books.

PRE-HERO MARVEL - A term used to describe *Strange Tales* #1-100 (pre-Human Torch), *Journey Into Mystery* #1-82 (pre-Thor), *Tales To Astonish* #1-35 (pre-Ant Man), and *Tales Of Suspense* #1-38 (pre-Iron Man).

PROVENANCE - When the owner of a book is known and is stated for the purpose of authenticating and documenting the history of the book. Example: A book from the Stan Lee or Forrest Ackerman collection would be an example of a value-adding provenance.

PULP - Cheaply produced magazine made from low grade newsprint. The term comes from the wood pulp that was used in the paper manufacturing process.

QUARTERLY - Published every three months (four times a year).

R - Abbreviation for Reprint.

RARE - 10-20 copies estimated to exist.

RAT CHEW - Damage caused by the gnawing of rats and mice. Just where are you storing your comics anyway?

RBCC - Abbreviation for Rockets Blast Comic Collector, one of the first and most prominent adzines instrumental in developing the early comic book market.

READING COPY - A comic that is in FAIR to

GOOD condition and is often used for research; the condition has been sufficiently reduced to the point where general handling will not degrade it further.

READING CREASE - Book-length, vertical front cover crease at staples, caused by bending the cover over the staples. Square-bounds receive these creases just by opening the cover too far to the left.

REILLY, TOM - A large high grade collection of 1939-1945 comics with 5000+ books.

REPRINT COMICS - In earlier decades, comic books that contained newspaper strip reprints; modern reprint comics usually contain stories originally featured in older comic books.

RESTORATION - Any attempt, whether professional or amateur, to enhance the appearance of an aging or damaged comic book. These procedures may include any or all of the following techniques: recoloring, adding missing paper, stain, ink, dirt or tape removal, whitening, pressing out wrinkles, staple replacement, trimming, re-glossing, etc. Amateur work can lower the value of a book, and even professional restoration has now gained a certain negative aura in the modern marketplace from some quarters. In all cases, except for some simple cleaning procedures, a restored book can never be worth the same as an unrestored book in the same condition.

REVIVAL - An issue that begins republishing a comic book character after a period of dormancy.

ROCKFORD - A high grade collection of 1940s comics with 2000+ books from Rockford, IL.

ROLLED SPINE - A spine condition caused by folding back pages while reading.

ROUND BOUND - Standard saddle stitch binding typical of most comics.

RUN - A group of comics of one title where most or all of the issues are present. See Complete Run.

S&K - Abbreviation for the legendary creative team of Joe Simon and Jack Kirby, creators of Marvel Comics' Captain America.

SADDLE STITCH - The staple binding of magazines and comic books.

SAN FRANCISCO COLLECTION - (see Reilly, Tom)

SCARCE - 20-100 copies estimated to exist.

SEDUCTION OF THE INNOCENT - An inflammatory book written by Dr. Frederic Wertham and published in 1953; Wertham asserted that comics were responsible for rampant juvenile deliquency in American youth.

SET - (1) A complete run of a given title; (2) A grouping of comics for sale.

SEMI-MONTHLY - Published twice a month, but not necessarily Bi-Weekly.

SEWN SPINE - A comic with many spine perforations where binders' thread held it into a bound volume. This is considered a defect.

SF - Abbreviation for Science Fiction (the other commonly used term, "sci-fi," is often considered derogatory or indicative of more "low-brow" rather than "literary" science fiction, i.e. "sci-fi television."

SILVER AGE - Comics published from approximately 1956 (*Showcase* #4) to 1969.

SILVER PROOF - A black and white actual size print on thick glossy paper hand-painted by an artist to indicate colors to the engraver.

SLAB - Colloquial term for the plastic enclosure used by grading certification companies to seal in certified comics.

SLABBING - Colloquial term for the process of encapsulating certified comics in a plastic enclosure.

SOTI - Abbreviation for Seduction of the Innocent.

SPINE - The left-hand edge of the comic that has been folded and stapled.

SPINE ROLL - A condition where the left edge of the comic book curves toward the front or back, caused by folding back each page as the comic was read.

SPLASH PAGE - A Splash Panel that takes up the entire page.

SPLASH PANEL - (1) The first panel of a comic book story, usually larger than other panels and usually containing the title and credits of the story; (2) An oversized interior panel.

SQUARE BACK or SQUARE BOUND - See Perfect Binding.

STORE STAMP - Store name (and sometimes address and telephone number) stamped in ink via rubber stamp and stamp pad.

SUBSCRIPTION COPY - A comic sent through the mail directly from the publisher or publisher's agent. Most are folded in half, causing a subscription crease or fold running down the center of the comic from top to bottom; this is considered a defect.

SUBSCRIPTION CREASE - See Subscription Copy.

SUBSCRIPTION FOLD - See Subscription Copy. Differs from a Subscription Crease in that no ink is missing as a result of the fold.

SUN SHADOW - Darker, usually linear area at the edge of some comics stored in stacks. Some portion of the cover was not covered by the comic immediately above it, and it suffered prolonged exposure to light. A serious defect, unlike a Dust Shadow, which can sometimes be removed. Also see Oxidation Shadow.

SUPER-HERO - A costumed crime fighter with powers beyond those of mortal man.

SUPER-VILLAIN - A costumed criminal with powers beyond those of mortal man; the antithesis of Super-Hero.

SWIPE - A panel, sequence, or story obviously borrowed from previously published material.

TEXT ILLO. - A drawing or small panel in a text story that almost never has a dialogue balloon.

TEXT PAGE - A page with no panels or drawings.

TEXT STORY - A story with few if any illustrations commonly used as filler material during the first three decades of comics.

3-D COMIC - Comic art that is drawn and printed in two color layers, producing a 3-D effect when viewed through special glasses.

3-D EFFECT COMIC - Comic art that is drawn to appear as if in 3-D but isn't.

TITLE - The name of the comic book.

TITLE PAGE - First page of a story showing the title of the story and possibly the creative credits and indicia.

TTA - Abbreviation for *Tales to Astonish*.

UK - Abbreviation for British edition (United Kingdom).

UNDER GUIDE - When a comic book is priced at a value less than Guide list.

UPGRADE - To obtain another copy of the same comic book in a higher grade.

VARIANT COVER - A different cover image used on the same issue.

VERY RARE - 1 to 10 copies estimated to exist.

VICTORIAN AGE - Comics published from approximately 1828-1899.

WANT LIST - A listing of comics needed by a collector, or a list of comics that a collector is interested in purchasing.

WAREHOUSE COPY - Originating from a publisher's warehouse; similar to file copy.

WHITE MOUNTAIN COLLECTION - A collection of high grade 1950s and 1960s comics which originated in New England.

X-OVER - Short for Crossover.

ZINE - Short for Fanzine.

COMIC B
DEFININ

By Arnold T. Blumberg & J.C. Vaughn
(with additional material and timeline graphics by Douglas Gillock)

OOK AGES:
G ERAS

In* The Official Overstreet Comic Book Price Guide *#33, we offered the beginnings of a discussion on Comic Book Ages. This article features the results of that discussion.

The search for agreement on comic book ages has proven to be one of those topics, the kind for which no one is without an opinion or two (or twelve). It has produced scores of animated e-mails, letters and even academic papers, all of them from collectors, dealers and historians who care deeply about where comics have been and where they're going.

In the pages of* Overstreet's Comic Price Review *and online in the* Scoop *newsletter, we've offered samplings of the fantastic, thought provoking feedback to the Comic Book Ages piece we offered in* The Official Overstreet Comic Book Price Guide *#33. As we worked to arrive at a consensus, we've heard from many different fans of the four-color medium in a wide variety of capacities. While there are still some elements to be decided, a great deal of agreement was found in some areas of understanding.

COMICS DIDN'T START IN 1933

More than 90 years before *New Fun* hit the stands, *The Adventures of Obadiah Oldbuck* presented a story in sequential comic form. Someone made the decision to publish it and influenced the next generation of cartoonists. More than 50 years before *New Fun*, Palmer Cox collected his Brownies cartoons into one publication, influencing 60 years of comics publishing during which a tremendous variety of packaging and presentations were tried out.

If you still think it's the comics themselves and not the creative and business people behind them that the Ages denote, consider these questions: If Vin Sullivan and his contemporaries hadn't been looking to try something different, would *Action Comics #1* ever have happened? If Julie Schwartz hadn't been interested in reviving the superheroes, would *Showcase #4* have witnessed the reinterpretation of the Flash? If Stan Lee hadn't stepped away from the day-to-day operations at Marvel, would Gwen Stacy have died? If the limited series format hadn't proved successful, how would *Crisis on Infinite Earths* have been handled?

It's simple: the comics we have come to recognize as indicators of significant changes, like those noted in the previous paragraph, are the manifestations of *editorial or publishing decisions* that were made several months before. It is actually these decisions we are marking when we note the importance of the publication of *The Adventures of Obadiah Oldbuck*, the collection of Palmer Cox's Brownies into their first book, or the introduction of the Barry Allen Flash. Bill Gaines, Harvey Kurtzman and Al Feldstein wouldn't have done anything that hadn't already been done. Denny O'Neil and Neal Adams wouldn't have told their classic Green Lantern/Green Arrow tales. Gwen Stacy never would have died, the Punisher never

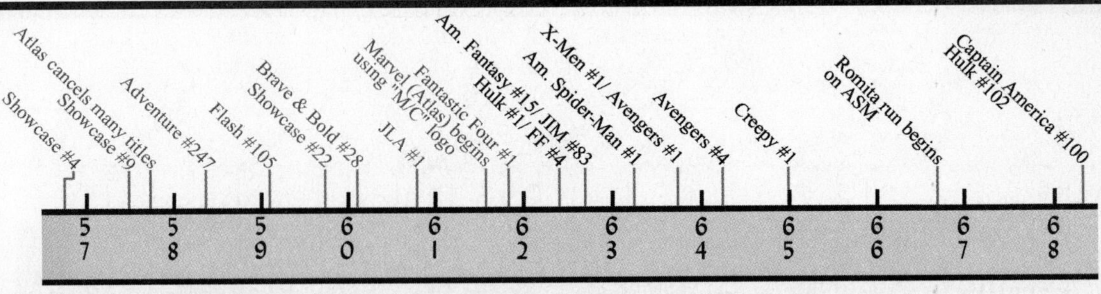

would have appeared, and Conan would never have been a licensed comic book title.

A SEARCH FOR THE AGES

We must first acknowledge that comic book Ages really exist only to facilitate the ease of conveying information to other parties. In other words, they help create a verbal shorthand to make it easier to explain the creative, editorial or publishing work involved in a specific comic or set of comics (or the present day value we attach to a specific comic or set of comics) in comparison to other comics.

The act of splitting comics up into groups creates the illusion that these are not part of a much bigger picture, but believing that illusion would be a mistake. Comics are just one part of the much larger world of comic character collectibles, and that world itself is just a piece of the even larger entire history of popular culture.

Comic book Ages are important and they're fun, but they're truly nothing more than an intellectual exercise. If it were more serious, we'd have to take a look at why the comic book Ages run backwards (Golden, Silver, Bronze instead of Bronze, Silver, Golden as does the rest of human history). Picking the landmarks by which we navigate comics history isn't easy though, as we have often discovered.

CODIFYING THE AGES

Does one incident or single comic book issue define an Age? Surely *Action Comics #1* begins the Golden Age just as *The Brownies* begin the Platinum Age, but some have observed that the Comics Code might be the deciding factor in dividing the various eras. That idea did in fact help to suggest an even more innovative way of looking at the whole Age issue that finally breaks away from the narrow-minded reliance on the superhero genre as the end-all be-all of Comic Book Age definition. In the final analysis, we determined that it was not the superheroes *alone* that dictated when these Ages began or ended. They were merely the superficial result of a much deeper motivating force that ultimately serves as the primary shaper of every Comic Book Age; namely, the editorial and publishing decisions that drive the industry and influence the content of the comics themselves. Seen from this perspective, the entire Age issue takes on even greater resonance and even the already established Ages fall neatly into place.

As we will see, the Comics Code can serve to illuminate this theory. Though the original incarnation of the Comics Code Authority and its system of strict self-regulation only existed for 16 years (Oct. 1954 to Jan. 1971), its influence on comic book history has been enormous. Primarily, the implementation of the CCA suggested – and perhaps necessitated – the resurrection of a stagnating superhero genre and heralded the beginnings of the Silver Age. But as this genre was given new life with the inclusion of a fresh, realism-based perspective and a growing social consciousness, creators quickly found themselves restricted by walls of content regulation that had been used in the '50s to protect an industry under public siege. It was this desire for greater content flexibility on the part of Silver Age creators that was the first sign of things to come.

Social issues had been creeping into the pages of comics for a few years, but by the end of 1970 there seems to have been a general consensus within the business that the CCA needed revision. In 1971, the Comics Magazine Association of America ratified a general overhaul of the Code, the first since its inception in 1954. Not only did this revision allow for the inclusion of content that for more than a decade had been absent from the pages of comic books, but it denoted a fundamental shift in thinking by the industry as a whole. From this point on, it was clear that the industry itself was in control of the specifics of the CCA. If they saw fit, they could change the Code to keep it current with their perception of public standards.

And change it they did. A mere three months after the original revision of the CCA, the members of the Association found themselves meeting once again to amend the specifics of the system of self-regulation. The topic at hand was the portrayal of drugs, and on April 15, 1971, an agreement was reached to allow stories depicting graphic drug use with the understanding that "narcotics addiction shall not be portrayed except as a vicious habit." This unexpected amendment was directly inspired by Stan Lee's decision at Marvel to distribute three issues of *Amazing Spider-Man* that failed to meet Code approval because of the portrayal of drug abuse. With the inconsistencies in the Code rectified, Carmine Infantino – then editor at DC – followed suit and released a Code-approved story in *Green Lantern* dealing with heroin addiction.

Just as the implementation of the Code can be seen as a defining aspect of the dawn of the Silver Age, the growing social consciousness of certain comic creators and the resulting decision to amend the CCA stands as a herald of the shift into the Bronze Age. With a revised Code, genres and topics that had been forbidden for years suddenly re-emerged in the pages of mainstream comics. The major publishers began

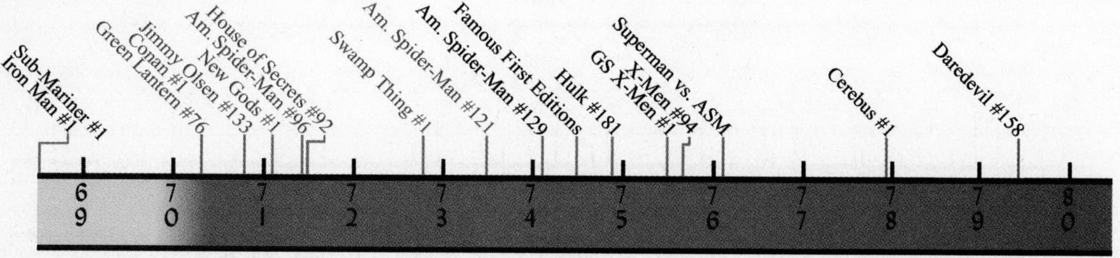

launching a multitude of new titles and re-invigorating others that had floundered under the original content restrictions. Without a conscious decision by the industry to expand the range of allowable material, many of the characters, titles, and stories that are now considered foundational to the Bronze Age never could have been published.

In looking beyond the Bronze Age to define the Copper Age, we can see another important reconsideration of the CCA playing a role. Just as publishers had realized in the early '70s that they themselves were in control of the particulars of the Code, in the mid-'80s they decided that for certain kinds of comics the restrictions were not necessary at all. These comics were targeted at an older audience, many of whom had grown up with the socially relevant comics of the '70s. This audience realized the potential the medium had for a broader type of storytelling and they demanded more "mature" content. Comics like Frank Miller's *Dark Knight Returns* and Alan Moore's *Watchmen* played a major role in defining this new Copper Age and pointed the way to yet another revision of the Code in 1989.

But just as we are suggesting that no single issue can be used to wholly define an era of comic book history, it is important to point out that the CCA was not the only factor in the evolution of the industry. Many creative, social, economic, and technological factors combined to make comics what they are today. But the Code does stand out as a profound, industry-wide influence that can be very helpful in charting the progression of the medium since the mid-'50s. Only now, almost fifty years after the CCA was first imposed, are the publishers of comic books moving away from a single system of content regulation. This "deregulation" of the industry will surely be a determining factor in Ages yet to be defined.

THE SHIFTING SANDS OF TIME

Another aspect of the debate was also clarified for us during this process. For years, we have struggled to define Comic Book Ages based on a single turning point – an individual issue of one comic book from one genre and one company that straddles the line between the end of one era and the start of the next. But since these Ages are arbitrary, applied to real-world developments that never truly reach an end, the flow of history often obscures any specific turning point and instead suggests that one era might subtly segue into another over a period of time. Therefore, we establish here that the later eras on the Comic Book Age scale can be defined through gradual transitions that have start and end points. For example, while *Showcase* #4 (1956) remains an undisputed watershed moment that heralds the coming of the Silver Age (and indeed adheres strongly to our editorial and publishing theory in that it represents a decision to revive a nearly-dead genre), we propose that the transition only *began* with *Showcase* #4...but it ended with *Fantastic Four* #1 (1961).

This same thinking can be applied to the later Ages as well. Perhaps one of the reasons the Bronze Age has been so difficult to nail down at either its beginning or conclusion is that it represents a volatile shift in editorial and publishing philosophy on both ends. Here we propose that the Bronze Age began arriving with *Green Lantern* #76 (1970), the first of a series of books in 1970 and 1971 to break boundaries, explore new editorial and publishing opportunities in storytelling and theme, and start a march toward maturity in the medium. But where did this transformation reach its *climax*, signaling the death of innocence embodied by the Silver Age and opening the door to a more adult era of heightened violence and heightened consequences? *Amazing Spider-Man* #121 (1973).

Finally, we introduce a new Age with this edition: the Copper Age, spanning the years from the end of the Bronze Age in 1985 to the debut of Image Comics in 1992. As before, we propose that the transition begins with Marvel's editorial and publishing decision to embark on a twelve-issue maxi-series that ties in their entire superhero universe while introducing changes to their primary characters that would echo forward for years to come. That series was *Marvel Super-Heroes: Secret Wars* (1984-85). The Copper Age then fully arrives when DC takes the notion one step further, utilizing the same editorial and publishing concept to completely remake their fictional universe and wash away the last vestiges of the Silver and Bronze Ages with *Crisis on Infinite Earths* (1985-86).

Now, with what is hopefully a much clearer understanding of this approach to the organization of comic book history, we look forward to the future, and countless other Ages to be explored, enjoyed and defined. The adventure continues...

Without further ado, some revisions:

AGE	YEARS	CATALYSTS
Silver	1956-1970	*Showcase* #4 (1956), *FF* #1 (1961)
Bronze	1970-1984	*GL* #76 (1970), *AMZ* #121 (1973)
Copper	1984-1992	*Secret Wars* (1984-85), *Crisis* (1985-86)
Modern	1992-Present	Image Comics debut

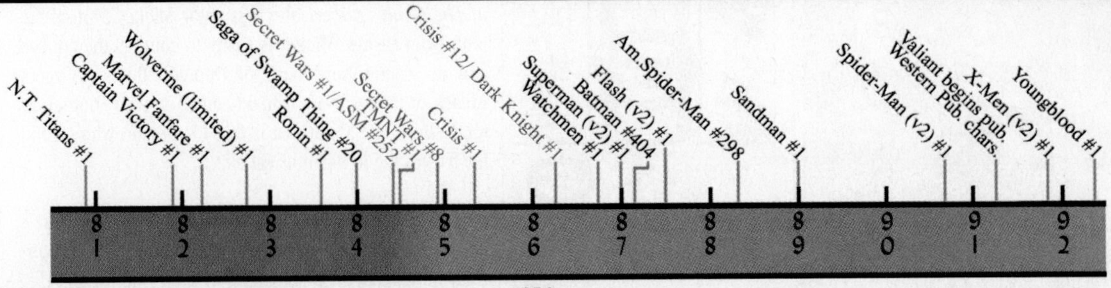

70 YEARS & STI

AN ANNIVERSARY LOO

He's an angry everyman, a frustrated character for whom the breaks never entirely fall the right way. He regularly comes oh-so-close to his dreams, only to see something go exasperatingly wrong. What's worse, he's seemingly overmatched by his three young nephews, who at least on the surface appear brighter than him.

And yet, he's also the personification of the gutsy never-give-up spirit of the pioneer, of the entrepreneur, of the working man, of the tired parents and of frustrated kids. From his rather inauspicious debut in the *Silly Symphony* short cartoon *The Wise Little Hen*, he has emerged to be one of the most collected, most documented comic characters in history.

If one hops on the internet, a Google search on the name Donald Duck brings back something like 977,000 possible websites to check out. Even discounting 95% of them, one is still faced with 48,850 web pages to scan for information about Walt Disney's 70-year-old fireball.

With so much written, it's a hard task to say something new about the character. It's even more difficult to say something new that is not merely conjecture, opinion, or a recitation of urban legend. With that in mind, we talked with John K. Snyder, Jr., President of Diamond International Galleries, one of the character's foremost collectors, with more than 1,000 Donald Duck items in his collection, for a fresh perspective.

J.C. Vaughn: The name Donald Duck popped up in Disney history before the character showed up. Where did that happen?

John K. Snyder, Jr.: Donald was first mentioned in *The Adventures of Mickey Mouse*, a book published by David McKay in 1931. He was mentioned for a second time in Mickey Mouse Annual #3, published by Dean & Son of London in 1932. There was a picture of a duck in both books that is not distinctly Donald. Whether or not this was intended to be him at the time is anyone's guess.

JCV: When did Donald first appear and when did he take on the look of the feisty Donald character we recognize today?

JKS: Donald made his definitive first appearance in one of the *Silly Symphony* series, *The Wise Little Hen*, June 9, 1934. In that movie short, he was sort of shiftless or just out for a good time. It wasn't the angry or frustrated personality that people came to know him for later. He also wore a sort of French-looking sailor cap in that film. In a cultural view, it's probably notable that he wore a yachting-type sailor suit, not a Navy uniform.

Orphan's Benefit, Donald's second appearance on screen, debuted August 11, 1934. In addition to the more familiar sailor's cap, Donald displayed some of his trademark aggravation. In a scene where he tried unsuccessfully to recite "Mary Had a Little Lamb," circumstances and misperceptions lead Donald to become increasingly agitated, leading to some of the film's best laughs. Of course many laughs were generated by Clarence "Ducky" Nash's voice for Donald, too, and the familiar aggravated look was developed by Dick Lundy, one of Disney's animators, and another noteworthy item is that this was the first Mickey Mouse cartoon in which he had a supporting role.

Mickey Mouse Magazine Volume 2 #5, the Dairy giveaway, featured Donald Duck on the front (and back) cover for the first time in any of the magazine's three series.

At that point, Donald was the classic second tier character. He basically was an enlivened foil for Mickey, as seen in *The Band Concert*, the first color Mickey Mouse cartoon from Disney. Mickey is trying to conduct the concert and no matter how many of Donald's flutes he takes, breaks or throws away, Donald comes up with another. An interesting note about that is that it's Donald who's doing the frustrating in this musical skit.

JCV: How did Donald first appear in newspapers?

JKS: *The Wise Little Hen* appeared in the *Silly Symphony* daily newspaper strip beginning in September of 1934.

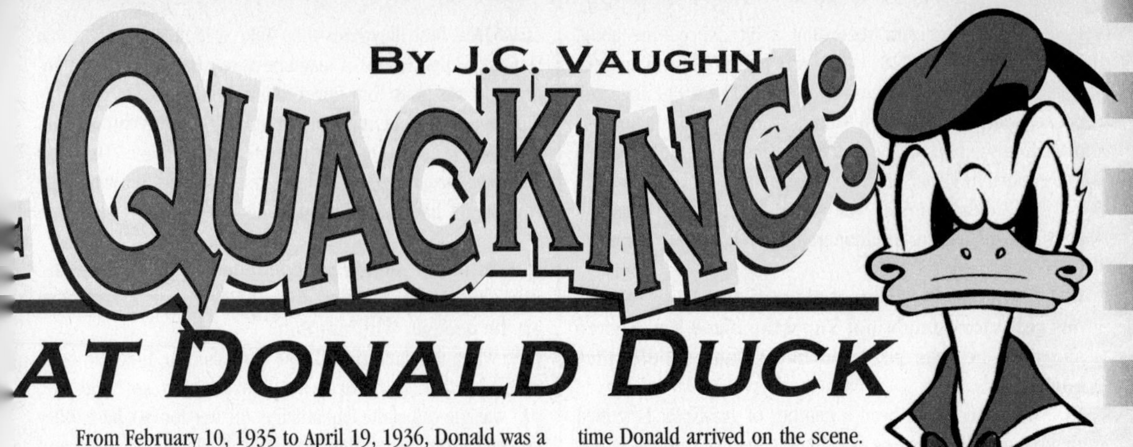

Quacking: At Donald Duck

By J.C. Vaughn

From February 10, 1935 to April 19, 1936, Donald was a frequent costar in Gottfredson's Mickey Mouse daily and Sunday strip. After a short break, a *Silly Symphony* Sunday page featuring Donald debuted August 30, 1936. The *Silly Symphony* strip ran through December 5, 1937 and originals from it are incredibly rare. In fact, there are only seven known to exist.

Donald got his own daily strip on February 7, 1938, and then his own Sunday page started on December 10, 1939. Al Taliaferro became famous for drawing the Donald strips, and did so until he died in 1969.

JCV: When did he start to become a force in licensed paper products?

JKS: *The Wise Little Hen* hard cover with dust jacket appeared in 1934 (and was reprinted in 1935), and it did feature Donald on the cover. He first appeared on *Mickey Mouse Magazine* on the front and back cover of volume 2, issue #5, which was a giveaway in March 1935. That was the second volume of the earlier, smaller series of *Mickey Mouse Magazine*, which were dairy giveaways. He also appeared on the Summer issue of the larger *Mickey Mouse Magazine* in 1935. He showed up in a self-titled linen book that summer. *The Wise Little Hen* was published as a linen book in 1937.

Grossett & Dunlap also published a Donald Duck book in 1936, which sold for 50¢. The standee promoting this book, the earliest known promotional item for a Donald book, recently sold in the Hake's Americana & Collectibles auction.

Walt Disney's Donald Duck, a no-number issue featuring Donald with a bubble pipe on the cover, was produced in 1938. The material included in it was reprinted from the Sunday strips from 1936-37. It included the October 17, 1937 strip with the appearances of Huey, Dewey & Louie, Donald's nephews, who were the children of Donald's unseen sister, Della.

Four Color Comics #4, and *Walt Disney's Comics & Stories #1*, which featured Donald on the cover, are fairly obvious choices as important developments in the comic book format in 1940 because they do reveal the character's increasing popularity and his importance to Disney at the time.

JCV: What do you think set the groundwork for Donald's success?

JKS: Mickey Mouse was already a staggering success by the time Donald arrived on the scene. In our current area, with its hyper media awareness, it might be difficult to fully put ourselves in the shoes of the people in 1928 and on into the Great Depression, but try to imagine it. Mickey debuted in 1928. The Depression hit at the end of '29 and it immediately created a serious need for cheap entertainment, for escapism. The timing is so providential that you might even call it "fate." Never before in so few years had a character moved so quickly into all the various categories of merchandise. Toys, food products, the cartoons themselves, you name it and Mickey Mouse was on it.

In 1935, Disney told *Time* that he was testing characters, looking for audience reaction to Donald and others, to see if they had staying power or appeal to the audience. Everything was being measured against Mickey's success.

JCV: It would seem that with that attitude perhaps Donald would have been held back a bit, like saying, "If you're not number one, why bother?" or something along those lines. Was that the case?

JKS: The simple answer is probably "yes." It makes sense, though. The Brownies had really pioneered licensing, and Felix the Cat would have been a relatively recent success in the minds of Disney's people, particularly Kay Kamen, who is the one who jump started the Disney licensing model. At one point, for instance, he had over 50 major department stores using Mickey as their Christmas theme for all of their toy departments. If there were that many major brand stores these days, can you imagine getting all of them to agree on something like that? So, yes, of course there was a lot invested in Mickey Mouse.

Donald, at least at first, was an unknown quantity. He's certainly something of an everyman, but here was Mickey with his plucky spirit and positive attitude, and he wasn't something that parents had to be concerned about their kids seeing.

Also, don't discount the importance of Mickey's momentum. In terms of dominance, the period of 1928 to 1938 was his golden age. The licensees wanted Mickey. The Mickey Mouse Club organization also really pumped up the demand for the character.

Donald's popularity did start to grow. As early as 1935, Donald was a balloon in Macy's parade, and 1936 saw the

Victor Young orchestra recording a hit dance tune about Donald (Decca disc 3285). It wasn't all smooth sailing once Donald got going in licensing, though. The 1939 Ingersoll pocket watch didn't sell well until an embossed Mickey was placed on the back of the watch, and the angry-faced Donald toys created by Fisher Price for toddlers as Easter toys in 1936 and 1937 didn't go over well either. It scared the kids and thereafter the toys featured the traditional happy face Donald.

JCV: To digress for moment, a lot of people, even serious collectors, might not know the name Kay Kamen and why he was so important. What should they know?

JKS: Well, there have been a number of great pieces written about Kamen, but his first big success was with products featuring the *Our Gang* characters. He also launched the Tim Club, which became the Superman-Tim Club later on, as a marketing effort for clothing manufacturers and retailers.

He teamed up with Walt Disney in what was truly an unprecedented move. On any licensing they did, Disney and Kamen split the first $100,000 in profits 60/40, respectively. Then everything else was split 50/50. Can you imagine how quickly he became a multi-millionaire? If you take The Brownies as a road map, he improved on that map and got Mickey Mouse and Disney characters about everywhere you would think to look. Unfortunately Kamen died in a plane crash in 1949.

JCV: What type of products?

JKS: In addition to toys, you had bread, milk, orange juice and other products. If you look at the history of successful marketing with characters, you'll find very often that the ones that have made it to the level of pop culture icon have been involved with the basics of milk, bread, beverages, candy, cereal or the other staples.

JCV: Going back to Donald specifically, when did he begin to emerge as an important character and why?

JKS: His personality had a lot to do with it, but again it's difficult to ignore the timing of his ascension at Disney. During World War II, Donald was the number one character on planes and patches worn by service men. Again, this goes back to his attitude. It's probably difficult for most people to imagine Mickey getting riled up enough to fight. Not so with Donald Duck. In fact, after Orphan's Benefit, it was pretty easy to visualize Donald getting mad concerning just about anything. His personality continued to emerge as feisty, even angry.

JCV: Donald also changed physically in a couple ways as the character evolved, didn't he?

JKS: Sure. Most serious collectors will spot the longer bill on the early Donald right away. It's a common way of identifying the earlier works even if one isn't familiar with the particular piece or story. What a lot of folks don't necessarily know, though, is that he didn't have hands right away. He used to have wings in place of hands. His appearance in *The Wise Little Hen* best illustrates this. Take a look and notice that Donald's *three* layers of feathers were what he used for fingers. He was given four-fingered hands in 1936. So, while his bill continued to be modified up until 1938, the end of 1935 was also the end of Donald's three-feathered-fingers. Orphan's Picnic (February 1936) was the first animated film where he consistently had four-fingered hands.

JCV: Donald's popularity continued to grow after the war, while other wartime niches like superheroes were on the decline. Why was that?

JKS: When the dads came home from the war, they had been instilled with a fairly strict sense of order. "Yes, sir," and "No, sir," was the call of the day. Much of the freedom we have today proceeds from the combined relative abundance of capital and free time and the immediacy of our media. In those days, rarely did those factors apply. Credit cards didn't exist yet. People just didn't buy things they couldn't afford. If you can imagine that, then it's not a big step to imagine that rebellion wasn't really tolerated. In a way, Donald represented something kids of the '40s and '50s couldn't get away with.

JCV: Any other factors?

JKS: In terms of storytelling, it's difficult to overstate the importance of Carl Barks. His work has had just about every positive adjective possible thrown at it, but maybe the best is "timeless." That's why so many of his stories can be reprinted today and still seem so fresh for new audiences. A great deal of credit goes to Another Rainbow and Bruce Hamilton for the wonderful job they did in reprinting and producing this material.

JCV: Did you discover Donald during that period?

JKS: Yes. I knew the character, of course, but I hadn't read any Donald Duck comics before "Sheriff of Bullet Valley," which was a great story in *Four Color #199*. Practically every kid I knew had cap guns and loved westerns, and here was a Donald Duck story with a western theme. It was a great fit. And I can still remember so vividly, almost impossibly so, the feeling I had when it looked like Donald had been shot in that issue. You had to turn the page to find out the bullets bounced of his badge, but I remember almost not being able to turn it because I thought they had killed him…

JCV: And that story came out in 1948?

JKS: Yes, and I was five years old.

JCV: What was the next step for you?

JKS: In 1950, the first time I ever sold and bought back issue comics, I found a store that sold old comics for 5¢ and bought them for 2¢. I saw comics I had never seen before, characters I vaguely recognized or didn't know. They had a *Superman #6*, for instance. I picked up *Four Color #62*, the "Frozen Gold" story, which had come out in 1945. I also took in 65 comics and got $1.30 for them. I was seven years old then and I had never made that much money on my own. I really liked that feeling.

JCV: Where did your Donald Duck collecting go from there?

JKS: July 14, 1974 I went to the Wheaton Armory Comic Book Convention in Silver Spring, Maryland. I met two dealers who were set up there, Walt Zimmerli and Steve Geppi. They both loved Disney comics and in particular the work of Carl Barks. I talked to Walt first, but he got busy with customers and I ended up talking to Steve. I told him that "Frozen Gold" was a book I wouldn't mind investing in. He said he thought he could come up with one. The following Thursday he had two of them for me. I picked them up on Friday and told him that was enough for the moment...but I started collecting comics seriously from that point.

JCV: As someone who was there, how did you see the back issue market developing back then?

JKS: By the mid-70s, at least 10 of the top 100 books featured Donald on the cover or in the stories. These included *Four Color #4*, *Four Color #9*, *Four Color #29*, *Walt Disney's Comics & Stories #1*, the Kite Giveaway, *March of Comics #4*, *March of Comics #20*, *March of Comics #41*, *Black & White #16*, and *Black & White #20*. I would also say that the "Bubble Pipe" feature book comic was probably just off the edge of that list.

With the high profile focus on superhero comics these days, and with a quarter century more of comics added to the mix, it's a testament to the power of the Disney characters that *Four Color #4* and *Walt Disney's Comics & Stories #1* are still in the Top 100 comics today. As the awareness of their history continues to increase, it would not be at all surprising to see some of the others work their way back onto the list as well.

JCV: Were the other areas of comic character collectibles keeping up with comics during this time?

JKS: Yes, Hake's Americana & Collectibles was already established in the business and experienced collector-dealers such as Malcom Willits, Harry Matetsky, Howard Bayliss, Russ Cochran, Bruce Hamilton, Leonard Brown, Richard Olson, Rex Miller, Jim Harmon, Bill Campbell, Jack Melcher and Don Phelps were already calling attention to radio, movie and newspaper memorabilia. Remember, though, the collectors who loved comics best could really concentrate on them because they were very affordable compared to today's prices.

JCV: As someone who has devoted a lot of effort to collecting this character, is it fun to play a part in bringing him back into the comic book world now that Gemstone is publishing the Disney comics?

JKS: It's great, and all the credit for that goes to Steve Geppi. For a long time now he's seen the decline in the number of comics suitable for children as a real problem not just for the moment, but for the future of our business and our hobby. *Happy Anniversary, Donald!*

Carl Barks wrote and illustrated "Sheriff of Bullet Valley," which originally appeared in Four Color #199, published in 1948. You had to turn the page to find out that Donald's badge saved him from an untimely death. (These panels are reprinted from The Carl Barks Library of Donald Duck Adventures in Color #9.)

GOING

THE BEST C

GREEN: THE HULK

BY ARNOLD T. BLUMBERG

The monstrous man-brute known as the Incredible Hulk has been leaping around the American southwest (and elsewhere) for over forty years now, and that covers a lot of territory. A newcomer to the gamma-spawned saga – someone who first encountered the Hulk via the new issues written by Bruce Jones, or who discovered the green gargantuan through the somewhat disappointing would-be-blockbuster 2003 film, The Hulk – would be hard-pressed to know just where to begin catching up with four decades of smashing, "thooming," and green-skinned adventuring. Worry not, O Fledgling Hulk-o-phile! We've assembled a brief overview of some of the best and most significant story arcs in Hulk history, and pretty soon you too will know everything there is to know about gamma bombs, grotesque villains, and gorgeous girlfriends from the tumultuous life of that misunderstood monster, the Incredible Hulk!

Tales to Astonish era (1965-1968, *TTA* #70-101) – True, the Hulk's adventures began with *Incredible Hulk* #1-6 in 1962-63, but the first truly distinct, mythos-building era for the character commenced with the cancellation of his own floundering title and his installation as a feature in this anthology series. During this run, which shared real estate with a Sub-Mariner solo series, the Hulk's speech patterns and behavior began to normalize…at least in terms of what later fans might consider 'normal' for ol' Greenskin. The formulaic pursuit of General Thunderbolt

RATHER, IT IS A PAIR OF MIGHTY GREEN PAWS--
--FOLLOWED CLOSELY BY THE MOST INCREDIBLE MAN-MONSTER OF ALL!

Ross and his Hulk-busting military team also really appeared here for the first time, as did recurring adversary (and rival for Betty's affections) Major Glenn Talbot. The Leader and the Abomination, two other gamma-spawned creatures who are to this day the Hulk's greatest foes, also debuted in *Tales to Astonish* and began long and fruitful careers plaguing the behemoth for countless issues to come. The popularity of the Hulk's adventures was proven beyond a shadow of a doubt when the series expanded to fill the entire title and *Tales to Astonish* transformed, as if caught in its own gamma explosion, into the new incarnation of *The Incredible Hulk* with issue #102.

The Herb Trimpe Years (1968-1975, *Incredible Hulk* #106-193) – The first major era of the character to be more clearly delineated by a dominant artistic style more than an editorial direction, the years in which the Hulk was illustrated by Herb Trimpe also represent the first long-term stability for the title. Trimpe's Neanderthal design for the Rampaging One, with his low brow and incredibly expansive upper lip region, lent a certain child-like pathos to the Hulk that was supported by a number of contemplative tales as well as the usual high-octane action adventure arcs. Trimpe had lent his talents to Hulk stories in *TTA*, but here his contribution reached its creative apex. One of the high points of this period was undoubtedly 1971's "The Brute That Shouted Love at the Heart of the Atom" (*Incredible Hulk* #140), a tale specially scribed by author Harlan Ellison that saw the introduction of the Hulk's sub-microscopic love interest, Princess Jarella. Trimpe's run was incredibly (heh) long, seeing the Hulk through his earliest days in his own title through the historic introduction of Wolverine in *Incredible Hulk* #181 and beyond. And then came…

The Sal Buscema Years (1975-1985, *Incredible Hulk* #194-309) – This is the second major era of the Hulk's career that is characterized more by the primary artist than the individual writers. Who knew that anyone would be able to trump Trimpe when it came to delineating the Green One's rampaging romps? But along came Sal Buscema, and for many his slavering, mop-topped Savage Hulk is the definitive incarnation. For years during Buscema's tenure, the stories were often run-of-the-mill, but the classic "Hulk smash!" dialogue and fist-shaking theatrics carried readers through and cemented Buscema's take on the character. Late in his run, Buscema was given the opportunity to push that visualization even further when the Hulk was left a mindless animal, bereft of Banner's inner guidance. Banished to the Crossroads, the *Truly* Savage Hulk embarked on a series of surreal alien escapades. While an intriguing footnote in Hulk history, the Crossroads saga is more significant for its insights into the Jade Giant's psyche than for any actual plotline offered during the arc, and it was during this very unusual time in the series that Buscema departed. Some years later, Buscema

would briefly return to the character, but his more recent effort is a mere footnote compared to the body of work generated in this substantial run.

The Peter David Era (1987-1998, *Inc. Hulk* #331-#467) – This is a bit of a cheat, since Peter David's historic run on the title really counts as several eras in one when you consider how many format-shattering changes David instituted in his long years on the series. From the Mr. Fixit period through to the "intelligent Hulk" saga, David's work on the Hulk may be second only to Lee and Kirby for sheer character development and mythos-building power. Drawing on all of the confusing elements at play in those first formative issues from the early 1960s, David reconciled all of the inconsistencies by crafting story arcs that only served to deepen and expand the psychological underpinnings of the character. Perhaps the high point of the era was the "Pantheon" saga, which definitely polarized fan opinion but provided the "intelligent Hulk" with a base of operations and a team that often exhibited more problems than they solved. During David's tenure (which actually began with a stand-alone scripting gig in #328), the series went from an almost forgotten part of the Marvel line-up to one of the most popular titles in the company's stable. Unfortunately, the end of David's run is marred by a series of publisher-mandated crossover events that hampered his ability to tell cohesive stories, but he still managed to craft a stunning concluding chapter to his version(s) of the Hulk in issue #467. For many fans of this run, that issue serves as a satisfying capper to the Hulk saga as a whole...but of course there was a lot more to come.

The Bruce Jones era (2002-Present, *Hulk* #34-Present): This latest arc, typified by suspense and shadowy intrigue instead of showy superheroism, centers on Banner's flight from a secret organization that has designs on the Hulk's blood. Throw in a mystery concerning the Hulk's alleged murder of a small boy and you have one of the darkest and arguably most emotionally charged storylines in the series' history. With undead secret agents, a Hulk-powered Bruce Banner, and a strange romantic liason between Banner and the wife of a long-time Hulk foe, Jones has crafted a strange but enthralling storyline that takes the series down a very different road – and that's saying something. In fact, it's an era we're tempted to call atypical of the Hulk, but that's not entirely fair since the entire series – to say nothing of the Hulk himself – has been in a near constant state of metamorphosis since Stan and Jack first tried to puzzle out what they were going to do with the brute in 1962. As such, we recommend you think of this as just another intriguing variation on a theme. At press-time the mystery surrounding the identities of all parties and the ultimate fate of Bruce Banner was still deepening.

And there you have it. So now that you've immersed yourself in Hulk lore, it's time to get outside and soak in some gamma rays – they give you that healthy green glow!

(JOE)

He created or co-created Captain America, Boys' Ranch, Fighting American, the Newsboy Legion, Manhunter, Boy Commandos, and the Fly. He edited for Fox, Harvey, and Crestwood, and served as publisher of Mainline Publications and* Sick *Magazine. He was the first editor-in-chief of Marvel Comics' predecessor, Timely.

During his long career, he worked for Timely, DC, Harvey, Archie, and others, and he played a key role in the launch of many different genres in comic book form. He played in the fields of superheroes, westerns, and he practically gave birth to romance comics. Most recently, Joe Simon contributed the Shazam cover featuring the original Captain Marvel for one of the Direct Market editions of this book – a re-creation of his own work on Special Edition Comics *#1.*

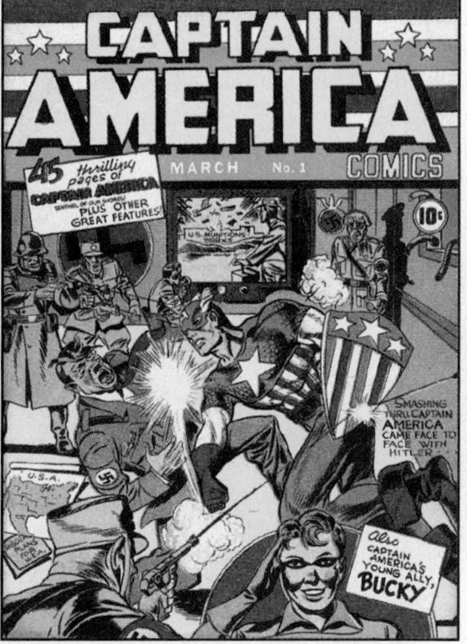

In 1939, Joe Simon made the leap from newspaper illustration to the fledgling comics industry, taking a free-lance assignment for Lloyd Jacquet's production studio, Funnies, Inc. During his stint there, he illustrated and wrote stories for Centaur, Novelty, and Fox Publications. A short time later, he pitched the idea for Captain America to Timely publisher Martin Goodman, setting the groundwork for many of his successes that followed.

The first thing that strikes many younger fans, though – even those who remember the Silver Age first-hand and who are now only young at heart – is that there was another "and Kirby" team who revolutionized the comic book field long before "Lee & Kirby" re-shaped the medium in the 1960s.

And make no mistake; the mark Simon made is indelible.

On his own or along with Jack Kirby, he created *Stuntman, Boy Explorers*, and *Boys' Ranch* for Harvey Publications, *The Fly* for Archie Comics, and *Fighting American, Bulls Eye*, and the entire romance genre for Prize Publications, besides editing for Timely, Fox, and Harvey. It is no overstatement to suggest his work influenced the subsequent generation of comic book creators – and collectors.

"I grew up on the Boy Commandos and the Newsboy Legion. They taught me to be the street urchin I am today!" says noted author Harlan Ellison. "I love Joe Simon."

"I think of Joe Simon as one of the all-time greats, one of the giants upon whose shoulders we stand," says former Marvel editor-in-chief Jim Shooter. "Not only was he a creative powerhouse who had a tremendous influence on the field, establishing visual storytelling conventions that all comics creators observe to this day, but he taught Jack Kirby a great deal of his craft. What else need be said?"

It's not that Simon himself or Simon & Kirby together had success all the time ("*Red Raven* was one of the worst things we ever put out," Simon told author and comics historian Will Murray a few years ago in *Comic Book Marketplace*), but that their overall rate of success remains staggering.

While they were working on Captain America at Timely, Simon and Kirby received a call from Fawcett, the home of Captain Marvel.

"Timely was on 42nd Street, about a block away from Fawcett," says Simon. "Fawcett was in the Paramount Building. They had a couple editors there who were new with the firm – John Beardsley and Eddie Herrin – and they called me and asked it we could come down there."

"Al Allard was the art director at Fawcett," Simon continues. "He was a real Hollywood type – the haircut, the suit, the tie, everything. He was in a class above us. He was the art director of the whole Fawcett line including the slick magazines. We were the bottom of the totem poll, but Jack Kirby and I were very well respected because we had one of the big hits at the time."

Fawcett, of course, had its own big hit with Captain Marvel.

"It was beautifully done and completely different than our style," says Simon. "Their style was more cartoonish. C.C. Beck

SIMON SAYS . . .

BY J.C. VAUGHN

was doing it. He was terrific, and we loved the character."

The Fawcett team asked Simon and Kirby if they could do an issue of the character.

"One of the reasons they called us was that we could get the stuff out quickly. We were really professional at that business ...unlike a lot of guys who would play with the drawing and show up two weeks late," Simon laughs. "That went on all the time."

Simon adds that the duo had to devise the script as well as illustrate the book, and they had to do it on their own time since they were working for publisher Martin Goodman at Timely during the day.

"We rented a hotel room," he says. "We just stayed there for several days. I forget exactly, but I think it was less than a week. We worked and worked. During the day we went and worked on Captain America and we worked on Captain Marvel at night."

Simon said that attorneys in the Captain America case asked him last year whether he felt it was fair to Martin Goodman that he and Kirby were working on Captain Marvel at night.

"I told them I didn't think it was any of his business what we did after hours," he laughs.

After the short hotel stay, they turned in their assignment.

"I didn't think we did very well with it, but they liked it and the book did very well. Our style was much more sketchy," he says. "I like both a lot, though."

The cover, of course, became a classic. Simon says that surprised him, but he enjoys the fact that people still like it and love the chance to revisit it.

"Re-creating is something a lot of us artists from the old days can't handle too well. We were used to working on a 10- or 12-inch board, sitting at our slanted drawing tables, with T-squares, compasses and everything else. It's easier to get into a lot of detail working like that," he laughs.

SPECIAL EDITION
NUMBER ONE
COMICS
64 PAGES—NEW ADVENTURES OF
CAPTAIN MARVEL
10¢
Featuring
Brand-New Stories of
CAPTAIN MARVEL
World's Mightiest Man

"The guys who had originally been painters or had some background in painting did a lot better than the cartoon guys because they were accustomed to working on easels, standing back and seeing the bigger work areas, making corrections, using smaller brushes, and everything that goes along with that," he adds. "I think re-creation is a little art by itself. I liked it, and I liked doing it. The re-creation I did had a lot of acrylic in it, and that's a brilliant color you can't get with washes."

He said that he and his colleagues never imagined the prices the re-creations or the originals would go for today.

"If we had imagined that, we would have saved some of the artwork! Nobody wanted to take the artwork home. They mopped the floor and we'd put the art boards down and walk on them. I never expected there to be any field like this."

He said he enjoys the reactions people have to re-creations.

"I love the impression they make," Simon says. "It has nothing to do with how old you are. They look at them and go, 'Wow!' They're a hell of a lot more spectacular than the originals and the color holds up for a long time. On the original sketch I did of Captain America, we used Dr. Martin's dyes, and that stuff fades, but these acrylics last much longer. I haven't seen any of them turn bad."

Joe Simon and his son Jim have recently re-issued The Comic Book Makers, *an autobiographical look at the early days of the industry and Joe's career. It is published by Vanguard.*

As seen above, Joe Simon painstakingly re-created the classic cover to Special Edition Comics *#1, featuring Captain Marvel astride a hurtling bomb. This indelible historic image from the Golden Age, pictured in its original comic book form on the previous page, is seen here completely unaltered. This painted*

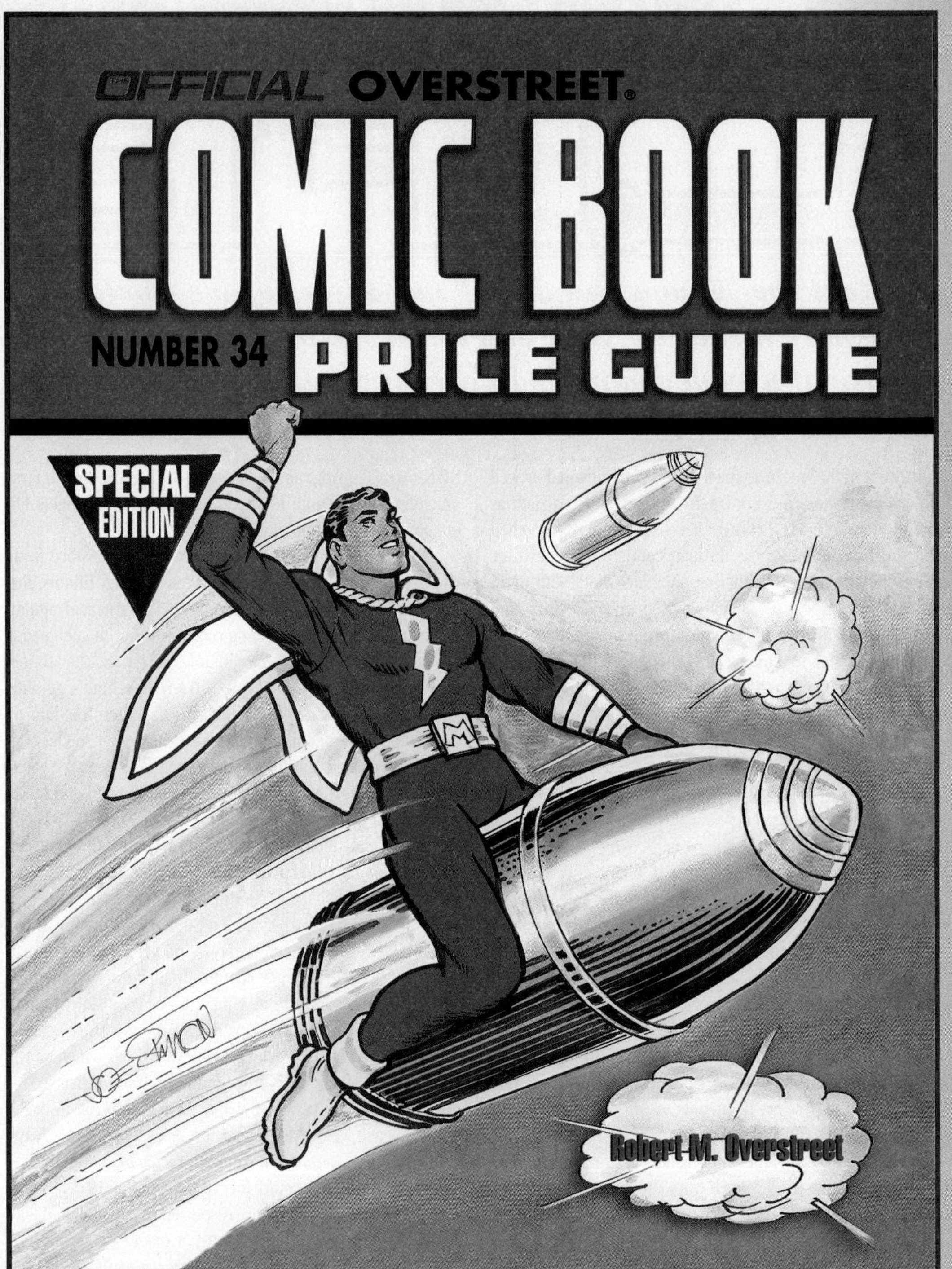

re-creation was then reworked to make it suitable for our own use as one of the direct market edition covers of this very guide. Above, we present the final version of the re-creation as seen on the cover of The Overstreet Comic Book Price Guide #34.

COMIC BOO[K] LIFE[...]

Now that the "gloom and doom" nay-sayers of the comic book world have turned to "grow and thrive" choir-preachers, there is a sense of urgency more than ever regarding charity services and their impact on the comic book industry at large.

The advent of the Internet, specifically eBay; personal as well as dealer websites; and third party grading services such as Comics Guaranty, LLC. (CGC), has brought unprecedented gains in disposable income through comic book sales over the past few years. Remembering the adage that "With Great Power Comes Great Responsibility," many collectors and dealers have joined forces with non-profit organizations that protect the First Amendment rights of creators, furnish a solid foundation from which to build basic English skills, and offer financial support to creators in their golden years.

It is important to note that not only industry giants are engaged in the support of these companies, but also regular people from all walks of life, many of whom have no interest in comic books. These people are interested in the effects of these groups and are willing to help them achieve their respected goals. Even in the leanest of times, a well-placed donation can make a world of difference. The intent of this article is to introduce all *Guide* readers to the non-profit charities of the comic book industry.

A non-profit/not-for-profit company, as defined by the *Sunrise Dictionary of Business & Finance Terms*, is "an organization that is generally intended to provide socially desirable services and that does not realize a profit, financed by taxes and/or contributions from constituents, and said contributions may be tax-deductible within certain limits." It is recommended that you check with your financial advisor before committing to a donation to such an organization. The three companies covered here are: The Comic Book Legal Defense Fund (CBLDF), Comics4Kids (C4K), and A Commitment To Our Roots (ACTOR). Most of the information here is culled from their websites and promotional materials, all of which is readily available to the public.

The Comic Book Legal Defense Fund (CBLDF)

Founded in 1986 by Denis Kitchen (Kitchen Sink Press), The Comic Book Legal Defense Fund is the Foxy Grandpa of the comic book non-profit world. It is a federally recognized I.R.S. 501 © 3 program, dedicated to the preservation of First Amendment (Freedom of Speech and Expression) rights for creators and comic book retailers as well.

Originally formed to defend Friendly Frank's store from charges of selling "obscene comics" in Lansing, Illinois, the CBLDF maintained its presence to protect others from similar unfair persecution. Maintaining relationships with such peers as The American Civil Liberties Union (ACLU) and the Motion Picture Association of America (MPAA), the fund's guiding principle is that comic books deserve the same freedom of expression accorded in film, literature, and other media.

The popularly distributed newsletter, *Busted*, is the voice of the CBLDF. It reports that they have coordinated and funded the legal defense of more than a dozen First Amendment cases, including those involving adults selling adult comics to other adults, cartoons poking fun at corporation logos, and restrictions of intellectual freedom on the Internet.

The CBLDF has many noted supporters, among them Frank Miller, Neil Gaiman, Jimmy Palmiotti, Amanda Conner, and Penn & Teller. So many people, too numerous to mention here, are generous with their time, money, and talent, contributing specially produced products such as T-shirts, comic books, and other merchandise. The CBLDF also maintain a presence at virtually every show in the convention season.

"Without the CBLDF, we would have absolutely no organized defense against the rising forces of oppression," says Chuck Rozanski of Mile High Comics, recipient of the CBLDF's Defender of Liberty Award for 2003. The Fund's Executive Director, Charles Brownstein (respected personality and staple at all major shows), elaborates in one of his company's newsletters that "comic books are approaching the front lines of America's cultural dialogue…and the Fund stands firm as the fields' most ardent advocate and its best line of defense."

Membership levels range from $25 (Member) to $1,000 (Angel), and all who donate receive an exclusive CBLDF member card featuring art by Jim Lee as well as a four-issue subscription to *Busted*.

CHARITIES:

LINES OF THE INDUSTRY

By Dale Moore (Comics4Kids)

Find out more at **www.cbldf.org**. Be sure to swim around their comprehensive site and read all the features, including a fascinating timeline of comic book case history.

Comics4Kids (C4K)

"I would never have been interested in reading," says Ron Lowy, an attorney in Miami Florida. "I would never have been able to become a lawyer without comic books as an influence."

Comics4Kids distributes donated comic books to children and other persons free of charge in order to promote literacy, capitalizing on the morality plays and wholesome images of Comics Code Authority-approved comics. Donated comic books are screened by the C4K staff and distributed accordingly. Those books found not suitable for kids are traded or sold to cover collection/overstock purchases, as well as transportation and advertising costs. Operating independently for years, the company became incorporated in the year 2000, its 501 © 3 recognition pending at press time. However, donors may use the I.R.S. 8283-Non Cash Charitable Contribution form if they so choose when donating comic books.

I saw the need for this service and understood that comic books are the number one contribution to literate society today. Like Lowy, hundreds of thousands of children saw the action in comic books and became curious as to what language drove the characters to respond to each other, forming interaction through dialogue. That curiosity led to learning, and the result is amazing. With multimedia at a fever pitch,

Dale Moore, President of Comics4Kids.org (with friend), is a vocal advocate of the power of comics.

even three-year olds know who Spider-Man and Batman are. They are the modern Pecos Bills and Paul Bunyans of the world (and Stan Lee is the Walt Disney of the 21st century).

An unexpected benefit of the program is that people learning English as a second language are using donated comic books to help them with learning the nuances and slang as presented in the pages of the comics. There is increasing awareness of the comic book industry crossing all ethnic boundaries.

Furthermore, hoping to follow Joe Field's Free Comic Book Day(s) success, in which publishers provided free comics to stores in anticipation of introducing new titles to customers and attracting new store clients, C4K wants to get millions of free comic books to kids everywhere, not just those who frequent shops. Fire departments, hospitals, public schools, libraries, and even orphanages are recipients of C4K-donated books, and the demand is growing every day.

We'd like to do more than just encourage kids to go to a comic store and spend Mom and Dad's money. We want to enable children everywhere to improve their English skills and at the same time stimulate their imagination. After all, these children may become the future law writers of the world.

Comic book luminaries such as Mitch O'Connell, Howard Greber, O'Leary's Books, Investment Collectibles, and Gary Barnes have helped C4K amass and distribute over 100,000 comics. The company hopes to receive more cash contributions to offset the overwhelming costs of ad space and show presentations. Eventually, C4K would like to produce its own comic book for free distribution, showcasing other non-profits as public service announcements, like the Meningitis Foundation and Chris Farley Foundation.

Visit the Comics4Kids web site at **www.comics4kids.org** for more information, and donate books now to Comics4Kids, P.O. Box 3977 Sarasota, Fl. 34230.

A Commitment To Our Roots (ACTOR)

Established in 2001, ACTOR is an association of CrossGen Entertainment, Dark Horse Comics, Marvel Comics, and *Wizard* Magazine. The company is dedicated to helping older comic creators in need. These creators worked during a time when salaries and benefits were low, and now in retirement they have been degraded to a sub-standard quality of life. ACTOR distributes donated monies to these persons, allowing them to live free of worry.

In the top-notch promotional material distributed by ACTOR, President Jim McLauchlin says the program is "loosely based on Major League Baseball's 'Baseball Assistance Program' (BAT), whose premise is that many players, coaches, and other personalities had worked in MLB.....for low pay and a non-existent pension plan, and that this parallel exists today in comics. Most Golden and Silver Age creators toiled to build today's industry, working only for page rate with no chance of ownership and no pension. ACTOR hopes to be a safety net for these creators, to whom today's comics owe so much."

ACTOR has two Boards of Directors. The Executive/Fund Raising Board features McLauchlin, Mark Alessi and Brian Pulido of CrossGen Entertainment, Joe Quesada of Marvel Comics, and Mike Richardson of Dark Horse Comics. The Fund Disbursement Board consists of George Perez, Roy Thomas, Dick Giordano, Joe Kubert, Dennis O'Neil, and John Romita Sr.

Jim McLauchlin of ACTOR, A Commitment To Our Roots

Raising over $100,000 so far, the company is a major presence at all trade shows and industry events. Miramax Films, Sony Corporation, Paul Dini, Alex Ross, and Kevin Smith are among the voluminous contributors to this worthy cause. ACTOR is an I.R.S. 501 © 3 recognized company.

To make a donation, send checks to ACTOR, 11301 Olympic Boulevard #587, Los Angeles, CA 90064.

Conclusion

A 'who's who' of comic book professionals have given their time, money, and comic books to these charities, including Steve Borock, Gemma Adel, Scott Talmadge, Korey Hall, and Paul Litch of CGC. Even the CGC website chat room members, led by David Matteini, raised over $1,100 for all three companies, starting with its DAM60 1st Annual CGC Forum Philanthropy Drive in 2003.

"Our industry has some wonderful charity organizations," says Litch. "I have been a supporter and member of CBLDF since 1998. I always try to buy something from them at any show. They are on the front lines, protecting this industry from censorship by defending our First Amendment rights. Comics4Kids is an amazing charity that I have happily donated over 600 comic books to, in order to help children learn how to read. By using comic books to help children learn to read, we are not only benefiting their education and boosting their self-esteem, we are adding to the next generation of fandom."

"ACTOR is another inspiring charity that provides financial aide for veteran comic book creators when they need it. It is our chance to give something back to the people who have inspired so many of us. I always try to bid generously during the art auction at Megacon. I have also had the opportunity to work with ACTOR through CGC in order to put together a wonderful CGC/ACTOR Signature Series signing last year at Wizard World Chicago with Mark Bagley."

It behooves all of us as comic book fans to consider making a donation to these charities. The great power and great responsibility are ours, and the time to act is now.

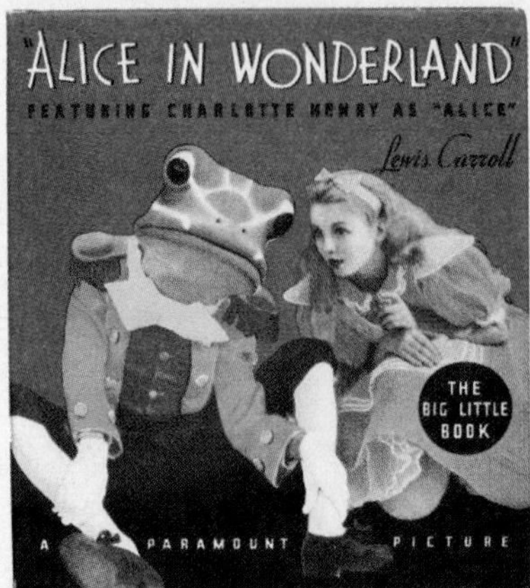

ALICE IN WONDERLAND
BLB #759 - 1933. © WDC

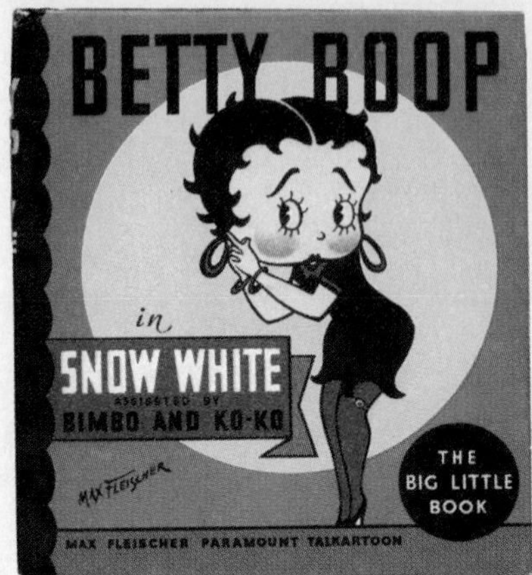

BETTY BOOP IN SNOW WHITE
BLB #1119 - 1934. © Paramount

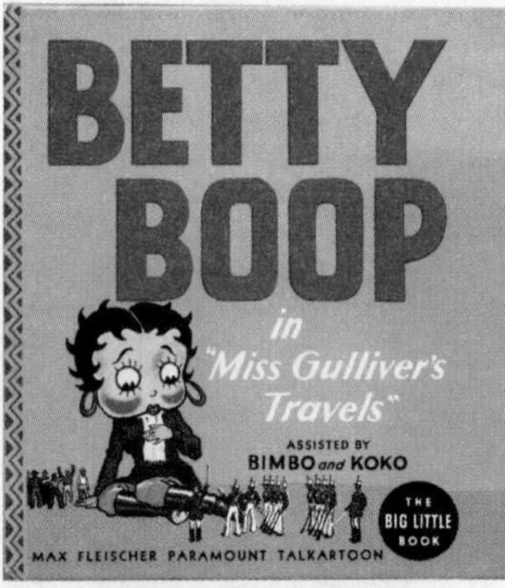

BETTY BOOP IN
"MISS GULLIVER'S TRAVELS"
BLB #1158 - 1935. © Paramount

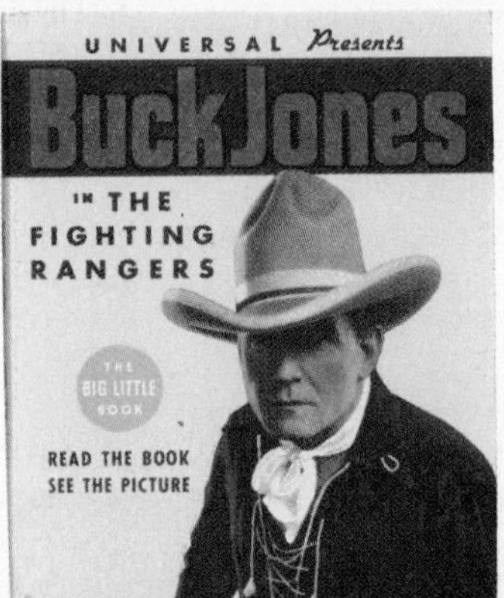

BUCK JONES IN
THE FIGHTING RANGERS
BLB #1188 - 1936. © Universal

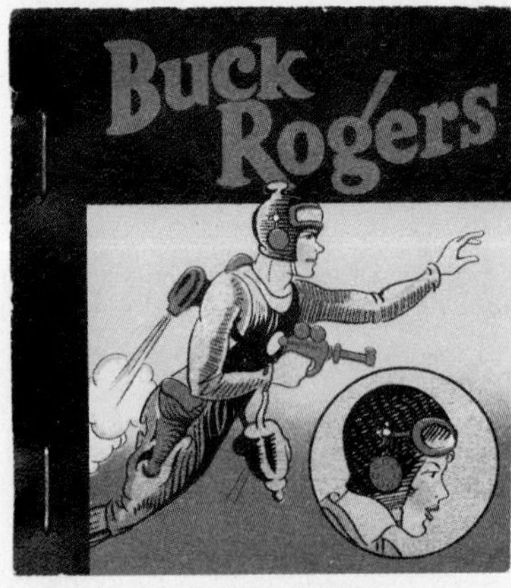

BUCK ROGERS
1935. Tarzan Ice Cream premium. © UFS

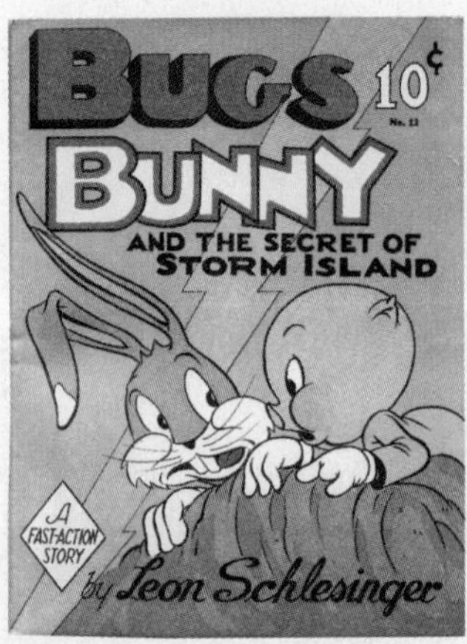

BUGS BUNNY AND THE SECRET
OF STORM ISLAND
Fast Action Story #13 - 1942. © WB

DICK TRACY
AND THE
FROZEN BULLET MURDERS
Fast Action Story #9 - 1941.
© NYNS

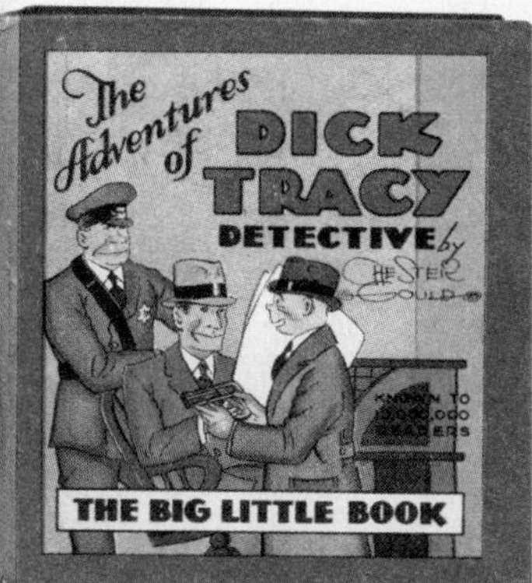

DICK TRACY,
THE ADVENTURES OF
BLB #W-707 - 1933.
The first Big Little Book.
© NYNS

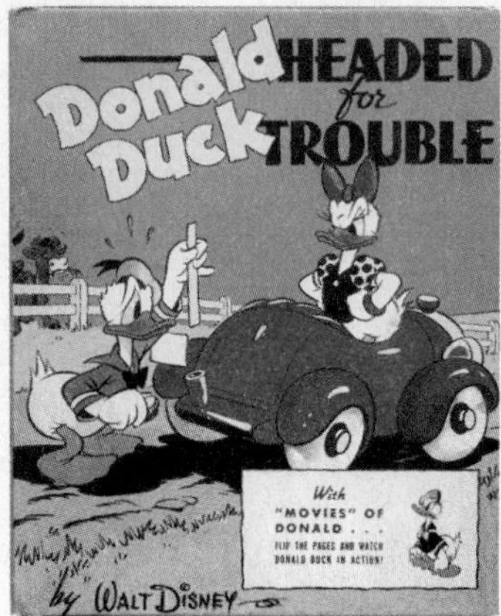

DONALD DUCK
HEADED FOR TROUBLE
BLB #1430 - 1942. © WDC

FELIX THE CAT
All Pictures Comics #1439 - 1943. © KING

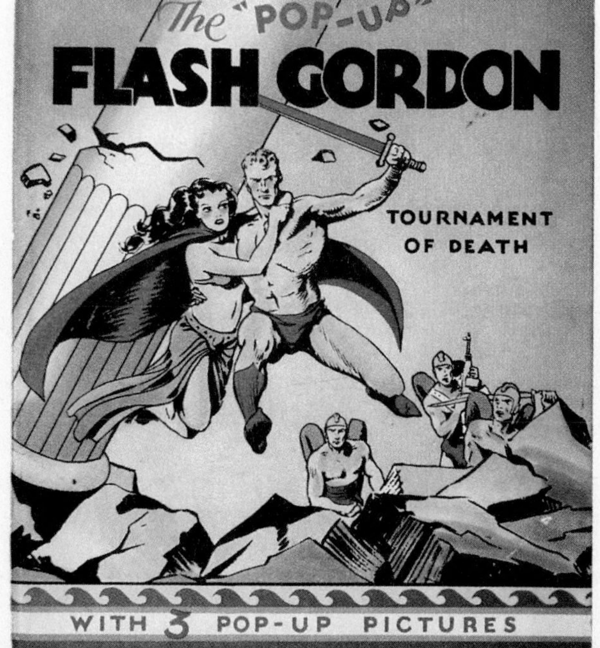

THE "POP-UP" FLASH GORDON
TOURNAMENT OF DEATH
Pop-Up #210 - 1935. © KING

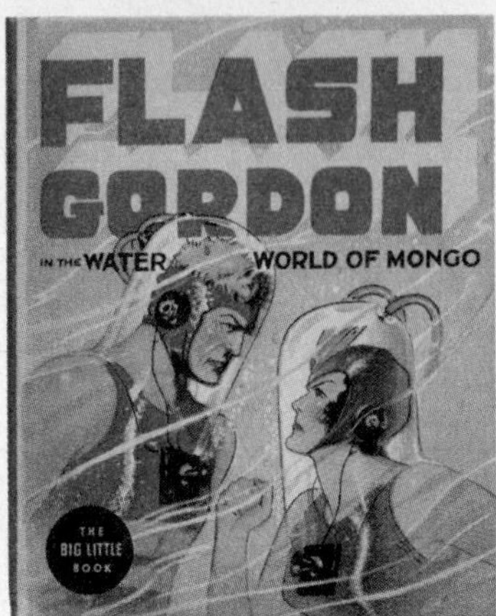

FLASH GORDON IN THE
WATER WORLD OF MONGO
1937. © KING

GANG BUSTERS
AND THE RADIO CLUES
Penny Book - 1938. © WHIT

GENE AUTRY IN
LAW OF THE RANGE
BLB #1483 - 1939. © Gene Autry

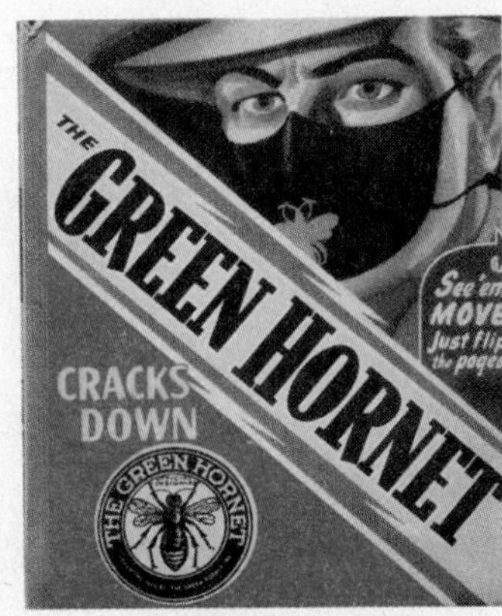

THE GREEN HORNET
CRACKS DOWN
BLB #1480 - 1942. © WHIT

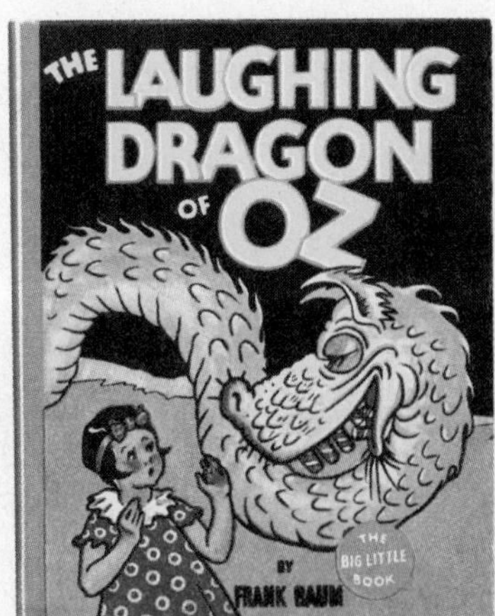

THE LAUGHING DRAGON OF OZ
BLB #1126 - 1934. © WHIT

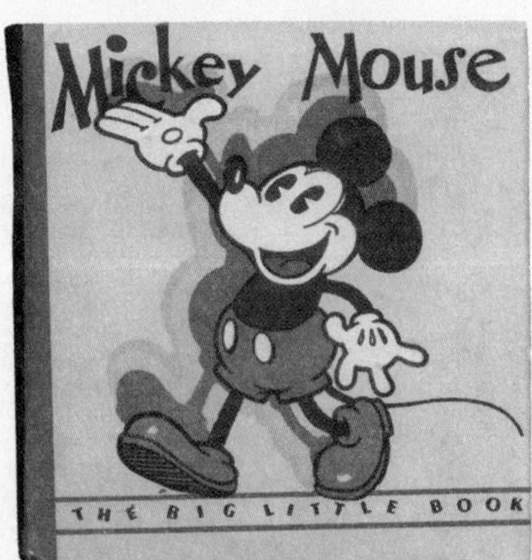

MICKEY MOUSE
BLB #717 - 1933.
The first Mickey Mouse BLB. © WDC

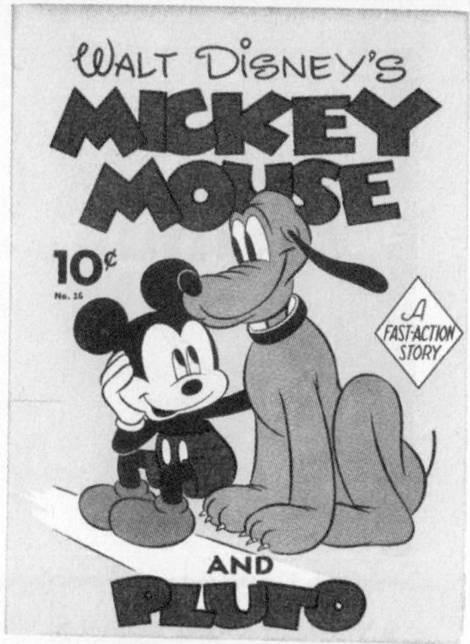

MICKEY MOUSE AND PLUTO
Fast Action Story #16 - 1942. © WDC

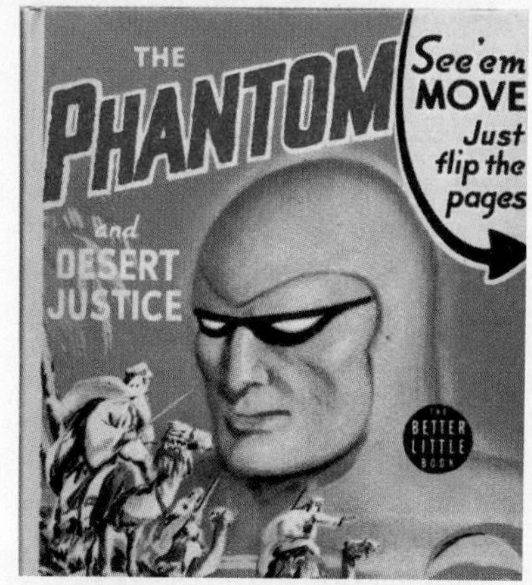

THE PHANTOM AND DESERT JUSTICE
BLB #1421 - 1941. © KING

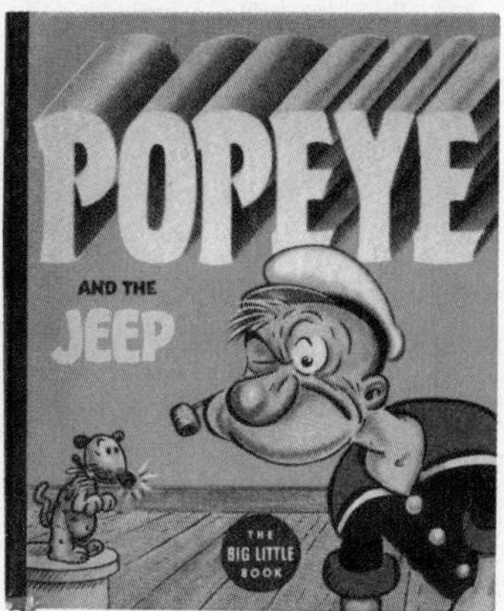

POPEYE AND THE JEEP
BLB #1405 - 1937. © KING

SMILIN' JACK
Penny Book - 1938. © WHIT

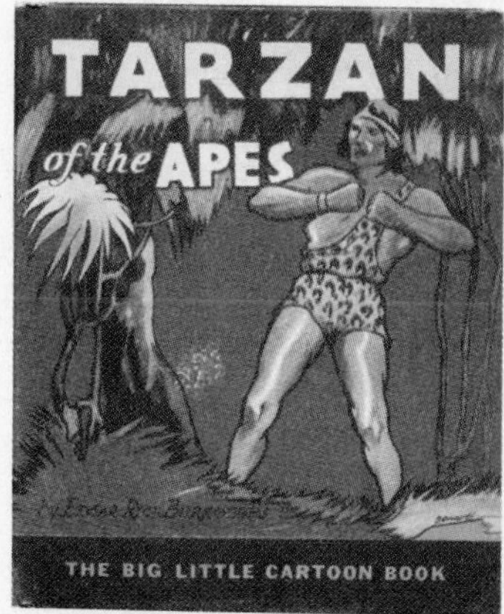

TARZAN OF THE APES
BLB #744 - 1933. © ERB

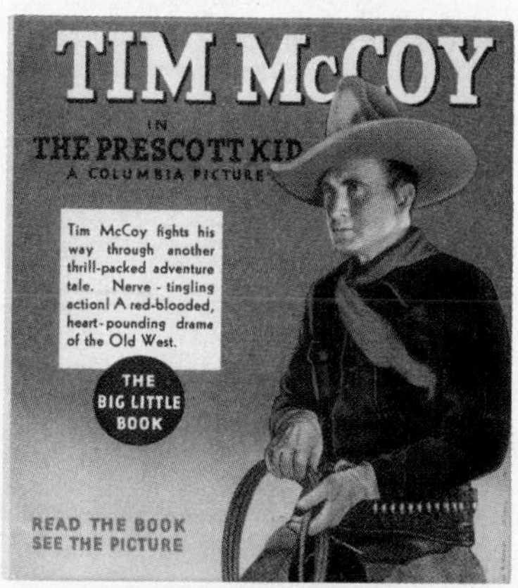

TIM McCOY IN THE
PRESCOTT KID
BLB #1152 - 1935. © WHIT

THE ADVENTURES OF
MR. OBADIAH OLDBUCK
1870s reprint of 1849 2nd printing.
© Dick & Fitzgerald, New York

BOB SCULLY, THE TWO-FISTED
HICK DETECTIVE
No date (1933).
© Humor Publ. Co.

BARKER'S "KOMIC" PICTURE SOUVENIR
Part I c.1901. © Barker, Moore & Mein Medicine Co.

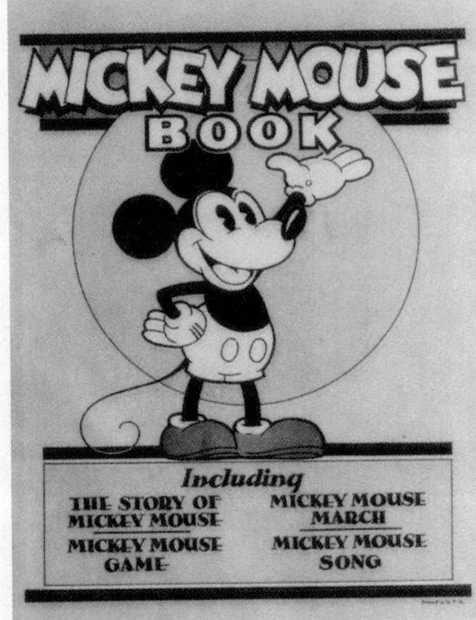

MICKEY MOUSE BOOK
1930 - 1931. © WDC

HANS UND FRITZ
1917. © Saalfield Publishing Co.

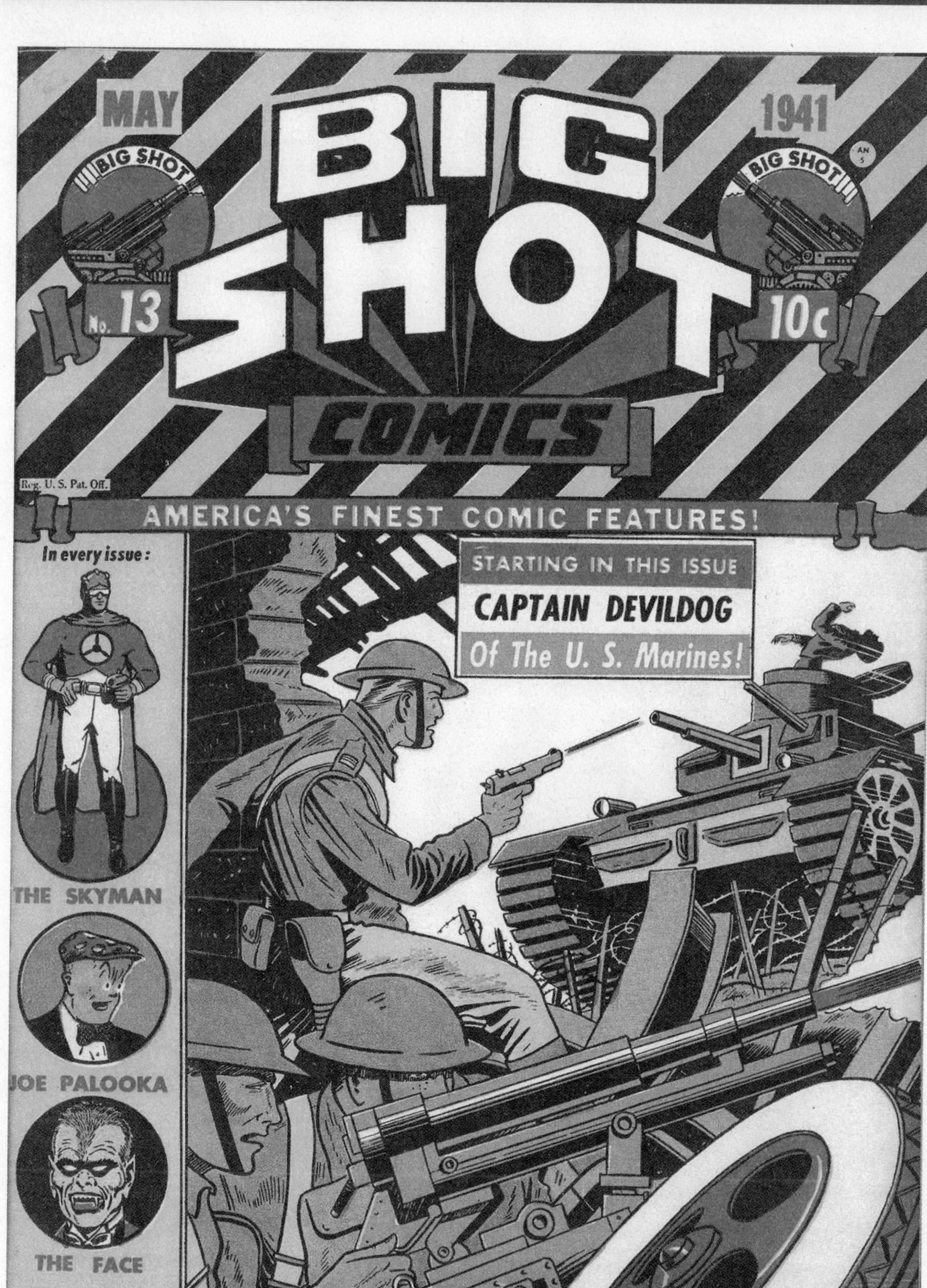

BIG SHOT COMICS #13
May 1941. From the Rockford collection. © CCG

CLASSIC COMICS #12
June 1943. First printing. © GIL

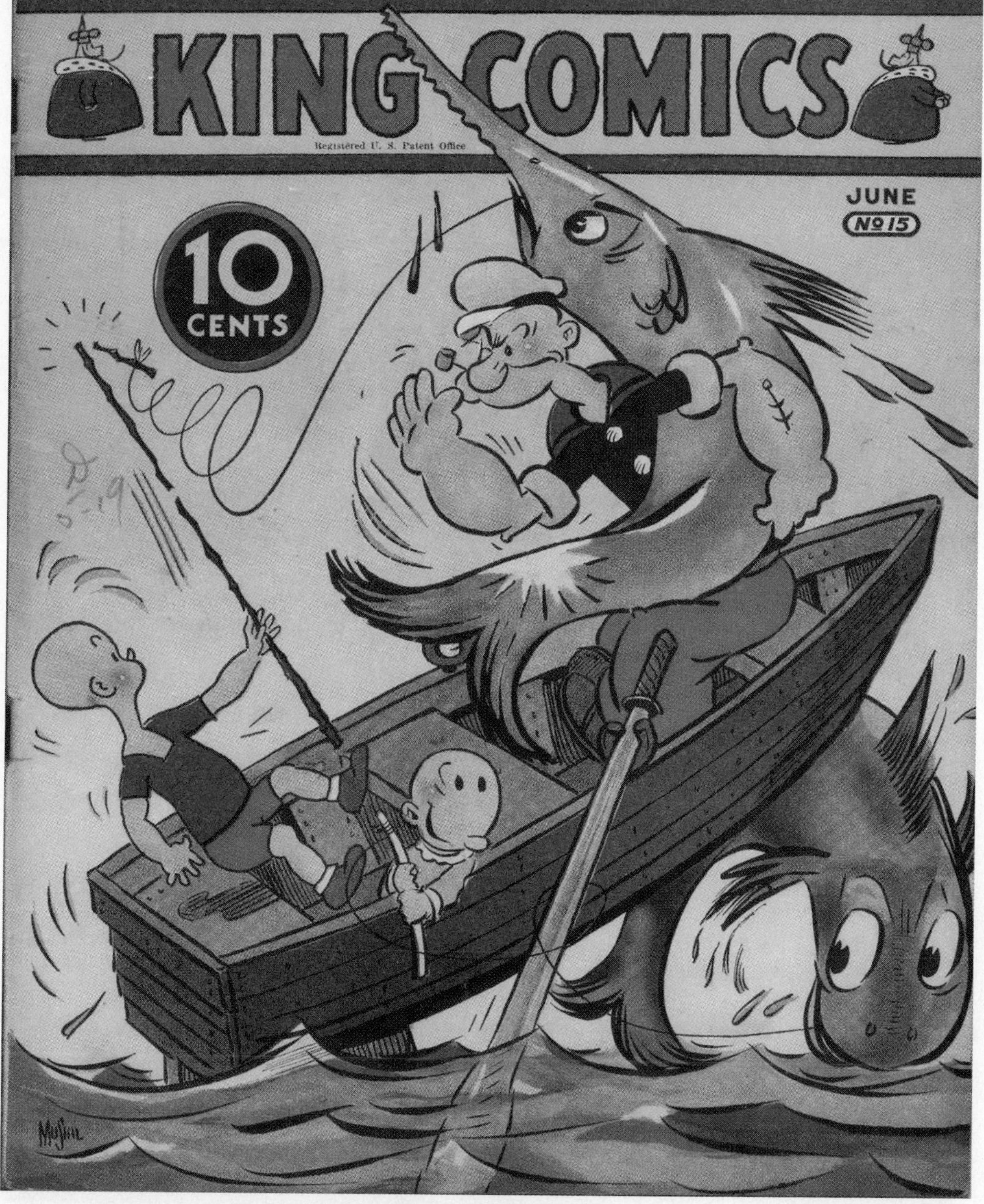

KING COMICS #15
June 1937. From the Mile High collection. © DMP

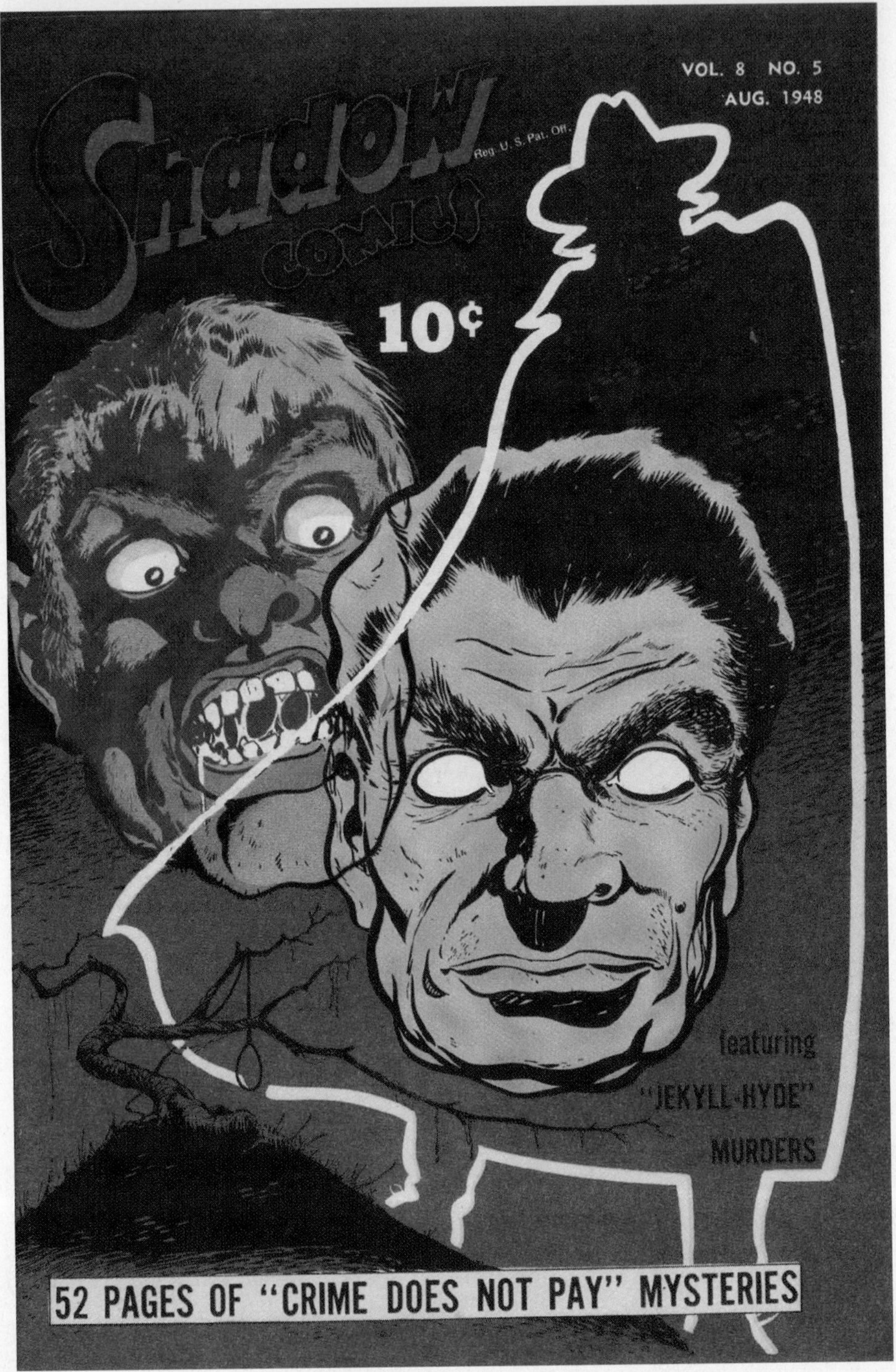

SHADOW COMICS V8 #5
August 1948. © CN

WALT DISNEY'S COMICS & STORIES #2
November 1940. © WDC

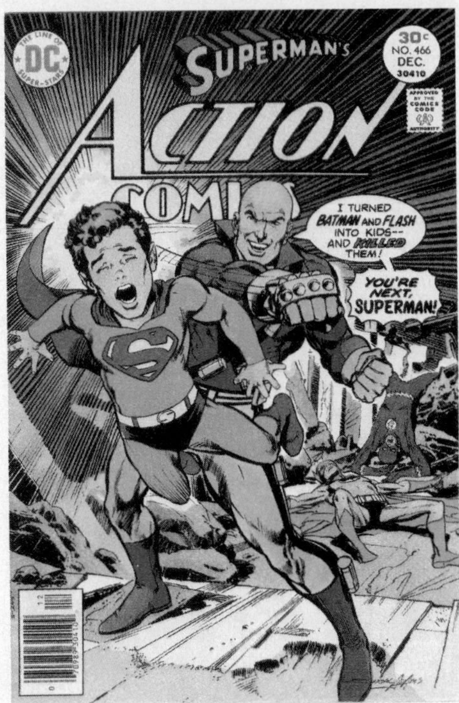

ACTION COMICS #466
December 1976. Neal Adams cover. © DC

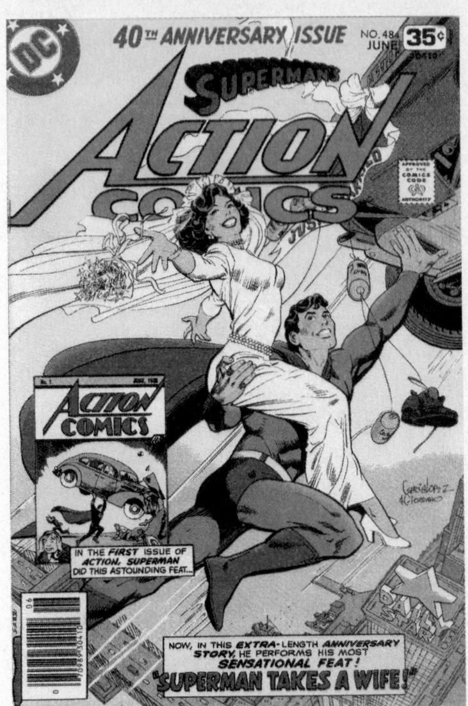

ACTION COMICS #484
June 1978. Superman of Earth-Two marries Lois Lane. © DC

ADVENTURE COMICS #462
March-April 1979. The death of The Batman of Earth-Two. © DC

ALL-STAR COMICS #17
June-July 1943. © DC

ALL-STAR COMICS #65
March-April 1977. Wally Wood cover. © DC

AMAZING SPIDER-MAN #1
March 1963. Stan Lee file copy. © MAR

AMAZING SPIDER-MAN #3
July 1963. First appearance of Doctor Octopus. © MAR

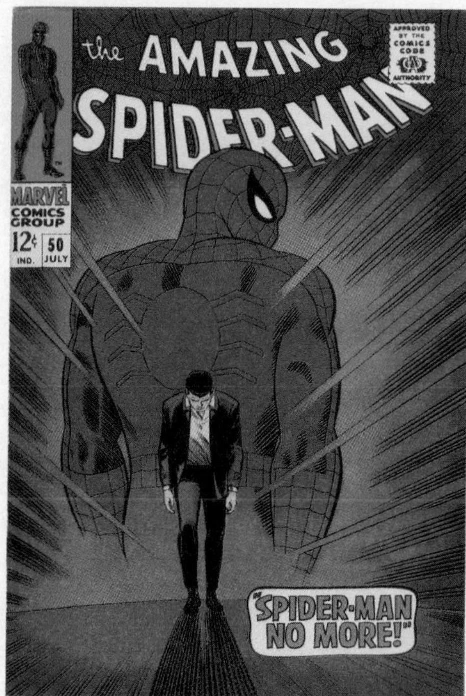

AMAZING SPIDER-MAN #50
July 1967. © MAR

AMAZING SPIDER-MAN ANNUAL #6
November 1969. © MAR

AMERICA'S BEST TV COMICS
1967. © ABC TV, Ltd.

AQUAMAN #40
August 1968. © DC

THE ATOM #7
July 1963. First Atom-Hawkman team-up. © DC

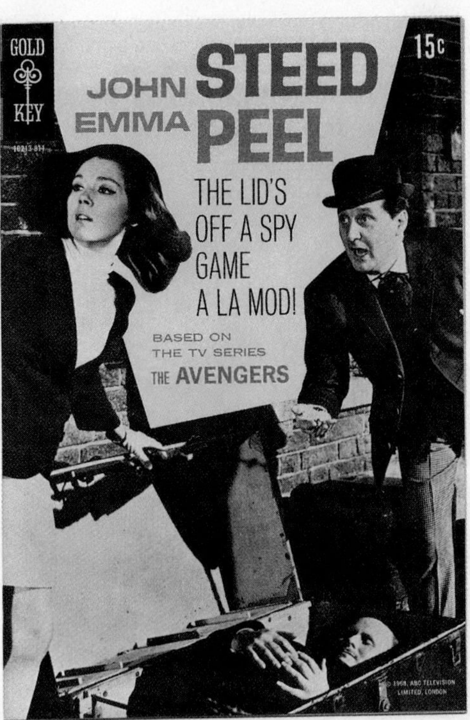

THE AVENGERS #1
November 1968. © ABC TV, Ltd.

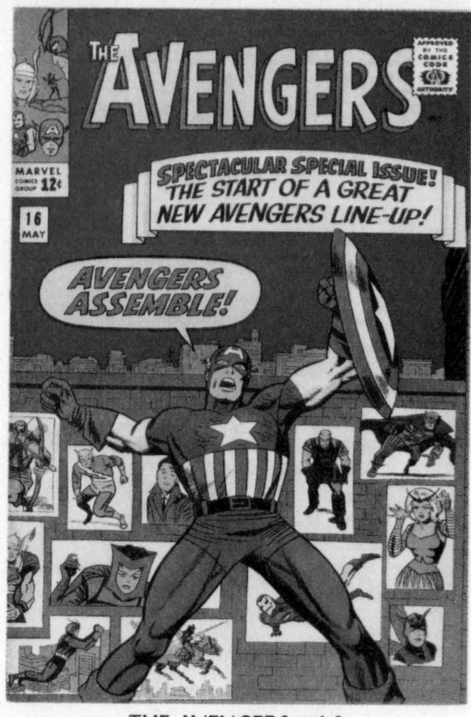

THE AVENGERS #16
May 1965. © MAR

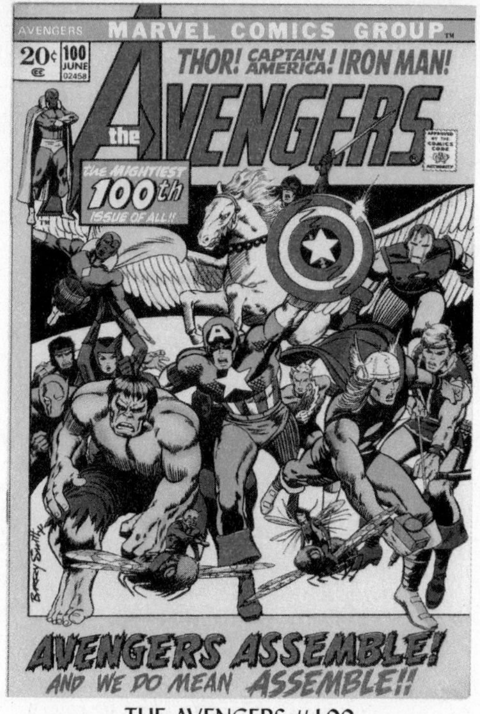

THE AVENGERS #100
June 1972. © MAR

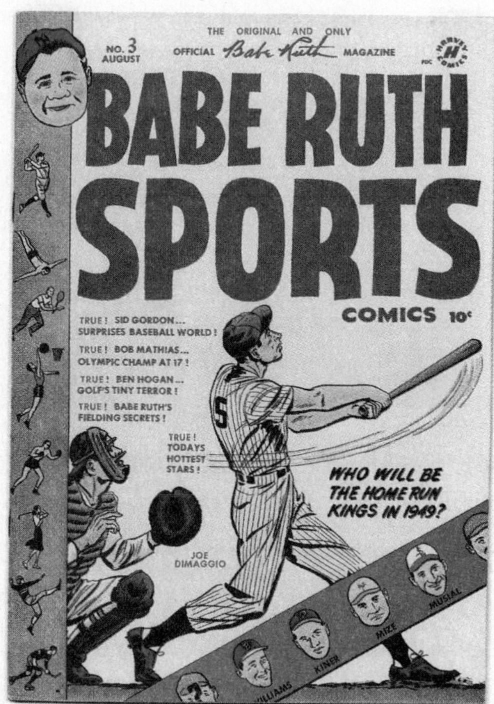

BABE RUTH SPORTS #3
August 1949. © HARV

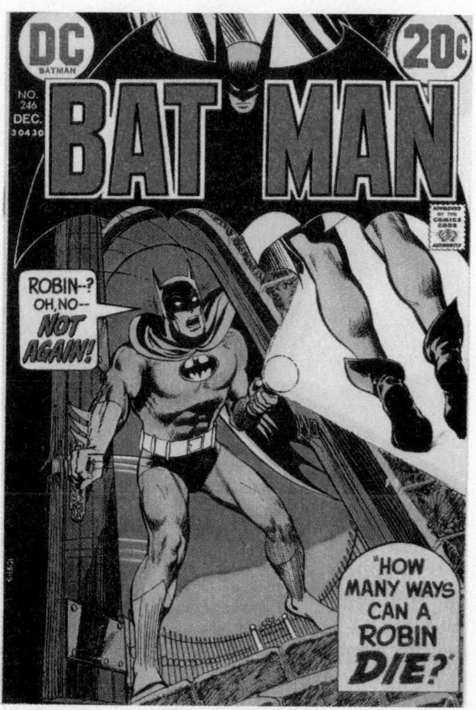

BATMAN #246
December 1972. © DC

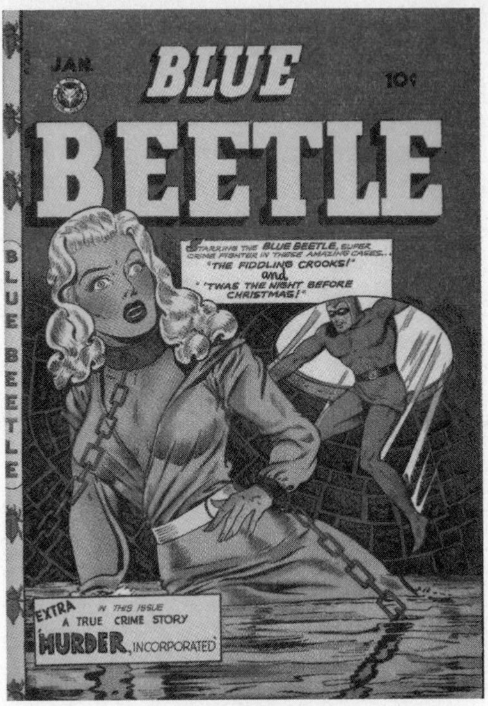

BLUE BEETLE #52
January 1948. Jack Kamen cover. © FOX

THE BRAVE AND THE BOLD #1
August-September 1955. © DC

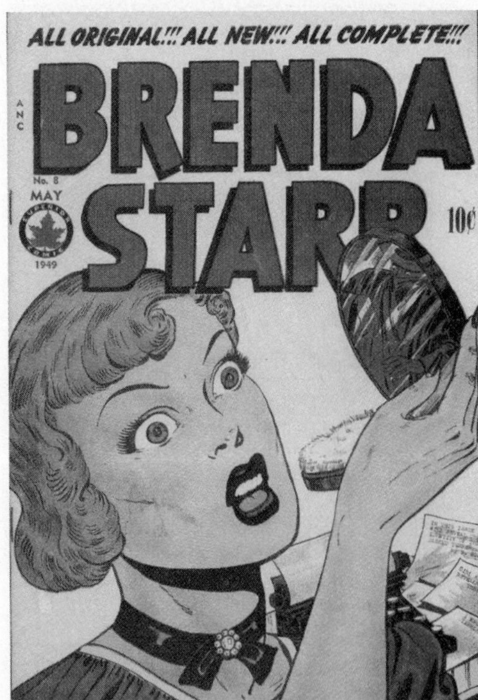

BRENDA STARR VOL. 2 #8
May 1949. From the Mile High collection. © SUPR

CAPTAIN ACTION #1
October-November 1968. © DC

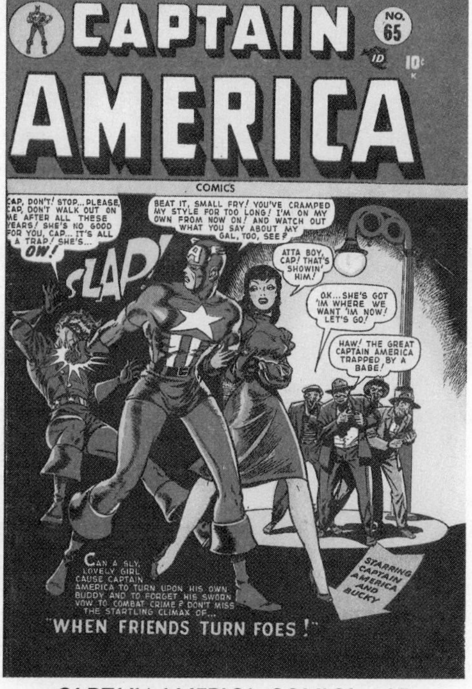

CAPTAIN AMERICA COMICS #65
January 1948. © MAR

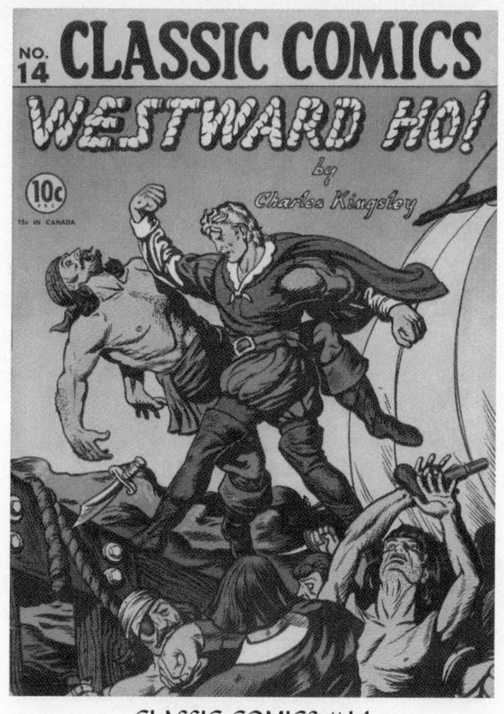

CLASSIC COMICS #14
September 1943. © GIL

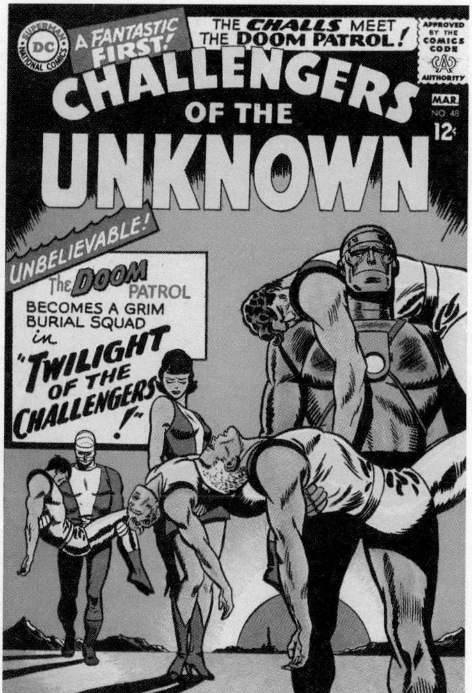

CHALLENGERS OF THE UNKNOWN #48
March 1966. First crossover with the Doom Patrol.
© DC

THE DOOM PATROL #102
March 1966. First crossover with the Challengers of the Unknown. © DC

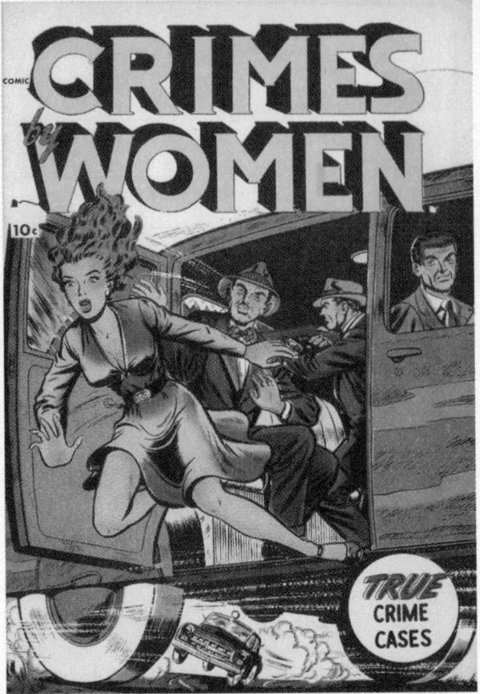

CRIMES BY WOMEN #54
1954. © M.S. Pub.

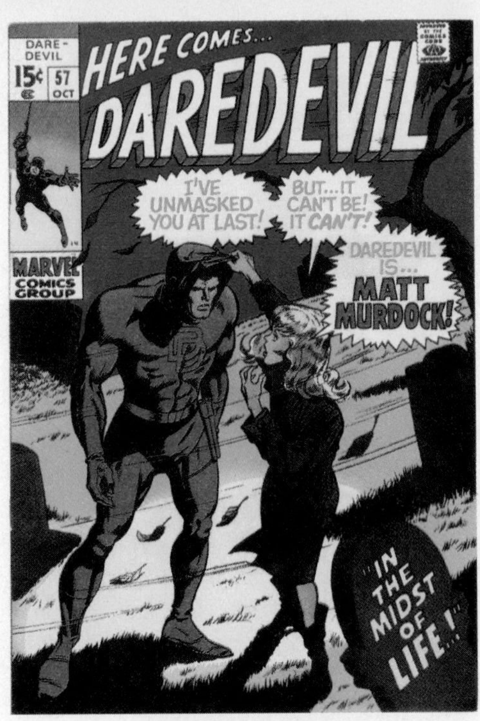

DAREDEVIL #57
October 1969. © MAR

DETECTIVE COMICS #225
November 1955. Debut of the Martian Manhunter.
© DC

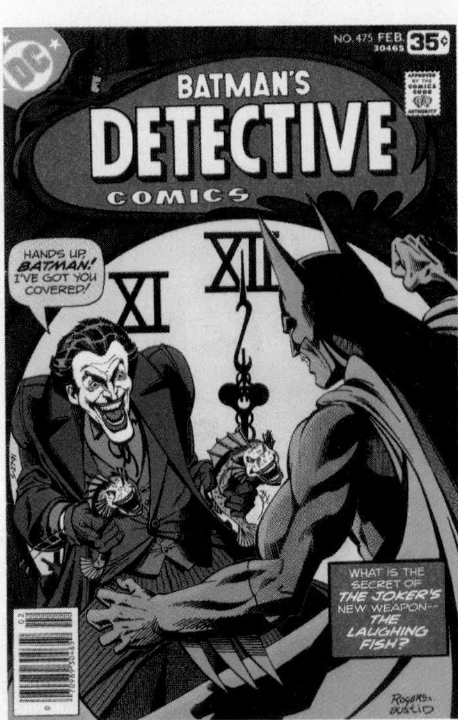

DETECTIVE COMICS #475
February 1978. © DC

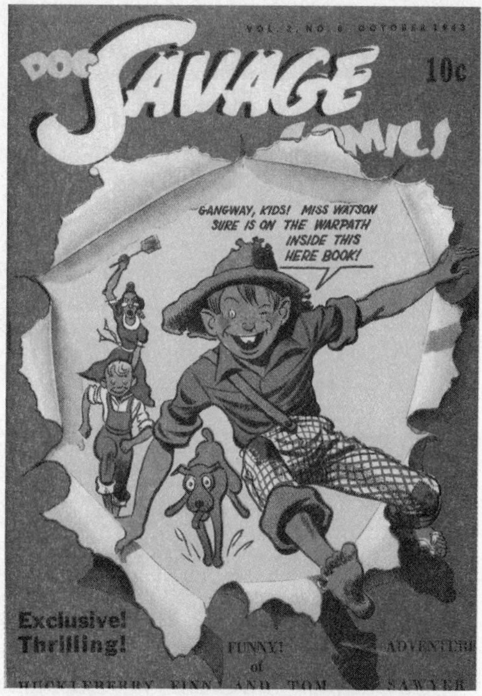

DOC SAVAGE COMICS VOL. 2 #8
October 1943. From the Mile High collection. © CN

DOCTOR STRANGE #169
June 1968. © MAR

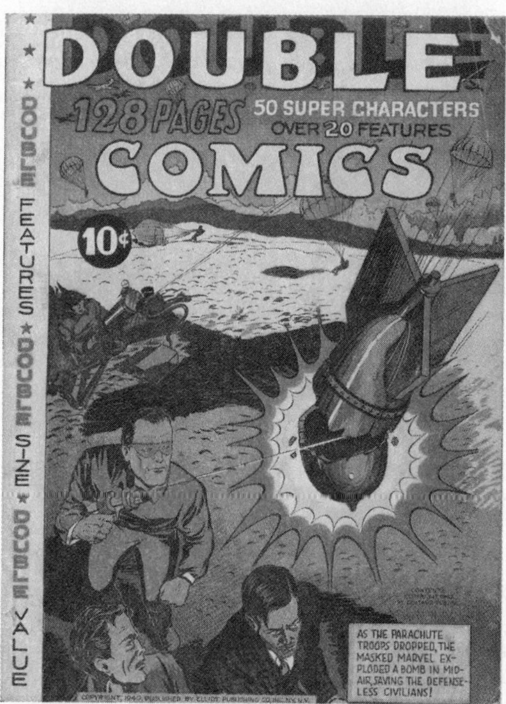

DOUBLE COMICS
1940. © Elliot Publ.

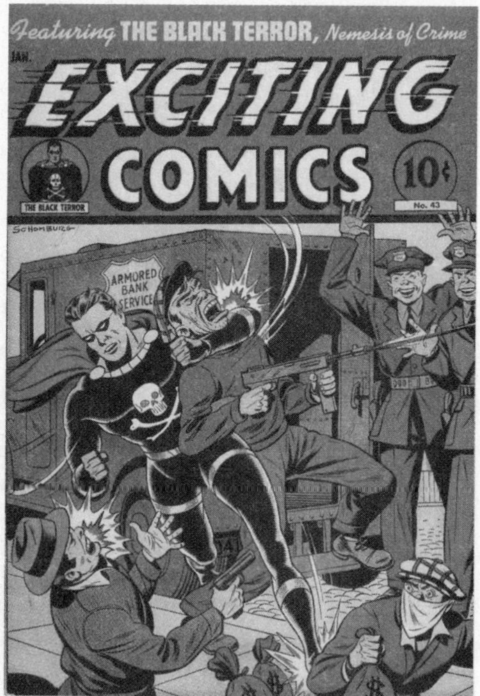

EXCITING COMICS #43
January 1946. © Nedor

G A L L E R Y

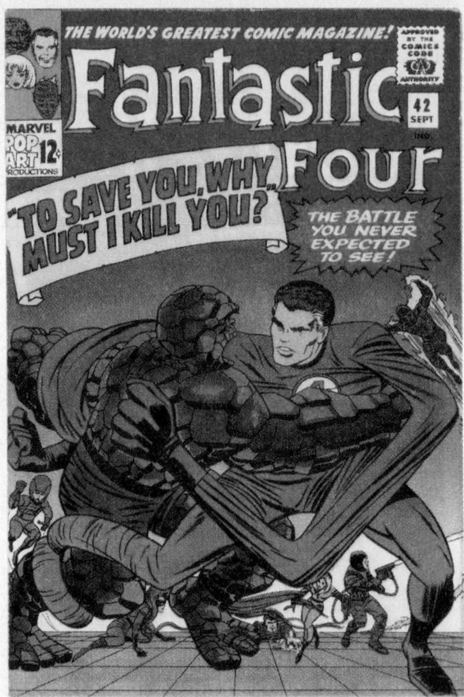

FANTASTIC FOUR #42
September 1965. © MAR

FANTASTIC FOUR #112
July 1971. © MAR

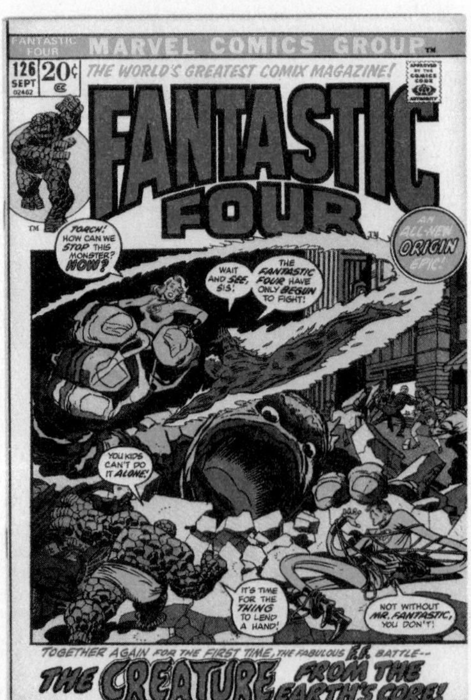

FANTASTIC FOUR #126
September 1972. © MAR

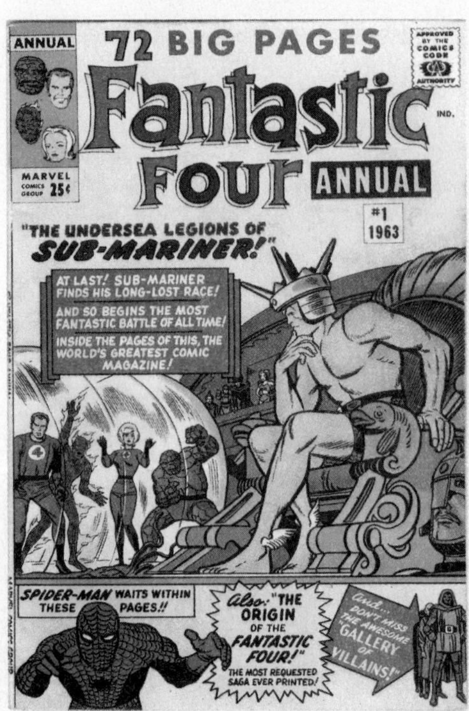

FANTASTIC FOUR ANNUAL #1
1963. © MAR

FIRESTORM #1
March 1978. © DC

THE FLASH #203
February 1971. © DC

THE FLASH #233
May 1975. © DC

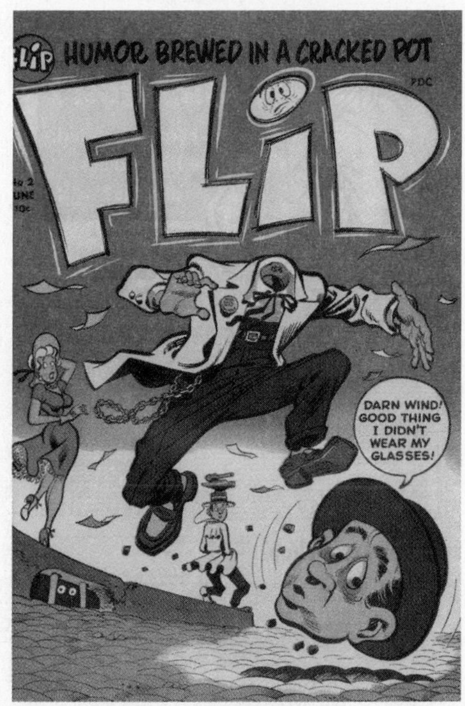

FLIP #2
June 1954. © HARV

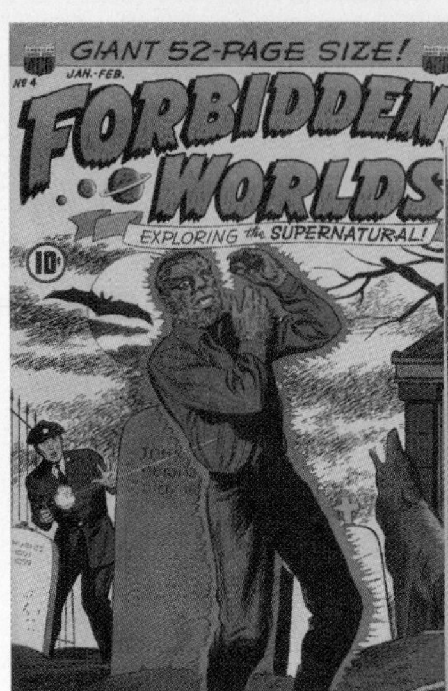

FORBIDDEN WORLDS #4
January-February 1952.
© ACG

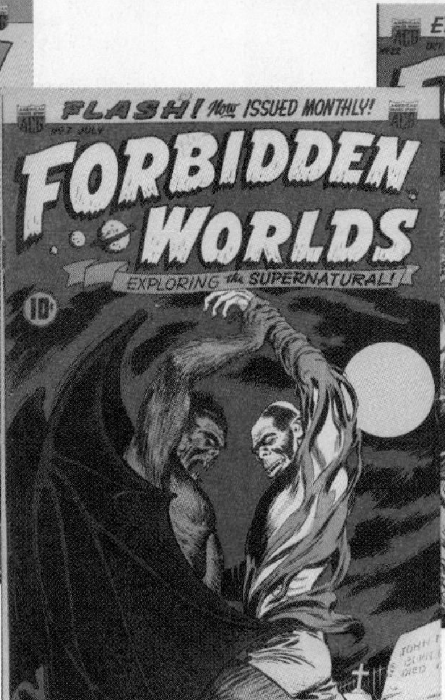

FORBIDDEN WORLDS #7
July 1952. From the Mile High collection.
© ACG

FORBIDDEN WORLDS #22
October 1953. From the
Big Apple collection. © ACG

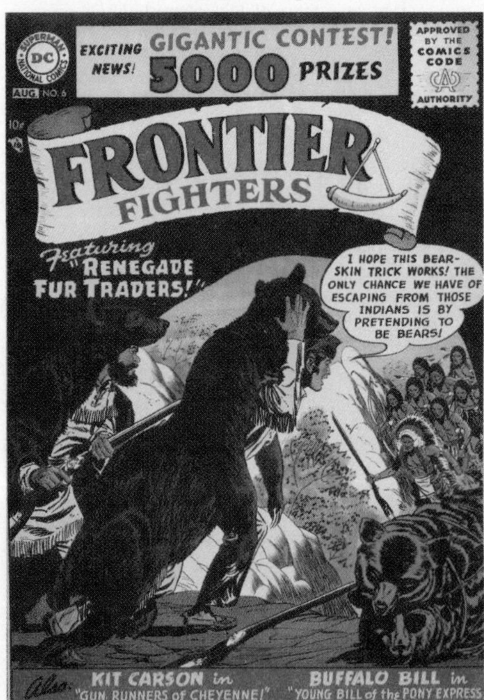

FRONTIER FIGHTERS #6
July-August 1956. © DC

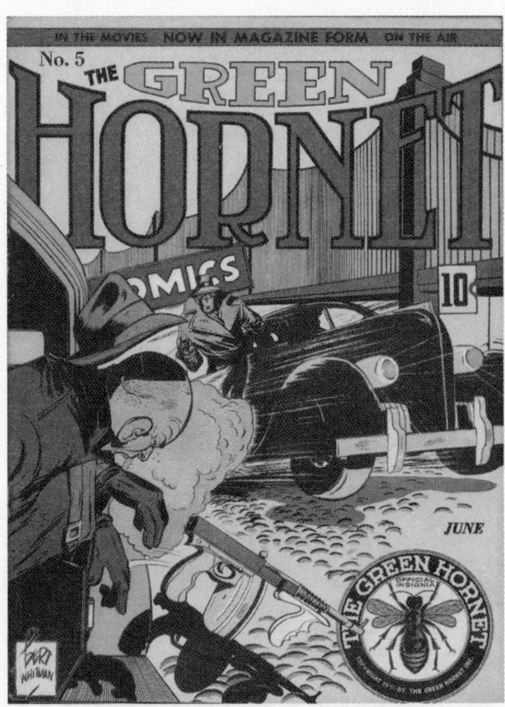

GREEN HORNET COMICS #5
June 1941. © HARV

GREEN LANTERN #68
April 1969. © DC

GREEN LANTERN #87
December 1971- January 1972.
First appearance of John Stewart. © DC

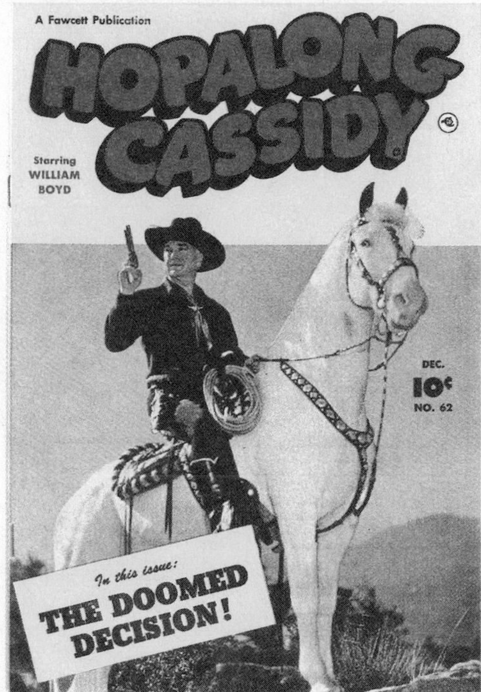

HOPALONG CASSIDY #62
December 1951. © DELL

H.R. PUFNSTUF #2
January 1971. © Sid & Marty Krofft

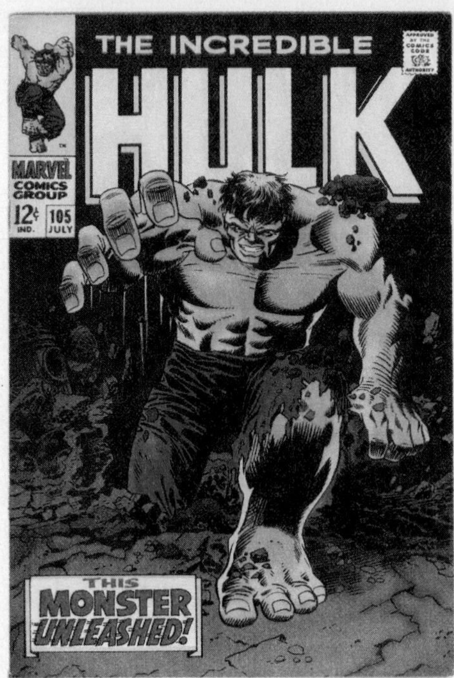

INCREDIBLE HULK #105
July 1968. © MAR

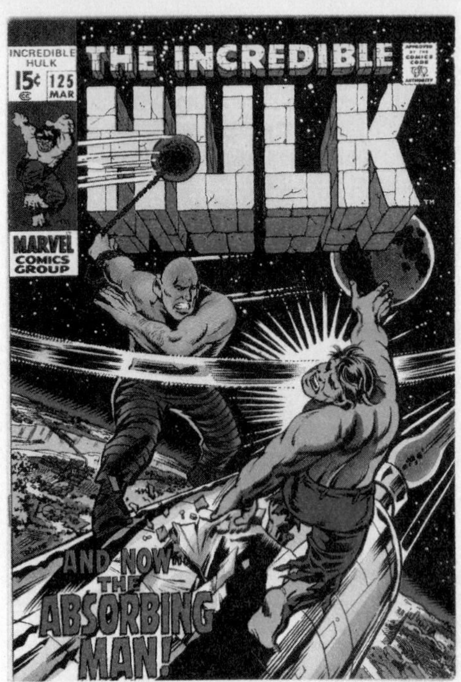

INCREDIBLE HULK #125
March 1970. © MAR

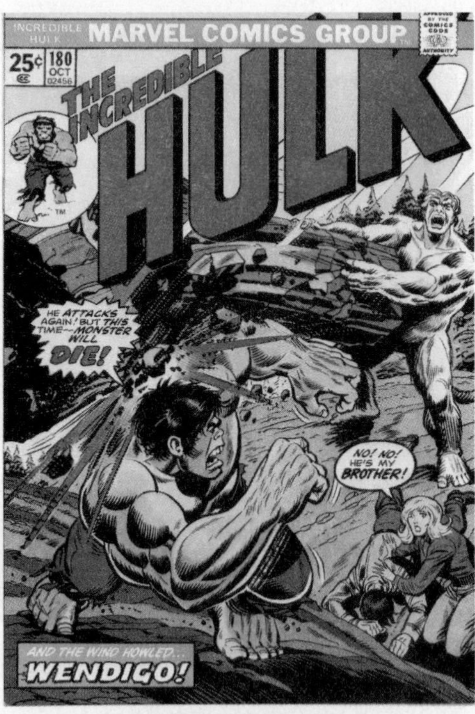

INCREDIBLE HULK #180
October 1974. Wolverine debuts in the final panel.
© MAR

INCREDIBLE HULK #181
November 1974. CGC 9.9, the highest graded copy known. First full appearance of Wolverine.
© MAR

IRON MAN #55
February 1973. First appearance of Thanos. © MAR

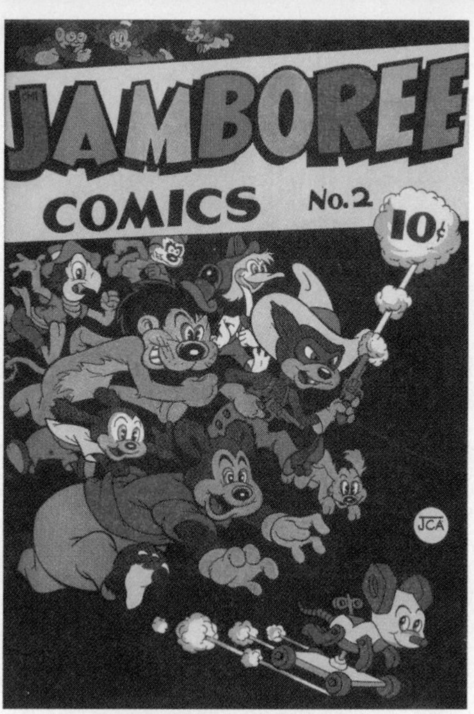

JAMBOREE COMICS #2
March 1946. © Round Publ.

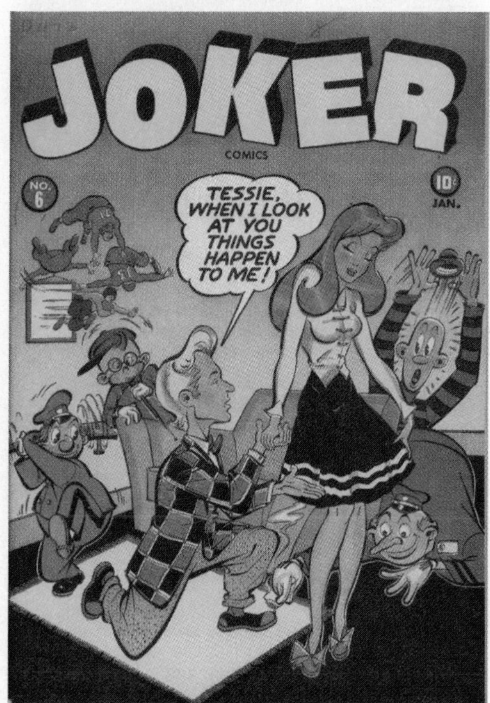

JOKER COMICS #6
January 1945. From the Mile High collection.
© MAR

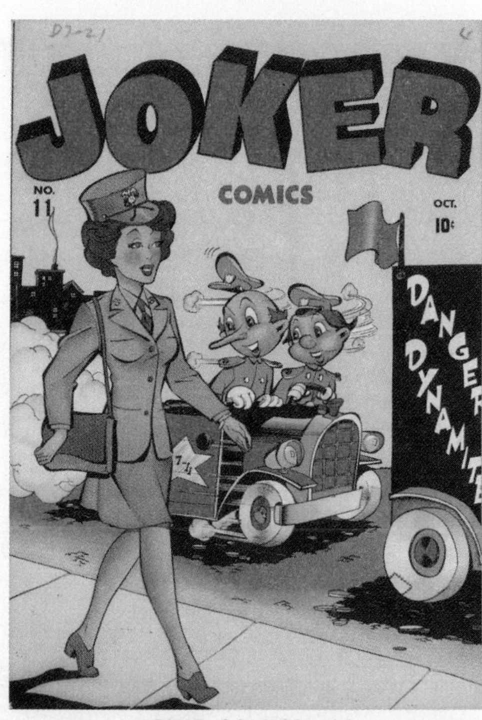

JOKER COMICS #11
October 1943. From the Mile High collection.
© MAR

JUGHEAD'S JOKES #4
March 1968. © AP

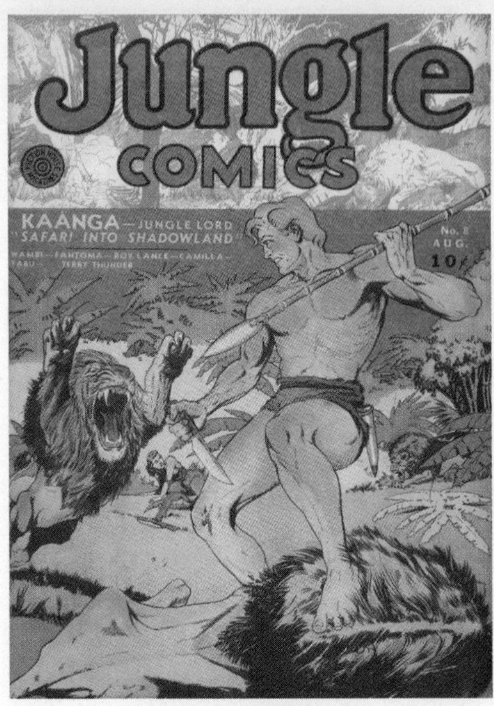

JUNGLE COMICS #8
August 1940. © FH

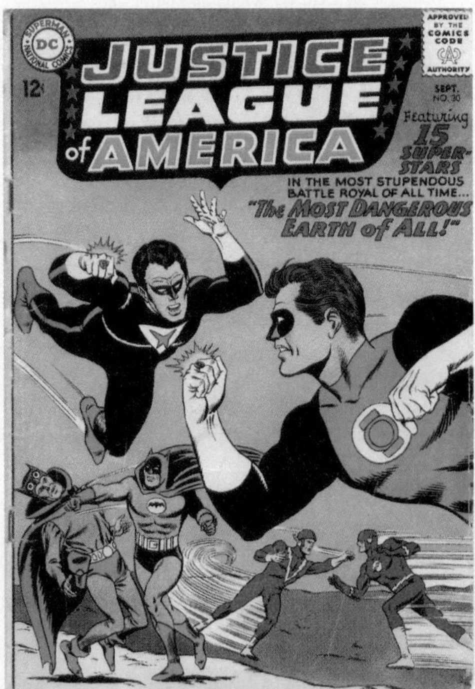

JUSTICE LEAGUE OF AMERICA #30
September 1964. Part 2 of the 2nd JLA/JSA team-up and the debut of Earth-Three's Crime Syndicate. © DC

JUSTICE LEAGUE OF AMERICA #138
January 1977. © DC

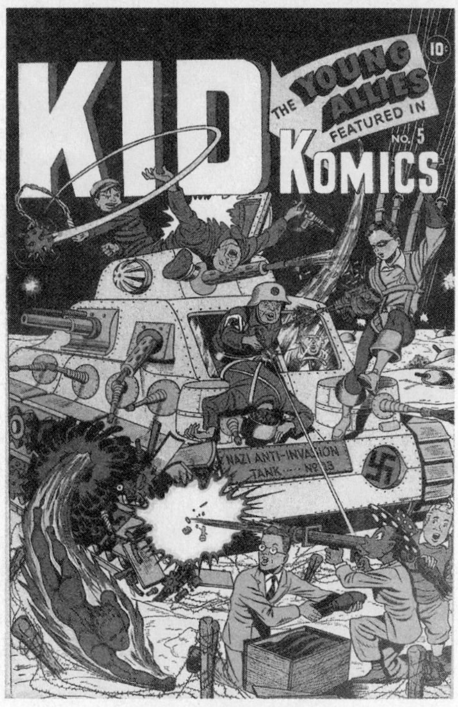

KID KOMICS #5
Summer 1944. © MAR

KOLYNOS PRESENTS THE WHITE GUARD #1
1949. This is the oldest comic graded as GEM MINT 10.0 by CGC. © Whitehall Pharmacal

THE ADVENTURES OF LASSIE
1949. Red Heart Dog Food giveaway. The first app. of Lassie in comics. © DELL

THE LONE RANGER COMICS BOOK #1
2nd version, 1939. © Lone Ranger, Inc.

MAGIC COMICS #3
October 1939. From the Mile High collection. © DMP

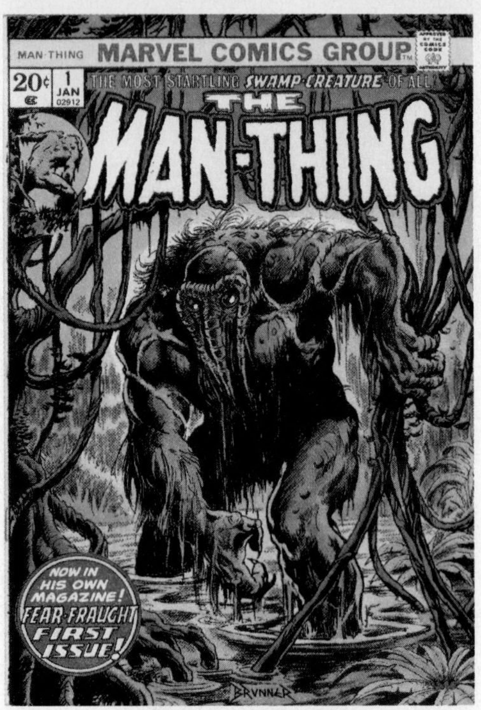

THE MAN-THING #1
January 1974. © MAR

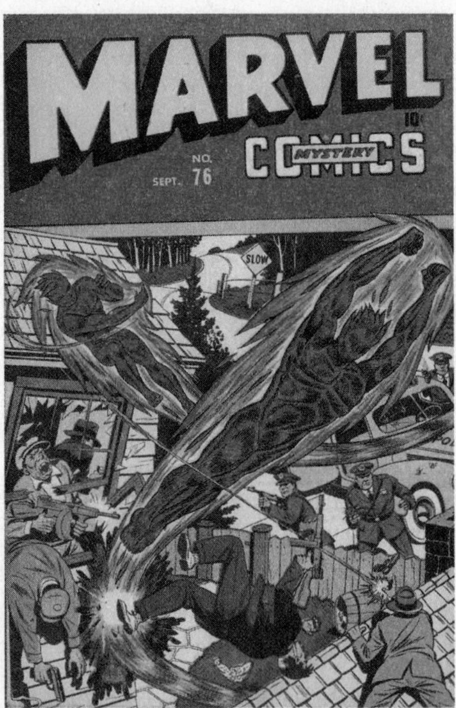

MARVEL MYSTERY COMICS #76
September 1946. The "D" copy. © MAR

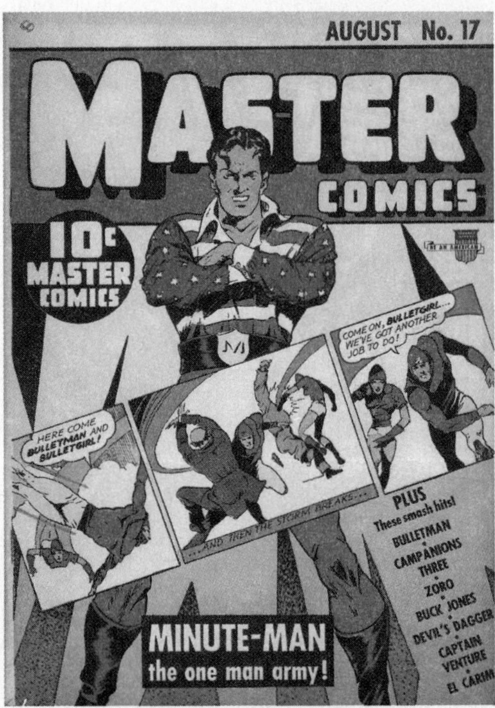

MASTER COMICS #17
August 1941. © FAW

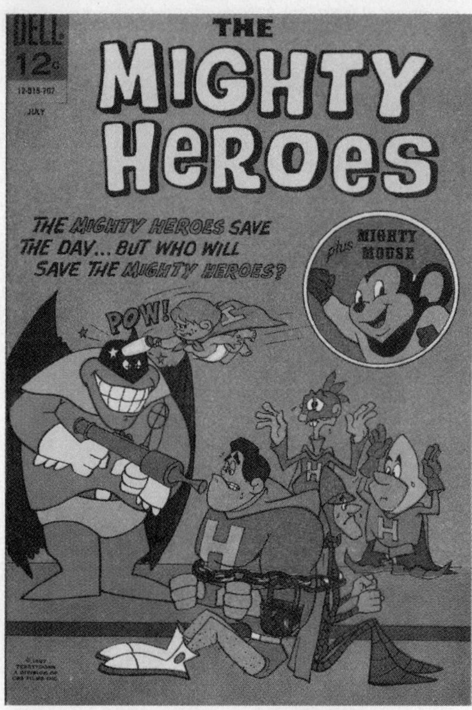

THE MIGHTY HEROES #4
July 1967. © Terrytoons

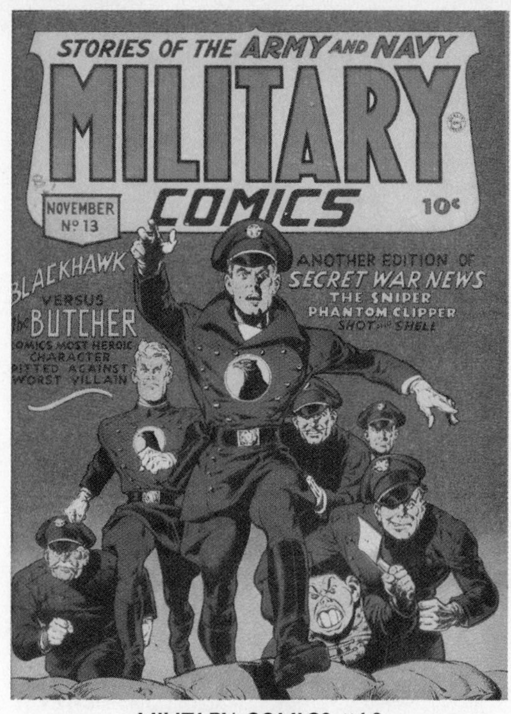

MILITARY COMICS #13
November 1942. © QUA

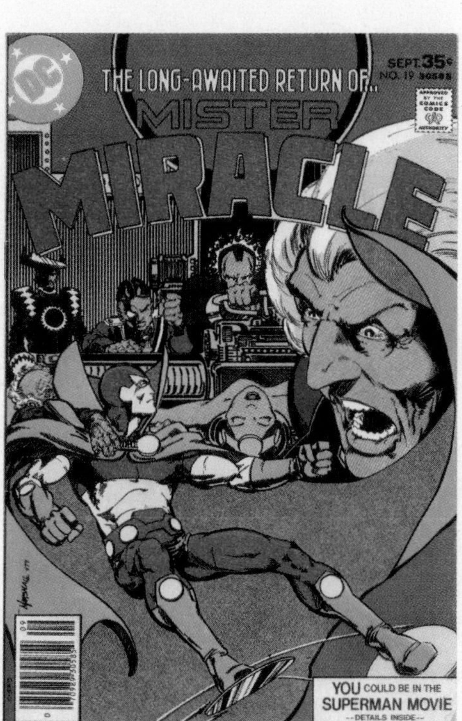

MISTER MIRACLE #19
September 1977. © DC

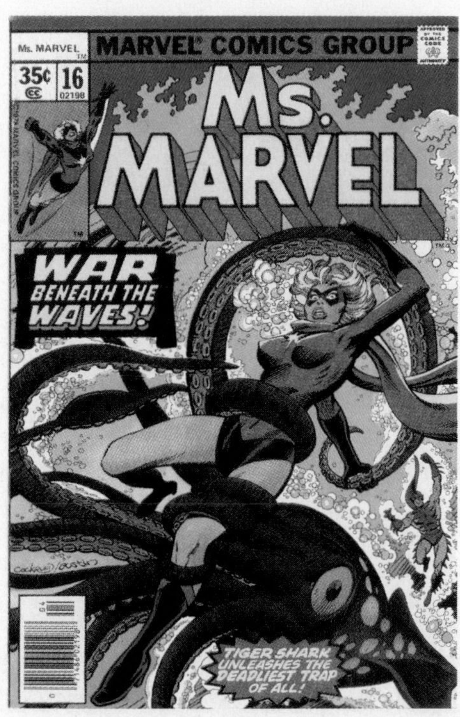

MS. MARVEL #16
April 1978. First cameo app. of Mystique. © MAR

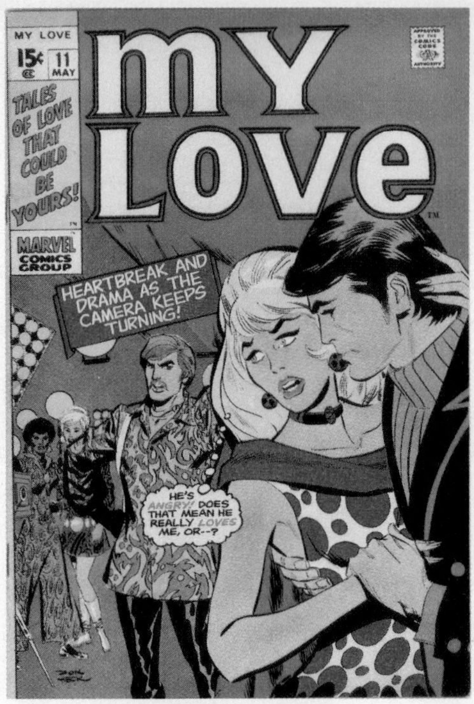

MY LOVE #11
May 1971. © MAR

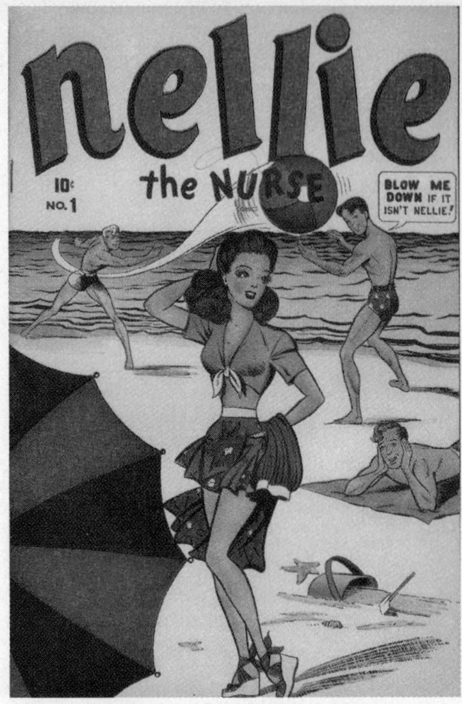

NELLIE THE NURSE #1
1945. © MAR

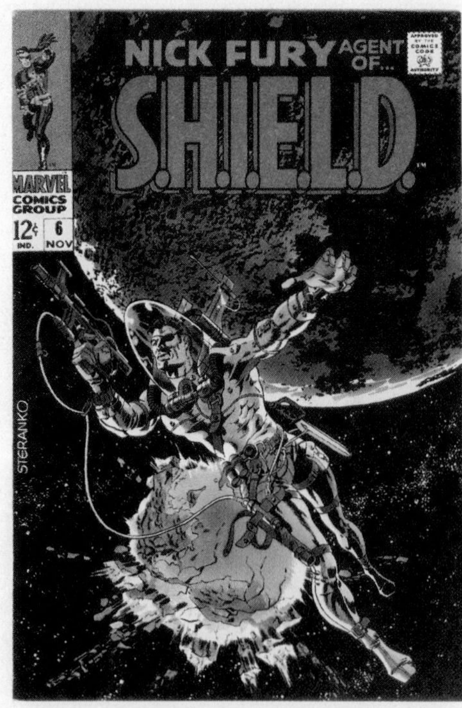

NICK FURY, AGENT OF SHIELD #6
November 1968. Jim Steranko cover. © MAR

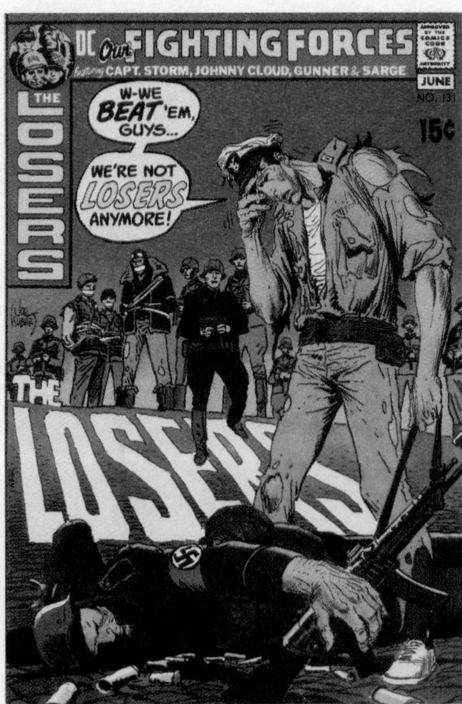

OUR FIGHTING FORCES #131
May-June 1971. © DC

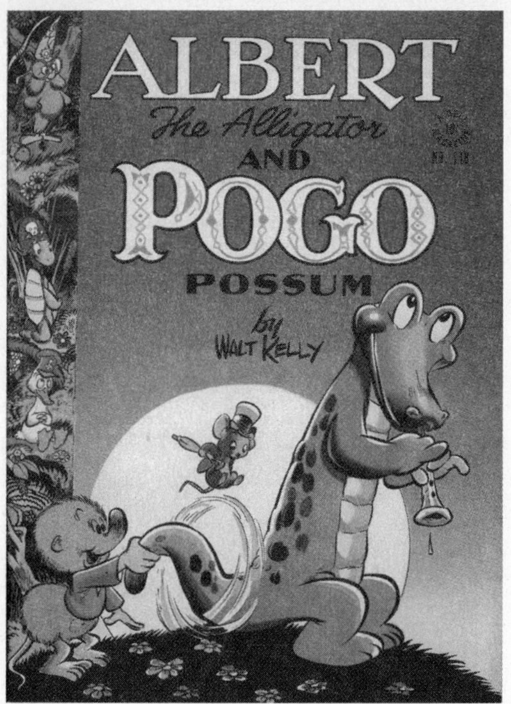

POGO FOUR COLOR #148
May 1947. © Walt Kelly

POLICE COMICS #21
August 1943. Jack Cole cover. © QUA

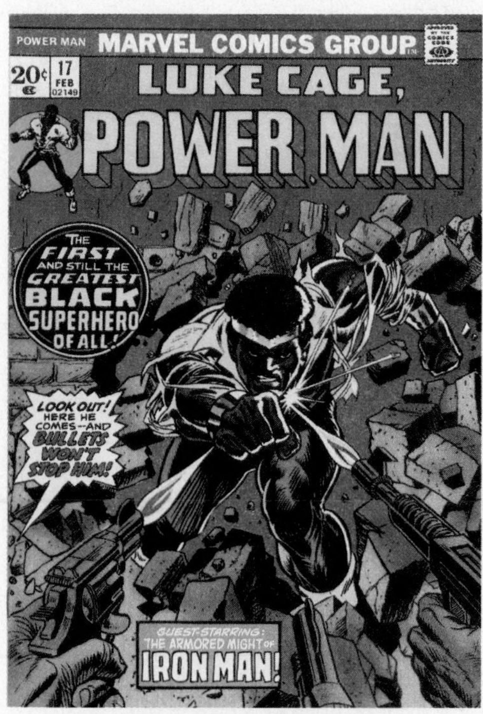

POWER MAN #17
February 1974. © MAR

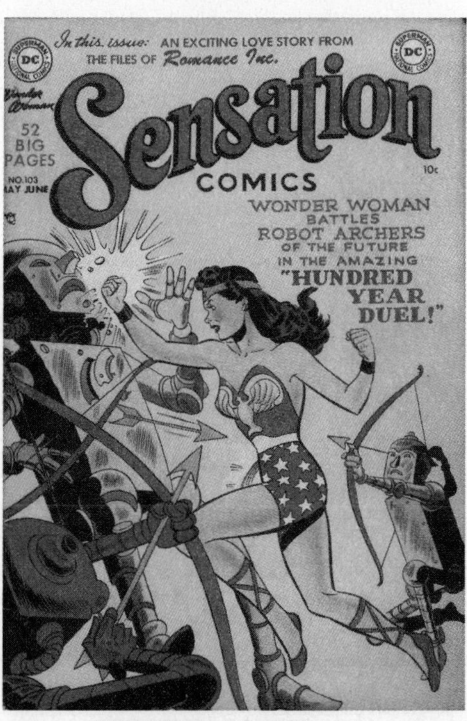

SENSATION COMICS #103
May-June 1951. © DC

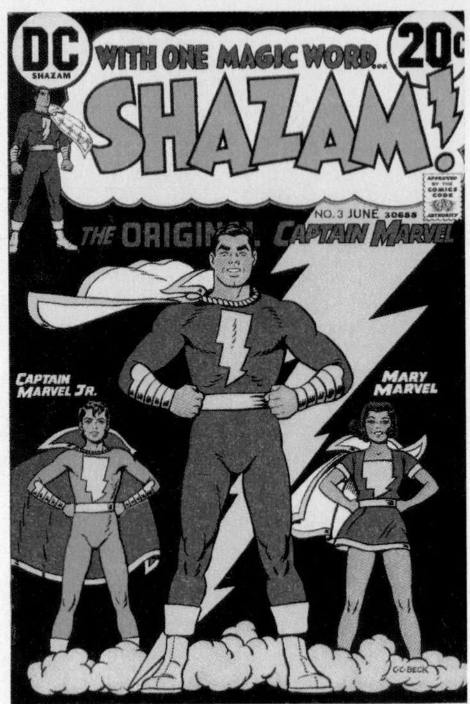

SHAZAM! #3
June 1973. C.C. Beck cover. © DC

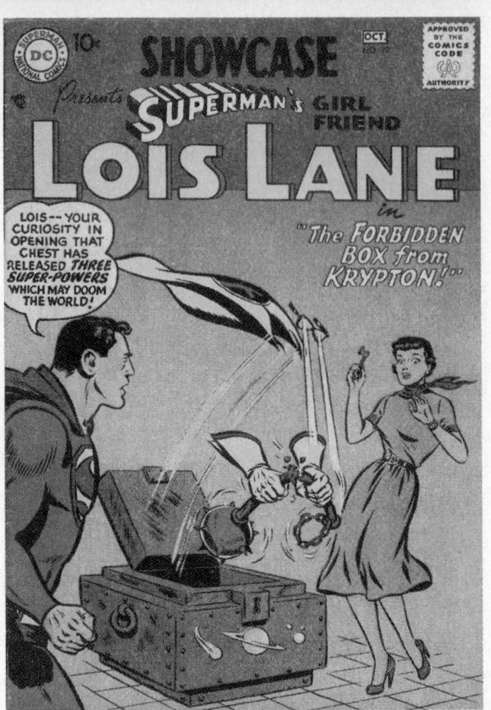

SHOWCASE #10
September-October 1957. © DC

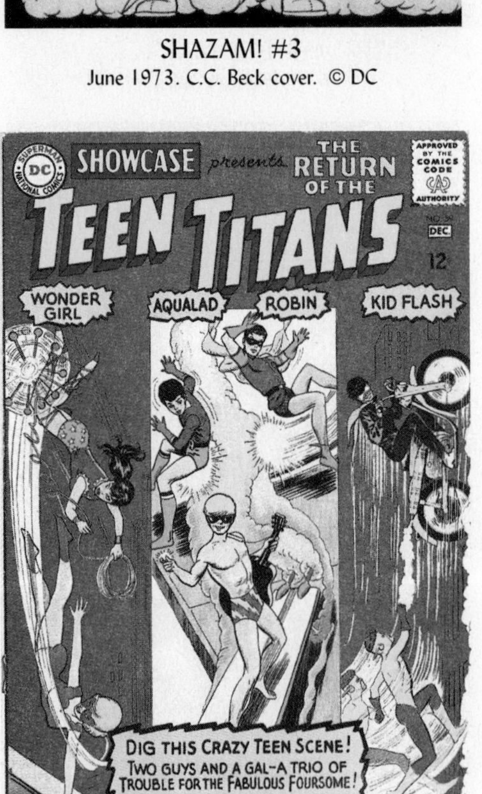

SHOWCASE #59
November-December 1965.
Third appearance of the Teen Titans. © DC

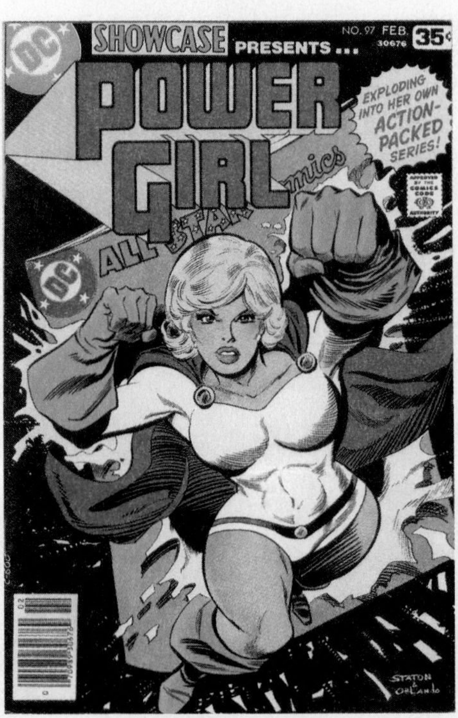

SHOWCASE #97
February 1978. © DC

SILVER SURFER #14
March 1970. © MAR

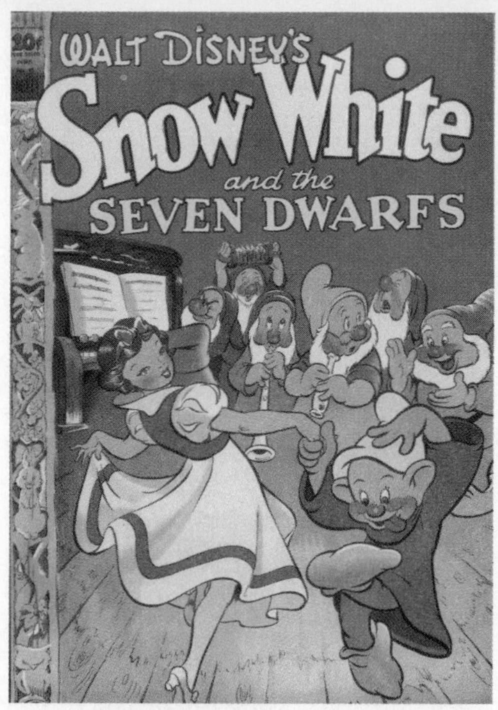

SNOW WHITE FOUR COLOR #49
July 1944. © WDC

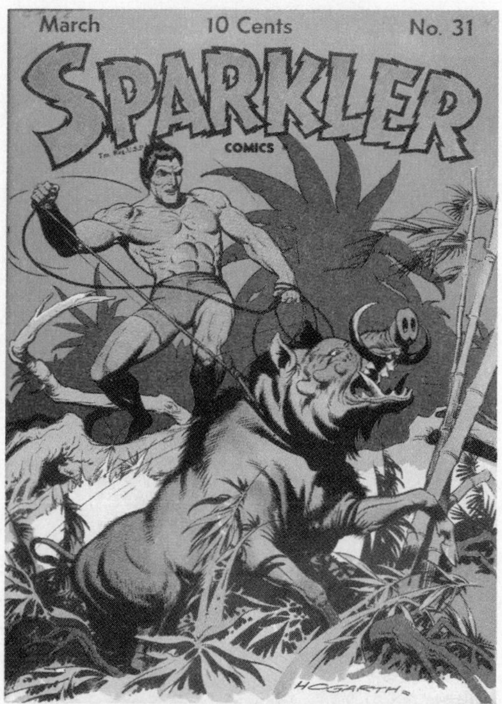

SPARKLER COMICS #31
March 1944. From the Mile High collection. © UFS

SPECIAL MARVEL EDITION #15
December 1973. First appearance of Shang-Chi, Master of Kung Fu. © MAR

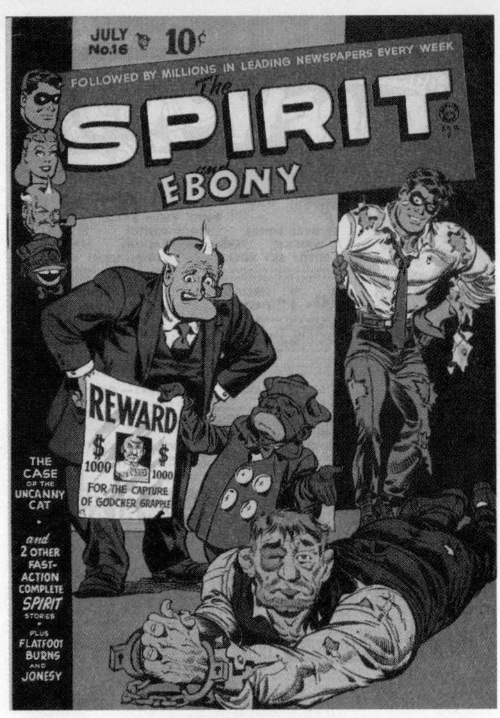

THE SPIRIT #16
July 1949. © Will Eisner

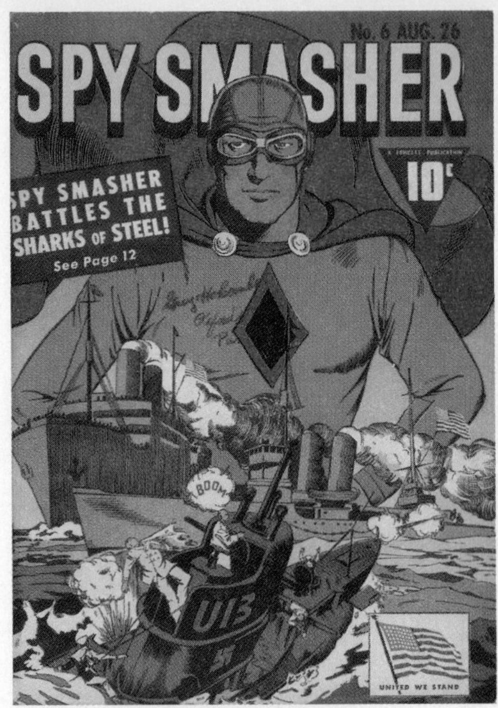

SPY SMASHER #6
August 1942. Mac Raboy cover. © FAW

STAR TREK #19
July 1973. © Paramount

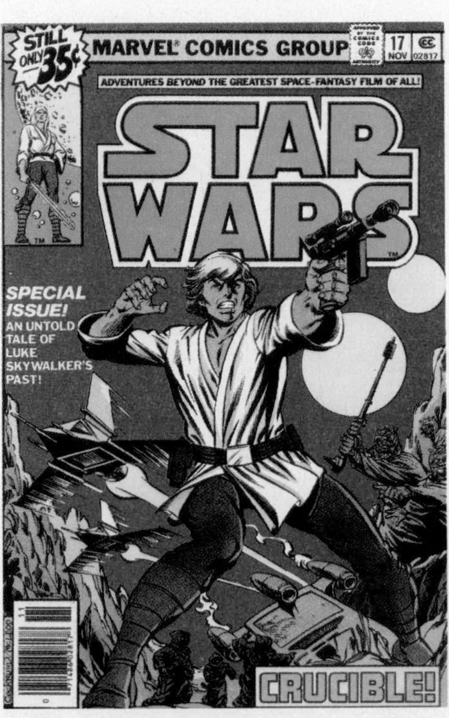

STAR WARS #17
November 1978. © Lucasfilm Ltd.

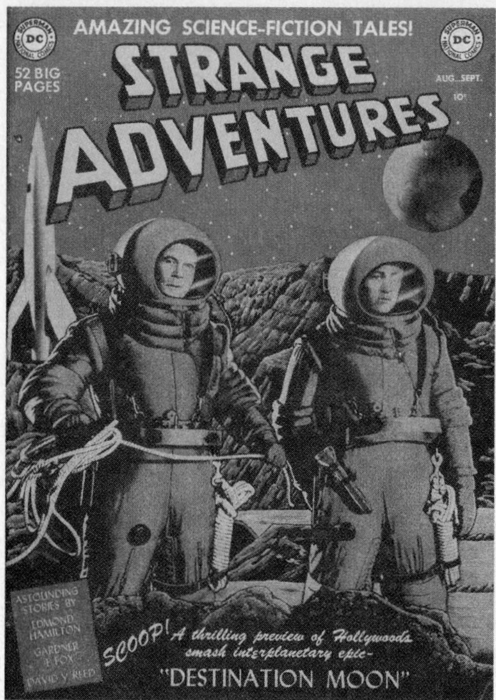

STRANGE ADVENTURES #1
August-September 1950. © DC

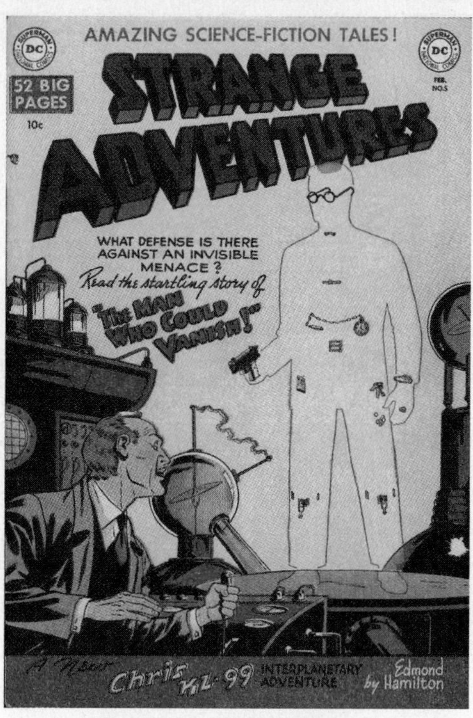

STRANGE ADVENTURES #5
February 1951. © DC

SUB-MARINER COMICS #34
June 1954. © MAR

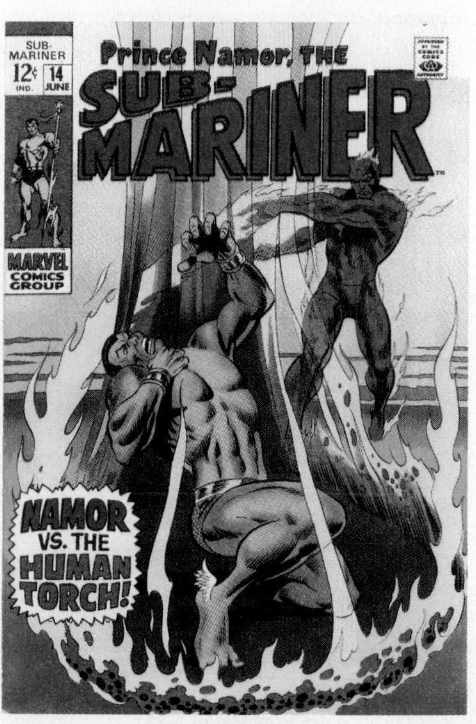

SUB-MARINER #14
June 1969. © MAR

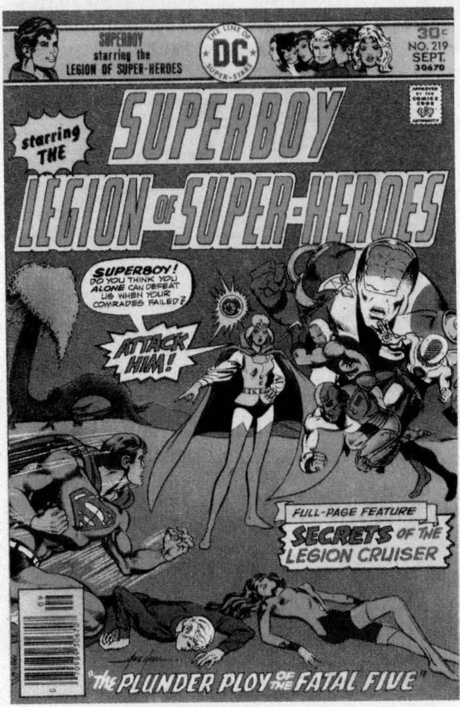

SUPERBOY #219
September 1976. © DC

SUPERMAN #1
Summer 1939. © DC

SUPERMAN #234
February 1971. © DC

SUPERMAN WORKBOOK
1945. © DC

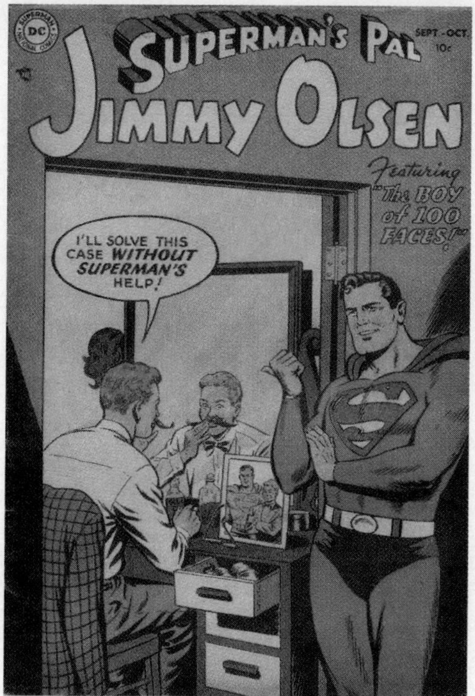

SUPERMAN'S PAL JIMMY OLSEN #1
September-October 1954. © DC

TARGET COMICS VOL. 3 #7
September 1942. From the Rockford collection.
© NOVP

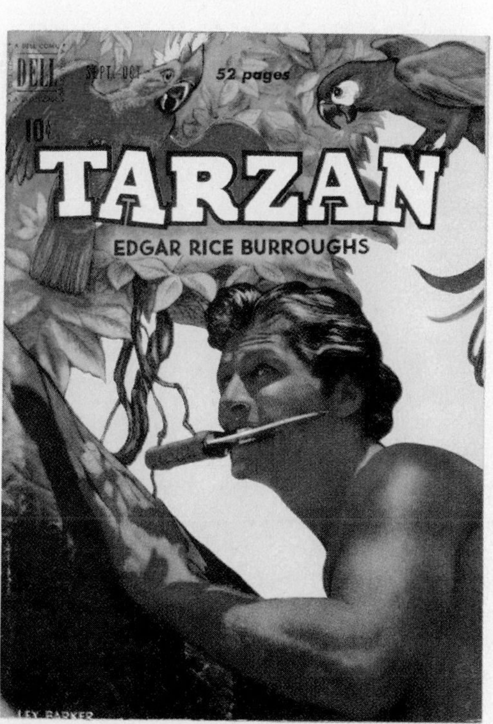

TARZAN #17
September-October 1950. © ERB

TARZAN #1
June 1977. © ERB

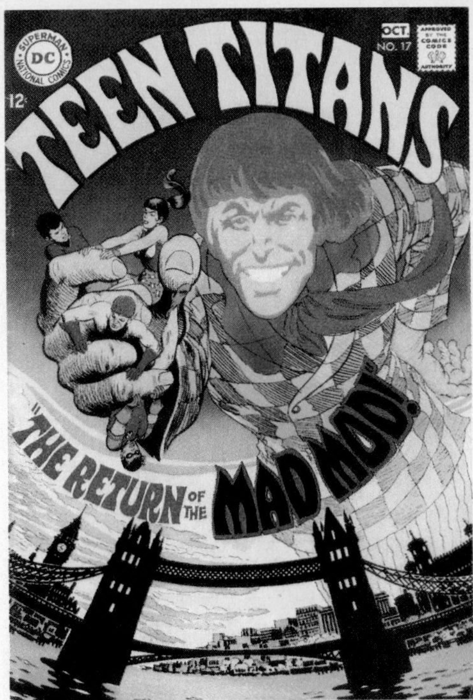

TEEN TITANS #17
September-October 1968. © DC

TEEN TITANS #23
September-October 1969. © DC

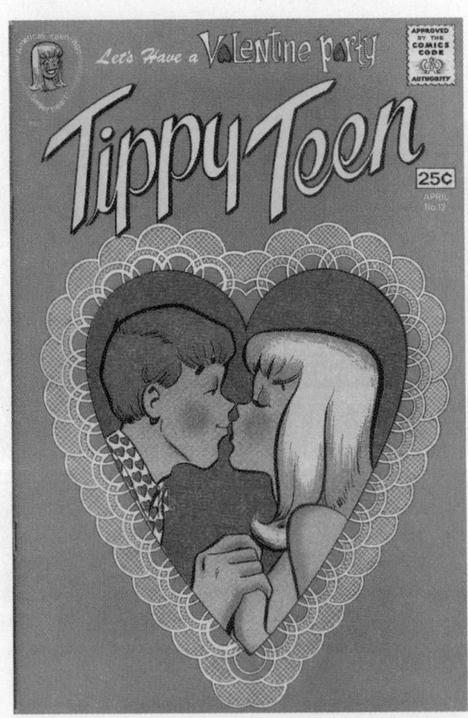

TIPPY TEEN #12
April 1967. © TC

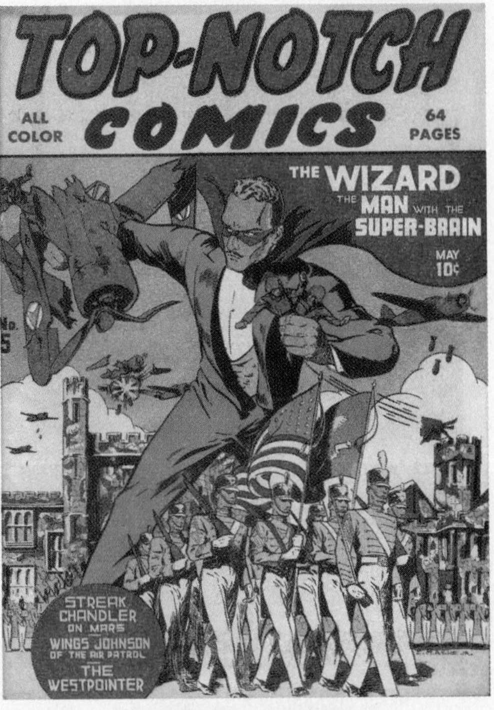

TOP-NOTCH COMICS #5
May 1950. © MLJ

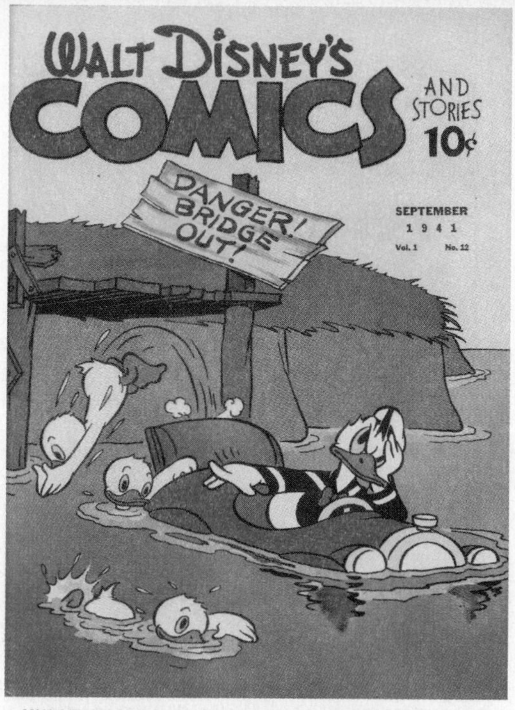

WALT DISNEY'S COMICS AND STORIES #12
September 1941. © WDC

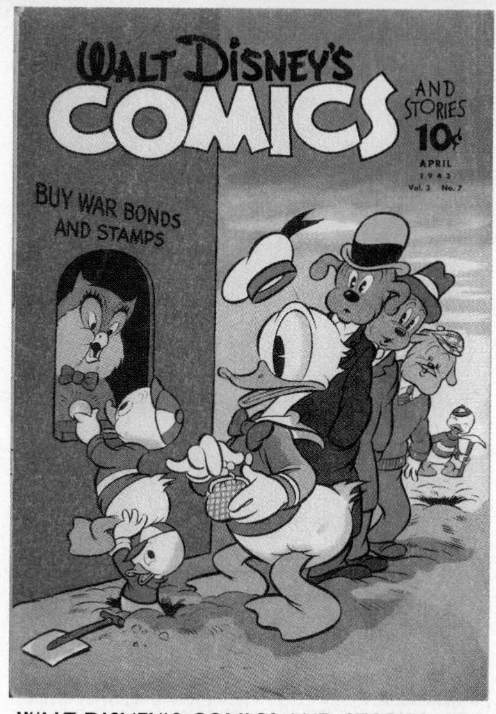

WALT DISNEY'S COMICS AND STORIES #31
April 1943. © WDC

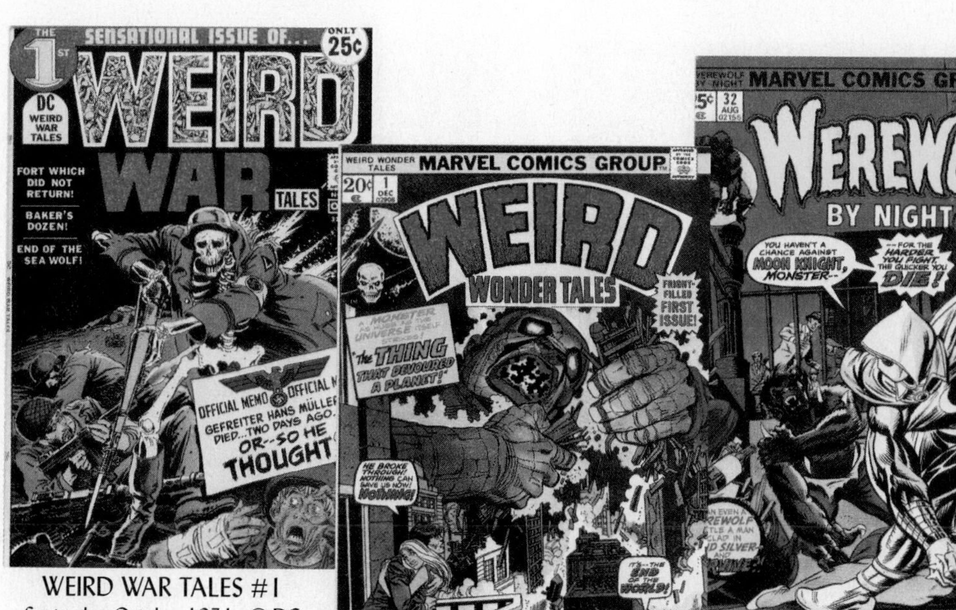

WEIRD WAR TALES #1
September-October 1971. © DC

WEIRD WONDER TALES #1
December 1973. © MAR

WEREWOLF BY NIGHT #32
August 1975. © MAR

WHIZ COMICS #20
August 1941. © FAW

WORLD'S FINEST COMICS #59
July-August 1959. © DC

WOW COMICS #29
September 1944. © FAW

X-MEN #104
April 1977. © MAR

Overstreet Price Guide Back Issues

The Overstreet® Comic Book Price Guide has held the record for being the longest running annual comic book publication. We are now celebrating our 34th anniversary, and the demand for the Overstreet® price guides is very strong. Collectors have created a legitimate market for them, and they continue to bring record prices each year. Collectors also have a record of comic book prices going back further than any other source in comic fandom. The prices listed below are for NM condition only, with GD-25% and FN-50% of the NM value. Canadian editions exist for a couple of the early issues.

Special thanks to Robert Rogovin of Four Color Comics for his assistance in researching the prices listed in this section. Abbreviations: SC-softcover, HC-hardcover, L-leather bound.

1970	#1 White SC $1800.00
1970	#1 Blue SC (2nd Printing) $1500.00
1972	#2 SC $650.00; #2 HC $1100.00
1973	#3 SC $300.00; #3 HC $950.00
1974	#4 SC $165.00; #4 HC $475.00
1975	#5 SC $155.00; #5 HC $260.00
1976	#6 SC $105.00; #6 HC $155.00
1977	#7 SC $145.00; #7 HC $230.00
1978	#8 SC $130.00; #8 HC $180.00
1979	#9 SC $130.00; #9 HC $180.00
1980	#10 SC $140.00; #10 HC $190.00
1981	#11 SC $85.00; #11 HC $115.00
1982	#12 SC $85.00; #12 HC $115.00
1983	#13 SC $85.00; #13 HC $115.00
1984	#14 SC $55.00; #14 HC $110.00; #14 L $170.00
1985	#15 SC $55.00; #15 HC $80.00; #15 L $160.00
1986	#16 SC $60.00; #16 HC $85.00; #16 L $170.00
1987	#17 SC $55.00; #17 HC $110.00; #17 L $160.00
1988	#18 SC $45.00; #18 HC $65.00; #18 L $160.00
1989	#19 SC $50.00; #19 HC $60.00; #19 L $170.00
1990	#20 SC $32.00; #20 HC $50.00; #20 L $135.00
1991	#21 SC $35.00; #21 HC $55.00; #21 L $145.00
1992	#22 SC $32.00; #22 HC $50.00

1993

#23 SC $32.00
#23 HC $50.00

1994

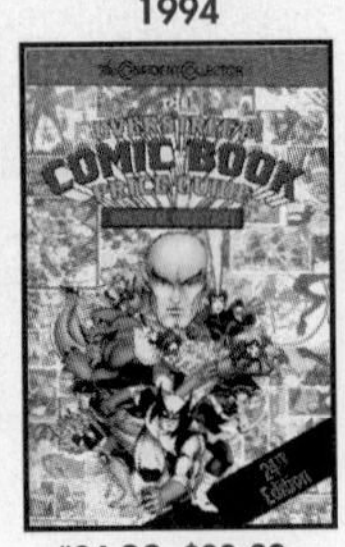

#24 SC $26.00
#24 HC $36.00

1995

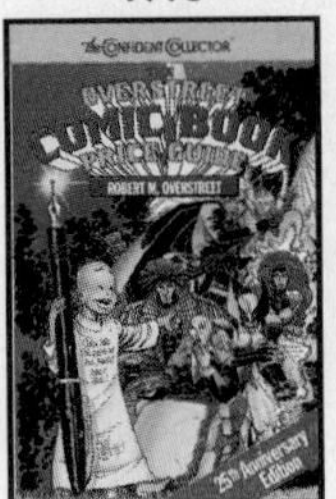

#25 SC $26.00
#25 HC $36.00
#25 L $110.00

1996

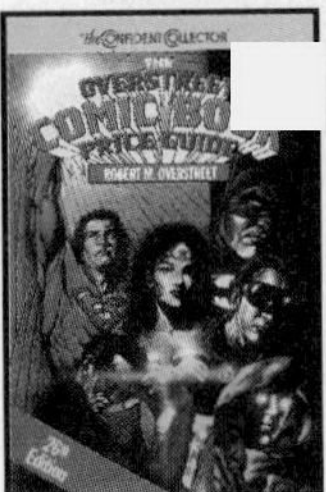

#26 SC $20.00
#26 HC $30.00
#26 L $100.00

1997

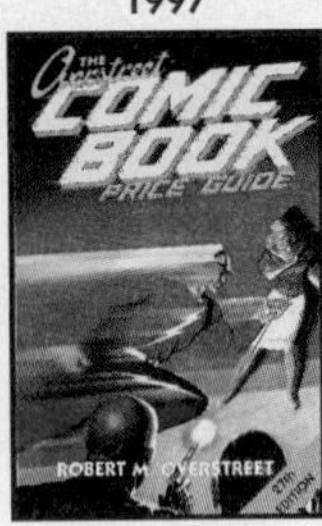

#27 SC $22.00
#27 HC $38.00
#27 L $125.00

1997

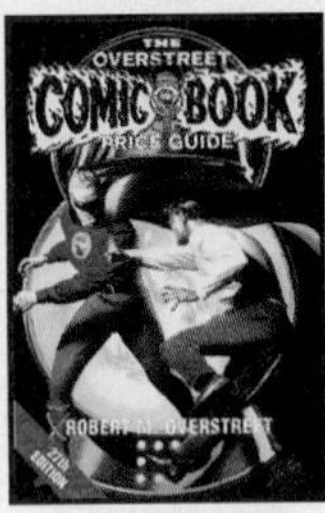

#27 SC $22.00
#27 HC $38.00
#27 L $125.00

1998

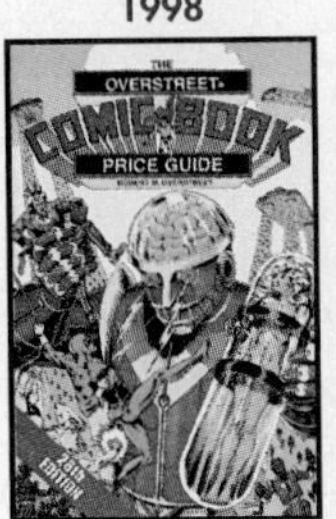

#28 SC $20.00
#28 HC $35.00

1998

#28 SC $20.00
#28 HC $35.00

1999

#29 SC $22.00
#29 HC $38.00

1999

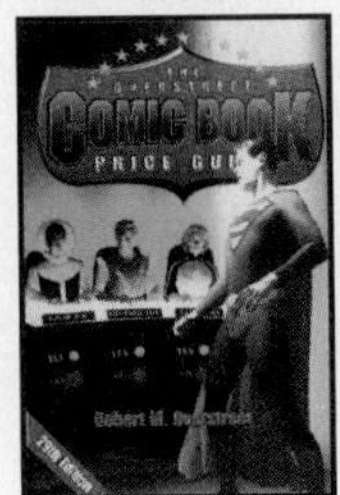

#29 SC $20.00
#29 HC $35.00

2000

#30 SC $22.00
#30 HC $32.00

2000

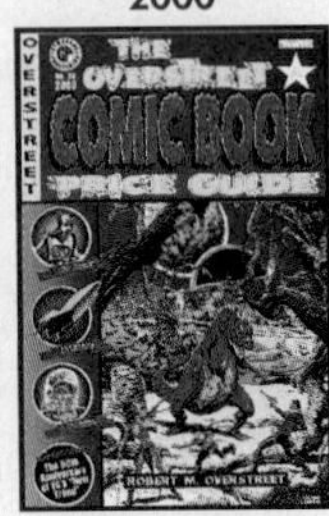

#30 SC $22.00
#30 HC $32.00

2001

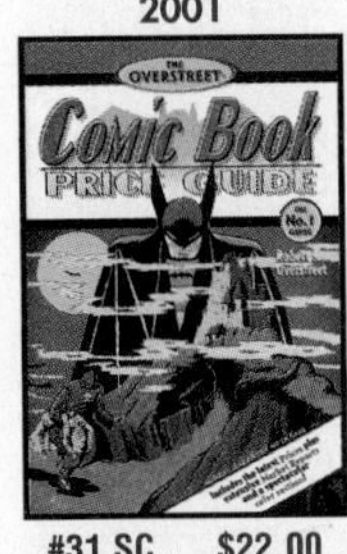

#31 SC $22.00
#31 HC $32.00

2001

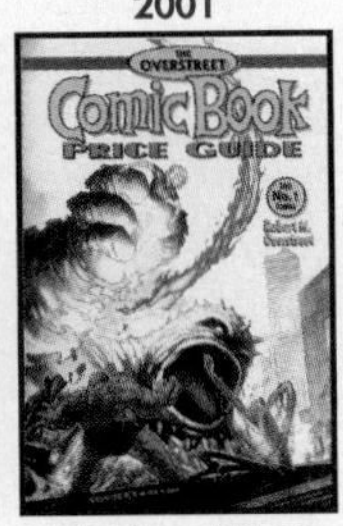

#31 SC $22.00
#31 HC $32.00

2001

#31 Bookstore Ed.
SC only $22.00

2002

#32 SC $22.00
#32 HC $32.00

2002

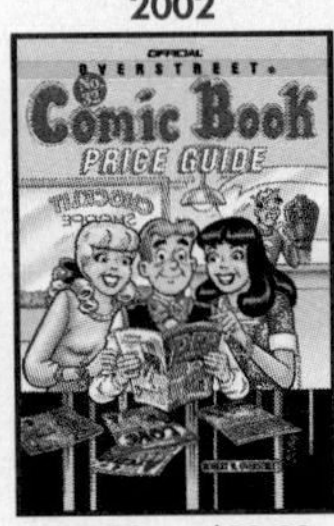

#32 SC $22.00
#32 HC $32.00

2002

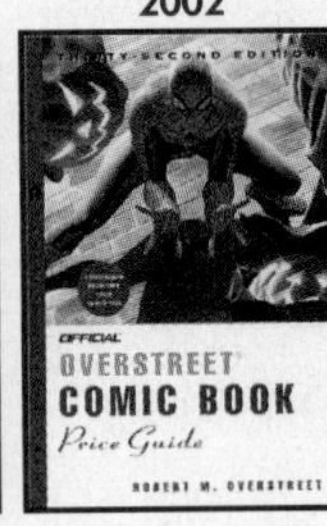

#32 Bookstore Ed.
SC only $22.00

2003

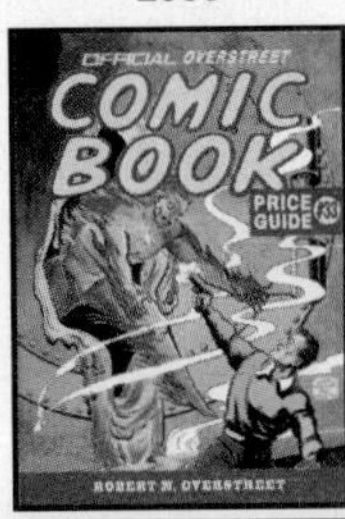

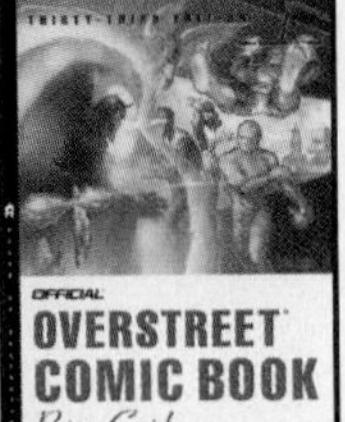

#33 SC $25.00
#33 HC $32.00

#33 Bookstore Ed.
SC only $25.00

2001

#31 Workbook
$35.00

2002

#32 Workbook
$35.00

2003

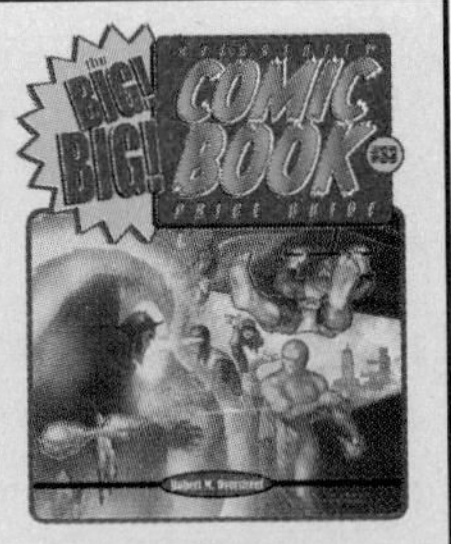

#33 Workbook
$37.00

Feature Article Index

Over the years, the **Overstreet Comic Book Price Guide** has grown into much more than a simple catalog of values. Almost since the very beginning, Bob has worked hard to make sure that the book reflects the latest information about the hobby, and this has resulted in some fascinating in-depth articles about aspects of the industry and the rich history of comics. Sadly, many of you may never have read a lot of these articles, or even knew they existed.

These two pages contain a comprehensive index to every feature article ever published in the **Overstreet Comic Book Price Guide**. From interviews with legendary creators to exhaustively researched retrospectives, it's all here. Enjoy this look back at the Overstreet legacy, and remember, many of these editions are still available through Gemstone and your local comic book dealer.

Note: The first three editions of the Guide had no feature articles, but from #4 on, a tradition was born that has carried through to the very volume you hold in your hands. This index begins with the 4th edition and lists all articles published up to and including last year's 32nd edition of the guide.

		1941: Comic Books Go To War!:	Harry B. Thomas	A-79-98
		Those fabulous comics of World War II	and Gary M. Carter	
#22	1992	Spider-Man - An Amazing Success Story	Steve Saffel	A-77-86
		Journey Into the Unknown World of Atlas Fantasy	Gary M. Carter & Pat S. Calhoun	A-87-103
#23	1993	Green Lantern's Light! A History by...	Thomas Andrae with Keif Fromm	A-71-79
		Silver Sagas of the Scarlet Speedster:	Gary M. Carter	A-80-86
		Whirlwind Adventures of the Fastest Man Alive! 1956-1960		
#24	1994	Three Uncanny Decades of X-Men!	John Townsend, Ph.D.	A-146-156
		Living on Borrowed Time! A Nostalgic Look at the Early Years	Pat S. Calhoun & Gary M. Carter	A-157-164
		of DC's Challengers of the Unknown!		
#25	1995	The Mystery of the 12 Missing ECs	Bruce Hamilton	A-99-106
		100 Years - A Century of Comics	Pat S. Calhoun	A-107-123
#26	1996	The American Comic Book: 1897-1932	Richard D. Olson, Ph.D.	pp. 1-2
		The Formative Years - The Platinum Age		
		The American Comic Book: 1933-Present	Richard D. Olson, Ph.D.	pp. 10-11
		The Modern Comic Book		
		The Golden Age and Beyond	Jerry Weist	652-667
		A Short History of Comic Book Fandom	Sotheby's Comic Book Consultant	
		& Comic Book Collecting in America		
#27	1997	Gotham Knights - A Conversation	Arnold T. Blumberg	A-25-27
			with Jerry Robinson	
		Strange Adventures - A Conversation with Murphy Anderson	Scott Braden	A-30-32
		The American Comic Book: 1897-1932	Robert L. Beerbohm	pp. 1-15
		The Beginning: The Platinum Age		
		The American Comic Book: 1933-Present	Richard D. Olson, Ph.D.	23-24
		The Golden Age and Beyond: The Modern Comic Book		
#28	1998	Friends of Lulu Sounds Off on Comics	Jackie Estrada	79-81
		The World of Tomorrow :	Arnold T. Blumberg	82-88
		How Comics of the Past Portrayed the 1990s		
		Invasion of the Giant (and Not So Giant) Robots!	Arnold T. Blumberg	83-87
		Built to Last	J. C. Vaughn and Scott Braden	89-102
		The American Comic Book: 1897-1932	J. C. Vaughn	201-203
		In the Beginning: The Platinum Age:		
		The American Comic Book: 1933-Present	Richard D. Olson, Ph.D.	211-212
		The Golden Age & Beyond: The Modern Comic Book (Revised)		
#29	1999	Special Feature: Grading - The Next Revolution for Comic Books	Bruce Hamilton	17-21
		Avenues of Collecting: A Walk Through the Comic Book Neighborhood	J. C. Vaughn	91-94
		Just Another Justice League?	J. C. Vaughn	95-100
		Legiondary Adventures	Mark Huesman	101-106
		One For All and All For One:	Arnold T. Blumberg	107-112
		A Brief History of Super-Teams: Top Ten Greatest Super-Teams	Benn Ray	108-112
		The American Comic Book: 1897-1932	Robert L. Beerbohm	211-218
		In the Beginning: The Platinum Age (Rev.)	& Richard D. Olson, PhD	
		The American Comic Book: 1933-Present	Robert L. Beerbohm	226-233
		The Golden Age & Beyond & The Origin of the Modern Comic Book	& Richard D. Olson, PhD	
#30	2000	History with a Twist	Arnold T. Blumberg	18-22
		EC, MAD and Beyond: Al Feldstein	J. C. Vaughn	24-28
		Flights to EC and Beyond with Al Williamson	J. C. Vaughn	36-39
		Bob's Bizarre Tales	Bob Overstreet	42-63
		The Marketing of a Medium	Arnold T. Blumberg	195-198
		New Discoveries Beyond the Platinum Age	Beerbohm & Olson	226-234
		The Golden Age & Beyond: Origins of the Modern Comic Book	Beerbohm & Olson	242-249
#31	2001	Why The Fantastic Four Made It To Forty	Arnold T. Blumberg	20-24
		Sixty Years of Wonder Woman	Charles S. Novinskie	26-29
		Brownie Points	Arnold T. Blumberg	30-32
		Re-Creations in a Flash (Murphy Anderson profile)	Arnold T. Blumberg	39-40
		Extraordinary! (John K. Snyder III profile)	J.C. Vaughn	42-44
		Bendis! (Brian Michael Bendis profile)	J.C. Vaughn	46-48
#32	2002	Superman: Patriotic Covers Through the Years	Arnold T. Blumberg	40-43
		Spidey Goes Hollywood	Arnold T. Blumberg	44-46
		Archie at 60	J. C. Vaughn	47-49
#33	2003	A Brief History of the Justice Society	J. C. Vaughn	850-852
		Mutant Movie Stars: The "New" X-Men Storm the Silver Screen	Arnold T. Blumberg	854-856
		Through Waves and Flame: The Elemental Entrance of the Sub-Mariner	Arnold T. Blumberg	858-860
		Variant Watch: Ultimate Spider-Man #1	J. C. Vaughn	862-863
		Comic Book Ages: Starting the Discussion	J. C. Vaughn & Arnold T. Blumberg	866-867

Overstreet Advisors

DAVID T. ALEXANDER
David Alexander Comics
Tampa, FL

LON ALLEN
Heritage Comics Auctions
Dallas, TX

DAVE ANDERSON
Want List Comics
Tulsa, OK

STEPHEN BARRINGTON
Collector
Chickasaw, AL

ROBERT BEERBOHM
Robert Beerbohm Comic Art
Fremont, NE

JON BERK
Collector
Hartford, CT

JASON BESSONETTE
Comics4Kids
Tacoma, WA

STEVE BOROCK
Primary Grader
Comics Guaranty, LLC

MICHAEL BROWNING
Collector
Delbarton, WV

MICHAEL CARBONARO
Neatstuffcollectibles.com
Englewood, NJ

GARY CARTER
Collector
Coronado, CA

JOHN CHRUSCINSKI
Tropic Comics
Lyndora, PA

GARY COLABUONO
Dealer/Collector
Elk Grove Village, IL

BILL COLE
Bill Cole Enterprises, Inc.
Randolph, MA

TIM COLLINS
RTS Unlimited, Inc.
Lakewood, CO

GARY DOLGOFF
Gary Dolgoff Comics
Easthampton, MA

BRUCE ELLSWORTH
Dealer
Las Vegas, NV

CONRAD ESCHENBERG
Collector/Dealer
Cold Spring, NY

RICHARD EVANS
Bedrock City Comics
Houston, TX

D'ARCY FARRELL
Pendragon Comics
Toronto, ONT

STEPHEN FISHLER
Metropolis Collectibles, Inc.
New York, NY

DAN FOGEL
Hippy Comix, Inc.
El Sobrante, CA

STEVEN GENTNER
Golden Age Specialist
Portland, OR

STEVE GEPPI
Diamond Int. Galleries
Timonium, MD

MICHAEL GOLDMAN
Motor City Comics
Southfield, MI

TOM GORDON
Gemstone Publishing
Timonium, MD

JAMIE GRAHAM
Graham Crackers
Chicago, IL

DANIEL GREENHALGH
Showcase New England
Northford, CT

ERIC J. GROVES
Dealer/Collector
Oklahoma City, OK

ROBERT HALL
Collector
Harrisburg, PA

JIM HALPERIN
Heritage Comics Auctions
Dallas, TX

BRUCE HAMILTON
Collector
Prescott, AZ

MARK HASPEL
Grader
Comics Guaranty, LLC

JOHN HAUSER
Dealer/Collector
New Berlin, WI

BILL HUGHES
Dealer/Collector
Flower Mound, TX

ROB HUGHES
Arch Angels
Manhattan Beach, CA

ED JASTER
Heritage Comics Auctions
Dallas, TX

PHIL LEVINE
Dealer/Collector
Three Bridges, NJ

PATRICK MARCHBANKS
Golden Age Comics & Games
Gulfport, MS

HARRY MATETSKY
Collector
Middletown, NJ

JON McCLURE
Dealer/Collector
Durango, CO

MIKE McKENZIE
Alternate Worlds
Cockeysville, MD

FRED McSURLEY
Heritage Comics Auctions
Dallas, TX

PETER MEROLO
Collector
Sedona, AZ

DALE MOORE
Comics4Kids
Bonney Lake, WA

MICHAEL NAIMAN
Silver Age Specialist
San Diego, CA

JOSHUA NATHANSON
ComicLink
Little Neck, NY

MATT NELSON
Classic Conservations
Dallas, TX

RICHARD OLSON
Collector/Academician
Poplarville, MS

TERRY O'NEILL
Terry's Comics
Orange, CA

GEORGE PANTELA
GPAnalysis for Comics
Hampton, Victoria, Australia

JIM PAYETTE
Golden Age Specialist
Bethlehem, NH

CHRIS PEDRIN
Pedrin Conservatory
Redwood City, CA

JOHN PETTY
Heritage Comics Auctions
Dallas, TX

JIM PITTS
Collector
El Sobrante, CA

RON PUSSELL
Redbeard's Book Den
Crystal Bay, NV

JO ANN REISNER
Collector
Vienna, VA

TODD REZNIK
Pacific Comic Exchange
Palos Verdes Peninsula, CA

ROBERT ROGOVIN
Four Color Comics
Scarsdale, NY

RORY ROOT
Comic Relief
Berkeley, CA

MARNIN ROSENBERG
Collectors Assemble
Great Neck, NY

ROBERT ROTER
Pacific Comic Exchange
Palos Verdes Peninsula, CA

CHUCK ROZANSKI
Mile High Comics
Denver, CO

MATT SCHIFFMAN
Bronze Age Specialist
Aloha, OR

DAVID SINCERE
Sincere Comics
Mobile, AL

DAVID SMITH
Fantasy Illustrated/Rocket Comics
Seattle, WA

JOHN SNYDER
Diamond Int. Galleries
Timonium, MD

TONY STARKS
Silver Age Specialist
Evansville, IN

TERRY STROUD
Dealer/Collector
Santa Monica, CA

DOUG SULIPA
"Everything 1960-1996"
Manitoba, Canada

MICHAEL TIERNEY
The Comic Book Store
Little Rock, AR

JOE VERENEAULT
JHV Associates
Woodbury Heights, NJ

BOB WAYNE
DC Comics
New York City, NY

JERRY WEIST
Sotheby's
Gloucester, MA

HARLEY YEE
Dealer/Collector
Detroit, MI

VINCENT ZURZOLO, JR.
Metropolis Collectibles, Inc.
New York, NY

Advertisers' Index

A

B

C

D

E

F

G

H

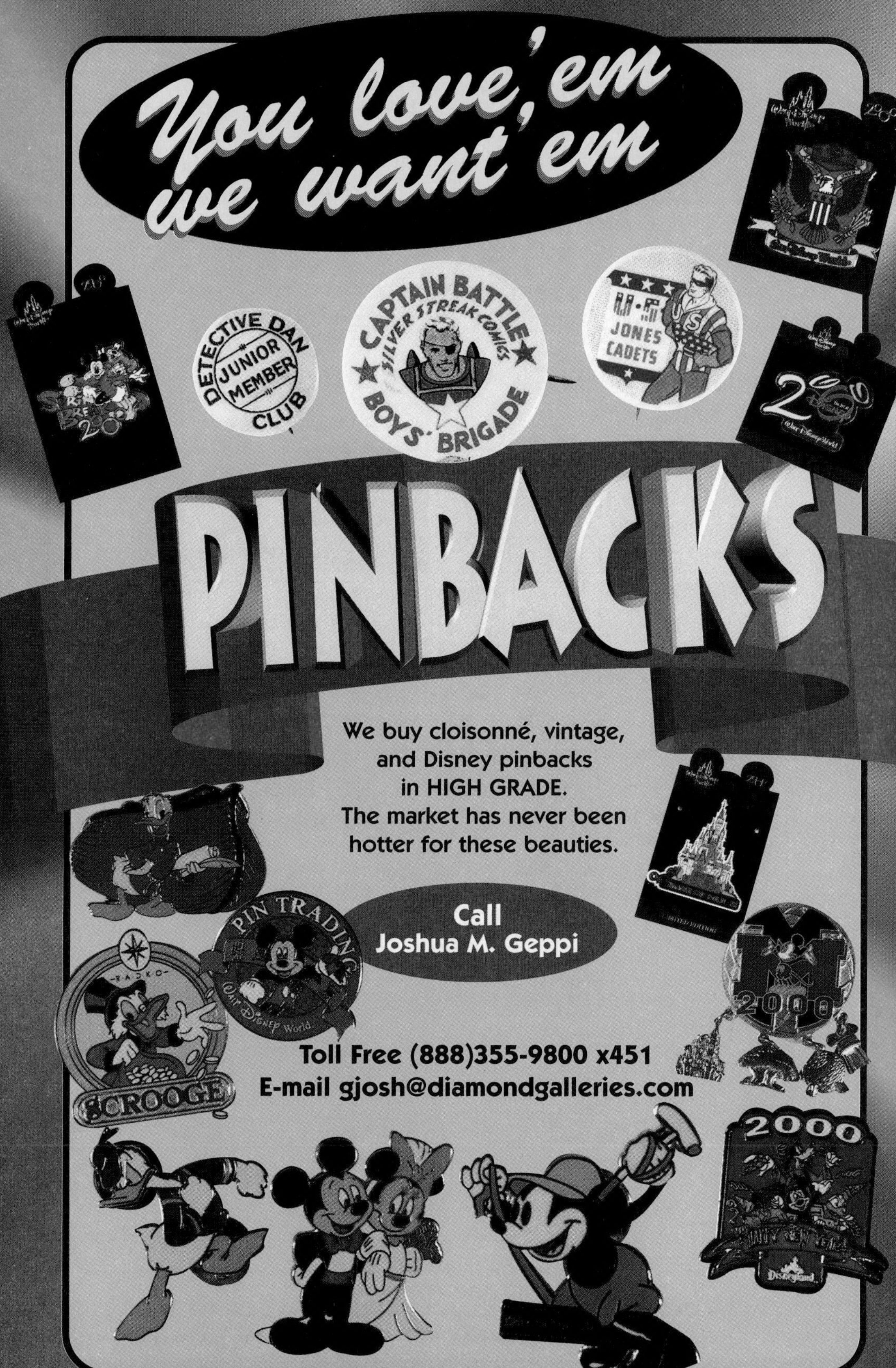

You love 'em
we want 'em
DETECTIVE DAN
JUNIOR MEMBER
CLUB
CAPTAIN BATTLE
SILVER STREAK COMICS
BOYS' BRIGADE
JONES CADETS
PINBACKS
We buy cloisonné, vintage,
and Disney pinbacks
in HIGH GRADE.
The market has never been
hotter for these beauties.
Call
Joshua M. Geppi
PIN TRADING
Walt Disney World
SCROOGE
2000
Toll Free (888)355-9800 x451
E-mail gjosh@diamondgalleries.com
2000

NOW OPEN
the online webstore!
We sell everything! CALL NOW!
800-903-7246
Website www.neatstuffcollectibles.com
Email neatstuffdeals@yahoo.com
mail Neatstuff Collectibles
704 76th St.
North Bergen, NJ 07047
Michael Carbonaro's
Neat Stuff Collectibles, LLC
Purchasing agents:
Michael Carbonaro Overstreet advisor
Alex Needleman
CGC
Comics Guaranty, LLC
Charter Member Dealer
Dealing in comics, comic art, toys, rock-n-roll, tv & movie memorabilia, warehouse lots, and all types of collectibles!
INFANTINO
McLAUGHLIN
SPURLOCK
© 2004 DC Comics. All rights reserved.
BUYING! BUYING! BUYING!
BUYING! BUYING! BUYING!
BUYING! BUYING! BUYING!
BUYING! BUYING! BUYING!
BUYING! BUYING! BUYING!
BUYING! BUYING! BUYING!